Greenland
(DENMARK)

Alaska
(U.S.A.)

REYKJAVÍK
ICELAND

C A N A D A

OTTAWA

St Pierre &
Miquelon
(FRANCE)

UNITED STATES
OF AMERICA

Chicago

New York

WASHINGTON

A t l a n t i c

Los Angeles

Bermuda
(U.K.)

O c e a n

MEXICO

Hawaii
(U.S.A.)

P a c i f i c

MEXICO
CITY

BELIZE

Cayman Is.
(U.K.)

BAHAMAS

CUBA

*Turks &
Caicos Is*
(U.K.)

Puerto
Rico
(U.S.A.)

British Virgin Is (U.K.)
U.S. Virgin Is (U.S.A.)
Anguilla (U.K.)
ST KITTS & NEVIS
ANTIGUA & BARBUDA
Montserrat (U.K.)
Guadeloupe (FRANCE)
DOMINICA
Martinique (FRANCE)
ST LUCIA
BARBADOS
ST VINCENT & THE GRENADINES
GRENADA

CAPE
VERDE

JAMAICA

HAITI

DOM.
REP.

MARSHALL
IS

O c e a n

GUATEMALA
EL SALVADOR
NICARAGUA

HONDURAS

Aruba
(NETH.)

*Neth.
Ant.*
(NETH.)

NAURU

KIRIBATI

SOLOMON
ISLANDS

TUVALU

Tokelau
(N.Z.)

COSTA RICA

PANAMA

CARACAS

VENEZUELA

TRINIDAD
& TOBAGO

GUYANA
SURINAME

BOGOTÁ

COLOMBIA

French Guiana
(FRANCE)

VANUATU

*Wallis &
Futuna Is*
(FRANCE)

SAMOA

*American
Samoa*
(U.S.A.)

Cook Is
(N.Z.)

QUITO
ECUADOR

*New
Caledonia*
(FRANCE)

FIJI

TONGA

Niue
(N.Z.)

French Polynesia
(FRANCE)

LIMA

PERU

B R A Z I L

LA PAZ

BRASÍLIA

BOLIVIA

Pitcairn Is
(U.K.)

PARAGUAY

Rio de Janeiro

ASUNCIÓN

São Paulo

Norfolk Is.
(AUSTRALIA)

CHILE

NEW ZEALAND

A R G E N T I N A

URUGUAY

SANTIAGO

WELLINGTON

BUENOS
AIRES

MONTEVIDEO

*Falkland
Islands*
(U.K.)

*South Georgia & the
South Sandwich Islands*
(U.K.)

Digital Cartography by: Map Creation Ltd
Woodlands Park Avenue,
Maidenhead, Berks., SL6 3LT

The Middle East
and
North Africa
2003

The Middle East and North Africa 2003

49th Edition

Europa Publications
Taylor & Francis Group

LONDON AND NEW YORK

First published 1948

Forty-Ninth Edition 2003

© Europa Publications 2002
11 New Fetter Lane, London EC4P 4EE, England
(A member of the Taylor & Francis Group)

ISBN 1-85743-132-4
ISSN 0076-8502

Library of Congress Catalog Card Number 48–3250

Editor: Joanne Maher
Statistics Editor: Andrew Thomas
Regional Organizations Editors: Catriona Appeatu Holman, Helen Canton
Technology Editor: Ian Preston
Assistant Editors: Lucy Dean, Iain Frame, Tiara Misquitta, Annamarie Rowe,
Daniel Ward
Contributing Editor: Philip McIntyre
Editorial Co-ordinator: Mary Hill
Editorial Clerical Assistant: Zoë Hood

Typeset by MPG Dataworld and printed by Unwin Brothers Limited
The Gresham Press
Old Woking, Surrey

FOREWORD

After a further year of deep crisis in the Middle East, during which suicide bombings were directed with increasing frequency at Israeli military and civilian targets not just by 'rejectionist' Islamist groups but also by militants of secular and nationalist Palestinian groups, while Israel's armed forces had reoccupied Palestinian-administered territories for prolonged periods, targeting 'terrorists' and infrastructure and on several occasions acting physically to isolate the Palestinian leader, prospects for quelling the al-Aqsa *intifada* seemed remote. Meanwhile, it had been clearly demonstrated that far greater engagement in attempts at resolving the Israeli–Palestinian conflict would be a prerequisite for the US Administration of George W. Bush if its principal regional policy objective—that of bringing about 'regime change' in Iraq—was to be achieved at least with a degree of acquiescence on the part of the Arab world, if not its support.

The 49th edition of THE MIDDLE EAST AND NORTH AFRICA, which went to press as preparations began for the return of weapons inspectors to Iraq, provides detailed commentary on issues that continue to feature prominently in world headlines: conflict between Israel and the Palestinians; perceptions and reality of militant Islamism; and the prospects for Iraq and for the wider Middle East should the USA and its allies seek to extend the 'war against terror' to target the incumbent regime in Baghdad. Also embraced are regional themes that have attracted less international attention, among them the progression to the first elections to take place in Morocco under King Muhammad, and preparations for legislative voting in Bahrain, proclaimed a constitutional monarchy in early 2002, and in Turkey, where economic stability has continued to be severely undermined by political turbulence.

The Editor would once again like to thank all the contributors for their articles and advice, and the various governmental and non-governmental and other organizations that have assisted in the revision of statistical and directory material for this edition.

October 2002

ACKNOWLEDGEMENTS

The editors gratefully acknowledge the interest and co-operation of all the contributors to this volume, and of numerous national statistical and information offices, and government departments, as well as embassies in London and throughout the region, whose kind assistance in updating the material contained in THE MIDDLE EAST AND NORTH AFRICA is greatly appreciated.

We acknowledge particular indebtedness for permission to reproduce material from the following publications: the United Nations' *Demographic Yearbook, Statistical Yearbook, Industrial Commodity Statistics Yearbook* and *International Trade Statistics Yearbook*; the United Nations' Educational, Scientific and Cultural Organization's *Statistical Yearbook*; the United Nations' Economic and Social Commission for Western Asia's *National Accounts Studies of the ESCWA Region*; the Food and Agriculture Organization of the United Nations' Statistical Database and *Yearbook of Fishery Statistics*; the International Labour Office's *Yearbook of Labour Statistics*; the World Bank's *World Bank Atlas, Global Development Finance, World Development Report* and *World Development Indicators*; the International Monetary Fund's *International Financial Statistics* and *Government Finance Statistics Yearbook*; the World Tourism Organization's *Yearbook of Tourism Statistics*; and *The Military Balance 2001–2002*, a publication of the International Institute for Strategic Studies, Arundel House, 13–15 Arundel Street, London WC2R 3DX. We are also grateful to the Israeli embassy, London, for the use of two maps illustrating the disengagement agreements between Israel and Egypt (1974) and Israel and Syria. Our thanks also go to the following for particular assistance: Bank Markazi, Islamic Republic of Iran; Saudi Arabian Monetary Agency, Riyadh; United Nations Relief and Works Agency for Palestine Refugees in the Near East.

The following publications have been of special value in providing regular coverage of the affairs of the Middle East and North Africa region: *Middle East Economic Digest*; and *Keesing's Record of World Events*.

HEALTH AND WELFARE STATISTICS: SOURCES AND DEFINITIONS

Fertility Source: WHO, *The World Health Report* (2001). The number of children that would be born per woman, assuming no female mortality at child-bearing ages and the age-specific fertility rates of a specified country and reference period.

Under-5 mortality rate Source: UNDP, *Human Development Report* (2002). The ratio of registered deaths of children under 5 years to the total number of registered live births over the same period.

HIV/AIDS Source: UNDP, *Human Development Report* (2002). Estimated percentage of adults aged 15 to 49 years living with HIV/AIDS. < indicates 'fewer than'.

Health expenditure Source: WHO, *The World Health Report* (2001).
US $ per head (PPP)
International dollar estimates, derived by dividing local currency units by an estimate of their purchasing-power parity (PPP) compared with the US dollar. PPPs are the rates of currency conversion that equalize the purchasing power of different currencies by eliminating the differences in price levels between countries.
% of GDP
GDP levels for OECD countries follow the most recent UN System of National Accounts. For non-OECD countries a value was estimated by utilizing existing UN, IMF and World Bank data.
Public expenditure
Government health-related outlays plus expenditure by social schemes compulsorily affiliated with a sizeable share of the population, and extrabudgetary funds allocated to health services. Figures include grants or loans provided by international agencies, other national authorities, and sometimes commercial banks.

Access to water and sanitation Source: WHO, *Global Water Supply and Sanitation Assessment* (2000 Report). Defined in terms of the type of technology and levels of service afforded. For water, this includes house connections, public standpipes, boreholes with handpumps, protected dug wells, protected spring and rainwater collection; allowance is also made for other locally defined technologies. 'Access' is broadly defined as the availability of at least 20 litres per person per day from a source within 1 km of the user's dwelling. Sanitation is defined to include connection to a sewer or septic tank system, pour-flush latrine, simple pit or ventilated improved pit latrine, again with allowance for acceptable local technologies. Access to water and sanitation does not imply that the level of service or quality of water is 'adequate' or 'safe'.

Human Development Index (HDI) Source: UNDP, *Human Development Report* (2002). A summary of human development measured by three basic dimensions: prospects for a long and healthy life, measured by life expectancy at birth; knowledge, measured by adult literacy rate (two-thirds' weight) and the combined gross enrolment ratio in primary, secondary and tertiary education (one-third weight); and standard of living, measured by GDP per head (PPP US $). The index value obtained lies between zero and one. A value above 0.8 indicates high human development, between 0.5 and 0.8 medium human development, and below 0.5 low human development. Countries with insufficient data were excluded from the HDI. In total, 173 countries were ranked for 2000.

CONTENTS

CONTENTS

CONTENTS

PART THREE

Regional Information

REGIONAL ORGANIZATIONS

THE CONTRIBUTORS

Simon Chapman. Editor of *The Middle East and North Africa*, 1989–97.

Stephanie Cronin. Iran Heritage Research Fellow, Department of History, University College, Northampton, England; Senior Research Associate, Department of History, School of Oriental and African Studies, University of London, England.

Alan J. Day. Former Editor of *The Annual Register,* London, England; former Joint Editor of the *Political Handbook of the World,* Binghamton University, New York, USA.

Toby Dodge. Research Fellow, Centre for the Study of Globalisation and Regionalisation, University of Warwick, England; Associate Research Fellow, Middle East Programme, Royal Institute of International Affairs, London, England.

Richard German. Writer and researcher on international political and economic affairs.

Richard I. Lawless. Emeritus Reader in Middle Eastern Studies, University of Durham, England; Research Associate, Queen Elizabeth House, University of Oxford, England.

Jon Lunn. Occasional Teacher at the Development Studies Institute, London School of Economics, England; human rights consultant.

Dr Kamil Mahdi. Lecturer in the Economics of the Middle East and Director of the Programme of Gulf and Arabian Peninsula Studies, Institute of Arab and Islamic Studies, University of Exeter, England.

Nur Masalha. Senior Lecturer and Director of Holy Land Studies, St Mary's College, University of Surrey, England; Research Associate, Centre for Islamic and Middle Eastern Law, School of Oriental and African Studies, University of London, England.

Malise Ruthven. Former Lecturer at the Centre for the Study of Religions, University of Aberdeen, Scotland.

Elizabeth Taylor. Writer and researcher on international economic affairs.

Rodney Wilson. Professor of Economics, University of Durham, England.

ABBREVIATIONS

AAHO	Afro-Asian Housing Organization
AAPSO	Afro-Asian People's Solidarity Organization
Acad.	Academy
AD	Algerian dinars
AD	anno Domini
ADB	African Development Bank
ADC	Aide-de-camp
AED	UAE dirhams
Admin.	Administrative, Administration, Administrator
Admin.-Gen	Administrator-General
Agric.	Agriculture
AH	anno Hegirae (year of the Hegira)
a.i.	ad interim
AIDS	acquired immunodeficiency syndrome
AIWO	Agudath Israel World Organization
ALF	Arab Liberation Front
AM	Amplitude Modulation
a.m.	ante meridiem (before noon)
Apdo	Apartado (Post Box)
API	American Petroleum Institute
approx.	approximately
apptd	appointed
ARE	Arab Republic of Egypt
AŞ.	Anonim Şirketi (Joint-Stock Company)
Ass.	Assembly
Asscn, assn	Association
Assoc.	Associate
Asst	Assistant
ATUC	African Trade Union Confederation
AU	African Union
auth.	authorized
AUXERAP	Société auxiliaire de la régie du pétrole
Ave	Avenue
Avda	Avenida
BADEA	Banque arabe pour le développement economique en Afrique (Arab Bank for Economic Development in Africa)
BC	before Christ
b/d	barrels per day
BD	Bahrain dinars
Bd	Board
Bde	Brigade
Bldg	Building
Blvd	Boulevard
BP	Boîte Postale (Post Box)
br.(s)	branch(es)
Brig.	Brigadier
BST	British Standard Time
Bul.	Bulvar (Boulevard)
C	Centigrade
c.	circa
Cad.	Caddesi (Street)
CAFRAD	Centre africain de formation et de recherches administratives pour le développement
cap.	capital
Capt.	Captain
CARE	Co-operative for American Relief Everywhere
Cdre	Commodore
CE	Common era
cen.	central
CEN-SAD	Community of Sahel-Saharan States
CEO	Chief Executive Officer
cf.	confer (compare)
Chair.	Chairman/person/woman
Cie	Compagnie (Company)
c.i.f.	cost, insurance and freight
C-in-C	Commander-in-Chief
circ.	circulation
CIS	Commonwealth of Independent States
cm	centimetre(s)
CMEA	Council for Mutual Economic Assistance
cnr	corner
c/o	care of
Co	Company
Col	Colonel

Comm.	Commission
Commdr	Commander
Commdt	Commandant
Commr	Commissioner
Conf.	Conference
Confed.	Confederation
Cons.-Gen.	Consul-General
COO	Chief Operating Officer
Corpn	Corporation
Cttee	Committee
cu	cubic
cwt	hundredweight
Del.	Delegate, Delegation
Dep.	Deputy
dep.	deposits
Dept	Department
Devt	Development
DFLP	Democratic Front for the Liberation of Palestine
Dir	Director
Div.	Division
DPA	Deutsche Presse-Agentur
Dr	Doctor
DU	depleted uranium
dwt	dead weight tons
E	East, Eastern
EC	European Community
ECOSOC	Economic and Social Council (UN)
ECU	European Currency Unit(s)
Ed.(s)	Editor(s)
edn	edition
EFTA	European Free Trade Association
e.g.	exempli gratia (for example)
est.	established; estimate(d)
excl.	excluding
EU	European Union
Exec.	Executive
F	Fahrenheit
f.	founded
FAO	Food and Agriculture Organization
FAPS	Framework Agreement on Permanent Status
FCM	Federation of Muslim Councillors
Fed.	Federal, Federation
FIDES	Fonds d'investissement pour le développement economique et sociale de la France d'outre-mer
Flt	Flight
FM	Frequency Modulation
fmr(ly)	former(ly)
f.o.b.	free on board
Fr.	Franc
ft	foot (feet)
g	gram(s)
GAFTA	Greater Arab Free Trade Agreement
GATT	General Agreements on Tariffs and Trade
GCC	Gulf Co-operation Council
GDA	Gas Distribution Administration
GDP	gross domestic product
Gen.	General
GHQ	General Headquarters
GMT	Greenwich Mean Time
GNP	gross national product
Gov.	Governor
Govt	Government
grt	gross registered ton(s)
GW	gigawatt(s)
GWh	gigawatt hour(s)
ha	hectare(s)
HE	His (or Her) Excellency, His Eminence
HIV	human immunodeficiency virus
hl	hectolitre(s)
HM	His (or Her) Majesty
Hon.	Honorary; Honourable
HQ	Headquarters
HRH	His (or Her) Royal Highness

ABBREVIATIONS

IAEA	International Atomic Energy Authority
IATA	International Air Transport Association
ibid	ibidem (from the same source)
IBRD	International Bank for Reconstruction and Development
ICAO	International Civil Aviation Organization
ICATU	International Conference of Arab Trade Unions
ICFTU-AFRO	International Confederation of Free Trade Unions—African Regional Organization
IDA	International Development Association
IDF	Israeli Defence Forces
i.e.	id est (that is to say)
IFC	International Finance Corporation
IISS	International Institute of Strategic Studies
ILO	International Labour Office/Organization
IMF	International Monetary Fund
in(s)	inch(es)
Inc	Incorporated
incl.	include, including
Ind.	Independent
Insp.	Inspector
Inst.	Institute; Institution
Int.	International
IRF	International Road Federation
Is	Islands
IT	information technology
ITU	International Telecommunication Union
ISIC	International Standard Industrial Classification
Jr	Junior
Jt	Joint
kg	kilogram(s)
KFAED	Kuwait Fund for Arab Economic Development
km	kilometre(s)
kV	kilovolt(s)
kW	kilowatt(s)
kWh	kilowatt hour(s)
lb	pound(s)
Legis.	Legislative
LNG	liquefied natural gas
LPG	liquefied petroleum gas
Lt	Lieutenant
Ltd	Limited
m	metre(s)
m.	million
Maj.	Major
Man.	Manager, Managing
MB	Bachelor of Medicine
MD	Doctor of Medicine
mem.(s)	member(s)
Mfg	Manufacturing
Mgr	Monseigneur, Monsignor
Mil.	Military
mm	millimetre(s)
MP	Member of Parliament
MSS	Manuscripts
Mt	Mount
MTBE	methyl tertiary butyl ether
MW	megawatt(s); medium wave
MWh	megawatt hour(s)
N	North, Northern
n.a.	not available
Nat.	National
NATO	North Atlantic Treaty Organization
NDRC	National Defence Research Council
NE	North-East
NECCCRW	Near East Christian Council Committee for Refugee Work
NEPAD	New Partnership for Africa's Development
n.e.s.	not elsewhere specified
NGLs	natural gas liquids
NGO(s)	non-governmental organization(s)
n.i.e.	not included elsewhere
no.	number
nr	near
nrt	net registered ton(s)
NW	North-West
OAPEC	Organization of Arab Petroleum Exporting Countries
OAU	Organization of African Unity

OECD	Organisation for Economic Co-operation and Development
OIC	Organization of the Islamic Conference
OPEC	Organization of the Petroleum Exporting Countries
Org.(s)	Organization(s)
oz	ounce(s)
p.	page
PA	Palestinian Authority
p.a.	per annum
Parl.	Parliament(ary)
PCC	Palestinian Central Council
PDFLP	Popular Democratic Front for the Liberation of Palestine
Perm.	Permanent
Perm. Rep.	Permanent Representative
PFLP	Popular Front for the Liberation of Palestine
PhD	Doctor of Philosophy
PLC	Palestinian Legislative Council; Public Limited Company
PLO	Palestine Liberation Organization
p.m.	post meridiem (after noon)
PNA	Palestinian National Authority
PNC	Palestine National Council
POB	Post Office Box
PPP	purchasing-power parity
Pres.	President
Prof.	Professor
Propr	Proprietor
Pty	Proprietary
p.u.	paid up
publ.(s)	publication(s)
Publr	Publisher
q.v.	quod vide (to which refer)
RCC	Revolutionary Command Council (Iraq, Libya)
RCD	Regional Co-operation for Development
Rd	Road
RDA	Rassemblement démocratique africain
regd	registered
Rep.	Representative
Repub.	Republic
res	reserves
retd	retired
Rev.	Reverend
ro-ro	roll-on roll-off
S	South, Southern
SDR(s)	special drawing right(s)
SE	South-East
Sec.	Secretary
Secr.	Secretariat
SITC	Standard International Trade Classification
Soc.	Society; Société
Sok.	Sokak (Street)
SpA	Società per Azioni (Limited Company)
sq	square (in measurements)
Sq.	Square
Sr	Senior
St	Saint; Street
Stn	Station
subs.	subscribed
Supt	Superintendent
SW	South-West
Tapline	Trans-Arabian Pipeline Company
TAŞ	Türk Anonim Şirketi (Turkish Joint-Stock Company)
tel.	telephone
Treas.	Treasurer
trans.	translated; translation
TV	Television
UA	Unit(s) of Account
UAE	United Arab Emirates
UAR	United Arab Republic
UBAF	Union des banques arabes et françaises
UHF	Ultra High Frequency
UK	United Kingdom
UN	United Nations
UNCTAD	United Nations Conference on Trade and Development
UNDOF	United Nations Disengagement Observer Force
UNDP	United Nations Development Programme
UNEF	United Nations Emergency Force

ABBREVIATIONS

UNEP	United Nations Environment Programme	UPAF	Union Postale Africaine (African Postal Union)
UNESCO	United Nations Educational, Scientific and Cultural Organization	UP	University Press
		UPI	United Press International
UNFICYP	United Nations Peace-keeping Force in Cyprus	USA (US)	United States of America (United States)
UNFPA	United Nations Population Fund	USIS	United States Information Services
UNICEF	United Nations Children's Fund	USSR	Union of Soviet Socialist Republics
UNIDO	United Nations Industrial Development Organization	UTA	Union de Transports Aériens
UNIFIL	United Nations Interim Force in Lebanon	VAT	Value-Added Tax
Univ.	University	VHF	Very High Frequency
UNMEM	United Nations Middle East Mission	vol.(s)	volume(s)
UNMOVIC	United Nations Monitoring, Verification and Inspection Commission	W	West, Western
UNRWA	United Nations Relief and Works Agency for Palestine Refugees in the Near East	WFTU	World Federation of Trade Unions
		WHO	World Health Organization
UNSCOM	United Nations Special Commission	WTO	World Trade Organization
UNTSO	United Nations Truce Supervision Organization	yr	year

INTERNATIONAL TELEPHONE CODES

To make international calls to telephone and fax numbers listed in *The Middle East and North Africa*, dial the international code of the country from which you are calling, followed by the appropriate country code for the organization you wish to call (listed below), followed by the area code (if applicable) and telephone or fax number listed in the entry.

	Country code	+ GMT*
Algeria	213	+1
Bahrain	973	+3
Cyprus	357	+2
'Turkish Republic of Northern Cyprus'	90 392	+2
Egypt	20	+2
Iran	98	+3½
Iraq	964	+3
Israel	972	+2
Jordan	962	+2
Kuwait	965	+3
Lebanon	961	+2
Libya	218	+1
Morocco	212	0

	Country code	+ GMT*
Oman	968	+4
Palestinian Autonomous Areas	970	+2
Qatar	974	+3
Saudi Arabia	966	+3
Spain (for Spanish North Africa)	34	+1
Syria	963	+2
Tunisia	216	+1
Turkey	90	+2
United Arab Emirates	971	+4
Yemen	967	+3

* Time difference in hours + Greenwhich Mean Time (GMT). The times listed compare the standard (winter) times. Some countries adopt Summer (Daylight Saving) Times—i.e. + 1 hour—for part of the year.

EXPLANATORY NOTE ON THE DIRECTORY SECTION

The Directory section of each chapter is arranged under the following headings, where they apply:

THE CONSTITUTION

THE GOVERNMENT
　HEAD OF STATE
　CABINET/COUNCIL OF MINISTERS
　MINISTRIES

LEGISLATURE

POLITICAL ORGANIZATIONS

DIPLOMATIC REPRESENTATION

JUDICIAL SYSTEM

RELIGION

THE PRESS

PUBLISHERS

BROADCASTING AND COMMUNICATIONS
　TELECOMMUNICATIONS
　RADIO
　TELEVISION

FINANCE
　CENTRAL BANK
　STATE BANKS
　COMMERCIAL BANKS
　DEVELOPMENT BANKS
　INVESTMENT BANKS

　SAVINGS BANKS
　ISLAMIC BANKS
　FOREIGN BANKS
　STOCK EXCHANGE
　INSURANCE

TRADE AND INDUSTRY
　GOVERNMENT AGENCIES
　DEVELOPMENT ORGANIZATIONS
　CHAMBERS OF COMMERCE AND INDUSTRY
　INDUSTRIAL AND TRADE ASSOCIATIONS
　EMPLOYERS' ORGANIZATIONS
　HYDROCARBONS
　UTILITIES
　MAJOR COMPANIES
　CO-OPERATIVES
　TRADE UNIONS

TRANSPORT
　RAILWAYS
　ROADS
　SHIPPING
　CIVIL AVIATION

TOURISM

DEFENCE

EDUCATION

TRANSCRIPTION OF ARABIC NAMES

The Arabic language is used over a vast area. Though the written language and the script are standard throughout the Middle East, the spoken language and also the pronunciation of the written signs exhibit wide variation from place to place. This is reflected, and even exaggerated, in the different transcriptions in use in different countries. The same words, names and even letters will be pronounced differently by an Egyptian, a Lebanese, or an Iraqi—they will be heard and transcribed differently by an Englishman, a Frenchman, or an Italian. There are several more or less scientific systems of transliteration in use, sponsored by learned societies and Middle Eastern governments, most of them requiring diacritical marks to indicate Arabic letters for which there are no Latin equivalents.

Arabic names occurring in the historical and geographical sections of this book have been rendered in the system most commonly used by British and American Orientalists, but with the omission of the diacritical signs. For the convenience of the reader, these are explained and annotated below. The system used is a transliteration—i.e. it is based on the writing, which is standard throughout the Arab world, and not on the pronunciation, which varies from place to place. In a few cases consistency has been sacrificed in order to avoid replacing a familiar and accepted form by another which, although more accurate, would be unrecognizable.

Consonants

d   represents two Arabic letters. The second, or emphatic *d*, is transliterated *ḍ*. It may also be represented, for some dialects, by *dh* and by *z*, e.g. Qāḍī, qadhi, qazi.

dh   in literary Arabic and some dialects, pronounced like English *th* in *this*. In many dialects pronounced *z* or *d*.

gh   A strongly guttural *g*—sometimes written *g*, e.g. Baghdād, Bagdad.

h   represents two Arabic letters. The second, more guttural *h*, is transliterated *ḥ*, e.g. Husain, Husein.

j   as English *j* in *John,* also represented by *dj* and *g*. In Egypt this letter is pronounced as a hard *g*, and may be thus transcribed (with *u* before *e* and *i*), e.g. Najib, Nadjib, Nagib, Naguib, Neguib.

kh   as *ch* in Scottish *loch,* also sometimes represented by *ch* and *h*, e.g. Khalīl, Chalil, Halil.

q   A guttural *k*, pronounced farther back in the throat. Also transcribed *ḳ, k,* and, for some dialects, *g*, e.g. Waqf, Waḳf, Wakf, wagf.

s   represents two Arabic letters. The second, emphatic *s*, is transliterated *ṣ*. It may also be represented by *ç*, e.g. Sāliḥ, Saleh, Çaleh.

sh   as in English *ship*. The French transcription *ch* is found in Algeria, Lebanon, Morocco, Syria and Tunisia, e.g. Shaikh, Sheikh, Cheikh.

t   represents two Arabic letters. The second, emphatic *t*, is transliterated *ṭ*.

th   in literary Arabic and some dialects, pronounced as English *th* in *through*. In many dialects pronounced *t* or *s*, e.g. Thābit, Tabit, Sabit.

w   as in English, but often represented by *ou* or *v*, e.g. Wādā, Vadi, Oued.

z   represents two Arabic letters. The second, or emphatic *z*, is transliterated *ẓ*. It may also be represented, for some dialects, by *dh* or *d*, e.g. Ḥāfiẓ, Hafidh, Hafid.

’   A glottal stop, as in Cockney *'li'l bo'ls'*. May also represent the sound transliterated ‘, a deep guttural with no English equivalent.

Vowels

The Arabic script only indicates three short vowels, three long vowels, and two diphthongs, as follows:

a   as in English *hat,* and often rendered *e,* e.g. balad, beled, emir, amir; with emphatics or gutturals usually pronounced as *u* in *but,* e.g. Khalīfa, Baghdād.

i   as in English *bit*. Sometimes rendered *e,* e.g. jihād, jehād.

u   as in English *good*. Often pronounced and written *o,* e.g. Muhammad, Mohammad.

In some Arabic dialects, particularly those of North Africa, unaccented short vowels are often omitted altogether, and long vowels shortened, e.g. Oued for Wādī, bled for balad, etc.

ā   Long *a,* variously pronounced as in *sand, dart* and *hall*.

ī   As *ee* in *feet*. In early books often rendered *ee*.

ū   As *oo* in *boot*. The French transcription *ou* is often met in English books, e.g. Maḥmūd, Mahmood, Mahmoud.

ai   Pronounced in classical Arabic as English *i* in *hide,* in colloquial Arabic as *a* in *take*. Variously transcribed as *ai, ay, ei, ey* and *ê,* e.g. sheikh, shaikh, shaykh, etc.

aw   Pronounced in classical Arabic as English *ow* in *town,* in colloquial Arabic as in *grow*. Variously rendered *aw, ew, au, ô, av, ev,* e.g. Tawfīq, Taufiq, Tevfik, etc.

Sun- and Moon-Letters

In Arabic pronunciation, when the word to which the definite article, *al,* is attached begins with one of certain letters called 'Sun-letters', the *l* of the article changes to the initial letter in question, e.g. *al-shamsu* (the sun) is pronounced *ash-shamsu; al-rajulu* (the man) is pronounced *ar-rajulu*. Accordingly, in this book, where the article is attached to a word beginning with a Sun-letter, it has been rendered phonetically.

There are 14 Sun-letters in the Arabic alphabet, which are transcribed as: d, dh, n, r, s, sh, t, th, z, zh (d, s, t and z, and their emphatic forms, ḍ, ṣ, ṭ and ẓ, are not differentiated in this book). The remaining 15 letters in the Arabic alphabet are known as 'Moon-letters'.

TURKISH ORTHOGRAPHY AND PRONUNCIATION

Turkish has been written in Roman characters since 1928. The following pronunciations are invariable:

c   hard *j*, as in *majority, jam*.

ç   *ch,* as in *church*.

g   hard *g*, as in *go, big*.

ğ   not voiced, or pronounced *y*; Ereğli is pronounced *erayly*.

ı   short vowel, as the second vowel of *'centre',* or French *'le'*.

i   *i* sound of *India, bitter* (NOT as in *bite, might*).

o   *o,* as in *hot, boss*.

ö   *i* sound of *'birth',* or French *'oeuvre'*.

ş   *sh,* as in *cash*.

u   as in *do, too,* German *'um'*.

ü   as in *burette,* German *'Hütte'*.

CALENDAR OF POLITICAL EVENTS IN THE MIDDLE EAST AND NORTH AFRICA, OCTOBER 2001–SEPTEMBER 2002

2001

OCTOBER

2 Maj.-Gen. Sheikh Rashid bin Abdullah al-Khalifa was appointed Chief of Staff of the Bahraini Defence Force.

Iran signed a military co-operation accord with Russia, reportedly entailing annual sales to Iran of Russian weaponry worth some US $300m.

Iraq claimed that at least two civilians were killed in the first of a number of aerial attacks carried out by US and British military aircraft during October on alleged Iraqi military installations in the southern and northern air exclusion zones.

US President George W. Bush explicitly stated for the first time that he was in favour of the eventual establishment of a 'viable' Palestinian state.

3 The Turkish Grand National Assembly approved a set of constitutional amendments, including a relaxation of restrictions on use of the Kurdish language. the amendments were in large part designed to facilitate Turkey's admission to the European Union. Further reforms were formally approved on 22 November and on 3 August 2002, most notably the abolition of the death penalty except in time of war.

8 Syria was elected for a two-year term as a non-permanent member of the UN Security Council.

10 The Turkish Grand National Assembly authorized the Government to send Turkish troops abroad to participate in the US-led military operation in Afghanistan against bases of the militant Islamist al-Qa'ida (Base) organization and the fundamentalist Taliban, in response to al-Qa'ida's presumed responsibility for the suicide attacks against the mainland USA in September 2001. The stationing of more foreign troops in Turkey was also authorized.

15 Yemen's Minister of the Interior confirmed that 21 individuals had been detained in Yemen on suspicion of involvement with the al-Qa'ida network.

17 The Israeli Minister of Tourism, Rechavam Ze'evi of the right-wing Haichud Haleumi-Israel B'Aitainu alliance, was assassinated in East Jerusalem by militants of the Popular Front for the Liberation of Palestine (PFLP), apparently in response to the killing of PFLP leader Abu Ali Moustafa in late August 2001.

18 The Israel Government suspended all contacts with the Palestinian (National) Authority (PA), and ordered the Israeli Defence Forces (IDF) to enter a number of Palestinian-administered population centres in the West Bank; 14 Palestinians were killed in the reoccupation of Bethlehem.

Morocco unexpectedly recalled its ambassador to Spain.

30–31 Prime Minister Tony Blair of the United Kingdom was received for talks in Damascus, Syria, by President Bashar al-Assad. Blair attempted to secure Syrian support for the US-led 'coalition against terror', but the two leaders openly disagreed over the concept of 'terrorism'.

NOVEMBER

5, 9 Changes to the composition and structure of the Omani Council of Ministers were implemented.

8 The Government of Lebanon announced its refusal to comply with US requests for the imposition of financial sanctions against Hezbollah, including the freezing of the organization's assets. Hezbollah had earlier in the month been included on a list issued by the US Department of State of 'terrorist' organizations, but the Lebanese authorities asserted that Hezbollah was a legitimate resistance movement, not a terrorist organization.

11 Iran's largest political trial since the Islamic Revolution began in Tehran. More than 30 activists of Nehzat-e Azadi-ye Iran charged with acting against national security and plotting to overthrow the Islamic regime. Custodial sentences of up to 10 years were imposed on the activists by the Revolutionary Court in late July 2002, and Nehzat-e Azadi was officially banned.

12 Iraqi troops were reported to have fired across the demilitarized zone into Kuwait, prompting the Kuwaiti authorities to refer the incident to the UN.

14 Israel announced that its recent military operation in the West Bank had achieved its objectives, and that a phased withdrawal would begin. Some 79 Palestinians had been killed during the Israeli incursions, and scores of arrests had been made.

19 US Secretary of State Colin Powell announced the appointment of Gen. (retd) Anthony Zinni as US envoy to the Middle East.

21 A major reorganization of the Egyptian Council of Ministers included the abolition of the Ministry of the Economy and the devolution of most of its power to conduct monetary policy to the Central Bank of Egypt.

23 King Abdullah of Jordan appointed a new Senate.

29 UN Security Council Resolution 1382 extended the oil-for-food programme for Iraq for a further six-month period, effective from 1 December; the resolution provided for the implementation at the end of this 11th phase of a new mechanism for the delivery of goods to Iraq.

DECEMBER

1–2 Responsibility for suicide bombings in West Jerusalem and Haifa, in which 25 Israelis were killed, was claimed by the militant Islamist Hamas in reprisal for the deaths in late November of five Palestinian youths in the Gaza Strip and of a senior Hamas military leader in the West Bank.

2 On the 30th anniversary of the creation of the United Arab Emirates (UAE), the Supreme Council of Rulers re-elected Sheikh Zayed bin Sultan an-Nahyan as President of the UAE for a seventh five-year term.

3 The IDF initiated attacks against PA infrastructure in the West Bank and Gaza, disabling PA President Yasser Arafat's helicopter fleet and destroying the runway at Gaza international airport. Israel stated that Arafat would only be able to leave Ramallah (to where the PA leader had relocated in anticipation of military action) once PA security forces had complied with requests for the arrest of those named on an Israeli list of militants suspected of planning attacks on Israel.

4 The first meeting in four years between the Greek Cypriot President, Glavkos Klerides, and Rauf Denktaş, President of the 'Turkish Republic of Northern Cyprus' ('TRNC'), resulted in an agreement to recommence direct talks, under UN auspices, on the future of the island 'without preconditions'.

10 Trial proceedings began against Azmi Bishara, the most prominent Arab Israeli deputy in the Knesset (legislature), on charges of supporting terrorism and of undermining the Jewish State; Bishara's parliamentary immunity had been revoked in November.

13 Extensive government changes were announced in Syria, with new ministers being appointed notably to the finance, economy and trade, and petroleum and mineral resources portfolios.

15 King Abdullah of Jordan issued a decree abolishing the Ministry of Information; the ministry was to be replaced by a Media High Council.

16 In a televised address, Yasser Arafat demanded a 'complete cessation of military activities' by Palestinian groups, condemning suicide bombings and ordering the closure of several institutions affiliated to Islamist organizations. Hamas and Islamic Jihad were reported to have agreed to cease armed operations inside Israel.

18 An armed assault by Yemeni security forces on villages in Harib province, in a stated effort to apprehend suspected al-Qa'ida activists, resulted in 12 reported deaths.

25 Hossein Loqmanian became the first serving member of the Iranian Majlis (parliament) to be gaoled since the 1979 Revolution. Loqmanian was sentenced to 10 months' imprisonment, having been found guilty of libel and slander against the judiciary, but was released on 15 January 2002, after protests by the Majlis Speaker and deputies led to the intervention of Iran's spiritual leader, Ayatollah Khamenei.

27 Minister of Defence Binyamin Ben-Eliezer was elected leader of the Israel's Labour Party.

29 A new General People's Committee Secretary for the Economy and Trade was appointed in Libya.

30–31 The 22nd summit meeting of the Co-operation Council for the Arab States of the Gulf (the Gulf Co-operation Council—GCC) approved the extension to Yemen of membership of several non-political committees of the organization.

2002

JANUARY

3 Israeli naval forces seized a freighter, the *Karine A,* in international waters of the Red Sea; the freighter was found to be carrying some 50 metric tons of weaponry, alleged to be en route from Iran for use by Palestinians in the Gaza Strip.

A brief lull in violence between Israel and the Palestinians, during which the PA had instructed Palestinian security forces to crack down on militant groups, came to an end with an attack by Hamas on an army outpost near the Gaza Strip, in which four Israeli soldiers and two assailants were killed. The IDF responded the following day with an incursion into the Rafah refugee camp, and with attacks on the international airport and against PA police and naval bases in the Gaza Strip.

10 Turkey's Constitutional Court banned the leader of the Islamist AK Partisi (Justice and Development Party), Reçep Tayyıp Erdogan, from contesting the next general election on the grounds that his conviction on a sedition charge in 1999 disqualified him from politics.

14 A new Jordanian Government was announced, under incumbent Prime Minster Ali Abu ar-Ragheb.

15 The Secretary-General of the PFLP, Ahmad Saadat, was arrested by Palestinian security forces.

19 Amr Muhammad Moussa, Secretary-General of the League of Arab States (the Arab League) held talks in Baghdad with President Saddam Hussain; Moussa thus became the first Iraqi head of the Arab League to visit Iraq since the Iraqi invasion of Kuwait in 1990.

21 Presidents Klerides and Denktaş commenced thrice-weekly formal negotiations on the Cyprus issue, hosted by the UN Secretary-General's Special Adviser, Alvaro de Soto.

21–22 Serious rioting broke out in Ma'an, in southern Jordan, following the death there of a youth in police custody; one police-officer died in the clashes.

22 Maj.-Gen. Hassan at-Turkmani was appointed Chief of Staff of the Syrian Armed Forces.

24 Elie Hobeika, former head of the Christian Lebanese Forces militia in Lebanon, was killed by a car bomb in Beirut.

19 Sheikh Zayed bin Sultan an-Nahyan, President of the UAE, formally endorsed a decree that sought to prohibit the 'laundering' of funds through the UAE banking sector; the decree also formally established a national commission to seek to combat such practices.

19 A suicide bombing in West Jerusalem, in which one Israeli was killed, was the first by a Palestinian woman; the bomber was acting on behalf of the nationalist al-Aqsa Martyrs Brigades.

29 In his State of the Union address, US President George W. Bush identified Iran and Iraq as forming (with the Democratic People's Republic of Korea) an 'axis of evil', responsible for harbouring terrorists and intent on developing weapons of mass destruction.

FEBRUARY

4 UN Secretary-General Kofi Annan announced that he had received, via the Secretary-General of the Arab League, a communication from President Saddam Hussain of Iraq expressing willingness to resume dialogue with the UN 'without preconditions'; talks had been suspended a year earlier.

6 US Secretary of State Colin Powell stated that the USA was prepared to act unilaterally, if necessary, to achieve 'regime change' in Iraq.

8 Antar Zouabri, national 'emir' of the militant Groupe islamique armé, was killed by Algerian security forces.

9 Kuwait's Council of Ministers accepted the resignation of the Minister of Oil, tendered following an explosion at the Raudhatain oilfield on 31 January in which four people were killed.

10 Salih ibn Humayd was appointed Chairman of the Saudi Majlis ash-Shoura, following the death of Sheikh Muhammad ibn Ibrahim al-Jubair on 24 January.

11 Jordan's State Security Court imposed a death sentence on Raed Hijazi, a Jordanian-US citizen convicted of plotting terrorist attacks; Hijazi had been convicted *in absentia* in 2000, and was retried following his detention in Syria and extradition to Jordan in late 2001.

12 Acting on intelligence gathered from suspected al-Qa'ida and Taliban members under detention at the US military base at Guantánamo Bay, Cuba, US intelligence officers published a list of 17 individuals with strong links to Yemen whom they believed to be engaged in efforts to perpetrate imminent acts of terrorism in the USA or against US targets in the Gulf region. The following day a suspected al-Qa'ida militant blew himself up as Yemeni security forces attempted to arrest him in the capital, San'a.

14 Sheikh Hamad bin Isa al-Khalifa declared Bahrain to be a constitutional monarchy and proclaimed himself King.

19 Israeli forces launched an assault on Yasser Arafat's headquarters in Gaza, in response to the shooting of

9 Lt-Gen. Moshe Ya'alon was named as Israel's armed forces Chief of Staff.

11–22 A crisis developed in Morocco's relations with Spain after 12 Moroccan troops occupied the uninhabited islet of Perejil (called Leila in Morocco), west of the Spanish North African enclave of Ceuta. Spanish troops forcibly removed the occupying troops on 17 July, and on the same day Spain withdrew its ambassador to Morocco. Following intensive mediation by the US Secretary of State, the Moroccan and Spanish Ministers of Foreign Affairs agreed to return to the *status quo ante* regarding the islet.

23 An Israeli air-strike on a residential building in Gaza City resulted in the deaths of some 15 Palestinians (including a leader of Hamas' military wing, as well as several children).

29 The Gesher leader, David Levy, withdrew from the Israeli Cabinet; Gesher had, along with the National Religious Party, joined Ariel Sharon's coalition in April.

31 Iran and Russia agreed a 10-year programme of bilateral co-operation in the nuclear power industry.

At least seven Israelis were killed in a Hamas suicide bombing at the Hebrew University in Jerusalem.

AUGUST

5 Following consultations with the Security Council, UN Secretary-General Kofi Annan rejected an invitation issued by Iraq, on 1 August, for senior UN weapons inspectors to visit Iraq for preliminary technical discussions on the resumption of inspections.

10 Turkey's political crisis deepened with the resignation of the Minister of State responsible for economic policy, Kemal Derviş.

13 President Muhammad Khatami of Iran became the first Iranian Head of State for 40 years to visit Afghanistan, where he held discussions with President Hamid Karzai.

Two people were killed in the worst factional fighting for several years at the Ain el-Hilweh Palestinian refugee camp in Lebanon.

15 A group representing 900 relatives of victims of the September 2001 suicide attacks on the US mainland filed a civil suit in Washington, DC, against senior Saudi officials and institutions (and the Government of Sudan), seeking compensation amounting to US $1,000,000m. for their alleged funding of al-Qa'ida activities.

18 Israel and the PA signed a security accord, termed the 'Gaza, Bethlehem First' plan; Israeli troops began withdrawing from Bethlehem the following day.

19 Iraq's National Assembly unanimously approved the RCC's nomination, four days earlier, of Saddam Hussain to serve a further seven-year term as President.

Reports emerged that Sabri Khalil al-Banna ('Abu Nidal'), who as head of the Palestinian Fatah Revolutionary Council had been held responsible for numerous terrorist attacks in the Middle East and Europe in the 1970s and 1980s, had been found dead in Baghdad. Iraqi officials subsequently stated that he had committed suicide.

SEPTEMBER

1 The Israeli Minister of Defence ordered an internal military investigation into the actions of Israeli soldiers, following the deaths of 12 West Bank Palestinians during a 24-hour period.

4 Violent clashes between the Lebanese army and Palestinian militants at the al-Jalil refugee camp in Lebanon resulted in the deaths of one soldier and three Palestinians.

5 Some 100 British and US military strike and support aircraft conducted an air attack on Iraq's western defence command centre at Anbar, with the stated objective of enforcing the air exclusion zones imposed following the 1990–91 Gulf crisis.

Trial proceedings against Marwan Barghouthi, the Fatah leader in the West Bank, were initiated in Tel-Aviv.

8 Leaders of the Patriotic Union of Kurdistan and the Kurdistan Democratic Party, meeting in Arbil, signed a political co-operation agreement providing for the full participation of both groups in the restored Iraqi Kurdistan National Assembly.

9 Talks in Paris, France, between Presidents Klerides and Denktaş, hosted by UN Secretary-General Kofi Annan, failed to break the impasse in negotiations on the future of Cyprus.

11 The entire Palestinian Cabinet resigned, in order to prevent a vote of 'no confidence' in the Palestinian Legislative Council.

16 Iraq indicated its willingness to readmit UN weapons inspectors 'without preconditions'.

19 Following the deaths of seven Israelis in two suicide attacks, Israeli forces again entered Arafat's Ramallah compound (where Israel alleged 'wanted' militants were sheltering) and began the systematic destruction of buildings there.

24 King Hamad of Bahrain enacted legislation allowing trade unions to operate in the kingdom.

The UN Security Council adopted Resolution 1435, demanding that Israel cease measures in and around Ramallah, and the 'expeditious withdrawal of Israeli occupying forces from Palestinian cities' towards positions held prior to September 2000, and calling on the PA to make good its expressed commitment to bring to justice those responsible for 'terrorist acts'.

27 The first legislative elections in Morocco since the accession of King Muhammad VI took place. Early results indicated that the Union socialiste des forces populaires, the party of Prime Minister Abd ar-Rahman el-Youssoufi, and its coalition partner Istiqlal had performed well, while the moderate Islamist Parti de la justice et du développement had made strong gains.

29 Yasser Arafat emerged from confinement in Ramallah, after Israeli forces redeployed some distance from the presidential compound.

30 Officials of UNMOVIC and the International Atomic Energy Agency began discussions in Vienna with Iraqi representatives to devise a comprehensive agreement for the return of weapons inspectors to Iraq.

PART ONE
General Survey

ARAB–ISRAELI RELATIONS 1967–2002

PAUL COSSALI

Israel's decisive victory in the June war of 1967 had resulted in the capture of considerable territory from its Arab neighbours. In addition to the Egyptian Sinai and the Syrian Golan Heights, Israel also occupied the last remaining areas of historic Palestine; the West Bank of the Jordan river (including Arab East Jerusalem) and the Gaza Strip. The conflict had created a further 380,000 refugees and brought a million Arabs under Israeli occupation. The overwhelming majority of these were Palestinian. The speed with which Israel's armed forces had routed their Arab adversaries dramatically underlined the Jewish State's military superiority. With its acquisition of Arab land Israel now possessed valuable bargaining chips for any future negotiations towards a settlement of the Middle East conflict. Israeli euphoria was mirrored by deep depression in the Arab world. The sense of national humiliation that had accompanied the 'loss' of Palestine in 1948 was now painfully revisited. For the Palestinians the June war had exposed the emptiness of Nasser's rhetoric when he had promised that Arab might would erase the Zionist entity and recover Palestinian rights.

RESOLUTION 242

At the end of August 1967 Arab leaders met for a summit conference in Khartoum, Sudan. The conference reiterated the opposition of the assembled states to recognition or direct negotiations with Israel. Israel's Prime Minister meanwhile affirmed that Israel would refuse to withdraw from any of the Arab territories occupied in June without negotiations. The gulf between the two parties bedevilled early attempts by the UN Security Council to agree on a resolution to address the crisis. While the Arab world, backed by the USSR, was adamant that the UN should demand the withdrawal of Israeli forces from occupied Arab territory, Israel and the USA were opposed to draft resolutions that did not provide adequate guarantees of Israel's security. A formula meeting the minimum demands of both sides eventually found expression in UN Resolution 242 (see Documents on Palestine, p. 57). Adopted unanimously by the Security Council on 22 November 1967, the resolution emphasized the 'inadmissibility' of the acquisition of territory by war; and called 'for a just and lasting peace in which every state in the area can live in security' and for a settlement of the 'refugee problem'. Resolution 242 called on Israel to withdraw from 'territories occupied in the recent conflict', but crucially did not specify the extent of the withdrawal. Arguments generated by the ambiguities and omissions of Resolution 242 were to be a theme of the Arab–Israeli debate for years to come.

Israel's Prime Minister, Levi Eshkol, did not reject Resolution 242, but stated his preference for direct negotiations leading to agreements between Israel and its neighbours. In late 1968 Israel presented a nine-point plan for a Middle East peace to the UN General Assembly, which did not offer an Israeli withdrawal but proposed mutually agreeable 'boundary settlements'. The proposal elicited no response from an Arab world that remained highly suspicious of Israeli intentions. Speculation that Israel planned to remain in control of conquered lands had been aroused by Israel's de facto annexation of Arab East Jerusalem in the summer of 1967 and the establishment of Jewish settlements on the West Bank in September of the same year. Despite the existence of a formal cease-fire, violent incidents continued to capture the headlines. There were frequent artillery duels across the Suez Canal, and in Gaza Palestinian fighters fought an increasingly desperate campaign against the occupying army. Raids by Palestinian irregulars across the Jordanian border were met with heavy Israeli reprisals, as were the increasing incidences of the hijacking of Israeli airliners by Palestinian radicals. In response to one of these attacks Israeli commandos raided Beirut airport in late 1968, destroying 13 aircraft. Israel drew international condemnation for its assault on Lebanon. Nevertheless, the newly installed Administration

under Richard Nixon in the USA went ahead with the earlier decision of Lyndon B. Johnson's Administration to supply the Israelis with 50 Phantom aircraft, a decision which confirmed the region as a major arena of US–Soviet rivalry. In July 1969, after continued fighting along both the Suez and Jordan fronts, Egypt's President Gamal Abd an-Nasir (Nasser) publicly gave up hope of a peaceful settlement and predicted that 'a war of attrition' would be necessary to dislodge Israel from the territories occupied in 1967.

Attempts by the USSR, the USA, France and the United Kingdom to obtain agreement on the implementation of Resolution 242 made little initial progress. The major obstacles remained Arab insistence that the resolution should be implemented in toto and did not require negotiation, and Israel's demand for direct negotiation to decide on new international boundaries. In December 1969 the US Secretary of State, William Rogers, produced a set of proposals designed to steer a middle course between the conflicting viewpoints. Known as the Rogers Plan, its most important aspect was that it made clear the US opinion that there should be only minor modifications to the pre-June 1967 boundaries. Although Israel's Minister of Foreign Affairs, Abba Eban, had assured the international community that 'everything was negotiable', Israel's initial response to Rogers was antagonistic, apparently revealing serious divisions within the Israeli Cabinet over the extent of compliance with Resolution 242. In January 1970 the Israeli air force launched a series of strikes on Egyptian targets, prompting Egypt to call for greater assistance from the USSR and for the USA to intensify diplomatic initiatives in the region. Israeli requests for more Phantoms were turned down by Nixon, and behind the scenes considerable pressure was placed on Israel to renew its cease-fire with Egypt and to promise a withdrawal from most of the territory occupied after the June war. No such undertaking on the latter issue was given publicly, but sufficient understanding was achieved in private for Rogers to relaunch his proposals with the backing of the four major powers. In July 1970 Nasser signalled Egyptian acceptance of US calls for a renewal of the cease-fire, to be followed by UN-mediated negotiations on the implementation of Resolution 242. A week later, after receiving assurances on the future supply of arms, the Israeli Government agreed to the US proposals. However, it added the provisos that Israel would never return to the pre-war borders and that none of its troops would be withdrawn from the cease-fire line until a binding peace agreement had been signed. The renewed cease-fire along the Suez Canal came into effect on 8 August and was to last for 90 days. During this time the two sides were to engage in indirect negotiations through the UN Special Representative, Dr Gunnar Jarring. These negotiations were suspended after a single meeting when Israel recalled its diplomats in protest at the movement of Soviet missiles behind the Egyptian lines.

'Black September'

In September 1970 the focus of attention in the Middle East shifted to Jordan. In the years since the radicalizing experience of the Six-Day War, thousands of Palestinians had flocked to the various guerrilla organizations that made up the nascent Palestine Liberation Organization (PLO). Mindful of the sensitivity of the Palestinian cause to the mass of their citizens, many Arab leaders had allowed Palestinian groups an unprecedented degree of freedom to organize and agitate. In Jordan, where perhaps half the population was of Palestinian origin, Palestinian groups had taken advantage of their freedom of movement to mount attacks against Israeli targets. Retaliation in the form of ground and air raids followed Palestinian infiltration. These had resulted in heavy casualties and served to depopulate parts of the East Bank of the Jordan. Ideological differences strained further the relations between Jordan's King Hussein and the Palestinian organizations. The latter's heady blend of revolutionary Marxism and radical Arab nationalism sat uneasily with a pro-Western monarchy. Moreover, while the Palestinian resistance movement had committed itself in 1968 in the Palestinian National Charter (the PLO Covenant—see Documents on Palestine, p. 57) to the dismantling of the 'Zionist' state and its replacement with a 'secular democratic Palestine', the Jordanian monarch had been swift to follow Egypt in signing up to the Rogers Plan with its implicit acceptance of the Jewish State. By mid-1970 it became difficult to see how the uneasy state of coexistence could last. Matters came to a head at the beginning of September when militants of the Popular Front for the Liberation of Palestine (PFLP), one of the more radical groupings of the PLO, hijacked and then blew up three airliners on an airfield in Jordan. Soon afterwards King Hussein appointed a military Government in Jordan, which mobilized against PLO bases in the kingdom. After 10 days of heavy fighting the Palestinian resistance movement in Jordan had been crushed. A cease-fire, ending what would be referred to by Palestinians as 'Black September', was signed in Cairo, Egypt, on 27 September. President Nasser suffered a heart attack the following day and died soon after.

Sadat assumes the Egyptian presidency

Egypt's new President, Anwar Sadat, agreed to the 90-day cease-fire renewal along the Suez front. After receiving the promise of US credits to the value of US $500m., the Israeli Government also agreed to return to the talks under Jarring's auspices. On 8 February 1971 Jarring wrote to the Governments of Israel and Egypt, inviting each to give firm commitments to resolve the deadlock. He suggested that Israel should withdraw to the international boundary as of 4 June 1967, and that Egypt should give a parallel undertaking to conclude a peace agreement explicitly ending the state of war with Israel and recognizing Israel's right to exist in peace and security. In effect, both parties were being asked formally to accept their principal obligations under Resolution 242. Egypt replied that it would be prepared to meet the requirements stipulated by Jarring as long as Israel agreed to withdraw its forces to the international boundary. Israel responded that while it was prepared to withdraw to 'secure, recognized and agreed boundaries to be established in the peace agreement', it would not retreat to the pre-war border. This embarrassed the US Administration, which had first withheld and then granted military and economic assistance to Israel in an attempt to persuade the Israeli Government to accept only 'minor rectification' of the armistice line. In December 1971 the UN General Assembly, in a resolution reaffirming the principles of Resolution 242, urged Israel to respond favourably to Jarring's February proposals. Only seven states, one of them being Israel, voted against the resolution. In a gesture of frustration with Israeli intransigence, the USA—which had usually sided with Israel on territorial questions—abstained. Nevertheless, the sale of US military aircraft to Israel continued during 1972, eliciting fierce criticism from the Egyptians. Sadat's failure to deliver the political settlement he had promised his people at the beginning of 1971 had left him frustrated and politically exposed. In July 1972 the Egyptian President unexpectedly requested the withdrawal from Egypt of Soviet military advisers. This was interpreted by observers as a final appeal to the Nixon Administration to bring pressure on Israel to accede to a settlement involving a withdrawal from the occupied Sinai.

Although the cease-fire along the Suez Canal was maintained during 1972, the absence of political progress sustained regular incidences of violent conflict elsewhere. In February Israeli forces launched a major incursion into southern Lebanon, in an attempt to destroy PLO guerrilla bases there; four months later Israeli air raids on Lebanese territory left more than 70 civilians killed or wounded. The war of terror and counter-terror continued to escalate. In mid-1972 several Palestinian leaders were killed or maimed by letter bombs in Beirut. In September Palestinian gunmen took several Israeli athletes hostage during the Olympic games in Munich, West Germany, in a declared attempt to win the freedom of Arab prisoners in Israeli jails. The athletes were later killed by their captors during an abortive rescue operation at Munich airport. Israel responded to the Munich events with a series of attacks on Palestinian targets in Lebanon and the assassination

in various European capitals of those PLO personnel it believed responsible for masterminding the operation. Israeli officials in various parts of the world were also targeted in a letter bombing campaign, presumably initiated by one of the PLO factions.

THE OCTOBER WAR

The beginning of 1973 saw further Israeli air-strikes on guerrilla bases in Lebanon and the shooting down of a Libyan airliner that had strayed over occupied Sinai. These two incidents caused a storm of protest in the Arab world and thwarted all expectations of progress at a US-hosted series of talks with Egyptian, Jordanian and Israeli leaders in Washington, DC. Instead, six years after the June war, a resolution of the Arab–Israeli conflict appeared further away than ever. Israel had ceded none of the land it had occupied in 1967, and had established some 50 civilian and paramilitary settlements in these territories. Although the Jordanian and Egyptian Governments had signalled that they would be prepared to recognize Israel in return for an Israeli withdrawal from Arab lands (not a position shared by the Syrians), Israel remained in defiance of those UN resolutions calling upon it to return to its pre-1967 borders. The USA meanwhile, found itself isolated in its support for Israel. In Europe, where the Jewish State had long benefited from a groundswell of popular sympathy, an increasing dependence on Arab oil and a frustration with what was regarded as the overly-partisan support for Israel in the USA saw members of the European Community (EC) becoming more critical of perceived Israeli intransigence. However, as long as the political support of the USA was forthcoming and its military superiority unchallenged, the Israeli Government appeared unconcerned either by the regional stalemate or by Israel's creeping political isolation. This complacency was dramatically challenged on 6 October 1973, when Egyptian and Syrian forces launched a full-scale assault on Israeli positions in the Golan Heights and along the Suez Canal. The timing of the assault was not accidental. With public services in Israel effectively suspended because of observation of Yom Kippur, the holiest day in the Jewish calendar, Israel's army found it difficult to mobilize its forces rapidly. By midnight on the first day of the war 400 Egyptian tanks had crossed the Suez Canal, outflanking the supposedly impregnable Israeli fortifications on the eastern bank known as the Bar Lev line. Meanwhile, the Israeli army and air force were struggling to contain a massive assault by Syrian tanks beyond the Golan Heights. Over the next three weeks Israel suffered heavy casualties but was able to reverse the early territorial losses. Counter-attacking forces pushed the Egyptians back across the Suez Canal and succeeded in isolating Egyptian armed forces on the western side of the canal around the city of Suez. In the north, Israel's troops had occupied further Syrian territory and had advanced towards Damascus. The UN Security Council, adopting Resolution 338 on 22 October, urged a cease-fire and reaffirmed the principles defined in Resolution 242. By the time a disengagement had been agreed at the end of October the military advantage lay clearly with the Israelis. It was the Arab world, however, that was considered to have gained the most politically from the conflict. Not only had the war demonstrated that the gap in military strength compared with Israel had narrowed, but it had also added a new dimension to the conflict. Soon after the outbreak of the war, there were calls from within the Arab world to deny oil to Israel's supporters. In mid-October Arab oil exporters, meeting in Kuwait, agreed to cut production, while Abu Dhabi took the lead in halting the export of oil to the USA. Western nations were soon experiencing rising fuel prices and growing shortages, underlining the extent of their dependency on oil produced in the Arab world. In early November the member states of the EC endorsed a statement calling for an Israeli withdrawal from the territories occupied in 1967 and asserting the need for any Middle East settlement to meet the legitimate rights of the Palestinians. Israel accused Europe of surrendering to Arab 'blackmail', a charge which it might also have levelled at the USA. Finding his nation more inconvenienced than envisaged by this rare show of Arab solidarity, President Nixon dispatched his Secretary of State, Dr Henry Kissinger, on a series of visits to Middle East capitals. His diplomacy led to disengagement agreements between Egypt and Israel (18 January 1974) and between Syria and Israel (31 May 1974). In June 1974 Nixon embarked on his own tour of the region. He reassured Israel of continuing US support, but also forecast a new era of co-operation with the Arab world. Arab leaders broadly welcomed Nixon's overtures, believing that at last US influence would be used to promote a settlement based on Israel's withdrawal. The embargo on the export of Arab oil to the USA was revoked, and diplomatic relations between Syria and the USA were re-established.

The Palestinian profile raised

Israel's international position had been weakened by the revelation of the extent to which the world was dependent upon Arab goodwill. Israel's Prime Minister Golda Meir was criticized for her Government's failure to anticipate the Arab attack; and while her Labour party won a narrow victory at the end of 1973, she was unable to rebuild her coalition in April 1974. Meir was succeeded by Itzhak Rabin as Labour leader and Prime Minister. Within the Arab world the effect of the war was to strengthen the position of the regimes in Cairo and Damascus and to give new authority to King Faisal of Saudi Arabia—whose control of the greatest share of the oil reserves of the Middle East made him a dominant figure in Arab politics. Satisfaction greeted Israel's relinquishing of small areas of Arab territory under the US-brokered disengagement agreements, but the central problem of the future of the Palestinians had been made no clearer by the October conflict. Nevertheless, the PLO and the Palestinians saw their international profile raised in the wake of the new Arab confidence. In November 1973 the Arab governments had recognized the PLO as 'the sole, legitimate representative of the Palestinian people', and the centrality of the Palestinians to the Middle East conflict was strikingly endorsed in September 1974 when the UN General Assembly voted for the first time since Israel's establishment to include 'the Palestine question' on its agenda. In the following month the PLO Chairman, Yasser Arafat, addressed the General Assembly, speaking of his vision of a unitary and secular Palestine for both Arabs and Jews. Also in October Arab heads of state, meeting in Rabat, Morocco, had formally affirmed the status of the PLO as the 'sole legitimate representative of the Palestinian people' (see Documents on Palestine, p. 62). The elevation of the PLO to the status of a principal player on the Middle East stage was welcomed by the Arab people, but served only to deepen the impasse with regard to a settlement. The Israeli Government refused to have any dealings with the PLO, dismissing it as a terrorist organization responsible for the deaths of many of its citizens. The PLO's position was in itself complicated by internal divisions over political objectives. Although committed through its Charter to the replacement of Israel with a 'secular democratic' Palestine, by the end of 1974 majority opinion within the PLO had reluctantly accepted the idea of a Palestinian state in the West Bank and Gaza with East Jerusalem as its capital. While this was also the preferred option of the 'conservative', Western-aligned Arab states headed by Egypt and Jordan, the Governments of Libya and Iraq continued to give their backing to the significant minority of 'rejectionists' within the Palestinian national movement who were bitterly opposed to any formula involving a compromise with 'Zionism' and 'imperialism'. These radical factions viewed the Arab-US *rapprochement* with disdain, and violently underscored their opposition to compromise with Israel through bloody assaults on targets inside Israel.

Arab hopes that the diplomatic initiative unleashed by the October war would lead to a breakthrough in the regional stalemate were frustrated through the latter part of 1974. The disengagement agreements had been honoured by both sides, but attempts by Henry Kissinger to further the process of disengagement on the Egyptian–Israeli front by securing a partial Israeli withdrawal in Sinai foundered on Israel's insistence that such an agreement be accompanied by a non-aggression pact with Egypt. Unwilling to risk the opprobrium of the Arab world by pursuing a separate peace treaty with Israel, Sadat rejected the Israeli conditions. The US Secretary of State blamed Israeli obstinacy for the failure of his shuttle diplomacy to build upon the initial disengagements. In a clear expression of displeasure with the Rabin Government, US President Gerald Ford intimated that the granting of increased military and economic aid to Israel would be dependent upon a more flexible

response to US initiatives. In the summer of 1975 Kissinger returned to Israel to promote a second disengagement agreement between Israel and Egypt. This time his efforts bore fruit: on 4 September both states signed an agreement in Geneva, Switzerland, that provided for an Israeli withdrawal from the Mitla and Gidi passes in Sinai and a return of the Abu Rudeis oilfields (on which Israel had depended for some 50% of its oil supplies). A UN buffer zone would be established between the two forces, along with five 'listening posts' to monitor troop movements on either side. Non-military cargoes sailing to and from Israel would be allowed to pass through the newly reopened Suez Canal. In addition, both sides agreed to respect the cease-fire and to resolve their conflict by peaceful means. Although greeted in the West as a triumph of US diplomacy, the agreement was viewed in most of the Arab world—and particularly by the Syrians and the PLO—as a dangerous capitulation to US and Israeli interests. The united Arab front presented during the October war was undermined, and Egypt had clearly aligned itself with Washington. Relations between Cairo and Moscow, strained for some years, deteriorated further during 1975 as Sadat repeatedly criticized Egypt's former ally. In March 1975 Sadat abrogated the 1971 Soviet-Egyptian Treaty of Friendship. Syria now assumed leadership of the Arab cause. In October 1975 Syria's President Hafiz al-Assad visited Moscow, securing the promise of increased arms supplies to match the deliveries made by the US to Israel.

In late 1975 and early 1976 the international position of the PLO was further enhanced through a series of debates at the UN. In November 1975 the General Assembly adopted three resolutions concerning Palestine: the first concerned the establishment of a 20-nation committee to devise plans for the implementation of Palestinian 'self-determination and national independence'; the second extended an invitation to the PLO to take part in future debates on the Middle East; and, most controversially, the third condemned Zionism as 'a form of racism and racial discrimination'. However, the USA blocked a resolution in January 1976 affirming the Palestinians' right to establish their own state, and again sided with Israel in March to defeat a resolution condemning Israel's actions in the Occupied Territories. However, the US delegate did issue a statement strongly critical of Israeli settlement policy. This policy continued to exacerbate tensions in Palestinian areas under Israeli control, prompting sustained rioting throughout the West Bank and Gaza in the spring of 1976. Israeli attempts to defuse unrest by allowing Palestinians on the West Bank municipal elections only confirmed the weight of nationalist sentiment when the electorate voted overwhelmingly for candidates closely identified with the PLO.

CIVIL WAR IN LEBANON

Palestinian militancy in the Occupied Territories had been intensified by the outbreak in April 1975 of full-scale civil war in Lebanon. This increasingly bloody conflict saw Palestinians allied with the forces of the Lebanese left against the conservative Christian establishment. Attempts by the USA, France and various Arab leaders to broker an end to the hostilities failed to produce anything more than temporary cease-fires in a cycle of violence where the civilian population, and particularly the Palestinians, were the principal victims. By May 1976 the leftist-Palestinian alliance was on the brink of a military victory. Fearing that such an outcome would prompt an Israeli intervention, Syria's President Assad won tacit US approval to send his troops across the border to prevent a Christian defeat. Following intensive lobbying by Kuwait and Saudi Arabia, a limited Arab summit was convened in Riyadh in October 1976, at which the leaders of Egypt, Syria, Lebanon and the PLO agreed to a cease-fire that would see the reform of the Lebanese political system and the stationing of an Arab peace-keeping force in the country. By the end of the year this force had established some semblance of order throughout most of the country.

Although the Arab focus on the civil war in Lebanon was welcomed in Israel, the Labour Government of Itzhak Rabin was beset by its own internal pressures. A weak economy and a series of scandals involving senior Labour politicians had combined to undermine the governing coalition. Street protests continued in the West Bank and Gaza throughout 1976, and were met by increasingly repressive measures by the Israeli security forces. The Israeli response to Palestinian unrest was roundly condemned by the international community. On 20 December, following the publication of a UN report critical of Israel, the General Assembly once again censured the Israeli Government for its treatment of the Palestinians. Settlement policy served to fuel Palestinian protests and lay at the core of international concern. The Rabin administration was itself divided over the issue of whether it should be controlling or facilitating Jewish settlement in the territories occupied in 1967. No such dilemma exercised the nationalist Likud opposition led by Menachem Begin. In the approach to the 1977 election Begin campaigned hard for the expansion of Jewish settlement and permanent Israeli control over the West Bank. However, on the issue of relations with the Palestinians and the PLO there was broad agreement between the major political blocs in Israel. Both were opposed to negotiation with a 'terrorist' organization and refused to accept the notion of an independent Palestinian state. The PLO, meanwhile, remained publicly committed to the replacement of Israel with a unitary secular democracy. The entrenched position of the conflict's two principal protagonists confirmed that the possibility of an overall settlement remained as remote as ever. Nevertheless, the ending of the Lebanese civil war and the election of Jimmy Carter to the US presidency gave new impetus to the search for a way out of the regional deadlock.

New diplomatic initiatives

With the Lebanese situation no longer consuming the political energies of the Arab world, attention once again turned to Israel. The common position of the Arab states was that an overall settlement should be predicated upon the withdrawal of Israeli forces from all lands occupied in 1967 and the establishment of a Palestinian state in the West Bank and Gaza. It would be necessary to enlist the support of Washington to put pressure on Israel to achieve these goals. Early indications certainly gave grounds for optimism in that the new US Administration had identified the Middle East conflict as a primary foreign policy concern and had promised more direct involvement in the region. In February 1977 President Carter sent his Secretary of State, Cyrus Vance, on a tour of the Middle East and invited Israeli and Arab leaders to visit him in Washington. Carter also stated that a 'homeland' for the Palestinians should be a goal of regional peace efforts. It was also reported that US officials were in contact with the PLO with the aim of persuading them to modify their position on Israel. In apparent response to both US and Arab lobbying, PLO representatives indicated willingness to establish a state 'on any part of Palestine' vacated by Israel.

US attempts to foster better relations between Israel and the Arab world faced an immediate challenge with the victory of the right-wing Likud coalition in Israel's May 1977 elections. President Carter issued an early invitation to the new Israeli Prime Minister, Menachem Begin, to visit Washington. Prior to the Israeli leader's arrival in July, the US Department of State reiterated the USA's support for UN Resolution 242 and reaffirmed Carter's belief in 'the need for a homeland for the Palestinians, whose exact nature should be negotiated between the parties'. (These sentiments were echoed in a declaration published by a meeting of EC heads of government at the end of June 1977. The EC Declaration also called for representatives of the Palestinian people to be included in any peace negotiations.) Begin's visit to the USA failed to generate an understanding on which to base a peace settlement. A tour of the Middle East by Cyrus Vance in August produced a brief sense of optimism when the Saudi Arabian Government reported that the PLO might accept Resolution 242 if it were amended to include provision for Palestinian self-determination. President Carter subsequently raised the possibility of the PLO's being represented in a reconvened Geneva Conference if the movement accepted Resolution 242. However, following the Begin Government's categorical rejection of either dialogue with the PLO or the notion of Palestinian self-determination, the PLO refused to amend its stance over Resolution 242. Within days of Vance's departure from the region, the Begin Government announced that it would be extending health, education and welfare services to the Palestinian populations of the West Bank and Gaza. Arab fears that this was in fact the precursor to Israeli annexation of the

two territories were deepened by the announcement that three new Jewish settlements were to be built on the West Bank, and by the unveiling of a draft Israeli proposal for a territorial settlement that envisaged the maintenance of the occupation throughout the West Bank and Gaza. Concerned that these measures would alienate the Arab world, the US sought to mollify Arab anger with a call for Palestinian representatives to be included in an Arab delegation to a future peace conference. This proposal was reluctantly accepted by the Israeli Government. On 1 October 1977 the USA and the USSR issued a joint statement urging a Middle East settlement that would ensure 'the legitimate rights of the Palestinians'. The inclusion of such a phrase signalled an important shift in the official US attitude to the Arab–Israeli conflict and clearly troubled the Begin Government. The PLO gave qualified acceptance of the US-Soviet statement as the basis for a reconvened peace summit.

Sadat visits Israel

The course of the Arab–Israeli conflict underwent fundamental change at the end of 1977. In a speech to the Egyptian parliament on 9 November President Sadat expressed his frustration with the lack of progress towards a peace settlement and announced that he would be prepared to go to Jerusalem to negotiate direct with Israel. His offer was immediately taken up by a delighted Israel, and on 19 November Sadat flew to Tel-Aviv. His initiative was warmly welcomed in the West, where it was regarded as a bold attempt to break with the sterile attitudes of the past. Within the Arab world Sadat's visit was viewed with a mix of scepticism and hostility. This reaction was centred on a conviction that the Egyptian leader was prepared fatally to undermine the cause of Arab unity for an initiative that was self-serving and unlikely to achieve its minimum expectations. Egypt's Minister of Foreign Affairs resigned in protest at the proposed visit. Arab fears were undimmed by the international euphoria that accompanied the Sadat trip, and appeared to be confirmed when it emerged that Israeli leaders had stated a readiness to withdraw from most Egyptian territory but were unprepared to cede all Arab lands captured in 1967. When negotiations between the two states resumed on 25 December in Egypt, at Ismailia, Menachem Begin produced a set of proposals for the West Bank and Gaza that offered the Palestinian population a modest degree of self-rule under the auspices of Israeli 'security and public order' control. Sadat's embarrassment at the limited scope of Israeli proposals on issues of territory and Palestinian self-determination was matched by a deepening Arab cynicism towards the motives of Egypt's ruler. Israeli-Egyptian talks on military and political issues affecting a settlement resumed in Cairo on 16 January 1978, but were suspended almost immediately because of Egyptian anger with Israel's insistence on retaining settlements in occupied Sinai.

ISRAEL INVADES SOUTHERN LEBANON

The Palestinians had been among the most vociferous in denouncing Sadat's overtures to Israel. In March 1978 PLO gunmen launched a sea-borne raid north of Tel-Aviv, killing 36 Israelis. Israel responded with a major land and air assault on Palestinian bases in southern Lebanon. The USA hurriedly introduced a resolution at the UN Security Council: Resolution 425, adopted on 19 March, demanded that Israel withdraw its troops, under UN supervision, and respect Lebanese territorial integrity, sovereignty and independence. Israel agreed to a cease-fire the following day, but by this time its forces were in occupation of nearly all Lebanese territory up to the Litani river. Israel's invasion was condemned internationally for its high human cost: an estimated 1,000 Lebanese and Palestinian civilians had been killed in the Israeli bombardments, and more than 200,000 had fled their homes. Friction soon developed over the role of the UN Interim Force in Lebanon (UNIFIL), the body mandated to supervise an Israeli withdrawal. The Israeli Defence Forces (IDF) undertook a partial withdrawal at the end of April, but Israeli leaders insisted that they would maintain an armed presence in the country until the UN force could ensure the security of northern Israel against Palestinian incursions. Although determined not to relinquish its presence in southern Lebanon, the PLO promised to co-operate with UNIFIL. Israeli forces eventually withdrew from Lebanese territory on 13 June, but handed over their positions to their right-wing Lebanese militia allies, rather than to UNIFIL. Alarmed at the instability caused by Israel's invasion of Lebanon and the prospect of the Sadat peace initiative unravelling, President Carter persuaded the Israeli and Egyptian foreign ministers to attend talks in the United Kingdom in July. When this meeting ended with the Egyptians announcing they would not take part in further negotiations unless Israel changed its positions, Carter invited Begin and Sadat to a final attempt to break the deadlock at the US presidential retreat at Camp David, Maryland, in September.

THE CAMP DAVID ACCORDS

The Camp David talks lasted for 12 days. At their conclusion on 17 September President Carter announced that the Egyptian and Israeli leaders had signed two documents providing a framework for peace in the Middle East (see Documents on Palestine, p. 63). The first committed Israel and Egypt to conclude a peace treaty that would provide for an Israeli withdrawal from Sinai and the establishment of normal relations. The second concerned the future of the West Bank and Gaza and proposed the election of a self-governing Palestinian authority to replace the existing military administration. Palestinian autonomy would last for a period of five years, during which time it was agreed there would be negotiations to determine the final status of the territories and to conclude a peace treaty between Israel and Jordan. The agreements were greeted in the West as a triumph of US politics and diplomacy. They were also given cautious approval in Israel, where there was satisfaction that a peace treaty could be completed with Egypt without substantive concessions on the issues of Israeli settlements and continued territorial control over the other lands conquered in 1967.

Jordan and Saudi Arabia, both key players in shaping regional opinion, declared strong reservations about the terms of the Camp David accords. The more radical Arab states, led by Syria, joined the PLO in declaring their outright rejection. In November 1978 representatives of the League of Arab States (the Arab League) convened in Baghdad, Iraq, to discuss action to be taken against Egypt—which was not invited to the session. After heated debate over measures to isolate the Sadat Government, it was agreed that formal sanctions would be postponed until such time as a peace treaty with Israel was actually signed. It was argued that this would allow Sadat to reconsider a political course that would lead to total dependence on the USA. Accelerated settlement construction in the Occupied Territories, coupled with Israel's reluctance to comply with Egyptian requests for a timetable for the implementation of autonomy proposals on the West Bank, led to increasingly bitter recriminations and the missing of the deadline, of 18 December, for the bilateral treaty to be signed. Ministerial meetings in Washington failed to break the deadlock, and on 7 March the US President flew to the Middle East. After intensive discussions Carter announced on his return to the USA that 'we have now defined the major components of a peace treaty'. On 26 March, and despite reports of a serious rift on the issue of Israeli settlement on the West Bank, the Israeli-Egyptian peace treaty was signed in Washington by Anwar Sadat and Menachem Begin (see Documents on Palestine, p. 65). The optimism in the West that was generated by the symbolism of an Arab and an Israeli leader shaking hands on the White House lawn was swiftly dispelled by the decision of the rest of the Arab world to impose an immediate political and economic boycott of Egypt, and to transfer the Arab League headquarters from Cairo to Tunis (see Documents on Palestine, p. 66). Sadat maintained that his treaty with Israel was the first step towards a comprehensive regional settlement that would restore the rights of the Palestinians. To the rest of the Arab world it appeared that Cairo had entered into a separate understanding that would see the return of Sinai to Egypt but would leave the rest of occupied Arab land under Israeli control. This perception was reinforced by a broadcast made by Begin on the anniversary of the creation of the State of Israel in which he asserted that no border would ever be drawn 'through the land of Israel' and that 'we shall never withdraw from the Golan Heights'.

Early agreements were reached between Israel and Egypt on the issue of border controls, oil sales and the return of Sinai's St Catherine's monastery to Egypt. However, discussion on the implementation of Palestinian autonomy continued to be soured by the Likud Government's settlement policy. In May 1979 Israel disclosed plans for an ambitious programme of settlement construction in the West Bank and Gaza, and in September the ban on Israeli citizens purchasing Arab land in the Occupied Territories was ended. Although the left-wing opposition in Israel, loosely organized under the banner of the Peace Now movement, was able to mount legal challenges to the proposed construction of certain settlements, the process of expropriation, land clearance and large-scale construction was leaving an ever larger imprint on the physical landscape of the West Bank and Gaza.

Western European governments became more vocal in their opposition to Israeli policy in the Occupied Territories. Their protests were accompanied by recognition of the centrality of the Palestinians, and the PLO, to the Arab–Israeli issue. In July 1979 Yasser Arafat held talks with the Austrian Chancellor, Bruno Kreisky, and two months later was officially received by King Juan Carlos of Spain and his Prime Minister. In the same month the EC representative at the UN called for a role for the PLO in the efforts to bring peace to the Middle East, while strongly criticizing Israeli policy. In November the PLO was awarded political recognition by the Italian Government. PLO leaders also held talks with government representatives in Portugal, Belgium, Italy and Greece. Speculation that the USA was itself engaging in dialogue with the PLO was repeatedly denied by President Carter. In September, however, the US ambassador to the UN, Andrew Young, met with the PLO observer, Labib Terzi. Protests from the Israeli Government forced Young to resign; the departing ambassador described Washington's refusal to talk to the PLO as 'ridiculous'. The influence of the Jewish lobby on US policy was again demonstrated in March 1980 when President Carter retracted an affirmative US vote on UN Security Council Resolution 465 (see Documents on Palestine, p. 66), which sought the dismantling of 'existing settlements' in the Occupied Territories. Carter explained the reversal by asserting his Administration's belief that dismantling was neither 'proper nor practical'. The EC states continued meanwhile to develop links with the PLO and to lend support to the idea of Palestinian self-determination. In June an EC summit meeting in Venice, Italy, issued a statement declaring collectively for the first time support for full Palestinian self-determination and a role for the PLO in the search for a comprehensive peace (see Documents on Palestine, p. 67). The statement also repeated opposition to Israeli settlements and any change to the status of Jerusalem.

Egyptian-Israeli talks on the issue of Palestinian autonomy failed to make any progress, despite the active facilitation of the USA. In the Occupied Territories opposition to the autonomy proposals remained as vehement as ever, and served to fuel regular protests against the Israeli authorities. In early 1980 six Jewish settlers were shot dead by PLO gunmen in Hebron; the Israelis responded by deporting two local mayors. Shortly afterwards militant Israeli settlers placed bombs in the cars of three other West Bank mayors, severely injuring two of them.

Ronald Reagan was elected US President at the end of 1980. Viewed as strongly sympathetic to the Jewish State, his appointment of a team of pro-Israeli foreign affairs advisers caused consternation in the Arab world. Concerns were heightened when the new President appeared to reverse existing US policy by declaring that Israeli settlements were 'not illegal'. The Reagan Administration faced an early test of its attitudes to the Arab–Israeli conflict following the shooting down of two Syrian helicopters by Israeli military aircraft over Lebanon. In response Syria deployed batteries of anti-aircraft missiles in the Beka'a valley. Israel demanded the withdrawal of the missiles, while the US Special Envoy to the Middle East, Philip Habib, urged Saudi Arabia to persuade Syria to withdraw the missiles. The Saudi Government, however, joined the rest of the Arab world in strongly supporting the Syrian position. In June 1981 Begin warned that if the USA failed to arrange the withdrawal of the missiles through diplomacy, then Israel would remove them by force. In the same month the Israeli Government dramatically underlined its willingness to resort to military measures by bombing and destroying an Iraqi nuclear installation near Baghdad. Israel justified the raid on the grounds of self-defence, although most experts, including the International

Atomic Energy Agency (IAEA) concurred that Iraq would not have the means to produce nuclear weapons for many years. President Reagan indicated his Administration's displeasure by suspending the sale of four F-16 fighter aircraft to Israel. He commented none the less that Israel had 'reason for concern' about Iraq's nuclear programme.

Menachem Begin's Likud coalition was returned to power in the June 1981 election. Ariel Sharon, one of the nation's foremost 'hawks', was appointed as defence minister. Ten days after the election Israel launched air-strikes against Palestinian targets in Lebanon, causing many deaths. The PLO retaliated with rocket fire against Israel's northern townships. Pressure from the USA on Israel, and from Saudi Arabia on the Palestinians, eventually brought about a cease-fire, which came into effect on 24 July.

Assassination of Anwar Sadat

In October 1981 President Anwar Sadat was killed by Islamist extremists during a military parade in Cairo. The assassination followed months of tension in Egypt as intercommunal fighting was followed by a clamp-down on the media and the detention of hundreds of Sadat's political opponents. The death of the Egyptian President marked the final chapter of the Camp David process. Sadat's successor, Hosni Mubarak, made it clear that although he would refrain from any political initiatives that could jeopardize the scheduled return of Sinai to Egypt, his principal strategic goal would be to mend fences with the rest of the Arab world. Sadat's funeral brought an impressive array of Western dignitaries to Cairo, but was largely ignored by the local population. The absence of public grief contrasted sharply with the scenes that had accompanied Nasser's funeral, and was interpreted as a telling symbol of Egyptian and Arab disaffection with Sadat's pro-Western foreign policy. Saudi Arabia had already attempted to fill the vacuum created by the failures of Camp David by launching its own peace initiative in August. Known as the 'Fahd Plan', after its author the Saudi Crown Prince, it promised recognition of Israel in return for the establishment of a Palestinian state in the Occupied Territories (see Documents on Palestine, p. 68). The EC states responded positively to the proposal, noting its similarities to their own Venice Declaration of the previous year, the USA less so. Prime Minister Begin dismissed the plan as a recipe for Israel's destruction, while the Arab world, with the exception of Libya, accorded it varied levels of approval. However, the tentative prospect of agreement on a joint Arab-European framework for a regional settlement quickly receded. Following a visit to Israel, the French Minister of Foreign Affairs distanced his Government from the European initiative. In November Syria led several Arab states in opposition to the timing—rather than the substance—of the Fahd plan. The regional political climate became even less receptive to peace initiatives at the end of the year when the Israeli Knesset (legislature) endorsed government legislature extending Israeli laws, jurisdiction and administration over the occupied Golan Heights. The UN Security Council, in Resolution 497, unanimously condemned the annexation of the Syrian territory and gave Israel two weeks to rescind its decision. Jordan introduced a resolution urging voluntary sanctions against Israel, but this was vetoed by the USA. The Reagan Administration did, however, make clear its opposition to Israel's action. Despite the regional disquiet over the Golan annexation, Israel proceeded with its scheduled withdrawal from Sinai on 25 April 1982. Prior to the evacuation Israeli troops had forcibly removed settlers who had occupied the Yamit settlement in the north of the peninsular.

ISRAEL'S REINVASION OF LEBANON

The dismissal of elected pro-PLO mayors in the West Bank in the spring of 1982 precipitated sustained street protests in Gaza and the West Bank against Israeli occupation. Several Palestinians were killed during the disturbances before the IDF were able to restore a semblance of order. In May the Israeli air force broke the cease-fire that had held along its northern border with Lebanon with strikes on Palestinian targets inside Lebanon. The attempted assassination of Israel's ambassador to the United Kingdom by radical Palestinians opposed to the PLO was followed by further Israeli air raids on targets in Lebanon, to which the PLO retaliated with rocket attacks on northern Israel.

Although the Palestinian counter-attack did not result in any casualties, it became the official pretext for a full-scale Israeli invasion of Lebanon designated 'Operation Peace for Galilee'. By 10 June, four days after 30,000 troops of the IDF had crossed into Lebanese territory, the main coastal cities had been captured and Israeli tanks had taken up positions on the outskirts of Beirut. Syrian ground forces stationed in Lebanon put up some resistance to the Israeli advance, while the Syrian air force suffered heavy losses as the Israelis demonstrated their overwhelming superiority in the air. A cease-fire between the two sides was brokered by the USA on 11 June, but fighting with Palestinian forces intensified as the Israeli army tightened its siege of west Beirut: water, electricity, food and medical supplies were cut, while Israeli artillery and aircraft maintained a relentless bombardment. Ariel Sharon announced that the siege would be lifted only if PLO combatants surrendered or left the city. This the PLO finally agreed to do on 21 August, as part of an arrangement that also provided for the deployment of a multinational force (MNF) to supervise the withdrawal and protect the civilians of west Beirut. By the end of the month the PLO had evacuated its forces from the city. A second Israeli objective was also achieved on 23 August, when the Lebanese National Assembly was persuaded to elect the pro-Israeli Phalangist commander, Bashir Gemayel, as the new Lebanese President. On 14 September Gemayel was assassinated in a bomb explosion at his party headquarters. Two days later the IDF command apparently allowed right-wing Christian militias into the Palestinian refugee camps of Sabra and Chatila to 'mop up' remaining resistance. Over a 48-hour period the militias killed an estimated 1,500 civilians. International outrage at the massacre forced the Israeli Government to launch an inquiry into the circumstances surrounding the events in the Palestinian camps. A report published in February 1983 considered Minister of Defence Sharon as principally responsible for the Sabra and Chatila operation. He resigned his post but remained in the Government as a minister without portfolio.

The Reagan Plan

In September 1982 US President Ronald Reagan formulated new proposals to settle the Arab–Israeli conflict. The Reagan Plan (see Documents on Palestine, p. 68) envisaged the restoration of the Occupied Territories to their Arab populations, but ruled out the creation of a Palestinian state. Instead it proposed Palestinian self-government in association with Jordan. The position of Jordan's King Hussein was crucial to the success of the US proposal. Visiting Washington in December, Hussein made it clear that he would only be prepared to explore the Reagan proposals if he received a mandate to that effect from the Palestinians. Although it emerged that Arafat and Palestinian moderates were not fundamentally opposed to the Reagan Plan, there was strong opposition from PLO factions backed by Syria.

On 17 May 1983 the Lebanese administration of President Amin Gemayel (brother of Bashir) and the Israeli Government signed a US-brokered agreement providing for the withdrawal of Israeli troops from Lebanon and the establishment of joint Israeli-Lebanese patrols along their common border. However, the Begin Government stressed that any withdrawal from southern Lebanon would be conditional upon a simultaneous withdrawal of Syrian troops from the Beka'a valley. The agreement was roundly condemned by President Assad of Syria, who was committed to ensuring that the Israelis would gain no influence over Lebanese affairs as a result of their 1982 invasion. To underline his regime's opposition to a softening of the Arab approach towards Israel, Assad subsequently gave his backing to a revolt by dissidents within Yasser Arafat's own Fatah movement. Under the command of Abu Musa, and supported by units of the Syrian army, the Fatah rebels captured loyalist positions in the Beka'a valley. In June Assad expelled Arafat from Syria. Meanwhile, Palestinian and Lebanese guerrilla attacks on the Israeli army had persuaded Israel's Cabinet to order a unilateral pull-back of Israeli forces behind the more easily defensible line of the Awali river. The withdrawal not only confirmed that the agreement of 17 May would not be implemented; it also exposed the weakness of the Gemayel regime. Shortly after the 4 September retreat of the IDF to the Awali, the pro-Syrian Druze militia led by Walid Joumblatt launched a full-scale assault on the Christian forces allied to the Lebanese President. The Druze made rapid and significant gains, prompting the US offshore fleet to shell Druze- and Syrian-controlled territory in the hills above Beirut. Saudi Arabia managed to mediate a cease-fire between the warring factions, which came into effect on 25 September. The terms of the cease-fire provided for a dialogue of national reconciliation with Syrian participation, effectively awarding Damascus a power of veto over political developments in Lebanon. Syria also continued its military support for Fatah rebels laying siege to Arafat's last remaining stronghold around the northern Lebanese port of Tripoli. The increasingly isolated PLO leader was only able to gain the neutrality of other opposition groups within the PLO by bowing to demands to submit to the Palestinian Central Council's denunciation of the Reagan Plan.

The growth of Syrian influence in Lebanese affairs and the delivery to Damascus of Soviet long-range surface-to-surface (SS) missiles in October 1983, alarmed the US Administration and encouraged the Department of State to view the Lebanese situation increasingly in the context of the Cold War. US intervention on the side of the Gemayel Government had concomitantly strengthened Lebanese Muslim—and wider Arab—perceptions that the USA lacked the credibility to be an honest regional broker. Deepening anger at the Western role in Lebanon found violent expression in simultaneous suicide bombings of the headquarters of the US and French contingents of the MNF in Beirut, in which 241 US Marines and 58 French soldiers were killed. Two extremist Shi'ite groups linked to Iran claimed responsibility for the attacks, although US officials also ascribed a degree of culpability to Syria and the USSR (both of which denied any involvement). Shortly afterwards a bomb attack on Israel's military headquarters in Tyre caused 60 deaths. Israeli military aircraft bombed Palestinian and Druze positions in retaliation for the attack, and the Israeli authorities appealed for closer military co-ordination with the USA. The announcement of a policy of 'strategic co-operation' between the USA and Israel was denounced by Syria, which demanded a general mobilization of its forces on 7 November. Continued faith in military support from the USA and Israel allowed Gemayel's Government to resist calls from Syria and its Lebanese allies for the abrogation of the 17 May agreement and for constitutional changes. Israeli air raids on Syrian-controlled territory continued through the latter part of 1983, and on 4 December two US aircraft were shot down in a direct clash with Syrian forces.

Arafat's departure from Lebanon

Although the Assad Government saw its prestige in the Arab world enhanced by its confrontational stance towards the USA and Israel, its military involvement in the bloody conflict between Arafat loyalists and Abu Musa's forces proved deeply unpopular. As the siege of Arafat's fighters in Tripoli became more desperate, residual sympathy for the initial aims of the dissidents—to challenge the autocratic and unprincipled style of Arafat's leadership—was replaced by the perception that Abu Musa had become little more than a Syrian 'puppet' and that the struggle had become one for PLO independence from external control. This was felt particularly strongly in the Occupied Territories. Arafat's standing was further enhanced when on 24 November he was able to exchange six Israeli prisoners for 4,800 Lebanese and Palestinians held by the Israelis. Lobbying by the USSR and the Arab Gulf states achieved Syrian agreement to end the Tripoli siege through the evacuation of Arafat and some 4,000 loyalists by sea. Their departure was, however, delayed until 20 December by an Israeli naval bombardment of Tripoli and refusal to guarantee the UN evacuation fleet safe passage.

Renewed attacks on the US contingent of the MNF in Lebanon, and further US bombardments of anti-Gemayel forces around Beirut, caused increasing disquiet among the USA's European partners in the MNF. At the beginning of February 1984 further heavy fighting in Lebanon prompted the resignation of the Lebanese Government and the disintegration of the Lebanese army along sectarian lines. With Druze and Shi'ite militiamen co-operating effectively against the embattled Gemayel, the role of the MNF became increasingly untenable. By the end of February US, Italian and the token British force had withdrawn from Beirut. French troops followed in March, leaving west Beirut, as in the days before the Israeli invasion,

under the control of left-wing and Muslim militias. On 5 March Gemayel abrogated the 17 May Lebanese-Israel agreement in return for guarantees of internal security from Syria. At the end of April a new government of national unity was installed in Lebanon. Gemayel retained the presidency, but the new Lebanese cabinet reflected Syrian influence and the growing importance of the Shi'a community. The new Government resolved to secure the complete and unconditional removal of Israeli forces from the country, and awarded responsibility for the southern region to the leader of the Shi'a Amal militia, Nabih Berri, whose fighters had been at the forefront of resistance to the IDF.

Menachem Begin unexpectedly resigned the Israeli premiership on 30 August 1983. He was succeeded by the equally hawkish Minister of Foreign Affairs, Itzhak Shamir. The new Israeli Prime Minister was faced by a series of pressing challenges. Spiralling inflation and massive debt had brought the country to the verge of bankruptcy, and forced the imposition of austerity measures including huge reductions in public spending, cuts in subsidies on basic commodities, and the devaluation of the national currency. Defence and settlement were not immune from the cuts, causing a backlash from Shamir's right-wing coalition partners who were eager to sustain the rapid colonization of the Occupied Territories initiated by his predecessor. The publication in February 1984 of a long-suppressed report by the Ministry of Justice into Jewish terrorism against Palestinians in the Occupied Territories also served to embarrass the Likud leader, detailing as it did the consistent failures of the Israeli Government to apprehend the perpetrators. At the end of April the security forces finally acted, arresting some 30 people suspected of planting bombs on Arab buses. At their trial the leaders of the so-called 'Jewish Underground' confessed to the attacks in 1980 on the West Bank mayors and to an armed assault on Hebron University in July 1983 that had left three students dead and wounded many others. Their stated aim was to force a mass Palestinian exodus from the West Bank. Statements from right-wing political leaders effectively condoning the actions of the extremists caused consternation among liberal Israeli opinion.

Abroad, Shamir was also having to come to terms with the scale of the failure of the Lebanese war. Far from securing a 'client regime' in Beirut, it had brought about the defeat of Israel's Christian allies and served to entrench Syrian influence. Despite the set-backs suffered by the PLO, the Israeli army and its militia allies of the self-styled South Lebanon Army (SLA) were now confronted by a Shi'a guerrilla foe which was proving to be a dedicated adversary. The human cost of the invasion and occupation—600 deaths and 3,000 wounded by June 1984—had led to domestic agitation for withdrawal, as well as deeper questioning of the wisdom of Israel's military adventure.

PLO-Jordanian initiatives

On leaving Tripoli in late 1983, Arafat travelled to Egypt for a meeting with President Mubarak. This was the first time a prominent Arab leader had set foot on Egyptian territory since the Camp David accords. The Palestinian leader's *de facto* ending of the Arab boycott of Cairo was followed by the signing of an Egyptian-Jordanian protocol in January 1984, raising expectations of the emergence of a moderate Arab alignment comprising Egypt, Jordan and the PLO. Syria and the left-wing PLO factions denounced the *rapprochement* with Egypt and the developing relationship between the PLO and Jordan. The Israeli Prime Minister also criticized the Arafat-Mubarak meeting as a 'severe blow to the peace process', but the US Administration welcomed the dialogue as a boost for the Reagan Plan. In a move that was interpreted as preparing the constitutional ground for a joint Palestinian-Jordanian initiative, King Hussein decided on 5 January to reconvene the Jordanian parliament (its representation theoretically divided the East and West Banks of the Jordan) which had been suspended since the 1974 Rabat summit decision to accord the PLO the status of sole representative of the Palestinian people. Israel refused an Egyptian request for 160 members of the Palestine National Council (PNC—the supreme organ of the PLO) to attend the proposed session.

In the spring of 1984 early elections were forced on the Shamir Government by the defection of a minor party from the ruling coalition. The precarious state of the economy became a principal election issue. With the occupation of Lebanon costing an estimated US $1m. per day, the pledge of the Labour leader, Shimon Peres, to bring Israeli troops home within 'three to six months' proved to be popular with the electorate. At the election, held on 23 July, the Likud and the Labour Party each secured one-third of Knesset seats, with the balance being held by several small left- and right-wing parties. The ensuing political deadlock was broken when Peres and Shamir agreed to form a government of national unity with a two-year rotation of the posts of Prime Minister and Minister of Foreign Affairs.

After securing the endorsement, in November 1984, of the 17th session of the PNC for further negotiations with Jordan on a common approach to a Middle East settlement, Yasser Arafat and King Hussein signed an accord in the Jordanian capital in February 1985. This provided for Palestinian self-determination within the framework of a Jordanian-Palestinian federation. It also called for peace negotiations involving all parties to the conflict and the five permanent members of the UN Security Council. The Amman agreement was opposed by Syria and Arafat's Damascus-based opposition. The USA viewed the raising of the Jordanian profile positively, but still refused to deal directly with the PLO. Visits to the Middle East by the US Secretary of State, George Schultz, in the spring of 1985 failed to resolve the central dilemma of Palestinian representation in future peace talks, and the prospect of a breakthrough receded in subsequent months. In the Occupied Territories Israel responded to violence and civil unrest with deportations of activists and lengthy closures of Palestinian universities. In October, in response to the PLO's killing of three Israelis in Cyprus, Israel's air force bombed the PLO headquarters in Tunis, killing 75 people. In the same month gunmen belonging to a pro-Arafat faction of the PLO hijacked an Italian cruise-liner, the *Achille Lauro*, murdering an elderly American Jewish passenger. Arafat's condemnation of the incident did not persuade the US Administration to compromise the official position that the PLO and personalities close to it should be excluded from the peace process. By the end of the year it was becoming clear that the Jordanian-PLO initiative had lost viability. The reluctance of the PLO to meet US preconditions for a dialogue, namely that it accept Resolution 242 in its entirety and recognize the State of Israel, had begun to frustrate King Hussein. Mindful also of a general lack of enthusiasm in the Arab world for the Jordanian-Palestinian accord, the King moved to ease the traditionally frosty relations with his northern neighbour. On 21 October Jordan signalled its intention to move away from further collaboration with Yasser Arafat by signing an agreement with Syria that included a pledge not to seek a separate peace with Israel. In February 1986 King Hussein announced the end of political co-ordination with the PLO leadership, citing his disappointment at the organization's preoccupation with self-determination at the expense of the 'liberation of the land', and at its refusal to accept Resolution 242.

Israeli withdrawal to the southern Lebanese 'security zone'

At the beginning of 1985, after failing to reach agreement in UN-brokered talks on a withdrawal from Lebanon, the Israeli Cabinet announced plans for a unilateral departure in three phases. By 10 June 1985 the Israelis had evacuated most of the territory they held, leaving in their wake fresh outbreaks of fighting between Christian and Muslim forces. Shi'ite militias harried the retreating IDF, their anger exacerbated by the revelation that the departing Israelis had secretly transferred more than 1,000 Lebanese Shi'ite prisoners to Israel. Israel retained a strip of Lebanese territory, 8–10 km wide, along its northern border as a self-declared 'security zone'. Responsibility for policing the zone would fall to the IDF and their allies in the SLA.

The 'war of the camps'

Syria was determined that Arafat's PLO should not re-establish itself in Lebanon after the Israeli withdrawal. In the spring of 1985 the pro-Syrian Amal militia began a bombardment of the Palestinian refugee camps in Beirut, besieging the inhabitants and causing hundreds of casualties. During 1986 the fighting spread to the southern cities of Tyre and Sidon, where PLO

forces—many of them loyal to Yasser Arafat—had once again developed a power base. The extended assault on the Palestinians would prove to be a political mistake for Assad. Confronted by a common enemy, the erstwhile pro-Syrian factions of the PLO joined forces with the Arafat loyalists to defend their Palestinian constituency. Crucially, none of the other leftist or Muslim militias shared Amal's enthusiasm for siding with Syria against the PLO. Several of the militias gave active support to the Palestinians, prompting a series of clashes with Amal at the beginning of 1987. With Western media attention arousing widespread international sympathy for the plight of the beleaguered Palestinians, Syria acted to end the sieges in February 1987.

The 'war of the camps' paved the way for the reunification of the PLO. The 18th session of the PNC, held in Algiers in April 1987, was attended by all principal factions of the organization. In return for factional fealty to his leadership Arafat agreed to abrogate the Amman accord with Jordan and to downgrade co-operation with Egypt until Cairo formally renounced the Camp David agreements. The unification was greeted with great enthusiasm among a Palestinian population tired of resistance to Israel being compromised by factional wrangling. The outcome of the 18th PNC was less welcome among the neighbouring Arab states, each of which saw its future ability to manipulate the PLO seriously undermined.

In September 1986, one month before he was ready to hand over the premiership to Likud's Itzhak Shamir, Shimon Peres travelled to Egypt for a two-day summit meeting with President Mubarak. The two leaders gave their endorsement to the idea of an international conference on the Arab–Israeli conflict to include the five permanent members of the UN Security Council. The critical issue of Palestinian representation was left untouched. On assuming the post of Prime Minster in October, Shamir made clear his opposition to such a proposal, despite the enthusiasm of US Secretary of State George Schultz. The US Administration appeared reluctant to pressure Shamir into adopting a more flexible line on the issue of the conference. However, following congressional pressure, the State Department arrogated to itself the right to close the PLO's observer mission at the UN headquarters in New York and the Palestine Information Office in New York. The decision caused consternation in Europe, where it was considered counter-productive to a proposed peace conference.

THE PALESTINIAN UPRISING

Throughout 1987 there was a steady rise in political tension in the Occupied Territories. Demonstrations against Israeli policy grew in frequency, as did incidences of armed attacks against Israel's security forces. Israel responded with widespread administrative detentions, house demolitions and other retaliatory measures. On 8 December four workers in Gaza were killed in a road traffic accident involving an Israeli military vehicle. Their funerals precipitated huge demonstrations in Gaza and prolonged assaults on Israeli security forces, whose increasing use of live ammunition in counter-operations caused a number of fatalities. The rioting quickly spread to the West Bank. As the number of Palestinian deaths mounted and the street protests intensified, the populations of the Occupied Territories began to refer to their revolt as the *intifada* (uprising). Initially spontaneous, the *intifada* soon became co-ordinated under the leadership of the clandestine Unified National Leadership of the Uprising (UNLU), an umbrella organization composed of the different PLO factions and the militant Islamic Jihad. Broadly loyal to the PLO, UNLU issued regular communiqués co-ordinating strikes and demonstrations and encouraging civil disobedience. That Israel was clearly caught off guard by the scale and the ferocity of the revolt was apparently reflected in its initial response. Shootings and beatings of unarmed demonstrators caused an international outcry, and mass arrests of activists and continued deportations of suspected ringleaders only appeared to fuel the rebellion.

Amid mounting international concern at events in the Occupied Territories, US Secretary of State George Schultz formulated proposals to end the conflict. His plan (see Documents on Palestine, p. 69) called for negotiations between Israel and a Jordanian-Palestinian delegation, based on Resolutions 242 and 338, to determine an interim form of autonomy for the Occupied

Territories. Such a transitional arrangement would last for three years and would provide for an Israeli military withdrawal on the West Bank and for municipal elections of Palestinian officials. Negotiations on a final settlement would begin within the year and be paralleled by an international conference involving the five permanent members of the UN Security Council and all other parties to the conflict. This latter conference would have no power to veto any agreements reached in the separate Israeli-Jordanian-Palestinian talks. Itzhak Shamir pronounced that the Schultz Plan had 'no prospect of implementation'. Jordan announced itself opposed to 'partial or interim solutions', although welcoming US acknowledgement of the legitimate rights of the Palestinians. However, Egypt and Syria gave no indication that they would support the Plan's implementation, while the PLO rejected it outright on the grounds that it failed to make provision for a Palestinian state or for the organization's own participation in the process. The PLO position won the backing of the Arab League, convened in an emergency summit meeting in Algiers in June, which promised financial support to sustain the 'heroic' Palestinian uprising.

By the spring of 1988 the *intifada* was firmly entrenched in the Occupied Territories. Suspension of fuel supplies, the cutting of telephone links with the outside world, the closure of media outlets and a daily round of arrests and shootings had failed to curb the protests. After reports of initial friction between UNLU and the external leadership over the co-ordination of the uprising, it had become clear that a good working relationship existed—with the PLO abroad taking responsibility for ensuring the passage of funds to the Occupied Territories and for overall political strategy. Arafat's deputy, Khalil al-Wazir (alias Abu Jihad), who had been accorded responsibility for co-ordinating strategy with cadres in the West Bank and Gaza, was killed by an Israeli assassination squad in Tunis on 16 April. His death led to furious protests in the Occupied Territories, to which the Israeli security forces' response was severe: 16 Palestinians were shot dead in a single day. By the end of July 1988 more than 290 had been killed in the *intifada*.

Declaration of Palestinian independence

King Hussein announced in July 1988 that he was severing Jordan's legal and administrative links with the West Bank. He explained his decision in terms of complying with the wishes of the PLO and the Arab League. The latter had long recognized the PLO as the Palestinians' sole representative. His action was interpreted partly as a response to the *intifada* and partly as an act of impatience with the PLO Chairman: observers believed that Hussein considered Arafat incapable of forwarding the peace process, and that he would be compelled at a later date actively to involve the Jordanians in any settlement. In the short term the King's decision dealt a blow to US peace plans, and also undermined the Israeli Labour Party's advocacy of a Jordanian-Palestinian federation. UNLU issued a statement applauding the Jordanian decision as the 'greatest accomplishment' of the *intifada*, while for the PLO it presented a serious challenge. The Occupied Territories (with the exception of Arab Jerusalem) were now claimed by no sovereign state as their territory, providing the PLO with an historic opportunity to assert sovereignty over a specific area. Arafat immediately began canvassing international support for a new peace strategy. Addressing the European Parliament in September 1988, he asserted the PLO's willingness to recognize Israel's right to security in return for Israeli recognition of an independent Palestinian state. He also declared his movement's opposition to armed action outside the Occupied Territories. In Algiers on 15 November, at the close of the 19th session of the PNC, an independent State of Palestine was unilaterally declared (see Documents on Palestine, p. 69), with the PLO's Executive Committee functioning as an *ad hoc* government. Although Arafat wanted the PNC to strengthen his diplomatic hand by granting recognition of Resolution 242 in isolation, the opposition of left-wing factions forced a compromise formula whereby the PNC would accept Resolution 242 in conjunction with the Palestinian right to self-determination. Addressing the UN General Assembly in December, Arafat went further, explicitly recognizing Israel and renouncing 'terrorism'. He also called for an international peace conference to be held on the basis of Resolutions 242 and 338. Israeli Prime Minster Shamir (who

had been returned to power in the previous month's election), dismissed Arafat's address as a 'public relations exercise'. After concerted mediation by the Swedish Government, the outgoing Reagan Administration acknowledged the PLO's concessions by holding the USA's first official talks with representatives of the movement. Despite reservations that too much had been conceded with too few firm guarantees, the declaration of Palestinian independence and the opening of a dialogue with the USA were regarded in the Occupied Territories as vindication of the sacrifices of the *intifada*.

Under pressure to respond to Arafat's diplomatic offensive with ideas of its own, the Shamir Government (a Likud-Labour coalition) produced its own initiative for a negotiated end to the conflict. Formally unveiled in April 1989, the Shamir proposals provided for elections in the West Bank and Gaza in return for an end to the *intifada*. The elections would produce a Palestinian delegation to conduct negotiations on a final settlement. As further details of the plan emerged in May (see Documents on Palestine, p. 72), it became clear that Shamir was offering little more than a reworking of the Camp David proposals. The declared opposition to a Palestinian state, and the proposed Israeli veto over any future changes to the status of the Occupied Territories, effectively ensured that the Shamir plan would be unacceptable to the PLO and to the wider Arab world. Attempts by Egypt's President Mubarak and by the US Secretary of State, James Baker, to make the proposals more acceptable to Arab opinion failed to produce an outcome that would meet minimum Palestinian demands. While the new US Administration of George Bush proved to be more critical of Israel than Reagan's, the PLO was angered by the failure of the USA to pressure the Israeli Government into adopting a less intransigent approach to the peace process. Shamir also encountered dissent within his coalition for his perceived lack of commitment to the peace issue. At the beginning of 1990 Deputy Prime Minister Shimon Peres warned that he would withdraw his Labour Party from the Government if there was no progress towards dialogue with the Palestinians. In March the coalition collapsed after Peres was dismissed from the Cabinet for stating his intention of supporting the opposition in a 'no confidence' motion.

Among the population of the Occupied Territories, there were signs of exhaustion with the efforts necessary to sustain the uprising. The mass character of the *intifada* had been gradually undermined by the lengthening lists of dead and injured and by the weight of punitive Israeli reprisals. The failure of Arafat's 'historic' concessions to achieve substantive political gains had come as a bitter disappointment and had led to fierce debate as to the wisdom of the PLO's peace strategy. This, in turn, had created a steady growth in factional tension and an alarming increase in killings of Palestinians suspected of 'collaboration' with the Israeli authorities. Disillusion within the territories, and political impasse without, had strengthened the hand of the radical resistance; foremost among these movements was the militant Hamas, a radical offshoot of the Muslim Brotherhood opposed to any accommodation with Israel. Palestinian despondency was further deepened by the relaxation of emigration controls in the USSR and the prediction of a huge increase in Soviet Jewish migration to Israel. Shamir had welcomed the prospect of new arrivals, commenting on the need for a 'big state' to absorb them, while Israeli officials stated they would not dissuade the estimated 150,000 new immigrants from settling in the Occupied Territories. This brought protest from the Arab League, but also a less predictable warning from the Bush Administration that it was opposed not only to the settling of new immigrants in Gaza and the West Bank but also in East Jerusalem. In June 1990 Shamir established a new governing coalition with a number of nationalist and religious parties which was viewed as one of the least conciliatory in recent Israeli history. There was a further set-back to the peace process later that month, when the US suspended its dialogue with the PLO after an abortive raid on the Israeli coast by guerrillas belonging to one of the organization's smaller factions.

THE GULF CONFLICT

In August 1990 Iraqi troops invaded Kuwait. A proposal by Iraq's President, Saddam Hussain, to link Iraq's withdrawal from Kuwait with an Israeli withdrawal from the Occupied Territories was greeted with great enthusiasm by Palestinians.

After early attempts to co-ordinate a pan-Arab response to the Iraqi invasion had led to confused acrimony, Yasser Arafat joined the small number of Arab states—principally Jordan, Yemen and Sudan—aligned with Baghdad against the deployment of a US-led multinational force in Saudi Arabia. Willing the opprobrium of the West and the 'conservative' Arab states through such close identification with Iraq was regarded by many observers as a grave political error. Palestinian commentators rejoined that such was the groundswell of popular support for an Arab leader portrayed as confronting Western hypocrisy and interference that Arafat had no other option. For Israel, the crisis in the region of the Persian (Arabian) Gulf could be argued to have created a welcome diversion of international attention from its suppression of the *intifada*. Moreover, the PLO's stance following the Kuwaiti invasion allowed the Shamir Government to argue that its decision not to negotiate with the PLO had been conclusively vindicated. The need to maintain the fragile Arab alliance against Baghdad was also forcing the Bush Administration to execute a delicate political balancing act. It was crucial to Western strategy to avoid scenarios that might involve the intervention of an explicit 'Israeli factor' in the impending conflict, as this would almost certainly signal the end of the uneasy Arab alliance against Saddam Hussain. Ensuring that Israel was not drawn into the conflict thus became an unswerving priority of the USA. There was a similar realization that those Arab states giving their reluctant support to the military build-up in Saudi Arabia would expect political reward for their loyalty in the form of movement towards a resolution of their conflict with Israel. The killing of 17 Palestinians by Israeli troops in Jerusalem's Old City in October 1990 provided an early test of Washington's ability to be seen to be paying due regard to Arab sensibilities while, at the same time, not overly antagonizing Israel. Amid Palestinian denunciation of perceived double standards, in supporting Resolution 672 the USA voted for the first time in the UN Security Council to censure Israel. Washington also endorsed the call for the dispatch of an investigative mission to Jerusalem. Israel denounced the resolution and the decision to send a fact-finding mission as interference in its internal affairs. Shamir castigated the US President for 'messing with Israel' and for not realizing that his country was the USA's 'only reliable ally' in the region.

On 19 January 1991, three days after the multinational force had begun its aerial bombardment of Iraq, Saddam Hussain carried out his threat to launch Scud missiles against Israel. Armed with conventional warheads, the strikes caused widespread panic and damage to buildings but only minor casualties. The attacks drew immediate demands for retaliation from senior Israeli political and military figures. The USA and the European members of the multinational force urged restraint, as Egypt and Syria made it clear they would not remain aligned against Saddam Hussain if Iraq were attacked by Israel. The USA reinforced its call for restraint with an airlift of Patriot anti-missile batteries to Israel and the concerted targeting of Scud missile launchers inside Iraq. The Bush Administration also assured Shamir that it would provide funding for the development of Israel's own anti-ballistic missile project.

The decisive defeat of Iraq by the multinational force left the PLO demoralized and dangerously isolated. The members of the Co-operation Council for the Arab States of the Gulf (Gulf Co-operation Council—GCC) punished the PLO for its support of Iraq by cutting off funds, and openly canvassed for a change in its leadership. Israel drew comfort from the PLO's vulnerability, and had attracted considerable international sympathy through its restraint following the Scud attacks. Shamir was none the less wary of the political pressures that might accompany the post-war search for a resolution of the Arab–Israeli conflict. As expected, US Secretary of State James Baker made several tours of the Middle East in the weeks following the end of the war. However, his attempts to procure support for a regional peace conference, to be sponsored jointly by the USA and USSR, failed to win the firm endorsement of either Israel or the front-line Arab states. Israel indicated that it would only support such a conference if it led directly to bilateral talks. Shamir also ruled out goodwill gestures to the populations of the Occupied Territories as long as the *intifada* continued. After lengthy talks in Damascus President Assad reaffirmed that Syria would only attend a peace conference held under UN auspices and based on Resolutions 242 and 338. Jordan and the PLO indicated they were in full agreement with Syria.

THE MADRID PEACE CONFERENCE

In May 1991 Syria and Lebanon signed a treaty of 'fraternity, co-operation and friendship', confirming Syria's dominant role in the affairs of its neighbour. Two months later the Lebanese army forced the PLO to surrender its heavy weaponry and positions around Sidon in a series of brief but decisive battles. This prompted speculation that, deprived of its Soviet sponsor, Syria had reached an understanding with the USA whereby the latter would tolerate Syrian control in Lebanon in return for President Assad's backing for the Bush Administration's Middle East peace plans. Both Syria and the USA, it was suggested, wanted to ensure that the PLO remained militarily weakened and diplomatically isolated. In mid-July it was announced that President Assad had abandoned his opposition to US conditions for the convening of a peace conference. Syria's volte-face was swiftly followed by Jordanian, Egyptian and Lebanese acceptance of the USA's proposals. Saudi Arabia also lent its support to the proposed conference, and to an Egyptian suggestion that the Arab states should end their trade boycott of Israel in return for a moratorium on settlement in the Occupied Territories. Shamir rejected the offer. Indeed, despite the *de facto* capitulation of the Arab world to Israeli conditions for an international conference, Shamir's Cabinet would only endorse the Prime Minister's acceptance on the understanding that Israel must hold a power of veto regarding the composition of any Palestinian representation. Yasser Arafat was placed in a difficult position by the proposed conference. It was clear that the PLO would not be represented officially, a situation that caused several factions to denounce the conference as a 'conspiracy aimed at bypassing the PLO and Palestinian rights'. However, the Palestinian leadership was concerned that to exclude the PLO from a process that might offer an opportunity to end the occupation of the West Bank and Gaza could be exceedingly dangerous. Attempts by Arafat, with Jordanian support, to co-ordinate Arab positions prior to the conference were rejected by Egypt and Syria. The PLO leader was no more successful in seeking the assurances from the Bush Administration that would allow the movement to sanction Palestinian participation. Although James Baker affirmed that the USA shared Arab interpretation of pertinent UN resolutions and of the status of East Jerusalem, he would offer no commitment on the Palestinian right to self-determination or to US pressure on Israel to freeze settlement in the Occupied Territories. The US Secretary of State also refused to allow the PLO formally to nominate a Palestinian delegation. But such was the pressure on the PLO from the USA and the Arab states to support the Baker proposals that by September Arafat had authorized Palestinian representation through a Jordanian-Palestinian delegation.

The peace conference, convened in Madrid, Spain, on 30 October 1991, excited considerable international attention. The Palestinian delegation was made up of personalities strongly identified with the PLO; the presence in Madrid of a high-level PLO delegation also left little doubt that the organization was representing the Palestinians in all but name. However, despite the intense media focus on the deliberations in Madrid, the talks produced little in the way of agreement. Syrian-Israeli negotiations ended in early deadlock and a Syrian undertaking not to attend the proposed multilateral negotiations on regional issues until Israel had committed itself to territorial concessions. There was scarcely more progress in the other bilateral sessions, although significantly the Palestinian side accepted that self-determination should follow a period of autonomy in the Occupied Territories. The Madrid Conference ended after three days without agreement on a venue or an agenda for the next round of negotiations. James Baker subsequently issued invitations to all parties to attend follow-up talks in Washington in December. This attempt to sustain momentum was broadly welcomed by the Arabs but brought a protest from the Israelis, who complained of 'American compulsion' and announced they would not be going to Washington until five days after the official start of the talks. The Israeli decision was held up in the Arab world as evidence of Shamir's contempt for the peace process. Palestinian and Arab scepticism deepened at the conclusion of the Washington talks. Little progress was made in any of the negotiations, with much time being consumed on procedural rather than substantive issues. Israeli talks with the Lebanese and Syrian delegations stalled on Israel's refusal to accept that Resolution 242 compelled it to withdraw from all occupied Arab territory, and by a Lebanese insistence that Resolution 425 was not negotiable. Appeals by the Arab delegations for some sort of US intervention to break the deadlock were met with Baker's assertion that the USA would be adopting a 'hands off' approach. By now it had become an article of faith in the Arab world that there would be no breakthrough in the peace process without US intervention. This perception became further entrenched after the third round of bilateral talks in January 1992, which once again broke up without any obvious signs of progress.

Palestinian support for participation in the peace process was also being eroded by a dramatic rise in settlement construction in the West Bank and Gaza. Work had begun on 13,500 housing units during 1991—a 65% increase over all the units established in the previous 23 years, boosting the Israeli population of the territories to an estimated 200,000. It was also reported that 13% of immigrants from the former USSR were being settled on occupied Arab land. The US Administration signalled its own displeasure at the scale of settlement building by informing Congress that Israel's request for US $10,000m. in loan guarantees would not be granted until there was a halt to settlement activity.

The prospect of a negotiated settlement receded further in January 1992 with the resignation of two right-wing parties from the governing coalition in Israel, leaving Shamir without a majority and thus making an early election inevitable. The forthcoming presidential election in the USA also suggested that George Bush would be unlikely to pressure Israel into breaking the deadlock. At the end of January multilateral talks on regional issues opened in Moscow. Syria and Lebanon carried out their threat to boycott these talks until progress had been made on the bilateral 'tracks'. The Palestinians also boycotted the Moscow talks in protest at the refusal of the USA to accept the presence of diaspora Palestinians on all of the five established working groups.

Negotiations on the issue of a proposed Palestinian autonomy dominated the fourth and fifth rounds of the bilateral talks between Israel and the Palestinians in the spring of 1992. The discussions confirmed the gulf between Israel and Arab-Palestinian aspirations. While the Palestinians called for the election of a legislative assembly, a halt to settlement and for the transfer of judicial and administrative authority prior to an Israeli withdrawal from the Occupied Territories and full Palestinian self-determination, the Israelis offered little more than phased municipal elections. Israel's continued rejection of territorial compromises also left negotiations with Syria and Jordan in stalemate.

Itzhak Rabin becomes Israel's Prime Minister

The Israeli general election of 23 June 1992 produced unexpectedly large gains for the opposition Labour Party headed by Itzhak Rabin. The inauguration of a Rabin-led Government in Israel was warmly welcomed in the USA and Europe, where it was widely considered that Shamir's stonewalling presented a major obstacle to the peace process. The Arabs were more equivocal in their reaction to the new Israeli Prime Minister. The prospect of improved US-Israeli relations resurrected fears of the kind of US partisanship that had characterized the Reagan presidency. Rabin's refusal to heed calls for a moratorium on settlement construction was also greeted with disappointment by the international community, despite the Labour leader's pledge that the forthcoming rounds of bilateral talks would yield progress on substantive issues. The sixth round of talks proved to be the longest thus far, but failed to achieve significant progress. The seventh round of talks—which coincided with the victory of the Democrat candidate, Bill Clinton, in the November US presidential election—also proved disappointing, with discussions between Israel and the Palestinian delegation mired in issues of the applicability of pertinent UN resolutions to the interim autonomy proposals for the Occupied Territories and the Lebanese refusal to agree to an Israeli proposal for the establishment of a joint military commission in southern Lebanon. Syrian-Israeli discussions foundered after Syria accused Israel of seeking to discuss only limited territorial

withdrawal from the Golan Heights. Only in the talks between Israel and Jordan was there a modicum of success, with both parties agreeing on a provisional agenda for the next round of talks.

Yasser Arafat encountered mounting pressure from his Palestinian constituency over the lack of progress in the peace process. Within the Occupied Territories the radical Hamas and Islamic Jihad movements had demonstrated their contempt for the political process sanctioned by the PLO leader with a series of armed attacks on Israeli forces in the West Bank and Gaza. Six Israeli soldiers were killed during the first two weeks of December 1992, prompting the Israeli Prime Minister to order the arrest of 1,600 alleged Islamist activists on 16–17 December; 413 of these were subsequently transported to Israel's northern border and expelled via the Israeli security zone into southern Lebanon. The mass deportation elicited strong international condemnation and the unanimous adoption of UN Security Council Resolution 799, demanding the immediate return of those expelled. Several Palestinians were killed in Gaza in demonstrations that flared in response to the expulsions. Concerted diplomatic activity by the USA helped defuse support in the UN Security Council for the imposition of sanctions on Israel for its non-compliance with Resolution 799. The Palestinians and most Arab states condemned the US moves as a further example of its complicity in safeguarding Israel from international law. Many observers viewed Rabin's vilification of Palestinian Islamist groups as paving the way for a future Israeli-PLO dialogue.

Clinton's Secretary of State, Warren Christopher, toured the Middle East in mid-February 1993, in an attempt to revive the peace process following the deportations. Syria and Lebanon stated they could separate the deportations issue from the peace process, but emphasized that regional peace would be impossible without a resolution of the Palestinian issue. Jordan's King Hussein proved less amenable to Christopher's urgings, indicating that it would be impossible for Jordan to attend the next round of talks in the absence of the Palestinians. It was clear that the Palestinian team would try to extract concessions from the USA in return for their continued attendance at the peace talks. During their meetings with the US Secretary of State they were reported to have sought, and gained, assurances including the Clinton Administration's reaffirmation of its commitment to Resolutions 242 and 338, and its acknowledgement of East Jerusalem as occupied territory. However, when Israel failed to confirm Christopher's assertion that deportation would no longer be employed against the Palestinian population of the West Bank and Gaza, the PLO ordered the Palestinian delegates not to attend the next round of negotiations. The USA and Egypt immediately urged the Rabin Government to adopt confidence-building measures to allow the Palestinians to resume participation. Rabin subsequently announced that mass deportation was not government policy and that he was withdrawing objections to Palestinians from East Jerusalem participating in bilateral negotiations. This latter point was particularly welcomed. Nevertheless, the consensus among Palestinians remained that there should be no return to the negotiating table as long as the deportees remained in their makeshift camp in Lebanon. Animosity towards Israel was heightened by the ongoing cycle of violence and repression in the Occupied Territories that saw a steady increase in Palestinian deaths and injuries. Against this background, and amid warnings of impending economic collapse, the PLO had unenviable choices to make. Domestic opposition to the Madrid peace process was counterpoised by pressure from the USA, the EC and moderate Arab states to resume the dialogue. To a chorus of Palestinian protest Arafat finally consented to Palestinian representation at the ninth round of talks. Disarray in the Palestinian ranks appeared to harden Israeli resolve against concessions on any of the contentious issues. The talks ended with Palestinian complaints that no progress had been made. The 10th round of negotiations opened in mid-June with commentators predicting a continuation of the impasse. Several Palestinian delegates demonstrated their lack of faith in the process by refusing to make the journey to Washington. Not for the first time the negotiations ended in mutual recrimination and deepening pessimism.

'Operation Accountability'

Lack of progress at the negotiating tables was reflected in volatility elsewhere. At the end of July 1993, following the killing of seven Israeli soldiers by Hezbollah fighters in southern Lebanon, the IDF launched 'Operation Accountability'. In the severest Israeli bombardment of Lebanese territory since 1982, scores were killed and 300,000 fled their homes. Coercing the Lebanese and Syrians to rein in Hezbollah militants by means of the deliberate targeting of civilians and the creation of a refugee crisis provoked international condemnation, and led Syria and the USA to mediate an 'understanding' between Israel and Hezbollah whereby the IDF would refrain from attacking civilian targets as long as Hezbollah confined its operations to Lebanese territory. Although Israel declared its attack on southern Lebanon a success, nine of its soldiers were killed in ambushes in the three weeks after their bombardment.

THE OSLO ACCORDS

At the end of August 1993, with the peace process begun in Madrid seemingly on the point of collapse, there came the dramatic revelation that Israel and the PLO had been engaged in parallel but secret negotiations in the Norwegian capital, Oslo. The two sides were reported to have reached agreement on mutual recognition and on staged Palestinian autonomy in the West Bank and Gaza. The precise details of these 'Oslo accords' were kept deliberately vague but were said to include an early withdrawal of Israeli forces from Gaza and the Jericho area of the West Bank; the redeployment of Israeli troops in other areas of the West Bank; the gradual transfer of civic power to a Palestinian authority; the creation of a Palestinian police force; and the election of a Palestinian council. Negotiations on what were termed 'permanent status' issues would begin within two years of the Gaza and Jericho withdrawals and be concluded within five years. Palestinian reaction to the Oslo agreements was decidedly mixed. Refugees in Lebanon decked their camps with the black flags of mourning, while one prominent Palestinian intellectual scorned Oslo for transforming the PLO from a liberation movement to a municipal council. Within the West Bank and Gaza, where the attrition of the five years of the *intifada* had left a collective exhaustion, many Palestinians expressed guarded approval. Notwithstanding, there was widespread concern among activists of all persuasions that the new agreements represented a capitulation to Israeli demands and a dangerous journey into the unknown. Egypt and Jordan were quick to give their backing to the PLO Chairman's gambit, and this was followed by cautious approval from the GCC states. However, Arafat failed to secure the endorsement of the Syrian leader for the Oslo accords during lengthy talks in Damascus. President Assad complained that the Israeli-PLO deal had made an Israeli withdrawal from the Golan Heights and Lebanon more difficult to achieve.

The Israeli Cabinet unanimously approved the Oslo accords. The opposition Likud accused the Rabin Government of laying the cornerstone of a Palestinian state, and representatives of the settler movement vowed to obstruct the implementation of the agreements. However, opinion polls suggested that a significant majority of Israelis supported their Government on Oslo. The emergence of the fundamentalist Hamas had made recognition of the PLO politically inevitable and psychologically acceptable, and few could justify the continued exposure of Israeli soldiers to the lethal and immutable hostility of Gaza's crowded slums and refugee camps. Agreement with the Palestinians also offered the prospect of an end to the Arab economic boycott of Israel and of normalized relations with the Arab states.

THE DECLARATION OF PRINCIPLES

The formal signing of the Israeli-PLO Declaration of Principles on Palestinian Self-Rule (see Documents on Palestine, p. 72) took place in Washington on 13 September 1993 and concluded with a brief but symbolic handshake between Itzhak Rabin and Yasser Arafat. The following day Rabin was received in Morocco by King Hassan, on the first official visit by an Israeli Prime Minister to any Arab country other than Egypt. The same day Jordanian and Israeli government representatives signed an agreement on an agenda for forthcoming negotiations between the two states. The PLO leader also benefited from the approbation with which the international community greeted the Oslo accords. Fêted by the media networks in the USA, Arafat enjoyed the kind of rehabilitation in the perception of the US public that would have been unthinkable only a few months previously. At an international donors' conference organized by the Clinton Administration in Washington, Arafat secured pledges of US $2,300m. in emergency aid for the West Bank and Gaza over the coming five years.

Israeli-Palestinian negotiations on the implementation of the first stages outlined in the Declaration of Principles began in Egypt on 13 October 1993. It swiftly became evident that there were serious differences between the two sides over the interpretation of key articles. An Israeli proposal for the troops withdrawn from the Palestinian areas in Gaza to be redeployed around the Strip's Jewish settlements elicited strong protest from the Palestinians. Similar disagreements arose over what constituted the geographical area referred to as Jericho. The Palestinians claimed that this area covered 390 sq km, while Israeli cartographers proposed just 25 sq km. The issue of Palestinian prisoners proved to be equally contentious. Israel refused a Palestinian request to draw up a timetable for prisoner releases. Although 617 detainees were released on 25 October, the majority of these were Fatah loyalists and represented a small fraction of the estimated 17,000 Palestinians held in Israeli gaols. An outcry from the Israeli right wing at the freeing of Palestinian prisoners led Rabin to suspend almost all prisoner releases shortly afterwards. Hopes that the Oslo agreements would end the violence in the Occupied Territories also proved to be unfounded. On the eve of the Washington signings Hamas gunmen had killed three Israeli soldiers on the outskirts of Gaza City, and attacks by Palestinian militants on soldiers and settlers in the Occupied Territories persisted throughout the autumn of 1993. Several Palestinians were killed in reprisal attacks by settlers. Meanwhile, Israel's security forces pursued their controversial policy of 'targeted killings' of Palestinians suspected of involvement in military operations. The continued instability made the prospect of a withdrawal from Gaza and Jericho by the 13 December deadline increasingly unlikely. Rabin appeared unperturbed by the delay, pointing out that the timetable laid out in the Declaration of Principles was not a rigid one. However, the failure to meet the deadline caused further erosion of Palestinian support for Arafat and his agreements with Israel. The initial enthusiasm that had greeted the prospect of an end to the occupation had now given way to a deepening concern that the PLO Chairman had overplayed his hand. The Rabin Government had demonstrated that it would be resolute in exploiting the ambiguities that underlay so much of the Declaration. The failure of the PLO to establish the principle of the illegality of the settlements, or even a moratorium on further construction, was regarded as a particularly grave error.

While the PLO's negotiations with Israel faltered, Jordanian and Israeli representatives, meeting in Washington, were reported to have laid the foundations for a formal peace treaty. In Syria, where official commentaries had been severe in their criticism of Arafat's deal with Israel, the news of the rapidly warming relations between the Jordanian regime and Israel was greeted with similarly harsh warnings of the price to be paid for unprincipled accommodation with Israel. In an attempt to draw Syria more fully into the peace process President Clinton met with President Assad in Geneva in January 1994. Assad reaffirmed that Syria would not countenance any normalization of relations with Israel until Israel had committed itself to full withdrawal from the Golan Heights. Although Rabin had stated that he was prepared to consider a partial withdrawal from occupied Syrian territory, Israeli opinion polls suggested that 90% of the population were opposed to a total evacuation.

After a series of meetings in early February 1994 it was announced that agreement had been reached between Israel and the PLO on the security and territorial arrangements for the Gaza Strip that would follow an Israeli redeployment. Under the terms of the agreement, Israel would maintain control of the settlement blocs and the border area with Egypt while the rest of the Strip would be transferred to the new Palestinian (National) Authority (PA). The perimeter area of the settlements and their access roads would be patrolled jointly by the IDF and the new Palestinian security force. The precise size of the Jericho enclave remained unresolved. Palestinian opposition groups—Hamas, Islamic Jihad and the left-wing factions of the PLO—denounced the security arrangements as a further capitulation to Israeli and US interests.

Arab–Israeli relations were plunged into further crisis on 25 February 1994 with the deaths of 29 Palestinians in an attack on the Ibrahimi mosque in Hebron by an extremist Jewish settler. A further 33 Palestinians were killed in demonstrations that erupted in the Occupied Territories in the eight days following the massacre. The PLO, Jordan, Syria and Lebanon declared the suspension of their participation in the peace process. The PLO initially demanded the removal of the 400 militant settlers living in central Hebron and the dispatch of an international protection force to the Occupied Territories as the price for a resumption of talks with Israel. After intense US lobbying, however, the Syrian and Jordanian Governments signalled a willingness to return to the negotiating tables. Syria justified its decision by reproving the PLO's 'isolationist' approach to the peace process, while it appeared Jordan had been swayed by a US undertaking to end the naval blockade of the Jordanian port of Aqaba (in place since the Iraqi invasion of Kuwait) as a reward for ending its suspension. Deprived of the support of the front-line Arab states, a continued PLO boycott of the peace process appeared untenable. At the UN the Security Council adopted Resolution 904, condemning the Hebron massacre and sanctioning the dispatch of a temporary 'observer' force 'to monitor Palestinian safety' in Hebron. The PLO was clearly dissatisfied with the limited remit and profile of the international force. Nevertheless, by the beginning of April Arafat had agreed to resume negotiations with Israel. His failure to extract any significant concessions from Israel on the settlement issue in the aftermath of the Hebron killings was viewed with dismay in the Occupied Territories. Meanwhile, violence in Israel and the Occupied Territories militated against the forging of trust. IDF rocket attacks in Hebron and Gaza killed several Palestinians, including Fatah cadres aligned with Arafat. In Israel 12 people were killed and many injured in car bombings claimed by Hamas as reprisals for the Hebron killings.

The Cairo Agreement

Israeli and Palestinian officials finally signed their agreement on autonomy proposals for the Gaza Strip and Jericho in Cairo on 4 May 1994 (see Documents on Palestine, p. 76). Contingents of the Palestinian police force began arriving soon afterwards, and by 17 May, amid Palestinian celebration, the IDF had completed their scheduled withdrawals in Jericho and Gaza. In Gaza the PAPA inherited administrative and economic chaos. Although the international community had promised substantial financial support for the Palestinian areas, there was a reluctance to disburse funds before proper accounting procedures had been established. After threats from Arafat that he would not visit the autonomous areas as long as funds were not forthcoming, the donor countries agreed to the immediate release of US $42m. and to take steps to finance the projected deficits for 1994. On 1 July Arafat finally made the journey to Gaza. In his first public address he acknowledged the lack of enthusiasm for the Oslo accords but reassured his audiences that Gaza and Jericho were the stepping stones to an independent Palestinian state with Jerusalem as its capital. Right-wing parties in Israel reacted to Arafat's visit with a protest rally in Jerusalem. Some 10,000 demonstrators broke away from the main rally and rampaged through East Jerusalem, causing widespread damage to Palestinian property and also embarrassment for the new Likud leader, Binyamin Netanyahu. The fragility of the new Palestinian-Israeli relationship was more seriously exemplified on 17 July when Palestinian workers wanting to cross into Israel at the Erez check-point in Gaza rioted in response to the lengthy security checks. There followed a prolonged gun battle between Israeli and Palestinian security forces, leaving two Palestinians dead and several Israeli soldiers injured.

JORDAN'S PEACE WITH ISRAEL

King Hussein confirmed the extent to which Jordan had travelled in peace talks with Israel by announcing on 9 July 1994 his readiness to meet Israeli Prime Minister Itzhak Rabin. The decision followed a US undertaking to work towards waiving Jordan's US $900m. debt to the USA and to persuade Saudi Arabia and the Gulf states to end their political and economic boycott of Jordan. On 25 July, at a ceremony in Washington, the leaders of Jordan and Israel formally ended the state of war between the two states. The overwhelming majority of Israelis warmly welcomed the development. Jordanians were less sanguine, conceding that the agreement with Israel was the price that would have to be paid if Jordan was to resolve the problems it had created by its stance following Iraq's invasion of Kuwait. Palestinians condemned the Israeli-Jordanian agreement as premature, with Arafat reserving especially strong criticism for a paragraph of the document signed by Rabin and King Hussein that acknowledged Jordan's 'special role' as guardian of Muslim holy sites in Jerusalem. The rest of the Arab world responded to the Israeli-Jordanian agreement and the PLO's quarrel with Jordan with a large measure of indifference. Although the Syrian leadership echoed the PLO's dissatisfaction with Jordan's action, other Arab states indicated a readiness to develop links with Israel. Morocco established ties in September, and Tunisia announced the opening of a special interest section at the Belgian embassy in Tel-Aviv. Also in September the six member states of the GCC announced an end to the 'secondary' economic boycott of Israel. On 26 October Israel and Jordan sealed their agreement with the signing of a peace treaty. A large Israeli delegation meanwhile attended a regional economic summit in Casablanca, Morocco.

By the autumn of 1994 Palestinian-Israeli negotiations on the implementation of the Declaration of Principles had become deadlocked. It became evident that Israel would not accede to further troop redeployments on the West Bank or the release of gaoled Palestinians until the PAPA had proved itself willing and able to halt the 'anti-Oslo' violence of Islamist militants and PLO 'rejectionists'. Palestinians accused Israel of using the 'security agenda' to ensure that the PAPA played the role of Israel's gendarme, while at the same time exploiting delays in agreed land transfers to pursue the infrastructural development—road building and settlement expansion—that would create the necessary 'facts' to prejudice the course and outcome of the 'final status' talks. Nevertheless, a series of killings and suicide bombings by Hamas and Islamic Jihad—most notoriously the killing of 22 Israelis in the bombing of a Tel-Aviv bus in October—bolstered Israeli demands that the PAPA must curb the violence before progress could be made on the implementation of the Oslo agreements. Under mounting Israeli and US pressure, Arafat ordered the detention of scores of activists connected to the Islamist movement. The arrests precipitated a serious crisis in the PA's relations with the Islamist opposition, which deepened dramatically on 18 November when Palestinian police opened fire on an Islamist demonstration in Gaza City, killing 12 protesters and wounding many others. The prospect of full-scale civil conflict was only averted by the hasty convening of mediation committees and lower-profile policing by the PA security forces. Reports that Rabin was seeking a revision of the timetable for the troop withdrawals stipulated in the Declaration of Principles added to the woes of the PLO Chairman, as did the continued expansion of existing settlements in the West Bank. Some 40,000 acres of Palestinian land had been confiscated since the signing of the Declaration, and work started on constructing an additional 400 km of access roads. A leading Israeli critic of successive governments' settlement policies in the Occupied Territories commented that Rabin was ensuring that in large expanses of the West Bank it would be 'impossible to implement any final arrangement except annexation to Israel'.

On 22 January 1995 Islamic Jihad suicide bombers killed 22 Israelis, most of them soldiers, in a suicide attack in Beit Lid. Rabin responded by sealing off the West Bank and Gaza and announcing the expansion of Jewish settlement around Jerusalem. Demands by Arafat to have the blockade lifted and for assurances on the redeployment of troops were disregarded by the Israeli Prime Minister, leading many observers to question the future viability of the peace process. Egypt and Jordan expressed their own disquiet with Israel's perceived obstructionism. Hosni Mubarak warned that Egypt would not sign the renewal of the 1970 Treaty on the Non-Proliferation of Nuclear Weapons (the Nuclear Non-Proliferation Treaty—NPT) unless

Israel, a non-signatory, also undertook to adhere to the NPT. (This decision was later reversed after the USA indicated that it would withhold aid to Cairo.) The Jordanian Prime Minister asserted that the key to improved Israeli-Jordanian relations lay in progress in Israel's negotiations with Syria and the Palestinians.

Israel relaxed its closure of the West Bank and Gaza in March 1995, granting permits for work in Israel to some 20,000 Palestinians. In the course of meetings with Yasser Arafat, however, the Israeli Minister of Foreign Affairs, Shimon Peres, insisted that further troop redeployments and the holding of scheduled elections for a Palestinian legislative assembly would be conditional on a cessation of Palestinian violence. Arafat continued his crack-down on opposition groups in Gaza, attracting condemnation from human rights organizations for what was perceived as the increasing authoritarianism of his rule. None the less, his measures failed to halt attacks on Israeli soldiers and settlers in Gaza.

Progress on the Israeli-Syrian track

After a period of deadlock in Israel's negotiations with Syria and the intensification of Hezbollah attacks on IDF and SLA targets in southern Lebanon, it was reported that Israel and Syria had succeeded in narrowing their differences over future arrangements on the Golan Heights. Emboldened by references made by Shimon Peres to the Golan as Syrian territory, President Assad hinted that he would be prepared to share the territory's water resources with Israel in the event of the latter's evacuation. In June 1995 Syria also conceded that a future demilitarized zone on either side of a new border would not have to be equal in size: Syria had hitherto insisted on 'symmetry' in all security arrangements. An attempt in Israel by opponents of a withdrawal to derail the negotiations, by introducing legislation requiring a withdrawal from the Golan to be subject to a referendum, was narrowly defeated in the Knesset.

OSLO II

Throughout the summer of 1995 Israeli and Palestinian negotiators attempted to forge an agreement on implementing the long-overdue second phase of Palestinian autonomy. Meeting in Washington on 28 September—after a succession of delays and the deaths of 11 Israelis in two Hamas suicide bombings—the Israeli Minister of Foreign Affairs, Shimon Peres, and the PLO leader, Yasser Arafat, put their signatures to a document detailing the interim stage of the Declaration of Principles. The Interim Agreement on the West Bank and Gaza Strip (see Documents on Palestine, p. 80), or Oslo II, committed Israel to redeploying its forces from the 440 villages of the West Bank and six of the seven cities (there was no agreement on redeployment from Hebron). Civil authority would be transferred to the PA in all these areas, but Israel would reserve the right to intervene militarily in the villages. An 88-member Palestinian Council was to be elected, with executive and some legislative powers. Israel would retain full or partial authority over much of central Hebron, including the Ibrahimi mosque and various locations where Jewish settlers and religious students were housed. There was no firm commitment on a timetable for the release of Palestinian prisoners still held in Israeli gaols. Oslo II was greeted with a mixture of indifference and resignation by the Israeli public; nationalist rallies to oppose the agreement were unusually muted and poorly attended. Among Palestinians there was anger at Arafat's acceptance of a continued settler and IDF presence in the heart of Hebron, and at his failure to secure guarantees on Palestinian detainees. IDF redeployment began in mid-October from West Bank villages, with Jenin on 25 October being the first city to be evacuated by Israeli troops. However, relief among the Palestinians at the removal of the Israeli military presence was tempered by the realization that in many localities the IDF withdrew not much further than municipal boundaries, leading some observers to comment that this was not so much an ending of an occupation but its reorganization.

Assassination of Itzhak Rabin

On 4 November 1995 the Israeli Prime Minister, Itzhak Rabin, was assassinated by a Jewish nationalist extremist while leaving a peace rally in Tel-Aviv. The manner and circumstances of Rabin's death completed his metamorphosis from warrior to peacemaker, and prompted an outpouring of popular grief in Israel. For the right-wing Likud leader the assassination was a major embarrassment. Binyamin Netanyahu came under fierce attack from the liberal establishment for not having distanced himself from the increasingly rancorous verbal attacks on Rabin by the settler lobby, while Rabin's widow accused Netanyahu of bearing moral responsibility for her husband's death. Rabin's funeral was attended by several Arab representatives, including high-ranking government ministers from Oman and Qatar. Yasser Arafat and King Hussein both paid effusive tribute to Rabin and his legacy to the peace process. In Western and Arab capitals there was concern that Rabin's successor as Prime Minister, Shimon Peres, failed to command sufficient trust on the centre-right of Israel's political spectrum to carry the peace process forward. Opinion polls conducted in Israel in the immediate aftermath of Rabin's assassination nevertheless revealed 54% support for Peres compared with just 20% for Netanyahu.

The IDF's redeployment in the West Bank was completed by the end of 1995, paving the way for elections to the Palestinian Legislative Council (PLC). The left-wing factions of the PLO urged a boycott of the process, and, after some prevarication, Hamas also stated it would not take part in the elections. Following talks between Hamas and the PA leadership in Cairo, none the less, a joint communiqué stressed the importance of national unity. The Islamists reportedly also undertook to refrain from attacks on Israeli targets until after the elections. The assassination—attributed to Israeli agents—in early January 1996 of Yahya Ayyash, a senior Hamas operative who was believed to have co-ordinated the previous year's suicide bombings in Israel, appeared to guarantee that the *de facto* cease-fire, which had lasted for several months, would not continue for much longer. As predicted, Arafat's official Fatah candidates put up a strong showing at the elections to the PLC held on 20 January, winning a comfortable majority of the seats in polling that was declared by international observers to be free and fair. It was unclear at this stage what the relationship would be between the PLC and the PNC, theoretically the Palestinians' supreme decision-making body. Arafat himself secured a resounding victory in the concurrent election for Palestinian Executive President, and was formally sworn into this office on 12 February.

Hamas carried out its threat to avenge the killing of Ayyash with several suicide attacks in Israeli cities in February and March 1996 that left 57 people dead and many more badly injured. The scale of the bloodshed led Peres to demand that Arafat act to dismantle Hamas's institutional base. The PLO leader was reluctant to risk full-scale internecine conflict by acceding to the Israel's demands, but having in effect so closely tied the success of the Oslo process to the fortunes of the Israeli Labour Party, it was inevitable that Arafat would need to take some action against the Islamist opposition to bolster Peres's chances of success in forthcoming elections. Hundreds of supporters of Hamas and Islamic Jihad were rounded up, and on 3 March five Palestinian militias were officially outlawed by the PA. With the co-operation of Palestinian security forces, the IDF arrested Islamist suspects in PA areas. Peres also declared an indefinite closure of the West Bank and Gaza. But despite these co-ordinated attempts at damage limitation and the unequivocal condemnation of the bombings by a broad spectrum of Palestinian opinion, polls conducted in the aftermath of the bombings revealed that Netanyahu had overturned the massive lead enjoyed earlier by the Labour leader.

'Operation Grapes of Wrath'

The resumption of talks between Israel and Syria in December 1995 had failed to achieve progress on the issue of the Golan Heights, despite Peres's assertions that peace with Syria would be a priority of his premiership. With talks again deadlocked, the two states' proxy war in Lebanon intensified. In April 1996, following the killing of two Lebanese children by Israeli tankfire and retaliatory rocket assaults on northern Israel by Hezbollah, Peres authorized intense aerial and artillery strikes, not only against suspected Hezbollah targets but also against power stations near Beirut and the main north–south arterial highway. Several Lebanese and Syrian troops were killed when Beirut's international airport was struck. Continued rocket attacks on northern Israel confirmed that Hezbollah's operational abilities remained largely unaffected by the Israeli onslaught. Furthermore, hundreds of Lebanese youths were reported to be volunteering to join the ranks of the Islamist militia. Peres's sense of unease at the palpable failure of 'Operation Grapes of Wrath' to achieve its objectives was magnified by strong criticism from abroad. This condemnation became even more forceful after Israeli shells landed on a UNIFIL base at Qana in southern Lebanon, killing 105 civilian refugees who had been sheltering there and wounding Fijian soldiers serving with the peace-keeping force. The deaths at Qana galvanized efforts to bring about a cease-fire. Mediation efforts by the USA and then France eventually brought an end to the hostilities and a reaffirmation of earlier 'understandings' on the non-targeting of civilians in the zone of conflict.

Netanyahu wins power

With its Middle East policy so firmly linked to the victory of the Labour Party in the forthcoming Israeli general election, the US Administration of Bill Clinton attempted to lend support to the embattled Peres. Promises of military and technological aid and the establishment of a formal defence treaty were made during a prime ministerial visit to Washington. Arafat also again answered calls to aid the Peres campaign, presiding over the 21st session of the PNC at which, on 24 April 1996, the articles in the Palestinian National Charter denying Israel's right to exist were formally abrogated. Peres expressed delight at the PNC decision, but neither this development nor the clear preference of the international community for his re-election was able to save him from a narrow defeat in the polls on 19 May.

Early statements by the new Israeli Prime Minister, Binyamin Netanyahu, confirmed that his Likud-led coalition would be adopting a less compromising approach to the peace process than its predecessor. Speaking in Washington in July 1996, he dismissed the 'land-for-peace' formula and confirmed that progress on the interim arrangements of the Oslo agreements would be conditional upon the PA's ceasing political activity in Jerusalem and on controlling its Islamist opposition. Netanyahu stated that his priority in future dialogue with Syria would be the cessation of guerrilla activity against the IDF in its southern Lebanese 'security zone'. After several weeks of disregarding PA attempts to resume the negotiations on autonomy issues, Netanyahu finally heeded Washington's urgings for an Israeli return to the negotiating table. Initial contacts in September failed to produce agreement on outstanding issues. At a meeting of Arab ministers of foreign affairs in Cairo, Arafat assessed that Netanyahu was not interested in peace and that the Oslo process had reached a critical juncture. The sense of crisis was heightened a few days later when the Israeli Prime Minister announced he would be reopening an ancient tunnel that ran under the Muslim quarter of Jerusalem's Old City and alongside the al-Aqsa mosque. With not untypical brinkmanship, Arafat denounced the reopening of the Hasmonean as a 'crime against our holy places', leaving Fatah cadres to call their supporters onto the streets to protest. Demonstrations on 25 September echoing those of the *intifada* were rapidly overtaken by armed clashes between Palestinian security personnel and the soldiers of the IDF. The three days that followed witnessed the most serious violence in the Occupied Territories since June 1967: some 55 Palestinians and 14 Israeli soldiers were killed before a cease-fire was mediated. To the international community, it was Netanyahu's intransigence, rather than Arafat's manipulation of the Palestinian 'street', that was deemed to be responsible for the violence. Arafat's reputation among his Palestinian constituency was enhanced by the stance he had taken on the issue of the tunnel. The PA President also boasted that he had succeeded in 'uniting the world against the Netanyahu government'. The Jordanian and Egyptian leaders meanwhile expressed their own fears for the future of the peace process under the Likud leader.

Agreement on Hebron

Several months of faltering negotiations between Israel and the PA eventually produced agreement on arrangements for the city of Hebron. Under the terms of the protocol, signed on 15 January 1997, Israel undertook to withdraw from 80% of the city but to remain in control of the settler enclave for a period of at least two years. The Israelis also agreed to begin immediate discussion of the outstanding interim issues of Oslo II: Palestinian detainees in Israeli gaols; the opening of a West Bank–Gaza 'corridor'; and the inauguration of Gaza airport.

Har Homa

Hopes that the peace process was back on track proved to be short lived. At the end of February 1997 Israel's Ministerial Committee on Jerusalem announced the construction of the 6,500-unit settlement of Har Homa, south-east of Jerusalem at Jabal Abu Ghunaim. The decision attracted strong condemnation. President Clinton, who had recently lauded the Hebron agreements, concurred with a statement by the European Union (EU, as the EC had become) to the effect that Har Homa was an obstacle to peace. PA officials warned that the proposed settlement could signify the end of the peace process, while Jordan's Crown Prince Hassan cancelled an official visit to Tel-Aviv in protest. Calls by opposition groups in Jordan for diplomatic ties with Israel to be severed were ignored by the Jordanian leadership, despite the fact that popular sentiment was increasingly hostile to the Kingdom's links with Israel under Netanyahu. On 11 March Arafat announced that he was suspending all contacts with Israel. One week later a Hamas suicide bomber killed three women in an attack on a café in Tel-Aviv. In contrast to the clamp-down on the Islamist movement orchestrated in the wake of the previous year's bombings, this time Israeli demands that Arafat take action went unheeded.

The spring and early summer of 1997 was punctuated by frequent Palestinian demonstrations against the Har Homa settlements. These were particularly fierce in the divided city of Hebron. US attempts to get Israel and the PA to restart negotiations continued to founder on Israel's rejection of Palestinian calls for an end to construction at Har Homa. In May the USA undermined the principal Israeli justification for continued settlement on occupied territory—namely that it was needed to relieve Israel's chronic housing shortage—by leaking an intelligence report claiming that many of the houses in Israeli settlements were standing empty. Netanyahu and settler leaders angrily dismissed the report. At the end of July it was finally announced that Israel and the PA would be resuming talks on the Oslo accords. It was reported that the breakthrough had been achieved following an Israeli promise to suspend construction at Har Homa for a period of three to six months, and indications from Washington that it would be assuming a more active part in the peace process. A sense of relief that the peace process might yet be salvaged was swiftly undermined when on 30 July Hamas bombers struck again in West Jerusalem, killing 14 and wounding more than 150 in the city's central market. Netanyahu accused Arafat of responsibility for the atrocity because of his failure to deal with Islamist extremism. Forthcoming negotiations with the Palestinians were cancelled. Netanyahu also announced the closure of Gaza and the West Bank, the withholding of tax revenues from the PA and the jamming of Palestinian radio and television broadcasts. Israeli officials were adamant that any relaxation of sanctions would be predicated upon Arafat's taking action against the Islamist opposition. Arafat once again ignored the demands, choosing instead to hold a 'national unity' conference in mid-August which was attended by both Hamas and Islamic Jihad. Clinton dispatched his new Secretary of State, Madeleine Albright, to the Middle East in mid-September. Albright supported Netanyahu's calls for Arafat to take action to prevent the Islamist extremist threat against Israel, but also backed Palestinian demands for an end to Israel's illegal withholding of Palestinian tax revenues. She was able to secure the commitment of both sides to resume talks in the near future.

Israel's relations with Jordan were further strained in September 1997 following the attempted assassination by Israeli agents of Khalid Meshaal, a Jordanian citizen and the chief of the Hamas political bureau in Amman. The two Israelis apprehended by the Jordanian security forces following the attack were subsequently returned to Israel—but not before King Hussein had unleashed a stinging attack on Netanyahu's handling of the peace process, and Israel had announced it would be releasing the Hamas spiritual leader, Sheikh Ahmad Yassin, from a long prison sentence. Israel's denials that it had done a deal with Jordan over Yassin's release had little credibility. Moreover, given Netanyahu's repeated demands for the PA to apprehend and contain Hamas activists, the release of the movement's leader by Israel could scarcely have had greater ironic resonance. Netanyahu's troubles were increased by Israeli reverses in Lebanon. Some 17 Israeli soldiers were killed in action in Lebanon during September, prompting public debate as to the wisdom of maintaining the 'security zone'. Opinion polls published in the wake of September's army losses suggested 60% of the population favoured an early withdrawal of the IDF from southern Lebanon.

The long hiatus in negotiations over implementation of the Oslo agreements ended in late September 1997 when the Israeli Minister of Foreign Affairs, David Levy, met with the Palestinian chief negotiator, Mahmoud Abbas, in Washington. This was followed on 8 October by a meeting between Netanyahu and Arafat (their first since the announcement of the Har Homa construction) at the Erez crossing-point. Although the resumption of negotiations was welcomed in Arab and Western capitals, progress proved limited. The principal obstacle remained the scale of the scheduled IDF redeployments in the West Bank. The lack of progress on this issue caused exasperation in Washington, where officials privately blamed the Israeli premier for a lack of commitment to the Oslo and subsequent agreements. In early 1998 the Clinton Administration proposed that Israeli forces redeploy from between 12% and 15% of the West Bank in return for a Palestinian commitment to 'fight terror and prevent violence'. While this was a far more modest territorial commitment than had been anticipated by the Palestinians, who believed a redeployment of 30%–40% would be needed to make up for Oslo's missed deadlines, the Israeli premier rejoined that a redeployment of more than 10% would jeopardize Israeli security. Yasser Arafat reluctantly accepted the US plan, less out of commitment than out of hope that by doing so it would lead to Netanyahu's diplomatic isolation. The Israeli Prime Minister continued to resist the US proposals throughout the first half of the year, declaring them 'neither desirable nor viable'. Arafat meanwhile risked growing unpopularity among the Palestinians by acting to appease the US Administration with arrests of opposition Islamists in areas under PA control. In April Jordan's King Hussein held an unscheduled meeting with the Israeli Prime Minister in Eilat, during which he urged Netanyahu to accept the US redeployment proposals. Commenting that not all of the meeting had been positive, Hussein warned that Netanyahu would be held responsible for the collapse of the peace process. The British Prime Minister, Tony Blair, invited US, Israeli and Palestinian leaders to London in early May, but these talks failed to produce agreements on redeployment. Arafat responded to the growing tide of domestic dismay at the parlous state of the peace process by stating his intention unilaterally to declare Palestinian statehood when the five-year interim period established by the Oslo accords expired on 4 May 1999. Netanyahu warned that such a declaration would provoke a stern Israeli response. He also reported to the Knesset that the PA was failing to honour its pledge to 'combat terrorism' and therefore bore responsibility for the delay in reaching agreement on the second-phase redeployment. Meanwhile, it was reported that the number of settlers in the West Bank and Gaza had risen by 12.4% in the 18 months to June 1998, to reach a total of 170,000.

THE WYE RIVER MEMORANDUM

Increasingly concerned by the lack of progress in the peace process, President Clinton hosted a bilateral summit meeting attended by the Israeli Prime Minister, Binyamin Netanyahu, and the PA President, Yasser Arafat, at the Wye Plantation, Maryland. Convened on 15 October 1998, with the expressed aim of reaching agreement on all the outstanding provisions of the interim phase of the Oslo accords, as defined in the Interim Agreement of September 1995, the negotiations between the Israeli and Palestinian teams concluded on 23 October with the signing of the Wye River Memorandum (see Documents on Palestine, p. 86). This committed Israel to withdraw from 13.1% of the West Bank, but to do so in three phases, each being contingent on the PA's meeting 'concrete and verifiable' security arrangements. Compliance was to be verified by the US Central Intelligence Agency (CIA). Oslo's putative third redeployment was to be discussed at sessions of a special committee, but

without commitment from Israel that it would ever be implemented. Negotiations on the 'final status' issues—*inter alia* refugees, settlements and Jerusalem—were to commence in November 1998 and continue until Oslo's scheduled expiry date of May 1999. Israel also agreed to a schedule of release dates for Palestinian detainees, and to facilitate the opening of Gaza international airport and the Gaza–West Bank corridor. The terms of the Wye Memorandum were viewed as more favourable to Israel than to the Palestinians, and opinion polls in Israel revealed 75% support for the agreements. Despite the positive interpretation of Arafat's spokesmen, Palestinians were concerned that Wye had committed them to entering the crucial 'final status' talks with Israel in absolute control of 60% of the West Bank and in security control of a further 22%. Given the linkage of redeployment with security issues, there was also a fear that the authoritarian character of the PA would become more pronounced.

Although the first redeployment agreed at Wye—the evacuation of territory around the town of Jenin—took place without significant delay, events precipitated by the agreement ensured no lessening in the climate of mistrust and suspicion. Hamas and Islamic Jihad militants demonstrated their rejection of the agreements with bomb attacks on Israeli targets in Israel and Gaza. In the West Bank there were several incidences of militant settlers seizing land in areas thought likely to be subject to negotiation in the 'final status' talks. The IDF did little to restrain the encroachments, and peace groups in Israel accused the Government of political and legal collusion with the land seizures. Disagreement over the release of detainees led to an upsurge in street protests that left a number of Palestinians dead. In early December 1998 Israel's Minister of Foreign Affairs informed US Secretary of State Albright that the second Israeli withdrawal, scheduled for that month, would be suspended because of Palestinian incitement. Meanwhile, the PA derived a measure of support from Bill Clinton's attendance at the inauguration of Gaza airport in December and an address to the PLC in which he called on Israel to develop an understanding of the Palestinians' 'history of dispossession and dispersal'. Arafat's pleasure at the Clinton visit was not shared by all PLC members, 28 of whom boycotted the US President's address to register their protest at the Wye Memorandum. The Israeli premier was also having to face domestic difficulties. Having failed to secure Knesset approval for the 1999 budget or to entice the opposition Labour Party into a national unity government, Netanyahu bowed to the inevitable and voted for early Knesset and prime ministerial elections.

The end of 1998 witnessed another escalation in the conflict in Lebanon, with seven Israeli soldiers killed in Hezbollah offensives in the occupied zone in November. In the following month Israel conducted air-strikes against the Beka'a valley and shelled power and water facilities in the south. One assault caused the deaths of eight civilians, to which Hezbollah fighters responded with rocket attacks on targets in northern Israel, causing widespread damage and a number of casualties. Four Israeli soldiers—including a brigadier-general in charge of IDF liaison with the SLA—were killed in early 1999, ensuring that the issue of the Israeli presence in Lebanon became a principal focus of the Labour and Likud electoral campaigns. Labour's candidate for the premiership, Ehud Barak, promised to effect an Israeli withdrawal from the Lebanese arena within a year of being elected.

Death of King Hussein of Jordan

Jordan's King Hussein died on 7 February 1999. World leaders paid affectionate tribute to a man who had been central to the search for a regional peace. Flags flew at half-mast in Israel, a telling symbol of the genuine public affection for the Jordanian monarch. Hussein was succeeded by his eldest son, Abdullah. In one of his first foreign policy statements, the new King announced his intention to foster closer relations with all Arab and Islamic nations. In early March full diplomatic relations were restored with Kuwait, and in mid-April Abdullah made a high-profile visit to Damascus where the Syrian and Jordanian leaders pledged to put aside their past differences and pursue relations that would 'safeguard...the Arab nation'.

Declaration of Palestinian statehood deferred

The forthcoming general election in Israel precluded progress on the implementation of the Wye Memorandum. During a tour of more than 50 nations in the spring of 1999, Yasser Arafat was warned that his proposed declaration of Palestinian statehood would aid the electoral fortunes of Israel's right wing. On 29 April a meeting of the PLO's Central Council reluctantly agreed to defer a decision on statehood; meanwhile, members acknowledged 'grave concern' that Oslo's interim period was to expire without the requirements of the phase having been implemented. Arafat was rewarded by the USA for postponing the declaration of statehood with a letter of assurances that reaffirmed President Clinton's support for Palestinians to 'determine their future as a free people on their own land'. US officials also accused Netanyahu of duplicity over the scale and extent of new settlement construction.

Ehud Barak elected

Israel's elections held on 17 May 1999 produced a convincing victory for Ehud Barak and the One Israel alliance over Binyamin Netanyahu and Likud (with the Labour leader taking some 56% of the votes cast in the election for Prime Minister). Netanyahu immediately resigned as Likud leader, leaving the veteran hardliner, Ariel Sharon, as caretaker leader. Barak's Cabinet was sworn in on 6 July, having secured the support of 77 members of the 120-member Knesset. In his inaugural address Barak stated that he desired peace with all of his Arab neighbours. At a joint press conference with Egypt's President Mubarak in Alexandria on 9 July, Barak vowed 'to turn every stone in order to find a way to go forward without risking our vital security interests'.

Wye Two

Early discussions between Israeli and Palestinian negotiators, encouraged by delegations from EU countries and by an official visit by US Secretary of State Madeleine Albright, culminated in an agreement in the Egyptian resort of Sharm esh-Sheikh to revise the timetable for the outstanding provisions of the 1998 Wye Memorandum. The Sharm esh-Sheikh Memorandum (or Wye Two—see Documents on Palestine, p. 88), signed on 4 September 1999, included a commitment to achieve a framework agreement on permanent status issues by February 2000 and for the phased 13% Israeli redeployment in the West Bank to be completed by 20 January 2000. 'Final status' negotiations were scheduled to be completed by September 2000, although Barak commented that these might result in a series of long-term interim arrangements rather than a permanent settlement. The transfer to the PA of 400 sq km (7%) of West Bank territory was initiated on 10 September, and the southern 'safe passage' between Gaza and the West Bank was opened on 5 October.

While Barak was more circumspect in his promises to the settler lobby than had been his Likud predecessor, the new Government did not delay in underlining that there would be no radical revision of settlement policy in the West Bank. Commitment to the concept of 'natural growth' saw the Ministry of Construction and Housing issue tenders for 2,600 units in the first three months of Barak's administration. It was also announced that a further five bypass roads were to be constructed in the West Bank. In mid-October the Cabinet also decided that the overwhelming majority of the 42 outpost settlements established in the final months of the Netanyahu administration would be allowed to remain *in situ*. Barak's settlement policy was condemned by the PA's chief negotiator, Yasser Abd ar-Rabbuh, as 'unprecedented colonialist aggression'. There was a further souring of relations when, on the eve of the commencement of the 'final status' talks in November, Barak informed his Cabinet that Resolution 242 did not apply to the West Bank and Gaza because it pertained to sovereign states and not organizations. Palestinian anger at these comments was exacerbated by differences over redeployment issues. The PA refused to sign maps approved by the Israeli Government detailing the remaining lands to be transferred under the interim agreements because it was claimed they were either sparsely populated or too far removed from the main areas of PA control. Mediation by the USA failed to break the impasse, and on 6 December the

PA announced that it was suspending involvement in the 'final status' talks because of the settlement issue.

Israeli–Syrian talks revived

Barak's pre-election commitment to effect an Israeli withdrawal from Lebanon, and his declared intention to achieve a peace treaty with Syria, had prompted speculation that there would be a swift resumption of the bilateral talks broken off in 1996. US intermediaries were informed that Syria's President Assad would only resume negotiations on the basis of the understandings purportedly reached with the Rabin Government (i.e. that Israel was committed to a withdrawal from the occupied Golan Heights). Irritated by this precondition but aware of Assad's desire to secure a deal with Israel on the Golan, Barak's administration attempted to pressure Damascus by conferring 'national priority' status on the Golan—enabling settlers there to benefit from extra government aid and tax benefits. Syria responded by accusing Israel of trying to sabotage the peace process. In December 1999 US Secretary of State Albright met with Israeli and Syrian leaders during a regional tour. Expectations that her diplomatic efforts might revive the Israeli-Syrian track of the peace process were deliberately downplayed. Nevertheless, her visit was followed by an announcement that the Israeli Prime Minister and the Syrian Minister of Foreign Affairs, Farouk ash-Shara', would be resuming negotiations 'from the point where they left off' in February 1996. The talks were formally reopened in Washington on 15 December. Syrian and Israeli delegations, led by ash-Shara' and Barak, convened in Shepherdstown, West Virginia, on 3 January 2000, amid optimism that a peace treaty might be concluded by the summer. The talks ended on 10 January with a commitment to resume discussions on the key areas of borders, water, security and diplomatic relations on 19 January. However, the leaking of a US framework document revealing that Israel had not committed itself to a withdrawal to the boundaries as of 4 June 1967 prompted Syria to announce that its negotiators would not be returning to Shepherdstown. Opinion polls in Israel had meanwhile suggested that 53% of the population opposed a comprehensive withdrawal from the Golan Heights in return for a 'full peace'. Two of Barak's coalition partners—the National Religious Party and Israel B'Aliyah—were also against an Israeli evacuation from the Golan. Despite the hiatus in formal negotiations, channels of communication between Syria and Israel were kept open, and in due course it was announced that President Clinton would be meeting with President Assad in Geneva on 26 March. Given the poor state of health of the Syrian leader, and his general reluctance to venture outside his country's borders, there was a strong expectation that Clinton would be conveying Barak's assurances on an Israeli withdrawal from the Golan. In the event, however, the US President reportedly brought a proposal from Barak that Israel retain sovereignty over the shores of Lake Tiberias (the Sea of Galilee) and the waters of the Jordan river following a withdrawal. This had already been rejected by Syria. The meeting ended with Syrian officials angrily claiming that the meeting had been designed to fail so that Barak could avoid the territorial concessions on the Golan that might precipitate the fall of his Government. Both Jordan and Oman postponed scheduled negotiations on economic initiatives with Israel in response to the breakdown on the Israeli-Syrian track.

Israeli redeployments

Having failed to persuade the USA to intervene in the dispute over the second redeployment, Arafat reluctantly abandoned his opposition to Israeli proposals. This was carried out on 6–7 January 2000. PA officials mitigated the reversal of the Palestinian position with suggestions that Barak had promised to transfer villages around Jerusalem as part of the interim final-phase redeployment, as well as other 'quality lands'. However, when Israel presented its redeployment maps at the beginning of February, these did not include the Jerusalem villages that both the Israeli media and the Palestinians had confidently predicted would be transferred to PA control. Barak also proposed that the target dates for achieving framework and 'final status' agreements be shifted to mid-August 2000 and mid-June 2001 respectively. He also called for the crucial third redeployment to be 'collapsed' into the 'final status' negotiations.

A furious Arafat rejected the redeployment proposals and revised timetables. Once again the USA refused to involve itself in the disagreement—asserting that its role was to facilitate the peace process, not to act as its guarantor. At talks with Barak, hosted by Egyptian President Hosni Mubarak at Sharm esh-Sheikh on 9 March, the PA leader agreed to accept Israel's proposed map for the delayed redeployment in exchange for Israel's abandoning its suggestion of extending framework and 'final status' deadlines(these were now set for mid-May and mid-September 2000). Negotiations on a framework agreement dragged on through the spring of 2000, and it became clear that no agreement would be achieved by the revised mid-May deadline. Frustration in the West Bank and Gaza at the lack of progress in the talks and with delays over prisoner releases found expression in renewed street demonstrations and violence in mid-May; that the protests, which claimed several Palestinian lives, were orchestrated by Fatah activists led to Israeli charges that the violence had been encouraged at the highest levels of the PA.

ISRAELI DEPARTURE FROM SOUTHERN LEBANON

On 6 March 2000 the Israeli Cabinet ratified its decision to effect a withdrawal of Israeli forces from Lebanon by early July 2000. In mid-May the IDF began redeploying in preparation for the final evacuation. Fortified positions were handed over to the SLA, but many of these were swiftly abandoned as Israel's proxy militia began to disintegrate. Hezbollah and its supporters quickly overran villages and military outposts in the occupation zone. Realizing that an orderly retreat was now impossible, Israeli commanders ordered an immediate withdrawal. By 24 May the last Israeli soldier had left Lebanese territory. There followed a largely peaceful take-over of the south by Lebanese security forces and various militia groups. Some 6,000 SLA fighters and their families were given refuge in Israel, while 1,500 surrendered to Hezbollah and the Lebanese police. Hezbollah's Secretary General, Hasan Nasrallah, urged restraint in dealing with collaborators, but insisted that the conflict would continue until the Lebanese prisoners held in Israeli detention were released and violations of Lebanese waters and airspace ended. Israeli claims to have withdrawn from all Lebanese territory were disputed by Lebanon's President Emile Lahoud, who asserted that Israel still controlled three parcels of land belonging to Lebanon, including the 25-sq km enclave of Shebaa Farms. (Most independent experts agreed that Shebaa Farms was Syrian rather than Lebanese territory.) Lebanese jubilation at the recovery of occupied territory was shared by the rest of the Arab world—not least by the Palestinians of the West Bank and Gaza, where comparisons were drawn between the successes of the Hezbollah-led resistance in forcing an Israeli withdrawal and the Palestinians' own achievements via the path of negotiation. Within Israel unease at the precipitate manner of the withdrawal was outweighed by relief that Israel's armed forces were no longer embroiled in the 'mini-Viet Nam' of southern Lebanon.

Death of President Hafiz al-Assad

President Assad of Syria died on 10 June 2000. He was succeeded by his eldest surviving son, Bashar. There were hopes in Europe and Washington that the new leader would liberalize the governing regime and open Syria up to the West. However, there seemed little immediate prospect that the accession of Bashar al-Assad to the Syrian presidency would facilitate a revival of negotiations on the Israeli-Syrian track of the peace process.

Camp David II

In mid-May 2000 it was disclosed that the PA and the Israeli Government had been involved in a secret dialogue in the Swedish capital, Stockholm. The negotiations had been facilitated by a US Administration apparently anxious to see an Israeli-Palestinian agreement on a future settlement before November's US presidential election. The sense of urgency within the Clinton Administration was heightened by a decision of the Palestinian Central Council on 3 July to empower Arafat to declare a Palestinian state on 13 September, and by an Israeli threat to annex settlement blocs in the West Bank in such an eventuality. On 5 July Bill Clinton invited Barak and Arafat to an open-ended summit meeting at Camp David to forge the all-important framework agreement on 'final status' issues. Complaining that they had not been consulted over the extent of the concessions that Barak would be prepared to make at Camp David, the leaders of three nationalist parties in the ruling coalition (Israel B'Aliyah, the NRP and Shas) withdrew their support for the Government, although the Israeli premier narrowly survived a Knesset vote of 'no confidence' prior to his departure for the USA. Both Barak and Arafat announced to their respective constituencies that any agreements on a permanent status would be subject to national referendums. Talks opened at Camp David on 11 July, and after 15 days of exhaustive negotiations, brinkmanship and a virtual news blackout, the summit broke up in acrimony, with the Israelis and the Palestinians each accusing the other of responsibility for the failure. Although it was reported that Barak had verbally made a number of significant concessions—including a proposal to transfer part of the Negev desert to the PA in exchange for annexation of settlement blocs in the West Bank—serious disagreements remained on the issues of refugees and the status of Jerusalem. An Israeli offer of PA control over some Arab districts of Jerusalem was turned down by the Palestinians, who insisted on sovereignty over all of East Jerusalem, with each religious denomination having control over its holy places. President Clinton made it clear that he believed Barak to have been the more flexible in the negotiations, and that Arafat bore the greater responsibility for the collapse of the talks. However, the PA President was warmly commended in the Arab world for having resisted US and Israeli pressure to conclude a 'dishonourable peace'. Sensitive to Barak's domestic political vulnerability, Clinton emphasized that the permanent status talks had been adjourned rather that ended. US influence was again apparent when on 10 September a meeting of the Palestinian Central Council endorsed Arafat's recommendation to postpone a decision on a declaration of statehood. This followed strong hints from the Clinton Administration that it was considering relocating the US embassy in Israel from Tel-Aviv to Jerusalem.

THE AL-AQSA UPRISING

Throughout the latter part of September 2000 there were conflicting signals from the Israeli Prime Minister as to his intentions regarding the resumption of negotiations with the PA. On 23 September Barak publicly questioned the usefulness of resuming contacts with Arafat, but the two did meet at the Israeli premier's home on 25 September and it was announced that they would meet again on 29 September. With both sides' positions apparently more deeply entrenched since the collapse of the Camp David summit, few observers predicted an easy or an early end to the stalemate in the peace process. The proposed meeting never materialized. On 28 September the controversial leader of the Likud opposition, Ariel Sharon, toured the al-Aqsa compound at Temple Mount/Haram ash-Sharif in Jerusalem's Old City. Regarded by many Palestinians as a provocative attempt to demonstrate Israeli sovereignty over one of Islam's holiest sites, the visit provoked scuffles and stone-throwing. The next day Palestinians in the al-Aqsa compound demonstrated at the conclusion of Friday's midday prayers. Israeli security forces responded with rubber bullets and live ammunition, leaving seven Palestinians dead and more than 200 wounded. Palestinians reacted to the deaths by taking to the streets in huge numbers to throw rocks and petrol bombs at Israeli soldiers. In a number of localities in Gaza and the West Bank Palestinian security forces engaged Israeli troops in prolonged gun battles. Mutual recriminations characterized proximity talks and direct encounters between Arafat and Barak hosted by US Secretary of State Madeleine Albright in Paris, France, on 4 October, and the Israeli premier did not proceed with Albright and Arafat to Sharm esh-Sheikh for further talks led by Hosni Mubarak. Meanwhile, Palestinian casualties mounted, with each death fanning the flames of a revolt that was soon being referred to as the al-Aqsa *intifada*. By 9 October 90 Palestinians, 18 of them children, had been shot dead in clashes with Israeli security forces, and more than 2,500 wounded; 13 of those killed were Arab citizens of Israel, as protests in support of Palestinians in the Occupied Territories were quelled with unprecedented force. Although mass street protests reminiscent of the early months of the previous *intifada* remained an important characteristic of this new rebellion, the uprising swiftly came under the leadership and direction of the Tanzim militias affiliated to Arafat's Fatah movement. The Tanzim concentrated firepower on Israel's more exposed military and civilian settlements in the West Bank and Gaza, notably forcing the evacuation of Israeli soldiers from the outpost at Joseph's Tomb in Nablus. Elsewhere, but primarily at the Netzarim crossroads in Gaza and around the settler enclave in Hebron, the IDF responded to Palestinian attacks with fire from tanks and helicopter gunships.

Barak did not delay in laying responsibility for the dramatic upsurge in violence at the door of the Palestinian leader. US-mediated efforts to broker a cease-fire were unsuccessful, despite a series of meetings between Israeli and Palestinian military commanders. Arafat asserted that Israel's refusal to withdraw its forces from around Palestinian population centres was at the heart of the failure to agree a cessation of hostilities. He also called for an international commission of inquiry to examine the cause of the violence, a proposal that was rejected by Israel. Alarmed by the scale of the violence, President Clinton invited Barak, Arafat and representatives from Jordan and Egypt to attend a crisis summit to be held at Sharm esh-Sheikh. Popular support within the Arab states for the plight of the Palestinians led to mass demonstrations—a reported 700,000 Moroccans marched in Rabat to show their solidarity with the *intifada*—and calls for Arab governments to take action. The uprising brought early pledges of support from the leadership of Lebanon's Hezbollah, which had long exhorted Palestinians to abandon the path of negotiation with Israel in favour of armed resistance. Both Israeli and Arab commentators cited the perceived successes of the Hezbollah guerrilla campaign against the Israeli occupation of southern Lebanon as having inspired the Palestinian revolt. In a potentially dangerous escalation of the regional crisis, Hezbollah fighters ambushed and abducted three Israeli soldiers from the disputed Shebaa Farms on 7 October 2000. Hezbollah leaders claimed that the abductions had been carried out to facilitate the release of Arab prisoners held in Israel and also out of support for the *intifada*. Israel threatened reprisals against Lebanon and Syria for the Shebaa Farms incident—leading the Syrian Government to inform the USA that it wanted no escalation, and Egypt to warn Israel that it would not tolerate any aggression against Syria. Popular anger at the bloodshed in the West Bank and Gaza persuaded Arab heads of state to bring forward the date of their scheduled summit from January 2001 to 21 October. Meanwhile, on 7 October the UN Security Council adopted Resolution 1322, which condemned the 'provocation carried out' at the al-Aqsa compound on 28 September and the 'excessive use of force' against Palestinians that had followed it. The US ambassador to the UN abstained in the vote on the Resolution, which was carried by 14 votes to none.

Crisis talks at Sharm esh-Sheikh

Following the mob killing on 12 October 2000 of two Israeli soldiers being held in a police station in Ramallah, Israel launched air and naval attacks on PA buildings and installations in the major cities of Gaza and the West Bank. Although there were no deaths in the bombardments, there were many casualties and heavy damage was inflicted. Polarization widened with these events and their aftermath, confirming convictions that neither the Israeli nor the Palestinian leader was in a mood to make a success of the Sharm esh-Sheikh summit—which both had agreed to attend following intense diplomacy by UN Secretary-General Kofi Annan—when it convened on 16 October. After a day of rancorous exchanges the predictions of failure appeared to be confirmed. Barak refused to revoke the military sieges in the West Bank and Gaza (which had been sealed off since 6 October), and only reluctantly agreed to an international investigation—by an inquiry panel to be appointed by the US President—into the causes of the violence. It was also clear that in advance of the Arab League summit there was little incentive for the PLO Chairman to act to calm the violence. The meeting ended on 17 October with an unsigned statement committing the two parties to take steps to return to the situation that had existed before 28 September. This 'compromise' was immediately rejected by militia leaders in the Occupied Territories for not meeting the 'minimal expectations' of the Palestinian people.

Israelis were also angered that 60 Islamist prisoners held in PA prisons in Gaza and Nablus had been freed during the bombardments of 12 October. There were growing signs of military co-operation and co-ordination between the Fatah militias and those owing allegiance to Hamas and Islamic Jihad. There was also a shift in tactics; by the end of the third week of the uprising there had been a steady rise in the number of 'hit-and-run' attacks on peripheral settlements and on settler traffic on the roads of the West Bank and Gaza. The aim, according to one Tanzim leader, was 'to persuade the settler that they would be safer within the Green Line than beyond it', and to convince the international community of the impossibility of peace as long as Israeli settlements remained in the Occupied Territories.

The Arab League summit

Arab heads of state met for their emergency summit in Cairo on 21–22 October 2000. Given that their meeting had been brought forward specifically to address the situation created by the new *intifada*, Palestinians hoped that the Arab leaders would adopt measures that would both deter Israel from military escalation and also raise the international profile of the conflict. To reinforce their demand for concerted Arab action, Fatah leaders ensured that the summit took place against a background of intensified protest in Gaza and the West Bank; 20 Palestinians were killed during 20–22 October. However, the outcome of the summit proved to be largely disappointing for Arafat and the Palestinians. Although Libya's Col Muammar al-Qaddafi and the more radical Arab leaders had urged the severing of all ties with Israel and the use of the oil 'weapon' to counterbalance US support for Israel, the summit's final communiqué reflected the determination of most Arab governments not to antagonize the US Administration. This was particularly true of the Egyptian host, Hosni Mubarak, who had earlier emphasized the need for Arab leaders to be 'reasonable and practical' and to avoid 'emotive' decisions. As expected, the summit document professed strong support for the Palestinians, but little in the way of tangible action. Avoiding calls for the closure of diplomatic missions, Arab leaders asked instead for a halt to the establishment of new ties with Israel. (Oman and Tunisia had shut their trade offices in Tel-Aviv prior to the Cairo meeting, and Morocco followed suit the day after the Arab declaration. In mid-November Qatar also formally succumbed to pressure to shut an Israeli mission in Doha.) Other measures adopted in Cairo—the halt to the already moribund multilateral negotiations with Israel on regional issues, and calls for the UN Security Council to form a tribunal on Israeli war crimes—were dismissed by Palestinians as mere tokenism. A Saudi Arabian proposal to set up two funds—one of US $800m. to preserve the Arab identity of Jerusalem, and the other of $200m. to support the families of those killed in the uprising, was warmly welcomed by the PA.

Violence continues

Several Israeli soldiers were killed in Palestinian attacks at the beginning of November 2000, with reprisal assaults on suspected militia targets claiming a further six Palestinian lives. Arafat had met with former Israeli Prime Minister Shimon Peres on 1 November, briefly raising hopes that a mechanism had been agreed to contain the violence, but the optimism proved short lived. On 2 November a car bombing by Islamic Jihad killed two Israelis in West Jerusalem. The PA leadership condemned the attack, and issued a statement calling on Palestinians to 'ensure that the *intifada* maintains its popular and peaceful course'. Such comments were seen as largely disingenuous. Most analysts shared the view that while Arafat was not in control of every action in the rebellion, he remained in charge of its strategic direction. Having so forcefully demonstrated the Palestinian rejection of the humiliations of the Oslo process, the PLO leader was not going to ease the pressure on Israel nor spare the discomfort of the USA by abandoning the revolt. After a brief lull in the fighting in mid-November the cycle of violence was once again renewed on 20 November when a mortar attack on a settler bus transporting pupils to a school in a Gaza settlement killed two people and seriously wounded several others, including a number of children. Arafat promised to 'investigate' the incident, but although his spokesman reiterated the PA's opposition to 'all kinds of violence in principle', retaliation appeared inevitable. That evening Israeli navy gunboats, tanks and helicopters sustained a three-hour-long assault on a variety of military and civilian targets in Gaza, leaving 120 injured and a Palestinian policeman dead. Many buildings belonging to the PA and its security forces were reduced to rubble in the bombardment. The Israeli action was condemned as 'state terror' by the PA, and was viewed with sufficient concern in Cairo for the Egyptian ambassador to be recalled for only the second time in 21 years (the first had been in response to the Sabra and Chatila massacres in Lebanon). Egypt's action was welcomed by Arafat. However, the Palestinian leader's attempt to capitalize on international condemnation of the Israeli attack by renewing calls for an international protection force to be sent to the West Bank and Gaza failed to shift either Bill Clinton or Kofi Annan from their previous position that the dispatch of an international force to the region would require the approval of the Israeli Government. With Israel historically determined to resist any Arab or Palestinian attempt to internationalize the Middle East conflict, Ehud Barak reiterated his Government's opposition to such a force.

At the end of November 2000 the Israeli Prime Minister gave up his battle to keep together a governing coalition that commanded only minority support in the Knesset. Confronted by an opposition-sponsored bill for dissolution and elections, Barak signalled his willingness to go to the polls early. The popularity he had enjoyed in the initial months of his premiership had been eroded by a series of broken promises: the perception was that his Government had failed to deliver on peace with the Palestinians or with Syria, and at home the country was suffering rising unemployment and an underfunded social welfare system. Although Israel's Arab citizens (some 20% of the electorate) had voted overwhelmingly for Barak in 1999, attracted by his twin pledges of regional peace and greater government funding for Arab municipalities, they had been alienated by the lethal response to their protests in solidarity with the Palestinian uprising and the rising toll of deaths and injuries in the Occupied Territories. Opinion polls conducted in November showed Barak trailing badly behind his Likud rival, Ariel Sharon. These same polls revealed that Barak's election prospects would be revived if he were able to use his remaining time in office to achieve a peace deal with the Palestinians. There seemed little hope of such a development. Nevertheless, two days after the election announcement Barak made public a proposal that Israel recognize Palestinian statehood and redeploy from a further 10% of the Occupied Territories in return for the annexation of some settlement blocs and the deferral of agreement on issues such as Jerusalem, settlements, refugees and borders. Barak himself conceded that these proposals rated 'not more than a 10%' chance of success. Given that Arafat had rejected a more generous offer at Camp David, it came as little surprise that the proposal was dismissed by a Palestinian leadership apparently disinclined to boost the electoral fortunes of Israel's Prime Minister. Speaking on 2 December, Marwan Barghouthi, a leader of the Fatah movement on the West Bank, pledged that the uprising and 'armed resistance' against soldiers and settlers would continue. Yasser Arafat was no more conciliatory the following day, when he in turn affirmed that 'our people' would continue their revolt against the Israeli presence in Gaza and the West Bank.

The Clinton plan

Palestinian and Israeli officials met in Washington on 19 December 2000 at the invitation of the outgoing US President. PA negotiators admitted that their attendance at the talks had been motivated by a desire not to be accused of intransigence, rather than through faith in the continuation of the Oslo process. The head of the Palestinian delegation, Saeb Erakat, commented that without an Israeli commitment to return to the borders of 4 June 1967 and to accept the principle of a return of refugees, 'there would be no point in conducting further negotiations'. Details of Bill Clinton's proposals appeared in the Israeli and Arab media in late December. Unlikely not to have been given prior approval by the Israeli premier, the Clinton plan envisaged a non-militarized Palestinian state in all of Gaza and 95% of the West Bank. Israel would annex 5% of the West Bank to incorporate the three settlement blocs of Ma'aleh Edomin, Ariel

and Gush Etzion. The Palestinians would be compensated by the acquisition of 3% of land from within Israel's 1967 borders. In East Jerusalem the Palestinians would be given sovereignty over Arab districts, but Israel would extend its sovereignty over the Jewish settlements built within the city's annexed and enlarged municipal boundaries. Israel would annex the Jewish quarter of the Old City and the Western Wall, and would have 'shared functional sovereignty under' the al-Aqsa compound, and 'behind' the Western Wall. On the issue of the 3.7m Palestinian refugees, Clinton proposed a right to return to their homeland in a West Bank-Gaza state but not to their original lands in what was now Israel. Those unwilling to accept this option would be entitled to compensation and resettlement. Although Arafat was wary of rejecting the proposal outright, his negotiating team submitted a detailed rebuttal of the Clinton plan on 1 January 2001. They argued that the provisions for Israeli annexation of settlement blocs on the West Bank and Jerusalem would 'cantonize' the Palestinian state and jeopardize its viability. Moreover, the Palestinians rejected the notion that refugees should forswear their right of return: 'There is no historical precedent for a people abandoning their fundamental right to return to their homes, whether they were forced to leave or fled in fear', explained the document; 'We will not be the first people to do so.' The publication of this text made anything other than a diplomatic rejection of the Clinton proposals very difficult for the PA President. Under pressure from Egypt and the EU not to dismiss the plan, Arafat met with the US President in Washington on 3 January to express reservations and ask for clarifications. Clinton rejoined that these proposals would only be on offer until he left office on 20 January. The Oslo experience had made Palestinians acutely aware of the dangers of endorsing vague agreements that lacked implementation guarantees and which Israel, as the stronger party, could reinterpret and renege upon without sanction. But despite Arafat's decision not to embrace the Clinton plan, he was equally mindful of Israel's impending prime ministerial election, scheduled for 6 February, and the importance of avoiding actions that would bolster the campaign of the Likud leader, Ariel Sharon. On 10 January Palestinian and Israeli negotiators agreed in Cairo to a CIA-devised plan to reduce the violence in the Occupied Territories. This produced a significant, albeit temporary, drop in shooting incidents. The two sides also agreed to a resumption of direct negotiations in the Egyptian resort of Taba on 21 January. Arafat's sanctioning of these developments was reputedly motivated not only through fear of an election victory for Sharon, but also by the Occupied Territories' parlous economic state. According to the PA's Minister of Finance, the Palestinian economy had lost US $2,900m. since Israel's sealing of the West Bank and Gaza in October 2000. With unemployment and poverty indices at unprecedentedly high levels, and the PA on the edge of bankruptcy, Arafat was clearly desperate for some respite for his beleaguered administration.

Ariel Sharon wins the Israeli premiership

A slight lessening of tension in the Occupied Territories was never likely to overturn the Likud leader's commanding lead in the opinion polls. Ariel Sharon's pledge to deal firmly with the Palestinian uprising—one of his campaign mottoes was 'Let the IDF Win'—struck a chord with the large number of electors who had lost all faith with the idea of Arafat as a peace partner. Until recently Sharon had been regarded as the unacceptable face of the nationalist right wing in Israel, but his 'rebranding' as a tough but benignly paternal politician had been sufficiently skilful for the Likud leader to appeal to Israel's notoriously fickle political centre ground. Aided by an unconvincing Barak campaign and a widely observed boycott of the polls by Israel's Arab voters, Sharon secured an overwhelming victory over his Labour rival in the prime ministerial election. In the run-up to the polls Sharon had made no secret of his preference for a government of national unity, and was quick to invite Labour politicians to join his coalition. After some prevarication Barak declined the invitation, but Shimon Peres accepted the post of Deputy Prime Minister and Minister of Foreign Affairs in a Cabinet that also included representatives of the extreme right of Israeli politics. Peres was criticized by many of his Labour colleagues for lending a veneer of respectability to a government headed by an uncompromising right-winger with a reputation for military adventurism. Binyamin Ben-Eliezer, a notably 'hawkish' Labour figure, also joined the Sharon Cabinet as Minister of Defence.

George W. Bush assumes the US presidency

The international community greeted Sharon's election victory with a mixture of stoicism and dismay. Given the new Prime Minister's pledge to increase Israeli settlement on the West Bank and to maintain undiluted sovereignty over all areas of Jerusalem, it was difficult to see how there could be a retreat from the bloodshed in Israel and the Occupied Territories and a revival of the peace process. In the Arab world and in Europe there was a general consensus that the policies of the new US Administration of George W. Bush would be critical in determining the parameters of the crisis in the Middle East. During his election campaign Bush had promised a less partisan approach to the Arab–Israeli conflict, but had also indicated that he did not advocate direct US involvement in negotiations between the Arabs and the Israelis and would not be appointing a special Middle East Co-ordinator to replace the outgoing Dennis Ross (who had been closely involved in the Oslo process under both the Administrations of George Bush, Sr and Bill Clinton). The appointment as Secretary of State of Gen. Colin Powell (who had been Chairman of the US Joint Chiefs of Staff at the time of the Gulf conflict) appeared to confirm commentators' belief that the containment of Saddam Hussain's regime in Iraq would henceforth be the principal objective of Washington's Middle East policy. In late February 2001, during his first tour of the Middle East as Secretary of State, Powell met both Barak and Sharon and reiterated pledges of US support for Israel; he also joined in their calls for an 'end to violence'. Keen perhaps to demonstrate Washington's new even-handedness, Powell then travelled to Ramallah to meet with Yasser Arafat. There he endorsed the PA President's demand for Israel to release millions of dollars of taxes withheld from the Authority. This appeal coincided with the publication of a report by the US Department of State that was strongly critical of Israel's policy of assassinating Palestinian political figures and of the ongoing closure of the West Bank and Gaza.

Hostilities continue

On 4 March 2001 a Hamas suicide bomber killed three Israelis and injured scores of others in an attack on the Israeli coastal town of Netanya. The previous day Hamas's military wing had warned that it had 10 volunteers ready to carry out suicide attacks against Israeli targets in retaliation for the continued killings of Palestinian civilians in the Occupied Territories. In a rare address to the PLC a week later, Yasser Arafat acknowledged that peace remained the 'strategic option' of the Palestinians but cautioned the new Israeli Prime Minister that he demanded a settlement based on 'international legitimacy'. In an interview with a Saudi newspaper the following day the PA President asserted that the '*intifada* would continue', and that future negotiations must resume from the point at which they had left off under the Barak Government. Ariel Sharon reiterated that he would not entertain negotiations while violence persisted in the Occupied Territories, and scorned the notion that his administration would be bound by any promises made by his Labour predecessor. Instead, the Likud leader revealed a new tactic to quell the rebellion—ordering the IDF to ring Palestinian population centres with a series of deep trenches and earth barricades. These measures added to the economic hardship in the territories, and briefly revitalized large-scale civilian protests, but had little obvious impact on the ability of the Palestinian militias to wage their guerrilla campaign. Drive-by shootings of soldiers and settlers on the West Bank, and mortar attacks on Israeli settlements in the Gaza Strip, had become almost daily occurrences. These attacks were often perpetrated by the Popular Resistance Committees (PRCs), which claimed cross-factional support. Inevitably such assaults on settlers brought their own response from a section of Israeli society that had been emboldened by Sharon's election victory and which was enjoying unprecedented sympathy from a hitherto antipathetic Israeli public. Human rights organizations estimated that in the first six months of the *intifada* settlers were responsible for an estimated 40 Palestinian deaths, in addition to widespread destruction of agricultural land and property.

The killing of a 10-month-old Jewish girl in a Palestinian gun attack on the settler enclave in Hebron on 26 March 2001 ensured that the cycle of violence was sustained. While armed settlers set fire to Palestinian houses in the PA-controlled parts of the city, Israeli tankfire targeted districts linked to the Palestinian militants. A number of Palestinians were seriously injured in the bombardments. Over the next two days militants from Hamas and Islamic Jihad used the indiscriminate weapon of the suicide bomb in three attacks on Israeli civilians. Two young students were killed and many injured in the explosions, which the bombers claimed were in reprisal for the assault on Hebron. At an emergency cabinet meeting convened to consider a response to the bombings, Sharon held Arafat responsible for the deaths and pledged 'no restraint in the war against terror'. On the night of 29 March Israeli helicopters attacked barracks of Arafat's Force 17 presidential guard in Gaza and Ramallah, killing three and wounding 64. The following day seven Palestinians were shot dead on the outskirts of Nablus and Ramallah during traditional Land Day protests. Battles between Palestinian militiamen and the IDF in Hebron and Beit Jala in the West Bank were reported to have lasted for many hours. Arafat was visibly shaken while touring the wreckage of the Force 17 bases in Gaza. While publicly invoking experience of the 1982 siege of Beirut to warn Sharon of Palestinian 'steadfastness', he was reported privately to have offered a cease-fire in return for an Israeli military pull-back from Palestinian population centres and a renewal of negotiations on 'final status' issues. The Israeli premier rejected the offer as a ploy to coerce Israel into negotiating 'under fire', something he had vowed he would not do. In a move destined to ensure no lessening in the political temperature, Israel's media reported that the Ministry of Construction and Housing was preparing to commence work on 6,000 new homes in the area between Bethlehem and Hebron.

The absence of tangible political support from the Arab world was a major contributory factor to Arafat's political vacillation. Arab League heads of state met in Amman on 27–28 March 2001, but (as in Cairo the previous October) the rhetorical expressions of support for the *intifada* were not translated into the actions hoped for by the Palestinians. Some measures were welcomed by the PA. These included the reinstatement of the secondary economic boycott of Israel; the commitment to sever relations with any country transferring its embassy from Tel-Aviv to Jerusalem; and the disbursement of emergency funds to Arafat's destitute administration.

Egyptian-Jordanian peace proposals

Israel continued its policy of assassinations of Palestinian activists and political leaders in early April, targeting both Islamists and Fatah members with some success. In response, PRC fighters intensified mortar attacks on Israeli settlements within Gaza, and also fired on the Israeli town of Sederot, just north of the Gaza Strip. This proved a provocation too far for the Sharon Government. On the night of 17 April Israeli gunboats and helicopters once again undertook rocket attacks on Palestinian installations in Gaza, while Israeli tanks and bulldozers crossed into PA-controlled areas in the north-east of the Gaza Strip, occupying the town of Beit Hanoun. The IDF announced that their occupation would last as long as was needed to deter Palestinian mortar fire. However, following a stern rebuke from the US Administration at what constituted Israel's most serious violation of PA territory, Sharon ordered the immediate withdrawal of Israeli forces—although he denied that he had acted in response to US pressure. The daily litany of violent incidents in the Occupied Territories overshadowed efforts by the Governments in Cairo and Amman to prevent the seemingly inexorable descent into full-scale military conflict. The Egyptian-Jordanian plan was essentially a modification of the proposals agreed, but never implemented, at the Sharm esh-Sheikh summit in October 2000. It urged the withdrawal of Israeli forces from Palestinian civilian areas; an end to the siege of the West Bank and Gaza; and the transfer by Israel of US $430m. in tax revenues to the PA. For its part, the PA would rein in the gunmen operating from its areas and resume security co-operation with the Israelis. After a six-week 'cooling-off' period, Israel and the PA would resume negotiations on 'final status' issues for a period lasting no more than 12 months. The USA and members of the EU were reported to have given strong backing to the plan. Arafat had also moved from a position of scepticism to one of support. To underline his stated commitment to the proposals, and in the wake of another suicide bombing that left one Israeli killed, Arafat ordered an end to attacks on Israelis from Palestinian civilian areas and authorized renewed contacts with Israeli security personnel. The PA President's rediscovered enthusiasm for the concepts outlined at Sharm esh-Sheikh was interpreted in Palestinian circles more as a ploy to isolate the Israeli premier than as an expression of belief in their viability. Sharon had initially rejected the Egyptian-Jordanian plan in a meeting with the Jordanian Minister of Foreign Affairs, Abd al-Ilah al-Khatib, on 16 April, but— apparently realizing the dangers of being exposed as the sole detractor—he revised his position on 25 April, characterizing the new initiative as 'important' but 'in need of some changes and improvements'. The Likud leader once again emphasized that negotiations could only take place once there had been a total cessation of violence. This remained an unlikely prospect. Despite Arafat's clear message that he believed it expedient, for the time being at least, to scale down the use of arms, the dynamic of the conflict dictated otherwise. On 26 April four Fatah activists, including the leader of the southern Gaza PRC, were killed near the Egyptian border. The circumstances surrounding their deaths remained mysterious, but Gaza's chief of police insisted that the men had been 'assassinated' by an explosive device. Fatah militiamen retaliated with renewed mortar fire against the Israeli settlements of Gush Qatif and Kfar Darom on 28–29 April; among those injured in the attacks were five children. Clearly embarrassed, Arafat ordered an end to such 'security breaches' and the disbanding of the PRCs. Both calls were quietly ignored, and Arafat refrained from attempting to impose his will through force of arms.

Tensions in Lebanon

Meanwhile, Hezbollah guerrillas maintained their sporadic attacks against the disputed Shebaa Farms region. On 16 February 2001 an attack on an Israeli patrol in the area resulted in a number of Israeli casualties. Two months later another Israeli soldier was killed in a Hezbollah rocket attack against an Israeli tank. Israel responded with the bombing of a Syrian radar station at Dahr al-Baydar, east of Beirut, killing and wounding an undisclosed number of Syrian military personnel. The attack was roundly condemned in Beirut and Damascus, with the Syrian Minister of Foreign Affairs promising a response 'at an appropriate time'. Israel denied that the attack represented an escalation of the situation, but a spokesman warned that the new Government would not follow the 'policy of restraint' exercised by Barak's administration. The attack on Dahr al-Baydar was justified by Israeli officials on the grounds that Syria allegedly remained the conduit for the flow of Iranian arms to Hezbollah, and that Syria should pay the price for facilitating aggression against Israel. The resurgence of tension along the Israeli–Lebanese border prompted further calls from Washington, the UN and EU members for the Lebanese army to deploy as far as the Israeli border and thus take control of the border region from Hezbollah. Despite this pressure, President Emile Lahoud insisted that the Lebanese state would not provide security for Israel until peace agreements were reached with both Lebanon and Syria. Lebanon's Prime Minister, Rafik Hariri, was less tolerant of the activities of the Hezbollah militias, having publicly decried the adverse impact of their paramilitary activities on foreign investment. Nevertheless, in a meeting with US President Bush in late April, he reportedly endorsed the presidential (and Syrian) line on Lebanese army deployment. UN officials meanwhile announced plans for the phased reduction of UNIFIL forces stationed in Lebanon.

The Mitchell Report

On 5 May 2001 the international fact-finding commission established by the previous October's Sharm esh-Sheikh summit to investigate the causes of the al-Aqsa *intifada* presented its initial findings. Chaired by former US Senator George Mitchell, the committee produced a report (the full text of which was published on 20 May—see Documents on Palestine, p. 90) that trod a finely balanced line between Israeli and Palestinian narratives of the conflict. The report absolved Ariel Sharon of

direct responsibility for precipitating the uprising, but criticized his September tour of the al-Aqsa compound as 'provocative'. The report also concluded that Israel had used excessive lethal force against Palestinian demonstrators, but rejected the PA's demands for an international protection force because the Israeli Government was so vehemently opposed to such a force. There was harsh condemnation of Palestinian 'terrorism' and criticism of Palestinian gunmen for firing at Israeli soldiers and settlers from PA-controlled areas. While these comments made uncomfortable reading for the PA leadership, there was considerable satisfaction in the commission's conclusion that Israel's settlements were obstacles to a search for a regional peace and that 'a cessation of Palestinian–Israeli violence will be particularly hard to sustain unless the Government of Israel freezes all settlement construction activity', and that Israel should 'freeze all settlement activity, including the "natural growth" of existing settlements'. The PA leadership endorsed the Mitchell recommendations, secure in the knowledge that the report had the backing of the USA, Russia, the EU, Jordan and Egypt but had caused consternation in Israeli government circles. Sharon and his Minister of Foreign Affairs, Shimon Peres, categorically rejected the link between a freeze on settlement and an end to violence as a 'reward' for 'terrorism'. In the two weeks following the release of the draft Mitchell report, Israel initiated an unusually high number of attacks on Palestinian targets, killing at least 17 and wounding hundreds more. The victims included a four-month-old baby killed during the shelling of a market at the Khan Younis refugee camp in Gaza, and five Palestinian policemen killed when an IDF unit inexplicably raked their check-point with automatic gunfire. There were also an estimated 24 incursions into PA-controlled territory, in what some observers interpreted as a clear attempt to heighten tension and provoke a response from the Palestinians at a time when international focus was on Israel's settlement policy. Two Israeli teenagers were battered to death in mid-May, and 15 mortars were fired at Israeli settlements on 11–13 May. A subsequent bombardment along Gaza's coastline destroyed several PA and Fatah positions.

On 19 May 2001 another Hamas suicide bomber penetrated the security cordons around the West Bank, killing five Israelis in the coastal town of Netanya. Shortly afterwards F-16 fighter jets of Israel's air force fired missiles at the PA's intelligence service headquarters in Ramallah and at its prison in Nablus, demolishing both buildings and killing 13 policemen in the process. While the PA leadership denounced Israel's first use of jet fighters against the West Bank since the June war of 1967, the US Administration did not selectively condemn the airstrikes—despite the high toll of Palestinian casualties. Instead, the US Vice-President, Dick Cheney, asked both sides to reflect on the dangers that flowed from taking the road of escalation. On the specific issue of Israel's use of F-16s against the Palestinian police, Cheney would only comment that it was a 'delicate situation'. Even more reassuring for Israel's Prime Minister was the apparent revision by Colin Powell of the international (and Palestinian) community's interpretation of the Mitchell Report's cease-fire recommendations. Speaking on 21 May the US Secretary of State opined that there was no link between the Mitchell Report's call for an immediate cessation of violence and the need for subsequent confidence-building measures which might well include a moratorium on settlement construction. Having earlier expressed his 'reservations' over this key element of Mitchell's findings, Sharon now declared his readiness to accept 'in principle' all the report's recommendations. In a bid to pressure Arafat and answer the critics of the airstrikes of 19 May, Sharon also declared on 22 May that the IDF would refrain from 'all initiated pre-emptive operations against Palestinians except in cases of extreme danger'. He urged the PA to reciprocate and to desist from further violence. His appeal was disregarded by Arafat, who embarked on a tour of Europe and the Far East to muster support for the Palestinian contention that a settlement freeze was integral to a cessation of violence in the West Bank and Gaza. On 27 May, during talks with William Burns, US ambassador to Jordan and designated Assistant Secretary of State for Near Eastern Affairs, Arafat outlined the preconditions for a Palestinian cease-fire. These consisted not only of a settlement freeze but also an end to the blockades of population centres, the implementation of Oslo's third redeployment and a resumption of 'final status' negotiations from the point they had reached under Barak's premiership. There was little likelihood that the Sharon Government would accede to any of these demands. What was more important from Arafat's point of view was that Washington recognize that calm in the Occupied Territories could only be brought about by means of substantive Palestinian political gains.

This assertion was rudely undermined on the night of 1 June 2001 with another Hamas suicide bombing outside a Tel-Aviv nightclub, as a result of which 20 young Israelis—most of them immigrants from the former USSR—were killed and more than 100 injured. It was widely predicted that the deadliest such outrage of the *intifada* would be answered with massive Israeli retaliation against Palestinian targets in the West Bank and Gaza. This did not materialize for two principal reasons. First, the Sharon Government was persuaded not to take action that would detract from the international sympathy accorded Israel in the wake of the bombing. Secondly, the PA came under intense pressure from the EU states and the USA to call an immediate cease-fire. The US Secretary of State reportedly warned Arafat that without such a declaration Washington would sever relations with the PLO and do nothing to moderate Israeli reprisals. On 2 June Arafat duly abandoned his earlier conditions for a cessation of violence and announced that the PA would 'do all that is necessary to achieve an immediate, unconditional, real and effective cease-fire'. This would not, however, include the arrests of Islamist militants demanded by Israel and the USA. To have done so would not only have shattered national unity, cited by many Palestinians as the major achievement of the uprising, but it would also have raised the spectre of civil war. Instead he appealed to factional leaders to recognize their predicament and endorse the calls for a cease-fire. Such entreaties from a leader renowned for his often autocratic approach to dissent were evidence of the extent to which the *intifada* had shifted the balance of power within the Palestinian national movement. It was equally telling that although Fatah agreed to an end to actions from within the PA-administered areas and inside Israel, the Islamist factions and the PFLP reserved the right to carry out 'resistance' activities anywhere.

Tenet's 'cease-fire'

The enforced cease-fire was a major political reverse for Arafat and his attempt to mobilize international opinion around the Mitchell Report's recommendations for a moratorium on settlements. President George W. Bush moved swiftly to consolidate the cease-fire declaration by sending the Director of the CIA, George Tenet, to the Middle East to mediate its terms. Following meetings with Israeli and Palestinian leaders on 9–10 June, Tenet presented his proposals on 12 June. In essence, these confirmed the Israeli position that there would need to be a cessation of violence for a significant period (six weeks according to the Israelis) before other confidence-building measures could be considered: these included a return to negotiations or a freeze on settlement construction. In order to facilitate an end to the violence, the PA would be required to 'arrest, question and incarcerate terrorists in the West Bank and Gaza'. Israel would also be allowed to maintain the 'buffer' zones it had created in the Palestinian territories during the course of the previous nine months. Arafat accepted the cease-fire conditions, albeit with grave reservations. It was evident to observers that he would not pursue its implementation with the energy or the focus demanded by the US Administration. Several Palestinians were arrested for continuing mortar assaults on settlements in Gaza, but the large-scale round-ups of Islamists that had been ordered after the suicide bombings of the mid-1990s did not materialize. The PA leadership might have felt under greater pressure to abide by 'Tenet's truce' if the Israeli side had itself exercised more restraint. Three sleeping Palestinian women were killed in Gaza by Israeli tankfire on 10 June, while three Islamic Jihad members were reportedly the subject of Israeli targeted killings in the West Bank in subsequent days. These deaths brought the inevitable Palestinian retaliation and a swift return to the dialogue of assassination and ambush. By the third week in June, and despite the professed commitment of both Israel and the PA to a reduction in violence, the cease-fire existed in name only. Three Israeli settlers were shot dead on

20–21 June in road ambushes in the West Bank; the following day a Hamas suicide bomber killed two soldiers in the Gaza Strip. On 23 June Israeli forces entered PA territory in southern Gaza and demolished a number of houses; on 24 June a Fatah activist was assassinated in Nablus.

The fiction of the cease-fire was maintained during Colin Powell's second visit to the region on 27–28 June 2001. Acknowledging that there had been no significant reduction in the levels of violence in the Occupied Territories, the US Secretary of State proposed that there should be a seven-day period of 'quiet' before the 'cooling-off period' itself began. His suggestion that the period of quiet should begin as soon as he had left the region had no impact in reality: five Palestinian activists from Hamas and Islamic Jihad were killed in targeted assassinations on 1 July. Two car bombs were detonated in Tel-Aviv, and three Israelis were killed in the West Bank in the first week in July, leading right-wing members of the Israeli Cabinet to demand an end to Sharon's policy of 'restraint'. Such calls intensified on 6 July, following the deaths of two Israeli soldiers in a suicide bombing in Tel-Aviv (the first attack of its kind since the nightclub bombing at the beginning of June). The deaths were followed by the shelling of the Palestinian towns of Jenin and Tulkarm and an assault by helicopter gunship on a farm in Bethlehem that left a Hamas activist and three others dead. On 12 July two settlers were gunned down outside the Kiryat Arba settlement near Jerusalem, and a week later an extremist settler organization claimed responsibility for an attack on a Palestinian vehicle near Hebron that killed three members of one family and wounded four others; among the dead was a 10-week-old baby, the youngest victim of the *intifada* to date. The following day missiles were fired at Fatah offices in PA-controlled Hebron, killing one person and injuring 10. With the Palestinian factions pronouncing the 'cease-fire' to be dead and the violence threatening to escalate into an ever more serious conflict, the leaders of the Group of Eight (G-8) industrialized nations, meeting in Genoa, Italy, announced that 'third party monitoring, accepted by both sides' would be the most effective way of implementing the Mitchell Report and the Tenet cease-fire. Opposed in principle to the presence of any kind of international force in the Occupied Territories, but discomforted by the settler attack near Hebron, Sharon reluctantly noted that he might be willing to see more CIA personnel involved in the dormant Israeli-Palestinian security committees. This was far removed from the ideas of the PA leader, who in recent weeks had devoted more and more of his political energies into securing the backing of the international community for an independent monitoring force to be dispatched to the West Bank and Gaza. Such a development would represent a significant milestone in the PA's determination to internationalize the conflict. It was also believed that Arafat would require a political gain of this magnitude if he was to be able to reassert his authority over the militia groups that were increasingly determining the course of the *intifada*. It was not just Arafat's ruling élite in the PA leadership that was watching the ascendancy of the armed militants with unease. Many Palestinians viewed the militarization of the uprising as not only detracting from attempts to develop its character as a popular revolt but also as an obstacle to the democratization of the Palestinian national movement.

Egypt's President Mubarak expressed his own fears with regard to the deterioration of the situation in the Palestinian territories in an unprecedented verbal attack on the Israeli premier in an interview carried by Egypt's official news agency on 19 July 2001. Describing Ariel Sharon as 'a man who knows only murder, violence and war', he despaired of any progress being made in the peace process under the incumbent Israeli leadership. Equally fearful of the possibility of the situation in the Occupied Territories developing into a wider conflict, the Saudi Arabian Government meanwhile attempted to pressure the Bush Administration into restraining its Israeli ally. Meanwhile, at a meeting with Colin Powell in Paris at the end of June, Crown Prince Abdullah voiced Riyadh's unhappiness with the USA's perceived pro-Israeli bias. In mid-July it was reported in *The New York Times* that the Saudi authorities had restricted the kind of ordnance that US forces were allowed to bring into the Prince Sultan military base (from where US aircraft patrolled Iraq's southern air exclusion zone). The newspaper also carried reports of increasing friction between US and Saudi military personnel at the Prince Sultan base. On 18 July, at a meeting in Cairo of the Arab League's committee to support the decisions of the October 2000 Arab summit on the Palestinian uprising, the USA was called upon 'to live up to its responsibility as a sponsor of the Middle East peace process by halting Israeli practices which threaten the chances of peace in the region'.

On 30 July 2001 six Fatah members were killed in an explosion at the Fara'a refugee camp in the West Bank. Palestinians accused Israel of responsibility for the bombing as part of its policy of assassination, a charge denied by Israel. On the same day in the Gaza Strip a PA policeman and an Islamic Jihad member were killed by IDF snipers at the Munzar crossing into Israel. The following day Israeli helicopters fired missiles into Hamas offices in Nablus, killing eight people—among them two leading Hamas activists, a visiting journalist and two young children. While a Fatah official described the two days of attrition as marking 'a point of no return' in the 10-month conflict, a Hamas spokesman warned of 'resistance against Israel by all means and in all places'. During the first week in August several settlers were injured and one killed in ambushes by Palestinian militias. On 5 August a lone gunman launched a machine-gun attack on the Ministry of Defence in Tel-Aviv, wounding nine soldiers and two civilians before being shot dead. Two attempts by Palestinians to detonate explosive devices on Israeli buses were also thwarted, heightening the vigilance of the Israeli public in the face of Islamist threats to avenge the deaths of those killed in Nablus. The expected retaliation came with brutal force on 9 August, when 15 Israelis were killed and many injured in the suicide bombing of a busy restaurant in the centre of West Jerusalem. Hamas claimed responsibility for the bombing, which it described as just retribution for 'terrorist Zionist attacks'. Although the PA leadership condemned the targeting of Israeli civilians, Arafat's spokesman blamed the policies of the Sharon Government for provocations that led Palestinians to commit such desperate acts. The US Administration, although not directly blaming the PA for the bombing, urged Arafat to 'act now to arrest those responsible and take immediate, sustained action to prevent future terrorist attacks'. There was little chance that Arafat would order his security forces—themselves frequent victims of Israeli missile and bomb attacks—to arrest those being lauded by many Palestinians as 'heroes of the resistance'. Israel's Prime Minister was once again caught between the conflicting pressures of international appeals for restraint and the urgings of cabinet ministers and a large section of the Israeli public to unleash a massive assault on Arafat's PA. In the event, Sharon's response was swift but not on the scale initially feared. On the night of 9 August Israeli fighter jets demolished a Palestinian police station in Ramallah. The station had been evacuated in anticipation of just such an attack, and few casualties were reported. More controversially, Sharon ordered his police to seize Orient House, the PLO's unofficial headquarters in East Jerusalem and for many years the most tangible symbol of the Palestinians' political claim to East Jerusalem. Orient House had long been regarded as a provocation by the nationalist right wing in Israel. Attempts by the previous Likud Prime Minister, Binyanim Netanyahu, to close down the building had been abandoned after strong warnings from the international community. The Jerusalem bombing had, however, provided the Sharon Government with a context in which to fly the Israeli flag over a compound described by an official spokesman as 'a virtual hub and nerve centre of terrorists'. Despite the strong expressions of revulsion in Washington and in Europe at the carnage visited by Hamas on the streets of Jerusalem, the seizure of Orient House was criticized by Western governments as unnecessary and as representing a political escalation of the conflict. Israeli peace groups also stated their opposition to the take-over; their protest vigils outside the newly occupied building were violently dispersed by Israeli police. Three days after the Jerusalem blast a suicide bombing carried out in the name of Islamic Jihad wounded 20 young Israelis outside a café in the northern city of Haifa. Israel responded to the attack by sending tanks and bulldozers into the heart of the Palestinian-controlled city of Jenin in the early hours of 14 August. There they demolished the main police station and several other PA offices. Israel justified the attack on the grounds that this northern West Bank city was the principal staging-post for suicide attacks on Israeli targets.

Palestinian leaders denounced the violation of their sovereignty, accusing Israel of engaging in a concerted campaign to destroy the institutions of the PA and to create chaos in the Occupied Territories. This interpretation of Sharon's policy was shared by influential Israeli defence analysts. 'This is a rolling war,' commented one security commentator, 'We are rolling towards an all-out war with the Palestinians. What happened in the last few days was that we were not making war against terrorist individuals but against the Palestinians'.

On 27 August 2001 the leader of the PFLP, Abu Ali Moustafa, was assassinated by Israeli troops in the West Bank. The assassination was roundly condemned in the Arab world. Although he had led an organization that had maintained uncompromising opposition to the Oslo process, unlike most recent victims of Israel's assassination policy Abu Ali was widely seen as a political personality with little involvement in his movement's military activities. The PFLP vowed 'qualitative revenge' for the killing. On the same night Palestinian gunmen in Beit Jala opened fire on the settlement of Gilo, prompting a temporary reoccupation by Israeli tanks of a town dubbed 'a sniper's nest' by an Israeli government spokesman. Similar incursions by the IDF into 'Area A' locations of the West Bank and Gaza (i.e. population centres under PA jurisdiction and security control) during the first week of September left 11 Palestinians dead and several homes demolished. Hamas and Islamic Jihad responded in predictably bloody fashion on 9 September, killing five Israeli civilians and wounding many more in a series of co-ordinated bomb and gun attacks in Israel and the Jordan Valley. Sharon dismissed the PA's condemnation of the attacks and ordered retaliatory strikes against PA and Fatah infrastructure targets across the West Bank and Gaza. In the early hours of 11 September Israeli tanks and bulldozers were again dispatched to Jenin, where they were met with uncommonly fierce resistance from numerically and technologically inferior Palestinian forces. There followed the most sustained Israeli ground assault on PA territory in the year-old *intifada*. Six Palestinians were killed, and every PA barracks and police station in Jenin was destroyed, during a seven-day campaign. The offensive was barely registered by the international media as attention focused on the suicide attacks on the USA of 11 September, and on related events in subsequent days.

GLOBAL INSECURITY

The events of 11 September 2001, and Washington's subsequent decision to prosecute a 'war against terror', presented the Administration of George W. Bush with a foreign policy challenge not dissimilar to that which had arisen during his father's presidency 11 years earlier. In its attempt to build regional support for military action against Iraq following that country's invasion of Kuwait in 1990, the USA had been required to appreciate the conflicting demands and sensitivities of Israel and the Arab states on the question of Palestine. In order to secure legitimacy for a military campaign to dismantle the al-Qa'ida (Base) network of the Saudi Arabian-born militant Islamist Osama bin Laden, held responsible for the attacks on the USA, and depose al-Qa'ida's Taliban hosts in Afghanistan, it was again required to manage the differing agendas of the Arabs and the Israelis. With the exception of Saddam Hussain, Arab leaders were swift to denounce the attacks in New York and Washington. But while it was evident that the Arab states did not wish to incur George W. Bush's displeasure by opposing his initiative on global terrorism, there were two issues on which they sought assurances: the scale and legal framework of any military action and the nature of future US engagement with the Arab-Israeli conflict, which the Arab nations had hitherto perceived as insufficient and favourable to Israel. Prior to 11 September there had been growing disquiet in the Arab world regarding the US role in the region. Speaking in Alexandria in August, President Mubarak had condemned 'the complete and utter American bias in Israel's favour', and in early September GCC foreign ministers released a statement accusing the US of threatening regional security by condoning what he described as Israel's 'racist' policy of aggression towards the Palestinians. It was also reported that Crown Prince Abdullah of Saudi Arabia had refused to accept an invitation to visit the USA because of perceived US detachment from the crisis in the Occupied Territories.

For Arafat the new political realities offered an exit strategy from the *intifada*, a rebellion which daily grew more threatening to the PA and its leader. Arafat believed that the US need to garner Arab support for an anti-terrorist front would exacerbate tensions in Israel's ruling coalition and lead to the elections that would return a premier less fundamentally opposed to Palestinian aspirations than was Sharon. In the days following the attacks the PA made every effort to demonstrate Palestinian readiness to accommodate US sensitivities. Greatly disturbed by television footage of small groups of Palestinians purportedly celebrating the attacks on the World Trade Center, Arafat invited journalists to witness his donation of blood to the US victims. Arafat also declared before an audience of foreign dignitaries on 17 September 2001 that he had 'issued strong and clear instructions for a full commitment to a cease-fire'. Predictions that US-Israeli relations would be strained by the countries' competing priorities following the attacks appeared to be supported by both governments' actions. Sharon's public comparison of Arafat with the al-Qa'ida leader, and his demand that the nascent 'coalition against terror' should target the 'terrorist organization led by Arafat' annoyed and embarrassed the US Administration. Israel's escalating assaults on the West Bank and Gaza further discomfited Bush. During the week following the attacks 28 Palestinians were killed in 18 separate incursions into the West Bank and Gaza. With the belief that Sharon was, on balance, detrimental to US strategy gaining currency in the US State Department, Secretary of State Colin Powell urged Israel to constrain its military operations against the PA and to respond positively to Arafat's cease-fire proposal. The Israeli premier reluctantly announced a halt to 'offensive actions', although initially at least he refused US and EU requests that the cease-fire be consolidated through a meeting between the PLO leader and Peres. While Sharon was to concede that the period of calm required before such a meeting could be sanctioned would be reduced from seven to two days, he vetoed the prospect of Arafat-Peres talks five times in the two weeks following 11 September. This was despite Israeli intelligence assessments that there had been a significant decrease in Palestinian armed activity following Arafat's cease-fire instruction on 17 September. Peres responded with vehemence to the obstacles being placed in the way of talks with Arafat, commenting that Sharon's insistence that a cessation of violence must precede negotiations on a cease-fire had made Israel a 'laughing stock in the eyes of the world'.

Peres finally met with Arafat on 26 September 2001. The cease-fire agreed by the two men lasted only a few hours. Later that day Palestinian guerrillas wounded three Israeli soldiers in an attack on an army base on Gaza's border with Egypt. Shortly afterwards Israeli tanks and bulldozers carried out a raid on the town of Rafah, killing four, wounding 30 and destroying a number of houses. Sources within the Labour party alleged that certain IDF commanders had colluded with Sharon to undermine the cease-fire. Even if this were the case, many observers believed it was unlikely that the tensions of a violent September could have been contained with the uprising's first anniversary approaching. A further 12 Palestinians died in violent incidents on 28–29 September; this number included four militants killed in a landmine explosion near Rafah. Subsequent rumours that the PA was sending policemen to quell anti-Israeli protests in Gaza led to the sacking of three police stations by angry crowds. There were further challenges to Arafat's authority at the beginning of October when suicide bombers and gunmen aligned to both Islamist groups and Fatah committed attacks on several civilian and military targets inside Israel and the Occupied Territories, killing six people. In Hebron Israeli forces killed nine as they staged a three-day occupation of a Palestinian district in response to the wounding of two Israeli women in the settler enclave. A further six Palestinians were killed in the north of Gaza after Palestinian gunmen killed two Israelis in a settlement at Gaza's northern border. Questioned over whether he believed Arafat was capable of preventing such attacks, Sharon ventured that he had no trust in the PLO leader and that he did not consider him 'a partner for anything'. Although the US and European assessment of Arafat was more generous, there was clear impatience with the PA's reluctance or inability to take action against the factions that targeted civilians inside Israel. The Palestinian leader once

again faced the choice of alienating the US or risking internecine conflict. Over the past year the PA had sought to preserve the notion of Palestinian unity and there had been few arrests of Islamist opponents. However, with Sharon's confident disregard of US calls for reduced tension in the West Bank and Gaza souring US-Israeli relations, and the imperatives for an expanded US role in the region appearing more urgent than they had for many months, Arafat's closest advisers calculated that they could not jeopardize the strategic objective of US involvement by refusing to act. Arafat ordered the arrest of three senior Hamas and Islamic Jihad activists, including the Hamas leader in Tulkarm. This was arguably the minimum he could to do to mollify the Bush Administration, but the arrests were unpopular with a domestic constituency that was increasingly scornful of Arafat's trust in the USA. While the PA leadership had welcomed the announcement by President Bush that his Government supported the creation of a 'viable Palestinian state', much of Palestinian opinion had interpreted the US Administration's renewed interest in the Middle East conflict as a cynical attempt to win support in the Arab and Islamic world for a military campaign in Afghanistan. On 8 October, the day after such military action began, students from the Islamic University in Gaza took to the streets to protest against what they perceived as 'the war against Islam'. PA police opened fire on the demonstrators, killing three and wounding several dozen. In the ensuing riots police stations were attacked and the office of the PA airline ransacked. The use of live ammunition on unarmed protesters was widely denounced. Demands for an investigation into the shootings were accompanied by the urgings of the Fatah movement for all factions to observe the 'unity of Palestinian blood'. Arafat reportedly ordered his security personnel to seize all footage of the incident.

Wary of the ambiguities and future direction of the US campaign against terrorism (the scope of which was not to be necessarily limited to Afghanistan, according to US sources), the Arab states had been reluctant to translate their avowed political support into military assistance. Despite intensive diplomacy by the US Secretary of Defense, Donald Rumsfeld, and by Powell, the USA's key allies in the region maintained a cautious distance from the military preparations. Both Oman and Saudi Arabia stated they would not be prepared for the USA to use their military bases for offensive actions. US-Israeli relations also remained strained in the prelude to military action against Afghanistan. Although the Sharon Government could have expected that the USA would turn down its offer of direct military assistance, the latter's overtures to Iran and Syria had engendered resentment—which grew following the perceived insult of Rumsfeld's electing not to visit Israel during his tour of the USA's regional allies in late September 2001. More irritating for the Israeli premier was the USA's expectation that the IDF should exercise restraint in its operations against Palestinian 'terrorism' in order that US forces might enjoy a favourable political climate for their own actions. Sharon's anger was expressed in characteristic fashion at a press conference in early October. Likening Israel's situation to that faced by Czechoslovakia in 1938, he urged the USA not to 'appease the Arab states at Israel's expense'. He added that 'Israel won't be another Czechoslovakia. Israel will fight terrorism'. US officials were surprised by the vehemence of Sharon's statement, and commented that his allegations were 'unacceptable'. Appreciating that his populist remarks risked alienating US government opinion, Sharon subsequently issued a statement emphasizing the depth and closeness of Israel's alliance with the USA.

Assassination of Rehavam Ze'evi

On 17 October 2001 Palestinian gunmen of the PFLP assassinated Israel's Minister of Tourism, Rehavam Ze'evi, in an East Jerusalem hotel. Ze'evi had led a party on the extreme right of the Israeli political spectrum, which advocated the expulsion of the Arab populations of Israel and the Occupied Territories. Ze'evi's killing, claimed as retribution for the death of Abu Ali Moustafa, came hours before he was due to withdraw from the Government in protest at Sharon's earlier admission that Palestinian sovereignty over parts of the West Bank was an inevitability. In a strongly worded condemnation of the assassination, Sharon stated that the killing of Ze'evi was 'Israel's own

Twin Towers'. He demanded that the PA either surrender those responsible for the assassination, including the new leader of the PFLP, or risk being defined as 'an entity that supports terror'. There was no possibility of the PA extraditing wanted Palestinians to Israel, nor was it likely that the PA's condemnation of Ze'evi's killing or its detention of numerous PFLP activists and the outlawing of its military wing would deflect Israel from the military reprisals presaged by Sharon's rhetoric. On 18 October Israeli tanks and bulldozers encircled Jenin and entered deep into Ramallah, in an operation that many analysts regarded as pre-planned and for which the Ze'evi killing had provided the necessary pretext. Following further Palestinian fire against Gilo, Israeli forces took control of Beit Jala and entered Bethlehem. On 20 October tanks also entered Qalqilya and Tulkarm. The fighting provoked by the Israeli advances proved fiercest in Bethlehem, where 14 Palestinians were killed over a five-day period. Arafat responded to this, the most serious assault on the PA, with statements urging his people 'to resist the invaders' and pleas to the USA and the international community to force restraint on Israel. On 22 October a US State Department spokesman urged Sharon to halt the IDF's offensive and withdraw forces from Palestinian areas. It was not a message that Sharon initially appeared ready to heed. He insisted that the IDF would remain in their zones of control until 'terrorism, violence and incitement' had ended. Expressions of unease at the escalation in violence were made during visits to the region by the German Minister of Foreign Affairs, Joschka Fischer, and the British Prime Minister, Tony Blair. There was particular disapproval of the daily battles around the Christian landmarks of Bethlehem, many of which were televised. On 28 October Sharon announced a withdrawal of troops from Bethlehem and Beit Jala. Elsewhere in the West Bank and Gaza the incursions, assassinations and mass arrests of suspected militants from all Palestinian factions continued. Palestinian groups also demonstrated their ability to penetrate Israeli security control and exact indiscriminate revenge against Israeli civilians. Four women were killed by Islamic Jihad in the town of Hadera on 28 October; a week later two youths were killed when their bus was fired on in a Jewish settlement of East Jerusalem. On 4 November, three weeks after an offensive that had left 79 Palestinians dead, scores detained and several hundred more injured, Israel's Minister of Defence announced that the incursions had achieved their military objectives. He authorized a phased withdrawal from Palestinian territory, 'subject to security assessments in each location'. The following day Sharon acknowledged that the USA was seeking a rapid Israeli retreat from the reoccupied areas, but denied that he was under any pressure from the Bush Administration to effect this. He did, however, cancel a visit to Washington scheduled for 4 November, thus avoiding the possibility of direct confrontation with the US President. EU mediation led to the arrangement of an informal meeting between Yasser Arafat and Shimon Peres in Belgium on 5 November. That Sharon was willing to tolerate his Minister of Foreign Affairs meeting with the man now routinely referred to by the Israeli Government as a 'terrorist' reflected renewed confidence in Israel's position. Only a few months previously the IDF's first incursion into an area of full PA control had ended abruptly after stern warnings from the Bush Administration that it was opposed to such operations. Now Israel had concluded a lengthy campaign against the PA which had provoked only relatively mild rebuke in the West, and the IDF remained in control of strategic areas at the heart of PA territory. Furthermore, although both Blair and Fischer had conveyed their belief that an enduring cease-fire was not sustainable unless Israel ended its policy of assassination, lifted its siege of Palestinian areas and returned to the negotiating table, the EU had joined the USA in echoing more forcefully Israel's demand that the neutralization of the factions that continued to commit acts of violence in Israel was the *sine qua non* of the revival of the peace process.

The West had ignored the Sharon's attempts to characterize Arafat as the 'Palestinian bin Laden'. However, any comfort the PLO leader might have derived from the perceived European and US belief that he remained their only interlocutor was offset by the knowledge that he could not rely indefinitely on the promise of US re-engagement to guarantee the Mitchell principles and provide support for the PA. October's incursions

had consolidated the cantonization of the West Bank and appeared to confirm the assessment of both Israeli and Palestinian analysts that Sharon's notion of a Palestinian state encompassed little more than the arrangements offered to the African 'homelands' under apartheid rule in South Africa. The Israeli Government's insistence that withdrawal from the recently reoccupied areas would be dependent on the conclusion of local security arrangements appeared to prefigure such a settlement. As it was, the steady attrition against the PA's infrastructure had meant that in some areas, most notably in Jenin on the West Bank and around Rafah and Khan Younis in the Gaza Strip, Arafat's PA exercised little control over the local populations. There, as elsewhere, groups of gunmen determined the course of the *intifada*. Opinion polls revealed that support for Hamas continued to grow at Arafat's expense, and there was mounting evidence of fighters who owed nominal allegiance to Arafat's Fatah organization co-operating militarily with Islamist militias. Arafat's failure to exert control over the uprising, to articulate his strategic vision, or to respond to calls for greater democracy and accountability within the PA, was also alienating political leaders who had hitherto been supportive of his stewardship. One of Arafat's principal lieutenants in Gaza, Muhammad Dahlan, tendered his resignation as head of preventive security in mid-November, in response to the executive's refusal to suspend the police chief responsible for the shooting of students on 8 October and in protest at the ongoing arrests of PFLP activists. He was, however, subsequently persuaded to withdraw his resignation and reaffirm loyalty to Arafat.

US policy defined

In early November 2001 George W. Bush outlined US policy on the Middle East in a speech to the UN General Assembly in New York. Before the speech he had declined to meet or even shake the hand of the PA President. There was, none the less, much in the speech to raise the spirits of the beleaguered Arafat. Citing the applicability of UN Security Council Resolutions 242 and 338 to any settlement, Bush also proclaimed that he was 'working towards a day when two states, Israel and Palestine, live peacefully within secure and recognized borders'. This was followed by a joint statement with the Russian President, Vladimir Putin, advocating the immediate resumption of talks between Israelis and Palestinians. In his own speech to the General Assembly Arafat offered his 'deepest appreciation' for the commitment of the US President. On 19 November Secretary of State Powell expanded upon Bush's words with a long-anticipated policy speech. He confirmed the US Administration's commitment to a 'just and lasting peace between Israel and its Arab neighbours' based on relevant Security Council Resolutions. Although stating that Israel's occupation of the West Bank, Gaza and East Jerusalem 'must end', he made it clear to listeners that the first stage in achieving this goal would necessarily be an end to violence in Israel and the Occupied Territories. He announced the appointment of Gen. (retd) Anthony Zinni as a new US envoy to the region. Zinni's 'immediate mission' would be the achievement of a cease-fire between Israelis and Palestinians. Primary responsibility for the success or failure of the Zinni mission, Powell confirmed, lay with Arafat's PA. He described the *intifada* as being 'mired in the quicksand of self-defeating violence and terror directed against Israel'. The Palestinian leadership, he contended, 'must make a 100% effort to end violence and to end terror. There must be real results, not just words and declarations. The Palestinian leadership must arrest, prosecute and punish perpetrators of acts of terror'. Developments in the West Bank and Gaza continued to remind Arafat of the difficulties of the problem assigned to him by the USA. In mid-November the arrest by the PA's security police in Jenin of an Islamic Jihad activist wanted on suspicion of planning a suicide-bombing operation in Israel led to the besieging of offices of the Preventive Security Force by a crowd of some 2,000. Another Islamic Jihad activist was freed from PA custody by an armed crowd in Gaza, and a committee to defend political prisoners won cross-factional support. The Palestinian High Court had also ordered the release of some of the detained PFLP members on the grounds that their arrests had been unlawful. Meanwhile, in elections to the student council at an-Najah University in Nablus, the first to be held since the beginning of the uprising, Islamist groups won 48 of the 81 seats—Fatah supporters winning only 28. This steady migration of the Islamist movements from the margins to the mainstream of Palestinian political life was perhaps the main factor militating against the success of any cease-fire initiative. Powell had unambiguously established the position for future progress in the peace process: the PA would be obliged to resume its commitment to an alliance with the IDF and the CIA against its Islamist opposition. Having recently been included by the US State Department on a list of organizations that would be subject to financial sanctions in the campaign against terrorism, it was evident that both Hamas and Islamic Jihad had a vested interest in subverting the formation of such an axis. Popularity on the Palestinian street, significantly greater than it had been during the bombing campaign of the mid-1990s, would be a major weapon in their defiance.

The US Administration's strong reaffirmation of its commitment to UN Resolutions 242 and 338 may have vexed Sharon, but was unlikely to have surprised him. Neither was Zinni's mission to the region regarded as especially troubling to the Israeli premier. Immediate responsibility for ensuring the success of the cease-fire lay with the embattled Palestinian leader's ability to impose authority over his fractured domain. There was no certainty that such an outcome could be achieved. To the annoyance of the USA and the EU, Sharon also announced that 'seven days of peace and quiet' would be necessary before the commencement of formalized talks on a cease-fire. In effect, commentators observed, this would bestow the power of veto on any Palestinian wielding a gun. Sharon's optimistic mood originated in part from developments outside the region. The sudden collapse of the Taliban regime in Afghanistan had rendered the US need for public Arab support less urgent. President Bush had also commented that the 'war against terror' 'could not wait for a Palestinian state'. While the USA had been cautious in being seen to lend validity to the Israeli-drawn parallels between the battles waged by the USA against the al-Qa'ida network and its own fight against the second *intifada*, Israeli officials expressed satisfaction that several Palestinian factions, as well as Lebanon's Hezbollah, had been formally listed as 'terrorist' organizations by the US State Department. Hezbollah received the support of the Lebanese and Syrian governments in rejecting the designation. Speaking on 6 November 2001 the Lebanese Minister of Finance echoed views expressed in Damascus during the recent visit of the British Prime Minister. He declared that he would not sequester the movement's assets, in accordance with US wishes, because the Lebanese Government 'views the group as a resistance movement and not a terrorist organization'. The US National Security Advisor, Condoleezza Rice, acknowledged that Hezbollah 'has a side which conducts social and political activities', but insisted that the movement also possessed a 'terrorist branch which is responsible for many problems in the Middle East'. For his part, the US ambassador in Beirut accused Hezbollah of having a global terrorist reach, and of fuelling the violence in Israel and the Occupied Territories through its assistance to Palestinian Islamist organizations. Following visits to Damascus and Beirut in mid-December, US envoy William Burns gave no sign that Washington would relinquish its demand that the Lebanese Government take action against Hezbollah. He did, however, add that USA would pursue its goals through 'a practical and quiet dialogue'. The omission of Hezbollah's military wing from the EU's list of terrorist organizations was warmly welcomed in Beirut and Damascus.

A period of comparative calm in the Occupied Territories came to an end on 22 November 2001 with the deaths of five Palestinian minors in Khan Younis, apparently after they activated a device intended for fighters operating in the area. The following day, the first Friday in the Muslim holy month of Ramadan, an Israeli missile attack on the West Bank resulted in the death of a senior Hamas military leader, Mahmoud Abu Hanoud, and two of his bodyguards. Hamas announced publicly that it would seek to avenge the assassination. Elsewhere in the Occupied Territories four other Palestinians were killed in violent incidents. Hamas fulfilled its threat of retribution for the death of Abu Hanoud with two devastating suicide bombings in West Jerusalem and Haifa on 1 and 2 December respectively. A total of 25 Israelis were killed and scores injured in the attacks. Hamas' spiritual leader, Sheikh Ahmad Yassin, defended the bombings as a just retaliation for the cycle of violence initiated by Israel on 22 November. He denied that they were intended to forestall Zinni's impending visit to the region. Sharon cut short a visit to the USA in response to the bombings, but not before receiving US approval to take stern action against the PA. On 3 December Sharon delivered a nation-wide address in which he accused the PA and Arafat of sole responsibility for 'this war of terror forced upon us'. The widely anticipated retaliatory actions against the PA were initiated the same day. F-16 fighters and helicopter gunships struck against numerous PA targets throughout the West Bank and Gaza. Arafat's helicopter fleet in Gaza was disabled in the operation and a number of fuel dumps were destroyed. During the night Israeli bulldozers tore up the runway at Gaza international airport. For once, the customary US pleas for restraint were not forthcoming. Speaking after the first round of attacks, US presidential spokesman Ari Fleischer stated that Israel 'had a right to defend itself'. Arafat meanwhile had moved to Ramallah in anticipation of Israeli attacks against his headquarters in Gaza. On 4 December, as Israeli tanks encircled Palestinian town and cities, Arafat's compound in the town was fired on by helicopter gunships. An IDF spokesman denied that they intended physically to harm the Palestinian leader, but confirmed that they would not allow him to move from Ramallah until he had complied with Israeli requests for the arrest of named militants wanted for allegedly planning attacks on Israel. To demonstrate the extent of the Palestinian leader's humiliation, an Israeli tank was positioned less than 200 m from the Arafat residence. The PA leadership had reiterated its opposition to the targeting of Israeli civilians in the immediate aftermath of the first suicide bombing in Jerusalem, and had ordered that all hostile operations against Israel should cease. More than 100 prominent Islamists were also arrested across the West Bank and Gaza in the week following the bombings. This proved insufficient not only for Israel and the USA, but also for EU leaders. On 10 December they urged Arafat to bring an end to the *intifada* and to 'dismantle the terrorist networks' of Hamas and Islamic Jihad. The following day Palestinian gunmen ambushed a settler convoy in the West Bank, killing 10 people. In the previous few days Sharon had ordered restraint on the IDF, apparently unwilling to expose Israel to accusations of excessive military force or to redirect international attention from the discomfort he had imposed on Arafat. However, these latest killings, in which Arafat's Fatah had been implicated, prompted a resumption of aggressive incursions. Scores of Palestinian activists were arrested, and many killed, in IDF sweeps across the Occupied Territories. Sharon also escalated his rhetoric against Arafat, declaring him to be 'irrelevant' to the political process. This, in turn, prompted EU leaders at their summit meeting in Laeken, Belgium, to issue a statement reminding the Israeli Prime Minister that Arafat was the partner Israel needed 'in order to eradicate terrorism and to work towards peace'. Sharon's words and deeds led to inevitable speculation as to his strategic intentions. If Arafat was no longer considered relevant to the search for a settlement to the conflict, which Palestinian figures did the Israeli Government view as viable—or even likely—alternatives? Analysts also pondered the logic of Israel's demanding that Arafat tackle the Islamist opponents of accommodation with Israel while at the same time targeting the physical and human resources needed to achieve such a goal. President Mubarak of Egypt attempted to ameliorate Arafat's isolation by sending his Minister of Foreign Affairs, Ahmad Maher, to Israel on 6 December. Maher failed to win any undertaking to lessen the pressure on the PA or its leader. A week later the USA vetoed a draft resolution at the UN Security Council, co-sponsored by Egypt, condemning 'all acts of violence and terror resulting in deaths and injuries among Palestinian and Israeli civilians'. The draft's proposed condemnation of breaches of the Geneva Conventions, was, furthermore, deemed by the US ambassador to the UN, John Negroponte, as being intended to 'isolate' Israel. On 5 December the Conference of the High Contracting Parties to the Fourth Geneva Convention, meeting in Geneva (but boycotted by Israel and the USA), had decided unanimously that the Conventions did apply to the Occupied Territories and that Israel was in serious violation of many of the articles.

On 16 December 2001 Arafat acceded to international opinion and, in a televised address, reiterated his demand 'for a complete cessation of military activities, especially suicide attacks, which we have always condemned'. He asserted that the PA would locate and punish 'planners', 'executors', and 'violators' of the cease-fire. He also ordered the closure of 30 institutions affiliated to the Islamist movement. Hamas spokesmen were highly critical of Arafat, stating that his announcement and the measures taken against their institutional bases were tantamount to 'legitimizing the occupation'. Similar sentiments were expressed also by Islamic Jihad and the PFLP. Nevertheless, recognizing the precariousness of Arafat's position, the two main Islamist organizations were reported to have given an undertaking to suspend military operations inside Israel. The attrition in the West Bank and Gaza continued, albeit at a lesser intensity. Israel forces assassinated a Hamas activist in Gaza on 17 December, and killed a policeman in Nablus the same day. Palestinian militants responded with mortar fire against settlements in Gaza and attacks on settlers on the West Bank. Arafat, meanwhile, remained confined to his Ramallah compound. President Mubarak reported that the Palestinian leader had been informed that his request to attend an emergency session of the Organization of the Islamic Conference in Doha, Qatar, on 10 December, convened in response to the crisis, would only be granted if he did not return. Sharon also refused to allow Arafat to attend the Christmas celebrations in Bethlehem, including midnight mass at the Church of the Nativity.

The year 2001 thus proved to be the bloodiest in Israel and Occupied Territories since 1967. More than 1,000 Palestinians and nearly 200 Israelis had now lost their lives in the 15 months of the second *intifada*. The prospect of Arafat's regaining his previous status seemed remote, and the apparent absence of an alternative leader with the will and the ability to command a broad base of Palestinian support indicated that the deterioration in relations in the early 2000s was unlikely to be attenuated in the immediate future.

On 3 January 2002 Israeli naval commandos seized the freighter *Karine A* in international waters of the Red Sea. The ship was carrying some 50 metric tons of weapons, including rockets and missiles, which Israel claimed were en route from Iran to the PA in Gaza. Both Iran and the Palestinian leadership denied knowledge of the *Karine A* or its cargo, although the vessel was skippered by a lieutenant-colonel in the PA naval police. Israeli officials held up the seizure of the arms as evidence of Arafat's commitment to a war of terror against Israel. This message was forcibly relayed to Anthony Zinni on his return visit to the region later on the same day. The US special envoy did not, however, comment publicly on Israeli claims of PA complicity in the *Karine A* affair, reflecting the reported uncertainty within the State Department regarding the stewardship of the project.

The gun-running charges were an embarrassment for the PA. However Arafat's standing in Washington had been improved by the Palestinian factions' continued observance of his appeal for a cease-fire in the previous month; this was despite the deaths of some 20 Palestinians in Israeli military operations in the three weeks following the declaration. On 6 January 2002 Zinni met with Israeli and Palestinian security officials to outline the confidence-building measures to be taken prior to the implementation of the Mitchell and Tenet recommendations for ending the violence and restarting the peace process: the PA was required to arrest and prosecute the 33 Palestinians named on an Israeli list of 'terrorist' suspects, while Israel would reciprocate by ending its sieges of Palestinian population centres. Additionally, Zinni made it clear in his discussions with Arafat that the Bush Administration expected the 'terrorist infrastructure' in Gaza and the West Bank to be dismantled. The formula was an old one, and no more palatable to a PA leadership reliant on the goodwill of Islamist and dissident PLO militias to maintain the calm in the Occupied Territories that Arafat believed necessary to expose the Israeli leader's lack of commitment to the implementation of the Mitchell principles. Nevertheless, Arafat instructed his security forces to target militant groups; six Islamic Jihad members, including one named on Israel's list, were detained in a large-scale PA security sweep in Jenin in early January. A week later Abu Ali Moustafa's successor as leader of the PFLP, Ahmad Saadat, who was

sought in connection with October's killing of Rehavam Ze'evi, was arrested in Ramallah, prompting the PFLP to make threats against the lives of PA security chiefs. A brief lull in the violence in the West Bank and Gaza came to an abrupt end on 9 January with a Hamas assault on an IDF base near Rafah. Four soldiers and two assailants were killed in the operation, which a Hamas spokesman claimed as retaliation for Israel's killing of three Palestinian children in the north of Gaza at the end of December. The following day Israeli troops launched a major incursion into the Rafah refugee camp, bulldozing 60 houses. Attacks were also launched against PA police and naval bases on Gaza's southern coast and against Gaza international airport. On 14 January the leader of Fatah's al-Aqsa Martyrs Brigades in Tulkarm was assassinated while nominally under the protective custody of the PA. The Brigades immediately joined the other militant factions in declaring 'the hoax of the cease-fire cancelled'. Three days later a gunman from the organization attacked a Bar Mitzvah celebration in the Israeli town of Hadera, killing six people and wounding 30 others. Israel responded with ground and air assaults on PA targets throughout the West Bank. Tanks were once again positioned outside Arafat's compound in Ramallah, and the broadcasting facilities of the PA's television station in the city were blown up.

The Israeli Prime Minister was subjected to unusually sharp media criticism for his perceived part in reigniting the intifada. An editorial in the conservative daily *Ma'ariv* charged Sharon with not being 'really interested in peace and quiet, only in gradually breaking the Palestinian Authority and its leader'. Editors also questioned the value of pursuing a policy of assassination when these actions invited such bloody retaliation as had occurred in Hadera. But although there was little evidence that the Israeli public believed that Sharon possessed a viable vision for his nation's future relations with the Palestinians, his coalition government remained solid. An attempt by the Labour 'dove' Yossi Beilin to force his party's withdrawal from the Likud-led coalition was roundly defeated at a meeting of its Central Committee in mid-January 2002, not least because Labour politicians appeared unwilling to give up on power, or Sharon, as long as the Prime Minister's military escalations against the PA did not destabilize relations with Washington. A rift appeared a distant prospect. George Bush's State of the Union address at the end of the month (*inter alia* characterizing Iraq, Iran and North Korea as forming an 'axis of evil') demonstrated that in the aftermath of the 11 September, his avowed commitment to wage war on terrorism and its sponsors was undiminished. The US Administration's rhetoric also sat increasingly uneasily with the Arab world's hopes of a less partisan approach to the Middle East conflict. Concerns that the US position was moving ever closer to the formulations of the Likud leader grew stronger with the hardening of criticisms directed at the PA and its leader. At the end of January the US President stated, 'I am disappointed in Yasser Arafat. He must make a fuller effort to root out terror in the Middle East'. Commenting on the recent Israeli attacks on PA territory, White House Press Secretary Ari Fleischer told assembled journalists that the US President 'understands the reason Israel has taken the action it takes and it is up to Chairman Arafat to demonstrate the leadership to combat terrorism'. Assurances that the USA would maintain pressure on the PA leader were given to Sharon during his visit to Washington in the first week of February. Although these fell short of a US commitment to cease dealing with the Palestinian leader, Israel's Minister of Defence, Ben Eliezer, none the less confided that Vice-President Dick Cheney's attitudes towards Arafat were 'more extreme' than his own.

European leaders shared Arab fears that Washington's willingness and ability to deal with the complexities of the continuing crisis in the Middle East had been dangerously compromised by the simplistic frameworks generated by the attacks of 11 September 2001. The most outspoken assessments came from Sweden's Minister of Foreign Affairs, Anna Lindh, who decried US policy towards the Middle East as 'stupid', and the Administration's equating of Arafat with terrorism as 'factually incorrect…and very dangerous'. EU foreign ministers met in Brussels in mid-February 2002 to discuss ideas for de-escalating the conflict and revitalizing the search for a political solution. Proposals reportedly included an early declaration of

Palestinian statehood and the convening of an international conference. Neither Israel nor the USA was prepared to extend its backing to the European plans, on the grounds that the security imperatives outlined by Mitchell and Tenet must have priority over restarting a political process. Lack of unanimity or clarity among EU nations, and in particular German and British opposition to undermining US policy, effectively scuppered the initiative, to the evident satisfaction of the Israeli Government. Sharon did meet with three of Arafat's deputies at the end of January. These sought the lifting of the siege of Palestinian towns, the ending of targeted killings and freedom of movement for the PA leader (who was still confined to his Ramallah compound). According to Israeli press reports Sharon replied that none of the requests could be granted until Arafat and the PA put an end to 'terrorism' and 'incitement' and carried out the arrest of named individuals.

With all the Palestinian factions having abandoned a cease-fire which Israeli forces had never observed, there was a steady escalation in violent incidents in the West Bank and Gaza and within Israel. On 22 January 2002 the IDF killed four wanted Hamas members in a raid on Nablus. Within a week several armed attacks had been carried out on Israeli civilians in Tel-Aviv and Jerusalem. On 27 January a Palestinian woman blew herself up in West Jerusalem. Her death represented another bloody milestone of the *intifada*, not only because she was the first female suicide bomber but also because it marked a commitment by the nationalists of the al-Aqsa Martyrs Brigades to emulate the Islamist organizations in employing this most feared and indiscriminate of weapons. (The avowed secularists and nominal Marxists of the PFLP would soon also be dispatching 'martyrs' against Israeli targets). In mid-February Hamas deployed a new weapon in the conflict, firing two home-made rockets from Gaza into Israel. Dubbed the *Qassam 2*, the weapons were crude in design, modest in performance and had little conventional military value: both fell harmlessly in fields. Nevertheless, their use was seized on by Sharon 'as an act of war'. Israeli military aircraft were sent to bomb PA buildings in Gaza City and suspected mortar factories in the Jabalia refugee camp. The IDF also launched a major ground assault in the central area of the Gaza Strip, taking over PA security bases and dividing the Strip into two northern and two southern enclaves. Several PA security police and militiamen were killed in the attacks. In an ambush reminiscent of the Hezbollah guerrilla war in southern Lebanon, an Israel tanks was blown up and three of its occupants killed in a landmine explosion during the incursion. In the West Bank attacks on military and settler targets were reported daily. The intensification of the conflict and the growing number of casualties on both sides had a polarizing effect on the political debate within Israel. In late January more than 50 IDF reservists signed a declaration announcing their intention of refusing to do military service in the West Bank and Gaza. They stated they would 'no longer fight in the war for the welfare of the settlements in the Territories. We will not continue to fight beyond the Green Line for the purpose of dominating, expelling, starving and humiliating an entire people'. The declaration served to revitalize the Israeli peace movement; rallies in Tel-Aviv brought together activists from Peace Now, Meretz and the 'dovish' wing of the Labour Party into a new 'Peace Coalition'. While there was a reluctance on the part of these representatives of the political mainstream to endorse the call of the 'refuseniks', opinion polls released in the weeks following the publication of the declaration revealed the reservists had the support of 15%–25% of the Israeli public. At the other end of the political spectrum, advocates of expulsion or 'transfer' of the Palestinian populations (the most high-profile of whom was Minister of Tourism Benny Eilon) were reported in an opinion poll published in the daily *Ma'ariv* to have the backing of 35% of Israeli Jews.

The Saudi initiative

In mid-February 2002 substance was given to rumours of a new Middle East peace plan with the announcement by Saudi Arabia's Crown Prince Abdullah of an initiative for a comprehensive resolution of the Arab–Israeli conflict. The central idea of the Saudi proposals was for the Arab states collectively to normalize relations with Israel within its pre-June 1967 borders in return for the establishment of a Palestinian state in the West Bank and Gaza with East Jerusalem as its capital. According to US and Arab media reports, the basic tenets of the Saudi plan had been formulated in Washington the previous November but had not been promoted by George W. Bush because he had felt that US credibility in the Arab world could not risk further harm through failure of an official peace initiative. Saudi Arabia had its own reasons for now accepting authorship of the proposals. It would help repair the rift in relations with Washington after revelations that many of those involved in the September 2001 attacks had come from the Kingdom. Moreover, Riyadh perceived sponsorship of a US-originated peace plan as strengthening its bid to rival Cairo as the West's favoured interlocutor in the Arab world. Fittingly, Crown Prince Abdullah stated that the plan would be officially launched at the summit meeting of Arab League heads of state to be held in Beirut at the end of March. EU ministers of foreign affairs praised the Saudi proposals as making a 'significant contribution' to the search for a regional peace. With the exception of Syria and Libya, Arab responses were also largely positive. Seeing Crown Prince Abdullah's plan as a chance to isolate Sharon internationally and exacerbate tensions within the Likud-led coalition, PA officials expressed full support for the Saudi formula; full acceptance, however, would be conditional on Israel's lifting of the siege of Yasser Arafat's Ramallah compound and allowing him to attend the Arab summit in Beirut. This stance was endorsed by GCC foreign ministers meeting with their EU counterparts in Granada, Spain, at the end of February. Oman's Minister of Foreign Affairs commented that if Arafat was not freed to attend, 'we shall all consider that Israel does not take the initiative seriously'. Indeed, that appeared to be the official attitude of the Sharon Government.

Encouraged by the lukewarm reception extended to the Saudi plan in Washington, and in particular the emphasis placed by spokesmen for the Bush Administration on the need for a cessation of violence to precede political dialogue, the Israeli Government appeared unwilling to engage with the Saudi offer. Nor was it predisposed to ease regional tensions. In a televised address on 22 February 2002 Sharon signalled the IDF's readiness to take the war against Palestinian militants to the 'terrorist nests' of the refugee camps. Six days later major assaults were launched against the Balata and Jenin refugee camps on the West Bank, killing 30 Palestinians, injuring more than 200, and causing widespread destruction. Balata was the West Bank stronghold of the al-Aqsa Martyrs Brigades, and the organization was quick to vow and exact retaliation. On 2 March responsibility was claimed for a suicide bombing in an ultra-orthodox Jewish district of Jerusalem in which nine Israelis, including four young children, were killed. The following day a lone Palestinian sniper shot dead seven soldiers and three settlers at an army check-point on the West Bank. Charging that the Palestinians would need to be 'hit hard...so that they understand that terrorism will achieve nothing', Sharon ordered gunboat, fighter aircraft and helicopter strikes against a variety of PA targets in the West Bank and Gaza and tank-led incursions against refugee camps in both areas. The PA called on Palestinians to 'confront the invaders', but despite fierce resistance from Palestinian policemen and assorted militia groups, the overwhelmingly superior forces of the IDF were able to reoccupy Ramallah and carry out arrests and weapons seizures throughout the Occupied Territories. By the end of the third week in March some 200 Palestinians, many of them civilians, had been killed in the Israeli assaults. Palestinian gun and bomb attacks inside Israel contributed to a rising toll of civilian deaths and a growing sense of vulnerability in the towns and cities that would marshal popular support behind the uncompromising military responses of the Israel Prime Minister.

Resolution 1397

The ferocity of Israel's attacks on the Palestinian territories caused alarm in the USA, not least because of the Bush Administration's renewed focus on achieving 'regime change' in Iraq. With Vice President Dick Cheney already scheduled to tour Middle East capitals to garner Arab acquiescence in, if not support for, military action against Baghdad, the US President announced that he would also be sending Anthony Zinni back to the region in an attempt to broker another cease-fire. Annoyed that Sharon's adventurism was apparently undermining his principal foreign policy objective, Bush was moved to direct rare criticism at his ally, declaring that, while he understood the need to defend against terrorism, Israel's 'recent actions aren't helpful'. Elsewhere, stronger words were directed against Israeli policies. The EU condemned Israel's excessive use of force, and warned that there was 'no military solution to the conflict'. The UN Secretary-General, Kofi Annan, was unusually forthright in attributing responsibility for the deepening of the conflict. He stated that the indiscriminate killing of civilians by Palestinian suicide bombings was 'morally repugnant' and politically counter-productive. He asserted that Israel had 'the right to live in peace and security within internationally recognized borders, but called on Israel to end 'illegal occupation'. 'More urgently,' he continued, Israel 'must stop the bombing of civilian areas, the assassinations, the unnecessary use of lethal force, the house demolitions, and the daily humiliations of ordinary Palestinians. Such actions gravely erode Israel's standing in the international community, and further fuel the fires of hatred, despair and extremism among Palestinians.' On 12 March the UN Security Council adopted Resolution 1397 (see Documents on Palestine, p. 98). This was the first UN Resolution to affirm the 'vision' of a Palestinian state. It was also noteworthy for being the first resolution on the Middle East to be sponsored by the USA for 25 years. Syria abstained in the vote. The Arab grouping at the UN had attempted to formulate a resolution calling for protection under the Fourth Geneva Convention (pertaining to protection for civilians in time of war) for the Palestinians of the Occupied Territories. This would have been unacceptable to the USA. However, rather than being seen to exercise yet another veto in Israel's favour at a time when the USA was canvassing Arab support for its policies against Iraq, the US ambassador drafted a compromise which would be adopted as Resolution 1397. The resolution also welcomed the recent Saudi peace initiative, demanded 'immediate cessation of all acts of violence', and called on the Israelis and Palestinians to co-operate in implementing the Tenet and Mitchell proposals with a view to resuming negotiations on a political settlement. Although the mention of a Palestinian state was welcomed by the PA and the Arab world, the enshrining of the security-based Tenet and Mitchell proposals in a UN plan of action was viewed by some Palestinian analysts as unwelcome.

The Beirut Declaration

Sharon ordered a pull-back of his forces from Palestinian population centres on the eve of Zinni's arrival on 15 March 2002. However, IDF tanks remained on the outskirts of Ramallah and other 'Area A' territories, while the IDF Chief of Staff, Shaul Mofaz, warned that he was prepared to call up reservists and occupy all PA territories if required to do so. Meanwhile, Vice-President Cheney's tour of Arab states failed to elicit support for military action against Iraq. Washington's key allies in the region, Egypt, Jordan and Saudi Arabia, all voiced strong opposition to a US strike on Iraq. King Abdullah of Jordan asserted that such a development would represent 'a catastrophe for Iraq and the region in general', while Saudi Arabia's Minister of Foreign Affairs stated that the Kingdom would not sanction the use of its airbases for an assault. Even Kuwaiti leaders were said to have informed Cheney that they preferred political dialogue to military action in dealing with the problem of their northern neighbour. Just as disconcerting for the US Vice-President was Arab unanimity in insisting that it was the issue of Palestine, not Iraq, that was the major cause of instability in the region. These priorities were forcibly underlined at the 14th Arab League summit in Beirut on 27–28 March. Responding to Crown Prince Abdullah's keynote speech in which he reiterated the principles of his peace plan, Arab leaders assented to a text calling for Israel's full withdrawal from lands occupied in 1967, and what were termed 'territories still occupied in southern Lebanon', the creation of a Palestinian state in the West Bank and Gaza Strip with East Jerusalem as its capital, and a 'just solution' to the refugee issue, based on the principles of repatriation or compensation in accordance with UN General Assembly Resolution 194 (see Documents on Palestine, p. 57). In return, the Arab world would 'consider the Arab–Israeli conflict at an end and enter into a peace agreement with Israel'. A snub was also delivered to Washington with the public reconciliation of Kuwaiti and Saudi delegation leaders with the Iraqi

Vice-President, Izzat Ibrahim. The summit declaration welcomed Iraq's assurances that it would respect the 'independence, sovereignty and security' of the state of Kuwait, and emphasized its rejection of 'threats of aggression against some Arab states, particularly Iraq'. Yasser Arafat did not attend the summit, having failed to secure Israeli guarantees that he would be able to return. Egypt's President Mubarak and Jordan's King Abdullah also stayed away, and were represented in Beirut by their respective prime ministers. Solidarity with the PA leader was cited as the official reason for their absence, however most commentators explained their decision not to attend the summit as a response to concerns that their continued diplomatic links with Sharon's Israel would come under an unwelcome spotlight.

'Operation Defensive Shield'

Undoubtedly mindful of the impending summit in Beirut, militant Islamist and nationalist organizations sought to heighten tension in the region with a series of deadly suicide attacks against Israelis, designed in the words of one Fatah leader 'to destroy Sharon' and 'create mayhem from Cairo to the Galilee'. On 20 March 2002 seven Israelis, including four soldiers, were killed by a suicide bomber acting for Islamic Jihad. Over the next week attacks in Jerusalem, Tel-Aviv and Haifa resulted in 16 civilian fatalities and many scores of injuries. Responsibility was claimed by Hamas and the al-Aqsa Martyrs Brigades, and the frequency of the attacks deepened the sense of panic and outrage among the Israeli population. On 27 March a Hamas bomber blew himself up in a restaurant in Netanya, causing the deaths of 29 mainly elderly Israelis gathered for a Passover celebration and injuring more than 100 others. This was the deadliest Palestinian attack of the 18 months of the *intifada*, and was destined to elicit a formidable response. At a crisis meeting of the Cabinet following the bombing Sharon authorized a major assault on PA-controlled areas of the West Bank. In the early morning of 29 March tanks and troops entered Ramallah and forced their way through the perimeter walls of Arafat's compound. With the exception of a couple of rooms in which the PA leader was allowed refuge with assorted advisers, security personnel and journalists, the compound was soon under tight Israeli control. After several hours of street fighting, and at a cost of some 30 Palestinian lives, the rest of the city was also placed under a tight curfew while Israeli troops carried out searches and arrested more than 700 people. Sharon subsequently appeared on Israeli television to announce that the country was at war and that the IDF were embarking on 'Operation Defensive Shield', a rolling campaign designed to 'vanquish the Palestinian terror infrastructure'. The PLO leader was declared an enemy who was to be 'isolated'—an apparent climbdown for the Israeli leader, who had only been deterred from his preferred option of arresting and expelling Arafat after stern warnings from the US Administration. In subsequent days, and with overwhelming domestic support, the IDF overran Qalqilya, Tulkarm and Bethlehem, causing widespread destruction and loss of life. More than 100 Palestinian police and militiamen sought refuge with clerics and other non-combatants inside Bethlehem's Church of the Nativity. With the central areas of the West Bank reconquered the Israelis turned their attention to the militant strongholds of Nablus and Jenin. After four days of stiff resistance to combined air and ground assaults, the militias of Nablus and its refugee camps surrendered to the IDF; 74 people, fighters and civilians alike, were killed in the offensive. Here, as in other parts of the West Bank, Palestinians reported that the IDF systematically destroyed educational, media and research facilities belonging to the PA and independent Palestinian organizations. But it was in the northern town of Jenin and its adjacent refugee camp where the IDF met the most sustained and fierce resistance. It took a week of house-to-house fighting and the loss of 28 of its soldiers before Israel's security forces were able to exert control over the refugee camp adjoining the town. Much of the central area of the Jenin camp was destroyed in the Israeli assault. Palestinian sources claimed a massacre had taken place, allegations that were strenuously denied by Israel, which continued to deny independent access to the area.

Having endorsed what they considered a comprehensive and historic peace offer to Israel at the Beirut summit, Arab states responded angrily to Israel's offensive on the West Bank.

Demonstrations took place across the Arab world. In Cairo and Alexandria at least one person was killed and many were injured as students clashed with riot police deployed to protect US multinationals. Responding to the mood of popular outrage, President Mubarak announced that Egypt would suspend all ties with Israel except those links that might 'help the Palestinian cause'. This was deemed insufficient by opposition groups, who demanded that Cairo sever its peace treaty with Israel and supply weapons to the Palestinians. Similar calls were made in Jordan, where protesters took to the streets to demand a firm Arab response to the unfolding crisis on the West Bank. Jordan's Minister of Foreign Affairs, Marwan al-Muasher, summoned the Israeli ambassador on 31 March 2002 and warned that action would be taken against Israel unless the IDF withdrew from the Palestinian areas it had recently occupied and the siege on Arafat's compound was lifted. Jordanian officials told reporters that measures under consideration included the severing of diplomatic ties and the closure of Israel's embassy in Amman and the Jordanian embassy in Tel-Aviv. Lebanon also witnessed joint Palestinian-Lebanese demonstrations organized by student, Islamist and professional groups. Significantly, Lebanon's Christian clerics and politicians, not normally known for their pro-Palestinian sentiments, also added their voices to the chorus of condemnation of Israeli aggression. On 7 April an officially sanctioned rally in support of the Palestinians in the Moroccan capital, Rabat, drew a crowd of some 500,000–800,000. Images conveyed via Arab satellite television stations of the destruction and bloodshed in the West Bank were regarded as having contributed to the scale and size of the anti-Israeli and anti-US protests. On Israel's northern border Hezbollah stepped up its attacks on the disputed Shebaa Farms enclave in an attempt to divert Israeli military attention from the Palestinian territories.

That the Bush Administration accorded a low-key reception to adoption by the Beirut summit of Crown Prince Abdullah's initiative was interpreted as reflecting anger at the rebuff delivered to Vice-President Cheney on his recent Middle East tour and the subsequent Arab reconciliation with Iraq in Beirut. Initial reaction to Israel's 'Operation Defensive Shield' was also muted, and contrasted sharply to the animated responses in European as well as Arab capitals. The carnage inflicted by Palestinian suicide bombers inside Israeli cities had a powerful resonance with a US public well versed in its leadership's policy and rhetoric on terrorism. The early comments from US officials appeared to confirm that the Israeli Prime Minister had received a degree of advance support from Washington for its assault on the West Bank. Speaking on consecutive days at the beginning of the attack, both Secretary of State Powell and President Bush placed the responsibility for initiating and also for easing the crisis on the beleaguered Arafat and his willingness to act against those Palestinians responsible for orchestrating the violence against Israelis. 'It's essential for the peace of the region and the world that we root out terrorist activities and condemn those activities,' Bush declared on 1 April, adding, 'the free world, the civilized world must band together to stop this kind of activity if we expect there to be peace and resolution in the Middle East.' Israel's role, in Bush's assessment, was to 'keep in mind there must be an avenue towards a peaceful settlement'. On 30 March 2002 the USA voted in favour of UN Security Council Resolution 1402, which expressed grave concern at the further deterioration of the situation, including the suicide bombings in Israel and the military attack against the headquarters of the PA President, and called *inter alia* for both Israelis and Palestinians to move immediately towards a 'meaningful' cease-fire and for Israel to withdraw troops from Ramallah and other Palestinian cities. There was some surprise that the USA was prepared to vote for a resolution nominally critical of Israel. However, analysts pointed out that the absence of detail on a timetable or enforcement rendered the resolution less problematic for Israel. Israel's ambassador to the UN, Yehuda Lancry, subsequently told Israel Army Radio that 'US officials' concurred with the Israeli view that his country did not have to act immediately.

With anti-US sentiment rising in the Arab world as the human and material costs of Israel's offensive spiralled, the Bush Administration signalled a volte-face in its support for Sharon's West Bank campaign. Addressing world media from the White House on 4 April, the US President urged Israeli forces to withdraw from Palestinian areas 'without delay'. Although once again castigating Yasser Arafat for lack of leadership and for betraying 'the hopes of his people', he also called for Israeli settlement activity to cease and for an end to the Israeli occupation in accordance with UN Resolutions 242 and 338. Recognizing, moreover, EU and Arab appeals for the USA to 're-engage' with the Middle East conflict, Bush announced that he would be dispatching his Secretary of State to the region with a brief to secure a cease-fire and restart the political process. His speech won immediate support from the EU, and deflected calls from some member states for an independent European initiative on the Arab–Israeli conflict—including the imposition of trade sanctions against Israel. The French Minister of Foreign Affairs, Hubert Védrine, considered to be a critic of the USA's Middle East policy, confirmed European backing for the Powell's peace mission as 'the best way of moving forward, the most intelligent thing we can do'. The Israeli Government appeared unconcerned by the implicit ultimatum from Washington, and responded to Bush's speech by reiterating that it would not halt its offensive on the West Bank until the objectives of 'Operation Defensive Shield' had been achieved. Although reportedly angry with Sharon's obduracy, the US President side-stepped a confrontation. It was announced that Powell's departure from the USA would not take place for several days; neither would he fly direct to the conflict zone, with stop-over visits to Morocco, Egypt, Jordan and Spain before arriving in Israel and the West Bank. The delay to the Powell mission and the circuitousness of his itinerary were interpreted in the Arab world as further evidence of US collusion with Israel's military goals on the West Bank. In talks with Arab leaders in Morocco, Egypt and Jordan, the US Secretary of State was urged to pressure Israel to end its offensive against the Palestinians and allow the free movement of the PA President. It was also reported that Jordan's King Abdullah emphasized to Powell that the stability of pro-Western Arab governments was threatened by the violence in the Occupied Territories.

By the time Powell arrived in Israel on 11 April 2002 the IDF had withdrawn from several areas of the West Bank, although troops continued to besiege Arafat's Ramallah compound and the Church of the Nativity in Bethlehem. Smaller-scale operations against other towns and villages in the West Bank continued, and Israeli forces remained in tight control of Jenin. Shortly before Powell's visit the rationale for 'Operation Defensive Shield' was violently reinforced with a suicide attack on a bus near Haifa in which eight people died. Several people were killed in a further bombing in Jerusalem on 12 April, perpetrated within the hearing of the visiting US Secretary of State. Powell's scheduled meeting with the PA leader was delayed in response to the latter attack, but after Arafat issued an explicit condemnation of the suicide bombings the US mission travelled on to Ramallah. The talks were said to be cordial, but there was little common ground. Arafat refused to countenance a cease-fire as long as Israeli forces remained in occupation of Area A Palestinian territories. In response to Powell's insistence that the PA crack-down on Palestinian militants, the PA's chief negotiator, Saeb Erakat, informed his guest that 'The Palestinian Authority has ceased to exist'. In his four-hour meeting with the Israeli Prime Minister, Powell also failed to wean Sharon away from his insistence that a cessation of military activity would only be secured through the destruction of the Palestinian militias and the PA's handing over of terrorist suspects, including those responsible for the assassination of Rehavam Ze'evi. After the failure of the Powell-Arafat talks on 14 April, Sharon proposed the convening of an international peace conference to be chaired by the USA and to include Palestinians and front-line Arab states, but not Yasser Arafat. In order for the conference to go ahead there would need to be a cessation of violence in Israel and the Occupied Territories. PA officials dismissed these ideas as unacceptable. On 15 April Israeli forces arrested the West Bank's Fatah leader Marwan Barghouthi, a veteran of the resistance to Israeli occupation frequently mentioned as a likely successor to Yasser Arafat.

After concentrating its military operation in the central and northern areas of the West Bank, in mid-April 2002 Israeli troops turned their attentions to the south, occupying the towns of Dura, Dhahiriya, Yatta and Sammu. The pattern of these operations mirrored those that had taken place in other areas of the West Bank, with large numbers of Palestinian casualties reported as well as mass arrests and the deliberate targeting of the infrastructural symbols of self-rule. On 29 April the PA-controlled areas of Hebron witnessed an invasion by 100 tanks and armoured personnel carriers. Nine Palestinians were reported to have been killed in the initial attack, and some 20 people on Israel's 'wanted' list were arrested. However the details of the IDF's incursions into Palestinian population centres in the south of the West Bank were overshadowed by the continued controversy surrounding Israel's 13-day assault on the Jenin refugee camp. On 16 April the first independent observers entered the camp to witness the massive scale of the destruction. Claim and counter-claim by Palestinians and Israelis over allegations of a massacre in Jenin dominated subsequent news reports. Preliminary investigations by outside agencies, including the International Committee of the Red Cross and the human rights organization Amnesty International, did not support Palestinian claims of a massacre but did suggest that serious violations of human rights had been committed by Israeli forces. On 19 April the UN Security Council adopted Resolution 1405, which expressed concern at the 'dire humanitarian situation of the Palestinian population, in particular reports from the Jenin refugee camp of an unknown number of deaths and destruction', and welcomed an initiative by the Secretary-General for a fact-finding team to be sent to Jenin to report on recent events in the camp. Although Israel initially agreed to co-operate with an independent mission, having conceived the idea with the USA in the first place, the Sharon Government swiftly adopted a less accommodating stance. There were a number of objections. First, Sharon considered that the proposed team, to be led by former Finnish President Martti Ahtisaari, had too much of a 'humanitarian' composition and too little military expertise objectively to evaluate the Jenin events. Second, there was strong Israeli opposition to the idea that the UN team would be allowed to make observations on what happened in Jenin in addition to reporting the strict facts. Finally, Israel was opposed to allowing team members free access to serving military personnel, and demanded a prior guarantee of immunity from prosecution by a third party. After a week of fitful negotiations and last minute delays to the dispatch of the team, the Israeli Government announced on 28 April that it would not co-operate with the mission and would deny its members entry. Relaying this decision to the media, Minister of Communications Reuven Rivlin explained, 'This awful United Nations committee is out to get us and is likely to smear Israel and to force us to do things which Israel is not prepared even to hear about, such as interrogating soldiers and officers who took part in the fighting. No country in the world would agree to such a thing'. Under US pressure, the Security Council chose not to try to send the team to Jenin without the co-operation of Israel. Instead, it was decided that the fact-finding mission on the Jenin events would be downgraded to a report compiled by UN staff commissioned by the Secretary-General.

The Bush Administration apparently lent its support for Israel's blocking of the UN investigation into Jenin in return for an Israeli promise of flexibility in resolving Yasser Arafat's continued incarceration in Ramallah and an end to the siege of the Church of the Nativity in Bethlehem. At the end of April Sharon agreed to lift the siege of the PA leader in return for guarantees that Palestinians who were sheltering in the compound and who had been convicted under PA jurisdiction for the assassination of Rehavam Ze'evi would serve their gaol terms under the supervision of US and British prison warders. A compromise deal between the PA and the Israeli Government on the fate of the wanted Palestinians in the Church of the Nativity was also brokered by US and European diplomats. The siege finally came to an end on 10 May with the transfer of 26 of the gunmen to the Gaza Strip and the transportation to Cyprus, under international guard, of the 13 higher-level cadres described by Israel as 'senior terrorists'. The latter were to be dispersed to permanent exile in various EU member states (one remained in Cyprus), while it was unclear that trial by a Palestinian court of those deported to the Gaza Strip, as envisaged under the agreement, would actually take place.

Pressure for reform of the PA

For most of the five weeks during which he was confined to a tiny enclave within his Ramallah headquarters, Yasser Arafat enjoyed his highest popularity ratings among the Palestinians of the West Bank and Gaza for many years. However, the tumultuous applause that he received when he emerged onto the streets of Ramallah at the beginning of May 2002 failed to conceal the dissatisfaction among political and civic leaders with the PA's leadership in the period leading up to Israel's rolling reoccupation of the self-rule areas. At an angry meeting of the Palestinian leadership on 3 May Fatah representatives lambasted the PA for its weakness in the face of the Israeli incursions and demanded elections to determine a new cabinet. Arafat walked out of the meeting, only to return to announce the appointment of committees to oversee political reform and national reconstruction. These were to be headed by two of Arafat's closest associates, Muhammad Rashid and Nabil Shaath. Both men had been tainted by charges of corruption, and neither had broad political support. Arafat's popularity declined further with the disclosure of the deal to end the siege of the Church of the Nativity. The PA President's approval of a formula that resulted in the exile of Palestinian militants was seen as breaching a central tenet of Palestinian nationalism and was widely condemned. A scheduled visit by Arafat to view the destruction in Jenin in mid-May was cancelled by his officials, fearing that Arafat would face too hostile a reception. Calls for the reform of the PA were also being made in the USA and in Israel. Speaking on 8 May after meeting with the visiting Israeli Prime Minister, George W. Bush echoed his guest's assertions that progress towards meaningful dialogue between Israel and the Palestinians could only be made if the PA's political, security and financial institutions were restructured to make them more democratic and accountable. Signalling that the attitude of his Administration had moved yet further towards Sharon's characterization of Arafat as an enemy, rather than an ally, in the search for peace, Bush declared, 'What is an accurate reflection of my opinion is that Mr Arafat has let the Palestinian people down. He hasn't led. And as a result, the Palestinian people suffer…'. Sharon was more strident, warning in an address to the Knesset on 14 May that there could be no peace with a 'corrupt, terror regime' and that 'everything must be overhauled' within the PA before political negotiations could resume. Palestinians regarded US and Israeli championing of democratization of the PA with heavy cynicism. Supporters of internal reform were quick to point out that successive US and Israeli governments had ignored the autocratic nature of Arafat's rule and the PA's human rights abuses as long as violence against Israelis was being contained. Nevertheless, caught between internal and external pressures for structural change within the PA, Arafat reluctantly proceeded with a reform programme. He approved the adoption of legislation intended to separate judicial and executive functions in the PA, and on May it was announced that municipal elections would be held by the end of 2002. It was also widely reported that the 13 different branches of the PA's security and police forces were to be streamlined and placed under the control of the Ministry of the Interior.

Meanwhile, on 7 May 2002 15 Israelis were killed in a Hamas suicide bombing in the town of Rishon Le Zion. The blast exposed the limitations of 'Operation Defensive Shield' and Sharon's exclusively security-based response to the Palestinian *intifada*. Cutting short his visit to Washington, and brushing aside Yasser Arafat's strong denunciation of the attack, Sharon convened an emergency cabinet meeting at Tel-Aviv's airport. The session was followed by an emergency call-up of IDF reservists and a movement of Israeli armour southwards. The Gaza Strip had thus far been spared the large-scale incursions visited on Palestinian population centres of the West Bank, but now military assault appeared to have been signposted. That it failed to materialize was explained by Israel's Minister of Defence as a response to 'too much public discussion of the scheduled operation, including details of targets'. However, it was felt to be more likely that the expected invasion had been deferred by the realization that any assault on the densely populated cities and camps of Gaza would result in unacceptably high casualties among the IDF and Palestinian civilians and would have uncertain political and military outcomes. Meanwhile, and despite consistently high levels of domestic support for his premiership, Sharon suffered a political defeat at the hands of his party rival, ex-Prime Minister Binyamin Netanyahu, at Likud's Central Committee Meeting. In a debate charged with personal acrimony the former Likud leader secured majority backing on a vote committing the party to oppose the creation of a Palestinian state, even the fragmented and vague entity envisaged by Sharon. The Israeli Prime Minister also had to face the problem of Israel's economic downturn. Foreign investment in Israel had declined in response to the continuing violence, and the transfer of capital out of the country had contributed to the national currency's losing 20% of its value in the first five months of 2002. Likud's coalition partners in the Shas party were thrown out of the Cabinet in May for opposing government proposals for budget cuts.

Israeli incursions and suicide attacks continued through the late spring of 2002. Qalqilya, Bethlehem, Tulkarm and Jenin were all reoccupied by Israeli forces in the last week of May 2002. The assaults had been preceded by a spate of suicide bombings which had killed 10 Israeli civilians. On 5 June an Islamic Jihad suicide bomber targeted a bus at the Megiddo junction in northern Israel, killing 17 Israelis—14 of them soldiers. The following day a Hamas attack on a West Bank settlement left three settlers dead. The Israelis responded by sending tanks once again onto the streets of Ramallah, where they carried out scores of arrests while the town's 120,000 inhabitants were confined to their houses under a tight curfew. This latest upsurge in the violence came amid renewed US diplomatic efforts to manage the crisis. On 4 June CIA Director George Tenet met with the Palestinian leader in Ramallah in an attempt to adopt US suggestions for the overhaul of Palestinian security forces. Tenet urged Arafat to amalgamate his security forces into one body, reporting to a national security council to be advised by US, European and Egyptian officials. The proposals were rejected by the PA President. On 8–9 June Egypt's President Mubarak attended talks with the US President at Camp David. At their post-summit media briefing Bush made it clear that although he shared the vision of a Palestinian state, internal reform of the PA and the fight against Palestinian 'terror' remained his Administration's principal focus. Mubarak's assertion that a timetable was needed for the creation of a Palestinian state went unacknowledged by his US host. Questioned directly on the possibility of Israel's expelling the Palestinian leader, Bush did not express US opposition to Arafat's removal but declared that he did not think Arafat was 'the issue'. After discussions with Israel's Prime Minister on 10 June the US President echoed Sharon's assessment that there was no obvious partner for peace on the Palestinian side. Referring to the PA President's recent unveiling of a new cabinet (which saw most ministries allocated to Fatah members or independents loyal to Arafat) Bush declared 'No one has confidence in the emerging Palestinian government'.

'Operation Determined Path'

The limitations of Israel's spring offensive in the West Bank to deliver security to its citizens was once again underlined in mid-June with two devastating suicide attacks in Jerusalem. On 18 June 2002 at least 19 people were killed in a bus bombing in Gilo; seven were killed the following day at a bus stop in another Jewish area of East Jerusalem. The attacks were claimed by Hamas and Fatah. On 20 June a gunman from the PFLP infiltrated a settlement near Nablus and shot dead five Israelis. These were provocations too far for the Israeli leader. After another crisis meeting of his Cabinet it was announced that the IDF was initiating 'Operation Determined Path', the indefinite reoccupation of any PA territory Israel deemed necessary to meet its security needs. Within days Israeli troops and armour had taken control of most of the major town and cities of the West Bank without encountering significant Palestinian resistance. Curfews were imposed on the newly occupied population centres, and the Ministry of Defence declared that the families of suicide bombers would be deported from the West Bank to the Gaza Strip. In a separate but related development, the Government confirmed that it had completed the first stage in the construction of a 'security wall' that was intended to follow the entire length of the West Bank and prevent would-be suicide bombers from penetrating Israeli cities.

Palestinian bombings prompted George W. Bush to delay a policy statement on the Middle East. The US Administration under his presidency had been repeatedly criticized for lack of coherence in its policy towards the Arab–Israeli conflict, and it was hoped that his speech would signal renewed US commitment to pursuit of a regional peace settlement. However, the vision elucidated outside the White House on 24 June 2002 was judged by most commentators to be too partisan to offer a workable way forward. Bush stated that he would offer US support for a 'provisional' Palestinian state once 'Palestinians embrace democracy, confront corruption and firmly reject terror'. It was made clear that this could not be achieved under Arafat's stewardship. 'Peace requires a new and different Palestinian leadership so that a Palestinian state can be born,' Bush opined, 'I call on the Palestinian people to elect new leaders, leaders not compromised by terror.' Only after the Palestinians had effected progress on security issues would Israel be required to stop its settlement activity and begin working towards a 'final status' agreement. At the end of this process Israel's occupation would be 'ended through a settlement negotiated between the parties, based on UN Resolutions 242 and 338, with Israeli withdrawal to secure and recognized borders'. The address was not well received in the Arab world. There was disappointment that Bush had not referred to the Arab initiative elaborated in Beirut in March, and that the Palestinians had not been given a timetable for independence, but rather the prospect of open-ended negotiations on the establishment of an entity with powers and borders that were undefined. That these negotiations would only commence once the Palestinians had ended resistance and installed a leadership acceptable to Washington was seen as particularly discouraging. By contrast, there was little in the Bush speech to concern Sharon, and much to cause satisfaction. Two key demands of the Israeli premier—for Palestinian resistance to end before negotiations could begin and for Yasser Arafat's removal as a political player—had now been adopted as US policy. Reference to Israeli withdrawal to 'secure borders', rather than to the lines of 4 June 1967, was also regarded as a concession to Sharon's interpretation of Resolution 242 as calling for a withdrawal within, but not from, the territories occupied in the June war. Indeed such was the perceived bias in the Bush speech that Israeli commentators suggested that it could easily have been penned by Sharon himself. Surprisingly, the Palestinian leader responded positively to Bush's statement, choosing to praise the vision of a Palestinian state and to interpret the call for a new leadership as an endorsement of the reform process currently under way within the PA—and not as a demand for him to step down. Arafat's welcome caught his Arab neighbours off guard. While Bush's stance was being vilified in the press and among the Arab people, Jordan's King Abdullah praised its positive elements and said that it represented 'the beginning of the end of the conflict between Arabs and Israelis'. In interviews with Arab newspapers on 29 June the Jordanian monarch was, however, more critical, rejecting the idea of a 'provisional' state and charging that it was up to the Palestinian people 'to determine the fate of Yasser Arafat'. President Mubarak of Egypt made similar assessments in his reaction to the Washington statement. Privately, EU leaders were reported to be dismayed by Bush's proposals. Gathered at the G-8 summit in Kananaskis, Canada, at the end of June French President Jacques Chirac and British Prime Minister Tony Blair made public their differences with the Bush Administration. Although in broad agreement on the need for reform of the PA, both distanced themselves from the US demand for 'regime change'. 'We have a simple position: it is for the Palestinians to designate their representatives,' stated Chirac, continuing, 'We cannot ask them to vote and then tell them who to elect'. EU officials insisted that the Union would remain in close contact with Arafat.

Meanwhile, there was a heightening of tension along Israel's northern border. On several occasions in mid-June 2002 Hezbollah militants fired anti-aircraft batteries at Israeli military aircraft overflying the country. Several shells fell in the waters of Lake Tiberias, leading a senior IDF commander to comment that an escalation in the simmering conflict with Hezbollah fighters and their Syrian sponsors was unavoidable. Israeli intelligence reports claimed, moreover, that Hezbollah had taken delivery of long-range *Fajr* rockets which it had stockpiled in caves in southern Lebanon. A US State Department official delivered warnings to Beirut, Damascus and Tehran in response to Israel's allegations of the new weaponry and further claims that al-Qa'ida operatives were based in the country's Palestinian refugee camps. These allegations were categorically denied by the Lebanese Minister of Foreign Affairs in a meeting with representatives of the five permanent members of the UN Security Council, and the US delegate declared himself satisfied with the assurances. Syria for its part continued to reject US demands that it should condemn Palestinian attacks on Israeli civilians and to clamp down on Hezbollah and Palestinian military organizations operating from Syria.

Arafat's domestic position was generally regarded as having been strengthened by the US Administration's apparent attempts to sideline him. Earlier speculation that the PA leader would face a serious challenge in forthcoming elections was now ended with all potential candidates, including those personalities favoured by Washington, declaring that they would not be seen to be doing the Bush Administration's bidding by standing against the PLO veteran. Arafat continued the tentative reform process within his administration, dismissing his head of security in the West Bank and Gaza's unpopular police chief. In mid-July 2002 Israeli and Palestinian ministers held their first meetings in three months to discuss ways of easing the humanitarian crisis caused by the curfews and travel bans on the West Bank. Shimon Peres agreed to increase access to besieged PA areas, to facilitate the withdrawal of troops from some of the towns currently under occupation, and also to release a proportion of the US $600m. in tax revenues owed to the PA. Saudi Arabia, Jordan, Egypt and the EU were reported to be mediating discussions between the different Palestinian factions, with the aim of reaching agreement on a cease-fire within Israel and the Occupied Territories. There were, however, few signs of Hamas, Islamic Jihad or the al-Aqsa Martyrs Brigades eschewing military attacks in the West Bank and Gaza: a Hamas gunman killed 10 Israelis in an ambush on a settler bus outside Nablus on 16 July, although Hamas leaders did state that they would call a halt to attacks on civilians inside Israel in return for the IDF's withdrawal from Palestinian cities, the release of prisoners and an end to the assassination policy. Doubts that the Israeli Prime Minister would respond to such an offer were confirmed in the early hours of 23 July, when an F-16 fighter of the Israeli air force fired a rocket into an apartment block in Gaza City, reducing it to rubble. The intended target of the attack, Hamas military leader Salah Shihada, was killed outright, as were 14 other Palestinians, nine of them children. Sharon lauded as a 'great success' an operation that drew international condemnation. UN Secretary-General Kofi Annan stated that Israel 'has the legal and moral responsibility to take all measures to avoid the loss of civilian life; it clearly failed to do so in using a missile against an apartment building'. Javier Solana, the EU's High Representative for foreign and security policy, implicitly questioned Israeli motivation for carrying out such a provocative action at a time 'when both Israelis and Palestinians were working very seriously to curb violence'. For the White House, spokesman Ari Fleischer commented that the

US President regretted the loss of innocent lives and believed that 'this heavy-handed action does not contribute to peace'. Arab reaction was far less circumspect. Both Yasser Arafat and Egypt's Minister of Foreign Affairs, Ahmad Maher, termed the Gaza killings a 'war crime'. Tens of thousands blocked the streets of Gaza for the funeral of the victims of the attack. Predictably, Hamas vowed to exact a terrible revenge. 'Every Israeli at any time and at any place, is now a target for strikes by the Palestinian resistance,' declared a spokesman for the movement in Gaza, 'Hamas will not accept any conditions for halting resistance operations to avenge the Palestinian martyrs.' In the days after the Shihada assassination several settlers were killed in the West Bank, despite the massive IDF presence in the territory and a strict regime of curfews and closures. On 31 July a bomb was detonated in a cafeteria of the Hebrew University in Jerusalem, killing at least seven students—five of them US citizens. A Hamas official asserted that this would be the first of many attacks. The PA leader added his voice to those condemning the bombing, but stated that the Israeli Prime Minister bore partial responsibility because of Israel's policy of 'destruction, killing and collective punishment'. On 4 August 2002 nine people were killed in a Hamas suicide bombing on a bus in northern Israel. Three people were killed in a gun battle outside the Old City of Jerusalem on the same day and two settlers were shot dead in an ambush on their car in the West Bank. Israel responded with a major incursion into the Old City of Nablus and the declaration of a total ban on Palestinians travelling in the northern sector of the West Bank. The IDF also continued its policy of destroying the homes of suicide bombers, and Israel's Minister of Defence confirmed that he would pursue the policy of deporting to Gaza relatives of Palestinians held responsible for attacks on Israelis. This was despite a legal challenge in the Israeli courts, as well as warnings from the EU and the USA that such measures were both illegal and counter-productive.

On 1 August 2002 the UN released its long awaited report into Israel's spring invasion of the West Bank, and in particular events in the Jenin camp. The report concluded that there was no evidence to support Palestinian claims of a massacre. It stated that 52 Palestinians had died during the days of the Israeli assault, the same number that had been reported by Israeli officials. In the period 1 March–7 May a recorded 497 Palestinians had been killed during Israeli incursions in the West Bank, over 1,400 had been wounded and more than 17,000 made homeless. More than 100 Israelis had died in Palestinian attacks within Israel during the same period. Israeli forces were criticized for the widespread destruction of Palestinian property, and both they and Palestinian militias were considered to have disregarded the safety of civilians. Although it had refused to co-operate with the reporting team and denied access to Jenin, the Israeli Government welcomed the findings as exposing Palestinian 'fabrication' and 'false propaganda'. The UN Secretary-General stated that he believed the report to be a 'fair representation of a complex situation', but added that Palestinians were still suffering severe 'humanitarian consequences' as a result of Israeli policies in the West Bank and Gaza.

THE JERUSALEM ISSUE

Updated for this edition by PAUL COSSALI

Based on an original article by MICHAEL ADAMS, with subsequent additions by DAVID GILMOUR, PAUL HARPER and STEVEN SHERMAN

The Arab sector of Jerusalem, including the old walled city, was captured during the Six-Day War in 1967 by Israeli forces, which went on to occupy all the Jordanian territory lying west of the Jordan river. Theoretically, there was no difference in status between Jerusalem and the rest of the West Bank; both were occupied territory. In practice, Israel immediately removed the walls and barriers dividing the western (Israeli) and eastern (Arab) sectors of the city, and at the end of June 1967 the Israeli Knesset (parliament) approved legislation incorporating the Arab sector into a reunited Jerusalem under Israeli sovereignty. At the same time the boundaries of the municipal area of Jerusalem were greatly extended, reaching to near Bethlehem in the south and incorporating Kalandia airport (close to Ramallah) in the north.

In response to Israel's effective annexation of the Arab sector, on 4 July 1967 the UN General Assembly ruled the annexation to be invalid, and called on Israel not to take any measures to alter the status of the city. Ten days later the Assembly adopted a second resolution 'reiterating' the earlier one and 'deploring' Israel's failure to implement it.

Before the first of these resolutions was passed, the Israeli authorities had embarked on a series of structural alterations and demolitions in the Old City of Jerusalem, which aroused strong Arab protests. The continuation of such activity was to lead to considerable international controversy. In clearing the area in front of the Western (Wailing) Wall, the dwellings of 50 Arab families were expropriated and demolished at very short notice, while in the Jewish Quarter a further 200 Arab families were dispossessed. In all, and before the end of June 1967, some 4,000 Arabs in Jerusalem had lost their homes. In some cases, but not all, they were provided with alternative accommodation.

In November 1967 the UN Security Council unanimously approved Resolution 242, setting out the basis for an overall settlement between Israel and its Arab neighbours. However, it was not until May 1968 that the Security Council adopted its first resolution dealing specifically with the Jerusalem issue. Resolution 252 of 21 May 1968 (see Documents on Palestine, p. 57) deplored Israel's failure to comply with the two General Assembly resolutions of 4 and 14 July 1967, confirmed that any measures taken by Israel to alter the status of Jerusalem were invalid, and called on Israel to rescind all such measures and to refrain from similar action in the future. The only visible effect of the declaration was to increase the haste with which Israel set about changing the face of the city. Bulldozers had been at work on Mount Scopus since February, and soon the first of the new housing estates began to take shape beside the Nablus Road leading northwards out of Jerusalem. In the absence of any progress towards a peace settlement, it became clear that the Israeli Government intended, by establishing a physical presence in the Arab sector of Jerusalem, to forestall any future attempt to challenge its sovereignty over the whole of the municipal area.

On 3 July 1969 the UN Security Council unanimously adopted (the USA had previously abstained from voting on the Jerusalem resolution) an even stronger resolution. Reaffirming the Security Council's earlier position, and deploring 'the failure of Israel to show any regard' for the previous resolutions both of the General Assembly and of the Security Council, Resolution 267 'censured in the strongest terms' all measures taken by Israel to change the status of Jerusalem, confirmed that all such measures were 'invalid', and again called on Israel to desist from taking any further action of a similar kind. Israel formally rejected the resolution, and the Israeli Minister of Information stated that it could not influence the 'facts' which had been intentionally created by Israel 'after due consideration of the political danger involved'.

The situation in Jerusalem itself was further aggravated in August 1969 by a disastrous fire in the al-Aqsa mosque, which at first sight appeared to confirm the fears of the Arabs for the safety of the Islamic and Christian shrines in the Old City. Israeli investigations showed that the fire had been caused by a deranged Australian religious fanatic, who was later brought to trial; but from that moment the concern of Muslim communities throughout the world reinforced the Arab sense of grievance at the loss of the Holy City.

In the following year Christian concern also began to make itself felt, especially after the publication of an Israeli 'master plan' for the future of Jerusalem. This plan envisaged the doubling of the Jewish population of the city by 1980, and an eventual total population of 900,000. An international conference of town planners, convoked by the Israeli municipal authorities at the end of 1970, was almost unanimous in condemning it's the plan's aesthetic implications. Early in 1971 a dispute also developed between the UN and the Israeli Government over the intention, announced in the 'master plan', to build another housing estate in the neighbourhood of Government House, the headquarters in Jerusalem of the UN. In March 1971 articles in the official Vatican newspaper *L'Osservatore Romano* and in the English Catholic weekly *The Tablet* revealed the strength of Catholic feeling over developments in the Holy City, and these feelings were strengthened when it became known that in the same month Israel had destroyed an Arab village on the hill of Nebi Samwil, north-west of Jerusalem, in preparation for the building on Arab land of yet another housing estate for immigrant Jews.

Israeli opinion was divided over the future of Jerusalem. Only a small minority of Israelis were in favour of relinquishing Israeli sovereignty over the Arab sector of the city, should negotiations for an overall settlement of the Arab–Israeli conflict ever materialize. In the absence of any sign of such negotiations, the issue remained a hypothetical one, and the Israeli Government made no secret of its determination to establish a hold on Jerusalem that would prove unbreakable. A further resolution by the UN Security Council (No. 298 of 25 September 1971—see Documents on Palestine, p. 59) was rejected by Israel as brusquely as its predecessors, and even a provision in the resolution that the UN Secretary-General, 'using such instrumentalities as he may choose', should report to the Council within 60 days on the implementation of the resolution, was ultimately fruitless, since the Secretary-General was unable to execute his mission for lack of co-operation from the Israeli authorities.

On purely aesthetic grounds, however, many Israelis were disturbed by the physical changes overtaking Jerusalem. Within five years of the 1967 Six-Day War the construction of large housing estates had transformed the appearance of Mount Scopus, where the Old City (and the whole of the Arab sector) was dominated by a row of apartment blocks breaking the historic skyline. There were acute disagreements between the Mayor of Jerusalem and the housing and tourism ministers over some of the implications of this building programme, but continuing uncertainty over the prospects for a political settlement with the Arabs gave encouragement to the 'activists' in Israel, and the creation of 'facts' continued, in Jerusalem as in the rest of the Occupied Territories, throughout 1972 and much of 1973.

Anxiety over the future of Jerusalem, and resentment at Israel's treatment both of the Arab population and of the physical fabric of the city, played a part in provoking the Arab decision to resort to war in October 1973. In particular, these feelings influenced King Faisal's decision to throw Saudi Arabia's weight behind the attempt to enforce Israel's withdrawal from the Occupied Territories, including Arab East Jerusalem. Henceforth, the restoration of Arab sovereignty over the Old City became one of the principal conditions demanded by the Arabs for a comprehensive peace settlement with Israel.

Immediately after the October War political and adverse economic conditions in Israel combined to slow down for a time the work of demolition and construction by which the face of the city was being transformed. In the course of 1974, however, the same general pattern as before was maintained, resulting in the steady eviction from the Old City of Arabs, whose houses were demolished and replaced by dwellings for Jewish immigrants. Between 1967 and 1977 some 6,300 Arab residents of Jerusalem were thus evicted from their homes in the Old City. Protests from the international community, stimulated by anxiety over the continuing exodus from Jerusalem of Christian Arabs, became more frequent but achieved only publicity.

Similar protests over excavations being conducted by the Israeli authorities in the vicinity of Islamic and Christian holy places in the Old City of Jerusalem brought to a head criticisms that had been voiced for more than five years by the UN Educational, Scientific and Cultural Organization (UNESCO). Recalling that urgent appeals previously addressed to the Israeli Government to suspend these excavations had been ignored, in June 1974 UNESCO's Executive Board voted 'to condemn the persistent violation by Israel of the resolutions and decisions adopted by the General Conference and the Executive Board'. In its turn the General Conference, meeting in November 1974, condemned Israel's attitude as 'contradictory to the aims of the Organization as laid down in its Constitution' and resolved to withhold assistance in the fields of education, science and culture until Israel agreed to respect previous conference resolutions in the matter.

The attitude previously expressed by both the UN Security Council and the General Assembly was reaffirmed in subsequent years, despite the failure to obtain the compliance of the Government of Israel with existing resolutions. In a 'consensus statement' adopted unanimously on 11 November 1976, the Security Council 'strongly deplored' Israel's actions in the Occupied Territories, including Jerusalem; required Israel once more to 'desist forthwith from any action which tends to alter the status of Jerusalem'; and called on Israel to comply with the terms of the 1949 Fourth Geneva Convention on the Protection of Civilians in Wartime.

Jerusalem once again became a controversial issue in May 1980, when Geula Cohen, a leader of the ultra-nationalist Tehiya party, tabled in the Israeli Knesset a bill with the object of confirming Jerusalem as Israel's indivisible capital. Despite strong protests from the Egyptian Government, which emphasized that it would not resume peace negotiations on Palestinian autonomy (see Arab–Israeli Relations 1967–2002) unless the bill was rejected, it was placed before a Knesset committee. Egypt was further antagonized when, on 23 June, Israeli Prime Minister Menachem Begin announced that he was moving his offices to the Arab sector of Jerusalem. At a time when the USA was endeavouring to produce some compromise on the Jerusalem issue that would enable Israel and Egypt to resume negotiations, the Knesset's legal committee voted in favour of giving a first reading of the bill which annexed status of the Arab sector of Jerusalem. As the originator of the legislation told *The Times* of London on 30 June, 'This Bill is designed to ensure that there will never be any compromise over the sovereignty of Jerusalem'. Nevertheless, a debate taking place in the UN Security Council the same day made it clear that this view would not be accepted by the international community. By a vote of 14 to none (the USA abstained), the Security Council adopted Resolution 476, denying Israel the right either to change the status of Jerusalem or to declare the city to be its capital. The action of the Security Council was followed by an emergency resolution of the UN General Assembly on 29 July 1980, which called upon Israel to withdraw completely and unconditionally from all territories occupied in 1967, including Jerusalem. The Resolution (ES-7/2) was passed by 112 votes to 7, with 24 abstentions. The following day Israel enacted its 'basic law' proclaiming Jerusalem to be its 'eternal capital'.

The Arab response to this law was swift. On 6 August 1980 Saudi Arabia and Iraq, the Middle East's two largest oil exporters, announced that they would sever economic and diplomatic relations with any country that recognized Jerusalem as Israel's capital. A fortnight later the UN Security Council adopted Resolution 478, declaring Israel's enactment of the 'basic law' to be a violation of international law and urging 'those states

that have established diplomatic missions in Jerusalem to withdraw such missions from the Holy City'. The Resolution was adopted by 14 votes to none, with the USA again abstaining. During the debate the US Secretary of State, Edmund Muskie, berated the Council for passing a 'series of unbalanced and unrealistic resolutions on Middle East issues'. Shortly afterwards the Netherlands and a number of Latin American countries with embassies in Jerusalem announced that they would be transferring them to Tel-Aviv.

Jerusalem continued to figure prominently in international efforts to promote an overall settlement of the Arab–Israeli conflict: the European Community's Venice Declaration of 13 June 1980 (see Documents on Palestine, p. 67) rejected any unilateral actions designed to change the status of the city, and in September 1982 proposals adopted in Fez, Morocco, by the League of Arab States (the Arab League) and a plan put forward by the Soviet leader, Leonid Brezhnev, both urged an Israeli withdrawal from the eastern sector of the city and its inclusion in a future Palestinian state. The initiative of US President Ronald Reagan, announced in the same month, declared only that the city must remain undivided and its final status be negotiable. Every indication remained, however, that Israel was not deterred from its resolve to ensure in advance the city's ultimate status by pursuing an accelerated programme of 'Judaization'. To the south and east of the Old City, plans to complete the encirclement of the Arab population with highrise, high-density housing complexes proceeded apace with the Neve Yaacov South, Gilo and Ma'aleh Edomin schemes, which were to comprise a total of 26,000 apartments. More than 10,000 dunums of land (1,000 dunums = 1 sq km) were seized for these schemes, virtually all of it expropriated from private Arab owners. In July 1981 the Knesset reaffirmed the designation of the whole of Jerusalem as Israel's 'eternal capital'.

The undiminished sensitivity to the issue of Arabs and the whole Islamic world was demonstrated following an indiscriminate gun attack on worshippers at the Dome of the Rock mosque by an Israeli soldier in April 1982, in which two Arabs were killed and more than 30 wounded. The day of protest urged by the Organization of the Islamic Conference (OIC) was observed throughout the Islamic world, while a UN Security Council draft resolution condemning the attack and deploring 'any act or encouragement of destruction or penetration of the holy places, religious buildings and sites in Jerusalem' was vetoed only by the USA. The threat posed by Jewish religious extremists increased throughout 1983 with the emergence of a clandestine group calling itself 'Terror against Terror', which claimed responsibility for a series of bomb attacks on Islamic and Christian sites around Jerusalem. This campaign culminated in January 1984 in an attempt to smuggle explosives into the al-Aqsa mosque, which was foiled at the last moment by security guards. The implications of the plot were particularly horrendous—not just because the attack had been timed to coincide with the congregation of thousands for Friday prayers the following day, but also because of evidence that the motive of the group, which was in possession of standard Israeli army-issue weapons, was to advance the reconstruction of the Jewish Temple by ridding the Temple Mount area of its 'encumbrance' of Islamic holy sites.

The dual threats to Jerusalem represented by Israeli settlement and Jewish religious fanaticism were overshadowed by another to the city's legal status, when it became clear that a number of countries, including most notably the USA, were prepared to signal their acceptance of Israel's claim to the city as its sovereign capital by transferring their embassies from Tel-Aviv to Jerusalem. Discussion of such a move on the part of the USA began in Washington, DC, in February 1984, and the proposal rapidly gained momentum—winning the sponsorship of over 180 members of the House of Representatives and some 37 senators. The Reagan Administration did not, however, lend its support to the move, and the Secretary of State, George Shultz, writing to the Senate Foreign Relations Committee, described the proposed legislation as 'damaging to the cause of peace' and contrary to the US position on Jerusalem of refusing 'to recognize unilateral acts by any party'. Such opposition was felt to spring more from fear of the anti-US backlash that relocating the embassy would provoke throughout the Islamic world than from respect for successive UN resolutions declaring East Jerusalem to be occupied territory, or for the Hague Convention of 1907 and the Fourth Geneva Convention, which held that purported annexations of territory occupied in war were a violation of international law. (As treaties of the USA, both these conventions are parts of 'the Supreme Law of the Land' under Article VI of the US Constitution, and for the US Government to assent to or condone Israel's violation of them would be unconstitutional.)

The extreme importance attached to the issue by Arab and Islamic interests was illustrated again when, in March 1984, El Salvador followed Costa Rica's decision of 1982 to relocate its embassy to Jerusalem—a move which, it had been led to believe, would result in the pro-Israel lobby in Congress facilitating US military assistance programmes for El Salvador. A meeting of the OIC in Fez in April, which emphasized the obligation to make Jerusalem an international, independent city open to all peoples and faiths, adopted a resolution to the effect that member states should sever all diplomatic, economic and cultural relations with any country that moved its embassy to Jerusalem. Egypt made a similar declaration and duly severed diplomatic ties with El Salvador and Costa Rica.

The US Administration remained firmly opposed to relocating its embassy in Israel to Jerusalem in the foreseeable future. US officials rejected as 'ridiculous' and potentially dangerous a formal statement issued on 4 April 1982 by leaders of the American Jewish Congress asserting that the status of the US consulate in Jerusalem was 'intolerable' and undermined US interests in the Middle East. For its part, the Israeli Government stood by its claim that Jerusalem was Israel's 'eternal capital', rejecting outright a proposal made by Pope John Paul II on 25 April for an internationally guaranteed status for Jerusalem in the interests of Christianity, Islam and Judaism.

Israeli settlement projects in the city proceeded apace in 1984–85, with many thousands of new apartments being built and occupied within the boundary of annexed East Jerusalem. Just outside the municipal line, in the occupied West Bank, there was also rapid construction of the satellite towns of Efrat, south of Bethlehem, Ma'aleh Edomin to the east, and Givat Zeev to the north, which were designed to provide, in total, housing for more than 50,000 Israelis. The completion of these new towns filled the last remaining gaps in the ring of settlements enclosing East Jerusalem as part of Israel's Metropolitan Plan, which aimed to achieve a Jewish majority of 120,000 over the Arab population in the Greater Jerusalem area by 1986.

The focus of the conflict over Jerusalem soon shifted back to the competing claims of possession of Jews and Muslims within the Old City. The increasing numbers of Jews settling in the Muslim Quarter, which before 1980 had housed no Jews at all, threatened to introduce strife to an area where relations between the two communities had long been exemplary. Cases of Jewish settlers intimidating Arab residents in order to establish proprietorial rights, and of Jewish-occupied buildings being illegally extended, greatly alarmed the Muslim population, who feared that the inroads could be the start of a campaign to expel the Old City's inhabitants. The new settlers, who by mid-1985 numbered some 200 among the Muslim Quarter's 20,000 Arabs, were nearly all religious-nationalist extremists, openly dedicated to rebuilding the Jewish Temple on the site of the Muslim sanctuary and mosques, the Haram ash-Sharif. Traditionally, the controversy over the Temple Mount issue had been minimized by Jewish religious rulings forbidding Jews even to enter the area, but the encroachment by Jewish zealots on Muslim areas bordering the shrine was a sign that this precept was now being challenged. In the Old City alone, seven *yeshivas* (Jewish religious colleges) had been set up expressly to study the issue of the Temple and how Jews could once again pray there.

In January 1986 members of the Israeli Knesset Interior Committee asked permission to visit the compound of al-Aqsa mosque, ostensibly to ensure that restoration work being undertaken by the Islamic authorities was not detrimental to the ancient remains of the Jewish Temple. Although it was known that the Knesset committee was acting at the instigation of Jewish extremists, who had been attempting to establish a foothold in the mosque compound by conducting prayers there, the Islamic Awqaf (religious endowments) department, entrusted with safeguarding the shrine, nevertheless gave permission for members of the committee to visit certain unused chambers beneath the al-Aqsa structure, known to Jews as

Solomon's Stables. On 7 January the Israeli parliamentarians arrived at the site accompanied by television crews and a number of religious and nationalist extremists, including the leader of the Temple Mount Faithful, a Jewish group dedicated to rebuilding the Temple in place of the al-Aqsa mosque. Deciding that the Israeli delegation intended a political demonstration of Jewish claims to the site rather than an inspection of restoration work, Muslim officials refused it entry, whereupon members of the group, led by the Tehiya party's Geula Cohen, attempted to force their way through. Calls for help were broadcast from the minarets of the Old City's mosques, and alarmed Muslims rushed to the site. The ensuing riot was brought under control only when police escorted the Israeli group away and fired tear gas into the crowd. A week later, despite an inspection of the site in the interim by the leader of the Knesset, Shlomo Hillel, and the Mayor of Jerusalem, Teddy Kollek, who testified that no structural changes had been made, the extremist group returned to the compound and attempted to pray inside it. More riots ensued, and were again dispersed by police using tear gas.

The al-Aqsa riots were seized upon by Israeli nationalists as an opportunity to publicize Jewish claims to the site, and there were signs that Temple Mount was increasingly becoming a nationalist, as well as a religious, issue in Israeli politics, in that it was a means of asserting Israeli sovereignty over what was internationally considered to be occupied territory. On 30 January 1986 the UN Security Council drafted a resolution strongly condemning Israel's 'provocative acts', which 'violated the sanctity of the sanctuary of the Haram ash-Sharif in Jerusalem' and constituted 'a serious obstruction to achieving a comprehensive, just and lasting peace in the Middle East'. The resolution, otherwise supported by all the Security Council members except Thailand, which abstained, was vetoed by the USA. Although the US Administration maintained its official position that East Jerusalem was occupied territory and that the ultimate status of the city should be determined through negotiation, it was clearly embarrassed by the reiteration of the UN's rejection of Israeli claims to sovereignty over the entire city. Despite the intense anger and alarm generated throughout the Arab and Muslim world by the perceived threat to Islam's third holiest shrine, Israel's Chief Rabbi, Mordechai Eliahu, shortly afterwards proposed the construction of a synagogue next to the mosques on Temple Mount. The proposed synagogue would be 'higher and more elevated' than the mosques of al-Aqsa and the Dome of the Rock, which would remain only 'to commemorate the Destruction' and the day when the Temple would be rebuilt.

There was a marked deepening in tension in the Old City in the autumn of 1986, with increasingly frequent acts of intimidation against Palestinians by religious extremists, as well as attacks against Israeli security personnel by Palestinians. The situation erupted in November after the stabbing of a *yeshiva* student (one of a group of religious nationalists that had resorted to the violent intimidation of neighbouring Palestinian families in an effort to force them to abandon their homes in the Aqbat al-Khaldi quarter). The subsequent backlash from Israeli extremists shocked even Israeli officials. For several days they pursued a campaign of burning and looting Palestinian homes and shops, and assaulting individual Palestinians throughout the Old City. In the days following the violence, vigilante groups were created to warn and protect the community against the Israeli extremists.

While the level of violence diminished in the early part of 1987, the attitude of the Palestinian population in East Jerusalem continued to harden. Demands for protest action, formerly heeded elsewhere in the Occupied Territories but only to a very limited extent in Jerusalem, began to win more active support. On that year's Land Day almost every shop in East Jerusalem closed in observance of the annual commemorative strike, marking a departure from previous years and a change in the political climate which prefigured confrontation on an increasing scale.

The heightened nationalist consciousness of Palestinians in East Jerusalem progressively involved them in an extension of the running conflict between the people of the Occupied Territories and the Israeli authorities, which began in December 1987. Clashes in Jerusalem grew more frequent in 1987, and the Palestinian *intifada* (uprising), although it began in Gaza and spread to the West Bank, took root in Jerusalem as firmly as elsewhere. The city's historical status has made it a centre of Palestinian resistance, notably during the first *intifada* for the Unified National Leadership of the Uprising (UNLU), whose organizational work was largely been conducted there.

The city's central importance to the international community was underlined at the summit meeting of the Arab League in Amman, Jordan, in November 1987. Jerusalem was cited as a 'symbol of peace' and as the 'embodiment of the historic ties between the Muslim and Christian faiths'. This description was contained in a little-noticed passage of the official communiqué at the end of the summit, in which King Hussein of Jordan, rather than the PLO, was mandated to undertake contacts with the Vatican on the Jerusalem issue.

The peace proposals first put forward by the Israeli Government in April 1989 (see Arab–Israeli Relations 1967–2002), while incorporating elections in the Occupied Territories, made no mention of the eligibility or otherwise of Palestinians in East Jerusalem to vote or stand as candidates in such elections. This question was repeatedly raised by those seeking to obtain more concessions from Israel in order to make the proposals more acceptable to Palestinians, but Israel's agreeing to allow the participation of residents of East Jerusalem would clearly have contradicted its formal annexation of the city in 1967.

At the 19th session of the Palestine National Council (PNC) in Algiers in November 1988, Jerusalem was named the capital of the newly declared independent state of Palestine, and in July 1989 was recognized as such by more than 60 countries.

Disagreements over the status of East Jerusalem and its residents continued to frustrate the progress of the various peace proposals put forward during 1989. US Secretary of State James Baker's preference for 'constructive ambiguity'—keeping the peace agenda deliberately vague in order not to snare progress on controversial issues—was sorely tested by the Israeli right wing's insistence that Palestinians from East Jerusalem be barred from prospective elections for the Occupied Territories. Moreover, after President Mubarak of Egypt had suggested that pre-election talks between an Israeli and a Palestinian delegation should be convened in Cairo, Israeli Prime Minister Itzhak Shamir made clear the opposition of the Likud Party to the inclusion of East Jerusalemites in the talks. Attempts by James Baker and Israel's Labour Party to coax Shamir into accepting a compromise formula, whereby Palestinians who had East Jerusalem identity papers but who lived in the West Bank would be allowed to participate in the talks, were unsuccessful. Indeed, in what was widely interpreted as a move to emphasize his opposition to such an arrangement, Shamir was said to have ordered the arrest in February 1990 of Faisal Husseini, a leading pro-PLO personality and East Jerusalem resident, on the charge that he had supplied funds for the purchase of uniforms by the Palestine Popular Army. An international outcry forced Husseini's prompt release, and at a press conference he subsequently alleged that his arrest had been meant to discredit him in view of his association with the proposed Cairo talks.

There was little doubt that Shamir's refusal to compromise on the issue of East Jerusalem stemmed as much from tactical as from ideological imperatives. Endless debate over the details of Palestinian representation seemed the least damaging way for Israel to stifle the peace process. However, such delaying tactics risked frustrating the USA to such an extent that it would be compelled, against Secretary of State James Baker's wishes, to state its position on East Jerusalem. However, it was not the stalled peace process that finally led the US Administration to reveal its hand, but the issue of Soviet Jewish emigration to Israel. Alarmed by the news that 10% of new Jewish immigrants from the USSR were being settled in East Jerusalem, US President George Bush unequivocally equated East Jerusalem with occupied territory during a telephone conversation with Prime Minister Shamir on 10 February 1990. One week later he commented that US foreign policy was opposed to any new settlements in either the West Bank or East Jerusalem. While President Bush's comment marked a radical departure from the strong pro-Israeli sentiments of the Reagan Administration, there were few signs that the Senate was about to abandon its traditional support for Israel. In March 1990 senators voted perfunctorily but overwhelmingly to recognize Jerusalem as the capital of Israel.

In 1989, as in 1988, the Palestinian *intifada* was waged with less ferocity in Jerusalem than in other cities in the West Bank and Gaza. Owing to the city's high profile and its importance to Israel's tourist industry, the Israelis were wary of employing the same kind of lethal force there as they did in Nablus or Gaza. The tactics of the security forces in Jerusalem were noticeably different from those employed elsewhere in the Occupied Territories. Whenever tensions ran high, or a nationalist anniversary approached, Israel was prepared to swamp Arab Jerusalem with huge numbers of police and border guards. Nevertheless, clashes between demonstrators and security forces in and around the city claimed a number of lives during 1989. There were also frequent confrontations between Palestinians living in the eastern suburbs of Jerusalem and Israelis from the settlement of Ma'aleh Edomin. At the end of 1989 Israeli riot police violently dispersed a legitimate rally for peace held by Palestinians, Israelis and Europeans in the eastern half of the city. Many people, including several foreigners, suffered injury.

The influx of Soviet Jews into Israel at the beginning of 1990 was regarded with dismay by Palestinians living in Jerusalem. The settlement of the new immigrants on Jewish housing estates, built on confiscated Arab lands in the eastern half of the city, resulted in a significant increase in street confrontations during the early part of the year. During Easter celebrations a force of some 120 Jewish religious nationalists forcibly occupied the St John's Hospice in the Christian quarter of the Old City, claiming they had purchased the building from an Armenian tenant for the sum of US $1.8m., most of which had been supplied by the Israeli Government. The Greek Orthodox Church, which owned the building, disputed the legality of the purchase and mounted an international campaign to have the 'settlers' removed. Anger among local Palestinian Christians was especially strong, not only because of the provocative timing of the action, but also because it was the first attempt by Israeli right-wingers to settle in the Christian quarter of Jerusalem. Demonstrations outside the Hospice by Greek Orthodox and Muslim clergy quickly developed into violent confrontation. The occupation of the Hospice was also condemned by the Israeli left and Jerusalem's Labour Mayor, Teddy Kollek, who reportedly threatened to resign unless the 'settlers' were evicted from the Hospice. While the Israeli courts eventually decided that most of the 'settlers' should leave the Hospice, 20 were given permission to remain until the ownership of the building was conclusively established.

The bloodiest incident yet of the Palestinian *intifada* occurred in Jerusalem on 8 October 1990, when members of the Temple Mount Faithful made one of their periodic and highly conspicuous attempts to lay the symbolic cornerstone of the Third Temple at the al-Aqsa mosque. Both the Israeli police and the Palestinian population had been forewarned and prepared accordingly. The police refused the members of the Temple Mount Faithful permission to enter the mosque compound, while Palestinians gathered at the site to defend it against the intruders. A full-scale riot rapidly developed. The paramilitary Border Guard opened fire indiscriminately on the crowds inside the compound and on medical staff called to treat casualties. By the time the violence had ceased, 17 Palestinians had been shot dead and many more had been injured. International condemnation was swiftly expressed in UN Security Council Resolution 672, adopted unanimously (i.e. with US support) on 12 October. However, a proposal to send a fact-finding mission to Jerusalem was rejected by the Israeli Government as interference in Israel's internal affairs. A commission of inquiry set up by the Israeli Government, and chaired by an ex-general and former chief of Mossad known for his right-wing views, predictably absolved the security forces of responsibility for the bloodshed. In the months following the killings there was a spate of 'revenge' stabbings in West Jerusalem that claimed several Israeli lives and led to further anti-Arab violence. Many Palestinians employed in the West Bank either gave up their jobs or were forced to leave by gangs of right-wing vigilantes. Not since the early days of the occupation had the city appeared so divided.

As, following the defeat of Iraq in the Gulf War in February 1991, efforts were renewed to settle the Arab–Israeli conflict,

Israel's Prime Minister Shamir took the opportunity of Jerusalem Day, the anniversary of the annexation of the city, to tell an audience of Soviet immigrants that 'Jerusalem has never been subject to negotiation. United Jerusalem is the capital of Israel'. This position was forcibly underlined by an ambitious programme of building for settlement in and around East Jerusalem, a policy that continued to exasperate both US President Bush and Secretary of State James Baker. Furthermore, the confiscation of Arab property in the Muslim quarter of the Old City continued.

The dispute over the status of East Jerusalem and its Palestinian inhabitants initially threatened to obstruct the Arab-Israeli peace talks that began in Madrid in October 1991. Israel had made it clear to the USA that it regarded the participation in the talks of Palestinian residents of East Jerusalem as unacceptable because this would represent an implicit challenge to Israel's claim that the city was not occupied territory. Such a condition was unacceptable to the Palestinians, not only because it would have established the principle of an Israeli veto over Palestinian representation, but also because it would have made it even more difficult for the Palestinians to force the issue of Jerusalem onto the agenda. James Baker assured the Palestinians that the USA did consider East Jerusalem to be occupied territory, but he cautioned that the Palestinians could not afford to be seen to be wrecking the peace talks by their inflexible attitude over representation. Similar warnings came from Egypt and Jordan and resulted in a compromise, supported by the USA and (somewhat reluctantly) by the PLO, whereby the official members of the Palestinian-Jordanian negotiating team would be accompanied by an advisory team composed primarily of East Jerusalem residents. At the Madrid conference, and subsequent rounds of bilateral talks in Washington, it became clear that the principal function of the advisory body was to co-ordinate negotiation tactics and positions with the PLO. In the course of the talks the meetings between East Jerusalem Palestinians and PLO representatives became more overt, and there was pressure from the Israeli establishment to bring charges against the offending Palestinians under anti-terrorism legislation which forbade such contact. But, although Faisal Husseini and Hanan Ashrawi (the PLO representatives) were questioned by the police, US opposition restrained any further action.

The Palestinian delegation tried unsuccessfully to raise the subject of Jerusalem during various rounds of the peace process. James Baker's attitude towards the Arab-Israeli talks was that their continuation depended upon avoiding the more intractable problems until progress had been made in less controversial areas. As progress under the Shamir premiership was agonizingly slow, Jerusalem did not come onto the negotiation agenda.

In 1991 Israel began its most aggressive programme of settlement construction in the Occupied Territories since 1967. The settlement drive was concentrated in the West Bank and in Gaza, but included considerable building activity in and around Arab Jerusalem. Palestinians were particularly disturbed by attempts to extend colonization to parts of the city hitherto regarded as exempt from settlement. In July 1991 security guards acting for a department of the Ministry of Housing took possession of a house in the Arab suburb of Sheikh Jarrah under orders from the Custodian of Absentee Property. Since the owners lived in the West Bank, the seizure set an ominous precedent by classifying West Bank residents as 'absentees'. On the eve of the Madrid conference Jewish settlers occupied seven houses in the Silwan district outside the Old City walls, evicting a number of families in the process. Court action forced them to leave six of the houses, but the settlers returned in December, assured by Israel's Attorney-General that he found nothing wrong with their titles to 20 houses in the district. These titles were based on the assertion that the properties had been owned by Jews in the 1930s. The Arab owners secured a temporary injunction for the eviction of some of the settlers, but the settlers appealed against this, guaranteeing a lengthy round of legal battles before ownership could be established. Jerusalem's Labour Mayor, Teddy Kollek, joined Palestinian leaders in condemning the settlers and their sponsors. The Government, he said, was sacrificing calm in the city 'on the altar of ideology'. Controversy over the Silwan incident was heightened by the

leaking of an Israeli housing ministry blueprint for extensive land expropriation in the Arab suburbs of the city.

The election of a Labour-led Government in Israel in July 1992 brought little hope that Jerusalem would be included on the agenda of the peace process. Although the new Government seemed sure to refrain from the ideological excesses of Likud when it came to settlement in traditional Arab areas of East Jerusalem, Prime Minister Itzhak Rabin repeated that Israeli sovereignty over the whole of Jerusalem would remain non-negotiable if the peace talks were revived. His promise was borne out by Israel's sustained refusal, during the sixth and subsequent rounds of the Middle East peace process, to discuss the issue of Jerusalem in negotiations on the period of interim self-rule for Palestinians in the Occupied Territories. Rabin's position received the tacit support of the Bush Administration when the latter declared that the USA would not deduct from the US $10,000m. in loan guarantees recently released to Israel sums that were spent on financing settlement construction in East Jerusalem. This appeared to be a clear retreat from earlier assurances given to the Palestinian peace delegation on the US position regarding Jerusalem, and was fundamental in strengthening Palestinian opposition to the peace process.

The election of Bill Clinton to the US presidency in November 1992 was greeted with some trepidation by the PLO. Both Clinton and his Vice-President, Al Gore, were regarded as committed Zionists. During the presidential campaign Gore had voiced his support for the transfer of the US embassy to Jerusalem. Although such a step was highly unlikely, given sensitivities surrounding the peace process, it was the view of the Palestinians that the new US Administration would be reluctant to pressure Israel into allowing Jerusalem onto the agenda of the bilateral negotiations. Attempts by Palestinian negotiators to extract from the USA a statement of principle regarding East Jerusalem produced conflicting signals. When US Secretary of State Warren Christopher visited East Jerusalem in the wake of the deportation affair (see Arab–Israeli Relations 1967–2002) to try to establish grounds for a restart of the peace process, he reassured members of the Palestinian delegation that President Clinton was committed to assurances on Jerusalem made by his predecessor—namely that it was considered to be occupied territory. However, during subsequent rounds of bilateral talks in Washington in the spring and early summer of 1993, US negotiators supported Israel in its insistence that Jerusalem would not be discussed until the so-called 'final status' negotiations took place some years hence. By the summer of 1993 the conflict over Jerusalem at the Washington talks was threatening to make progress on any other issue an impossibility.

Palestinians feared that the Rabin Government was adopting the same approach to negotiations on Jerusalem as had the Shamir Government towards the Occupied Territories as a whole—i.e. avoiding discussion of fundamental issues at the negotiating table while creating 'facts' on the ground. There was increasing evidence to support this view. In March 1993 Rabin sealed off the West Bank and Gaza from Israel proper, including annexed East Jerusalem, following the killing of two young Israelis by a Palestinian in West Jerusalem. As the cultural, political, geographical and economic capital of the Occupied Territories, the isolation of East Jerusalem from the West Bank was extremely disruptive to Palestinian populations on both sides of the divide (it was possible, although very difficult in practice, for West Bank and Gaza residents to get permits to visit Jerusalem). Most worrying from the Palestinian point of view were the political implications of the new measure. There was a widespread conviction that the closure heralded an attempt to 'cantonize' the Occupied Territories and bring about the permanent separation of East Jerusalem from the West Bank. In June it was also revealed that, for the first time since 1967, there were more Israelis than Palestinians living in East Jerusalem.

The Declaration of Principles (see Documents on Palestine, p. 72), agreed in Oslo and signed by Yasser Arafat and Itzhak Rabin in September 1993, stipulated that issues relating to Jerusalem would be left until 'final status' negotiations took place. Given the polarized positions of Palestinians and Israel on the future of the city, it was hardly surprising that discussion of Jerusalem would not take place during the interim negotiations. Palestinians were far less comfortable with this than were their Israeli counterparts. A highly visible and ambitious programme of settlement and road-building in and around the occupied east side of the city appeared as irrefutable confirmation that Israel was transforming East Jerusalem into a ghetto, isolated from its West Bank hinterland. The rapid physical transformation suggested that by the time Jerusalem joined the negotiation agenda, the proposed capital of a future Palestinian state would be dwarfed by a ring of Jewish suburbs and a major ring road. The deposition of the moderate Teddy Kollek as Mayor of Jerusalem by the Likud candidate, Ehud Olmert, in late 1993 implied that this process of encirclement would be hastened. Kollek had tried to avoid a Likud victory in the municipal polls by appealing to Palestinians in East Jerusalem to vote. Significantly, however, the city's Arab population observed its customary boycott of Israeli elections: only 6% of Jerusalem's Palestinians exercised their voting rights.

Palestinians attempted to use the political space conferred by the legalization of the PLO to push their own claim to sovereignty over East Jerusalem. Orient House, the property of the family of Faisal Husseini and once home to the Arab Studies centre, became the semi-official headquarters of the PLO in the Occupied Territories, and there were moves to establish similar quasi-governmental offices in the city. This largely symbolic attempt to create the 'fact' of a Palestinian 'capital' was viewed with suspicion by the Israeli Government and the new Likud administration in the city. Indeed, public pronouncements about Jerusalem by Israeli leaders continued to be united by the common thread of a refusal to countenance any compromise on Israeli sovereignty. While the Israeli position was clear to the PLO, it was dismayed at what appeared to be a shift in the USA's policy towards Jerusalem. During the 1992 presidential campaign there had been unconfirmed rumours that Clinton and Gore had promised Jewish leaders that they would revise US policy on the status of Jerusalem by excluding reference to Jerusalem as occupied territory—a formulation that the USA had accepted in UN resolutions since 1971. However, during a UN Security Council vote on a resolution (No. 904) condemning the massacre of worshippers in Hebron, the USA abstained on a preambulary clause defining Jerusalem as occupied Palestinian territory; the USA stated, furthermore, that it would have voted against if the definition had been in an operative paragraph. The US ambassador to the UN defended this apparent shift in policy by saying that Israel and the Palestinians had agreed, under the Declaration of Principles, to negotiate the city's 'final status' and the Clinton Administration did not wish to prejudice the outcome of those negotiations.

The conclusion of the first stage of the Declaration of Principles, with the redeployment of Israeli troops in Gaza and Jericho, once again focused attention on Jerusalem. Yasser Arafat was criticized in Israel when he appealed for a *jihad* (holy war) to free Jerusalem. Although Arafat later attempted a clarification by insisting that he meant a peaceful crusade, his comment was acknowledged to be a public relations disaster. Israeli leaders responded to Arafat's gaffe with an offensive of their own. The Jerusalem municipality announced its intention to begin the process of demolishing an estimated 2,000 Arab dwellings in East Jerusalem that had been built without licences. Rabin, meanwhile, instructed his Government's legal experts to explore the possibility of drawing up legislation that would forestall the PLO's plans to develop its institutional base in East Jerusalem. A confidential cabinet report leaked to the Israeli press in July 1994 detailed plans to reinforce Israeli control of Jerusalem during the approach to the 1996 talks on the status of the city. It proposed the adoption of measures to stop the 'illegal' ingress of outsiders—presumably Arabs—to the city and the creation of job opportunities for Arabs outside the city boundaries. The inescapable conclusion was that the Israeli Government was trying to engineer a further change in the demographic balance, not just by settling Jews in the eastern half of the city but also by trying to exclude its non-Jewish population.

Palestinian despondency over the developing battle for Jerusalem deepened with Israel's agreement with Jordan, on 25 July, formally to end the state of war that had existed between the two countries. One of the articles in the Israeli-Jordanian agreement acknowledged the special role of Jordan in guarding Muslim sites in Jerusalem. Responding to Palestinian objections

to the implications of such an agreement, Jordan's King Hussein stated that 'religious and political sovereignty over the holy city were two separate issues'. Further comments from Jordanian officials that the motivation for the controversial clause was a desire to save the holy sites from Israeli control before the 'final status' negotiations did little to allay Palestinian fears that Jordan was being used by Israel to undermine Palestinian claims to sovereignty over East Jerusalem. Although the PLO had until this point declined to challenge Jordan's custodianship of the Muslim holy sites, King Hussein's agreement with Israel revived speculation that the Palestinians would work towards the creation of a Palestinian *waqf* (religious endowment fund) department to replace the existing Jordanian one. A furious Arafat insisted that only Palestinians could decide the fate of East Jerusalem, and called a meeting of the Arab League to discuss the Jerusalem clause. There were also reports that King Hassan of Morocco had been asked to mediate between King Hussein and Arafat. Commentaries in the Arab press were generally critical of the Jordanian monarch's agreement with Israel on Jerusalem. Israel, meanwhile, appeared to take particular delight at the disarray. Speaking in Washington, Rabin commented, 'It wouldn't bother me at all if there is a little friction between Jordanians and Palestinians over Jerusalem'.

Israeli and Palestinian sensitivity over Jerusalem ensured that the city would continue to be an issue of contention between the Israeli Government and the Palestinian (National) Authority (PA) in the period leading up to 'final status' talks. In September 1994 the World Bank was obliged to cancel a donor's conference in Paris after Israel and the Palestinians became entangled in a bitter dispute over whether foreign aid for the PA could be used to fund development projects in East Jerusalem. Israel adamantly refused to accept that such aid was authorized in the Declaration of Principles. Further controversy followed in November when the Turkish Prime Minister, Tansu Çiller, visited Orient House, the PA's *de facto* headquarters in Jerusalem. The visit had not been approved by the Israeli Government and provoked strong protests. Israel insisted that any discussion on Palestinian self-rule had to take place in Gaza City or Jericho. Faisal Husseini, the principal PA spokesperson on Jerusalem (whose office was located in Orient House), rejoined that what was being discussed with the Turkish Prime Minister was the wider issue of the Middle East. The visit was followed by others by French, Czech and South African diplomats. The Israeli Government claimed that the Palestinians were trying to 'create facts' to prejudice the outcome of 'final status' talks, and stationed Israeli troops outside the building. Draft legislation to restrict PLO activity in Jerusalem was given its first reading in the Knesset in November, and was approved on 26 December. This was despite the assertion, made by the Israeli Minister of Foreign Affairs, Shimon Peres, in 1993 to his Norwegian counterpart, that 'All the Palestinian institutions of East Jerusalem, including the economic, social, educational and cultural...will be preserved. Needless to say, we will not hamper their activity; on the contrary, the fulfilment of this important mission is to be encouraged'.

By the end of 1994 it had also become apparent that Jordan would have to revise its position on Jerusalem. The clause it had signed with Israel concerning Jordanian custodianship of the Muslim holy sites in the city was not popular on either bank of the Jordan river, largely because the rift that it had created in relations with the PLO was seen as divisive to Arab interests and of benefit only to Israel. More importantly, at a meeting of the OIC in Casablanca, Morocco, in mid-December, King Hussein spectacularly failed to win recognition of his country's role in Jerusalem. Jordanian officials later conceded that they had mishandled the Jerusalem issue with Israel, and stated that defusing the conflict with the PLO over the city would become a priority. In January 1995 Jordan's Minister of Foreign Affairs assured Arafat that Jordan would support all steps taken to ensure Palestinian sovereignty over the east of the city, and that the patronage of the holy sites was never intended to prejudice this eventuality. A mollified Arafat agreed not to raise the issue in a forthcoming visit to Jordan.

The construction of exclusively Jewish housing in East Jerusalem and around the city boundaries continued to provoke Palestinian and international concern. Commitment to the notion of a Jerusalem 'united under Israeli sovereignty' was once again underlined in the aftermath of the Beit Lid bombings (see Arab–Israeli Relations 1967–2002), when the Ministry of Housing won the Cabinet's support for the construction of an additional 5,000 housing units in the dormitory settlements of Greater Jerusalem. When the Meretz party leader enquired where the expanding Palestinian population of East Jerusalem was going to live, Rabin answered bluntly, 'I am worried about Israelis, not the Arabs'. Meretz claimed that of the 70,000 dunums of land in East Jerusalem, 23,000 had been confiscated since 1967. Of these expropriations, 85% had been of Arab land; but of the 35,000 apartments subsequently constructed, not one had been for Jerusalem's Arab citizens. 'Whoever thinks we can go on with this policy,' commented Yair Tzaban, a prominent Meretz member, 'is making a grave mistake'. This was not an opinion that would deflect Rabin from his drive to assert Israel's territorial and demographic domination. In April 1995 the Labour leader authorized the confiscation of a further 500 dunums of Arab land in Jerusalem and the construction of an additional 7,000 new homes. Ehud Olmert, the city's Likud Mayor, expressed his warm support for the Government's plans, while his deputy stated that this was the first stage of a wider design to confiscate up to 4,400 dunums of East Jerusalem. The original expropriation proposals were eventually 'frozen' following a threat by the Arab parties represented in the Knesset to bring down the Israeli Government. An earlier Security Council resolution demanding that Israel should rescind the land confiscation had been vetoed by the USA. The US ambassador to the UN, Madeleine Albright, had defended the US action on the grounds that the issue was a local matter that would have to be resolved within the framework of the Declaration of Principles. The US veto was unremarkable and largely symptomatic of the increasingly pro-Israel leaning informing the policies and discourse of both Democratic and Republican parties. The views of the Clinton Administration were well known; the US President had received 60% of his funding from Jewish sources and 80% of the Jewish vote in his 1992 campaign. What was more alarming from an Arab perspective was a movement among Republican leaders to co-ordinate their attempts to court the Jewish vote with a campaign to have the US embassy in Israel moved from Tel-Aviv to Jerusalem. In February 1995 the Republican Speaker in the US House of Representatives, Newt Gingrich, stated that he 'strongly favoured' moving the embassy. His comments prompted politicians in both the Senate and the House of Representatives to express support for his position. By May the leader of the Republicans in the Senate, Bob Dole, who had recently argued in favour of a reduction in US aid to Israel, had garnered bipartisan support for a bill requiring the USA to build a new embassy in Jerusalem. Clinton's embarrassment at having to oppose the measure was pre-empted, for the time being, by Rabin's decidedly lukewarm response to the Dole initiative. There were two reasons for this. First, Rabin was concerned that such a gesture was untimely given the precarious state of negotiations on Palestinian autonomy. Second, and relatedly, the US Republicans' novel enthusiasm for the transfer of the embassy originated from the activities of the American Israel Public Affairs Committee (Aipac), the most influential and increasingly intransigent pro-Israel lobby group. Ideologically, Aipac had far more in common with the Israeli right wing than with the Labour Party, and Rabin suspected that however welcome a transfer of embassy might be in theory, the sabotage of the autonomy talks was Aipac's hidden agenda.

An opinion poll published in June 1995 provided some comfort for Palestinians. It revealed that there was a significant decline in support among Jerusalem's Jewish citizens for the nationalist doctrine of exclusive Israeli sovereignty over Jerusalem. According to the findings, support for this notion had decreased from 57.4% in 1993 to 45.8%. There was a big difference in opinion between secular and religious voters, with the latter more strongly in favour of exclusive sovereignty. However, the preponderance of secular opinion nationally seemed to suggest that there was a greater readiness for some compromise with the Palestinians over the status of East Jerusalem than had previously been thought.

The PA secured a small but significant victory on the issue of Jerusalem during the negotiation of interim-phase agreements (see Documents on Palestine, p. 80) with Israel, within the framework of the Oslo accords. According to a deal concluded by the two sides in the Egyptian resort of Taba in September 1995, the Palestinian villages on the municipal borders of the city were to enjoy the same status as the rest of the West Bank villages; i.e. civic authority and responsibility for 'public order' there would be transferred to the PA, while Israel would remain in charge of 'overriding security'. Israel also agreed to allow residents of East Jerusalem to vote in the forthcoming elections to the Palestinian Legislative Council (PLC), and to stand as candidates provided they also had residency in the West Bank. In the view of one of the Palestinian negotiators at the Taba talks, the agreement on the Jerusalem villages meant that Israel's dream of a Greater Jerusalem had come to an end. Despite these concessions, Israel gave notice that it would not tolerate any PA activity in East Jerusalem. As a prelude to the closure of Orient House, the unofficial PA headquarters in the city, Israel's Chief of Police shut down three Palestinian institutions in the city (the Palestinian Health Council, Broadcasting Corporation and Bureau of Statistics). Arafat was able to forestall their closure by allowing the three institutions to sign declarations stating that they were independent of the PA.

Meanwhile, US Senator Bob Dole, by now the leading Republican candidate for the US presidency, had won an overwhelming majority in the US Congress for his bill to have the US embassy in Israel transferred from Tel-Aviv to Jerusalem by May 1999. The PA reacted sharply to the decision, with Yasser Arafat angrily condemning the proposed move as 'incompatible with the spirit of the peace process'. President Bill Clinton's embarrassment at this transparent electioneering by his Republican rival was partially allayed when he secured a last-minute amendment to the bill. This allowed the US President to certify every six months that it would not be in the national interest to transfer the embassy. The certification could be employed indefinitely.

Palestinians were noticeably less enthusiastic about registering for the 1996 PLC elections in Jerusalem than they were in the towns and villages of the West Bank and the Gaza Strip, despite the PA urging them to do so. Their reluctance originated partly through fear that by registering to vote they would jeopardize their status as Jerusalem identity-card holders, and partly through lack of faith in a process that was being conducted under continued Israeli occupation. However, just as the PA had a vested interest in ensuring that the turn-out for the elections to the PLC was as high as possible, so Israel was happy to see as few Palestinians as possible take part. Israeli police established blockades to prevent candidates for Jerusalem's seven seats from canvassing during the election campaign, and insisted on restricting polling stations to a number that Palestinians argued was far less than could realistically accommodate the expected number of voters. On 20 January 1996 some 40% of potential voters cast their ballots, a turn-out that was lower than in any other area of the territories occupied in 1967 except Hebron (significantly, the only other Palestinian population centre also under partial Israeli control). This was a disappointment for the PA, but the fact that Jerusalem had participated at all was declared by one of the successful Jerusalem candidates as signifying 'the beginning of the re-emerging of Jerusalem, legally, politically and structurally within the Palestinian system'.

In Israel's prime ministerial and legislative elections in May 1996 both the Labour and Likud leaders reiterated their commitment to a unified Jerusalem under Israeli sovereignty. Their pronouncements were given added resonance by the fact that the talks about to resume between Israel and the PA on the 'final status' of the territories occupied in 1967 would focus on the need to reconcile opposing claims to the Arab areas of Jerusalem. Despite the ritualized utterings of successive Labour leaders on the need to preserve Israeli domination of all sections of the city, the fact that a two-thirds' majority of Labour Party members in Jerusalem were reportedly willing to accept something less than full Israeli sovereignty implied that most Palestinians supported Shimon Peres and the Labour Party. The victory of Binyamin Netanyahu and his Likud Party was perceived, not just by the Palestinians and Arab states but by much of the international community, as a set-back to hopes of achieving a compromise on Jerusalem. Initial policy statements by the victorious Likud leader appeared to confirm the international pessimism. In his first meeting with Yasser Arafat, Israel's newly appointed Minister of Foreign Affairs, David Levy, stated that the PA would have to shut down all of its institutions in Jerusalem—including its headquarters, Orient House—before negotiations could be resumed on 'final status' agreements. In a further statement of intent to limit the Palestinians' room for manoeuvre in Jerusalem, the Israeli police summoned the seven PLC deputies who represented Jerusalem to question them about 'their political activity'. The seven refused to respond, claiming immunity under agreements previously signed between Israel and the PA. In late June the Israeli press revealed plans for the seizure of large tracts of land belonging to two Palestinian villages with the purpose of building new housing units, an industrial zone, a public park and a swimming pool. Observers pointed out that if the proposals proceeded, it would effectively mean the encirclement of East Jerusalem. Palestinians were angered again at the end of July when the Israeli High Court granted members of the extremist Temple Mount Faithful permission to enter the compound of the al-Aqsa mosque. Hundreds of Palestinians converged on the scene and a bloody confrontation was only narrowly avoided. Commenting on the incident, the PA's Minister of Awqaf declared, 'We know well that the hour of confrontation with the Jews is getting closer, and we must be willing to die and shed blood for our rights and for the holy places'.

Netanyahu underlined his Government's opposition to Palestinian attempts at institutional development in East Jerusalem with an order in late August 1996 for the closure of further institutions (including the Geographical Office and the Youth and Sports Department) loosely connected to the PA. Just days after compliance with the order, Israeli bulldozers demolished a Palestinian centre for the elderly and handicapped in Jerusalem's Old City, on the grounds that the five-year-old building had been constructed without a licence. This development provoked strong protests from the PA and from the city's PLC members, who advocated a four-hour general strike to demonstrate opposition to the measure.

On 23 September 1996 the Likud Prime Minister announced the opening of the 500-m Hasmonean tunnel that runs through the heart of the Old City, alongside the compound of the al-Aqsa mosque. Given the existing political climate and Muslim sensitivities over any perceived threat to Islamic holy sites, Netanyahu's decision was widely viewed as somewhat rash. King Hussein of Jordan, whose 1994 peace treaty with Israel recognized Jordanian custodianship of *waqf* property in the city, was extremely critical of Netanyahu's failure to consult or inform him regarding the move. Yasser Arafat, meanwhile, denounced the decision as a 'crime against our holy places' and he urged Palestinians to protest against what he termed the 'Judaization of Jerusalem'. The response was immediate and overwhelming. Three Palestinians were shot dead and more than 120 were injured after Friday prayer demonstrations at the al-Aqsa mosque on 27 September. Elsewhere in the Occupied Territories, 52 Palestinians and 15 Israelis died in the bloodiest series of confrontations since the June war of 1967. While the scale of the violence unleashed in September injected an urgency into the peace process that had hitherto been lacking under the Netanyahu Government, there was no evidence of any reversal of Israel's policy of extending control over the east of the city while denying Palestinians either the physical or the political space to preserve residual autonomy. In November 50 prominent Palestinians organized a sit-down demonstration outside Jerusalem's interior ministry to draw attention to two aspects of Israel's rule that they claimed were having a particularly insidious impact on the status and livelihoods of the city's Palestinian residents. The first of these was the 'general' closure imposed on the West Bank and Gaza in 1993. This had required non-resident Palestinians to obtain Israeli permission to enter the city and had effectively detached East Jerusalem from its Arab hinterland. Many of the city's businesses had subsequently relocated to the West Bank. The result, according to Palestinian economists, had been a 50% decline in trade among its merchants and steadily rising unemployment. Of equal concern to the protesters was a policy of the Ministry of the Interior of redefining the parameters under which Palestinians could live in Jerusalem. Since 1994 Palestinians' right of residency in Jerusalem had become increasingly determined by whether or not

their so-called 'centre of life' was in the city. By the end of 1996 more than 1,000 Palestinians had been relieved of their rights of residency because they failed to meet this criterion. Many of these individuals were people who had moved to the West Bank in response to the economic downturn.

Construction of Jewish apartments in East Jerusalem continued at a steady pace. In December 1996 the Jerusalem District Housing Committee approved the construction of 132 housing units in the Palestinian village of Ras al-Amud, just outside the Old City walls. Financed by Irving Moskowitz, a US-based millionaire, and intended for Orthodox Jews, it had yet to receive ministerial sanction but was regarded as a particularly provocative proposal. According to the Israeli group Peace Now, which supported Palestinian opposition to the development, its inauguration would mean that for the first time since 1967 an Israeli government had 'decided to plan a settlement in the heart of a Palestinian neighbourhood'. While the international community was pondering the likely effect on the peace process of such a development, Prime Minister Netanyahu gave his support to the construction of a massive new settlement on Jabal Abu Ghunaim, a forested hilltop straddling the southeastern municipal borders of Jerusalem and belonging to the Palestinian town of Beit Sahur. Construction of the new development (Har Homa), which was expected to comprise 6,500 housing units, would represent the completion of Arab Jerusalem's encirclement by exclusively Jewish settlements. Despite united local and international opposition to Har Homa, work began on its construction in March 1997. Under US pressure the Netanyahu Government also announced that it would be granting 3,015 building permits to Palestinians in East Jerusalem to ensure 'equal rights and development for Jews and Arabs' in the city. But this intended palliative did little to lessen Palestinian opposition to Har Homa. It was observed that the granting of permits would be conditional on infrastructural development in Palestinian areas, something for which successive Israeli governments had an extremely poor track record.

Yasser Arafat's PA responded to the commencement of work on Har Homa by calling a halt to negotiations on the Oslo accords. Arafat stated that their resumption would be conditional on suspension of the project. The Clinton Administration in the USA also supported the international community's expression of opposition to Israeli settlements in East Jerusalem. Nevertheless, Washington vetoed a UN resolution condemning the Har Homa decision because its wording categorized East Jerusalem as occupied territory. This, according to the US ambassador to the UN, prejudged future Israeli-Palestinian negotiations on the 'final status' of the city and was thus at odds with US policy. His remarks were considered disingenuous by many independent observers, since developments such as Har Homa, together with ongoing Jewish housing construction in other parts of East Jerusalem, were already creating the 'facts on the ground' that contravened the spirit, if not the letter, of the Oslo accords.

With an increasing sense that the battle to preserve East Jerusalem as the future capital of an independent Palestinian state was being lost, there were belated signs of resistance. In April and May 1997 a campaign to raise US $100m. for real estate development was conducted among Palestinian, Jordanian and Egyptian businessmen. In June Palestinian merchants also staged a one-day strike in protest against tax raids initiated by Likud Mayor Ehud Olmert, who claimed that the merchants owed the municipality $38m. In response, Palestinians claimed that their tax burden was too high, given that they comprised around 30% of the city's population but received only 7% of municipal funds. After the strike the Jerusalem Chamber of Commerce announced that it would maintain the tax boycott and would consider an indefinite strike if the raids continued.

The interruption to negotiations on the Oslo accords caused by the Har Homa construction resulted in US pressure on the Netanyahu Government to take steps to ease tension over the settlement issue. In May 1997 Olmert announced a six-month moratorium on the demolition of unlicensed Palestinian dwellings in Jerusalem, and in July the Israeli Prime Minister declared his opposition to the controversial settlement of Ras al-Amud. This latter concession, together with reports that a temporary 'freeze' was being considered on the Har Homa development, was instrumental in an agreement by the Israeli

Government and the PA to restart formal negotiations which had been suspended since March. The day after the announcement 13 Israelis were killed in West Jerusalem's Mahane Yehuda market in a double suicide bombing by Islamist militants. Netanyahu immediately imposed a blockade of all PA-controlled areas, and announced that further negotiations on the Oslo accords would be suspended until Arafat had satisfied Israeli demands for the apprehension of militant Islamist suspects. By the end of July the prospect of a solution to the Har Homa problem appeared to have receded. There were further suicide bombings in Jerusalem at the beginning of September. Three suspected Islamist bombers killed four Israelis and themselves in a co-ordinated attack in the west of the city.

The Jerusalem bomb attacks and the deepening crisis in the Oslo peace process provided a sombre backdrop to the first official trip to the region by the new US Secretary of State, Madeleine Albright. While in Israel in September 1997 she cautioned Israel against provocative settlement activity in the territories occupied by Israel in 1967. Within 48 hours of her leaving Israel, however, Jerusalem was once again the focus of media attention owing to settler action in the east of the city. On 14 September three Jewish families, escorted by armed settlers, occupied buildings in Ras al-Amud. The settler families claimed legitimacy of tenancy on the grounds that the buildings had been rented from Irving Moskowitz, the Miami-based financier who had initiated earlier plans for a settlement in the village and who had already bankrolled the activities of militant settlers in the Old City. Residents of the village, for their part, fiercely disputed Moskowitz's claim to ownership of the occupied buildings. After the Government negotiated with lawyers representing Moskowitz, Netanyahu announced a 'compromise' deal to end the stand-off whereby the Jewish families agreed to vacate the buildings on the understanding that they would be occupied by 10 *yeshiva* students. The agreement was denounced in the strongest terms by Arafat and the Israeli peace movement. It sustained fears that the village would continue to be a target for settlers and their allies in the Israeli Government. The Israeli Minister of National Infrastructure, Ariel Sharon, noted that the creation of a Jewish settlement in Ras al-Amud was critical if the Israeli state was to prevent 'Arab contiguity' between the Old City and the Palestinian villages that served as its hinterland. Palestinian-Israeli negotiations concerning the implementation of the Oslo accords, effectively stalled since the inauguration of work on the Har Homa project, remained deadlocked for much of 1997 and early 1998. Israel's refusal to undertake the scheduled redeployment of its forces in the West Bank was justified by the Israeli Government in terms of the continuing threat posed to Israel's security. However, there was also a widely held belief that Netanyahu was hoping to secure an accelerated transition to 'final status' talks in which land settlements and the future of Jerusalem would be the most intractable issues for negotiation. Predictably, there was little sign that either Netanyahu's Government or the Labour opposition was prepared to countenance anything less than full Israeli sovereignty over the entire city. A corollary of this position was Israeli determination to undermine attempts by the PA to develop an institutional base in the city. Indeed, a crucial precondition of the Netanyahu Government for moving towards redeployment in the West Bank was that the PA end all political activity in East Jerusalem. Heightened political sensitivities over the Jerusalem issue were clearly underlined in March 1998 during a visit to the city by the British Secretary of State for Foreign and Commonwealth Affairs, Robin Cook. Cook's decision to visit the site of the Har Homa settlement provoked barely concealed outrage from the Israeli Government: not only would the visit refocus world attention on Israel's settlement policy, but Cook announced that he intended to view the controversial building work in the company of Faisal Husseini, the Palestinian Minister responsible for Jerusalem Affairs. Netanyahu declared such a visit 'unacceptable', and eventually it was agreed that Cook would visit the site accompanied by Israel's cabinet secretary, a compromise that dismayed the Palestinians and appeared to do little to mollify Netanyahu. The British politician was jeered and jostled at the site by right-wing settlers and was forced to make a swift retreat. However, Cook later met Husseini in East Jerusalem, where he laid a wreath to the victims of the 1948 massacre of Palestinians at Deir Yassin.

Netanyahu reacted to the clear symbolism of Cook's itinerary by cancelling a planned dinner together, agreeing only to a brief 15-minute meeting with the visitor. At subsequent press conferences the Israeli Prime Minister promised 'thousands of homes in Har Homa'. For his part, Cook reiterated the position of the European Union (EU). 'My visit to Har Homa was symbolic,' he declared, 'one of the biggest obstacles to the peace process is the expansion of settlements...there has been no progress in the peace process since the decision to build Har Homa was made.'

If Cook's visit served to reinforce the Israeli Government's belief that it could expect little backing from Europe for Israel's claim to exclusive sovereignty over Jerusalem, tours of the USA undertaken by Netanyahu in the first half of 1998 confirmed that there was no diminution in such support from US congressional leaders. Netanyahu won repeated standing ovations for a series of uncompromising statements on Israeli attitudes towards relations with the Palestinians, none more enthusiastic than that which he received when he pledged that Israel would never give up a part of Jerusalem. In May the city became the principal focus of Israel's 50th anniversary celebrations, during which time the city's West Bank borders were once again sealed to Palestinians. Large numbers of security personnel were deployed on the streets of Arab Jerusalem and the Old City to thwart Palestinian disruption of the celebrations. Nevertheless, serious rioting broke out in Arab quarters later in the month as Palestinians commemorated *an-Nakba*, the 'catastrophe' of 1948 that had resulted in their dispossession.

On 23 May 1998 Israelis celebrated the 31st 'Jerusalem Day'. Sharing a platform with Irving Moskowitz, the Israeli Prime Minister reaffirmed his pledge that Jerusalem would remain united under Israeli sovereignty in perpetuity. The day also witnessed a march by some 13,000 Israeli troops through West Jerusalem, and symbolic attempts by right-wing extremist groups to occupy both the al-Aqsa mosque and Orient House. The following day members of the Ateret Kohanim movement (one of the most active settler organizations in East Jerusalem, largely funded by Moskowitz) began to lay the foundations of a new *yeshiva* in the Muslim quarter of the Old City. The site had originally housed a Palestinian charitable organization, but this had been one of the buildings demolished 21 months previously by the Jerusalem municipality on the grounds that they had been built without a licence. Ateret Kohanim had reportedly been interested in purchasing the site for several months and had been in illegal occupation since the beginning of May. Two days after the building work began seven temporary homes had been erected and supplied with water and electricity. Although the construction work was patently illegal, since no building permit had been granted, the site was protected throughout by units of the paramilitary Border Police. Israeli radio also broadcast reports that the settlers had been encouraged to build on the plot by Ariel Sharon. On 26 May members of the PLC attempted to enter the building compound; the ensuing scuffles with the Border Police resulted in injury to several Palestinian politicians (including Faisal Husseini) and the destruction of one of the homes. Israel's internal security ministry subsequently announced that the Jerusalem municipality and the Israeli Antiquities Department had obtained a restraining order on further building—this announcement was made after the latter body had cautioned that the construction work was endangering the perimeter wall of the Old City. In discussions with local police chiefs and Mayor Olmert the settlers agreed to halt development on the site on condition that their members would remain *in situ* to provide security for any excavation work carried out by the Antiquities Department. A tender would later be submitted by Ateret Kohanim to build a *yeshiva* and 12 apartments for 400 religious students. Expectation was high that the tender would be approved. Left-wing Israelis and Palestinians criticized the agreement, describing it as a capitulation to religious nationalism and a further significant set-back to the peace process.

On 21 June 1998 the Israeli Cabinet approved a proposal to create a 'Greater Jerusalem'. The plan envisaged the extension of the city's municipal boundaries westwards to incorporate Israeli commuter towns, and therefore guarantee a Jewish majority within the city. More controversially, the proposal also contained provision for the creation of an 'umbrella municipality' over eight Jewish settlements bordering the city but currently occupying the territories of the West Bank. These settlements would continue paying local property taxes and voting in their own jurisdictions but would fall under Jerusalem's municipal authority for certain services, including building and planning. The US Department of State described the plan as 'extremely provocative', and Ahmad Tibi, Yasser Arafat's economic adviser, deemed it 'a total violation of the Oslo Agreement' and an attempt 'to annex Palestinian land'. Similar concerns were expressed by the EU. Netanyahu responded to the mounting chorus of local and international criticism by stating that the proposal was 'entirely municipal, entirely administrative, with no political implications'.

In July 1998 the Arab representatives on the UN Security Council successfully lobbied for a debate on Israeli plans for the extension of Jerusalem's boundaries. The USA's ambassador to the UN, Bill Richardson, reiterated his country's belief that the proposals were 'unhelpful', but added that the Security Council should not 'interject itself into issues' that needed to be resolved by the two parties concerned. The inevitability of the US veto being exercised to block a resolution critical of Israel led the Council to issue instead a strongly worded statement condemning the Jerusalem plan. Notwithstanding these minor diplomatic achievements at the UN, Palestinians continued to accuse the Netanyahu Government of pursuing policies designed to ensure Israeli hegemony over the whole city. The 'Greater Jerusalem' plan was the most obvious example of Israel's intent to facilitate new political and demographic realities, but the PA also complained of a steady erosion of Palestinian civil rights. Of prime concern was the removal of the right of residency for Palestinians for whom the Israeli authorities judged East Jerusalem not to be the centre of life. According to Israel's interior ministry, 436 Palestinians had their Jerusalem identity cards confiscated in the first half of 1998. It was also reported that the Ministry of the Interior refused to issue such cards to West Bank Palestinians who had married Jerusalem residents, or to the children of their union. By the end of 1998 some 4,000 families were reported to have been affected by this policy.

The Wye River Memorandum of October 1998 (see Documents on Palestine, p. 86) committed Israel and the PA to commence negotiations on Oslo's 'final status' arrangements, including the future of Jerusalem, in November 1998. Israeli accusations that the PA was not complying with its security commitments, coupled with a Knesset vote in December for early prime ministerial and parliamentary elections, effectively stalled the peace process. The resulting hiatus added to a growing sense of Palestinian vulnerability. With the Oslo process suspended and the US Government eager for 'final status' negotiations to begin as soon as possible after the elections due in May 1999, there was a clear imperative for the Netanyahu Government and its allied settler groups to consolidate control over Jerusalem. In January 1999 the Israeli Prime Minister gave his consent for construction to begin on the Har Homa settlement at the cleared site of Jabal Abu Ghunaim, and final approval for the development of high-rise apartments at Ras al-Amud in East Jerusalem. At the same time there was mounting evidence that the Jerusalem municipality was preparing to shift the city's borders southwards and westwards, to encompass the territory between Jerusalem and Bethlehem. Shopkeepers and restaurant owners in the area complained that they had been instructed henceforth to pay taxes to the Jerusalem municipality, while residents of the village of Walaja received notification that the Israeli Defence Forces (IDF) were to demolish several buildings in the village, including the local mosque. Further land seizures and confiscations were reported around Bethlehem in February. The ability of the Palestinians to challenge Likud's vision of a 'Greater Jerusalem' was undermined by the consensus within the Israeli political establishment. Labour leader and premiership hopeful Ehud Barak subscribed to the same notion of a Jerusalem united in perpetuity under Israeli sovereignty as his predecessors. In mid-March Netanyahu once again soured relations with the EU by instructing foreign delegations not to visit the *de facto* PLO headquarters at Orient House. The German Government, as holder at that time of the EU presidency, responded with the dispatch of a letter to the Israeli Ministry of Foreign Affairs, reaffirming the European position that Jerusalem was a divided city and that Israeli sovereignty

over occupied East Jerusalem was not recognized. As Netanyahu's fortunes suffered a reversal in the weeks prior to the elections, he appeared determined to make the closure of Orient House a centrepiece of his election campaign. Despite pleas from the international community to show restraint in the matter, he instructed the Minister of Internal Security to order the closure of Orient House by the evening of 9 May. The Palestinians refused to comply, and on the morning of 10 May hundreds of members of Arafat's Fatah movement formed a protective cordon around the building. As last-minute efforts to broker a compromise failed in the face of Palestinian determination to defy Netanyahu, violent confrontation appeared to be inevitable. Meanwhile, in a co-ordinated effort with the PA, a group of Israeli peace activists was petitioning Israel's Supreme Court to delay the closure order on the grounds that it was 'motivated by electoral considerations' and 'could lead to bloodshed'. Their argument was accepted, and on 11 May a temporary injunction was served on the Israeli Government, preventing it from closing any offices at Orient House. Although the Supreme Court only delivered a stay of execution, the Palestinians regarded the verdict as a rare victory.

It was thought unlikely that Ehud Barak, who went on to secure a convincing victory in the elections held on 17 May 1999, would devote energy to the kind of ideological brinkmanship that Netanyahu had willingly engaged in over Orient House. It was equally evident, none the less, that neither would he waver in the drive to consolidate Israeli control over Jerusalem. On 14 September, the day after the conclusion of the ceremony marking the beginning of 'final status' talks between Israel and the PA, Barak visited the settlement of Ma'aleh Edomin to the east of the city. He informed the assembled leaders that the 25,000-strong township was part of 'Greater Jerusalem'. He also promised, 'Every tree planted here, every house and stone here is part of the State of Israel for ever'. Later in the month tenders were awarded for the construction of 2,600 housing units in the settlement. Palestinian spokesmen accused Israel of trying to create a 'Jewish demographic continuity' by expanding Ma'aleh Edomin westwards to link with Jerusalem proper. The underlying goal, it was claimed, was to render any future division of Jerusalem impossible.

Lobbyists for a unified Jerusalem under Israeli sovereignty scored victories in the US political arena during the summer of 1999 by securing public declarations of support for their position from leading Democratic and Republican candidates for the US presidency. Hillary Clinton (wife of the incumbent and herself a future New York Senator), who had earlier attracted criticism from the pro-Israel lobby for her declared support for a Palestinian state, also voiced commitment to Jerusalem as the 'eternal and indivisible capital of Israel'. Elsewhere, the opposition of the international community to Israeli policy on Jerusalem remained unchanged. In voting in the UN General Assembly in early December, only Israel voted against reaffirming that the annexation and extension of Israeli rule to East Jerusalem was illegal. The USA abstained, commenting that it was not appropriate for the General Assembly to 'interject' at a time when the city's future was being discussed between the Israelis and the PA during the 'final status' talks. International attention was once again focused on the city during the visit of Pope John Paul II, the head of the Roman Catholic Church, in March 2000. Yasser Arafat had achieved a minor political coup in the weeks prior to the visit with the signing, in mid-February, of a PLO-Vatican accord. The agreement, finalized in Rome, stated that policies affecting the 'specific character and status of Jerusalem are morally and legally unacceptable'. The Israeli Ministry of Foreign Affairs summoned the apostolic delegate to Jerusalem and Palestine to protest at the timing and tenor of the sentiments expressed in the document. Predictably, the papal visit itself was marred by controversy as both Israel and the PA were less than discreet in their respective attempts to make political capital from the pilgrimage. The Palestinians complained that the massive Israeli security presence during the Pope's tour of the Old City was aimed at preventing ordinary Palestinians from coming into contact with the Pontiff. It was also claimed by prominent Palestinian Christian Hanan Ashrawi that 'international political figures' such as herself had been warned to stay away from the papal mass at the Church of the Holy Sepulchre unless they wanted 'the entire Israeli Cabinet' also to turn up. The Grand Mufti of Jerusalem, a PA appointee, drew sharp international criticism for using the occasion of the Pope's visit to the Holocaust memorial at Yad Vashem to belittle Jewish suffering during the Nazi era.

As Israeli-Palestinian negotiations on 'final status' issues inched painfully towards their September 2000 deadline, the reaching of an understanding on Jerusalem's future was regarded by all parties as particularly problematic. The thickening of Israeli settlement in and around the city boundaries had led Yasser Arafat to lobby hard in Washington, as well as in his meetings with Ehud Barak, for areas of Palestinian population close to the city to be transferred to full PA control. This was in conformity with the redeployment agreements reached at Wye (see above) and at the September 1999 summit at Sharm esh-Sheikh (see Documents on Palestine, p. 88). Despite the opposition of the more nationalist of his coalition partners to a PA presence on the outskirts of the city, Barak told a meeting of the Israeli Cabinet that he was not opposed in principle to exclusive Palestinian control of villages bordering Jerusalem (most notably Abu Dis, Sawahara and Azariya) because he had no desire to incorporate a further 50,000 Palestinians into a Jerusalem under Israeli sovereignty. There were other factors nudging Barak into handing over the three villages. The Minister of Justice, Yossi Beilin, one of the more 'dovish' of Barak's Labour Party colleagues, had advanced the idea that Palestinian aspirations in Jerusalem could be accommodated by the creation of a 'substitute Jerusalem' based in the areas overlooking the Old City, citing the ongoing construction in Abu Dis of a new Palestinian parliament. It was pointed out that, on completion, this building would be geographically equidistant from the holy sites of the Old City as the Israeli Knesset. Barak was reported to be in favour of Beilin's suggestion. He won narrow backing in the Knesset for the transfers, but froze implementation in response to the violent protests in the West Bank and Gaza in mid-May (see Arab–Israeli Relations 1967–2002). The Palestinians dismissed the Beilin proposal as completely unacceptable.

In July 2000 the Israeli and Palestinian leaders accepted Bill Clinton's invitation to attend a peace summit at the Camp David US presidential retreat in Maryland. Clinton expressed hope that the two sides would reach a framework agreement on all the major issues, including the future status of Jerusalem. Arafat and Barak prefaced their attendance at the summit by reiterating their seemingly irreconcilable positions on the city, thus confirming the centrality and intractability of Jerusalem in respect of the wider conflict. Fears that this issue would prove the major obstacle to the achievement of a framework agreement on permanent status were confirmed by Israeli and Palestinian spokesmen when the talks collapsed after 15 days of intensive negotiations. According to press reports, the USA had attempted to broker a compromise over Jerusalem that would provide the Palestinians with a form of enhanced autonomy in the Arab areas of the city, including the Muslim and Christian quarters of the Old City. In return, Israel would formally annex the suburban settlement blocs they had constructed around East Jerusalem, including Ma'aleh Edomin. Arafat, mindful of expectation in the Arab and Islamic world that there must be no compromise over Jerusalem, rejected the plan. He insisted that East Jerusalem must be the sovereign capital of the future Palestinian state, with individual religions having control over their own holy places.

Arafat's stance on Jerusalem was regarded as unduly inflexible by the US Administration. The PA leader's refusal to give up claims to Palestinian sovereignty over East Jerusalem in exchange for the promise of a Palestinian state clearly irked the US President. In an interview on Israeli television on 27 July 2000 Bill Clinton remarked that as a result of the failures at Camp David he was considering a move of the US embassy to West Jerusalem. Washington's reproach was mirrored by plaudits for the PA President in the Arab world. Although Egypt's President Mubarak was normally guarded in his comments on regional issues, he gave unusually strong backing to the Palestinian claim to East Jerusalem. Commenting for the first time on the collapse of the Camp David summit, he opined, 'No single person in the Arab or Muslim world can give away East Jerusalem or al-Aqsa mosque...In this context, even Arafat himself will not dare to sign a deal to give up these Muslim

holy sites...We will not dictate to him any decision that he does not accept and that is not compatible with his Palestinian people's demands'. Buoyed by Arab support, Yasser Arafat delivered an address to the OIC's Al-Quds (Jerusalem) Committee on 28 August, in which he vowed that the Palestinians would never offer concessions on Jerusalem.

With the focus of the debate on the stalemate in the Middle East peace process firmly centred on the issue of Jerusalem, the Israeli Government reaffirmed its readiness to pursue its own vision of a Jerusalem united under Israeli sovereignty. On 18 September 2000 the Ministry of the Interior approved the confiscation of a swathe of Arab land in East Jerusalem to facilitate the completion of an eastern ring road connecting Israeli settlements in East Jerusalem to each other and also to West Jerusalem. The announcement heightened the tension between the PA and Barak's Government, but it was the actions of the uncompromising leader of the Likud opposition, Ariel Sharon, that were dramatically to underline the city's ability to fire the passions of Arabs and Jews. On 28 September Sharon attempted to assert Israeli claims to sovereignty over the Old City's religious sites by entering the al-Aqsa compound (Haram ash-Sharif/Temple Mount) accompanied by a large retinue of bodyguards and security personnel. His clearly provocative visit had reportedly been sanctioned by Ehud Barak. The presence at Islam's third holiest shrine of an Israeli politician long reviled by Palestinians for his part in the 1982 massacres at Sabra and Chatila (see Arab–Israeli Relations 1967–2002), led to scuffles and stone-throwing, which were easily contained by the Israeli police. However, at the conclusion of Friday prayers the following day, Palestinian worshippers at al-Aqsa spilled out of the compound to confront Israel's security forces. The violent protests that raged through the Old City quickly spread to the towns and refugee camps of the West Bank. By the end of the day six Palestinians had been shot dead. Their funerals became the rallying points for further demonstrations, which quickly engulfed all areas of the Occupied Territories. After three days of sustained conflict, which saw Palestinian militants engaged in prolonged gun battles with the Israeli army, the rebellion was being referred to as the al-Aqsa *intifada*. Further demonstrations broke out at al-Aqsa after Friday prayers on 6 October, leading to the storming of the compound by Israeli riot police. The following day the UN Security Council adopted Resolution 1322, which reaffirmed 'the need for full respect by all of the Holy Places of the City of Jerusalem' and deplored 'the provocation carried out' at Haram ash-Sharif on 28 September. The US ambassador to the UN abstained in the vote.

The Israeli decision to seal off the West Bank and Gaza in early October 2000 failed to stifle the Palestinian revolt there, but did ensure that Jerusalem did not see the daily clashes witnessed elsewhere. Nevertheless, in the locations where Israeli settlements at the edge of Jerusalem abutted Palestinian towns and villages on the West Bank, there were frequent gun battles. This was particularly true of the southern districts of Jerusalem, where Palestinian gunmen frequently fired on the suburban Israeli settlement of Gilo. On 30 October a security guard was shot dead, and another wounded, in an attack on an Israeli National Insurance office in East Jerusalem. Two days later a car bomb explosion in West Jerusalem killed two Israelis, one of them the daughter of the leader of the National Religious Party. The Palestinian leadership issued a condemnation of the bombing in West Jerusalem but remained silent over the attack in East Jerusalem. At the emergency summit meeting of the Arab League, convened in Cairo on 21–22 October, Arab leaders endorsed a Saudi Arabian proposal to establish of fund of US \$800m. to be dedicated to preserving the Arab identity of Jerusalem.

In December 2000 the outgoing US President, Bill Clinton, formulated a new plan aimed at ending the Israeli–Palestinian conflict. On the issue of Jerusalem it proposed that Israel should extend its sovereignty over the 11 settlements that lay inside the annexed and expanded municipal boundaries. The Palestinians would be granted sovereignty over the Arab districts of East Jerusalem and the Christian and Muslim quarters of the Old City. The residential area of the Armenian quarter would also come under Palestinian control, with Israel extending sovereignty over the Jewish quarter, the Western Wall and the roads through the Armenian quarter leading to them. The proposals for the Haram ash-Sharif/Temple Mount area attempted to accommodate the religious-nationalist sensibilities of both Palestinians and Israelis, but were described by many observers as overly complex: the Palestinians would be awarded sovereignty over the 'surface' of the Haram, and Israel would be given 'shared functional sovereignty under' the Haram and 'behind' the Western Wall. Palestinian negotiators submitted a detailed rebuttal of the Clinton plan. On the articles relating to Jerusalem, they commented that Clinton's proposals legalized Israeli control over 85% of East Jerusalem and divided the sovereign Palestinian areas into districts unconnected to each other or to the rest of a Palestinian state.

The Likud leader, Ariel Sharon, became Israel's new Prime Minister following the election of 7 February 2001. He had campaigned on a platform of a Jerusalem united under Israeli sovereignty, and his political track record suggested that his national unity Government would not consider the kind of concessions on Jerusalem that had reportedly been offered by his Labour predecessor. There was also a new incumbent in the US White House. The Republican George W. Bush had been sworn in as US President in January, and Gen. Colin Powell, a veteran of the 1991 war against Iraq, had been appointed Secretary of State. Conscious of the perception in the Arab world that the Clinton Administration was too pro-Israeli to fulfil the role of 'honest broker', President Bush had promised a more even-handed approach to the Middle East. This message was conveyed to Arab leaders during Powell's first tour of the region in late February. The Arab world was therefore taken by surprise when, on his return to Washington, Powell told the Senate Foreign Relations Committee that the Bush Administration was committed to moving the US embassy 'to the capital of Israel, which is Jerusalem'. After strong protests from Arab-US organizations, the State Department contradicted Powell, confirming that US policy on Jerusalem remained unchanged. A spokesman reiterated that Bush believed the final status of the city would be determined by negotiations between Israel and the PA.

The radical Islamic Jihad and Hamas movements continued to target Israeli civilians in Jerusalem. On 27 March 2001 a car bomb exploded in West Jerusalem, wounding five Israelis. Six hours later a suicide bomber injured 32 at a bus stop in the French Hill settlement of East Jerusalem. But by far the deadliest assault on Israeli civilians occurred on 9 August, when a young Hamas suicide bomber detonated his bomb in a West Jerusalem restaurant popular with Orthodox Jews; 15 people were killed and scores more wounded. Many of the dead and injured were young children. The scale of the atrocity provoked widespread international condemnation. The PA leadership also condemned the attack, but blamed the Sharon Government for creating the climate that provoked such acts of terrorism. The Likud leader strongly rejected such assertions, laying the blame for the bombing with Arafat and his failure to act decisively to suppress the Islamist movement in areas under PA control. The Israeli Cabinet met for several hours to consider an appropriate response. In the early hours of 10 August—while an Israeli F-16 fighter aircraft was razing the Palestinian police station in Ramallah—a large contingent of Israel's paramilitary border police seized Orient House and other Palestinian offices in East Jerusalem. The unofficial PLO headquarters in the city had long been regarded as a political provocation by nationalist politicians in Israel, with both Israelis and Palestinians viewing it as a symbol of the Palestinian claim to East Jerusalem. The previous Likud leader, Binyamin Netanyahu, had tried and failed to have Orient House shut down, amid warnings from the international community that such a step would be regarded very negatively. Sharon calculated that in the aftermath of the Jerusalem bombing, and with the expectation of massive and possibly bloody Israeli retaliation, the conditions were as favourable as they would ever be for the forcible closure of the Orient House complex. In the event, the move was criticized in European capitals and in Washington. A State Department official commented, 'Orient House has long symbolized the importance of political dialogue and reconciliation between Israelis and Palestinians. These actions represent a political escalation, undermine faith and confidence in a negotiated settlement of this conflict and increase the risk of further deterioration of the political situation'. The Israeli Government answered the

censure with allegations that Orient House had been 'a nerve centre of terrorists'. The claim was ridiculed by much of the mainstream media in Israel, and no evidence was produced to support it. Activists from Israeli peace organizations joined Palestinians and foreign human rights groups in demonstrations on 13 August to protest against the occupation of Orient House; these were violently dispersed by the Israeli police.

Palestinian personalities in the city were critical of the PA leadership over the Israeli take-over of Orient House. They pointed out that since the death, at the end of May 2001, of Faisal Husseini, the PA's charismatic minister responsible for Jerusalem, the Israeli authorities had stepped up land confiscations and house demolitions in East Jerusalem. Yasser Arafat's failure to reconstitute political leadership in the city meant that these encroachments had gone largely unchallenged and had paved the way for the seizures on August. The moderate scale of the protests that followed was seen as further evidence of a deepening crisis and the tension between the city's symbolic importance to the Palestinian national cause and its current political neglect. 'Palestinians in Jerusalem need a face, an address and a sense of where Jerusalem now fits in the Palestinian national agenda,' commented a prominent Palestinian figure in the city in the aftermath of the Israeli confiscations, 'in short they need leadership. Currently they don't have one.'

The Israeli premier continued to restate Israeli sovereignty over East Jerusalem, confirming in an interview with the *Jerusalem Post* in mid-September 2001 that none of the city would be relinquished to Palestinian control. Meanwhile, Jerusalem remained a principal stage in the spiralling violence of the al-Aqsa *intifada*. The Palestinian areas of the city did not witness the widespread street protests that had characterized the early days of the uprising, but Jerusalem's profile and its relative ease of access for West Bank Palestinians ensured the city's Jewish neighbourhoods were regular targets of suicide bombers and gunmen. On 17 October gunmen belonging to the Popular Front for the Liberation of Palestine (PFLP) assassinated Israel's right-wing Minister of Tourism, Rehavam Ze'evi, in an hotel in East Jerusalem. In one of the bloodiest attacks, at the beginning of December an explosion in the commercial heart of West Jerusalem killed several Israelis, most of them teenagers, and wounded scores of others. The impact of the violence on the city's economy, particularly the tourist trade, was substantial. According to a spokesman for the Jerusalem Hotel Association, 60% of hotel employees in the city had been laid off in the 12 months since the beginning of the al-Aqsa *intifada*. The Sharon Government responded to its citizens' heightened vulnerability with a proposal in early 2002 to construct an electronic fence between Jerusalem and the main Palestinian population centres of the West Bank. This barrier would extend east of the city, and both the settlement of Ma'aleh Edomin and several Palestinian Area B villages (under PA civil, but Israeli security, control) would fall inside its perimeter. A statement from the office of the Prime Minister denied that there were plans to alter the legal status of the Palestinian villages enveloped by the new security wall, but claimed that these areas 'must be considered part of the greater Jerusalem area'. Palestinians protested that the proposals prefigured the annexation of further areas of the West Bank into an expanded Jerusalem. Israeli commentators, while critical of the cost and likely effectiveness of an electronic fence, viewed it as consistent with the Government's assertion of the need to demonstrate that terrorism must be proven to be counter-productive.

Palestinian bombings in the city intensified in 2002. Nine Israelis were killed in a suicide attack in the ultra-Orthodox Meir Sharim quarter of West Jerusalem on 2 March. On 12 April, while Israeli forces were engaged in Operation Defensive Shield, a major military offensive against the Palestinian militias on the West Bank (see Arab–Israeli Relations 1967–2002), a bus bomb in the heart of West Jerusalem claimed a further five lives. The aftermath of the bombing was witnessed by visiting US Secretary of State Colin Powell, who postponed a meeting with Yasser Arafat in response. This was despite Arafat's reiteration of his condemnation of 'violent operations' against all civilians. Two further bombings in the suburbs of Jerusalem on 18 and 19 June killed 25 Israelis and were the stated provocation for Israel's decision to reoccupy seven of the eight major population centres on the West Bank. Seven people. five of whom held US passports, were killed on 31 July by a bomb planted in a cafeteria at the Hebrew University. The bombing was claimed by militant Hamas Islamists. Regarded as one of the few areas of the city where Jews and Arabs could interact in relative harmony, the University had hitherto avoided the violence that had affected so many other parts of the city.

DOCUMENTS ON PALESTINE

DECLARATION OF FIRST
WORLD ZIONIST CONGRESS

The Congress, convened in Basle by Dr Theodor Herzl in August 1897, adopted the following programme.*

The aim of Zionism is to create for the Jewish people a home in Palestine secured by public law.

The Congress contemplates the following means to the attainment of this end:

1. The promotion on suitable lines, of the settlement of Palestine by Jewish agriculturists, artisans and tradesmen.

2. The organization and binding together of the whole of Jewry by means of appropriate institutions, local and general, in accordance with the laws of each country.

3. The strengthening of Jewish sentiment and national consciousness.

4. Preparatory steps towards obtaining government consent as are necessary, for the attainment of the aim of Zionism.

McMAHON CORRESPONDENCE†

Ten letters passed between Sir Henry McMahon, British High Commissioner in Cairo, and Sherif Husain of Mecca from July 1915 to March 1916. Husain offered Arab help in the war against the Turks if Britain would support the principle of an independent Arab state. The most important letter is that of 24 October 1915, from McMahon to Husain:

... I regret that you should have received from my last letter the impression that I regarded the question of limits and boundaries with coldness and hesitation; such was not the case, but it appeared to me that the time had not yet come when that question could be discussed in a conclusive manner.

I have realized, however, from your last letter that you regard this question as one of vital and urgent importance. I have, therefore, lost no time in informing the Government of Great Britain of the contents of your letter, and it is with great pleasure that I communicate to you on their behalf the following statement, which I am confident you will receive with satisfaction:

The two districts of Mersina and Alexandretta and portions of Syria lying to the west of the districts of Damascus, Homs, Hama and Aleppo cannot be said to be purely Arab, and should be excluded from the limits demanded.

With the above modification, and without prejudice to our existing treaties with Arab chiefs, we accept those limits.

As for those regions lying within those frontiers wherein Great Britain is free to act without detriment to the interest of her ally, France, I am empowered in the name of the Government of Great Britain to give the following assurances and make the following reply to your letter:

(1) Subject to the above modifications, Great Britain is prepared to recognize and support the independence of the Arabs in all the regions within the limits demanded by the Sherif of Mecca.

(2) Great Britain will guarantee the Holy Places against all external aggression and will recognize their inviolability.

(3) When the situation admits, Great Britain will give to the Arabs her advice and will assist them to establish what may appear to be the most suitable forms of government in those various territories.

(4) On the other hand, it is understood that the Arabs have decided to seek the advice and guidance of Great Britain only, and that such European advisers and officials as may be required for the formation of a sound form of administration will be British.

(5) With regard to the *vilayets* of Baghdad and Basra, the Arabs will recognize that the established position and interests of Great Britain necessitate special administrative arrangements in order to secure these territories from foreign aggression, to promote the welfare of the local populations and to safeguard our mutual economic interests.

I am convinced that this declaration will assure you beyond all possible doubt of the sympathy of Great Britain towards the aspirations of her friends the Arabs and will result in a firm and lasting alliance, the immediate results of which will be the expulsion of the Turks from the Arab countries and the freeing of the Arab peoples from the Turkish yoke, which for so many years has pressed heavily upon them. ...

ANGLO-FRANCO-RUSSIAN AGREEMENT
(SYKES—PICOT AGREEMENT)

April-May 1916

The allocation of portions of the Ottoman empire by the three powers was decided between them in an exchange of diplomatic notes. The Anglo-French agreement‡ dealing with Arab territories became known to Sherif Husain only after publication by the new Bolshevik Government of Russia in 1917:

1. That France and Great Britain are prepared to recognize and protect an independent Arab State or a Confederation of Arab States in the areas (A) and (B) marked on the annexed map (*not reproduced here—Ed.*), under suzerainty of an Arab Chief. That in area (A) France, and in area (B) Great Britain shall have priority of right of enterprises and local loans. France in area (A) and Great Britain in area (B) shall alone supply foreign advisers or officials on the request of the Arab State or the Confederation of Arab States.

2. France in the Blue area and Great Britain in the Red area shall be at liberty to establish direct or indirect administration or control as they may desire or as they may deem fit to establish after agreement with the Arab State or Confederation of Arab States.

3. In the Brown area there shall be established an international administration of which the form will be decided upon after consultation with Russia, and after subsequent agreement with the other Allies and the representatives of the Sherif of Mecca.

4. That Great Britain be accorded

(*a*) The ports of Haifa and Acre;

(*b*) Guarantee of a given supply of water from the Tigris and the Euphrates in area (A) for area (B).

His Majesty's Government, on their part, undertake that they will at no time enter into negotiations for the cession of Cyprus to any third Power without the previous consent of the French Government.

5. Alexandretta shall be a free port as regards the trade of the British Empire and there shall be no discrimination in treatment with regard to port dues or the extension of special privileges affecting British shipping and commerce; there shall be freedom of transit for British goods through Alexandretta and over railways through the Blue area, whether such goods are going to or coming from the Red area, area (A) or area (B); and there shall be no differentiation in treatment, direct or indirect, at the expense of British goods on any railway or of British goods and shipping in any port serving the areas in question.

Haifa shall be a free port as regards the trade of France, her colonies and protectorates, and there shall be no differentiation

* Text supplied by courtesy of Josef Fraenkel.
† British White Paper, Cmd. 5957, 1939.

‡ E. L. Woodward and Rohan Butler (Eds.). *Documents on British Foreign Policy 1919–1939*. First Series, Vol. IV, 1919. London, HMSO, 1952.

in treatment or privilege with regard to port dues against French shipping and commerce. There shall be freedom of transit through Haifa and over British railways through the Brown area, whether such goods are coming from or going to the Blue area, area (A) or area (B), and there shall be no differentiation in treatment, direct or indirect, at the expense of French goods on any railway or of French goods and shipping in any port serving the areas in question.

6. In area (A), the Baghdad Railway shall not be extended southwards beyond Mosul, and in area (B), it shall not be extended northwards beyond Samarra, until a railway connecting Baghdad with Aleppo along the basin of the Euphrates will have been completed, and then only with the concurrence of the two Governments.

7. Great Britain shall have the right to build, administer and be the sole owner of the railway connecting Haifa with area (B). She shall have, in addition, the right in perpetuity and at all times of carrying troops on that line. It is understood by both Governments that this railway is intended to facilitate communication between Baghdad and Haifa, and it is further understood that, in the event of technical difficulties and expenditure incurred in the maintenance of this line in the Brown area rendering the execution of the project impracticable, the French Government will be prepared to consider plans for enabling the line in question to traverse the polygon formed by Banias-Umm Qais-Salkhad-Tall 'Osda-Mismieh before reaching area (B).

Clause 8 referred to customs tariffs.

9. It is understood that the French Government will at no time initiate any negotiations for the cession of their rights and will not cede their prospective rights in the Blue area to any third Power other than the Arab State or Confederation of Arab States, without the previous consent of His Majesty's Government who, on their part, give the French Government a similar undertaking in respect of the Red area.

10. The British and French Governments shall agree to abstain from acquiring and to withhold their consent to a third Power acquiring territorial possessions in the Arabian Peninsula; nor shall they consent to the construction by a third Power of a naval base in the islands on the eastern seaboard of the Red Sea. This, however, will not prevent such rectification of the Aden boundary as might be found necessary in view of the recent Turkish attack.

11. The negotiations with the Arabs concerning the frontiers of the Arab State or Confederation of Arab States shall be pursued through the same channel as heretofore in the name of the two Powers.

12. It is understood, moreover, that measures for controlling the importation of arms into the Arab territory will be considered by the two Governments.

BALFOUR DECLARATION

2 November 1917

Balfour was British Foreign Secretary, Rothschild the British Zionist leader.

Dear Lord Rothschild,

I have much pleasure in conveying to you on behalf of His Majesty's Government the following declaration of sympathy with Jewish Zionist aspirations, which has been submitted to and approved by the Cabinet.

'His Majesty's Government view with favour the establishment in Palestine of a national home for the Jewish people, and will use their best endeavours to facilitate the achievement of this object, it being clearly understood that nothing shall be done which may prejudice the civil and religious rights of existing non-Jewish communities in Palestine, or the rights and political status enjoyed by Jews in any other country.'

I should be grateful if you would bring this declaration to the knowledge of the Zionist Federation.

Yours sincerely,
Arthur James Balfour.

HOGARTH MESSAGE*

4 January 1918

The following is the text of a message which Commander D. G. Hogarth, CMG, RNVR, of the Arab Bureau in Cairo, was instructed on 4 January 1918 to deliver to King Husain of the Hijaz at Jeddah:

1. The *Entente* Powers are determined that the Arab race shall be given full opportunity of once again forming a nation in the world. This can only be achieved by the Arabs themselves uniting, and Great Britain and her Allies will pursue a policy with this ultimate unity in view.

2. So far as Palestine is concerned, we are determined that no people shall be subject to another, but—

(a) In view of the fact that there are in Palestine shrines, Wakfs and Holy places, sacred in some cases to Moslems alone, to Jews alone, to Christians alone, and in others to two or all three, and inasmuch as these places are of interest to vast masses of people outside Palestine and Arabia, there must be a special régime to deal with these places approved of by the world.

(b) As regards the Mosque of Omar, it shall be considered as a Moslem concern alone, and shall not be subjected directly or indirectly to any non-Moslem authority.

3. Since the Jewish opinion of the world is in favour of a return of Jews to Palestine, and inasmuch as this opinion must remain a constant factor, and, further, as His Majesty's Government view with favour the realization of this aspiration, His Majesty's Government are determined that in so far as is compatible with the freedom of the existing population, both economic and political, no obstacle should be put in the way of the realization of this ideal.

In this connection the friendship of world Jewry to the Arab cause is equivalent to support in all States where Jews have political influence. The leaders of the movement are determined to bring about the success of Zionism by friendship and co-operation with the Arabs, and such an offer is not one to be lightly thrown aside.

ANGLO-FRENCH DECLARATION†

7 November 1918

The object aimed at by France and Great Britain in prosecuting in the East the war let loose by the ambition of Germany is the complete and definite emancipation of the peoples so long oppressed by the Turks and the establishment of national Governments and Administrations deriving their authority from the initiative and free choice of the indigenous populations.

In order to carry out these intentions France and Great Britain are at one in encouraging and assisting the establishments of indigenous Governments and Administrations in Syria and Mesopotamia, now liberated by the Allies, and in the territories the liberation of which they are engaged in securing and recognizing these as soon as they are actually established.

Far from wishing to impose on the populations of these regions any particular institutions they are only concerned to ensure by their support and by adequate assistance the regular working of Governments and Administrations freely chosen by the populations themselves. To secure impartial and equal justice for all, to facilitate the economic development of the country by inspiring and encouraging local initiative, to favour the diffusion of education, to put an end to dissensions that have too long been taken advantage of by Turkish policy which the two Allied Governments uphold in the liberated territories.

---

* British White Paper, Cmd. 5964, 1939.

† Report of a Committee set up to consider Certain Correspondence between Sir Henry McMahon and the Sherif of Mecca in 1915 and 1916, 16 March 1939 (British White Paper, Cmd. 5974).

RECOMMENDATIONS OF
THE KING—CRANE COMMISSION*

28 August 1919

The Commission was set up by President Wilson of the USA to determine which power should receive the Mandate for Palestine. The following are extracts from their recommendations on Syria:

1. We recommend, as most important of all, and in strict harmony with our Instructions, that whatever foreign administration (whether of one or more Powers) is brought into Syria, should come in, not at all as a colonising Power in the old sense of that term, but as a Mandatory under the League of Nations with the clear consciousness that 'the well-being and development' of the Syrian people form for it a 'sacred trust'.

2. We recommend, in the second place, that the unity of Syria be preserved, in accordance with the earnest petition of the great majority of the people of Syria.

3. We recommend, in the third place, that Syria be placed under one mandatory Power, as the natural way to secure real and efficient unity.

4. We recommend, in the fourth place, that Amir Faisal be made the head of the new united Syrian State.

5. We recommend, in the fifth place, serious modification of the extreme Zionist program for Palestine of unlimited immigration of Jews, looking finally to making Palestine distinctly a Jewish State.

(1) The Commissioners began their study of Zionism with minds predisposed in its favor, but the actual facts in Palestine, coupled with the force of the general principles proclaimed by the Allies and accepted by the Syrians have driven them to the recommendation here made.

(2) The Commission was abundantly supplied with literature on the Zionist program by the Zionist Commission to Palestine; heard in conferences much concerning the Zionist colonies and their claims; and personally saw something of what had been accomplished. They found much to approve in the aspirations and plans of the Zionists, and had warm appreciation for the devotion of many of the colonists, and for their success, by modern methods in overcoming great, natural obstacles.

(3) The Commission recognised also that definite encouragement had been given to the Zionists by the Allies in Mr Balfour's often-quoted statement, in its approval by other representatives of the Allies. If, however, the strict terms of the Balfour Statement are adhered to—favoring 'the establishment in Palestine of a national home for the Jewish people', 'it being clearly understood that nothing shall be done which may prejudice the civil and religious rights of existing non-Jewish communities in Palestine'—it can hardly be doubted that the extreme Zionist program must be greatly modified. For 'a national home for the Jewish people' is not equivalent to making Palestine into a Jewish State; nor can the erection of such a Jewish State be accomplished without the gravest trespass upon the 'civil and religious rights of existing non-Jewish communities in Palestine'. The fact came out repeatedly in the Commission's conference with Jewish representatives, that the Zionists looked forward to a practically complete dispossession of the present non-Jewish inhabitants of Palestine, by various forms of purchase.

In his address of 4 July 1918, President Wilson laid down the following principle as one of the four great 'ends for which the associated peoples of the world were fighting': 'The settlement of every question, whether of territory, of sovereignty, of economic arrangement, or of political relationship upon the basis of the free acceptance of that settlement by the people immediately concerned, and not upon the basis of the material interest or advantage of any other nation or people which may desire a different settlement for the sake of its own exterior influence or mastery.' If that principle is to rule, and so the wishes of Palestine's population are to be decisive as to what is to be done with Palestine, then it is to be remembered that the non-Jewish

population of Palestine—nearly nine-tenths of the whole—are emphatically against the entire Zionist program. The tables show that there was no one thing upon which the population of Palestine were more agreed than upon this. To subject a people so minded to unlimited Jewish immigration, and to steady financial and social pressure to surrender the land, would be a gross violation of the principle just quoted, and of the people's rights, though it kept within the forms of law.

It is to be noted also that the feeling against the Zionist program is not confined to Palestine, but shared very generally by the people throughout Syria, as our conferences clearly showed. More then 72%—1,350 in all—of all the petitions in the whole of Syria were directed against the Zionist program. Only two requests—those for a united Syria and for independence—had a larger support. This general feeling was duly voiced by the General Syrian Congress in the seventh, eighth and tenth resolutions of their statement.

The Peace Conference should not shut its eyes to the fact that the anti-Zionist feeling in Palestine and Syria is intense and not lightly to be flouted. No British officer, consulted by the Commissioners, believed that the Zionist program could be carried out except by force of arms. The officers generally thought that a force of not less than 50,000 soldiers would be required even to initiate the program. That of itself is evidence of a strong sense of the injustice of the Zionist program, on the part of the non-Jewish populations of Palestine and Syria. Decisions requiring armies to carry out are sometimes necessary, but they are surely not gratuitously to be taken in the interests of serious injustice. For the initial claim, often submitted by Zionist representatives, that they have a 'right' to Palestine, based on an occupation of 2,000 years ago, can hardly be seriously considered.

There is a further consideration that cannot justly be ignored, if the world is to look forward to Palestine becoming a definitely Jewish State, however gradually that may take place. That consideration grows out of the fact that Palestine is the Holy Land for Jews, Christians, and Moslems alike. Millions of Christians and Moslems all over the world are quite as much concerned as the Jews with conditions in Palestine, especially with those conditions which touch upon religious feelings and rights. The relations in these matters in Palestine are most delicate and difficult. With the best possible intentions, it may be doubted whether the Jews could possibly seem to either Christians or Moslems proper guardians of the holy places, or custodians of the Holy Land as a whole.

The reason is this: The places which are most sacred to Christians—those having to do with Jesus—and which are also sacred to Moslems, are not only not sacred to Jews, but abhorrent to them. It is simply impossible, under those circumstances, for Moslems and Christians to feel satisfied to have these places in Jewish hands, or under the custody of Jews. There are still other places about which Moslems must have the same feeling. In fact, from this point of view, the Moslems, just because the sacred places of all three religions are sacred to them, have made very naturally much more satisfactory custodians of the holy places than the Jews could be. It must be believed that the precise meaning in this respect of the complete Jewish occupation of Palestine has not been fully sensed by those who urge the extreme Zionist program. For it would intensify, with a certainty like fate, the anti-Jewish feeling both in Palestine and in all other portions of the world which look to Palestine as the Holy Land.

In view of all these considerations, and with a deep sense of sympathy for the Jewish cause, the Commissioners feel bound to recommend that only a greatly reduced Zionist program be attempted by the Peace Conference, and even that, only very gradually initiated. This would have to mean that Jewish immigration should be definitely limited, and that the project for making Palestine distinctly a Jewish commonwealth should be given up.

There would then be no reason why Palestine could not be included in a united Syrian State, just as other portions of the country, the holy places being cared for by an international and inter-religious commission, somewhat as at present, under the oversight and approval of the Mandatory and of the League of Nations. The Jews, of course, would have representation upon this commission.

---

* US Department of State. *Papers Relating to the Foreign Relations of the United States. The Paris Peace Conference 1919.* Vol. XII. Washington, 1947.

ARTICLE 22 OF THE
COVENANT OF THE LEAGUE OF NATIONS

1. To those colonies and territories which as a consequence of the late War have ceased to be under the sovereignty of the States which formerly governed them and which are inhabited by peoples not yet able to stand by themselves under the strenuous conditions of the modern world, there should be applied the principle that the well-being and development of such peoples form a sacred trust of civilization and that securities for the performance of this trust should be embodied in this Covenant.

2. The best method of giving practical effect to this principle is that the tutelage of such peoples should be entrusted to advanced nations who by reason of their resources, their experience or their geographical position can best undertake this responsibility, and who are willing to accept it, and that this tutelage should be exercised by them as Mandatories on behalf of the League.

3. The character of the Mandate must differ according to the stage of the development of the people, the geographical situation of the territory, its economic conditions and other similar circumstances.

4. Certain communities formerly belonging to the Turkish Empire have reached a stage of development where their existence as independent nations can be provisionally recognized subject to the rendering of administrative advice and assistance by a Mandatory until such time as they are able to stand alone. The wishes of these communities must be a principal consideration in the selection of the Mandatory.

7. In every case of Mandate, the Mandatory shall render to the Council an annual report in reference to the territory committed to its charge.

8. The degree of authority, control, or administration to be exercised by the Mandatory shall, if not previously agreed upon by the Members of the League, be explicitly defined in each case by the Council.

9. A permanent Commission shall be constituted to receive and examine the annual reports of the Mandatories and to advise the Council on all matters relating to the observance of the Mandates.

MANDATE FOR PALESTINE*

24 July 1922

The Council of the League of Nations:

Whereas the Principal Allied Powers have agreed, for the purpose of giving effect to the provisions of Article 22 of the Covenant of the League of Nations to entrust to a Mandatory selected by the said Powers the administration of the territory of Palestine, which formerly belonged to the Turkish Empire, within such boundaries as may be fixed by them; and

Whereas the Principal Allied Powers have also agreed that the Mandatory should be responsible for putting into effect the declaration originally made on 2 November 1917 by the Government of His Britannic Majesty, and adopted by the said Powers, in favour of the establishment in Palestine of a National Home for the Jewish people, it being clearly understood that nothing should be done which might prejudice the civil and religious rights of existing non-Jewish communities in Palestine, or the rights and political status enjoyed by Jews in any other country; and

Whereas recognition has thereby been given to the historical connection of the Jewish people with Palestine and to the grounds for reconstituting their National Home in that country; and

Whereas the Principal Allied Powers have selected His Britannic Majesty as the Mandatory for Palestine; and

Whereas the Mandate in respect of Palestine has been formulated in the following terms and submitted to the Council of the League for approval; and

Whereas His Britannic Majesty has accepted the Mandate in respect of Palestine and undertaken to exercise it on behalf of

* British White Paper, Cmd. 1785.

the League of Nations in conformity with the following provisions; and

Whereas by the aforementioned Article 22 (paragraph 8), it is provided that the degree of authority, control or administration to be exercised by the Mandatory, not having been previously agreed upon by the Members of the League, shall be explicitly defined by the Council of the League of Nations;

Confirming the said Mandate, defines its terms as follows:

ARTICLE 1. The Mandatory shall have full powers of legislation and of administration, save as they may be limited by the terms of this Mandate.

ARTICLE 2. The Mandatory shall be responsible for placing the country under such political, administrative and economic conditions as will secure the establishment of the Jewish National Home, as laid down in the preamble, and the development of self-governing institutions, and also for safeguarding the civil and religious rights of all the inhabitants of Palestine, irrespective of race and religion.

ARTICLE 3. The Mandatory shall, so far as circumstances permit, encourage local autonomy.

ARTICLE 4. An appropriate Jewish Agency shall be recognized as a public body for the purpose of advising and co-operating with the Administration of Palestine in such economic, social and other matters as may affect the establishment of the Jewish National Home and the interests of the Jewish population in Palestine, and, subject always to the control of the Administration, to assist and take part in the development of the country.

The Zionist organization, so long as its organization and constitution are in the opinion of the Mandatory appropriate, shall be recognized as such agency. It shall take steps in consultation with His Britannic Majesty's Government to secure the co-operation of all Jews who are willing to assist in the establishment of the Jewish National Home.

ARTICLE 5. The Mandatory shall be responsible for seeing that no Palestine territory shall be ceded or leased to, or in any way placed under the control of, the Government of any foreign Power.

ARTICLE 6. The Administration of Palestine, while ensuring that the rights and position of other sections of the population are not prejudiced, shall facilitate Jewish immigration under suitable conditions and shall encourage, in co-operation with the Jewish Agency referred to in Article 4, close settlement by Jews on the land, including State lands and waste lands not required for public purposes.

ARTICLE 7. The Administration of Palestine shall be responsible for enacting a nationality law. There shall be included in this law provisions framed so as to facilitate the acquisition of Palestinian citizenship by Jews who take up their permanent residence in Palestine.

ARTICLE 13. All responsibility in connection with the Holy Places and religious buildings or sites in Palestine, including that of preserving existing rights and of securing free access to the Holy Places, religious buildings and sites and the free exercise of worship, while ensuring the requirements of public order and decorum, is assumed by the Mandatory, who shall be responsible solely to the League of Nations in all matters connected herewith, provided that nothing in this Article shall prevent the Mandatory from entering into such arrangements as he may deem reasonable with the Administration for the purpose of carrying the provisions of this Article into effect; and provided also that nothing in this Mandate shall be construed as conferring upon the Mandatory authority to interfere with the fabric of the management of purely Moslem sacred shrines, the immunities of which are guaranteed.

ARTICLE 14. A special Commission shall be appointed by the Mandatory to study, define and determine the rights and claims in connection with the Holy Places and the rights and claims relating to the different religious communities in Palestine. The method of nomination, the composition and the functions of this Commission shall be submitted to the Council of the League for its approval, and the Commission shall not be appointed or enter upon its functions without the approval of the Council.

ARTICLE 28. In the event of the termination of the Mandate hereby conferred upon the Mandatory, the Council of the League of Nations shall make such arrangements as may be deemed necessary for safe-guarding in perpetuity, under guarantee of the League, the rights secured by Articles 13 and 14, and shall use its influence for securing, under the guarantee of the League, that the Government of Palestine will fully honour the financial obligations legitimately incurred by the Administration of Palestine during the period of the Mandate, including the rights of public servants to pensions or gratuities.

CHURCHILL MEMORANDUM*
3 June 1922

The Secretary of State for the Colonies has given renewed consideration to the existing political situation in Palestine, with a very earnest desire to arrive at a settlement of the outstanding questions which have given rise to uncertainty and unrest among certain sections of the population. After consultation with the High Commissioner for Palestine the following statement has been drawn up. It summarizes the essential parts of the correspondence that has already taken place between the Secretary of State and a Delegation from the Moslem Christian Society of Palestine, which has been for some time in England, and it states the further conclusions which have since been reached.

The tension which has prevailed from time to time in Palestine is mainly due to apprehensions, which are entertained both by sections of the Arab and by sections of the Jewish population. These apprehensions, so far as the Arabs are concerned, are partly based upon exaggerated interpretations of the meaning of the Declaration favouring the establishment of a Jewish National Home in Palestine, made on behalf of His Majesty's Government on 2 November 1917. Unauthorized statements have been made to the effect that the purpose in view is to create a wholly Jewish Palestine. Phrases have been used such as that Palestine is to become 'as Jewish as England is English.' His Majesty's Government regard any such expectation as impracticable and have no such aim in view. Nor have they at any time contemplated, as appears to be feared by the Arab Delegation, the disappearance or the subordination of the Arabic population, language or culture in Palestine. They would draw attention to the fact that the terms of the Declaration referred to do not contemplate that Palestine as a whole should be converted into a Jewish National Home, but that such a Home should be founded *in Palestine*. In this connection it has been observed with satisfaction that at the meeting of the Zionist Congress, the supreme governing body of the Zionist Organization, held at Carlsbad in September 1921, a resolution was passed expressing as the official statement of Zionist aims 'the determination of the Jewish people to live with the Arab people on terms of unity and mutual respect, and together with them to make the common home into a flourishing community, the upbuilding of which may assure to each of its peoples an undisturbed national development.'

It is also necessary to point out that the Zionist Commission in Palestine, now termed the Palestine Zionist Executive, has not desired to possess, and does not possess, any share in the general administration of the country. Nor does the special position assigned to the Zionist Organization in Article IV of the Draft Mandate for Palestine imply any such functions. That special position relates to the measures to be taken in Palestine affecting the Jewish population, and contemplates that the Organization may assist in the general development of the country, but does not entitle it to share in any degree in its Government.

Further, it is contemplated that the status of all citizens of Palestine in the eyes of the law shall be Palestinian, and it has never been intended that they, or any section of them, should possess any other juridical status.

So far as the Jewish population of Palestine are concerned, it appears that some among them are apprehensive that His Majesty's Government may depart from the policy embodied in the Declaration of 1917. It is necessary, therefore, once more to affirm that these fears are unfounded, and that the Declaration, re-affirmed by the Conference of the Principal Allied Powers at

San Remo and again in the Treaty of Sèvres, is not susceptible of change.

During the last two or three generations the Jews have recreated in Palestine a community, now numbering 80,000, of whom about one-fourth are farmers or workers upon the land. This community has its own political organs; an elected assembly for the direction of its domestic concerns; elected councils in the towns; and an organization for the control of its schools. It has its elected Chief Rabbinate and Rabbinical Council for the direction of its religious affairs. Its business is conducted in Hebrew as a vernacular language, and a Hebrew Press serves its needs. It has its distinctive intellectual life and displays considerable economic activity. This community, then, with its town and country population, its political, religious and social organizations, its own language, its own customs, its own life, has in fact 'national' characteristics. When it is asked what is meant by the development of the Jewish National Home in Palestine, it may be answered that it is not the imposition of a Jewish nationality upon the inhabitants of Palestine as a whole, but the further development of the existing Jewish community, with the assistance of Jews in other parts of the world, in order that it may become a centre in which the Jewish people as a whole may take, on grounds of religion and race, an interest and a pride. But in order that this community should have the best prospect of free development and provide a full opportunity for the Jewish people to display its capacities, it is essential that it should know that it is in Palestine as of right and not on sufferance. That is the reason why it is necessary that the existence of a Jewish National Home in Palestine should be internationally guaranteed, and that it should be formally recognized to rest upon ancient historic connection.

This, then, is the interpretation which His Majesty's Government place upon Declaration of 1917, and, so understood, the Secretary of State is of opinion that it does not contain or imply anything which need cause either alarm to the Arab population of Palestine or disappointment to the Jews.

For the fulfilment of this policy it is necessary that the Jewish community in Palestine should be able to increase its numbers by immigration. This immigration cannot be so great in volume as to exceed whatever may be the economic capacity of the country at the time to absorb new arrivals. It is essential to ensure that the immigrants should not be a burden upon the people of Palestine as a whole, and that they should not deprive any section of the present population of their employment. Hitherto the immigration has fulfilled these conditions. The number of immigrants since the British occupation has been about 25,000. . . .

REPORT OF PALESTINE ROYAL COMMISSION (PEEL COMMISSION)†
July 1937

The Commission under Lord Peel was appointed in 1936. The following are extracts from recommendations made in Ch. XXII:

Having reached the conclusion that there is no possibility of solving the Palestine problem under the existing Mandate (or even under a scheme of cantonization), the Commission recommend the termination of the present Mandate on the basis of Partition and put forward a definite scheme which they consider to be practicable, honourable and just. The scheme is as follows:

The Mandate for Palestine should terminate and be replaced by a Treaty System in accordance with the precedent set in Iraq and Syria.

Under Treaties to be negotiated by the Mandatory with the Government of Transjordan and representatives of the Arabs of Palestine on the one hand, and with the Zionist Organization on the other, it would be declared that two sovereign independent States would shortly be established—(1) an Arab State consisting of Transjordan united with that part of Palestine allotted to the Arabs, (2) a Jewish State consisting of that part of Palestine allotted to the Jews. The Mandatory would undertake to support any requests for admission to the League of Nations made by the Governments of the Arab and Jewish States. The Treaties would include strict guarantees for the

---

* Palestine, Correspondence with the Palestine Arab Delegation and the Zionist Organization (British White Paper, Cmd. 1700), pp. 17–21.

† *Palestine Royal Commission: Report,* 1937 (British Blue Book, Cmd. 5479).

protection of minorities. Military Conventions would be attached to the Treaties.

A new Mandate should be instituted to execute the trust of maintaining the sanctity of Jerusalem and Bethlehem and ensuring free and safe access to them for all the world. An enclave should be demarcated to which this Mandate should apply, extending from a point north of Jerusalem to a point south of Bethlehem, and access to the sea should be provided by a corridor extending from Jerusalem to Jaffa. The policy of the Balfour Declaration would not apply to the Mandated Area.

The Jewish State should pay a subvention to the Arab State. A Finance Commission should be appointed to advise as to its amount and as to the division of the public debt of Palestine and other financial questions.

In view of the backwardness of Transjordan, Parliament should be asked to make a grant of £2,000,000 to the Arab State.

WHITE PAPER*
May 1939
The main recommendations are extracted below:

10. . . . His Majesty's Government make the following declaration of their intentions regarding the future government of Palestine:

(i) The objective of His Majesty's Government is the establishment within ten years of an independent Palestine State in such treaty relations with the United Kingdom as will provide satisfactorily for the commercial and strategic requirements of both countries in the future. This proposal for the establishment of the independent State would involve consultation with the Council of the League of Nations with a view to the termination of the Mandate.

(ii) The independent State should be one in which Arabs and Jews share in government in such a way as to ensure that the essential interests of each community are safeguarded.

(iii) The establishment of the independent State will be preceded by a transitional period throughout which His Majesty's Government will retain responsibility for the government of the country. During the transitional period the people of Palestine will be given an increasing part in the government of their country. Both sections of the population will have an opportunity to participate in the machinery of government, and the process will be carried on whether or not they both avail themselves of it.

(iv) As soon as peace and order have been sufficiently restored in Palestine steps will be taken to carry out this policy of giving the people of Palestine an increasing part in the government of their country, the objective being to place Palestinians in charge of all the Departments of Government, with the assistance of British advisers and subject to the control of the High Commissioner. With this object in view His Majesty's Government will be prepared immediately to arrange that Palestinians shall be placed in charge of certain Departments, with British advisers. The Palestinian heads of Departments will sit on the Executive Council, which advises the High Commissioner. Arab and Jewish representatives will be invited to serve as heads of Departments approximately in proportion to their respective populations. The number of Palestinians in charge of Departments will be increased as circumstances permit until all heads of Departments are Palestinians, exercising the administrative and advisory functions which are at present performed by British officials. When that stage is reached consideration will be given to the question of converting the Executive Council into a Council of Ministers with a consequential change in the status and functions of the Palestinian heads of Departments.

(v) His Majesty's Government make no proposals at this stage regarding the establishment of an elective legislature. Nevertheless they would regard this as an appropriate constitutional development, and, should public opinion in Palestine hereafter show itself in favour of such a development, they will be prepared, provided that local conditions permit, to establish the necessary machinery.

* British White Paper, Cmd. 6019.

(vi) At the end of five years from the restoration of peace and order, an appropriate body representative of the people of Palestine and of His Majesty's Government will be set up to review the working of the constitutional arrangements during the transitional period and to consider and make recommendations regarding the Constitution of the independent Palestine State.

(vii) His Majesty's Government will require to be satisfied that in the treaty contemplated by sub-paragraph (i) or in the Constitution contemplated by sub-paragraph (vi) adequate provision has been made for:

(a) the security of, and freedom of access to, the Holy Places, and the protection of the interests and property of the various religious bodies;

(b) the protection of the different communities in Palestine in accordance with the obligations of His Majesty's Government to both Arabs and Jews and for the special position in Palestine of the Jewish National Home;

(c) such requirements to meet the strategic situation as may be regarded as necessary by His Majesty's Government in the light of the circumstances then existing.

His Majesty's Government will also require to be satisfied that the interests of certain foreign countries in Palestine, for the preservation of which they are presently responsible, are adequately safeguarded.

(viii) His Majesty's Government will do everything in their power to create conditions which will enable the independent Palestine State to come into being within ten years. If, at the end of ten years, it appears to His Majesty's Government that, contrary to their hope, circumstances require the postponement of the establishment of the independent State, they will consult with representatives of the people of Palestine, the Council of the League of Nations and the neighbouring Arab States before deciding on such a postponement. If His Majesty's Government come to the conclusion that postponement is unavoidable, they will invite the co-operation of these parties in framing plans for the future with a view to achieving the desired objective at the earliest possible date.

14. . . . they believe that they will be acting consistently with their Mandatory obligations to both Arabs and Jews, and in the manner best calculated to serve the interests of the whole people of Palestine by adopting the following proposals regarding immigration:

(i) Jewish immigration during the next five years will be at a rate which, if economic absorptive capacity permits, will bring the Jewish population up to approximately one-third of the total population of the country. Taking into account the expected natural increase of the Arab and Jewish populations, and the number of illegal Jewish immigrants now in the country, this would allow for the admission, as from the beginning of April this year, of some 75,000 immigrants over the next five years. These immigrants would, subject to the criterion of economic absorptive capacity, be admitted as follows:

(a) For each of the next five years a quota of 10,000 Jewish immigrants will be allowed, on the understanding that a shortage in any one year may be added to the quotas for subsequent years, within the five-year period, if economic absorptive capacity permits.

(b) In addition, as a contribution towards the solution of the Jewish refugee problem, 25,000 refugees will be admitted as soon as the High Commissioner is satisfied that adequate provision for their maintenance is ensured, special consideration being given to refugee children and dependants.

(ii) The existing machinery for ascertaining economic absorptive capacity will be retained, and the High Commissioner will have the ultimate responsibility for deciding the limits of economic capacity. Before each periodic decision is taken, Jewish and Arab representatives will be consulted.

(iii) After the period of five years no further Jewish immigration will be permitted unless the Arabs of Palestine are prepared to acquiesce in it.

(iv) His Majesty's Government are determined to check illegal immigration, and further preventive measures are being adopted. The numbers of any Jewish illegal immigrants who, despite these measures, may succeed in coming into the country and cannot be deported will be deducted from the yearly quotas.

15. His Majesty's Government are satisfied that, when the immigration over five years which is now contemplated has taken place they will not be justified in facilitating, nor will they be under any obligation to facilitate, the further development of the Jewish National Home by immigration regardless of the wishes of the Arab population.

16. The Administration of Palestine is required, under Article 6 of the Mandate, 'while ensuring that the rights and position of other sections of the population are not prejudiced,' to encourage 'close settlement by Jews on the land,' and no restriction has been imposed hitherto on the transfer of land from Arabs to Jews. The Reports of several expert Commissions have indicated that, owing to the natural growth of the Arab population and the steady sale in recent years of Arab land to Jews, there is now in certain areas no room for further transfers of Arab land, whilst in some other areas such transfers of land must be restricted if Arab cultivators are to maintain their existing standard of life and a considerable landless Arab population is not soon to be created. In these circumstances, the High Commissioner will be given general powers to prohibit and regulate transfers of land. These powers will date from the publication of this statement of Policy and the High Commissioner will retain them throughout the transitional period.

17. The policy of the Government will be directed towards the development of the land and the improvement, where possible, of methods of cultivation. In the light of such development it will be open to the High Commissioner, should he be satisfied that the 'rights and position' of the Arab population will be duly preserved, to review and modify any orders passed relating to the prohibition or restriction of the transfer of land.

BILTMORE PROGRAMME*

11 May 1942

The following programme was approved by a Zionist Conference held in the Biltmore Hotel, New York City:

1. American Zionists assembled in this Extraordinary Conference reaffirm their unequivocal devotion to the cause of democratic freedom and international justice to which the people of the United States, allied with the other United Nations, have dedicated themselves, and give expression to their faith in the ultimate victory of humanity and justice over lawlessness and brute force.

2. This Conference offers a message of hope and encouragement to their fellow Jews in the Ghettos and concentration camps of Hitler-dominated Europe and prays that their hour of liberation may not be far distant.

3. The Conference sends its warmest greetings to the Jewish Agency Executive in Jerusalem, to the Va'ad Leumi, and to the whole Yishuv in Palestine, and expresses its profound admiration for their steadfastness and achievements in the face of peril and great difficulties. . . .

4. In our generation, and in particular in the course of the past twenty years, the Jewish people have awakened and transformed their ancient homeland; from 50,000 at the end of the last war their numbers have increased to more than 500,000. They have made the waste places to bear fruit and the desert to blossom. Their pioneering achievements in agriculture and in industry, embodying new patterns of co-operative endeavour, have written a notable page in the history of colonization.

5. In the new values thus created, their Arab neighbours in Palestine have shared. The Jewish people in its own work of national redemption welcomes the economic, agricultural and national development of the Arab peoples and states. The Conference reaffirms the stand previously adopted at Congresses of the World Zionist Organization, expressing the readiness and the desire of the Jewish people for full co-operation with their Arab neighbours.

6. The Conference calls for the fulfilment of the original purpose of the Balfour Declaration and the Mandate which

'recognizing the historical connexion of the Jewish people with Palestine' was to afford them the opportunity, as stated by President Wilson, to found there a Jewish Commonwealth.

The Conference affirms its unalterable rejection of the White Paper of May 1939 and denies its moral or legal validity. The White Paper seeks to limit, and in fact to nullify Jewish rights to immigration and settlement in Palestine, and, as stated by Mr Winston Churchill in the House of Commons in May 1939, constitutes 'a breach and repudiation of the Balfour Declaration'. The policy of the White Paper is cruel and indefensible in its denial of sanctuary to Jews fleeing from Nazi persecution; and at a time when Palestine has become a focal point in the war front of the United Nations, and Palestine Jewry must provide all available manpower for farm and factory and camp, it is in direct conflict with the interests of the allied war effort.

7. In the struggle against the forces of aggression and tyranny, of which Jews were the earliest victims, and which now menace the Jewish National Home, recognition must be given to the right of the Jews of Palestine to play their full part in the war effort and in the defence of their country, through a Jewish military force fighting under its own flag and under the high command of the United Nations.

8. The Conference declares that the new world order that will follow victory cannot be established on foundations of peace, justice and equality, unless the problem of Jewish homelessness is finally solved.

The Conference urges that the gates of Palestine be opened; that the Jewish Agency be vested with control of immigration into Palestine and with the necessary authority for upbuilding the country, including the development of its unoccupied and uncultivated lands; and that Palestine be established as a Jewish Commonwealth integrated in the structure of the new democratic world.

Then and only then will the age old wrong to the Jewish people be righted.

UN GENERAL ASSEMBLY RESOLUTION ON THE FUTURE GOVERNMENT OF PALESTINE (PARTITION RESOLUTION)

29 November 1947

The General Assembly,

Having met in special session at the request of the mandatory Power to constitute and instruct a special committee to prepare for the consideration of the question of the future government of Palestine at the second regular session;

Having constituted a Special Committee and instructed it to investigate all questions and issues relevant to the problem of Palestine, and to prepare proposals for the solution of the problem, and

Having received and examined the report of the Special Committee (document A/364) including a number of unanimous recommendations and a plan of partition with economic union approved by the majority of the Special Committee,

Considers that the present situation in Palestine is one which is likely to impair the general welfare and friendly relations among nations;

Takes note of the declaration by the mandatory Power that it plans to complete its evacuation of Palestine by 1 August 1948;

Recommends to the United Kingdom, as the mandatory Power for Palestine, and to all other Members of the United Nations the adoption and implementation, with regard to the future government of Palestine, of the Plan of Partition with Economic Union set out below;

Requests that

(a) The Security Council take the necessary measures as provided for in the plan for its implementation;

(b) The Security Council consider, if circumstances during the transitional period require such consideration, whether the situation in Palestine constitutes a threat to the peace. If it decides that such a threat exists, and in order to maintain international peace and security, the Security Council should supplement the authorization of the General Assembly by taking measures, under Articles 39 and 41 of the Charter, to empower the United Nations Commission, as provided in this resolution,

---

* Text supplied by courtesy of Josef Fraenkel.

to exercise in Palestine the functions which are assigned to it by this resolution;

(c) The Security Council determine as a threat to the peace, breach of the peace or act of aggression, in accordance with Article 39 of the Charter, any attempt to alter by force the settlement envisaged by this resolution;

(d) The Trusteeship Council be informed of the responsibilities envisaged for it in this plan;

Calls upon the inhabitants of Palestine to take such steps as may be necessary on their part to put this plan into effect;

Appeals to all Governments and all peoples to refrain from taking any action which might hamper or delay the carrying out of these recommendations . . .

Official Records of the second session of the General Assembly, Resolutions, p. 131.

UN GENERAL ASSEMBLY RESOLUTION 194 (III)
11 December 1948

The resolution's terms have been reaffirmed every year since 1948.

11. . . . the refugees wishing to return to their homes and live at peace with their neighbours should be permitted to do so at the earliest practicable date, and that compensation should be paid for the property of those choosing not to return and for the loss of or damage to property which, under principles of international law or in equity, should be made good by the Governments or authorities responsible;

Official Records of the third session of the General Assembly, Part I, Resolutions, p. 21.

UN GENERAL ASSEMBLY RESOLUTION ON THE INTERNATIONALIZATION OF JERUSALEM
9 December 1949

The General Assembly,

Having regard to its resolution 181 (II) of 29 November 1947 and 194 (III) of 11 December 1948,

Having studied the reports of the United Nations Conciliation Commission for Palestine set up under the latter resolution,

I. Decides

In relation to Jerusalem,

Believing that the principles underlying its previous resolutions concerning this matter, and in particular its resolution of 29 November 1947, represent a just and equitable settlement of the question,

1. To restate, therefore, its intention that Jerusalem should be placed under a permanent international regime, which should envisage appropriate guarantees for the protection of the Holy Places, both within and outside Jerusalem, and to confirm specifically the following provisions of General Assembly resolution 181 (II): (1) The City of Jerusalem shall be established as a *corpus separatum* under a special international regime and shall be administered by the United Nations; (2) The Trusteeship Council shall be designated to discharge the responsibilities of the Administering Authority . . .; and (3) The City of Jerusalem shall include the present municipality of Jerusalem plus the surrounding villages and towns, the most eastern of which shall be Abu Dis; the most southern, Bethlehem; the most western, Ein Karim (including also the built-up area of Motsa); and the most northern, Shu'fat, as indicated on the attached sketchmap; . . . [*map not reproduced: Ed.*]

Official Records of the fourth session of the General Assembly, Resolutions, p. 25.

TEXT OF UN SECURITY COUNCIL RESOLUTION 242
22 November 1967

The Security Council,

Expressing its continued concern with the grave situation in the Middle East,

Emphasizing the inadmissibility of the acquisition of territory by war and the need to work for a just and lasting peace in which every state in the area can live in security,

Emphasizing further that all Member States in their acceptance of the Charter of the United Nations have undertaken a commitment to act in accordance with Article 2 of the Charter

1. *Affirms* that the fulfilment of Charter principles requires the establishment of a just and lasting peace in the Middle East which should include the application of both the following principles:

(i) Withdrawal of Israel armed forces from territories occupied in the recent conflict;

(ii) Termination of all claims or states of belligerency and respect for the acknowledgement of the sovereignty, territorial integrity and political independence of every State in the area and their right to live in peace within secure and recognized boundaries free from threats or acts of force.

2. *Affirms further* the necessity

(a) For guaranteeing freedom of navigation through international waterways in the area;

(b) For achieving a just settlement of the refugee problem;

(c) For guaranteeing the territorial inviolability and political independence of every State in the area, through measures including the establishment of demilitarized zones;

3. *Requests* the Secretary-General to designate a Special Representative to proceed to the Middle East to establish and maintain contacts with the States concerned in order to promote agreement and assist efforts to achieve a peaceful and accepted settlement in accordance with the provisions and principles in this resolution;

4. *Requests* the Secretary-General to report to the Security Council on the progress of the efforts of the Special Representative as soon as possible.

UN Document S/RES/242 (1967).

UN SECURITY COUNCIL RESOLUTION 252
21 May 1968

Resolution 252 was the first Security Council resolution dealing specifically with the issue of Jerusalem. It was adopted by 13 votes to none; the USA and Canada abstained in the vote. [The two General Assembly resolutions, the Jordanian Permanent Representative's letter and the report of the Secretary-General, to which the introductory section refers, are not repro-duced here.]

The Security Council,

Recalling General Assembly resolutions 2253 (ES-V) of 4 July 1967 and 2254 (ES-V) of 14 July 1967,

Having considered the letter of the Permanent Representative of Jordan on the situation in Jerusalem (S/8560) and the report of the Secretary-General (S/8146),

Having heard the statements made before the Council,

Noting that since the adoption of the above-mentioned resolutions Israel has taken further measures and actions in contravention of those resolutions,

Bearing in mind the need to work for a just and lasting peace,

Reaffirming that acquisition of territory by military conquest is inadmissible,

1. *Deplores* the failure of Israel to comply with the General Assembly resolutions mentioned above;

2. *Considers* that all legislative and administrative measures and actions taken by Israel, including expropriation of land and properties thereon, which tend to change the legal status of Jerusalem are invalid and cannot change that status;

3. *Urgently calls upon* Israel to rescind all such measures already taken and to desist forthwith from taking any further action which tends to change the status of Jerusalem;

4. *Requests* the Secretary-General to report to the Security Council on the implementation of the present resolution.

PALESTINIAN NATIONAL CHARTER (PLO COVENANT)

Resolutions of the Palestine National Council, July 1–17, 1968

In September 1993 Yasser Arafat declared those articles of the PLO Covenant which deny Israel's right to exist or are inconsis-

tent with the PLO's commitments to Israel under the terms of subsequent accords to be invalid. Revision of those articles, presented here in italics, was to be undertaken as part of the ongoing peace process.

The following is the complete and unabridged text of the Palestinian National Covenant, as published officially in English by the PLO.

Article I:

Palestine is the homeland of the Arab Palestinian people; it is an indivisible part of the Arab homeland, and the Palestinian people are an integral part of the Arab nation.

Article II:

Palestine, with the boundaries it had during the British Mandate, is an indivisible territorial unit.

Article III:

The Palestinian Arab people possess the legal right to their homeland and have the right to determine their destiny after achieving the liberation of their country in accordance with their wishes and entirely of their own accord and will.

Article IV:

The Palestinian identity is a genuine, essential, and inherent characteristic; it is transmitted from parents to children. The Zionist occupation and the dispersal of the Palestinian Arab people, through the disasters which befell them, do not make them lose their Palestinian identity and their membership in the Palestinian community, nor do they negate them.

Article V:

The Palestinians are those Arab nationals who, until 1947, normally resided in Palestine regardless of whether they were evicted from it or have stayed there. Anyone born, after that date, of a Palestinian father—whether inside Palestine or outside it—is also a Palestinian.

Article VI:

The Jews who had normally resided in Palestine until the beginning of the Zionist invasion will be considered Palestinians.

Article VII:

That there is a Palestinian community and that it has material, spiritual, and historical connection with Palestine are indisputable facts. It is a national duty to bring up individual Palestinians in an Arab revolutionary manner. All means of information and education must be adopted in order to acquaint the Palestinian with his country in the most profound manner, both spiritual and material, that is possible. He must be prepared for the armed struggle and ready to sacrifice his wealth and his life in order to win back his homeland and bring about its liberation.

Article VIII:

The phase in their history, through which the Palestinian people are now living, is that of national (watani) struggle for the liberation of Palestine. Thus the conflicts among the Palestinian national forces are secondary, and should be ended for the sake of the basic conflict that exists between the forces of Zionism and of imperialism on the one hand, and the Palestinian Arab people on the other. On this basis the Palestinian masses, regardless of whether they are residing in the national homeland or in diaspora (mahajir) constitute—both their organizations and the individuals—one national front working for the retrieval of Palestine and its liberation through armed struggle.

Article IX:

Armed struggle is the only way to liberate Palestine. This is the overall strategy, not merely a tactical phase. The Palestinian Arab people assert their absolute determination and firm resolution to continue their armed struggle and to work for an armed popular revolution for the liberation of their country and their return to it. They also assert their right to normal life in Palestine and to exercise their right to self-determination and sovereignty over it.

Article X:

Commando action constitutes the nucleus of the Palestinian popular liberation war. This requires its escalation, comprehensiveness, and the mobilization of all the Palestinian popular and educational efforts and their organization and involvement in

the armed Palestinian revolution. It also requires the achieving of unity for the national (watani) struggle among the different groupings of the Palestinian people, and between the Palestinian people and the Arab masses, so as to secure the continuation of the revolution, its escalation, and victory.

Article XI:

The Palestinians will have three mottoes: national (wataniyya) unity, national (qawmiyya) mobilization, and liberation.

Article XII:

The Palestinian people believe in Arab unity. In order to contribute their share toward the attainment of that objective, however, they must, at the present stage of their struggle, safeguard their Palestinian identity and develop their consciousness of that identity, and oppose any plan that may dissolve or impair it.

Article XIII:

Arab unity and the liberation of Palestine are two complementary objectives, the attainment of either of which facilitates the attainment of the other. Thus, Arab unity leads to the liberation of Palestine, the liberation of Palestine leads to Arab unity; and work towards the realization of one objective proceeds side by side with work towards the realization of the other.

Article XIV:

The destiny of the Arab nation, and indeed Arab existence itself, depend upon the destiny of the Palestine cause. From this interdependence springs the Arab nation's pursuit of, and striving for, the liberation of Palestine. The people of Palestine play the role of the vanguard in the realization of this sacred (qawmi) goal.

Article XV:

The liberation of Palestine, from an Arab viewpoint, is a national (qawmi) duty and it attempts to repel the Zionist and imperialist aggression against the Arab homeland, and aims at the elimination of Zionism in Palestine. Absolute responsibility for this falls upon the Arab nation—peoples and governments—with the Arab people of Palestine in the vanguard. Accordingly, the Arab nation must mobilize all its military, human, moral, and spiritual capabilities to participate actively with the Palestinian people in the liberation of Palestine. It must, particularly in the phase of the armed Palestinian revolution, offer and furnish the Palestinian people with all possible help, and material and human support, and make available to them the means and opportunities that will enable them to continue to carry out their leading role in the armed revolution, until they liberate their homeland.

Article XVI:

The liberation of Palestine, from a spiritual point of view, will provide the Holy Land with an atmosphere of safety and tranquility, which in turn will safeguard the country's religious sanctuaries and guarantee freedom of worship and of visit to all, without discrimination of race, color, language, or religion. Accordingly, the people of Palestine look to all spiritual forces in the world for support.

Article XVII:

The liberation of Palestine, from a human point of view, will restore to the Palestinian individual his dignity, pride, and freedom. Accordingly the Palestinian Arab people look forward to the support of all those who believe in the dignity of man and his freedom in the world.

Article XVIII:

The liberation of Palestine, from an international point of view, is a defensive action necessitated by the demands of self-defense. Accordingly the Palestinian people, desirous as they are of the friendship of all people, look to freedom-loving, and peace-loving states for support in order to restore their legitimate rights in Palestine, to re-establish peace and security in the country, and to enable its people to exercise national sovereignty and freedom.

Article XIX:

The partition of Palestine in 1947 and the establishment of the state of Israel are entirely illegal, regardless of the passage of time, because they were contrary to the will of the Palestinian people and to their natural right in their homeland, and inconsistent with the principles embodied in the Charter of the United Nations, particularly the right to self-determination.

Article XX:

The Balfour Declaration, the Mandate for Palestine, and everything that has been based upon them, are deemed null and void. Claims of historical or religious ties of Jews with Palestine are incompatible with the facts of history and the true conception of what constitutes statehood. Judaism, being a religion, is not an independent nationality. Nor do Jews constitute a single nation with an identity of its own; they are citizens of the states to which they belong.

Article XXI:

The Arab Palestinian people, expressing themselves by the armed Palestinian revolution, reject all solutions which are substitutes for the total liberation of Palestine and reject all proposals aiming at the liquidation of the Palestinian problem, or its internationalization.

Article XXII:

Zionism is a political movement organically associated with international imperialism and antagonistic to all action for liberation and to progressive movements in the world. It is racist and fanatic in its nature, aggressive, expansionist, and colonial in its aims, and fascist in its methods. Israel is the instrument of Zionist movement, and geographical base for world imperialism placed strategically in the midst of the Arab homeland to combat the hopes of the Arab nation for liberation, unity, and progress. Israel is a constant source of threat vis-à-vis peace in the Middle East and the whole world. Since the liberation of Palestine will destroy the Zionist and imperialist presence and will contribute to the establishment of peace in the Middle East, the Palestinian people look for the support of all the progressive and peaceful forces and urge them all, irrespective of their affiliations and beliefs, to offer the Palestinian people all aid and support in their just struggle for the liberation of their homeland.

Article XXIII:

The demand of security and peace, as well as the demand of right and justice, require all states to consider Zionism an illegitimate movement, to outlaw its existence, and to ban its operations, in order that friendly relations among peoples may be preserved, and the loyalty of citizens to their respective homelands safeguarded.

Article XXIV:

The Palestinian people believe in the principles of justice, freedom, sovereignty, self-determination, human dignity, and in the right of all peoples to exercise them.

Article XXV:

For the realization of the goals of this Charter and its principles, the Palestine Liberation Organization will perform its role in the liberation of Palestine in accordance with the Constitution of this Organization.

Article XXVI:

The Palestine Liberation Organization, representative of the Palestinian revolutionary forces, is responsible for the Palestinian Arab people's movement in its struggle—to retrieve its homeland, liberate and return to it and exercise the right to self-determination in it—in all military, political, and financial fields and also for whatever may be required by the Palestine case on the inter-Arab and international levels.

Article XXVII:

The Palestine Liberation Organization shall co-operate with all Arab states, each according to its potentialities; and will adopt a neutral policy among them in the light of the requirements of the war of liberation; and on this basis it shall not interfere in the internal affairs of any Arab state.

Article XXVIII:

The Palestinian Arab people assert the genuineness and independence of their national (wataniyya) revolution and reject all forms of intervention, trusteeship, and subordination.

Article XXIV:

The Palestinian people possess the fundamental and genuine legal right to liberate and retrieve their homeland. The Palestinian people determine their attitude toward all states and forces on the basis of the stands they adopt vis-à-vis to the Palestinian revolution to fulfil the aims of the Palestinian people.

Article XXX:

Fighters and carriers of arms in the war of liberation are the nucleus of the popular army which will be the protective force for the gains of the Palestinian Arab people.

Article XXXI:

The Organization shall have a flag, an oath of allegiance, and an anthem. All this shall be decided upon in accordance with a special regulation.

Article XXXII:

Regulations, which shall be known as the Constitution of the Palestinian (sic) Liberation Organization, shall be annexed to this Charter. It will lay down the manner in which the Organization, and its organs and institutions, shall be constituted; the respective competence of each; and the requirements of its obligation under the Charter.

Article XXXIII:

This Charter shall not be amended save by [vote of] a majority of two-thirds of the total membership of the National Congress of the Palestine Liberation Organization [taken] at a special session convened for that purpose.

English rendition as published in Basic Political Documents of the Armed Palestinian Resistance Movement; Leila S. Kadi (Ed.), Palestine Research Centre, Beirut, December 1969, pp. 137–141.

UN SECURITY COUNCIL RESOLUTION ON JERUSALEM

25 September 1971

The resolution, No. 298 (1971), was passed nem. con., with the abstention of Syria.

The Security Council,

Recalling its resolutions 252 (1968) of 21 May 1968, and 267 (1969) of 3 July 1969, and the earlier General Assembly resolution 2253 (ES-V) and 2254 (ES-V) of 4 and 14 July 1967, concerning measures and actions by Israel designed to change the status of the Israeli-occupied section of Jerusalem,

Having considered the letter of the Permanent Representative of Jordan on this situation in Jerusalem and the reports of the Secretary-General, and having heard the statements of the parties concerned in the question,

Recalling the principle that acquisition of territory by military conquest is inadmissible,

Noting with concern the non-compliance by Israel with the above-mentioned resolutions,

Noting with concern also that since the adoption of the above-mentioned resolutions Israel has taken further measures designed to change the status and character of the occupied section of Jerusalem.

1. *Reaffirms* its resolutions 252 (1968) and 267 (1969);

2. *Deplores* the failure of Israel to respect the previous resolutions adopted by the United Nations concerning measures and actions by Israel purporting to affect the status of the City of Jerusalem;

3. *Confirms* in the clearest possible terms that all legislative and administrative actions taken by Israel to change the status of the City of Jerusalem, including expropriation of land and properties, transfer of populations and legislation aimed at the incorporation of the occupied section, are totally invalid and cannot change that status;

4. *Urgently calls upon* Israel to rescind all previous measures and actions and to take no further steps in the occupied section of Jerusalem which may purport to change the status of the City, or which would prejudice the rights of the inhabitants and the interests of the international community, or a just and lasting peace;

5. *Requests* the Secretary-General, in consultation with the President of the Security Council and using such instrumentalities as he may choose, including a representative or a mission, to report to the Council as appropriate and in any event within 60 days on the implementation of the present resolution.

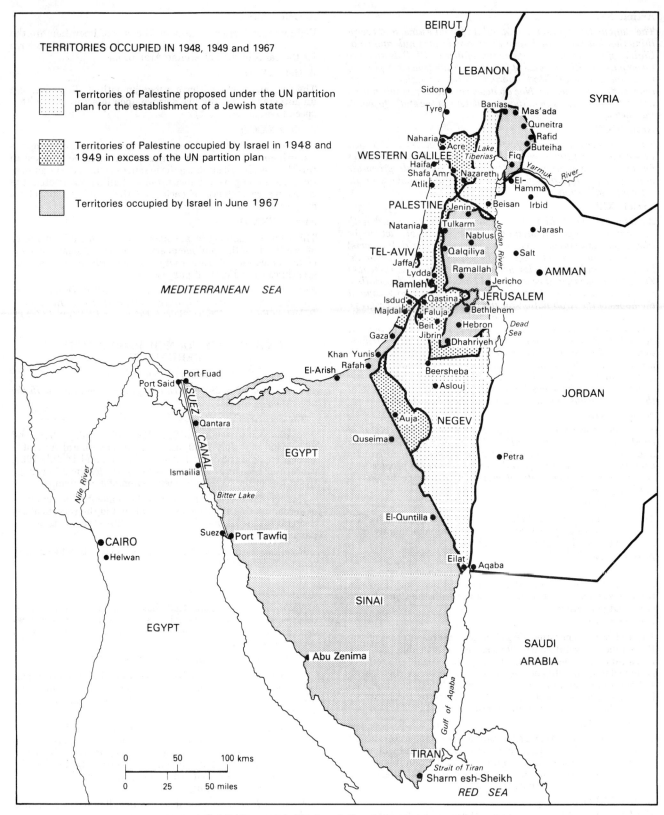

TERRITORIES OCCUPIED IN 1948, 1949 and 1967

Territories of Palestine proposed under the UN partition plan for the establishment of a Jewish state

Territories of Palestine occupied by Israel in 1948 and 1949 in excess of the UN partition plan

Territories occupied by Israel in June 1967

Territories occupied by Israel. See also maps on page 63

UN Document S/RES/298 (1971).

UN SECURITY COUNCIL RESOLUTION 338
22 October 1973

UN Resolutions between 1967 and October 1973 reaffirmed Security Council Resolution 242 (see above). In an attempt to end the fourth Middle East war, which had broken out between the Arabs and Israel on 6 October 1973, the UN Security Council passed the following Resolution:

The Security Council,

1. *Calls upon* all parties to the present fighting to cease all firing and terminate all military activity immediately, not later than 12 hours after the moment of the adoption of the decision, in the positions they now occupy;

2. *Calls upon* the parties concerned to start immediately after the ceasefire the implementation of Security Council Resolution 242 (1967) in all of its parts;

3. *Decides that,* immediately and concurrently with the cease-fire negotiations start between the parties concerned under appropriate auspices aimed at establishing a just and durable peace in the Middle East.

UN Document PR/73/29 (1973).

UN SECURITY COUNCIL RESOLUTION 340
25 October 1973

The Security Council,

Recalling its Resolutions 338 (1973) of 22 October 1973 and 339 (1973) of 23 October 1973,

Noting with regret the reported repeated violations of the ceasefire in non-compliance with Resolutions 338 (1973) and 339 (1973),

Noting with concern from the Secretary-General's report that the UN military observers have not yet been enabled to place themselves on both sides of the ceasefire line,

1. *Demands* that an immediate and complete ceasefire be observed and that the parties withdraw to the positions occupied by them at 16.50 hours GMT on 22 October 1973;

2. *Requests* the Secretary-General as an immediate step to increase the number of UN military observers on both sides;

3. *Decides* to set up immediately under its authority a UN emergency force to be composed of personnel drawn from member states of the UN, except the permanent members of the Security Council, and requests the Secretary-General to report within 24 hours on the steps taken to this effect.

4. *Requests* the Secretary-General to report to the Council on an urgent and continuing basis on the state of implementation of this Resolution, as well as Resolutions 338 (1973) and 339 (1973);

5. *Requests* all member states to extend their full co-operation to the UN in the implementation of this Resolution, as well as Resolutions 338 (1973) and 339 (1973).

UN Document PR/73/31 (1973).

DECLARATION OF EEC FOREIGN MINISTERS ON THE MIDDLE EAST SITUATION
6 November 1973

The Nine Governments of the European Community have exchanged views on the situation in the Middle East. While emphasizing that the views set out below are only a first contribution on their part to the search for a comprehensive solution to the problem, they have agreed on the following:

1. They strongly urge that the forces of both sides in the Middle East conflict should return immediately to the positions they occupied on 22 October in accordance with Resolutions 339 and 340 of the Security Council. They believe that a return to these positions will facilitate a solution to other pressing problems concerning prisoners of war and the Egyptian Third Army.

2. They have the firm hope that, following the adoption by the Security Council of Resolution 338 of 22 October, negotiations will at last begin for the restoration in the Middle East of a just and lasting peace through the application of Security Council Resolution 242 in all of its parts. They declare them-

selves ready to do all in their power to contribute to that peace. They believe that those negotiations must take place in the framework of the United Nations. They recall that the Charter has entrusted to the Security Council the principal responsibility for international peace and security. The Council and the Secretary-General have a special role to play in the making and keeping of peace through the application of Council Resolutions 242 and 338.

3. They consider that a peace agreement should be based particularly on the following points:

(i) the inadmissibility of the acquisition of territory by force;

(ii) the need for Israel to end the territorial occupation which it has maintained since the conflict of 1967;

(iii) respect for the sovereignty, territorial integrity and independence of every state in the area and their right to live in peace within secure and recognized boundaries;

(iv) recognition that in the establishment of a just and lasting peace account must be taken of the legitimate rights of the Palestinians.

Article 4 calls for the dispatch of peace-keeping forces to the demilitarized zones.

Bulletin of the European Communities Commission, No. 10, 1973, p. 106.

EGYPTIAN-ISRAELI AGREEMENT ON DISENGAGEMENT OF FORCES IN PURSUANCE OF THE GENEVA PEACE CONFERENCE
(signed by the Egyptian and Israeli Chiefs of Staff, 18 January 1974)

This agreement was superseded by the second Interim Peace Agreement signed in September 1975 (see p. 62) and then by the Peace Treaty between Egypt and Israel signed on 26 March 1979 (see p. 65). A map showing the boundaries of the first agreement is reproduced in this edition (see p. 63) and the terms can be found in the 1975–76 edition of The Middle East and North Africa.

DISENGAGEMENT AGREEMENT BETWEEN SYRIAN AND ISRAELI FORCES
AND
PROTOCOL TO AGREEMENT ON UNITED NATIONS DISENGAGEMENT OBSERVER FORCE (UNDOF)
(signed in Geneva, 31 May 1974)

(Annex A)

A.   Israel and Syria will scrupulously observe the cease-fire on land, sea and air and will refrain from all military actions against each other, from the time of signing this document in implementation of the United Nations Security Council Resolution 338 dated 22 October 1973.

B.   The military forces of Israel and Syria will be separated in accordance with the following principles:

1. All Israeli military forces will be west of a line designated line A on the map attached hereto (*reproduced below*), except in Quneitra (Kuneitra) area, where they will be west of a line A-1.

2. All territory east of line A will be under Syrian administration and Syrian civilians will return to this territory.

3. The area between line A and the line designated as line B on the attached map will be an area of separation. In this area will be stationed UNDOF established in accordance with the accompanying Protocol.

4. All Syrian military forces will be east of a line designated as line B on the attached map.

5. There will be two equal areas of limitation in armament and forces, one west of line A and one east of line B as agreed upon.

C.   In the area between line A and line A-1 on the attached map there shall be no military forces.

D.   *Paragraph D deals with practical details of signing and implementation.*

E.   Provisions of paragraphs A, B and C shall be inspected by personnel of the United Nations comprising UNDOF under the Agreement.

F. *Paragraphs F and G deal with repatriation of prisoners and return of bodies of dead soldiers.*

H. This Agreement is not a peace agreement. It is a step towards a just and durable peace on the basis of the Security Council Resolution 338 dated 22 October 1973.

A Protocol to the Disengagement Agreement outlined the functions of the United Nations Disengagement Observer Force (UNDOF).

RESOLUTION OF CONFERENCE OF ARAB HEADS OF STATE

Rabat, 28 October 1974

The Conference of the Arab Heads of State:

1. *Affirms* the right of the Palestinian people to return to their homeland and to self-determination.

2. *Affirms* the right of the Palestinian people to establish an independent national authority, under the leadership of the PLO in its capacity as the sole legitimate representative of the Palestine people, over all liberated territory. The Arab States are pledged to uphold this authority, when it is established, in all spheres and at all levels.

3. *Supports* the PLO in the exercise of its national and international responsibilities, within the context of the principle of Arab solidarity.

4. *Invites* the kingdom of Jordan, Syria and Egypt to formalize their relations in the light of these decisions and in order that they be implemented.

5. *Affirms* the obligation of all Arab States to preserve Palestinian unity and not to interfere in Palestinian internal affairs.

Sources: *Le Monde: Problèmes Politiques et Sociaux*, 7 March 1975; *Arab Report and Record.*

UN GENERAL ASSEMBLY RESOLUTION 3236 (XXIX)

22 November 1974

The General Assembly,

Having considered the question of Palestine,

Having heard the statement of the Palestine Liberation Organization, the representative of the Palestinian people,

Having also heard other statements made during the debate,

Deeply concerned that no just solution to the problem of Palestine has yet been achieved and recognizing that the problem of Palestine continues to endanger international peace and security,

Recognizing that the Palestinian people is entitled to self-determination in accordance with the Charter of the United Nations,

Expressing its grave concern that the Palestinian people has been prevented from enjoying its inalienable rights, in particular its right to self-determination,

Guided by the purposes and principles of the Charter,

Recalling its relevant resolutions which affirm the right of the Palestinian people to self-determination,

1. *Reaffirms* the inalienable rights of Palestinian people in Palestine, including:

   (a) The right to self-determination without external interference;

   (b) The right to national independence and sovereignty;

2. *Reaffirms also* the inalienable right of the Palestinians to return to their homes and property from which they have been displaced and uprooted, and calls for their return;

3. *Emphasizes* that full respect for and the realization of these inalienable rights of the Palestinian people are indispensable for the solution of the question of Palestine;

4. *Recognizes* that the Palestinian people is a principal party in the establishment of a just and durable peace in the Middle East;

5. *Further Recognizes* the right of the Palestinian people to regain its rights by all means in accordance with the purposes and principles of the Charter of the United Nations;

6. *Appeals* to all States and international organizations to extend their support to the Palestinian people in its struggle to restore its rights, in accordance with the Charter;

7. *Requests* the Secretary-General to establish contacts with the Palestinian Liberation Organization on all matters concerning the question of Palestine;

8. *Requests* the Secretary-General to report to the General Assembly at its thirtieth session on the implementation of the present resolution;

9. *Decides* to include the item 'Question of Palestine' in the provisional agenda of its thirtieth session.

Source: UN Document BR/74/55 (1974).

SECOND INTERIM PEACE AGREEMENT BETWEEN EGYPT AND ISRAEL

(signed 4 September 1975)

This agreement was superseded by the Peace Treaty between Egypt and Israel signed on 26 March 1979 (see p. 65). A map showing the boundaries of the Second Interim Peace Agreement is reproduced in the 1979–80 edition and the terms can be found in the 1978–79 edition of The Middle East and North Africa.

DEVELOPMENTS 1975–78

At the 30th Meeting of the UN General Assembly in November 1975, General Assembly Resolution 3236 (XXIX) was reaffirmed and a 20-nation Committee (the Committee on Palestine Rights) was set up to report on the 'Exercise of the Inalienable Right of the Palestine People' by 1 June 1976.

At the UN Security Council a draft resolution which would have affirmed the rights of the Palestinian people to self-determination, including the right to establish an independent state, was vetoed by the USA on 26 January 1976. A Security Council draft resolution criticizing Israeli policies in East Jerusalem and on the West Bank of the Jordan was also vetoed by the USA on 25 March 1976.

The Committee on Palestine Rights presented its report in June 1976 and recommended that Israel should withdraw from all occupied territories by June 1977. A resolution in the Security Council, stemming from the report, affirmed the 'inalienable rights of the Palestinians' and called for the creation of a 'Palestine entity' in the West Bank and Gaza. This resolution was vetoed by the USA on 29 June 1976. The Committee on Palestine Rights then submitted its report to the UN General Assembly in November 1976 in the form of a resolution. The resolution (No. 20, of 24 November 1976) was adopted by a vote of 90 to 16 (30 members abstained; 10 were absent). The USA and 10 other Western countries (including the UK) opposed the resolution.

Other General Assembly resolutions in December 1976 called for the reconvening of the Geneva Middle East peace conference by March 1977 and the participation in the negotiations of the PLO. Neither of these resolutions was implemented.

After a meeting in London of the nine EC heads of government at the end of June 1977, a statement was issued reaffirming earlier statements and stating that 'The Nine have affirmed their belief that a solution to the conflict in the Middle East will be possible only if the legitimate rights of the Palestinian people to give effective expression to its national identity is translated into fact, which would take into account the need for a homeland for the Palestinian people. . . . In the context of an overall settlement Israel must be ready to recognize the legitimate rights of the Palestinian people; equally, the Arab side must be ready to recognize the right of Israel to live in peace within secure and recognized boundaries'.

A UN General Assembly Resolution of 25 November 1977 (32/ 30) 'called anew' for the early convening of the Geneva Middle East peace conference.

A further UN General Assembly Resolution (33/29 of 7 December 1978) repeated the call for the convening of the Geneva Middle East peace conference. The main focus of attention, however, had now moved away from the UN. President Sadat of Egypt visited Jerusalem in November 1977, and after protracted negotiations, President Sadat and Menachem Begin first of all signed two agreements at Camp David in the USA under the auspices of the US President, Jimmy Carter, and subsequently signed a Peace Treaty in Washington on 26 March 1979. The

Disengagement Agreement of 18 January 1974 between Israel and Egypt.

Disengagement Agreement of 31 May 1974 between Israel and Syria.

Arab League Council, angry at Egypt's unilateral action, met in Baghdad on 27 March and passed a series of resolutions aimed at isolating Egypt from the Arab world.

CAMP DAVID: THE FRAMEWORK FOR PEACE IN THE MIDDLE EAST

Muhammad Anwar as-Sadat, President of the Arab Republic of Egypt, and Menachem Begin, Prime Minister of Israel, met with President Carter of the USA at Camp David from 5 September to 17 September 1978, and agreed on the following framework for peace in the Middle East. They invited other parties to the Arab–Israeli conflict to adhere to it.

Preamble:

The search for peace in the Middle East must be guided by the following:

The agreed basis for a peaceful settlement of the conflict between Israel and its neighbours is UN Security Council Resolution 242 in all its parts.

The historic initiative by President Sadat in visiting Jerusalem and the reception accorded to him by the Parliament, Government and people of Israel, and the reciprocal visit of Prime Minister Begin to Ismailia, the peace proposals made by both leaders, as well as the warm reception of these missions by the peoples of both countries, have created an unprecedented opportunity for peace which must not be lost if this generation and future generations are to be spared the tragedies of war.

The provisions of the Charter of the UN and the other accepted norms of international law and legitimacy now provide accepted standards for the conduct of relations between all states.

To achieve a relationship of peace, in the spirit of article 2 of the UN Charter, future negotiations between Israel and any neighbour prepared to negotiate peace and security with it, are necessary for the purpose of carrying out all the provisions and principles of Resolutions 242 and 338.

Peace requires respect for the sovereignty, territorial integrity and political independence of every state in the area and their right to live in peace within secure and recognized boundaries free from threats or acts of force. Progress toward that goal can accelerate movement towards a new era of reconciliation in the Middle East marked by co-operation in promoting economic development, in maintaining stability and in assuring security....

Framework

Taking these factors into account, the parties are determined to reach a just, comprehensive and durable settlement of the Middle East conflict through the conclusion of peace treaties based on Security Council Resolutions 242 and 338 in all their parts. Their purpose is to achieve peace and good neighbourly relations. They recognize that, for peace to endure, it must involve all those who have been most deeply affected by the conflict. They therefore agree that this framework as appropriate is intended by them to constitute a basis for peace not only between Egypt and Israel but also between Israel and each of its other neighbours which is prepared to negotiate peace with Israel on this basis. With that objective in mind, they have agreed to proceed as follows:

A. West Bank and Gaza

1. Egypt, Israel, Jordan and the representatives of the Palestinian people should participate in negotiations on the resolution of the Palestinian problem in all its aspects to achieve that objective, negotiations relating to the West Bank and Gaza should proceed in three stages.

(A) Egypt and Israel agree that, in order to ensure a peaceful and orderly transfer of authority, and taking into account the security concerns of all the parties, there should be transitional arrangements for the West Bank and Gaza for a period not exceeding five years. In order to provide full autonomy to the inhabitants, under these arrangements the Israeli military government and its civilian administration will be withdrawn as soon as a self-governing authority has been freely elected by the inhabitants of these areas to replace the existing military government.

To negotiate the details of transitional arrangement, the Government of Jordan will be invited to join the negotiations on the basis of this framework. These new arrangements should give due consideration to both the principle of self-government by the inhabitants of these territories and to the legitimate security concerns of the parties involved.

(B) Egypt, Israel and Jordan will agree on the modalities for establishing the elected self-governing authority in the West Bank and Gaza. The delegations of Egypt and Jordan may include Palestinians from the West Bank and Gaza or other Palestinians as mutually agreed. The parties will negotiate an agreement which will define the powers and responsibilities of the self-governing authority to be exercised in the West Bank and Gaza. A withdrawal of Israeli armed forces will take place and there will be a redeployment of the remaining Israeli forces into specified security locations.

The negotiations shall be based on all the provisions and principles of UN Security Council Resolution 242. The negotiations will resolve, among other matters, the location of the boundaries and the nature of the security arrangements. The solution from the negotiations must also recognize the legitimate rights of the Palestinian people and their just requirements. In this way, the Palestinians will participate in the determination of their own future through:

(i) The negotiations among Egypt, Israel, Jordan and the representatives of the inhabitants of the West Bank and Gaza to agree on the final status of the West Bank and Gaza and other outstanding issues by the end of the transitional period.

(ii) Submitting their agreement to a vote by the elected representatives of the inhabitants of the West Bank and Gaza.

(iii) Providing for the elected representatives of the inhabitants of the West Bank and Gaza to decide how they shall govern themselves consistent with the provisions of their agreement.

(iv) Participating as stated above in the work of the committee negotiating the peace treaty between Israel and Jordan.

The agreement will also include arrangements for assuring internal and external security and public order. A strong local police force will be established, which may include Jordanian citizens. In addition, Israeli and Jordanian forces will participate in joint patrols and in the manning of control posts to assure the security of the borders.

(C) When the self-governing authority (administrative council) in the West Bank and Gaza is established and inaugurated, the transitional period of five years will begin. As soon as possible, but not later than the third year after the beginning of the transitional period, negotiations will take place to determine the final status of the West Bank and Gaza and its relationship with its neighbours, and to conclude a peace treaty between Israel and Jordan by the end of the transitional period. These negotiations will be conducted among Egypt, Israel, Jordan and the elected representatives of the inhabitants of the West Bank and Gaza.

Two separate but related committees will be convened; one committee, consisting of representatives of the four parties which will negotiate and agree on the final status of the West Bank and Gaza, and its relationship with its neighbours, and the second committee, consisting of representatives of Israel and representatives of Jordan to be joined by the elected representatives of the inhabitants of the West Bank and Gaza, to negotiate the peace treaty between Israel and Jordan, taking into account the agreement reached on the final status of the West Bank and Gaza.

2. All necessary measures will be taken and provisions made to assure the security of Israel and its neighbours during the transitional period and beyond. To assist in providing such security, a strong local police force will be constituted by the self-governing authority. It will be composed of inhabitants of the West Bank and Gaza. The police will maintain continuing liaison on internal security matters with the designated Israeli, Jordanian and Egyptian officers.

3. During the transitional period, the representatives of Egypt, Israel, Jordan and the self-governing authority will constitute a continuing committee to decide by agreement on the modalities of admission of persons displaced from the West Bank and Gaza in 1967, together with necessary measures to prevent disruption and disorder. Other matters of common concern may also be dealt with by this committee.

4. Egypt and Israel will work with each other and with other interested parties to establish agreed procedures for a prompt, just and permanent implementation of the resolution of the refugee problem.

B. Egypt-Israel

1. Egypt and Israel undertake not to resort to the threat or the use of force to settle disputes. Any disputes shall be settled by peaceful means in accordance with the provisions of article 33 of the Charter of the UN.

2. In order to achieve peace between them, the parties agree to negotiate in good faith with a goal of concluding within three months from the signing of this framework a peace treaty between them, while inviting the other parties to the conflict to proceed simultaneously to negotiate and conclude similar peace treaties with a view to achieving a comprehensive peace in the area. The framework for the conclusion of a peace treaty between Egypt and Israel will govern the peace negotiations between them. The parties will agree on the modalities and the timetable for the implementation of their obligations under the treaty.

Associated principles

1. Egypt and Israel state that the principles and provisions described below should apply to peace treaties between Israel and each of its neighbours—Egypt, Jordan, Syria and Lebanon.

2. Signatories shall establish among themselves relationships normal to states at peace with one another. To this end, they should undertake to abide by all the provisions of the Charter of the UN. Steps to be taken in this respect include:

(a) Full recognition.

(b) Abolishing economic boycotts.

(c) Guaranteeing that under their jurisdiction the citizens of the other parties shall enjoy the protection of the due process of law.

3. Signatories should explore possibilities for economic development in the context of final peace treaties, with the objective of contributing to the atmosphere of peace, co-operation, and friendship which is their common goal.

4. Claims commissions may be established for the mutual settlement of all financial claims.

5. The United States shall be invited to participate in the talks on matters related to the modalities of the implementation of the agreements and working out the time-table for the carrying out of the obligation of the parties.

6. The UN Security Council shall be requested to endorse the peace treaties and ensure that their provisions shall not be

violated. The permanent members of the Security Council shall be requested to underwrite the peace treaties and ensure respect for their provisions. They shall also be requested to conform their policies and actions with the undertakings contained in this framework.

The second agreement signed at Camp David was a framework for the conclusion of a peace treaty between Egypt and Israel. The actual Treaty was signed on 26 March 1979, and is reproduced below.

THE PEACE TREATY BETWEEN EGYPT AND ISRAEL SIGNED IN WASHINGTON ON 26 MARCH 1979

The Government of the Arab Republic of Egypt and the Government of the State of Israel:

Preamble

Convinced of the urgent necessity of the establishment of a just, comprehensive and lasting peace in the Middle East in accordance with Security Council Resolutions 242 and 338:

Reaffirming their adherence to the 'Framework for Peace in the Middle East agreed at Camp David', dated 17 September 1978:

Noting that the aforementioned framework as appropriate is intended to constitute a basis for peace not only between Egypt and Israel but also between Israel and each of the other Arab neighbours which is prepared to negotiate peace with it on this basis:

Desiring to bring to an end the state of war between them and to establish a peace in which every state in the area can live in security:

Convinced that the conclusion of a treaty of peace between Egypt and Israel is an important step in the search for comprehensive peace in the area and for the attainment of the settlement of the Arab–Israeli conflict in all its aspects:

Inviting the other Arab parties to this dispute to join the peace process with Israel guided by and based on the principles of the aforementioned framework:

Desiring as well to develop friendly relations and co-operation between themselves in accordance with the UN Charter and the principles of international law governing international relations in times of peace:

Agree to the following provisions in the free exercise of their sovereignty, in order to implement the 'framework for the conclusion of a peace treaty between Egypt and Israel'.

Article I

1. The state of war between the parties will be terminated and peace will be established between them upon the exchange of instruments of ratification of this treaty.

2. Israel will withdraw all its armed forces and civilians from the Sinai behind the international boundary between Egypt and Mandated Palestine, as provided in the annexed protocol (annexed), and Egypt will resume the exercise of its full sovereignty over the Sinai.

3. Upon completion of the interim withdrawal provided for in Annex 1, the parties will establish normal and friendly relations, in accordance with Article II (3).

Article II

The permanent boundary between Egypt and Israel is the recognized international boundary between Egypt and the former Mandated Territory of Palestine, as shown on the map at Annex 2 (*not reproduced here—Ed.*), without prejudice to the issue of the status of the Gaza Strip. The parties recognize this boundary as inviolable. Each will respect the territorial integrity of the other, including their territorial waters and airspace.

Article III

1. The parties will apply between them the provisions of the Charter of the UN and the principles of international law governing relations among states in times of peace.

In particular:

A. They recognize and will respect each other's sovereignty, territorial integrity and political independence.

B. They recognize and will respect each other's right to live in peace within their secure and recognized boundaries.

C. They will refrain from the threat of use of force, directly or indirectly, against each other and will settle all disputes between them by peaceful means.

2. Each party undertakes to ensure that acts or threats of belligerency, hostility, or violence do not originate from and are not committed from within its territory, or by any forces subject to its control or by any other forces stationed on its territory, against the population, citizens or property of the other party. Each party also undertakes to refrain from organizing, instigating, inciting, assisting or participating in acts or threats of belligerency, hostility, subversion or violence against the other party, anywhere, and undertakes to ensure that perpetrators of such acts are brought to justice.

3. The parties agree that the normal relationship established between them will include full recognition, diplomatic, economic and cultural relations, termination of economic boycotts and discriminatory barriers to the free movement of people and goods, and will guarantee the mutual enjoyment by citizens of the due process of law. The process by which they undertake to achieve such a relationship parallel to the implementation of other provisions of this treaty is set out in the annexed protocol (Annex 3).

Article IV

1. In order to provide maximum security for both parties on the basis of reciprocity, agreed security arrangements will be established including limited force zones in Egyptian and Israeli territory, and UN forces and observers, described in detail as to nature and timing in Annex 1, and other security arrangements the parties may agree upon.

2. The parties agree to the stationing of UN personnel in areas described in Annex 1, the parties agree not to request withdrawal of the UN personnel and that these personnel will not be removed unless such removal is approved by the Security Council of the UN, with the affirmative vote of the five members, unless the parties otherwise agree.

3. A joint commission will be established to facilitate the implementation of the treaty, as provided for in Annex 1.

4. The security arrangements provided for in paragraphs 1 and 2 of this article may at the request of either party be reviewed and amended by mutual agreement of the parties.

Article V

Article V deals with rights of passage of shipping through the Suez Canal, the Strait of Tiran and the Gulf of Aqaba.

Article VI

1. This treaty does not affect and shall not be interpreted as affecting in any way the rights and obligations of the parties under the Charter of the UN.

2. The parties undertake to fulfil in good faith their obligations under this treaty, without regard to action or inaction of any other party and independently of any instrument external to this treaty.

3. They further undertake to take all the necessary measures for the application in their relations of the provisions of the multilateral conventions to which they are parties. Including the submission of appropriate notification to the Secretary-General of the UN and other depositories of such conventions.

4. The parties undertake not to enter into any obligation in conflict with this treaty.

5. Subject to Article 103 of the UN Charter, in the event of a conflict between the obligations of the parties under the present treaty and any of their other obligations, the obligations under this treaty will be binding and implemented.

Article VII

1. Disputes arising out of the application or interpretation of this treaty shall be resolved by negotiations.

2. Any such disputes which cannot be settled by negotiations shall be resolved by conciliation or submitted to arbitration.

Article VIII

The parties agree to establish a claims commission for the mutual settlement of all financial claims.

Article IX

1. This treaty shall enter into force upon exchange of instruments of ratification.

2. This treaty supersedes the agreement between Egypt and Israel of September 1975.

3. All protocols, annexes, and maps attached to this treaty shall be regarded as an integral part hereof.

4. The treaty shall be communicated to the Secretary-General of the UN for registration in accordance with the provisions of Article 102 of the Charter of the UN.

Annex 1—military and withdrawal arrangements:

Israel will complete withdrawal of all its armed forces and civilians from Sinai within three years of the date of exchange of instruments of ratification of the treaty. The withdrawal will be accomplished in two phases, the first, within nine months, to a line east of Al Arish and Ras Muhammad; the second to behind the international boundary. During the three-year period, Egypt and Israel will maintain a specified military presence in four delineated security zones (see map—*not reproduced here—Ed.*), and the UN will continue its observation and supervisory functions. Egypt will exercise full sovereignty over evacuated territories in Sinai upon Israeli withdrawal. A joint commission will supervise the withdrawal, and security arrangements can be reviewed when either side asks but any change must be by mutual agreement.

Annex 2—maps (*not reproduced here*).

Annex 3—normalization of relations:

Ambassadors will be exchanged upon completion of the interim withdrawal. All discriminatory barriers and economic boycotts will be lifted and, not later than six months after the completion of the interim withdrawal, negotiations for a trade and commerce agreement will begin. Free movement of each other's nationals and transport will be allowed and both sides agree to promote 'good neighbourly relations'. Egypt will use the airfields left by Israel near Al Arish, Rafah, Ras an-Naqb and Sharm ash-Shaikh, only for civilian aircraft. Road, rail, postal, telephone, wireless and other forms of communications will be opened between the two countries on completion of interim withdrawal.

Exchange of letters

Negotiations on the West Bank and Gaza—Negotiations on autonomy for the West Bank and Gaza will begin within one month of the exchange of the instruments of ratification. Jordan will be invited to participate and the Egyptian and Jordanian delegations may include Palestinians from the West Bank and Gaza, or other Palestinians as mutually agreed. If Jordan decides not to take part, the negotiations will be held by Egypt and Israel. The objective of the negotiations is the establishment of a self-governing authority in the West Bank and Gaza 'in order to provide full autonomy to the inhabitants'.

Egypt and Israel hope to complete negotiations within one year so that elections can be held as soon as possible. The self-governing authority elected will be inaugurated within one month of the elections at which point the five year transitional period will begin. The Israeli military Government and its civilian administration will be withdrawn, Israeli armed forces withdrawn and the remaining forces redeployed 'into specified security locations'.

MAIN POINTS OF THE RESOLUTIONS PASSED BY THE ARAB LEAGUE COUNCIL IN BAGHDAD ON 27 MARCH 1979

—To withdraw the ambassadors of the Arab states from Egypt immediately.

—To recommend the severance of political and diplomatic relations with the Egyptian Government. The Arab governments will adopt the necessary measures to apply this recommendation within a maximum period of one month from the date of the issue of this decision, in accordance with the constitutional measures in force in each country.

—To consider the suspension of the Egyptian Government's membership in the Arab League as operative from the date of the Egyptian Government's signing of the peace treaty with the Zionist enemy. This means depriving it of all rights resulting from that membership.

—To make the city of Tunis, capital of the Tunisian Republic, the temporary headquarters of the Arab League, its general secretariat, the competent ministerial councils and the permanent technical committees, as of the date of signing of treaty between the Egyptian Government and the Zionist enemy. This shall be communicated to all international and regional organizations and bodies. They will also be informed that dealings with the Arab League will be conducted with its secretariat in its new temporary headquarters.

—To condemn the policy that the United States is practising regarding its role in concluding the Camp David agreements and the Egyptian-Israeli treaty.

The Arab League Council, at the level of Arab Foreign and Economy Ministers, has also decided the following:

—To halt all bank loans, deposits, guarantees or facilities, as well as all financial or technical contributions and aid by Arab Governments or their establishments to the Egyptian Government and its establishments as of the treaty-signing date.

—To ban the extension of economic aid by the Arab funds, banks and financial establishments within the framework of the Arab League and the joint Arab co-operation to the Egyptian Government and its establishments.

—The Arab governments and institutions shall refrain from purchasing the bonds, shares, postal orders and public credit loans that are issued by the Egyptian Government and its financial foundations.

—Following the suspension of the Egyptian Government's membership in the Arab League, its membership will also be suspended from the institutions, funds and organisations deriving from the Arab League.

—In view of the fact that the ill-omened Egyptian-Israeli treaty and its appendices have demonstrated Egypt's commitment to sell oil to Israel, the Arab states shall refrain from providing Egypt with oil and its derivatives.

—Trade exchanges with the Egyptian state and with private establishments that deal with the Zionist enemy shall be prohibited.

Source: *MEED Arab Report,* 11 April 1979, p. 9.

UN SECURITY COUNCIL RESOLUTION ON ISRAELI SETTLEMENTS
1 March 1980

The resolution, No. 465, was adopted unanimously by the 15 members of the Council. The USA repudiated its vote in favour of the resolution on 3 March 1980 (see below).

The Security Council, taking note of the reports of the Commission of the Security Council established under resolution 446 (1979) to examine the situation relating to the settlements in the Arab territories occupied since 1967, including Jerusalem, contained in documents S/13450 and S/13679,

—Taking note also of letters from the permanent representative of Jordan (S/13801) and the permanent representative of Morocco, Chairman of the Islamic Group (S/13802),

—Strongly deploring the refusal by Israel to co-operate with the Commission and regretting its formal rejection of resolutions 446 (1979) and 452 (1979),

—Affirming once more that the fourth Geneva Convention relative to the protection of civilian persons in time of war of 12 August 1949 is applicable to the Arab territories occupied by Israel since 1967, including Jerusalem,

—Deploring the decision of the Government of Israel to officially support Israeli settlement in the Palestinian and other Arab territories occupied since 1967,

—Deeply concerned over the practices of the Israeli authorities in implementing that settlement policy in the occupied Arab territories, including Jerusalem, and its consequences for the local Arab and Palestinian population,

—Taking into account the need to consider measures for the impartial protection of private and public land and property, and water resources,

—Bearing in mind the specific status of Jerusalem and, in particular, the need for protection and preservation of the unique spiritual and religious dimension of the holy places in the city,

—Drawing attention to the grave consequences which the settlement policy is bound to have on any attempt to reach a comprehensive, just and lasting peace in the Middle East,

—Recalling pertinent Security Council resolutions, specifically resolutions 237 (1967) of 14 June 1967, 252 (1968) of 21 May 1968, 267 (1969) of 3 July 1969, 271 (1969) of 15 September 1969 and 298 (1971) of 25 September 1971, as well as the consensus statement made by the President of the Security Council on 11 November 1976,

—Having invited Mr Fahd Qawasmah, Mayor of Al-Khalil (Hebron), in the occupied territories, to supply it with information pursuant to rule 39 of provisional rules of procedure,

1. Commends the work done by the Commission in preparing the report contained in document S/13679,

2. Accepts the conclusions and recommendations contained in the above-mentioned report of the Commission,

3. Calls upon all parties, particularly the Government of Israel, to co-operate with the Commission,

4. Strongly deplores the decision of Israel to prohibit the free travel of Mayor Fahd Qawasmah in order to appear before the Security Council, and requests Israel to permit his free travel to the United Nations headquarters for that purpose,

5. Determines that all measures taken by Israel to change the physical character, demographic composition, institutional structure or status of the Palestinian and other Arab territories occupied since 1967, including Jerusalem, or any part thereof, have no legal validity and that Israel's policy and practices of settling parts of its population and new immigrants in those territories constitute a flagrant violation of the Fourth Geneva Convention relative to the protection of civilian persons in time of war and also constitute a serious obstruction to achieving a comprehensive, just and lasting peace in the Middle East,

6. Strongly deplores the continuation and persistence of Israel in pursuing those policies and practices and calls upon the Government and people of Israel to rescind those measures, to dismantle the existing settlements and in particular to cease, on an urgent basis, the establishment, construction and planning of settlements in the Arab territories occupied since 1967, including Jerusalem,

7. Calls upon all states not to provide Israel with any assistance to be used specifically in connection with settlements in the occupied territories,

8. Requests the Commission to continue to examine the situation relating to settlements in the Arab territories occupied since 1967 including Jerusalem, to investigate the reported serious depletion of natural resources, particularly the water resources, with a view of ensuring the protection of those important natural resources of the territories under occupation, and to keep under close scrutiny the implementation of the present resolution,

9. Requests the Commission to report to the Security Council before 1 September 1980, and decides to convene at the earliest possible date thereafter in order to consider the report and the full implementation of the present resolution.

PRESIDENT CARTER'S STATEMENT REPUDIATING US VOTE IN SUPPORT OF UN SECURITY COUNCIL RESOLUTION 465

3 March 1980

I want to make it clear that the vote of the US in the Security Council of the UN does not represent a change in our position regarding the Israeli settlements in the occupied areas nor regarding the status of Jerusalem.

While our opposition to the establishment of the Israeli settlements is long-standing and well-known, we made strenuous efforts to eliminate the language with reference to the dismantling of settlements in the resolution. This call for dismantling was neither proper nor practical. We believe that the future disposition of the existing settlements must be determined during the current autonomy negotiations.

As to Jerusalem, we strongly believe that Jerusalem should be undivided with free access to the holy places for all faiths, and that its status should be determined in the negotiations for a comprehensive peace settlement.

The US vote in the UN was approved with the understanding that all references to Jerusalem would be deleted. The failure to communicate this clearly resulted in a vote in favour of the resolution rather than abstention.

EEC STATEMENT ON THE MIDDLE EAST

Issued in Venice, 13 June 1980

1. The heads of state and government and the ministers of foreign affairs held a comprehensive exchange of views on all aspects of the present situation in the Middle East, including the state of negotiations resulting from the agreements signed between Egypt and Israel in March 1979. They agreed that growing tensions affecting this region constitute a serious danger and render a comprehensive solution to the Israeli–Arab conflict more necessary and pressing than ever.

2. The nine member-states of the European Community consider that the traditional ties and common interests which link Europe to the Middle East oblige them to play a special role and now require them to work in a more concrete way towards peace.

3. In this regard, the nine countries of the Community base themselves on Security Council Resolutions 242 and 338 and the positions which they have expressed on several occasions, notably in their declarations of 29 June 1977, 19 September 1978, 26 March and 18 June 1979, as well as the speech made on their behalf on 25 September 1979, by the Irish Minister of Foreign Affairs at the thirty-fourth United Nations General Assembly.

4. On the bases thus set out, the time has come to promote the recognition and implementation of the two principles universally accepted by the international community: the right to existence and to security of all the states in the region, including Israel, and justice for all the peoples which implies the recognition of the legitimate rights of the Palestinian people.

5. All of the countries in the area are entitled to live in peace within secure, recognized and guaranteed borders. The necessary guarantees for a peace settlement should be provided by the United Nations by a decision of the Security Council and, if necessary, on the basis of other mutually agreed procedures. The Nine declared that they are prepared to participate within the framework of a comprehensive settlement in a system of concrete and binding international guarantees, including (guarantees) on the ground.

6. A just solution must finally be found to the Palestinian problem, which is not simply one of refugees. The Palestinian people, which is conscious of existing as such, must be placed in a position, by an appropriate process defined within the framework of the comprehensive peace settlement, to exercise fully its right to self-determination.

7. The achievement of these objectives requires the involvement and support of all the parties concerned in the peace settlement which the Nine are endeavouring to promote in keeping with the principles formulated in the declaration referred to above. These principles apply to all the parties concerned, and thus the Palestinian people, and to the PLO, which will have to be associated with the negotiations.

8. The Nine recognize the special importance of the role played by the question of Jerusalem for all the parties concerned. The Nine stress that they will not accept any unilateral initiative designed to change the status of Jerusalem and that any agreement on the city's status should guarantee freedom of access for everyone to the holy places.

9. The Nine stress the need for Israel to put an end to the territorial occupation which it has maintained since the conflict of 1967, as it has done for part of Sinai. They are deeply convinced that the Israeli settlements constitute a serious obstacle to the peace process in the Middle East. The Nine

consider that these settlements, as well as modifications in population and property in the occupied Arab territories, are illegal under international law.

10. Concerned as they are to put an end to violence, the Nine consider that only the renunciation of force or the threatened use of force by all the parties can create a climate of confidence in the area, and constitute a basic element for a comprehensive settlement of the conflict in the Middle East.

11. The Nine have decided to make the necessary contacts with all the parties concerned. The objective of these contacts would be to ascertain the position of the various parties with respect to the principles set out in this declaration and in the light of the result of this consultation process to determine the form which such an initiative on their part could take.

Subsequent UN Resolutions (General Assembly Resolutions ES-7/2, 29 July 1980; Security Council Resolution 478, 20 August 1980; General Assembly Resolutions 35-169 and 35-207 of 15 and 16 December 1980, etc.) have reaffirmed earlier resolutions and condemned the Israeli 'Jerusalem Bill' of July 1980, which stated explicitly that Jerusalem should be for ever the undivided Israeli capital and seat of government, parliament and judiciary. A UN General Assembly Resolution of 6 February 1982, condemned Israel's annexation of the Golan Heights. UN Resolutions in June 1982 condemned the Israeli invasion of Lebanon, and called for the withdrawal of Israeli forces.

THE FAHD PLAN

In August 1981 Crown Prince Fahd of Saudi Arabia launched an 8-point peace plan for the Middle East. During the remainder of 1981 some Arab states showed their support, but failure to agree on the 'Fahd Plan' caused the break-up of the Fez Arab Summit in November only a few hours after it had opened. The plan is as follows:

1. Israel to withdraw from all Arab territory occupied in 1967, including Arab Jerusalem.

2. Israeli settlements built on Arab land after 1967 to be dismantled.

3. A guarantee of freedom of worship for all religions in holy places.

4. An affirmation of the right of the Palestinian Arab people to return to their homes, and compensation for those who do not wish to return.

5. The West Bank and Gaza Strip to have a transitional period under the auspices of the United Nations for a period not exceeding several months.

6. An independent Palestinian state should be set up with Jerusalem as its capital.

7. All states in the region should be able to live in peace.

8. The UN or member-states of the UN to guarantee carrying-out of these principles.

THE REAGAN PLAN

After the Israeli invasion of Lebanon in June 1982, and the consequent evacuation of the PLO from Beirut, the US Government made strenuous efforts to continue the Camp David peace process and find a permanent solution that would ensure peace in the Middle East. On 1 September 1982 President Reagan outlined the following proposals in a broadcast to the nation from Burbank, California:

'. . . First, as outlined in the Camp David accords, there must be a period of time during which the Palestinian inhabitants of the West Bank and Gaza will have full autonomy over their own affairs. Due consideration must be given to the principle of self-government by the inhabitants of the territories and to the legitimate security concerns of the parties involved.

The purpose of the 5-year period of transition, which would begin after free elections for a self-governing Palestinian authority, is to prove to the Palestinians that they can run their own affairs and that such Palestinian autonomy poses no threat to Israel's security.

The United States will not support the use of any additional land for the purpose of settlements during the transition period. Indeed, the immediate adoption of a settlement freeze by Israel, more than any other action, could create the confidence needed for wider participation in these talks. Further settlement activity is in no way necessary for the security of Israel and only diminishes the confidence of the Arabs that a final outcome can be freely and fairly negotiated.

I want to make the American position well understood: The purpose of this transition period is the peaceful and orderly transfer of authority from Israel to the Palestinian inhabitants of the West Bank and Gaza. At the same time, such a transfer must not interfere with Israel's security requirements.

Beyond the transition period, as we look to the future of the West Bank and Gaza, it is clear to me that peace cannot be achieved by the formation of an independent Palestinian state in those territories. Nor is it achievable on the basis of Israeli sovereignty or permanent control over the West Bank and Gaza.

So the United States will not support the establishment of an independent Palestinian state in the West Bank and Gaza, and we will not support annexation or permanent control by Israel.

There is, however, another way to peace. The final status of these lands must, of course, be reached through the give-and-take of negotiations. But it is the firm view of the United States that self-government by the Palestinians of the West Bank and Gaza in association with Jordan offers the best chance for a durable, just and lasting peace.

We base our approach squarely on the principle that the Arab-Israeli conflict should be resolved through negotiations involving an exchange of territory for peace. This exchange is enshrined in UN Security Council Resolution 242, which is, in turn, incorporated in all its parts in the Camp David agreements. UN Resolution 242 remains wholly valid as the foundation stone of America's Middle East peace effort.

It is the United States' position that—in return for peace—the withdrawal provision of Resolution 242 applies to all fronts, including the West Bank and Gaza.

When the border is negotiated between Jordan and Israel, our view on the extent to which Israel should be asked to give up territory will be heavily affected by the extent of true peace and normalization and the security arrangements offered in return.

Finally, we remain convinced that Jerusalem must remain undivided, but its final status should be decided through negotiations.

In the course of the negotiations to come, the United States will support positions that seem to us fair and reasonable compromises and likely to promote a sound agreement. We will also put forward our own detailed proposals when we believe they can be helpful. And, make no mistake, the United States will oppose any proposal—from any party and at any point in the negotiating process—that threatens the security of Israel. America's commitment to the security of Israel is ironclad. And, I might add, so is mine.'

FEZ SUMMIT PEACE PROPOSAL

A further Fez Arab Summit was held in September 1982, and produced a set of peace proposals. The following excerpts are from the official English-language text of the final declaration on 9 September 1982, and are reproduced from American Arab Affairs, No 2:

I. The Israeli-Arab conflict:

The summit adopted the following principles:

1. The withdrawal of Israel from all Arab territories occupied in 1967 including Arab Al Qods (East Jerusalem).

2. The dismantling of settlements established by Israel on the Arab territories after 1967.

3. The guarantee of freedom of worship and practice of religious rites for all religions in the holy shrine.

4. The reaffirmation of the Palestinian people's right to self-determination and the exercise of its imprescriptible and inalienable national rights under the leadership of the Palestine Liberation Organization (PLO), its sole and legitimate representative, and the indemnification of all those who do not desire to return.

5. Placing the West Bank and Gaza Strip under the control of the United Nations for a transitory period not exceeding a few months.

6. The establishment of an independent Palestinian state with Al Qods as its capital.

7. The Security Council guarantees peace among all states of the region including the independent Palestinian state.

8. The Security Council guarantees the respect of these principles.

II. The Israeli aggression against Lebanon:

The summit was informed of the Lebanese Government's decision to put an end to the mission of the Arab deterrent forces in Lebanon. To this effect, the Lebanese and Syrian governments will start negotiations on measures to be taken in the light of the Israeli withdrawal from Lebanon.

JOINT JORDAN–PLO PEACE PROPOSALS

After a series of negotiations which began in January 1984, establishing a platform for joint action, King Hussein of Jordan and Yasser Arafat, Chairman of the PLO, announced their proposals for a Middle East peace settlement in Amman, on 23 February 1985. The failure of these proposals to further the peace process was acknowledged by King Hussein on 19 February 1986, when he abandoned Jordan's political collaboration with the PLO. The PLO did not formally abrogate the Amman agreement until the 18th session of the PNC in Algiers in April 1987. The following is the entire text of the joint agreement in an English-language version distributed by the Jordanian Government.

A PLAN OF JOINT ACTION

Proceeding from the spirit of the Fez summit resolutions approved by the Arab states and from UN resolutions on the Palestinian question, in accordance with international legitimacy, and proceeding from a common understanding on the building of a special relationship between the Jordanian and Palestinian peoples, the Government of the Hashemite Kingdom of Jordan and the Palestine Liberation Organization have agreed to work together with a view to a just and peaceful settlement of the Middle East crisis and to the termination of the occupation by Israel of the occupied Arab territories, including Jerusalem, on the basis of the following principles:

1. The return of all territories occupied in 1967 in exchange for a comprehensive peace, as stipulated in the resolutions of the United Nations and its Security Council.

2. The right of the Palestinian people to self-determination: in this respect the Palestinians will exercise their inalienable right to self-determination within the context of the formation of the proposed confederated states of Jordan and Palestine.

3. The solution of the Palestinian refugee problem in accordance with United Nations resolutions.

4. The solution of all aspects of the Palestinian question.

5. On this basis, negotiations should be undertaken under the auspices of an international conference to be attended by the five permanent members of the United Nations Security Council and all parties to the conflict, including the Palestine Liberation Organization, which is the sole legitimate representative of the Palestinian people, in the form of a joint delegation (a joint Jordanian–Palestinian delegation).

THE SHULTZ PLAN

At the beginning of February 1988 the Government of the USA announced a new plan for the resolution of the Palestine issue, which came to be known as the 'Shultz Plan', after the US Secretary of State, George Shultz. The presentation of the plan followed more than a year of diplomatic activity during which the idea of an international peace conference under the auspices of the UN, which had been agreed in principle by Shimon Peres, the Israeli Minister of Foreign Affairs, and King Hussein of Jordan, had won increasing support. The main provisions of the plan, as they were subsequently clarified, were for a six-month period of negotiations between Israel and a joint Jordanian/ Palestinian delegation, to determine the details of a transitional autonomy arrangement for the West Bank and the Gaza Strip, which would last for three years; during the transitional period a permanent settlement would be negotiated by the Israeli and Jordanian/Palestinian delegations; both sets of negotiations

would run concurrently with and, if necessary, with reference to, an international peace conference, involving the five permanent members of the UN Security Council and all the interested parties (including the Palestinians in a joint Jordanian/Palestinian delegation), which, like the separate Israeli-Jordanian/Palestinian negotiations, would be conducted on the basis of all the participants' acceptance of UN Security Council Resolutions 242 and 338, but would have no power to impose a settlement.

On 6 March 1988, the Israeli newspaper, Yedioth Aharonoth, published a photocopy of a letter from George Shultz to the Israeli Prime Minister, Itzhak Shamir, containing details of his peace proposals. The contents of the letter, identical versions of which were believed to have been delivered to the governments of Egypt, Jordan and Syria, were as follows:

Dear Mr. Prime Minister,

I set forth below the statement of understandings which I am convinced is necessary to achieve the prompt opening of negotiations on a comprehensive peace. This statement of understandings emerges from discussions held with you and other regional leaders. I look forward to the letter of reply of the government of Israel in confirmation of this statement.

The agreed objective is a comprehensive peace providing for the security of all the States in the region and for the legitimate rights of the Palestinian people.

Negotiations will start on an early date certain between Israel and each of its neighbors which is willing to do so. Those negotiations could begin by May 1, 1988. Each of these negotiations will be based on United Nations Security Council Resolutions 242 and 338, in all their parts. The parties to each bilateral negotiation will determine the procedure and agenda of their negotiation. All participants in the negotiations must state their willingness to negotiate with one another.

As concerns negotiations between the Israeli delegation and Jordanian-Palestinian delegation, negotiations will begin on arrangements for a transitional period, with the objective of completing them within six months. Seven months after transitional negotiations begin, final status negotiations will begin, with the objective of completing them within one year. These negotiations will be based on all the provisions and principles of the United Nations Security Council Resolution 242. Final status talks will start before the transitional period begins. The transitional period will begin three months after the conclusion of the transitional agreement and will last for three years. The United States will participate in both negotiations and will promote their rapid conclusion. In particular, the United States will submit a draft agreement for the parties' consideration at the outset of the negotiations on transitional arrangements.

Two weeks before the opening of negotiations, an international conference will be held. The Secretary-General of the United Nations will be asked to issue invitations to the parties involved in the Arab-Israeli conflict and the five permanent members of the United Nations Security Council. All participants in the conference must accept United Nations Security Council Resolutions 242 and 338, and renounce violence and terrorism. The parties to each bilateral negotiations may refer reports on the status of their negotiations to the conference, in a manner to be agreed. The conference will not be able to impose solutions or veto agreements reached.

Palestinian representation will be within the Jordanian-Palestinian delegation. The Palestinian issue will be addressed in the negotiations between the Jordanian-Palestinian and Israeli delegations. Negotiations between the Israeli delegation and the Jordanian-Palestinian delegation will proceed independently of any other negotiations.

This statement of understandings is an integral whole. The United States understands that your acceptance is dependent on the implementation of each element in good faith.

Sincerely yours,
George P. Shultz.

DECLARATION OF PALESTINIAN INDEPENDENCE

In November 1988, the 19th session of the Palestine National Council (PNC) culminated in the declaration 'in the name of God and the Palestinian Arab people' of the independent State of Palestine, with the Holy City of Jerusalem as its capital. The opportunity for the PLO to assert sovereignty over a specific area arose through the decision of King Hussein of Jordan, in July 1988, to sever Jordan's 'administrative and legal links' with the West Bank. The Declaration of Independence cited United Nations General Assembly Resolution 181 of 1947, which partitioned Palestine into two states, one Arab and one Jewish, as providing the legal basis for the right of the Palestinian Arab people to national sovereignty and independence. At the end of the session, the PNC issued a political statement. Details of the Declaration of Independence, and of the political statement, set out below, are taken from an unofficial English-language translation of the proceedings, distributed by the PLO.

'The National Council proclaims, in the name of God and the Palestinian Arab people, the establishment of the State of Palestine on our Palestinian land, with the Holy City of Jerusalem as its capital.

The State of Palestine is the state of Palestinians wherever they may be. In it they shall develop their national and cultural identity and enjoy full equality in rights. Their religious and political beliefs and their human dignity shall be safeguarded under a democratic parliamentary system of government built on the freedom of opinion; and on the freedom to form parties; and on the protection of the rights of the minority by the majority and respect of the decisions of the majority by the minority; and on social justice and equal rights, free of ethnic, religious, racial or sexual discrimination; and on a constitution that guarantees the rule of law and the independence of the judiciary; and on the basis of total allegiance to the centuries-old spiritual and civilizational Palestinian heritage of religious tolerance and coexistence.

The State of Palestine is an Arab state, an integral part of the Arab nation and of that nation's heritage, its civilization and its aspiration to attain its goals of liberation, development, democracy and unity. Affirming its commitment to the Charter of the League of Arab states and its insistence on the reinforcement of joint Arab action, the State of Palestine calls on the people of its nation to assist in the completion of its birth by mobilizing their resources and augmenting their efforts to end the Israeli occupation.

The State of Palestine declares its commitment to the principles and objectives of the United Nations, and to the Universal Declaration of Human Rights, and to the principles and policy of non-alignment.

The State of Palestine, declaring itself a peace-loving state committed to the principles of peaceful coexistence, shall strive with all states and peoples to attain a permanent peace built on justice and respect of rights, in which humanity's constructive talents can prosper, and creative competition can flourish, and fear of tomorrow can be abolished, for tomorrow brings nothing but security for the just and those who regain their sense of justice.

As it struggles to establish peace in the land of love and peace, the State of Palestine exhorts the United Nations to take upon itself a special responsibility for the Palestinian Arab people and their homeland; and exhorts the peace-loving, freedom-cherishing peoples and states of the world to help it attain its objectives and put an end to the tragedy its people are suffering by providing them with security and endeavouring to end the Israeli occupation of the Palestinian territories.

The State of Palestine declares its belief in the settlement of international and regional disputes by peaceful means in accordance with the Charter and resolutions of the United Nations; and its rejection of threats of force or violence or terrorism and the use of these against its territorial integrity and political independence or the territorial integrity of any other state, without prejudice to its natural right to defend its territory and independence.

The Palestine National Council resolves:

First: On the escalation and continuity of the *intifada*

A. To provide all the means and capabilities needed to escalate our people's *intifada* in various ways and on various levels to guarantee its continuation and intensification.

B. To support the popular institutions and organizations in the occupied Palestinian territories.

C. To bolster and develop the Popular Committees and other specialized popular and trade union bodies, including the attack

group and the popular army, with a view to expanding their role and increasing their effectiveness.

D. To consolidate the national unity that emerged and developed during the *intifada*.

E. To intensify efforts on the international level for the release of the detainees, the repatriation of the deportees, and the termination of the organized, official acts of repression and terrorism against our children, our women, our men, and our institutions.

F. To call on the United Nations to place the occupied Palestinian land under international supervision for the protection of our people and the termination of the Israeli occupation.

G. To call on the Palestinian people outside our homeland to intensify and increase their support, and to expand the family-assistance program.

H. To call on the Arab nation, its people, forces, institutions and governments, to increase their political, material and informational support of the *intifada*.

I. To call on all free and honorable people worldwide to stand by our people, our revolution, our *intifada* against the Israeli occupation, the repression, and the organized, fascist official terrorism to which the occupation forces and the armed fanatic settlers are subjecting our people, our universities, our institutions, our national economy, and our Islamic and Christian holy places.

Second: In the political field

Proceeding from the above, the Palestine National Council, being responsible to the Palestinian people, their national rights and their desire for peace as expressed in the Declaration of Independence issued on November 15, 1988; and in response to the humanitarian quest for international entente, nuclear disarmament and the settlement of regional conflicts by peaceful means, affirms the determination of the Palestine Liberation Organization to arrive at a political settlement of the Arab–Israeli conflict and its core, the Palestinian issue, in the framework of the UN Charter, the principles and rules of international legitimacy, the edicts of international law, the resolutions of the United Nations, the latest of which are Security Council Resolutions 605, 607 and 608, and the resolutions of the Arab summits, in a manner that assures the Palestinian Arab people's right to repatriation, self-determination and the establishment of their independent state on their national soil, and that institutes arrangements for the security and peace of all states in the region.

Towards the achievement of this, the Palestine National Council affirms:

1. The necessity of convening an international conference on the issue of the Middle East and its core, the Palestinian issue, under the auspices of the United Nations and with the participation of the permanent members of the Security Council and all parties to the conflict in the region, including, on an equal footing, the Palestine Liberation Organization, the sole legitimate representative of the Palestinian people; on the understanding that the international conference will be held on the basis of Security Council Resolutions 242 and 338 and the safeguarding of the legitimate national rights of the Palestinian people, foremost among which is the right to self-determination, in accordance with the principles and provisions of the UN Charter as they pertain to the right of peoples to self-determination, and the inadmissibility of the acquisition of others' territory by force or military conquest, and in accordance with the UN resolutions relating to the Palestinian issue.

2. The withdrawal of Israel from all the Palestinian and Arab territories it occupied in 1967, including Arab Jerusalem.

3. The annulment of all expropriation and annexation measures and the removal of the settlements established by Israel in the Palestinian and Arab territories since 1967.

4. Endeavouring to place the occupied Palestinian territories, including Arab Jerusalem, under the supervision of the United Nations for a limited period, to protect our people, to create an atmosphere conducive to the success of the proceedings of the international conference toward the attainment of a comprehensive political settlement and the achievement of peace and security for all on the basis of mutual consent, and to enable

the Palestinian state to exercise its effective authority in these territories.

5. The settlement of the issue of the Palestinian refugees in accordance with the pertinent United Nations resolutions.

6. Guaranteeing the freedom of worship and the right to engage in religious rites for all faiths in the holy place in Palestine.

7. The Security Council shall draw up and guarantee arrangements for the security of all states concerned and for peace between them, including the Palestinian state.

The Palestine National Council confirms its past resolutions that the relationship between the fraternal Jordanian and Palestinian peoples is a privileged one and that the future relationship between the states of Jordan and Palestine will be built on confederal foundations, on the basis of the two fraternal peoples' free and voluntary choice, in consolidation of the historic ties that bind them and the vital interests they hold in common.

The National Council also renews its commitment to the United Nations resolutions that affirm the right of peoples to resist foreign occupation, imperialism and racial discrimination, and their right to fight for their independence; and it once more announces its rejection of terrorism in all its forms, including state terrorism, emphasizing its commitment to the resolutions it adopted in the past on this subject, and to the resolutions of the Arab summit in Algiers in 1988, and to UN Resolutions 42/159 of 1967 and 61/40 of 1985, and to what was stated in this regard in the Cairo Declaration of 7/11/85.

Third: In the Arab and international fields

The Palestine National Council emphasizes the importance of the unity of Lebanon in its territory, its people and its institutions, and stands firmly against the attempts to partition the land and disintegrate the fraternal people of Lebanon. It further emphasizes the importance of the joint Arab effort to participate in a settlement of the Lebanese crisis that helps crystallize and implement solutions that preserve Lebanese unity. The Council also stresses the importance of consecrating the right of the Palestinians in Lebanon to engage in political and informational activity and to enjoy security and protection; and of working against all the forms of conspiracy and aggression that target them and their right to work and live; and of the need to secure the conditions that assure them the ability to defend themselves and provide them with security and protection.

The Palestine National Council affirms its solidarity with the Lebanese nationalist Islamic forces in their struggle against the Israeli occupation and its agents in the Lebanese South; expresses its pride in the allied struggle of the Lebanese and Palestinian peoples against the aggression and toward the termination of the Israeli occupation of parts of the South; and underscores the importance of bolstering this kinship between our people and the fraternal, combative people of Lebanon.

And on this occasion, the Council addresses a reverent salute to the long-suffering people of our camps in Lebanon and its South, who are enduring the aggression, massacres, murder, starvation, air raids, bombardments and sieges perpetrated against the Palestinian camps and Lebanese villages by the Israeli army, air force and navy, aided and abetted by hireling forces in the region; and it rejects the resettlement conspiracy, for the Palestinians' homeland is Palestine.

The Council emphasizes the importance of the Iraq–Iran cease-fire resolution toward the establishment of a permanent peace settlement between the two countries and in the Gulf Region; and calls for an intensification of the efforts being exerted to ensure the success of the negotiations toward the establishment of peace on stable and firm foundations; affirming, on this occasion, the price of the Palestinian Arab people and the Arab nation as a whole in the steadfastness and triumphs of fraternal Iraq as it defended the eastern gate of the Arab nation.

The National Council also expresses its deep pride in the stand taken by the peoples of our Arab nation in support of our Palestinian Arab people and of the Palestine Liberation Organization and of our people's *intifada* in the occupied homeland; and emphasizes the importance of fortifying the bonds of combat among the forces, parties and organizations of the Arab national liberation movement, in defense of the right of the Arab nation and its peoples to liberation, progress, democracy and unity. The Council calls for the adoption of all measures needed to reinforce the unity of struggle among all members of the Arab national liberation movement.

The Palestine National Council, as it hails the Arab states and thanks them for their support of our people's struggle, calls on them to honour the commitments they approved at the summit conference in Algiers in support of the Palestinian people and their blessed *intifada*. The Council, in issuing this appeal, expresses its great confidence that the leaders of the Arab nation will remain, as we have known them, a bulwark of support for Palestine and its people.

The Palestine National Council reiterates the desire of the Palestine Liberation Organization for Arab solidarity as the framework within which the Arab nation and its states can organize themselves to confront Israel's aggression and American support of that aggression, and within which Arab prestige can be enhanced and the Arab role strengthened to the point of influencing international policies to the benefit of Arab rights and causes.

The Palestine National Council expresses its deep gratitude to all the states and international forces and organizations that support the national rights of the Palestinians; affirms its desire to strengthen the bonds of friendship and co-operation with the Soviet Union, the People's (Republic of) China, the other socialist countries, the non-aligned states, the Islamic states, the African states, the Latin American states and the other friendly states; and notes with satisfaction the signs of positive evolution in the positions of some West European states and Japan in the direction of support for the rights of the Palestinian people, applauds this development, and urges intensified efforts to increase it.

The National Council affirms the fraternal solidarity of the Palestinian people and the Palestine Liberation Organization with the struggle of the peoples of Asia, Africa and Latin America for their liberation and the reinforcement of their independence; and condemns all American attempts to threaten the independence of the states of Central America and interfere in their affairs.

The Palestine National Council expresses the support of the Palestine Liberation Organization for the national liberation movements in South Africa and Namibia . . . .

The Council notes with considerable concern the growth of the Israeli forces of fascism and extremism and the escalation of their open calls for the implementation of the policy of annihilation and individual and collective expulsion of our people from their homeland, and calls for intensified efforts in all areas to confront this fascist peril. The Council at the same time expresses its appreciation of the role and courage of the Israeli peace forces as they resist and expose the forces of fascism, racism and aggression, support our people's struggle and their valiant *intifada* and back our people's right to self-determination and the establishment of an independent state. The Council confirms its past resolutions regarding the reinforcement and development of relations with these democratic forces.

The Palestine National Council also addresses itself to the American people, calling on them all to strive to put an end to the American policy that denies the Palestinian people's national rights, including their sacred right to self-determination, and urging them to work toward the adoption of policies that conform to the Declaration of Human Rights and the international conventions and resolutions and serve the quest for peace in the Middle East and security for all its peoples, including the Palestinian people.

The Council charges the Executive Committee with the task of completing the formation of the Committee for the Perpetuation of the Memory of the Martyr-Symbol Abu Jihad, which shall initiate its work immediately upon the adjournment of the Council.

The Council sends its greetings to the United Nations Committee on the Exercise of the Inalienable Rights of the Palestinian People, and to the fraternal and friendly international and non-governmental institutions and organizations, and to the journalists and media that have stood and still stand by our people's struggle and *intifada*.

The National Council expresses deep pain at the continued detention of hundreds of combatants from among our people in a number of Arab countries, strongly condemns their continued detention, and calls upon those countries to put an end to these abnormal conditions and release those fighters to play their role in the struggle.

In conclusion, the Palestine National Council affirms its complete confidence that the justice of the Palestinian cause and of the demands for which the Palestinian people are struggling will continue to draw increasing support from honorable and free people around the world; and also affirms its complete confidence in victory on the road to Jerusalem, the capital of our independent Palestinian state.'

THE ISRAELI PEACE INITIATIVE

In May 1989 the Government of Israel approved a four-point peace initiative for a resolution of the Middle East conflict, the details of which had first been announced during a meeting between US President George Bush and Israeli Prime Minister, Itzhak Shamir, in Washington on 6 April. Based largely on peace proposals made by Israeli Defence Minister, Itzhak Rabin, in January 1989, the new plan followed increased international diplomatic pressure on Israel to respond to the uprising in the Occupied Territories with constructive action to end the conflict. The main proposals of the Israeli initiative were that elections should be held in the West Bank and Gaza Strip in order to facilitate the formation of a delegation of appropriate interlocutors (i.e. non-PLO representatives) to take part in negotiations on a transitional settlement, when a self-ruling authority might be established. The transitional period would serve as a test of co-operation and coexistence and would be followed by negotiations on a final agreement in which Israel would be prepared to discuss any option presented; that Israel, Egypt and the USA should reconfirm their commitment to the Camp David Agreements of 1979; that the USA and Egypt should seek to persuade Arab countries to desist from hostility towards Israel; and that an international effort should be made to solve the 'humanitarian issue' of the inhabitants of refugee camps in Judaea, Samaria and the Gaza Strip. In July 1989 four amendments to the Israeli peace initiative were approved by the central committee of the Likud. These stipulated that residents of East Jerusalem would not be allowed to take part in the proposed elections in the West Bank and Gaza; that violent attacks by Palestinians must cease before elections could be held in the Occupied Territories; that Jewish settlement should continue in the Territories and that foreign sovereignty should not be conceded in any part of Israel; and that the establishment of a Palestinian state west of the River Jordan was out of the question, as were negotiations with the PLO. At the end of July, however, the Israeli Cabinet once again endorsed the peace initiative in its original form.

In September 1989 President Mubarak of Egypt sought ten assurances from the Israeli Government with regard to its peace initiative: (i) a commitment to accept the results of the elections proposed by the peace initiative; (ii) the vigilance of international observers at the elections; (iii) the granting of immunity to all elected representatives; (iv) the withdrawal of the Israel Defence Force from the balloting area; (v) a commitment by the Israeli Government to begin talks on the final status of the Occupied Territories on a specific date within three to five years; (vi) an end to Jewish settlement activities in the Occupied Territories; (vii) a ban on election propaganda; (viii) a ban on the entry of Israelis into the Occupied Territories on the day of the proposed elections; (ix) permission for residents of East Jerusalem to participate in the elections; (x) a commitment by the Israeli Government to the principle of exchanging land for peace. Mubarak also offered to host talks between Palestinian and Israeli delegations prior to the holding of the elections, but a proposal by the Labour component of the Israeli Government to accept his invitation was rejected by Israel's 'inner' Cabinet in October 1989. In the same month the US Secretary of State, James Baker, put forward a series of unofficial proposals which aimed to give new impetus to the Israeli peace initiative and the subsequent clarification proposed by President Mubarak. On the basis of its understanding that a dialogue between Israeli and Palestinian delegations would take place, the USA, through the 'Baker plan', sought assurances that Egypt could not and would not substitute itself for the Palestinians in any future negotiations, and that

both Israel and the Palestinians would take part in any future dialogue on the basis of the 'Shamir plan'.

THE 1991 MIDDLE EAST PEACE CONFERENCE

On 30 October 1991 the first, symbolic session of a Middle East peace conference, sponsored by the USA and the USSR and attended by Israeli, Syrian, Egyptian, Lebanese and Palestinian / Jordanian delegations, commenced in Madrid, Spain. The text of the invitation sent to the participants by the US and Soviet Presidents is reproduced from Al-Hayat, London

After extensive consultations with Arab states, Israel and the Palestinians, the US and the Soviet Union believe that an historic opportunity exists to advance the prospects for genuine peace throughout the region. The US and the Soviet Union are prepared to assist the parties to achieve a just, lasting and comprehensive peace settlement, through direct negotiations along two tracks, between Israel and the Palestinians, based on UN Security Council resolutions 242 and 338. The objective of this process is real peace.

Towards that end, the president of the US and the president of the USSR invite you to a peace conference, which their countries will co-sponsor, followed immediately by direct negotiations. The conference will be convened in Madrid on 30 October 1991.

President Bush and President Gorbachev request your acceptance of this invitation no later than 6.00pm Washington time, 23 October 1991, in order to ensure proper organisation and preparation of the conference.

Direct bilateral negotiations will begin four days after the opening of the conference. Those parties who wish to attend multilateral negotiations will convene two weeks after the opening of the conference to organise those negotiations. The co-sponsors believe that those negotiations should focus on regionwide issues such as arms control and regional security, water, refugee issues, environment, economic development, and other subjects of mutual interest.

The co-sponsors will chair the conference which will be held at ministerial level. Governments to be invited include Israel, Syria, Lebanon and Jordan. Palestinians will be invited and attend as part of a joint Jordanian-Palestinian delegation. Egypt will be invited to the conference as a participant. The EC will be a participant in the conference alongside the US and Soviet Union and will be represented by its presidency. The GCC will be invited to send its secretary-general to the conference as an observer, and GCC member states will be invited to participate in organising the negotiations on multilateral issues. The UN will be invited to send an observer, representing the secretary-general.

DECLARATION OF PRINCIPLES ON PALESTINIAN SELF-RULE

13 September 1993

The Government of the State of Israel and the Palestinian team (in the Jordanian-Palestinian delegation to the Middle East Peace Conference) (the 'Palestinian Delegation') representing the Palestinian people, agree that it is time to put an end to decades of confrontation and conflict, recognize their mutual legitimate and political rights, and strive to live in peaceful coexistence and mutual dignity and security and achieve a just, lasting and comprehensive peace settlement and historic reconciliation through the agreed political process.

Accordingly, the two sides agree to the following principles:

Article I

Aim of the negotiations

The aim of the Israeli-Palestinian negotiations within the current Middle East peace process is, among other things, to establish a Palestinian Interim Self-Government Authority, the elected Council, (the 'Council') for the Palestinian people in the West Bank and the Gaza Strip, for a transitional period not exceeding five years, leading to a permanent settlement based on Security Council Resolutions 242 and 338.

It is understood that the interim arrangements are an integral part of the overall peace process and that final status negotiations will lead to the implementation of Security Council Resolutions 242 and 338.

Article II

Framework for the interim period

The agreed framework for the interim period is set forth in the Declaration of Principles.

Article III

Elections

1. In order that the Palestinian people in the West Bank and Gaza Strip may govern themselves according to democratic principles, direct, free and general political elections will be held for the Council under agreed supervision and international observation, while the Palestinian police will ensure public order.

2. An agreement will be concluded on the exact mode and conditions of the elections in accordance with the protocol attached as Annex I, with the goal of holding the elections not later than nine months after the entry into force of this Declaration of Principles.

3. These elections will constitute a significant interim preparatory step toward the realization of the legitimate rights of the Palestinian people and their just requirements.

Article IV

Jurisdiction of the Council will cover West Bank and Gaza Strip territory, except for issues that will be negotiated in the permanent status negotiations. The two sides view the West Bank and the Gaza Strip as a single territorial unit, whose integrity will be preserved during the interim period.

Article V

Transitional period and permanent status negotiations

1. The five-year transitional period will begin upon the withdrawal from the Gaza Strip and Jericho area.

2. Permanent status negotiations will commence as soon as possible, but not later than the beginning of the third year of the interim period, between the Government of Israel and the Palestinian people representatives.

3. It is understood that these negotiations shall cover remaining issues, including Jerusalem, refugees, settlements, security arrangements, borders, relations and co-operation with other neighbours, and other issues of common interest.

4. The two parties agree that the outcome of the permanent status negotiations should not be prejudiced or pre-empted by agreements reached for the interim period.

Article VI

Preparatory transfer of powers and responsibilities

1. Upon the entry into force of this Declaration of Principles and the withdrawal from the Gaza Strip and Jericho area, a transfer of authority from the Israeli military government and its Civil Administration to the authorized Palestinians for this task, as detailed herein, will commence. This transfer of authority will be of preparatory nature until the inauguration of the Council.

2. Immediately after the entry into force of this Declaration of Principles and the withdrawal from the Gaza Strip and Jericho area, with the view to promoting economic development in the West Bank and Gaza Strip, authority will be transferred to the Palestinians in the following spheres: education and culture, health, social welfare, direct taxation, and tourism. The Palestinian side will commence in building the Palestinian police force, as agreed upon. Pending the inauguration of the Council, the two parties may negotiate the transfer of additional powers and responsibilities as agreed upon.

Article VII

Interim agreement

1. The Israeli and Palestinian delegations will negotiate an agreement on the interim period (the 'Interim Agreement').

2. The Interim Agreement shall specify, among other things, the structure of the Council, the number of its members, and the transfer of powers and responsibilities from the Israeli military government and its Civil Administration to the Council. The Interim Agreement shall also specify the Council's executive authority, legislative authority in accordance with Article IX below, and the independent Palestinian judicial organs.

3. The Interim Agreement shall include arrangements, to be implemented upon the inauguration of the Council, for the assumption by the Council of all of the powers and responsibilities transferred previously in accordance with Article VI above.

4. In order to enable the Council to promote economic growth, upon its inauguration, the Council will establish, among other things, a Palestinian Electricity Authority, a Gaza Sea Port Authority, a Palestinian Development Bank, a Palestinian Export Promotion Board, a Palestinian Environmental Authority, a Palestinian Land Authority and a Palestinian Water Administration Authority, and any other authorities agreed upon, in accordance with the Interim Agreement that will specify their powers and responsibilities.

5. After the inauguration of the Council, the Civil Administration will be dissolved, and the Israeli military government will be withdrawn.

Article VIII

Public order and security

In order to guarantee public order and internal security for the Palestinians of the West Bank and the Gaza Strip, the Council will establish a strong police force, while Israel will continue to carry the responsibility for defending against external threats, as well as the responsibility for overall security of the Israelis to protect their internal security and public order.

Article IX

Laws and military orders

1. The Council will be empowered to legislate, in accordance with the Interim Agreement, within all authorities transferred to it.

2. Both parties will review jointly laws and military orders presently in force in remaining spheres.

Article X

Joint Israeli-Palestinian liaison committee

In order to provide for a smooth implementation of this Declaration of Principles and any subsequent agreements pertaining to the interim period, upon the entry into force of this Declaration of Principles, a Joint Israeli-Palestinian Liaison Committee will be established in order to deal with issues requiring co-ordination, other issues of common interest, and disputes.

Article XI

Israeli-Palestinian co-operation in economic fields

Recognizing the mutual benefit of co-operation in promoting the development of the West Bank, the Gaza Strip and Israel, upon the entry into force of this Declaration of Principles, an Israeli-Palestinian Economic Co-operation Committee will be established in order to develop and implement in a co-operative manner the programmes identified in the protocols attached as Annex III and Annex IV.

Article XII

Liaison and co-operation with Jordan and Egypt

The two parties will invite the Governments of Jordan and Egypt to participate in establishing further liaison and co-operation arrangements between the Government of Israel and the Palestinian representatives, on one hand, and the Governments of Jordan and Egypt, on the other hand, to promote co-operation between them. These arrangements will include the constitution of a Continuing Committee that will decide by agreement on the modalities of the admission of persons displaced from the West Bank and Gaza Strip in 1967, together with necessary measures to prevent disruption and disorder. Other matters of common concern will be dealt with by this Committee.

Article XIII

Redeployment of Israeli forces

1. After the entry into force of this Declaration of Principles, and not later than the eve of elections for the Council, a redeploy-

ment of Israeli military forces in the West Bank and the Gaza Strip will take place, in addition to withdrawal of Israeli forces carried out in accordance with Article XIV.

2. In redeploying its military forces, Israel will be guided by the principle that its military forces should be redeployed outside the populated areas.

3. Further redeployments to specified locations will be gradually implemented commensurate with the assumption of responsibility for public order and internal security by the Palestinian police force pursuant to Article VIII above.

Article XIV

Israeli withdrawal from the Gaza Strip and Jericho area

Israel will withdraw from the Gaza Strip and Jericho area, as detailed in the protocol attached as Annex II.

Article XV

Resolution of disputes

1. Disputes arising out of the application or interpretation of this Declaration of Principles, or any subsequent agreements pertaining to the interim period, shall be resolved by negotiations through the Joint Liaison Committee to be established pursuant to Article X above.

2. Disputes which cannot be settled by negotiations may be resolved by a mechanism of conciliation to be agreed upon by the parties.

3. The parties may agree to submit to arbitration disputes relating to the interim period, which cannot be settled through conciliation. To this end, upon the agreement of both parties, the parties will establish an Arbitration Committee.

Article XVI

Israel-Palestinian co-operation concerning regional programs

Both parties view the multilateral working groups as an appropriate instrument for promoting a 'Marshall Plan,' the regional programs and other programs, including special programs for the West Bank and Gaza Strip, as indicated in the protocol atttached as Annex IV.

Article XVII

Miscellaneous provisions

1. This Declaration of Principles will enter into force one month after its signing.

2. All protocols annexed to this Declaration of Principles and Agreed Minutes pertaining thereto shall be regarded as an integral part hereof.

Annex 1—protocol on the mode and conditions of elections

1. Palestinians of Jerusalem who live there will have the right to participate in the election process, according to an agreement between the two sides.

2. In addition, the election agreement should cover, among other things, the following issues:

   a. the system of elections,

   b. the mode of the agreed supervision and international observation and their personal composition, and

   c. rules and regulations regarding election campaign, including agreed arrangements for the organizing of mass media, and the possibility of licensing a broadcasting and TV station.

3. The future status of displaced Palestinians who were registered on 4th June 1967 will not be prejudiced because they are unable to participate in the election process due to practical reasons.

Annex 2—protocol on withdrawal of Israeli forces from the Gaza Strip and Jericho Area

1. The two sides will conclude and sign within two months from the date of entry into force of this Declaration of Principles, an agreement on the withdrawal of Israeli military forces from the Gaza Strip and Jericho area. This agreement will include comprehensive arrangements to apply in the Gaza Strip and the Jericho area subsequent to the Israeli withdrawal.

2. Israel will implement an accelerated and scheduled withdrawal of Israeli military forces from the Gaza Strip and Jericho area, beginning immediately with the signing of the agreement on the Gaza Strip and Jericho area and to be completed within a period not exceeding four months after the signing of this agreement.

3. The above agreement will include, among other things:

   a. Arrangements for a smooth and peaceful transfer of authority from the Israeli military government and its Civil Administration to the Palestinian representatives.

   b. structure, powers and responsibilities of the Palestinian authority in these areas, except, external security, settlements, Israelis, foreign relations, and other subjects mutually agreed upon.

   c. Arrangements for assumption of internal security and public order by the Palestinian police force consisting of police officers recruited locally and from abroad (holding Jordanian passports and Palestinian documents issued by Egypt). Those who will participate in the Palestinian police force coming from abroad should be trained as police and police officers.

   d. A temporary international or foreign presence, as agreed upon.

   e. Establishment of a joint Palestinian-Israeli co-ordination and co-operation committee for mutual security purposes.

   f. An economic development and stablization program, including the establishment of an Emergency Fund, to encourage foreign investment, and financial and economic support. Both sides will co-ordinate and co-operate jointly and unilaterally with regional and international parties to support these aims.

   g. Arrangements for a safe passage for persons and transportation between the Gaza Strip and Jericho area.

4. The above agreement will include arrangements for co-ordination between both parties regarding passages:

   a. Gaza – Egypt; and

   b. Jericho – Jordan.

5. The offices responsible for carrying out the powers and responsibilities of the Palestinian authority under this Annex II and Article VI of the Declaration of Principles will be located in the Gaza Strip and in the Jericho area pending the inauguration of the Council.

6. Other than these agreed arrangements, the status of the Gaza Strip and Jericho area will continue to be an integral part of the West Bank and Gaza Strip, and will not be changed in the interim period.

PROTOCOL ON ISRAELI-PALESTINIAN CO-OPERATION IN ECONOMIC AND DEVELOPMENT PROGRAMS

The two sides agree to establish an Israeli-Palestinian Continuing Committee for Economic Co-operation, focusing, among other things, on the following:

1. Co-operation in the field of water, including a Water Development Program prepared by experts from both sides, which will also specify the mode of co-operation in the management of water resources in the West Bank and Gaza Strip, and will include proposals for studies and plans on water rights of each party, as well as on the equitable utilization of joint water resources for implementation in and beyond the interim period.

2. Co-operation in the field of electricity, including an Electricity Development Program, which will also specify the mode of co-operation for the production, maintenance, purchase and sale of electricity resources.

3. Co-operation in the field of energy, including an Energy Development Program, which will provide for the exploitation of oil and gas for industrial purposes, particularly in the Gaza Strip and in the Negev, and will encourage further joint exploitation of other energy resources. This Program may also provide for the construction of a Petrochemical industrial complex in the Gaza Strip and the construction of oil and gas pipelines.

4. Co-operation in the field of finance, including a Financial Development and Action Program for the encouragement of

international investment in the West Bank and the Gaza Strip, and in Israel, as well as the establishment of a Palestinian Development Bank.

5. Co-operation in the fields of transport and communications, including a Program, which will define guidelines for the establishment of a Gaza Sea Port Area, and will provide for the establishing of transport and communications lines to and from the West Bank and the Gaza Strip to Israel and to other countries. In addition, this Program will provide for carrying out the necessary construction of roads, railways, communications lines, etc.

6. Co-operation in the field of trade, including studies, and Trade Promotion Programs, which will encourage local, regional and inter-regional trade, as well as a feasibility study of creating free trade zones in the Gaza Strip and in Israel, mutual access to these zones, and co-operation in other areas related to trade and commerce.

7. Co-operation in the field of industry, including industrial Development Programs, which will provide for the establishment of joint Israeli-Palestinian Research and Development Centers, will promote Palestinian-Israeli joint ventures, and provide guidelines for co-operation in the textile, food, pharmaceutical, electronics, diamonds, computer and science-based industries.

8. A program for co-operation in, and regulation of, labour relations and co-operation in social welfare issues.

9. A Human Resources Development and Co-operation Plan, providing for joint Israeli-Palestinian workshops and seminars, and for the establishment of joint vocational training centres, research institutes and data banks.

10. An Environmental Protection Plan, providing for joint and/or co-ordinated measures in this sphere.

11. A program for developing co-ordination and co-operation in the field of communication and media.

12. Any other programs of mutual interest.

PROTOCOL ON ISRAELI-PALESTINIAN CO-OPERATION CONCERNING REGIONAL DEVELOPMENT PROGRAMS

1. The two sides will co-operate in the context of the multilateral peace efforts in promoting a Development Program for the region, including the West Bank and the Gaza Strip, to be initiated by the G-7. The parties will request the G-7 to seek the participation in this program of other interested states, such as members of the Organization for Economic Co-operation and Development, regional Arab states and institutions, as well as members of the private sector.

2. The Development Program will consist of two elements:
   a) an Economic Development Program for the West Bank and the Gaza Strip;
   b) a Regional Economic Development Program

A. The Economic Development Program for the West Bank and the Gaza Strip will consist of the following elements:
   (1) A Social Rehabilitation Program, including a Housing and Construction Program.
   (2) A Small and Medium Business Development Plan.
   (3) An Infrastructure Development Program (water, electricity, transportation and communications, etc.)
   (4) A Human Resources Plan.
   (5) Other programs.

B. The Regional Economic Development Program may consist of the following elements:
   (1) The establishment of a Middle East Development Fund, as a first step, and a Middle East Development Bank, as a second step.
   (2) The development of a joint Israeli-Palestinian-Jordanian Plan for co-ordinated exploitation of the Dead Sea area.
   (3) The Mediterranean Sea (Gaza)—Dead Sea Canal.
   (4) Regional Desalinization and other water development projects.
   (5) A regional plan for agricultural development, including a co-ordinated regional effort for the prevention of desertification.
   (6) Interconnection of electricity grids.
   (7) Regional co-operation for the transfer, distribution and industrial exploitation of gas, oil and other energy resources.
   (8) A regional Tourism, Transportation and Telecommunications Development Plan.
   (9) Regional co-operation in other spheres.

3. The two sides will encourage the multilateral working groups, and will co-ordinate towards its success. The two parties will encourage international activities, as well as pre-feasibility and feasibility studies, within the various multilateral working groups.

AGREED MINUTES TO THE DECLARATION OF PRINCIPLES ON INTERIM SELF-GOVERNMENT ARRANGEMENTS

A. General Understandings and Agreements

Any powers and responsibilites transferred to the Palestinians pursuant to the Declaration of Principles prior to the inauguration of the Council will be subject to the same principles pertaining to Article IV, as set out in these Agreed Minutes below.

B. Specific Understandings and Agreements

Article IV

It is understood that:

1. Jurisdiction of the Council will cover West Bank and Gaza Strip territory, except for issues that will be negotiated in the permanent status negotiations: Jerusalem, settlements, military locations and Israelis.

2. The Council's jurisdiction will apply with regard to the agreed powers, responsibilities, spheres and authorities transferred to it.

Article VI (2)

It is agreed that the transfer of authority will be as follows:

(1) The Palestinian side will inform the Israeli side of the names of the authorized Palestinians who will assume the powers, authorities and responsibilities that will be transferred to the Palestinians according to the Declaration of Principles in the following fields: education and culture, health, social welfare, direct taxation, tourism, and any other authorities agreed upon.

(2) It is understood that the rights and obligations of these offices will not be affected.

(3) Each of the spheres described above will continue to enjoy existing budgetary allocations in accordance with arrangements to be mutually agreed upon. These arrangements also will provide for the necessary adjustments required in order to take into account the taxes collected by the direct taxation office.

(4) Upon the execution of the Declaration of Principles, the Israeli and Palestinian delegations will immediately commence negotiations on a detailed plan for the transfer of authority on the above offices in accordance with the above understandings.

Article VII (2)

The Interim Agreement will also include arrangements for co-ordination and co-operation.

Article VII (5)

The withdrawal of the military government will not prevent Israel from exercising the powers and responsibilities not transferred to the Council.

Article VIII

It is understood that the Interim Agreement will include arrangements for co-operation and co-ordination between the two parties in this regard. It is also agreed that the transfer of powers and responsibilities to the Palestinian police will be accomplished in a phased manner, as agreed in the Interim Agreement.

Article X

It is agreed that, upon the entry into force of the Declaration of Principles, the Israeli and Palestinian delegations will exchange the names of the individuals designated by them as members of the Joint Israeli-Palestinian Liaison Committee.

It is further agreed that each side will have an equal number of members in the Joint Committee. The Joint Committee will reach decisions by agreement. The Joint Committee may add other technicians and experts, as necessary. The Joint Committee will decide on the frequency and place or places of its meetings.

Annex II

It is understood that, subsequent to the Israeli withdrawal, Israel will continue to be responsible for external security, and for internal security and public order of settlements and Israelis. Israeli military forces and civilians may continue to use roads freely within the Gaza Strip and the Jericho area.

Article XVI

Israeli-Palestinian Co-operation Concerning Regional Programs

Both parties view the multilateral working groups as an appropriate instrument for promoting a 'Marshall Plan,' the regional programs and other programs, including special programs for the West Bank and Gaza Strip, as indicated in the protocol attached as Annex IV.

Article XVII

Miscellaneous Provisions

1. This Declaration of Principles will enter into force one month after its signing.

2. All protocols annexed to this Declaration of Principles and Agreed Minutes pertaining thereto shall be regarded as an integral part hereof.

THE CAIRO AGREEMENT ON THE GAZA STRIP AND JERICHO
4 May 1994

The Government of the State of Israel and the Palestine Liberation Organization (hereinafter 'the PLO'), the representative of the Palestinian people;

Preamble

Within the framework of the Middle East peace process initiated at Madrid in October 1991;

Reaffirming their determination to live in peaceful co-existence, mutual dignity and security, while recognizing their mutual legitimate and political rights;

Reaffirming their desire to achieve a just, lasting and comprehensive peace settlement through the agreed political process;

Reaffirming their adherence to the mutual recognition and commitments expressed in the letters dated September 9, 1993, signed by and exchanged between the Prime Minister of Israel and the Chairman of the PLO;

Reaffirming their understanding that the interim self-government arrangements, including the arrangements to apply in the Gaza Strip and the Jericho Area contained in this Agreement, are an integral part of the whole peace process and that the negotiations on the permanent status will lead to the implementation of Security Council Resolutions 242 and 338;

Desirous of putting into effect the Declaration of Principles on Interim Self-Government Arrangements signed at Washington, D.C. on September 13, 1993, and the agreed minutes thereto (hereinafter 'The Declaration of Principles'), and in particular the protocol on withdrawal of Israeli forces from the Gaza Strip and the Jericho Area:

Hereby agree to the following arrangements regarding the Gaza Strip and the Jericho Area:

Article I
Definitions

For the purpose of this Agreement:
a. The Gaza Strip and the Jericho Area are delineated on Map Nos. 1 and 2 attached to this Agreement (*Maps not reproduced—Ed.*);
b. 'The settlements' means the Gush Katif and Erez settlement areas, as well as the other settlements in the Gaza Strip, as shown on attached Map No. 1;
c. 'The military installation area' means the Israeli military installation area along the Egyptian border in the Gaza Strip, as shown on Map No. 1; and
d. The term 'Israelis' shall also include Israeli statutory agencies and corporations registered in Israel.

Article II
Scheduled withdrawal of Israeli military forces

1. Israel shall implement an accelerated and scheduled withdrawal of Israeli military forces from the Gaza Strip and from the Jericho Area to begin immediately with the signing of this Agreement. Israel shall complete such withdrawal within three weeks from this date.

2. Subject to the arrangements included in the Protocol concerning withdrawal of Israeli military forces and security arrangements attached as Annex I, the Israeli withdrawal shall include evacuating all military bases and other fixed installations to be handed over to the Palestinian Police, to be established pursuant to Article IX below (hereinafter 'the Palestinian Police').

3. In order to carry out Israel's responsibility for external security and for internal security and public order of settlements and Israelis, Israel shall, concurrently with the withdrawal, redeploy its remaining military forces to the settlements and the military installation area, in accordance with the provisions of this Agreement. Subject to the provisions of this Agreement, this redeployment shall constitute full implementation of Article XIII of the Declaration of Principles with regard to the Gaza Strip and the Jericho Area only.

4. For the purposes of this Agreement, 'Israeli military forces' may include Israeli police and other Israeli security forces.

5. Israelis, including Israeli military forces, may continue to use roads freely within the Gaza Strip and the Jericho Area. Palestinians may use public roads crossing the settlements freely, as provided for in Annex I.

6. The Palestinian Police shall be deployed and shall assume responsibility for public order and internal security of Palestinians in accordance with this Agreement and Annex I.

Article III
Transfer of authority

1. Israel shall transfer authority as specified in this Agreement from the Israeli military government and its Civil Administration to the Palestinian Authority, hereby established, in accordance with Article V of this Agreement, except for the authority that Israel shall continue to excercise as specified in this Agreement.

2. As regards the transfer and assumption of authority in civil spheres, powers and responsibilities shall be transferred and assumed as set out in the Protocol concerning civil affairs attached as Annex II.

3. Arrangements for a smooth and peaceful transfer of the agreed powers and responsibilities are set out in Annex II.

4. Upon the completion of the Israeli withdrawal and the transfer of powers and responsibilities as detailed in Paragraphs 1 and 2 above and in Annex II, the Civil Administration in the Gaza Strip and the Jericho Area will be dissolved and the Israeli military government will be withdrawn. The withdrawal of the military government shall not prevent it from continuing to excercise the powers and responsibilities specified in this Agreement.

5. A joint Civil Affairs Co-ordination and Co-operation Committee (hereinafter 'the CAC') and two joint regional civil affairs subcommittees for the Gaza Strip and the Jericho Area respectively shall be established in order to provide for co-ordination and co-operation in civil affairs between the Palestinian Authority and Israel, as detailed in Annex II.

6. The offices of the Palestinian Authority shall be located in the Gaza Strip and the Jericho Area pending the inauguration of the council to be elected pursuant to the Declaration of Principles.

Article IV
Structure and composition of the Palestinian Authority

1. The Palestinian Authority will consist of one body of 24 members which shall carry out and be responsible for all the legislative and executive powers and responsibilities transferred to it under this Agreement, in accordance with this article, and shall be responsible for the excercise of judicial functions in accordance with Article VI, subparagraph 1.b of this Agreement.

2. The Palestinian Authority shall administer the departments transferred to it and may establish, within its jurisdiction, other departments and subordinate administrative units as necessary for the fulfilment of its responsibilities. It shall determine its own internal procedures.

3. The PLO shall inform the Government of Israel of the names of the members of the Palestinian Authority and any change of members. Changes in the membership of the Palestinian Authority will take effect upon an exchange of letters between the PLO and the Government of Israel.

4. Each member of the Palestinian Authority shall enter into office upon undertaking to act in accordance with this Agreement.

Article V
Jurisdiction

1. The authority of the Palestinian Authority encompasses all matters that fall within its territorial, functional and personal jurisdiction, as follows:
   a. The territorial jurisdiction covers the Gaza Strip and the Jericho Area territory, as defined in Article I, except for settlements and the military installation area.
   Territorial jurisdiction shall include land, subsoil and territorial waters, in accordance with the provisions of this Agreement.
   b. The functional jurisdiction encompasses all powers and responsibilities as specified in this Agreement. This jurisdiction does not include foreign relations, internal security and public order of settlements and the military installation area and Israelis, and external security.
   c. The personal jurisdiction extends to all persons within the territorial jurisdiction referred to above, except for Israelis, unless otherwise provided in this Agreement.

2. The Palestinian Authority has, within its authority, legislative, executive and judicial powers and responsibilities, as provided for in this Agreement.

3.a. Israel has authority over the settlements, the military installation area, Israelis, external security, internal security and public order of settlements, the military installation area and Israelis, and those agreed powers and responsibilities specified in this Agreement.
   b. Israel shall exercise its authority through its military government, which for that end, shall continue to have the necessary legislative, judicial and executive powers and responsibilities, in accordance with international law. This provision shall not derogate from Israel's applicable legislation over Israelis in personam.

4. The exercise of authority with regard to the electromagnetic sphere and airspace shall be in accordance with the provisions of this Agreement.

5. The provisions of this article are subject to the specific legal arrangements detailed in the Protocol concerning legal matters attached as Annex III. Israel and the Palestinian Authority may negotiate further legal arrangements.

6. Israel and the Palestinian Authority shall co-operate on matters of legal assistance in criminal and civil matters through the legal subcommittee of the CAC.

Article VI
Powers and responsibilities of the Palestinian Authority

1. Subject to the provisions of this Agreement, the Palestinian Authority, within its jurisdiction:
   a. has legislative powers as set out in Article VII of this Agreement, as well as executive powers;
   b. will administer justice through an independent judiciary:
   c. will have, inter alia, power to formulate policies, supervise their implementation, employ staff, establish departments, authorities and institutions, sue and be sued and conclude contracts; and
   d. will have, inter alia, the power to keep and administer registers and records of the population, and issue certificates, licenses and documents.

2.a. In accordance with the Declaration of Principles, the Palestinian Authority will not have powers and responsibilities in the sphere of foreign relations, which sphere includes the establishment abroad of embassies, consulates or other types of foreign missions and posts or permitting their establishment in the Gaza Strip or the Jericho Area, the appointment of or admission of diplomatic and consular staff, and the exercise of diplomatic functions.
   b. Notwithstanding the provisions of this paragraph, the PLO may conduct negotiations and sign agreements with states or international organizations for the benefit of the Palestinian Authority in the following cases only:
      (1) Economic agreements, as specifically provided in Annex IV of this Agreement;
      (2) Agreements with donor countries for the purpose of implementing arrangements for the provision of assistance to the Palestinian Authority;
      (3) Agreements for the purpose of implementing the regional development plans detailed in Annex IV of the Declaration of Principles or in agreements entered into in the framework of the multilateral negotiations; and
      (4) Cultural, scientific and education agreements.
   c. Dealings between the Palestinian Authority and representatives of foreign states and international organizations, as well as the establishment in the Gaza Strip and the Jericho Area of representative offices other than those described in subparagraph 2.a, above, for the purpose of implementing the agreements referred to in subparagraph 2.b above, shall not be considered foreign relations.

Article VII
Legislative powers of the Palestinian Authority

1. The Palestinian Authority will have the power, within its jurisdiction, to promulgate legislation, including basic laws, laws, regulations and other legislative acts.

2. Legislation promulgated by the Palestinian Authority shall be consistent with the provisions of this Agreement.

3. Legislation promulgated by the Palestinian Authority shall be communicated to a legislation subcommittee to be established by the CAC (hereinafter 'the Legislation Subcommittee'). During a period of 30 days from the communication of the legislation, Israel may request that the Legislation Subcommittee decide whether such legislation exceeds the jurisdiction of the Palestinian Authority or is otherwise inconsistent with the provisions of this Agreement.

4. Upon receipt of the Israeli request, the Legislation Subcommittee shall decide, as an initial matter, on the entry into force of the legislation pending its decision on the merits of the matter.

5. If the Legislation Subcommittee is unable to reach a decision with regard to the entry into force of the legislation within 15 days, this issue will be referred to a Board of Review. This Board of Review shall be comprised of two judges, retired judges or senior jurists (hereinafter 'Judges'), one from each side, to be appointed from a compiled list of three judges proposed by each.

6. Legislation referred to the Board of Review shall enter into force only if the Board of Review decides that it does not deal with a security issue which falls under Israel's responsibility, that it does not seriously threaten other significant Israeli interests protected by this Agreement and that the entry into force of the legislation could not cause irreparable damage or harm.

7. The Legislation Subcommittee shall attempt to reach a decision on the merits of the matter within 30 days from the date of the Israeli request. If this subcommittee is unable to

reach such a decision within this period of 30 days, the matter shall be referred to the joint Israeli-Palestinian Liaison Committee referred to in Article XV below (hereinafter 'the Liaison Committee'). This Liaison Committee will deal with the matter immediately and will attempt to settle it within 30 days.

8. Where the legislation has not entered into force pursuant to paragraphs 5 or 7 above, this situation shall be maintained pending the decision of the Liaison Committee on the merits of the matter, unless it has decided otherwise.

9. Laws and military orders in effect in the Gaza Strip or the Jericho Area prior to the signing of this Agreement shall remain in force, unless amended or abrogated in accordance with this Agreement.

Article VIII
Arrangements for security and public order

1. In order to guarantee public order and internal security for the Palestinians of the Gaza Strip and the Jericho Area, the Palestinian Authority shall establish a strong police force, as set out in Article IX below. Israel shall continue to carry the responsibility for defence against external threats, including the responsibility for protecting the Egyptian border and the Jordanian line, and for defence against external threats from the sea and from the air, as well as the responsibility for overall security of Israelis and settlements, for the purpose of safeguarding their internal security and public order, and will have all the powers to take the steps necessary to meet this responsibility.

2. Agreed security arrangements and co-ordination mechanisms are specified in Annex I.

3. A Joint Co-ordination and Co-operation committee for mutual security purposes (hereinafter 'the JSC'), as well as three joint district co-ordination and co-operation offices for the Gaza District, the Khan Younis District and the Jericho District respectively (hereinafter 'the DCOS') are hereby established as provided for in Annex I.

4. The security arrangements provided for in this Agreement and in Annex I may be reviewed at the requests of either party and may be amended by mutual agreement of the parties. Specific review arrangements are included in Annex I.

Article IX
The Palestinian Directorate of Police Force

1. The Palestinian Authority shall establish a strong police force, the Palestinian Directorate of Police Force (hereinafter 'the Palestinian Police'). The duties, functions, structure, deployment and composition of the Palestinian Police, together with provisions regarding its equipment and operation, are set out in Annex I, Article III. Rules of conduct governing the activities of the Palestinian Police are set out in Annex I, Article VIII.

2. Except for the Palestinian Police referred to in this article and the Israeli military forces, no other armed forces shall be established or operate in the Gaza Strip or the Jericho Area.

3. Except for the arms, ammunition and equipment of the Palestinian Police described in Annex I, Article III, and those of the Israeli military forces, no organization or individual in the Gaza Strip and the Jericho Area shall manufacture, sell, acquire, possess, import or otherwise introduce into the Gaza Strip or the Jericho Area any firearms, ammunition, weapons, explosives, gunpowder or any related equipment, unless otherwise provided for in Annex I.

Article X
Passages

Arrangements for co-ordination between Israel and the Palestinian Authority regarding the Gaza–Egypt and Jericho–Jordan passages, as well as any other agreed international crossings, are set out in Annex 1.

Article XI
Safe passage between the Gaza Strip and the Jericho Area

Arrangements for safe passage of persons and transportation between the Gaza Strip and the Jericho Area are set out in Annex I, Article IX.

Article XII
Relations between Israel and the Palestinian Authority

1. Israel and the Palestinian Authority shall seek to foster mutual understanding and tolerance and shall accordingly abstain from incitement, including hostile propaganda, against each other and, without derogating from the principle of freedom of expression, shall take legal measures to prevent such incitement by any organizations, groups or individuals within their jurisdiction.

2. Without derogating from the other provisions of this agreement, Israel and the Palestinian Authority shall co-operate in combating criminal activity which may affect both sides, including offences related to trafficking in illegal drugs and psychotropic substances, smuggling, and offences against property, including offences related to vehicles.

Article XIII
Economic relations

The economic relations between the two sides are set out in the Protocol on Economic Relations signed in Paris on April 29, 1994 and the appendixes thereto, certified copies of which are attached as Annex IV, and will be governed by the relevant provisions of this agreement and its annexes.

Article XIV
Human rights and the rule of law

Israel and the Palestinian Authority shall exercise their powers and responsibilities pursuant to this Agreement with due regard to internationally-accepted norms and principles of human rights and the rule of law.

Article XV
The Joint Israeli-Palestinian Liaison Committee

1. The Liaison Committee established pursuant to Article X of the Declaration of Principles shall ensure the smooth implementation of this Agreement. It shall deal with issues requiring co-ordination, other issues of common interest and disputes.

2. The Liaison Committee shall be composed of an equal number of members from each party. It may add other technicians and experts as necessary.

3. The Liaison Committee shall adopt its rules of procedure, including the frequency and place or places of its meetings.

4. The Liaison Committee shall reach its decision by agreement.

Article XVI
Liaison and Co-operation with Jordan and Egypt

1. Pursuant to Article XII of the Declaration of Principles, the two parties shall invite the governments of Jordan and Egypt to participate in establishing further Liaison and Co-operation Arrangements between the Government of Israel and the Palestinian Representatives on the one hand, and the governments of Jordan and Egypt on the other hand, to promote co-operation between them. These arrangements shall include the constitution of a Continuing Committee.

2. The Continuing Committee shall decide by agreement on the modalities of admission of persons displaced from the West Bank and the Gaza Strip in 1967, together with necessary measures to prevent disruption and disorder.

3. The Continuing Committee shall deal with other matters of common concern.

Article XVII
Settlement of differences and disputes

Any difference relating to the application of this agreement shall be referred to the appropriate co-ordination and co-operation mechanism established under this agreement. The provisions of Article XV of the Declaration of Principles shall apply to any such difference which is not settled through the appropriate co-ordination and co-operation mechanism, namely:

1. Disputes arising out of the application or interpretation of this agreement or any subsequent agreements pertaining to the

interim period shall be settled by negotiations through the Liaison Committee.

2. Disputes which cannot be settled by negotiations may be settled by a mechanism of conciliation to be agreed between the parties.

3. The parties may agree to submit to arbitration disputes relating to the interim period, which cannot be settled through conciliation. To this end, upon the agreement of both parties, the parties will establish an arbitration committee.

Article XVIII
Prevention of hostile acts

Both sides shall take all measures necessary in order to prevent acts of terrorism, crime and hostilities directed against each other, against individuals falling under the other's authority and against their property, and shall take legal measures against offenders. In addition, the Palestinian side shall take all measures necessary to prevent such hostile acts directed against the settlements, the infrastructure serving them and the military installation area, and the Israeli side shall take all measures necessary to prevent such hostile acts emanating from the settlements and directed against Palestinians.

Article XIX
Missing persons

The Palestinian Authority shall co-operate with Israel by providing all necessary assistance in the conduct of searches by Israel within the Gaza Strip and the Jericho Area for missing Israelis, as well as by providing information about missing Israelis. Israel shall co-operate with the Palestinian Authority in searching for, and providing necessary information about, missing Palestinians.

Article XX
Confidence-building measures

With a view to creating a positive and supportive public atmosphere to accompany the implementation of this agreement, and to establish a solid basis of mutual trust and good faith, both parties agree to carry out confidence-building measures as detailed herewith:

1. Upon the signing of this agreement, Israel will release, or turn over, to the Palestinian Authority within a period of 5 weeks, about 5,000 Palestinian detainees and prisoners, residents of the West Bank and the Gaza Strip. Those released will be free to return to their homes anywhere in the West Bank or the Gaza Strip. Prisoners turned over to the Palestinian Authority shall be obliged to remain in the Gaza Strip or the Jericho Area for the remainder of their sentence.

2. After the signing of this Agreement, the two parties shall continue to negotiate the release of additional Palestinian prisoners and detainees, building on agreed principles.

3. The implementation of the above measures will be subject to the fulfilment of the procedures determined by Israeli law for the release and transfer of detainees and prisoners.

4. With the assumption of Palestinian Authority, the Palestinian side commits itself to solving the problem of those Palestinians who were in contact with the Israeli authorities. Until an agreed solution is found, the Palestinian side undertakes not to prosecute these Palestinians or to harm them in any way.

5. Palestinians from abroad whose entry into the Gaza Strip and the Jericho Area is approved pursuant to this agreement, and to whom the provisions of this article are applicable, will not be prosecuted for offences committed prior to September 13, 1993.

Article XXI
Temporary international presence

1. The parties agree to a temporary international or foreign presence in the Gaza Strip and the Jericho Area (hereinafter 'the TIP'), in accordance with the provisions of this article.

2. The TIP shall consist of 400 qualified personnel, including observers, instructors and other experts, from 5 or 6 of the donor countries.

3. The two parties shall request the donor countries to establish a special fund to provide finance for the TIP.

4. The TIP will function for a period of 6 months. The TIP may extend this period, or change the scope of its operation, with the agreement of the two parties.

5. The TIP shall be stationed and operative within the following cities and villages: Gaza, Khan Younis, Rafah, Deir al-Balah, Jabalya, Absan, Beit Hanun and Jericho.

6. Israel and the Palestinian Authority shall agree on a special protocol to implement this article, with the goal of concluding negotiations with the donor countries contributing personnel within two months.

Article XXII
Rights, liabilities and obligations

1.a. The transfer of all powers and responsibilities to the Palestinian Authority, as detailed in Annex II, includes all related rights, liabilities and obligations arising with regard to acts or omissions which occurred prior to the transfer. Israel will cease to bear any financial responsibility regarding such acts or omissions and the Palestinian Authority will bear all financial responsibility for these and for its own functioning.

b. Any financial claim made in this regard against Israel will be referred to the Palestinian Authority.

c. Israel shall provide the Palestinian Authority with the information it has regarding pending and anticipated claims brought before any court or tribunal against Israel in this regard.

d. Where legal proceedings are brought in respect of such a claim, Israel will notify the Palestinian Authority and enable it to participate in defending the claim and raise any arguments on its behalf.

e. In the event that an award is made against Israel by any court or tribunal in respect of such a claim, the Palestinian Authority shall reimburse Israel the full amount of the award.

f. Without prejudice to the above, where a court or tribunal hearing such a claim finds that liability rests solely with an employee or agent who acted beyond the scope of the powers assigned to him or her, unlawfully or with willful malfeasance, the Palestinian Authority shall not bear financial responsibility.

2. The transfer of authority in itself shall not affect rights, liabilities and obligations of any person or legal entity, in existence at the date of signing of this Agreement.

Article XXIII
Final clauses

1. This Agreement shall enter into force on the date of its signing.

2. The arrangements established by this Agreement shall remain in force until and to the extent superseded by the Interim Agreement referred to in the Declaration of Principles or any other Agreement between the parties.

3. The five-year Interim Period referred to in the Declaration of Principles commences on the date of the signing of this Agreement.

4. The parties agree that, as long as this Agreement is in force, the security fence erected by Israel around the Gaza Strip shall remain in place and that the line demarcated by the fence, as shown on attached Map No. 1, shall be authoritative only for the purpose of this Agreement.

5. Nothing in this Agreement shall prejudice or pre-empt the outcome of the negotiations on the Interim Agreement or on the Permanent Status to be conducted pursuant to the Declaration of Principles. Neither party shall be deemed, by virtue of having entered into this Agreement, to have renounced or waived any of its existing rights, claims or positions.

6. The two parties view the West Bank and the Gaza Strip as a single territorial unit, the integrity of which will be preserved during the Interim Period.

7. The Gaza Strip and the Jericho Area shall continue to be an integral part of the West Bank and the Gaza Strip, and their

status shall not be changed for the period of this Agreement. Nothing in this Agreement shall be considered to change this status.

8. The preamble to this Agreement, and all Annexes, Appendices and Maps attached hereto, shall constitute an integral part hereof.

ISRAELI-PALESTINIAN INTERIM AGREEMENT ON THE WEST BANK AND THE GAZA STRIP

28 September 1995

The Interim Agreement was signed by the Chairman of the PLO, Yasser Arafat, and the Israeli Minister of Foreign Affairs, Shimon Peres, in Washington, DC, USA. The Agreement was witnessed by representatives of the USA, Russia, Egypt, Jordan, Norway and the European Union (EU). Considerable additional detail was contained in seven annexes (not reproduced here) to the Agreement (the most expansive of which—Annex I—concerned redeployment and security arrangements) and a map (also not reproduced here) in which the boundaries of first-phase redeployment areas 'A' and 'B' were defined.

The Government of the State of Israel and the Palestine Liberation Organization (hereinafter the 'PLO'), the representative of the Palestinian people;

Preamble

WITHIN the framework of the Middle East peace process initiated at Madrid in October 1991;

REAFFIRMING their determination to put an end to decades of confrontation and to live in peaceful coexistence, mutual dignity and security, while recognizing their mutual legitimate and political rights;

REAFFIRMING their desire to achieve a just, lasting and comprehensive peace settlement and historic reconciliation through the agreed political process;

RECOGNIZING that the peace process and the new era that it has created, as well as the new relationship established between the two Parties as described above, are irreversible, and the determination of the two Parties to maintain, sustain and continue the peace process;

RECOGNIZING that the aim of the Israeli-Palestinian negotiations within the current Middle East peace process is, among other things, to establish a Palestinian Interim Self-Government Authority, i.e. the elected Council (hereinafter 'the Council' or 'the Palestinian Council'), and the elected Ra'ees of the Executive Authority, for the Palestinian people in the West Bank and the Gaza Strip, for a transitional period not exceeding five years from the date of signing the Agreement on the Gaza Strip and the Jericho Area (hereinafter 'the Gaza-Jericho Agreement') on May 4, 1994, leading to a permanent settlement based on Security Council Resolutions 242 and 338;

REAFFIRMING their understanding that the interim self-government arrangements contained in this Agreement are an integral part of the whole peace process, that the negotiations on the permanent status, that will start as soon as possible but not later than May 4, 1996, will lead to the implementation of Security Council Resolutions 242 and 338, and that the Interim Agreement shall settle all the issues of the interim period and that no such issues will be deferred to the agenda of the permanent status negotiations;

REAFFIRMING their adherence to the mutual recognition and commitments expressed in the letters dated September 9, 1993, signed by and exchanged between the Prime Minister of Israel and the Chairman of the PLO;

DESIROUS of putting into effect the Declaration of Principles on Interim Self-Government Arrangements signed at Washington, DC on September 13, 1993, and the Agreed Minutes thereto (hereinafter 'the DOP') and in particular Article III and Annex I concerning the holding of direct, free and general political elections for the Council and the Ra'ees of the Executive Authority in order that the Palestinian people in the West Bank, Jerusalem and the Gaza Strip may democratically elect accountable representatives;

RECOGNIZING that these elections will constitute a significant interim preparatory step toward the realization of the legitimate rights of the Palestinian people and their just requirements and will provide a democratic basis for the establishment of Palestinian institutions;

REAFFIRMING their mutual commitment to act, in accordance with this Agreement, immediately, efficiently and effectively against acts or threats of terrorism, violence or incitement, whether committed by Palestinians or Israelis;

FOLLOWING the Gaza-Jericho Agreement; the Agreement on Preparatory Transfer of Powers and Responsibilities signed at Erez on August 29, 1994 (hereinafter 'the Preparatory Transfer Agreement'); and the Protocol on Further Transfer of Powers and Responsibilities signed at Cairo on August 27, 1995 (hereinafter 'the Further Transfer Protocol'); which three agreements will be superseded by this Agreement;

HEREBY AGREE as follows:

CHAPTER 1—THE COUNCIL

ARTICLE I
Transfer of Authority

1. Israel shall transfer powers and responsibilities as specified in this Agreement from the Israeli military government and its Civil Administration to the Council in accordance with this Agreement. Israel shall continue to exercise powers and responsibilities not so transferred.

2. Pending the inauguration of the Council, the powers and responsibilities tranferred to the Council shall be exercised by the Palestinian Authority established in accordance with the Gaza-Jericho Agreement, which shall also have all the rights, liabilities and obligations to be assumed by the Council in this regard. Accordingly, the term 'Council' throughout this Agreement shall, pending the inauguration of the Council, be construed as meaning the Palestinian Authority.

3. The transfer of powers and responsibilities to the police force established by the Palestinian Council in accordance with Article XIV below (hereinafter 'the Palestinian Police') shall be accomplished in a phased manner, as detailed in this Agreement and in the Protocol concerning Redeployment and Security Arrangements attached as Annex I to this Agreement (hereinafter 'Annex I').

4. As regards the transfer and assumption of authority in civil spheres, powers and responsibilities shall be transferred and assumed as set out in the Protocol Concerning Civil Affairs attached as Annex III to this Agreement (hereinafter 'Annex III').

5. After the inauguration of the Council, the Civil Administration in the West Bank will be dissolved, and the Israeli military government shall be withdrawn. The withdrawal of the military government shall not prevent it from exercising the powers and responsibilities not transferred to the Council.

6. A Joint Civil Affairs Co-ordination and Co-operation Committee (hereinafter 'the CAC'), Joint Regional Civil Affairs Sub-committees, one for the Gaza Strip and the other for the West Bank, and District Civil Liaison Offices in the West Bank shall be established in order to provide for co-ordination and co-operation in civil affairs between the Council and Israel, as detailed in Annex III.

7. The offices of the Council, and the offices of its Ra'ees and its Executive Authority and other committees, shall be located in areas under Palestinian territorial jurisdiction in the West Bank and the Gaza Strip.

ARTICLE II
Elections

1. In order that the Palestinian people of the West Bank and the Gaza Strip may govern themselves according to democratic principles, direct, free and general political elections will be held for the Council and the Ra'ees of the Executive Authority of the Council in accordance with the provisions set out in the Protocol concerning Elections attached as Annex II to this Agreement (hereinafter 'Annex II').

2. These elections will constitute a significant interim preparatory step towards the realization of the legitimate rights of the Palestinian people and their just requirements and will provide a democratic basis for the establishment of Palestinian institutions.

3. Palestinians of Jerusalem who live there may participate in the election process in accordance with the provisions contained in this Article and in Article VI of Annex II (Election Arrangements concerning Jerusalem).

4. The elections shall be called by the Chairman of the Palestinian Authority immediately following the signing of this Agreement to take place at the earliest practicable date following the redeployment of Israeli forces in accordance with Annex I, and consistent with the requirements of the election timetable as provided in Annex II, the Election Law and the Election Regulations, as defined in Article I of Annex II.

ARTICLE III
Structure of the Palestinian Council

1. The Palestinian Council and the Ra'ees of the Executive Authority of the Council constitute the Palestinian Interim Self-Government Authority, which will be elected by the Palestinian people of the West Bank, Jerusalem and the Gaza Strip for the transitional period agreed in Article I of the DOP.

2. The Council shall possess both legislative power and executive power, in accordance with Articles VII and IX of the DOP. The Council shall carry out and be responsible for all the legislative and executive powers and responsibilities transferred to it under this Agreement. The exercise of legislative powers shall be in accordance with Article XVIII of this Agreement (Legislative Powers of the Council).

3. The Council and the Ra'ees of the Executive Authority of the Council shall be directly and simultaneously elected by the Palestinian people of the West Bank, Jerusalem and the Gaza Strip, in accordance with the provisions of this Agreement and the Election Law and Regulations, which shall not be contrary to the provisions of this Agreement.

4. The Council and the Ra'ees of the Executive Authority of the Council shall be elected for a transitional period not exceeding five years from the signing of the Gaza-Jericho Agreement on May 4, 1994.

5. Immediately upon its inauguration, the Council will elect from among its members a Speaker. The Speaker will preside over the meetings of the Council, administer the Council and its committees, decide on the agenda of each meeting, and lay before the Council proposals for voting and declare their results.

6. The jurisdiction of the Council shall be as determined in Article XVII of this Agreement (Jurisdiction).

7. The organization, structure and functioning of the Council shall be in accordance with this Agreement and the Basic Law for the Palestinian Interim Self-Government Authority, which Law shall be adopted by the Council. The Basic Law and any regulations made under it shall not be contrary to the provisions of this Agreement.

8. The Council shall be responsible under its executive powers for the offices, services and departments transferred to it and may establish, within its jurisdiction, ministries and subordinate bodies, as necessary for the fulfillment of its responsibilities.

9. The Speaker will present for the Council's approval proposed internal procedures that will regulate, among other things, the decision-making processes of the Council.

ARTICLE IV
Size of the Council

The Palestinian Council shall be composed of 82 representatives and the Ra'ees of the Executive Authority, who will be directly and simultaneously elected by the Palestinian people of the West Bank, Jerusalem and the Gaza Strip.

ARTICLE V
The Executive Authority of the Council

1. The Council will have a committee that will exercise the executive authority of the Council, formed in accordance with paragraph 4 below (hereinafter 'the Executive Authority').

2. The Executive Authority shall be bestowed with the executive authority of the Council and will exercise it on behalf of the Council. It shall determine its own internal procedures and decision making processes.

3. The Council will publish the names of the members of the Executive Authority immediately upon their initial appointment and subsequent to any changes.

4.a. The Ra'ees of the Executive Authority shall be an ex officio member of the Executive Authority.

b. All of the other members of the Executive Authority, except as provided in subparagraph c. below, shall be members of the Council, chosen and proposed to the Council by the Ra'ees of the Executive Authority and approved by the Council.

c. The Ra'ees of the Executive Authority shall have the right to appoint some persons, in number not exceeding twenty percent of the total membership of the Executive Authority, who are not members of the Council, to exercise executive authority and participate in government tasks. Such appointed members may not vote in meetings of the Council.

d. Non-elected members of the Executive Authority must have a valid address in an area under the jurisdiction of the Council.

ARTICLE VI
Other Committees of the Council

1. The Council may form small committees to simplify the proceedings of the Council and to assist in controlling the activity of its Executive Authority.

2. Each committee shall establish its own decision-making processes within the general framework of the organization and structure of the Council.

ARTICLE VII
Open Government

1. All meetings of the Council and of its committees, other than the Executive Authority, shall be open to the public, except upon a resolution of the Council or the relevant committee on the grounds of security, or commercial or personal confidentiality.

2. Participation in the deliberations of the Council, its committees and the Executive Authority shall be limited to their respective members only. Experts may be invited to such meetings to address specific issues on an ad hoc basis.

ARTICLE VIII
Judicial Review

Any person or organization affected by any act or decision of the Ra'ees of the Executive Authority of the Council or of any member of the Executive Authority, who believes that such act or decision exceeds the authority of the Ra'ees or of such member, or is otherwise incorrect in law or procedure, may apply to the relevant Palestinian Court of Justice for a review of such activity or decision.

ARTICLE IX
Powers and Responsibilities of the Council

1. Subject to the provisions of this Agreement, the Council will, within its jurisdiction, have legislative powers as set out in Article XVIII of this Agreement, as well as executive powers.

2. The executive power of the Palestinian Council shall extend to all matters within its jurisdiction under this Agreement or any future agreement that may be reached between the two Parties during the interim period. It shall include the power to formulate and conduct Palestinian policies and to supervise their implementation, to issue any rule or regulation under powers given in approved legislation and administrative decisions necessary for the realization of Palestinian self-government, the power to employ staff, sue and be sued and conclude contracts, and the power to keep and administer registers and records of the population, and issue certificates, licenses and documents.

3. The Palestinian Council's executive decisions and acts shall be consistent with the provisions of this Agreement.

4. The Palestinian Council may adopt all necessary measures in order to enforce the law and any of its decisions, and bring proceedings before the Palestinian courts and tribunals.

5.a. In accordance with the DOP, the Council will not have

powers and responsibilities in the sphere of foreign relations, which sphere includes the establishment abroad of embassies, consulates or other types of foreign missions and posts or permitting their establishment in the West Bank or the Gaza Strip, the appointment of or admission of diplomatic and consular staff, and the exercise of diplomatic functions.

b. Notwithstanding the provisions of this paragraph, the PLO may conduct negotiations and sign agreements with states or international organizations for the benefit of the Council in the following cases only:

(1) Economic agreements, as specifically provided in Annex V of this Agreement;

(2) Agreements with donor countries for the purpose of implementing arrangements for the provision of assistance to the Council;

(3) Agreements for the purpose of implementing the regional development plans detailed in Annex IV of the DOP or in agreements entered into in the framework of the multilateral negotiations; and

(4) Cultural, scientific and educational agreements.

c. Dealings between the Council and representatives of foreign states and international organizations, as well as the establishment in the West Bank and the Gaza Strip of representative offices other than those described in subparagrah 5.a above, for the purpose of implementing the agreements referred to in subparagraph 5.b above, shall not be considered foreign relations.

6. Subject to the provisions of this Agreement, the Council shall, within its jurisdiction, have an independent judicial system composed of independent Palestinian courts and tribunals.

CHAPTER 2—REDEPLOYMENT AND SECURITY ARRANGEMENTS

ARTICLE X
Redeployment of Israeli Military Forces

1. The first phase of the Israeli military forces redeployment will cover populated areas in the West Bank—cities, towns, villages, refugee camps and hamlets—as set out in Annex I, and will be completed prior to the eve of the Palestinian elections, i.e., 22 days before the day of the elections.

2. Further redeployments of Israeli military forces to specified military locations will commence after the inauguration of the Council and will be gradually implemented commensurate with the assumption of responsibility for public order and internal security by the Palestinian Police, to be completed within 18 months from the date of the inauguration of the Council as detailed in Articles XI (Land) and XIII (Security), below and in Annex I.

3. The Palestinian Police shall be deployed and shall assume responsibility for public order and internal security for Palestinians in a phased manner in accordance with Article XIII (Security) below and Annex I.

4. Israel shall continue to carry the responsibility for external security, as well as the responsibility for overall security of Israelis for the purpose of safeguarding their internal security and public order.

5. For the purpose of this Agreement, 'Israeli military forces' includes Israeli Police and other Israeli security forces.

ARTICLE XI
Land

1. The two sides view the West Bank and the Gaza Strip as a single territorial unit, the integrity and status of which will be preserved during the interim period.

2. The two sides agree that West Bank and Gaza Strip territory, except for issues that will be negotiated in the permanent status negotiations, will come under the jurisdiction of the Palestinian Council in a phased manner, to be completed within 18 months from the date of the inauguration of the Council, as specified below:

a. Land in populated areas (Areas A and B), including

government and Al Waqf land, will come under the jurisdiction of the Council during the first phase of redeployment.

b. All civil powers and responsibilities, including planning and zoning, in Areas A and B, set out in Annex III, will be transferred to and assumed by the Council during the first phase of redeployment.

c. In Area C, during the first phase of redeployment Israel will transfer to the Council civil powers and responsibilities not relating to territory, as set out in Annex III.

d. The further redeployments of Israeli military forces to specified military locations will be gradually implemented in accordance with the DOP in three phases, each to take place after an interval of six months, after the inauguration of the Council, to be completed within 18 months from the date of the inauguration of the Council.

e. During the further redeployment phases to be completed within 18 months from the date of the inauguration of the Council, powers and responsibilities relating to territory will be transferred gradually to Palestinian jurisdiction that will cover West Bank and Gaza Strip territory, except for the issues that will be negotiated in the permanent status negotiations.

f. The specified military locations referred to in Article X, paragraph 2 above will be determined in the further redeployment phases, within the specified time-frame ending not later than 18 months from the date of the inauguration of the Council, and will be negotiated in the permanent status negotiations.

3. For the purpose of this Agreement and until the completion of the first phase of the further redeployments:

a. 'Area A' means the populated areas delineated by a red line and shaded in brown on attached map No. 1 (*not reproduced here—Ed.*);

b. 'Area B' means the populated areas delineated by a red line and shaded in yellow on attached map No. 1, and the built-up area of the hamlets listed in Appendix 6 to Annex I; and

c. 'Area C' means areas of the West Bank outside Areas A and B, which, except for the issues that will be negotiated in the permanent status negotiations, will be gradually transferred to Palestinian jurisdiction in accordance with this Agreement.

ARTICLE XII
Arrangements for Security and Public Order

1. In order to guarantee public order and internal security for the Palestinians of the West Bank and the Gaza Strip, the Council shall establish a strong police force as set out in Article XIV below. Israel shall continue to carry the responsibility for defence against external threats, including the responsibility for protecting the Egyptian and Jordanian borders, and for defence against external threats from the sea and from the air, as well as the responsibility for overall security of Israelis and Settlements, for the purpose of safeguarding their internal security and public order, and will have all the powers to take the steps necessary to meet this responsibility.

2. Agreed security arrangements and co-ordination mechanisms are specified in Annex I.

3. A Joint Co-ordination and Co-operation Committee for Mutual Security Purposes (hereinafter 'the JSC'), as well as Joint Regional Security Committees (hereinafter 'RSCs') and Joint District Co-ordination Offices (hereinafter 'DCOs'), are hereby established as provided for in Annex I.

4. The security arrangements provided for in this Agreement and in Annex I may be reviewed at the request of either Party and may be amended by mutual agreement of the Parties. Specific review arrangements are included in Annex I.

5. For the purpose of this Agreement, 'the Settlements' means, in the West Bank—the settlements in Area C; and in the Gaza Strip—the Gush Katif and Erez settlement areas, as well as the other settlements in the Gaza Strip, as shown on attached map No. 2 (*not reproduced—Ed.*).

ARTICLE XIII
Security

1. The Council will, upon completion of the redeployment of Israeli military forces in each district, as set out in Appendix 1 to Annex I, assume the powers and responsibilities for internal security and public order in Area A in that district.

2.a. There will be a complete redeployment of Israeli military forces from Area B. Israel will transfer to the Council and the Council will assume responsibility for public order for Palestinians. Israel shall have the overriding responsibility for security for the purpose of protecting Israelis and confronting the threat of terrorism.

   b. In Area B the Palestinian Police shall assume the responsibility for public order for Palestinians and shall be deployed in order to accommodate the Palestinian needs and requirements in the following manner:

   (1) The Palestinian Police shall establish 25 police stations and posts in towns, villages, and other places listed in Appendix 2 to Annex I and as delineated on map No. 3 (*not reproduced—Ed.*). The West Bank RSC may agree on the establishment of additional police stations and posts, if required.

   (2) The Palestinian Police shall be responsible for handling public order incidents in which only Palestinians are involved.

   (3) The Palestinian Police shall operate freely in populated places where police stations and posts are located, as set out in paragraph b(1) above.

   (4) While the movement of uniformed Palestinian policemen in Area B outside places where there is a Palestinian police station or post will be carried out after co-ordination and confirmation through the relevant DCO, three months after the completion of redeployment from Area B, the DCOs may decide that movement of Palestinian policemen from the police stations in Area B to Palestinian towns and villages in Area B on roads that are used only by Palestinian traffic will take place after notifying the DCO.

   (5) The co-ordination of such planned movement prior to confirmation through the relevant DCO shall include a scheduled plan, including the number of policemen, as well as the type and number of weapons and vehicles intended to take part. It shall also include details of arrangements for ensuring continued co-ordination through appropriate communication links, the exact schedule of movement to the area of the planned operation, including the destination and routes thereto, its proposed duration and the schedule for returning to the police station or post.

   The Israeli side of the DCO will provide the Palestinian side with its response, following a request for movement of policemen in accordance with this paragraph, in normal or routine cases within one day and in emergency cases no later than 2 hours.

   (6) The Palestinian Police and the Israeli military forces will conduct joint security activities on the main roads as set out in Annex 1.

   (7) The Palestinian Police will notify the West Bank RSC of the names of the policemen, number plates of police vehicles and serial numbers of weapons, with respect to each police station and post in Area B.

   (8) Further redeployments from Area C and transfer of internal security responsibility to the Palestinian Police in Areas B and C will be carried out in three phases, each to take place after an interval of six months, to be completed 18 months after the inauguration of the Council, except for the issues of permanent status negotiations and of Israel's overall responsibility for Israelis and borders.

   (9) The procedures detailed in this paragraph will be reviewed within six months of the completion of the first phase of redeployment.

ARTICLE XIV
The Palestinian Police

1. The Council shall establish a strong police force. The duties, functions, structure, deployment and composition of the Palestinian Police, together with provisions regarding its equipment and operation, as well as rules of conduct, are set out in Annex I.

2. The Palestinian police force established under the Gaza-Jericho Agreement will be fully integrated into the Palestinian Police and will be subject to the provisions of this Agreement.

3. Except for the Palestinian Police and the Israeli military forces, no other armed forces shall be established or operate in the West Bank and the Gaza Strip.

4. Except for the arms, ammunition and equipment of the Palestinian Police described in Annex I, and those of the Israeli military forces, no organization, group or individual in the West Bank and the Gaza Strip shall manufacture, sell, acquire, possess, import or otherwise introduce into the West Bank or the Gaza Strip any firearms, ammunition, weapons, explosives, gunpowder or any related equipment, unless otherwise provided for in Annex I.

ARTICLE XV
Prevention of Hostile Acts

1. Both sides shall take all measures necessary in order to prevent acts of terrorism, crime and hostilities directed against each other, against individuals falling under the other's authority and against their property, and shall take legal measures against offenders.

2. Specific provisions for the implementation of this Article are set out in Annex I.

ARTICLE XVI
Confidence Building Measures

With a view to fostering a positive and supportive public atmosphere to accompany the implementation of this Agreement, to establish a solid basis of mutual trust and good faith, and in order to facilitate the anticipated co-operation and new relations between the two peoples, both Parties agree to carry out confidence building measures as detailed herewith:

1. Israel will release or turn over to the Palestinian side, Palestinian detainees and prisoners, residents of the West Bank and the Gaza Strip. The first stage of release of these prisoners and detainees will take place on the signing of this Agreement and the second stage will take place prior to the date of the elections. There will be a third stage of release of detainees and prisoners. Detainees and prisoners will be released from among categories detailed in Annex VII (Release of Palestinian Prisoners and Detainees). Those released will be free to return to their homes in the West Bank and the Gaza Strip.

2. Palestinians who have maintained contact with the Israeli authorities will not be subjected to acts of harassment, violence, retribution or prosecution. Appropriate ongoing measures will be taken, in co-ordination with Israel, in order to ensure their protection.

3. Palestinians from abroad whose entry into the West Bank and the Gaza Strip is approved pursuant to this Agreement, and to whom the provisions of this Article are applicable, will not be prosecuted for offences committed prior to September 13, 1993.

CHAPTER 3—LEGAL AFFAIRS
ARTICLE XVII
Jurisdiction

1. In accordance with the DOP, the jurisdiction of the Council will cover West Bank and Gaza Strip territory as a single territorial unit, except for:

   a. Issues that will be negotiated in the permanent status negotiations: Jerusalem, settlements, specified military locations, Palestinian refugees, borders, foreign relations and Israelis; and

b. Powers and responsibilities not transferred to the Council.

2. Accordingly, the authority of the Council encompasses all matters that fall within its territorial, functional and personal jurisdiction, as follows:

a. The territorial jurisdiction of the Council shall encompass Gaza Strip territory, except for the Settlements and the Military Installation Area shown on map No. 2, and West Bank territory, except for Area C which, except for the issues that will be negotiated in the permanent status negotiations, will be gradually transferred to Palestinian jurisdiction in three phases, each to take place after an interval of six months, to be completed 18 months after the inauguration of the Council. At this time, the jurisdiction of the Council will cover West Bank and Gaza Strip territory, except for the issues that will be negotiated in the permanent status negotiations.

Territorial jurisdiction includes land, subsoil and territorial waters, in accordance with the provisions of this Agreement.

b. The functional jurisdiction of the Council extends to all powers and responsibilities transferred to the Council, as specified in this Agreement or in any future agreements that may be reached between the Parties during the interim period.

c. The territorial and functional jurisdiction of the Council will apply to all persons, except for Israelis, unless otherwise provided in this Agreement.

d. Notwithstanding subparagraph a. above, the Council shall have functional jurisdiction in Area C, as detailed in Article IV of Annex III.

3. The Council has, within its authority, legislative, executive and judicial powers and responsibilities, as provided for in this Agreement.

4.a. Israel, through its military government, has the authority over areas that are not under the territorial jurisdiction of the Council, powers and responsibilities not transferred to the Council and Israelis.

b. To this end, the Israeli military government shall retain the necessary legislative, judicial and executive powers and responsibilities, in accordance with international law. This provision shall not derogate from Israel's applicable legislation over Israelis in personam.

5. The exercise of authority with regard to the electromagnetic sphere and air space shall be in accordance with the provisions of this Agreement.

6. Without derogating from the provisions of this Article, legal arrangements detailed in the Protocol Concerning Legal Matters attached as Annex IV to this Agreement (hereinafter 'Annex IV') shall be observed. Israel and the Council may negotiate further legal arrangements.

7. Israel and the Council shall co-operate on matters of legal assistance in criminal and civil matters through a legal committee (hereinafter 'the Legal Commmittee'), hereby established.

8. The Council's jurisdiction will extend gradually to cover West Bank and Gaza Strip territory, except for the issues to be negotiated in the permanent status negotiations, through a series of redeployments of the Israeli military forces. The first phase of the redeployment of Israeli military forces will cover populated areas in the West Bank—cities, towns, refugee camps and hamlets, as set out in Annex I—and will be completed prior to the eve of the Palestinian elections, i.e. 22 days before the day of the elections. Further redeployments of Israeli military forces to specified military locations will commence immediately upon the inauguration of the Council and will be effected in three phases, each to take place after an interval of six months, to be concluded no later than eighteen months from the date of the inauguration of the Council.

ARTICLE XVIII
Legislative Powers of the Council

1. For the purposes of this Article, legislation shall mean any primary and secondary legislation, including basic laws, laws, regulations and other legislative acts.

2. The Council has the power, within its jurisdiction as defined in Article XVII of this Agreement, to adopt legislation.

3. While the primary legislative power shall lie in the hands of the Council as a whole, the Ra'ees of the Executive Authority of the Council shall have the following legislative powers:

a. The power to initiate legislation or to present proposed legislation to the Council;

b. The power to promulgate legislation adopted by the Council; and

c. The power to issue secondary legislation, including regulations, relating to any matters specified and within the scope laid down in any primary legislation adopted by the Council.

4.a. Legislation, including legislation which amends or abrogates existing laws or military orders, which exceeds the jurisdiction of the Council or which is otherwise inconsistent with the provisions of the DOP, this Agreement, or of any other agreement that may be reached between the two sides during the interim period, shall have no effect and shall be void ab initio.

b. The Ra'ees of the Executive Authority of the Council shall not promulgate legislation adopted by the Council if such legislation falls under the provisions of this paragraph.

5. All legislation shall be communicated to the Israeli side of the Legal Committee.

6. Without derogating from the provisions of paragraph 4 above, the Israeli side of the Legal Committee may refer for the attention of the Committee any legislation regarding which Israel considers the provisions of paragraph 4 apply, in order to discuss issues arising from such legislation. The Legal Committee will consider the legislation referred to it at the earliest opportunity.

ARTICLE XIX
Human Rights and the Rule of Law

Israel and the Council shall exercise their powers and responsibilities pursuant to this Agreement with due regard to internationally-accepted norms and principles of human rights and the rule of law.

ARTICLE XX
Rights, Liabilities and Obligations

1.a. Transfer of powers and responsibilities from the Israeli military government and its civil administration to the Council, as detailed in Annex III, includes all related rights, liabilities and obligations arising with regard to acts or omissions which occurred prior to such transfer. Israel will cease to bear any financial responsibility regarding such acts or omissions and the Council will bear all financial responsibility for these and for its own functioning.

b. Any financial claim made in this regard against Israel will be referred to the Council.

c. Israel shall provide the Council with the information it has regarding pending and anticipated claims brought before any court or tribunal against Israel in this regard.

d. Where legal proceedings are brought in respect of such a claim, Israel will notify the Council and enable it to participate in defending the claim and raise any arguments on its behalf.

e. In the event that an award is made against Israel by any court or tribunal in respect of such a claim, the Council shall immediately reimburse Israel the full amount of the award.

f. Without prejudice to the above, where a court or tribunal hearing such a claim finds that liability rests solely with an employee or agent who acted beyond the scope of the powers assigned to him or her, unlawfully or with willful malfeasance, the Council shall not bear financial responsibility.

2.a. Notwithstanding the provisions of paragraphs 1.d through 1.f above, each side may take the necessary measures, including promulgation of legislation, in order to ensure that such claims by Palestinians, including pending claims in which the hearing of evidence has not yet begun, are brought only before Palestinian courts or tribunals in the West Bank and the Gaza Strip, and are not brought before or heard by Israeli courts or tribunals.

b. Where a new claim has been brought before a Palestinian court or tribunal subsequent to the dismissal of the claim pursuant to subparagraph a. above, the Council shall defend it and, in accordance with subparagraph 1.a above, in the event that an award is made for the plaintiff, shall pay the amount of the award.

c. The Legal Committee shall agree on arrangements for the transfer of all materials and information needed to enable the Palestinian courts or tribunals to hear such claims as referred to in sub-paragraph b. above, and, when necessary, for the provision of legal assistance by Israel to the Council in defending such claims.

3. The transfer of authority in itself shall not affect rights, liabilities and obligations of any person or legal entity, in existence at the date of signing of this Agreement.

4. The Council, upon its inauguration, will assume all the rights, liabilities and obligations of the Palestinian Authority.

5. For the purpose of this Agreement, 'Israelis' also includes Israeli statutory agencies and corporations registered in Israel.

ARTICLE XXI
Settlement of Differences and Disputes

Any difference relating to the application of this Agreement shall be referred to the appropriate co-ordination and co-operation mechanism established under this Agreement. The provisions of Article XV of the DOP shall apply to any such difference which is not settled through the appropriate co-ordination and co-operation mechanism, namely:

1. Disputes arising out of the application or interpretation of this Agreement or any related agreements pertaining to the interim period shall be settled through the Liaison Committee.

2. Disputes which cannot be settled by negotiations may be settled by a mechanism of conciliation to be agreed between the Parties.

3. The Parties may agree to submit to arbitration disputes relating to the interim period, which cannot be settled through conciliation. To this end, upon the agreement of both Parties, the Parties will establish an Arbitration Committee.

CHAPTER 4—CO-OPERATION
ARTICLE XXII
Relations between Israel and the Council

1. Israel and the Council shall seek to foster mutual understanding and tolerance and shall accordingly abstain from incitement, including hostile propaganda, against each other and, without derogating from the principle of freedom of expression, shall take legal measures to prevent such incitement by any organizations, groups or individuals within their jurisdiction.

2. Israel and the Council will ensure that their respective educational systems contribute to the peace between the Israeli and Palestinian peoples and to peace in the entire region, and will refrain from the introduction of any motifs that could adversely affect the process of reconciliation.

3. Without derogating from the other provisions of this Agreement, Israel and the Council shall co-operate in combating criminal activity which may affect both sides, including offenses related to trafficking in illegal drugs and psychotropic substances, smuggling, and offenses against property, including offenses related to vehicles.

ARTICLE XXIII
Co-operation with Regard to Transfer of Powers and Responsibilities

In order to ensure a smooth, peaceful and orderly transfer of powers and responsibilities, the two sides will co-operate with regard to the transfer of security powers and responsibilities in accordance with the provisions of Annex I, and the transfer of civil powers and responsibilities in accordance with the provisions of Annex III.

ARTICLE XXIV
Economic Relations

The economic relations between the two sides are set out in the Protocol on Economic Relations, signed in Paris on April 29, 1994, and the Appendices thereto, and the Supplement to the Protocol on Economic Relations, all attached as Annex V, and will be governed by the relevant provisions of this Agreement and its Annexes.

ARTICLE XXV
Co-operation Programmes

1. The Parties agree to establish a mechanism to develop programmes of co-operation between them. Details of such co-operation are set out in Annex VI.

2. A Standing Co-operation Committee to deal with issues arising in the context of this co-operation is hereby established as provided for in Annex VI.

ARTICLE XXVI
The Joint Israeli-Palestinian Liaison Committee

1. The Liaison Committee established pursuant to Article X of the DOP shall ensure the smooth implementation of this Agreement. It shall deal with issues requiring co-ordination, other issues of common interest and disputes.

2. The Liaison Committee shall be composed of an equal number of members from each Party. It may add other technicians and experts as necessary.

3. The Liaison Committee shall adopt its rules of procedures, including the frequency and place or places of its meetings.

4. The Liaison Committee shall reach its decisions by agreement.

5. The Liaison Committee shall establish a subcommittee that will monitor and steer the implementation of this Agreement (hereinafter 'the Monitoring and Steering Committee'). It will function as follows:

a. The Monitoring and Steering Committee will, on an ongoing basis, monitor the implementation of this Agreement, with a view to enhancing the co-operation and fostering the peaceful relations between the two sides.

b. The Monitoring and Steering Committee will steer the activities of the various joint committees established in this Agreement (the JSC, the CAC, the Legal Committee, the Joint Economic Committee and the Standing Co-operation Committee) concerning the ongoing implementation of the Agreement, and will report to the Liaison Committee.

c. The Monitoring and Steering Committee will be composed of the heads of the various committees mentioned above.

d. The two heads of the Monitoring and Steering Committee will establish its rules of procedures, including the frequency and places of its meetings.

ARTICLE XXVII
Liaison and Co-operation with Jordan and Egypt

1. Pursuant to Article XII of the DOP, the two Parties have invited the Governments of Jordan and Egypt to participate in establishing further liaison and co-operation arrangements between the Government of Israel and the Palestinian representatives on the one hand, and the Governments of Jordan and Egypt on the other hand, to promote co-operation between them. As part of these arrangements a Continuing Committee has been constituted and has commenced its deliberations.

2. The Continuing Committee shall decide by agreement on the modalities of admission of persons displaced from the West Bank and the Gaza Strip in 1967, together with necessary measures to prevent disruption and disorder.

3. The Continuing Committee shall also deal with other matters of common concern.

ARTICLE XXVIII

Missing Persons

1. Israel and the Council shall co-operate by providing each other with all necessary assistance in the conduct of searches for missing persons and bodies of persons which have not been recovered, as well as by providing information about missing persons.

2. The PLO undertakes to co-operate with Israel and to assist it in its efforts to locate and to return to Israel Israeli soldiers who are missing in action and the bodies of soldiers which have not been recovered.

CHAPTER 5—MISCELLANEOUS PROVISIONS

ARTICLE XXIX

Safe Passage between the West Bank and the Gaza Strip

Arrangements for safe passage of persons and transportation between the West Bank and the Gaza Strip are set out in Annex 1.

ARTICLE XXX

Passages

Arrangements for co-ordination between Israel and the Council regarding passage to and from Egypt and Jordan, as well as any other agreed international crossings, are set out in Annex I.

ARTICLE XXXI

Final Clauses

1. This Agreement shall enter into force on the date of its signing.

2. The Gaza-Jericho Agreement, the Preparatory Transfer Agreement and the Further Transfer Protocol will be superseded by this Agreement.

3. The Council, upon its inauguration, shall replace the Palestinian Authority and shall assume all the undertakings and obligations of the Palestinian Authority under the Gaza-Jericho Agreement, the Preparatory Transfer Agreement, and the Further Transfer Protocol.

4. The two sides shall pass all necessary legislation to implement this Agreement.

5. Permanent status negotiations will commence as soon as possible, but not later than May 4, 1996, between the Parties. It is understood that these negotiations shall cover remaining issues, including: Jerusalem, refugees, settlements, security arrangements, borders, relations and co-operation with other neighbours, and other issues of common interest.

6. Nothing in this Agreement shall prejudice or preempt the outcome of the negotiations on the permanent status to be conducted pursuant to the DOP. Neither Party shall be deemed, by virtue of having entered into this Agreement, to have renounced or waived any of its existing rights, claims or positions.

7. Neither side shall initiate or take any step that will change the status of the West Bank and the Gaza Strip pending the outcome of the permanent status negotiations.

8. The two Parties view the West Bank and the Gaza Strip as a single territorial unit, the integrity and status of which will be preserved during the interim period.

9. The PLO undertakes that, within two months of the date of the inauguration of the Council, the Palestinian National Council will convene and formally approve the necessary changes in regard to the Palestinian Covenant, as undertaken in the letters signed by the Chairman of the PLO and addressed to the Prime Minister of Israel, dated September 9, 1993 and May 4, 1994.

10. Pursuant to Annex I, Article IX of this Agreement, Israel confirms that the permanent checkpoints on the roads leading to and from the Jericho Area (except those related to the access road leading from Mousa Alami to the Allenby Bridge) will be removed upon the completion of the first phase of redeployment.

11. Prisoners who, pursuant to the Gaza-Jericho Agreement, were turned over to the Palestinian Authority on the condition that they remain in the Jericho Area for the remainder of their sentence, will be free to return to their homes in the West Bank and the Gaza Strip upon the completion of the first phase of redeployment.

12. As regards relations between Israel and the PLO, and without derogating from the commitments contained in the letters signed by and exchanged between the Prime Minister of Israel and the Chairman of the PLO, dated September 9, 1993 and May 4, 1994, the two sides will apply between them the provisions contained in Article XXII, paragraph 1, with the necessary changes.

13.a. The Preamble to this Agreement, and all Annexes, Appendices and maps attached hereto (*not reproduced—Ed.*), shall constitute an integral part hereof.

   b. The Parties agree that the maps (*not reproduced—Ed.*) attached to the Gaza-Jericho Agreement as:

   a. map No. 1 (The Gaza Strip), an exact copy of which is attached to this Agreement as map No. 2 (in this Agreement 'map No. 2');

   b. map No. 4 (Deployment of Palestinian Police in the Gaza Strip), an exact copy of which is attached to this Agreement as map No. 5 (in this Agreement 'map No. 5'); and

   c. map No. 6 (Maritime Activity Zones), an exact copy of which is attached to this Agreement as map No. 8 (in this Agreement 'map No. 8');

   are an integral part hereof and will remain in effect for the duration of this Agreement.

14. While the Jeftlik area will come under the functional and personal jurisdiction of the Council in the first phase of redeployment, the area's transfer to the territorial jurisdiction of the Council will be considered by the Israeli side in the first phase of the further redeployment phases.

THE WYE RIVER MEMORANDUM

The Wye River Memorandum was signed by Israeli Prime Minister Binyamin Netanyahu and PA President Yasser Arafat, and witnessed by US President Bill Clinton, on 23 October 1998 at the Wye Plantation, Maryland, USA. The Memorandum was to enter into force 10 days after this date. An attachment to the Memorandum detailed a 'time line' for the implementation of the terms of the Interim Agreement and the Memorandum.

The following are steps to facilitate implementation of the Interim Agreement on the West Bank and Gaza Strip of September 28, 1995 (the 'Interim Agreement') and other related agreements including the Note for the Record of January 17, 1997 (hereinafter referred to as 'the prior agreements') so that the Israeli and Palestinian sides can more effectively carry out their reciprocal responsibilities, including those relating to further redeployments and security respectively. These steps are to be carried out in a parallel phased approach in accordance with this Memorandum and the attached time line. They are subject to the relevant terms and conditions of the prior agreements and do not supersede their other agreements.

I. FURTHER REDEPLOYMENTS

A. Phase One and Two Further Redeployments

1. Pursuant to the Interim Agreement and subsequent agreements, the Israeli side's implementation of the first and second F.R.D. will consist of the transfer to the Palestinian side of 13% from Area C as follows:

1% to Area (A)

12% to Area (B)

The Palestinian side has informed that it will allocate an area/areas amounting to 3% from the above Area (B) to be designated as Green Areas and/or Nature Reserves. The Palestinian side has further informed that they will act according to the established scientific standards, and that therefore there will be no changes in the status of these areas, without prejudice to the rights of the existing inhabitants in these areas including Bedouins; while these standards do not allow new construction in these areas, existing roads and buildings may be maintained.

The Israeli side will retain in these Green Areas/Nature Reserves the overriding security responsibility for the purpose of protecting Israelis and confronting the threat of terrorism.

Activities and movements of the Palestinian Police forces may be carried out after co-ordination and confirmation; the Israeli side will respond to such requests expeditiously.

2. As part of the foregoing implementation of the first and second F.R.D., 14.2% from Area (B) will become Area (A).

B. Third Phase of Further Redeployments

With regard to the terms of the Interim Agreement and of Secretary Christopher's letters to the two sides of January 17, 1997 relating to the further redeployment process, there will be a committee to address this question. The United States will be briefed regularly.

II. SECURITY

In the provisions on security arrangements of the Interim Agreement, the Palestinian side agreed to take all measures necessary in order to prevent acts of terrorism, crime and hostilities directed against the Israeli side, against individuals falling under the Israeli side's authority and against their property, just as the Israeli side agreed to take all measures necessary in order to prevent acts of terrorism, crime and hostilities directed against the Palestinian side, against individuals falling under the Palestinian side's authority and against their property. The two sides also agreed to take legal measures against offenders within their jurisdiction and to prevent incitement against each other by any organizations, groups or individuals within their jurisdiction.

Both sides recognize that it is in their vital interests to combat terrorism and fight violence in accordance with Annex I of the Interim Agreement and the Note for the Record. They also recognize that the struggle against terror and violence must be comprehensive in that it deals with terrorists, the terror support structure, and the environment conducive to the support of terror. It must be continuous and constant over a long-term, in that there can be no pauses in the work against terrorists and their structure. It must be co-operative in that no effort can be fully effective without Israeli-Palestinian co-operation and the continuous exchange of information, concepts, and actions.

Pursuant to the prior agreements, the Palestinian side's implementation of its responsibilities for security, security co-operation, and other issues will be as detailed below during the time periods specified in the attached time line:

A. Security Actions

1. Outlawing and Combating Terrorist Organizations

a. The Palestinian side will make known its policy of zero tolerance for terror and violence against both sides.

b. A work plan developed by the Palestinian side will be shared with the U.S. and thereafter implementation will begin immediately to ensure the systematic and effective combat of terrorist organizations and their infrastructure.

c. In addition to the bilateral Israeli-Palestinian security co-operation, a U.S.-Palestinian committee will meet biweekly to review the steps being taken to eliminate terrorist cells and the support structure that plans, finances, supplies and abets terror. In these meetings, the Palestinian side will inform the U.S. fully of the actions it has taken to outlaw all organizations (or wings of organizations, as appropriate) of a military, terrorist or violent character and their support structure and to prevent them from operating in areas under its jurisdiction.

d. The Palestinian side will apprehend the specific individuals suspected of perpetrating acts of violence and terror for the purpose of further investigation, and prosecution and punishment of all persons involved in acts of violence and terror.

e. A U.S.-Palestinian committee will meet to review and evaluate information pertinent to the decisions on prosecution, punishment or other legal measures which affect the status of individuals suspected of abetting or perpetrating acts of violence and terror.

2. Prohibiting Illegal Weapons

a. The Palestinian side will ensure an effective legal framework is in place to criminalize, in conformity with the prior agreements, any importation, manufacturing or unlicensed sale, acquisition or possession of firearms, ammunition or weapons in areas under Palestinian jurisdiction.

b. In addition, the Palestinian side will establish and vigorously and continuously implement a systematic programme for the collection and appropriate handling of all such illegal items in accordance with the prior agreements. The U.S. has agreed to assist in carrying out this programme.

c. A U.S.-Palestinian-Israeli committee will be established to assist and enhance co-operation in preventing the smuggling or other unauthorized introduction of weapons or explosive materials into areas under Palestinian jurisdiction.

3. Preventing Incitement

a. Drawing on relevant international practice and pursuant to Article XXII (1) of the Interim Agreement and the Note for the Record, the Palestinian side will issue a decree prohibiting all forms of incitement to violence or terror, and establishing mechanisms for acting systematically against all expressions or threats of violence or terror. This decree will be comparable to the existing Israeli legislation which deals with the same subject.

b. A U.S.-Palestinian-Israeli committee will meet on a regular basis to monitor cases of possible incitement to violence or terror and to make recommendations and reports on how to prevent such incitement. The Israeli, Palestinian and U.S. sides will each appoint a media specialist, a law enforcement representative, an educational specialist and a current or former elected official to the committee.

B. Security Co-operation

The two sides agree that their security co-operation will be based on a spirit of partnership and will include, among other things, the following steps:

1. Bilateral Co-operation

There will be full bilateral security co-operation between the two sides which will be continuous, intensive and comprehensive.

2. Forensic Co-operation

There will be an exchange of forensic expertise, training, and other assistance.

3. Trilateral Committee

In addition to the bilateral Israeli-Palestinian security co-operation, a high-ranking U.S.-Palestinian-Israeli committee will meet as required and not less than biweekly to assess current threats, deal with any impediments to effective security co-operation and co-ordination and address the steps being taken to combat terror and terrorist organizations. The committee will also serve as a forum to address the issue of external support for terror. In these meetings, the Palestinian side will fully inform the members of the committee of the results of its investigations concerning terrorist suspects already in custody and the participants will exchange additional relevant information. The committee will report regularly to the leaders of the two sides on the status of co-operation, the results of the meetings and its recommendations.

C. Other Issues

1. Palestinian Police Force

a. The Palestinian side will provide a list of its policemen to the Israeli side in conformity with the prior agreements.

b. Should the Palestinian side request technical assistance, the U.S. has indicated its willingness to help meet their needs in co-operation with other donors.

c. The Monitoring and Steering Committee will, as part of its functions, monitor the implementation of this provision and brief the U.S.

2. PLO Charter

The Executive Committee of the Palestine Liberation Organization and the Palestinian Central Council will reaffirm the letter of 22 January 1998 from PLO Chairman Yasser Arafat to President Clinton concerning the nullification of the Palestinian

National Charter provisions that are inconsistent with the letters exchanged between the PLO and the Government of Israel on 9–10 September 1993. PLO Chairman Arafat, the Speaker of the Palestine National Council, and the Speaker of the Palestinian Council will invite the members of the PNC, as well as the members of the Central Council, the Council, and the Palestinian Heads of Ministries to a meeting to be addressed by President Clinton to reaffirm their support for the peace process and the aforementioned decisions of the Executive Committee and the Central Council.

3. *Legal Assistance in Criminal Matters*

Among other forms of legal assistance in criminal matters, the requests for arrest and transfer of suspects and defendants pursuant to Article II (7) of Annex IV of the Interim Agreement will be submitted (or resubmitted) through the mechanism of the Joint Israeli-Palestinian Legal Committee and will be responded to in conformity with Article II (7) (f) of Annex IV of the Interim Agreement within the twelve week period. Requests submitted after the eighth week will be responded to in conformity with Article II (7) (f) within four weeks of their submission. The U.S. has been requested by the sides to report on a regular basis on the steps being taken to respond to the above requests.

4. *Human Rights and the Rule of Law*

Pursuant to Article XI (1) of Annex I of the Interim Agreement, and without derogating from the above, the Palestinian Police will exercise powers and responsibilities to implement this Memorandum with due regard to internationally accepted norms of human rights and the rule of law, and will be guided by the need to protect the public, respect human dignity, and avoid harassment.

III. INTERIM COMMITTEES AND ECONOMIC ISSUES

1. The Israeli and Palestinian sides reaffirm their commitment to enhancing their relationship and agree on the need actively to promote economic development in the West Bank and Gaza. In this regard, the parties agree to continue or to reactivate all standing committees established by the Interim Agreement, including the Monitoring and Steering Committee, the Joint Economic Committee (JEC), the Civil Affairs Committee (CAC), the Legal Committee, and the Standing Co-operation Committee.

2. The Israeli and Palestinian sides have agreed on arrangements which will permit the timely opening of the Gaza Industrial Estate. They also have concluded a 'Protocol Regarding the Establishment and Operation of the International Airport in the Gaza Strip During the Interim Period'.

3. Both sides will renew negotiations on Safe Passage immediately. As regards the southern route, the sides will make best efforts to conclude the agreement within a week of the entry into force of this Memorandum. Operation of the southern route will start as soon as possible thereafter. As regards the northern route, negotiations will continue with the goal of reaching agreement as soon as possible. Implementation will take place expeditiously thereafter.

4. The Israeli and Palestinian sides acknowledge the great importance of the Port of Gaza for the development of the Palestinian economy, and the expansion of Palestinian trade. They commit themselves to proceeding without delay to conclude an agreement to allow the construction and operation of the port in accordance with the prior agreements. The Israeli-Palestinian Committee will reactivate its work immediately with a goal of concluding the protocol within sixty days, which will allow commencement of the construction of the port.

5. The two sides recognize that unresolved legal issues adversely affect the relationship between the two peoples. They therefore will accelerate efforts through the Legal Committee to address outstanding legal issues and to implement solutions to these issues in the shortest possible period. The Palestinian side will provide to the Israeli side copies of all of its laws in effect.

6. The Israeli and Palestinian sides will launch a strategic economic dialogue to enhance their economic relationship. They will establish within the framework of the JEC an Ad Hoc Committee for this purpose. The committee will review the

following four issues: (1) Israeli purchase tax; (2) co-operation in combating vehicle theft; (3) dealing with unpaid Palestinian debts; and (4) the impact of Israeli standards as barriers to trade and the expansion of the A1 and A2 lists. The committee will submit an interim report within three weeks of the entry into force of this Memorandum, and within six weeks will submit its conclusions and recommendations to be implemented.

7. The two sides agree on the importance of continued international donor assistance to facilitate implementation by both sides of agreements reached. They also recognize the need for enhanced donor support for economic development in the West Bank and Gaza. They agree jointly to approach the donor community to organize a Ministerial Conference before the end of 1998 to seek pledges for enhanced levels of assistance.

IV. PERMANENT STATUS NEGOTIATIONS

The two sides will immediately resume permanent status negotiations on an accelerated basis and will make a determined effort to achieve the mutual goal of reaching an agreement by May 4, 1999. The negotiations will be continuous and without interruption. The U.S. has expressed its willingness to facilitate these negotiations.

V. UNILATERAL ACTIONS

Recognizing the necessity to create a positive environment for the negotiations, neither side shall initiate or take any step that will change the status of the West Bank and the Gaza Strip in accordance with the Interim Agreement.

SHARM ESH-SHEIKH MEMORANDUM ON THE IMPLEMENTATION TIMELINE OF OUTSTANDING COMMITMENTS OF AGREEMENTS SIGNED AND THE RESUMPTION OF PERMANENT STATUS NEGOTIATIONS (WYE TWO)

The implementation of the Wye River Memorandum having stalled under the Netanyahu administration in Israel, in September 1999 the new Israeli Prime Minister, Ehud Barak, and the PA President, Yasser Arafat, met in the Egyptian resort of Sharm esh-Sheikh to discuss the possible reactivation of the Memorandum. On 4 September the two leaders signed the Sharm esh-Sheikh Memorandum (also known as Wye Two), which detailed a revised timetable for the outstanding provisions of the October 1998 Memorandum. The Memorandum was witnessed by President Hosni Mubarak for Egypt, Secretary of State Madeleine Albright for the USA, and King Abdullah of Jordan.

The Government of the State of Israel and the Palestine Liberation Organization (PLO) commit themselves to full and mutual implementation of the Interim Agreement and all other agreements concluded beween them since September 1993 (hereinafter 'the prior agreements'), and all outstanding commitments emanating from the prior agreements. Without derogating from the other requirements of the prior agreements, the two sides have agreed as follows:

1. Permanent Status Negotiations

a. In the context of the implementation of the prior agreements, the two sides will resume the Permanent Status negotiations in an accelerated manner and will make a determined effort to achieve their mutual agenda, i.e. the specific issues reserved for Permanent Status negotiators and other issues of common interest;

b. The two sides reaffirm their understanding that the negotiations on the Permanent Status will lead to the implementation of Security Council Resolutions 242 and 338;

c. The two sides will make a determined effort to conclude a Framework Agreement on all Permanent Status issues in five months from the resumption of the Permanent Status negotiations;

d. The two sides will conclude a comprehensive agreement on all Permanent Status issues within one year from the resumption of the Permanent Status negotiations;

e. Permanent Status negotiations will resume after the implementation of the first stage of release of prisoners and the second stage of the First and Second Further Redeployments and not later than September 13, 1999.

In the Wye River Memorandum, the United States has expressed its willingness to facilitate these negotiations.

2. Phase One and Phase Two of the Further Redeployments

The Israeli side undertakes the following with regard to Phase One and Phase Two of the Further Redeployments:

a. On September 5, 1999, to transfer 7% from Area C to Area B;

b. On November 15, 1999, to transfer 2% from Area B to Area A and 3% from Area C to Area B;

c. On January 20, 2000, to transfer 1% from Area C to Area A, and 5.1% from Area B to Area A.

3. Release of Prisoners

a. The two sides shall establish a joint committee that shall follow up on matters related to the release of Palestinian prisoners;

b. The Government of Israel shall release Palestinian and other prisoners who committed their offences prior to September 13, 1993, and were arrested prior to May 4, 1994. The Joint Committee shall agree on the names of those who will be released in the first two stages. Those lists shall be recommended to the relevant Authorities through the Monitoring and Steering Committee;

c. The first stage of release of prisoners shall be carried out on September 5, 1999 and shall consist of 200 prisoners. The second stage of release of prisoners shall be carried out on October 8, 1999 and shall consist of 150 prisoners;

d. The joint committee shall recommend further lists of names to be released to the relevant Authorities through the Monitoring and Steering Committee;

e. The Israeli side will aim to release Palestinian prisoners before next Ramadan.

4. Committees

a. The Third Further Redeployment Committee shall commence its activities not later than September 13, 1999;

b. The Monitoring and Steering Committee, all Interim Committees (i.e. Civil Affairs Committee, Joint Economic Committee, Joint Standing Committee, legal committee, people to people), as well as Wye River Memorandum committees shall resume and/or continue their activity, as the case may be, not later than September 13, 1999. The Monitoring and Steering Committee will have on its agenda, inter alia, the Year 2000, Donor/PA projects in Area C, and the issue of industrial estates;

c. The Continuing Committee on displaced persons shall resume its activity on October 1, 1999 (Article XXVII, Interim Agreement);

d. Not later than October 30, 1999, the two sides will implement the recommendations of the Ad-hoc Economic Committee (article 111-6, Wye River Memorandum).

5. Safe Passage

a. The operation of the Southern Route of the Safe Passage for the movement of persons, vehicles, and goods will start on October 1, 1999 (Annex I, Article X, Interim Agreement) in accordance with the details of operation, which will be provided for in the Safe Passage Protocol that will be concluded by the two sides not later than September 30, 1999;

b. The two sides will agree on the specific location of the crossing point of the Northern Route of the Safe Passage as specified in Annex I, Article X, provision c-4, in the Interim Agreement not later than October 5, 1999;

c. The Safe Passage Protocol applied to the Southern Route of the Safe Passage shall apply to the Northern Route of the Safe Passage with relevant agreed modifications;

d. Upon the agreement on the location of the crossing point of the Northern Route of the Safe Passage, construction of the needed facilities and related procedures shall commence and shall be ongoing. At the same time, temporary facilities will be established for the operation of the Northern Route not later than four months from the agreement on the specific location of the crossing-point;

e. In between the operation of the Southern crossing point of the Safe Passage and the Northern crossing point of the Safe Passage, Israel will facilitate arrangements for the movement between the West Bank and the Gaza Strip, using non-Safe Passage routes other than the Southern Route of the Safe Passage;

f. The location of the crossing points shall be without prejudice to the Permanent Status negotiations (Annex I, Article X, provision e, Interim Agreement).

6. Gaza Sea Port

The two sides have agreed on the following principles to facilitate and enable the construction works of the Gaza Sea Port. The principles shall not prejudice or pre-empt the outcome of negotiations on the Permanent Status:

a. The Israeli side agrees that the Palestinian side shall commence construction works in and related to the Gaza Sea Port on October 1, 1999;

b. The two sides agree that the Gaza Sea Port will not be operated in any way before reaching a joint Sea Port protocol on all aspects of operating the Port, including security;

c. The Gaza Sea Port is a special case, like the Gaza Airport, being situated in an area under the responsibility of the Palestinian side and serving as an international passage. Therefore, with the conclusion of a joint Sea Port Protocol, all activities and arrangements relating to the construction of the Port shall be in accordance with the provisions of the Interim Agreement, especially those relating to international passages, as adapted in the Gaza Airport Protocol;

d. The construction shall ensure adequate provision for effective security and customs inspection of people and goods, as well as the establishment of a designated checking area in the Port;

e. In this context, the Israeli side will facilitate on an ongoing basis the works related to the construction of the Gaza Sea Port, including the movement in and out of the Port of vessels, equipment, resources, and material required for the construction of the Port;

f. The two sides will co-ordinate such works, including the designs and movement, through a joint mechanism.

7. Hebron Issues

a. The Shuhada Road in Hebron shall be opened for the movement of Palestinian vehicles in two phases. The first phase has been carried out, and the second shall be carried out not later than October 30, 1999;

b. The wholesale market Hasbahe will be opened not later than November 1, 1999, in accordance with arrangements which will be agreed upon by the two sides;

c. A high-level Joint Liaison Committee will convene not later than September 13, 1999 to review the situation in the Tomb of the Patriarchs/Al Haram Al Ibrahimi (Annex I, Article VII, Interim Agreement and as per the January 15, 1998 US Minute of Discussion).

8. Security

a. The two sides will, in accordance with the prior agreements, act to ensure the immediate, efficient and effective handling of any incident involving a threat or act of terrorism, violence or incitement, whether committed by Palestinians or Israelis. To this end, they will co-operate in the exchange of information and co-ordinate policies and activities. Each side shall immediately and effectively respond to the occurrence of an act of terrorism, violence or incitement and shall take all necessary measures to prevent such an occurrence;

b. Pursuant to the prior agreements, the Palestinian side undertakes to implement its responsibilities for security, security co-operation, ongoing obligations and other issues emanating from the prior agreements, including, in particular, the following obligations emanating from the Wye River Memorandum:

1. continuation of the programme for the collection of the illegal weapons, including reports;

2. apprehension of suspects, including reports;

3. forwarding of the list of Palestinian policemen to the Israeli side not later than September 13, 1999;

4. beginning of the review of the list by the Monitoring and Steering Committee not later than October 15, 1999.

9. The two sides call upon the international donor community to enhance its commitment and financial support to the Palestinian economic development and the Israeli-Palestinian peace process.

10. Recognizing the necessity to create a positive environment for the negotiations, neither side shall initiate or take any step that will change the status of the West Bank and the Gaza Strip in accordance with the Interim Agreement.

11. Obligations pertaining to dates which occur on holidays or Saturdays shall be carried out on the first subsequent working day.

This memorandum will enter into force one week from the date of its signature.

It is understood that, for technical reasons, implementation of Article 2a and the first stage mentioned in Article 3c will be carried out within a week from the signing of this Memorandum.

REPORT OF THE SHARM ESH-SHEIKH FACT-FINDING COMMITTEE (THE MITCHELL REPORT)

Violence between Israeli forces and Palestinians broke out in late September 2000, following a visit by the leader of Israel's Likud party, Ariel Sharon, to the site of the Temple Mount/ Haram ash-Sharif, in East Jerusalem. A period of intense international diplomatic activity ensued, in an attempt to bring about an end to the violent confrontations which had swiftly spread throughout the West Bank and Gaza Strip. On 14 October UN Secretary-General Kofi Annan secured the agreement of the Israeli Prime Minister, Ehud Barak, and the PA President, Yasser Arafat, to lead delegations to a summit meeting in Sharm esh-Sheikh, Egypt, with mediation by US President Bill Clinton. The summit duly proceeded on 16 October, concluding the following day with what Clinton termed agreement on 'immediate concrete measures' to end the violence. (Subsequent truce agreements, based on understandings brokered by Clinton at Sharm esh-Sheikh, failed to hold, and violence continued in mid-2001.) Agreement was reached at the summit on the formation of a US-appointed international fact-finding commission to investigate the clashes. The committee—chaired by former US Senator George Mitchell and comprising also former President Süleyman Demirel of Turkey, Norwegian Minister of Foreign Affairs Thorbjørn Jagland, former US Senator Warren Rudman, and the High Representative for the Common Foreign and Security Policy of the European Union, Javier Solana—was appointed by Clinton in early November. Reproduced is the full text of the committee's report, published on 20 May 2001. [Footnotes to the report—principally references to statements and submissions of the Government of Israel and the PLO, which made submissions to the committee on behalf of the Palestinians—have been omitted].

SUMMARY OF RECOMMENDATIONS

The Government of Israel and the Palestinian Authority (PA) must act swiftly and decisively to halt the violence. Their immediate objectives then should be to rebuild confidence and resume negotiations.

During this mission our aim has been to fulfil the mandate agreed at Sharm esh-Sheikh. We value the support given our work by the participants at the summit, and we commend the parties for their co-operation. Our principal recommendation is that they recommit themselves to the Sharm esh-Sheikh spirit and that they implement the decisions made there in 1999 and 2000. We believe that the summit participants will support bold action by the parties to achieve these objectives.

The restoration of trust is essential, and the parties should take affirmative steps to this end. Given the high level of hostility and mistrust, the timing and sequence of these steps are obviously crucial. This can be decided only by the parties. We urge them to begin the process of decision immediately.

Accordingly, we recommend that steps be taken to:

END THE VIOLENCE

The Government of Israel and the PA should reaffirm their commitment to existing agreements and undertakings and should immediately implement an unconditional cessation of violence.

The Government of Israel and PA should immediately resume security co-operation.

REBUILD CONFIDENCE

The PA and Government of Israel should work together to establish a meaningful 'cooling-off period' and implement additional confidence-building measures, some of which were detailed in the October 2000 Sharm esh-Sheikh Statement and some of which were offered by the US on January 7, 2001 in Cairo [see Recommendations section for further description].

The PA and Government of Israel should resume their efforts to identify, condemn and discourage incitement in all its forms.

The PA should make clear through concrete action to Palestinians and Israelis alike that terrorism is reprehensible and unacceptable, and that the PA will make a 100 percent effort to prevent terrorist operations and to punish perpetrators. This effort should include immediate steps to apprehend and incarcerate terrorists operating within the PA's jurisdiction.

The Government of Israel should freeze all settlement activity, including the 'natural growth' of existing settlements.

The Government of Israel should ensure that the IDF [*Israeli Defence Forces*] adopt and enforce policies and procedures encouraging non-lethal responses to unarmed demonstrators, with a view to minimizing casualties and friction between the two communities.

The PA should prevent gunmen from using Palestinian populated areas to fire upon Israeli populated areas and IDF positions. This tactic places civilians on both sides at unnecessary risk.

The Government of Israel should lift closures, transfer to the PA all tax revenues owed, and permit Palestinians who had been employed in Israel to return to their jobs; and should ensure that security forces and settlers refrain from the destruction of homes and roads, as well as trees and other agricultural property in Palestinian areas. We acknowledge the Government of Israel's position that actions of this nature have been taken for security reasons. Nevertheless, the economic effects will persist for years.

The PA should renew co-operation with Israeli security agencies to ensure, to the maximum extent possible, that Palestinian workers employed within Israel are fully vetted and free of connections to organizations and individuals engaged in terrorism.

The PA and Government of Israel should consider a joint undertaking to preserve and protect holy places sacred to the traditions of Jews, Muslims, and Christians.

The Government of Israel and PA should jointly endorse and support the work of Palestinian and Israeli non-governmental organizations involved in cross-community initiatives linking the two peoples.

RESUME NEGOTIATIONS

In the spirit of the Sharm esh-Sheikh agreements and understandings of 1999 and 2000, we recommend that the parties meet to reaffirm their commitment to signed agreements and mutual understandings, and take corresponding action.This should be the basis for resuming full and meaningful negotiations.

INTRODUCTION

On October 17, 2000, at the conclusion of the Middle East Peace Summit at Sharm esh-Sheikh, Egypt, the President of the United States spoke on behalf of the participants (the Government of Israel, the Palestinian Authority, the Governments of Egypt, Jordan, and the United States, the United Nations, and the European Union). Among other things, the President stated that:

The United States will develop with the Israelis and Palestinians, as well as in consultation with the United Nations Secretary-General, a committee of fact-finding on the events of the past several weeks and how to prevent their recurrence. The committee's report will be shared by the US President with the UN Secretary-General and the parties prior to publication. A final report shall be submitted under the auspices of the US President for publication.

On November 7, 2000, following consultations with the other participants, the President asked us to serve on what has come to be known as the Sharm esh-Sheikh Fact-Finding Committee. In a letter to us on December 6, 2000, the President stated that:

The purpose of the Summit, and of the agreement that ensued, was to end the violence, to prevent its recurrence, and to find a path back to the peace process. In its actions and mode of operation, therefore, the Committee should be guided by these overriding goals ... [T]he Committee should strive to steer clear of any step that will intensify mutual blame and finger-pointing between the parties. As I noted in my previous letter, 'the Committee should not become a divisive force or a focal point for blame and recrimination but rather should serve to forestall violence and confrontation and provide lessons for the future.' This should not be a tribunal whose purpose is to determine the guilt or innocence of individuals or of the parties; rather, it should be a fact-finding committee whose purpose is to determine what happened and how to avoid it recurring in the future.

After our first meeting, held before we visited the region, we urged an end to all violence. Our meetings and our observations during our subsequent visits to the region have intensified our convictions in this regard. Whatever the source, violence will not solve the problems of the region. It will only make them worse. Death and destruction will not bring peace, but will deepen the hatred and harden the resolve on both sides. There is only one way to peace, justice, and security in the Middle East, and that is through negotiation.

Despite their long history and close proximity, some Israelis and Palestinians seem not to fully appreciate each other's problems and concerns. Some Israelis appear not to comprehend the humiliation and frustration that Palestinians must endure every day as a result of living with the continuing effects of occupation, sustained by the presence of Israeli military forces and settlements in their midst, or the determination of the Palestinians to achieve independence and genuine self-determination. Some Palestinians appear not to comprehend the extent to which terrorism creates fear among the Israeli people and undermines their belief in the possibility or co-existence, or the determination of the Government of Israel to do whatever is necessary to protect its people.

Fear, hate, anger, and frustration have risen on both sides. The greatest danger of all is that the culture of peace, nurtured over the previous decade, is being shattered. In its place there is a growing sense of futility and despair, and a growing resort to violence.

Political leaders on both sides must act and speak decisively to reverse these dangerous trends; they must rekindle the desire and the drive for peace. That will be difficult. But it can be done and it must be done, for the alternative is unacceptable and should be unthinkable.

Two proud peoples share a land and a destiny. Their competing claims and religious differences have led to a grinding, demoralizing, dehumanizing conflict. They can continue in conflict or they can negotiate to find a way to live side-by-side in peace.

There is a record of achievement. In 1991 the first peace conference with Israelis and Palestinians took place in Madrid to achieve peace based on UN Security Council Resolutions 242 and 338. In 1993, the Palestine Liberation Organization (PLO) and Israel met in Oslo for the first face-to-face negotiations; they led to mutual recognition and the Declaration of Principles (signed by the parties in Washington, D.C. on September 13, 1993), which provided a road map to reach the destination agreed in Madrid. Since then, important steps have been taken

in Cairo, in Washington, and elsewhere. Last year the parties came very close to a permanent settlement.

So much has been achieved. So much is at risk. If the parties are to succeed in completing their journey to their common destination, agreed commitments must be implemented, international law respected, and human rights protected. We encourage them to return to negotiations, however difficult. It is the only path to peace, justice and security.

DISCUSSION

It is clear from their statements that the participants in the summit of last October hoped and intended that the outbreak of violence, then less than a month old, would soon end. The US President's letters to us, asking that we make recommendations on how to prevent a recurrence of violence, reflect that intention.

Yet the violence has not ended. It has worsened. Thus the overriding concern of those in the region with whom we spoke is to end the violence and to return to the process of shaping a sustainable peace. That is what we were told, and were asked to address, by Israelis and Palestinians alike. It was the message conveyed to us as well by President Mubarak of Egypt, King Abdullah of Jordan, and UN Secretary-General Annan.

Their concern must be ours. If our report is to have effect, it must deal with the situation that exists, which is different from that envisaged by the summit participants. In this report, we will try to answer the questions assigned to us by the Sharm esh-Sheikh summit: What happened? Why did it happen?

In light of the current situation, however, we must elaborate on the third part of our mandate: How can the recurrence of violence be prevented? The relevance and impact of our work, in the end, will be measured by the recommendations we make concerning the following:

Ending the Violence.

Rebuilding Confidence.

Resuming Negotiations.

WHAT HAPPENED?

We are not a tribunal. We complied with the request that we do not determine the guilt or innocence of individuals or of the parties. We did not have the power to compel the testimony of witnesses or the production of documents. Most of the information we received came from the parties and, understandably, it largely tended to support their arguments.

In this part of our report, we do not attempt to chronicle all of the events from late September 2000 onward. Rather, we discuss only those that shed light on the underlying causes of violence.

In late September 2000, Israeli, Palestinian, and other officials received reports that Member of the Knesset (now Prime Minister) Ariel Sharon was planning a visit to the Haram ash-Sharif/Temple Mount in Jerusalem. Palestinian and US officials urged then Prime Minister Ehud Barak to prohibit the visit. Mr Barak told us that he believed the visit was intended to be an internal political act directed against him by a political opponent, and he declined to prohibit it.

Mr Sharon made the visit on September 28 accompanied by over 1,000 Israeli police officers. Although Israelis viewed the visit in an internal political context, Palestinians saw it as highly provocative to them. On the following day, in the same place, a large number of unarmed Palestinian demonstrators and a large Israeli police contingent confronted each other. According to the US Department of State, 'Palestinians held large demonstrations and threw stones at police in the vicinity of the Western Wall. Police used rubber-coated metal bullets and live ammunition to disperse the demonstrators, killing 4 persons and injuring about 200.' According to the Government of Israel, 14 Israeli policemen were injured.

Similar demonstrations took place over the following several days. Thus began what has become known as the 'Al-Aqsa Intifada' (Al-Aqsa being a mosque at the Haram ash-Sharif/ Temple Mount).

The Government of Israel asserts that the immediate catalyst for the violence was the breakdown of the Camp David negotiations on July 25, 2000 and the 'widespread appreciation in the international community of Palestinian responsibility for the impasse'. In this view, Palestinian violence was planned by the PA leadership, and was aimed at 'provoking and incurring Palestinian casualties as a means of regaining the diplomatic initiative.'

The Palestine Liberation Organization (PLO) denies the allegation that the intifada was planned. It claims, however, that 'Camp David represented nothing less than an attempt by Israel to extend the force it exercises on the ground to negotiations,' and that 'the failure of the summit, and the attempts to allocate blame on the Palestinian side only added to the tension on the ground ...'

From the perspective of the PLO, Israel responded to the disturbances with excessive and illegal use of deadly force against demonstrators; behavior which, in the PLO's view, reflected Israel's contempt for the lives and safety of Palestinians. For Palestinians, the widely seen images of the killing of 12-year-old Muhammad ad-Durra in Gaza on September 20, shot as he huddled behind his father, reinforced that perception.

From the perspective of the Government of Israel, the demonstrations were organized and directed by the Palestinian leadership to create sympathy for their cause around the world by provoking Israeli security forces to fire upon demonstrators, especially young people. For Israelis, the lynching of two military reservists, First Sergeant Vadim Novesche and First Corporal Yosef Avrahami, in Ramallah on October 12, reflected a deep-seated Palestinian hatred of Israel and Jews.

What began as a series of confrontations between Palestinian demonstrators and Israeli security forces, which resulted in the Government of Israel's initial restrictions on the movement of people and goods in the West Bank amd Gaza Strip (closures), has since evolved into a wider array of violent actions and responses. There have been exchanges of fire between built-up areas, sniping incidents and clashes between Israeli settlers and Palestinians. There have also been terrorist acts and Israeli reactions thereto (characterized by the Government of Israel as counter-terrorism), including killings, further destruction of property and economic measures. Most recently, there have been mortar attacks on Israeli locations and IDF ground incursions into Palestinian areas.

From the Palestinian perspective, the decision of Israel to characterize the current crisis as 'an armed conflict short of war' is simply a means 'to justify its assassination policy, its collective punishment policy, and its use of lethal force.' From the Israeli perspective, 'The Palestinian leadership have instigated, orchestrated and directed the violence. It has used, and continues to use, terror and attrition as strategic tools.'

In their submissions, the parties traded allegations about the motivation and degree of control exercised by the other. However, we were provided with no persuasive evidence that the Sharon visit was anything other than an internal political act; neither were we provided with persuasive evidence that the PA planned the uprising.

Accordingly, we have no basis on which to conclude that there was a deliberate plan by the PA to initiate a campaign of violence at the first opportunity; or to conclude that there was a deliberate plan by the Government of Israel to respond with lethal force.

However, there is also no evidence on which to conclude that the PA made a consistent effort to contain the demonstrations and control the violence once it began; or that the Government of Israel made a consistent effort to use non-lethal means to control demonstrations of unarmed Palestinians. Amid rising anger, fear, and mistrust, each side assumed the worst about the other and acted accordingly.

The Sharon visit did not cause the 'Al-Aqsa Intifada'. But it was poorly timed and the provocative effect should have been foreseen; indeed it was foreseen by those who urged that the visit be prohibited. More significant were the events that followed: the decision of the Israeli police on September 29 to use lethal means against the Palestinian demonstrators; and the subsequent failure, as noted above, of either party to exercise restraint.

WHY DID IT HAPPEN?

The roots of the current violence extend much deeper than an inconclusive summit conference. Both sides have made clear a profound disillusionment with the behavior of the other in failing to meet the expectations arising from the peace process launched in Madrid in 1991 and then in Oslo in 1993. Each side has accused the other of violating undertakings and undermining the spirit of their commitment to resolving their political differences peacefully.

Divergent Expectations:

We are struck by the divergent expectations expressed by the parties relating to the implementation of the Oslo process. Results achieved from this process were unthinkable less than 10 years ago. During the latest round of negotiations, the parties were closer to a permanent settlement than ever before.

None the less, Palestinians and Israelis alike told us that the promise on which the Oslo process is based—that tackling the hard 'permanent status' issues be deferred to the end of the process—has gradually come under serious pressure. The step-by-step process agreed to by the parties was based on the assumption that each step in the negotiating process would lead to enhanced trust and confidence. To achieve this, each party would have to implement agreed-upon commitments and abstain from actions that would be seen by the other as attempts to abuse the process in order to predetermine the shape of the final outcome. If this requirement is not met, the Oslo road map cannot successfully lead to its agreed destination. Today, each side blames the other for having ignored this fundamental aspect, resulting in a crisis in confidence. This problem became even more pressing with the opening of permanent status talks.

The Government of Israel has placed primacy on moving toward a Permanent Status Agreement in a non-violent atmosphere, consistent with commitments contained in the agreements between the parties. 'Even if slower than was initially envisaged, there has, since the start of the peace process in Madrid in 1991, been steady progress towards the goal of a Permanent Status Agreement without the resort to violence on a scale that has characterized recent weeks.' The 'goal' is the Permanent Status Agreement, the terms of which must be negotiated by the parties.

The PLO view is that delays in the process have been the result of an Israeli attempt to prolong and solidify the occupation. Palestinians 'believed that the Oslo process would yield an end to Israeli occupation in five years,' the time frame for the transitional period specified in the Declaration of Principles. Instead there have been, in the PLO's view, repeated Israeli delays culminating in the Camp David summit, where, 'Israel proposed to annex about 11.2% of the West Bank (excluding Jerusalem)...' and offered unacceptable proposals concerning Jerusalem, security and refugees. 'In sum, Israel's proposals at Camp David provided for Israel's annexation of the best Palestinian lands, the perpetuation of Israeli control over East Jerusalem, a continued Israeli military presence on Palestinian territory, Israeli control over Palestinian natural resources, airspace and borders, and the return of fewer than 1% of refugees to their homes.'

Both sides see the lack of full compliance with agreements reached since the opening of the peace process as evidence of a lack of good faith. This conclusion led to an erosion of trust even before the permanent status negotiations began.

Divergent Perspectives:

During the last seven months, these views have hardened into divergent realities. Each side views the other as having acted in bad faith; as having turned the optimism of Oslo into the suffering and grief of victims and their loved ones. In their statements and actions, each side demonstrates a perspective that fails to recognize any truth in the perspective of the other.

The Palestinian Perspective:

For the Palestinian side, 'Madrid' and 'Oslo' heralded the prospect of a State, and guaranteed an end to the occupation and a resolution of outstanding matters within an agreed time frame. Palestinians are genuinely angry at the continued growth of settlements and at their daily experiences of humiliation and disruption as a result fo Israel's presence in the Palestinian territories. Palestinians see settlers and settlements in their midst not only as violating the spirit of the Oslo process, but also as an application of force in the form of Israel's overwhelming military superiority, which sustains and protects the settlements.

The Interim Agreement provides that 'the two parties view the West Bank and Gaza as a single territorial unit, the integrity and status of which will be preserved during the interim period.' Coupled with this, the Interim Agreement's prohibition on taking steps which may prejudice permanent status negotiations denies Israel the right to continue its illegal expansionist settlement policy. In addition to the Interim Agreement, customary international law, including the Fourth Geneva Convention, prohibits Israel (as an occupying power) from establishing settlements in occupied territory pending an end to the conflict.

The PLO alleges that Israeli political leaders 'have made no secret of the fact that the Israeli interpretation of Oslo was designed to segregate the Palestinians in non-contiguous enclaves, surrounded by Israeli military-controlled borders, with settlements and settlement roads violating the territories' integrity.' According to the PLO, 'In the seven years since the [Declaration of Principles], the settler population in the West Bank, excluding East Jerusalem and the Gaza Strip, has doubled to 200,000, and the settler population in East Jerusalem has risen to 170,000. Israel has constructed approximately 30 new settlements, and expanded a number of existing ones to house these new settlers.'

The PLO also claims that the Government of Israel has failed to comply with other commitments such as the further withdrawal from the West Bank and the release of Palestinian prisoners. In addition, Palestinians expressed frustration with the impasse over refugees and the deteriorating economic circumstances in the West Bank and Gaza Strip.

The Israeli Perspective:

From the Government of Israel perspective, the expansion of settlement activity and the taking of measures to facilitate the convenience and safety of settlers do not prejudice the outcome of permanent status negotiations.

Israel understands that the Palestinian side objects to the settlements in the West Bank and Gaza Strip. Without prejudice to the formal status of the settlements, Israel accepts that the settlements are an outstanding issue on which there will have to be agreement as part of any permanent status resolution between the sides. This point was acknowledged and agreed upon in the Declaration of Principles of 13 September 1993 as well as other agreements between the two sides. There has in fact been a good deal of discussion on the question of settlements between the two sides in the various negotiations toward a permanent status agreement.

Indeed, Israelis point out that at the Camp David summit and during subsequent talks the Government of Israel offered to make significant concessions with respect to settlements in the context of an overall agreement.

Security, however, is the key Government of Israel concern. The Government of Israel maintains that the PLO has breached its solemn commitments by continuing the use of violence in the pursuit of political objectives. 'Israel's principal concern in the peace process has been security. This issue is of overriding importance ... [S]ecurity is not something on which Israel will bargain or compromise. The failure of the Palestinian side to comply with both the letter and spirit of the security provisions in the various agreements has long been a source of disturbance in Israel.'

According to the Government of Israel, the Palestinian failure takes several forms: institutionalized anti-Israel, anti-Jewish incitement; the release from detention of terrorists; the failure to control illegal weapons; and the actual conduct of violent operations, ranging from the insertion of riflemen into demonstrations to terrorist attacks on Israeli civilians. The Government of Israel maintains that the PLO has explicitly violated its renunciation of terrorism and other acts of violence, thereby significantly eroding trust between the parties. The Government of Israel perceives 'a thread, implied but nonetheless clear, that runs throughout the Palestinian submissions. It is that Palestinian violence against Israel and Israelis is somehow explicable, understandable, legitimate.'

END THE VIOLENCE

For Israelis and Palestinians alike the experience of the past several months has been intensely *personal*. Through relation-

ships of kinship, friendship, religion, community and profession, virtually everyone in both societies has a link to someone who has been killed or seriously injured in the recent violence. We were touched by their stories. During our last visit to the region, we met with the families of Palestinian and Israeli victims. These individual accounts of grief were heart-rending and indescribably sad. Israeli and Palestinian families used virtually the same words to describe their grief.

When the widow of a murdered Israeli physician—a man of peace whose practice included the treatment of Arab patients—tells us that it seems that Palestinians are interested in killing Jews for the sake of killing Jews, Palestinians should take notice. When the parents of a Palestinian child killed while in his bed by an errant .50 calibre bullet draw similar conclusions about the respect accorded by Israelis to Palestinian lives, Israelis need to listen. When we see the shattered bodies of children we know it is time for adults to stop the violence.

With widespread violence, both sides have resorted to portrayals of the other in hostile stereotypes. This cycle cannot be easily broken. Without considerable determination and readiness to compromise, the rebuilding of trust will be impossible.

Cessation of Violence:

Since 1991, the parties have consistently committed themselves, in all their agreements, to the path of non-violence. They did so most recently in the two Sharm esh-Sheikh summits of September 1999 and October 2000. To stop the violence now, the PA and Government of Israel need not 'reinvent the wheel'. Rather, they should take immediate steps to end the violence, reaffirm their mutual commitments, and resume negotiations.

Resumption of Security Co-operation:

Palestinian security officials told us that it would take some time—perhaps several weeks—for the PA to reassert full control over armed elements nominally under its command and to exert decisive influence over other armed elements operating in Palestinian areas. Israeli security officials have not disputed these assertions. What is important is that the PA make an all-out effort to enforce a complete cessation of violence and that it be clearly seen by the Government of Israel as doing so. The Government of Israel must likewise exercise a 100 percent effort to ensure that potential friction points, where Palestinians come into contact with armed Israelis, do not become stages for renewed hostilities.

The collapse of security co-operation in early October reflected the belief by each party that the other had committed itself to a violent course of action. If the parties wish to attain the standard of 100 percent effort to prevent violence, the immediate resumption of security co-operation is mandatory.

We acknowledge the reluctance of the PA to be seen as facilitating the work of Israeli security services absent an explicit political context (i.e., meaningful negotiations) and under the threat of Israeli settlement expansion. Indeed, security co-operation cannot be sustained without such negotiations and with ongoing actions seen as prejudicing the outcome of negotiations. However, violence is much more likely to continue without security co-operation. Moreover, without effective security co-operation, the parties will continue to regard all acts of violence as officially sanctioned.

In order to overcome the current deadlock, the parties should consider how best to revitalize security co-operation. We commend current efforts to that end. Effective co-operation depends on recreating and sustaining an atmosphere of confidence and good personal relations.

It is for the parties themselves to undertake the main burden of day-to-day co-operation, but they should remain open to engaging the assistance of others in facilitating that work. Such outside assistance should be by mutual consent, should not threaten good bilateral working arrangements, and should not act as a tribunal or interpose between the parties. There was good security co-operation until last year that benefited from the good offices of the US (acknowledged by both sides as useful), and was also supported indirectly by security projects and assistance from the European Union. The role of outside assistance should be that of creating the appropriate framework, sustaining goodwill on both sides, and removing friction where possible. That framework must be seen to be contributing to the safety and welfare of both communities if there is to be acceptance by those communities of these efforts.

REBUILD CONFIDENCE

The historic handshake between Chairman Arafat and the late Prime Minister Rabin at the White House in September 1993 symbolized the expectation of both parties that the door to the peaceful resolution of differences had been opened. Despite the current violence and mutual loss of trust, both communities have repeatedly expressed a desire for peace. Channelling this desire into substantive progress has proved difficult. The restoration of trust is essential, and the parties should take affirmative steps to this end. Given the high level of hostility and mistrust, the timing and sequence of these steps are obviously crucial. This can be decided only by the parties. We urge them to begin the process of decision immediately.

Terrorism:

In the September 1999 Sharm esh-Sheikh Memorandum, the parties pledged to take action against 'any threat or act of terrorism, violence or incitement.' Although all three categories of hostilities are reprehensible, it was no accident that 'terrorism' was placed at the top of the list.

Terrorism involves the deliberate killing and injuring of randomly selected non-combatants for political ends. It seeks to promote a political outcome by spreading terror and demoralization throughout a population. It is immoral and ultimately self defeating. We condemn it and we urge that the parties co-ordinate their security efforts to eliminate it.

In its official submissions and briefings, the Government of Israel has accused the PA of supporting terrorism by releasing incarcerated terrorists, by allowing PA security personnel to abet, and in some cases to conduct, terrorist operations, and by terminating security co-operation with the Government of Israel. The PA vigorously denies the accusations. But Israelis hold the view that the PA's leadership has made no real effort over the past seven months to prevent anti-Israeli terrorism. The belief is, in and of itself, a major obstacle to the rebuilding of confidence.

We believe that the PA has a responsibility to help rebuild confidence by making clear to both communities that terrorism is reprehensible and unacceptable, and by taking all measures to prevent terrorist operations and to punish perpetrators. This effort should include immediate steps to apprehend and incarcerate terrorists operating within the PA's jurisdiction.

Settlements:

The Government of Israel also has a responsibility to help rebuild confidence. A cessation of Palestinian–Israeli violence will be particularly hard to sustain unless the Government of Israel freezes all settlement construction activity. The Government of Israel should also give careful consideration to whether settlements that are focal points for substantial friction are valuable bargaining chips for future negotiations or provocations likely to preclude the onset of productive talks.

The issue is, of course, controversial. Many Israelis will regard our recommendation as a statement of the obvious, and will support it. Many will oppose it. But settlement activities must not be allowed to undermine the restoration of calm and the resumption of negotiations.

During the half-century of its existence, Israel has had the strong support of the United States. In international forums, the US has at times cast the only vote on Israel's behalf. Yet, even in such a close relationship there are some differences. Prominent among those differences is the US Government's long-standing opposition to the Government of Israel's policies and practices regarding settlements. As the then Secretary of State, James A. Baker, III, commented on May 22, 1991:

Every time I have gone to Israel in connection with the peace process, on each of my four trips, I have been met with the announcement of new settlement activity. This does violate United States policy. It's the first thing that Arabs—Arab Governments, the first thing that the Palestinians in the territories—whose situation is really quite desperate—the first thing they raise when we talk to them. I don't think there is any bigger obstacle to peace than the settlement activity that continues not only unabated but at an enhanced pace.

The policy desribed by Secretary Baker, on behalf of the Administration of President George H.W. Bush, has been, in essence, the policy of every American administration over the past quarter century.

Most other countries, including Turkey, Norway, and those of the European Union, have also been critical of Israeli settlement activity, in accordance with their views that such settlements are illegal under international law and not in compliance with previous agreements.

On each of our two visits to the region there were Israeli announcements regarding expansion of settlements, and it was almost always the first issue raised by Palestinians with whom we met. During our last visit, we observed the impact of 6,400 settlers on 140,000 Palestinians in Hebron and 6,500 settlers on over 1,100,000 Palestinians in the Gaza Strip. The Government of Israel describes its policy as prohibiting new settlements but permitting expansion of existing settlements to accommodate 'natural growth'. Palestinians contend that there is no distinction between 'new' and 'expanded' settlements; and that, except for a brief freeze during the tenure of Prime Minister Itzhak Rabin, there has been a continuing, aggressive effort by Israel to increase the number and size of settlements.

The subject has been widely discussed within Israel. The *Ha'aretz* English Language Edition editorial of April 10, 2001 stated:

A government which seeks to argue that its goal is to reach a solution to the conflict with the Palestinians through peaceful means, and is trying at this stage to bring an end to the violence and terrorism, must announce an end to construction in the settlements.

The circumstances in the region are much changed from those which existed nearly 20 years ago. Yet, President Reagan's words remain relevant: 'The immediate adoption of a settlement freeze by Israel, more than any other action, could create the confidence needed [...]'

Beyond the obvious confidence-building qualities of a settlement freeze, we note that many of the confrontations during this conflict have occurred at points where Palestinians, settlers, and security forces protecting the settlers, meet. Keeping both the peace and these friction points will be very difficult.

Reducing Tension:

We were told by both Palestinians and Israelis that emotions generated by the many recent deaths and funerals have fuelled additional confrontations, and, in effect, maintained the cycle of violence. We cannot urge one side or the other to refrain from demonstrations. But both sides must make clear that violent demonstrations will not be tolerated. We can and do urge that both sides exhibit a greater respect for human life when demonstrators confront security personnel. In addition, a renewed effort to stop the violence might feature, for a limited time, a 'cooling off' period during which public demonstrations at or near friction points will be discouraged in order to break the cycle of violence. To the extent that demonstrations continue, we urge that demonstrators and security personnel keep their distance from one another to reduce the potential for lethal confrontation.

Actions and Responses:

Members of the Committee staff witnessed an incident involving stone throwing in Ramallah from the perspectives, on the ground, of both sides. The people confronting one another were mostly young men. The absence of senior leadership on the IDF side was striking. Likewise, the absence of responsible security and other officials counselling restraint on the Palestinian side was obvious.

Concerning such confrontations, the Government of Israel takes the position that 'Israel is engaged in an armed conflict short of war. This is not a civilian disturbance or a demonstration or a riot. It is characterized by live-fire attacks on a *significant scale* [emphasis added]...[T]he attacks are carried out by a well-armed and organized militia...' Yet, the Government of Israel acknowledges that of some 9,000 'attacks' by Palestinians against Israelis, 'some 2,700 [about 30 percent] involved the use of automatic weapons, rifles, hand guns, grenades, [and] explosives of other kinds.'

Thus, for the first three months of the current uprising, most incidents *did not* involve Palestinian use of firearms and explosives. B'Tselem *[the Israeli Information Centre for Human Rights in the Occupied Territories]* reported that, 'according to IDF figures, 73 percent of the incidents [from September 29 to December 2, 2000] did not include Palestinian gunfire. Despite this, it was in these incidents that most of the Palestinians [were] killed and wounded...' Altogether, nearly 500 people were killed and over 10,000 injured over the past seven months; the overwhelming majority in both categories were Palestinian. Many of these deaths were avoidable, as were many Israeli deaths.

Israel's characterization of the conflict, as noted above, is overly broad, for it does not adequately describe the variety of incidents reported since late September 2000. Moreover, by thus defining the conflict, the IDF has suspended its policy of mandating investigations by the Department of Military Police Investigations whenever a Palestinian in the territories dies at the hands of an IDF soldier in an incident not involving terrorism. In the words of the Government of Israel, 'Where Israel considers that there is reason to investigate particular incidents, it does so, although, given the circumstances of armed conflict, it does not do so routinely.' We believe, however, that by abandoning the blanket 'armed conflict short of war' characterization and by re-instituting mandatory military police investigations, the Government of Israel could help mitigate deadly violence and help rebuild mutual confidence. Notwithstanding the danger posed by stone-throwers, an effort should be made to differentiate between terrorism and protests.

Controversy has arisen between the parties over what Israel calls the 'targeting of individual enemy combatants.' The PLO describes these actions as 'extra-judicial executions', and claims that Israel has engaged in an 'assassination policy' that is 'in clear violation of Article 32 of the Fourth Geneva Convention...' The Government of Israel states that, 'whatever action Israel has taken has been taken firmly within the bounds of the relevant and accepted principles relating to the conduct of hostilities.'

With respect to demonstrations, the Government of Israel has acknowledged 'that individual instances of excessive response may have occurred. To a soldier or a unit coming under Palestinian attack, the equation is not that of the Israeli army versus some stone throwing Palestinian protesters. It is a personal equation.'

We understand this concern, particularly since rocks can maim or even kill. It is no easy matter for a few young soldiers, confronted by large numbers of hostile demonstrators, to make fine legal distinctions on the spot. Still, this 'personal equation' must fit within an organizational ethic; in this case, *The Ethical Code of the Israel Defence Forces*. which states, in part:

> *The sanctity of human life in the eyes of the IDF servicemen will find expression in all of their actions, in deliberate and meticulous planning and in safe and intelligent training and in proper execution of their mission. In evaluating the risk to self and others, they will use the appropriate standards and will exercise constant care to limit injury to life to the extent required to accomplish the mission.*

Those required to respect the IDF ethical code are largely draftees, as the IDF is a conscript force. Active duty enlisted personnel, non-commissioned officers and junior officers—the categories most likely to be present at friction points—are young, often teenagers. Unless more senior career personnel or reservists are stationed at friction points, no IDF personnel present in these sensitive areas have experience to draw upon from previous violent Israeli–Palestinian confrontations. We think it is essential, especially in the context of restoring confidence by minimizing deadly confrontations, that the IDF deploy more senior, experienced soldiers to these sensitive points.

There were incidents where IDF soldiers have used lethal force, including live ammunition and modified metal-cored rubber rounds, against unarmed demonstrators throwing stones. The IDF should adopt crowd-control tactics that minimize the potential for deaths and casualties, withdrawing metal-cored rubber rounds from general use and using instead rubber baton rounds without metal cores.

We are deeply concerned about the public safety implications of exchanges of fire between populated areas, in particular

between Israeli settlements and neighbouring Palestinian villages. Palestinian gunmen have directed small arms fire at Israeli settlements and at nearby IDF positions from within or adjacent to civilian dwellings in Palestinian areas, thus endangering innocent Israeli and Palestinian civilians alike. We condemn the positioning of gunmen within or near civilian dwellings. The IDF often responds to such gunfire with heavy calibre weapons, sometimes resulting in deaths and injuries to innocent Palestinians. An IDF officer told us at the Ministry of Defence on March 23, 2001 that, 'When shooting comes from a building we respond, and sometimes there are innocent people in the building.' Obviously, innocent people are injured and killed during exchanges of this nature. We urge that such provocations cease and that the IDF exercise maximum restraint in its responses if they do occur. Inappropriate or excessive uses of force often lead to escalation.

We are aware of IDF sensitivities about these subjects. More than once we were asked: 'What about Palestinian rules of engagement? What about a Palestinian code of ethics for their military personnel?' These are valid questions.

On the Palestinian side there are disturbing ambiguities in the basic areas of responsibility and accountability. The lack of control exercised by the PA over its own security personnel and armed elements affiliated with the PA leadership is very troubling. We urge the PA to take all necessary steps to establish a clear and unchallenged chain of command for armed personnel operating under its authority. We recommend that the PA institute and enforce effective standards of conduct and accountability, both within the uniformed ranks and between the police and the civilian political leadership to which it reports.

Incitement:

In their submissions and briefings to the Committee, both sides expressed concerns about hateful language and images emanating from the other, citing numerous examples of hostile sectarian and ethnic rhetoric in the Palestinian and Israeli media, in school curricula and in statements by religious leaders, politicians and others.

We call on the parties to renew their formal commitments to foster mutual understanding and tolerance and to abstain from incitement and hostile propaganda. We condemn hate language and incitement in all its forms. We suggest that the parties be particularly cautious about using words in a manner that suggests collective responsibility.

Economic and Social Impact of Violence:

Further restrictions on the movement of people and goods have been imposed by Israel on the West Bank and the Gaza Strip. These closures take three forms: those which restrict movement between the Palestinian areas and Israel; those (including curfews) which restrict movement within the Palestinian areas; and those which restrict movement from the Palestinian areas to foreign countries. These measures have disrupted the lives of hundreds of thousands of Palestinians; they have increased Palestinian unemployment to an estimated 40 percent, in part by preventing some 140,000 Palestinians from working in Israel; and have stripped away about one-third of the Palestinian gross domestic product. Moreover, the transfer of tax and customs duty revenues owed to the PA by Israel has been suspended, leading to a serious fiscal crisis in the PA.

Of particular concern to the PA has been the destruction by Israeli security forces and settlers of tens of thousands of olive and fruit trees and other agricultural property. The closures have had other adverse effects, such as preventing civilians from access to urgent medical treatment and preventing students from attending school.

The Government of Israel maintains that these measures were taken in order to protect Israeli citizens from terrorism. Palestinians characterize these measures as 'collective punishment'. The Government of Israel denies the allegations:

> *Israel has not taken measures that have had an economic impact simply for the sake of taking such measures or for reasons of harming the Palestinian economy. The measures have been taken for reasons of security. Thus, for example, the closure of the Palestinian territories was taken in order to prevent, or at least minimize the risks of, terrorist attacks...The*

Palestinian leadership has made no attempt to control this activity and bring it to an end.

Moreover, the Government of Israel points out that violence in the last quarter of 2000 cost the Israeli economy $1.2 billion [US $1,200m.], and that the loss continues at a rate of approximately $150 million per month.

We acknowledge Israel's security concerns. We believe, however, that the Government of Israel should lift closures, transfer to the PA all revenues owed, and permit Palestinians who have been employed in Israel to return to their jobs. Closure policies play into the hands of extremists seeking to expand their constituencies and thereby contribute to escalation. The PA should resume co-operation with Israeli security agencies to ensure that Palestinian workers employed within Israel are fully vetted and free of connections to terrorists and terrorist organizations.

International development assistance has from the start been an integral part of the peace process, with an aim to strengthen the socio-economic foundations for peace. This assistance today is more important than ever. We urge the international community to sustain the development agenda of the peace process.

Holy Places:

It is particularly regrettable that places such as the Temple Mount/Haram ash-Sharif in Jerusalem, Joseph's Tomb in Nablus, and Rachel's Tomb in Bethlehem have been the scenes of violence, death and injury. These are places of peace, prayer and reflection which must be accessible to all believers.

Places deemed holy by Muslims, Jews, and Christians merit respect, protection and preservation. Agreements previously reached by the parties regarding holy places must be upheld. The Government of Israel and the PA should create a joint initiative to defuse the sectarian aspect of their political dispute by preserving and protecting such places. Efforts to develop inter-faith dialogue should be encouraged.

International Force:

One of the most controversial subjects raised during our inquiry was the issue of deploying an international force to the Palestinian areas. The PA is strongly in favour of having such a force to protect Palestinian civilians and their property from the IDF and from settlers. The Government of Israel is just as adamantly opposed to an 'international protection force', believing that it would prove unresponsive to Israeli security concerns and interfere with bilateral negotiations to settle the conflict.

We believe that to be effective such a force would need the support of both parties. We note that international forces deployed in this region have been or are in a position to fulfil their mandates and make a positive contribution only when they were deployed with the consent of all of the parties involved.

During our visit to Hebron we were briefed by personnel of the Temporary International Presence in Hebron (TIPH), a presence to which both parties have agreed. The TIPH is charged with observing an explosive situation and writing reports on their observations. If the parties agree, as a confidence-building measure, to draw upon TIPH personnel to help them manage other friction points, we hope that TIPH contributors could accommodate such a request.

Cross-Community Initiatives:

Many described to us the near absolute loss of trust. It was all the more inspiring, therefore, to find groups (such as the Parent's Circle and the Economic Co-operation Foundation) dedicated to cross-community understanding in spite of all that has happened. We commend them and their important work.

Regrettably, most of the work of this nature has stopped during the current conflict. To help rebuild confidence, the Government of Israel and PA should jointly endorse and support the work of Israeli and Palestinian non-governmental organizations (NGOs) already involved in confidence-building through initiatives linking both sides. It is important that the PA and Government of Israel support cross-community organizations and initiatives, including the provision of humanitarian assistance to Palestinian villages by Israeli NGOs. Providing travel permits for participants is essential. Co-operation between the humanitarian organizations and the military/security services of the parties should be encouraged and institutionalized.

Such programmes can help build, albeit slowly, constituencies for peace among Palestinians and Israelis and can provide safety nets during times of turbulence. Organizations involved in this work are vital for translating good intentions into positive actions.

RESUME NEGOTIATIONS

Israeli leaders do not wish to be perceived as 'rewarding violence'. Palestinian leaders do not wish to be perceived as 'rewarding occupation'. We appreciate the political constraints on leaders of both sides. Nevertheless, if the cycle of violence is to be broken and the search for peace resumed, there needs to be a new bilateral relationship incorporating both security co-operation and negotiations.

We cannot prescribe to the parties how best to pursue their political objectives. Yet the construction of a new bilateral relationship solidifying and transcending an agreed cessation of violence requires intelligent risk-taking. It requires, in the first instance, that each party again be willing to regard the other as a *partner*. Partnership, in turn, requires at this juncture something more than was agreed in the Declaration of Principles and in subsequent agreements. Instead of declaring the peace process to be 'dead', the parties should determine how they will conclude their common journey along their agreed 'road map' a journey which began in Madrid and continued in spite of problems—until very recently.

To define a starting point is for the parties to decide. Both parties have stated that they remain committed to their mutual agreements and undertakings. It is time to explore further implementation. The parties should declare their intention to meet on this basis, in order to resume full and meaningful negotiations, in the spirit of their undertakings at Sharm esh-Sheikh in 1999 and 2000.

Neither side will be able to achieve its principal objectives unilaterally or without political risk. We know how hard it is for leaders to act—especially if the action can be characterized by political opponents as a concession—without getting something in return. The PA must—as it has at previous critical junctures—take steps to reassure Israel on security matters. The Government of Israel must—as it has in the past—take steps to reassure the PA on political matters. Israelis and Palestinians should avoid, in their own actions and attitudes, giving extremists, common criminals and revenge seekers the final say in defining their joint future. This will not be easy if deadly incidents occur in spite of effective co-operation. Notwithstanding the daunting difficulties, the very foundation of the trust required to re-establish a functioning partnership consists of each side making such strategic reassurances to the other.

RECOMMENDATIONS

The Government of Israel and the PA must act swiftly and decisively to halt the violence. Their immediate objectives then should be to rebuild confidence and resume negotiations. What we are asking is not easy. Palestinians and Israelis—not just their leaders, but two publics at large—have lost confidence in one another. We are asking political leaders to do, for the sake of their people, the politically difficult: to lead without knowing how many will follow.

During this mission our aim has been to fulfil the mandate agreed at Sharm esh-Sheikh. We value the support given our work by the participants at the summit, and we commend the parties for their co-operation. Our principal recommendation is that they recommit themselves to the Sharm esh-Sheikh spirit, and that they implement the decisions made there in 1999 and 2000. We believe that the summit participants will support bold action by the parties to achieve these objectives.

END THE VIOLENCE

The Government of Israel and the PA should reaffirm their commitment to existing agreements and undertakings and should immediately implement an unconditional cessation of violence.

Anything less than a complete effort by both parties to end the violence will render the effort itself ineffective, and will likely be interpreted by the other side as evidence of hostile intent.

The Government of Israel and PA should immediately resume security co-operation.

Effective bilateral co-operation aimed at preventing violence will encourage the resumption of negotiations. We are particularly concerned that, absent effective, transparent security co-operation, terrorism and other acts of violence will continue and may be seen as officially sanctioned whether they are or not. The parties should consider widening the scope of security co-operation to reflect the priorities of both communities and to seek acceptance for these efforts from those communities.

We acknowledge the PA's position that security co-operation presents a political difficulty absent a suitable political context, i.e., the relaxation of stringent Israeli security measures combined with ongoing, fruitful negotiations. We also acknowledge the PA's fear that, with security co-operation in hand, the Government of Israel may not be disposed to deal forthrightly with Palestinian political concerns. We believe that security co-operation cannot long be sustained if meaningful negotiations are unreasonably deferred, if security measures 'on the ground' are seen as hostile, or if steps are taken that are perceived as provocative or as prejudicing the outcome of negotiations.

REBUILD CONFIDENCE

The PA and Government of Israel should work together to establish a meaningful 'cooling-off period' and implement additional confidence-building measures, some of which were proposed in the October 2000 Sharm esh-Sheikh Statement and some of which were offered by the US on January 7, 2001 in Cairo.

The PA and Government of Israel should resume their efforts to identify, condemn and discourage incitement in all its forms.

The PA should make clear through concrete action to Palestinians and Israelis alike that terrorism is reprehensible and unacceptable, and that the PA will make a 100 percent effort to prevent terrorist operations and to punish perpetrators. This effort should include immediate steps to apprehend and incarcerate terrorists operating within the PA's jurisdiction.

The Government of Israel should freeze all settlement activity, including the 'natural growth' of existing settlements.

The kind of security co-operation desired by the Government of Israel cannot for long co-exist with settlement activity described very recently by the European Union as causing 'great concern' and by the US as 'provocative'.

> *The Government of Israel should give careful consideration to whether settlements which are focal points for substantial friction are valuable bargaining chips for future negotiations, or provocations likely to preclude the onset of productive talks.*
>
> *The Government of Israel may wish to make it clear to the PA that a future peace would pose no threat to the territorial contiguity of a Palestinian State to be established in the West Bank and the Gaza Strip.*

The IDF should consider withdrawing to positions held before September 28, 2000 which will reduce the number of friction points and the potential for violent confrontations.

The Government of Israel should ensure that the IDF adopt and enforce policies and procedures encouraging non-lethal responses to unarmed demonstrators, with a view to minimizing casualties and friction between the two communities. The IDF should:

> *Re-institute, as a matter of course, military police investigations into Palestinian deaths resulting from IDF actions in the Palestinian territories in incidents not involving terrorism. The IDF should abandon the blanket characterization of the current uprising as 'an armed conflict short of war', which fails to discriminate between terrorism and protest.*
>
> *Adopt tactics of crowd-control that minimize the potential for deaths and casualties, including the withdrawal of metal-cored rubber rounds from general use.*
>
> *Ensure that experienced, seasoned personnel are present for duty at all times at known friction points.*
>
> *Ensure that the stated values and standard operating procedures of the IDF effectively instil the duty of caring for*

Palestinians in the West Bank and Gaza Strip as well as Israelis living there, consistent with The Ethical Code of the IDF.

The Government of Israel should lift closures, transfer to the PA all tax revenues owed, and permit Palestinians who had been employed in Israel to return to their jobs; and should ensure that security forces and settlers refrain from the destruction of homes and roads, as well as trees and other agricultural property in Palestinian areas. We acknowledge the Government of Israel's position that actions of this nature have been taken for security reasons. Nevertheless, their economic effects will persist for years.

The PA should renew co-operation with Israeli security agencies to ensure, to the maximum extent possible, that Palestinian workers employed within Israel are fully vetted and free of connections to organizations and individuals engaged in terrorism.

The PA should prevent gunmen from using Palestinian populated areas to fire upon Israeli populated areas and IDF positions. This tactic places civilians on both sides at unnecessary risk.

The Government of Israel and IDF should adopt and enforce policies and procedures designed to ensure that the response to any gunfire emanating from Palestinian populated areas minimizes the danger to the lives and property of Palestinian civilians, bearing in mind that it is probably the objective of gunmen to elicit an excessive IDF response.

The Government of Israel should take all necessary steps to prevent acts of violence by settlers.

The parties should abide by the provisions of the Wye River Agreement prohibiting illegal weapons.

The PA should take all necessary steps to establish a clear and unchallenged chain of command for armed personnel operating under its authority.

The PA should institute and enforce effective standards of conduct and accountability, both within the uniformed ranks and between the police and the civilian political leadership to which it reports.

The PA and Government of Israel should consider a joint undertaking to preserve and protect holy places sacred to the traditions of Muslims, Jews, and Christians. An initiative of this nature might help to reverse a disturbing trend: the increasing use of religious themes to encourage and justify violence.

The Government of Israel and PA should jointly endorse and support the work of Palestinian and Israeli non-governmental organizations (NGOs) involved in cross-community initiatives linking the two peoples. It is important that these activities, including the provision of humanitarian aid to Palestinian villages by Israeli NGOs, receive the full backing of both parties.

RESUME NEGOTIATIONS

We reiterate our belief that a 100 percent effort to stop the violence, an immediate resumption of security co-operation and an exchange of confidence-building measures are all important for the resumption of negotiations. Yet none of these steps will long be sustained absent a return to serious negotiations.

It is not within our mandate to prescribe the venue, the basis or the agenda of negotiations. However, in order to provide an effective political context for practical co-operation between the parties, negotiations must not be unreasonably deferred and they must, in our view, manifest a spirit of compromise, reconciliation and partnership, notwithstanding the events of the past seven months.

In the spirit of the Sharm esh-Sheikh agreements and understandings of 1999 and 2000, we recommend that the parties meet to reaffirm their commitment to signed agreements and mutual understandings, and take corresponding action. This should be the basis for resuming full and meaningful negotiations.

The parties are at a crossroads. If they do not return to the negotiating table, they face the prospect of fighting it out for years on end, with many of their citizens leaving for distant shores to live their lives and raise their children. We pray they make the right choice. That means stopping the violence now. Israelis and Palestinians have to live, work, and prosper together. History and geography have destined them to be neighbours. That cannot be changed. Only when their actions are guided by this awareness will they be able to develop the vision and reality of peace and shared prosperity.

UN SECURITY COUNCIL RESOLUTION 1397
12 March 2002

Resolution 1397 affirmed for the first time the UN Security Council's 'vision' of both Israeli and Palestinian states. It was the first US-sponsored resolution on the Middle East for some 25 years, and was adopted by 14 votes to none; Syria abstained in the vote.

The Security Council,

Recalling all its previous relevant resolutions, in particular resolutions 242 (1967) and 338 (1973),

Affirming a vision of a region where two States, Israel and Palestine, live side by side within secure and recognized borders,

Expressing its grave concern at the continuation of the tragic and violent events that have taken place since September 2000, especially the recent attacks and the increased number of casualties,

Stressing the need for all concerned to ensure the safety of civilians,

Stressing also the need to respect the universally accepted norms of international humanitarian law.

Welcoming and encouraging the diplomatic efforts of special envoys from the United States of America, the Russian Federation, the European Union and the United Nations Special Coordinator and others, to bring about a comprehensive, just and lasting peace in the Middle East,

Welcoming the contribution of Saudi Crown Prince Abdullah,

1. *Demands* immediate cessation of all acts of violence, including all acts of terror, provocation, incitement and destruction;

2. *Calls upon* the Israeli and Palestinian sides and their leaders to cooperate in the implementation of the Tenet work plan and Mitchell Report recommendations with the aim of resuming negotiations on a political settlement;

3. *Expresses* support for the efforts of the Secretary-General and others to assist the parties to halt the violence and to resume the peace process;

4. *Decides* to remain seized of the matter.

UN Document S/Res/1397 (2002).

IRAQ, SANCTIONS AND THE 'WAR AGAINST TERROR'

TOBY DODGE

INTRODUCTION

By mid-2002 the US Administration of George W. Bush appeared determined to tackle the issue of Iraq and its possession of weapons of mass destruction in the next stage of its 'war' against terrorism—initiated against al-Qa'ida and its Taliban hosts in Afghanistan following the suicide attacks on New York and Washington, DC, in September 2001. It had by now become a question not of whether military action was to be taken against Baghdad, but when and how.

Success in a new war against Saddam Hussain's Iraq would be a defining moment in the evolution of the 'Bush doctrine'. In the aftermath of the horrific attacks on the Pentagon and the World Trade Center there has been a growing coherence and confidence in this strategy of 'offensive defence'. In many respects the doctrine is an attempt to codify international relations in the post-Cold War era, recognizing and institutionalizing the political effects of globalization.

Since the September 2001 attacks uncompromising figures in the US Administration—principal among them Vice-President Richard Cheney, Secretary of Defense Donald Rumsfeld and his deputy, Paul Wolfowitz—have been reworking the US understanding of state sovereignty in the developing world. Concerns with democracy and human rights that apparently dominated foreign policy under the presidency of Bill Clinton (1993–2001) never sat comfortably with right-wing Republican promotion of US interests to the exclusion of all else. Under this new doctrine, states in the developing world are not to be subject to US strictures as to how their populations may be treated, as long as they conform to certain rules. These concern the suppression of all terrorist activity on their territory, the transparency of banking and trade arrangements, and the disavowal of weapons of mass destruction.

For the Bush Administration, the incumbent regime in Baghdad is a potent symbol of a defiance. Despite invasion, continuous bombing and more than a decade of the most stringent sanctions ever imposed, it has continued to reject the demands of the USA and the international community. By engineering what has increasingly been termed 'regime change' in Baghdad, Washington would clearly signal its commitment to the Bush doctrine as well as the lengths to which it would go to achieve its core foreign policy goals.

However, military action against Iraq would be much more complicated than that undertaken in Afghanistan. Pentagon staff attempting to draw up credible plans of action encounter various geographic and strategic problems. The diplomatic task is, if anything, even harder. A sustained attack on Iraq would be very unpopular in the Middle East. Arab public opinion has been inflamed by what it sees as the Bush Administration's unwillingness to restrain Israeli attacks on Palestinians. Almost 12 years after the end of Operation Desert Storm, there is also a great deal of international sympathy for the extended suffering of the Iraqi population under sanctions.

By tracing the birth and evolution of UN sanctions against Iraq over the last decade, the roots of US plans to attack Iraq and the possible resulting instability in the Gulf region become apparent. Iraq's relations with the international community over the past 12 years are explained by the UN as an extended exercise in coercive diplomacy. The sanctions imposed on Iraq in 1990 in order to force its armed forces to leave Kuwait were conceived of by the international community as a temporary measure. The sanctions failed to realize their initial aim, and 500,000 troops were needed to reclaim Kuwait's sovereignty. Since that time sanctions have been used to try to obtain a series of overt and covert aims. Overtly, they were supposed to offer the regime in Baghdad incentives to change its behaviour and rejoin the international community. Covertly, however, it was hoped by key members of the UN Security Council (most notably the USA) that the economic hardship caused by the blockade would lead to a change of leadership in Iraq. It is the

failure of sanctions to realize either of these key aims that has led Washington to consider renewed military action.

For sanctions and, more broadly, coercive diplomacy to succeed, the demands made of the targeted government need to be precise, limited and deliverable. The problem that has dominated policy towards Iraq is the extent and nature of the results sanctions were designed to produce. Since the Gulf crisis, arising from Iraq's invasion of Kuwait in 1990, and especially since September 2001, it has been made abundantly clear (especially to Baghdad) that the ultimate aim of US policy has always been a change of regime in Iraq. On this basis it became increasingly apparent to President Saddam Hussain and his Government that there was no incentive to co-operate with the UN, as sanctions would remain in place as long as they remained in power. Indeed the regime's survival is dependent upon Iraq's effective defiance and evasion of the blockade. With this fundamental flaw at the heart of UN and US policy towards Iraq, the perception of the Administration of George W. Bush has been that it is left with very little choice but to intervene by force.

SANCTIONS, THE INTERNATIONAL COMMUNITY AND IRAQ

In response to Iraq's invasion of Kuwait in August 1990, the UN, in a series of resolutions adopted by the Security Council in New York, placed Iraq under the most draconian economic blockade in modern international history. On an economic level, Iraq's dependence on oil exports meant that the effects of sanctions were immediate. The swift and almost total curtailment of trade resulted in widespread food shortages and rampant inflation. However, the Iraqi regime—as opposed to its society—had been set up to withstand intense domestic and international pressure. Emerging from an eight-year conflict with Iran, and still very much on a war footing, the Baghdad Government was able to continue functioning despite stringent sanctions. Crucially, the rapid collapse in the living standards of the Iraqi population was not translated into effective domestic political pressure on the Government to withdraw from Kuwait.

In the event, it took six weeks of intensive aerial bombing and then a lightning four-day military ground campaign to force Iraqi troops from Kuwait. The unconditional cease-fire was formally agreed on 3 March 1991, but it was UN Resolution 687, adopted one month later, that set the terms Iraq had to meet for a final end to the second Gulf War. In the aftermath of the victory this resolution set eight specific tasks that the Iraqi Government had to fulfil before sanctions could be revoked—most contentiously the elimination of weapons of mass destruction and secondarily the return of Kuwaiti prisoners of war and property. A UN Special Commission (UNSCOM) was then established to certify that Iraq had rid itself entirely of its chemical, biological and nuclear weapons capability along with all ballistic missiles with a range exceeding 150 km.

DISARMAMENT AND CONFLICT

With Iraqi forces so completely vanquished, and with the regime facing such a seemingly uncertain future, the assumption among the victorious coalition was that Saddam Hussain's Government, or its successor, would have little choice but to implement its demands. However, the failure to meet the terms of Resolution 687 has remained the overt reason why sanctions have not been revoked, and why the US has been planning to use military action to unseat Saddam Hussain.

The stand-off and stalemate that have developed between the international community and Iraq have destabilized the Gulf region over the past decade and fuelled the rise of anti-Western sentiment. The evolution of this relationship can be divided into the three distinct phases: from 1991 until 1995; from 1995 to 1997; and from 1997 to the present. During this time two different arenas for Iraq's interaction with the international community have developed, one marked by conflict and one that has become broadly co-operative. Firstly, at the core of Resolution 687, and the main reason for Iraq's continued isolation, is the ongoing attempt to force the regime to give up its weapons of mass destruction. Iraq's attitude to this process has ranged from begrudging tolerance to outright hostility. Secondly, as it became widely appreciated that the Iraqi population was subject to undeniable economic suffering, a large-scale humanitarian relief operation was put in place allowing Iraq to sell oil under UN supervision in return for controlled imports of food and consumer goods. On the whole, the Iraqi Government has co-operated with the humanitarian operation, which over the past 10 years has developed into a complex mechanism for feeding the Iraqi population, restoring Iraqi infrastructure and ministering to the wider needs of society.

UNSCOM was created in April 1991 as the means to deliver Iraq's weapons of mass destruction. It was acknowledged by both Baghdad and the UN Security Council that UNSCOM stood between Iraq and its goal of a complete end to sanctions. However, UNSCOM's task soon evolved from simply verifying the Iraqi regime's compliance with UN demands to taking an active role in the search for weapons of mass destruction across Iraq and installing equipment to ensure those weapons were not re-created when the inspectors left. UNSCOM's first inspection teams entered Iraq in May 1991. From then until mid-1995 they made slow but steady progress. By 1995 the commission had reported positive progress on the destruction of Iraq's military nuclear, chemical and ballistic missile capabilities. It had also begun to set up the machinery needed to monitor Iraq's continued compliance. Iraq had reluctantly co-operated with UNSCOM's work, and there were good reasons to praise the commission's success and be optimistic about its future results.

In August 1995, however, this mood of optimism was shattered by a dramatic defection from the highest ranks of the Iraqi regime. After a violent disagreement at the centre of the ruling élite Saddam Hussain's sons-in-law, Lt-Gen. Hussain Kamel al-Majid and Col Saddam Kamel Hussain, defected to Jordan where they were extensively debriefed by US intelligence officials. Lt-Gen. Hussain Kamel, a member of the Iraqi Council of Ministers since 1988, had been head of the Ministry of Industry and Military Industrialization: he knew more than any other government official about Iraq's extensive weapons programme. Hussain Kamel informed his debriefers in Jordan, and through them UNSCOM, that Iraq had a much more extensive programme for the development of weapons of mass destruction than anyone had suspected, and that it had managed to keep much of this hidden from UN inspections.

From 1995 onwards relations between UNSCOM and the Iraqi Government were characterized by mistrust and conflict. As relations deteriorated Baghdad accused the inspection teams of being confrontational and of spying for the USA and Israel. UNSCOM countered that it was faced with a deliberate campaign of evasion and obstruction. Matters reached a head in October 1997 when UNSCOM published a report stating that Iraq was still concealing chemical and, especially, biological weapons. Throughout 1998 relations between Iraq and the UN remained tense, culminating in the withdrawal of all weapons inspectors in December 1998 and the start of Operation Desert Fox. The operation involved four days of intensive bombardment by US and British military aircraft—justified by the assertion that Iraq had never seriously engaged in the task of disarmament, and coercion was thus needed to make it do so.

There has been an enduring stalemate between Iraq and the UN from the commencement of Operation Desert Fox in 1998 to the present day. Ever since 1991 Iraq had been assured by Russian and French diplomats that if it co-operated with disarmament efforts then they would use their influence within the UN Security Council to secure the revocation of sanctions. By 1998 Iraq had begun to doubt the ability of France and Russia to deliver on this promise. After seven years of weapons inspections Iraq came to the conclusion that the USA would never agree an end to sanctions as long as the Government of Saddam Hussain remained in power. Citing abuse of its sovereignty, Iraq has therefore refused to countenance the renewal of weapons inspections. With the USA very much committed to a change of regime in Iraq, discord within the Security Council has largely prevented the UN from offering Iraq any meaningful incentives to facilitate the resurrection of a disarmament programme.

The four-year stand-off between the UN and Iraq has done much to undermine support for sanctions across the Gulf region. The aim of disarming Iraq has widespread support among the states and populations of the Gulf. Iran had suffered from an eight-year war with Iraq, and the states of the Co-operation Council for the Arab States of the Gulf (the Gulf Co-operation Council—GCC), after the invasion of Kuwait, were very much aware of their vulnerability to a militarily resurgent Iraq. But with disarmament efforts ending in 1998, it has been the continuing suffering of the Iraqi population, and even the possible fragmentation of Iraq itself, that has come to dominate regional discussions.

OIL-FOR-FOOD AND CO-OPERATION

The sanctions regime imposed on Iraq has proved to be extremely efficient. A complete embargo on the export of oil was imposed in 1990, along with the prohibition of all flights and non-humanitarian trade. With 75% of its GDP and 95% of foreign-exchange earnings accruing from oil sales, the Iraqi economy was extremely vulnerable to the imposition of an economic blockade. Coming only two years after the end of a gruelling eight-year war with Iran, the rapid economic slump caused by the imposition of sanctions caused massive suffering across the whole of Iraqi society.

For the first five years of sanctions the Government in Baghdad maintained a reasonably efficient rationing system across the southern and central parts of Iraq under its control. By 1995 the realization that sanctions were not going to be revoked for many years, along with rampant inflation and looming bankruptcy, caused the Iraqi regime to agree to negotiate with the UN, with the aim of alleviating its own economic woes and the suffering of the population. The result was the 'oil-for-food' accord signed in April 1995 but eventually implemented in December 1996. Under the terms of this agreement Iraq was allowed to export oil to the value of US $1,000m. every three months, in return for importing food and humanitarian supplies. The UN set up a complex monitoring operation that continues to oversee the selling of Iraqi oil and the import and distribution of humanitarian aid to the Iraqi people. The limit on oil exports was gradually raised to allow Iraq to sell all the oil it can pump.

With the signing of the oil-for-food agreement and the subsequent deadlock over arms inspection, the conflict between Iraq and the international community has shifted to a propaganda war—with each side attempting to blame the other for the undoubted and continuing suffering of ordinary Iraqis. This battle is aimed at international public opinion, primarily in the Gulf region but also wider in the Middle East and Western world. Surprisingly, given the reputation of the Iraqi regime, the diplomatic efforts of Baghdad have gained the upper hand. The UN, and behind it US intransigence, are widely believed—throughout the Middle East and beyond—to be to blame for the poor state of health and nutrition of the Iraqi population. The propaganda battle over the effects of sanctions has now become the main arena in which Iraq fights for the revocation of sanctions.

Propaganda aside, it is clear that from 1990 until today Iraq has suffered from hyperinflation and a rapid rise in poverty and malnutrition. Historically generous state welfare provision and a large and educated middle class have both been decimated by the post-war stalemate. The fact that pre-war economic and social progress were overwhelmingly state driven and funded by oil has caused the impoverishment of Iraqi society. Post-1991 Iraq is a country that has undergone a profound and continuing macroeconomic shock of enormous proportions.

Before the imposition of sanctions Iraq's average imports per person put it in the high-middle-income bracket of World Bank classification. However, the rapid ending of imports and exports has driven annual inflation since 1991 to levels as high as 500%. The civilian sectors of the state once employed 21% of the active work-force, with 40% of Iraqi households directly dependent on government payments. A further 50% of the work-force were employed in the services sector. This meant the population as a whole was brutally exposed to inflation and extreme austerity measures. The middle class has been devastated to the extent that it is barely discernible as a category. A UN survey estimated for example that 63% of professionals are now engaged in menial labour.

Combined with the suffering of the Iraqi people, it is the possible fragility of political authority in Iraq that has caused the continuation of UN sanctions to be questioned by governments of the Gulf region and wider Middle East. Since independence in 1932 the power of central government in Baghdad has always been contested by organized groups within society. Successive regimes have ruled over a population whose allegiances are defined by either local sub-state or religious and cultural supra-state loyalties. This socio-political situation has been greatly exacerbated over the past decade. By the end of the Gulf War the Iraqi Government appeared on the verge of collapse. The dramatic effects of societal conflict on Iraqi society were personified by the post-war uprisings in 1991 of the Shi'as in the south and the Kurds to the north. The spectre of Iraq's fracturing along religious or ethnic lines into three separate 'statelets' has tempered the neighbouring states' attitudes towards the regime of Saddam Hussain. Whatever the current Iraqi regime did in the past, the destabilizing possibility of the country's fragmenting if the regime were to be removed has greatly reduced regional opposition to it.

IRAQI KURDISTAN SINCE 1990

It is the political fate of the Kurdish population in northern Iraq that has played a key role in highlighting the fragility of the state and the dangerous possibilities inherent in its break-up. Historically, the Kurds have been the main challenge to the authority of the central administration in Iraq since its creation in the 1920s. Twice in recent times—from 1960 until 1975 and from 1983 until 1988—Kurdish organizations, primarily the Kurdistan Democratic Party (KDP) and Patriotic Union of Kurdistan (PUK), have risen in open rebellion against Baghdad. Both uprisings were supported by Iran. Once this external help had been withdrawn the Kurds were crushed by overwhelming military force.

The evolution of the third Kurdish rebellion, from 1991 onwards, has threatened the territorial integrity of the Iraqi state and removed a large section of the Kurdish population from Baghdad's direct control. As the Gulf War approached US President George Bush, Snr, urged the Iraqi people to rise up and overthrow Saddam Hussain. In early March 1991, following the defeat of the Iraqi army in Kuwait, sections of the Shi'a and Kurdish populations took him at his word and launched an armed rebellion against the central Government.

In the north of Iraq the Kurdish revolt was short lived. Two weeks after capturing Kirkuk, the main oil centre of the region, Kurdish forces were pushed back by Iraqi government troops. The reaction of the Kurdish population to this reverse was dramatic: 500,000–700,000 civilians fled the advancing troops, heading into the mountains that border Iran and Turkey. The spectacle of so many civilians fleeing into such inhospitable terrain provoked public outrage across the Western world. In response, the USA, the United Kingdom and France launched Operation Provide Comfort, using US and allied troops to set up a 'safe haven' for the Kurds in the north. Although allied troops withdrew, they had set up—and continue to protect—a separate jurisdiction whose survival is guaranteed by the USA's force of arms.

From its inception in 1991 the Kurdish enclave was perceived as offering an example of what an Iraq without Saddam Hussain might look like. The Kurds were eager to show that their bid for autonomy, if not outright independence, would be run along democratic lines. In 1992 elections were held across the enclave for a Kurdish regional parliament and government to sit at Arbil. The reasonably free elections emphasized the polarized nature of Kurdish political life, with the KDP and PUK both securing roughly 50% of the votes cast. In an indication of tensions to come, the leaders of each party refused to take direct part in the coalition government that was formed. Each party concentrated on consolidating its regional support-base, building what became in effect two competing administrations whose very existence sabotaged the chances of a strong, enclave-wide government.

The tensions and rivalries between the PUK and KDP, both trying to dominate the political life of the enclave, erupted into violence and civil war at the end of 1993. By 1994 PUK forces had seized Arbil, bringing to an end hopes of a united regional government. The creation of the Kurdish enclave had fuelled fears of instability among Iraq's northern neighbours, especially Turkey and Iran. This was greatly exacerbated by the civil war between the KDP and PUK. Regional powers began to be drawn into the conflict in order to gain some influence among the warring parties on their borders.

The conflict between the two Kurdish parties, and outside interference, reached a peak of destructiveness in mid-1996. The KDP, fearing it was losing the struggle to the PUK, appealed to Baghdad for military assistance, and at the end of August 30,000 Iraqi troops entered the Kurdish enclave in support of the KDP. With this help the KDP captured Arbil, Sulaimaniyah and the strategic town of Koi Sanjak. In addition to forcing 39,000 refugees to flee the area, the incursion of Iraqi troops into the Kurdish 'safe haven' greatly weakened opposition organizations sheltering in the north.

The USA launched a sustained cruise-missile attack against Iraq for its incursion into the northern 'safe haven'. But the fighting between the PUK and KDP, the increased involvement of neighbouring states in the north of Iraq, and the resulting regional insecurity, served to emphasize the difficulties involved in supporting active military action against the Iraqi Government. The USA went on to invest a great deal of energy in brokering an accommodation between the PUK and KDP. The result was the Washington Accords, signed between the two parties in September 1998. None the less, the Kurdish enclave is in effect divided between the KDP and PUK. Each party has a separate administration, raises separates taxes and has separate armed forces. The Kurds, as the only effective opposition to Baghdad, are going to have to form the basis to any increased US commitment to a change of regime in Iraq. However, the conflict between the Kurdish movements, and the uneasy truce that exists today, mean that over the past decade they have proved to be unreliable allies. The instability in northern Iraq has done much to hasten a diplomatic *rapprochement* between Baghdad and most of its neighbours.

IRAQ'S REGIONAL RELATIONS

Iraq's relations with the majority of its neighbours have been slowly transformed since the late 1990s. This has in part been due to a sustained diplomatic campaign by Baghdad aimed at ending its regional isolation. Key to the campaign's success has been the strategic use of its oil exports to seal better diplomatic relations. In addition, Iraq has opened up its substantial markets to those states in the region sympathetic to its demand for an unconditional end to sanctions. The governments in the region have not forgotten the instability brought by two wars in the past 20 years. But, for differing sets of geopolitical and economic reasons, they all have good reason to fear the uncertainty that would accompany a violent and externally driven change of regime in Baghdad.

Economically, it is Jordan and Turkey that benefit the most from trade with Iraq. Iraq exports 100,000 barrels per day (b/d) of crude oil and petrol to Jordan, half of it free and with the other half heavily discounted. Jordan has since 1990 acted (with UN agreement) as Iraq's economic conduit to the world. Over the past two years Jordan's dominant position has been threatened as Iraq's other neighbours have opened up their borders. This has led to Jordan's becoming increasingly vulnerable to Iraqi economic pressure. With important parts of Jordan's industry, banking and transport sectors dependent upon continued trade with Iraq, the Jordanian Government has found it problematic to alienate Baghdad. Turkey also benefits from trade with Iraq, but unlike the case of Jordan this trade has flourished without UN endorsement. Turkey receives an estimated 100,000 b/d of oil from Iraq, trucked across its northern border and sold to Turkish traders at discounted rates. Turkey has also positioned itself to be a major trading partner with Iraq once the sanctions are officially revoked, signing hundreds of trade development deals with the Government in Baghdad.

Syria's economic and diplomatic *rapprochement* with Iraq has been the most dramatic. It was only in 1998 that Iraq reopened its trade office in Damascus, but business between the two countries amounted to US $500m. in 2000 and was expected to have increased to $1,000m. in 2001. Like Jordan, Syria is a party to regional moves to establish free-trade agreements encompassing Iraq. Furthermore, the reopening of an oil pipeline between Iraq and Syria at the end of 2000 marked Baghdad's greatest diplomatic coup for many years and the biggest blow to UN sanctions to date. The Iraqi–Syrian pipeline, closed since 1982, thereafter pumped 100,000 b/d of oil to Syrian refineries—payment for which went directly to the Iraqi Government, beyond the scrutiny of the UN.

There are several geo-strategic reasons for the increased economic and diplomatic ties between Iraq and its neighbours. Generally, the continuing violence between Israel and the Palestinians has driven an upsurge in Arab nationalist sentiment across the region. The UN and the Western powers are seen as hypocritical in their harsh treatment of Iraq in comparison to Israel.

Although Syria joined the Gulf War coalition against Iraq, it was disappointed with the benefits supplied by the Gulf states in the aftermath of the campaign. Furthermore, Jordan's peace treaty and Turkey's alliance with Israel increased Syria's sense of regional isolation. In these circumstances Syria would much rather see the present regime in power in Baghdad than a pro-US alternative. Damascus, in improving its relations with Baghdad, can signal its discontent with the present political situation while highlighting Syria's own importance to regional stability. In addition the regime of President Bashar al-Assad fears that with Saddam Hussain gone, Washington will turn its attentions towards Damascus. Syria has of late instigated attempts to forge better relations between Iraq and Iran, in the eventual hope that all three states can create a bulwark to what it regards as increased US and Israeli influence in the region.

Turkey, on the other hand, is closely aligned with the USA and has a loose security arrangement with Israel. The US and British military aircraft that provide protection for the Kurdish 'safe haven' in Iraq use Turkish airbases. Turkey's dependence on the USA has been heightened by its own ongoing economic crisis and its need for financial support from the IMF and World Bank. However, Turkey's stable relations with Iraq must also be understood in terms of its own domestic problems with Kurdish insurgency. The creation in 1991 of a semi-independent Kurdish enclave on its borders was a great worry to the authorities in Ankara. Although instability within Iraqi Kurdistan has greatly increased its ability to control events, it is still the case that Baghdad's control over all of Iraqi territory would be welcomed by Turkey.

Relations between Iran and Iraq have also been improving steadily. After a bitter eight-year war the progress of this diplomatic initiative is slow and complex. None the less, Iranian pilgrims are now frequent visitors to Shi'a holy shrines in Iraq, bringing with them much-needed foreign exchange. Iran's inclusion, along with Iraq (and North Korea), in George W. Bush's 'axis of evil', defined in the US President's State of the Union address in January 2002, has highlighted a mutual vulnerability of both regimes to a more interventionist foreign policy emanating from Washington. Iraq's relations with Iran are, however, constrained by mutual distrust and the fact that each supports armed opponents of the other's regime. This is indicative of continuing mistrust over and above any geo-strategic gains to be made by an alliance.

Iraq's relations with the states that make up the GCC can be ranked on the basis of geographic proximity. Clearly, with the trauma of 1990–91 still largely undressed, Kuwait's policy is understandably militant. For Saudi Arabia, the United Arab Emirates (UAE), Bahrain, and Oman, the current domestic and regional status quo poses much less of a strategic threat and so they feel they have the scope to argue forcibly against US plans for regime change in Baghdad. Qatar, while it has actively supported an end to UN sanctions against Iraq, and has pursued contacts with representatives of the Iraqi Government, has since late 2001 allowed a significant increase in US military personnel and equipment on its territory. It is these differing approaches, along with the USA's seeming inability to deliver any solutions, that have sown discord on the issue of Iraq within the ranks of the GCC.

The GCC's inception and evolution are intimately linked to the fortunes of Iraq. Officially inaugurated in May 1981, the GCC was formed during the Iran–Iraq War to ensure that if Iraq emerged victorious its regional dominance would be tempered by the collective action of the Arab Gulf states. However, the GCC has been unable to capitalize on this collective feeling of vulnerability during the 20 years of its existence. Economic integration among its members remains limited, and progress towards collective security is even less impressive. The Damascus Declaration—the security alliance formed in 1991 by the GCC and its two Arab Gulf War allies, Egypt and Syria—has also foundered on fears of each member state for its national sovereignty. With a distinct lack of unity among its members, the GCC states have had to rely on the USA to guarantee their security. In return, the USA gets help in meeting the cost of its military presence in the region and—more importantly—it gets military bases in the Gulf to station its troops and equipment.

Although of late there has been increasing disagreement about how to deal with Iraq, the GCC has in the past developed a common and coherent position. This revolves around an insistence that Iraq must abide by all pertinent UN resolutions. The GCC has in return undertaken to recognize and strive to preserve the territorial integrity of Iraq while agreeing not to interfere in Iraqi domestic politics. Thus even Kuwait has refused residency to active members of the Iraqi opposition.

Kuwait none the less remains at the centre of the anti-Saddam coalition in the region. Along with the USA, it insists that Iraq must fully disarm and return Kuwaiti prisoners and property before international sanctions can be revoked. But even in Kuwait there is a growing realization that some means of dealing with Iraq in the future will have to be found. As US plans for regime change in Baghdad gain coherence, Kuwait is caught between Washington and its fellow GCC members. It would welcome regime change, but does not have the confidence unilaterally to back US action. This tension was highlighted at the summit meeting of the League of Arab States (the Arab League) in Beirut, Lebanon, in late March 2002. With the prospect of US military action against Baghdad overshadowing the conference, Arab leaders joined together to oppose any possible attack. The Vice-Chairman of Iraq's Revolutionary Command Council, Izzat Ibrahim, spearheaded attempts to forestall US action. He pledged in Beirut that his country would recognize Kuwaiti sovereignty, never invade it again, and work towards resolving the issue of Kuwaiti missing persons. Although privately favouring efforts to depose the Iraqi President, Kuwait felt bound not to oppose these regional diplomatic manoeuvres by Iraq.

The suffering of the Iraqi population, combined with widespread popular anger at US support of Israel, has led the Government of Saudi Arabia actively to oppose US military plans for an assault on Iraq. With a large and potentially troublesome Shi'a population of its own, the Saudi Government has been concerned about the growth of Shi'a radicalism in Iraq and the potential this gives for increased Iranian influence. Prince Nayef ibn Abd al-Aziz, Saudi Arabia's Minister of the Interior, asserted in early 2002 that 'Saudi Arabia is against resolving disputes through violence...If this happens, God forbid, the kingdom will not in any circumstances be for any war against any Arab country'. In effect, this implies that the Saudi Government would not allow US forces to use the Prince Sultan airbase, previously the hub of the US military's command-and-control operations in the Gulf region.

The UAE—and especially its President, Sheikh Zayed—has taken a leading role in expressing humanitarian concerns about the suffering of the Iraqi people. This was accompanied by the restoration of full diplomatic ties with Baghdad in April 2000. Geo-strategically, the UAE's long-standing dispute with Iran over the sovereignty of the islands of Abu Musa and the Tunbs has led it to investigate the diplomatic reintegration of Iraq as a possible counterbalance to Iran.

In 1991 the majority of Iraq's neighbours joined the Gulf War coalition to force its armed forces from Kuwait. In the years that have elapsed since then a combination of astute Iraqi diplomacy and 'sanctions-fatigue' has undermined that unity of purpose. With the exception of Kuwait (and possibly Qatar), every state in the region apparently regards the present regime in Baghdad as the lesser of two evils. All governments in the region are concerned about the potential for instability in an Iraq splintered into different groups vying for power. With this scenario uppermost in their minds, the relative certainty provided by Saddam Hussain and the regime he commands becomes the best of a limited set of alternatives. Baghdad has worked hard through political and economic diplomacy to improve relations with its neighbours. In the absence of any viable new peaceful initiative from the UN or the USA to change the status quo, Iraq's neighbours have been learning to live with their 'rogue' neighbour.

THE POSSIBILITY OF US MILITARY ACTION

The clamour within the Bush Administration for military action against Saddam Hussain has been driven by recognition that the policy of 'containing' Iraq has become increasingly ineffective. Under the terms of successive UN Security Council resolutions Iraq had grown to become the third largest oil producer in OPEC and the sixth largest exporter of oil to the USA itself. However, it is the import and export of goods outside the terms of sanctions regulations that have threatened attempts to sustain Iraq's economic isolation.

Since the late 1990s the smuggling of oil out of Iraq has increased dramatically. In addition to the oil exported illegally to Turkey and Syria, it is now estimated that 100,000 barrels per day (b/d) of oil are smuggled illegally out of Iraq by ship, via the Shatt al-Arab waterway, and into the Gulf. In effect, the growth of illicit exports means that the regime in Baghdad has independently gained US $1,000m. each year to spend as it likes—irrespective of UN sanctions. Along with the progressive undermining of economic sanctions, Baghdad has also successfully challenged its diplomatic isolation.

In an attempt to halt the economic and political undermining of sanctions, the Bush Administration decided, as its first major foreign policy initiative, that 'smart' sanctions were the answer to the problem of Iraq. US Secretary of State Colin Powell hoped that by reforming the sanctions regime he could once again rally international support behind a renewed UN embargo. After more than a year of diplomatic efforts a resolution (No. 1409) instituting a form of 'smart' sanctions was unanimously adopted by the UN Security Council on 14 May 2002. The limited nature of the new initiative, amounting to little more than a reform of the mechanisms for importing goods into Iraq, represented a defeat for Colin Powell and his more moderate approach to the problem of Iraq. The result was an increase in influence of 'hawkish' policy prescriptions in Washington.

Discussions within the Pentagon about extending the 'war against terror' to Iraq are also a direct result of the perceived success of the campaign against the Taliban. However, continued political and military instability in Afghanistan suggest that the US-led action there is far from being a long-term success. Overwhelming weapons superiority does not necessarily guarantee victory. As with Iraq in 1990, an underestimation of the problems—and the tenacity of the enemy—could mean that political, as opposed to strategic, success may yet elude Washington. More important, military action again the Taliban and al-Qa'ida in Afghanistan brings with it few lessons for a future campaign in Iraq.

Firstly, Afghanistan was a weak state struggling to control a very strong society. The Taliban regime was confronted by a number of armed groups operating against it from within. As its rapid fall indicates, even in the territory it controlled it remained a coalition of armed groups rather than a coherent governing force. Once military pressure was applied, and Pakistani support removed, it fell apart.

Iraq, on the other hand, is a strong state dominating a very weak society. Since seizing power in 1968, the regime has been highly successful in either co-opting or breaking any group that could challenge its control. The result has been the 'atomizing' of the population: individuals are linked directly to the State with no vestiges of civil society to shelter them from its power. This has, if anything, been exacerbated by 12 years of sanctions. The population is dependent for at least half its nutritional needs on the monthly state ration. This means that dissent can be punished economically as well as militarily.

Since 1990 Baghdad has no formal regional or international allies. In contrast to the build-up to the campaign in Afghanistan, there is very little that the USA can do to isolate or weaken it further. War and sanctions have drastically reduced the power of the army, denying it ammunition and spare parts. However, with an estimated army strength of 375,000 men, and well-equipped élite regiments like the Republican Guard, the regime in Baghdad appears more than capable of maintaining its rule in the face of domestic uprising.

There is no equivalent to the Afghan Northern Alliance in Iraq. The only military forces outside the direct control of Baghdad are the KDP and the PUK. Having suffered international indifference in the past, both Jalal Talabani of the PUK and Masoud Barzani of the KDP have expressed deep misgivings about a US attack.

With this in mind, the US military planners have developed three possible options. The first is an extended bombing campaign that would target the heart of the regime and its most trusted troops. The Republican Guard, largely stationed on the outskirts of Baghdad, would be encouraged to move against the Government to avoid becoming the focus of further bombing. For a decade, the USA has favoured a *coup d'état* and has concentrated all its efforts on achieving one. The Iraqi regime itself used the military to achieve power, and has long been aware of the danger it poses. Numerous coup attempts have been foiled since 1991. Although this still remains the most likely scenario for regime change, Saddam Hussain has hitherto successfully deployed huge resources to prevent this happening.

The second scenario would involve a limited invasion of special forces and a sustained bombing campaign. US forces would seize small amounts of territory in the north and south of the country and set up an alternative government composed of exiles and Kurdish parties. This enclave would be used to organize defecting Iraqi troops into an alternative army. If Baghdad struck back, this would precipitate a much larger US invasion. If not, the enclave could be slowly enlarged until opposition forces backed by US troops controlled the whole country.

This plan has been widely criticized for being flawed militarily. The fear is that it would lead to what has been dubbed a 'Bay of Goats' fiasco, with small numbers of US troops and ill-prepared opposition forces tied down in sparsely populated desert areas in the south. In addition, it would take a long time to succeed and it would be unpopular with Iraq's neighbours. Arab states, primarily Saudi Arabia, think it could cause regional political instability and ultimately lead to the break-up of Iraq.

The final option is a massive land invasion by more than 200,000 US troops, similar to Operation Desert Storm. This also carries great political and strategic risks. It is doubtful that Saudi Arabia would agree to its territory being used by US troops. Osama bin Laden's hatred of the US military presence has found widespread support among ordinary Saudis, and a new and even greater build-up would hold many risks for the present leadership.

If the USA were to launch a sustained ground invasion, those loyal to the current regime would have nowhere to go. The danger is that they would concentrate their last stand on the urban areas of Baghdad, using all possible means to fend off the final stages of a US-led attack. The price of Bush's plans could be huge. Enormous civilian and military casualties might be accompanied by widespread destruction.

Since January 2002 Baghdad has also intensified its diplomatic offensive across the Middle East and at the UN in New York. There has been speculation that this may yet result in its acceptance of renewed UN arms inspections. A diplomatic master stroke of this nature, combined with the collective hostility of Arab states to military action, would not prevent the USA targeting Saddam Hussain, but it would undoubtedly make the task much more difficult.

CONCLUSIONS

After 12 years the international coalition that expelled Iraqi forces from Kuwait is no more. The sanctions designed to 'keep Saddam in his box' are now largely ineffective. The regime in Baghdad appears stronger than at any time since it invaded Kuwait, and the USA is having to make difficult decisions when plotting regime change. Regionally, US policy towards the Israeli–Palestinian conflict has made it extremely unpopular. Although none of Iraq's Arab neighbours conform to the democratic criteria prescribed by Washington, they cannot ignore public opinion. A successful campaign against Iraq would certainly make governments across the Middle East much more responsive to US demands. However, it would also fuel popular resentment towards the USA and encourage support for al-Qa'ida's brand of anti-Western militancy.

Against this background, the removal of Saddam Hussain, could if possible cause greater regional instability than his continued rule. The question that is worrying both regional and European allies of the USA is whether the Bush Administration, after engineering regime change, is ready to commit itself to the expensive and time-consuming task of post-Saddam state building. This is something to which US Republicans in the past have appeared ideologically averse. This task, last unsuccessfully undertaken in Iraq by the British in the 1920s, could entail a military and financial commitment for up to a generation. If this commitment is not forthcoming, then Afghanistan may well offer a convincing comparison—not the Afghanistan of today but the Afghanistan of the 1990s, cast aside after becoming the expedient of Cold War politics, to descend into a collapsed state and a centre for global insecurity.

On the other hand, Iraqi foreign policy continues to be rational and is clearly driven by the attainment of two goals—an end to sanctions and the ultimate survival of the regime. If the international community is serious about disarmament, then it has to offer the Iraqi Government guarantees about its future survival along with a realistic mechanism for the lifting of sanctions in return for letting the weapons inspectors back in: anything less is not enough to bring the Iraqis to the table. However unpalatable this may be to those in Washington and elsewhere, it is the only alternative to the destabilizing and unpredictable policy of violent regime change.

SELECT BIBLIOGRAPHY

Aburish, Said K. *Saddam Hussein: The Politics of Revenge*. New York, Bloomsbury, 1999.

Cockburn, Andrew, and Cockburn, Patrick. *Saddam Hussein: An American Obsession*, London, Verso, 2002.

Dawod, Hosham, and Jabar, Faleh (Eds). *Tribes and Power: Nationalism and Ethnicity in the Middle East*. London, Saqi Books, 2002.

Jabar, Faleh. *Ayatollahs, Sufis and Ideologues: State, Religion and Social Movements*. London, Saqi Books, 2002.

Niblock, Tim. *'Pariah States' in the Middle East: Iraq, Libya, Sudan*. Boulder, CO, Lynne Rienner, 2001.

Ritter, Scott. *Endgame: Solving the Iraq Problem—Once and for All*. New York, Simon & Schuster, 1999.

Tripp, Charles. *A History of Iraq*. Cambridge University Press, 2000.

THE ISLAMIST MOVEMENT IN THE MIDDLE EAST AND NORTH AFRICA

MALISE RUTHVEN

Revised for this edition by the Editorial staff

More than two decades after the proclamation of an Islamic revolution in Iran the Islamist political fervour afflicting the Middle East and North Africa shows little sign of abating. In Algeria the civil war between Islamists and the Government has devastated the country at the cost of more than 100,000 lives. In Egypt, where the Government still appears to have the upper hand, the estimated casualty rate is much lower—about one-tenth of the Algerian figure—but the cost has been prodigious, with tourism, the country's largest foreign currency earner, devastated and the country's ancient Christian minority increasingly fearful of its future. For many years before the al-Aqsa *intifada*, which erupted in late September 2000, Islamist militants in Gaza and the West Bank had adopted the 'rejectionist' position abandoned by the PLO since 1988, threatening to undermine the peace process—in ironic collusion with Jewish fundamentalists who also believe themselves to be acting on divine instructions. With Islamists entrenched in Iran, Afghanistan and Sudan and challenging for power in Algeria, alarm bells were ringing on both sides of the Atlantic long before the suicide attacks on the USA in September 2001, when militants apparently acting in the name of Islam caused more than 3,000 deaths, and the ensuing prosecution of the US-led 'war against terror', targeted first against the al-Qa'ida (Base) organization of Osama bin Laden—the USA's prime suspect in the attacks—and al-Qa'ida's Taliban hosts in Afghanistan. Was a revitalized 'fundamentalist' Islam and its concept of *jihad* the new menace that would replace communism as the principal 'threat' to the secular, liberal, democratic values of the West?

This view, put forward among others by Samuel Huntington, the influential Harvard political scientist, and Willy Claes, the former Secretary-General of NATO, is based on the premise that the difference between 'Islamic' and 'Western' civilizations and value systems are as fundamental, in terms of economic management and social organization, as those which formerly divided the Eastern and Western blocs. It is seriously disputed by many leading scholars and journalists who argue that, despite its rhetorical excesses, the Islamist movement is not so much a 'threat' to the West or the regimes supported by it as a reflection of a crisis—or series of crises—internal to the Islamic world. On closer inspection, these crises reveal themselves to be little different from those afflicting non-Islamic nations in the developing world.

In theory Islam is an inherently political religion. As well as being the bearer of divine revelation, the Prophet Muhammad founded a state which his successors, the caliphs, transformed into an empire stretching from the Atlantic to the Indus valley. Although the empire rapidly lost its political cohesion as rival claimants fought each other for the leadership, the elaboration of the laws derived from the Koran and the Hadith (reports of the sayings and deeds of the Prophet) by the *'ulama* (specialists in the interpretations of texts) came to supply the unchallenged, and unchallengeable, rules of daily social life. After the first disputes, resulting in the split between Sunni and Shi'a, the Muslim ruler's legitimacy came to depend less on his lineage than his role as protector of the Umma, or Islamic community, and preserver of the *Shari'a*, divine law, according to the Koranic command to 'enjoin the good and forbid the evil'. Despite many regional variations, the application of the *Shari'a* over the course of 15 centuries produced a remarkably homogenous international society, bound by common customs and procedures, which contrasted strikingly with the tribalism operating at the level of power politics. Islamic identity *vis-à-vis* the rest of the world became a matter of practice as much as belief; orthopraxy as distinct from orthodoxy. Whereas the Christian road to salvation was determined mainly by faith and moral outlook, Muslims, additionally, lived in a world of legal exacti-

tude where rules were specified, together with the means of enforcing them.

However, although comprehensive in theory, the system was never complete. In theory the rulers (sultans or emirs) ruled according to the *Shari'a*, with *'ulama* support. In practice the *'ulama* were often forced to acquiesce in the loss of their legal monopoly. Islamic law was supplemented by the decrees of rulers in substantial areas of commerce, taxation, public and criminal law. Moreover, since the *qadis* (*Shari'a* judges) were appointed by the rulers, they were powerless to enforce decisions that went against those rulers' interests. A *de facto* separation of politics and religion came into existence. However, it was not formally acknowledged by the religious establishment, which continued to uphold the principle that sovereignty belonged to God alone. A major consequence has been the continuance of 'Islam' as a political factor: for so long as the principle has continued to exist that Islam is a 'total way of life' that makes no distinction between God and Caesar, people have sought to realize the Islamic ideal through political action—or, to express the same idea more cynically, they have tried to achieve political power by exploiting Islam's rich symbolic repertoire.

The principal intellectual forebears of the modern fundamentalist or 'Islamist' political movements which would challenge governments from the Maghreb to Malaysia during the latter decades of the 20th century CE were to be found in the Middle East and South Asia, with increasing cross-fertilization between the two regions. From the 18th century CE Islamic reformers, such as Shah Wali Ullah in India and Muhammad ibn Abd al-Wahhab in Arabia, had prepared the ground for a modernist movement by seeking to purge Islamic belief and ritual of the accretions and innovations acquired over the centuries, particularly the cults surrounding the Sufi *walis* or 'saints', living and dead. An Islam pruned of its medieval accretions was better able to confront the challenge of foreign power than a local cult bounded by the intercessional power of a particular saint or family of saints. The movements of resistance to European rule during the 19th and early 20th centuries were led or inspired by renovators (*mujaddids*), most of them members of Sufi orders, who sought to emulate the Prophet Muhammad's example by purifying the religion of their day and waging war on corruption and infidelity.

Both modernists, like Sir Sayyid Ahmad Khan, founder of the Anglo-Oriental College (later University) of Aligarh in India, and reformers like Muhammad 'Abduh (d. 1906), founder of the *Salafiyya* movement in Egypt, were inspired by the same example. Their problem was not, as 'Abduh's patron Lord Cromer (virtual ruler of Egypt between 1882 and 1908) would argue, that 'reformed Islam is no longer Islam'; but rather that there was no institutional hierarchy comparable to a Christian priesthood through which theological and legal reforms could be effected. Reformist *'ulama* like 'Abduh or his more conservative disciple Rashid Rida had no special authority through which they could impose their views, and the *'ulama*, for the most part, have remained unreconstructed traditionalists up to the present.

Rida became the first important advocate of a modernized Islamic state. He formulated his views during the crisis surrounding the abolition of the Ottoman Caliphate by Kemal Atatürk and the Turkish National Assembly in 1924, a move which, blamed on the colonial victors over the Ottoman Empire during the 1914–18 war, had led to a mass agitation among Muslims in India. Though originally a supporter of the Ottoman Caliphate, Rida came to accept its demise as a symptom of Muslim decadence; and, while no advocate of secularism, he saw the Assembly's decision as a genuine expression of the Islamic principle of consultation (*shura*). The ideal caliph, according to Rida, was an independent interpreter of the Law (*mujtahid*) who would work in concert with the *'ulama*. In the absence of a suitable candidate, and of *'ulama* versed in the modern sciences, the best alternative was an Islamic state ruled by an enlightened élite in consultation with the people, and able to interpret the *Shari'a* and legislate when necessary.

Many of Rida's ideas were taken up by the most influential Sunni reform movement, the Muslim Brotherhood, founded in 1928 by Hassan al-Banna, an Egyptian schoolteacher. The Brotherhood's original aims were moral as much as political: it sought to reform society by encouraging Islamic observance and opposing western cultural influences, rather than by attempting to capture the state by direct political action. However, in the mounting crisis over Palestine during and after the Second World War the Brotherhood became increasingly radicalized. In 1948 the Egyptian Prime Minister, Nuqrashi Pasha, was assassinated by a Brotherhood member, and Hassan al-Banna paid with his life in a retaliatory killing by the security services the following year.

The Brotherhood played a leading part in the disturbances that led to the overthrow of the Egyptian monarchy in 1952, but after the revolution it came into increasing conflict with the nationalist Government of Gamal 'Abdul Nasser. In 1954, after an attempt on Nasser's life, the Brotherhood was again suppressed, its members imprisoned, exiled or driven underground. It was during this period that the Brotherhood became internationalized, with affiliated movements springing up in Jordan, Syria, Sudan, Pakistan, Indonesia and Malaysia. In Saudi Arabia, under the vigorous leadership of Amir (later King) Faisal ibn 'Abdul 'Aziz, the Brotherhood found refuge, and political and financial support, with funds for the Egyptian underground and salaried posts for exiled intellectuals.

It was a radical member of the Brotherhood, Sayyid Qutb, executed in 1966 for an alleged plot to overthrow the Egyptian Government, who would prove to be the Arab world's most influential Islamist theorist. Some of Qutb's key ideas, however, are directly attributable to the Indian scholar and journalist, Abu'l 'Ala (Maulana) Maududi (1906–79), whose works became available in Arabic translation during the 1950s. One of Maududi's doctrines, in particular, would have a major impact on Islamic political movements. It was the idea that the struggle for Islam was not for the restoration of an ideal past, but for a principle vital to the here and now: the vice-regency of man under God's sovereignty. The *jihad* was therefore not just a defensive war for the protection of the Islamic territory or *Dar al-Islam*. It might also be waged against governments which prevent the preaching of true Islam, for the condition of *jahiliyya* (the state of ignorance before the coming of Islam) was to be found currently, in the here and now.

During his years in prison Qutb, who had spent some time in the USA as a member of an Egyptian educational delegation, wrote a comprehensive account of the modern *jahiliyya* in his book *Ma'alim fi'l-tariq* ('Signposts along the Road'):

'Today we are in the midst of a *jahiliyya* similar to or even worse than the *jahiliyya* that was 'squeezed out' by Islam. Everything about us is *jahiliyya*, the ideas of mankind and their beliefs, their customs and traditions, the sources of their culture, their arts and literature, and their laws and regulations. [This is true] to such an extent that much of what we consider to be Islamic culture and Islamic sources, and Islamic philosophy and Islamic thought...is nevertheless the product of that *jahiliyya*'.

Qutb advocated the creation of a new élite among Muslim youth that would fight the new *jahiliyya* as the Prophet had fought the old one. Like the Prophet and his Companions, this élite must choose when to withdraw from the *jahiliyya* and when to seek contact with it. His ideas set the agenda for Islamic radicals, not just in Egypt but throughout the Sunni Muslim world. Those influenced by them included Shukri Mustafa, a former Muslim Brotherhood activist and leader of a group known as *Takfir wa Hijra* ('excommunication and emigration') who followed the early Kharijites in designating their enemies (in this case the Government) as *kafirs* (infidels); Khalid Islambuli and Abd as-Salaam Farraj, executed for the murder of President Anwar Sadat in October 1981; and the *Hizb at-Tahrir* (Islamic Liberation Party), founded in 1952 by Sheikh Taqi ad-Din an-Nabahani (1910–1977), a graduate of al-Azhar whose writings lay down detailed prescriptions for a restored Caliphate.

While Qutb's writings remained an important influence on Islamic radicals, or 'Islamists', from Algeria to Pakistan, a major boost to the movement came from Iran, where Ayatollah Khomeini came to power after the collapse of the Pahlavi regime in February 1979. During the final two decades of the 20th century CE the Iranian Revolution remained the inspiration for 'Islamists' from Morocco to Indonesia. Despite this universalist appeal, however, the Revolution never succeeded in spreading beyond the confines of Shi'i communities and even among them its capacity to mobilize the masses remained limited. During the eight-year war that followed Iraq's invasion of Iran in 1980 the Iraqi Shi'is, who form about 50% of the population, conspicuously failed to support their co-religionists in Iran. The Revolution did spread to Shi'i communities in Lebanon, Saudi Arabia, Bahrain, Afghanistan and Pakistan, but generally proved unable to cross the sectarian divide. The new Shi'i activism in these countries either stirred up sectarian conflicts or stimulated severe repression by Sunni governments (as in Iraq and Bahrain).

Within Iran the success of the Revolution had rested on three factors usually absent from the Sunni world: the mixing of Shi'i and Marxist ideas among the radicalized urban youth during the 1970s; the autonomy of the Shi'i religious establishment which, unlike the Sunni *'ulama*, disposed of a considerable amount of social power as a body or 'estate'; and the eschatological expectations of popular Shi'ism surrounding the return of the Twelfth Imam.

The leading Shi'i exponent of Islam as a revolutionary ideology comparable to Marxism was 'Ali Shari'ati (d. 1977), a historian and sociologist who had been partly educated in Paris. Though without formal religious training, Shari'ati reached large numbers of youth from the traditional classes through his popular lectures at the Husayniyah Irshad, an informal academy which he established in Tehran. Shari'ati's teachings contain a rich mix of ideas in which theosophical speculations of mystics like Ibn al-'Arabi and Mulla Sadra were blended with the insights of Marx, Sartre, Camus and Fanon. The result was an eclectic synthesis of Islamic and leftist ideas. God was virtually identified with the People, justifying revolutionary action in the name of Islam; the *kafirs* (infidels) excoriated in the Koran were identified with those who refused to take action against injustice. An outspoken critic of those members of the clergy who acquiesced in the Shah's tyranny, Shari'ati drew a distinction between the official Shi'ism of the Safavid dynasty (1501–1722), which made Shi'ism the state religion in Iran, and the 'revolutionary' commitment of such archetypal Shi'i figures as the Imams 'Ali and Husain and Abu Dharr al-Ghifari (a Companion of the Prophet often credited with having socialist principles). Shari'ati's ideas, disseminated through photocopies and audio tapes, provided a vital link between the student vanguard and the more conservative forces which brought down the Shah's regime. The latter were mobilized by Sayyid Ruhallah Khomeini, an Ayatollah or senior cleric from Qom who had come to prominence as the leading critic of Shah Muhammad Reza Pahlavi's 'White Revolution' during the early 1960s. This was a series of agricultural and social reforms which threatened the interest of the religious establishment, not least because the estates from which many of the *'ulama* drew their incomes were expropriated or divided up. Exiled to Najaf in Iraq, Khomeini developed his theory of government—the *Velayet-e-faqheh* (jurisconsult's trusteeship)—which radically broke with tradition by insisting that government be entrusted directly to the religious establishment:

'The slogan of the separation of religion and politics and the demand that Islamic scholars should not intervene in social or political affairs have been formulated and propagated by the imperialists; it is only the irreligious who repeat them. Were religion and politics separate at the time of the Prophet?'

Popular Shi'ism focuses on the martyred figures of 'Ali and Husain and the expected return of the Twelfth Imam to restore justice and peace in the world. These motifs were skilfully deployed in the mass demonstrations preceding the fall of the Shah in 1978–79. Though Khomeini never formally claimed to be the Hidden Imam, there can be no doubt that by allowing his followers to address him as 'Imam', a title normally reserved by Shi'is for the Imams of the Prophet's house (*Ahl al-bait*), Khomeini deliberately allowed popular eschatological expectations to work on his behalf.

Contrary to the view widely held in the West, however, Khomeini did not impose a fully 'Islamic' system of government (comparable, for example to Saudi Arabia, where the Government rules in accordance with the *Shari'a*, supplemented by royal decrees). The 1979 Constitution is really a hybrid of Islamic and western liberal concepts. As the sociologist Sami Zubaida points out, there is a 'contradictory duality of sovereignties'. Article 6 refers to the 'sovereignty of the popular will' in line with democratic national states, but the principle of *Velayet-e-faqheh* gave sweeping powers to Khomeini as 'chief jurisconsult' or trustee. The Constitution is the keystone of a range of institutions, including the *majlis-e-shura* (consultative assembly) composed of elected members under the supervision of a *shura-e-nigahban* (council of guardians). Although the *Shari'a* is supposed to be the basis for all law and legislation, many of the civil codes from the previous regime were retained: there were three court systems, the *madani* (civil) courts, the *Shari'a* courts and the 'revolutionary courts' which handed out often arbitrary punishments by the *komitehs* or revolutionary guards. 'Islamization' was introduced in a number of areas. Women were forced to wear 'Islamic' clothing and removed from certain professions, including the law; interest-bearing loans were forbidden and education was altered to include Islamic doctrines. In practice the *shura-e-nigahban* proved an embarrassment by vetoing, as contrary to the *Shari'a*, various measures passed by the Majlis, including a major land reform. In January 1988 Khomeini ruled decisively in favour of the Majlis, pronouncing that the power of the Islamic State was comparable to that enjoyed by the Prophet Muhammad and took precedence over *Shari'a*. Now that the Islamic State had been won, religious obligations were 'secondary' to government decrees. By giving the state priority over Islamic law from within the religious tradition, Khomeini ironically initiated a process that could open the way to a *de facto* secular regime in which the power of the clergy as a separate estate was effectively neutralized. The reduced status of the Shi'i hierarchy became apparent on Khomeini's death in June 1989, with the election, by the *majlis-e-khobregan* (council of experts), of the then President, Ali Khamenei, as Khomeini's successor to the position of Wali Faqih, supreme jurisconsult. As Khamenei was only *hojatoleslam* at the time (i.e. a middle-ranking cleric), the choice in effect negated the Revolution's most significant achievement, which had been to place government under the moral and juridical authority of the supreme spiritual leadership—known in Shi'i terminology as the *marja'iyya*, (after the highest clerical office, the *marja' at-taqlid*, source of imitation, of whom there are several). The succession was legitimized by an amendment to the Constitution sanctioning the eventual separation of the *marja'iyya* as theological authority from the *velaya* (guardianship or legal authority), by allowing any faqih with 'scholastic qualifications for issuing religious decrees' to assume the leadership. The result was a divorce of political and religious functions at the highest level in blatant contradiction of Khomeini's doctrine. Since then Iran has witnessed an increasingly open conflict between the spiritual authority of the senior clergy and the politico-religious leadership exercised by the clerics actually in power. In January 1995, in an open letter to the authorities, Ayatollah Ruhani declared that life in Iran had become 'unbearable' for those who adhered to true Islamic principles. He felt he 'could not remain a spectator while Islam is violated daily' and the 'true religious leaders' were silenced in a country claiming to be an Islamic republic. He claimed that his home had been attacked by armed criminals who threatened to kill him unless he pledged allegiance to Khamenei; in July of the same year his residence was raided again and his son was arrested. Other senior clerics, or their spokesmen, articulated similar views. Sayed Muhammad Qomi, a son of Ayatollah Sayed Hasan Qomi-Tabataba'i, asserted that state and religion were incompatible, and must be separated. Since governments were bound to commit immoral acts, it was counter to the interests of religion that they be run by clerics. The experience of Iran since 1979 had done damage to Islam and its religious leaders. 'Terrorism, torture, bombing, explosions and hostage-taking', which had no place in Islam, were now identified with

it. The rule of the clerics had only brought disgrace to Islam. The same critique has been articulated even more forcefully by one of Iran's leading intellectuals, the philosopher Abd al-Karim Soroush, a professor at the University of Tehran. Adopting a view of religion in line with Western phenomenology, Soroush argues that religion, unlike ideology, cannot be cast in any one shape, but bears interpretations that vary in accordance with time and circumstance. Religion is richer, more comprehensive and more humane than mere ideology. It can generate weapons, instruments and ideals, but itself transcends all of these things. Imposing a fixed interpretation on religion—any religion—makes it rigid, superficial, dogmatic and one-dimensional. Khomeini's movement, according to Soroush, will not bear the 'appropriate fruits' unless his followers nurture 'a new understanding of the faith'. Soroush has been physically attacked on several occasions and has been subjected to harassment and intimidation by militants, such as the Ansar-e Hezbollah, assumed to have links with Khamenei and the right-wing elements associated with the Society of Combatant Clergy (Jameh-e-Ruhaniyat Mobarez—JRM) in the Majlis. Recent developments, however, indicate that Soroush is far from isolated, and that the political tide is moving in his direction. In April 1996 elections to the Majlis revealed a decline in support for the JRM and advanced the cause of its more moderate challengers, the Servants of Iran's Construction. An even more decisive shift in public opinion was demonstrated a year later, in May 1997, with the unexpected election of Sayed Muhammad Khatami to the presidency with a massive majority (more than 20m. votes to 7.2m.) over his leading rival, the 'conservative' Speaker of the Majlis, Ali Akbar Nateq Nouri. A former Minister of Culture and Islamic Guidance, noted for his support for the film industry, Khatami was supported by a broad coalition of forces, including industrialists, urban professionals, university students, educated women and technocrats. The right-wing elements surrounding Khamenei, however, remained determined to retain their collective grip on power. In 1998–99 the conflict between 'conservatives' and 'liberals', dogmatists and pragmatists raged in the Iranian courts, and 'conservatives' in the Majlis sought, with varying success, to impeach government ministers whom they considered unacceptably tolerant of liberal or reformist attitudes.

Increasingly, the issue of press freedom became inseparable from the struggle between conservative and reformist elements in Iran, with the closure during 1998 of several publications and the prosecution of journalists associated with them. Endorsement by the conservative-controlled Majlis in July 1999 of draft legislation seeking to curb the activities of the 'liberal' press was the catalyst for what were reportedly the most serious demonstrations in Tehran since the Islamic Revolution. Several days of rioting, in which pro-reform students and other 'liberal' activists clashed with security forces and Ansar-e Hezbollah vigilantes, attracted considerable international media coverage. As elections to the Majlis, due in early 2000, approached, 'conservative' elements redoubled their efforts to curb the activities of the 'liberal' press. Not least because the process of scrutinizing candidates apparently resulted in the disqualification of many 'reformists', the extent of the successes achieved by 'liberal' and 'moderate' candidates was not widely predicted. However, while 'reformists' and 'liberals' nominally formed a sizeable majority in the new Majlis, which was inaugurated in late May, it was considered likely that the continuing dominance of the 'conservative' clergy in the judicial and other organs of the Islamic State would severely restrict their actual legislative power. For its part, the judiciary pursued its actions against the 'reformist' press: the outgoing, 'conservative'-controlled Majlis had endorsed restrictive legislation making criticism of the Constitution illegal and increasing judicial powers to close newspapers. The Majlis had also approved legislation effectively depriving the legislature of authority to call to account security organizations under the control of Ayatollah Khamenei. Khamenei's personal intervention to block the new legislature's efforts to amend the press law, on the grounds that such reforms would endanger state security and religious faith, appeared to sanction a more vigorous campaign against 'liberal' interests in the approach to the presidential election, scheduled for June 2001. In late 2000, notably, the trial took place of a group of prominent 'reformists', accused of 'acting against national security and propagandizing against the regime' by attending a conference on political reform in Iran, held in Berlin, Germany, earlier in the year. Among the accused were a dissident cleric, Hassan Yousefi Eshkevari, who had also been tried before the Special Clerical Court on charges including apostasy. That Khatami's convincing victory in the 2001 presidential election represented an endorsement by the electorate of his reformist political programme—and a mandate for further change—could not be ignored by his 'conservative' detractors; however, these same 'conservative' forces remained firmly entrenched in the Islamic State at the commencement of the 21st century and seemed no less likely to seek to restrict moves towards 'liberalization' perceived as detrimental to the interests of fundamentalist Islam.

In the immediate aftermath of the September 2001 suicide attacks on the USA, there was considerable speculation among Western observers as to Iran's likely response to US prosecution of a campaign against al-Qa'ida and the Taliban regime in Afghanistan. President Khatami was swift to offer his 'deep sympathy. . .to the American nation,' asserting that terrorism was 'condemned' and urging the international community to take 'effective measures against it'. In a letter to the UN Secretary-General, Khatami stated that he regarded the UN as the most appropriate mechanism to achieve the eradication of terrorism. Ayatollah Khamenei, for his part, condemned the atrocities in the strongest terms but cautioned against a military offensive against Afghanistan which might result in the deaths of innocent civilians and create a new refugee exodus, asserting that Iran would similarly condemn any 'catastrophe' brought about in Afghanistan by US-led conflict; he warned, furthermore, that the USA's problems would multiply if the country sought to establish a presence in Pakistan and send troops into Afghanistan. Khamenei's views were echoed in Iran's 'conservative' press. Both 'liberals' and 'conservatives' in the Iranian regime strongly condemned the commencement of hostilities in early October, and the immediate impact of the US-led military campaign in Afghanistan was to unite all sides in condemnation. Iranian influence and interests were, however, evident in the establishment, following the defeat of the Taliban, of the new Afghan administration led by Hamid Karzai. The rallies that took place in Tehran and elsewhere in February 2002 to mark the anniversary of the 1979 Revolution were larger than usual, with a notable increase in angry demonstrations of hostility towards the USA, and discourse within Iran was dominated by the possibility that the Bush Administration's anti-Iran rhetoric might be galvanized into military action. At much the same time, Iran took steps to counter US accusations that defeated al-Qa'ida and Taliban fighters had found sanctuary in Iran, and closed down the offices of Gulbuddin Hekmatyar, the *mujahidin* commander who had been involved in the destruction of Kabul in the early 1990s. However, despite a general preoccupation with events in Afghanistan, the struggle between Iran's 'reformists' and 'conservatives' continued. In the latter part of 2001 and into 2002 the main focus of this struggle was, once again, the judiciary—often in conflict with the Majlis and the 'reformist' press.

The gap between the regime's Islamic rhetoric and its political realities has been demonstrated in one of the most sensitive cultural areas, namely gender and family life. In opposition and exile, Khomeini had opposed the female franchise introduced by the Shah and bitterly denounced the Family Protection Laws introduced in 1967 and 1976 which limited the rights of men in divorce cases, improved the rights of women and raised the age of marriage to 18. Khomeini declared that divorces obtained according to these laws would not be recognized and marriages subsequently contracted would be punished as adulterous. Chador-clad women were among the most active participants in the Revolution: the rhetoric of the time stressed that 'true Islam' fully protected female rights, while granting them a dignity and status denied by Western sexual exploitation which reduced them to the condition of prostitutes. After coming to power with much female support, however, the mullahs were in no position to remove the female franchise. Islamic legal practice was restored to the extent that the age of marriage for girls was lowered to 13, and in some cases to nine, the official age of maturity. However most of the provisions of the Shah's laws protecting the rights of women in marriage were retained.

A new family law enacted in 1992 represents, in the view of the anthropologist Homa Hoodfar, 'one of the most advanced marriage laws in the Middle East (after Tunisia and Turkey) without deviating from any of the major conventional assumptions of Islamic law'. Evidently under clerical pressure, female employment in the public sector decreased, and women are prevented by law from occupying certain senior offices of state. None the less, in 2000 it was conceded by Iran's clerics that a woman could lead other women in prayer, and the restoration of the full right of women to become judges (revoked after the Revolution) was being debated. Women's votes were particularly influential in the election of Muhammad Khatami to the presidency in 1997 and in his re-election in June 2001, and women have themselves held high political office and achieved notable electoral successes under his administration. Thus, while under Islamic law Iranian women remain subject to strict dress code and their rights are undoubtedly restricted, it can be argued that in Iran, more than any other Middle Eastern country, the highly contentious issue of women's rights is being debated on the basis of contested interpretations of Islamic law, within the forum of an elected assembly. This may not be a fully fledged democracy according to Western models, but such open and public debate would be unthinkable in an Islamic society such as that which prevails in Saudi Arabia.

Outside Iran, however, the factors that contributed to the Islamic Revolution continued to sustain the Islamist movements, accounting for the continuing popularity of their ideologies. The collapse of communism and the failure of Marxism to overcome the stigma of 'atheism' made Islam seem an attractive ideological weapon against regimes grown increasingly corrupt, authoritarian and sometimes tyrannical. The rhetoric of national liberation, appropriated by monopolist ruling parties, became discredited as those parties failed to address fundamental economic and structural problems, and were increasingly seen to be controlled by tribal coteries or political cliques indifferent to the needs of the majority. In countries such as Egypt and Algeria, qualified successes achieved by governments in the field of education turned against them, as graduates from state universities found career opportunities blocked. As centres of opposition, the mosques enjoy privileged status, and the efforts of governments to subject them to state control are usually incomplete. If they close down 'rebel' mosques they merely confirm the charges of disbelief directed against them by their opponents. At the same time, the explosion of information technology and particularly the revolution in communications media undercut the authority of the literate élites. The effect of this has been twofold. While such media expose ever-growing numbers of people to transgressive and often salacious images created by the Western entertainment and advertising industries, video and audio cassettes, and increasingly the internet, enable radical preachers to evade government controls on radio and television.

In many Middle Eastern countries an exponential leap in the rate of urbanization has decisively altered the cultural and demographic balance between urban and rural populations, creating a vast new proletariat of recently urbanized migrants susceptible to the messages of populist preachers and demagogues. The Islamist movements, through their welfare organizations, have been able to fill the gaps caused by government failure to deal with housing shortages and other social problems. Housing shortages are forcing young people to delay marriage in societies where extra-marital sexual activity is strictly forbidden. The resulting frustration, it may be argued, accounts for the obsessive manner with which the Islamists seek to enforce their rigid sexual codes. Restrictions on government spending imposed by the IMF have tended to exacerbate housing and welfare problems by forcing cuts in social spending, leading to the withdrawal of the state from some areas and its replacement by Islamic welfare organizations and charitable associations. Such voluntary organizations have found generous sources of funds in Saudi Arabia and the Gulf. The Islamic financial sector provides employment opportunities and an avenue for building networks of patronage, religious orthodoxy and political mobilization able to compensate for the disappearance of older communal bonds and patronage. With rapid urbanization and the growth of slums and shanty towns, the old systems have ceased to function, as sheikhs and notables, local and party leaders have become detached from their previous clients. The former nationalist rhetoric, whether Nasserist or Baathist, has been discredited. 'It is into this vacuum of organization and power,' writes Sami Zubaida, 'that the Islamic groups have stepped to impose their authority and discipline. The organization they impose is not one of popular participation. The activists and militants remain in charge, and the common people, to whom they provide services against modest payments, are considered as subjects of ethical reform, to be converted to orthodox conformity and mobilized in political support.'

Though inspired by local conditions, the international factors affecting the Islamist movement should not be ignored. Veterans of the Afghan war against the Soviet occupation have formed the core of armed Islamist groups not just in Afghanistan but also in Algeria, Yemen and Egypt. At the height of the conflict there are said to have been between 10,000 and 12,000 *mujahidin* from Arab countries financed from mosques and private contributions in Saudi Arabia and the Gulf states. Many of them, ironically, are reported to have been trained by the US Central Intelligence Agency (CIA) in the camps of Gulbuddin Hekmatyar. The Saudi-born militant Islamist Osama bin Laden (whose citizenship was revoked in 1994 because of his alleged activities against the royal family) was believed to have organized large groups of Arab volunteers in the Afghan *jihad*, before his campaign of direct sponsorship of terrorist attacks against Western targets took him and a loyal band of 'Afghan Arabs' to Sudan (from where they were expelled in 1996) and finally back to Afghanistan (where they were once considered a great inconvenience for the Taliban regime, frustrating its attempts to secure recognition from the international community).

Saudi influence also operates at the religious or ideological level. Many of the Islamists active in Egypt and Algeria spent time in Saudi Arabia as teachers or exiles where they became converted to the rigid, puritanical version of Islam practised in that country. Thus a prominent (currently imprisoned) leader of the Front islamique du salut (FIS) in Algeria, Ali Belhadj, far from operating within the regional Maliki school of jurisprudence, which allows for considerable latitude of interpretation 'in the public interest', is trying to impose the rigid tenets of the Hanbali school prevailing in Saudi Arabia on the leadership of the FIS.

The responses of governments to the challenge of political Islam range from outright repression to co-optation and accommodation. In the Syrian city of Hama a rebellion by the Muslim Brotherhood in 1982 was suppressed by the Government of President Hafiz al-Assad at a human cost estimated at between 5,000 and 20,000 lives.

In Algeria the army's cancellation of the second round of the national elections after the FIS won the first round in December 1991 led to a bloody civil war that came to resemble, in its barbarity and carelessness for the lives of non-combatants, the campaign fought by the French against Algerian nationalists nearly two generations earlier. Although it organized meetings with some of its Islamist opponents, the administration under Liamine Zéroual refused to countenance outside mediation by France, or by the European Union, initiatives which might present the possibility of an end to this terrible conflict on Europe's southern borders. The prospects for a solution have been undermined by internal divisions on both sides. Zéroual's freedom of manoeuvre was restricted by the powerful faction of senior army generals known as the 'eradicators', headed by the Chief of Staff Lt-Gen. Muhammad Lamari, who favour a military solution; the Islamist cause is even more riven by factionalism, with increasingly bitter rivalry between the FIS and its military wing, the Armée islamique du salut (AIS) on one side, and the extremist Groupe islamique armé (GIA) on the other, as well as by divisions within the political leadership of the FIS.

After secret dialogue between the Algerian Government and FIS leaders Abbasi Madani and Ali Belhadj in the spring of 1995 ended in failure and mutual recrimination, the Government sought to legitimize its own position and to discredit that of its Islamist opponents by holding a presidential election in November 1995 (the first multi-party election since independence), to be followed by the creation of a new National Assembly. The strategy was successful, despite a boycott by all the main opposition parties, to the extent that it improved the Government's international standing by means of a sizeable—if disputed—majority of 61% for President Zéroual. During the campaign, registered opposition candidates including Mahfoud Nahnah, leader of the moderate Islamist Hamas party, were free to organize political rallies and to express criticism of the Government in televised broadcasts. The relatively large showing for Nahnah (25.6%, according to official figures) indicated that many FIS supporters had voted for him. Observers noted the high proportion of women voters, who had taken part in defiance of Islamist threats.

Political advances towards participatory democracy and constitutional government in Algeria were, however, vitiated by the deteriorating security situation, and in particular by the spiralling cost in human lives. The death toll among civilians, terrorists and armed forces since the conflict began in 1992 was finally admitted by the new President, Abdelaziz Bouteflika, in August 1999 to be at least 100,000. In the complex and highly unstable patterns of terror and counter-terror, attributing responsibility for the massacres in which unarmed civilians have been the principal victims has become increasingly difficult. Initially, both of the armed Islamist organizations aimed to weaken the foundations of the state by striking at its economic infrastructure and its officials. Army officers, government employees and politicians were among the primary targets, as were religious functionaries who dared to condemn the insurgents' activities as being contrary to Islam. Increasingly, however, the GIA expanded its activity to embrace a much broader 'culture war', in which anything with 'Western' or 'secular' associations was liable to attack. The view that the education system serves an 'impious state' has resulted in the destruction of more than a thousand schools. Students have been warned to stay away, and occasionally schoolchildren have been the targets of violence. Journalists and media personnel have also been targeted. In their war against the *'jahiliyya'* state, the Islamists have murdered hundreds of artists and journalists accused of collaborating with the enemy or of peddling Western 'filth'; technicians responsible for installing television satellite dishes, through which Algerians can receive French and Italian programmes, have had their throats cut. Musicians specializing in the formerly popular *rai* music (a blend of Arabic music and Western rock) have been assassinated, along with other representatives of 'Western' or hybrid culture, including scientists, athletes and foreign personnel. The assault on 'Western' culture is seen by some observers as an attack on culture itself. One foreign journalist noted that the GIA's war against 'intellectuals' had begun to resemble 'not so much an Islamic uprising but a Khmer-Rouge style slaughter of the élite'. Women, particularly those suspected of having 'Western' educations, have been singled out for attack, along with all those who refuse to wear the veil.

The counter-measures initiated by the army have been no less brutal, and in the distorted world where terrorism and counter-terrorism meet, accusations that sections of the armed forces have themselves perpetrated atrocities in order to 'discredit' the Islamists have appeared increasingly plausible. Amnesty International, noting in a report on Algeria published in November 1997 that the Government blamed the violence on terrorist groups, drew attention to the fact that most of the attacks on unarmed villagers had occurred 'in areas around the capital in the most heavily militarized region of the country and often in close proximity to army barracks and security force outposts'. It also commented that 'on no occasion have the army and security forces intervened to stop or prevent the massacres, or to arrest those responsible'. In the case of one of the worst incidents of the conflict, the murders of some 300 people in three villages in the Blida region in August 1997, Amnesty noted that there were two military barracks within 6 km of the scene of the massacres, while there were security force posts within 'a few hundred yards'. The report concluded that 'at the very least' the Government was culpable for its failure to provide adequate protection for the population. It also suggested that there was a growing concern that death squads working in conjunction with elements in the security forces 'may have been responsible for some of the massacres'.

Although many observers were encouraged by the conciliatory campaign pledges of the country's new President (Abdelaziz Bouteflika—elected in April 1999), some concern was expressed at his alleged close relations with the powerful commercial organizations associated with the security services. Meanwhile, the scale of the conflict appeared to have lessened: the GIA continued its campaign of violence, but a unilateral cease-fire declared by the AIS in September 1997 (apparently to expose the GIA as responsible for recent atrocities against civilians) had been maintained, and the strength of the Islamist opposition was clearly undermined by the deep divisions within its own ranks. President Bouteflika swiftly established contacts with the FIS, and in June the AIS agreed to make permanent its cease-fire. Some 5,000 Islamist detainees were pardoned in July 1999, although Abbasi Madani remained under house arrest. There was considerable scepticism in certain quarters that a national referendum, in September, to endorse the new Law on Civil Concord, which offered an amnesty for Islamist militants who surrendered to the authorities within a six-month deadline, was principally a device to legitimize Bouteflika's election (a detailed account of the Law on Civil Concord and its application is given in the chapter on Algeria). In January 2000, following the expiry of the six-month deadline, the Government announced that 80% of members of armed groups had surrendered to the authorities. However, the amnesty apparently caused further divisions in the Algerian militant Islamist movement. In November 1999 Abdelkader Hachani, the most senior leader of the FIS still at liberty, was assassinated, to which crime a member of the main GIA faction was reported by the authorities to have confessed. Indications by Bouteflika early in 2000 that an amnesty agreement with a breakaway movement from the GIA, the Groupe salafiste pour la prédication et le combat (or Da'wa wal Djihad), was under consideration, on the grounds that the organization's offensives targeted the security forces rather than civilians, were apparently rejected by the group's leader, Hassan Hattab. In May of that year the Government implied, in refusing to accord legal status to a new political party, al-Wafa wa al-Adl, led by Ahmed Taleb Ibrahimi, that the party was essentially a reconstitution of the FIS.

The questions both of reintegrating those who surrendered under the terms of the Law on Civil Concord, and of the extent to which political legitimacy might be granted to the Islamist movement, were ones that remained to be addressed. Furthermore, thousands of Islamist fighters remained at large. Anti-guerrilla operations by the armed and security forces continued, and there were almost daily reports of continued violence. In July 2000 an article in the daily *Jeune Indépendant*, citing unofficial sources, claimed that some 1,100 civilians and an estimated 2,000 Islamist fighters had been killed in Algeria since the expiry of the general amnesty in January. Later that month another newspaper stated that it had calculated the number of people killed by militants' operations whose deaths had been reported in the press to total 777 between July 1999 and June 2000.

A sharp escalation in violence from late 2000 added weight to the arguments of those who believed that the civil conflict in Algeria, after nine years, was far from resolution. Meanwhile, there were persistent rumours of tensions between Bouteflika and the *éradicateurs* of the military high command, with some commentators suggesting that the army generals regarded the President as too willing to make concessions to the Islamists. There were also indications that the military was increasingly uneasy at efforts by human rights organizations to investigate 'disappearances' and secret detentions during the period of the conflict. Amnesty International had in late 2000 stated that the authorities had made no response to requests for meetings with officers of the security forces. In May 2001 Algeria's Minister of State for the Interior and Local Authorities informed the legislature that some 4,480 people had disappeared since 1992; he stated that enquiries were underway and that the results would be publicized, but rejected accusations that the security forces might be implicated in the disappearances. International human rights organizations, which, having been banned from visiting Algeria for several years, were finally readmitted in 2000, disputed the official figures (the head of the Amnesty International delegation that visited in mid-2000 had referred to some 22,000 missing persons), and some sources estimated that as many as 7,000 disappearances could be attributed to the security forces.

In the aftermath of the September 2001 attacks against the USA both the GIA and Da'wa wal Djihad appeared on the list of international terrorist organizations published by the US Administration whose assets were to be frozen. Shortly after the attacks, Da'wa wal Djihad's leader, Hassan Hattab, declared that if the USA attacked Muslims it could expect reprisals that would be far worse than those inflicted on New York and Washington, DC. In subsequent weeks a number of arrests were made in Europe of alleged members of Da'wa wal Djihad cells who were said to have links with Osama bin Laden and al-Qa'ida. Several Algerian sources suggested that close links had existed between bin Laden and the Algerian Islamist movement from the early 1990s, and that several Algerians working directly for al-Qa'ida ran a series of 'charitable' organizations and Islamic centres in Europe which acted as 'fronts' for the organization's activities. A number of sources claimed that bin Laden had been instrumental in the schism in the GIA in 1998 that led to the establishment of Da'wa wal Djihad. The Algerian authorities declared that they felt that there was now greater understanding in the West of their own 'battle' against Islamist terrorism. Great emphasis was placed on the level of co-operation between the Algerian security services and the US Federal Bureau of Investigation (FBI) in tracking down terrorists of Algerian origin based in Europe. The growing *rapprochement* with the USA in particular was regarded as furthering Algeria's successful emergence from a decade of diplomatic isolation. The US-led bombing of Afghanistan was, however, strongly condemned by prominent political parties within Algeria, notably the Front de libération nationale, while a senior member of the FIS declared that all Arab and Muslim allies of the USA were traitors to their religion, people and nation. In contrast with the 1991 Gulf conflict, there were no street protests or demonstrations against the US military action in Afghanistan or in support of bin Laden and his allies, but there was speculation that the silence was deceptive and that events in Afghanistan had merely served to strengthen the anti-US sentiment of many ordinary Algerians that was only likely to deepen as the USA apparently moved to make the regime of Saddam Hussein in Iraq the next target of its 'war against terror'. For their part, the *éradicateurs* within the Algerian ruling élite demanded Algeria's active engagement in the US-led coalition against 'Islamic terrorism', praising the tough stance adopted by the Bush Administration, and also took the opportunity once again to condemn Bouteflika for maintaining a dialogue with the country's radical Islamists.

Violence escalated in Algeria in early 2002, with unofficial reports indicating that some 150 people were killed by armed Islamist groups during the month of January alone, and there was a particular upsurge of violence in advance of the legislative elections which took place at the end of May. (Of the 'moderate' Islamist parties participating in the elections, the Mouvement de la société pour la paix—as Hamas was now styled—secured only 38 seats, compared with 69 in 1997; Sheikh Abdallah Djaballah's Mouvement de la réforme nationale took 43 seats; and Djaballah's former party, Nahdah, which had won 34 seats in 1997, retained just one.) There were, meanwhile, reports that some members of armed Islamist groups who had surrendered to the authorities under the Civil Concord had again taken up arms in the name of Da'wa wal Djihad, which according to one estimate had some 800–1,000 militants in Algeria. By contrast, the GIA appeared to have been greatly weakened not just by the actions of the security forces but also by its increasing factionalism. There were suggestions that the group, discredited in the view of most Algerians because of the extreme cruelty of its methods, had no more than 100 members, while a senior military source claimed that it had only 40 members but that these were highly mobile and well-armed. When, in February, the security forces found and killed GIA leader Antar Zouabri, there were rumours that they had acted on information received from Da'wa wal Djihad. Rachid Abou Tourab, subsequently named as Zouabri's successor, pledged to continue the violent campaign of his predecessor until the establishment of an Islamic state in Algeria had been achieved.

In Tunisia the regime of President Zine al-Abidine Ben Ali, a former security chief, has responded to the perceived Islamist threat in an uncompromising manner. The main Islamist party, an-Nahda ('Renaissance', formerly the Islamic Tendency Movement) has been banned along with all other parties based on religion, and its membership subjected to a ruthless campaign of repression leading to accusations of human rights abuses by Amnesty International and the UN Commission on Human Rights. The Government refuses to accept declarations by an-Nahda's leader, Rached Ghanouchi (who was granted political asylum in the United Kingdom in 1993) that his party is committed to pluralism and representative government, although an-Nahda has joined with other, non-Islamist opposition parties in proposing a dialogue with the regime. Ghanouchi emphasizes that 'the Islamists should accept a democratic coalition rule that might encompass only part of their programme' while believing that, far from being incompatible, Islamic and Western values can accommodate each other. 'Once the Islamists are given a chance to comprehend the values of Western modernity, such as democracy and human rights, they will search within Islam for a place for these values.' Non-Islamist opposition parties, meanwhile, have accused the Government of using the struggle against the Islamists to reinforce its authoritarian powers. President Ben Ali, however, insists that he is not dealing with the Islamists by security methods alone, but is adopting policies 'which tackle the economic and social problems, by taking care of the poorer regions and helping the poorest sections of society'. In this he has been helped by Tunisia's relatively prosperous economy. Stringent security measures, including road-blocks on all main routes leading to Algeria and the presence of undercover police-officers on cross-border trains appear to have prevented the Algerian conflict from spilling over into Tunisia. Like their Algerian counterparts, the Tunisian authorities have since 2001 shown themselves willing to co-operate with US and European intelligence in tracking down Islamists of Tunisian origin with alleged links to Da'wa wal Djihad and al-Qa'ida. Assertions made by Tunisia's pro-Government press that an-Nahda has links with al-Qa'ida have been strongly denied by Ghanouchi and his representatives. Responsibility for an explosion outside a synagogue on the island of Djerba in April 2002, in almost 20 people were killed, was later attributed by al-Qa'ida to a Tunisian acting in the name of the organization.

In Morocco King Muhammad (like Hassan before him) derives much legitimacy from his descent from the Prophet Muhammad and his caliphal title 'Commander of the Faithful'. The vast Hassan II mosque in Casablanca, completed in 1993 and one of the largest in the world, provides a tangible, if flamboyant symbol of the regime's Islamic credentials. Morocco's public discourse is replete with Islamic symbolism; more secure in its identity than its neighbours, there is, despite much higher levels of poverty and serious social problems, less space in the 300-year-old kingdom for an 'Islamic alternative' that challenges the status quo. The principal Islamist leader, Abd as-Salam Yassin, head of the banned *Al-Adl wa-'l Ihsan* (Justice and Charity movement) was placed under house arrest in 1989 'for his own protection' pending 'judicial investigations' into his activities. However, he was allowed to preach on at least one occasion, although the Government insisted that he refrain from political statements. Restrictions on Yassin's movements were removed in May 2000, although the ban on his party, and on publications associated with it, remained in force. Meanwhile, fundamentalist Islamists expressed outrage at social reforms proposed by the Government apparently at the behest of the new King, Muhammad VI, that would notably improve the social status and legal rights of Moroccan women. Islamic financial institutions have been refused licences. But compared to their Algerian counterparts, the Moroccan Islamists who, as elsewhere in the Arab world are active on university campuses, have taken a relatively moderate line, avoiding confrontation with the state or direct challenges to the authority of the monarch. According to one of Morocco's leading sociologists, there are at least 30 different Islamist groups in the country, but only four of them have a significant following and influence; security forces of the Ministry of the Interior constantly monitor their activities. Periodically weapons caches are discovered. In a few instances death sentences have been handed down by the courts.

In October 2001 16 Moroccan ulema (religious scholars appointed by the Ministry of Religious Endowments and Islamic Affairs) issued a *fatwa* condemning the Moroccan Government for participating in a multi-faith ceremony to commemorate the victims of the previous month's suicide attacks on the USA, and

warned against any Moroccan participation in a US-led military alliance against a Muslim state or group. The Moroccan security services co-operated with US intelligence in tracking down terrorists of Maghreb origin based in Europe, and reportedly in interrogating detainees transferred from Afghanistan to US custody at Guantánamo Bay, Cuba. Although King Muhammad has expressed measured criticism of US policy towards the Israeli–Palestinian conflict and of the Bush Administration's apparent preoccupation with bringing about 'regime change' in Iraq, Paul Wolfowitz, the 'hawkish' US Deputy Secretary of Defense, has named Morocco as one of the Muslim states most closely involved in the war against 'terrorism' and 'religious obscurantism'. In mid-2002 the Moroccan authorities announced that they had arrested a group of Saudi nationals who were alleged to be members of an Islamist cell linked to al-Qa'ida that was preparing imminent attacks on US and British vessels in the Strait of Gibraltar, similar to that perpetrated against the USS *Cole* in Yemen in October 2000 (see below).

The Jordanian monarchy, which also claims descent from the Prophet, has been relatively successful in containing Islamist militancy within a parliamentary system. In the elections of November 1993—the first multi-party elections for 36 years—an Islamist victory was confidently predicted until a change in the electoral rules was introduced, with King Hussein's warm approval, substituting the plural voting system in multi-member constituencies for one limiting each voter to a single vote. The result was a reduction in representation of the main Islamist party, the Islamic Action Front (IAF—the political wing of the Muslim Brotherhood) in the National Assembly from 22 seats to 16. At the July 1997 elections, however, the Islamic Action Front, in common with other opposition parties, boycotted the poll in protest against the 1994 Peace Treaty between Jordan and Israel and against censorship laws placing restrictions on Islamist publications. In March 1996 a prominent Islamist and former parliamentary deputy, Leith Shbeilat (also head of the Engineers' Association—and the Treaty's most outspoken critic), was sentenced to three years' imprisonment after being found guilty of 'slandering the royal family'. He had publicly criticized Queen Noor for weeping before the television cameras at the funeral of the assassinated Israeli Prime Minister, Itzhak Rabin. Six months later, in a conciliatory gesture to the opposition, Shbeilat was granted a royal pardon, the King personally driving him from Swaqa prison, 100 km south of Amman, to his mother's home in the capital. Shbeilat was arrested and imprisoned again in early 1998 following allegations that he had organized a number of proscribed demonstrations in support of Iraq (at a time of increased US military pressure in the Persian (Arabian) Gulf) but was released, once again, following the intervention of King Hussein. It was considered unlikely that the succession of King Abdullah following the death of his father in February 1999 would result in any significant change in the general policy of containment. Security trials involving radical Islamists in Jordan multiplied in frequency in late 2001 and early 2002, and Jordanian officials were swift to emphasize that the country had for several decades been 'struggling against terrorism', increasingly emanating from radical and militant Islamist groups. Most notably, Raed Hijazi, a Jordanian-US national of Palestinian origin (named by the FBI on its list of wanted 'terrorists'), was sentenced to death in February 2002, having been convicted of plotting terrorist attacks in Jordan; the State Security Court did, however, dismiss a charge that Hijazi was a member of al-Qa'ida. Hijazi, who had been detained in Syria and extradited to Jordan, had previously been sentenced to death *in absentia* by the State Security Court in 2000, in a case involving 28 Islamists accused of planning 'terrorist attacks' and of having links to al-Qa'ida.

In Israel, the Occupied Territories and in the areas controlled by the Palestinian (National) Authority (PA), Hamas and its counterpart Islamic Jihad have continued to challenge the authority of Yasser Arafat. During the 1990s the Islamist movement was divided between rejectionists who sustained the 'armed struggle' and accommodationists who gave conditional support to Arafat in order to ensure an Israeli withdrawal from part of the Occupied Territories in accordance with the 1993 Oslo accords. In the aftermath of the assassination of Prime Minister Itzhak Rabin by a right-wing Israeli extremist, in November 1995, the rejectionists appeared to gain the upper hand. A series of suicide bombings in Jerusalem, Ashkelon and Tel-Aviv (in which dozens of Israeli civilians were killed) helped to bring down the Labour Government of Rabin's successor, Shimon Peres, and elect the Likud coalition which, under Binyamin Netanyahu, effectively stalled the peace process by ending the moratorium on building new Jewish settlements. In order to appease the Israelis, Arafat was forced to clamp down on the rejectionists. While this appeared to confirm Islamist charges that he was, in effect, an Israeli stooge, the Hamas majority were prepared to bide their time, having no desire to take responsibility for an Israeli reoccupation of Palestinian territory. Hamas scored a moral victory when, following a bungled attempt by Israeli agents to murder one of its principal officers, Khalid Meshaal in Amman in September 1997, the Jordanian Government secured the release from an Israeli gaol of the Hamas spiritual leader, Sheikh Ahmad Yassin, in exchange for returning the Mossad agents apprehended following the attempted assassination. Under the terms of the Wye Memorandum, brokered by the US Government and signed by Yasser Arafat and Binyamin Netanyahu in October 1998, the Palestinians undertook to intensify anti-terrorist activities in the Occupied Territories and to remove all clauses from the PLO Covenant that urged the armed destruction of the State of Israel. (A list of suspected Palestinian terrorists who were to be arrested forthwith was attached to the memorandum.) In late November (in a largely symbolic gesture), following an increase in Hamas terrorist activity, Arafat announced that Sheikh Yassin had been placed under house arrest for making declarations disadvantageous to the Palestinian national interest. By December of the same year, however, he had been released. At the end of August 1999, in an atmosphere of renewed expectation and hopes for peace proceeding from the election of a new Labour Prime Minister in Israel, the Jordanian authorities moved to close the headquarters of Hamas in Amman, and to suppress the activities of its members there. Warrants were issued for the arrest of senior Hamas figures, including Meshaal and the Hamas spokesman, Ibrahim Ghosheh; these last were detained in late September, on their return from a visit to Iran, and were deported to Qatar. (The Jordanian authorities granted permission for Ghosheh to enter the country at the end of June 2001, after he had agreed to end his involvement with Hamas.)

A notable dimension of the al-Aqsa *intifada* swiftly emerged in moves towards a national unity—reflected in the formation of the Palestinian National and Islamic Forces (PNIF) embracing all the Palestinian factions from the 'nationalists' of the PLO (predominantly Yasser Arafat's own Fatah movement) to the 'rejectionist' Islamist elements, including Hamas and Islamic Jihad. However, a distinction remained that for Fatah and most of the other PLO factions armed resistance should be confined to acts against soldiers and settlers in the Occupied Territories, while the Islamist groups did not explicitly accept this distinction between Israeli military and civilian targets. The Islamist groups were vocal in their denunciation of the tentative truce agreement brokered at Sharm-esh-Sheikh in mid-October, and of subsequent peace initiatives based on this accord, and the issue of the rearrest in particular of Hamas and Islamic Jihad militants who had been released from Palestinian detention shortly after the outbreak of violence became a key demand of the Israelis and a key recommendation of international mediators.

The violent actions of rejectionist Islamist organizations, and a perceived 'migration' of the Islamist movements from the margins towards the mainstream of Palestinian political life, has perhaps been the main factor militating against the success of any cease-fire initiative since the eruption of violence in late 2000. Additionally, they have arguably provided Israel with a pretext for its increasingly protracted incursions into Palestinian-administered territory in 2001–02, as well as justification for its often-repeated claim that Arafat, through his alleged failure to act decisively to rein in Hamas and Islamic Jihad (as well as the nationalists of the al-Aqsa Martyrs Brigades and the secularist Popular Front for the Liberation of Palestine, whose militants were by 2002 emulating the suicide bombings of the Islamists), had become an 'irrelevance' as leader of the PA. In the USA the Administration of George W. Bush has for its part emphasized in its at times reluctant dealings with the PA that it requires the 'terrorist infrastructure' in Gaza and the West Bank to be dismantled, placing the responsibility for initiating and also for easing the crisis on the beleaguered Arafat. While Israel expressed satisfaction that several Palestinian 'rejectionist' factions were listed as 'terrorist' organizations by the US Department of State in late 2001, the USA has shown itself unwilling to lend validity to the Israeli-drawn parallels between the USA's 'war against terror' and Israel's own offensives against the *intifada*.

In Egypt the Government initially adopted a strategy broadly similar to Jordan's, co-opting the moderates by allowing the Muslim Brotherhood to be represented through other parties in the National Assembly while seeking to eliminate the extremists by police methods. The more militant Islamist elements, led by Islamic Jihad and Jama'ah al-Islamiyah, active on university campuses since the 1970s, continued to wage a sporadic war of attrition against the regime, attacking Christians, government officials and foreign tourists. The violence was mainly concentrated in the southern part of the country, and was complicated by the still widely-practised tradition of blood-vengeance: when policemen, state officials or members of the Coptic minority were attacked or murdered, their families were honour-bound to respond in kind, and violence against the state rapidly became entangled in blood feuds. There were many reports of police-officers taking hostage the relatives of Islamist fugitives, destroying their homes and burning their crops. Attacks on tourists were deliberately designed to cripple the country's economy by undermining its most important source of foreign currency. Tourists were also viewed as spies for Israel and the West, and a source of corruption. Tal'at Fu'ad Qasim, a Jama'ah spokesman, has declared tourism in its present form to be 'an abomination', and 'a means by which prostitution and AIDS are spread by Jewish women tourists', and 'a source of all manner of depravities, not to mention a means of collecting information on the Islamic movement'. The campaign against tourism had the desired effect of crippling the industry. In April 1996 17 Greek tourists were killed and 15 others injured in an attack outside a Cairo hotel. In November 1997 68 tourists (mainly Swiss and Japanese) were shot dead outside the Temple of Queen Hatshepsut at Luxor. As in April 1996, Jama'ah al-Islamiyah accepted responsibility for the attack; however, they claimed that the casualties had been the result of bungling by the police, their intention having been to take the tourists hostage and attempt to force the release of the movement's spiritual leader, Sheikh Omar Abd ar-Rahman, currently serving a prison sentence for his involvement in the bombing of the World Trade Center in New York in February 1993. Survivors of the massacre, however, rejected this, stating that the gunmen, disguised as security officers, had begun firing automatic weapons at the tourists as soon as they arrived at the scene. (In December 2001 Syria agreed to extradite to Egypt Rifa'i Ahmad Taha of Jama'ah al-Islamiyah, who had been sentenced to death *in absentia* for his part in the Luxor killings.)

As the 1993 attack on the World Trade Center demonstrated, Islamists based in Egypt did not confine their attacks to Egyptian territory. In June 1995 President Mubarak's motorcade was attacked as he was driving from the airport to attend a conference of the Organization of African Unity in Addis Ababa, Ethiopia. Two Islamist organizations linked to Jama'ah al-Islamiyah claimed responsibility. The following November at least 15 people were killed and 60 injured when a car bomb exploded in the Egyptian embassy compound in Islamabad, Pakistan. The Government's response to these attacks was to increase pressure not only on the militants, but also on so-called moderate elements within the mainstream Muslim Brotherhood. In 1994 the Government introduced a 50% majority rule for elections to the country's professional associations—moderate Islamists at this time dominated the largest of these, including the medical, engineering and legal syndicates—hoping thereby to secure a secularist majority in future elections. In 1995 they took the additional step of granting the judiciary wide powers to supervise union elections, including the right to disqualify candidates. Brotherhood activists were arrested and detained, with dozens referred to military courts for rapid trials. The judiciary in Egypt, however, is relatively independent, and contains its share of Islamist sympathizers at senior level. In a number of celebrated cases, the Egyptian courts became battle grounds for the culture wars conducted between the Islamists and their secular critics. Nasir Hamid Abu Zayd, a professor of Arabic at the University of Cairo, was denied tenure and accused of apostasy after a colleague attacked his work in analysing the Koran from a literary-historical perspective. Not content with depriving Abu Zayd of his livelihood, some extreme Islamists demanded that his wife divorce him on the grounds that he was an 'apostate' who could not be married to a Muslim. While a lower court rejected their demands, a higher court ruled against Abu Zayd on appeal. Similarly, an attempt by a fundamentalist lawyer to have a feminist writer forcibly divorced from her husband on the grounds of apostasy was dismissed by Egypt's Prosecutor-General in April 2001, and by a family affairs tribunal in July. Such cases, which have received widespread publicity, reveal the clear affinities between what might be called 'intellectual Islamism' and Protestant fundamentalism in the USA—where fundamentalists also object to the Bible being treated as a literary-historical text.

Between 1992 and mid-1998 106 death sentences were conferred by Egyptian courts on militant Islamists, of which number 72 were reported to have been carried out. In February 1999 Egypt's largest ever trial of suspected Islamist terrorists began in a military court, when legal proceedings were initiated against 107 alleged members of Islamic Jihad. In April the court imposed death sentences on nine of those accused (who were among 62 of the total number being tried *in absentia*) and prison sentences ranging from three years to life to a further 78. In an unexpected development in March, one of the leaders of Jama'ah al-Islamiyah announced that the organization was abandoning its armed struggle and would henceforth seek to express opposition to the Government through political channels. Some 1,000 Jama'ah detainees were subsequently released by the Government in a conciliatory gesture designed to help consolidate the cease-fire. Although there were fears for the continuation of the cease-fire after security forces in Giza shot dead four alleged members of Jama'ah al-Islamiyah, including the organization's military leader, a further 1,200 prisoners linked to the movement were released in December. However, there were reports in late 1999 of a power-struggle within the Jama'ah leadership (not least involving the accession to the chairmanship of the organization's Shura Council of the principal suspect in the 1995 attempt on Mubarak's life). In June 2000, moreover, it was reported that Sheikh Omar Abd ar-Rahman, who remained in detention in the USA, had withdrawn his support for the cease-fire. Meanwhile, in February following recent reports of a 'coup' within the organization's high command (in which one of the leaders of the organization, Ayman az-Zawahri, had been deposed—allegedly owing to his links with Osama bin Laden), senior members of the leadership of Islamic Jihad made an apparently unprecedented call for cessation of the organization's armed activities, appealing to militants to concentrate their activities instead on the liberation of the al-Aqsa mosque in Jerusalem. In the following month between 500 and 1,000 Islamists, mainly members of Jama'ah al-Islamiyah and Islamic Jihad, were released from detention, and a further 500 were freed in July. By contrast, an increase in the rate of arrest of alleged members of the Muslim Brotherhood was generally perceived as being linked to the approaching legislative elections, scheduled for late 2000. Of some 100 pro-Brotherhood candidates who contested the elections to the People's Assembly as 'independents', 17 were reportedly elected. In November, shortly after the conclusion of the elections, 15 alleged members of the Muslim Brotherhood—who had been arrested in late 1999 on charges of plotting to overthrow the Government and of infiltrating professional syndicates (among those detained were leading members of the doctors', engineers' and veterinarians' organizations) in order to undermine national security—were convicted and sentenced to between three and five years' imprisonment; five were acquitted. For more than a year, meanwhile, actions by the authorities to delay elections to the governing council of the Lawyers' Syndicate had been interpreted in some quarters as reflecting official concern regarding likely successes by Islamist candidates. Indeed, when the elections eventually proceeded, in February 2001, supporters of the Muslim Brotherhood won all but two of the 24 available seats. Like the Jordanian authorities, the Egyptian Government stated that the September 2001 attacks on the USA justified Egypt's own long-running 'war on terror', and President Mubarak asserted that the country offered a model 'responsible democracy' in response to the threat posed by radical Islam. Several members of Egyptian Islamic Jihad were alleged to have assumed significant roles in the suicide attacks. Ayman az-Zawahri, said to be one of bin Laden's closest associates, was presumed by US investigators to have been responsible for the organization of the attacks, and another Egyptian, Muhammad Atef, who was reportedly killed by US forces in Afghanistan in November, was, according to US intelligence, believed to have been al-Qa'ida's chief military planner. (An Egyptian national was, furthermore, suspected of having piloted one of the hijacked aircraft that destroyed the World Trade Center in New York.) Following the events of 11 September more than 260 suspected Islamists were arrested in Egypt, and in December the trial commenced of 22 members of the Muslim Brotherhood charged with leading or belonging to an illegal organization. In November the trial by military court commenced of 94 Islamists accused of conspiring to assassinate President Mubarak and overthrow the Government; 51 of the accused were convicted in September 2002 and sentenced to terms of imprisonment ranging from two to 15 years' duration. In late 2001, meanwhile, the trial began of 22 members of the Muslim Brotherhood on charges of incitement to violence and belonging to an illegal organization. While open reaction in Egypt to the commencement of US military action against targets in Afghanistan in October 2001 was generally muted, Israel's effective reoccupation of Palestinian-controlled areas of the West Bank in March 2002 provoked mass street demonstrations, and the Muslim Brotherhood condemned the Government for failing to sever diplomatic ties with Israel at all levels.

In Yemen the Islamist Yemeni Islah Party (YIP), consisting mainly of the northern Hashed tribe with support from the Muslim Brotherhood, strengthened its position after the 1994 civil war with the south. Its rather narrow tribal base, however, prevented the YIP from securing more than 53 seats in the legislative elections of April 1997, compared with the 187 seats secured by the governing General People's Congress (GPC). A small extremist Islamist group, the Islamic Aden-Abyan Army, achieved some prominence in the international press in late 1998 and early 1999 following its involvement in a highly-publicized kidnapping (16 foreign tourists were taken hostage; four of them were later killed during an attempt to free them) and its alleged links to a number of foreign nationals who were arrested in Yemen in early 1999, allegedly intent on perpetrating terrorist attacks on Western targets in Aden. Three men were sentenced to death, and a fourth to 20 years' imprisonment, convicted in May 1999 of responsibility for the kidnapping; two of the sentences were eventually commuted, but the organization's leader, Abu al-Hassan, was executed in October. Meanwhile, in August 10 men, eight of whom held British citizenship, received custodial sentences, having been convicted on terrorism charges. Kidnappings of foreign nationals continued, and in October 2000 Hatim Muhsin bin Farid, alleged to be the new leader of the Islamic Aden-Abyan Army, was convicted on kidnapping charges and sentenced to seven years' imprisonment. International attention on militant activities in Yemen was abruptly heightened in that month, when a suicide bomb attack on a US destroyer, the USS *Cole*, in Aden harbour resulted in the deaths of 17 US naval personnel. The bombing was linked by many commentators to the escalating crisis in the Middle East. The Yemeni authorities responded by arresting several alleged Islamist militants, among them leading members of Islamic Jihad from Yemen, Egypt, Algeria and other Arab states. The USA held agents of Osama bin Laden responsible for the attack, and claimed to have evidence that the two suicide bombers were Saudi nationals.

After the September 2001 terrorist attacks on New York and Washington many US commentators frequently named Yemen as one of the states harbouring militant Islamists, suggesting the country might be a possible target in the 'war against terror'. President Saleh, however, immediately promised full support for the US-led campaign. Security forces were instructed to detain any Yemeni suspected of having links with Osama bin Laden, and many Arab 'Afghans' (i.e. veterans of Arab origin of the Western-supported *jihad* against Soviet occupation of Afghanistan) were arrested and deported. In subsequent months several religious institutes were closed down, and their foreign students deported, as the Yemeni authorities began implementing 1992 legislation bringing 'independent' religious institutes under control of the Ministry of Education. In January 2002 the private al-Iman University, run by Sheikh Abd al-Majid az-Zindani, the chairman of the Shura Council of the Yemeni Islah Party, was briefly closed down. The University, where many students from other Muslim countries were enrolled, was regarded by many as attracting Islamist extremists. By early 2002 it was reported that some 600 foreign students enrolled in religious institutes had been deported. However, President Saleh played down the threat from organizations such as the 'Sympathizers of al-Qa'ida', which claimed responsibility for a series of explosions targeting the offices of the Yemeni secret police, and insisted that the small number of al-Qa'ida activists in Yemen were being carefully watched. In February 2002 it was reported that the trial of the eight suspects in the bombing of the USS *Cole* had been postponed at the request of the US authorities, because of the possibility that new information about the case would be obtained during interrogation of al-Qaida and Taliban prisoners captured in Afghanistan and held at Guantánamo Bay. In that month a team of Yemeni investigators visited the Guantánamo base in order to assist in questioning some Yemenis being detained there. In the following month a US official stated that Washington was preparing to send troops to Yemen to assist Yemeni forces in locating members of al-Qa'ida.

Even Saudi Arabia, the most traditionalist and religiously observant of Muslim states, was subjected to criticism from Islamist quarters, with the circulation of a manifesto in 1992 by mainly Nejdi *'ulama* complaining that the religious leaders were not sufficiently consulted by the Government, which, it complained, was 'inefficient, obsolete and corrupt in its upper reaches'. While the attack on princely corruption found an echo in some liberal circles, the ultra-traditionalist character of some of Saudi Arabia's religious protesters was evidenced by the fact that a leading member of the principal opposition group, the Committee for the Defence of Legal *(Shari'a)* Rights, demanded that the whole of the country's Shi'ite minority be put to death. In mid-1995, in an attempt to counter publicly a perceived spread of Islamist zealotry, King Fahd replaced one-half of the members of the Council of Ulema (the country's most senior Islamic authority) and six of the country's seven university chancellors. Terrorist attacks against Western targets, encouraged by the prolonged US military presence in the region in the aftermath of the 1990–91 Gulf War, have been variously attributed to Sunni extremist factions and Saudi Shi'a groups operating with or without foreign support.

Saudi Arabia severed ties with the Taliban regime in Afghanistan in late September 2001 (hitherto Saudi Arabia had been, with Pakistan and the United Arab Emirates, one of the few countries ever to have maintained diplomatic relations with the Taliban). However, notably in response to revelations that as many as 15 of the hijackers involved in the attacks were apparently of Saudi origin, sections of the US media subsequently conducted an unprecedented campaign of vilification against Saudi Arabia, alleging complicity in the rise of Islamist global terror networks. The authorities in Saudi Arabia declared their determination to uncover supporters of bin Laden, and took action to freeze their financial assets. However, under evident pressure from internal Islamist groups implacably opposed to the US military presence on Saudi territory and to any military action against another Islamic state, the Saudi Government refused permission for the use of its airbases for military action against Afghanistan (although an air 'command-and-control' base in the kingdom was made available to support the military operation). In early 2002 the Saudi authorities sought the return of all Saudi nationals (reported to number at least 100) captured in Afghanistan while apparently fighting for the Taliban and subsequently transferred to the US base at Guantánamo Bay.

In Bahrain, where a Sunni dynasty rules over an underprivileged Shi'i majority, the authorities have notably sought to suppress the activities of Hezbollah Bahrain, recruited from Bahraini Shi'i students at Qom, in Iran, and trained in Lebanon. There has been considerable speculation as to whether Bahrain's Shi'i might secure a degree of political representation as a result of the constitutional reforms undertaken by the new Amir (who proclaimed himself King in early 2002).

In Kuwait Islamists in the National Assembly have been pressing for legislation to enforce greater adherence to the *Shari'a* as the only source of law and to outlaw coeducation in the University, where two-thirds of the student body is female. The strong presence of Islamists in the legislature following elections in 1999 was regarded as likely to hinder the passage of 'reformist' laws. Notably, a decree promulgated by the Government following the dissolution of the previous assembly that would have permitted women to contest and vote in elections from 2003 was rejected by the new legislature in late 1999. In late 2001, in response to the attacks on the USA, Kuwait's Central Bank implemented measures designed to prevent Islamic charitable organizations from using Kuwait's financial institutions to channel funds to al-Qa'ida. Meanwhile, in October the Kuwaiti authorities revoked the citizenship of the official spokesman of al-Qa'ida, Sulayman Abu Ghaith.

The legitimacy of the territorial governments established after decolonization was always open to challenge on Islamic grounds. The new national states were in most cases being imposed on societies where the culture of public institutions was weak and where ties of kinship prevailed over allegiances to corporate bodies. In most Middle Eastern countries and many others beyond the Muslim heartlands, the ruling institutions fell victim to manipulation by factions based on kinship, regional or sectarian loyalties. Even when the army took power, as the only corporate group possessing internal cohesion, the élite corps buttressing the leadership were often drawn from a particular family, sect or tribe. In the period following decolonization the new élites legitimized themselves by appealing to nationalist goals. Their failure to 'deliver the goods' either economically or militarily (especially in the case of the states confronting Israel) led to an erosion of their popular bases and the rise of movements pledged to 'restore' Islamic forms of government after years of *jahiliyya* rule.

Following the collapse of communism, Islamism is likely to dominate the political discourse in Muslim lands for the foreseeable future. But, for all the anxieties expressed in the West about a 'clash of civilizations', it for many years seemed unlikely to effect significant external political change. Existing Muslim states are locked into the international system. Despite the turbulence in Algeria and episodes of violence in Egypt, there have been fewer violent changes of government in the Middle East since 1970 than in the preceding two decades when different versions of Arab nationalism competed for power. At the same time the political instability in Pakistan and the conflict in Afghanistan have demonstrated that 'Islam' in its current political or ideological forms has hitherto been unable to transcend ethnic and sectarian divisions. The territorial state, though never formally sanctified by Islamic tradition, has proved highly resilient, not least because of the support it receives, militarily and economically, through the international system. For all the protests by Islamist movements that Saddam Hussain's invasion of Kuwait in August 1990 was a 'Muslim affair', and in spite of the evident *rapprochement* between Iraq and many Arab states at the opening of the new century, the result of Operation Desert Storm (in which the Muslim armies of Morocco, Egypt, Pakistan, Syria and Saudi Arabia took part) demonstrated, at this time at least, that where major economic and political interests are at stake, the status quo would prevail.

In the long term, the globalization of culture through the revolution in communications technology must lead to a form of secularization in Muslim societies, not least because of the increasing availability of religious and cultural choice. A significant factor will be the presence of a large and growing Muslim diaspora educated in the West and able to rediscover in Islam a voluntary faith freed from the imperatives of enforcement, while finding an outlet for Islamic values through voluntary activity. Although the political currents of Shari'ati (exoteric) Islam appear to be in the ascendant, it is the pietistic and mystical traditions that promise to open up the 'straight path' *(sirat al-mustaqim)* in the future. There is evidence that quietist versions of Islam have been able to gain ground. The *Tablighi Jama'at*, originally founded in India, has spread to more than 90 countries from Malaysia to Canada and is now becoming thoroughly internationalized. Though active in promoting the faith, it is explicitly non-political. Both Maududi and Hassan al-Banna built pietism into their systems, believing that society must be converted before the state could be conquered. However, the militants and activists who followed them, obsessed with the corruption of governments and embittered by the appalling treatment many of them received at the hands of the State, have tended to focus on action, not least because killings and bombings are bound to attract attention in an international culture dominated by instant media coverage—whether by the press, television or the internet.

With globalization eroding the classic distinction between *Dar al-Islam* and *Dar al-Harb*, the coming decades could see a retreat from direct political action and a renewed emphasis on the personal and private aspects of faith. But so long as government corruption persists, and governments such as those of Egypt and Algeria find it more expedient to respond to the Islamist challenge by repression than reform, the Islamists, however inept their political programmes, will find a ready audience.

SELECT BIBLIOGRAPHY

Ahmed, Akbar S., and Donnan, Hastings (Eds). *Islam, Globalization and Postmodernity*. London, Routledge, 1994.

Ali, Tariq. *The Clash of Fundamentalisms: Crusades, Jihads and Modernity*. London, Verso, 2002.

Al-Azmeh, Aziz. *Islams and Modernities*. London, Verso, 1993.

Beinin, Joel, and Stork, Joe (Eds). *Political Islam: Essays from The Middle East Report*. London, I. B. Tauris, 1997.

Binder, Leonard. *Islamic Liberalism: A Critique of Development Ideologies*. Chicago, 1988.

Brown, L. Carl. *Religion and State: The Muslim Approach to Politics*. New York, Columbia University Press, 2000.

Burgat, François, and Dowell, William. *The Islamic Movement in North Africa*. Austin, Texas, University of Texas Press, 1993.

Cantwell Smith, W. *Islam in Modern History*. Princeton University Press, 1957.

Choueiri, Youssef M. *Islamic Fundamentalism*. Boston, Twayne Books, 1990.

Cooley, John K. *Unholy Wars: Afghanistan, America, and International Terrorism*. London, Pluto Press, 3rd edn, 2002.

Cooper, John and Nettler, Ronald L., and Mahmoud, Mohamed (Eds). *Islam and Modernity: Muslim Intellectuals Respond*. London, I. B. Tauris, 1998.

Easterman, Daniel. *New Jerusalems: Reflections on Islam, Fundamentalism and the Rushdie Affair*. London, Grafton Books, 1993.

Eickelman, Dale F., and Piscatori, James. *Muslim Politics*. Princeton University Press, 1996.

El Fadl, Khaled Abou. *Rebellion and Violence in Islamic Law*. Cambridge University Press, 2002.

Esposito, John L. (Ed.). *Islam and Development*. Syracuse University Press, 1980.

The Islamic Threat: Myth or Reality? New York, Oxford University Press, Inc., 3rd edn, 1999.

(Ed.). *The Oxford Encyclopaedia of the Modern Islamic World*. Oxford University Press, 1995.

(Ed.). *The Oxford History of Islam*. New York, Oxford University Press, Inc. 2000.

Unholy War: Terror in the Name of Islam. New York, Oxford University Press, Inc., 2002.

Gellner Ernest. *Postmodernism, Reason and Religion*. London, Routledge, 1992.

Gilsenan, Michael. *Recognizing Islam—Religion and Society in the Modern Middle East*. London, I. B. Tauris, revised edn, 2000.

Halliday, Fred. *Islam and the Myth of Confrontation: Religion and Politics in the Middle East*. London, I. B. Tauris, revised edn, 2002.

Heikal, Muhammad. *Autumn of Fury: The Assassination of Sadat*. London, André Deutsch, 1983.

Hiro, Dilip. *War Without End: The Rise Of Islamist Terrorism And Global Response*. London, Routledge, 2002.

Hourani, Albert. *Arabic Thought in the Liberal Age*. Oxford University Press, 1969.

Keddie, N. R. (Ed.). *Scholars, Saints and Sufis: Muslim Religious Institutions since 1500*. University of California Press, 1972.

Kepel, Gilles (trans. Jon Rothschild). *The Prophet and Pharaoh: Muslim Extremism in Egypt*. London, Saqi Books, 1985.

(trans. Antony Roberts) *Jihad: The Trail of Political Islam*. London, I. B. Tauris, 2002.

Lawrence, Bruce B. *Shattering the Myth: Islam beyond Violence*. Princeton University Press, 1998.

Lewis, Bernard. *What Went Wrong?: Western Impact and Middle Eastern Response*. New York, Oxford University Press, Inc., 2001.

Mernissi, Fatima. *Islam and Democracy—fear of the modern world*. London, Virago, 1993.

Mortimer, Edward. *Faith and Power: The Politics of Islam*. Faber, 1982.

Pipes, Daniel. *In the Path of God: Islam and Political Power*. New York Basic Books, 1983.

Piscatori, James (Ed.). *Islam in the Political Process*. Cambridge University Press, 1983.

Islam in a World of Nation States. Cambridge, 1986.

Rahman, Fazlur. *Islam*. Chicago University Press, 1979.

Rippin, Andrew. *Muslims—Their Religious Beliefs and Practices*. Vol II, The Contemporary Period, London, Routledge, 1993.

Roy, Olivier. *The Failure of Political Islam*. London, I. B. Tauris, 1994.

Ruthven, Malise. *Islam in the World*. London, Penguin, 1991.

Islam: A Very Short Introduction. Oxford University Press, 1997.

A Fury for God: The Islamist Attack on America. London, Granta Books, 2002.

Said, Edward W: *Covering Islam: How the Media and the Experts Determine How We See the Rest of the World*. Vintage, revised edn, 1997.

Sivan, Emmanuel. *Radical Islam: Medieval Theology and Modern Politics*. Yale University Press, 1985.

Tamimi, Azzam (Ed.). *Islam and Secularism in the Middle East*. London, C. Hurst & Co, 2000.

Third World Quarterly. Vol. 10, No. 2, *Islam and Politics*. April 1988.

Zubaida, Sami. *Islam, The People and The State: Essays on Political Ideas and Movements in the Middle East*. London, I. B. Tauris, 1993.

OIL IN THE MIDDLE EAST AND NORTH AFRICA

SIMON CHAPMAN

Based on an original essay by RICHARD JOHNS

OWNERSHIP OF THE INDUSTRY AND SUPPLY CONTRACTS

The first concessions

Until the end of 1972 most of the Middle East's and North Africa's petroleum was produced under the traditional concession agreements. The first concession was granted in 1901 in Iran by Muzzaffareddin Shah to William Knox D'Arcy, for £20,000 in cash and the promise of a further £20,000 in shares. Oil was discovered in 1908 at Masjid-i-Sulaiman, and just before the beginning of the First World War the Anglo-Persian Oil Company—formed to take over the concession—began exports through the port of Abadan. (APOC was renamed the Anglo-Iranian Oil Company in 1935 and British Petroleum in 1954.)

During the 1920s and 1930s further concessions were granted in Iraq and in the states of the Arabian Peninsula. In every case the concessionaire companies were chiefly members of the seven major oil companies that dominated the world oil business throughout much of the 20th century. In approximate order of size these were: Standard Oil of New Jersey (which changed its name to Exxon in 1972 and markets its products in Europe under the name Esso), the Royal Dutch/Shell Group, Texaco, Standard Oil of California (known as Socal and marketed as Chevron), Mobil, Gulf and British Petroleum (BP). The only other company to participate in the early days was Compagnie Française des Pétroles (CFP—marketing as Total. Totalfina, as the company became, merged with Elf Aquitaine in 2000 to become TotalFinaElf, the fourth largest oil company worldwide.)

Initially, these companies held exclusive rights for drilling, production, sales, the ownership at the wellhead of all oil produced, and immunity from taxes and customs dues. The governments' receipts, apart from an initial downpayment and a rental, came either as a share of profits (which is how Iran's income was calculated until 1933, when Iran negotiated a fixed-royalty-plus-share-of-company-dividends formula) or as a fixed royalty of four gold shillings per ton (22 US cents per barrel).

In view of the vast amounts of oil discovered during the 1930s and 1940s, and the extremely low cost of production, the Middle Eastern governments by the later 1940s no longer regarded the companies' terms as generous.

Reforming the concessions

Major changes in the financial terms of the concessions that followed did not, however, stem from events in the Middle East, but from Venezuela, where in November 1948 the Accíon Democrática party enacted income tax legislation giving the Government 50% of the companies' profits. Realizing that such a revolutionary change could not be confined to one country, the companies offered the same deal to the Middle Eastern governments. Under the new system, introduced in Saudi Arabia at the end of 1950 and in Iraq and Kuwait in 1951, the companies' 'profits', were divided equally between the companies and the governments.

Iran was the only country not to receive the 50:50 profit split at this time, but in 1949 Anglo-Iranian and the Iranian Government concluded a Supplemental Agreement giving Iran royalty and profit-sharing terms as good as those achieved in the Arab states 18 months later. In December 1950, however, as a result of dissatisfaction within the Iranian legislature, the Government was forced to renounce the deal altogether. Then, in May 1951, the Shah of Iran was forced to assent to the nationalization of the Iranian oil industry.

After a period of political turmoil, in subsequent negotiations the companies recognized the principle of nationalization. However, the National Iranian Oil Company (NIOC) was forced to grant a lease (effectively a concession) incorporating the 50:50 profit split to Iranian Oil Participants (known as 'the Consortium'), made up of BP, Shell, CFP and the five US majors—which

the US Government later obliged to give a 5% shareholding to a group of US independents.

Partnership, contracts and production sharing

From 1957 the concession concept was superseded by arrangements giving the State a degree of direct participation, and placing heavier financial burden and greater risks on the companies. The first of the new arrangements was the partnership of Société Irano-Italienne des Pétroles (SIRIP) between NIOC and the Italian state concern ENI. ENI's subsidiary, AGIP, agreed to bear all exploration costs (only to be repaid one-half if oil was found), and to spend at least US $22m. on exploration. One-half of any oil produced would be owned by NIOC and sold by AGIP on Iran's behalf, while half would be owned by the Italian company and taxed at the normal 50% rate—giving the Government a 75:25 profit split.

One year later Iran improved its terms when it formed IPAC, a partnership with Amoco (a subsidiary of Standard Oil of Indiana). During the early 1960s and early 1970s it signed further partnerships, four of which eventually struck oil.

With certain variations, Iran's example was followed in the allocation of new acreage by Saudi Arabia and Kuwait in the Neutral Zone in 1957. Other countries that copied Iran were Kuwait, Egypt and Algeria. In Qatar, Abu Dhabi, Tunisia and Kuwait (with its offshore areas granted to Shell), the governments concluded carried-interest arrangements, where acreage was let originally as a concession, the State retaining the right to negotiate a shareholding once oil was discovered. These ventures rarely succeeded, so the carried-interest charges seldom applied. Tax terms were universally adjusted to reflect prevailing OPEC rates.

In 1966 Iran introduced the more radical idea of service contracts, relinquishing Consortium acreage to a French group, SOFIRAN. SOFIRAN agreed to bear all of the exploration costs, but if oil was struck it was to be refunded completely. NIOC, which was to provide all development capital, was to be the sole owner of any oil produced, while the foreign contractor was to act as a broker for the national company on a commission of 2% of the realized price, being paid by the guaranteed purchase of 35%–45% of production at cost plus 2%. Of the difference between this sum and the realized price, 50% was to be payable as income tax—although when oil was brought on stream the financial terms were to be adjusted.

Iran signed seven more service contracts, the last (in 1974) allowing foreign companies to purchase about one-half of production at discounts of up to 5%. None of the other Middle Eastern or North African states concluded service contracts.

Similar to service contracts are 'production-sharing' arrangements, which were pioneered by Indonesia. Production-sharing arrangements were concluded by Egypt in 1973, and by Libya in 1974. In the mid-1970s Syria also signed a number of production-sharing agreements. This type of agreement generally involves the compensation of the foreign company for its share of expenditure in cash or kind, or by favourable tax terms, while production is divided in a ratio of between 75:25 and 85:15 in favour of the state.

After the Islamic Revolution in Iran, the new regime decided to end its four successful production partnerships—SIRIP, IPAC (with Amoco), LAPCO (with Arco, Murphy, Sun and Unocal) and IMINOCO (with AGIP, Phillips and the Indian Oil and Natural Gas Commission). The Government acquired the foreign partners' shareholdings, and in August 1980 announced that these would be run by a new Continental Shelf Oil Company.

The drive for participation, and Algerian take-overs

In the 1960s producer governments sought participation in existing concessions. Originally put by Saudi Arabia to Aramco in 1964, this idea was given formal voice in 1968 in OPEC's

Declaratory Statement of Petroleum Policy. However, it was not until July 1971, after the appearance of a seller's market and its success in the Tehran price negotiations in February of that year, that OPEC decided to call the companies to formal talks on participation.

Algeria had by this time set a precedent, having nationalized its US concessionaires and Shell in 1967. This left the French companies, CFP and ERAP, which were in a special position under the 1965 Franco-Algerian Evian Agreement. In 1969, under the terms of the agreement, Algeria opened negotiations for higher prices.

In July 1970, after inconclusive talks, Algeria increased its prices unilaterally. After further fruitless discussions, it seized 51% of the two French companies in February 1971. France sponsored an effective boycott, but both CFP and ERAP later came to terms.

While the take-over of CFP and ERAP was purely a Franco-Algerian affair, it increased the other producers' confidence when they began negotiations with the companies in 1972. The countries concerned in these negotiations were the five Arab producers in the Gulf (Venezuela and Indonesia having already achieved a degree of participation or close involvement in their oil industries, and Iran, Libya and Nigeria determined to pursue their own negotiations). The producers initially demanded an immediate 25% share, rising to 51%, with compensation to be at net book value, and that part of the government share of production sold back to the companies should be priced between the posted price and the tax-paid cost (government revenue plus production cost). In March the companies agreed in principle to surrender 20% of their operations, and in October, by which time Iraq, having nationalized the Iraq Petroleum Company (IPC), was no longer involved in the negotiations, an outline agreement was reached.

The General Agreement of 1972

The General Agreement on Participation was finalized in December 1972, and ratified by Saudi Arabia, Qatar and Abu Dhabi at the beginning of 1973. Under the Agreement the producers took an immediate 25% stake in the concessionaire companies. The earliest date for majority participation laid down was 1 January 1982, with the initial shareholding rising by 5% per year in 1978, 1979, 1980 and 1981 and by 6% in 1982.

The need to ease company problems accounted for the complex arrangements for pricing and disposing of the states' 25% share of production. The 75% companies' entitlement, which became known as 'equity crude', remained subject to the Tehran Agreement of February 1971, but the balance belonging to the producing states was divided into three categories, each priced differently. A small proportion of production (only 10% of the states' share, or 2.5% of total output in 1973) the governments undertook to sell on the open market for whatever price they could get. The other two categories of crude were 'bridging crude' and 'phase-in crude', both priced above the normal tax-paid cost and set to decline in volume as the states' direct sales increased. The Gulf producers subsequently decided that both bridging and phase-in crude should be treated similarly, and priced at 93% of the posting. For compensation the criterion adopted was 'updated book value', taking account of the cost of replacing company assets.

Iraqi nationalization

Iraq's involvement in the participation negotiations ceased in 1972, when it nationalized IPC. In June 1971, as part of the agreement on Iraqi Mediterranean crude prices which followed the Tehran pact in February, the IPC group undertook to increase production, but in the following spring the company was obliged to cut the throughput of its pipeline from Kirkuk to the Mediterranean terminals of Banias (Syria) and Tripoli (Lebanon). The Iraqi Government claimed that the cut-back was due to political, not economic, reasons, and presented IPC with alternatives: either the company was to restore Kirkuk production to normal levels and cede the extra production to the Government, or it was to surrender the field entirely and concentrate production on the Basra Petroleum Company's (BPC) acreage in the south. On 31 May 1972 IPC presented its answers to the Iraqi ultimatum. These did not satisfy the Government, and the next day IPC was nationalized. IPC's

affiliates, BPC and the Mosul Petroleum Company (MPC), were not immediately affected.

Negotiations commenced in July 1972, and on 28 February 1973 IPC and the Government reached agreement. IPC accepted expropriation that had taken place in 1961 and the nationalization of the Kirkuk producing area. At the same time it relinquished the MPC and paid the Government US $41m. in outstanding royalty backpayments. In return it was promised 15m. tons of oil and received some assurance of the long-term security of its investment and growth of output from BPC's southern fields, where it agreed to more than double production.

In the event, it was only seven months before BPC suffered the seizure, during the October (1973) War, of the holdings of Exxon and Mobil, and 60% of Shell's share as a political gesture against the USA's and the Netherlands' association with Israel. Later the 5% share of the Participations and Explorations Corporation (owned by the Gulbenkian family) was seized on the grounds that the company was registered in Portugal, which was pursuing racist policies in Africa. Thereafter the Government watched the progress of take-over negotiations in Saudi Arabia and Kuwait, and after a final agreement had been signed in Kuwait, it nationalized the remaining Western-owned share in BPC.

Iranian Sales and Purchase Agreement

Although it was already clear in January 1972 that Iran was not interested in the type of participation envisaged by the Gulf states, the Shah did not decide what Iran would demand instead until January 1973. The Consortium received an ultimatum: Iran would not extend its lease, and the companies could either continue under existing arrangements until the expiry of their lease in 1979, or they could negotiate a new agency agreement immediately. The Consortium chose the latter plan, and, under the Iranian Sales and Purchase Agreement signed in Tehran in May 1973, NIOC took control of the management of the Consortium's production operation and the Abadan refinery. NIOC was to provide 60% of the capital for expanding production, while the companies would contribute 40% of the funds needed in the first five years in return for a discount of 22 cents per barrel on their liftings.

Although NIOC became owner/manager, the Consortium members established a service company, the Oil Service Company of Iran (OSCO), to undertake operations on NIOC's behalf for an initial (and renewable) period of five years. NIOC agreed to raise total installed production capacity to 8m. barrels/day (b/d) by October 1976. The national company was also entitled to take the oil needed for internal consumption and a 'stated quantity' for export, which was to rise from 200,000 b/d in 1973 to 1.5m. b/d in 1981 and therefore, except in certain cases of *force majeure*, would remain in the same proportion to total crude available for export as 1.5m. b/d represented to oil available for export in 1981. The balance of crude production went to the Consortium members, which were guaranteed secure supplies for 20 years.

Libya asserts 51% control

Only weeks after OPEC had demanded participation in July 1971, Libya announced that it would be interested in nothing less than an immediate 51% share. For the next year, however, the Libyan Government made no move while it awaited the outcome of the participation negotiations in the Gulf.

Talks on Libya's demand began in early 1973, with the Government negotiating on a company-by-company basis as usual. In June Libya nationalized outright the US independent Nelson Bunker Hunt. This company had been BP's 50% partner in the Sarir field (Libya had nationalized outright BP's half-share of the Sarir field in December 1971), and the Government had chosen it for its first negotiations because it had no source of oil outside the USA and therefore seemed especially vulnerable.

In August 1973, following the nationalization of Bunker Hunt, the Libyan Government seized 51% of Occidental's operations. Faced with losing its assets and its most vital source of oil outside the USA, Occidental announced its 'acquiescence' in the measure. For the other companies the significance of this 'acquiescence' lay in the fiscal terms. The companies had in fact been prepared to offer Libya a nominal 51% provided that the financial results gave parity with those deriving from the participation agreements with the Gulf producers and Nigeria—but this was not so in the terms settled with Occidental. Compensation was agreed on at book value, rather than the updated book value formula used in the Gulf, and the buy-back price was set above the posting, rather than between the posting and the tax-paid cost.

Five days after the Occidental seizure three independent companies in the Oasis group—Continental, Marathon and Amerada Hess—accepted similar take-over terms, though Shell, the only major in Oasis, refused them. Then, in September 1973 the Libyan Government announced 51% take-overs of all the other significant producing groups. Gelsenberg, a German concern in partnership with Mobil, and W. R. Grace, a small shareholder in the Esso Sirte venture, agreed to Libya's terms; but Atlantic Richfield (another partner in Esso Sirte) and the majors, Mobil, Esso and the Texaco-Socal company, Amoseas, joined Shell in resisting any arrangement that might have undermined their participation agreements in the Gulf.

In February 1974 Libya seized all of the remaining assets of Texaco, Socal and Atlantic Richfield; and in the following month Shell too was nationalized. Finally Mobil, in March, and Esso, in April, accepted the 51% seizure of the previous September.

Gulf states achieve 60% participation

The General Agreement on Participation concluded at the end of 1972 had satisfied the Kuwaiti Government, and had been signed at the beginning of January 1973; but the Kuwait National Assembly refused its approval. By the summer of 1973 it was clear that the Government would not, as it had originally hoped, be able to rally sufficient support to get the General Agreement accepted. In June the Amir formally requested a revision of the accord, and during the autumn, when Libya announced its series of 51% take-overs, the other Gulf producers followed Kuwait's example. In November the Saudi Arabian oil minister, Sheikh Ahmad Zaki Yamani, announced that Saudi Arabia would not accept a simple majority holding, and it was made clear early in 1974 that the Saudi Government would negotiate a complete take-over of Aramco's operations.

Negotiations between the Kuwaiti Government and the Kuwait Oil Company (KOC) shareholders, BP and Gulf, resulted at the end of January 1974 in the State's gaining a holding of 60%. The new agreement, ratified in May, was to last for six years. The compensation formula agreed was net book value, rather than updated book value, but there was no settlement of buy-back terms. In fact, Kuwait did not conclude a buy-back deal with BP and Gulf until after it had rejected all bids for its 60% crude share at an auction in July.

Before the ratification of the Kuwaiti participation agreement, Qatar had concluded a similar accord with its concessionaires—the Qatar Petroleum Company (QPC) and Shell—in February 1974, and in April it settled buy-back arrangements for the following six months. Then in June, after the Kuwait ratification, Saudi Arabia concluded an 'interim' 60% participation agreement with Aramco, with undisclosed buy-back arrangements. Finally, in September Abu Dhabi negotiated a 60% share in the Abu Dhabi Petroleum Company and Abu Dhabi Marine Areas, backdated to the beginning of the year.

Aramco take-over negotiations

Not until early 1974 (shortly before the Government took 60% of Aramco as an interim measure in June) did it become clear that the Saudi Arabian Government sought a complete take-over of Aramco. This was to be limited to sales and contracting arrangements similar to those agreed between Iran and the Consortium in May 1973. However, changing circumstances in the Middle East, in Saudi Arabia and in the world oil market over the next six years continually postponed the conclusion of an agreement.

Two principal issues in dispute—the companies' fee and their crude entitlements—were apparently resolved early in 1980. In April the Government transferred to the companies the final instalment of compensation for their assets—US $1,500m., in respect of the 40% share in Aramco retained by the companies since the second participation accord of 1974. At the same time, the Government completed its take-over of the Ras Tanura refinery and natural gas liquids (NGLs) facility which had been excluded from the 60% participation deal and for several years

after 1974 had remained 100% Aramco-owned. The Government then announced in April 1981 that it was taking 50% of Tapline, in which the Aramco partners each had the same shares as they had in Aramco itself.

Exactly what commitments the Government had given the companies on crude oil entitlements were not revealed. However, it was known that as of 1980 the Aramco partners were receiving a fee of 27 cents per barrel produced—although again there was no announcement of the details of the formula. Nor was there any announcement on the form of the new state oil corporation which would hold the Government's production assets.

In practice, while the negotiations with Aramco were in progress the oil industry in Saudi Arabia was run as if the Government had total control. The process of participation had involved the Government's acquisition of the company's assets in Saudi Arabia and its decision-making powers over exploration, the development of production capacity and the volume and allocation of output. Technically, Aramco remained wholly US-owned and US-registered. Before the completion of the take-over it was part owner of the Saudi production operation; after the signing of the take-over agreement it was assumed in 1981 that its status would change to that of owner of a service company.

Take-over in Kuwait

On 5 March 1975 Kuwait announced that as of that date it had taken over all assets of KOC and would begin negotiations to settle the terms with BP and Gulf retroactively. Kuwait made it clear that it wanted a continuing relationship with the KOC owners, but that it was capable of running the production operations itself. Negotiations, however, stuck on the problems of compensation, the service fee and credit terms, but at the beginning of December 1975 an agreement was announced. This involved: compensation of US $66m.; a discount on the 93% of postings third-party selling price of 15 cents per barrel—reflecting BP's and Gulf's continuing provision of technical services and technical personnel, the large size of their purchases and their undertakings to buy Kuwait's bunker fuel and use Kuwait's tankers; and commitments by BP to take an average of 450,000 b/d between 1 January 1976 and 1 April 1980 and by Gulf to take 500,000 b/d over the same period. The two companies received an option on a further 400,000 b/d. All of these quantities were subject to plus or minus 12.5% variations.

Take-overs in the Lower Gulf

The take-over in Kuwait in 1975 opened the way for other producers to take 100% of their former concessionaires. In December 1975 Iraq nationalized the BPC, and in February 1976 Kuwait began negotiations for the take-over of Aminoil in its half of the Neutral Zone. Negotiations did not go well, and in September 1977 Kuwait nationalized the company. In April 1978 it was decided that KOC should take over the production operation while the Kuwait National Petroleum Company (KNPC) should take control of the Mina Abdullah refinery, which had processed Aminoil's entire output.

Starting in June 1976 Qatar negotiated the complete take-over of its two concessionaires, signing broadly similar agreements with QPC in September and with Shell in February 1977. Compensation was calculated by net book value, involving the payment of US $14m. for Shell's remaining assets and $18m. for QPC's; both companies accepted a fee of 15 cents per barrel of oil produced. Furthermore, Shell was to receive an unspecified lump sum bonus as a condition of its undertaking further exploration (for gas) for the Qatar General Petroleum Corporation (QGPC, now Qatar Petroleum—QP) on a contracting basis.

In Bahrain the Government announced the take-over of the production operations of the Bahrain Petroleum Company (BAPCO) in April 1978, backdated to the beginning of January. BAPCO retained the Sitra refinery until May 1980, when the Government took a stake of 60%.

In Abu Dhabi, meanwhile, the Government made clear its conviction that the emirate's big potential for further discoveries and the technical problems involved in its offshore production made it very much in the State's interest for the companies to retain an equity participation and that the 60:40 agreement would be maintained. The policy of retaining the concessionaire as a partner also applied in Oman.

The end of the Iranian Consortium

It was not long before most of the Iranian Sales and Purchase Agreement became out of date. Whereas at one stage in 1973 the Shah had suggested that Iran's reserves might exceed 100,000m. barrels, it came to be realized quite suddenly that this was grossly over-optimistic. To add anything to the country's recoverable reserves beyond 65,000m. barrels, or even to recover that volume of oil, Iran realized that it would have to invest huge sums in a gas injection secondary recovery system.

At the end of 1975 the Consortium ceased contributing the 40% of development capital which it was supposed to invest under the Agreement, and in return NIOC reduced the Consortium's 22 cents per barrel discount to take account of interest accruing on the capital which NIOC saw itself as investing on the Consortium's behalf. Unsuccessful talks on a revision of the Agreement were held in late 1975 and early 1976. It was not until the beginning of 1978 that the two sides sat down to work out a complete replacement for the Agreement, and these negotiations were subsequently made irrelevant by the Iranian Revolution in 1979.

Early sales contracts after the Revolution were with former direct customers of NIOC and the Consortium and former Consortium members, though by mid-May 1979 NIOC was talking to new companies. In total the Consortium members, who had been lifting 3.3m. b/d before the Revolution, got 1.1m. b/d, of which BP took 450,000 and Shell 235,000 b/d. Up to 1.9m. b/d was allocated for about 50 other companies. All buyers soon found their contracts subject to volume reductions, which NIOC made in order to have more crude available for new customers.

THE DEVELOPMENT OF PRICES

Throughout the 1930s and the first half of the 1940s oil was priced on the basis of the anomalous 'US Gulf Plus' system, which stipulated that the price of oil throughout the world should be the same as that obtaining in the Gulf of Mexico, but that the price at the point of delivery should comprise the Gulf of Mexico price plus the cost of freight to that point from the Gulf of Mexico—regardless of the actual origin of the oil. This system gave way to variants that equalized the world price of oil first at the Persian Gulf and then at New York, USA. Thereafter, in the early 1950s the supply and demand situation in Europe became the determinant of the price of Gulf crudes.

In 1959 the closure of the Suez Canal caused all prices to rise. However, the companies subsequently implemented reductions about which the governments of the Middle Eastern producer states and Venezuela were not consulted and which reduced their budgets and damaged their development prospects. In September 1960, one month after a further reduction of Middle Eastern prices, the oil ministers of Iran, Iraq, Saudi Arabia, Kuwait and Venezuela convened an emergency meeting in the Iraqi capital, Baghdad, where it was decided to create the Organization of the Petroleum Exporting Countries—OPEC.

OPEC in the 1960s

With the aim of restoring posted prices to their pre-August 1960 level, OPEC member states, which now also included Qatar, Libya and Indonesia, decided to attempt to raise market prices by limiting the annual growth in their production. A joint production programme pursued from mid-1965 to mid-1967 was ineffective owing to the over-estimation of overall growth in demand for OPEC oil and to the flouting of quotas. However, OPEC did succeed in increasing its members' share of profits during the 1960s by forcing the companies to accept, in 1963, a cut in the marketing allowance; and by negotiating two agreements on the expensing of royalties in 1964 and 1968.

Tehran and Tripoli Agreements

In 1970 the Libyan Government was pursuing a claim for higher prices which would accurately reflect the freight advantage enjoyed by Libyan crude since the closure of the Suez Canal, as well as Libyan crude's high quality. In May Libya ordered Occidental, an independent deriving almost one-third of its earnings from its Libyan concession, to reduce its production. By September the imposition of further reductions on Occidental and other companies had deprived the industry of about 1m. b/d of Libyan production, and freight rates soared as extra supplies were shipped from the Gulf. One by one the independ-

ents, followed by the majors, conceded Libya's claim for higher prices. Libya achieved a price rise of US $0.30, rising to $0.40 over the next five years, and its tax rate rose from 50% to one of 54%–58% in payment for what Libya claimed should have been higher prices since 1965. Realizing that these changes would be bound to result in higher prices in the Gulf, the majors promptly resolved to pay Gulf producers a higher tax rate of 55% and an extra $0.09 on heavier crudes which were in particularly high demand in 1970. Then, in Venezuela in December, at OPEC's 21st conference, the members decided that the Gulf states should seek further price increases.

Talks with the producers' representatives, which began in Tehran in January 1971, culminated on 14 February in the companies' surrender to OPEC's demands. The producers received: an immediate US $0.33 basic increase, $0.02 for freight disparities, half a cent for every degree API by which any crude fell below 40° API, the elimination of all remaining discounts and allowances, and provision for prices to increase by 2.5% and $0.05 on 1 June 1971, and 1 January 1973, 1974 and 1975. The companies, meanwhile, received assurances that there would be no further claims before 31 December 1975, no more 'leap-frogging' if the Mediterranean producers concluded better terms, and no embargoes.

In March 1971 negotiations resumed in Libya, and on 2 April an agreement was signed giving Libya US $0.90, a uniform 55% tax rate, and provision for annual price increases of 2.5% and $0.07. Subsequent negotiations secured similar terms for Iraqi and Saudi Arabian crude delivered to Mediterranean terminals.

The price explosion

It was only months before the Tehran and Tripoli Agreements came under strain. In August 1971 the floating of the US dollar (leading to a formal devaluation in December) prompted OPEC to claim compensation. In February 1973 the dollar was devalued by a further 10%, leading, in June, to the signing of a second dollar compensation agreement.

By the summer of 1973 the Tehran Agreement was, additionally, being undermined by US demand. Falling production in the USA after 1970 had caused that country to turn to the eastern hemisphere not only to make good its domestic shortfall, but also for an annual increment in supplies that was nearly as big as the annual increase demanded by the whole of Western Europe. In 1973 prices on the open market began to rise accordingly. With the fiscal terms applied to the bulk of their production still tied to modified 1971 prices, the OPEC states were largely excluded from sharing in this boom.

Collective action pursued by OPEC to address this situation culminated in the decision of the producers, on 16 October 1973, to raise posted prices by 70%. (Libya subsequently raised its price by 94%.) The size of the October increase, and the fact that it was unilateral, signalled the final complete transfer of control over the price system into the hands of the producers. However, a meeting of Arab producers in Kuwait on 17 October was of far greater significance.

Meeting under the aegis of the Organization of Arab Petroleum Exporting Countries (OAPEC), they decided to use the 'oil weapon' to support Egypt and Syria in their war against Israel. With Iraq opting out, the other nine members of OAPEC decided on a policy of 5% cumulative monthly cuts in production from the levels of September. Within days all of the Arab producers (including Iraq) placed embargoes on the USA and the Netherlands and reduced their production by equivalent additional amounts, while Saudi Arabia and Kuwait also incorporated the 5% reduction scheduled for November into their initial cut-back. The Arab producers then decided at a meeting in Kuwait on 4 November to reduce output across the board by 25% of the September level, and gave notice of a further 5% cut in December. In practice, the cut-back turned out to be greater than it appeared on paper, and by mid-November output in the two biggest Arab producers—Saudi Arabia and Kuwait—had fallen by 30%–40%. The Arab cuts had a dramatic effect on the market. Cargoes of Algerian and Nigerian short-haul crude fetched up to US $16 per barrel, and in December NIOC sold oil at the staggering price of $17.40.

The production cuts effectively ended in December 1973 when the Arab states decided not to impose a further 5% reduction in January 1974, and to run production as normal for most of the European Community (EC) and Japan. However, it was only in March that they lifted the embargo on the USA and not until July that it was lifted for the Netherlands. The resumption of normal exports to the USA was accompanied by a decision to restore output to September 1973 levels. Market prices weakened accordingly over the following months.

1974: changing the tax system

Excess of supply now assumed critical importance for a struggle within OPEC over pricing policy. In June 1974 Saudi Arabia's oil minister, Sheikh Yamani, formally proposed that the marker (i.e. reference) crude posting should be lowered by US $2.50. However, at the next OPEC meeting, held in Ecuador in the same month, the other members proposed formulas which would have raised the price of oil for consumers by as much as $1.50. Saudi Arabia's objection to this led to the decision to increase the royalty rate on the companies' 40% crude entitlement (known as equity oil) from 12.5% to 14.5%.

At the same time, 60% participation agreements, concluded in mid-1974 but backdated to the beginning of the year, increased the governments' take considerably. In 1973, under a 25% regime, the overall effect of participation had been fairly small. In mid-1974, however, under the 60% regime, the weighted average revenue amounted, in theory, to some US $2 more than the government revenue on equity crude (which after the December 1973 increases was about $7). In practice, there were considerable variations between the different producers in the amount by which the weighted average revenue exceeded the take on equity crude; in every case the actual weighted average was lower than it appeared to be in theory. One reason for the variations between the states was the different percentages of postings charged to the companies for buy-back crude.

One consequence of this dual pricing system was that the companies got their crude on average at a price well below that demanded by governments for their direct sales. The companies were thus able to undercut state prices, causing the failure of auctions and giving the companies large windfall profits. At OPEC's meeting in September 1974 in Vienna, Austria, the members decided to increase the royalty rate on equity crude to 16.67%, and to increase the tax rate on equity crude from 55% to 65.65%.

In November 1974 a Saudi Arabian delegation met with the Qatari and Abu Dhabi oil ministers in Abu Dhabi and agreed to raise the royalty rate on equity crude to 20% and the tax rate to 85%, with effect from the beginning of the month. At the same time postings were cut by US $0.40. At OPEC's final conference of 1974, held in Vienna in December, OPEC members endorsed these changes, and decided that from 1 January 1975 all of the Gulf states would apply the new weighted average cost to all of their production exported by their concessionaires, and that the new price levels should be frozen for nine months. The distinction between equity and participation crude, and the possibility of variations in the weighted average cost being caused by alterations in the ratio between the two crudes, therefore ceased to exist—although a notional 40:60 split was still used to calculate the new cost, or 'acquisition price'. The new single price system increased government revenue, not only because it was partly based on the higher tax and royalty rates agreed at Abu Dhabi, but also because it was based on a 40:60 equity-participation crude ratio which had not previously existed. Government revenue on marker crude rose to $10.13, and the acquisition price for the companies to $10.25, reflecting the notional marker production cost of $0.12. The gap between the acquisition price and the 93% of postings, $10.46, which remained the official sale price, narrowed to $0.21. Over the following years the acquisition price applied only in countries where the companies retained a 40% equity stake—which soon meant just Abu Dhabi and Saudi Arabia, among the bigger producers. In practice it was the state selling prices, in all countries, that became the important prices for OPEC.

Differentials: 1975–78, OPEC split and reconciliation

December 1974 marked the end of the oil price explosion; within 15 months government revenues and the consumer price of oil had multiplied almost exactly five times. From then until 1 January 1979 there were only two OPEC price rises—one, of 10%, in September 1975, and the second, also of 10%, agreed

by the majority of OPEC members in December 1976. The latter increase was opposed by Saudi Arabia and the UAE, both of which opted for an immediate 5% increase for the whole of 1977, while the other members decided on 10% for the first six months of the year with an additional 5% to take effect on 1 July. In June 1977 Saudi Arabia's acceptance of a formula whereby Saudi Arabia and the UAE would raise their prices by 5% in July, and the remaining OPEC members at the same time would forgo their own scheduled 5% increase, effectively healed the rift.

For much of 1975–78 markets characterized by weak demand and glut caused OPEC's tendency to focus mainly on differentials—the different margins between crudes of different qualities in different locations. Inability to agree on any comprehensive new system meant that adjustments were generally made unilaterally. Other recurrent issues addressed during this period were production programming and the protection of prices against dollar fluctuations.

The second oil crisis: 1979

OPEC assumed that conditions of glut prevailing during most of 1978 would begin to come to an end late that year or in 1979. Members also assumed that a subsequent period of balance would be succeeded by conditions of shortage some time in the 1980s. However, this transformation occurred much sooner. At the end of October 1978 strikes in Iran began to affect oil production. At the end of December Iranian production, normally about 5.8m. b/d, fell to 235,000 b/d, remaining at that level until March 1979. Up to the end of 1978 the companies made good the shortfall by increasing liftings elsewhere. The Iranian crisis added little impetus to the OPEC meeting held in Abu Dhabi in December, when it was decided to raise prices for 1979 by 10% in quarterly instalments. These would raise the marker crude selling price from US $12.70 in December 1978 to $14.54 in October 1979—an average increase for 1979 of 10%. Although this was an extremely modest increase and followed a long period of stability, Western governments were outraged.

During January 1979 spot market prices began to climb at a rate that was to destroy the price programme agreed at Abu Dhabi and, by mid-May, to cause the West to talk of a 'second oil crisis'. By the middle of February, when OPEC announced that an extraordinary meeting would be held in Geneva, Switzerland, at the end of March, spot prices for light Gulf crudes had risen to US $21 and higher, involving premiums of more than $7.50.

The resumption of Iranian exports in March 1979 caused spot premiums to decline from their end-February peak of US $23, but market pressure for a production increase was still impossible for Saudi Arabia to resist when the extraordinary meeting of OPEC was held. All producers agreed to bring forward their scheduled 1979 last-quarter increase to the second quarter, and it was decided that producers could impose any additional surcharges they deemed justifiable.

In April 1979 it became known that Saudi Arabia was not maintaining in the second quarter the increase in production of 1m. b/d implemented in order to compensate for lost Iranian production. Shortly thereafter the effect of the Iranian stoppage finally began to affect the market, as oil companies reduced their deliveries. In May these developments caused another jump in the spot market price for light crudes, which by mid-May had risen to levels in the region of US $33 per barrel. Iran subsequently led two further rounds of 'leap-frogging' increases.

At the OPEC meeting held in Geneva in June 1979 Saudi Arabia raised its marker price to US $18, while the other members were allowed to impose surcharges up to $23.50. It was not until September that Nigeria broke the $23.50 ceiling by imposing a further premium on the price of its crude, thus triggering another round of increases.

Saudi attempts to reunify prices: December 1979–September 1980

Attempts to bring about the reunification of prices, initiated by Saudi Arabia from December 1979, made little progress. At the OPEC meeting held in Algeria in June 1980, for instance, the only agreement reached was to accept a two-tier price system. It was not until the OPEC meeting held in September in Vienna that the Saudi Arabian delegation was able to make what seemed to be real progress towards reunification and agreement on a proper system of differentials. It was agreed that the price of Arabian Light should be raised by US $2 to $30 per barrel and that this should be regarded as the official marker price. Other OPEC crudes, aligned on a theoretical $32 marker, were to remain frozen until the next OPEC conference in December.

Iran–Iraq War: renewed price discord

The outbreak of the Iran–Iraq War in September 1980 led to the removal of 4m. b/d from the international market. In October the oil ministers of the four Arabian OPEC members agreed on a programme of compensatory increases in production, though given the pre-war surplus of 2m. b/d–2.5m. b/d the amounts involved were modest. Arabian producers' output was raised by only some 1m. b/d, Saudi Arabia accounting for about 700,000 b/d–800,000 b/d of this. The additional Saudi crude was sold to state-owned oil companies of industrialized and developing countries at a US $2 premium to the official Arabian Light price of $30. Spot market prices nevertheless rose gradually: by the end of November some Arabian Light and African oils were trading at $42–$43.

At the OPEC meeting held in Indonesia in December 1980 Saudi Arabia agreed to raise the price of Arabian Light by US $2 to $32, and the conference set a theoretical marker crude price of $36 on which increases in the prices of other crudes were to be based. A differentials limit of $5 was set, giving an OPEC ceiling price of $41.

1981: price reunification

During December 1980 both Iran and Iraq recommenced exports of crude, offering substantial discounts. In response, Abu Dhabi ceased its output of 80,000 b/d of war-relief crude, but Saudi Arabia maintained its output at 10.3m. b/d, thus accounting for 43% of total OPEC output and attaining a position of unprecedented influence.

Contrary to Saudi Arabian wishes, however, no progress was made towards the reunification of prices at the OPEC conference held in Geneva in May 1981. Instead, members agreed to freeze the theoretical marker price at US $36 and the maximum OPEC price at $41 until the end of 1981. Excluding Saudi Arabia, Iran and Iraq, the members also agreed to cut their output by 10% in an attempt to reduce the surplus on world markets. This was the first time since the 1960s that OPEC had taken a decision on production levels.

At the end of October 1981, when OPEC convened in Geneva, members were finally able to agree on reunification—at US $34, a figure that involved Saudi Arabia's increasing its price by $2 and the other OPEC members' cutting theirs by $1–$2. At a subsequent meeting in Abu Dhabi in December new, more realistic differentials were also agreed upon.

OPEC's first production programme

Only weeks after the reunified price structure and the new differentials took effect, OPEC found itself confronted by the worst crisis in its history. Continued recession in the industrialized countries and a run-down on stocks reduced demand for OPEC oil in February 1982 to just 20.5m. b/d, compared with a forecast of 23m. b/d. The prices of Iranian and North Sea crudes were reduced in response, while the spot market price for Arabian Light fell to US $28.50—$5.50 below the government selling price.

At a full, extraordinary OPEC meeting held in March 1982 in Vienna, Saudi Arabia ruthlessly imposed discipline on the members by warning them that if they did not seriously defend the US $34 marker price, then it would, among other measures, reduce the price of Arabian Light to $24 per barrel, increase its output to 10m. b/d–11m. b/d and sell substantial quantities of crude on the spot market. In response, members agreed on a set of quotas involving an 18m. b/d ceiling, accompanied by a further lowering of light crude prices in Africa and the Gulf, and the establishment of a ministerial committee to monitor the market and the implementation of quotas.

By mid-June 1982, however, it was clear that the ceiling had been exceeded. In that month production averaged nearly 18m. b/d, even though Saudi Arabia's output was only about 6m. b/d and Iraq was fulfilling just over two-thirds of its quota. By July, when ministers gathered in Vienna for an extra-

ordinary conference planned two months earlier, the production programme was disintegrating. That the extraordinary ministerial conference was suspended—rather than ended without agreement—indicated the extent of its failure. Apart from a common commitment to the US $34 reference price and to the need to restrain production within a 17.5m. b/d ceiling, Iran, Libya and Algeria insisted that Saudi Arabia should further cut its production to accommodate other producers, in particular Iran. Saudi Arabia's response was that it still refused to discuss its level of output with other members and that it had already made substantial sacrifices.

Subsequent ministerial meetings, some within the context of the Co-operation Council for the Arab States of the Gulf (the Gulf Co-operation Council—GCC), from December 1982 failed to produce a concerted strategy. When the chief delegates of OPEC convened in formal session in London, United Kingdom, in March 1983 there had been no recovery in demand for OPEC oil. Rather, destocking by the oil companies was generally estimated to have surged to more than 4.5m. b/d during the first quarter of 1983, while members' output of oil and NGLs dropped to about 15.5m. b/d. The prospect of a general price collapse resulted in an arrangement of which the essential elements were: a 15% cut in the reference price, from US $34 to $29 per barrel; and a new production programme under a ceiling on collective output of 17.5m. b/d.

By the time of the next ministerial conference, held in Helsinki, Finland, in July 1983, the market had strengthened considerably. With demand for OPEC oil clearly starting to grow, it was hoped that economic recovery and heightened demand for oil might permit an increase in output. As it was, however, OPEC production surged well above the ceiling to pass 19m. b/d, an average rate now maintained until the end of 1983. Saudi Arabia was mainly responsible for the increase. Saudi Arabia had not, in fact, agreed to any limitation on its production, and at the end of the London meeting in March 1983 had done no more than commit itself to being OPEC's 'swing producer' (i.e. meeting any increase in demand for OPEC crude above the 17.5m. b/d ceiling or absorbing any drop below it). When OPEC's market-monitoring committee asked Saudi Arabia late in October 1983 to explain its high output, the Kingdom's response was that it could not perform its role as 'swing producer' if other members did not observe quotas and price commitments. OPEC's collective output exceeded 17.5m. b/d by a clear margin over the 12-month period following the conclusion of the pact on production and prices, but no precise figures were available. Indeed, the failure of member countries to report accurately rendered more difficult the job of OPEC's market-monitoring committee, which was to supervise adherence to quotas. The Paris-based International Energy Agency (IEA) calculated average OPEC production during April 1983–March 1984 (not including NGLs) at 18.1m. b/d.

OPEC's production-monitoring scheme

Rising consumption, evident in the winter of 1983/84, led OPEC to hope that it might be possible to raise the ceiling on output to as much as 19m. b/d for the final quarter of 1984. The expectation was that, by then, demand for OPEC crude might amount to as much as 20m. b/d, depending on how far stocks were drawn down. In the spring of 1984 the market had revived to the extent that spot rates for Brent, the North Sea reference crude, marginally exceeded the official selling rate of US $30 per barrel at the end of April. It was strengthened by fears of serious disruption of supplies from the Gulf resulting from the continued conflict between Iran and Iraq. By the summer of 1984, however, these fears had largely subsided, causing the average spot rate for Brent, now established as the all-important market indicator, to fall below the official selling price in late May. OPEC's hopes that there would be an appreciable rise in demand for its oil in the second half of the year were also confounded. With available supplies greatly exceeding demand and (for the most part) selling at a discount to official prices, the market continued to sag.

In October 1984, at a full, extraordinary ministerial conference held in Geneva, in order to defend itself against a potentially vicious downward price spiral precipitated by North Sea producers and Nigeria, OPEC again lowered the ceiling on collective production, to 16m. b/d, and agreed a new allocation of quotas. This time the limit was intended to be temporary, to be raised when the supply situation tightened up and spot market prices aligned themselves with official rates. No progress was made, however, on the increasingly critical issue of OPEC's price differentials, by now glaringly misaligned with market realities. Nothing more was achieved than the appointment of a three-member committee to deal with this problem, and it was not until the extraordinary ministerial conference held in Geneva in January 1985 that anything like a coherent system was elaborated.

Another OPEC monitoring scheme

At a ministerial conference held in Geneva in December 1984 OPEC took a major step towards enforcing more effectively the pact on production, pricing and sales by establishing a supervisory body, the Ministerial Executive Council (MEC), which was empowered to employ independent auditors whom member states agreed to allow 'to check on member countries' petroleum sales, tanker nominations, shipments, pricing, quantities, etc.'.

In February 1985 the market strengthened, largely owing to lower OPEC output and a measure of confidence arising from revised differentials and the new production-policing measures. However, despite a forecast slump in demand in the spring, OPEC's pricing and production discipline remained slack. Co-operation with the MEC in the first quarter of 1985 was assessed as reasonable, but the MEC was far from exposing the scale of price discounting prevalent at this time.

The harsh fact was that the US $5 per barrel price cut of March 1983 had not stimulated demand for OPEC's oil. Such growth in world demand as had occurred had only benefited non-members, whose investment in exploration and development had been boosted by the price escalation of 1979–81. The extent of the damage was reflected in the fall of OPEC's output from a peak of more than 31m. b/d in 1979 to about 18.5m. b/d (including NGLs) in 1984, a drop of 40%. In the same period OPEC's share of the market fell from 60% to 40%.

During the summer of 1985 it became increasingly clear that, on the one hand, OPEC would not be able to raise the 16m. b/d production ceiling, and that, on the other, several members could not live comfortably with their quotas under the pact agreed in 1984. It became clear, too, that control of production was not in itself enough to strengthen the market, and that drastic action on the issue of price was imperative.

When OPEC met in Vienna in July 1985 spot prices had fallen to a level US $2–$3 per barrel below official selling rates, even though output continued to stagnate. The need to restore a measure of credibility to official OPEC rates was more urgent than ever, and this meant resisting a drift towards market prices. At a subsequent consultative meeting in Vienna OPEC members agreed that they should cease direct discounting and phase out price-cutting methods such as 'net-back' arrangements and counter-trade deals. At the next of OPEC's two annual ordinary conferences in Geneva in July a decision to widen the differential between the price of heavy Gulf crudes and ultra-light, North African crudes reduced the weighted average official price for all OPEC crudes from US $27.96 to $27.82 per barrel.

In September 1985 Saudi Arabia's decision—apparent in July—to renounce the role of 'swing producer', and its determination to enjoy the maximum entitlement of 4.35m. b/d allowed it under the OPEC output-sharing agreement, manifested itself in the Kingdom's abandonment of its previously strict adherence to official selling prices by reverting to (officially unacknowledged) 'net-back' deals. Saudi Arabia's categorical insistence on its full portion of OPEC's diminishing share of the oil market was, in itself, enough to ensure the failure of the next OPEC meeting, held in Vienna in October 1985. The conference was forced to reaffirm the ceiling on collective output of 16m. b/d, with the economic experts' optimum estimate of demand for OPEC crude amounting to only 15.6m. b/d, despite the onset of winter. The meeting foreshadowed the abandonment of any real effort to control production, despite the fact that discipline over output had become vital if prices were to be maintained.

OPEC's 'fair' market share policy

OPEC met again in Geneva on 7 December 1985 in a mood of growing desperation at the possibility of a 'price war'. Its decision

'to secure and defend a fair share of the world oil market' had enormous implications for prices. While the 16m. b/d ceiling and official selling rates remained notionally in force, in practice most members had abandoned them both in favour of a strategy aimed at forcing other producers to collaborate with OPEC in maintaining prices and to concede to them a part of their market share.

By the end of January 1986 the price of Brent had fallen to US $18.80 per barrel on the spot market. In the period from November 1985 to March 1986 spot market prices for widely traded crudes plummeted by 60%–75%, to their lowest level, in real terms, since 1973. At the OPEC ministerial conference held in Geneva in March 1986 it nevertheless proved impossible to agree on what the level of OPEC production should be and how it should be shared. The only agreement reached was with a group of non-member producers (Mexico, Egypt, Oman, Malaysia and Angola), who committed themselves, in principle, to reducing their own output, with the implicit proviso that OPEC should first establish a workable system of quotas. The conference was adjourned and reconvened in Geneva in April. Eventually a majority of 10 members agreed that a production rate of 16.3m. b/d in the third quarter of 1986, and 17.3m. b/d in the fourth, would be compatible with the aim of restoring market stability. The critical question of quotas, however, remained unresolved.

In June 1986 OPEC oil ministers met in Yugoslavia in another, unsuccessful, attempt to agree production levels and quotas. It was recognized that the big surplus overhanging the market, which had resulted from a surge in OPEC production in June (to 19m. b/d, nearly 2m. b/d more than actual demand), would immediately depress prices. In fact, they fell below US $10 per barrel, the Brent blend falling to a low of $8.60. OPEC's collective production remained in excess of 18.5m. b/d well into July.

The reintroduction of quotas

The next OPEC meeting, held in Geneva in July 1986, achieved a breakthrough by effectively setting a limit for the 12 members, excluding Iraq, of 14.8m. b/d. However, the resolution adopted stressed that 'this agreement is temporary and does not constitute a basis for any fair distribution of national quotas in any future negotiations thereon, nor does it bear any prejudice on OPEC's appropriate and rightful production'.

At the next OPEC meeting in October 1986 the majority of members were in favour of extending the two-month interim agreement until the end of the year. However, Saudi Arabia insisted that a redistribution of quotas was 'absolutely essential'. The other matter to be settled was the GCC's insistence on the establishment of prices in a US $17–$19 per barrel range. Agreement was ultimately reached on a complex formula under which a higher production ceiling for OPEC members (excluding Iraq) of 14.961m. b/d was set for November and one of 15.039m. b/d for December. At a subsequent, emergency meeting in Ecuador in November OPEC's pricing committee urged 'a prompt return to the system of fixing officially the prices for OPEC', as the appropriate means to restore to the Organization its capacity for controlling the price structure and maintaining stability in the world oil market. The committee also recommended that a reference price of $18 should not be fixed solely on the basis of 34° API Arabian Light (which Saudi Arabia did not want to be the marker crude) but on a 'basket' of seven crudes—Arabian Light, Dubai (UAE), Minas (Indonesia), Bonny Light (Nigeria), Saharan Blend (Algeria), Tia Juana Light (Venezuela) and Isthmus (Mexico).

At OPEC's next meeting, in Geneva in December 1986, the 12 members agreed on a 4.7% reduction in the limit on collective production from 15.039m. b/d in December to 14.334m. b/d for the first half of 1987. A theoretical quota of 1.466m. b/d was allocated to Iraq, giving a notional ceiling for OPEC as a whole of 15.8m. b/d. It was agreed that fixed prices should be imposed from 1 February. Differential prices were fixed for the 17 most important crudes, apart from those in the basket, varying from US $18.87 per barrel for Algeria's ultra-light Zarzaitine, to $16.67 for Kuwait's Export.

The cost of the 'price war'

The reason for the effective abandonment of OPEC's 'fair' market share strategy at the meeting in Yugoslavia in June

1986, despite the fact that its two leading proponents (Saudi Arabia and Kuwait) were still cushioned by substantial, if diminishing, financial reserves, was that it was too costly. Prior to the Yugoslavia meeting OPEC experts had estimated the overall annual loss of revenue by the 13 members at US $50,000m.–$60,000m. Despite stronger prices in the second half of 1986, actual losses were probably much greater.

OPEC's efforts to control prices and production during 1987

By the end of March 1987 the agreement of December 1986 had boosted the price of Brent to US $17.55 per barrel, compared with an average of $16.20 during February. Before the OPEC conference in Vienna in June 1987, however, collective output rose to 17.3m. b/d, significantly greater than demand, and there were signs of growing indiscipline. (At least, when OPEC did convene, prices on the spot market were more or less aligned with official selling rates.) The conference agreed to raise the limit on OPEC output by 800,000 b/d to 16.6m. b/d for the rest of the year. (Iraq, once again, refused to participate in the agreement.) The level was calculated to be significantly lower than actual demand to allow for Iraq's likely output and quota violations by other members.

In mid-1987 OPEC was able to derive some comfort from a marked reduction in stocks, which had been built up to an inordinately high level by members' over-production in the autumn and summer of 1986. It appeared, too, that spot market prices would continue to be supported by tension in the Gulf arising from the prospect of a military confrontation between the USA and Iran. However, that remained a matter of speculation: the Iran–Iraq war had made surprisingly little difference to the oil market, notwithstanding sustained aggravation that had prompted Kuwait to seek assistance from both the USSR and the USA. There was confidence that, in the event of a confrontation, official selling rates of around US $18 per barrel could be maintained, though it was realized that any serious development in the Gulf might send spot market prices soaring.

When the Iran–Iraq war did escalate in late 1987, Iran's resilience and flexibility in its selling arrangements undermined prices. By mid-November it was estimated that there were some 20m. barrels of unsold Iranian crude in storage, and another 14m. at sea. The market was, additionally, awash with excess supplies from other producers. By December OPEC production was running at about 19m. b/d. The growing surplus inevitably affected price levels: by mid-November the spot rate for Brent had fallen to US $17.37, and it was consistently below $18 throughout the month. As OPEC prepared for its end-of-year ministerial conference, it was clear that the price structure was coming under grave strain, largely as a result of the Iran–Iraq war.

The Vienna meeting commenced amid considerable despondency and scepticism as to what could be done to stop the downward drift of prices from the US $18 per barrel target, set over a year earlier. Only six months previously the issue had been whether OPEC could or should raise the reference price to a level higher than $18 per barrel. General prospects for a successful meeting were blighted by deteriorating relations between Iran and Saudi Arabia, which would almost certainly make impossible the kind of compromises reached in August and December 1986, as well as June 1987. The only possible outcome was a continuation of the output-sharing accord concluded the previous June. Despite Iranian reluctance, the accord was renewed and the existing quotas of the 12 retained. The only difference was that any pretence about Iraq's having a notional allocation was abandoned. OPEC reaffirmed official selling prices based on the US $18 reference level, but the Organization was, in reality, about to abandon any pretence or effort at maintaining them. The emphasis had switched decisively towards concentration on output control, which—if effectively applied—would keep prices around $18 per barrel.

1988: no progress on prices or production

During January 1988 OPEC's output dropped to about 17m. b/d. At the end of the month the spot rate for Brent blend had fallen to US $16.25 per barrel, compared with $17.95 at the beginning. By the end of February Brent had dropped to only $14.77, even though collective production had averaged only 17.4m. b/d. Nevertheless, it was not until 19 April that OPEC's price-monitoring committee met in Vienna. It did so mainly in response to an initiative by a group of non-member producers: Angola, the People's Republic of China, Egypt, Malaysia, Mexico and Oman. Mexico had indicated that the group would be prepared to cut its exports by 5% in return for a comparable reduction by OPEC. At an OPEC consultative conference held at the end of April, however, divisions regarding the proposal meant that no more could be decided than to maintain contact with the group, with the aim of long-term collaboration.

At the next OPEC ordinary ministerial conference, held in Vienna in June 1988, the Organization's crude output was reckoned to have risen above 18.5m. b/d in May, compared with a modest 17.5m. b/d in the second quarter. In mid-May OPEC's rate of output was still some 500,000 b/d above the stipulated ceiling and, in the circumstances, a decision to roll over the current agreement on quotas seemed to be a foregone conclusion. In July 1988, in the wake of the June conference, prices fell to around US $14 per barrel, and, with stocks high, appeared likely to weaken further in the third quarter. Having failed to make positive progress towards a collaborative production programme with the non-OPEC group, which might have stabilized prices, OPEC's $18 target now seemed somewhat chimerical.

The acceptance, in July 1988, by Iraq and Iran of UN cease-fire terms opened up new prospects for OPEC to take a firmer grip on oil supply and tackle other outstanding issues. As the cease-fire became a reality, Saudi Arabia reversed its former opposition to an emergency meeting of OPEC's pricing committee, the group charged with convening the 13-nation conference if prices were deviating too far from the official target. When the pricing committee convened in August, it was realistic enough to recognize that there was little it could do until Iran and Iraq had begun to tackle directly the issues dividing them. None the less, despite the scepticism of market operators and of some ministers, the session was to prove important in setting a realistic agenda for the 'reconstruction' of OPEC.

The pricing committee also recognized that issues related to the Iran–Iraq conflict were not the only problem impeding unity among the oil exporters. Indeed, the long-standing issue of over-production by the UAE dominated the discussions in August. Assurances that the UAE would always 'endeavour' to act in the best interests of OPEC as a whole lay oddly with a claim for a quota more than 50% higher than that assigned by the rest of the group. The contradiction damaged market confidence at this time.

As prices continued to slide towards US $10 per barrel, and with Iran and Iraq still unable to agree on quotas, as well as on territorial and other war-related issues, OPEC's Middle Eastern members took matters into their own hands and began to raise production to compensate for lower prices, which were therefore subjected to further pressure.

In September 1988 OPEC's pricing committee met again, in Madrid, Spain, where its decision to reconstitute the Organization's Long-Term Strategy Committee led to the addition to OPEC's steering group of three crucial Middle Eastern oil exporters: Iran, Iraq and Kuwait. Their statement, that a review of objectives and strategies in the context of current circumstances, *'especially concerning the price of oil and the production mechanism to support it'*, was necessary, was a clear warning to all oil exporters that OPEC would either have to tackle outstanding issues or give up all attempts to control prices and production.

By the end of October 1988 OPEC production had soared to more than 22m. b/d, far above most estimates of demand. The Gulf Arab states increased their production markedly and made it clear that they would not observe their official quotas unless there was total discipline.

When the Long-Term Strategy Committee reassembled in Vienna in November 1988 Iran appeared to have adopted a more flexible approach to the vexed issue of quota parity with Iraq. Having commenced major pipeline expansion schemes and the repair of its Gulf export facilities, Iraq would, unless it agreed to observe its quota, be able to meet all of the likely increase in world demand for OPEC crude oil over the coming year and was likely to do so anyway, if growth in demand declined, at the expense of other exporters' market share. The choice appeared simple. If Iraq's demand for a quota of about

2.5m. b/d was not met, it would undermine the market for all other exporters with production of around 4m. b/d in the coming year.

In the resulting distribution, Iran's quota was 125,000 b/d higher than it would have been under a distribution proposed by the GCC. Iraq was granted the same amount while the other 11 members of OPEC sacrificed pro-rata 250,000 b/d out of the 18.5m. b/d ceiling agreed for the first half of 1989.

Very high production in November and December 1988—after the OPEC agreement had been signed but before the new 18.5m. b/d ceiling took effect—underlined that most exporters intended to abide by the letter of the agreement. In the final weeks of 1988 production reached 23m. b/d, 4.5m. b/d above the ceiling agreed for the first six months of 1989 and 6m. b/d in excess of the ceiling then officially in force.

As it became clear that demand for oil had surged in late 1988 and was continuing to do so, oil prices strengthened to a level close to, and in some cases above, the official US $18 target price.

In January 1989 representatives of 13 non-OPEC oil exporters met with counterparts from six OPEC nations to indicate their willingness to support OPEC's efforts to stabilize prices. Saudi Arabia insisted that OPEC, by setting a ceiling of 18.5m. b/d for the first half of 1989, had taken an important step that the non-members should match. In late February the non-OPEC producers announced that they would reduce exports by 5% (or freeze them at 5% below planned levels) for the April–June period at least.

At a meeting of OPEC's price-monitoring committee, held in late March 1989 ostensibly to review how closely the membership had adhered to the agreement signed in November, Kuwait dramatically announced its intention of seeking a higher market share for itself, for the UAE and for the three smallest exporters—Gabon, Ecuador and Qatar. When oil ministers convened in June 1989 many were unable to believe that Kuwait would insist on a quota increase larger than the 5%–8% increase in the OPEC total which was under discussion for the second half of the year. However, Kuwait was unique within OPEC, having made greater production sacrifices, in percentage terms, during the 1980s than any other member. Leaving no room for doubt as to his intentions, the Kuwaiti oil minister proposed an amendment to the final OPEC resolution, exempting Kuwait from the agreed production quotas. To take account of additional Kuwaiti production, which was now regarded as inevitable, the production ceiling was raised by only 1m. b/d to 19.5m. b/d, correspondingly reducing the extra volumes to which other members were entitled.

In September 1989 a meeting of OPEC's Long-Term Strategy Committee was due to attempt to solve the perennial problems of quota distribution, oil prices and the likely impact on producers of 'environmentalist' movements in Western countries. In the event, with the eight permanent members of the Committee being joined by ministers from all other OPEC adherents, a full-scale quota and pricing meeting took place. The outcome was an unconvincing revival of the old pro rata quota formula, within a new ceiling of 20.5m. b/d: just 1m. b/d lower than the previous level. Kuwait duly rejected its quota of 1.149m. b/d for the final quarter of 1989.

At the next full OPEC meeting, held in November 1989, OPEC's production ceiling was raised to 22m. b/d, although most members regarded this as insignificant since *de facto* production was already 24m. b/d. Kuwait was allocated 6.82% of total output, compared with 5.61% previously. Iran, Algeria and Indonesia all relinquished quota share in Kuwait's favour, although they were probably more suitable candidates for increases themselves. The immediate result was that the UAE, inspired by Kuwait's disregard of the needs of poorer members, felt obliged to follow suit. Thus the November 1989 agreement left the overall situation largely unchanged, with Kuwait adhering to its quota but the UAE producing 100% more than its allocation. Overall production continued at almost 24m. b/d. Having risen to their highest level for two years in January 1990, prices subsequently fell steadily in the period to May. The potential stabilizing factor—adherence to quotas—was forgotten.

With the market behaving unpredictably, a meeting of the ministerial monitoring committee in March 1990 took no action,

opting to wait for the situation to clarify. At a subsequent meeting, held in May, it was agreed to reduce production by 1.445m. b/d from an average level of 23.5m. b/d. This measure brought production to just within the previously agreed ceiling and had little more than a token effect on the market. While producers all willingly pledged to reduce their output, some weeks later the overall cut was only around half that which had been agreed.

Conflict in the Gulf and its aftermath

The full OPEC meeting which began on 25 July 1990 took place in an atmosphere of tension caused by Iraq's threats of military action against countries that failed to observe production quotas. (Iraq had accused both the UAE and Kuwait of flouting their quotas.) At the meeting Iraq sought to raise OPEC's minimum reference price to US $25 per barrel, but in the event a new price of $21 per barrel was adopted and a new production ceiling of 22.5m. b/d fixed for the remainder of 1990. The immediate effect of Iraq's invasion—and subsequent annexation—of Kuwait at the beginning of August, and of the economic sanctions imposed on Iraq by the UN in response, was the loss of about 8% of world oil production. By late August prices had risen to about $30 per barrel.

Within weeks many OPEC members had decided that it was in the best interests of all to make good the 4.5m. b/d loss. Saudi Arabia raised production considerably, partly to pay for foreign military assistance to defend its borders and partly as a quid pro quo. Other OPEC members, mindful that non-OPEC sources might be used to compensate for the loss of Iraqi and Kuwaiti supplies, followed suit.

The *de facto* raising of production by a number of OPEC member states duly became *de jure* on 29 August 1990, when 10 OPEC oil ministers met in Vienna and agreed to compensate for 3.0m.–3.5m. b/d of lost production. By this time the price of some crudes had risen as high as US $32 per barrel. A further meeting took place in December 1990, when it was agreed to retain the suspension of quotas until the Iraq–Kuwait conflict was resolved.

The next meeting of OPEC, held in Geneva in March 1991, confirmed that whatever decisions OPEC took, the market remained the dominant force. Oil producers had by this time increased production to such an extent that, even with the loss of Iraqi and Kuwaiti supplies, prices had plummeted and storage capacity had become scarce. With supplies abundant and demand moving from winter to summer levels, prices fell by about 50% from their peak of US $32 per barrel. Saudi Arabia, whose production had peaked at more than 9m. b/d, reduced its output so that by April 1991 the market had become more balanced, with prices having recovered to around $4 below the target price of $21. It was decided at the OPEC meeting in March to reduce production by about 5%, from 23.4m. b/d to 22.298m. b/d. However, individual OPEC members had already taken account of falling demand, and the true level of production was little above the newly targeted level.

By formalizing new quotas the March 1991 OPEC meeting allowed most producers to maintain output at a level close to capacity. At a further meeting held in Vienna in June it was agreed to retain the quotas set in March until September, when a further meeting would decide if adjustments were needed. Ironically, Iraq's invasion of Kuwait had had the effect of stabilizing the market, but neither Iraq nor Kuwait could take advantage of the new equilibrium. At the September meeting, in Geneva, OPEC set a new production ceiling of 23.6m. b/d. In fact, OPEC production had averaged 23.636m. b/d during the first half of 1991, far above the production ceiling agreed in March; while in the second half of that year it had averaged 24.741m. b/d. Clearly, OPEC members were seeking to maximize production regardless of quota allocations, and prices remained far below the targeted US $21.

By the end of 1991 Kuwait had succeeded in restoring its production to 550,000 b/d. It was clear that if Kuwait continued to restore capacity at this rate, other OPEC producers would have to reduce theirs. Meanwhile, the market began to dictate production levels. The situation was complicated by a steep decline in production by the former Soviet republics, although this was offset by continued economic recession in many consuming countries. As a result, total demand for oil declined by

1.1% and it became clear that, without a voluntary reduction in production, the market would enforce a collapse in prices.

Before the OPEC meeting of February 1992 took place, nine of the 13 members announced reductions in production totalling 400,000 b/d. At the February meeting, held in Geneva, a new production quota of 22.982m. b/d was formally established. Iraq was allocated a quota which, at 505,000 b/d, was sufficient to satisfy domestic demand. Kuwait was granted a quota of 812,000 b/d, although it was unclear whether it would be able to achieve this level of production. Despite quota violations, market forces meant that overall OPEC production remained more or less in line with the production ceiling.

At the next OPEC meeting, held in Vienna in May 1992, it was agreed to maintain the production ceiling at 22.982m. b/d, although Kuwait was allowed to produce more than its previous quota of 812,000 b/d in order to compensate for losses arising from the Iraqi occupation.

Spot prices firmed in the immediate aftermath of the May 1992 meeting, reaching their highest level for seven months in late June. On the whole, prices remained firm in July, August and early September. By mid-September, however, when the ministerial monitoring committee met in Geneva, concern was being expressed at the margin by which spot prices were falling short of the targeted US $21, especially since market conditions were regarded as fundamentally favourable. By this time OPEC production was substantially greater than the previously agreed level. A statement issued at the conclusion of the meeting indicated that OPEC's market share in the final quarter of 1992 should be 24.2m. b/d in order to achieve the target price, and reaffirmed the Organization's earlier decision to allow for unspecified additional Kuwaiti production.

With demand for OPEC crude rising, total production averaged some 24.75m. b/d in September 1992. However, as seasonal demand for oil began to reach its peak in early October, prices remained below the anticipated level.

At the OPEC meeting held in November 1992 in Vienna measures were taken that were designed to remove some 400,000 b/d of OPEC crude from the market in December. These included the establishment of a total OPEC production level of slightly less than 24.6m. b/d for the first quarter of 1993; and the establishment of new production allocations for member states, with effect from 1 December 1992. By mid-December a feared collapse in the price of oil had apparently been averted. However, by early January 1993 prices had fallen to almost the lowest levels recorded in 1992 as a result of weak demand and production that remained in excess of the levels agreed the previous November. It was reported that OPEC production had averaged 25.27m. b/d in December 1992, its highest level since 1980.

At the next full OPEC meeting, held in Vienna in February 1993, it was agreed to make pro rata reductions in production that would effectively remove almost 1.5m. b/d from the market. The reductions, which pertained to the second quarter of 1993, were to take effect from 1 March. However, OPEC's declared commitment to maintaining a production ceiling of 23.58m. b/d met with the strongest scepticism from most observers, who believed that the new agreement would only begin to support prices in mid-March when it would be clear whether or not it was being observed. By late February 1993 the price of crude petroleum had reached a three-month peak as it appeared that OPEC's biggest producers would observe the agreement. Prices did, in fact, remain firm during March, even though it appeared that production had averaged 24m. b/d–24.3m. b/d. This compared with estimated production of 25.35m. b/d in February and the reduction was greater than most observers had expected.

At the beginning of May 1993 the market was reported to be broadly in balance and prices were steady though below the levels OPEC producers had hoped for. The spot price of a selection of OPEC crudes was reported to have averaged US $18.20 per barrel in May, almost 1.5% lower than in March and April. Production in May was reportedly 230,000 b/d lower than in April, but, at an estimated 24.1m. b/d, still higher than OPEC's second-quarter output ceiling of 23.58m. b/d.

During June 1993 oil prices remained below the targeted level of US $21 per barrel that OPEC had sought to achieve by reintroducing—in all but name—the quota system it had abandoned during the 1990–91 Gulf crisis. Nobody involved in the industry believed that the member states would be able to summon sufficient discipline to observe the production ceiling of 23.58m. b/d introduced in February 1993 and extended, in June, to the third quarter of 1993. (In 1993, overall, OPEC production reportedly rose by 2.9%, to an average of just under 25m. b/d, while world oil prices declined by some 30%. In December prices fell to their lowest level for five years as a consequence of OPEC's failure, in late November, to modify the production ceiling of 24.52m. b/d first fixed in September.)

In early July 1994 oil prices were strengthening in response to OPEC's undertaking, made at a meeting of member states' oil ministers in Vienna in mid-June, to freeze production at 24.52m. b/d for the remainder of 1994 and to cancel its regular September meeting. OPEC's decision consolidated a recovery in the price of world crude oil, which had risen by some 25% between the end of March and mid-May 1994. This recovery was in contrast to the trend that had prevailed for most of the previous 12 months. Indeed, OPEC's decision, in March 1994, to maintain production at 24.52m. b/d had led to fears of a collapse in the world price of oil and to speculation that OPEC might take emergency measures if prices fell any closer to US $10 per barrel in the spring and summer.

In late July 1994 prices were firm, owing to OPEC member states' observance of the Organization's combined production quota, and to the loss of some Nigerian supplies after industrial action. During August OPEC producers did not attempt to compensate for the lost Nigerian production by raising their output, with the result that the distance between supply and demand continued to increase, contributing to an increase in the average price of crude oil during the second quarter of the year. During the third week of August the price of the OPEC 'basket' of crudes was reported to have averaged US $16.70 per barrel, about $0.40 higher than one year earlier. At the OPEC ministerial conference, in Bali, Indonesia, in November, the unanimous decision was taken to adhere to the existing level of production of 24.52m. b/d in the hope that this would cause prices to rise towards the desired level of US $21 per barrel. The average price of OPEC crudes in October had been only $15.36 per barrel.

At the beginning of 1995 prices remained firm, despite further evidence of excessive production within OPEC and increased competition from non-OPEC suppliers. In January average OPEC production was estimated at 25m. b/d, while the average price for OPEC crudes was US $17 per barrel, compared with $16 per barrel in December 1994. Prices remained stable in mid-March, but increases achieved since production had been frozen at the beginning of 1995 had been cancelled out by a decline in the value of the US dollar. OPEC production was reported to have risen further, to 25.1m. b/d, in February. In the final week of March prices rose to their highest level that year, owing to a combination of strong demand and uncertainty as to whether the USA would succeed in imposing an embargo on sales of Libyan oil. These factors, combined with reduced production in Iran and Saudi Arabia in March, had by mid-April raised prices to more than $18 per barrel, their highest level since August 1994. At a ministerial meeting held in Vienna in June 1995 OPEC member states chose to retain the production quota of 24.52m. b/d for the remainder of the year.

By July 1995, however, markets for oil were weak, with prices falling to their lowest levels for the year early in the month. Speculation about the future marketing of Iraqi oil was responsible for a further weakening of prices in mid-August, amid predictions that weaker economic growth in the coming months would reduce demand for OPEC oil and that non-OPEC producers would capture most future growth that did occur. The London-based news agency Reuters reported that OPEC production in August was at its highest level for 15 years, averaging 25.72m. b/d. Average OPEC production was thus 1.2m. b/d higher than the quota level of 24.52m. b/d. During January–August 1995 the price of the OPEC 'basket' of crudes averaged US $17 per barrel. At the next OPEC ministerial meeting, held in Vienna in November, it was agreed to maintain production at its current level for a further six months from 1 January 1996.

Stimulated by fundamental factors, demand in the northern hemisphere remained strong during December 1995 and into 1996. Earlier predictions of a sharp decline in prices in 1996 seemed unlikely to be realized during the early part of the year as stocks—especially in the USA—remained low, this factor combining with strong seasonal demand to support prices.

High seasonal demand continued to combine with low stocks to support prices during February 1996, a process reinforced at the end of the month by the conclusion without agreement of a first round of negotiations between Iraq and the UN on the sale of a limited quantity of Iraqi oil. The Iraqi issue continued to influence markets, however. In early March it appeared that Iraq was moving closer to accepting the UN's terms for a resumption of sales, and there was widespread scepticism among observers that OPEC would be able, or indeed willing, to accommodate Iraqi supplies except in the event of a drastic decline in prices. Continued flouting of quotas reportedly caused OPEC production to rise to 26m. b/d in February.

The resumption of Iraqi supplies

On 20 May 1996 the UN and Iraq concluded an agreement whereby Iraq was permitted to sell petroleum to the value of US $2,000m. over a 180-day period in order to finance the purchase of humanitarian supplies and UN operations in Iraq and its northern Kurdish governorates. Predictably, it was Iraq that dominated the OPEC ministerial meeting held in Vienna in June. Despite speculation prior to the meeting that OPEC would act to curb over-production by its members, the production quota of 24.52m. b/d in force during the first half of the year was renewed, with a supplementary allowance of 800,000 b/d required by Iraq to sell, at prevailing price levels, in order to generate the maximum revenue permitted under the agreement with the UN. OPEC production was estimated to have averaged 26m. b/d in May, and in view of this already considerable overproduction it was arguable that the conference had done nothing that was likely to be effective to manage the return of Iraqi supplies.

By the beginning of July 1996 it was clear that there was going to be some delay before Iraqi exports recommenced, the USA having rejected Iraq's proposed procedures in late June. From now almost until the end of 1996 prices rose consistently, mainly but not exclusively in response to the delay in implementing the so-called 'oil-for-food' agreement between Iraq and the UN. OPEC production was estimated to have amounted to 25.64m. b/d in June, some 600,000 b/d above the expanded quota announced that month. OPEC reported that the 'basket' price of member states' crudes had averaged US $18.83 per barrel in the first half of 1996, compared with $16.86 per barrel in the whole of 1995.

US missile attacks on Iraqi targets in early September 1996 raised oil prices to their highest levels since the conflict in the Gulf in 1991. Perceived shortages of heating oil in the USA and Europe began to assume more significance in forecasts of oil price developments for the final quarter of the year, the possibility of shortages in the absence of Iraqi supplies lifting prices to their highest levels for the year in the second week of September. In Europe the price of the Brent reference blend rose above US $23 per barrel. With prices having risen by almost 30% since June, and with many observers indicating the possibility of shortages before the end of 1996, it was no surprise that the revived OPEC monitoring committee, meeting in Vienna in September, decided—despite earlier warnings—to take no action against member states that continued to produce and market oil in excess of their quotas. Prices were supported in early October by continued predictions of a shortage of heating oil in the northern hemisphere in the coming winter months, and by continued forecasts of strong demand in the final quarter of 1996.

The strength of crude oil prices in the second half of 1996 had led some observers to claim that a new trading range, one of US $24–$25, had established itself, compared with that of $15–$20 hitherto regarded as the long-term, sustainable trend. Some 15 months later, by the end of March 1998, world markets for crude oil appeared to be on the verge of collapse. Venezuela, generally considered to be OPEC's most extravagant quotabuster, had been instrumental, together with Saudi Arabia and Mexico, in obtaining the agreement of producers, both OPEC and non-OPEC, to begin to reduce supplies by 1.245m. b/d from 1 April. To many observers this agreement, coming so soon after the formal revision of OPEC quotas in November 1997,

represented a significant step towards a free market in oil. For all its novelty, it was, initially at least, received with indifference by markets, and prices remained doggedly low.

One factor behind the unexpected decline in the price of oil was the resumption, from December 1996, of Iraqi exports for the first time (officially) since the Gulf War of 1990–91. By April 1997 the 'basket' price for OPEC crudes had fallen to about US $16 per barrel, compared to some $24 per barrel at the end of 1996. The imminence of Iraq's return to the market had probably supported prices in the second half—particularly the final quarter—of 1996, since some producers were thought to have prepared for it by restraining output. This, together with lower-than-anticipated output by some non-OPEC producers and low stocks world-wide, meant that prices were at an artificially high level when Iraq's return to the market coincided with mild winter weather conditions in the northern hemisphere to effect an unusually sharp adjustment.

As 1997 progressed it became clear that the resumption of Iraqi exports had introduced an element of volatility into an otherwise stable market. However, the contribution of Iraqi exports to the decline in prices in the first quarter of 1998 may have been exaggerated. The main factor at work then was excess of supply, on such a scale that while the availability of Iraqi exports and the timing of their return to the market could make a bad situation worse, their suspension would do little to bring about any recovery.

Over-production within OPEC

Supplies of crude oil were already regarded as more than adequate before the financial difficulties of some East Asian countries in late 1997 began to be perceived as an economic crisis, reducing world demand for oil. In early and mid-1997 attention focused on the extent of over-production within OPEC. According to the IEA, OPEC production had reached 27.13m. b/d in April 1997, compared with the official quota of 25.03m. b/d. In its mid-year report the IEA referred to the continued strength of demand, led by economic growth in the USA, Asia and Latin America, but nevertheless forecast weaker prices and substantial growth in inventories in the second half of the year, unless there was a significant reduction in OPEC output. At the ministerial conference held in Vienna in June OPEC's response to predictions of steady, weaker prices was to renew its official production quota of 25.03m. b/d for a further six months.

OPEC raises its quota

In view of what happened in early 1998, OPEC's decision, taken at the ministerial conference held in Jakarta, Indonesia, in November 1997, to raise its production quota (for the first time in four years) to 27.5m. b/d from 1 January 1998, was later deemed a misjudgement. Without the benefit of hindsight, however, there appeared to be strong arguments in its favour. The producer states of the Gulf—the principal advocates of raising the quota—considered that in abiding by their quotas (relatively speaking) they were not benefiting fully from growing world demand for oil. They continued to forfeit market share to other OPEC members, especially Venezuela, with apparently fewer scruples about quota observance. At the time of the decision actual OPEC production was already estimated at about 28m. b/d, and was forecast to average some 27.5m. b/d in 1997. The crucial factor left unconsidered was the seriousness of the developing economic crisis in East Asia, the region which in 1990–97 was estimated to have accounted for some 70% of growth in world demand for oil.

In early December 1997 the price of some crudes fell to their lowest level since June, and from the beginning of January 1998 began to decline rapidly. That of Brent, for instance, fell below US $15 per barrel in the first week of 1998, compared with more than $17 per barrel in late December 1997. By mid-January 1998 prices had fallen to their lowest levels for more than three years. Estimated growth in demand for oil in East Asia had by this time been revised downwards by some 300,000 b/d.

At the beginning of February 1998 Iraq began to exert a more negative influence on oil markets, following the announcement of a possible future increase in the value of Iraqi oil exports. Estimates of OPEC production published in the same month suggested that it had increased to more than 28m. b/d in December 1997 and January 1998. By late March oil prices had fallen to their lowest levels for 10 years. Arabian Light, for instance, was trading below US $10 per barrel. On 22 March a plan, initiated by Saudi Arabia, Venezuela and non-OPEC Mexico, was announced to reduce world oil supplies by some 2m. b/d from 1 April 1998. To summarize, the market conditions to which producers were attempting to co-ordinate a response comprised the following factors: forecasts that world production of oil would exceed demand by 1.5m. b/d–2m. b/d in 1998; a possible fall in East Asian demand of more than 300,000 b/d, whereas previous forecasts had predicted it to rise by some 1m. b/d in 1998; mild winter weather conditions in the northern hemisphere, which, together with surplus supplies, had increased fuel inventories at a time when they usually declined, undermining futures prices as well as spot prices; uncertainty as to whether the continuing reintegration of Iraq into world markets would support or weaken prices; the possibility of Iraqi exports approaching 2m. b/d by mid-1998; uncertainty about the level of non-OPEC output; OPEC production estimated at about 2m. b/d in excess of demand in January 1998, and—given the scale of over-production—doubts about the Organization's ability to reduce it.

At a meeting of OPEC oil ministers in Vienna on 30 March 1998 the reductions announced a week earlier were supplemented by further commitments that would bring about a total reduction in world oil production of 1.5m. b/d, to which OPEC would contribute cuts totalling 1.245m. b/d and non-OPEC producers (Mexico, Oman, Norway and Egypt) 260,000 b/d.

Oil prices declined in early April 1998 to the levels prevailing before 22 March. In mid-April, with markets remaining oversupplied, Brent was trading at about US $12.50 per barrel. Prices rose in mid-May as it appeared that OPEC producers were reducing output in line with their agreement. By mid-June 1998, however, the price of Saudi Arabia's marker crude, Arabian Light, was only just above the level it had fallen to in 1986. This was despite the announcement in early June of an agreement between Saudi Arabia, Venezuela and Mexico to reduce production by a further 450,000 b/d from 1 July 1998. Quite simply, the market did not believe that OPEC and its allies would be able to make the new reduction effective, compliance with production cuts agreed in March 1998 being estimated at only about 75%.

Friction within OPEC

At the ministerial conference held in Vienna in June 1998 OPEC agreed to reduce production by a further 1.355m. b/d (to 24.387m. b/d) from 1 July 1998 for a period of 12 months. However, the consensus of opinion among analysts was that this would not be enough to reverse the decline in prices. In mid-August markets remained subject to the burden of very substantial over-supply. On 11 August the price of the September contract of Brent—US $11.55 per barrel—was barely above its lowest level ever. High stocks were the cause of this latest collapse: world-wide, stores were almost full. By the end of August Reuters estimated that OPEC had achieved 90% compliance with the June 1998 agreement, production having averaged 27.11m. b/d in that month. In September, according to the same source, compliance improved further, to 94%, as OPEC production declined to an estimated average of 27m. b/d. However, the market remained largely resistant to OPEC's efforts.

By the time of the next OPEC ministerial conference, held in Vienna in November 1998, there were still no signs that the measures hitherto adopted by the Organization had been—or would be—successful. It had been hoped that the agreements to reduce production concluded earlier in the year would bring about a recovery in prices to US $17–$18 per barrel by November. Instead, they remained below $12 per barrel and there was increasing concern that OPEC would no longer be able to sustain the discipline necessary to continue implementing the cuts in production already agreed, to say nothing of further reductions.

Market calls OPEC's bluff

On the positive side, while prices had not even approached the levels hoped for earlier in the year, they did, by November 1998, appear to have stabilized. Forecasts for demand in 1999 had also improved. The IEA, for example, predicted that it would

rise to an average of 75.6m. b/d, compared with the average of 74.3m. b/d forecast for 1998. Nevertheless, one week before the November ministerial conference, prices sank to their lowest levels of the year, with Arabian Light trading at US $8.28 per barrel. On the opening day of the ministerial conference London futures prices fell to their lowest level—$10.65 per barrel—for 12 years. The ministerial conference was unable to agree to extend for a further six months, to the end of 1999, the production cuts agreed in June 1998. Instead, OPEC undertook to improve compliance with the June agreement, which had been estimated at about 90% in October. The average price of the OPEC 'basket' of crudes had reportedly fallen to $12.71 per barrel during the first nine months of 1998, compared with $18.81 per barrel during the corresponding period of 1997.

High stocks remain key influence

At the beginning of 1999 the key influence on global markets for oil remained the very high levels of crude and products in storage: sufficient, by some estimates, to meet industrial demand for about 60 days during the first half of 1999. OPEC's failure to implement a further reduction in production at the ministerial conference in November 1998 was regarded as another misjudgement, and it was noted that compliance with the cuts in production already agreed had averaged only about 70% up to the end of December. More positively, low prices had led to reductions in non-OPEC supplies, and this was expected to affect stock levels during the second half of 1999.

In January 1999 OPEC's ability to implement reductions already agreed was further called into question. According to Reuters, compliance with existing agreements was only 66% during the month, with production totalling 27.81m. b/d, compared with 27.45m. b/d in December 1998. This, in combination with higher Iraqi production, meant that OPEC's output had fallen only 1m. b/d below the level of production in February 1998 from which the cuts were measured. Continued near-record levels of stocks of crude and products in the industrialized countries of the Organisation for Economic Co-operation and Development (OECD) emphasized the urgent need for further action.

In March 1999 OPEC (excluding Iraq) agreed, at a ministerial meeting in Vienna, to reduce output by a further 1.7m. b/d, to 22.976m. b/d, for a period of 12 months from 1 April 1999. Voluntary cuts in production by non-OPEC Mexico, Norway, Oman and Russia were to consolidate the latest reduction at 2.1m. b/d. Despite the absence of any other alteration to the fundamentally bearish factors that had caused the collapse of world markets for oil from late 1997, the response to this agreement was immediate, with prices rising by some US $3.50 per barrel during the remainder of March 1999. By June it was estimated that OPEC production had declined to an average of some 23.25m. b/d.

The March 1999 undertaking had a dramatic impact on world markets for oil during the remainder of the year and into 2000. By the end of 1999 the price of Brent crude had recovered to almost US $26 per barrel, compared with less than $10 per barrel one year earlier. The average price in 1999 was more than $18 per barrel, compared with only $12.76 per barrel in 1998, the lowest average price recorded in the 1990s. Having brought supply and demand more nearly into equilibrium, the agreement concluded in March 1999 had, in one respect, been a resounding success. It did nothing, however, to restore stability to world markets for oil. By March 2000, as the agreement approached its term, OPEC was confronted with a problem that was precisely the opposite of the one it had faced one year earlier: how to bring about a swift reduction in the price of oil. Prices had risen far beyond what had formerly been considered as the long-term sustainable trading range of $20–$25 per barrel. In mid-July 2000 the Organization remained unable even to establish its new preferred trading range of $22–$28, and found itself the focus of political pressure to raise production more emphatically.

It was generally agreed that the key factor behind the effectiveness of the March 1999 agreement had been an unprecedented degree of compliance by the principal producers. By mid-July 1999, as world oil prices rose to their highest levels for some 20 months, a new discipline was already apparent within OPEC. By October compliance had become the key determinant of markets' upward movements: in March 2000 it was estimated that compliance had averaged 80%–90% over the past year.

One of the principal causes of the collapse in world oil prices from late 1997 had been the very high stocks of crude oil and petroleum products held world-wide. By some estimates these had risen to their highest levels ever in 1998, and in their public statements after March 1999 OPEC representatives focused repeatedly on the level of inventories as the measure of the effectiveness of the March 1999 agreement. At a ministerial meeting held in Vienna in September 1999 OPEC justified its decision to postpone any revision of quotas until early 2000 with reference to the high level of inventories. By early 2000, however, it was clear that inventories had declined substantially as a result of OPEC's production cuts. There was a consensus within the industry that so-called depressive inventories had been eliminated in the third quarter of 1999, and any demurral by OPEC was dismissed as a bluff on the part of an interest group intent on maximizing its revenues. By March 2000 the price of oil had risen above US $30 per barrel: markets were clearly overheating as a result of the rapid decline in stocks.

OPEC's challenge as the ministerial meeting on 27 March 2000 approached was to devise a strategy to bring prices down sufficiently to reduce the threat to global economic growth, while maintaining revenues at the level necessary to meet member states' budgetary requirements. Political pressure on the Organization had begun to intensify. It had been suggested, for instance, that the USA should release crude from its strategic reserve in order to bring down the price of oil.

At the ministerial meeting held in Vienna in March 2000 nine of the Organization's 11 members agreed to increase production by a total of 1.45m. b/d with effect from 1 April, and to review this decision in June. The decision was made at the expense of the unity of purpose that had been responsible for the recovery of oil markets over the previous 12 months. Iran refused to endorse the agreement, but did announce that it would in any case raise its production in order not to forfeit market share. Such an increase by Iran would boost the agreed 1.45m. b/d to 1.7m. b/d, while the London-based Centre for Global Energy Studies (CGES) estimated that 'cheating' would bring about a total increase in production of some 2.1m. b/d. Iraqi production remained constrained by UN sanctions.

By early June 2000, as prices remained above US $30 per barrel, it was clear that OPEC's March decision to increase production had not been effective. Furthermore, although the Organization had undertaken in March to raise production by 500,000 b/d when a 20-day moving average of prices remained above the $22–$28 trading range, it had not implemented its pledge when these conditions prevailed. In response to further political pressure from the USA, and anxious not to encourage increased investment in new, non-OPEC production, OPEC ministers, meeting in Vienna, agreed in June to a further increase in production, of a total of 708,000 b/d. One month later this decision had had no significant effect, and Saudi Arabia threatened unilaterally to increase production by 500,000 b/d unless prices fell below $30 per barrel, thus alienating its partners in the Organization—who complained that such a decision was in violation of previous agreements. On 17 July OPEC announced that it was ready to increase production by a further 500,000 b/d in order to depress prices. This increase was to take effect if prices remained above $28 per barrel for 20 business days from 1 July 2000. There was no immediate positive response by markets to the news of OPEC's revised quota, however, and analysts questioned whether the Organization—excepting Saudi Arabia and the Gulf States—would be able to effect the latest proposed increases in production, since most member states were thought to be already producing at or close to capacity. Under continuing strong pressure from Western governments, OPEC ministers meeting in Vienna on 10–11 September agreed to a further increase in production of 800,000 b/d, bringing total output to 25.4m. b/d effective from 1 October. However, the announcement did little to reverse the upward trend in prices, which continued to reach their highest levels for 10 years. On 22 September the USA announced that it would release some 30m. barrels of crude from its strategic reserve, emphasizing that this was in order to address concerns regarding low domestic and corporate stocks. However, a decline in prices as stocks began to be released was short-lived, as the political crisis in the Middle East which erupted at the end of that month prompted a further series of increases: by 12 October the London Brent price had exceeded $35 per barrel for the first time since 1990, and OPEC came under considerable pressure to announce a further increase in output ahead of its ministerial meeting scheduled for November. On 31 October OPEC made good its pledge to increase production by 500,000 b/d after prices had remained above $28 per barrel for 20 consecutive business days.

OPEC members' heads of state and government convened in the Venezuelan capital on 27–28 November 2000 to commemorate the 40th anniversary of the Organization's foundation. (The summit was only the second in OPEC's history, the first having taken place in 1975.) The 'Caracas Declaration', issued by the summit, included a resolution to promote market stability by developing 'remunerative, stable and competitive' pricing policies in conjunction with implementing a production policy that would secure member states an equitable share of world supply; by strengthening co-operation with non-member oil exporters; and by developing communication between producers and consumers. The host of the summit, Venezuela's President Hugo Chávez Frías, distanced OPEC members from the prevailing high prices, blaming market speculation and high rates of taxation in consumer countries. Having already increased production four times in 2000, by a total of 3.7m. b/d, OPEC ministers meeting in Vienna on 13 November postponed any decision to raise output again until January 2001, thereby fortifying the continued upward trend of prices. This deferral was reportedly prompted by concerns within the Organization that any further increase in supplies might cause prices to decline sharply in the second quarter of 2001. Prices in mid-November remained just below the 10-year peak attained in mid-October, with Brent trading at slightly less than US $34 per barrel. By late November prices had fallen slightly in response to OPEC's earlier increases in production and the release of oil from the US strategic reserve. The effect of these measures was also apparent in a continual rise up to the end of the month in US stocks. A dispute between Iraq and the UN in early November, after Iraq announced that it would henceforth require payment for petroleum exports under the oil-for-food programme in euros rather than in US dollars, had little sustained effect on markets.

In the first week of December 2000 the effect of increased supplies became more marked, with prices falling by more than 10%. The declines occurred in spite of Iraq's suspension of exports in early December as a consequence of a new confrontation with the UN over pricing: Iraq was seeking a lower price for its oil sales, in compensation for which it would require purchasers to pay a surcharge into an Iraqi-controlled account. Although Iraqi oil sales effectively remained suspended for 12 days, prices continued to fall—in total by an average of more than US $6 per barrel—until mid-December, when a limited recovery was attributed to seasonal demand for heating oil. Some OPEC ministers had by this time reportedly begun to give serious consideration to reducing supplies further in early 2001 if prices fell below the $22–$28 trading range. Further declines in prices throughout the remainder of December, to below the lower limit of OPEC's targeted $22–$28 trading range, were attributed mainly to higher stocks world-wide, particularly in the USA.

In response to the sharp decline in prices in December 2000, Saudi Arabia let it be known that it would seek agreement to reduce production by some 1.5m. b/d at OPEC's forthcoming extraordinary ministerial conference in January 2001. However, the task of the conference was widely recognized as a difficult one: how to prevent stocks rising to such an extent that prices would collapse in the second quarter of the year—a decision complicated by a lack of clear evidence to indicate the direction of the US economy, and the realization that reducing production excessively could compound the economic downturn in the USA and thereafter cause prices to collapse. Uncertainty over the likely future level of Iraqi exports had also to be factored into the equation. In the event, OPEC's oil ministers, meeting in Vienna on 17 January, opted to reduce production by 1.5m. b/d, to 25.2m. b/d, from 1 February. OPEC was also reported to be considering the possibility of further reductions in the second quarter of 2001. By late January 2001 OPEC appeared to have assessed market conditions correctly, prices having stabilized at around the targeted level of $25 per barrel. An upward trend in oil prices was maintained until mid-February, when increased stocks in the USA, in combination with renewed concerns about the prospects for the US economy, caused a decline towards the middle of OPEC's targeted trading range.

Another factor behind the relative strength of prices from mid-February 2001 was the apparent growing conviction, expressed at the highest level within OPEC, that it would be necessary to reduce output further, possibly by as much as 1m. b/d, in March in order to prevent a price collapse in the second quarter of the year. Against this, as in January, had to be weighed the possibility that too sharp a reduction would damage the prospects of the US and other Western economies. At the OPEC ministerial meeting held on 17 March in Vienna, it was duly decided to reduce supplies by 1m. b/d, to 24.2m. b/d. This had no immediate supportive effect on prices, however, and within days OPEC had indicated that it would consider a further reduction, if necessary, to support the target price. Prices remained under pressure throughout the rest of the month, with OPEC crudes generally trading at close to the lower limit of the targeted trading range. Depressive factors were a reported increase in US stocks of crude and continued uncertainty about the direction of the US economy.

OPEC's second reduction in supplies, agreed in March 2001, was implemented on 1 April, with no immediately discernible effect. A decline in US gasoline stocks in the first week of April, combined with a sharp reduction in Iraqi exports, did cause prices to strengthen, but they did not begin to approach the target of US $25 per barrel that OPEC's second reduction in supplies of the year was designed to establish as the reference price for the Organization's crudes. By late April, however, prices had risen towards and, briefly beyond, the upper limit of the $22–$28 trading range. They came under renewed pressure in early May after the American Petroleum Institute (API) reported a substantial increase in US stocks of both crude oil and gasoline, and it appeared likely that US summer demand would be easily met. From mid-May, however, an upward trend established itself, and Saudi Arabia indicated that it might now be necessary to raise production in order to prevent subsequent shortages. In the USA, where the price of gasoline had risen to record levels, the new US Administration under George W. Bush had made clear its view that OPEC should raise production in order to counteract recessionary pressure.

By mid-June 2001 prices were approaching US $30 per barrel, following a reported substantial decline in US crude stocks. Another factor was Iraq's decision to curtail exports from early June in protest at attempts to alter the terms of the UN oil-for-food programme. The difficulty of gauging the likely future level of Iraqi exports was cited as an important factor behind OPEC's decision, at an extraordinary conference held in Vienna on 5 June, to defer a possible adjustment to its production level for one month. While noting that stocks of both crude oil and products were at a satisfactory level, that the market was in balance and that the year-to-date average of the OPEC reference 'basket' of crudes had been $24.8 per barrel (i.e. within the targeted trading range), OPEC nevertheless decided to hold a further extraordinary conference in early July in order to take account of future developments.

In late June 2001 OPEC's Secretary-General, Dr Alí Rodríguez Araque, issued a statement in response to criticism that the Organization's determination to maintain 'high' oil prices had contributed to increased inflationary pressure in the global economy. Noting that fluctuations in oil prices have a 'much smaller impact on inflation nowadays than was the case in the 1970s', and that 'economic cycles are a constant in the world's economic system', Rodríguez reaffirmed OPEC's 'commitment to a policy aimed at stabilizing the oil market. With this goal in mind, we have designed our price band mechanism, in order to prevent prices from rising too high and hurting consumers, or from falling too low, making producers suffer'.

At the extraordinary OPEC conference, held on 3 July 2001 in Vienna, ministers once again opted to maintain production at the prevailing level, emphasizing that they would continue to monitor the market and take further measures, if deemed necessary, to maintain prices within the US $22–$28 trading range. The conference appealed to other oil exporters to continue to collaborate with OPEC in order to minimize price volatility

and safeguard stability. Towards the end of the month, as prices declined steadily towards (and briefly below) $23 per barrel, Rodríguez indicated that he was consulting OPEC ministers regarding the possibility of holding a further extraordinary conference early in August—ahead of the next ordinary session scheduled for September. Two days later, on 25 July, OPEC agreed to reduce production by a further 1m. b/d, to 23.2m. b/d, with effect from 1 September; the Organization reiterated that it was retaining the option to convene an extraordinary meeting if the market warranted it (this latest reduction, which had been agreed without a full meeting, had been ratified by oil ministers by telephone). The Organization again expressed confidence that its action in reducing output would be matched by non-OPEC producing/exporting countries, and recognized in particular Mexico's support for its efforts. While there was broad agreement that the production cut would reduce inventories, the consensus remained that demand would also decline in view of the prevailing world economic outlook. The extent of this decline remained the subject of much speculation, with a statement by Rodríguez in mid-July that growth in demand would average 850,000 b/d in 2001 seeking to counter a forecast by the IEA of demand growth averaging 450,000 b/d.

A decline of 1.1% in US inventories of crude oil, reported by the API in late July 2001, apparently indicated that US demand was resisting, for the time being, a deceleration in economic growth, and was cited as the main reason for a recovery in the price of Brent, to US $24.97 per barrel, on 1 August. A further decline of the same order, reported on 7 August, raised the price of Brent to $27.94 per barrel, and that of the OPEC 'basket' of crudes to $24.99 per barrel. Throughout most of the remainder of August declining US inventories of both crude and refined products appeared to suggest a strength of demand that belied pessimistic assessments of US (and global) economic prospects in the near term, combining with anticipation of the reduction of OPEC production by 1m. b/d from 1 September, to support the price of the Brent reference blend and the OPEC 'basket' of crudes.

OPEC's policy at this time of adjusting its production in order to maintain oil prices within a trading range of US $22–$28 per barrel appeared to have been successful, although it had proved more difficult to stabilize prices at OPEC's targeted mid-range reference price of $25 per barrel. The difficulty of fine-tuning the market to such a degree was widely recognized, and, furthermore, OPEC has to balance its common interest with those economies in ensuring that recession does not lead to much lower demand, and consequently much lower prices, for oil with the potential disruption that downside volatility can inflict on its members' economies.

As recently as 1998, for instance, prices averaged only US $12.76 per barrel. Even before the suicide attacks on New York and Washington, DC, on 11 September 2001 prompted speculation that the much-discussed world-wide economic recession could not now be averted—with a further downturn in demand from retrenching Western economies conflicting with fears of disruption to supply from a potential escalation of insecurity in the Middle East region—many analysts were questioning the sustainability of the currently targeted trading range beyond 2002–03.

Leaving other considerations aside, the suicide attacks carried out against US targets in New York and Washington, DC, on 11 September 2001 could hardly have come at a worse time for OPEC, whose ministers, having just begun to implement a cut in production of 1m. b/d, were due to meet on 26 September to assess the direction of markets for crude and fix the level of the Organization's production for the rest of 2001. As the price of Brent rose above US $30 per barrel immediately following the attacks, OPEC's Secretary-General was swift to emphasize the Organization's commitment to 'strengthening market stability and ensuring that sufficient supplies are available to satisfy market needs', by utilizing its spare capacity, if necessary. With the benefit of only very little hindsight, Dr Rodríguez Araque's reassurances seemed curiously irrelevant, for no sooner had the attacks taken place than there was virtual unanimity among commentators that their effect would be to worsen the prospects of the global economy, if not plunge it into recession, causing a considerable decline in demand for oil. The task of assessing the direction of markets for crude was instantly simplified, since any upward movements of US inventories of crude and refined products could henceforth be taken unambiguously to mean (unlike those that had occurred in late August and early September) that demand was falling.

By mid-October 2001 the price of the OPEC 'basket' of crudes had remained below US $22 per barrel—the minimum price the Organization's market management strategy was designed to sustain—since late September, and it was clear that, at the risk of adding to recessionary pressures, OPEC would have to implement a further cut in production if it was to bring the price back into its preferred trading range. In late October Venezuela, Iran, Saudi Arabia, the UAE and non-OPEC Oman all declared themselves in favour of a further cut in production. However, diplomacy undertaken by President Chávez of Venezuela and Saudi Arabia's Minister of Petroleum and Mineral Resources, Ali ibn Ibrahim an-Nuaimi, had apparently made no progress in achieving its objective of persuading Mexico, Norway and Russia, all key non-OPEC producers, to support the Organization's management strategy.

In the first week of November 2001 the price of Brent fell to fractionally above US $19 per barrel, while that of OPEC's 'basket' of crudes declined to $17.56 per barrel. An extraordinary meeting of the OPEC conference convened in Vienna on 14 November observed that 'as a result of the global economic slowdown and the aftermath of the tragic events of 11 September 2001, in order to achieve a balance in the oil market, it will be necessary to reduce the supply from all oil producers by a further 2m. b/d, bringing the total reduction in oil supply to 5.5m. b/d from the levels of January 2001, including the 3.5m. b/d reduction already effected by OPEC this year. In this connection, and reiterating its call on other oil exporters to co-operate so as to minimize price volatility and ensure market stability, the Conference decided to reduce an additional volume of 1.5m. b/d, effective 1 January 2002, subject to a firm commitment from non-OPEC oil producers to cut their production by a volume of 500,000 b/d simultaneously'. The meeting 'welcomed the positive responses expressed by some non-OPEC producers, especially Mexico and Oman, to co-operate in balancing the market'. However, it was widely recognized that the success of a collaboration of the kind envisaged depended on the co-operation of Russia. Prior to the extraordinary meeting in Vienna, Russia had indicated that it would be willing to reduce its production, estimated at more than 7m. b/d, by no more than 30,000 b/d, far less than would be necessary for OPEC's strategy to be effective. It was not until early December that Russia's Prime Minister announced its commitment to reducing its exports of crude by up to 150,000 b/d, and it was uncertain, in any case, whether a reduction of that magnitude could be enforced, owing to the Russian Government's lack of control over the oil industry.

On 18 December 2001 the price of the OPEC 'basket' of crudes fell to US $16.62 per barrel. Thereafter, in December, however, the price recovered, in response to commitments by major non-OPEC producers to collaborate with the Organization by reducing either output or exports. On 28 December, at a consultative meeting of the OPEC conference, convened in Cairo, OPEC confirmed its decision to implement a reduction of 1.5m. b/d in its overall production from 1 January 2002, having received assurances that Angola, Mexico, Norway, Oman and Russia would reduce their output—or, in the case of Russia, exports—of crude by a total of 462,500 b/d. OPEC members agreed to reduce their output as follows—in theory at least, since overproduction by members had compounded the Organization's problems since September 2001: Algeria from 741,000 b/d to 693,000 b/d; Indonesia from 1.2m. b/d to 1.1m. b/d; Iran from 3.4m. b/d to 3.2m. b/d; Kuwait from 1.9m. b/d to 1.7m. b/d; Libya from 1.24m. b/d to 1.16m. b/d; Nigeria from 1.9m. b/d to 1.8m. b/d; Qatar from 601,000 b/d to 562,000 b/d; Saudi Arabia from 7.5m. b/d to 7.1m b/d; the UAE from 2.0m. b/d to 1.9m. b/d; and Venezuela from 2.7m. b/d to 2.5m. b/d. Adherence to these revised quotas would reduce OPEC's total production from 23.2m. b/d to 21.7m. b/d. BP's *Statistical Review of World Energy 2002* noted that for the whole of 2001 the price of Brent had averaged $24.77 per barrel. The average price of the reference blend was substantially less than $20 per barrel in October–December 2001, however. For 2001 as a whole OPEC's production of crude had declined by 720,000 b/d, or 2.7%, com-

pared with 2000, with a fall in Saudi Arabian production of some 350,000 b/d accounting for almost 50% of the total reduction within OPEC. In 2001, for the first time since 1993, consumption of oil world-wide declined, albeit marginally.

In January 2002 the decline in the price of the OPEC 'basket' of crudes was halted for the first time since the suicide attacks of September 2001. According to the Organization's own data, the 'basket' price rose by 4.6% in January 2002, compared with December 2001, but was 24% lower when considered on a year-on-year basis. The price of Brent, meanwhile, averaged US $19.48 per barrel in January. Reviewing the state of the market in January 2002, OPEC noted that it was still too early to assess the reduction in output and exports that had begun on 1 January. The recovery in the average price of the OPEC 'basket' had been uneven throughout the month. Low demand, as indicated by data published by the US Department of Energy's Energy Information Administration (EIA) and the API, recording rises in US crude inventories and either increases or lower-than-expected declines in inventories of distillate products, combined in the second week of January with uncertainty regarding Russia's expressed commitment to reducing its exports by 150,000 b/d to exert pressure on prices. During the third week of January, however, prices were supported, according to OPEC, by the strength of product prices, and by the USA's decision to add 22m. barrels of crude to its strategic reserve. Apparently good adherence by OPEC members to the revised quotas announced in December 2001 was among other factors helping to sustain the upward trend in the final week of January 2002.

In February 2002 the average price of the OPEC 'basket' of crudes rose for the second consecutive month, recording an increase of 3.1% compared with January. As OPEC noted in its review of crude price movements in February, however, the average price of the 'basket' was 25.7% lower when considered on a year-on-year basis. The price of the OPEC 'basket' rose steadily during the first two weeks of February, supported, *inter alia*, by reports of an explosion at oil-gathering facilities in Kuwait that was initially expected to remove some 600,000 b/d from the market; and by increased political tension between the USA and Iraq. In the third week of February the OPEC 'basket' price moved up and down, but, overall, was weaker compared with the previous week. Continued doubts over Russia's commitment to reducing its exports was one element exerting downward pressure on prices. In the final week of the month prices strengthened considerably as a result of the interplay between reportedly higher product inventories, renewed political tension between the West and Iraq, and a dispute between the Venezuelan Government and employees of Petróleos de Venezuela.

In early March 2002 a meeting took place between a delegation of senior OPEC representatives and Russian government and energy officials. OPEC's objective at the meeting was to persuade Russia to continue to limit its exports of crude to 150,000 b/d during the second quarter of 2002. OPEC regarded the continued limitation of Russian exports as imperative if market stability was to be maintained at a time of seasonally weak markets for oil. Russia's initial commitment to reduce its exports, however, applied only to the first quarter of 2002, with any continuation of the restriction subject to a review of market conditions. Norway had, by this time, already agreed to continue to restrict its production of crude to 150,000 b/d during April–June 2002. Moreover, it was clear in March that the market stability measures undertaken since the beginning of the year had been successful. The price of the OPEC 'basket' of crudes rose by 20% in March, compared with the previous month, although it was 5% lower when considered on a year-on-year basis. As OPEC noted in its review of markets for crude in March, prices rose consistently throughout the month. Evidence of economic recovery in the USA was a positive factor in early March—data published by the API indicated declining US inventories of gasoline and distillate products—as was the apparent likelihood of Russia's agreeing to carry over into the second quarter the restriction applied to its exports of crude. In the second week of March an intensification of the conflict between Israel and the Palestinians, and OPEC's announcement that it would maintain production at the prevailing level until the end of June at least, were additional factors that supported prices. In the third week of March prices rose above US $25 per barrel, owing, according to OPEC, to technical factors that were subsequently cancelled out by profit-taking. The upward movement continued towards the end of March, when positive inventory data combined with optimism regarding the sustainability of economic recovery in the USA to support prices.

From late March 2002 the escalating Israeli–Palestinian crisis was cited as a key factor supporting crude prices. On 1 April, for the first time since 11 September 2001, the price of the OPEC 'basket' of crudes rose above US $25 per barrel. On 8 April Iraq added to the increased political tension in the Middle East by suspending its exports of crude for a period of 30 days in response to assaults by Israeli armed forces against Palestinian targets in the West Bank. Although Iraq's action was of little real consequence for crude markets, since other producers could if necessary easily compensate for the loss of its exports, it came at a time when a number of countries, including Iraq itself, Iran and Libya, had expressed their support for an embargo to be placed on the supply of oil by OPEC in support of the Palestinian struggle against Israeli occupation. It was generally acknowledged in April that prices were inflated by a so-called 'war premium' of some $4–$6 per barrel, without which they would decline towards the lower end of OPEC's preferred trading range. Political upheaval in Venezuela also lent a degree of volatility to prices in mid-April, when the brief removal from power of Hugo Chávez caused them to decline sharply. Following Chávez's reinstatement as President, the key market influence for the remainder of the month was the perception, supported by a reported decline in US inventories of crude, that demand for oil was growing in response to improved economic conditions in the USA.

A combination of apparently stronger US demand and tighter supplies was regarded as the most significant determinant of the direction of markets for crude in early May 2002. On 7 May the API announced that US inventories of crude had declined by some 4.5m. barrels in the week to 3 May, and on the day of this announcement the price of the Brent reference blend reached US $27.14 per barrel, an increase of more than $1 per barrel compared with the previous week. Among other factors contributing to the tightening of supplies at this time was OPEC's apparent decision not to compensate for the 30-day suspension of Iraqi exports. In the second week of May prices declined somewhat in response to data published by the US Department of Energy that indicated an increase in US inventories of crude. Towards the end of the month prices weakened again, in response to the publication of data that appeared to cast doubt on the strength of the US economic recovery.

Prices remained under pressure at the beginning of June 2002, owing to the publication of data indicating a further, unexpected increase in US inventories of crude and of distillate products in late May. Iraqi exports had also risen substantially in late May and early June. Most commentators appeared to agree with OPEC, representatives of whose members referred to a balanced market for crude in statements released early in the month, and indicated that OPEC would not alter its production quotas at its forthcoming extraordinary ministerial confer-

ence. In its assessment of the oil market in June, the IEA noted that geopolitical factors (i.e. violence in the Middle East) were now perceived as less of a risk to supplies of crude and predicted that prices would continue to weaken. US inventories of crude and gasoline were reported to have declined slightly in the first week of June. Crude stocks fell again during the second week, but this decline was balanced by substantial increases in inventories of gasoline and distillate products, indicating the ongoing weakness of economic recovery in the USA. At an extraordinary ministerial conference held in Vienna on 26 June, OPEC, as expected, agreed to maintain production at the prevailing level until the end of September 2002. The Organization noted that its 'reduction measures during 2001 and 2002, supported by similar measures from some non-OPEC producers over the first half of the year, had restored relative market balance'. At the same time OPEC observed that 'the relative strength in current market prices is partially a reflection of the prevailing political situation rather than solely the consequence of market fundamentals', and undertook to continue carefully to monitor market conditions and to take further action, if necessary, to maintain market stability. At the extraordinary meeting held in June Alvaro Silva Calderón was appointed as Secretary-General of OPEC, with effect from 1 July 2002 until 31 December 2003. The average price of the OPEC 'basket' of crudes was US $23.80 per barrel in June, compared with $24.76 per barrel in May.

In July 2002 the average price of the OPEC 'basket' of crudes rose by US $1.33 per barrel to $25.13 per barrel. However, in its monthly report OPEC noted that while this was the second highest July average in 1998–2002, the year-to-date average, at $22.57 per barrel, remained lower than that ($24.79 per barrel) of the same period of the previous year. The 'spot' market quotation of the Brent reference blend also increased in July, averaging $25.79 per barrel, compared with $24.04 per barrel in June. These increases occurred in spite of increasingly pessimistic forecasts of world economic growth in 2002. Political tension in the Middle East continued to support prices, especially in the third week of July when, as OPEC noted in its monthly report, US rhetoric regarding Iraq became less compromising.

The price of the OPEC 'basket' of crudes eased in the final week of July and the first week of August 2002, but rose to about US $26 per barrel in the second week of August owing to increased political tension in the Middle East. The threat of US military action against Iraq continued to support prices during the remainder of August and the first two weeks of September. Prior to the OPEC ministerial conference held in Osaka, Japan, on 19 September, Iraq's expressed willingness to allow the return of UN weapons inspectors caused prices to weaken, but they were subsequently supported by OPEC's decision to maintain production at the prevailing level until 12 December 2002, when the conference would meet again to review the market. The conference noted that since its previous meeting in June the average weekly price of the OPEC 'basket' of crudes had stabilized at $25–$27 per barrel and was thus well within the Organization's targeted trading range.

Oil Statistics

CRUDE OIL PRODUCTION[1] (million barrels per day)

	1999	2000	2001
Middle East OPEC:			
Saudi Arabia	8.549	9.115	8.768
Kuwait	2.038	2.169	2.142
Neutral Zone[2]	0.590	0.628	n.a.
Iran	3.552	3.772	3.688
Iraq	2.581	2.624	2.414
UAE	2.299	2.491	2.422
Qatar	0.724	0.796	0.783
North Africa OPEC:			
Libya	1.425	1.475	1.425
Algeria	1.515	1.579	1.563
Other OPEC:			
Venezuela	3.249	3.321	3.418
Nigeria	2.028	2.103	2.148
Indonesia	1.408	1.456	1.410
Other Middle East and North Africa:			
Oman	0.911	0.961	0.959
Bahrain	0.102[3]	0.102[3]	n.a.
Syria	0.584	0.555	0.551
Egypt	0.827	0.781	0.758
Tunisia	0.086	0.080	0.073
Turkey	0.056	0.057	n.a.
Yemen	0.396	0.438	0.458
Other producers:			
USA	7.731	7.733	7.717
Canada	2.604	2.721	2.763
Mexico	3.343	3.450	3.560
Ecuador	0.382	0.409	0.416
Trinidad and Tobago	0.141	0.139	0.135
Colombia	0.838	0.711	0.627
Argentina	0.843	0.811	0.822
Brazil	1.133	1.268	1.337
Brunei	0.182	0.193	0.195
India	0.788	0.788	0.782
Malaysia	0.791	0.791	0.788
Australia	0.577	0.812	0.733
United Kingdom	2.903	2.667	2.503
Norway	3.132	3.347	3.414
Ex-USSR	7.551	8.013	8.652
China, People's Rep.	3.213	3.252	3.308
Gabon	0.340	0.327	0.301
World total (incl. others)	71.832	74.482	74.493
OPEC total	29.368	30.901	30.181

[1] Includes shale oil, oil sands and natural gas liquids.

[2] Shared equally between Saudi Arabia and Kuwait.

[3] Includes production from the Abu Saafa oilfield situated between Bahrain and Saudi Arabia; from 1996 Saudi Arabia agreed to allocate Bahrain all revenue from Abu Saafa.

Source: mainly BP, *Statistical Review of World Energy 2002*.

Conversion factors based on world average crude oil gravity:

1 long ton = 7.42 barrels

1 short ton = 6.63 barrels

1 metric ton = 7.30 barrels

1 barrel = 35 imperial gallons

1 barrel = 42 US gallons

To convert metric tons per year into b/d divide by 50.0

To convert long tons per year into b/d divide by 49.2

**PROVEN PUBLISHED WORLD OIL RESERVES AS AT
1 JANUARY 2002** ('000 million barrels)

	Reserves	Years of production* at 2001 levels
Middle East and North Africa		
Saudi Arabia.	261.8	85.0
Kuwait	96.5	†
Neutral Zone.	5.0	21.8
Iran .	89.7	67.4
Iraq .	112.5	†
UAE .	97.8	†
Qatar .	15.2	55.5
Oman .	5.5	15.8
Bahrain .	0.1	4.0
Syria.	2.5	12.5
Algeria .	9.2	17.6
Libya .	29.5	57.3
Egypt .	2.9	11.1
Tunisia .	0.3	11.6
Yemen .	4.0	24.2
Middle East and North Africa total	724.5	n.a.

	Reserves	Years of production* at 2001 levels
Other leading producers		
Other OPEC		
Venezuela	77.7	63.5
Nigeria .	24.0	30.8
Indonesia.	5.0	10.1
Total OPEC	818.8	76.6
Rest of World:		
USA .	30.4	10.7
Canada .	6.6	8.8
Mexico .	26.9	21.7
Ecuador .	2.1	14.0
United Kingdom .	4.9	5.6
Norway .	9.4	7.8
Ex-USSR.	65.4	21.1
Other Eastern Europe	2.0	n.a.
China, People's Repub.	24.0	19.9
Gabon	2.5	22.8
World total (incl. others)	1,050.0	40.3

* Including crude oil, shale oil, oil sands and natural gas liquids.   † More than 100.

Sources: BP, *Statistical Review of World Energy 2002, Oil and Gas Journal,* December 2000.

Note: Reserve figures are subject to wide margins of error, and there are considerable differences between sources—including oil companies and governments. Proven reserves do not denote 'total oil in place', but only that proportion of the oil in a field that drilling has shown for certain to be there and to be recoverable with current technology and at present prices. Normally recoverable reserves amount to about a third of the oil in place. Because the potential of fields is continually being reassessed in the light of production experience and because the production characteristics of a field can (and often do) change as it gets older, proven reserves figures may sometimes be revised upwards or downwards by quite dramatic amounts without any new discoveries being made. Price rises tend inevitably to increase reserves figures by making small fields or more complex recovery techniques economic.

The only exception to the proven commercially recoverable reserves formula used in this table applies to the ex-USSR figures, which, as reported by *Oil and Gas Journal,* refer to 'explored reserves', which include proven, probable and some possible reserves.

OILFIELDS IN THE MIDDLE EAST WITH RESERVES OF MORE THAN 5,000 MILLION BARRELS

		Year of discovery	Age of principal reservoirs	Estimated reserves ('000 million barrels)
Ghawar	Saudi Arabia	1948	Jurassic	83
Burgan	Kuwait	1948	Cretaceous	72
Safaniyah-Khafji	Saudi Arabia (Neutral Zone)	1951	Cretaceous	30
Rumaila	Iraq	1953	Cretaceous	20
Ahwaz	Iran	1958	Oligocene, Miocene, Cretaceous	17.5
Kirkuk	Iraq	1927	Oligocene-Eocene, Cretaceous	16
Marun	Iran	1964	Oligocene-Miocene	16
Gach Saran	Iran	1928	Oligocene-Miocene, Cretaceous	15.5
Agha Jari	Iran	1938	Oligocene-Miocene, Cretaceous	14
Abqaiq	Saudi Arabia	1940	Jurassic	12.5
Berri	Saudi Arabia	1964	Jurassic	12
Zakum	Abu Dhabi	1964	Cretaceous	12
Manifah	Saudi Arabia	1957	Cretaceous	11
Fereidoon-Marjan	Iran/Saudi Arabia	1966	Cretaceous	10
Bu Hasa	Abu Dhabi	1962	Cretaceous	9
Qatif	Saudi Arabia	1945	Jurassic	9
Khurais	Saudi Arabia	1957	Jurassic	8.5
Zuluf	Saudi Arabia	1965	Cretaceous	8.5
Raudhatain	Kuwait	1955	Cretaceous	7.7
Shayban	Saudi Arabia	1968	Cretaceous	7
Abu Saafa	Saudi Arabia/Bahrain	1963	Jurassic	6.6
Asab	Abu Dhabi	1965	Cretaceous	6
Bab	Abu Dhabi	1954	Cretaceous	6
Umm Shaif	Abu Dhabi	1958	Jurassic	5

Source: *Oilfields of the World,* E.N. Tiratsoo (Scientific Press Ltd).

OPEC CRUDE OIL EXPORT REVENUES, 1991–2001 (US $ '000m.)

	1991	1992	1993	1994	1995	1996	1997	1998	1999	2000	2001
Algeria	8.82	8.25	6.99	6.54	7.23	9.30	8.85	5.68	8.02	13.01	11.04
Iran	14.13	15.16	13.29	13.71	15.24	18.07	16.70	10.79	15.07	25.67	21.79
Iraq	0.28	0.55	0.68	0.64	0.66	0.93	4.71	6.54	11.59	19.60	14.92
Kuwait	0.57	5.78	9.13	10.03	11.51	13.18	12.40	8.04	10.00	17.75	11.44
Libya	10.11	9.47	7.74	7.26	7.90	9.78	9.32	5.98	7.97	13.53	10.96
Qatar	2.68	2.98	2.54	2.44	2.75	3.63	3.90	3.21	4.53	7.99	6.71
Saudi Arabia	44.85	48.04	40.55	40.62	45.69	53.66	51.72	32.85	42.37	72.45	54.90
UAE	14.81	14.51	12.33	12.00	13.04	15.82	15.46	10.07	12.97	22.39	18.04

Source: US Energy Information Administration.

NATURAL GAS IN THE MIDDLE EAST
AND NORTH AFRICA

CHRIS CRAGG

Revised for this edition by SIMON CHAPMAN

The Middle East now accounts for more than 35% of the world's proven reserves of natural gas. With the addition of Algeria, Libya, Tunisia and Egypt, the figure rises to more than 40%. This amounts to 62,740,000m. cu m (excluding Tunisia), according to a 2002 industry survey, but even this figure should be regarded as conservative. The eastern part of the region lies in a trend that most geologists now believe contains the bulk of Eurasia's hydrocarbons. This runs from the Yamal peninsula in Russian Siberia to the Caspian Sea, across the 'fertile crescent' into Saudi Arabia, and across the Red Sea towards Sudan. Proven reserves in the region have more than doubled since 1981. Indeed, since the early 1990s they have increased by nearly 50%, the additional amount alone sufficient for almost nine years of global gross consumption. At current levels of production, proven reserves in the Middle East could last well into the second century of the new millennium, and proven reserves underestimate potential reserves, sometimes by as much as a factor of two.

In spite of huge reserves, natural gas was, until quite recently, an under-utilized resource in much of the Middle East and North Africa. In contrast to oil, it was difficult to export, requiring either large pipeline systems or very expensive conversion into liquefied natural gas (LNG). Since, in terms of volume, oil has a far greater thermal content than gas, gas produced far less reward than oil for a given capital expenditure. Local markets were generally either dominated by oil burning, or else did not exist. As a result, oil companies looking for oil and finding gas shut in the gas and went elsewhere. Where gas was found with oil—'associated' gas—the oil was used and the gas flared. In 1973 Saudi Arabia was flaring as much as 86% of its gross production, and its flare stacks were visible to the early astronauts. Some producers, notably Algeria, Libya and Abu Dhabi, did export by liquefying the gas for European, US or Japanese consumption. Yet this was a formidable technical undertaking, requiring liquefaction plants to cool the gas to −165°C, each costing as much as US $2,000m., and special ships costing over $100m. Constructed in the late 1970s, these plants came into operation at an inopportune moment, since between 1979 and 1982 world gas consumption actually fell. In the USA there was a huge surplus of domestically-produced gas, while in Europe large volumes of Soviet gas from Siberia reached the market. Only Japan, with no resources of its own, remained faithful to its supplier in Abu Dhabi. Much of the extremely expensive Algerian LNG capacity was idle for a time after a series of disputes with US distributors.

Many countries, however, perhaps motivated by this experience, began to realize the value of what was being flared. As a substitute for oil, gas could be burnt in power stations, desalination plants, and wherever heat was required. This, in an era of high oil prices, would free crude for export. As a result, the flaring of associated gas was gradually cut, a process which, in the case of Saudi Arabia, required a major offshore and onshore gathering grid. By 1991 flaring in that country had been reduced to only 6% of total—greatly increased—production. Compared with 1983, when Saudi Arabia used some 4,000m. cu m of natural gas and flared 26,900m. cu m, in 1991 it used 32,000m. cu m and flared only 4,400m. cu m. From 1991 until 1997, when it was overtaken by Iran, Saudi Arabia was the second largest regional producer after Algeria. Saudi Arabian reserves have been boosted substantially by new discoveries in recent years, most notably in 2000. In 2002 Saudi Arabia was engaged in negotiations with international oil companies regarding the development of a major gas production and exploration project, focused on reserves at the Shaybah and South Ghawar oilfields, and potential resources on the Red Sea coast. The total cost of the project has been estimated at US $25,000m.

Iran, too, realized the waste involved in flaring gas and had begun to use reinjection techniques in order to assist the recovery of oil. In 1991, having increased its production of natural gas by 97% since 1983, Iran reinjected into the ground more gas than it had actually been using a decade earlier. In the Middle East and North Africa generally, however, flaring remained high, involving 52,420m. cu m in 1991—an amount almost double Norway's marketed production—compared with 43,840m. cu m in 1980. A sudden increase in 1991 was largely due to events in Kuwait, where the Iraqi invasion and subsequent war brought about the flaring of 96% of total production in that year. Over the same period gross production in the region had increased by 110%. A greater achievement was to have found a commercial use for the gas. In 1991 the Middle East and North Africa used or exported some 179,760m. cu m of natural gas, more than double the level of consumption seven years earlier. Iran, Abu Dhabi, Saudi Arabia, Bahrain, Oman, Egypt, Libya and Qatar have all more than doubled domestic consumption of natural gas since the mid-1980s, water desalination plants, power stations and even town distribution grids having been constructed near where the gas used to be flared. Equally, regional petrochemical and metal industries have increasingly utilized gas rather than oil. By 1991 the Middle East and North Africa had more gas-fired power stations than both Western Europe and North America combined.

The increase in demand for natural gas has not only occurred in the countries that produce it. By 1999 the countries of the Middle East and North Africa were exporting some 77,000m. cu m of natural gas (including LNG), compared with only 2,300m. cu m in the early 1980s. In 1990 Algeria, which had found it difficult to export natural gas in the early 1980s, received orders from Italy, Germany, Yugoslavia, Spain and France and had fully to utilize its previously idle LNG capacity. By 2000 the annual capacity of the Transmediterranean (Transmed, or Enrico Mattei) pipeline to Italy via Libya had risen to more than 25,000m. cu m. To the west, Spain and Morocco had agreed, in the late 1990s, to begin constructing another pipeline to Spain, passing beneath the Strait of Gibraltar (see below). Algerian exports of natural gas had risen to 33,900m. cu m by 1991, compared with about 17,000m. cu m annually in the mid-1980s. Indeed, by mid-1992 European dependency on Algerian supplies had begun to cause alarm, owing to political unrest in that country. Yet, with its rapidly increasing, youthful population, the Algerian Government could not afford to reduce its exports. By late 1996 Algeria was supplying some 25% of gas imported into Europe, and aimed to retain its market share in the face of future competition from Libya, which has supply contracts with Italy, and Egypt, which is emerging as an exporter (see below). In the mid-1990s it was estimated that natural gas would meet about 25% of Europe's energy requirements in 2010, compared with 20% in 1996, of which some 50% would be imported. However, industry figures published in 2002 suggested that this assessment had underestimated growth in Europe's consumption of natural gas, which by 2001 was already reckoned to meet 22.3% of primary energy requirements. In 2000 Algeria supplied about 20% of all gas imported by the European Union (EU). In late 1996 Algeria began to supply gas to Córdoba in southern Spain via the Maghreb–Europe (or Pedro Duran Farrell) pipeline, which runs through Morocco and beneath the Strait of Gibraltar. By 2001 the Maghreb–Europe line was capable of transporting about 8,070m. cu m annually to Spain and Portugal, and in that year more than 60% of Spain's total natural gas requirements were met by Algerian imports. In December 2001 SONATRACH, Algeria's state energy operator, and an international consortium comprising Cepsa and Endesa of Spain, and the French companies TotalFinaElf and Gaz de France, reportedly agreed to proceed with the construction of a third pipeline, the Medgaz line, between Algeria and Europe. Medgaz is expected to connect to the existing south European pipeline at Almería in Spain, and could commence operations as early as 2006. SONATRACH was also reported to be studying, in collaboration with Enel of Italy and Wintershall of Germany, the feasibility of building a fourth pipeline, initially connecting Algeria with the Italian mainland, via Sicily, and then extending to southern France. Currently the two existing pipelines have insufficient excess capacity to cope with rapidly rising demand for gas within the EU. Algerian exports of natural gas totalled about 60,000m. cu m in 1999, and it is planned to increase this to 75,000m. cu m in the short term and 100,000m. cu m in the medium term.

Algeria is actively seeking increased foreign investment in order to share the cost of developing its oil and gas industries, which was forecast at more than US $17,000m. in 1996–2000. At an estimated cost of $1,000m., SONATRACH is developing the Ohanet field—four wet gas reservoirs in Algeria's Illizi province—as a joint venture with, among others, Australian, Japanese and US partners. Production from the field is expected to begin in 2004. SONATRACH has also signed contracts with the French distributor Gaz de France for the marketing (in a joint venture) of some 1,000m. cu m of natural gas annually in the Mediterranean and southern Europe, as well as for the exploration and development of new resources globally. In early 2001 SONATRACH, Gaz de France and Petronas of Malaysia signed an agreement to develop a gasfield in the Ahnet region of southern Algeria, in which total investment may eventually rise as high as $2,000m. Reserves in the Ahnet region have been estimated at 140,000m. cu m. Production from Algeria's In Salah gas development project (In Salah Gas)—where annual capacity is expected eventually to amount to 9,000m. cu m—is expected to begin in mid-2004. Almost all of the gas produced from the project, which encompasses seven of In Salah's 12 fields, will be exported. Foreign participants in In Salah Gas include British Petroleum (BP) of the United Kingdom and Bechtel of the USA.

Algeria is not alone in having come to regard exports of natural gas as a major source of revenue. In the Gulf Abu Dhabi has long been a major supplier of LNG to Japan. Recent initiatives to expand production capacity include the Khuff development project, which aims to exploit a gas reservoir beneath the Abu al-Bakhoosh and Umm Shaif oilfields. In mid-2002 Abu Dhabi Gas Industries Company was seeking to tender management contracts for the third phase of its Onshore Gas Development project (OGD-3), and for the second phase of its Asab Gas Development project (AGD-2). Qatar, which has huge reserves—estimated at 14,400,000m. cu m, 9.3% of total world reserves, at the beginning of 2002—has spent US $3,500m. on constructing an LNG plant and export facilities which include an industrial port (at Ras Laffan), offshore platforms and ships to transport the LNG. This project was completed in 1997 and now supplies almost 6,000m. cu m of natural gas annually, mainly to electricity producers in the Far East, and now Europe, under long-term contracts—although some is also sold on European 'spot' markets. A second LNG project commenced in 1997, as did the expansion of associated petrochemicals programmes. Qatargas aims to raise the annual production capacity of its liquefaction plant as Ras Laffan to 9.2m. metric tons by 2005, as part of an effort to increase Qatar's total production of LNG to 30m. tons annually by 2006. In mid-2001 the Ras Laffan Liquefied Natural Gas Company (RasGas) became the first Gulf-based producer of LNG to conclude a long-term supply contract with a European customer—Edison International of Italy. Under the terms of the agreement, RasGas will supply Edison with 3.5m. tons of LNG annually in 2005–30. RasGas is currently constructing a third export train at its Ras Laffan complex, in order to meet a commitment to supply Petronet LNG of India with 7.5m. tons of LNG annually. Meanwhile, the Dolphin gas project, which involves the construction of a submarine pipeline to supply some 60m. cu m of Qatari gas daily to the UAE, at an estimated total cost of $3,500m., is scheduled for completion in 2005. The Dolphin project is also intended to supply Oman and, eventually, Pakistan. Oman LNG supplies LNG to customers in Japan and the Republic of Korea. In 2001 the company concluded a contract to supply customers of the

Royal Dutch/Shell Group in Spain with 700,000 tons of LNG annually for five years. In mid-2002 the Omani Government was reportedly assessing the feasibility of a project to construct a third LNG train, with a view to exporting to destinations in Europe, Asia and the USA. However, the project, which would raise Oman's LNG capacity—currently 6.6m. tons annually—by 50%, will not proceed without the prior commitment of foreign buyers to purchase the gas.

The development of Iran's South Pars field began in 1993, but has not proceeded smoothly owing to the huge cost of the project and to obstructive US legislation that penalizes companies investing in Iran. The field is being developed in 25 phases—each costing some US $1,000m.—over 25 years, and by August 2000 contracts had been awarded for the first eight phases. Iran's reserves of natural gas are second only to those of the former USSR, and are regularly boosted by new discoveries. The South Pars field alone accounts for about 30% of Iranian and about 7% of world reserves. The Government is keen to develop exports of natural gas, and has committed itself to a substantial export programme that began in mid-2001. At that time plans were announced to implement the so-called IGAT-4 project to complement Iran's gas transportation network. If deemed feasible, IGAT-4 will ultimately involve the pumping of greater quantities of gas northwards from the offshore South Pars and onshore Tabnak fields for possible export to Turkey, Europe and the Far East. Iranian domestic demand still uses only a tiny fraction of potential production, although in 2001 consumption outstripped actual production. In 1998 Iran began to seek new foreign investment in its hydrocarbons sectors, including its gasfields, generally on a 'buy-back' basis. Production of natural gas increased by 0.6% in 2001 to 60,600m. cu m.

It is possible that plans to transport Iranian natural gas to India and to Pakistan will be realized in the early years of the 21st century. In October 2000 BG International of the United Kingdom was reported to have established a joint venture with Oil Industry Engineering & Construction Company of Iran in order to develop facilities for the export of LNG to Gujarat state in north-west India. If constructed, the plant is expected to utilize all of the gas from any one phase of the South Pars field and, on completion, to have an annual capacity of 6m.–7m. metric tons. The question of constructing pipelines in the opposite direction is more complex politically, but Iran's ambitions have been boosted by the disintegration of the USSR. The USSR achieved its export links with western Europe with a system that took little account of the real investment costs of the very long Siberian pipelines. These pipelines, and the reserves that filled them, were in poor condition, but the construction of new capacity was likely to be extremely expensive. The collapse of the communist system freed Eastern European countries and the republics of the former USSR to seek alternative suppliers of fuel. Iran now has two options for expanding its sales of natural gas in Europe. It can either conclude agreements with Turkey, or it can enter Eastern Europe through Ukraine. In May 1997 Iran, Turkey and Turkmenistan agreed on plans to export as much as 30,000m. cu m of Turkmen gas to Turkey via Iran. This was in addition to plans to connect Turkey and Turkmenistan to the Iranian gas pipeline system. In August 2000 Iran and Turkey signed an agreement under which Iran would supply Turkey with 228,000m. cu m of natural gas over a 25-year period, commencing in July 2001.

If Iran appears likely to become a major exporter of natural gas in the 21st century, then the underlying reason is the increasing importance of gas to the global economy. Growth in world consumption has remained fairly steady (although a slight decrease was recorded in 1997) and 2,164.3m. metric tons of oil equivalent were consumed world-wide in 2001, compared with 2,157.5m. tons in 2000. The market for natural gas, in terms of energy equivalence, is approaching two-thirds of the size of that for crude oil. Gas has a number of advantages over oil in an era of environmental concern. In contrast to coal or oil, gas produces less carbon dioxide on combustion and generally contains less sulphur. Any carbon tax thus discriminates against gas rather less than it does against rival fuels. In addition, the use of gas for generating electricity has greatly increased and will continue to increase because the fuel can be used in combined-cycle turbines. Such turbines generate power with a 50% rate of efficiency, compared with the 34% generally achieved by standard, single-cycle oil- or coal-fired power stations. The International Energy Agency (IEA) forecast that the consumption of gas for power generation alone would increase from 32,000m. cu m in 1989 to at least 81,000m. cu m by 2000. Apart from nuclear energy, gas is the fuel best suited to this process. Natural gas is also a major petrochemical feedstock. With environmental awareness growing, the region has quickly realized the value of gas for production of methanol and, from it, methyl-tertiary-butyl ether (MTBE). With the search now on for cleaner fuels, methanol itself may one day become an important vehicle fuel and it requires a gas feedstock.

As the role of Middle Eastern gas in world trade has grown, increasing exporters' revenues, countries with smaller reserves have developed them to make a significant contribution to domestic requirements. Compared with Iran's resources, Jordan's reserves are minute, but gas from the al-Lisheh region now supplies more than 15% of Jordan's electricity. In Syria local supplies have rapidly been put to use for the production of electricity; future projects include the construction of a pipeline to transport gas from the newly developed Palmyra fields in order to supply a new 1,000-MW power station at Aleppo. In Egypt, in the western desert, offshore of Alexandria and in the Red Sea, small fields have all yielded quantities that would probably not have been developed in the Gulf region. These are now used to supply industry and the Cairo gas distribution system. Since the mid-1980s pipeline development has doubled Egyptian consumption, but diligent exploration has discovered sufficient natural gas to produce a healthy reserves-to-production ratio—47.5 years at the beginning of 2002. By late 1996 most Egyptian power stations were gas fired, and in 1997–98 an exportable surplus became available when new fields north of the Nile Delta commenced production. In late 2000 four projects to export LNG were under way. One of these involves Unión Fenosa of Spain, which is constructing two LNG trains, each with an annual capacity of 4,000m. cu m, at the Egyptian Mediterranean port of Damietta. Another, to construct an LNG export complex at Idku, near Alexandria, and to develop gasfields to supply it, is being undertaken by Egyptian LNG, in which BG International of the United Kingdom and Italy's Edison International each have a 35.5% share. In 2002 Gaz de France committed itself to purchasing all of the output from the first train at the Idku complex, thereby boosting Egypt's ambition to become a significant global exporter of natural gas. Egypt has also announced plans to construct a submarine export pipeline from el-Arish to Ceyhan in Turkey, with, possibly, branches connected to Israel and Lebanon. In early 2001 the Israel Electric Corporation entered into negotiations with East Mediterranean Gas, an Egyptian-Israeli joint venture, with a

view to concluding a supply agreement for its natural gas requirements over a 15-year period. In December 2000 Egypt, Syria and Lebanon were reported to have signed a memorandum of understanding for the construction of a regional gas pipeline costing an estimated US $1,000m. Lebanon has announced its intention to import some 9m. cu m of gas daily from Egypt and a further 3m. cu m daily from Syria. In early 2002 a contractor was being sought to undertake the construction of a transmission pipeline linking Egypt with Jordan, at a cost of $300m. In mid-2001 Egypt agreed to supply Jordan with about 1,000m. cu m of gas annually from 2003. However, the new pipeline's total capacity will also permit future exports to Syria, Lebanon and Cyprus. At the end of 2001 Egypt's proven reserves of natural gas totalled 1,000,000m. cu m. Libya has proven reserves of natural gas that are comparable in size with those of Egypt. Libya's reserves-to-production ratio was estimated at more than 100 years at the beginning of 2002, and, in fact, production declined in 2000, although it is not unusual for Libyan output to fluctuate slightly. In 2002 Libya's National Oil Corporation (NOC) and Eni of Italy were engaged, as Agip Gas, in a $4,500m. venture, the Western Desert gas project, to supply some 8,000m. cu m of gas to European markets annually, from 2005, via the Greenstream pipeline to Sicily, currently under construction.

The importance of natural gas to the future of the Middle East and North Africa has thus increased enormously since the early 1970s. A new appreciation of the fuel as clean-burning has created potential demand that has been seen to be a major element in the region's development. In recognition of this, a new spirit of co-operation has developed. Unlike crude oil, the production of which is controlled by OPEC and thus dominated by the politics of oil pricing and the organization's internal disputes, gas diplomacy is largely free of past East–West recriminations. The development of reserves, pipelines, liquefaction units and power plants in the region is being aided by Western multinational companies—Royal Dutch/Shell Group, Total-FinaElf, Agip, BG International and others—while Japanese trading groups such as Mitsui and Mitsubishi have also established a foothold in the industry. Gas remains a capital-intensive business, and external assistance is required in both the financial and technical spheres. Gas supply is a central element in the Gulf Co-operation Council's plans for economic development. Iran trades with its northern neighbours. Trade in natural gas with Europe has made a major contribution to Algeria's economic development, and one which has been mutually beneficial. Despite their apparent vulnerability to civil commotion, the long gas pipelines that are beginning to spread across the region and on into Europe have become links that the beneficiaries are reluctant to break.

GAS: RESERVES AND PRODUCTION
(t.c.m. = trillion cu metres)

Country	Reserves 1 Jan. 2002 (t.c.m.)	Production 2001 (m. tons oil equivalent)
Saudi Arabia	6.2	48.3
Kuwait	1.5	8.6
Iran	23.0	54.5
Iraq	3.1	n.a.
UAE	6.0	37.2
Qatar	14.4	29.3
Libya	1.3	4.9
Algeria	4.5	70.4
Nigeria	3.5	12.1
Indonesia	2.6	56.6
Venezuela	4.2	26.0
Ecuador	0.1	n.a.
USA	5.0	499.9
Canada	1.7	154.8
Mexico	0.8	31.3
United Kingdom	0.7	95.2
Norway	1.3	51.7
Netherlands	1.8	55.2
Italy	0.2	13.9
Germany	0.3	15.3
Russian Federation	47.6	488.2
Asia Pacific (excl. Indonesia)	9.7	195.4
World total (incl. others)	155.1	2,217.7
OPEC total	70.3	347.9
OPEC % World total	45.3	15.7

Source: BP, *Statistical Review of World Energy 2002.*

Notes: Figures in the Reserves column are for gas recoverable with present technology and at present prices. Figures for reserves of gas—like reserves of oil—may be subject to wide margins of error.

Definitions: Natural gas may be found on its own ('unassociated' gas) or with oil ('associated' gas). 'Associated' gas exists partly as a gas cap above the oil and partly dissolved in oil—it is the presence of gas under pressure in new oil fields which drives the oil to the surface. 'Associated' gas is unavoidably produced with oil and may be flared, reinjected or used as fuel.

Natural gas is a mixture of numerous hydrocarbons and varying amounts of inert gases, including nitrogen, carbon dioxide and sulphur compounds. (Gas containing large quantities of sulphur is know as *sour* gas; gas without sulphur is *sweet* gas.) By far the biggest component of all natural gas by volume (at least 75%) is methane, CH_4. Other components are ethane—C_2H_6, propane—C_3H_8, and butane—C_4H_{10}. All of these hydrocarbons are gases at normal temperatures and pressures. Suspended in the gas are various heavier hydrocarbons, pentane (C_5H_{12}), octane etc., which are liquids at normal temperatures and pressures. Gas with a relatively high proportion of propane, butane and the heavier hydrocarbons is known as *wet* gas. 'Associated' natural gas tends to be wetter than 'unassociated' gas.

Methane is the normal pipeline natural gas used for domestic and industrial purposes. It liquefies at very low temperatures (−160°C) and very high pressures, and in this condition is known as *liquefied natural gas,* LNG.

Ethane is either kept with methane and used as a fuel, or is separated and used as a feedstock for petrochemicals production. Ethane is not traded on its own internationally.

Propane and butane are used as cylinder gases for a large number of industrial and domestic purposes—camping gas and cigarette lighter gas is either propane or butane. The two gases liquefy at higher temperatures and lower pressures than methane. In their liquid state they are known as *liquefied petroleum gases*—LPGs.

Pentane and other heavier liquids are used for a variety of purposes, including the spiking of heavy crude oils and as petrochemical feedstocks. These hydrocarbons, liquid at normal temperatures and pressures, are known as *natural gasolines* or *condensate.*

Together, liquefied petroleum gases and natural gasolines are referred to as *natural gas liquids*—NGLs.

NATURAL GAS CONSUMPTION
(millions of metric tons of oil equivalent*)

	1999	2000	2001
USA	559.6	582.4	554.6
Canada	65.4	69.8	65.4
Mexico	30.4	31.4	30.4
North America Total	655.4	683.6	650.4
Belgium-Luxembourg	13.3	13.4	13.2
Netherlands	34.1	35.3	35.3
France	33.9	35.7	36.6
Germany	72.1	71.5	74.6
United Kingdom	83.2	86.4	85.9
Romania	15.5	15.4	15.8
Europe Total	399.9	412.9	423.0
Middle East	163.5	173.4	181.3
South and Central America	78.8	83.7	87.2
Africa	45.1	50.0	54.1
Australia	17.8	19.1	20.3
Japan	67.1	68.6	71.1
Former USSR	480.6	492.3	493.6
China, People's Republic	19.3	22.1	24.9
World Total	2,069.2	2,157.5	2,164.3

* One metric ton of oil equivalent = 1,120 cu m of gas.

Source: BP, *Statistical Review of World Energy 2002.*

ISLAMIC BANKING AND FINANCE

RODNEY WILSON

Revised for this edition by the Editorial staff

The development of modern commercial banking has been relatively slow in the Middle East and, even today, many people do not use banks. To some extent this reflects the historical underdevelopment of the region as, for ordinary people, the monetization of transactions has been a relatively recent phenomenon. In other Third World societies there were no moral objections to the replacement of barter with cash and credit transactions. Due to the Islamic code of ethics, however, there has been popular resistance to modern financial developments in many parts of the Muslim world, including the Middle East. Saudi Arabia, for example, did not issue its own banknotes until the 1960s, as before then gold and silver coins were the major instruments for transactions. Although most people no longer regard paper money as being un-Islamic, the use of cheques, commercial bank credit and other banking instruments were for many years viewed with suspicion by many devout Muslims.

Arab-owned commercial banks were only founded in the Middle East in the 1920s, the first being Banque Misr of Egypt and the Arab Bank, a Palestinian institution. Most financial activity up until then was handled by foreign banks, and even banks such as the Ottoman Bank or the National Bank of Egypt were foreign-owned. As these banks were largely involved in trade finance or arranging government loans, they were not dealing directly with ordinary local Muslims. In any case, trade was often in the hands of non-Muslims; the Egyptian cotton trade, for example, being largely handled by foreigners resident in Alexandria. Hence, banks were regarded as institutions serving infidels, and not organizations with which the devout Muslim should become involved. This attitude has persisted, and despite the development of indigenous commercial banking, it tends to be only the more Westernized elements in Muslim societies that use modern banking services.

Principles of Islamic Finance

Perhaps the most widely known tenet of Islamic finance in the West is the prohibition of *riba*. What constitutes *riba* has long been the subject of debate among Islamic scholars. Some believe that *riba* refers to usury, and make a distinction between this and the (lawful) earning of profit (*ribh*), whereas others believe that all interest is *riba*. Certainly, one Muslim objection to interest payments is on the grounds of equity. It is the poor and needy who are often forced to borrow, whereas the rich have surplus funds to save. Interest thus penalizes the poor and benefits the rich. To the devout Muslim this is anathema, as it results in hardship and increasing social polarization. Such practices could not be tolerated in a community of believers.

A further objection to interest is that it corrupts the recipient. It is viewed as an unearned income, a reward without productive effort. Interest can be a deterrent to honest toil, as it may be tempting to rely on unearned income rather than working for a wage or salary. Western neo-classical economics sees interest as a reward for waiting or deferring consumption until a future time. The Protestant ethic which underlies Western capitalism regarded saving as virtuous. Time is treated as a type of commodity by Western economists, which has a price. There is believed to be a trade-off between earnings and leisure, and wages are a reward for forgoing leisure. Muslim scholars reject such notions. The just wage reflects the workers' contribution to society, not the time spent working. Time itself is valueless. Hence there can be no justification in a reward for time.

To the devout Muslim abstinence needs no material reward. The earth's bounty is to be used, but Allah demands certain sacrifices, such as fasting during the month of Ramadan. The rewards for such abstinence are spiritual, and the introduction of monetary incentives would only undermine the spiritual value of such practices. Furthermore, an incentive for saving may result in underconsumption, and a lack of effective demand in the economy. Hoarding is viewed as socially undesirable in Muslim societies, as it can result in unemployment and idle

capacity. In this sense Muslim ideals are consistent with Keynesian views on economic management. Currency must circulate, and the accumulation of the means of exchange for its own sake is seen as undesirable. In the view of Muslim economists, capitalism does not achieve the right balance. Too much power is vested in the suppliers of capital; and the loanable fund market is distorted. A market system is viewed as natural: it is capitalism that is unnatural.

Application of Islamic Ideals

Although there is little disagreement over the principles of Islamic finance, the interpretation of the prohibition of *riba* in practice has been subject to much greater controversy. Should the prohibition apply to all interest, or does it merely mean that interest rates should be constrained at moderate levels? Are interest charges for business loans permissible, as the borrowers are seeking to use their credit to generate profits? Are fixed-interest loans preferable to those subject to interest-rate variations, as at least the borrower knows the exact charges in advance, and there is no element of uncertainty? Finally, under inflationary conditions, should interest rewards be allowed to compensate savers for the depreciation of the value of their savings? A prohibition of nominal interest to compensate for inflation would penalize lenders and subsidize borrowers. It could be argued that the prohibition of *riba* applies to real interest, not nominal interest, as with inflation a ban on the latter may result in negative real interest.

Most Islamic states in practice have tried to restrain nominal interest rates. As inflation results in social strains in any Muslim community, and also poses moral dilemmas, the control of price increases has been an important economic priority for Muslim governments. In the Middle East inflation has been a major worry most persistently in Turkey, and until the early 1990s was a cause of concern in Lebanon, Iran, Egypt and Syria. The consequences of inflation for nominal interest rates appalled the majority of devout Muslims. Double-figure nominal interest rates became all too prevalent in these countries, and even where action against price rises has succeeded problems can remain. As there are some lags in adjustment, it is possible to have high real rates, especially as inflation starts to fall.

Some states, such as Saudi Arabia, have a prohibition on all interest payments and receipts under their Islamic laws. Arrangement fees and service charges are permitted, however, on bank loans, and in practice, as they are calculated on a percentage basis, they resemble interest in many respects. The service charges are fixed, however, and hence borrowers are not subject to the uncertainty over the future costs of debt-servicing which arises when interest rates vary. In Saudi Arabia most bank deposits are in current accounts which earn no income, but even deposits in savings accounts only earn a modest fixed return, not an interest receipt.

Modern Islamic Banking

In Islamic states where commercial banks are free to charge and receive interest, many Muslim businessmen felt obliged to participate in *riba* transactions, even though they felt a moral guilt in doing so. To overcome this dilemma of conscience, specifically Islamic banks were founded which could compete with conventional commercial banks but which adhered to Islamic principles. The movement was started in Pakistan in the 1950s, but soon spread to the Arab world, with the opening of the Mitr Ghams Savings Bank in Egypt in 1963, which later was superseded by the Nasser Social Bank. The impact of these institutions was modest, as the major state-owned banks continued to account for most of the banking business in Egypt. Nevertheless, the Nasser Social Bank attracted deposits from an influential group of pious farmer landlords, and backed some significant agro-industrial ventures.

It was, however, the devout Muslim merchants of the Gulf who were largely responsible for the subsequent rapid expansion of Islamic banking. These conservative merchants were reluctant to use the services of conventional commercial banks yet, with the rapid business expansion in the Gulf following the oil price rises of 1973–74, some type of financial intermediation was clearly needed. Institutions such as the Dubai Islamic Bank (founded 1975), the Kuwait Finance House (KFH—1977), and the Bahrain Islamic Bank (1979) were established to serve such clients, while at the same time avoiding *riba* transactions. There was some government encouragement, with the states taking a minority shareholding in each of the institutions, but most of the finance came from the merchants themselves, especially in the case of the Dubai Islamic Bank which was 80% privately owned.

The Islamic banks in the Gulf account for around 10% of total bank deposits. Although their role in Gulf finance is modest, the banks' market penetration is considered a success, given that they represent a new type of institution adopting innovative financial techniques. Although there have been set-backs, notably as a result of dealings in precious metals, the track record of the Islamic banks has been favourable so far, and the returns to investors have been competitive with those offered by more conventional banks. As most deposits are of modest amounts, the total number of depositors is higher than their share of total deposits indicates. Many customers maintain accounts with both the new Islamic banks and conventional commercial banks. In this sense the Islamic banks complement rather than replace conventional banks. Nevertheless, the ultimate objective for the Islamic banks is to provide a comprehensive range of banking services as a complete alternative to *riba* finance.

In terms of domestic market penetration, KFH has enjoyed particular success, accounting for almost one-fifth of total bank deposits in Kuwait. Its activities are more diverse than those of the commercial banks in Kuwait, as it is heavily involved in housing loans and car-purchase financing, in addition to trade and commerce. The extent of its involvement in real estate means that, in many respects, it resembles a building society. Islamic services are provided in a modern fashion, with computerized accounts, fully automatic telling facilities and even Islamic debit and credit cards. During Iraq's occupation of Kuwait in 1990–91 KFH refused to remain open for business, unlike other Kuwaiti banks. Following the country's liberation, KFH reopened, having gained much respect by its refusal to collaborate with the Iraqis in any way. KFH reported net profits of some US \$172.5m. in 2001, an increase of some 10% compared with 2000.

In Saudi Arabia there has been considerable support for Islamic banking, even though the Kingdom had no specifically Islamic banks until recently. As all banks in Saudi Arabia are supposed to operate according to Islamic principles, the Saudi Arabian Monetary Agency saw no need to license a specially designated Islamic bank. Indeed it was thought that granting such a licence would place the commercial banks in an invidious position. Hence the only Islamic financial institution in the Kingdom was the Jeddah-based Islamic Development Bank (IDB), but this is a development assistance agency, and not a bank dealing with the general public. Its principal aim is to provide *riba*-free finance for Islamic countries, especially those with low per caput income levels.

Money-lenders as Islamic Banks

Many Saudi citizens do not maintain accounts with the commercial banks in the Kingdom. Instead they resort to money-lenders and money-changers for their financial requirements. Some of these informal bankers offer a wide range of financial services, including the exchange of currency, the handling of overseas remittances, deposit facilities and loans. Interest is not earned on loans, which are often in kind rather than cash. For example, if a client needs some item of equipment, the money-lender will usually purchase it on behalf of the client, and then either collect instalments from the client, or else enter a leasing arrangement. In either case the payments over a period will exceed the initial cost of the item, the difference representing the money-lender's profit.

One Saudi Arabian money-lending and money-changing family, the ar-Rajhis, has grown to become one of the largest commercial financial institutions in the Kingdom. In 2001 Ar-Rajhi Banking and Investment Corporation's assets amounted to SR 51,742m., an increase of 6.3% compared with the previous year. The bank's profitability owes much to its substantial non-interest-bearing deposits. All of the business has been built up on the basis of *riba*-free transactions. In 1983 there were pressures on the ar-Rajhis to register as a commercial bank, as, unlike the other banks, they did not hold reserves with the Saudi Arabian Monetary Agency and were completely unregulated. Rather than register as a conventional commercial bank, the ar-Rajhis decided to seek Islamic banking status, as they claimed their business methods conformed to Koranic principles in any case.

There was some hesitation on the part of the Saudi Arabian Monetary Agency, given the implications for the other banks and the problems in acting as a lender of the last resort for this type of financial institution. In the end, however, the Saudi Arabian Monetary Agency decided to license the ar-Rajhis officially in 1985 as deposit-takers and exchange dealers, largely in order to help safeguard the stability of the domestic financial system. In 1988 the ar-Rajhis decided to increase their capital base by becoming a public company and sold one-half of their shares outside the family. Although the Monetary Agency is not obliged to act as lender of the last resort with respect to institutions such as the ar-Rajhis, it is widely believed that it would if the need arose. It is only the unregistered money-changers, who refuse to submit properly audited annual accounts, that lie outside the Monetary Agency's protective net. With the registration of the money-lenders as Islamic banks, the Monetary Agency has conceded that Islamic financial principles can be interpreted in different ways. Plurality exists as both the conventional commercial banks and the money-lenders claim to conform with Islamic principles, even though their methods of operation differ considerably.

Islamic Banks in International Markets

Prince al-Faisal as-Sa'ud of Saudi Arabia is one of the leading activists in the Islamic banking movement. Although he has not established a domestic banking operation within Saudi Arabia, he was the prime instigator of the Faisal Islamic Banks of Egypt and Sudan, both of which were founded in 1977. Both banks received some local deposits, but much of their funds for lending came from Saudi Arabia. Hence, in this sense, the institutions represented a vehicle for the intra-regional diversion of petroleum revenue to less affluent Muslim states. Prince al-Faisal as-Sa'ud, however, decided that it would be desirable to have an Islamic banking presence in Western financial markets. It was felt necessary to provide some mechanism whereby investors from Saudi Arabia and elsewhere in the Gulf could participate in Western markets on the basis of *riba*-free transactions. Consequently Dar al-Maal al-Islami (DMI), the House of Islamic Funds, was founded in Geneva, Switzerland, in 1981, with a paid-up capital of US \$316m.

Despite some initial problems, and losses during the 1983/84 financial year, DMI seems to have established a sound deposit base, and is widening its lending and investment activities. The major difficulty has been to identify *riba*-free projects to back profitably in Western markets. There is no objection to dealing with institutions that participate in *riba* transactions, however, as long as the Islamic institution is not directly involved, though in the longer term it is hoped to avoid such dealings. In practice, DMI functions as a kind of investment company, deploying most of its funds in equity markets and in property, though it also holds short-term assets in the form of cash and commodities. It is the appropriate choice of liquid financial instruments that has caused greatest difficulty, as Islamic institutions cannot hold government bills or bonds which yield interest.

Constraints in Secular Societies

Problems inevitably arise when Islamic financial institutions operate in a non-Islamic environment. As the Islamic banks do not hold Western government securities as part of their liquid assets, they cannot be registered in Western Europe or the USA as fully-fledged commercial banks. Commodity holdings are not recognized as liquid assets, and the maintenance of a large proportion of non-earning cash reserves would substantially reduce the banks' returns on their assets. One possible solution in the West is to act as a kind of building society, lending to Muslims for house purchases.

The Bank of England has been reluctant even to register the Islamic banks as licensed deposit-takers, largely owing to their inability to provide a guaranteed rate of return on deposits and a perceived opacity of transactions and procedures, and those operating in the United Kingdom are regarded as investment companies rather than banks. The lack of banking status has drawbacks. Islamic institutions cannot solicit for deposits from Muslim investors who reside in the United Kingdom, nor can they carry out normal banking operations. The Islamic financial institutions in London are mainly engaged in the finance of Euro-Arab trade. Clients of British banks exporting to the Islamic world are often referred to Islamic institutions in London. One new development has been for Western commercial banks to offer Islamic financial services to their Muslim clients. The Union Bank of Switzerland, for example, offers an Islamic investment fund. The Saudi International Bank in London offers Islamic trade finance and is also offering Islamic portfolio management services for clients of substantial means. The United Bank of Kuwait has opened a specialized Islamic Investment Banking Unit in London. Citibank has offered Islamic banking services since 1994, its Bahrain branch being the centre for these activities.

Indebtedness and Shari'a Law

Sudden fluctuations in the world price for oil can result in vulnerable loan agreements and the creation of bad debts. Many borrowers argue that they should not be liable for interest payments when they fall into debt. The *Shari'a* courts have usually sided with the debtors rather than with the banks, and in Saudi Arabia there is some doubt if even service charges can be legally enforced.

In the United Arab Emirates the courts have ruled that simple interest is permissible, but that borrowers are not liable for compound interest payments. As *Shari'a* law does not follow case precedent, there is much confusion about the situation. Commercial banks operating in the Gulf are increasingly reluctant to take debtors to court, and many are trying to reach out-of-court settlements by granting payment moratoriums. Rolling over credits is regarded as preferable to writing down the value of bank assets.

In order to avoid problems of this kind in the future the commercial banks in Saudi Arabia are now offering Islamic finance. Some, including the Kingdom's largest bank, the National Commercial, have opened separate branches for women, a move favoured by some Islamic theologians, who advocate the sexual segregation of finance in accordance with Islamic inheritance laws. The National Commercial Bank has also opened new Islamic branches, and converted some existing branches to Islamic branches. By 2001 more than 60 of its 257 branches had been 'Islamized'. This is partly in response to clients' wishes, but also because, in the event of repayments failure, restitution can be more easily sought through the courts. Trade credit is granted through resale and leasing arrangements, and the profit-sharing principle covers medium- and long-term finance. It seems likely that an increasing proportion of commercial banking business in the Gulf will be 'Islamized', even though it requires much more work by the banks. The emphasis switches from mere risks appraisal to the fuller evaluation of returns which is necessary with Islamic finance.

'Islamization' of Banking

In post-revolutionary Iran a major policy objective has been the 'Islamization' of the nation's institutions. In an Islamic society it is felt that all institutions should operate in accordance with Islamic principles, including banks and financial institutions. Merely permitting Islamic banks to operate alongside Westernized commercial banks is unsatisfactory. In a society of believers there is no place for *riba* financial institutions, indeed the workings of commercial banks are an affront to the faithful. Instead, to ensure conformity with Koranic ideas and the spirit of Shi'ism, the Tehran authorities have 'Islamized' the entire banking system, precluding the operation of commercial banks using principles of Western finance.

Iranian commentators have repeatedly attacked the Arab Islamic banking movement as a camouflage for capitalism.

Merely using the word 'Islamic' does not change the nature of the banks themselves. The expression 'Islamic banking' is itself a contradiction in terms according to these critics. The word 'bank' comes from the Italian 'banco', meaning 'table', as in the past money-changers from Lombardy used to place money on a table. Such practices are inappropriate in Islamic financial transactions, which are based on trust. The word of a devout Muslim is believed, and he has no need to produce proof of his worth. This explains why even some Arab Islamic institutions are called houses rather than banks, KFH and DMI being notable examples.

Merely providing interest-free transactions, though a welcome development, is insufficient, according to Iranian critics. Islamic financial institutions cannot be limited-liability companies as obligations between Muslims who enter transactions must be absolute. There can be no evading personal liability, and institutions can have no personality of their own in any case.

Implementation of Islamic Financial Law

Iran's Islamic financial laws were approved by the Majlis (Islamic Consultative Assembly) in February 1984. They provided for the 'Islamization' of all Iran's financial institutions by 22 March 1985, although the implementation of the new regulations took four years to complete. Interest has been phased out of the system, and the banks now offer either interest-free current and savings deposits, or long-term investment deposits. With current account deposits customers can use chequing facilities, but only those with savings deposits are given preferential treatment with respect to loan applications. Incentives are also offered on savings deposits, including the possibility of a funded pilgrimage to Mecca. Those with long-term investment deposits cannot withdraw their funds without several months' notice, but they are entitled to share in the bank's profits in accordance with the Islamic *mudaraba* (speculation) system. Borrowers are encouraged to enter into partnership arrangements with the banks, under which they share any profits arising as a result of the investments financed by the bank. The partnership arrangement may be only in respect of one project which the bank backs, or it may be with the business as a whole. In the case of a limited partnership the profits shared are only those which arise from the specific project for which funds have been obtained. Under a full partnership arrangement all profits are shared. Machinery purchases are often financed by the bank purchasing the item required on behalf of the client, who repays by instalments. In this case the ownership is transferred on payment of the first instalment. An alternative arrangement is leasing conditioned to purchase, whereby the ownership is only transferred when the final instalment is paid.

Under the Islamic banking laws banks may also finance trade through forward purchases on a client's behalf. There is a distinction drawn between such purchases and futures trading, which is regarded as speculative and therefore prohibited. Under a forward purchase the bank pays for the commodity being traded on behalf of the import agent or wholesaler, who will repay the bank when he resells the merchandise to the retailer or final customer. The Arab Islamic banks have similar resale contracts, the time period for this type of credit typically being 90 or 180 days.

Employee Attitudes

In practice, there was some opposition in Iran to the new laws from existing bankers, and many bank employees were less than enthusiastic about the new systems. To facilitate implementation the banks were reorganized into three groups, Melat, Melli and Tejarat. A Council of Money and Credit Regulation was established to supervise the banking system, the Council consisting of representatives from the banks themselves, independent financial experts and religious advisers (two of whom are mullahs). The Central Bank retains its executive role, but the Council is responsible for bank policy, and the implementation of the new code. In 1994 it was announced that foreign banks could operate in Iran again, and not be confined solely to maintaining representative offices. It remains to be seen how they will be regulated under the Islamic banking laws.

The Arab Islamic financial institutions have had fewer personnel problems. All of the staff recruited by the Islamic banks are practising Muslims, apart from some employees in Europe. Many are experienced bankers who took salary cuts to join the new institutions because they wished to work in an Islamic environment and refrain from participation in *riba* transactions. Their attitude is extremely positive, and they are genuinely seeking to make Islamic principles work. The bank employees view their jobs as part of their religious devotion, and there is little doubt that in many respects a voluntary system of Islamic banking is preferable to compulsion.

Monetary Policy Issues

Islamic financial principles are not only applicable to banking activity, but also to government finance and management of the economy at the national level. The prohibition of *riba* precludes the use of interest-rate changes as an instrument of monetary policy. Islamic economists believe it is unfair to penalize borrowers by raising interest rates merely for the sake of demand management, when the problems which resulted in such an action were not the fault of individual borrowers. Hence, even in Muslim economies where interest is permitted, it is felt desirable to keep rates stable, and preferably at low levels. Other instruments of monetary policy can be used, including control of the money supply and the regulation of bank lending through reserve requirements and special deposits. Indeed a strict monetary policy is thought to be essential in order to keep inflation under control. High and unpredictable rates of price increase result in social strains and uncertainty which can undermine the cohesion of Islamic societies.

Many Islamic economists urge balanced budgets, as if government expenditure exceeds tax receipts, borrowing then becomes necessary. If resort is made to bill or bond issues, this implies the government is dependent on *riba* finance—an undesirable state of affairs for any government in the Islamic world. In Saudi Arabia the authorities have attempted to avoid interest by issuing government securities at a discount below their redeemable value. The difference represents the return to purchasers of the securities. A large number of Islamic economists object to this practice, however, as the yield on the securities resembles interest. Indeed the price at which this type of Saudi Government security has been traded has been influenced by interest-rate developments in Western markets. This is a result of the openness of the Kingdom's economy, and the ease with which foreign assets can be substituted for domestic assets.

Fiscal Policy Constraints

The public sector borrowing requirement can of course be controlled through fiscal policy, by restraining government expenditure or increasing taxation. The governments of many of the poorer Islamic states find great difficulty in restraining expenditure, especially on items such as food subsidies, given the pressing social needs. Many face a dilemma, as the reduction of the food subsidies results in inflationary pressures, causing Islamic critics to assert that they are penalizing the poor and acting contrary to the spirit of Islamic brotherhood. On the other hand, if the subsidies are maintained, the governments are forced to borrow—not only from their own citizens, but also from Western infidels, or non-believers.

In the poorer Islamic states the tax base is extremely restricted, as most of the population do not earn enough to pay income tax, and purchase taxes on basic commodities would penalize the needy. Import duties usually constitute the major source of government revenue, except in the oil-producing and exporting states. Islamic law provides for *zakat*, a type of wealth tax, which is on the statutes of all Muslim countries. This is levied annually on both businesses and individuals at a rate of 2.5% of their total net value. *Zakat* is a unique tax, as contributions are entirely voluntary, but most believers pay as it is regarded as one of the five central obligations of the Islamic faith.

In countries such as Saudi Arabia *zakat* collection is encouraged, and the funds are collected by a special ministry which uses the revenue for social purposes. *Zakat* has to be administered separately from other tax revenue and cannot be used for general government spending, even on development projects. For this reason some governments have done little to encourage *zakat*. In pre-Revolution Iran many of the bazaar merchants paid *zakat*, but not to the secular Tehran authorities. Instead they paid *zakat* to local relief agencies organized by the mullahs through the local mosques. Most of the revenue was used to help poor rural immigrants to the cities who had difficulty in finding employment and who often lived in appalling conditions. Since the Revolution the Islamic Government has taken over the administration of the tax, and there has been much debate about whether it should be made compulsory given the great social problems inherited from the Shah's regime.

Islamic Investment

Perhaps the most interesting recent development has been the widening of the scope of Islamic finance to encompass equity investment. Such participatory finance is acceptable under *Shari'a* law but until recently the major constraints have been the unacceptability of many Western companies because of their involvement in *haram* activities such as alcohol or pork production and distribution. Drawing from the experience of the ethical investment movement in the West, criteria have now been established for Islamically-acceptable equity investment. By early 2002, according to the London-based *Middle East*, there were some 105 Islamic equity funds world-wide, with total managed assets of some US $3,324m., compared with just 29 funds (with assets of $800m.) in 1996. Bahrain's central bank, the Bahrain Monetary Agency (BMA), issued the first of a series of short-term Islamic bonds, with each issue valued at some $25m., in June 2001. This was followed in October of that year by the listing on the Bahrain Stock Exchange of the BMA's first issue of Islamic five-year leasing securities; issued with a total value of $100m., the securities were each worth $10,000 at issue in the previous month.

In 1999 Dow Jones & Co Inc, the US international business news publisher, launched an Islamic Market Index covering more than 600 companies around the world. Companies are listed only if their debt-to-asset level is less than one-third, if receivable accounts are less than one-half of total assets, and if interest income is less than 10% of operating income. These screening criteria are acceptable to many *Shari'a* scholars, providing an amount equivalent to the interest-generated income is donated to charitable causes as a means of income 'purification'. Similarly, the FTSE Global Islamic Index Series, also launched in 1999, covers 1,000 approved stocks. These listings, together with the proliferation of internet websites dedicated to Islamic finance, not only reflect, but also contribute to, the increasingly high profile of the Islamic financial sector.

Prospects for the Future

The prospects for Islamic finance were dealt several blows in the late 1980s, most notably the collapse in 1988 of the Egyptian Islamic investment house, Ar-Rayan. The Central Bank refused to intervene; thousands of small investors lost their savings, and—although Egypt's Islamic banks were not directly involved—confidence in the whole sector was shaken. This had implications well beyond Egypt, as did the difficulties of the Jordan Islamic Bank, which were caused by the effect on the Jordanian economy of the 1990–91 Gulf crisis. Investors in the Ar-Rayan company were eventually compensated by an anonymous Gulf source and confidence among depositors with Islamic banks in Egypt was restored. The four principal state-owned commercial banks in Egypt (all of which are scheduled for privatization) now offer Islamic banking facilities to their clients. More recently, the collapse in Turkey in early 2001 of the Islamic finance house Ihlas Finans (blamed by the country's banking regulators on a long history of mismanagement and abuse of creditors' funds), and the resultant losses to some 200,000 investors, prompted concern that depositors would lose confidence in other Islamic financial institutions in Turkey at a time of severe economic instability in that country.

Despite these reversals, and despite concern in some quarters regarding the adequacy of earlier regulatory mechanisms for the sector, the outlook for Islamic banking in the early years of the 21st century is encouraging. Islamic financial assets world-wide (including those held by insurance companies) were estimated to amount to more than US $150,000m. by 2002. Existing Islamic financial institutions are now well established, and Islamic financial instruments are widely recognized as a viable alternative to *riba* finance.

Recent political developments in the Gulf may favour Islamic finance. Governments' fear of the perceived rise of Islamist fundamentalism has brought a political response, but has also made the authorities there more concerned than ever to emphasize their own Islamic credentials. This can be done with little controversy in the economic and banking sphere by accepting and even encouraging Islamic finance. Financial 'Islamization' may be seen as preferable to political 'Islamization', and as a way of meeting at least some of the aspirations of citizens of the Gulf.

Especially in view of the international scrutiny of the financial affairs of individuals and organizations allegedly linked to the suicide attacks on targets in the USA in September 2001, representatives of the Islamic financial community have been keen to defend the probity and transparency of the sector and to emphasize full co-operation with local and international regulatory authorities. In January 2002 Bahrain became the first country to publish a full set of regulations, including requirements in terms of capital adequacy, risk management, asset quality, liquidity management and corporate governance, for its Islamic banking sector. Bahrain's increasing status as the main regional centre for Islamic finance was further enhanced by the establishment there in August 2002 of the International Islamic Financial Market, a joint venture by the IDB and the monetary authorities of Bahrain, Brunei, Indonesia, Malaysia and Sudan. The same agencies, together with the central banks of Iran, Kuwait, Lebanon, Pakistan, Saudi Arabia and the UAE, had also agreed in April to establish an Islamic Financial Services Board, to be based in Kuala Lumpur, Malaysia, with the aim of promoting good regulatory and supervisory practices and uniform prudential standards for Islamic financial institutions. The new body was intended to complement the activities of the Accounting and Auditing Organization of Islamic Financial Institutions.

In the early years of the 21st century future prospects for Islamic banking were continuing to improve, with the establishment of several new banks as well as what appeared to be a trend towards mergers and acquisitions, and also conversions. Notably, Faysal Islamic Bank of Bahrain and Islamic Investment Company of the Gulf merged in June 2000 to form the Shamil Bank of Bahrain (SBB), with a paid-up capital of US $230m. and assets exceeding $2,900m. The main banking subsidiary of the DMI group, SBB (hitherto an 'offshore' banking unit) shortly afterwards changed its status to that of a full commercial bank, immediately taking its place among Bahrain's foremost commercial banks. In 2001 (its first full year of operations) SBB forecast profits approaching $11m. In March 2001 shareholders in the National Bank of Sharjah (NBS) approved its conversion to Islamic bank status; this was facilitated by an amendment to the bank's constitution to allow another bank from a GCC state to hold up to 20% of NBS capital, thus enabling KFH to acquire an initial 10% stake in the bank.

Meanwhile, there had been speculation that the enactment in the USA, in late 1999, of legislation (the Gramm-Leach-Bliley Act) that effectively repealed the 1933 Glass-Steagall Banking Act would facilitate the eventual establishment of truly Islamic banks there. In early 2001 the US Federal Home Loan Mortgage Corporation began to invest in financing contracts acceptable under US and Islamic law, with the intention of facilitating wider home ownership among Muslim families in the USA. US banks were also planning to promote not just home financing but also Islamically-correct current accounts and allied banking facilities. In March 2002, furthermore, the Bahrain-based First Islamic Investment Bank announced the establishment of its third real estate concern, in the assisted-living sector, in the USA.

The financial contributions of KFH to the ambitious Equate petrochemical plant project in Kuwait, and in the Shuweihat power and water project in Abu Dhabi (UAE) have also demonstrated the possibilities for Islamic financing of large develop-ment projects. In January 2002 the IDB Infrastructure Fund was launched, sponsored by the IDB in partnership with DMI, Bahrain, Brunei and the Saudi Arabian state pension fund. With initial financing of US $980m., it was aimed to raise, over 10 years, $1,000m. for equity investments in infrastructure projects in member countries of the IDB, as well as $500m. as a complementary finance facility to promote, underwrite and syndicate Islamic finance. Expansion in both the scale and the scope of the sector was thus predicted for the new millennium.

SELECT BIBLIOGRAPHY

Abdeen, Adnan M., and Shook, Dale N. *The Saudi Financial System in the Context of Western and Islamic Finance.* Chichester, John Wiley, 1984.

Ali, S. Nazim, and Ali, Naseem N. *Information Sources on Islamic Banking and Economics.* London, Kegan Paul International, 1994.

Beaugé, Gilbert, (Ed.). *Les Capitaux de l'Islam.* Paris, Presses du CNRS, 1990.

Chapra, M. Umer. *Islam and the Economic Challenge.* Leicester, Islamic Foundation, 1992.

Cunningham, Andrew. *Banking in the Middle East.* London, FT Finance, 1997.

Institute of Islamic Banking and Insurance. *Directory of Islamic Banking.* London, 2000.

   Directory of Islamic Insurance (Takaful). London, 2000.

   Encyclopaedia of Islamic Banking and Insurance. London, 1995.

Iqbal, Munawar, and Llewellyn, David T. (Eds). *Islamic Banking and Finance.* Cheltenham, Edward Elgar, 2002.

Kazarian, Elias. *Islamic Banking in Egypt.* Lund Economic Studies, 1991.

Lewis, Mervin K., and Algaoud, Latifa M. *Islamic Banking.* Cheltenham, Edward Elgar, 2001.

Mallat, Chibli, (Ed.). *Islamic Law and Finance.* London, Graham and Trotman, 1988.

Mannan, Muhammad Abd al-. *Islamic Economics: Theory and Practice.* Sevenoaks, Hodder and Stoughton, 1986.

Mayer, Ann Elizabeth. 'Islamic Banking and Credit Policies in the Sadat Era: The Social Origins of Islamic Banking'. *Arab Law Quarterly.* Vol. 1, part 1, 1985.

Mills, Paul S., and Presley, John R. *Islamic Finance: Theory and Practice.* New York, St. Martin's Press, 1999.

Naqvi, Syed Nawab Haider. *Islam, Economics and Society.* London, Kegan Paul International, 1994.

Nomani, Farhad, and Rahnema, Ali. *Islamic Economic Systems.* London, Zed Books, 1994.

Piccinelli, Gian Maria, (Ed.). *Banche Islamiche in Contesto Non-Islamico.* Rome, Istituto per l'Oriente, 1994.

Rodinson, Maxime. *Islam and Capitalism.* Harmondsworth, Penguin Books, 1979.

Roy, Delwin. *Islamic Banking. Middle Eastern Studies.* Vol. 27, 1991.

Sadeq, Abul Hasan M., (Ed.). *Financing Economic Development: Islamic and Mainstream Approaches.* Longman Malaysia, 1992.

Siddiqi, Muhammad N. *Banking Without Interest.* Leicester, The Islamic Foundation, 1983.

Vogel, Frank, and Hayes, Samuel. *Islamic Law and Finance.* The Hague, Kluwer, 1998.

Wilson, Rodney J. A. *Banking and Finance in the Arab Middle East.* London, Macmillan, 1983.

   Islamic Finance. London, Financial Times Publications, 1997.

   Islamic Financial Markets. London, Routledge, 1990.

THE RELIGIONS OF THE MIDDLE EAST AND NORTH AFRICA

Islam

R. B. SERJEANT

Islam is a major world religion and the faith predominating throughout the Middle East (with the exception of Israel) and North Africa. There are substantial Christian minorities in some countries (e.g. Lebanon) and communities of oriental Jews and other faiths, for centuries integrated with the Muslim majority. Islam is not only a highly developed religious system, but also an established and distinctive culture embracing every aspect of human activity from theology, philosophy and literature to the visual arts and even the individual's routine daily conduct. Its characteristic intellectual manifestation, therefore, is in the field of Islamic law, the *Shari'a*. Though in origin a Semitic Arabian faith, Islam was also the inheritor of the legacy of classical Greek and Roman civilization and, in its major phase of intellectual, social and cultural development after its emergence from its Arabian womb, it was affected by Christian, Jewish and Persian civilization. In turn, Greek scientific and philosophical writings—in the form of direct translations into Arabic or as a principal element in the books of Arab scholars—began to enter medieval Europe in Latin renderings about the early 12th century from the brilliant intellectual circles of Islamic Spain, and formed a potent factor in the little Renaissance of western Europe.

Islamic civilization had, by about the 18th century, clearly lost its initiative to the ascendant West and has not since regained it. Today, however, certain oil-rich Arab states, notably Saudi Arabia and Kuwait, have made significant progress in the world of international finance and mercantilism, engaging in activities such as the provision of Islamic banking services—for which since the latter part of the 20th century there has been an increase in demand.

HISTORY

The founder of the religion of Islam was the Prophet Muhammad b. 'Abdullah, born about AD 570, a member of the noble house of Hashim, belonging to the 'Abd Manaf clan, itself a part of the Quraish tribal confederation of Mecca. 'Abd Manaf may be described as semi-priestly, since they had the privilege of certain functions during the annual pilgrimage to the Meccan Ka'ba—a cube-shaped temple set in the sacred enclave (*haram*). Quraish controlled this enclave which was maintained inviolate from war or killing, and they had established a pre-eminence and loose hegemony even, over many Arabian tribes which they had induced to enter a trading alliance extending over the main Arabian land routes, north and south, east and west. Muhammad clashed with the powerful Quraish leaders in Mecca (temple guardians, chiefs, merchant adventurers), when, aged about 40, he began to proclaim the worship of one God, Allah, as against their multiplicity of gods. The Quraish leaders were contemptuous of his mission.

While his uncle Abu Talib, head of the house of Hashim, lived, he protected Muhammad from physical harm, but after his death Muhammad sought protection from tribes outside Mecca. However, even after asking to remain quietly without preaching, they would not accept him and Thaqif of Taif (at-Ta'if) drove him roughly away. Ultimately pilgrims of the Aws and Khazraj tribes of Yathrib (Medina), some 200 miles north of Mecca, agreed to protect him there, undertaking to associate no other god with Allah and accepting certain moral stipulations. Muhammad left Mecca with his Companion, Abu Bakr, in the year 622—this is the year of the *hijra* or hegira.

Arriving in Yathrib, Muhammad formed a federation or community (*umma*) of Aws and Khazraj known as the 'Supporters' (*Ansar*), followed by their Jewish client tribes, and the 'Emigrants' (*Muhajirun*—his refugee Quraish adherents) with himself as the ultimate arbiter of the *umma* as a whole. However, there remained a local opposition covertly antagonistic to him, the *Munafiqun*, rendered as 'Hypocrites'. Two internal issues had now to be fought by Muhammad—the enforcement of his position as theocratic head of the federation, and the acquisition of revenue to maintain his position; externally, he adopted an aggressive attitude towards the Meccan Quraish.

In Yathrib his disposal of the Jewish tribes who made common cause with the 'Hypocrites' improved his financial position. Muhammad overcame the Meccan Quraish more as a result of skilful political manoeuvre than of occasional armed clashes, and in year 8 he entered Mecca peacefully. He had previously declared Yathrib a sacred enclave (*haram*), renaming it Medina, the City (of the Prophet)—the two cities known as al-Haraman have become the holy land of Islam. Muhammad was conciliatory towards his defeated Quraish kinsmen, and after his success in at-Ta'if, south of Mecca, deputations came from the Arabian tribes to make terms with the Prophet—the heritor of the influence of the Meccan Quraish.

Early Islam

The two main tenets of Islam are embodied in the formula of the creed, 'There is no god but Allah and Muhammad is the Apostle of God'. Unitarianism (*tawhid*), as opposed to polytheism (*shirk*) or making partners with God, is Islam's basic principle, coupled with the authority conferred on Muhammad by God. Muhammad made little change to the ancient Arabian religion—he abolished idolatry but confirmed the pilgrimage to the Ka'ba; the Koran, the sacred Book in Arabic revealed to Muhammad for his people, lays down certain social and moral rules. Among these are the condemnation of usury or interest (*riba*) on loans and the prohibition of wine (*khamr*)—both ordinances have always been difficult to enforce. In many respects, the similarities between the old and new faiths enabled Arabia to embrace Islam with relative ease. While there is incontrovertible evidence of Muhammad's contact with Judaism, and even with Christianity, and the Koran contains versions of narrative known to the sacred books of these faiths, yet these are used to point purely Arabian morals. The limited social law laid down by the Koran is supplemented by a body of law and precept derived from the *Hadith* or Tradition of Muhammad's practice (*Sunna*) at Medina, and welded into the Islamic system, mainly in its second and third centuries.

Subsequent History

Immediately after Muhammad's death in 632, Abu Bakr, delegated by the Prophet to lead the prayer during his last indisposition, became his successor or Caliph. Some Medinan 'Supporters' had attempted a breakaway from Quraish overlordship but Abu Bakr adroitly persuaded them to accept his succession. Office in Arabia, generally speaking, is hereditary within a family group, though elective within that group, and Abu Bakr's action had taken no account of the claims of 'Ali, the Prophet's cousin and son-in-law. The house of Hashim, to which Muhammad and 'Ali belonged, was plainly aggrieved that a member of a minor Quraish clan, not of the 'house' (*Bait*) of their ancestor, Quṣaiy, the holder of religious offices in Mecca which he bequeathed to his descendants, should have snatched supreme power. Muhammad's Arabian coalition also weakened, the tribes particularly objecting to paying taxes to Medina, but Abu Bakr's uncompromising leadership reasserted cohesion. Expansionist campaigns beyond Arabia undertaken during his Caliphate were continued under his successors 'Umar and 'Uthman, diverting tribal energies to profitable warfare in Mesopotamia, Palestine-Syria, Egypt and Persia. Muslim armies were eventually to conquer North Africa, much of Spain, parts of France, and even besiege Rome, while in the east they later penetrated to Central Asia and India.

During 'Uthman's tenure the pace of conquest temporarily slackened and the turbulent tribes, now settled in southern Iraq and Egypt, began to dispute the Caliph's disposal of plunder and revenue, maintaining that he favoured members of his own house unduly. A delegation of tribal malcontents from Egypt murdered 'Uthman in the holy city of Medina, and in the resultant confusion 'Ali, Muhammad's cousin, was elected Caliph with the support of the tribesmen responsible for murdering 'Uthman. This raised grave constitutional problems for the young Muslim state, and is regarded as the origin of the first and greatest schism in Islam.

If legitimist arguments were the sole consideration 'Ali's claims to succession would appear to be superior, but his claim had already been superseded by 'Uthman—whose father belonged to the Umaiya clan which had opposed Muhammad, but whose mother was of Hashim. 'Uthman naturally appointed Umaiya men loyal to him to commands in the Empire, notably Mu'awiya—the son of Abu Sufyan who had led Quraish opposition to Muhammad at Mecca, but was later reconciled with him—as governor of Syria. Mu'awiya demanded 'Uthman's murderers be brought to justice in accordance with the law, but 'Ali, unable to deliver the murderers from among his supporters, was driven by events to take up arms against Mu'awiya. When they clashed at Siffin, in Syria, 'Ali was forced, against his better judgement, to submit to the arbitration of the Koran and *Sunna*, thus automatically losing the position of supreme arbiter, inherited by the Caliphs from Muhammad. Although history is silent as to what the arbiters actually judged upon, it was most likely as to whether 'Ali had broken the law established by Muhammad, and that he was held to have sheltered unprovoked murderers. The arbiters deposed him from the Caliphial office, though historians allege trickery entered into their action.

'Ali was murdered shortly after by one of a group of his former supporters which had come out against the arbitration it had first urged upon him. This group, the Khawarij, is commonly held to be the forerunner of the Ibadis of Oman and elsewhere. Mu'awiya became Caliph and founder of the Umaiyad dynasty with its capital at Damascus. The ambitions of the Hashim house were not, however, allayed, and when Umaiyad troops slew 'Ali's son Husain at Karbala' in southern Iraq they created the greatest Shi'a martyr (see Religious Groupings, p. 147).

The house of Hashim also included the descendants of 'Abbas the Prophet's uncle, but 'Abbas had opposed Muhammad until late in his life. The 'Abbasids made common cause with the 'Ali-id Shi'a against the Umaiyads, but were evidently abler in the political field. In the Umaiyad empire the Arabian tribes formed a kind of military élite but were constantly at factious war with one another. The Hashimites rode to power on the back of a rebellion against the Umaiyads which broke out in Khurasan in eastern Persia, but it was the 'Abbasid branch of Hashim which assumed the Caliphate and ruled from the capital they founded at Baghdad.

The 'Abbasid Caliphate endured up to the destruction of Baghdad in 1258 by the devastating Mongol invaders of the eastern empire, but the Caliphs had long been mere instruments in the hands of Turkish and other mercenaries, and the unwieldy empire had fragmented into independent states which rose and fell, though they mostly conceded nominal allegiance to the 'Abbasid Caliphs.

The Mongol Ilkhanid sovereigns, now turned Muslim, were in turn displaced by the conquests of Tamerlane at the end of the 14th century. In fact the Islamic empire had largely been taken over by Turkic soldiery. The Mameluke or Slave rulers of medieval Egypt who followed the Aiyubid (Kurdish) dynasty of Salah ud-Din (Saladin) were mainly Turks or Circassians. It was they who checked the Mongol advance at 'Ain Jalut in Palestine (1260). The Ottoman Turks captured Constantinople in 1453, and took Egypt from the Mamelukes in 1516, subsequently occupying the Hijaz where the Ashraf, descendants of the Prophet, ruled in Mecca and Medina, under first Mameluke then Turkish suzerainty. In 1533 the Turks took Baghdad, and Iraq became part of the Ottoman Empire. The Ottoman Sultans assumed the title of Caliph—though in Islamic constitutional theory it is not easy to justify this. The Ottoman Caliphs endured until the Caliphate was abolished by Mustafa Kemal (later called Atatürk) in 1924. The Turks have always been characterized by their adherence to Sunni orthodoxy.

Throughout history the 'Ali-ids have constantly asserted their right to be the Imams or leaders of the Muslim community—this in the religious and political senses, since Islam is funda-

mentally theocratic. The Shi'a, or followers of 'Ali and his descendants, were in constant rebellion against the 'Abbasids and came to form a distinct schismatic group of legitimist sects—at one time the Fatimid Shi'a rulers of Egypt were near to conquering the main part of the Islamic world. The main Shi'a sects today are the Ithna'asharis, the Isma'ilis, and the near-orthodox Zaidis of Yemen. The Safavids who conquered Persia at the beginning of the 16th century brought it finally into the Shi'a fold. Sunni Hashimite dynasties flourish today in Jordan and Morocco as they did until fairly recently in Iraq and Libya, and the Shi'a Zaidi ruler of Yemen was only displaced in 1962. The main difference between Sunnis and Shi'a concerns the Imamate, i.e. the temporal and spiritual leadership of Islam; for Sunnis, while they respect the Prophet's house, do not consider the Imam must be a member of it—the Shi'a insist on an Imam of the descendants of 'Ali and his wife Fatima, daughter of the Prophet.

It has been too readily assumed that, during the later Middle Ages and long Turkish domination, the Islamic Middle East was completely stagnant. The shift in economic patterns after the discovery of the New World and the Cape route to India, coupled with widening Western intellectual horizons and the development of science and technology, did push European culture far ahead of the Muslim Middle East. It was confronted by a vigorous and hostile Christianity intent on proselytizing in its very homelands. Muslims had to face the challenge of the ideas and attitudes of Christian missionaries. Muslim thinkers like Muhammad 'Abduh (1849–1905) of Egypt and his school asserted that Islam had become heavily overlaid with false notions—hence its decline; like earlier reformers they were convinced that present difficulties could be resolved by reversion to an (idealized) pure, primitive Islam. Sometimes, in effect, this meant reinterpreting religious literature to suit attitudes and ideas of modern times—as for instance when the virtual prohibition of polygamy was identified in the restrictions which define the practice. Since the earlier modern days political leaders like Atatürk have often taken drastic measures, secularizing the state itself even in the sensitive field of education, and accusing the more conservative forms of Islam of blocking progress. In recent years the Islamic Middle East has witnessed regimes ranging from the strong supporters of traditional Islam—like Saudi Arabia and Libya—to the anti-religious Marxist group which controlled Aden (the People's Democratic Republic of Yemen) until 1990. In Libya, nevertheless, Col Muammar al-Qaddafi has published *The Green Book*, embodying his personal, socialist solution of problems of democracy and economics. Theocratic Shi'a Iran has a distinctive character of its own.

ISLAMIC LAW

Orthodox Sunni Islam finds its main expression in *Shari'a* law, which it regards with great veneration. The Sunnis have crystallized into four schools or rites (*madhhab*), all of which are recognized as valid. Although in practice the adherents of one school can sometimes be at loggerheads with another, in modern times it is claimed that the law of any one of the rites can be applied to a case. The schools, named after their founders, are the Hanbali, regarded as the strictest, with adherents mainly in Saudi Arabia; the Shafi'is, the widest in extent with adherents in Egypt, Palestine-Syria, South Arabia and the Far East; the moderate Hanafi school, which was the official rite of the Ottoman Turkish empire and to which most Muslims in the Indian sub-continent belong; and the Malikis of the North African states, Nigeria and Sudan. The Shi'ite sects have developed their own law and give prominence to *ijtihad*, the forming of independent judgement, whereas the Sunnis are more bound by *taqlid* or following ancient models. However, as the law of Sunnis, the moderate Shi'a and the Ibadis is basically derived from the same sources, the differences are generally more of emphasis than principle.

The completely Islamic state as the theorists envisage it, run in conformity with the rules of the *Shari'a*, has probably never been achieved, and people's practice is often at variance with some or other requirements of *Shari'a*. The imprint of Islam is nevertheless unmistakably evident, in one way or another, on almost every country in this volume.

Civil Courts

In modern states of the Islamic world there exists, side by side with the *Shari'a* court (judging cases on personal status, marriage, divorce, etc.), the secular court which has a wide jurisdiction (based on Western codes of law) in civil and criminal matters. This court is competent to give judgment irrespective of the creed or race of the defendant.

Islamic Law as Applying to Minorities

In cases of minorities (Christian or Jewish) residing as a community in Muslim countries, spiritual councils are established where judgment is passed according to the law of the community, in matters concerning personal status, under the jurisdiction of the recognized head of that community.

Tribal Courts

In steppe and mountain areas of some countries a proportion of the population maintain tribal courts which administer law and justice in accordance with ancient custom and tribal procedure. Among tribes these courts are often more popular than *Shari'a* courts, because justice is swifter. Conciliation (*sulh*) is generally their objective. There is, nonetheless, constant pressure to eliminate customary practices where they are unequivocally seen to be contrary to Islamic principles.

Awqaf

In Muslim countries the law governing *awqaf* (singular, *waqf*), called in North Africa *habous* (*hubus*), is the law applied to religious and charitable endowments, trust and settlements. This important Islamic institution is administered in most Muslim countries by a special ministry of *awqaf*. *Awqaf*, or endowments, are pious bequests made by Muslims for the upkeep of religious institutions, public benefits, etc. Family *awqaf* provide an income partly for religious purposes and partly for the original donor's family.

SUFIS

In common with other religions where simple observance of a code of law and morals proves spiritually unsatisfying, some Muslims have turned to mysticism. From early times Islamic mystics existed known as Sufis, allegedly owing to their wearing a woollen garment. They seek complete identification with the Supreme Being, and annihilation of the self—the existence of which they term polytheism (*shirk*). The learned doctors of Islam often think ill of the Sufis, and indeed rogues and wandering mendicants found Sufism a convenient means of livelihood. Certain Sufi groups allowed themselves dispensations and, as stimulants, even used hashish and opium, which are not sanctioned by the Islamic moral code. The Sufis became organized in what are loosely called brotherhoods (*turuq*; singular, *tariqa*), and have to a large extent been incorporated into the structure of orthodox Islamic society. Some *turuq* induce ecstatic states by their performance of the *dhikr*, meaning, literally, the mentioning (of Allah). Today there is much disapproval of the more extravagant manifestations of the Sufis and in some places these have been banned entirely.

BELIEF AND PRACTICE

'Islam' means the act of submitting or resigning oneself to God, and a Muslim is one who resigns or submits himself to God. Muslims disapprove of the term 'Muhammadan' for the faith of Islam, since they worship Allah, and Muhammad is only the Apostle of Allah whose duty it was to convey revelation, though he is regarded as the 'Best of Mankind'. He is the Seal (*Khatam*) of the prophets, i.e. the ultimate Prophet in a long series in which both Moses and Jesus figure. They are revered, but, like Muhammad the Prophet, they are not worshipped.

Nearly all Muslims agree on acceptance of six articles of the faith of Islam: (i) Belief in God; (ii) in His angels; (iii) in His revealed books; (iv) in His Apostles; (v) in the Resurrection and Day of Judgement; and (vi) in His predestination of good and evil.

Faith includes works, and certain practices are obligatory on the believing Muslim. These are five in number:

1. The recital of the creed (*Shahada*)—'There is no god but God (Allah) and Muhammad is the Apostle of God.' This formula is embodied in the call to prayer made by the *muezzin* (announcer) from the minaret of the mosque before each of the five daily prayers.

2. The performance of the Prayer (*Salat*) at the five appointed canonical times—in the early dawn before the sun has risen above the horizon, in the early afternoon when the sun has begun to decline, later when the sun is about midway in its course towards setting, immediately after sunset, in the evening between the disappearance of the red glow in the west and bedtime. In prayer Muslims face towards the Ka'ba in Mecca. They unroll prayer mats and pray in a mosque (place of prostration), at home, or wherever they may be, bowing and prostrating themselves before God and reciting set verses in Arabic from the Koran. On Fridays it is obligatory for men to attend congregational Prayer in the central mosque of the quarter in which they live—women do not normally attend. On this occasion formal prayers are preceded by a sermon.

3. The payment of the legal alms (*Zakat*). In early times this contribution was collected by officials of the Islamic state, and devoted to the relief of the poor, debtors, travellers and to other charitable and state purposes, and it often became, in effect, a purely secular tax on crops. Nowadays the fulfilment of this religious obligation is left to the conscience of the individual believer. The *zakat* given at the breaking of the fast at the end of Ramadan, for example, is a voluntary gift of provisions.

4. The 30 days of the fast in the month of Ramadan, the ninth month in the lunar year. As the lunar calendar is shorter by 11 days than the solar calendar, Ramadan moves from the hottest to the coldest seasons of the solar year. It is observed as a fast from dawn to sunset each day by all adults in normal health, during which time no food or drink may be taken. The sick, pregnant women, travellers and children are exempt; some states exempt students, soldiers and factory workers. The fast ends with one of the two major Muslim festivals, 'Id al-Fitr.

5. The pilgrimage (*Hajj*) to Mecca. Every Muslim is obliged, circumstances permitting, to perform this at least once in his lifetime, and when accomplished he may assume the title, *Hajji*. More than two million pilgrims go each year to Mecca, but the holy cities of Mecca and Medina are prohibited to non-Muslims.

Before entering the sacred area around Mecca by the seventh day of Dhu'l-Hijja, the 12th month of the Muslim year, pilgrims must don the *ihram*, consisting of two unseamed lengths of white cloth, indicating that they are entering a state of consecration and casting off what is ritually impure. The pilgrims circumambulate the Ka'ba seven times, endeavouring to kiss the sacred Black Stone. Later they run seven times between the nearby twin hills of Safa and Marwah (now covered in by an immense hall), thus recalling Hagar's desperate search for water for her child Ishmael (from whom the Arabs claim descent). On the eighth day of the month the pilgrims leave the city for Mina, a small town six miles to the east. Then, before sunrise of the next day, all make for the plain below Mount 'Arafat, some 12 miles east of Mecca, where they pass the day in prayers and recitation until sunset. This point is the climax of the pilgrimage when the whole gathering returns, first to Muzdalifah where it spends the night, then to Mina where pilgrims stone the devil represented by three heaps of stones (*jamra*). The devil is said to have appeared to Abraham here and to have been driven away by Abraham throwing stones at him. This day, the 10th of Dhu'l-Hijja, is 'Id al-Adha, the Feast of the Sacrifice, and the pilgrims sacrifice an animal, usually a sheep, and have their heads shaved by one of the barbers at Mina. They return to Mecca that evening. In recent years the increasing number of pilgrims arriving (especially by air) has presented the Saudi authorities, guardians of the Holy Places, with major problems of organization, supply, health and public order. In 1988, following the tragic events of July 1987, when 402 people, including 275 Iranian pilgrims, lost their lives in clashes between the Iranians and Saudi security forces, and in order to reduce overcrowding, the Saudi Government imposed national quotas for the numbers of pilgrims performing the *Hajj*. However, overcrowding has continued to present serious problems, and tragic incidents similar to that of 1988 have not been infrequent in recent years.

The Holy War (*Jihad*) against the infidel was the means whereby Arab Muslim rule made its immense expansion in the first centuries of Islam, but despite pressures to do so, it has never been elevated to form a sixth Pillar of Islam. Today some theologians interpret *jihad* in a less literal sense as the combating of evil, but it is significant that the Afghan guerrillas who resisted the Soviet presence in their country called themselves *mujahidin*, i.e. those who wage the *jihad* against the enemies of Islam.

The Koran (*Qur'an*—'recital', 'reading') is for Muslims the very Word of God. The Koran consists of 114 chapters (*surah*) of uneven length, the longest coming first after the brief opening chapter called *al-Fatiha*. (The Koran is about as long as the New Testament). *Al-Fatiha* (The Opener) commences (as does every chapter) with the words, '*Bismillahi 'l-Rahmani 'l-Rahim*', 'In the name of God, the Compassionate, the Merciful', and forms part of the ritual five prayers (*salat*). Other special verses and chapters are also used on a variety of occasions, and Muslim children are taught to recite by heart a portion of the Koran or, preferably, the whole of it. The Koran has been the subject of vast written commentaries, but translation into other languages is not much approved by Muslims, though interlinear translations (a line of Koran underneath which is a line of translation) are used, and a number of modern translations into English and most other languages exist. The earlier (Meccan) chapters of the Koran speak of the unity of God and his wonders, of the Day of Judgement and Paradise, while the Medinan chapters tend to be occupied more with social legislation for marriage, divorce, personal and communal behaviour. The definitive redaction of the Koran was ordered by the Caliph 'Uthman (644–56).

HOLY PLACES

Mecca (Makkah): Hijaz province of Saudi Arabia. Mecca is centred around the Ka'ba, the most venerated building in Islam, traditionally held to have been founded by Abraham, recognized by Islam also as a prophet. It stands in the centre of the vast courtyard of the Great Mosque and has the form of a cube; its construction is of local grey stone and its walls are draped with a black curtain embroidered with a strip of writing containing verses from the Koran. In the eastern corner is set the famous Black Stone. The enlarging of the Great Mosque commenced under the second Caliph 'Umar. Both the Ka'ba and Great Mosque have undergone many renovations, notably since 1952. Mecca is the centre of the annual pilgrimage from all Muslim countries.

Al-Medina (*Al-Madinah—The City*, i.e. of the Prophet): Hijaz province of Saudi Arabia. Medina, formerly called Yathrib, was created as a sacred enclave (*haram*) by Muhammad, who died there in the year 11 of the *hijra* and was buried in the Mosque of the Prophet. Close to his tomb are those of his companions and successors, Abu Bakr and 'Umar, and a little further away, that of his daughter Fatima. Frequently damaged, restored and enlarged, the mosque building was extensively renovated by the Saudi Government in 1955.

Jerusalem (Arabic *al-Quds* or *Bait al-Maqdis, The Hallowed / Consecrated*): West Bank (annexed by Israel). Jerusalem is Islam's next most holy city after al-Haraman (Mecca and Medina), not only because it is associated with so many pre-Islamic prophets, but because Muhammad himself is popularly held to have made the 'Night Journey' there. Jerusalem contains the magnificent Islamic shrine, the Dome of the Rock (688–91), built by the Caliph 'Abd al-Malik, and the famous al-Masjid al-Aqsa.

Hebron (Al-Khalil): West Bank. The Mosque of Abraham, called al-Khalil, the 'Friend of God', is built over the tomb of Abraham, the Cave of Machpelah; it also contains the tombs of Sarah, Isaac, Rebecca, Jacob, and Leah. The shrine is revered by Muslims and Jews, and is also important to Christians.

Qairawan: Tunisia. The city is regarded as a holy place for Muslims, seven pilgrimages to the Great Mosque of Sidi 'Uqbah b. Nafi' (an early Muslim general who founded Qairawan as a base for the Muslim invaders of North Africa) being considered the equivalent of one pilgrimage to Mecca.

Muley Idris: Morocco. The shrine at the burial-place of the founder of the Idrisid dynasty in the year 687, at Walili, near Fez.

Every Middle Eastern country has a multitude of shrines and saints' tombs held in veneration, except Wahhabi states which consider saint cults to be polytheism (*shirk*). In Turkey, however, the policy of secularization led to Aya Sofya Mosque (St Sophia) being turned into a museum.

The following shrines are associated with the Shi'a or Legitimist sects of Islam.

Mashad (Meshed): Iran. The city is famous for the shrine of Imam 'Ali ar-Rida/Riza, the eighth Imam of the Ithna'ashari group, which attracts some hundred thousand pilgrims each year. The shrine is surrounded by buildings with religious or historical associations.

Qom: Iran. A Shi'a centre, it is venerated as having the tomb of Fatima, the sister of Imam ar-Rida/Riza, and those of hundreds of saints and kings including Imams 'Ali b. Ja'far and Ibrahim, Shah Safi and Shah 'Abbas II. Following the Iranian Revolution it became the centre favoured by Ayatollah Khomeini.

Najaf: Iraq. Mashhad 'Ali, reputed to be constructed over the place where 'Ali b. Abi Talib, fourth Caliph, the cousin and son-in-law of Muhammad, is buried, is a most venerated Shi'a shrine, drawing many pilgrims.

Karbala': Iraq. The shrine of Husain b. 'Ali where, at Mashhad Husain, he was slain with most of his family, is today more venerated by the Shi'a than the Mashhad 'Ali. 'Ashoura Day (10th Muharram) when Husain was killed is commemorated by passion plays (*ta'ziya*) and religious processions during which the drama of his death is re-enacted with extravagant expressions of emotion.

Baghdad: Iraq. The Kazimain/Kadhimain Mosque is a celebrated Shi'a shrine containing the tomb of Musa al-Kazim/Kadhim, the seventh Imam of the Ithna'asharis.

RELIGIOUS GROUPINGS

Sunnis

The great majority, probably over 80% of Muslims, are Sunni, followers of the *Sunna*, i.e. the way, course, rule or manner of conduct of Prophet Muhammad; they are generally called 'Orthodox'. The Sunnis recognize the first four Caliphs (Abu Bakr, 'Umar, 'Uthman, 'Ali) as Rashidun, i.e. following the right course. They base their *Sunna* upon the Koran and 'Six Books' of Traditions, and are organized in four Orthodox schools or rites (*madhhab*), all of equal standing within the Orthodox fold. Many Muslims today prefer to avoid identification with any single school and simply call themselves Muslim or Sunni.

Wahhabis

The adherents of 'Wahhabism' strongly disapprove of this title by which they are known outside their own group, for they call themselves Muwahhidun or Unitarians. In fact they belong to the strict Hanbali school following its noted exponent, the 13th/14th century Syrian reformer Ibn Taimiyah. The founder of 'Wahhabism', Muhammad b. 'Abd al-Wahhab of Arabian Najd (1703–87), sought to return to the pristine purity of early Islam freed from all accretions and what he regarded as innovations contrary to its true spirit, such as saint worship, lax sexual practices, and superstition. His doctrine was accepted by the chief Muhammad b. Sa'ud of Dar'iya (near ar-Riyadh). Ibn Sa'ud and his son 'Abd al-'Aziz—who proved a capable general—conquered much of Arabia. Medina fell in 1804 and Mecca in 1806 to Sa'ud, son of 'Abd al-'Aziz, but after his death in 1814 the Wahhabis were gradually broken by the armies of the Pasha of Egypt, Muhammad 'Ali, acting nominally on behalf of the Ottoman Sultan of Turkey. After varying fortunes in the 19th century the Wahhabis emerged as an Arabian power in the opening years of the 20th century. By the close of 1925 they held the Holy Cities and Jeddah and are today the strongest power in the Arabian Peninsula. Though Wahhabism remains the strictest of the Orthodox groups, Saudi Arabia has made some accommodation to modern times.

The Turuq or Religious Orders

In many Middle Eastern countries the religious orders (*turuq*) have important political-cum-religious roles in society. There are the widely spread Qadiriya who, with Tijaniya, are found in North Africa, the Khatmiya in Sudan, the Rifa'iya in Egypt and Syria, to pick out a few at random. The West has no organizations exactly equivalent to these Sufi orders into which an individual has to be initiated, and in which, by dint of ascetic exercises and study, he may attain degrees of mystical enlightenment—this can also bring moral influence over his fellow men. The Orders may be Sunni or Shi'a; some few Orders are even so unconventional as to be hardly Islamic at all. Although Sufism is essentially uninterested in worldly politics, the *turuq* have, nonetheless, at times been drawn into the political arena. It was the Orthodox reformist Sanusi Order that played the most significant role in our time. The Grand Sanusi, Muhammad b. 'Ali, born at Mustaghanem in Algeria of a Sharif family, founded the first *zawiya* or lodge of the Sanusis in 1837. The Sanusi *tariqa* is distinguished for its exacting standards of personal morality. The Sanusis set up a network of lodges in Cyrenaica (Libya) and put up strong resistance to Italian colonization. The Grand Sanusi was recognized as King Idris of Libya in 1951, but lost his throne in the military revolt led by Col Qaddafi in 1969.

The Muslim Brothers (al-Ikhwan al-Muslimun)

Founded in Egypt by Hasan al-Banna in 1928, the career of the Muslim Brothers (or Brotherhood) in Middle East political history has been active and often violent. Al-Banna considered westernizing influences and intellectual emancipation in Egypt to be weakening Islam, itself in decline since the ideal age of the first four Caliphs. So, the movement has a rigidity and intolerant attitude towards Christians and Jews, but this may even extend to other Muslim groups. Al-Banna was a member of a *tariqa* and the Brothers (*Ikhwan*) were initially organized along *tariqa* lines with a graded membership. This membership is not restricted to particular social classes but finds support especially among Azhar students, particularly those graduates of the Azhar who hold teaching and minor religious office. By 1939 the Brothers were one of the most important political groups in Egypt.

In 1944 a 'secret apparatus' was formed, rationalized as for the *jihad* in defence of Islam but used to defend the movement against the Government. The *Ikhwan* became involved in acts of terrorism and murder, but in 1949 al-Banna himself was murdered by the political police. At first the *Ikhwan* supported the Egyptian revolution but, falling out with the republican Government, they attempted the assassination of Nasser in 1954 following which he put down the society with a stern hand. The society opened branches in other Arab states—one of their emissaries was implicated in the 1948 Revolution in Yemen—and the movement flourishes in these states.

Ideologically the *Ikhwan* seeks a return to Islam and the *Shari'a*; it accepts all orthodox Islamic groups but it is anti-Qadiyani and Bahá'í. In Egypt it provided certain welfare projects and it has been active in publishing its views. A section of 'Muslim Sisters' was set up in 1933.

Shi'a

The Legitimist Shi'a pay allegiance to 'Ali as mentioned above. 'Ali's posterity, which must number at least hundreds of thousands scattered all over the Muslim world, are customarily called Sharifs if they trace descent to his son al-Hasan, and Saiyids if descended from al-Husain, but while the Sharifs and Saiyids, the religious aristocracy of Islam, traditionally are accorded certain privileges in Islamic society, not all are Shi'a, many being Sunnis. By the ninth century many strange sects, and even pagan beliefs, had become associated with the original Shi'a or Party of 'Ali, but these extremist sects called *ghulat* have mostly vanished except for a few, often practising a sort of quietism or dissimulation (*taqiyya*) for fear of persecution. All Shi'a accord 'Ali an exalted position, the extreme (and heretical) Shi'a at one time even according him a sort of divinity. Shi'ite Islam does not in the main differ on fundamental issues from the Sunni Orthodox since they draw from the same ultimate sources, but Shi'a *mujtahids* have, certainly in theory,

greater freedom to alter the application of law since they are regarded as spokesmen of the Hidden Imam.

The Ithna'asharis (Twelvers)

The largest Shi'a school or rite is the Ithna'ashariya or Twelvers, acknowledging a succession of 12 Imams. From 1502 Shi'ism became the established school in Iran under the Safavid ruler Sultan Shah Isma'il, who claimed descent from Musa al-Kazim (see below). There are also Ithna'ashariya in southern Iraq, al-Hasa, Bahrain and the Indian sub-continent.

The last Shi'a Imam, Muhammad al-Mahdi, disappeared in 878, but the Ithna'asharis believe he is still alive and will re-appear in the last days before the Day of Judgement as the Mahdi (Guided One)—a sort of Messiah—who will rule personally by divine right.

The 12 Imams recognized by the Twelver, Ithna'ashari Shi'a are:

(1) 'Ali b. Abi Talib, cousin and son-in-law of the Prophet Muhammad.

(2) Al-Hasan, son of 'Ali.

(3) Al-Husain, second son of 'Ali.

(4) 'Ali Zain al-'Abidin, son of Husain.

(5) Muhammad al-Baqir, son of 'Ali Zain al-'Abidin.

(6) Ja'far as-Sadiq, son of Muhammad al-Baqir.

(7) Musa al-Kazim, son of Ja'far as-Sadiq.

(8) 'Ali ar-Rida, son of Musa al-Kazim.

(9) Muhammad at-Taqi, son of 'Ali ar-Rida.

(10) 'Ali an-Naqi, son of Muhammad at-Taqi.

(11) Al-Hasan az-Zaki, son of 'Ali an-Naqi, al-'Askari.

(12) Muhammad al-Mahdi, son of al-Hasan b. 'Ali, al-'Askari, known as al-Hujja, the Proof.

Isma'ilis

This group of the Shi'a does not recognize Musa al-Kazim as seventh Imam, but holds that the last Imam visible on earth was Isma'il, the other son of Ja'far as-Sadiq. For this reason they are also called the Sab'iya or Seveners. There is, however, much disagreement among the Seveners as to whether they recognized Isma'il himself as seventh Imam, or one of his several sons, and the Fatimids of Egypt (10th–12th centuries) in fact recognized a son of Isma'il's son Muhammad. Schismatic offshoots from the Fatimid-Isma'ili group are the Druzes, the Musta'lians first settled in Yemen but now with their main centre in Mumbai (Bombay), India—where the Daudi section, under the chief 'missionary' (Da'i al-Du'a), is known as Bohoras, but who are properly called the Fatimi Taiyibi Da'wa, and the Nizari Isma'ilis of whom the Agha Khan is the spiritual head. These sects have a secret literature embodying their esoteric philosophies. Both groups are very active and a large Isma'ili Institute, sponsored by the Agha Khan, was opened in London, United Kingdom, in 1985. Small groups of Isma'ilis are to be found in north-west Syria, Iran, Afghanistan, East Africa and Zanzibar, and larger numbers in India and Pakistan.

'Alawis (Nusairis)

The 'Alawis believe Muhammad was a mere forerunner of 'Ali and that the latter was an incarnation of Allah. This Shi'a extremist sect established in the ninth century has also adopted practices of both Christian and pagan origin. Most of its members today live in north-west Syria.

Druze

The Druze are heretics, an offshoot of the Fatimid Isma'ilis (see above), established in Lebanon and Syria. Their name (Duruz) derives from ad-Darazi, a missionary of Persian origin who brought about the conversion of these Syrian mountaineers to the belief of the divine origin of the Fatimid Caliph al-Hakim. The origins of this sect and its subsequent expansion are still obscure. Hamza b. 'Ali, a Persian contemporary of ad-Darazi, is the author of several of the religious treatises of the Druze. This community acknowledges one God and believes that he has on many occasions become incarnate in man. His last appearance was in the person of the Fatimid Caliph al-Hakim (disappeared 1020). The Druze have played a distinctive role in the political and social life of their country and are renowned for their independence of character. They engaged ardently in *jihad* against the Israeli invaders of Lebanon and their Christian allies. Druze morale is reinforced by the inspiration of the Islamic Revolution in Shi'ite Iran.

Zaidis

The Zaidis are a liberal and moderate sect of the Shi'a, close enough to the Sunnis to call themselves the 'Fifth School' (*al-madhhab al-khamis*). Their name is derived from a grandson of al-Husain b. 'Ali called Zaid b. 'Ali whom they recognize as fifth Imam. They reject religious dissimulation (*taqiyya*) and are extremely warlike. Zaidism is the dominant school of Islam in Yemen, its main centres being San'a and Dhamar, but Shafi'is form roughly half the population.

Ibadis

The Ibadis are commonly held to have their origins in the Khawarij who dissociated themselves from 'Ali b. Abi Talib when he accepted arbitration in his quarrel with Mu'awiya, but this is open to question. They broke off early from the main stream of Islam and are usually regarded as heretics though with little justification. Groups of the sect, which has often suffered persecution, are found in Oman where Ibadism is the majority religion, Zanzibar, Libya and Algeria, mainly in the Mzab.

THE ISLAMIC REVIVAL

In a number of Muslim countries revivalist or reactionary Islamic movements are taking place. Islam makes no essential distinction between religion and politics so this affects not only the whole Muslim community but also those of other faiths residing in an Islamic state. In one sense it may be said that there is a common basis to the revival in all the Islamic states in that people believe that a reversion to an idealized Islamic community, or the substitution of the principles embodied in *Shari'a* law for the practice of a secular state, will resolve current problems and tensions. Each country, however, seems to differ as to what it expects the Islamic revival to react against. Since imported ideologies like socialism, communism, etc., have not solved political, social and economic problems besetting the Islamic world, in the popular return to the indigenous cultural heritage, Islam has tended to become the ideology of political opposition to existing political establishments and to be regarded as the means to link current development with the traditions of the past.

Saudi Arabia, the heartland of Islam, has always maintained a strict formal adherence to traditional Islam. The late King Faisal, though tactfully curbing the extreme tendencies of Saudi Arabia's Mutawwa' 'clergy', initiated and financed a policy of promoting Islam to counter President Nasser's alignment with socialist propaganda to subvert monarchic regimes elsewhere. King Faisal's initiative took the form of subsidizing the building of mosques in Muslim countries (and, later, also in Europe and other parts of the world), the publication of Islamic books and religious tracts, and the founding or support of such institutions as the Islamic Council of Europe.

In general, the Western concept of a 'permissive society' is rejected with distaste by all Muslim countries. Saudi Arabia's financial and moral strength has enabled it to take practical steps to pressure other Islamic states to conform, sometimes if they fear only to be out of line, to such Islamic prescriptions as the prohibition of liquor. Even in Egypt alcoholic beverages are not served at public occasions or in public places. On the other hand, banks and insurance companies, which depend on taking interest on loans, are regarded as earning profit (*ribh*), which is lawful to a Muslim, not taking usury (*riba*), which is unlawful. Since the recent wide revivalist trend that has reasserted itself in Islamic countries, the ethics of banking have troubled the conscience of certain Muslim states, and experiments have been made with Islamic banks which, formally at least, avoid interest. In Libya Col Qaddafi has also been making highly original experiments in the monetary field which he would regard as Islamic. To the West certain Islamic laws and penalties for their infringement, such as floggings, amputations and public beheadings, are undoubtedly repugnant. In Algeria the revival of conservative Islam was manifest in 1990 with the success in the local elections in the main cities of the Front islamique du salut (FIS). In the following year demonstrations and riots in Algiers by supporters of the FIS led to the dismissal of the Algerian Government by President Chadli, the postponement of the general election and the deployment of the army to restore order. After the FIS achieved an unassailable position in the first round of voting of the rescheduled general election in December 1991, the Algerian armed forces acted to stem its success by suspending the second round of voting and imposing a form of military rule. Algeria subsequently fell into a state of civil conflict between militant Islamist groups and their supporters on the one hand, and the security forces on the other.

In Iran the motivation of Islamic reaction, as was symbolized by Ayatollah Khomeini, was in part that of the conservative, even chauvinistic, provinces against a secular monarch who introduced foreigners who brought with them Western manners distasteful to Islamic society. This found expression in the destruction of bars, cinemas, etc., the banning of music on the radio, and the attempt, by imposing the veil, to reverse the tide of female emancipation. Persecution of the Bahá'ís was reminiscent of the late 19th century. In 1982, all courts established prior to the Islamic Revolution of 1979 were abolished, and all laws not conforming with Islam were revoked. Although interest-free banking is being introduced, there are difficulties in applying Islamic law to economic policy as there seems to be fundamental disagreement on how to apply it. In practice, too, *Shari'a* penalties are not easy to enforce.

Khomeini aimed to return to the ideal 'Islamic' state as conceived by the Shi'a mullahs. The emphasis on the concept that the *ulema* (mullahs) have had trusteeship over the entire community deputed to them by the invisible Imam has led to rule by them of a theocratic type, but Khomeini maintained that they must share in the Islamic ideology as interpreted by his group. Khomeini considered Islam's contemporary state as decadent and deviating from Islamic principles. He was critical of other Muslim governments, in part, as they were affected by Western influences, and his dictum, 'we should try hard to export our revolution to the world', though he considered this 'revolution' a spiritual, not a nationalistic one, had an aggressive overtone. The actions and practice of the new state were at times of an extremity rejected by Muslims and non-Muslims alike. Yet, if, on the one hand, some Muslim countries criticized the Khomeini regime for actions difficult to reconcile with the spirit of Islam, on the other there has been a widespread sentiment of sympathy among ordinary Muslims for the 'Islamic' government of Iran in its opposition to the 'Great Satan' USA, as supporter of Israel, etc.

Atatürk aimed at a complete separation of religion and state—in this secular state women were accorded equal rights with men. It is now clear that secularization in Turkey did not penetrate deep into the urban and (particularly) the rural population. After the Second World War resentment against the Government for financial hardship was fanned by religious leaders, and ever increasing religious freedom has had to be conceded within the secular state. Many women have, illegally, resumed the veil. The upper classes tend to favour a secular state, but religious feeling combined with chauvinism are behind the popular revival of Islam. In the legislative elections of 1995 the pro-Islamic Refah Partisi (RP—Welfare Party) won the largest number of seats in the National Assembly, though not sufficient for it to govern alone. Its success was widely regarded as an expression of the electorate's disillusionment with the established political parties rather than an endorsement of Refah's Islamist policies, however. Indeed, in 1996 the RP leader, Necmettin Erbakan, assumed the premiership of the country at the head of a coalition administration but was forced to resign 12 months later following repeated accusations (proceeding chiefly from the armed forces) that he was attempting to undermine the secular State through the promotion of Islamist interests. (The RP was later banned, as was the party's effective successor, the Fazilet Partisi—Virtue Party).

In no way was the interdependence of religion and politics in Islam better illustrated than in the condemnation of Israel by 40 Islamic states, over the question of Jerusalem, a city sacred to Muslims from which the Prophet made his celebrated Night Ascent to Heaven. Intensity of feeling over the Palestine issue varies in degree from one Islamic country to another and has often been far overshadowed by local issues, but it remains everywhere a major obstacle to East-West understanding. Israel's invasion of Lebanon in 1982 and the horrific massacre perpetrated by a Christian Lebanese group at the Sabra and Chatila Palestinian refugee camps in Beirut, with Israeli connivance, and the Israeli suppression of the Palestinian *intifada* (uprising) which began in the Occupied Territories at the end of 1987, exacerbated an already tense situation, persuading the Islamic world at large of the West's underlying hostility. To many Muslims the attempt by President Saddam Hussain to link Iraq's occupation of Kuwait in August 1990 with the Israeli occupation of Arab territories was justifiable. The vigour with which Western governments reacted against the Iraqi occupation, having effectively condoned the Israeli occupations for so long, appeared to them to be blatant hypocrisy. A decade later the catalyst for the renewed uprising—swiftly termed the al-Aqsa *intifada*—was a highly symbolic visit by Israel's right-wing Likud leader, Ariel Sharon, to Haram ash-Sharif, or Temple Mount in September 2000. The ensuing violence between Palestinians and Israeli armed forces seemingly brought to an end in all but name the peace process under the Oslo accords, and notably united the Arab world, and Palestinian 'nationalist' and fundamentalist 'rejectionist' groups, once again in condemnation of Israel. The suicide attacks perpetrated against targets in New York and Washington, DC, in September 2001, for which the USA held the fundamentalist Islamist al-Qa'ida (Base) organization of Osama bin Laden primarily responsible, were widely interpreted as a devastating symbol of Muslim perception of US sponsorship of Israel's continued occupation of Palestinian territory.

A Muslim writer recently distinguished between 'Westernization' and 'modernization', describing the latter as broadly acceptable, except to a reactionary minority. If the distinction between the two is a little blurred, the idea has some validity. In general, however, the Islamic revival among ordinary Muslims is bound up with factors, simple conservatism apart, varying from country to country and class to class, and it may oppose either governments conducted on a secular basis, or those claiming to be 'Islamic'.

Christianity

DEVELOPMENT IN THE MIDDLE EAST

Christianity was adopted as the official religion of the Roman empire in AD 313, and the Christian Church came to be based on the four leading cities, Rome, Constantinople (capital from AD 330), Alexandria and Antioch. From the divergent development of the four ecclesiastical provinces there soon emerged four separate churches: the Roman Catholic or Latin Church (from Rome), the Greek Orthodox Church (from Constantinople), the Syrian or Jacobite Church (from Antioch) and the Coptic Church (from Alexandria).

Later divisions resulted in the emergence of the Armenian (Gregorian) Church, which was founded in the fourth century, and the Nestorian Church, which grew up in the fifth century in Syria, Mesopotamia and Iran, following the teaching of Nestorius of Cilicia (d. 431). From the seventh century onwards followers of St Maron began to establish themselves in northern Lebanon, laying the foundations of the Maronite Church.

Subsequently the Uniate Churches were brought into existence by the renunciation by formerly independent churches of doctrines regarded as heretical by the Roman Church and by the acknowledgement of Papal supremacy. These churches—the Armenian Catholic, Chaldean (Nestorian) Catholic, Greek Catholic, Coptic Catholic, Syrian Catholic and Maronite Church—did, however, retain their Oriental customs and rites. The independent churches continued in existence alongside the Uniate Churches with the exception of the Maronites, who reverted to Rome.

HOLY PLACES

Bethlehem: West Bank. The traditional birthplace of Jesus is enclosed in the Basilica of the Nativity, revered also by Muslims. Christmas is celebrated here by the Roman and Eastern Rite Churches on 25 December, by the Greek Orthodox, Coptic and Syrian Orthodox Churches on 6 and 7 January, by the Ethiopian

Church on 8 January, and by the Armenian Church on 19 January. The tomb of Rachel, important to the three faiths, is just outside the town.

Jerusalem: West Bank (annexed by Israel). The most holy city of Christianity has been a centre for pilgrims since the Middle Ages. It is the seat of the patriarchates of the Roman, Greek Orthodox and Armenian Churches, who share the custodianship of the Church of the Holy Sepulchre and who each own land and buildings in the neighbouring area.

The Church of the Holy Sepulchre stands on the hill of Golgotha in the higher north-western part of the Old City. In the central chamber of the church is the Byzantine Rotunda built by 12th century crusaders, which shelters the small shrine of the traditional site of the tomb. Here the different patriarchates exercise their rights in turn. Close by is the Rock of Calvary, revered as the site of the Crucifixion.

Most pilgrims devoutly follow the Way of the Cross, leading from the Roman Praetorium through several streets of the Old City to the Holy Sepulchre. Franciscan monks, commemorating the journey to the Crucifixion, follow the course of this traditional route each Friday; on Good Friday this procession marks a climax of the Easter celebrations of the Roman Church.

Outside the Old City stands the Mount of Olives, the scene of Jesus' Ascension. At the foot of its hill is the Garden of Gethsemane, which is associated with the vigil on the eve of the Crucifixion. The Cenaculum, or traditional room of the Last Supper, is situated on Mount Zion in Israel.

Nazareth: Israel. This town, closely associated with the childhood of Jesus, has been a Christian centre since the fourth century AD. The huge, domed Church of the Annunciation has recently been built on the site of numerous earlier churches to protect the underground Grotto of the Annunciation. Nearby the Church of St Joseph marks the traditional site of Joseph's workshop.

Galilee: Israel. Many of the places by this lake (the Sea of Galilee, or Lake Tiberias) are associated with the life of Jesus: Cana, scene of the miracle of water and wine, which is celebrated by an annual pilgrimage on the second Sunday after Epiphany; the Mount of Beatitudes; Tabgha, scene of the multiplication of the loaves and fish; and Capurneum, scene of the healing of the Centurion's servant.

Mount Tabor: Israel. The traditional site of the Transfiguration, which has drawn pilgrims since the fourth century, is commemorated by a Franciscan Monastery and a Greek Basilica, where the annual Festival of the Transfiguration is held.

Jericho: West Bank. The scene of the baptism of Jesus; nearby is the Greek Monastery of St John the Baptist.

Nablus (*Samaria*): West Bank. This old town contains Jacob's Well, associated with Jesus, and the Tomb of Joseph.

Qubaibah (*Emmaus*): Jordan. It was near this town that two of the Disciples encountered Jesus after the Resurrection.

'Azariyyah (*Bethany*): Jordan. A town frequented by Jesus, the home of Mary and Martha, and the scene of the Raising of Lazarus.

Mount Carmel: Haifa, Israel. The Cave of Elijah draws many pilgrims, including Muslims and Druzes, who celebrate the Feast of Mar Elias on 20 July.

Ein Kerem: Israel. Traditional birthplace of John the Baptist, to whom a Franciscan church is dedicated; nearby is the church of the Visitation.

Ephesus: Turkey. The city, formerly a great centre of pagan worship, where Paul founded the first of the seven Asian Churches. The Basilica, built by Justinian, is dedicated to John the Evangelist, who legend claims died here; a fourth-century church on Aladag Mountain commemorating Mary's last years spent here now draws an annual pilgrimage in August.

Judaism

There are two main Jewish communities, the Ashkenazim and the Sephardim, the former from east, central and northern Europe, the latter from Spain, the Balkans, the Middle East and North Africa. The majority of immigrants into Israel were from the Ashkenazim, and their influence predominates there, though the Hebrew language follows Sephardim usage. There is no doctrinal difference between the two communities, but they observe distinct rituals.

HOLY PLACES

Wailing Wall: Jerusalem. This last remnant of the western part of the wall surrounding the courtyard of Herod's Temple, finally destroyed by the Romans in 70 AD, is visited by devout Jews, particularly on the Fast Day of the ninth of Av, to grieve at the destruction of the First and Second Temples which had once stood on the same site.

Mount Zion: Israel. A hill south-west of the Old City of Jerusalem, venerated particularly for the tomb of David, acknowledged by Muslims as Abi Dawud (the Jebuzite hill on which David founded his Holy City is now known as Mount Ophel, and is in Jordan, just to the east of the modern Mount Zion). Not far from the foot of the hill are the rock-cut tombs of the family of King Herod.

Cave of Machpelah: West Bank. The grotto, over which was built a mosque, contains the tombs of Abraham and Sarah, Isaac and Rebecca, Jacob and Leah.

Bethlehem: West Bank. The traditional tomb of Rachel is in a small shrine outside the town, venerated also by Muslims and Christians.

Mount Carmel: Israel. The mountain is associated with Elijah, whose Cave in Haifa draws many pilgrims. (See Christianity, above).

Safad: Israel. Centre of the medieval Cabbalist movement, this city contains several synagogues from the 16th century associated with these scholars, and many important tombs, notably that of Rabbi Isaac Louria.

Meiron: Israel. The town contains the tombs of Shimon bar Yohai, reputed founder in the second century of the medieval Cabbalist movement, and his son Eleazer. A yearly Hassidic pilgrimage is held to the tomb to celebrate Lag Ba'Omer with a night of traditional singing and dancing in which Muslims also participate.

Tiberias: Israel. An ancient city containing the tombs of Moses Maimonides and Rabbi Meir Baal Harness. Famous as an historical centre of Cabbalist scholarship, it is—with Jerusalem, Safad and Hebron—one of the four sacred cities of Judaism, and once accommodated a university and the Sanhedrin.

Other Communities

ZOROASTRIANS

Zoroastrianism developed from the teaching of Zoroaster, or Zarathustra, who lived in Iran some time between 700 and 550 BC. Later adopted as the official religion of the Persian empire, Zoroastrianism remained predominant in Iran until the rise of Islam. Many adherents were forced by persecution to emigrate, and the main centre of the faith is now Mumbai, where followers are known as Parsees. Technically a monotheistic faith, Zoroastrianism retained some elements of polytheism. It later became associated with fire-worship.

Yazd: Iran. This city was the ancient centre of the Zoroastrian religion, and was later used as a retreat during the Arab conquest. It contains five fire temples and still remains a centre for this faith, of which some 28,000 adherents live in Iran.

BAHÁ'ÍS

Bahá'ísm developed in the mid-19th century from Babism. The Bab, or Gateway (to Truth), Saiyid Ali Muhammad of Shiraz (1821–1850), was opposed to the corrupt Shi'a clergy in the Iran of his day and was executed in 1850. His remains were later taken to Haifa and buried in a mausoleum on the slopes of Mount Carmel. Mirza Husain Ali Bahá'ullah ('Splendour of Allah', 1817–92), a follower of Babism, experienced a spiritual revelation while in prison and in 1863 declared himself to be 'he whom Allah shall manifest' as predicted by the Bab. A member of the Persian nobility, he devoted his life to preaching against the corruption endemic in Persian society and as a result spent many years in exile. He died at Acre in Palestine in 1892 and is buried in a shrine adjacent to the mansion in which the Bab died, at Bahji, some miles north of Acre on the road to Beirut.

It was in the will and testament of Abdul Bahá, the eldest son and successor of Bahá'ullah, that after his death (in 1921) the head of the Bahá'í faith would be Shoghi Effendi known as the Guardian of the Bahá'í faith ('Guardian of Allah's Command') and that he would be the 'President' of the Universal House of Justice which would be elected in due course. In fact Shoghi Effendi died in London in November 1957 after 36 years as Guardian, but the Universal House of Justice was not elected from the Bahá'í world until 1963. The presidency was never assumed and there is no possibility of a second Guardian being appointed.

In 1846 the Babis declared their secession from Islam, and the Bahá'ís claim independence from all other faiths. They believe that the basic principles of the great religions of the world are in complete harmony and that their aims and functions are complementary. Other tenets include belief in the brotherhood of man, opposition to racial and colour discrimination, equality of the sexes, progress towards world peace, monogamy, chastity and the encouragement of family life. Bahá'ísm has no priesthood and discourages asceticism, monasticism and mystic pantheism. Most of Bahá'ísm's Middle Eastern adherents live in Iran and—on a temporary basis—Israel, but since the Islamic Revolution those in Iran have suffered from severe official persecution. Some 2m. Bahá'ís live in India and in fact Bahá'ís are established in some 235 countries and territories world-wide.

Haifa: Israel. Shrine and gardens of the Bab on Mount Carmel, world centre of the Bahá'í faith. Pilgrims visit the Bahá'í holy places in Haifa and in and around Acre. The Pilgrimage lasts for nine days and the pilgrimage period extends over the whole year with the exception of the months of August and September.

SAMARITANS

Mount Gerazim: Jordan. The mountain is sacred to this small sect, who celebrate Passover here. The Samaritan High Priest lives at Nablus.

PART TWO
Country Surveys

ALGERIA

Physical and Social Geography

Algeria is the largest of the three countries in north-west Africa that comprise the Maghreb, as the region of mountains, valleys and plateaux that lies between the sea and the Sahara desert is known. It is situated between Morocco and Tunisia, with a Mediterranean coastline of nearly 1,000 km and a total area of some 2,381,741 sq km, over four-fifths of which lies south of the Maghreb proper and within the western Sahara. Its extent, both from north to south and west to east, exceeds 2,000 km. The Arabic name for the country, el-Djezaïr (the Islands), is said to derive from the rocky islands along the coastline.

The total population of Algeria increased from 23,038,942 in April 1987 to 29,272,343 (according to provisional figures) at the census of June 1998. The great majority of the inhabitants reside in the northern part of the country, particularly along the Mediterranean coast where both the capital, Algiers or el-Djezaïr (population, not including suburbs, 1,519,570 at the 1998 census), and the second largest town, Oran or Ouahran (655,852), are located. Many settlements reverted to their Arabic names in 1981. The population is almost wholly Muslim. A majority speak Arabic and the remainder Tamazight, the principal language of the Berber minority who were the original inhabitants of the Maghreb. Many Algerians also speak French.

PHYSICAL FEATURES

The major contrast in the physical geography of Algeria is between the mountainous, relatively humid terrain of the north, which forms part of the Atlas mountain system, and the vast expanse of desert to the south, which is part of the Saharan tableland. The Atlas Mountains extend from south-west to north-east across the whole of the Maghreb. Structurally they resemble the 'Alpine' mountain chains of Europe and, like them, they came into existence during the Tertiary era. They remain unstable and liable to severe earthquakes, such as those which devastated el-Asnam in 1954 and 1980. The mountains consist of rocks, now uplifted, folded and fractured, that once accumulated beneath an ancestral Mediterranean sea. Limestone and sandstone are particularly extensive and they often present a barren appearance in areas where the topsoil and vegetation is thin or absent altogether.

In Algeria the Atlas mountain system comprises three broad zones running parallel to the coast: the Tell Atlas, the High Plateaux and the Saharan Atlas. In the north, and separated from the Mediterranean only by a narrow and discontinuous coastal plain, is the complex series of mountains and valleys that encompass the Tell Atlas. Here individual ranges, plateaux and massifs vary in height from about 500 m to 2,500 m above sea-level and are frequently separated from one another by deep valleys and gorges which divide the country into self-contained topographic and economic units. Most distinctive of these are the massifs of the Great and Little Kabyle between Algiers and the Tunisian frontier, which have acted as mountain retreats where Berber ways of village life persist.

South of the Tell Atlas lies a zone of featureless plains known as the High Plateaux of the Shotts. To the west, near the Moroccan frontier, they form a broad, monotonous expanse of level terrain about 160 km across and more than 1,000 m above sea level. They gradually narrow and descend eastward to end in the Hodna basin, a huge enclosed depression, the bottom of which is only 420 m above sea level. The surface of the plateaux consists of alluvial debris from erosion of the mountains to the north and south. The plateaux owe their name to the presence of several vast basins of internal drainage, known as shotts, the largest of which is the Hodna basin. During rainy periods water accumulates in the shotts to form extensive shallow lakes which give way, as the water is absorbed and evaporated, to saline mudflats and swamps.

The southern margin of the High Plateaux is marked by a series of mountain chains and massifs that form the Saharan Atlas. They are more interrupted than the Tell Atlas and present no serious barrier to communication between the High Plateaux and the Sahara. From west to east the chief mountain chains are the Ksour, Amour, Ouled Naïl, Ziban and Aurès. The latter, the most impressive massif in the whole Algerian Atlas system, includes the highest peak: Djebel Chelia, 2,328 m (7,638 ft). The relief of the Aurès is extremely bold, with narrow gorges cut between sheer cliffs surmounted by steep bare slopes, and to the east and north of the Hodna basin its ridges merge with the southernmost folds of the Tell Atlas. North-eastern Algeria thus forms therefore, a compact block of high relief in which the two Atlas mountain systems cease to be clearly separated. Here there are a number of high plains studded with salt flats but their size is insignificant compared with the enormous shotts to the west.

CLIMATE AND VEGETATION

The climate of northernmost Algeria, including the narrow coastal plain and the Tell Atlas southward to the margin of the High Plateaux, is of 'Mediterranean' type with warm, wet winters and hot, dry summers. Rainfall varies from over 1,000 mm annually on some coastal mountains to less than 130 mm in sheltered, lee situations, and occurs mostly during the winter. Complete drought lasts for three to four months during the summer, when the notorious sirocco (Chehili) also occurs. It is a scorching, dry and dusty southerly wind blowing from the Sahara, prevailing for some 40 days a year over the High Plateaux but nearer the coast its duration is closer to 20 days. With the arrival of the sirocco, shade temperatures often rise rapidly to more than 40°C (104°F), while vegetation and crops, unable to withstand the intensity of evaporation, may die within a few hours. As a result of low and uneven rainfall combined with high rates of evaporation, the rivers of the Tell tend to be short and to suffer large seasonal variations in flow. Many run completely dry during the summer and are full only for brief periods following heavy winter rains. The longest perennially flowing river is the Oued Chélif, which rises in the High Plateaux and crosses the Tell to reach the Mediterranean Sea east of Oran.

Along the northern margin of the High Plateaux 'Mediterranean' conditions give way to a semi-arid or steppe climate, in which summer drought lasts from five to six months and winters are colder and drier. Rainfall is limited to 200 mm–400 mm annually and tends to occur in spring and autumn rather than in winter. It is, moreover, variable from year to year, and under these conditions the cultivation of cereal crops without irrigation becomes unreliable. South of the Saharan Atlas annual rainfall decreases to below 200 mm and any regular cultivation without irrigation becomes impossible. There are no permanent rivers south of the Tell Atlas and any surface run-off following rain is carried by temporary watercourses towards local depressions, such as the shotts.

The soils and vegetation of northern Algeria reflect the climatic contrast between the humid Tell and the semi-arid lands farther south, but they have also suffered widely from the destructive effects of over-cultivation, over-grazing and deforestation. In the higher, wetter and more isolated parts of the Tell Atlas relatively thick soils support forests of Aleppo pine, cork-oak and evergreen oak, while the lower, drier, and more accessible slopes tend to be bare or covered only with thin soils and a scrub growth of thuya, juniper and various drought-resistant shrubs. Only a few remnants survive of the once extensive forests of Atlas cedar, which have been exploited for timber and fuel since classical times. They are found chiefly above 1,500 m in the eastern Tell Atlas. South of the Tell there is very little woodland except in the higher and wetter parts of the Saharan Atlas. The surface of the High Plateaux is bare or covered only with scattered bushes and clumps of esparto and other coarse grasses.

SAHARAN ALGERIA

South of the Saharan Atlas, Algeria extends for over 1,500 km into the heart of the desert. Structurally, this huge area consists of a resistant platform of geologically ancient rocks against which the Atlas Mountains were folded. Over most of the area relief is slight, with occasional plateaux, such as those of Eglab, Tademaït and Tassili-n-Ajjer, rising above vast spreads of gravel, such as the Tanezrouft plain, and huge sand accumulations, such as the Great Western and Eastern Ergs. In the south-east, however, the great massif of Ahaggar rises to a height of 2,918 m (9,573 ft). Here, erosion of volcanic and crystalline rocks has produced a lunar landscape of extreme ruggedness. Southward from the Ahaggar the massifs of Adrar des Iforas and Aïr extend into neighbouring Mali and Niger.

The climate of Saharan Algeria is characterized by extremes of temperature, wind and aridity. Daily temperature ranges reach 32°C, and maximum shade temperatures of over 55°C have been recorded. Sometimes very high temperatures are associated with violent dust storms. Mean average rainfall, although extremely irregular, is everywhere less than 130 mm, and in some of the central parts of the desert it falls to less than 10 mm. These rigorous conditions are reflected in the extreme sparseness of the vegetation and in a division of the population into settled cultivators, who occupy oases dependent on permanent supplies of underground water, and nomadic pastoralists who make use of temporary pastures which appear after rain.

History

RICHARD I. LAWLESS

EARLY HISTORY

The Berber people have comprised the majority of the population of this part of Africa since the earliest times. From 208 to 148 BC Numidia occupied most of present-day Algeria north of the Sahara. After the destruction of Carthage in 146 BC Numidia, greatly reduced in extent, was transformed into a Roman vassal-state, while the rest of the area formed a loose confederacy of tribes, which maintained their independence by frequent revolt. After a brief period of Vandal dominance, Roman rule was restored in the provinces of Africa (modern Tunisia) and Numidia, and parts of the coast. Elsewhere, the Berber confederacies, centred in the Aurès and the Kabyle, maintained their independence.

The rise of Islam in Arabia was soon followed by its penetration of North Africa, the first Arab raids taking place about the middle of the seventh century. Qairawan (in present-day Tunisia) was founded by the Arabs in 670 as a base; the other towns remained under Byzantine control, and the Berber tribes set up a state centred on the eastern Maghreb. Increasing Arab immigration towards the end of the seventh century finally overcame Berber and Byzantine resistance, the Berbers gradually converted to Islam, and the whole of the area was incorporated into the Ummayad Empire. In 756 the Berbers freed themselves from the control of the recently established Abbasid Caliphate, and for the next three centuries power was disputed between various Arab dynasties and Berber tribes. After the invasion in c. 1050 of the Banu Hilal, a confederation of nomadic Arab tribes dislodged from Egypt, a period of anarchy ensued, but the Berber dynasty of the Almoravids, from Morocco, temporarily restored order in the area of modern Algiers and Oran. In c. 1147 the Almoravids were succeeded by the Almohads, who unified the whole of the Maghreb and Muslim Spain, bringing cultural and economic prosperity to North Africa. From the middle of the 13th century, however, the region entered a period of decline, both economic and in terms of its political influence, which persisted for more than two centuries.

In the closing years of the 15th century the Spanish monarchy carried its crusade against Muslim power to North Africa, the fragmented political state of that area offering little resistance. On the death of Ferdinand of Castile in 1516, the Algerines sought the assistance of the Turkish corsair Aruj, who took possession of Algiers and proclaimed himself Sultan. In 1518 he was succeeded by his brother Khayr ad-Din (Barbarossa), who placed all his territories under the nominal protection of the Ottoman Sultan. This decisive act may be said to mark the emergence of Algiers as a political entity. After numerous efforts to re-establish their position, the Spanish finally withdrew in 1541 and Algeria was left for three centuries to the Muslims. Power in Algiers lay in the hands of the dey and there was a rapid succession of deys, often due to assassinations. Each dey established his relationship with the Sultan by sending him tribute. Real power in Algiers was held by two bodies—the janissary corps and the guild of corsair captains. The Regency

of Algiers reached its peak in the 17th century, the profitable trade of piracy bringing great wealth. Despite Turkish attempts to control the interior, several Berber tribes most distant from Algiers retained their independence. During the 18th century the growth of European sea power in the Mediterranean brought a period of decline to the littoral, while in the interior a period of relative economic prosperity ensued.

THE FRENCH CONQUEST

On 5 July 1830 Algiers fell to a French expedition, and the dey and most of the Turkish officials were sent into exile. The pretext for intervention was an insult offered by the dey to the French consul in 1827: the real cause was the pressing need of Polignac, the chief minister under Charles X, to secure some credit for his administration from the French public and to provide employment for the Napoleonic veterans. However, the Bourbon dynasty and its government were subsequently overthrown by revolution and Polignac's plan to hand over the rest of the country, and the decision on its future, to a European congress was abandoned. In Algeria the absence of any central authority increased the prestige of the tribal chiefs. In 1834, however, the French decided upon the further conquest and annexation of Algeria, and a governor-general was appointed.

Over the next quarter of a century, France pursued its conquest of Algeria, despite bitter opposition. Constantine, the last Turkish stronghold, was captured in 1837, and by 1841 French rule had been consolidated in most of the ports and their immediate environs. By 1844 much of the eastern part of Algeria was under French control, but in the west the conquerors encountered the formidable Abd al-Kadir, a skilful diplomat and military commander, who at first concluded treaties with the French, consolidating his position as leader of the Berber confederacies in the west. In 1839, however, he declared war on France and united Berbers and Arabs against the invaders. Resistance was maintained until 1847, when Abd al-Kadir was defeated by Gen. Bugeaud, the real architect of French rule in Algeria. During the late 1840s and 1850s the tribes on the edge of the Sahara were pacified, while the conquest was effectively completed by the submission of the hitherto independent Berber confederacies of the Kabyle in 1857. Notwithstanding, further rebellions were to occur throughout the 19th century.

Meanwhile, a policy of colonization, with widespread confiscation of land and the transference thereof to settler groups, had been adopted. Bugeaud at first encouraged colonization in the coastal plains, and after 1848 the influx of colonists accelerated. Further stimulus to colonization was provided by the widespread confiscation of lands after an unsuccessful Muslim rebellion in 1871. French settlers had, by that time, become the dominant power in Algeria, owning much of the best land and initiating extensive agricultural development.

After the revolt of 1871 the situation was regularized by a new French administration under Adolphe Thiers. A civil administration with the status of a French *département* was established for much of Algeria, while the area of territory under military rule steadily declined. From 1871 to 1900 there was considerable economic development in Algeria and increasing European immigration, notably from Italy. A feature of this period was the growth of large-scale agricultural and industrial enterprises, which further concentrated power in the leaders of the settler groups. In 1900 Algeria secured administrative and financial autonomy, to be exercised through the so-called 'Financial Delegations', composed of two-thirds European and one-third Muslim members, which were empowered to set the annual budget and to raise loans for economic development.

Within 70 years the Muslim people of Algeria had been reduced from relative prosperity to economic, social and cultural subordination. Some 3m. inhabitants had died, tribes had been disbanded and the traditional economy altered during the prolonged 'civilizing' campaigns. In particular, the production of wine for export had replaced the growing of cereals for domestic consumption. By contrast, the settlers enjoyed a high level of prosperity in the years before the First World War.

BIRTH OF NATIONALISM

The spirit of nationalism, which was spreading throughout the Middle East, emerged among Algerian Muslims after the First World War. Nationalist aspirations were voiced not only by Algerian veterans of the war in Europe but also by those Algerians who had gone to France to study or work. In 1924 one of these students, Messali Hadj, in collaboration with the French Communist Party, founded in Paris the first Algerian nationalist newspaper; the link with the Communists was, however, severed in 1927. Messali Hadj and his movement were forced into hiding by the French Government, but re-emerged in 1933 to sponsor a congress on the future of Algeria—demanding full independence, the recall of French troops, the establishment of a revolutionary government, large-scale reforms in land ownership and the nationalization of industrial enterprises.

More moderate doctrines were advanced by an influential body of French-educated Muslims, formalized in 1930 as the Federation of Muslim Councillors. Under the leadership of Ferhat Abbas, it sought integration with France on a basis of complete equality. The victory of the Popular Front in the French elections of 1936 gave rise to the hope that some of these aspirations might be peaceably achieved. However, the Blum-Viollet Plan, which would have granted full rights of citizenship to an increasing number of Algerian Muslims, was abandoned by the French Government as it was fiercely opposed by French settlers and the Algerian civil service.

The years immediately prior to the Second World War were characterized by growing nationalist discontent, in which Hadj played a significant part with the formation of the Party of the Algerian People (PPA). The outbreak of war in 1939 suspended the nationalists' activities, but the war greatly strengthened their position. Although the Vichy administration in Algeria, strongly supported by the French settlers, was antipathetic to nationalist sentiment, the Allied landings in North Africa in 1942 provided an opportunity for the Algerian nationalists to present constitutional demands. A group led by Abbas submitted to the French authorities and the Allied military command a memorandum demanding the post-war establishment of an Algerian constituent assembly, to be elected by universal suffrage. However, no demand was made for Algerian independence outside the French framework.

These proposals, to which the French authorities remained unresponsive, were followed early in 1943 by the 'Manifesto of the Algerian People', which demanded immediate reforms, including the introduction of Arabic as an official language and the end of colonization. Further proposals, submitted in May, envisaged the post-war creation of an Algerian state with a constitution to be determined by a constituent assembly, and anticipated an eventual North African Union, comprising Tunisia, Algeria and Morocco. The newly-established Free French administration in Algiers categorically rejected the Manifesto and the subsequent proposals.

Confronted with growing Muslim discontent, and following a visit to Algiers by Gen. Charles de Gaulle, a new statute for Algeria came into effect in March 1944. Membership of the French electoral college was opened to 60,000 Muslims, but

there were still 450,000 European voters, and only 32,000 Muslims registered to vote. The Muslim share of the seats in the *communes mixtes* was restricted to 40%. All further discussion of Algeria's future relationship with France was rejected.

Shortly afterwards, Abbas founded the Friends of the Manifesto of Freedom (AML), which aimed to establish an autonomous Algerian republic linked federally with France. The movement was based mainly on the support of middle-class Muslims, and also gained a certain following among the masses, who comprised the main support of the PPA during 1944–45.

FRENCH INTRANSIGENCE

All possibility of a gradually negotiated settlement was destroyed by blunders of post-war French policy and the opposition of the French settlers to any concessions to Muslim aspirations. Riots at Sétif in May 1945 were ruthlessly suppressed; it was estimated that 8,000–40,000 Muslims were killed. This suppression, the subsequent arrest of Abbas and the dissolution of the AML convinced many nationalist leaders that force was the only means of gaining their objective.

Nevertheless, attempts to reach a compromise continued. In March 1946 Abbas, released under an amnesty, launched the Democratic Union of the Algerian Manifesto (UDMA), with a programme providing for the creation of an autonomous, secular Algerian state within the French Union. Despite successes in elections to the French Assembly, the UDMA failed to achieve its objectives. It withdrew from the Assembly in September and refused to participate in the next elections. The breach was filled by the more radical Movement for the Triumph of Democratic Liberties (MTLD), formed by Hadj at the end of the war, which demanded the creation of a sovereign constituent assembly and the withdrawal of French troops.

In another attempt at compromise, the French Government introduced a new Constitution, adopted on 20 September 1947, granting French citizenship, and therefore the right to vote, to all Algerian citizens, both men and women, and recognizing Arabic as equal in status to French. The proposed new Algerian Assembly, however, was to be divided into two colleges, each of 60 members, one to represent the 1.5m. resident Europeans, the other the 9m. Algerian Muslims. Other provisions excluded any legislation contrary to the interest of the colonists.

The new Constitution was never brought fully into operation. Following MTLD successes in the municipal elections of October 1947, the elections to the Algerian Assembly were openly interfered with: many candidates were arrested and polling stations were improperly operated. As a result only one-quarter of the members returned to the second college in April 1948 belonged to the MTLD or the UDMA; the remainder, known as the 'Béni-Oui-Oui', were nominally independent, but easy to manipulate. Such methods continued to be employed in local and national elections during the next six years, as well as in the Algerian elections to the French National Assembly in June 1951. Some of the improvements envisaged under the 1947 Constitution were never put into effect. The aim was to destroy, or at least render harmless, opposition to French rule; the result was to compel the main forces of nationalism to operate clandestinely.

As early as 1947 several of the younger members of the MTLD had formed the 'Secret Organization' (OS), which collected arms and money and organized a network of cells throughout Algeria in preparation for armed insurrection and the establishment of a revolutionary government. Two years later the OS felt itself strong enough to launch a terrorist attack in Oran. The movement was discovered subsequently and most of its leaders were arrested. A nucleus survived, however, in the Kabyle region and the organizer of the attack, Ahmed Ben Bella, escaped to Cairo in 1952.

A decisive split was opening in the ranks of the MTLD, and the veteran Hadj, who now embraced nebulous doctrines of Pan-Arabism, was gradually losing control of the party organization to more activist members. In March 1954 nine former members of the OS formed the Revolutionary Council for Unity and Action (CRUA) to prepare for an immediate revolt against French rule.

WAR OF INDEPENDENCE

Plans for the insurrection were formulated at a series of CRUA meetings in Switzerland during March–October 1954. Algeria was divided into six *wilaya* (administrative districts) and a military commander was appointed for each. When the revolt was launched on 1 November the CRUA changed its name to the National Liberation Front (Front de libération nationale—FLN), its armed forces being known as the National Liberation Army (Armée de libération nationale—ALN). Beginning in the Aurès, by early 1955 the revolt had spread to the Constantine area, the Kabyle and the Moroccan frontier, west of Oran. By the end of 1956 the ALN was active throughout the settled areas of Algeria.

Abbas and Ahmad Francis of the more moderate UDMA and the religious leaders of the *ulema* (Muslim scholar/lawyers) joined the FLN in April 1956, thereby integrating all sectors of Algerian nationalist feeling with the exception of Hadj's Algerian National Movement (MNA). In August a secret congress of the FLN, convened at Soummam in the Kabyle, established a central committee and formed the National Council of the Algerian Revolution. A socialist programme for the future Algerian republic and plans for a terrorist offensive in Algiers were also approved.

Between September 1956 and June 1957 bomb explosions engineered by the FLN caused great loss of life. This terrorism was halted only by severe French repression of the Muslim population, including the use of torture and internment. Guerrilla activities continued, but electrified barriers were erected along the Tunisian and Moroccan borders and ALN bands attempting to cross into Algeria suffered heavy losses.

In June 1957 the French Government introduced legislation to link Algeria indissolubly with France, but the measure was not approved. Following the Soummam conference, a joint Moroccan-Tunisian plan had been announced for the establishment of a North African federation linked with France. FLN leaders began negotiations in Morocco in October 1957. However, Ben Bella and his companions were kidnapped *en route* from Morocco to Tunisia, when the French pilot of their aircraft landed at Algiers. The French authorities could hardly ignore this *fait accompli*, and the hijacked leaders were arrested and interned in France. Neither the internment of FLN leaders nor the bombing by French aircraft, in February 1958, of a Tunisian border village, in which 79 villagers were killed, weakened the resolve or the capacity of the FLN to continue fighting, and the failure of these desperate measures only made the possibility of French negotiations with the FLN more likely. This, in turn, provoked a violent reaction from the Europeans in Algeria (only about one-half of whom were of French origin).

In May 1958 the colonists rebelled and installed 'committees of public safety' in the major Algerian towns. Supported by the army and exploiting the fear of civil war, the colonists prompted the overthrow of the discredited Fourth French Republic and celebrated de Gaulle's return to power, in the belief that he would further their aim of complete integration of Algeria with France. Although de Gaulle intensified military action against the FLN, this was achieved only at the cost of increased terrorism in Algiers and of growing tension on the Tunisian and Moroccan borders. The FLN responded in August by establishing the Provisional Government of the Algerian Republic (GPRA) in Tunis, headed by Abbas and including Ben Bella and the other leaders who had been interned in France. Already de Gaulle was beginning to recognize the strength of Algerian nationalism and was moving cautiously towards accepting FLN demands.

NEGOTIATIONS AND THE COLONISTS' OPPOSITION

Initially de Gaulle's public statements on Algeria were vague. When he did make an unequivocal pronouncement in September 1959, upholding the right of Algerians to determine their own future, the colonists reacted swiftly. In January 1960 they rebelled again, this time against de Gaulle, and erected barricades in Algiers. However, without the support of the army the insurrection collapsed within nine days. Provisional talks between French and FLN delegates took place in secret near Paris in mid-1960 but were inconclusive.

In November 1960 de Gaulle announced that a referendum was to be held on the organization of government in Algeria, pending self-determination, and the following month he visited Algeria to prepare the way. In the referendum the electorate was asked to approve a draft law providing for self-determination and immediate reforms to give Algerians the oppor-

tunity to participate in government. There were mass abstentions from voting in Algeria, however, and in February 1961 new French approaches to the FLN were made through the President of Tunisia. Direct negotiations between French and FLN representatives began at Evian, on the Franco-Swiss border in May but foundered in August over the question of the Sahara and because of a French attack on the blockaded French naval base at Bizerta (Tunisia), which resulted in the deaths of 800–1,300 Tunisians.

Europeans in Algeria and sections of the French army, meanwhile, had formed the Secret Army Organization (OAS) to resist a negotiated settlement and the transfer of power from European hands. In April 1961 four generals organized the seizure of Algiers, but this attempt at an army coup proved abortive as most regular officers remained loyal to de Gaulle. Offensive operations against the Algerian rebels, suspended upon the commencement of the Evian talks, were resumed by the French Government and fighting continued, although on a reduced scale. At the same time, the OAS initiated a campaign of indiscriminate terrorist violence against native Algerians. The Mayor of Evian had already been killed by an OAS bomb, and attacks were now also mounted in Paris.

Secret contacts between the French Government and the FLN were re-established in October 1961. Negotiations resumed in December and in January 1962 in Geneva and Rome, the five members of the GPRA interned in France taking part through a representative of the King of Morocco. Ministerial-level meetings were held in strict secrecy in Paris in February and the negotiations were concluded at Evian in March with the signing of a cease-fire agreement and a declaration of future policy, which provided for the establishment of an independent Algerian state after a transitional period, and for the safeguarding of individual rights and liberties. Other declarations issued subsequently dealt with the rights of French citizens in Algeria and with future Franco-Algerian co-operation. In the military sphere, France was to retain the naval base at Mers el-Kebir for 15 years and the nuclear testing site in the Sahara, together with various landing rights, for five years.

In accordance with the Evian accords, a provisional Government was formed on 28 March 1962, with Abderrahman Farès as President and an executive composed of FLN members, other Muslims and Europeans. The USSR and many East European, African and Asian countries quickly gave *de jure* recognition to the GPRA.

The signing of the Evian accords provoked renewed opposition by the OAS. A National Council of French Resistance in Algeria was formed, with Gen. Raoul Salan (one of the leaders of the attempted coup in 1961) as Commander-in-Chief. OAS commando units launched attacks on the Muslim population and on public buildings in an attempt to prompt a general breach of the cease-fire. After the failure of the OAS to establish an 'insurrectional zone' in the Orléansville (El-Asnam) area and Salan's capture in April 1962, and with a renewal of FLN terrorist activity and reprisals, increasing numbers of Europeans began to leave Algeria for France. Secret negotiations between OAS leaders and the FLN, aimed at securing guarantees for the European population, revealed a division in the OAS, heralding the virtual end of European terrorist activity. By late June more than one-half of the European population of Algeria had left the country.

The final steps towards Algerian independence were taken at a referendum on 1 July 1962 at which 91% of participants voted for independence. Algerian independence was proclaimed by Gen. de Gaulle on 3 July.

THE INDEPENDENT STATE

The achievement of power by the FLN revealed serious tensions within the Government, while the problems facing the new state after eight years of civil war were formidable.

The dominant position in the GPRA of the 'centralist' group, headed by Ben Khedda and comprising former members of the MTLD, was threatened by the release in March 1962 of the five GPRA members who had been detained in France—Ben Bella, Muhammad Khider, Muhammad Boudiaf, Hocine Aït Ahmed and Rabah Bitat. Boudiaf and Aït Ahmed rallied temporarily to the support of Ben Khedda, while the others formed yet another opposition faction besides that of Abbas, who had been removed from the GPRA leadership in 1961.

The ALN leadership was also split, with the commanders of the main armed forces in Tunisia and Morocco opposing the politicians of the GPRA, and the commanders of the internal guerrilla groups hostile to all external and military factions.

Serious differences emerged when the National Council of the Algerian Revolution met in Tripoli, Libya, in May 1962 to consider policies for the new state. A commission headed by Ben Bella produced a programme envisaging large-scale agrarian reform through expropriation and the establishment of peasant co-operatives and state farms; a state monopoly of external trade; and a foreign policy aimed towards Maghreb unity, neutrality and anti-colonialism, especially in Africa. Despite the opposition of Ben Khedda's group, the Tripoli programme became the official FLN policy.

After independence the GPRA Cabinet, with the exception of Ben Bella, flew to Algiers, where they installed themselves alongside the official Provisional Executive. Ben Khedda attempted to reassert control over the ALN by dismissing the Commander-in-Chief, Col Houari Boumedienne. Ben Bella, however, flew to Morocco to join Boumedienne, and in July 1962 they crossed into Algeria and established headquarters in Tlemcen, where Ben Bella instituted the Political Bureau as the chief executive organ of the FLN and a rival to the GPRA. After negotiations, he was joined by some of the GPRA leaders, leaving Ben Khedda isolated in Algiers, with Boudiaf and Aït Ahmed in opposition.

Several *wilaya* leaders, however, felt that, having provided the internal resistance, they represented the true current of the revolution, and were opposed to the Political Bureau and Boumedienne. While ALN forces loyal to the Bureau occupied Constantine and Bône (Annaba) in the east in July 1962, Algiers remained in the hands of the leadership of *wilaya* IV, who refused the Bureau entry. When Boumedienne's forces marched on Algiers from Oran in September there were serious clashes with *wilaya* IV troops. Total civil war was averted, partly because of mass demonstrations against the fighting which were organized by the Algerian General Workers' Union (UGTA).

The struggle for power proved costly for Ben Khedda. Before the elections were held on 20 September 1962, one-third of the 180 candidates on the single list drafted in August had been purged (including Ben Khedda himself) and replaced with lesser-known figures. Some 99% of the electorate were declared to have voted in favour of the proposed powers of the Constituent Assembly. The functions of the GPRA were transferred to the Assembly when it convened on 25 September, and Abbas was elected its President. The Algerian Republic was proclaimed, and on the following day Ben Bella was elected Prime Minister. He subsequently appointed a Cabinet comprising his personal associates and former ALN officers.

BEN BELLA IN POWER

The new Government immediately acted to consolidate its position. Hadj's PPA (formerly the MNA), the Algerian Communist Party, and Boudiaf's Party of the Socialist Revolution were all banned in November 1962; the *wilaya* system was abolished the following month, and, apart from the UGTA, all organizations affiliated to the FLN were brought firmly under control.

The country's economic plight was severe. Some 90% (1m.) of the Europeans, representing virtually all the entrepreneurs, technicians, administrators, teachers, doctors and skilled workers, had left the country. Factories, farms and shops had closed, leaving 70% of the population unemployed. Public buildings and records had been destroyed by the OAS. At the end of the war, in which more than 1m. people had died, there had been 2m. people in internment camps and 500,000 refugees in Tunisia and Morocco. An austerity plan was formulated in December 1962, and large loans and technical assistance from France, plus other emergency foreign aid, enabled the Government to remain in power.

By packing the first UGTA congress with FLN militants and unemployed, the FLN managed in January 1963 to gain control of the UGTA executive, which had been opposed to the dictatorial nature of the new Government. In March the workers' committees which, aided by the UGTA, had taken over the operation of many of the abandoned European estates were

legalized; the remaining estates were nationalized in 1963. The system of workers' management, known as *autogestion*, under which the workers elected their own management board to work alongside a state-appointed director, became the basis of 'Algerian socialism'.

In April 1963 Ben Bella assumed the post of Secretary-General of the FLN. In August he secured the adoption by the Assembly of a draft constitution providing for a presidential regime, with the FLN as the sole political party. The new Constitution was approved by referendum, and on 13 September Ben Bella was elected President for a five-year period, taking the title of Commander-in-Chief of the Armed Forces as well as becoming Head of State and head of government. These moves towards dictatorial government aroused opposition. Abbas, the leading proponent of a more liberal policy, resigned from the presidency of the Assembly and was subsequently expelled from the FLN.

THE BOUMEDIENNE ERA

On 19 June 1965 Ben Bella was deposed and arrested in a swift and bloodless military *coup d'état*, led by the Minister of Defence, Col Boumedienne, whose army had brought Ben Bella to power in 1962. Supreme political authority in Algeria passed to the Council of the Revolution, consisting mostly of military figures and presided over by Boumedienne. The Boumedienne regime enjoyed a remarkable degree of stability after the debilitating rivalries and uncertainties of the early years of independence. The majority of the Algerian population greeted the new regime with indifference, and most active opposition was crushed after an abortive coup in 1967. There was no real attempt to democratize the structure of political control, and Algeria continued to be governed by a few men and a few institutions—with the army and the administration having central importance as executors. The FLN, once a successful mass political movement, ceased to play an effective role, and although a number of attempts were made to revive it, the heavy hand of the state and the army denied it any independent political activity. Although elected local and provincial assemblies were created in the late 1960s, their role was essentially advisory and they operated within a framework determined by the central Government.

The personal authority of Boumedienne increased in the 1970s, and in 1975 he announced that elections for a National Assembly and a President were to be held, and that a national charter would be drafted to provide the state with a new constitution. Public discussion of the national charter was vigorous and often critical of local and central government, but it received the approval of 98.5% of the population at a referendum held in June 1976. The essence of the charter was the irreversible commitment of Algeria to socialism, albeit a socialism specifically adapted to Third World conditions. The dominant role of the FLN was reasserted, but, as a concession to conservative elements, Islam was recognized as the state religion. In November a new Constitution, embodying the principles of the charter, was also approved by referendum, and in December Boumedienne was elected unopposed as President, with 99% of votes cast. To complete the new formal structure of power, a 261-member National People's Assembly was elected in February 1977 from 783 candidates selected by a committee of the FLN.

During the Boumedienne era Algeria's activities in international affairs were as ambitious as its development strategy. In any conventional analysis Algeria ranks as a small power, yet the record of its diplomacy was impressive. Boumedienne's ministers often expressed a grand concept of Algeria's role in the world, and the Minister of Foreign Affairs, Abdelaziz Bouteflika, described Algeria as the 'central country' in the Maghreb, on the borders of the Mediterranean, with an attachment to both Africa and the Arab world, and thus ideally placed at the crossroads of Europe, Asia and Africa. The country's major successes in world affairs during the 1970s were in oil politics and within the Non-aligned Movement. Algeria joined the Organization of the Petroleum Exporting Countries (OPEC) in 1969 and, and as a minor producer, quickly became one of the organization's leading 'hawks', consistently campaigning for the maintenance of high prices for the commodity. Among the Non-aligned states, Algeria argued persuasively in favour of nationalization and producer cartels and used the example of its own experience to demonstrate that the struggle for development should be seen as an extension of the struggle for liberation. These policies were promoted energetically at the fourth conference of Non-aligned states held in Algiers in September 1973, and again in April 1974 when Boumedienne addressed a special session of the UN General Assembly. His call for a 'new international economic order' to redress the economic disparities between the Western industrialized countries and the developing world heralded Algeria's efforts to establish an international forum to tackle these problems through dialogue rather than confrontation. Algeria's mobilization of the Non-aligned world, the 'seventy-seven' developing countries, the UN and OPEC in support of these initiatives, even though the practical outcome was negligible, won it new prestige and almost universal recognition as a diplomatic leader of the Third World.

In spite of the militancy of Algerian rhetoric in international affairs and its vociferous support for liberation movements, in practice Algeria's foreign relations have been tempered by a good deal of pragmatism. Anxieties in the West that Algeria might fall within the Soviet sphere of influence proved unfounded, and co-operation with the USSR was limited essentially to the supply of military equipment for Algeria's armed forces, while technology for its economic development programme was purchased mainly from the USA and Western Europe. Although Algeria was critical of US actions in Latin America, the Middle East and Viet Nam, by 1976 the USA had replaced France as Algeria's principal trading partner. Increasing contact with the English-speaking world inevitably produced new strains in Algeria's intense but uneasy relations with its former colonial power. Bilateral relations had already been aggravated by the nationalization, in 1971, of French oil interests—responsible for some two-thirds of Algeria's total production—and France's decision to impose a boycott of Algerian petroleum, and by the inability, or unwillingness, of the French police to protect Algerian workers living in France. In 1973, following a series of racially-motivated incidents in the south of France directed against Algerians, the Algerian Government suspended all new emigration to France.

The dispute over French oil interests was resolved in late 1974, and in April 1975 Valéry Giscard d'Estaing became the first French President to visit Algeria since independence. However, a new source of friction arose later in 1975 when Spanish Sahara was annexed by Morocco and Mauritania following their Tripartite Agreement with Spain. Algeria denounced the annexation and gave active support to the Saharan liberation movement, the Frente Popular para la Liberación de Saguia el-Hamra y Río de Oro (the Polisario Front), which proclaimed the Sahrawi Arab Democratic Republic (SADR) in 1976. France, on the other hand, supported Morocco, and in May 1978 French military aircraft intervened by carrying out bombing raids against Polisario guerrillas. The prospect of full-scale war between Morocco and Algeria over Western Sahara quickly receded; however, Algeria continued to provide military and diplomatic assistance to Polisario and refuge for displaced persons and Polisario fighters near Tindouf.

CHADLI IN POWER

Boumedienne died suddenly on 27 December 1978 without naming a successor. The choice of Col Ben Djedid Chadli, the commander of the Oran military district, as the new President—rather than Minister of Foreign Affairs Bouteflika, or Muhammad Salah Yahiaoui, the administrative head of the FLN, both of whom had been regarded as more obvious potential candidates—came as a surprise both inside and outside the country, but unquestionably reaffirmed the political primacy of the armed forces. Chadli was inaugurated as President on 9 February 1979, after his candidature had been approved by 94% of the electorate.

Initially the Chadli Government was in a weak position, as the President's own supporters were in a minority. However, the existence of a number of factions within the regime gave Chadli some room for manoeuvre and enabled him gradually to exert his control over the state apparatus. Bouteflika, Yahiaoui and other influential personalities from the Boumedienne era were dismissed first from the Political Bureau and then from the Central Committee of the FLN, paving the way for the removal of potential opponents at lower levels of the system. For the first time since independence a Prime Minister was named: Col Muhammad ben Ahmed Abd al-Ghani. This nomination preceded constitutional changes, adopted by the National People's Assembly in June 1979, which made the appointment of a Prime Minister obligatory and also reduced the President's term of office from six to five years, to coincide with five-yearly party congresses.

Following his re-election as party Secretary-General at the FLN's fifth party congress in December 1983, Chadli automatically became the party's candidate in the presidential election held in January 1984 at which he was re-elected for a second five-year term, with 95% of the vote. After his re-election Chadli quickly strengthened his position by carrying out a major reallocation of both party and government posts.

On coming to power Chadli had declared that he would uphold the policies of his predecessor, but it soon became clear that, despite the official rhetoric about 'continuity', Boumedienne's policies were to be revised, reversed or abandoned. In foreign affairs Boumedienne's aim of presenting Algeria as one of the leaders of the developing world was abandoned, together with the policy of distracting attention from domestic problems by stridency abroad. Chadli forged close links with conservative states while attempting not to alienate radicals. Algeria earned high regard as a mediator, notably in negotiations that secured the release of US hostages detained in Iran after the 1979 Islamic Revolution, and in the brokering of an agreement in 1989 between Chad and Libya over the disputed Aozou Strip. Much attention was paid to improving relations with Algeria's Maghreb neighbours, especially Morocco, and in February 1989 Algeria signed the treaty creating the Union du Maghreb arabe (UMA—Union of the Arab Maghreb) with Libya, Mauritania, Morocco and Tunisia.

In domestic politics the Chadli regime devoted most of its attention to the economy, introducing a range of reforms. Some analysts interpreted these as a pragmatic attempt to deal with the country's economic problems, while others accused the Chadli regime of consolidating the gains of the new industrial bourgeoisie and encouraging the gradual 'compradorization' of the Algerian economy and society. What is not in doubt is that the impact of the liberalization programme was uneven and had unintended consequences. Restructuring state-owned industrial enterprises did not improve productivity. Far from transforming the pattern of trade, the country became almost completely dependent on petroleum and gas for its export revenues. The liberalization of the deeply troubled agricultural sector failed to stimulate food production, although it paved the way for the enrichment of certain private farmers specializing in speculative products. By the early 1990s Algeria had the most precarious food security situation in the region, with as much as 80% of its food supply being imported. The private sector, formal and informal, legal and illegal, expanded dramatically. The entrepreneurs who benefited most from economic liberalization were those close to the state who could avoid the stifling bureaucracy because of their association with government officials. This produced serious corruption at the highest levels, led by what Algerians refer to as the 'mafia', within the informal economy.

The dramatic collapse in oil prices in 1986, together with the depreciation of the US dollar, had a devastating effect on the Algerian economy. Receipts from sales of crude oil dropped by 80% in real terms and, as prices for Algeria's exports of natural gas were linked to that of crude petroleum, overall hydrocarbon export receipts fell from US $12,970m. in 1985 to $7,633m. in 1986 and remained depressed for the rest of the decade. Algeria was particularly vulnerable because it had incurred heavy foreign debt during the 1970s in order to finance its ambitious development programme and, following the fall in petroleum prices, debt-servicing costs accounted for a growing proportion of the country's export revenues. The Government responded to the crisis by taking measures to reduce both imports and public spending. A second phase of reforms was introduced to accelerate economic liberalization. Subsidies on basic consumer goods were reduced and price controls lifted from state industrial and agricultural sectors in order to allow market forces to regulate resource distribution. The social costs of these reforms were high, particularly for the vulnerable strata of society. Inequalities in income widened and, while a privileged minority was enriched, the vast majority of Algerians were severely affected by rising prices and cuts in both social benefits and public sector jobs. Unemployment rose and the purchasing power of the majority of families declined drastically.

THE 1988 RIOTS AND THE RE-EMERGENCE OF THE ISLAMIST MOVEMENT

The tensions that had been mounting in Algerian society erupted in widespread rioting in October 1988. The disturbances, affecting Algiers and other cities, proved difficult to control, and the eventual deployment of the army incurred intense popular anger at the brutal manner in which the rioters were subdued. Hundreds were killed and thousands injured and there were reports of the torture of some detainees. It was rumoured at the time that the clandestine communist party, the Parti d'avant-garde socialiste (PAGS—renamed Ettahaddi in 1993), which was influential in the main trade union, the Union Générale des Travailleurs Algériens (UGTA), had been responsible for provoking these disturbances in an attempt to force the Government to decelerate its economic liberalization programme. The riots rapidly became an opportunity for the release of feelings of intense frustration and alienation among the Algerian youth against a regime that was perceived to have marginalized and abandoned them.

The riots also saw the re-emergence of the Islamist movement in mainstream Algerian political life. Islamist militants had not instigated the riots but they represented the only organized movement to voice the frustration of those involved, and Islamists became prominent targets for the security forces in the subsequent repression. There is evidence that at first the Chadli regime quietly encouraged the Islamists in order to intimidate the left and the Berberists. Unlike their opposition rivals, the Islamists did not hesitate to employ violence to promote their cause. Many state-controlled mosques were taken over by force and hundreds of unofficial mosques beyond state control were established. In their desire to uphold public morality, stocks of alcohol were destroyed and brothels were attacked in several towns. In particular the universities became the scenes of violent confrontation between militant Islamists and the left and the Berberists. The first armed resistance was launched by a former FLN war veteran, Mustafa Bouiali, who during 1981–1987 embarked on an armed struggle against 'the impious state' in the name of *jihad* (holy war). By reviving the old *maquis* traditions in the mountains, the rebels evaded the security forces for over a year before Bouiali was finally killed.

INTRODUCTION OF A MULTI-PARTY SYSTEM

Chadli responded to the October 1988 riots by accelerating economic reforms and introducing wide-ranging political changes. In late October 1988 he proposed that the identification of the state with the FLN be ended by allowing non-party candidates to contest elections. Furthermore, the Prime Minister and the Government would no longer be responsible to the President, who would stand above party politics, but to the National People's Assembly. To demonstrate that these measures would not be merely superficial, five days later Chadli dismissed his uncompromising FLN deputy, Muhammad Cherif Messaadia, replacing him with the more liberal Abd al-Hamid Mehiri, who had been the Algerian ambassador to France and Morocco. On 3 November the proposed reforms were approved at a referendum by 92.3% of the votes cast (in a turn-out of 83.1% of eligible voters).

After Chadli's re-election as President in December 1988 (when he received 81% of the votes cast) further constitutional changes were approved by 73.4% of the votes cast at a referendum in February 1989, signalling a clear ideological break with the past. The 'irreversible commitment to socialism' was abandoned, and freedoms of expression, association and organization were guaranteed, as were the rights to unionize and strike. Executive, legislative and judicial functions were separated and no longer controlled by the FLN; instead they were to be supervised by a Constitutional Council. Mouloud Hamrouche, hitherto a senior figure in the presidential office, was appointed Prime Minister in September 1989.

Most notable of the changes in progress, however, 'associations of a political nature' were allowed to compete with the FLN providing their platforms were neither religious nor region-

alist. A law on political associations was passed in July 1989, and a new electoral law adopted later that month paved the way to a controlled multi-party system. Within a short time some 30 political parties, representing a wide range of ideological tendencies, had been officially registered. Apart from the previously outlawed Front des forces socialistes (FFS), led by Hocine Aït Ahmed (one of the *chefs historiques* of the Algerian revolution), and Saïd Saâdi's newly created Rassemblement pour la culture et la démocratie, both of which drew their support predominantly from the Berber-speaking Kabyle region, together with Ben Bella's Mouvement pour la démocratie en Algérie (MDA), most parties were relatively small and insignificant—with the exception of the fundamentalist Front islamique du salut (FIS), which quickly emerged as the only serious nation-wide competitor to the FLN. Although other Islamist parties emerged, the FIS gathered together the major, yet diverse, elements of the Islamist movement into a political coalition which had a well-organized and well-financed party network, strongly rooted at the local level in the many neighbourhood mosques. The party attracted support from the so-called 'pious bourgeoisie', some members of the technical and intellectual élite, and from the deprived and frustrated urban youth from the city slums, the main victims of the regime's economic reforms.

LOCAL AND NATIONAL ELECTIONS

The new multi-party system was put to the test in June 1990 when municipal and provincial elections were held—the first free elections in Algeria since independence. Disregarding a high rate of voter abstention (estimated at between 35% and 40%), the FIS won a sweeping victory—obtaining some 55% of votes cast and gaining control of 853 municipalities, including the three major cities, Algiers, Oran and Constantine, and 32 *wilayat*. Only in the Berber-speaking Kabyle and in the south did the FIS fail to win convincingly. In contrast, its chief rival, the FLN, which had entered the elections deeply divided, was comprehensively defeated, obtaining only 32% of the votes and taking control of only 487 municipalities and 14 *wilayat*. Prior to the elections, the former Prime Minister, Abd al-Hamid Brahimi, had alleged that FLN and government officials had received US $26,000m. ($2,000m. more than the entire national debt) in bribes during the previous decade. The FIS's victory was widely interpreted as a crushing rejection of rule by the FLN establishment, rather than an endorsement for the project and world view of radical Islamism.

In December 1990 the National People's Assembly approved a vote of confidence in Prime Minister Hamrouche, the first such vote for 20 years. At the end of the month the Assembly approved a law stipulating that, after 1997, Arabic would become Algeria's official language and that the use of the French and Berber languages by private companies and by political parties would thereafter incur heavy fines. The new law was regarded as an attack on Algeria's Western-educated élite and the Berber people, and some 500,000 people demonstrated in Algiers against religious and political intolerance. The FIS regarded the adoption of the 'Arabization' law as a political triumph, but it no longer held a monopoly on Islamist activism. There were now two new political parties which aimed to recruit people dissatisfied with the intolerance of the FIS and those who saw no incompatibility between Islam and liberal economics. Sheikh Abdallah Djaballah founded the Islamic Renaissance Movement (Nahdah), while Sheikh Mahfoud Nahnah founded Hamas. The FIS, which was also losing support to the MDA, claimed that these new parties had been sponsored by the Government. The FIS itself appeared to be undermined by divisions between the organization's leader, Abassi Madani, and another senior figure, Ali Belhadj, notably on the issue of the crisis arising from Iraq's invasion of Kuwait: while the latter urged his supporters to prepare to give military support to Iraq in the face of the US-led military build-up in the Gulf region, Madani argued that military training should be restricted to the army and that the FIS should achieve power through electoral means.

In early April 1991 the Government announced that the long-awaited parliamentary elections would be held in two rounds in June and July, and introduced major revisions to the country's electoral law. In constituencies where no candidate achieved an absolute majority in the first round of voting, second ballots were to be conducted; campaigning in mosques and proxy voting were to be restricted; and the number of constituencies was increased from 290 to 542. The FIS regarded these changes as a deliberate ploy to reduce its chances of victory in the forthcoming elections, and demanded that a presidential election be held concurrently with the legislative elections. In protest at the new electoral law, in May the FIS urged an indefinite general strike and numerous FIS supporters took to the streets of Algiers as part of a campaign of peaceful protest. However, when riot police were ordered to clear the streets fierce fighting erupted as armed FIS supporters set up barricades in two of the city's main squares.

At the beginning of June 1991 Chadli declared a 'state of siege' and suspended the elections indefinitely. Tanks were deployed in Algiers and a curfew was imposed. Armed with extensive powers, the military subsequently restored relative calm on the streets of the capital. Shortly afterwards the FIS leadership abandoned the general strike, declaring that the President had agreed to hold both legislative and presidential elections before the end of the year and to change the disputed electoral laws to ensure that elections would be 'clean and fair'. What appeared to be a victory for the FIS antagonized elements within the army bitterly hostile to the Islamists. Army leaders demanded a crack-down on the radical fringe of the Islamist movement, and later in June, when troops removed Islamic slogans from FIS-controlled municipal buildings, further violent clashes erupted as FIS militants confronted the security forces. At the end of June Madani, Belhadj and some 2,500 of their supporters (8,000 according to opponents of the Government) were arrested. The two FIS leaders were accused of having led an armed conspiracy against the state in an attempt to take power. Despite rumours that an army-backed regime was to be installed, the army did not take power at this time but waited a further six months before intervening decisively. Some analysts have argued that leading members of the military hierarchy were persuaded that the FIS would not be able to repeat their success in the forthcoming legislative elections; others maintained that the army leadership was poised to take over but that, aware of international opinion, the military was waiting until it could claim that the incompetent Chadli regime had allowed the political situation to escalate out of control and that it had been forced to intervene to protect the integrity of the state against the threat of an Islamist take-over.

In October 1991 the National People's Assembly approved amendments to the electoral law, establishing the number of single-member parliamentary constituencies at 430. Independent candidates would in future need to obtain only 300 (rather than 500) supporters of their candidacy, and the minimum age of parliamentary candidates was lowered from 35 to 28 years. President Chadli announced that the first round of voting in the general election would take place on 26 December, with a second round of voting on 16 January 1992 in constituencies where there had been no outright winner at the first round. The FIS threatened to boycott the elections unless its leaders were released, but agreed to participate at the last minute.

The 430 seats in the National People's Assembly were contested by 5,712 candidates representing 49 political parties and by more than 1,000 independents. In the first round of voting, in which some 59% of the electorate participated, the FIS took an apparently unassailable lead, winning 188 seats outright, although it had obtained just 3.2m. votes (1.5m. fewer than in the municipal elections) from an electorate of 13.3m. The FFS took 25 seats, while the former ruling party, the FLN, was relegated to a humiliating third place with only 15 seats (although it won about half as many votes as the FIS). The FLN complained of intimidation and malpractice in 340 constituencies in which officials of FIS-controlled municipalities had distributed voting papers. A second round of voting was required for 199 seats, with the FIS needing to win only 20 to gain an absolute majority in the Assembly. The other three Islamist parties, Nahdah, Hamas and El-Oumma, instructed their supporters to vote for the FIS against the FLN in the second round, but the secular parties failed to declare their support for the FLN. President Chadli, who had resigned from the FLN the previous year, reaffirmed that he would respect the election results and indicated his willingness to 'cohabit' with an FIS government. The FIS however, confident of winning at least

two-thirds of seats in the new Assembly, rejected the possibility of power-sharing and demanded the appointment of Abassi Madani as Prime Minister and the immediate holding of a presidential election. Meanwhile, there were widespread demonstrations in defence of democracy and against the potential establishment of an 'Iranian-style' fundamentalist regime.

THE MILITARY TAKE-OVER

On 4 January 1992 the National Assembly was dissolved by presidential decree. One week later, and five days before the scheduled second round of the election, President Chadli, apparently under intense pressure from the army chiefs, resigned 'to safeguard the interests of the country'. Tanks and heavily-armed troops were deployed around key buildings in the capital, and the High Security Council, dominated by three senior generals—the Minister of Defence, Khaled Nezzar, the Minister of the Interior, Larbi Belkheir, and Abd al-Malek Guenaizia, the armed forces chief-of-staff—and also including the Prime Minister, and the Ministers of Justice and Foreign Affairs—took power with the declared aim of preserving public order and national security. They appointed Abd al-Malek Benhabiles, the Chairman of the Constitutional Council, as acting Head of State. The second round of the elections was cancelled and a 'state of exception' was announced.

On 14 January 1992 a five-member High Council of State (HCS) was appointed to operate as a collegiate presidency until the expiry of Chadli's term of office in December 1993. The leading figure in the Council was clearly Nezzar, but its Chairman was Muhammad Boudiaf, one of the historic leaders of the War of Independence who now returned from self-imposed exile in Morocco where he had lived since 1964. Some analysts argued that the military take-over put an end to Algeria's inevitable transformation from a one-party authoritarian state to a liberal multi-party democratic polity and that the 1992 *coup d'état* marked a retreat to Algeria's authoritarian past. However, others insisted that the elections themselves had been deeply flawed and expressed serious doubts that an FIS-dominated government would have preserved democracy once it came to power. They emphasized that much of the political rhetoric of the FIS was highly intolerant and that the statements of its leaders left no doubt that the party's aim was the creation of an Islamic state and an end to multi-party democracy.

On taking power, the military junta moved swiftly against municipalities, newspapers and mosques controlled by the FIS. Security forces seized control of the FIS offices and arrested leading FIS officials, who were accused of inciting soldiers to desert. Violent clashes broke out between the army and demonstrators across the country, and on 9 February 1992 the HCS declared a 12-month state of emergency giving the security services sweeping powers of arrest and detention. Thousands of FIS supporters were arrested, and by the end of March some 9,000 were being held in special detention camps set up in remote parts of the Sahara. Already, more than 100 people had been killed in clashes between Islamist militants and the security forces.

In early March 1992, following a court ruling, the FIS was outlawed 'for pursuing by subversive means goals that endanger public order'. Madani and Belhadj were brought before a military court in late June, accused of aggression and conspiracy against the state, and were subsequently sentenced to 12 years in prison. The security situation continued to deteriorate, and at the end of August a series of bombings, including an attack on Algiers international airport which killed nine people and injured 120, marked a dangerous escalation in the cycle of violence. Tough new security laws were introduced as the authorities declared 'total war' against supporters of the proscribed FIS. A curfew was imposed in Algiers and surrounding areas, and was later extended to 10 other provinces. Three state security courts were established with the authority to impose harsh sentences including the death penalty. In January 1993 the first two Islamist militants, both of them former soldiers, were put to death, and more executions followed—including that of Hocine Abderramane, a close associate of Madani. In February the state of emergency was renewed indefinitely. The London-based human rights organization Amnesty International reported a dramatic increase in the use of torture by the security forces. These tough policies found support among some elements within Algerian society, but for the vast majority of the population, especially the urban poor, the crude techniques of mass repression provoked popular resentment and merely increased their support for the Islamists.

EMERGENCE OF ARMED ISLAMIST GROUPS

Following the proscription of the FIS and the dismantling of its political organization in early 1992, the Islamist initiative passed to a number of armed clandestine opposition groups, some of which derived from the earlier phase of armed Islamist resistance led by Mustafa Bouiali in the 1980s. The precise relationship of these groups with the FIS political leadership was unclear. The Mouvement de l'état islamique (MEI), under the leadership of Abdelkader Chebouti, a former associate of Bouiali, and Said Mekhloufi, a founder member of the FIS, attracted a certain number of militants from the dissolved FIS. Well organized and with a clear command structure, the MEI directed its struggle primarily against the state and its representatives. Its more radical rival, the Groupe islamique armé (GIA), linked together several largely autonomous cells, including many so-called 'Afghanists'—Algerian Islamists who had fought with the *mujahidin* in Afghanistan against the Soviet occupation—and groups that had opposed the electoral strategy of the political wing of the FIS. The GIA had its power base in the eastern suburbs of Algiers and in nearby towns such as Blida, while other cells were active around Sidi Bel Abbès in the west and the Jijel district in the north-east. It condemned as impious those pacifist FIS members who refused to take up arms, calling for a *jihad*, following the Afghan model, to establish a 'caliphate' in Algeria. The GIA targeted not only the security services but also sought to remove prominent public figures, intellectuals, journalists and teachers, not all of whom were linked to the regime, as well as 'impious' foreign nationals. Its warning that all foreigners should leave the country or die accelerated the exodus of foreign nationals. However, there were rumours that some of the more spectacular assassinations were the work of military security, which some analysts believed had infiltrated GIA factions as a means of eliminating those critical of the military junta. Armed Islamist groups attracted mainly young men from the poor urban quarters. At first they received voluntary contributions from members of the 'pious bourgeoisie' hostile to a regime that had robbed them of electoral victory. But they quickly resorted to extortion and intimidation, alienating their middle-class supporters and thus dividing and eventually weakening the Islamist movement.

THE ASSASSINATION OF BOUDIAF

Muhammad Boudiaf, who had been installed as chairman of the HCS to give a measure of legitimacy to the new regime, was assassinated on 29 June 1992 while opening a cultural centre in the eastern city of Annaba. Widely respected as a man of integrity, he had begun to give indications of a personal political agenda. In particular, his efforts to eradicate corruption had threatened many at the highest levels of the ruling establishment, and he had ensured that at least one senior army officer, Maj.-Gen. Mustafa Beloucif, was charged before a military tribunal for the embezzlement of millions of dinars. Although there was television footage of Boudiaf's killing, and the assassin was seized on the spot, it was by no means certain whether the assassination was the action of a lone killer or part of a conspiracy; nor was the motive for the killing clear. The HCS declared seven days of mourning and cancelled planned celebrations to commemorate the 30th anniversary of independence on 5 July; it also ordered a commission of inquiry into the assassination. Islamist extremists applauded the killing but did not claim credit for it. The inquiry's report was made available to the media in December, but with 76 of its 111 pages missing. Its conclusion was that the killer had not acted alone but on behalf of an unspecified organization that was increasingly identified with the FLN. One of the demands of those taking part in a demonstration in March 1993, the first permitted for more than a year, was for the truth about the murder of Boudiaf to be published. It was not until June 1995 that Lt Lembarek Boumâarafi, a member of the special anti-terrorist unit responsible for the President's security on the day of his assassination, was sentenced to death for Boudiaf's murder. Little new information was revealed at the trial, and the authorities maintained that Boumâarafi had acted alone. However, popular suspicion fell on the 'mafia' and its allies in the administration and army, often referred to as the *hizb fransa*—the 'party of France'.

There was speculation that Maj.-Gen. Nezzar would succeed Boudiaf as Chairman of the HCS, but he was in poor health and apparently unwilling to make too obvious the military's control of the state. After consulting with party leaders, another member of the HCS, Ali Kafi, the head of the Algerian War Veteran's Organization, was nominated for the chairmanship of the HCS. Kafi pledged adherence to Boudiaf's programme but showed no signs of enacting it. Sid-Ahmed Ghozali, who had been Prime Minister since mid-1991, resigned and was replaced by Belaid Abd es-Salam, who had been in charge of Algeria's hydrocarbons and industrial policy under Boumedienne. On the anniversary of the military take-over, Kafi promised that a new Constitution would be drafted, after consultation with groups not committed to violence, and that the resultant document would be pluralist and allow genuinely democratic elections. There would be a referendum on the balance of power between the President and the Government. Regarded as a further pretext for postponing elections, this proposal was greeted with scepticism by the main political parties.

In July 1993 Maj.-Gen. Nezzar was replaced as Minister of Defence by Gen. Liamine Zéroual, although he remained a member of the HCS. Gen. Muhammad Lamari, who had been responsible for organizing anti-terrorist units, was appointed Chief of Staff. In August 1993, after only a year in office, Abd es-Salam was replaced as Prime Minister by the Minister of Foreign Affairs, Redha Malek, a former career diplomat. There had been speculation for some weeks about the departure of Abd es-Salam, who had opposed economic liberalization policies, and both the French and US governments were reported to have favoured Malek's appointment. The appointment of Mourad Benachenhou, a former Algerian representative at the World Bank, as Minister of the Economy, apparently signalled a return to the reform programme. A senior army officer, Col Sélim Saâdi, was appointed Minister of the Interior, and this was followed by the reorganization of the security forces and the creation of a unified command between the military and police forces in the effort to combat Islamist violence.

LIAMINE ZÉROUAL BECOMES HEAD OF STATE

The mandate of the HCS was scheduled to expire on 31 December 1993, and in October the formation of an eight-member National Dialogue Commission (NDC) was announced, to oversee the transition to an elected government. The appointment of three generals to the commission openly brought the military into the political process for the first time. However, little progress was made by the NDC in its negotiations with opposition parties regarding the creation of a transitional regime. The only significant legal parties, the FLN and FFS, had strongly opposed the 1992 *coup d'état* and the interruption of the electoral process and had refused to co-operate with the military-backed governments installed since then. Since 1992 the power structure had become deeply divided, with two tendencies confronting one another: the so-called *éradicateurs*—who rejected any compromise with the FIS and the Islamist militants and insisted on the brutal suppression of the Islamist movement—and the *conciliateurs*, who believed that the political crisis could only be solved by compromise and dialogue with the Islamist opposition. The main *éradicateurs* were those senior army officers who had served in the French army before independence and who had occupied key positions in the army high command since 1988. Support outside the army for this hardline tendency was limited to the leadership of the trade union movement, the Berber Rassemblement pour la culture et la démocratie (RCD), the former communist party, Ettahaddi, women's groups and most of the francophone press. The *conciliateurs* could count on less formal support among the senior officer class, but included all the main political parties, human rights activists, and intellectuals and journalists grouped around the journal *Naqd* and the weekly *La Nation*.

In mid-December 1993 the HCS stated that it would not disband itself until a new presidential body had been inaugurated. It proposed the convening of a national dialogue conference in January 1994 to choose a new collective leadership. The conference proved to be an abject failure as it was boycotted by almost all the main political parties. The HCS then appeared to have abandoned the idea of a presidential triumvirate to rule during the transitional period from 1994–96, in favour of a single strong hand intended to restore confidence and coherence to government policy. Hard-liners in the regime, such as Gens Nezzar, Belkheir, Benabbes Gheziel and Muhammad Mediene, favoured Abdelaziz Bouteflika, Boumedienne's Minister of Foreign Affairs, but he declined the invitation to take control. Eventually the HCS named the Minister of Defence, Liamine Zéroual, as Head of State. Zéroual, who was inaugurated on 31 January 1994, was one of the most respected members of the senior officer corps and was believed to share the views of the *conciliateurs*. Zéroual derived a measure of personal legitimacy from the fact that he had joined the ALN at the age of 16 and fought in the guerrilla struggle inside Algeria for independence. In his first public statement the new President appealed for 'serious dialogue' to find a way out of the country's crisis and made cautious overtures to those members of the banned FIS who renounced violence. In April he removed the *éradicateur* Redha Malek from the premiership, and also dismissed the hard-line Minister of the Interior, Sélim Saâdi, appointing a new government team, comprised mainly of technocrats and senior civil servants, headed by Mokdad Sifi, hitherto Minister of Equipment. The following month he made changes to senior posts in the military, but security operations remained under the control of hard-liners such as Gens Lamari, Mediene and Muhammad Touati.

DIALOGUE FAILS

Efforts to promote dialogue proved cautious. In May 1994 Zéroual inaugurated the National Transition Council (NTC), an interim legislature of 200 appointed members intended to provide a forum for debate until new parliamentary elections were held. Of the main political parties, only the 'moderate' Islamist Hamas agreed to participate in the new body, which became the target of ridicule in the media. Indeed, the regime consistently failed to involve a majority of the leading legalized political parties in its efforts to promote dialogue. It was not until August that the President managed to persuade five leading legalized parties to join dialogue talks aimed at drawing up an acceptable peace formula, and then there was disagreement among the parties over whether or not to include the banned FIS. Earlier in the year two high-ranking FIS members—Ali Djeddi and Abdelkader Boukhamkham—had been released from prison in order to explore the possibilities for dialogue with the Islamist opposition, but little progress was made. Finally, in late August a breakthrough appeared to have been made. In a letter to Zéroual, imprisoned FIS leader Abassi Madani agreed to respect the 1989 Constitution and the principle of the alternation of power, and, while not explicitly renouncing violence, referred to the possibility of a truce. In early September Zéroual ordered the release of both Madani and Belhadj from prison and their transfer to house arrest.

Several factors are thought to have prompted the change in the FIS's intransigent stance towards the military-backed regime, but most important may have been its fear of marginalization by the extremist GIA. In May 1994 the MEI and a number of other armed groups linked to the FIS had agreed to merge with the GIA and accept the leadership of the GIA's 'national emir', Cherif Gousmi. However, unwilling to let the extremists gain the upper hand, the head of the FIS Executive Committee Abroad, Rabah Kebir, rejected the agreement and in July announced the creation of the Armée islamique du salut (AIS) under the leadership of Madani Merzag. The AIS brought together, under the authority of the FIS and its imprisoned leadership, armed Islamist groups active in the west and east of Algeria. Thus the FIS political leadership sought to create its own armed wing, distinct from the radical GIA, in order to negotiate with the military-backed regime from a position of strength. The GIA, which had its stronghold in the centre of the country, especially in and around Algiers, immediately denounced the FIS leadership's decision to negotiate with Zéroual's Government, and opposed the establishment of democracy by means of a moderate Islamic regime. There was to be no truce and no dialogue. Instead, the country had to be purified of the 'impious' and an Islamic state established by *jihad*.

The transfer of the two FIS leaders to house arrest failed to break the impasse between the regime and the FIS. In October 1994 Zéroual announced that neither Madani nor Belhadj was willing to renounce violence or participate in negotiations. Prior to his release from prison Madani had stated that he was willing to consider terminating the military campaign if certain conditions were met. Zéroual was unable to concede on a number of points: rescinding the ruling that outlawed the FIS in order to restore the party to legality; releasing all imprisoned FIS members; and allowing the armed wing of the FIS to participate in talks. In a speech in late October, Zéroual spoke of the failure of dialogue with the FIS, and of announced his decision to hold a presidential election in 1995 before the end of his mandate. He also used the occasion to announce the promotion of Gen. Muhammad Lamari, a leading opponent of dialogue with the Islamists, to the highest rank in the Algerian military.

THE SANT' EGIDIO PACT

The plan to hold a presidential election towards the end of 1995, announced by Zéroual in October 1994, was rejected by many leading legalized opposition parties and condemned by the exiled FIS leadership. Unexpectedly, the opposition parties seized the initiative and—after talks in Rome, Italy, under the aegis of the Sant' Egidio Roman Catholic community in November 1994 and again in January 1995—the main Algerian opposition parties agreed a 'platform for a national contract', presenting the basis for a negotiated end to the conflict and a return to democracy. The document was signed by representatives of the FIS, the FLN and the FFS, together with the MDA, Nahdah, the Parti des travailleurs (PT) and the Algerian League for the Defence of Human Rights (ALDHR).

The Sant' Egidio pact made an urgent appeal to all parties in the conflict to end their hostilities and allow the restoration of civil peace. It recommended the establishment of a transitional government, in which both the regime and the political parties would be represented, to prepare the way for free multi-party elections. All parties were asked to guarantee to respect the results of the elections. Before any negotiations, the participants appealed for the release of the FIS leadership and of all political detainees, the restoration of the FIS to legality, and an immediate end to the use of torture and of attacks on civilians, foreigners and public property. The participants also agreed certain general principles including the renunciation of violence as a means to achieve or retain power, together with respect for human rights, popular legitimacy, multi-party democracy and the alternation of power, and the guarantee of fundamental liberties. They recognized the importance of Islamic, Arab and Berber culture in Algeria, and demanded that both the Arab and Berber languages be recognized as national languages. Finally, they appealed for the withdrawal of the army from politics. Belhadj and Madani endorsed the Sant' Egidio pact, whereas the GIA condemned it and reaffirmed its commitment to the establishment of a 'caliphate' by armed struggle.

Zéroual's regime condemned the Sant' Egidio meeting even before it had begun, claiming foreign interference in its national affairs, and after the pact was announced a government spokesman categorically rejected its proposals. The French, Italian, Spanish and US Governments expressed support for the Rome talks. Whereas some analysts argued that the Sant' Egidio pact confirmed that the FIS was distancing itself from the Islamist radicals, anti-Islamist organizations in Algeria saw the pact as no more than a ploy by the Islamists to take power; with the army neutralized they would abandon all pretence at democracy and impose fundamentalist rule.

Meanwhile, President Zéroual continued to prepare for a presidential election. In April 1995 he attempted the regain the initiative by resuming talks with the legalized opposition parties. However, talks with the FLN and the FFS quickly collapsed when Zéroual again refused to include the FIS in any dialogue. The FLN and FFS agreed to take part in the presidential election only if the FIS was allowed to participate. The Government reiterated its demand that the FIS would have to renounce violence and accept the Constitution before it could participate in the election. There was speculation that unofficial talks were continuing between the Government and the FIS leadership, but in mid-July Zéroual issued a statement confirming the collapse of dialogue with the FIS. In early June

Abassi Madani and Ali Belhadj had once again been returned to prison.

THE DIRTY WAR

For all the talk of dialogue during 1994, the descent into civil war continued, and some of the barbarous acts reported recalled the worst days of the struggle for independence. Indiscriminate terror tactics by both Islamist guerrillas and the security forces turned the conflict into a dirty war. The regime admitted in September 1994 that 10,000 people had died in the conflict since early 1992. Amnesty International estimated the death toll at 20,000, one-half of them ordinary civilians who bore the brunt of the violence. These figures almost certainly underestimated the scale of the death toll, as daily killings went unreported in the heavily-censored media. As many as 30,000 lives had probably been lost since February 1992, with around 1,000 killed every week by the end of 1994.

An Amnesty International report released in October 1994 painted the grim picture of a country where civilians were living in a state of fear, threatened and killed by Islamists for not obeying their orders, and by the security forces in retaliation for Islamist raids. Damage to the country's infrastructure as a result of the conflict was estimated at US $3,000m. Certain towns, and entire neighbourhoods in some cities, were virtually controlled by armed Islamist groups, and Islamist attacks on government officials, politicians, judges, intellectuals, journalists and teachers continued. In addition to their campaign of assassinations, Islamist guerrillas burnt down schools and colleges and instituted a reign of terror in areas under their control; anyone violating Islamist diktats risked mutilation or murder. Foreign nationals continued to be targeted; the exodus of foreigners continued at an even faster rate, and some countries closed their embassies and consulates (making it difficult for Algerians to travel abroad).

The security forces intensified their campaign against armed Islamist groups, undertaking air attacks using napalm, and conducting punitive raids, torture and psychological warfare in their efforts to eradicate the militants. Army repression was particularly harsh in the more densely populated quarters of Algiers and other large cities, where many young men suspected of Islamist sympathies were apprehended in raids by the security forces, tortured and summarily executed. 'Death squads' emerged, carrying out 'revenge' killings against victims selected at random. In the Kabyle, a region traditionally alienated from the regime but strongly opposed to the Islamists, Berber villages began organizing their own armed militias. After the failure of dialogue with the Islamist opposition, the army embarked on the most extensive military operations of the conflict, seemingly having abandoned all restraint in its efforts to uncover Islamist sympathizers and guerrilla units. Some analysts argued that the main reason for the regime's new intransigence was that it could depend on the undivided support of France, fearful of the consequences of an Islamist victory in its former colony. In October 1994 Djamel Zitouni became the GIA's new 'national emir', following the murder of Gousmi the previous month.

On 24 December 1994 four GIA guerrillas hijacked an Air France airbus at Algiers airport and murdered three passengers. The aircraft was stormed by French counter-terrorist police after it landed at Marseille and the hijackers were killed. It was claimed that the guerrillas had intended to blow up the aircraft over Paris. The GIA called for war on France and in the summer and autumn of 1995 carried out a series of terrorist attacks including the bombing of the Paris metro. By launching a terrorist campaign in France, the GIA sought to demonstrate that the FIS had no control over the armed struggle and was therefore incapable of negotiating an agreement with the military junta that would end the violence. In mid-April 1995 security measures were reinforced in the four 'exclusion zones' at Ouargla, Laghouat, El Oued and Illizi—established to protect the Saharan oil- and gasfields, which provided 95% of Algeria's export revenues. Nevertheless, in May five foreign oil workers were killed by the GIA at an industrial zone near Ghardaia in the heart of the Sahara desert.

THE PRESIDENTIAL ELECTION OF NOVEMBER 1995

Algeria's first multi-party presidential election since independence was held on 16 November 1995 and resulted in a clear

victory for the incumbent President Zéroual, who won 61.0% of the votes cast. Sheikh Mahfoud Nahnah, the leader of Hamas, took 25.6% of the votes, followed by Saïd Saâdi, Secretary-General of the RCD (9.6%) and Nourreddine Boukrouh, leader of the Parti du renouveau algérien—PRA—(3.8%). The FIS, the FLN and the FFS had all urged a boycott of the election. Notwithstanding their demand, and threats by Islamist militants to turn the ballot-boxes into coffins, official figures stated that 75.7% of the electorate participated in the election. The main legal opposition parties, together with the proscribed FIS, were forced to acknowledge the political implications of the election, and there were appeals for a renewal of dialogue. At his inauguration on 27 November Zéroual reiterated his commitment to national dialogue and pledged to hold pluralist legislative and municipal elections, although he offered no precise timetable. The FFS announced that it would end its boycott of the electoral process and participate in legislative elections. The FLN, under a new leader, Boualem Benhamouda, was publicly reconciled with Zéroual and also indicated that it was prepared to contest future elections. Immediately after the presidential election, Rabah Kebir, the senior FIS spokesman in exile, acknowledged Zéroual's victory and appealed for new negotiations with the regime. In April and July 1996 Zéroual held talks with leaders of the main opposition parties, the UGTA and other associations, culminating in a national conference in September to ratify his political reform programme.

A referendum followed on 28 November 1996 to amend the 1989 Constitution in preparation for general and local elections in 1997. The proposed changes included the creation of a bicameral parliament with the new upper house, the Council of the Nation, appointed either directly or indirectly by the President, a ban on political parties based on religion or language, and the introduction of voting by proportional representation. According to official figures, some 79.8% of the electorate participated in the referendum, with 85.9% voting in favour of the constitutional changes. A number of opposition parties claimed that the results had been manipulated by the Government. Opposition to the proposed reforms was particularly strong in the Kabyle, where residents staged protests against the designation of Arabic as the sole 'national language'.

THE GENERAL AND LOCAL ELECTIONS OF 1997

Some 39 political parties qualified to take part in legislative elections held on 5 June 1997, when more than 7,000 candidates contested the 380 seats in the National People's Assembly. They included a new political party, the Rassemblement national démocratique (RND), created only a few months before and led by Abdelkader Bensalah, former President of the NTC. The RND brought together a range of anti-Islamist organizations, self-defence groups, trade unions and women's associations, and its electoral lists included Ahmed Ouyahia, who had replaced Mokdad Sifi as Prime Minister in December 1995, and numerous other government ministers. The party was permitted to use official buildings for its electoral campaign and benefited from other public facilities, drawing accusations of favouritism from opposition parties. According to official results, the RND won 156 of the 380 seats contested; the Mouvement de la société pour la paix (MSP—as Hamas had been renamed in May, in compliance with new legislation) 69, the FLN 62, Nahdah 34, the FFS 20, the RCD 19, and the PT four, with the remainder taken by independent candidates and other small political groupings. The RND did not achieve an overall majority in the new lower house, but it was generally assumed that it could rely on the support of the FLN. The two Islamist parties, the MSP and Nahdah, won more than 100 seats and, according to official figures, received over 20% of all votes cast. In contrast, the centre-left parties, especially the FFS, failed to gain as many seats as they had in the previous election. The level of voter participation was officially put at 65.5%, although less than one-half of eligible voters in Algiers took part in the election. Opposition parties insisted that the turn-out had been lower than the official figures indicated, and complained of numerous and deliberate abuses. An editorial in the French daily *Le Monde*, referred to 'an election without true debate for an assembly without real power'. In mid-June President Zéroual asked Ouyahia to form a government; the FLN and MSP received seven portfolios in the new Council of Ministers, while the RND took the remainder.

Elections to restore regional and municipal councils, which had not existed since 1992, followed in October 1997. The RND won more than one-half of the seats contested, with seven other parties winning seats on the regional councils and 33 securing representation on municipal councils. According to official results, some 62.7% of the electorate participated in regional elections and 67.7% in municipal elections. The Government expressed satisfaction at the result, and sought to portray the polls as the final stage in the restoration of the democratic process in Algeria. All major political parties complained of widespread electoral fraud, and in the weeks following the elections opposition parties organized mass demonstrations on a scale not seen for many years. President Zéroual refused to annul the results, and street protests continued. In late December an electoral college selected two-thirds of the seats in the new 144-member Council of the Nation, from members of the regional and municipal councils; of the 96 seats, the RND took 80, the FLN 10, the FFS four and the MSP two. The remaining 48 members were nominated by Zéroual. Henceforth, legislation drafted by the lower house would not be promulgated unless approved by two-thirds of members in the Council of the Nation. In April 1998 a new Constitutional Council was installed.

POLITICAL VIOLENCE INTENSIFIES

The presidential election of November 1995 did not bring an end to political violence, which continued to claim an estimated 100 victims every week. Nevertheless, military analysts argued that the new strategies introduced by the security forces were more efficient than in the past, that anti-terrorist intelligence was better co-ordinated, and that the self-defence groups—numbering some 18,000 men—had become increasingly integrated with the regime's security apparatus. They claimed that the security forces had made it more difficult for Islamist guerrilla bands to regroup and obtain weapons, and that they had fragmented into small groups unable to mount operations against major military targets. As a result, Islamist militants increasingly favoured the use of car bombs: it was estimated that in the six weeks after the start of Ramadan in January 1996 some 80 car bombs had exploded. After the presidential election the internment camp in the Sahara for alleged Islamist militants was closed and its inmates were released. However, some 17,000 Algerians remained imprisoned—the majority without trial—for alleged terrorist activities. Human rights organizations continued to condemn both the Islamist militants and the security forces for human rights abuses. Journalists still suffered violence and intimidation from Islamist militants and harassment by the authorities, and several were killed in a wave of car bomb attacks in early 1996.

Meanwhile, the armed Islamist movement remained deeply divided, and, under the leadership of Djamel Zitouni, the GIA was characterized by growing internal dissent. During 1995 several senior figures in the group—notably Ezzedine Baa, Abderrazaq Redjem and Muhammad Said—were eliminated after they defected to the AIS. Zitouni had earlier accused them of attempting a 'coup' against him. Further defections followed after the GIA murdered and mutilated seven French Trappist monks who had been kidnapped from their monastery near Médéa in May. A number of local GIA commanders abandoned their support for Zitouni, and in June 1996 the GIA's principal ideologues, the Palestinian Abu Qatada and the Syrian Abu Mous'ab, both based in London, United Kingdom, announced that they were withdrawing support from Zitouni, who was killed the following month following clashes between rival factions. The FIS leadership and several independent commentators asserted that under Zitouni's leadership the GIA had been infiltrated by Algerian secret services and manipulated by them in order to discredit and divide the Islamist movement.

As the violence intensified, support for the Islamists' armed struggle diminished and the population became increasingly weary of a conflict which appeared to be leading nowhere. Zitouni was succeeded as the GIA's 'national emir' by Antar Zouabri, a close ally. Zouabri carried out further purges within the GIA, eliminating those who challenged his authority. Early in 1997 Zouabri acquired a new ideologue in the form of the London-based Egyptian militant Abu Hamza who published a pamphlet, entitled *Le sabre tranchant*, in which he admitted that *jihad* had become unpopular and that only a tiny minority of Algerians affirmed their religion by participating in the armed struggle. Under Zouabri's leadership many of the violent acts perpetrated by the GIA factions were aimed at punishing the civilian population for betraying the cause. In 1997 acts of brutality against civilians occurred on a scale hitherto unprecedented in the civil war. Beginning in January and February and intensifying in August and September, a series of massacres took place in villages to the south and west of Algiers. In some villages several hundred people—men, women and children, even babies—were slaughtered. Some victims had their throats cut or were burnt alive, and many were horribly mutilated. The security forces appeared unable or unwilling to prevent the bloodshed; on several occasions the military failed to assist the local population during attacks that took place in the vicinity of army barracks.

In September 1997, in a communiqué published by Abu Hamza in the periodical *Al-Ansar*, Zouabri claimed responsibility for the massacres in the name of the GIA and justified them by declaring all Algerians who did not join the GIA to be 'impious'. Shortly afterwards Abu Hamza ended his support for Zouabri and the GIA for pronouncing *takfir* (excommunication) against the whole of Algerian society. In the opinion of some commentators, from the end of 1997 the GIA ceased to have a coherent command structure at the national level and fragmented into a number of 'autonomous' factions, some reduced to simple banditry. Nevertheless, the violence continued unabated. Further massacres were perpetrated in December in the days preceding the start of Ramadan, and during the holy month more than 1,300 civilians were killed—including 400 civilians slaughtered in one night in villages near Rélizane. In September, meanwhile, the AIS leader, Madani Merzag, called for all militants under his command to observe a unilateral cease-fire effective from 1 October. Although details of the agreement struck between the military high command and the AIS that led to the cease-fire were not revealed, there was speculation that it included the incorporation of some AIS fighters into regular units of the armed forces. Always much weaker militarily than its rival the GIA, the AIS considered a cease-fire preferable to defeat or surrender. In spite of official claims that the conflict was nearly over and that GIA groups had incurred significant losses as a result of operations by the security forces, massacres, ambushes and bomb attacks continued during late 1998 and into 1999, although not on the scale experienced during 1997 and early 1998.

In April 1998 more than 100 people, including policemen, leaders of self-defence groups and local government officials, were arrested for alleged involvement in the massacres of civilians. Those arrested were alleged to have been involved not only in eliminating suspected Islamists but also in killings linked to criminal activities and tribal rivalries. While officials admitted that some abuses were committed by the security forces and their allies, they insisted that such incidents were rare. The horrific massacres of civilians in 1997 had led to appeals from several European states for international intervention to resolve the conflict. Two European Union (EU) delegations visited Algiers in early 1998, but Algerian officials continued to reject all offers of foreign mediation or assistance for the victims of violence and opposed any form of independent inquiry into the massacres. A senior-level UN 'fact-finding' mission, led by former Portuguese President Mário Soares, visited Algiers in July 1998 and, in addition to consultations with government officials and representatives of political parties and civil society, it was allowed access to sites of recent massacres. The mission's report was strongly criticized by Amnesty International for failing to address the human rights crisis.

ZÉROUAL RESIGNS: THE PRESIDENTIAL ELECTION OF APRIL 1999

In a dramatic television address in September 1998, President Zéroual announced that he would stand down after a presidential election to be held in February 1999, almost two years before the end of his five-year term of office. Subsequently the date of the election was postponed until April, officially to give political parties time to participate fully in the electoral process.

Although suffering from poor health, it was widely acknowledged that Zéroual was being forced out as a result of renewed infighting in the army high command. His announcement followed a series of vitriolic articles in sections of the press against Gen. Muhammad Betchine, Zéroual's presidential adviser and closest political ally, clearly aimed at the President himself. Betchine resigned in October, as did the Minister of Justice, Muhammad Adami, another of Zéroual's allies. Both strongly denied allegations made by the press of corruption. The episode was regarded as a victory for the 'clan' led by Lt-Gen. Muhammad Lamari and the powerful head of military security, Gen. Muhammad Mediene. In mid-December 1998 Prime Minister Ouyahia resigned and was replaced by Smail Hamdani. A new, largely unaltered Council of Ministers was appointed.

Of 47 would-be candidates for the presidential election, only seven made it to the final list: Abdelaziz Bouteflika; Ahmed Taleb Ibrahimi, a leading member of the establishment's Arab/Islamic wing; Sheikh Abdallah Djaballah, who had formed the Mouvement de la réforme nationale (MRN) after being ousted as leader of Nahdah by members who supported Bouteflika's candidacy; Hocine Aït Ahmed; Mouloud Hamrouche, the leader of the FLN's liberal reformist wing; former premier Mokdad Sifi; and Youcef Khateb, a hero of the war of independence reported to have close links with some of the 'patriot' militias. This time the senior generals did not present one of their own members for the post, as they had Zéroual, deciding that the new President should be a civilian. During the electoral campaign Bouteflika swiftly emerged as the leading candidate and was widely seen as the '*candidat privilégié*'. Two days before the first round of the presidential election (scheduled to be held on 15 April 1999) a crisis developed when four of the candidates—Aït Ahmed, Hamrouche, Ibrahimi and Djaballah—issued a communiqué accusing the authorities of initiating a 'massive fraud' in favour of Bouteflika. They claimed that a large number of additional voting papers in the name of Bouteflika had been deposited in the *wilayat*, and that the security forces had been instructed to prevent representatives of the other candidates from being present at polling stations on the day of the first round of voting. The next day they were joined in their allegations by Khateb and, unexpectedly, Sifi. The Minister of Interior rejected the allegations of fraud, accusing the candidates of trying to discredit the administration and mislead public opinion. The protesting candidates responded by withdrawing from the election. Bouteflika decided to continue as the sole candidate, but on the day of the election he announced that he would not assume the presidency unless he received substantial support from the electorate.

According to official results, Bouteflika won 73.8% of the votes cast at the presidential election of 15 April 1999, followed by Ibrahimi (12.5%), Djaballah (4.0%), Aït Ahmed (3.2%), Hamrouche (3.1%), Sifi (2.2%) and Khateb (1.2%). Although Bouteflika's opponents had withdrawn, they did not make a formal appeal for a boycott and voting papers for all seven contestants were provided at the polling stations. The rate of voter participation was officially stated to be 60.9% of the electorate, but there were sharp regional disparities. On 16 April Bouteflika accepted the presidency, and he was sworn in to office on 27 April. The opposition, which had already rejected the legitimacy of the results, immediately challenged the official rate of voter participation, with the FFS claiming that a mere 23.3% of the electorate had voted. The French daily *Le Monde*, quoting a military source, estimated turn-out at 23%, with Bouteflika obtaining only 28% of votes cast (little more than 1m.), Ibrahimi 20%, Aït Ahmed 13.3%, Djaballah 12.8% and Hamrouche 12.2%. The opposition called for a peaceful protest march in Algiers against military dictatorship, but the rally was banned by the authorities. Clashes took place between demonstrators and security forces in central Algiers, and several arrests were made.

BOUTEFLIKA'S PRESIDENCY

Bouteflika's first priority on assuming the presidency was the restoration of peace in the country. He established contacts with senior members of the outlawed FIS, and in June the movement's military wing, the AIS, agreed to make its ceasefire (in place since October 1997) permanent. Furthermore, it offered to co-operate with the security forces against other armed Islamist groups, notably its rival the GIA, which had refused to join the truce. Abbasi Madani, the FIS leader, who remained under house arrest, and the FIS Constitutional Council endorsed the agreement, but some FIS supporters complained that it did not provide a political solution to the conflict. Others demanded that *jihad* should continue until an Islamic state was finally achieved. On 5 July—Independence Day—the President pardoned 5,000 imprisoned Islamist sympathizers and drew up a Law on Civil Concord, which was unanimously adopted by the National People's Assembly on 13 July. The new legislation offered an amnesty for Islamist militants not implicated in mass killings, rapes, or bomb attacks on public places, and reduced sentences for those who had taken part in such crimes provided they surrendered to the authorities within a period of six months (i.e. by 13 January 2000). At a referendum held on 16 September, according to official figures, 98.6% of voters endorsed the President's peace initiative, with turn-out reported at 85% of the registered electorate. (The opposition FFS insisted that the rate of participation had been only 45%). Families of victims of Islamist attacks denounced the new Law on Civil Concord, which was condemned by the French-language press as 'a shameful capitulation to Islamist violence'. An editorial in the independent daily *Le Matin* accused Bouteflika of handing the 'terrorists' a political victory 'on a silver platter' just when they had been defeated militarily. Given the controversial circumstances of his election, some politicians accused Bouteflika of using the referendum to bolster his own legitimacy. After the results of the vote were announced the President called for those members of armed groups who surrendered to be welcomed back into society without question.

At a press conference in October 1999 the Minister of the Interior announced that 531 'terrorists' had surrendered under the Law on Civil Concord, and that the vast majority who were thus exempted from prosecution belonged to the GIA. Some commentators argued that the numbers coming forward were disappointing because although the legal status of those Islamists surrendering to the authorities was addressed by the new legislation, the practicalities of their reintegration into society had not been resolved. In some cases it was proposed to resettle former militants away from their places of origin owing to fears of possible revenge attacks, especially by the self-defence groups. Despite official optimism regarding the amnesty programme, by the end of 1999 the response to it had not been encouraging. In early January 2000, following urgent high-level negotiations between the Government and the AIS leadership, which had reportedly threatened to withdraw from the President's peace initiative, a new agreement was reached providing for a full amnesty for the group's estimated 3,000 fighters, financial compensation for their families, housing for those whose homes had been destroyed by the security forces, and assistance in securing employment. Furthermore, Saudi Arabia was reported to have granted US $800m. to help rehabilitate former members of the AIS. For its part, the AIS agreed to disband permanently, although in the short term several hundred fighters were to be enrolled in an 'auxiliary unit' and would assist the security forces in their attempts to apprehend members of the GIA and a breakaway group from the GIA, the Groupe salafiste pour la prédication et le combat (GSPC), or Da'wa wal Djihad, led by Hassan Hattab. On 19 January the Minister of the Interior announced that 80% of the members of armed groups had surrendered to the authorities. At the same time a pro-Government newspaper, *El Khabar*, reported that in addition to the AIS fighters, some 4,200 militants may have given themselves up. Other sources put the total figure at 6,000. The amnesty for AIS fighters prompted one FIS official abroad to urge the President to begin implementing the political clauses of the agreement that led to the 1997 AIS cease-fire. While Bouteflika indicated that the FIS might be allowed to re-form under another name and with a new structure, he insisted that it must be headed by new leaders, as the incumbent leadership was implicated in inciting political violence.

In late November 1999, meanwhile, Abdelkader Hachani, the third most senior figure in the FIS hierarchy and the most senior member of the leadership still at liberty and politically active, was assassinated in Algiers by a lone gunman. Hachani had favoured dialogue with all political forces and was rumoured to have been involved in secret political contacts between the Government and the FIS. In the following month Fouad Boulemia, a member of the main GIA faction headed by Antar Zouabri, was reported to have confessed to the murder, after having been found in possession of the alleged murder weapon and identity documents belonging to Hachani. Early in 2000 there were reports that the new agreement between the AIS and the Government had further divided the FIS both inside the country and abroad, and that the leaders of the AIS were planning to establish their own political party.

In the months following his inauguration Bouteflika gave numerous speeches across the country and participated in several interviews on national and foreign radio and television in which he pronounced on a wide range of issues, some of them highly controversial, and made promises, some of which appeared contradictory. The new President denounced weaknesses in the country's educational system, spoke out on the sensitive language issue, promised to reform the justice system, urged that national reconciliation should include Algeria's Jewish community, the 'pieds-noirs' (the pre-independence population of French origin) and the 'harkis' (those Algerians who had served in the French army prior to independence), and in particular condemned corruption which he stated paralysed the administration and undermined the economy. In August 1999 Bouteflika dismissed 22 of the country's 48 *walis* (prefects or provincial governors) on the grounds of alleged corruption or other abuses of power. He used the installation of the country's first female *wali*, at Tipasa, to denounce corruption, mentioning specifically the security and customs services. Although Bouteflika gave his first speech to the nation in late May in classical Arabic (poorly understood by the majority of Algerians), he later used French in many of his speeches both within Algeria and abroad. This angered those seeking to promote 'Arabization' and provoked one of their number, Abdelkader Hadjar, an influential FLN deputy, to address a lengthy private letter to the President strongly criticizing his lack of commitment to 'Arabization' and accusing him of promoting French at the expense of Arabic. Bouteflika published the letter in October, a move seen by some observers as an attempt to confront these factions within the FLN and the army hostile to him. Following this incident Hadjar was expelled from the FLN and forced to resign as President of the Parliamentary Commission for Foreign Affairs.

During his first months in power much attention focused on the new President's relations with the army high command. While frequently praising the army for its loyalty and for preserving 'territorial integrity', Bouteflika repeatedly emphasized that he did not intend to be manipulated by the generals, and that he was determined to exercise power as Head of State following the model of his mentor, the late President Boumedienne. However, six months after assuming office there were few signs that Bouteflika exercised real power. Both the Algerian and foreign media commented on his repeated delays in forming a new government, and in early October 1999 it was reported that the military had rejected Bouteflika's proposed formation of a government composed of personalities drawn from his own entourage, insisting that he select his ministers from the political parties and thereby ensuring the continuation of the practice whereby the different army factions placed their own 'clients' in ministerial office.

In late December 1999 Bouteflika finally announced the composition of a new Government. Ahmed Benbitour, a former Minister of Finance and more recently president of a parliamentary economic and financial committee, was appointed Prime Minister at the head of a 33-member Council of Ministers. The new administration included several of the President's close aides and some technocrats, but was predominantly composed of politicians representing those political parties that had supported Bouteflika at the presidential election. The various army factions thus appeared to have achieved their aim of getting their nominees into the new cabinet. Nevertheless, Bouteflika did succeed in placing members of his own entourage in a number of key positions: Abdellatif Benachenhou replaced Abelkrim Harchaoui as Minister of Finance; Chakib Khelil, Algeria's representative at the World Bank, replaced Youcef Yousfi as Minister of Energy and Mines (Yousfi assumed the foreign affairs portfolio); Yazid Zerhouni, a former ambassador to the USA, succeeded Abdelmalek Sellal as Minister of the Interior (Sellal was appointed Minister of Youth and Sport); and Hamid

Temmar was assigned the new post of Minister of Participation and Co-ordination of Reforms. Seven political parties shared 20 cabinet posts. The RND, with by far the largest number of deputies in the National People's Assembly, saw its ministerial strength reduced from 19 to eight; however, its Secretary-General, former premier Ahmed Ouyahia, took over the important justice portfolio and became the Government's only Minister of State. Both the FLN and MSP each retained only three of their four portfolios, while four political parties that had not participated in the previous administration secured cabinet posts. The 'moderate' Islamist party, Nahdah, and the staunchly anti-Islamist RCD each received two posts; a further anti-Islamist party, Redha Malek's Alliance nationale républicaine (ANR), took one post, while PRA leader Noureddine Boukrouh was appointed Minister of Small and Medium-sized Enterprises. The President called on the new Government to consolidate national reconciliation in order to achieve a comprehensive solution to the current crisis. Bouteflika had also appointed his team of presidential advisers. Ali Benflis, who had run his presidential campaign, was appointed Director of the President's Private Office; El Eulmi Muhammad Kamal became Secretary-General of the Presidency, and Mezhoud Djamal Eddine was allocated the post of Director of General Administration. Furthermore, the appointment of a former communications minister, Hamraoui Habib Chawki, regarded as an opponent of a free press, as head of the state-owned television company ENTV, was interpreted as a sign of Bouteflika's determination that state television should support and defend government policies and not become a platform for opposition parties to air their views. One of Bouteflika's senior economic advisers, Abdelhak Bouhafs, a former energy minister, was appointed chairman of the state hydrocarbons company, SONATRACH, a position he had previously held from 1989 to 1995.

In late February 2000 President Bouteflika announced what were the most wide-ranging changes to the military high command since 1988. These included the replacement of the commanders of four of the country's six military regions. Significantly, however, the most senior positions remained unchanged. Lt-Gen. Muhammad Lamari (who remained Chief of Staff), Maj.-Gen. Tawfik Medienne (head of military intelligence and security), and Maj-Gen. Smain Lamari (head of counter-espionage and internal security) were regarded as the principal architects of the repressive policies against Islamist movement after 1992. New appointees included Gen. Ali Djamai as Commander of the Republican Guard, Gen. Brahim Dadci as Commander of the Naval Forces, Maj.-Gen. Ahmed Bousteila as Commander of the National Gendarmerie, and Gen. Abdelaziz Madjahed as Chief of Staff of the Land Forces. The reorganization appeared to reinforce the dominant position within the military high command of those officers who had begun their careers in the French army, only joining the ALN towards the end of the war of independence, and their allies, at the expense of those senior officers who had fought in the *maquis*. Two close allies of Lt-Gen. Lamari were appointed to command the two most important military regions: Brahim Fodhil Cherif assumed command at Blida and Said Bey at Constantine. Later in 2000 the appointment of two generals to the presidential team, Gen. (retd) Belkheir as Director of the President's Office and Gen. Touati with responsibility for military affairs, was interpreted by some as an attempt by senior military figures to exert greater control over Bouteflika.

Meanwhile, the Government gave permission for the independent private press to set up its own printing and distribution network, in effect removing the state monopoly on printing houses. The Minister of Communications and Culture described the change as part of a plan to reform the unpopular information code. In May 2000 the Minister of the Interior and Local Authorities told a press conference that the authorities would not grant legal recognition to Ahmed Taleb Ibrahimi's new political party, Wafa, insinuating that the party was simply a reconstitution of the banned FIS under another name. In response Wafa claimed that former FIS members made up only a tiny fraction of the party's leadership. Some observers considered that Bouteflika was keen to launch his own political party, and regarded Wafa as a potential rival especially in securing popular support within Islamist circles. However, other sources claimed that Bouteflika was in favour of legalizing Wafa but that the move had been opposed by the military. Following the publication, in July, of a government-endorsed report on the judiciary, which urged action against corruption and interference in the system, the President appointed 311 new judges and prosecutors. New emergency measures were introduced to enforce the rule of law in all public institutions, and the Ministry of Justice was allocated new funds to improve conditions inside the country's prisons.

A new Government was formed in late August 2000, following the resignation of Ahmed Benbitour. The French daily *Le Monde* commented that the outgoing premier had considered himself to be excluded by Bouteflika from the decision-making process; furthermore, the President had not refrained from public criticism of the Government's '*immobilisme*'. In addition, there were known to be fundamental differences between the Head of State and Prime Minister on economic policy, not least on the issue of the privatization of state concerns (Benbitour, concerned not to exacerbate social tensions, favoured a cautious approach). Bouteflika appointed one of his closest associates, Ali Benflis, as Prime Minister. The composition of the new Government was little changed from that of the Benbitour administration: most senior ministers retained their posts, the most notable exception being Yousfi (redesignated Minister-delegate to the Prime Minister) who was replaced as Minister of Foreign Affairs by Abdelaziz Belkhadem, a well-known reformist, former head of the legislature and a principal architect of the Sant' Egidio pact.

In November 2000 the Minister of State for the Interior and Local Authorities ordered the closure all of Wafa's offices. The decision was condemned by the FIS, which criticized the authorities for their reluctance to allow the full participation of all opposition groups and for reneging on their pledges under the Civil Concord. In December a new political alliance emerged, with the stated aim of challenging Bouteflika in presidential elections scheduled for 2004, led by four unlikely allies: Hocine Aït Ahmed of the FIS; Abdallah Djaballah of the MRN; Gen. Muhammad Betchine, a leading adviser to former President Zéroual; and Wafa's Ahmed Taleb Ibrahimi. Elections in December 2000 for one-half of the 96 elected members of the Conseil de la Nation, the country's upper house, produced few changes: the RND comfortably retained its majority, now holding a total of 74 seats. Also in December Bouteflika announced a two-stage programme of reform of the judiciary, including measures to strengthen the rights of detainees and to improve the professional and social conditions of those practising law. He also established a 70-member committee to examine the workings of state institutions and to propose changes—among which, notably, was a move towards greater decentralization.

In mid-December 2000 a new wave of massacres, attributed to the GIA but on which the authorities and the official media declined to comment (see below), provoked the strongest public criticism of President Bouteflika since he took office, articulated not only in the private press but also by several political parties, including two members of the governing coalition, the RCD and ANR. Sections of the press declared that the massacres demonstrated that the President's peace initiative had failed, and some claimed that the amnesty had actually encouraged terrorism. At the same time some analysts attributed the resurgence in violence to the latest power struggle between Bouteflika and the senior generals (see below). The country's military *décideurs*, it was claimed, had lost confidence in Bouteflika, accusing him of seeking to make peace with the Islamists at the military's expense. Rumours circulated that the senior generals were planning to replace Bouteflika, naming former premier Ghozali as his most likely successor. It was suggested that matters had reached a climax when in November a delegation from Amnesty International, which had been granted permission by Bouteflika to visit Algiers, requested to hear from Gens Muhammad Lamari, Tawfik Medienne and Smain Lamari about human rights abuses in Algeria and the question of the disappeared—a request reported to have caused indignation and panic among senior military figures. The generals, it was claimed, considered that Bouteflika was using Amnesty International against them and had decided that he had to be replaced. In September Bouteflika had decided to publish the full version of a confidential memorandum by Amnesty International which referred openly to abuses of power, disappearances and unlawful killings. There were also reports of tensions over the President's

determination to reform state institutions and establish control over the economy, moves which challenged the vested interests carefully built up by the military over many years.

At the beginning of 2001 Bouteflika appeared to be more isolated than ever, and was subject to continued criticism of his autocratic style both in the press and from within the coalition Government. In late February the Minister of Justice, Ahmed Ouyahia, announced that amendments to the penal code would be submitted to the legislature proposing harsh penalties for articles or caricatures judged defamatory; under the new measures authors of articles considered defamatory risked three years' imprisonment and fines of AD 100,000, while fines of up to AD 5m. could be imposed for offending the Head of State. President Bouteflika had earlier called for tougher penalties to be imposed anyone who insulted the state and damaged its prestige either inside the country or abroad, and at the end of February Muhammad Lamari had criticized the local press for its 'shameless comments, caricatures, excesses and insanities' with regard to the army and its leaders. In late May, after the National People's Assembly had approved the amendments, more than 1,000 journalists protested in Algiers against the new laws, and for the first time in a decade the French- and Arabic-language press, usually divided in their attitude to political Islam, joined forces. Islamist members of the governing coalition, who had voted against the amendments, also took part in the demonstration, as did students, and similar protests took place in 11 other cities across the country.

During the early part of the year local sources reported growing frustration and disillusionment with Bouteflika among ordinary Algerians, as a result of the continuing violence and his failure to implement effective economic and social reforms. According to a survey published in *El Watan* in mid-April 2001 popular support for the President had fallen from 65% to 42% in a year. Moreover, 37% of those interviewed stated that they were opposed to Bouteflika's peace initiative, with only 31% expressing their support for it. Relations between the President and the Government also became increasingly strained. Bouteflika accused several members of the Government of being more interested in their ministerial portfolios and privileges than the welfare of the country, while the coalition parties, for their part, criticized the President for excluding them from the decision-making process and marginalizing the National People's Assembly. In an interview with *Le Monde* in early April, Ahmed Taleb Ibrahimi described the situation in the country as one of misery and despair, asserting that, with 14m. Algerians living below the poverty line, the social situation was explosive. He accused Bouteflika of failing to tackle the serious problems of persistent violence, unemployment, housing shortages, and questions of identity and human rights. He also expressed doubt that there were in truth serious disagreements between Bouteflika and the senior generals, and claimed that it was not in the interests of either the generals or the President to see the current crisis resolved. He also argued that the military *décideurs* and the President were in agreement on the question of Algeria's identity, insisting that both wished to cut Algeria off from the Arab Muslim world and from its roots. Ibrahimi maintained that the President's attitude towards the Islamists was unclear, and that the majority of Algerians were unsure of his true stance on this issue. Furthermore, Ibrahimi suggested that the President might be trying to win the support of a part of the FIS political wing, but questioned both whether this strategy had the support of the generals and how the rank and file of the FIS would react. Finally, he condemned the authorities' decision to ban Wafa, declaring that they did not want credible opposition and were only prepared to tolerate parties that conformed to their demands.

In late May 2001 President Bouteflika announced a number of cabinet changes. Abdellatif Benachenou was replaced as Minister of Finance by Mourad Medelci, who had hitherto held the commerce portfolio. Hammid Temmar, Minister of Participation and Co-ordination of Reforms, was transferred to the Ministry of Commerce and was replaced by Noureddine Boukrouh, formerly Minister of Small and Medium-sized Enterprises. Some analysts considered that the reshuffle removed the remaining ministers responsible for economic affairs who were regarded as Bouteflika's allies, thus reducing the President's direct control over economic decision-making and highlighting a further weakening in his position.

In early November 2001 coastal regions of the country were hit by torrential rain, which caused widespread destruction and loss of life. Official figures indicated that 764 people had been killed, mainly in Algiers; 170 had disappeared and some 24,000 had been made homeless. The total cost of the damage was estimated at US $300m. Two days of torrential storms led to flash floods and mudslides, which destroyed houses, buried cars and severed power supplies to some of the most densely populated parts of the capital, notably the low-income districts of Bab el-Oued, Oued Koriche and El-Kittan, which were devastated. President Bouteflika, who immediately declared three days of national mourning, received a hostile reception from local residents when he toured the worst affected areas of the capital. Residents and some sections of the press denounced the authorities for their negligence and incompetence and called on the Government to resign. Demonstrations outside the seat of the Council of Ministers by young people from Bab el-Oued were dispersed by the security forces. Algiers had experienced years of rapid and unplanned urban growth. Overpopulation, lack of effective planning controls, illegal construction and deforestation of the high ground around the city all contributed to the scale of the catastrophe. Locals also insisted that the disaster had been aggravated by the authority's decision in the early 1990s to seal the entrances of key sections of the capital's underground drainage system to prevent them from being used as hiding places by armed Islamist groups. There were also allegations that the country's meteorological service had issued advance warnings of exceptionally heavy rain and strong winds but that neither the presidency nor the interior ministry had taken any action. Foreign emergency assistance arrived swiftly and in great quantities from France and other EU countries, as well as from other Arab countries. Promises from the Algerian authorities of financial help to rehouse those made homeless, to rebuild damaged houses and to provide compensation for the families of those killed in the disaster failed to assuage the anger of local residents. Strong criticism was levelled at both the Minister of the Interior and the *wali* of Algiers for the way in which they handled relief operations. The catastrophe merely served to strengthen popular resentment towards the military-backed regime.

VIOLENCE ERUPTS IN THE KABYLE

In mid-April 2001 violent clashes broke out between young protesters and security forces in several villages in the Kabyle following the killing of a secondary school student while he was being held in police custody at Beni Douala near the regional capital, Tizi Ouzou. Several protesters were injured during the rioting. The local head of the gendarmerie referred to a 'regrettable shooting incident', claiming that the victim had been among a group of youths apprehended for committing an assault during a robbery. This version of events angered both local inhabitants and the family of the victim, and thousands of people signed a petition demanding a full inquiry into the incident. Three days after the student was killed the situation was further inflamed when three other young Kabyles were brutally assaulted by gendarmes near Béjaïa. The incidents coincided with demonstrations traditionally held to mark the anniversary of the 'Berber Spring' of protests in 1980. Appeals by the two main political parties in the region, the FFS and RCD, failed to calm an increasingly tense situation, and the violence quickly escalated. By the end of April over 60 people were reported to have been killed, and more than 600 wounded, in the rioting which spread from the Béjaïa area to the *wilayat* of Bouira, Tizi Ouzou, Borj Bou Arreridj and parts of Sétif. Tensions also increased in the capital—especially on university campuses, where meetings were organized to condemn the killings in the Kabyle, and the extreme brutality employed, especially by the gendarmerie, to restore order was widely denounced. In the past resentment in the Kabyle had focused on the Government's refusal to recognize the Berber Tamazight as a national language, but some observers argued that despair born out of lack of economic opportunities and mounting hostility to the central Government were the underlying causes of the rioting. For many Kabyles the gendarmerie, in particular, was seen as the representative of the central Government and an occupying force which regularly committed abuses against the local population, and public buildings as symbols of the state became the main target for the rioters' anger.

On 30 April 2001 President Bouteflika made an address to the nation on the crisis in Kabyle and announced the establishment of a national commission of inquiry, which would include representatives of civil society, to investigate recent events. He indicated that the question of the Tamazight language would be considered as part of his future plans to revise the Constitution, and that he intended to adopt a proposal making instruction in the Berber language compulsory in the Berber-speaking areas. Bouteflika subsequently appointed Mohand Issad, a lawyer originally from the Kabyle, to head the commission of inquiry. The President's address was, however, strongly criticized by the main political groupings in the Kabyle, and in early May the leader of the RCD, Saïd Saâdi, announced his party's withdrawal from the coalition Government. The two RCD ministers, Amara Benyounes (public works) and Hamid Lounaouci (transport), immediately resigned their posts. The National People's Assembly subsequently announced that it would establish its own parliamentary inquiry into the events in the Kabyle.

In early May 2001 the FFS organized a demonstration in Algiers, attended by some 10,000–30,000 predominantly young people, to condemn the authorities and denounce the repression in the Kabyle. A large force of anti-riot police had been deployed in the capital, but the demonstration passed without incident. By this time the violence in the Kabyle had subsided and become more sporadic, although tensions remained high in the region and later in the month rioting again intensified and spread. Young Kabyles continued to attack symbols of state authority such as *daira* (sub-prefecture) headquarters, offices of the state airline and shipping company and houses of local government officials. The gendarmerie responded by using tear gas and live ammunition. The protests appeared to have been organized by local committees without links to the traditional political parties represented in the region. In the face of a mounting cycle of rioting and repression the authorities remained silent until late May, when President Bouteflika made a second speech in which he called for vigorous sanctions against those who had instigated the tragic events in the Kabyle and against all those responsible for excesses, irrespective of their origins. He also announced that a second *baccalauréat* examination would be organized in September, as demanded by secondary school students in the Kabyle. Furthermore, Bouteflika emphasized that Islam united all Algerians and referred to a 'plot hatched from inside and outside the country to destabilize the entire nation'. Certain groups or individuals, who were not named, sought to 'undermine national unity, the unity of the people and territorial integrity' while others used the 'confused situation to profit by robberies, looting and rackets'. The speech did little to reduce tensions in the region, and sections of the press strongly criticized the authorities for their handling of the situation. Earlier the heads of the gendarmerie and civil police, as well as the Ministry of the Interior, had admitted the existence of abuse in the Kabyle but denied that it was systematic and widespread. Thousands of women from the Kabyle subsequently gathered in Tizi Ouzou to demand justice, medical staff there staged a silent protest against the 'barbarous repression', and at the end of May some 300,000 people (600,000 according to the organizers) took part in a 'march of democratic hope' in Algiers organized by the FFS: in addition to calls for an international inquiry into events in the Kabyle, there were demands for an immediate end to repression and provocation; for Tamazight to be acknowledged as a national and official language; for the arrest of those responsible for assassinations; for the immediate withdrawal of amendments to the penal code (see above); and for an end to the 'plundering of the national heritage'. The scale of the demonstration surprised many commentators; over the last decade only the Islamists of the FIS had succeeded in mobilizing such large numbers.

In early June 2001 security forces dispersed a demonstration in central Algiers by 3,000 Berbers who were protesting against the situation in the Kabyle. Scores of protesters were arrested, and some 20 people were wounded. The demonstration, which had not been authorized by the authorities, was organized by the Coordination nationale pour la défense des libertés démocratiques and supported by a number of political parties, notably the PT, the MDC and the RCD. A week later the Coordination des aarchs, dairas et communes (CADC) organized a large demonstration in Algiers to protest against repression and injustice. Village committees (*aarush*), which have traditionally played a key role in the social fabric of the Kabyle, began to assume a political role in an effort to assert their authority over the currents of protest in the region. While the two main political parties active in the Kabyle, the FFS and the RCD, appeared remote from the daily concerns of marginalized youths in the region, the CADC explicitly identified itself with their main demand, namely the withdrawal of all gendarmerie brigades from the region and the demonstration, the largest since independence, attracted some 500,000 people. Although intended as a peaceful protest, the demonstration degenerated into violence after the route was blocked by the security forces, and there was rioting and looting of shops in the capital's main commercial street. Hundreds of protesters were injured as police broke up the demonstrations. State television broadcast pictures showing the damage caused by the rioters, and the Ministry of the Interior and Local Authorities praised the young people of the capital who had 'defended their honour' in the face of acts of sabotage by the protesters. Several newspapers claimed that the police had encouraged militant groups from certain quarters of the capital to attack the Kabyle demonstrators and journalists covering the event. Appeals for calm from the main political parties in the region and from local popular committees went unheeded. By the end of June the unrest had spread beyond the Kabyle to the Berber-speaking Aurès region (where rioting broke out in Khenchala and demonstrations were held in Batna, the provincial capital), as well as to Annaba and to Biskra in the south of the country. Reports suggested that at least 100 people had been killed, and several hundred more wounded, since the violence first erupted. Local commentators spoke of disturbing signs of a more generalized revolt of the country's marginalized youth, with rioters seeking revenge against the state and local notables. Meanwhile, in a joint statement Wafa leader Ahmed Taleb Ibrahimi, Gen (retd) Rachid Benyelles—who had resigned from the post of permanent under-secretary at the Ministry of Defence after the riots of October 1988, and ALDHR leader Ali Yahia Abdennour held Bouteflika entirely responsible for the chaos and anarchy prevailing in the country and for the loss of life. The press repeatedly demanded the President's resignation in order to restore peace to the country, but on a visit to Tamanrasset in the Sahara in late June Bouteflika declared that he would not resign and again urged the rioters not to participate in an external plot to undermine the security of the country. In early July the security forces prevented some 4,000–5,000 delegates of the CADC from entering Algiers, amid fears that a planned protest march would ignite a new round of rioting after a week of relative quiet. Later in July several thousand people demonstrated in Bouira, demanding political and social reforms and the recognition of the rights of the Kabyle community; there was a large security presence and the march took place without incident.

Mounting evidence that deliberate provocations by the security forces had helped to reignite rioting in many places led to accusations by some opposition politicians that the 'Kabyle threat' was being used by the regime in the same way it had used the 'Islamist threat'—namely to justify its actions. There was speculation among some commentators that senior generals may have deliberately sabotaged efforts by civilian politicians to restore order and that the unrest may have been manipulated in order to put pressure on Bouteflika to resign. However, in an interview with *Le Monde* in mid-June, Benyelles declared that there was no conflict between Bouteflika and the generals, insisting that the country's military *décideurs* had given Bouteflika room to manoeuvre in dealing with the crisis in the Kabyle and would not have prevented him from taking action against the gendarmes held responsible for recent events. Benyelles claimed that Bouteflika had been 'overtaken' by events in the Kabyle, and accused him of incompetence. Furthermore, he explicitly advocated Bouteflika's resignation and the holding of free presidential, legislative and local elections.

At the end of July 2001 the provisional report of the Issad commission into the violence in the Kabyle was made public. It strongly criticized the gendarmerie for the violent methods used against unarmed civilians and stated that its actions had

deliberately provoked and prolonged the violence. The report concluded that either the senior gendarmerie commanders in the Kabyle had lost control of the situation, or they were being exploited by 'external forces'. As the commission dismissed any foreign involvement in the crisis, the reference to external forces appeared to point to one of the clans within the military hierarchy. The report was criticized by the FFS and local leaders in the Kabyle, who insisted that the commission should have named those individuals responsible for the repression. There was also no reference in the report to the failure of the country's political leadership to take early action to halt the repression. Nevertheless, this was the first time that an official report had condemned part of the armed forces for excesses against the civilian population. The commission resumed its work in late August, but, lacking the authority to insist that politicians and military officers give evidence before it, it was unable to make further progress, and in December it declared that its task was at an end.

On 20 August 2001 more than 100,000 people (1m. according to the organizers, the CADC) staged a peaceful protest march in the Soummam Valley near Ifri. The protesters, mainly young Kabyles, condemned the 'Republic of generals' and called for a democratic Algeria. They succeeded in forcing the abandonment of planned official celebrations there to mark the 45th anniversary of the holding of a secret FLN congress that had resulted in the formation of the National Council of the Algerian Revolution. The official ceremony to mark the anniversary took place in Mascara in the west of the country. At the end of October RCD leader Saïd Saâdi accused the security services of plotting his assassination. He told a local newspaper that one of his party's activists had been arrested and tortured by men presumed to be members of military security and ordered to deliver a parcel bomb to Saâdi's home.

In October 2001, after months of political paralysis, Bouteflika announced that Tamazight would be designated a national language alongside Arabic in a forthcoming constitutional amendment, and gave Prime Minister Benflis, a Berber from the Aurès region, responsibility for dealing with the crisis in the Kabyle. Benflis sought dialogue with CADC, but by this time the citizens' movement was deeply divided and it was sometimes unclear who was authorized to speak on behalf of the protesters. In December Benflis held talks with one of the movement's factions but the so-called 'radicals', who appeared to be in the majority, rejected all negotiations with the Government. One of the leading radicals, Belaid Abrika, described the *dialoguistes* as 'government agents'. Algeria's military *décideurs*, for their part, seemed to be opposed to any significant political compromise.

In January 2002 Benflis reported that a series of resolutions had been adopted during discussions with the *dialoguistes* of the CADC, including the establishment of a special ministerial council to implement the Kabyles' main demands as set out in their 15-point 'El-Kseur platform'; notably the creation of decentralized government councils at *wilaya* level in the Kabyle and the granting of 'martyr of citizenship' status to victims of the crisis. However no reference was made to the Kabyles' demand that the gendarmerie be withdrawn from the region. The radicals continued to insist that their demands were not negotiable, and maintained the pressure on the authorities by means of strikes and demonstrations. They also threatened to boycott legislative elections scheduled for May 2002. Meanwhile, the Kabyle was slowly descending into anarchy as the authority of the central Government in the region weakened. Sporadic rioting continued, people refused to pay their taxes or their utility bills, and notification of military service was ignored. The gendarmes remained confined to their barracks, and the police appeared unwilling to intervene against the protesters in case this unleashed violent reactions.

The final report of the Issad commission was leaked to the press in early January 2002. It expressed deep pessimism regarding the immediate future of the Kabyle and emphasized the difficulties of carrying out an in-depth study of recent events in the region because many witnesses were afraid to come forward. At a broader level the report highlighted the weakening of the powers of the civil authorities in Algeria in favour of the military since 1992, and claimed that during the last decade there had been a subtle slide from a state of emergency to a state of siege. On questions of public order the responsibilities of civil and military authorities had become blurred, and respect for the law had not yet become part of the culture of the country's officials. Finally, the report suggested that the spontaneous and rapid appearance of a citizen's movement in the Kabyle emphasized the urgent need for Algerians to have real and effective political representation. In early February 2002 Benflis declared that the authorities had no intention of sending military units to restore order in the Kabyle, and insisted that the Government was committed to resolving the crisis through dialogue. The Prime Minister held another meeting with the *dialoguistes* from the CADC, but this faction appeared to have little influence over actual events in the region. On 12 February the region was paralysed by a general strike called by the CADC in protest at the reappearance of units of the gendarmerie, which had begun to man roadblocks in some parts of the region.

In early March 2002 in a televised address before a gathering of state officials, political parties and *dialoguistes* from the CADC, President Bouteflika announced the formal recognition of Tamazight as a national language without putting the issue to a referendum; local sources suggested that he feared that Algerians might not support the proposal. However, Bouteflika rejected demands for the withdrawal of the gendarmerie from the Kabyle, although he indicated that he might consider re-examining the deployment of the force at some future date. For the moment he stated that there was no question of withdrawing the gendarmerie while the entire country 'continued to fight against terrorism'. Furthermore, he reported that 24 gendarmes, including five officers, had been jailed for murder and the misuse of firearms during the riots in the spring of 2001. Victims of the rioting would be compensated but they would not be granted the status of 'martyrs'. In mid-March there were reports of fresh clashes between young protesters and gendarmes in the Kabyle. Meanwhile, the radical faction of the CADC rejected the conciliatory gestures made by President Bouteflika, and announced that they would prevent legislative elections being held in the region.

In late March 2002 a young protester was killed near Béjaïa, the first death since the commencement of the rioting in 2001. The CADC claimed that the youth had been shot in the head after clashes with the gendarmerie. Three other youths were killed shortly afterwards in clashes between security forces and demonstrators, while a gendarmerie barracks at Azazgua was ransacked by rioters. Tensions had mounted after four members of the CADC, including Ali Gherbi, a member of the movement's radical wing, were arrested outside the courthouse in Béjaïa where they were taking part in a sit-in in solidarity with five protesters arrested at the beginning of the month and given one-year prison sentences. At this time some 15 gendarmerie units were withdrawn from the Kabyle and replaced by police. Official sources insisted that other units would be withdrawn and that this was part of a 'redeployment'. While some sections of the press welcomed the move, others, notably the Arabic-language papers, declared that it was a concession that risked playing into the hands of 'extremists' and 'separatists'. Some commentators saw the withdrawal as an attempt to diffuse tensions in the region in the run-up to parliamentary elections. However, both the RCD and the FFS maintained that they would boycott the elections. The RCD leader Saïd Saâdi, described the actions of the security forces in the Kabyle as 'worse than under the French occupation'. On 8 April the National People's Assembly voted almost unanimously in favour of amending the constitution to grant Tamazight the status of national language. The FFS described the amendment as a 'masquerade' and, together with the RCD, boycotted the meeting. In late April, on the anniversary of the 1980 'Berber spring', numerous demonstrations were held across the Kabyle, the largest in the regional capital, Tizi Ouzou, which was attended by some 100,000 people.

Unrest was not, however, limited to the Kabyle. The deepening socio-economic crisis led to rioting in several small towns in different parts of the country in late 2001 and early 2002, as youths took to the street to protest about lack of employment opportunities, housing shortages, inadequate infrastructure and corruption among local officials. In some places rioters attacked public buildings and mounted road-blocks. The security forces were called in to restore order and made several arrests. Particularly disturbing for the authorities was the fact that the unrest

had spread to the south of the country, which had previously been relatively peaceful. In the Saharan town of Djanet, for example, youths attacked the town hall and rioting continued for several days before the security forces were able to restore order.

THE LEGISLATIVE ELECTIONS OF MAY 2002

In late February 2002 President Bouteflika announced that parliamentary elections would be held on 30 May, and expressed his determination to respect the results of the poll and to guarantee that voters had freedom of choice. To ensure that the elections were free and fair he called on the Government to put in place legal and constitutional mechanisms to control voting procedures. In addition he announced that a supervisory committee would be created, made up of representatives drawn from the political parties and civil society, and gave instructions for the Government to begin consultations without delay. Furthermore, Benflis was given the task of establishing a government commission responsible for co-ordinating all measures required for the preparation and conduct of the elections. This caused disquiet in some political circles, where it was argued that there was a conflict of interest as, in addition to being Prime Minister, Benflis was also Secretary-General of the FLN, a post he had assumed in September 2001. Benflis, for his part, strongly denied this, maintaining that his two political roles were quite separate.

In mid-April 2002 the President announced the establishment of a national commission to supervise the legislative elections (the Commission politique nationale de surveillance des élections législatives—CPNSEL). The commission was to be free from government influence, with its membership drawn entirely from members of opposition parties and independent personalities. Saïd Bouchair, President of the Constitutional Council, was appointed head of the CPNSEL. Meanwhile, three prominent political personalities—Ali Yahia Abdennour, president of the ALDHR, Gen. Rachid Benyelles, former chief of staff of the navy, and Wafa leader Ahmed Taleb Ibrahimi—joined the FFS leader, Hocine Aït Ahmed, in signing a declaration calling on Algerians to reject the forthcoming 'electoral masquerade' and demanding a radical change of regime that would give the country institutions deriving their legitimacy and authority from the free expression of the people.

Official campaigning for the elections began on 9 May 2002, with 23 political parties taking part together with 129 independent lists. The number of seats in the National People's Assembly was increased from 380 to 389 to take account of population growth. Amid general indifference on the part of the majority of Algerians more concerned with their everyday problems and hardships, the main issue debated in political circles was the scale of participation in the forthcoming poll. President Bouteflika embarked on a nation-wide campaign in an effort to counter appeals from the FFS, RCD and the CADC for Algerians to boycott the elections. Campaigning was a lacklustre affair, with only the FLN and MSP reported to have made any significant impact. Ali Benflis visited 35 of the country's 48 *wilaya*, attracting crowds of some 5,000–8,000 people. Meetings addressed by Sheikh Mahfoud Nahnah, the MPS leader, were also well attended, although not on the same scale of those organized by the FLN. The most notable feature of the election was the low rate of voter participation: the Minister of Interior and Local Authorities announced that only 46.2% of the 18m. eligible voters had participated—compared with 65.5% in 1997 and 59% in 1991—the lowest rate since independence.

The lowest levels of voter participation were recorded in the Kabyle where the boycott organized by the CADC, FFS and RCD proved highly effective. The participation rates in Tizi Ouzou and Béjaïa were 1.8% and 2.6%, respectively. Most polling stations in the Kabyle remained closed, and some came under attack by rioters who burnt ballot boxes. There were disturbances throughout the region as riot police clashed with demonstrators, reportedly resulting in the death of at least one person; several others were injured. Tensions in the region were increased when more than 110 people campaigning for a boycott were arrested in the Kabyle in the days immediately preceding the election. According to the Ministry of the Interior and Local Authorities, 707 out of 880 polling stations in the Tizi Ouzou *wilaya* and 455 out of 488 in Béjaïa remained closed. The CADC had announced its intention to use all means to prevent the election taking place. Elsewhere, voting proceeded peacefully, with participation rates highest in the south and lowest in the major cities. In the national capital, where polling stations were heavily guarded because of fears of attacks by armed Islamist groups, the participation rate, traditionally low, was recorded at only 30%. Both the FFS and RCD challenged the official figures on voter turn-out, claiming that it had reached no more than 15%–20%,and declaring that for the first time since independence part of the Algerian people (those of Kabyle) would be excluded from parliamentary representation. Ibrahimi argued that the nation-wide low rate of participation was a sign of solidarity with the people of the Kabyle.

The election results proved surprising as the FLN secured 199 of a total of 389 seats, giving the former single party an absolute majority in the new National People's Assembly. The FLN had finished third in the 1997 elections, after the RND and MSP, and held only 62 seats in the outgoing legislature. The RND was relegated to second place, retaining only 48 seats (compared with 155 in 1997). Of the two Islamist parties, the MSP (which had won 69 seats in 1997) secured only 38 seats, while Sheikh Abdallah Djaballah's MRN took 43 seats (Djaballah's former party, Nahdah, had won 34 seats in 1997). Independent candidates won 30 seats (compared with only 11 in 1997) while the PT increased its representation from four to 21. Political commentators attributed the FLN's success to the energetic leadership of Benflis and to the changes introduced since he became the party's Secretary-General, notably his efforts to open the party to young people and women. (Some 19 of the FLN's seats in the new Assembly were won by women.) They also believed the record level of abstentions had worked in favour of the FLN, which also benefited from the collapse of the RND—seen as the voice of the military *décideurs* and held responsible for the bad management of the many municipalities it controlled. Leaders of opposition parties stated that voting had been sullied by fraud, and that the results had no significance because they would not help to resolve the political, economic and social difficulties confronting the country. The FFS, the RCD and the CADC called for the elections to be annulled. Some political analysts, however, argued that the results had not been manipulated and reflected the country's true political landscape. After the FLN's victory Benflis stated that this was no time for 'triumphalism' and that no one party could solve the complex crisis facing the country and eliminate the damaging effects on the economy and society.

On 10 June 2001 Karim Younès, who had been Minister for Vocational Training in the previous administration, was elected President of the National People's Assembly, defeating Muhammad Djadid Younsi of the MRN by 271 votes to 52. In mid-June Benflis formed a new coalition Government of 38 ministers, mainly FLN deputies but with the RND and MSP retaining some portfolios. However, the Prime Minister failed to persuade other political parties, notably the PT and MRN, to join the new administration. Almost half of the ministers were new appointees, but the ministerial posts that remained unchanged included Noureddine Yazid Zerhouni, a close ally of Bouteflika, who retained the interior portfolio despite widespread criticism of his handling of the crisis in the Kabyle, and Abdelaziz Belkhadem, a strong supporter of dialogue with the Islamists, as Minister of State for Foreign Affairs. Several appointments—notably Noureddine Salah as Minister of National Education, Rachid Harraoubia, a reformist close to former Prime Minister Hamrouche, as Minister of Higher Education and Scientific Research, and Khalida Toumi-Messaoudi, an ex-RCD member and an outspoken campaigner for women's rights, as Minister of Communications and Culture and Government Spokesperson, were interpreted by some observers as signs of a desire for greater openness. This was the first time women had achieved this level of representation in government in Algeria: Toumi-Messaoudi was one of five women appointed to the new cabinet. There was general agreement that the new appointments suggested that Benflis had been given somewhat greater room to manoeuvre in forming his new administration.

ARMED ISLAMIST GROUPS REMAIN ACTIVE

Despite President Bouteflika's peace initiative, launched in July 1999, the killing of civilians, soldiers and policemen by the GIA and its splinter groups continued during the second half 1999,

albeit at a much lower level than in previous years. An estimated 150 people were reported killed during the month of Ramadan— only a fraction of the killings recorded during the same period in the years since the conflict began. The security forces continued to mount increasingly successful offensives against GIA strongholds, and greatly reduced, although did not eliminate, the threat posed by radical Islamist forces. The GIA itself, while apparently weakened and more divided than ever, remained extremely dangerous. In response to the AIS announcement in June that it was to make its cease-fire (in place since October 1997) permanent, the main GIA faction, headed by Antar Zouabri, threatened to intensify its campaign of violence inside Algeria and abroad. GIA violence intensified in the run up to the September referendum on the Law on Civil Concord, and the group pledged to continue its attacks until Algeria became an Islamic state. Nevertheless, official sources claimed that by the mid-January 2000 deadline large numbers of GIA militants had surrendered to the authorities under the President's amnesty programme. Immediately after the expiry of the deadline the Minister of the Interior and Local Authorities announced that 80% of members of armed groups had surrendered to the authorities. Also in mid-January all AIS fighters were granted a full amnesty, in return for which the force agreed to disband permanently. In the short term several hundred former AIS fighters were to be enrolled in an 'auxiliary unit' under army command and deployed against those Islamist militants (primarily the GIA) who remained active; local reports suggested they would number some 1,500. President Bouteflika declared that after the amnesty deadline had expired rebels who had not surrendered would be hunted down relentlessly. In the second half of January the security forces mounted a major offensive against GIA strongholds in the west of the country, with the local media reporting the deaths of a number of soldiers, rebels and civilians. In February Bouteflika indicated that he might be prepared to offer an amnesty to members of Hassan Hattab's Da'wa wal Djihad (which had broken away from the GIA in October 1998), on the grounds that its attacks had targeted the security forces rather than civilians. For some months there had been speculation that Hattab would seek a deal with the authorities and disband his group, although a statement to news organizations claiming to come from Hattab denied that any talks had taken place or indeed that the group intended to surrender. In late March Gen. (retd) Muhammad Attalila, a close and influential ally of Bouteflika, asserted that only a general amnesty covering all the armed groups still active would bring the violence to an end—a proposal opposed by the RND and the FLN. Despite numerous security force offensives against rebel Islamist groups' strongholds throughout 2000, in July of that year, 12 months after the launch of Bouteflika's initiative for national reconciliation, thousands of Islamist guerrillas remained at large. Bouteflika had acknowledged in August 1999 that at least 100,000 people had died in the previous seven years as a result of the civil conflict (rather than the 30,000 previously claimed by the Government), and the number of victims continued to rise during 2000. There were regular reports in the Algerian media of killings of Islamist rebels, security force members and civilians, and scepticism remained about the success of Bouteflika's initiative.

In May 2000 the Tunisian authorities announced that their security forces had repulsed a cross-border attack by militants belonging to Da'wa wal Djihad, and throughout that year there were reports of joint Algerian-Moroccan military operations along the western border against the GIA. In mid-November it was reported that Ali Belhadj, second-in-command in the FIS hierarchy had written from detention to Bouteflika promising that if released he would attempt to persuade the remaining armed Islamist groups to end their hostilities.

Although relative calm prevailed in the capital and in most major cities, large areas of the countryside remained insecure, with around 200 civilians killed every month. At the end of the 2000, however, there was a marked upsurge in the level of violence, with some 300 civilians killed during the first two weeks of December, including the massacre of 16 students at a technical college in Médéa; the renewed violence was attributed to the GIA, especially to the faction led by Antar Zouabri. The authorities released no information about the latest atrocities, but they were widely reported in the independent press—which voiced strong criticisms of the President and claimed that certain Islamist militants had taken advantage of the amnesty to re-establish their networks. Questions were raised about the high degree of mobility of the armed groups and their apparent access to sophisticated weapons. Some analysts argued that the resurgence of violence reflected the latest power struggle between Bouteflika and the high-ranking military *éradicateurs*, suggesting that the GIA was the creation of military security and was acting on orders to discredit Bouteflika's policy of reconciliation (see above).

In his book *Qui a tué à Bentalha?*, published in November 2000, Nesroulah Yous, a survivor (now living in France) of the massacre—attributed to Islamist extremists acting on the orders of the GIA—of almost 400 people in a suburb of Algiers in September 1997, implied that a special death squad attached to the security forces was in fact behind the killings. Furthermore, in February 2001 a former lieutenant in the Algerian army, Habib Souaïdia, who had also taken refuge in France, published *La sale guerre*, a book in which he presented what were claimed to be first-hand accounts of military operations against isolated hamlets by soldiers often out of uniform, the massacre of civilians by soldiers disguised as 'terrorists', summary executions and the burning of bodies, and the routine torture of suspected Islamists at one of the army's interrogation centres. This was the first time that a former officer had revealed allegedly personal experiences of military operations against the Islamists, and apparently provided hitherto unknown insights into the internal organization of the Algerian army. Souaïdia concluded that those responsible for these abuses should be brought to justice, and asserted that he was prepared to appear before a court to answer for his actions while a serving officer. There were reports that following the revelations by Yous and Souaïdia, members of their families living in Algeria had been interrogated by the security forces. Souaïdia and his book became the objects of vilification in the official Algerian press, and Chief of Staff Muhammad Lamari condemned the book as an attempt to destabilize the army and the security forces.

In February 2001 a former senior member of the GIA, Omar Chikhi, declared in an interview with the review *El-Youm* that he did not regret the killing of journalists and that the GIA had deliberately targeted French interests in an attempt to force France to withdraw its support for the military regime in Algiers. Chikhi had been pardoned under Bouteflika's Civil Concord, and claimed that he had decided to surrender after differences with GIA leader Antar Zouabri over the killing of civilians. The interview provoked a furious reaction in the Algerian press, which condemned the fact that Chikhi had been pardoned despite admitting that he had murdered journalists.

In an interview with the French daily *Le Figaro* in April 2001, former Minister of Defence Khaled Nezzar categorically rejected the allegations made by Habib Souaïdia, dismissing them as lies which had created unease among the Algerian community in France. When asked why the army had not intervened during the massacre at Bentalha, Nezzar stated that as there were relatively few soldiers available in the region on the night of the attack, any intervention would only have aggravated an already confused situation. It was his opinion that at the present time the only way to deal with those militants who refused to lay down their arms was to 'eradicate' them. With regard to Bouteflika's Civil Concord, Nezzar suggested that it was too early to speak of failure, and that with a presidential mandate of five years there was still time for the peace initiative to succeed. He defended the army's decision to intervene in January 1992, arguing that victory of the FIS in the elections would have introduced the 'reign of the Talibans' in Algeria. In late August 2001 Nezzar announced his intention to sue Souaïdia in France, following a French television programme in which Souaïdia accused Nezzar of responsibility for the assassination of thousands of Algerians. Nezzar referred to a media plot against the Algerian regime by the proscribed FIS, the Socialist International and FFS leader Hocine Aït Ahmed, accusing them of using Souaïdia as part of their campaign. Nezzar also denounced allegations made via the Qatar-based satellite television company Al-Jazeera by Col Mohammed Samraoui, a former Algerian military attaché in Germany, now living in exile, that

the GIA had been created by military security before the army annulled the 1991 legislative elections.

While Nezzar was in Paris in late April 2001 a group of Algerians resident in France—a family whose son had died under torture and two former detainees who had also been tortured by the army after the military take-over in 1992—commenced legal proceedings against him for torture. Nezzar was reported to have left France immediately by private jet before the police had opportunity to question him. The Fédération internationale des ligues des droits de l'homme (FIDH) described the general's hasty departure as a confession of guilt. According to the French Ministry of Foreign Affairs, Nezzar had been on an 'official visit' to France and was travelling on a diplomatic passport. However, Nezzar had himself previously stressed that he had retired from the army and had no involvement in Algerian politics. Lawyers for the plaintiffs accused the French authorities of ignoring their obligations under international conventions—notably the 1984 UN Convention against Torture and Other Cruel, Inhuman or Degrading Treatment or Punishment—by allowing Nezzar to leave. This was the first time that a legal complaint had been lodged in France against a former Algerian official, and many believed that had Nezzar been detained to face legal proceedings, the affair would have provoked a major crisis in France's uneasy relations with Algeria. At the beginning of May, after the Algerian press published the names of the plaintiffs—accusing them of belonging to the Islamist movement—lawyers for the three Algerians appealed to the French Government to ensure their protection. In early 2002 Nezzar returned to Paris voluntarily and informed police investigating the case that he strongly rejected allegations made against him. He stated that, as Minister of Defence, he had not had responsibility for internal security and that one of the complaints made against him referred to a period when he was already retired. At the end of April one of the plaintiffs withdrew his complaint against Nezzar after the former's son was arrested in Algiers by the security services as part of an operation to break up an alleged terrorist 'cell'. Meanwhile, in late April 2001 the French judge responsible for the inquiry into the bombing of a Paris metro station in July 1995 referred two Algerians, Boualem Bensaïd and Rachid Ramada, for trial for their alleged involvement in the attack. Bensaïd was alleged to have been in charge of the operation and to have received his instructions direct from senior members of the GIA in Algeria. Ramada, who was living in the United Kingdom, was accused of financing preparations for the attack; he had been arrested in London in November 1995, but hitherto the French authorities had been unable to obtain his extradition for trial.

In early January 2001 the authorities discovered the bodies of four Russian engineers employed by a state fertilizer company outside a village close to Annaba. The murders—the first killings of foreign nationals since 1996—were attributed to Islamist rebels. Some 27 armed Islamists were reported to have been killed by the security forces during two major army operations in Aïn Defla and Mascara in late February 2001. In mid-March some 26 people were massacred in two villages near Tipaza, and in Médéa in attacks presumed to have been perpetrated by armed Islamists. In one of the villages 11 members of the same family, including a two-month-old baby, had been slaughtered. At the same time 15 armed Islamists were killed by security forces during a major army operation in the Djelfa region. In late April more than 40 members of the security forces were killed, and 38 wounded, in eastern Algeria when they were attacked by a large group of heavily armed Islamists. Reports in the local press indicated that during April more than 150 people had been killed in attacks involving armed Islamist groups and that over 1,000 people, including more than 400 Islamists, had been killed since the beginning of the year. In early May state television reported that eight policemen had been killed by armed Islamists at Tigzirt, east of Algiers. Both the GIA faction led by Antar Zouabri and Da'wa wal Djihad were known to be active in this part of the Kabyle. Later that month security forces killed seven members of Da'wa wal Djihad following the murder of four civilians in an ambush near Batna. In mid-June there were reports in the local press that as many as 27 soldiers had been killed when armed Islamists ambushed a military convoy in the Chlef region, to the west of Algiers. As the rioting in the Kabyle intensified (see above) and gendarmerie brigades stationed there were confined to their barracks, there were reports that the GIA and Da'wa wal Djihad had strengthened their operations in the region now that many roads and numerous isolated villages were no longer protected. In early June 10 people were assassinated by an armed group near Médéa. It was reported that more than 110 people, including 40 members of the security forces, had been killed by armed Islamists since the beginning of June. Rumours of a *rapprochement* between armed Islamists and rioters in the Kabyle were strongly denied by the CADC, which stated that it wished to see the fall of the military-backed regime but not at the price of the establishment of a theocratic state.

There was a renewed resurgence of violence in late August and early September 2001, when some 80 people were killed during a two-week period. Massacres again took place in areas that were understood to have been 'pacified' and new bomb attacks were carried out in Algiers, following a two-year period of relative calm in the capital. In late August a bomb planted in the Casbah wounded 35 people, a number of them seriously, and in late November a large bomb explosion at an Algiers bus station resulted in numerous casualties. At the beginning of September the sense of insecurity in the capital was heightened when seven people were killed and 11 wounded in an attack on the tourist complex of Zeralda, in a high security zone west of Algiers. In late September 12 civilians, most of them children, were brutally murdered by masked men at Larbaa, a former AIS stronghold near Algiers, suggesting a revenge attack by the GIA. At the end of October 13 people, mostly *gardes communaux* were killed in an ambush near Relizane, and two *gardes communaux* and seven armed Islamists were killed in clashes during November. According to the opposition, around 1m. people had been displaced in rural areas as a result of a decade of violence, with the majority now encamped in shanty towns on the edges of the main cities.

Ongoing criticism in the francophone press of the President's Civil Concord intensified after the terrorist attacks on New York and Washington, DC, on 11 September 2001, as the *éradicateurs* condemned Bouteflika for maintaining a dialogue with the country's radical Islamists. In the aftermath of the attacks against the USA, both the GIA and Da'wa wal Djihad appeared on the USA's list of alleged international terrorist organizations whose assets were to be frozen. Da'wa wal Djihad's leader, Hassan Hattab, warned shortly after the attacks that if the Americans attacked Muslims they could expect reprisals that would be much worse than those inflicted on New York and Washington. At the end of September Spanish security forces arrested six Algerians living in various Spanish cities and charged them with belonging to a Da'wa wal Djihad terrorist cell. The Spanish interior minister stated that the Da'wa wal Djihad cell received financial support from the exiled Saudi Arabian-born dissident Osama bin Laden, whose al-Qa'ida (Base) organization was held by the USA to be principally responsible for the September attacks, and that Da'wa wal Djihad members had undergone military training in Afghanistan. All the suspects were described as being well-integrated into Spanish society. They were found to have sophisticated equipment for producing false documents, chemicals that could be used for making explosives, and some 30 videos portraying violent terrorist attacks in Algeria, Chechnya, Afghanistan and the Israeli Occupied Territories, which they used for recruitment purposes among North African immigrants in Spain. The group specialized in producing false papers, which were supplied to other terrorist cells in Europe linked to al-Qa'ida.

In October 2001 four men believed to be part of a Da'wa wal Djihad cell were arrested in France. Police were reported to have discovered false papers, weapons and instruction manuals for manufacturing explosives. This was the first apparent evidence of Da'wa wal Djihad activities in France. In early November five Algerians were arrested in Strasbourg on suspicion of belonging to a terrorist cell that was preparing an attack against the city's cathedral and Christmas market. They appeared to have been part of an alleged Da'wa wal Djihad cell based in Frankfurt, Germany, which had been dismantled by police in December 2000. The Algerian leader of the Frankfurt cell Muhammad Bensakhria, fled to Spain where he was arrested in June 2001 and subsequently extradited to France.

Meanwhile, in April 2001 Italian police had begun to dismantle a Da'wa wal Djihad cell in Milan that was alleged to have been preparing an attack on the US embassy in Rome. For three months the Italian police had intercepted telephone calls to and from the group's headquarters which revealed that the Milan cell was in close contact with a network of other Da'wa wal Djihad cells in Germany, Belgium, Spain, the United Kingdom and Algeria. The Italian investigations indicated that the Da'wa wal Djihad network in Europe, whose membership included not only Algerians but also Tunisians and Moroccans, was providing logistical support for al-Qa'ida and for the Algerian *maquis* and was said to have been planning terrorist attacks in Europe under directions from the al-Qa'ida leadership. The Italian police alleged that Tarek Maaroufi, a Belgian national of Tunisian origin arrested by Belgian police in December, was the head of the Da'wa wal Djihad network in Europe and a prominent member of Al-Qa'ida. The Italian and US authorities believed that he may have played a role in the 11 September attacks and in other actions against US interests, notably the foiled attack planned against the US embassy in Rome at the beginning of 2001.

After the events of 11 September 2001 a number of Algerian sources suggested that close links had existed between Osama bin Laden and the Algerian Islamist movement from the early 1990s, and that several Algerians working directly for al-Qa'ida ran a series of 'charitable' organizations and Islamic centres in Europe which acted as 'fronts' for the organization's activities. According to one report, bin Laden had become more interested in the Islamist movement in Algeria after the military takeover in 1992 and designated Sheikh Abu Qatada, a Palestinian Islamist and alleged al-Qa'ida member based in London, as the spiritual guide to the GIA. (Together with Abu Mous'ab, a Syrian with Spanish nationality, Abu Qatada had edited a weekly bulletin, *Al Ansar—The 'Partisans' of Jihad in Algeria and the World*—which acted as the 'voice' of the GIA abroad between 1993 and 1996.) A number of sources, including the Algerian Arabic-language newspaper, *El-Khabar*, claimed that bin Laden had engineered the schism in the GIA in 1998 that had led to the establishment of Da'wa wal Djihad. Italian intelligence sources claimed that Da'wa wal Djihad had become an integral part of the al-Qa'ida network in Europe, and that it was composed of an Algerian and a Tunisian network.

After a period of relative calm during Ramadan in late 2001, violence erupted again in Algeria in early 2002. Unofficial reports indicated some 150 people were killed by armed Islamist groups during January alone, predominantly in the so-called 'triangle of death' between Blida, Aïn Defla and Médéa. There were reports that some *repentis* (members of armed Islamist groups who had surrendered to the authorities under the Civil Concord) had taken up arms again and returned to the *maquis* where they joined Da'wa wal Djihad, which according to one estimate had some 800–1,000 militants in Algeria. Its rival, the GIA, in contrast appeared to have been greatly weakened by internal divisions (some asserted that it was made up of several different factions with no overall command structure) and by the actions of the security forces, and was said to have become totally discredited among Algerians owing to its cruel and barbarous methods. Some commentators suggested that the group had no more than 100 members, while a senior military source claimed that it had only 40 members, but that these were highly mobile, well armed and capable of continuing to mount terrorist actions.

In early February 2002 security forces killed Antar Zouabri, the GIA 'national emir' since 1996, along with two other senior members of the organization at the house of a *repenti* in Boufarik, near Algiers. (The GIA immediately murdered six members of the same family in a revenge attack.) There were rumours that the security forces had acted on information received from Da'wa wal Djihad. Rachid Abou Tourab, named as the GIA's 'national emir' in late March, gave an undertaking to continue the violent methods of his predecessor until the establishment of an Islamic state in Algeria had been achieved, later reiterating that there would be no respite in the killings and massacres. At the beginning of April 21 soldiers were killed by an armed group in an ambush in mountainous terrain near Saïda while engaged in a military operation against the GIA. In mid-April it was estimated that 380 people, including more than 100 armed Islamists, had been killed since the beginning of the year. Later in April 15 people, mainly women and children, were murdered by an armed group near Tiaret. According to official sources this was the worst massacre of civilians by the GIA since the beginning of the year. Meanwhile, there were reports that armed forces had surrounded Hassan Hattab and his senior lieutenants in the Kabyle in mid-April when they met to discuss the problems facing Da'wa wal Djihad, following the dismantling of many of the group's cells in Europe.

Prior to the elections at the end of May 2002, Algerian officials confirmed that there had been an upsurge in the number of attacks by armed Islamist groups. In early May 31 people were killed in two separate attacks by armed extremists near Tiaret, and later that month 15 government troops were killed after being ambushed in the Kabyle. In July, on the 40th anniversary of Algeria's independence from France, some 50 people were killed when a bomb exploded in a busy market in Larba, southeast of Algiers. A further 100 people were estimated to have been injured in the incident, which was reported to be the single most deadly attack in Algeria since 1992.

Meanwhile, in late 1999 President Bouteflika agreed to allow Amnesty International to send a delegation to Algeria. The organization had been banned from visiting the country for some four years. The delegation visited Algeria in May 2000, and another mission followed in November. The organization criticized the President's peace initiative, arguing that in practice neither side in the conflict would be punished for acts of brutality, and urged the authorities to investigate all past and present atrocities, make public the results of the investigations, and bring those responsible to justice. After the November mission Amnesty International highlighted the fact that families of victims were frustrated at what they considered a lack of political will by the authorities to establish the truth about human rights abuses committed by the security forces, self-defence militias and armed groups. The organization welcomed plans for reforming the judiciary (see above), but reminded the authorities that such measures had to be accompanied by a determination to enforce existing laws. During the year there were also visits from other international human rights groups, notably the FIDH, Human Rights Watch and Reporters sans Frontières.

In early May 2001 the Minister of State for the Interior and Local Authorities informed the National Assembly that some 4,480 people had 'disappeared' since 1992. Furthermore, he stated that inquiries were under way into the disappearances and that the results would be made public, but rejected accusations that the security forces might be implicated in the disappearances. Human rights organizations disputed the official figures, estimating that as many as 7,000 disappearances could be attributed to the security forces.

FOREIGN RELATIONS AFTER THE 1992 COUP

Following the army's cancellation of the second round of parliamentary elections in January 1992, Western governments were reluctant to be seen to offer political support to the new military-backed regime. Nevertheless, mindful of the consequences of an Islamist victory in Algeria—EU member states in particular were afraid of a massive influx of Algerian immigrants—discreet contacts were maintained and the junta was provided with urgently needed financial assistance by Western governments and by international agencies such as the IMF. Relations, were however, frequently strained, and Algerian officials repeatedly criticized Western governments for granting Algerian Islamists political asylum and allowing Islamist groups in their countries to raise funds to support terrorist activities in Algeria. The GIA in particular developed extensive support networks in several European countries to raise money and purchase weapons for the armed struggle in Algeria. France, the former colonial power, quickly became Algeria's leading supporter in the West, lending political and economic support to the military regime, although persistent reports of French military assistance were strongly denied by French officials. After the hijacking of a French airliner by GIA militants in December 1994, the GIA issued a statement declaring war on France because of its 'support to the oppressive regime, in addition to its military presence in Algeria'. During July–October 1995 the GIA launched a series of bomb attacks in France, in which seven people were killed

and 160 wounded, with the aim of persuading the French Government to withdraw its support for the junta and thus hasten its collapse. The plan had the opposite effect. The French authorities increased their support for the military-backed regime and quickly moved to dismantle FIS and GIA cells and support networks across France and elsewhere in Europe. In July 1996 the French Minister of Foreign Affairs made an official visit to Algiers, the first ministerial-level visit for three years.

After the election of a socialist Government in France in 1997, there was speculation that the French authorities might adopt a more critical approach towards the regime in Algiers, but comments made by the new French Minister of Foreign Affairs suggested that official policy towards Algeria remained unchanged. In response to allegations of massive fraud in the 1999 Algerian presidential election, the French authorities expressed concern and regretted that the electoral process was not as transparent and pluralist as promised. For his part, President-elect Bouteflika accused France of regarding his country as a 'protectorate', asserting that it should abandon its 'fixation' with Algeria.

France none the less remained Algeria's chief interlocutor with the EU. In December 1996 the EU agreed to begin talks on the admission of Algeria to the Euro-Mediterranean free-trade zone, although Algerian and EU officials admitted that they expected the negotiations to be difficult. In January 1998 the EU presidency expressed grave concern at the dramatic increase in violence in Algeria and later that month sent a delegation of ministers from the United Kingdom, Luxembourg and Austria to Algiers. Yet despite growing unease in Europe at the escalating violence in Algeria, and concerns that the Algerian authorities might have been involved in the bloodshed, the EU appeared reluctant to antagonize the Algerian regime and risk jeopardizing member states' substantial economic interests there.

There was speculation in 1994 that the USA was adjusting its policy towards Algeria and that, in order to avoid the mistakes made in the case of Iran, it was preparing for a possible Islamist regime to assume power there in the future. In June US President Bill Clinton confirmed that there had been low-level contacts between US officials and the FIS in the USA and Germany, and stated that his Administration was not opposed to some form of power sharing between the Zéroual regime and 'dissident groups who are not involved in terrorism'. However, during 1995 the US Administration appeared to adopt a tougher policy on radical Islamists, and it was reported that the Pentagon maintained that Islamist forces could not win an overall victory over the military-backed regime. In March 1996 US Assistant Secretary of State Robert Pelletreau visited Algiers, the first visit by a senior US official since 1992, and reaffirmed his country's support for Zéroual's policy of dialogue. It was also reported that the US Department of State had ended contacts with FIS spokesman Anwar Haddam, and in December 1996 Haddam was taken into custody by US immigration officials pending his deportation.

Algeria's North African neighbours, particularly Tunisia, did not disguise their relief that a possible Islamist take-over had been averted by the military's intervention in 1992. Nevertheless, relations with Morocco remained strained owing to Algeria's continued support of the Polisario Front, while each country accused the other of sponsoring terrorism to destabilize its neighbour. President Zéroual declared Algeria's commitment to working towards Maghreb unity, but strained relations with Morocco, civil conflict in Algeria, and UN sanctions against Libya meant that the UMA was virtually moribund. Elsewhere in the Middle East, those Arab states that had their own problems, or perceived problems, with militant Islamists, generally welcomed the new regime in Algiers. Iran, however, which had previously warned that force should not be used against the FIS, declared the postponement of the second round of voting to be illegal. Algeria accused Iran of interfering in its internal affairs and severed relations completely in March 1993.

FOREIGN RELATIONS UNDER THE BOUTEFLIKA PRESIDENCY

In July 1999, less than three months after Bouteflika assumed the presidency, Algeria hosted a summit meeting of the Organization of African Unity (OAU, now the African Union—AU) in

Algiers, which was attended by representatives of 43 of the 53 member states and which was widely regarded as a success. Algeria assumed the presidency of the organization for the next year, and in the following months Algerian envoys were dispatched on peace initiatives to various parts of Africa where conflicts remained unresolved. In May 2000 President Bouteflika, in his capacity as Chairman of the OAU Assembly of Heads of State, visited the Horn of Africa to mediate in the war between Ethiopia and Eritrea. Representatives of both countries subsequently attended peace talks in Algiers, and a peace agreement was eventually signed there in mid-December.

During the 1999 election campaign Bouteflika pledged to restore Algeria to its role as a leading regional power. However, on assuming the presidency he adopted a more conciliatory stance towards Algeria's Maghreb neighbours, especially Morocco. Bouteflika responded positively to King Hassan's message of congratulation on his election victory, and following the King's death in late July the Algerian President held talks with his successor, Muhammad VI, in Rabat after attending Hassan's funeral. However, despite an undertaking to work towards a further improvement in bilateral relations, this co-operation proved short-lived. In August, following the GIA's massacre of 29 civilians in the Béchar region near the Moroccan border, Bouteflika accused Morocco of providing sanctuary for those responsible for the attack and also extended accusations to drugs-trafficking and arms-dealing on the joint border. Renewed tensions prevented the long-awaited reopening of the land border between the two countries, scheduled for late August.

Algeria's generals, and not the President, apparently dictated policy on the Western Sahara issue. While Algeria continued to support a solution to the conflict by means of the UN referendum process, many Moroccans remained convinced that the Polisario Front was only a force to be reckoned with because of Algerian backing. However, in February 2000 both Algeria and Morocco expressed a desire to improve relations, and Algeria's Minister of Foreign Affairs, Youcef Yousfi, declared that the contention over Western Sahara should not be an obstacle to this goal. Although Bouteflika held talks with King Muhammad at the EU-OAU summit held in the Egyptian capital in April, relations remained strained, not least by the revelation in mid-July that Qatar had purchased weapons from the United Kingdom worth US $7.5m. which the Moroccan Government declared might be destined for Polisario. Meanwhile, in an interview with the US *Time* magazine, King Muhammad asserted that the Western Sahara dispute was of Algeria's creation. Nevertheless, the Algerian and Moroccan interior ministers subsequently held a number of meetings, and after talks in Rabat in November they announced that a preparatory committee would assemble soon in Algiers as a preliminary to the reopening of the land border between the two countries. Progress towards the normalization of relations was, however, expected to be slow, especially as the Western Sahara peace process remained stalled. In December Polisario threatened to end the nine-year cease-fire early in 2001 if Morocco allowed that year's Paris–Dakar rally to pass through the disputed territory, but, after appeals by the UN, the OAU and Algeria, it did not reopen hostilities. Although Polisario warned that its forces remained in a state of war, it was thought unlikely that Algeria would allow Polisario to break the truce.

Algeria did not support the autonomy proposals for Western Sahara put forward by the UN Security Council in late June 2001 and based on a report by UN Special Envoy James Baker (detailed in the chapter on Morocco). Subsequent discussions between Baker and Algerian ministers failed to make any progress. However, there were reports in the local Algerian press that Bouteflika had accepted the Baker plan at a meeting with US President George W. Bush in Washington, DC, in November. Algerian officials denied these reports, and during a meeting in Algiers in January 2002 with the newly-appointed head of the UN Mission for the Referendum in Western Sahara (MINURSO), William Lacy Swing, Abdelkader Messahel, a junior minister at the Algerian Ministry of Foreign Affairs, reaffirmed Algeria's support for the principle of self-determination and the right of the Sahrawi people to independence. Nevertheless, there was some speculation that as a result of its growing *rapprochement* with the West following the suicide

attacks on New York and Washington in September 2001, Algeria might abandon the Sahrawi cause.

In February 2002, following a report to the Security Council by UN Secretary-General, Kofi Annan, in which he stated that partition was one option in the Western Sahara issue, relations between Algeria and Morocco deteriorated further. Morocco categorically rejected the proposal, claiming that it was an Algerian plan designed to create a Sahrawi 'mini-state' under Algerian protection, thus providing Algeria with an outlet to the Atlantic Ocean. Algeria's representative at the UN denied that he had formulated the proposal, but there was speculation that it had been a personal initiative of President Bouteflika. On 27 February Bouteflika became the first Algerian President to visit the Sahrawi refugee camps around Tindouf in south-western Algeria. The visit, on the 26th anniversary of the establishment of the SADR, was described by Morocco as 'provocative'. In late April, in response to US efforts to persuade members of the UN Security Council to accept the Moroccan-backed option of autonomy for the Western Sahara, Algeria wrote to all members of the Security Council stating that the only reasonable solution was one accepted unanimously by the Council and by interested parties.

Despite much rhetoric about reviving the virtually moribund UMA, little progress was made—largely because of continuing tensions between Algeria and Morocco. Bouteflika regarded a revived UMA as essential because it would enable the Maghreb states to bargain collectively with the EU, thus strengthening their hand. However, a UMA summit meeting scheduled for the end of 1999 was cancelled. In September 2000 Bouteflika stated that efforts to revive the UMA remained deadlocked even though Algeria and Morocco had agreed to regard the Western Sahara conflict as a separate issue. In mid-March 2001 the UMA's council of foreign ministers met in Algiers to prepare for a summit of heads of state, but Morocco was only represented at the meeting by its secretary of state for foreign affairs. The Moroccan Minister of Foreign Affairs, Muhammad Benaissa, did, however, attend a meeting of UMA foreign ministers in Algiers in January 2002 at which Habib Boularès of Tunisia was elected as the organization's new Secretary-General. However, on the sensitive issue of Western Sahara, Benaissa made it clear that there was no question of Morocco sacrificing its 'national cause for the sake of building a Greater Maghreb'. A summit meeting of UMA heads of state, the first since 1994, was scheduled to take place in Algiers in late June 2002. However, the summit was postponed indefinitely just days before it was due to open, after King Muhammad of Morocco announced his refusal to attend.

President Zine al-Abidine Ben Ali of Tunisia made an official visit to Algiers in February 2002 to discuss bilateral relations and measures to revive the UMA. In April and November 2001 Gen. Muhammad Lamari, Algeria's Chief of Staff, had held talks in Tunis with Ben Ali and his military and security officials on issues of intensifying the campaign against Islamist militants, improving border surveillance—notably to prevent Algerian and Tunisian members of al-Qa'ida from returning to their country of origin—and dismantling North African Islamist cells in Europe. It was reported that numerous alleged Islamist activists from Tunisia who had taken refuge in Algeria and joined local GIA groups had been arrested by the Algerian authorities and handed over to the Tunisian security forces.

Algeria's negotiations with the EU over admission to the Euro-Mediterranean free-trade zone resumed after the 1999 presidential election. At the close of the sixth session of talks, in December 2000, Algeria declared that the need for discussions on the free movement of people, and not just goods, had to be recognized by the EU, as did the fact that during the establishment of a free-trade zone the Algerian economy would require a transitional period to enable it to adjust to growing competition from EU member states. Hopes were expressed that negotiations could be concluded by 2002, but it was acknowledged that ratification of the agreement by all the individual EU member states was likely to take much longer. Romano Prodi, President of the European Commission, held talks in Algiers in January 2001 to review progress on the negotiations. During the visit three financial protocols, to the value of €30m., were signed to assist with the reform of the posts and telecommunications sector; to enhance to role of the private press; and to raise professional and technical standards in the police force. Prodi was making his first visit to the Maghreb region in order to revitalize the Euro-Mediterranean partnership programme. He pledged to encourage EU investment but emphasized the importance of reviving the UMA.

Following further discussions in February and March 2001, officials from Algeria and the EU stated that substantial progress had been made. President Bouteflika signed an association agreement at the European Commission headquarters in Brussels, Belgium, in December and a formal signing took place in April 2002. Until the agreement has been ratified by all EU member states, an interim accord will allow Algeria to benefit from tariff concessions. The accord obliges Algeria to respect democracy and human rights, but some human rights activists argued that little pressure would be exerted by the EU on the Algerian authorities to implement these clauses. During his visit to Brussels in December 2001 Bouteflika became the first Algerian Head of State to visit the NATO headquarters, where he met the organization's Secretary-General, Lord Robertson. Bouteflika promised to maintain closer relations with NATO 'for the sake of regional stability'. Algeria was to negotiate an accord with NATO for the secure exchange of military information. Among a senior-level EU delegation that visited Algiers in early June 2002 was the Spanish Minister of Foreign Affairs, who stated that discussions had been very useful and that Algeria had recorded a clear improvement in the sphere of human rights. In an open letter to the EU, however, Amnesty International stated that there was no sign of improvement in Algeria's human rights situation and criticized the EU for failing to impose changes on the Algerian authorities.

Tensions that had developed between Algeria and France following the presidential election soon eased. In what was regarded as a significant development, in June 1999 the French National Assembly voted unanimously to abandon the official claim that the French role in the Algerian war of independence had been no more than a peace-keeping operation. French Minister of the Interior Jean-Pierre Chevènement and Minister of Foreign Affairs Hubert Védrine visited Algiers later in June and in July, respectively. In September Bouteflika met the French President, Jacques Chirac, at the UN in New York (the first meeting between the leaders of the two countries since 1992). To mark the improvement in bilateral relations, Paris agreed to increase substantially the number of visas issued to Algerians wishing to visit France. A delegation from the French Senate visited Algeria in December, and in late January 2000 Algeria's new Minister of Foreign Affairs, Youcef Yousfi, became the first member of an Algerian government to make an official visit to France in six years when, acting as Bouteflika's special envoy, he held talks with Prime Minister Jospin in Paris. France subsequently initiated discussions on bilateral military co-operation, and in May the French naval commander for the Mediterranean, Vice-Adm. Paul Habert, visited Algiers for talks.

Bouteflika made a full state visit to Paris in mid-June 2000—the first of its kind by an Algerian President—during which he was received with full ceremony, including a personal welcome by Chirac at the airport and an invitation to address the French National Assembly. Sections of the French press none the less published unflattering assessments of Bouteflika's presidency and highlighted criticism of his country's human rights record. The visit produced few tangible results, but was interpreted in Algiers as an important step towards ending the diplomatic isolation imposed on Algeria after the 1992 military take-over. In mid-February 2001 Védrine again visited Algiers. However, since Bouteflika's state visit relations between Algiers and Paris had not witnessed the expected improvement, and a climate of reciprocal disenchantment had set in. Both governments emphasized that they wished to improve bilateral relations, although several important issues remained unresolved. According to the French Ministry of Foreign Affairs, Védrine's visit was aimed at renewing dialogue and exchanges between the two countries. It was, however, overshadowed by the publication in France earlier in the month of a controversial book, *La sale guerre*, by a former Algerian army officer (see above). At the same time a group of leading French intellectuals accused the French Government of supporting an Algerian regime which they claimed was, under the guise of an anti-terrorist campaign, seeking the political and physical eradication of all opposition,

and demanded that an international commission of inquiry should be sent to Algeria to investigate the massacres of civilians.

In early May 2001, in response to the rioting in the Kabyle (see above), Védrine told the French National Assembly that France could not remain silent about the violent repression by the Algerian authorities of demonstrations at which many young people had been killed, and called for 'political dialogue'. His Algerian counterpart, Abdelaziz Belkhadem, described the remarks as 'unacceptable'. Védrine had earlier reaffirmed that an official visit to Algeria by President Chirac and Prime Minister Jospin had been agreed in principle but would not take place in the immediate future. At the end of April some 2,000 people, mainly from France's large Kabyle community, demonstrated in Paris to condemn violence in the Kabyle. The protesters denounced the 'colonial' Government in Algiers, directing much of their anger at senior military figures. The French Ligue des droits de l'homme staged a demonstration outside the Algerian embassy in Paris, demanding an end to 'armed intervention' in the Kabyle and to human rights violations. Also in late April the Paris-based FIDH deplored the fact that the French authorities had allowed former Algerian Minister of Defence Khaled Nezzar to leave France before he could be questioned about allegations of torture made against him by a group of Algerians currently resident in France (see above). At the beginning of May Chirac condemned torture, summary executions and assassinations committed by France during Algeria's war of independence. His comments followed revelations in a book (*Services spéciaux Algérie 1955–1957: Mon témoignage sur la torture*) by a retired French general, Paul Aussaresses, former head of special services in Algeria, about actions that he had ordered, notably during the battle of Algiers in 1957. Chirac stated that he had been appalled by these revelations and demanded that disciplinary action be taken against Aussaresses. In mid-June 2001 the French authorities announced that Aussaresses, who had been deprived of his military rank, would stand trial on charges of 'apologizing for war crimes'. He was convicted in January 2002 and fined €7,500.

Meanwhile, in mid-June 2001 the French Secretary of State for Foreign Trade, François Huwart, visited the Algiers International Fair (where some 260 French companies were represented) and held meetings with Algerian ministers. He stated that despite the difficult political situation in Algeria, France reaffirmed its support for the country's economic development. The journalists of the leading French dailies *Le Monde*, *Le Figaro* and *Libération* were refused visas by the Algerian authorities to cover the event. The Algerian embassy in Paris urged the French media to respect 'truth and objectivity' in the reporting on events in the Kabyle (see above) and in Algeria in general, emphasizing that as millions of Algerians listened to broadcasts from France, this gave the French media a 'considerable responsibility'. Two days later thousands of people demonstrated in Paris to express their anger at the conduct of the Algerian regime, and there were calls for an end to the military junta and the departure of President Bouteflika. Shortly afterwards, during a speech at Illizi in southern Algeria, Bouteflika—without explicitly naming France—blamed the former colonial power for the violence in the Kabyle. Since rioting broke out in that region in mid-April Bouteflika had repeatedly claimed the existence of a plot or conspiracy in part directed from abroad to exploit Kabyle separatism. However, Bouteflika subsequently stated that the accusations of French involvement in the rioting in the Kabyle were not directed at the French people or the French Government but at 'secret business circles' and their networks in Algeria.

In early July 2001 France and Algeria signed an agreement granting new rights to the 0.5m. Algerian nationals resident in France. The status of Algerians in France had been governed by a 1968 accord, but as the situation of other foreigners in France had improved Algerians considered themselves to be in a less favourable situation. The new accord would bring the status of Algerians in line with that of other foreign nationals: in particular, Algerian parents of children holding French nationality were to be accorded full residency rights in France. The changes, which would enter force when the accord had been ratified by the legislatures of both countries, were generally welcomed—despite some criticisms from associations campaigning for immigrants' rights.

There was a marked improvement in relations between France and Algeria following the suicide attacks on the USA in September 2001. At the end of September Nicolas Sarkozy became the first French deputy to visit Algeria since 1998. He expressed the view that the Algerian Government had been criticized too harshly and that there were no alternatives to the policy being pursued by President Bouteflika. Hubert Védrine visited Algiers in early October 2001, as part of a tour of the Maghreb to discuss co-operation in the fight against terrorism. Both Algeria and France agreed that in response to the attacks on New York and Washington, DC, the USA and its allies were justified in taking reprisals. Védrine's Algerian counterpart supported a strengthening of co-operation with France against terrorism in all areas, notably the dismantling of transnational networks, the freezing of their sources of finance and the exchange of information on the prevention of terrorist crimes. In December Jacques Chirac became the first French President to visit Algeria since 1989. The visit was part of a rapid tour of the Maghreb capitals to discuss the US-led military campaign against al-Qa'ida and the Taliban regime in Afghanistan, and the international repercussions of this so-called 'war against terror'. President Chirac stated that the French and Algerian authorities were in full agreement on the need to eradicate international terrorism, including al-Qa'ida and its leader bin Laden, and both rejected the notion of a 'clash of civilisations', which the French President described as 'absurd, dangerous and unfounded', as well as any attempt to equate Islam with terrorism. The French President also recognized that in Europe there had been 'great weaknesses' in dealing with 'terrorists', and pledged to take tough measures against such 'criminals' who sought refuge there. During his brief visit to Algiers, in addition to holding talks with President Bouteflika and other Algerian officials, Chirac visited the Bab el-Oued district of the capital which had been devastated by flash floods in early November (see above) where he was warmly welcomed by a large crowd.

In February 2002 AirLib inaugurated a twice-daily service from Paris to Algiers, the first time that a French airline had made scheduled flights to Algeria since the hijacking of an Air France Airbus by the GIA in December 1994. The French Minister of Capital Works, Transport and Housing, Jean-Claude Gayssot, travelled on the inaugural flight and held talks with President Bouteflika in Algiers. Gayssot stated that security at Algiers international airport was 'satisfactory' while the president of AirLib declared that the airport was one of the most secure in the world. Also in February 2002 President Bouteflika was one of 13 African heads of state who attended a meeting in Paris with President Chirac to launch the New Partnership for Africa's Development (NEPAD) initiative.

During 2001 a number of Algerians and French nationals of Algerian origin were arrested during a crack-down on Islamist networks operating in France and suspected of having links with al-Qa'ida. Shortly before the attacks on the USA a Franco-Algerian was arrested in Dubai, United Arab Emirates, and extradited to France on suspicion of involvement in a plot to attack the US embassy in Paris. He was believed to be a key figure in directing bin Laden's terrorist campaign in Europe, with a network extending to several other European countries. In October four men believed to be part of a Da'wa wal Djihad cell were arrested by French police, and during subsequent investigations false papers, equipment for producing false documents, weapons, and instruction manuals for making explosives were discovered. In November five Algerians were arrested in Strasbourg on suspicion of belonging to an Islamist network linked to bin Laden. Later that month, despite opposition from human rights organizations, the French Minister of the Interior ordered the deportation of two Algerians who had served prison sentences for their involvement in GIA cells in France during the early 1990s. On their arrival in Algiers both men were immediately arrested by the security services.

Algerians reacted with horror and disbelief when the extreme right-wing National Front leader, Jean-Marie Le Pen, came second to the incumbent Jacques Chirac at the first round of the French presidential election in late April 2002 (defeating the Socialist Prime Minister Lionel Jospin and thus proceeding to the second round). For four decades Le Pen's name had been associated with bitter memories of the Algerian war of independence, and his views on immigration aroused particular fears for the future of Algerians and their families living in France.

Meanwhile, Germany reopened its visa and consular divisions in Algeria, and Denmark announced that from February 2000 its new embassy in Algiers would become the regional base for diplomatic services covering Morocco, Libya, Tunisia and Mauritania. A British Minister of the Foreign and Commonwealth Office visited Algiers in October 2001 to discuss security and co-operation in the fight against terrorism, and in early February 2002 Ahmed Ouyahia, Algeria's Minister of Justice, made an official visit to London. For some years Algeria had criticized the British Government for granting refuge to its Islamist opponents. At least 20 Algerians condemned to death for acts of terrorism were living in the United Kingdom. Ouyahia was reported to be particularly concerned about the networks that allegedly continued to supply the Algerian *maquis* with arms and explosives and provide logistical support for terrorists in Europe.

The US Department of State welcomed President Bouteflika's peace initiative, and stated that the successful outcome of the referendum on the Law on Civil Concord represented an important step in achieving a lasting peace. Martin Indyk, the USA's Assistant Secretary for Near Eastern Affairs, held talks with Bouteflika in Algiers in September 1999 and pledged US support for Algeria's economic and political reform programme. Later that month, as Bouteflika attended the UN General Assembly in New York, he held talks with President Clinton. In January 2000, however, two Algerians, suspected of having links with the GIA and with Osama bin Laden, were arrested in the USA and charged with conspiring to carry out a bomb attack. In December 1999 another Algerian national had been arrested while attempting to cross the US–Canadian border carrying bomb-making equipment. The US authorities believed the two incidents were linked to a millennium bomb plot involving bin Laden and other Islamist extremists. In February 2000 US Secretary of Defense William Cohen announced that the USA intended to expand military co-operation with Algeria.

During 2000 there were visits to Algiers by a number of senior US officials to discuss political, economic and military issues, and President Bouteflika met Susan Rice, the US Assistant Secretary of State for African Affairs, at the OAU summit at Lomé, Togo, in July. President Clinton subsequently praised Bouteflika's domestic leadership and Algeria's role in securing an end to the conflict between Ethiopia and Eritrea in 2000. President Bouteflika made an official visit to the USA in mid-July 2001 (the first visit by an Algerian head of state for more than a decade), accompanied by several government ministers. Talks between Bouteflika and the new US President, George W. Bush, were described as 'very positive'. The discussions were reported to have included energy co-operation, the fight against terrorism and the Western Saharan dispute. There were also reports of increased intelligence co-operation between Algeria and the USA, with Algerian military security providing information to the US officials regarding suspected Algerian members of al-Qa'ida.

President Bouteflika condemned in the strongest terms the suicide attacks on New York and Washington, DC, of 11 September 2001, and sent a message of condolence to President Bush. Shortly after the attacks the two radical Algerian Islamist groups, the GIA and Da'wa wal Djihad, both of which were alleged to have close links with al-Qa'ida, appeared on an official US list of terrorist organizations whose assets were to be frozen (see above). Algeria voiced support for the US-led international 'coalition against terror', but did not participate in military operations. The *éradicateurs* among the ruling élite demanded Algeria's active participation in the US-led campaign against 'Islamic terrorism', and praised the tough stance adopted by the Bush Administration. The US-led bombing of Afghanistan was, however, condemned by several political parties in Algeria, notably the FLN, while a senior member of the proscribed FIS declared that all Arab and Muslim allies of the USA were traitors to their religion, people and nation. Algeria's Muslim leaders recalled that it was forbidden for a Muslim state to support or assist in an attack against another Muslim state. In contrast to the 1991 Gulf War, however, there were no street protests or demonstrations against the US-led military action in Afghanistan or in support of bin Laden and his allies. Some observers claimed that the silence was deceptive, and that events in Afghanistan had merely served to strengthen the deep-seated anti-US sentiment among ordinary Algerians who regarded bin Laden as a hero because he had dared defy the USA. Others contended that although Algerians followed events in Afghanistan with great interest, it was not an Arab country and therefore did not evoke the same passions as events in the Palestinian territories or Iraq.

President Bouteflika made a second official visit to Washington, DC, in November 2001, where he reiterated his support for the US-led military campaign in Afghanistan. The Algerian authorities declared that they felt less isolated after the 11 September attacks, and considered that there was now greater understanding in the West of their own 'struggle' against terrorism. This growing *rapprochement* with the West, notably the USA, apparently exemplified Algeria's successful emergence from a decade of diplomatic isolation after the military takeover in 1992. The US Assistant Secretary for Near Eastern Affairs, William Burns, visited Algiers in December 2001 for

talks with President Bouteflika and his officials as part of a regional tour. He reaffirmed Washington's interest in Maghreb development, and thanked the Algerian authorities for their expressions of solidarity following the terrorist attacks. Co-operation between the Algerian security services and the US Federal Bureau of Investigation in tracking down terrorists of Algerian origin based in Europe continued. The USA declared that the Algerian parliamentary elections held at the end of May 2002 were evidence of the 'development of democracy'.

President Bouteflika visited Moscow, Russia, in April 2001, and in June, after his return from a visit to Algiers, the Russian vice-premier, Ilya Klebanov, announced the beginning of a 10-year programme of military and technical co-operation. In December Algeria took delivery of a number of new Russian military aircraft, under the first part of a major military contract with Russia to modernize and upgrade the country's ageing air force. Visiting Moscow in April 2002, Algeria's Chief of Staff, Gen. Muhammad Lamari, signed a new agreement on arms purchases.

Diplomatic relations with Iran were restored in January 2001 after a meeting between Bouteflika and President Muhammad Khatami at the UN Millennium Summit in New York, USA, in September 2000.

Economy

ALAN J. DAY

With subsequent revisions by RICHARD I. LAWLESS. Revised for this edition by RICHARD GERMAN

Algeria covers an area of 2,381,741 sq km (919,595 sq miles), of which a large part is desert. At the census of February 1977 the population (excluding Algerians abroad) was 16,948,000. At the census of April 1987 the population had reached 23,038,942, in addition to about 1m. Algerians living abroad (mainly in France). The overall population growth rate averaged 3.1% per annum during 1970–80 and 2.8% per annum in 1980–92. Provisional results of the June 1998 census gave a population of 29,276,767 (subsequently revised to 29,272,343) and indicated a decline in the annual rate of population growth from 3.2% in 1987 to 2.2% in 1997. The proportion of the Algerian population living in urban areas increased from 40% in 1970 to 54% in 1992, the average urban growth rate having risen from 4.1% per annum during the 1970s to 4.9% per annum in 1980–92. Nearly 54% of Algerians were aged less than 15 years in 1992. Political violence in recent years, often affecting isolated rural communities, is believed to have forced many thousands of rural dwellers into the cities. The populations of the main cities were enumerated by the 1998 census as 1.52m. in the capital, Algiers (el-Djezaïr), 0.66m. in Oran (Ouahran), 0.46m. in Constantine (Qacentina) and 0.24m. in Annaba. According to the World Bank, in 2000 60.3% of the population were living in urban areas. The estimated average life expectancy at birth in 1990–95 was 67.1 years, increasing to 69.7 years in 2000. By 2001 the population was estimated to have reached 32,000,000. The country is divided into 48 *wilayat* (departments) for administrative purposes.

Algeria has varied natural resources. In the coastal region are fertile plains and valleys, where profitable returns are made from cereals, wine, olives and fruit. The remainder of the country supports little agriculture, though in the mountains grazing and forestry produce a small income, and dates are cultivated in the oases of the Sahara. Mineral resources, in particular petroleum and natural gas, are abundant and dominate Algeria's export trade.

GOVERNMENT STRATEGY

From independence in 1962 Algerian governments sought to promote economic growth as a foundation for a future socialist society. They acquired either a complete or a controlling interest in most foreign-owned companies. In 1966 the Government nationalized foreign-owned mines, land which had been abandoned by Europeans at independence, and insurance companies.

In 1971 it assumed control of the hydrocarbons sector. This sector accounted for 43.3% of Algeria's gross domestic product (GDP) in 2000. In that year, according to estimates by the World Bank, Algeria's gross national product (GNP), measured at average 1998–2000 prices, was US $48,325m., equivalent to $1,590 per head (or $5,040 on an international purchasing-power parity basis).

The Government's strategy for development traditionally involved a high degree of austerity, with heavy restrictions placed on the import of luxury and consumer goods. The first Four-Year Plan, covering the period 1970–73, emphasized the establishment of a capital-intensive sector, involving the hydrocarbons, iron and steel, chemical and engineering industries, and an annual growth rate of 9.7% was achieved. The second Plan, for 1974–77, aimed to establish a sound industrial base and also put emphasis on better agricultural methods, housing, health, job-creation and training. A high level of investment (40% of GDP) was maintained, and the Government aimed to achieve an average annual growth rate of 10%. Total expenditure, originally projected at AD 52,000m., was later increased to AD 110,000m., on the basis of increased income, owing to higher petroleum prices. The country's GDP grew by an average annual rate of 6%–6.5% in the 1970s, reaching AD 120,825m. in 1979.

During the 1980–84 planning period total investment was estimated to have reached AD 345,000m. (nearly 14% below the Government's target figure), while GDP growth averaged 4.5% per year (compared with a planning target of 8.2% per year). Under a policy of gradual economic liberalization introduced during the planning period, light industries producing consumer goods were opened up to private investment, the private sector being responsible for an estimated AD 3,400m. of investment for the creation of 20,000 jobs (notably in the textile and leather-ware industries). A new investment code was instituted in 1982 to stimulate private enterprise in areas such as retailing, hotels and catering, housing, handicrafts and light industry. Tax concessions were introduced to attract foreign partners into private-sector joint ventures. Within the state sector, efforts were made from 1981 to increase productivity and efficiency, notably by reorganizing 90 of Algeria's giant state corporations into 300 more specialized units, many with decentralized management away from Algiers.

The 1985–89 Development Plan, which required total investment of AD 550,000m., reflected the Government's new priorities for development, shifting investment away from industry and into agriculture and irrigation projects. Industry was to receive 32% of the total investment, compared with 38% in the previous Five-Year Plan. Agriculture and hydraulics were to receive 14% of investment, compared with 11% in 1980–84. About 30% of total investment spending in the Plan was allocated to social infrastructure, with projects for the development of housing, education, health and transport receiving particular emphasis. The targeting of these sectors reflected the need to satisfy the requirements of a rapidly expanding population, and to compensate for the imbalances of previous plans. More than one-half of the credits in the new Plan were to be allocated to the completion of existing projects.

The diversification of government revenue away from dependence on sales of crude petroleum to include refined products, natural gas and condensates—each contributing about one-quarter of total revenue by 1983—helped Algeria to adjust to the falls in prices and quotas sponsored by the Organization of the Petroleum Exporting Countries (OPEC). During the 1985–89 Development Plan the Government aimed to increase non-hydrocarbon exports, particularly those of agricultural produce, other minerals and manufactured goods, which in 1984 accounted for only about 2% of total exports. In late 1985 a further slump in petroleum prices gave added urgency to the promotion of non-hydrocarbon exports. By 1988, however, revenue from the export of non-hydrocarbons had reached only AD 2,500m., just over 50% of the target figure. Meanwhile, the erosion of government income in 1986, as a result of the collapse in petroleum prices, had prevented the achievement of the investment targets of the 1985–89 Plan. Algeria entered this planning period with the highest foreign debt of any country in the Arab world (an estimated $18,500m. at the end of 1985), having financed many development projects through borrowings on the international capital markets since the 1970s. In 1986 Algeria borrowed from commercial banks to finance import spending; in 1987 it sought official export credit lines to finance imports; and in 1988–89 it had to raise major new medium- and long-term syndicated loans to finance current spending. Legislation enacted in December 1987 eased restrictions on commercial bank lending to private companies and opened the way for public-sector enterprises to adopt their own annual plans, to determine the prices of their products and to invest their profits freely. By mid-1989 three-quarters of Algeria's state-controlled enterprises, including banks, insurance companies and industrial, commercial and service organizations, had become autonomous *entreprises publiques économiques* (EPEs). Formal ownership of state shareholdings in EPEs was vested in eight state holding companies (*fonds de participation*), established in 1988 to take responsibility for different sectors (agriculture, fisheries and food; mining, hydrocarbons and hydraulics; equipment; construction; chemicals, petrochemicals and pharmaceuticals; electronics, telecommunications and computers; textiles, footwear and furnishings; and service industries). Regulations restricting access to convertible currency were modified in 1988 to attract investment in productive sectors and improve the export marketing capabilities of EPEs.

In June 1989 Algeria made its first ever use of IMF resources, securing a 12-month stand-by credit worth US $187m. (to support the Government's economic programme) and a compensatory financing allocation of $378m. (to assist with trade financing). In 1990 the importing of goods for resale on the Algerian domestic market ceased to be a state monopoly. Foreign manufacturers and traders who established import businesses in Algeria were offered tax incentives to reinvest their profits in the country's production facilities. Under the old import rules there had been frequent supply shortages and widespread black-marketeering. Devaluation reduced the exchange rate of the dinar from around 8 dinars per US dollar at the end of 1990 to around 22 per dollar at the end of 1992. In June 1991 the IMF agreed to make $404m. of stand-by credit available in the period to March 1992, while the World Bank approved a $350m. structural adjustment loan to be disbursed in two instalments (one available immediately). In March 1992 a group of international banks agreed to refinance $1,457m. of Algeria's short-term commercial debt.

Prime Minister Sid-Ahmed Ghozali's 'recovery programme', announced in February 1992 included details of recent economic statistics highlighting the seriousness of Algeria's crisis. Reflecting the radical devaluation of the dinar, GDP had declined, in dollar terms, by 26.9% in 1991. GDP per head declined from US $2,752 in 1987 to $1,607 in 1991. Production in 1991 was only 8% higher than in 1984, even though agricultural GDP and hydrocarbons output had risen substantially. Industrial production, in contrast, had fallen by 5.5% between 1987 and 1991. Consumer prices were increasing by about 28% annually. The debt-service ratio had risen from 35% in 1985 to 72.7% in 1991. Unemployment stood at 21% in 1991. Ghozali's recovery programme gave priority to key sectors of the economy, such as agriculture, public works and construction, which were targeted in a carefully structured import programme. Priority was also to be given to purchases of pharmaceuticals, essential consumer goods, food and spare parts. Ambitious plans were announced to develop small and medium-sized companies and to restructure public companies. While the programme envisaged a strong public sector at the centre of the economy, Ghozali favoured the private management of tourism, agriculture and trade. Financing the programme depended on the availability of international credit and success in attracting international petroleum companies to invest in the hydrocarbons sector.

In July 1992, addressing the nation for the first time since becoming Prime Minister, Belaid Abd es-Salam declared that Algeria had deviated from the principles of the revolution over the previous decade, and expressed strong reservations about Ghozali's economic reforms. He warned that a period of austerity lay ahead, stating that he intended to reduce imports to the bare minimum and to close some factories, if necessary, in order to service the foreign debt of US $25,000m. He rejected debt rescheduling, devaluation and further trade liberalization. In September the Government imposed controls on imports, indicating that preference would be given in foreign-exchange allocations to basic foods, spare parts and construction materials. In November the Government suspended indefinitely imports of luxury goods in order to conserve foreign exchange. Hydrocarbon earnings had fallen from AD 68,412m. ($3,096m.) in the second quarter of 1992 to AD 58,457m. ($2,645m.) in the third quarter, as a result of lower petroleum prices and changes in dollar exchange rates.

In August 1993 the decision of the High Council of State (HCS) to dismiss Abd es-Salam and to appoint Redha Malek to the premiership resulted in a further change of economic policy. Mourad Benachenhou, formerly Algeria's representative at the World Bank and an advocate of debt rescheduling, was appointed Minister of the Economy in the new Government. It became clear that important decisions on economic policy would only be taken when the HCS, the Government and a majority of the conflicting pressure groups could agree on a suitable strategy. The new Government introduced an investment code (whose implementation had been postponed during Abd es-Salam's premiership), intended to stimulate foreign and domestic private investment in areas outside the mining and hydrocarbons sectors (which were covered by separate legislation introduced in late 1991), and providing protection for investors who were to be offered a range of tax and duty reductions for certain categories of investment. A new body, the Agence de Promotion et de Suivi des Investissements (APSI), was established in November to accelerate investment applications.

In December 1993 talks recommenced with the IMF concerning a loan to be linked to an economic stabilization programme, and government statements indicated a return to a more liberal economic policy. Officials stated that there were plans to ease import controls and to dissolve the committee established under the previous Government to allocate hard currency. The economic situation was exacerbated as this time by the depressed price of petroleum on world markets. In January 1994 Algeria ceased repayment of most of its medium- to long-term debt insured by European export credit agencies, including payments to its largest creditors. Talks on a stand-by loan from the IMF continued and, although the Government was still advocating bilateral rescheduling, most creditors were convinced that a rescheduling by the 'Paris Club' of official creditors had become inevitable.

In March 1994 Algeria further reduced its forecast of export revenues for the current year, and in April the Government formally requested the 'Paris Club' to consider rescheduling up to US $13,500m. of Algerian debt. In the same month the IMF approved a stand-by package for Algeria and requested donor agencies to provide substantial new loans over the next year. Over the next 12 months the IMF was to provide a $500m. stand-by loan and a $300m. compensatory and contingency financing facility (CCFF). The IMF agreement committed Algeria to a number of reforms, including a 40% devaluation and a sharp increase in interest rates, which had already been implemented in early April.

In June 1994 the 'Paris Club' creditor governments agreed to refinance a total of about US $5,400m. of sovereign debt incurred by Algeria up to September 1993, with repayments to be rescheduled over a period of 15 years following a four-year grace period. Finalization of the rescheduling arrangements was completed in March 1995. In July 1994 Saudi Arabia (not a 'Paris Club' member) rescheduled $500m. of official debt on similar terms. In October the Banque d'Algérie (the central bank) began talks with the 'London Club' of creditor banks to reschedule $3,200m. of long-term commercial debt contracted by Algerian state-owned banks and by the state energy company, the Société Nationale pour la Recherche, la Production, le Transport, la Transformation et la Commercialisation des Hydrocarbures (SONATRACH—see below). An agreement was reached in principle in May 1995 and finalized in July 1996 whereby repayments were rescheduled to start between September 1998 and September 2000.

In April 1994 Benachenhou became Minister of Industrial Restructuring and Participation, with responsibility for managing the reform of the public sector as required by the new IMF programme. Later in the year the IMF indicated its approval of current government initiatives to contain the budget deficit and acknowledged that the overall performance of the economy in 1994 had to be seen against a background of escalating violence and political uncertainty which continued to discourage investment. Algeria's GDP declined by 1.8% in real terms in 1994 (the ninth consecutive year of negative growth), compared with a planning target of 3% positive growth. In January 1995 the World Bank approved a US $150m. economic rehabilitation support loan to provide urgent assistance for current reform policies, including, in particular, privatization initiatives and the restructuring of public enterprises.

In February 1995 the IMF commenced talks with Algeria to agree a follow-up to the stand-by arrangement which was due to expire at the end of March. In May the IMF approved a US $1,800m. three-year extended Fund facility for Algeria. The Government undertook to continue to pursue a wide-ranging programme of structural reforms, including privatization, rationalization of the public sector, trade liberalization, monetary and fiscal reforms to reduce inflation and encourage investment and private enterprise, and the elimination by the end of 1996 of subsidies on food and other commodities.

In advance of the IMF agreement, the Government submitted a draft privatization law to public and private organizations for consultation purposes, and in early 1995 invited bids for five state-owned hotels as a pilot project for the privatization programme. Private capital participation had been permitted in public-sector companies since 1994, but no ownership transfer had actually taken place. A comprehensive privatization law was enacted in August 1995. Legislation was introduced later in the year to allow local councils to employ private contractors to manage water resources and related services.

Under a balance-of-payments support contract signed in May 1995, the European Union (EU) agreed to lend Algeria US $268m. on conditions similar to those of the IMF. In July the 'Paris Club' agreed to a refinancing of debts worth over $7,000m. Payments due between June 1995 and May 1997 were rescheduled over 15 years from 1999. Unlike the June 1994 'Paris Club' agreement, which dealt only with repayments of debt principal, the July 1995 agreement included some rescheduling of interest payments. Finalization of the rescheduling arrangements under this agreement was completed in July 1996. In April 1996 the World Bank approved a further loan of $300m. to support the Government's structural adjustment programme, together with a loan of $50m. in support of job-

creation and other social welfare measures to offset some of the negative social effects of the adjustment programme. Higher agricultural output and stronger international petroleum prices contributed to a 3.8% increase in real GDP in 1995 (the first year of real growth since 1985).

To expedite the restructuring of public-sector enterprises, the system of ownership through *fonds de participation*, dating from 1988 (see above) was replaced in October 1996 by a new ownership structure. The former holding companies, which had been conceived as permanent fiduciary institutions, were replaced by 11 holding companies authorized not merely to hold shares in state enterprises but also to offer shares for sale and to take action to close unprofitable enterprises. Once they had fulfilled their roles as vehicles for the transfer of state assets to the private sector and into independent public companies, the holding companies would disappear.

The World Bank stated in February 1997 that a total of 138 public-sector 'industrial units' had been disposed of to date, although 87 of these were liquidated rather than sold as going concerns and 13 others were construction companies rather than industrial enterprises. The World Bank noted that a further 134 public-sector companies had been offered for sale, and that the Government's privatization programme was currently running somewhat ahead of the agreed schedule. The 134 companies in the most recent round of privatization offers included 60 industrial units (many of them individual plants owned by larger public enterprises) as well as commercial, agricultural and tourism companies. Some were offered for outright or partial sale, while others were tendered to the private sector on a management contract basis. The next round of privatizations was to focus on 1,300 small and medium-sized companies.

In December 1996 the Government published a series of amendments to the August 1995 privatization law, designed to stimulate private-sector interest in the purchase of fully operational companies. Eligibility for privatization (hitherto limited to EPEs) was to be extended to enterprises controlled by Algerian local government bodies; purchasers were no longer to be required to take on a legal duty to maintain pre-privatization staffing levels (although financial incentives would be available to buyers who gave voluntary undertakings to this effect); mechanisms were to be introduced to facilitate sales of shares to retail investors as well as to corporate buyers, and to open up the possibility of direct share sales to companies' staff members; and the administration of the privatization process (including the pricing of share offers) was to become more flexible.

There was a fall in the end-year inflation rate to 15% in 1996, compared with 22% in 1995 and 39% in 1994, reflecting the economy's adjustment to more stable conditions after the large 1994 currency devaluation and the subsequent withdrawal of price subsidies. The dinar's end-year exchange rate against the US dollar (AD 24.10 in 1993, AD 42.90 in 1994 and AD 52.20 in 1995) underwent a relatively small decline to AD 56.20 in 1996. The freeing of prices had by early 1997 produced what the World Bank described as 'one of the most liberal trade regimes in the region'. Increases in both the volume and unit value of hydrocarbon exports, coupled with a record cereals harvest, gave Algeria a significant trade surplus and a positive current-account balance in 1996, underpinning the achievement of 4% real GDP growth in that year. Most hydrocarbon exploration and production operations were relatively remote from centres of terrorist activity, which was not regarded as a major risk factor by petroleum companies operating in Algeria. Following the rescheduling agreements with foreign creditors, debt-servicing as a proportion of export earnings (which had reached 77.7% in 1993, 48.3% in 1994 and 34.8% in 1995) fell to 27.9% in 1996, when the country's total external indebtedness amounted to US $33,421m. (of which $31,062m. was long-term public debt). Foreign-exchange reserves doubled during 1996 and were sufficient to cover six months' imports in the first quarter of 1997. A greatly reduced budget deficit was achieved in 1996, and the 1997 budget estimates (see Finance, below) were said by the Government to include an 'underlying surplus'.

Against these and other positive macroeconomic achievements had to be set the fact that the output of non-hydrocarbon industries fell by 8% in 1996, contributing to a rise in Algeria's official unemployment rate to 28.3% of the work-force. More than 56% of the unemployed were aged under 24 years, and about 80% were aged under 30 years. The removal of price subsidies had caused hardship for the poorest sections of society, who were also those worst affected by acute housing shortages in Algiers and other urban centres. Given the continuing volatility of the internal security situation, the Government was fully aware in 1997 that many entrenched structural problems remained to be solved before Algeria could claim to have made a genuinely successful transition to a free-market economy. GDP grew by an estimated 1.3% in 1997, well below the official target of 5%, as a result of a decline in both agricultural and industrial production. Non-hydrocarbons exports fell by 50% in that year.

Following an agreement with the powerful Union Générale des Travailleurs Algériens (UGTA) in March 1998, it was reported that the Government had pledged to stop the closure of public-sector companies and promised to re-examine the position of some enterprises that had been closed. The agreement was reached after a two-day strike, organized by the UGTA to protest against the high level of redundancies resulting from the closure of many loss-making public-sector companies, and delays in the payment of salaries. Industrial relations nevertheless remained strained, and there was a succession of strikes later in the year. In early 1999 officials reported that the reform of public-sector companies was nearly complete. Firms had either been closed, restructured or sold to employees. In May 1998 the Minister of Finance, Abdelkrim Harchaoui, stated that Algeria would not seek to extend the IMF credit facility when it expired later that month because the economy could be supported by private investment. He insisted, however, that the Government would continue to maintain fiscal discipline even though its economic policies would no longer be under the formal scrutiny of the IMF. There were reports that the IMF had wanted Algeria to make a new agreement. Some financial analysts argued that even though there had been an improvement in Algeria's macroeconomic situation, the Government would experience problems in raising finance cheaply from international capital markets. In May Prime Minister Ahmed Ouyahia signed a decree listing the first 89 companies to be privatized from June, affecting enterprises in the tourism, construction, services, agribusiness and transport sectors. The Government hoped to raise some US $1,000m. from the sales. Despite the announcement of further privatization plans, later in the year the head of the National Privatization Council admitted that it was proving difficult to interest local or foreign investors in the programme. Early in 1999 the partial privatization of the state-owned pharmaceuticals company, SAIDAL, and the cereals distributor, Eriad-Sétif, raised more than AD 4,000m. for the Government.

Foreign investment outside the energy sector remained limited. A World Bank study in mid-1998 identified the inefficiency of the local banking system, property disputes, the threat of currency devaluation and the tax burden as the major obstacles deterring investment in the private sector. An independent report published in that year identified the informal economy as Algeria's most dynamic sector, accounting for over one-third of non-agricultural employment and one-fifth of household income.

After his appointment as premier in December 1998, Smail Hamdani announced a one-year economic programme that largely continued the work of the outgoing administration. He pledged a radical reform of the banking system, a more efficient privatization policy and increased local and foreign private investment. On the sensitive issue of labour relations, Hamdani stated that the Government would seek solutions through dialogue but warned that escalating pay rises for public-sector workers could increase the budget deficit and lead to inflationary pressures. Hamdani stated that the projected 1999 growth rate of 6.2% was 'realistic'. Projected real GDP growth in 1999 was later revised downwards to around 5% to take account of weak oil prices in the early part of the year. The official figure for growth in 1998 was 5.1%, but independent sources claimed that it was probably half that figure and stated that the Government's forecast for 1999 was optimistic.

Following a 'fact-finding' mission to Algeria in March 1999, the Arab Monetary Fund agreed to provide a loan of US $131m. to help finance economic reforms in 1999–2000 and provide balance-of-payments support. In May the IMF approved a credit of $300m. under the CCFF to help Algeria offset the sharp decline in its hard currency earnings as a result of low oil prices in 1998. The loan was to be repaid over three to five years.

Although Abdelaziz Bouteflika, who assumed the presidency in April 1999, was seen as a strong supporter of state institutions, he promised an acceleration in the privatization programme—insisting that only competitive firms in the public sector would not be sold off. The new President emphasized the importance of reducing unemployment, of fighting poverty and providing adequate housing, and stated that peace and national reconciliation would only be achieved if these issues were successfully addressed. Bouteflika made attracting foreign investment one of his priorities, targeting Arab countries—especially the Gulf states where he had many business connections. The new Government appointed in late December 1999—headed by Ahmed Benbitour, a former Minister of Finance and more recently president of a parliamentary economic and financial commission—was expected to speed up economic liberalization. Close aides of Bouteflika were appointed to the ministries of finance, and energy and mining and to head the state hydrocarbons company, SONATRACH.

In January 2001 the Minister of Participation and Co-ordination of Reforms announced that 184 public enterprises, most of them in the services, construction, public works and food processing sectors, would be offered for sale over the following three years, of which 121 would be completely privatized. Legislation ending the state's monopoly of the posts and telecommunications sector was approved in mid-2000, and new legislation was enacted in 2002 to open the mining and power sectors to private investment. Furthermore, a draft hydrocarbons bill proposed the total liberalization of upstream and downstream sectors to national and international investors, although the privatization of SONATRACH was ruled out at least in the medium term. Despite a great deal of rhetoric from successive governments on the urgency of implementing economic reforms, key political figures have not been in agreement on the precise content of the reforms. One of the reasons for the resignation of Prime Minister Benbitour in August 2000, after only eight months in office, was his differences with President Bouteflika over economic policy: the two had drafted sharply contrasting economic programmes. Furthermore, partisans of economic reform continued to encounter strong resistance from the bureaucracy, the labour movement and from powerful commercial cartels linked to senior figures in the military. In January 2001 Benbitour's successor as Prime Minister, Ali Benflis, announced the establishment of a ministerial commission to reform the banking sector.

Early in 2001 the Banque d'Algérie reported real GDP growth of 3.2% in 1999 and of 3.8% in 2000. Growth for the latter year had been officially projected at 5.6%; however, the positive impact of sustained high international prices for oil was offset by the decline in agriculture owing to drought and by low investment in the industrial sector. The Banque d'Algérie estimated that growth of 6%–7% would be required in order significantly to reduce unemployment. Official statistics indicated that some 2.4m. Algerians were unemployed at mid-2000—representing almost 30% of the active population—with an estimated two-thirds of the unemployed under the age of 30. Other sources have estimated that 40% of the country's workforce is either unemployed or underemployed. Furthermore, reports in the local press in early 2001 claimed that 12m. Algerians, some 40% of the total population, were living below the poverty line. The average rate of inflation fell from 5% in 1998 to 2.6% in 1999 and to just over 1% in 2000, a trend reflecting weak domestic demand.

In April 2001 the Government unveiled an economic recovery plan, committing US $700m. in expenditure to stimulate growth for the period 2001–04. The IMF endorsed the programme but cautioned that fiscal policy should be adjusted to future developments in the oil market. It commended the Government for its fiscal discipline, careful monetary policy and its management of the exchange rate float. However, it emphasized the need for privatization and banking reform to sustain growth while lowering tariffs aimed at protecting domestic industry and reducing dependence on hydrocarbons. The 2001 privatization programme included the sale of assets in the steel sector and the award of a Global Standard for Mobiles (GSM) licence (see Telecommunications). The power generation sector has been deregulated under Bouteflika, and the hydrocarbons law was expected to be ratified during 2002. The Government has also committed sizeable funds to the housing and water sectors. The 2002 privatization schedule proposed the sale of some 100 state concerns. Following the signing of an association agreement with the EU, the Government introduced reductions in tariffs and a new incentive structure to attract foreign investors.

Real GDP growth was expected to reach 4.4% in 2002, following estimated growth of 3.8% in 2001. During 2001 the rate of unemployment stood at 30%, with an estimated 70% of the unemployed under the age of 25. The average rate of inflation rose to 4%.

AGRICULTURE

The agricultural sector employed 24.3% of Algeria's labour force in mid-2000, and accounted for 8.4% of GDP in that year. In 1998 the value of domestic agricultural production reached US $8,000m., according to official figures. More than 90% of the land consists of arid plateaux, mountains or desert, supporting herds of sheep, goats or camels. Only the northern coastal strip, 100 km–200 km wide, is suitable for arable farming. There are about 7.6m. ha of cultivable land, representing less than 1 ha per rural inhabitant. Forests cover about 4.4m. ha. Most of the Sahara is devoted to semi-desert pasturage. A total of 3.6m. ha were under cultivation in 1998/99, of which only 400,000 ha were irrigated. The Government planned to increase the irrigated area to 1m. ha. Most of the cultivated area is devoted to cereals, principally wheat and barley; other crops include citrus fruits, vegetables, grapes, olives and dates.

Scarcity of food is an acute problem in Algeria. In 1969 the country was 73% self-sufficient in food. However, by 1986 it was importing 75% of its food requirements, and by 1990 Algeria produced only 25% of its domestic cereal requirements. In 1991 food and live animals comprised about 24% of total imports. The recovery programme announced by the Ghozali administration in February 1992 drew attention to a dangerous level of dependence on strategic products such as cereals, animal feed and milk and stated that efforts to raise agricultural production were central to economic policy. Spending on imported foodstuffs amounted to US $2,502m. (28.8% of total imports) in 1997, $2,200m. in 1998, $2,438m. (27.2% of imports) in 1999 and $2,356m. (25.2% of imports) in 2000.

AGRICULTURAL REFORM

By October 1963 state-owned farm land accounted for 2.7m. ha, roughly one-half of the cultivable land in Algeria. In May 1966 all remaining unoccupied property that had been evacuated by settlers was finally expropriated by the state; the land was turned into state farms run by workers' committees.

In 1971 President Boumedienne announced an agrarian reform programme which provided for the break-up of large, state-owned farms and their redistribution to families of landless peasants, or *fellahin*, who would be organized in co-operatives. The 1972 census showed that one-quarter of cultivable land was in the hands of 16,500 large landowners who represented only 3% of the total number of farmers. In 1973 the reform programme entered its second phase, that of redistributing over 650,000 ha of private land to 60,000 *fellahin*. Those receiving land were granted permanent use of it, on condition that they belonged to one of the new co-operatives. Through these they were to be given state loans and assistance in the form of seed, fertilizers and equipment. By early 1979 some 22,000 absentee landowners had been obliged either to cultivate their land or to cede it to peasant farmers, and more than 6,000 agricultural co-operatives of various kinds had been established.

Following Boumedienne's death, there was a gradual change of priorities and the private sector was given freedom to produce and market agricultural goods. The Chadli administration encouraged private, small-scale farmers by supplying equipment, loans and assistance, while investment in agricultural infrastructure, particularly the construction of dams, was increased in an attempt to reduce the need for food imports. Moreover, to discourage rural drift (particularly among young people), farmers' earnings were more closely related to those of their industrial counterparts.

A new Banque de l'Agriculture et du Développement Rural (BADR) was established in 1982, expressly to serve the rural sector. The BADR's first project was a lending programme which aimed to make Algeria self-sufficient in eggs and poultry. In the same year the Government relaxed price controls, allowing farmers to sell directly to markets or to private vendors and across *wilaya* boundaries. After 1983 farmers who brought desert land under cultivation automatically received a title to own the land. In 1987 the Government introduced major reforms whereby the *fellahin* were allowed to form autonomous collectives, comprising at least three members, and to lease land units formed from the subdivision of the existing 3,347 co-operatives. The *fellahin* were to be allowed to transfer or trade their leases after five years, to control their own operations, to work directly with banks and to make a profit. The state, as owner of the land, was to restrict its role to the provision of aid and to mediation in disputes over land division. By October the reforms were being implemented in 41 *wilayat*, and by the end of the following year 3,000 state farms were controlled by private entrepreneurs. Meanwhile, subsidies on staple foods were drastically reduced. In January 1989 Banque Nationale de Paris (BNP) agreed to channel an agro-industrial loan of almost US $750m. for 1989 through the BADR. In 1990 the Government announced plans to encourage agricultural producers to form a new type of co-operative to market goods directly, thereby promoting price competition between the co-operatives. A public fund to protect farmers against natural disasters became operational in May. The Government also released $107m. to support farmers affected by drought. State subsidies for agriculture totalled $1,000m. in 1990. In late 1994 the Government announced the creation of a lending agency, Crédit Mutuel Agricole, to provide private-sector farmers with financial assistance and measures to reschedule their outstanding debts. Land-reform legislation was presented to the National People's Assembly in early 1998 to allow the privatization of state-owned farms. Land reform was one of the measures insisted upon by the World Bank under its structural adjustment loan agreement with the Algerian Government. By clarifying land rights, the Government hoped to encourage greater investment in agriculture and create new jobs. Little progress was made, however, largely owing to the influence of powerful political factions opposed to privatization.

CROPS

Wines were one of Algeria's principal agricultural exports during and immediately preceding the French colonial era. However, Algeria's annual output of wine declined from 8m. hl in the early 1970s to around 3m. hl by the end of the decade. The Government planned to maintain production at the latter level for the rest of the century, while developing the production of better-quality wines which are more easily marketable in the EU. By the early 1980s annual production had fallen to less than 2m. hl, and this trend continued with production during 1992 totalling only 410,000 hl and a mere 248,000 hl in 1996. Whereas some 370,000 ha were devoted to vines in 1962, by 1990 a mere 38,531 ha were harvested.

Production of cereals, grown principally in the Constantine, Annaba, Sétif and Tiaret areas, fluctuates considerably, largely due to drought, and grains have to be imported—particularly from Canada, France and the USA. Wheat and barley are the most important cereals. Yields are very low, averaging some 810 kg per hectare (kg/ha) in the late 1990s, compared with average US yields of more than 5,500 kg/ha. In 1995 the harvest was badly affected by drought, producing only 2.1m. tons of cereals; however, in 1996 the cereals harvest totalled 4.6m. tons, including 2.8m. tons of wheat and 1.8m. tons of barley and oats. After a serious drought in 1997 cereal production fell to only 869,300 tons. Officials reported that 2.3m. ha of farmland (of a total of 3.5m. ha) had been designated as drought-affected. Although cereal production rose to just over 3m. tons in 1998, this figure was still well below the level achieved in 1996. As a result of drought conditions affecting the west of the country the 1999 cereals harvest fell to 2.2m. tons. Severe drought in the main cereal producing areas led to a further sharp fall in cereal production in 2000, to 922,000 tons (including 480,000 tons of durum wheat, 272,000 tons of soft wheat and 162,000 tons of barley), and to a 12% increase in cereal imports to 7.3m.

tons. It was announced that in 2001–02 some 750,000 ha of marginal lands currently devoted to cereals to the south of the main coastal plains were to be converted to tree crops in order to prevent desertification. This was the first phase of an ambitious four-year plan to convert some two-thirds of lands devoted to cereals in these areas to other crops. In order to compensate for lost output, efforts would be made to intensify cereals production in those areas receiving higher rainfall.

Olives are grown mainly in the western coastal belt and in the Kabyle. Output fluctuates because of the two-year flowering cycle of the olive. According to data published by FAO, production of olives totalled 217,000 metric tons in 2000, but increased to an estimated 300,000 tons in 2001. The citrus crop, grown in the coastal districts, increased from 416,000 tons in 1998 to 451,000 tons in 1999, but fell slightly, to 431,000 tons, in 2000 and 440,780 tons in 2001. Production of potatoes fluctuated during the late 1990s, but reached 1.2m. tons in 2001. About 400,000 tons of dried onions are produced annually. Algeria is among the world's largest producers of dates, although production fell from 428,000 tons in 1999 to an estimated 370,000 tons in 2001. While much of the crop is consumed locally, dates form one of the country's most important non-hydrocarbon exports. About 7,000 tons of tobacco leaves are produced each year.

Overall agricultural output increased by 14.1% in volume in 1995 and by 18.0% in 1996. Although output declined by 20.0% in 1997, it rose by 13.9% in 1998; a smaller increase, of 3.4%, in 1999 was followed by a decline of 4.5% in 2000, but output increased by an estimated 8.9% in 2001.

LIVESTOCK, FORESTRY AND FISHING

Sheep, goats and cattle are raised, but great improvements are needed in stock-raising methods, grassland, control of disease and water supply if the increasing demand for meat is to be satisfied. The cost of raising milk production is prohibitive, and a high level of imports is likely to continue. By 1990 60% of milk requirements were imported. However, there has been a notable success in increasing production of white meat, in which the country was self-sufficient by 1984. About 1m. eggs, or one-half of total consumption, are imported annually. FAO figures for 2001 estimated that there were 3.5m. goats, 1.4m. cattle and 17.6m. sheep. Private farmers produce 90% of local meat.

The area covered by forests declined rapidly during 1970–90 in spite of the Government's plans to reafforest 364,000 ha in the 1985–89 Plan period. In 1975 work began to grow a 'green wall' of pines and cypresses 20 km wide, planted along 1,500 km on the northern edge of the Sahara from the Moroccan to the Tunisian frontier in order to arrest steady northward desertification. The project, which encountered numerous problems, also involved the construction of roads, reservoirs and plantations of fruit trees and vegetables. Large areas of forest covering the mountainous regions along the Mediterranean coast have been destroyed in recent years, some as a result of operations carried out by the security forces against Islamist militants active in these regions.

During the 1990s the Government sought to exploit its fishing potential and made attempts to increase the annual catch. The total catch in 1998 was 92,600 metric tons (compared with a potential annual estimated catch of 170,000 tons). The catch increased to 105,900 tons in 1999. Most local fishing activity is carried out in small, family-owned boats and commercial fishing remains marginal. Under legislation enacted in 1994 foreign fishing vessels may apply to fish in Algeria's territorial waters.

METALLIC MINERALS

Algeria has rich deposits of iron ore, phosphates, lead, zinc and antimony. Legislation adopted in December 1991 allowed local private sector and foreign investment in the mining sector, which had been nationalized in 1966. The aim was to increase exploration and reverse declining production. Under the terms of the law, foreign companies could form joint ventures and benefit from tax concessions. The Office de Recherche Géologique et Minière was created to co-ordinate the various enterprises, state and private, involved in this sector. In September 1993 the Government authorized the allocation of mineral research permits to local companies, and included for the first time enterprises from outside the mining sector.

In 1999 the Government amended the mining law in an attempt to attract further private investment into the sector, and a number of partnership agreements with foreign companies for exploration and development of minerals were signed. In March 2000 the Minister of Energy and Mines announced that, as a first step in the privatization programme, 48 small mines (producing gold, semi-precious stones and marble) would be put out to tender for local investors. At the end of the first phase of the programme 24 licences—mainly for marble, sand and gold projects—had been awarded to local private investors. In May 2001 bids were received from 237 private investors for exploitation permits for 178 small and medium-sized mines. In 2001 a new mining law provided for the creation of two organizations— the Agence Nationale du Patrimoine Minier and the Agence Nationale du Contrôle des Mines—to manage the mining sector, leaving the state to act as a regulator rather than an operator. The legislation puts all investors—local and foreign, public and private—on an equal footing, and no longer insists on the state's taking a 51% stake in all discoveries.

Iron ore is mined at Beni-Saf, Zaccar, Timezrit and near the eastern frontier at Ouenza and Bou Khadra. The average grade of ore is 50%–60%. Production has fluctuated greatly since independence, reaching 2.1m. metric tons (metal content) in 1974, falling to 897,000 tons in 1981, and totalling an estimated 1.6m. tons in 2000. The deposits at Ouenza represent 75% of total production. Important deposits were found in 1975 at Djebel Bouari in Batna *wilaya*. Italy is the biggest customer, followed by the United Kingdom. Production of bituminous coal, mined at Colomb Béhar-Kenadza and Ksiksou, declined steadily from 153,000 tons in 1958 to about 5,000 tons in 1978. Production was estimated at 23,000 tons in 2000.

The main deposits of lead and zinc ores are at el-Abed, on the Algerian–Moroccan frontier, and at the Kherzet Youcef mine, in the Sétif region. Total zinc output (metal content of concentrates) declined from 12,200 metric tons in 1988 to 3,690 tons in 1997, although production recovered to 10,452 tons in 2000. Production of lead in 2000 was estimated at 1m. tons.

Exploitation of large phosphate deposits at Djebel-Onk, 340 km from Annaba, began in 1960. Total phosphate rock output reached 1.1m. metric tons in 1999, declining to 877,000 tons in 2000. About one-half of phosphate production is exported, mainly to France and Spain.

Algeria's other mineral resources include tungsten, manganese, mercury, copper and salt. Output of mercury was estimated at 216 metric tons in 2000. Production of marble at Bendjerah in Guelma amounted to 730,000 tons in that year. According to studies carried out by the state owned Enterprise d'Exploitation des Mines d'Or (ENOR), gold deposits at Tirek and Amessmessa in the Haggar region are capable of producing yields of 25.1 grams per ton. ENOR was in 1996 joined by SONATRACH, Société Algérienne d'Assurance and the Banque d'Algérie in a joint venture to develop the Tirek gold deposits. In 1998 the Minister of Energy and Mines stated that some US $40m. had been invested in the Amessmessa gold mine, and that co-operation in the mining sector with South Africa, which was already involved in the exploitation of gold and diamond mines in southern Algeria, was to be strengthened.

PETROLEUM PRODUCTION AND REFINING

Production of crude petroleum in the Algerian Sahara began, on a commercial scale, in 1958. The principal producing areas were at Hassi Messaoud, in central Algeria, and around Edjeleh-Zarzaitine in the Polignac Basin, near the Libyan frontier. Algeria's production of crude petroleum increased from 1.2m. metric tons in 1959 to 26m. tons per year in 1964 and 1965, with output limited by the capacity of the two pipelines to the coast, one from the eastern fields through Tunisia to La Skhirra, and the other from Hassi Messaoud to Béjaia on the Algerian coast. The Government established a state-controlled company, SONATRACH, to be responsible for the construction of a third pipeline from Hassi Messaoud to Arzew on the coast. This pipeline came into operation in early 1966. In that year Algeria's production of crude petroleum was increased by substantial quantities from oilfields at Gassi Touil, Rhourde el-Baguel and Rhourde Nouss. Subsequent discoveries of petroleum were made at Nezla, Hoaud Berkaoui, Ouargla, Mesdar, el-Borma, Hassi Keskessa, Guellala, Tin Fouyé and el-Maharis, and by early

1989 there were some 50 oilfields in operation. Export pipelines link the oilfields to Algiers, to supply the refinery at el-Harrach, and to Skikda. Increased production of condensates and liquefied petroleum gas (LPG) prompted the construction of special pipelines to Arzew. In 2000 contracts were awarded for the construction of a major new 822-km pipeline (OZ2) linking Haoud el-Hamra in the Berkine basin, and Arzew for the modernization of the existing 801-km pipeline. The two pipelines will have a total capacity of 680,000 barrels per day (b/d), and will handle increased production expected from new fields in the Berkine and Illizi basins (see below). COSIDER, a local engineering and construction firm, and Brown and Root Condor of the USA are responsible for the first section of the new pipeline linking Haoud el-Hamra to the PC5 centre based at Laghouart, and Russia's Stroytransgaz for the second, linking the PC5 centre and Arzew. In 2001 a consortium of Spie Capag of France and Saipem of Italy was selected to build six pumping stations to increase the capacity of the pipeline.

Output of crude petroleum reached around 1.2m. b/d in 1979. Thereafter output of crude petroleum was restricted in order to prolong the life of the oilfields and, after 1983, to conform to the production quotas set by OPEC. Production of other hydrocarbons, particularly gas, liquefied natural gas (LNG), natural gas liquids (NGLs—a category including condensates) and refined products, assumed greater importance as a source of government revenues. By 1986 production of crude petroleum had decreased to an average of 670,000 b/d, mainly from the Hassi Messaoud oilfield, representing 56% of Algeria's total oil production in that year. By the mid-1990s, as new oilfields came into production, output began to rise. Algeria produces a light crude with a low sulphur content which is attractive to foreign refiners. Algeria's proven and recoverable petroleum reserves at the end of 2001 totalled 9,200m. barrels, equivalent to 17.6 years' output at 2001 levels. Although Algeria agreed to decrease production by 80,000 b/d from July 1998 (as part of an overall OPEC reduction totalling 2.6m. b/d to offset sharply falling oil prices), its actual cut-back was much smaller and production during 1998, according to industry figures, averaged as much as 1.46m. b/d, compared with its revised quota of 788,000 b/d. From 1 April Algeria's OPEC quota was reduced to 731,000 b/d as part of a new round of cuts agreed by OPEC ministers in March. Algeria's Minister of Energy and Mines instructed SONATRACH to negotiate with its foreign partners over sharing the production cuts. In practice, Algeria's crude oil production averaged 1.52m. b/d during 1999. At its meeting in Vienna, Austria, in March 2000, when OPEC agreed to restore output to pre-March 1999 levels, Algeria's production quota was raised to 788,000 b/d from April 2000. The quota was further increased to 811,000 b/d in July, to 836,000 b/d in October and to 852,000 b/d in November. By December output had risen to 850,000 b/d. For 2000 as a whole crude oil production averaged 1.58m. b/d. Following production cuts agreed at OPEC's meeting in January 2001 (at which Algeria's Minister of Energy and Mines, Chakib Khelil, assumed the chairmanship of the Organization's Conference), Algeria's quota was reduced to 805,000 b/d. Further cuts in April and September that year reduced Algeria's quota further, to 741,000 b/d. From January 2002 the quota was reduced again, to 693,000 b/d, significantly below production capacity: oil industry figures put average production for 2001 at 1.56m. b/d. Most of Algeria's oil exports go to Western Europe and the USA.

There are refineries at Algiers, Hassi Messaoud, Skikda, Arzew and In Amenas. SONATRACH issued a tender for the construction and operation of a new refinery at Adrar in the Sbaa basin near the In Salah gasfield in 2001. Also in that year the Ministry of Energy and Mines and the state petroleum refining company, Naftec, issued an international tender to upgrade the refinery at In Amenas.

Algeria's domestic fuel prices were very low by international standards until March 1994, when the Government doubled the retail price of diesel fuel and petrol. In April 1995 the price of petrol for car-users was increased by 8%–11% as part of the Government's efforts to raise more revenue and control energy consumption.

NATURAL GAS PRODUCTION AND EXPORTS

At 31 December 2001 Algeria's published proved reserves of natural gas—mostly unassociated with oilfields—totalled 4,520,000m. cu m, equivalent to 57.8 years' output at current rates. Most of the gas was in the Hassi R'Mel region, 400 km south of Algiers. The field was discovered in 1956, and is still considered to be one of the largest in the world. Unassociated gas is also found near In Amenas, Alrar, Gassi Touil, Rhourde Nouss, Tin Fouyé and In Salah. The Government invested heavily in the development of these gasfields. Pipelines were laid to the coast, to supply local gas distribution systems, and LNG has been exported since 1965. The export of dry natural gas to Italy began in 1983 following the inauguration of the Transmediterranean (Transmed, or Enrico Mattei) pipeline, running from Algeria to Sicily via Tunisia and the Mediterranean. By 1997 gas products comprised 40% of Algeria's total export receipts. Total natural gas production reached 89,300m. cu m in 2000.

Before 1962 Algeria exported relatively small amounts of LNG from the Camel liquefaction plant at Arzew. The second phase of Algeria's gas development began in the early 1970s with the negotiation of major new export contracts with companies including the USA's Distrigas, Trunkline and El Paso, Belgium's Distrigaz, Enagas of Spain, and Italy's SNAM (a subsidiary of the Italian state energy group, Ente Nazionale Idrocarburi—ENI). Exports of LNG to the United Kingdom continued, and new contracts were signed with Gaz de France. The price of the gas to be delivered under the contracts was calculated according to the value of equivalent amounts of refined petroleum products (on a calorific basis). In 1978 there was a shift to a more aggressive pricing policy. The Algerian Government argued that the old pricing terms did not fully compensate Algeria for the massive investments in LNG facilities and transportation that it had made. The central feature of the change in Algerian gas policy was the demand that natural gas prices be linked to the then rapidly rising price of crude petroleum. The change in policy was strongly opposed by Algeria's customers, but the Government was able to persuade several clients to accept the terms, using various economic and political sanctions.

SONATRACH nevertheless lost several customers—El Paso, British Methane (after 1981) and Trunkline, which suspended purchases at the end of 1983. Other countries, such as the Federal Republic of Germany and Austria, considered buying Algerian gas but then obtained cheaper supplies from the USSR and Norway. SONATRACH therefore became more flexible on the link between crude oil and gas prices in order to win new customers, while insisting on the existing index with current buyers. In April 1987 the US Panhandle Eastern Corpn, the parent company of Trunkline, agreed to resume shipments of Algerian LNG in late 1988. The price of deliveries was to be based on a flexible formula which would preserve SONATRACH's interests while taking account of developments in the international market. In late 1987 Distrigas resumed shipments at the spot market price, after reaching a short-term agreement with SONATRACH in November. Distrigas had gone into liquidation under the US federal bankruptcy code in 1985, when its previous long-term contract with SONATRACH had proved to be too expensive. In February 1988 SONATRACH and Distrigas signed a 15-year contract for the supply of LNG, whereby gas would be sold at 'market-responsive' prices. Distrigas was to pay for shipping and regasification, after which the gas would be sold at market prices and the profits divided on the basis of a ratio of 63:37 in SONATRACH's favour. In early 1988 SONATRACH reached similar long-term agreements with DEP of Greece and Botaş of Turkey. Meanwhile, the signing of an agreement with Ruhrgas of the Federal Republic of Germany over purchases of LNG, discussed in late 1987, was delayed until early 1989. In 1991 a gas export agreement with ENI of Italy envisaged an increase of nearly 60% in the volume of SNAM's gas purchases from Algeria over the next 25 years.

In October 1992 Ente Nazionale per l'Energia Elettrica (ENEL) of Italy signed a 20-year supply contract with SONATRACH, starting in the last quarter of 1994, to lift 4,000m. cu m of gas annually through the enlarged Transmed pipeline and 1,000m. cu m–2,000m. cu m of LNG. The agreement helped to diversify gas exports and to strengthen Algeria's position in the Italian market. Gas sales to France increased from 1996, and Algeria was Gaz de France's second largest supplier in 1998, accounting for 27% of its supplies. In 2000 SONATRACH and Gaz de France agreed to extend two LNG contracts, due to expire in 2002, to 2013. The two companies also signed a co-operation accord enabling them to undertake joint projects in marketing gas. In June 1992 SONATRACH signed a contract with Enagas of Spain to supply 6,000m. cu m of natural gas per year over 25 years via a new Maghreb–Europe pipeline (see below). In April 1994 the Portuguese consortium Transgas signed a 25-year contract with SONATRACH to take 2,500m. cu m of natural gas annually via the same pipeline. Under the terms of a co-operation agreement signed with SONATRACH in October 1994, ENI made a commitment to purchase 26,000m. cu m of natural gas per year by 1997, almost double the current amount. In late 1995 SONATRACH announced that it had signed an agreement to supply a further 1,000m. cu m of LNG to Botaş of Turkey in addition to the 2,000m. cu m already supplied. In May 1996 it was reported that Algeria's gas exports to the EU increased by 24% in 1995 to 1.6m. metric tons of oil equivalent, representing one-quarter of all EU gas imports. Algeria supplied one-half of Italy's natural gas imports in 1995.

In 1990 contracts were signed for the renovation of gas lique-faction facilities at Skikda and Arzew, which had been con-structed in the 1970s. The renovation programme, which was completed in 1999, was expected to prolong the units' life by some 20 years. LPG exports, which totalled 5.8m. metric tons in 1997, were projected to increase to 6.8m. tons in 1999. In February 2000 the fifth train on the Rhourde Nouss gas plant south of Hassi Messaoud was inaugurated, enabling the plant to produce 3,860 tons of LPG, 612 tons of condensed gas and 46m. cu m of LNG per day. (The original plant was built in the 1980s.)

The annual capacity of the Transmed gas pipeline between Algeria and Italy was due to increase from 16,000m. cu m to 24,000m. cu m during 1997, on completion of expansion work. In December 2001 SONATRACH signed an agreement with ENEL and Germany's Wintershall to undertake a feasibility study for a second natural gas pipeline from Algeria via Sicily to the Italian mainland.

In November 1996 a new Maghreb–Europe (or Pedro Duran Farrell) gas pipeline, running 1,365 km from Algeria to Spain via Morocco and the Mediterranean, carried its first supplies of Algerian dry gas to Spain. Portugal was linked to the pipeline in early 1997. Initially operating at a capacity of 7,000 cu m per year, plans were announced in 2000 to increase the annual capacity of the Maghreb–Europe line to 11,000m. cu m. In addition, the construction of new compression stations will raise the capacity of the Transmed pipeline by a further 5,000 cu m per year. Plans for another gas pipeline linking Algeria to Spain were announced in August 2000. The 450 km pipeline, a joint venture between SONATRACH and Cepsa of Spain, is expected to run from Beni Saf in Algeria to Almería and have a capacity of 20,000m. cu m per year. It is scheduled to be completed by 2006. In September 2001 Algeria signed a memorandum with Nigeria to investigate the feasibility of a 4,000-km pipeline linking the two countries, estimated to cost between US $5,000m. and $7,000m.

In order to bring Algeria's expanded export pipeline capacity into full use, there was a requirement to increase supplies from the Hassi R'Mel gasfield by building an additional 970-km trunkline within Algeria. In late 1997 the European Investment Bank (EIB) announced a US $300m. loan for SONATRACH towards the $1,000m. project, known as the GR2 pipeline. The Government envisaged that exports of natural gas, which reached 54,000m. cu m in 1998 and 60,340m. cu m in 1999, will increase to 75,000m. cu m in the short term and 100,000m. cu m in the medium term as a result of new discoveries. In 2000 Algeria exported 60,200m. cu m of natural gas—57,500m. cu m of which to Western Europe (notably 25,100m. cu m to Italy; 10,300m. cu m. to France and 9,800m. cu m to Spain). Just over one-half of the exports (32,800m. cu m) were delivered via the Transmed and Maghreb–Europe pipelines, with the remainder in the form of LNG (making Algeria the second largest LNG exporter that year with 20% of the world total).

In line with SONATRACH's plans for further integration in international downstream activities, the company announced in March 2000 that it had agreed in principle to take a stake in the Spanish LNG regasification terminal to be built at Ferrol in Galicia. SONATRACH stated that its participation in the project would enable the company to sell additional quantities of LNG to Spain on a long-term basis by 2004. Gas will be derived from the In Salah project. In December 2000 SONATRACH acquired a 10% stake in one of the consortia developing the US $2,000m. Camisea gasfield project in Peru, and the company will be involved in the transportation of natural gas and liquids from the Camisea field to Lima and Callao. Also in December SONATRACH and Conoco of the USA signed a memorandum of understanding to evaluate the potential use of Algerian gas in Algeria, Spain and Turkey. A feasibility study is to be carried out for a $3,000m. integrated energy project involving installation of gas production facilities and the con-struction of a 1,200-MW power station.

FOREIGN PARTICIPATION IN THE PETROLEUM AND GAS SECTOR

In 1970 the Algerian oil interests of Shell, Phillips, Elwerath and AMIF were nationalized, after protracted negotiations had failed to achieve agreement on tax reference prices, and SONA-TRACH thus became Algeria's largest producer. In 1971 Algeria nationalized French petroleum companies operating in the country, as well as pipeline networks and natural gas deposits. Later in the year President Boumedienne issued a decree ban-ning concession-type agreements and laying down the conditions under which foreign oil companies could operate in Algeria. As a result, SONATRACH gained control of virtually all of Algeria's petroleum production, having held only 31% in 1970. After 1979 SONATRACH attempted to bring foreign oil companies back to Algeria to explore, in view of its declining existing petroleum reserves. Some companies, such as Italy's Agip and France's Total, made small discoveries. In 1986 the Government intro-duced a new oil exploration law, offering better terms for foreign exploration companies, with the aim of encouraging those that had made discoveries to develop their finds. In addition, some new companies, including US oil firms, expressed an interest in acquiring rights to operate in Algerian concessions. In December 1987 Agip became the first foreign company to sign an explora-tion and production agreement with SONATRACH under the new law. A further agreement was signed by the Spanish company Cepsa in January 1988, and a contract with the Australian group BHP Petroleum was concluded in December 1988. An agreement with the US company Anadarko Petroleum Corpn was signed in June 1989.

In late 1991 a new hydrocarbons law was promulgated, with the aim of encouraging greater participation by foreign com-panies in Algeria's oil and gas industry. It marked the most radical change in energy policy since the nationalizations in 1971. The legislation sought to stimulate exploration, but the most notable feature was that it allowed foreign companies to participate in existing oilfields in order to improve recovery rates and thus increase production. The Government hoped to encourage the participation of the major oil companies, which were expected to pay substantial front-end bonuses in return for a share of the output. Equally significant was the fact that foreign companies would be allowed a stake in gas reserves discovered under exploration and production-sharing agree-ments, though not in existing fields. Gas had hitherto been a national monopoly, and foreign companies had been excluded from benefiting from the discovery of gas in their oil acreage. New investment from the participation of foreign companies was regarded as essential to reverse falling oil output.

In July 1994 it was announced that negotiations were in progress with the US company Atlantic Richfield Co (Arco) on the terms of an enhanced oil recovery (EOR) contract, valued at US $1,300m., to raise output in the Rhourde el-Baguel field. US firms were expected to take a leading role in future EOR contracts. Several contracts with international companies had been concluded in 1992–93 for new exploration work. In 1994 the Anadarko (Algeria) Petroleum Corpn of the USA announced plans to drill two more exploration wells in the Hassi Berkine field. Cepsa and Repsol of Spain and BHP Petroleum of Australia were also engaged in drilling projects. In late 1993 British Petroleum (BP) announced that it would drill its first exploration well in 1994 as part of a nine-year programme during which the company was committed to drill five wells. Despite the deteriorating security situation and the withdrawal of some expatriate staff and dependants, international petroleum companies stated that they were continuing operations. In January 1994 SONATRACH opened a second round of exploration bidding and announced that it was pursuing plans to allocate at least four new exploration permits; in May plans were announced to drill 51 exploration wells. In June Pluspetrol of Argentina signed an exploration agreement, and in November a group of South Korean companies signed a contract to explore and drill wells in the central Illizi basin. In May 1995 Italy's Agip signed an exploration and production sharing agreement to undertake work in the Zemoul al-Kbar concession, where three discoveries had already been made. Production facilities were under construction, and a 230-km pipeline was being built to link the new wells to the existing pipeline system. It was anticipated that total production would eventually rise to some 60,000 b/d. The agreement also included production tests at Agip's oil discovery at Rhourde Messaoud. Petro-Canada, which had signed a 10-year exploration and production-sharing accord in April 1993, announced in September 1994 an oil and gas find in its Tinhrert acreage in the Illizi basin, and in March 1995 sought approval to develop the field. In early 1995 Anadarko (Algeria) sought permission to develop two oilfields in the Hassi Berkine block following the announcement in December 1994 of a third oil discovery.

In December 1995 SONATRACH signed a gas exploration and production agreement with BP, the country's first gas production-sharing agreement with a private company. SONATRACH agreed that the gas would be marketed with BP in a 50:50 joint-venture company. The project (estimated to cost US $2,700m.) to develop seven unexploited fields in the In Salah region was expected to bring a further 9,000m. cu m of gas on stream by 2004. Production was due to commence in 2002–03, after the drilling of up to 200 production wells and construction of a $1,000m. pipeline link to Hassi R'Mel. However, progress has been slowed due to several factors, including the depressed price of gas (which remained linked to that of oil) in the early months of 1999 and the need to sign more gas purchase agreements. Although by 1999 In Salah Gas (the joint venture created by SONATRACH and BP Amoco) had signed agreements to supply 4,000m. cu m to ENEL, Italy's state power generator, and the same volume to Edison Gas, also of Italy, negotiations with other European countries were stalled by the 1998 EU Gas Directive. This opened up the European market to foreign competition, but has caused conflict over its 'destination clause', which prevents the original importer reselling the gas to another EU country. To resolve the problem of securing gas sales, SONATRACH signed an agreement to buy back BP's share until further gas contracts could be concluded. In August 2001 contracts were awarded to enable the project to go ahead—Japan's JGC Corpn and US-based Kellogg Brown and Root were selected for the main engineering, procurement and construction project; Bechtel of the USA for in-field pipelines and a 460-km pipeline link to Hassi R'Mel; and the SONATRACH subsidiary Enefor for the drilling development programme. Production is expected to commence in 2004 following the completion of the development of the first three fields.

In January 1996 Total of France, together with Repsol of Spain, signed a production agreement with SONATRACH to develop the Tin Fouye Tabankort gasfield, the second agreement of its kind between the state energy company and private investors. After a total investment of US $700m. by the three partners, the gasfield officially came on stream in May 1999. Production was expected to reach 20m. cu m of wet gas a day, to be separated into dry gas, 23,000 b/d of condensate and 26,000 b/d of LPG.

In March 1996 Arco signed a contract with SONATRACH to rehabilitate the Rhourde el-Baguel oilfield, the country's second largest field, for which a preliminary agreement had been reached in July 1994 (see above). This was the country's first EOR scheme, and involved the drilling of additional wells and the use of gas injection techniques to gradually increase production from 25,000 b/d to 125,000 b/d within 10 years. The field was expected to produce more than 500m. barrels over a period of 25 years. Arco would take 49% of the field's output. In October 1995 Anadarko Petroleum announced that it was proceeding with plans to develop the Hassi Berkine South field, including

processing units and a link with an existing pipeline used by Agip.

In November 1995 Mobil of the USA, which had signed a production-sharing and exploration agreement in February, announced that it had found oil at its first exploration well and was evaluating the results to decide whether or not the discovery was commercially viable. In December Agip of Italy, which had signed a US $25m. exploration agreement with SONATRACH in May, discovered oil in the Zemoul el-Kbar concession in the Hassi Berkine North field. A second discovery was made in May 1996, and Agip planned to develop both wells and connect them to existing production facilities at the Bir Rebaa North field. Production from the concession was to be increased from 46,000 b/d to 70,000 b/d. In March 1996 Cepsa of Spain announced that it was to develop a second field (Rhourde el-Krouf) in its Rhourde Yacoub concession, with the aim of achieving production of 70,000 b/d by the end of the year. Estimated recoverable reserves at the field were 74m.–125m. barrels of light crude. Also in March 1996 the Minister of Energy and Mines urged international oil companies to invest $3,500m. in hydrocarbons projects in the following five years. Algeria aimed to exploit all gas reserves and to increase oil production at many existing fields by as much as 50% by introducing enhanced oil recovery technology, similar to the project signed with Arco. The minister stated that EOR projects being discussed with other companies, which had been deliberately suspended, would be reopened in order to try to secure more deals in fields such as Rhourde el-Baguel. He said that $18,000m. was to be invested in the oil and gas industries in the following five years, of which the Government hoped as much as 20% might be covered by the private sector.

In January 1998 Oryx Energy, a US independent company, signed an exploration and production-sharing agreement with SONATRACH, whereby it would invest US $28.8m. in exploration work in the Timissit region, south of Hassi Messaoud, over the following five years. Anadarko announced a major investment programme in the country during 1998 to develop three oilfields and continue exploration work. In May Anadarko began producing oil at Hassi Berkine South, the company's first production in Algeria. Production rose from 5,000 b/d to 30,000 b/d in July. The Hassi Berkine South processing plant, built at a cost of $222m., formally commenced operations in May 1999. By late 2000 production at the field had reached 53,000 b/d and was expected to reach 135,000 b/d by August 2001 upon completion of the second production train. In 2000 the Export-Import Bank of the USA approved a nine-year loan worth $120m. to SONATRACH to finance part of the second phase of the Hassi Berkine South project, which is being jointly funded by the state company (with a 51% share) and a group led by Anadarko, Lasmo and Maersk Olie Algérie. By early 1999 Arco and SONATRACH had invested over $1,000m. in the redevelopment of the Rhourde el-Baguel oilfield. The main construction phase was virtually complete, but there were plans to build a gas plant capable of recovering some 150m. barrels of LPG, as well as to upgrade gas- and oil-handling facilities. In 2000 Arco announced that it expected to raise production capacity at Rhourde el-Baguel from 20,000 b/d to 50,000 b/d by 2005, and eventually to 125,000 b/d. In April 1998 Cepsa of Spain announced investment of over $1,000m. to develop the new Oughroud field, previously known as Qoubba. Cepsa was working with companies operating adjacent blocks, and development plans were being prepared for production to begin in 2002, rising to a target of 230,000 b/d.

In early 1999 Mobil announced that as a result of depressed world petroleum markets it had stopped all exploration and production in Algeria. However, following a sharp rise in oil prices later that year a number of international oil companies announced that they were proceeding with major development projects in Algeria. Anadarko signed agreements with contractors for the development of stage-two facilities for the Hassi Berkine South field; the agreements comprised the construction of a collection station and a 75,000-b/d crude treatment plant, and similar facilities at Hassi Berkine North, which were completed in January 2002. Total output capacity at Hassi Berkine South and Hassi Berkine North was thus increased to 210,000 b/d. Following completion of the further expansion of the complex, scheduled for later in 2002, total output from the field will reach 285,000 b/d. Early in 2001 SONATRACH awarded the Italian arm of ABB, Lummus Global, a US $69m. contract to extend the oil pipeline linking Hassi Berkine to the main oil terminal facility at Haoud el-Hamra, and to construct an oil stocking unit and a crude pumping station at Nezla, 154 km north of Hassi Berkine. An agreement announced in September 1999 between Arco and France's Elf Aquitaine to give Elf a 40% stake in the Rhourde el-Baguel oilfield was subsequently blocked by SONATRACH. The agreement would have marked Elf's return to Algeria after an absence of almost 30 years. Elf sought to play down SONATRACH's decision, stating that as the company intended to merge with France's TotalFina it would continue to have interests in Algeria. In late January 2000 Burlington Resources of the USA announced a major new oil and gas discovery in the Berkine basin. After more than two years of negotiations Amerada Hess of the USA signed an agreement with SONATRACH in April 2000 to invest $500m. over the next 25 years on enhanced recovery from the Zotti, El-Gassi and El-Agreb fields, south-east of Hassi Messaoud, with production scheduled to rise to 45,000 b/d by 2003. SONATRACH was to retain a 51% stake in the production-sharing contract. Under the terms of a second agreement, Amerada Hess was also to invest $28.5m. in exploration work. In February 2000 the Islamic Development Bank approved a loan of $13.34m. to SONATRACH to help finance the development of the Mesdar oilfield near Hassi Messaoud which includes the installation of a gas-injected station. As part of this project, in early April 2001 Sofresid of France was awarded a $36m. contract to expand the Mesdar oil pipeline terminal which is used to transfer hydrocarbons from the Rhourde el-Baguel, el-Borma, Bordj Rbaa North and Mesdar fields.

In July 2000 Australia's BHP acquired a 60% stake in the Ohanet gas condensate project, which is being developed with Japan Ohanet Oil and Gas, and Petrofac Resources. With reserves estimated at 96,300m. cu m, the project is expected to produce 30,400 b/d of condensate, 27,700 b/d of LPG and 665m. cu m of natural gas commencing in October 2003. The contract, worth US $74m., to design and build a gas processing plant and a 236-km pipeline for the project was awarded to ABB of Switzerland and Petrofac International of the United Kingdom. BHP also announced that it was proceeding with the $500m. Rhourde Ouled Djemma integrated development project near Ohanet in partnership with Agip Algeria Exploration and SONATRACH. Reserves are estimated at 300m. barrels and production is expected to reach 80,000 b/d by 2003. In July 2000 Burlington Resources of the USA and Talisman Energy of Canada announced plans to develop the Menzel Ledjmat MLN field, with the first phase of the project to be completed in 2002. This will include construction of a central production facility and a 16,000 b/d oil-export pipeline. In October 2000 SONATRACH opened its first public licensing round for six exploration blocks—four in the Berkine Basin and one each at In Salah and Constantine. In March 2001 the Ministry of Energy and Mines awarded contracts for three of the exploration blocks—to the Russian companies Rosneft and Stroytransgaz in the Illizi basin; Gulf Keystone Petroleum of the United Arab Emirates (UAE) in the Constantine region; and Anadarko of the USA in the Berkine Basin—but no bids were received for the remaining three blocks. A second international bidding round for 15 oil and gas blocks was launched in May 2001 with awards due to be made in October of that year. The turn-out was lower than expected, and there were no offers for blocks in frontier areas outside Berkine. Companies receiving blocks included Anadarko, Burlington Resources, First Calgary Petroleum, TotalFinaElf, and Repsol-YPF. In December a third bidding round was launched for the development of five oil and gas projects in the Illizi basin for which 14 international oil companies have submitted proposals.

Meanwhile, in January 2001 SONATRACH signed an agreement with Gaz de France and Petronas of Malaysia to develop seven blocks in the Ahnet region, which has gas reserves estimated at 140,000m cu m. In February a Japanese consortium of JGC Corpn and Itochu Corpn was awarded a US $372m. contract for the construction of the first phase of the Hassi R'Mel gas boosting project, to help combat falling pressure at the field and enable LPG and condensate to be extracted beyond 2020. The total cost of the project, which is due for completion in

2006, is projected to be $951m. In March 2001 Petro-Canada, which had been involved in talks with SONATRACH for two years about the development of a major gas project in the Tihert region capable of producing up to 11.3m. cu m per day, broke off the negotiations. SONATRACH subsequently announced that it would issue a tender for the gas reserve at a later date. The new hydrocarbons law expected to be in place by the end of 2002 (see SONATRACH, below) was expected to boost foreign investment in the hydrocarbons sector, and the Minister of Energy and Mines has stated that it was hoped to double the number of foreign operators in the country by 2004. There are also plans to accelerate the process of awarding concessions and contracts, addressing long-standing complaints from foreign companies about the lengthy delays in securing contracts. Furthermore, foreign operators will be given financial incentives to reduce the time they take to recover oil and gas from their concessions.

By the late 1990s revenue from hydrocarbons exports had been expected to increase substantially, but a sharp fall in oil prices resulted in receipts from hydrocarbon exports falling from US $13,600m. in 1997 to $9,700m. in 1998, according to the Banque d'Algérie. As a result of higher petroleum prices from the second half of 1999, oil and gas exports during 1999 were valued at $11,800m. and in 2000 at $21,000m., according to the Algerian authorities. The structure of hydrocarbon exports has also changed since the 1980s, as Algeria has successfully diversified the hydrocarbon sector. By 2000 crude petroleum accounted for only 23% of total hydrocarbons exports, and natural gas and liquefied gas for 33%, with the remainder being accounted for by petroleum products. It was reported that production of all hydrocarbon products fell by 1.5% in the first six months of 2001, representing a 2.2% decrease in total hydrocarbon exports.

SONATRACH

Following its establishment in 1963, SONATRACH expanded to become the largest, most complex and economically most important state company in Algeria. In May 1980 the Government decided that SONATRACH should be rationalized into smaller, specialized and more autonomous units. Thirteen such units were eventually formed, including SONATRACH itself. In January 1998 the National Energy Council, chaired by President Liamine Zéroual, approved a long-standing restructuring plan for SONATRACH under which non-core activities were to be detached as separate companies and the downstream oil and gas sector would be open to foreign investment. In March SONATRACH was converted into a joint-stock company by presidential decree, with a capital of AD 245,000m. entirely subscribed by the state (to prevent foreign investors acquiring stakes). The company was to be headed by a director-general answerable to a board of directors chaired by the Minister of Energy and Mines. The corporate status received international recognition in 2001 when a consortium of Japanese banks extended a US $254m. loan without a government guarantee for the Hassi R'Mel gas boosting project (see below). SONATRACH sought to become a global energy company by forging links with multinational and state-oil companies in petrochemicals, refining and power generation. In October 1998 Belgium's Générale de Banque SA signed a credit line of US $57.5m. to finance the modernization of SONATRACH's pipeline infrastructure by Belgian firms, and the Banque Extérieure d'Algérie (BEA) provided a seven-year loan of AD 15,000m. to the company to finance new investments. In May 1999 SONATRACH signed a memorandum of understanding with Agip of Italy on joint oil exploration and production projects outside Algeria. Under the agreement, SONATRACH would take a 40% stake in an oilfield operated by Agip in Yemen. During 2000 SONATRACH continued to seek investment opportunities overseas, as part of its strategy to become a truly international company. These included investment in Angola's oil industry, the expansion of its operations in Yemen with Agip, and an energy co-operation agreement signed with Equatorial Guinea at the end of the year. In early 2002 SONATRACH signed an agreement to carry out exploration in the neighbouring state of Mali and a 15-year contract to supply 1,000m. cu m annually of gas to the Spanish energy company Iberdrola.

In April 2000 SONATRACH and SONELGAZ, the state power company, signed a framework agreement to create a new body to carry out integrated energy projects with local and foreign partners. In October SONATRACH's chairman announced the appointment of four new vice-presidents dealing with upstream activity, commercialization, transport and downstream activity as part of organizational changes to streamline the company's operations. The restructuring of the company was aimed at improving its competitive position among other international oil companies in the world market. As part of this process a new international holding section for overseas subsidiaries and expansion was also established.

In 2001 the Minister for Energy and Mines, Chakib Khelil, pressed ahead with a new hydrocarbons law which would end SONATRACH's monopoly in the domestic petroleum market. The new legislation envisages the total liberalization of the upstream, downstream and transportation sectors to national and international investors, and aims to transfer SONATRACH's regulatory and negotiating roles to two independent agencies: one would be responsible for promoting exploration and production investment; the other, a regulatory body, would apply technical, safety and environmental rules, make recommendations for the award of pipeline concessions, and assume responsibility for issuing construction and operating permits for downstream activities. While SONATRACH would continue as the national oil company, it would have to compete on an equal footing with international companies for new acreage and would be responsible for securing its finances without resorting to Government guarantees. However, the legislation would not apply to production-sharing agreements, which SONATRACH would continue to administer. It is envisaged that SONATRACH will eventually become fully independent of the state, but any plans to privatize the company have been ruled out, at least in the medium term. The proposed reforms were welcomed by international oil companies, which considered that the new measures would provide fresh momentum to the exploration and production sector, but were condemned by union leaders, who declared that the draft law would result in the loss of national sovereignty over national resources and seriously undermine the country's future. In late March 2001 several unions organized a one-day strike to protest against the proposed reforms. Responding with redrafted proposals later in 2001, the Government stated that although the new law would open the energy sector to private (including foreign) investment, the state would retain control of the oil and gas market, inviting the criticism from some analysts that the bill had been diluted somewhat from its original form.

In April 1989 Algeria's first nuclear reactor came into operation. Following international press speculation in April 1991 that the 15 MW nuclear reactor at Aïn Oussera was for military use, officials of the Ministry of Research and Technology stressed its peaceful application and asserted Algeria's willingness to allow an inspection by the International Atomic Energy Agency. At the inauguration of the reactor, in December 1993, it was announced that Algeria would sign the Treaty on the Non-Proliferation of Nuclear Weapons.

SONATRACH, with Air Liquide of France, operates a helium plant, Helios, near Arzew, which exports 75% of its production to Europe. In 2002 the company selected Germany's Linde AG to build and operate a new US $80m. helium plant with a capacity of 17m. cu m at Skikda. SONATRACH is to provide $15m. of the investment for the project, which is expected to be completed in 2005. Algeria has proven helium reserves of 6,000m. cu m.

ELECTRICITY AND WATER

By the early 1990s Algeria had an installed electricity capacity of 4,771 MW, most of which was provided by gas-fired power plants at the three major cities, Algiers, Annaba and Oran, although there were also a number of small hydroelectric stations in the Kabyle. In 1998 the state power company, SONELGAZ, awarded a construction contract for a 460-MW gas turbine plant at Hamma, near Algiers, to Ansaldo Energia of Italy. The US $150m. Arab-financed plant began generation from the first turbine in early 2002, with the second turbine expected to be commissioned later in the year. In 1999 SONATRACH awarded GE Nuovo Pignone a contract to build a 300-MW gas turbine plant in the Hassi Berkine area. The $107m. plant, part of Algeria's first independent power project, is sched-

uled to be completed in stages, commencing in 2001. In early 2000 the Arab Fund for Economic and Social Development (AFESD) agreed to provide a $98m. loan to SONELGAZ to help finance a $260m. programme to improve the country's electricity distribution network.

Power demand is expected to rise by 5% over the 10 years from 2000, requiring estimated investment by the Government of at least US $12,000m. In January 2002 new legislation to deregulate the power sector and open it up to private investment was ratified by the National People's Assembly. SONELGAZ will lose its monopoly status and will be restructured into a joint-stock company in which the state will retain a majority shareholding, with 30% open to private investment. The state will retain control of transmission and distribution but generation will be open to competition. The company has a three-year respite, during which period an independent regulatory authority, the Commission de régulation de l'électricité et du gaz, will be established to ensure transparency, competition and free access to the networks.

The Algerian Energy Company (AEC), established as a joint venture in 2001 between SONELGAZ and SONATRACH, is responsible for a range of projects to generate 1,200 MW of power capacity for export and a further 800 MW for domestic consumption. Recent international power agreements include a joint venture signed in 2001 with the Italian network operator, Gestore della Rete di Trasmissione Nazionale, to examine the feasibility of an undersea electricity link with Italy (via Sardinia); and the award to CESI (of Italy) of a contract to investigate an undersea cable to export power directly to Spain. Other power projects include the Hadjret Ennous plant near Tipaza, scheduled for completion in 2003–04; the Terga plant near Oran Tipaza, scheduled for completion in 2005–06; and the Koudiat Draouch plant near Annaba, scheduled for completion in 2003–04. SONELGAZ has awarded a US $30m. contract to ABB to install new energy management systems to control the 247 power stations and sub-stations that make up the electricity supply network. The project, designed to improve monitoring and control of power generation resources and transmission systems, is scheduled to start operation in 2004.

In October 2001 the Government announced plans to invest US $3,500m. in the water sector to ease severe shortages, of which $1,200m. would provide an emergency fund for projects in the north of the country. These include a $482m. water transfer system at Taksebt to supply water to Algiers and other towns in the region. Eight international companies were bidding for the construction of an 84-km conduit and treatment and pumping works, which was expected to commence in 2002 (with completion by 2006). Smaller projects include a wastewater treatment facility to serve Mila province, and two water treatment plants for the Sidi Abdellah new town, which is being built on the outskirts of the capital.

HOUSING AND SOCIAL INFRASTRUCTURE

A key feature of the 1980–84 and the 1985–89 Development Plans, and a priority for the regime of President Ben Djedid Chadli, was a concerted effort to address Algeria's chronic housing shortage. Additional expenditure was also allocated for other aspects of social infrastructure, notably health and education facilities, which, like housing, had been neglected in the 1970s. Under the 1985–89 Plan 8% of total investment was allocated to transport infrastructure and nearly 16% to housing. More than 300,000 new homes were to be built and some 350,000 homes started under the previous Plan were to be completed.

According to official estimates, at least 100,000 new homes were built in 1982–83. Building, traditionally the province of state concerns, was facilitated by two independent factors: the 30,000 and more homes believed to have been started—frequently without official permission—by the thriving private domestic construction industry; and the prefabricated construction techniques which had been introduced by foreign companies under the aegis of the Office National de la Promotion de la Construction en Préfabriqué (ONEP), a state concern founded in March 1982, following the successful use of imported prefabricated building techniques to repair earthquake damage in el-Asnam. By the end of that year, ONEP had signed contracts for its entire construction programme of almost 5m. sq m, at a total cost of almost US $2,800m. It was the world's largest prefabricated construction programme, and was chosen as a costly but speedy and efficient way of satisfying urgent demand. ONEP drew most of its contractors from France, Spain, Italy, Denmark, Belgium, the United Kingdom, Switzerland, Portugal and Sweden, financing the bulk of its work through export credits. The 1982 programme included 21,000 homes (about one-half of that number being attached to hospitals), 34 fully equipped hospitals, 60 polyclinics, 83 vocational training centres, 41 technical schools, 122 secondary schools, six biological research centres and six university residence areas. ONEP contractors worked directly for local *wilayat*, but negotiated through ONEP and received tax and customs dispensations.

Although prefabricated construction was, on average, almost one-half the cost of traditional methods, it was a drain on Algeria's foreign exchange because of the high proportion of imported work. ONEP awarded no new contracts in 1983, and was disbanded in the following year. By then traditional construction methods were being used to build most of the extra housing.

In 1983 the Government launched its other main scheme to expedite building, namely the use of foreign contractors under bilateral agreements with foreign governments. After the dissolution of ONEP, however, there was a general shift in government policy towards housing construction. Contracts were awarded to companies from Eastern Europe, often to accompany barter agreements, because they could complete the work more cheaply. The Government also urged local construction companies to become involved in the housing programme. Foreign companies were asked to form joint ventures with local companies if they wished to be awarded more work, but these requirements proved unpopular. After the collapse of petroleum prices in 1986 the Government began to search for cheaper methods of solving the housing crisis, encouraging local companies to undertake housing projects. The private sector was given more freedom to undertake developments on its own, and those who had built their houses illegally were offered an amnesty. However, the Government remained determined to prevent housing development on potential farming land. In 1989 it was estimated that about 100,000 new homes needed to be built each year in order to resolve the housing crisis.

Announcing the outlines of the Government's recovery programme in February 1992, Prime Minister Ghozali stated that priority would be given to spending on imports for public works and construction and that foreign participation would be encouraged in the production of construction materials. The Government's stated aim was to eliminate shanty towns, especially in the major cities. In April 1993 the World Bank approved a US $200m. loan to support the Government's emergency programme to build 130,000 public housing units. The EU also approved a parallel structural adjustment grant of ECU 70m. to finance imports needed for the construction of 100,000 social housing units. In July a loan was agreed with the Saudi Fund for Development to finance the construction of 2,000 homes in Algiers. Following agreement on a new accord with Algeria in 1994, the IMF asked other donors to concentrate additional funding on social spending projects, especially housing.

A radical review of housing policy was in progress in early 1997 with a view to introducing reforms based on current IMF and World Bank criteria for structural adjustment loans. By this time the country's housing stock was estimated at 4m. units for a population exceeding 29m.—one of the highest occupancy rates in the world. About one-half of all dwellings had been built more than 35 years earlier, the housing stock as a whole was of poor quality and rents in public housing were well below market prices. Agreement in principle with the World Bank was reached in March on an outline programme that envisaged a reform of the public-sector housing fund (Caisse Nationale d'Epargne et de Prévoyance—CNEP); privatization of state-run construction firms; privatization of the housing development sector, including the introduction of a mortgage market; and significant increases in rents for public-sector housing. In July the CNEP was restructured and converted into a state-owned commercial bank, the Banque de l'Habitat. At the same time new auxiliary financial institutions were created by the Government to open housing finance to the entire banking sector and to better control related risks. They included a mortgage refinancing company (Société de Refinancement Hypo-

thécaire), a mortgage guarantee company (Société de Garantie du Crédit Immobilier) and a fund to provide guarantees to housing companies (Fonds de Garantie et de Caution Mutuelle de la Promotion Immobilière). The Government continued its progressive withdrawal from direct involvement in housing construction and the participation of the private sector in the provision of housing increased substantially. By 1997 many public construction companies had been liquidated and the work-force of those remaining substantially reduced. During 1995–97 some 93,000 construction workers, or just over one-half of current employment in public construction companies, were made redundant. Public enterprises increasingly turned to private sub-contractors, especially in the finishing stages of public housing projects. By 1997 the private sector, mainly small local construction firms, accounted for more than 50% of work on public housing projects, compared with only 20% in 1994. Subsidized public rents were increased substantially between March 1994 and December 1997. Further rises were envisaged, while the Government aimed to establish a system of direct subsidies to assist low-income tenants. In 1997–98 plans were announced to liquidate or restructure public rental companies responsible for the supply of most rental housing, with the aim of privatizing the existing stock of public housing for rent and subcontracting its maintenance to the private sector. At the same time a shift was planned from rental public housing to the promotion of owner occupation.

By the end of 1997 the IMF reported that 79,000 housing units, out of 142,000 approved in 1995 (under a social construction programme) had been completed. The supplementary budget for 1998 envisaged a new social construction programme of 80,000 units to be built by both private and public contractors, with 5,000 units completed during 1998. In late 1997 a US company, Omnitek, signed a joint-venture agreement with COSIDER to build a factory in Algiers to produce prefabricated houses. In early 1998 it was reported that Royal Building Systems of Canada was to establish a similar plant with the capacity to produce 12,500 housing units per year. In early 2000 it was reported that a group of Australian companies had signed a partnership agreement with the Conseil supérieur du patronat algérien to construct 100,000 low-income housing units. The Australian Government would provide 80% of the financing of the US $100m. project, 40% of which would be in the form of an interest-free loan repayable over 10 years. AFESD subsequently agreed a loan of $114m. for housing projects in the central region. In July of that year popular frustration caused by acute housing shortages led to riots in Sidi-bel-Abbès over housing allocation. In August some 96 families in an Algiers neighbourhood threatened to go on hunger strike after they were not allocated new housing units for which they had been given ownership documents six years previously.

Devastating floods in coastal regions of the country in November 2001 worsened the acute housing shortage. An estimated 23,000 houses were destroyed, and in Algiers, which sustained most of the damage, more than 700 people were killed. The Government pledged additional funding for the housing sector and plans to build 35,000 units in 2002 financed by the sale of social housing homes (70% of the housing supply) to the private sector. The project will be carried out on a build-own-lease basis. Furthermore, some 800,000 housing units were expected to be constructed by private sector companies during 2002.

TRANSPORT

At the start of the 1980s Algeria's state railway company, the Société Nationale des Transports Ferroviaires (SNTF), announced ambitious plans to double the length and the freight-carrying capacity of its 3,900-km network within 10 years. After 1985, however, SNTF revised its investment priorities in order to concentrate on the maintenance and upgrading of existing track and equipment. A local company was established in 1986 to implement the upgrading programme in co-operation with foreign firms, while most expansion projects were postponed or cancelled. In 1991 SNTF carried 58m. passengers and 12m. metric tons of freight. Rail routes within Algeria include Algiers–Oran, Béchar–Mohammedia (narrow-gauge), Mohammedia–Mostaganem, Algiers–Annaba, Constantine–Touggourt, Constantine–Skikda, Algiers–Tizi Ouzou, Annaba–Tebessa and

Djelfa–Blida (narrow-gauge). There are international rail links to Morocco and Tunisia.

In September 1994 the Government announced plans to restructure SNTF, including a proposed privatization of 12 subsidiary companies. Disagreements about corporate restructuring had earlier delayed the full utilization of a 1989 World Bank loan for railway projects. Contracts were awarded in 1996 for the construction of a 5.2-km tunnel at El-Achir, part of the north bypass railway system on the main east–west line between Constantine and Algiers near the town of Bourj Bou-Arreridj (where a new railway station was opened in July 2000), to be part-financed by an African Development Bank (ADB) loan approved in 1991. Excavation work was completed two years behind schedule in 2001 because of delays caused by unforeseen geological difficulties, travel limitations and regulations governing the use of explosives imposed on the contractor, Lesi Dipenta Group of Italy. The ADB provided a supplementary US $27.9m. loan in 2000 to cover the revised costs.

Upgrading of the south-western (Béchar–Mohammedia) line, on which the narrow-gauge track dated from 1912, was given high priority in the late 1990s. A long-standing (and repeatedly postponed) proposal to build a new east–west railway across the high plateaux of southern Algeria was in 1996 again rejected for the foreseeable future because of the high cost of the project (an estimated US $3,000m. at 1996 prices). The Government's most serious rail financing problem in 1996 arose out of the need to replace the 250 passenger carriages and 20 locomotives destroyed or damaged by Islamist guerrillas. In 2000 it was reported that SNTF was to be opened to private investment, although only after long-delayed restructuring has been carried out to enable the company to concentrate on its core business activities. With much of the rolling-stock needing replacement, and track and signalling in need of urgent upgrading, SNTF announced plans to renovate its fleet of locomotives in a project led by General Motors of the USA, which includes upgrading of onboard electro-mechanical equipment to electronic systems.

Construction of a proposed Algiers metro system began in the early 1980s but was suspended for some years, owing to financial constraints. Although work resumed in 1989, government efforts to attract international contractors proved unsuccessful and the project was abandoned in 1996. It was revived early in 2000 when the Entreprise Métro d'Alger invited international construction companies to bid for two projects: a 9-km underground network with 10 stations and a 4.3-km network with four stations. One of the financial options was a build-operate-transfer (BOT) arrangement. The Government appointed the French consulting firm Ingerop/Semaly to conduct a feasibility study for a tramway system in Algiers as part of its 2002 economic recovery package to carry up to 200,000 passengers, on an eastbound link to Aïn Taya and Borj El Kiffan and westbound to Bab el-Oued and Aïn Benian.

The national airline, Air Algérie, was restructured in 1984, with domestic routes being passed to the newly-formed Air Inter Services. Algeria purchased its first two European Airbus A310 aircraft in 1984. The number of passengers carried by Air Algérie fell from 4.2m. in 1986 to 3.7m. in 1991. The company's outstanding debt was calculated to have risen to AD 9,000m. in 1991 and debt due in 1992 equalled one-third of the company's turnover. The company's problems arose from the effects of devaluation, a reduction in traffic (due to the introduction of new visa regulations for Algerians visiting Europe) and increased operating costs. In 1991 Air Algérie raised its international fares by 50% and suspended plans to renew its aircraft fleet over the next 10 years. In 1992 a three-year reform programme, designed to improve the management and performance of the airline, was initiated. Air Algérie reported profits of US $14.5m. in 1992, but in December 1994 the company's director-general reported further losses of revenue, owing to the security crisis and tougher visa restrictions imposed by France and other countries.

In September 1994, as part of a radical review of all state transport undertakings, the Government indicated its intention to reform the structure of Air Algérie in order to improve its efficiency and competitiveness as the Government moved towards its medium-term goal of opening the air and sea transport sectors to private competition. Meanwhile, Air Algérie's aircraft purchase plans remained obstructed because of a lack of funds, the Government's stated preference at this time being for the airline to lease or charter additional aircraft while this remained a cost-effective option. During 1999 Air Algérie reported a sharp decline in the number of passengers (to 1.3m. from 1.7m in 1998), flying on its internal routes, and announced that in response the company would extend its international services. In January 2001 the Government announced plans to appoint consultants to advise on the partial privatization of the company and in June Booz Allen & Hamilton of the USA was appointed to recommend strategies for offering up to 49% of Air Algérie's capital to private investors. Meanwhile, Air Algérie took delivery of two Boeing 737s aircraft, as part of a US $600m. order for 12 new passenger aircraft by 2002.

A number of private airlines have been granted operating licences since the Government's decision in 1998 to liberalize this sector. Khalifa Airways began domestic services in August 1999 and commenced daily flights to Marseille and Lyon in France in the following month. New flights were introduced to Spain in 2000 and to South Africa in 2001. In March 2001 the airline announced that it had ordered 18 aircraft from Europe's Airbus Industrie at a cost of US $1,700m. The first aircraft is to be delivered in 2004, and will be used to increase the airline's domestic and regional services. It was reported in December 2001 that Khalifa Airways had commenced discussions regarding a possible merger with Air Algérie. Eco Air offers a service from the western city of Oran to Alicante and Palma de Mallorca, and Antinea Airlines is introducing services to Charleroi in Belgium and Mulhouse in France. Saharan Airlines, based in Touggourt, provides services on domestic routes. In June 2001 Tassili Airlines, a joint venture established in 1998 by SONATRACH and Air Algérie, launched an international tender to expand its fleet. The airline, based in Hassi Messaoud, carries passengers and freight related to the hydrocarbons industry. Meanwhile, in the latter half of 1999 several major airlines, notably Alitalia, Turkish Airlines and Saudi Arabian Airlines, announced they had resumed flights to Algeria.

Airport upgrading projects undertaken in the early 1990s included the construction of new runways at Tamanrasset, El-Achouet, Aïn-Arnet and Hassi R'Mel and the completion of basic structural work on a new international terminal at Algiers Houari Boumedienne airport. However, funding was not available in 1996 to equip the terminal building and bring it into operation, the need for new facilities having become less pressing because of a decrease in passenger numbers (attributable to Algeria's internal security problems). In late 1996 the Government examined the scope for negotiating a partnership agreement to attract overseas project finance for the terminal. By late 2000 an AD 5,600m. state-led project was underway at Houari Boumedienne international airport to repair mistakes made during previous construction phases of the upgrading programme scheduled to be completed by the end of 2002. The project will enable the airport to handle an extra 3m. passengers per year. In 2001 the airport handled 4.3m. passengers, representing a 40% increase in domestic use and an 18% increase in international use. At the same time the Société d'investissement, d'exploitation et de gestion aéroportuaire commenced its search for a co-investor to help fund a new terminal at the airport, representing the first phase of an expansion programme to increase capacity to 12m. passengers per year. In April 2001 it was announced that the US-based Sterling Merchant Finance had been selected to advise the Government on the private concession to operate the airport. The company is charged with defining the strategy and conditions under which a private company will operate the airport. Meanwhile, the heavily protected Hassi Messaoud airport in the Sahara has become a busy centre for charter traffic serving the oil industry, and a new runway was opened at Hassi R'Mel to support oil and gas developments in that region. In 1998 the Minister of Transport announced plans to extend and modernize the small airport serving Touggourt. In late 1999 the Etablissement national de navigation aérienne awarded an Italian company the contract to set up six radar stations and satellite links for air-traffic control. In 2000 the EIB approved a loan of €30m. to support the modernization of air-traffic control.

In 1993 Japan's International Co-operation Agency completed a major survey of development priorities for the seaports of

Algiers, Oran and Annaba. It recommended that facilities for unloading cereals and containers should be upgraded at the ports of Annaba and Oran. In 1991 the three ports handled 71% of all traffic: Algiers 32%, Annaba 23% and Oran 16%. A new port at Djen-Djen, near Jijel, would serve Algeria's first free-zone development, and was scheduled to open in 1998 (see Manufacturing, below). In October 1995, as part of a World Bank scheme to reduce oil pollution in the southern Mediterranean, contractors were invited to bid for the supply and installation of maritime traffic control equipment at the ports of Algiers, Skikda and Arzew. In 1996 a 375,000-metric ton multi-purpose container terminal opened at Annaba. By the end of 2000 a new 17.5 ha container terminal had opened at Algiers, and when the current expansion programme has been completed in 2005 the port will be able to handle some 450,000 containers per year, more than double its present capacity. In early 2002 it was reported that the Government was intending to sell a 49% stake in the shipping company Société Nationale de Transport Maritime et Compagnie Nationale Algérienne de Navigation (SNTM-CNAN), which owns a fleet of 26 ships and carried 2.7m. tons of merchandise in 2001.

From 1992 the Government revived plans for an east–west motorway system linking Annaba and Tlemcen and forming part of a trans-Maghreb motorway. In December 1993 the EIB made a loan of US $24.2m. for a section of the 1,400-km trans-Algerian highway between Lakhdaria and Bouira, and an agreement for a further loan of $97m. was concluded in late 1994. In December 1995 the ADB agreed a loan of $39m. to finance construction of a motorway to bypass Constantine, with the 11 km six-lane highway being integrated into the east–west motorway system.

By the end of 2000 the Government had announced plans to privatize all road transport and indicated that it was seeking private investment in the national road system. A new €45m. loan from the EIB was approved in September 2000 to support the further development of the country's motorway network. The loan will be used to finance the construction of an 80-km motorway in the Algiers region.

In August 2001 the World Bank approved a US $8.72m. loan towards Algeria's Transport Technical Assistance Project to develop the country's infrastructure. This includes two subways and a ports project on a BOT basis, upgrading of the railway network and the creation of an institutional framework to facilitate private-public partnerships.

TELECOMMUNICATIONS

In August 2000 a posts and telecommunications bill was ratified by parliament, removing the state's monopoly over this sector and redefining its role to that of a supervisory authority. The new legislation provided for the appointment of an independent regulator and opened up both the fixed-line and mobile sectors to foreign competition. The Ministry of Posts and Telecommunications selected Detcom of Germany, Optec of Canada and the United Kingdom's Arthur Andersen for the consultancy contract for the restructuring of this sector, while the Gide Loyrette Nouel group of France was appointed to negotiate the consultancy contract for the implementation of the sector's regulatory framework. A loan of US $9m. was approved by the World Bank to support the reforms. The Ministry of Posts and Telecommunications also invited Cisco Systems of the USA to establish a centre in Algeria to train telecommunications staff specifically for the development of the country's internet infrastructure. To date there are relatively few personal computers in the country, limiting uptake of the internet; however, over the next 10 years the Government plans to increase fixed-line density from five lines to 20 lines per 100 persons. Some 120,000 new lines were installed in Algiers during 2001. In February Pirelli Submarine Telecoms systems of Italy was awarded a $15m. contract to supply and install a 320-km fibre optic cable between Algiers and Palma de Mallorca, as part of a joint project between France Télécom, Telefónica of Spain, Telecom Italia and Algeria's Ministry of Posts and Telecommunications, which—when completed in 2002—will provide a fast and reliable link between Algeria and the rest of the European network via Spain. In March 2001 the Government announced of a new joint-stock company, Algérie Télécoms, to be responsible for the country's fixed-line services and existing GSM licence—functions previously undertaken by the Ministry of Posts and Telecommunications.

In July 2001 the second GSM licence, valued at US $737m., was awarded to the Egyptian company Orascom Telecom, to provide services in Algiers and in 11 other cities in the northeast. Orascom selected Alcatel of France to install the $372m. GSM network. The service, which was named Djezzy GSM, was officially launched in February 2002 and hoped to obtain 1m. subscribers by 2003. The first instalment of the licence fee has been submitted to the Government, and the second part is due at the end of 2003. In August Algérie Telecoms opened a tender for the installation of a GSM network with a subscriber capacity of 500,000. In April 2002 the Ministry of Higher Education and Scientific Research reported that Algeria was to launch its first small telecommunications satellite, ALSAT 1, by the end of the year.

MANUFACTURING

Industrial development has long been a priority area of Algerian economic policy, and the major investment effort in the 1970–73 Development Plan was devoted to this end. Under the 1974–77 Plan industry received about 43.5% of total allocations. In the 1980–84 Plan it was allocated 38% of total investment, and 32% in the 1985–89 Plan.

At independence the Algerian industrial sector was very small, being confined mainly to food processing, building materials, textiles and minerals. The departure of the French entailed loss of demand, capital and skill, thereby decelerating the industrialization process. Foreign firms became increasingly reluctant in the 1960s to invest in Algeria because of the danger of nationalization. By 1978 about 300 state-owned manufacturing plants had been established, but productivity was very low, with some factories operating at only 15%–25% of design capacity. The early 1980s were a time of increasing emphasis on productivity and efficiency, and nowhere more so than in the manufacturing sector.

In 1983 the Government began to encourage foreign and domestic manufacturers to supply the larger *sociétés nationales*, such as SONACOME. Foreign companies would be junior partners to state concerns, but local businesses would receive the finance from state banks that was normally available to state concerns. The Government also sought to encourage companies to establish joint ventures, in order to stimulate foreign investment and to ensure closer working relations with foreign companies, thus enabling Algerian enterprises to monitor the progress of projects and gain a genuine transfer of technology.

In the late 1980s the Ministry of Light Industries considered that the basic network of small-scale manufacturing was complete, and it intended to concentrate in future on improving the integration of the sector. The private sector was to be accorded a greater role in establishing manufacturing industries to process raw materials produced in the state sector. Instead of investing in new cement works, the ministry was to concentrate on increasing output at existing works, and to carry out small extensions to satisfy any increase in demand. Beyond 1990 the ministry planned to develop high technology industries. In 1992 the Government announced radical measures to open state-sector industries, which accounted for some 80% of industrial production, to local (private) and foreign participation. Officials acknowledged that many state industries were operating at below 50% capacity, and recognized that as income from hydrocarbons was insufficient to finance the recovery of its industrial base, privatization was essential to provide investment and new markets as well as technology. The only exceptions would be industries classified as strategic, such as the Entreprise Nationale de Sidérurgie (SIDER), SONELGAZ and agro-industrial companies. After an audit of major state companies carried out as part of Algeria's World Bank structural adjustment programme, the following were identified as viable, if non-profit-making: Entreprise Nationale des Véhicules Industriels, Entreprise Nationale des Matériaux de Travaux Publics, Entreprise Nationale de Production de Matériel Agricole and Entreprise Nationale de Production de Matériel Hydraulique. In April 1994 a new ministry was created to oversee the restructuring of state companies as required by the agreements signed with the IMF in May 1994 and May 1995 (see Government Strategy, above).

According to a report published by the Ministry of Industrial Restructuring and Participation in May 1996, four years of civil strife had reduced industrial capacity by 10%, but the decline was being stemmed, and industrial production fell by only 0.5% in 1995, compared with 8% in 1994. Also in May 1996 the state-owned Entreprise Nationale de Distribution et de Commercialisation des Produits Pétroliers (NAFTAL) indicated that sabotage, allegedly by Islamist extremists, had inflicted damage assessed at AD 3,000m. to the company's facilities; NAFTAL reported a deficit of AD 11,700m., and demanded urgent government assistance.

Government efforts to attract foreign investment in the manufacturing industry had only limited success, but in October 1997 Daewoo of South Korea signed a memorandum of understanding with the Ministry of Industry and Restructuring to invest some US $2,000m. over a five-year period, including acquiring a share of a range of state-owned manufacturing industries such as fertilizers, car assembly and electrical goods. However, progress with this investment programme (representing more than twice the total foreign investment in the non-hydrocarbons sector over the previous three years) was threatened by South Korea's financial crisis which began in late 1997.

In February 1999 the Minister of Industry and Restructuring presented a report outlining major policy objectives for the manufacturing sector during the period to 2015. The report emphasized the need to achieve sustained industrial growth, improve the competitiveness of industrial enterprises, diversify products and promote a competitive export sector. In the following month the minister announced that industrial production had increased by 10.5% in 1998 compared with 1997, representing the first recorded growth since 1991. He attributed the increase to a reduction in the work-force by some 15,000 and measures taken to protect the domestic economy. Production rises had been strongest in electronics (18.3%) and food (13.1%), with more modest increases in building materials (5%), chemicals and pharmaceuticals (2.3%) and textiles (1.1%). Nevertheless, public companies remained heavily indebted to state banks. The minister also revealed that foreign investment contracts totalling US $220m. had been signed in 1997 and 1998, of which $161m. was in chemicals and pharmaceuticals. Of all investment outside the hydrocarbons sector, only pharmaceuticals projects were making progress. According to official sources, turnover in the private sector recorded a 33% increase in 1998, notably in food and food-processing, pharmaceuticals, chemicals, construction equipment and leather. However, industrial production fell by 1.5% in 1999 according to the Ministry of Industry and Restructuring.

Overall industrial production increased by 1.2% in 2000, reflecting a 6.4% increase in output in the private sector, although production in the public sector recorded a fall of 2.3%. Output was disappointing in the sectors most subject to competition from imports, such as leather (which decreased by 3.6%), textiles (a decline of 13.5%), paper and timber (–0.6%) and food (–9.4%). However, increases were recorded in the steel-making (which rose by 5.1%), electronics (3.4%), chemical and pharmaceutical (6.4%) and building materials (5.1%) sectors. The work-force in the public sector was reduced, resulting in 5,848 job losses.

The iron and steel industry is crucial to the development of other industries. In 1988 the state-owned steel company, SIDER, announced proposals to increase output of long-steel products to meet 70%, rather than 30%, of local demand and thus reduce imports of steel, which totalled 1.9m.–2m. metric tons per year. Plans were also made to increase SIDER's annual flat-steel capacity to 1.8m. tons from 1.4m. tons. Huge investments were made in the el-Hadjar complex at Annaba, although output, which has averaged 800,000 tons per year, has fallen well below the 1.8m.-ton production capacity. The el-Hadjar operation was restructured as Societé Algérienne de Fabrication Sidérurgique (ALFASID) in 1999. It required significant financial resources to implement a plant modernization programme, including the contract awarded for the upgrading of the hot-rolling mill. In 2001 India's Ispat International, part of the LNM Group, acquired a 70% stake in ALFASID and some subsidiaries of the state iron and phosphate company Ferphosin in a transaction valued at US $400m. Metalsider, Algeria's first private steelmaker, started operations in 1992. A merchant bar mill with a capacity of 100,000 tons per year commenced production in 1993, and a third bar/rod combination mill commenced operations in 1996.

Although ambitious plans were announced to expand the country's petrochemical industries, technical and financial problems have hindered progress. A vast petrochemical complex at Skikda produces polyethylene, PVC, caustic soda and chlorine. In 1991 a project to build a high-density polyethylene plant at Skikda was announced, with an annual capacity of 130,000 metric tons. ENIP (Entreprise Nationale d'Industrie Pétrochimique) formed a joint-venture company (Polymed) with Spain's Repsol Química to build the plant, but a series of problems delayed the start of construction work until mid-1997. The plant came into operation in late 1999. There is a nitrogenous fertilizer plant at Arzew, utilizing natural gas, with an annual capacity of 800,000 tons, and a complex for the manufacture of intermediate petrochemical products. In May 1991 ENIP established a joint venture with Repsol of Spain and Rhône-Poulenc of France to build a polyester resins plant at Arzew with an annual production of 10,000 tons. In early 1999 ENIP announced ambitious plans for a number of major new petrochemicals plants, mainly at Skikda and Arzew, to be developed with foreign partners; however, attracting investors appeared highly problematic for most of the projects listed.

Since the early 1970s fertilizer and associated phosphate industries have been developed at Annaba and later at Arzew. By the late 1990s the Annaba complex had the annual capacity to produce 164,000 metric tons of nitric acid, 330,000 tons of ammoniac, 330,000 tons of ammonium nitrate, 550,000 tons of phosphate fertilizers and 40,000 tons of soda tripolyphosphate. The Arzew complex had the annual capacity to produce 396,000 tons of nitric acid, 660,000 tons of ammoniac and 495,000 tons of ammonium nitrate, while a single superphosphate complex (with capacity of 600,000 tons per year) came on stream in 1998. In early 1999 it was reported that foreign investment was being sought for several major new projects including complexes for diammonium phosphate, phosphoric acid (900,000 tons per year), ammonia (1,221,000 tons per year), urea (594,000 tons per year) and superphosphate (300,000 tons per year).

Following a Government decision in early 1998 to open the downstream oil and gas sector to foreign investment, Prime Minister Ouyahia announced in March that the Government had commenced negotiations with several international companies wishing to invest in petrochemicals. In early 1998 a US $500m. joint venture was agreed between Fertiberia of Spain and SONATRACH, together with the EPE Asmidal and the Entreprise Nationale du Fer et du Phosphate (Ferphos) (state-owned fertilizer and phosphate companies), to produce fertilizers and ammonia products for the Algerian market and for export. Both Asmidal and Ferphos were to be opened to foreign investors under the privatization programme. In 2001 Asmidal, in a joint venture with Fritz Werner Industrie of Germany and Transammonia Inc. of the USA, announced plans to add a 675,250-metric tons-per-year capacity unit to its existing ammonia plant at Arzew. The facility was scheduled to be completed by 2003,.

The assembly of industrial vehicles in Algeria began in 1974 at a plant in Rouiba, established by a state-run company in association with the French manufacturer Berliet. In 1992 work began at Ain Bouchekif, near Tiaret, to build a Fiat car assembly plant, to be 64.4% owned by an Algerian public-sector company, Fatia, and 35.6% owned by Fiat of Italy. The plant was to have the capacity to produce 30,000 cars per year. By mid-1999 work on the project remained stalled as a result of financial difficulties, and it was reported that a US $50m. line of credit provided through Italy's Crediop was blocked, despite the fact that almost 80% of work on the plant had been completed. Later in 1999 talks with Fiat resumed in an attempt to resolve the difficulties. The local manufacture of vehicle components by Algerian companies and joint ventures with other countries has been encouraged by the Government since 1987. A plant for the overhaul of Peugeot engines was established near Algiers in 1990. The importing of vehicles to meet Algeria's annual demand for about 100,000 cars and light vans was opened to the private sector in 1990–91, allowing foreign manufacturers (including Peugeot, Renault, Fiat, Daewoo, Honda and Nissan) to establish local distribution agencies. Tax incentives were offered to encourage such manufacturers to make future investments in Algerian production facilities. In early 1999 negotiations with Daewoo to assume part of SNVI's Rouiba operations were still continuing (although Daewoo was declared bankrupt in 2000) and it was reported that both MAN and Renault were engaged in talks about proposals to build a new production plant for SNVI. In mid-1999 an agreement was signed by Dacia-Romania of Romania and the local Dacia-Algeria to manufacture cars from kits. In early 2000 plans for the construction of the assembly plant in the suburbs of Algiers, capable of producing 30,000 cars per year, were reported to be on target. Exports of some of the cars produced were expected to commence in 2002.

There are 12 cement works, with a total installed capacity of about 11.5m. metric tons, accounting for 70% of annual consumption. In 2001 HSBC Investment Banking was selected to advise the Government on the sale of strategic stakes in three cement plants at Meftah, Hadjar Essoud and Zahanna. Construction work began in early 2002 on a 3.6m.-tons-per-year cement plant in the M'Sila region south-east of Algiers by Egypt's Orascom Construction Industries. Further projects under evaluation include the expansion of the Tebessa, Djelfa and El-Kseur plants and construction of a 125,000m.-tons-per-year white cement plant at Beni-Saf.

A pharmaceuticals industry was developed in Algeria after 1991, when international companies were encouraged to invest in local manufacturing facilities in return for licences to sell products on the local market. Several new joint ventures, including one between Rhône-Poulenc Rorer of France and the Entreprise Nationale de Production de Produits Pharmaceutiques (SAIDAL, the state-owned pharmaceutical company), were announced in early 1998. Early in 2000 Tabuk Pharmaceutical of Saudi Arabia announced that it planned to establish a pharmaceuticals plant in Algeria producing a wide range of drugs and scheduled to commence operations in 2001. In 2000 the International Finance Corpn (IFC) announced that it would invest US $89m. in Adalph, a joint venture with Laboratoires Pierre Fabre of France and Denmark's Novo Nordisk. The investment includes a $7.5m. loan, a $1,500m. equity investment and a syndicated loan of a further $6.5m. to promote competition in the pharmaceuticals sector. In May 2002, the Arab consortium Taphco, which includes SAIDAL, contracted with the German company Pharmaplan to build a $30m. pharmaceuticals factory at the Rouiba industrial park, due for completion in 2004.

The privatization offers announced by the Government during 1996 included a management contract for the SIDER steel mill; a management contract for the Ghardaia plant of the Entreprise Nationale de Tubes et de Transformation des Produits Plats (ENTTPP or ANABIB, the company supplying pipes for the Maghreb–Europe gas pipeline); a management contract for the Médéa plant of SAIDAL; the offer for sale of 17 textile manufacturing units currently owned by five state enterprises; management contracts for five cement units owned by two state enterprises; the offer for sale of six fertilizer units owned by Asmidal, with two further units offered on a management contract basis; and offers of shareholdings in several food companies, including the Office Régional des Produits Oléicoles (producing olive oil) and the Entreprise Nationale des Jus et Conserves Alimentaíres (ENAJUC, producing fruit juice and other food products). In early 1999 it was announced that the sale of brickworks and breweries had earned US $150m., of which $100m. was in foreign investment. Later in the year the SAIDAL and the cereals distributor Eriad-Sétif were part-privatized, raising some AD 4,000m.

Algeria's first 'free zone' area for industrial development opened in 1998 on a site at Bellara, near Jijel international airport and 40 km from a new harbour. Basic infrastructure had previously been installed on the 500 ha site as part of a plan (otherwise unimplemented) to build a steel complex. Figures released by the then national investment agency APSI in mid-1997 showed that foreign companies invested a total of AD 56,800m. in non-hydrocarbons sectors of the Algerian economy between November 1993 and May 1997.

TRADE

Algeria had a consistent foreign trade deficit, with the exception of small surpluses recorded in 1967 and 1968, until the huge increases in petroleum prices in 1973. Exports of petroleum and natural gas have transformed the pattern of Algerian exports, previously limited to agricultural products and some minerals—mainly wine, citrus fruit and iron ore. Prior to the liberalization of trading policy in the mid-1990s the Government fixed an annual budget for imports and strictly controlled the import requirements of public-sector companies. The visible trade account turned from a state of chronic deficit to surplus in 1974, alternating annually between deficit and surplus thereafter. Increases in the price of petroleum in 1979, however, put Algeria in credit and kept the trade balance in surplus. In order to preserve this surplus (which reached AD 16,500m. in 1985), the Government introduced new import controls. However, the sharp fall in the price of petroleum in 1986 resulted in a trade deficit of AD 6,567m. for that year. In 1987 the price of petroleum recovered slightly and there was a trade surplus of US $2,413m. There was a trade surplus of $946m. in 1988. In 1990, although imports increased by almost 22%, exports increased further, by 42%. This produced a trade surplus of AD 11,497m., compared with a deficit of AD 1,835m. in 1989. A trade surplus of $4,107m. was recorded in 1991, although in 1992 the surplus declined to $2,489m., owing to a 12.6% rise in expenditure on imports. In February 1994 officials of the Ministry of Commerce stated that a ban on imports of consumer goods imposed by the Government in late 1992 had been revoked.

Algeria's overall trade balance (including trade in services as well as visible commodities) evolved as follows between 1993 and 1996. In 1993 there was a surplus of US $756m. (imports $10,004m.; exports $10,760m., including $9,760m. from hydrocarbons). In 1994 there was a deficit of $1,500m. (imports $11,090m.; exports $9,590m., including $8,610m. from hydrocarbons). In 1995 there was a deficit of $1,260m. (imports $12,200m.; exports $10,940m., including $9,370m. from hydrocarbons). In 1996 there was a surplus of $3,030m. (imports $11,240m.; exports $14,270m., including $12,640m. from hydrocarbons). Foodstuffs accounted for 28.7% of visible imports in 1996 (25.6% in 1995); raw materials and semi-finished products constituted 26.3% of visible imports in 1996 (30.5% in 1995); capital equipment accounted for 33.5% of visible imports in 1996 (27.7% in 1995); and consumer goods constituted 11.5% of visible imports in 1996 (16.2% in 1995). By the end of 1996 all restrictions on external trade had been eliminated, allowing public and private importers to finance their transactions from their own foreign-exchange holdings or through official cash and credit lines. At the end of 1996 Algerian customs statistics indicated that more than 25,000 private enterprises and about 300 public enterprises were involved in foreign trading operations. In 1997 the Government established an export promotion agency (PROMEX), to be funded by receipts from taxes on imported luxury goods) and introduced a range of financial incentives to stimulate the growth of non-hydrocarbons exports. In 1997 there was a trade surplus of $5,790m., with exports totalling $14,140m. and imports restricted to $8,350m. In September 1997 the ADB approved a 20-year loan of $215m. to finance imports. In early 1998 it was reported that terms had been issued to enable Algerian exporters to draw on new short-term state credit insurance facilities. As a result of a sharp fall in oil and gas revenues, exports totalled only $10,910m. in 1998, with imports rising slightly to $10,940m.—resulting in a small trade deficit. According to Algerian customs data, the value of exports rose to $12,300m. in 1999 ($11,800 of which was from hydrocarbons), mainly due to the sharp increase in oil prices during the second half of the year, with imports falling to $9,000m.—giving a trade surplus of $3,300m. With oil prices averaging $28 per barrel in 2000, the value of exports rose sharply, to $22,030m. ($18,800m. of which was from hydrocarbons), while imports rose slightly, to $9,170m.—leading to a significant rise in the trade surplus, to $12,860m. The overall value of exports fell to $20,040m. in 2001 as a result of the decrease in world prices for petroleum over the year, with imports increasing to $9,760m., narrowing the trade surplus to $10,280m., equivalent to 12.5% of GDP.

Before independence France purchased 81% of Algeria's exports and provided 82% of its imports. In 1998 France remained Algeria's largest supplier of imports (with a 29.8% market share), but took only 14.3% of Algeria's 1998 exports. In 1996 hydrocarbons accounted for 96.3% of Algerian exports to France, while capital goods remained the single largest element in French exports to Algeria, followed by agro-industrial products and consumer goods. In April 1995 the French export agency, Coface, confirmed that it was continuing to provide normal cover for French export contracts despite the serious security situation in Algeria. The only modification to the agency's policy on Algeria concerned infrastructure projects involving expatriate staff working in areas known to present a security problem. The agency, then covering contracts worth US $6,144m., was making every effort to ensure that projects in the oil and gas sector were covered in order to maintain Algeria's export capacity. Apart from France, Algeria's largest trading partners in 1998 were Italy (accounting for 19.5% of exports and supplying 9.2% of imports), the USA (17.4% of exports and 9.0% of imports), Spain (10.2% of exports and 7.8% of imports), Turkey, Germany, Canada and Belgium. Since 1995, when an agreement to supply Algerian gas to Turkey came into effect, trade between the two countries increased rapidly and in 1997 Turkey emerged as Algeria's fifth largest export market. Algerian exports to Turkey, valued at $49.5m. in 1994, had risen to $828.8m. by 1997. Imports from Turkey also increased although at a more modest rate (from $250.5m. in 1994 to $306.6m. in 1997). In early 1999 the authorities made efforts to promote trade with the rest of the Arab world, which currently accounts for only 5% of Algeria's imports.

The finalization in July 1996 of debt rescheduling arrangements under the 1995 'Paris Club' and 'London Club' agreements (see Government Strategy, above) opened the way for a relaxation of export-credit guarantee restrictions that had been introduced by several of Algeria's major trading partners. Agencies making announcements included Eximbank of the USA (short- and medium-term cover for Algerian public-sector importers resumed from August 1996); SACE of Italy (resumption of cover from late 1996, subject to strict conditions); the Belgian Government (reopening in November 1996 of a line of credit for Algerian transport projects which has been in abeyance since 1994); and the United Kingdom's Export Credits Guarantee Department (resumption of cover for Algerian petroleum and gas projects from early 1997).

In February 1989 the Union of the Arab Maghreb (UMA) was formed by Algeria, Libya, Mauritania, Morocco and Tunisia. A focus of discussion has been industrial unity and economic integration; co-operation in the mining, textiles, electronics, domestic appliances, leather and construction industries is also under consideration. The UMA aimed to establish a customs union and a single monetary exchange currency. The ultimate aim was to allow all UMA members to establish industries in each of the five countries. But despite a great deal of rhetoric little progress was recorded in the late 1990s and the early years of the 21st century (see History).

In 1998 the EU made a grant of US $70m. to stimulate the development of small and medium-sized companies in Algeria, as part of a strategy to bring Algerian businesses closer to European standards, and in late 1999 it provided a loan of $25m. to support reforms in the Algerian financial sector. The EU also provided humanitarian aid to Algeria's Red Crescent Society. On his first visit to Algiers in January 2001 Romano Prodi, President of the European Commission, reviewed progress of the negotiations (commenced in 1997) for an association agreement between Algeria and the EU, and signed three financial protocols providing investment of €30m. over four years. Negotiations were concluded in December 2001 and in April 2002 the EU-Algeria Euro-Mediterranean Association Agreement was formally signed in Valencia, Spain. It is subject to ratification by the parliaments of Algeria and the member states of the EU. With Algerian manufactures already having duty-free access to the EU, the main focus of the free-trade component of the agreement is the phasing out of Algerian import duties on EU manufactures over 12 years. Algeria is to introduce tariff reductions on EU agricultural products. Other elements include economic co-operation, capital transfers, the establishment of companies, and social and cultural co-operation. President Bouteflika has indicated that Algeria will pursue its application for membership of the World Trade Organization, which has been under negotiation since 1987.

In December 2001 the Government introduced a number of new incentives for foreign investors. These reduced customs duties and tax on capital goods for new projects and gave tax relief on profits for 10 years. The Government also established the Agence Nationale de Développement de l'Investissement (ANDI) to advise on attracting foreign investment.

BANKING SYSTEM

The Banque Centrale d'Algérie (Banque d'Algérie from 1990) started its operations on 1 January 1963; it issued currency, regulated and licensed banks and supervised all foreign transactions. A state monopoly on all foreign financial transactions was imposed in November 1967; this followed a similar monopoly imposed on insurance in June 1966. State-run banks include the Banque Nationale d'Algérie (BNA), founded in 1966, traditionally service-sector based; Crédit Populaire d'Algérie, founded in 1966, strong in the construction sector; the BEA, founded in 1967, dealing with foreign trade; the Caisse Nationale d'Epargne et de Prévoyance, specializing in savings and housing loans; the BADR, founded in 1982, providing finance for the agricultural sector; and the Banque de Développement Local (BDL), founded in 1985, which has traditionally provided loans for companies run by local government. Legislation on banking and credit was introduced in 1986 to define the role of these institutions and of the central bank, and to improve their project-assessment capabilities, in addition to guaranteeing banking secrecy. In 1987 legislation was introduced to enable local commercial banks to provide credit directly to state-owned enterprises, as well as to private companies. The criteria for authorizing credit were modified, requiring the bank to assess a project primarily by its economic viability (including the company's ability to make repayments), rather than its social value. This legislation allowed banks to compete against each other for business, although they were not allowed to determine their own interest rates. In the same year the Conseil National de Crédit was established to supervise the implementation of the banking reforms and to determine the level of Algeria's foreign borrowing. In October 1988 banks were included in the group of more than 70 state-controlled companies which became EPEs. The BEA was the first state bank to become fully autonomous under the scheme. In 1998 the central bank authorized a transfer of US $8.13m. by the BEA to raise its stake in the Paris-based Union des Banques Arabes et Françaises.

Under the terms of the IMF accord signed in May 1995, five state-owned banks signed performance contracts of between one and three years with the Government in which they pledged to adhere to Bank for International Settlements' standards and to make their operations more transparent. The Government, for its part, would increase the banks' capital to help them restructure, but would phase out further subsidies over the contract period. The Ministry of Finance was to cease intervening in the running of the banks. The Government's aim was to prepare for privatization, encouraging banks to lessen their emphasis on lending and seek to expand their customer base. In April 1996 the Minister of Finance announced that the Government planned to restructure the five state-owned banks into five separate holdings, each with four subsidiaries specializing in financing areas such as leasing and equity participation. In March 1997 the Government announced that the first state bank to be opened to private investment would be the BDL, which drew 75% of its current clients from small and medium-sized private businesses. In mid-1999 the Minister of Finance stated that the bank was to be divided up into 10 regionally-based divisions, each of which was to be sold off to private investors. At the end of 1998 plans were announced to sell a 30% share in the country's largest bank, the BNA, to local and foreign investors. The process of exchanging foreign currency—hitherto monopolized by the state banks—was opened to the private sector in 1997. Following the drafting of regulations to permit private companies to enter the Algerian insurance market, a new insurance venture, Trust Algeria, was announced in mid-1997. Trust Insurance Co (of Bahrain) and Qatar General Insurance and Reinsurance Co were to hold 65% of the shares; the remainder was to be held by the state-owned Compagnie Algérienne d'Assurance et de Réassurance.

Algeria has also formed joint institutions with other countries. In 1974 an Algerian-Libyan bank, the Banque Internationale Arabe, opened in Paris to finance trade and investment between

France and Arab countries. Possible joint financial institutions have been discussed with Kuwait, Saudi Arabia and the UAE. The Banque de Coopération du Maghreb Arabe was established with Tunisia, in order to promote joint projects. In 1988 Algeria and Libya agreed to establish a joint bank, the Banque du Maghreb Arabe pour l'Investissement et le Commerce. In March 1990 a banking and investment law was approved that, for the first time since independence, permitted foreign investors, in most sectors, to own up to 100% of companies and to repatriate all of their profits. Foreign banks were to be allowed to establish representative branches. Three French banks had already opened 'liaison offices' in Algiers under the terms of earlier legislation. In June 1991 Al-Baraka Bank of Algeria, the country's first joint-venture bank, opened. It was also Algeria's first Islamic bank, and the two partners were the BADR and Dallah Al-Baraka (of Saudi Arabia). In June 1993 the Banque d'Algérie reported that legislation permitting the establishment of local private banks was in place and that applications to set up new institutions were being considered. The country's first local private bank, the Union Bank, was established in 1995 and had assets of AD 1,591m. at the end of 1997. Two further local private banks were authorized in early 1998: the El-Khalifa Bank, set up entirely by local investors (with 45 branches by 2001), and the El-Mouna Bank, established in Oran. By late 1998 Citibank of the USA had upgraded its representative office in Algiers to a full branch, and the Arab Banking Corpn (ABC) of Bahrain had become the first major international Arab bank to open an office in Algiers. ABC plans to establish a leasing firm—ABC-Algeria—in Algiers in partnership with IFC and local business interests. France's Natexis Groupe, Société Générale, SA and BNP received clearance to set up operations in Algeria, as did the Algerian-Saudi Leasing Co. In 2000 IFC announced that it would acquire a 20% stake in Algiers Investment Partnership, the first specialized full-service investment bank; Cairwood Group of the USA would hold 60% and local management the remaining 20%. In 2001 Banque d'Algérie gave approval for the establishment of BNP Paribas El-Djazair, a wholly-owned subsidiary of BNP Paribas, with capital of AD 500m. EFG Hermes of Egypt applied for a licence to open a commercial bank in Algeria in 2001. In early 2002 it was reported that the EU ambassador to Algeria had announced the establishment of the first Euro-Mediterranean bank to finance small businesses.

In January 1996 the Government announced the creation of two new financial institutions, an inter-bank foreign exchange market, the Bourse des Valeurs Mobilières, and a monitoring organization to control the new Algiers stock exchange, the Commission d'Organisation et de Surveillance des Opérations de Bourse (Cosob). The inter-bank foreign exchange market was to set the dinar's rate of exchange, based on bidding for currency by banks, other financial institutions and authorized intermediaries, bringing to an end the flexible system of fixing the value of the dinar (introduced in October 1994 under the IMF stand-by agreement). All dinar and convertible currency transactions were to pass through the inter-bank market, but the central bank was to retain control over the use of foreign exchange by intermediaries in order to prevent undue capital flight and large imports of luxury and other consumer goods. Non-hydrocarbons exports were expected to provide most of the receipts, and it was anticipated that the size of the market would increase in line with the growth of non-hydrocarbons exports, which were forecast to rise threefold by 1999. Cosob was entrusted with co-ordinating the establishment of the market and representing Algeria's nascent investment industry abroad. The new Algiers stock exchange began trading in July 1999, although only four securities were listed by early 2002. Amendments to the 1990 banking and investment law had given foreign investors free access to the stock exchange and the right to expatriate profits from stock trading.

In May 2000 the Minister of Finance informed the National People's Assembly that the current banking and financial system represented 'a real danger for national security', a comment which provoked an angry reaction from many deputies and from the finance workers' union, which condemned his remarks as 'defamatory and unacceptable'. Despite opposition from powerful interest groups, in November, in an address to the National Economic and Social Council, Prime Minister Ali Benflis declared that one of his Government's major priorities would be to intensify reforms to the banking sector. He admitted that the sector urgently needed modernization and that poor management and standard of service presented obstacles to the privatization programme. He also acknowledged that foreign and private investors were essential in order to diversify and enlarge the banking and financial sectors, and proceeded to outline a strategy aimed at consolidating existing reforms including the modernization and improvement of auditing procedures, training for staff and management, and the creation of new financial institutions and structures. In January 2001 Benflis announced that a ministerial commission had been established to reform the banking sector. Many observers regard the current banking system as one of the major obstacles to economic reform, and privatization of the state-owned banking system is unlikely to be pursued before far-reaching reforms to this sector have been achieved.

BUDGET

Statistics published in 1994 revealed that Algeria's budget was in deficit by more than AD 74,000m. in 1992 and by AD 192,000m. in 1993. The 1992 budget had introduced new corporate, income and value-added taxes; provided for higher investment in agriculture, mining and energy; and sought to limit the impact of price rises on poor families, partly by maintaining price subsidies on 10 essential food items. The 1993 budget included sharply higher defence and internal security spending. The original budget estimates for 1994 provided for a deficit of AD 125,300m. (9.6% of forecast GDP). However, Algeria's 1994 currency devaluation, together with lower-than-expected world petroleum prices, contributed to an actual deficit of some AD 160,000m. in 1994. In 1995 the Government originally budgeted for a deficit of AD 148,400m. (8.3% of forecast GDP), but subsequently undertook to curb the deficit through tighter fiscal policies when it agreed a structural reform programme with the IMF in May 1995.

In 1996 the Government originally budgeted for a deficit of AD 99,400m. (revenue AD 749,200m.; expenditure AD 848,600m.), and introduced various measures to improve revenues, including price increases for bread and petrol and steps to counter the evasion of an estimated AD 2,000m. of taxes each year. In the event, the actual deficit in 1996 was only about AD 31,500m., reflecting a rise in the average oil export price to US $22 per barrel, compared with the Government's original estimate of $16.50 per barrel. Provisional out-turn statistics for 1996 showed that AD 485,600m. had been raised in hydrocarbons taxes out of total revenue of AD 810,100m., while spending had totalled AD 841,600m. (slightly less than originally budgeted).

The 1997 budget provided for revenue of AD 829,400m., including AD 451,000m. from hydrocarbons taxes, and for expenditure of AD 914,100m., producing a deficit of AD 84,700m. However, the Government argued that there was in effect an underlying surplus of AD 7,400m., given that the expenditure total included an allowance for amortization of domestic debt (not included in previous years' budget calculations) and a once-only allocation of AD 78,000m. for a fund to restructure public-sector enterprises. The budget assumed an average 1997 petroleum export price of US $17.50 per barrel, and forecast an increase in the economic growth rate to 5% (compared with 4% in 1996), while the annual inflation rate was expected to fall to 10% (compared with an end-year rate of 15% in 1996). Capital spending was to be 10.3% higher than in 1996 and was to emphasize the completion of existing projects, while new projects would be required to demonstrate good growth potential. There was a reduction in the rate of value-added tax (VAT) for companies. The 1997 budget was revised in August 1997, setting revenues at AD 881,500m. (of which AD 507,000m. was anticipated from oil and gas) and expenditure at AD 946,200m., giving a deficit of AD 64,700m. The 1998 budget, given parliamentary approval in December 1997, projected revenues of AD 901,500m. (of which AD 528,000m. was anticipated from oil and gas) and set expenditure at AD 980,200m., giving a deficit of AD 78,700m.—representing 2.6% of GDP. Revenues from oil and gas were based on oil prices averaging $17 per barrel in 1998. To balance a sharp increase in current expenditure in 1998, capital spending was reduced substantially. As a result of falling oil prices, the 1998 budget was revised mid-year, increasing projected expenditure slightly to AD 1,022,000m. while setting projected revenues at AD 882,000m. (of which AD 460,000m. was anticipated from oil and gas, based on a forecast oil price of $15 per barrel), giving a much larger deficit of AD 140,000m. Towards the end of the year, despite a decline in oil prices to just over $10 per barrel, the Minister of Finance insisted that the budget remained under control, adding that the deficit could have been reduced but that this would have meant less spending on urgently-needed housing, capital equipment and water projects.

The 1999 budget projected spending at AD 1,098,000m. and revenue at AD 937,100m. (of which AD 480,000m. was expected from oil and gas, again based on a forecast oil price of US $15 per barrel), giving a deficit of AD 161,500m. According to the Minister of Finance, the higher projected deficit was to take account of higher debt repayments. Education and vocational training, and agriculture and irrigation accounted for the bulk of projected expenditure. As the price of oil did not exceed $11.75 per barrel during the early months of 1999, some observers forecast that the deficit could reach AD 184,400m. Later in 1999, as prospects for world oil prices improved, analysts forecast a budget deficit of AD 133,000m. In February there were reports that the Minister of Finance had instructed ministries to restrict their expenditure to 70% of allocations under the 1999 budget in order to avoid the necessity of formally adopting a revised budget. However, owing to the sharp rise in oil prices during the second half of 1999, official estimates suggested that the budget deficit was lower than projected—equivalent to 1.5% of GDP. The 2000 budget, approved by the National People's Assembly in late December 1999, projected spending at AD 1,252,000m. and revenue at AD 1,032,000m. (of which AD 524,000m. was expected from hydrocarbons, and was based on an average oil price of $15 per barrel), resulting in a deficit of AD 220,000m. Defence and education received the highest ministerial allocations. The outgoing Minister of Finance, Abdel-krim Harchaoui, stated that if higher oil prices during 2000 resulted in additional revenues, part of the excess would be used to reduce the budget deficit. In June 2000 parliament approved a revised budget for 2000 based on an average oil price of $19 per barrel. Although current spending was increased from AD 290,240m. to AD 346,010m., the revised budget projected a sharp fall in the budget deficit to AD 132,620m. (equivalent to 3.9% of GDP). Earlier the Minister of Finance had stated that to help finance the budget deficit, the Government was negotiating with international financial institutions to raise between $526m. and $875m. in loans and would seek $263m.–$394m. in domestic loans. The 2001 budget, approved in December 2000, projected spending at AD 1,251,000 and revenue at AD 1,234,000m., based on an average oil price of $19 per barrel, resulting in a expected deficit of AD 17,000m. Oil prices, however, were expected to be well in excess of $19 per barrel, and any revenues above the projected level were to be transferred to a stabilization fund established within the treasury in 2000 to support the budget should oil prices fall in the future. It was reported in September 2000 that the Banque d'Algérie had transferred some $3,000m. to the fund. The budget included a 33% increase to the monthly minimum wage effective from 1 January 2001 and a 15% increase in the monthly salaries of public-sector workers. Furthermore, VAT was to be simplified, and shopkeepers and small vendors were now to be exempt from the tax. In December 2001 parliament approved the 2002 budget, which projected spending at AD 1,559,850m. and revenue at AD 1,475,750m. (63% of which was to be derived from hydrocarbons revenues, based on an average oil price of $22 per barrel).

FOREIGN DEBT

During the 1970s Algeria borrowed heavily on the international markets to finance development, especially in its gas industry. Borrowing on the Euromarket, principally by SONATRACH, in one peak year, 1978, amounted to US $2,515m. In 1979 total borrowing declined by almost one-third. The total borrowing requirement for the 1980–84 Plan was estimated at $10,000m. Algeria avoided the Euromarkets during 1980–83, but after 1983 the country again began to borrow heavily on the international markets, owing to a steady erosion of its earnings from

hydrocarbons. Algeria's return to the international capital markets in 1983 ended a period during which the Government had managed to effect a net repayment of its external debt. The Organisation for Economic Co-operation and Development estimated that total external debt rose from $17,924m. at the end of 1983 to $26,020m. at the end of 1993. The cost of servicing the debt in the latter year was equivalent to 78% of Algeria's export earnings.

As detailed in the section on Government Strategy above, major rescheduling of sovereign debt (through the 'Paris Club') and of commercial debt (through the 'London Club') had been completed by 1996, temporarily eliminating the short-term component within Algeria's external debt and leaving a total long-term debt of US $33,421m. at the end of 1996. Statistics published by the World Bank in mid-1996 gave Algeria's 'financing gap' for 1995 as $6,000m., which was covered by $3,770m. of 'Paris Club' rescheduling, $1,010m. of 'London Club' rescheduling and $1,220m. of balance-of-payments support from the IMF, World Bank and other sources. In 1996 a gap of $4,780m. was covered by 'Paris Club' rescheduling ($2,810m.), 'London Club' rescheduling ($920m.) and balance-of-payments support ($1,050m.). By 1998 the World Bank expected the financing gap to be below $1,000m., and to be covered by $560m. of 'Paris Club' rescheduling and $400m. of balance-of-payments support. The first repayment of Algeria's 'London Club' debt was made in March 1998. During 1998, as the grace period in the 'Paris Club' and 'London Club' rescheduling agreements neared an end, debt-service repayments were forecast to rise to $5,210m. Algeria's total foreign debt stood at $30,894m. at the end of 1997, equivalent to 68% of GNP, down from 76% in 1996. In May 1998 the Minister of Finance stated that, despite falling petroleum prices, external debt-servicing would not absorb more than 50% of foreign-exchange reserves over the following three years. Total external debt fell slightly in 1998, to $30,676m., equivalent to 62% of GNP. Debt-servicing payments rose more sharply than had been expected, from $4,418m. in 1997 to $5,131m. in 1998. In 1999 the external debt fell to $28,005m., of which $25,903m. was long-term debt. Debt-servicing payments totalled $5,196m. There was a further decline in debt in 2000, to $25,002m. (according to World Bank data), equivalent to 49% of GNP. At the end of that year the Governor of the Banque d'Algérie forecast that most of the foreign debt would be erased by 2011—provided that no new borrowing was undertaken. The debt-service ratio was assessed by the World Bank at 37.0% of the value of exports of goods and services in 1999, falling markedly, to 19.6%, in 2000, with payments in the latter year totalling $4,467m. Principal repayments—$3,386m. in 1999, and $2,812m. in 2000—were expected to remain high but were predicted to decline gradually.

In March 1999 a Russian delegation visited Algeria; discussions included the issue of repayment of debt incurred with the former USSR, estimated at US $3,000m. In early 2000 Algeria came to an agreement with Poland to reschedule debts under 'Paris Club' terms. In June, following President Bouteflika's visit to France, the French Government agreed to convert Algerian debt to the value of 400m. French francs into investment. During a visit by the Spanish Prime Minister to Algeria in July, Spain also agreed a further debt conversion, although the amount of Algeria's debt to Spain to be converted into investments was not publicly released. Algeria was also to repay $60m. in debt (originally incurred in the 1980s to the former Czechoslovakia) to the Czech Republic over three years.

FOREIGN-EXCHANGE RESERVES

According to IMF data, Algeria's foreign-exchange reserves minus gold amounted to only US $404m. in July 1991, as the Government came under pressure to meet debt repayments, but rose to $1,094m. in October. In June 1993 officials of the Banque d'Algérie stated that reserves had been increased to $2,000m., the highest level since 1986, as a result of the Government's austerity programme. By the end of 1993, however, they had decreased again to $1,510m. Subsequent end-year reserves levels were $2,674m. (1994), $2,005m. (1995) and $4,235m. (1996). At the end of June 1997 the reserves totalled $6,440m., representing around nine months' import cover, and the end-year total was $8,047m. In May 1998 the Minister of Finance stated that foreign-exchange reserves currently stood at

$8,800m., but reserves contracted sharply, to $6,846m. by the end of the year, reflecting a draw-down to meet Algeria's debt repayment obligations. Reserves had fallen to $4,000m. by September 1999, but following the sharp increase in oil prices rose

to $4,526m. by the end of that year and $12,024m. by the end of 2000. By the end of 2001 foreign reserves had increased to $18,081m.

Statistical Survey

Source (unless otherwise stated): Office National des Statistiques, 8 rue des Moussebiline, BP 55, Algiers; tel. (2) 64-77-90; e-mail ons@onssiege.ons.dz; internet www.ons.dz.

Area and Population

AREA, POPULATION AND DENSITY

Area (sq km)	2,381,741*
Population (census results)†	
20 April 1987	23,038,942
25 June 1998 (provisional)	
Males	14,471,318
Females	14,801,025
Total	29,272,343
Population (official estimates at mid-year)	
1999	29,950,000
2000	30,386,000
2001	30,836,000
Density (per sq km) at mid-2001	12.9

* 919,595 sq miles.
† Excluding Algerian nationals residing abroad, numbering an estimated 828,000 at 1 January 1978.

POPULATION BY WILAYA (ADMINISTRATIVE DISTRICT)
(provisional, 1998 census)

	Area (sq km)	Population	Density (per sq km)
Adrar	439,700	311,615	0.7
Aïn Defla	4,897	660,342	134.9
Aïn Témouchent	2,379	327,331	137.6
Algiers (el-Djezaïr) . . .	273	2,562,428	9,386.2
Annaba	1,439	557,818	387.6
Batna	12,192	962,623	79.0
el-Bayadh	78,870	168,789	2.1
Béchar	162,200	225,546	1.4
Béjaïa	3,268	856,840	262.2
Biskra (Beskra)	20,986	575,858	27.4
Blida (el-Boulaïda) . . .	1,696	784,283	462.4
Borj Bou Arreridj . . .	4,115	555,402	135.0
Bouira	4,439	629,560	141.8
Boumerdes	1,591	647,389	406.9
Chlef (ech-Cheliff) . . .	4,795	858,695	179.1
Constantine (Qacetina) . .	2,187	810,914	370.8
Djelfa	66,415	797,706	12.0
Ghardaïa	86,105	300,516	3.5
Guelma	4,101	430,000	104.9
Illizi	285,000	34,108	0.1
Jijel	2,577	573,208	222.4
Khenchela	9,811	327,917	33.4
Laghouat	25,057	317,125	12.7
Mascara (Mouaskar) . . .	5,941	676,192	113.8
Médéa (Lemdiyya) . . .	8,866	802,078	90.5
Mila	9,375	674,480	71.9
Mostaganem	2,175	631,057	290.1
M'Sila	18,718	805,519	43.0
Naâma	29,950	127,314	4.3
Oran (Ouahran)	2,121	1,213,839	572.3
Ouargla	211,980	445,619	2.1
el-Oued	54,573	504,401	9.2
Oum el-Bouaghi	6,768	519,170	76.7
Relizane (Ghilizane) . . .	4,870	642,205	131.9
Saïda	6,764	279,526	41.3
Sétif	6,504	1,311,413	201.6
Sidi-bel-Abbès	9,096	525,632	57.8
Skikda	4,026	786,154	195.3

—continued	Area (sq km)	Population	Density (per sq km)
Souk Ahras	4,541	367,455	80.9
Tamanrasset (Tamanghest) . .	556,200	137,175	0.3
el-Tarf	3,339	352,588	105.6
Tebessa	14,227	549,066	38.6
Tiaret	20,673	725,853	35.1
Tindouf	159,000	27,060	0.2
Tipaza	2,166	506,053	233.6
Tissemsilt	3,152	264,240	83.8
Tizi Ouzou	3,568	1,108,708	310.7
Tlemcen	9,061	842,053	92.9
Total*	**2,381,741**	**29,100,867**	**12.2**

* Excluding Sahrawi refugees in camps (171,476 in 1998).

PRINCIPAL TOWNS (provisional, population at 1998 census)

Algiers (el-Djezaïr, capital) . .	1,519,570	Djelfa	154,265
		Tébassa (Tbessa) .	153,246
Oran (Ouahran) .	655,852	Blida (el-Boulaïda) .	153,083
Constantine (Qacentina) . . .	462,187	Skikda . . .	152,335
Batna . . .	242,514	Béjaia	147,076
Annaba . . .	215,083	Tiaret (Tihert) . .	145,332
Sétif (Stif) . .	211,859	Chlef	133,874
Sidi-bel-Abbès .	180,260	el-Buni . . .	133,471
Biskra (Beskra) .	170,956	Béchar . . .	131,010

BIRTHS, MARRIAGES AND DEATHS*

	Registered live births†		Registered marriages		Registered deaths†	
	Number	Rate (per 1,000)	Number	Rate (per 1,000)	Number	Rate (per 1,000)
1993 . .	775,000	28.2	153,137	5.7	168,000	6.3
1994 . .	776,000	28.2	147,954	5.4	180,000	6.6
1995 . .	711,000	25.3	152,786	5.5	180,000	6.4
1996 . .	654,000	22.9	156,870	5.5	172,000	6.0
1997 . .	654,000	22.5	157,831	5.4	178,000	6.1
1998 . .	620,000	21.0	158,298	5.4	172,000	5.8
1999 . .	605,000	21.2	163,126	5.5	168,000	5.6
2000 . .	600,000	19.8	177,548	5.8	166,000	5.5

* Figures refer to the Algerian population only. Birth registration is estimated to be at least 90% complete, but the registration of marriages and deaths is incomplete. According to UN estimates, the average annual rates per 1,000 in 1995–2000 were: births 25.9; deaths 7.5.
† Excluding live-born infants dying before registration of birth.

Expectation of life (WHO estimates, years at birth, 2000): Males 68.1; Females 71.2. (Source: WHO, *World Health Report*).

ECONOMICALLY ACTIVE POPULATION (1987 census)*

	Males	Females	Total
Agriculture, hunting, forestry and fishing	714,947	9,753	724,699
Mining and quarrying	64,685	3,142	67,825
Manufacturing	471,471	40,632	512,105
Electricity, gas and water.	40,196	1,579	41,775
Construction.	677,211	12,372	689,586
Trade, restaurants and hotels.	376,590	14,399	390,990
Transport, storage and communications	207,314	9,029	216,343
Financing, insurance, real estate and business services	125,426	17,751	143,178
Community, social and personal services	945,560	234,803	1,180,364
Activities not adequately defined	149,241	83,718	232,959
Total employed	3,772,641	427,183	4,199,824
Unemployed	1,076,018	65,260	1,141,278
Total labour force	4,848,659	492,443	5,341,102

* Employment data relate to persons aged 6 years and over; those for unemployment relate to persons aged 16 to 64 years. Estimates have been made independently, so the totals may not be the sum of the component parts.

1997 (sample survey, '000 persons, July–September): Agriculture, hunting, forestry and fishing 884; Mining and quarrying, manufacturing, electricity, gas and water 584; Construction 588; Trade, restaurants and hotels 838; Government services 1,317; Other services 1,496; Total employed 5,708 (males 4,819, females 889); Unemployed 2,049 (males 1,769, females 280); Total labour force 7,757 (males 6,588, females 1,169). Figures refer to males aged 15 to 60 years and females aged 15 to 55 years.

Mid-2000 (estimates in '000): Agriculture, etc. 2,545; Total labour force 10,458 (Source: FAO).

Health and Welfare

KEY INDICATORS

Fertility (births per woman, 2000).	3.0
Under-5 mortality rate (per 1,000 live births, 2000).	65
HIV/AIDS (% of persons aged 15–49, 1999).	0.10
Physicians (per 1,000 head, 1995) .	0.85
Hospital beds (per 1,000 head, 1994)	2.1
Health expenditure (1998): US $ per head (PPP)	148
% of GDP	4.1
public (% of total)	80.2
Access to water (% of persons, 2000)	94
Access to sanitation (% of persons, 2000)	73
Human Development Index (2000): ranking	106
value	0.697

For sources and definitions, see explanatory note on p. vi.

Agriculture

PRINCIPAL CROPS ('000 metric tons)

	1998	1999	2000
Wheat	2,280	1,470	760
Barley	700	510	163
Oats	45	40	8
Potatoes.	1,100	996	1,208
Broad beans, dry.	21	22	13
Chick-peas	18	13	7
Almonds	22	26	26
Olives	124	363	217
Rapeseed*	100	100	100
Cabbages	19	22	19
Artichokes	45	30	39
Tomatoes	752	955	800*
Cauliflowers	39	40	44
Pumpkins, squash and gourds	87	92	95
Cucumbers and gherkins .	42	46	53
Aubergines (Eggplants) .	31	34	38
Chillies and green peppers	157	156	175
Dry onions	393	382	316
Garlic	30	30	36
Green beans.	22	26	26
Green peas	47	45	47
Green broad beans	102	119	78
Carrots .	141	135	149
Other vegetables*	216	266	251
Oranges .	280	307	300
Tangerines, mandarins, clementines and satsumas .	111	115	102
Lemons and limes	25	29	29
Apples	75	87	97
Pears	60	82	74
Apricots.	58	74	56
Peaches and nectarines	45	61	59
Plums	21	25	26
Grapes	147	178	204
Watermelons	502	538	399
Figs.	42	51	54
Dates	387	428	366
Other fruits .	45	52	57
Pimento and allspice*	7	7	8
Tobacco (leaves) .	7	6	7

* FAO estimate(s).

Source: FAO.

LIVESTOCK ('000 head, year ending September)

	1998	1999	2000
Sheep	17,900	18,200	19,500
Goats	3,257	3,400	3,400
Cattle	1,317	1,650	1,650
Horses	46	46	47*
Mules	50	50*	50*
Asses	183	180*	180*
Camels	154	220	235
Chickens (million)	125	105	110*

* FAO estimate.

Source: FAO.

LIVESTOCK PRODUCTS ('000 metric tons)

	1998	1999	2000
Beef and veal	103	117	133
Mutton and lamb	167	163	164
Goat meat	12	12	12
Poultry meat	220	210	210
Rabbit meat	7	7	7
Other meat	4	4	3
Cows' milk	984	1,040	1,170
Sheep's milk	180	220	180
Goats' milk	160	143	153
Poultry eggs*	112	125	127
Honey	2	2	2
Wool: greasy	22	23	24
scoured*	11	12	12
Cattle hides	11	13	13
Sheepskins	22	24	24
Goatskins	2	2	2

* FAO estimates.

Source: FAO.

Forestry

ROUNDWOOD REMOVALS
(FAO estimates, '000 cubic metres, excl. bark)

	1997	1998	1999
Sawlogs, veneer logs and logs for sleepers	68	68	68
Pulpwood	85	85	85
Other industrial wood	285	291	298
Fuel wood	2,239	2,291	2,344
Total	2,677	2,735	2,795

2000: Production as in 1999 (FAO estimates).

Sawnwood production ('000 cubic metres, incl. railway sleepers): 13 per year (FAO estimates) in 1980–2000.

Source: FAO.

Fishing

('000 metric tons, live weight)

	1997	1998	1999
Capture	91.6	92.3	105.7
Bogue	1.6	3.2	3.5
Jack and horse mackerels	5.5	4.8	6.2
Sardinellas	15.7	10.0	11.4
European pilchard (sardine)	49.1	49.3	56.7
European anchovy	1.9	3.5	3.1
Northern bluefin tuna	0.3	0.5	5.0
Crustaceans and molluscs	2.9	3.6	3.3
Aquaculture	0.3*	0.3	0.3
Total catch	91.9*	92.6	105.9

* FAO estimate.

Source: FAO, *Yearbook of Fishery Statistics.*

Mining

('000 metric tons, unless otherwise indicated)

	1998	1999	2000*
Crude petroleum ('000 barrels)	454,750	457,158	476,288
Natural gas (million cu m)†	125,971	128,783	139,499
Iron ore:			
gross weight	1,783	1,336	1,645
metal content	900	680	n.a.
Lead concentrates (metric tons)‡	730	1,215	818
Zinc concentrates (metric tons)‡	4,555	9,808	10,452
Mercury (metric tons)‡	224	240	216
Phosphate rock§	1,155	1,096	877
Barite (Barytes)	37	51	52
Salt (unrefined)	172	164*	182
Gypsum (crude)*	275	1,316	1,341

* Provisional or estimated data.

† Figures refer to gross volume. Production on a dry basis (in million cu m) was: 96,873 in 1998; 97,151 in 1999; 100,092 in 2000.

‡ Figures refer to the metal content of ores or concentrates.

§ Figures refer to gross weight. The estimated phosphoric acid content (in '000 metric tons) was 358 in 1998; 340 in 1999; 265 in 2000.

Source: US Geological Survey.

Industry

SELECTED PRODUCTS ('000 metric tons, unless otherwise indicated)

	1997	1998	1999
Olive oil (crude)*	46	15	57
Refined sugar	68	58	48
Wine*	26	34	42
Beer ('000 hectolitres)	379	382	383
Soft drinks ('000 hectolitres)	599	375	315
Footwear—excl. rubber ('000 pairs)	2,542	1,249	1,167
Nitrogenous fertilizers (a)†	28‡	41‡	57
Phosphate fertilizers (b)†	118	183	201
Naphthas‡	4,043	3,855	n.a.
Motor spirit (petrol)	1,989	2,037‡	n.a.
Kerosene‡	325	317	n.a.
Jet fuel‡	1,197	970	n.a.
Gas-diesel (distillate fuel) oils	6,523	6,198‡	n.a.
Residual fuel oils	5,556	5,061‡	n.a.
Lubricating oils‡	98	104	n.a.
Petroleum bitumen (asphalt)‡	183	171	n.a.
Liquefied petroleum gas:			
from natural gas plants‡	6,186	7,089	n.a.
from petroleum refineries‡	477	466	n.a.
Cement	7,146	7,836	7,587
Pig-iron for steel-making§	526	757	807
Crude steel (ingots)§	361	581	675
Zinc—unwrought	31.4	23.7	24.9
Refrigerators for household use ('000)	175	215	181
Telephones (million)	3	30	151
Television receivers ('000)	172	251	173
Buses and coaches—assembled (number)	264	307	529
Lorries—assembled (number)	1,293	1,798	1,583
Electric energy (million kWh)	21,489	23,615‡	n.a.

2000 (FAO estimates, '000 metric tons)*: Olive oil (crude) 50‡; Wine 36.

* Data from FAO.

† Production in terms of (a) nitrogen or (b) phosphoric acid.

‡ Provisional or estimated figure(s).

§ Data from the US Geological Survey.

Source: mainly UN, *Industrial Commodity Statistics Yearbook.*

Finance

CURRENCY AND EXCHANGE RATES

Monetary Units

100 centimes = 1 Algerian dinar (AD).

Sterling, Dollar and Euro Equivalents (31 May 2002)

£1 sterling = 117.36 dinars;
US $1 = 80.01 dinars;
€1 = 75.11 dinars;
1,000 Algerian dinars = £8.521 = $12.498 = €13.314

Average Exchange Rate (dinars per US $)

1999	66.574
2000	75.260
2001	77.215

BUDGET ('000 million AD)*

Revenue	1998	1999	2000
Hydrocarbon revenue. . . .	425.9	588.2	1,213.2
Export taxes	328.6	510.1	n.a.
Domestic receipts . . .	50.0	50.0	n.a.
Dividends and entry rights . .	47.3	28.1	40.0
Other revenue	348.7	358.4	364.9
Tax revenue	329.8	314.8	349.5
Taxes on income and profits .	88.1	72.2	82.0
Taxes on goods and services .	154.9	149.7	165.0
Customs duties . . .	75.5	80.2	86.3
Non-tax revenue . . .	18.9	43.6	15.4
Total	774.6	950.5	1,578.1

Expenditure†	1998	1999	2000
Current expenditure . . .	664.1	774.7	856.2
Personnel expenditure . . .	268.6	286.1	289.6
War veterans' pensions . . .	37.9	59.9	57.7
Material and supplies . . .	47.5	53.6	54.6
Public services . . .	75.2	81.9	92.0
Hospitals . . .	28.8	31.2	33.0
Current transfers . . .	124.1	166.8	200.0
Family allowances . .	42.5	36.2	29.0
Public works and social assistance. . . .	13.6	14.2	8.6
Food subsidies . . .	0.2	0.4	0.5
Housing	19.0	14.5	8.6
Interest payments . . .	110.8	126.4	162.3
Capital expenditure . . .	211.9	187.0	321.9
Total	875.7	961.7	1,178.1

* Figures refer to operations of the central Government, excluding special accounts. The balance (revenue less expenditure) on such accounts (in '000 million AD) was: –6.9 in 1998; –5.6 in 1999; –0.7 in 2000.
† Excluding net lending by the Treasury ('000 million AD): 0.1 in 1998; –0.3 in 1999; 0.5 in 2000.

Source: IMF, *Algeria: Statistical Appendix* (September 2001).

CENTRAL BANK RESERVES (US $ million at 31 December)

	1999	2000	2001
Gold*	268	255	246
IMF special drawing rights . .	2	3	11
Reserve position in IMF . .	117	111	107
Foreign exchange	4,407	11,910	17,963
Total	4,794	12,278	18,327

* Valued at SDR 35 per troy ounce.

Source: IMF, *International Financial Statistics.*

MONEY SUPPLY (million AD at 31 December)

	1999	2000	2001
Currency outside banks . . .	440,263	484,948	577,355
Demand deposits at deposit money banks.	352,707	460,267	524,731
Checking deposits at post office .	87,428	89,090	96,998
Private sector demand deposits at treasury	9,384	7,066	9,435
Total money (incl. others) . .	889,784	1,044,020	1,210,250

Source: IMF, *International Financial Statistics.*

COST OF LIVING (Consumer Price Index; base: 1990 = 100)

	1999	2000	2001
Foodstuffs, beverages and tobacco	471.6	461.6	481.7
All items (incl. others) . . .	467.7	464.8	481.1

Source: UN, *Monthly Bulletin of Statistics.*

NATIONAL ACCOUNTS (million AD at current prices)

National Income and Product

	1998	1999	2000
Compensation of employees . .	785,838.1	846,679.2	882,826.4
Operating surplus	1,289,716.7	1,544,284.9	2,085,199.8
Domestic factor incomes . .	2,075,554.8	2,390,964.1	2,968,026.2
Consumption of fixed capital .	218,993.4	262,852.8	357,371.6
Gross domestic product (GDP) at factor cost .	2,294,548.2	2,653,816.9	3,325,397.8
Indirect taxes, *less* subsidies .	515,576.2	561,308.2	753,277.5
GDP in purchasers' values .	2,810,124.4	3,215,125.1	4,078,675.3
Factor income received from abroad	25,958.0	19,920.2	37,700.8
Less Factor income paid abroad	140,715.5	167,254.2	211,390.2
Gross national product .	2,695,366.9	3,067,791.1	3,904,985.9
Less Consumption of fixed capital	218,993.4	262,852.8	357,371.6
National income in market prices	2,476,373.5	2,804,938.3	3,547,614.3
Other current transfers from abroad	97,071.0	101,473.8	106,247.8
Less Other current transfers paid abroad	3,152.6	3,423.8	29,201.3
National disposable income .	2,570,291.9	2,902,988.3	3,624,660.8

Expenditure on the Gross Domestic Product

	1998	1999	2000
Government final consumption expenditure	503,630.7	543,603.9	560,193.1
Private final consumption expenditure . . .	1,555,370.7	1,667,199.8	1,713,206.5
Increase in stocks . . .	26,191.1	35,114.8	15,232.3
Gross fixed capital formation .	728,754.1	789,798.6	869,325.6
Total domestic expenditure .	2,813,946.6	3,035,717.1	3,157,957.5
Exports of goods and services .	652,257.3	918,889.0	1,748,978.7
Less Imports of goods and services .	656,079.5	739,481.0	828,260.9
GDP in purchasers' values .	2,810,124.4	3,215,125.1	4,078,675.3

Gross Domestic Product by Economic Activity

	1998	1999	2000†
Agriculture, forestry and fishing .	304,479.6	338,233.8	325,751.1
Hydrocarbons*	673,692.8	927,361.2	1,666,235.5
Mining (excl. hydrocarbons) . .			
Manufacturing (excl. hydrocarbons) . . .	256,821.0	4,710.7 / 225,624.6	5,021.6 / 234,623.9
Electricity and water . . .		40,037.2	44,108.0
Construction	265,412.0	271,257.7	292,046.3
Wholesale and retail trade . .	380,362.2	406,307.2	431,909.9
Hotels and restaurants . . .	38,795.5	46,384.6	46,930.0
Transport and communications .	206,470.2	238,856.0	272,696.8
Finance, real estate and business services	114,895.1	126,989.5	136,590.7
Government services . . .	333,092.8	353,930.8	359,744.4
Other services to households .	48,003.1	51,731.2	58,106.6
Sub-total	2,622,024.3	3,031,424.4	3,873,764.8
Import duties	226,924.8	226,271.7	250,063.4
Less Imputed bank service charges	38,824.7	42,571.0	45,152.9
GDP in purchasers' values .	2,810,124.4	3,215,125.1	4,078,675.3

* Extraction and processing of petroleum and natural gas, including related services and public works.

† Provisional.

BALANCE OF PAYMENTS (US $ million)

	1998	1999	2000
Exports of goods f.o.b. . . .	10,126	12,325	21,650
Imports of goods f.o.b. . . .	−8,629	−8,960	−9,030
Trade balance	1,497	3,365	12,620
Exports of services . . .	777	720	910
Imports of services . . .	−2,311	−2,560	−2,360
Balance on goods and services .	−37	1,525	11,170
Other income received . . .	340	220	380
Other income paid	−2,286	−2,510	−3,090
Balance on goods, services and income	−1,983	−765	8,460
Transfers (net)	1,064	790	790
Current balance	−919	25	9,250
Direct investment (net) . . .	505	460	420
Official capital (net) . . .	−1,104	−1,957	−1,960
Short-term credit (net), net errors and omissions	352	−995	−147
Overall balance	−1,166	−2,467	7,563

Source: Ministry of Finance.

External Trade

Note: Data exclude military goods. Exports include stores and bunkers for foreign ships and aircraft.

PRINCIPAL COMMODITIES (distribution by SITC, US $ million)

Imports c.i.f.	1997	1998	1999
Food and live animals . .	2,502.3	2,438.3	2,222.1
Dairy products and birds' eggs .	442.7	481.8	437.9
Milk and cream . . .	384.4	411.1	365.9
Cereals and cereal preparations .	1,270.9	1,025.9	908.4
Wheat and meslin (unmilled) .	730.4	691.2	660.8
Meal and flour of wheat, etc. .	318.6	112.5	8.4
Crude materials (inedible) except fuels	307.5	273.2	263.4
Animal and vegetable oils, fats and waxes	214.9	312.9	230.5
Chemicals and related products	853.0	1,051.0	1,073.7
Medicinal and pharmaceutical products	373.4	503.8	534.8
Medicaments (incl. veterinary) .	336.3	468.9	499.9
Basic manufactures . .	1,502.6	1,681.8	1,666.6
Iron and steel	547.5	594.5	654.2
Tubes, pipes and fittings . .	203.4	191.5	301.7

Imports c.i.f. — *continued*	1997	1998	1999
Machinery and transport equipment	2,725.6	3,040.2	3,034.9
Power-generating machinery and equipment	216.6	296.4	255.2
Machinery specialized for particular industries . .	246.7	325.2	342.1
General industrial machinery, equipment and parts . .	796.6	800.7	859.6
Electrical machinery, apparatus, etc.	704.9	748.7	705.5
Road vehicles and parts* . .	537.0	648.8	666.1
Miscellaneous manufactured articles	407.6	422.7	459.6
Total (incl. others) . . .	8,688.4	9,403.4	9,161.9

* Excluding tyres, engines and electrical parts.

Exports f.o.b.	1997	1998	1999
Mineral fuels, lubricants, etc. .	13,504.1	9,544.0	12,167.2
Petroleum, petroleum products, etc.	7,952.8	5,502.1	6,940.0
Crude petroleum oils, etc. . .	5,646.5	4,084.2	4,975.1
Refined petroleum products .	2,185.0	1,340.4	1,882.6
Gas oils (distillate fuels) . .	627.7	378.6	515.6
Residual fuel oils . . .	695.2	390.9	596.3
Gas (natural and manufactured) .	5,548.3	4,041.8	5,227.2
Liquefied petroleum gases .	3,487.6	2,791.0	2,888.1
Petroleum gases, etc., in the gaseous state	2,061.2	1,250.8	2,339.2
Total (incl. others) . . .	13,894.1	9,838.6	12,525.3

Source: UN, *International Trade Statistics Yearbook*.

2000 (US $ million): Total imports c.i.f. 9,173; Total exports f.o.b. 22,031.
2001 (US $ million): Total imports c.i.f. 9,910; Total exports f.o.b. 19,132.

PRINCIPAL TRADING PARTNERS (US $ million)*

Imports c.i.f.	1997	1998	1999
Argentina	52.9	87.9	122.8
Austria	90.7	102.1	108.2
Belgium†	228.8	247.8	192.9
Brazil	87.1	57.7	104.8
Canada	489.1	523.2	385.8
China, People's Republic .	163.8	211.7	229.5
Côte d'Ivoire	54.9	105.2	77.4
France (incl. Monaco) . .	2,009.5	2,241.3	2,086.1
Finland	77.9	81.5	97.4
Germany	482.6	645.1	678.7
Italy	750.7	845.8	907.4
Japan	318.5	205.7	356.6
Korea, Republic . . .	99.2	209.4	308.8
Mexico	40.1	28.1	104.4
Netherlands	204.6	189.1	164.0
Poland	94.6	69.6	40.5
Russia	110.9	122.5	135.7
Spain	603.7	547.3	507.6
Sweden	101.1	105.0	75.4
Switzerland-Liechtenstein .	68.4	105.3	107.8
Syria	240.3	135.8	65.4
Turkey	313.9	410.8	337.6
Ukraine	57.9	75.2	122.7
United Kingdom . . .	280.6	250.4	218.6
USA	921.0	991.7	769.7
Total (incl. others) . . .	8,688.4	9,403.4	9,161.9

Exports f.o.b.	1997	1998	1999
Austria .	185.3	66.3	5.8
Belgium† .	504.1	420.8	327.4
Brazil .	746.6	632.2	964.0
Canada .	470.2	358.9	405.0
France (incl. Monaco)	2,189.1	1,675.9	1,719.1
Germany .	309.5	166.7	198.4
Italy .	2,866.3	1,841.6	2,942.2
Netherlands .	1,170.4	806.8	1,021.3
Portugal.	74.4	61.5	154.0
Singapore .	139.6	8.0	18.7
Spain .	1,247.2	960.3	1,329.0
Turkey .	810.9	579.3	605.3
United Kingdom .	252.4	258.4	233.2
USA .	2,221.8	1,520.0	1,755.1
Total (incl. others)	13,894.7	9,838.6	12,525.3

* Imports by country of production; exports by country of last consignment.
† Figures for 1997 and 1998 include trade with Luxembourg.

Source: UN, *International Trade Statistics Yearbook.*

Transport

RAILWAYS (traffic)

	1997	1998	1999
Passengers carried ('000) .	38,101	34,132	32,027
Freight carried ('000 metric tons) .	7,927	8,292	7,842
Passenger-km (million) .	1,360	1,163	1,069
Freight ton-km (million) .	2,892	2,174	2,033

ROAD TRAFFIC (motor vehicles in use at 31 December)

	1998	1999	2000
Passenger cars .	1,634,394	1,676,784	1,692,148
Lorries .	295,106	296,660	296,145
Vans .	589,042	604,644	609,617
Buses and coaches .	32,602	37,932	42,791
Motorcycles .	9,025	9,119	9,198

SHIPPING

Merchant Fleet (registered at 31 December)

	1999	2000	2001
Number of vessels .	148	142	143
Total displacement ('000 grt) .	1,004.7	960.8	963.9

Source: Lloyd's Register-Fairplay, *World Fleet Statistics.*

International Sea-borne Freight Traffic ('000 metric tons)

	1997	1998	1999
Goods loaded .	74,300	75,500	77,900
Goods unloaded .	15,200	16,000	16,600

Note: Figures are rounded to the nearest 100,000 metric tons.

CIVIL AVIATION (traffic on scheduled services)

	1996	1997	1998
Kilometres flown (million) .	31	34	31
Passengers carried ('000) .	3,494	3,518	3,382
Passenger-km (million) .	2,863	3,130	3,012
Total ton-km (million) .	274	299	292

Source: UN, *Statistical Yearbook.*

Tourism

FOREIGN TOURIST ARRIVALS BY COUNTRY OF ORIGIN*

	1998	1999	2000
France .	38,357	49,559	64,839
Germany .	1,721	3,168	4,784
Italy .	3,419	4,483	7,158
Libya .	4,305	4,117	4,851
Mali .	7,105	9,878	8,857
Morocco .	2,399	2,949	3,805
Spain .	5,518	4,652	7,048
Tunisia .	20,056	22,779	32,481
Total (incl. others) .	107,202	140,861	175,538

* Excluding arrivals of Algerian nationals resident abroad: 571,234 in 1998; 607,675 in 1999; 690,446 in 2000.

Source: World Tourism Organization, *Yearbook of Tourism Statistics.*

Tourism receipts (US $ million): 74 in 1998; 80 in 1999; 102 in 2000.

Communications Media

	1999	2000	2001
Television receivers ('000 in use)	3,300	3,400	n.a.
Telephones ('000 main lines in use)	1,600.0	1,761.3	1,880.0
Mobile cellular telephones (subscribers) .	72	86	100
Personal computers ('000 in use)	180	200	220
Internet users ('000) .	20	50	60

1990: Non-daily newspapers 37 (average circulation 1,409,000 copies); Other periodicals 48 (average circulation 803,000 copies).

1996: Book production (titles)* 670; Daily newspapers 5 (average circulation 1,080,000 copies).

1997: Radio receivers ('000 in use): 7,100; Facsimile machines (number in use) 7,000.

* Excluding pamphlets.

Sources: UNESCO, *Statistical Yearbook*; International Telecommunication Union.

Education

(1996/97, unless otherwise indicated)

	Institutions	Teachers	Pupils
Pre-primary. .	n.a.	1,333	33,503
Primary .	15,426	170,956	4,674,947
Secondary			
General .	} 4,138 {	145,160	2,480,168
Vocational .		6,788	138,074
Higher			
Universities, etc.* .	n.a.	14,364	267,142
Distance-learning institutions* .	n.a.	3,213	60,095
Other* .	n.a.	2,333	20,173

* 1995/96.

Sources: UNESCO, *Statistical Yearbook,* and Ministère de l'Education nationale.

1998/99 (Pre-primary and primary): 15,729 institutions; 170,562 teachers; 4,843,313 pupils.

Adult literacy rate (UNESCO estimates): 66.7% (males 76.2%; females 57.1%) in 2000 (Source: UN Development Programme, *Human Development Report*).

Directory

The Constitution

A new Constitution for the Democratic and People's Republic of Algeria, approved by popular referendum, was promulgated on 22 November 1976. The Constitution was amended by the National People's Assembly on 30 June 1979. Further amendments were approved by referendum on 3 November 1988, on 23 February 1989, and on 28 November 1996. On 8 April 2002 the National People's Assembly approved an amendment, which granted Tamazight, the language spoken by the Berber population of the country, the status of a national language. The main provisions of the Constitution, as amended, are summarized below:

The preamble recalls that Algeria owes its independence to a war of liberation which led to the creation of a modern sovereign state, guaranteeing social justice, equality and liberty for all. It emphasizes Algeria's Islamic, Arab and Amazigh (Berber) heritage, and stresses that, as an Arab Mediterranean and African country, it forms an integral part of the Great Arab Maghreb.

FUNDAMENTAL PRINCIPLES OF THE ORGANIZATION OF ALGERIAN SOCIETY

The Republic

Algeria is a popular, democratic state. Islam is the state religion and Arabic and Tamazight are the official national languages.

The People

National sovereignty resides in the people and is exercised through its elected representatives. The institutions of the State consolidate national unity and protect the fundamental rights of its citizens. The exploitation of one individual by another is forbidden.

The State

The State is exclusively at the service of the people. Those holding positions of responsibility must live solely on their salaries and may not, directly or by the agency of others, engage in any remunerative activity.

Fundamental Freedoms and the Rights of Man and the Citizen

Fundamental rights and freedoms are guaranteed. All discrimination on grounds of sex, race or belief is forbidden. Law cannot operate retrospectively, and a person is presumed innocent until proved guilty. Victims of judicial error shall receive compensation from the State.

The State guarantees the inviolability of the home, of private life and of the person. The State also guarantees the secrecy of correspondence, the freedom of conscience and opinion, freedom of intellectual, artistic and scientific creation, and freedom of expression and assembly.

The State guarantees the right to form political associations (on condition that they are not based on differences in religion, language, race, gender or region), to join a trade union, the right to strike, the right to work, to protection, to security, to health, to leisure, to education, etc. It also guarantees the right to leave the national territory, within the limits set by law.

Duties of Citizens

Every citizen must respect the Constitution, and must protect public property and safeguard national independence. The law sanctions the duty of parents to educate and protect their children, as well as the duty of children to help and support their parents. Every citizen must contribute towards public expenditure through the payment of taxes.

The National Popular Army

The army safeguards national independence and sovereignty.

Principles of Foreign Policy

Algeria subscribes to the principles and objectives of the UN. It advocates international co-operation, the development of friendly relations between states, on the basis of equality and mutual interest, and non-interference in the internal affairs of states.

POWER AND ITS ORGANIZATION

The Executive

The President of the Republic is Head of State, Head of the Armed Forces and responsible for national defence. He must be of Algerian origin, a Muslim and more than 40 years old. He is elected by universal, secret, direct suffrage. His mandate is for five years, and is renewable once. The President embodies the unity of the nation. The President presides over meetings of the Council of Ministers. He decides and conducts foreign policy and appoints the Head of Government, who is responsible to the National People's Assembly. The Head of Government must appoint a Council of Ministers. He drafts, co-ordinates and implements his government's programme, which he must present to the Assembly for ratification. Should the Assembly reject the programme, the Head of Government and the Council of Ministers resign, and the President appoints a new Head of Government. Should the newly-appointed Head of Government's programme be rejected by the Assembly, the President dissolves the Assembly, and a general election is held. Should the President be unable to perform his functions, owing to a long and serious illness, the President of the Council of the Nation assumes the office for a maximum period of 45 days (subject to the approval of a two-thirds' majority in the National People's Assembly and the Council of the Nation). If the President is still unable to perform his functions after 45 days, the Presidency is declared vacant by the Constitutional Council. Should the Presidency fall vacant, the President of the Council of the Nation temporarily assumes the office and organizes presidential elections within 60 days. He may not himself be a candidate in the election. The President presides over a High Security Council which advises on all matters affecting national security.

The Legislature

The legislature consists of the Assemblée Populaire Nationale (National People's Assembly) and the Conseil de la Nation (Council of the Nation, which was established by constitutional amendments approved by national referendum in November 1996). The members of the lower chamber, the National People's Assembly, are elected by universal, direct, secret suffrage for a five-year term. Two-thirds of the members of the upper chamber, the Council of the Nation, are elected by indirect, secret suffrage from regional and municipal authorities; the remainder are appointed by the President of the Republic. The Council's term in office is six years; one-half of its members are replaced every three years. The deputies enjoy parliamentary immunity. The legislature sits for two ordinary sessions per year, each of not less than four months' duration. The commissions of the legislature are in permanent session. The two parliamentary chambers may be summoned to meet for an extraordinary session on the request of the President of the Republic, or of the Head of Government, or of two-thirds of the members of the National People's Assembly. Both the Head of Government and the parliamentary chambers may initiate legislation. Legislation must be deliberated upon respectively by the National People's Assembly and the Council of the Nation before promulgation. Any text passed by the Assembly must be approved by three-quarters of the members of the Council in order to become legislation.

The Judiciary

Judges obey only the law. They defend society and fundamental freedoms. The right of the accused to a defence is guaranteed. The Supreme Court regulates the activities of courts and tribunals, and the State Council regulates the administrative judiciary. The Higher Court of the Magistrature is presided over by the President of the Republic; the Minister of Justice is Vice-President of the Court. All magistrates are answerable to the Higher Court for the manner in which they fulfil their functions. The High State Court is empowered to judge the President of the Republic in cases of high treason, and the Head of Government for crimes and offences.

The Constitutional Council

The Constitutional Council is responsible for ensuring that the Constitution is respected, and that referendums, the election of the President of the Republic and legislative elections are conducted in accordance with the law. The Constitutional Council comprises nine members, of whom three are appointed by the President of the Republic, two elected by the National People's Assembly, two elected by the Council of the Nation, one elected by the Supreme Court and one elected by the State Council. The Council's term in office is six years; the President of the Council is appointed for a six-year term and one-half of the remaining members are replaced every three years.

The High Islamic Council

The High Islamic Council is an advisory body on matters relating to Islam. The Council comprises 15 members and its President is appointed by the President of the Republic.

Constitutional Revision

The Constitution can be revised on the initiative of the President of the Republic (subject to approval by the National People's Assembly and by three-quarters of the members of the Council of the Nation), and must be approved by national referendum. Should the Constitutional Council decide that a draft constitutional amendment does not in any way affect the general principles governing Algerian society, it may permit the President of the Republic to promulgate the amendment directly (without submitting it to referendum) if it has been approved by three-quarters of the members of both parliamentary chambers. Three-quarters of the members of both parliamentary chambers, in a joint sitting, may propose a constitutional amendment to the President of the Republic who may submit it to referendum. The basic principles of the Constitution may not be revised.

The Government

HEAD OF STATE

President and Minister of Defence: ABDELAZIZ BOUTEFLIKA (inaugurated 27 April 1999).

COUNCIL OF MINISTERS
(September 2002)

Prime Minister: ALI BENFLIS.

Minister of State, Personal Representative of the President of the Republic: AHMED OUYAHIA.

Minister of State for the Interior and Local Authorities: NOUREDDINE YAZID ZERHOUNI.

Minister of State for Foreign Affairs: ABDELAZIZ BELKHADEM.

Minister of Justice and Attorney-General: MUHAMMAD CHARFI.

Minister of Participation and Investment Promotion: Prof. ABDELHAMID TEMMAR.

Minister of Commerce: NOUREDDINE BOUKROUH.

Minister of Energy and Mines: Prof. CHAKIB KHELIL.

Minister of Religious Affairs and Endowments: Prof. BOUAB-DELLAH GHLAMALLAH.

Minister of War Veterans: MUHAMMAD CHERIF ABBAS.

Minister of Town Planning and the Environment: CHERIF RAHMANI.

Minister of Transport: ABDELMALEK SELLAL.

Minister of Youth and Sports: Prof. BOUBEKEUR BENBOUZID.

Minister of Agriculture and Rural Development: Dr SAÏD BERKAT.

Minister of Tourism: LAKHDAR DORBANI.

Minister of Public Works: Dr OMAR GHOUL.

Minister of Health, Population and Hospital Reform: Prof. ABDELMADJID ABERKANE.

Minister of Finance: MUHAMMAD TERBECHE.

Minister of Communications and Culture, and Government Spokesperson: KHALIDA TOUMI-MESSAOUDI.

Minister of Water Resources: ADBELMADJID ATTAR.

Minister of Small and Medium-sized Enterprises and Handicrafts: MUSTAPHA BENBADA.

Minister of National Education: NOUREDDINE SALAH.

Minister of Higher Education and Scientific Research: Dr RACHID HARROUBIA.

Minister of Postal Services, Telecommunications and Information Technology: Prof. ZINE EDDINE YOUBI.

Minister of Vocational Training: Dr ABDELHAMID ABAD.

Minister of Housing and Urban Development: MUHAMMAD NADIR HAMIMID.

Minister of Industry: EL-HACHEMI DJAABOUB.

Minister of Labour and Social Security: TAYEB LOUH.

Minister of Employment and National Solidarity: TAYEB BELAIZ.

Minister in charge of Relations with Parliament: NOUREDDINE TALEB.

Minister of Fisheries and Marine Resources: Dr SMAIL MIMOUNE.

Minister-delegate to the Minister of State for Foreign Affairs, in charge of Maghreb and African Affairs: ABDELKADER MESSAHEL.

Minister-delegate to the Minister of State for the Interior and Local Authorities, responsible for Local Authorities: DAHO OULD KABLIA.

Minister-delegate to the Prime Minister, in charge of Family and Women's Affairs: Prof. BOUTHEINA CHERIET.

Minister-delegate to the Prime Minister, in charge of the Algerian Expatriate Community: FATMA ZOHRA BOUCHELMA.

Minister-delegate to the Minister of Justice, in charge of Prison Reform: ABDELKADER SALLAT.

Minister-delegate to the Minister of Agriculture and Rural Development, in charge of Rural Development: Dr RACHID BENAISSA.

Minister-delegate to the Minister of Higher Education and Scientific Research, in charge of Scientific Research: Prof. LEILA HAMMOU BOUTLELIS.

Minister-delegate to the Minister of Finance, responsible for Financial Reform: FATIHA MENTOURI.

Secretary-General of the Government: AHMED NOUI.

MINISTRIES

Office of the President: Présidence de la République, el-Mouradia, Algiers; tel. (21) 69-15-15; fax (21) 69-15-95.

Office of the Prime Minister: rue Docteur Saâdane, Algiers; tel. (21) 73-23-40; fax (21) 71-79-27.

Ministry of Agriculture and Rural Development: 4 route des Quatre Canons, Algiers; tel. (21) 71-17-12; fax (21) 61-57-39.

Ministry of Commerce: rue Docteur Saâdane, Algiers; tel. (21) 73-23-40; fax (21) 73-54-18; internet www.ministereducommerce-dz.org.

Ministry of Communications and Culture: Palais de la Culture, Les Annassers, Kouba, Algiers; tel. (21) 69-22-01; fax (21) 68-40-41.

Ministry of Defence: Les Tagarins, el-Biar, Algiers; tel. (21) 71-15-15; fax (21) 64-67-26.

Ministry of Employment and National Solidarity: Palais du Government, Algiers; tel. (21) 71-91-38; fax (21) 73-59-96.

Ministry of Energy and Mines: 80 ave Ahmed Ghermoul, Algiers; tel. (21) 67-33-00; fax (21) 67-03-66; e-mail info@mem-algeria.org; internet www.mem-algeria.org.

Ministry of Finance: Immeuble Maurétania, place du Pérou, Algiers; tel. (21) 71-13-66; fax (21) 73-42-76; e-mail algeriafinance @multimania.com; internet www.multimania.com/algeriafinance.

Ministry of Fisheries and Marine Resources: Algiers.

Ministry of Foreign Affairs: place Mohamed Seddik Benyahia, el-Mouradia, Algiers; tel. (21) 69-23-33; fax (21) 69-21-61; internet www.mae.dz.

Ministry of Health, Population and Hospital Reform: 125 rue Abd ar-Rahmane Laâla, el-Madania, Algiers; tel. (21) 68-29-00; fax (21) 66-24-13; www.ands.dz.

Ministry of Higher Education and Scientific Research: 11 rue Doudou Mokhtar, Algiers; tel. (21) 91-12-56; fax (21) 91-11-97; e-mail mesrs@ist.cerist.dz; internet www.mesrs.edu.dz.

Ministry of Housing and Urban Development: 137 rue Didouche Mourad, Algiers; tel. (21) 74-07-22; fax (21) 74-53-83.

Ministry of Industry: Immeuble le Colisée, 4 rue Ahmed Bey, Algiers; tel. (21) 60-11-44; fax (21) 69-32-35; e-mail info@mir-algeria.org; internet www.mir-algeria.org.

Ministry of the Interior and Local Authorities: 18 rue Docteur Saâdane, Algiers; tel. (21) 73-23-40; fax (21) 73-43-67.

Ministry of Justice: 8 place Bir Hakem, el-Biar, Algiers; tel. (21) 92-41-83; fax (21) 92-25-60.

Ministry of Labour and Social Security: 40–44 blvd Mohamed Belouizdad, Algiers; tel. (21) 65-99-99; fax (21) 66-26-08; e-mail mtps@wissal.dz.

Ministry of National Education: 8 ave de Pékin, Algiers; tel. (21) 60-67-57; fax (21) 60-57-82; e-mail men@meducation.edu.dz; internet www.meducation.edu.dz.

Ministry of Participation and Investment Promotion: Chemin Ibn Badis el-Mouiz, El-Biar, Algiers; tel. (21) 92-98-85; fax (21) 92-17-55.

Ministry of Postal Services, Telecommunications and Information Technology: 4 blvd Krim Belkacem, Algiers; tel. (21) 71-12-20; fax (21) 71-92-71; internet www.barid.dz.

Ministry of Public Works: Algiers.

Ministry of Religious Affairs and Endowments: 4 rue de Timgad, Hydra, Algiers; tel. (21) 60-85-55; fax (21) 60-09-36.

Ministry of Small and Medium-sized Enterprises and Handicrafts: Immeuble le Colisée, 4 rue Ahmed Bey, Algiers; tel. (21) 69-73-63; fax (21) 23-00-94.

Ministry of Tourism: 7 rue des Frères Ziata, el-Mouradia, 16000 Algiers; tel. (21) 60-33-55; fax (21) 59-13-15.

Ministry of Town Planning and the Environment: Algiers.

Ministry of Transport: 119 rue Didouche Mourad, Algiers; tel. (21) 74-06-99; fax (21) 74-33-95.

Ministry of Vocational Training: Algiers.

Ministry of War Veterans: 2 ave du Lt. Med Benarfa, el-Biar, Algiers; tel. (21) 92-23-55; fax (21) 92-35-16.

Ministry of Water Resources: BP 86, Ex Grand Séminaire, Algiers; tel. (21) 68-95-00; fax (21) 58-63-64.

Ministry of Youth and Sports: 3 rue Mohamed Belouizdad, Algiers; tel. (21) 66-33-50; fax (21) 68-41-71.

President and Legislature

PRESIDENT

Presidential Election, 15 April 1999

Candidate*	Votes	% of votes
Abdelaziz Bouteflika	7,445,045	73.76
Ahmed Taleb Ibrahimi	1,265,594	12.54
Sheikh Abdallah Djaballah	400,080	3.96
Hocine Aït Ahmed	321,179	3.18
Mouloud Hamrouche	314,160	3.11
Mokdad Sifi	226,139	2.24
Youcef Khateb	121,414	1.20
Total†	10,093,611	100.00

* Six of the seven presidential candidates withdrew prior to the election, leaving Abdelaziz Bouteflika as the only remaining official contestant.
† Excluding 559,012 invalid votes.

LEGISLATURE
National People's Assembly

President: KARIM YOUNÈS.

General Election, 30 May 2002

	Seats
Front de libération nationale (FLN)	199
Rassemblement national démocratique (RND)	47
Mouvement de la réforme nationale (MRN)	43
Mouvement de la société pour la paix (MSP)	38
Parti des travailleurs (PT)	21
Front national algérien	8
Nahdah	1
Parti du renouveau algérien (PRA)	1
Mouvement de l'entente nationale (MEN)	1
Independents	30
Total	389

Council of the Nation

President: ABDELKADER BENSALAH.

Elections, 25 December 1997 and 30 December 2000*

	Seats*
Rassemblement national démocratique (RND)	74
Front de libération nationale (FLN)	15
Front des forces socialistes (FFS)	4
Mouvement de la société pour la paix (MSP)	3
Appointed by the President†	48
Total	144

* Deputies of the Council of the Nation serve a six-year term; one-half of its members are replaced every three years. Elected representatives are selected by indirect, secret suffrage from regional and municipal authorities.
† Appointed on 4 January 2001.

Political Organizations

Until 1989 the FLN was the only legal party in Algeria. The February 1989 amendments to the Constitution permitted the formation of other political associations, with some restrictions. The right to establish political parties was guaranteed by constitutional amendments in November 1996; however, political associations based on differences in religion, language, race, gender or region were proscribed. Some 39 political parties contested the legislative elections that took place in June 1997. The most important political organizations are listed below.

Alliance nationale républicaine (ANR): Algiers; f. 1995; anti-Islamist; Leader REDHA MALEK.

Congrès national algérien: Algiers; f. 1999; Leader ABDELKADER BELHAYE.

Front démocratique: Algiers; f. 1999; Leader SID-AHMED GHOZALI.

Front des forces socialistes (FFS): 56 ave Souidani Boudjemaâ, 16000 Algiers; tel. (21) 59-33-13; fax (21) 59-11-45; internet www .f-f-s.com; f. 1963; revived 1990; Leader HOCINE AÏT AHMED.

Front islamique du salut (FIS): Algiers; e-mail mail @fisalgeria.org; internet www.fisalgeria.org; f. 1989; aims to emphasize the importance of Islam in political and social life; formally dissolved by the Algiers Court of Appeal in March 1992; Leader ABBASI MADANI.

Front de libération nationale (FLN): 7 rue du Stade, Hydra, Algiers; tel. (21) 59-21-49. 1954; sole legal party until 1989; socialist in outlook, the party is organized into a Secretariat, a Political Bureau, a Central Committee, Federations, Kasmas and cells; under the aegis of the FLN are various mass political organizations, including the Union Nationale de la Jeunesse Algérienne (UNJA) and the Union Nationale des Femmes Algériennes (UNFA); Sec.-Gen. ALI BENFLIS.

Front national algérien: Algiers; f. 1999; advocates eradication of poverty and supports the Govt's peace initiative; Pres. MOUSSA TOUATI.

Front national de renouvellement (FNR): Algiers; Leader ZINEDDINE CHERIFI.

Mouvement algérien pour la justice et le développement (MAJD): Villa Laibi, Lot Kapiot No. 5, Bouzaréah, Algiers; tel. (21) 60-58-00; fax (21) 78-78-72; f. 1990; reformist party supporting policies of fmr Pres. Boumedienne; Leader MOULAY HABIB.

Mouvement pour la démocratie et la citoyenneté (MDC): Tizi-Ouzou; f. 1997 by dissident members of the FFS; Leader SAÏD KHELIL.

Mouvement démocratique et social (MDS): Algiers; internet www.mds.pol.dz; f. 1998 by fmr mems of Ettahaddi; left-wing party; 4,000 mems; Sec.-Gen. HACHEMI CHERIF.

Mouvement pour la liberté: Algiers; f. 1999; in opposition to Pres. Bouteflika; Leader MOULOUD HAMROUCHE.

Mouvement de la réforme nationale (MRN): Algiers; f. 1998; Leader Sheikh ABDALLAH DJABALLAH.

Mouvement de la société pour la paix (MSP): 163 Hassiba Ben Bouali, Algiers; e-mail bureau@hms-algeria.net; internet www .hms-algeria.net; f. as Hamas; adopted current name in 1997; moderate Islamic party, favouring the gradual introduction of an Islamic state; Leader Sheikh MAHFOUD NAHNAH.

Nahdah: Algiers; fundamentalist Islamist group; Sec.-Gen. HABIB ADAMI.

Parti démocratique progressif (PDR): Algiers; f. 1990 as a legal party; Leader SACI MABROUK.

Parti national pour la solidarité et le développement (PNSD): BP 110, Staouéli, Algiers; tel. and fax (21) 39-40-42; e-mail cherif_taleb@yahoo.fr; f. 1989 as Parti social démocrate; Leader MOHAMED CHERIF TALEB.

Parti du renouveau algérien (PRA): Algiers; tel. (21) 56-62-78; Sec.-Gen. YACINE TERKMANE; Leader NOUREDDINE BOUKROUH.

Parti républicain progressif (PRP): 10 rue Ouahrani Abou-Mediêne, Cité Seddikia, Oran; tel. (41) 35-79-36; f. 1990 as a legal party; Sec.-Gen. SLIMANE CHERIF.

Parti des travailleurs (PT): Algiers; workers' party; Leader LOUISA HANOUNE.

Rassemblement pour la concorde nationale: Algiers; f. 2001 to support the policies of President Bouteflika; Chair. SID AHMED ABACHI.

Rassemblement pour la culture et la démocratie (RCD): 40 rue Muhammad Chabane, el-Biar, Algiers; tel. (21) 92-50-76; fax (21) 92-51-01; internet www.rcd-algerie.org; f. 1989; secular party; advocates inclusion of Berber traditions into the Algerian identity; Pres. SAÏD SAÂDI.

Rassemblement national démocratique (RND): Algiers; f. 1997; centrist party; Sec.-Gen. AHMED OUYAHIA.

Union pour la démocratie et les libertés (UDL): Algiers; f. 1997; Leader ABDELKRIM SEDDIKI.

Wafa wa al-Adl (Wafa): Algiers; f. 1999; Leader AHMED TALEB IBRAHIMI.

The following groups are in armed conflict with the Government:

Da'wa wal Djihad—Groupe salafiste pour la prédication et le combat (GSPC): f. 1998; breakaway group from the GIA; particularly active in the east of Algiers and in the Kabyle; responds to preaching by Ali Belhadj, the second most prominent member of the proscribed FIS; Leader Hassan Hattab.

Groupe islamique armé (GIA): the most prominent and radical Islamist militant group; Leader Rachid Abou Tourab.

Diplomatic Representation

EMBASSIES IN ALGERIA

Angola: 14 rue Marie Curie, el-Biar, Algiers; tel. (21) 92-54-41; fax (21) 79-74-41; Ambassador: José César Augusto.

Argentina: 7 rue Hamami, 16000 Algiers; tel. (21) 71-86-83; fax (21) 64-38-43; e-mail emargentin@djazair-connect.com; Ambassador: Jorge Alberto Rafael Vehils.

Austria: 17 chemin Abdel Kader Gadouche, 16035 Hydra, Algiers; tel. (21) 69-10-86; fax (21) 69-12-32; e-mail obalgier@mail.com; Ambassador: Thomas Michael Baier.

Belgium: 22 chemin Youcef Tayebi, el-Biar, Algiers; tel. (21) 92-24-46; fax (21) 92-50-36; Ambassador: Dirk Lettens.

Benin: 36 Lot du Stade, Birkhadem, Algiers; tel. (21) 56-52-71; Ambassador: Leonard Adjin.

Brazil: 10 chemin Laroussi Messaoud Les Glycines, BP 186, Algiers; tel. (21) 74-95-75; fax (21) 74-96-87; Ambassador: Sérgio Thompson-Flores.

Bulgaria: 13 blvd Col Bougara, Algiers; tel. (21) 23-00-14; fax (21) 23-05-33; Ambassador: Peter Gradev.

Burkina Faso: 23 Lot el-Feth, Poirson, el-Biar, BP 212 Didouche Mourad, Algiers; tel. (21) 92-33-39; fax (21) 92-73-90; e-mail abf@wissal.dz.

Cameroon: 26 chemin Cheikh Bachir El-Ibrahimi, 16011 el-Biar, Algiers; tel. (21) 92-11-24; fax (21) 92-11-25; ambacam_alger@yahoo.fr; Chargé d'affaires: Jean Missoup.

Canada: 18 rue Mustapha Khalef, Ben Aknoun, BP 48, 16000 Alger-Gare, Algiers; tel. (21) 91-49-51; fax (21) 91-49-73; Ambassador: Richard Belliveau.

Chad: Villa No. 18, Cité DNC, chemin Ahmed Kara, Hydra, Algiers; tel. (21) 69-26-62; fax (21) 69-26-63; Ambassador: El-Hadj Mahamoud Adji.

China, People's Republic: 34 blvd des Martyrs, Algiers; tel. (21) 69-27-24; fax (21) 69-29-62; Ambassador: Zheng Aquan.

Congo, Democratic Republic: BP 302, Algiers; tel. (21) 59-12-27; Ambassador: Ikaki Bomele Molingo.

Congo, Republic: 111 Parc Ben Omar, Kouba, Algiers; tel. (21) 58-68-00; Ambassador: Pierre N'Gaka.

Côte d'Ivoire: Immeuble 'Le Bosquet', Le Paradou, BP 260 Hydra, Algiers; tel. (21) 69-23-78; fax (21) 69-36-83; Ambassador: Gustave Ouffoue-Kouassi.

Cuba: 22 rue Larbi Alik, Hydra, Algiers; tel. (21) 69-21-48; fax (21) 69-32-81; Ambassador: Rafael Polanco Brahojos.

Czech Republic: BP 358, Villa Koudia, 3 chemin Ziryab, Alger-Gare; Algiers; tel. (21) 23-00-56; fax (21) 23-01-03; e-mail algiers@embassy.mzv.cz; Ambassador: Jaromír Marek.

Denmark: 12 ave Emile Marquis, Lot Djenane el-Malik, 16035 Hydra, BP 384, 16000 Alger-Gare, Algiers; tel. (21) 69-27-55; fax (21) 69-28-46; e-mail ambadane@djazair-connect.com; Ambassador: Bo Eric Weber.

Egypt: BP 297, 8 chemin Abdel-Kader Gadouche, 16300 Hydra, Algiers; tel. (21) 60-16-73; fax (21) 60-29-52; Ambassador: Ibrahim Youssri.

Finland: BP 256, 16035 Hydra, Algiers; tel. (21) 69-29-25; fax (21) 69-16-37; e-mail finamb@wissal.dz.

France: chemin Abd al-Kader Gadouche, Hydra, Algiers; tel. (21) 69-24-88; fax (21) 69-13-69; Ambassador: Daniel Bernard.

Gabon: BP 125, Rostomia, 21 rue Hadj Ahmed Mohamed, Hydra, Algiers; tel. (21) 69-24-00; fax (21) 60-25-46; Ambassador: Yves Ongollo.

Germany: BP 664, Alger-Gare, 165 chemin Sfindja, Algiers; tel. (21) 74-19-56; fax (21) 74-05-21; e-mail amballemagne@djazair-connect.com; Ambassador: Hans Peter Schiff.

Ghana: 62 rue des Frères Benali Abdellah, Hydra, Algiers; tel. (21) 60-64-44; fax (21) 69-28-56; Ambassador: George A. O. Kugblenu.

Greece: 60 blvd Col Bougara, Algiers; tel. (21) 92-34-91; fax (21) 69-16-55; Ambassador: Ioannis Drakoularakos.

Guinea: 43 blvd Central Saïd Hamdine, Hydra, Algiers; tel. (21) 69-20-66; fax (21) 69-34-68; Ambassador: Mamady Condé.

Guinea-Bissau: 17 rue Ahmad Kara, BP 32, Colonne Volrol, Hydra, Algiers; tel. (21) 60-01-51; fax (21) 60-97-25; Ambassador: José Pereira Batista.

Holy See: 1 rue Noureddine Mekiri, 16090 Bologhine, Algiers (Apostolic Nunciature); tel. (21) 95-45-20; fax (21) 95-40-95; e-mail nuntiusalger@hotmail.com; Apostolic Nuncio: Most Rev. Augustine Kasujja, Titular Archbishop of Caesarea in Numidia.

Hungary: BP 68, 18 ave des Frères Oughlis, el-Mouradia, Algiers; tel. (21) 69-79-75; fax (21) 69-81-86; e-mail huembalg@yahoo.com; Chargé d'affaires: László Szabó.

India: 14 rue des Abassides, BP 108, el-Biar, 16030 Algiers; tel. (21) 92-04-11; fax (21) 92-32-88; e-mail indemb@wissal.dz; Ambassador: (vacant).

Indonesia: BP 62, 16 chemin Abd al-Kader Gadouche, 16070 el-Mouradia, Algiers; tel. (21) 69-20-11; fax (21) 69-39-31; Ambassador: Lillahi Grahana Sidharta.

Iraq: 4 rue Abri Arezki, Hydra, Algiers; tel. (21) 69-31-25; fax (21) 69-10-97; Ambassador: Abd al-Karim al-Mulla.

Italy: 18 rue Muhammad Ouidir Amellal, el-Biar, 16030 Algiers; tel. (21) 92-23-30; fax (21) 92-59-86; e-mail ambitalgeri@ambitalgeri.org; Ambassador: Romualdo Bettini.

Japan: 1 chemin el-Bakri, el-Biar, Algiers; tel. (21) 91-20-04; fax (21) 91-20-46; Ambassador: Urabe Akira.

Jordan: 6 rue du Chenoua, Algiers; tel. (21) 60-20-31; Ambassador: Khaled Abidat.

Korea, Democratic People's Republic: 49 rue Hamlia, Bologhine, Algiers; tel. (21) 62-39-27; Ambassador: Pak Ho Il.

Korea, Republic: BP 92, 17 chemin Abdelkader Gadouche, Hydra, Algiers; tel. (21) 69-36-20; fax (21) 69-16-03; Ambassador: Heung-Sik Choi.

Kuwait: chemin Abd al-Kader Gadouche, Hydra, Algiers; tel. (21) 59-31-57; Ambassador: Shamlan Abd-al-Aziz Muhammad ar-Rumi.

Lebanon: 9 rue Kaïd Ahmad, el-Biar, Algiers; tel. (21) 78-20-94; Ambassador: Salhad Nasri.

Libya: 15 chemin Cheikh Bachir Ibrahimi, Algiers; tel. (21) 92-15-02; fax (21) 92-46-87; Ambassador: Abdel-Moula el-Ghadhbane.

Madagascar: 22 rue Abd al-Kader Aouis, 16090 Bologhine, BP 65, Algiers; tel. (21) 95-03-89; fax (21) 95-17-76; Ambassador: Laurent Radaody-Rakotondravao.

Mali: Villa 15, Cité DNC/ANP, chemin Ahmed Kara, Hydra, Algiers; tel. (21) 69-13-51; fax (21) 69-20-82; Ambassador: Cheick S. Diarra.

Mauritania: 107 Lot Baranès, Air de France, Bouzaréah, Algiers; tel. (21) 79-21-39; fax (21) 78-42-74; Ambassador: Sid Ahmed Ould Babamine.

Mexico: BP 329, 21 rue du Commandant Amar Azzouz (ex rue Général Lapperine), el-Biar, 16030 Algiers; tel. (21) 92-40-23; fax (21) 92-34-51; e-mail mexiarl@ist.wissal.dz; Ambassador: Franciso Correa Villalobos.

Morocco: 8 rue des Cèdres, el-Mouradia, Algiers; tel. (21) 69-14-08; fax (21) 69-29-00; Ambassador: Abderrazak Doghmi.

Netherlands: BP 72, el-Biar, Algiers; tel. (21) 92-28-28; fax (21) 92-37-70; e-mail nldalg@wissal.dz; Ambassador: J. W. de Waal.

Niger: 54 rue Vercors Rostamia Bouzaréah, Algiers; tel. (21) 78-89-21; fax (21) 78-97-13; Ambassador: Gourouza Oumarou.

Nigeria: BP 629, 27 bis rue Blaise Pascal, Algiers; tel. (21) 69-18-49; fax (21) 69-11-75; Ambassador: Aliyu Mohammed.

Oman: 53 rue Djamel Eddine, El Afghani, Bouzaréah, Algiers; tel. (21) 94-13-10; fax (21) 94-13-75; Ambassador: Hellal as-Siyabi.

Pakistan: BP 404, 62A Djenane el-Malik, Le Pardou, Hydra, Algiers; tel. (21) 69-37-81; fax (21) 69-22-12; e-mail parepalgiers@gwissal.dz; Ambassador: M. Aslam Rizvi.

Poland: 37 ave Mustafa Ali Khodja, el-Biar, Algiers; tel. (21) 92-25-53; fax (21) 92-14-35; e-mail lupina@wissal.dz; Ambassador: Andrzej Michal Lupina.

Portugal: 4 rue Mohamed Khoudi, el-Biar, Algiers; tel. (21) 92-53-13; fax (21) 92-54-14; e-mail portemdz@hotmail.com; Ambassador: Eduardo Farinha Fernandes.

Qatar: BP 118, 7 chemin Doudou Mokhtar, Algiers; tel. (21) 92-28-56; fax (21) 92-14-15; Ambassador: Hussain Ali ed-Dousri.

Romania: 24 rue Abri Arezki, Hydra, Algiers; tel. (21) 60-08-71; fax (21) 69-36-42; Ambassador: Dumitru Olaru.

Russia: 7 chemin du Prince d'Annam, el-Biar, Algiers; tel. (21) 92-31-39; fax (21) 92-28-82; Ambassador: Aleksandr Adsenyonok.

Saudi Arabia: 62 rue Med. Drafini, chemin de la Madeleine, Hydra, Algiers; tel. (21) 60-35-18; Ambassador: Hasan Faqqi.

Senegal: BP 379, Alger-Gare, 1 chemin Mahmoud Drarnine, Hydra, Algiers; tel. (21) 69-16-27; fax (21) 69-26-84; Ambassador: Saïdou Nourou.

Slovakia: BP 84, 7 chemin du Ziryab, Didouche Mourad, 16006 Algiers; tel. (21) 23-01-31; fax (21) 23-00-51; e-mail amb.slovaque .alger@centrum.sk; Chargé d'affaires a.i.: Dr JÁN DÖMÖK.

South Africa: Sofitel Hotel, 172 rue Hassuba Ben Bouali, Algiers; tel. (21) 68-52-10; fax (21) 66-21-04.

Spain: 46 bis rue Mohamed Chabane, el-Biar, Algiers; tel. (21) 92-27-13; fax (21) 92-27-19; Ambassador: EMILIO FERNÁNDEZ-CASTAÑO.

Sudan: Algiers; tel. (21) 56-66-23; fax (21) 69-30-19; Ambassador: YOUCEF FADUL AHMED.

Sweden: rue Olof Palme, Nouveau Paradou, Hydra, Algiers; tel. (21) 69-23-00; fax (21) 69-19-17; Ambassador: ANDREAS ADAHL.

Switzerland: BP 443, 2 rue Numéro 3, 16035 Hydra, Algiers; tel. (21) 60-04-22; fax (21) 60-98-54; Ambassador: ANDRÉ VON GRAFFEN-INED.

Syria: Domaine Tamzali, 11 chemin Abd al-Kader Gadouche, Hydra, Algiers; tel. (21) 91-20-26; fax (21) 91-20-30; Ambassador: HAMMADI SAID.

Tunisia: 11 rue du Bois de Boulogne, el-Mouradia, Algiers; tel. (21) 60-13-88; fax (21) 69-23-16; Ambassador: MOHAMED EL FADHAL KHALIL.

Turkey: Villa dar el Ouard, chemin de la Rochelle, blvd Col Bougara, Algiers; tel. (21) 23-00-04; fax (21) 23-01-12; e-mail cezayir.be@mfa .gov.tr; Ambassador: ATTILA UZER.

Ukraine: 199 rue des Frères Belhafid, Hydra, Algiers; tel. (21) 69-13-87. Ambassador: (vacant).

United Arab Emirates: BP 165, Alger-Gare, 14 rue Muhammad Drarini, Hydra, Algiers; tel. (21) 69-25-74; fax (21) 69-37-70; Ambassador: HAMAD SAÏD AZ-ZAABI.

United Kingdom: BP 08, Alger-Gare, 16000 Algiers, 6 ave Souidani Boudjemaa, Algiers; tel. (21) 23-00-68; fax (21) 23-00-67; Ambassador: GRAHAM HAND.

USA: BP 549, 4 chemin Cheikh Bachir Ibrahimi, 16000 Alger-Gare, Algiers; tel. (21) 60-11-86; fax (21) 60-39-79; e-mail amembalg@ist .cerist.dz; Ambassador: JANET SANDERSON.

Venezuela: BP 297, 3 impasse Ahmed Kara, Algiers; tel. (21) 69-38-46; fax (21) 69-35-55; Ambassador: EDUARDO SOTO ALVAREZ.

Viet Nam: 30 rue de Chenoua, Hydra, Algiers; tel. (21) 69-27-52; fax (21) 69-37-78; Ambassador: TRAN XUAN MAN.

Yemen: Villa 19, Cité DNC, rue Ahmed Kara, Hydra, Algiers; tel. (21) 69-30-85; fax (21) 69-17-58; Ambassador: GASSEM ASKAR DJEBRANE.

Yugoslavia: BP 561, 7 rue des Frères Ben-hafid, Hydra, Algiers; tel. (21) 69-12-18; fax (21) 69-34-72; e-mail yuga@wissal.dz; Chargé d'affaires a.i.: JOVAN DASIĆ.

Judicial System

The highest court of justice is the Supreme Court (Cour suprême) in Algiers, established in 1963, which is served by 150 judges. Justice is exercised through 183 courts (tribunaux) and 31 appeal courts (cours d'appel), grouped on a regional basis. New legislation, promulgated in March 1997, provided for the eventual establishment of 214 courts and 48 appeal courts. The Cour des comptes was established in 1979. Algeria adopted a penal code in 1966, retaining the death penalty. In February 1993 three special courts were established to try suspects accused of terrorist offences; however, the courts were abolished in February 1995. Constitutional amendments introduced in November 1996 provided for the establishment of a High State Court (empowered to judge the President of the Republic in cases of high treason, and the Head of Government for crimes and offences), and a State Council to regulate the administrative judiciary. In addition, a Conflicts Tribunal is to be established to adjudicate in disputes between the Supreme Court and the State Council.

Supreme Court: ave du 11 décembre 1960, Ben Aknoun, Algiers; tel. and fax (21) 92-44-89.

President of Supreme Court: MUHAMMAD ZAGHLOUL BOUTERENE.

Attorney-General: MUHAMMAD CHARFI.

Religion

ISLAM

Islam is the official religion, and the whole Algerian population, with a few exceptions, is Muslim.

High Islamic Council: place Cheikh Abd al-Hamid ibn Badis, Algiers.

President of the High Islamic Council: (vacant).

CHRISTIANITY

The European inhabitants, and a few Arabs, are generally Christians, mostly Roman Catholics.

The Roman Catholic Church

Algeria comprises one archdiocese and three dioceses (including one directly responsible to the Holy See). In December 2000 there were an estimated 3,450 adherents in the country.

Bishops' Conference: Conférence des Evêques de la Région Nord de l'Afrique (CERNA), 13 rue Khélifa-Boukhalfa, 16000 Alger-Gare, Algiers; tel. (21) 63-35-62; fax (21) 63-38-42; e-mail seercerna@ yahoo.fr; f. 1985; Pres. Most Rev. HENRI TEISSIER, Archbishop of Algiers; Sec.-Gen. Fr BERNARD LEFEBVRE.

Archbishop of Algiers: Most Rev. HENRI TEISSIER, 22 Chemin d'Hydra, 16030 El Biar, Algiers; tel. (21) 92-56-67; fax (21) 92-55-76; e-mail evechealger@yahoo.fr.

Protestant Church

Protestant Church of Algeria: 31 rue Reda Houhou, 16000 Alger-Gare, Algiers; tel. and fax (21) 71-62-38; three parishes; 1,500 mems; Pastor Dr HUGH G. JOHNSON.

The Press

DAILIES

L'Authentique: Algiers; internet www.authentique-dz.com; French.

Ach-Cha'ab (The People): 1 place Maurice Audin, Algiers; e-mail ech-chaab@ech-chaab.com; internet www.ech-chaab.com; f. 1962; FLN journal in Arabic; Dir KAMEL AVACHE; circ. 24,000.

La Dépêche de Kabylie: f. 2002; Dir AMARA BENYOUNES.

Al-Djeza'ir El-Ghad (Algeria of Tomorrow): Algiers; f. 1999; Arabic; Editor MUSTAPHA HACINI.

Echourouk El Yaoumi: Algiers; f. 2000; Arabic.

L'Expression, Le Quotidien: Maison de la Presse, Kouba, Algiers; tel. (21) 23-37-97; fax (21) 23-25-80; e-mail direction@ lexpressiondz.com; internet www.lexpressiondz.com; f. 2000; French; Editor AHMED FATTANI; circ. 70,000.

El Fedjr: Algiers; f. 2000; Arabic.

Horizons: 20 rue de la Liberté, Algiers; tel. (21) 73-47-25; fax (21) 73-61-34; e-mail admin@horizons-dz.com; internet www .horizons-dz.com; f. 1985; evening; French; circ. 35,000.

Le Jeune Indépendant: Algiers; tel. (21) 67-07-48; fax (21) 67-07-46; e-mail redaction@jeune-independant.com; internet www.jeune -independant.com; f. 1997; French; circ. 60,000.

Al-Joumhouria (The Republic): 6 rue Bensenouci Hamida, Oran; f. 1963; Arabic; Editor BOUKHALFA BENAMEUR; circ. 20,000.

Le Journal: Algiers; f. 1992; French.

El Khabar: Maison de la Presse 'Tahar Djaout', 1 rue Bachir Attar, place du 1er mai, Algiers; tel. (21) 67-07-05; fax (21) 67-07-10; e-mail admin@elkhabar.com; internet www.elkhabar.com; f. 1990; Arabic; Gen. Man. ALI DJERRI; circ. 450,000.

Liberté: 37 rue Larbi Ben M'Hidi, BP 178, Alger-Gare, Algiers; tel. (21) 69-25-88; fax (21) 69-35-46; e-mail webmaster@liberte-algeria .com; internet www.liberte-algerie.com; French; independent; Dir-Gen ABROUS OUTOUDERT; circ. 20,000.

Al-Massa: Maison de la Presse, Abd al-Kader Safir, Kouba, Algiers; tel. (21) 59-54-19; fax (21) 59-64-57; f. 1977; evening; Arabic; circ. 45,000.

Le Matin: Maison de la Presse, 1 rue Bachir Attar, 16016 Algiers; tel. (21) 66-07-08; fax (21) 66-20-97; e-mail info@lematin-dz.com; internet www.lematin-dz.com; French; Dir MUHAMMAD BENCHICOU.

El-Moudjahid (The Fighter): 20 rue de la Liberté, Algiers; tel. (21) 73-70-81; fax (21) 73-90-43; e-mail redchef@elmoudjahid-dz.com; internet www.elmoudjahid-dz.com; f. 1965; govt journal in French and Arabic; Dir ADBELMAJID CHERBAL; circ. 392,000.

An-Nasr (The Victory): BP 388, Zone Industrielle, La Palma, Constantine; tel. (31) 93-92-16; f. 1963; Arabic; Editor ABDALLAH GUETTAT; circ. 340,000.

La Nouvelle République: Algiers; French.

Ouest Tribune: Oran; e-mail redact@ouest-tribune.com; internet www.ouest-tribune.com; French.

Le Quotidien d'Oran: 63 ave de l'ANP, BP 110, Oran; (41) 32-63-09; fax (41) 32-51-36; www.quotidien-oran.com; French.

Le Soir d'Algérie: Algiers; e-mail info@lesoirdalgerie.com; internet www.lesoirdalgerie.com; f. 1990; evening; independent information journal in French; Editors ZOUBIR SOUISSI, MAAMAR FARRAH; circ. 80,000.

La Tribune: Algiers; e-mail latribune@latribune-online.com; internet www.latribune-online.com; f. 1994; current affairs journal in French; Editor BAYA GACEMI.

El Watan: Maison de la Presse, 1 rue Bachir Attar, 16016 Algiers; tel. (21) 68-21-83; fax (21) 68-21-87; e-mail infos@elwatan.com; internet www.elwatan.com; French; Dir OMAR BELHOUCHET.

El-Youm: 1 rue Bachir Attar, place du 1er mai, Algiers; tel (21) 67-39-37; fax (21) 67-39-49; e-mail info@el-youm.com; internet www.el-youm.com; Arabic; circ. 54,000.

WEEKLIES

Algérie Actualité: 2 rue Jacques Cartier, 16000 Algiers; tel. (21) 63-54-20; f. 1965; French; Dir KAMEL BELKACEM; circ. 250,000.

Al-Hadef (The Goal): Algiers; tel. (21) 93-92-16; f. 1972; sports; French; Editor-in-Chief LARBI MOHAMED ABBOUD; circ. 110,000.

Libre Algérie: Algiers; French; organ of the FFS.

La Nation: 33 rue Larbi Ben M'hidi, Algiers; f. 1993; French; Editor SALIMA GHEZALI; circ. 35,000.

Révolution Africaine: Algiers; tel. (21) 59-77-91; fax (21) 59-77-92; current affairs journal in French; socialist; Dir FERRAH ABDELLALI; circ. 50,000.

El Wadjh al-Akhar (The Other Face): Algiers; Arabic.

OTHER PERIODICALS

Al-Acala: 4 rue Timgad, Hydra, Algiers; tel. (21) 60-85-55; fax (21) 60-09-36; f. 1970; published by the Ministry of Religious Affairs and Endowments; fortnightly; Editor MUHAMMAD AL-MAHDI.

Algérie Médicale: Algiers; f. 1964; publ. of Union médicale algérienne; 2 a year; circ. 3,000.

Alouan (Colours): 119 rue Didouche Mourad, Algiers; f. 1973; cultural review; monthly; Arabic.

Bibliographie de l'Algérie: Bibliothèque Nationale d'Algérie, BP 127, Hamma el-Annasser, 16000 Algiers; tel. (21) 67-18-67; fax (21) 67-29-99; f. 1963; lists books, theses, pamphlets and periodicals published in Algeria; 2 a year; Arabic and French; Dir-Gen. MOHAMED AÏSSA OUMOUSSA.

Ach-Cha'ab ath-Thakafi (Cultural People): Algiers; f. 1972; cultural monthly; Arabic.

Ach-Chabab (Youth): Algiers; journal of the UNJA; bi-monthly; French and Arabic.

Al-Djeich (The Army): Office de l'Armée Nationale Populaire, Algiers; f. 1963; monthly; Algerian army review; Arabic and French; circ. 10,000.

Journal Officiel de la République Algérienne Démocratique et Populaire: BP 376, Saint-Charles, Les Vergers, Bir Mourad Raïs, Algiers; tel. (21) 54 35 06; fax (21) 54-35-12; f. 1962; French and Arabic.

Nouvelles Economiques: 6 blvd Amilcar Cabral, Algiers; f. 1969; publ. of Institut Algérien du Commerce Extérieur; monthly; French and Arabic.

Révolution et Travail: Maison du Peuple, 1 rue Abdelkader Benbarek, place du 1er mai, Algiers; tel. (21) 66-73-53; journal of UGTA (central trade union) with Arabic and French editions; monthly; Editor-in-Chief RACHIB AÏT ALI.

Revue Algérienne du Travail: Algiers; f. 1964; labour publication; quarterly; French.

Ath-Thakafa (Culture): 2 place Cheikh ben Badis, Algiers; tel. (21) 62-20-73; f. 1971; every 2 months; cultural review; Editor-in-Chief CHEBOUB OTHMANE; circ. 10,000.

NEWS AGENCIES

Agence Algérienne d'Information: Maison de la Presse Tahar Djaout, 1 rue Bachir Attar, place de 1er mai, Algiers; tel. (21) 67-52-34; fax (21) 67-07-32; e-mail aai@aai-online.com; internet www.aai-online.com; f. 1999.

Algérie Presse Service (APS): 2 rue Farid Zouieche, Kouba, 16050 Algiers; tel. (21) 68-94-43; fax (21) 68-91-45; e-mail aps@wissal.dz; internet www.aps.dz; f. 1962; provides news reports in Arabic, English, French and Spanish.

Foreign Bureaux

Agence France-Presse (AFP): 6 rue Abd al-Karim el-Khettabi, Algiers; tel. (21) 72-16-54; fax (21) 72-14-89; Chief MARC PONDAVEN.

Agencia EFE (Spain): 4 ave Pasteur, 15000 Algiers; tel. (21) 71-85-59; fax (21) 73-77-62; Chief MANUEL OSTOS LÓPEZ.

Agenzia Nazionale Stampa Associata (ANSA) (Italy): 4 ave Pasteur, Algiers; tel. (21) 63-73-14; fax (21) 61-25-84; Rep. CARLO DI RENZO.

Associated Press (AP) (USA): BP 769, 4 ave Pasteur, Algiers; tel. (21) 63-59-41; fax (21) 63-59-42; Rep. RACHID KHIARI.

Informatsionnoye Telegrafnoye Agentstvo Rossii—Telegrafnoye Agentstvo Suverennykh Stran (ITAR—TASS) (Russia): 21 rue de Boulogne, Algiers; Chief KONSTANTIN DUDAREV.

Rossiiskoye Informatsionnoye Agentstvo—Novosti (RIA—Novosti) (Russia): Algiers; Chief Officer YURII S. BAGDASAROV.

Xinhua (New China) News Agency (People's Republic of China): 32 rue de Carthage, Hydra, Algiers; tel. and fax (21) 69-27-12; Chief WANG LIANZHI.

Wikalat al-Maghreb al-Arabi (Morocco), the Middle East News Agency (Egypt) and Reuters (UK) are also represented.

Publishers

Entreprise Nationale du Livre (ENAL): 3 blvd Zirout Youcef, BP 49, Algiers; tel. and fax (21) 73-58-41. 1966 as Société Nationale d'Edition et de Diffusion, name changed 1983; publishes books of all types, and imports, exports and distributes printed material, stationery, school and office supplies; Pres. and Dir-Gen. HASSEN BENDIF.

Office des Publications Universitaires: 1 place Centrale de Ben Aknoun, Algiers; tel. (21) 78-87-18; publishes university textbooks.

Broadcasting and Communications

TELECOMMUNICATIONS

New legislation approved by the National People's Assembly in August 2000 removed the state's monopoly over the telecommunications sector and redefined its role to that of a supervisory authority. Under the legislation an independent regulator for the sector was created, and both the fixed-line and mobile sectors were opened to foreign competition.

Algérie Télécoms: f. 2001 to manage and develop telecommunications infrastructure.

Autorité de Régulation de la Poste et des Télécommunications (ARPT): 4 blvd Col Krim Belkacem, 16027 Algiers; e-mail arpt.lic@postelecom.dz; f. 2001; Dir-Gen. AHMAD GACEB.

Djezzy GSM: Orascom Telecom Algérie, Algiers; tel. (21) 54-00-53; e-mail souheila.battou@otalgerie.com; internet www.otalgerie.com; f. 2002; operates mobile cellular telephone network; Group Chair. NAGUIB SAWIRIS.

Entreprise Nationale des Télécommunications (ENTC): 1 ave du 1er novembre, Tlemcen; tel. (43) 20-76-71; fax (43) 26-39-51; f. 1978; national telecommunications org; jt venture with Sweden; Dir-Gen. SIBAWAGHI SAKER.

BROADCASTING
Radio

Arabic Network: transmitters at Adrar, Aïn Beïda, Algiers, Béchar, Béni Abbès, Djanet, El Goléa, Ghardaia, Hassi Messaoud, In Aménas, In Salah, Laghouat, Les Trembles, Ouargla, Reggane, Tamanrasset, Timimoun, Tindouf.

French Network: transmitters at Algiers, Constantine, Oran and Tipaza.

Kabyle Network: transmitter at Algiers.

Radiodiffusion Algérienne: 21 blvd des Martyrs, Algiers; tel. (21) 69-12-81; fax (21) 23-08-23; e-mail info@algerian-radio.dz; internet www.algerian-radio.dz; govt-controlled; Dir-Gen. ABDELKADER LALMI.

Television

The principal transmitters are at Algiers, Batna, Sidi-Bel-Abbès, Constantine, Souk-Ahras and Tlemcen. Television plays a major role in the national education programme.

Télévision Algérienne (ENTV): 21 blvd des Martyrs, Algiers; tel. (21) 60-23-00; fax (21) 60-19-22; internet www.entv.dz; Dir-Gen. HAMRAOUI HABIB CHAWKI.

Finance

(cap. = capital; res = reserves; dep. = deposits; brs = branches; m. = million; amounts in Algerian dinars)

BANKING
Central Bank

Banque d'Algérie: 38 ave Franklin Roosevelt, 16000 Algiers; tel. (21) 23-00-23; fax (21) 23-01-50; e-mail bacom@ist.cerist.dz; internet www.bank-of-algeria.dz; f. 1963 as Banque Centrale d'Algérie; present name adopted 1990; cap. 40m.; bank of issue; Gov. MUHAMMAD LAKSACI; 50 brs.

Nationalized Banks

Banque Al-Baraka d'Algérie: Haï Bouteldja Houidef, Villa n°1 Rocades Sud, Ben Aknoun, Algiers; tel. (21) 91-64-50; fax (21) 91-64-57; e-mail info@albaraka-bank.com; internet www.albaraka-bank.com; f. 1991; cap. 500m., res 532.8m., dep. 9,771.3m. (Dec. 2000); Algeria's first Islamic financial institution; owned by the Jeddah-based Al-Baraka Investment and Development Co (50%) and the local Banque de l'Agriculture et du Développement Rural (BADR) (50%); Chair. ADNANE AHMAD YOUCEF; Gen. Man. MUHAMMAD SEDDIK HAFID.

Banque Extérieure d'Algérie (BEA): 11 Blvd Col Amirouche, 16000, Algiers; tel. (21) 23-93-30; fax (21) 23-90-99; e-mail bea@algerianetwork.net; internet www.bea.algerianetwork.net; f. 1967; cap. 5,600m., res 12,417m., dep. 362,283m. (Dec. 1999); chiefly concerned with energy and maritime transport sectors; Chair. M. TERBECHE; Dir-Gen. HOCINE HANNACHI; 81 brs.

Banque du Maghreb Arabe pour l'Investissement et le Commerce: 7 rue de Bois, Hydra, Algiers; tel. (21) 59-07-60; fax (21) 59-02-30; owned by the Algerian Govt (50%) and the Libyan Govt (50%); Pres. M. HAKIKI; Dir-Gen. IBRAHIM ALBISHARY.

Banque Nationale d'Algérie (BNA): 8 blvd Ernesto Ché Guévara, 16000 Algiers; tel. (21) 71-55-64; fax (21) 71-47-59; e-mail dg-bna@bna.com.dz; internet www.bna.com.dz; f. 1966; cap. 8,000m., res 10,227m., dep. 68,920m. (Dec. 1995); specializes in industry, transport and trade sectors; Chair. and Man. Dir MUHAMMAD TERBECHE; 163 brs.

Crédit Populaire d'Algérie (CPA): BP 1031, 2 blvd Col Amirouche, 16000 Algiers; tel. (21) 64-13-34; fax (21) 64-11-79; e-mail cpadmc@gecos.net; internet www.cpa-bank.com; f. 1966; cap. 13,600m., total assets 353,863m. (Dec. 1996); specializes in light industry, construction and tourism; partial privatization pending; Chair. ABD AL-MADJID NASSOU; Dir-Gen. EL HACHEMI MEGHAOUI; 117 brs.

Development Banks

Banque de l'Agriculture et du Développement Rural (BADR): 17 blvd Col Amirouche, 16000 Algiers; tel. (21) 63-49-22; fax (21) 63-51-46; internet www.badr-dz.com; f. 1982; cap. 33,000m., res 1,473m., dep. 368,560m. (Dec. 1999); finance for the agricultural sector; Chair. and Man. Dir FAROUK BOUYAKOUB; 270 brs.

Banque Algérienne de Développement (BAD): Lot Mont-Froid, Zonka, Birkhadem, BP 36, 13336 Algiers; tel. (21) 55-22-89; fax (21) 55-48-63; e-mail bad@ist.cerist.dz; f. 1963; cap. 100m., total assets 152,082.0m. (Dec. 1999); a public establishment with fiscal sovereignty; aims to contribute to Algerian economic devt through long-term investment programmes; Chair. and Dir-Gen. SADEK ALILAT; 4 brs.

Banque de Développement Local (BDL): 5 rue Gaci Amar, Staouéli, Algiers; tel. (21) 39-37-55; fax (21) 39-37-57; f. 1985; regional devt bank; cap. 7,140m., dep. 108,708m. (2000); Pres. and Dir-Gen. AMAR DAOUDI; 15 brs.

Caisse Nationale d'Epargne et de Prévoyance (CNEP): 42 blvd Khélifa Boukhalfa, Algiers; tel. (21) 71-33-53; fax (21) 71-41-31; f. 1964; 206,915.8m. (Dec. 1992); savings and housing bank; Pres. and Dir-Gen. ABDELKRIM NAAS.

Private Banks

Arab Algérie Leasing: Algiers; f. 2001.

Banque Commerciale et Industrielle d'Algérie (BCIA): 4 chemin Doudou Mokhtar, Ben Aknoun, 16030 Algiers; tel. (21) 91-30-06; fax (21) 91-17-13; internet www.bciabank.com; f. 1998; cap. and res 436.7m., dep. 2,768.8m.; Pres. AHMED KHERROUBI; Chair. MUHAMMAD-ALI KHERROUBI; Gen. Man. BADREDDINE KHERROUBI.

BNP-Paribas El Djazair: 10 rue Abou Nouass, Hydr, Algiers; tel. (21) 60-39-42; fax (21) 60-39-29; f. 2001; cap 500m.; Chair FATHI MESTIRI; Man. Dir JEAN-FRANÇOIS CHAZU

EFG Hermes SPA: Algiers; f. 2000.

El Khalifa Bank: 61 Lot Ben Haddadi, Dar Diaf, Chéraga, 16800 Algiers; tel. (21) 36-97-70; fax (21) 36-98-04; e-mail ek_bank@ist.cerist.dz; internet www.elkhalifbank.com; f. 1998; cap. 125m., total assets 11,659.4m. (Dec. 1999); Pres. RAFIK ABDELMOUMENE KHELIFA.

El Mouna Bank: 22 rue Boudjellad Ahmad Hai el-Moudjahidine, Oran; tel. (41) 41-15-90; fax (41) 41-18-08; f. 1998; cap. 260m.; Pres. AHMED BENSADOUN.

Al-Rayan Algerian Bank: 29 rue Ahmad Kara, Bir Mourad Rais, Algiers; tel. (21) 44-99-00; fax (21) 44-92-05; internet www.alrayan-bank.com; f. 2001.

Trust Bank: Algiers; f. 2001.

Union Bank: 5 bis chemin Mackley, el-Biar, 16030 Algiers; tel. (21) 91-45-49; fax (21) 91-45-48; internet www.ub-alger.com; f. 1995; cap. 250m., total assets 1,591m. (Dec. 1997); principal shareholder BRAHIM HADJAS; Pres. SELIM BENATA.

Foreign Banks

Arab Banking Corpn (Bahrain): 54 ave des Trois Frères Bouaddou, BP 367, Bir Mourad Rais, Algiers; tel. (21) 54-15-15; fax (21) 54-16-04; e-mail abcbank@ist.cerist.dz; total assets US $1,477.2m.

Natexis Al-Amana Banque (France): 62 chemin Drareni, Hydra, Algiers; tel. (21) 69-40-11; fax (21) 69-40-00; f. 1999; owned by Natexis Banques Populaires; Man. Dir HOCINE MOUFFOK121

STOCK EXCHANGE

The Algiers Stock Exchange began trading in July 1999.

Commission d'Organisation et de Surveillance des Opérations de Bourse (COSOB): Algiers; tel. (21) 71-27-25; fax (21) 71-21-98; e-mail infos@cosob.com.dz; internet www.cosob.com.dz; Chair. BELKACEM IRATNI; Gen. Sec. ABDELHAKIM BERRAH.

INSURANCE

Insurance is a state monopoly; however, in 1997 regulations were drafted to permit private companies to enter the Algerian insurance market.

Caisse Nationale de Mutualité Agricole: 24 blvd Victor Hugo, Algiers; tel. (21) 73-46-31; fax (21) 73-34-79; f. 1972; Dir-Gen. YAHIA CHERIF BRAHIM; 47 brs.

Cie Algérienne d'Assurance et de Réassurance (CAAR): 48 rue Didouche Mourad, 16000 Algiers; tel. (21) 72-71-90; fax (21) 72-71-97; e-mail caaralg@caar.com.dz; www.caar.com.dz; f. 1963 as a public corpn; partial privatization pending; Pres. ALI DJENDI.

Cie Centrale de Réassurance (CCR): Lot No 1, Saïd-Hamdine-Bmr, Algiers; tel. (21) 54-69-33; fax (21) 54-75-06; f. 1973; general; Chair. DJAMEL-EDDINE CHOUAÏB CHOUITER.

Société Nationale d'Assurances (SNA): 5 blvd Ernesto Ché Guévara, Algiers; tel. (21) 71-47-60; fax (21) 71-22-16; f. 1963; state-sponsored co; Pres. KACI AISSA SLIMANE; Chair. and Gen. Man. LATROUS AMARQ.

Trust Algeria: 70 chemin Larbi Allik, Hydra, Algiers; tel. (21) 54-74-83; fax (21) 54-71-36; e-mail info@trust-algeria.com; internet www.trust-algeria.algeriainfo.com; f. 1997; 65% owned by Trust Insurance Co (Bahrain) and Qatar General Insurance and Reinsurance Co, 35% owned by Compagnie Algérienne d'Assurance; Gen. Man. HORI MOHD BOUZIANE.

Trade and Industry

GOVERNMENT AGENCIES

Centre Algérien pour la Promotion des Investissements (CALPI): Algiers; f. 1994 to promote investment; offices in the 48 administrative districts.

Conseil National des Participations de L'Etat (CNPE): Algiers; supervises state holdings; participants include the Prime Minister and reps of 16 govt ministries; Sec.-Gen. AHMED EL-ANTRI TIBAOUI.

DEVELOPMENT ORGANIZATIONS

Agence Nationale pour l'Aménagement du Territoire (ANAT): 30 ave Muhammad Fellah, Algiers; tel. (21) 58-48-12; fax (21) 68-85-03; f. 1980; Pres. and Dir-Gen. KOUIDER DJEBLI.

Engineering Environment Consult (EEC): BP 395, Alger-Gare, 50 rue Khélifa Boukhalfa, Algiers; tel. (21) 23-64-86; fax (21) 23-72-49; e-mail eec@wissal.dz; internet www.eec.com; f. 1982; Dir-Gen. MUHAMMAD BENTIR.

Institut National de la Production et du Développement Industriel (INPED): 126 rue Didouche Mourad, Boumerdès; tel. (21) 41-52-50.

Office Algérien de Promotion du Commerce Extérieur (PROMEX): route nationale 5, Muhammadia, Algiers; tel. (21) 52-20-82; fax (21) 52-11-26; e-mail promex@wissal.dz; internet www.promex.com.dz.

CHAMBERS OF COMMERCE

Chambre Française de Commerce et d'Industrie en Algérie (CFCIA): 1 rue Lt Mohamed Touileb, Algiers; tel. (21) 73-28-28; fax (21) 63-75-33; internet www.cfcia.org; f. 1965; Pres. JEAN-PIERRE DEQUEKER; Dir JEAN-FRANÇOIS HEUGAS.

Chambre Algérienne de Commerce et d'Industrie (CACI): BP 100, Palais Consulaire, 6 blvd Amilcar Cabral C.P., 16003 Algiers;

tel. (21) 57-55-55; fax (21) 57-70-25; e-mail caci@wissal.dz; internet www.caci.com.dz; f. 1980; Dir-Gen. MUHAMMAD CHAMI.

INDUSTRIAL AND TRADE ASSOCIATIONS

Association Nationale des Fabrications et Utilisateurs d'Emballages Métalliques: BP 245, rue de Constantine, Algiers; Pres. OTHMANI.

Centre National des Textiles et Cuirs (CNTC): BP 65, route du Marché, Boumerdès; tel. (21) 81-13-23; fax (21) 81-13-57.

Entreprise Nationale de Développement des Industries Alimentaires (ENIAL): RN 5, 16110 Bab Ezzouar, Algiers; tel. (21) 76-21-06; fax (21) 75-77-65; f. 1982; Dir-Gen. ARESKI LAKABI.

Entreprise Nationale de Développement des Industries Manufacturières (ENEDIM): 22 rue des Fusillés, El Anasser, Algiers; tel. (21) 68-13-43; fax (21) 67-55-26; f. 1983; Dir-Gen. FODIL.

Entreprise Nationale de Développement et de Recherche Industriels des Matériaux de Construction (ENDMC): BP 78, 35000 Algiers; tel. (21) 41-50-70. 1982; Dir-Gen. A. TOBBAL.

Groupement pour l'Industrialisation du Bâtiment (GIBAT): BP 51, 3 ave Col Driant, 55102 Verdun, France; tel. 29-86-09-76; fax 29-86-20-51; Dir JEAN MOULET.

Institut Algérien de la Propriété Industrielle (INAPI): 42 rue Larbi Ben M'hidi, 16000 Algiers; tel. (21) 73-23-58; fax (21) 73-55-81; e-mail info@inapi.org; internet www.inapi.org; f. 1973; Dir-Gen. M. BOUHNIK AMOR.

Institut National Algérien du Commerce Extérieur (COMEX): 6 blvd Anatole-France, Algiers; tel. (21) 62-70-44; Dir-Gen. SAAD ZER-HOUNI.

Institut National des Industries Manufacturières (INIM): 35000 Boumerdès; tel. (21) 81-62-71; fax (21) 82-56-62; f. 1973; Dir-Gen. HOCINE HASSISSI.

State Trading Organizations

Since 1970 all international trading has been carried out by state organizations, of which the following are the most important:

Entreprise Nationale d'Approvisionnement en Bois et Dérivés (ENAB): BP 166, Alger-Gare, 2 blvd Muhammad V, Algiers; tel. (21) 63-75-35; fax (21) 63-77-17; e-mail info@enab-dz.com; internet www.enab-dz.com; import and distribution of wood and derivatives and other building materials; Dirs OMAR BENOUNICHE, OMAR SADAOUI, SMAÏL EL-ROBRINI.

Entreprise Nationale d'Approvisionnement en Outillage et Produits de Quincaillerie Générale (ENAOQ): 5 rue Amar Semaous, Hussein-Dey, Algiers; tel. (21) 23-31-83; fax (21) 47-83-33; tools and general hardware; Dir-Gen. SMATI BAHIDJ FARID.

Entreprise Nationale d'Approvisionnements en Produits Alimentaires (ENAPAL): Algiers; tel. (21) 76-10-11; f. 1983; monopoly of import, export and bulk trade in basic foodstuffs; brs in more than 40 towns; Chair. LAID SABRI; Man. Dir BRAHIM DOUAOURI.

Entreprise Nationale d'Approvisionnement et de Régulation en Fruits et Légumes (ENAFLA): BP 42, 12 ave des Trois Frères Bouadou, Bir Mourad Rais, Algiers; tel. (21) 54-10-10; fax (21) 56-79-59; f. 1983; division of the Ministry of Commerce; fruit and vegetable marketing, production and export; Man. Dir REDHA KHELEF.

Entreprise Nationale de Commerce: 6–9 rue Belhaffat-Ghazali, Hussein-Dey, Algiers; tel. (21) 77-43-20; Dir-Gen. MUHAMMAD LAÏD BELARBIA.

Office Algérien Interprofessionel des Céréales (OAIC): 5 rue Ferhat-Boussaad, Algiers; tel. (21) 73-26-01; fax (21) 73-22-11; f. 1962; monopoly of trade in wheat, rice, maize, barley and products derived from these cereals; Gen. Man. LAÏD TALAMALI.

Office National de la Commercialisation des Produits Viti-Vinicoles (ONCV): 112 Quai-Sud, Algiers; tel. (21) 73-72-75; fax (21) 73-72-97; e-mail info@oncv-dz.com; internet www.oncv-dz.com; f. 1968; monopoly of importing and exporting products of the wine industry; Man. Dir SAÏD MEBARKI.

UTILITIES

Commission de Régulation de l'Electricité et du Gaz: Algiers; f. 2002; regulatory authority.

Société Nationale de l'Electricité et du Gaz (SONELGAZ): 2 blvd Col Krim Belkacem, Algiers; tel. (21) 72-31-01; fax (21) 61-54-77; internet www.sonelgaz.com.dz; f. 1969; production, distribution and transportation of electricity and transportation and distribution of natural gas; Gen. Man. AÏSSA ABDELKRIM BENGHANEM.

Electricity

Entreprise de Travaux d'Electrification (KAHRIF): Villa Malwall, Ain d'Heb, Médéa; tel. (25) 50-26-96; fax (25) 58-31-14; e-mail kahrif@ixiissal.dz; f. 1982; study of electrical infrastructure; Pres. and Dir-Gen. HOCINE RAHMANI.

Gas

Entreprise Nationale de Production et de Distribution des Gaz Industriels (ENGI): 23 route de l'ALN, 16040 Husein-Dey, Algiers; tel. (21) 49-85-99; fax (21) 49-71-94; e-mail boucherit@usa.net; internet www.gaz-ind.com; f. 1972; production and distribution of gas; Gen. Man. LAHOCINE BOUCHERIT.

Water

Agence Nationale de l'Eau Potable et Industrielle et de l'Assainissement (AGEP): rue Chemseddine Hafid-Kouba, 16000 Algiers; tel. (21) 28-30-96; fax (21) 28-30-33; f. 1985; state water co.

STATE HYDROCARBONS COMPANIES

Société Nationale pour la Recherche, la Production, le Transport, la Transformation et la Commercialisation des Hydrocarbures (SONATRACH): 10 rue du Sahara, Hydra, Algiers; tel. (21) 54-80-11; fax (21) 54-77-00; e-mail sonatrach@sonatrach.dz; internet www.sonatrach.dz; f. 1963; exploration, exploitation, transport and marketing of petroleum, natural gas and their products; Chair. ABDELMALEK ZITOUNI; Vice-Pres ALI HACHED (Marketing), ABDELHADI ZERGUINE (Transport), BACHIR ACHOUR (Liquefaction), DJAMEL EDINE KHENE (Exploration and Production).

Since 1980 the following associated companies have shared SONATRACH's functions:

Entreprise Nationale de Canalisation (ENAC): Muhammadia, rue Benyoucef Khattab, El Harrach, Algiers; tel. (21) 53-85-49; fax (21) 53-85-53; piping; Dir-Gen. RACHID HAMADOU.

Entreprise Nationale d'Engineering Pétrolier (ENEP): 2 blvd Muhammad V, Algiers; tel. (21) 64-08-37; fax (21) 63-71-83; design and construction for petroleum-processing industry; Gen. Man. MUSTAPHA MEKIDECHE.

Entreprise Nationale de Forage (ENAFOR): BP 211, 30500 Hassi Messaoud, Algiers; tel. (21) 73-71-35; fax (21) 73-22-60; drilling; Dir-Gen. ABD AR-RACHID ROUABAH.

Entreprise Nationale de Génie Civil et Bâtiments (GCB): BP 23, route de Corso, Boudouaou, Algiers; tel. (21) 84-65-26; fax (21) 84-60-09; civil engineering; Dir-Gen. ABD EL-HAMID ZERGUINE.

Entreprise Nationale de Géophysique (ENAGEO): BP 140, 30500 Hassi Messaoud, Ouargla; tel. (29) 73-77-00; fax (29) 73-72-12; f. 1981; e-mail enageoh1@wissal.dz; seismic crews, geophysics; Dir-Gen. RÉDA RAHAL.

Entreprise Nationale des Grands Travaux Pétroliers (ENGTP): BP 09, Zone industrielle, Reghaïa, Boumerdès; tel. (24) 80-06-80; fax (24) 85-14-70; f. 1980; major industrial projects; Dir-Gen. B. DRIAD.

Entreprise Nationale des Services aux Puits (ENSP): BP 83, 30500 Hassi Messaoud, Ouargla; tel. (29) 73-73-33; fax (29) 73-82-01; f. 1970; e-mail info@enspgroup.cominternet www.enspgroup.com; oil-well services; Dir-Gen. AZZEDINE GASMI.

Entreprise Nationale des Travaux aux Puits (ENTP): BP 206, 30500 Hassi Messaoud, Ouargla; tel. (29) 73-87-78; fax (29) 73-84-06; f. 1981; oil-well construction; Dir-Gen. ABD AL-AZIZ KRISSAT.

Groupe Industriel des Plastiques & Caoutchoucs: BP 452–453, Zone industrielle, 19000 Sétif; tel. (36) 90-75-45; fax (36) 93-05-65; f. 1967; e-mail grenpc@el-hidhab.cerist.dz; production and marketing of rubber and plastics products; Dir-Gen. BELKACEM SAMAT.

Société Nationale de Commercialisation et de Distribution des Produits Pétroliers (NAFTAL, SpA): BP 73, route des Dunes, Cheraga, Algiers; tel. (21) 36-09-69; fax (21) 36-07-86; e-mail naf-div-bp@wissal.dz; internet www.naftal-dz.com; f. 1987; international marketing and distribution of petroleum products; Gen. Man. NOREDINE CHEROUATI.

NATIONALIZED INDUSTRIES

A large part of Algerian industry is nationalized. Following the implementation of an economic reform programme in the 1980s, privatizations were undertaken during the 1990s, and it was further planned to transfer more than 180 companies to private control by 2004.

The following are some of the most important nationalized industries, each controlled by the appropriate ministry.

Centre National d'Etudes de Recherches Appliquées et de Travaux d'Art (CNERATA): BP 279, 114 rue de Tripoli, Hussein-Dey, Algiers; tel. (21) 77-50-22; Gen. Man. REMILI SMIDA.

Entreprise des Eaux Minérales de l'Algérois (EMAL): 21 rue Bellouchat Mouloud, 16040 Hussein-Dey, Algiers; tel. (21) 23-13-

94; fax (21) 23-14-01; f. 1983; mineral water, carbonated beverages and beer; Dir-Gen. RABAH CHENNOUFI.

Entreprise Nationale d'Approvisionnement en Bois et Dérivés (ENAB): BP 166, 2 blvd Muhammad V, 16026 Algiers; tel. (21) 63-77-35; fax (21) 63-77-37; f. 1970; e-mail enab@algeria info.com; internet www.enab.algeriainfo.com; import and distribution of wood and wood products; Pres. EL HADJ REKHROUKH.

Entreprise Nationale d'Ascenseurs (ENASC): 86 rue Hassiba Ben Bouali, 16014 Algiers; tel. (21) 65-99-40; fax (21) 65-99-44; f. 1989; manufacture of elevators; Dir-Gen. ACHOUR AROUDJ.

Entreprise Nationale de Bâtiments Industrialisés (BATI-METAL): BP 88, Zone industrielle de Oued-Smar, 16270 Algiers; tel. (21) 51-68-21; fax (21) 51-64-60; e-mail batimetal@wissal.dz; internet www.batimetal.com.dz; f. 1983; study and commercialization of buildings; Dir-Gen. ABD AL-KADER RAHAL.

Entreprise Nationale de la Cellulose et du Papier (CELPAP): BP 628, Mont Plaisir, 27000 Mostaganem; tel. (45) 26-30-58; fax (45) 26-31-00; f. 1985; pulp and paper; Chair. MUSTAPHA MERZOUK.

Entreprise Nationale de Charpentes et de Chaudronnerie (ENCC): BP 1547, 35 rue Tabet Muhammad, 31000 Oran; tel. (41) 33-29-32; fax (41) 33-57-05; e-mail encceng@wissal.dz; f. 1983; manufacture of boilers; Dir-Gen. CHEMSEDINE KARADJA.

Entreprise Nationale de Construction de Matériaux et d'Equipements Ferroviaires: BP 63, route d'El Hadjar, Annaba; tel. (38) 85-74-06; fax (38) 85-23-98; f. 1983; production, import and export of railway equipment; Dir-Gen. MELEK SALAH.

Entreprise Nationale de Développement et de Coordination des Industries Alimentaires (ENIAL): Bab Ezzouar, route nationale 5, 16110 Algiers; tel. (21) 76-21-06; fax (21) 75-77-65; f. 1965; semolina, pasta, flour and couscous; Dir-Gen. ARESKI LAKABI.

Entreprise Nationale de Distribution du Matériel Electrique (EDIMEL): 4–6 blvd Muhammad V, Algiers; tel. (21) 63-70-82; fax (21) 74-86-00; f. 1983; distribution of electrical equipment; Dir-Gen. YAHIA MOUNSI.

Entreprise Nationale de Produits Métalliques Utilitaires: BP 25, carrefour de Meftah, Oued Smar, Algiers; tel. (21) 51-65-12; fax (21) 51-68-44; f. 1983; manufacture of metal products; Dir-Gen. YACHIR EL HADI.

Entreprise Nationale de Produits Miniers Non-Ferreux et des Substances Utiles (ENOF): 31 rue Muhammad Hattab Belfort BP 183, 16200 El Harrach; tel. (21) 76-62-42; fax (21) 75-77-73; f. 1983; production and distribution of minerals; Dir-Gen. MUHAMMAD LALAMI.

Entreprise Nationale des Appareils de Mesure et de Contrôle (AMC): BP 248, route de Djeinila, El Eulma; tel. (5) 87-34-24; fax (5) 87-49-72; f. 1984; production of measuring equipment; Dir-Gen. MOKHTAR TOUIMER.

Entreprise Nationale des Corps Gras (ENCG): BP 126, 13 ave Mustapha Sayed el-Ouali, 16006 Algiers; tel. (21) 74-49-99; fax (21) 74-79-67; f. 1982 to replace SOGEDIA; oils, margarines, soaps and food packaging; Pres. SAHLI AÏSSA.

Entreprise Nationale des Industries de Confection et de Bonneterie (ECOTEX): BP 324, Zone industrielle Ilhaddaden, 06000 Béjaia; tel. (34) 21-28-84; fax (34) 22-00-08; f. 1982; consortium of textiles and clothing manufacturers; Dir-Gen. AMAR CHERIF.

Entreprise Nationale des Industries de l'Electroménager (EPE-ENIEM): BP 71A, Chikhi, Tizi-Ouzou; tel. (26) 21-87-45; fax (26) 21-87-44; consortium of manufacturers of household equipment; Dir-Gen. BELKACEM BERRADAII.

Entreprise Nationale des Jus et Conserves Alimentaires (ENAJUC): BP 108, Zone industrielle Ben-Boulaid, 09000 Blida; tel. (25) 41-78-90; fax (25) 41-74-91; e-mail enajuc@enterprises -dz.com; internet www.enterprises-dz.com/enajuc; f. 1983; manufacture of food products; Dir-Gen. MUHAMMAD BELKADI.

Entreprise Nationale de la Pêche Hauturière et Océanique (ENOCEP): quai d'Aigues Mortes, Port d'Alger; tel. (21) 71-52-68; fax (21) 71-52-67; f. 1979, as Entreprise Nationale des Pêches, to replace (with ECOREP, which is responsible for fishing equipment) former Office Algérien des Pêches; production, marketing, importing and exporting of fish; Man. Dir HACHANI MADANI.

Entreprise Nationale de Sidérurgie (SIDER): BP 342, Chaiba, el-Hadjar, 23000 Annaba; tel. (38) 87-22-11; fax (38) 87-29-22; f. 1964 as Société Nationale de Sidérurgie, restructured 1983; steel, cast iron, zinc and products; Man. Dir SLIMANE TAHARI.

Entreprise Nationale de Tubes et de Transformation de Produits Plats (ENTTPP): BP 131, route de la Gare, Reghaia, Algiers; tel. (21) 80-91-86. 1983; manufacture and distribution of tubing; Dir-Gen. RACHID BELHOUS.

Enterprise Nationale des Véhicules Industriels (SNVI): BP 153, route nationale 5, 35300 Rouiba; tel. (21) 85-19-70; fax (21) 85-

13-45; internet www.snvimkt@ist.cerist.dz; f. 1981; manufacture of industrial vehicles; Dir-Gen. MOKHTAR CHAHBOUB.

Entreprise Nationale du Fer et du Phosphate (FERPHOS): BP 122, 12000 Tebessa; tel. (38) 49-31-97; fax (38) 49-43-50; e-mail ferphos@ferphos.com; f. 1983; production, import and export of iron and phosphate products; Dir-Gen. AHMAD BENSLIMANE.

Entreprise Publique Economique Asmidal, SpA: BP 326, route des Salines, 23000 Annaba; tel. (38) 83-20-22; fax (38) 84-47-20; f. 1985; production of ammonia, fertilizers, pesticides and sodium tripolyphosphate.

Entreprise Publique Economique des Manufactures de Chaussures et Maroquinerie (EMAC): route de Sidi Bel-Abbès, Sig 29300; tel. (48) 83-82-15; fax (48) 83-84-51; f. 1983; manufacture of shoes and leather goods; Dir-Gen. DJELLOUL BENDJEDID.

Entreprise de Transformation de Produits Longs (TPL): BP 1005, 19 rue Mekki Khelifa, El Manouar, Oran; tel. (41) 34-37-05; fax (41) 34-19-50; e-mail tplsiege@algeriecom.com; internet www .tpl-algeria.com; f. 1983; production and distribution of girders; Dir-Gen. ABDAL-HAMID BENAHMED.

Ministère de l'Agriculture: Direction Générale des Forêts, chemin Doudou Mokhtar, Ben Aknoun, Algiers; tel. (21) 91-52-90; fax (21) 91-53-14; e-mail dgf.dpff@wissal.dz; f. 1971; production of timber, care of forests.

Office Régional du Centre des Produits Oléicoles (ORECPO): route de Ain Bessem Bouira, 10000 Algiers; tel. (21) 92-92-11; fax (21) 92-00-88; f. 1982; production and marketing of olives and olive oil; Dir-Gen. CHABOUR MUSTAPHA.

SAIDAL Production Pharmaceutique: BP 141, 11 route de Wilaya, A16100 Dar el-Beida; tel. (21) 50-58-18; fax (21) 50-57-37; f. 1983; production of pharmaceuticals; partially privatized in early 1999; Dir-Gen. ALI ALOUN.

Société Nationale de Constructions Mécaniques (SONACOME): Algiers; tel. (21) 65-93-92; f. 1967; to be reorganized into 11 smaller cos, most of which will specialize in manufacture or distribution of one of SONACOME's products; Dir DAOUD AKROUF.

Société Nationale de Constructions Métalliques (SN METAL): 110 rue de Tripoli, Hussein-Dey, Algiers; tel. (21) 77-28-10; fax (21) 77-28-38; f. 1968; production of metal goods; Chair. HACHEM MALIK; Man. Dir ABD AL-KADER MAIZA.

Société Nationale de Fabrication et de Montage du Matériel Electrique (SONELEC): 4–6 blvd Muhammad V, Algiers; tel. (21) 63-70-82; electrical equipment.

Société Nationale des Emballages et Arts Graphiques, SpA (EMBAG): BP 490, route d'Alger, 34000 Bordj-Bou-Arreridj; tel. (35) 68-58-09; fax (35) 67-34-72; f. 1985; wrapping paper and cardboard containers.

Société Nationale des Industries Chimiques (SNIC): BP 641, route des 5 Maisons, El Harrach, Algiers; tel. (21) 76-37-82; fax 67-55-55; f. 1986; production and distribution of chemical products; Dir-Gen. SAADNA KHALED.

Société Nationale des Industries des Lièges et du Bois (SNLB): BP 61, 1 rue Kaddour Rahim, Hussein-Dey, Algiers; tel. (21) 77-99-99. 1973; production of cork and wooden goods; Chair. MALEK BELLANI.

Société Nationale des Industries des Peaux et Cuirs (SONIPEC): BP 113, 100 rue de Tripoli, Hussein-Dey, Algiers; tel. (21) 77-20-42; fax (21) 77-76-11; f. 1967; hides and skins; Chair. MUHAMMAD CHERIF AZI; Man. Dir NACERI ABDENOUR.

Société Nationale des Matériaux de Construction (SNMC): Algiers; tel. (21) 64-35-13; f. 1968; production and import monopoly of building materials; Man. Dir ABD AL-KADER MAIZI.

Société Nationale de Recherches et d'Exploitations Minières (SONAREM): 127 blvd Salah Bouakouiz, Algiers; tel. (21) 63-15-55; f. 1967; mining and prospecting; Dir-Gen. OUBRAHAM FERHAT.

Société Nationale des Tabacs et Allumettes (SNTA): 40 rue Hocine-Nourredine, Algiers; tel. (21) 68-43-95; fax (21) 65-41-80; f. 1963; monopoly of manufacture and trade in tobacco, cigarettes and matches; Chair. MESSAI HACENE.

TRADE UNIONS

Union Générale des Travailleurs Algériens (UGTA): Maison du Peuple, place du 1er mai, Algiers; tel. (21) 66-89-47. 1956; 800,000 mems; Sec.-Gen. ABDELMADJID SIDI SAID.

There are 10 national 'professional sectors' affiliated to the UGTA:

Secteur Alimentation, Commerce et Tourisme (Food, Commerce and Tourist Industry Workers): Gen. Sec. ABD AL-KADER GHRIBLI.

Secteur Bois, Bâtiments et Travaux Publics (Building Trades Workers): Gen. Sec. LAIFA LATRECHE.

Secteur Education et Formation Professionnelle (Teachers): Gen. Sec. SAÏDI BEN GANA.

Secteur Energie et Pétrochimie (Energy and Petrochemical Workers): Gen. Sec. ALI BELHOUCHET.

Secteur Finances (Financial Workers): Gen. Sec. MUHAMMAD ZAAF.

Secteur Information, Formation et Culture (Information, Training and Culture).

Secteur Industries Légères (Light Industry): Gen. Sec. ABD AL-KADER MALKI.

Secteur Industries Lourdes (Heavy Industry).

Secteur Santé et Sécurité Sociale (Health and Social Security Workers): Gen. Sec. ABD AL-AZIZ DJEFFAL.

Secteur Transports et Télécommunications (Transport and Telecommunications Workers): Gen. Sec. EL-HACHEMI BEN MOUHOUB.

Al-Haraka al-Islamiyah lil-Ummal al-Jazarivia (Islamic Movement for Algerian Workers): Tlemcen; f. 1990; based on teachings of Islamic faith and affiliated to the FIS.

Ittahad as-Sahafiyin al-Jaza'iriyin (Algerian Journalists Union): Algiers; f. 2001.

Union Nationale des Paysans Algériens (UNPA): f. 1973; 700,000 mems; Sec.-Gen. AÏSSA NEDJEM.

Transport

RAILWAYS

Entreprise Métro d'Alger: 4 chemin de Wilaya 13, Kouba, Algiers; tel. (21) 28-94-64; fax (21) 28-01-83; construction of a 26.5-km metro railway line began in 1991; initial 12.5-km section (16 stations) scheduled to open in two stages, starting in 2006; Dir-Gen. A. MERKEBI.

Infrafer (Entreprise Publique Economique de Réalisation des Infrastructures Ferroviaires): BP 208, 35300 Rouiba; tel. (21) 85-27-47; fax (21) 85-17-55; f. 1987; responsible for construction and maintenance of track; Pres. and Dir-Gen. K. BENMAMI.

Société Nationale des Transports Ferroviaires (SNTF): 21–23 blvd Muhammad V, Algiers; tel. (21) 71-15-10; fax (21) 74-81-90; f. 1976 to replace Société Nationale des Chemins de Fer Algériens; 4,820 km of track, of which 304 km are electrified and 1,156 km are narrow gauge; daily passenger services from Algiers to the principal provincial cities and services to Tunisia and Morocco; Dir-Gen. ABD AL-ADIM BENALLEGUE.

ROADS

In 1996 there were an estimated 104,000 km of roads and tracks, of which 640 km were motorways, 25,200 km were main roads and 23,900 km were secondary roads. The French administration built a good road system (partly for military purposes), which, since independence, has been allowed to deteriorate in parts. New roads have been built linking the Sahara oil fields with the coast, and the Trans-Sahara highway is a major project. In 1996 it was estimated that the cost of renovating the national road system would amount to US $4,124m.

Société Nationale des Transports Routiers (SNTR): 27 rue des Trois Frères Bouadou, Bir Mourad Rais, Algiers; tel. (21) 54-06-00; fax (21) 54-05-35; e-mail dg-sntr@sntr-dz.com; internet www.groupe-sntr.com; f. 1967; holds a monopoly of goods transport by road; Chair. and Dir-Gen. ABDALLAH BENMAAROUF.

Société Nationale des Transports des Voyageurs (SNTV): Algiers; tel. (21) 66-00-52. 1967; holds monopoly of long-distance passenger transport by road; Man. Dir M. DIB.

SHIPPING

Algiers is the main port, with anchorage of between 23 m and 29 m in the Bay of Algiers, and anchorage for the largest vessels in Agha Bay. The port has a total quay length of 8,380 m and is expected to be able to handle 250,000 containers per year by 2005. There are also important ports at Annaba, Arzew, Béjaia, Djidjelli, Ghazaouet, Mostaganem, Oran, Skikda and Ténès. Petroleum and liquefied gas are exported through Arzew, Béjaia and Skikda. Algerian crude petroleum is also exported through the Tunisian port of La Skhirra. In December 2001 Algeria's merchant fleet totalled 143 vessels, with an aggregate displacement of 963,824 grt.

Cie Algéro-Libyenne de Transports Maritimes (CALTRAM): 19 rue des Trois Frères Bouadou, Bir Mourad Rais, Algiers; tel. (21) 57-17-00; fax (21) 54-21-04; e-mail caltram@wissal.dz; f. 1974; Man. Dir A. KERAMANE.

Entreprise Nationale de Réparation Navale (ERENAV): quai no. 12, Algiers; tel. (21) 42-37-83; fax (21) 42-30-39; internet www .erenav.com.dz; f. 1987; ship repairs; Dir-Gen. MUHAMMAD FARES.

Entreprise Nationale de Transport Maritime de Voyageurs—Algérie Ferries (ENTMV): BP 467, 5–6 rue Jawharlal Nehru, 16001 Algiers; tel. (21) 74-04-85; fax (21) 64-88-76; e-mail entmv@ algerieferries.com; f. 1987 as part of restructuring of SNTM-CNAN; responsible for passenger transport; operates car ferry services between Algiers, Annaba, Skikda, Alicante, Marseilles and Oran; Dir-Gen. BOUDJEMA CHERIET.

Entreprise Portuaire d'Alger (EPAL): BP 16, 2 rue d'Angkor, Alger-Gare, Algiers; tel. (21) 71-54-39; fax (21) 71-54-52; e-mail portalg@ist.cerist.dz; internet www.portalger.com.dz; f. 1982; responsible for management and growth of port facilities and sea pilotage; Dir-Gen. ALI FERRAH.

Entreprise Portuaire d'Annaba (EPAN): BP 1232, Môle Cigogne-Quai nord, Annaba; tel. (38) 86-31-31; fax (38) 86-54-15; e-mail epan@annaba-port.com; internet www.annaba.port.com; Man. Dir DJILANI SALHI.

Entreprise Portuaire d'Arzew (EPA): BP 46, 7 rue Larbi Tebessi, Arzew; tel. (41) 37-24-91; fax (41) 47-49-90; Man. Dir CHAIB OUMER.

Entreprise Portuaire de Béjaia (EPB): 13 ave des Frères Amrani, BP 94, 06000 Béjaia; tel. (34) 21-18-07; fax (34) 22-03-46; e-mail portbj@wissal.dz; internet www.portdebejaia.com.dz; Man. Dir M. BOUMSILLA.

Entreprise Portuaire de Djen-Djen (EPDJ): BP 87,18000 Jijel; tel. (34) 44-06-90; fax (34) 44-02-72; e-mail epijdjendjen@wissal.dz; f. 1984; Man. Dir MUHAMMAD ATMANE.

Entreprise Portuaire de Ghazaouet (EPG): BP 217, route du Phare, 13400 Ghazaouet; tel. (43) 32-33-45; fax (43) 32-31-75; Man. Dir B. ABDELMALEK.

Entreprise Portuaire de Mostaganem (EPM): BP 131, quai du Port, Mostaganem; tel. (45) 21-14-11; fax (45) 21-78-05; Dir-Gen. M. LAKEHAL.

Entreprise Portuaire d'Oran (EPO): 1 rue du 20 août, 31000 Oran; tel. (41) 33-24-41; fax (41) 33-24-98; e-mail webmaster@oran -port.com; internet oran-port.com; Man. Dir M. S. LOUHIBI.

Entreprise Portuaire de Skikda (EPS): BP 65, 46 ave Rezki Rahal, Skikda; tel. (38) 75-68-50; fax (38) 75-20-15; e-mail info@ skikda-port.com; internet skikda-port.com; Man. Dir M. LEMRABET.

Entreprise Portuaire de Ténès (EPT): BP 18, 02200 Ténès; tel. (27) 76-72-76; fax (27) 76-61-77; Man. Dir K. EL-HAMRI.

NAFTAL Division Aviation Marine: BP 70, Aéroport Houari Boumedienne, Dar-el-Beïda, Algiers; tel. (21) 50-95-50; fax (21) 50-67-09; e-mail avm@ist.cerist.dz; Dir MESNOUS NOUREDINE.

Société Générale Maritime (GEMA): 2 rue J. Nehru, Algiers; tel. (21) 74-73-00; fax (21) 74-76-73; gemadg@gema-groupe.com; f. 1987 as part of restructuring of SNTM-CNAN; shipping, ship-handling and forwarding; Dir-Gen. BELKADI BOUALEM.

Société Nationale de Transport Maritime et Cie Nationale Algérienne de Navigation (SNTM-CNAN): BP 280, 2 quai no. 9, Nouvelle Gare Maritime, Algiers; tel. (21) 71-14-78; fax (21) 73-02-33; f. 1963; state-owned co which owns and operates fleet of freight ships; rep. office in Marseilles (France) and rep. agencies in Antwerp (Belgium), Valencia (Spain) and the principal ports in many other countries; Gen. Man. ABDELHAMID KARA.

Société Nationale de Transports Maritimes des Hydrocarbures et des Produits Chimiques (SNTM-HYPROC): BP 60, Arzew, 31200 Oran; tel. (41) 47-48-55; fax (41) 47-34-45; e-mail hyproc@hyproc.com; internet www.hyproc.com; f. 1982; Pres. and Dir-Gen. MUSTAPHA ZENASNI.

CIVIL AVIATION

Algeria's principal international airport, Houari Boumedienne, is situated 20 km from Algiers. At Constantine, Annaba, Tlemcen and Oran there are also airports that meet international requirements. There are, in addition, 65 aerodromes, of which 20 are public, and a further 135 airstrips connected with the petroleum industry.

Air Algérie (Entreprise Nationale d'Exploitation des Services Aériens): BP 858, 1 place Maurice Audin, Immeuble el-Djazair, Algiers; tel. (21) 74-24-28; fax (21) 61-05-53; e-mail contact@ airalgerie.dz; internet www.airalgerie.dz; f. 1953 by merger; state-owned from 1972; partial privatization pending; internal services and extensive services to Europe, North and West Africa, and the Middle East; Chair. and Dir-Gen. TAYEB BENOUIS; Sec.-Gen. NOUREDDINE MERROUCHE.

Desert Aviation Co: Touggourt; f. 1999; private co; internal flights; Exec. Dir CHOKRI MIAADI.

Ecoair International: 12 rue Branly, El Mouradia, Algiers; tel. (21) 69-82-00; f. 1998; private co operating domestic and international passenger flights to Europe and North Africa.

Khalifa Airways: chemin de la Petite Province, Lot 11 décembre 1960, Hydra, Algiers; tel. (21) 50-63-70; f. 1999; e-mail contact@ khalifaairways-dz.com; internet www.khalifaairways-dz.com; private airline operating domestic and international passenger flights to destinations in Europe, Africa and the Middle East.

Saharan Airlines: Cité Ezzahra, Touggourt; tel. (29) 68-35-34; fax (29) 68-22-85; f. 1999; domestic passenger services; CEO MIADI CHOUKRI.

Tassili Airlines: blvd Mustapha Ben Boulaid, 301 Hassi Messaoud; tel. (29) 73-84-25; fax (29) 73-84-24; f. 1997; jt venture between SONATRACH and Air Algérie; domestic passenger services.

Tourism

Algeria's tourist attractions include the Mediterranean coast, the Atlas mountains and the desert. In 1999 a total of 748,536 tourists visited Algeria, compared with 722,682 in 1991. Receipts from tourism totalled US $20m. in 1997. In 1996 there were 737 hotels, with a total of 64,695 beds.

Agence Nationale de Développement Touristique (ANDT): BP 151, Sidi Fredj Staoueli, Algiers; tourism promotion; Dir-Gen. ABDELKRIM BOUCETTA.

Office National du Tourisme (ONT): 2 rue Ismail Kerrar, Algiers; tel. (21) 71-29-81; fax (21) 71-30-59; e-mail info@algeria-tourism.org; internet www.algeria-tourism.org; f. 1990; state institution; oversees tourism promotion policy; Dir-Gen. SALAH MOUHOUB.

ONAT-TOUR (Opérateur National Algérien de Tourisme): 126 bis A, rue Didouche Mourod, 16000 Algiers; tel. (21) 74-44-48; fax (21) 74-32-14; e-mail onat@onat-dz.com; www.onat-dz.com; f. 1962; Dir-Gen. BELKACEMI HAMMOUCHE.

Société de Développement de l'Industrie Touristique en Algérie (SODITAL): 72 rue Asselah Hocine, Algiers; f. 1989; Dir-Gen. NOUREDDINE SALHI.

TCA-TOUR (Touring Club d'Algérie): BP 18, Birkhamden; rue Hacéne Benaamane, quartier les vergers, Algiers; tel. (21) 56-90-16; fax (21) 54-19-39; Dir-Gen. ABDERAHMANE ABD-EDDAIM.

Defence

Chief of Staff of the Army: Lt-Gen. MUHAMMAD LAMARI.
Commander of the Land Force: Gen. ABDELAZIZ MADJAHED.

Commander of the Air Force: Maj.-Gen. MUHAMMAD BENSLIMANE.
Commander of the Naval Forces: Gen. BRAHIM DADCI.
Defence Budget (2000): AD 138,000m.
Military Service: 18 months national service (army only).
Total Armed Forces (August 2001): 124,000: army 107,000 (75,000 conscripts); navy 7,000; air force 10,000.
Paramilitary Forces: 181,200 (including an estimated 100,000 self-defence militia and communal guards, and a gendarmerie of 60,000).

Education

Education, in the national language (Arabic), is officially compulsory for a period of nine years, for children between six and 15 years of age. Primary education begins at the age of six and lasts for six years. Secondary education begins at 12 years of age and lasts for a maximum of six years, comprising two cycles of three years each. In 1996 the total enrolment at primary and secondary schools was equivalent to 86% of the school-age population (90% of boys; 82% of girls). Primary enrolment in that year included 94% of children in the relevant age-group (boys 97%; girls 91%). The comparable ratio for secondary enrolment was 56% (boys 58%; girls 54%). Some 12.5% of total planned expenditure in the 1997 administrative budget was allocated to education and training.

There were some 4,778,870 pupils at primary schools in 1997/98, compared with about 800,000 in 1962. Most education at primary level is in Arabic, but at higher levels French is still widely used. In 1999 provision was made to allow the use of the Berber language, Tamazight, as a language of instruction in Algerian schools. The majority of foreign teachers in Algeria come from Egypt, Syria, Tunisia and other Arab countries.

In 1995/96 the number of students receiving higher education was 347,410. In addition to the 10 main universities there are seven other *centres universitaires* and a number of technical colleges. Several thousand students go abroad to study. Efforts have been made to combat adult illiteracy by means of a large-scale campaign in which instruction is sometimes given by young people who have only recently left school, and in which the broadcasting services are widely used.

Bibliography

Ageron, Charles-Robert. *Modern Algeria: A History from 1830 to the present*. London, Hurst, 1992.

Aissaoui, Ali. *Algeria—The Political Economy of Oil and Gas*. New York/Oxford, Oxford University Press, 2001.

Aït-Chaalal, Amine. *Algérie–Etats-Unis; des relations denses et complexes*. Louvain-la-Neuve, CERMAC, 1998.

Al-Ahnaf, M., Botiveau, B., and Frégosi, F. *L'Algérie par ses islamistes*. Paris, Editions Karthala, 1992.

Alazard, J., and others. *Invitation à l'Algérie*. Paris, 1957.

Allais, M. *Les Accords d'Evian, le référendum et la résistance algérienne*. Paris, 1962.

Amin, Samir. *The Maghreb in the Modern World: Algeria, Tunisia, Morocco*. Harmondsworth, Penguin, 1970.

Amrane-Minne, Danièle Djamila. *Des Femmes dans la Guerre d'Algérie*. Paris, Editions Karthala, 1996.

Aron, Raymond. *La Tragédie Algérienne*. Paris, 1957.

Aussaresses, Gen. Paul. *Services spéciaux Algérie 1955–1957: Mon témoignage sur la torture*. Paris, Perrin, 2001.

Baduel, Pierre R. *L'Algérie incertaine*. Aix-en-Provence, Edisud, 1993.

Barakat, H. *Contemporary North Africa. Issues of development and integration*. London, Croom Helm, 1985.

Bedjaoui, Youcef, et al (Eds). *An inquiry into the Algerian massacres*. Geneva, Hoggar, 1999.

Belarbi, Ahcene. *Demain, la mémoire: chroniques de l'Algérie massacrée*. Paris, Editions des Ecrivains, 2000.

Bencherif, Osman. *The Image of Algeria in Anglo-American Writings 1785–1962*. Lanham MD, University Press of Algeria, 1997.

Bennoune, M. *The Making of Contemporary Algeria (1830–1987)*. Cambridge, Cambridge University Press, 1988.

Bonora, C. *France and the Algerian Conflict*. Aldershot, Ashgate Publishing Ltd, 2000.

Boudiaf, Muhammad. *Où va l'Algérie?* Algeria, Rahma, 1992.

Boukhobza, M'Hammed. *Ruptures et transformations sociales en Algérie*. Algiers, OPU 1989.

Boukra, Liess. *Algérie: la terreur sacrée*. Paris, Favre, 2002.

Bourdieu, Pierre. *The Algerians*. Boston, 1962.

Sociologie de l'Algérie. Paris, Que Sais-je, 1958.

Brace, R. and J. *Ordeal in Algeria*. New York, 1960.

Burgat, F., and Dowell, W. *The Islamic Movement in North Africa*. Austin, Texas, University of Texas Press, 1993.

Chaliand, G. *L'Algérie, est-elle Socialiste?* Paris, Maspéro, 1964.

Charrad, Mounira M., *States and Women's Rights—The Making of Postcolonial Tunisia, Algeria and Morocco*. Berkeley, CA, University of California Press, 2000.

Ciment, James. *Algeria*. London, Facts on File Inc., 1997.

De Gaulle, Charles. *Mémoires d'espoir: Le Renouveau 1958–1962*. Paris, Plon, 1970.

Derradji, A. *The Algerian Guerrilla Campaign: Strategy and Tactics*. Edwin Mellen Press, 1997.

Dillmann, Bradford D. *State and Private Sector in Algeria: The Politics of Rent-seeking and Failed Development*. Boulder, CO, Westview Press, 2000.

Duquesne, Jacques. *Pour Comprendre la Guerre d'Algérie*. Paris, Perrin, 2002.

El-Hadi, Chalabi. *La Presse Algérienne Au-dessus de tout Soupçon*. Algiers/Paris, Hina-Yas, 1999.

Encyclopaedia of Islam. *Algeria*. New edition, Vol. I. London and Leiden, 1960.

Eveno, P., and Planchais, J. *La Guerre d'Algérie*. Paris, La Découverte, 1989.

Faivre, Maurice. *Les archives inédites de la politique algérienne 1958–1962*. Paris, L'Harmattan, 2000.

Faksh, Mahmud A. *The Future of Islam in the Middle East.* London, Praeger Publishers, 1997.

Favrod, Ch.-H. *Le FLN et l'Algérie.* Paris, 1962.

First, Ruth. *The Barrel of a Gun: Political Power in Africa and the Coup d'Etat.* London, Allen Lane, The Penguin Press, 1970.

Forestier, Patrick, with Salam, Ahmed. *Confession d'un émir du GIA.* Grasset et Fasquelle, Paris, 1999.

Francos, Avia, and Séréri, J.-P. *Un Algérien nommé Boumedienne.* Paris, 1976.

Fuller, Graham E. *Algeria: The Next Fundamentalist State.* Rand Corporation, 1996.

Gacemi, Baya. *Moi, Nadia, femme d'un émir du GIA.* Seuil, Paris, 1999.

Garon, Lise. *L'obsession unitaire et la Nation trompée: la fin de l'Algérie socialiste.* Montreal, University of Laval Press, 1993.

Gillespie, Joan. *Algeria.* London, Benn, 1960.

Gordon, David. *North Africa's French Legacy, 1954–1963.* London, 1963.

   The Passing of French Algeria. Oxford, 1966.

Goytisolo, Juan. *Argelia en el vendaval.* Madrid, El País-Aguilar, 1994.

Harbi, Muhammad. *L'Algérie et son destin.* Paris, Arcantère, 1992.

Hassan. *Algérie, histoire d'un naufrage.* Paris, Seuil, 1995.

Henissart, Paul. *Wolves in the City: The Death of French Algeria.* London, Hart-Davis, 1971.

Horne, Alistair. *A Savage War of Peace: Algeria 1954–1962.* London, Macmillan, 1977.

Humbaraci, Arslan. *Algeria—A Revolution that Failed.* London, Pall Mall, 1966.

Ibrahimi, A. Taleb. *De la Décolonisation à la Révolution Culturelle (1962–72).* Algiers, SNED, 1973.

Jeanson, F. *La Révolution Algérienne; Problèmes et Perspectives.* Milan, 1962.

Joesten, Joachim. *The New Algeria.* New York, 1964.

Julien, Charles-André. *Histoire de l'Algérie contemporaine, conquête et colonisation, 1827–1871.* Paris, Presses Universitaires de France, 1964.

Kettle, Michael. *De Gaulle and Algeria.* London, Quartet, 1993.

Khelladi, A. *Les islamistes algériens face au pouvoir.* Algiers, Alfa, 1992.

Lacheraf, Mostepha. *L'Algérie, Nation et Société.* Paris, Maspéro, 1965.

Laffont, Pierre. *L'Expiation: De l'Algérie de papa à l'Algérie de Ben Bella.* Paris, Plon, 1968.

Lakehal, M. *Algérie: De l'indépendance à l'Etat d'urgence.* Paris, L'Harmattan, 1992.

Lambotte, R. *Algérie, naissance d'une société nouvelle.* Paris, Editions Sociales, 1976.

Laremont, Ricardo René. *Islam and the Politics of Resistance in Algeria 1783–1992.* Trenton, NJ, Africa World Press, 2000.

Lassassi, Assassi. *Non-alignment and Algerian Foreign Policy.* Aldershot, Dartmouth, 1988.

Lawless, Richard I. *Algeria.* World Bibliographical Series Vol. 19. Denver, CO, Clio Press, 1995.

Lazseg, Marnia (Ed.). *The Eloquence of Silence: Algerian Women in Question.* London, Routledge, 1994.

Le Sueur, James D. *Uncivil War: Intellectuals and Identity Politics during the Decolonzation of Algeria.* Philadelphia, PA, University of Pennsylvania Press, 2001.

Lebjaoui, Mohamed. *Vérités sur la Révolution Algérienne.* Paris, Gallimard, 1970.

Leca, Jean, and Vatin, Jean-Claude. *L'Algérie politique, institutions et régime.* Paris, Fondation nationale des sciences politiques, 1974.

López, B., Martín Muñoz, G., and Larramendi, M. *Elecciones, participación y transiciones políticas en el norte de Africa.* Madrid, ICMA, 1992.

Lorcin, Patricia M. E. Imperial Identities: *Stereotyping, Prejudice and Race in Colonial Algeria.* London and New York, I. B. Tauris, 1999.

Lyotard, Jean-François. *La Guerre des Algériens Ecrits 1956–1963.* Paris, Galilée, 1989.

Mallarde, Etienne. *L'Algérie depuis.* Paris, La Table Ronde, 1977.

Malley, Robert. *The Call from Algeria: Third Worldism, Revolution and the Turn to Islam.* University of California Press, 1996.

Mandouze, André. *La Révolution Algérienne par les Textes.* Paris, 1961.

Martens, Jean-Claude. *Le modèle algérien de développement (1962–1972).* Algiers, SNED, 1973.

Martin, Claude. *Histoire de l'Algérie Française 1830–1962.* Paris, 1962.

Martín Muñoz, G. *Democracia y derechos humanos en el mundo árabe.* Madrid, ICMA, 1994.

Martinez, Luis. *The Algerian Civil War, 1990–1998.* London, C. Hurst and Co., 2000.

Mouilleseaux, Louiz. *Histoire de l'Algérie.* Paris, 1962.

Nabi, Muhammad. *L'Algérie aujourd'hui ou l'absence d'alternatives à l'Islam politique.* Paris, L'Harmattan, 2000.

Nyssen, Hubert. *L'Algérie en 1970.* 1970.

Ottaway, David and Marina. *Algeria. The Politics of a Socialist Revolution.* Berkeley, University of California Press, 1970.

Ouzegane, Amar. *Le Meilleur Combat.* Paris, Julliard, 1962.

Pierre, Andrew J., and Quandt, William B. *The Algerian Crisis, Policy Options for the West.* Washington, DC, The Brookings Institution, 1997.

Quandt, William B. *Revolution and Political Leadership: Algeria, 1954–1968.* MIT Press, 1970.

   Between Ballots and Bullets: Algeria's Transition from Authoritarianism. Brookings Institution Press, 1998.

Redjala, R. *L'opposition en Algérie depuis 1962.* Paris, L'Harmattan, 1988.

Reudy, John D. *Land Policy in Colonial Algeria: The Origins of the Rural Public Domain.* Berkeley, University of California Press, 1967.

Rey-Goldzeiguer, Annie. *Aux origines de la guerre d'Algérie 1940–1945. De Mers el-Kébir aux massacres du Nord-Constantinois.* Paris, La Découverte, 2002.

Rivet, Daniel. *Le Maghreb à l'épreuve de la colonisation.* Paris, Hachette Littératures, 2002.

Robson, P., and Lury, D. *The Economics of Africa.* London, Allen & Unwin, 1969.

Ruedy, J. *Modern Algeria: The origins and development of a nation.* Bloomington, Indiana University Press, 1992.

Sa'dallah, A. Q. *Studies on Modern Algerian Literature.* Beirut, Al Adab, 1966.

Sanderson, H. *Laïcité islamique en Algérie.* Paris, CNRS, 1983.

Schiemla, E. *Unbowed: An Algerian Woman Confronts Islamic Fundamentalism. Interviews with Khalida Messaoudi.* Philadelphia, PA, University of Pennsylvania Press, 1998.

Segura i Mas, Antoni. *El Magreb, del colonialismo al islamismo.* Barcelona, Universidad de Barcelona, 1994.

Shade, Poulsen Marc. *Men and Popular Music in Algeria: The Social Significance of Rai.* Austin, University of Texas Press, 1999.

Sivan, Emmanuel. *Communisme et Nationalisme en Algérie (1920–1962).* Paris, 1976.

Smith, Tony. *The French Stake in Algeria 1945–1962.* Cornell University Press, 1978.

Souaïda, Habib. *La sale guerre.* Paris, La Découverte, 2001.

Stone, Martin. *The Agony of Algeria.* London, C. Hurst & Co Ltd, 1998.

Stora, Benhamin. *Historie de l'Algérie coloniale.* Cheltenham, Gallimard-Jenmesse, 1998.

Sulzberger, C. L. *The Test, de Gaulle and Algeria.* London and New York, 1962.

Talbott, John. *France in Algeria, 1954–1962.* New York, Knopf, 1980.

Vatin, Jean-Claude. *L'Algérie politique, histoire et société.* Paris, Fondation nationale des sciences politiques, 1974.

Vidal-Naquet, Pierre. *L'Affaire Audin.* Paris, Les éditions de Minuit, 1989.

   Face à la Raison d'Etat: Un Historien dans la Guerre d'Algérie. Paris, La Découverte, 1989.

Wall, Irwin M. *France, the United States and the Algerian War,* Berkeley, CA, University of California Press, 2001.

Willis, Michael. *The Islamist Challenge in Algeria.* Reading, Ithaca Press, 1996.

Yous, Nesroulah. *Qui a tué à Bentalha?* Paris, La Découverte, 2000.

Zahraoui, Saïd. *Entre l'horreur et l'espoir 1990–1999: Chronique de la nouvelle guerre d'Algérie.* Paris, Laffont, 2000.

BAHRAIN

Geography

The Kingdom of Bahrain consists of a group of some 36 islands, situated midway along the Persian (Arabian) Gulf, about 24 km from the east coast of Saudi Arabia, and 28 km from the west coast of Qatar.

The total area of the Bahrain archipelago is 711.9 sq km. Bahrain itself, the principal island, is about 50 km long and between 13 km and 25 km wide. To the north-east of Bahrain, and linked to it by causeway and road, lies Muharraq island, which is approximately 6 km long. A causeway also links Bahrain island to Sitra island. Other islands in the state include Nabih Salih, Jeddah, Hawar, Umm Nassan and Umm Suban. A causeway linking Bahrain and Saudi Arabia was opened in November 1986. The construction of a causeway linking eastern Bahrain to Qatar (the Friendship Bridge) is also planned.

Between April 1971 and the latest census of 7 April 2001 the total population of Bahrain increased from 216,078 to 650,604, of whom 405,667 (62.4%) were Bahraini citizens. About 80% of the population are thought to be of Arab ethnic origin, and 20% Iranian. In 2001 the port of Manama (on Bahrain island), the capital and seat of government, had a population of 153,395. Bahrain's Muslim population (82% of the total in 1991) is estimated to consist of more than 40% of the Sunni sect and almost 60% of the Shi'ite sect. The ruling family are Sunnis. The Bahraini labour force was forecast to have doubled between 1989 and the end of the 20th century: some 62% of the working population were estimated to be of non-Bahraini origin in 2001.

History

EARLY HISTORY

After several centuries of independence, Bahrain passed first under the rule of the Portuguese (1521–1602) and then under periodic Persian rule (1602–1782). The Persians were expelled in 1783 by the Utub tribe from Arabia, whose leading family, the al-Khalifas, became the independent sheikhs of Bahrain and have ruled Bahrain ever since, except for a brief period before 1810. Nevertheless, claims based on the Persian occupation of the islands were renewed intermittently.

In the 19th century European powers began to take an interest in the Gulf area. Britain was principally concerned with preventing French, Russian and German penetration towards India, and suppressing the trade in slaves and weapons. In 1861 the Sheikh of Bahrain undertook to abstain from the prosecution of war, piracy and slavery by sea, in return for British support in case of aggression. In 1880 and 1892 the Sheikh also pledged not to cede, mortgage or otherwise dispose of parts of his territories to anyone except the British Government, nor to enter into relations with any other government without British consent. A convention acknowledging Bahrain's independence was signed by the British and Ottoman Governments in 1913, although the islands remained under British control.

Under Sheikh Sulman bin Hamad al-Khalifa (who became ruler of Bahrain in 1942) social services and public works were considerably extended. Sheikh Sulman was succeeded on his death in November 1961 by his eldest son, Sheikh Isa bin Sulman al-Khalifa. In February 1956 elections were held for members of an Education and Health Council (the first election in Bahrain had been held in 1919 for the Municipal Council). Shortly after the 1956 elections a strike was held at the petroleum refinery, alleged to be partly a protest against the paternalism of the British adviser to the Sheikh; there were further disturbances during the Suez crisis. Other symbols of Bahrain's growing independence included the establishment of Bahraini, as opposed to British, legal jurisdiction over a wide range of nationalities (1957), the issue of Bahrain's own postage stamps (1960) and the introduction of a separate currency (1965). Bahrain also pioneered free education and health services in the Gulf region. In 1967 the United Kingdom transferred its principal Arabian military base from Aden to Bahrain, but by 1968 the British Government had decided to withdraw all forces 'East of Suez' before the end of 1971. In October 1973, at the time of the Arab–Israeli war, the Bahrain Government gave one year's 'notice to quit' to the US navy, whose ships had docking facilities in Bahrain. However, it was not until July 1977 that Bahrain finally took over the base.

Extensive administrative and political reforms came into effect in January 1970, when a 12-member Council of State was established. The formation of this new body, which became the state's supreme executive authority, represented the first formal derogation of the ruler's powers. Sheikh Khalifa bin Sulman al-Khalifa, the ruler's eldest brother, became President of the Council. Only four of the initial 12 'Directors' were members of the royal family, but all were Bahrainis, and the British advisers were reduced to the status of civil servants. Equal numbers of Sunni and Shi'ite Muslims were included (the royal family apart) to reflect Bahrain's religious balance. When Bahrain became fully independent, in August 1971, the Council of State became the Cabinet of the State of Bahrain (with Sheikh Khalifa as Prime Minister), with authority to direct the country's internal and external affairs.

After 1968 Bahrain was officially committed to membership of the embryonic Federation of Arab Emirates. The Bahrain Government, however, failed to agree on the terms of the federal constitution with the richer, but less developed, sheikhdoms in the region. Bahrain's position was strengthened in May 1970 when Iran accepted the findings of a UN report that the Bahraini people overwhelmingly favoured complete independence rather than union with Iran.

DOMESTIC POLITICS AND INTERNAL UNREST

On 15 August 1971 Bahrain's full independence was proclaimed; a new treaty of friendship was signed with the United Kingdom, and Sheikh Isa took the title of Amir. Bahrain became a member of the League of Arab States (the Arab League) and of the UN. In December 1972 elections were held for a Constituent Assembly. This body drafted a new Constitution, which came into force on 6 December 1973. Elections to a 44-member National Assembly took place the following day. Of its members, 30 were chosen by the all-male electorate, the rest being members of the Government. A delay in the establishment of trade unions, for which the Constitution made provision, and a sharp rise in the cost of living provoked industrial unrest in 1974. In August 1975 the Prime Minister submitted his resignation, complaining that the National Assembly was preventing the Government from exercising its functions. The Amir invited him to form a new government, and, two days later, dissolved the National Assembly and suspended the Constitution. Although the traditional administrative system of *majlis* (assembly), where citizens and non-citizens present petitions to the Amir, remained, it was not until November 1992 that the Amir announced the formation of a new, 30-member Consultative Council. The Council, whose establishment met with little popular enthusiasm, had little scope to question or alter government policy, and power remained with the Amir and the ruling al-Khalifa family.

In September 1979 Iranian Shi'ite elements exhorted Bahraini Shi'ites, who are in the majority and many of whom are of Iranian descent, to demonstrate against the Sunni Amir. Calm was restored, but it was apparent that the new regime in Iran was interested in reviving the Iranian claim to Bahrain, which the Shah of Iran had not renounced until 1975. In December 1981 at least 50 people, mainly Bahrainis, were arrested in Bahrain on charges of conspiring to overthrow the Government. Bahrain's Minister of the Interior alleged that the plot was the work of Hojatoleslam Hadi al-Mudarasi, an Iranian cleric who was operating in the name of the Islamic Front for the Liberation of Bahrain (IFLB). In 1984 the discovery of a cache of weapons in a Bahraini village renewed fears of Iranian attempts to disrupt the island's stability, and in June 1985 concern grew when a further plot to overthrow the Government was discovered. Despite subsequent reassurances from President Hashemi Rafsanjani of Iran, and cordial relations with his successor, President Muhammad Khatami, Bahrain has continued to monitor carefully both domestic stability and the political situation in Tehran. Strict censorship is imposed, and political parties and trade unions are banned. The Government has been severely criticized by human rights organizations for its alleged use of torture and detention without trial.

Fears of unrest among Bahrain's Shi'ite majority have continued to preoccupy the ruling regime and to motivate an uncompromising response to popular disaffection. In December 1993 a prominent human rights organization, Amnesty International, published a highly critical report, claiming that Bahraini Shi'ites had been deprived of their nationality and forcibly exiled by their own Government. In response to such criticism, the Amir issued a decree in March 1994 pardoning 64 Bahrainis exiled since the 1980s and permitting them to return to Bahrain. Unrest continued during 1994 as young men demonstrated against rising unemployment among Bahraini nationals, particularly the Shi'ite population. In November 12 Shi'ite villagers were reported to have been arrested in Jidd Hafs, to the west of Manama, following the violent disruption of a charity running event in which a group of expatriate men and women was participating. In early December police arrested a young Shi'ite cleric, Sheikh Ali Salman, imam of the main Shi'ite mosque in Manama, who had demanded the release of those arrested at Jidd Hafs and had also condemned the participation of women in the race. He had, moreover, appealed for the restitution of the National Assembly and criticized the ruling family, the large number of foreign workers employed on the island, and the decline of moral standards. Despite an attempt by the Amir to defuse the crisis, widespread rioting ensued, especially in Shi'ite areas where demonstrators appealed for the release of Sheikh Salman; several people died in clashes with armed police. The crisis was particularly embarrassing for the Government as it occurred as Bahrain was about to host a summit meeting of the Co-operation Council for the Arab States of the Gulf (Gulf Co-operation Council—GCC). The authorities acknowledged the existence of political unrest and blamed Sheikh Salman and certain 'foreign interests'—a coded reference to Iran. The police proceeded to make a large number of arrests: according to opposition sources, some 2,500 Bahrainis, mainly Shi'ites, had been arrested by mid-January 1995. While some observers pointed to the role of Shi'ite clerics—many of whom received their religious training in the Iranian city of Qom—in instigating the unrest, others emphasized that these disturbances were very different from the events of 1981, when the new regime in Tehran had urged Bahraini Shi'ites to overthrow the Amir. Indeed, the political slogans employed during the 1994 demonstrations were not urging the establishment of an Islamic republic in Bahrain but, rather, the restoration of parliamentary life through the re-establishment of the National Assembly. Sheikh Salman had been active in supporting a petition (which had been circulating since October 1994) appealing for the restoration of the Assembly, the involvement of women in the democratic process and the organization of free elections. According to opposition sources, some 21,000–25,000 signatures had been obtained, including those of Sunnis and Shi'ites from the professional classes, despite the vigilance of the security services. The thwarted aspirations of the Shi'ite majority—

primarily a result of socio-economic factors, especially rising unemployment—also contributed to the crisis. Shi'ite workers felt threatened by the recruitment of cheap and well-qualified Asian labour, a practice encouraged by several members of the royal family who benefited financially from immigration; they also resented the presence of a large number of highly-paid expatriates employed mainly in the financial sector.

In mid-January 1995 Sheikh Salman, together with two associates, was deported from Bahrain. He arrived in the United Kingdom seeking political asylum, whereupon the Bahraini Minister of Foreign Affairs, Sheikh Muhammad bin Mubarak al-Khalifa, was dispatched to London to demand that Salman's request be denied. Crown Prince Sheikh Hamad bin Isa al-Khalifa accused the British authorities of sheltering 'terrorists and saboteurs'. The Government confirmed that the demonstrators detained during the unrest in December 1994 would stand trial, but denied foreign press reports of renewed civil disturbances.

Throughout the crisis the Amir received the full support of Saudi Arabia, which, according to Bahraini opposition sources, had rapidly dispatched two brigades of its National Guard (around 4,000 men) across the causeway to Bahrain to assist the local police in quelling the rioting. During a visit to Manama in late December 1994 the Saudi Minister of the Interior, Prince Nayef ibn Abd al-Aziz as-Sa'ud, reiterated his country's support for the Bahrain Government's firm stance against the demonstrators, as Saudi Arabia was particularly concerned that any unrest among the Shi'ites of Bahrain should not spread to its own Shi'ite population.

In early March 1995 the Amir ordered the release of 100 detainees, including some of those arrested during the disturbances in December 1994—300 of whom reportedly remained in prison. At least two people died in further violence at the end of March 1995, and there were renewed protests during the first week of April. The Prime Minister blamed 'foreign groups' for what he claimed were premeditated 'acts of sabotage'. In May and July several Bahrainis were sentenced to prison terms ranging from one year to life imprisonment for their role in the protests, and one Bahraini was sentenced to death for his part in the murder of a policeman in March (see below). In mid-August the Amir issued a decree pardoning 150 people detained since the disturbances. In the same month the Government initiated talks with Shi'ite opposition leaders in an apparent attempt at reconciliation, although by mid-September the talks had collapsed. Nevertheless, in late September an influential Shi'ite clergyman, Sheikh Abd al-Amir al-Jamri (imprisoned in April), was released from detention; more than 40 other Shi'ite detainees were released shortly afterwards.

At the end of June 1995 the Prime Minister, Sheikh Khalifa bin Sulman al-Khalifa, announced the first major cabinet reshuffle in nearly 20 years. Cabinet changes had been expected since the outbreak of political unrest in December 1994, although the regime insisted that the reallocation of portfolios had been planned for some time. There were no changes, however, to the key defence, foreign affairs, finance and national economy and interior portfolios. Within the new 16-member Cabinet, seven posts were retained by members of the ruling family and five by Shi'ites. It was also announced that the Bahraini Defence Force would be expanded. The opposition denounced the reshuffle as purely cosmetic, and accused the Government of ignoring new political developments.

Meanwhile, the opposition maintained that the authorities had agreed, in the course of the reconciliation talks initiated in mid-1995, to release all detainees and to allow the return of political exiles. In return, the opposition pledged to exert its influence in an attempt to end the violence. By early October some 400 political prisoners had been released. However, accusing the Government of having failed to fulfil its promise to release all detainees, in October seven opposition leaders led by Sheikh Abd al-Amir al-Jamri began a hunger strike. They demanded the release of all political prisoners, as well as permission for those dissidents who had been deported to return to Bahrain and an agreement by the authorities to resume open talks with the opposition regarding the restoration of the 1973 Constitution; the Government had denied that earlier meetings with the opposition had actually taken place. Sheikh al-Jamri and the other protesters ended their hunger strike at the beginning of November 1995 without achieving their objectives.

Disturbances erupted again in November 1995 (especially among students) and, according to opposition sources, the police made hundreds of arrests. The authorities sought assistance from Saudi Arabia, and it was reported that Saudi security officers were again dispatched to reinforce the Bahraini police. In January and February 1996 the conflict escalated when a number of bombs exploded in Manama's business district. The security forces had closed mosques where prominent leaders had continued to urge the authorities to restore democracy, and in late January eight opposition leaders, including Sheikh al-Jamri, had been rearrested. They were expected to stand trial on charges of inciting unrest. For the first time in the recent disturbances the authorities also detained a prominent Sunni member of the Committee for Popular Petition: Ahmad ash-Shamlan, a lawyer, was arrested after distributing a statement criticizing the Government's authoritarian action. Ash-Shamlan was released in May, following strong representation by international organizations. The closure of mosques provoked renewed clashes between protesters and police. Mass arrests were reported, and at the beginning of February the Ministry of the Interior admitted that some 600 people had been detained; the opposition estimated the number of arrests at 2,000. Reports suggested that most of those detained (including women and children) were held without charge or trial. A report published in September 1995 by Amnesty International had emphasized what it claimed to be the systematic use of torture by the security services when interrogating political prisoners. Previously, civil disturbances had been dealt with by the Ministry of the Interior, but in a statement issued at the end of January 1996 the Ministry of Defence announced that it was prepared to introduce martial law and to deploy the Bahraini Defence Force to restore effective order in the future.

In March 1996, as unrest continued, seven Bangladeshi workers were killed in the worst arson attack since the disturbances began— a fire-bomb at a restaurant in Sitra. Within days the Ministry of the Interior announced that it had arrested a number of individuals who had confessed to the attack, but many Bahrainis suspected the involvement of government agents. The opposition condemned the attack, while the Bangladeshi Government was critical of the Bahrain security forces' handling of the case. The Amir subsequently issued a decree transferring jurisdiction for a range of offences from ordinary courts to the Higher Court of Appeal, sitting as the State Security Court. This effectively introduced a 'fast-track' system, denying the accused any right of appeal and greatly limiting the role of the defence. In late March Isa Ahmad Hassan Qambar was executed by firing squad for killing a police-officer during clashes with security forces in March 1995. This was the first execution in Bahrain for almost 20 years. The Bahraini opposition described it as a 'political murder' intended to prompt popular compliance. There were allegations that the case against Qambar had been based on confessions made in detention and under torture. The execution provoked mass protests, with police using tear gas to disperse young Shi'ite protesters. In April 1996 the Government announced the creation of a Higher Council of Islamic Affairs, appointed by the Prime Minister and headed by the Minister of Justice and Islamic Affairs, to supervise religious activities in the country, including those of the Shi'ite population. Leading Shi'ites immediately condemned the move as an attempt to interfere in their affairs. At the end of April the Government announced that the State Security Court had imprisoned 11 people on charges connected with the disturbances, including arson, sabotage and membership of illegal organizations. It was reported that large numbers of defendants had been tried in groups and sentenced to long terms of imprisonment by the Court. At the beginning of May, following the death of a demonstrator after security forces opened fire on a crowd of protesters, a number of bombs exploded throughout the country, killing several people (including two policemen). Most observers consider that the pro-democracy movement is locally-rooted, unifying various trends and sections of Bahraini society with no outside support, despite the insistence of the authorities that the dissidents have foreign backers.

At the beginning of June 1996, at a press conference in Manama, the Government announced that some 10 prisoners had confessed to belonging to the military branch of Hezbollah Bahrain, a previously unknown organization. According to the authorities, the prisoners had admitted that this terrorist group had been created on the instruction of, and had received financial support from, Iran's Revolutionary Guards. They alleged that young Bahraini Shi'ites had received military training in the Iranian holy city of Qom and in guerrilla bases in the Beka'a valley in Lebanon. They also claimed that the previous 18 months of unrest had been the culmination of a 'terrorist programme of sabotage' perpetrated by Hezbollah Bahrain in order to overthrow the regime and replace it with a pro-Iranian government. However, the authorities were satisfied that they had arrested the movement's leaders. The day after the press conference, as the prisoners made their confessions before television cameras, one of them claimed that Sheikh al-Jamri had 'sanctioned' two bomb attacks carried out in July 1995. However, an opposition spokesman in the United Kingdom rejected claims that a Hezbollah group sponsored by Iran was active in Bahrain. Independent sources also cast doubt on the validity of the confessions, claiming that the prisoners had been denied legal representation during their detention, and referred to Amnesty International's report in September 1995 which alleged that political detainees were systematically tortured. They also pointed out that recent acts of sabotage were not professionally executed and therefore not consistent with the presence of a well-trained and well-armed movement such as Hezbollah. This was the first time that the Bahrain Government had directly accused Iran of supporting the unrest, allegations which Iran persistently denied. Bahrain recalled its ambassador to Tehran and downgraded its diplomatic representation there.

In July 1996 the State Security Court imposed death sentences on three of the eight young Bahrainis convicted of the arson attack in Sitra. Another four men were sentenced to life imprisonment. The death sentences provoked widespread protests, and, after international criticism, the Government agreed to allow an appeal against the ruling. In October the Court of Cassation ruled that it had no jurisdiction to overturn the verdict, and the fate of the three men seemed likely to be decided by the Amir. There were more anti-Government demonstrations in July and August, and a campaign of civil disobedience organized by the exiled Bahrain Freedom Movement (BFM) was reported to have been well supported, notably among the Shi'ite population. Towards the end of the year government plans to close a number of Shi'ite mosques resulted in further unrest. Demonstrators gathered at the Ras Roman mosque in central Manama became involved in a violent confrontation with the security forces during which police fired tear gas at worshippers. Meanwhile, rumours circulated that the ruling family was divided over how to respond to the civil unrest.

In September 1996, in what was interpreted as a move to counter opposition demands, the Amir expanded the membership of the government-appointed Consultative Council from 30 to 40 and allowed up to one-half of the members to be elected indirectly through professional and cultural organizations. The new Council comprised 22 members of the previous body and 18 new members nominated by the Amir. Appointed for a four-year term, the Council was to comment on most areas of government policy (the previous Council had been restricted to consideration of Cabinet-proposed legislation) but would still enjoy very limited powers since its recommendations would continue to be non-binding on the Government. A new decree, issued by the Amir in June, divided Bahrain into four new administrative regions, or *mohafadat*, with the aim of improving services and making officials more accountable. However, opponents argued that the new system would enable the Ministry of the Interior to intensify security measures, particularly following reports that the ministry was to be reorganized and the intelligence service expanded. In January 1997 the Amir issued a decree establishing a National Guard to provide support for the Bahraini Defence Force and the security forces of the interior ministry. Crown Prince Hamad, already Commander-in-Chief of the Defence Force, was also appointed to command the new force, and there was speculation that its primary duty would be to protect the ruling family.

Unrest continued, and in March 1997 a week of anti-Government protests marked the first anniversary of the execution of Isa Ahmad Hassan Qambar. Although stricter security measures had resulted in fewer public demonstrations, arson attacks increased substantially, especially against commercial premises in Manama. During 1994–97 more than 30 people were killed in arson attacks and small-scale bombings. Two car bomb explosions in the capital, in June and October 1997, were considered by some observers to signal the beginning of a heightened campaign of violence on the part of the opposition. A pronounced increase in the number of Asian workers targeted by arsonists between 1996 and early 1998 was attributed, in part, to mounting frustration among less privileged sections of Bahraini society at rising unemployment.

In April 1997 the US military command in Bahrain placed its forces on alert after reports of possible terrorist operations against US navy personnel by Hezbollah Bahrain. In January the security forces had successfully contained large-scale anti-Government demonstrations organized by opponents of the regime on the occasion of the second anniversary of the arrest of Sheikh Abd al-Amir al-Jamri. The cleric's deteriorating state of health lent a sense of urgency to the occasion. In July, following the death in custody of another senior Shi'ite dissident cleric, the US-based Human Rights Watch published a report condemning the security practices of the Bahrain Government. Growing concern for human rights in Bahrain resulted in unprecedented scrutiny of its internal affairs by the international community (the European Parliament in particular urged the Bahrain Government to release political prisoners and to grant access to human rights organizations), and sentences imposed on political opponents became noticeably more lenient. In mid-April 1997 the trial of 81 Bahrainis accused of membership of Hezbollah Bahrain ended unexpectedly with relatively light sentences: the maximum terms of imprisonment imposed (on the alleged leaders) were 15 years. A lawsuit filed by the Government in October against eight Shi'ite members of the opposition resident abroad followed a similar course. Despite the severity of the charges, which included inciting violence, establishing Hezbollah Bahrain, and attempting to overthrow the regime, the dissidents, who were tried *in absentia*, received prison sentences of between five and 15 years. During 1997 the authorities released a substantial number of political detainees (some 3,000, according to unofficial sources).

In January 1998 the Amir announced plans further to enlarge the Consultative Council. Media coverage of Council proceedings, meanwhile, increased substantially, and access to its sessions was granted to the press and to state-controlled television. In addition, during 1997 the Ministry of Information relaxed publishing restrictions considerably. Administrative reorganization of state continued, and two members of the ruling family were appointed to the governorships of Manama and Muharraq island in 1997 and 1998; they were to be directly responsible to the Ministry of the Interior. These new developments were interpreted as further evidence of an ongoing power struggle between the Prime Minister and the Crown Prince. In February 1998 Ian Henderson, the long-serving British-born head of the State Security Investigation Directorate, was replaced by Khalid bin Muhammad al-Khalifa, a close associate of the Crown Prince. The dismissal of Henderson, considered to be central to the apparatus of state repression, was welcomed by opponents of the Government, who stated that a precondition for dialogue with the Government was the 'Bahrainization' of the security forces: in 1997 opposition sources estimated that as many as 50,000 non-Bahrainis were employed in the country's security services.

During 1998 the security forces were increasingly successful in containing internal unrest. Harsh sentences were imposed on political opponents by the State Security Court, in contrast to the leniency displayed during the previous year. Although the International Committee of the Red Cross (ICRC) reported an improvement in prison conditions, opposition figures continued to voice concerns about security practices, particularly the alleged extraction of confessions under torture and the enforced signing of pre-drafted documents. Renewed protests followed the death in government custody of a young Shi'ite in July 1998, and in late 1998 the death of a political activist recently released from detention provoked confrontations between Shi'ite demonstrators and police in Sitra. Also in July the death in Lebanon, in mysterious circumstances, of a Bahraini national, Tawfiq Abd an-Nabi Ibrahim al-Baharinah, prompted speculation about

efforts on the part of the Bahrain Government to trace links between the internal opposition and Hezbollah. Initial reports, endorsed by the Lebanese Minister of Foreign Affairs, suggested that al-Baharinah had been a Bahraini intelligence agent, although Bahrain subsequently denied this. Independent observers suggested that al-Baharinah might have been a member of the opposition IFLB, believed to have a strong support base in Lebanon. Renewed government concerns over the possible involvement of Lebanese Hezbollah in Bahrain's internal affairs coincided with the explosion of a car bomb in central Manama in November. A few days earlier a Lebanese Shi'ite had been arrested, together with five Bahraini citizens, on terrorist charges; it was alleged that the six had smuggled explosives into Bahrain via Syria and Saudi Arabia following intensive training at a Hezbollah camp in southern Lebanon. In November the Bahrain Government announced its willingness to allow a UN human rights working party to visit Bahrain in order to investigate the application of the 1974 Decree Law on State Security Measures. Following widespread international media attention focusing on criticism of alleged legal abuses in Bahrain, in February 1999 the State Security Court finally began legal proceedings against Sheikh al-Jamri, the opposition spiritual leader imprisoned in 1996. (Under the terms of the security legislation, which provided for the imprisonment of suspects without trial for a period of up to three years, Sheikh al-Jamri was due to be released early in 1999.) In July 1999 the Court sentenced al-Jamri to 10 years' imprisonment and imposed a substantial fine on him, although the new Amir (see below) granted him an official pardon the following day. In June the Amir had granted an amnesty to a number of detainees being held on security-related charges.

ACCESSION OF SHEIKH HAMAD AND POLITICAL REFORM

On 6 March 1999 Crown Prince Sheikh Hamad bin Isa al-Khalifa was appointed Amir upon the death of his father. His accession apparently encouraged expectations of political change among the opposition, which welcomed the change of leadership as an opportunity to renew negotiations with the Government and urged a temporary cessation of popular protest as a gesture of respect for the late Amir. Although diplomatic sources in Bahrain predicted that the new Amir would adopt a more conciliatory position with regard to security issues, Sheikh Hamad's first official address to the nation, in mid-March, was emphatic in its high regard for the armed forces as the guardians of both internal security and regional stability. At the end of May Sheikh Hamad effected a cabinet reorganization. Sheikh Khalifa bin Sulman al-Khalifa remained Prime Minister, despite his long-standing power struggle with the new Amir. Abdullah Hassan Saif, formerly Governor of the Bahrain Monetary Agency (BMA), entered the Cabinet as Minister of Finance, while Majid Jawad al-Jishi was appointed to the new post of Minister of State. Sheikh Salman bin Hamad al-Khalifa, eldest son of the Amir, became Crown Prince.

Relations between the Amir and the Prime Minister remained strained during 1999. Sheikh Hamad made efforts to establish both his reputation and that of the Crown Prince; Sheikh Salman deputized for his father in high-profile meetings with foreign diplomats, and made a much-publicized four-day visit to the USA in January 2000. In a National Day address in December 1999, Sheikh Hamad stated his intention to hold elections for municipal councils, on the basis of universal suffrage. However, no timetable was announced for these elections, and the extent of the Amir's desire to introduce some form of democracy remained unclear, particularly in the light of the military credentials of the new governors of Manama and Muharraq, appointed in September. The Government's nomination of 18 mayors with responsibility for districts of Manama raised further concerns as to the authorities' security agenda.

The opposition continued to voice concerns about the real substance of planned reforms, despite the Amir's promises of an expanded role for the Consultative Council and the creation of a human rights committee in early October 1999. The release of 320 political detainees and the pardon of 42 exiles between June and November was welcomed by the opposition as a response to calls for national reconciliation. However, the opposition's spiritual leader, Sheikh Abd al-Amir al-Jamri, remained effectively under house arrest, despite receiving a pardon from the new Amir.

In May 2000 Prime Minister Sheikh Khalifa bin Sulman al-Khalifa announced that women, as well as a number of non-Muslims, would for the first time be appointed to the Consultative Council, which was to be elected by popular vote from 2004. This unexpected announcement intensified the struggle between the Prime Minister and the Amir over issues of domestic policy and placed the extension of political participation at the top of the Government's agenda. At the end of September 2000 the appointment by Sheikh Hamad of a Jewish businessman, together with a Bahraini of Indian origin and four women (one of whom a Christian), to the Consultative Council was welcomed by foreign governments, especially the US Administration. A climate of religious tolerance was further promoted when, in October, the Amir invited Christian leaders to visit Bahrain.

Progress towards political reform gathered momentum in late November 2000, when the Amir appointed a 46-member Supreme National Committee (SNC), charged with drafting a document outlining the further evolution of Bahrain's political system. The proposed National Action Charter (NAC), published in late December, included recommendations by the SNC that there should be a transition from an emirate to a constitutional monarchy, with a directly elected bicameral parliament (with women allowed both to vote and to seek election), a consultative chamber appointed by the Government from all sections of society, and an independent judiciary. The Amir, who approved the proposals, announced that the reforms outlined in the NAC would be submitted to a national referendum. However, the British-based opposition questioned the legal basis for the Charter, and urged the reinstatement of the 1973 Constitution as the legitimate framework for democratic development.

The referendum (in which Bahraini women voted for the first time) was conducted on 14–15 February 2001. Having secured a resounding popular endorsement of the NAC, with some 98.4% of those who participated approving its terms, the Government announced that the first parliamentary elections would be held by 2004. This was widely understood to be a significant victory for Sheikh Hamad, as it overruled the proposed elections for the Consultative Council that the Prime Minister had announced in May 2000. In late February 2001 Sheikh Hamad formed two committees. The first, the Committee for the Activation of the National Charter, chaired by Crown Prince Sheikh Salman, was charged with implementing the NAC and with defining the respective responsibilities of the parliament and the monarchy. The second committee, chaired by the Minister of Justice and Islamic Affairs, Sheikh Abdullah bin Khalifa Khalid al-Khalifa, was required to oversee amendments to the Constitution and, in the view of many commentators, was to act as a crucial arbiter on the role of the Consultative Council, whose likely position with regard to the future legislature has sparked fierce debate within Bahrain.

The national referendum won the praise of the international community and of human rights organizations, and received an unprecedented degree of support from Bahraini opposition groups. Moreover, in late February 2001 the 1974 Decree Law on State Security Measures was, together with the State Security Court (see above), abolished. Shortly before the referendum the Amir ordered the release of all political prisoners, including those who had been imprisoned for their involvement in the civil unrest of the mid-1990s and the Shi'ite cleric Sheikh al-Jamri, who had been under house arrest since July 1999. After the Cabinet removed travel restrictions for members of the opposition, by mid-March 2001 dozens of political exiles had returned to Bahrain, among them Sheikh Ali Salman, the Shi'ite cleric deported to the United Kingdom in 1995, and Abd ar-Rahman an-Naimi, the former leader of the Bahrain Popular Liberation Front. In early March 2001, prior to a visit by representatives of Amnesty International, the Government licensed the independent Bahrain Society for Human Rights and announced that henceforth it would look favourably on the establishment of non-governmental organizations (NGOs). Full Bahraini citizenship was also to be granted to Shi'ite Muslims of Iranian descent whose ancestors had lived in Bahrain for several generations.

In mid-April 2001 Nabil Yaqub al-Hamer was appointed Minister of Information, and Muhammad Jassim al-Ghatam became Minister of Education, as part of a government reorganization aimed at consolidating the political reforms already undertaken by the Amir. Five new ministers were appointed to the Cabinet, and several ministries were restructured, although the key ministerial portfolios remained unchanged. In early October Sheikh Abdullah bin Salman bin Khalid al-Khalifa, the former Chief of Staff of the Bahraini Defence Force and a close ally of Sheikh Hamad, was appointed Minister of Electricity and Water; he replaced Sheikh Daij bin Khalifa bin Muhammad al-Khalifa, who had died in early August. The new Chief of Staff was named as Maj.-Gen. Sheikh Rashid bin Abdullah al-Khalifa. Meanwhile, in late 2001 the formation of a Supreme Council for Bahraini Women was announced, to be chaired by the wife of the Amir.

In June 2001 Mansour al-Jamri, leader of the London-based BFM, endorsed the NAC during his first visit to Bahrain for 15 years. Al-Jamri's support for the charter boosted domestic and international confidence in the Government's commitment to reform, despite several restrictions imposed by the authorities on public gatherings. During 2001 the Government addressed outstanding popular grievances in an attempt, many observers have argued, to keep public discourse on political change within the framework outlined by the NAC. In May Sheikh Hamad separated the Public Prosecution Office from the Ministry of the Interior, in a further step to dismantle the state security system after the abolition of the relevant legislation in February. In October the Committee for the Activation of the National Charter put forward two proposals to tackle corruption in public administration: the formation of a body to control state spending and the drafting of a general Tenders Law to ensure transparency and fair competition in government tenders.

In the aftermath of the events of 11 September 2001 (see below), the Bahrain Government lent its support to the US-led coalition against the militant Islamist al-Qa'ida (Base) organization of Osama bin Laden. During a visit by the Crown Prince to Washington, DC, in November, a Bahraini journalist voiced concerns about the negative influence of the USA on the process of national reconciliation, foreseeing the exclusion of Islamists, both Sunni and Shi'ite, from the political arena. Even before the attacks on New York and Washington, the Minister of Information, Nabil Yaqub al-Hamer, had denied the sectarian nature of Bahrain's opposition in an official statement which also urged the media to support what he termed 'Bahrain's national objectives'. However, despite Sheikh Hamad's announcement that political activities would be restricted to broadly based, non-sectarian political parties, in October 2001 the Government began to grant licences to local NGOs irrespective of their religious orientation. From early 2002 the al-Wefaq National Islamic Society—headed by Sheikh Ali Salman, the Shi'ite cleric whose arrest in 1994 provoked widespread unrest—emerged as a leading opposition group. It was widely considered that the establishment of political groups under the aegis of local NGOs represented a significant step towards the formation of a multi-party system. During the first months of 2002 the Government also authorized the publication of two independent newspapers, al-Mithaq and al-Wasat.

During 2001 the Government continued to remain silent over the constitutional aims of the NAC, particularly with regard to the responsibilities of the elected parliament (House of Representatives) and of the Consultative Council (Majlis ash-Shoura). In early October the Amir renewed pledges to convene parliamentary and municipal elections, and announced the drafting of a new municipal law before the end of the year. In an announcement on state-owned television on 14 February 2002—the first anniversary of the referendum in which the NAC proposals were approved—Sheikh Hamad declared Bahrain to be a constitutional monarchy and proclaimed himself King. The new King signed the constitutional amendments into law and set the dates of the municipal and legislative elections for 9 May and 24 October 2002, respectively.

The prospect of imminent parliamentary elections (which had not been expected until 2004) received universal praise from the international media but encountered substantial criticism in Bahraini opposition circles. King Hamad's decision to enact an amended Constitution and to grant the new Consultative Council legislative powers equal to those of the elected Chamber of Deputies was rebuffed by members of the opposition as a 'constitutional putsch' in betrayal of the spirit of the 1973 Constitution (under which the National Assembly was unicameral and included exclusively elected members). Furthermore, Article 73 of the new Constitution gives the King the right to make amendments without the approval of the two chambers. Soon after Sheikh Hamad's historic announcement Mary Robinson, the UN High Commissioner for Human Rights, echoed widespread popular concerns over the democratic credentials of the new National Assembly.

Municipal elections took place on 9 May 2002, with run-off voting one week later. A decree issued in December 2001 added new responsibilities to Bahrain's municipal councils, while for electoral purposes the country was divided into five districts, with each district to provide 10 elected representatives. Despite concerns over the 'sectarian approach' employed by the Government in the distribution of seats, in March 2002 five of the major NGO-based political organizations, including al-Wefaq, stated their intention to take part in the ballot. Groups of Islamist orientation performed well, while nationalist and leftist currents failed to win consistent support. Female candidates—for the first time permitted to stand for public office, and who reportedly constituted some 10% of candidates—failed to win any seats on the new regional councils.

In preparation for the forthcoming legislative elections, in late June 2002 a draft electoral law was approved by the Bahrain Government; however, the new legislation was criticized by opposition groups since it barred all trade unions and overtly political organizations from participating in the ballot. In early July King Hamad ordered the establishment of an independent financial auditing court with far-reaching powers to monitor state spending. Later in that month the creation of a Constitutional Court was also approved by the Government, while legislation allowing the establishment of independent trade unions was enacted in late September.

TERRITORIAL DISPUTE WITH QATAR

In April 1986 a long-standing territorial dispute between Bahrain and Qatar erupted into military confrontation. Qatari military forces raided the island of Fasht ad-Dibal, a coral reef situated midway between Bahrain and Qatar, over which both claimed sovereignty. During the raid Qatar seized 29 foreign workers (all of whom were subsequently released), who were constructing a coastguard station for Bahrain on the island. Officials of the GCC attempted to reconcile the two states and avoid a split within the organization. Fasht ad-Dibal was the third area of contention, the others being Zubarah, on mainland Qatar, and the Hawar islands. In July 1991 Qatar instituted proceedings at the International Court of Justice (ICJ) in The Hague, Netherlands, in an attempt to resolve the dispute over the potentially oil-rich Hawar islands, the shoals of Dibal and Qit'at Jaradah and the delineation of the maritime boundary. In mid-1992 Qatar rejected Bahrain's attempt to broaden the issue to include its claim to part of the Qatari mainland, around Zubarah, which had been Bahraini territory until the early 20th century. Following preliminary deliberations, the ICJ declared that it did have authority to adjudicate in the dispute, even though Qatar had applied unilaterally to the Court. Bahrain continued to insist that a bilateral solution be sought, rejected the jurisdiction of the ICJ in the matter and welcomed a Saudi Arabian offer to act as mediator.

Relations with Qatar deteriorated further at the end of 1995. Qatar criticized Bahrain's decision to build a tourist resort on the Hawar islands, and urged co-operation with the ICJ on the resolution of the dispute. Bahrain, however, maintained that the islands were 'sovereign territory', and again refused to accept the ICJ's jurisdiction on this issue. Bahrain boycotted the GCC annual summit convened in the Qatari capital, Doha, in December 1996, at which it was decided to establish a quadripartite committee (comprising those GCC countries not involved in the dispute) to facilitate a solution. Attempts by the committee to foster improved relations between Bahrain and Qatar achieved a degree of success, and meetings between prominent government ministers from both countries in the United Kingdom and in Manama in February and March 1997 resulted in the announcement that they were to establish diplomatic relations at ambassadorial level by mid-1997. However, while the Qatari Government swiftly appointed its diplomatic representative, Bahrain did not name its representative to Doha. There were renewed bilateral tensions in mid-1997, when the Bahraini authorities opened a new hotel on the Hawar islands; plans to build a housing complex there were also announced, and in February 1998 the Amir made a widely publicized visit to the islands. There were repeated regional attempts to find a solution to the dispute, particularly by Saudi Arabia and the United Arab Emirates (UAE), whose opposition to Qatar's stance encouraged Bahrain to emphasize its belief in its territorial rights there by increasing its occupancy of the islands. Bahrain repeatedly stated that it would disregard any final decision made by the ICJ, and dismissed as forgeries a series of documents submitted to the Court by the Qatari Government in support of its own claim. In September Qatar presented a report to the ICJ in support of the legitimacy of these documents, although it subsequently agreed to withdraw them from evidence. In mid-1998 Bahrain's plans to build a causeway linking the islands to the mainland fuelled speculation about a future military escalation between the two countries, and in October the Qatari Government retaliated by including Zubarah and the Hawar islands among the listed constituencies at municipal elections. The Bahrain Government publicly denounced this action as a violation of Bahrain's territorial integrity, and accused Qatar of undermining Bahrain's internal stability.

Relations with Qatar remained tense following the accession of Sheikh Hamad in March 1999. In June Bahrain notably attempted to pressure other GCC members into censuring the Qatar-based Al-Jazeera satellite television station, which had broadcast interviews with members of the Bahraini opposition. In late 1999, however, there was a marked *rapprochement*, and the Amir of Qatar made his first official visit to Manama. In the course of the visit it was agreed that a joint committee, headed by the Crown Princes of Bahrain and Qatar, would be established to encourage co-operation and to seek a bilateral solution to the territorial disputes. A second senior-level meeting was held in early January 2000, when Sheikh Hamad made his first visit to Qatar. The two countries agreed to expedite the opening of embassies in Manama and Doha. In February, following the first meeting of the Bahrain-Qatar Supreme Joint Committee, it was announced that the possibility of constructing a causeway to link the two states was to be investigated; Qatar officially named its ambassador to Bahrain on the same day. In May, however, Bahrain unilaterally suspended the Supreme Joint Committee pending the ruling of the ICJ.

Hearings by the ICJ began in late May 2000 and were completed by the end of June. The Court's final verdict was delayed until March 2001, when it confirmed Bahrain's sovereignty over the Hawar islands and Qit'at Jaradah, while Zubarah, Janan island and Fasht ad-Dibal were to remain under Qatari control. This arbitration, which ended the 60-year dispute, was accepted by both sides and hailed by Bahrain's Amir as an 'historic victory'. In late March the two countries agreed to resume the activities of the Supreme Joint Committee, after a high-profile visit by Sheikh Hamad to Doha. Future projects to be considered included the establishment of a joint investment fund, the development of joint industrial plans, and the construction of a pipeline to supply Bahrain with Qatari gas. After the ICJ ruling Prime Minister Sheikh Khalifa bin Sulman al-Khalifa led a high-level Bahraini delegation to Hawar to make a preliminary assessment of the infrastructure needed for future development.

From early 2002 international oil companies were invited to submit bids to drill for oil and gas off the Hawar islands. Moreover, after the ICJ ruling Sheikh Hamad renewed pledges to transform the area into a major tourist resort. In late September 2001 the two countries commissioned a feasibility study for the Bahrain–Qatar causeway (known as the Friendship Bridge) from a Danish consortium; the project is expected to be completed by 2006. The two Governments also signed a protocol establishing a joint committee to oversee the construction of the pipeline intended to transport gas from Qatar to Kuwait via Bahrain.

OTHER INTERNATIONAL RELATIONS

Concern over regional security was one of the reasons why Bahrain joined five other Gulf states in forming the GCC in 1981. Bahrain's intention to maintain its security through collective defence has also been emphasized by the country's participation in joint naval manoeuvres with Qatar and other Gulf states, and in the GCC's 'Peninsula Shield' military exercises. Bahrain provides onshore facilities for US forces, and there is a large US navy presence.

In August 1990 Bahrain's position assumed new strategic importance as a result of Iraq's occupation and annexation of Kuwait. Following the annexation, Bahrain firmly supported the implementation of UN economic sanctions against Iraq, and permitted the stationing of US combat aircraft in Bahrain. British armed forces participating in the multinational force for the defence of Saudi Arabia and the liberation of Kuwait were also stationed in Bahrain during 1990–91. In May 1991 representatives of the Bahrain Government met defence officials from the USA, the United Kingdom and Germany to discuss post-war security arrangements, and the role that the USA should play in the implementation of any regional security plan. In June the Amir visited Kuwait for talks on regional security, and it was announced that Bahrain would remain a regional support base for the USA but would not become the headquarters of a Gulf-based US military command and control centre. At the end of October Bahrain and the USA signed a defence co-operation agreement allowing for joint military exercises, the storage of equipment and the use of Bahraini port facilities by US forces. In January 1994 memorandums on military co-operation were signed with the USA and the United Kingdom.

In July 1992 Bahrain's Prime Minister expressed the hope that the country's relations with Iraq would improve and that, eventually, both Iraq and Iran would be incorporated into the GCC. This was the first time that a government of a GCC state had openly promoted the restoration of contacts with Iraq. However, at the GCC summit held in Riyadh, Saudi Arabia, in December 1993 there was criticism of both Iraq and Iran. In the final communiqué the six Heads of State demanded that international pressure on Iraq to observe all UN resolutions pertaining to it should be maintained, and that the sovereignty of Kuwait should be respected. It was also decided to double the size of the Saudi-based 'Peninsula Shield' joint defence force. In October 1994, when Iraqi troops were again positioned in the Iraq–Kuwait border area, Bahrain deployed combat aircraft and naval units to join GCC and US forces in the defence of Kuwait.

Throughout the 1990s Bahrain received support from Pakistan, Egypt, Syria and Jordan, but Saudi Arabia has remained its most steadfast ally, in both political and economic respects. Increasingly, Saudi Arabia has linked Bahrain's stability to its own internal security, owing to the large Shi'ite population in its oil-rich Eastern Province. A number of GCC countries have offered their support for maintaining the status quo in Bahrain, but it is unclear whether they accept Bahrain's argument that if the dissidents succeed there, unrest will spread to other states in the region. However, regional tensions have continued to arise. An appeal made by a number of leading Kuwaiti personalities to the Amir to renew dialogue with the opposition resulted in an official Bahraini protest to the Kuwait Government, while the UAE's request for an end to UN sanctions against Iraq was similarly rejected by Bahrain (which supports Saudi Arabia's uncompromising stance on this issue).

Bahrain attended the Arab League summit meeting in Cairo, Egypt, at the end of June 1996, where the final communiqué criticized Iran for its 'interference in the internal affairs of Bahrain'. Relations have, however, improved steadily since the election of Sayed Muhammad Khatami as President of Iran in May 1997. The new Iranian Minister of Foreign Affairs, Kamal Kharrazi, visited Bahrain in November and discussed the expansion of diplomatic, cultural and economic relations between the two countries with his Bahraini counterpart. In March 1998 Iran's former President Rafsanjani was received for talks with the Amir during a two-day visit to Manama. It was noted that Saudi Arabia actively encouraged increased diplomatic contacts between Bahrain and Iran, which culminated in the nomination of an Iranian ambassador to Bahrain in December 1998. Bahrain's Minister of Labour and Social Affairs, Abd an-Nabi ash-Shula, had visited Iran in October, when he met representatives of a number of Shi'ite religious foundations that the Bahrain Government has accused of providing financial support to the Bahraini opposition. The Iranian Government has come under increasing pressure from Saudi Arabia to control the activities of uncompromising Shi'ite clerics in Bahrain, particularly following the tentative *rapprochement* between Saudi Arabia and Iran which gathered momentum during 1998.

Following talks in December 1999, relations at ambassadorial level were re-established between Bahrain and Iran, and in late March 2000 the Ministers of Foreign Affairs of the two countries met in Manama to discuss regional security as well as political and economic co-operation. A joint economic commission held its first meeting in that month. Moreover, a visit by the Iranian Deputy Minister of Foreign Affairs for Education and Research Affairs to Manama in November 2000 was expected to lead to further bilateral co-operation.

The first official Israeli delegation to visit Bahrain arrived in late September 1994, and in the following month the Israeli Minister of the Environment, Yossi Sarid, attended multilateral regional talks on environmental issues held in Manama. During his visit Sarid met with Bahrain's Minister of Foreign Affairs, marking the first contact at ministerial level between Bahrain and Israel. Despite further ministerial-level contacts, however, it is thought that Bahrain will follow the example of Saudi Arabia and refuse a move towards diplomatic relations until there is a comprehensive Middle East peace settlement involving a solution to the problem of the status of Jerusalem. Bahrain, unlike Qatar and Oman, declined to send a representative to the funeral of Israeli Prime Minister Itzhak Rabin, assassinated in November 1995, and denied that there had been any contact between the Bahraini Minister of Commerce and his Israeli counterpart at the Middle East and North Africa Economic Summit conducted in Jordan during the previous month. Allegations in late 1999 of secret diplomatic and commercial contacts between the Bahrain Government and Israel were promptly denied by Manama. In early 2000 Crown Prince Salman held semi-official talks with former Israeli Prime Minister Shimon Peres during the World Economic Forum summit in Davos, Switzerland. After widespread criticism in the Arab press, on this occasion the Bahrain Government made it clear that the meeting was contingent on progress in the Middle East peace process.

In December 1995, with some reluctance, Bahrain agreed to a request from the USA to allow the temporary stationing of US military aircraft in Bahrain. In March 1996 an agreement was reached with the USA to supply Bahrain with an advanced frigate and air defence system. The USA condemned Iran for interfering in Bahrain's internal affairs, and in June 1996, after the Bahraini authorities announced the discovery of an alleged Iranian-backed plot to destabilize the archipelago, Bahrain made public US President Bill Clinton's assurances to the Amir that the USA pledged its 'total support to his Government, his sovereignty and the security of Bahraini territories'. In late 1997 the USA supported Bahrain's candidature to the UN Security Council. However, relations between the two countries deteriorated subsequently; in early 1998 a US Department of State review of human rights was extremely critical of Bahrain's record, and relations deteriorated further in February when Bahrain opposed any military intervention in Iraq and advocated a diplomatic solution to the impasse between weapons inspectors of the UN Special Commission (UNSCOM) and the Iraqi authorities. In March the Bahrain Government agreed to accommodate a continued US military presence, and in April US forces replaced their combat and air support units using Bahrain as a base, in order to strengthen US offensive capabilities; Bahraini forces also participated in naval exercises with both US and British units. However, following a visit by the Amir to the USA in June, it seemed that the US Administration was intending to reduce its military presence in the region. Talks with President Clinton and UN Secretary-General Kofi Annan in Washington, DC, in early June emphasized Bahrain's support for the implementation of Middle East peace accords in line with the policy of the Arab League. Following a meeting of Bahraini and US officials in Washington in October, the US Secretary of Defense, William Cohen, visited Bahrain in an attempt to promote the purchase of a US anti-ballistic missile system. Although the Bahrain Government supported the US-led military campaign against Iraq in December (the operation was centred in Manama, where the Fifth Fleet is headquartered), it maintained a low profile and refrained from any public endorsement of the air-strikes.

Since his accession in March 1999 Sheikh Hamad has strengthened military co-operation with the USA in an attempt to consolidate his international credentials. In mid-1999, however, it was reported that Bahrain desired both a reduction of the US military presence in Bahrain, particularly the Fifth Fleet, and the closure of the UNSCOM office in Manama. Despite local discontent, a prolonged visit by Secretary of Defense William Cohen in early April 2000 confirmed the importance of Bahrain to US regional policy. The renewed Palestinian *intifada* (uprising) against Israel in late 2000 channelled popular opinion in Bahrain against the USA, and riot police intervened to disperse demonstrations outside the US embassy in Manama. In June 2001 US forces in Bahrain were again alerted following the indictment of 13 Saudi Shi'ites by the US Department of Justice for a 1996 bombing launched against US military personnel in the Saudi town of al-Khobar, which is linked to Bahrain by the King Fahd Causeway.

In common with the other GCC states, Bahrain condemned the devastating suicide attacks on New York and Washington, DC, on 11 September 2001, and pledged to co-operate with the USA's attempts to forge an international 'coalition against terror', notably by freezing the financial assets of individuals or organizations allegedly linked to Osama bin Laden and al-Qa'ida, held by the USA to be principally responsible for the attacks. As elsewhere in the region, however, there was concern that US-led military action should not be directed against any Muslim target in the Middle East (with Iraq being seen as a possible target). Bahrain joined the US-led military offensive against al-Qa'ida and the fundamentalist Taliban regime in Afghanistan (which began in early October), contributing a frigate for rescue and humanitarian operations. The extent of Bahrain's support for Washington's ' war on terror' has won the praise of the US Administration of George W. Bush, which, in November, described Bahrain as a 'major non-NATO ally'. Nevertheless, in the aftermath of the suicide attacks small demonstrations and 'bomb-scare' telephone calls to US firms based in Bahrain indicated renewed antipathy towards the USA in some quarters. In April 2002 anti-US slogans featured prominently in a large demonstration organized in support of the Palestinians during Israeli military operations in the Palestinian autonomous areas.

Relations with the United Kingdom were somewhat strained by the election there, in May 1997, of a Labour Government which announced its intention to place greater importance on human rights considerations in its foreign policy dealings. None the less, in October 1998 the British Secretary of State for Defence, George Robertson, visited Bahrain to rally support for

a planned renewal of the military campaign against Iraq. At the end of 1998 the British Government attempted to improve military relations with Bahrain by actively encouraging an accord that would lead to the establishment of a British-sponsored military college in the archipelago. The activities of the London-based opposition, meanwhile, continued to test diplomatic relations between the two countries. In September a British government delegation encountered considerable opposition to a decision by the British authorities to grant refugee status to three prominent Bahraini opposition figures; earlier in September Ali Salman Ahmed, Hamza Ali ad-Dayri and Haidar Hasan as-Sitri, who had each been sentenced *in absentia* to five years' imprisonment by a Bahraini court in November 1997, were allowed to extend their period of residence in the United Kingdom. A report produced by the British Broadcasting Corporation during the delegation's visit alleged discrimination by the Bahrain Government against the local Shi'ite population, and was publicized by the local media as evidence of continued British support for 'terrorist activities'. Visiting London in April 1999, Bahrain's Minister of Foreign Affairs, Sheikh Muhammad bin Mubarak al-Khalifa, demanded the immediate expulsion of his Government's political opponents from the United Kingdom.

The announcement in July 1999 of a new military co-operation accord between Bahrain and France was widely interpreted as an indication of Bahrain's growing dissatisfaction with the United Kingdom's attitude towards members of the exiled Bahrain opposition. None the less, official sources described the first visit as Amir of Sheikh Hamad to the United Kingdom in November as 'constructive', despite renewed protests from human rights groups. During 2000 bilateral relations improved considerably, particularly after dissidents were allowed to return to Bahrain. A new bilateral agreement on military co-operation was expected to facilitate an increase in joint exercises and the sale to Bahrain of defence systems and equipment produced in the United Kingdom. In July 2001 Bahrain signed a number of bilateral agreements with the United Kingdom. Meanwhile, military agreements with the USA and the United Kingdom apparently mirrored efforts to increase military capability and co-operation in the region, an issue which was discussed during the 21st GCC summit, held in Manama in December 2000.

Bahrain established diplomatic ties with the Democratic People's Republic of Korea (North Korea) in May 2001. In March 2002 a delegation from the Bahrain Chamber of Commerce and Industry visited Iraq to enhance trade and economic co-operation between the two countries. During a visit to Damascus in April, Prime Minister Sheikh Khalifa bin Sulman al-Khalifa signed various co-operation accords with Syria within the framework of the Higher Joint Committee Agreement signed by the two states in September 2000.

Economy

ALAN J. DAY

Based on an earlier article by Dr P. T. H. UNWIN, with subsequent revision by RICHARD I. LAWLESS

INTRODUCTION

During the 1970s and 1980s the exploitation of Bahrain's hydrocarbon resources was the basis for considerable economic diversification, particularly in the construction, industry and banking sectors, as a result of which Bahrain has become the Gulf region's leading banking and financial centre. Having encountered some difficulties in the wake of the 1990–91 Gulf crisis, Bahrain regained economic momentum in the late 1990s, with gross domestic product (GDP) increasing by 3.1% in 1997, 4.8% in 1998, 4.3% in 1999 and 5.3% in 2000. Nevertheless, a rapid rate of population growth—currently around 3% a year, having exceeded the GDP growth rate until 1997—has resulted in a persistent problem of unemployment, which in mid-2001 was

officially given as 3.5% but was unofficially estimated at 16.5% of the available work-force of some 200,000.

In 1991 the Government established the Bahrain Development Bank to provide long-term loans and venture capital to attract investors, and the Bahrain Marketing and Promotions Office to encourage companies to establish a base in the region. Incentives to new investors introduced in the 1993 Government Incentive Programme included major tax concessions, rebates on rent and power charges to small and medium-sized companies, and a subsidy for every Bahraini national employed. Official procedures were simplified, and full foreign ownership of companies was allowed provided that they were engaged in industrial activities or were establishing a base for the sale of manufactured goods and services in the Gulf region. There was also duty-free access to the wider market of the Co-operation Council for the Arab States of the Gulf (Gulf Co-operation Council, GCC—of which Bahrain is a member) for Bahrain-based industries whose products met GCC eligibility criteria.

Having encouraged new private industrial investment, Bahrain was forced to consider the crucial future expansion of infrastructure, including water and electricity supply systems in need of additional capacity to meet rising demand. The Government was, however, reluctant to embark on a major capital spending programme as long as it continued to experience problems in containing the existing budget deficit. Approval for several major development projects was postponed during 1994 and 1995, when it was widely predicted that the Government would eventually seek foreign private investment for key infrastructure developments. During 1996, however, the Government's financial situation (already benefiting from higher oil export prices) was greatly strengthened by Saudi Arabia's decision to allocate its share of the 1996 annual output of petroleum from the jointly-owned Abu Saafa oilfield to Bahrain (see Petroleum and Gas, below). By early 1997 the Government had approved a medium-term investment programme totalling more than US $3,000m., including a new port and industrial area and additional water and power plants, giving rise to expectations of a period of strong growth after several years of relative stagnation. However, the decline in world petroleum prices resulted in a budget deficit of 3% of GDP in 1998, the largest for many years. Some development projects were cancelled or scaled down, and more than BD 70m. was borrowed during 1999 to finance essential infrastructure projects. According to a report published by the UN Conference on Trade and Development (UNCTAD) in 2000, Bahrain attracted foreign direct investment of $329m. in 1997, $181m. in 1998 and $300m. in 1999.

On his accession to power in March 1999, the new Amir, Sheikh Hamad bin Isa al-Khalifa, declared his intention to continue to promote established lines of economic policy, including the privatization of state assets, while adopting a more interventionist approach to economic decision-making. Bahrain benefited from the sharp upturn in world oil prices in late 1999, which had the effect of reducing the budget deficit and stimulating a resumption of economic growth. In April 2000 a Supreme Council for Economic Development was established under the chairmanship of the Prime Minister; it was transformed into the Economic Development Board (EDB) in April 2001. Its stated priorities include the privatization of some state-owned industries and economic diversification so as to create more jobs for Bahraini nationals.

Bahrain's GDP per head in 1999 was estimated to be US $10,410 (or $13,700 per head on an international purchasing-power parity basis). During 1990–99, it was estimated, GDP per head increased, in real terms, at an average rate of 0.8% per year. In 2000 Bahrain's GDP, on a conventional exchange-rate basis, was $7,739m., equivalent to $11,055 per head. Boosted by high world oil prices, real GDP growth remained high in 2001, at 4.6%, although the rate was projected to slow to 3.5% in 2002.

AGRICULTURE AND FISHING

Agriculture has declined rapidly since the 1960s, and in 2001 contributed only 0.7% of GDP. The Bahrain islands are largely barren and thus have never been able to support farming on more than a limited scale. About three-quarters of the agricultural land in traditional farming areas in the north had been abandoned by the end of the 1970s. By 2000 only 1% of the labour force was engaged in agriculture. This reduction in agricultural activity was caused both by the increasing salinity of traditional supplies of water and by the attractions of other sectors of the economy. The Government was, nevertheless, keen to develop the archipelago's agricultural potential. By 1988 milk production had risen sufficiently to satisfy 50% of local demand, and vegetable production had increased to meet 75% of requirements. Self-sufficiency in egg production had also been achieved. In 2000 there were an estimated 11,000 cattle, 18,000 sheep, 16,000 goats and 1,000 camels in the country. In order to increase the national agricultural area, the Government initiated a two-stage irrigation project, costing an estimated

BD 12m., which entailed ozonizing and storing treated sewage at the Tubli sewage works for distribution and application to fields. A major extension of the Tubli works, in progress in 1999–2000, was intended in part to benefit local agriculture, as were four new desalination projects due to come on stream between 2000 and 2006. The value of agricultural output rose to BD 14.2m. in 2000, from BD 13.8m. in 1999.

In 1979 the Bahrain Fishing Company was forced to cease its operations because pollution had led to the virtual disappearance of shrimps from the Gulf. In 1981 the Government initiated a five-year plan to revive the industry by acquiring more sophisticated equipment and establishing training schemes. In 1985 the Government announced an investment of BD 20,000 to revive the pearling industry. In December 1988 a fisheries development programme, with a projected cost of BD 19m., was initiated, but in mid-1989 about 75% of the country's fish resources remained unexploited, and one-third of local fish requirements were being supplied by imports. There are plans to modernize the fishing fleet and processing facilities at Mina Salman, which could eventually supply 25% of the local market for fish products. The value of fishing output fell from BD 8.4m. in 1996 to BD 7.3m. in 1997, but recovered to BD 7.9m. in 2000.

PETROLEUM AND GAS

Bahrain's petroleum and gas industries are controlled by the state-owned Bahrain Petroleum Company (BAPCO), created by royal decree in December 1999 as a merger of the upstream and marketing roles of the Bahrain National Oil Company (BANOCO) and the downstream activities of the previous Bahrain Petroleum Company (BAPCO). Overall policy for the sector is determined by the Supreme Oil Council. The functional merger of day-to-day oil industry operations was phased in from 2001 and officially implemented in mid-2002.

Bahrain's average production of crude petroleum from the onshore Awali field peaked at 76,639 barrels per day (b/d) in 1970 and subsequently decreased steadily as reserves were depleted. Since the 1980s output has generally been kept below a 42,000 b/d ceiling in order to regulate the rate of depletion. Production averaged 37,674 b/d in 1998 and was estimated to have fallen to around 30,000 b/d in 1999, before rising to 37,250 b/d in 2000. At 1 January 2001 Bahrain's proven published reserves of petroleum were estimated at only 100m. barrels, sufficient to maintain production (at 2000 levels) for just four years. As a result of high international oil prices, the value of oil and gas production rose sharply in 2000 to BD 836m., from BD 448m. in 1999 and BD 311m. in 1998.

Between 1981 and 1984 the Government spent US $20m. on exploration and drilling, but no significant discoveries were made. Offshore exploration in the 1990s was similarly unproductive. In February 1998 BANOCO signed an agreement with the US Chevron Corporation for renewed exploration of the northern and western offshore areas, involving drilling in three new exploration areas covering 5,900 sq km. In January 2000 Chevron moved its headquarters for Middle East and North African operations from the United Kingdom to Bahrain. A further exploration rights agreement was signed with Texaco in August 1999, whereby the US company was to conduct technical studies to evaluate the potential for oil and gas exploration using the most advanced technology. This was followed in November 2001 by BAPCO's signature of exploration and production-sharing agreements with the recently merged ChevronTexaco company and with Petronas of Malaysia, respectively covering one and two oil-bearing blocks near the Hawar islands. Subject to successful drilling and acceptance of field development plans by the Ministry of Oil, commercial production from the blocks was expected to start in 2004.

Although not a significant oil producer itself, Bahrain has a long-standing entitlement to a 50% share in revenues from the Abu Saafa field, situated between Bahrain and Saudi Arabia and operated by Saudi Aramco. In the mid-1990s the field was producing an average of 140,000 b/d. Saudi Arabia increased Bahrain's allocation to 100,000 b/d for two years at the beginning of 1993, and in early 1996 agreed to allocate the entire Abu Saafa revenue to Bahrain, this decision apparently being unconditional and open-ended. Estimated production at Abu Saafa in 2000 was 145,000 b/d.

A 250,000-b/d refinery at Sitra, established in 1936 and therefore the oldest operational refinery in the Gulf, processes all Bahrain's onshore output and supplies the country's domestic requirements of around 10,000 b/d. However, most of its crude supply is imported via pipeline from Saudi Arabia and the bulk of its product output is exported. With storage facilities for 14m. barrels and operating a six-berth export terminal, the refinery achieved record output of 262,000 b/d in 1999, up from 248,600 b/d in 1998. It was originally operated by BAPCO, owned from 1981 by the Bahrain Government (60%) and Caltex (40%) until in April 1997 the Government acquired the Caltex shareholding to become sole owner. The Government thus assumed complete control of Bahrain's oil exports and became the sole decision-maker on the question of implementing a major refinery modernization programme—which was repeatedly deferred during the 1990s. Eventually, in July 1998 the Supreme Oil Council approved a US $900m. refurbishment and expansion programme for the Sitra refinery, including a low-sulphur diesel production (LSDP) project, tenders for which were under evaluation in mid-2000. Other components of the Sitra upgrade include a new sulphur recovery unit, sour water treatment facilities, instrument modernization, a new keromerox plant and an unleaded gasoline project. A new in-line blending facility was commissioned in June 2000. By November of that year technology licensing agreements were in place for all the main components of the Sitra expansion programme, beginning with a 40,000 b/d LSDP hydrocracker intended to reduce the sulphur content in diesel produced by the refinery from 7,500 parts per million (ppm) to 50 ppm. Front-end engineering and design studies on the LSDP project were submitted by Bechtel of the USA in October 2001, following which bids were invited for the $600m. contract. The Government remained publicly confident that at least the first phase of the Sitra upgrade would be completed by 2004.

A development proposal from the Saudi Arabian Petroma Refining and Marketing Company for a 500,000-b/d refinery at Hidd, valued at some US $2,500m., and an associated petrochemicals plant costing $2,200m., was given notice to proceed in March 1998. However, in late 1998 the US Hutchinson Group withdrew from the project, and by mid-2002 no progress had been reported on the selection of another international oil company as a partner.

Bahrain's proven reserves of natural gas totalled 90,000m. cu m at the end of 2001, sufficient to sustain production at current rates for 10.3 years. In 2001 8,900m. cu m of gas was produced, an increase of 1.4% compared with the previous year. Nearly one-third of Bahrain's gas output is reinjected, the remainder being used by power stations, by the Aluminium Bahrain (ALBA) aluminium smelter (see Industry and Manufacturing, below), by the Sitra oil refinery and (as feedstock) by the local petrochemicals industry. The 75% state-owned Bahrain National Gas Company (BANAGAS) has the capacity to process 4.8m. cu m of gas per day to produce liquefied products (propane, butane and naphtha) for export, and dry gases (mainly methane and ethane) for local use as industrial fuels.

In February 2002 BANAGAS formed a joint venture with Dynegy Global Liquids of the USA, to be called DANAGAS, to invest in gas extraction, processing, storage and transportation worldwide. The joint venture was to concentrate on midstream opportunities in gas production in the Middle East and North Africa, offering technical and operational solutions to foreign clients.

INDUSTRY AND MANUFACTURING

In the mid-1990s government efforts were concentrated on encouraging private foreign investment in the industrial sector to achieve greater diversification and to promote more export-orientated industries. Investment is being sought in downstream industries related to aluminium and pharmaceuticals, as well as in new activities. The Government's Incentive Programme, introduced in 1993, offers a wide range of concessions and incentives to attract foreign investment, and official procedures have been greatly simplified. In 1996 there were seven designated industrial areas offering competitively-priced leases on manufacturing units with infrastructural support services in place. Manufacturing accounted for 11.0% of GDP in 2001.

The aluminium industry remains central to the Government's strategy to expand the country's export-orientated industries, aluminium currently accounting for about one-half of Bahrain's non-oil exports by value. The development of Bahrain's aluminium industry began in 1969, when the Government formed a consortium with British, Swedish, French and US companies to construct and operate an aluminium smelter with a capacity of 120,000 metric tons per year. Production at the ALBA smelter began in 1972, using alumina imported from Australia. The Bahrain Government now owns 77% of ALBA, the Public Investment Fund of Saudi Arabia 20% and Breton Investments of Germany 3%. A US $1,500m. expansion programme to increase the annual capacity of the smelter to 460,000 tons was completed in November 1992, making it one of the largest in the world. ALBA's output increased to 461,245 tons in 1996, the first year in which the smelter operated above its nominal design capacity. At the start of 1997 a third potline came on stream, increasing annual capacity to 496,500 tons from the middle of the year. Following the addition of a fourth potline, ALBA's total production was 500,921 tons in 1999, a marginal increase on 1998 output. Infrastructural facilities within the ALBA production complex include two desalination plants with a combined capacity of 3,000 cu m per day, an 800-MW main power plant and an additional 164-MW gas turbine (added in 1997). In July 1998 ALBA secured a $400m. loan to build a new coke-calcinating plant to enable the company not only to meet its own requirement of 250,000 tons per year, which is currently imported from the USA and Argentina, but also to export a further 200,000 tons per year. The project further includes construction of an associated 43,000-cu m-per-day sea water desalination plant at an estimated cost of $24m., and improvements to existing facilities, including construction of a new jetty capable of handling ships of up to 80,000 dwt.

In May 2000 a feasibility study was commissioned into a proposed expansion programme, including a fifth potline, to increase ALBA's annual capacity by 50%, to 750,000 tons, in order to meet anticipated rising export demand and to facilitate the expansion of downstream industries in Bahrain. On completion of the feasibility study in November, the expansion (which would make the smelter one of the largest in the world) was approved in principle by ALBA's board and the Bahraini Government, which initiated a study of the options for raising the estimated US $1,700m. required to finance the expansion. In March 2002 bids for the contract to build the fifth potline were received from Bechtel of the USA and from SNC Lavalin and Hatch Kaiser Light Metals of Canada. ALBA's output was marketed abroad by the Bahrain-Saudi Aluminium Marketing Company (BALCO) until June 1999, when ALBA itself assumed responsibility for marketing operations. About two-thirds of ALBA's production in 2001 was sold within Bahrain and other GCC countries. GCC efforts to secure the elimination or reduction of the 6% tariff imposed by the European Union (EU) on aluminium imports from GCC states had made no progress by early 2002.

Seven major secondary enterprises, related to aluminium, now exist in Bahrain. The first downstream venture was Bahrain Atomizers International, established in 1973 with 51% government ownership in association with Eckart Werke of Germany. It produces 7,000 metric tons of atomized aluminium powder per year, which is marketed in Japan, Germany, the United Kingdom and the USA.

The Bahrain Aluminium Extrusion Company (BALEXCO, established in state ownership in 1977 and transferred to the private sector in 1995) produces aluminium profiles and sections for domestic and foreign markets. In 1997 it completed a third extrusion line, which brought its total capacity up to 21,000 metric tons per year. During 1996 BALEXCO added a 12,000-tons-per-year scrap recycling plant and a powder-coating facility to its operations. In 2000 BALEXCO was selling about 18% of its output in Europe, 15% in Bahrain, and the remainder in other GCC counties as well as in Algeria, Yemen and Lebanon. The company held the Middle East licence for the production of a leading French range of materials for the construction industry, and was represented in Qatar and Kuwait by service centres operated as 50:50 joint ventures with local partners. BALEXCO's development plans included a shift of emphasis away from mass-produced items (for which there was currently excess capacity world-wide) towards non-standard, specialized applications.

Midal Cables, established under private ownership in 1978, was producing around 50,000 metric tons per year of aluminium rods and coils (including overhead transmission conductors) in 1997 and planned to add more capacity in the future. Its subsidiary, Metal Form, was set up in 1994 to produce products from Midal's own aluminium rods. Another subsidiary, Aluwheel, established in 1991, produces semi-finished aluminium wheel hubs for European car manufacturers; its 1996 output was around 600,000 units.

Gulf Aluminium Rolling Mill Company (GARMCO, established in 1981 under the auspices of the Gulf Organization for Industrial Consulting) had a total production capacity of 120,000 metric tons per year of aluminium plate and sheet products in 1997, following a major expansion of its plant.

Bahrain Alloys Manufacturing Company, established by overseas investors in 1994, produces alloys for the automotive and aerospace industries.

The Gulf Petrochemical Industries Corpn (GPIC) built a petrochemicals plant at Sitra in 1985 with a capacity of 1,200 metric tons per day each of ammonia and methanol. The complex was a joint venture between BANOCO, the Saudi Basic Industries Corpn and Kuwait's Petrochemical Industries Corpn. Output of ammonia and methanol totalled 777,000 tons in 1996, when GPIC recorded an operating profit of US $52m. A new plant, currently under construction, is designed to produce urea using ammonia feedstock from the existing GPIC facility.

In June 1993 the National Chemical Industries Corpn (NACIC) signed a US $13.1m. contract with United Engineers International of the USA to build a sulphur derivatives plant near the refinery at Sitra. The plant was to produce 18,000 metric tons of sodium sulphite and sodium metabisulphite each year. NACIC is owned by the Bahraini United Gulf Industries Corpn (55%), together with the Qatar Industrial Manufacturing Company (15%), the Saudi Arabian Industry Development Company (10%) and the United Group for the Development of Riyadh (5%).

The Arab Shipbuilding and Repair Yard (ASRY) Company's dry dock, financed by the members of the Organization of Arab Petroleum Exporting Countries (OAPEC), was opened in 1977, and first recorded a full year's profitable trading in 1987. In 1992 ASRY invested US $61m. in two floating docks, giving the yard (which originally had a single 500,000-metric ton graving dock) increased flexibility. However, an $87m. expansion project for the shipyard was suspended in 1998, owing to continuing growth in overseas competition and falling trade volumes. Although the number of vessels repaired rose from 104 in 1994 to 119 in 1998, repair revenues registered a decline in the latter year. A partial recovery in both numbers and revenue in 1999 revived interest in the expansion project, on which initial designs were completed, although implementation depended on a further increase in demand for ASRY's services. This failed to materialize in 2000, when ASRY indicated that it did not expect to return to profitability before 2002. Price competition from Chinese shipyards was cited as the main threat to the financial viability of ASRY's general repair and maintenance business, notwithstanding the achievement of cost reductions of up to 20% in recent years. Under these market conditions, ASRY's policy has been to diversify into higher-value 'niche' markets for specialized services, including the conversion and fitting out of vessels for the offshore oil and gas industry. In 2001 ASRY developed plans for a major expansion, potentially involving the addition of 1,500 m of berth space and associated docking facilities. The Bahrain Ship Repairing and Maintenance Company specializes in smaller-scale ship repairs.

In 1985 the Gulf Acid Industries Company began production of sulphuric acid and distilled water. Light industry, including the production of supplementary gas supplies, asphalt, prefabricated buildings, plastics, soft drinks, air-conditioning equipment and paper products, also continued to develop during 1986. In 1987 the Government imposed a 20% tariff on competing imported goods for a trial period of 12 months, as part of a programme to support the expansion of light industry. In 1987 Wires International became the first Bahraini company to export an industrial product (aluminium fly mesh) to the Far East. In 1988 the Government announced plans to increase

import substitution to a level of 30%, with guaranteed state protection of markets. Following the introduction of the Government's Incentive Programme in 1993, two joint ventures were agreed: a tissue-paper mill—a joint venture between Olayan of Saudi Arabia and Kimberly-Clark of the USA—and a factory producing prefabricated pipeline systems, a joint venture between Shaw Industries of the USA and the local Ahmad Nass Industrial Services. The tissue-paper mill started production in March 1995. Output is marketed in the Gulf states, mainly in Saudi Arabia. It was announced in January 2000 that a consortium of Egon Eertz of Germany and private GCC investors had secured a preliminary licence for a US $47m. joint venture steel mill in the Hidd industrial zone, with an annual capacity of 300,000 metric tons of iron beams and rods for the construction industry.

In early 1994 Bahrain became the first Gulf state to secure access to EU equity investment funds for small and medium-sized industrial joint ventures. Up to 20% of the equity for joint ventures between local and European partners can be provided by the EU, as well as concessional funding for feasibility studies and human resource development. In January 1995 the Government launched a programme to encourage investment in medium-scale industrial projects in order to strengthen economic diversification. Some 13 projects were identified in food, engineering, textiles and health care. As the new projects were of a modest scale, the Government hoped to attract investment from Bahraini entrepreneurs and provide more employment and training for Bahraini nationals.

In September 1999 plans were confirmed for the construction of Bahrain's first television-manufacturing factory, as a joint venture of the local United Commercial Agencies and Videocon of India; the start of production was projected for late 2000, initially at the rate of 100,000 units annually, with the manufacture of refrigerators and air-conditioning units being envisaged for later phases. In January 2000 Pakistani-owned Manama Textile announced a new US $21m. spinning unit in the ALBA industrial zone, intended to produce 8.7m. metric tons of cotton yarn annually using raw cotton imported from Pakistan. Manama Textile already operated two weaving units at Sitra with a combined capacity of 90,000 m of unbleached cloth per day. Bahrain's exports of textiles and textile articles were valued at BD 158.2m. in 2001, exceeding imports by some BD 64m.

POWER AND WATER

Industrial expansion and rapid population growth have put increasing pressure on electricity and water supplies. Until 1999 Bahrain had four power stations: a gas-fired 126-MW station at Manama, a steam-fired 120-MW station at Sitra, a 38-MW station on Muharraq and the largest station, an open-cycle gas turbine plant at Rifa'a, with capacity of 700 MW. In 1991 plans for an increase in electricity supplies were activated. The Sitra power station was refurbished, and in 1994 the ALBA aluminium complex's 1,500-MW power plant was linked to the national grid, giving the Ministry of Electricity and Water access to an additional 250 MW of generating capacity for a period of 10 years. However, peak electricity demand was close to the national grid's maximum supply capability, and in June 1999 the Government issued an urgent appeal to consumers to reduce their electricity consumption—as demand increased to within 10 MW of available supply of 1,260 MW. The Government was forecasting an increase in electricity demand to 1,600 MW by 2005.

In January 1997 the Government signed a US $530m. contract to construct a 280-MW power station and associated desalination plant with a capacity of 30m. gallons (136,380 cu m) per day on reclaimed land at Hidd. The first of two 140-MW gas turbines was commissioned at Hidd in July 1999 and the second in mid-2000, while four 7.5m. gallons-per-day desalination units were also installed. In 2001 bids were evaluated for a major second-phase expansion of the complex to add between 630 MW and 750 MW of new generating capacity (230 MW in 2003, a further 230 MW in 2004 and the balance in 2005). The successful bidder was Alston Power of France, which in September 2001 signed a $300m. engineering, procurement and construction (EPC) contract. In April 2002 the Government and a group of regional and international banks concluded a $255m. financing package agreement for the second phase of the Hidd expansion.

A third phase was to involve the installation of 60m. gallons per day of new desalination capacity, to be accomplished once the bulk of the new generating capacity was in place. In preparation for the planned expansion of generating capacity at Hidd, the Government in 2001 initiated various projects to upgrade the country's power transmission network. Financing estimated at $90m. was to be provided by the Arab Fund for Economic and Social Development, the Islamic Development Bank (IDB) and the Bahrain Government.

In January 2002 Siemens of Germany was awarded a US $22m. EPC contract to carry out the first phase of an upgrade of the Rifa'a power station, to extend the operational life of five 50-MW gas turbines which are over 30 years old. Designs for the Rifa'a upgrade had been submitted in March 2000 by the US Kuljian Engineering Corporation. In January 2001 a consultancy contract was awarded for the modernization of the newer (second-phase) capacity at Rifa'a, comprising six 75-MW turbines commissioned in 1983–84. In May 1999 tender documents were issued for the BD 16m. refurbishment of the power and desalination plant at Sitra, to extend its life by 10 years.

In 1999 the Gulf Council Interconnection Authority (GCIA) was formed by the GCC to oversee the connection of the national grids of its six member states. The first phase will establish a link between Bahrain, Kuwait, Qatar and Saudi Arabia at an estimated cost of US $2,500m., of which Bahrain will contribute almost $100m.

In early 1994 the Bahrain Centre for Studies and Research warned that the island's primary water resources could be exhausted by 2010 unless measures were taken to limit the rate of extraction from the underground aquifer. Extraction rates had in past decades been so far in excess of the natural replenishment rate of about 67.5m. gallons (306,820 cu m) per day that it was estimated that full regeneration of the aquifer could take centuries. Water pumped from underground had become increasingly saline, affecting crop yields in agriculture and necessitating an increasing admixture of desalinated water for domestic use. In 1994 the Ministry of Electricity and Water imposed a ceiling on total water use which had the effect of reducing the groundwater extraction rate to about 29.2m. gallons (132,500 cu m) per day. Tariffs were introduced for agricultural water use in 1997. In 1999 domestic use accounted for 60% of water consumption, industry 36% and agriculture 4%.

Extensive renovation work was undertaken in 1999 to allow Bahrain's three desalination plants to operate at full capacity; the multi-stage flash plant at Sitra, with a capacity of 25m. gallons (113,650 cu m) per day, is awaiting refurbishment. A consultant has been appointed to raise the capacity of the reverse osmosis plant at Abu Jajour from 3m. to 10m. gallons per day, and a BD 7.6m. contract has been awarded to expand the capacity of a second reverse osmosis plant at Ad-Dur from the current 10m. to 15m. gallons per day. Construction has begun for the first stage of the Tubli sewerage plant expansion project, which involves raising the capacity of the secondary effluent plant from the current 120,000 cu m per day to 200,000 cu m per day. Two contracts to link the power and desalination plant at Hidd to the existing water network have also been awarded.

In December 2001 three international companies submitted bids to the Ministry of Electricity and Water for the contract to build a desalination plant to supply fresh water for projected tourism developments on the Hawar islands (see Tourism, below). In May 2002, however, the Ministry announced that the award of the contract had been postponed indefinitely.

TRANSPORT AND COMMUNICATIONS

Bahrain's role as a major financial centre has been associated with an expansion of the country's air and telephone services. Bahrain International Airport was opened in 1971 on Muharraq island, and it has also become the headquarters of Gulf Air, which is owned jointly by the Governments of Bahrain, Oman and Abu Dhabi (part of the United Arab Emirates—UAE). In 1996 the airport (in the fourth phase of an expansion programme) handled almost 56,600 flights and about 3.4m. passengers (about 55% of them transit passengers). In 1995 the airport handled around 100,000 metric tons of cargo, about 30% of which was transhipment cargo.

In 1995, as a result of fierce regional competition, Gulf Air recorded an annual loss of BD 61.9m. (US $164m.), prompting a programme of aircraft disposals and route cuts designed to eliminate some of the 60 destinations previously served. In 1995 Gulf Air carried more than 5m. passengers and 170,000 metric tons of cargo. Its finances had been depleted by a large loan-servicing burden in respect of aircraft purchased in the late 1980s. During 1996 measures were adopted that reduced operating costs by 5% and increased operating revenue by a similar amount, but the airline nevertheless reported an annual loss of BD 25.2m. ($66.8m.). Recommendations to increase the airline's capital from BD 150m. to BD 250m. were discussed by the shareholder Governments in January 1997. An offer by Abu Dhabi to inject more capital in return for an increased shareholding was rejected by Oman and Qatar (a joint owner until it withdrew its stake in 2002), and it was instead agreed that the shareholder Governments should provide 'discretionary loans' totalling $200m. to Gulf Air. The shareholders' respective contributions were not specified. By early 1997 Gulf Air had sold seven Boeing 767s and reduced its total number of destinations to 50. In that year the company recorded an operating profit of $8m. In June 1999 Gulf Air received the first of six A330 Airbuses as part of a $550m. investment initiative to renew its fleet.

Plans for a US $80m. expansion of facilities at Bahrain International Airport (BIA), delayed in 1998 owing to the then decline in international petroleum prices, were pursued in 1999–2000, including the construction of a new airport hotel, the acquisition of firefighting vehicles and the construction of an aircraft repair and maintenance facility as a joint venture between Bahrain Air Services and the Abu Dhabi-based Gulf Air Maintenance Company (GAMCO). The airport handled some 4m. passengers in 2000, an increase of about 10% over 1999, and reaffirmed its target of achieving 8m. passengers by 2005. In September 2001 the Department of Civil Aviation Affairs received consultants' proposals for the construction of an additional terminal at BIA, while plans were also under consideration for a new duty-free hall, a multi-storey car park and a shopping mall.

The Bahrain Telecommunications Company (BATELCO), in which the Bahrain Government has a 39% stake and the British Cable & Wireless a 20% stake, was formed in July 1981 with capital of BD 60m. At the beginning of 1986 Bahrain became the 45th member of the International Maritime (now Mobile) Satellite Organization (INMARSAT), and during 1986 BATELCO also introduced a cellular telephone system. The digitalization of Bahrain's 120,000-line domestic network was completed in 1992. There is also a digital international exchange. In March 1996 it was announced that BD 100m. was to be invested in the network over the next five years. Projects contained in the BD 27m. investment budget for 1996 included work on a regional fibre-optic link between Bahrain, Qatar, Kuwait and the UAE. An International Services Digital Network (ISDN) capability was in place in Bahrain in 1997. BATELCO's profits rose by 33% in 1998, to BD 43.1m., owing to a 57% increase in mobile telephone users and a 53% increase in internet subscribers.

In 1999 BATELCO embarked on a US $118m. investment programme to increase its mobile telephone capacity from 130,000 to 230,000 'lines' by the end of 2001 and to upgrade its internet access service. In 1999 BATELCO's profits surged by 11.6% to BD 48.1m., again principally on the strength of increased demand for mobile and internet services. Prospects for international investment in information technology projects in Bahrain were enhanced by the country's removal in March 1999 from the US Government's list of countries tolerating copyright piracy. In November 1999 a subsidiary of BATELCO formed a joint venture with two Jordanian internet service providers to develop services within Jordan. The same subsidiary acquired a controlling interest in an Egyptian data services network. BATELCO invested BD 35m. in telecommunications infrastructure in 2000. It reported a net profit of BD 52.5m. in the same year. In February 2001 a contract was awarded to expand further BATELCO's mobile subscriber capacity to 340,000. The Bahrain Government announced in that month that plans were being drawn up to end BATELCO's monopoly in Bahrain's telecommunications sector, which was to be opened up to other (including foreign) companies.

From 1 January 2002 BATELCO reduced its mobile telephone tariffs by 16% and its registration fees by 43%, with the result that by April it had 330,000 mobile subscribers—equivalent to a 50% penetration of the available market. Under a US $26m. expansion programme being carried out by Ericsson of Sweden, BATELCO's Global Standard for Mobiles (GSM) network was to have a capacity of 400,000 subscribers by 2004 and the company would be able to offer a wider range of advanced internet services. BATELCO reported net profits of BD 54.3m. in 2001, while the first quarter of 2002 showed a 20% increase in turnover and a 16% increase in profits compared with the same period of 2001.

Since 1979 Bahrain has had a container terminal at the port of Mina Salman, with a 400-m quay allowing simultaneous handling of two 180-m vessels as well as 14 conventional berths and a roll-on roll-off berth. In March 2002 the Prime Minister laid the foundation stone for the first phase of a new US $420m. port complex and industrial development zone on 110 ha of reclaimed land at south Hidd, to be carried out by the US Great Lakes Dredge and Dock Company and involving the construction of a 1,800-m quay wall. On its completion in late 2004 or early 2005, the new port will have an annual handling capacity of 234,000 20-ft equivalent units (TEUs) and will include a general cargo berth and two container berths with roll-on roll-off facilities. The Abu Dhabi Development Fund has agreed to provide $100m. of loan financing for the Hidd development project. The inauguration in February 1987 of a causeway between Bahrain and Saudi Arabia led to increased motor traffic in Bahrain, in the light of which the road network has been upgraded and traffic management studies have been undertaken. The causeway was used by 1.3m. vehicles in its first year of operation. There were more than 176,000 cars and around 36,000 goods vehicles and buses registered in Bahrain at the end of 2000. Following the completion of a 2.5-km causeway from Manama to Muharraq in early 1997, a project (the Sheikh Khalifa bin Sulman project) for a second causeway, linking Hidd (on Muharraq island) and Manama, completed its design stage in 2000. Bids for the construction of the 3.6-km causeway's main section—a 404-m bridge—were under evaluation in mid-2001, with a target completion date of 2003. Following the settlement, in March 2001, of Bahrain's long-standing territorial dispute with Qatar (see History), the two Governments accelerated plans to build a 50-km causeway (the Friendship Bridge) between their countries, at an estimated cost of $2,000m. In February 2002 the Government invited companies to prequalify for the contract for a $40m. project to expand the main arterial road and flyover north of Manama.

In December 1999 the UAE-based Naif Marine Services began a weekly ferry service from Bahrain to the Iraqi port of Umm Qasr. In mid-2000 a sea link was also established between Bahrain and the Iranian port of Bushehr.

BUDGET, INVESTMENT AND FINANCE

The Bahrain Monetary Agency (BMA), established in 1973 to replace the Bahrain Currency Board, has exercised all the powers of a central bank since 1975. The BMA oversees the issuing of currency, regulates exchange control and credit policy, and licenses and controls the banking and financial system. The Bahraini dinar is formally linked to the special drawing right (SDR), with the US dollar as intervention currency. Since 1975 a licensed status of 'offshore banking unit' (OBU) has been available to banks using Bahrain as a base from which to conduct exclusively offshore business (such companies being exempt from the shareholder nationality requirements applicable to banks providing services within Bahrain). There was a rapid expansion of offshore banking activities in the late 1970s and early 1980s, with Bahrain taking advantage of the boom in bank lending to the major petroleum exporters to become the region's principal financial centre, assisted by the BMA's reputation for proper regulation. In July 1999 the BMA announced plans to curb money-laundering activities in Bahrain, while in April 2002 responsibility for the management and regulation of the insurance sector and capital markets was transferred to the BMA, with the aim of improving standards of financial probity in accordance with international standards. An independent central bank is to replace the BMA in the near future.

The number of OBUs licensed in Bahrain peaked at 74 in 1985, when—in addition to the 20 locally-incorporated commercial banks within Bahrain's domestic banking system—there were also 60 representative offices, more than 12 licensed investment banks, six money brokers and 43 money changers. In subsequent years the number of OBUs declined as financial institutions adjusted to changing regional economic conditions at a time of declining oil prices. However, forecasts of a major decline in Bahrain's offshore financial services sector proved to be unfounded, with the combined assets of the remaining OBUs (numbering 65 in 1988) reaching a new record level of US $68,100m. in 1988. The annual contribution of OBUs to Bahrain's economy was officially estimated to be in excess of $500m. in that year.

The second half of the 1980s was also a period of readjustment for Bahrain's domestic commercial banks, some of which recorded reduced profits or net losses in 1986 and 1987 after making large provisions for loan defaults by recession-hit borrowers. By 1989 banking profits were generally much improved. The Gulf crisis of 1990–91 had a strong impact on Bahrain's banking sector as funds were withdrawn on a large scale. However, the BMA ensured that dinar liquidity was maintained, and by October 1990 the outflow of capital had been stemmed. Between 1992 and 1999 the number of financial institutions in Bahrain increased from 155 to 176, the latter total including 19 commercial banks serving the domestic market, 48 OBUs, 33 investment banks, 13 Islamic banks, 36 representative offices and 19 money changers.

As part of its efforts to promote Bahrain as a centre for Islamic banking, the BMA announced in April 2000 that capital adequacy requirements would be introduced for Islamic banks, similar to the ratios currently applicable to conventional banks. An Islamic Credit Card Company was licensed by the BMA in May 2001, following which the world's first International Islamic Financial Market, with a liquidity management centre and Islamic ratings agency, was officially established in Bahrain in August 2002 as a joint venture by the IDB and the monetary authorities of Bahrain, Brunei, Indonesia, Malaysia and Sudan. In September 2001 the BMA made an inaugural issue of five-year 'Islamic leasing instruments' worth a total of US $100m., with the aim of developing the ability of the Islamic financial community to handle medium- to long-term exposures. In January 2002 the BMA introduced more comprehensive regulations for its Islamic banks, covering capital adequacy ratios, risk management, asset quality, liquidity management and auditing.

Important investment banks in Bahrain—owned by shareholders in the Gulf but having most of their earning assets outside the region—included in 1999 Gulf International Bank (1999 assets US $15,680m.), Investcorp (end-1998 assets $2,490m.) and Bahrain Middle East Bank ($765m.). In October 1999 the Dubai-based Cupola Group announced that, subject to BMA approval, it planned to establish a new investment bank in Bahrain in the second half of 2000, to be called CIBIC. Foreign life insurance companies, whose entry into Bahrain had been restricted to representative offices since 1987, were to be permitted to set up branch offices from 1997. At the end of 2001 the consolidated balance sheet of banks operating in Bahrain was $102,700m., of which OBUs accounted for $88,370m., commercial banks for $3,883m. and investment banks for $4,034m.

In 1982, when oil provided 80% of Bahrain's budgetary revenues, there was a budget surplus of BD 46.4m.—the latest in a succession of such surpluses. In 1983 a budget deficit of a similar margin was recorded, mainly because of a 17% decline in oil revenue. Thereafter, budget deficits have recurred, despite the Government's efforts to moderate its spending programmes and despite the receipt of annual grant aid from Kuwait and Saudi Arabia (each providing about US $50m.). Moreover, from 1993 Saudi Arabia waived part (and from 1996 waived all) of its entitlement to 50% of the revenue from oil produced in the shared Abu Saafa field (see Petroleum and Gas, above).

Bahrain's two-year budget for 1995–96 provided for deficits of BD 65.2m. in 1995 and BD 114.0m. in 1996. In 1995 there was provision for total revenue of BD 560.8m. (57% from petroleum) and total expenditure of BD 626m. (83% recurrent and 17% capital). In 1996 there was provision for total revenue of BD 530m. (48% from oil) and total expenditure of BD 644m.

(81% recurrent and 19% capital). In view of advantageous developments subsequent to publication of the 1996 budget (increased Abu Saafa revenues and relatively strong world oil prices in 1996), actual revenue in 1996 was BD 615.5m., with expenditure of BD 581.3m., resulting in a surplus of BD 34.2m. The two-year budget for 1997–98, drawn up at the end of 1996, provided for a deficit of BD 75m. in each year. However, after showing a small surplus in 1997 on revenues of BD 706m. (including oil revenue of BD 423m.), the budget account went into heavy deficit in 1998, as oil revenue dropped by almost 40%—to BD 259m. in total revenue of BD 554m.—whereas expenditure remained constant at BD 705m.

In March 1996 the Government approved a public-expenditure management strategy for the period 1997–2006, outlining a wide range of actions to eliminate the budget deficit within 10 years. The strategy document did not consider the introduction of a direct income tax, the absence of which was regarded as an important factor in Bahrain's appeal to foreign investors. The two-year budget for 1999–2000 forecast deficits of BD 160m. for both 1999 and 2000; however, the sharp upturn in world oil prices in 1999 produced an unexpected recovery in the Government's oil revenues, to more than three times their 1998 level, so that the 1999 budget deficit was expected to be less than half the amount originally anticipated. In 2000 there was provision for total revenue of BD 572m. (BD 256m. from oil) and total expenditure of BD 732m. that deficit, equivalent to 6.4% of GDP, was covered by issues of treasury bills. Negative inflation of 1% was recorded in 2000 and 2001.

The two-year budget for 2001–2002, finalized in November 2000, provided for a deficit of BD 154m. in 2001 (expenditure BD 823m., revenue BD 669m.) and a deficit of BD 160m. in 2002 (expenditure BD 835m., revenue BD 675m.). Allocations of BD 160m. per year were made for public-sector development projects in 2001 and 2002, with the main emphasis on infrastructure, the enhancement of which was seen as essential to stimulating private investment in Bahrain's economy.

The Bahrain Stock Exchange (BSE) opened in June 1989 with an initial market capitalization of BD 1,121m. Since the end of 1994 the stock exchanges of Bahrain and Oman have listed each other's shares under a reciprocal agreement. Bahrain and Jordan made similar reciprocal listing arrangements in March 1996. Under liberalized rules introduced in 1997, and further amended by decree in March 1999, non-GCC investors may hold up to 49% of shares in any listed company provided that they have resided in Bahrain for at least one year or are resident outside Bahrain; GCC nationals may hold up to 100% of companies listed on the BSE. An electronic trading system was introduced on a trial basis at the end of 1999, during which the BSE share index rose by only 1.1%. The volume of shares traded on the BSE fell steadily from 630.1m. in 1997 (from 38 listed companies) to 335.3m. in 2001 (from 36 listed companies), while the value of traded shares fell from a high of BD 217.3m. in 1998 to BD 72.2m. in 2001. At the end of 2001 market capitalization of stocks traded on the BSE stood at BD 2,489m., compared with a peak level of BD 2,954m. at the end of 1997. The BSE share index, which had reached 2,310 points at the end of 1997, stood at 1,761 at the end of 2001, subsequently recovering to 1,810 by mid-May 2002. Analysts attributed the post-1997 decline in the market partly to local investors turning their attention to US and other international markets.

Bahrain's first private placement of shares was announced in April 2001, one month after the introduction of a property law permitting non-GCC nationals to acquire limited ownership rights in designated sites in Bahrain. The shares offered were in a property company set up to undertake a BD 60m. development scheme on a waterfront site at Ghalali. In December the National Bank of Bahrain and the TAIB Bank combined to provide direct-access online share-trading services for investors.

FOREIGN TRADE AND BALANCE OF PAYMENTS

Trade figures for 1996 indicated a surplus of US $508m. (exports $4,437m., imports $3,929m.). Bahrain's imports of Saudi Arabian crude petroleum in that year were valued at $1,710m., while exports of petroleum products were valued at $3,180m. Manufactured goods accounted for 21.4% of 1996 exports, while re-exports represented just 1% of the total. In 1997 the trade surplus fell to BD 134.6m., from total exports of BD 1,648.2m.

(including BD 1,020.7m. in oil products) against total imports of BD 1,513.6m. (including BD 984.4m. in non-oil items). In 1998 falling world oil prices resulted in a trade deficit of BD 111.3m., from total exports of BD 1,229.6m. (including BD 664m. in oil products) against total imports of BD 1,240.3m. (including BD 905.4m. in non-oil items). In 1999 the sharp recovery in oil prices contributed to a return to a healthy surplus of BD 166.5m. in the trade balance, from total exports of BD 1,556.8m. (including BD 960.1m. in oil products) against total imports of BD 1,390.3m. (including BD 921.2m. in non-oil items).

Trade statistics for 2000 showed that the surplus had increased sharply, to BD 402.3m., principally because of a year-on-year rise of 49% in Bahrain's surplus on oil trade, to BD 727.6m. (oil product exports BD 1,498.9m.; crude oil imports BD 771.3m.), while the deficit on non-oil trade increased slightly, to BD 356.1m., and re-exports rose to BD 30.8m. The current-account of the balance of payments showed a surplus of BD 42.5m. in 2000, compared with deficits of BD 128.1m. and BD 292.3m. in 1999 and 1998 respectively. Figures for 2001 showed a further rise in the trade surplus, to BD 482.0m., from exports of BD 2,084.8m. (including BD 1,394.8m. in oil exports and BD 27.8m. in re-exports) and imports of BD 1,602.8m. Apart from Saudi Arabia, significant suppliers of imports in 2001 included Australia, Japan, the USA and the United Kingdom. Important export markets in that year included the USA, Saudi Arabia, Taiwan and Malaysia. Foreign currency reserves stood at US $1,630m. in February 2002.

In November 1999 Bahrain was a signatory of a GCC agreement providing for the creation of a full customs union by 2005, with a common external tariff of 5.5% on basic goods and of 7.5% on luxury items. From January 2000 the Government abolished import duties on foodstuffs and applied a 25% reduction in tariffs on 53 essential commodities, including duties on garments, electrical appliances and computers. In December of that year Bahrain announced its intention to implement the GCC's proposed external tariff rates by 2003. The six GCC member states anticipated the creation of a single market and currency by January 2010.

TOURISM

Tourism has been systematically promoted by the Government since 1985, with increasing emphasis from the mid-1990s, as various major projects have been initiated seeking to capitalize on Bahrain's island location in warm waters. Spanning both the recreational and conference markets, tourism contributed 9.2% of GDP and employed 16.7% of the work-force in 1995, in which year spending by visitors was estimated at US $870m., about one-half of which was classed as 'direct income to Bahrain's economy'. In 1998 Saudi Arabian citizens, travelling to Bahrain across the causeway between the two countries, accounted for 1.9m. of Bahrain's estimated 2.9m. visitor arrivals. Total visitor numbers were estimated to have risen to almost 3.9m. in 2000. Early in 2001 the Government's five-year forecast was that the tourism sector would expand by 10% a year and that tourist arrivals would reach 7m.–8m. by 2006.

Events at the Bahrain International Exhibition Centre attracted nearly 250,000 visitors in 1996. Inaugurated in 1991, the purpose-built centre underwent a major expansion programme in 1998–99, as a result of which a 6,300-sq m extension, constructed at a cost of US $6.6m., was officially inaugurated in September 1999, to coincide with the opening of the first Bahrain International Electronics Fair. A new International Convention Centre was opened at Bahrain's Gulf Hotel in 1997. In 1999 the local EBH Holdings and India's Oberoi Group announced plans for the development of a luxury hotel and resort, at a cost of $70m., on the man-made Lulu Island. The development was to include a five-star hotel, restaurants, conference facilities and a marina; the island was to be linked to the mainland by a new causeway.

In November 1999 the Government signed an agreement with the private Dallah Real Estate and Tourism Development Company of Saudi Arabia for the 50:50 joint-venture Durrat al-Bahrain tourism development project on the southern Gulf coast, costing an anticipated US $800m. and featuring a new five-star hotel, recreational facilities, shopping malls and residential apartments. The first phase of development work on the resort, involving the reclamation of 20 sq km of land to create the site of a 'self-contained city' capable of accommodating 250,000 Saudi visitors annually, was completed in late 2001 and scheduled to be officially opened in August 2002.

In January 2001 the Government announced that it was setting up a holding company, with a paid-up capital of BD 100m. (20% to be invested by the Government and the remainder raised through share offers to local and foreign investors), as a vehicle for joint-venture projects to develop tourism facilities on three sites on Manama island. In May 2002 the EDB invited bids for the Al-Jazair project on a beach site in south-west Bahrain, involving the creation of a wide range of family leisure and tourism facilities in units which investors would be able to lease for 35 years for a minimum annual rent of US $270,000. As part of its strategy of making Bahrain a centre for international sporting events, the Government also invited bids for the contract to build a $80m. multi-purpose racetrack complex near Manama, featuring a motor-racing circuit, a drag-racing track and permanent seating for up to 62,000 spectators. Contacts were initiated with the Formula One authorities with a view to Bahrain's eventual inclusion in the international Grand Prix circuit.

The confirmation of Bahrain's sovereignty over the Hawar islands in March 2001 accelerated the elaboration of plans by the South Area Development Company for the development on these and adjacent islands for tourism, at a projected total cost of some US $100m. In March 2002 seven international companies submitted bids for the first-phase dredging and reclamation work on the islands, involving the reclamation from the sea of 300,000 sq m of land with the aim of creating 32 islets and one large new island, on which building plots would be created for sale to private investors, including non-Bahraini nationals. It was also envisaged that the development would include a five-star hotel, marina village and other facilities on the main existing island.

In May 2002 plans were announced for the US $130m. Fanar Beach tourism complex on the western side of the artificially created Amwaj islands, as the first phase of real estate development covering a 2.8m. sq m plot at Ghalali, north-east of Muharraq island. Scheduled to be completed in 2003, the project will involve the construction of two five-star hotels, four four-star hotels, a marina and an aquatic theme park.

ECONOMIC PROSPECTS

Although not a significant oil or gas producer itself, Bahrain is well placed, as the region's best-regulated banking and financial centre, to benefit from post-1999 buoyancy in the regional oil market and resultant investment flows, albeit with a perceived need for consolidation in the heavily-populated banking sector. At the same time, Bahrain's well-developed oil-refining and aluminium industries provide a solid basis for further development of the manufacturing sector, while tourism has also been identified by the Government as a potential growth industry, with the potential to ameliorate a persistent problem of high unemployment. A major additional bonus would be some success in the new search for hydrocarbon resources in unexplored offshore areas being undertaken by ChevronTexaco of the USA and Petronas of Malaysia.

Bahrain is committed to enhancing its reputation for providing a compatible environment for foreign investors and for the operation of market forces, and has not ruled out the opening up of core infrastructure to private investors. However, the creation, in April 2000, of a new Supreme Council for Economic Development (now the EDB) and the merger of the main state-owned oil industry enterprises in the new BAPCO were interpreted as signs of the Government's desire to continue to direct Bahrain's economic policy. Progress on several major infrastructure development projects (some of which had remained at the pre-bidding stage for a considerable time) was accelerated in 2001–02, as the Bahraini authorities responded to the favourable conditions offered by sustained high prices on international oil markets.

Statistical Survey

Sources (unless otherwise stated): Central Statistics Organization, POB 5835, Manama; tel. 725725; fax 728989; e-mail cso@bahrain.gov.bh; Bahrain Monetary Agency, POB 27, Bldg 96, Block 317, Rd 1702, Manama; tel. 547777; fax 534170; e-mail bmalbr@batelco.com.bh; internet www.bma.gov.bh; Ministry of Finance and National Economy, POB 333, Diplomatic Area, Manama; tel. 530800; fax 532853; e-mail mofne@batelco.com.bh; internet www.mofne.gov.bh.

AREA AND POPULATION

Area (2001): 711.9 sq km (274.9 sq miles).

Population: 508,037 at census of 16 November 1991; 650,604 (males 373,649; females 276,955), comprising 405,667 Bahrainis (males 204,623; females 201,044) and 244,937 non-Bahraini nationals (males 169,026; females 75,911), at census of 7 April 2001.

Density (2001): 913.9 per sq km.

Principal Towns (population in 2001): Manama (capital) 153,395; Muharraq Town 91,939; Riffa 79,985.

Births, Marriages and Deaths (2000): Registered live births 13,947 (birth rate 20.2 per 1,000); Registered marriages 3,963 (marriage rate 5.7 per 1,000); Registered deaths 2,045 (death rate 3.0 per 1,000).

Expectation of Life (WHO estimates, years at birth, 2000): Males 72.7; Females 74.7. Source: WHO, *World Health Report*.

Economically Active Population (persons aged 15 years and over, 1991 census): Agriculture, hunting, forestry and fishing 5,108; Mining and quarrying 3,638; Manufacturing 26,618; Electricity, gas and water 2,898; Construction 26,738; Trade, restaurants and hotels 29,961; Transport, storage and communications 13,789; Financing, insurance, real estate and business services 17,256; Community, social and personal services 83,944; Activities not adequately defined 2,120; *Total employed* 212,070 (males 177,154; females 34,916); Unemployed 14,378 (males 9,703; females 4,675); *Total labour force* 226,448 (males 186,857; females 39,591), comprising 90,662 Bahrainis (males 73,118; females 17,544) and 135,786 non-Bahraini nationals (males 113,739; females 22,047). *Mid-2000* (estimates): Agriculture, etc. 3,000; Total 299,000 (Source: FAO).

HEALTH AND WELFARE
Key Indicators

Fertility (births per woman, 2000): 2.5.

Under-5 Mortality Rate (per 1,000 live births, 2000): 16.

HIV/AIDS (% of persons aged 15–49, 2001): 0.26.

Physicians (per 1,000 head, 2000): 1.53.

Hospital Beds (per 1,000 head, 2000): 2.6.

Health Expenditure (1998): US $ per head (PPP): 611.
%of GDP: 4.7.
public (% of total): 70.6.

Human Development Index (2000): ranking: 39.
value: 0.831.

For sources and definitions, see explanatory note on p. vi.

AGRICULTURE, ETC.

Principal Crops ('000 metric tons, 2000): Cabbages 1.1; Tomatoes 4.2; Dry onions 1.6; Other vegetables 4.9*; Dates 16.5; Other fruits (excl. melons) 5.0*. Source: FAO.

Livestock (FAO estimates, '000 head, year ending September 2000): Cattle 11.0; Sheep 17.5*; Goats 16.3*. Source: FAO.

Livestock Products ('000 metric tons, 2000): Mutton and lamb 5.4; Goat meat 1.8*; Poultry meat 5.4*; Milk 14.4*; Poultry eggs 3.0*. Source: FAO.
* FAO estimate.

Fishing (metric tons, live weight, 1999): Capture 10,290 (Groupers 525, Grunts and sweetlips 325, Emperors 1,227, Porgies and seabreams 582, Goatfishes 413, Spinefeet 1,241, Carangids 524, Portunus swimcrabs 2,090, Penaeus shrimps 1,413); Aquaculture 5; Total catch 10,295. Source: FAO, *Yearbook of Fishery Statistics.*

MINING

Production (2000): Crude petroleum 13,766,000 barrels; Natural gas 8,970 million cubic metres (excluding associated gas: 2,700 million cubic metres).

INDUSTRY

Production ('000 barrels, 2000, unless otherwise indicated): Liquefied petroleum gas 346; Naphtha 12,899; Motor spirit (Gasoline) 7,090; Kerosene and jet fuel 18,445; Fuel oil 21,278; Diesel oil and gas oil 32,389; Petroleum bitumen (asphalt) 1,078; Electric energy (2001) 6,779.3 million kWh; Aluminium (unwrought) 509,038 metric tons (Source: US Geological Survey).

FINANCE

Currency and Exchange Rates: 1,000 fils = 1 Bahraini dinar (BD). *Sterling, Dollar and Euro Equivalents* (31 May 2002): £1 sterling = 551.5 fils; US $1 = 376.0 fils; €1 = 353.0 fils; 100 Bahraini dinars = £181.33 = $265.96 = €283.33. *Exchange Rate:* Fixed at US $1 = 376.0 fils (BD 1 = $2.6596) since November 1980.

Budget (BD million, 1998): *Revenue:* Taxation 204.1 (Taxes on income and profits 34.4, Social security contributions 72.4, Domestic taxes on goods and services 19.3, Import duties 63.4); Entrepreneurial and property income 277.6; Other current revenue 34.8; Capital revenue 0.1; Total 516.6, excl. grants from abroad (37.6). *Expenditure:* General public services 97.7; Defence 111.2; Public order and safety 94.7; Education 85.3; Health 57.8; Social security and welfare 27.7; Housing and community amenities 22.8; Recreational, cultural and religious affairs and services 11.8; Economic affairs and services 111.5 (Fuel and energy 83.6, Transport and communications 20.2); Interest payments 24.1; Total 644.6 (Current 528.0, Capital 116.6), excl. lending minus repayments (26.1). Source: IMF, *Government Finance Statistics Yearbook.*

1999 (BD million): Revenue 622.8 (excl. grants 37.6); Expenditure 723.8.
2000 (BD million): Revenue 1,028.4 (excl. grants 18.8); Expenditure 1,042.0.
2001 (forecasts, BD million): Revenue 669; Expenditure 823.
2002 (forecasts, BD million): Revenue 675; Expenditure 835.

International Reserves (US $ million at 31 December 2001): Gold (valued at $44 per troy oz) 6.6; IMF special drawing rights 1.1; Reserve position in IMF 84.4; Foreign exchange 1,598.5; Total 1,690.6. Source: IMF, *International Financial Statistics.*

Money Supply (BD million at 31 December 2001): Currency outside banks 122.9; Demand deposits at commercial banks 429.1, Total money 552.0. Source: IMF, *International Financial Statistics.*

Cost of Living (Consumer Price Index; base: 1994–95 = 100): 102.8 in 1999; 102.1 in 2000; 100.9 in 2001.

Expenditure on the Gross Domestic Product (BD million, 2000): Government final consumption expenditure 526.2; Private final consumption expenditure 1,411.8; Increase in stocks 100.1; Gross fixed capital formation 404.6; *Total domestic expenditure* 2,442.7; Exports of goods and services 2,455.4; *Less* Imports of goods and services 1,901.1; *GDP in purchasers' values* 2,996.9.

Gross Domestic Product by Economic Activity (provisional, BD million at current prices, 2001): Agriculture, hunting, forestry and fishing 21.7; Mining and quarrying 739.9; Manufacturing 358.1; Electricity and water 42.8; Construction 119.4; Trade, restaurants and hotels 319.6; Transport, storage and communications 224.2; Finance, insurance, real estate and business services 842.7; Government services 505.7; Other community, social and personal services 77.6; *Sub-total* 3,251.6; *Less* Imputed bank service charge 325.8; *GDP at factor cost* 2,925.8; Import duties 57.6; *GDP in purchasers' values* 2,983.4.

Balance of Payments (US $ million, 2000): Exports of goods f.o.b. 5,700.5; Imports of goods f.o.b. −4,373.4; *Trade balance* 1,327.1; Exports of services 830.1; Imports of services −682.7; *Balance on goods and services* 1,474.5; Other income received 5,902.4; Other income paid −6,273.7; *Balance on goods, services and income* 1,103.2; Current transfers received 22.3; Current transfers paid −1,012.8; *Current balance* 112.8; Capital account (net) 50.0; Direct investment abroad 0.3; Direct investment from abroad 357.7; Portfolio investment assets −83.5; Portfolio investment liabilities 282.4; Other investment assets −3,833.8; Other investment liabilities 3,268.6; Net errors and omissions 45.6; *Overall balance* 200.1. Source: IMF, *International Financial Statistics.*

EXTERNAL TRADE

Total Trade (BD million): *Imports c.i.f.:* 1,390.3 in 1999; 1,742.2 in 2000; 1,602.8 in 2001. *Exports:* 1,556.8 in 1999; 2,144.5 in 2000; 2,084.8 in 2001. Source: IMF, *International Financial Statistics.*

Principal Commodities (BD million, 2001): *Imports c.i.f.:* Live animals and animal products 47.3; Vegetable products 55.6; Prepared foodstuffs; beverages, spirits and vinegar; tobacco and manufactured substitutes 76.6; Mineral products 66.9; Products of chemical or allied industries 146.4; Plastics, rubber and articles thereof 32.3; Textiles and textile articles 93.9; Articles of stone, plaster, cement, asbestos, mica, etc.; ceramic products; glass and glassware 33.4; Base metals and articles thereof 59.5; Machinery and mechanical appliances; electrical equipment; sound and television apparatus 189.3; Vehicles, aircraft, vessels and associated transport equipment 108.8; Miscellaneous manufactured articles 31.0; Total (incl. others) 1,015.8. *Exports f.o.b.:* Mineral products 90.8; Products of chemicals and allied industries 40.9; Textiles and textile articles 158.2; Base metals and articles of base metal 313.3; Total (incl. others) 662.2, excl. re-exports (27.8). Note: Figures exclude trade in petroleum (BD million): Imports 587.0; Exports 1,394.8.

Principal Trading Partners (BD million, 2001): *Imports c.i.f.:* Argentina 11.8; Australia 101.4; Belgium 15.6; Brazil 25.1; China, People's Repub. 51.2; France 36.2; Germany 61.4; India 40.9; Italy 33.3; Japan 84.3; Korea Repub. 24.0; Malaysia 14.7; Netherlands 19.0; Pakistan 18.2; Saudi Arabia 91.2; Spain 12.3; Sweden 10.2; Switzerland 22.5; Thailand 13.2; United Arab Emirates 40.2; United Kingdom 64.7; USA 79.4; Total (incl. others) 1,015.8. *Exports f.o.b.:* Algeria 9.5; China, People's Repub. 12.5; India 29.1; Indonesia 19.1; Iran 17.7; Italy 21.5; Japan 22.5; Republic of Korea 8.1; Kuwait 13.9; Malaysia 30.0; Netherlands 13.6; Oman 6.9; Qatar 24.2; Saudi Arabia 97.8; Taiwan 67.4; United Arab Emirates 21.9; USA 164.1; Total (incl. others) 662.2. Note: Figures exclude trade in petroleum.

TRANSPORT

Road Traffic (registered motor vehicles, 31 December 2000): Passenger cars 176,261; Buses and coaches 5,473; Lorries and vans 30,758; Motorcycles 2,159.

Shipping (international sea-borne freight traffic, '000 metric tons, 1990): *Goods loaded:* Dry cargo 1,145; Petroleum products 12,140. *Goods unloaded:* Dry cargo 3,380; Petroleum products 132. Source: UN, *Monthly Bulletin of Statistics. Merchant Fleet* (31 December 2001): Registered vessels 121; Total displacement 338,091 grt. Source: Lloyd's Register-Fairplay, *World Fleet Statistics.*

Civil Aviation (1998): Kilometres flown (million) 19; Passengers carried ('000) 1,207; Passenger-km (million) 2,653; Total ton-km (million) 357. Figures include an apportionment (equivalent to one-quarter) of the traffic of Gulf Air, a multinational airline with its headquarters in Bahrain. Source: UN, *Statistical Yearbook.*

TOURISM

Tourist Arrivals (2000): 3,868,738*.

Tourist Receipts (2001): BD 130.3 million.

* Figure refers to arrivals at frontiers of visitors from abroad (excluding Bahraini nationals residing abroad).

Source: partly World Tourism Organization, *Yearbook of Tourism Statistics.*

COMMUNICATIONS MEDIA

Radio Receivers ('000 in use, 1997): 338.

Television Receivers ('000 in use, 2000): 275.

Telephones ('000 main lines in use, 2001): 173.9.

Facsimile Machines (1999): 6,928 in use.

Mobile Cellular Telephones ('000 subscribers, 2001): 299.6.

Personal Computers ('000 in use, 2001): 100.

Internet Users ('000, 2001): 140.

Book Production (1996, titles, first editions only): 40.

Daily Newspapers (1996): 4 (circulation 67,000 copies).

Non-daily Newspapers (1993): 5 (circulation 17,000 copies).

Other Periodicals (1993): 26 (circulation 73,000 copies).

Source: mainly UNESCO, *Statistical Yearbook,* and International Telecommunication Union.

EDUCATION

Pre-primary: 90 schools (1996/97); 449 teachers (1995/96); 12,308 pupils (1996/97). Source: UNESCO, *Statistical Yearbook.*

Primary (2000/01): 62,917 pupils* (males 31,374; females 31,543).

Intermediate (2000/01): 28,972 pupils* (males 14,211; females 14,761).

General Secondary (2000/01): 11,974 pupils (males 3,941; females 8,033).

Commercial Secondary (2000/01): 7,870 pupils (males 3,622; females 4,248).

Technical Secondary (2000/01): 2,566 pupils.

Vocational Secondary (2000/01): 956 pupils.

Source: Ministry of Education.

Adult literacy rate (UNESCO estimates): 87.6% (males 90.9%; females 82.6%) in 2000 (Source: UN Development Programme, *Human Development Report*).

* Figures relate to government schools only and exclude pupils of religious education.

Directory

The Constitution

A 108-article Constitution was ratified in June 1973. It states that 'all citizens shall be equal before the law' and guarantees freedom of speech, of the press, of conscience and of religious beliefs. Other provisions include the outlawing of the compulsory repatriation of political refugees. The Constitution also states that the country's financial comptroller should be responsible to the legislature and not to the Government, and allows for national trade unions 'for legally justified causes and on peaceful lines'. Compulsory free primary education and free medical care are also laid down in the Constitution. The Constitution, which came into force on 6 December 1973, also provided for a National Assembly, composed of 14 members of the Cabinet and 30 members elected by popular vote, although this was dissolved in August 1975.

A National Action Charter was approved in a nation-wide referendum held on 14–15 February 2001. The Charter had been prepared by a Supreme National Committee, created by Amiri decree in late 2000 with the task of outlining the future evolution of Bahrain's political system. Principal among the Committee's recommendations were that there should be a transition from an emirate to a constitutional monarchy (the Amir proclaimed himself King on 14 February 2002), with a bicameral parliament (comprising a directly elected legislature and an appointed consultative chamber). Bahraini women were to be permitted for the first time to hold public office and to vote in elections. In mid-2002 it was decreed that representatives of both the new legislature (or House of Representatives) and the Consultative Council (Majlis ash-Shoura) are to serve four-year terms. Members of the lower house were to be Bahraini nationals of at least 30 years of age, while those of the appointed chamber—who must also be Bahraini citizens—are to be aged at least 35.

The Government

HEAD OF STATE

King: HM Sheikh Hamad bin Isa al-Khalifa (acceded as Amir 6 March 1999; proclaimed King 14 February 2002).

Crown Prince and Commander-in-Chief of Bahraini Defence Force: Sheikh Salman bin Hamad al-Khalifa.

CABINET
(September 2002)

Prime Minister: Sheikh Khalifa bin Sulman al-Khalifa.

Minister of Justice and Islamic Affairs: Sheikh Abdullah bin Khalid al-Khalifa.

Minister of Foreign Affairs: Sheikh Muhammad bin Mubarak bin Hamad al-Khalifa.

Minister of the Interior: Sheikh Muhammad bin Khalifa bin Hamad al-Khalifa.

Minister of Transport: Sheikh Ali bin Khalifa bin Salman al-Khalifa.

Minister of Housing and Agriculture: Sheikh Khalid bin Abdullah bin Khalid al-Khalifa.

Minister of Public Works: Fahmi Ali al-Jouder.

Minister of Finance and National Economy: Abdullah Hassan Saif.

Minister of Defence: Maj.-Gen. Sheikh Khalifa bin Ahmad al-Khalifa.

Minister of Cabinet Affairs: Muhammad Ibrahim al-Mutawa.

Minister of Information: Nabil Yaqub al-Hamer.

Minister of Oil: Sheikh Isa bin Ali al-Khalifa.

Minister of Commerce and Industry: Ali Saleh Abdullah as-Saleh.

Minister of Education: Dr Muhammad Jassim al-Ghatam.

Minister of Health: Dr Faisal Radhi al-Mousawi.

Minister of Electricity and Water: Sheikh Abdullah bin Salman bin Khalid al-Khalifa.

Minister of Labour and Social Affairs: Abd an-Nabi Abdullah ash-Shula.

Minister of Royal Court Affairs: Sheikh Ali bin Isa bin Sulman al-Khalifa.

Ministers of State: Brig.-Gen. Abd al-Aziz Muhammad al-Fadhil (Consultative Council Affairs), Dr Muhammad Abd al-Ghaffar Abdullah (Foreign Affairs), Jawad Salim al-Arrayedh (Municipalities and Environment Affairs), Sheikh Khalid bin Ahmad al-Khalifa (Royal Court Affairs), Muhammad Hassan Kamaleldine.

MINISTRIES

Royal Court: POB 555, Riffa Palace, Manama; tel. 666666; fax 663070.

Office of the Prime Minister: POB 1000, Government House, Government Rd, Manama; tel. 253361; fax 533033.

Ministry of Cabinet Affairs: POB 26613, Manama; tel. 223366.

Ministry of Commerce and Industry: POB 5479, Diplomatic Area, Manama; tel. 531531; fax 530455; e-mail drmansoor@commerce.gov.bh; internet www.commerce.gov.bh.

Ministry of Defence: POB 245, West Rifa'a; tel. 653333; fax 663923.

Ministry of Education: POB 43, Isa Town; tel. 685558; fax 680161; e-mail info@batelco.com.bh; internet www.education.gov.bh.

Ministry of Electricity and Water: POB 2, Manama; tel. 533133; fax 533035.

Ministry of Finance and National Economy: POB 333, Diplomatic Area, Manama; tel. 530800; fax 532853; e-mail mofne@batelco.com.bh; internet www.mofne.gov.bh.

Ministry of Foreign Affairs: POB 547, Government House, Government Rd, Manama; tel. 227555; fax 212603.

Ministry of Health: POB 12, Sheikh Sulman Rd, Manama; tel. 255555; fax 252569; e-mail webmaster@health.gov.bh; internet www.moh.gov.bh.

Ministry of Housing and Agriculture: POB 5802, Diplomatic Area, Manama; tel. 533000; fax 534111; e-mail mohvip@batelco.com.bh.

Ministry of Information: POB 572, Manama; tel. 781888; fax 682777; e-mail brtcnews@batelco.com.bh; internet www.moi.gov.bh.

Ministry of the Interior: POB 13, Police Fort Compound, Manama; tel. 272111; fax 262169.

Ministry of Justice and Islamic Affairs: POB 450, Diplomatic Area, Manama; tel. 531333; fax 536343.

Ministry of Labour and Social Affairs: POB 32333, Isa Town; tel. 687800; fax 686954; e-mail jamalq@bah-molsa.com; internet www.bah-molsa.com.

Ministry of Oil: POB 1435, Manama; tel. 291511; fax 293007.

Ministry of Public Works: POB 5, Muharraq Causeway Rd, Manama; tel. 535222; fax 533095.

Ministry of State for Municipalities and Environment Affairs: POB 26909, Manama; tel. 293693; fax 293694.

Ministry of Transport: POB 10325, Diplomatic Area, Manama; tel. 534534; fax 534041.

Legislature

The National Assembly provided for in the 1973 Constitution was dissolved in August 1975. Among the recommendations of the National Action Charter, approved in a referendum in February 2001, was that there should be a bicameral parliament, comprising a directly elected legislature and an appointed consultative chamber. Elections to a 40-member legislature (House of Representatives) were subsequently scheduled for 24 October 2002. The establishment of a 40-seat Consultative Council (Majlis ash-Shoura) was also anticipated, with members to be appointed by the King.

Political Organizations

Political parties are still prohibited in Bahrain. However, several political and civic societies (many of which were previously in exile) are now active in the country, and a number of new groups have been established since 2001.

Diplomatic Representation

EMBASSIES IN BAHRAIN

Algeria: POB 26402, Villa 579, Rd 3622, Adliya, Manama; tel. 713669; fax 713662; e-mail abdemyh@hotmail.com; Ambassador: LAHSSAN BOUFARES.

Bangladesh: POB 26718, House 2280, Rd 2757, Area 327, Adliya, Manama; tel. 714717; fax 710031; e-mail bangla@batelco.com.bh; Ambassador: ANWAR UL-ALAM.

China, People's Republic: POB 3150, Bldg 158, Road 382, Juffair Ave, Block 341, Manama; tel. 723800; fax 727304; Ambassador: YANG HONGLIN.

Egypt: POB 818, Adliya, Manama; tel. 720005; fax 721518; e-mail jawad1eg@yahoo.com; Ambassador: MAHMOUD ABD AL-JAWAD.

France: POB 11134, Road 1901, Building 51, Block 319, Diplomatic Area, Manama; tel. 291734; fax 293655; e-mail consulfr@batelco .com.bh; Ambassador: ANITA LIMIDO.

Germany: POB 10306, Al-Hasan Bldg, Sheikh Hamad Causeway, Manama; tel. 530210; fax 536282; Ambassador: WOLFGANG LERKE.

India: POB 26106, Bldg 182, Rd 2608, Area 326, Adliya, Manama; tel. 712785; fax 715527; e-mail indemb@batelco.com.bh; internet www.indianembassy-bah.com; Ambassador: BHASKAR KUMAR MITRA.

Iran: POB 26365, Entrance 1034, Rd 3221, Area 332, Mahooz, Manama; tel. 722400; fax 722101; Ambassador: MUHAMMAD JALAL FIROUZNIA.

Iraq: POB 26477, Ar-Raqib Bldg, No 17, Rd 2001, Comp 320, King Faysal Ave, Manama; tel. 741472; fax 720756; Chargé d'affaires: AWAD FAKHRI.

Japan: POB 23720, 55 Salmaniya Ave, Manama Tower 327, Manama; tel. 716565; fax 715059; e-mail embjap@batelco.com.bh; Ambassador: ONO YASUAKI.

Jordan: POB 5242, Villa 43, Rd 915, Area 309, Hoora, Manama; tel. 291109; fax 291980; e-mail jordemb@batelco.com.bh; Ambassador: Dr SHAKER ARABIAT.

Kuwait: POB 786, Rd 1703, Diplomatic Area, Manama; tel. 534040; fax 530278; Ambassador: ABD AL-MUHSIN SALIM AL-HARUN.

Lebanon: POB 32474, Manama; tel. 786994; fax 784998; Ambassador: ZUHAIR A. QAZAZ.

Morocco: POB 26229, Manama; tel. 740566; fax 740178; Ambassador: OMER AN-NAJEY.

Oman: POB 26414, Bldg 37, Rd 1901, Diplomatic Area, Manama; tel. 293663; fax 293540; Ambassador: SALIM ALI OMAR BAYAQOOB.

Pakistan: POB 563, Bldg 261, Rd 2807, Block 328, Segeiya, Manama; tel. 244113; fax 255960; e-mail parep@batelco.com.bh; Ambassador: Lt-Gen. (retd) MUHAMMAD SHAFIQ.

Philippines: POB 26681, Manama; tel. 710200; fax 710300; e-mail ambaphil_manama@hotmail.com; Ambassador: RODOLFO I. DUMA-PIAS.

Qatar: Manama; Ambassador: ABDULLAH BIN THAMIR ATH-THANI.

Russia: POB 26612, House 877, Rd 3119, Block 331, Zinj, Manama; tel. 725222; fax 725921; e-mail rusemb@batelco.com.bh; Ambassador: VALERII VLASOV.

Saudi Arabia: POB 1085, Bldg 1450, Rd 4043, Area 340, Juffair, Manama; tel. 537722; fax 533261; Ambassador: ABDULLAH BIN ABD AR-RAHMAN ASH-SHEIKH.

Sudan: POB 5438, Villa 690, Rd 1219, Block 312, Manama; tel. 252558; fax 252594; e-mail sudanimanama@hotmail.com; Ambassador: SALAH ALDIN KARAR.

Syria: Manama; Ambassador: MAJID ABU SALEH.

Tunisia: POB 26911, House 54, Rd 3601, Area 336, Manama; tel. 714149; fax 715702; e-mail tunisemb@batelco.com.bh; Ambassador: MUHAMMAD AOUITI.

Turkey: POB 10821, Flat 10, Bldg 81, Rd 1702, Area 317, Manama; tel. 533448; fax 536557; e-mail tcbahrbe@batelco.com.bh; Ambassador: HILAL BASKAL.

Ukraine: Manama; Ambassador: I. V. TYMOFYEYEV.

United Arab Emirates: POB 26505, Manama; tel. 723737; fax 727343; Ambassador: SULTAN AL-QARTASI AN-NUAIMI.

United Kingdom: POB 114, 21 Government Ave, Area 306, Manama; tel. 534404; fax 536109; e-mail britemb@batelco .com.bh; internet www.ukembassy.gov.bh; Ambassador: PETER FORD.

USA: POB 26431, Bldg 979, Rd 3119, Block 331, Zinj, Manama; tel. 273300; fax 272594; e-mail consularmanama@state.gov; internet www.usembassy.com.bh; Ambassador: RONALD E. NEUMANN.

Yemen: POB 26193, House 1048, Rd 1730, Area 517, Saar; tel. 277072; fax 262358; Ambassador: NASSER M. Y. ALGAADANI.

Judicial System

Since the termination of British legal jurisdiction in 1971, intensive work has been undertaken on the legislative requirements of Bahrain. The Criminal Law is at present contained in various Codes, Ordinances and Regulations. All nationalities are subject to the jurisdiction of the Bahraini courts, which guarantee equality before the law irrespective of nationality or creed. The 1974 Decree Law on State Security Measures and the State Security Court were both abolished in February 2001. A Constitutional Court and independent financial auditing court are both to be established.

Directorate of Courts: POB 450, Government House, Government Rd, Manama; tel. 531333.

Religion

At the November 1991 census the population was 508,037, distributed as follows: Muslims 415,427; Christians 43,237; others 49,373.

ISLAM

Muslims are divided between the Sunni and Shi'ite sects. The ruling family is Sunni, although the majority of the Muslim population (estimated at almost 60%) are Shi'ite.

CHRISTIANITY

The Anglican Communion

Within the Episcopal Church in Jerusalem and the Middle East, Bahrain forms part of the diocese of Cyprus and the Gulf. There are two Anglican churches in Bahrain: St Christopher's Cathedral in Manama and the Community Church in Awali. The congregations are entirely expatriate. The Bishop in Cyprus and the Gulf is resident in Cyprus, while the Archdeacon in the Gulf is resident in Qatar.

Provost: Very Rev. KEITH W. T. W. JOHNSON, St Christopher's Cathedral, POB 36, Al-Mutanabi Ave, Manama; tel. 253866; fax 246436; e-mail decani@batelco.com.bh; internet www .stchcathedral.org.bh.

Roman Catholic Church

A small number of adherents, mainly expatriates, form part of the Apostolic Vicariate of Arabia. The Vicar Apostolic is resident in the United Arab Emirates.

The Press

DAILIES

Akhbar al-Khaleej (Gulf News): POB 5300, Manama; tel. 620111; fax 624312; e-mail editor@akhbar-alkhaleej.com; internet www.akhbar-alkhaleej.com; f. 1976; Arabic; Chair. IBRAHIM AL-MOAYED; Man. Dir and Editor-in-Chief Dr HILAL ASH-SHAIJI; circ. 42,000.

Al-Ayam (The Days): POB 3232, Manama; tel. 727111; fax 729009; e-mail alayam@batelco.com.bh; internet www.alayam.com; f. 1989; Arabic; publ. by Al-Ayam Establishment for Press and Publications; Editor KHALIL YOUSUF; circ. 21,000.

Bahrain Tribune: POB 3232, Manama; tel. 827111; fax 827222; e-mail tribune@batelco.com.bh; internet www.bahraintribune.com; f. 1997; English; Editor-in-Chief NABIL YAQUB AL-HAMER; circ. 12,500.

Gulf Daily News: POB 5300, Manama; tel. 620222; fax 622141; e-mail info@gulf-daily-news.com; internet www.gulf-daily-news.com; f. 1978; English; Editor-in-Chief GEORGE WILLIAMS; Deputy Editor LES HORTON; circ. 50,000.

Khaleej Times: POB 26707, City Centre Bldg, Suite 403, 4th Floor, Government Ave, Manama; tel. 213911; fax 211819; f. 1978; English; circ. 72,565.

WEEKLIES

Al-Adhwaa' (Lights): POB 250, Old Exhibition Rd, Manama; tel. 290942; fax 293166; f. 1965; Arabic; publ. by Arab Printing and

Publishing House; Chair. RAID MAHMOUD AL-MARDI; Editor-in-Chief MUHAMMAD QASSIM SHIRAWI; circ. 7,000.

Al-Bahrain ath-Thaqafia: POB 2199, Manama; tel. 290210; fax 292678; e-mail aqaqeel@batelco.com.bh; internet www.al-thaqafia.com; Arabic; publ. by the Ministry of Information; Editor MAI BINT MUHAMMAD AL-KHALIFA.

BAPCO News: Bahrain Refinery, Sitra; tel. 755049; fax 755047; e-mail kathleen_croes@bapco.net.bh; bi-weekly; English and Arabic; publ. by the Bahrain Petroleum Co BSC; Editors KATHLEEN CROES, KHALID F. MEHMAS; circ. 4,000.

Gulf Economic Monitor: POB 224, Exhibition Ave, Manama; tel. 293131; fax 293400; e-mail hilalmag@tradearabia.net; English; publ. by Al-Hilal Publishing and Marketing Group; Man. Dir RONNIE MIDDLETON.

Huna al-Bahrain (Here is Bahrain): POB 26005, Isa Town; tel. 731888; fax 681292; f. 1957; Arabic; publ. by the Ministry of Information; Editor HAMAD AL-MANNAI; circ. 3,000.

Al-Mawakif (Attitudes): POB 1083, Manama; tel. 231231; fax 271720; f. 1973; Arabic; general interest; Editor-in-Chief MANSOOR M. RADHI; circ. 6,000.

Oil and Gas News: POB 224, Bldg 149, Exhibition Ave, Manama; tel. 293131; fax 293400; e-mail hilalmag@batelco.com.bh; f. 1983; English; publ. by Al-Hilal Publishing and Marketing Co; Editor-in-Chief CLIVE JACQUES; circ. 5,000.

Sada al-Usbou (Weekly Echo): POB 549, Manama; tel. 291234; fax 290507; f. 1969; Arabic; Owner and Editor-in-Chief ALI ABDULLAH SAYYAR; circ. 40,000 (in various Gulf states).

OTHER PERIODICALS

Arab Agriculture: POB 10131, Manama; tel. 213900; fax 211765; e-mail fanar@batelco.com.bh; f. 1984; annually; English and Arabic; publ. by Fanar Publishing WLL; Editor-in-Chief ABD AL-WAHED ALWANI; Gen. Man. FAYEK AL-ARRAYED; circ. 13,000.

Arab World Agribusiness: POB 10131, Manama; tel. 213900; fax 211765; e-mail fanar@batelco.com.bh; f. 1985; nine per year; English and Arabic; publ. by Fanar Publishing WLL; Editor-in-Chief ABD AL-WAHED ALWANI; Gen. Man. FAYEK AL-ARRAYED; circ. 16,618.

Bahrain This Month: POB 20461, Manama; tel. 244455; fax 242229; e-mail redhouse@batelco.com.bh; internet www.bahrainthismonth.com; f. 1997; monthly; English; Publ. Dir GEORGE F. MIDDLETON; Editor ROY KIETZMAN; circ. 9,948.

Discover Bahrain: POB 10704, Manama; tel. 534587; fax 531296; f. 1988; English; publ. by G. and B. Media Ltd; Publr and Editor ROBERT GRAHAM.

Gulf Construction: POB 224, Exhibition Ave, Manama; tel. 293131; fax 293400; e-mail editor@gulfconstructiononline.com; internet www.gulfconstructiononline.com; f. 1980; monthly; English; publ. by Al-Hilal Publishing and Marketing Group; Editor BINA PRABHU GOVEAS; circ. 12,485.

Gulf Panorama: POB 3232, Manama; tel. 727111; fax 727552; f. 1983; monthly; Arabic; Editor IBRAHIM BASHMI; circ. 10,000.

Al-Hayat at-Tijariya (Commerce Review): POB 248, Manama; tel. 229555; fax 224985; e-mail bahcci@batelco.com.bh; monthly; English and Arabic; publ. by Bahrain Chamber of Commerce and Industry; Editor KHALIL YOUSUF; circ. 7,500.

Al-Hidayah (Guidance): POB 450, Manama; tel. 727100; fax 729819; f. 1978; monthly; Arabic; publ. by Ministry of Justice and Islamic Affairs; Editor-in-Chief ABD AR-RAHMAN BIN MUHAMMAD RASHID AL-KHALIFA; circ. 5,000.

Middle East Expatriate: POB 224, Manama; tel. 293131; fax 292400; e-mail info@middleeastexpatonline.com; internet www.middleeastexpatonline.com; monthly; English; publ. by Al-Hilal Publishing and Marketing Group; Editor BABU KALYANPUR; circ. 16,816.

Al-Mohandis (The Engineer): POB 835, Manama; e-mail mohandis@batelco.com.bh; internet www.mohandis.org; f. 1972; quarterly; Arabic and English; publ. by Bahrain Society of Engineers; Editor ISA ALI JANAHI.

Al-Musafir al-Arabi (Arab Traveller): POB 10131, Manama; tel. 213900; fax 211765; e-mail fanar@batelco.com.bh; f. 1984; six per year; Arabic; publ. by Fanar Publishing WLL; Editor-in-Chief ABD AL-WAHED ALWANI; Gen. Man. FAYEK AL-ARRAYED.

Profile: POB 10243, Manama; tel. 291110; fax 294655; f. 1992; monthly; English; publ. by Bahrain Market Promotions; Editor ISA KHALIFA AL-KHALIFA.

Al-Quwwa (The Force). POB 245, Manama; tel. 291331; fax 659596; f. 1977; monthly; Arabic; publ. by Bahrain Defence Force; Editor-in-Chief Maj. AHMAD MAHMOUD AS-SUWAIDI.

Gulf Industry: POB 224, Manama; tel. 293131; fax 293400; e-mail salvador.almeida@tradearabia.net; English; journal of industry and transport; publ. By Al-Hilal Publishing and Marketing Group; Editor SALVADOR ALMEIDA.

Travel and Tourism News Middle East: POB 224, Exhibition Ave, Manama; tel. 293131; fax 293400; e-mail hilalmag@tradearabia.net; internet www.ttnonline.com; f. 1983; monthly; English; travel trade; publ. by Al-Hilal Publishing and Marketing Group; Editorial Man. KAMLESHKUMAR DESAI; circ. 6,621.

NEWS AGENCIES

Bahrain News Agency (BNA): Ministry of Information, POB 26613, Government House, Government Rd, Manama; f. 2001.

Gulf News Agency (GNA): POB 5421, Manama; tel. 689044; fax 683825; e-mail brtcnews@batelco.com.bh; internet www.gna.gov.bh; f. 1978; transmits news to the Gulf region in Arabic and English; Chief Editor KHALID ABDULLAH AZ-ZAYANI.

Foreign Bureaux

Agence France-Presse (AFP): POB 5890, Kanoo Tower, Phase 3, Tijaar Ave, Manama; tel. and fax 403446; Dir JEAN-PIERRE PERRIN.

Associated Press (AP) (USA): POB 26940, Mannai Bldg, Manama; tel. 530101; fax 530249.

Deutsche Presse-Agentur (dpa) (Germany): POB 26695, Manama; tel. 716655; fax 714119.

Reuters (United Kingdom): POB 1030, UGB Bldg, 6th Floor, Diplomatic Area, Manama; tel. 536111; fax 536192; Bureau Man. KENNETH WEST.

PRESS ASSOCIATION

Bahrain Journalists' Association: Manama; f. 2000; Chair. NABIL YAQUB AL-HAMER; 250 mems.

Publishers

Arab Communicators: POB 551, 6th Floor, Almoayyed Bldg, Government Ave, Manama; tel. 534664; fax 531837; f. 1981; publrs of annual Bahrain Business Directory; Dirs AHMAD A. FAKHRI, HAMAD A. ABUL.

Fanar Publishing WLL: POB 10131, Manama; tel. 213900; fax 211765; e-mail fanar@batelco.com.bh.

Gulf Advertising: POB 5518, Manama; tel. 226262; fax 228660; e-mail gulfad@batelco.com.bh; f. 1974; advertising and marketing communications; Chair. and Man. Dir KHAMIS AL-MUQLA.

Al-Hilal Publishing and Marketing Group: POB 224, Exhibition Ave, Manama; tel. 293131; fax 293400; e-mail hilalpmg@tradearabia.net; f. 1977; specialist magazines and newspapers of commercial interest; Chair. A. M. ABD AR-RAHMAN; Man. Dir R. MIDDLETON.

Manama Publishing Co WLL: POB 1013, Manama; tel. 213223; fax 211548.

Al-Masirah Journalism, Printing and Publishing House: POB 5981, Manama; tel. 258882; fax 276178; e-mail almasera@batelco.com.bh.

Tele-Gulf Directory Publications, WLL: POB 2738, 3rd Floor, Bahrain Tower, Manama; tel. 213301; fax 210503; e-mail telegulf@batelco.com.bh; f. 1977; publrs of annual *Gulf Directory* and *Arab Banking and Finance*.

Government Publishing House

Directorate of Publications: POB 26005, Manama; tel. 689077; Dir MUHAMMAD AL-KHUZAI.

Broadcasting and Communications

TELECOMMUNICATIONS

Regulatory Authority

Telecommunications Directorate: POB 11170, Manama; tel. 534534; fax 533544; Dir Dr RASHID JASSIM ASHOOR.

Bahrain Telecommunications Co BSC (BATELCO): POB 14, Manama; tel. 884557; fax 611898; e-mail batelco@btc.com.bh; internet www.batelco.com.bh; f. 1981; operates all telecommunications services; cap. BD 100m.; 80% owned by Government of Bahrain, financial institutions and public of Bahrain, 20% by Cable and Wireless PLC (United Kingdom); launched mobile cellular telecommunications service, Sim Sim, in 1999; Chair. Sheikh ALI BIN KHALIFA BIN SALMAN AL-KHALIFA; CEO TONY HART.

BROADCASTING

Radio

Bahrain Radio and Television Corpn: POB 702, Manama; tel. 781888; fax 681544; internet www.gna.gov.bh/brtc/radio.html;

f. 1955; state-owned and -operated enterprise; two 10-kW transmitters; programmes are in Arabic and English, and include news, drama and discussions; Dir of Broadcasting ABD AR-RAHMAN ABDULLAH.

Radio Bahrain: POB 702, Manama; tel. 629085; fax 780911; e-mail brtcnews@batelco.com.bh; f. 1977; commercial radio station in English language; Head of Station SALAH KHALID.

Television

Bahrain Radio and Television Corpn: POB 1075, Manama; tel. 686000; fax 681544; e-mail ceobrtc@batelco.bh; internet www.gna .gov.bh/brtc/bah-tv.html; commenced colour broadcasting in 1973; broadcasts on five channels, of which the main Arabic and the main English channel accept advertising; covers Bahrain, eastern Saudi Arabia, Qatar and the UAE; an Amiri decree in early 1993 established the independence of the Corpn, which was to be controlled by a committee; Dir H. AL-UMRAN.

Finance

(cap. = capital; res = reserves; dep. = deposits; m. = millions; brs = branches; amounts in Bahraini dinars unless otherwise stated)

BANKING
Central Bank

Bahrain Monetary Agency (BMA): POB 27, Bldg 96, Block 317, Rd 1702, Manama; tel. 547777; fax 534170; e-mail bmalbr@batelco .com.bh; internet www.bma.gov.bh; f. 1973, in operation from January 1975; controls issue of currency, regulates exchange control and credit policy, organization and control of banking and insurance systems and bank credit; cap. and res 290.9m., dep. 136.0m. (May 2000); Gov. Sheikh AHMAD BIN MUHAMMAD AL-KHALIFA.

Locally-incorporated Commercial Banks

Ahli United Bank (AUB): Manama; f. 2001 by merger of Al-Ahli Commercial Bank and Commercial Bank of Bahrain; CEO ADEL EL-LABBAN.

Bahrain Islamic Bank BSC: POB 5240, Government Rd, Manama; tel. 535888; fax 535808; e-mail bahisl@batelco.com.bh; internet www.bahisl.com.bh; f. 1979; cap. 23.0m., res 15.4m., dep. 153.6m. (Dec. 2000); Chair. Sheikh ABD AR-RAHMAN AL-KHALIFA; Gen. Man. ABD AL-LATIF ABD AR-RAHIM JANAHI; 5 brs.

Bahraini Saudi Bank BSC (BSB): POB 1159, As-Saddah Bldg, Government Ave, Manama; tel. 211010; fax 210989; e-mail bsbbahr@batelco.com.bh; internet www.bahrainisaudibank.com; f. 1983; commenced operations in early 1985; licensed as a full commercial bank; cap. 20.0m., res 8.7m., dep. 159.6m. (Dec. 2000); Chair. Sheikh IBRAHIM BIN HAMAD AL-KHALIFA; Gen. Man. MANSOOR A. AS-SAYED; 5 brs.

Bank of Bahrain and Kuwait BSC (BBK): POB 597, 43 Government Ave, Manama 309; tel. 207400; fax 210636; e-mail monaa@bbkonline.com; internet www.bbkonline.com; f. 1971; cap. 56.9m., res 34.0m., dep. 922.3m. (Dec. 2000); Chair. HASSAN KHALIFA AL-JALAHMA; Gen. Man. and CEO MURAD ALI MURAD; 21 local brs, 4 brs overseas.

National Bank of Bahrain BSC (NBB): POB 106, Government Ave, Manama; tel. 228800; fax 228998; e-mail nbb@nbbonline.com; internet www.nbbonline.com; f. 1957; 49% govt-owned; cap. 40.0m., res 70.0m., dep. 896.7m. (Dec. 2000); Chair. ABDULLAH ALI KANOO; Gen. Man. ABD AR-RAZAK A. HASSAN; 25 brs.

Shamil Bank of Bahrain EC (SBB): POB 3005, Chamber of Commerce Bldg, King Faysal Rd, Manama; tel. 227040; fax 224872; e-mail alshamil@shamilbank.com.bh; f. 1982 as Massraf Faysal Al-Islami of Bahrain EC; renamed Faysal Islamic Bank of Bahrain in 1987 and as above in 2000; cap. US $100.0m., res US $15.7m., dep. US $162.0m. (Dec. 1999); CEO NABIL A. NASSIEF; 3 brs.

Foreign Commercial Banks

Arab Bank PLC (Jordan): POB 395, Government Rd, Manama; tel. 229988; fax 210443; internet www.arabbank.com; Chair. ABD AL-MAJEED SHOMAN; 4 brs.

Bank Melli Iran: POB 785, Government Rd, Manama; tel. 229910; fax 224402; e-mail bmibah@batelco.com.bh; Gen. Man. MOHAMMAD TAGHI TAVAKULI; 2 brs.

Bank Saderat Iran: POB 825, 106 Government Rd, Manama; tel. 210003; fax 210398; Man. MUHAMMAD JAVAD NASSIRI; 2 brs.

Banque du Caire, SAE (Egypt): POB 815, Government Ave, Manama; tel. 227454; fax 213704; Man. MOUSTAFA ES-SAYED ED-DOKMAWEY.

Citibank NA (USA): POB 548, Bab al-Bahrain Bldg, Government Rd, Manama; tel. 223344; fax 211323; internet www.citibank.com /bahrain; Gen. Man. MUHAMMAD ASH-SHROOGI; 1 br.

Habib Bank Ltd (Pakistan): POB 566, Government Ave, Manama; tel. 224746; fax 224749; e-mail maziz@batelco.com.bh; f. 1941; Exec. Vice-Pres. and Gen. Man. ASHRAF BIDIWALA; 5 brs.

HSBC Bank Middle East (United Kingdom): POB 57, 93 Al-Khalifa Ave, Manama 304; tel. 224555; fax 226822; e-mail hsbcmnm@batelco.com.bh; internet www.banking.middle east.hsbc.com; CEO SALEH AL-KOWARY; 4 brs.

Rafidain Bank (Iraq): POB 607, Heaya House Bldg, Government Rd, Manama; tel. 275796; fax 255656; f. 1969; Man. IBTISAM NAJEM ABOUD; 1 br.

Standard Chartered Bank (United Kingdom): POB 29, Government Rd, Manama; tel. 223636; fax 225001; internet www.standard chartered.com/bh/index.html; f. in Bahrain 1920; Man. PETER RAWLINGS; 5 brs.

United Bank Ltd (Pakistan): POB 546, Government Rd, Manama; tel. 224030; fax 224099; e-mail ublbah@batelco.com.bh; Gen. Man. M. A. RAUF; 3 brs.

Specialized Financial Institutions

Bahrain Development Bank (BDB): POB 20501, Manama; tel. 537007; fax 534005; f. 1992; invests in manufacturing, agribusiness and services; cap. 10.0m., res 1.8m., dep. 0.1m. (Dec. 1999); Chair. Sheikh IBRAHIM BIN KHALIFA AL-KHALIFA.

The Housing Bank: POB 5370, Diplomatic Area, Manama; tel. 534443; fax 533437; f. 1979; provides housing loans for Bahraini citizens and finances construction of commercial properties. Chair. Sheikh KHALID BIN ABDULLAH BIN KHALID AL-KHALIFA; Gen. Man. ISA SULTAN ADH-DHAWADI.

'Offshore' Banking Units

Bahrain has been encouraging the establishment of 'offshore' banking units (OBUs) since 1975. An OBU is not permitted to provide local banking services, but is allowed to accept deposits from governments and large financial organizations in the area and make medium-term loans for local and regional capital projects. At the end of 2001 there were 48 OBUs in operation in Bahrain.

Allied Banking Corporation (Philippines): POB 20493, Bahrain Tower, 11th Floor, Govt Ave, Manama; tel. 224707; fax 210506; e-mail ally3540@batelco.com.bh; f. in Bahrain 1980; Chair. LUCIO C. TAN; Gen. Man. RAMON R. LANDINGIN.

Alubaf Arab International Bank EC: POB 11529, UGB Tower, Diplomatic Area, Manama; tel. 531212; fax 523100; f. 1982; cap. US $50.0m., dep. US $82.3m. (Dec. 1999); Chair. RASHID AZ-ZAYANI.

Arab Bank PLC (Jordan): POB 813, Manama; tel. 212255; fax 224475; e-mail cib@arabbank.com.bh; f. 1930; Senior Vice-Pres. and Man. HANI FADAYEL.

Arab Banking Corporation BSC: POB 5698, ABC Tower, Diplomatic Area, Manama; tel. 543000; fax 533062; e-mail webmaster@ arabbanking.com; internet www.arabbanking.com; f. 1980; cap. US $1,000m., res US $913m., dep. US $21,544m. (Dec. 2000); Chair. KHALIFA AL-KINDI; Pres. and CEO GHAZI ABD AL-JAWAD.

Arab Investment Co. S.A.A. (Saudi Arabia): POB 5559, Bldg 2309, Rd 2830, As-Seef District 428, Manama; tel. 588888; fax 588885; e-mail taicone@batelco.com.bh; Dir-Gen. Dr SALEH AL-HUMAIDAN.

Bahrain International Bank E.C.: POB 5016, As-Salam Tower, Government Ave, Manama; tel. 538777; fax 535141; f. 1982; cap. US $182.1m., res US $31.1m., dep. US $450.5m. (Dec. 2000); Chair. FAISAL YOUSUF AL-MARZOUK; Vice-Chair. SAMI SALMAN KAIKSOW.

Bank of Tokyo-Mitsubishi, Ltd. (Japan): POB 5850, Government Ave, Manama; tel. 227518; fax 225013; Regional and Gen. Man. KAN SATOH.

Banque de Commerce et de Placements (Switzerland): POB 11720, BDB Bldg, Diplomatic Area, Manama; tel. 530500; fax 532400; e-mail bcpsa@batelco.com.bh; Man. WAQAR AL-ISLAM.

Banque Française de l'Orient (France): POB 5820, Zina Complex, Tijar Rd, Manama; tel. 229995; fax 229994; Regional Man. HERMAN DOM.

BNP Paribas (France): POB 5253, UGB Bldg, 10th Floor, Diplomatic Area, Manama; tel. 531152; fax 531237; e-mail jean -christophe.durand@mideastbnpparibas.com; Regional Man. JEAN-CHRISTOPHE DURAND.

Chase Manhattan Bank N.A. (USA): POB 368, 368 Sheraton Complex, Government Ave, Manama; tel. 535388; fax 535135; Man. STEVEN J. FULLENKAMP.

Crédit Agricole Indosuez (France): POB 5410, Manama; tel. 531345; fax 531476; Reg. Man. MUHAMMAD SALEH.

Gulf International Bank BSC (GIB): POB 1017, Ad-Duwali Bldg, 3 Palace Ave, Manama 317; tel. 534000; fax 522633; e-mail info @gibbah.com; internet www.gibonline.com; cap. US $1,000m., res US $206.0m., dep. US $12,624.0m. (Dec. 2000); Chair. Sheikh IBRAHIM BIN KHALIFA AL-KHALIFA; CEO Dr KHALID AL-FAYEZ.

Woori Bank (Repub. of Korea): POB 1151, Government Rd, Manama; tel. 223503; fax 224429; e-mail bahrain@wooribank.com; internet www.wooribank.com; formerly Hanvit Bank; Gen. Man. OK YOUNG KANG.

Korea Exchange Bank (Repub. of Korea): POB 5767, Manama; tel. 229333; fax 225327; e-mail kebbn002@batelco.com.bh; Gen. Man. JONG-HO YOON.

Korfezbank (Turkey): POB 1937, UNITAG House, 6th Floor, Govt Ave, Manama; tel. 216161; fax 214477.

Mashreq Bank PSC (UAE): POB 20654, Manama Centre, Govt Ave, Manama; tel. 211241; fax 213516; Branch Man. ADEL AL-MANNAI.

Muslim Commercial Bank Ltd (Pakistan): POB 10164, Dipl. Area, Manama; tel. 533306; fax 533308; Gen. Man. FAQIR EIAZ ASGHER.

National Bank of Abu Dhabi (UAE): POB 5886, Manama 304; tel. 214450; fax 210086.

National Bank of Kuwait S.A.K.: POB 5290, Bahrain BMB Centre, Dipl. Area, Manama; tel. 532225; fax 530658; e-mail nbkbah @batelco.com.bh; Gen. Man. ALI Y. FARDAN.

Pamukbank T.A.S. (Turkey): POB 11378, BDB Bldg, Dipl. Area, Manama; tel. 537711; fax 535463.

National Commercial Bank (Saudi Arabia): POB 10363, Manama; tel. 531182; fax 530657; Man. SALEH HUSSEIN.

Standard Chartered Bank PLC (United Kingdom): POB 29, Manama; tel. 223636; fax 225001; CEO RUPERT KEELEY.

State Bank of India: POB 5466, Bahrain Tower, Govt Ave, Manama; tel. 224956; fax 224692; CEO ASHWINI KUMAR SHARMA.

Yapi ve Kredi Bankasi A.S (Turkey): POB 10615, c/o Bahrain Development Bank, Dipl. Area, Manama; tel. 530313; fax 530311; Dir SABAH TUZCU.

Investment Banks

Al-Baraka Islamic Bank BSC (EC): POB 1882, Diplomatic Area, Manama; tel. 535300; fax 533993; e-mail baraka@batelco.com.bh; internet www.barakaonline.com; f. 1984 as Al-Baraka Islamic Investment Bank BSC (EC); current name adopted in 1998; cap. US $50.0m., res US $4.3m., dep. US $48.8m. (Dec. 2000); Chair. MAHMOUD JAMEEL HASSOUBAH; Gen. Man. SALAH AHMAD ZAINALABEDIN; 17 brs.

ANZ Investment Bank: POB 5793, 14th Floor, Al-Jasra Tower, Bldg 95, Road 1702, Block 317, Diplomatic Area, Manama; tel. 549292; fax 532319; Regional Man. GEOFFREY BIRON.

BMB Investment Bank: POB 797, BMB Centre, Diplomatic Area, Manama; tel. 532345; fax 530526; e-mail corpcom@bmb.com.bh; internet www.bmb.com.bh; formerly Bahrain Middle East Bank EC; cap. US $90.8m., res US $–47.6m., dep. US $458.2m. (Dec. 2001); Chair. Sheikh ALI JARRAH AS-SABAH; CEO ALBERT KITTANEH.

INVESTCORP Bank EC: POB 5340, Investcorp House, Diplomatic Area, Manama; tel. 532000; fax 530816; e-mail info@investcorp.com; internet www.investcorp.com; f. 1982 as Arabian Investment Banking Corpn (INVESTCORP) EC, current name adopted in 1990; cap. US $100.0m., res US $79.1m., dep. US $762.2m. (Dec. 1999); Pres. and CEO NEMIR A. KIRDAR.

Nomura Investment Banking (Middle East) EC: POB 26893, 7th Floor, BMB Centre, Diplomatic Area, Manama; tel. 530531; fax 530365; f. 1982; cap. US $25m., res US $107.1m., dep. US $37.1m. (Dec. 1997); Chair. TAKASHI TSUTSUI.

TAIB Bank EC: POB 20485, Sehl Centre, 81 Rd 1702, Diplomatic Area, Manama 317; tel. 533334; fax 533174; e-mail taib@taib.com; internet www.taib.com; f. 1979 as Trans-Arabian Investment Bank EC; current name adopted in 1994; cap. US $84.4m., res US $18.8m., dep. US $328.6m. (Dec. 1999); Chair. ABD AR-RAHMAN AL-JERAISY; Vice-Chair. and CEO IQBAL G. MAMDANI.

United Gulf Bank (BSC) EC: POB 5964, UGB Tower, Diplomatic Area, Manama; tel. 533233; fax 533137; e-mail ugbbah @batelco.com.bh; internet www.ugbbh.com; f. 1980; cap. US $171.4m., res US $19.9m., dep. US $385.5m. (Dec. 2000); Chair. FAISAL HAMAD M. AL-AYYAR; CEO WILLIAM KHOURI.

Other investment banks operating in Bahrain include the following: ABC Islamic Bank EC, Amex (Middle East) EC, Arab Financial Services Co EC, Bahrain Investment Bank BSC, Bahrain Islamic Investment Co BSC, Capital Union EC, Daiwa Middle East EC, Faysal Investment Bank of Bahrain EC, First Islamic Investment Bank EC, Man-Ahli Investment Bank EC, Merrill Lynch Int. Bank Ltd, Nikko Europe PLC, Okasan Int. (Middle East) EC, Turk-Gulf Merchant Bank EC.

STOCK EXCHANGE

Bahrain Stock Exchange (BSE): POB 3203, Manama; tel. 261260; fax 256362; e-mail info@bahrainstock.com; internet www .bahrainstock.com; f. 1989; nine mems; linked to Muscat Securities Market (Oman) in 1995, and to Amman Financial Market (Jordan) in 1996; Dir-Gen. Sheikh AHMAD BIN MUHAMMAD AL-KHALIFA.

INSURANCE

Abdullah Yousuf Fakhro Corpn: POB 39, Government Ave, Manama; tel. 275000; fax 256999; internet www.fakhro.com; general; Man. Dir ADEL FAKHRO.

Al-Ahlia Insurance Co BSC: POB 5282, 4th Floor, Chamber of Commerce Bldg, King Faysal Rd, Manama; tel. 225860; fax 224870; e-mail alahlia@alahlia.com; internet www.alahlia.com; f. 1976; Chair. ABDULLATIF MUHAMMAD SHARIF AR-RAYES; Gen. Man. YAHYA NOORUDDIN.

Arab Insurance Group BSC (ARIG): POB 26992, Arig House, Diplomatic Area, Manama; tel. 544444; fax 531155; e-mail info@arig.com.bh; internet www.arig.com.bh; f. 1980; owned by Governments of Kuwait, Libya and the UAE (49.5%), and other shareholders; reinsurance and insurance; Chair. NASSER M. AN-NOWAIS; CEO UDO KRUEGER.

Arab International Insurance Co EC (AIIC): POB 10135, Manama; tel. 295395; fax 294059; f. 1981; non-life reinsurance; Chair. and Man. Dir Sheikh KHALID J. AS-SABAH.

Bahrain Kuwait Insurance Co BSC: POB 10166, Diplomatic Area, Manama; tel. 542222; fax 530799; e-mail bkicbah@batelco .com.bh; internet www.bkic.com; f. 1975; CEO A. HAMEED AN-NASSER; Gen. Man. SAMEER E. AL-WAZZAN.

Bahrain National Insurance (BNI): POB 843, Manama; tel. 227800; fax 224385; e-mail bnic@batelco.com.bh; internet www .bnigroup.com; f. 1998 by merger of Bahrain Insurance Co and National Insurance Co; all classes including life insurance; Chair. QASSIM MUHAMMAD FAKHRO; Gen. Man. PATRICK IRWIN.

Gulf Union Insurance and Reinsurance Co: POB 10949, Ground Floor, Manama Centre, Manama; tel. 215622; fax 215421; e-mail guirco@batelco.com.bh; internet www.gulfunion-bah.com; Chair. Sheikh IBRAHIM BIN HAMAD AL-KHALIFA.

Trade and Industry

GOVERNMENT AGENCIES

Economic Development Board (EDB): POB 11299, Manama; tel. 583311; fax 583322; e-mail edb@bahrainedb.com; internet www.bahrainedb.com; f. 2000; assumed duties of Bahrain Promotions and Marketing Board (f. 1993) and Supreme Council for Economic Development (f. 2000) in 2001; provides national focus for Bahraini marketing initiatives; attracts inward investment; encourages development and expansion of Bahraini exports; Chair. Sheikh SALMAN BIN HAMAD AL-KHALIFA; CEO JAMAL ALI AL-HAZEEM.

Supreme Oil Council: Manama; formulates Bahrain's petroleum policy; Chair. Prime Minister.

CHAMBER OF COMMERCE

Bahrain Chamber of Commerce and Industry: POB 248, Manama; tel. 229555; fax 224985; e-mail bahcci@batelco.com.bh; f. 1939; 7,300 mems (1996); Chair. KHALID MUHAMMAD KANOO; Sec.-Gen. JASSIM MUHAMMAD ASH-SHATTI.

STATE HYDROCARBONS COMPANIES

Bahrain National Gas Co BSC (BANAGAS): POB 29099, Rifa'a; tel. 756222; fax 756991; e-mail bng@banagas.com.bh; internet www.banagas.com.bh; f. 1979; responsible for extraction, processing and sale of hydrocarbon liquids from associated gas derived from onshore Bahraini fields; ownership is 75% Government of Bahrain, 12.5% Caltex and 12.5% Arab Petroleum Investments Corpn (APICORP); produced 202,955 metric tons of LPG and 189,803 tons of naphtha in 1996; Chair. Sheikh HAMAD BIN IBRAHIM AL-KHALIFA; Gen. Man. Dr Sheikh MUHAMMAD BIN KHALIFA AL-KHALIFA.

Bahrain Petroleum Co BSC (BAPCO): POB 25555, Awali; tel. 704040; fax 704070; e-mail info@bapco.net; f. 2000 by merger of Bahrain National Oil Co (f. 1976) and Bahrain Petroleum Co (f. 1980); fully integrated co responsible for exploration, drilling and production of oil and gas; supply of gas to power-generating plants and industries, refining crude oil, international marketing of crude oil and refined petroleum products, supply and sale of aviation fuel at Bahrain International Airport, and local distribution and marketing of petroleum products; Pres. and Man. Dir MUHAMMAD SALEH SHEIKH ALI; CEO JOHANN LUBBE.

Gulf Petrochemical Industries Co BSC (GPIC): POB 26730, Sitra; tel. 731777; fax 731047; f. 1979 as a joint venture between the Governments of Bahrain, Kuwait and Saudi Arabia, each with one-third equity participation; a petrochemical complex at Sitra, inaugurated in 1981; produces 1,200 metric tons of both methanol and ammonia per day (1990); Chair. Sheikh ISA BIN ALI AL-KHALIFA; Gen. Man. MUSTAFA AS-SAYED.

UTILITIES

Ministry of Electricity and Water: (see Ministries, above); provides electricity and water throughout Bahrain.

Electricity

Directorate of Electricity: POB 2, King Faysal Rd, Manama; tel. 533133; supplies domestic and industrial power and street lighting.

Water

Directorate of Water Supply: POB 326, Manama; tel. 727009; responsible for water supply to all areas except Awali.

MAJOR COMPANIES

Aluminium Bahrain BSC (ALBA): POB 570, Manama; tel. 830000; fax 830083; e-mail alba@alba.com.bh; internet www.aluminiumbahrain.com; f. 1971; operates a smelter owned by the Government of Bahrain (77%), Saudi Public Investment Fund (20%) and Breton Investments Ltd (3%); capacity 500,000 metric tons per year; Chair. Sheikh ISA BIN ALI AL-KHALIFA; CEO BRUCE HALL; 2,400 employees.

Bahrain Aluminium Extrusion Co BSC (BALEXCO): POB 1053, Manama; tel. 730073; fax 736924; e-mail balexco@batelco.com.bh; internet www.balexco.com.bh; f. 1977; supplies aluminium profiles in mill finish, powder coated and anodized; capacity 21,000 metric tons per year; cap. BD 10m.; Chair. A. RAHMAN MUHAMMAD JAMSHEER; Gen. Man. MAHMOUD AS-SOUFI; 302 employees.

Bahrain Atomizers International BSC: POB 5328, Manama; tel. 830880; fax 830025; e-mail bai1@batelco.com.bh; f. 1973; produces 7,000 metric tons of atomized aluminium powder per year; owned by the Government of Bahrain (51%) and Eckart Austria GmbH (49%); Chair. Y. SHIRAWI; Gen. Man. LEON FABRIKANOV; 56 employees.

Bahrain Danish Dairy Co WLL: POB 601, Manama; tel. 591591; fax 591150; e-mail bddc@batelco.com.bh; f. 1963; sales BD 7.0m. (1999); cap. and res BD 1.5m.; processing, packaging and distribution of milk, ice cream and fruit juice; Chair. IBRAHIM MUHAMMAD ALI ZAINAL; Gen. Man. PAUL MIKKELSEN; 240 employees.

Bahrain Light Industries Co BSC: POB 26700, Manama; tel. 830222; fax 830399; e-mail blico@batelco.com.bh; f. 1979; cap. and res BD 5m.; manufacture of solid wood and veneered furniture, internal partitions and doors; Chair. HAMID R AZ-ZAYANI; Gen. Man. N. NATARAJAN; 190 employees.

Gulf Aluminium Rolling Mill Co BSC (GARMCO): POB 20725, Manama; tel. 731000; fax 730542; e-mail sales@garmco.com; internet www.garmco.com; f. 1981 as a joint venture between the Governments of Bahrain, Saudi Arabia, Kuwait, Iraq, Oman and Qatar; produced 120,000 metric tons of rolled aluminium in 1997; Chair. and Man. Dir Sheikh IBRAHIM BIN KHALIFA AL-KHALIFA; Gen. Man. ANTHONY D. LEWIS; 800 employees.

Al-Khajah Establishment and Factories: POB 5042, Sitra Industrial Area; tel. 730611; fax 731340; e-mail alkhajah@batelco.com.bh; f. 1972; sales BD 6m. (1999); cap. and res BD 2.3m.; contracting, trading and manufacture of switchgear and light fittings; numerous subsidiaries within the Gulf; Chair. and Man. Dir JASSIM AL-KHAJAH; 375 employees.

Maskati Brothers and Co: POB 24, Manama; tel. 729911; fax 725454; e-mail maskati@batelco.com.bh; internet www.maskatibros.com; f. 1957; sales BD 9.0m. (1995); cap. and res BD 9m.; paper converters, polyethylene manufacture, injection moulders; Chair. HUSSAIN M. MASKATI; Man. Dir KHALID H. MASKATI; 600 employees.

Midal Cables Ltd: POB 5939, Manama; tel. 830111; fax 830168; e-mail midalcbl@batelco.com.bh; internet www.midalcable.com; f. 1978; cap. US $21.1m.; sales US $141.1m. (2001); manufacture of aluminium and aluminium alloy electrical rods and conductors for overhead transmission and distribution lines; Man. Dir HAMID R. AZ-ZAYANI; CEO SALMAN ASH-SHEIKH; 350 employees.

TRADE UNIONS

There are currently no trade unions in Bahrain. However, in September 2002 legislation was enacted to permit the establishment of independent trade unions.

Transport

RAILWAYS

There are no railways in Bahrain.

ROADS

In 2000 Bahrain had 3,261 km of roads, including 421 km of highways, main or national roads, 410 km of secondary or regional roads and 1,650 km of other roads; about 78% of roads were paved. A modern network of dual highways is being developed, and a 25-km causeway link with Saudi Arabia was opened in 1986. A three-lane dual carriageway links the causeway to Manama. Other causeways link Bahrain with Muharraq island and with Sitra island. In March 1997 the Government approved the construction of the Sheikh Khalifa bin Sulman Causeway, linking Hidd on Muharraq island with the port of Mina Salman; the new causeway was scheduled to be completed in 2003. A second, 2.5-km Manama-to-Muharraq causeway was opened in early 1997. It is planned to construct a causeway (the Friendship Bridge) linking eastern Bahrain with Qatar by 2006.

Directorate of Roads: POB 5, Manama; tel. 545555; fax 532565; responsible for traffic engineering and planning, traffic control and safety, bridges, road design, maintenance and construction supervision; Dir WALEED Y. AS-SAIE.

SHIPPING

Numerous shipping services link Bahrain and the Gulf with Europe, the USA, Pakistan, India, the Far East and Australia.

The deep-water harbour of Mina Salman was opened in 1962; it has 13 conventional berths, two container terminals (one of which has a 400-m quay—permitting two 180-m container ships to be handled simultaneously) and a roll-on roll-off berth. Two nearby slipways can accommodate vessels of up to 1,016 tons and 73 m in length, and services are available for ship repairs afloat. During 2000 906 vessels called at Mina Salman, and in that year the port handled 1,954,396 metric tons of cargo.

By 1999 work had begun on the construction of a new port and industrial zone at Hidd, on Muharraq island. The port, Mina Khalifa bin Salman, which is scheduled to become operational in 2005 (at an estimated cost of US $330m.), is to have an annual handling capacity of 234,000 TEUs and to include a general cargo berth and two container berths with roll-on roll-off facilities.

Directorate of Customs and Ports: (Customs) POB 15, Manama; tel. 725333; fax 727556; e-mail customs@batelco.com.bh; internet www.bahraincustoms.com.bh; (Ports) POB 453, Manama; tel. 725555; fax 725534; internet www.bahrainports.com.bh; responsible for customs activities and acts as port authority; Pres. of Customs and Ports EID ABDULLAH YOUSUF; Dir-Gen. of Ports Capt. MAHMOOD Y. AL-MAHMOOD; Dir-Gen. of Customs JASSIM JAMSHEER.

Arab Shipbuilding and Repair Yard Co (ASRY): POB 50110, Hidd; tel. 671111; fax 670236; e-mail asryco@batelco.com.bh; internet www.asry.net; f. 1974 by OAPEC members; 500,000-ton dry dock opened 1977; two floating docks in operation since 1992; repaired 104 ships in 2001; Chair. EID ABDULLAH YOUSUF; CEO MUHAMMAD M. AL-KHATEEB.

Principal Shipping Agents

Bahrain Enterprises Co Ltd: POB 2661, Manama; tel. 731224.

Dilmun Shipping Co Ltd E.C.: POB 11664, Manama; tel. 534530; fax 531287; e-mail dilmunbh@batelco.com.bh; Chair. Capt. PHILIP G. CARR.

The Gulf Agency Co (Bahrain) WLL: POB 412, Manama; tel. 827927; fax 827928; e-mail bahrain.ops@gulfagencycompany.com; internet www.gacbahrain.com; f. 1957; Man. Dir Capt. BJORN SVANHOLM.

Al-Jazeera Shipping Co WLL: POB 302, Manama; tel. 728837; fax 728217; Dir ALI HASSAN MAHMOUD.

Abdullah Ahmad Nass: POB 669, Manama; tel. 254856.

Al-Sharif Group: POB 1322, Manama; tel. 530535; fax 537637; e-mail general@bahragents.com; Dirs ALI ABDULRASOOL AL-SHARIF, KHALID ABDULRASOOL AL-SHARIF.

UCO Marine Contracting WLL: POB 1074, Manama; tel. 5730816; fax 5732131; e-mail ucomarin@batelco.com.bh; Man. Dirs BADER A. KAIKSOW, HASSAN AS-SABAH, ALI AL-MUSALAM.

Yusuf bin Ahmad Kanoo: POB 45, Al-Khalifa Ave, Manama; tel. 220800; fax 229122; e-mail kanoomgt@batelco.com.bh; air and shipping cargo services, commercial and holiday services; Chair. and CEO ABDULLAH ALI KANOO.

CIVIL AVIATION

Bahrain International Airport (BIA) has a first-class runway, capable of taking the largest aircraft in use. In 2000 there were 60,072 flights to and from the airport, and some 3.9m. passengers were carried. Extension work to the airport's main terminal building was undertaken during the 1990s, in order to increase the airport's cargo-handling facilities. Construction of a new terminal is planned, to give BIA an annual passenger capacity of 8m. by 2005.

Department of Civil Aviation Affairs: POB 586, Bahrain International Airport, Muharraq; tel. 321000; fax 325757; e-mail caa info@bahrainairport.com; internet www.bahrainairport.com; Under-Sec. IBRAHIM ABDULLAH AL-HAMER.

Gulf Air Co GSC (Gulf Air): POB 138, Manama; tel. 322200; fax 338033; e-mail gfpr@batelco.com.bh; internet www.gulfairco .com.; f. 1950; jointly owned by Govts of Bahrain, Oman and Abu Dhabi (part of the United Arab Emirates) since 1974; services to the Middle East, South-East Asia, the Far East, Australia, Africa and Europe; Chair. Sheikh HAMDAN BIN MUBARAK AN-NAHYAN (UAE); Pres. and CEO JAMES HOGAN.

Tourism

There are several archaeological sites of importance in Bahrain, which is the site of the ancient trading civilization of Dilmun. There is a wide selection of hotels and restaurants, and a new national museum opened in 1989. The Government is currently promoting Bahrain as a destination for sports and leisure activities. In 2000 Bahrain received about 3.9m. foreign visitors (excluding Bahraini nationals residing abroad). Income from tourism totalled some BD 130m. in 2001.

Bahrain Tourism Co (BTC): POB 5831, Manama; tel. 530530; fax 530867; e-mail btc@alseyaha.com; internet www.alseyaha.com; Chair. MUHAMMAD YOUSUF JALAL.

Tourism Affairs: Ministry of Information, POB 26613, Manama; tel. 201203; fax 229787; e-mail btour@bahraintourism.com; internet www.bahraintourism.com; Asst Under-Sec. for Tourism Dr KADHIM RAJAB.

Defence

Commander-in-Chief of Bahraini Defence Force: Sheikh SALMAN BIN HAMAD AL-KHALIFA.

Chief of Staff of the Bahraini Defence Force: Maj.-Gen. Sheikh RASHID BIN ABDULLAH AL-KHALIFA.

Commander of the National Guard: Lt-Gen. Sheikh MUHAMMAD BIN ISA BIN SALMAN AL-KHALIFA.

Estimated Defence Budget (2001): BD 119m.

Military Service: voluntary.

Total Armed Forces (August 2001): 11,000 (army 8,500; navy 1,000; air force 1,500).

Paramilitary Forces: estimated 10,160 (police 9,000; national guard some 900; coastguard 260).

Education

Although education is not compulsory, it is provided free of charge up to the secondary level. Basic education, from the ages of six to 14, is divided into two levels; children attend primary school from six to 11 years of age and intermediate school from 12 to 14. Secondary education, beginning at the age of 15, lasts for three years; students choose to follow a general (science or literary), commercial, technical or vocational curriculum. As part of a reform programme initiated in 2001, human rights studies has been incorporated into the school curriculum. In 1996 enrolment at primary level included 98% of children in the relevant age-group (males 97%; females 99%) and enrolment at the intermediate level included 96% of children in the relevant age-group (males 97%; females 96%). In that year enrolment at secondary level included 83% (males 79%; females 87%) of children in the relevant age-group. In 2000/01 115,715 pupils were receiving education in 193 government-operated schools, which employed 7,172 teachers. Private and religious education are also available. Budget forecasts for 2001 allocated BD 93.1m. (11.3% of total government expenditure) on education.

The University of Bahrain, established by Amiri decree in 1986, comprises five colleges: the College of Engineering, the College of Arts, the College of Science, the College of Education and the College of Business Administration. About 9,665 students were enrolled at the University in 1999. Higher education is also provided by the College of Health Sciences (610 students in 1999). The Arabian Gulf University (AGU), funded by seven Arab Governments, also provides higher education. In 1999 it comprised two colleges: the College of Medicine and Medical Sciences, and the College of Graduate Studies. The University campus is due to be completed at the end of 2006, and will accommodate 5,000 students. In 1999 569 students were enrolled at the AGU.

Bibliography

Adamiyat, Fereydoun. *Bahrain Islands: A Legal and Diplomatic Study of the British-Iranian Controversy*. New York, Praeger, 1955.

Belgrave, Charles. *Personal Column*. 2nd edn, Beirut, Librarie du Liban, 1972.

Belgrave, James H. D. *Welcome to Bahrain*. 4th edn, Stourbridge, Mark and Moody, 1960.

Burton, Paul, and Hassan, Omar. *Bahrain and its Development Philosophy*. London, Gulf Centre for Strategic Studies, 1998.

Clarke, Angela. *Bahrain: Oil and Development, 1929–1989*. London, Immel, 1998.

Cordesman, Anthony H. *Bahrain, Oman, Qatar and the UAE: Challenges of Security*. Boulder, CO, Westview Press, 1997.

Crawford, Harriet (Ed.). *The Dilmun Temple at Saar: Bahrain and its Archeological Inheritance*. London, Kegan Paul International, 1997.

Dilmun and its Gulf Neighbours. Cambridge University Press, 1998.

Dabrowska, Karen. *Bahrain Briefing: The Struggle for Democracy*. London, Colourmast, 1997.

Farah, Talal T. *Protection and Politics in Bahrain, 1869–1915*. Beirut, American University of Beirut, 1985.

Faroughby, Abbas. *The Bahrain Islands*. New York, 1951.

Hakima, A. M. *Eastern Arabia: Bahrain*. International Book Centre, 1984.

The Rise and Development of Bahrain and Kuwait. Beirut, 1965.

Hamad bin Isa al-Khalifa, Sheikh. *First Light: Modern Bahrain and its Heritage*. London, Kegan Paul International, 1995.

Hassan, Omar. *Border Dispute Between Bahrain and Qatar and the Challenges of Gulf Co-operation*. London, Gulf Centre for Strategic Studies, 1997.

Hay, Sir Rupert. *The Persian Gulf States*. Washington, DC, Middle East Institute, 1959.

Khuri, F. I. *Tribe and State in Bahrain*. Chicago University Press, 1981.

Larsen, Curtis. *Life and Land Use on the Bahrain Islands*. Chicago, University of Chicago Press, 1983.

Lawson, Fred H. *The Modernization of Autocracy*. Boulder, CO, Westview Press, 1989.

Marlowe, John. *The Persian Gulf in the 20th Century*. London, Cresset Press, 1962.

Miles, S. B. *The Countries and Tribes of the Persian Gulf*. 3rd edn, London, Cass, 1970.

Mojtahed-Zadeh, Pirouz. *Security and Territoriality in the Persian Gulf: A Maritime Political Geography*. Richmond, Curzon Press, 1999.

Nakhleh, Emile A. *Bahrain: Political Development in a Modernizing Society*. Lexington, MA, Lexington Books, 1976.

Nugent, Jeffrey, and Thomas, Theodore. *Bahrain and the Gulf: Prospects for the Future*. London, Croom Helm, 1985.

Routine Abuse, Routine Denial: Civil Rights and the Political Crisis in Bahrain. New York, Human Rights Watch, 1997.

Rumaihi, Mohammed al-. *Bahrain: Social and Political Change since the First World War*. Durham Univ., Bowker, in association with the Centre for Middle Eastern and Islamic Studies, 1977.

Shirawi, May al-Arrayed. *Education in Bahrain: Problems and Progress*. Reading, Ithaca Press, 1989.

Wheatcroft, Andrew. *The Life and Times of Sheikh Salman bin Hamad al-Khalifa: Ruler of Bahrain 1942–61*. London, Kegan Paul International, 1995.

Yateem, Aisha. *Bahrain Memories: Glimpses of the Past*. Bosphorus Press, 1992.

Zahlan, Rosemarie Said, and Owen, Roger. *The Making of the Modern Gulf States: Kuwait, Bahrain, Qatar, the UAE and Oman*. Reading, Ithaca Press, 1997.

CYPRUS

Physical and Social Geography

W. B. FISHER

The island of Cyprus, with an area of 9,251 sq km (3,572 sq miles), is situated in the north-eastern corner of the Mediterranean Sea, closest to Turkey (which is easily visible from its northern coast), but also less than 160 km (100 miles) from the Syrian coast. Its greatest length (including the long, narrow peninsula of Cape Andreas) is 225 km. The census of 1 October 1982, which was held in Greek Cypriot areas only, recorded a total population (including an estimate for the Turkish-occupied region) of 642,731. The census of 1 October 2001 (excluding the Turkish-occupied region) recorded a total population of 689,471. According to an official estimate, the population was 759,100 (including 87,800 in the Turkish-occupied region) at 31 December 2000. However, these figures exclude settlers from Turkey in the 'Turkish Republic of Northern Cyprus' ('TRNC'), who are regarded as illegal residents by the Greek Cypriot authorities. This group was believed to total some 114,000 in 1998. According to a census conducted in the 'TRNC' on 15 December 1996, the population of the region was 200,587, and an official estimate by the 'TRNC' authorities put the population at 208,886 at the end of 2000.

PHYSICAL FEATURES

Cyprus owes its peculiar shape to the occurrence of two ridges that were once part of two much greater arcs running from the mainland of Asia westwards towards Crete. The greater part of these arcs has disappeared, but remnants are found in Cyprus and on the eastern mainland, where they form the Amanus range of Turkey. In Cyprus the arcs are visible as two mountain systems—the Kyrenia range of the north, and the much larger and imposing Troödos massif in the centre. Between the two mountain systems lies a flat lowland, open to the sea in the east and west and spoken of as the Mesaoria. Here also lies the chief town, Nicosia (Lefkoşa in Turkish).

The mountain ranges are actually very different in structure and appearance. The Kyrenia range is a single narrow fold of limestone, with occasional deposits of marble, and its maximum height is 900 m. As it is mainly porous rock, rainfall soon seeps below ground; and so its appearance is rather arid, but very picturesque, with white crags and isolated pinnacles. The soil cover is thin. The Troödos, on the other hand, has been affected by folding in two separate directions, so that the whole area has been fragmented, and large quantities of molten igneous rock have forced their way to the surface from the interior of the earth, giving rise to a great dome that reaches 1,800 m above sea level. As it is impervious to water, there are some surface streams, rounder outlines, a thicker soil, especially on the lower slopes, and a covering of pine forest.

CLIMATE

The climate in Cyprus is strongly 'Mediterranean' in character, with the usual hot dry summers and warm, wet winters. As an island with high mountains, Cyprus receives a fair amount of moisture, and up to 1,000 mm of rain falls in the mountains, with the minimum of 300 mm–380 mm in the Mesaoria. Frost does not occur on the coast, but may be sharp in the higher districts, and snow can fall fairly heavily in regions over 900 m in altitude. In summer, despite the proximity of the sea, temperatures are surprisingly high, and the Mesaoria, in particular, can experience over 38°C (100°F). A feature of minor importance is the tendency for small depressions to form over the island in winter, giving a slightly greater degree of changeability in weather than is experienced elsewhere in the Middle East.

Cyprus is noteworthy in that between 50% and 60% of the total area is under cultivation—a figure higher than that for most Middle Eastern countries. This is partly to be explained by the relatively abundant rainfall, the expanses of impervious rock that retain water near the surface, and the presence of rich soils derived from volcanic rocks which occur around the Troödos massif. The potential of the tourist trade and the export markets in wine and early vegetables add to the incentives to development. In the southern (Greek) part of the island economic recovery after partition has been considerable; far less so in the north.

History

Revised for this edition by ALAN J. DAY

EARLY HISTORY

Cyprus first became important in recorded history when the island fell under Egyptian control in the second millennium BC. After a long period during which the Phoenicians and the people of Mycenae founded colonies there, Cyprus, in the eighth century BC, became an Assyrian protectorate at a time when the Greeks of the mainland were extending their settlements in the island. From the sixth century BC it was a province of the Persian empire and took part in the unsuccessful Ionian revolt against Persian rule in 502 BC. Despite the Greek triumph over Xerxes in 480 BC, subsequent efforts by the Greek city states of the mainland to free Cyprus from Persian control met with little success, largely because of dissension among the Greek cities of Cyprus itself. For more than two centuries after 295 BC the Ptolemies of Egypt ruled in Cyprus until it became part of the Roman Empire.

Cyprus prospered under the enlightened Roman rule of Augustus, for trade flourished while the Romans kept the seas free of piracy. When Jerusalem fell to the Emperor Titus in AD 70, many Jews found refuge in Cyprus where they became numerous enough to undertake a serious revolt in AD 115. Christianity, apparently introduced into the island in the reign of the Emperor Claudius (AD 41–54), grew steadily in the next three centuries, during which Cyprus, isolated from a continent frequently ravaged by barbarian inroads, continued to enjoy a relative degree of prosperity. From the time of Constantine the Great, Cyprus was a province governed by officials appointed from Antioch and formed part of the diocese of the East. In the reign of Theodosius I (379–395) the Greek Orthodox Church was firmly established there and in the fifth century proved strong enough to resist the attempts of the Patriarchs of Antioch to control the religious life of the island.

The Arab attack of 649 began a new period in the history of Cyprus, which now became, for more than 300 years, the object of dispute between the Byzantines and the Muslims. Whenever the Byzantine fleet was weak, Cyprus remained a doubtful possession of the Empire. After the decisive Byzantine reconquest of 964–65, Cyprus enjoyed, for more than two centuries, a period of relative calm.

WESTERN RULE

In 1192 King Richard I of England, having taken the island from the Greek usurper Comnenus, sold it to the Knights Templar, who, in turn, sold it to Guy de Lusignan, formerly King of Jerusalem. Thus began almost 400 years of Western rule, which saw the introduction of Western feudalism and of the Latin Church into a land which hitherto had been Greek in its institutions and Orthodox in its religious beliefs.

In the period from 1192 to 1267 (when the direct line of the Lusignan house became extinct) the new regime was gradually elaborated. The Lusignan monarchy was limited in character, for the royal power was effective only in the military sphere, all other important business of state being decided in a high court, which consisted of the nobles, the fief-holders, and the great officers of state. This court applied to the island a highly developed code of feudal law derived from the Assizes of Jerusalem, the Cypriots being allowed to retain their own laws and customs in so far as these did not conflict with the feudal law. The period was also marked by the determined efforts of the Latin clergy, supported by the Papacy, to establish complete control over the Orthodox Church—a policy carried out with much harshness, which the Crown and the feudal nobility often sought to mitigate in order to keep the loyalty of the subject population. The dominance of the Latin Church was finally assured by the Bulla Cypria of Pope Alexander IV (1260).

During the second half of the 13th century the kingdom of Cyprus (now ruled by the house of Antioch-Lusignan) played an important role in the last struggle to maintain the Latin states in Syria against the Mamluk offensive. The influence of the monarchy was further strengthened in this period, and when, in 1324, Hugues IV became king, the great age of feudal Cyprus had begun. Cyprus was now of great importance in the commerce that the Italian republics maintained with the East, and Famagusta became a flourishing port. The Papacy, however, always anxious to weaken the power of Mamluk Egypt, placed severe limitations on the trade of the Italian republics with that state and charged Cyprus and Rhodes with their enforcement. Thus began a conflict between the kings of Cyprus and the great republics of Venice and Genoa, which did not endanger Cyprus provided the Papacy could mobilize sentiment in the West to support the crusading state of the Lusignans. When, as the 14th century advanced, the Papacy lost its power to command such support in the West, Cyprus was left to face unaided, and was powerless to withstand, the ambitions of Genoa and Venice.

Before this decline began, Cyprus enjoyed a brief period of great brilliance under the crusading King Peter I (1359–69). In 1361 he occupied the port of Adalia on the south coast of Asia Minor, then held by the Turkish emirate of Tekke, and in 1362–65 he toured Europe in an effort to win adequate support for a new crusade. His most memorable exploit came in 1365, when he captured Alexandria in Egypt, sacking it so completely that even as late as the 16th century it had not recovered its former splendour. With his assassination in 1369 the great period of the Lusignan house was ended.

The reign of King Janus I (1398–1432) was a long struggle to drive out the Genoese, who had seized Famagusta during the war with Cyprus in 1372–74, and to repel the attacks of Mamluk Egypt, which had become weary of the repeated sea-raids undertaken from the ports of Cyprus. After plundering Larnaca and Limassol in 1425 the Mamluks crushed the army of Cyprus in a battle at Khoirakoitia in 1426, King Janus himself being captured, and his capital, Nicosia, sacked. The king was released in 1427, when he had promised the payment of a large ransom and of an annual tribute. The last years of Lusignan power were marked by dissension in the ruling house and by the increasing domination of Venice, which, with the consent of Caterina Cornaro, the Venetian widow of the last Lusignan king, annexed Cyprus in 1489.

TURKISH RULE

Venice held Cyprus until 1570, when the Ottoman Turks began a campaign of conquest which led to the fall of Nicosia in September 1570 and of Famagusta in August 1571. The Turks now restored to the Greek Orthodox Church its independence and ended the former feudal status of the peasantry. The Cypriots paid a tax for the freedom to follow their own religion, and were allowed to cultivate their land as their own and to hand it to their descendants on payment of a portion of the produce. About 30,000 Turkish soldiers were also given land on the island, thus forming a Turkish element in the population, which was later reinforced by immigration from Asia Minor.

The 17th and 18th centuries were a melancholy period in the history of Cyprus. Repeated droughts and ravages of locusts preceded a famine in 1640 and an outbreak of plague in 1641. In 1660 the Ottoman Government, in order to limit the extortions of its officials and of the tax-farmers, recognized the Orthodox Archbishop and his three suffragans as guardians of the Christian peasantry, but this step did not prevent revolts in 1665 and 1690. A great famine in 1757–58 and a severe plague in 1760 reduced the numbers of the peasantry very considerably, causing widespread distress which culminated in the revolt of 1764–66. From 1702 Cyprus had been a fief of the Grand Vizier, who normally sold the governorship to the highest bidder—usually for a period of one year. This practice created great opportunities for financial oppression. Perhaps the most striking development of the period was the continued rise in the power of the Orthodox bishops, whose influence was so great in the late 18th century that the Turkish administration depended on their support for the collection of revenues. The Turkish elements in Cyprus, resenting the dominance of the Orthodox bishops, accused them in 1821 of having a secret understanding with the Greeks of the Morea (who had revolted against Turkish rule) and carried out a massacre of the Christians at Nicosia and elsewhere, which brought the supremacy of the bishops to an end.

In 1833 the Sultan granted Cyprus to Muhammad Ali, Pasha of Egypt, who was forced to renounce possession of it in 1840 at the demand of the Great Powers. During the period of reforms initiated by Sultan Mahmud II (1808–39) and continued by his immediate successors, efforts were made to improve the administration of the island. The practice of farming out taxes was abolished (although later partially re-introduced) and the Governor became a salaried official, ruling through a *divan* that was half-Turkish and half-Christian in composition.

BRITISH RULE

At the Congress of Berlin of 1878 the Great Powers endorsed an agreement between the United Kingdom and the Sultan of Turkey whereby Cyprus was put under British control, to be used as a base from which to protect the Ottoman Empire against the ambitions of Russia. Control of Cyprus was now regarded as vital, since the opening of the Suez Canal (1869) had made the eastern Mediterranean an area of great strategic importance. Under the 1878 agreement Cyprus remained legally a part of the Ottoman Empire, to which a tribute was paid, consisting of the surplus revenues of the island, calculated at less than £93,000 per annum.

From 1882 until 1931 the island had a legislative council that was partly nominated and partly elected. Various reforms were carried out in this first period of British rule: the introduction of an efficient judicial system and of an effective police force, and considerable improvements in agriculture, roads, education and other public services.

When Turkey joined the Central Powers in the First World War, the United Kingdom immediately annexed Cyprus (1914) and then offered it to Greece (1915), provided the latter joined the Allies: this offer was refused, however, and was not repeated when Greece eventually joined the hostilities in 1917. Under the terms of the Treaty of Lausanne of 1923, both Greece and Turkey recognized British sovereignty over Cyprus, which became a Crown Colony in 1925. Thereafter, discontent among the Greek Cypriots began to assume serious proportions, culminating in anti-British riots in 1931 and the suspension of constitutional rule.

In the period after 1931 the desire to achieve self-government within the British Commonwealth grew stronger, but the movement for *Enosis* (union with Greece) became the dominant influence in the political life of the island. Following the Second World War, during which Cypriot troops served notably in Libya and in the Greek campaign of 1941, Cyprus was used as a place of detention for illegal Jewish immigrants into Palestine, the last of such detention camps being closed in 1949. Following his election as head of the Orthodox Church of Cyprus in 1950, Archbishop Makarios III assumed the leadership of the *Enosis* movement. An unofficial plebiscite, conducted by the Church in that year, demonstrated overwhelming support for *Enosis* among Greek Cypriots.

CONSTITUTIONAL PROPOSALS

In July 1954 the United Kingdom made known its intention to prepare a restricted form of constitution for Cyprus, with a legislature containing official, nominated and elected members. The Greek Cypriots, insisting that their ultimate goal was *Enosis*, viewed the proposed constitution with disfavour, whereas the Turkish Cypriots declared their readiness to accept it. The Greek Government in Athens now brought the problem of Cyprus before the UN. It was the view of the United Kingdom, however, that the question was one with which it alone was competent to deal. In December 1954 the UN resolved to take no immediate action in the matter.

The more extreme advocates of *Enosis*, grouped together in EOKA (National Organization of Cypriot Combatants) under the leadership of Gen. George Grivas (Dhigenis), now began a campaign of terrorist activities against the British administration. A conference including British, Greek and Turkish representatives met in London, United Kingdom, in August 1955. The British offer of substantial autonomy for Cyprus failed to win the approval of Greece, since it held out no clear prospect of self-determination for the island, and the conference ended in frustration.

A new and more violent wave of terrorism swept Cyprus in November 1955. A state of emergency was declared on 27 November whereby the death penalty was imposed for the bearing of arms; life imprisonment for sabotage; and lesser sentences for looting and the harbouring of terrorists. All public assemblies of a political nature were forbidden; the British troops in Cyprus (about 10,000 in all) assumed the status of active service in wartime. The Governor now ruled the island through an executive council consisting of four officials from the administration, two Greek Cypriots and one Turkish Cypriot.

At the beginning of 1956 the Governor, Sir John Harding, discussed the situation with Archbishop Makarios. Since the United Kingdom was now willing to accept the principle of ultimate independence for Cyprus, agreement seemed to be within reach. In March 1956, however, the discussions were suspended, and Archbishop Makarios, implicated in the activities of EOKA, was deported to the Seychelles.

RELEASE OF MAKARIOS

In March 1957 Archbishop Makarios was released from detention in the Seychelles and, since he was not allowed to return to Cyprus, went to Athens. The British authorities also relaxed some of the emergency laws, such as the censorship of the press and the mandatory death penalty for the bearing of arms. These measures facilitated the holding of further discussions, but little progress was made.

The tide of violence ran high in Cyprus during the first half of 1958. EOKA carried out an intensive campaign of sabotage, especially in Nicosia and Famagusta. Meanwhile, strife between the Greek Cypriots and the Turkish Cypriots was becoming more frequent and severe, with particularly serious outbreaks in June 1958. There was increased tension, too, between the Greek and Turkish Governments.

It was amid this situation that in June 1958 the United Kingdom made public a new scheme for Cyprus, which came into force in October. The island was to remain under British control for seven years; full autonomy in communal affairs would be granted, under separate arrangements, to the Greek Cypriots and the Turkish Cypriots; internal administration was to be reserved for the Governor's Council, which would include representatives of the Greek Cypriot and Turkish Cypriot communities and also of the Greek and Turkish Governments in Athens and Ankara.

INDEPENDENCE

As a result of a conference held in Zürich, Switzerland, it was announced in February 1959 that Greece and Turkey had devised a compromise settlement concerning Cyprus. A further conference in London decided that Cyprus was to become an independent republic with a Greek Cypriot President and a Turkish Cypriot Vice-President. There would be a Council of Ministers (seven Greeks, three Turks) and a House of Representatives (70% Greek, 30% Turkish) elected by universal suffrage for a term of five years. Communal Chambers—one Greek, one Turkish—were to exercise control in matters of religion, culture and education. The Turkish inhabitants in five of the main towns would be allowed to establish separate municipalities for a period of four years. Cyprus was not to be united with another state, nor was it to be subject to partition. The United Kingdom, Greece and Turkey guaranteed the independence, the territorial integrity and the Constitution of Cyprus. Greece received the right to station a force of 950 men on the island, and Turkey a force of 650 men. The United Kingdom retained under its direct sovereignty two base areas in Cyprus—at Akrotiri and at Dhekelia.

In November 1959 agreement was attained in regard to the delimitation of the executive powers to be vested in the President and Vice-President of Cyprus. A further agreement defined the composition of the Supreme Constitutional Court. In December the state of emergency came to an end, and Archbishop Makarios was elected to be the first President of Cyprus. The post of Vice-President was awarded, unopposed, to the Turkish Cypriot leader, Dr Fazil Küçük. After lengthy negotiations, concluded in July 1960, the United Kingdom and Cyprus reached agreement over the precise size and character of the two military bases to be assigned to British sovereignty.

Cyprus formally became an independent republic on 16 August 1960, and was admitted to the UN in the following month and to the Commonwealth in March 1961.

CONSTITUTIONAL PROBLEMS

As Cyprus achieved independence, serious problems began to arise over the interpretation and working of the Constitution. There was divergence of opinion between Greek and Turkish Cypriots over the formation of a national army, in accordance with provisions of the Zürich agreement of 1959 (2,000 men: 60% Greek; 40% Turkish); the main point of dispute being the degree of integration to be established between the two components. In October 1961 Vice-President Küçük used his power of veto to ban full integration, which President Makarios favoured at all levels of the armed forces. Difficulties also arose over the implementation of the 70:30 ratio of Greek Cypriot to Turkish Cypriot personnel in the public services.

1962 saw the development of a serious crisis over the system of separate Greek and Turkish municipalities in the five main towns of Cyprus—Nicosia, Famagusta, Limassol, Larnaca and Paphos. In December the Turkish Communal Chamber passed a law maintaining the Turkish municipalities in the five towns from 1 January 1963, and also establishing a similar municipality in the predominantly Turkish town of Lefka. President Makarios issued a decree stating that, from 1 January 1963, government-appointed bodies would control municipal organizations throughout the island—a decree which the Turkish Cypriots denounced as an infringement of the Constitution.

The Constitutional Court of Cyprus, sitting in judgment on the financial disputes, ruled in February 1963 that, in view of the veto exercised by the Turkish members of the House of Representatives since 1961, taxes could be imposed on the people of the island, but that no legal mechanism existed for the collection of such taxes. In April the court declared that the Government had no power to control the municipalities through bodies of its own choosing, and that the decision of the Turkish Communal Chamber to maintain separate Turkish municipalities in defiance of the Cyprus Government was also invalid.

Negotiations between President Makarios and Vice-President Küçük to resolve the deadlock broke down in May 1963. Accordingly, in November, Archbishop Makarios put forward proposals for a number of reforms. However, these proved to be unacceptable to the Turkish Cypriots.

CIVIL WAR

Meanwhile, underground organizations, prepared for violence, had been formed among both the Greek and the Turkish communities. In December 1963 serious conflict broke out. The United Kingdom suggested that a joint force composed of British, Greek and Turkish troops should be established to restore order. The Cyprus, Greek and Turkish Governments gave their assent to this scheme. At this time the forces of Turkey serving in the island occupied a strong position, north of Nicosia, which gave them control of the important road to Kyrenia on the northern coast—a road which was to become the scene of much conflict. As a result of the December crisis, co-operation between the Greek Cypriots and the Turkish Cypriots in government and in other sectors of public life came almost to an end, most notably in the Turkish Cypriot boycott of the House of Representatives.

There was renewed violence in February 1964, especially in Limassol. Arms in considerable quantities were being brought secretly into the island for both sides, and the number of armed 'irregulars' was increasing rapidly. These developments also gave rise to friction between Athens and Ankara.

ESTABLISHMENT OF UN PEACE-KEEPING FORCE

In January 1964, following a request by the Cyprus Government, the UN nominated Lt-Gen. Prem Gyani of India to act as its representative to the island. Later in the same month the Cyprus Government informed the UN Secretary-General it would be glad to see a UN force established in the island; on 4 March the UN Security Council adopted a resolution establishing the UN Peace-keeping Force in Cyprus (UNFICYP). Advance units reached the island in March, and by 22 May the UN headquarters at Nicosia controlled 6,931 military personnel.

There was more fighting between Greek and Turkish Cypriots in March and April 1964. On 1 June the Cyprus House of Representatives approved legislation establishing a National Guard and rendering all male Cypriots between the ages of 18 and 59 liable to six months' service. Only members of the National Guard, of the regular police and of the armed forces would now have the right to bear arms. One purpose of the legislation was to suppress the irregular bands which increasingly tended to escape the control of the established regime.

Under the agreements concluded for the independence of Cyprus in 1959–60, Turkey maintained a contingent of troops on the island, the personnel of this force being renewed from time to time on a system of regular rotation. A new crisis arose in August–September 1964 when the Cyprus Government refused to allow such a rotation of personnel. After much negotiation through the UN officials on the island, the Government agreed to raise its existing blockade of the Turkish Cypriots entrenched in the Kokkina district and to allow the normal rotation of troops for the Turkish force stationed at Cyprus. The Turkish Government now consented that this force should come under UN command in Cyprus.

GENERAL GRIVAS

There was further tension in Cyprus during March 1966 over the position of Gen. Grivas, the former head of EOKA. Grivas had returned to the island in June 1964 at a time when it was felt that he might be able, with his high personal prestige, to bring to order the small 'private armies' and 'irregular bands' which had emerged among the Greek Cypriots and which were violently defying the Cyprus Government.

In March 1966 President Makarios attempted to limit the functions of Gen. Grivas in Cyprus and so to end a situation whereby political control was vested in himself while command of the armed forces (both the Greek Cypriot National Guard and also the 'volunteer' Greek troops stationed in Cyprus) rested with the General, who took his orders from Greece. The President's proposal that the National Guard should be transferred to the control of the Cyprus Minister of Defence found favour neither with Gen. Grivas nor in Athens, where it provoked a serious political crisis. The whole affair underlined the distrust separating President Makarios and Gen. Grivas and the doubts existing in Athens regarding the ultimate intentions of the Cyprus President.

The military coup in Greece in April 1967 was followed by a brief improvement in Greco-Turkish relations. The Prime Ministers and Foreign Ministers of Greece and Turkey met in Thrace in September, but failed to reach an agreement on Cyprus, Greece rejecting any form of partition, which was implicit in the Turkish proposal to accept *Enosis* in return for military bases and 10% of the island's territory.

TURKISH CYPRIOT ADMINISTRATION

On 29 December 1967 the Turkish Cypriot community announced the establishment of a 'Transitional Administration' to administer its affairs until the provisions of the 1960 Constitution were implemented. Measures were approved to establish separate executive, legislative and judicial authorities, and Fazil Küçük, who remained the official Vice-President of Cyprus, was appointed President of the Transitional Administration, with Rauf Denktaş as Vice-President. A legislative body was established, consisting of the Turkish Cypriot members of the House of Representatives elected in 1960 and the members of the Turkish Communal Chamber. The Executive Council's nine members functioned as the administration. President Makarios described the Transitional Administration as 'totally illegal', but it continued to function as the *de facto* Government of the Turkish community in Cyprus.

INTERCOMMUNAL TALKS, 1968–74

Between January and April 1968 the Cypriot Government gradually relaxed the measures it had adopted against the Turkish community. With the exception of the Turkish area in Nicosia, freedom of movement for Turkish Cypriots was restored, checkpoints were removed and unrestricted supplies to Turkish areas were permitted. In April Rauf Denktaş, the Vice-President of the Turkish Cypriot Administration, was permitted to return from exile, and in May he began talks with Glavkos Klerides, the President of the House of Representatives. These negotiations were intended to form the basis of a settlement of the constitutional differences between the Greek and Turkish communities, but very little progress was made. After years of intermittent discussion there was still an impasse—the Turks demanding local autonomy and the Greeks rejecting any proposals tending towards a federal solution, fearing that this might lead to partition. In June 1972 the UN Secretary-General, Dr Kurt Waldheim, attended the talks, stressing the need for a peaceful settlement and expressing a hope that UNFICYP might be withdrawn in the near future. By the end of 1973 the Greek Cypriot representative seemed to have accepted the principle of local autonomy, but no acceptable compromise had been found on the scope of local autonomy or the degree of control to be exercised by the central Government over local authorities. A statement by the Prime Minister of Turkey, Bülent Ecevit, calling for a federal settlement of the constitutional problem, caused the talks to break down in April 1974. The Greek and Cypriot Governments claimed that the negotiations had been conducted on the understanding that any solution would be in terms of a unitary state, while Denktaş declared that federation would not necessarily mean partition. Denktaş also feared that the Greek Government was giving support to the *Enosis* movement. Each side accused the other of trying to sabotage the talks.

TERRORISM AND ELECTIONS, 1969–70

There was a marked reduction in intercommunal violence while the talks between the Greek and Turkish communities continued. However, the Greek population of the island was divided between supporters of Makarios, and his aim of an independent unitary state, and those who demanded union with Greece. In 1969 the National Front, an organization advocating immediate *Enosis*, embarked on a campaign of terrorism, raiding police stations to steal arms, bombing British military buildings and vehicles, shooting and wounding the chief of police, and making several unsuccessful bomb attacks on government ministers. An attempt in March 1970 to assassinate President Makarios was attributed to the National Front, and a week later Polykarpos Georghadjis, a former Minister of the Interior, was found shot dead. At the trial of the President's would-be assassins, Georghadjis was named as a party to the conspiracy.

Despite the activities of the National Front, the Government decided to hold a general election on 5 July 1970. The dissolved House of Representatives had been in existence since 1960, and the elections which should have been held in 1965, according to the Constitution, had been postponed from year to year. The continued absence of the 15 Turkish members, who met as part of the Turkish Legislative Assembly, meant that the Greek Cypriot House of Representatives contained only 35 members. Fifteen of the Greek Cypriot seats were won by the Unified

Party, led by Glavkos Klerides, with a policy of support for President Makarios and a united independent Cyprus. The communist Anorthotiko Komma Ergazomenou Laou (AKEL—Progressive Party of the Working People) won nine seats, to become the second largest in the House. None of the candidates of the Demokratikon Ethnikon Komma (DEK—Democratic National Party—which advocated *Enosis*), won a seat. The elections held at the same time by the Turkish Cypriots resulted in a victory for the National Solidarity Party, led by Rauf Denktaş.

RETURN OF GRIVAS AND EOKA-B, 1971–72

The ideal of *Enosis* was still attractive to many Greek Cypriots, despite the lack of success for pro-union candidates in the election. Greek Cypriot students condemned President Makarios's support for the creation of an independent unitary state, and demanded an end to the intercommunal talks. Gen. Grivas denounced the President in an article in an Athens newspaper, calling for his resignation on the grounds that, by abandoning *Enosis*, the President had betrayed EOKA's struggle for freedom.

At the beginning of September 1971 Grivas returned secretly to Cyprus and began to hold meetings with the leaders of the National Front and his followers in the EOKA movement of the 1950s. President Makarios threatened to arrest the General for setting up armed bands, and declared his opposition to the achievement of *Enosis* by violent means. For their part pro-*Enosis* Greek Cypriots condemned the intercommunal talks and rejected the idea of a negotiated compromise with the Turkish community. The Cyprus Government imported a considerable quantity of arms as a precautionary measure, but after protests from Greece and Turkey that the distribution of these arms would serve only to aggravate an already tense situation, the consignment was placed under the custody of UNFICYP.

Makarios had been under pressure for some time from the Greek Government to dismiss ministers considered hostile to Athens. In February 1972 it was suggested in Athens that a Cypriot government of national unity should be formed, including moderate representatives of Gen. Grivas. For some months the President resisted this pressure, and it seemed that the Greek Government, in alliance with dissident bishops and. Grivas, was intent on forcing his resignation. In May the Minister of Foreign Affairs, Spyros Kyprianou, who had been the main target of Greek hostility and one of the President's closest associates, resigned, and in June the President capitulated and carried out an extensive reorganization of his Cabinet.

Gen. Grivas organized a new guerrilla force, which became known as EOKA-B, and launched a series of attacks on the Makarios Government similar to those against British rule in the 1950s. While the Committee for the Co-ordination of the *Enosis* Struggle, Grivas's political front organization, demanded a plebiscite on *Enosis* and rejected intercommunal agreement as a means of settling the future of Cyprus, EOKA-B raided police stations, quarries and warehouses, stealing arms, ammunition, dynamite and radio transmitters.

1973 PRESIDENTIAL ELECTION

The demand for a plebiscite from supporters of Gen. Grivas was put forward as an alternative to the election for the presidency, called by President Makarios as a test of strength. The President's speech of 8 February 1973 set out his position: while believing in *Enosis*, he considered that talks with the Turkish community on the basis of an independent Cyprus were the only practical possibility. He condemned terrorism and violence as counter-productive, likely to lead to Turkish intervention and unsupported by the Greek and Cypriot authorities. The Greek Government also repudiated terrorism and expressed its support for a constitutional solution.

On 8 February 1973 Makarios was returned unopposed for a third five-year term as President, and in the Turkish quarter of Nicosia Rauf Denktaş was declared elected Vice-President, following the withdrawal of Ahmet Berberoğlu.

EOKA-B continued its terrorist activities throughout 1973, concentrating on bombings and raids on police stations. In July the Minister of Justice, Christos Vakis, was kidnapped, prompting an escalation in violence. The President refused to submit to violence or to blackmail, rejecting the terms put

forward by Grivas for the release of Vakis. Numerous police and National Guard officers, suspected of being Grivas sympathizers, were dismissed, and Vakis was released in August. Action by security forces against secret EOKA bases resulted in many arrests, the seizure of quantities of munitions and the discovery of plans to assassinate the President. President Georgios Papadopoulos of Greece publicly condemned the activities of 'the illegal organization of Gen. Grivas', which undermined the Greek policy of 'support for the finding of a solution to the Cyprus problem through the enlarged local talks aimed at ensuring an independent, sovereign and unitary state'.

ABORTIVE MILITARY COUP OF 1974

The deposition of three bishops of the Orthodox Church of Cyprus for attempting to remove Archbishop Makarios from the Church, and the resultant demonstrations of popular support for the President, enabled the Cyprus Government to take strong measures against other supporters of Gen. Grivas. Forces loyal to the President waged guerrilla war against EOKA-B, and carried out a purge of the armed forces and police—some of whose members had collaborated with EOKA and helped in their raids. The Grivas campaign of terrorism seemed to have been checked by the beginning of 1974, and when Gen. Grivas died as a result of a heart attack in January the President granted an amnesty to 100 of his imprisoned supporters, hoping to restore normality in Cyprus.

In June 1974 President Makarios ordered a purge of EOKA supporters in the police, civil service, schools and National Guard, and on 2 July he wrote to President Phaidon Ghizikis of Greece, accusing the Greek military regime of giving arms and subsidies to EOKA and of using the Greek army officers attached to the Cyprus National Guard for subversion. The President demanded that the Greek officers who had collaborated with EOKA should be withdrawn, and began to take steps to ensure that the Guard was loyal to Cyprus, rather than to Greece and *Enosis*. The National Guard, apparently with Greek support, then staged a coup, and on 15 July a former EOKA militant, Nikos Sampson, was appointed President. Makarios fled to the United Kingdom, the resistance of his supporters was crushed, and Greece sent more officers to reinforce the National Guard.

Rauf Denktaş, the Turkish Cypriot leader, called for military action by the United Kingdom and Turkey, as guarantors of Cypriot independence, to prevent Greece imposing *Enosis*. Having failed to induce the United Kingdom to intervene, Turkey acted unilaterally. Turkish troops landed in Cyprus on 20 July and seized the port of Kyrenia and a corridor connecting it to the Turkish sector in Nicosia. A cease-fire on 22 July did not prevent further Turkish advances, and the UN peace-keeping force had little success in its efforts to interpose itself between the two Cypriot communities. Massacres and other atrocities were reported from many bi-communal villages, reinforcing the hostility between the Greeks and Turks.

TURKEY OCCUPIES NORTHERN CYPRUS

The successful Turkish invasion had foiled Greek plans to take over Cyprus using the National Guard, and when the military Government in Greece resigned on 23 July 1974, Sampson did likewise. Glavkos Klerides, the moderate Speaker of the House of Representatives who had led the Greek Cypriot delegation to the intercommunal talks, was appointed President, and began negotiations with Rauf Denktaş. The United Kingdom, Greece and Turkey also held talks (in Geneva, Switzerland), but negotiations broke down following Turkish demands for the establishment of a cantonal federation giving almost one-third of the area of Cyprus to the Turkish Cypriots.

On 14 August 1974, the day after the Geneva talks ended, the war was renewed. Turkish forces seized the whole of Cyprus north of what became the 'Attila line', running from Morphou through Nicosia to Famagusta, and the new civilian Government in Greece announced its inability to intervene. Turkey proclaimed that, by this *fait accompli*, the boundaries of an autonomous Turkish Cypriot administration had been established. For his part, Denktaş spoke of establishing a completely independent Turkish Cypriot state north of the 'Attila line' and of encouraging the immigration of Turkish Cypriots from areas still under Greek Cypriot control, to produce a permanent ethnic and political partition of the island. UN Secretary-General Waldheim succeeded in arranging talks between Klerides and Denktaş, but was unable to bring about any constructive results from these negotiations. An important round of peace talks on the Cyprus problem began in Vienna, Austria, between Klerides and Denktaş in January 1975, under the aegis of Dr Waldheim. The success of the negotiations depended on whether the two sides could reach agreement on the political future of the island: the Turkish Cypriots sought a Greek-Turkish bi-regional federation with strong regional governments, whereas the Greeks, while not ruling out a bi-zonal solution, favoured a multi-regional or cantonal federation with strong central government. Both parties stressed the need for an independent, non-aligned, demilitarized Cyprus.

On 13 February 1975 a 'Turkish Federated State of Cyprus' ('TFSC') was proclaimed in the part of the island under Turkish occupation. The new state was not proclaimed as an independent republic, but as a restructuring of the Autonomous Turkish Cypriot Administration, a body established after the invasion, 'on the basis of a secular and federated state until such time as the 1960 Constitution of the Republic...is amended in a similar manner to become the Constitution of the Federal Republic of Cyprus'. Rauf Denktaş was appointed President of the new 'state'. Greece denounced this move as a threat to peace and declared that the issue would be taken to the UN Security Council, which, in March, adopted a resolution (No. 367) regretting the unilateral decision to establish a Federated Turkish State. Talks were resumed in April, and the foundation was laid for intercommunal reconciliation and co-operation, when the Cypriot leaders agreed to form an expert committee, under the auspices of Dr Luis Weckmann-Muñoz, Special Representative of the UN Secretary-General, to consider the powers and functions of a central government for Cyprus and present their findings in June to the Cypriot negotiators in Vienna.

The flight of Turkish Cypriots to British bases after the National Guard coup, and the withdrawal of Greek Cypriot civilians before the advancing Turkish army, had created a major problem in Cyprus. In August 1974 the UN estimated that there were some 225,600 refugees in Cyprus, of whom 183,800 were Greek Cypriots. In the southern part of Cyprus, under Greek Cypriot control, were 198,800 of these refugees, of whom 35,000 were Turkish Cypriots, including prisoners of war. This problem remained unsolved in 1976, with an estimated 200,000 refugees on the island. However, 9,000 Turkish Cypriots were given the opportunity to move to the northern sector in August 1975. In return, the Turkish Cypriot authorities allowed 800 relatives of Greeks who remained in the north to join them in the Turkish sector. The concern over the treatment of Greeks in the Turkish-occupied area gave rise in August 1975 to an investigation by the European Commission of Human Rights, which in a report published in January 1977 found Turkey guilty of committing atrocities in Cyprus.

In December 1974 Archbishop Makarios returned to Cyprus and resumed the presidency. In January 1975 the United Kingdom decided to permit the resettlement of more than 9,000 Turkish Cypriot refugees from the British Sovereign Base at Akrotiri. In retaliation for the alleged ill-treatment of Turkish Cypriots still living in Greek areas, and in order to force a decision on the release of the refugees and their resettlement, the Turks threatened to expel all remaining Greek Cypriots in northern Cyprus and launched a massive scheme to colonize the area, bringing thousands of farmers and peasants from mainland Turkey and settling them in Greek-owned property.

ELECTIONS AND INTERCOMMUNAL TALKS, 1975–76

In September 1975 talks between the two sides resumed in New York. However, these and further discussions in February 1976 were completely unproductive. In April 1976 the divergence in the policies of Archbishop Makarios and Glavkos Klerides, the Greek Cypriot negotiator, eventually led to the resignation of the latter and his replacement by Tassos Papadopoulos.

During 1976 general elections were held on both sides of the 'Attila line'. In June Rauf Denktaş was elected President of the 'TFSC'. His election placed him constitutionally above party politics but in fact his position depended upon the support of the Ulusal Bırlık Partisi (UBP—National Unity Party). Under the terms of the Constitution promulgated by the Turkish Cypriot authorities, 40 deputies were elected to a legislative assembly, with the UBP gaining a majority. Nejat Konuk, the Secretary-General of the UBP, was appointed Prime Minister. In September a general election was conducted in the government-controlled area. A new party under Spyros Kyprianou, the Democratic Front (supporting the policies of Archbishop Makarios), won a decisive victory, taking 21 of the 35 seats. The party of Glavkos Klerides, the Dimokratikos Synagermos (DISY—Democratic Rally), failed to secure representation.

In January 1977 Denktaş initiated a meeting with Archbishop Makarios to establish preliminaries for resuming intercommunal talks (suspended since February 1976); Makarios made it clear that he was prepared to accept a bi-zonal federation provided the Turkish authorities made territorial concessions, and only if there was provision for a central government with adequate powers. A sixth round of talks, which opened in Vienna in March, broke down, was resumed in Nicosia in May, but was then suspended until after the general election due in Turkey in June.

DEATH OF MAKARIOS, ACCESSION OF KYPRIANOU

The death of Archbishop Makarios, on 3 August 1977, put an end to hopes for an immediate continuation of negotiations, and gave rise to fears about the stability of the Greek Cypriot regime in his absence—especially since there was no obvious successor. Spyros Kyprianou, the President of the House of Representatives, was elected on 31 August to serve the remainder of Makarios's presidential term. In the presidential election of January 1978 he was returned to office unopposed. Shortly afterwards EOKA-B announced its dissolution, but in April, after the discovery of a destabilization plot, 22 of its members were arrested. In the same month, following criticism in the Turkish Cypriot press about rising prices, Nejat Konuk resigned as Prime Minister of the 'TFSC' and was replaced by Osman Orek, former President of the National Assembly, who formed a new Cabinet.

In April and July 1978 President Kyprianou was subjected to criticism from within his own Government, both from the powerful left wing and from the followers of the late President Makarios. This resulted in the dismissal of Tassos Papadopoulos, his chief negotiator with the Turkish Cypriots. In December there was a crisis in the 'TFSC' as a result of factional disputes within the UBP. Amid widespread rumours about the establishment of a multinational company to which the Turkish Cypriot trade unions were opposed, all nine cabinet ministers, followed by the Prime Minister, Osman Orek, resigned. A new Cabinet was formed under Mustafa Çağatay, formerly Minister of Labour, Social Affairs and Health. In April 1979 a new party, the Democratic Party, was formed by Nejat Konuk, the former Prime Minister, as the UBP lost support in the legislature.

On 19 May 1979 Kyprianou and Denktaş drew up a 10-point agenda, based on the Makarios-Denktaş agreement of February 1977. However, intercommunal talks in June were adjourned after a week, over differences in the interpretation of the agreement, which Turkish Cypriots saw as providing for bi-zonality on the island. Meanwhile, the UNFICYP mandate continued to be extended at six-monthly intervals.

On 9 September 1980 a reorganization of the Greek Cypriot Government led to the appointment of seven new ministers. As a result, President Kyprianou again came under criticism from the communist AKEL and from the right-wing opposition under Klerides, thus losing his overall majority in the House of Representatives. During the next three months three new 'centrist' political parties were established: the Pankyprio Ananeotiko Metopo (PAME—Pancyprian Renewal Front), the Dimokratiko Komma (DIKO—Democratic Party) and the Enosi Kentrou (Centre Union).

ELECTIONS AND FURTHER TALKS, 1980–81

On 16 September 1980, in the shadow of the military coup in Turkey, the intercommunal peace talks were resumed after an interval of 15 months. These were to be held within the framework of a procedural formula proposed by Hugo Gobbi, the UN Special Representative for Cyprus. The negotiators for the Greek and Turkish sides were, respectively, George Ioannides and Umit Süleyman Onan. There were to be four main areas of discussion: the resettlement of Varosha (the Greek area of

Cyprus, showing the 'Turkish Republic of Northern Cyprus'

Famagusta); constitutional aspects; territorial aspects; and 'initial practical measures by both sides to promote goodwill, mutual confidence and the return to normal conditions'. The talks continued intermittently, but by the spring of 1981 no concrete results had been achieved. In March negotiations with the United Kingdom about outstanding development payments to Cyprus, which, according to the Cypriots, amounted to £150m. since 1960, were resumed.

Growing criticism of Kyprianou's Government for its failure to avert an economic crisis or to make any real progress in the intercommunal talks led the House of Representatives to vote almost unanimously on 16 April for the dissolution of the Government. In the subsequent parliamentary elections, held on 24 May 1981, under a system of proportional representation, the communist AKEL and Klerides' DISY each won 12 of the 35 Greek Cypriot seats in the House of Representatives, while President Kyprianou's DIKO took only eight seats. In the elections held in the 'TFSC' in June, President Rauf Denktaş was returned to office, but with only 52% of the vote. His right-wing UBP won 18 out of 40 seats, compared with 23 at the previous elections.

The intercommunal talks continued throughout 1981, but little progress was made. In August there was optimism when fresh proposals were put forward by the Turkish Cypriots. These envisaged handing back 3%–4% of the 35.8% of land now controlled by them, as well as the buffer zone between the two communities, and allowing some 40,000 of the 200,000 Greek Cypriot refugees to return to the Famagusta area. The constitutional issue remained the main problem: the Greek Cypriots wanted a federation with a strong central government and freedom of movement throughout the island; the Turkish Cypriots favoured something similar to a partition within a confederation, equal representation in government and strong links with the mother country. The Greek Cypriots, while agreeing to the principle of an alternating presidency, objected to disproportionate representation of the Turkish community, who formed less than 20% of the population. The Turkish proposals were rejected by the Greek Cypriots, but it was agreed that the talks should continue.

NEW UN PEACE PROPOSAL

In November 1981 the UN put forward a new peace plan, or 'evaluation', for a federal, independent and non-aligned Cypriot state. Although more favourable to the Greek side than the

Turkish Cypriot proposals had been, this was only accepted reluctantly as a basis for negotiation by the Greek Cypriots, in the face of opposition from the Church and some political groups. The Turkish Cypriots accepted the plan.

The socialist Government of Greece, elected in October 1981, pledged more active support for the Greek Cypriots than its predecessors. Andreas Papandreou, the Greek Prime Minister, who visited Cyprus early in 1982, wanted to see the withdrawal of all Greek and Turkish troops from the island, and favoured an international conference on Cyprus rather than the continuation of the intercommunal talks.

With presidential elections in view, President Kyprianou and his DIKO party formed an alliance with AKEL in April 1982, based on a 'minimum programme' of continuance of the non-aligned *status quo*, defence of the mixed economy and support for the intercommunal talks. This put a strain on relations with the Greek Government, since it was contrary to the policy recently laid down by Athens and Nicosia. The alliance with AKEL involved a wide-ranging cabinet reorganization.

In the 'TFSC' the Çağatay Government resigned in December 1981. A period of political crisis ensued, and it was not until March 1982 that a coalition Government was formed by Çağatay between his own UBP, the Democratic People's Party and the Turkish Unity Party.

In February 1983 President Kyprianou was re-elected, with 56.5% of the vote, for a five-year term. The DISY candidate, Glavkos Klerides, polled 34%, and Vassos Lyssarides, of the Socialistiko Komma Kyprou EDEK (EDEK—EDEK Socialist Party of Cyprus), 9.5%.

In May 1983 the UN General Assembly voted overwhelmingly in favour of the withdrawal of Turkish troops from Cyprus, although the USA and the United Kingdom abstained in protest against the partisan wording of the resolution. In retaliation, Rauf Denktaş threatened to boycott any further intercommunal talks and to call a referendum in the 'TFSC' to decide whether to make a unilateral declaration of independence and seek international recognition. The Cyprus pound was replaced by the Turkish lira as legal tender in the 'TFSC'.

Informal talks continued in August 1983 under the auspices of the UN, but no agreement was reached, and in September the Greek Cypriot Minister of Foreign Affairs resigned because of policy differences with President Kyprianou over the proposed resumption of the intercommunal talks. UN proposals for a summit meeting between Denktaş and Kyprianou in late 1983 were unsuccessful.

DECLARATION OF 'TURKISH REPUBLIC OF NORTHERN CYPRUS'

On 15 November 1983 the 'TFSC' made a unilateral declaration of independence as the 'Turkish Republic of Northern Cyprus' ('TRNC'), with Denktaş as President. Later that month, Mustafa Çağatay resigned as Turkish Cypriot Prime Minister and as leader of the UBP. On 2 December the Legislative Assembly of the 'TRNC' adopted legislation for the establishment of a 70-member constituent assembly (comprising the 40 elected members of the Legislative Assembly and 30 others appointed from representative groups within the community), which met for the first time on 6 December. The following day President Denktaş appointed Nejat Konuk (Prime Minister of the 'TFSC' in 1976–78 and at this time President of the 'TRNC' Legislative Assembly) to be Prime Minister in an interim Cabinet, pending elections in 1984. Like the 'TFSC', the 'TRNC' was recognized only by Turkey, and the declaration of independence was condemned (in Resolution 541) by the UN Security Council. However, the European Community (EC, now European Union—EU) resolved not to apply trade sanctions against the 'TRNC'. Conciliatory proposals that were made by the 'TRNC', including the resettlement of 40,000 Greek Cypriot refugees, were rejected by the Cyprus Government in January 1984, while the 'TRNC' in turn refused to accept President Kyprianou's proposal that the Turkish Cypriots should be allowed to administer 25% of the island (despite the fact that they comprised only 18% of the population) on condition that the declaration of independence be withdrawn before talks resumed.

In April 1984 Turkey and the 'TRNC' exchanged ambassadors, and plans were made for a referendum on 19 August to approve a new constitution, to be followed by a general election on 4 November to elect members for the Constituent Assembly. (These elections were subsequently postponed.) The establishment of diplomatic links with Turkey was followed by a formal rejection of UN proposals for a 'freezing' of independence as a pre-condition for peace talks, along with a continued refusal to return the Varosha (Greek Cypriot) area of Famagusta.

FAILED 1985 KYPRIANOU-DENKTAŞ SUMMIT

In August and September 1984 the Greek and Turkish Cypriots conferred separately with the UN Secretary-General, Javier Pérez de Cuéllar, whose aim was to bring the two sides together for direct negotiations. The Turkish Cypriots reiterated that they would accept the proposed creation of a bi-zonal federation only if power were to be shared equally between the north and the south. The third round of negotiations, begun in November, was seen as being crucial to any long-term solution of the problem but, despite some concessions on the part of the Turkish Cypriots, an impasse was reached. In December, after the third round of talks had ended, the leaders of the two communities, Spyros Kyprianou and Rauf Denktaş, agreed to hold a summit meeting in January 1985. No agreement was reached at the meeting, however, and Denktaş subsequently declared that a further summit meeting could not be arranged until after the elections due to be held in the 'TRNC' in June. The new Constitution of the 'TRNC' was approved by a referendum in May, and this was followed by a presidential election on 9 June, at which Rauf Denktaş was returned to power with more than 70% of the vote. A general election followed on 23 June, with the UBP, led by Dr Derviş Eroğlu, winning more seats than any other party (24) but failing to win an overall majority in the 50-seat Legislative Assembly.

In July 1985 the UN Secretary-General drew up further proposals, which the Greek Cypriots accepted. The new UN proposals were for a bi-zonal federal Cyprus (with the Turkish Cypriots occupying 29% of the land) in which the government would be led by a Greek Cypriot president and a Turkish Cypriot vice-president, both having limited power of veto over federal legislation. Ministers would be appointed in a ratio of seven Greek Cypriots to three Turkish Cypriots. One 'major' ministry would always be held by a Turkish Cypriot, and a special working party would consider demands that the Minister of Foreign Affairs should always be a Turkish Cypriot. There would be two assemblies: an upper house, with a 50:50 community representation, and a lower house, weighted 70:30 in favour of the Greek Cypriots. Legislation on important issues would require 'separate majorities in both chambers'. A tripartite body, including one non-Cypriot voting member, would have the final say in constitutional clashes concerning the extent of federal power. However, serious problems remained over the crucial questions of a timetable for the withdrawal of Turkey's troops and the nature of international guarantees for a newly united Republic of Cyprus. This plan was underwritten by foreign governments (in effect the USA), which were to subsidize two funds: one to help the poorer Turkish Cypriot community, and the other to aid both Greek and Turkish Cypriots who had been displaced as a result of the events of 1974. However, the Turkish Cypriots did not accept the revised plan, as they wanted Turkish troops to remain on the island indefinitely, to protect their interests, and felt that any peace settlement must include Turkey as a guarantor. They had also revised their opinion on allowing Greek Cypriot refugees to return to the 'TRNC'.

1985 GREEK CYPRIOT ELECTIONS

President Kyprianou had come under severe criticism within the House of Representatives over the failure of the summit in January 1985. He reshuffled the Council of Ministers and terminated his alliance with AKEL, which had become increasingly strained, mainly because of Kyprianou's unyielding attitude to the intercommunal talks. In November, following an acrimonious debate over Kyprianou's leadership, the House of Representatives was dissolved. A general election was not due to be held until May 1986, but the two largest parties, AKEL and the conservative DISY, had formed an alliance with the intention of achieving a two-thirds' majority in the House, which would enable them, under Article 44, to amend the Constitution and so force an early presidential election. However, they were one vote short of the required majority.

A general election was held on 8 December 1985 for an enlarged House of 56 Greek Cypriot seats (compared with 35 previously), while the nominal allocation of seats to the Turkish Cypriot community was increased from 15 to 24. Significant gains were made by DIKO, although it remained short of a majority. It won 16 seats and increased its share of the vote to 27.6% (compared with 19.5% in the 1981 election). AKEL suffered a reverse, taking only 15 seats, while its share of the vote fell to 27.4% from 32.8% in 1981. This ended a communist ascendancy in Greek Cypriot politics which dated back to independence in 1960 (although AKEL partially recovered its position in the local elections in May 1986). DISY replaced AKEL as the largest party in the House by winning 19 seats, with 33.6% of the vote, compared with 31.9% in 1981. The socialist EDEK, which supported Kyprianou's stand on peace negotiations, won six seats with 11.1% of the vote, compared with 8.2% in 1981. Campaigning had been dominated by two issues: the proposed peace plan and Kyprianou's argument that, constitutionally, the President was not bound by the decisions of the House. The result of the election was interpreted as evidence of widespread support for Kyprianou's policies.

Further meetings to discuss the UN peace plan were conducted in March 1986. On this occasion the Turkish Cypriots accepted the draft peace plan (which was still based on the idea of establishing a bi-zonal federal republic, with specified posts and ratios for the Greek and Turkish Cypriot participants in the federal government), while the Greek Cypriots stated that it was the same as that put forward in January 1985 (which they had rejected). The Greek Cypriots' principal objections were that the plan failed to envisage the withdrawal of the Turkish troops prior to implementation of the plan; the removal from Cyprus of settlers from the Turkish mainland; the provision of suitable international guarantors for the settlement, with the exclusion of Turkey; and the assurance of the 'three basic freedoms', namely the right to live, move and work anywhere in Cyprus. Kyprianou and other Greek Cypriot leaders, as well as Prime Minister Papandreou of Greece, were all opposed to the plan but were careful not to reject it absolutely. They sought a summit meeting between the two leaders (Kyprianou and Denktaş) or an international conference to discuss the matter. President Denktaş, however, later stated that he would not accept an international conference that treated the Greek Cypriots as the official government of Cyprus and the

Turkish Cypriots as a minority population, and that should such a conference be arranged, he would seek international recognition of the 'TRNC'.

In July 1986 Turgut Özal, the Prime Minister of Turkey, made his first visit to the 'TRNC' and urged the adoption of an economic model similar to that in Turkey. The Toplumcu Kurtuluş Partisi (Communal Liberation Party) disagreed with this policy, and in August it withdrew from the 'TRNC' coalition Government. In September the Prime Minister, Derviş Eroğlu, formed a new administration in coalition with the Yeni Doğuş Partisi (YDP—New Dawn Party).

In July 1987 it was reported that the Cyprus Government had proposed to the UN Secretary-General that the Cypriot National Guard be dissolved, and orders for military equipment cancelled, in exchange for the withdrawal of Turkish forces from the island. In an address to the UN General Assembly in October, President Kyprianou proposed an international peace-keeping force to replace the armed forces of both the Greek and Turkish Cypriots. President Denktaş, however, maintained that negotiations on the establishment of a federal bi-zonal republic should precede any demilitarization.

ELECTION OF VASSILIOU AS PRESIDENT

The first round of voting in a presidential election took place in the Greek Cypriot zone on 14 February 1988. There were four main candidates, including Kyprianou, who was seeking his third consecutive five-year term. The three other main candidates were: Georghios Vassiliou, who presented himself as an independent, but who (although not himself a communist) was unofficially backed by AKEL; Glavkos Klerides, the leader of the conservative DISY; and Dr Vassos Lyssarides, leader of the socialist EDEK. Since no candidate received more than 50% of the total vote, a second round was held a week later to decide between the two leading candidates at the first round—Glavkos Klerides, with 33.3% of the total vote, and Georghios Vassiliou, with 30.1%. Kyprianou was third, with 27.3% of the total vote. This unexpected defeat was widely interpreted as a result of the failure of Kyprianou's uncompromising policies for the reunification of Cyprus. In the second round of voting, Georghios Vassiliou, with the backing of EDEK and a significant number of Kyprianou supporters (the outgoing President had declared that he would not support either candidate), was elected as the new President by a narrow margin, taking 51.6% of the total votes cast.

Although it was predicted that President Vassiliou would promote his predecessor's policies regarding a settlement for the divided island, he, unlike Kyprianou, quickly expressed his willingness to enter into direct informal dialogue with the Turkish Cypriot leader. Vassiliou also promised to re-establish the National Council, which was to include representatives from all the main Greek Cypriot parties, to negotiate plans for the settlement of the Cyprus problem. On 28 February 1988 Vassiliou was officially sworn in as the new President and named a new Council of Ministers. The same day President Vassiliou proposed a meeting with the Turkish Prime Minister, Turgut Özal, to discuss the withdrawal of Turkish troops from Cyprus. Özal responded by claiming that Vassiliou's priority, as regards the Cyprus problem, should be to talk with President Denktaş of the 'TRNC'. In March Denktaş submitted a series of goodwill proposals to President Vassiliou, via Oscar Camilión, the new Special Representative of the UN Secretary-General. Vassiliou immediately rejected the proposals, which included a plan to form committees to study the possibilities of intercommunal co-operation. In the same month President Vassiliou held talks in Athens with the Greek Prime Minister, Andreas Papandreou, to examine the prospects for a Cyprus settlement.

RESUMPTION OF INTERCOMMUNAL TALKS

After a meeting with the newly revived National Council in June 1988, President Vassiliou agreed to a proposal by the UN Secretary-General to resume intercommunal talks, without pre-conditions, with President Denktaş of the 'TRNC', in the capacity of the respective leaders of two communities. Following a meeting with the Turkish Government in July, Denktaş also approved the proposal. Consequently, the impasse between the two sides was ended and a Cyprus summit meeting proceeded in Geneva on 24 August, under the auspices of the UN. At this summit, which was the first such meeting between Greek and Turkish Cypriot leaders since January 1985, Vassiliou and Denktaş resumed direct talks on a settlement of all aspects of the Cyprus problem. As a result of this meeting, the two leaders began the first formal round of substantive direct negotiations, under UN auspices, in Nicosia on 15 September 1988. Despite several rounds of intensive, UN-sponsored direct talks, held in Nicosia and New York, it became apparent by the end of June 1989 that no progress had been achieved as a result of the discussions. The general consensus seemed to be that although the two leaders expressed their willingness that Cyprus should be reunited as a bi-zonal federation, they disagreed on what form an eventual government should take. In addition, attitudes regarding three issues that had caused the collapse of previous talks (i.e. the withdrawal of Turkish troops, the right of Turkey to intervene as a guarantor, and the assurance of the 'three basic freedoms'—see above) appeared irreconcilable. Vassiliou and Denktaş agreed to hold another meeting with the UN Secretary-General to review the intercommunal talks in New York in September.

In mid-May 1989, under the supervision of the UNFICYP, a deconfrontation agreement (reached at the end of March) was implemented, which involved the withdrawal of Greek Cypriot and Turkish Cypriot troops from 24 military posts along the central Nicosia sector of the 'Attila line'. It was hoped that this limited withdrawal would reduce the tension that persisted in this troubled area (five fatal shootings had been reported during the period May–December 1988). In July 1989, however, crowds of Greek Cypriot women held angry demonstrations at the buffer zone to protest against the continuing partition of Cyprus. There was a dramatic escalation in tension when more than 100 protesters were arrested by the Turkish Cypriot forces during the demonstration and were detained for several days.

ABORTIVE 1990 VASSILIOU-DENKTAŞ SUMMIT

Despite a relaxation, in November 1989, of entry restrictions for Greek Cypriots with compelling reasons to travel to the 'TRNC', no significant progress was made towards a political settlement in the first half of 1990. A new round of UN-sponsored talks, which began in late February in New York, came to a premature end in early March, following disagreement arising from demands by Rauf Denktaş that the right to self-determination of the Turkish Cypriots be recognized by the Greek Cypriot community. President Vassiliou accused Denktaş of deliberately frustrating hopes of a settlement by introducing new conditions to the negotiations and implicitly advocating some form of partition or secession. Denktaş in turn accused Vassiliou of refusing to consider any form of compromise. A resolution approved by the UN Security Council later in March rejected Denktaş's stance and reaffirmed the UN's commitment to a resolution based on a bicommunal federal republic.

Later in March 1990 Denktaş resigned the presidency and called an early presidential election for 22 April. Denktaş, standing as an independent, received 66.7% of the votes cast, while İsmail Bozkurt, who also stood as an independent, received about 32%, and Alpay Durduran of the Yeni Kıbrıs Partisi (YKP—New Cyprus Party) slightly more than 1%. Denktaş's victory was widely interpreted as a sign of Turkish Cypriot approval of the President's stance throughout the recent negotiations with President Vassiliou, although opposition parties advocating a more conciliatory approach commanded significant support in the 'TRNC'.

The UBP retained its majority in the 'TRNC' Legislative Assembly at a general election on 6 May 1990, when it received 55% of the votes cast, thereby securing 34 of the 50 available seats. In June Denktaş approved the appointment of several newcomers to the Council of Ministers, which Derviş Eroğlu continued to head as Prime Minister. In local elections on 24 June the UBP consolidated its position when its candidates were elected to 14 out of a total of 22 mayoral positions.

Rumours in the Greek Cypriot zone of widespread disaffection within AKEL were apparently substantiated in early 1990, when resignations and dismissals from the party's central committee and politburo followed calls for democratic reform of the party structure. At least five of the party's 15 parliamentary representatives were thought to belong to the dissident faction. A new party, the Ananeotiko Demokratiko Sosialistiko Kinima

(ADISOK—Democratic Socialist Reform Movement), was formed in April 1990, and was expected to attract many dissatisfied supporters of AKEL.

In July 1990 Cyprus formally applied for full membership of the EC. International observers regarded the political division within the island as a major obstacle to Cyprus's achieving member status, while President Denktaş declared that the 'unilateral' application by the Greek Cypriots on behalf of the whole island would further complicate the search for a political settlement for Cyprus.

In July and October 1990, in retaliation for the EC application, the 'TRNC' Government and Turkey signed an agreement envisaging the creation of a customs union, the abolition of passport controls and the introduction of a 'TRNC' currency backed by the Turkish central bank. These 'unilateral' steps were condemned by the Greek Cypriot Government, which claimed that the 'TRNC' was also actively planning to settle sensitive northern areas, such as Varosha, with Palestinians and Bulgarian Turkish immigrants. (In June 1989 President Denktaş had advocated the transfer of Bulgarian Turkish refugees from Turkey to the 'TRNC', but the Turkish Government had declined the offer.)

UN-sponsored efforts to revive intercommunal talks on the Cyprus question were hindered by international preoccupation with the conflict in the Persian (Arabian) Gulf after August 1990. As a supporter of the multinational coalition against Iraq, the Vassiliou Government drew parallels between the Iraqi invasion of Kuwait and the Turkish occupation of northern Cyprus in 1974. The 'TRNC' and Turkish authorities, however, maintained that any similarities lay rather with the attempted Greek military takeover of Cyprus in 1974, which had precipitated the Turkish action. Of the obstacles to an outline agreement as proposed by the UN, the most intractable remained the demands of the Turkish Cypriots for recognition as a 'people' with the right to self-determination in UN terms, a demand interpreted by the Greek Cypriots as a desire for distinct sovereignty. Another major point of contention remained each side's rejection of the other's preferred negotiating framework: whereas the Greek Cypriots, with support from Greece, advocated a UN-chaired conference to be attended by the five permanent members of the UN Security Council, the Turkish Cypriots, with Turkish support, favoured a conference at which participation would be limited to representatives of the Turkish and Greek Cypriot sectors as well as Turkey and Greece.

1991 GREEK CYPRIOT ELECTIONS

In general elections for the 56 Greek Cypriot seats in the House of Representatives held on 19 May 1991, campaigning focused on economic and social issues, there being only marginal policy differences between the parties regarding the Cyprus issue. The conservative DISY, in alliance with the Komma ton Phileleftheron (Liberal Party), received 35.8% of the votes cast (2.2% more than in 1985) and secured 20 seats (a gain of one seat). The AKEL communists, despite competition from ADISOK, unexpectedly achieved the biggest advance, with 30.6% of the vote and 18 seats (a gain of three seats). The EDEK socialists also gained ground by securing seven seats in the House, while support for the 'centrist' DIKO decreased from 27.6% of votes cast and 16 seats in 1985 to 19.5% of the vote and just 11 seats in 1991. Both ADISOK and the Pankyprio Komma Prosfygon ke Pligenton (PAKOP—Pancyprian Party of Refugees and Stricken Persons) failed to win a seat in the House.

On 30 May 1991, at the inaugural meeting of the newly-constituted House of Representatives, Alexis Galanos (the former parliamentary spokesman for DIKO) was elected President of the House in succession to the EDEK leader, Dr Vassos Lyssarides.

RESUMPTION OF UN-SPONSORED TALKS, 1991–92

US diplomatic efforts resulted in an announcement by US President George Bush in August 1991 that the Greek and Turkish Prime Ministers had confirmed their willingness to attend a UN-sponsored conference in New York with the aim of finding a solution to the Cyprus question. However, although Presidents Vassiliou and Denktaş declared their support for this initiative, hopes of a breakthrough receded when the UN Secretary-General, Javier Pérez de Cuéllar, made it clear that

the conference would not be convened unless progress had been made on resolving outstanding differences. No such progress being immediately apparent, the Bush schedule for a conference in September was not met.

On taking office on 1 January 1992, the new UN Secretary-General, Dr Boutros Boutros-Ghali, initiated another attempt to establish the basis for a high-level conference on Cyprus. To this end, UN envoys visited Cyprus, Turkey and Greece in February, and Boutros-Ghali held meetings in New York with Vassiliou and Denktaş in January and March. However, in a report to the Security Council in April, the UN Secretary-General advised that no progress had been made towards resolving basic disagreements and that 'there has even been regression'. Although there was a measure of agreement on the shape of a federal government structure, the issues of 'territorial adjustment' and the return of displaced persons remained serious obstacles. In Resolution 750, adopted on 10 April, the Security Council reaffirmed that a settlement 'must be based on a state of Cyprus with a single sovereignty and international personality and a single citizenship, with its independence and territorial integrity safeguarded, and comprising two politically equal communities'.

In accordance with Security Council instructions, Boutros-Ghali held further separate talks with Vassiliou and Denktaş in New York in June 1992, when deliberations centred on UN proposals for the demarcation of Greek Cypriot and Turkish Cypriot areas of administration under a federal structure. In view of the reluctance of the parties to discuss lines on a map, the cartographic ideas put forward by Boutros-Ghali were described as a 'non-map'. Although both sides undertook to observe a news black-out on the talks, pending a further round in mid-July, the Boutros-Ghali 'non-map' was published by the Turkish Cypriot press on 30 June. It showed that the area of Turkish administration would be about 25% smaller than the 'TRNC', from whose present territory the Greek Cypriots would recover Morphou and Varosha (although not old Famagusta) and a total of 34 villages. According to the published details, the new division would, *inter alia*, create a Turkish enclave to the east of Nicosia and a Greek enclave in the north-eastern tip of the island. It was estimated that under the UN plan some 60,000 displaced Greek Cypriots would be able to return to their pre-1974 homes and remain under Greek Cypriot administration.

While denying that he had leaked details of the 'non-map' (which was eventually released by the UN in August 1992), Denktaş seized the opportunity presented by its publication to assert that its proposals were totally unacceptable to the 'TRNC' Government. On the Greek Cypriot side, government spokesmen took the view that the disclosure of the UN plan was a ploy by which the Turkish Cypriots hoped to gain negotiating leverage.

Following further unsuccessful UN-sponsored talks, conducted in New York during October and November 1992, the Secretary-General took the unusual step of publishing a tabulation of the respective responses to his settlement ideas. This revealed that, whereas the Greek Cypriot side accepted the proposals and the UN map as the basis for a negotiated settlement, the Turkish Cypriot side had reservations with regard to nine of the 100 articles, all of which dealt with crucial matters. The tabulation demonstrated that, apart from the basic issues of sovereignty and territorial division, the Turkish Cypriots were continuing to insist that the posts of federal President and Vice-President should rotate between the two communities and that the federal Government should comprise an equal number of Greek Cypriot and Turkish Cypriot ministers. The Greek Cypriots proposed that the two premier positions should be decided by 'federation-wide and weighted universal suffrage', and also endorsed the UN proposal that there should be a 7:3 ratio of Greek Cypriot and Turkish Cypriot ministers, although they accepted that a Turkish Cypriot should normally hold one of the three main portfolios of foreign affairs, finance and defence. Moreover, while both sides accepted the 'security and guarantees' section of the UN proposals (including provisions for the withdrawal of all non-Cypriot forces), considerable disagreement persisted as to whether or not the 1959 treaty of guarantee afforded Turkey a unilateral right of intervention in Cyprus.

Reporting to the UN Security Council on the failure of the latest round of negotiations, Dr Boutros-Ghali noted that a 'lack of political will...continues to block the conclusion of an agreement', adding that 'it is essential that the Turkish Cypriot side adjust its position'. This assessment was reflected in the resultant Security Council Resolution 789, adopted in late November 1992, which also incorporated a set of proposed confidence-building measures. These included a reduction in the level of armed forces on both sides, the extension of the UN security zone to include the disputed Varosha suburb of Famagusta, the easing of restrictions on 'people to people' contacts, and the reopening of Nicosia international airport.

GREEK CYPRIOT AND TURKISH CYPRIOT ELECTIONS, 1993

The veteran DISY leader, Glavkos Klerides, was the unexpected victor in Greek Cypriot presidential elections conducted in two rounds on 7 and 14 February 1993, narrowly defeating Vassiliou's bid for a second term. Again standing as an independent with AKEL support, Vassiliou headed the first-round voting with 44.2%, compared with 36.7% for Klerides and 18.6% for a joint DIKO-EDEK candidate, Paschalis Paschalides. Although DISY had previously declared its support for the Government's conduct of the settlement negotiations, in the election campaign Klerides distanced himself from Vassiliou's stance. This enabled DIKO and EDEK, both strongly opposed to the UN plan, to transfer their support to Klerides, who won 50.3% of the second-round vote. The new Government, appointed by the President-elect on 25 February, contained six DISY ministers and five from DIKO.

Despite his long-standing personal relationship with Denktaş, Klerides failed to obtain any significant compromise in the Turkish Cypriots' declared objections to the confidence-building measures at reconvened talks in New York during May and June 1993. Denktaş submitted counter-proposals urging international recognition of certain other parts of Turkish-controlled northern Cyprus, but these were interpreted by Klerides as an attempt to obtain a degree of international acceptance of the division of Cyprus, in opposition to the Greek Cypriot (and UN) insistence that the island should remain a single state.

Despite the recommendation of the new Turkish President, Süleyman Demirel, that Denktaş should adopt a more conciliatory approach to the negotiations, Denktaş failed to meet the Secretary-General's proposed deadline of mid-June 1993 for acceptance of the confidence-building measures. A mission to Athens, Cyprus and Ankara, undertaken by the UN Secretary-General's new Special Representative in Cyprus, Joe Clark, failed to foster any significant new initiative for peace.

An early general election in the 'TRNC' on 12 December 1993 partially resolved a long power-struggle between Denktaş and the Prime Minister, Derviş Eroğlu, in the former's favour. The UBP, once led by Denktaş but now advocating Eroğlu's openly pro-partition stance, remained the largest party in the Legislative Assembly, but failed to win an overall majority. The pro-Denktaş Demokrat Parti (DP—Democrat Party) and the left-wing Cumhuriyetçi Türk Partisi (CTP—Republican Turkish Party) thereupon agreed to form a coalition under the premiership of Hakki Atun, the DP leader (hitherto the Speaker of the Assembly). The new coalition supported the Denktaş policy that talks should continue, while at the same time confirming policy positions likely to ensure continued stalemate.

DEADLOCK ON CONFIDENCE-BUILDING MEASURES

Negotiations in the first half of 1994 on the UN-sponsored confidence-building measures centred on the proposed transfer to UN administration of the Turkish-held Varosha suburb of Famagusta (so that its former Greek Cypriot inhabitants might then return) and the reopening of Nicosia airport for use by both sides. Despite a further visit by Clark in May, no agreement could be reached, in particular because Denktaş claimed that the proposals envisaged greater concessions by the Turkish Cypriots than by the Greek Cypriots. In a report submitted to the Security Council in May, the UN Secretary-General again censured the Turkish Cypriot side for failing to show the political will needed to produce a settlement. In the following month, however, he amended this verdict by stating that there was 'a very substantial measure of agreement' and that the only obstacle to implementation of the confidence-building measures was disputed methodology. The Greek Cypriots countered that this assessment did not give 'the true picture' of the persisting differences between the two sides.

In a concurrent deterioration, at the end of May 1994 Denktaş warned that if Greek Cyprus was admitted to the EU without reference to the Turkish Cypriots, the 'TRNC' would opt for integration with Turkey. However, this warning did not deter Greek Cypriot spokesmen from welcoming an EU decision, in June, to include Cyprus in the next phase of enlargement. The Greek Cypriot Government was also gratified in July by a ruling of the European Court of Justice banning EU members from importing goods from the 'TRNC'. This ruling was condemned by the 'TRNC' authorities, who proceeded to organize large-scale public celebrations to commemorate the 20th anniversary of the Turkish invasion of the island. In late August the 'TRNC' Legislative Assembly sought co-ordination with Turkey on defence and foreign policy, and rejected a federal solution, urging instead 'political equality and sovereignty' for the Turkish Cypriots.

In Resolution 939, adopted on 29 July 1994, the UN Security Council effectively conceded that confidence-building measures were not a realistic possibility in the absence of agreement on fundamental issues. Yet another round of UN-sponsored talks reached deadlock by September, whereupon President Klerides demanded coercive UN measures to achieve a settlement and appealed for the support of the UN General Assembly. Pursuant to a November 1993 agreement placing Cyprus within 'the Greek defence area', joint Greek-Greek Cypriot military exercises were held for the first time in October 1994, matching similar military co-operation between the 'TRNC' and Turkey.

TURKISH CYPRIOT PRESIDENTIAL ELECTION, 1995

Atun resigned as 'TRNC' Prime Minister on 24 February 1995, after the CTP had opposed Denktaş's offer, made in advance of the scheduled presidential election, to distribute to 'TRNC' citizens the title deeds to property in the north owned by Greek Cypriots; however, after the UBP leader, Eroğlu, had rejected an invitation to form a government, the DP leader was reappointed in the following month. At the presidential election, conducted on 15 and 22 April, Denktaş for the first time failed to win an outright majority in the first round (receiving only 40.4% of the votes), although he achieved a comfortable 62.5% victory over Eroğlu in the second round of voting. Protracted interparty negotiations were then needed to produce a new Government, which was a further DP-CTP coalition under Atun's premiership.

In a forceful statement issued on 2 May 1995, Denktaş opined that war might result from unilateral Greek Cypriot accession to the EU, because this would constitute a form of *Enosis* with Greece (already an EU member) and would be in breach of international treaty stipulations that Cyprus was barred from joining any supranational grouping that did not include both Greece and Turkey. Two days later President Klerides led a visit to Athens by the Greek Cypriot National Council (consisting of the main party leaders) for a 'unity' meeting with Greek government leaders, at which he expressed gratitude for Greek support for his Government's EU application.

1996 GREEK CYPRIOT ELECTIONS—NEW 'TRNC' GOVERNMENT

In the wake of its success in achieving the Dayton peace accord for Bosnia and Herzegovina in November 1995, the US Administration under President Bill Clinton gave renewed attention to the Cyprus issue, regarding it as the remaining major source of instability in the eastern Mediterranean region to affect the allied countries. However, political instability in Turkey and the impending Greek Cypriot legislative elections precluded any progress being made in the early months of 1996.

Greek Cypriot elections to the House of Representatives were held on 26 May 1996. DISY remained the largest single party, with 20 seats (34.5% of the vote), slightly ahead of the opposition AKEL, which took 19 seats (33.0%). DIKO lost one of its 11 seats (16.4%), while the EDEK socialists retained only five seats (8.1%) and the new Kinema ton Eleftheron Dimokraton (KED—Movement of Free Democrats), led by ex-President Vassiliou, won the remaining two seats (3.7%). DISY accordingly remained the dominant party in a further coalition Government with DIKO. KED subsequently merged with ADISOK to form the Enomeni Dimokrates (EDE—United Democrats).

US diplomatic efforts on Cyprus gathered pace in June 1996, partly owing to Bill Clinton's desire to make substantive progress towards a settlement before the US presidential election in November. UN and EU endeavours to bring the sides together continued parallel to the US initiative, while in May the British Government appointed Sir David Hannay, the United Kingdom's former ambassador to the UN, to be its own special representative for Cyprus. President Klerides had talks with Clinton in Washington, DC, in mid-June, and at the end of the month the UN Security Council, unanimously adopting Resolution 1062, urged both sides to respond 'positively and urgently' to the Secretary-General's efforts to break the deadlock.

Following policy disagreements, the DP-CTP coalition Government in the 'TRNC' resigned in July 1996; the UBP authorized Eroğlu to begin talks with the DP, now headed by Serdar Denktaş (the President's son, who had been elected to this post in May), on forming a new government. After a successful conclusion to the negotiations, the protocol of the new DP-UBP coalition Government was signed in mid-August; ministers assumed their duties shortly thereafter, with Eroğlu replacing Atun as Prime Minister and Serdar Denktaş becoming Deputy Prime Minister.

1996 VIOLENCE IN THE UN BUFFER ZONE—CRISIS OVER RUSSIAN MISSILES

From mid-1996 intercommunal relations descended to some of their most hostile levels since 1974, as the result of a series of violent incidents in the UN buffer zone. In early June Turkish Cypriot forces shot and killed an unarmed Greek Cypriot soldier in the Nicosia sector, and in August a Greek Cypriot anti-partition demonstrator was beaten to death by Turkish nationalist extremists during a protest rally, at which an estimated 50 people were injured. The victim's funeral was followed by further violence, in which a Greek Cypriot was shot dead by Turkish Cypriot guards (as he attempted to remove a Turkish flag at a fortified post in the buffer zone), and a further 11 people, including two UN officials, were injured. Greek Cypriot outrage at the killings intensified when the Turkish Minister of Foreign Affairs, Tansu Çiller, visited the 'TRNC' the following day and warned that Turkey would continue to retaliate with force against those who insulted the Turkish flag. Tensions were further exacerbated in September when a Turkish Cypriot soldier was shot and killed, and another wounded, across the buffer zone, in the south-eastern sector, and in October another Greek Cypriot was shot dead by Turkish Cypriot forces near the British military base at Dhekelia.

In a landmark judgment delivered on 18 December 1996, the European Court of Human Rights (ECHR) ruled that Turkey, as the effective power in the 'TRNC', had breached the European Convention on Human Rights by denying a Greek Cypriot woman, Titina Loizidou, access to her property in Kyrenia since the 1974 invasion. Applauded by the Greek Cypriot Government, the ruling opened the way for compensation claims against Turkey by other displaced persons, although Turkey rejected the ruling and also refused to comply with the ECHR's decision in 1998 to award some US $900,000 to Loizidou in damages and costs.

A further severe crisis developed in January 1997, when it was confirmed that the Greek Cypriot Government had signed an agreement to purchase Russian S-300 surface-to-air missiles. Amid international criticism of the purchase, particularly by the USA, the 'TRNC' authorities described the agreement as an 'act of aggression', while the Turkish Government warned that it would be prepared to use military force to prevent deployment of the system. Mediation by the USA and other foreign governments succeeded in defusing the immediate crisis on the basis of an assurance by the Greek Cypriot Government that the missiles would not be deployed for at least 13 months. However, indications of continuing tension included a 'TRNC'-Turkish commitment to a joint defence strategy, whereby an attack on the 'TRNC' would be regarded as an attack on Turkey itself.

1997 KLERIDES–DENKTAŞ TALKS—EU ACCESSION NEGOTIATIONS SCHEDULED

Renewed international attempts at mediation prompted by the intercommunal crisis of mid-1996 in Cyprus resulted in meetings between Sir David Hannay and the two Cypriot leaders in October, as a result of which the British special representative announced that sufficient progress had been made to enable direct negotiations to resume, under UN auspices, in 1997. At the same time senior military commanders from both sides began UN-sponsored talks with the aim of defusing tension along the demarcation line.

In April 1997 major changes to the Greek Cypriot Government included the appointment of Yiannakis Kasoulides as Minister of Foreign Affairs. Two months later, Kasoulides welcomed President Clinton's appointment of Richard Holbrooke as US mediator on Cyprus, in the hope that Holbrooke would be able to repeat his success as the chief broker of the Dayton peace accord for Bosnia. Following proximity talks which had begun in March, Klerides and Denktaş attended their first direct discussions for three years on 9–12 July at Troutbeck, New York State (USA). The meetings were chaired by UN Special Envoy Diego Córdovez and were attended by the UN Secretary-General, Kofi Annan, and other Security Council representatives. Sufficient progress was made for further direct talks to be held by the two leaders in late July, in Nicosia, where agreement was reached regarding the implementation of measures to establish the fate of persons missing since the hostilities both prior to and during the 1974 invasion.

Meanwhile, the Greek Cypriot Government's objective of EU membership became a critical source of dissension in July 1997, when an EU summit in the Netherlands formally agreed that Cyprus would be included in the next phase of EU enlargement, on which negotiations were to begin in 1998. The decision was to apply to Cyprus as a whole, and was regarded by the EU as a possible device for bringing about a settlement that would preserve Cyprus as a single sovereignty. However, the Turkish Cypriot authorities categorically rejected any EU negotiations not based on Turkish Cypriot sovereignty, while the Turkish Government also opposed any accession by Cyprus to the EU that did not accommodate Turkish Cypriot demands or preceded the admittance of Turkey itself. On 20 July, at celebrations to mark the 23rd anniversary of Turkish military intervention on the island, President Denktaş and the Turkish Deputy Prime Minister, Bülent Ecevit, signed a joint declaration threatening to integrate the 'TRNC' into Turkey if EU negotiations with the Greek Cypriot administration commenced as planned.

Further formal intercommunal talks, which took place in Switzerland on 11–15 August 1997, demonstrated that the conceptual gulf between the two sides remained as wide as ever, notably in that Denktaş continued to insist on recognition of separate Turkish Cypriot sovereignty, while accusing both Klerides and the EU of having disregarded the rights of the Turkish Cypriot community. Talks broke down on 15 August, with Denktaş claiming that the Cypriot application for EU membership was illegal since it had not been made on behalf of the population of the whole island. Further meetings between Klerides and Denktaş were conducted in Nicosia on 26 September and 11 November—the latter hosted by Holbrooke during his first visit to Cyprus as official US mediator—but failed to break the deadlock. Relations worsened in December when an EU summit in Luxembourg issued a formal invitation to Cyprus to begin accession negotiations in 1998; the 'TRNC' responded by suspending its participation in intercommunal talks.

RE-ELECTION OF KLERIDES, 1998—MILITARY TENSIONS

The five DIKO ministers resigned from the coalition Greek Cypriot Government in early November 1997 (and were replaced by non-partisan technocrats), following an announcement by Klerides that he intended to seek a second presidential term with the endorsement of DISY. In the first round of the presidential election, conducted on 8 February 1998, Georghios Iacovou (with the support of AKEL and DIKO) won a narrow victory over Klerides; five other candidates, among them Vasos Lyssarides for EDEK and former President Vassiliou for EDE, were eliminated. However, in the second round of voting, conducted on 15 February, Klerides defeated Iacovou with 50.8% of the votes. The decision of EDEK, whose candidate had taken 10.6% of the votes in the first round of the election, to support Klerides in the second round had been crucial to his success. A new Government of national unity was sworn in on 28 February, including ministers from DISY, EDEK and EDE as well as several DIKO dissidents, although DIKO itself joined AKEL in opposition. Vassiliou was appointed chief negotiator for Cyprus at the EU accession talks, which were formally inaugurated on 31 March.

Meanwhile, there had been renewed tensions in January 1998 following the completion of a new Greek Cypriot military airfield at Paphos. In the absence of a Cypriot air force, the new airfield was intended to be an emergency base for Greek war planes, and was to be protected by the controversial missiles being purchased from Russia. Vociferous opposition from Denktaş prompted the Greek Government to emphasize that the new site had the status of a Greek military base, and thus any assault on the site would be regarded as an attack on a mainland military installation. There was further tension in mid-June when six Turkish war planes landed at a 'TRNC' airfield, in response to the landing of Greek military aircraft at Paphos the previous week. While Greek Cypriot and Greek spokesmen described the Turkish action as 'completely illegal', the US Department of State condemned both deployments as unhelpful to the peace process and urged an end to such actions.

At the end of June 1998, President Konstantinos Stefanopoulos of Greece paid an official visit to Cyprus (the first such visit by a Greek head of state since independence in 1960), during which he publicly envisaged 'a free and truly independent Cyprus', with equality for all its citizens; Stefanopoulos also appealed to the Turkish Cypriots to seize the opportunity offered by the prospective accession to the EU. Denktaş responded in August by elaborating his proposal for a confederation based on two sovereignties, and by again rejecting the resumption of intercommunal talks unless the Greek Cypriot Government suspended accession negotiations with the EU. In the following month the UN Secretary-General announced that efforts to resolve the differences between the two sides were to be renewed by the UN Deputy Special Representative for Cyprus, Dame Ann Hercus, who co-ordinated indirect talks between Klerides and Denktaş in October.

Parliamentary elections in the 'TRNC', conducted on 6 December 1998, resulted in gains for the UBP, which won 24 of the 50 contested seats, followed by the DP with 13, the Toplumcu Kurtuluş Partisi (TKP—Communal Liberation Party) with seven and the CTP with six. At the end of the month UBP leader Eroğlu was reappointed Prime Minister at the head of a new Government formed in coalition with the TKP.

NON-DEPLOYMENT OF RUSSIAN MISSILES—IMPACT OF 1999 KOSOVO CRISIS

Following intense pressure from the UN, the USA and the countries of the EU, on 29 December 1998 President Klerides announced that Russian-supplied S-300 missiles would not after all be deployed in Cyprus. A crucial factor in this decision had been the adoption by the UN Security Council (on 22 December) of two new resolutions pertaining to Cyprus: Resolution 1217 renewed the UNFICYP mandate and urged reunification as a single sovereign state (apparently dismissing notions of a confederation), while Resolution 1218 expressed 'grave concern at the lack of progress towards an overall political settlement' based on UN resolutions, and advocated a phased demilitarization of the island. For the first time the resolutions incorporated a requirement for compliance by the parties involved, although they contained no timetable for a settlement. After consultations with the Greek and Russian authorities, in January 1999 the Greek Cypriot Government confirmed that the missiles would instead be deployed on the Greek island of Crete, after the necessary preparations had been made to install them. Turkey claimed to have won a political victory over the decision to relocate the missiles, but maintained that it was equally opposed to their deployment on Crete. Klerides' decision aroused strong domestic criticism and prompted the withdrawal from the ruling coalition of EDEK, which had favoured adherence to the original plan. As a result, new Ministers of Defence and of Education and Culture were appointed to replace the EDEK representatives. A

further reorganization was announced in March following the resignation of the Minister of the Interior, Dinos Michaelides, as a result of allegations of corruption, which he strenuously denied.

During talks in Washington in February 1999, the Greek Cypriot Minister of Foreign Affairs, Yiannakis Kasoulides, secured an agreement from the US Government that a new diplomatic initiative on Cyprus would be launched following the Turkish general election scheduled for April. However, the ongoing political and humanitarian crisis in the Yugoslav province of Kosovo and resultant NATO air assaults on Yugoslavia, from late March, served to divert international attention from the Cyprus problem. While the 'TRNC' followed Turkey's lead in backing the Kosovan ethnic Albanians, the Greek Cypriot Government responded to massive popular support for the Serbian cause, aligning itself with Greece in urging a prompt negotiated solution that would preserve the territorial integrity of Yugoslavia. Although in May the Greek Cypriot Government agreed to observe sanctions against Yugoslavia proposed by NATO and the EU, it was emphasized that this decision had been taken in the 'national interest', given the paramountcy of eventual accession to the EU.

UN-SPONSORED PROXIMITY TALKS—RE-ELECTION OF DENKTAŞ, 1999–2000

An improvement in relations between Greece and Turkey following the Greek response to a major earthquake in north-west Turkey in August 1999 (see the chapter on Turkey) increased hopes of a settlement for Cyprus. Denktaş and Klerides attended UN-sponsored proximity talks in New York on 3–14 December, intended to lead to 'meaningful negotiations' and ultimately to a comprehensive settlement. The talks focused on the key issues of the distribution of powers, property rights, territorial issues and security arrangements. However, not least because of the continuing insistence of the Turkish Cypriots on recognition of 'TRNC' sovereignty, no substantive progress was made. The negotiations were also undermined by the EU summit in Helsinki, Finland, in December 1999, which, while calling for a settlement of the Cyprus issue, agreed that Turkey (now accorded official candidate status for membership of the union) could not block the accession of Cyprus to the EU if the island were to remain divided. However, the Turkish Cypriots continued to voice their objections to the ongoing EU-Cyprus negotiations, reiterating that the Greek Cypriot Government had no right to negotiate for the whole of Cyprus. A second round of talks followed in Geneva on 31 January–8 February 2000, but failed to break the deadlock.

A presidential election held in the 'TRNC' in April 2000 went to a second round of voting after Denktaş won 43.7% of the votes in the first round, conducted on 15 April, thus failing to secure the 50% necessary for an outright victory. However, Denktaş was subsequently declared to have won the election by default after his second-round challenger, Eroğlu, withdrew three days before the vote, scheduled for 22 April, in protest at what he alleged was 'interference' in the electoral process. In July thousands of Turkish Cypriots joined a demonstration in Nicosia to demand that Denktaş resign. The demonstration followed the arrest, some 10 days previously, of six people (including the editor and three journalists of a daily newspaper) on charges of spying for the Greek Cypriots; shortly before the arrests the newspaper had criticized the role of the Turkish military in the running of the 'TRNC'. The six were released shortly before the demonstration began.

The UNFICYP mandate had continued to be renewed at six-monthly intervals, and on 14 June 2000 the UN Security Council approved a further six-month renewal, calling on all states to respect the sovereignty, independence and territorial integrity of Cyprus. However, the approval of Resolution 1303 caused some controversy after the UN altered its wording to accommodate Greek Cypriot concerns that it implicitly recognized the legitimacy of the 'TRNC'. In protest at the altered wording (the resolution excluded any reference to the authority of the 'TRNC'), Turkish troops in early July advanced 300 m into the UN buffer zone near the Greek Cypriot village of Strovilia and established a check-point on the main road, refusing to withdraw despite UN and other appeals for a return to the *status quo ante*.

A third round of proximity talks opened in Geneva on 5 July 2000 (they had initially been scheduled for New York in May, but were postponed to allow Klerides to recuperate after major surgery). The talks were chaired by Alvaro de Soto, the Special Adviser on Cyprus to the UN Secretary-General, who indicated that the talks, which were adjourned on 12 July, had moved from procedural issues to a more substantive phase; however, although the talks resumed on 24 July–4 August, it appeared that no progress was made. A fourth round of negotiations, held on 12–26 September, was described as positive by de Soto, but a fifth round, on 1–10 November, highlighted familiar fundamental differences between the two sides.

TURKISH CYPRIOT WITHDRAWAL FROM TALKS— GREEK CYPRIOT ELECTIONS, 2001

The UN-sponsored peace process came to a halt on 24 November 2000 when the Turkish Cypriots announced they would not participate in the sixth round of proximity talks scheduled to begin in late January 2001. Denktaş cited the continuing refusal of the international community to accord recognition to the 'TRNC' as the reason for his withdrawal, which was decided at a 'TRNC'-Turkish summit in Ankara. A further crucial factor in determining the withdrawal was Ankara's expressed annoyance at the inclusion in newly published draft EU requirements for Turkish accession to the EU of a stipulation that Turkey should expedite a settlement of the Cyprus problem. In December Turkey secured adjustments to the EU text specifying that the Cyprus impasse would be covered by EU-Turkish 'dialogue' rather than in accession negotiations, although the Turkish side subsequently remained unyielding to international pressure in its refusal to rejoin the UN talks. It also took an increasingly belligerent line against the Greek Cypriot Government's EU accession course—on which rapid progress was being made—warning in April 2001 that unilateral EU entry by the Greek Cypriots would be a 'Pyrrhic victory' because the Turkish reaction would have 'no limits'.

The stalemate thus continued in the approach to Greek Cypriot parliamentary elections in May 2001, an additional negative factor being that the new US Administration of George W. Bush adopted a lower diplomatic profile than its predecessor on the Cyprus problem. The gulf between the Cypriot sides was further emphasized by an ECHR judgment on 10 May that found Turkey guilty of extensive violations of human rights in the Turkish-occupied area—in which it was deemed to have 'effective overall control'. Whereas the Greek Cypriot Government described the ruling as 'historic', and as its most significant legal victory over Turkey since the 1974 invasion, Turkey dismissed it as 'wrong', while Denktaş claimed that it justified his refusal to participate in further talks.

The Greek Cypriot general election, held on 27 May 2001, produced small but significant changes in the composition of the House of Representatives. AKEL became the largest single party, with 20 of the 56 seats (and 34.7% of the votes cast), overtaking DISY, which retained 19 seats (with 34.0% of the vote). DIKO's representation was reduced to nine seats (14.8%), the Kinima Sosialdimokraton (KISOS—Movement of Social Democrats, the successor party to EDEK) held only four seats (6.5%) and EDE one (2.6%). Three other parties won one seat each. When the new House convened in June, the AKEL leader, Demetris Christofias, was elected as its new president in succession to Spyros Kyprianou of DIKO (who had retired at the election), receiving crucial support from the DIKO members to defeat the DISY leader, Nicos Anastasiades. Observers saw the outcome of this contest (for the second most important post in the Greek Cypriot state hierarchy) as indicating the likely alignment of political forces in the presidential election due in 2003.

In the 'TRNC' the ruling coalition between the UBP and the TKP was terminated by the UBP in May 2001. It was replaced the following month by a coalition of the UBP and the DP, with Eroğlu continuing as Prime Minister and Salih Coşar (who had succeeded Serdar Denktaş as DP leader) becoming Minister of State and Deputy Prime Minister in a Government more firmly committed than its predecessor to the policy of President Denktaş on the Cyprus question.

RESUMPTION OF UN-SPONSORED TALKS—ISSUE OF EU ACCESSION, 2001–02

International diplomatic pressure on Turkey resulted in an agreement on the part of the Turkish Cypriot side to return to UN-sponsored negotiations, on the basis of the 'Nicosia Agreement' concluded between Klerides and Denktaş on 4 December 2001. This specified that there would be no pre-conditions to renewed talks; that all issues would be open for discussion; that the negotiations would continue 'in good faith' until a comprehensive settlement had been reached; and that 'nothing will be agreed until everything is agreed'. Formal, direct talks between the two leaders began on 16 January 2002 in the UN buffer zone in Nicosia, with Alvaro de Soto in attendance. In February the UN Security Council expressed the hope that a settlement would be reached by June, and this target date for a resolution of 'core' issues—defined as governance, security, territory and property—was reiterated by Secretary-General Kofi Annan during an official visit to Cyprus in May, despite growing pessimism regarding the progress of the talks. Although Klerides and Denktaş had held 51 separate negotiating sessions by the end of August, they failed to make any breakthrough, with the key obstacle continuing to be the Turkish Cypriot side's insistence on separate sovereignty for the 'TRNC'. Talks in Paris, France, in early September, hosted by Annan, similarly failed to break the impasse. Although the UN Secretary-General again expressed confidence that mutually acceptable elements of a comprehensive settlement did exist, it was generally considered that no substantive progress would be made before the legislative elections due to take place in Tukey at the beginning of November. Amid growing pressure for a settlement that would avert a potential crisis over wider EU enlargement, further talks between Annan and the Greek and Turkish Cypriot leaders were planned for early October in New York.

Parallel to, but separate from, the resumed UN talks, the Cyprus Government continued its EU accession negotiations, and by the end of August 2002 had finalized all but three of the 31 negotiating chapters. The expectation was that the negotiations would be completed by the end of 2002 and that Cyprus's accession treaty would be signed in the first half of 2003, leading to formal admission to the EU on 1 January 2004. EU leaders continued to stress that, while a pre-accession political settlement was highly desirable, it was not a precondition for the admission of Cyprus: in the absence of a settlement, the *acquis communautaire* would not apply to the Turkish-occupied area. However, the Turkish Government remained resolutely opposed to EU accession by the Greek Cypriot Government, claiming that such a course would be 'illegal' and repeatedly warning that it would take drastic countermeasures against any such 'unilateral' action.

Meanwhile, tensions had developed in Cyprus over activities at the British sovereign base area (SBA) at Akrotiri, where violent clashes occurred in July 2001 when local residents protested against the installation of a new communications antenna suspected of emitting dangerous radiation. The confrontation was defused by an agreement whereby experts would monitor radiation levels, but the British authorities subsequently rejected Greek Cypriot demands that the antenna should not be completed without the consent of the Greek Cypriot Government. Further tensions emerged in March 2002, when the Greek Cypriot Government expressed strong opposition to any British move to upgrade the Akrotiri and Dhekelia SBAs, following reports of plans to develop them into a 'forward operating base' for British and allied forces. The United Kingdom responded that under the 1960 independence settlement it was under no obligation to inform the Cyprus Government about any plans for the SBAs, and also confirmed that the SBAs would remain outside the EU upon Cyprus's accession.

In May 2002 Cyprus assumed a key role in the resolution of the prolonged siege by Israeli forces of the Church of Nativity in Bethlehem. Under agreement ending the crisis, 13 Palestinian militants who had been sheltering in the church were flown under international guard to Cyprus, prior to the dispersal of 12 of them into permanent exile in various EU countries (the 13th remained in Cyprus). It was widely considered that a principal motivation for the Greek Cypriot authorities in agreeing to receive the Palestinians was to demonstrate the strategic regional benefit that would result from Cyprus's admission to the EU. In the same month the Minister of the Interior, Christodoulos Christodoulou, was appointed as Governor of the Central Bank. He was directly replaced in the cabinet by Andreas Panayiotou.

In late July 2002 more than 90% of delegates at a special AKEL congress voted to support the candidacy of the DIKO leader, Tassos Papadopoulos, in the election for the Greek Cypriot presidency, due to be held in February 2003. AKEL's Secretary-General, Demetris Christofias, regarded as one of the most popular politicians in the Greek Cypriot region, stated that he had decided not to contest the presidency in the interests of avoiding political 'polarization'.

Economy

ALAN J. DAY

Geographically, Cyprus may be divided into four regions, distinguished by their natural and climatic features. These are the northern coastal belt, including the narrow Kyrenia mountain chain; the central plain, known as the Mesaoria, from Famagusta and Larnaca to Morphou Bay; the mountainous area of the south-centre, dominated by the Troödos massif, with the summit of Mt Olympus (1,951 m above sea-level) as its highest point; and the coastal plain of the south, running from a point west of Larnaca to Limassol and Paphos.

Since the middle of 1974, however, the most important division in Cyprus has been that between the areas to the north and south of the 'Attila line' which divides the island (see map, p. 247). The northern two-fifths of the country, under Turkish Cypriot control, is closely linked to the economy of Turkey, and has almost no economic contact with the south of the island. The unilateral declaration of independence by the 'Turkish Republic of Northern Cyprus' ('TRNC') in November 1983 reinforced the economic embargo, which has caused serious problems for the northern sector. Both areas suffered severe disruption as a result of the events of 1974. As well as the physical damage caused by the fighting, more than one-third of the total population of around 640,000 became refugees, some 180,000 Greek Cypriots fleeing to the south and about 45,000 Turkish Cypriots moving to the north. The collapse of essential services in many places reduced economic activity to a low level. Crops were not harvested, tourism ceased, and industrial buildings and plants were destroyed or lost their work-force.

THE SOUTHERN ECONOMY

Since 1974 the economies to the north and the south of the 'Attila line' have diverged sharply. The economy of the south made a remarkable recovery, despite having lost 38% of the island's territory, 70% of its productive resources, 30% of its factories, 60% of the tourist installations, the main port (Famagusta), 66% of the grain-producing land and 80% of the citrus fruit groves, all of which were on the northern side of the line. In 1975 the gross domestic product (GDP) was only two-thirds of the 1973 level, but during 1976 and 1977 production rose at an average of 18% per year. Even with the growth rate falling to an average 7% annually during 1978 and 1979, at the end of that period production in the southern part of the island was 12% higher than for the whole of Cyprus in 1973. Unemployment was reduced from almost 25% of the labour force in late 1974 to 1.8% in 1979, partly by the emigration of workers but largely through the promotion of labour-intensive industry and massive expansion of the construction sector, both for private housing and for development projects.

By 1980, however, it was clear that the post-1976 boom in the Cypriot economy would not continue at the same level. This was partly the result of the disappearance of short-term factors that had favoured growth: in 1977 market conditions in the Middle East and Europe were advantageous to Cypriot exports, and petroleum prices were temporarily stable, whereas by 1979 it was becoming difficult for agricultural products from Cyprus to penetrate the European market, while petroleum prices were once more rising sharply. However, there was also a deeper instability in the economy. Recovery was based on labour-intensive production by a low-wage work-force—wages in 1976 were lower than in 1973—but, with full employment from 1977, wage rises escalated. Between 1976 and 1979 real wages increased by an average of 10% annually, and in 1980 average wages nominally rose by 20% (6.5% in real terms). Rising wages

and the increasing cost of imported petroleum, among other factors, helped to increase inflation from an annual average of 4% in 1976–77 to 9.8% in 1979 and 13.4% in 1980. The Cyprus Government was also faced with widening balance-of-payments and budgetary deficits. Economic growth had been stimulated by tax incentives and direct government investment in development projects. Consequently, revenue failed to keep pace with expenditure. Despite loans from international agencies and foreign governments, and extensive borrowing abroad, Cyprus's reserves in 1980 were perilously low. The Government adopted a stabilization programme designed to reduce imports, to cut the budget deficit and to limit inflation. As a result, inflation declined from 10.8% in 1981 to 5% in 1985.

The 1980s saw a diversification of the Greek Cypriot economy, with less reliance being placed on the agricultural sector and increased emphasis on the development of more broadly-based services and industrial sectors—particularly tourism, shipping and financial services. Real GDP increased by an annual average of 5.6% in 1980–1985, and of 6.8% in 1985–90. The rate of growth was only 0.9% in 1991, but rose sharply to 9.9% in 1992 (partly a consequence of the introduction of value-added tax—VAT, see below). The Government's Five-Year Economic Plan for the period 1989–93, adopted in June 1989, envisaged annual growth of 5%. However, in 1993 the growth rate was only 1.8%, owing to the effects on the Cyprus economy of the European recession, before approaching the Government's 5% target in 1994 and 1995. The annual growth rate then decreased to 2.8% in 1996, and to 1.7% in 1997, before recovering to 5.0% in 1998, 4.5% in 1999, 4.8% in 2000 and 4% in 2001. Following more difficult economic conditions, particularly a slow-down in the tourist industry partly produced by the September 2001 suicide attacks on the USA, the GDP growth rate in 2002 was projected at 2.5%–3%.

In August 1991, in view of the government-controlled area's encouraging economic performance, the World Bank removed Cyprus from its official list of developing countries, thereby ending Cyprus's qualification for development loans at preferential rates. Nominal GDP in the Greek Cypriot sector increased from C£4,161.0m. in 1996 to C£4,370.6m. in 1997, C£4,693.7m. in 1998, C£5,017.5m. in 1999, C£5,486.9m. in 2000 and to a provisional C£5,867.2m. in 2001. At purchasing-power parity (PPP), GDP in the Greek Cypriot area increased from US $9,100m. in 1999 to $9,700m. in 2000, while in the Turkish Cypriot area GDP at PPP was estimated at $830m. in 1999.

The average level of unemployment decreased steadily from 3.6% of the registered labour force in 1986 to 1.8% in 1990; it fluctuated during the early 1990s and stood at 2.6% in 1995, before rising to 3.1% by December 1996 and to 3.4% by December 1997. It increased slightly, to 3.5% by December 1998, and rose again to 3.8% (11,785 persons) by December 1999. By December 2000 the rate had fallen to 3.4% (10,911 persons), but increased marginally, to 3.6% (11,365 persons), by December 2001 and continued to rise in the first half of 2002.

After a reduction in the average annual rate of inflation to 1.2% in 1986 (its lowest level for 20 years), an increase in economic activity caused the rate to rise again, reaching an annual average of 4.7% during 1990–95. The rate fell to 2.6% in 1995, before rising to 3.0% in 1996 and to 3.6% in 1997. In 1998 inflation declined to 2.2%, well within the 2.7% necessary for participation in the single European currency, and fell further to 1.6% in 1999. Inflation accelerated sharply to 4.2% in 2000, owing to higher energy and food prices, the depreciation of the Cyprus pound (because of its link with the euro) and an increase in the VAT rate from 8% to 10% on 1 July. Minimal price increases for local products and many imports resulted in the overall inflation rate being reduced to its underlying core rate of 2% in 2001, while by mid-2002 the annual inflation rate for the year was projected at 2%–2.5%.

A feature of economic policy since 1992 has been the gradual adaptation of economic practices and procedures to prepare for full membership of the European Community (EC, now European Union—EU), for which the Cyprus Government had applied in July 1990 (having achieved customs union with the EC from 1 January 1988). In addition to the introduction of VAT, in June 1992 the Government linked the Cyprus pound to the narrow band of the EC's exchange rate mechanism (ERM). Both the Vassiliou administration and its successor expressed support for a policy of economic harmonization with EC guidelines, including those detailed in the Treaty on European Union (which had been agreed by EC heads of government at Maastricht, the Netherlands, in December 1991) for eventual economic and monetary union. Full achievement of the Maastricht 'convergence' criteria was identified as a central objective of the Government's Strategic Development Plan for the period 1994–98, the three 'axes' of which were the preparation for Cyprus's accession to the EU; the technological upgrading, restructuring and modernization of the economy, with the general aim of creating the necessary conditions for a satisfactory growth rate within a climate of external and internal stability; and the improvement of the quality of life in Cyprus, with particular emphasis on the environment and on cultural development. Within the framework of the Plan, in October 1995 the Government announced a US $2,000m. programme of infrastructural projects.

In May 1993 the new Klerides Government announced a programme of austerity measures designed to reduce the budget deficit and the public debt (which totalled C£2,400m.). An increase in the rate of VAT from 5% to 8% was to take effect from October 1993, while higher taxes were to be imposed on petrol and cigarettes. A proposed end to the index-linking of wages to inflation encountered considerable opposition from trade unions. However, the economic stance of the new Government received endorsement from an IMF report, published in July, which warned that wage increases were surpassing productivity gains and eroding competitiveness, and from the Governor of the Central Bank of Cyprus, who later in the month urged broader deregulation of capital markets and speedier progress towards trade liberalization.

To signify its commitment to EU accession, the Greek Cypriot Government welcomed the introduction, on 1 January 1999, of the euro as the new unit of currency of 11 EU members, and maintained the existing parity of the Cyprus pound against the European currency at C£1 = €1.7086. EU accession was also the principal objective of the Government's Strategic Development Plan for 1999–2003. The Plan aimed to achieve the highest possible rate of growth consistent with macroeconomic stability, to restructure and modernize economic sectors to exploit comparative advantages and enhance competitiveness, to develop Cyprus as an international business and services centre, to improve the quality of life and the environment, and to modernize the public sector. GDP growth of an average of 4% per year was envisaged for the period of the Plan.

A report published by the IMF in May 2000 praised the Cyprus economy but warned that important policy decisions were needed if Cyprus was to qualify for accession to the EU. It also highlighted a number of negative indicators, including an inflation rate well above the EU average and the rising current-account and budget deficits. The Government was therefore urged to give priority to restoring macroeconomic stability, in particular by reducing the budget deficit to no more than 3% of GDP by 2001, by reducing credit growth and increasing indirect taxation, and by liberalizing capital markets. The Government responded by taking corrective measures to reduce the budget and current-account deficits (see Budget, Investment and Finance, below).

A report on the economy issued by the Greek Cypriot Government in May 2001 noted that unemployment, inflation and the budget deficit were all showing downward trends. The report also listed the country's recent economic achievements,

including average annual GDP growth in 1998–2000 of 4.8% (compared with an average of 2.7% in the EU and 3.7% globally), PPP income per caput of some US $16,000 in 2000 (the 16th highest in the world) and creation of the strongest economy among the 13 EU applicant countries. By June 2002 Cyprus had finalized all but three of the 31 policy chapters in its accession negotiations with the EU. The Government expected that the negotiations would be completed in the second half of 2002 and that it would sign a formal treaty early in 2003, providing for accession on 1 January 2004. Independent assessments agreed that, among the EU applicant countries, Cyprus was in joint lead with Slovenia in undertaking the required harmonization of domestic laws and regulations with the EU's *acquis communautaire*.

The regional financial importance of Cyprus was signalled by the opening of a stock exchange in Nicosia in March 1996. In February 1997 the Government approved a number of relaxations to the rules governing foreign investment in Cyprus and investment by Cypriots overseas—the aim being to create an environment of minimum intervention, in accordance with EU legislation. Allowing foreign investment in Cyprus provided that it 'does not pose a national risk, has no negative environmental impact and is not a burden on the economy', the new rules permitted foreigners to own 100% of share capital in companies in the clothing, footwear, furniture, wholesale and retail sectors, and up to 49% of share capital in those in the primary sector (agriculture, fisheries and forestry) and in the tourism and leisure sectors. From January 2000 most of the remaining restrictions on foreign investment in Cyprus were revoked for nationals of EU member states, although with the continued exceptions of the banking sector (where a 49% foreign ownership limit remained in force) and immovable property. Most restrictions on investment abroad by Cypriots were also lifted at the same time, except for portfolio investment in overseas companies and deposits with foreign banks. In March 2001, moreover, Cyprus-EU negotiators agreed that the remaining restrictions on capital movement would be abolished when Cyprus became a member of the EU.

The recovery of the tourist industry in 1997, combined with optimistic economic projections for 1998, produced a significant increase in investment activity on the Cyprus Stock Exchange (CSE) from December 1997, assisted by the announcement that the Bank of Cyprus would have a listing on the London Stock Exchange (the first such foreign listing of a Cypriot concern). The annual volume of CSE transactions doubled in 1998 compared with 1997, reaching a record value of C£337m. and generating a 17% increase in share prices overall. In May 1999 the CSE introduced electronic trading of shares, a further step towards the creation of a regional financial and business centre in Cyprus. The CSE continued to increase in value in 1999; share transactions in that year achieved a record value of C£3,858m. and aggregate capitalization of CSE-quoted companies reached a high of C£13,433m. in November. Under legislation adopted in December, a special levy was imposed on CSE share transactions in 2000–01, at a rate of 1% for legal entities and 0.6% for individual investors.

However, declining share prices in early 2000 culminated in a major correction in late March, when the CSE index fell to half its 1999 high and market capitalization of quoted companies decreased to less than C£8,000m. Further slides in the following months effectively wiped out the 1999 gains and inflicted heavy losses on new investors, some of whom staged angry demonstrations in protest against what they alleged were fraudulent activities by brokers with the connivance of the CSE authorities. The Government responded in August by announcing various measures to restore investor confidence, including a strengthening of the CSE's legal framework and the introduction of greater transparency in its operations. Nevertheless, the CSE all-share index continued on a downward trend, which accelerated following the September 2001 attacks on the USA. By mid-June 2002 the index had fallen below 100—compared with a high point of 848 at the end of November 1999.

THE NORTHERN ECONOMY

Since 1974 the economy of the area north of the 'Attila line' has not made nearly as much progress as the Greek Cypriot area, despite an extensive programme of development, based on aid from Turkey (estimated to amount to some 20% of projected budget expenditure in recent years). The cost to Turkey of maintaining its forces in northern Cyprus and supporting the northern economy is currently estimated at the equivalent of US $2,000m. per year, so that by 2001 the 27-year occupation was believed to have cost Turkey in excess of $50,000m.

Initial development priorities of the 'TRNC' authorities were the improvement of communications, irrigation, and the restoration of damaged citrus groves, in the pursuit of which the methods of central planning were used for some years. Beginning in 1978 successive development plans aimed, according to official statements, 'to secure the achievement of the highest rate of growth compatible with the maintenance of economic stability'. Other goals included increased capital investment, particularly in tourism and industry, balance-of-payments improvement, 'the more equitable distribution of economic burdens and national income', and 'the further expansion and improvement of the financial sector and social services'. From 1987, however, the emphasis switched to the encouragement of free-market economic activity, with priority being given to the development of trade, tourism, banking, education, transportation and the industrial sector.

Assessment of the real performance of the 'TRNC' economy has been notoriously difficult, because of the lack of objective data. Much of the statistical material issued by the northern authorities is not regarded as accurate by the Greek Cypriot side (or by many independent observers). According to official 'TRNC' figures, northern gross national product (GNP) increased by 87% in the period 1977–92, measured at constant 1977 prices. However, the annual growth target of 7.5% during the first Five-Year Plan (1978–82) was not thought to have been achieved: in 1981, for example, the 'TRNC' economy contracted by 7.5%. By the final year of the second Five-Year Plan (1983–87) GNP had officially risen to TL 5,684m. (at 1977 prices), compared with TL 3,810.5m. in 1977.

The targets of the third Five-Year Plan (1988–92) included an annual growth rate of 7%, but the out-turn was officially assessed at 4.6%, in part because of an actual 5.3% decline in 1991. Measured at 1977 prices, total GNP reached TL 7,125m. in 1992, according to official figures, which also claimed that GNP per head had increased by 66.4% over the period of the plan, to stand at US $3,343 in 1992 (compared with $2,009 in 1987). The sectors that were reported to have contributed most to economic growth in 1988–92 were manufacturing, construction, tourism and services, which yielded average annual growth rates of 9.2%, 7.7%, 9.6% and 7.2% respectively. After a 7.8% increase in 1992, GNP expanded by 5.9% in 1993 (well above the original projection), but contracted by 3.7% in 1994, to $554m., yielding a GNP per head of $3,093. According to official statistics, aggregate GNP rose to $755.7m. in 1995 and to $773.9m. in 1996, the latter figure resulting in annual GNP per caput of $4,222. In 1999 trade and tourism contributed 17.3% of GDP, industry 11.7%, agriculture 9.1% and transport and communications 11.6%. According to official statistics, aggregate GNP increased further, to $757.7m. in 1997, to $885.3m. in 1998, to $963.9m. in 1999 and to an estimated $1,099.3m. in 2000, when GNP per head was given as $5,263. Economic growth of 3.8% was recorded in 1997, increasing to 5.1% in 1998 before declining marginally, to an estimated 4.9%, in 1999 and to 4% in 2000.

The 'TRNC' has experienced a persistently high level of inflation, much of it 'imported' from Turkey, in that the Turkish lira is the currency in use and the local authorities have no control over the money supply. Having reached 93% in 1980, the annual inflation rate fell to 33% in 1982; it then rose again to an estimated 69% in 1990, before dipping to 61% in 1993. A further inflationary surge in 1994, to 215%, was reversed in 1995 to 72.2%, although the rate rose again in 1996 to 87.5% and declined slightly to 81.7% in 1997, before subsiding to 66.5% in 1998, 55.3% in 1999 and 53.2% in 2000. However, the rate increased to 76.8% in 2001. The official unemployment rate remained low in the 'TRNC', despite an increase of 11.8% in the working population in the period 1987–92, to a total of 74,037 (increasing to 76,454 in 1995). According to official figures, the unemployment rate declined from 1.8% of the labour force in 1987 to 0.9% (or 704 persons) in 1994 and to 0.7% (567 persons) in 1995. The official unemployment rate for 1996 was 1.2% of a

total labour force of some 79,400 people. In the period 1997–99 the unemployment rate was officially put at around 1%, the total work-force in 1999 being just under 87,000. In 2000 average unemployment rose slightly, to 1.3%, in a working population of 89,000.

The liberal trade policies adopted by the 'TRNC' since 1987 have resulted in the establishment of trading relations with over 60 countries—mostly via Turkey, owing to the non-recognition of the 'TRNC' as a political entity. Its volume of trade was officially said to have increased from US $276.1m. in 1987 to $426m. in 1992, with imports increasing by 68% from $221m. to $371.4m. and exports decreasing from $55.1m. to $54.6m., with the result that the trade deficit grew from $165.9m. in 1987 to $316.8m. in 1992. Net tourism revenues rose from $103.5m. in 1987 to $175.1m. in 1992 (i.e. by an average of 11% annually), while other invisible earnings increased by 15% per annum, so that the current-account deficit in 1992 was only $23.4m. Moreover, a positive capital movements balance, of $41.7m. in 1992, produced an overall balance-of-payments surplus of $18.3m. in 1992, compared with $23.1m. in 1987. After falling to $275m. in 1993, the trade deficit showed a further official contraction to $233.2m. in 1994, when net receipts from tourism were $172.9m. and from other invisibles $56.1m., so that the current-account deficit was only $4.2m. In 1995 both exports and imports increased, and the deficit widened to $298.8m.; net receipts from tourism were $218.9m., and other invisibles yielded $67.6m., resulting in a current-account deficit of only $12.3m. In 1996 imports of $318.4m. and exports of $70.5m. resulted in a crude trade deficit of $247.9m., although net receipts from tourism of $175.6m. and other invisibles reduced the current-account deficit to $2m. Foreign-exchange reserves at the end of 1996 totalled $510.9m. In 1997 the trade deficit increased to $298.9m. (from imports of $356.6m. and exports of $57.7m.), while in 1998 the trade deficit expanded to $377.1m. (from imports of $430.5m. and exports of only $53.4m.). The current-account deficit in 1997 was $41.0m., but the overall balance of payments (including net capital movement of $54.9m.) was $13.9m. in surplus. In 1998 a current-account deficit of $103.1m. was more than offset by net capital movement of $194.4m., yielding an overall balance-of-payments surplus of $91.3m. Official figures for 1999 gave the trade deficit as $360.3m. (from imports of $412.7m. and exports of $52.4m.) and the current-account deficit as $90.3m., the corresponding provisional figures for 2000 being $424.9m. and $74.6m.

From August 1990 the northern economy encountered major difficulties as a result of the collapse, with debts of some £1,300m., of Polly Peck International, a fruit-packaging, tourism and publishing conglomerate based in the United Kingdom but with substantial interests in the 'TRNC'. In December 1990 charges of theft and fraud were preferred against the Turkish Cypriot chairman of the conglomerate, Asil Nadir, whose various companies were estimated to have provided more than one-third of the GDP in the 'TRNC', accounting for 60% of total exports. Pending Nadir's trial, British administrators of the collapsed concern attempted to locate the conglomerate's assets in the 'TRNC', but encountered legal and political obstacles. Further complications arose when Greek Cypriot authorities claimed that several of Polly Peck's major properties in the 'TRNC' had been expropriated from Greek Cypriots after 1974. In May 1993 Nadir fled to the 'TRNC', claiming that he could not expect a fair trial from the British authorities. It was reported that he intended to revive the remnants of the Polly Peck empire in northern Cyprus. Whether or not he had the official support of the 'TRNC' authorities in this endeavour remained unclear. In mid-2001 legal and other efforts by British administrators to recover Polly Peck assets in the 'TRNC' were still in progress.

Further damage was done to the 'TRNC' economy by a European Court of Justice ruling in July 1994 whereby EU member states were banned from importing goods originating from the 'TRNC'. Under an earlier decision, the Council of Ministers of the then EC had enjoined in 1983 that exports from the Turkish-controlled area of Cyprus would be allowed to enter EC countries only if accompanied by documents from the Greek Cypriot Government, and that such goods also had to pass through ports controlled by that administration. However, this restriction had been evaded by the 'TRNC' by use of Turkey as an export channel, and the United Kingdom, in particular, had been prepared to import goods from northern Cyprus as long as the export documents did not bear the stamp of the 'TRNC'. The court ruling stated, *inter alia*, that 'co-operation is excluded with the authorities of an entity such as that established in the northern part of Cyprus, which is recognized neither by the Community nor by the member states'. It was subsequently reported that the United Kingdom and other EU governments were taking measures to ensure compliance with the ruling, one consequence of which was that hundreds of 'TRNC' textile workers were made redundant.

Agreements signed by Turkey and the 'TRNC' in 1990 envisaged the eventual replacement of the Turkish lira in the 'TRNC' by a local currency, backed by the Turkish central bank (as well as the creation of a full customs union between the two entities), but progress on achieving these goals was slow. In January 2000 the Turkish Ministry of Finance issued a decree setting an official exchange rate between the Turkish lira and the Cyprus pound (TL 952,000 = C£1) for the first time since 1974. The main factor in this decision was the need to discourage Turkish Cypriots from changing Cyprus pounds (in which they are often paid) on the black market.

The major financial crisis in Turkey in February 2001 and the 30% devaluation of the Turkish lira directly affected the 'TRNC', where resultant price increases and non-payment of state salaries and pensions provoked protest demonstrations and opposition calls for the Government to move away from economic dependence on Turkey. The crisis therefore strengthened Turkish Cypriot elements that favoured participation in Cyprus's accession negotiations with the EU and the restoration of economic unity in the island. The new Government that took office in June 2001 undertook to pursue free-market polices and to accelerate privatization, while 'keeping in mind the country's social structure', and also to pursue the creation of a joint economic zone with Turkey.

AGRICULTURE

Until quite recently agriculture was the single most important economic activity in Cyprus, but in the Greek Cypriot sector agriculture has in recent years been superseded in importance by tourism, manufacturing and financial services. In 1974 agriculture employed 33% of the island's labour force. In 2000 some 20% of the northern sector's working population were engaged in agriculture, a sector which contributed 9.1% of GDP in 2001, according to provisional figures; in the south the corresponding figures were 9% (in 2000) and 3.7% (according to provisional 2001 figures), respectively. The chief crops in both parts of the island are citrus fruits, potatoes, olives, carobs, tobacco, wheat and barley.

After the division of the island in 1974, the Government of the Republic of Cyprus initiated a series of emergency development plans in which agriculture and irrigation featured prominently. Loans were given to farmers, and agricultural production responded rapidly. Most of the island's citrus trees were in the north, so they were replaced as the main agricultural product in the south by potatoes and other vegetables. Total exports of agricultural products (mainly citrus fruits and potatoes) accounted for more than one-third of the value of all domestic exports from the government-controlled area in 1977. Following a disappointing year in 1978, exports of fruit and vegetables recovered in 1979, largely owing to an increase in the production and export of citrus fruits, grapes and wine. Although potatoes remained the single most important crop, the importance of fruits and wine continued to grow throughout the 1980s, and, despite periodic drought conditions, agricultural production increased by an annual average of 1.5% in 1989–92.

After expanding by 13% in 1995, agricultural production fell by 3% in 1996 and by 19% in 1997. Severe drought in 1997 caused production of cereals to decrease to 47,780 metric tons, while the potato crop was badly hit by frost, with the result that exports fell dramatically, to 35,218 tons. Exports of citrus fruits, at 80,410 tons, were slightly below 1996 levels. The total value of raw agricultural exports fell by 32.6% in 1997 to C£35.9m., although meat production expanded by 4.5%, the largest increases being recorded in the production of beef and poultry. Agricultural output recovered partially in 1998, increasing by about 14% over the previous year, mainly owing to a large increase in production of cereals (to 67,000 tons), while

livestock production remained static. Although exports of citrus fruit contracted to 59,221 tons, exports of potatoes more than doubled in 1998, to 89,000 tons, contributing to a 13% increase in the value of raw agricultural exports, to C£40.5m., of which potatoes accounted for C£19m. and citrus fruit C£12.7m. The agricultural production index (1995 = 100) declined to 88.0 in 1997, but rose to 96.3 in 1998.

Despite continuing water shortages, the agricultural production index rose to 103.4 in 1999, during which year the value of aggregate output rose to C£357m., including C£174.1m. in crop production and C£139m. in livestock production. A further substantial increase in cereals production in 1999, to 127,100 metric tons, was supplemented by a rise in production of potatoes to 161,500 tons (of which 116,831 tons were exported), of citrus fruits to 119,100 tons (of which 68,253 tons were exported), and of olives to 14,000 tons. However, the value of raw agricultural exports fell to C£36.5m. in 1999, with potatoes accounting for C£14m. and citrus fruits for C£13.8m. In 2000 the agricultural production index fell by 12% compared with 1999, with potato exports falling sharply to 71,836 tons (worth C£12.3m.) and citrus fruit exports to 61,391 tons (worth C£11.7m.). Official figures released in December 2000 showed that in the period 1993–2000 the Government had committed C£430m. to supporting the agricultural sector, it being stated that all possible assistance would continue to be given to farmers with the aim of restructuring and upgrading the sector to meet modern challenges. Agricultural output recovered strongly in 2001, when the production index showed a 9% rise over 2000 and the value of raw agricultural exports increased by 29%, to C£41.7m., of which potatoes accounted for C£17.5m. and citrus fruits C£13.7m. Exports of products of agricultural origin fell slightly in value in 2001, to C£25.6m. (from C£26.2m. in 2000), of which halloumi cheese was the most important item—with exports worth C£6.8m.

The Paphos project, completed in 1983 at a cost of C£24m., involved the irrigation of some 5,000 ha along the south-western coast, to facilitate the production of tropical fruits such as mango, avocado and papaya, as well as grapes and early vegetables. The Government is currently working on the Southern Conveyor Project, the completed first phase of which carries water from the mountainous region of western Cyprus to the main potato-growing area in the south-east of the island. The next phase of the project, completed in 1994, increased water supplies to Nicosia, Larnaca and Limassol, and in April 2000 a further phase was completed with the inauguration of a water conveyor from the Tersephanou treatment plant to Nicosia. The project is the largest water treatment and irrigation programme ever undertaken on the island, and total costs are expected to amount to C£200m. Another major investment is the Pitsilia Integrated Rural Development Project, which aims to stem the tide of rural depopulation by doubling the irrigated area in the mountainous central regions of the island.

In early 1992 the Greek Cypriot Government approved initial plans for the construction of a number of desalination plants, intended to compensate for the shortfall in water resources resulting from inconsistent rainfall. The first such plant, at Dhekelia on the southern coast, became operational in 1997, providing 20,000 cu m of water per day. By mid-1998 one of the most protracted droughts of the 20th century had reduced reservoirs to their lowest ever levels, obliging the authorities to institute stringent rationing and conservation measures. Government backing was also given to promising new research by the Cyprus Higher Technical Institute into the use of applied solar energy in reducing the high energy costs of the desalination process. In April 2000, following winter rainfall one-third below the normal average, the Government announced that restrictions would be placed on water supply for households and agriculture during the summer. In May plans were announced for the creation of a floating desalination unit as a two-year transitional measure to increase water supply.

A second permanent desalination plant, located near Larnaca airport and having a capacity of 52,000 cu m per day, was inaugurated in April 2001, and was said by government ministers to herald a new era in which water supply would be assured to domestic consumers—although the agricultural sector would continue to depend mainly on rainfall for some time to come. The Government stressed that other areas of water policy would continue to be pursued, including treatment of waste water for irrigation, enrichment of aquifers, exploitation of subterranean brackish water, and development of crops that require less water to flourish. After several years of semi-drought conditions for agriculture, heavy rainfall during the winter of 2001/02 replenished reservoirs and created the conditions for a further recovery in crop output. On the inauguration of the Tamassos Dam in Nicosia district in May 2002, the Government claimed that in proportion to its size and population Cyprus ranked first among EU member countries and applicants in the number of its water reservoir dams.

In February 2002 the Government announced a new 10-year strategy for the sustainable development of forests aimed at achieving wider participation in afforestation and preservation measures on both state-owned and privately-owned land. Particular objectives included the development of tourism and leisure facilities in forest areas and the promotion of a 'green conscience' in villages adjacent to forests. Against the plan's annual cost of some C£10m., potential indirect financial gains were estimated at C£40m. a year by the Government.

The Turkish Cypriot north inherited about 80% of the island's citrus groves, all the tobacco fields, 40% of the carobs, 80% of carrots and 10%–15% of potatoes. Nevertheless, agriculture in the north has lagged behind that of the south. In the chaos that followed the fighting, many citrus trees were neglected and died, or contracted diseases. Production resumed gradually, with exports of citrus fruit rising from 66,174 metric tons in 1976/77 to 96,637 tons in 1980 and 115,163 tons in 1982. The growing importance of citrus fruit in the Turkish Cypriot economy was reflected in the fact that the value of citrus fruit exports in 1986 totalled US $28.5m. (54.8% of total export revenue), although in 1987 the value of citrus fruit exports declined to $22.5m. and the proportion of total export revenue derived from citrus fruit decreased to 40.9%. In 1990–91 the collapse of Polly Peck International (see above) seriously disrupted the northern citrus fruit industry, resulting in the closure of some processing plants and severely reducing export volumes. Agricultural exports from the 'TRNC' were valued at $24.3m. in 1993, representing 44.6% of total exports, and increased to $25.7m. and 48.1%, respectively, in 1994. However, the European Court of Justice ruling in July 1994, effectively barring the import of 'TRNC' goods and produce by EU countries unless certificated by the recognized Cypriot authorities, had damaging consequences. In 1995 figures showed that agricultural exports had decreased to 40.0% of the total, valued at $26.9m., although in 1996 there was a partial recovery to $31.0m., representing 44.0% of total export value. In 1998 the total value of agricultural production in the 'TRNC' increased to TL 18,075,858.1m. from TL 8,278,463.6m. in 1997. In 1999 this figure increased again, to TL 32,647,771.2m. The share of agricultural products in total exports was 37.0% in 2001. In that year 16.6% of the working population were engaged in agriculture.

Water shortage has also been a persistent problem in the 'TRNC', necessitating the importation of water from Turkey by tanker and other means. In January 2000 a Turkish-led international consortium announced that construction of a 78-km water pipeline between Turkey and the 'TRNC' would begin in late 2000. Since the new pipeline's annual capacity of 75m. cu m would be well in excess of 'TRNC' requirements, it was expected that the consortium would seek to sell any surplus water to the Greek Cypriots.

INDUSTRY, MANUFACTURING AND SERVICES

Industry, also, was severely affected by the war of 1974. It was estimated that the Greek Cypriots lost 70% of gross domestic manufacturing output, yet the growth of this sector from 1975 was spectacular. Government incentives for investment, combined with a decline in real wages, stimulated a rapid expansion of manufacturing industry, especially in small-scale labour-intensive plants producing goods for export. The most striking success in manufacturing in the late 1970s and 1980s was achieved by the textiles and footwear sectors, with exports rising from C£3.2m. in 1974 to C£82m. in 1991, representing some 30% of total domestic export earnings. During the period 1979–88 output in the industrial sector increased by an annual average of 3% (and in the manufacturing sector by 4.5%),

although the sector's share of overall GDP fell from 33% in 1979 to 27% in 1989.

In the period 1989–92 the output of the manufacturing sector increased at an average rate of 3% per year, compared with the planning target of 5% annually. Failure to attain the projected growth rate was attributed to adverse conditions in major markets, such as the United Kingdom and the Arab states. From the late 1980s the service industries, such as banking, insurance and consultancy, grew at a remarkable rate and emerged as an important part of the Greek Cypriot economy. By the end of 1994 more than 17,000 foreign companies were registered in the Greek Cypriot sector, although only about 10% maintained offices on the island. In the period 1989–92 the services sector expanded at an average annual rate of 8% in real terms, exceeding the original planning target of 5.7%. In this period all service areas, both those directly connected with tourism (e.g. hotels, restaurants and transport) and other activities (e.g. commerce, communications, banking and professional services), expanded at substantially higher rates than had been projected. By 1995 the services sector was providing 69.8% of GDP and engaging 64% of the employed labour force, while industry contributed 24.7% of GDP and engaged 25.3% of the employed labour force.

Over the 10-year period 1989–98 the average annual rate of expansion of the industrial sector slowed to 2% (and that of manufacturing to 0.4%), so that in 1998 it contributed 22.4% of aggregate GDP and engaged 22% of the employed labour force (as against 71.3% and 68% respectively for services). The aggregate value of manufacturing output at current market prices rose from C£1,296m. in 1995 to C£1,553m. in 2000, although the manufacturing production index (1995 = 100) fell to 95.4 in 1998 before rising to 96.3 in 1999 and to 100.1 in 2000. Within the sector, food products, beverages and tobacco formed substantially the largest component in 2000, contributing output valued at C£573m., followed by refined petroleum products (C£162m.), other non-metallic mineral products (C£124m.) and basic metals and fabricated metal products (C£109m.). During 1995–2000 clothing and textiles lost their status as the largest manufacturing category, the value of output at current market prices falling from C£150.3m. to C£97.5m., while footwear and leather, in decline since the late 1980s because of Asian competition based on cheaper labour, fell from an output value of C£31m. in 1995 to C£22m. in 2000. The value of domestic manufactured exports rose from C£164m. in 1995 (including C£44m. from clothing and textiles as the largest category) to C£187m. in 2000 (when the most important category was pharmaceuticals, at C£31m.).

In 2001 the manufacturing production index fell by 2.6%, to 97.5, with the food, beverages and tobacco sectors showing a 7.3% decrease and textiles a decline of 3.4%. However, the value of domestic exports of manufactured goods increased slightly, to C£137.8m., with declines in exports of textiles and cigarettes, to C£18.5m. and C£10.1m. respectively, being offset by a 27% increase in the value of exports of pharmaceutical products to C£35.9m.

The construction sector grew rapidly after the 1974 Turkish invasion, with an average annual growth of 40% in 1975–79. The most important growth area was the housing sector, which provided accommodation for refugees. A record 9,449 units of housing were constructed in 1979. The manufacturing and construction sectors were hampered, in the early 1980s, by the adverse effects of the Government's measures to deflate the economy and by the accumulated results of wage inflation over several years. However, the construction sector enjoyed a period of rapid growth in the late 1980s, contributing C£240m. (10%) to GDP in 1990; in that year authorized building permits increased by 47% in value and by 22% in volume, in comparison with 1989. The number of authorized building permits decreased from 7,259 in 1995, to 7,156 in 1996 and to 6,614 in 1997. Construction activity showed a sharp decline in 1997, as indicated by the quantity index of the main construction materials for local use, which during 1997 fell by 6% (compared with a marginal decline of 0.2% in 1996). There was a further decline in authorized building permits in 1998, to 6,558. This particularly affected the hotel and tourist apartment sector, which declined by 59% in 1998, although there was a substantial increase in the volume of permits granted for commercial buildings. Gross output of the construction sector at current market prices was valued at C£650m. in 1998, in which year 6,599 new dwellings were completed (compared with 7,148 in 1997). The number of building permits granted fell further, to 6,429 in 1999 and 6,096 in 2000, but increased to 6,499 in 2001, in which year local sales of cement increased by 12%, to 1.1m. metric tons. Mining and quarrying output was valued at C£19.7m. in 1995, increasing to C£26.4m. in 2000, while the sector's production index (1995 = 100) rose from 122.8 in 1998 to 135.2 in 2000. It fell to 131.7 in 2001, when production was valued at C£25.3m. (compared with C£26.4m. in 2000). Production of sand, gravel and road aggregate (the bulk of this sector's output) increased from 6.2m. tons in 1995 to 9.6m. tons in 2000, valued at C£20.1m., and to just under 10m. tons in 2001, also valued at C£20.1m.

Although the labour market loosened somewhat in the early 1980s, an increase in economic activity, beginning in 1986, resulted in a shortage of skilled labour. In conditions of effective full employment in 1990, the Government authorized the recruitment of 1,600 additional foreign workers (mainly from Bulgaria and Poland) to fill vacancies in the construction and manufacturing sectors. In the early years after 1974 the Government encouraged the temporary emigration of workers as a solution to unemployment. Now the emphasis is more on encouraging workers to return, although their remittances are still important to Cyprus's foreign reserves. By mid-1992 renewed labour shortages had induced the Greek Cypriot Government to authorize the recruitment of another 8,000 foreign workers (some 2%–3% of the labour force), although the maximum contract period was restricted to two years because of fears that permanent immigration might engender social problems. In 1999 the Government imposed a moratorium on the issuing of work permits to foreigners, announcing in July 2000 that the freeze would be maintained for the foreseeable future, although with some exceptions for the tourism industry and certain other sectors. Because of these exceptions, the number of foreign workers in the government-controlled area rose sharply in 2001, to 34,500, over 30% higher than in 2000 and equivalent to 10% of the total labour force.

The Turkish-occupied area has few industrial resources. The share of industrial exports in total 'TRNC' exports, however, increased from 28.3% (US $14.7m.) in 1986 to 55.0% ($30.0m.) in 1993, before falling slightly to 51.3% ($27.4m.) in 1994. The textile and clothing industry has grown rapidly since the early 1980s (although most of the raw material has to be imported), overtaking citrus fruit as the largest source of export revenue, with earnings of $21.5m. (40.2% of the total) in 1998. The share of manufacturing in total exports rose from 61.2% in 1999 to 68.0% in 2000.

It is estimated that 90% of Cyprus's mining operations are in the Greek zone, while the Turkish zone has no petroleum refinery. Hitherto also lacking electricity-generating capacity, the 'TRNC' was reported, in July 1994, to be about to open its first power plant, located near Kyrenia and financed by Turkey; however, an explosion at the site rendered the start-up date uncertain. Meanwhile, the Cyprus Electricity Authority was continuing to supply electricity to both zones and the Turkish north's debt for unbilled consumption had reached some US $270m. by the end of 1993. A successful energy conservation programme is under way in the Greek Cypriot sector, involving the exploitation of solar and wind energy and the development of hydroelectricity potential. Gross electricity production in the government-controlled area rose from 3,139m. kWh in 1999 to 3,370m. kWh in 2000, while billed consumption rose from 2,785m. kWh in 1999 to 3,011 kWh in 2000. In 2001 gross electricity production increased to 3,551m. kWh and billed consumption to 3,125m. kWh.

In January 2001 the Greek Cypriot Government approved plans for the concentration of all refining and energy production facilities at Vassiliko on the southern coast. The Vassiliko Energy Centre would be completed by 2008 and would host all existing and new electricity generation and oil refining installations from 2010. The Government subsequently confirmed that on cost and environmental grounds Cyprus would eventually switch to the use of natural gas rather than oil for generating electricity. To that end, it entered into talks with Syria and Egypt on the supply of Egyptian natural gas to Cyprus via Syria and an underwater pipeline, stating that this was its preferred solution. However, the option of importing liquefied gas by tanker was also being investigated.

TRANSPORT AND COMMUNICATIONS

As part of a programme of economic diversification, the Greek Cypriot sector has become a major maritime trading centre. From 1989 to mid-1992 the number of shipping companies registered in Cyprus doubled to more than 700, making the Cyprus registry the fastest growing in the world. By the end of 1996 Cyprus had climbed to fifth position in terms of displacement, which totalled more than 23m. grt. By December 2000 Cyprus had slipped to sixth position, having 1,475 ocean-going ships on its registry with a combined displacement of 23.2m. grt. Under a new policy introduced in January 2000 to improve the safety record of Cyprus-registered ships, the age-limit for registration was reduced from 17 to 15 years. These and other quality improvements resulted in the Cyprus registry increasing to some 2,200 vessels by mid-2002, including 1,675 ocean-going ships. In 2001 the shipping sector contributed 2% of GDP, earning some C£100m., and employed about 5,000 people. The Government points out that the accession of Cyprus to the EU will boost the EU's combined shipping fleet by 25% and increase its share of world shipping from 16% to 20%.

Famagusta formerly handled 83% of Cyprus's freight traffic but now that it is in Turkish hands it has been largely superseded by Larnaca and Limassol. In 1996 a total of 5,109 vessels visited Greek Cypriot ports, of which 3,747 visited Limassol. The number of vessels calling at Greek Cypriot ports rose to 4,858 in 1999 from 4,476 in 1998. Unloadings of sea freight fell to 5.2m. metric tons in 2001 (from 5.3m. tons in 2000), while loadings declined to 1.4m. tons (from 1.6m. tons in 2000). Port development schemes have been instituted at Larnaca and Limassol, and a new port is also under development at Paphos.

The two international airports in the Greek Cypriot area, at Larnaca and Paphos, handled more than 1,100 scheduled flights per week by 36 international airlines in 1999, as well as flights by 84 charter companies. Aircraft landings rose from 23,590 in 1998 to 24,86 in 1999, 26,540 in 2000 and 29,195 in 2001. In November 2001 the Government secured parliamentary approval for plans to privatize the operation and development of the two international airports, following which a short-list of five international consortia was drawn up for the award of the contract in September 2002. It was expected that the first phase of the development of Paphos airport, increasing its capacity to 2m. passengers a year, would be completed by 2004 at a cost of C£50m. and that the first phase of the Larnaca development, increasing its capacity to 7.5m. passengers a year, would be completed by 2005 at a projected cost of C£170m. Second-phase development of the two airports, to be completed by 2010, was expected to cost a further C£50m. Motor vehicle registrations totalled 459,106 in the Greek Cypriot area by the end of 2001, in which year the number of new vehicle registrations rose significantly to 38,075 (compared with 32,165 in 2000), with registrations of private saloon cars increasing by 19%.

The Greek Cypriot Government has given priority to establishing Cyprus as a centre for regional telecommunications and as a staging-post for satellite communications between Europe, the Middle East and Asia. The sector is currently dominated by the state-owned Cyprus Telecommunications Authority (CYTA), although plans were confirmed in 1999 for opening the sector to competition and private participation in accordance with the requirements of eventual accession to the EU. In 1998 the number of direct exchange lines in the government-controlled area reached 404,710, corresponding to 61% of the population (well above the EU average), while mobile telephone subscribers rose to 108,183. In 1999 there were 636 telephone lines per 1,000 people and five internet service providers (ISPs).

In March 2002 the Government unveiled plans to ensure that Cyprus maintained its prominent position in the digital economy, including special incentives for small and medium-sized companies to embrace digital information technology (IT) and electronic commerce. Official figures showed that IT investment had increased by an average of 15% per year in the period 1996–2000 and that 33% of households possessed a personal computer, with 20% having access to the internet.

TOURISM

Tourism was one of the areas of the Greek Cypriot economy that was most adversely affected by the 1974 war, as 90% of the island's hotels came under Turkish Cypriot control. Following the introduction of a government loan plan, however, the number of hotel beds increased from a low point of 3,880 in 1975 to 18,197 in 1985. Tourist receipts rose to C£71m. in 1980, with 353,375 visitors. The sector continued to expand rapidly in the 1980s, becoming the Republic of Cyprus's largest source of income, with receipts totalling C£257m. in 1986 from 900,727 tourist arrivals. There were an estimated 47,500 tourist beds (many of them in self-catering accommodation) in 1988, with projects to provide a further 15,500 already in progress. Employment in the hotel and restaurant sector increased to 24,000 in 1990, accounting for almost 10% of the employed labour force.

By 1990 the annual total of tourist arrivals had increased to 1,561,479 (of whom 44% were from the United Kingdom). Receipts from tourism in that year totalled C£573m., representing an increase of 13% over the 1989 total (compared with a 27% increase between 1988 and 1989). In promoting the industry, the Greek Cypriot authorities laid emphasis on the desirability of developing 'high-value' tourism (as opposed to the 'package' holiday trade) and on sustainable tourist development. In 1996 efforts were mounted to attract more tourists from the USA, although the United Kingdom, Scandinavia and Germany continued to provide the majority of visitors to the island. Although tourist arrivals in that year declined slightly, to 1,950,000, with receipts from tourism totalling C£780m. (compared with 2,100,000 arrivals and receipts of C£813m. in 1995), tourism revived in 1997, largely owing to the strength of sterling against the Cyprus pound, the economic upswing in most EU countries and the restrained pricing policy followed by Cypriot hoteliers. Total tourist arrivals increased to 2,088,000, of which 40.5% came from the United Kingdom, and large increases were recorded in arrivals from Russia, Switzerland and Israel. Foreign-exchange earnings from tourism in 1997 totalled C£843m., with the sector accounting for 20% of GDP and 12% of employment. In 1998 total tourist arrivals increased to 2,222,701, providing foreign-exchange earnings of C£878m.

In 1999 tourist arrivals increased to a record level of 2,434,300, producing revenue of C£1,022m., so that the Government was on course for its target of 3m. tourist arrivals by 2003. The United Kingdom continued to be the largest source of tourists in 1999 (47.4%), followed by Germany (9.8%). Other areas that provided a large number of tourists included Scandinavia (with 10.9%) and the former USSR (5.5%). In May 2000 approval was given for the construction of six new marinas by the end of 2002, as part of the Government's strategy of promoting 'high-value' tourism. Another record year was achieved in 2000, with tourist arrivals rising to 2,686,202 (of whom 50.7% came from the United Kingdom) and revenue to C£1,200m., representing about 20% of GDP. Under a 10-year strategic plan for tourism adopted in January 2001, the Government aimed to increase the annual number of tourists to 4m. by 2010 and the number of available hotel beds from 105,000 to 130,000.

The upward trend in tourism continued in the first half of 2001, when arrivals were 8% higher than in the corresponding period in 2000. However, it slowed dramatically in the wake of the September 2001 suicide attacks on the USA, with the result that tourist arrivals for the year as a whole, at 2,696,732, were only 0.4% higher than in 2000, although revenue from tourism increased by 7.5% to C£1,283m., according to provisional figures. The downturn continued in the first half of 2002, in which tourist arrivals were around 15% lower than in the first half of 2001, despite the allocation by the Government of additional funds for the promotion of Cyprus as a tourist destination.

Tourism in the north has also expanded, giving rise to a shortage of hotel beds. The best hotels still exist in the Turkish sector, but most remained unused and derelict after the invasion. Some have, however, been taken over, much against the will of the Greek Cypriot owners. The number of non-Turkish visitors rose steadily from 8,172 in 1978 to 36,372 in 1987. Turkish visits from the mainland remained fairly constant between 1978 (when they totalled 104,738) and 1986, increasing to 147,965 in 1987, when net income from tourism totalled US $103.5m. By 1990 tourism receipts had increased to $224.8m. (from 243,269 Turkish visitors and 57,541 others),

then declined to $172.9m. (from 256,549 Turkish visitors and 95,079 others) in 1994. Total tourist arrivals increased to 399,364 (including 326,364 from Turkey) in 1997, but declined to 393,027 (315,797 from Turkey) in 1998, yielding net revenue of $186.0m. The upward trend resumed in 1999, when tourist arrivals totalled 414,015 (including 334,400 from Turkey) and net earnings from tourism were $192.8m., and continued in 2000, when 433,000 tourist arrivals and net revenues of $208.1m. were recorded. The number of hotels and other tourist accommodation in the 'TRNC' increased from 99 in 1996 to 116 in 2000, with total bed capacity rising from 8,267 to 10,520 over the same period.

BUDGET, INVESTMENT AND FINANCE

The budget for 1994 envisaged expenditure and net lending of C£1,221.6m., against revenue and grants of C£1,108.9m. The main items of development expenditure under the 1994 budget were the road network (C£43.5m.), water development (C£19.4m.), education (C£17.5m.), public construction (C£13.6m.) and airports (C£10.2m.). The fiscal deficit fell to 1.4% of GDP in 1994 (from 2.4% in 1993). The 1995 budget provided for expenditure of C£1,306m. and revenue of C£1,267m. (a deficit equivalent to 1.0% of GDP), while the 1996 budget (designed to encourage 'stability and modernization') set expenditure at C£1,349m. and anticipated revenue of C£1,321m., resulting in a deficit estimated to be equivalent to 0.6% of GDP for that year. A reduction in the performance of the economy in 1996 was attributable mainly to a decline in tourism and in investment and private consumption expenditure. The 1997 budget, adopted in February, forecast net expenditure of C£1,689m. against revenue of C£1,106m., and was accompanied by a series of measures designed to boost tourism, manufacturing, exports, investment and agriculture. In May 1997 the Government approved a plan of action for 'the harmonization, adjustment and convergence of the Cyprus economy with the EU *acquis*', the aim being to prepare the ground for the opening of formal accession negotiations in 1998.

The 1998 budget, approved in January of that year, provided for total net expenditure of C£1,603m. and revenues of C£1,080m. Following an IMF warning in June that the fiscal deficit was on the verge of becoming unsustainable, the Government drafted further proposals designed to reduce government spending and to increase revenues. Nevertheless, the budget deficit, expressed as a percentage of GDP, increased to 5.6% in 1998 (from 5.3% in 1997), while government debt rose to 59.3% of GDP (from 57.6% in 1997). As finally adopted, the 1999 budget provided for total expenditure of C£1,707m., against forecast revenue of C£1,106m., projecting an increased deficit of 5.1% of GDP, which was in fact reduced to 4.1%.

The 2000 budget unified the three traditional budget accounts (ordinary, development and resettlement) into a single measure, providing for expenditure of C£2,007.4m., net revenues of C£1,348.1m. and a projected budget deficit equivalent to 4.3% of GDP (although in the event the deficit was contained at 2.7% of GDP as a result of subsequent austerity measures). In May the Government secured approval for a programme of tax cuts and other measures designed to compensate the lower paid for an increase in VAT from 8% to 10%, which came into effect on 1 July, as a step towards a 15% rate by 2002 in accordance with the requirements of EU accession. In the same context, legislation adopted in December 1999 provided for the existing 9% statutory ceiling on interest rates to be removed with effect from 1 January 2001.

The budget for 2001, as finally approved in January 2001, provided for expenditure of C£2,426m. and net revenue of C£1,553m., envisaging a fiscal deficit of 2.5%–3% of GDP. In March 2001 the Government set itself the objective of reducing the fiscal deficit to 2% in 2002 and achieving a balanced budget in 2004. At that stage public debt as a proportion of GDP had been brought down to 59.8%, from more than 62% in mid-2000. In its 2002 budget, as adopted in January 2002, the Government retained the objective of reducing the deficit to 2% of GDP (compared with an out-turn of 2.9% in 2001) as a stage towards achieving a balanced budget in 2004, the anticipated first year of EU membership. Against anticipated net revenue of C£2,400m., total expenditure was set at C£2,700m., including C£348m. for development and infrastructure projects.

In light of deteriorating international economic conditions in the latter part of 2001, the Central Bank of Cyprus applied three successive 0.5% cuts in interest rates, bringing the Lombard (commercial bank lending) rate down to 5.5% with effect from 5 November 2001 and the overnight deposit facility rate to 2.5%. Also in November 2001, the Government announced major reforms in taxation policy, including reductions in personal income tax, an increase in VAT from 10% to 13% in the course of 2002 and a reduction of corporation tax to a standard rate of 10%. Offshore companies would lose their preferential 4.5% corporation tax rate and be required to pay the 10% rate, although the Government stated that it would seek EU authority to delay its full application until the expiry of existing offshore laws.

In January 2002 the Government announced that it expected to award contracts worth some C£600m. over the next five years under a public-private partnership programme. Representing a major departure from previous state financing practice, the public-private programme was to be aimed primarily at facilitating the rapid improvement of infrastructure and service provision while ensuring that government finances remained within the EU's Maastricht criteria for participation in the single currency. Under constitutional amendments enacted in June 2002, the Central Bank became fully independent from the Government on 1 July, in accordance with the norm in EU member states. The newly appointed Governor of the Central Bank, Christodoulos Christodoulou, stated that his priority would be the maintenance of monetary stability in preparation for the adoption of the euro upon Cypriot accession to the EU.

Total local revenues in the 'TRNC', according to official reports, showed 'an ascending tendency' during the period 1987–92, with an average annual growth rate of 5.9%. During the same period total budgetary expenditures increased by 3% annually, while as a proportion of GNP they declined from 36.7% to 33.9%. As a result, the ratio of budget deficit to GNP was reduced from 16.3% to 12.2%, and to total budget from 44.3% to 36%. On 1 July 1992, in partial parallel to Greek Cypriot policy, the 'TRNC' Government introduced VAT on consumer goods at a rate of 10% (compared with the introductory rate of 5% in the south). The 1993 budget envisaged a 9.9% increase in total local revenues, while expenditure and the budget deficit were projected to increase by 7.6% and 3.5% respectively; these targets implied a ratio of revenue, expenditure and deficit to GNP of 23.5%, 35.9% and 12.4% respectively. In the 1994 Annual Programme total local revenues were projected to increase by 5.4% at 1993 prices, the growth targets for expenditure and budget deficit being 4.6% and 3% respectively. Actual local revenues in 1994 were officially reported as the equivalent of US \$137.7m. and budgeted expenditure as \$198.6m., the shortfall being covered by foreign aid and loans of \$60.8m. The 1995 budget provided for expenditure of TL 14,450,000m. against local revenue of TL 8,000,000m., with the shortfall to be covered by foreign aid and loans of TL 6,450,000. The 1996 budget envisaged expenditure of TL 24,380,624.4m. against local revenue of TL 15,528,392.7m., with the shortfall to be met by foreign aid and loans of TL 8,852,231.7m.

Budgeted expenditure in 1997 was TL 50,160,862m., compared with income of TL 34,385,090m., the corresponding figures in 1998 (following a sharp depreciation of the Turkish lira) being TL 105,910,700m. and TL 62,798,400m. In US dollar terms, budgeted expenditure rose from \$323.8m. in 1997 to \$403.6m. in 1998, while budgeted income increased from \$220.0m. to \$239.3m. In 1999 budgeted expenditure rose to TL 190,254,477m. (\$455.1m.), against budget revenue of TL 114,458,200m. (\$268.1m.), with the shortfall to be met by foreign aid and loans of TL 75,795,279m. (\$187.0m.). In 2000 budgeted expenditure was the equivalent of \$495m. (including capital expenditure of \$60m.), against anticipated revenue of \$294m.

FOREIGN TRADE AND BALANCE OF PAYMENTS

Cyprus has experienced a persistent trade deficit for many years (with imports regularly being three or four times as great as exports in terms of value), offset by an increasingly healthy 'invisible' balance—arising mainly from earnings from tourism. The effect in recent years has been a manageable current-account deficit, which stood at C£99.4m. in 1995 (while there was an overall balance-of-payments deficit of C£111m.), with a net invisible surplus of C£889.8m. being exceeded by a trade deficit of C£989.2m. (from exports of C£510.2m. and imports of C£1,499.4m.). In 1996 the current-account balance deteriorated to produce a deficit of C£228.2m. (with the overall balance-of-payments deficit amounting to C£219.7m.), as the result of a crude trade deficit of C£1,070.3m. (from exports of C£597.1m. and imports of C£1,667.4m.) and a reduced surplus on the invisible account of C£842.1m. Nevertheless, at the end of 1996 foreign-exchange reserves totalled C£2,249.7m. (compared with C£1,861.4m. at the end of 1995), mainly as the result of a large increase in non-resident deposits.

In 1997, due to restrained domestic demand, total imports (excluding imports of military equipment) recorded a small increase of less than 3%, to C£1,704.7m., with increases in imports of consumer goods and of fuels and lubricants of 14.9% and 3%, respectively, being offset in particular by a 7.6% decrease in imports of transport equipment. During 1997 EU countries supplied 47.6% of total imports (including 11.4% from the United Kingdom), other European countries 8.1%, the USA 19% and Asian countries 16%. Total exports declined to C£605.7m., so that the crude trade deficit (excluding military imports) widened to C£1,099m. In that year both the current-account deficit and the overall balance-of-payments deficit decreased, to C£187.8m. and C£119.1m. respectively, the trade deficit being offset by a surplus on invisibles of C£911.3m. and a net capital movement surplus of C£94.4m. Strong economic growth in 1998 resulted in an increase in imports to C£1,807.4m., while exports declined to C£519.9m., yielding a crude trade deficit of C£1,287.5m. Categories of imports showing the highest growth rates were capital goods (24.2%), transport equipment (22.5%) and consumer goods (21.2%), while the value of imports of fuel and lubricants fell by 21.6% owing to the decline in world petroleum prices. A sharp increase in exports of agricultural products offset a decline in manufactured exports, while a 21.5% decline in re-exports was mainly attributable to a sharp fall in re-exports of cigarettes, particularly to Russia.

In 1998 the current-account deficit and the overall balance-of-payments deficit were C£314.3m. and C£189.3m. respectively, the trade deficit being offset by a surplus on invisibles of C£973.2m. and a net capital movement surplus of C£155.6m. In 1999 the crude trade deficit increased to C£1,428.0m (from imports of C£1,970.9m. and exports of C£542.9m.), although an improved invisibles balance resulted in the deficits on the current account and balance of payments overall being reduced to C£117.9m. and C£152.1m. respectively. The crude trade deficit widened further in 2000, to C£1,810m. (from imports of C£2,401.9m. and exports of C£591.9m.); however, a further advance in the invisibles balance contained the current-account deficit at C£284m., while a strong recovery in net capital inflows resulted in an overall balance-of-payments deficit of C£57.5m. In 2001 the primary trade deficit increased further, to C£1,907.4m., from imports of C£2,536.6m. and exports of C£629.2m. However, continuing advances in earnings from invisibles and in net capital inflows produced an overall balance-of-payments surplus of C£217m.

Having risen to C£2,607.6m. at the end of 1997, foreign-exchange reserves declined to C£2,315.7m. by the end of 1998, but rose to C£2,960.5m. by the end of 1999, to C£4,009.7m. by the end of 2000 and to C£5,023.4m. by the end of 2001. One of the main problems confronting the economy, however, is the continuing high level of foreign debt. Total outstanding external debt (government, semi-government and private) increased from C£736m. in 1988 to C£1,042.2m. in 1993, then decreased to an estimated C£1,029.5m. in 1994. By 1997 it had declined further, to an estimated C£825m., but it rose again to C£1,587.7m. in 1998 and to C£1,796.0m. in 1999.

There was a significant alteration in the Greek Cypriot trading pattern in the mid-1980s, with EC countries taking over the dominant role from Arab countries (chiefly Lebanon, Egypt, the states of the Arabian peninsula, and Libya), although exports to the latter rose again in the early 1990s. The Arab countries' share of total Greek Cypriot exports was reduced from 48% in 1985 to 28% in 1990, largely as a result of the crisis in the Persian (Arabian) Gulf region following Iraq's invasion of Kuwait in August of that year; thereafter they recovered to some 40% in 1991–93, with the economic revival of Lebanon, in particular, providing an expanding market. Greek Cypriot exports to EC countries, on the other hand, increased from 32.4% of total domestic export revenue in 1985 to 53.2% in 1990, although they declined in the succeeding years, to 41.7% in 1993. In 1987 the Greek Cypriot Government established a Council for the Promotion of Exports (COPE), one of the main aims of which was to promote exports to Europe. EC countries were also the main suppliers of goods to the Greek Cypriot sector, their share of the region's total imports, by value, increasing to 60.8% in 1986, before decreasing slightly, to 57% in 1987 and 54% in 1990, only to increase again to 58% in 1992. Imports from Arab countries, in turn, declined after 1985 (when they accounted for 10.1% of total import costs), to 6.1% in 1987 and to 5% in 1993. In 1994 the United Kingdom remained Cyprus's largest individual trading partner, supplying 11.4% of its imports and taking 27.1% of total Cypriot exports. A feature of Cypriot trade in 1995 was the rapid growth in imports from and exports to the USA, although the EU countries (particularly the United Kingdom) remained the dominant trading partners. In 2001 EU countries received 52.3% of Greek Cypriot exports and supplied 50.8% of imports.

In November 1985 the EC Council of Ministers approved the admission of Cyprus to a customs union with the EC. Accordingly, a protocol with the EC was signed in October 1987 and entered effect on 1 January 1988. The protocol defined an initial 10-year phase (1988–98), during which time tariffs on imports to Cyprus were to be reduced by 10% annually—leading to their complete removal by 1998. For some products that are important to the island's economy (e.g. clothing and footwear), tariffs were to fall by only 4% annually in the first phase. The EC agreed to waive quantitative restrictions on exports to the EC of Cypriot garments and to make concessions to Cypriot agricultural exports, particularly potatoes, grapes, wine and citrus fruit. Cyprus, in turn, agreed to dismantle its quantitative restrictions on imports of industrial products from EC countries, yet was to be allowed to retain a 20% tariff on up to 15% of imports that competed with local products. A second phase, of four to five years' duration, which was to be introduced after a review of the first phase, was to remove all remaining restrictions and trade barriers on products covered by the agreement. Cyprus was then expected to adopt the EC's common customs tariff, in accordance with its third-country provisions, freeing it of restrictions within the EC. The President of the 'TRNC', Rauf Denktaş, denounced the customs union, claiming that the EC was not entitled to negotiate the agreement without consulting representatives of the Turkish sector of the island. The EC, however, made it clear that the union would apply to the whole island, reiterating this assertion in a report published by the Commission in June 1993, which confirmed Cyprus's eligibility for EC membership.

Under the fourth EU-Cyprus financial protocol, signed in June 1995 in the framework of the existing association agreement, the island was to receive €74m. in loans and grants over five years, in support of efforts to promote economic integration and to prepare for EU membership. In December 2000 agreements were signed whereby Cyprus would receive €57m. in pre-accession assistance from the EU.

ECONOMIC PROSPECTS

The economy of Cyprus and its future are inextricably linked with the political deadlock in the island, which, despite the intensive negotiations during 2002, seems unlikely to be resolved by diplomacy in the near future. The Turkish Cypriot opposition to ongoing accession negotiations with the EU aggravates the problem. Meanwhile, both sides are proceeding with their own plans for development on either side of the 'Attila line', although the Turkish Cypriot economy remains heavily dependent on financial aid from Turkey and thus is directly affected by the periodic economic crises in Turkey.

Boosted by the rapid development of the tourist industry, the Greek Cypriot economy recovered quickly from the damaging effects of the 1990–91 Gulf crisis, and it seems likely to receive increasing economic benefit from its geographical location as an entrepôt between Europe and the Middle East and from its long-standing connections in Eastern Europe and the former Soviet republics. Nevertheless, trade with the EU is certain to have an increasingly predominant share of both the imports and the exports of the Greek Cypriots in the years ahead, thus providing new opportunities for local industries, while at the same time presenting them with the challenge of competing with EU exports to Cyprus.

For the Greek Cypriot Government, entry into the EU remains a cardinal goal, in which context it welcomed the formal opening of accession negotiations in March 1998 and urged the 'TRNC' to participate; this invitation was, however, refused. Questions over the legitimacy of Greek Cypriot accession while the island remains divided have been raised, although in December 1999 the EU gave a formal assurance that the absence of a political settlement would not be a barrier to Greek Cypriot accession prior to reunification. Internally, the harmonization of domestic legislation and economic arrangements with the EU's *acquis communautaire* has been accelerated, although the associated deregulation or privatization of state-owned sectors such as telecommunications is politically controversial despite almost universal support for EU membership.

The Greek Cypriot economy quickly felt the impact of the international economic slow-down partly attributed to the September 2001 attacks on the USA. Most notably, the tourist industry went into recession after a long period of rapid expansion. The difficulties have resulted in GDP growth forecasts for 2002 and 2003 being pitched lower than the buoyant expansion rates of previous years, although measures taken by the Government to ward off any general recession appear likely to prove effective.

One important potential source of future economic growth is the possible existence of major oil and gas deposits in the eastern Mediterranean south of Cyprus and within its 200-mile exclusive economic zone. In February 2001 the Government responded to press reports of promising initial surveys of the area by confirming that 25 foreign oil companies had so far made approaches for exploration rights, and by disclosing that international legal experts had been called in to assist with the detailed mapping of the economic zone. The Government subsequently entered into detailed negotiations with other eastern Mediterranean countries on the delimitation of their economic zones, while maintaining an official silence on the probability of recoverable hydrocarbon reserves being found in the area.

Statistical Survey

Source (unless otherwise indicated): Department of Statistics and Research, Ministry of Finance, Nicosia; tel. (2) 309301; fax (2) 374830; internet www.pio.gov.cy/dsr/index.htm.

Note: Since July 1974 the northern part of Cyprus has been under Turkish occupation. As a result, some of the statistics relating to subsequent periods do not cover the whole island. Some separate figures for the 'TRNC' are given on pp. 265–266.

AREA AND POPULATION

Area: 9,251 sq km (3,572 sq miles), incl. Turkish-occupied region; 5,896 sq km (2,276 sq miles), government-controlled area only.

Population: 602,025 (males 299,614; females 302,411), excl. Turkish-occupied region, at census of 1 October 1992; 759,100, incl. 87,800 in Turkish-occupied region, at 31 December 2000 (official estimate); 689,471, excl. Turkish-occupied region, at census of 1 October 2001. Note: Figures for the Turkish-occupied region exclude settlers from Turkey, estimated at 114,000 in 1998.

Density (at census of 1 October 2001): 116.9 per sq km (government-controlled area).

Ethnic Groups (estimates, 31 December 1998): Greeks 639,200 (85.1%), Turks 88,200 (11.7%), others 24,100 (3.2%); Total 751,500.

Principal Towns (population at 1 October 1992): Nicosia (capital) 181,234 (excl. Turkish-occupied portion); Limassol 139,424; Larnaca 62,178; Famagusta (Gazi Mağusa) 39,500 (mid-1974); Paphos 33,246; (estimated population at 31 December 1998): Nicosia 195,000 (excl. Turkish-occupied portion); Limassol 154,400; Larnaca 68,500; Paphos 38,800.

Births, Marriages and Deaths (government-controlled area, 2000): Registered live births 8,447 (birth rate 12.6 per 1,000); Registered marriages 9,282 (marriage rate 13.8 per 1,000); Registered deaths 5,355 (death rate 8.0 per 1,000).

Expectation of Life (WHO estimates, years at birth, 2000): Males 74.8; Females 79.0 (Source: WHO, *World Health Report*).

Employment (government-controlled area, provisional figures, '000 persons aged 15 years and over, excl. armed forces, 1999): Agriculture, hunting, forestry and fishing 26.9; Mining and quarrying 0.6; Manufacturing 38.6; Electricity, gas and water 1.5; Construction 24.2; Trade, restaurants and hotels 83.6; Transport, storage and communications 19.4; Financing, insurance, real estate and business services 28.5; Community, social and other services 66.9; *Total* 290.2. Figures exclude employment on British sovereign bases. Source: IMF, *Cyprus: Selected Issues and Statistical Appendix* (September 2000).

HEALTH AND WELFARE
Key Indicators

Fertility (births per woman, 2000): 2.0.

Under-5 Mortality Rate (per 1,000 live births, 2000): 7.

HIV/AIDS (% of persons aged 15–49, 2001): 0.25.

Physicians (per 1,000 head, 1996): 2.55.

Hospital Beds (per 1,000 head, 1996): 5.09.

Health Expenditure (1998): US $ per head (PPP): 966.
% of GDP: 6.3.
public (% of total): 37.9.

Human Development Index (2000): ranking: 26.
index: 0.883.

For sources and definitions, see explanatory note on p. vi.

AGRICULTURE, ETC.

Principal Crops (government-controlled area, '000 metric tons, 2000): Wheat 10.0; Barley 37.6; Potatoes 120.0; Olives 21.0; Cabbages 5.3; Tomatoes 34.0; Cucumbers and gherkins 14.5; Dry onions 7.7; Bananas 8.5; Oranges 42.7; Tangerines, mandarins, etc. 42.7; Lemons and limes 20.9; Grapefruit and pomelos 28.1; Apples 11.0; Grapes 110.7; Cantaloupes and other melons 10.0. Source: FAO.

Livestock (government-controlled area, '000 head, year ending September 2000): Cattle 54.0; Sheep 233.0; Goats 346.0; Pigs 418.5; Chickens 3,200; Asses 5.2 (estimate). Source: FAO.

Livestock Products (government-controlled area, '000 metric tons, 2000): Beef and veal 4.5; Mutton and lamb 4.2; Goat meat 6.3; Pig meat 52.3; Poultry meat 34.8; Cows' milk 146.6; Sheep's milk 18.0; Goats' milk 29.2; Cheese 4.8; Hen eggs 10.6. Source: FAO.

Forestry (government-controlled area, '000 cubic metres, 2000): Roundwood removals (excl. bark) 25.1; Sawnwood production (incl. railway sleepers) 8.7. Source: FAO.

Fishing (government-controlled area, metric tons, live weight, 1999): Capture 5,273 (Bogue 259, Picarels 546, Jack and horse mackerels, 1,034, Sardinellas 613, Argentine anchovy 845, Chub

mackerel 256); Aquaculture 1,422 (European seabass 298, Gilthead seabream 986); Total catch 6,695. Source: FAO, *Yearbook of Fishery Statistics*.

MINING AND QUARRYING

Selected Products (government-controlled area, provisional figures, metric tons, 2000): Sand and gravel 9,570,000; Gypsum 138,076; Bentonite 126,313; Umber 12,258.

INDUSTRY

Selected Products (government-controlled area, 1999): Wine 42.1m. litres; Beer 40.5m. litres; Soft drinks 60.0m. litres; Cigarettes 4,783m.; Footwear 1,710,000 pairs; Bricks 50m.; Floor and wall tiles 804,000 sq m.; Cement 1,157,000 metric tons; Electricity 2,954m. kWh (estimate, 1998). Source UN, *Industrial Commodity Statistics Yearbook*.

FINANCE

Currency and Exchange Rates: 100 cents = 1 Cyprus pound (Cyprus £). *Sterling, Dollar and Euro Equivalents* (31 May 2002): £1 sterling = 90.58 Cyprus cents; US $1 = 61.76 Cyprus cents; €1 = 57.97 Cyprus cents; Cyprus £100 = £110.40 sterling = $161.92 = €172.49. *Average Exchange Rate* (US $ per Cyprus £): 1.8440 in 1999; 1.6107 in 2000; 1.5559 in 2001.

Budget (government-controlled area, Cyprus £ million, 2000): *Revenue:* Taxation 1,455.6 (Direct taxes 558.1, Indirect taxes 653.5, Social security contributions 244.0); Other current revenue 406.7; Capital revenue 0.7; Total 1,863.0, excl. grants from abroad (2.5). *Expenditure:* Current expenditure 1,789.8 (Wages and salaries 526.3, Other goods and services 160.9, Social security payments 304.0, Subsidies 79.5, Interest payments 311.8); Capital expenditure 215.8 (Investments 153.2, Capital transfers 62.6); Total 2,005.6.

International Reserves (US $ million at 31 December 2001): Gold (national valuation) 127.6; IMF special drawing rights 1.4; Reserve position in IMF 44.4; Foreign exchange 2,221.9; Total 2,394.3. Source: IMF, *International Financial Statistics*.

Money Supply (government-controlled area, Cyprus £ million at 31 December 2001): Currency outside banks 356.5, Demand deposits at deposit money banks 724.2; Total money (incl. others) 1,081.4. Source: IMF, *International Financial Statistics*.

Cost of Living (government-controlled area, Retail Price Index; base: 1995 = 100): 110.8 in 1999; 115.4 in 2000; 117.7 in 2001. Source: IMF, *International Financial Statistics*.

Gross Domestic Product in Purchasers' Values (government-controlled area, Cyprus £ million): *GDP at current prices:* 5,017.5 in 1999; 5,486.9 (provisional) in 2000; 5,867.2 (provisional) in 2001.

Expenditure on the Gross Domestic Product (government-controlled area, provisional, Cyprus £ million at current prices, 2001): Government final consumption expenditure 1,016.8; Private final consumption expenditure 4,030.1; Increase in stocks 70.0; Gross fixed capital formation 1,012.8; Statistical discrepancy 24.3; *Total domestic expenditure* 6,154.0; Exports of goods and services 2,743.7; *Less* Imports of goods and services 3,030.5; *GDP in purchasers' values* 5,867.2.

Gross Domestic Product by Economic Activity (government-controlled area, provisional, Cyprus £ million at current prices, 2001): Agriculture and hunting 207.8; Fishing 11.6; Mining and quarrying 15.0; Manufacturing 562.7; Electricity, gas and water supply 115.2; Construction 398.5; Wholesale and retail trade 723.0; Restaurants and hotels 544.7; Transport, storage and communications 557.8; Financial intermediation 410.5; Real estate, renting and business activities 783.8; Public administration and defence 514.8; Education 294.6; Health and social work 200.5; Other community, social and personal services 230.2; Private households with employed persons 32.5; *Sub-total* 5,603.2; Import duties 152.3; Value-added tax 344.7; *Less* Imputed bank service charges 233.0; *GDP in purchasers' values* 5,867.2.

Balance of Payments (government-controlled area, US $ million, 2001): Exports of goods f.o.b. 976.5, Imports of goods f.o.b. −3,526.9; *Trade balance* −2,550.4; Exports of services 3,352.9; Imports of services −1,185.2; *Balance on goods and services* −382.7; Other income received 563.8; Other income paid −597.6; *Balance on goods, services and income* −416.4; Current transfers received 49.3;

Current transfers paid –27.7; *Current balance* –394.8; Direct investment abroad –217.7; Direct investment from abroad 163.3; Portfolio investment assets –443.2; Portfolio investment liabilities 524.0; Other investment asests –540.5; Other investment liabilities 1,359.8; Net errors and omissions 161.4; *Overall balance* 612.3.
Source: IMF, *International Financial Statistics*.

EXTERNAL TRADE

Total Trade (government-controlled area, Cyprus £ million): *Imports c.i.f.:* 1,970.9 in 1999; 2,401.9 in 2000; 2,528.7 in 2001. *Exports f.o.b.* (incl. re-exports): 542.9 in 1999; 591.9 in 2000; 628.0 in 2001.

Principal Commodities (government-controlled area, Cyprus £ '000, 2001): *Imports c.i.f.:* Consumer goods 793,223 (Food and beverages 145,038; Other non-durable 358,207; Semi-durable 173,714; Durable 116,265); Intermediate inputs 736,688 (Construction and mining 124,721; Manufacturing 443,184); Capital goods 269,550; Transport equipment and parts thereof 328,866 (Passenger motor vehicles 160,398; Motor vehicles for the transport of goods 85,864); Fuels and lubricants 302,471; Total (incl. others) 2,528,723. *Exports f.o.b.:* Potatoes 17,511; Citrus fruit 14,717; Cheese 8,558; Cigarettes 10,768; Cement 8,396; Pharmaceutical products 39,411; Clothing 19,700; Total (incl. others) 233,944. Figures for exports exclude re-exports (Cyprus £ '000): 381,039. Also excluded are domestic exports of stores and bunkers for ships and aircraft (Cyprus £ '000): 13,046.

Principal Trading Partners (government-controlled area, Cyprus £ million, 2001): *Imports c.i.f.:* China, People's Repub. 91.0; France 127.3; Germany 172.7; Greece 225.2; Israel 99.7; Italy 223.2; Japan 153.7; Netherlands 52.8; Russia 78.9; Spain 96.5; Syria 96.6; Taiwan 27.3; Thailand 31.4; United Kingdom 222.2; USA 237.9; Total (incl. others) 2,528.7. *Exports f.o.b.* (incl. re-exports): Egypt 16.8; France 6.2; Germany 18.4; Greece 52.6; Iraq 9.5; Israel 8.8; Lebanon 23.3; Netherlands 10.7; Romania 6.5; Russia 54.1; Saudi Arabia 5.9; Spain 10.2; Syria 37.4; United Arab Emirates 49.0; United Kingdom 117.6; USA 10.7; Total (incl. others) 530.3, excluding stores and bunkers for ships and aircraft (97.7).

TRANSPORT

Road Traffic (government-controlled area, licensed motor vehicles, 31 December 2001): Private passenger cars 270,348; Taxis and self-drive cars 9,721; Buses and coaches 3,003; Lorries and vans 117,942; Motor cycles 41,985; Total (incl. others) 459,106.

Shipping (government-controlled area, freight traffic, '000 metric tons, 2001): Goods loaded 1,406, Goods unloaded 5,237. At 31 December 2001 a total of 1,407 merchant vessels (combined displacement 22,761,778 grt) were registered in Cyprus (Source: Lloyd's Register-Fairplay, *World Fleet Statistics*).

Civil Aviation (government-controlled area, 2001): Overall passenger traffic 6,415,225; Total freight transported 32,446 metric tons.

TOURISM

Foreign Tourist Arrivals (government-controlled area, '000): 2,434.3 in 1999; 2,686.2 in 2000; 2,696.7 in 2001.

Arrivals by Country of Residence (government-controlled area, 2001): Germany 214,149; Greece 89,758; Norway 61,614; Russia (incl. other ex-USSR countries) 128,504; Sweden 127,415; Switzerland 76,608; United Kingdom 1,486,700; Total (incl. others) 2,696,732. Source: Cyprus Tourism Organization.

Tourism Receipts (government-controlled area, Cyprus £ million): 1,025 in 1999; 1,194 in 2000; 1,283 (provisional) in 2001..

COMMUNICATIONS MEDIA

Radio Receivers (government-controlled area, 1997): 310,000 in use.

Television Receivers (government-controlled area, 2000): 122,000 in use.

Telephones (main lines in use, 2001): 435,000.

Facsimile Machines (provisional or estimated figure, number in use, 1993): 7,000.

Mobile Telephones (subscribers, 2001): 314,400.

Personal Computers ('000 in use, 2001): 170.

Internet Users ('000, 2001): 150.

Book Production (government-controlled area, 1996): 930 titles and 1,776,000 copies.

Newspapers (1996): 9 daily (circulation 84,000 copies); 31 non-daily (circulation 185,000 copies).

Sources: mainly UNESCO, *Statistical Yearbook*, UN, *Statistical Yearbook*, and International Telecommunication Union.

EDUCATION

1997/98 (government-controlled area): Kindergarten: 665 institutions, 1,461 teachers, 26,517 pupils; Primary schools: 372 institutions, 3,521 teachers, 64,592 pupils; Secondary schools (Gymnasia and Lyceums): 114 institutions, 4,438 teachers, 56,872 pupils; Technical colleges: 11 institutions, 594 teachers, 4,831 pupils; University of Cyprus: 196 teachers, 2,311 students; Other post-secondary: 33 institutions, 639 teachers, 8,216 students.

1999/2000 (government-controlled area): students: 26,155 pre-primary; 63,715 primary; 63,043 secondary; 10,414 post-secondary; 327 special.

Adult literacy rate (UNESCO estimate): 97.1% (males 98.7%; females 95.4%) in 2000 (Source: UN Development Programme, *Human Development Report*).

'Turkish Republic of Northern Cyprus'

Sources: Statistics and Research Dept, State Planning Organization, Prime Ministry, Lefkoşa (Nicosia), Mersin 10, Turkey; tel. (22) 83141; fax (22) 85988; e-mail trnc-spo@management.emu.edu.tr; internet www.devplan.org; Office of the London Representative of the 'Turkish Republic of Northern Cyprus', 29 Bedford Sq., London WC1B 3EG; tel. (20) 7631-1920; fax (20) 7631-1948.

AREA AND POPULATION

Area: 3,355 sq km (1,295 sq miles).

Population (census, 15 December 1996): 200,587 (males 105,978; females 94,609). Official estimate at 31 December 2000: 208,886.

Density: (2000): 62.3 per sq km.

Ethnic Groups (census, 15 December 1996): Turks 197,264, English 627, Greeks 384, Maronites 173, Russians 130, Germans 106, Others 1,903; Total 200,587.

Principal Towns (population within the municipal boundary, census, 15 December 1996): Lefkoşa (Nicosia) 39,176 (Turkish-occupied area only); Gazi Mağusa (Famagusta) 27,637; Girne (Kyrenia) 14,205.

Births, Marriages and Deaths (registered, 1999): Live births 2,422 (birth rate 11.7 per 1,000); Marriages 1,146 (marriage rate 5.5 per 1,000); Deaths 717 (death rate 3.5 per 1,000).

Expectation of life (years at birth, 2000): Males 70.9; Females 75.1.

Employment (provisional, 2001): Agriculture, forestry and fishing 14,931; Industry 8,715; Construction 14,104; Trade and tourism 9,630; Transport and communications 8,104; Financial institutions 2,275; Business and personal services 13,818; Public services 18,162; *Total employed* 89,739. Total unemployed 1,508; *Total labour force* 91,247.

HEALTH AND WERLFARE

Key Indicators

Physicians (per 1,000 head, 2000): 1.7.

Hospital Beds (per 1,000 head, 2000): 5.4.

AGRICULTURE, ETC.

Principal Crops ('000 metric tons, 1999): Wheat 21.2; Barley 79.1; Potatoes 11.2; Legumes 2.0; Tomatoes 5.4; Onions 2.1; Artichokes 1.1; Watermelons 5.2; Melons 2.8; Cucumbers 2.0; Carobs 4.4; Olives 8.8; Lemons 11.8; Grapefruit 25.0; Oranges 91.1; Tangerines 2.1.

Livestock ('000 head, 1999): Cattle 28.3; Sheep 210.1; Goats 55.6; Chickens 4,125.3.

Livestock Products ('000 metric tons, unless otherwise indicated, 1999): Sheep's and goats' milk 12.8; Cows' milk 50.3; Mutton and lamb 3.5; Goat meat 0.8; Beef 1.6; Poultry meat 6.2; Wool 0.2; Eggs (million) 11.6.

Fishing (metric tons, 1994): Total catch 400.

FINANCE

Currency and Exchange Rates: Turkish currency: 100 kuruş = 1 Turkish lira (TL) or pound. *Sterling, Dollar and Euro Equivalents*

(31 May 2002): £1 sterling = 2,114,216 liras; US $1 = 1,441,478 liras; €1 = 1,353,115 liras; 10,000,000 Turkish liras = £4.730 = $6.937 = €7.390. *Average Exchange Rate* (liras per US dollar): 418,783 in 1999; 625,219 in 2000; 1,225,588 in 2001.

Budget (provisional, '000 million Turkish liras, 2001): *Revenue:* Internal revenue 253,300 (Direct taxes 96,200, Indirect taxes 74,000, Other income 55,100, Fund revenues 28,000); Aid from Turkey 118,411; Aid from other countries 90; Loans 107,410; Total 479,211. *Expenditure:* Personnel 137,000; Other goods and services 27,000; Transfers 230,900; Investments 45,442; Defence 38,869; Total 479,211.

Cost of Living (Retail Price Index at December; base: December of previous year = 100): 155.3 in 1999; 153.2 in 2000; 176.8 in 2001.

Expenditure on the Gross Domestic Product (provisional, '000 million Turkish liras at current prices, 2001): Government final consumption expenditure 235,571; Private final consumption expenditure 627,327; Increase in stocks 15,700; Gross fixed capital formation 150,972; *Total domestic expenditure* 1,029,570; Exports of goods and services, *less* Imports of goods and services −58,538; *GDP in purchasers' values* 971,032; *GDP at constant 1977 prices* (million liras) 8,707.9.

Gross Domestic Product by Economic Activity (provisional, '000 million Turkish liras, 2001): Agriculture, forestry and fishing 80,580; Industry 105,835 (Mining and quarrying 6,109; Manufacturing 52,181; Electricity and water 47,545); Construction 41,344; Wholesale and retail trade 106,159; Restaurants and hotels 61,909; Transport and communications 126,669; Finance 54,606; Ownership of dwellings 26,997; Business and personal services 86,673; Government services 197,603; *Sub-total* 888,376; Import duties 82,656; *GDP in purchasers' values* 971,032.

Balance of Payments (provisional, US $ million, 2001): Merchandise exports f.o.b. 46.0; Merchandise imports c.i.f. −301.0; *Trade balance* −255.0; Services and unrequited transfers (net) 210.4; *Current balance* −44.6; Capital movements (net) 133.1; Net errors and omissions −29.2; *Total* (net monetary movements) 59.3.

EXTERNAL TRADE

Principal Commodities (provisional, US $ million, 2001): *Imports c.i.f.:* Food and live animals 49.2; Beverages and tobacco 19.2; Mineral fuels, lubricants, etc. 26.5; Chemicals 28.5; Basic manufactures 70.5; Machinery and transport equipment 102.2; Miscellaneous manufactured articles 25.6; Total (incl. others) 329.0. *Exports f.o.b.:* Agricultural products 17.0 (Citrus fruit 10.7); Indus-trial products 28.8 (Processed agricultural goods 11.9); Total (incl. others) 46.0.

Principal Trading Partners (US $ million, 1999): *Imports c.i.f.:* Belgium 4.5; Germany 19.4; Hong Kong 4.3; Italy 11.4; Japan 19.8; Netherlands 5.8; Turkey 256.4; United Kingdom 47.4; USA 6.3; Total (incl. others) 412.7. *Exports f.o.b.:* Germany 3.5; Kuwait 1.5; Netherlands 0.9; Russia 0.8; Turkey 27.9; United Kingdom 15.9; Total (incl. others) 52.4. *2001* (provisional): Imports c.i.f.: Turkey 196.0; United Kingdom 31.2.; USA 4.5; Total (incl. others) 301.0. Exports f.o.b.: Turkey 16.7; United Kingdom 12.2; Total (incl. others) 46.0.

TRANSPORT

Road Traffic (registered motor vehicles, 1999): Saloon cars 70,494; Estate cars 8,919; Pick-ups 3,731; Vans 8,420; Buses 1,879; Trucks 776; Lorries 5,755; Motor cycles 15,618; Agricultural tractors 6,288; Total (incl. others) 123,986.

Shipping (1999): Freight traffic ('000 metric tons): Goods loaded 284.5, Goods unloaded 957.2; Vessels entered 3,868.

Civil Aviation: Kilometres flown (Turkish Cypriot Airlines) 1,126,848 (1985); Passenger arrivals and departures 624,189 (1994); Freight landed and cleared (metric tons) 6,585 (1999).

TOURISM

Visitors (2000): 432,953 (including 347,712 Turkish); **Accommodation** (2000): Hotels 116, Tourist beds (in all tourist accommodation, including pensions and hotel-apartments) 10,520; **Net Receipts** (US $ million, 2000): 198.3.

COMMUNICATIONS MEDIA

Radio Receivers (1994, provisional): 56,450 in use.

Television Receivers (1994, provisional): 52,300 in use.

Telephones (31 December 1999): 84,815 subscribers.

EDUCATION

2000/01: *Pre-primary schools:* 147 institutions, 253 teachers, 3,859 pupils; *Primary schools:* 93 institutions, 1,052 teachers, 15,493 pupils; *Junior high schools:* 28 institutions, 837 teachers, 9,713 students; *General high schools:* 22 institutions, 677 teachers, 5,593 students; *Vocational schools:* 13 institutions, 436 teachers, 2,071 students; *Universities:* 5 institutions, 22,924 students.

Adult literacy rate (census, 15 December 1996): 93.5%.

Directory

The Constitution

The Constitution, summarized below, entered into force on 16 August 1960, when Cyprus became an independent republic.

THE STATE OF CYPRUS

The State of Cyprus is an independent and sovereign Republic with a presidential regime.

The Greek Community comprises all citizens of the Republic who are of Greek origin and whose mother tongue is Greek or who share the Greek cultural traditions or who are members of the Greek Orthodox Church.

The Turkish Community comprises all citizens of the Republic who are of Turkish origin and whose mother tongue is Turkish or who share the Turkish cultural traditions or who are Muslims.

The official languages of the Republic are Greek and Turkish.

The Republic shall have its own flag of neutral design and colour, chosen jointly by the President and the Vice-President of the Republic.

The Greek and the Turkish Communities shall have the right to celebrate respectively the Greek and the Turkish national holidays.

THE PRESIDENT AND VICE-PRESIDENT

Executive power is vested in the President and the Vice-President, who are members of the Greek and Turkish Communities respectively, and are elected by their respective communities to hold office for five years.

The President of the Republic as Head of the State represents the Republic in all its official functions; signs the credentials of diplomatic envoys and receives the credentials of foreign diplomatic envoys; signs the credentials of delegates for the negotiation of international treaties, conventions or other agreements; signs the letter relating to the transmission of the instruments of ratification of any international treaties, conventions or agreements; confers the honours of the Republic.

The Vice-President of the Republic, as Vice-Head of the State, has the right to be present at all official functions; at the presentation of the credentials of foreign diplomatic envoys; to recommend to the President the conferment of honours on members of the Turkish Community, which recommendation the President shall accept unless there are grave reasons to the contrary.

The election of the President and the Vice-President of the Republic shall be direct, by universal suffrage and secret ballot, and shall, except in the case of a by-election, take place on the same day but separately.

The office of the President and of the Vice-President shall be incompatible with that of a Minister or of a Representative or of a member of a Communal Chamber or of a member of any municipal council including a Mayor or of a member of the armed or security forces of the Republic or with a public or municipal office.

The President and Vice-President of the Republic are invested by the House of Representatives.

The President and the Vice-President of the Republic in order to ensure the executive power shall have a Council of Ministers composed of seven Greek Ministers and three Turkish Ministers. The Ministers shall be designated respectively by the President and the Vice-President of the Republic who shall appoint them by an instrument signed by them both. The President convenes and presides over the meetings of the Council of Ministers, while the Vice-President may ask the President to convene the Council and may take part in the discussions.

The decisions of the Council of Ministers shall be taken by an absolute majority and shall, unless the right of final veto or return is exercised by the President or the Vice-President of the Republic or both, be promulgated immediately by them.

The executive power exercised by the President and the Vice-President of the Republic conjointly consists of:

Determining the design and colour of the flag.

Creation or establishment of honours.

Appointment of the members of the Council of Ministers.

Promulgation by publication of the decisions of the Council of Ministers.

Promulgation by publication of any law or decision passed by the House of Representatives.

Appointments and termination of appointments as in Articles provided.

Institution of compulsory military service.

Reduction or increase of the security forces.

Exercise of the prerogative of mercy in capital cases.

Remission, suspension and commutation of sentences.

Right of references to the Supreme Constitutional Court and publication of Court decisions.

Address of messages to the House of Representatives.

The executive powers which may be exercised separately by the President and Vice-President include: designation and termination of appointment of Greek and Turkish Ministers respectively; the right of final veto on Council decisions and on laws concerning foreign affairs, defence or security; the publication of the communal laws and decisions of the Greek and Turkish Communal Chambers respectively; the right of recourse to the Supreme Constitutional Court; the prerogative of mercy in capital cases; and addressing messages to the House of Representatives.

THE COUNCIL OF MINISTERS

The Council of Ministers shall exercise executive power in all matters, other than those which are within the competence of a Communal Chamber, including the following:

General direction and control of the government of the Republic and the direction of general policy.

Foreign affairs, defence and security.

Co-ordination and supervision of all public services.

Supervision and disposition of property belonging to the Republic.

Consideration of Bills to be introduced to the House of Representatives by a Minister.

Making of any order or regulation for the carrying into effect of any law as provided by such law.

Consideration of the Budget of the Republic to be introduced to the House of Representatives.

THE HOUSE OF REPRESENTATIVES

The legislative power of the Republic shall be exercised by the House of Representatives in all matters except those expressly reserved to the Communal Chambers.

The number of Representatives shall be 50, subject to alteration by a resolution of the House of Representatives carried by a majority comprising two-thirds of the Representatives elected by the Greek Community and two-thirds of the Representatives elected by the Turkish Community.

Out of the number of Representatives 70% shall be elected by the Greek Community and 30% by the Turkish Community separately from amongst their members respectively, and, in the case of a contested election, by universal suffrage and by direct and secret ballot held on the same day.

The term of office of the House of Representatives shall be for a period of five years.

The President of the House of Representatives shall be a Greek, and shall be elected by the Representatives elected by the Greek Community, and the Vice-President shall be a Turk and shall be elected by the Representatives elected by the Turkish Community.

THE COMMUNAL CHAMBERS

The Greek and the Turkish Communities respectively shall elect from amongst their own members a Communal Chamber.

The Communal Chambers shall, in relation to their respective Community, have competence to exercise legislative power solely with regard to the following:

All religious, educational, cultural and teaching matters.

Personal status; composition and instances of courts dealing with civil disputes relating to personal status and to religious matters.

Imposition of personal taxes and fees on members of their respective Community in order to provide for their respective needs.

THE PUBLIC SERVICE AND THE ARMED FORCES

The public service shall be composed as to 70% of Greeks and as to 30% of Turks.

The Republic shall have an army of 2,000 men, of whom 60% shall be Greeks and 40% shall be Turks.

The security forces of the Republic shall consist of the police and gendarmerie and shall have a contingent of 2,000 men. The forces shall be composed as to 70% of Greeks and as to 30% of Turks.

OTHER PROVISIONS

The following measures have been passed by the House of Representatives since January 1964, when the Turkish members withdrew:

The amalgamation of the High Court and the Supreme Constitutional Court (see Judicial System section).

The abolition of the Greek Communal Chamber and the creation of a Ministry of Education.

The unification of the Municipalities.

The unification of the Police and the Gendarmerie.

The creation of a military force by providing that persons between the ages of 18 and 50 years can be called upon to serve in the National Guard.

The extension of the term of office of the President and the House of Representatives by one year intervals from July 1965 until elections in February 1968 and July 1970 respectively.

New electoral provisions; abolition of separate Greek and Turkish rolls; abolition of post of Vice-President, which was re-established in 1973.

The Government*

HEAD OF STATE

President: GLAVKOS KLERIDES (took office 28 February 1993; re-elected 15 February 1998).

COUNCIL OF MINISTERS
(September 2002)

A coalition Government, comprising DISY, EDE (United Democrats) and Independents (Ind.).

Minister of Foreign Affairs: YIANNAKIS KASOULIDES (DISY).

Minister of Defence: SOKRATIS HASIKOS (DISY).

Minister of Finance: TAKIS KLERIDES (Ind.).

Minister of the Interior: ANDREAS PANAYIOTOU (DISY).

Minister of Justice and Public Order: NIKOS KOSHIS (DISY).

Minister of Commerce, Industry and Tourism: NIKOS ROLANDIS (DISY).

Minister of Education and Culture: OURANIOS IOANNIDES (DISY).

Minister of Health: FRIXOS SAVVIDHIS (Ind.).

Minister of Labour and Social Insurance: ANDREAS MOUSHATTAS (Ind.).

Minister of Communications and Works: AVEROF NEOPHITOU (DISY).

Minister of Agriculture, Natural Resources and the Environment: KOSTAS THEMISTOKLEOUS (EDE).

* Under the Constitution of 1960, the vice-presidency and three posts in the Council of Ministers are reserved for Turkish Cypriots. However, there has been no Turkish participation in the Government since December 1963. In 1968 President Makarios announced that he considered the office of Vice-President in abeyance until Turkish participation in the Government is resumed, but the Turkish community elected Rauf Denktaş Vice-President in February 1973.

MINISTRIES

Office of the President: Presidential Palace, Dem. Severis Ave, 1400 Nicosia; tel. (22) 661333; fax (22) 665016.

Ministry of Agriculture, Natural Resources and the Environment: Loukis Akritas Ave, 1411 Nicosia; tel. (22) 300807; fax (22) 781156; e-mail minagre@cytanet.com.

Ministry of Commerce, Industry and Tourism: 6 Andreas Araouzos St, 1424 Nicosia; tel. (22) 867100; fax (22) 375120; e-mail mcitrade@cytanet.com.cy.

Ministry of Communications and Works: 28 Achaion St, 1424 Nicosia; tel. (22) 800106; fax (22) 776248; e-mail permsec@mcw.gov.cy.

Ministry of Defence: 4 Emmanuel Roides Ave, 1432 Nicosia; tel. (22) 807622; fax (22) 675289.

Ministry of Education and Culture: Kimonos & Thoukydidou, Akropolis, 1434 Nicosia; tel. (22) 800600; fax (22) 427559; e-mail moec@moec.gov.cy; internet www.moec.gov.cy.

Ministry of Finance: Ex Secretariat Compound, 1439 Nicosia; tel. (22) 803640; fax (22) 302168; e-mail minfinresearch@cytanet.com.cy.

Ministry of Foreign Affairs: 18–19 Dem. Severis Ave, 1447 Nicosia; tel. (22) 300600; fax (22) 665778; e-mail minforeign1@cytanet.com.cy.

Ministry of Health: Byron Ave, 1448 Nicosia; tel. (22) 309526; fax (22) 305803.

Ministry of the Interior: Dem. Severis Ave, Ex Secretariat Compound, 1453 Nicosia; tel. (22) 867629; fax (22) 671465.

Ministry of Justice and Public Order: 125 Athalassa Ave, 1461 Nicosia; tel. (22) 805955; fax (22) 518356; e-mail registry@mjpo.gov.cy.

Ministry of Labour and Social Insurance: Byron Ave, 1463 Nicosia; tel. (22) 303481; fax (22) 670993.

President and Legislature

PRESIDENT

Election, First round, 8 February 1998

Candidate	Votes	%
Glavkos Klerides (Democratic Rally)	158,763	40.1
Georghios Iacovou (Independent, with AKEL-DIKO support)	160,918	40.6
Vassos Lyssarides (EDEK—Socialist Party*)	41,978	10.6
Alexis Galanos (Independent)	16,003	4.0
Georghios Vassiliou (United Democrats)	11,908	3.0
Nikos Koutsou (New Horizons)	3,625	0.9
Nikos Rolandis (Liberal Party†)	3,104	0.8
Total	396,299	100.0

* Became Kinima Sosialdimokraton (KISOS) in 2000.
† Subsequently merged with DISY.

Second round, 15 February 1998

Candidate	Votes	%
Glavkos Klerides (Democratic Rally)	206,879	50.8
Georghios Iacovou (Independent, with AKEL-DIKO support)	200,222	49.2
Total	407,101	100.0

HOUSE OF REPRESENTATIVES

The House of Representatives originally consisted of 50 members, 35 from the Greek community and 15 from the Turkish community, elected for a term of five years. In January 1964 the Turkish members withdrew and set up the 'Turkish Legislative Assembly of the Turkish Cypriot Administration' (see p. 270). At the 1985 elections the membership of the House was expanded to 80 members, of whom 56 were to be from the Greek community and 24 from the Turkish community (according to the ratio of representation specified in the Constitution).

President: Demetris Christofias.

Elections for the Greek Representatives, 27 May 2001

Party	Votes	% of Votes	Seats
AKEL (Progressive Party of the Working People)	142,648	34.7	20
DISY (Democratic Rally)	139,721	34.0	19
DIKO (Democratic Party)	60,986	14.8	9
KISOS (Movement of Social Democrats)	26,767	6.5	4
NEO (New Horizons)	12,333	3.0	1
EDE (United Democrats)	10,635	2.6	1
ADIK (Fighting Democratic Movement)	8,860	2.2	1
Movement of Ecologist and Environmentalists	8,129	2.0	1
Independents	908	0.1	—
Total	410,987	100.0	56

Political Organizations

Agonistiko Dimokratiko Kinima (ADIK) (Fighting Democratic Movement): POB 216095, 80 Arch. Makariou III St, Flat 401, 1077 Nicosia; tel. (22) 765353; fax (22) 375737; e-mail info@adik.org.cy; internet www.adik.org.cy; f. 1999; centre-right; supports independent and united Cyprus and a settlement based on UN resolutions; advocates accession of Cyprus to the European Union; Pres. DINOS MICHAELIDES; Gen. Sec. YIANNIS PAPADOPOULOS.

Anorthotiko Komma Ergazomenou Laou (AKEL) (Progressive Party of the Working People): POB 21827, 4 E. Papaioannou St, 1513 Nicosia; tel. (22) 761121; fax (22) 761574; e-mail k.e.akel@cytanet.com.cy; internet www.akel.org.cy; f. 1941; successor to the Communist Party of Cyprus (f. 1926); Marxist-Leninist; supports demilitarized, non-aligned and independent Cyprus; over 14,000 mems; Sec.-Gen. DEMETRIS CHRISTOFIAS.

Dimokratiko Komma (DIKO) (Democratic Party): POB 23979, 50 Grivas Dhigenis Ave, 1080 Nicosia; tel. (22) 666002; fax (22) 666488; e-mail diko@diko.org.cy; internet www.diko.org.cy; f. 1976; absorbed Enosi Kentrou (Centre Union, f. 1981) in 1989; supports settlement of the Cyprus problem based on UN resolutions; Pres. TASSOS PAPADOPOULOS; Gen. Sec. ANDREAS ANGELIDES.

Dimokratikos Synagermos (DISY) (Democratic Rally): POB 25303, 25 Pindarou St, 1061 Nicosia; tel. (22) 883164; fax (22) 753821; e-mail epikinonia@disy.org.cy; internet www.disy.org.cy; f. 1976; absorbed Democratic National Party (DEK) in 1977, New Democratic Front (NEDIPA) in 1988 and Liberal Party in 1998; advocates entry of Cyprus into the European Union and greater active involvement by the EU in the settlement of the Cyprus problem; advocates market economy with restricted state intervention and increased state social role; 27,000 mems; Pres. NIKOS ANASTASIADES; Dir-Gen. GEORGE LIVERAS.

Enomeni Dimokrates (EDI) (United Democrats): POB 23494, 8 Iassonos St, 1683 Nicosia; tel. (22) 663030; fax (22) 664747; e-mail edicy@spidernet.com.cy; internet www.edi.org.cy; f. 1996 by merger of Ananeotiko Dimokratiko Socialistiko Kinema (ADISOK—Democratic Socialist Reform Movement) and Kinema ton Eleftheron Dimokraton (KED—Movement of Free Democrats); Pres. GEORGHIOS VASSILIOU; Gen. Sec. KOSTAS THEMISTOKLEOUS.

Epalxi Anasygrotisis Kentrou (EAK) (Political Forum for the Restructuring of the Centre): POB 22119, Lambousa St, 1095 Nicosia; tel. (22) 773564; fax (22) 779939; e-mail kchrysos@logos.cy.net; f. 1998; aims to achieve a wider grouping of all centrist social-democratic movements; supports a settlement to the Cyprus problem based on the principles of the Rule of Law, international law and respect for human rights for all citizens, and the establishment of a democratic federal system of government.

Kinima Ekologon-Perivallontiston (Movement of Ecologists and Environmentalists): POB 29682, 1722 Nicosia, tel. (22) 518787; fax (22) 512710; e-mail greenpar@cytanet.com.cy; internet www.cycentral.com/greens; f. 1996; opposed to any geographical division of the island; supports entry into the European Union; Gen. Co-ordinator SAVVAS PHILIPPOU.

Kinima Sosialdimokraton (KISOS) (Movement of Social Democrats): POB 21064, 40 Byron Ave, 1096 Nicosia; tel. (22) 670121; fax (22) 678894; e-mail info@kisos.org; internet www.kisos.org; f. 2000 as successor to Socialistico Komma Kyprou (EDEK—Socialist Party of Cyprus, f. 1969); supports independent, non-aligned, unitary, demilitarized Cyprus; advocates accession of Cyprus to the European Union; Pres. Dr VASSOS LYSSARIDES; Dep. Pres. YIANNAKIS OMIROU.

Kinisi Politikou Eksychronismou (Movement for Political Reforms): 22 Stasikratous St, 1065 Nicosia; tel. (22) 668894; fax (22) 6698892; f. 1995; aims to contribute to realignment of the parties of the Centre; supports settlement of the Cyprus problem based on UN resolutions; supports accession of Cyprus to the European Union.

Komma Evrodimokratikis Ananeosis (KEA) (Eurodemocratic Renewal Party): 176 Athalassa Ave, Office 402, 2025 Nicosia; tel. (22) 514551; fax (22) 513565; f. 1998; supports entry into the European Union and federal settlement to the Cyprus problem based on UN resolutions; Pres. TAKIS HADJIOANNOU (acting).

Neoi Orizontes (NEO) (New Horizons): POB 22496, 3 Trikoupi St, 1522 Nicosia; tel. (22) 761476; fax (22) 761144; e-mail neo@neoiorizontes.org; internet www.neoiorizontes.org; f. 1996; supports settlement of the Cyprus problem through political means and the establishment of a non-federal unitary state with single sovereignty throughout the whole territory of the island; Pres. NIKOS KOUTSOU; Gen. Sec. MARIA ROSSIDOU.

Diplomatic Representation

EMBASSIES AND HIGH COMMISSIONS IN CYPRUS

Australia: 4 Annis Komninis St, 2nd Floor, 1060 Nicosia; tel. (22) 753001; fax (22) 766486; e-mail auscomm@logos.cy.net; High Commissioner: FRANZ JOHANN INGRUBER.

Bulgaria: POB 24029, 13 Konst. Paleologos St, 2406 Engomi, Nicosia; tel. (22) 672486; fax (22) 676598; e-mail bulgaria@cytanet .com.cy; Ambassador: KRASSIMIR STEFANOV.

China, People's Republic: POB 4531, 28 Archimedes St, 2411 Engomi, Nicosia; tel. (22) 352182; fax (22) 353530; Ambassador: SONG AIGUO.

Cuba: 7 Yiannis Taliotis St, Strovolos 2014, Nicosia; tel. (22) 512332; fax (22) 512331; e-mail embacuba@spidernet.com.cy; Ambassador: MANUEL PARDIÑAS AJENO.

Czech Republic: POB 5202, 48 Arsinois St, 1307 Nicosia; tel. (22) 421118; fax (22) 421059; e-mail nicosia@embassy.mzv.cz; Ambassador: VEŘA JEŘÁBIKOVÀ.

Egypt: POB 21752, 3 Egypt Ave, 1097 Nicosia; tel. (22) 680650; fax (22) 664265; Ambassador: OMAR METWALLY.

France: POB 21671, 12 Ploutarchou St, Engomi, Nicosia; tel. (22) 779910; fax (22) 781052; e-mail ambachyp@spidernet.com.cy; internet www.ambafrancechypre.org; Ambassador: JACQUES DESAIGNE.

Germany: POB 25705, 10 Nikitaras St, Ay. Omoloyitae, 1311 Nicosia; tel. (22) 451145; fax (22) 665694; e-mail info@german embassy-nicosia.org.cy; internet www.germanembassy-nicosia .org.cy; Ambassador: Dr JOCHEN TREBESCH.

Greece: POB 1799, 8/10 Byron Ave, Nicosia; tel. (22) 680670; fax (22) 680649; Ambassador: CHRISTOS PANAGOPOULOS.

Holy See: POB 21964, Holy Cross Catholic Church, Paphos Gate, 1010 Nicosia (Apostolic Nunciature); tel. (22) 662132; fax (22) 660767; e-mail holcross@logos.cy.net; Apostolic Nuncio: Most Rev. PIETRO SAMBI, Titular Archbishop of Belcastro (with residence in Jerusalem).

India: POB 25544, 3 Indira Gandhi St, Engomi, 2413 Nicosia; tel. (22) 351741; fax (22) 350402; e-mail india@spidernet.com.cy; High Commissioner: SHYAMALA B. COWSIK.

Iran: POB 8145, 42 Armenias St, Akropolis, Nicosia; tel. (22) 314459; fax (22) 315446; Ambassador: BAHMAN AGHA-RAZI.

Israel: POB 1049, 4 I. Gryparis St, Nicosia; tel. (22) 445195; fax (22) 453486; Ambassador: MICHAEL ELIGAL.

Italy: POB 27695, 11 25th March St, Engomi 2432, Nicosia; tel. (22) 357635; fax (22) 358112; e-mail italian.embassy@cytanet.com.cy; internet italian.embassy.cyprus.homepage.com; Ambassador: FRANCESCO BASCONE.

Lebanon: POB 21924, 1 Vasilissis Olgas St, Nicosia; tel. (22) 776845; fax (22) 776662; Ambassador: SAMIRA HANNA ED-DAHER.

Libya: POB 3669, 14 Estias St, 1041 Nicosia; tel. (22) 317366; fax (22) 316152; Ambassador: KHALIFA AHMAD BAZELYA.

Poland: 11 Acharnon St, 2027 Strovolos, Nicosia; tel. (22) 427077; fax (22) 510611; Ambassador: TOMASZ LIS.

Romania: POB 2210, 83 Kennedy Ave, 1077 Nicosia; tel. (22) 379303; fax (22) 379121; e-mail romemb@globalsoftmail.com; Ambassador: COSTIN GEORGESCU.

Russia: Ay. Prokopias St and Archbishop Makarios III Ave, Engomi, Nicosia; tel. (22) 772141; fax (22) 774854; Ambassador: VLADIMIR PRYGIN.

Slovakia: POB 21165, 4 Kalamatas St, 2002 Strovolos, Nicosia; tel. (22) 879681; fax (22) 311715; e-mail skembassy@cytanet.com.cy; Ambassador: DUŠAN ROZBORA.

Switzerland: POB 20729, MEDCON Bldg, 6th Floor, 46 Themistoklis Dervis St, 1663 Nicosia; tel. (22) 766261; fax (22) 766008; e-mail swiemnic@spidernet.com.cy; Chargé d'affaires a.i.: MARGRITH BIERI.

Syria: POB 21891, 24 Nikodimos Mylona St, Ay. Antonios, 1071 Nicosia; tel. (22) 764481; fax (22) 756963; Chargé d'affaires a.i.: Dr AHMAD HAJ-IBRAHIM.

United Kingdom: POB 21978, Alexander Pallis St, 1587 Nicosia; tel. (22) 861100; fax (22) 861125; e-mail infobhc@cylink.com.cy; internet www.britain.org.cy; High Commissioner: LYN PARKER.

USA: POB 24536, 7 Ploutarchou, 2407 Engomi, Nicosia; tel. (22) 776400; fax (22) 780944; e-mail amembass@spidernet.com.cy; internet www.americanembassy.org.cy; Ambassador: DONALD K. BANDLER.

Yugoslavia: 2 Vasilissis Olgas St, Nicosia; tel. (22) 445511; fax (22) 445910; Ambassador: SVETISLAV BASARA.

Judicial System

Supreme Council of Judicature: Nicosia. The Supreme Council of Judicature is composed of the President and Judges of the Supreme Court. It is responsible for the appointment, promotion, transfer, etc., of the judges exercising civil and criminal jurisdiction in the District Courts, the Assize Courts, the Family Courts, the Military Court, the Rent Control Courts and the Industrial Dispute Court.

SUPREME COURT

Supreme Court: Char. Mouskos St, 1404 Nicosia; tel. (22) 865716; fax (22) 304500. The Constitution of 1960 provided for a separate Supreme Constitutional Court and High Court but in 1964, in view of the resignation of their neutral presidents, these were amalgamated to form a single Supreme Court.

The Supreme Court is the final appellate court in the Republic and the final adjudicator in matters of constitutional and administrative law, including recourses on conflict of competence between state organs on questions of the constitutionality of laws, etc. It deals with appeals from Assize Courts, District Courts and other inferior Courts as well as from the decisions of its own judges when exercising original jurisdiction in certain matters such as prerogative orders of *habeas corpus, mandamus, certiorari,* etc., and in admiralty cases.

President: GEORGHIOS M. PIKIS.

Judges: I. C. CONSTANTINIDES, T. ELIADES, CHR. C. ARTEMIDES, G. NIKOLAOU, P. KALLIS, FR. G. NIKOLAIDES, S. NIKITAS, P. CH. ARTEMIS, M. KRONIDES, A. KRAMVIS, R. GAVRIELIDES, Y. CHRYSOSTOMIS.

Attorney-General: ALEKOS MARKIDES.

OTHER COURTS

As required by the Constitution a law was passed in 1960 providing for the establishment, jurisdiction and powers of courts of civil and criminal jurisdiction, i.e. of six District Courts and six Assize Courts. In accordance with the provisions of new legislation, approved in 1991, a permanent Assize Court, with powers of jurisdiction in all districts, was established.

In addition to a single Military Court, there are specialized Courts concerned with cases relating to industrial disputes, rent control and family law.

'Turkish Republic of Northern Cyprus'

The Turkish intervention in Cyprus in July 1974 resulted in the establishment of a separate area in northern Cyprus under the control of the Autonomous Turkish Cypriot Administration, with a Council of Ministers and separate judicial, financial, police, military and educational machinery serving the Turkish community.

On 13 February 1975 the Turkish-occupied zone of Cyprus was declared the 'Turkish Federated State of Cyprus', and Rauf Denktaş declared President. At the second joint meeting held by the Executive Council and Legislative Assembly of the Autonomous Turkish Cypriot Administration, it was decided to set up a Constituent Assembly which would prepare a constitution for the 'Turkish Federated State of Cyprus' within 45 days. This Constitution, which was approved by the Turkish Cypriot population in a referendum held on 8 June 1975, was regarded by the Turkish Cypriots as a first step towards a federal republic of Cyprus. The main provisions of the Constitution are summarized below:

The 'Turkish Federated State of Cyprus' is a democratic, secular republic based on the principles of social justice and the rule of law. It shall exercise only those functions that fall outside the powers and functions expressly given to the (proposed) Federal Republic of Cyprus. Necessary amendments shall be made to the Constitution of the 'Turkish Federated State of Cyprus' when the Constitution of the Federal Republic comes into force. The official language is Turkish.

Legislative power is vested in a Legislative Assembly, composed of 40 deputies, elected by universal suffrage for a period of five years. The President is Head of State and is elected by universal suffrage for a period of five years. No person may be elected President for more than two consecutive terms. The Council of Ministers shall be composed of a prime minister and 10 ministers. Judicial power is exercised through independent courts.

Other provisions cover such matters as the rehabilitation of refugees, property rights outside the 'Turkish Federated State', protection of coasts, social insurance, the rights and duties of citizens, etc.

On 15 November 1983 a unilateral declaration of independence brought into being the 'Turkish Republic of Northern Cyprus', which, like the 'Turkish Federated State of Cyprus', was not granted international recognition.

The Constituent Assembly, established after the declaration of independence, prepared a new constitution, which was approved by the Turkish Cypriot electorate on 5 May 1985. The new Constitution is very similar to the old one, but the number of deputies in the Legislative Assembly was increased to 50.

HEAD OF STATE

President of the 'Turkish Republic of Northern Cyprus': RAUF R. DENKTAŞ (assumed office as President of the 'Turkish Federated State of Cyprus' 13 February 1975; became President of the 'TRNC' 15 November 1983; re-elected 1985, 1990, 1995 and 15 April 2000).

COUNCIL OF MINISTERS
(September 2002)

A coalition of the Ulusal Bırlık Partisi (UBP) and the Demokrat Parti (DP).

Prime Minister: Dr DERVİŞ EROĞLU (UBP).

Minister of State and Deputy Prime Minister: SALIH COŞAR (dp).

Minister of Foreign Affairs and Defence: TAHSIN ERTUĞRUL-OĞLU (UBP).

Minister of the Interior, Rural Affairs and Housing: Dr MEHMET ALBAYRAK (UBP).

Minister of Finance: MEHMET BAYRAM (UBP).

Minister of National Education and Culture: İLKAY KAMIL (UBP).

Minister of Agriculture and Forestry: İRSEN KÜÇÜK (UBP).

Minister of Communications and Works: SALIH MIOĞLU (UBP).

Minister of Tourism and Environment: SERDAR DENKTAŞ (DP).

Minister of Health and Social Welfare: Dr MUSTAFA ARABACI-OĞLU (DP).

Minister of Labour, Social Security, Youth Affairs and Sports: Dr AHMET KAŞIF (DP).

MINISTRIES

Prime Minister's Office: Lefkoşa (Nicosia), Mersin 10, Turkey; tel. (22) 83141; fax (22) 75281; e-mail pressdpt@brimnet.com.

Ministry of State and Deputy Prime Minister's Office: Lefkoşa (Nicosia), Mersin 10, Turkey; tel. (22) 86838; fax (22) 85204; e-mail kktcb3@kktc.net; internet www.Turizm.TRNC.net.

Ministry of Agriculture and Forestry: Lefkoşa (Nicosia), Mersin 10, Turkey; tel. (22) 83735; fax (22) 86945.

Ministry of Communications and Works: Lefkoşa (Nicosia), Mersin 10, Turkey; tel. (22) 83666; fax (22) 81891.

Ministry of Finance: Lefkoşa (Nicosia), Mersin 10, Turkey; tel. (22) 83116; fax (22) 85204; e-mail ekonomi@ebim .com.tr.

Ministry of Foreign Affairs and Defence: Lefkoşa (Nicosia), Mersin 10, Turkey; tel. (22) 83241; fax (22) 84290; e-mail bakan lik@pubinfo.org; internet www.trncinfo.com.

Ministry of Health and Social Welfare: Lefkoşa (Nicosia), Mersin 10, Turkey; tel. (22) 78765; fax (22) 76349.

Ministry of the Interior, Rural Affairs and Housing: Lefkoşa (Nicosia), Mersin 10, Turkey; tel. (22) 85453; fax (22) 83043.

Ministry of Labour, Social Security, Youth Affairs and Sports: Lefkoşa (Nicosia), Mersin 10, Turkey; tel. (22) 83136; fax (22) 82334.

Ministry of National Education and Culture: Lefkoşa (Nicosia), Mersin 10, Turkey.

Ministry of Tourism and Environment: Lefkoşa (Nicosia), Mersin 10, Turkey; tel. (22) 83173; fax (22) 83893; e-mail tur izm@dbby.trnc.net; internet www.tourism.trnc.net.

PRESIDENT
Election, 15 April 2000*

Candidates	Votes	%
Rauf R. Denktaş (Independent) . . .	42,819	43.67
Dr Derviş Eroğlu (UBP)	29,505	30.14
Mustafa Akinci (TKP)	11,469	11.70
Mehmet Ali Talat (CTP)	9,834	10.03
Arif Hasan Tahsin (YBH)	2,545	2.60
Sener Levet (Independent) . . .	899	0.92
Turgut Afsaroglu (Independent) . .	553	0.56
Ayhan Kaymak (Independent) . . .	369	0.38
Total	97,993†	100.00

* Although Denktaş did not gain the 50% of the votes necesary to be elected in the first round, he was declared the winner after

Eroğlu withdrew from a second round of voting, scheduled for 22 April 2000.

† Excluding invalid votes.

LEGISLATIVE ASSEMBLY

Speaker: ERTUĞRUL HASIPOĞLU (UBP).

General Election, 6 December 1998

Party	% of votes	Seats
Ulusal Birlik Partisi	40.3	24
Demokrat Parti	22.6	13
Toplumcu Kurtuluş Partisi	15.4	7
Cumhuriyetçi Türk Partisi	13.4	6
Others*	8.3	—
Total	100.0	50

* The other parties that contested the election were the National Revival Party, which won 4.6% of the votes; the Patriotic Unity Movement, which obtained 2.5%; and Our Party, which won 1.2%.

POLITICAL ORGANIZATIONS

Cumhuriyetçi Türk Partisi (CTP) (Republican Turkish Party): 99A Şehit Salahi, Şevket Sok., Lefkoşa (Nicosia), Mersin 10, Turkey; tel. (22) 73300; fax (22) 81914; e-mail ctp@cypronet.net; f. 1970 by members of the Turkish community in Cyprus; socialist principles with anti-imperialist stand; district organizations at Gazi Mağusa (Famagusta), Girne (Kyrenia), Güzelyurt (Morphou) and Lefkoşa (Nicosia); Leader MEHMET ALI TALAT; Gen. Sec. MUSTAFA FERD SOYER.

Demokrat Parti (DP) (Democrat Party): Lefkoşa (Nicosia), Mersin 10, Turkey; tel. (22) 83795; fax (22) 87130; e-mail yenidem@kktc.net; f. 1992 by disaffected UBP representatives; merged with the Yeni Doğuş Partisi (New Dawn Party; f. 1984) and Sosyal Demokrat Partisi (Social Democrat Party) in May 1993; Leader SALIH COŞAR; Sec.-Gen. HURSIT EMINER.

Hür Demokrat Parti (Free Democrat Party): Lefkoşa (Nicosia), Mersin 10, Turkey; f. 1991; Leader ÖZEL TAHSIN.

Toplumcu Kurtuluş Partisi (TKP) (Communal Liberation Party): 44 İkinci Selim Sok., Lefkoşa (Nicosia), Mersin 10, Turkey; tel. (22) 72555; internet www.cm.gov.nc.tr/tkp; f. 1976; merged with the Atılımcı Halk Partisi (Progressive People's Party, f. 1979) in 1989; democratic left party; wants a solution of Cyprus problem as an independent, non-aligned, bi-zonal and bi-communal federal state; Leader MUSTAFA AKINCI; Gen. Sec. HÜSEYIN ANGOLEMLI.

Ulusal Bırlık Partisi (UBP) (National Unity Party): 9 Atatürk Meydanı, Lefkoşa (Nicosia), Mersin 10, Turkey; tel. (22) 73972; f. 1975; right of centre; based on Atatürk's reforms, social justice, political equality and peaceful co-existence in an independent, bi-zonal, bi-communal, confederate state of Cyprus; Leader Dr DERVİŞ EROĞLU; Sec.-Gen. SUHA TURKOZ.

Ulusal Dirilis Partisi (UDP) (National Revival Party): Lefkoşa (Nicosia), Mersin 10, Turkey; f. 1997; Leader ENVER EMIN.

Unity and Sovereignty Party (BEP): Lefkoşa (Nicosia), Mersin 10, Turkey; Leader ARIF SALIH KIRDAĞ.

Yeni Doğus Partisi (YDP) (New Dawn Party): Lefkoşa (Nicosia); f. 1984; merged with DP in May 1993, revived 1997.

Yurtsever Bırlık Hareketi (YBH) (Patriotic Unity Movement): Lefkoşa (Nicosia), Mersin 10, Turkey; tel. (22) 74917; fax (22) 88931; e-mail ybh@north-cyprus.net; f. 1989; Leader RASIH KESKINER.

DIPLOMATIC REPRESENTATION
Embassy in the 'TRNC'

Turkey: Bedrettin Demirel Cad., T.C. Lefkoşa Büyükelçisi, Lefkoşa (Nicosia), Mersin 10, Turkey; tel. (22) 72314; fax (22) 85118; e-mail tclefkbe@cc.emu.edu.tr; Ambassador: HAYATI GÜVEN.

Turkey is the only country officially to have recognized the 'Turkish Republic of Northern Cyprus'.

JUDICIAL SYSTEM

Supreme Court: Lefkoşa (Nicosia), Mersin 10, Turkey; tel. (22) 87535; fax (22) 85265; e-mail mahkeme@kktc.net. The highest court in the 'TRNC' is the Supreme Court. The Supreme Court functions as the Constitutional Court, the Court of Appeal and the High Administrative Court. The Supreme Court, sitting as the Constitutional Court, has exclusive jurisdiction to adjudicate finally on all matters prescribed by the Constitution. The Supreme Court, sitting as the Court of Appeal, is the highest appellate court in the 'TRNC'. It also has original jurisdiction in certain matters of judicial review.

The Supreme Court, sitting as the High Administrative Court, has exclusive jurisdiction on matters relating to administrative law.

The Supreme Court is composed of a president and seven judges.

President: SALIH S. DAYIOĞLU.

Judges: CELÂL KARABACAK, TANER ERGINEL, METIN A. HAKKI, NEVVAR NOLAN, MUSTAFA ÖZKÖK, GÖNÜL ERÖNEN, SEYT A. BENSEN.

Subordinate Courts: Judicial power other than that exercised by the Supreme Court is exercised by the Assize Courts, District Courts and Family Courts.

Supreme Council of Judicature: The Supreme Council of Judicature, composed of the president and judges of the Supreme Court, a member appointed by the President of the 'TRNC', a member appointed by the Legislative Assembly, the Attorney-General and a member elected by the Bar Association, is responsible for the appointment, promotion, transfer and matters relating to the discipline of all judges. The appointments of the president and judges of the Supreme Court are subject to the approval of the President of the 'TRNC'.

Attorney-General: SAIT AKIN.

Religion

Greeks form 77% of the population and most of them belong to the Orthodox Church, although there are also adherents of the Armenian Apostolic Church, the Anglican Communion and the Roman Catholic Church (including Maronites). Most Turks (about 18% of the population) are Muslims.

CHRISTIANITY
The Orthodox Church of Cyprus

The Autocephalous Orthodox Church of Cyprus, founded in AD 45, is part of the Eastern Orthodox Church; the Church is independent, and the Archbishop, who is also the Ethnarch (national leader of the Greek community), is elected by representatives of the towns and villages of Cyprus. The Church comprises six dioceses, and in 1995 had an estimated 600,000 members.

Archbishop of Nova Justiniana and all Cyprus: Archbishop CHRYSOSTOMOS, POB 1130, Archbishop Kyprianos St, Nicosia; tel. (22) 430696; fax (22) 432470.

Metropolitan of Paphos: Bishop CHRYSOSTOMOS.

Metropolitan of Kitium: Bishop CHRYSOSTOMOS, POB 40036, 6300 Larnaca; fax (4) 655588; e-mail mlarnaca@logosnet.cy.net.

Metropolitan of Kyrenia: Bishop PAULUS.

Metropolitan of Limassol: Bishop ATHANASIOS.

Metropolitan of Morphou: Bishop NEOPHYTIOS.

The Roman Catholic Church

Latin Rite

The Patriarchate of Jerusalem covers Israel, Jordan and Cyprus. The Patriarch is resident in Jerusalem (see the chapter on Israel).

Vicar Patriarchal for Cyprus: Fr UMBERTO BARATO, Holy Cross Catholic Church, Paphos Gate, POB 21964, 1515 Nicosia; tel. (22) 662132; fax (22) 660767; e-mail holcross@logos.cy.net.

Maronite Rite

Most of the Roman Catholics in Cyprus are adherents of the Maronite rite. Prior to June 1988 the Archdiocese of Cyprus included part of Lebanon. At December 2000 the archdiocese contained an estimated 10,000 Maronite Catholics.

Archbishop of Cyprus: Most Rev. BOUTROS GEMAYEL, POB 22249, Maronite Archbishop's House, 8 Ayios Maronas St, Nicosia; tel. (22) 678877; fax (22) 668260.

The Anglican Communion

Anglicans in Cyprus are adherents of the Episcopal Church in Jerusalem and the Middle East, officially inaugurated in January 1976. The Church has four dioceses. The diocese of Cyprus and the Gulf includes Cyprus, Iraq and the countries of the Arabian peninsula.

Bishop in Cyprus and the Gulf, President Bishop of the Episcopal Church in Jeruselam and the Middle East: Most Rev. CLIVE HANDFORD, c/o POB 22075, Diocesan Office, 2 Grigoris Afxentiou St, 1517 Nicosia; tel. (22) 671220; fax (22) 674553; e-mail georgia@spidernet.com.cy.

Other Christian Churches

Among other denominations active in Cyprus are the Armenian Apostolic Church and the Greek Evangelical Church.

ISLAM

Most adherents of Islam in Cyprus are Sunni Muslims of the Hanafi sect. The religious head of the Muslim community is the Mufti.

Mufti of Cyprus: AHMET CEMAL İLKTAÇ (acting), PK 142, Lefkoşa (Nicosia), Mersin 10, Turkey.

The Press
GREEK CYPRIOT DAILIES

Alithia (Truth): POB 21695, 26A Pindaros and Androklis St, 1060 Nicosia; tel. (22) 763040; fax (22) 763945; e-mail alithia@spidernet .com.cy; f. 1952 as a weekly, 1982 as a daily; morning; Greek; right-wing; Dir SOCRATIS HASIKOS; Chief Editor ALEKOS KONSTANTINIDES; circ. 11,000.

Apogevmatini (Afternoon): POB 25603, 5 Aegaleo St, Strovolos, Nicosia; tel. (22) 353603; fax (22) 353223; f. 1972; afternoon; Greek; independent; Dirs EFTHYMIOS HADJIEFTHIMIOU, ANTONIS STAVRIDES; Chief Editor COSTAKIS ANTONIOY; circ. 8,000.

Cyprus Mail: POB 21144, 24 Vassilios Voulgaroktonos St, Nicosia; tel. (22) 818585; fax (22) 676385; e-mail mail@cyprus-mail.com; internet www.cyprus-mail.com; f. 1945; morning; English; independent; Dir KYRIACOS IAKOVIDES; Editor STEVEN MYLES; circ. 4,000.

Epilogi: 19 Nikitara St, Ay. Omologies, Nicosia; tel. (22) 367345; fax (22) 367511; f. 1997; Greek; Chief Editor COSTAS ZACHARIADES.

Haravghi (Dawn): POB 21556, ETAK Bldg, 6 Akamantos St, Nicosia; tel. (22) 766666; fax (22) 765154; f. 1956; morning; Greek; organ of AKEL (Communist Party); Dir NIKOS KATSOURIDES; Chief Editor ANDREAS ROUSOS: circ. 9,000.

Machi (Combat): POB 27628, 4A Danaes, Engomi, Nicosia; tel. (22) 356676; fax (22) 356701; f. 1961; morning; Greek; right-wing; Dir SOTIRIS SAMPSON; Chief Editor MINA SAMPSON; circ. 4,750.

Phileleftheros (Liberal): POB 21094, Commercial Centre, 1 Diogenous St, 3rd, 6th–7th Floor, Engomi, 1501 Nicosia; tel. (22) 744000; fax (22) 590122; e-mail artemiou@phileleftheros.com; internet www.phileleftheros.com.cy; f. 1955; morning; Greek; independent, moderate; Dir N. PATTICHIS; Editorial Dir ANTHOS LYKAVGIS; Chief Editor TAKIS KOUNNAFIS; circ. 28,000.

Politis (Citizen): 12 Makhera St, Engomi, Nicosia; tel. (22) 861861; fax (22) 861871; e-mail info@politis-news.com; internet www .politis-news.com; f. 1999; morning; Greek; independent; Chief Editor ARISTOS MICHAELIDES.

Simerini (Today): POB 21836, 31 Archangelos Ave, Strovolos, Nicosia; tel. (22) 353532; fax (22) 352298; internet www.odyssey .com.cy/simerini; f. 1976; morning; Greek; right-wing; supports DISY party; Dir KOSTAS HADJIKOSTIS; Chief Editor SAVVAS IAKOVIDES; circ. 17,000.

TURKISH CYPRIOT DAILIES

Afrika: Lefkoşa (Nicosia), Mersin 10, Turkey; tel. (22) 71338; fax (22) 74585; e-mail avrupa@cc.emu.edu.tr; frmly Avrupa; independent; Editor ŞENER LEVENT; circ. 3,000.

Bırlık (Unity): 43 Yediler Sok., PK 841, Lefkoşa (Nicosia), Mersin 10, Turkey; tel. (22) 72959; fax (22) 83959; f. 1980; Turkish; organ of UBP; Editor LÜTFI ÖZTER.

Halkın Sesi (Voice of the People): 172 Kyrenia Sok., Lefkoşa (Nicosia), Mersin 10, Turkey; tel. (22) 73141; f. 1942; morning; Turkish; independent Turkish nationalist; Editor AKAY CEMAL; circ. 6,000.

Kıbrıs: Dr Fazıl Küçük Bul., Lefkoşa (Nicosia), Mersin 10, Turkey; tel. (22) 52555; fax 52934; e-mail kibris@cypronet.net; Editor MEHMET ALI AKPINAR; circ. 13,000.

Ortam (Political Conditions): 158A Girne Cad., Lefkoşa (Nicosia), Mersin 10, Turkey; tel. (22) 74872; Turkish; organ of the TKP; Editor ÖZAL ZIYA; circ. 1,250.

Vatan (Homeland): 46 Mufti Ziyai Sok., PK 842, Lefkoşa (Nicosia), Mersin 10, Turkey; tel. (22) 77557; fax (22) 77558; e-mail vatan@ kktc.net; f. 1991; Editor ERTEN KASIMOĞLU.

Yeni Demokrat (New Democrat): 1 Cengiz Han Cad., Kösklüçiftlik, Lefkoşa (Nicosia), Mersin 10, Turkey; tel. (22) 81485; fax (22) 72558; Turkish; organ of the DP; Editor MUSTAFA OKAN; circ. 450.

Yeni Düzen (New System): Yeni Sanayi Sok., Lefkoşa (Nicosia), Mersin 10, Turkey; tel. (22) 56658; fax (22) 53240; e-mail yeniduzen@ defne.net; Turkish; organ of the CTP; Editor BURHAN ERASUAN; circ. 1,250.

GREEK CYPRIOT WEEKLIES

Athlitiki tis Kyriakis: 5 Epias, Engomi, Nicosia; tel. (22) 352966; fax (22) 348835; f. 1996; Greek; athletic; Dir PANAYIOTIS FELLOUKAS; Chief Editor SAWAS KOSHARIS; circ. 4,000.

Cyprus Financial Mirror: POB 24280, 80B Thermopylon St, 2007 Nicosia; tel. (22) 495790; fax (22) 495907; e-mail shavasb@ financialmirror.com; internet www.financialmirror.com; f. 1993; English (with Greek-language supplement); independent; Dirs MASIS DER PARTHOGH, SHAVASB BOHDJALIAN; circ. 3,500.

Cyprus Weekly: POB 24977, Suite 102, Trust House, Gryparis St, 1306 Nicosia; tel. (22) 666047; fax (22) 668665; e-mail weekly@ spidernet.com.cy; internet www.cyprusweekly.com.cy; f. 1979; English; independent; Dirs GEORGES DER PARTHOGH, ALEX EFTHYVOULOS, ANDREAS HADJIPAPAS; Chief Editor MARTYN HENRY; circ. 18,000.

Ergatiki Phoni (Workers' Voice): POB 25018, SEK Bldg, 23 Alkeou St, Engomi, Nicosia; tel. (22) 441142; fax (22) 476360; f. 1947; Greek; organ of SEK trade union; Dir MICHALAKIS IOANNOU; Chief Editor XENIS XENOFONTOS; circ. 10,000.

Ergatiko Vima (Workers' Tribune): POB 21885, 31–35 Archemos St, Nicosia 1045; tel. (22) 349400; fax (22) 349382; f. 1956; Greek; organ of the PEO trade union; Chief Editor KOSTAS GREKOS; circ. 14,000.

Official Gazette: Printing Office of the Republic of Cyprus, Nicosia; tel. (22) 302202; fax (22) 303175; f. 1960; Greek; published by the Government of the Republic of Cyprus; circ. 5,000.

Paraskinio (Behind the Scenes): 6 Psichikou St, Strovolos, Nicosia; tel. (22) 322959; fax (22) 322940; f. 1987; Greek; Dir and Chief Editor D. MICHAEL; cir. 3,000.

Selides (Pages): POB 21094, 1501 Nicosia; tel. (22) 590000; fax (22) 590122; e-mail selides@phileleftheros.com; internet www .phileleftheros.com; f. 1991; Greek; Dir N. PATTICHIS; Chief Editor STAVROS CHRISTODOLOU; circ. 16,500.

Super Flash: POB 23647, 11 Kolokotronis St, Kaimakli, Nicosia; tel. (22) 316674; fax (22) 316582; f. 1979; youth magazine; Greek; Dir DEMETRIS ALONEFTIS; circ. 4,000.

Ta Nea (News): POB 4349, 40 Vyronos Ave, Nicosia; tel. (22) 476575; fax (22) 476512; f. 1968; Greek; organ of EDEK (Socialist Party); Chief Editor PHYTOS SOCRATOUS; circ. 3,000.

Tharros (Courage): POB 27628, 4A Danaes, Engomi, Nicosia; tel. (22) 356676; fax (22) 356701; f. 1961; Greek; right-wing; Dir SOTIRIS SAMPSON; Chief Editor MINA SAMPSON; circ. 5,500.

To Periodiko: POB 21836, Dias Bldg, 31 Archangelos Ave, Strovolos, Nicosia; tel. (22) 353646; fax (22) 352268; f. 1986; Greek; Dir KOSTAS HADJIKOSTIS; Chief Editor ANDREAS DEMETROPOULOS; circ. 16,000.

TURKISH CYPRIOT WEEKLIES

Cyprus Today: Dr Fazil Küçük Bul., PK 831, Lefkoşa (Nicosia), Mersin 10, Turkey; tel. (22) 52555; fax (22) 52934; e-mail cyprustoday@yahoo.com; f. 1991; English; political, social, cultural and economic; Editor GILL FRASER; circ. 5,000.

Ekonomi (The Economy): Bedrettin Demirel Cad. No.90, Lefkoşa (Nicosia), Mersin 10, Turkey; tel. (22) 83760; fax (22) 83089; f. 1958; Turkish; published by the Turkish Cypriot Chamber of Commerce, Editor-in-Chief SAMI TAŞARKAN; circ. 3,000.

Safak: PK 228, Lefkoşa (Nicosia), Mersin 10, Turkey; tel. (22) 71472; fax (22) 87910; f. 1992; Turkish; circ. 1,000.

Yeni Çağ: 28 Ramadan Cad., Lefkoşa (Nicosia), Mersin 10, Turkey; tel. (22) 74917; fax (22) 71476; e-mail yenicag@8m.com; internet www.north-cyprus.net/ybh; f. 1990; Turkish; publ. of the YBH; circ. 500.

OTHER WEEKLIES

The Blue Beret: POB 21642, HQ UNFICYP, 1590 Nicosia; tel. (22) 864550; fax (22) 864461; e-mail blueberetcyprus@hotmail.com; internet www.unficyp.org; English; circ. 1,500.

Lion: 55 AEC Episkopi, British Forces Post Office 53; tel. (25) 262445; fax (25) 263181; e-mail wolves1@cytanet.com.cy; distributed to British Sovereign Base Areas, United Nations Forces and principal Cypriot towns; weekly; includes British Forces Broadcasting Services programme guide; Editor SARA WOOTTON; circ. 5,000.

Middle East Economic Survey: Middle East Petroleum and Economic Publications (Cyprus), POB 24940, Flat 24, 31 Evergoras Ave, Evergoras Complex, 1355 Nicosia; tel. (22) 665431; fax (22) 671988; e-mail info@mees.com; internet www.mees.com; f. 1957 (in Beirut, Lebanon); weekly review and analysis of petroleum, finance and banking, and political developments; Publr BASIM W. ITAYIM; Editor WALID KHADDURI.

GREEK CYPRIOT PERIODICALS

Cool: POB 8205, 86 Iphigenias St, 2091 Nicosia; tel. (22) 378900; fax (22) 378916; f. 1994; Greek; youth magazine; Chief Editor PROMETHEAS CHRISTOPHIDES; circ. 4,000.

Cypria (Cypriot Woman): POB 28506, 56 Kennedy Ave, 11th Floor, 1076 Nicosia; tel. (22) 494907; fax (22) 427051; f. 1983; every 2 months; Greek; Owner MARO KARAYIANNI; circ. 7,000.

Cyprus P.C.: POB 24989, 6th Floor, 1 Kyriakou Matsi St, 1306 Nicosia; tel. (22) 765999; fax (22) 765909; e-mail pc@infomedia .cy.net; internet www.infomedia.com.cy; f. 1990; monthly; Greek; computing magazine; Dir LAKIS VARNAVA; circ. 5,000.

Cyprus Time Out: POB 3697, 4 Pygmalionos St, 1010 Nicosia; tel. (22) 472949; fax (22) 360668; f. 1978; monthly; English; Dir ELLADA SOPHOCLEOUS; Chief Editor LYN HAVILAND; circ. 8,000.

Cyprus Today: c/o Ministry of Education and Culture, Nicosia; tel. (22) 800933; fax (22) 518042; e-mail cycult@cytanet.com.cy; f. 1963; quarterly; English; cultural and information review; published and distributed by Press and Information Office; Dir of Cultural Services Dr STELIOS ACH. HADJISTYLLIS; circ. 12,000.

Cyprus Tourism: POB 51697, Limassol; tel. (25) 337377; fax (25) 337374; f. 1989; bimonthly; Greek; English; tourism and travel; Man. Dir G. EROTOKRITOU; circ. 250,000.

Dimosios Ypallilos (Civil Servant): 3 Dem. Severis Ave, 1066 Nicosia; tel. (22) 667260; fax (22) 665189; fortnightly; published by the Cyprus Civil Servants' Association (PASYDY); circ. 14,000.

Enosis (Union): 71 Piraeus & Tombazis, Nicosia; tel. (22) 756862; fax (22) 757268; f. 1996; monthly; Greek; satirical; Chief Editor VASOS FTOCHOPOLILOS; circ. 2,000.

Eso-Etimos (Ever Ready): POB 4544, Nicosia; tel. (22) 443587; f. 1913; quarterly; Greek; publ. by Cyprus Scouts' Asscn; Editor TAKIS NEOPHYTOU; circ. 2,500.

Eva: 6 Psichikou St, Strovolos, Nicosia; tel. (22) 322959; fax (22) 322940; f. 1996; Greek; Dir DINOS MICHAEL; Chief Editors CHARIS PONTIKIS, KATIA SAVVIDOU; circ. 4,000.

Hermes International: POB 24512, Nicosia; tel. (22) 570570; fax (22) 581617; f. 1992; quarterly; English; lifestyle, business, finance, management; Chief Editor JOHN VICKERS; circ. 8,500.

I Kypros Simera (Present Day Cyprus): Apellis St, 1456 Nicosia; tel. (22) 801196; fax (22) 666123; e-mail pioxx@cytanet.com.cy; internet www.pio.gov.cy; f. 1983; fortnightly; Greek; published by the Press and Information Office of the Ministry of the Interior; Principal Officers E. HADJIPASCHALIS, A. LYRITSAS; circ. 3,500.

Nicosia This Month: POB 21015, Nikoklis Publishing House, Ledras and Pygmalionos St, Nicosia; tel. (22) 673124; fax (22) 663363; f. 1984; monthly; English; Chief Editor ELLADA SOPHOCLEOUS; circ. 4,000.

Omicron: POB 25211, 1 Commercial Centre Diogenous, 2nd Floor, 1307 Nicosia; tel. (22) 590110; fax (22) 590410; f. 1996; Greek; Dir NIKOS CHR. PATTICHIS; Chief Editor STAVROS CHRISTODOULOU; circ. 8,000.

Paediki Chara (Children's Joy): POB 136, 18 Archbishop Makarios III Ave, 1065 Nicosia; tel. (22) 817585; fax (22) 817599; e-mail poed@ cytanet.com.cy; f. 1962; monthly; for pupils; publ. by the Pancyprian Union of Greek Teachers; Editor SOFOCLES CHARALAMBIDES; circ. 15,000.

Synergatiko Vima (The Co-operative Tribune): Kosti Palama 5, 1096 Nicosia; tel. (22) 680757; fax (22) 660833; e-mail coop.confeder@ cytanet.com.cy; f. 1983; monthly; Greek; official organ of the Pancyprian Co-operative Confederation Ltd; circ. 5,000.

Synthesis (Composition): 6 Psichikou St, Strovolos, Nicosia; tel. (22) 322959; fax (22) 322940; f. 1988; every 2 months; Greek; interior decorating; Dir DINOS MICHAEL; circ. 6,000.

Tele Ores: POB 28205, 4 Acropoleos St, 1st Floor, 2091 Nicosia; tel. (22) 513300; fax (22) 513363; f. 1993; Greek; fortnightly; television guide; Chief Editor PROMETHEAS CHRISTOPHIDES; circ. 17,000.

TV Kanali (TV Channel): POB 25603, 5 Aegaleo St, Strovolos, Nicosia; tel. (22) 353603; fax (22) 353223; f. 1993; Greek; Dirs A. STAVRIDES, E. HADJIEFTHYMIOU; Chief Editor CHARIS TOMAZOS; circ. 13,000.

TURKISH CYPRIOT PERIODICALS

Güvenlik Kuvvetleri Magazine: Lefkoşa (Nicosia), Mersin 10, Turkey; tel. (22) 75880; publ. by the Security Forces of the 'TRNC'.

Halkbilimi: Has-Der, PK 199, Lefkoşa (Nicosia), Mersin 10, Turkey; tel. (22) 83146; fax (22) 84125; e-mail mesan@north-cyprus.net; internet www.cypnet.com/ncyprus/gifs/halkbil.gif; f. 1986; annual; publ. of Folk Arts Assoc.; academic; Turkish; Chief Editor KANI KANOL; circ. 1,500 (2000).

Kıbrıs—Northern Cyprus Monthly: Ministry of Foreign Affairs and Defence, Lefkoşa (Nicosia), Mersin 10, Turkey; tel. (22) 83365; fax (22) 84847; e-mail pio@trncpio.org; internet www.trncpio.org; f. 1963; Editor GÖNÜL ATANER.

Kıbrıslı Türkün Sesi: 44 Mecidiye St, Lefkoşa (Nicosia), Mersin 10, Turkey; tel. (22) 78520; fax (22) 87966; internet www

.medyatext.com/kibrisli/; monthly; political; Exec. Dir DOGAN HARMAN; Gen. Co-ordinator CEVDET ALPARSLAN.

Kültür Sanat Dergisi: Girne Cad. 92, Lefkoşa (Nicosia), Mersin 10, Turkey; tel. (22) 83313; e-mail info@turkishbank.com; internet www.turkishbank.com; publ. of Türk Bankası; circ. 1,000.

Kuzey Kıbrıs Kültür Dergisi (North Cyprus Cultural Journal): PK 157, Lefkoşa (Nicosia), Mersin 10, Turkey; tel. (22) 31298; f. 1987; monthly; Turkish; Chief Editor GÜNSEL DOĞASAL.

NEWS AGENCIES

Cyprus News Agency: POB 23947, 7 Kastorias St, 2002 Strovolos, 1687 Nicosia; tel. (22) 499662; fax (22) 492697; e-mail cna@cytanet .com.cy; internet www.cna.org.cy; f. 1976; English and Greek; Dir THEMIS THEMISTOCLEOUS.

Kuzey Kıbrıs Haber Ajansı (Northern Cyprus News Agency): Alirizin Efendi Cad., Vakiflar Işhani, Kat 2, No. 3, Ortaköy, Lefkoşa (Nicosia), Mersin 10, Turkey; tel. (22) 81922; fax (22) 81934; f. 1977; Dir-Gen. M. ALI AKPINAR.

Papyrus General Press Distribution Agency: POB 12669, 5 Arch. Kyprianou, Latsia, Nicosia; tel. (22) 488855; fax (22) 488883; e-mail papyrus@spidernet.com.cy.

TürkAjansı-Kıbrıs (TAK) (Turkish News Agency of Cyprus): POB 355, 30 Mehmet Akif Cad., Lefkoşa (Nicosia), Mersin 10, Turkey; tel. (22) 71818; fax (22) 71213; e-mail tak@cc.emu.edu.tr; internet www.emu.edu.tr/~tak; f. 1973; Dir EMIR HÜSEYN ERSOY.

Foreign Bureaux

Agence France-Presse (AFP) (France): POB 7242, Loizides Centre, 7th Floor, 36 Kypranoros St, Nicosia; tel. (22) 754050; fax (22) 768977; e-mail nicosie.redaction@afp.com; Bureau Chief PIERRE TAILLEFER.

Agencia EFE (Spain): 64 Metochiou St, Office 401, Nicosia; tel. (22) 775725; fax (22) 781662; Correspondent DOMINGO DEL PINO.

Agenzia Nazionale Stampa Associata (ANSA) (Italy): Middle East Office, 10 Katsonis St, Ayii Omoloyites, Nicosia; tel. (22) 491699; fax (22) 492732; Rep. VITTORIO FRENQUELLUCCI.

Associated Press (AP) (USA): POB 4853, Neoelen Marina, 10 Katsonis St, Nicosia; tel. (22) 492599; fax (22) 491617; Correspondent ALEX EFTY.

Athinaikon Praktorion Eidiseon (Greece): Flat 64, Tryfonos Bldg, Eleftherias Sq., 1011 Nicosia; tel. (22) 441110; fax (22) 457418; Rep. GEORGE LEONIDAS.

Informatsionnoye Telegrafnoye Agentstvo Rossii—Telegrafnoye Agentstvo Suverennykh Stran (ITAR—TASS) (Russia): POB 2235, 5–6 Evangelias St, Archangelos, Nicosia; tel. (22) 382486; Rep. ALEXEI YEROVTCHENKOV.

Iraqi News Agency: POB 1098, Flat 201, 11 Ippocratous St, Nicosia; tel. (22) 472095; fax (22) 472096; Correspondent AHMAD SULEYMAN.

Jamahiriya News Agency (JANA) (Libya): Flat 203, 12 Kypranoros, Nicosia; tel. (22) 361129; Rep. MUHAMMAD ALI ESHOWEIHIDI.

Reuters (United Kingdom): POB 25725, 5th Floor, George and Thelma Paraskevaides Foundation Bldg, 36 Grivas Dhigenis Ave, Nicosia; tel. (22) 469607; fax (22) 662487; Correspondent MICHELE KAMBAS.

Sofia-Press Agency (Bulgaria): 9 Roumeli St, Droshia, Larnaca; tel. (4) 494484; Rep. IONKA VERESIE.

United Press International (UPI) (USA): 24A Heroos Ave, Nicosia 171; tel. (22) 456643; fax (22) 455998; Rep. GEORGES DER PARTHOGH.

Xinhua (New China) News Agency (People's Republic of China): 12 Byzantiou St, Flat 201, Ayios Dhometios, Nicosia; tel. (22) 590133; fax (22) 590146; Rep. HUANG JIANMING.

Publishers

GREEK CYPRIOT PUBLISHERS

Action Publications: POB 24676, 35 Ayiou Nicolaou St, Engomi, 1302 Nicosia; tel. (22) 590555; fax (22) 358443; e-mail chris.c@ actionprgroup.com; f. 1971; travel; Pres. TONY CHRISTODOULOU.

Andreou Chr. Publications: POB 22298, 67A Regenis St, 1520 Nicosia; tel. (22) 666877; fax (22) 666878; e-mail andreou2@cytanet .com.cy; f. 1979; biography, literature, history, regional interest.

James Bendon Ltd: POB 56484, 3307 Limasol; tel. (25) 633181; fax (25) 632352; e-mail jbendon@attglobal.net; internet www .jamesbendon.com; philately; Pres. JAMES BENDON; Vice-Pres. RIDA BENDON.

Chrysopolitissa: 27 Al. Papadiamantis St, 2400 Nicosia; tel. (22) 353929; f. 1973; theatre, literature.

Costas Epiphaniou: Ekdoseis Antiprosopies Ltd, POB 2451, 1521 Nicosia; tel. (22) 750873; fax (22) 759266; f. 1973; Dir COSTAS EPIPHANIOU.

Foundation 'Anastasios G. Leventis': 40 Gladstonos St, POB 22543, 1095 Nicosia; tel. (22) 667706; fax (22) 675002; e-mail leventcy@zenon.logos.cy.net; internet www.leventisfoundation.org.

KY KE M: POB 4108, Nicosia; tel. (22) 450302; fax (22) 463624; Pres. NIKOS KOUTSOU.

MAM Ltd (The House of Cyprus and Cyprological Publications): POB 21722, 1512 Nicosia; tel. (22) 753536; fax (22) 375802; e-mail mam@mam.cy.net; internet www.mam.cy.net; f. 1965.

Nikoklis Publishing House: POB 23697, Nicosia; tel. (22) 672949; fax (22) 330218; ethnicity, travel; Man. ELLADA SOPHOCLEOUS.

Omilos Pnevmatikis Ananeoseos: 1 Omirou St, 2407 Engomi, Nicosia; tel. (22) 775854; literature.

Pierides Foundation: Larnaca; tel. (4) 651345; fax (4) 657227.

POLTE (Pancyprian Organization of Tertiary Education): c/o Higher Technical Institute, Nicosia; tel. (22) 305030; fax (22) 494953; Pres. KOSTAS NEOKLEOUS.

TURKISH CYPRIOT PUBLISHERS

Birlik Gazetesi: Yediler Sok., Lefkoşa (Nicosia), Mersin 10, Turkey; tel. (22) 72959; f. 1980; Dir MEHMET AKAR.

Bolan Matbaası: 35 Pençizade Sok., Lefkoşa (Nicosia), Mersin 10, Turkey; tel. (22) 74802.

Devlet Basımevi (Turkish Cypriot Government Printing House): Şerif Arzik Sok., Lefkoşa (Nicosia), Mersin 10, Turkey; tel. (22) 72010; Dir S. KÜRŞAD.

Halkın Sesi Ltd: 172 Girne Cad., Lefkoşa (Nicosia), Mersin 10, Turkey; tel. (22) 73141.

Kema Matbaası: 1 Tabak Hilmi Sok., Lefkoşa (Nicosia), Mersin 10, Turkey; tel. (22) 72785.

North Cyprus Research and Publishing Centre (CYREP): PK 327, Lefkoşa (Nicosia), Mersin 10, Turkey; tel. (22) 78914; fax (22) 72592; Man. Editor AHMET C. GAZIOĞLU.

K. Rüstem & Bro.: 22–24 Girne Cad., Lefkoşa (Nicosia), Mersin 10, Turkey; tel. (22) 71418.

Sebil International Press: PK 421, Lefkoşa (Nicosia), Mersin 10, Turkey; tel. (22) 46805; fax (22) 310804; e-mail ics@analiz.net; f. 1985; technical and scientific; Principal Officer E. BAŞARAN.

Tezel Matbaası: 35 Şinasi Sok., Lefkoşa (Nicosia), Mersin 10, Turkey; tel. (22) 71022.

Broadcasting and Communications

TELECOMMUNICATIONS

Cyprus Telecommunications Authority (CYTA): POB 24929, 1396 Nicosia; tel. (22) 701000; fax (22) 494940; e-mail pr@cyta .cytanet.com.cy; internet www.cyta.com.cy; provides national, international and cellular services in Cyprus.

Telekomünikasyon Diaresi Müdürlügü (Directorate of Telecommunications): Lefkoşa (Nicosia), Mersin 10, Turkey; tel. (22) 81888; fax (22) 88666; f. 1963; state-owned; responsible to Ministry of Communications, Works and Tourism; admin. and operation of telecommunications services; Gen. Man. SALIH KARA.

BROADCASTING

Radio

British Forces Broadcasting Service, Cyprus: Akrotiri, British Forces Post Office 57; tel. (25) 252009; fax (25) 268580; e-mail Dusty.Miller@bfbs.com; internet www.bfbs.com; f. 1948; broadcasts a two-channel 24-hour radio service in English on VHF; Station Man. DUSTY MILLER; Engineering Man. JON FORDHAM.

Cyprus Broadcasting Corporation (CyBC): POB 24824, Broadcasting House, 1397 Nicosia; tel. (22) 422231; fax (22) 314050; e-mail rik@cybc.com.cy; internet www.cybc.com.cy; radio f. 1952; Programme I in Greek, Programme II in Greek, Turkish, English and Armenian, Programme III in Greek; two medium-wave transmitters of 100 kW in Nicosia with relay stations at Paphos and Limassol; three 10-kW ERP VHF FM stereo transmitters on Mount Olympus; and three relay stations; Chair. MARIOS ELIADES; Dir-Gen. MICHAEL STYLIANOU; Head of Radio KYRIACOS CHARALAMBIDES.

Logos: Church of Cyprus, POB 27400, 1644 Nicosia; tel. (22) 355444; fax (22) 355737; e-mail director@logos.cy.net; Chair. ANDREAS PHILIPPOU; Dir-Gen. CHRISTODOULOS PROTOPAPAS.

Radio Astra: 145 Athalassas Ave, Strovolos, 2045 Nicosia; tel. (22) 313200; fax (22) 319261; e-mail info@astra.com.cy; internet www .astra.com.cy; Dir TAKIS HADJIGEORGIOU.

Radio Proto: POB 21836, 31 Archangelos St, Parissinos, 2054 Nicosia; tel. (22) 353545; fax (22) 352266; e-mail pavlos@radiopro to.com; internet www.radioproto.com; Chair. KOSTAS HADJIKOSTIS; Gen. Man. PAVLOS PAPACHRISTODOULOU.

Bayrak Radio and TV Corpn (BRTK): Atatürk Sq., Lefkoşa (Nicosia), Mersin 10, Turkey; tel. (22) 85555; fax (22) 81991; e-mail brt@cc.emu.edu.tr; internet www.brt.gov.nc.tr; in July 1983 it became an independent Turkish Cypriot corpn, partly financed by the Govt; Radio Bayrak f. 1963; home service in Turkish, overseas service in Turkish, Greek, English, Arabic and German; broadcasts 52.5 hours per day; Chair. GÜNAY YORGANCIOĞLU; Dir ISMET KOTAK; Head of Radio ŞIFA NESIM.

First FM and Interfirst FM: Lefkoşa (Nicosia), Mersin 10, Turkey; f. 1996.

Kıbrıs FM: Dr Fazil Küçük Blvd, Yeni Sanayi Bolgesi, Lefkoşa (Nicosia), Mersin 10, Turkey; tel. (22) 81922; fax (22) 81934; Dir MEHMET ALI AKPINAR.

Radio Emu: Gazi Mağusa (Famagusta), Mersin 10, Turkey; e-mail radioemu@cc.emu.edu.tr; internet www.emu.edu.tr/~radioemu.

Television

Greek Cypriot viewers have access to Greek television channels via satellite. Several Turkish channels are transmitted to the 'TRNC'.

Antenna T.V.: POB 20923, 1655 Nicosia: tel. (22) 311111; fax (22) 314959; Chair. LOUKIS PAPAPHILIPPOU; Man. Dir STELIOS MALEKOS.

British Forces Broadcasting Service, Cyprus: Akrotiri, British Forces Post Office 57; tel. (25) 252009; fax (25) 268580; e-mail dusty.miller@bfbs.com; f. 1948; broadcasts a daily TV service; Station Man. DUSTY MILLER; Engineering Man. JON FORDHAM.

Cyprus Broadcasting Corporation (CyBC): POB 24824, Broadcasting House, 1397 Nicosia; tel. (22) 422231; fax (22) 314050; e-mail rik@cybc.com.cy; internet www.cybc.com.cy; television f. 1957; **Pik 1 (CyBC 1):** one Band III 100/10-kW transmitter on Mount Olympus. **Pik 2 (CyBC 2):** one Band IV 100/10-kW ERP transmitter on Mount Olympus. **ET 1:** one Band IV 100/10-kW ERP transmitter on Mount Olympus for transmission of the ETI Programme received, via satellite, from Greece. The above three TV channels are also transmitted from 80 transposer stations; Chair. MARIOS ELIADES; Dir-Gen. MICHAEL STYLIANOU.

Lumiere TV Ltd: POB 25614, 2063 Nicosia; tel. (22) 357272; fax (22) 354622; e-mail administration@ltv.com.cy; internet www .lumieretv.com; f. 1992; encoded signal; Chair. and Man. Dir AKIS AVRAAMIDES; Gen. Man. GEORGE XINARIS.

O Logos: POB 27400, 1644 Nicosia; tel. (22) 355444; fax (22) 355737; e-mail director@logos.cy.net; Chair. ANDREAS PHILIPPOU; Dir CHRISTODOULOS PROTOPAPAS.

Sigma Radio TV Ltd: POB 21836, 2054 Nicosia; tel. (22) 357070; fax (22) 358640; island-wide coverage; Chair. and Dir KOSTAS HAD-JICOSTIS; Man. DINOS ODYSSEOS; New Business Devt Dir ANDY HAD-JICOSTIS.

Bayrak Radio and TV Corpn (BRTK): Atatürk Sq., Lefkoşa (Nicosia), Mersin 10, Turkey; tel. (22) 85555; fax (22) 81991; e-mail brt@cc.emu.edu.tr; internet www.brt.gov.nc.tr; in July 1983 it became an independent Turkish Cypriot corpn, partly financed by the Govt; Bayrak TV f. 1976; transmits programmes in Turkish, Greek, English and Arabic on nine channels; Chair. GÜNAY YORGANCI-OĞLU; Dir ISMET KOTAK; Head of Television TÜLIN URAL.

Gene TV: Bevel Yusuf Cad. 8, Yenişehir, Lefkoşa (Nicosia), Mersin 10, Turkey; tel. (22) 80790; fax (22) 76363; Dir ERTAN BIRINCI.

Kanal T: Dr Fazıl Küçük Cad. Foto Filiz Binaları, Göçmenköy, Lefkoşa (Nicosia), Mersin 10, Turkey; tel. (22) 37678; fax (22) 34257; Owner ERSIN FATAR.

Finance

(brs = branches; cap. = capital; res = reserves; dep. = deposits; m. = million; amounts in Cyprus pounds, except for Turkish Cypriot banks)

BANKING
Central Bank

Central Bank of Cyprus: POB 25529, 80 Kennedy Ave, 1395 Nicosia; tel. (22) 714100; fax (22) 378153; e-mail cbcinfo@ centralbank.gov.cy; internet www.centralbank.gov.cy; became fully independent from govt control in July 2002; f. 1963; cap. 15m., res 15m., dep. 1,209m. (Dec. 2000); Gov. CHRISTODOULOS CHRISTODOULOU.

Greek Cypriot Banks

Alpha Bank Ltd: POB 21661, Yiorkion Bldg, 1 Prodromou St, 1596 Nicosia; tel. (22) 888888; fax (22) 773766; e-mail secretariat@

alphabank.com.cy; internet www.alphabank.com.cy; f. 1960 as Lombard Banking (Cyprus) Ltd; name changed to Lombard NatWest Banking Ltd in 1989 and as above in 1998; locally incorporated although foreign-controlled; cap. 16.8m., res 50.8m., dep. 633.0m. (Dec. 2000); Chair. M. G. COLOCASSIDES; Dir ELEFTHERIOS IOANNOU; Man. Dir A. DEMETRIADES; 24 brs.

Bank of Cyprus Group: POB 21472, 51 Stassinos St, Ayia Paraskevi, 2002 Strovolos 140, 1599 Nicosia; tel. (22) 378000; fax (22) 378111; e-mail info@cy.bankofcyprus.com; internet www .bankofcyprus.com; f. 1899, reconstituted 1943 by the amalgamation of Bank of Cyprus, Larnaca Bank Ltd and Famagusta Bank Ltd; cap. 216.1m., res 254.9m., dep. 5,350.4m. (Dec. 2000); Chair. SOLON A. TRIANTAFYLLIDES; Group Chief Exec. CHR. S. PANTZARIS; 180 brs.

Co-operative Central Bank Ltd: POB 24537, 8 Gregoris Afxentiou St, 1389 Nicosia; tel. (22) 743000; fax (22) 670261; e-mail coopbank.gm@cytanet.com.cy; f. 1937 under the Co-operative Societies Law; banking and credit facilities to member societies, importer and distributor of agricultural requisites, insurance agent; cap. 3.6m., dep. 873.6m. (Dec. 2001); Chair. D. STAVROU; Sec.-Gen. D. PITSILLIDES; 4 brs.

The Cyprus Popular Bank Ltd: POB 22032, Laiki HQ, 154 Limassol Ave, 1598 Nicosia; tel. (22) 752000; fax (22) 811250; e-mail laiki.telebank@laiki.com; internet www.laiki.com; f. 1901; full commercial banking; cap. 149.1m., res 220.1m. dep. 3,438.5m. (Dec. 2000); Chair. and Pres. KIKIS N. LAZARIDES; 121 brs.

Hellenic Bank Ltd: POB 24747, 1394 Nicosia; tel. (22) 860000; fax (22) 754074; e-mail hellenic@hellenicbank.com; internet www .hellenicbank.com; f. 1974; financial services group; cap. 58.4m., res 123.8m., dep. 1,890.5m. (Dec. 2001); Chair. and Chief Exec. PANOS CHR. GHALANOS; 93 brs.

Housing Finance Corpn: POB 23898, 41 Themistoklis Dervis St, Hawaii Tower, Nicosia; tel. (22) 761777; fax (22) 762870; f. 1980; provides long-term loans for home-buying; cap. 12m., dep. 213m. (June 2000); Gen. Man. CH. SHAMBARTAS; 6 brs.

National Bank of Greece (Cyprus) Ltd: 15 Arch. Makarios III Ave, 1065 Nicosia; tel. (22) 840000; fax (22) 762080; e-mail cloizou@nbg.com.cy; f. 1994 by incorporating all local business of the National Bank of Greece SA; full commercial banking; cap. 23m. (Nov. 2000); Chair. TH. KARATZAS; Man. Dir M. TAGAROULIAS; 30 brs.

Universal Bank: 6th Floor, Universal Tower, 85 Dhigeni Akrita Ave, 1070 Nicosia; tel. (22) 883333; fax (22) 358702; e-mail unimai-l@usb.com.cy; internet www.universalbank.com.cy; f. 1925 as Yial-ousa Savings Ltd (closed 1974, reopened 1990), renamed as above 1996; cap. 15.0m., res 12.9m., dep. 91.1m. (Dec. 2000); Chair. GEORGE SYRIMIS; Gen. Man. Dr SPYROS EPISKOPOU; 15 brs.

Turkish Cypriot Banks
(amounts in Turkish liras unless otherwise indicated)

Akdeniz Garanti Bankası Ltd: PK 149, 2–4 Celaliye Sok. Inönu Meydan, Lefkoşa (Nicosia), Mersin 10, Turkey; tel. (22) 86742; fax (22) 86741; f. 1989 as Mediterranean Guarantee Bank; cap. and res 605,600m., dep. 22,867,000m. (Dec. 1999); Chair. ERDOĞAN NAIM.

Asbank Ltd: 8 Mecidiye Sok., PK 448, Lefkoşa (Nicosia), Mersin 10, Turkey; tel. (22) 83023; fax (22) 81244; internet www.asbank .com.tr; f. 1986; cap. 1,200,000m., res 782,148m., dep. 19,423,752m. (Dec. 2000); Chair. ALTAY ADADEMIR; Dep. Gen. Man. T. M. ALTUNER; 7 brs.

First Merchant Bank OSH Ltd: 25 Serif Arzik Sok., Lefkoşa (Nicosia), Mersin 10, Turkey; tel. (22) 75373; fax (22) 75377; e-mail fmb@firstmerchantbank.com; internet www .firstmerchantbank.com; f. 1993; also provides offshore services; cap. US $10m., res US $6.2m., dep. US $2,123.8m. (Dec. 2000); Chair. and Gen. Man. Dr H. N. YAMAN.

Kibris Altinbaş Bank Ltd (Cyprus Altinbaş Bank Ltd): PK 843, 2 Müftü Ziyai Efendi Sok., Lefkoşa (Nicosia), Mersin 10, Turkey; tel. (22) 88222; fax (22) 71623; e-mail kibrisaltinbasbank@yahu.com; internet www.altinbasbank.com.tr; f. 1993; cap. 748,100m., res 81,330m., dep. 7,822,563m. (Dec. 2000); Chair. VAKKAS ALTINBAŞ; Gen. Man. ÖZKAN TEKGUMUS.

Kıbrıs Endüstri Bankası Ltd: (Industrial Bank of Cyprus Ltd): Bedrettin Demirel Cad., Başbakanlık Kavşağı, Lefkoşa (Nicosia), Mersin 10, Turkey; tel. (22) 83770; fax (22) 71830; administrators appointed in May 2000.

Kıbrıs Eurobank Ltd: PK 35, 18 Mecidiye Sok., Lefkoşa (Nicosia), Mersin 10, Turkey; tel. (22) 87550; fax (22) 87670; e-mail eurobank@ kktc.net; internet www.eurobank.cjb.net; f. 1993; cap. US $2.0m., dep. US $2.5m. (Dec. 1999); Pres. and Chair. BEDI TUNASOY; Gen. Man. NUR SENLET SELHEP.

Kıbrıs İktisat Bankası Ltd (Cyprus Economy Bank Ltd): 151 Bedreddin Demirel Cad., Lefkoşa (Nicosia), Mersin 10, Turkey; tel. (22) 85300; fax (22) 81311; e-mail info@iktisatbank.cc; internet www.iktisatbank.cc; f. 1990; cap. 900,000m., res 2,495,006m., dep.

32,696,936m. (Dec. 2001); Chair. and Gen. Man. METE ÖZMERTER; 12 brs.

Kıbrıs Kredi Bankası Ltd (Cyprus Credit Bank Ltd): 5–7 İplik Pazarı Sok., Lefkoşa (Nicosia), Mersin 10, Turkey; tel. (22) 83667; fax (22) 76999; f. 1978; administrators appointed in May 2000; cap. 30,930m., res 164,131m., dep. 2,628,193m. (Dec. 1994); Chair. SALIH BOYACI; Gen. Man. YÜKSEL YAZGIN; 12 local brs.

Kıbrıs Ticaret Bankası Ltd (Cyprus Commercial Bank Ltd): 111 Bedrettin Demirel Ave, Lefkoşa (Nicosia), Mersin 10, Turkey; tel. (22) 83180; fax (22) 82278; e-mail cycom@kktc.net; f. 1982; cap. 500,000m., res 833,934m., dep. 10,679,115m. (Dec. 1998); Chair. YÜKSEL AHMET RAŞIT; Gen. Man. HÜSEYIN HARMANCI; 8 brs.

Kıbrıs Türk Kooperatif Merkez Bankası Ltd (Cyprus Turkish Co-operative Central Bank): 49–55 Mahmut Paşa Sok., PK 823, Lefkoşa (Nicosia), Mersin 10, Turkey; tel. (22) 83207; fax (22) 76787; e-mail info@koopbank.com; internet www.koopcb.com; f. 1959; cap. and res 4,344,363m., dep. 117,722,019m. (Dec. 2000); banking and credit facilities to member societies and individuals; Chair. AHMET ALPER; Gen. Man. Dr TUNCER ARIFOĞLU; 12 brs.

Kıbrıs Vakiflar Bankası Ltd (Cyprus Vakiflar Bank Ltd): 58 Yediler Sok., PK 212, Lefkoşa (Nicosia), Mersin 10, Turkey; tel. (22) 75109; fax (22) 75169; e-mail kvb@kktc.net; f. 1982; cap. 300,000m., res 1,391,816m., dep. 46,475,912m. (Dec. 2000); Pres. and Chair. LATIF ARAN; Gen. Man. ALPAY R. ADANIR; 7 brs.

Limassol Turkish Co-operative Bank Ltd: 10 Orhaneli Sok., Kyrenia, PK 247, Mersin 10, Turkey; tel. (22) 8156786; fax (22) 8156959; e-mail fordept@kktc.net; internet www.limasolbank.com; f. 1939; cap. 6,993,213.8m., res 601,679.6m, dep. 96,734,104.4m. (Dec. 2001); Chair. GÜZEL HALIM; Gen. Man. TANER EKDAL.

Türk Bankası Ltd (Turkish Bank Ltd): 92 Girne Cad., PK 242, Lefkoşa (Nicosia), Mersin 10, Turkey; tel. (22) 83313; fax (22) 82432; e-mail info@turkishbank.com; internet www.turkishbank.com; f. 1901; cap. 12,600,245m., res 9,367,102m., dep. 172,201,574m. (Dec. 2000); Chair. M. TANJU ÖZYOL; Gen. Man. C. YENAL MUSANNIF; 12 brs.

Universal Bank Limited: POB 658, 57 Mehmet Akif ave, Lefkoşa (Nicosia), Mersin 10, Turkey; tel. (22) 86262; fax (22) 87826; e-mail univers@kktc.net; internet www.bankunivers.com; f. 1997; cap. 821,100.0m., res 261,023.3m., dep. 6,118,885.4m. (Dec. 2000); Chair. ILHAN KÖSEOĞLU; Gen. Man. MÜNIR ALTUNER.

Viyabank Ltd: Ataturk Cad., 16 Muhtar Yusuf Galleria, Lefkoşa (Nicosia), Mersin 10, Turkey; tel. (22) 88902; fax (22) 85878; e-mail viyabank@future.com.tr; internet www.viyabank.com; f. 1998; cap. US $0.6m., res US $0.4m., dep. US $2.8m. (Dec. 2000); Pres. SALVO TARAGANO; Chair. ERDOĞAN SEVINÇ; 3 brs.

Yakin Dogu Bank Ltd (Near East Bank Ltd): POB 47, 1 Girne Caddesi, Lefkoşa (Nicosia), Mersin 10, Turkey; tel. (22) 83834; fax (22) 84180; cap. 1,110,000.0m., res 331,051.6m., dep. 10,057,425.0m. (Dec 2000); Chair. Dr SUAT I. GÜNSEL; Gen. Man. KAZIM M. OLGU.

Yeşilada Bank Ltd: POB 626, 11 Atatürk ave, Lefkoşa (Nicosia), Mersin 10, Turkey; tel. (22) 81999; fax (22) 81962; e-mail yesil ada@north-cyprus.net; cap. 599,550m., res 281,600m., dep. 4,520,516m. (Dec. 2000); Chair. and Pres. BURHAN YETKILI; Gen. Man. DERVIŞ TÜRKER.

Turkish Cypriot Bankers' Association

Northern Cyprus Bankers' Association: 92 Girne Cad., PK 242, Lefkoşa (Nicosia), Mersin 10, Turkey; f. 1987; tel. (22) 83180; fax (22) 82278; e-mail info@turkishbank.com; internet www.turkish bank.com; 31 mems (1998).

Investment Organization

Cyprus Investment and Securities Corpn: POB 20597, 1660 Nicosia; tel. (22) 881700; fax (22) 757737; f. 1982 to promote the development of capital market; member of Bank of Cyprus Group; issued cap. 20m. (2001); Chair. S. A. TRIANTAFYLLIDES; Gen. Man. STELIOS CHRISTODOULOU.

Development Bank

The Cyprus Development Bank Ltd: POB 21415, Alpha House, 50 Archbishop Makarios III Ave, 1508 Nicosia; tel. (22) 846500; fax (22) 846603; e-mail info@cdb.com.cy; internet www.cyprusdevelopmentbank.com; f. 1963; cap. 12.4m., res 34.0m., dep. 16.5m. (Dec. 2001); aims to accelerate the economic development of Cyprus by providing medium- and long-term loans for productive projects, developing the capital market, encouraging joint ventures and providing technical and managerial advice to productive private enterprises; Chair. ANDREAS MOUSKOS; Gen. Man. JOHN G. JOANNIDES; 1 br.

Foreign Banks

Arab Bank PLC: POB 25700, 1 Santaroza Ave, 1393 Nicosia; tel. (22) 899100; fax (22) 760890; e-mail info@arabbank.com.cy; f. 1984; commercial; Area Exec. TOUFIC J. DAJANI; 15 brs.

Commercial Bank of Greece SA: POB 25151, 4 Ionos St, 2015 Nicosia; tel. (22) 363646; fax (22) 663923; f. 1992; Country Man. G. KANTIANIS; 3 brs.

Türkiye Cumhuriyeti Ziraat Bankası: Girnekapi Cad., Ibrahimpaşa Sok. 105, Lefkoşa (Nicosia), Mersin 10, Turkey; tel. (22) 83050; fax (22) 82041.

Türkiye Halk Bankası AŞ: Osman Paşa Cad., Ümit Office, Lefkoşa (Nicosia), Mersin 10, Turkey; tel. (22) 72145; fax (22) 72146.

Türkiye İş Bankası AŞ: Girne Cad. 9, Lefkoşa (Nicosia), Mersin 10, Turkey; tel. (22) 83133; fax (22) 78315; f. 1924; Man. KEMAL AĞANOĞLU.

'Offshore' (International) Banking Units

Cyprus-based Offshore Banking Units (OBUs) are fully-staffed units which conduct all forms of banking business from within Cyprus with other offshore or foreign entities and non-resident persons. (OBUs are not permitted to accept deposits from persons of Cypriot origin who have emigrated to the United Kingdom and taken up permanent residence there.) Although exempt from most of the restrictions and regulatory measures applicable to 'onshore' banks, OBUs are subject to supervision and inspection by the Central Bank of Cyprus. OBUs may conduct business with onshore and domestic banks in all banking matters which the latter are allowed to undertake with banks abroad. OBUs are permitted to grant loans or guarantees in foreign currencies to residents of Cyprus (conditional on obtaining an exchange control permit from the Central Bank of Cyprus). Interest and other income earned from transactions with residents is subject to the full rate of income tax (20%), but the Minister of Finance is empowered by law to exempt an OBU from the above tax liability if satisfied that a specific transaction substantially contributes towards the economic development of the Republic. In 1999 there were 29 OBUs operating in Cyprus.

Agropromstroybank: POB 55297, Maximos Court B, 17 Leontiou St, Limassol; tel. (25) 384747; fax (25) 384858; Man. ALEXANDER MOKHONKO.

Allied Business Bank SAL: POB 54232, 3rd Floor, Flat 31, Lara Court, 276 Archbishop Makarios III Ave, Limassol; tel. (25) 363759; fax (25) 372711; Local Man. NAJIBA HAWILLA.

Arab Bank PLC: POB 25700, 1 Santaroza Ave, 1393 Nicosia; tel. (22) 899100; fax (22) 760890; e-mail arabbank@spidernet.com.cy; OBU licence granted 1997; Area Exec. TOUFIC J. DAJAN.

Arab Jordan Investment Bank SA: POB 54384, Libra Tower, 23 Olympion St, Limassol; tel. (25) 351351; fax (25) 360151; e-mail ajib@cy.net; internet www.ajib.com; f. 1978; cap. and dep. US $388m., total assets US$410m. (Dec. 1999); Man. ABED ABU-DAYEH.

AVTOVAZBANK: POB 22025, Office 201, Stefanie Court, 301A Saint-Andrews, 3035 Limassol; tel. (25) 354594; fax (25) 362582; Local Man. A. TSELOUNOV.

Banca Română de Comerţ Exterior (Bancorex) SA: POB 22538, Margarita House, 5th Floor, 15 Them. Dervis St, 1309 Nicosia; tel. (22) 677992; fax (22) 677945; Local Man. GRIGORE IOAN BUDISAN.

Bank of Beirut and the Arab Countries SAL: POB 56201, Emelle Bldg, 1st Floor, 135 Archbishop Makarios III Ave, Limassol; tel. (25) 381290; fax (25) 381584; Man. O. S. SAAB.

Banque du Liban et d'Outre-Mer SAL: POB 53243, P. Lordos Centre Roundabout, Byron St, Limassol; tel. (25) 376433; fax (25) 376292; Local Man. S. FARAH.

Banque Nationale de Paris Intercontinentale SA: POB 50058, Kanika Business Centre, 319 28th October St, 3600 Limassol; tel. (25) 340840; fax (25) 840698; e-mail bnpi.cyprus@bnpparibas.com; internet www.bnpi.com.cy; Local Man. CHRISTIAN ARLOT.

Banque SBA: 8C Iris House, Kanika Enaerios Complex, John Kennedy St, Limassol; tel. (25) 588650; fax (25) 581643; e-mail sba.ibu@banque-sba.com; branch of Banque SBA (fmrly Société Bancaire Arabe), Paris; Local Man. ADNAN NUWAYHED.

Barclays Bank PLC International Banking Unit: POB 27320, 88 Dhigenis Akritas Ave, 1644 Nicosia; tel. (22) 764777; fax (22) 754233; e-mail barclays@spidernet.co.cy; Head of IBU JONATHAN PINE.

BEMO—Banque Européenne pour le Moyen-Orient SAL: POB 6232, Doma Court, 1st–2nd Floors, 227 Archbishop Makarios III Ave, Limassol; tel. (25) 583628; fax (25) 588611; e-mail bemolobu@ spidernet.com.cy; Local Man. N. A. HCHAIME.

Byblos Bank SAL: POB 50218, Loucaides Bldg, 1 Archbishop Kyprianou St/St Andrew St, 3602 Limassol; tel. (25) 341433; fax (25) 367139; e-mail byblos@spidernet.com.cy; internet www.byblosbank .com.lb; Man. ANTOINE SMAIRA.

Commercial Bank of Greece SA: 1 Iona Nicolaou, POB 27587, Engomi, 2431 Nicosia; tel. (22) 663686; fax (22) 663688; Man. G. KANTIANIS.

Crédit Libanais SAL: POB 53492, Chrysalia Court, 1st Floor, 206 Archbishop Makarios III Ave, 3030 Limassol; tel. (25) 376444; fax (25) 376807; e-mail credub@inco.com.lb; Local Man. HAYAT HARFOUCHE.

Crédit Suisse First Boston (Cyprus) Ltd: POB 57530, 199 Christodolou Hadsipavlou Ave, 3316 Limassol; tel. (25) 341244; fax (25) 817424; internet www.csfb.com; f. 1996, OBU status granted 1997; Gen. Man. ANTONIS ROUVAS.

DePfa Investment Bank Ltd: POB 20909, 2nd Floor, 178 Athalassa Ave, 1665 Nicosia; tel. (22) 879300; fax (22) 318978; e-mail mail@depfacy.com; internet www.depfa.com; IBU licence granted 1998; Gen. Mans FRANK OTTERSBACH, LAMBROS CHARIDEMOU.

Federal Bank of the Middle East Ltd: POB 25566, J&P Bldg, 90 Archbishop Makarios III Ave, 1391 Nicosia; tel. (22) 888444; fax (22) 888555; e-mail mail@fbme.com; internet www.fbme.com; f. 1983; cap. US $46.0m., dep. $281.1m. (Dec. 2001); Chair. AYOUB-FARID M. SAAB; 2 brs.

First Investment Bank Ltd: POB 16023, cnr of Kennedy Ave & 39 Demoforitos St, 4th Floor, Flat 401, 2085 Nicosia; tel. (22) 760150; fax (22) 376560; Gen. Man. ENU NEDELE.

HSBC Republic Bank (Cyprus) Ltd: POB 25718, Para Bldg. Block C, 7 Dositheou St, 1311 Nicosia; tel. (22) 376116; fax (22) 376121; internet www.hsbc.com; f. 1984, as Wardley Cyprus Ltd; Man. Dir T. TAOUSHANIS; 1 br.

Jordan Kuwait Bank: Nicosia; business licence granted 2001.

Karić Banka: POB 26522, Flat 22, Cronos Court, 66 Archbishop Makarios III Ave, Nicosia; tel. (22) 374980; fax (22) 374151; Man. Dir O. ERDELIJANOVIĆ.

Lebanon and Gulf Bank SAL International Banking Unit: POB 40337, Akamia Centre, 3rd Floor, Flat 309, cnr of G. Afxentiou and Archbishop Makarios III Ave, 6303 Larnaca; tel. (4) 620500; fax (4) 620708; Local Man. F. SAADE.

Mega Euro Banka AD: c/o Tassos Papadopoulos and Co., Law Offices, 2 Safouli, Nicosia; OBU licence granted 1998.

Russian Commercial Bank (Cyprus) Ltd: POB 56868, 2 Amathuntos St, 3310 Limassol; tel. (25) 837300; fax (25) 342192; e-mail rcbib1@cytanet.com.cy; f. 1995; cap. US $10.8m., res US $5.2m., dep. US $497m. (Dec. 2000); Gen. Man. KONSTANTIN E. BUROWLEV.

Société Générale Cyprus Ltd: POB 25400, 7–9 Grivas Dhigenis Ave, 1309 Nicosia; tel. (22) 817777; fax (22) 764471; internet www.socgen.com; cap. US $2.0m., res US $5.9m., dep. US $105.2m. (Dec. 2000); Chair. MAURICE SEHNAOUI; Gen. Man. GÉRARD MALHAME.

STOCK EXCHANGE

Cyprus Stock Exchange: POB 5427, 54 Grivas Dhigenis Ave, 1309 Nicosia; tel. (22) 668782; fax (22) 668790; e-mail cyse@zenon.logos.cy.net; internet www.cse.com.cy; official trading commenced in March 1996; 60 companies listed in 1999; Chair. PAVLOS SAVVIDES; Gen. Man. NONDAS METAXAS.

INSURANCE

Insurance Companies Control Service: Ministry of Finance, POB 23364, 1682 Nicosia; tel. (22) 303256; fax (22) 302938; e-mail insurance.control@cytanet.co.cy; f. 1969 to control insurance companies, insurance agents, brokers and agents for brokers in Cyprus.

Greek Cypriot Insurance Companies

Aegis Insurance Co Ltd: POB 23450, 7 Klimentos St, Ayios Antonios, 1061 Nicosia; tel. (22) 343644; fax (22) 343866; Chair. ARISTOS KAISIDES; Principal Officer PANTELAKIS SOUGLIDES.

Aetna Insurance Co Ltd: POB 8909, 19 Stavrou St, 2035 Strovolos; tel. (22) 510933; fax (22) 510934; f. 1966; Chair. KONSTANTINOS L. PRODROMOU; Principal Officer KONSTANTINOS TSANGARIS.

Agrostroy Insurance Co Ltd: POB 6624, 89 Kennedy Ave, Office 201, 1077 Nicosia; tel. (22) 379210; fax (22) 379212; f. 1996; offshore captive company operating outside Cyprus; Chair. VALERIE V. USHAKOV; Principal Officer IOANNIS ELIA.

Akelius Insurance Ltd: POB 23415, 36 Laodikias St, 1683 Nicosia; tel. (22) 318883; fax (22) 318925; e-mail info@akelius.com; internet www.akelius.com; f. 1987; offshore company operating outside Cyprus; Chair. ROGER AKELIOUS; CEO IOANNIS LOIZOU; Principal Officer DEMETRIS SYLLOURIS.

Allied Assurance & Reinsurance Co Ltd: POB 5509, 66 Grivas Dhigenis Ave, 1310 Nicosia; tel. (22) 672235; fax (22) 677656; f. 1982; offshore company operating outside Cyprus; Chair. HENRI J. G. CHALHOUB; Principal Officer DEMETRIOS DEMETRIOU.

Alpha Insurance Ltd: POB 26516, cnr Kennedy Ave and Stasinou St, 1640 Nicosia; tel. (22) 379999; fax (22) 379097; e-mail customer_service@alphainsurance.com.cy; f. 1993; Chair. DOUKAS PALEOLOGOS: Principal Officer EVANGELOS ANASTASIADES.

Antarctic Insurance Co Ltd: POB 613, 199 Archbishop Makarios III Ave, Neokleou Bldg, 3030 Limassol; tel. (25) 362818; fax (25) 359262; offshore captive company operating outside Cyprus; Principal Officer ANDREAS NEOKLEOUS.

Apac Ltd: POB 25403, 5 Mourouzi St, Apt 1, 1055 Nicosia; tel. (22) 343086; fax (22) 343146; f. 1983; captive offshore company operating outside Cyprus; Chair. KYPROS CHRYSOSTOMIDES; Principal Officer GEORGHIOS POYATZIS.

Asfalistiki Eteria I 'Kentriki' Ltd: POB 25131, Kentriki Tower, 33 Clementos St, 1061 Nicosia; tel. (22) 745745; fax (22) 745746; e-mail kentriki@logosnet.com.cy; internet www.kentriki.com.cy; f. 1985; Chair. ARISTOS CHRYSOSTOMOU; Principal Officer GEORGHIOS GEORGALLIDES.

Aspis Pronia Insurance Co Ltd: POB 25183, 101 Acropolis Ave, 2012 Strovolos; tel. (22) 871087; fax (22) 492402; e-mail aspis@spidernet.com.cy; f. 1996; Chair. P. PSOMIADES; Principal Officer CHRISTAKIS ELEFTHERIOU.

Atlantic Insurance Co Ltd: POB 24579, 37 Prodromou St, 2nd Floor, 1090 Strovolos; tel. (22) 664052; fax (22) 661100; f. 1983; Chair. and Man. Dir ZENIOS PYRISHIS; Principal Officer EMILIOS PYRISHIS.

Axioma Insurance (Cyprus) Ltd: POB 24881, 2 Ionni Klerides St, Demokritos No. 2 Bldg, Flat 83, 1070 Nicosia; tel. (22) 374197; fax (22) 374972; offshore company operating outside Cyprus; Principal Officer KONSTANTINOS KYAMIDES.

B & B Marine Insurance Ltd: POB 22545, 46 Gladstonos St, 1095 Nicosia; tel. (22) 666599; fax (22) 676476; f. 1996; offshore company operating outside Cyprus; Chair. DMITGRI MOLTCHANOV; Principal Officer GEORGHIOS YIANGOU.

Berytus Marine Insurance Ltd: POB 50132, 284 Archbishop Makarios III Ave, 3105 Limassol; tel. (25) 369404; fax (25) 377871; f. 1997; offshore company operating outside Cyprus; Principal Officer CHRIS GEORGHIADES.

Cathay Insurance Co Ltd: POB 54708, 21 Vasili Michailidi, 3727 Limassol; f. 1997; offshore captive company operating outside Cyprus; Principal Officer ARETI CHARIDEMOU.

Commercial Union Assurance (Cyprus) Ltd: POB 21312, Commercial Union House, 101 Archbishop Makarios III Ave, 1071 Nicosia; tel. (22) 377373; fax (22) 376155; e-mail mailbox@commercial-union.com.cy; internet www.commercial-union.com.cy; f. 1974; Chair. ANDREAS ARTEMIS; Man. Dir KONSTANTINOS P. DEKATRIS.

Cosmos (Cyprus) Insurance Co Ltd: POB 21770, 1st Floor, Flat 12, 6 Ayia Eleni St, 1060 Nicosia; tel. (22) 441235; fax (22) 457925; f. 1982; Chair. and Gen. Man. ANDREAS K. TYLLIS.

Crown Insurance Co Ltd: POB 24690, Royal Crown House, 20 Mnasiadou St, Nicosia 136; tel. (22) 673333; fax (22) 670757; f. 1992; Chair. W. R. ROWLAND; Principal Officer PHILIOS ZACHARIADES.

Cygnet Insurance Ltd: POB 58482, 56 Grivas Dhigenis Ave, Anna Tower, 4th Floor, Office 42, 3101 Limassol; tel. (25) 583253; fax (25) 584514; e-mail tcsl@logos.cy.net; f. 1997; offshore captive company operating outside Cyprus; Principal Officer MARIOS LOUKAIDES.

Cyprialife Ltd: POB 20819, 64 Archbishop Makarios III Ave and 1 Karpenisiou St, 1077 Nicosia; tel. (22) 887300; fax (22) 374450; e-mail cyprialife@cytanet.com.cy; f. 1995; Chair. KIKIS LAZARIDES; Principal Officer DIMIS MICHAELIDES.

Direct Insurance Company Ltd: POB 22274, 35–37 Byzantium St, 1585 Nicosia; tel. (22) 664433; fax (22) 665139; Chair. STAVROS DAVERONAS.

E.F.U. General Insurance Ltd: POB 1612, 3 Themistoklis Dervis St, Julia House, Nicosia; tel. (22) 453053; fax (22) 475194; offshore company; Chair. ROSHEN ALI BHIMJEE; Principal Officer CHARALAMBOS ZAVALLIS.

Emergency Market Insurance Ltd: POB 613, 199 Archbishop Makarios Ave, Neokleous Bldg, 3030 Limassol; tel. (25) 362818; fax (25) 359262; f. 1997; offshore captive company operating outside Cyprus; Principal Officer ANDREAS NEOKLEOUS.

Eurolife Ltd: POB 21655, Eurolife House, 4 Evrou, 1511 Nicosia; tel. (22) 474000; fax (22) 341092; internet www.bankofcyprus.com/eurolife; Chair. E. XENOPHONTOUS; Principal Officer ANDREAS KRITOTIS.

Eurosure Insurance Co Ltd: POB 21961, Eurosure Tower, 5 Limassol Ave, 2112 Aglantzia, 1515 Nicosia; tel. (22) 882500; fax (22) 882599; e-mail info@eurosure.com; internet www.eurosure.com; Chair. EFTHYVOULOS PARASKEVAIDES.

Excelsior General Insurance Co Ltd: POB 6106, 339 Ayiou Andreou St, Andrea Chambers, Of. 303, Limassol; tel. (25) 427021; fax (25) 312446; f. 1995; Chair. CLIVE E. K. LEWIS; Principal Officer MARIA HADJIANTONIOU.

FAM Financial and Mercantile Insurance Co Ltd: POB 50132, 284 Archbishop Makarios III Ave, Fortuna Bldg, Block 'B', 2nd Floor, 4007 Limassol; tel. (25) 362424; fax (25) 370055; f. 1993; offshore captive company operating outside Cyprus; Chair. VLADIMIR MOISSEEV; Principal Officer CHR. GEORGHIADES.

General Insurance of Cyprus Ltd: POB 21668, 2–4 Themistoklis Dervis St, 1066 Nicosia; tel. (22) 848700; fax (22) 671355; e-mail finance@gic.bankofcyprus.com; f. 1951; Chair. V. ROLOGIS; Gen. Man. A. STYLIANOU.

Geopolis Insurance Ltd: POB 8530, 6 Neoptolemou St, 2045 Strovolos, Nicosia; tel. (22) 490094; fax (22) 490494; f. 1993; Chair. MARIOS PROIOS; Principal Officer NIKOS DRYMIOTIS.

Granite Insurance Co Ltd: POB 613, 199 Archbishop Makarios III Ave, Neokleou Bldg, 3030 Limassol; tel. (25) 362818; fax (25) 359262; captive offshore company operating outside Cyprus; Chair. and Gen. Man. KOSTAS KOUTSOKOUMNIS; Principal Officer ANDREAS NEOKLEOUS.

Greene Insurances Ltd: POB 132, 4th Floor, Vereggaria Bldg, 25 Spyrou Araouzou St, 3036 Limassol; tel. (25) 362424; fax (25) 363842; f. 1987; Chair. GEORGHIOS CHRISTODOULOU; Principal Officer JOSIF CHRISTOU.

Hermes Insurance Ltd: POB 24828, 1st Floor, Anemomylos Bldg, 8 Michalakis Karaolis St, 1095 Nicosia; tel. (22) 666999; fax (22) 667999; e-mail cyprus-credit-insurance@cytanet .com.cy; f. 1980; Chair. and Man. Dir P. G. VOGAZIANOS.

I.G.R. Co Ltd: POB 21343, 20 Vasilissias Friderikis St, El Greco House, Office 104, 1066 Nicosia; tel. (22) 473688; fax (22) 455259; f. 1996; offshore company operating outside Cyprus; Principal Officer CHRISTODOULOS VASSILIADES.

Laiki Insurance Co Ltd: POB 22274, 45 Vyzantiou St, Strovolos, 1585 Nicosia; tel. (22) 664792; e-mail laiki.tele bank@laiki.com; internet www.laiki.com; f. 1981; Chair. K. N. LAZARIDES; Gen. Man. STEPHIE DRACOS.

LCF Reinsurance Co Ltd: POB 60479, Abacus House, 58 Grivas Dhigenis Ave, 8103 Paphos, Nicosia; tel. (22) 555000; fax (22) 555001; f. 1984; Chair. ALAIN COPINE; Principal Officer SOPHIA XINARI.

Ledra Insurance Ltd: POB 23942, 66 Griva Dhigeui Ave, 1080 Nicosia; tel. (22) 743700; fax (22) 677656; f. 1994; Chair. CONSTANTINOS LOIZIDES; Principal Officer ALECOS PULCHERIOS.

Liberty Life Insurance Ltd: POB 26070, 75 Limassol Ave, 5th Floor, Nicosia; tel. (22) 319300; fax (22) 429134; f. 1994; Chair. KONSTANTINOS KITTIS; Principal Officer EURIPIDES NEOKLEOUS.

Marketrends Insurance Ltd: POB 24841, corner Kennedy Ave and 7 Epaninonda St, 1076 Nicosia; tel. (22) 796600; fax (22) 768065; e-mail markins@cytanet.com.cy; Man. Dir PANOS JOAHNOU.

Medlife Insurance Ltd: POB 21675, Themistoklis Dervis-Florinis St, 1512 Nicosia; tel. (22) 675181; fax (22) 671889; e-mail office@ medlife.net; internet www.medlife.net; f. 1995; Chair. Dr WOLFGANG GOSCHNIK.

Minerva Insurance Co Ltd: POB 20866, 8 Epaminondas St, 1684 Nicosia 137; tel. (22) 445134; fax (22) 455528; f. 1970; Chair. and Gen. Man. K. KOUTSOKOUMNIS.

Pancyprian Insurance Ltd: POB 21352, Mepa Tower, 66 Grivas Dhigenis Ave, 1080 Nicosia; tel. (22) 672235; fax (22) 677656; f. 1993; Chair. HENRI CHALHOUB; Principal Officer SOCRATES DEMETRIOU.

Paneuropean Insurance Co Ltd: POB 553, 88 Archbishop Makarios III Ave, 1660 Nicosia; tel. (22) 377960; fax (22) 377396; f. 1980; Chair. N. K. SHACOLAS; Gen. Man. POLIS MICHAELIDES.

Philiki Insurance Co Ltd: POB 22274, 35–37 Byzantium St, 2026 Strovolos, 1585 Nicosia; tel. (22) 664433; fax (22) 665139; f. 1982; Chair. NIKOS SHAKOLAS; Principal Officer DOROS ORPHANIDES.

Progressive Insurance Co Ltd: POB 22111, 44 Kallipoleos St, 1071 Nicosia; tel. (22) 758585; fax (22) 754747; e-mail progressive@ cytanet.com.cy; Chair. ANDREAS HADJIANDREOU; Principal Officer TAKIS HADJIANDREOU.

Saviour Insurance Co Ltd: POB 23957, 8 Michalakis Karaolis St, Anemomylos Bldg, Flat 204, 1687 Nicosia; tel. (22) 675085; fax (22) 676097; f. 1987; Chair. ROBERT SINCLAIR; Principal Officer KONSTANTINOS KITTIS.

Sunlink Insurance Co Ltd: POB 3585, 3 Themistoklis Dervis St, Julia House, 1066 Nicosia; tel. (22) 453053; fax (22) 475194; f. 1995; offshore captive company operating outside Cyprus; Chair. ANDREAS STYLIANOU; Principal Officer MARIA LAMBROU.

Technolink Insurance Services Ltd: POB 7007, 70 Kennedy Ave, Papavasiliou House, 1076 Nicosia; tel. (22) 496000; fax (22) 493000; f. 1996; offshore captive company operating outside Cyprus; Principal Officer GEORGHIOS YIALLOURIDES.

Tercet Insurance Ltd: POB 2545, 46 Gladstones St, 1095 Nicosia; tel. (22) 466456; fax (22) 466476; f. 1994; Chair. ANDREAS STYLIANOU; Principal Officer MARIA PIPINGA.

Triada Insurance Ltd: POB 21675, corner Themistoklis Dervis & Florinis St, Stadyl Bldg, 6th Floor, 1512 Nicosia; tel. (22) 675182; fax (22) 675926; f. 1996; offshore captive company operating outside Cyprus; Principal Officer ANDREAS STYLIANOU.

Trust International Insurance Co (Cyprus) Ltd: POB 54857, 284 Archbishop Makarios III Ave, Fortuna Bldg, 2nd Floor, 4007 Limassol; tel. (25) 369404; fax (25) 377871; f. 1992; Chair. GHAZI K. ABU NAHL; Principal Officer CHR. GEORGHIADES.

Universal Life Insurance Company Ltd: POB 21270, Universal Tower, 85 Dhigenis Akritas Ave, 1505 Nicosia; tel. (22) 882222; fax (22) 882200; e-mail unilife@unilife.com.cy; internet www .universallife.com.cy; f. 1970; Chair. ANDREAS GEORGHIOU.

UPIC Ltd: POB 57237, Nicolaou Pentadromos Centre, 10th Floor, Ayias Zonis St, 3314 Limassol; tel. (25) 347664; fax (25) 347081; e-mail upic@spidernet.com.cy; f. 1992; Principal Officer POLAKIS SARRIS.

Veritima Insurance Ltd: POB 956, 2B Orpheus St, Office 104, 1070 Nicosia; tel. (22) 375646; fax (22) 375620; f. 1996; offshore captive company operating outside Cyprus; Principal Officer SANDROS DIKEOS.

VTI Insurance Co Ltd: POB 50613, 199 Archbishop Makarios III Ave, Neokleou Bldg, 4004 Limassol; tel. (25) 362818; fax (25) 359262; f. 1994; Chair. SOTERIS PITTAS; Principal Officer ANDREAS NEOKLEOUS.

Turkish Cypriot Insurance Companies

Akfinans Sigorta Insurance AŞ: 16 Osman Paşa Cad., Lefkoşa (Nicosia), POB 451, Mersin 10, Turkey; tel. (22) 84506; fax (22) 85713; e-mail akfinans@akfinans.com; internet www.akfinans.com; f. 1996; Gen. Man. MEHMET KADER.

Altınbaş Sigorta Ltd: Müftü Ziya Sok. 2, Lefkoşa (Nicosia), Mersin 10, Turkey; tel. (22) 88222; fax (22) 76648.

Anadolu Anonim: 1-7-9 Girne Cad., Lefkoşa (Nicosia), Mersin 10, Turkey; tel. (22) 83133; fax (22) 79596.

Ankara Sigorta: PK 551, Bedrettin Demirel Cad., Lefkoşa (Nicosia), Mersin 10, Turkey; tel. (22) 85815; fax (22) 83099.

Başak Sigorta AŞ: Mehmet Akif Cad. 95, Lefkoşa (Nicosia), Mersin 10, Turkey; tel. (22) 80208; fax (22) 86160.

Bey Sigorta Ltd: Atatürk Cad. 5, Yenişehir, Lefkoşa (Nicosia), Mersin 10, Turkey; tel. (22) 88241; fax (22) 87362.

Birinci Sigorta Ltd: Tekin Yurdabak Cad., Tekin Birinci Binaları, Göçmenköy, Lefkoşa (Nicosia), Mersin 10, Turkey; tel. (22) 83200; fax (22) 83498.

Gold Insurance Ltd: Salih Mecit Sok. 12/B, Lefkoşa (Nicosia), Mersin 10, Turkey; tel. (22) 86500; fax (22) 86300.

Güneş Sigorta AŞ: Vakıflar İş Hanı 1C Girne Cad., Lefkoşa (Nicosia), Mersin 10, Turkey; tel. (22) 87333; fax (22) 81585.

Güven Sigorta (Kıbrıs) Sirketi AŞ: Mecidiye Sok. 8, Lefkoşa (Nicosia), Mersin 10, Turkey; tel. (22) 83023; fax (22) 81431.

İnan Sigorta TAŞ: Mehmet Akif Cad. 98, Kumsal, Lefkoşa (Nicosia), Mersin 10, Turkey; tel. (22) 83333; fax (22) 81976.

İşlek Sigorta: Bahçelievler Bul., Güzelyurt (Morphou), Mersin 10, Turkey; tel. (71) 42473; fax (71) 45507.

İsviçre Sigorta AŞ: Arkom Ltd, PK 693, Lefkoşa (Nicosia), Mersin 10, Turkey; tel. (22) 82125; fax (22) 88236.

Kıbrıs Sigorta: Osman Paşa Cad., Yağcıoğlu Işhanı 4, Lefkoşa (Nicosia), Mersin 10, Turkey; tel. (22) 83022; fax (22) 79277.

Limassol Sigorta Ltd: PK 267, Orhaneli Sok., Girne, Mersin 10, Turkey; tel. (81) 56786; fax (81) 58773.

Ray Sigorta AŞ: Bedrettin Demirel Cad. Arabacıoğlu Apt. 7, Lefkoşa (Nicosia), Mersin 10, Turkey; tel. (22) 70380; fax (22) 70383.

Saray Sigorta: 182 Girne Cad., Lefkoşa (Nicosia), Mersin 10, Turkey; tel. (22) 72976; fax (22) 79001.

Şeker Sigorta (Kıbrıs) Ltd: Mahmut Paşa Sok. 14/A, PK 664, Lefkoşa (Nicosia), Mersin 10, Turkey; tel. (22) 85883; fax (22) 74074.

Zirve Sigorta Ltd: Gültekin Şengör Sok., Abahorlu Türk Apt. 9, Lefkoşa (Nicosia), Mersin 10, Turkey; tel. (22) 75633; fax (22) 83600.

Trade and Industry

GREEK CYPRIOT CHAMBERS OF COMMERCE AND INDUSTRY

Cyprus Chamber of Commerce and Industry: POB 21455, 38 Grivas Dhigenis Ave, 1509 Nicosia; tel. (22) 889800; fax (22) 669048; e-mail chamber@ccci.org.cy; internet www.ccci.org.cy; f. 1927; Pres. VASSILIS ROLOGIS; Sec.-Gen. PANAYIOTIS LOIZIDES; 8,000 mems, 100 affiliated trade asscns.

Famagusta Chamber of Commerce and Industry: POB 53124, 339 Ayiou Andreou St, Andrea Chambers Bldg, 2nd Floor, Office

No 201–202, 3300 Limassol; tel. (25) 370165; fax (25) 370291; e-mail chamberf@cytanet.com.cy; internet www.ccci.org.cy; f. 1952; Pres. PHOTIS PAPATHOMAS; Sec. IACOVOS HADJIVARNAVAS; 450 mems.

Larnaca Chamber of Commerce and Industry: POB 287, 12 Gregoriou Afxentiou St, Skouros Bldg, Apt 43, 4th Floor, 6302 Larnaca; tel. (4) 655051; fax (4) 628281; Pres. IACOVOS DEMETRIOU; Sec. OTHON THEODOULOU; 450 mems.

Limassol Chamber of Commerce and Industry: POB 55699, 1st Floor, 166 Franklin Rossevelt, 3781 Limassol; tel. (25) 662556; fax (25) 661655; e-mail chamberl@cylink.com.cy; f. 1962; Pres. TONY ANTONIOU; Sec. and Dir CHRISTOS ANASTASSIADES; 770 mems.

Nicosia Chamber of Commerce and Industry: POB 21455, 38 Grivas Dhigenis Ave, Chamber Bldg, 1509 Nicosia; tel. (22) 889600; fax (22) 667433; e-mail ncci@ccci.org.cy; f. 1962; Pres. MANTHOS MAVROMATIS; Sec. SOCRATES HERACLEOUS; 1,200 mems.

Paphos Chamber of Commerce and Industry: POB 82, Athinon Ave & corner Alexandrou Papayou Ave, 8100 Paphos; tel. (6) 235115; fax (6) 244602; Pres. THEODOROS ARISTODEMOU; Sec. KENDEAS ZAMPIRINIS; 450 mems.

TURKISH CYPRIOT CHAMBERS OF COMMERCE AND INDUSTRY

Turkish Cypriot Chamber of Industry: 14 Osman Paşa Cad., PK 563, Köşklüçiftlik, Lefkoşa (Nicosia), Mersin 10, Turkey; tel. (22) 84596; fax (22) 84595; Pres. EREN ERTANIN.

Turkish Cypriot Chamber of Commerce: Bedrettin Demirel Cad., PK 718, Lefkoşa (Nicosia), Mersin 10, Turkey; tel. (22) 83645; fax (22) 83089; f. 1958; more than 6,000 regd mems; Chair. SALIH BOYACI; Sec.-Gen. JANEL BURCAN.

GREEK CYPRIOT EMPLOYERS' ORGANIZATION

Cyprus Employers' & Industrialists' Federation: POB 21657, 30 Grivas Dhigenis Ave, 1511 Nicosia; tel. (22) 665102; fax (22) 669459; e-mail oeb@oeb.com.cy; internet www.oeb-eif.org; f. 1960; 45 member trade associations, 400 direct and 3,000 indirect members; Dir-Gen. MICHAEL PILIKOS; Chair. BYRON KRANDIDIOTIS. The largest of the trade association members are: Cyprus Building Contractors' Association; Land and Building Developers' Association; Association of Cyprus Tourist Enterprises; Cyprus Shipping Association; Cyprus Footwear Manufacturers' Association; Cyprus Metal Industries Association; Cyprus Bankers Employers' Association; Cyprus Association of Business Consultants; Mechanical Contractors Association of Cyprus; Union of Solar Energy Industries of Cyprus.

TURKISH CYPRIOT EMPLOYERS' ORGANIZATION

Kıbrıs Türk İşverenler Sendikası (Turkish Cypriot Employers' Association): PK 674, Lefkoşa (Nicosia), Mersin 10, Turkey; tel. (22) 73673; fax (22) 77479; Chair. HASAN SUNGUR.

GREEK CYPRIOT UTILITIES
Electricity

Electricity Authority of Cyprus (EAC): POB 24506, 1399 Nicosia; tel. (22) 845000; fax (22) 767658; e-mail eac@eac.com.cy; internet www.eac.com.cy; generation, transmission and distribution of electric energy in government-controlled area; total installed capacity 988 MW in 2002.

Water

Water Development Department: Dem. Severis Ave, 1413 Nicosia; tel. (22) 803100; fax (22) 675019; e-mail waterdep@cytanet.com.cy; dam storage capacity 300m. cu m; Dir CHR. MARCOULLIS.

TURKISH CYPRIOT UTILITIES
Electricity

Cyprus Turkish Electricity Corpn: Lefkoşa (Nicosia), Mersin 10, Turkey; tel. (22) 83648; fax (22) 83851.

MAJOR COMPANIES
Greek Cypriot Companies

Covotsos Textiles Ltd: POB 1090, Limassol; tel. (25) 391344; fax (25) 390754.

Cyprus Canning Co Ltd: POB 21, Limassol; tel. (25) 392078; fax (25) 392083.

Cyprus Forest Industries Ltd: POB 24043, Nicosia; tel. (22) 832121; fax (22) 833564; e-mail cfi@cytanet.com.cy.

Cyprus Phassouri Plantations Ltd: POB 180, Limassol; tel. (25) 252211; fax (25) 252225.

Cyprus Trading Corporation Ltd: POB 1744, Nicosia; tel. (22) 482800; fax (22) 485385.

Keo Ltd: POB 50209, 1 Franklin Roosevelt Ave, 3602 Limassol; tel. (25) 853100; fax (25) 573429; e-mail keo@keogroup.com; f. 1927; cap. C£7.1m; manufacturers of wine, beer and spirits, fruit juices, canned vegetables and mineral water; Chair. E. PANTELIDES; Man. Dir A. M. ZAMBARTAS; 662 employees.

Vassiliko Cement Works Ltd: POB 22281, 1519 Nicosia; tel. (4) 817100; fax (4) 332651; f. 1963; cap. C£10.7m; cement manufacturers; Exec. Chair. PANOS CHR. GHALANOS; Gen. Man. GEORGE A. SIDERIS; 220 employees.

Turkish Cypriot Companies

Cypfruvex Ltd: Güzelyurt, PK 433, Lefkoşa (Nicosia), Mersin 10, Turkey; tel. (22) 43495; state-owned; fruit exporters; Gen. Man. MUSTAFA REFIK.

Eti Ltd: Abdi İpekci Cad., PK 452, Lefkoşa (Nicosia), Mersin 10, Turkey; tel. (22) 71222; state-owned; import and distribution of foodstuffs.

Hilmi Toros Industry Ltd: Mehmet Akif Ave, PK 526, Lefkoşa (Nicosia), Mersin 10, Turkey; tel. (22) 72412; fax (22) 87574; textile and clothing manufacturers.

Kıbrıs Türk Petrolleri Ltd, Şti (Turkish Cypriot Petroleum Co Ltd): Gazi Mağusa (Famagusta), PK 117, Mersin 10, Turkey; tel. (36) 63260; fax (36) 65230; import, storage and distribution of petroleum and petroleum derivatives.

Kıbrıs Türk Tütün Endüstri Ltd (Turkish Cypriot Tobacco Industry Ltd): 27 Atatürk Cad., Lefkoşa (Nicosia), Mersin 10, Turkey; tel. (22) 73403; state-owned; cigarette manufacturers.

Learned Ltd: Lefkoşa (Nicosia), Mersin 10, Turkey; hotels, packaging, fruit processing; Dir SIDIKA ATALAY.

TAŞEL (Turkish Spirits and Wine Enterprises Ltd): Gazi Mağusa (Famagusta), PK 48, Mersin 10, Turkey; tel. (36) 65440; fax (36) 66330; f. 1961; state-owned; manufacturers of alcoholic beverages; Gen. Man. HASAN YUMUK.

Toprak Ürünleri Kurumu: 11 Şehit Mustafa Hacı Sok., Yenişehir, Lefkoşa (Nicosia), Mersin 10, Turkey; tel. (22) 83211; state-owned; potato exporters.

TRADE UNIONS
Greek Cypriot Trade Unions

Cyprus Civil Servants' Trade Union: 3 Dem. Severis Ave, Nicosia; tel. (22) 662337; fax (22) 665199; e-mail pasydy@spidernet.com.cy; f. 1949, registered 1966; restricted to persons in the civil employment of the Government and public authorities; 6 brs with a total membership of 15,383; Pres. ANDREAS PAPAPOLYUIOU; Gen. Sec. GLAFKOS HADJIPETROU.

Dimokratiki Ergatiki Omospondia Kyprou—DEOK (Democratic Labour Federation of Cyprus): POB 21625, 40 Byron Ave, Nicosia; tel. (22) 676506; fax (22) 670494; e-mail deok@cytanet.com.cy; f. 1962; 5 workers' unions with a total membership of 7,316; Gen. Sec. DIOMEDES DIOMEDOUS.

Pankypria Ergatiki Omospondia—PEO (Pancyprian Federation of Labour): POB 21885, 31–35 Archermos St, Nicosia 1045; tel. (22) 886400; fax (22) 349382; e-mail peo@cytanet.com.cy; internet www.cytanet.com.cy/peo; f. 1946, registered 1947; previously the Pancyprian Trade Union Committee f. 1941, dissolved 1946; 8 unions and 176 brs with a total membership of 75,000; affiliated to the WFTU; Gen. Sec. PAMBIS KYRITSIS.

Pankyprios Omospondia Anexartition Syntechnion (Pancyprian Federation of Independent Trade Unions): 4B Dayaes St, 2369 Ay. Dhometios; POB 7521, 2430 Nicosia; tel. (22) 356414; fax (22) 354216; f. 1956, registered 1957; has no political orientations; 8 unions with a total membership of 798; Gen. Sec. KYRIACOS NATHANAEL.

Synomospondia Ergaton Kyprou (Cyprus Workers' Confederation): POB 25018, 11 Strovolos Ave, 2018 Strovolos, 1306 Nicosia; tel. (22) 849849; fax (22) 849850; e-mail sek@org.cy.net; f. 1944, registered 1950; 7 federations, 5 labour centres, 47 unions, 12 brs with a total membership of 62,559; affiliated to the ICFTU and the ETUC; Gen. Sec. DEMETRIS KITTENIS; Deputy Gen. Sec. NIKOS MOESEOS.

Union of Cyprus Journalists: POB 23495, 2 Kratinos St, Strovolos, 1082 Nicosia; tel. (22) 664680; fax (22) 664598; e-mail cyjourun@logosnet.cy.net; f. 1959; Chair. ANDREAS KANNAOUROS.

Turkish Cypriot Trade Unions

In 1998 trade union membership totalled 24,864.

Devrimci İşçi Sendikaları Federasyonu (Dev-İş) (Revolutionary Trade Unions' Federation): 6 Şerabioğlu Sok., Lefkoşa

(Nicosia), Mersin 10, Turkey; tel. (22) 72640; e-mail devis@defne.net; f. 1976; four unions with a total membership of 1,850 (2002); affiliated to WFTU; Pres. ALI GULLE; Gen. Sec. BAYRAM ÇELIK.

Kıbrıs Türk İşçi Sendikaları Federasyonu (TÜRK-SEN) (Turkish Cypriot Trade Union Federation): POB 829, 7–7A Şehit Mehmet R. Hüseyin Sok., Lefkoşa (Nicosia), Mersin 10, Turkey; tel. (22) 72444; fax (22) 87831; f. 1954, regd 1955; 12 unions with a total membership of 5,250 (1998); affiliated to ICFTU, ETUC, CTUÇ and the Confederation of Trade Unions of Turkey (Türk-İş); Pres. ÖNDER KONULOĞLU; Gen. Sec. ASLAN BIÇAKLI.

Transport

RAILWAYS

There are no railways in Cyprus.

ROADS

In 1999, according to data published by the International Road Federation, there were 11,009 km of roads in the government-controlled areas, of which 216 km were motorway and 2,131 km were highways and other main roads; some 87.4% of the road network was paved. The Nicosia–Limassol four-lane dual carriageway, which was completed in 1985, was subsequently extended with the completion of the Limassol and Larnaca bypasses. Highways also connect Nicosia and Larnaca, Larnaca and Kophinou, Aradippo and Dhekelia, and Nicosia and Anthoupolis-Kokkinotrimithia. The first section of the Limassol–Paphos highway opened in 1997, and work on the remainder was scheduled to be completed in 2000. In 1997 work began on a Dhekelia–Ammochostos (Famagusta) highway. The north and south are now served by separate transport systems, and there are no services linking the two sectors.

SHIPPING

Until 1974 Famagusta, a natural port, was the island's most important harbour, handling about 83% of the country's cargo. Since its capture by the Turkish army in August 1974 the port has been officially declared closed to international traffic. However, it continues to serve the Turkish-occupied region.

The main ports that serve the island's maritime trade at present are Larnaca and Limassol, which were constructed in 1973 and 1974 respectively. Both ports have since been expanded and improved. There is also an industrial port at Vassiliko and there are three specialized petroleum terminals, at Larnaca, Dhekelia and Moni. A second container terminal became operational at Limassol in 1995.

In 1998 4,475 vessels, with a total net registered tonnage of 15,963,000, visited Cyprus, carrying 7,017,000 metric tons of cargo to and from Cyprus. In addition to serving local traffic, Limassol and Larnaca ports act as transhipment load centres for the Eastern Mediterranean, North Adriatic and Black Sea markets and as regional warehouse and assembly bases for the Middle East, North Africa and the Persian (Arabian) Gulf. Containerized cargo handled at Cypriot ports amounted to 1,722,300 metric tons in 1998.

Both Kyrenia and Karavostassi are under Turkish occupation and have been declared closed to international traffic. Karavostassi used to be the country's major mineral port, dealing with 76% of the total mineral exports. However, since the war minerals have been passed through Vassiliko which is a specified industrial port. A hydrofoil service operates between Kyrenia and Mersin on the Turkish mainland. Car ferries sail from Kyrenia to Taşucu and Mersin, in Turkey.

At 31 December 2001 the Greek Cypriot shipping registry comprised 1,407 vessels, with an aggregate displacement of 22.76m. grt.

Department of Merchant Shipping: POB 56193, Kyllinis St, Mesk Geitonia, 4405 Limassol; tel. (25) 848100; fax (25) 848200; e-mail dms@cytanet.com.cy; internet www.shipping.gov.cy; Dir SERGHIOS SERGHIOU.

Cyprus Ports Authority: POB 22007, 23 Crete St, 1516 Nicosia; tel. (22) 756100; fax (22) 765420; e-mail cpa@cpa.gov.cy; internet www.cpa.gov.cy; f. 1973; Chair. CHRISTOS HADJIMANOLIS; Gen. Man. Dr ANTONIS TOUMAZIS.

Cyprus Shipping Council: POB 56607, 3309 Limassol; tel. (25) 360717; fax (25) 358642; e-mail csc@csc-cy.org; internet www.csc-cy.org; Gen. Sec. THOMAS A. KAZAKOS.

Greek Cypriot Shipping Companies

Amer Shipping Ltd: POB 27363, 6th Floor, Ghinis Bldg, 58–60 Dhigenis Akritas Ave, 1061 Nicosia; tel. (22) 751707; fax (22) 751460; e-mail amer@spidernet.com.cy; internet www.amershipping.com; Man. Dir ANIL DESHPANDE.

C. F. Ahrenkiel Shipmanagement (Cyprus) Ltd: POB 53594, 4th Floor, O & A Tower, 25 Olympion St, 3033 Limassol; tel. (25) 854000; fax (25) 854001; Man. Dir VASSOS STAVROU.

Columbia Shipmanagement Ltd: POB 51624, Columbia House, Dodekanissou and Kolonakiou Corner, 3507 Limassol; tel. (25) 843100; fax (25) 320325; e-mail shipmanagement@csmcy.com; internet www.columbia.com.cy; f. 1978; Chair H. SCHOELLER, Man. Dir D. FRY.

Hanseatic Shipping Co Ltd: POB 127, 111 Spyrou Araouzou St, Limassol; tel. (25) 345111; fax (25) 342879; f. 1972; Man. Dirs A. J. DROUSSIOTIS, R. GROOL.

Interorient Navigation Co Ltd: POB 51309, 3 Thalia St, 3504 Limassol; tel. (25) 840300; fax (25) 575895; e-mail management@interorient.com.cy; internet www.interorient.com; Man. Dir JAN LISSOW.

Louis Cruise Lines: POB 21301, 54-58 Evagoras I Ave, Nicosia; tel. (22) 678000; fax (22) 679800; e-mail egavrielldes@louisgroup.com; internet www.louiscruises.com; Exec. Chair. KOSTAKIS LOIZOU; Man. Dir EURIPIDES GAVRIELIDES.

Marlow Navigation Co Ltd: POB 4077, Marlow Bldg, cnr 28th October St and Sotiris Michaelides St, Limassol; tel. (25) 348888; fax (25) 748222; e-mail marlow@marlow.com.cy; Gen. Man. ANDREAS NEOPHYTOU.

Oldendorff Ltd, Reederei 'Nord' Klaus E: POB 56345, Libra Tower, 23 Olympion St, 3306 Limassol; tel. (25) 841400; fax (25) 345077; e-mail rnkeo@spidernet.com.cy; internet www.rnkeo.com; Chair. and Man. Dir KLAUS E. OLDENDORFF.

Seatankers Management Co Ltd: POB 3562, Flat 411, Deana Beach Apartments, Promachon Eleftherias St, 4103 Limassol; tel. (25) 326111; fax (25) 323770; Man. Dir DANIEL IONNIDES; Gen. Man. DEMETRIS HANNAS.

Turkish Cypriot Shipping Companies

Armen Shipping Ltd: Altun Tabya Yolu No. 10–11, Gazi Mağusa (Famagusta), Mersin 10, Turkey; tel. (36) 64086; fax (36) 65860; e-mail armen@armenshipping.com; Dir VARGIN VARER.

Compass Shipping Ltd: Seagate Court, Gazi Mağusa (Famagusta), Mersin 10, Turkey; tel. (36) 66393; fax (36) 66394.

Denko Koop Marine Cargo Department: PK 4, 12 Canbulat St, Gazi Mağusa (Famagusta), Mersin 10, Turkey; tel. (36) 65419; fax (36) 62773; e-mail info@koopbank.com; internet www.koopbank.com; Dir HASAN TRANSTURK.

Ertürk Ltd: Kyrenia (Girne), Mersin 10, Turkey; tel. (81) 55834; fax (81) 51808; Dir KEMAL ERTÜRK.

Fergun Maritime Co: Kyrenia (Girne), Mersin 10, Turkey; tel. (81) 54993; ferries to Turkish ports; Owner FEHIM KÜÇÜK.

Kıbrıs Türk Denizcilik Ltd, Şti (Turkish Cypriot Maritime Co Ltd): 3 Bülent Ecevit Bul., Gazi Mağusa (Famagusta), Mersin 10, Turkey; tel. (36) 65995; fax (36) 67840; e-mail cypship@superonline.com.

Medusa Marine Shipping Ltd: Aycan Apt, Gazi Mağusa (Famagusta), Mersin 10, Turkey; tel. (36) 63945; fax (36) 67800; Dir ERGÜN TOLAY.

Orion Navigation Ltd: Seagate Court, Gazi Mağusa (Famagusta), Mersin 10, Turkey; tel. (36) 62643; fax (36) 64773; e-mail orion@analiz.net; f. 1976; shipping agents; Dir O. LAMA; Shipping Man. L. LAMA.

Özari Shipping Ltd: Seagate Court, Gazi Mağusa (Famagusta), Mersin 10, Turkey; tel. (36) 66555; fax (36) 67098; Dir YALÇIN RUHI.

Tahsin Transtürk ve Oğlu Ltd: 11 Kizilkule Yolu, Gazi Mağusa (Famagusta), Mersin 10, Turkey; tel. (36) 65409.

CIVIL AVIATION

There is an international airport at Nicosia, which can accommodate all types of aircraft, including jet-engined airliners. It has been closed since 1974, following the Turkish invasion. A new international airport was constructed at Larnaca, from which flights operate to Europe, the USA, the Middle East and the Gulf. Another international airport at Paphos began operations in 1983. A C£210m. expansion and modernization of Larnaca and Paphos airports was proposed in late 2001 and was due for completion by 2010.

Avistar: POB 5532, Nicosia; tel. (22) 459533; fax (22) 477367; f. 1990; freight; Chief Exec. Dr WALDEMAR HAAS.

Cyprus Airways: 21 Alkeou St, Engomi 2404, POB 21903, 1514 Nicosia; tel. (22) 663054; fax (22) 663167; e-mail marketing@cyprusair.com.cy; internet www.cyprusair.com.cy; f. 1947; jointly owned by Cyprus Government (66%) and local interests; wholly-owned subsidiaries Cyprair Tours Ltd, Eurocypria Airlines Ltd, Duty Free Shops Ltd and Zenon NDC Ltd; Chair. HARIS LOIZIDES; Gen. Man. CHRISTOS KYRIAKIDES; services throughout Europe and the Middle East.

Eurocypria Airlines (ECA): POB 970, 97 Artemidos Ave, Artemis Bldg, Larnaca; tel. (4) 658001; fax (4) 658008; services to European destinations from Larnaca and Paphos; Chair. HARIS LOIZIDES; Gen. Man. GEORGE SOUROULLAS.

In 1975 the Turkish authorities opened Ercan (formerly Tymbou) airport, and a second airport was opened at Geçitkale (Lefkoniko) in 1986.

Kıbrıs Türk Hava Yolları (Cyprus Turkish Airlines): Bedrettin Demirel Cad., PK 793, Lefkoşa (Nicosia), Mersin 10, Turkey; tel. (22) 83901; fax (22) 81468; e-mail info@kthy.net; internet www .kthy.net; f. 1974; jointly owned by the Turkish Cypriot Community Assembly Consolidated Improvement Fund and Turkish Airlines Inc; services to Turkey and five European countries; Gen. Man. M. ZEKI ZIYQ.

Tourism

In 2001 a total of 2,696,700 foreign tourists visited the Greek Cypriot area and receipts from tourism amounted to C£1,283m., according to provisional figures. In the same year there were 88,302 hotel beds in the Greek-Cypriot area. In 2000 432,953 tourists visited the Turkish Cypriot area, and revenue from tourism reached $198.3m.

Cyprus Tourism Organisation (CTO): POB 24535, 19 Limassol Ave, 1390 Nicosia; tel. (22) 691100; fax (22) 331644; e-mail cytour@cto.org.cy; internet www.visitcyprus.org.cy; Chair. CHRYSIS PRENTZAS; Dir-Gen. PHRYNE MICHAEL.

Defence

The House of Representatives authorized the formation of the National Guard in 1964, after the withdrawal of the Turkish members. Men aged between 18 and 50 years are liable to 26 months' conscription. At 1 August 2001 the National Guard comprised an army of 10,000 regulars, mainly composed of Cypriot conscripts (some 8,700) but with an estimated 200 seconded Greek Army officers and NCOs, and 60,000 reserves. A further 1,250 Greek army personnel were stationed in Cyprus at that time. There is also a Greek Cypriot paramilitary police force of 750. In 2001 the defence budget for the Greek Cypriot area was C£212m. At 1 August 2001 the 'TRNC' had an army of about 5,000 regulars and 26,000 reserves. There was also a paramilitary armed police force of about 150. Men between 18 and 50 years of age are liable to 24 months' conscription. The 'TRNC' forces were being supported by an estimated 36,000 Turkish troops. In 1999 the defence expenditure of the 'TRNC' was TL 22,421,093m. Cyprus also contains the UN Peace-keeping Force and the British military bases at Akrotiri and Dhekelia.

Commander of the Greek Cypriot National Guard: Lt-Gen. ATHANASIOS NICOLODEMUS.

Commander of 'TRNC' Security Forces: Brig.-Gen. GALIP MENDI.

UNITED NATIONS PEACE-KEEPING FORCE IN CYPRUS (UNFICYP)

Headquarters at POB 1642, Nicosia; tel. (22) 464000.

Set up for a three-month period in March 1964 by Security Council resolution (subsequently extended at intervals of three or six months by successive resolutions) to keep the peace between the Greek and Turkish communities and help to solve outstanding issues between them. In mid-1993, following an announcement by troop-providing countries that they were to withdraw a substantial number of troops, the Security Council introduced a system of financing UNFICYP by voluntary and assessed contributions. At 31 May 2002 the Force comprised 1,241 military and police personnel (compared with 2,078 at November 1992), drawn from 14 countries.

Commander: Maj.-Gen. JIN HA HWANG (South Korea).

Special Adviser to the UN Secretary-General: ALVARO DE SOTO (Peru).

See also the section on UN Peace-keeping Operations in the Regional Organizations section of Part Three.

BRITISH SOVEREIGN BASE AREAS
Akrotiri and Dhekelia

Headquarters British Forces Cyprus, British Forces Post Office 53; tel. (5) 263395; fax (5) 211593.

Under the Cyprus Act 1960, the United Kingdom retained sovereignty in two sovereign base areas and this was recognized in the Treaty of Establishment signed between the United Kingdom, Greece, Turkey and the Republic of Cyprus in August 1960. The base areas cover 99 square miles. The Treaty also conferred on Britain certain rights within the Republic, including rights of movement and the use of specified training areas. In August 2001 an estimated 3,250 military personnel were resident in the sovereign base areas.

Administrator: Maj.-Gen. ANGUS RAMSAY.

Chief Officer of Administration: DAVID BONNER.
Senior Judge of Senior Judge's Court: RONALD J. D. LIVESEY.
Resident Judge of Judge's Court: DENIS B. PAIN.

Education

Until 1965 each community in Cyprus managed its own schooling through a Communal Chamber. On 31 March, however, the Greek Communal Chamber was dissolved and a Ministry of Education was established to take its place. Intercommunal education has been placed under this Ministry. Government expenditure on education in 1999 amounted to C£286.8m., equivalent to 5.7% of GDP.

GREEK CYPRIOT EDUCATION

Primary education is compulsory and is provided free in six grades to children between 5½ and 12 years of age. In some towns and large villages there are separate junior schools consisting of the first three grades. Apart from schools for the deaf and blind, there are also seven schools for handicapped children. In 1997/98 there were 665 Kindergartens (including privately run pre-primary schools) for children aged 3–5½ years of age. There were 372 primary schools, with 3,521 teachers and 64,592 pupils in 1997/98. In 1999/2000 enrolment in primary education included 97% of children in the relevant age-group.

Secondary education is also free for all years of study and lasts six years, three years at the Gymnasium being followed by three years at technical school or the Lyceum. Attendance for the first cycle of secondary education is compulsory. Pupils at the Lyceums may choose one of five main fields of specialization: humanities, science, economics, commercial/secretarial and foreign languages. At technical schools students may undertake one of several specializations offered within two categories of courses—technician and craft; the school-leaving certificate awarded at the end of the course is equivalent to that of the Lyceum. In 1997/98 there were 114 secondary schools (gymnasia, lyceums and technical schools) with 4,438 teachers and 56,872 pupils. In addition, there were numerous privately-operated secondary schools, where instruction is in English. In 1999/2000 enrolment in secondary education included 97% of children in the relevant age-group.

Post-Secondary education is offered at the University of Cyprus, which was inaugurated in September 1992 with 440 undergraduates. There are currently schools in the humanities and social sciences, pure and applied sciences, and economics and management. The University is expected to reach its full operational level of 4,000 students by 2000. In addition, there are five other public third-level institutions. The Higher Technical Institute offers sub-degree courses, leading to a diploma, in civil, electrical, mechanical and marine engineering and in computer studies. Other specialized training is provided at the Forestry College, the Higher Hotel Institute, the Mediterranean Institute of Management and the School of Nursing. There are also a number of private third-level institutions, registered with the Ministry of Education and Culture, offering courses in various fields. In 1998/99 enrolment in third-level education in Cyprus included 23% of people in the relevant age-group.

In 1994/95, 9,188 students were studying at universities abroad, mainly in Greece, the USA, and the United Kingdom.

TURKISH CYPRIOT EDUCATION

With the exception of private kindergartens, a vocational school of agriculture attached to the Ministry of Agriculture, a training school for nursing and midwifery attached to the Ministry of Health and Social Welfare, and a school for hotel catering attached to the Ministry of Communications, Public Works and Tourism, all schools and educational institutes are administered by the Ministry of National Education and Culture.

Education in the Turkish Cypriot zone is divided into two sections, formal and adult education. Formal education covers nursery, primary, secondary and higher education. Adult (informal) education caters for special training outside the school system.

Formal education is organized into four categories: pre-primary, primary, secondary and higher education. Pre-primary education is provided by kindergartens for children between the ages of 5 and 6. In 2000/01 there were 147 public kindergartens with 253 teachers catering for 3,859 children. Primary education is provided at two stages. The first stage (elementary) lasts five years and caters for children aged 7–11. The second stage (junior), lasting three years, is intended for pupils aged 12–14. Both stages of primary education are free and compulsory. In 2000/01 there were 93 elementary primary schools with 1,052 teachers and 15,493 pupils. In that year there were 28 junior schools with 837 teachers and 9,713 pupils. Secondary education consists of a three-year programme of instruction for pupils aged 15–17. Pupils elect either to prepare for higher education, to prepare for higher education with vocational training, or to prepare for vocational training only. Secondary education is free, but not compulsory. In 2000/01 there were 22 schools and lycées, with 677 teachers and 5,593 pupils. There were also 13 lycées and technical secondary schools, with 436 teachers and 2,071 pupils.

Cyprus's first university, The Eastern Mediterranean University, which is located near Gazi Mağusa (Famagusta), was opened in October 1986. The university has four main faculties: Engineering, Arts and Sciences, Tourism and Hotel Management, and Economics and Business Administration. A total of 13,304 students attended the university in 2000/01. There are a further seven institutions which provide higher education in the Turkish Cypriot zone: the Near East University College in Lefkoşa (Nicosia), attended by 6,290 students in 2000/01; the Girne (Kyrenia) American University, with 1,442 students; the Anadolu Open University, with 3,073; Lefke (Levka) University, with 1,365; the International Cyprus University, with 523; the Teachers' Training College in Lefkoşa (Nicosia), which trains teachers for the elementary school stage, with 91 (1999/2000); and the International American University, with 1,123 (in 1998/99). In 1982 an Institute of Islamic Banking and Economics was opened to provide postgraduate training.

In 1998/99 2,749 students were pursuing higher education studies abroad, mainly in Turkey, the USA and the United Kingdom.

Bibliography

Alastos, D. *Cyprus in History*. London, 1955.

Arnold, Percy. *Cyprus Challenge*. London, Hogarth Press, 1956.

Barker, Dudley. *Grivas*. London, Cresset Press, 1960.

Borowiec, Andrew. *Cyprus: A Troubled Island*. Westport, CT, Praege Publishers, 2000.

Brewin, Christopher. *The European Union and Cyprus*. Huntingdon, Eothen Press, 1999.

Byford-Jones, W. *Grivas and the Story of EOKA*. London, Robert Hale, 1960.

Calotychos, Vangelis (Ed.). *Cyprus and its People: Nation, Identity and Experience in an Unimaginable Community, 1955–97*. Boulder, CO, Westview Press, 1998.

Casson, S. *Ancient Cyprus*. London, 1937.

Crawshaw, Nancy. *The Cyprus Revolt: An Account of the Struggle for Union with Greece*. London, Allen and Unwin, 1978.

Denktaş, Rauf R. *The Cyprus Triangle*. London, K. Rüstem and Bros, 1988.

Dodd, Clement H. *The Cyprus Imbroglio*. Huntingdon, Eothen Press, 1998.

  Storm Clouds Over Cyprus (A Briefing). Huntingdon, Eothen Press, 2001.

  (Ed.). *The Political, Social and Economic Development of Northern Cyprus*. Huntingdon, Eothen Press, 1993.

  (Ed.). *Cyprus: The Need for New Perspectives*. Huntingdon, Eothen Press, 1999.

Edbury, Peter W. *Kingdoms of the Crusaders: From Jerusalem to Cyprus*. Aldershot, Ashgate Publishing, 1999.

Emilianides, Achille. *Histoire de Chypre*. Paris, 1963.

Esin, Emel. *Aspects of Turkish Civilization in Cyprus*. Ankara, Ankara University Press, 1965.

Foley, Charles. *Island in Revolt*. London, Longmans Green, 1962.

  Legacy of Strife. London, Penguin, 1964.

Foot, Sylvia. *Emergency Exit*. London, Chatto and Windus, 1960.

Foot, Sir Hugh. *A Start in Freedom*. London, 1964.

Green, Pauline (with Collins, Ray). *Embracing Cyprus: The Path to Unity in the New Europe*. London, I. B. Tauris, 2002.

Grivas (Dhigenis), George. *Guerrilla Warfare and EOKA's Struggle*. London, Longman, 1964.

  Memoirs of General Grivas. London, Longman, 1964.

Harbottle, Michael. *The Impartial Soldier*. Oxford University Press, 1970.

Hill, Sir George. *A History of Cyprus*. 4 vols, London, 1940–1952.

Hitchens, Christopher. *Hostage to History: Cyprus from the Ottomans to Kissinger*. London, Verso Books, 1997.

Holland, Robert. *Britain and the Revolt in Cyprus, 1954–59*. Oxford, Clarendon Press, 1998.

House, William J. *Cypriot Women in the Labour Market: An Exploration of Myths and Reality*. London, International Labour Office, 1985.

Joseph, Joseph S. *Cyprus: Ethnic Conflict and International Politics: From Independence to the Threshold of the European Union*. New York, St Martin's Press, 1999.

Koumoulides, John A. *Cyprus: The Legacy*. University Press of Maryland, 1999.

Kyle, Keith. *Cyprus*. London, Minority Rights Group, 1984.

Kyriakides, S. *Cyprus—Constitutionalism and Crisis Government*. Philadelphia, University of Pennsylvania Press, 1968.

Lavender, D. S. *The Story of Cyprus Mines Corporation*. San Marino, Calif., 1962.

Luke, Sir H. C. *Cyprus under the Turks 1571–1878*. Oxford, 1921.

  Cyprus: A Portrait and an Appreciation. London, Harrap, 1965.

Meyer, A. J. (with Vassiliou, S.). *The Economy of Cyprus*. Harvard University Press, 1962.

Mirbagheri, Farid. *Cyprus and International Peacemaking, 1964–86*. London, Routledge, 1998.

Moran, Michael (Ed.). *Rauf Denktash at the United Nations: Speeches on Cyprus*. Huntingdon, Eothen Press, 1997.

Newman, Philip. *A Short History of Cyprus*. 1940.

O'Malley, Brendan, and Craig, Ian. *The Cyprus Conspiracy: America, Espionage and the Turkish Invasion*. New York, St Martin's Press, 2000.

Panteli, Stavros. *The Making of Modern Cyprus*. Interworld, 1990.

  Historical Dictionary of Cyprus. Lanham, MD, Scarecrow Press, 1995.

Papadopoullos, T. *The Population of Cyprus (1570–1881)*. Nicosia, 1965.

Purcell, H. D. *Cyprus*. London, Benn, 1969.

Richard, J. *Chypre sous les Lusignan*. Paris, 1962.

Richmond, Oliver P. *Mediating in Cyprus: The Cypriot Communities and the United Nations*. London, Frank Cass, 1998.

Richmond, Oliver P., and Ker-Lindsay, James. *The Work of the UN in Cyprus: Promoting Peace and Development*. New York, Palgrave, 2001.

Rossides, Eugene T. (Ed.). *The United States, Cyprus and the Rule of Law: Twenty Years of Turkish Aggression and Occupation*. Melissa Media, 1999.

Sevcenko, Nancy P., and Moss, Christopher F. *Medieval Cyprus*. Princeton, NJ, Princeton University Press, 1999.

Sonyel, Salahi R. *Cyprus: The Destruction of a Republic. British Documents 1960–65*. Huntingdon, Eothen Press, 1997.

Spyridakis, Dr C. *A Brief History of Cyprus*. Nicosia, 1964.

Stefanidis, Ioannis D. *Isle of Discord: Nationalism, Imperialism and the Making of the Cyprus Problem*. New York University Press, 1999.

Storrs, Sir Ronald. *A Chronology of Cyprus*. Nicosia, 1930.

Streissguth, Thomas. *Divided Island*. Lerner Publications, 1998.

Stylianou, A., and Stylianou, J. *Byzantine Cyprus*. Nicosia, 1948.

Theophylactou, Demetrios A. *Security, Identity and Nation Building: Cyprus and the European Union in Comparative Perspective*. Avebury, 1995.

Xydis, S. G. *Cyprus—Conflict and Conciliation 1945–58*. Columbus, OH, Ohio State University Press, 1967.

Official Books of Reference:

Cyprus: Documents relating to Independence of Cyprus and the Establishment of British Sovereign Base Areas. London, Cmnd 1093, HMSO, July 1960.

Cyprus: Treaty of Guarantee, Nicosia, 16 August 1960.

EGYPT

Physical and Social Geography

W. B. FISHER

SITUATION

The Arab Republic of Egypt occupies the north-eastern corner of the African continent, with an extension across the Gulf of Suez into the Sinai region which is usually regarded as lying in Asia. The area of Egypt is 1,002,000 sq km (386,874 sq miles) but only 5.5% can be said to be permanently settled or cultivated, the remainder being desert or marsh. Egypt lies between Lat. 22°N and 32°N; the greatest distance from north to south is about 1,024 km (674 miles), and from east to west is 1,240 km (770 miles), giving the country a roughly square shape, with the Mediterranean and Red Seas forming, respectively, the northern and eastern boundaries. Egypt has political frontiers on the east with Israel, on the south with the Republic of Sudan, and on the west with Libya. The actual frontiers run, in general, as straight lines drawn directly between defined points, and do not normally conform to geographical features. Between June 1967 and October 1973 the *de facto* frontier with Israel was the Suez Canal. As a result of the 1979 Peace Treaty, the frontier reverted to a line much further to the east (see p. 00).

PHYSICAL FEATURES

The remarkable persistence of cultural cohesion amongst the Egyptian people may largely be explained by the geography of the country. Egypt consists essentially of a narrow, trough-like valley, some 3 km–15 km wide, cut by the Nile river in the plateau of north-east Africa. At an earlier geological period a gulf of the Mediterranean Sea probably extended as far south as Cairo, but deposition of silt by the Nile has entirely filled this gulf, producing the fan-shaped Delta region (22,000 sq km in area), through which flow two main distributary branches of the Nile—the eastern, or Damietta branch (240 km long), and the western, or Rosetta branch (235 km), together with many other minor channels. As deposition of silt takes place, large stretches of water are gradually impounded to form shallow lakes, which later become firm ground. At present there are four such stretches of water in the north of the Delta: from east to west are, and, in order of size, lakes Menzaleh, Brullos, Idku and Mariut.

Upstream from Cairo the Nile Valley is at first 10 km–15 km in width, and, as the river tends to lie close to the eastern side, much of the cultivated land, and also most of the major towns and cities, lie on the western bank. Towards the south the river valley gradually narrows until, at about 400 km from the border with Sudan, it is no more than 3 km wide. Near Aswan there is an outcrop of resistant rock, chiefly granite, which the river has not been able to erode as quickly as the rest of the valley. This gives rise to a region of cascades and rapids which is known as the First Cataract. Four other similar regions occur on the Nile, but only the First Cataract lies within Egypt. The cataracts form a barrier to human movement upstream and serve to isolate the Egyptian Nile from territories further south. In Ancient Egypt, when river communications were of paramount importance, there was a traditional division of the Nile Valley into Lower Egypt (the Delta), Middle Egypt (the broader valley above the Delta), and Upper Egypt (the narrower valley as far as the cataracts). Now it is usual to speak merely of Upper and Lower Egypt, with the division occurring at Cairo.

The fertile strip of the Nile Valley is separated to the south by the cataracts and by the deserts and swamps of Sudan; to the north by the Mediterranean Sea; and to the east and west by desert plateaux. The land immediately to the east of the Nile Valley, known as the Eastern Highlands, is a complex region with peaks that rise 1,800 m to 2,100 m but also deep valleys which make travel difficult. Owing to aridity the whole region is sparsely populated, with a few partly nomadic shepherds, one or two monasteries and a number of small towns associated

chiefly with the exploitation of minerals—petroleum, iron, manganese and granite—that occur in this region. Difficult landward communications mean that contact is mostly by sea, except in the case of the ironfields. The Sinai, separated from the Eastern Highlands by the Gulf of Suez, is structurally very similar, but the general plateau level is tilted, giving the highest land (again nearly 2,100 m in elevation) in the extreme south, where it rises in bold scarps from sea-level. Towards the north the land gradually slopes down, ultimately forming the low-lying sandy plain of the Sinai desert which fringes the Mediterranean Sea. Because of its low altitude and accessibility, the Sinai, in spite of its desert nature, has been for many centuries an important corridor linking Egypt with Asia.

West of the Nile occur the vast expanses known as the Western Desert. Though by no means uniform in height, the land surface is much lower than that to the east of the Nile, and within Egypt rarely exceeds 300 m above sea-level. Parts are covered by extensive masses of light, shifting sand which often form dunes; but in addition there are a number of large depressions, some of which actually reach to below sea level. These depressions seem to have been hollowed out by wind action, breaking up rock strata that were weakened by the presence of underground water, and most hollows still contain supplies of artesian water. In some instances (as, for example, the Qattara depression, and the Wadi Natrun, respectively south-west and south-east of Alexandria) the subterranean water is highly saline and consequently useless for agriculture; but in others—notably the oases of the Fayum, Siwa, Dakhlia, Behariya and Farafra—the water is suitable for irrigation purposes, and settlements have grown up within the desert.

CLIMATE

The main feature of the Egyptian climate is the almost uniform aridity. Alexandria, the wettest part, receives only 200 mm of rain annually, and most of the south has 80 mm or less. In many districts rain may fall in quantity only once every two or three years; consequently, throughout most of Egypt, including Cairo itself, the majority of the people live in houses made of unbaked, sun-dried brick. During the summer, temperatures are extremely high, sometimes reaching 38°C–43°C and even 49°C in the southern and western deserts. The Mediterranean coast has cooler conditions, with a maximum of 32°C; as a result the wealthier classes tend to move to Alexandria for the three months of summer. Winters are generally warm, with very occasional rain, but cold spells occur from time to time and light snow is not unknown. Owing to the large expanse of desert, hot dry sand-winds (called *khamsin*) are fairly frequent, particularly in spring, and much damage can be caused to crops; it has been known for the temperature to rise by 20°C in two hours, and the wind to reach 150 km per hour. Another unusual condition is the occurrence of early morning fog in Lower Egypt during spring and early summer. This has a beneficial effect on plant growth since it supplies moisture and is a partial substitute for rainfall.

IRRIGATION

With insufficient rainfall over the entire country, human existence in Egypt is heavily dependent on irrigation from the Nile. It may be stated, in summary, that the river rises in the highlands of East Africa, with its main stream issuing from Lakes Victoria and Albert. In southern Sudan it flows sluggishly across a flat, open plain, where the fall in level is only 1:100,000. Here the shallow waters become a vast swamp, full of dense masses of papyrus vegetation, and this section of the Nile is called the Sudd ('blockage'). Finally, in the north of Sudan, the Nile flows in a well-defined channel and enters Egypt. In Upper

Egypt the river is in the process of cutting its bed deeper into the rock floor; but in the lower part of its course silt is deposited, and the level of the land is rising—in some places by as much as 10 cm per century.

The salient feature of the Nile is its annual flood, which is caused by the onset of summer rains in East Africa and Ethiopia. The flood waters travel northward, reaching Egypt during August, and within Egypt the normal rise in river level was at first 6.4 m, declining to 4.6 m as irrigation works developed. This cycle of flooding had been maintained for several thousand years until, in 1969, construction of the Aswan High Dam made it a feature of the past (see below) so far as Egypt is concerned.

Originally, the flood waters were simply retained in specially prepared basins with earthen banks, and the water could then be used for three to four months after the flood. Within the last century, the building of large barrages, holding water all the year round, has allowed cultivation in any season. The old (basin) system allowed one or two crops per holding per year; the newer (perennial) system, allows three or even four. In the past, barley and wheat were the main crops; under perennial irrigation maize and cotton, which can tolerate the great summer heat, provided they are watered, have assumed equal importance.

The transfer from basin to perennial irrigation allowed a considerable population increase in Egypt, from about 2.5m. in 1800 to 67.9m. in 2001, giving rural densities of over 2,500 per sq km in some areas; and, as 99% of all Egyptians live within the Nile valley (only 4% of the country's area), there is considerable pressure on the land.

With most Egyptians entirely dependent upon Nile water, almost all the water entering Egypt is fully utilized. However, there are enormous losses by evaporation which at present amount to some 70% of the total flow. Difficulties and opportunities over use of Nile water were exemplified by the High Dam scheme at Aswan, which created a lake 500 km in length and 10 km wide which extends southwards across the Sudanese border. The High Dam is 3,600 m across, with a girth of 980 m

at the river bed and 40 m at the top. It holds back one of the largest artificial lakes in the world (Lake Nasser), and enables large-scale storage of water from year to year, and the regular planned use of all Nile water independently of the precise amount of annual flood. The irrigation potential of the High Dam is 2m. feddans for Lower Egypt alone, and the provision for the Nile valley (including Upper Egypt) was expected to add 30% to the total cultivable area of Egypt. Furthermore, 12 generator units incorporated into the dam give considerable quantities of low-cost electric power. This power has been a most important aid to industrialization, especially for the new metal industries. The dam was completed in July 1970 and officially inaugurated in January 1971.

However, adverse effects were soon noticed: scouring of the Nile bed below the dam; increased salinity in the lower stretches; reduced sedimentation below the dam and heavy deposition within the basin, resulting in the need for greater use of artificial fertilizers, which must be imported; and, perhaps more seriously, the disappearance of fish (particularly sardines) off the Mediterranean coast of Egypt. Possibly the most serious effect of all was a notable rise in the water-table in some areas, owing to hydrostatic pressures, and the year-round presence of water. Besides disturbing irrigation systems (which are adapted to pre-existing conditions), salinity and gleying of a more permanent nature began to appear; reports of bilharzia and other parasitic diseases increased; and the appearance of the plant water hyacinth threatened to choke irrigation systems.

LANGUAGE
Arabic is the language of almost all Egyptians, although there are very small numbers of Berber-language-speaking villages in the western oases. This is a reflection of the traditional French interest in Egypt, which is reciprocated: government decrees are sometimes published in French, as well as Arabic, and newspapers in French have an important circulation in Cairo and Alexandria. Small colonies of Greeks and Armenians are also a feature of the larger Egyptian towns. The Arabic name for Egypt, Misr, is always used within the country itself.

History

Revised for this edition by JON LUNN

PRE-ARAB EGYPT
Egypt's relative isolation, with the majority of the population living in the Nile Valley and the Nile Delta, with desert on either side, has produced a high degree of cultural individuality. Pharaonic Egypt lasted from the end of the fourth millennium BC until conquest by the Assyrians in 671 BC. The building of the pyramids and other works in the third millennium BC indicate a powerful monarchy commanding great resources. After the rule of Rameses II (c. 1300–1234 BC), Egypt entered a decline, but after the Assyrian conquest in 671 native rule was soon restored until 525, when Persia conquered Egypt.

The Persian kings patronized the religion of their subjects and were officially regarded as pharaohs. Another change occurred in 332 when the Persian satrap surrendered to Alexander the Great, who was recognized as a pharaoh and founded the city of Alexandria. After Alexander's death Egypt fell to his general, Ptolemy, and his dynasty was Greek in origin and outlook.

On the death of Cleopatra in 30 BC Egypt passed under Roman rule and became a province of a great Mediterranean empire. Christianity was introduced, and the Coptic church of Egypt clung to its monophysite beliefs in the face of Byzantine opposition.

THE COMING OF THE ARABS
Except for a brief Sasanian (Persian) invasion in 616, Egypt remained under Byzantine rule until, with the birth and advance of Islam in the seventh century AD, the Arab army under 'Amr ibn al-As invaded Egypt from Syria. The conquest was

virtually complete by 641, but for some centuries Egypt remained an occupied rather than a Muslim country. The Copts, who disliked Byzantine rule, had not opposed the conquest. In the course of time, however, Egypt became an Arabic-speaking country with a Muslim majority, although there remained a Coptic Christian minority. For over two centuries Egypt was administered as part of the Abbasid caliphate of Baghdad, but the Tulunid and Ikshidid dynasties functioned in virtual independence of the caliph between 868 and 969. Ikshidid rule was ended in 969 by a Fatimid invasion from Tunisia. The Fatimids were Shi'a Muslims, and Egypt was to remain under Shi'ite (as opposed to orthodox Sunni) rule until 1171.

Under the early Fatimids, Egypt enjoyed a golden age. The country was a well-administered absolute monarchy and it formed the central portion of an empire which, at its height, included North Africa, Sicily and western Arabia. The city of Cairo was developed and the mosque of al-Azhar founded. However, by the long reign of al-Mustansir (1035–94) decay had set in, and when the Kurdish Salah ad-Din ibn Ayyub, known to Europe as Saladin, rose to prominence as he opposed the Syrian Crusader states in the 12th century, he was able to become sultan over Egypt and almost the whole of the former Crusader territory.

When Saladin died in 1193, his Empire was divided amongst his heirs, one branch of which, the Egyptian Ayyubids, reigned in Cairo. Louis IX of France led an attack on Egypt in 1249, but was stopped at the battle of al-Mansura in 1250. Thereafter Egypt was ruled by Mamluk sultans until the Ottoman advance at the beginning of the 16th century.

OTTOMAN EGYPT: 1517–1798

By the beginning of the 16th century the Ottoman Turks had made dramatic advances. Constantinople was captured by them in 1453, and in their expansion southwards the Turks defeated the Mamluks at the battle of Marj Dabiq, north of Aleppo, in 1516, and overthrew the last Mamluk sultan at a second battle, outside Cairo, in 1517. Egypt became a province of the Ottoman Empire, but the Turks usually interfered little with the Egyptian administration.

At the end of the 18th century Egypt became a pawn in the war between France and Britain. Napoleon wanted to disrupt British commerce and eventually overthrow British rule in India. He landed at Alexandria in 1798, but in 1801 the French were forced to capitulate by a British and Ottoman force. French interest in Egyptian affairs and culture continued, however.

INCREASED EUROPEAN INFLUENCE

The expulsion of the French was followed by a struggle for power in which the victor was an Albanian officer in the Ottoman forces, Muhammad Ali. In 1807 he defeated a British force that had occupied Alexandria, and between 1820 and 1822 his army conquered most of northern Sudan.

In 1824 Muhammad Ali sent his son Ibrahim with an Egyptian force to help the Sultan suppress the Greek struggle for independence, but European intervention in 1827 led to the destruction of the Turkish and Egyptian fleets at Navarino. On the rejection by the Sultan of Muhammad Ali's demand that he should be given Syria in recompense, Ibrahim invaded Syria in 1831. Ibrahim was eventually defeated and Muhammad Ali's dominion was restricted to Egypt and the Sudan, but his governorship was made hereditary. He died in 1849, having been predeceased by Ibrahim. Muhammad Ali introduced many features of Western intellectual life into Egypt, and a Western-educated class began to emerge. Muhammad Ali was succeeded by his grandson, Abbas I (1849–54), under whom Westernization was reduced, and he by Said (1854–64), Muhammad Ali's surviving son.

In 1854 Said granted a concession to a French engineer, Ferdinand de Lesseps, to build the Suez Canal; work began in 1859 and the canal was opened in 1869. By this time Said had been succeeded by Ibrahim's son, Ismail. Ismail extended his Sudanese dominions, built railways and constructed telegraph lines. Moreover, his personal expenses were high, and between 1863 and 1876 Egyptian indebtedness rose from £7m. to nearly £100m. In 1875 Ismail averted a financial crisis by selling his Suez Canal shares to the British Government. As part of the Ottoman Empire, Egypt was bound by the Capitulations—treaties with European powers giving European communities in Ottoman territories a considerable degree of autonomy under the jurisdiction of their consuls, and, under conditions of indebtedness and the necessity of loans from the European powers, financial control by outsiders increased.

Ismail was succeeded by his son, Tawfiq, who ostensibly governed through a responsible Egyptian ministry, but strict financial control was exercised by a French and a British controller. Meanwhile a nationalist outlook was developing among those Egyptians who had been touched by Western influences, many of whom regarded Tawfiq as a puppet maintained by France and Britain. In 1881 a group of army officers, led by Arabi Pasha, forced Tawfiq to form a new ministry and to summon the Chamber of Notables, a consultative body originally set up by Ismail. France opposed any concessions to placate Egyptian opinion, and Britain concurred in this. Feelings in Egypt hardened, and in 1882 Tawfiq had to appoint a nationalist ministry with Arabi as Minister for War. France and Britain sent naval squadrons, but France subsequently withdrew support and a British expeditionary force landed at Ismailia and routed the Egyptian army at Tel el-Kebir. Cairo was occupied and Tawfiq's prerogatives were restored, to be subsequently exercised under British control.

INCREASED BRITISH INFLUENCE

From 1883 to 1907 the Egyptian Government was dominated by the British Agent and Consul-General, Sir Evelyn Baring, who in 1891 became Lord Cromer. Tawfiq was succeeded by his son Abbas II in 1892. He resented Cromer's authority and a new nationalist movement developed under Mustafa Kamil, a young lawyer. A series of puppet governments preserved a façade of constitutionalism, but educated youth turned increasingly to opposition. British officials increased from about 100 in 1885 to over 1,000 in 1905, and were out of touch with the growing strength of nationalist feeling.

Cromer was succeeded in 1907 by Sir Eldon Gorst, who established better relations with Abbas II, and Gorst was in turn followed by Lord Kitchener in 1911. When Turkey entered the First World War in November 1914 on the side of Germany, Egypt was still nominally a province of the Ottoman Empire. Egypt was declared a British protectorate, with a British High Commissioner, and Britain assumed responsibility for the defence of the Suez Canal. In December Abbas II was deposed and the British Government offered the title of Sultan to Hussain Kamil, the brother of Tawfiq. When Hussain died in 1917 he was succeeded by his brother Fouad. The nationalist movement flourished under wartime conditions, and in November 1918 the nationalist leader Saad Zaghloul presented the High Commissioner, Sir Reginald Wingate, with a demand for autonomy, which Britain refused. The nationalists became known as the *Wafd* (Delegation), but a negotiated settlement was not forthcoming and on 28 February 1922 Britain unilaterally abolished the protectorate and recognized Egypt as an independent sovereign state. Britain, however, maintained its control over the security of the Suez Canal and the defence of Egypt. In March 1922 Fouad took the title of King of Egypt.

INDEPENDENCE

The years between independence and the Second World War brought a triangular struggle between the King, the Wafd and the British Government. The Wafd wanted a revolution, but the King owed his throne to the British. Elections usually gave the Wafd a majority, but a Wafd ministry was unacceptable to King Fouad, who normally had the concurrence of the British Government. In 1935 Fouad was succeeded by his son Farouk, and in 1936 an Anglo-Egyptian treaty of 20 years' duration was signed which terminated British occupation but empowered Britain to station forces in the Suez Canal Zone until the Egyptian army was in a position to ensure the security of the canal.

During the Second World War Egypt played a vital strategic role as the British base in the Middle East. Egyptian support for the Allied cause was by no means total. The Wafd favoured co-operation with the British, and Britain forced Farouk's acquiescence in the formation of a Wafdist Government under Nahas Pasha in 1942. Nahas became increasingly enthusiastic about Arab unity and was instrumental in establishing the League of Arab States (the Arab League). In 1944 his Government fell.

Egypt joined Iraq, Syria and Jordan in military action following the declaration of the State of Israel in May 1948. However, military failure resulted. The King's early popularity had vanished; the Ikhwan al-Muslimun, or Muslim Brotherhood, a puritanical religious body, had become a threat, and communism had gained new adherents. The discredited regime made a last bid for royal and popular support when Nahas, again in power, abrogated the 1936 Treaty with Britain. Terrorism and economic sanctions were then employed in an attempt to compel the British forces to withdraw from the Canal Zone.

THE REVOLUTION: 1952–56

On 23 July 1952 a group of young army officers, the 'Free Officers', who had long been planning a *coup d'état*, seized power in Cairo. They invited the veteran politician Ali Maher to form a government under their control, and secured the abdication of King Farouk in favour of his infant son, Ahmad Fuad II, on 26 July.

Gen. Muhammad Neguib, an associate of the Free Officers who had incurred the enmity of King Farouk and who had earlier made himself popular by his condemnation of the British action in 1942, was made Commander-in-Chief of the Armed Forces and head of the military junta. A Council of Regency was formed in August. On 7 September, after an attempt by the Wafd and other parties to resume the political battle on their own terms, a new Cabinet, with Gen. Neguib as Prime Minister, replaced that of Ali Maher. Real power, however, lay with the nine officers who formed the Revolutionary Command Council (RCC).

The Revolution soon gained momentum. On 10 December the Constitution was abolished, and on 16 January 1953 all political parties were dissolved. It was announced that there would be a three-year transitional period before representative government was restored. On 18 June the monarchy was abolished and Egypt was declared a republic, with Neguib as President and Prime Minister as well as Chairman of the RCC. Col Gamal Abd an-Nasir (Nasser), who, although leader of the Free Officers, had hitherto remained in the background, became Deputy Prime Minister and Minister of the Interior, and Abd al-Hakim Amer was appointed Commander-in-Chief of the Armed Forces.

A struggle for power soon developed between Gen. Neguib, whose personal tendencies were Islamic and conservative, and Col Nasser. On 25 February 1954 Neguib was relieved of his posts as President, Prime Minister and Chairman of the RCC, accused of having attempted to concentrate power in his own hands. Nasser became Prime Minister and Chairman of the RCC in his place for a few days but Neguib was restored as President and reassumed both the other posts, only to be ousted again as Prime Minister by Nasser in April. When in October a member of the Muslim Brotherhood attempted to assassinate Nasser, its leaders and several thousand alleged supporters were arrested and in subsequent trials a number of death sentences were imposed. On 14 November 1954 Neguib was relieved of the office of President and accused of being involved in a Muslim Brotherhood conspiracy against the regime. He was placed under house arrest and Nasser became acting Head of State.

A settlement of the Sudan and Suez problems had been facilitated by the expulsion of King Farouk. The claim to the joint monarchy of Egypt and Sudan was dropped and negotiations with Sudanese leaders were facilitated because Neguib himself was half-Sudanese and popular in Sudan. An Anglo-Egyptian agreement, signed on 12 February 1953, ended the Condominium and offered the Sudanese the choice of independence or union with Egypt. Egyptian expectation that they would choose the latter was disappointed; the overthrow of Neguib and the suppression of the Muslim Brotherhood fed the century-old suspicion of Egyptian motives.

An Anglo-Egyptian agreement on Suez was signed on 19 October 1954; this provided for the withdrawal of British troops from the Canal Zone within 20 months. The agreement recognized the international importance of the Suez Canal (which was described as 'an integral part of Egypt') and expressed the determination of both parties to uphold the 1888 Constantinople Convention.

Under Nasser Egypt began to assert its importance in world affairs. He sought influence in three circles: the Islamic, the African and the Arab, and his visit to the Bandung Conference of April 1955 added a fourth: the 'non-aligned'. Egypt led the opposition among certain Arab states to the Baghdad Pact (later to become the Central Treaty Organization). In October 1955 Egypt concluded defence agreements with Syria and with Saudi Arabia, and in April 1956 a military pact was signed between Egypt, Saudi Arabia and Yemen. Tension with Israel, however, remained high. In September 1955 Nasser announced an arms deal with Czechoslovakia, which was to supply large quantities of military equipment—including Soviet tanks and aircraft—in return for cotton and rice.

In 1956 a constitutional basis for Nasser's authority was established. A new Constitution providing for a strong presidency was proclaimed in January and on 23 June approved in a plebiscite in which the citizens of the Egyptian Republic also elected Nasser as President.

THE SUEZ CRISIS AND ITS CONSEQUENCES: 1956–57

President Nasser's policy of non-alignment, which implied willingness to deal with both power blocs, was followed by the Egyptian attempt to obtain funds for the ambitious High Dam project at Aswan. By this project the Egyptian Government aimed to increase cultivable land and generate electricity for industrialization, which was seen as the main solution to Egypt's increasing population problem. Following offers of assistance from the USA and the United Kingdom and, separately, from the USSR, the World Bank offered a loan of US $200m. in

February 1956, on condition that the USA and Britain lent a total of $70m. and that the agreement of the riparian states to the scheme was obtained; Egypt was to provide local services and material.

The last British troops were withdrawn from Egypt in June 1956, in accordance with the 1954 agreement. Relations with the West were impeded, however, by Egyptian opposition to the Baghdad Pact and strong propaganda attacks on Britain, France and the USA. On 20 July the USA and Britain withdrew their offers of finance for the High Dam, noting that agreement between the riparian states had not been achieved and that Egypt's ability to devote adequate resources to the scheme was doubtful. The USSR made no compensating move. On 26 July President Nasser announced that the Suez Canal Company had been nationalized and that revenue from the Canal would be used to finance the High Dam.

The United Kingdom, France and the USA protested strongly at this action, and, after an international conference had met in London, United Kingdom, in August, a committee, under the chairmanship of the Prime Minister of Australia, went to Cairo to submit proposals for the operation of the Canal under an international system. These were rejected by the Egyptian Government. At a second London conference, in September, a Suez Canal Users' Association was formed; it was later joined by 16 states. On 13 October the UN Security Council voted on an Anglo-French resolution embodying basic principles for a settlement agreed earlier between the British, French and Egyptian Ministers of Foreign Affairs in the presence of the UN Secretary-General. The first part of this, outlining the agreed principles, was adopted unanimously; the second, endorsing the proposals of the first London conference and inviting Egypt to make prompt proposals providing no less effective guarantees to users, was vetoed by the USSR.

Britain and France, frustrated in their attempts to retain some measure of control over the Suez Canal, reached a secret understanding with Israel involving military action. Following the disclosure on 24 October that a unified military command had been formed by Egypt, Jordan and Syria, Israeli forces crossed into Sinai on 29 October, ostensibly to attack Egyptian *fedayin* bases, and advanced towards the Suez Canal. On 30 October France and Britain called on Israel and Egypt to cease warlike action and withdraw their forces from either side of the Canal; Egypt was requested to agree to an Anglo-French force moving temporarily into key positions at Port Said, Ismailia and Suez; Israel agreed but Egypt refused. The same day, at a meeting of the UN Security Council, Britain and France vetoed US and Soviet resolutions requesting an immediate Israeli withdrawal and calling on all UN members to refrain from the use of force or the threat of force.

Anglo-French air operations against Egypt began on 31 October but paratroops and sea-borne forces landed in the Port Said area only on 5 November. Meanwhile, on 2 November, the UN General Assembly called for a cease-fire and two days later adopted a Canadian proposal to create a UN Emergency Force to supervise the ending of hostilities. On 6 November, following considerable US pressure, the British Prime Minister, Sir Anthony Eden, announced that, subject to confirmation that Egypt and Israel had accepted an unconditional cease-fire, the armed conflict would end at midnight.

The organization of the UN force was rapidly undertaken, and the first units reached Egypt on 15 November. The withdrawal of the Anglo-French forces was completed in December. Israeli forces, which had occupied the entire Sinai peninsula, withdrew from all areas except the Gaza Strip, which they wished to prevent becoming a base for more raids, and Sharm esh-Sheikh at the entrance to the Gulf of Aqaba, which commanded the seaway to the port of Eilat. These areas were returned to Egyptian control in March 1957 after pressure on Israel by the USA.

The Suez Canal, which had been blocked by the Egyptians, was cleared by a UN salvage fleet and reopened in late March 1957. The terms under which the Canal reopened were full control by the Egyptian Canal Authority and respect for the Constantinople Convention of 1888, which provided that the Suez Canal should be open to vessels of all nationalities, in war and peace. Disputes would be settled in accordance with the UN Charter or referred to the International Court of Justice.

UNION OF EGYPT AND SYRIA

Elections to the Egyptian National Assembly, provided for in the 1956 Constitution, were held in July 1957. Only candidates approved by President Nasser and his colleagues were permitted to stand, and it was clear that the 350 elected members (who included women) were not expected to exert much influence on the Government.

Following the defence agreement in 1955, discussions had been held in the following two years on union between Egypt and Syria. Both countries were aligned against the West and looked to the USSR and the communist bloc for support, and in Syria pro-Egyptian elements were in the ascendant. On 1 February 1958 the union of Egypt and Syria, under the title of the United Arab Republic (UAR), was announced, but it was not until 21 July 1960 that the first National Assembly of the UAR, consisting of deputies from both Egypt and Syria, was opened in Cairo by President Nasser.

EXTERNAL RELATIONS: 1958–61

An invitation was extended to other Arab states to join the new union, and in March 1958 the UAR and Yemen entered into a loose association called the United Arab States. This association did not prosper, however, and was terminated by the UAR in December 1961.

President Nasser's antipathy towards the West found favour with the USSR, with which the UAR established closer ties during these years. Soviet military and industrial aid was granted and in December 1958 an agreement was concluded that ensured Soviet assistance for the building of the Aswan High Dam. Work on the first stage of the High Dam began in January 1960.

Relations with the West improved during 1959 and 1960. Through the mediation of the World Bank an agreement with the United Kingdom was signed on 1 March 1959 providing for the payment by the UAR of £27.5m. as compensation for British private property taken over at the time of the Suez crisis in 1956. Diplomatic relations with Britain were resumed at chargé d'affaires level in December 1959 and raised to ambassadorial level in early 1961. A loan of US $56.5m. to improve the Suez Canal was obtained from the World Bank in 1959, and other aid came from the USA in 1960.

SYRIAN WITHDRAWAL FROM UAR

President Nasser replaced the two Regional Executive Councils and the Central Cabinet of the UAR with a single central government in August 1961. Syria had by now become dissatisfied with the union and on 28 September the Syrian army seized control in Damascus and Syria withdrew from the UAR. Nasser at first called for resistance to the Syrian *coup d'état*, but, when the insurgents were seen to be in firm control, said on 5 October that he would not oppose recognition of Syria's independence. The loss of Syria was a bitter blow to President Nasser and his Egyptian colleagues, who now set about a re-examination of their policies which resulted in a renewal of revolutionary fervour.

The UAR Government (Egypt retained the full title) was re-formed on 18 October 1961 and a National Congress of Popular Forces, consisting of 1,750 delegates, representing economic and professional interests and other social groups, rather than geographical areas, met in Cairo on 21 May 1962. President Nasser presented the National Congress with a draft National Charter outlining his programme for developing the UAR according to Arab socialist principles. A new democratic system of government was introduced, based on the Arab Socialist Union (ASU) (replacing the National Union) and including popular councils of which at least one-half of the members would be workers or *fellahin*.

MORE ATTEMPTS AT UNION

The Syrian *coup d'état* had been preceded by the overthrow in February 1963 of the regime of Gen. Kassem in Iraq. These changes in power brought Syria and Iraq into closer alignment with Egypt, and it was announced on 17 April that agreement had been reached on the formation of a federation of the three countries under the name of the United Arab Republic. Rivalries, however, arose in both Baghdad and Damascus between supporters of the Baath Party and 'Nasserists', and by August President Nasser had withdrawn from the agreement, claiming that the Baathists had established one-party dictatorships in Syria and Iraq and ignored his insistence on wider nationalist representation.

A month later President Aref of Iraq called for a Baathist union of the three countries but, after the expulsion of Baath leaders from Iraq in November 1963 and the consolidation of power in Aref's hands, the unity movement between Iraq and Syria collapsed and Iraq and Egypt again moved closer together. A Unified Political Command between Iraq and Egypt began work in early 1965, but progress towards unity was slow.

During 1964 President Nasser took an important initiative in Arab League affairs by convening two Arab summit meetings in Egypt, which determined Arab policy on the use of water from the River Jordan and also strengthened the armies of Syria, Lebanon and Jordan. A further £E1m. was set aside for the formation of the Palestine Liberation Organization (PLO).

The Arab reconciliation and presentation of a united front lasted until the spring of 1965. Iraq, Kuwait, Yemen (Arab Republic), Algeria and Lebanon continued to follow President Nasser's lead, with only Syrian critics complaining that UAR policy was not sufficiently anti-Israeli. Relations between the UAR and Jordan improved markedly and, after a conference of heads of Arab governments in Cairo in January 1965 to discuss co-ordination of Arab policies, Jordan's King Hussein, previously denounced by the UAR, visited Cairo.

In Yemen, despite Egyptian support, the republican regime seemed no closer to victory over the royalists, who held the mountainous regions of the north-east and were assisted by Saudi Arabian finance and supplies of arms. This military stalemate and the financial burden of maintaining some 50,000 troops in Yemen moved President Nasser to attempt to disengage, but negotiations ended in deadlock and Egyptian troops remained in Yemen. On 22 February 1966, the day the British Government announced that British forces would leave Aden and South Arabia when that territory became independent in 1968, President Nasser stated that Egyptian troops would not be withdrawn until the Revolution in Yemen could 'defend itself against the conspiracies of imperialism and reactionaries'.

CHANGES OF INTERNATIONAL ALIGNMENT

1964 and 1965 saw a deterioration of UAR relations with the West, in particular the USA and the United Kingdom, and increasing dependence on the USSR. Relations with the USSR had been strengthened in May 1964 when the Soviet leader, Nikita Khrushchev, made a 16-day visit to Egypt to attend the ceremony marking the completion of the first stage of the Aswan High Dam, being built with Soviet aid. President Nasser paid his third visit to the USSR in August 1965 and the new Soviet leader, Alexei Kosygin, visited the UAR in May 1966, expressing support for UAR policies and again demonstrating Soviet interest in the Middle East.

DOMESTIC TROUBLES

Although Nasser obtained over 99% of the votes cast in the presidential referendum in March 1965, there were subsequently more signs of discontent in the UAR than at any time since he had come to power. In a speech to Arab students during his visit to Moscow in August, he disclosed that a plot against his life had been discovered, in which the proscribed Muslim Brotherhood was thought to have been involved.

In September 1965 a new Government headed by Zakaria Mohi ed-Din replaced that of Ali Sabri, who became Secretary-General of the ASU. Thereafter, administrative changes were made and the security system was improved. Taxation was increased and measures of retrenchment were introduced because of increasing economic difficulties, particularly the acute shortage of foreign exchange. US wheat supplies were continued, credits from France, Japan and Italy and a loan from Kuwait were obtained and there were increased drawings from the IMF. Nevertheless, the level of imports, particularly food to sustain the growing population, and the debt-service burden resulting from the first Five-Year Plan represented a continuing drain on foreign-exchange reserves, and the UAR faced a balance of payments crisis. Zakaria Mohi ed-Din's replacement in September 1966 by Sidki Sulaiman (a technocrat who retained his post as Minister of the High Dam) was seen as the outcome of disagreement over retrenchment measures. When the UAR defaulted on repayments due to the IMF in December 1966, the country was on the verge of bankruptcy.

WIDENING RIFT WITH SAUDI ARABIA

The rift between the UAR and Saudi Arabia widened. In February 1966 Nasser expressed opposition to an Islamic grouping that King Faisal was promoting, and in subsequent months propaganda warfare between the two countries was intensified. In October Tunisia severed relations with the UAR in response to continued differences over Arab League policies.

In Yemen Egyptian forces had been withdrawn from northern and eastern areas and concentrated in the triangle between San'a, Hodeida and Taiz. Egyptian control over the republican armed forces and administration was increased, and when in September 1966, after President Sallal had returned to Yemen from a year's absence in Cairo, the republican Prime Minister, Hassan al-Amri, and seven senior members of his Cabinet visited Egypt to make a plea for greater independence, they were arrested and detained there. In the following month about 100 senior Yemeni officials were dismissed, and arrests and executions were carried out.

WAR WITH ISRAEL

The events of May 1967 were to transform the Middle East. There had been an increase in Syrian guerrilla activities in Israel during the previous six months, and in April the tension led to fighting in the Tiberias area during which six Syrian aircraft were shot down. Israeli warnings to the Syrian Government, culminating on 12 May in the threat by Prime Minister Levi Eshkol of severe reprisals if terrorist activities were not controlled, prompted Syrian allegations that Israel was about to mount a large-scale attack on Syria. President Nasser, who had been reproached for not aiding Syria in the April fighting in accordance with the mutual defence agreement, responded immediately, moving large numbers of troops to the Israeli border. He secured the dissolution of the UN Emergency Force, which depended on Egyptian permission for its presence on the Egyptian side of the frontier, and reoccupied the gun emplacement at Sharm esh-Sheikh on the Straits of Tiran. He later justified these steps by claiming that he had received Syrian and Soviet warnings that Israeli troops were concentrated on the Syrian border (an allegation subsequently disproved by reports of UN truce observers) and that an invasion of Syria was imminent. When on 23 May President Nasser closed the Straits of Tiran to Israeli shipping, thereby effectively blockading the Israeli port of Eilat, his prestige in the Arab world increased considerably. The United Kingdom and the USA protested that the Gulf of Aqaba was an international waterway; Israel regarded the blockade of the Straits as an unambiguous act of war. As tension increased, King Hussein of Jordan concluded a mutual defence pact with the UAR and was immediately joined by Iraq. On 5 June Israel launched large-scale air attacks on Egyptian, Jordanian, Syrian and Iraqi airfields, and Israeli ground forces made rapid advances into the Gaza Strip, Sinai and western Jordan; there was also fighting on the Israeli–Syrian border. The outcome was decided within hours by the air-strikes, which destroyed the bulk of the Arab air forces, and the Israeli ground forces were everywhere successful. By 10 June, when all participants had accepted the UN Security Council's demand for a cease-fire, Israeli troops were in control of the Sinai peninsula as far as the Suez Canal (including Sharm esh-Sheikh), the West Bank of the Jordan (including the Old City of Jerusalem), the Gaza Strip and Syrian territory extending 12 miles from the Israeli border. The Suez Canal was blocked by Egypt in the course of the fighting. President Nasser offered to resign, but popular support led him to withdraw his resignation. He dismissed a number of senior army officers and took over himself the duties of Prime Minister and Secretary-General of the ASU.

The implications of the catastrophe were only gradually realized. It was estimated that the loss of revenue from the Suez Canal, from oil produced in Sinai and from tourism amounted to some £E12.5m. per month, or almost half Egypt's foreign currency earnings. Also, the withdrawal of a large part of the Egyptian force in Yemen reduced Nasser's ability to influence

affairs both in that country and in Aden and South Arabia (which became independent as the Republic of Southern Yemen on 30 November 1967, after the withdrawal of British troops).

The USSR, which had given the Arab cause strong verbal support throughout the crisis, continued to take a strong pro-Arab stand at the UN, and President Nikolai Podgornii paid a lengthy visit to Cairo to discuss future Egyptian policy. The USSR replaced about half the lost Egyptian aircraft and provided other military supplies and instructors.

After repeated violations of the cease-fire by both sides, on 22 November 1967 the UN Security Council adopted a resolution laying down the principles for a just and lasting peace in the Middle East and authorizing the appointment of a UN special representative to assist in achieving a settlement. This was Resolution 242 (see Documents on Palestine, p. 57), which has subsequently formed the basis of most attempts to restore peace to the Middle East.

THE UAR AFTER THE JUNE WAR

Meanwhile, President Nasser faced daunting economic difficulties and an unstable political situation in Egypt. An austerity budget had been framed in July 1967. The cost of re-equipping the armed forces required reductions in investment, despite Soviet aid and assistance from other Arab governments. Socialist policies were still pursued, as demonstrated by the decision, announced in October, to nationalize the wholesale trade. The continuing shortage of foreign exchange made it desirable to improve the UAR's relations with the West, and in December diplomatic relations with the United Kingdom were resumed. A bridging loan from British, West German and Italian banks, obtained in February 1968, enabled the UAR to make the repayments to the IMF that had been outstanding since the end of 1966, and in March the Fund approved further drawings.

Demonstrations by students and workers took place in Cairo and Helwan towards the end of February 1968. Initially organized to protest against the leniency of court sentences passed against senior air force officers for their failure to prevent the destruction of the UAR air force on 5 June 1967, they revealed widespread discontent. Several people were killed in clashes with police, and the universities were closed; nevertheless, President Nasser realized the need for immediate conciliatory action. Retrials were ordered and comprehensive changes to the Cabinet were announced, including the introduction of a number of civilian experts. Ali Sabri, who had been reinstated as Secretary-General of the ASU in January, was also included, but Zakaria Mohi ed-Din left the Government. President Nasser retained the premiership.

Deprived of foreign exchange by the continued closure of the Canal and the reduction in the tourist trade, the UAR remained dependent on the regular aid payments from Saudi Arabia, Kuwait and Libya and on Soviet assistance. There were signs that the civilian economy ministers favoured some relaxation of over-rigid state control in industry and more encouragement of private enterprise and foreign investment. Meanwhile, military expenditure in 1968 and 1969 remained high; Soviet arms deliveries continued, as did the presence in Egypt of some 3,000 Soviet military advisers and instructors.

A pattern of sporadic action, involving artillery duels across the Suez Canal, commando raids and air combat developed throughout 1969 and into 1970, with growing Soviet involvement in Egypt's defence. In the summer of 1970 the US Secretary of State, William Rogers, presented a set of proposals for solving the continuing Middle East crisis. An uneasy cease-fire, but no permanent solution, resulted.

EGYPT AFTER NASSER

Although President Nasser had clear differences with the Palestinian guerrillas over their rejection of the US peace proposals and the hijacking of Western airliners at the beginning of September 1970, one of his final acts was to secure agreement in Cairo between King Hussein of Jordan and the Palestinian leader, Yasser Arafat, for an end to the fighting between the Jordanian army and the guerrillas.

Nasser's sudden death on 28 September 1970 came as a profound shock, precipitating fears that peace prospects for the Middle East would now be jeopardized. A close associate of Nasser, and Vice-President at the time of his death, Col Anwar

Sadat, was immediately appointed provisional President by the Cabinet and the ASU, later being elected President in a national referendum; by mid-1971 he was firmly in control of the Government.

In November 1970 President Sadat had agreed to the creation of a federation with Sudan and Libya. Sudan, however, later postponed its membership of the union. In April 1971 Syria agreed to become the third member of the federation. The federation proposals, together with Sadat's plan for the re-opening of the Canal, precipitated a crisis in the leadership, which led to a comprehensive purge by Sadat of opponents at all government levels. In July new elections were held, not only for all levels of the ASU, but also for trade unions and professional bodies. The first permanent Constitution since the 1952 revolution was approved in September. It contained important clauses governing personal freedoms and replaced the name of the United Arab Republic with that of the Arab Republic of Egypt.

Egypt was becoming increasingly dependent on the USSR, both militarily and economically. Student riots at the beginning of 1972 prompted assurances from President Sadat that an armed confrontation with Israel was definitely intended. Against this background of increasing internal unease Egypt intensified efforts to diversify sources of development aid and armaments. The Suez–Alexandria (Sumed) pipeline received promises of Western backing, and in May 1972 a five-year preferential trade agreement was concluded with the European Community (EC, now European Union—EU).

CRISIS IN RELATIONS WITH THE USSR

The most striking event of 1972 was the dismissal of Soviet military advisers from Egypt in July. This did not lead to a rupture in Egyptian-Soviet relations but neither did it result in any significant *rapprochement* with the West. A new round of diplomacy to state Egypt's case, particularly in the West and the Far East, ensued, and arms supplies were requested from France and Britain. With the announcement on 2 August 1972 of Egypt's plan to merge with Libya, France stated that supplies of *Mirage* fighters to Libya would continue, since Libya was not in direct conflict with Israel.

Contacts with the USSR continued and economic relations appeared unaffected by the events of July, although it was clear that the USSR was looking elsewhere to maintain its presence in the Mediterranean. It was unclear to what extent Sadat's hand had been forced in ordering the Soviet withdrawal.

INTERNAL UNREST

A law enacted in August 1972 provided for penalties as severe as life imprisonment for offences endangering national unity, including opposing the Government by force and inciting violence between Muslims and the Coptic minority. Clashes between these two communities were becoming more frequent and, along with growing student unrest, were seen as an expression of dissatisfaction with the state of 'no-peace-no-war'. The Government resorted to repeated assurances of military preparations. Indeed, in December 1972 Sadat ordered preparations for war, after strong criticism in the People's Assembly (the new legislative body comprising 350 elected members and 10 presidential nominees—instituted by the new Constitution, and elected in October and November 1971) of the Government's policies. Another cause of unease was the proposed merger with Libya, which many felt might give Col Muammar al-Qaddafi, the Libyan leader, excessive control over Egypt's destiny.

In January 1973 there were violent clashes between police and students. In February a number of left-wing elements, including several journalists, were expelled from the ASU; student unrest continued and in March President Sadat took over from Aziz Sidqi (who was appointed in January 1972 in succession to Dr Mahmoud Fawzi, 1970–72) as Prime Minister.

RELATIONS WITH LIBYA

Egypt and Libya had agreed a programme providing for full union by stages at a meeting between the two Heads of State in Benghazi, Libya, in August 1972, and a merger of the two countries was planned for 1 September 1973. The Libyan leader, Col Qaddafi, demonstrated greater enthusiasm than President

Sadat for total union, and in July 1973 Qaddafi organized a 40,000-strong Libyan march on Cairo, in order to bring pressure to bear on Egypt. The march was turned back about 200 miles from Cairo, however, and Sadat, although still supportive of eventual union, stated that 'enthusiasm and emotional impulses are not a sufficient basis for unity'. An agreement in principle was nevertheless signed on 29 August, but few practical steps were taken to ensure its prompt implementation.

Throughout 1974 and early 1975 relations between the two countries deteriorated to such an extent that President Sadat openly vilified Qaddafi in April 1975, at which time Libya had been threatening to take action against Egyptians working in Libya. Relations worsened when a Soviet-Libyan arms agreement was revealed later in the month. In July 1977 open warfare broke out on the border between Egypt and Libya, and when Sadat visited Israel in November 1977 (see below) relations deteriorated even further, with Egypt severing diplomatic relations with Libya in December. Libya joined the rest of the Arab world in condemning the Egypt-Israel peace treaty in March 1979, and it was reported that renewed outbreaks of fighting on the Egypt-Libya border were prevented only by the intervention of the USA. In March 1980 Libya constructed airfields and fortifications on the border with Egypt, and in June 1980 Egypt declared martial law in the border area with Libya for a period of one year.

THE OCTOBER WAR AND ITS AFTERMATH

Between the June 1967 war and October 1973 Egyptian leaders frequently stated that the war against Israel would be resumed, but when Egyptian forces crossed the Suez Canal on 6 October 1973, it came as a surprise both to Israel and the rest of the world. For President Sadat the war was a considerable triumph; it appeared to end the years of stalemate with Israel, and his personal reputation was greatly enhanced. As a result of the Disengagement Agreement signed by Israel and Egypt, Egyptian forces regained a strip of territory to the east of the Suez Canal (see map on p. 63).

After the war extensive and far-reaching changes took place in Egypt. An amnesty was granted to many important political prisoners in January 1974, and in April was further extended to more than 2,000 persons who had been imprisoned for political or criminal offences. Press censorship was ended in February, and in May, at a national referendum, some 8.5m. voters gave a 99.95% endorsement to a programme of economic and social reform which concentrated on reconstruction, attracting foreign investment, the introduction of a private enterprise sector in the economy (while still maintaining the public sector), and limiting police interference in everyday life.

One result of the October War was Egypt's improved relations with the USA. Diplomatic relations between the two countries were restored in November 1973 and the US Secretary of State, Dr Henry Kissinger, maintained a cordial relationship with President Sadat during the disengagement talks. US initiatives in peacemaking were generally welcomed by Egypt, while the USA became more conscious of the extent of its dependence on Arab oil.

RETURN TO STALEMATE

The euphoria engendered by the crossing of the Suez Canal began to dissipate during 1974. Increases in the cost of living, and the slow pace of economic reform, provoked riots in Cairo on 1 January 1975, and further disturbances among textile workers in March, when the textile complex at el-Mahalla el-Koubra was closed for several days after violent clashes over pay demands.

As a result of these disturbances Dr Abd al-Aziz Higazi, who had succeeded President Sadat as Prime Minister in September 1974, resigned the premiership and was replaced in April 1975 by Gen. Mamdouh Muhammad Salem, the former Minister of the Interior and Deputy Prime Minister. On 1 May 1975 President Sadat announced that all lower-paid public-sector employees would receive additional cost-of-living allowances equal to 30% of their pay.

During the first eight months of 1975 Dr Kissinger engaged in considerable 'shuttle diplomacy' and in September Egypt and Israel signed the Second Interim Peace Agreement (see Documents on Palestine, p. 62). In brief, Israel withdrew from the Giddi and Mitla passes and Egypt recovered the Abu Rudeis oilfield in Sinai, while Article I of the Agreement stated that Egypt and Israel agreed that 'the conflict between them and in the Middle East shall not be resolved by military force but by peaceful means'. This agreement brought upon President Sadat the strong disapproval of other Arab interests, particularly Syria, Jordan, Iraq and the PLO, as it appeared to them that Egypt was seeking to commit the whole Arab world to a policy of peace with Israel. The position had also been complicated by the fact that, at the Arab League summit in Rabat, Morocco, in October 1974, the PLO had achieved formal recognition as the sole legitimate representative of the Palestinian people. In May 1976 Egypt attempted to consolidate an improvement in relations with the PLO by asking the Arab League to admit the PLO as a full member. The rest of the Arab world was also aware that Egypt was establishing closer links with the USA at the expense of the USSR. In March 1976 Sadat abrogated the Treaty of Friendship with the USSR, which Egypt had signed in 1971. In a speech to the Egyptian People's Assembly, Sadat accused the USSR of exerting political, economic and military pressure on Egypt by criticizing his Middle East policies, refusing to reschedule Egypt's debts, and declining to provide supplies of weapons and spares.

POLITICAL ADVANCE AND DOMESTIC DIFFICULTIES

During 1976 and for most of 1977 President Sadat was forced to concentrate increasingly on domestic issues. In March 1976 three political 'platforms' were allowed to form within the ASU, and in the November 1976 elections to the People's Assembly the 'platforms' entered the contest as full-scale political parties. The Arab Socialists (a party of the centre, supporting Sadat) won 280 seats, while the Liberal Socialists (supporting political and economic liberalization) won 12 seats. The left-wing National Progressive Unionist Party (NPUP) won two seats. After the elections President Sadat announced that the ASU would take a less active political role in the future, acting more as a supervisory body for the three parties' activities.

During 1976 Egypt's economy was experiencing severe difficulty, and when in January 1977 Sadat announced a budget that outlined significant price increases, severe riots erupted in Cairo and other centres. Consequently Sadat revoked the price increases, and in February he introduced a law that made a wide range of new offences (including some relating to industrial action) punishable by hard labour for life. The legislation was subsequently endorsed by a national referendum.

By June 1977 Sadat considered the internal situation in Egypt to be sufficiently under control to address the introduction of regulations to permit the creation of new political parties. A law was adopted by the People's Assembly stipulating that each prospective new party must include at least 20 members of the People's Assembly (existing parties excepted), and must have no history of political activity during the time of the monarchy. This effectively excluded the Communist Party, the Muslim Brotherhood and the New Wafd Party.

TOWARDS A PEACE TREATY WITH ISRAEL

In November 1977, however, domestic issues were completely overshadowed by Sadat's visit to Israel and his address to the Knesset, the Israeli legislature. No significant breakthrough was made immediately, with the status of any future Palestinian state presenting the main obstacle. Talks continued in 1978, in spite of the opposition of much of the Arab world, which regarded Egypt's unilateral bid for peace with Israel as detrimental to Arab unity. Egypt had pre-empted action being considered by Syria, Libya, Algeria, Iraq and the People's Democratic Republic of Yemen, by severing diplomatic relations with these countries in December 1977. In September 1978 an unexpected breakthrough was achieved when, after talks at the US presidential retreat at Camp David, Maryland, under the auspices of US President Jimmy Carter, Sadat and the Israeli Prime Minister, Menachem Begin, signed two agreements. The first was a 'framework for peace in the Middle East' (see Documents on Palestine, p. 63) and the second was a 'framework' for the conclusion of a peace treaty between Egypt and Israel'. The first agreement provided for a five-year transitional period during which the inhabitants of the Israeli-occupied West Bank of the

Jordan and the Gaza Strip would obtain full autonomy and self-government, and the second provided for the signing of a peace treaty within three months. In the event, the signing of the peace treaty was delayed because of the question of whether there should be any linkage between the conclusion of the peace treaty and progress towards autonomy in the Israeli-occupied areas, but on 26 March 1979, after another intervention by President Carter, the signing took place. The treaty (see Documents on Palestine, p. 65) provided for a phased Israeli withdrawal from Sinai over a period of three years. This withdrawal went according to plan, and, for the first time, diplomatic relations between Egypt and Israel were established on 26 February 1980 and the two countries exchanged ambassadors.

Proposals for Palestinian autonomy were contained in a separate letter published with the treaty, and provided for both sides to attempt to complete negotiations within 12 months. There would then be elections of Palestinian local councils, and a five-year transitional period would follow during which the final status of the West Bank and Gaza would be negotiated. The autonomy negotiations began in May 1979, but the deadline of 26 May 1980 passed without agreement being reached. The main obstructions were the presence and growth of Israeli settlements on the West Bank, Israel's increasing insistence that Jerusalem was its eternal indivisible capital, and a fundamental difference between Egyptian ideas of Palestinian autonomy, which were tantamount to an independent state, and those of Israel, which envisaged a limited form of self-government.

The Camp David agreements and the subsequent peace treaty resulted in Egypt's isolation in the Arab world. Syria, Algeria, Libya and the PLO had met in Damascus in September 1978 and strongly condemned the Camp David agreements, and in March 1979, after the signing of the peace treaty, the Arab League Council met in Baghdad, Iraq, and passed a series of resolutions (see Documents on Palestine, p. 66) comprising the withdrawal of Arab ambassadors to Egypt, the severing of economic and political links with Egypt, the withdrawal of Arab aid and the removal of the headquarters of the Arab League from Cairo to Tunis. Some Arab states were reluctant to implement these decisions, but when Saudi Arabia also severed diplomatic relations with Egypt in late April, Egypt's isolation became potentially serious, although private Arab investment continued. (Only Oman, Sudan and Somalia now maintained diplomatic relations with Egypt.) As a result, Egypt became increasingly dependent on financial and military aid from the USA. During 1980 the damage inflicted by the economic measures imposed against Egypt was offset by the growing strength of Egypt's own economy. The exchange of ambassadors between Egypt and Sudan, and Egypt's sale of arms worth US $25m. to Iraq in the same month, were indicative of its reduced isolation.

INTERNAL POLITICAL CHANGE

Since 1976 President Sadat had been trying to allow the formation of political parties while at the same time ensuring that dangerous opposition did not achieve too much influence. In a law of June 1977 political parties were legalized. Disturbed by the revival of the Wafd Party (as the New Wafd Party) and the criticisms of the NPUP, Sadat won approval in a referendum for new regulations on political parties which resulted in the disbanding of the New Wafd Party and the suspension of the NPUP. In July Sadat announced the creation of a new political party, the National Democratic Party (NDP), with himself as leader, which in practice replaced the Arab Socialist Party. In September 1978 an official opposition party, the Socialist Labour Party (SLP), was formed.

The signing of the Camp David agreements in September 1978, although causing the resignation of the Egyptian Minister of Foreign Affairs, Muhammad Ibrahim Kamel, was generally popular in Egypt, and in October Sadat appointed a new Government, designed to further the peace process, with Mustafa Khalil as Prime Minister. Khalil also became Minister of Foreign Affairs in February 1979. The signing of the peace treaty in March was followed by a referendum in April at which 99.95% of the voters approved the document. A simultaneous referendum gave Sadat a mandate for fresh general elections and for future constitutional changes. The elections, held in June, resulted in a convincing win for Sadat's NDP, which obtained 302 seats in the expanded 392-seat People's Assembly. On 30 April 1980 the People's Assembly approved a number of amendments to the Constitution, the most important of which provided Sadat with the opportunity to seek further terms as President and recognized that Islamic jurisprudence was the basis of Egyptian law.

On 12 May 1980 the Prime Minister, Mustafa Khalil, offered his resignation. Two days later, Sadat appointed a Government in which he himself became Prime Minister. The constitutional amendments were approved by more than 98% of the voters at a further referendum. One of these amendments provided for the election of a 210-member Majlis ash-Shura (Advisory Council) to replace the former Central Committee of the ASU. Elections took place in September 1980, at which the NDP won all 140 elective seats. The remaining 70 members were appointed by the President. The NDP also increased in strength in the People's Assembly in 1980 and early 1981, as at least 13 members of the official opposition SLP defected to the NDP or became independents.

MUBARAK SUCCEEDS SADAT

Although political parties had been allowed by Sadat, power had remained with his own NDP, yet opposition was never far beneath the surface. In the summer of 1981 there were clashes between Copts and militant Islamists, resulting in numerous arrests and the closure of various newspapers. Sadat was trying to stifle the opposition, of whatever religious or political persuasion.

On 6 October 1981, while attending a military parade, Sadat was assassinated by a group of militant Islamists led by Lt Khaled Islambouli, who was executed with four associates on 15 April 1982. An Islamist rebellion, which began in Asyout immediately after the assassination, was quickly suppressed, and Vice-President Muhammad Hosni Mubarak was confirmed as President in a referendum on 13 October.

Following his sudden rise to power, although many of the late President's religious and political detainees were released, Mubarak continued to arrest Islamist fundamentalists, several hundred of whom were tried on charges of belonging to the extreme Islamist organization al-Jihad (or Islamic Jihad), which plotted to overthrow the Government in 1981. In September 1984 174 of the 302 people arrested in connection with Sadat's murder were acquitted of conspiring to overthrow the Government; 16 were sentenced to hard labour for life; and the remainder received prison sentences ranging from two to 15 years. The state of emergency declared after the assassination of President Sadat was subsequently extended at regular intervals.

In his first government reshuffle, in January 1982, Mubarak replaced Dr Ali Abd ar-Razzaq Abd al-Majid (the architect of Egypt's 'open door policy') as Deputy Prime Minister for Finance and Economy, signalling a concern to correct the great inequalities of wealth in Egypt. A second reshuffle in August, including the dismissal of three Deputy Prime Ministers, was intended to secure an improved economic performance.

In foreign affairs, the early months of Mubarak's presidency were preoccupied with the question of the return of Sinai by Israel under the Camp David process. After many last-minute problems, the last section was returned to Egypt on 25 April 1982—although a dispute persisted until 1989 concerning the 1 sq km of the Taba enclave on the Egypt–Israel border, north of the Gulf of Aqaba, which was still occupied by Israel. Relations between the two countries were subsequently soured, most significantly, by Israel's invasion of Lebanon in June 1982, in protest at which Egypt withdrew its ambassador from Tel-Aviv; and by Israel's suppression of the Palestinian uprising in the Occupied Territories (see below). There were signs during 1983—such as the readiness of Iraq and the PLO to restore normal diplomatic links, the resumption of trade with Jordan and with Iraq, and the increased flow of Arab money into Egyptian banks—that the period of the country's ostracism by other Arab states (with the exception of those with the most uncompromising regimes, such as Algeria, Libya and Syria) was drawing to a close. President Mubarak had openly supported Yasser Arafat when a Syrian-inspired revolt against his leadership of the PLO erupted in 1983, in the Beka'a Valley, in Lebanon. In recognition of Egypt's support, Arafat visited Mub-

arak for talks in Cairo in December 1983, his first visit to Egypt for six years, marking the end of the rift between Egypt and the PLO. Substantial proof of Egypt's rehabilitation was provided by its readmission to the Organization of the Islamic Conference (OIC) in March 1984, although several countries, notably Libya and Syria, opposed the move.

RELATIONS WITH SUDAN: 1982–87

A joint Egypt-Sudan Nile Valley Parliament, a Higher Integration Council and a Joint Fund, based on the two countries' common interests in the River Nile, were established by charter in October 1982. The Parliament, comprising 60 Egyptian and 60 Sudanese members, was inaugurated in May 1983. Relatively powerless in itself, it was designed as the first step towards economic integration and an ultimate federation of the two states. The Higher Integration Council was to meet regularly to organize and review joint economic projects and to plan all aspects of the transition to the hoped-for federation. It was also to be used as a forum to co-ordinate policy on Pan-Arab questions.

In October 1984 Egypt unilaterally withdrew from the confederation agreement for a 'Union of Arab Republics', which it had entered into with Syria and Libya in 1971, saying it was no longer relevant. In April 1985 President Nimeri of Sudan was deposed by Lt-Gen. Abd ar-Rahman Swar ad-Dahab in a bloodless coup, which was endorsed by Col Qaddafi of Libya, who urged Arabs to overthrow other 'reactionary' regimes, implicitly including Egypt. Lt-Gen. Swar ad-Dahab reaffirmed Sudan's commitment to the integration agreement of 1982 during a visit to Egypt in October, but the Sudanese Government, led by Sadiq al-Mahdi (who became Prime Minister in May 1986), sought to improve its relations with Libya. It was also feared that relations between Egypt and the new Sudanese regime would be embittered by the presence of ex-President Nimeri in Egypt, where he had been granted political asylum. Bilateral links were placed on a more secure footing in February 1987, when Sadiq al-Mahdi and his Egyptian counterpart, Atif Sidqi (appointed in November 1986, see below), signed a 'Brotherhood Charter' in Cairo. This was understood to supersede the integration charter of October 1982 and to form the basis for future relations between the two countries. It was agreed in July 1987 that the issue of Nimeri's political asylum in Egypt should not be permitted to jeopardize bilateral links.

THE RE-EMERGENCE OF THE NEW WAFD PARTY

The right-wing New Wafd, as the Wafd Party, had led the Egyptian nationalist movement against Britain between 1919 and 1952. In the slightly more liberal atmosphere developing under Mubarak, the New Wafd reformed in August 1983, and Muhammad Fouad Serag ed-Din emerged from political retirement to lead the party. Alarmed at the New Wafd's potential for popular support, Mubarak's Government refused to recognize the party, but its legality was finally established by the courts in January 1984. In its modern guise, the New Wafd was more heterogeneous than before, comprising Copts, Nasserites, Islamist fundamentalists, former army officers (both pro- and anti-Nasser) and socialist and liberal businessmen.

THE GENERAL ELECTION OF 1984

In April 1984, in the hope that he could consolidate his authority and also (by restoring a measure of real democracy) establish himself as a popular leader who was tolerant, within limits, of opposition, Mubarak promised the first 'free, honest and sincere' elections in Egypt for more than 30 years. Safe passage in these elections for the ruling NDP had effectively been assured by an electoral law passed in July 1983 that required parties to gain a minimum 8% of the total vote in order to be represented in the People's Assembly, which was to be increased from 392 elected seats to 448 from 48 constituencies. Elections to the People's Assembly took place on 27 May, and the NDP accordingly took 72.9% of the total vote (the official turn-out was only 43.14% of eligible voters), entitling it to 389 seats. Of the four other participating parties, only the New Wafd, with 15.1% of the vote, crossed the 8% threshold, winning 59 seats in the Assembly. The opposition parties claimed that the elections had been undemocratic, accusing the Government of widespread fraud and intimidation of voters. The electoral alliance of the New Wafd and the fundamentalist Muslim Brotherhood was thought to have alienated many of Egypt's 6m. Copts, potentially a major constituency for the New Wafd.

The Assembly elections left Mubarak firmly in power, with a viable, yet politically brittle, opposition in the New Wafd, and the subversive Muslim Brotherhood in a relatively open political role, in which their activities could more easily be monitored. The Prime Minister, Fuad Mohi ed-Din, died on 5 June 1984, and in mid-July Mubarak reshuffled his Council of Ministers.

DIPLOMATIC DEVELOPMENTS

As if to signal its progress back into the Arab fold, Egypt severed diplomatic relations with El Salvador and Costa Rica in May 1984, in compliance with a call by the Al-Quds (Jerusalem) Committee of the OIC after both countries had transferred their embassies in Israel from Tel-Aviv to Jerusalem. Egypt and Morocco agreed, in principle, to resume diplomatic relations, while President Mubarak and King Hassan of Morocco discussed moves to end Egypt's suspension from the Arab League, the last major obstacle to Egypt's reintegration into the Arab community of states.

The full resumption of diplomatic relations with the USSR was also achieved during 1984, following the visit to Cairo in May of Vladimir Polyakov, the last Soviet ambassador to Egypt, who had been expelled with 1,000 or more experts by President Sadat in 1981. Mubarak had previously allowed the experts to return, and had signed trade and cultural agreements with the USSR. While it sought improved relations with the USSR, Egypt now stood second only to Israel in the amount of economic and military aid that it received from the USA.

Egypt's renewed commitment to issues affecting the entire Arab community (in particular, as concerning its relations with Israel, the Palestinian question) gave it the confidence to use its influence with both sides in the Arab–Israeli conflict to try to achieve a general peace in the Middle East. Israel repeatedly accused Egypt of contraventions of the military provisions of the 1979 peace treaty, and the question of ownership of the disputed Taba region was a further obstacle to any improvement in bilateral relations. In January 1986 Israel agreed to submit the dispute to international arbitration, provided that this was preceded by a period of conciliation (during which arbitrators would try to secure a compromise solution before delivering a binding decision). The process of arbitration began in December. In May 1987 each side presented its case for sovereignty to the arbitration panel, and in September a three-member 'conciliation chamber' was established. This failed to formulate a compromise solution in the 60 days allotted to it. In January 1988 Israel rejected a US plan whereby Egypt would be granted sovereignty over Taba while Israel was given access to the area, and in July Egypt rejected further attempts at compromise which failed to establish Egyptian sovereignty. The arbitration panel effectively awarded sovereignty to Egypt on 29 September, but left a key border undefined. Discussions on the final arrangements for the Taba enclave were held in January 1989, and Egypt assumed control over the area in March.

EGYPT'S REHABILITATION AND MIDDLE EAST PEACE INITIATIVES

In September 1984 Jordan resumed diplomatic relations with Egypt. The gradual rehabilitation of Egypt as a political force in the Middle East was deeply frustrating to Libya and Syria, as it was progressing without Egypt having to renounce the Camp David agreements or the 1979 treaty with Israel, which had been the cause of its ostracism. Furthermore, Egypt's rehabilitation suggested the emergence of a moderate alignment in Arab politics which could bring its influence to bear on the seemingly intractable problems facing the region, in opposition to the particular aims of Syria. Egypt's confidence in its role in international affairs was demonstrated by Mubarak's active involvement in attempts to find a diplomatic solution to the Iran–Iraq War. The division of loyalties in this conflict reflected the wider split in the Arab world, with Egypt, Jordan, Saudi Arabia and, less vocally, the other Gulf states supporting Iraq, while Libya and Syria, hoping to usurp Egypt's traditional role as leader of the Arab community, backed Iran. Relations with Libya continued to deteriorate. In July 1985 Col Qaddafi barred

Egyptian workers (of whom there were some 100,000 in the country at the time) from Libya, in retaliation against a similar Egyptian measure preventing Libyans from working in Egypt.

Consolidating the contacts first made between them after Yasser Arafat's expulsion from Lebanon at the end of 1983, following the revolt against his leadership of Fatah, the PLO leader, King Hussein of Jordan and President Mubarak continued their discussions on the Palestinian issue during 1984 and 1985, in Cairo and Amman. In February 1985 Hussein and Arafat agreed, in principle, that a joint Jordanian-Palestinian delegation could take part in a Middle East peace conference that would include the members of the UN Security Council, although issues regarding the composition of such a delegation and the basis on which peace talks would proceed were not resolved. The PLO rejected UN Resolution 242 as a basis for negotiation and it was not clear whether the Palestinian representation in the joint delegation would comprise members of the PLO. The US Administration of Ronald Reagan, for its part, maintained that it would not negotiate with the PLO unless it accepted Resolution 242 and therefore, implicitly, Israel's right to exist; King Hussein voiced equivocal approval only, standing by the agreement he had made with Arafat.

A series of terrorist incidents during the second half of 1985, in which factions of the PLO loyal to Arafat were implicated, damaged the PLO's credibility as a participant in peace negotiations and virtually assured the failure of the Jordanian-PLO peace initiative. In November, in Cairo, Arafat, responding to pressure from King Hussein and President Mubarak, called for the PLO to renounce violence, reiterated a PLO decision of 1974 to confine military operations to Israel and the Occupied Territories; this was hardly the unequivocal statement that the two leaders had sought, and was immediately repudiated by Arafat's aides.

In September 1986 President Mubarak met with Israel's Prime Minister, Shimon Peres, in Alexandria to discuss ways of reviving the Middle East peace process. After the summit meeting (the first between Egypt and Israel since August 1981), and following the signing of the Taba arbitration agreement (see above), Mubarak appointed Muhammad Bassiouni, Egypt's former chargé d'affaires in Tel-Aviv, as ambassador to Israel. The previous Egyptian Ambassador had been recalled from Israel in 1982, following the Israeli invasion of Lebanon.

It was largely as a result of its links with Israel that a new rift occurred between Egypt and the PLO in 1987. The crisis in relations was precipitated by the reunification of the Palestinian movement that took place at a session of the Palestine National Council (PNC) in Algiers in April 1987. One of the conditions that dissident PLO factions exacted as the price for their return to the mainstream of the movement, under Arafat's leadership, was the weakening of Arafat's links with Egypt. The Popular Front for the Liberation of Palestine (PFLP) initially demanded the immediate severance of relations, but the PNC finally adopted a compromise resolution urging the reappraisal of PLO links with Egypt and making future contacts dependent on Egypt's abrogation of the Camp David accord and the 1979 peace treaty with Israel. President Mubarak responded by closing all the PLO's offices in Egypt at the end of April 1987.

INTERNAL DISSENSION

While conscious of the need to relieve the country's finances of the crippling burden of state subsidies, President Mubarak was also aware of the dangers to social stability inherent in increasing the prices of basic commodities. These dangers were demonstrated by riots in the town of Kafr ad-Dawar in September 1984, which were prompted by modest price increases in staple foodstuffs. The Government, nevertheless, continued gradually to reduce subsidies on food, electricity and oil.

The campaign by Islamist fundamentalists for the legal system fully to adopt the principles of the *Shari'a* (Islamic law) intensified and became part of a wider resurgence of Islamic consciousness in Egypt. An amendment to the Constitution, endorsed by the People's Assembly in 1980, made Islamic law the basis of national law, and this was largely, but not fully, implemented. As well as taking account of the views of a potentially volatile Islamist section of the community, Mubarak was anxious not to alienate the country's Coptic Christians (many of whom occupied important positions in commerce, industry and the professions). Mubarak did make concessions to purist doctrine by imposing tighter censorship on books and films and by restricting the progress of female emancipation. However, he continued to adopt measures to prevent agitation by fundamentalists from destabilizing the country: banning Islamic rallies, arresting militant Islamic leaders and, in July 1985, placing all mosques under the control of the Ministry of Awqaf (Islamic Endowments).

A further threat to public order arose from Egypt's poor economic condition, which exaggerated the already wide discrepancy in living standards between the vast and growing numbers of people who lived in great poverty, and a rich minority. Seeking to prioritize this issue, President Mubarak appointed Dr Ali Lutfi, a former Minister of Finance under President Sadat, as Prime Minister on 4 September 1985, following the resignation of Gen. Kamal Hassan Ali and his Council of Ministers. Ali Lutfi presided over a Council of Ministers containing nine new appointees and three members who, while retaining their portfolios, were elevated to the rank of Deputy Prime Minister, making four in all.

On 25 February 1986, reacting to speculation that their period of service was to be extended by one year, to four years, some 17,000 poorly-paid conscripts to the Central Security Force (CSF) staged violent protests in and around Cairo, destroying two luxury hotels and damaging other buildings used by tourists in the Pyramids area of the city. The disturbances lasted for three days and there were clashes between the conscripts and the army, which was attempting to regain control of the city. According to government figures, 107 people died as a result of the mutiny, and 1,324 members of the CSF were arrested.

In November 1986 President Mubarak accepted the resignation of Prime Minister Ali Lutfi. A new Council of Ministers, containing, among several changes, a new Minister of Finance and three other new ministers in positions related to economic matters, was appointed under a new premier, Dr Atif Sidqi. President Mubarak was believed to have been critical of Ali Lutfi's apparent readiness to accede to demands from the IMF for the introduction of far-reaching economic reforms, in return for financial aid, and yet dissatisfied with the pace of reform to combat the continuing deterioration of the economy.

THE 1987 GENERAL ELECTION

Agitation by militant Islamists led to student riots in Asyout in October 1986 (in protest against the university authorities' refusal to allow women to veil their faces on university premises) and in February 1987. In December 1986 it was revealed that, three or four months earlier, four reserve army officers and 29 civilians, allegedly linked with Islamic Jihad, had been arrested in Cairo, accused of plotting to overthrow the Government. This was the first known case of fundamentalist infiltration of the armed forces since the assassination of President Sadat in 1981. Another, communist-inspired, coup plot was reportedly foiled in December.

A referendum was held on 12 February 1987, to decide whether the People's Assembly should be dissolved prior to the holding of a general election on the basis of a new electoral law, providing for a total of 48 seats for independent candidates in the 458-seat Assembly. The new law had been quickly adopted in December 1986 to pre-empt a ruling by the Supreme Constitutional Court that the general election of 1984 had been unconstitutional, as independent candidates had not been allowed to stand. An overwhelming vote in the referendum in favour of the dissolution of the People's Assembly facilitated the holding of a general election on 6 April. Mubarak hoped that the election would establish his Government on a firm constitutional basis and effectively secure him a second term as President. The SLP, the Liberal Socialist Party (LSP) and the Muslim Brotherhood (which was legally barred from forming its own political party) decided to form an electoral alliance, principally in order to overcome the requirement for political parties to win at least 8% of the total vote before they qualified for seats in the People's Assembly, a requirement that effectively prevented a single opposition party from gaining significant representation. The doctrine of wholesale application of Islamic law, the Muslim Brotherhood's principal tenet, was a prominent element in the alliance's campaign.

The election campaign was marred by sectarian clashes between Muslims and Christians in several towns in February and March 1987, and the opposition parties accused the Government of electoral fraud, the intimidation of opposition candidates and other forms of corruption.

Polling resulted in a large, though reduced, majority for the NDP in the People's Assembly. The ruling party won 346 seats (compared with 389 at the previous election in 1984), the opposition parties won a total of 95, and independents seven. The SLP-LSP-Muslim Brotherhood alliance won a combined total of 60 seats, of which the Brotherhood took 37, making it the largest single opposition group in the new Assembly. The New Wafd Party, which, with 58 seats, had been the only opposition party to be represented in the previous Assembly, won only 35 seats.

In July 1987 Mubarak was nominated by the necessary two-thirds' majority of People's Assembly members to seek a second six-year term as President. Mubarak, the sole candidate, was duly confirmed in office by national referendum on 5 October, polling 97.1% of the votes cast.

The principal threat to Mubarak's position remained the activities of Islamist militants. More than 500 Islamist fundamentalists, mostly members of Islamic Jihad and Jama'ah al-Islamiyah, were reportedly arrested after the attempted assassination of former Minister of the Interior Maj.-Gen. Hassan Abou Basha and two US diplomats in May 1987, and of a left-wing magazine editor in June. Egypt severed its remaining diplomatic ties with Iran in May, closing the Iranian interests section at the Swiss embassy, which, it was alleged, maintained contacts with Islamist extremists.

RELATIONS RESTORED WITH THE ARAB LEAGUE

President Mubarak and Yasser Arafat held two sessions of discussions in Addis Ababa, Ethiopia, in July 1987; the PLO's offices in Egypt, closed since April, were unofficially reopened at the end of July, and formally at the end of November. At the talks, both leaders endorsed proposals (already supported by Egypt and Jordan) for the convening of an international peace conference on the Middle East, under UN auspices, involving the five permanent members of the UN Security Council and all parties to the conflict, including the PLO. President Mubarak and the Israeli Minister of Foreign Affairs, Shimon Peres, had agreed in principle on the need for an international conference when the latter visited Egypt in February, although the issue of PLO representation remained an obstacle to further progress. The Israeli Prime Minister, Itzhak Shamir, was opposed to a peace conference in any form, and suggested direct talks between Israel, Egypt, a Jordanian-Palestinian delegation, and the USA. President Mubarak urged the PLO to devise a formula for its inclusion in an international peace conference, and, during a visit to Israel in July (the first by a high-ranking Egyptian since 1982), the Egyptian Minister of Foreign Affairs, Dr Esmat Abd al-Meguid, appealed to the Israeli Government to participate in such a conference.

In November 1987, at a summit conference in Amman, Jordan, which was attended by the majority of Arab leaders (excluding Col Qaddafi of Libya), the Syrian President, Hafiz al-Assad, obstructed proposals to readmit Egypt to membership of the Arab League. However, recognizing Egypt's support for Iraq in its war against Iran and acknowledging the influence that Egypt (as the most populous and, militarily, the most powerful Arab nation) could bring to bear on the problems of the region, the conference approved a resolution putting the establishment of diplomatic links with Egypt at the discretion of member governments. One week after the conference ended, nine Arab states (the United Arab Emirates, Iraq, Kuwait, Morocco, the Yemen Arab Republic, Bahrain, Saudi Arabia, Mauritania and Qatar) had re-established full diplomatic relations with Egypt. Of the remaining 12 members of the League, three (Sudan, Somalia and Oman) had maintained diplomatic links with Egypt throughout the period of the boycott, Jordan and Djibouti had re-established them in 1985 and 1986, respectively, and the PLO (to which the League accorded nation status) had recently begun to settle its differences with Egypt. In February 1988 the People's Democratic Republic of Yemen restored full diplomatic relations with Egypt, leaving Algeria, Lebanon, Libya and Syria as the only Arab League members not to have done so. Libya was the most outspoken critic of the change in the League's policy towards Egypt, on the grounds that the 1979 peace treaty with Israel, the original reason for Egypt's ostracism, remained in force. In November Algeria announced that it would re-establish diplomatic relations with Egypt, and in June 1989 full diplomatic relations with Lebanon were restored.

Following Jordan's decision, in July 1988, to sever its legal and administrative links with the West Bank region (annexed by Jordan in 1950 but, like the Gaza Strip, under Israeli occupation since 1967), President Mubarak urged the PLO to exercise caution in its plans to declare an independent Palestinian state and to form a government-in-exile. However, in November Egypt granted full recognition to the newly-declared Palestinian state.

The visit of King Fahd of Saudi Arabia to Cairo in March 1989 was a further sign of the rehabilitation of Egypt's standing in the Arab world. In May President Mubarak represented Egypt at an emergency summit meeting of the Arab League in Casablanca, Morocco. The meeting, convened to rally support for the diplomatic initiatives of Yasser Arafat following the Palestinian declaration of independence, was preceded by a meeting of foreign ministers of the majority of the League's members, which endorsed Egypt's formal readmission to the Arab League after an absence of 10 years. Despite Libya's opposition to Egypt's readmission to the League, Col Qaddafi attended the meeting, and held separate talks with President Mubarak. In June 1989 it was announced that Egypt was preparing to reopen its border with Libya, and in October Col Qaddafi visited Egypt, the first such visit for 16 years, for further discussions with President Mubarak.

MIDDLE EAST PEACE MOVES

Egypt was hopeful that its improved standing in the Arab world would enhance its role as a mediator in the Middle East peace process. In February 1989, during a tour of five Middle Eastern countries, Eduard Shevardnadze made the first visit to Egypt by a Soviet Minister of Foreign Affairs for 15 years, and held talks with both President Mubarak and Moshe Arens, the Israeli Minister of Foreign Affairs. In the wake of the Israeli peace initiative announced in April 1989 (see Documents on Palestine, p. 72), Egypt directed its diplomatic efforts towards activating preliminary negotiations between Palestinian and Israeli delegations. In September President Mubarak sought to persuade the Israeli Government to accept 10 points clarifying its peace initiative (the 'Mubarak plan') so that direct Palestinian-Israeli negotiations could begin. The 10 points in question were: a commitment by Israel to accept the results of the elections proposed under its initiative; the supervision of the elections by international observers; the granting of immunity to elected representatives; the withdrawal of the Israeli Defence Force from the balloting area; a commitment by Israel to begin negotiations within three to five years after the proposed elections; the ending of Israeli settlement of the West Bank; complete freedom as regards election propaganda; a ban on entry of all Israelis to the Occupied Territories on the day of the proposed elections; the participation of residents of East Jerusalem in the elections; and a commitment by Israel to the principle of exchanging land for peace. In early December, following two months of US diplomatic support for (and development of) the Mubarak plan, Egypt accepted a five-point US framework for the holding of elections in the Occupied Territories. By early 1990, however, there had been no appreciable progress in the peace process, which had been further complicated by Israel's apparent intention to settle in the Occupied Territories some of the Soviet Jewish immigrants who had arrived in the country in large numbers throughout 1989 and continued to do so in 1990.

Egypt's increasing frustration at the lack of progress in the peace process and its concern about the escalation of the Palestinian *intifada* led it to assume a more critical stance towards the Israeli Government in the first half of 1990. In June, after the formation of a new Israeli Government by Itzhak Shamir, the Egyptian Government suggested that Israel was preparing for war in the region. Following the suspension by the US Government of its dialogue with the PLO in June 1990, Egypt again attributed the disintegration of the peace process to 'Israeli intransigence' and urged the resumption of the US-PLO dialogue.

In March 1988 Egypt signed an arms co-operation agreement with the USA, replacing the memorandum of understanding signed in 1979. The new five-year agreement placed Egypt on the same footing with the USA as Israel and the members of NATO, giving it access to US defence contracts and to the latest weaponry, as well as exempting Egyptian military exports from US import duties. However, the arrest, in July, of an Egyptian with US citizenship, who was charged with stealing US missile parts and attempting to smuggle them to Egypt, placed arms sales by the USA to Egypt in doubt.

SOCIAL REPERCUSSIONS OF ECONOMIC CRISIS

The extreme caution with which Egypt implemented economic reforms was largely due to fears that they would provoke further social unrest and increase the threat to social stability posed by Islamist activists. In December 1988 more than 500 militant Islamist students in Cairo and Asyout were arrested on suspicion of involvement in 'anti-state activities'; and in April and May 1989, facing mounting popular discontent over price increases and food shortages, the Government acted to pre-empt disturbances during the month of Ramadan by detaining more than 2,000 Islamist extremists. In June elections to the 210-member Advisory Council were contested by opposition parties (the 'Islamic Alliance', consisting of the Muslim Brotherhood, the LSP and the SLP) for the first time since the establishment of the Council in 1980. Other political parties, however, boycotted the elections in protest at the prevailing state of emergency. None of the candidates from the 'Islamic Alliance' was elected, and it was subsequently alleged that the NDP had achieved its victory by fraudulent means.

In July and August 1989, in a further attempt by the Government to suppress political opposition, members of the proscribed Egyptian Communist Workers' Party and Shi'ite Muslims, including prominent members of the Muslim Brotherhood, were arrested on charges of subversion. By early September, following international protests, it was reported that most of the detainees had been released. In December there was speculation that Islamist fundamentalists had been responsible for the attempted assassination of the Minister of the Interior, Maj.-Gen. Zaki Badr, who had conducted the Government's ruthless campaign against political dissent. In January 1990 Badr was dismissed from his post and replaced by Muhammad Abd al-Halim Moussa. In the same month the Egyptian Organization for Human Rights (EOHR) condemned the violence that, it alleged, was routinely inflicted on political detainees by the Egyptian security forces.

In April 1990 three new political parties, the Green Party, the Democratic Unionist Party (DUP) and the Young Egypt Party (YEP), were legalized, bringing the total number of officially recognized political parties in Egypt to nine.

THE 1990 GENERAL ELECTION

In May 1990 a constitutional crisis arose after Egypt's Supreme Constitutional Court ruled that elections to the People's Assembly in 1987 had been unconstitutional because the electoral law promulgated in 1986 unfairly discriminated against independent candidates. Legislation subsequently passed by the Assembly was deemed to be valid, but the Court declared that any new laws approved after 2 June 1990 could not be endorsed. In September President Mubarak announced that a popular referendum would be held on 11 October in order to decide whether the People's Assembly should be dissolved; and that the electoral law would be amended with regard to the limited number of independent candidates previously permitted to participate in elections. (The People's Assembly, in recess since 4 June, had granted the President permission to legislate by decree in its absence.) Of the 58.6% of the electorate who subsequently participated in the referendum, 94.34% voted for the dissolution of the People's Assembly; this duly occurred on 12 October.

Campaigning for the elections to a new Assembly took place amid tensions resulting from the crisis in the Gulf (see below) and from the threat to Egypt's security posed by Islamist extremists hostile to the Government's pro-Western stance over Iraq's invasion of Kuwait. The assassination of Dr Rifa'at el-Mahgoub, the Speaker of the People's Assembly, on 12 October increased tensions and led to the most comprehensive security operation since President Sadat's murder in 1981, with hundreds of suspected Islamists arrested and detained. The Ministry of the

Interior claimed that eight members of Islamic Jihad had been responsible for the assassination.

At the legislative elections, held on 29 November and 6 December 1990, the former requirement for political parties to win a minimum of 8% of the total vote in order to gain representation in the Assembly was abolished, and restrictions on independent candidates were removed. However, the Government refused to concede to the opposition parties' demands that the elections be removed from the supervision of the Ministry of the Interior, and that the emergency regulations (in force since 1981) be repealed. The elections resulted in a clear victory for the ruling NDP: of the 444 elective seats in the new Assembly, the NDP won 348 (compared with 346 at the 1987 general election), the NPUP six, and independent candidates (of whom 56 were affiliated to the NDP, 14 to the New Wafd Party, eight to the SLP and one to the LSP) 83. Voting in the remaining seven seats was suspended. President Mubarak exercised his right to appoint 10 additional deputies, including five Copts. The turn-out of voters was estimated at only 20%–30%; four of the main opposition groups, the New Wafd Party, the SLP, the LSP and the prohibited—but officially tolerated—Muslim Brotherhood, boycotted the elections after the Government refused their demands concerning the conduct of the polls.

THE CRISIS IN THE GULF IN 1990–91

In December 1989 Egypt and Syria restored full diplomatic relations after a rift of 12 years. The *rapprochement* between Egypt and Syria was widely regarded as signalling a shift away from the balance of power that had prevailed in the Arab world throughout the 1980s.

In November 1989 reports of widespread acts of violent discrimination against Egyptian expatriate workers in Iraq threatened the special relationship which had developed between Egypt and Iraq during the Iran–Iraq War, when Egypt provided Iraq with military equipment and advisers. Prior to the crisis in the Persian (Arabian) Gulf region precipitated by Iraq's invasion and annexation of Kuwait in August 1990, Egypt had attempted to mediate between Iraq and Kuwait. Following the invasion of Kuwait, Egypt sought initially to maintain its role as a mediator, immediately proposing the convening of—and subsequently hosting—a summit meeting of Arab leaders. At the meeting, held on 10 August, Egypt firmly demanded the withdrawal of Iraqi forces from Kuwait, and 12 of the 20 Arab League member states participating in the meeting voted to send an Arab deterrent force to the Gulf in support of the USA's effort to deter an Iraqi invasion of Saudi Arabia. By late August about 5,000 Egyptian troops were reported to be in Saudi Arabia.

Egypt's quick success in mobilizing the support of 'moderate' Arab states for the economic sanctions imposed on Iraq by the UN, and for the defence of Saudi Arabia, emphasized the extent of the improvement in relations with Syria. While Iraq called on the Egyptian people to overthrow the Egyptian Government, there was no evidence of widespread popular support in Egypt for President Saddam Hussain of Iraq, and the Government's action was judged to have bolstered its domestic popularity. While it condemned Iraq's invasion of Kuwait, however, the Muslim Brotherhood, demanded the immediate withdrawal of US forces from the Gulf and opposed the dispatch of Egyptian troops to Saudi Arabia as part of an Arab deterrent force. It was feared, too, that Egyptian expatriate workers (totalling some 800,000 in Iraq and some 100,000 in Kuwait before the Iraqi invasion) returning in large numbers from Iraq and Kuwait to almost certain unemployment in Egypt might have a destabilizing effect. Some 600,000 were reported to have returned to Egypt by January 1991.

Following the outbreak of hostilities between Iraq and the UN multinational force in January 1991, the Egyptian Government continued to support the anti-Iraq coalition. Egypt's contingent within the multinational force, eventually 35,000-strong, sustained only light casualties in the fighting. On the domestic front, there were few disturbances during the war, and the opposition's predictions of popular unrest proved unfounded. In fact, Egypt emerged from the conflict in the Gulf with its international reputation enhanced, largely as a result of President Mubarak's firm leadership of 'moderate' Arab opinion. Moreover, the economy benefited from the waiving of almost US $14,000m. of Egypt's debts to the USA and other Western

and Gulf states at an early stage in the crisis, and by the signing of an agreement with the IMF in May 1991, which, later in the same month, led to the rescheduling of $10,000m. of Egypt's debt to the 'Paris Club' of Western creditor governments, and the cancellation of the remaining $10,000m. over a three-year period.

Following the conclusion of the war in February 1991, Egypt took part in a meeting of the eight Arab nations (the six GCC member states, Egypt and Syria) that had participated in the UN multinational force, held on 5–6 March in the Syrian capital. The statement issued after the meeting, known as the Damascus Declaration, called for 'a new Arab order to bolster joint Arab action'. It proposed, *inter alia*, that Egyptian and Syrian troops already deployed in Saudi Arabia and the Gulf states should constitute the nucleus of an Arab regional security force. However, in early May Egypt unexpectedly announced that its forces in Saudi Arabia and Kuwait were to be withdrawn. No Arab regional security force as envisaged in the Damascus Declaration has since been formed.

EGYPT AND THE MIDDLE EAST PEACE PROCESS

After the end of the Gulf crisis the Government's foreign policy continued to focus on the twin themes of Arab reconciliation and a settlement of the Arab–Israeli dispute, with particular emphasis being given to the Palestinian dimension. Egypt participated in the inaugural meeting of the Middle East peace conference in Madrid, Spain, in October 1991. In later stages it attended bilateral sessions as an observer and multilateral sessions as a participant. Despite the procedural delays and the slow progress of the negotiations, Egypt felt that the conference represented the best hope for a durable peace in the region and considered that Egypt had an important role to play in co-ordinating Arab strategy and providing diplomatic expertise. The choice of Egypt's former Deputy Prime Minister, Dr Boutros Boutros-Ghali, as the new Secretary-General of the UN was regarded by Egypt as recognition of its moderating regional influence. President Mubarak welcomed the change of government in Israel in June 1992, and in July the Israeli Prime Minister, Itzhak Rabin, visited Cairo for talks with President Mubarak, who reportedly emphasized to him his opinion that progress in the peace process was dependent on a halt to Jewish settlement construction in the Occupied Territories.

Egyptian mediators played an active role during the secret negotiations that led to the signing of the Declaration of Principles on Palestinian Self-rule between Israel and the PLO on 13 September 1993 (see Documents on Palestine, p. 73). The agreement made provision for limited Palestinian self-rule in the Gaza Strip and the town of Jericho on the West Bank. Once the agreement was announced, Egypt was the first Arab state that the PLO looked to for support. In October PLO and Israeli negotiating teams began meeting regularly in Cairo, or at Taba on the Red Sea, to discuss the detailed implementation of the agreement. In November King Hussein of Jordan visited Cairo for talks on the Middle East peace process—his first visit since the Gulf crisis of 1990–91, which had strained relations between the two countries. In December, when talks between the PLO and Israel became deadlocked, President Mubarak convened an emergency summit meeting in Cairo between the Israeli Prime Minister and the PLO leader, Yasser Arafat. However, the meeting failed to achieve an agreement on the withdrawal of Israeli armed forces from Gaza and Jericho, which had been scheduled to begin on 13 December.

The massacre of more than 40 Palestinians in Hebron on the West Bank by an Israeli settler on 25 February 1994 provoked several days of angry demonstrations in Cairo. Egypt withdrew its ambassador from Israel for consultations, but Egyptian diplomats tried to persuade both the PLO and Israel to resume their negotiations. Talks between Israel and the PLO recommenced in Cairo on 29 March. On 4 April President Assad of Syria visited Cairo for talks with President Mubarak, reportedly concerning Syria's dissatisfaction with Egypt's support for the Israeli-PLO agreement. On 4 May, after months of negotiations, an agreement on Palestinian self-rule in Gaza and Jericho was signed in Cairo by the Israeli Prime Minister and the PLO Chairman at a ceremony presided over by President Mubarak (see Documents on Palestine, p. 76). Under the terms of the

Cairo agreement, Israeli forces withdrew from Gaza on 13 May and from Jericho on 17 May.

OTHER REGIONAL ISSUES

Egypt's relations with Libya at this time were dominated by the repercussions of the 'Lockerbie affair' (see the chapter on Libya). With an estimated 1m. Egyptians working in Libya, Egypt used its diplomacy to try to avert a confrontation between Libya and the West, which could not only threaten the jobs of its workers but also undermine a steadily growing market for its exports. Egypt also regarded the Qaddafi regime as a useful ally in its struggle against Islamist militancy in the region. At the beginning of November 1993, as the UN Security Council was being urged by the USA, the United Kingdom and France to impose tougher economic sanctions on Libya, President Mubarak met Col Qaddafi, although Egyptian mediation efforts failed to produce a compromise.

In March 1994 Egypt attempted to mediate between rival Yemeni leaders, and hosted peace talks in Cairo between rival Somali factions. However, UN-sponsored talks in Cairo in June failed to achieve a cease-fire in the Yemeni civil war, and Egypt was accused by the northerners of favouring the breakaway south. In May, at the 11th ministerial conference of the Non-aligned Movement, which took place in Cairo, the Egyptian Minister of Foreign Affairs met his Iranian counterpart, Ali Akbar Velayati, who was the first senior Iranian minister to visit Egypt since the Iranian Revolution. However, there was no improvement in relations between the two countries; Egypt maintained that Iran was assisting Egypt's Islamist militants. Following an increase in commercial and economic exchanges during 1993, Egypt resumed diplomatic relations with South Africa in May 1994, one month before President Mubarak stood down as Chairman of the Organization of African Unity (OAU). Egypt's relations with its southern neighbour, Sudan, deteriorated following the visit to Khartoum, in December 1991, of a large Iranian delegation led by President Hashemi Rafsanjani. Acutely aware of the dangers posed by its own Islamist militants, Egypt was alarmed by Iran's support for Sudan's military regime, which is dominated by the National Islamic Front, and by the dangerous escalation of Islamist violence in Algeria. In June 1993 President Mubarak held private talks in Cairo with the Sudanese President, Lt-Gen. Omar al-Bashir, in an attempt to reduce tensions between Egypt and Sudan.

THE UPSURGE IN ISLAMIST VIOLENCE

From the early part of 1992 militant Islamist groups intensified their campaign to overthrow the Government and establish an Islamic state. Militant Islamists were particularly active in Asyout governorate in Upper Egypt, the traditional stronghold of Islamic militancy, and also in the poorer districts of Cairo, such as Imbaba. At the beginning of June 1992 some 5,000 members of the security forces were deployed in Asyout governorate in the most extensive military operation against militant Islamists for many years, and at the end of July the People's Assembly adopted new anti-terrorism legislation which imposed the death sentence for some crimes. In December an Egyptian military court sentenced to death eight Islamist fundamentalists, after finding them guilty of conspiring to overthrow the Government. It was reported that during the previous 12 months some 70 people, including several foreign tourists, had been killed as a result of Islamist violence. The leader of Jama'ah al-Islamiyah publicly denounced the very concept of foreign tourism in Egypt and threatened to destroy the country's major tourist attractions, the Pharaonic sites. Tourist numbers were reported to have fallen by 40% by the end of 1992, with a loss of foreign currency earnings of US $1,500m. Among those killed during 1992 was the writer Farag Fouda, one of Egypt's most outspoken critics of militant Islam, who was assassinated in June by members of Islamic Jihad, the group believed to have been responsible for the assassinations of President Sadat and the Speaker of the People's Assembly, Rifa'at el-Mahgoub. A year later, at the trial of those charged with Fouda's murder, Sheikh Muhammad el-Ghazali, a leading Islamist scholar, claimed that it was legitimate to kill any Muslim who opposed the application of Islamic law.

The problem of Islamist violence became more acute in 1993 and attempts to control it came to dominate the domestic political agenda. In April 1993 Safwat Muhammad ash-Sharif, the Minister of Information, narrowly escaped death when his car was ambushed. Ironically, the Minister had been criticized by liberals for filling the television schedules with religious programmes, which was regarded as a crude and unconvincing attempt to appease Islamist opinion. The new Minister of the Interior, Hassan Muhammad al-Alfi (see below), was seriously wounded in an assassination attempt in August. Officials stated that the attack had been carried out by the Vanguards of Conquest, a faction of Islamic Jihad. In November the Prime Minister, Atif Sidqi, escaped unharmed when a car bomb exploded near his residence, killing a schoolgirl and injuring 18 other people. The police stated that the attack was once again the work of the Vanguards of Conquest, although Islamic Jihad claimed responsibility. Attacks on foreign tourists occurred regularly during 1993, seriously damaging the country's vital tourist industry. As a result of the Islamists' campaign of violence, many international tour operators withdrew from Egypt, and revenues from tourism fell by about US $800m. in 1993, to $1,300m.

Harsh measures were employed by the security forces to counter the escalation in Islamist violence, and those arrested were increasingly tried by military courts which were seen as more effective than the civil courts in securing quick convictions. During 1993 military courts sentenced 38 militant Islamists to death and 29 were hanged. This was the largest number of political executions in Egypt's recent history.

In April 1993 President Mubarak had dismissed the Minister of the Interior, Muhammad Abd al-Halim Moussa, because he had indicated that he was willing to start a dialogue with imprisoned leaders of Islamic Jihad and Jama'ah al-Islamiyah. He was replaced by Gen. Hassan Muhammad al-Alfi, who immediately reaffirmed the Government's uncompromising commitment to suppressing militant Islamist groups. However, the new minister won approval in some quarters for favouring a more subtle approach to the security question. He pledged to stop the security forces carrying out indiscriminate mass arrests—a policy strongly criticized by human rights organizations—and stressed the need for greater efforts to improve social conditions. The crude methods employed by the police were revealed in August when a panel of eight judges found the 24 defendants on trial for the assassination of Rifa'at el-Mahgoub not guilty of murder. The court strongly criticized police practices and revealed that medical reports had shown that 16 of the defendants had been tortured (this claim was later denied by the Minister of the Interior). Safwat Abd al-Ghani, the political leader of Jama'ah al-Islamiyah, one of 10 defendants convicted of lesser offences, stated that the Mahgoub case highlighted the injustice of the military courts which accepted police evidence unchallenged. In December a civil court acquitted Abd al-Ghani on the charge of ordering the assassination of Farag Fouda from his prison cell.

Policing methods and the use of military courts in the campaign against Islamist violence provoked widespread international criticism. In May 1993 the human rights organization Amnesty International published a report in which it strongly condemned the 'frightening brutality' of the Egyptian security forces and alleged that, in response to the increased killings of police-officers and others, the security forces appeared to have been given 'a licence to kill with impunity'. It labelled the military courts 'a travesty of justice'. In November the UN Committee against Torture accused the Egyptian security forces of carrying out systematic torture against suspects in security cases and in ordinary criminal cases. The EOHR issued a statement endorsing the UN's accusations, and claimed that 13 people had died under torture in gaols, police stations or state security headquarters during 1993. The EOHR also drew attention to the 221 cases of torture that it had documented since July 1986 when Egypt ratified the UN Convention against Torture and Other Cruel, Inhuman or Degrading Treatment or Punishment. Nevertheless, in January 1994 the EOHR admitted that the major responsibility for all acts of violence in the country lay with militant Islamist groups, and produced figures showing that Islamist groups were responsible for the deaths of 137 people in 1993. The EOHR also accused the Government of acceding to Islamist pressure to ban books and of permitting the state-controlled media and education system to promote Islamist ideas. The Government moved to take some action in these areas. Already in February 1993 a trade union election law had been enacted requiring the participation of at least 50% of the members for an election to be valid. Earlier, the Muslim Brotherhood had gained control of the Lawyers', Engineers' and Doctors' Syndicates. Press censorship was increased and a number of high-profile corruption cases were prosecuted.

Following the bombing of the World Trade Center in New York in February 1993, investigations by the US Federal Bureau of Investigation led to the dismantling of some of the Islamist networks in the USA and the arrest of the spiritual leader of Jama'ah al Islamiyah, Sheikh Omar Abd ar-Rahman. At the beginning of July the Government (unsuccessfully) requested the extradition of Sheikh Abd ar-Rahman so that he could face charges of inciting violence in Egypt. Meanwhile, leaders of the Islamist militant groups continued to operate in some European countries. For example, it was reported that Tala'at Muhammad Tala'at, one of the leaders of the Vanguards of Conquest, was living in Denmark and that Egyptian requests for his extradition had been rejected. Ayman az-Zawari, the leader of Islamic Jihad, sentenced to death *in absentia* for his part in the assassination of President Sadat, was reported to be living in Switzerland where he had applied for political asylum.

In November 1993 it was reported that a preliminary agreement had been reached between the leaderships of Islamic Jihad and Jama'ah al-Islamiyah, urging joint action and greater co-ordination between the two groups in confronting the security forces. It was also agreed that Sheikh Abd ar-Rahman should be the leader of the Islamist movement as a whole.

MUBARAK'S THIRD TERM

President Mubarak was formally nominated for a third six-year term of office in July 1993. Although his nomination was supported by 439 of 448 votes cast in the People's Assembly, none of the opposition parties, nor the proscribed but officially tolerated Muslim Brotherhood, endorsed his candidature. Mubarak's nomination was approved by nation-wide referendum on 4 October. According to official figures, he secured 96.3% of the valid votes cast in an 84% turn-out. However, despite an intensive publicity campaign by the ruling NDP, independent observers commented on the low numbers of people voting. Mubarak immediately promoted the Minister of Defence, Gen. Muhammad Hussain Tantawi, to the rank of Field Marshal, an honour accorded to only four other generals since the revolution. Senior air force and air defence officers were also promoted. Some observers saw this as a move to placate the army, the ultimate power behind the regime, after Mubarak's refusal to appoint a Vice-President, a post that the military had tradition-ally regarded as its own. In a newspaper interview in October, Tantawi stated that he would deploy the army against Islamist extremists if they threatened the security of the State. This was the first time that the army had publicly declared its readiness to involve itself in the campaign against militant Islamist groups. Hitherto, operations against Islamist extremists had been car-ried out by forces under the command of the Ministry of the Interior.

During his third term of office President Mubarak continued to set strict limits on the extent of political reform. There was considerable internal and external pressure for fundamental changes to the Government in order to meet the challenge of economic reform and to counter the Islamist threat. However, when the new Council of Ministers was sworn in, in October 1993, Dr Atif Sidqi—first appointed in 1986—was retained as Prime Minister and the strategic portfolios of foreign affairs, defence, the interior and information remained unchanged. The President announced that the priorities of his third term would be security and stability, economic reform, social justice, educa-tional reform, combating unemployment, dealing with the problem of high population growth and improving Egypt's unwieldy bureaucracy. He made no reference to political reform.

However, Mubarak did propose a 'broad national dialogue' involving all parties that rejected violence and terrorism and supported democracy. The idea was first broached by the Presi-dent at the end of September 1993, and at the beginning of December Egypt's 10 principal legal political parties, together with the Muslim Brotherhood and the Communists, issued a

statement welcoming dialogue but insisting that the discussions should be comprehensive and focus on the question of political reform. Officials of the ruling NDP, headed by the Deputy Prime Minister, Yousuf Wali, eventually indicated that they would be willing to hold wide-ranging discussions covering political, social and economic reforms, but that the dialogue would be confined to the principal political parties in the first instance. There seemed little doubt that the decision not to include professional and trade unions was taken because several of them were controlled by the Muslim Brotherhood. The national dialogue meetings were scheduled to start in February 1994, but were postponed until April and then again until late May. In April President Mubarak stated that he would nominate a 25-member preparatory committee composed of party and trade union leaders to prepare a report on the terms of reference for dialogue.

When the President inaugurated the first session of the 40-member preparatory committee of the National Dialogue Con-ference, it was heavily dominated by the NDP. The Communist Party, the Muslim Brotherhood and various Coptic groups were not allocated seats on the committee, and the opposition parties claimed that the Government had no intention of seriously discussing political change but was merely using the conference to isolate the main Islamist political movement. The New Wafd Party and the Nasserist Arab Democratic Party announced that they were withdrawing from the conference, and the Chairman of the New Wafd Party, Muhammad Fouad Serag ed-Din, accused the Government of monopolizing the planning of the conference and of deliberately excluding from discussion impor-tant topics such as constitutional reform.

Despite these criticisms the first session of the National Dialogue Conference took place on 25 June 1994. President Mubarak told the 276 participants—including delegates from 10 political parties, deputies in the People's Assembly, trade union leaders, journalists, academics, businessmen, economists and, predominantly, NDP members—that dialogue was neces-sary not only to forge a united front against terrorism, but also to make the opposition feel that it was part of the system of government and that its views would be taken into account. The conference's political, economic and social and cultural committees completed their deliberations on 7 July and recom-mended only limited changes, reflecting the Government's suc-cess in controlling the agenda.

In January 1995 the NDP announced that the parliamentary elections planned for November of that year would not be contested on the party list system as recommended by the National Dialogue Conference, but that the individual list system would be retained. Most opposition parties, including the banned Muslim Brotherhood, indicated that they would not boycott the elections as in 1990. Pope Shenouda III urged all Copts to vote in the forthcoming elections to the People's Assembly and to become more involved in the country's political life. In the approach to the elections there was a government crack-down on the activities of the Muslim Brotherhood, including the arrest of a number of prominent officials of the organization (see below). The authorities also acted to reduce the Brotherhood's influence within key professional organizations.

At the beginning of June 1995 the NDP won all but two of the 90 vacant seats in elections for the 210-member Advisory Council. Independent candidates won the remaining two seats. The SLP and the LSP had offered only 29 candidates, and most of the remaining opposition parties had decided not to contest the elections.

THE CAMPAIGN AGAINST MILITANT ISLAMISTS INTENSIFIES

In February 1994 militant Islamist groups intensified their attacks on tourists and also targeted foreign investors. Jama'ah al-Islamiyah sent a series of warnings to international news agencies warning that tourists and foreign investors should leave Egypt, and that anyone helping a regime that opposed Islam would receive 'the same punishment as the oppressors'. This policy, however, was condemned by the Vanguards of Conquest which, in a statement from Islamabad in Pakistan, declared that targeting foreigners and foreign investors would only increase the hardships of the Muslim people. Earlier there had been reports of differences between the two extremist groups and of their failure to establish a joint advisory council (as agreed in November 1993). In February and March 1994 there were several attacks on tourist trains in Upper Egypt, and in early March a German tourist was killed when shots were fired at Nile cruise ships. Jama'ah al-Islamiyah also carried out a series of bomb attacks on banks in Cairo and towns in Upper Egypt. The organization had issued a warning to Egyptians to close their accounts at banks practising *riba* (usury). On 9 April Maj.-Gen. Raouf Khairat, a prominent state security officer and a key figure in the campaign against Islamist violence, was assassinated. Jama'ah al-Islamiyah claimed responsibility for the attack. In February suspected militant Islamists had shot dead the chief prosecution witness in the trial of those arrested for the attempted assassination of the Prime Minister, Atif Sidqi.

The crack-down by the security forces was unrelenting. Figures released by the Ministry of the Interior showed that 29,000 Islamist militants had been incarcerated following mass arrests. The security forces claimed to have arrested 900 Islamist suspects in a single week in February 1994. Adil Awad Siyam, the military commander of Islamic Jihad, was killed during an operation by security forces in Giza in April, and in the same month Tala'at Yasin Himam, believed to be the military commander of Jama'ah al-Islamiyah, died in a gun battle in Asyout along with four of his associates. In March two army officers were executed for their part in a plot to assassinate President Mubarak.

On 10 April 1994 a new law was enacted abolishing local elections and granting the Ministry of the Interior powers to appoint village *omdas* or mayors. In response to criticism from opposition deputies, the Government claimed that many *omdas* had refused to co-operate in security matters and were corrupt. The following day the emergency laws, which gave the security forces wide powers to arrest and detain suspects, were renewed for a further three years. The authorities also redoubled their efforts to curb the activities of leaders of extremist groups living abroad. In early April an extradition treaty was signed with Pakistan, and there were reports that the authorities in Yemen and Saudi Arabia were co-operating with Egypt in security matters. Local and Western journalists were warned to ensure that their articles on the Islamist issue conformed with official guide-lines or they would face arrest or expulsion. A propaganda offensive against the Islamists launched in the state-controlled media included televised confessions by former members of clandestine Islamist groups. Allegations that several senior police-officers were being investigated for supplying arms to Islamist militants were strongly denied by the Minister of the Interior in March.

The major battle between the security forces and the armed Islamist movement continued unabated in the southern governorate of Asyout, one of the poorest in the country. The political violence there was believed to have intensified because of the widespread tradition of *thaar*, or blood feud, strongly rooted in local culture. Asyout became the scene of almost daily clashes between security forces and armed Islamists, with police reports stating that 54 people were killed, and 67 wounded, between January and March 1994. In March an Islamist gunman fired into a crowd of Coptic Christians outside the Muharraq monastery, killing five people and wounding three others. In April the Minister of the Interior announced that the province was to be divided into four zones, each headed by a senior officer, in order to assist the security forces in controlling the area. At the same time it was reported that several development projects were under way to improve basic services there. Following the death in police custody of Abd el-Harith Madani, a lawyer acting for the Islamist militants, the Ministry of the Interior claimed that he was a 'terrorist' who had acted as an intermediary between imprisoned Islamist militants and those still at liberty. Madani's death provoked widespread protests and demands for a public inquiry, and following the threat of a general strike by several professional unions the Government reluctantly agreed to investigate claims of torture.

Claims by the Government that the security forces had suppressed the Islamist groups responsible for the violence proved premature. Towards the end of 1994 Jama'ah al-Islamiyah appeared to have regrouped and to have renewed its attacks, but, owing to tight police control over its traditional stronghold in Asyout, the conflict moved to the neighbouring governorates,

in particular the areas around the towns of Mallawi and Samalut in Menia governorate, much of which was under curfew. Clashes between militant Islamists and the security forces in Upper Egypt claimed 87 lives in January 1995, the highest figure for any month in three years. Moreover, in August 1994 Jama'ah al-Islamiyah had resumed its attacks on foreign tourists, striking for the first time at the country's Red Sea resorts.

Meanwhile, the Government moved to isolate the more moderate Muslim Brotherhood and to weaken its political influence in the approach to the parliamentary elections planned for November 1995. Several leading members of the Brotherhood were arrested in late January of that year, and both President Mubarak and the Minister of the Interior claimed that there was evidence of links between it and more extreme groups. At the end of March five members of the Doctors' Syndicate, which is controlled by the Muslim Brotherhood, were detained on charges of using medical relief operations as a cover for military training abroad. The Government acted to exert more control over other professional organizations, in order to counter Islamist influence within them. In February the People's Assembly passed an amendment to legislation governing professional organizations, giving the judiciary wide powers to intervene in trade-union elections and to prevent Muslim Brotherhood members from standing.

GROWING CRITICISM OF HUMAN RIGHTS VIOLATIONS BY THE SECURITY FORCES

Stringent security measures remained in force, and the continued use of special military courts to try suspected Islamists was criticized by human rights groups. Some 62 Islamists had been sentenced to death by military courts since 1992. Mass arrests continued: among those detained in December 1994 was the Secretary-General of the pro-Islamist SLP, Adel Hussein, a former Marxist turned Islamist, who was accused of having links with militant extremist groups and of supporting Jama'ah al-Islamiyah in its efforts to overthrow the Government. A prominent journalist, Hussein had written several articles vehemently denouncing official corruption. He was detained for one month and only released after strong protests from journalists, intellectuals and opposition leaders. In the early months of 1995 some 20 members of the SLP were arrested in Menia and charged with distributing anti-Government leaflets and of supporting Jama'ah al-Islamiyah. In December the EOHR warned that harsh security measures would not solve the problem of violence, asserting that only freedom of opinion and organization and democratic access to power would prevent the same kind of conflict developing in Egypt as in Algeria. The security forces were accused of torture and summary executions, and of intimidating the relatives of suspected Islamists. According to the US-based Middle East Watch, more than 8,000 political prisoners were being held in detention, most of them accused of being Islamist militants. In February 1995 the US Department of State also published a report that was highly critical of the methods employed by the Egyptian security forces.

On 26 June 1995 President Mubarak escaped an assassination attempt while he was travelling from the airport in Addis Ababa, Ethiopia, to attend the opening session of the OAU summit meeting. Mubarak, who was being driven in his own bullet-proof car, was unharmed and returned immediately to Cairo. On 29 June, addressing a meeting of workers in Cairo, the President claimed that Sudan was responsible for the attempt on his life and denounced the Sudanese regime. Sudan strenuously denied the allegation. In early July Jama'ah al-Islamiyah claimed responsibility for the assassination attempt. Two of the President's assailants who were killed during the attack, and a further three who were killed in subsequent raids by Ethiopian security forces, were believed to be Egyptians. In September the Ethiopian authorities stated that nine members of Jama'ah al-Islamiyah formed the team that had plotted the President's assassination, and a further two members had controlled the operation from Sudan. Ethiopia accused the Sudanese security forces of complicity in the attack, claiming that the assailants had safe houses in Sudan and that they had received training in special camps near Khartoum. Egypt had long claimed that Egyptian Islamist militants were being armed and trained in Sudan. Mounting evidence of Sudan's complicity in the assassination attempt against Mubarak was one of the factors prompting the UN to impose sanctions against Sudan in 1996 (see below).

By the end of 1995 the militants appeared to be under strong pressure from the security forces. In August it had been reported that Jama'ah al-Islamiyah was planning to revive its terrorist campaign in Cairo, which had been largely unaffected by Islamist militancy for more than a year, and in the following months several groups of extremists were arrested, allegedly for planning to assassinate leading politicians. At the end of November security forces arrested a large group of alleged militants belonging to Islamic Jihad who were accused of planning to explode a car bomb in the Khan al-Khalili, Cairo's main tourist bazaar, and to assassinate leading public figures. In November, during a visit to Paris, France, President Mubarak deplored the fact that certain European countries, including the United Kingdom and Germany, had offered political asylum to Islamist 'criminals'. In January 1996, after a US court sentenced Sheikh Omar Abd ar-Rahman, the spiritual leader of Jama'ah al-Islamiyah, to life imprisonment for terrorist plots including the bombing of the World Trade Center in 1993, Jama'ah threatened revenge attacks on US interests.

In February 1996 violence erupted once again in Asyout governorate, after some two years of relative calm, when Jama'ah al-Islamiyah launched a violent campaign in revenge for the killing of two of its members by the police in neighbouring Menia. Observers remarked that some four years of political violence had intensified local feuds and that, as a result, the periodic upsurge of violence was virtually impossible to control. By the end of February some 24 people had died in Asyout in clashes between the police, Jama'ah militants and rival families supporting either the security forces or the militant Islamists. In contrast, in mid-March the Government felt sufficiently confident that the security situation in and around Mallawi in Menia governorate was under control to lift a 20-month curfew imposed on the town. Mass arrests by the security forces across the country were reported in March and April, including the detention of some 245 men alleged to be members of the extremist Takfir wal-Higara group—inactive since the 1970s, but which the Ministry of the Interior claimed was regrouping and planning a campaign of violence. In September 1995 the EOHR issued a report condemning the harsh conditions under which Islamists were being detained in certain desert prisons, claiming that almost 20 had died in two prisons in less than a year. The allegations were dismissed by the Ministry of the Interior. Following the attempt on President Mubarak's life in Addis Ababa in June 1995 (see above), Islamist militants continued their struggle abroad. In October Jama'ah al-Islamiyah claimed responsibility for a car bomb explosion in the Croatian port of Rijeka, while just before the legislative elections in Egypt in November an Egyptian diplomat was assassinated in Geneva, Switzerland. A few days later a suicide bomber killed 16 people, including five Egyptians, and wounded 60 in an attack on the Egyptian embassy in Islamabad, Pakistan. The Group for International Justice (GIJ), believed to be part of Jama'ah al-Islamiyah, claimed responsibility for the murder of the Egyptian diplomat, while the GIJ, Jama'ah al-Islamiyah and Islamic Jihad all claimed responsibility for the bombing of the Egyptian embassy.

In November 1995, as Egypt's peak winter tourism season began, militants of Jama'ah al-Islamiyah advised all foreign tourists to leave the country and resumed their attacks on trains carrying tourists to sites in the south. In April 1996 four gunmen perpetrated the first major attack on tourists in the Cairo region since 1993 after they opened fire on a group of Greek tourists outside an hotel in Cairo, killing 17 of them and one Egyptian, and wounding another 15. Jama'ah al-Islamiyah claimed responsibility for the attack, stating that it had planned to strike at a group of Israeli tourists in revenge for Israeli attacks on Hezbollah bases in Lebanon. In the aftermath of the attack the security forces conducted raids on Islamist hide-outs in and around Cairo, arresting many alleged militants. In March three Egyptians had hijacked an EgyptAir aircraft carrying tourists from Luxor to Cairo and forced it to fly to Libya. None of the passengers was hurt and the hijackers were extradited at the end of March, although the breach in security was an embarrassment for the authorities.

In mid-1996 the Ministry of the Interior claimed that militant Islamist activities were now largely confined to parts of Menia, Asyout and Suhag governorates in Upper Egypt, where tight security measures remained in place. The security services reported that despite a series of violent robberies carried out by activists of Jama'ah al-Islamiyah, a sharp decline in high-profile attacks on foreign tourists and senior government officials indicated that the group had been effectively isolated from its overseas leadership and funds. In early May the offer of a ceasefire by Jama'ah was rejected by the Minister of the Interior, who insisted that there would be no dialogue with 'killers and assassins'. Later that month his ministry announced that the security forces had killed one of Jama'ah's leaders and arrested 33 of the group's activists. Further arrests of Islamist extremists were announced in June, and in September and October police launched major operations in Asyout and Suhag governorates to trace militants who had taken refuge there. The Government claimed to have made many arrests, but other sources reported that most of the militants had evaded capture. In September official sources announced the arrest of 16 leading members of the military wing of Islamic Jihad, and in October the detention of more than 50 members of a clandestine Shi'a group was reported. Earlier that month President Mubarak had accused Iran of both providing support for Egyptian Islamist militants and of involvement in his attempted assassination in June 1995. Iranian officials rejected the President's allegations and claimed that he was attempting to transfer responsibility for Egypt's internal problems. As the Government continued its campaign to suppress Islamist militancy, the large number of political prisoners held in Egyptian gaols provoked criticism from human rights groups. The Arab Organization for Human Rights claimed that 17,000 political prisoners, most of them Islamists, had been detained since 1991. By January 1997 83 Islamist militants had been sentenced to death by military courts since 1992, of whom 54 had been executed.

In September 1996 Egypt urged the British Government to prohibit the organization of a large international conference of militant Islamist groups, due to have been held in London that month, claiming that the United Kingdom was indirectly supporting international terrorism. The Egyptian media also criticized the United Kingdom for harbouring Islamist extremists, including Yasser Tawfiq as-Sirrim, alleged to be a leading strategist of Islamic Jihad.

At the end of February 1997 the People's Assembly approved a presidential decree whereby emergency law provisions were extended for a further three years. Human rights groups insisted that the emergency measures were being used not only to counter Islamist militancy but also to undermine support for political groups opposed to the regime. In the early months of 1997 there were a number of reports of attacks by militant Islamist groups against Coptic Christians in Upper Egypt. Indeed, militant groups were believed to be targeting the Christian minority in Upper Egypt as a source of funds in order to maintain their armed struggle against the Government. In March Islamic Jihad and the Vanguards of Conquest announced that they had merged, proclaiming their commitment to continuing a campaign of violence.

ATTACKS ON FOREIGN TOURISTS IN CAIRO AND LUXOR

In mid-September 1997 a military court in Haekstep, north of Cairo, held Egypt's largest trial to date of suspected Islamist militants; 98 people were convicted on charges of subversion, four of whom were sentenced to death and eight to life imprisonment. A few days later, in the first such attack for almost 18 months, suspected Islamist militants attacked a tourist bus in Cairo, killing nine German tourists and injuring 11 others. Although the perpetrators were widely believed to be members of Jama'ah al-Islamiyah, the Government, in an apparent attempt to protect the country's vital tourist industry, claimed that the attack was an isolated incident that had no connection with terrorism. The reports of eye-witnesses to the attack, which differed from the Government's account in some respects, were dismissed, and military prosecutors subsequently prohibited the publication of articles that challenged the official version of events. In May 1998 two men were hanged, having been convicted in October 1997 of conducting the attack.

In November 1997 the Government's campaign against the armed Islamist movement suffered a devastating reverse when 70 people, including 58 foreign tourists, were massacred by members of Jama'ah al-Islamiyah near the tomb of Queen Hatshepsut in the ancient city of Luxor. The damage to the Egyptian tourist industry was apparent in the immediate aftermath of the attack as foreign tour operators cancelled bookings and foreign governments advised their citizens to leave the country. It was generally agreed that the armed Islamist movement in Egypt was profiting from the deadlock in the Arab–Israeli peace process, from frustrations felt in Egypt at the lack of legitimate means to express political opposition, from economic hardship which had resulted from the country's programme of fiscal reform, and from the corruption resulting from that programme. A spokesman of the Egyptian Muslim Brotherhood condemned the attack at Luxor but emphasized the need for the Government to engage in dialogue with those among its political opponents who rejected violence, as part of a wider process of political, economic and social reform.

Following the attack at Luxor, the Minister of the Interior, Hassan Muhammad al-Alfi, who had conceived the Government's uncompromising strategy to eradicate Islamist militancy, was replaced by Habib Ibrahim el-Adli, hitherto the head of the state security services. President Mubarak ordered a heightened security presence at all tourist sites, and placed the Prime Minister at the head of a special committee that was to devise a plan to safeguard the tourist industry. In June 1998 two senior police-officers (the first to stand trial for 18 years) who had been responsible for security at Luxor's tourist sites were dismissed and fined, after a police disciplinary hearing found them guilty of gross negligence.

Prior to the Luxor attack, evidence had emerged of a willingness among the jailed leadership of both Jama'ah al-Islamiyah and Islamic Jihad to cease the movements' armed operations. In early December 1997 a statement that had apparently been approved by an exiled leader of Jama'ah al-Islamiyah condemned the attack at Luxor, thereby fuelling speculation that a rift had developed between the exiled leadership and those in command of armed units within Egypt. It also undermined the Government's claim that exiles had been responsible for planning the atrocity. It was not, therefore, clear whether an order to cease all attacks on foreign tourists, reportedly issued in early December by the exiled leadership, would be observed by all Jama'ah armed units. In May 1999 security officials in Switzerland alleged that the massacre had been organized and financed by the Afghan-based Saudi militant Islamist Osama bin Laden.

THE GENERAL ELECTION OF 1995

As elections to the People's Assembly in November 1995 approached, the political opposition remained weak and divided. After many months of negotiations the different parties were unable to agree on terms for a united front against the ruling NDP, failing to draw up an 'opposition charter' that was to have demanded the right for political parties to organize and campaign without hindrance, that elections be placed under judicial scrutiny, and that legal controls placed on the media be ended. The main disagreement appeared to be between the secular and pro-Islamist opposition parties. The Muslim Brotherhood spokesman, Maamoun al-Hodaiby, for example, insisted that his party would only support a common agenda that explicitly demanded the application of *Shari'a* law by the government in power.

Despite the opposition's outspoken lack of confidence in the electoral process, in August 1995 the New Wafd Party formally announced that it would participate in the elections and the other parties quickly followed suit. Following the attempted assassination of President Mubarak in June, pre-election security operations against the Muslim Brotherhood intensified. In the months preceding the election 19 members of the Brotherhood's Shura Council were arrested, accused of colluding with Sudan to promote terrorism. In a separate raid a further 200 members were arrested in several cities, representing the largest single operation against the movement since the assassination of President Sadat in 1981. At the end of August President Mubarak's decision to refer 49 leading members of the Brotherhood for trial by military courts attracted widespread

criticism, even from the movement's political opponents. Tagammu, the Nasserist Party and the New Wafd Party, among others, endorsed a statement of protest against the military trials, observing that the Muslim Brotherhood was committed to dialogue. Just days before the election, some 54 of the Brotherhood's members, including many parliamentary candidates, received prison sentences of three to five years for 'unconstitutional activities' from a military court which also closed down the movement's headquarters in central Cairo. In November the Minister of the Interior repeated his claim to have evidence of close links between the Brotherhood and the Islamist militants, and accused the Brotherhood, Jama'ah al-Islamiyah and Islamic Jihad of being, ultimately, part of one single organization. More than 1,000 Brotherhood members, including several hundred due to monitor the polls and witness the counting of votes, were arrested on the eve of the elections. The SLP also complained that the police had arrested some of its members in the approach to the elections and accused the regime of intimidation.

The combined results of the first and second rounds of voting, held on 29 November and 6 December, respectively, were announced by the Minister of the Interior on 7 December. The NDP won 316 of the total 444 seats, independent candidates 115 and the opposition parties combined just 13—the New Wafd Party six, Tagammu five, and the LSP and the Nasserist Party one each. For the first time the NDP pitted powerful government ministers against prominent Islamist candidates, most of whom were defeated in the first round. After the vote 99 independent deputies were reported to have joined the NDP, giving the ruling party an overwhelming victory with 93% of all parliamentary seats. Five women won seats, all candidates of the NDP. The Independent Commission for Electoral Review (ICER—newly formed by a group of prominent Egyptians and organizations active in civil society) noted that 56 Coptic candidates contested the elections, but that no Copts were included on NDP nomination lists. No Copts were elected, but of the 10 deputies appointed by the President six were Copts. Voter participation was officially registered at 50% in the first round of voting—out of 21m. registered voters—and 49.73% in the second round; the ICER claimed that fear of violence and lack of faith in the fairness of the elections had resulted in a considerable increase in voter abstention in the second round. Despite government assurances that the elections would be fair, and official press releases during the elections confirming the Government's neutrality and the efficiency of the police in securing and regulating the electoral process, they were widely denounced as the most fraudulent in Egypt's recent history. Furthermore, the ICER and other sources claimed that they had been characterized by unprecedented violence and bloodshed. Figures for casualties varied, but the Egyptian Centre for Human Rights and Legal Aid recorded that 51 people were killed and 878 injured during the electoral campaign. Prior to the first round of voting, the ICER, which employed some 600 volunteers to monitor 88 electoral districts, received numerous complaints about faulty voting lists and about the illegal, but widespread, practice of mass registration. Some opposition candidates complained that they had been assigned negative symbols, such as a sword or a pistol, so that voters would think that they supported the Islamists. On the first day of the poll the ICER received 1,240 complaints of irregularities from candidates, election agents and voters, more than one-half of them from Muslim Brotherhood and SLP members. They reported ballot-box stuffing, refusal to admit election agents into polling areas and, in some cases, physical abuse. Particularly disturbing were complaints by Coptic candidates citing examples of the NDP urging people not to vote for Christians. The revival of old traditions of tribalism among the supporters of various candidates and their re-emergence in the country's major cities was identified as perhaps the most dangerous outcome of the elections.

DOMESTIC DEVELOPMENTS: 1996–99

At the beginning of January 1996 President Mubarak appointed the Deputy Prime Minister and Minister of Planning, Dr Kamal al-Ganzouri, to head a new Government in place of the long-serving Dr Atif Sidqi. After the parliamentary elections Mubarak had come under pressure to improve the Government's image by creating a more efficient administration with less ministerial conflict. With the President maintaining firm personal control over the strategic portfolios of defence, the interior and foreign affairs, the Prime Minister's role was to take charge of economic affairs, to hasten economic reform, especially privatization, and to raise living standards. Although regarded as an economic conservative, international institutions expressed the hope that with strong support from the President, the new Prime Minister would prove more decisive than Sidqi in implementing reforms. Al-Ganzouri, who retained the planning portfolio, stated that he would give priority to job creation, to accelerating economic development and to encouraging foreign investment. In the reshuffle of the Council of Ministers that followed his appointment, the main changes were to the economic portfolios. In January the President also replaced 17 of the country's 26 provincial governors, appointing new governors to Asyout and Menia, regarded as the strongholds of Islamist militancy, while retaining the governors of key provinces such as Cairo, Giza and Alexandria.

After several cases in which Islamist lawyers had instituted legal proceedings against prominent Egyptians for contravening what they claimed to be Islamic morality, in January 1996 the People's Assembly passed a new *jesba* law to limit such claims of un-Islamic conduct. In March a new draft of a controversial proposed law governing the media was agreed which went some way towards reducing the harsh penalties for slander and libel proposed in the original draft; however, journalists expressed concern that the new version did not remove the threat of state intimidation of the press. In June the decision of the Advisory Council to reintroduce the harsh penalties from the original press law into the new draft encountered strong opposition from the Press Syndicate, prompting President Mubarak to intervene and annul most of the amendments by presidential decree. The People's Assembly endorsed the revised press law in mid-June. With a few exceptions, including criticism of the President and his family, journalists no longer faced lengthy prison sentences for libel and slander, although they continued to risk heavy fines. In September 1997 an Egyptian journalist at the Saudi Arabian-owned daily newspaper *Asharq al-Awsat* was sentenced to six months' imprisonment after having been convicted of libelling the President's two sons, and in October, following the attack on German tourists in Cairo (see above), strict controls were imposed on the reporting of attacks on tourists by both foreign and local journalists. In February 1998 Magdi Hussein, the chief editor of the pro-Islamist *Ash-Shaab*, and a journalist employed by the paper were each sentenced to one year in prison, with hard labour, convicted of libel, slander and defamation against two sons of the former Minister of the Interior, Hassan al-Alfi. In March the Government banned more than 30 foreign-registered companies from printing in industrial 'free zones' around Cairo. The prohibition was subsequently overruled by the Prime Minister, although restrictions remained on the printing of the *Cairo Times* and the *Middle East Times*. In March the Government ordered the closure of *Ad-Dustur* for publishing comments by a Jama'ah al-Islamiyah sympathizer. In July Magdi Hussein and his colleague were released from prison after their sentences were overturned. Further charges were brought against Hussein and three other *Ash-Shaab* journalists in April 1999, following accusations that they had libelled the Deputy Prime Minister and Minister of Agriculture and Land Reclamation, Dr Yousuf Wali, by claiming that his ministry was maintaining close links with Israel. In August Hussein and two of the journalists were sentenced to two years' imprisonment with hard labour, while the other received a £E20,000 fine.

The Government's intimidation of the Muslim Brotherhood continued after the parliamentary elections. In April 1996 12 leading members of the Brotherhood were arrested and charged with trying to re-establish the movement's clandestine activities and its links with extremist groups. For the first time the authorities arrested a member of the movement's Supreme Guidance Council. Three of those arrested were founder members of a new political grouping, the Al-Wasat (Centre) Party, and included Abu-Ela Mada, a former Deputy Secretary-General of the Engineers' Syndicate, who had campaigned to obtain official recognition of the new party. Mada was accused of trying to use Al-Wasat as a cover for Brotherhood activities, but the founders of the new party, including young Islamist, Christian, leftist and Nasserist activists, claimed that they were trying to

create a political movement occupying the middle ground between the State and the Islamist militants. In April 1996 the Government moved once again to reduce Islamist control over professional associations. Following allegations of financial mismanagement, the Lawyers' Syndicate, which had been dominated by members of the Muslim Brotherhood, was placed under the control of court-appointed custodians, leaving the Doctors' Syndicate as the only major professional union controlled by Islamists. In May the Supreme Constitutional Court upheld a decree, issued by the Minister of Education in July 1994, prohibiting girls from wearing the *niqab* (veil) in schools. Also in May the Advisory Council's Political Parties' Committee rejected Al-Wasat's application for a political licence. (In May and September 1998, and again in June 1999, Al-Wasat was denied legal status on the grounds that the party's political agenda was not sufficiently different from that of existing political groups.) In August 1996, however, Mada and the two other founder members of Al-Wasat were acquitted after trial by a military court. In contrast, seven members of the Muslim Brotherhood were sentenced to up to three years' imprisonment for supporting the new party. Some observers argued that the authorities were trying to exacerbate existing divisions within the Muslim Brotherhood between the young reformers of Al-Wasat and the older, more conservative, leadership. In October the three founder members of Al-Wasat were among 13 members who resigned from the Brotherhood. In December the People's Assembly made it an offence to preach in a mosque that had not been licensed by the Ministry of Awqaf. The Government thereby intended to extend its control over the country's many private mosques, which it claimed were used by fundamentalist Islamist groups, such as the Brotherhood, for their political activities. In March 1997 the Brotherhood announced that it would not contest the forthcoming elections because it did not expect them to be free or fair. The other main opposition party, the New Wafd, also indicated that it would boycott the elections.

As expected, at the local elections held on 7 April 1997 the ruling NDP won the vast majority of seats. Official sources indicated that the NDP took almost 45% of the 47,382 seats unopposed. The Minister of Information expressed the opinion that potential opponents had declined to come forward because of the violence surrounding the 1995 parliamentary elections, while local human rights organizations suggested that the electorate had simply lost faith in the electoral process. Although the Government declared that voter attendance was 40% in urban areas and 75% in the countryside, independent sources maintained that it was much lower: between 5% and 20%. Although the NDP faced little or no opposition, there were widespread claims of electoral fraud. Two days before the elections the State Security Prosecutor ordered the arrest of 27 members of the Muslim Brotherhood, which claimed that hundreds of its followers had been detained to prevent them from participating. No comprehensive monitoring of the voting took place, but human rights groups and opposition sources claimed that electoral malpractice had once again been widespread.

In June 1998 the NDP secured 85 of the 88 contested seats at mid-term elections to the Advisory Council. The remaining three seats were won by independent candidates. Most opposition parties had decided not to contest the election. In November 1998 Ahmad Fathi Surur, regarded as a close political ally of President Mubarak, was re-elected Speaker of the People's Assembly for the ninth time in succession.

In December 1998 the EOHR announced the suspension of its activities in protest at the arrest of its Secretary-General, Hafiz Abu Sa'ada. The arrest followed allegations made by the weekly *al-Usbu'* newspaper that Sa'ada had been paid some US $25,000 by a British parliamentary human rights committee, via the British embassy in Cairo, to write a false report exposing alleged police brutality against Copts in Upper Egypt during August of that year. A British embassy official maintained that the payment was intended for a legal aid project, which had been funded from Britain in this way since 1996. Human rights activists, meanwhile, claimed that the Government and security services (with which *al-Usbu'* was alleged to have connections) were seeking to punish the EOHR for having exposed institutionalized ill-treatment of Egypt's Coptic minority.

By early 1999 labour unrest in Egypt had reached its highest level since the 1952 revolution. Despite legal restrictions on strike action, an estimated 80 protests were staged by public sector workers in 1998, and 10 strikes were organized in February 1999 alone. This increase in industrial action, which affected the road and air transport and textiles sectors, as well as several state enterprises, was believed to reflect public concerns about a proposed labour law that would facilitate the termination of employment contracts. Meanwhile, legislation concerning the activities of non-governmental organizations (NGOs), approved by the People's Assembly in May, attracted strong criticism from both the committee charged with preparing recommendations on the proposed law and from human rights groups who claimed that the legislation would compromise the independence of the organizations. The new Law on Associations and Civil Institutions imposed stringent state regulation on such bodies, including the right of state intervention to dismiss board members and appoint government representatives in their place, and prevented NGOs from receiving funding from abroad.

Attempts by the Government to suppress the activities of Islamist groups intensified during 1998, with further arrests and security trials. By June of that year 106 death sentences had been received by militant Islamists since 1992, of which 72 had been carried out. However, new measures regarding state security, adopted by the Ministry of the Interior in 1998, included a relaxation of the criteria on which affiliation to Islamist groups was assumed, and the release of some 5,000 Islamist prisoners who had renounced connections with illegal organizations and the use of violence. The release of prisoners was interpreted by some observers as a goodwill gesture by the Government towards Jama'ah al-Islamiyah, which appeared to be moving towards the declaration of a cease-fire.

Internal dissent within Jama'ah al-Islamiyah remained evident meanwhile: in October 1998 one of the group's imprisoned leaders urged all Islamist groups to form a 'world Islamic front', employing exclusively peaceful means; however, reports of a change in the group's political strategy were later denied by another senior member. In early 1999 one of Jama'ah al-Islamiyah's founders denied reports that the organization was planning to establish a political party. Nevertheless, speculation continued during 1999, and it was predicted that the political programme of the new party (reportedly to be called Al-Islah or Reform) would soon be presented to the Political Parties Committee. Meanwhile, in late March 1999 Jama'ah al-Islamiyah declared a unilateral cease-fire and announced a new strategy of exerting maximum political pressure on the Egyptian Government without the use of violence. The cease-fire had reportedly been endorsed by the organization's imprisoned spiritual leader, Sheikh Omar Abd ar-Rahman, its Shura Council and the historical leaders in exile. However, it remained unclear as to whether Jama'ah's military commanders, led by Rifai at-Taha from his base in Afghanistan, would end their campaign of violence. Although the Government gave no formal acknowledgement of the cease-fire, there followed an acceleration in the release of imprisoned Islamist militants, in an apparent attempt to consolidate the peace. In late April the Ministry of the Interior released some 1,200 Jama'ah al-Islamiyah prisoners (reportedly including two of the group's leaders who were implicated in the assassination of President Sadat); government officials strongly denied that a deal had been concluded with the proscribed organization.

Despite the apparent development of a fragile truce between the Government and Islamists, the arrest and trial of suspected Islamist militants continued in 1999. In February it was reported that three men suspected of belonging to Jama'ah al-Islamiyah and of involvement in the 1997 Luxor attack were arrested on the Uruguayan–Brazilian border; the Egyptian authorities subsequently demanded their extradition in order to face trial in Cairo. In the same month proceedings began against 107 alleged members of Islamic Jihad who were charged with conspiring to overthrow the Government, in the largest security trial in Egypt since militant Islamist groups launched their campaign against the State in 1992. In April 1999 nine of the accused were sentenced to death for having led an illegal organization and for plotting attacks on state officials and the police; 78 received prison sentences of between one year and

life, all with hard labour, while 20 were acquitted. Among those sentenced to death, having been tried *in absentia* (as were most of the defendants), was a senior leader of Islamic Jihad, Ayman el-Zawahri. In response to the verdicts, the group pledged to continue its actions against the State, despite Jama'ah al-Islamiyah's cease-fire declaration in March. The EOHR, meanwhile, claimed that there had been insufficient evidence for the defendants to be sentenced. In May the security services detained 23 suspects on the grounds that they were seeking to revive the activities in Egypt of the Jihad splinter group, the Vanguards of Conquest. In June 20 members of Jama'ah al-Islamiyah were given prison sentences for a planned bomb attack on President Mubarak's Alexandria residence in 1996. However, the military court's decision not to impose the death sentence was interpreted by the organization's lawyers as a positive response to Jama'ah's recent cease-fire declaration. In September 1999 the Government claimed that it had released more than 5,000 Islamist detainees since the beginning of the year. Human rights groups claimed that this still left 15,000 in detention, two-thirds of whom had no extremist Islamist connections, and that most of these detainees were being held without charge or trial. In the same month security forces in Giza shot dead four alleged members of Jama'ah al-Islamiyah, including the commander of its military wing, Farid Salem al-Kedwani. This was the Government's first security action against the group since Jama'ah declared its cease-fire in March.

EGYPT STRIVES TO REASSERT ITS REGIONAL STATUS

The Middle East peace process continued to dominate Egypt's foreign policy. In July 1994 President Mubarak travelled to Damascus in an effort to break the deadlock in the negotiations between Syria and Israel, and before returning to Cairo he met the Israeli Prime Minister, Itzhak Rabin, at Taba. Mubarak reportedly urged Rabin to effect a full Israeli withdrawal from the occupied Golan Heights. Despite the first official visit to Egypt by the Israeli President, Ezer Weizman, in December, relations between Egypt and Israel began to deteriorate. Egypt was concerned that the peace process might collapse unless Israel showed more flexibility in the negotiations and the Palestinians quickly secured some real benefits from the peace agreement.

During a visit to Cairo in January 1995 the Israeli Minister of Foreign Affairs, Shimon Peres, was informed that Egypt had no desire to obstruct the normalization of relations between Israel and the Arab states. However, tension remained as Mubarak reiterated his threat that Egypt would not sign the Treaty on the Non-Proliferation of Nuclear Weapons (the Non-Proliferation Treaty—NPT), which was due for renewal in April, unless Israel also agreed to sign it; and urged other Arab states to follow Egypt's example. Israel, meanwhile, accused Egypt of attempting to use the non-proliferation issue to disrupt its efforts to normalize relations with other Arab states. In March 1995 Israel offered to sign the NPT once it had concluded peace treaties with all the Arab states and Iran, and to allow Egypt to inspect its research nuclear reactor at Nahal Shorek but not the nuclear facility at Dimona. Egypt rejected both offers, but adopted a more conciliatory stance on the issue. Both states appeared anxious to avoid a major crisis in their relations.

Egypt's position regarding the NPT antagonized the USA, which insisted that the continuation of US aid depended on Egypt's signing the Treaty. Egypt remained concerned about its relations with the USA, and feared that, weakened as he was after the recent Republican victory in the US Congress, President Bill Clinton might become even more dependent on the support of the pro-Israel lobby. When President Mubarak visited Washington, DC, in April 1995, Egypt's relations with the USA had reached their lowest level for many years. The dispute with Israel over the NPT dominated discussions during the visit, at the end of which President Mubarak pledged that Egypt would not withdraw from the Treaty nor persuade other states to suspend their membership. However, the possibility of a reduction in US aid to Egypt continued to be openly discussed.

As the dispute over the NPT came to a head at the UN in New York in May 1995, Egypt led the Arab states in demanding a resolution requiring Israel to sign the Treaty. However, under US pressure, the Arab states agreed to a resolution that did not mention Israel by name but instead urged all states in the Middle East without exception to sign the NPT and accept inspection of their nuclear facilities by the International Atomic Energy Agency (IAEA). Egypt also led the Arab states in condemning Israel's planned land seizures in occupied East Jerusalem, and demanded the convening of an emergency Arab League summit meeting on the question. However, at the end of May the Israeli Government decided to suspend the confiscation, and at the beginning of June, after a meeting in Cairo between President Mubarak, Itzhak Rabin and US Secretary of State Warren Christopher, the US official claimed that relations between Egypt and Israel had been 'rejuvenated'. However, relations deteriorated again in August when it was revealed that Israeli soldiers had killed large numbers of Egyptian prisoners of war during the Suez crisis in 1956 and the Six-Day War in 1967. After the discovery of mass graves in Sinai, President Mubarak demanded that the Israeli Government investigate these crimes. At first Israel refused, offering instead to pay compensation to the families of the victims.

In spite of this dispute, Egypt continued its intermediary role in the complex negotiations that eventually led to the signing of the Israeli-Palestinian Interim Agreement on the West Bank and the Gaza Strip in Washington, DC, in September 1995 (see Documents on Palestine, p. 80). On 6 November Mubarak made his first visit to Israel as President of Egypt, in order to attend the funeral of the assassinated Prime Minister Itzhak Rabin. Egypt also participated in meetings leading to the start of more substantive talks between Israel and Syria at the end of 1995. However, disputes over Israel's nuclear capability and the execution of Egyptian prisoners of war continued. In April 1996, following reports of a possible leak of nuclear waste from Israel's Dimona reactor, Egypt's Minister of Foreign Affairs, Amr Moussa, urged that the reactor should be dismantled and rejected any co-operation on security with Israel while it retained a nuclear capability. In that month the African Nuclear-Weapon-Free Zone Treaty (or Pelindaba Treaty) was signed in Cairo. At the signing ceremony, President Mubarak urged all Middle East countries to make the region a nuclear-free zone by signing the NPT.

President Mubarak met King Hussein of Jordan at Aqaba in January 1995, in his first visit to Jordan since the Gulf crisis. The visit was regarded as signalling an improvement in relations between the two countries now that Jordan had signed a peace treaty with Israel. However, Egypt's relations with Jordan deteriorated once again in August 1995, when King Hussein changed policy on Iraq, granted asylum to Saddam Hussain's two defecting sons-in-law and their wives, and broke decisively with the Iraqi leader. King Hussein's appeal for political change in Iraq was strongly criticized by the Egyptian regime, which expressed its opposition to any kind of outside intervention to depose Saddam Hussain. In reply, Jordan claimed that Egypt resented the more active role that Jordan was now playing in the Middle East region.

In March 1996, in response to a number of devastating suicide bomb attacks in Israel, Egypt, together with the USA, co-hosted a hastily arranged 'Summit of Peacemakers' in March 1996 at the Red Sea resort of Sharm esh-Sheikh, which was attended by 29 world leaders. Little of substance was achieved at the meeting, which was widely regarded as a move to reassure Israel and to lend support to Prime Minister Peres during the approach to the Israeli legislative elections in May. Egypt's relations with Israel deteriorated further in April when Israeli forces began air and artillery attacks on Hezbollah bases in Lebanon (q.v.), inflicting heavy casualties on Lebanese civilians. The Lebanese Prime Minister, Rafik Hariri, visited Cairo to seek assistance against Israeli aggression; however, diplomatic efforts by the Egyptian Minister of Foreign Affairs to achieve a cease-fire were unsuccessful, and in exasperation he complained that Israel's actions threatened the credibility of the entire peace process. Relations did not improve when it was announced, in April, that Israel and Turkey had concluded a military agreement in February allowing Israeli aircraft to fly from Turkish airbases and Israeli warships to use Turkish ports during joint naval manoeuvres. The Egyptian Minister of Foreign Affairs denounced the agreement, arguing that it did not serve the interests of peace or stability in the region. Military strategists in Egypt regarded it as the creation of 'a second front against the

Arabs', while other observers maintained that a new strategic partnership was emerging in the region between Israel, the USA, Jordan and Turkey that could only serve to increase Egypt's marginalization.

There was surprise in some quarters when it was announced in November 1994 that Egypt had applied for permanent observer status and possible membership of the Union of the Arab Maghreb (Union du Maghreb arabe—UMA), a regional economic and security grouping of Algeria, Libya, Mauritania, Morocco and Tunisia. Egypt had collaborated for some time with Algeria and Tunisia in the struggle against Islamist militancy, but the reasons behind the application appeared to be linked to its desire to reassert its central role in the Middle East as Israel successfully normalized its relations with a growing number of Arab states, and, by emphasizing its Mediterranean role, to give a higher priority to diplomatic relations with Europe in the hope of securing economic benefits from the EU. In April 1999 Egypt, Morocco and Tunisia announced that they were discussing the establishment of a free-trade area.

Relations with neighbouring Sudan, always uneasy, deteriorated in August 1994 when each side accused the other of mistreating its nationals. In the following month Sudan alleged that Egyptian troops had entered the disputed border area of Halaib and, in response, impounded the Aswan–Wadi Halfa ferry, claiming that it was carrying troops. Relations worsened sharply in June 1995, after the assassination attempt on President Mubarak in Addis Ababa (see above). The Egyptian Government accused Sudan of complicity in the attack, and Egypt immediately strengthened its control of the Halaib triangle. In July, in contravention of an agreement concluded with Sudan in 1978, Egypt imposed visa and permit requirements on Sudanese nationals visiting or resident in Egypt. Relations deteriorated further in September 1995, when the OAU accused Sudan of direct involvement in the attempted assassination, and in December, when it demanded that Sudan should immediately extradite three individuals sought in connection with the attack. In February 1996 Sudan introduced permit requirements for Egyptian nationals resident in Sudan. Presidents Mubarak and al-Bashir met at the Arab League summit meeting in Cairo in May. In July, however, Egypt accused Sudan of harbouring Egyptian terrorists, contrary to an agreement concluded at the summit meeting. None the less, Egypt opposed the imposition of more stringent economic sanctions against Sudan by the UN (in addition to diplomatic sanctions and an embargo on international flights operated by Sudan Airways), on the grounds that they would harm the Sudanese people more than the Sudanese regime.

THE PEACE PROCESS STAGNATES

During the approach to the May 1996 Israeli elections President Mubarak did not disguise his preference for a Labour victory, while the semi-official *Al-Ahram* newspaper warned that the Arabs should prepare for tough negotiations in the event of a Likud victory. After the victory of Likud leader Binyamin Netanyahu was confirmed, it was reported that President Mubarak had telephoned the new Israeli Prime Minister and invited him to visit Cairo. At the end of June, however, after Netanyahu had repeated his rejection of the principle of 'land for peace', President Mubarak convened an emergency summit meeting of the Arab League in Cairo—the first full-scale summit meeting for six years. (Iraq was not invited because of what President Mubarak referred to as 'continuing sensitivities'.) The summit reaffirmed Egypt's central role in the Arab world, where Egyptian efforts at reconciliation created some semblance of unity. The summit's final communiqué reaffirmed the Arabs' commitment to peace, but warned that peace and any further *rapprochement* between the Arabs and Israel depended on the return by Israel of all of Arab land occupied in 1967. Israel immediately rejected all of the resolutions adopted at the summit meeting, and Prime Minister Netanyahu declared that unilateral demands had to cease if the peace process was to continue successfully.

Although Netanyahu was invited for talks with President Mubarak in Cairo in July 1996, relations with Israel became increasingly strained. The Egyptian Government argued that it had worked hard to restrain some of the more militant Arab states, but that the Israeli Prime Minister had not reciprocated:

he had neither moderated his uncompromising stance nor fulfilled Israel's commitments to the Palestinians under the Oslo accords. In September there were popular demonstrations in Egypt after the Israeli Government opened the ancient Hasmonean tunnel in East Jerusalem, close to Muslim religious sites. Violent clashes erupted between Israeli troops and Palestinians and public anger prevented Egypt from acting as mediator in the crisis. Although Prime Minister Netanyahu, King Hussein of Jordan and the President of the Palestinian (National) Authority (PA), Yasser Arafat, attended a summit meeting in Washington to try to defuse the crisis, President Mubarak resisted US pressure to participate, stating that an immediate resolution was unlikely to be achieved. Despite a goodwill visit to Cairo by the President of Israel, Ezer Weizman, in October, his reassurances about Israel's peace commitments failed to ease tensions between the two countries. In December a new dispute arose when the Israeli Minister of Foreign Affairs, David Levy, accused Egypt of interfering in talks between Israel and the Palestinians on the partial withdrawal of Israeli troops from the town of Hebron on the West Bank. President Mubarak insisted that Prime Minister Netanyahu had invited Egypt to act as mediator in the talks, but Levy stated that Egypt's involvement would only complicate the negotiations.

When the Ministers of Foreign Affairs of the Arab League member states met in Cairo at the end of March 1997, it was decided to reintroduce the economic boycott of Israel and to halt the normalization of relations. Egypt was exempt from the boycott, however, because of its peace treaty with Israel. In early April President Mubarak insisted that relations with Israel would remain secure. Indeed, Egypt wished to maintain its intermediary role and its economic links with the country. Nevertheless, there were many signs of popular dissatisfaction with the normalization of relations with Israel. In late April a large political rally in Cairo in protest against Israeli policies in Jerusalem was attended by representatives from across Egypt's political spectrum.

At the end of May 1997 President Mubarak met the Israeli Prime Minister at Sharm esh-Sheikh in order to try to reactivate the peace process. President Mubarak agreed to contact the Palestinian leader, Yasser Arafat, who had refused to meet with Netanyahu after Israel confirmed its intention to proceed with the controversial construction of a new Jewish settlement at Har Homa on the outskirts of Arab East Jerusalem—a decision which had effectively stalled the peace process. In early June Osama el-Baz, President Mubarak's senior adviser, conferred with Israeli and Palestinian negotiators in Cairo. However, Israel's continued building of settlements in East Jerusalem appeared to prolong the deadlock, and for the remainder of the year the Egyptian Government, in its role as principal mediator, attempted unsuccessfully to revive the peace process. Increasingly, official announcements on the stalled negotiations were made in a tone of desperation, not least because Israel's intransigence, to which the Egyptian Government frequently referred, strengthened the position of the armed militant Islamist opposition in Egypt.

In September 1997 Egypt's relations with Israel were further impaired when an Egyptian State Security Court sentenced an Israeli Arab, Azam Azam, to 15 years' imprisonment, with hard labour, having convicted him of spying for the Israeli intelligence services. The Israeli Government denied that Azam had been involved in espionage and described the sentence as an 'outrage'. In October Egypt announced a prohibition of imports of Israeli goods produced in the Occupied Territories. In the same month President Mubarak stated that the peace process had never before 'reached such an impasse'. In November Egypt, together with several other Arab countries, boycotted the fourth Middle East and North Africa economic conference in Doha, Qatar, in protest at Israel's failure to honour its commitments to the Palestinians under the terms of the Oslo accords. It was not clear to what extent Egypt's abstention was responsible for a subsequent deterioration in relations with Qatar. In November Qatar accused Egypt of involvement in an attempted *coup d'état* against the Qatari Government in 1996.

In April 1998, in their first meeting for 11 months, President Mubarak and Prime Minister Netanyahu of Israel held talks in Cairo. The focus of their discussions was reportedly a US initiative to restart the peace process, which proposed that Israel

should withdraw from a further 13.1% of West Bank territory. Prior to his meeting with President Mubarak, Netanyahu had rejected the US proposal, and the renewed strain in relations between Egypt and Israel became apparent. In Mubarak's view, Israel's acceptance of the proposal would facilitate the resumption of 'final status' negotiations between Israel and the Palestinians, as well as Israel's negotiations with Syria and Lebanon. In June, after talks were held with Arafat to discuss an Israeli proposal for a new Madrid peace conference, President Mubarak accused Netanyahu of 'destroying the peace process' by seeking to annul the first Madrid agreement. By July bilateral relations were reported to have deteriorated to their worst level since 1979. President Mubarak cautiously welcomed the Wye River Memorandum signed by Arafat and Netanyahu in Maryland, USA in October 1998 (see Documents on Palestine, p. 86). However, in January 1999 the Egyptian Government froze all contacts with Israel's Likud Government over its decision to suspend the implementation of the agreement.

President Mubarak attended the funeral of King Hussein of Jordan in February 1999. In March, following a trilateral meeting with Palestinian representatives, Egypt and Jordan made a joint declaration in support of the Palestinians' right to declare an independent state after the expiry of the Oslo accords on 4 May. However, in the light of an increasingly volatile security situation in the Occupied Territories, and of the Israeli general election scheduled for 17 May, Egypt and Jordan subsequently joined the USA, the EU and other countries in urging Arafat to postpone the planned declaration of Palestinian statehood. The election in Israel of Labour leader Ehud Barak and his One Israel alliance was generally welcomed in Egypt. Shortly afterwards President Mubarak held talks with Arafat in Cairo, hoping to devise a formula to restart the peace process, and at the end of May Mubarak met with Jordan's new King Abdullah. In July the Egyptian Minister of Foreign Affairs, Amr Moussa, emphasized none the less that there could be no normalization of Egyptian–Israeli relations prior to the resumption of comprehensive peace talks. In early July Prime Minister Barak held talks with Egyptian, Jordanian, Palestinian and US leaders to seek to advance the peace process. It was considered to be a clear sign of Egypt's crucial role in the negotiations—especially after the death of King Hussein—that President Mubarak should be chosen as the first Arab leader to meet the new Israeli premier. After their meeting Mubarak announced that he had 'great hopes' that Ehud Barak could revitalize the stalled peace process.

OTHER DIPLOMATIC DEVELOPMENTS

Relations with the USA remained strained, with Egypt convinced that the Clinton Administration had forfeited its role as impartial mediator in the Middle East peace process because of its close alliance with Israel. Visiting Cairo in April 1996, the US Secretary of Defense, William Perry, denied rumours that the USA had signed a secret defence agreement with Israel. He was reported to have shown President Mubarak firm evidence that Libya was building a huge chemical weapons factory at Tarhuna. However, the President doubted the US claims and, while offering to mediate with Col Qaddafi on this issue, warned against any further US military action against Libya. Perry did, however, announce that the USA would supply advanced military equipment to Egypt, including 21 F-16 fighter aircraft, in acknowledgement of its key role in the peace process. In September US missile attacks against military targets in southern Iraq provoked criticism from the Egyptian authorities. Egypt indicated that it strongly opposed moves to partition Iraq and condemned Turkish attempts to establish a security zone inside the northern region. In December the US veto of a second term of office as UN Secretary-General for Boutros Boutros-Ghali provoked widespread outrage in the Egyptian media.

In August 1998 Egypt was highly critical of US military airstrikes against alleged terrorist strongholds in Afghanistan, and a pharmaceuticals factory in Khartoum, Sudan, which the US Government claimed was being used by associates of the Saudi Arabian-born militant Islamist, Osama bin Laden (in exile in Afghanistan), to manufacture chemical weapons' components. Moreover, air-strikes against Iraq undertaken by US and British forces in December 1998 exacerbated existing tensions between Egypt and the USA, since Mubarak had consistently urged a diplomatic solution to the crisis. Tensions persisted as the US Secretary of Defense, William Cohen, visited Cairo and other regional capitals in March 1999 to seek support for a renewed air campaign against Iraq. During his visit to Egypt Cohen agreed to supply Egypt with US $3,200m. of weaponry, including a further 24 F-16 fighter jets, a *Patriot* missile battery and 200 M1-A1 battle tanks. President Mubarak visited Washington in late June—his first visit to the USA for two years—and the two countries made significant progress on proposals for the resumption of Middle East peace talks. Differences remained, none the less, over the issue of sanctions imposed by the USA against Iraq and Libya.

Egypt has sought to mediate in disputes between Iraq and the UN since 1991. In September 1997, in a joint declaration with Russia, Egypt urged the restoration of Iraq's status as a full member of the international community, while insisting that it should comply with pertinent UN resolutions. In February 1998, following consultations with other Arab leaders, President Mubarak presented the US Secretary of State, Madeleine Albright, with an 'integrated' Arab plan to resolve Iraq's latest conflict with the UN over weapons inspections. Mubarak subsequently warned the US Secretary of State that further military action against Iraq might provoke Islamist militancy against secular Arab governments and thus destroy the Arab-Israeli peace process. Despite strong criticism of US and British air-strikes carried out against Iraq in December 1998, President Mubarak maintained that Saddam Hussain was responsible for the crisis between the UN and Iraq. In January 1999 the Egyptian Minister of Foreign Affairs, Amr Moussa, accused the Iraqi leader of urging the Egyptian people to overthrow their Government. In the same month Arab League foreign affairs ministers, meeting in Cairo, made a formal request for Iraq to comply with all pertinent UN Security Council resolutions and apologize to Kuwait for the 1990 invasion.

Egypt's relations with Libya slowly improved after 1996. Egypt played an important role as mediator in Libya's discussions with the USA and the United Kingdom over the Lockerbie affair, the repercussions of which had dominated Egyptian-Libyan relations. In April 1999, following further mediation by Saudi Arabia and South Africa, the two Libyans suspected of organizing the Lockerbie bomb were extradited to the Netherlands to stand trial. In the same month, as a result of this development, UN sanctions imposed against Libya in 1992 were suspended indefinitely.

In January 1997 Egypt refused to provide the Sudanese Government with military support in its struggle against rebel advances in southern Sudan. In June Sudan accused Egypt of providing the opposition with military training, and in October the Sudanese press reported that Egypt was obstructing imports of medical supplies to Halaib. Despite such accusations, from mid-1997 attempts were made to improve bilateral relations. In August security talks between the two countries resumed after a year-long suspension, and in October the Sudanese First Vice-President, Maj.-Gen. Zubair Muhammad Salih, visited Egypt to discuss the normalization of relations. Egypt continued to oppose the potential partition of Sudan that it feared might result from an eventual conclusion of the conflict in southern Sudan, and in November John Garang, the leader of the Sudan People's Liberation Movement, the principal rebel faction opposing the Sudanese Government, visited Cairo for talks with President Mubarak. In January 1998 elements of the Sudanese opposition expressed their concern at the ongoing improvement in Egyptian-Sudanese relations, claiming that the Sudanese regime continued to lend support to the armed Islamist movement in Egypt. In February, as part of the process of normalization, river transport resumed on the Aswan–Wadi Halfa route. In April the two countries agreed on the establishment of a joint ministerial committee, comprising their respective ministers responsible for higher education, defence and irrigation. An increase in diplomatic activity was evident in 1999. Although Sudan considered the presence of Sudanese opposition leaders in Egypt an obstacle to the normalization process, a meeting in Cairo, in May, between Sudan's former President Nimeri and a Sudanese government delegation to discuss arrangements for his return from exile represented significant progress on this issue.

There were signs from late 1997 of a possible improvement in Egypt's relations with Iran. In December the Egyptian Minister of Foreign Affairs attended the eighth Conference of the OIC, held in Tehran, where he met with Iranian President Sayed Muhammad Khatami. It was reported that Egypt had stipulated no conditions for the restoration of diplomatic relations with Iran, which had been severed in 1979. Although this process of normalization appeared to suffer a set-back in early 1998, when Egypt described Iranian criticism of the Algerian regime as 'blatant interference in the affairs of a fraternal Arab country', by early 1999 there were signs of an improvement in bilateral relations, with both sides declaring their readiness to restore full diplomatic ties.

Egypt remained distrustful of military co-operation between Israel and Turkey, in spite of an assurance, made by President Süleyman Demirel of Turkey during a visit to Egypt in September 1997, that such co-operation posed no threat to Egypt. In October 1998 cross-border military exchanges between Turkey and Syria over alleged Syrian support for Kurdish separatists operating in Turkey and Syria's suspicions regarding Turkish-Israeli co-operation were narrowly averted, largely owing to mediation efforts by President Mubarak and the Iranian Minister of Foreign Affairs, Kamal Kharrazi.

MUBARAK'S FOURTH TERM

In early June 1999 President Mubarak was formally nominated for a fourth six-year term of office. His nomination was endorsed by all 443 attending deputies in the People's Assembly, and was to be put to the electorate in a nation-wide referendum. Of the four main opposition parties, only the Nasserist Party refused to endorse Mubarak's candidature. Mubarak presented himself as the man who had brought Egypt political stability and economic prosperity. In early September a triumphal procession by President Mubarak in Port Said was disrupted when a man armed with a knife lunged at the presidential car. The President sustained only a superficial wound in the attack, for which, according to the Government, no political motive was uncovered; the assailant was killed by presidential aides immediately after the attack. The incident led to the replacement of the Chief of State Security and disciplinary action being taken against local police-officers.

In the national referendum, held on 26 September 1999, President Mubarak's re-election was approved by some 93.8% of the valid votes cast. The turn-out among eligible voters was reported to be 79.2%. In August opposition parties and human rights groups had urged the President to carry out radical constitutional and political reforms, notably the abolition of emergency laws and restrictions on the formation of political parties and trade unions, increased press freedom and the guarantee of free and fair elections. There was, however, to be little substantive change to reinforce hopes of political liberalization in the coming year. Modernizers found more to welcome in the economic sphere. On 5 October Mubarak appointed Dr Atif Muhammad Obeid, previously the Minister of the Public Enterprise Sector and responsible for the Government's programme of privatization, as the new Prime Minister. The appointment of Obeid was widely interpreted as an indication that economic reforms would be accelerated, since the new premier was viewed in business circles as being far more pro-liberalization and pro-privatization than his predecessor. This view appeared to be confirmed by the appointment of other younger technocrats to senior posts. (By mid-2000, however, several business leaders expressed their doubts that the Obeid Government was truly committed to economic reform; this was partly due to the fact that many important privatization projects had been postponed.) When, on 10 October 1999, Obeid announced his new Council of Ministers, which included 13 new ministers, Mubarak's trusted 'old guard' retained control over the strategic defence, interior and foreign affairs portfolios.

In political terms, the first year of Mubarak's fourth term was characterized by far more continuity than change. The overturning in December 1999, on procedural grounds, of the August convictions of editor Magdi Hussein and two other journalists of *Ash-Shaab* was almost a repeat of events that took place in 1998 (see above). The three journalists were released from prison pending a retrial. Meanwhile, a court order compelling the Government to allow fresh elections to the

Governing Council of the Lawyers' Syndicate, which had been under direct government supervision since 1996 as part of efforts to eradicate Islamist domination of the Syndicate, provoked a wave of arrests and the alleged harassment of potential candidates during October 1999. In mid-October 20 members of the Muslim Brotherhood were arrested on charges of plotting to overthrow the Government and of infiltrating professional syndicates (including the Doctors' and Engineers' Syndicates), in order to undermine national security. At the end of November the defendants' charges were modified from merely 'belonging' to the Brotherhood to 'participating in the founding and management' of the organization; the new charges were likely to result in harsher sentences for the accused. The trial—the biggest against the Muslim Brotherhood since 1995—opened in December but was postponed for procedural reasons and resumed in mid-January 2000 at a military base outside Cairo. Also in October 1999 the EOHR drew attention to the campaign of arrests against moderate Islamists, claiming that 200 members of the Brotherhood had been arrested between January and October, of whom 100 remained in detention.

At the end of October 1999 a British-based newspaper, *Ash-Sharq al-Awsat*, claimed that a new military leadership of Jama'ah al-Islamiyah had been established under Ala Abd ar-Raziq, following the killing of Farid al-Kedwani and three other Islamists in September (see above). In early December a further 1,200 Jama'ah al-Islamiyah prisoners began to be released by the authorities. During that month there were reports of a renewed power struggle within the Jama'ah leadership. It was reported that the new Chairman of its Shura Council was Moustafa Hamzah, the prime suspect in the 1995 assassination attempt on President Mubarak. In late January 2000 there were also rumours that a 'coup' had occurred within Islamic Jihad whereby one of the leaders of the organization, Dr Ayman az-Zawahri, had been removed (allegedly owing to his links with Osama bin Laden). In early February it was reported that the Jihad leadership had called on its members both in Egypt and abroad to cease their military activities, and instead to concentrate all their efforts on liberating the al-Aqsa Mosque in Jerusalem. This was the first time that Islamic Jihad leaders had called for a cease-fire, and it was reportedly backed by the group's imprisoned leaders. This appeared to be confirmed when, in mid-July, 11 leaders of Jihad's military wing, who were imprisoned in Egypt, officially declared an end to their armed operations against the Government. Meanwhile, in mid-June the cease-fire that had been declared by Jama'ah al-Islamiyah was called into question when the group's spiritual leader, Sheikh Omar Abd ar-Rahman, announced from detention in the USA that he was withdrawing his support for it, claiming that the cease-fire had achieved nothing. Although some of the group's founders stressed subsequently that Jama'ah remained committed to pursuing solely peaceful means, some observers feared a return to violence.

At the end of February 2000 police arrested eight prominent Islamists on charges of seeking to revive the Muslim Brotherhood. Among them was Muhammad Ibrahim Badawi, who had been released in August 1999 after serving a three-year prison sentence for the same offence. The continued hostility of the Government to virtually all independent and peaceful manifestation of Islamist sentiment was further illustrated by its unwillingness to recognize apparent initiatives by radical Islamists to renounce their armed struggle and enter the political mainstream. (Applications for official recognition by Jama'ah al-Islamiyah's Al-Islah party and the Shari'a Party in October 1999 had been refused.) Nevertheless, in mid-March 2000 it was reported that between 500 and 840 Islamist prisoners, mostly members of Jama'ah al-Islamiyah and Islamic Jihad, had been released. A further 500 Islamist prisoners were freed in late July, after they renounced their aim of overthrowing the Government.

The new Obeid Government also appeared to be continuing the campaign against human rights groups. In mid-February 2000 it was announced that the EOHR's Secretary-General, Hafiz Abu Sa'ada, was to stand trial before the Higher State Security Court for having accepted US $25,000 from the British embassy in Cairo without obtaining official permission from the Ministry of Social Affairs—the same alleged offence for which he had been detained for six days in 1998. Sa'ada, who was

abroad at the time of the announcement, returned to Egypt in May 2000, but no judicial process was immediately initiated.

Some observers saw a connection between this development and the EOHR's investigations into the worst incidence of sectarian violence in Egypt for decades. In early January 2000 three days of violent clashes took place between Muslims and Coptic Christians in the predominantly Christian village of el-Kosheh in Upper Egypt. An estimated 21 people, 19 Copts and two Muslims, died as a result of the violence, and more than 30 others were injured. There were also reports that the violence had spread to other villages in the vicinity. The EOHR's report, released in mid-February, identified the primary cause of the violence as 'economic inequalities' between the relatively prosperous Coptic majority and the poorer Muslim minority. The EOHR claimed that during 1991–98 about 99 Copts were killed by militant Islamist organizations. The report criticized the security forces and drew attention to allegations that they had used oppressive measures against the Coptic community during investigations in mid-1998 into the murder of two Copts in el-Kosheh, which the EOHR felt had contributed to communal tensions. (The security forces were subsequently exonerated in official inquiries into the 1998 allegations.) In early June 2000 the trial began of 96 men in connection with January's violence. In February 2001 the Coptic Church announced that it would appeal against the criminal court verdict: four Muslim men were sentenced to between one and 10 years' imprisonment, while the remaining 92 defendants were acquitted.

In early February 2000 President Mubarak appointed his son, Gamal, to the general secretariat of the ruling NDP, as part of a wider reorganization of the party. Gamal Mubarak, however, later denied rumours that he was preparing to stand for the People's Assembly in the forthcoming general election. On 26 February a presidential decree was issued extending until 2003 the state of emergency in place since President Sadat's assassination in 1981. It was reported in early March 2000 that the establishment of a new political party, Hizb al-Wifaq al-Qawmi or the National Accord Party, had been approved by the Government.

In late May 2000 the state-controlled Political Parties Committee suspended the Islamist-orientated SLP and its newspaper *Ash-Shaab*, on the grounds that the party had exceeded its political mandate. This followed a campaign by *Ash-Shaab* against *Banquet of Seaweed*, a book (first published in 1983) by the Syrian author Haidar Haidar, which the newspaper claimed was blasphemous. The SLP was held responsible for clashes in early May outside the Al-Azhar Islamic University between police and hundreds of students protesting at the decision, taken in November 1999 by the Ministry of Culture, to approve the reprinting of the book, which had been banned in most other Islamic countries. As a result of the riots, in which up to 50 students as well as six policemen were wounded when police used rubber bullets and tear gas, the Government removed the book from sale. Charges issued against several students for crimes such as rioting and vandalism were later abandoned. In mid-July 2000 charges were initiated against leaders of the SLP, including the editor of *Ash-Shaab*, Magdi Hussein; these included having links with the Muslim Brotherhood and disturbing public order. However, in late July a court ruling stated that the action of banning the party and closing down its newspaper were unconstitutional. The SLP's activities remained officially frozen, but in early September 2000 a Judicial Administrative Court ruled against the suspension of *Ash-Shaab* and referred the issue of the disbandment of the SLP to the High Administrative Court.

Continuing public opposition to any liberalization in the spheres of culture and family relations was demonstrated by the 'watering down' in the People's Assembly in late January 2000 of government proposals to improve the status of women. The draft Personal Status Law had proposed that women be given the right to divorce their husband 'immediately and unilaterally', in return for giving up all financial claims upon him. It also proposed permitting women to travel abroad without their husband's consent. Many parliamentarians, however, declared the bill to be un-Islamic, and important amendments were added. Although the bill passed into law, its final provisions included a requisite three-month period of arbitration before women could divorce their husband, while any provision for independent travel rights was abandoned.

There were, by contrast, minor successes for human rights groups and other NGOs in 2000. In May the Arab Organization for Human Rights, a regional group unofficially based in Cairo since 1989, was legalized. Moreover, in early June the Supreme Constitutional Court annulled the controversial Law on Associations and Civil Institutions, enacted in May 1999, declaring it to be 'unconstitutional'; the decision followed a judicial challenge by a local NGO. Nevertheless, at the end of June 2000 the Government ordered the closure of the Ibn Khaldoun Center for Social and Development Studies in Cairo and arrested five of its members, including the academic and democracy activist, Prof. Sa'adeddin Ibrahim. It was alleged that Ibrahim had accepted more than US $220,000 from the European Commission to produce a documentary on the electoral process in Egypt ahead of the parliamentary elections scheduled for late 2000. (One of those arrested was released in late July.) Western governments condemned the action, and expressed renewed concerns over the Egyptian authorities' apparent crack-down on human rights activists in the approach to the elections. In early August Prof. Ibrahim was also charged by the Egyptian Government of involvement in espionage activities on behalf of the USA. Ibrahim and his colleagues were released on bail in the same month. In late June 2000, after a trial which began in early 1997, the State Security Court in Cairo sentenced three parliamentary deputies from the ruling NDP (including a former tourism minister) each to a 10-year prison sentence, with hard labour, for their role in what had become Egypt's largest corruption scandal in two decades—involving the embezzlement of a reported £E1,600m. from five Egyptian banks during the early 1990s. A fourth NDP deputy received a one-year custodial sentence. The trial also implicated 28 businessmen and bank officials who were sentenced to terms of imprisonment ranging from one to 15 years, many with hard labour.

In early July 2000 the scheduled elections to the Governing Council of the Lawyers' Syndicate were abruptly cancelled by the government-controlled committee overseeing them. This occurred after it became clear that official efforts to frustrate campaigning by candidates aligned with the Muslim Brotherhood had failed. More than 100 suspected Brotherhood activists had been arrested and detained over the previous month (see above). The official pretext offered for the cancellation was that the issue of whether voting should take place within the offices of the Syndicate or (as the Government wanted) outside was still unresolved. Although a Judicial Administrative Court ruled in September that the offices of the Syndicate were the appropriate location for voting to take place it was apparent by this time that the elections could not realistically take place before the impending general election. The long-delayed elections finally took place in February 2001, when supporters of the Muslim Brotherhood won 22 of the 24 contested seats. A Nasserist candidate was elected Chairman of the Association. On 8 July 2000 the Supreme Constitutional Court ruled that the incumbent People's Assembly, elected in 1995, was invalid since the constitutional requirement that the judiciary have sole responsibility for the supervision of elections had been ignored. In response, President Mubarak held an extraordinary session of the Assembly on 16 July 2000, at which deputies unanimously approved two amendments to the existing electoral law in order to allow judges to oversee the forthcoming general election. The amendments were welcomed by opposition leaders. The Government announced in early September that the elections were to be held in three stages during October and November, with the first round of voting scheduled for 18 October, the second round for 29 October and the final round for 8 November.

THE GENERAL ELECTION OF 2000

The amendments to the electoral law providing for sole judicial supervision raised hopes that the 2000 elections would be the most transparent and credible for more than a decade. However, the announcement in September that the Minister of the Interior had been given the authority to name the judges who would chair local election committees, and that the Prosecutor-General—a government official—would chair the National Election Committee, prompted protests from the judiciary, which claimed that this decision violated the Supreme Constitutional Court

ruling. The Government furthermore announced that the presence of judges would be restricted to the counting stations. Ongoing arrests of Muslim Brotherhood activists also demonstrated the limits that remained upon free electoral campaigning.

Almost one-half of the ruling NDP's candidates were contesting seats in the legislature for the first time, while 100 of its candidates for the 444 elective seats in the People's Assembly were reported to be under 40 years of age. Nevertheless, despite these efforts to create the impression that a new generation was entering politics that would renew the NDP, the 'old guard' remained solidly in control of the party. It was noted that there were only two Copts among the NDP candidates, and that (contrary to wide expectation) Gamal Mubarak, the President's son, was not seeking election. Many nominally independent candidates were believed to be NDP sympathizers, while the Muslim Brotherhood fielded almost 100 candidates as 'independents', apparently in an effort to avert official harassment. Those parties established in 1999 by Islamists who had renounced violence were unable to present candidates, having had their applications for legal recognition denied. The New Wafd contested the elections under the leadership of Nu'man Jum'ah, following the death on 1 September 2000 of Muhammad Fouad Serag ed-Din.

While the new system of judicial supervision was considered to have had a positive impact in terms of improving the fairness of the elections, it did not prevent numerous incidents of harassment, aimed particularly at candidates believed to be sympathetic to the Muslim Brotherhood. At least 14 people reportedly died in election-related violence, and hundreds of others were injured. The NDP once again secured a resounding victory, with (according to official results) candidates of the ruling party taking 353 seats. Nominally independent candidates secured 72 seats, but it was reported that 35 of these had either joined or rejoined the NDP shortly after the elections; 17 other 'independents' were reported to be Muslim Brotherhood supporters. The New Wafd party won seven seats, the NPUP six, the Nasserist Party three, and the LSP one seat. (Voting for the two seats in one constituency in Alexandria was postponed following the arrest of some 20 Muslim Brotherhood activists.) The rate of participation by voters at the three stages was officially stated to be between 15% and 40%.

RECENT DOMESTIC DEVELOPMENTS

In mid-November 2000 the trial of 20 members of the Muslim Brotherhood arrested in October 1999 on charges of plotting to overthrow the Government and of infiltrating professional syndicates (including the Doctors' and Engineers' Syndicates), in order to undermine national security, ended with 15 being sentenced to between three and five years' imprisonment; the remaining defendants were acquitted. This constituted a clear signal from the Government that it would not acquiesce in the apparent growth of Islamist political support and representation. At the end of January 2001, however, writer Salah ed-Din Mohsin was sentenced by the State Security Court to three years' imprisonment for 'offending religion'; he had, in a book published privately in early 2000, described the Koran as promoting 'ignorance'. His original trial had resulted in July of that year in a six-month suspended sentence, but the authorities had ordered a retrial on the grounds that the sentence was too lenient.

Much attention in the immediate aftermath of the 2000 general election focused on what the strategy and tactics of the Muslim Brotherhood would be now that it had succeeded once again in achieving significant representation in the People's Assembly. Many commentators judged that, in concentrating excessively on cultural and religious issues at the expense of wider political and economic concerns, it had failed to make the most of previous periods of parliamentary influence. Its first intervention suggested that this might again be its approach. In January 2001 the Muslim Brotherhood members of the People's Assembly complained about the publication by the Ministry of Culture of three allegedly 'blasphemous' novels, to which the minister, Farouk Abd al-Aziz Hosni, responded by quickly withdrawing all three novels from sale and dismissing a senior official. The vulnerability to such pressure of the Minister of Culture had apparently been increased by the conviction in mid-January of his senior adviser, Muhammad Foda, to five years' imprisonment for accepting bribes. The incident indicated that the Government, while still opposed to independent Islamist political activity, might be obliged to show greater sensitivity to Islamist views in the cultural and religious spheres. However, an attempt by a fundamentalist lawyer to have a feminist writer, Nawal es-Sadawi, forcibly divorced from her husband on the grounds of apostasy, after she had allegedly criticized aspects of orthodox Muslim beliefs in a newspaper article, was dismissed by Egypt's Prosecutor-General in April, and by a family affairs tribunal in July.

Partial elections were held to the Advisory Council, the upper house of the legislature, on 16 and 22 May 2001. In the weeks leading up to the election, there were a number of arrests involving alleged members of the Muslim Brotherhood. In the elections to the Council the NDP won 74 of the 88 contested seats, while independent candidates won the remaining 14 seats. The opposition parties failed to win any seats. In mid-May 2001 Ahmad Maher was named as Egypt's new Minister of Foreign Affairs, to succeed Amr Moussa, who had been appointed Secretary-General of the Arab League (see below).

In late May 2001 Prof. Ibrahim was sentenced to seven years' imprisonment, with hard labour, having been convicted on charges of defaming Egypt, embezzlement, forgery and receiving unauthorized funds. A further 27 employees of the Ibn Khaldoun Center were given sentences of between one and seven years' imprisonment. In February 2002 the Court of Cassation overturned the convictions of Ibrahim and six others on appeal and ordered a retrial, which commenced in April. In July, following the conclusion of the retrial, Ibrahim was again sentenced to seven years' imprisonment. In July 2001 the long-running controversy surrounding the acquittal of the majority of the defendants in connection with the sectarian clashes in el-Kosheh in January 2000 (see above), came to prominence again when the Court of Cassation revoked the original verdict on procedural grounds and ordered a retrial.

Following the suicide attacks on New York and Washington, DC, in September 2001, for which the USA held the militant Islamist al-Qa'ida (Base) organization of Osama bin Laden principally responsible, President Mubarak asserted that the attacks justified Egypt's own long-running 'war' against fundamentalist Islamism, and stated that the country offered a model of the kind of 'responsible democracy' necessitated by the radical Islamist threat. Western pressure with regard to human rights issues in Egypt, particularly in relation to cases involving alleged Islamists, undoubtedly relaxed as the USA moved to forge a global 'coalition against terror'. In November 22 members of the Muslim Brotherhood were arrested on charges of incitement to violence and belonging to an illegal organization. In the same month, the trial, by military court, commenced of 94 Islamists accused of conspiring to assassinate President Mubarak and seize power. Guilty verdicts were passed against 51 of the defendants in September 2002: three were sentenced to 15 years' imprisonment, having been convicted of financing an illegal group to assassinate public figures; three were gaoled for seven years, with hard labour; and the remainder were sentenced to between two and five years' custody. Also in November 2001 23 men were convicted to between one and five years' imprisonment on charges of 'habitual debauchery'—a euphemism for homosexuality. In December Syria agreed to extradite Rifa'i Ahmad Taha of Jama'ah al-Islamiya to Egypt. He had been sentenced to death *in absentia* for his part in the 1997 killing of 58 tourists and four Egyptians in Luxor.

In contrast to the relatively muted domestic reaction to the commencement of US-led military action against al-Qa'ida and the Taliban regime in Afghanistan in October 2001, Israel's military offensive against the West Bank in late March 2002 provoked an angry response within Egypt. During mass street demonstrations the Muslim Brotherhood condemned the Government for failing to sever all diplomatic ties with Israel. The authorities' initial response to domestic pressure on this issue was low-key, and arrests of demonstrators were minimal.

In November 2001 President Mubarak implemented a major reorganization of the Council of Ministers, abolishing the Ministry of the Economy and devolving most of its power to conduct monetary policy to the Central Bank of Egypt. The incumbent Minister, Youssuf Boutros Ghali, retained the post of Minister of Foreign Trade.

In February 2002 373 people died in Egypt's worst railway disaster following a fire on a train travelling between Cairo and Luxor. Amid public indignation regarding persistently poor safety standards on the railways, the Minister of Transport, Dr Ibrahim ad-Dumeiri, resigned. (The preliminary report of an official inquiry recommended urgent action to improve safety standards and recommended that US $283m. be spent over the next two years to that end.) In a further reshuffle of the Council of Ministers in March Hamdy ash-Shayeb was named Minister of Transport, Gen. Ahmad Muhammad Shafiq Zaki was appointed to head the newly created Ministry of Civil Aviation (responsibility for which had been devolved from the Ministry of Transport), and Muhammad Awad Afifi Tag ed-Din replaced Dr Ismail Salam as Minister of Health and Population. Later in March the Grand Mufti, Nasr Wassel, announced his retirement. The Government appointed Ahmad at-Tayeb to succeed him.

In May 2002 President Mubarak, apparently in response to international pressure, overturned the convictions of 21 of the 23 men convicted of 'habitual debauchery' in late 2001, on the grounds that they had been tried by the wrong court; a retrial was subsequently ordered. The guilty verdicts against two men who had additionally been convicted of displaying 'contempt for religion' were, however, upheld.

In the context of international pressure for greater efforts to be made to control the flow of money suspected to be derived from terrorist networks, in May 2002 the Egyptian Parliament approved new anti-money laundering legislation. None the less, Egypt was included on the list of removed from list of 'non-cooperative countries and territories' issued by the Financial Action Task Force on Money Laundering in June 2002.

MUBARAK'S FOURTH TERM: REGIONAL AND INTERNATIONAL DEVELOPMENTS

The Middle East peace process continued to be a central preoccupation of Egypt's foreign policy under President Mubarak's fourth term. Mubarak placed strong emphasis on ensuring that any final settlement would be truly comprehensive. He was particularly concerned to avoid the Israeli-Syrian track becoming separated from the Israeli-Palestinian track. The poor state of Palestinian–Syrian relations meant that this could never be fully ruled out as a possibility. Egypt reiterated its stance that until a comprehensive peace settlement had been achieved in the region, the full normalization of relations with Israel was impossible. As the Israeli-Palestinian track reached crisis point in late 2000, Egypt sought to balance its solidarity with the Palestinian cause with desperate efforts to revive the peace process.

Egypt hosted the signing of the revised Wye River Memorandum by Ehud Barak and Yasser Arafat, which took place at Sharm esh-Sheikh in early September 1999. The Sharm esh-Sheikh agreement (or Wye Two—see Documents on Palestine, p. 88), effectively removed the obstacles to an Israeli transfer of a further 5% of the West Bank to the PA. Egyptian mediation had been influential in the discussions between Israeli and Palestinian negotiators that led to an agreement, and Mubarak called for immediate moves towards negotiations on a final peace settlement.

Nevertheless, relations between the Egyptian and Israeli Governments remained strained in late 1999. In early November Egypt declined an invitation to take part in a two-day summit meeting in Oslo, Norway, with US President Clinton and the then Russian Prime Minister, Vladimir Putin, stating that the meeting should focus on the growing number of Jewish settlements in the Occupied Territories, and that the USA and Russia should deal directly with the Palestinian leadership on the issue. Although 'final status' negotiations between Israel and the Palestinians opened at Ramallah on the West Bank on 8 November, they were broken off once again in early December.

In January 2000 Mubarak made an unscheduled visit to Damascus, amid increased optimism that substantive negotiations on both tracks in the Middle East peace process were about to resume once again. However, the momentum did not last. The resumption of peace negotiations between the Israeli Prime Minister and the Syrian Minister of Foreign Affairs,

Farouk ash-Shara', had taken place at Shepherdstown, West Virginia, USA, on 15 December and continued on 3–10 January 2000. Nevertheless, further negotiations were postponed indefinitely, owing to a lack of agreement regarding a possible Israeli withdrawal from the Golan Heights. In April 2000 Mubarak again met Syria's President Assad, in an effort to revive the Israeli-Syrian track following the failure of a summit meeting between the Syrian leader and US President Clinton in Geneva in March. The death of President Assad of Syria on 10 June 2000 further stalled the Israeli-Syrian track of the peace process. Mubarak attended Assad's funeral on 13 June, where he pledged his support to the late President's son and designated successor, Bashar.

After Israel launched a series of air raids on infrastructural targets in Lebanon in early February 2000, destroying three major power stations, President Mubarak made his first ever visit to Beirut on 19 February, where he held talks with Lebanese President Emile Lahoud. The purpose of the visit was ostensibly to demonstrate Egypt's solidarity with Lebanon. The Minister of Foreign Affairs, Amr Moussa, had described the Israeli attacks as 'extremely serious', while Mubarak denounced them as 'criminal acts' which required an 'urgent global response'.

Over the next two months Egypt's involvement in the peace process increased. In early March 2000 President Mubarak hosted a tripartite summit meeting at Sharm esh-Sheikh between PA President Yasser Arafat and Israeli Prime Minister Ehud Barak, at which both sides gave a commitment to meet in the USA in April and announced a timetable for achieving a framework peace agreement by the end of May—this as a step towards the final settlement due to be agreed by September. However, as adherence to the timetable quickly slipped again, Mubarak emphasized that Egypt would recognize the unilateral declaration of Palestinian statehood in September that was being threatened by Arafat if no final settlement had been negotiated by then.

On 10 July 2000 Barak held talks with Mubarak in Cairo prior to entering into a summit meeting with Yasser Arafat at Camp David, hosted by Bill Clinton, at which efforts would be made to reach final agreement ahead of the agreed 13 September deadline. Egyptian foreign minister Amr Moussa urged Israel to make concessions for peace. At the Cairo meeting Barak raised the case of Israeli businessman Azam Azam, who had been sentenced by an Egyptian court in 1997 to 15 years' imprisonment on espionage charges (see above). However, Mubarak indicated that there could be no possibility of an early release. Following the failure of the Camp David talks, which took place on 11–25 July, Mubarak continued to consult other Arab and Western leaders in the hope that the momentum of peace talks could be maintained. However, the Egyptian President emphasized that he would not pressure Arafat into making concessions over the status of Jerusalem, which had proved to be the principal stumbling-block in the talks. He appealed for a united Arab stance in support of the Palestinians until they regained all their legitimate rights in accordance with the pertinent UN resolutions. As the 13 September deadline for a final settlement passed without a declaration of independent statehood, Mubarak proposed a resolution of the dispute over Jerusalem that would make it an 'open city', with Israeli sovereignty over the West and Palestinian sovereignty over the East of the city.

From late September 2000 President Mubarak played a leading role in the intense international diplomacy aimed at preventing what was the most serious violence for many years between Israeli forces and Palestinians in the West Bank and Gaza Strip from escalating into a major regional conflict. A US-brokered summit meeting between Barak and Arafat was convened at Sharm esh-Sheikh on 16 October. A statement was issued at the end of the summit in which both sides were said to have agreed measures to end the violence. However, this fragile agreement was rapidly overtaken by further escalations in violence in what had become known as the al-Aqsa *intifada*. On 21–22 October an emergency meeting of Heads of State of Arab League countries was convened in Cairo. Mubarak's main objective was to promote a unified Arab position in support of the Palestinians. However, he was keen to avoid any decision to sever diplomatic relations with Israel. Measures adopted at the summit—including a call for an international tribunal to investigate Israeli 'war crimes'—were regarded by the Palestinians as 'tokenism', although the establishment of an Arab solidarity fund to support the families of Palestinian victims of the conflict was welcomed. The summit's final communiqué held Israel solely to blame for the violence, and 'for any steps taken in regard to relations with Israel by Arab countries, including their cancellation'.

As the violence escalated, President Mubarak found it increasingly difficult to justify to the Egyptian public his unwillingness to implement diplomatic sanctions against Israel. Finally, on 21 November 2000, following Israeli air attacks on offices of the PA in the Gaza Strip, Egypt withdrew its ambassador to Israel. Egypt also gave its support to Palestinian efforts to secure a UN resolution that would send a UN protection force to the region. In the approach to the premiership election scheduled to take place in Israel in February 2001, Mubarak and the outgoing US President, Bill Clinton, engaged in intensive (but ultimately unsuccessful) diplomatic efforts to sustain the peace process and secure an accommodation ahead of the expected electoral victory of the right-wing Likud leader, Ariel Sharon. At an Arab League summit on the Palestinian situation, held in Jordan on 26–28 March 2001, President Mubarak was again successful in dampening demands from more radical Arab states that Egypt and Jordan should break off diplomatic relations with Israel entirely. The summit appointed Egypt's Minister of Foreign Affairs, Amr Moussa, as the new Secretary-General of the Arab League.

In April 2001 Egypt and Jordan tabled a joint peace plan that called for an immediate halt to Israeli construction of settlements and a withdrawal of Israeli forces to pre-*intifada* positions, as a basis for both sides taking steps to end the violence and with a view to the resumption of 'final status' talks. This initiative was an attempted revival of the 'understandings' first reached by Israel and the Palestinians at the Sharm esh-Sheikh meeting in October 2000. Israel argued that it would be willing only to restrict settlement building to one of 'natural growth', and claimed that the plan did not place enough weight upon the responsibility of the Palestinian security forces to end what it called 'terrorist attacks' on Israel. However, the plan was supported by the new US Republican Administration of President George W. Bush, the EU and the Arab world. President Mubarak urged the Bush Administration to adopt a more active engagement in the Middle East peace process. Egypt had criticized the USA's use of its veto in the UN Security Council in late March to defeat the long-awaited resolution to send an international protection force to the region. Following a meeting in Cairo between Mubarak and the Israeli Deputy Prime Minister and Minister of Foreign Affairs, Shimon Peres, on 29 April, Mubarak claimed that he had secured the agreement of both Israel and the Palestinians to the Egyptian-Jordanian proposal plan. However, it was subsequently announced that this claim was premature. Egypt welcomed the conclusions and recommendations published in May by the Mitchell Commission, which had been established following the October 2000 Sharm esh-Sheikh summit to investigate the causes of the violence between Israel and the Palestinians (see Documents on Palestine, p. 90).

However, escalating violence rather than diplomatic progress characterized the following months. Egypt condemned the use by Israel of F-16 fighter aircraft to bomb Palestinian targets in mid-May 2001, and President Mubarak warned that the violence was close to reaching a 'point of no return'. Arab foreign ministers met in Egypt on 19 May and agreed to suspend all political contacts with Israel until Israel's attacks on Palestinians halted. Once again, with Egyptian influence evident, they stopped short of breaking diplomatic ties entirely.

The Egypt-Jordan peace plan fell into abeyance during the second half of 2001 as all parties struggled with little success to promote a durable cease-fire. President Mubarak periodically urged dispatch of international monitors in the event of a future cease-fire and argued against calls for a further Arab League summit on the Palestinian situation. In December the Egyptian Minister of Foreign Affairs, Ahmad Maher, met with Ariel Sharon in an unsuccessful attempt to persuade him to abandon his demand that there be 'seven days of calm' before political negotiations could begin. In response to Israeli declarations that Yasser Arafat had become 'irrelevant', Maher warned Israel not to destroy Arafat's credibility as a negotiating partner. For his part, Mubarak expressed frustration at Yasser Arafat's failure to take decisive measures to prevent suicide bombings by Palestinian militants against Israeli civilians.

The Egyptian response to a new Middle East peace plan first proposed in February 2002 by Saudi Arabia's Crown Prince Abdullah was ambivalent, partly because it threatened to displace Egypt from its accustomed central mediating role. In March President Mubarak made apparent moves in support of the plan—which essentially proposed Arab recognition of Israel in return for a 'final status' agreement between Israel and the Palestinians based on a Palestinian state with East Jerusalem as its capital—by hosting a meeting in Cairo between Arafat and Sharon at which an unsuccessful attempt was made to agree a cease-fire. At a summit meeting of Arab League heads of state, held in Beirut on 26–28 March, Egypt supported the final version of the Saudi Arabian peace plan, devised to ensure that the Israeli-Syrian track and the Palestinian right of return remained part of any future agreement. (Ostensibly in solidarity with Yasser Arafat, neither President Mubarak nor King Abdullah of Jordan attended the summit, both being represented in Beirut by their respective prime ministers; however, their decision not to attend the summit was widely interpreted as a response to concerns that their countries' continued diplomatic links with Israel would be subject to unwelcome scrutiny.) However, Israel's categorical rejection of the Abdullah plan, and its *de facto* reoccupation of the West Bank, again placed all peace initiatives on hold. Egypt suspended all non-diplomatic contacts with Israel at the beginning of April.

President Mubarak met with the US Secretary of State, Colin Powell, in Cairo in early April 2002, demanding Israel's immediate and unconditional withdrawal from the West Bank. Mubarak responded cautiously to US and Israeli proposals for a Middle East peace conference, concerned that it would simply be another 'talking shop'. In early June he met with President Bush at Camp David and put forward a peace plan of his own, in which he proposed a sequence of events beginning with political and security reform within the PA and parliamentary and presidential elections in the Palestinian territories by late 2002. Thereafter, a Palestinian state would be declared in early 2003 based on land controlled by the PA under the Oslo accords, further to which Palestine would be admitted to the UN. Negotiations would then be held with Israel for a total withdrawal from lands occupied in 1967. The Mubarak plan was widely interpreted as a rival to both the US-Israeli proposal and Crown Prince Abdullah's initiative. In July 2002, following an Israeli air force attack on Gaza City, which resulted in the death of some 15 Palestinians, including a senior Hamas military figure and nine children, Mubarak denounced the actions of the Israeli military and accused Sharon of deliberately ordering the attacks in order to sabotage Palestinian peace efforts.

Egypt's relations with the USA remained close, but often uneasy, during Mubarak's fourth term in office. At the end of October 1999 an EgyptAir Boeing 767, travelling from New York to Cairo, mysteriously crashed into the Atlantic Ocean, off the east coast of the USA, killing all 217 passengers and the crew. Bilateral relations were complicated after US investigators claimed that the crash might have been the result of a suicide mission by the flight's Egyptian co-pilot. Egypt's state-owned media dismissed such allegations, claiming that the crash had occurred as a result of mechanical failure; nevertheless, mutual accusations by Egypt and the USA that the other country was seeking to absolve its nationals from blame continued into mid-2000. In early April of that year the US Secretary of Defense, William Cohen, visited Cairo for talks with President Mubarak. Following the meeting, it was announced that the USA would supply Egypt with a new air defence weapons system.

With the installation of a new US Administration, led by President George W. Bush, in January 2001, it appeared inevitable that US-Egyptian relations would have to be renegotiated. Egypt expressed frustration at the new Administration's apparent reluctance to become fully engaged in diplomatic efforts to revive the Middle East peace process. During a visit to the USA in early April President Mubarak met with Bush for the first time and urged the USA to support the Egyptian-Jordanian peace plan (see above). Meanwhile, Bush, who had indicated

that Iraq would be his administration's priority in terms of Middle East policy, expressed his unease at Egypt's lack of support for continuing international sanctions against Saddam Hussain; he also urged Egypt to return its ambassador to Israel. A further irritant to relations was the conviction in May 2001 of civil rights activist Sa'adeddin Ibrahim (see above), who held US citizenship.

Relations with the USA were further complicated by the suicide attacks against New York and Washington, DC, on 11 September 2001, which President Mubarak was swift to condemn. However, the Egyptian Government was unwilling to participate directly in the US-led military campaign against Osama bin Laden and the Taliban regime in Afghanistan which commenced in October, although it pronounced itself satisfied that US evidence establishing responsibility for the attacks was compelling. In October Egypt submitted a list of 150 Egyptian dissidents abroad that it wanted returned to the country either to stand trial or serve terms of imprisonment imposed *in absentia*. President Mubarak expressed concern that the phrase 'war on terror' was being used too indiscriminately by the USA to shape its foreign policy. He particularly opposed its use as a template for the Israeli-Palestinian conflict or for resolving tensions with Iraq. During a meeting with the US Vice-President, Dick Cheney, in Cairo in late March 2002, President Mubarak urged the US Administration not to embark on a military campaign to overthrow the Iraqi President, Saddam Hussain, asserting that the priority must be to ensure the return to Iraq of UN weapons inspectors. Egypt undertook to exert pressure on the Iraqi Government to readmit weapons inspectors. Following the renewed conviction of Sa'adeddin Ibrahim (see above) President Bush announced that the USA would withhold additional unilateral aid from Egypt in protest at the Egyptian courts' verdict.

Despite such tensions, however, the USA remained committed to maintaining Egypt as a close ally in the Arab world. In September 2001 Egypt took delivery of a consignment of four F-16 fighter jets. (The full consignment of 24 F-16 fighters was scheduled to be delivered by the end of 2002.) In October 2001 US and Egyptian forces conducted joint military exercises, and in December the USA agreed to sell Egypt advanced naval vessels and missile systems. In November, meanwhile, the US Department of State declared that it considered that the conditions were right for talks on an Egypt-USA free-trade agreement. In January 2002 Egypt and Israel joined together to urge the USA not to implement a proposal to withdraw almost all its troops from the force that serves as a buffer between the two countries in the Sinai Peninsula; the USA subsequently agreed to defer the proposal.

Relations between Egypt and Iraq improved markedly during Mubarak's fourth term, and Egypt became a principal advocate of an end to the international sanctions in force since 1990 and a critic of US-British air-strikes against Iraqi targets. In January 2001 the Iraqi Vice-President, Taha Yassin Ramadan, visited Cairo; he was the highest ranking Iraqi official to visit Egypt since 1990. The two countries signed a trade agreement during the visit. In February 2001 a delegation of Egyptian officials and businessmen flew to Iraq to discuss the activation of the trade agreement, which came into effect in August. By early 2002 Iraq had become an increasingly important market for Egyptian exporters. In June 2001, meanwhile, following a meeting in Baghdad of the Council of Arab Economic Unity, plans were advanced for a quadripartite free-trade zone encompassing Egypt, Iraq, Libya and Syria, in the context of a long-standing commitment to establish a regional common market under the auspices of the Council.

Egypt intensified its efforts to act as a mediator in the civil war in Sudan during Mubarak's fourth term. In late December 1999 Egypt and Sudan had agreed to a full normalization of diplomatic relations, and to co-operate to resolve the dispute over the border area of Halaib in an 'integrational brotherly context'. The announcement came at the end of an official two-day visit by Sudan's President al-Bashir to Cairo. Sudanese efforts to persuade the UN to lift the sanctions imposed against it in 1996 appeared by mid-2000 to have won the support of Egypt. On 14 May 2001 President Mubarak visited Khartoum, where he and President al-Bashir committed themselves to further improving relations between the two countries. In June, in co-operation with Libya, Egypt sought to relaunch a peace initiative that it had first put forward in 1999. However, its emphasis on Sudan's territorial unity was not acceptable to armed opposition groups in the south of the country, and once again its impact was limited. Although further attempts to mediate in the conflict were made during 2001–02, Egypt played no role in the brokering of a provisional peace accord between the warring Sudanese factions in Kenya in July 2002.

Improving ties with Libya were also demonstrated by the announcement in early July 2000 that EgyptAir was to resume regular flights to Tripoli, following the suspension of UN sanctions against Libya in April 1999. Libyan flights to Egypt resumed in the same month.

Economy

Revised for this edition by ELIZABETH TAYLOR

INTRODUCTION

Over the past few decades Egypt's economy has been fundamentally influenced by various political vicissitudes. In particular, relations with Israel have had major repercussions on the nature of expenditure and foreign aid, while the Government has moved away from state socialism and towards a market economy. Underneath these changes of direction, however, lie the important physical constraints of a large and rapidly growing population, and the dearth of land available for agriculture and water for irrigation.

The total area of Egypt is 1,002,000 sq km, but more than 90% of the country is desert. With no forested land, and hardly any permanent meadows or pastures, the arable land available is greatly overcrowded. Relating the population, numbering 38.2m. at the 1976 census, to the inhabited area (about 35,200 sq km), a density of 1,085 persons per sq km gave 5.7 persons per acre of arable land, representing one of the highest person/ land ratios in the world. Since then, the root of Egypt's poverty has remained the rapid rise in the population, of 2.8% per year between 1976 and 1986, which added about 1.3m. people per year. According to the results of the 1986 census, the population had risen to 48.2m., and only 4% of the land area was occupied. The average annual rise in population in the 1980s was 2.4% and World Bank figures estimated an average annual rate of increase in population of 2.0% during 1990–2000. The census of December 1996 recorded a permanently resident Egyptian population of 59,312,914. According to official mid-year estimates, this population was 67,886,000 in 2001. Family planning has been heavily promoted by the Government since the establishment of a National Population Council in 1985. An estimated 48% of families were practising contraception in 1992, when the average number of births per mother fell below four for the first time since records have been kept. The Government's long-term aim is to extend the practice of contraception to 70% of Egyptian families by 2010.

Lack of employment opportunities drove people from the country into already overcrowded cities, which grew at a rate of 3.4% per year in the late 1970s (the population of Greater Cairo increased from 7m. in 1976 to more than 10m. in 1985), and hastened the emigration of qualified personnel the country could ill afford to lose. In 1983 3.28m. Egyptians were working abroad. Many originally went to much better-paid jobs in the rich Gulf states and Libya, although a considerable number were forced to return from the former in the 1980s, owing to a downturn in the oil industry, and from the latter because of a government order of 1985 prohibiting the employment of Egyptian workers. Poor job prospects were not improved by the return of thousands of expatriate workers (including about 5,000 from Libya in 1985, and about 250,000 who left Iraq in the first half of 1986, when new restrictions were imposed on the amount of money they were allowed to send home). This trend also helped swell the bureaucracy, since the Government had been committed to giving a post to every Egyptian graduate who could not find other employment. By the time of the census in late 1996 the number of Egyptians resident abroad had fallen to an estimated 2.18m. In February 1998 the Egyptian Mobilization and Statistics Agency estimated that there were 3.0m. Egyptians living abroad, 720,000 of whom were permanent immigrants. In 1998 unemployment was an estimated 8.2% of the total labour force, and by 2001 this figure had increased

marginally, to 8.4%. Also in 1998 the Government was requested to review its policy on child labour, after a report compiled by the National Centre for Social Research claimed that children comprised 70% of the rural work-force. Although it is illegal to employ children under the age of 14, the report found that many employers were exploiting a rule allowing children to be trained from the age of 12 years. According to the 1996 census, 43% of the population was estimated to be urban, compared with the 44% comprising the urban population at the 1976 census and 41% in 1965. The number of Egyptians resident in new industrial cities rose from 200,214 (in nine cities) in 1986 to 618,665 (in 19 cities) in 1996. One of the objectives of a long-term development strategy proposed by the Government in 1997 was to reduce the undeveloped proportion of Egypt's land area (used neither for habitation, agriculture nor industry) to 75% by 2017, compared with more than 95% in 1997. Despite high rates of economic growth in the latter part of the 1990s, by the beginning of the 21st century Egypt's fundamental problem remained that the continued increase in population tended to offset the modest annual rates of economic growth, leading to a decline in real terms in average standards of living. Likewise, the continuing trend of migration from rural to urban areas continued unabated, severely testing already limited metropolitan amenities. Opposition leaders criticized President Mubarak for doing little to rectify disparities in wealth between the country's richest and poorest citizens. Moreover, Egypt continued to rely on foreign aid, especially from Arab states and the USA.

During the 1960s Egypt, under Nasser, followed an economic policy based on socialist planning. However, the wars with Israel in 1967 and 1973, and Nasser's death in 1970, heralded a major period of change in Egypt's economic relations, both with its Arab neighbours and with the superpowers. From 1973 great efforts were made to repair the war damage, and the replacement of Nasser's socialist planning by an 'open door policy' (*infitah*) encouraged foreign investment. The economic implications of Sadat's assassination in October 1981 were slight at first, but his successor, Hosni Mubarak, gradually encouraged the private sector. Basic tax on company profits was reduced from 40% to 32% in early 1982, while the enactment in 1990 of Law No. 230 was regarded as a sign of the Government's commitment to the growth of private enterprise and deregulation. This shift from an essentially centrally controlled economy to one that was much more open to private enterprise and foreign investment itself caused considerable strain on the economy. The 1970s saw a great increase in aid from the oil-rich Arab states. Much of this aid came from the Gulf Organization for the Development of Egypt (GODE), established by Saudi Arabia, Kuwait, the United Arab Emirates (UAE) and Qatar in 1977.

By signing the peace treaty with Israel in March 1979, however, Sadat undertook the risk of losing this Arab aid. The League of Arab States (the Arab League), meeting in Baghdad immediately after the signing of the peace treaty, agreed on a policy of economic and political isolation of Egypt. At first it seemed unlikely that the economic sanctions would be stringently observed by some of the Arab countries, but, following Saudi Arabia's break in diplomatic relations with Egypt, some of the more 'moderate' Arab states implemented the boycott. The Arab Fund for Economic and Social Development (AFESD) suspended all future aid and credit relations with Egypt, although honouring transactions already in progress, and Saudi Arabia, Qatar and the UAE withdrew from the Arab Organization for Industrialization (AOI), which was an Egypt-based Arab arms enterprise, causing its collapse. Egypt, however, responded by planning to establish its own arms industry with Western capital (see Manufacturing Industry, below). During 1980 Egypt and Israel signed agricultural, trade, aviation and health agreements, and their common border was opened to commercial and tourist traffic towards the end of the year. While the loss of Saudi military aid, estimated at an annual rate of just under US $2,000m., was undoubtedly significant, the fact that only about 7% of Egypt's total trade was with Arab countries implied that the Arab trade boycott would probably not be of major importance. The loss of Arab aid from the GODE was significant, however, although Egypt ceased to pay interest due on sums already loaned in 1979. By 1987 the resulting arrears in interest on GODE loans totalled almost $2,000m. Sadat hoped that Egypt's economic difficulties would be alleviated by the 'Carter Plan', by which Egypt would receive $12,250m. over a period of five years, mainly from the USA, western Europe and Japan. The USA promised that it would be no less generous to Egypt after the peace treaty with Israel than it was to Israel itself in terms of economic aid; as a result, Egypt became the second largest recipient of US aid, after Israel. The return of multinationals such as Coca-Cola and Cadbury Schweppes, associated with the normalization of relations with Israel, clearly demonstrated the increased readiness of foreign capital to invest in Egypt.

In February 1989 Egypt was a founder member of the Arab Co-operation Council (ACC), together with Jordan, Iraq and the Yemen Arab Republic (YAR), and in May, Egypt was formally readmitted to the Arab League and its various economic committees. However, hopes that the ACC would provide a framework for increased economic co-operation were dissipated, at least temporarily, by the impact of the Gulf crisis of 1990–91. Egypt's bid for membership of the Union of the Arab Maghreb (the Union du Maghreb arabe—UMA) appeared to be a more promising option, especially since in April 1999 Libya was invited to join the European Union (EU) Euro-Mediterranean initiative (see Foreign Trade and Payments, below). Participation in the EU-Mediterranean free-trade area planned for 2010 would offer Egypt good prospects for economic integration with both Europe and neighbouring countries. In mid-1998 Egypt was admitted to the Common Market for Eastern and Southern Africa (COMESA). In June 2001 Egypt signed an association agreement with the EU, which envisaged that trade barriers would be dismantled over a 12-year period (see Foreign Trade and Payments, below).

In 1990, according to estimates by the World Bank, Egypt's gross national product (GNP) per head was US $600, having increased at an average rate of 4.1% per year, in real terms, since 1965. The World Bank's estimates for 2000, at average 1998–2000 prices, gave GNP per head as $1,490, or $3,690 on a purchasing-power parity basis. The average annual growth of gross domestic product (GDP) was 7.3% in 1965–80, slowing to 5.4% in 1980–90 and 4.4% in 1990–2000. Egypt's GDP increased by 6.1% in the financial year ending 30 June 1999, by 6.5% in 1999/2000 and by 7.0% in 2000/01. According to the IMF, GDP growth of 2.0% was predicted for 2001/02.

POLICY AND PLANNING

Measures introduced by the socialist regime that assumed power in 1952 included agrarian reform, land reclamation, the Aswan High Dam scheme, wide-scale nationalization, and a programme of industrialization (which was accelerated in 1960). After 1967 the Government introduced restrictive measures aimed at curbing consumer demand, including a variety of taxes, forced savings and compulsory contributions out of wages and salaries. Following Nasser's death in 1970, however, President Sadat embarked on a gradual distancing from old-style socialist economic policies. Under what was termed 'denasserization', the sequestrations of the 1960s were ruled illegal, new laws were passed to allow private-sector participation in former state preserves such as exporting and importing and transport, and foreign investment was seen as the key to development.

Under President Mubarak, economic policy sought to increase exports and employment through meticulous planning for the public, private and co-operative sectors. Particular attention was to be paid to social problems. Investment resources were to be increased through new channels for private investment, increasing the contribution of the banking sector, improving the efficiency of the tax system, increasing indigenous financial resources, reducing government expenditure, and limiting the consumption of imported goods. A long-term national socio-economic development programme (broken down into medium-term five-year Plans) was devised. The strategy behind the 1982–87 Plan was to reduce the proportion of private consumption and of imports in total expenditure, so as to mobilize domestic resources for investment and to reduce the growing trade deficit, which had developed as a result of the policy of *infitah*. The Plan's objectives could be achieved, however, only if there was an improvement in Egypt's balance of payments. In this regard, the progressive decline in world oil demand (petroleum being Egypt's principal export commodity) undermined the viability of the Plan's targets. These doubts were confirmed by the collapse in the price of oil in 1986. The annual rate of growth of GDP during the Plan reached about 5%, well short of its target of 7.9%. It was reported that only 15% of projects outlined in the Plan had actually been carried out when it ended in June 1987, owing to inadequate funding.

The next Five-Year Plan (1987–92) was designed to encourage public-sector production, to increase the manufacturing of commodities and to raise the level of exports. It also devoted more resources to the development of the private sector. Another important feature of the new Plan was the improvement of agricultural output, so as to minimize food imports, which accounted for 60% of Egypt's requirements. To this end, it was intended to bring an extra 100,000 feddans of land into production during each year of the Plan. However, even before the onset of the 1990–91 Gulf crisis (precipitated by Iraq's invasion of Kuwait), the Plan's targets had been placed in serious doubt by the lack of funds available to finance development projects. According to one Egyptian newspaper, the shortage of foreign-currency reserves forced the Government to order the National Investment Bank to halt financing of the Plan in March 1988 and to cancel imports of a number of foodstuffs. The Gulf crisis reduced foreign-exchange earnings from tourism and remittances from Egyptian nationals working in Iraq and Kuwait. Losses in these two areas were officially estimated by the Government at US $1,500m. in the 1990–91 tourist season (see Tourism) and $2,400m. in the 1990 calendar year, respectively. After a decline in the mid-1980s a new boom in the oil-producing Gulf states had resulted in total remittances increasing to $4,235m. in 1989, a large proportion of which derived from the estimated 1.5m. Egyptians then working in Iraq and Kuwait. By late 1990 about 400,000 workers had returned to Egypt (the total rising to more than 600,000 following the outbreak of hostilities between Iraq and the US-led multinational force in January 1991); their return caused serious social problems for the Egyptian authorities and led to an increase in the existing level of unemployment of around 20%. On the other hand, an anticipated fall in Suez Canal revenues in 1990, because of the UN embargo on trade with Iraq, failed to materialize; instead, earnings increased by 14% over 1989 (see The Suez Canal). Moreover, increased world oil prices in the third quarter of 1990 almost doubled Egypt's revenues from oil exports to $210m. per month (compared with average monthly receipts of $138m. in 1989–90), thereby offsetting losses from suspended trade with Iraq and Kuwait. A further consequence of the crisis was an increase in the budget deficit, to 17% of GDP in 1990–91.

The Iraqi invasion of Kuwait did, however, result in a sharp increase in aid to Egypt, in addition to the waiver or rescheduling of certain Egyptian debts to other countries. Emergency aid was allocated through the Gulf Financial Crisis Co-ordinating Group (GFCCG), which by March 1991 had arranged funding amounting to US $11,741m. for Egypt, Turkey and Jordan. Saudi Arabia also announced that it had written off outstanding Egyptian debts of $4,000m. Moreover, in November 1990 the US Congress finally consented to waive some $7,000m. in Egyptian debts for arms purchases in the 1970s. With smaller amounts being written off by other Western and Gulf states, Egypt's debt was reduced from some $50,000m. before the Gulf crisis to around $36,000m. by early 1991. Despite the non-fulfilment of the 1987–92 Plan and the general move to a market economy, a further Five-Year Plan was drawn up for the period beginning 1 July 1992.

Draft planning proposals for the 1997–2002 period envisaged total investment of around £E400,000m. over five years, including £E58,000m. (60% from the private sector) during the fiscal year beginning July 1997. The target rate of economic growth for the 1997–2000 period was an average 6.8% per year. At the same time the Government outlined targets for the 20 years up to 2017. These envisaged a doubling of GDP between 1997 and 2007 and the same rate of increase between 2007 and 2017, eventually totalling £E1,100,000m. The target for GDP per head in 2017 was 'at least £E13,750'. It was hoped that economic growth would average 7.6% per year after 2002, while the rate of price inflation was to be kept below 5% from 1997 to 2017. The budget deficit was to be eliminated and, if possible, replaced by a surplus before the end of the 20-year period, while the target rate for the creation of new jobs was 550,000 per year throughout this period. In the event, the target rate of economic growth for 1997–2000 was overly ambitious. Annual growth was around 5%, largely reflecting the economic crisis in Asia, the decline in world prices for petroleum and reduced revenues from tourism following the 1997 terrorist attack at Luxor (see History). Nevertheless, the rate of growth was considerably higher than the 1990–99 average of 2.4%. Moreover, in 2000 the annual rate of price inflation, at only 2.7%, was reported to be at its lowest level for 30 years. This followed an average increase in consumer prices of some 3.5% in 1998 and of 5.3% in 1999 (all except in 1999 below the target of 5%). During 1990–2000 the annual rate of inflation averaged 8.4%. In an attempt to boost economic growth, the Government planned to raise Egypt's investment ratio from 18% of GDP (in 1997) to 23% in the near future by encouraging a higher level of savings. In 1997 gross domestic savings were only 13% of GDP. World Bank figures show that private consumption rose from 69% of GDP in 1980 to 76% in 1999.

The Five-Year Plan for 2002–07 envisages a total investment of £E445,000m., including £E73,000m. from the private sector. The target annual growth rate for 2002–03 is 4.6%, with an average rate of 6.2% for 2003–07. The Plan includes a £E7,000m. allocation for infrastructure projects, a reduction in the trade deficit by increasing export capacity, a reduction in the rate of unemployment, and an increase of service revenues by 7.5%. Revenues from the Suez Canal and from workers' remittances are targeted to increase by 2.2% and 7% respectively.

DEBT-SERVICING, THE IMF AND PRIVATIZATION

Following the collapse of world petroleum prices in 1986 and an increasingly heavy burden of debt-servicing, the Government was forced to negotiate a US $325m. stand-by credit with the IMF in 1987. This led to a major rescheduling of Egyptian debt, including $12,000m. in civilian and military debt over 10 years with the 'Paris Club' of Western creditors. However, the Government proved unable to adhere to the austerity measures demanded by the IMF reform programme, mainly out of concern for the domestic repercussions, and the programme collapsed in late 1988 after only half of the agreed support had been disbursed. Eventually, in 1990 the Government took some steps towards fulfilling the conditions stated by the IMF; in particular, subsidies applicable to a wide range of basic commodities were reduced, causing sharp price increases. Despite these steps, and provision for a budget deficit again within 10% of the country's GDP for 1990–91, the IMF remained dissatisfied and further discussions were overtaken by the onset of the Gulf crisis (see above).Negotiations with the IMF resumed after the end of the Gulf conflict, and were conducted in a more sympathetic climate in view of Egypt's active participation in the anti-Iraq coalition. Progress was also expedited by the following factors: the introduction in February 1991 of new market-related currency exchange arrangements, as a prelude to a single unified rate and full convertibility no later than February 1992; trade liberalization measures, under which most existing tariff and other barriers were to be phased out over three years; publication in April of a further list of 60 state-owned enterprises that the Government sought to privatize; price increases in April, ranging from 14% to 66% on petroleum products, gas and electricity; the introduction in May of new sales taxes of between 5% and 30% on most goods and services (although certain basic items were exempted); and the adoption of a budget for 1991/ 92 providing for a deficit of 9.3% of GDP, falling to 6.5% in 1992/ 93 and to 3.5% in 1993/94. The new exchange-rate arrangements resulted in an effective devaluation of some 38% by May 1991, while interest rates underwent a consequential significant rise (see Banking and Exchange Rates, below).

Against this background, a new stand-by facility was formally approved by the IMF in mid-May 1991, under which some US $372m. would be made available to Egypt over a period of 18 months to provide balance-of-payments assistance for its economic reform programme. This was rapidly followed by a decision of the 'Paris Club' of Western creditors to write off, over a three-year period, $10,000m. of the $20,000m. owed by Egypt to creditor nations and to reschedule repayment of the remaining $10,000m. on favourable terms. In early 1992 the World Bank concluded that the Egyptian economic reform programme was broadly on course. Remaining obstacles were the slow pace of privatization, investment authorization and deregulation. Accordingly, in March the General Authority for Investments introduced five new measures to facilitate investment. An initial 15% of Egypt's US $20,000m. 'Paris Club' debt was cancelled shortly after the formal announcement of the 1991 IMF stand-by arrangement, with cancellation of a further 15% scheduled to take effect at such time as the IMF formally approved the terms of a follow-up arrangement. (The remainder of the promised write-off, amounting to 20% of the original debt, was scheduled to take effect half-way through the duration of such a follow-up arrangement, provided that the IMF was broadly satisfied with government economic policy at that point.)

Notwithstanding Egypt's announcement that it did not intend to draw on the final tranche of the 1991 stand-by facility because of strong growth in the country's foreign-exchange reserves during 1992, formal expiry of the facility (originally set for the end of November 1992) was postponed by the IMF for two successive periods of three months. Meanwhile, the World Bank delayed from June 1992 to March 1993 the release of the second half of a US $300m. structural adjustment loan, eventually announcing the release of the funds shortly after the Government had announced the start of the active phase of its long-awaited privatization programme. The 20 firms whose shares were offered to local and foreign private investors in this initial privatization exercise included hotels, a cement company, beverage producers and vineyards.

Also in March 1993 the IMF's executive board formally declared that Egypt had fulfilled its commitments under the 1991 stand-by arrangement. This opened the way for negotiations on the terms of a follow-up arrangement. In July the Government announced that it would aim eventually to privatize public-sector assets with an estimated market value totalling £E40,000m., and it hoped to be able to complete around 25% of the privatization programme within three years. On trade liberalization (reportedly the most contentious issue in negotiations with the IMF), the Government's declared aim was to reduce Egypt's maximum import tariff from 80% (to which the maximum tariff had been cut from 100% earlier in 1993) to 50% over a four-year period. As an apparent gesture to IMF negotiators who had sought a much swifter cut in the top rate, the Government acted in mid-July to revoke certain import restrictions and to abolish preferential tariffs for public-sector industries. In September the IMF approved an extended fund facility of US $560m., to be drawn down in six-monthly tranches over a period of three years. Earlier in September the Egyptian Government had reached 'substantial agreement' with the World Bank on the monitoring of the process of structural economic reform over the same period. In view of the recent strengthening of the country's balance-of-payments position (attributed mainly to the attractive rates of return on local currency deposits), no new World Bank loan was associated with this agreement.

Having secured implementation of the second phase of the 'Paris Club' debt waiver in September 1993, the Egyptian Government was in mid-1994 seeking formal approval from the Bretton Woods institutions for the current economic position and outlook in order to activate the final phase of the promised debt write-off. The only perceived obstacle to the early achievement of this goal was a difference of opinion between the Government and the IMF on the currency exchange rate (which stood at US $1 = £E3.38 in May 1994). In the Fund's economic judgement, some devaluation was desirable, whereas the Government regarded exchange-rate stability as an important factor in maintaining investor confidence in the economy. Otherwise, the Government's monetary and fiscal policies were broadly on course to satisfy IMF targets, while the World Bank-monitored restructuring programme was gathering momentum, with up to £E3,200m. of public-sector assets scheduled for sale during the second half of 1994.

However, many of the businesses offered for sale in the initial privatization exercise had failed to attract adequate bids from single buyers, prompting the Government to modify its privatization strategy to include sales of share stakes in state enterprises through the local securities market. It was also decided that 10% of the shares in about 100 public-sector companies should be earmarked for sale to employee shareholders' associations over a period of years. The state shareholding in the Commercial International Bank (Egypt) was reduced from 70% to 43% in September 1993 by means of a (heavily over-subscribed) issue of new shares, and state-owned banks were recommended to reduce their shareholdings in joint-venture banks to 25% by the end of 1995.

The maximum import tariff was lowered to 70% in February 1994, as part of a wide-ranging reform package which included substantial tariff reductions for many raw materials, coupled with various fiscal incentives to exporters. By mid-1994 price subsidies had been eliminated or substantially reduced throughout the public sector, and schedules existed for the removal of the remaining subsidies.

By mid-1995 share offers were being brought to the market at the rate of about two per month, the Government's aim being to achieve a total of 50 such disposals during the course of the year. The Government strongly defended its gradualist approach to the privatization process, which had attracted public criticism from representatives of the World Bank and other interested organizations in October 1994. With the Government also maintaining its resistance to IMF pressure for a currency devaluation of around 30%, Egypt did not secure formal endorsement from the IMF and World Bank of its economic policy in the 1994/95 fiscal year, with the result that the final phase of the 'Paris Club' debt write-off remained in abeyance in July 1995. The World Bank estimated Egypt's total external indebtedness in 1994 at US $32,314m. and its 1994 debt-service payments at $2,22,223m. (a debt-service-to-export ratio of 14.6%).

In October 1995 the IMF withdrew its objections to the Government's exchange-rate policy following the release of trade statistics showing strong export growth in the first nine months of the 1994/95 fiscal year. Egypt's new Government under Kamal Ahmad Sidqi, appointed in January 1996, undertook to accelerate the process of structural economic reform by introducing measures to stimulate private investment in new projects (including major industrial developments) while setting revised targets for the sale of shares in state enterprises. Of the 314 companies within the public sector at the end of 1995, 224 were trading profitably in the 1994/95 fiscal year. However, the aggregate liabilities of public-sector companies at this time amounted to £E70,000m., settlement of which was a high priority in the Government's allocation plans for projected privatization receipts. As part of its drive to stimulate industrial investment, the Government cut import tariffs on capital goods (hitherto at 20%–40%) to 10% in January 1996. In the same month the Investment Authority approved 131 mainstream projects involving total investment of US $7,790m. and 13 free-trade zone projects involving total investment of $2,025m.

In October 1996 the IMF approved a US $391m. two-year stand-by arrangement (although in view of the strength of the Egypt's reserves position the Government had no plans to make any drawings on it). This arrangement prompted renewed discussion on activating the outstanding final stage of the 'Paris Club' debt write-off. Egypt, meanwhile, repaid $300m. to 'Paris Club' creditors in January 1997, in accordance with existing arrangements. An IMF review in that month concluded that most aspects of Egypt's current economic performance were satisfactory, while some were 'more than satisfactory'. A total

of $2,500m. ($1,500m. in grants and $1,000m. in long-term development loans) was pledged to Egypt for 1997/98 by major aid donors at a World Bank-sponsored meeting in May 1997. A new investment law adopted in May 1997 reaffirmed basic guarantees to investors and unified and rationalized the framework for investment incentives. Its provisions included 10-year tax exemptions for projects in designated 'new industrial areas' and 'remote areas' and 20-year tax exemptions for projects in the proposed New Valley development area (see The High Dam, below). In 1998 Egypt decided not to renew its arrangement with the IMF. At the end of 1998 Egypt's external debt totalled $32,268m., of which $27,622m. was long-term public debt. The cost of debt-servicing in that year was equivalent to 9.4% of export earnings. The external debt had declined to $30,802m. by the end of 1999, of which $26,026m. was long-term public debt. The debt-service ratio in that year represented 9.0% of export earnings. In 2000 the external debt was further reduced to $28,957, of which $24,279 was long-term public debt. The cost of debt-servicing in that year was equivalent to 8.4% of export earnings. Foreign debt totalled £E26,560m. in 2001.

In May 1998 the IMF expressed concern that inefficient bureaucracy and inadequate industry and export facilities could result in a minimal rate of increase in GDP over the next five years. Subsequently the IMF urged the Government to increase exports, to attract further foreign investment, and to complete its structural reform. In early 1998 the Government announced that it was to facilitate the establishment of new companies: new legislation would allow new ventures to be automatically approved within 10 days of the founders' submitting an application, subject to the approval of the regulatory body.

Despite the Government's gradualist approach, the stock exchange increased its trading volume from 200,000 investors in 1995 to 1.1m. in 1997. In late 1997 the Government announced that it was to invest its £E77,000m. state pension fund surplus on the stock market as part of a move to encourage domestic sources of investment capital. The Government also launched reforms to computerize the stock exchange in order to create a real-time trading system, so as to accelerate trading. A fully automated and integrated trading, clearing and settlement system (ATS) was launched in 2000.

By January 1999 119 public companies had, at least partly, come under private ownership, and an estimated £E10,000m. had been generated by the divestment programme. However, in mid-1999 the public sector still accounted for almost 70% of GDP and the pace of privatization had slowed appreciably. In October the new Government under Dr Atif Obeid stressed the importance of privatization as a means of generating economic growth, and it sought to reactivate the programme. Assuming that a simple market flotation would raise insufficient funds for the Government, the Public Enterprise Office considered a range of alternative options. Among these were: more stringent bid evaluations prior to flotation; sale by a process of electronic bidding or sealed bid offers; providing a dynamic database of company information on the internet; and the restructuring of about 80 companies prior to their sale. Opposition politicians suggested that the Government was using privatization as a short-term expedient to raise capital for servicing Egypt's mounting foreign debt. It was also pointed out, conversely, that by transforming the Egyptian Electricity Authority into a holding company—a first step towards flotation, as announced in May 2000—the Government would lose much-needed tax revenues. By December 2001 the Government had sold controlling interests in 167 companies and minority interests in another 18, raising total proceeds of £E16,813m. However, despite two substantial currency devaluations and the issue of a sovereign Eurobond, losses sustained after the September terrorist attacks in the USA caused the Government to seek further funding. Following a donors' conference in Sharm esh-Sheikh, finance totalling US $10,300m. was pledged over three years by the IMF, the Arab Monetary Fund and the Islamic Development Bank (IDB); however, negotiations with the IMF over a fast payment of $2,000m. stalled in early 2002.

THE NATIONAL BUDGET

Price increases and a new sales tax introduced in April–May 1991 were incorporated in the Government's budget for fiscal year 1991/92, which provided for a gross deficit equivalent to

9.3% of GDP. In the event, the deficit was trimmed to 7.1% of GDP, compared with 17% of GDP in 1990/91. Budgeted expenditure in 1991/92 showed a notional increase of more than one-third compared with the previous year, but much of this rise reflected a 38% depreciation of the Egyptian pound since the move to market-determined exchange rates in February 1991 (a rate of US $1 = £E3.24 being used for the budget). The 1992/93 budget provided for total expenditure of £E62,533m. and total revenue of £E53,389m., the resulting deficit of £E9,144m. representing less than 5% of GDP. Calculated at an exchange rate of $1 = £E3.33 (virtually unchanged from 1992/93), the 1993/94 budget provided for expenditure totalling £E65,313m. and revenue totalling £E56,330m., leaving a gross deficit of £E8,983m. (3.5% of GDP). After financing, there remained a net deficit (to be covered by treasury bills) of £E1,338m., compared with £E2,298m. in 1992/93. The 1994/95 budget (calculated at an exchange rate of US $1 = £E3.38) provided for an 8.4% increase in total expenditure to £E70,790m. (broadly in line with the rate of inflation), coupled with a 4.3% reduction in the gross deficit (to £E8,600m.) and a 63.5% reduction (to £E488m.) in the net budget deficit after financing. The 1995/96 budget provided for total expenditure of £E71,492m. (9.9% higher than actual expenditure in 1994/95) and a gross deficit of £E5,297m. (5.3% higher than the actual gross deficit in 1994/95). The net budget deficit after financing was expected to amount to £E407m. in 1995/96. The budget included social spending totalling £E24,997m. (with particular emphasis on education and health). Total public-sector wages were set to reach £E15,720m. in 1995/96, while just over £E2,000m. was budgeted for subsidies on basic goods. Revenue targets included £E18,262m. from general taxation, £E10,043m. from sales taxes and £E8,110m. from customs duties, the Government's objective being to achieve a current-account surplus of around £E4,000m. within the overall budget for 1995/96. The target for real GDP growth in 1995/96 was 5.4%. The overall investment target for 1995/96 was £E42,000m. (53% of this from the private sector), while the target for the creation of new jobs was stated as 498,000 (which would increase the officially estimated labour force to 16.9m.).

The 1996/97 budget provided for total expenditure of £E66,826m. and total revenue of £E64,498m., leaving a gross deficit of £E2,328m., equivalent to about 0.9% of GDP. Total public-sector wages reached £E15,368m., while £E4,134m. was to be allocated for subsidies on basic goods.

The 1997/98 budget provided for a 5.9% increase in total expenditure to £E70,783m., while total revenue increased by 5.4% to £E67,963m. The gross deficit of £E2,820m. was stated to be equivalent to about 1.0% of GDP. Total public-sector wages reached £E17,025m., while £E4,161m. was to be allocated for subsidies on basic goods.

The 1998/99 budget provided for a 6.4% increase in total expenditure to £E75,285m., while revenue increased by 4.9% to £E71,295m., leaving a gross domestic deficit of £E3,990m., equivalent to about 1.3% of GDP. GDP growth for the financial year 1998/99 was 6.1%. The budget included social spending totalling some £E34,500m. (with health and education being of central importance). Total public-sector wages reached £E18,833m., whilst £E4,498m. was to be allocated for subsidies on basic goods.

The 1999/2000 budget provided for total expenditure of £E99,453m. and total revenue of £E90,593m. The deficit of £E8,860m. was expected to be equivalent to some 1% of GDP. Increased revenues were to be derived from an expanded tax base and from greater encouragement of investment and production. Social spending was forecast to increase by 11.3%, to £E38,400m. The budget proposals were based on estimates of economic growth of 6.0% for that fiscal year. The 2000/01 budget provided for total expenditure of £E111,700m. and total revenue of £E97,700m., leaving a deficit of £E14,000m. The Central Bank reported, however, that after just three months of the fiscal year the deficit had reached £E14,300m., compared with £E7,900m. in the corresponding period of 1999/2000. The 2001/02 budget provided for total expenditure of £E126,800m. and total revenue of £E106,100m. The deficit was expected to be equivalent to some 3.3% of GDP. The 2002/03 budget provided for an 11% increase in total expenditure, to £E141,600m. and total revenue of £E111,400m. Social spending was allocated

£E57,800m., and public-sector wages were to increase by 9%, to £E34,000m. Subsidies were to rise by 9%, to £E6,700m., and £E19,300m. was allocated for infrastructure projects. The net budget deficit was expected to be £E17,200m. (equivalent to 4% of GDP), compared with £E9,600m. in 2001/02. Revenues were to be financed from taxation and income from the Suez Canal, the Egyptian General Petroleum Corporation (EGPC) and Telecom Egypt.

AGRICULTURE

Egyptian agriculture is dominated by the river Nile and the necessity for irrigation. The main summer crops are cotton, rice, maize and sorghum, and in winter the chief crops are wheat, beans, berseem (Egyptian clover, used for animal feed) and vegetables. While there is self-sufficiency in fruit and vegetables (some of which are exported to the EU), it is with the basic grains that shortages are encountered. During the 1970s agriculture's contribution to GDP remained fairly constant at just less than 30%, but fell steadily in the 1980s, to reach 17% by 1990. The agricultural sector contributed 16.1% of GDP in 2000/01 (measured at constant 1996/97 prices), and it employed an estimated 33.3% of the economically active population in 2000. In 1979 the sector accounted for approximately 50% of total export earnings, but by 1990 this had fallen to around 10%. During the 1970s the increase in agricultural production was clearly outstripped by population growth, and this reflected a diminishing emphasis on agriculture in government plans. Between 1970 and 1976 food imports, in terms of weight, more than doubled, and exports of rice declined to one-third of their former weight. Agricultural production averaged an annual increase of 3.1% in 1980–90, resulting in a continued dependence on substantial imports of foodstuffs. From a position of self-sufficiency in food during the early 1970s, Egypt now has to import more than one-half of its food. The difficulties in the agricultural sector were well illustrated by the riots against the increases in the prices of basic foodstuffs in Kafr ed-Dawar in September 1984, and by the heavy subsidies on bread and flour; these emphasized the critical problem that the Government faced in attempting to reduce basic subsidies. During 1990–99 agricultural GDP increased at an average annual rate of 3.1%. Over the same period output expanded by an average of 4.5% per year. Agricultural GDP grew by 3.8% in 1999/2000 and by 3.9% in 2000/01.

The increase in the rate of wheat consumption exemplified the problems faced by the agricultural sector. The annual consumption of wheat by Egyptians rose from 80 kg per head in 1960, to 197 kg in 1970 and 300 kg in 1986/87, making Egyptians the world's biggest consumers of wheat per head of population. On several occasions during the 1980s Egypt bought wheat and wheat flour from the USA on preferential terms, although it also bought subsidized grain from the EU. Other grain suppliers included Australia and Canada. Egyptian wheat production totalled 4.62m. metric tons in 1992 (the third successive record harvest), and production steadily increased in subsequent years. Farmers were encouraged to expand the area under wheat to 2.45m. feddans in 1995 (an increase of about one-fifth compared with the previous year) as part of a drive to attain 60% self-sufficiency in wheat production. A harvest of 5.7m. tons was achieved in 1995, when the yield per feddan stood at twice its 1980 level. Wheat production continued to rise to 6.3m. tons in 1999, 6.6m. tons in 2000 and 7.0m. tons in 2001.

Strong growth in crop production from 1990 onwards was attributed to changes in producer price policy, greater use of multiple cropping and a shift in land use from berseem to vegetables, while the relative stagnation of livestock output over the same period was linked to problems in introducing new supply and pricing arrangements for animal feedstuffs. The Egyptian Ministry of Agriculture estimated the value of farm output in the 1994/95 fiscal year at £E32,500m. The value of agricultural exports in that year was $615.5m. (representing about 14% of Egypt's total export earnings).

The arable area is about 5% of the total land area, and not much more than two-fifths of this is serviced by main and secondary drains. This deficiency is significant because an unforeseen effect of the High Dam (see below) was to make the water-table rise (because of more abundant water and more intensive cropping) and led to widespread waterlogging and high soil salinity. Insufficient attention to drainage has therefore been a serious problem with agricultural planning.

The extension of the cultivable area through reclamation has been slow, difficult and costly, but remains at the forefront of government policy. The increasing pressure of people on the land has led to an intensification of cultivation almost without parallel anywhere. Dams, barrages, pumps and an intricate network of canals and drains bring perennial irrigation to almost the whole area. The strict pursuit of crop rotation, lavish use of commercial fertilizer and pesticides, and the patient application of manual labour not only make multiple cropping possible, but also raise land yields to high levels. Despite the difficulties concerning reclamation, early in 1981 the Government announced plans to reclaim 1.2m. ha of land at a rate of 63,000 ha per year over the next 20 years. The largest planned development was at West Nuberiya near Alexandria where, in the first phase, 10,100 ha of land were to be irrigated and drained. A second major agricultural reclamation project has been in progress in the northern Tahrir region; a third project was intended for the region south of Port Said, and further long-term plans included the New Valley project from Aswan to the Qattara depression. While these developments look promising on paper, there is nevertheless much scepticism over official figures relating to the amount of land that has so far been reclaimed. Moreover, the reclamation programme is counterbalanced by the fact that about 20,000 ha of agricultural land has been lost each year owing to urban growth and the depredations of the red clay brick manufacturing industry, which paid farmers large sums for the rich, red topsoil from their fields to be used as raw material (a ban on the manufacture of red bricks was introduced in August 1985). In June 1989 the Government announced plans, within the framework of the socio-economic development plan for 1989/90, to reclaim a further 175,000 feddans of land for agriculture. A record cereal harvest in 1991 was officially attributed, in part, to the reclamation of some 125,000 feddans of land in Sinai and the Alexandria region. At the end of 1996 Egypt's cultivated area was estimated to total 7.6m. feddans, including 2.4m. feddans of reclaimed land. Between 1952 and 1998, an estimated 2,641,800 feddans were reclaimed. The bulk of agricultural production from reclamation is intended for the market place and not for subsistence. Nearly three-quarters of agricultural income comes from field crops, the remainder deriving from fruit, vegetables, livestock and dairy products.

Long-staple cotton is the most important field crop but the area under cultivation has declined since the late 1960s. Egypt produces about one-third of the world crop of long-staple cotton (1.125 in and longer) and is the world's largest exporter of the premium grades that have been least affected by competition from man-made fibres. Cotton provides 15% of all agricultural employment and helps to support a substantial textile industry. Many factors combine to give the high yields and excellent quality of Egyptian cotton. Among these are climatic, soil and labour conditions, and a long experience of careful planting, watering and picking. Government assistance and supervision have always been important. Fertilizers and pesticides are distributed through the government-sponsored agricultural credit banks and agricultural co-operatives. However, investment in cotton has been inadequate to develop the full potential of the industry. Plans were announced at the beginning of 1993 to liberalize Egypt's internal trade in cotton and to end the public-sector monopoly of cotton exports in force for over 30 years. Forming part of a deregulation programme agreed with the World Bank, the cotton industry reforms were designed to improve the crop's financial appeal to farmers and to encourage wider use of high-yield cultivation techniques. During recent years the Egyptian textile industry has absorbed about 80% of the country's cotton crop, and the volumes available for export have often fallen some way short of the prevailing levels of world demand.

Draft legislation was introduced in mid-1994 to revive the Alexandria Cotton Exchange, which had been closed down in 1961. Following allegations that raw cotton prices (initially driven up by the production shortfall) were being further inflated by speculative hoarding of stocks, in October 1995 the Government imposed a price ceiling on ginned cotton supplied to local textile mills, and banned the export of cotton until domestic

demand had been met. This temporary export ban was revoked in February 1996, while in the following month the cotton export trade was opened up to the private sector. At the same time Egypt's cotton import trade was opened up to all countries, with all shipments to be fumigated and sterilized at the point of entry into Egypt. Egyptian textile mills were expected to turn increasingly to competitively priced imports of short-staple cotton from such suppliers as Turkey and Syria, leaving the bulk of Egypt's long-staple crop available for export to Japan, Switzerland, Italy and other markets with a strong demand for premium-grade cotton. Production of cotton lint in 1998 totalled 229,700 metric tons, and production increased to 233,100 tons in 1999. The cotton crop for 2000 fell slightly, to 228,000 tons.

Rice is another important crop and is now, after cotton, almost as important as fruit in the agricultural sector as a foreign-currency earner. Rice exporters were among the main beneficiaries of a lifting of export licensing regulations for farm produce in late 1993. In 1998 rice exports generated an impressive £E242m., following a significant increase in productivity in recent years. Rice production in 1998 was 4.5m. metric tons. Production increased to 5.8m. tons in 1999 and to 6.0m. tons in 2000.

Another high yielding crop is sugar cane. In 1992 the state-owned sugar-refining company (which currently supplies two-thirds of Egypt's annual consumption of 1.5m. metric tons) was 90% reliant on cane as a raw material, the balance of its input being beet and corn. Although the company's plans for the future expansion of sugar production were mainly based on beet rather than cane, it was also planning to add new value to its cane-based operations by developing a plant to manufacture newsprint from *bagasse* (cane waste). Total production of sugar cane in 2000 was 15.7m. tons. Other crops include lucerne (alfalfa), a nitrogen-fixing fodder, beans, potatoes, onions and garlic. A pilot project to produce palm oil in the Western Desert began in 1993.

The many kinds of fruit, vegetables and horticultural products grown are capable of some expansion and are increasingly important as exports. Particular efforts are being made to promote the production of these items, especially citrus fruit, and special areas are being allocated along the Mediterranean coast for their cultivation. Output of fruit totalled 6.3m. metric tons in 1998, 6.6m. tons in 1999 and 6.6m. tons in 2000. Tomato production totalled 6.4m. tons and other vegetable production totalled an estimated 13.6m. tons in 2000. There was particularly rapid growth in production of high-value items for which there was strong export demand, such as peaches and strawberries. The value of vegetable and fruit exports totalled US $134.4m. in 1999 and $590m. in 2000/01.

Recent attention has been given to animal husbandry in an attempt to raise dairy and meat production, but there has so far been little increase in either number of livestock or productivity. Egypt is a net importer of meat to supplement its own output of around 800,000 metric tons per year. Increases in animal-feed prices to world levels were partly responsible for some well-publicized problems in 1992/93, including a fall in poultry production to as little as 55% of capacity as the industry adjusted to a new cost structure. In early 1996 the SDF allocated £E100m. for livestock development projects designed to increase annual output of red meat and dairy products by more than 20m. tons. In 1997 the Government ended a 10-year prohibition on poultry imports but placed an 80% tariff on a minimum price of US $1,600 per ton of the produce, to be reduced at a rate of 2.4% per year. Importers will be charged duties totalling some $1,200 per ton of poultry.

In 1988 measures were announced to conserve water supplies owing to the fall in the level of the Nile. These included a reduction in the area planted with rice to 900,000 feddans; a moratorium on the allocation of land for the cultivation of sugar cane; and a ban on the extension of the area planted to crops requiring large amounts of water. Major irrigation and drainage projects in preparation in 1992 included the 'Suez Siphon', which was intended to convey Nile water under the Suez Canal into the Sinai desert, and a scheme to update the drainage of about 720,000 feddans of existing cultivated land (about 10% of the country's total cultivable area). The Siphon project, which was expected to be completed in late 1996, involved the construction of a system whereby water (mostly recycled from agricultural drainage) would be pumped into North Sinai at a rate of 160 cu m per second over a distance of 150 km. In August 1997 the Government announced plans to convert 265,000 ha of orchards to drip irrigation from flood irrigation in an attempt to save 1,000m. cu m of water per year. Farmers making the conversions, costing £E1,500–£E4,000 per feddan, were to be assisted by subsidized loans from the Government.

Regarding the system of land tenure, the first agrarian reform law was issued in 1952, and was aimed at breaking the feudal power of the deposed regime. This law and subsequent measures limited individual and family landholding and widened the land ownership base, so that by 1985/86 1,072,000 feddans were stated to have been redistributed to 440,000 families. A further land reform law, introduced in 1997, met with widespread disapproval owing to its abolition of fixed rents and security of inherited tenure.

THE HIGH DAM

The decision to invest more than £E400m. in the Aswan High Dam project (including Soviet credits of £E194m.) was partly informed by the possibility of developing cheap hydroelectric energy for industry. The project was started in January 1960, completed in July 1970, and officially inaugurated in January 1971, with a generating capacity of 10,000m. kWh, compared with the 6,012m. kWh produced in all Egypt in 1967. By 1974 revenue from the dam had exceeded the cost of its construction. Transmission lines carried the current from the dam site to Cairo and further north, and a scheme aimed at the complete electrification of Egypt's villages was in progress. The Aswan II hydroelectric power station started up in early 1986, adding 270 MW of capacity to the national grid. In August 1991 a US $140m. contract was signed with a west European consortium for the renovation of the High Dam's older generating turbines and related installations. In 2001 Germany's Kreditanstalt für Wiederaufbau (KfW) financed consultancy work for further rehabilitation of the turbines.

The dam's primary purpose was to store the annual Nile flood which reaches its peak in August, allowing yearly control of the downstream flow, and, therefore, the possibility of perennial irrigation and further land reclamation. Between 1964 and 1978 Lake Nasser (maximum capacity 169,000m. cu m) behind the dam gradually filled and ensured that Egypt did not suffer the worst effects of the drought experienced in much of north-east Africa. Under the terms of an agreement signed with Sudan in 1959, Egypt was allocated 55,500m. cu m of Nile water a year out of an estimated 84,000m. cu m annual average flow as measured at Aswan. Sudan receives 18,500m. cu m and the remainder is calculated to be the annual evaporation loss from Lake Nasser. By June 1988, more than 10 years of drought at the source of the Blue Nile in Ethiopia (which provides approximately 70% of the flow at Aswan) had reduced the water level in Lake Nasser to 153 m, just above the 150 m point at which the High Dam's hydroelectricity turbines would be affected—and approaching the 147 m level at which they would have to be shut down completely. However, an exceptionally high flood after torrential rainfall on the Ethiopian plateau in August 1988 raised the water beyond this critical level. In September 1990 the water level in Lake Nasser was 167 m and live storage was calculated to be 83,700m. cu m. In October 1993, following inflows from an above-average flood, the water level reached 174 m, while storage behind the dam amounted to 116,110m. cu m of water. In September 1994 the water level reached 176.2m, and the stored volume 127,580m. cu m, when a very high Nile flood occurred in the aftermath of a reduction of 5m. cu m per day in farmers' irrigation requirements (a result of early planting in the previous growing season). During the 1996 Nile flood the water level behind the dam reached an unprecedented 178 m, increasing storage in Lake Nasser to 137,000m. cu m by the start of October, at which point water from the lake began to overflow into the Toshka reservoir to the west.

Lake Nasser was expected to become a major fisheries resource, the development of which would replace the sardine catch in the Mediterranean lost as a result of the building of the dam.

In January 1997 the Government inaugurated a 'New Valley' project to build a 30-m-wide canal from Lake Nasser to the oasis regions in the central Western Desert. In March 1998 a contract was signed to build a new £E1,200m. pumping station to extract water from Lake Nasser, just north of the outfall of the Toshka reservoir to the west, in order to fill the canal, which was to be the central feature of a scheme to irrigate up to 500,000 feddans (210,000 ha) of land and to open up adjacent areas for development. The pumping station is scheduled for completion in 2002. Overall, the Southern Egypt Development Project was designed to resettle 3m. Egyptians around the oases over the subsequent 20 years at a cost of up to £E300,000m. A total of £E5,800m. in government funding was allocated to the project for 1997–2002.

In addition to the Toshka project, two other schemes were under way: the Oweinat project aimed to irrigate some 80,000 ha in the most southerly part of the Western Desert, while the as-Salaam canal would be used to irrigate at least 168,000 ha in the Sinai desert with water from the Nile Delta.

THE SUEZ CANAL

After the October 1973 war, the most pressing need was to restore and reopen the Suez Canal and, at Sadat's initiative, the Canal was reopened in June 1975, on the eighth anniversary of the outbreak of war which led to its closure in 1967. Expansion was made all the more urgent because of the vast increase in oil-tanker sizes after June 1967 which the closure of the Canal helped to provoke. The Canal Authority set the dues for ships using the Canal 90%–100% higher than in 1967, and revenue in the first year of operation was US $230m. In December 1980 the first phase of work to widen and deepen the southern end of the Canal was completed at an estimated cost of $1,275m. In 1982 Suez Canal revenue was reported to have reached $1,000m. for the first time, with $956m. being derived from transit tolls and $44m. coming from services to ships in transit. Earnings from Suez Canal tolls were reported to have been $974m. in 1983/84 (in which year other services raised overall revenue to more than $1,000m.), but fell to $897m. in 1984/85. Revenue in 1984 totalled only $960m., $100m. less than had been projected, owing to reduced tanker traffic and the dangers posed by mines in the Red Sea approaches to the Canal, which deterred shipping from using it in the summer months. In 1986 revenue totalled $1,107m., compared with $929m. in 1985. Total revenue from tolls and other services in 1987 was a record $1,222m. The Chairman of the Suez Canal Authority attributed the increase to the Authority's success in attracting large oil tankers and container vessels by offering them a 17% reduction in transit fees. A $400m. development scheme, which was nearing completion in mid-1993, was designed to allow passage of vessels of 56 ft draught, or up to 170,000 dwt, compared with 130,000 dwt previously. A further scheme to deepen the canal to 72 ft (to accommodate vessels of up to 300,000 dwt) remained in abeyance in 1993 after feasibility studies had shown it to be uneconomic at current levels of world trade.

Reconstruction of the canal cities, some of them up to 80% destroyed, was also undertaken and by 1979 more than 1m. Egyptians had returned to Port Said, Ismailia and Suez. In November 1979 construction of the as-Salaam canal, to take water from the East Nile to Sinai, was started and in October 1980 the 1.64-km Ahmad Hamdi tunnel was opened, thus providing the first road link under the Suez Canal.

Despite initial forecasts that the Gulf crisis of 1990–91 would adversely affect the Canal, revenue in the 1990/91 financial year increased by 14% compared with 1989/90, to reach US $1,664m. From 1 January 1991 transit tolls were increased by 6% (4% for dry bulk carriers), while an average 3% increase in 1992 was below the rate of inflation of the Suez Canal Authority's operating costs. A carefully structured programme of selective discounts—e.g. for southbound tankers in ballast—kept the Canal keenly competitive with rival shipping routes, and the Suez Canal Authority's 1994 tariff schedule incorporated average toll increases of about 4%, coupled with further refinements of the structure of selective discounts. In addition to the commercially determined discounts for different categories of cargo vessel, a 35% discount was introduced for passenger cruise-ships in support of the Government's campaign to bolster the tourism industry. The number of vessels using the Canal fell from 17,318 (including 3,185 tankers) in 1993 to 16,370 (including 2,722 tankers) in 1994. Transit tolls were frozen, and some new discounts offered, in 1995. In 1995 the Canal handled 15,051 vessels and generated total revenue of $1,942m. At the start of 1996 the Canal Authority responded to a recent decline in tanker traffic by introducing substantial discounts for northbound oil tankers that discharged part of their cargo at the Ain Sukhna terminal of the Sumed pipeline, later reloading it at the northern end of the pipeline. These vessels would benefit from a new charging system based on the tonnage of their residual cargo. Operators of tanker fleets were offered volume discounts linked to the total annual tonnage that they routed via the Canal. In mid-1996 the Canal Authority finalized a new discount scheme to attract iron-ore and coal carriers away from the Cape route. During 1996 the Canal was used by 14,731 vessels. Revenue for the first 10 months of that year was 7.8% lower than in the corresponding period of 1995, and in November 1996 the Canal Authority announced new discounts for oil tankers, LNG carriers and container vessels. Basic transit fees remained unchanged in 1997. The number of vessels using the Canal during 1997 was 14,430, generating a revenue of $1,822m. In 1998 the Government placed the Suez Canal Authority under the auspices of the Prime Minister as part of an initiative to improve the efficiency of the Canal. During 1998 the Canal handled 13,472 vessels (including 2,135 tankers), with a net total displacement of 386m. tons. In 1999 13,490 vessels (including 1,987 tankers) used the Canal; their aggregate net displacement was 385m. tons. Notwithstanding the negative impact of the Asian economic crisis in the late 1990s on the transport sector, greater efficiency was required since the Canal was experiencing a slow decline in revenue due to increased competition from pipelines as a means of transporting oil. In 2000 14,141 vessels (including 2,563 tankers), with a net total displacement of 439m. tons, used the Canal. Revenue from the Suez Canal increased to $1,868m. in 1999/2000 and $1,947m. in 2000/01.

MANUFACTURING INDUSTRY

Food processing and textiles traditionally dominated the industrial sector, contributing 55%–60% of the total value of industrial output in the mid-1970s. With the growing importance of oil, however, this situation changed. Employment data for 1998 indicated a work-force of 2,111,200 in manufacturing and mining, 1,287,100 in construction, and 203,400 in electricity, gas and water, totalling 22.3% of employed labour. In the year ending June 2001 the mining and manufacturing sector accounted for 25.8% of GDP (at 1996/97 prices), while industry as a whole accounted for 33.6% of GDP (compared with 45% in 1990 and 27% in 1965). According to World Bank data, the GDP of the manufacturing sector increased at an average annual rate of 9.4% in 1990–2000, while that of industry as a whole expanded by an average of 4.7% a year: this lower overall rate largely reflecting the sharp decline in international petroleum prices in 1998 and the first half of 1999. According to official sources, industrial sector production was expected to increase from £E155,200m. in 2000/01 to £E166,100m. in 2001/02, a growth rate of 7.0%.

The manufacturing sector has long suffered from considerable inefficiency. A World Bank report published in 1987 showed that returns on investment were low and that, despite considerable investment, the industrial sector was neither diversified nor efficient, and, therefore, was unable to compete in international markets. Among the problems identified by the report were overstaffing and excessive government protection from foreign competition. The Egyptian authorities admitted that productivity was low, as was plant utilization (only 30% of capacity in some cases), but blamed the international recession and the lack of foreign exchange, in addition to problems of poor incentives and low salary levels among the work-force. In addition, private-sector investment was attracted to service industries rather than manufacturing industry. Nevertheless, private firms were responsible for about 50% of Egypt's US $2,000m.-worth of manufactured exports in 1992.

In the manufacturing industry textiles, having once accounted for about one-third of total output, contributed only 16% in 1989, although exports of textile fibres and products still contributed about 27% of total export revenue in 1990. The Government has embarked on a three-stage rehabilitation of the cotton-ginning industry costing US $40.4m. AFESD was to lend Egypt

$40m. to finance a spinning and weaving project at Kafr ed-Dawar and Bayda. Finished garments accounted for nearly 30% of Egypt's total textile exports in 1994, as the industry shifted increasingly towards value-added products. By 1997 private-sector manufacturers predominated in the dyeing, knitting and finished clothing industries, whereas the public sector was responsible for about 90% of the spinning industry and 60% of weaving activity (state textile enterprises having so far been a low priority for privatization because of widespread financial problems in this sector). Exports of textile fibres and waste amounted to $245.8m. in 1999 (7.0% of total exports), textile yarns to $355.1m. (10.1%) and clothing to $278.1m. (7.9%). In 2001 textile exports totalled $282m.

Developments in the food-processing industry included a major expansion of sugar refining, undertaken to reduce an import requirement of 600,000 metric tons per year, costing an estimated US $60m. Annual consumption per head more than doubled between the 1960s and the 1990s.

The heavy industry sector has been gradually developed since the 1970s. The Egyptian Iron and Steel Co complex at Helwan, developed around a Soviet-built plant first opened in 1973, was by late 1993 producing at its design capacity of 1.2m. metric tons per year, following a 10-year upgrading programme financed by the World Bank and Germany. The Japanese-built Alexandria Iron and Steel Co complex at ed-Dikheila—in production since the end of 1986—produced 1.1m. tons of high-quality steel reinforcing bars and wire rods in 1993. In 2000 Ezz Steel Rebars (ESR) acquired a 28% stake in that company and the two companies consolidated their marketing operations under the name Ezz-Dikheila Steel (EZDK), giving them control of over 50% of the market. A long-term growth strategy for the steel industry was under discussion by public- and private-sector experts in 1994, and in October 1997 a contract was signed for the construction of a giant steel plant in Suez, to produce some 1m. tons of flat steel sheets annually, 40% of which would be exported. Investment in the plant was expected to total some £E2,000m. Production capacity was estimated at 4.6m. tons in 2000 and 5.4m. tons in 2001. In April 1998 the Government announced plans to establish a £E500m. company to develop iron ore deposits south of Aswan. The Aswan Iron and Steel Co subsequently began construction of a £E2,600m. plant. In June the Aswan Development and Mining Co (Adamco) signed an agreement to mine iron ore and construct an integrated iron and steel plant south of Aswan to produce 1.42m. tons per year of steel billets. The Aluminium Co of Egypt, whose complex at Naga Hammadi opened in 1975 (having been developed to take advantage of power supplied from the Aswan High Dam), was in 1993 in the process of upgrading its annual production capacity from 180,000 tons to 250,000 tons, with no extra power use. Egypt exported £E405.4m. worth of aluminium rods and sections and £E94.4m. worth of unwrought aluminium in 1994/95. The new 60,000 tons-per-year rolling mill began production in 1995. In 1997 the company underwent a partial privatization.

Egypt's cement industry underwent rapid expansion in the 1980s. Annual consumption of cement rose from 4.1m. metric tons in 1977 to about 16m. tons in 1986. Four cement works began production in 1985, and the conversion of a Soviet-built cement works at Asyout created the largest production line in Africa, with a nominal output capacity of 5,000 tons per day. Under the 1987–92 Five-Year Plan, five new works were built, and steps were taken to expand output at existing plants. By the early 1990s local supply had been brought more closely into balance with demand. By 1997 cement production had increased to 15m. tons per year. According to the Ministry of Industry, output was equivalent to 19.7m. tons per year by mid-1998, and the construction of three new ventures was forecast to increase production by a further 4.2m. tons per year by 1999, although official figures estimated that production in 1998/99 decreased to just 11.9m. tons. Nevertheless, production is expected to reach 35m. tons by 2004. The proliferation of new projects was prompted by prospects of increased demand, owing to construction projects such as the Toshka irrigation scheme and new tourist developments. In the largest privatization of 2001, the Helwan Portland Cement Company was sold to the local ASEC Cement for an estimated US $300m. The sector has also attracted foreign investment—Lafarge, as a result of its acquisition of Blue Circle, controls the Alexandria Portland Cement

Company (and 25% of the market) and plans to double capacity at its Beni Suef plant, privatized in 1999; and Ciments Français has purchased a 25% stake in the Suez Cement Company, which itself acquired Tourah Cement, Egypt's oldest producer.

In 2001 the Government announced plans to re-issue the tender to sell its stake in the Egyptian Glass Company since the original bid from a shareholder (Pilkington) failed to win sufficient acceptances. The Al-Ahram Beverages Company (ABC, which was privatized in 1997) and the Saudi Dairy & Food Stuffs Company (Sadafco) formed a strategic alliance for the distribution of ABC's products.

Within the field of the motor industry, Egypt has been assembling and manufacturing parts of Italian Fiat passenger cars since the early 1960s. The En-Nasr Automotive Manufacturing Co (NASCO) produces these cars at a rate of 12,000 per year, as well as buses, trucks and other vehicles. General Motors Egypt (GME) was established in 1985 to build light commercial vehicles at 6 October City, south-west of Cairo. By the mid-1990s GME was also assembling passenger cars for Opel. Other companies were meanwhile developing local assembly plants for makes of passenger and commercial motor vehicles such as Hyundai, Suzuki, Peugeot, Citroen, Mercedes, Skoda, Daewoo, Nissan and BMW.

In early 1997 Egypt had seven car assembly plants in operation with a total capacity of 85,000 units per year, although current output was only about one-third of capacity. In 1996 the Egyptian market for cars was around 65,000 units, of which about one-half were assembled locally. The export of locally assembled cars was not permitted under licensing agreements between foreign parent manufacturers and Egyptian assembly plants, whose financial viability depended on substantial tariff protection in the Egyptian domestic market. Egyptian tariffs on vehicle imports—specifically excluded from the general reductions in tariffs in 1996 and 1997—ranged in mid-1997 from 40% on the smallest cars to 135% on cars with engine capacities of 1.6 litres or more. According to some industry estimates in 1996, a further 15 years of tariff protection would be needed for Egyptian vehicle plants to develop internationally competitive cost structures. In 2002 the Egyptian-German Auto Company agreed to export cars to the People's Republic of China and the Russian company AvtoVAZ announced plans to open an assembly plant.In the automotive parts sector, two export-orientated companies have been established by Lucasvarity of the UK (in 1998) and the Alexandria Automotive Castings Company backed by the International Finance Corporation (in 2001).

Early in 1983 the Chief of Staff of the Armed Forces stated that Egypt was interested in the joint manufacture of weapons with other countries, and in November 1987 Egypt began to press its former partners in the AOI (Saudi Arabia, Qatar and the UAE) to revive their involvement in a regional Arab defence industry. The AOI was established in 1974 to provide an Arab challenge to Israel's advanced defence industry but Egypt's three co-founders withdrew from the organization in 1979, after Egypt signed a peace treaty with Israel. The armaments industry was seen in Egypt as a possible source of revenue to offset the decline in receipts from the traditional revenue earners, and the decision of its former partners to re-establish diplomatic relations with Egypt after the Arab League summit meeting in Amman, Jordan, in November 1987 gave rise to hopes that new Arab investment in the AOI might be forthcoming. Sales of armaments earned a reported US $1,000m. in 1982, when Iraq, at a critical stage in its war with Iran, turned to Egypt for spare parts and ammunition for its mainly Soviet-built equipment, and bought battle tanks from Egypt's strategic reserves. Egypt acquired licences to rebuild and modify old Soviet tanks, and its most ambitious project involved the assembly, under licence, of US General Dynamics Land System's M1-A1 Abrams battle tanks. Some 75 of the latter had been produced by the beginning of 1994, when production was proceeding at the rate of 10 tanks per month towards a cumulative target of 540 tanks (all intended for use by the Egyptian armed forces). In 2001 the Government signed a $400m. contract with Boeing to upgrade its Apache helicopter fleet and received US government approval for Lockheed to supply the army with extended-range multiple launch rocket system pods.

To provide for the large number of Egyptians returning from the Gulf in 1990–91, the Government announced the creation of eight project zones, some of them free zones for tariff purposes, designed to provide factory employment for displaced workers. By March 1994, the total population of new industrial cities around Cairo was officially given as 265,000, and plans were announced to encourage their further growth by providing incentives for workers to take up residence in them. New incentives for investment in the economically-deprived Upper Egypt region were announced in January 1995. Industrial zones in Beni-Suef (120 km south of Cairo) and five population centres further to the south (Menia, Asyout, Suhag, Luxor and Aswan) became subject to accelerated planning procedures and other measures to attract new investors. In December 1997 the International Development Association (the concessionary lending arm of the World Bank) pledged credits worth US $15m. to settle 26,000 low-income families on reclaimed land east of the Delta. The Government's co-operative housing authority aimed to attract new residents by subsidizing approximately 50% of the cost of a house with a loan to be repaid over a period of 30–40 years. There were plans to build new towns to accommodate 5m. people by 2000 and relieve the pressures on existing urban centres of a rapidly increasing population, although these provisions were in danger of becoming obsolete in the face of an ever-accelerating birth rate. The Government expected its investment in new towns to reach £E142,000m. by 2017. The construction of a $50m. industrial park near Kampala was completed in early 2001. New water and wastewater projects commenced in 2002 under the secondary cities utilities programme, scheduled for completion in 2005. These were being supported by $315m. in grants from the US Agency for International Development (USAID), which is also providing funding for a $100m. programme for similar projects in central Egypt.

ELECTRICITY

The needs of heavy industry, and the plan to extend electric power to all Egypt's rural communities underlined the need for more power generation than that supplied by the Aswan High Dam. The dam represented some 2,000 MW of total installed capacity of 3,700 MW at the start of the 1982–87 Five-Year Plan. The Plan provided for the expansion of installed capacity by 3,430 MW, of which 270 MW was to be obtained through the Aswan II scheme, and the remainder from thermal power stations and eight nuclear plants, which were to be completed by 2005 at a cost of US $36,000m. Total net installed capacity rose to 5,850 MW in 1985. However, the nuclear programme) was cancelled following the disaster at the Chornobyl plant in the USSR in April 1986, and in view of the collapse of oil prices; while some of the thermal units, which were intended to be oil- and gas-fired, were redesigned to burn coal from Australia. It was proposed that a 2,600-MW plant, costing $1,800m. to construct, and ultimately using 15m. metric tons of Australian coal per year, would be built at Zaafarana on the Gulf of Suez during the 1987–92 Five-Year Plan, with an associated port capable of handling 7m.–8m. tons of coal per year initially, rising to 12m.–15m. tons. Annual consumption of electricity was given at 34,000m. kWh in 1985 and was expected to increase threefold by the end of the century. Hence, plans to implement the Qattara depression scheme to generate energy by flooding the depression with waters from the Mediterranean were given the final go-ahead late in 1980, at an estimated cost of at least $2,600m. In 1980 the USA agreed to provide a $102m. loan to modernize and expand the electricity grid, and in 1985 the US Agency for International Development also agreed to provide $55m. of an estimated $156m. required for the fourth power unit at Shoubra el-Kheima power station in Cairo. The station, whose first three units, costing $604m., became operational in early 1986, provides up to 75% of Cairo's electricity. The fourth unit was completed in the late 1980s, bringing total capacity to more than 1,000 MW. To guard against severe power shortages arising from low water levels at the Aswan High Dam (see above), the Government announced, in January 1988, that 20 thermal power plants, with a combined capacity of 5,500 MW, would be built by the end of 1992. By 1991 Egypt's total installed capacity was 10,938 MW. It was planned to add a further 6,000 MW by 2000, including the commissioning of a 400-MW combined cycle plant at Damietta, east of Alexandria, and the rehabilitation of an old Soviet-built plant at Suez, which would increased capacity by 185 MW. Annual output of electricity totalled 84,870m. kWh in 1997 and was expected to reach 100,000m. kWh in 1998. Meanwhile, the sector aimed to reduce oil consumption: where possible, power stations were being converted to use natural gas in the early 1990s, the Government's target being to increase the contribution of gas to thermal power generation from 60% in 1992 to 80% by 1997 (thus minimizing domestic use of petroleum that could be used to generate valuable export revenue). In 1997 thermal power stations accounted for 79% of electricity output. In March 1998 a contract was signed for the construction of five new power transformer stations with a total capacity of 250,000 kWh. The £E56m. project would provide electricity in rural areas of Abu el-Matamir, Motobus, Tel el-Kebir, Dekernes, and Samalout. As part of a regional inter-connection project financed by AFESD, the Egyptian and Jordanian electricity grid was inaugurated at the Jordanian port of Aqaba in March 1999, work having been completed in 1998.

As part of the restructuring of the power sector, the Egyptian Electricity Authority (EEA) was converted into Egyptian Electric Holding Company (EEHC) in 2000 in preparation for partial privatization. Future reforms include the separation of generation (under the control of EEHC) and distribution (with the distribution companies being privatized). New generation provided from privately-funded projects include major Build-Own-Operate-Transfer (BOOT) projects—a US $450m. gas-fired steam power plant with two 650-MW generating units, located at Sidi Kerir on the Gulf of Suez, and two 650-MW plants at Suez and Port Said. Planned future projects include two 750-MW plants at Nubariya, near Alexandria, and a 750-MW addition to the Cairo North combined cycle power complex. The foreign currency costs of the latter project are being covered by loans from the European Investment Bank (EIB) ($134m.), AFESD ($88m.) and the IDB ($41m.). A hydroelectric project is planned at Asyut and a 64-MW hydroelectric power plant is to be included in the Naga Hammadi barrage project, to be constructed 3.5 km downstream on the Nile from the existing barrage (financed by Germany's KfW and the EIB). Construction began in 2001. USAID is financing the construction of three substations to be located at El-Fayoum, Qesna and the Delta town of Kafr el-Shaikh. In 2001 construction began on a 60-MW wind-powered electricity farm in Zaafarana and plans were announced to build a part-solar power plant at Kureimat as a BOOT project with financing from the World Bank.

PETROLEUM AND GAS

The development of Egypt's hydrocarbons sector has had a major impact on the economy, although petroleum production in Egypt remains relatively small by Middle Eastern standards. Production of crude petroleum at the end of 1980 averaged approximately 600,000 barrels per day (b/d), and continued to rise thereafter. Petroleum revenue was US $3,431m. in 1981/82 (representing about 60% of total export earnings), compared with $960m. in 1979. Of average daily output, about 50% was used locally and between 25%–30% was taken by foreign oil companies, leaving only about one-quarter of output or less available for export. In 1986 the effect of the collapse in oil prices, coupled with Egypt's decision voluntarily to reduce production, was to limit average output to about 770,000 b/d, while exports fell to a rate of only 150,000 b/d.

Domestic consumption of hydrocarbons, was, until 1984, rising at a rate of 12%–15% each year, while oil production was rising by only 7% annually. Subsidies on petroleum placed a considerable strain on the nation's finances: the estimated US $3,600m. spent on them in 1983 kept oil products at less than one-fifth of their price on the world market. Substitution of natural gas for fuel oil helped to slow the rate of increase in domestic oil consumption during the latter part of the 1980s, while sharp reductions in price subsidies in 1991 helped to stabilize domestic hydrocarbon consumption, and in 1995 total hydrocarbon consumption was 29.3m. metric tons, comprising 19.4m. tons of petroleum products and 9.9m. tons of natural gas. The most significant factors in explaining the great increases in oil production so far are the return by Israel of the Alma Oilfield, renamed the Shaab Ali field, in the Gulf of Suez, in November 1979 and, in 1982, the Sinai oilfields (notably the Abu Rudeis

area), and the increase in concessions and finds particularly in the Gulf of Suez and the Western Desert. At the end of 2001, according to industry figures, Egypt's proven oil reserves totalled 2,900m. barrels, equivalent to 11.1 years' production at 2001 output levels.

Egypt, not being a member of Organization of the Petroleum Exporting Countries (OPEC), has maintained a flexible pricing policy. In 1983 and 1984, by maintaining a higher price for its oil (as much as US $28.50 per barrel for the premium Suez 33° API oil blend, which accounts for about 60% of all oil exports), Egypt's policy was consistent with its support for OPEC's programme to prevent a collapse in world oil prices. In February 1985, however, Egypt dissociated itself from OPEC's policies, steadily reducing the price of its oil, as demand remained slack. A decline in the value of the US dollar and a reduction in Iranian oil exports led to increases in all blends (including the 26° API Belayim blend and Râs Ghârib, the heaviest Egyptian crude) during late 1985. During 1986, however, the oil price, already weakened by the glut of oil on world markets, fell sharply after OPEC decided to increase production, in order to secure a 'fair' share of the reduced market. In order to remain competitive, Egypt was forced to cut production and make a series of reductions in the price of its oil. After OPEC decided in August 1986 to reintroduce a production ceiling, the price of petroleum on world markets began to increase again. Egypt's production rose after August 1986, reaching 940,000 b/d in December, but it agreed to restrict its output to 870,000 b/d for the first half of 1987, in support of OPEC's new production and prices strategy. However, according to the Egyptian General Petroleum Corporation (EGPC), average output exceeded 900,000 b/d during this period, and reached 904,000 b/d in the year as a whole. By mid-1988, with the world market once more oversupplied with petroleum, the price of the Suez and Ras al-Bihar blends had been reduced to $12.75 per barrel. Net petroleum revenues, which had totalled $2,630m. in 1985, declined to $704m. in 1986 and rose to $1,446m. in 1987, following an improvement in world oil prices. By 1990/91 oil exports totalled $2,539m. and oil imports $978m., making a surplus of $1,561m. In 1997 oil exports totalled $2,483m. and imports $1,606m., resulting in a surplus of $877m. In 1998 Egypt had an oil trade surplus of $113m. (exports $1,236m., imports $1,123m.). However, an oil trade deficit of $81m. was reported for 1999 (exports $1,182m., imports $1,263m.). In 2000/01 a payments' surplus of $510m. was recorded.

The plan for the hydrocarbon sector in 1982/83–1986/87 envisaged an increase in oil and gas production by 85% from 34m. metric tons in 1981 to 63m. tons by 1987. However, these plans had to be revised owing to the crisis in the world oil market. Actual production totalled 44.6m. tons in 1986 (oil 40.3m. tons; gas 4.3m. tons), rising to 50m. tons in 1987 (oil 45.2m. tons; gas 4.8m. tons). Production amounted to 49.6m. tons in 1988 and rose to 50.4m. tons in 1989, 50.0m. tons in 1990 and 51.6m. tons in 1991. In 1992 total hydrocarbon production of 53.6m. tons comprised 44.2m. tons of crude oil, 7.6m. tons of natural gas, 1.1m. tons of condensates and 0.7m. tons of butane. Total output was 56.4m. tons in 1993 (oil 45.5m. tons, gas 8.8m. tons, condensates 1.3m. tons, butane 0.8m. tons); and 56.2m tons in 1994 (oil 44.8m. tons, gas 9.3m. tons, condensates 1.3m. tons and butane 0.8m. tons). The 1995 production total was 56.65m. tons (oil 44.6m. tons, gas 9.9m. tons, condensates 1.3m. tons and butane 0.85m. tons). Data for 1996 indicated a decline of 3% in oil production and an increase of 5.6% in oil consumption, while natural gas production rose by 4.7% and gas consumption increased by 4.1%. In 2001 oil production was recorded at 37.3m. tons and consumption at 26.2m. tons. Natural gas production totalled 21.0m. tons and consumption was 18.9m. tons. Petroleum and petroleum products accounted for 36.0% of total export earnings in 1999. Total revenues from crude oil and natural gas reached £E16,780m. in 2000/01.

Egypt has made numerous oil concession and exploration agreements with foreign companies. The US company, Amoco, was responsible for nearly 50% of all Egyptian crude output in the early 1990s. Exploration was greatly stimulated by the oil price rises of the early 1970s, leading to new oil finds in the Gulf of Suez, on the Red Sea coast and in the Eastern and Western Deserts. Western Desert oilfields contributed 6.5% of national output in 1987 (compared with more than 90% for the

Gulf of Suez), when 41 of Egypt's oilfields were situated in the Gulf of Suez and 26 in the Western Desert.

Exploration continued, and in early 1983 four new major production-sharing agreements were signed by the Egyptian General Petroleum Corporation (EGPC) with Shell Winning, Getty Oil, Deminex, and a partnership of BP, Elf Aquitaine, Occidental Petroleum and IEOC (the Egyptian affiliate of Italy's ENI). Expansion continued during 1984, with petroleum flowing ashore from the first of the Deminex Egyptian Oil Company's platforms in the Ras Fanar field, in the Gulf of Suez. Further concessions were also signed with Deminex in the Zeit area; with Marathon, Aminoil and IEOC in the southern part of the Gulf of Suez; and with Shell Winning in the East Gamsa area of the Gulf of Suez and in the Qaraouan area of the Western Desert. The Zeit Bay oilfield came 'on stream' in 1984, with an initial output of 10,000 b/d, which had risen to 65,000 b/d by April 1985. The third oilfield in the Gulf of Suez to begin production during 1984 was Ras al-Bihar, the largest field yet struck by EGPC, with an initial output of 12,000 b/d. A consortium of Western oil companies, including Total-CFP and BP, discovered oil in Egyptian waters off the coast of North Sinai in early 1986. Texas International Inc and Conoco made two discoveries of oil in a 200,000-ha concession 325 km west of Alexandria in mid-1985. More than 350 exploratory wells were drilled in the Gulf of Suez, and some 40 fields discovered. During 1986 new discoveries were reported in the Western Desert by Khalda Petroleum (a joint venture of the EGPC, Texas International and Conoco). New exploration agreements were signed with BP, Shell, Amoco and Agip in mid-1987 for concessions in the Gulf of Suez and the Sinai desert, reflecting more advantageous production-sharing terms being offered by the EGPC to encourage foreign participation. In September 1987 the EGPC announced that 78 oil deposits had been discovered since 1982, of which 41 were in production and 31 were to begin production during the next five years. According to the EGPC, a record 49 exploration agreements with foreign oil companies were approved by the Egyptian Government in 1989.

The results of exploration in the late 1980s were generally disappointing, especially in the Western Desert, and a new round of invitations to bid for concessions issued by the EGPC in 1990 elicited only a limited response. Partly as a result, BP announced in November 1991 that it would sell its 16.6% stake in the Suez Petroleum Company (SUCO), while other Western companies scaled down their activities in Egypt. Nevertheless, several new oil and gas finds were announced in 1990–92, one by British Gas in December 1990, in its offshore North Zaafarana concession in the Gulf of Suez, being described as 'the most significant in the area for nearly a decade'. Other finds announced in early 1992 included strikes of both oil and gas in the Western Desert, the Gulf of Suez and the Nile delta, close to existing fields. According to government sources, there was known potential for the proving of a further 2,000m. barrels of oil reserves in Egypt, although it was conceded that they were in relatively small pockets that would be difficult to exploit.

In June 1989 Egypt was readmitted to the Organization of Arab Petroleum Exporting Countries (OAPEC), and it subsequently sought to increase co-operation with Libya, Syria, Jordan, Oman, Yemen and the other Gulf states. Companies from Kuwait and the UAE invested in exploration concessions in Egypt. In 1993 the EGPC made strenuous efforts to revitalize oil exploration activity, concluding seven new agreements in February for blocks in the Western Desert and the Gulf of Suez; the companies involved included British Gas, Amoco, Mobil and Agip. Bids for a further five blocks (two of them in the Delta region) were being evaluated in mid-1993, while bidding for 15 more blocks (five of them in the Mediterranean region) was to close near the end of the year. Reported improvements in terms included increased block sizes, improved cost-recovery formulas and flexible withdrawal options. Production-sharing terms (which were negotiable on a case-by-case basis) reportedly envisaged a reduction in the EGPC's share of output to between 70% and 80%, compared with its entitlements of between 80% and 89% under existing production-sharing agreements. Egypt's Minister of Petroleum and Mineral Wealth said that it was essential to adopt a flexible negotiating stance in an environment of 'intense international competition'. In a demonstration of its pragmatic approach to oil development, the Government

agreed in 1993 to allow Agip's local affiliate to merge a total of 14 separate agreements, of widely differing terms and lengths, into one unified agreement with an extended expiry date, thereby improving the viability of the company's capital investment programme. (The Agip-affiliated International Egyptian Oil Co was Egypt's second largest oil producer and largest gas producer in 1992.) Nine exploration blocks (including the last available blocks in the Gulf of Suez) were opened to bids in 1995, after which only 40% of Egyptian territory (including the 15% without any sedimentary rocks) would remain unallocated for exploration. The Government's intention was to have exploration agreements in place in every geologically appropriate area by 1998. Having concluded concession agreements in respect of eight of the nine blocks offered in 1995, the Government opened a further nine blocks to bids in 1996. In 1997 the EGPC offered 12 exploration blocks, 11 of which were awarded in mid-1998. Participating companies envisage drilling 63 wells in total, with total investment of US $208m. Nine exploration blocks were opened to bids in early 1998, and bids for a further nine blocks were to be opened later in the year. The auction of 32 exploration blocks planned in 2001 was postponed until 2002 to allow for reorganization in the oil and gas sector. This entailed restructuring EGPC into a holding company with responsibility for oil activities, leaving the newly created Egyptian Natural Gas Holding Company to oversee the gas sector (see below).

New discoveries were made in 2001 in the north-east Abu Gharadiq concession, in the Western Desert by Shell Egypt and Apache Corporation, in the Gulf of Suez by Ocean Energy of the USA (in the East Zeit block) and by Canada's Cabre Exploration in the West Esh el-Mallaha block.

The 320-km Suez–Mediterranean (Sumed) crude pipeline, operated by the Arab Petroleum Pipeline Co (owned 50% by Egypt and 50% by Saudi Arabia, Kuwait, Qatar and Abu Dhabi, mostly through state oil companies), opened in 1977 with an initial throughput capacity of 1.6m. b/d. Terminals at Ain Sukhna (near Suez) and Sidi Krier (near Alexandria) can accommodate tankers otherwise too large to navigate the Suez Canal. In 1998 the Sumed pipeline transported 2.4m. b/d, and revenues earned by the Arab Petroleum Pipeline Co totalled US $235m. As well as providing an oil transit service, the Sumed company does some trading on its own account (buying crude at the Red Sea terminal for resale at the Mediterranean terminal).

Annual output of refined products from Egypt's oil refineries— at Suez (two), Mosturud (near Cairo), Ameriya and Mex (near Alexandria), Tanta and Wadi Feirân—totalled 26.3m. metric tons in 1995 with the main population centres served by an extensive network of product pipelines. Downstream development initiatives for the mid-1990s were expected to include refinery modernization to bring the local industry's product mix more closely into line with the pattern of domestic demand.

In 1997 a contract was awarded to an Egyptian-Israeli joint venture to construct the 100,000 b/d Midor refinery as an export-orientated project at Sidi Kerir, near Alexandria. When it started trial production in 2001, Arab countries refused to supply oil until the Israeli company Merhav sold its 20% stake in Midor to the National Bank of Egypt. The Government announced plans in 2001 to build five additional refineries at a cost of US $2.500m. This includes a 35,000-b/d, $450m.hydrocracker at the El Nasr Petroleum Company refinery in Suez, for which a new financing proposal from Crédit Lyonnais is under consideration with a pledged $100m. loan from the EIB. Having brought its first natural gas field on stream in 1974 at a rate of 3.5m. cu m per day (cu m/d), Egypt was producing around 6m. cu m/d by the early 1980s, when the country's proven gas reserves totalled around 85,000m. cu m. Substantial new discoveries in succeeding years helped to increase proven reserves to 400,000m. cu m by the end of 1992, during which year Egyptian gas output averaged 31.15m. cu m/d (having increased by nearly 25% since 1990 and by nearly 50% since 1987). Until the late 1980s gas pipelines were developed primarily to serve industrial plants (including the Helwan iron and steel complex). Thereafter, power stations became the largest consumers of Egyptian gas, most of the steep rise in gas consumption in the early 1990s being attributable to a national strategy to substitute gas for oil wherever possible.

Almost 40% of Egypt's gas output in 1992 came from the Abu Madi and El Qara fields in the Nile Delta (foreign participant

Agip), while about 25% came from the Badr ed-Din field in the Western Desert (foreign participant Shell). The most important new gas discovery of 1992 was made by Shell Egypt in the coastal region of the Western Desert, involving the Obaiyed field, which was expected to add between 40,000m. cu m and 250,000m. cu m to the country's proven reserves when fully appraised. Other companies with major Egyptian gas interests include BP and Phillips Petroleum. Having significantly improved its financial terms for gas development and production in 1988, the Government further enhanced the return to producing companies in 1993, when it raised its main reference price by 12.5%, bringing it roughly into line with European gas prices. Egypt's gas production averaged 36.83m. cu m/d in 1994. At the end of 1994 the EGPC, Amoco and the Agip-affiliated International Egyptian Oil Co signed an agreement to establish an Egypt Trans-Gas Co to take charge of a project to build a 500-km gas pipeline from Port Said to Gaza and Israel, to handle proposed exports of gas to these markets, and to assess the potential for the eventual development of further markets in Lebanon and Turkey. Reflecting the entry into production in the late 1990s of new offshore fields north of the Nile Delta, Egypt's proven reserves at the end of 2001 totalled 1,000,000m. cu m, compared with 350,000m. cu m 10 years earlier. During 1998 considerable progress was made by the EGPC and Italy's ENI on development proposals for a pipeline linking the Nile Delta with El-Arish on the border with Palestinian-controlled Gaza. A provisional agreement with the Palestinian National Authority on the delivery of gas to the region was signed in October, although this would ultimately depend on the future political situation in the region. In August 1999 two Egyptian companies joined British Gas (BG) and Italy's Edison International in a joint venture, the Nile Valley Gas Co, which proposed to build the first natural gas pipeline to Upper Egypt. In June 2001 a project was announced to construct a US gas pipeline between Egypt and Jordan, Syria and Lebanon. The link between Egypt and Jordan is scheduled for inauguration in 2003.

New discoveries of natural gas deposits off the Nile Delta continued to be made in 2000–01. In 2001 Shell Egypt announced a second round of drilling in the north-east Mediterranean Deepwater (Nemed) block; meanwhile, BP was to drill its first well in the west Mediterranean Deepwater concession, and reported a new find in the offshore North Alexandria concession. Also in 2001 BG brought the Rosetta oil- and gasfield on stream and is developing new fields in the West Delta Deep Marine Concession. New discoveries were reported by Apache Corporation in the Khalda concession in the Western Desert and by Canadian Centurion Energy in the El Manzala concession, in the Nile Delta.

The gas discoveries, and the imminent launch of the Jordanian pipeline, have led to a search for further export options, since the Government believes that one-third of reserves will be sufficient to meet domestic needs. To manage the sector, the Government established the Egyptian Natural Gas Holding Company in 2002. The company is to be responsible for the assets previously held by the EGPC and for a programme to export 8.6m. metric tons per year of gas to Europe by 2005, with the start-up of a number of liquefied natural gas (LNG) export terminals along the Mediterranean coast. Unión Fenosa (Spain) plans to export 4,000m. cu m of LNG per year to power six new power stations in Spain from Egypt's first export terminal in Damietta. The contract for the US $1,000m. first train is scheduled to be completed by 2004. BP and ENI (Italy) plan to construct a two-train LNG plant in the Nile Delta province, with the capacity to process 31m. cu m/d. The project would also include a facility to produce liquefied petroleum gas (LPG). Shell is proposing a dual-use facility linked to the Nemed block, involving both an export terminal and a facility for gas-to-liquids production of petroleum products. Additionally, Electricité de France plans to construct and operate two natural gas 680-MW steam generation plants in Suez and East Port Said. The Government benefited from revisions to gas purchase agreements with three of the leading foreign operators—Shell, BP and ENI—in 2001. These entailed the creation of a ceiling and a floor to the crude oil reference prices for the purchases to prevent paying surcharges when oil prices reach more than $20 per barrel. The Egyptian Gas Company (Gasco) earned $41m. from propane exports in the first nine months of 2000/01. It also produced 235,000 metric tons of LPG for the domestic market, saving some $54m. in import costs.

There are five main fertilizer plants using Egypt's hydrocarbon feedstocks: Talkha I in Lower Egypt, producing 380,000 metric tons per year of nitrogenous fertilizers; Talkha II producing 396,000 tons per year of ammonia, which is then used for making urea (both plants use gas from the Abu Madi field); Suez, producing 250,000 tons per year of nitrogenous fertilizer, using gas from Abu Gharadeq; the plant at Dikheila, using Abu Qir gas, with a capacity of 500,000 tons per year of urea and 100,000 tons per year of ammonium nitrate; and the Abu Qir fertilizer works, in Alexandria, producing 450,000 tons per year of ammonia/urea. An extension to the Abu Qir plant is scheduled to come on stream in 2005. In January 1998 a contract was signed for the construction of a fertilizer complex in Suez, to produce 1,200 tons per day of urea and 1,925 tons per day of ammonia. In 1997 bids were invited for the development of Egypt's first polyethylene complex, to produce 200,000 tons per year, using feedstock from an ethylene plant already under construction. In 2001 the Oriental Petrochemicals Company announced plans to build a second polypropylene plant in Alexandria, which will utilize natural gas from Western Desert fields as feedstock. Other projects include a polyester plant in Alexandria and an ethylene plant with a 331,000-ton capacity.

OTHER MINERALS

Iron ore was traditionally mined from the Aswan area, but new and better quality reserves were discovered in the Bahariya Oasis region. Phosphate production from mines at Isna, Hamrawein and Safaga exceeded 600,000 metric tons per year in the 1980s, and exports reached around 300,000 tons in 1992/93. A new phosphate mine at Abu Tartur in the Western Desert was due to be brought into production at a rate of 2.2m. tons per year at the end of 1994, rising to twice that rate by 1996, when 600,000 tons of its output would be earmarked for export. However, production had still not begun in 1997, when the Government announced that private-sector investment would be sought to complete the project. Manganese was mined in the Eastern Desert and Sinai, there were chromium deposits in the Eastern Desert, and uranium was discovered in Sinai. In 1985 a British company, Minex Minerals Egypt, was awarded concessions to prospect for gold in two areas at Barramiya and es-Sid. In 1997 an Australian company, Pharaoh Gold Mines, was preparing to open a mine in the Eastern Desert, while a new gold discovery was announced in the far south-west of Egypt at Jabal Kamel, where Egyptian geologists had been prospecting for iron ore. In 2001 substantial gold reserves were discovered by Centamin Egypt in its Sukari concession in the Eastern Desert. The Gippsland consortium formed a joint venture, Tantalum Egypt, with the Egyptian Geological Survey & Mining Authority to extract tantalite deposits (at Abu Dabbab on the Red Sea) for the production of the metal tantalum used in electronic components.

There are extensive coal deposits in Sinai, including an estimated 21m. tons at Maghâra, where a deep mine (disused since 1967), was reopened in the mid-1990s. The company responsible, Sinai Coal Co, was under parliamentary investigation in 1997 following allegations of 'financial, operational and environmental shortcomings'.

BANKING AND EXCHANGE RATES

A reorganization of the banking system in 1971 entrusted the National Bank of Egypt with foreign trade, the Misr Bank with home trade, including agricultural finance, the Bank of Alexandria with manufacturing, Crédit Foncier Egyptien with construction and housing, and the Bank of Cairo with operations of the public sector. However, in 1975, in line with the liberalization of the banking system, these restrictions on the sectoral operations of the major banks were removed. A new bank, the Nasser Social Bank, was created to deal with pensions and other forms of social security. The Egyptian International Bank for Foreign Trade and Development was also created in 1971 to promote foreign trade and attract foreign investment but was later transformed into the Arab International Bank for Foreign Trade and Development with Egypt, Libya and other Arab investors holding shares. These banks are additional to the

Central Bank of Egypt, which was created from the issue department of the National Bank of Egypt in 1960, and the Public Organization for Agricultural Credit and Co-operatives, which the Crédit Agricole became in 1964.

Foreign banks have been welcome in Egypt since it began liberalizing its economy in earnest in 1974, and about 50 of them now operate in the country. The biggest impact on the Egyptian banking system from foreign banks, however, came from the joint ventures established with Egyptian banks. Other developments included the opening in Cairo in July 1979 of the Faisal-Islamic bank, with 49% Saudi and Gulf equity participation. This was the first Egyptian bank to do business according to the *Shari'a* (Islamic law). By 1987, however, the major public-sector banks (National Bank of Egypt, Banque Misr, Banque du Caire, and Bank of Alexandria) all had Islamic banking facilities. Some Islamic investment companies also appeared, although they encountered problems owing to excessive dividend payments. As a result, the Central Bank tightened its control over the banking sector in early 1987. In 2001 HSBC increased its stake in the Egyptian British Bank (renamed HSBC Bank Egypt) and Crédit Agricole Indosuez acquired a controlling stake in Crédit International d'Egypte from HSBC. However, Standard Chartered Bank's attempt to enter the market through the acquisition of a 75% stake in Egyptian American Bank collapsed in 2002.

During 1980 Egypt's first international bank, the Egyptian International Bank, was opened with a capital of US $100m. Of this capital 50% was subscribed by the country's four main banks: the National Bank of Egypt, Bank of Alexandria, Banque de Caire, and Banque Misr, with the other half being provided by the Central Bank of Egypt. In addition a National Investment Bank was established earlier in that year to monitor public investment, and there were also plans to establish an import-export bank. The fiscal year was also changed from a calendar year to begin in July.

For some years the Government had been concerned about the growth of Islamic investment companies, which attracted a significant proportion of private savings, including remittances from Egyptians working abroad, and channelled domestic funds and foreign exchange away from the official banking system—thus, in the view of the authorities, effectively constituting a large, unregulated financial sector in competition with the official banking institutions. According to the Islamic precepts under which these investment companies operate, they are not permitted to charge or pay interest (*riba*). Instead, they pay depositors out of profits, at a high rate of return (compared with the interest available from banks), from their speculations and investments at home and abroad. In June 1988 legislation was enacted requiring Islamic investment companies to become regular shareholding companies (issuing share certificates in exchange for deposits, rather than simple receipts) and placing a limit of £E50m. on their authorized capital. All companies were forbidden to take new deposits for three months, while they decided whether to comply with the new regulations or to go into liquidation. The measures provoked strong resistance among the Islamic investment companies, and many leading executives protested that they would not be able to continue in business if they complied with them. With the collapse in that year of a number of Islamic finance houses, thousands of small investors lost their savings. The Central Bank refused to intervene, and—although Egypt's Islamic banks were not directly involved—confidence in the whole sector was shaken for some time. None the less, Egypt's four principal state banks continued to offer Islamic financial services.

A new banking law, presented to parliament in November 1991, tightened the financial regulations relating to banks and strengthened the supervisory powers of the Central Bank. Under the measure, Egyptian banks were required to have paid-up capital of at least £E50m. (as against £E500,000 previously), while foreign banks had to have at least US $10m. An amendment was introduced in March 1993 to allow branches of foreign banks to take deposits and give loans in Egyptian pounds, regardless of whether they were locally incorporated or had local shareholders. By the beginning of 1997 sales of state shares had reduced the number of joint-venture banks in majority state ownership from nine to four. A committee was formed in January 1997 to plan the establishment of a new bank to provide unsecured loans to families on very low incomes. The new bank (inspired by similar institutions pioneered in Bangladesh) was to be covered by a special law. In January 1998 the Government introduced a new law to prevent banks and businesses from securing a double tax exemption by taking out loans carrying tax relief to invest in treasury bills on which earnings are tax-free. The legislation, stipulating that banks and businesses could only purchase treasury bills with their own funds, immediately prompted concern that profits would drop, owing to a significant increase in their tax burdens; share prices subsequently dropped as investors speculated on a decrease in earnings. Clarification of the law, issued in June, demonstrated that the effects of the new system were less severe than anticipated, and that banks that did not depend heavily on treasury bills and corporate bonds would not be liable to large tax increases.

In May 1998 legislation was adopted allowing the Egyptian or international private sector to invest in Egypt's four most prestigious wholly state-owned commercial banks. A similar law to privatize the four largest public insurance companies was also endorsed. Further legislation in June of that year restricted private-sector shares in the state-owned banks to just 10%, in response to concerns that conflicts between multinational and Egyptian interests might arise. In April 2000 draft legislation was approved allowing banks to extend loans for the purchase of houses under a mortgage system. The new law was viewed as a major breakthrough for the construction sector.

An incentive exchange rate was introduced in December 1984 in an effort to check a slide in the value of the Egyptian pound against the US dollar and to undercut the 'black' market in currency, which had grown following a major devaluation of the Egyptian pound, by one-half, against the US dollar in 1979. (Egypt maintained different exchange rates for specific purposes, e.g. for basic commodity transactions, for workers' remittances, for public sector purchases etc.) A series of measures by successive finance ministers, including the authorization of preferential exchange rates at Egypt's four public sector banks, failed to attract remittances from Egyptians working abroad who preferred to deal on the black market, where the rate of exchange on the US dollar remained above the official level. It was estimated that only about 40% of the estimated US $4,000m. generated annually in remittances reached Egyptian banks. In January 1985 the Minister of Finance, Dr Mustafa as-Said, established a 'floating' exchange rate to reflect more accurately the value of the Egyptian pound against the US dollar, to restrain rising imports, and to counter black market transactions by attracting remittances to the banks. However, the official rate of exchange remained some 10% below the free-market level and failed to divert remittances. Meanwhile, measures restraining imports, including the obligation to purchase letters of credit in Egyptian pounds, proved too restrictive, causing long delays for importers, particularly in the private sector, who were competing for short supplies of currency in the banks. Dr as-Said resigned at the end of March 1985 after a banking scandal arising from his 1983 decree banning banks from dealing with certain black market operators. His replacement, Dr Sultan Abu Ali, immediately withdrew the currency regulations of his predecessor, which meant that importers were once again able to fund imports by securing hard currency from the black market without having to declare the source and relaxed import restrictions.

By 1987 Egypt was under considerable pressure, particularly from the IMF, to unify its multiple exchange rates. In May 1987 the Government acted to curb the black market in currency and announced the partial 'flotation' of its currency, with a daily ('free pool') exchange rate being set by a panel consisting of representatives of eight banks, in order to attract foreign currency. The unofficial market rate persisted, but the new floating rate was much closer to it and made the federal banking system more accessible to foreign exchange. The fixed Central Bank rate was adjusted from US $1 = £E0.70 to $1 = £E1.10 in September 1989. However, the old rate was still applied to revenues from the Suez Canal and the EGPC. The commercial bank exchange rate ($1 = £E1.35 in May 1987), which was used to finance public sector imports and customs duties, was phased out by the end of March 1988, having been allowed to depreciate in order to merge with the 'free pool' rate. The IMF then requested the unification of the remaining exchange rates: the Central

Bank rate; the bank 'free pool' rate; the $1 = £E0.40 rate used for barter deals with the communist bloc; and a new rate of $1 = £E1.89, introduced in April 1988, for customs duties. Under reforms agreed with the IMF, which became operative in late February 1991, a new exchange system was introduced. It provided for the determination by the commercial banks of a free-market rate of exchange, although an 'official' Central Bank rate continued to be set at not more than 5% less (in terms of the Egyptian pound's free-market value) than the commercial bank rate. This two-tier system resulted in an effective devaluation of nearly 40% compared with the official rate in the previous year, and was officially stated to be a prelude to a unified exchange rate and full currency convertibility commencing in February 1992.

Total deposits in the Egyptian banking system stood at £E159,000m. (nearly two-thirds of this in local currency) at the beginning of February 1993—an increase of almost 50% over the previous six months, as depositors took advantage of the first opportunity for decades to earn a positive return on their money (Egypt's inflation rate having fallen to around 10% while bank deposit rates stood at 15%). The attractiveness of the local currency (which had maintained a stable exchange rate for over a year in conditions of virtually free convertibility) was such that the Central Bank was buying about US $1,000m. of 'surplus' foreign exchange each month—a development which helped to boost Egypt's foreign-exchange reserves to a record $14,300m. during the first quarter of 1993. By mid-1994 the country's foreign-exchange reserves had reached $16,600m. The amount of surplus liquidity in the Egyptian banking system was estimated at around £E4,400m. in the first half of 1994. Surplus liquidity in the banking system was substantially reduced in April 1995 when a £E3,000m. issue of five-year treasury bonds was fully subscribed. A 49% ceiling on foreign banks' shareholdings in some local joint-venture and private banks was abolished in June 1995. The same amending legislation increased the maximum amount that any bank could lend to a single creditor (hitherto defined as a sum equal to 25% of the bank's capital) to a sum equal to 30% of its capital. At the end of 1996 Egypt's official reserves exceeded $18,000m., representing nearly 15 months' import cover.

The drive towards liberalization during the late 1990s came at a cost. In January 1999 the stock market index was more than 25% higher than in January 1998. However, after a sharp rise in January 2000, the market stagnated, reflecting Egypt's ongoing liquidity crisis—the major causes of which were the government arrears to the private sector, increased expenditure by the Government of Kamal Ahmad al-Ganzouri on major infrastructure projects, and a depletion in the main sources of hard currency (principally petroleum sales, tourism, and Suez Canal revenues). Market capitalization declined from £E138,000m. in January to under £E120,000m. in June. In February Dr Atif Obeid promised to restore growth by injecting an extra £E2,500m. per month into the economy. The Prime Minister's plan was immediately criticized as being unrealistic, especially as the National Investment Bank (the usual source of short-term capital) was refusing to issue bridging loans for the first time since 1981. Eventually, intervention by the Government and the Central Bank in mid-2000 resulted in the informal abandonment of the Egyptian pound's fixed exchange rate against the US dollar. The value of the national currency subsequently declined substantially, from $1 = £E3.40 in May 2000 to $1 = £E4.09 at the beginning of January 2001. Government assertions that currency volatility in the second half of 2000 had been caused by speculative activities by money-changers were generally dismissed by many observers, who largely held fundamental weaknesses in exchange-rate policy and in the execution of the programme for the divestment of state assets as being responsible for the recent depreciations. In late January 2001 Obeid announced a series of fiscal reforms, including the transfer of control of the rate of exchange to the Central Bank. On 30 January the Central Bank introduced a new 'managed peg' system whereby the currency would be allowed to fluctuate within a narrow band (initially of 1%) either side of the official rate set by the Central Bank: this rate was initially established at $1 = £E3.85. While the adoption of what was considered a more appropriate official rate of exchange was broadly welcomed, the trading band was considered by some

analysts as being too restrictive to eradicate the black market for the currency: it was predicted that frequent intervention by the Central Bank would be required. On 5 August the Bank apparently moved decisively, adjusting the official rate to $1 = £E4.15, and widening the trading band to 3% either side of the new rate. The immediate impact of this was to allow an official trading rate, at its highest level, exceeding the prevailing black-market rate

Having appointed a new governor in October 2001, the Government granted the Central Bank of Egypt independent status with sole discretion over monetary policy and an extension of its supervisory role. The following month the Ministry of Economy was disbanded and its functions transferred to the Central Bank. In December, in response to the difficulties caused by the collapse in tourism after the September terrorist attacks in the USA in September, the Central Bank announced a further 7.5% devaluation in the currency to a central rate of $1 = £E4.50, with the trading band maintained and proposals to inject $500m. into the market immediately and a further $1,500m. over the next six months.

In 2001 a debut sovereign Eurobond was issued; heavily oversubscribed, it raised a total of US $1,500m. Also, a law promoting the development of a mortgage market with provisions for strengthening the potential claim of lenders over property collateral was passed. Following a review of existing financial legislation, a draft money-laundering law was approved in 2002.

FOREIGN TRADE AND PAYMENTS

Despite careful government examination of all external payments, the pressure of population on resources is the crucial factor responsible for keeping the balance of payments in a precarious state. Although the development of the petroleum sector has alleviated the difficulties to some extent, food and live animal imports have continued to be substantial, accounting for 20.5% of the value of total imports in 1997 (compared with 26% in 1965), while imports of machinery and transport equipment accounted for 26.9% in 1997 (compared with 23.0% in 1965). Exports were traditionally agricultural goods, with raw cotton accounting for almost one-third of the value in 1977. However, by 1979 a change was apparent, with crude petroleum accounting for 30% of the exports against raw cotton's 21%. However, while by 1982 crude oil accounted for 55% of exports, this proportion fell to 40% by 1990, as domestic requirements outstripped production, and in 1997 crude petroleum accounted for only 17.1% of exports, while raw cotton accounted for only 2.8%.

In 1995/96 there was a visible trade deficit of US $9,498m. (exports $4,4,609m., imports $14,017m.), a surplus of $5,791.5m. on services (payments $4,845m., receipts $10,636m.), and net inward transfers totalling $3,521m. (of which private transfers accounted for $2,798m.). There was an overall current-account deficit of $185m. Petroleum revenues contributed 48.3% of merchandise export earnings, while Suez Canal charges contributed 17.7%, and tourism 28.3%, of income from services in 1995/96. The 1996/97 balance-of-payments statistics showed a visible trade deficit of $10,219m. (exports $5,345m., imports $15,565m.), a surplus of $6,193m. on services (payments $5,048m., receipts $11,241m.), and net inward transfers totalling $4,145m. (of which private transfers accounted for $3,256m.). The overall current account reverted to a surplus, totalling $118.6m. Petroleum revenues contributed 48.2% of merchandise export earnings, while Suez Canal charges contributed 16.4%, and tourism 32.4%, of income from services. In 1997/98 Egypt recorded a visible trade deficit of $11,771m. (exports $5,128m., imports $16,899m.), a surplus of $4,692m. on services (payments $5,764m., receipts $10,455m.), and net inward transfers totalling $4,600m. (of which private transfers accounted for $3,718m.). The overall current account was in deficit, at $2,479m. As world oil prices declined, the contribution of petroleum revenues fell to 33.7% of merchandise export earnings; Suez Canal charges accounted for 16.9% of income from services, and tourism for 28.1%. The visible trade deficit widened further in 1998/99, to $12,563m. (exports $445m., imports $17,008m.), although the surplus on services increased to $5,970m. (payments $5,056m., receipts $11,026m.) and net inward transfers to $4,869m. (private transfers $3,772m.). The overall current-account deficit narrowed to $1,724m. In that year petroleum revenues declined to $999.7m. (22.5% of merchandise export earnings), compared with $2,577.8 in 1996/97. Suez Canal charges contributed 16.1% of services receipts, and tourism 29.3%. The strong recovery in petroleum in the second half of 1999 boosted petroleum receipts within the balance of payments to $2,272.9m. in 1999/2000—or 35.6% of export earnings of $6,387.7m.—and was reflected in a narrowing of the visible trade deficit in that year, to $11,472.3m., despite increased spending on imports ($17,860.0m.). The surplus on services was $5,629.7m. (payments $5,795.9m., receipts $11,425.6m.), while net inward transfers totalled $4,679.5m. (private transfers $3,747.1m.). The current-account deficit narrowed further, to $1,163.1m. Suez Canal receipts (at $1,780.8m.) contributed 15.5% of services income, and tourism receipts (at $4,313.8m.) 37.8%. Preliminary figures for 2000/01 indicated a further marked improvement in the balance of payments, with the overall current account in deficit of just $33.1m. The visible trade deficit was recorded at $9,353.6m. (exports $7,078.2m., imports $16,431.8m.); net services income at $5,578.4m. (payments $6,118.0m., receipts $11,696.4m.), and net transfers at $3,742.2m. (private transfers $2,972.9m.). Revenue from petroleum, at $2,632.4m., contributed 37.2% of export receipts, while Suez Canal receipts ($1,842.5m.) and tourism ($4,316.9m.) accounted for 15.8% and 36.9%, respectively, of services income. The overall balance of payments showed a surplus of $575m. and a small deficit on the current account in the first quarter of 2001/02. Free zone exports increased to $947m. in 2001 from $601m. in 2000 and were expected to exceed $1,000m. in 2002.

Negotiations were in progress between Egypt and the EU in 1997 for a partnership agreement within the framework of the EU's Euro-Mediterranean initiative to phase out most trade barriers between the EU and Mediterranean countries, which would be eligible for EU grants and 'soft' loans during the transition period. The EU's reluctance to move towards completely free trade in agricultural produce as well as manufactures was strongly challenged by Egypt, which emphasized that it was currently the world's 12th largest importer of European farm produce. On 25 June 2001 Egypt signed the partnership agreement with the EU, having concluded negotiations in June 1999. During the initial 12–16 year transitional period, the EU will lift quotas on imports of Egyptian textiles and agricultural goods. The agreement will also phase out tariffs on EU exports; tariffs on exports of raw materials and capital goods will be eliminated over the first three years, those on intermediate goods will be phased out between years four and nine, and duties on finished goods will be removed between years six and 13.

TRANSPORT AND TELECOMMUNICATIONS

Egypt's principal ports are at Alexandria, Port Said and Suez. In April 2001 work began on the expansion of both the Mediterranean and Red Sea port capacities to cope with traffic passing through the Suez Canal. Alexandria port was being expanded, aided by a US $95m. loan from the World Bank, and a completely new port was planned, west of Alexandria, at ed-Dikheila, with a capacity of 20m. metric tons per year, compared with Alexandria's capacity of 13m. tons. Safaga on the Red Sea was also being developed, but mainly to handle mineral imports and exports. The first stage of a port situated 16 km west of the Nile's Damietta tributary, and capable of handling up to 16m. tons of cargo per year, was opened in July 1986. A second stage would increase the port's capacity to 25m. tons per year. In 1998 the Government announced the formation of the Egyptian Company for Port Said Area Ports, to develop a huge hub port on the east bank of the bypass channel of the Suez Canal. The company would also be responsible for the construction of an industrial and storage zone in the area. The first 1.2-km section of container quay was due to open in late 2002. Plans for the construction of a port at Sharq et-Tafrea to provide tranship-ments to the eastern Mediterranean, and the construction of a port to cater primarily for industrial and distribution interests in the Suez zone, were also under discussion.

River transport is being expanded to relieve the load on roads and railways for internal distribution. Navigable waterways total about 3,100 km, of which about one-half is the Nile and the rest canals. Canals such as the Nubariya canal in the delta and the Bahr Yousuf, between Fayoum and Asyout, make it possible to link Alexandria with Upper Egypt through Cairo.

Egypt has over 5,000 km of railway. A project using loans from various sources is being undertaken to modernize the railway system and expand its carrying capacity, as well as to draw up a comprehensive national transport survey. This includes modernization of the line from Cairo to Upper Egypt, for which funding of US $300m. was sought from the World Bank in 1990, the repair of 300 km of the railway network in the south of the country, and the replacement of all locomotives in the country with modern rolling stock. Under active consideration in the early 1990s was a plan to upgrade the 160-km railway link between the Tabbia industrial zone to the south of Cairo and areas of mineral deposits in the Western Desert. Work began in mid-1995 on a project to create a rail link from Ismailia across Sinai to the town of Rafah in the Palestinian-administered Gaza Strip.

Construction of the first stage of the French-designed Cairo metro system, consisting of a 44-km line running from el-Marg in the north to Helwan in the south, began in 1982. Incorporating 34 stations, including six underground on a 4.2-km line tunnelled beneath the centre of Cairo (the first underground transport system in the Middle East and North Africa), this section connected with an existing line to Helwan; it was opened in September 1987. Construction work began in 1992 on Cairo's second metro line, running 18.3 km from the suburb of Shoubra el-Kheima to Cairo University, and was completed in three sections, in 1996, 1997 and 2000; it serves 18 stations, two of which interconnect with the first line. The US $63m. contract for an extension of the second line was awarded to a French consortium in 2001. Tenders for the construction of a third line, totalling 34.2 km, to run from Cairo International Airport to Imbaba, will be issued in 2002. The initial phase of construction of a new metro project in Alexandria began in 1999. The 55-km Alexandria Metro line was to be constructed in three phases; the first stage would be a 22-km line from Abu Qir in the east to Misr Station in the west, with the capacity to carry up to 60,000 passengers an hour; the second section, an 8-km tunnel connecting Misr Station to El-Mex, was due for completion in 2010. The final section, expected to be completed in 2015, would continue west from El-Mex for a further 15 km.

Good roads connect Cairo with Alexandria, the canal towns and Upper Egypt. In 1997 international companies were invited to submit proposals for the design, construction and maintenance of six major new highways running from Alexandria to Aswan and serving oases in the Western Desert. The routes concerned were Alexandria to Fayoum (199 km), Fayoum to Dayrout (21 km), Dayrout to Aswan (433 km), Dayrout to Al-Farafra (263 km), Al-Khârga to East Oweinat (520 km) and As-Sallum to Wadi en-Nâtrun (508 km).

In 1998 construction work began on a 2.9 km suspension bridge over the Suez Canal, designed to relieve congestion and to improve infrastructure for repopulation and industrial purposes. The bridge opened in 2001. The Government also approved the construction of two 2.6-km road tunnels beneath Old Cairo, again to facilitate the flow of traffic and to preserve the architecture in the city; the £E400m. project was completed in 2000.

EgyptAir, the state airline, operates a network of domestic and international routes. Cairo International Airport handled more than 7m. of the 11m. passengers who travelled through Egyptian airports in 1995. In 2001 plans for the construction of a new airport to the west of the city were shelved in favour of a long-delayed project to build a third passenger terminal and a new runway (costing US $550m.) at Cairo to increase the airport's annual handling capacity from 9m. to 20m. passengers. Other airport projects include the expansion of Borg el-Arab, with a high-speed rail link to Alexandria; a new terminal at Sharm esh-Sheikh; and a new cargo airport at Assiut.

In November 1997 the Government announced several measures to open up the aviation sector as part of an initiative to make the transport system more effective and improve services for exporters. The Government would abolish its 10% sales tax on imported aircraft and spare parts, no longer apply customs duties on imported aircraft, permit the private sector to utilize airports for ground services, and reduce its 45% customs duty on refrigerated airfreight to 5%.

The Egyptian telephone network was controlled by the National Telecommunications Organization (Arento—subsequently Telecom Egypt). In the late 1990s the telecommunications sector was viewed as an important area of growth and a potential magnet for foreign investment. The first private Global Standard for Mobiles (GSM) licence was awarded to Vodafone for US $516m. in 1998; and the second to ECMS (formerly the Egyptian Company for Mobile Services) at the same price. In October 1999 Egypt created a Ministry of Communications and Information Technology. In August 2000 the new ministry announced a US $1,000m. plan to modernize Egypt's telecommunications infrastructure over a three-year period. Telecom Egypt was prepared for privatization, but the transaction was suspended because of market conditions. In 2001 the Telecommunications Regulatory Authority (TRA) granted the company a $470m. licence to launch its own GSM service, which is scheduled to commence operations in December 2002 when the four-year exclusivity agreement with the existing operators expires. To attract foreign investment and expand the fixed-line system, Telecom Egypt selected the US-Kuwaiti Raneen consortium to set up a wireless local loop system at a cost of $700m.–$900m., on a revenue-sharing basis. Orascom Telecom, whose $320m. international public offering was 1.7 times over-subscribed in 2000, has emerged as the largest GSM network operator in the Middle East, Africa, and Indian sub-continent. With 21 licenses covering the region, it manages GSM networks in Algeria, Jordan, Syria, Yemen. In 2002 the company was awarded the GSM license in Tunisia. In 1998 the Government announced plans to establish a 3,000-acre zone for technological production called the Sinai Technology Valley (STV). The Government expected the zone to increase technology exports from US $200m. per year in 1998 to $2,000m. per year by 2002. Companies establishing in the STV would be entitled to tax incentives for a 10-year period. In September 2000 the Minister of Communications and Information Technology announced a three-year, $1,000m. plan to develop every aspect of information technology in Egypt.

TOURISM

The number of tourists visiting Egypt reached 2.5m. in 1990, slightly above the 1989 level, but below the original target of 2.9m. because of the impact of the Gulf crisis. Revenue from tourism was about US $2,500m. by 1989/90, making tourism one of the most dynamic sectors of the Egyptian economy. The management of several public-sector hotels has been transferred to international groups, legislation to reduce land speculation enacted, and the aviation industry liberalized. However, the industry remains one of the most immediately vulnerable to instability in the region. An increase in terrorist activity in the Middle East during the second half of 1985 and the anti-American reaction in the region, following the US air-strikes on targets in Libya in April 1986, combined to deter tourists, particularly US citizens, from visiting Egypt. The prospect of renewed and protracted instability in the region following the Iraqi invasion of Kuwait in August 1990 and the subsequent international response accordingly posed a serious threat to the sector's vital contribution to Egypt's reserves of foreign exchange. In February 1991 tourist arrivals slumped to 57,000, compared with 208,000 in February 1990. Following the end of the Gulf conflict, tourist numbers recovered rapidly, totalling 276,000 in August 1991 and reached the record figure of some 3m. in the 12 months to June 1992, over which period tourism's total contribution to the economy (including the indirect benefits not quantified in simple balance-of-payments analyses) was officially estimated at $3,500m.

None the less, the tourism industry experienced a sharp downturn in 1992/93, when a violent campaign by Islamist militants included foreign tourists as targets. The number of tourists visiting Egypt fell by about 22% in 1993, while revenue fell by 38% because the length of the average stay was shorter. Having failed to eradicate the problem of terrorism through its campaign against militant Islamists, the Government allocated US $25m. for a venture to promote tourism in 1994, with the aim of restoring revenue from this sector to its 1992 level. However, the number of visitors in the first three months of 1994 was 15% down on the 1993 level, while the average length of stay was rather shorter than in 1993. Upper Egypt (hardest hit by the terrorist campaign) reported little sign of a recovery, whereas Cairo hotels had a 60% occupancy rate and most Red Sea and Sinai resorts reported some upturn in tourist business. A similar pattern was evident in the first half of 1995, when many Upper Egypt hotels were operating at one-third of capacity, as against a two-thirds' occupancy rate in Cairo and virtually full utilization of the increasingly popular Sinai resorts. In January 1993 the World Bank had approved a $130m. loan for the development of new tourism infrastructure, within the framework of a programme, valued at some $805m., the main focus of which was the development of new resorts on Egypt's Red Sea coast. By mid-1995 work had begun on a major resort development in the Abu Soma area, while plans were well advanced for another development further up the Red Sea coast at Sahl Hashish. The Tourism Development Authority had meanwhile approved 27 new projects at locations on the south Sinai coast, where it was also inviting proposals for the development of a yacht harbour.

In 1995 there was a 24% increase in tourist arrivals, to 3.205m. (with the sharpest upturn in the last quarter of the year), followed by further growth in the first quarter of 1996. The total number of nights visitors spent in the country rose markedly, from 15.431m. in 1994 to 20.517m. in 1995. In 1996 Egypt's tourism industry recorded very strong growth, with some 3.9m. visitors spending a total of 23.8m. nights in the country and generating revenue of around £E5,043m.

Growth in the tourism industry suffered a dramatic reversal in late 1997. Fears for the safety of travellers after a terrorist attack on a German tour bus in Cairo in September, which resulted in the deaths of nine Germans and an Egyptian, were exacerbated the following month by the massacre of 58 tourists and four Egyptians in Luxor (see History). Many travel companies cancelled operations to the region, while other travellers were advised to leave immediately. In response to the attacks, in December the Government inaugurated a '100-day plan' to encourage internal tourism in the region. EgyptAir, which lost 85,000 passengers owing to cancellations in the aftermath of the attack, reduced its domestic fares by 50%; the airline announced a loss of £E240m. in 1997/98. The Government also announced a three-month moratorium on debt-service repayments by tourist ventures. Tourism companies offered discounted rates in order to entice visitors back to the region. In January 1998 68,000 tourists visited Egypt, 55% fewer than in January 1997; the number of visitors in October 1998 was 380,000, compared with 391,000 a year earlier. In 1997 Egypt's tourism industry had recorded growth, with some 4.0m. visitors spending a total of 26.6m. nights in the country and generating revenue of around £E5,847m. However, in 1998 the number of tourist arrivals fell to around 3.5m. (a total of 20.2m. nights), while tourism receipts decreased significantly, to some £E2,564m. By 1999 the tourism sector was showing signs of recovery, with the construction of new hotels and resorts continuing. Almost 4.8m. tourists visited Egypt in that year, spending 31.0m. nights in the country and generating revenue of some £E3,903m.

In the late 1990s tourism employed some 2.2m. people. In 1999 one of Egypt's leading attractions, the Great Pyramid of Cheops, was reopened following restoration. In 2001 a contract was awarded to develop a US $2,000m. luxury holiday resort planned for Port Ghaleb on the Red Sea. The resort is to include a marina for 1,000 yachts and an airport.

Tourist arrivals increased to 5.5m. in 2000/01, raising US $4,317m. in revenue. However, the Government launched a programme to support the airline industry and to expand the domestic travel market in 2002 to offset the anticipated sharp losses of tourist income arising from the September 2001 attacks on the USA. In 2002 UNESCO was to sponsor a $350m. project to design the Great Egyptian Museum to be built near the Pyramids at Giza.

Statistical Survey

Sources (unless otherwise stated): Central Agency for Public Mobilization and Statistics, POB 2086, Cairo (Nasr City); tel. (2) 4024632; fax (2) 4024099; internet www.capmas.gov.eg; Research Department, National Bank of Egypt, Cairo.

Area and Population

AREA, POPULATION AND DENSITY

Area (sq km) .	1,002,000*
Population (census results)†	
17–18 November 1986 .	48,254,238
31 December 1996	
Males .	30,351,390
Females .	28,961,524
Total .	59,312,914
Population (official estimates at mid-year)	
2001 .	67,886,000
Density (per sq km) at mid-2001 .	67.8

* 386,874 sq miles. Inhabited and cultivated territory accounts for 55,039 sq km (21,251 sq miles).

† Excluding Egyptian nationals abroad, totalling an estimated 2,250,000 in 1986 and an estimated 2,180,000 in 1996.

GOVERNORATES (estimated population at 1 January 2001)

Governorate	Area (sq km)*	Population ('000)	Capital
Cairo .	214.20	7,283	Cairo
Alexandria .	2,679.36	3,577	Alexandria
Port Said .	72.07	506	Port Said
Ismailia .	1,441.59	789	Ismailia
Suez .	17,840.42	452	Suez
Damietta .	589.17	995	Damietta
Dakahlia .	3,470.90	4,570	El-Mansoura
Sharkia. .	4,179.55	4,691	Zagazig
Kalyoubia .	1,001.09	3,584	Banha
Kafr esh-Sheikh.	3,437.12	2,403	Kafr esh-Sheikh
Gharbia .	1,942.21	3,661	Tanta
Menoufia .	1,532.13	2,994	Shebien el-Kom
Behera .	10,129.48	4,339	Damanhour
Giza .	85,153.56	5,208	Giza
Beni-Suef .	1,321.50	2,062	Beni-Suef
Fayoum .	1,827.10	2,208	El-Fayoum
Menia .	2,261.70	3,687	El-Menia
Asyout .	1,553.00	3,122	Asyout
Suhag .	1,547.20	3,401	Suhag
Qena .	1,795.60	2,697	Qena
Luxor .	55.00	392	Luxor
Aswan .	678.45	1,043	Aswan
Red Sea .	203,685.00	172	Hurghada
El-Wadi el-Gidid .	376,505.00	156	El-Kharga
Matruh. .	212,112.00	240	Matruh
North Sinai. .	27,574.00	280	El-Areesh
South Sinai. .	33,140.00	60	Et-Tour

* The sum of these figures is 997,738.40 sq km, compared with the official national total of 1,002,000 sq km.

PRINCIPAL TOWNS (population at 1996 census)*

Cairo (Al-Qahirah, the capital) .	6,789,479	Asyout (Asyut) . .	343,498
		Zagazig (Az-Zaqaziq) .	267,351
Alexandria		El-Fayum (Al-Fayyum)	260,964
(Al-Iskandariyah) .	3,328,196	Ismailia (Al-Ismailiyah)	254,477
Giza (Al-Jizah) .	2,221,868	Kafr ed-Dawar	
Shoubra el-Kheima		(Kafr ad-Dawwar) .	231,978
(Shubra al-Khaymah)	870,716	Aswan . .	219,017
Port Said (Bur Sa'id) .	469,533	Damanhour (Damanhur)	212,203
Suez (As-Suways) .	417,610	El-Menia (Al-Minya) .	201,360
El-Mahalla el-Koubra		Beni-Suef (Bani-Suwayf)	172,032
(Al-Mahallah al-Kubra)	395,402	Qena (Qina) . .	171,275
Tanta . .	371,010	Suhag (Sawhaj) . .	170,125
El-Mansoura		Shebien el-Kom	
(Al-Mansurah). .	369,621	(Shibin al-Kawn) .	159,909
Luxor (Al-Uqsor). .	360,503		

* Figures refer to provisional population. Revised figures include: Cairo 6,800,992; Alexandria 3,339,076; Port Said 472,335; Suez 417,527.

BIRTHS, MARRIAGES AND DEATHS

	Registered live births		Registered marriages		Registered deaths	
	Number	Rate (per 1,000)	Number	Rate (per 1,000)	Number	Rate (per 1,000)
1993 .	1,622,000	29.4	432,000	7.8	382,000	6.9
1994 .	1,636,000	29.0	452,000	8.0	388,000	6.9
1995 .	1,605,000	27.9	471,000	8.2	385,000	6.7
1996 .	1,662,000	28.3	489,000	8.3	380,000	6.5
1997 .	1,655,000	27.5	493,000	8.2	389,000	6.5
1998 .	1,687,000	27.5	504,000	8.2	399,000	6.5
1999 .	1,693,000	27.0	520,000	8.3	401,000	6.4
2000* .	1,753,000	27.4	579,000	9.1	406,000	6.4

* Provisional figures.

Expectation of life (WHO estimates, years at birth, 2000): Males 65.4; Females 69.1 (Source: WHO, *World Health Report*).

ECONOMICALLY ACTIVE POPULATION
(sample surveys, '000 persons aged 15 years and over)

	1997	1998	1999
Agriculture, hunting and forestry	4,860.0	4,723.1	4,684.4
Fishing	90.9	99.6	122.6
Mining and quarrying . .	42.0	69.0	47.4
Manufacturing . .	2,133.5	2,042.2	2,207.6
Electricity, gas and water supply	192.7	203.4	207.0
Construction. . .	1,152.9	1,287.1	1,320.1
Wholesale and retail trade; repair of motor vehicles, motorcycles and personal and household goods . .	1,745.8	1,949.9	2,020.2
Hotels and restaurants . .	217.1	277.0	299.6
Transport, storage and communications . .	923.2	954.1	1,060.2
Financial intermediation . .	180.0	174.3	185.2
Real estate, renting and business activities . . .	207.0	266.2	273.0
Public administration and defence; compulsory social security . .	1,565.3	1,628.6	1,631.7
Education . . .	1,715.1	1,665.2	1,764.5
Health and social work . .	410.4	485.8	531.1
Other community, social and personal service activities . .	304.4	316.3	356.5
Private households with employed persons . .	39.5	40.3	38.0
Activities not adequately defined	50.1	1.2	0.9
Total employed . .	15,830.0	16,183.0	16,750.2
Unemployed . . .	1,446.4	1,447.5	1,480.5
Total labour force . .	17,276.4	17,630.5	18,230.7
Males . . .	13,514.5	13,890.0	14,337.2
Females. . . .	3,761.9	3,740.5	3,893.5

Source: ILO, *Yearbook of Labour Statistics*.

Health and Welfare

KEY INDICATORS

Fertility (births per woman, 2000)	3.1
Under-5 mortality rate (per 1,000 live births, 2000). . .	43
HIV/AIDS (% of persons aged 15–49, 2001)	0.10
Physicians (per 1,000 head, 1996)	20.2
Hospital beds (per 1,000 head, 1997)	2.1
Health expenditure (1998): US $ per head (PPP) . . .	144
% of GDP	4.6
public (% of total) . . .	30.8
Access to water (% of persons, 2000)	95
Access to sanitation (% of persons, 2000)	94
Human Development Index (2000): ranking . . .	115
value	0.642

For sources and definitions, see explanatory note on p. vi.

Agriculture

PRINCIPAL CROPS ('000 metric tons)

	1998	1999	2000
Wheat	6,093.2	6,346.6	6,564.1
Rice (paddy)	4,474.1	5,817.0	6,000.5
Barley	148.0	114.0	99.4
Maize	6,336.8	6,143.4	6,474.5
Sorghum	887.3	954.2	941.2
Potatoes.	1,984.0	1,808.9	1,783.6
Sweet potatoes . . .	225.6	253.1	275.9
Taro (Coco yam) . . .	76.9	47.1	44.1
Sugar cane	14,352.8	15,253.6	15,668.3
Sugar beet	1,951.2	2,559.7	2,890.4
Dry broad beans . . .	523.1	307.1	353.9
Other pulses. . . .	63.5	72.1	75.3*
Groundnuts (in shell). . .	132.4	180.8	187.2
Olives	200.0	287.1	289.1*
Cottonseed	385.2	367.6	367.6*
Cabbages	525.7	497.9	574.8
Artichokes	40.3	43.8	87.9
Lettuce	165.5	159.6	176.4*
Tomatoes	5,753.3	6,273.8	6,354.4
Cauliflowers	114.7	110.8	113.2
Pumpkins, squash and gourds .	616.3	648.8	649.6
Cucumbers and gherkins* .	258.0	260.0	260.0
Aubergines (Eggplants)* . .	560.0	562.0	562.0
Chillies and green peppers .	410.8	388.1	369.0*
Dry onions	722.7	889.8	763.0
Garlic	173.6	224.1	266.6
Green beans	179.4	200.0	202.8
Green peas	158.8	189.1	340.1
Carrots	129.5	122.1	137.7
Okra*	75.0	76.0	76.0
Other vegetables* . . .	501.0	498.7	502.9
Bananas	655.8	729.0	736.0
Oranges	1,441.2	1,636.6	1,640.1
Tangerines, mandarins, clementines and satsumas .	421.8	420.0*	420.0*
Lemons and limes . .	252.5	278.6	282.6
Apples	388.5	415.6	418.6
Peaches and nectarines . .	429.9	301.2	302.7
Strawberries. . . .	52.3	53.7	70.7
Grapes	957.7	1,009.6	1,013.1
Watermelons	1,409.4	1,670.3	1,507.0
Cantaloupes and other melons .	467.4	773.6	718.1
Figs	220.8	203.0	204.5
Mangoes	222.7	287.2	289.2
Dates	839.8	906.0	890.3*
Other fruits and berries* . .	464.3	459.6	466.5
Cotton (lint)	229.7	233.1	228.0

* FAO estimate(s).   † Unofficial figure.

Source: FAO.

LIVESTOCK ('000 head, year ending September)

	1998	1999	2000
Cattle	3,216.7	3,417.6	3,450.0*
Buffaloes	3,149.4	3,329.7	3,350.0*
Sheep	4,351.8	4,390.7	4,450.0*
Goats	3,261.0	3,308.2	3,300.0*
Pigs*	28.5	29.0	29.5
Horses*	45.0	45.5	45.7
Asses*	2,995.0	3,000.0	3,050.0
Camels*	113.0	116.0	120.0
Rabbits*	9,000.0	9,200.0	9,250.0
Chickens	86,000.0	87,000.0*	88,000.0*
Ducks*	9,100.0	9,200.0	9,200.0
Geese*	8,921.0	9,000.0	9,100.0
Turkeys*	1,450.0	1,800.0	1,850.0

* FAO estimate(s).

Source: FAO.

LIVESTOCK PRODUCTS ('000 metric tons)

	1998	1999	2000
Beef and veal	252.0	232.8	238.5
Buffalo meat	266.2	277.0	285.3*
Mutton and lamb . . .	65.0	82.3	84.7*
Goat meat	30.0	30.4	31.3*
Pig meat*	3.0	3.0	3.0
Camel meat	25.0	33.6	33.9*
Rabbit meat	67.8	69.3	69.6
Poultry meat	534.9	536.8	563.9
Other meat*	9.6	9.8	10.0
Cows' milk	1,351.9	1,596.9	1,644.8*
Buffaloes' milk . . .	2,022.4	2,018.2	2,078.7*
Sheep's milk* . . .	92.5	93.0	93.0
Goats' milk*	14.5	15.0	15.0
Butter	91.4	96.1	96.1*
Cheese	427.0	464.3	464.3
Hen eggs	168.1	168.3	169.9*
Honey	8.2	8.1	8.1*
Wool: greasy	7.0	7.2	7.3*
scoured* . . .	3.2	3.3	3.3
Cattle hides	22.1	20.4	27.0
Buffalo hides	23.1	24.0	34.0
Sheepskins	8.0	10.1	10.3
Goatskins	4.2	4.3	4.4

* FAO estimate(s).

Source: FAO.

Forestry

ROUNDWOOD REMOVALS
(FAO estimates, '000 cubic metres, excluding bark)

	1997	1998	1999
Industrial wood	129	131	134
Fuel wood	2,647	2,698	2,749
Total	2,776	2,829	2,883

2000: Annual removals as in 1999 (FAO estimates).

Source: FAO.

SAWNWOOD PRODUCTION
('000 cubic metres, incl. railway sleepers)

	1997	1998	1999
Total	—	101	101*

* FAO estimate.

2000: Production as in 1999 (FAO estimate).

Source: FAO.

Fishing

('000 metric tons, live weight)

	1997	1998	1999
Capture .	345.2	365.6	380.5
Nile tilapia	131.0	128.4	112.8
Mudfish	22.4	21.6	21.5
Other mullets .	16.6	18.0	20.8
Sardinellas	16.3	28.9	44.9
Aquaculture .	73.5	139.4	226.3
Common carp .	22.3	50.8	73.7
Nile tilapia	30.4	52.8	104.0
Flathead grey mullet	16.0	28.4	43.0
Total catch	418.7	505.0	606.8

Source: FAO, *Yearbook of Fishery Statistics.*

Mining

('000 metric tons, year ending 30 June)

	1997/98	1998/99	1999/2000*
Crude petroleum .	40,000	4,000	n.a.
Natural gas .	10,434	11,872	14,500
Iron ore†	3,001	3,002	2,932
Salt (unrefined) .	2,488	2,588	1,990
Phosphate rock .	1,059	1,165	1,177
Gypsum (crude) .	2,423	2,666	3,027
Kaolin .	286	314	205

* Figures are provisional.
† Figures refer to gross weight. The estimated iron content is 50%.

Industry

SELECTED PRODUCTS

('000 metric tons, unless otherwise indicated, year ending 30 June)

	1997/98	1998/99	1999/2000
Cottonseed oil (refined) .	306	290	260
Cigarettes (million) .	52	51	53
Jute yarn .	15	10	5
Jute fabrics .	13	9	4
Wool yarn .	12	12	15
Rubber tyres and tubes ('000)† .	3,502	3,598	2,662
Caustic soda (Sodium hydroxide) .	51	58	44
Phosphate fertilizers‡	365	378	390
Jet fuels .	860	939	920
Kerosene .	1,260	1,072	1,011
Distillate fuel oils .	5,889	6,007	5,989
Residual fuel oil (Mazout) .	12,700	12,773	11,785
Petroleum bitumen (asphalt) .	714	954	957
Cement .	15,480	11,933*	n.a.
Passenger motor cars—assembly (number) .	13,337	11,629*	n.a.
Electric energy (million kWh) .	62,300	62,300*	n.a.

* Estimate(s).
† Tyres and inner tubes for road motor vehicles (including motorcycles) and bicycles.
‡ Production in terms of phosphoric acid.

Finance

CURRENCY AND EXCHANGE RATES

Monetary Units

1,000 millièmes = 100 piastres = 5 tallaris = 1 Egyptian pound (£E).

Sterling, Dollar and Euro Equivalents (31 May 2002)

£1 sterling = £E6.600;
US $1 = £E4.500;
€1 = £E4.224;
£E100 = £15.15 sterling = $22.22 = €23.67.

Note: From February 1991 foreign-exchange transactions were conducted through only two markets, the primary market and the free market. With effect from 8 October 1991, the primary market was eliminated, and all foreign-exchange transactions are effected through the free market. In January 2001 a new exchange rate mechanism was introduced, whereby the value of the Egyptian pound would be allowed to fluctuate within narrow limits: initially, as much as 1% above or below a rate that was set by the Central Bank of Egypt but would be adjusted periodically in response to market conditions. For external trade purposes, the average value of the Egyptian pound was 29.452 US cents in 1999, 28.796 US cents in 2000 and 25.237 cents in 2001.

STATE PUBLIC BUDGET (£E million, year ending 30 June)

Revenue	1998/99	1999/2000*	2000/01†
Current revenue .	67,207	71,898	86,294
Central Government	62,758	66,890	64,348
Tax revenue .	48,096	50,869	62,909
Taxes on income and profits .	15,641	17,550	27,788
Domestic taxes on goods and services .	14,313	16,000	18,000
Customs duties .	10,108	10,000	13,000
Stamp duties .	3,342	3,324	4,121
Other current revenue .	14,662	16,021	21,946
Profit transfers .	9,802	10,856	13,406
Petroleum Authority .	2,227	2,901	4,575
Suez Canal Authority .	2,914	3,000	3,500
Central Bank of Egypt	3,222	3,500	3,200
Local government .	4,449	2,879	1,404
Service authorities .	1,576	2,129	35
Capital revenue .	6,072	4,833	11,644
Total	73,279	76,731	97,938

Expenditure	1998/99	1999/2000*	2000/01†
Current expenditure .	61,117	68,610	85,688
Wages .	18,833	22,459	28,767
Pensions .	5,009	6,228	8,090
Goods and services .	3,888	3,946	3,884
Defence .	8,290	8,321	3,727
Public debt interest .	16,406	18,735	20,400
Local .	14,081	16,435	18,400
Foreign .	2,325	2,300	2,000
Subsidies .	4,498	5,387	5,789
Capital expenditure (net) .	24,892	20,452	26,011
Total	86,009	89,062	111,699

* Provisional figures. † Projections.

INTERNATIONAL RESERVES (US $ million at 31 December)

	1999	2000	2001
Gold* .	475	511	488
IMF special drawing rights .	41	48	35
Reserve position in IMF .	165	156	—
Foreign exchange .	14,278	12,913	12,891
Total	14,959	13,629	13,414

* Valued at market-related prices.

Source: IMF, *International Financial Statistics.*

MONEY SUPPLY (£E million at 31 December)

	1999	2000	2001
Currency outside banks . .	35,310	37,902	40,548
Demand deposits at deposit money banks.	20,506	21,747	23,515
Total money (incl. others) . .	59,066	62,195	67,078

Source: IMF, *International Financial Statistics*.

COST OF LIVING (Consumer Price Index; base: 1990 = 100)

	1998	1999	2000
Food, beverages and tobacco . .	190.9	203.4	208.5
Fuel and light . . .	324.1	313.6	336.1
Clothing and footwear . .	220.8	226.6	232.2
Rent	154.8	155.0	155.2
All items (incl. others) . . .	207.5	218.4	224.4

Source: ILO, *Yearbook of Labour Statistics*.

2001: Food 210.7; All items 229.4 (Source: UN, *Monthly Bulletin of Statistics*).

NATIONAL ACCOUNTS (£E million, year ending 30 June)

Expenditure on the Gross Domestic Product (at current prices)

	1997/98	1998/99	1999/2000
Government final consumption expenditure	28,250	30,420	32,800
Private final consumption expenditure	208,620	220,830	245,500
Increase in stocks . . .	5,610	7,950	7,500
Gross fixed capital formation .	66,100	69,170	72,900
Total domestic expenditure .	308,580	328,370	358,700
Exports of goods and services .	45,540	45,780	54,300
Less Imports of goods and services	73,900	71,700	76,500
GDP in purchasers' values .	280,200*	302,400*	336,500

* Including statistical discrepancy.

Source: IMF, *International Financial Statistics*.

Gross Domestic Product by Economic Activity (at constant 1996/97 factor cost)

	1998/99	1999/2000	2000/01
Agriculture, hunting, forestry and fishing	45,530	47,260	49,110
Mining and quarrying . . } Manufacturing . . . . }	67,401	72,324	78,871
Electricity	4,855	5,228	5,634
Construction	15,580	16,753	18,261
Transport and communications .	24,874	26,179	27,616
Tourism, restaurants and hotels .	3,709	4,687	5,228
Trade, finance and insurance .	58,441	62,704	67,491
Government services and social insurance	21,088	22,134	23,252
Other services	26,951	28,579	30,308
Total	268,429	285,848	305,771

BALANCE OF PAYMENTS (US $ million)

	1999	2000	2001
Exports of goods f.o.b. . . .	5,237	7,061	7,025
Imports of goods f.o.b. . . .	−15,165	−15,382	−13,960
Trade balance	−9,928	−8,321	−6,935
Exports of services . . .	9,494	9,803	9,042
Imports of services . . .	−6,452	−7,513	−7,037
Balance on goods and services	−6,886	−6,031	−4,929
Other income received . .	1,788	1,871	1,468
Other income paid . . .	−1,045	−983	−885
Balance on goods, services and income	−6,143	−5,143	−4,346
Current transfers received . .	4,564	4,224	4,056
Current transfers paid . .	−55	−52	−98
Current balance	−1,635	−971	−388
Direct investment abroad. .	−38	−51	−12
Direct investment from abroad .	1,065	1,235	510
Portfolio investment assets .	−22	−3	−2
Portfolio investment liabilities	617	269	1,463
Other investment assets . .	−1,805	−2,991	−1,261
Other investment liabilities .	−1,240	−105	−509
Net errors and omissions . .	−1,558	587	−1,146
Overall balance	−4,614	−2,030	−1,345

Source: IMF, *International Financial Statistics*.

External Trade

Note: Figures exclude trade in military goods.

PRINCIPAL COMMODITIES (distribution by SITC, US $ million)

Imports c.i.f.	1997	1998	1999
Food and live animals . . .	2,698.6	2,658.3	2,917.5
Cereals and cereal preparations .	1,257.6	1,253.4	1,298.2
Wheat and meslin (unmilled) .	821.0	813.9	602.8
Maize (unmilled) . . .	385.4	388.1	652.5
Crude materials (inedible) except fuels	1,119.8	1,182.0	1,068.3
Cork and wood . . .	538.1	589.3	509.5
Simply worked wood and railway sleepers.	502.2	553.3	473.2
Simply worked coniferous wood	410.3	444.8	369.6
Mineral fuels, lubricants, etc.	243.4	801.3	977.9
Petroleum, petroleum products, etc.	88.8	611.0	695.2
Crude petroleum oils, etc. .	0.0	439.9	417.3
Animal and vegetable oils, fats and waxes	484.3	534.7	415.8
Fixed vegetable oils and fats .	444.7	467.0	369.3
Chemicals and related products	1,727.2	1,785.6	1,830.9
Artificial resins, plastic materials, etc.	584.2	545.7	584.4
Products of polymerization, etc.	469.5	431.5	461.8
Basic manufactures . . .	2,574.7	3,148.6	2,876.5
Paper, paperboard and manufactures	388.7	511.8	452.8
Iron and steel	919.8	1,162.8	887.7
Machinery and transport equipment	3,547.0	4,311.4	4,187.6
Machinery specialized for particular industries . .	768.0	1,143.9	936.5
General industrial machinery, equipment and parts . .	791.2	861.3	974.1
Electrical machinery, apparatus, etc.	796.2	1,063.2	1,143.3
Road vehicles and parts* . .	596.0	665.7	582.9
Miscellaneous manufactured articles	533.7	681.8	664.6
Total (incl. others)	13,168.5	16,478.6	15,962.1

* Excluding tyres, engines and electrical parts.

Exports f.o.b.	1997	1998	1999
Food and live animals	269.6	364.4	276.4
Cereals and cereal preparations	77.1	140.3	95.9
Rice	71.4	135.2	87.6
Vegetables and fruit	140.4	184.3	134.5
Crude materials (inedible) except fuels	202.9	240.4	315.4
Textile fibres (excl. wool tops) and waste	117.4	163.8	245.8
Cotton	111.1	158.3	239.5
Raw cotton (excl. linters)	110.2	158.2	239.5
Mineral fuels, lubricants, etc.	1,772.3	943.4	1,292.3
Petroleum, petroleum products, etc.	1,731.8	911.6	1,261.3
Crude petroleum oils, etc.	668.2	162.0	293.0
Refined petroleum products	968.4	733.5	960.3
Residual fuel oils	886.2	685.5	908.5
Chemicals and related products	197.8	265.5	264.0
Basic manufactures	1,003.9	825.6	697.2
Textile yarn, fabrics, etc.	533.4	440.9	355.1
Textile yarn	285.0	230.1	128.1
Cotton yarn	280.6	225.6	123.5
Other non-metal mineral manufactures	121.2	54.9	65.0
Iron and steel	108.5	113.8	72.6
Non-ferrous metals	151.1	137.7	117.8
Aluminium and aluminium alloys	148.7	136.1	115.4
Unwrought aluminium and alloys	125.5	120.9	100.8
Miscellaneous manufactured articles	395.2	428.0	423.3
Clothing and accessories (excl. footwear)	258.9	333.4	278.1
Total (incl. others)	3,908.0	3,195.3	3,500.9

Source: UN, *International Trade Statistics Yearbook*.

PRINCIPAL TRADING PARTNERS
(countries of consignment, US $ million)

Imports c.i.f.	1997	1998	1999
Argentina	339.4	373.4	196.3
Australia	480.3	291.3	435.0
Belgium	206.4	232.3	—
Brazil	257.3	332.5	318.2
China, People's Repub.	295.6	418.5	620.6
Finland	177.4	237.4	206.1
France (incl. Monaco)	805.4	923.6	786.6
Germany	1,141.8	1,408.0	1,382.1
India	223.1	296.7	269.2
Indonesia	95.9	192.7	196.4
Ireland	140.2	187.4	214.1
Italy	929.9	1,111.1	1,049.3
Japan	446.5	502.0	520.9
Korea, Republic	233.1	364.7	349.9
Malaysia	232.5	248.5	196.5
Netherlands	379.2	361.4	373.6
Romania	218.5	224.1	211.7
Russia	379.2	374.8	402.5
Saudi Arabia	440.3	612.7	698.4
Spain	221.4	252.2	334.1
Sweden	299.8	349.7	310.4
Switzerland-Liechtenstein	340.8	281.1	245.1
Turkey	174.1	487.1	356.6
Ukraine	230.9	299.4	224.0
United Kingdom	427.0	516.2	477.5
USA	1,719.8	2,073.9	2,295.8
Total (incl. others)	13,168.5	16,478.6	15,962.1

Exports f.o.b.	1997	1998	1999
Belgium-Luxembourg	62.8	65.0	—
France (incl. Monaco)	150.2	126.2	134.4
Germany	265.6	127.6	108.5
Greece	175.0	90.2	103.3
India	44.0	41.7	134.5
Iraq	20.0	38.5	59.9
Israel	327.9	140.4	186.9
Italy	438.0	319.9	352.5
Japan	90.8	55.6	44.5
Korea, Republic	60.4	48.0	33.7
Libya	69.6	75.0	42.1
Netherlands	264.4	249.3	249.3
Portugal	40.4	31.4	28.5
Romania	64.3	35.5	21.6
Saudi Arabia	138.5	176.3	97.7
Singapore	152.7	62.8	110.7
Spain	111.9	61.5	118.9
Syria	34.6	45.5	41.7
Turkey	96.6	117.5	96.5
United Arab Emirates	34.2	40.5	33.2
United Kingdom	90.2	110.7	88.5
USA	447.2	389.7	435.7
Total (incl. others)	3,908.0	3,195.3	3,500.9

Source: UN, *International Trade Statistics Yearbook*.

Transport

RAILWAYS (traffic, year ending 30 June)

	1996/97	1997/98	1998/99*
Passengers (million)	1,218	1,314	1,395
Passenger-km (million)	52,929	56,667	n.a.

* Estimate.

1995/96: Freight ton-km (million): 4,117 (Source: UN, *Statistical Yearbook*).

ROAD TRAFFIC (licensed motor vehicles in use at 31 December)

	1995*	1996	1997
Passenger cars	1,280,000	1,099,583	1,154,753
Buses and coaches	36,630	39,781	43,740
Lorries and vans	387,000	489,542	510,766
Motorcycles and mopeds	397,000	427,864	439,756

* Estimates from IRF, *World Road Statistics*.

SHIPPING
Merchant Fleet (registered at 31 December)

	1999	2000	2001
Number of vessels	374	372	364
Displacement ('000 grt)	1,368.0	1,346.3	1,350.4

Source: Lloyd's Register-Fairplay, *World Fleet Statistics*.

International sea-borne freight traffic ('000 metric tons, incl. ships' stores, 1998): Goods loaded 23,868; Goods unloaded 31,152 (Source: UN, *Monthly Bulletin of Statistics*).

Suez Canal Traffic

	1998	1999	2000
Transits (number)	13,472	13,490	14,141
Displacement ('000 net tons)	386,069	384,994	438,962
Northbound goods traffic ('000 metric tons)	160,346	153,582	209,446
Southbound goods traffic ('000 metric tons)	118,107	153,088	158,535
Net tonnage of tankers ('000)	89,976	67,872	105,237

Source: Suez Canal Authority, *Yearly Report*.

CIVIL AVIATION (traffic on scheduled services)

			1996	1997	1998
Kilometres flown (million)	.	.	62	65	63
Passengers carried ('000) .	.	.	4,282	4,416	4,022
Passenger-km (million)	.	.	8,742	9,018	8,036
Total ton-km (million)	.	.	993	1,029	989

Source: UN, *Statistical Yearbook*.

Tourism

ARRIVALS BY NATIONALITY ('000)*

						1998	1999	2000
France .	.	.	.	.	.	175.3	313.0	379.9
Germany	.	.	.	.	.	273.8	547.9	786.3
Israel .	.	.	.	.	.	372.1	415.3	326.5
Italy .	.	.	.	.	.	373.1	667.5	752.2
Jordan .	.	.	.	.	.	78.2	72.4	78.5
Kuwait .	.	.	.	.	.	69.8	70.2	64.0
Libya .	.	.	.	.	.	186.0	145.7	152.5
Netherlands .	.	.	.	.	.	107.6	123.6	142.1
Palestine	.	.	.	.	.	195.9	160.1	149.8
Saudi Arabia	.	.	.	.	.	233.6	240.7	240.2
Syria .	.	.	.	.	.	74.2	60.2	67.4
United Kingdom .	.	.	.	.	.	239.9	336.4	378.4
USA .	.	.	.	.	.	153.6	196.1	235.3
Total (incl. others)	.	.	.	.		3,453.9	4,796.5	5,506.2

* Figures refer to arrivals at frontiers of visitors from abroad. Excluding same-day visitors (excursionists), the total number of tourist arrivals (in '000) was: 3,213 in 1998; 4,489 in 1999; 5,116 in 2000.

Source: World Tourism Organization, mainly *Yearbook of Tourism Statistics*.

Tourism receipts (US $ million): 2,564 in 1998; 3,903 in 1999; 4,345 in 2000 (Source: World Tourism Organization).

Communications Media

	1999	2000	2001
Television receivers ('000 in use)	11,400	12,000	n.a.
Telephones ('000 main lines in use)	4,686.4	5,483.6	6,650.0
Facsimile machines ('000 in use)	34.2	n.a.	n.a.
Mobile cellular telephones ('000 subscribers)	481.0	1,359.9	2,793.8
Personal computers ('000 in use)	750	1,400	1,000
Internet users ('000)	200	450	600

1995: Book production 2,215 titles; 92,353,000 copies.

1996: Daily newspapers 17 (average circulation 2,400,000 copies).

1997: Radio receivers ('000 in use) 20,500.

Sources: UNESCO, *Statistical Yearbook*; International Telecommunication Union.

Education

(provisional figures, 1999/2000, unless otherwise indicated)

	Schools	Teachers†	Students
Pre-primary	3,172†	14,894	289,995*
Primary	15,533	314,528	7,224,989
Preparatory	7,544	193,469	4,345,356
Secondary			
General	1,595	79,218	1,039,958
Technical	1,826	145,050	1,913,022
Higher	356†‡	n.a.	1,316,491*

* 1996/97 figure. Source: partly UNESCO, *Statistical Yearbook*.

† 1998/99 figure(s).

‡ Official estimate.

Source: Ministry of Education.

Al-Azhar (provisional figures, 1999/2000): *Primary:* 2,631 schools; 707,633 students. *Preparatory:* 1,805 schools; 316,108 students. *Secondary:* 1,081 schools; 269,469 students.

Adult literacy rate (UNESCO estimates): 55.3% (males 66.6%; females 43.8%) in 2000 (Source: UNDP, *Human Development Report*).

Directory

The Constitution

A new Constitution for the Arab Republic of Egypt was approved by referendum on 11 September 1971.

THE STATE

Egypt is an Arab Republic with a democratic, socialist system based on the alliance of the working people and derived from the country's historical heritage and the spirit of Islam.

The Egyptian people are part of the Arab nation, who work towards total Arab unity.

Islam is the religion of the State; Arabic is its official language and the Islamic code is a principal source of legislation. The State safeguards the freedom of worship and of performing rites for all religions.

Sovereignty is of the people alone which is the source of all powers.

The protection, consolidation and preservation of the socialist gains is a national duty: the sovereignty of law is the basis of the country's rule, and the independence of immunity of the judiciary are basic guarantees for the protection of rights and liberties.

THE FUNDAMENTAL ELEMENTS OF SOCIETY

Social solidarity is the basis of Egyptian society, and the family is its nucleus.

The State ensures the equality of men and women in both political and social rights in line with the provisions of Muslim legislation.

Work is a right, an honour and a duty which the State guarantees together with the services of social and health insurance, pensions for incapacity and unemployment.

The economic basis of the Republic is a socialist democratic system based on sufficiency and justice in a manner preventing exploitation.

Ownership is of three kinds: public, co-operative and private. The public sector assumes the main responsibility for the regulation and growth of the national economy under the development plan.

Property is subject to the people's control.

Private ownership is safeguarded and may not be sequestrated except in cases specified in law nor expropriated except for the general good against fair legal compensation. The right of inheritance is guaranteed in it.

Nationalization shall only be allowed for considerations of public interest in accordance with the law and against compensation.

Agricultural holding may be limited by law.

The State follows a comprehensive central planning and compulsory planning approach based on quinquennial socio-economic and cultural development plans whereby the society's resources are mobilized and put to the best use.

The public sector assumes the leading role in the development of the national economy. The State provides absolute protection of this sector as well as the property of co-operative societies and trade unions against all attempts to tamper with them.

PUBLIC LIBERTIES, RIGHTS AND DUTIES

All citizens are equal before the law. Personal liberty is a natural right and no one may be arrested, searched, imprisoned or restricted in any way without a court order.

Houses have sanctity, and shall not be placed under surveillance or searched without a court order with reasons given for such action.

The law safeguards the sanctities of the private lives of all citizens; so have all postal, telegraphic, telephonic and other means of communication which may not therefore be confiscated, or perused except by a court order giving the reasons, and only for a specified period.

Public rights and freedoms are also inviolate and all calls for atheism and anything that reflects adversely on divine religions are prohibited.

The freedom of opinion, the Press, printing and publications and all information media are safeguarded.

Press censorship is forbidden, so are warnings, suspensions or cancellations through administrative channels. Under exceptional circumstances, as in cases of emergency or in wartime, censorship may be imposed on information media for a definite period.

Egyptians have the right to permanent or provisional emigration and no Egyptian may be deported or prevented from returning to the country.

Citizens have the right to private meetings in peace provided they bear no arms. Egyptians also have the right to form societies that have no secret activities. Public meetings are also allowed within the limits of the law.

SOVEREIGNTY OF THE LAW

All acts of crime should be specified together with the penalties for the acts.

Recourse to justice is a right of all citizens. Those who are financially unable will be assured of means to defend their rights.

Except in cases of *flagrante delicto,* no person may be arrested or their freedom restricted unless an order authorizing arrest has been given by the competent judge or the public prosecution in accordance with the provisions of law.

SYSTEM OF GOVERNMENT

The President, who must be of Egyptian parentage and at least 40 years old, is nominated by at least one-third of the members of the People's Assembly, approved by at least two-thirds, and elected by popular referendum. His term is for six years and he 'may be re-elected for another subsequent term'. He may take emergency measures in the interests of the State but these measures must be approved by referendum within 60 days.

The People's Assembly, elected for five years, is the legislative body and approves general policy, the budget and the development plan. It shall have 'not less than 350' elected members, at least half of whom shall be workers or farmers, and the President may appoint up to 10 additional members. In exceptional circumstances the Assembly, by a two-thirds' vote, may authorize the President to rule by decree for a specified period but these decrees must be approved by the Assembly at its next meeting. The law governing the composition of the People's Assembly was amended in May 1979 (see People's Assembly, below).

The Assembly may pass a vote of no confidence in a Deputy Prime Minister, a Minister or a Deputy Minister, provided three days' notice of the vote is given, and the Minister must then resign. In the case of the Prime Minister, the Assembly may 'prescribe' his responsibility and submit a report to the President: if the President disagrees with the report but the Assembly persists, then the matter is put to a referendum: if the people support the President the Assembly is dissolved; if they support the Assembly the President must accept the resignation of the Government. The President may dissolve the Assembly prematurely, but his action must be approved by a referendum and elections must be held within 60 days.

Executive Authority is vested in the President, who may appoint one or more Vice-Presidents and appoints all Ministers. He may also dismiss the Vice-Presidents and Ministers. The President has 'the right to refer to the people in connection with important matters related to the country's higher interests.' The Government is described as 'the supreme executive and administrative organ of the state'. Its members, whether full Ministers or Deputy Ministers, must be at least 35 years old. Further sections define the roles of Local Government, Specialized National Councils, the Judiciary, the Higher Constitutional Court, the Socialist Prosecutor-General, the Armed Forces and National Defence Council and the Police.

POLITICAL PARTIES

In June 1977 the People's Assembly adopted a new law on political parties, which, subject to certain conditions, permitted the formation of political parties for the first time since 1953. The law was passed in accordance with Article Five of the Constitution which describes the political system as 'a multi-party one' with four main parties: 'the ruling National Democratic Party, the Socialist Workers (the official opposition), the Liberal Socialists and the Unionist Progressive'. (The legality of the re-formed New Wafd Party was established by the courts in January 1984.)

1980 AMENDMENTS

On 30 April 1980 the People's Assembly passed a number of amendments, which were subsequently massively approved at a referendum the following month. A summary of the amendments follows:

(i) the regime in Egypt is socialist-democratic, based on the alliance of working people's forces.

(ii) the political system depends on multiple political parties; the Arab Socialist Union is therefore abolished.

(iii) the President is elected for a six-year term and can be elected for 'other terms'.

(iv) the President shall appoint a Consultative Council to preserve the principles of the revolutions of 23 July 1952 and 15 May 1971.

(v) a Supreme Press Council shall safeguard the freedom of the press, check government censorship and look after the interests of journalists.

(vi) Egypt's adherence to Islamic jurisprudence is affirmed. Christians and Jews are subject to their own jurisdiction in personal status affairs.

(vii) there will be no distinction of race or religion.

The Government

THE PRESIDENCY

President: MUHAMMAD HOSNI MUBARAK (confirmed as President by referendum, 13 October 1981, after assassination of President Anwar Sadat; re-elected and confirmed by referendum 5 October 1987, 4 October 1993 and 26 September 1999).

COUNCIL OF MINISTERS
(September 2002)

Prime Minister: Dr ATIF MUHAMMAD OBEID.

Deputy Prime Minister and Minister of Agriculture and Land Reclamation: Dr YOUSUF AMIN WALI.

Minister of Defence and Military Production: Field Marshal MUHAMMAD HUSSAIN TANTAWI.

Minister of Information: MUHAMMAD SAFWAT ESH-SHARIF.

Minister of Foreign Affairs: AHMAD MAHER ES-SAYED.

Minister of Justice: FAROUK MAHMOUD SAYF AN-NASR.

Minister of Culture: FAROUK ABD AL-AZIZ HOSNI.

Minister of Education: Dr HUSSAIN KAMAL BAHA ED-DIN.

Minister of Foreign Trade: Dr YOUSUF BOUTROS-GHALI.

Minister of Tourism: Dr MUHAMMAD MAMDOUH AHMAD EL-BELTAGI.

Minister of Housing, Utilities and New Urban Communities: Dr Eng. MUHAMMAD IBRAHIM SULAYMAN.

Minister of Labour and Migration: AHMAD AHMAD EL-AMAWI.

Minister of Awqaf (Islamic Endowments): Dr MAHMOUD HAMDI ZAKZOUK

Minister of Health and Population: MUHAMMAD AWAD AFIFI TAG ED-DIN.

Minister of Higher Education and Scientific Research: Dr MUFID MAHMOUD SHEHAB.

Minister of Irrigation and Water Resources: Dr MAHMOUD ABD AL-HALIM ABU ZEID.

Minister of the Interior: Maj.-Gen. HABIB IBRAHIM EL-ADLI.

Minister of Local Development: MOUSTAFA MUHAMMAD ABD AL-QADIR.

Minister of Insurance and Social Affairs: Dr AMINAH HAMZEH MAHMOUD AL-JUNDI.

Minister of Industry and Technological Development: Dr ALI FAHMI IBRAHIM AS-SA'IDI.

Minister of Electricity and Energy: Eng. HASSAN YOUNIS

Minister of Transport: HAMDY ASH-SHAYEB.

Minister of Youth: Dr ALI AD-DIN HELAL AD-DASUQI.

Minister of Supply and Internal Trade: Dr HASSAN ALI KHIDR.

Minister of Planning: Dr AHMAD MAHRUS AD-DARSH.

Minister of Public Enterprise: Dr MUKHTAR ABD AL-MUN'IM KHATTAB.

Minister of Finance: Dr MUHAMMAD MIDHAT ABD AL-ATTI HASANAYN.

Minister of Communications and Information Technology: Dr AHMAD MAHMOUD MUHAMMAD NAZIF.

Minister of Petroleum: Dr AMIN SAMIH SAMIR FAHMI.

Minister of Civil Aviation: Gen. AHMAD MUHAMMAD SHAFIQ ZAKI.

Minister of State for Parliamentary Affairs: KAMAL MUHAMMAD ASH-SHAZLI.

Minister of State for Foreign Affairs: FAIZA ABUL NAGA.

Minister of State for Administrative Development: Dr MUHAMMAD ZAKI ABU AMER.

Minister of State for Environmental Affairs: Eng. MAMDOUH RIAD TADROS.

Minister of State for Military Production: Dr SAID ABDUH MOUSTAFA MASH'AL.

Cabinet Secretary: AHMAD HASSAN ABU TALEB.

MINISTRIES

Office of the Prime Minister: Sharia Majlis ash-Sha'ab, Cairo; tel. (2) 7958014; fax (2) 7958016; e-mail primemin@idsc.gov.eg.

Ministry of Administrative Development: Sharia Salah Salem, Cairo (Nasr City); tel. (2) 4022910; fax (2) 2614126.

Ministry of Agriculture and Land Reclamation: Sharia Nadi es-Sayed, Cairo (Dokki), Giza; tel. (2) 3772566; fax (2) 3498128; e-mail sea@idsc.gov.eg; internet www.agri.gov.eg.

Ministry of Awqaf (Islamic Endowments): Sharia Sabri Abu Alam, Bab el-Louk, Cairo; tel. (2) 3929403; fax (2) 3900362; e-mail mawkaf@idsc1.gov.eg.

Ministry of Civil Aviation: Sharia Matar, Cairo; tel. (2) 3555566; fax (2) 3555564.

Ministry of Communications and Information Technology: 1 Sharia Mahmoud el-Hossary, Mohandessin, Cairo (Giza); tel. (2) 3444533; fax (2) 34446088; e-mail anazif@mcit.gov.eg; internet www.mcit.gov.eg.

Ministry of Culture: 2 Sharia Shagaret ed-Dor, Cairo (Zamalek); tel. (2) 7380761; fax (2) 7356449; e-mail mculture@idsc.gov.eg.

Ministry of Defence and Military Production: Sharia 23 July, Kobri el-Kobra, Cairo; tel. (2) 2602566; fax (2) 2916227; e-mail mod@idsc.gov.eg.

Ministry of Education: 4 Sharia Ibrahim Nagiv, Cairo (Garden City); tel. (2) 5787643; fax (2) 7962952; e-mail moe@idsc.gov.eg; internet home.moe.edu.

Ministry of Electricity and Energy: Sharia Ramses, Abbassia, Cairo (Nasr City); tel. (2) 2616317; fax (2) 2616302; e-mail mee@idsc.gov.eg.

Ministry of Environmental Affairs: 30 Sharia Helwan, Cairo; tel. (2) 5256463; fax (2) 5256461.

Ministry of Finance: Justice and Finance Bldg, Sharia Majlis ash-Sha'ab, Lazoughli Sq., Cairo; tel. (2) 3541055; fax (2) 3551537; e-mail mofinance@idsc1.gov.eg.

Ministry of Foreign Affairs: Corniche en-Nil, Cairo (Maspiro); tel. (2) 5749820; fax (2) 5749533; e-mail minexter@idsc1.gov.eg; internet www.mfa.gov.eg.

Ministry of Foreign Trade: 8 Sharia Adly, Cairo; tel. (2) 3919661; fax (2) 3903029; e-mail moft@moft.gov.eg; internet www.moft.gov.eg.

Ministry of Health and Population: Sharia Majlis ash-Sha'ab, Lazoughli Sq., Cairo; tel. (2) 7941507; fax (2) 7953966; e-mail moh@idsc.gov.eg.

Ministry of Higher Education and Scientific Research: 101 Sharia Qasr el-Eini, Cairo; tel. (2) 7956962; fax (2) 7941005; e-mail mheducat@idsc.gov.eg; internet www.egy-mhe.gov.eg.

Ministry of Housing, Utilities and New Urban Communities: 1 Ismail Abaza, Sharia Qasr el-Eini, Cairo; tel. (2) 3553468; fax (2) 3557836; e-mail mhuuc@idsc1.gov.eg.

Ministry of Industry and Technological Development: 2 Sharia Latin America, Cairo (Garden City); tel. (2) 7946589; fax (2) 7955025; e-mail moindust@idsc.gov.eg.

Ministry of Information: Radio and TV Bldg, Corniche en-Nil, Cairo (Maspiro); tel. (2) 5748984; fax (2) 5748981; e-mail rtu@idsc.gov.eg.

Ministry of Insurance and Social Affairs: Sharia Sheikh Rihan, Bab el-Louk, Cairo; tel. (2) 3370039; fax (2) 3375390; e-mail msi@idsc.gov.eg.

Ministry of the Interior: Sharia Sheikh Rihan, Bab el-Louk, Cairo; tel. (2) 3557500; fax (2) 5792031; e-mail moi2@idsc.gov.eg.

Ministry of Irrigation and Water Resources: Sharia Corniche en-Nil, Imbaba, Cairo; tel. (2) 3123304; fax (2) 3123357; e-mail mpwwr@idsc.gov.eg; internet www.starnet.com.eg/mpwwr.

Ministry of Justice: Justice and Finance Bldg, Sharia Majlis ash-Sha'ab, Lazoughli Sq., Cairo; tel. (2) 7951176; fax (2) 7955700; e-mail mojeb@idsc1.gov.eg.

Ministry of Labour and Migration: 3 Sharia Yousuf Abbas, Abbassia, Cairo (Nasr City); tel. (2) 4042910; fax (2) 2609891; e-mail mwlabor@idsc1.gov.eg; internet www.emigration.gov.eg.

Ministry of Local Development: Sharia Nadi es-Seid, Cairo (Dokki); tel. (2) 3497470; fax (2) 3497788.

Ministry of Military Production: 5 Sharia Ismail Abaza, Qasr el-Eini, Cairo; tel. (2) 3552428; fax (2) 3548739.

Ministry of Parliamentary Affairs: Sharia Majlis ash-Sha'ab, Lazoughli Sq., Cairo; tel. (2) 3557750; fax (2) 3557681.

Ministry of Petroleum: Sharia el-Mokhayem ed-Dayem, Cairo (Nasr City); tel. (2) 2626060; fax (2) 2636060; e-mail mop@egyptonline.com.

Ministry of Planning: Sharia Salah Salem, Cairo (Nasr City); tel. (2) 4014615; fax (2) 4014733.

Ministry of Public Enterprise: Sharia Majlis ash-Sha'ab, Lazoughli Sq., Cairo; tel. (2) 3558026; fax (2) 3555882; e-mail mops@idsc.gov.eg.

Ministry of Supply and Internal Trade: 99 Sharia Qasr el-Eini, Cairo; tel. (2) 3557598; fax (2) 3544973; e-mail msit@idsc.gov.eg.

Ministry of Tourism: Misr Travel Tower, Abbassia Sq., Cairo; tel. (2) 2828439; fax (2) 2859551; e-mail mol@idsc.gov.eg; internet www.touregypt.net.

Ministry of Transport: 105 Sharia Qasr el-Eini, Cairo; tel. (2) 3555566; fax (2) 3555564; e-mail garb@idsc.gov.eg.

Legislature

MAJLIS ASH-SHA'AB
(People's Assembly)

There are 222 constituencies, which each elect two deputies to the Assembly. Ten deputies are appointed by the President, giving a total of 454 seats.

Speaker: Dr AHMAD FATHI SURUR.

Deputy Speakers: Dr ABD AL-AHAD GAMAL AD-DIN, AHMAD ABU ZEID, Dr AMAL UTHMAN.

Elections, 18 and 29 October and 8 November 2000

	Seats
National Democratic Party*	353
New Wafd Party	7
National Progressive Unionist Party	6
Nasserist Party	3
Liberal Socialist Party	1
Independents	72
Total†	442‡

* Official candidates of the National Democratic Party (NDP) won 353 seats in the three rounds of voting. However, after the elections it was reported that 35 of the 72 candidates who had successfully contested the elections as independents had either joined or rejoined the NDP.
† There are, in addition, 10 deputies appointed by the President.
‡ The results for the two seats in one constituency in Alexandria were annulled by a court ruling. (Elections were scheduled to be reheld there in 2001.)

MAJLIS ASH-SHURA
(Advisory Council)

In September 1980 elections were held for a 210-member **Shura (Advisory) Council**, which replaced the former Central Committee of the Arab Socialist Union. Of the total number of members, 140 are elected and the remaining 70 are appointed by the President. The opposition parties boycotted elections to the Council in October 1983, and again in October 1986, in protest against the 8% electoral threshold. In June 1989 elections to 153 of the Council's 210 seats were contested by opposition parties (the 'Islamic Alliance', consisting of the Muslim Brotherhood, the LSP and the SLP). However, all of the seats in which voting produced a result (143) were won by the NDP. NDP candidates won 88 of the 90 seats on the Council to which mid-term elections were held in June 1995. The remaining two elective seats were gained by independent candidates. On 21 June new appointments were made to 47 vacant, non-elective seats. Partial elections to the Council were held again in June 1998. The NDP won 85 of the 88 contested seats, while independent candidates won the remaining three seats. Most opposition parties chose not to contest the elections. In partial elections to the Council, held on 16 and 22 May 2001, the NDP won 74 of the 88 seats in question, while independent candidates won the remaining 14 seats.

Speaker: Dr MUSTAFA KAMAL HELMI.

Deputy Speakers: THARWAT ABAZAH, AHMAD AL-IMADI.

Political Organizations

Democratic People's Party: f. 1992; Chair. ANWAR AFIFI.

Democratic Unionist Party: f. 1990; Pres. IBRAHIM ABD AL-MONEIM TURK.

Et-Takaful (Solidarity): f. 1995; advocates imposition of 'solidarity' tax on the rich in order to provide needs of the poor; Chair. Dr USAMA MUHAMMAD SHALTOUT.

Green Party: f. 1990; Chair. Dr ABD AL-MONEIM EL-AASAR.

Hizb al-Wifaq al-Qawmi (National Accord Party): f. 2000.

Liberal Socialist Party (LSP): Cairo; f. 1976; advocates expansion of 'open door' economic policy and greater freedom for private enterprise and the press; Leader (vacant).

Misr el-Fatah (Young Egypt Party): f. 1990; Chair. GAMAL RABIE.

Nasserist Party: Cairo; f. 1991; Chair. DIAA ED-DIN DAOUD.

National Democratic Party (NDP): Cairo; f. 1978; government party established by Anwar Sadat; absorbed Arab Socialist Party; Leader MUHAMMAD HOSNI MUBARAK; Sec.-Gen. Dr YOUSUF AMIN WALI; Political Bureau: Chair. MUHAMMAD HOSNI MUBARAK.

National Progressive Unionist Party (Tagammu): 1 Sharia Karim ed-Dawlah, Cairo; f. 1976; left-wing; Leader KHALED MOHI ED-DIN; Sec. Dr RIFA'AT ES-SAID; 160,000 mems.

New Wafd Party (The Delegation): Cairo; original Wafd Party f. 1919; banned 1952; re-formed as New Wafd Party Feb. 1978; disbanded June 1978; re-formed 1983; Leader NU'MAN JUM'AH; Sec.-Gen. IBRAHIM FARAG.

Social Justice Party: f. 1993; Chair. MUHAMMAD ABD AL-AAL.

Socialist Labour Party (SLP): 12 Sharia Awali el-Ahd, Cairo; f. 1978; official opposition party; pro-Islamist; Leader IBRAHIM SHUKRI.

The following organizations are proscribed by the Government:

Islamic Jihad (al-Jihad—Holy Struggle): militant Islamist grouping established following the imposition of a ban on the Muslim Brotherhood.

Jama'ah al-Islamiyah (Islamic Group): militant Islamist group founded following the imposition of a ban on the Muslim Brotherhood; declared a cease-fire in March 1999; Spiritual Leader Sheikh OMAR ABD AR-RAHMAN; Chair. of the Shura Council MOUSTAFA HAMZAH; Mil. Cmmdr ALA ABD AR-RAQIL.

Muslim Brotherhood (Ikhwan al-Muslimun): internet www.um mah.org.uk/ikhwan; f. 1928 with the aim of establishing an Islamic society; banned in 1954; moderate; advocates the adoption of the *Shari'a*, or Islamic law, as the sole basis of the Egyptian legal system Dep. Supreme Guide MA'MUN AL-HUDA BI.

Vanguards of Conquest: militant Islamist grouping; breakaway group from Islamic Jihad; Leader YASIR AS-SIRRI.

Diplomatic Representation

EMBASSIES IN EGYPT

Afghanistan: 59 Sharia el-Orouba, Cairo (Heliopolis); tel. (2) 666653; fax (2) 662262; Ambassador: SAYED FAZLULLAH FAZIL.

Albania: 29 Sharia Ismail Muhammad, Cairo (Zamalek), tel. (2) 3415651; fax (2) 3413732; Ambassador: ARBEN PANDI CICI.

Algeria: 14 Sharia Bresil, Cairo (Zamalek); tel. (2) 3418527; fax (2) 3414158; Ambassador: MOUSTAFA CHERIF.

Angola: 12 Midan Fouad Mohi ed-Din, Mohandessin, Cairo; tel. (2) 3377602; fax (2) 708683; Ambassador: HERMINO JOAQUIM ESCORCIO.

Argentina: 1st Floor, 8 Sharia es-Saleh Ayoub, Cairo (Zamalek); tel. (2) 7351501; fax (2) 7364355; e-mail argemb@idsc.gov.eg; Ambassador: OSVALDO SANTIAGO PASCUAL.

Armenia: 20 Sharia Muhammad Mazhar, Cairo (Zamalek); tel. (2) 3424157; fax (2) 3424158; e-mail armenemb@idsc.gov.eg; Ambassador: Dr EDWARD NALBANDIAN.

Australia: 11th Floor, World Trade Centre, Corniche en-Nil, Cairo 11111 (Boulac); tel. (2) 5750444; fax (2) 5781638; e-mail cairo .austremb@dfat.gov.au; Ambassador: VICTORIA OWEN.

Austria: 5th Floor, Riyadh Tower, 5 Sharia Wissa Wassef, cnr of Sharia en-Nil, Cairo 11111 (Giza); tel. (2) 5702975; fax (2) 5702979; e-mail aec@gega.net; Ambassador: FERDINAND TRAUTTMANSDORFF.

Bahrain: 15 Sharia Bresil, Cairo (Zamalek); tel. (2) 3407996; fax (2) 3416609; Ambassador: EBRAHIM AL-MAJED.

Bangladesh: 47 Sharia Ahmad Heshmat, Cairo (Zamalek); tel. (2) 3412645; fax (2) 3402401; e-mail bdoot@wnet1.worldnet.com.eg; Ambassador: RUHUL AMIN.

Belarus: 19–1 Sharia Muhammad el-Ghazali, Cairo (Dokki); tel. (2) 3375782; fax (2) 3375845; Ambassador: IGOR LESHCHENYA.

Belgium: POB 37, 20 Sharia Kamal esh-Shennawi, Cairo 11511 (Garden City); tel. (2) 7947494; fax (2) 7943147; e-mail cairo@diplo bel.org; Ambassador: PAUL PONJAERT.

Bolivia: 2 Sharia Hod el-Labban, Cairo (Garden City); tel. (2) 3546390; fax (2) 3550917; Ambassador: HERNANDO VELASCO.

Bosnia and Herzegovina: 42 Sharia Sawra, Cairo (Dokki); tel. (2) 7499191; fax (2) 7499190; e-mail ebihebosnia@isdc.gov.eg; Ambassador: SRBOLJUB LALOVIĆ.

Brazil: 1125 Corniche en-Nil, Cairo 11221 (Maspiro); tel. (2) 5756938; fax (2) 5761040; e-mail brasemb@soficom.com.eg; Ambassador: CELSO MARCOS VIEIRA DE SOUZA.

Brunei: 24 Sharia Hassan Assem, Cairo (Zamalek); tel. (2) 7360097; fax (2) 7386375; e-mail ebdic@mail.link.net; Ambassador: Dato' Paduka Haji ALI BIN Haji HASSAN.

Bulgaria: 6 Sharia el-Malek el-Ajdal, Cairo (Zamalek); tel. (2) 7363025; fax (2) 7363826; e-mail bulembcai@link.net; Ambassador: ALEXANDAR OLSHEVSKI.

Burkina Faso: POB 306, Ramses Centre, 9 Sharia el-Fawakeh, Mohandessin, Cairo; tel. (2) 3758956; fax (2) 3756974; Ambassador: MAHAMOUDOU OUÉDRAOGO.

Burundi: 22 Sharia en-Nakhil, Madinet ed-Dobbat, Cairo (Dokki); tel. (2) 3373078; fax (2) 3378431; Ambassador: GERVAIS NDIKUMAGNEGE.

Cambodia: 2 Sharia Tahawia, Cairo (Giza); tel. (2) 3489966; Ambassador: IN SOPHEAP.

Cameroon: POB 2061, 15 Sharia Muhammad Sedki Soliman, Mohandessin, Cairo; tel. (2) 3441101; fax (2) 3459208; Ambassador: MOUCHILI NJI MFOUAYO ISMAILA.

Canada: POB 1667, 6 Sharia Muhammad Fahmi es-Said, Cairo (Garden City); tel. (2) 7943110; fax (2) 7963548; e-mail cairo@dfait -maeci.gc.ca; Ambassador: MICHEL DE SALABERRY.

Central African Republic: 41 Sharia Mahmoud Azmy, Mohandessin, Cairo (Dokki); tel. (2) 3446873; Ambassador: HENRY KOBA.

Chad: POB 1869, 12 Midan ar-Refaï, Cairo 11511 (Dokki); tel. (2) 3373379; fax (2) 3373232; Ambassador: AMIN ABBA SIDICK.

Chile: 5 Sharia Shagaret ed-Dor, Cairo (Zamalek); tel. (2) 3408711; fax (2) 3403716; e-mail chilemb@idsc.gov.eg; Ambassador: NELSON HADAD HERESI.

China, People's Republic: 14 Sharia Bahgat Ali, Cairo (Zamalek); tel. (2) 3411219; fax (2) 3409459; e-mail chinaemb@idsc.gov.eg; Ambassador: AN HUIHOU.

Colombia: 6 Sharia Gueriza, Cairo (Zamalek); tel. (2) 3414203; fax (2) 3407429; e-mail colombemb@idsc.gov.eg; Ambassador: JAIME GIRÓN DUARTE.

Congo, Democratic Republic: 5 Sharia Mansour Muhammad, Cairo (Zamalek); tel. (2) 3403662; fax (2) 3404342; Ambassador: KAMIMBAYA WA DJONDO.

Côte d'Ivoire: 9 ave Shehab, rue Abdel Meguid Omar Mohandessine, Cairo; tel. (2) 3034373; fax (2) 3050148; Ambassador: KONAN N. MARCEL.

Croatia: 3 Sharia Abou el-Feda, Cairo (Zamalek); tel. (2) 7383155; fax (2) 7355812; e-mail croem@soficom.com.eg; Ambassador: Dr IVICA TOMIĆ.

Cuba: Apartment 4, 14 Sharia Madinah Munawarah, Cairo (Dokki), tel. (2) 3371649; fax (2) 3350390; e-mail cubaemb@idsc.gov.eg; Ambassador: LUIS E. MARISY FIGUEREDO.

Cyprus: 23A Sharia Ismail Muhammad, 1st Floor, Cairo (Zamalek); tel. (2) 3411288; fax (2) 3415299; Ambassador: CHARALAMBOS KAPSOS.

Czech Republic: 1st Floor, 4 Sharia Dokki, Cairo 12511 (Giza); tel. (2) 3485531; fax (2) 3485892; e-mail caiembcz@intouch.com; Ambassador: DANA HUŇÁTOVÁ.

Denmark: 12 Sharia Hassan Sabri, Cairo 11211 (Zamalek); tel. (2) 7357411; fax (2) 7361780; e-mail rdemb@commnet.com.eg; internet www.danemb.org.eg/cairo-dk.html; Ambassador: CHRISTIAN OLDENBURG.

Djibouti: 11 Sharia el-Gazaer, Aswan Sq., Cairo (Agouza); tel. (2) 3456546; fax (2) 3456549; Ambassador: Sheikh MOUSSA MOHAMED AHMED.

Ecuador: Suez Canal Bldg, 4 Sharia Ibn Kasir, Cairo (Giza); tel. (2) 3496782; fax (2) 3609327; e-mail ecuademb@idsc.gov.eg; Ambassador: FRANKLIN BAHAMONDE.

Ethiopia: 6 Sharia Abd ar-Rahman Hussein, Midan Gomhuria, Cairo (Dokki); tel. (2) 3353696; fax (2) 3353699; Ambassador: GIRMA AMARE.

Finland: 3 Sharia Abou el-Feda, Cairo (Zamalek); tel. (2) 7363722; fax (2) 7355170; Ambassador: AAPO POLHO.

France: POB 1777, 29 Sharia Giza, Cairo (Giza); tel. (2) 5703916; fax (2) 5710276; e-mail info@ambafrance-eg.org; internet www.diplo -france.org.eg/; Ambassador: FRANÇOIS DOPFFER.

Gabon: 17 Sharia Mecca el-Moukarama, Cairo (Dokki); tel. (2) 3379699; Ambassador: MAMBO JACQUES.

Germany: 8B Sharia Hassan Sabri, Cairo (Zamalek); tel. (2) 7399600; fax (2) 7360530; e-mail germemb@gega.net; internet www.german-embassy.org.eg; Ambassador: PAUL VON MALTZAHN.

Ghana: 1 Sharia 26 July, Cairo (Zamalek); tel. (2) 3444455; fax (2) 3032292; Ambassador: BON OHANE KWAPONG.

Greece: 18 Sharia Aicha at-Taimouria, Cairo (Garden City); tel. (2) 3551074; fax (2) 3563903; Ambassador: GEORGE ASIMAKOPOULOS.

Guatemala: POB 346, 11 Sharia 10, Maadi, Cairo; tel. (2) 3802914; fax (2) 3802915; e-mail guatemb@infinity.com.eg; Ambassador: FLORIDALMA FRANCO PAIZ.

Guinea: 46 Sharia Muhammad Mazhar, Cairo (Zamalek); tel. (2) 7358109; fax (2) 7361446; Ambassador: el Hadj OUSMANE CAMARA.

Guinea-Bissau: 37 Sharia Lebanon, Madinet el-Mohandessin, Cairo (Dokki).

Holy See: Apostolic Nunciature, Safarat al-Vatican, 5 Sharia Muhammad Mazhar, Cairo (Zamalek); tel. (2) 7352250; fax (2) 7356152; e-mail nunteg@rite.com; Apostolic Nuncio: Most Rev. MARCO DINO BROGI, Titular Archbishop of Citta Ducale.

Honduras: 21 Sharia Aicha at-Taimouria, Cairo (Garden City); tel. (2) 3409510; fax (2) 3413835.

Hungary: 29 Sharia Muhammad Mazhar, Cairo (Zamalek); tel. (2) 7358659; fax (2) 7358648; e-mail huembcai@soficom.com.eg; Ambassador: LÁSZLÓ KÁDÁR.

India: 5 Sharia Aziz Abaza, Cairo (Zamalek); tel. (2) 3413051; fax (2) 3414038; e-mail indiaemb@idsc.gov.eg; Ambassador: KENWAL GIBAL; also looks after Iraqi interests at 5 Sharia Aziz Abaza, Cairo (Zamalek) (tel. (2) 3409815).

Indonesia: POB 1661, 13 Sharia Aicha at-Taimouria, Cairo (Garden City); tel. (2) 3547200; fax (2) 3562495; Ambassador: Dr BOER MAUNA.

Iraq: *Interests served by India.*

Ireland: POB 2681, 3 Sharia Abou el-Feda, Cairo (Zamalek); tel. (2) 7358264; fax (2) 7362863; e-mail irishemb@rite.com; Ambassador: PETER GUNNING.

Israel: 6 Sharia Ibn el-Malek, Cairo (Giza); tel. (2) 7610380; fax (2) 7610414; Ambassador: ZVI MAZEL.

Italy: 15 Sharia Abd ar-Rahman Fahmi, Cairo (Garden City); tel. (2) 7943194; fax (2) 7940657; e-mail ambcairo@brainy1.ie-eg.com; internet www.italemb.org.eg; Ambassador: MARIO SICA.

Japan: Cairo Centre Bldg, 2nd and 3rd Floors, 2 Sharia Abd al-Kader Hamza or 106 Sharia Qasr el-Eini, Cairo (Garden City); tel. (2) 7953962; fax (2) 7963540; e-mail center@embjapan.org.eg; internet www.mofa.go.jp/embjapan/egypt; Ambassador: TAKAYA SUTO.

Jordan: 6 Sharia Juhaini, Cairo; tel. (2) 3485566; fax (2) 3601027; Ambassador: NABIH AN-NIMR.

Kazakhstan: 4 Sharia Abay Kunanbayuli, New Maadi, Cairo; tel. and fax (2) 5194522; e-mail kazaemb@ids.gov.eg; Ambassador: BOL-ATKHAN K. TAIZHANOV.

Kenya: POB 362, 7 Sharia el-Mohandes Galal, Cairo (Dokki); tel. (2) 3453628; fax (2) 3443400; Ambassador: MUHAMMAD M. MAALIM.

Korea, Democratic People's Republic: 6 Sharia as-Saleh Ayoub, Cairo (Zamalek); tel. (2) 3408219; fax (2) 3414615; Ambassador: JANG MYONG-SON.

Korea, Republic: 3 Sharia Boulos Hanna, Cairo (Dokki); tel. (2) 3611234; fax (2) 3611238; Ambassador: SHIM KYOUNG-BO.

Kuwait: 12 Sharia Nabil el-Wakkad, Cairo (Dokki); tel. (2) 3602661; fax (2) 3602657; Ambassador: ABD AR-RAZAK ABD AL-KADER AL-KANDRI.

Lebanon: 22 Sharia Mansour Muhammad, Cairo (Zamalek); tel. (2) 7382823; fax (2) 7382818; Ambassador: SAMI KRONFOL.

Lesotho: 10 Sharia Bahr al-Ghazal, Sahafeyeen, Cairo; tel. (2) 3447025; fax (2) 3025495.

Liberia: 11 Sharia Bresil, Cairo (Zamalek); tel. (2) 3419864; fax (2) 3473074; Ambassador: Dr BRAHIMA D. KABA.

Libya: 7 Sharia as-Saleh Ayoub, Cairo (Zamalek); tel. (2) 3401864; Ambassador: JUM'AH AL-MAHDI AL-FAZZANI.

Lithuania: Cairo.

Malaysia: 29 Sharia Taha Hussein, Cairo (Zamalek); tel. (2) 3410863; fax (2) 3411049; Ambassador: Dato RAJA MANSUR RAZMAN.

Mali: 3 Sharia al-Kawsar, Cairo (Dokki); tel. (2) 3371641; fax (2) 3371841; Ambassador: ALLAYE ALPHADY CISSÉ.

Malta: 25 Sharia 12, Maadi, Cairo; tel. (2) 3804451; fax (2) 3804452; e-mail maltaemb@link.net; Ambassador: GAETAN NAUDI ACIS.

Mauritania: 114 Mohi ed-Din, Abou-el Ezz, Mohandessin, Cairo; tel. (2) 3490671; fax (2) 3489060; MUHAMMAD LEMINE OULD.

Mauritius: 156 Sharia es-Sudan, Mohandessin, Cairo; tel. (2) 7618102; fax (2) 7618101; e-mail embamaur@thewayout.net; Ambassador: SOOROOJDEV PHOKEER.

Mexico: 5th Floor, 17 Sharia Port Said, 11431 Cairo (Maadi); tel. (2) 3500258; fax (2) 3511887; e-mail mexemb@idsc.gov.eg; Ambassador: HÉCTOR CÁRDENAS.

Mongolia: 3 Midan en-Nasr, Cairo (Dokki); tel. (2) 3460670; Ambassador: SONOMDORJIN DAMBADARJAA.

Morocco: 10 Sharia Salah ed-Din, Cairo (Zamalek); tel. (2) 3409849; fax (2) 3411937; e-mail morocemb@idsc.gov.eg; Ambassador: ABD AL-LATIF MOULINE.

Mozambique: 9th Floor, 3 Sharia Abu el-Feda, Cairo (Zamalek); tel. (2) 3320647; fax (2) 3320383; e-mail emozcai@intouch.com; Ambassador: DANIEL EDUARDO MONDLANE.

Myanmar: 24 Sharia Muhammad Mazhar, Cairo (Zamalek); tel. (2) 3404176; fax (2) 3416793; Ambassador: U AUNG GYI.

Nepal: 9 Sharia Tiba, Madinet el-Kobah, Cairo (Dokki); tel. (2) 3603426; fax (2) 704447; Ambassador: JITENDRA RAJ SHARMA.

Netherlands: 36 Sharia Hassan Sabri, Cairo (Zamalek); tel. (2) 7356434; fax (2) 7365249; e-mail az-cz@hollandemb.org.eg; internet www.hollandemb.org.eg; Ambassador: SJOERD LEENSTRA.

Niger: 101 Sharia Pyramids, Cairo (Giza); tel. (2) 3865607; Ambassador: MAMANE OUMAROU.

Nigeria: 13 Sharia Gabalaya, Cairo (Zamalek); tel. (2) 3406042; fax (2) 3403907; Chargé d'affaires a.i.: P. S. O. EROMOBOR.

Norway: 8 Sharia el-Gezirah, Cairo (Zamalek); tel. (2) 7353340; fax (2) 7370709; e-mail embcai@mfa.no; internet www.norway.org.eg; Ambassador: BJØRN FRODE ØSTERN.

Oman: 52 Sharia el-Higaz, Mohandessin, Cairo; tel. (2) 3036011; fax (2) 3036464; Ambassador: ABDULLAH BIN HAMED AL-BUSAIDI.

Pakistan: 8 Sharia es-Salouli, Cairo (Dokki); tel. (2) 7487806; fax (2) 7480310; Ambassador: ANWAR KEMAL.

Panama: POB 62, 4A Sharia Ibn Zanki, 11211 Cairo (Zamalek); tel. (2) 3400784; fax (2) 3411092; Chargé d'affaires a.i.: ROY FRANCISCO LUNA GONZÁLEZ.

Peru: 8 Sharia Kamel esh-Shenawi, Cairo (Garden City); tel. (2) 3562973; fax (2) 3557985; Ambassador: MANUEL VERAMENDI I. SERRA.

Philippines: 14 Sharia Muhammad Saleh, Cairo (Dokki); tel. (2) 7480396; fax (2) 7480393; e-mail cairope@dfa.gov.ph; Ambassador: MENANDRO P. GALENZOGA.

Poland: 5 Sharia el-Aziz Osman, Cairo (Zamalek); tel. (2) 3409583; fax (2) 3405427; Ambassador: ROMAN CZYZYCKI.

Portugal: 1 Sharia es-Saleh Ayoub, Cairo (Zamalek); tel. (2) 7350779; fax (2) 7350790; e-mail embpcai@link.com.eg; Ambassador: MANUEL TAVARES DE SOUSA.

Qatar: 10 Sharia ath-Thamar, Midan an-Nasr, Madinet al-Mohandessin, Cairo; tel. (2) 3604693; fax (2) 3603618; Ambassador: BADIR AD-DAFA.

Romania: 6 el-Khamel Muhammad, Cairo (Zamalek); tel. (2) 7360107; fax (2) 7360851; e-mail roembegy@access.com.eg; Ambassador: DORU COSTEA.

Russia: 95 Sharia Giza, Cairo (Giza); tel. (2) 3489353; fax (2) 3609074; Ambassador: VLADIMIR GOUDEV.

Rwanda: 23 Sharia Babel, Mohandessin, Cairo (Dokki); tel. (2) 3350532; fax (2) 3351479; Ambassador: CÉLESTIN KABANDA.

San Marino: 5 Sharia Ramez, Mohandessin, Cairo; tel. (2) 3602718.

Saudi Arabia: 2 Sharia Ahmad Nessim, Cairo (Giza); tel. (2) 3490775; Ambassador: ASSAD ABD AL-KAREM ABOU AN-NASR.

Senegal: 46 Sharia Abd al-Moneim Riad, Mohandessin, Cairo (Dokki); tel. (2) 3460946; fax (2) 3461039; Ambassador: MAMADOU SOW.

Sierra Leone: *Interests served by Saudi Arabia.*

Singapore: 40 Sharia Babel, Cairo (Dokki); tel. (2) 7490468; fax (2) 7481682; e-mail singemb@link.com.eg; Ambassador: TEE TUA BA.

Slovakia: 3 Sharia Adel Hussein Rostom, Dokki, Cairo (Giza); tel. (2) 3358240; fax (2) 3355810; e-mail zukahira@gega.net; Ambassador: JOZEF CIBULA.

Slovenia: 5 es-Saraya el-Kobra Sq., Cairo (Garden City); tel. (2) 3555798; Ambassador: ANDREJ ZLEBNIK.

Somalia: 27 Sharia es-Somal, Cairo (Dokki), Giza; tel. (2) 3374577; Ambassador: ABDALLA HASSAN MAHMOUD.

South Africa: 18th Floor, Nile Tower Bldg, 21–23 Sharia Giza, Cairo (Giza); tel. (2) 5717238; fax (2) 5717241; e-mail saembcai@gega.net; Ambassador: JUSTUS DE GOEDE.

Spain: 41 Sharia Ismail Muhammad, Cairo (Zamalek); tel. (2) 3406397; fax (2) 3405829; e-mail spainemb@idsc.gov.eg; Ambassador: PEDRO LÓPEZ AGUIRREBENGOA.

Sri Lanka: POB 1157, 8 Sharia Sri Lanka, Cairo (Zamalek); tel. (2) 7350047; fax (2) 7367138; e-mail slembare@menanet.net; internet www.lankaemb-egypt.com; Ambassador: D. SERASINGHE.

Sudan: 4 Sharia el-Ibrahimi, Cairo (Garden City); tel. (2) 3545043; fax (2) 3542693; Ambassador: AHMAD ABD AL-HALIM.

Sweden: POB 131, 13 Sharia Muhammad Mazhar, Cairo (Zamalek); tel. (2) 3414132; fax (2) 3404357; e-mail sveamcai@link.com.eg; Ambassador: CHRISTER SYLVÉN.

Switzerland: POB 633, 10 Sharia Abd al-Khalek Sarwat, Cairo; tel. (2) 5758284; fax (2) 5745236; e-mail vertretung@cai.rep.admin.ch; Ambassador: BLAISE GODET.

Syria: 18 Sharia Abd ar-Rehim Sabry, POB 435, Cairo (Dokki); tel. (2) 3358806; fax (2) 3377020; Ambassador: YUSUF AL-AHMAD.

Tanzania: 9 Sharia Abd al-Hamid Lotfi, Cairo (Dokki); tel. (2) 704155; Ambassador: MUHAMMAD A. FOUM.

Thailand: 2 Sharia al-Malek el-Afdal, Cairo (Zamalek); tel. (2) 7358356; fax (2) 7360094; e-mail royalthia@link.net; Ambassador: Dr WARAWIT KANITHASEN.

Tunisia: 26 Sharia el-Jazirah, Cairo (Zamalek); tel. (2) 3418962; Ambassador: ABD AL-HAMID AMMAR.

Turkey: 25 Sharia Felaki, Cairo (Bab el-Louk); tel. (2) 3563318; fax (2) 3558110; Ambassador: YAŞAR YAKIŞ.

Uganda: 9 Midan el-Messaha, Cairo (Dokki); tel. (2) 3486070; fax (2) 3485980; Ambassador: IBRAHIM MUKIIBI.

Ukraine: 9 Sharia es-Saraya, Appt 31–32, Cairo (Dokki); tel. (2) 3491030; fax (2) 3360159; e-mail vlost@eis.com.eg.

United Arab Emirates: 4 Sharia Ibn Sina, Cairo (Giza); tel. (2) 3609721; e-mail uaeembassyca@online.com.eg; Ambassador: AHMAD AL-MAHMOUD MUHAMMAD.

United Kingdom: 17 Sharia Ahmad Ragheb, Cairo (Garden City); tel. (2) 7940852; fax (2) 7940859; e-mail info@britishembassy.org.eg; internet www.britishembassy.org.eg; Ambassador: JOHN SAWERS.

USA: 5 Sharia Latin America, Cairo (Garden City); tel. (2) 7973300; fax (2) 7973200; internet usembassy.egnet.net; Ambassador: C. DAVID WELCH.

Uruguay: 6 Sharia Lotfallah, Cairo (Zamalek); tel. (2) 3415137; fax (2) 3418123; Ambassador: JULIO CÉSAR FRANZINI.

Venezuela: 15A Sharia Mansour Muhammad, Cairo (Zamalek); tel. (2) 3413517; fax (2) 3417373; e-mail eov@idsc.gov.eg; Ambassador: DARIO BAUDER.

Viet Nam: 39 Sharia Kambiz, Cairo (Dokki); tel. (2) 3371494; fax (2) 3496597; Ambassador: NGUYEN LE BACH.

Yemen: 28 Sharia Amean ar-Rafai, Cairo (Dokki); tel. (2) 3614224; fax (2) 3604815; Ambassador: ABD AL-GHALIL GHILAN AHMAD.

Yugoslavia: 33 Sharia Mansour Muhammad, Cairo (Zamalek); tel. (2) 3404061; fax (2) 3403913; Ambassador: Dr IVAN IVEKOVIĆ.

Zambia: 6 Abd ar-Rahman Hussein, Mohandessin, Cairo (Dokki); tel. (2) 3610282; fax (2) 3610833; Ambassador: Dr ANGEL ALFRED MWENDA.

Zimbabwe: 40 Sharia Ghaza, Mohandessin, Cairo; tel. (2) 3030404; fax (2) 3059741; Ambassador: Dr HENRY V. MOYANA.

Judicial System

The Courts of Law in Egypt are principally divided into two juridical court systems: Courts of General Jurisdiction and Administrative Courts. Since 1969 the Supreme Constitutional Court has been at the top of the Egyptian judicial structure.

THE SUPREME CONSTITUTIONAL COURT

The Supreme Constitutional Court is the highest court in Egypt. It has specific jurisdiction over: (i) judicial review of the constitutionality of laws and regulations; (ii) resolution of positive and negative jurisdictional conflicts and determination of the competent court between the different juridical court systems, e.g. Courts of General Jurisdiction and Administrative Courts, as well as other bodies exercising judicial competence; (iii) determination of disputes over the enforcement of two final but contradictory judgments rendered by two courts each belonging to a different juridical court system; (iv) rendering binding interpretation of laws or decree laws in the event of a dispute in the application of said laws or decree laws, always provided that such a dispute is of a gravity requiring conformity of interpretation under the Constitution.

COURTS OF GENERAL JURISDICTION

The Courts of General Jurisdiction in Egypt are basically divided into four categories, as follows: (i) The Court of Cassation; (ii) The Courts of Appeal; (iii) The Tribunals of First Instance; (iv) The District Tribunals; each of the above courts is divided into Civil and Criminal Chambers.

(i) **Court of Cassation:** Is the highest court of general jurisdiction in Egypt. Its sessions are held in Cairo. Final judgments rendered by Courts of Appeal in criminal and civil litigation may be petitioned to the Court of Cassation by the Defendant or the Public Prosecutor

in criminal litigation and by any of the parties in interest in civil litigation on grounds of defective application or interpretation of the law as stated in the challenged judgment, on grounds of irregularity of form or procedure, or violation of due process, and on grounds of defective reasoning of judgment rendered. The Court of Cassation is composed of the President, 41 Vice-Presidents and 92 Justices.

President: Hon. ABD AL-BORHAN NOOR.

(ii) **The Courts of Appeal:** Each has geographical jurisdiction over one or more of the governorates of Egypt. Each Court of Appeal is divided into Criminal and Civil Chambers. The Criminal Chambers try felonies, and the Civil Chambers hear appeals filed against such judgment rendered by the Tribunals of First Instance where the law so stipulates. Each Chamber is composed of three Superior Judges. Each Court of Appeal is composed of President, and sufficient numbers of Vice-Presidents and Superior Judges.

(iii) **The Tribunals of First Instance:** In each governorate there are one or more Tribunals of First Instance, each of which is divided into several Chambers for criminal and civil litigations. Each Chamber is composed of: (a) a presiding judge, and (b) two sitting judges. A Tribunal of First Instance hears, as an Appellate Court, certain litigations as provided under the law.

(iv) **District Tribunals:** Each is a one-judge ancillary Chamber of a Tribunal of First Instance, having jurisdiction over minor civil and criminal litigations in smaller districts within the jurisdiction of such Tribunal of First Instance.

PUBLIC PROSECUTION

Public prosecution is headed by the Attorney-General, assisted by a number of Senior Deputy and Deputy Attorneys-General, and a sufficient number of chief prosecutors, prosecutors and assistant prosecutors. Public prosecution is represented at all levels of the Courts of General Jurisdiction in all criminal litigations and also in certain civil litigations as required by the law. Public prosecution controls and supervises enforcement of criminal law judgments.

Attorney-General: MAHIR ABD AL-WAHID.

Prosecutor-General: MUHAMMAD ABD AL-AZIZ EL-GINDI.

ADMINISTRATIVE COURTS SYSTEM
(CONSEIL D'ETAT)

The Administrative Courts have jurisdiction over litigations involving the State or any of its governmental agencies. The Administrative Courts system is divided into two courts: the Administrative Courts and the Judicial Administrative Courts, at the top of which is the High Administrative Court. The Administrative Prosecutor investigates administrative crimes committed by government officials and civil servants.

President of Conseil d'Etat: Hon. MUHAMMAD HILAL QASIM.

Administrative Prosecutor: Hon. RIFA'AT KHAFAGI.

THE STATE COUNCIL

The State Council is an independent judicial body which has the authority to make decisions in administrative disputes and disciplinary cases within the judicial system.

THE SUPREME JUDICIAL COUNCIL

The Supreme Judicial Council was reinstituted in 1984, having been abolished in 1969. It exists to guarantee the independence of the judicial system from outside interference and is consulted with regard to draft laws organizing the affairs of the judicial bodies.

Religion

According to the 1986 census, some 94% of Egyptians are Muslims (and almost all of these follow Sunni tenets). According to government figures published in the same year, there are about 2m. Copts (a figure contested by Coptic sources, whose estimates range between 6m. and 7m.), forming the largest religious minority, and about 1m. members of other Christian groups. There is also a small Jewish minority.

ISLAM

There is a Higher Council for the Isamic Call, on which sit: the Grand Sheikh of al-Azhar (Chair); the Minister of Awqaf (Islamic Endowments); the President and Vice-President of Al-Azhar University; the Grand Mufti of Egypt; and the Secretary-General of the Higher Council for Islamic Affairs.

Grand Sheikh of al-Azhar: Sheikh MUHAMMAD SAYED ATTIYAH TANTAWI.

Grand Mufti of Egypt: AHMAD AT-TAYEB.

CHRISTIANITY
Orthodox Churches

Armenian Apostolic Orthodox Church: 179 Sharia Ramses, Cairo, POB 48-Faggalah; tel. (2) 5901385; fax (2) 906671; Archbishop ZAVEN CHINCHINIAN; 7,000 mems.

Coptic Orthodox Church: St Mark Cathedral, POB 9035, Anba Ruess, 222 Sharia Ramses, Abbassia, Cairo; tel. (2) 2857889; fax (2) 2825683; e-mail coptpope@tecmina.com; internet www.copticpope .org; f. AD 61; Patriarch Pope SHENOUDA III; c. 13m. followers in Egypt, Sudan, other African countries, the USA, Canada, Australia, Europe and the Middle East.

Greek Orthodox Patriarchate: POB 2006, Alexandria; tel. (3) 4868595; fax (3) 4875684; e-mail goptalex@tecmina.com; internet www.greekorthodox-alexandria.org; f. AD 64; Pope and Patriarch of Alexandria and All Africa His Beatitude PETROS VII; 3m. mems.

The Roman Catholic Church

Armenian Rite

The Armenian Catholic diocese of Alexandria, with an estimated 1,276 adherents at 31 December 2000, is suffragan to the Patriarchate of Cilicia. The Patriarch is resident in Beirut, Lebanon.

Bishop of Alexandria: (vacant), Patriarcat Arménien Catholique, 36 Sharia Muhammad Sabri Abou Alam, 11121 Cairo; tel. (2) 3938429; fax (2) 3932025; e-mail pacal@gega.net.

Chaldean Rite

The Chaldean Catholic diocese of Cairo had an estimated 500 adherents at 31 December 2000.

Bishop of Cairo: Rt Rev. YOUSSEF IBRAHIM SARRAF, Evêché Chaldéen, Basilique-Sanctuaire Notre Dame de Fatima, 141 Sharia Nouzha, 11316 Cairo (Heliopolis); tel. and fax (2) 6355718.

Coptic Rite

Egypt comprises the Coptic Catholic Patriarchate of Alexandria and five dioceses. At 31 December 2000 there were an estimated 217,444 adherents in the country.

Patriarch of Alexandria: Cardinal STEPHANOS II (ANDREAS GHATTAS), Patriarcat Copte Catholique, POB 69, 34 Sharia Ibn Sandar, Koubbeh Bridge, 11712 Cairo; tel. (2) 2571740; fax (2) 4545766.

Latin Rite

Egypt comprises the Apostolic Vicariate of Alexandria (incorporating Heliopolis and Port Said), containing an estimated 10,500 adherents at 31 December 2000.

Vicar Apostolic: Rt Rev. GIUSEPPE BAUSARDO (Titular Bishop of Ida in Mauretania), 10 Sharia Sidi el-Metwalli, Alexandria; tel. (3) 4876065; fax (3) 4838169; e-mail latinvic@link.net.

Maronite Rite

The Maronite diocese of Cairo had an estimated 5,000 adherents at 31 December 2000.

Bishop of Cairo: Rt Rev. JOSEPH DERGHAM, Evêché Maronite, 15 Sharia Hamdi, Daher, 11271 Cairo; tel. (2) 5939610.

Melkite Rite

His Beatitude GRÉGOIRE III LAHAM (resident in Damascus, Syria) is the Greek-Melkite Patriarch of Antioch, of Alexandria and of Jerusalem.

Patriarchal Exarchate of Egypt and Sudan: Patriarcat Grec-Melkite Catholique d'Alexandrie, 16 Sharia Daher, 11271 Cairo; tel. (2) 5904697; fax (2) 5935398; e-mail grecmelkitecath_egy@hotmail.com; 6,500 adherents (31 December 2000); Auxiliary Most Rev. JOSEPH JULES ZEREY, Titular Archbishop of Damietta.

Syrian Rite

The Syrian Catholic diocese of Cairo had an estimated 1,709 adherents at 31 December 2000.

Bishop of Cairo: Rt Rev. CLÉMENT-JOSEPH HANNOUCHE, Evêché Syrien Catholique, 46 Sharia Daher, 11271 Cairo; tel. (2) 5901234.

The Anglican Communion

The Anglican diocese of Egypt, suspended in 1958, was revived in 1974 and became part of the Episcopal Church in Jerusalem and the Middle East, formally inaugurated in January 1976. The Province has four dioceses: Jerusalem, Egypt, Cyprus and the Gulf, and Iran, and its President is the Bishop in Egypt. The Bishop in Egypt has jurisdiction also over the Anglican chaplaincies in Algeria, Djibouti, Eritrea, Ethiopia, Libya, Somalia and Tunisia.

Bishop in Egypt: Rt Rev. Dr MOUNEER HANNA ANIS, Diocesan Office, POB 87, 5 Sharia Michel Lutfalla, 11211Cairo (Zamalek); tel. (2) 7380829; fax (2) 7358941; e-mail diocese@intouch.com; internet www.geocities.com/dioceseofegypt.

Other Christian Churches

Coptic Evangelical Organization for Social Services: POB 162-11811, Panorama, Cairo; tel. (2) 2975901; fax (2) 2975878; e-mail gm@ceoss.org.eg.

Other denominations active in Egypt include the Coptic Evangelical Church (Synod of the Nile) and the Union of the Armenian Evangelical Churches in the Near East.

JUDAISM

The 1986 census recorded 794 Jews in Egypt.

Jewish Community: Office of the Community, President ESTHER WEINSTEIN, 13 Sharia Sebil el-Khazindar, Abbassia, Cairo; tel. (2) 4824613; internet www.geocities.com/rain/forest/vines/5855.

The Press

Despite a fairly high illiteracy rate in Egypt, the country's press is well developed. Cairo is one of the region's largest publishing centres.

All newspapers and magazines are supervised, according to law, by the Supreme Press Council. The four major publishing houses of al-Ahram, Dar al-Hilal, Dar Akhbar al-Yawm and Dar at-Tahrir operate as separate entities and compete with each other commercially.

The most authoritative daily newspaper is the very long-established *Al-Ahram.*

DAILIES
Alexandria

Bareed ach-Charikat (Companies' Post): POB 813, Alexandria; f. 1952; Arabic; evening; commerce, finance, insurance and marine affairs; Editor S. BENEDUCCI; circ. 15,000.

Al-Ittihad al-Misri (Egyptian Unity): 13 Sharia Sidi Abd ar-Razzak, Alexandria; f. 1871; Arabic; evening; Propr ANWAR MAHER FARAG; Dir HASSAN MAHER FARAG.

Le Journal d'Alexandrie: 1 Sharia Rolo, Alexandria; French; evening; Editor CHARLES ARCACHE.

La Réforme: 8 Passage Sherif, Alexandria; French.

As-Safeer (The Ambassador): 4 Sharia as-Sahafa, Alexandria; f. 1924; Arabic; evening; Editor MUSTAFA SHARAF.

Tachydromos-Egyptos: 4 Sharia Zangarol, Alexandria; tel. (3) 35650; f. 1879; Greek; morning; liberal; Publr PENNY KOUTSOUMIS; Editor DINOS KOUTSOUMIS; circ. 2,000.

Cairo

Al-Ahram (The Pyramids): Sharia al-Galaa, Cairo 11511; tel. (2) 5801600; fax (2) 5786023; e-mail ahramdaily@ahram.org.eg; f. 1875; Arabic; morning, incl. Sundays (international edition published in London, England; North American edition published in New York, USA); Chair. and Chief Editor IBRAHIM NAFEH; circ. 900,000 (weekdays), 1.1m. (Friday).

Al-Ahram al-Misaa' (The Evening *Al-Ahram*): Sharia al-Galaa, Cairo 11511; f. 1990; Arabic; evening; Editor-in-Chief MORSI ATALLAH.

Al-Ahrar: 58 Manshyet as-Sadr, Kobry al-Kobba, Cairo; tel. (2) 4823046; fax (2) 4823027; f. 1977; organ of Liberal Socialist Party; Editor-in-Chief SALAH QABADAYA.

Al-Akhbar (The News): Dar Akhbar al-Yawm, 6 Sharia as-Sahafa, Cairo; tel. (2) 5782600; fax (2) 5782520; f. 1952; Arabic; Chair. IBRAHIM ABU SADAH; Man. Editor GALAL DEWIDAR; circ. 780,000.

Arev: 3 Sharia Sulayman Halabi, Cairo; tel. (2) 754703; f. 1915; Armenian; evening; official organ of the Armenian Liberal Democratic Party; Editor AVEDIS YAPOUDJIAN.

The Egyptian Gazette: 24–26 Sharia Zakaria Ahmad, Cairo; tel. (2) 5783333; fax (2) 5781110; e-mail 100236.3241@compuserve.com; f. 1880; English; morning; Chair. SAMIR RAGAB; Editor-in-Chief MUHAMMAD ALI IBRAHIM; circ. 90,000.

Al-Gomhouriya (The Republic): 24 Sharia Zakaria Ahmad, Cairo; tel. (2) 5783333; fax (2) 5781717; f. 1953; Arabic; morning; mainly economic affairs; Chair. and Editor-in-Chief SAMIR RAGAB; circ. 900,000.

Al-Misaa' (The Evening): 24 Sharia Zakaria Ahmad, Cairo; tel. (2) 5781010; fax (2) 5784747; f. 1956; Arabic; evening; political, social and sport; Editor-in-Chief MUHAMMAD FOUDAH; Man. Dir ABD AL-HAMROSE; circ. 450,000.

Phos: 14 Sharia Zakaria Ahmad, Cairo; f. 1896; Greek; morning; Editor S. PATERAS; Man. BASILE A. PATERAS; circ. 20,000.

Le Progrès Egyptien: 24 Sharia Zakaria Ahmad, Cairo; tel. (2) (2) 5783333; fax (2) 5781110; f. 1890; French; morning including Sundays; Chair. SAMIR RAGAB; Editor-in-Chief KHALED ANWAR BAKIR; circ. 60,000.

Al-Wafd: 1 Sharia Boulos Hanna, Cairo (Dokki); tel. (2) 3482079; fax (2) 3602007; f. 1984; organ of the New Wafd Party; Editor-in-Chief GAMAL BADAWI; circ. 360,000.

PERIODICALS
Alexandria

Al-Ahad al-Gedid (New Sunday): 88 Sharia Said M. Koraim, Alexandria; tel. (3) 807874; f. 1936; Editor-in-Chief and Publr GALAL M. KORAITEM; circ. 60,000.

Alexandria Medical Journal: 4 G. Carducci, Alexandria; tel. (3) 4829001; fax (3) 4833076; internet www.who.sci.eg; f. 1922; English, French and Arabic; quarterly; publ. by Alexandria Medical Asscn; Editor Prof. TOUSSOUN ABOUL AZM.

Amitié Internationale: 59 ave el-Hourriya, Alexandria; tel. (3) 23639; f. 1957; publ. by Asscn Egyptienne d'Amitié Internationale; Arabic and French; quarterly; Editor Dr ZAKI BADAOUI.

L'Annuaire des Sociétés Egyptiennes par Actions: 23 Midan Tahrir, Alexandria; f. 1930; annually in Dec.; French; Propr ELIE I. POLITI; Editor OMAR ES-SAYED MOURSI.

L'Echo Sportif: 7 Sharia de l'Archevêché, Alexandria; French; weekly; Propr MICHEL BITTAR.

Egyptian Cotton Gazette: POB 1772, 12 Sharia Muhammad Tala'at Nooman, Alexandria 21111; tel. (3) 4806971; fax (3) 4873002; e-mail alcotexa@idsc.gov.eg; internet www.alcotexa.org; f. 1947; organ of the Alexandria Cotton Exporters' Association; English; 2 a year; Chief Editor GALAI EL REFAI.

Informateur des Assurances: 1 Sharia Sinan, Alexandria; f. 1936; French; monthly; Propr ELIE I. POLITI; Editor SIMON A. BARANIS.

La Réforme Illustré: 8 Passage Sherif, Alexandria; French; weekly; general.

Sina 'at en-Nassig (L'Industrie Textile): 5 rue de l'Archevêché, Alexandria; Arabic and French; monthly; Editor PHILIPPE COLAS.

Voce d'Italia: 90 Sharia Farahde, Alexandria; Italian; fortnightly; Editor R. AVELLINO.

Cairo

Al-Ahali (The People): Sharia Kareem ad-Dawli, Tala'at Harb Sq., Cairo; tel. (2) 7786583; fax (2) 3900412; f. 1978; weekly; publ. by the National Progressive Unionist Party; Chair. LOTFI WAKID; Editor-in-Chief ABD AL-BAKOURY.

Al-Ahram al-Arabi: Sharia al-Galaa, Cairo 11511; f. 1997; Arabic; weekly; political, social and economic affairs; Chair. IBRAHIM NAFIE; Editor-in-Chief OSAMA SARAYA.

Al-Ahram Hebdo: POB 1057, Sharia al-Galaa, Cairo 11511; tel. (2) 5783104; fax (2) 5782631; e-mail hebdo@ahram.org.eg; internet www.ahram.org.eg/hebdo; f. 1993; French; weekly; Editor-in-Chief MUHAMMAD SALMAWI.

Al-Ahram al-Iqtisadi (The Economic *Al-Ahram*): Sharia al-Galaa, Cairo 11511; tel. (2) 5786100; fax (2) 5786833; Arabic; weekly (Monday); economic and political affairs; owned by Al-Ahram publrs; Chief Editor ISSAM RIFA'AT; circ. 93,798.

Al-Ahram Weekly (The Pyramids): Al-Ahram Bldg, Sharia al-Galaa, Cairo 11511; tel. (2) 5786100; fax (2) 5786833; e-mail weeklyweb@ahram.org.eg; internet www.ahram.org.eg/weekly; f. 1989; English; weekly; publ. by Al-Ahram publications; Editor-in-Chief HOSNI GUINDY; circ. 150,000.

Akhbar al-Adab: 6 Sharia as-Sahafa, Cairo; tel. (2) 5795620; fax (2) 5782510; e-mail akhbarelyom@akhbarelyom.org; www.akhbare lyom.org.eg/eladab; f. 1993; literature and arts for young people; Editor-in-Chief GAMAL AL-GHITANI.

Akhbar al-Hawadith: 6 Sharia as-Sahafa, Cairo; tel. (2) 5782600; fax (2) 5782510; f. 1993; weekly; crime reports; Editor-in-Chief MUHAMMAD BARAKAT.

Akhbar an-Nogoome: 6 Sharia as-Sahafa, Cairo; tel. (2) 5782600; fax (2) 5782510; f. 1991; weekly; theatre and film news; Editor-in-Chief AMAL OSMAN.

Akhbar ar-Riadah: 6 Sharia as-Sahafa, Cairo; tel. (2) 5782600; fax (2) 5782510; f. 1990; weekly; sport; Editor-in-Chief IBRAHIM HEGAZY.

Akhbar al-Yom (Daily News): 6 Sharia as-Sahafa, Cairo; tel. (2) 5782600; fax (2) 5782520; www.akhbarelyom.org.eg; f. 1944; Arabic; weekly (Saturday); Chair. and Editor-in-Chief IBRAHIM ABU SEDAH; circ. 1,184,611.

Akher Sa'a (Last Hour): Dar Akhbar al-Yawm, Sharia as-Sahafa, Cairo; tel. (2) 5782600; fax (2) 5782530; f. 1934; Arabic; weekly (Sunday); independent; consumer and news magazine; Editor-in-Chief MAHMOUD SALAH; circ. 150,000.

Aqidaty (My Faith): 24–26 Sharia Zakaria Ahmad, Cairo; tel. (2) 5783333; fax (2) 5781110; weekly; Muslim religious newspaper; Editor-in-Chief ABD AR-RAOUF ES-SAYED; circ. 300,000.

Al-Arabi an-Nassiri: Cairo; f. 1993; publ. by the Nasserist Party; Editor-in-Chief MAHMOUD EL-MARAGHI.

Al-Azhar: Idarat al-Azhar, Sharia al-Azhar, Cairo; f. 1931; Arabic; Islamic monthly; supervised by the Egyptian Council for Islamic Research of Al-Azhar University; Dir MUHAMMAD FARID WAGDI.

Al-Bitrul (Petroleum): Cairo; monthly; publ. by the Egyptian General Petroleum Corporation.

Cairo Today: POB 2098, 1079 Corniche en-Nil, Cairo (Garden City); monthly.

Computerworld Middle East: World Publishing Ltd (Egypt), 41A Masaken al-Fursan Bldg, Sharia Kamal Hassan Ali, Cairo 11361; tel. (2) 3460601; fax (2) 3470118; English; monthly; specialist computer information.

Contemporary Thought: University of Cairo, Cairo; quarterly; Editor Dr Z. N. MAHMOUD.

Ad-Da'wa (The Call): Cairo; Arabic; monthly; organ of the Muslim Brotherhood.

Ad-Doctor: 8 Sharia Hoda Sharawi, Cairo; f. 1947; Arabic; monthly; Editor Dr AHMAD M. KAMAL; circ. 30,000.

Droit al-Haqq: Itihad al-Mohameen al-Arab, 13 Sharia Itihad, Cairo; publ. by the Arab Lawyers' Union; 3 a year.

Echos: 1–5 Sharia Mahmoud Bassiouni, Cairo; f. 1947; French; weekly; Dir and Propr GEORGES QRFALI.

The Egyptian Mail: 24–26 Sharia Zakaria Ahmad, Cairo; weekly; Sat. edn of *The Egyptian Gazette*; English; circ. 40,000.

El-Elm Magazine (Sciences): 24 Sharia Zakaria Ahmad, Cairo; tel. (2) 5781010; fax (2) 5784747; f. 1976; Arabic; monthly; publ. with the Academy of Scientific Research in Egypt; circ. 70,000.

Al-Fusoul (The Seasons): 17 Sharia Sherif Pasha, Cairo; Arabic; monthly; Propr and Chief Editor SAMIR MUHAMMAD ZAKI ABD AL-KADER.

Al-Garidat at-Tigariyat al-Misriya (The Egyptian Business Paper): 25 Sharia Nubar Pasha, Cairo; f. 1921; Arabic; weekly; circ. 7,000.

Hawa'a (Eve): Dar al-Hilal, 16 Sharia Muhammad Ezz el-Arab, Cairo 11511; tel. (2) 3625450; fax (2) 3625469; f. 1892; women's magazine; Arabic; weekly (Sat.); Chief Editor EKBAL BARAKA; circ. 210,502.

Al-Hilal Magazine: Dar al-Hilal, 16 Sharia Muhammad Ezz el-Arab, Cairo 11511; tel. (2) 3625450; fax (2) 3625469; f. 1895; Arabic; literary monthly; Editor MOUSTAFA NABIL.

Horreyati: 24 Sharia Zakaria Ahmad, Cairo; tel. (2) 5781010; fax (2) 5784747; f. 1990; weekly; social, cultural and sport; Editor-in-Chief MUHAMMAD NOUR ED-DIN; circ. 250,000.

Huwa wa Hiya (He and She): Middle East Foundation, POB 525, Cairo 11511; tel. (2) 5167400; fax (2) 5167325; e-mail editor@huwa wahiya.com; f. 1977; monthly; news, leisure, sport, health, religion, women's issues; Dir GEORGE TAWFIK.

Industrial Egypt: POB 251, 26A Sharia Sherif Pasha, Cairo; tel. (2) 3928317; fax (2) 3928075; f. 1924; quarterly bulletin and year book of the Federation of Egyptian Industries in English and Arabic; Editor ALI FAHMY.

Informateur Financier et Commercial: 24 Sharia Sulayman Pasha, Cairo; f. 1929; weekly; Dir HENRI POLITI; circ. 15,000.

Al-Iza'a wat-Television (Radio and Television): 16 Sharia Muhammad Ezz el-Arab, Cairo 11511; tel. (2) 3643314; fax (2) 3543030; f. 1935; Arabic; weekly; Man. Editor MAHMOUD ALI; circ. 80,000.

Al-Kerazeh (The Sermon): Cairo; Arabic; weekly newspaper of the Coptic Orthodox Church.

Al-Kawakeb (The Stars): Dar al-Hilal, 16 Sharia Muhammad Ezz el-Arab, Cairo 11511; tel. (2) 3625450; fax (2) 3625469; f. 1952; Arabic; weekly; film magazine; Editor-in-Chief RAGAA AN-NAKKASH; circ. 86,381.

Kitab al-Hilal: Dar al-Hilal, 16 Sharia Muhammad Ezz el-Arab, Cairo 11511; tel. (2) 3625450; fax (2) 3625469; monthly; Founders EMILE and SHOUKRI ZEIDAN; Editor MOUSTAFA NABIL.

Al-Kora wal-Malaeb (Football and Playgrounds): 24 Sharia Zakaria Ahmad, Cairo; tel. (2) 5783333; fax (2) 5784747; f. 1976; Arabic; weekly; sport; circ. 150,000.

Al-Liwa' al-Islami (Islamic Standard): 11 Sharia Sherif Pasha, Cairo; f. 1982; Arabic; weekly; govt paper to promote official view of

Islamic revivalism; Propr AHMAD HAMZA; Editor MUHAMMAD ALI SHETA; circ. 30,000.

Lotus Magazine: 104 Sharia Qasr el-Eini, Cairo; f. 1992; English, French and Arabic; quarterly; computer software magazine; Editor BEREND HARMENS.

Magallat al-Mohandessin (The Engineer's Magazine): 28 Sharia Ramses, Cairo; f. 1945; publ. by The Engineers' Syndicate; Arabic and English; 10 a year; Editor and Sec. MAHMOUD SAMI ABD AL-KAWI.

Al-Magallat az-Zira'ia (The Agricultural Magazine): Cairo; monthly; agriculture; circ. 30,000.

Mayo (May): Sharia al-Galaa, Cairo; f. 1981; weekly; organ of National Democratic Party; Chair. ABDULLAH ABD AL-BARY; Chief Editor SAMIR RAGAB; circ. 500,000.

Medical Journal of Cairo University: Qasr el-Eini Hospital, Sharia Qasr el-Eini, Cairo; tel. and fax (2) 3655768; f. 1933; Qasr el-Eini Clinical Society; English; quarterly; Editor SALEH A. BEDIR.

MEN Economic Weekly: Middle East News Agency, 4 Sharia Hoda Sharawi, Cairo; tel. (2) 3933000; fax (2) 3935055.

The Middle East Observer: 41 Sharia Sherif, Cairo; tel. (2) 3926919; fax (2) 3939732; e-mail inquri@miobserver.com; f. 1954; English; weekly; specializing in economics of Middle East and African markets; also publishes supplements on law, foreign trade and tenders; agent for IMF, UN and IDRC publications, distributor of World Bank publications; Man. Owner AHMAD FODA; Chief Editor HESHAM A. RAOUF; circ. 20,000.

Middle East Times Egypt: 2 Sharia el-Malek el-Afdal, Cairo (Zamalek); tel. (2) 3419930; fax (2) 3413725; e-mail met@ritsec1.com.eg; f. 1983; English; weekly; Man. Editor ROD CRAIG; circ. 6,000.

Al-Musawar: Dar al-Hilal, 16 Sharia Muhammad Ezz el-Arab, Cairo 11511; tel. (2) 3625450; fax (2) 3625469; f. 1924; Arabic; weekly; news; Chair. and Editor-in-Chief MAKRAM MUHAMMAD AHMAD; circ. 130,423.

Nesf ad-Donia: Sharia al-Galaa, Cairo 11511; tel. (2) 5786100; f. 1990; weekly; women's magazine; publ. by Al-Ahram Publications; Editor-in-Chief SANAA AL-BESI.

October: Dar al-Maaref, 1119 Sharia Corniche en-Nil, Cairo; tel. (2) 5777077; fax (2) 5744999; f. 1976; weekly; Chair. and Editor-in-Chief RAGAB AL-BANA; circ. 140,500.

Al-Omal (The Workers): 90 Sharia al-Galaa, Cairo; publ. by the Egyptian Trade Union Federation: Arabic; weekly; Chief Editor AHMAD HARAK.

PC World Middle East: World Publishing Ltd (Egypt), 41A Masaken al-Fursan Bldg, Sharia Kamal Hassan Ali, Cairo 11361; tel. (2) 34606; fax (2) 3470118; monthly; computers.

Le Progrès Dimanche: 24 Sharia al-Galaa, Cairo; tel. (2) 5781010; fax (2) 5784747; French; weekly; Sunday edition of *Le Progrès Egyptien*; Editor-in-Chief KHALED ANWAR BAKIR; circ. 35,000.

Rose al-Yousuf: 89A Sharia Qasr el-Eini, Cairo; tel. (2) 3540888; fax (2) 3556413; f. 1925; Arabic; weekly; political; circulates throughout all Arab countries; Chair. of Board and Editor-in-Chief MUHAMMAD ABD AL-MONEIM; circ. 35,000.

As-Sabah (The Morning): 4 Sharia Muhammad Said Pasha, Cairo; f. 1922; Arabic; weekly (Thurs.); Editor RAOUF TAWFIK.

Sabah al-Kheir (Good Morning): 89A Sharia Qasr el-Eini, Cairo; tel. (2) 3540888; fax (2) 3556413; f. 1956; Arabic; weekly (Thurs.); light entertainment; Chief Editor RAOUF TAWFIK; circ. 70,000.

Ash-Shaab (The People): 313 Sharia Port Said, Sayeda Zeinab, Cairo; tel. (2) 3909716; fax (2) 3900283; e-mail elshaab@idsc.gov.eg; f. 1979; organ of Socialist Labour Party; bi-weekly (Tues. and Fri.); Editor-in-Chief MAGDI AHMAD HUSSEIN; circ. 130,000.

Shashati (My Screen): 24 Sharia Zakaria Ahmad, Cairo; tel. (2) 5781010; fax (2) 5784747; weekly; art, culture, fashion and television news.

As-Siyassa ad-Dawliya: Al-Ahram Bldg, 12th Floor, Sharia al-Galaa, Cairo 11511; tel. (2) 5786022; fax (2) 5786833; e-mail siyassa@ahram.org.eg; quarterly; politics and foreign affairs; Editor-in-Chief Dr OSAMA AL-GHAZALI.

Tabibak al-Khass (Family Doctor): Dar al-Hilal, 16 Sharia Muhammad Ezz el-Arab, Cairo; tel. (2) 3625473; fax (2) 3625442; monthly.

At-Tahrir (Liberation): 5 Sharia Naguib, Rihani, Cairo; Arabic; weekly; Editor ABD AL-AZIZ SADEK.

At-Taqaddum (Progress): c/o 1 Sharia Jarim ed-Dawlah, Cairo; f. 1978; weekly; organ of National Progressive Unionist Party.

Tchehreh Nema: 14 Sharia Hassan el-Akbar (Abdine), Cairo; f. 1904; monthly; political, literary and general; Editor MANUCHEHR TCHEHREH NEMA MOADEB ZADEH.

Up-to-Date International Industry: 10 Sharia al-Galaa, Cairo; Arabic and English; monthly; foreign trade journal.

Watani (My Country): 27 Sharia Abd al-Khalek Sarwat, Cairo; tel. (2) 3927201; fax (2) 3935946; e-mail watani@tecmina.com; internet www.watani.com.eg; f. 1958; Arabic and English; independent Sun. newspaper addressing Egyptians in general and the Christian Copts in particular; Editor-in-Chief YOUSSEF SIDHOM; circ. 60,000–100,000.

Yulio (July): July Press and Publishing House, Cairo; f. 1986; weekly; Nasserist; Editor ABDULLAH IMAM; and a monthly cultural magazine, Editor MAHMOUD AL-MARAGHI.

NEWS AGENCIES

Middle East News Agency (MENA): 17 Sharia Hoda Sharawi, Cairo; tel. (2) 3933000; fax (2) 3935055; e-mail newsroom@mena.org.eg; internet www.mena.org.eg; f. 1955; regular service in Arabic, English and French; Chair. and Editor-in-Chief MOUSTAFA NAGUIB.

Foreign Bureaux

Agence France-Presse (AFP): POB 1437-15511, 2nd Floor, 10 Misaha Sq., Cairo; tel. (2) 3481236; fax (2) 3603282; Chief SAMMY KETZ.

Agencia EFE (Spain): 35A Sharia Abou el-Feda, 4th Floor, Apt 14, Cairo (Zamalek); Correspondent DOMINGO DEL PIÑO.

Agenzia Nazionale Stampa Associata (ANSA) (Italy): 19 Sharia Abd al-Khalek Sarwat, Cairo; tel. (2) 3929821; fax (2) 3938642; Chief ANTONELLA TARQUINI.

Allgemeiner Deutscher Nachrichtendienst (ADN) (Germany): 17 Sharia el-Brazil, Apt 59, Cairo (Zamalek); tel. (2) 3404006; Correspondent RALF SCHULTZE.

Associated Press (AP) (USA): POB 1077, 1117 Sharia Corniche en-Nil, (Maspiro), Cairo 11221; tel. (2) 5784091; fax (2) 5784094; internet www.ap.org; Chief of Middle East Services EARLEEN FISHER.

Deutsche Presse-Agentur (dpa) (Germany): 1st Floor, 8 Sharia Dar esh-Shefaa, Cairo (Garden City); tel. (2) 7956842; fax (2) 7956318; e-mail dpa@gega.net; Chief ANN-BÉATRICE CLASMANN.

Informatsionnoye Telegrafnoye Agentstvo Rossii—Telegrafnoye Agentstvo Suverennykh Stran (ITAR—TASS) (Russia): 30 Sharia Muhammad Mazhar, Cairo (Zamalek); tel. (2) 3419784; fax (2) 3417268; Dir MIKHAIL I. KROUTIKHIN.

Jiji Press (Japan): 9 Sharia el-Kamal Muhammad, Cairo (Zamalek); tel. (2) 7356237; fax (2) 7355244; e-mail jijipresscairo@yahoo.com; Chief TETSUYA KATAYAMA.

Kyodo News (Japan): Flat 301, 15 Sharia Hassan Sabri, Cairo 11211 (Zamalek); tel. (2) 7361756; fax (2) 7356105; e-mail kyodo@intouch.com; Chief SHINGO KINIWA.

Reuters (United Kingdom): POB 2040, 21st Floor, Bank Misr Tower, 153 Sharia Muhammad Farid, Cairo; tel. (2) 5777150; fax (2) 5771133; e-mail cairo.newsroom@reuters.com; internet www.reuters.com; Chief ALISTAIR LYON.

United Press International (UPI) (USA): POB 872, 4 Sharia Eloui, Cairo; tel. (2) 3928106.

Xinhua (New China) News Agency (People's Republic of China): 2 Moussa Galal Sq., Mohandessin, Cairo; tel. (2) 3448950.

The Iraqi News Agency (INA) and the Saudi Press Agency (SPA) are also represented in Cairo.

PRESS ASSOCIATIONS

Egyptian Press Syndicate: Cairo; Chair. IBRAHIM NAFEH.

Foreign Press Association: Room 2037, Marriott Hotel, Cairo; tel. (2) 3419957.

Publishers

General Egyptian Book Organization: POB 1660, 117 Sharia Corniche en-Nil, Boulac, Cairo; tel. (2) 5775371; fax (2) 5754213; e-mail ssarhan@idsc.gov.eg; f. 1961; editing, publishing and distribution; organizer of Cairo International Book Fair; affiliated to the Ministry of Culture; Chair. Dr SAMIR SARHAN; Commercial Dir SAMIR SAAD KHALIL.

Alexandria

Alexandria University Press: Shatby, Alexandria.

Dar al-Matbo al-Gadidah: 5 Sharia St Mark, Alexandria; tel. (3) 4825508; fax (3) 4833819; agriculture, information sciences; social sciences.

Egyptian Printing and Publishing House: Ahmad es-Sayed Marouf, 59 Safia Zaghoul, Alexandria; f. 1947.

Maison Egyptienne d'Editions: Ahmad es-Sayed Marouf, Sharia Adib, Alexandria; f. 1950.

Maktab al-Misri al-Hadith li-t-Tiba wan-Nashr: 7 Sharia Noubar, Alexandria; also at 2 Sharia Sherif, Cairo; Man. AHMAD YEHIA.

Cairo

Al-Ahram Establishment: Al-Ahram Bldg, 6 Sharia al-Galaa, Cairo 11511; tel. (2) 5786100; fax (2) 5786023; e-mail ahram@ahram.org.eg; internet www.ahram.org.eg; f. 1875; publ. newspapers, magazines and books, incl. *Al-Ahram*; Chair. and Chief Editor IBRAHIM NAFEI; Dep. Chair. and Gen. Man. ALI GHONEIM.

Akhbar al-Yawm Publishing Group: 6 Sharia as-Sahafa, Cairo; tel. (2) 5748100; fax (2) 5748895; f. 1944; publ. *Al-Akhbar* (daily), *Akhbar al-Yawm* (weekly), and colour magazine *Akher Sa'a* (weekly); Pres. IBRAHIM SAAD.

Boustany's Publishing House: 29 Sharia Faggalah, Cairo 11271; tel. (2) 5915315; fax (2) 5908025; e-mail boustany@idsc.net.eg; internet www.boustanys.com; f. 1900; fiction, poetry, history, biography, philosophy, language, literature, politics, religion, archaeology, Egyptology; Chief Exec. FADWA BOUSTANY.

Cairo University Press: Al-Giza, Cairo; tel. (2) 846144.

Dar al-Gomhouriya: 24 Sharia Zakaria Ahmad, Cairo; tel. (2) 5781010; fax (2) 5784747; affiliate of At-Tahrir Printing and Publishing House; publications include the dailies, *Al-Gomhouriya*, *Al-Misaa', Egyptian Gazette* and *Le Progrès Egyptien*; Pres. SAMIR RAGAB.

Dar al-Hilal Publishing Institution: 16 Sharia Muhammad Ezz el-Arab, Cairo 11511; tel. (2) 3625450; fax (2) 3625469; f. 1892; publ. *Al-Hilal, Riwayat al-Hilal, Kitab al-Hilal, Tabibak al-Khass* (monthlies); *Al-Mussawar, Al-Kawakeb, Hawaa, Samir, Mickey* (weeklies); Chief Exec. MAKRAN MUHAMMAD AHMAD.

Dar al-Kitab al-Masri: POB 156, 33 Sharia Qasr en-Nil, Cairo 11511; tel. (2) 3922168; fax (2) 3924657; e-mail hlelzein@datum.com.eg; f. 1929; publishing, printing and distribution; publishers of books on Islam and history, as well as dictionaries, encyclopaedias, textbooks, children's books and books of general interest; Pres. and Man. Dir HASSAN EZ-ZEIN.

Dar al-Maaref: 1119 Sharia Corniche en-Nil, Cairo; tel. (2) 5777077; fax (2) 5744999; e-mail maaref@idselgov.eg; f. 1890; publishing, printing and distribution of wide variety of books in Arabic and other languages; publishers of *October* magazine; Chair. and Man. Dir RAGAB AL-BANA.

Dar an-Nahda al-Arabia: 32 Sharia Abd al-Khalek Sarwat, Cairo; tel. (2) 3926931; f. 1960; literature, law.

Dar an-Nashr (formerly Les Editions Universitaires d'Egypte): POB 1347, 41 Sharia Sherif, Cairo 11511; tel. (2) 3934606; fax (2) 3921997; f. 1947; university textbooks, academic works, encyclopaedia.

Dar ash-Shorouk Publishing House (Egyptian Publishers Association): 8 Sharia Sebaweh el-Masri, Rabaa el-Adawia; Nasr City, Cairo 11371; tel. (2) 4023399; fax (2) 4037567; e-mail imoallem@shorouk.com; f. 1968; publishing, printing and distribution; publishers of books on politics, history, Islamic studies, economics, literature, art and children's books; Chair. IBRAHIM EL-MOALLEM.

Dar ath-Thakafah al-Gadidah: 32 Sharia Sabry Abou Alam, Cairo; tel. (2) 42718; f. 1968; Pres. MUHAMMAD YOUSUF ELGUINDI.

Editions le Progrès: 6 Sharia Sherif Pasha, Cairo; Propr WADI SHOUKRI.

Egyptian Co for Printing and Publishing: 40 Sharia Noubar, Cairo; tel. (2) 21310; Chair. MUHAMMAD MAHMOUD HAMED.

Elias Modern Publishing House: 1 Sharia Kenisset ar-Rum el-Kathulik, Daher, Cairo; tel. (2) 5903756; fax (2) 5880091; e-mail eliaspub@gega.net; internet www.eliaspublishing.com; f. 1913; publishing, printing and distribution; publs dictionaries, children's books and books on linguistics, poetry and arts; Man. Dir LAURA KFOURY; Gen. Man. NADIM ELIAS.

Al-Khira Press: 8 Sharia Soliman el-Halabi, Cairo; tel. and fax (2) 5744809; Owner ABD AL-MEGUID MUHAMMAD.

Lagnat at-Taalif wat-Targama wan-Nashr (Committee for Writing, Translating and Publishing Books): 9 Sharia el-Kerdassi (Abdine), Cairo.

Librairie La Renaissance d'Egypte (Hassan Muhammad & Sons): POB 2172, 9 Sharia Adly, Cairo; f. 1930; religion, history, geography, medicine, architecture, economics, politics, law, philosophy, psychology, children's books, atlases, dictionaries; Man. HASSAN MUHAMMAD.

Maktabet Misr: POB 16, 3 Sharia Kamal Sidki, Cairo; tel. (2) 5898553; fax (2) 5907593; f. 1932; publs wide variety of fiction, biographies and textbooks for schools and universities; Man. AMIR SAID GOUDA ES-SAHHAR.

Middle East Book Centre: 45 Sharia Qasr en-Nil, Cairo; tel. (2) 910980; f. 1954; biography, fiction, history, language, literature, religion, philosophy, sciences; Man. Dir Dr A. M. MOSHARRAFA.

National Centre for Educational Research and Development: 12 Sharia Waked, el-Borg el-Faddy, POB 836, Cairo; tel. (2) 3930981; f. 1956; formerly Documentation and Research Centre for Education (Ministry of Education); bibliographies, directories, information and education bulletins; Dir Prof. ABD EL-FATTAH GALAL.

National Library Press (Dar al-Kutub): Midan Ahmad Maher, Cairo; bibliographic works.

Senouhy Publishers: 54 Sharia Abd al-Khalek Sarwat, Cairo; f. 1956; history, poetry, regional interests, religion, non-fiction; Man. Dir LEILA A. FADEL.

At-Tahrir Printing and Publishing House: 24 Sharia Zakaria Ahmad, Cairo; tel. (2) 5781222; fax (2) 2784747; e-mail eltahrir@eltahrir.net; internet www.eltahrir.net; f. 1953; affil. to Shura (Advisory) Council; Pres. and Chair. of Bd SAMIR RAGAB.

Watani (My Country): 27 Sharia Abd al-Khalek Sarwat, Cairo; tel. (2) 3927201; fax (2) 3935946; e-mail watani@tecmina.com; internet www.watani.com.eg; f. 1958; Arabic and English; Editor-in-Chief YOUSSEF SIDHOM.

Broadcasting and Communications

TELECOMMUNICATIONS

Telecommunications Regulatory Authority (TRA): 3 Burg Abu-el Feda, Cairo (Zamalek); e-mail tra@mcit.gov.eg; f. 2000.

Telecom Egypt: POB 2271, Sharia Ramses, Cairo 11511; tel. (2) 5793444; fax (2) 5744244; internet www.telecomegypt.com.eg; f. 1957; sole provider of fixed-line telephones; due to begin mobile telecommunications operations in 2002; partial privatization scheduled for 2002; Chair. AKIL HAMED BESHIR.

Egyptian Company for Mobile Services (MobiNil): Cairo; e-mail customercare@mobinil.com; internet www.mobinil.com; began operation of the existing state-controlled mobile telecommunications network in early 1998; owned by France Telecom and Orascom Telecom; CEO OSMAN SULTAN.

Orascom Telecom: 160 Sharia 26 July, POB 1191, Cairo (Agouza); tel. (2) 3026930; fax (2) 3440201; e-mail info@orascom.com; internet www.orascom.com; Chair. NAGUIB SAWARIS.

Vodafone Egypt: 7A Corniche en-Nil, Maadi, 11431 Cairo; tel. (2) 5292000; e-mail customer-service@vodafone.com.eg; internet www.vodafone.com/eg; f. 1998 by the MisrFone consortium; mobile telephone service provider; majority-owned by Vodafone International (UK); Chair. MUHAMMAD NOSSAIR; CEO and Man. Dir IAN GRAY.

BROADCASTING

Radio

Egyptian Radio and Television Union (ERTU): POB 11511, Cairo 1186; tel. (2) 5787120; fax (2) 746989; internet www.sis.gov.eg/vidaudio/html/audiofm.htm; f. 1928; home service radio programmes in Arabic, English and French; foreign services in Arabic, English, French, Swahili, Hausa, Bengali, Urdu, German, Spanish, Armenian, Greek, Hebrew, Indonesian, Malay, Thai, Hindi, Pushtu, Persian, Turkish, Somali, Portuguese, Fulani, Italian, Zulu, Shona, Sindebele, Lingala, Afar, Amharic, Yoruba, Wolof, Bambara; Pres. AMIN BASSIOUNI.

Middle East Radio: Société Egyptienne de Publicité, 24–26 Sharia Zakaria Ahmad, Cairo; tel. (2) 5781010; fax (2) 5784747; internet www.tahriv.net.

Television

Egypt had two direct television broadcast satellites. The second satellite, Nilesat 102, was launched in August 2000.

Egyptian Radio and Television Union (ERTU): (see Radio).

Finance

(cap. = capital; res = reserves;
dep. = deposits; m. = million; brs = branches;
amounts in Egyptian pounds unless otherwise stated)

BANKING

Central Bank

Central Bank of Egypt: 31 Sharia Qasr en-Nil, Cairo; tel. (2) 3931514; fax (2) 3926361; e-mail research@cbe.org.eg; internet www.cbe.org.eg; f. 1961; controls Egypt's monetary policy and supervises the banking and insurance sectors; dep. 101,904m., total assets 146,001m. (June 2000); Gov. and Chair. ISMAIL HASSAN MUHAMMAD; Dep. Gov. MAHMOUD IBRAHIM ABOUL-EIOUN; 3 brs.

Commercial and Specialized Banks

Alexandria Commercial and Maritime Bank, SAE: POB 2376, 85 ave el-Hourriya, Alexandria 21519; tel. (3) 3921237; fax (3) 3913706; f. 1981; cap. 84.1m., res 87.0m., dep. 1,386.2m. (Dec. 2001); Chair. and Man. Dir MUHAMMAD ADEL EL-BARKOUKI; 6 brs.

Bank of Alexandria: 49 Sharia Qasr en-Nil, Cairo; (2) 3911203 (Cairo); fax (2) 3919805 (Cairo); e-mail foreign@alexbank.com; internet www.alexbank.com; f. 1957; privatization pending; cap. 700m., res 486.8m., dep. 19,196.7m. (June 2000); Chair. MAHMOUD ABD AS-SALAM OMAR; 184 brs.

Bank of Commerce and Development (At-Tegaryoon): POB 1373, 13 Sharia 26 July, Mohandessin, Cairo (Agouza); tel. (2) 7472063; fax (2) 3023963; f. 1980; cap. 205.9m., res 0.7m., dep. 734.2m. (Dec. 2000); Chair. and Man. Dir SAMIR MUHAMMAD FOUAD EL-QASRI; 6 brs.

Banque du Caire, SAE: POB 1495, 30 Sharia Rushdi, Cairo (Abdin); tel. (2) 3904554; fax (2) 3908992; e-mail for eign@bdc.com.eg; internet www.bdc.com.eg; f. 1952; state-owned; cap. 750.0m., res 629.3m., dep. 30,785.0m. (June 2001); Chair. AHMAD MONIR EL-BARDAI; Vice-Chair. MONA YASSEN; 239 brs in Egypt, 4 abroad.

Banque Misr, SAE: 151 Sharia Muhammad Farid, Cairo; tel. (2) 3912711; fax (2) 3919779; internet www.banquemisr.com; f. 1920; privatization pending; cap. 1,000m., res 940.2m., dep. 50,687.4m. (June 2000); Chair. BAHAA ED-DIN HELMY; 438 brs.

Commercial International Bank (Egypt), SAE: POB 2430, Nile Tower Bldg, 21–23 Sharia Charles de Gaulle, Cairo (Giza); tel. (2) 5703043; fax (2) 5703172; e-mail info@cibeg.com; internet www .cibeg.com; f. 1975 as Chase National Bank (Egypt) SAE; adopted present name 1987; National Bank of Egypt has 19.91% interest, Bankers Trust Co (USA) 18.76% interest, International Finance Corpn 5%; cap. 650m., res 813.5m., dep. 12,152.1m. (Dec. 2000); Exec. Chair. and Man. Dir MAHMOUD HELAL; 27 brs.

Egyptian Arab Land Bank: 78 Sharia Gamet ad-Duwal al-Arabia, Mohandessin, Cairo (Giza); (2) 3383691; fax 3383561; e-mail albcd@starnet.com.eg; internet www.ealb.com.eg; f. 1880; cap. 211.9m., res 162.8m., dep. 12,488.4m. (Dec. 2001); Chair. ALAA AL-OUSSIYA; 26 brs in Egypt, 25 abroad.

Export Development Bank of Egypt (EDBE): 108 Mohyee el-Din Abou al-Ezz, Cairo 12311 (Dokki); tel. (2) 7480587; fax (2) 3385940; f. 1983 to replace National Import-Export Bank; cap. 250.0m., res 257.8m., dep. 4,958.9m. (June 2000); Chair. MAHMOUD MUHAMMAD MAHMOUD; Vice-Chair. SALAH ED-DIN FAHMY; 14 brs.

HSBC Bank Egypt, SAE: POB 126, Abou el-Feda Bldg, 3 Sharia Abou el-Feda, Cairo (Zamalek); tel. (2) 3409186; fax (2) 3414010; f. 1982 as Hongkong Egyptian Bank; changed name to Egyptian British Bank in 1994; changed name to above in 2001; the Hongkong and Shanghai Banking Corporation has a 90% shareholding, other interests 10%; cap. 168.2m., res 88.7m., dep. 3,188.4m. (Dec. 2000); Chair. ANDREW DIXON; Deputy Chair. and Man. Dir ABD AS-SALAM EL-ANWAR; 7 brs.

Mohandes Bank: 3–5 Sharia Mossadek, Cairo; tel. (2) 3362760; fax (2) 3362741; internet www.mohandesbank.com; f. 1979; cap. 161.0m., res 5.8m., dep. 4,320.6m. (Dec. 1999); Pres. and Man. Dir MUHAMMAD ADEL HASHISH; 10 brs.

National Bank for Development (NBD): POB 647, 5 Sharia el-Borsa el-Gedida, Cairo 11511; tel. (2) 7963505; fax (2) 7964966; e-mail nbd@internetegypt.com; internet www.nbdegypt.com; f. 1980; cap. 242.0m., res 183.0m., dep. 6,151.0m. (Dec. 2001); Chair. MUHAMMAD ZAKI EL-ORABI; 67 brs; there are affiliated National Banks for Development in 16 governorates.

National Bank of Egypt: POB 11611, National Bank of Egypt Tower, 1187 Corniche en-Nil, Cairo; tel. (2) 5749101; fax (2) 5762672; e-mail nbe@nbe.com.eg; internet www.nbe.com.eg; f. 1898; privatization pending; handles all commercial banking operations; cap. 1,000m., res 2,698m., dep. 63,454m. (June 2000); Chair. AHMAD DIAA ED-DIN FAHMY; Dep. Chair. HUSSEIN ABD AL-AZIZ HUSSEIN; 343 brs.

Principal Bank for Development and Agricultural Credit: POB 11669, 110 Sharia Qasr el-Eini, Cairo; tel. (2) 7951204; fax (2) 7948337; f. 1976 to succeed former credit organizations; state-owned; cap. 1,406m., res 275m., dep. 7,293m. (June 2001); Chair. Dr YOUSSEF A. RAHMAN HOSNI; 167 brs.

Société Arabe Internationale de Banque (SAIB): POB 54, 56 Sharia Gamet ed-Dowal al-Arabia, Mohandessin, Cairo (Giza); tel. (2) 3499463; fax (2) 3603497; f. 1976; the Arab International Bank has a 41.1% share, other interests 58.9%; cap. US $42.0m., res US $36.5m., dep. US $379.7m. (Dec. 2000); Chair. Dr HASSAN ABBAS ZAKI; Man. Dir MUHAMMAD NOUR; 4 brs.

United Bank of Egypt (UBE): Cairo Center, 106 Sharia Kasr el-Eini, Cairo; tel. (2) 7920146; fax (2) 7920153; e-mail info@ube.net;

internet www.ube.net; f. 1981 as Dakahlia National Bank for Development; current name adopted in 1997; cap. 200m., res 20.3m., dep 2,761.8m. (Dec. 2000); Chair. and Man. Dir SEIF COUTRY; 9 brs.

Social Bank

Nasser Social Bank: POB 2552, 35 Sharia Qasr en-Nil, Cairo; tel. (2) 3924484; fax (2) 3921930; f. 1971; state-owned; interest-free savings and investment bank for social and economic activities, participating in social insurance, specializing in financing co-opera-tives, craftsmen and social institutions; cap. 20m.; Chair. NASSIF TAHOON.

Multinational Banks

Arab African International Bank: 5 Midan as-Saray el-Koubra, POB 60, Majlis el-Sha'ab, Cairo 11516 (Garden City); tel. (2) 7945094; fax (2) 7958493; internet www.aaibank.com; f. 1964 as Arab African Bank, renamed 1978; cap. US $100.0m., res US $231m., dep. US $769m. (Dec. 2001); commercial investment bank; shareholders are Govts of Kuwait, Egypt, Algeria, Jordan and Qatar, Bank Al-Jazira (Saudi Arabia), Rafidain Bank (Iraq), individuals and Arab institutions; Chair. and Man. Dir Dr FAHED MOHAMMED AR-RASHED; Gen. Man. HASSAN E. ABDALLA; 6 brs in Egypt, 4 abroad.

Arab International Bank: POB 1563, 35 Sharia Abd al-Khalek Sarwat, Cairo; tel. (2) 3918794; fax (2) 3916233; internet www.aib_egypt.com; f. 1971 as Egyptian International Bank for Foreign Trade and Investment, renamed 1974; cap. US $262.0m., res US $143.2m., dep. US $2,314.7m. (June 2001); offshore bank; aims to promote trade and investment in shareholders' countries and other Arab countries; owned by Egypt, Libya, UAE, Oman, Qatar and private Arab shareholders; Chair. Dr MUSTAFA KHALIL; Man. Dir ALI GAMAL AD-DIN DABBOUS; 7 brs.

Commercial Foreign Venture Banks

Alwatany Bank of Egypt: POB 63, 13 Sharia Semar, Dr Fouad Mohi ed-Din Sq., Gameat ed-Dewal al-Arabia, Mohandessin, Cairo 12655; tel. (2) 3388816; fax (2) 3379302; e-mail watany@alwatany .com.eg; internet www.alwatany.com.eg; f. 1980; cap. 157.5m., res 171.9m., dep. 3,568.3m. (Dec. 2000); Chair. ADEL HUSSEIN EZZI; Man. Dir FATMA I. LOTFY; 13 brs.

BNP PARIBAS Le Caire: POB 2441, 3 Latin America St, Cairo (Garden City); tel. (2) 7948323; fax (2) 7940619; e-mail bcp egypt@bcpegypt.com; f. 1977 as Banque du Caire et de Paris SAE; name changed in 2001; BNP Group Paribas has 76% interest and Banque du Caire 19.8%; cap. 50.5m., res 30.6m., dep. 933.9m. (Dec. 2000); Chair. JEAN THOMAZEAU; Man. Dir NOUR NAHAURI; 6 brs.

Cairo Barclays Bank, SAE: POB 110, 12 Midan esh-Sheikh Yousuf, Cairo (Garden City); tel. (2) 3662600; fax (2) 3662810; f. 1975 as Cairo Barclays Int. Bank; name changed to Banque du Caire Barclays International in 1983; renamed in 1999; Barclays Bank has 60%, Banque du Caire 40%; cap. 106.0m., res 118.5m., dep. 2,741.6m. (Dec. 2000); Chair. ANDREW ROBERT BUXTON; Man. Dir COLIN MCCORMACK; 5 brs.

Cairo Far East Bank, SAE: POB 757, 104 Corniche en-Nil, Cairo (Dokki); tel. (2) 3362516; fax (2) 3483818; f. 1978; cap. 62.5m., res 13.6m., dep. 282.9m. (Dec. 2000); Chair. Dr HASSAN FAG EN-NOUR; Man. Dir FAWZIA YOUSUF; 3 brs.

Crédit Agricole Indosuez (Egypt), SAE: 46 Sharia el-Batal Ahmad Abd al-Aziz, Mohandessin, Cairo; tel. (2) 3361897; fax (2) 3608673; e-mail caie@eg.ca-indosuez.com; internet www.ca -indosuez.com; f. 1978 as Crédit International d'Egypte; renamed in 2001; Crédit Agricole Indosuez has 75% interest, el-Mansour & el-Maghraby for Financial Investment 25%; cap. 60.2m., res 33.5m., dep. 634.9m. (Dec. 2001); Chair. MUHAMMAD LOTFI MANSOUR; Man. Dir ADRIAN PHARES; 3 brs.

Delta International Bank: POB 1159, 1113 Corniche en-Nil, Cairo; tel. (2) 5753492; fax (2) 5743403; e-mail dib bank@mst1.mist.com.eg; f. 1978; cap. 300m., res 156m., dep. 1,556m. (Dec. 2001); Chair. and Man. Dir ALI MUHAMMAD NEGM; 17 brs.

Egyptian American Bank: POB 1825, 4 & 6 Sharia Hassan Sabri, Cairo (Zamalek); tel. (2) 7380126; fax (2) 7380609; e-mail ibadran@eab-online.com; internet www.eab-online.com; f. 1976; Amex Holdings Inc. has 40.8% interest, Bank of Alexandria 32.5%, others 26.7%; cap. 144.0m., res 381.0m., dep. 5,305.3m. (Dec. 2000); Chair. MAHMOUD ABD AS-SALAM OMAR; Man. Dir RODERICK RICHARDS; 30 brs.

Egyptian Commercial Bank: POB 92, 4th Floor, Evergreen Bldg, 10 Sharia Talaat Harb, Majlis ash-Sha'ab, Cairo; tel. (2) 5779766; fax (2) 5799862; f. 1978 as Alexandria-Kuwait International Bank, name changed as above in 1997; cap. 150m., res 15.4m., dep. 1,713.9m. (Dec. 2000); Chair. MUHAMMAD ABD AL-WAHAD; Gen. Man. AHMAD NABIL EL-MINOUFI; 6 brs.

Egyptian Gulf Bank: POB 56, El-Orman Plaza Bldg, 8–10 Sharia Ahmad Nessim, Cairo (Giza); tel. (2) 7606640; fax (2) 7606512; e-mail h.r.egb@mst1.mist.com.eg; f. 1981; Misr Insurance Co has 24.9% interest; cap. 217.7m., res 25.8m., dep. 1,675.1m. (Dec. 2000); Chair. JAWAD BU KHAMSEEN; Man. Dir MUHAMMAD BARAKAT; 5 brs.

Egyptian-Saudi Finance Bank: POB 445, 60 Sharia Mohy ad-Din Abu al-Ezz, Cairo (Dokki); tel. (2) 7481777; fax (2) 7611436; internet www.esf-bank.com; f. 1980 as Pyramids Bank; cap. 119.1m., res 24.5m., dep. 1,845.9m. (Dec. 2000); Chair. Sheikh SALEH ABDULLAH KAMAL; Man. Dir SOBHY BADAWY YAHIA; 7 brs.

Faisal Islamic Bank of Egypt, SAE: POB 2445, 1113 Corniche en-Nil, Cairo 11511; tel. (2) 5753109; fax (2) 777301; e-mail fi salbnk@internetegypt.com; f. 1977; all banking operations conducted according to Islamic principles; cap. 263.7m., res 80.6m., dep. 8,301.0m. (Dec. 2001); Chair. Prince MUHAMMAD AL-FAISAL AS-SA'UD; 14 brs.

Misr-America International Bank: POB 1003, 12 Sharia Nadi es-Seid, Cairo 11511 (Dokki); tel. (2) 7616623; fax (2) 7616610; e-mail maib@instinct.net; f. 1977; Misr Insurance Co has 50% interest, Banque du Caire 33%, Industrial Development Bank of Egypt 17%, S.A. for Investments, Luxembourg 1.2%; cap. 75.0m., res 37.9m., dep. 939.6m. (Dec. 2000); Chair. and Man. Dir AHMED MOUNIR EL-BARDAIE; 8 brs.

Misr Exterior Bank, SAE: Cairo Plaza Bldg, Corniche en-Nil, Boulaque, Cairo; tel. (2) 778701; fax (2) 762806; e-mail meb2@rite.com; internet www.misrext.com; f. 1981; Misr International Bank has 30.1% interest, Banque Misr 19.5%; cap. 51.1m., res 214.8m., dep. 5,026.2m. (Dec. 2000); Chair. and Man. Dir ABDULLAH TAYEL; 9 brs.

Misr International Bank, SAE: POB 218, 54 Sharia el-Batal Ahmad Abd al-Aziz, Mohandessin, Cairo 12411; tel. (2) 7497255; fax (2) 3489796; f. 1975; the Banque Misr has 26.0% interest, Banco di Roma 10%, UBAF London 8.5%, Europartners 7.9%; cap. 112.5m., res 792.1m., dep. 9,691.1m. (Dec. 2000); Chair. Dr BAHAA AD-DIN HELMY; 18 brs.

Misr Romanian Bank: 54 Sharia Lebanon, Mohandessin, Cairo (Giza); tel. (2) 3039825; fax (2) 3039804; e-mail mrbeg@ie-eg.com; internet www.mrb.com.eg; f. 1977; Banque Misr has 33% interest, Romanian Commercial Bank (Bucharest) 19%, Bank of Agriculture (Bucharest) 15%, and Romanian Bank for Development (Bucharest) 15%; cap. 81.5m., res 219.0m., dep. 2,270.7m. (Dec. 2001); Chair. Dr AHMAD METWALLY HUSSAIN; 6 brs in Egypt, 3 in Romania.

Mohandes Bank: POB 170, 3–5 Sharia Mossadek, Cairo (Dokki); tel. (2) 3373110; fax (2) 3362741; internet www.mohandesbank.com; f. 1979; cap. 161.0m., res 5.9m., dep. 4,768.9m. (Dec. 2000); Chair. and Man. Dir MUHAMMAD ADEL HASHISH; 10 brs.

Nile Bank, SAE: POB 2741, 35 Sharia Ramses, Abd al-Moneim Riad Sq., Cairo; tel. (2) 5741417; fax (2) 5756296; e-mail nilebank@egyptonline.com; f. 1978; cap. 32.2m., res 88.3m., dep. 1,365.0m. (Dec. 2000); Chair. ISSA EL-AYOUTY; Man. Dir MUHAMMAD ES-SABAGH; 18 brs.

Suez Canal Bank, SAE: POB 2620, 7 Abd el-Kader Hamza St, Cairo (Garden City); tel. (2) 7943433; fax (2) 7942526; e-mail info@scbank.com.eg; internet www.scbank.com.eg; f. 1978; cap. 230.0m., res 505.4m., dep. 9,831.3m. (Mar. 2002); Chair. and Man. Dir MOUSTAFA FAYEZ HABLAS; 20 brs.

Non-Commercial Banks

Arab Banking Corporation—Egypt: POB 61, Majlis ash-Sha'ab, 5 Midan es-Saray, al-Koubra, Cairo 11511 (Garden City); tel. (2) 7950948; fax (2) 7966239; e-mail abcegypt@arabbanking.com.eg; internet www.arabbanking.com.eg; f. 1982 as Egypt Arab African Bank; acquired by Arab Banking Corporation (Bahrain) in 1999; Arab Banking Corporation has 93% interest, other interests 7%; cap. 75m., res 80m., dep. 1,220.6m. (Dec. 2000); merchant and investment bank services; Chair. ESSA MUHAMMAD GHANEM ELSWEDY; Vice-Chair. FAHARTO MEKDARI; 7 brs.

Arab Investment Bank: POB 826, Cairo Sky Center Bldg, 8 Sharia Abd al-Khalek Sarwat, Cairo; tel. (2) 768097; fax (2) 770329; e-mail arinbank@mst1.mist.com.eg; internet www.arab-investment-bank.egypt.com; f. 1978 as Union Arab Bank for Development and Investment; Egyptian/Syrian/Libyan joint venture; cap. 85.8m., res 2.5m., dep. 1,720.7m. (Dec. 2000); Chair. Prof. Dr MUHAMMAD AHMAD AR-RAZAZ; 14 brs.

Housing and Development Bank, SAE: POB 234, 12 Sharia Syria, Mohandessin, Cairo (Giza); tel. (2) 7492013; fax (2) 7600712; e-mail hdbank@internetegypt.com; internet www.hdb-eg.com; f. 1979; cap. 54m., res 213.6m., dep. 1,329.6m. (Dec. 2000); Chair. and Man. Dir MUHAMMAD TALA'AT ABOU SEDA; 24 brs.

Islamic International Bank for Investment and Development: POB 180, 4 Sharia Ali Ismail, Mesaha Sq., Cairo (Dokki); tel.

(2) 7489983; fax (2) 3600771; e-mail ibid@infinitycom.eg; internet www.iibid.com; f. 1980; cap. 133.8m., res -25.3m., dep. 3,389.5m. (Dec. 2000); Chair. BADAWY HASAN HASSANAIN; Gen. Man. SAYED MUHAMMAD EL-MENSHAWY; 8 brs.

Misr Iran Development Bank: POB 219, Nile Tower Bldg, 21–23 Charles de Gaulle Ave, Cairo 12612 (Giza); tel. (2) 5727311; fax (2) 5701185; e-mail midb@mst1.mist.com.eg; f. 1975; the Bank of Alexandria has 39.73% interest, Misr Insurance Co 39.73%, Iran Foreign Investment Co 20.54%; cap. 211.9m., res 129.6m., dep. 1,077.1m. (Dec. 2000); Chair. and Man. Dir ISMAIL HASSAN MUHAMMAD; 7 brs.

National Société Générale Bank, SAE: POB 2664, Evergreen Bldg, 10 Sharia Tala'at Harb, Cairo; tel. (2) 5749376; fax (2) 5776249; e-mail nsgb.info@socgen.com; internet www.nsgb.co.eg; f. 1978; the Société Générale de Paris has 51% interest, National Bank of Egypt 18%, other interests 31%; cap. 220m., res 252.9m., dep. 4,615.8m. (Dec. 2000); Chair. MUHAMMAD MADBOULY; CEO JEROME GUIRAUD; 9 brs.

STOCK EXCHANGES

Capital Market Authority: 20 Sharia Emad ed-Din, Cairo; tel. (2) 5741000; fax (2) 5755339; e-mail cmauth@idsc.gov.eg; f. 1979; Chair. ABDELHAMID IBRAHIM; Dep. Chair. ASHRAF SHAMS ED-DIN.

Cairo and Alexandria Stock Exchanges (CASE): 4 Sharia esh-Sherifein, Cairo; tel. (2) 3921447; fax (2) 3928526; 11 Sharia Talaat Harb, Menshia, Alexandria; tel. (3) 4835432; fax (3) 4823039; internet www.egyptse.com; f. 1861; Chair. Dr SAMEH AT-TORGOMAN.

INSURANCE

Al-Ahly Insurance: Cairo; state-owned; scheduled for privatization.

Arab International Insurance Co: POB 2704, 28 Sharia Talaat Harb, Cairo; tel. (2) 5746322; fax (2) 5760053; e-mail aiic@aiic.com.eg; internet www.aiic.co.eg; f. 1976; a joint-stock free zone company established by Egyptian and foreign insurance companies; Chair. and Man. Dir HASSAN MUHAMMAD HAFEZ.

Ach-Chark Insurance Co: 15 Sharia Qasr en-Nil, Cairo; tel. (2) 5740455; fax (2) 5753316; e-mail ins_chark@frcu.eun.eg; f. 1931; scheduled for privatization; general and life; Chair. ANWAR ZEKRY.

Egyptian Reinsurance Co, SAE: POB 950, 7 Sharia Abd al-Latif Boltia, Cairo (Garden City); tel. (2) 3543354; fax (2) 3557483; e-mail egyptre@intouch.com; internet www.egyptre.com.eg; f. 1957; scheduled for privatization; Chair. MUHAMMAD HAMMAM BADR.

Al-Iktisad esh-Shabee, SAE: 11 Sharia Emad ed-Din, Cairo; f. 1948; Man. Dir and Gen. Man. W. KHAYAT.

Misr Insurance Co: POB 261, 44A Sharia Dokki, Cairo (Dokki); tel. (2) 3355350; fax (2) 3370428; e-mail micfin@frcu.eun.eg; internet www.frcu.eun.eg; f. 1934; all classes of insurance and reinsurance; scheduled for privatization; Chair.MOAWAD HASSANEIN.

Mohandes Insurance Co: POB 62, 3 El-Mesaha Sq., Cairo (Dokki); tel. (2) 3352162; fax (2) 3352697; e-mail mohandes@mist1.mist.com.eg; f. 1980; privately-owned; insurance and reinsurance; Chair. and Man. Dir SAMIR MOUSTAFA METWALLI.

Al-Mottahida: POB 804, 9 Sharia Sulayman Pasha, Cairo; f. 1957.

National Insurance Co of Egypt, SAE: POB 592, 41 Sharia Qasr en-Nil, Cairo; tel. (2) 3910731; fax (2) 3909133; e-mail omr-nice@eis.co.eg; f. 1900; cap. 100m.; scheduled for privatization; Chair. MUHAMMAD ABUL-YAZEED.

Provident Association of Egypt, SAE: POB 390, 9 Sharia Sherif Pasha, Alexandria; f. 1936; Man. Dir G. C. VORLOOU.

Trade and Industry

GOVERNMENT AGENCY

Egyptian Geological Survey and Mining Authority (EGSMA): 3 Tarik Salah Salem, Abbassia, Cairo; tel. (2) 2855660; fax (2) 4820128; e-mail egsma@idsc.gov.eg; internet www.egsma.gov.eg; f. 1896; state supervisory authority concerned with geological mapping, mineral exploration and other mining activities; Chair. M. E. EL-HENAWY.

DEVELOPMENT ORGANIZATION

General Authority for Investment and Free Zones (GAFI): POB 1007, 8 Sharia Adly, Cairo; tel. (2) 3906163; fax (2) 3907315; e-mail gafi@idsc.gov.eg; www.gafi.gov.eg; Chair. Dr Eng. MUHAMMAD EL-GHAMRAWI DAWOUD.

CHAMBERS OF COMMERCE

Federation of Chambers of Commerce: 4 el-Falaki Sq., Cairo; tel. (2) 3551164; fax (2) 3557940; Pres. MAHMOUD EL-ARABY.

Alexandria

Alexandria Chamber of Commerce: 31 Sharia el-Ghorfa Altogariya, Alexandria; tel. (3) 809339; fax (2) 808993; Pres. MOUSTAFA EN-NAGGAR.

Cairo

American Chamber of Commerce in Egypt: Cairo; e-mail web@ amcham.org.eg; internet www.amcham.org.eg.

Cairo Chamber of Commerce: 4 el-Falaki Sq., Cairo; tel. (2) 3558261; fax (2) 3563603; f. 1913; Pres. MAHMOUD EL-ARABY; Sec.-Gen. MOSTAFA ZAKI TAHA.

In addition, there are 20 local chambers of commerce.

EMPLOYERS' ORGANIZATION

Federation of Egyptian Industries: 1195 Cornich en-Nil, Ramlet Boulal, Cairo; and 65 Gamal Abd an-Nasser Ave, Alexandria; tel. (2) 5796950; fax (2) 5796953 (Cairo), tel. and fax (3) 4916121 (Alexandria); e-mail feind@idsc.net.eg; internet www.fei.org.eg; f. 1922; Pres. MUHAMMAD FARID KHAMIS; represents the industrial community in Egypt.

PETROLEUM AND GAS

Arab Petroleum Pipelines Co (SUMED): POB 158, Es-Saray, 431 El-Geish Ave, Louran, Alexandria; tel. (3) 5864138; fax (3) 5871295; f. 1974; Suez–Mediterranean crude oil transportation pipeline (capacity: 117m. metric tons per year) and petroleum terminal operators; Chair. and Man. Dir Eng. HAZEM AMIN HAMMAD.

Belayim Petroleum Co (PETROBEL): POB 7074, Sharia el-Mokhayam, Cairo (Nasr City); tel. (2) 2621738; fax (2) 2609792; f. 1977; capital equally shared between EGPC and International Egyptian Oil Co, which is a subsidiary of ENI of Italy; petroleum and gas exploration, drilling and production; Chair. and Man. Dir FAROUK KENAWY.

Egyptian General Petroleum Corporation (EGPC): POB 2130, 4th Sector, Sharia Palestine, New Maadi, Cairo; tel. (2) 7065956; fax (2) 7028813; e-mail info@egpc.com.eg; internet www.egpc.com.eg; state supervisory authority generally concerned with the planning of policies relating to petroleum activities in Egypt with the object of securing the development of the petroleum industry and ensuring its effective administration; Chair. MOUSTAFA SHAARAWI; Dep. Chair. HASAB EN-NABI ASAL.

> **General Petroleum Co (GPC):** POB 743, 8 Sharia Dr Moustafa Abou Zahra, Cairo (Nasr City); tel. (2) 4030975; fax (2) 4037602; f. 1957; wholly-owned subsidiary of EGPC; operates mainly in Eastern Desert; Chair. HUSSEIN KAMAL.

Egyptian Natural Gas Holding Co: Cairo; f. 2001 as part of a restructuring of the natural gas sector; Chair. MUHAMMAD TAWILA.

GASCO: Sheraton Heliopolis, 6A Sharia Moustafa Rifaat, Cairo (Heliopolis); tel. (2) 2666458; fax (2) 2666469; e-mail gasco@gasco.com.eg; internet www.gasco.com.eg; f. 1997; Gen. Man. Eng. MUHAMMAD IBRAHIM.

Gulf of Suez Petroleum Co (GUPCO): POB 2400, 4th Sector, Sharia Palestine, New Maadi, Cairo 11511; tel. (2) 3520985; fax (2) 3531286; f. 1965; partnership between EGPC and BP Egypt (UK/USA); developed the el-Morgan oilfield in the Gulf of Suez, also holds other exploration concessions in the Gulf of Suez and the Western Desert; Chair. AHMED SHAWKY ABDINE; Man. Dir L. D. MCVAY.

Western Desert Petroleum Co (WEPCO): POB 412, Borg eth-Thagr Bldg, Sharia Safia Zagloul, Alexandria; tel. (3) 4928710; fax (3) 4934016; f. 1967 as partnership between EGPC (50% interest) and Phillips Petroleum (35%) and later Hispanoil (15%); developed Alamein, Yidma and Umbarka fields in the Western Desert and later Abu Qir offshore gasfield in 1978 followed by NAF gas field in 1987; Chair. Eng. MUHAMMAD MOHI ED-DIN BAHGAT.

UTILITIES

Electricity

In 1998 seven new electricity generation and distribution companies were created, under the direct ownership of the Egyptian Electricity Authority (EEA). In 2000 the EEA was restructured into a holding company controlling five generation and seven distribution companies. A specialized grid company was to manage electricity transmission. The Government planned partial privatizations of the generation and distribution companies in 2001–02, while retaining control of the hydroelectric generation and grid management companies.

Egypt Electricity Holding Co: Sharia Ramses, Cairo (Nasr City); tel. (2) 2616301; fax (2) 2616512; formerly the Egyptian Electricity Authority, renamed as above in 2000; Chair. NABIL YOUNES.

Alexandria Electricity Distribution: 9 Sharia Sidi el-Liban, Alexandria; tel. (3) 4935726; fax (3) 4933223.

Cairo Electricity Co: 53 Sharia 26 July, Cairo; tel. (2) 766612.

Cairo Electricity Distribution: 53 Sharia 26 July, Cairo; tel. (2) 766612; fax (2) 760383; Gen. Man. LOFTY EL-MOSHTLY.

Gas

Egypt Gas Company: Corniche en-Nil, 2 Geziret Muhammad, Warak-Imbaba, Cairo; tel. and fax (2) 3126081; email egyptgas@ hotmail.com; f. 1983; Chair and Man. Dir NABIL HASHEM.

Water

National Association for Potable Water and Sanitary Drainage (NOPWASD): 6th Floor, Mogamma Bldg, et-Tahrir Sq., Cairo; tel. (2) 3557664; fax (2) 3562869; f. 1981; water and sewerage authority; Chair. MUHAMMAD KHALED MOUSTAFA.

TRADE UNIONS

Egyptian Trade Union Federation (ETUF): 90 Sharia al-Galaa, Cairo; tel. (2) 5740362; fax (2) 5753427; f. 1957; 23 affiliated unions; 5m. mems; affiliated to the International Confederation of Arab Trade Unions and to the Organization of African Trade Union Unity; Pres. MUHAMMAD ES-SAYED RASHID; Gen. Sec. MUHAMMAD ES-SAYED MORSI.

General Trade Union of Air Transport: G2, Osman Ibn Affoun, Sofin Sq., Cairo; tel. (2) 2413165; fax (2) 6336149; 11,000 mems; Pres. Eng. CHEHATA MUHAMMAD CHEHATA; Gen. Sec. MUHAMMAD HUSSEIN.

General Trade Union of Banks and Insurance: 2 Sharia el-Kady el-Fadel, Cairo; 56,000 mems; Pres. MAHMOUD MUHAMMAD DABBOUR; Gen. Sec. ABDOU HASSAN MUHAMMAD ALI.

General Trade Union of Building and Wood Workers: 9 Sharia Emad ed-Din, Cairo; tel. (2) 5913486; fax (2) 5915849; 500,000 mems; Pres. TAHA HASSAN SAGED; Gen. Sec. YEHIA EMAM ABDEL GAWAD.

General Trade Union of Chemical Workers: 90 Sharia al-Galaa, Cairo; fax (2) 5750490; 120,000 mems; Pres. IBRAHIM EL-AZHARY; Gen. Sec. GAAFER ABD EL-MONEM.

General Trade Union of Commerce: 54D Sharia el-Gomhouriya, Alfy Borg, Cairo; tel. (2) 5903159; fax (2) 5914144; f. 1903; 120,000 mems; Pres. FOUAD TOMA; Gen. Sec. SAMIR A. SHAFI.

General Trade Union of Food Industries: 3 Sharia Housni, Hadaek el-Koba, Cairo; 111,000 mems; Pres. SAAD M. AHMAD; Gen. Sec. ADLY TANOUS IBRAHIM.

General Trade Union of Health Services: 22 Sharia esh-Sheikh Qamar, es-Sakakiny, Cairo; 56,000 mems; Pres. IBRAHIM ABOU EL-MUTI IBRAHIM; Gen. Sec. AHMAD ABD AL-LATIF SALEM.

General Trade Union of Hotels and Tourism Workers: POB 606, 90 Sharia al-Galaa, Cairo; tel. and fax (2) 773901; 70,000 mems; Pres. MUHAMMAD HILAL ESH-SHARKAWI.

General Trade Union of Maritime Transport: 36 Sharia Sharif, Cairo; 46,000 mems; Pres. THABET MUHAMMAD ES-SEFARI; Gen. Sec. MUHAMMAD RAMADAN ABOU TOR.

General Trade Union of Military Production: 90 Sharia al-Galaa, Cairo; 64,000 mems; Pres. MOUSTAFA MUHAMMAD MOUNGI; Gen. Sec. FEKRY IMAM.

General Trade Union of Mine Workers: 5 Sharia Ali Sharawi, Hadaek el-Koba, Cairo; 14,000 mems; Pres. ABBAS MAHMOUD IBRAHIM; Gen. Sec. AMIN HASSAN AMER.

General Trade Union of Petroleum Workers: 5 Sharia Ali Sharawi, Hadaek el-Koba, Cairo; tel. (2) 4820091; fax (2) 4834551; 60,000 mems; Pres. FAUZI ABD AL-BARI; Gen. Sec. AMIR ABD ES-SALAM.

General Trade Union of Postal Workers: 90 Sharia al-Galaa, Cairo; 80,000 mems; Pres. HASSAN MUHAMMAD EID; Gen. Sec. SALEM MAHMOUD SALEM.

General Trade Union of Press, Printing and Information: 90 Sharia al-Galaa, Cairo; tel. (2) 740324; 55,000 mems; Pres. MUHAMMAD ALI EL-FIKKI; Gen. Sec. AHMAD ED-DESSOUKI.

General Trade Union of Public and Administrative Workers: 2 Sharia Muhammad Haggag, Midan et-Tahrir, Cairo; tel. (2) 5742134; fax (2) 5752044; 250,000 mems; Pres. Dr AHMAD ABDEL-ZAHER; Gen. Sec. MUKHTAR HAMOUDA.

General Trade Union of Public Utilities Workers: POB 194, 6 Sharia Ramsis, Cairo; tel. (2) 5799614 fax (2) 5799616; 290,000 mems; Pres. MUHAMMAD ES-SAYED MORSI ALY; Gen. Sec. USAMA GAMAL ABDUL SAMIEE.

General Trade Union of Railway Workers: POB 84 (el-Faggalah), 15 Sharia Emad ed-Din, Cairo; tel. (2) 5930305; fax (2) 5917776; 90,000 mems; Pres. SABER AHMAD HUSSAIN; Gen. Sec. YASIN SOLUMAN.

General Trade Union of Road Transport: 90 Sharia al-Galaa, Cairo; tel. (2) 5752955; fax (2) 5754919; 245,000 mems; Pres. SABRY EL-GUERIDI; Gen. Sec. SAYED RADURAN.

General Trade Union of Telecommunications Workers: POB 651, Cairo; 60,000 mems; Pres. KHAIRI HACHEM; Sec.-Gen. IBRAHIM SALEH.

General Trade Union of Textile Workers: 327 Sharia Shoubra, Cairo; 244,000 mems; Pres. ALI MUHAMMAD DOUFDAA; Gen. Sec. HASSAN TOULBA MARZOUK.

General Trade Union of Workers in Agriculture and Irrigation: 31 Sharia Mansour, Cairo (Bab el-Louk); tel. (2) 3541419; 150,000 mems; Pres. MUKHTAR ABD AL-HAMID; Gen. Sec. FATHI A. KURTAM.

General Trade Union of Workers in Engineering, Metal and Electrical Industries: 90 Sharia al-Galaa, Cairo; tel. (2) 742519; 160,000 mems; Pres. SAID GOMAA; Gen. Sec. MUHAMMAD FARES.

Transport

RAILWAYS

The area of the Nile Delta is well served by railways. Lines also run from Cairo southward along the Nile to Aswan, and westward along the coast to Salloum.

Egyptian National Railways: Station Bldg, Midan Ramses, Cairo 11794; tel. (2) 5751000; fax (2) 5740000; f. 1852; length 8,600 km; 42 km electrified; a 346-km line to carry phosphate and iron ore from the Bahariya mines, in the Western Desert, to the Helwan iron and steel works in south Cairo, was opened in 1973, and the Qena–Safaga line (length 223 km) came into operation in 1989; Chair. EID ABDELKADER.

Alexandria Passenger Transport Authority: POB 466, Aflaton, esh-Shatby, Alexandria 21111; tel. (3) 5975223; fax (3) 5971187; e-mail chrmapta@cns-egypt.com; f. 1860; controls City Tramways (28 km), Ramleh Electric Railway (16 km), suburban buses and minibuses (1,688 km); 121 tram cars, 42 light railway three-car sets; Chair. and Tech. Dir Eng. MEDHAT HAFEZ.

Cairo Metro: National Authority for Tunnels, POB 466, Ramses Bldg, Midan Ramses, Cairo 11794; tel. (2) 5742968; fax (2) 5742950; construction of the first electrified, 1,435 mm gauge underground transport system in Africa and the Middle East began in Cairo in 1982. Line 1 has a total of 34 stations (5 underground), connects el-Marg with Helwan and is 44 km long with a 4.2-km tunnel beneath central Cairo; Line 2 links Shoubra el-Kheima with Giza, totalling 19km. (13 km in tunnel), and with 18 stations (12 underground), two of which interconnect with Line 1; Line 2 was to be extended a further 2.5 km south to el-Monib; construction of Line 3 which will connect Imbaba and Mohandeseen with Cairo International Airport and will total 34.2 km (30.3 km in tunnel) with 29 stations (27 underground) was due to commence in mid-2003; Chair. Eng. SAAD HASSAN SHEHATA.

Cairo Transport Authority: POB 254, Madinet Nasr, Cairo; tel. (2) 830533; length 78 km (electrified); gauge 1,000 mm; operates 16 tram routes and 24 km of light railway; 720 cars; Chair. M. E. ABD ES-SALAM.

Lower Egypt Railway: El-Mansoura; f. 1898; length 160 km; gauge 1,000 mm; 20 diesel railcars.

ROADS

There are good metalled main roads as follows: Cairo–Alexandria (desert road); Cairo–Banha–Tanta–Damanhour–Alexandria; Cairo–Suez (desert road); Cairo–Ismailia–Port Said or Suez; Cairo–Fayoum (desert road); in 1997 there were some 41,300 km of roads, including 22,000 km of highways. The total length of road network at the end of 1999 was 44,000 km. The Ahmad Hamdi road tunnel (1.64 km) beneath the Suez Canal was opened in 1980. A 320-km macadamized road linking Mersa Matruh, on the Mediterranean coast, with the oasis town of Siwa was completed in 1986. A second bridge over the Suez Canal was completed in mid-2001.

General Authority for Roads, Bridges and Land Transport—Ministry of Transport: 105 Sharia Qasr el-Eini, Cairo; tel. (2) 3557429; fax (2) 3550591; e-mail garb@idsc.gov.eg; Chair. MUHAMMAD NABIL EL-KOUSSY.

SHIPPING

Egypt's principal ports are Alexandria, Port Said and Suez. A port constructed at a cost of £E315m., and designed to handle up to 16m. metric tons of grain, fruit and other merchandise per year (22% of the country's projected imports by 2000) in its first stage of development, was opened at Damietta in 1986. The second stage will increase handling capacity to 25m. tons per year. A ferry link

between Nuweibeh and the Jordanian port of Aqaba was opened in 1985.

Alexandria Port Authority: 106 ave el-Horreia, Alexandria; Head Office: 106 Sharia el-Hourriya, Alexandria; tel. (3) 4871640; fax (3) 4869714; e-mail alexportinfo@internetalex.com; internet www.alexandriaportauthority.com; f. 1966; Chair. R. Adm. MUHAMMAD FARAG LOTRY; Vice-Chair. R. Adm. MUHAMMAD M. ZAKI.

Major Shipping Companies

Alexandria Shipping and Navigation Co: POB 812, 557 ave el-Hourriya, Alexandria; tel. (3) 62923; services between Egypt, N. and W. Europe, USA, Red Sea and Mediterranean; 5 vessels; Chair. Eng. MAHMOUD ISMAIL; Man. Dir ABD AL-AZIZ QADRI.

Arab Maritime Petroleum Transport Co (AMPTC): POB 143, 9th Floor, Nile Tower Bldg, 21 Sharia Giza, 12211 Giza; tel. (2) 5701311; fax (2) 3378080; e-mail amptc.cairo@amptc.net; internet www.amptc.net; 11 vessels; Chair. Dr RAMADAN ES-SANOUSSI BELHAG; Gen. Man. SULAYMAN AL-BASSAM.

Egyptian Navigation Co: POB 82, 2 Sharia en-Nasr, Alexandria 21511; tel. (3) 4800050; fax (3) 4871345; e-mail enc@dataxprs .com.eg; internet www.enc.com.eg; f. 1930; owners and operators of Egypt's mercantile marine; international trade transportation; 24 vessels; Chair. ABDALLA ALI FAHIM; Man. Dir ABU ZID ES-SAADANY.

Memnon Tours Co: POB 2533, 18 Sharia Hoda Sharawi, Cairo; tel. (2) 3930195; fax (2) 3917410; 7 vessels.

Misr Petroleum Co: POB 228, Misr Petroleum House, 6 Sharia Orabi, Cairo; tel. (2) 5755000; fax (2) 5745436; 8 vessels; Chair. Eng. SALAH ED-DIN HASSAN.

Misr Shipping Co: POB 157, 13 Sharia Masgid en-Nasr, Soumoha, Sidi Gaber, Alexandria; tel. (3) 4270227; fax (3) 4288425; e-mail insp@misrshipping.com; internet www.misrshipping.com; 9 vessels; Chair. and Man. Dir Adm. YOUSRI HANAFY.

National Navigation Co: 4 Sharia Ehegaz, Cairo (Heliopolis); tel. (2) 4525575; fax (2) 4526171; 11 vessels; Chair. and Man. Dir MUHAMMAD SHAWKI YOUNIS.

Pan-Arab Shipping Co: POB 39, 404 ave el-Hourriya, Rushdi, Alexandria; tel. (3) 5468835; fax (3) 5469533; f. 1974; Arab League Co; 5 vessels; Chair. Adm. MUHAMMAD SHERIF ES-SADEK; Gen. Man. Capt. MAMDOUH EL-GUINDY.

As-Salam Shipping & Trading Establishment: Apartment 203, 24 Sharia Ahmad Talceer, Cairo (Heliopolis); tel. (2) 908535; fax (2) 4175390; 6 vessels.

Samatour Shipping Co: As-Salam Bldg, 4 Sharia Naguib er-Rihani, Rami Station, Alexandria; tel. (3) 4822028; fax (3) 4832003; 5 vessels; Chair. SALEM A. SALEM.

Sayed Nasr Navigation Lines: 5 Sharia Dr Ahmad Amin, Cairo (Heliopolis); tel. (2) 2457643; fax (2) 2457736; 6 vessels.

Société Coopérative des Pétroles: Cooperative Bldg, 94 Sharia Qasr el-Eini, Cairo; tel. (2) 7360623; fax (2) 7956404; Chair. Dr TAMER ABU BAKR; Gen. Dir OSAMA IBRAHIM.

THE SUEZ CANAL

In 2000 a total of 14,141 vessels, with a net displacement of 439m. tons, used the Suez Canal, linking the Mediterranean and Red Seas.

Length of canal 190 km; maximum permissible draught: 17.68 m (58 ft); breadth of canal at water level and breadth between buoys defining the navigable channel at −11 m: 365 m and 225 m, respectively, in the northern section and 305 m and 205 m in the southern section.

Suez Canal Authority (Hay'at Canal as-Suways): Irshad Bldg, Ismailia; tel. (64) 330000; fax (64) 320784; e-mail scanal-b@idsc.net.eg; Cairo Office: 6 Sharia Lazoughli, Cairo (Garden City); f. 1956; Chair. Adm. AHMAD ALI FADEL.

Suez Canal Container Handling Company: Cairo; f. 2000 with 30-year concession to operate the East Port Said container terminal, scheduled to begin operations in late 2002.

CIVIL AVIATION

The main international airports are at Heliopolis (23 km from the centre of Cairo) and Alexandria (7 km from the city centre). An international airport was opened at Nuzhah in 1983. In early 2001 the Ministry of Transport announced the restructure and modernization of the civil aviation sector. In that year airports were under construction at el-Alamein, west of Alexandria, and at Assiut, however, plans for the construction of a new airport in west Cairo were suspended in late 2001. The existing Cairo airport was to be expanded, with a third terminal and a new runway, while the Sharm esh-Sheikh airport was also scheduled for expansion.

In the 12-month period ending 30 June 1997 an estimated 14m. passengers and 109,000 metric tons of cargo passed through Egypt's airports.

Cairo Airport Authority (CAA): Cairo International Airport, Cairo (Heliopolis); tel. (2) 2474245; fax: (2) 2432522; responsible for management of Cairo International Airport.

EgyptAir: Administration Complex, Cairo International Airport, Cairo (Heliopolis); tel. (2) 2674700; fax (2) 2663773; internet www.egyptair.com.eg; f. 1932 as Misr Airwork; known as United Arab Airlines 1960–1971; operates internal services in Egypt and external services throughout the Middle East, Far East, Africa, Europe and the USA; Chair. Eng. MUHAMMAD FAHIM RAYAN.

Egyptian Civil Aviation Holding Co: Cairo; f. 2001; responsible for management and development of all Egyptian airports, excluding Cairo International; Pres. ABD AL-FATTAH KATTU.

Egyptian Airports Co: Cairo; f. 2001; responsible for new airport projects; Pres. NAGI SAMUEL.

Egyptian Civil Aviation Authority: ECAA Complex, Sharia Airport, Cairo 11776; tel. (2) 2677610; fax (2) 2470351; e-mail ego ca@idsc.gov.eg; f. 2000; Chair. Dr IBRAHIM MUHAMMAD MUTAWALLI AD-DUMEIRI.

Commander-in-Chief of the Armed Forces: Field Marshal MUHAMMAD ABD AL-HALIM ABU GHAZALAH.

Chief of Staff of the Armed Forces: Lt-Gen. SAFIY ED-DIN ABU SHINAF.

Commander of the Air Force: Air Marshal MUHAMMAD ABD AL-HAMID HELMI.

Commander of Air Defence: Maj.-Gen. MUSTAFA AHMAD ESH-SHADHILI.

Commander of the Navy: Admiral MUHAMMAD SHARIF ES-SADIQ.

Budgeted Defence Expenditure (2000/01): £E3,727m.

Military service: 18 months–three years, selective.

Total armed forces (August 2001): 443,000; army 320,000; air defence command 75,000; navy (estimated) 19,00; air force 29,000. Reserves 254,000. Paramilitary forces: 325,000 (Central Security Forces 250,000, National Guard 60,000, Border Guard 15,000 and Coast Guard (estimated) 2,000).

Tourism

Tourism is currently Egypt's second largest source of revenue, generating US $3,903m. in 1999. Traditionally the industry has attracted tourists to its pyramids and monuments. Recently the industry has diversified; the Red Sea coastline has 1,000 km of beaches along which developments, including two international airports at Taba and Suba Bay, are under construction. A further luxury resort was planned for Port Ghaleb, equipped with a marina for 1,000 yachts and an airport. In early 2001 the Biblioteca Alexandrina opened in Alexandria. The tourism industry was adversely affected in the mid-1990s by the campaign of violence by Islamist fundamentalists; although some recovery in tourist numbers was recorded by the end of the decade, the sector was again adversely affected by the crisis in Israeli–Palestinian relations from late 2000, and by the repercussions of the suicide attacks on the USA in September 2001.

Ministry of Tourism: Misr Travel Tower, Abbassia Sq., Cairo; tel. (2) 2828439; fax (2) 2859551; e-mail mol@idsc.gov.eg; internet www.touregypt.net; f. 1965; brs at Alexandria, Port Said, Suez, Luxor and Aswan; Minister of Tourism Dr MAMDOUH EL-BELTAGI.

Egyptian General Authority for the Promotion of Tourism: Misr Travel Tower, Abbassia Sq., Cairo; tel. (2) 2853576; fax (2) 2854363; Chair. ADEL ABD AL-AZIZ.

Egyptian General Co for Tourism and Hotels: 4 Sharia Latin America, Cairo (Garden City); tel. (2) 3542914; fax (2) 3564830; f. 1961; affiliated to the holding co for Housing, Tourism and Cinema; Chair. Dr ALI ISMAIL EL-EMBABY.

Defence

Supreme Commander of the Armed Forces: President MUHAMMAD HOSNI MUBARAK.

Education

Education is compulsory for eight years between six and 14 years of age. Primary education, beginning at six years of age, lasts for five years. Secondary education, beginning at 11 years of age, lasts for a further six years, comprising two cycles (the first being preparatory) of three years each. In 1997 primary enrolment included 95.2% of children in the relevant age-group (males 99.8%; females 90.6%), while the comparable ratio for secondary enrolment was 75.1% (males 80.1%; females 70.1%). There are 14 universities. During 1986–96 the number of university graduates increased by 3%, to 7.3% of the population. The Al-Azhar University and its various preparatory and associated institutes provide instruction and training in several disciplines, with emphasis on adherence to Islamic principles and teachings. In 1996/97 some 166,000 students were enrolled at the University. Education is free at all levels. The 2000/01 budget forecast spending on education of £E18,100m. (some 16% of total expenditure).

ADMINISTRATION

Responsibility for education and training lies with the Ministry of Education, except for the ministries that train manpower for their own specialized needs. The 14 universities are outside ministerial jurisdiction.

The Ministry of Education is responsible for primary, preparatory, secondary general, secondary technical (commercial, agricultural and industrial), primary teacher training and higher education.

The universities, however, maintain their individual independence even though the President of the Supreme Council is the Minister of Education. The Council is a planning and co-ordinating body and comprises the Rectors, Vice-Rectors and some representatives of different disciplines of university education.

Bibliography

GENERAL

Abdel-Malek, Anwar. *Egypte, société militaire.* Paris, 1962.

Idéologie et renaissance nationale / L'Egypte moderne. Paris, 1969.

Ahmed, J. M. *The Intellectual Origins of Egyptian Nationalism.* London, Royal Institute of International Affairs, 1960.

Aldridge, James. *Cairo: Biography of a City.* London, Macmillan, 1970.

Armbrust Walter. *Mass Culture and Modernism in Egypt.* Cambridge University Press, 1996.

Ayrout, H. H. *The Egyptian Peasant.* Boston, 1963.

Baddour, Abd. *Sudanese-Egyptian Relations. A Chronological and Analytical Study.* The Hague, Nijhoff, 1960.

Badeau, J. S. *The Emergence of Modern Egypt.* New York, 1953.

Baer, Gabriel. *A History of Landownership in Modern Egypt 1800–1950.* London, Oxford University Press, 1962.

The Evolution of Landownership in Egypt and the Fertile Crescent, the Economic History of the Middle East 1800–1914. Chicago and London, University of Chicago Press, 1966.

Studies in the Social History of Modern Egypt. Chicago and London, University of Chicago Press, 1969.

Baker, Raymond William. *Egypt's Uncertain Revolution under Nasser and Sadat.* Cambridge, MA, Harvard University Press, 1979.

Berger, Morroe. *Bureaucracy and Society in Modern Egypt: a Study of the Higher Civil Service.* Princeton University Press, 1957.

Islam in Egypt Today: Social and Political Aspects of Popular Religion. Cambridge University Press, 1970.

Berque, Jacques. *Egypt: Imperialism and Revolution.* London, Faber, 1972.

Boktor, Amin. *The Development and Expansion of Education in the UAR.* Cairo, The American University, 1963.

Cannuyer, Christian. *Les Coptes.* Turnhout, Editions Brepol 1991.

Chevillat, Alain and Evelyne. *Moines du désert d'Egypte.* Lyons, Editions Terres du Ciel, 1991.

Coult, Lyman H. *An Annotated Bibliography of the Egyptian Fellah.* University of Miami Press, 1958.

Cromer, Earl of. *Modern Egypt.* 2 vols, London, 1908.

Dawisha, A. I. *Egypt in the Arab World.* London, Macmillan, 1976.

Dodwell, H. *The Founder of Modern Egypt.* Cambridge, 1931, reprinted 1967.

Driault, E. *L'Egypte et l'Europe.* 5 vols, Cairo, 1935.

Garzouzi, Eva. *Old Ills and New Remedies in Egypt.* Cairo, Dar al-Maaref, 1958.

Harris, C. P. *Nationalism and Revolution in Egypt: the Role of the Muslim Brotherhood.* The Hague, Mouton and Co, 1964.

Harris, J. R. (Ed.). *The Legacy of Egypt.* 2nd edn Oxford University Press, 1972.

Holt, P. M. *Egypt and the Fertile Crescent.* London, Longman, 1966.

Hopkins, Harry. *Egypt, The Crucible.* London, Secker and Warburg, 1969.

Hurst, H. E. *The Nile.* London, 1952.

    The Major Nile Projects. Cairo, 1966.

Kepel, Gilles. *The Prophet and the Pharaoh: Muslim Extremism in Egypt.* London, Al Saqi Books, 1985.

King, Joan Wucher (Ed.). *An Historical Dictionary of Egypt.* Metuchen, NJ, Scarecrow Press, 1984.

Lacouture, Jean and Simonne. *Egypt in Transition.* London, Methuen, 1958.

Lauterpacht, E. (Editor). *The Suez Canal Settlement.* London, Stevens and Sons, 1960, under the auspices of the British Institute of International and Comparative Law.

Lengye, Emil. *Egypt's Role in World Affairs.* Washington, DC, Public Affairs Press, 1957.

Little, Tom. *Modern Egypt.* London, Ernest Benn, 1967, New York, Praeger, 1967.

Lloyd, Lord. *Egypt since Cromer.* 2 vols, London, 1933–34.

Marlowe, J. *Anglo-Egyptian Relations.* London, 1954.

Nasser, Gamal Abdel. *Egypt's Liberation: The Philosophy of the Revolution.* Washington, 1955.

Neguib, Mohammed. *Egypt's Destiny: A Personal Statement.* New York, 1955.

Owen, Robert, and Blunsum, Terence. *Egypt, United Arab Republic, The Country and its People.* London, Queen Anne Press, 1966.

Pick, Christopher. *Egypt: A Traveller's Anthology.* London, John Murray, 1991.

Riad, Hassan. *L'Egypte Nassérienne.* Paris, Editions de Minuit, 1964.

Robin, Barry. *Islamic Fundamentalism in Egyptian Politics.* London, Macmillan, 1990.

Stewart, Desmond. *Cairo.* London, Phoenix House, 1965.

Vaucher, G. *Gamal Abdel Nasser et son Equipe.* 2 vols, Leiden, Brill, 1950.

Viollet, Roger, and Doresse, Jean. *Egypt.* New York, Cromwell, 1955.

Waterfield, Gordon. *Egypt.* London, Thames and Hudson, 1966.

Watt, D. C. *Britain and the Suez Canal.* London, Royal Institute of International Affairs, 1956.

Wavell, W. H. *A Short Account of the Copts.* London, 1945.

Weaver, Mary Ann. *A Portrait of Egypt: A Journey Through the World of Militant Islam.* New York, Fawar, Straus and Giroux, 1998.

Wilbur, D. N. *The United Arab Republic.* New York, 1969.

Wilson, John A. *The Burden of Egypt.* Chicago, IL, 1951.

Wynn, Wilton. *Nasser of Egypt: The Search for Dignity.* Cambridge, MA, 1959.

MODERN HISTORY

Al-Ali, Nadje. *Secularism, Gender and the State in the Middle East: the Egyptian Women's Movement.* Cambridge University Press, 2000.

Avram, Benno. *The Evolution of the Suez Canal State 1869–1956.* A Historico-Juridical Study. Geneva, Paris, Librairie E. Droz, Librairie Minard, 1958.

Badrawi, Malak. *Political Violence in Egypt 1910–1925: Secret Societies, Plots and Assassinations.* Richmond, Curzon Press, 1999.

Baker, Raymond William. *Sadat and After: struggles for Egypt's political soul.* London, I. B. Tauris, 1990.

Baraway, Rashed El-. *The Military Coup in Egypt.* Cairo, Renaissance Bookshop, 1952.

Barraclough, Geoffrey (Ed.). *Suez in History.* London, 1962.

Bibars, Iman. *Victims and Heroines: Women, Welfare and the Egyptian State.* London, Zed Books, 2002.

Blunt, Wilfred Scawen. *Secret History of the English Occupation of Egypt.* London, Martin Secker, 1907.

Brown, Nathan J. *Peasant Politics in Modern Egypt: the struggle against the state.* New Haven and London, Yale University Press, 1990.

Carter, B. L. *The Copts in Egyptian Politics.* London, Croom Helm, 1986.

Chih, Rachida. *Le Soufisme au Quotidien: Confréries d'Egypte au XXe siècle.* Arles, Sinbad: Actes Sud, 2000

Cohen, Raymond. *Culture and Conflict in Egyptian-Israeli Relations: A Dialogue of the Deaf.* Indiana University Press, 1994.

Connell, John. *The Most Important Country. The Story of the Suez Crisis and the Events leading up to It.* London, Cassell, 1957.

Cooper, Mark N. *The Transformation of Egypt.* London, Croom Helm, 1982.

Efendi, Husein. *Ottoman Egypt in the Age of the French Revolution* (trans. and with introduction by Stanford J. Shaw). Cambridge, MA, Harvard Univ. Press, 1964.

Farnie, D. A. *East and West of Suez. The Suez Canal in history, 1854–1956.* Oxford, Clarendon Press, 1969.

Fawzi, Mahmoud. *Suez 1956.* London, Shorouk International, 1986.

Finklestone, Joseph. *Anwar Sadat: Visionary Who Dared.* London, Frank Cass, 1998.

Heikal, Muhammad. *The Road to Ramadan.* London, Collins, 1975.

    Sphinx and Commissar: The Rise and Fall of Soviet Influence in the Arab World. London, Collins, 1978.

    Autumn of Fury: The Assassination of Sadat. London, André Deutsch, 1983.

    Cutting the Lion's Tail: Suez through Egyptian eyes. London, André Deutsch, 1986.

Hirst, David, and Beeson, Irene. *Sadat.* London, Faber, 1981.

Holt, P. M. *Political and Social Change in Modern Egypt.* Oxford University Press, 1967.

Hussein, Mahmoud. *La Lutte de Classes en Egypte de 1945 à 1968.* Paris, Maspero, 1969.

Ismael, Tareq Y., and El-Said, Rifa'at. *The Communist Movement in Egypt 1920–1988.* Syracuse University Press, 1990.

Issawi, Charles. *Egypt in Revolution.* Oxford, 1963.

Joesten, Joachim. *Nasser: The Rise to Power.* London, Odhams, 1960.

Kamel, Muhammad Ibrahim. *The Camp David Accords: A Testimony by Sadat's Foreign Minister.* London, Routledge and Kegan Paul, 1986.

Karam, Azza M. *Women, Islamism and the State: Contemporary Feminism in Egypt.* London, Macmillan, 1998.

Kienle, Eberhard. *A Grand Delusion: Democracy and Economic Reform in Egypt.* London, I. B. Tauris, 2001.

Kinross, Lord. *Between Two Seas: The Creation of the Suez Canal.* London, John Murray, 1968.

Kyle, Keith. *Suez.* London, Weidenfeld, 1991.

Lacouture, Jean. *Nasser: A Biography.* London, Secker and Warburg, 1973.

Lane-Poole, S. *History of Egypt in the Middle Ages.* 4th edn, reprinted, London, Frank Cass, 1967.

Love, K. *Suez: the Twice-fought War.* Longman, 1970.

Mansfield, Peter. *Nasser's Egypt.* London, Penguin, 1965.

    Nasser. London, Methuen, 1969.

    The British in Egypt. London, Weidenfeld and Nicolson, 1971.

Marlowe, John. *Cromer in Egypt.* London, Elek Books, 1970.

Marsot, Afaf Lutfi as-Sayyed. *A Short History of Modern Egypt.* Cambridge University Press, 1985.

Nutting, Anthony. *No End of a Lesson; the Story of Suez.* London, Constable, 1967.

    Nasser. London, Constable, 1972.

O'Ballance, E. *The Sinai Campaign 1956.* London, Faber, 1959.

Quandt, William B. *Camp David: Peacemaking and Politics.* Washington, DC, Brookings Institution, 1986.

Raymond, André. *Artisans et commerçants au Caire au XVIIIe siècle.* 2 vols Paris, Librairie Adrien-Maisonneuve 1973–74.

Richmond, J. C. B. *Egypt, 1798–1952: Her Advance towards a Modern Identity.* London, Methuen, 1977.

Al-Sadat, Anwar. *Revolt on the Nile.* London, Allen Wingate, 1957.

Safran, Nadav. *Egypt in Search of Political Community. An analysis of the intellectual and political evolution of Egypt, 1804–1952.* Cambridge, MA, Harvard University Press, London, Oxford University Press, 1961.

Al-Sayyid, Afaf Lutfi. *Egypt and Cromer: A Study in Anglo-Egyptian Relations.* London, John Murray, New York, Praeger, 1968.

Schonfield, Hugh A. *The Suez Canal in Peace and War, 1869–1969.* London, Vallentine, Mitchell, 2nd revised edn, 1969.

Shaw, Tony. *Eden, Suez and the Mass Media: Propaganda and Persuasion During the Suez Crisis.* London, I. B. Tauris, 1995.

El-Shazly, Gen. Saad. *The Crossing of Suez: The October War (1973).* London, Third World Centre for Research and Publishing, 1980.

Stephens, R. *Nasser.* London, Allen Lane, Penguin, 1971.

Takeyh, Ray. *The Origins of the Eisenhower Doctrine: The US, Britain and Nasser's Egypt, 1953–57.* London, Macmillan, 2000.

Tignor, R. L. *Modernization and British Colonial Rule in Egypt 1882–1914*. Princeton, 1966.

Vatikiotis, P. J. *A Modern History of Egypt*. New York, Praeger, 1966; London, Weidenfeld and Nicolson, 1969, revised edn, 1980.

The Egyptian Army in Politics. Bloomington, Indiana University Press, 1961.

Waterbury, John. *The Egypt of Nasser and Sadat: The Political Economy of Two Regimes*. Princeton University Press, 1983.

Zaki, Abdel Rahman. *Histoire Militaire de l'Epoque de Mohammed Ali El-Kebir*. Cairo, 1950.

ECONOMY

El Ghonemy, M. Riad. *Economic and Industrial Organization of Egyptian Agriculture since 1952, Egypt since the Revolution*. London, Allen and Unwin, 1968.

Hopkins, Nicholas and Westergaard, Kirsten (Eds). *Directions of Change in Rural Egypt*. Columbia University Press, 1999.

Hvidt, Martin. *Water, Technology and Development: Upgrading Egypt's Irrigation System*. London, Tauris Academic Studies, 1997.

El Kammash, M. M. *Economic Development and Planning in Egypt*. London, 1967.

Kardouche, G. S. *The UAR in Development*. New York, Praeger, 1967.

Mabro, Robert. *The Egyptian Economy 1952–1972*. London, Oxford University Press, 1974.

Mead, Donald C. *Growth and Structural Change in the Egyptian Economy*. Homwood, IL, Irwin, 1967.

O'Brien, Patrick. *The Revolution in Egypt's Economic System 1952–65*. Oxford, 1966.

Posusney, Marsha Pripstein. *Labour and the State in Egypt: Workers, Unions and Economic Restructuring*. New York, Columbia University Press, 1998.

Saab, Gabriel S. *The Egyptian Agrarian Reform 1952–1962*. London and New York, Oxford University Press, 1967.

Warriner, Doreen. *Land Reform and Economic Development*. Cairo, 1955.

Land Reform and Development in the Middle East—A Study of Egypt, Syria and Iraq. London, 2nd edn, Oxford University Press, 1962.

IRAN

Physical and Social Geography

W. B. FISHER

SITUATION

The Islamic Republic of Iran is bounded on the north by the Caspian Sea, Azerbaijan and Turkmenistan, on the east by Afghanistan and Pakistan, on the south by the Persian (Arabian) Gulf and Gulf of Oman, and on the west by Iraq and Turkey.

PHYSICAL FEATURES

Structurally, Iran is an extremely complex area and, owing partly to political difficulties and partly to the difficult nature of the terrain itself, complete exploration and investigation have not so far been achieved. In general, Iran consists of an interior plateau, 1,000 m to 1,500 m above sea-level, ringed on almost all sides by mountain zones of varying height and extent. The largest mountain massif is that of the Zagros, which runs from the north-west, where the frontiers of Iran, Azerbaijan, Turkmenistan, Turkey and Iraq meet, first south-westwards to the eastern shores of the Persian Gulf, and then eastwards, fronting the Arabian Sea, and continuing into Baluchistan (Pakistan). Joining the Zagros in the north-west, and running along the southern edge of the Caspian Sea, is the narrower but equally high Elburz range; whilst along the eastern frontier of Iran are several scattered mountain chains, less continuous and imposing than either the Zagros or the Elburz, but sufficiently high to act as a barrier.

The Zagros range begins in north-west Iran as an alternation of high tablelands and lowland basins, the latter containing lakes, the largest of which is Lake Urmia. This lake, having no outlet, is saline. Further to the south-east the Zagros becomes much more imposing, consisting of a series of parallel hog's-back ridges, some of which reach over 4,000 m in height. In its southern and eastern portions the Zagros becomes distinctly narrower, and its peaks much lower, though a few exceed 3,000 m. The Elburz range is very much narrower than the Zagros, but equally, if not more, abrupt, and one of its peaks, the volcanic cone of Mt Damavand, at 5,604 m, is the highest in the country. There is a sudden drop on the northern side to the flat plain occupied by the Caspian Sea, which lies about 27 m below sea-level and is shrinking rapidly in size. The eastern highlands of Iran consist of isolated massifs separated by lowland zones, some of which contain lakes from which there is no outlet, the largest being the Hirmand Basin, on the border with Afghanistan.

The interior plateau of Iran is partly covered by a remarkable salt swamp (termed *kavir*) and partly by loose sand or stones (*dasht*), with stretches of better land mostly round the perimeter, near the foothills of the surrounding mountains. In these latter areas much of the cultivation of the country is practised, but the lower-lying desert and swamp areas, towards the centre of the plateau, are largely uninhabited. The Kavir is an extremely forbidding region, consisting of a surface formed by thick plates of crystallized salt, which have sharp, upstanding edges. Below the salt lie patches of mud, with, here and there, deep drainage channels—all of which are very dangerous to travellers and are hence unexplored. Because of the presence of an unusually intractable 'dead heart', it has proved difficult to find a good central site for the capital of Iran—many towns, all peripheral to a greater or lesser degree, have in turn fulfilled this function, but none has proved completely satisfactory. The choice of the present capital, Tehran, dates only from the end of the 18th century.

Iran suffers from occasional earthquakes, which can cause severe loss of life, damage to property and disruption of communications. A particularly bad earthquake occurred around Tabas in the north-eastern Khurasan province in September 1978, when an estimated 20,000 lives were lost; severe damage was inflicted, extending over 2,000 sq km. Even more devastating was the major earthquake which struck north-western Iran (principally the provinces of Gilan and Zanjan) in June 1990. Estimates put the number of those killed during the first quake and a series of severe tremors and aftershocks at some 40,000, while more than 60,000 were reportedly injured.

The climate of Iran is one of great extremes. Owing to its southerly position, adjacent to Arabia and near the Thar Desert, the summer is extremely hot, with temperatures in the interior rising possibly higher than anywhere else in the world—certainly a temperature exceeding 55°C has been recorded. In winter, however, the great altitude of much of the country and its continental situation result in far lower temperatures than one would expect to find in such low latitudes. Temperatures of −30°C have been recorded in the north-west Zagros, and −20°C is common in many places.

Another unfortunate feature is the prevalence of strong winds, which intensify the temperature contrasts. Eastern Iran is subject to the so-called 'Wind of 120 Days', which blows regularly throughout the summer, occasionally reaching a velocity of more than 160 km per hour and raising sand to such an extent that the stone walls of buildings are sometimes scoured away and turn to ruins.

Most of Iran is arid; but in contrast, parts of the north-west and north receive considerable rainfall—up to 2,000 mm along parts of the Caspian coast, producing very special climatic conditions in this small region, recalling conditions in the lower Himalayas. The Caspian coast has a hot, humid climate and this region is by far the most densely populated of the whole country. Next in order of population density comes the north-west Zagros area—the province of Azerbaijan, with its capital, Tabriz, the fourth city of Iran. Then, reflecting the diminished rainfall, next in order come the central Zagros area, and adjacent parts of the interior plateau, around Esfahan, Hamadan, Shiraz and Kermanshah, with an extension as far as Tehran. The extreme east and south, where rainfall is very scarce, were historically extremely lightly populated, except, in the few parts where water is available, by nomadic groups. Over the past few years, however, a development programme has been initiated, and the effects are seen in the expansion of towns, some of which have grown by 30%–40% since 1972.

ECONOMIC LIFE

Owing to the difficulties of climate and topography, there are few districts, apart from the Caspian plain, that are continuously cultivated over a wide area. Settlement tends to occur in small clusters, close to water supplies, or where there are especially favourable conditions—a good soil, shelter from winds, or easy communications. Away from these cultivated areas, which stand out like oases among the barren expanses of desert or mountain, most of the population live as nomads, by the herding of animals. The nomadic tribesmen have had great influence on the life of Iran. Their principal territory is the central Zagros, where the tribal system is strongly developed; but nomads are found in all the mountain zones, though their numbers are very few in the south and east. Reza Shah (see History) made considerable efforts to break the power of the nomadic tribes and to force them to settle as agriculturalists. Now, with the development of the economy, many nomads have moved into towns (though some still remain).

Economic activity has suffered from the handicaps of topography and climate, prolonged political and social insecurity (with constant pressure by foreign powers), and widespread devastation in the later Middle Ages by Mongol invaders. Agricultural methods in particular are primitive, so that yields are low; but the drawbacks to efficient production—archaic systems of land tenure, absentee landlords, lack of education, and

348

shortage of capital—are gradually being overcome. In the north and west, which are by far the most productive regions, a wide variety of cereals (including wheat, barley and rice) and much fruit are grown, but in the south and east dates are the principal source of food.

Iran has a number of mineral resources, some of which are exploited on a commercial scale. Copper deposits at Sar Cheshmeh are among the largest in the world. Iran also has very significant oil and natural gas resources; and there are large deposits of good-quality coal and iron ore near Kerman. Iranians have always had a good reputation as craftsmen—particularly in metalwork and carpet making. Although Reza Shah attempted to develop modern mechanized industry by siting state-owned factories in most large towns—some of which proved successful, others not—bazaar manufactures have retained their importance. Tehran is now a major manufacturing centre, with a considerable spread of activities from the processing of foodstuffs to the manufacture of consumer and construction goods as well as an increasing range of more complex items: electronic and motor manufactures and high-grade chemicals.

The adverse nature of geographical conditions has greatly restricted the growth of communications in Iran. The country is very large in relation to the size of its population—it is 2,250 km from north-west to south-west—and, because of the interior deserts, many routes must follow a circuitous path instead of attempting a direct crossing. Moreover, the interior is isolated by ranges that are in parts as high as the Alps of Europe, but far less broken up by river valleys. Road construction is generally difficult, but since the mid-1960s increasing effort has been devoted to providing all-weather trunk routes between major cities for which special allocations have been made in the five-year plans. An important link is the railway constructed with great effort before the Second World War between the Caspian coast, Tehran and the Gulf. Other rail links with bordering countries already exist or are under construction. Although there are mountain streams, many flowing in deep, inaccessible gorges, only one, the Karun river, is navigable. The Caspian ports are subject to silting, while most of the harbours in the south are either poorly sheltered or difficult of access

from the interior. However, there has been a deliberate focusing of development on the Gulf, in response to the enhanced economic and political status of the region, now one of the wealthiest in the world. Development was undertaken in the region of the Shatt al-Arab during the last years of the Shah's regime. However, the war between Iran and Iraq, beginning in September 1980, greatly impeded economic prospects, both there and in the Persian Gulf. Overall, the effect of the Revolution of 1979 was to reduce, though not entirely to terminate, the sophisticated industrial developments that were initiated under the Shah, and to shift external trading more towards imports of basic raw materials and food, balanced (often by direct exchange approaching barter) by exports of petroleum.

RACE AND LANGUAGE

Iran has numerous ethnic groups of widely differing origin. In the central plateau there occurs a distinctive sub-race, termed by some anthropologists Iranian or Irano-Afghan. In the mountain districts there are many other smaller groups of separate racial composition. A number of nomads, including the Bakhtiari tribes, would seem to be of Kurdish stock; whilst Turki (Mongoloid) strains are apparent in others, such as the Qashqai tribes. Smaller groups from the Caucasus (Georgians and Circassians) are represented in Azerbaijan and the Caspian provinces, while Turki influence is again apparent in the racial composition of the eastern districts of Iran, especially round Meshed. The southern Zagros near the Arabian Sea has a small population that tends to be of mixed Iranian, Afghan and Hindu stock. Some observers have suggested that in this region there may also be representatives of a primitive negrito race, related to the hill-tribes of India and of south-east Asia.

Several languages are current in Iran. Persian (Farsi), an Indo-Aryan language related to the languages of western Europe, is spoken in the north and centre of the country, and is the only official language of the state. As the north is by far the most densely populated region of Iran, the Persian language has an importance somewhat greater than its territorial extent would suggest. Various dialects of Kurdish are current in the north and central Zagros mountains, and alongside these are found several Turki-speaking tribes. Baluchi is spoken in the extreme south-east.

History

Updated for this edition by STEPHANIE CRONIN

EARLY HISTORY

The Achaemenid empire, the first Persian empire, was founded by Cyrus, who revolted against the Median empire in 533 BC. After the defeat of the Median empire, Babylon was taken in 529 BC, and in 525 BC under Cambyses, the successor of Cyrus, Egypt was conquered. The period of conquest was completed by Darius, who reduced the tribes of the Pontic and Armenian mountains and extended Persian dominion to the Caucasus. The main work of Darius, however, lay not in the conquest but in the organization that he gave to the empire. During his reign wars with Greece broke out and in 490 BC the Persian army suffered a major defeat at Marathon; an expedition under Xerxes, the successor of Darius, which set out to avenge this defeat was, after initial successes, defeated at Salamis in 480 BC. The empire was finally overthrown by Alexander, who defeated the Persian army at Arbela in 331 BC and then burnt Persepolis, the Achaemenid capital; the last Darius fled and was killed in 330 BC. Alexander thereafter regarded himself as the head of the Persian empire. The death of Alexander was followed by a struggle between his generals, one of whom, Seleucus, took the whole of Persia, apart from northern Media, and founded the Seleucid empire. About 250 BC a reaction against Hellenism began with the rise of the Parthian empire of the Arsacids. Although by origin nomads from the Turanian steppe, the Arsacids became the wardens of the north-east marches and were largely preoccupied in defending themselves in the east against the Scythians who, with the Tocharians and Sacae,

repeatedly attacked the Parthian empire, while in the west they were engaged in fending off attacks by the Romans.

The Arsacids were succeeded by the Sasanians, who, like the Achaemenids, came from Fars and, like them, were Zoroastrians. Ardashir b. Babak, after subduing the neighbouring states (c. AD 212), made war on the Arsacid, Artabanus V, whom he eventually defeated. The empire which he founded largely continued the traditions of the Achaemenids, although it never equalled the Achaemenid empire in extent. The monarchy of the Sasanian period was a religious and civil institution. The monarch, who ruled by divine right, was absolute but his autocracy was limited by the powers of the Zoroastrian hierarchy and the feudal aristocracy. In the reign of Qubad (488–531) a movement of revolt, partly social and partly religious, led by Mazdak, gained ground. Under Qubad's successor Anushiravan (531–79) orthodoxy was restored, but at the cost of the imposition of a military despotism. Like the Arsacids before them, the Sasanians were occupied in the west with wars against Rome and in the east with repelling the advances of nomads from Central Asia.

MUSLIM PERSIA

By the beginning of the seventh century AD Persia had been greatly weakened by these wars, and when the Muslim Arabs attacked, little effective resistance was offered. The decisive battles were fought at Qadisiyya (637) and Nihavand (c. 641). Persia did not re-emerge as a political entity until the 16th century, although with the decline of the Abbasid empire semi-independent and independent dynasties arose in different parts of Persia and at times even incorporated under their rule an area extending beyond the confines of present-day Iran. As a result of the Arab conquest Persia became part of the Muslim world. Local administration remained largely in the hands of the indigenous population, and many local customs continued to be observed. In due course a new civilization developed in Persia, the unifying force of which was Islam.

With the transfer of the capital of the Islamic empire from Damascus to Baghdad (*c.* 750), Persian influence began to be strongly felt in the life of the empire. Islam had already replaced Zoroastrianism and by the 10th century modern Persian, written in the Arabic script and including a large number of Arabic words in its vocabulary, had established itself. Its emergence was of immense importance; the literary tradition for which it became the vehicle has perhaps more than any other factor kept alive a national consciousness among the Iranians and preserved the memory of the great Persian empires of the past.

By the eighth century the Abbasid caliphate had begun to disintegrate and when in the 11th century control of the north-eastern frontiers broke down, the Ghuzz Turks invaded Persia. This movement, of which the Seljuqs became the leaders, was ethnologically important since it altered the balance of population, the Turkish element from then on being second only to the Persian in numbers and influence. Secondly, it was in the Seljuq empire that the main lines of the politico-economic structure, which was to last in Persia in a modified form until the 20th century, were developed. The basis of this structure was the land assignment, the holder of which was often virtually a petty territorial ruler, who was required, when called upon to do so, to provide the ruler with a military contingent.

The Seljuq empire itself disintegrated in the 12th century into a number of succession states; the 13th century saw the Mongol invasion and in 1258 Hulagu, the grandson of Chinghiz (Jenghiz) Khan, sacked Baghdad and destroyed the caliphate. For some years the Ilkhan dynasty, founded by Hulagu, ruled Persia as vassals of the Great Khan in Qaraqorum, but from the reign of Abaqa (1265–81) onwards they became virtually a Persian dynasty. Their empire, like that of the Seljuqs before them—and for the same reason—broke up at the beginning of the 14th century into a number of succession states. Towards the end of the century Persia again fell under the dominion of a military conqueror, when Timur, who had started his career as the warden of the marches in the Oxus-Jaxartes basin against the nomads of Central Asia, undertook a series of military campaigns against Persia between 1381 and 1387. The kingdom founded by him was short-lived and rapidly disintegrated on the death of his son Shahrukh, the western part falling first to the Turkomans of the Black Sheep and then to the Turkomans of the White Sheep, while Transoxania passed into the hands of the Uzbegs.

THE PERSIAN MONARCHY

The 16th century saw the foundation of the Safavid empire, which was accompanied by an eastward movement of the Turkomans from Asia Minor back into Persia. For the first time since the Muslim conquest Persia re-emerged as a political unit. The foundations of the Safavid empire were laid by Isma'il Safavi (1502–24). He deliberately fostered a sense of separateness and of national unity *vis-à-vis* the Ottoman Turks, with whom the Safavids were engaged in a struggle for supremacy in the west, and the main weapon he used to accomplish his purpose was Shi'ism. Not only the Turks but the majority of his own subjects were at the time Sunni Muslims—nevertheless he imposed Shi'ism upon them by force and created among the population of his dominions, many of whom, especially among his immediate followers, were Turks, a sense of national unity as Persians. Apart from a brief interlude under Nadir Shah, Shi'ism has remained the majority rite in Persia and is the official rite of the country today. Under Shah Abbas (1587–1629) the Safavid empire reached its zenith, and Persia enjoyed a power and prosperity which it has not achieved since.

GREAT POWER RIVALRY

During the Safavid period contact with Europe increased. Various foreign embassies interested mainly in the silk trade reached the Safavid court via Russia and the Persian (Arabian) Gulf. In the early years of the 16th century a struggle for supremacy developed between the British and the Dutch in the Gulf, where 'factories' began to be established by the East India Company.

Under the later Safavids internal decline set in and from 1722–30 Persia was subject to Afghan invasion and occupation, while in the west and north it was threatened by Turkey and Russia. After the death of Peter the Great there was a temporary slackening of Russian pressure, but the Turks continued to advance and took Tabriz in 1725, peace being made eventually at Hamadan in 1727. The Afghans were finally evicted by Nadir Shah Afshar, whose reign (1736–47) was remarkable chiefly for his military exploits. The Afsharids were succeeded by Karim Khan Zand (1750–79) whose relatively peaceful reign was followed by the rise of the Qajars, who continued to reign until 1925. Under them the capital was transferred from Esfahan to Tehran. During the Qajar period events in Persia became increasingly affected by Great Power rivalry, which came to dominate not only Persia's foreign policy but its internal politics also.

With the growth of British influence in India in the late 18th and early 19th centuries the main emphasis in Anglo-Persian relations began to shift from commerce to strategy. The region of Persia and the Persian Gulf came to be regarded as one of the main bastions protecting British India, and the existence of an independent Persia as a major British interest. In the early 19th century fear of a French invasion of India through Persia exercised the minds of the British in India and Whitehall. French envoys were active in Persia and Mesopotamia from 1796 to 1809, and to counter possible French activities Captain (later Sir) John Malcolm was sent to Persia in 1800 by the Governor-General of India. He concluded a political and commercial treaty with Fath Ali Shah, the main purpose of which was to ensure that the Shah should not receive French agents and would do his utmost to prevent French forces from entering Persia. With the defeat of Napoleon in Egypt the matter was no longer regarded as urgent, and the agreement was not ratified. Subsequently the French made proposals to Persia for an alliance against Russia, and in 1807 Persia concluded the Treaty of Finkenstein with France, after which a military mission under General Gardanne came to Persia. In 1808 another British mission was sent under Malcolm. Its object was 'first, to detach the Court of Persia from the French alliance and to prevail on that Court to refuse the passage of French troops through the territories subject to Persia, or the admission of French troops into the country. If that cannot be obtained, to admit English troops with a view of opposing the French army in its progress to India, to prevent the creation of any maritime post, and the establishment of French factories on the coast of Persia'. Malcolm's task was complicated by the almost simultaneous arrival of a similar mission from Whitehall. In 1809 after the Treaty of Tilsit, which debarred the French from aiding the Shah against Russia, Gardanne was dismissed.

WARS WITH RUSSIA AND TURKEY

Meanwhile, the formal annexation of Georgia by Russia in 1801 had been followed by a campaign against Russia. This proved disastrous to Persia and was temporarily brought to an end by the Treaty of Gulistan (1813), by which Persia ceded Georgia, Qara Bagh and seven other provinces. British policy continued to be concerned with the possibility of an invasion of India via Persia, and in 1814 the Treaty of Tehran was concluded with Persia—by which Great Britain undertook to provide troops or a subsidy in the event of unprovoked aggression against Persia. Although the treaty provided for defence against any European power, it was primarily intended to counteract the designs of Russia. In fact it proved ineffective: when the Perso–Russian war recommenced in 1825 Great Britain did not interfere except as a peacemaker and discontinued the subsidy to Persia, which was technically the aggressor. The war was concluded in 1828 by the Treaty of Turkomanchai, under the terms of which Persia ceded Erivan and Nakhjivan and agreed to pay an indemnity;

in addition, it was prohibited from having armed vessels on the Caspian.

During this period Persia was also engaged in hostilities with Turkey. Frontier disputes in 1821 culminated in the outbreak of war, which was concluded by the Treaty of Erzerum (1823).

By the 19th century the Persian Government had ceased to exercise effective control over the greater part of Khurasan. Russian policy, which became conciliatory towards Persia during the 25 years or so after the Treaty of Turkomanchai, encouraged the Shah to reimpose Persian rule on the eastern provinces. British policy, on the other hand, having come to regard Afghanistan as an important link in the defence of India, urged moderation upon the Persian Government. After the accession of Muhammad Shah in 1834, an expedition was sent against Herat. The siege of Herat began in 1837 but was raised when the Shah was threatened with British intervention. Subsequently local intrigues enabled the Persians to enter Herat. The seizure of the city by Persia led to the outbreak of the Anglo–Persian war in 1856, which was terminated by the Treaty of Paris (1857) after a British force had occupied the island of Kharg in the Persian Gulf.

In the second half of the century the subjection of the Turkoman tribes by Russia, its capture of Marv in 1854, and the occupation of the Panjeh, meant that Russian influence became dominant in Khurasan in the same way as the advance of Russia to the Araxes after the Persian wars in the early part of the 19th century had made Russian influence dominant in Azerbaijan.

INCREASED FOREIGN INTERVENTION

Internally, the second half of the 19th century was remarkable chiefly for the beginnings of the modernist movement, which was stimulated on the one hand by internal misgovernment and on the other by increased intervention in the internal affairs of the country by Russia and Britain. Towards the end of the century numerous concessions were granted to foreigners, largely in order to pay for the extravagances of the court. The most fantastic of these was the Reuter concession. In 1872 a naturalized British subject, Baron de Reuter, was given by the Shah a monopoly for 70 years of railways and tramways in Persia, all the minerals except gold, silver and precious stones, irrigation, road, factory and telegraph enterprises, and the farm of customs dues for 25 years. Eventually this concession was cancelled and permission given instead for the foundation of a Persian state bank with British capital, which was to have the exclusive right to issue banknotes: thus in September 1889 the Imperial Bank of Persia began trading. In the same year Dolgoruki obtained for Russia the first option of a railway concession for five years. In November 1890 the railway agreement with Russia was changed into one interdicting all railways in Persia. By the turn of the century there had been 'a pronounced sharpening of Anglo–Russian hostility as a consequence of a whole series of Russian actions, not only in northern Persia, where Russian ascendancy to a large extent had to be admitted, but as well in southern and eastern Persia which had hitherto been predominantly British preserves'. In 1900 a Russian loan was given. Subsequently various short-term advances and subsidies from the Russian treasury including advances to the heir apparent, Muhammad Ali, were made so that by 1906 some £7.5m. was owing to the Russians. Under the 1891 Russo-Persian tariff treaty bilateral trade had increased, and when, under the 1901 Russo-Persian commercial treaty, a new customs tariff was announced in 1903, Russian exports to Persia were considerably aided, and, up to 1914, Russian commerce with Persia continued to grow.

The grant of these various concessions to foreigners and the raising of foreign loans gave rise to growing anxiety on the part of the Persian public. Furthermore, large numbers of Persians had fled the country and were living in exile. When a tobacco monopoly was granted to a British subject in 1890, various elements of the population, including the intellectuals and religious classes, combined to oppose it. Strikes and riots threatened and the monopoly was rescinded. No effective steps, however, were taken to allay popular discontent. In 1901 protests were made against the loans and mortgages from Russia which were being contracted to pay for Muzaffar ud-Din Shah's journeys to Europe. Demand for reform increased, and finally on 5 August

1906, after 12,000 persons had taken sanctuary in the British legation, a constitution was granted. A long struggle then began between the constitutionalists and the Shah. The Cossack Brigade, formed during the reign of Nasir ud-Din Shah, which was under Russian officers and was the most effective military force in the country, played a major part in this struggle and was used by Muhammad Ali Shah to suppress the National Assembly in 1908. Civil war ensued, and Muhammad Ali Shah's abdication was forced in 1909.

Meanwhile, in 1907 the Anglo-Russian convention had been signed. The convention, which included a mutual undertaking to respect the integrity and independence of Persia, divided the country into three areas: that lying to the north of a line passing from Qasr-e-Shirin to Kakh, where the Russian, Persian and Afghan frontiers met in the east; that lying to the south of a line running from Qazik, on the Perso–Afghan frontier, through Birjand and Kerman to Bandar Abbas on the Persian Gulf; and that lying outside these two areas. Great Britain gave an undertaking not to seek or support others seeking political or economic concessions in the northern area, while Russia gave a similar undertaking with reference to the southern area. In the central area the freedom of action of the two parties was not limited, and their existing concessions (which included the oil concession granted to William Knox D'Arcy in 1901) were maintained. The conclusion of this convention—which had taken place partly because of a change in the relative strength of the Great Powers and partly because the British Government hoped thereby to terminate Anglo–Russian rivalry in Persia and to prevent further Russian encroachments—came as a shock to Persian opinion which had hoped for much from the support which the British Government had given to the constitutional movement. It was felt that Persian interests had been bartered away by Great Britain for a promise of Russian support in the event of a European war. In fact, the convention failed in its object. Russian pressure continued to be exercised on Persia directly and indirectly, leading, in 1911, to the suspension of the National Assembly and the forced resignation of the American Administrator-General of the Finances, Shuster, who had been appointed in the hope of bringing order to Persia's finances.

THE FIRST WORLD WAR

During the First World War (1914–18) Persia was nominally neutral but, in fact, pro-Turkish. By the end of the war the internal condition of Persia was chaotic. To the British Government the restoration of order was desirable; with this end in view the Agreement of 1919 was drawn up whereby a number of men were to be lent to reorganize the Persian army and to reform the Ministry of Finance, and a loan of £2m. was to be given. There was opposition to this agreement in the USA and France and in Persia itself, and the treaty was not ratified. A *coup d'état* took place in 1921, Reza Khan (later Reza Shah) becoming Minister of War. In February 1921 the Soviet-Persian Treaty was signed whereby the USSR declared all treaties and conventions concluded with Persia by the Tsarist Government null and void. Under Article VI the USSR was permitted 'to advance her troops into the Persian interior for the purpose of carrying out the military operations necessary for its defence' in the event of a third party attempting 'to carry out a policy of usurpation by means of armed intervention in Persia, or if such a Power should desire to use Persian territory as a base of operations against Russia...'

REZA SHAH, 1925–41, AND AFTER

In 1923 Reza Khan became Prime Minister, and finally in 1925 the crown of Persia was conferred upon him. His first task was to restore the authority of the central Government throughout the country, and the second to place Persia's relations with foreign countries on a basis of equality. All extra-territorial agreements were terminated from 1928. Lighterage and quarantine duties on the Persian littoral of the Persian (Arabian) Gulf, hitherto performed by Great Britain, were transferred to the Persian Government in 1930. The Indo-European Telegraphy Company, which had been in operation since 1872, had almost entirely been withdrawn by 1931, and the British coaling stations were transferred from Basidu and Henjam to Bahrain in 1935.

In 1932 the cancellation of the Anglo-Persian Oil Co's concession was announced by Persia. The original concession obtained by D'Arcy in 1901 had been taken over by the Anglo-Persian Oil Co (later the Anglo-Iranian Oil Co) in 1909 and the British Government had acquired a controlling interest in the company in 1914. The Persian Government's action in cancelling the concession was referred to the League of Nations. Eventually an agreement was concluded in 1933 for a new concession whereby the concession area was materially reduced and the royalty to be paid to the Persian Government increased. The concession was to run until 1993.

Internally Reza Shah's policy aimed at modernization and autarchy. In the later years of his reign the Government became increasingly totalitarian in nature. Compulsory military service was introduced and the army much increased in size. Communications were greatly improved, and the construction of a trans-Persian railway was begun. Education was remodelled on Western lines. Women were no longer obliged to wear the veil after 1936. Foreign trade was made a state monopoly, and currency and clearing restrictions were established. These arrangements were compatible with the economy of Germany, and, by the outbreak of the Second World War in 1939, Germany had acquired considerable commercial and political influence in Persia.

At the outbreak of war Persia declared its neutrality. In 1941 the Allies demanded a reduction in the number of Germans in the country, and when this was not fulfilled sent another communication demanding the expulsion of all German nationals, except those who were essential to the Persian economy and harmless to the Allies. This demand was not complied with, and on 26 August Persia was invaded. Hostilities lasted some two days. On 16 September Reza Shah abdicated in favour of his son Muhammad Reza. In January 1942 a Tripartite Treaty of Alliance was concluded with Great Britain and the USSR whereby those countries undertook jointly and severally 'to respect the territorial integrity, sovereignty and political independence of Persia' and 'to defend Persia by all means in their command from aggression'. The Persian Government undertook to give the Allies, for certain military purposes, the unrestricted right to use, maintain and guard, and in the case of military necessity, to control, all means of communications in Persia. Allied forces were to be withdrawn not later than six months after the conclusion of hostilities between the Allied Powers and Germany and its associates. In so far as the establishment of communications with the USSR was concerned the Treaty was effective; its operation in other respects was less satisfactory. In the Russian zone of occupation the Persian authorities were denied freedom of movement, and effective administration made impossible. American advisers were appointed by the Persian Government in 1942 and 1943, in the hope of reorganizing certain aspects of the administration, but little success was achieved.

In 1943 a British company applied for an oil concession in south-east Persia, and in 1944 the Socony Vacuum and Sinclair Oil Cos made various proposals to the Persian Government. In September the Persian Cabinet issued a decree deferring the granting of oil concessions until after the war. The USSR, meanwhile, asked for an oil concession in the north and brought heavy, though unavailing, pressure to bear on the Persian Government to accede to this demand. Persian security forces were prevented by Soviet forces from entering Azerbaijan or the Caspian provinces, and an autonomous government was set up in Azerbaijan, with Soviet support, in December 1945. In January 1946 the Persian Government had recourse to the UN Security Council. In March the Tripartite Treaty expired and British and US forces evacuated Persia, Soviet forces remaining. The Persian Government again presented a note to the Security Council. In April an understanding was reached whereby a joint Soviet-Persian company to exploit the oil in the northern provinces was to be formed. In May Soviet forces evacuated the country. Soviet pressure, however, continued to be exerted through the communist Tudeh party, the Democrat movement in Azerbaijan and the Kurdish autonomy movement, and the Persian Government was unable to re-enter Azerbaijan until December. In October the Soviet Oil Agreement was presented to the National Assembly but was not ratified. In October 1947 an agreement was signed with the USA, providing for a US military mission in Persia to co-operate with the Persian Ministry of War in 'enhancing the efficiency of the Persian army'.

NATIONALIZING THE OIL INDUSTRY

Meanwhile, unrest and discontent at internal misgovernment increased, culminating in the nationalist movement of 1950–51. In July 1949 a Supplemental Oil Agreement with the Anglo-Iranian Oil Co was initialled. Opposition to this agreement (whereby Persia was offered considerable financial gains) was strong. In November 1950 the oil commission of the National Assembly recommended its rejection. Meanwhile, Persia had received a loan of US $25m. from the Export & Import Bank of Washington and a grant of $500,000 under the Point IV allocation. Subsequently in 1952 the Point IV aid programme was expanded. In April 1951 the National Assembly enacted legislation for the nationalization of the oil industry, and in May Dr Muhammad Musaddiq, who had led the campaign for nationalization of oil, became Prime Minister. In spite of efforts to involve the International Court of Justice (ICJ), the *status quo* could not be maintained in Persia and the Anglo-Iranian Oil Co, unable to continue operations, evacuated the country.

In July 1952 the ICJ found that it had no jurisdiction in the oil dispute. This decision, however, was not a decision on the merits of the case. Anglo-Iranian accordingly maintained its claim to be entitled to all crude oil and oil products derived from the area covered by its concession agreement, and stated its intention to take such action as was necessary to protect its interests. US policy showed an increasing interest in Persian affairs. In subsequent weeks considerable correspondence passed between the British, US and Persian Governments in the oil dispute, culminating in a joint offer by Sir Winston Churchill and President Harry S Truman concerning proposals to assess the compensation to be paid to the Anglo-Iranian Oil Co and the resumption of the flow of oil to world markets. The Persian Government rejected these proposals and put forward counter-proposals that were unacceptable. In October the Persian Government broke off diplomatic relations with Great Britain. Further Anglo-American proposals for an oil settlement were put forward in February 1953, which the Persian Government rejected. Meanwhile, dissension between Musaddiq and some of his supporters broke out, and a rift also developed between him and the Shah. Persia's economic situation began to deteriorate rapidly, culminating in the overthrow of Musaddiq by General Zahedi in August 1953. Musaddiq was tried and sentenced to three years' solitary confinement for allegedly trying to overthrow the regime and illegally dissolving the Majlis-e-Shura (Consultative Assembly).

The new Government resumed diplomatic relations with the United Kingdom in December 1953, and negotiations with British and US oil interests began for the solution of the oil problem. An agreement was signed in September, and ratified by the Majlis and Senate in October, granting a concession to a consortium of eight companies (subsequently increased to 17) on a percentage basis. It was also agreed that the counter-claims of the Anglo-Iranian Oil Co and the Persian Government were to be settled by the payment of a lump sum to the former, which was also to receive compensation from the other members of the consortium. The profits arising within Persia from the oil operations were to be equally shared between the Persian Government and the consortium. The agreement was for a period of 25 years with provision for three five-year extensions, conditional upon a progressive reduction of the original area. The National Iranian Oil Co (NIOC) was to operate the Naft-i Shahr oilfield and the Kermanshah refinery, to meet some of Persia's own needs and to handle the distribution of oil products in Persia and manage all facilities and services not directly part of the producing, refining, and transport operations of the two operating companies set up under the agreement. The greater part of the cost of these facilities and services, which would include industrial training, public transport, road maintenance, housing, medical care, and social welfare, would be recovered by NIOC from the operating companies.

GROWING POWER OF THE SHAH

Internally, order was restored. The communist Tudeh Party was proscribed, but continued to exist underground. The failure of the Government to push forward actively with reform, however, led in due course to a reappearance of civil unrest. In April 1955 Zahedi resigned and was succeeded by Hussein Ala, the Shah henceforward taking a more active part in the administration. In October Persia joined the Baghdad Pact. In November an attempt was made on the Prime Minister's life. The country had not recovered from the financial difficulties brought on by the Musaddiq regime, in spite of considerable financial aid granted by the USA to enable the country to carry on until oil revenues were received. More than US $800m. were poured into Iran between the end of the Second World War and September 1960. In March 1959 a bilateral defence agreement was signed in Ankara, Turkey, between the USA and Iran. Under the agreement, the US Government would 'in case of aggression, take such appropriate action, including the use of armed force, as may be mutually agreed, and as envisaged in the Joint Resolution to promote peace and security in the Middle East'. (The Joint Resolution refers to the 'Eisenhower Doctrine'.)

Relations with the USSR in the years following the fall of Musaddiq were not cordial, but in December 1954 an agreement providing for the repayment by the USSR of its war debts to Persia for goods supplied and services rendered, and mapping of the revised frontiers, was signed.

In April 1957 Hussein Ala resigned; he was succeeded as Prime Minister by Dr Manoutchehr Egbal, who formed a new Government. Immediately after taking office Dr Egbal issued a decree ending martial law and declared his intention of forming a democratic two-party system, in accordance with the wishes of the Shah. In February 1958 a pro-Government Nation Party was formed. An opposition People's Party had been formed in 1957. Elections contested by both these political parties disclosed electoral irregularities, and in August 1960 Dr Jaafar Sharif-Emami replaced Egbal as Prime Minister. In May 1961, however, Emami resigned as a result of criticism of his handling of a teachers' strike, and the Shah called upon Dr Ali Amini, the leader of the opposition, to form a new government.

Dr Amini quickly took uncompromising measures to halt the political and economic chaos in Iran. A drive against corruption in the government and civil service was coupled with policies of land reform, decentralization of administration, control of government expenditure and limitation of luxury imports. Both houses of parliament were dissolved pending the enactment of a new electoral law that would make free and fair elections possible. Postponement of elections, in July 1962, led to disorder in Tehran, and the added difficulty of producing a reasonably balanced budget led Dr Amini to tender his resignation.

A new Government was quickly formed by Assadollah Alam, the leader of the Mardom (People's) Party. Alam, one of Iran's largest landowners and administrator of the Pahlavi Foundation, had previously distributed much of his land voluntarily amongst the peasants. He stated that Iran would remain closely linked to the West, and that he would continue the land reform programme and the struggle against internal political corruption.

REFORMS OF THE SHAH

In 1950 the Shah had begun distributing his estate amongst the peasants. By the end of 1963 he had disposed of all his Crown Properties. The Pahlavi Foundation was established in 1958 and received considerable gifts from the Shah for the purpose of improving standards of education, health and social welfare among the poorer classes. In October 1961 the Shah created the £40m. Pahlavi Dynasty Trust, the income of which was also used for social, educational and health services. In January 1963 a referendum gave overwhelming approval to the Shah's six-point plan, which included the distribution of lands among the peasants, the promotion of literacy and the emancipation of women. The dismantling of great estates began almost immediately, and the programme was finally completed in September 1971. Another important measure was the formation of the Literacy Corps (and later of the Health Corps), in which students could spend their period of national service as teachers, working in the villages.

Elections in September 1963 resulted in an overwhelming victory for Alam's National Union. The elections, at which women were allowed to vote for the first time, were held in the face of strong opposition from the left-wing parties of Iran, notably the National Front and the Tudeh Party, which cam-

paigned unsuccessfully for a boycott. The Shah called on the new Parliament to inaugurate a 20-year programme of economic and social reform and political development, and he also announced a second phase of the land reform programme, whereby it was hoped that another 20,000 villages would be added to the 10,000 already ceded to the tenants. The Alam Government continued until March 1964, when, without offering any reason, Alam resigned. The new leader was Hassan Ali Mansur, a former minister and founder of the Progressive Centre, which had played a prominent part in Alam's coalition the previous year. In December 1963 he had formed the New Iran Party, which by now had the support of some 150 members of the Majlis. The second stage of the land reform plan was placed before the Majlis in May 1964, aiming to break down the great estates more thoroughly: the maximum permissible size was to range from 120 ha in arid regions to 30 ha in more fertile areas.

On 21 January 1965 Mansur was assassinated by members of the right-wing religious sect Fedayin Islam. The assassins were reportedly followers of the Ayatollah Ruhollah Khomeini, a Shi'ite Muslim religious leader who had been exiled in 1964 for his opposition to the Shah's reforms. Amir Abbas Hoveida, the Minister of Finance, was immediately appointed Prime Minister, while retaining his ministerial post. He pledged the continuation of his predecessor's policies, and was given the massive support of the Majlis. Elections took place in 1967, 1971 and 1975. Hoveida continued as Prime Minister until August 1977, when he was succeeded by Dr Jamshid Amouzegar.

FOREIGN RELATIONS

It had been an avowed part of Mansur's policy that Iran should be as interested in maintaining links with the USSR as with the West. During 1964–65 various bilateral trade and technical agreements were signed, and a regular air service was established between Tehran and Moscow. In June 1965 the Shah visited Moscow, and in October an agreement was signed for the construction by Soviet engineers of a steel mill.

The coronation of the Shah in October 1967 seemed to augur forthcoming prosperity, and the apparent stability of Iran was emphasized not only by economic development and by the organization of international gatherings, but also by the formal ending in November of US economic aid under the Point IV programme. Iran, which had been the first country to accept this aid in 1951, was now the second (after the Taiwan Province of China) able to dispense with it. Military aid, however, was to continue. At the same time economic co-operation with the USSR was developed, and an agreement was made for the purchase of £40m. of munitions, the first occasion on which the USSR had concluded an arms transaction with a member of the Western bloc.

In January 1968 the British Government announced its decision to withdraw all of its forces from the Gulf by the end of 1971. Since these forces had apparently helped to preserve the local *status quo*, a revival of the ancient rivalry between Arabs and Persians over supremacy in the Gulf seemed a likely prospect following their removal. The Iranian Government's reiteration of its claim to Bahrain in February 1968 did not facilitate relations with the Arab world, but Iran cautiously welcomed the proposed Federation of Arab Emirates (which it was thought would incorporate Bahrain). A UN mission visiting Bahrain in early 1970 found that the large Arab majority overwhelmingly preferred full independence to joining Iran or remaining a British protectorate. Iran had previously agreed to accept the mission's findings, and it did so without complaint, though expressing concern for the future of Iranians in the Gulf states. In June 1970 a dispute with other Gulf states also arose over Iran's claim to the islands of Abu Musa and the Tunbs—belonging to Sharjah and Ras al-Khaimah respectively. The dispute was only settled in December 1971. The Sheikh of Sharjah agreed to share sovereignty of Abu Musa with Iran. The Sheikh of Ras al-Khaimah was less accommodating, so Iran invaded his possessions of the Greater and Lesser Tunbs and took them by force. After occupying Abu Musa and the Tunbs, Iran developed them as military bases to command the Strait of Hormuz at the neck of the Gulf. Iran regarded the maintenance of freedom of passage through the Strait of Hormuz as vital to its strategic and economic interests.

Iran's relations with the more radical Arab states were less friendly under the Shah. These states had long been suspicious of Iran's close ties with the West, and especially of the generous US military aid to the powerful Iranian armed forces. Moreover, the Arab states distrusted Iran's attitude to Israel. Although no formal diplomatic links existed, trade, particularly in oil, was conducted with Israel. One of the first actions of the Khomeini regime in early 1979 was to end any ties with Israel and to align Iran firmly with the Arab cause, by allowing, for example, the opening by the Palestine Liberation Organization (PLO) of an office in Tehran.

Iran's only frontier with an Arab state is with Iraq. Near the Gulf the border is delineated by the 185-km Shatt al-Arab waterway, the estuary of the Tigris and Euphrates, which flows into the Gulf. By the terms of the 1937 treaty, the frontier followed the eastern—i.e. Iranian—bank: thus, Iraq legally had sovereignty over the whole waterway. Iran resented this provision, and in 1966 a series of border incidents erupted. In April 1969 Iran decided to abrogate the treaty, sending Iranian vessels through the waterway while heavy naval forces stood ready to intervene. The aim was apparently to force a renegotiation of the treaty. There were further border clashes in September. In January 1970 Iraq accused the Iranian Government of supporting an abortive coup in Iraq, and diplomatic relations between the two countries were severed. Links were restored soon after the outbreak of the Arab–Israeli war in October 1973, but border incidents continued. In March 1975, however, it was announced at a meeting of the Organization of the Petroleum Exporting Countries (OPEC) in Algiers that the Shah and Saddam Hussein (then Vice-President of the Iraqi Revolutionary Command Council) had signed an agreement which 'completely eliminated the conflict between the two brotherly countries'. Not only did this agreement settle the outstanding border differences, but it also deprived the Kurds in Iraq of the help that they had been receiving from Iran in their struggle against the Iraqi Government, thus causing a Kurdish collapse and a virtual end to the Kurdish rebellion.

The border agreement provided that Iran and Iraq would define their frontiers on the basis of the Protocol of Constantinople of 1913 (which allowed the Ottoman Empire to retain control over the Shatt al-Arab but granted sovereignty over the east bank to Persia) and the verbal agreement on frontiers of 1914, and that the Shatt al-Arab frontier would be defined according to the Thalweg Line (i.e. the middle of the deepest shipping channel). The treaty giving effect to this agreement was signed on 15 June 1975 and later became one of the key issues of the war that broke out in September 1980 (see below).

INTERNAL PROBLEMS

Signs of domestic opposition to the Shah's regime, never far from the surface of Iranian life, became more and more evident as the celebrations for the 2,500th anniversary of the Persian monarchy were in preparation for October 1971. The combination of the very unequal distribution of the enormous earnings from oil and the suppression of any sign of dissent was made more politically explosive as the lavishness of the celebrations and the huge extent of the accompanying security precautions became apparent. From then until the final fall of the Shah in early 1979 there were countless stories of the stifling of opposition by the ruthless activities of SAVAK, the government security agency.

In March 1975 the Shah, dissatisfied with the current structure of party politics in Iran and seeking to weld together all those who supported the principles of his 'White Revolution' policy (later known as the 'Revolution of the Shah and People'), announced the formation of a single party system, the Iran National Resurgence Party (Rastakhiz), with the Prime Minister, Amir Abbas Hoveida, as Secretary-General. By 1978 it became clear that the single-party Rastakhiz system was not solving the problem of internal opposition in Iran, but few in early 1978 would have forecast that, within a year, a completely new political system would take its place.

FALL OF THE SHAH

During 1977 and 1978 demonstrations centred around the universities, and acts of political violence increased. Attempts by the Shah to control the situation, first by greater liberalization and then through firmer suppression, proved ineffective. In August 1977 Dr Jamshid Amouzegar, who had become Secretary-General of Rastakhiz, replaced the long-serving Amir Abbas Hoveida as Prime Minister, but he resigned a year later. In August 1978 Jaafar Sharif-Emami was appointed Prime Minister (an office he had previously held in 1960–61) and, in response to the emerging mood of the country, promised that his Government would observe Islamic tenets. However, unrest continued; martial law was introduced in September, and in November the Shah established a military Government headed by the army Chief of Staff, Gen. Gholamreza Azhari. Censorship was imposed, but industrial action undertaken by workers in the oil industry and public services left the Shah in a desperate situation, and in early January 1979 he charged Dr Shapour Bakhtiar, a former deputy leader of the National Front, with forming a 'last-chance' government. Dr Bakhtiar undertook to dissolve SAVAK, to halt the export of oil to South Africa and Israel, and to support the Palestinians. However, opposition to the Shah continued to such an extent that he left the country on 15 January, never to return.

The opposition within Iran had stemmed from two main sources, with little in common except their desire to overthrow the Shah. By the time of the Shah's departure opposition from the left and the more 'liberal' National Front had been overshadowed by the success of the opposition movement surrounding the exiled fundamentalist leader Ayatollah Khomeini. He conducted his campaign from France, where he had arrived in October 1978 after 14 years of exile in Iraq for opposing the Shah's 'White Revolution'.

In January 1979 Khomeini formed an Islamic Revolutionary Council from his base near Paris, and in Iran pressure grew for his return. The Bakhtiar Government tried to delay this for as long as possible, but on 1 February Khomeini arrived in Tehran from Paris to a tumultuous welcome from the Iranian people. Bakhtiar refused to recognize Khomeini, but, after several demonstrations and outbreaks of violence, the army withdrew its support from Dr Bakhtiar and he resigned on 11 February. Dr Mehdi Bazargan, named 'Provisional Prime Minister' by Khomeini on 6 February, formed a provisional government later in the month; however, it was evident that real power rested with Khomeini's 15-man Islamic Revolutionary Council.

IRAN UNDER AYATOLLAH KHOMEINI

Although Khomeini became the *de facto* leader of Iran, the difficulties of putting into practice the ideals of the Islamic Revolution severely tested the Revolutionary Government. From the very outset conflict arose between the Islamic Revolutionary Council, which gave effect to its policies through a network of *Komitehs*, and the Prime Minister, Dr Bazargan.

Tension over Iran's ethnic minorities, either not in evidence or stifled under the Shah, became a problem after the Revolution. Most serious was the demand for autonomy from the Kurds in the north-west, which often led to open warfare in that area. Other minorities also demanded autonomy. These included the Baluchis in the south-east, the Turkomans in the north-east and the Azerbaijanis in the north-west. Conflict with the Arabs in the south-west also interacted with hostile relations with Iraq, which later descended into the Iran–Iraq War in September 1980 (see below). The position was complicated by the fact that these minorities were Sunni Muslims, while the Khomeini regime and the majority of Iranians were Shi'ite.

Khomeini's regime from the outset condemned previous US interference in Iranian affairs, and when, on 4 November 1979, Iranian students seized 53 hostages in the US embassy in Tehran, Khomeini was quite ready to offer his support to the students who demanded the return of the Shah (then in the USA) to Iran to face trial. This problem dominated relations with the USA for the next 14 months, and was not resolved by the death of the Shah in Egypt on 27 July 1980. The USA launched an airborne military operation to free the hostages, landing a commando force in eastern Iran. The operation was aborted at an early stage, however, owing to equipment failure, and eight men died when a helicopter collided with a transport aircraft as the force prepared to abandon the mission. Internal disagreements meant that the first Islamic Majlis, elected in March and May 1980, was slow to address the problem of the hostages, who were not released until 20 January 1981 (after Ronald Reagan succeeded Jimmy Carter as US President).

Another problem was the intensity of Islamist fervour in Iran. Ayatollah Khalkhali, at one time Chief Justice of the Islamic Revolutionary Courts, set about his task with extraordinary zeal, and by May 1980 claimed to have ordered more than 300 executions. Moreover, in May 1980 he destroyed the tomb of Reza Shah, an action which was later condemned by President Bani-Sadr, who pointed out that such actions were counter-productive to the Revolution. Not all Iranians approved of the ardour with which the 'Bureau to Stop Bad Acts' set about cleaning up the moral lapses in Iranian society.

CONSTITUTIONAL DEVELOPMENT

At the end of March 1979 Ayatollah Khomeini held a referendum to ascertain the level of popular support for the creation of an Islamic republic. The result was almost unanimously in favour, and on 1 April the Islamic Republic of Iran was declared. A draft constitution proposed that Iran be governed by a president, prime minister and a single-chamber Islamic Consultative Assembly (Majlis-e-Shura) of 270 deputies. Although there was pressure in Iran to submit the draft constitution to a newly-elected Constituent Assembly, Khomeini submitted it for revision to a 'Council of Experts', comprising 75 members who were elected on 3 August. After prolonged deliberations the revised Constitution was submitted to a referendum at the beginning of December. The most important change from the draft Constitution was provision for a *Wali faqih* (supreme religious leader), whose extensive powers accorded him the most important executive influence in Iran. Votes against the Constitution were negligible.

Presidential elections followed on 25 January 1980, and resulted in a convincing victory for Abolhasan Bani-Sadr, with about 75% of the votes. All this time the Islamic Revolutionary Council had effectively been administering the country, although there was a Government headed by Dr Mehdi Bazargan until his resignation in mid-November 1979 over Khomeini's support for the retention of the US hostages. Thereafter the Islamic Revolutionary Council (chaired by President Bani-Sadr from February 1980) ruled more openly, appointing ministers to run the country until elections to the Majlis—which took place, in two rounds, on 14 March and 9 May 1980. A total of 3,300 candidates contested 270 seats, 30 of which were in Tehran. Disturbances in Kurdish areas and various allegations of fraud resulted in the fact that, when the Majlis convened, in late May, only 234 deputies had been decided, and, of those, only 213 had received their credentials. It was clear, however, that the Islamic Republican Party (IRP), the party identified with the policies of Ayatollah Khomeini, was in a majority, claiming 130 seats. The IRP leader, Ayatollah Beheshti, was perceived as a threat to the leadership of President Bani-Sadr. On 7 May Khomeini had given Bani-Sadr authority to appoint a Prime Minister until the Majlis convened, but Beheshti successfully prevented this, insisting that this appointment be the responsibility of the Majlis.

The Islamic Revolutionary Council was dissolved on 18 July 1980, but there followed a delay in forming a government. Many of the candidates for ministerial office who were proposed by the Majlis and supported by the IRP were unacceptable to President Bani-Sadr. The President agreed to the appointment of Muhammad Ali Rajai as Prime Minister only with reluctance, doubting his competence. The ministries of finance and economic affairs, commerce and foreign affairs were left without ministers for some months, and a feud developed between President Bani-Sadr, on the one hand, and Rajai and the IRP, on the other. In June 1981 Khomeini dismissed Bani-Sadr as Commander-in-Chief of the Armed Forces; soon afterwards Bani-Sadr was deprived of the presidency, and he later fled to France, where he formed a 'National Council of Resistance' in alliance with Massoud Rajavi, the former leader in Iran of the opposition guerrilla group, the Mujahidin-e-Khalq. (Bani-Sadr left the Council in 1984 because of his objection to Rajavi's increasing co-operation with the Iraqi Government.) A three-man Presidential Council replaced Bani-Sadr until new presidential elections

could be held. On 28 June, however, a bomb exploded at the headquarters of the IRP, killing Ayatollah Beheshti (the Chief Justice and head of the IRP), four cabinet ministers, six deputy ministers and 20 parliamentary deputies.

The presidential election, on 24 July 1981, resulted in a victory for Muhammad Ali Rajai. Muhammad Javad Bahonar then succeeded Rajai as Prime Minister. A further bomb, on 29 August, killed both the President and the Prime Minister. Ayatollah Muhammad Reza Mahdavi Kani became Prime Minister in September, and another round of presidential elections was held on 2 October. Hojatoleslam Ali Khamenei, a leading figure of the IRP, was elected President, winning more than 16m. of the 16.8m. votes cast. At the end of October, after the resignation of Ayatollah Muhammad Reza Mahdavi Kani, Mir Hossein Moussavi was appointed Prime Minister.

THE IRAN–IRAQ WAR

Outside Iran, it was widely held at this time that the Islamic Revolution was about to disintegrate. In addition to internal troubles, Iran had been at war with Iraq for over a year. Fighting between the two countries had begun after Iran ignored Iraqi demands for the withdrawal of Iranian forces from Zain ul-Qos, in Diali province on their joint border. Iraq maintained that this territory should have been returned to it under the 1975 Shatt al-Arab agreement with Iran. Iraq therefore abrogated the agreement and invaded Iran on 22 September 1980. Most observers now consider that this was no more than a pretext on Iraq's part, the real objective of its President, Saddam Hussain, being to topple what he regarded as the threatening but vulnerable Iranian regime.

Iranian resistance was spirited, and a position of stalemate was soon reached along a 480-km front. Various international peace missions failed, and in the spring of 1982 Iran's forces broke the stalemate by launching two offensives, the first in the Shush-Dezful area in March, and the second on a 60-mile front south of Susangerd to the port of Khorramshahr at the end of April. Both offensives achieved considerable success, with Iran recapturing Khorramshahr in May. It then carried the war into Iraqi territory, but the speedy conclusion for which Iran had hoped did not materialize. In February 1983 Iran began a major offensive in the area of Iraq's Misan province, but the impetus was soon lost, and a fresh Iranian assault in April was similarly indecisive. A further Iranian offensive in July (combined with operations to suppress renewed activity by Kurdish guerrillas in the area) saw its forces entrenched 15 km within northern Iraq. The attack seemed to be consistent with Iran's policy of waging a war of attrition, keeping Iraq on a war footing and thereby exerting pressure on the weakening Iraqi economy which might topple the regime of Saddam Hussain. Action by Iran prevented Iraq from exporting oil through the Gulf, and a pipeline through Syria was cut off. Iraq was able to continue the war only with financial aid from Saudi Arabia and Kuwait.

During the second half of 1983 Iraq stepped up missile and aircraft raids against Iranian towns and petroleum installations, and, furthermore, took delivery of five French-built *Super Etendard* fighter aircraft. With these, and with the *Exocet* missiles already in its possession, Iraq threatened to destroy Iran's oil export industry, centred on Kharg Island in the Gulf, which financed the Iranian war effort. Iran countered by declaring its intention to make the Gulf impassable to all shipping (one-sixth of the Western world's petroleum requirement passed through the Gulf) if Iraqi military action rendered it unable to export oil from the Gulf via the Strait of Hormuz. In retaliation for the sale of *Super Etendard* aircraft to Iraq, Iran severed most of its economic ties with France.

In March 1984 a further Iranian offensive succeeded in taking part of the marshlands around the southern Iraqi island of Majnoun, the site of rich oilfields, though only at a great human cost. Iraq subsequently retook some of the territory it had lost, but seemed more intent on consolidating its defences than making further ground. A team of UN observers, sent in at the request of the Iranian Government, found that Iraq had used mustard gas to counter the offensive. A long-awaited Iranian offensive against Basra failed to materialize. While Iran delayed, Iraq developed a formidable network of defensive fortifications along its southern border.

Although it had earlier declared a maritime exclusion zone at the north-east end of the Gulf around Kharg Island and made sporadic attacks against shipping (not only oil-tankers), in some cases well outside the zone, Iraq refrained from attacking tankers using the Kharg Island oil terminal until May 1984. Iran retaliated with assaults against Saudi and Kuwaiti tankers in the Gulf.

INTERNAL DEVELOPMENTS

At the time of the bomb outrages in mid-1981 the Iranian regime appeared to the rest of the world to be on the point of collapse. Subsequent events, however, demonstrated that it possessed greater resilience than was at one time thought possible. An extended, and often ferocious, campaign against the main anti-government guerrilla group, the Mujahidin-e-Khalq, eventually achieved some success, and in February 1982 the Mujahidin leader in Iran, Musa Khiabani, was killed. In April an anti-Government plot was uncovered in which Ayatollah Shariatmadari, one of Iran's leading mullahs, was accused of involvement. He denied this, but admitted knowledge of the plot, in which the former Minister of Foreign Affairs, Sadeq Ghotbzadeh, was deeply implicated. Ghotbzadeh was tried and executed in September. Ayatollah Shariatmadari died in April 1986, after two years of house arrest in Qom.

In 1983 the Iranian Government turned its attention to the communist Tudeh Party, which had been banned under the Shah but had re-emerged after the 1979 Revolution. In February the party's Secretary-General, Nour ed-Din Kianuri, was arrested on charges of spying for the USSR. Kianuri was subsequently the first of a number of Tudeh members publicly to confess on television to this and other crimes against the state. Further arrests of Tudeh Party members followed, bringing the total to about 1,000, and 18 Soviet diplomats were expelled. The party was officially banned again in April.

An intense rivalry within the Government, reflecting a wider divergence of views in the country, became increasingly apparent after the Revolution. The two rival groups were the right-wing Hojjatieh, identified with the traditionalist clerical and merchant ('bazaari') communities, and the radical technocrats. The Hojjatieh were opposed, on grounds of religion and self-interest, to radical economic reforms such as the nationalization programme and the reform of laws governing land ownership (the clergy are extensive landowners), as advocated by the technocrats—who were motivated by more secular, socialist concerns. The Hojjatieh had extensive representation in the first Majlis.

Elections to the second Majlis took place on 15 April and 17 May 1984, significantly altering the distribution of influence in the assembly. Slightly more than one-half of the outgoing Majlis were clerics, and that majority had given them the power to determine policy according to largely religious considerations. A high proportion of the 1,230 or more candidates who contested the elections were more secular: they included doctors, scientists and engineers. The elections were boycotted by former Prime Minister Dr Mehdi Bazargan's Liberation Movement opposition party (the only party recognized by the ruling IRP), in protest against what he considered to be the undemocratic conditions prevailing in Iran. It was estimated that more than 50% of the seats in the new assembly were filled by new members, giving rise to speculation that a more sympathetic Majlis might allow Moussavi greater success in implementing his economic programme. However, the Council of Guardians, which exists to determine whether Majlis legislation is both constitutional and Islamic, was of a 'conservative', clerical nature and proved to be a major obstacle to economic reform.

Islamic codes of correction were introduced in 1983, including the dismembering of a hand for theft; flogging for more than 50 offences including forgery, consumption of alcohol, fornication and violations of the strict code of dress for women; and stoning to death for adultery. These began to be more rigidly enforced in 1985, in response to demonstrations in April by young fundamentalists demanding stricter adherence to Islamic law. There were clashes between opponents of the regime and fanatical *hezbollahi* (members of the Party of God) who supported the continuation of the Iran–Iraq War and the rigid observance of Islamic codes of behaviour. Widespread active opposition to the Tehran regime was not conspicuous until 1985. Dissatisfaction

with the conduct of the war with Iraq and with austere economic conditions provoked demonstrations and rioting in several cities, including Tehran. Government supporters staged numerous counter-demonstrations.

Suppression of opposition to the Government continued. In 1985, according to Amnesty International, 399 people were executed in Iran in the period to the end of October, bringing the total to 6,426 since the Revolution. A report by the UN Commission on Human Rights, published in February 1987, estimated the number of executions at a minimum of 7,000 between 1979 and 1985.

President Ali Khamenei was due to complete his four-year term of office in September 1985, and a presidential election was held on 16 August, with only three candidates, including the incumbent, taking part. The Council of Guardians rejected almost 50 candidatures, including that of Dr Mehdi Bazargan. Ali Khamenei was re-elected President, with 85.7% of the votes cast.

Although 99 deputies either voted against him or abstained, Hossein Moussavi was confirmed as Prime Minister by the Majlis on 13 October 1985. A dispute over the composition of the new Council of Ministers, which President Khamenei considered to be too radical (he initially withheld approval of one half of Moussavi's appointees), was not resolved until the intervention of Ayatollah Khomeini on Moussavi's behalf, so that the list submitted to the Majlis contained only two changes. All but seven members of the new Council of Ministers had served in the previous Government.

DEVELOPMENTS IN THE IRAN–IRAQ WAR: 1985–86

A resumption of Iraqi raids on Iranian petroleum installations and oil tankers in the Gulf in December 1984 had the effect of reducing Iranian oil exports to an estimated 1.1m. barrels per day (b/d) and causing the Tehran Government to suspend imports temporarily. However, the Kharg Island oil terminal remained in operation, largely undamaged, and Iran's economy appeared to be capable of sustaining the cost of continuing the war, albeit under severe pressure. Iraq had an estimated 580 combat aircraft and 130 armed helicopters at the beginning of 1985, compared with Iran's 110 combat aircraft (of which only 50–60 were thought to be operational), but it failed fully to exploit its superiority. The People's Republic of China became the leading supplier of military equipment to Iran during the war, and it was estimated that businesses or governments in 44 countries, including both the USA and the USSR, had sold armaments to Iran during the war. Other major suppliers included the Democratic People's Republic of Korea and Israel.

Iran mounted an assault in the region of the al-Hawizah marshes in southern Iraq, east of the Tigris, in March 1985. This did not appear to be the long-awaited decisive thrust, as it involved, at the most, only 50,000 troops. The Iranian forces crossed the Tigris and succeeded, for a time, in closing the main road between Baghdad and Basra. The Iraqis launched a counter-offensive, repulsing the Iranians, with heavy casualties sustained by both sides. Iraq was again accused of using chemical weapons during this battle.

The UN had painstakingly engineered an agreement between Iran and Iraq in June 1984 to suspend attacks on civilian targets, but after the failure of the Iranian offensive in March 1985, and with the war on the ground once more at stalemate, Iraq resumed its assaults on Iranian cities. The first Iraqi air raid on Tehran for four years took place in March. Iran retaliated, shelling Basra and other Iraqi towns, and hit Baghdad with ground-launched missiles, but Iraq, in this instance making full use of its air superiority, hit more than 30 Iranian population centres by mid-1985, killing hundreds of civilians. President Saddam Hussain's stated intention was to carry the war to every part of Iran until Khomeini agreed to negotiate.

In April 1985 the UN Secretary-General, Javier Pérez de Cuéllar, visited both Tehran and Baghdad in an attempt to establish a basis for peace negotiations, but Iran's terms remained the same. The Iranian claim for Iraqi war reparations was US $350,000m., and although there was less official insistence on the removal of Hussain and his Baathist regime from power as a condition of peace, it was accepted by the Iranian Government that, if all the other conditions (the payment of reparations, an Iraqi admission of responsibility for starting the war, and the withdrawal of Iraqi troops from all Iranian territory) were met, he would fall anyway. Iran did not respond when Hussain ordered the suspension of air raids on Iranian towns in order to give Iran the opportunity to declare a cease-fire and begin negotiations. After six weeks, at the end of May Iraqi air raids resumed with greater intensity, prompting retaliatory air-strikes by Iran. A 16-day moratorium in June achieved the same result.

Iraq had hitherto failed to launch attacks against the main Iranian oil export terminal on Kharg Island of sufficient frequency or intensity seriously to threaten the continuation of oil exports. In August 1985, however, Iraq made the first of a concentrated series of raids upon Kharg, causing a reduction in Iranian oil exports from 1.2m.–1.5m. b/d in the months prior to the raids to less than 1m. b/d in September. By the end of 1985 it was reported that exports from Kharg had virtually ceased. In February 1986 Iraq announced an expansion of the area from which it would try to exclude Iranian shipping. Previously confined to the waters around Iran's Gulf ports, the area was broadened to include the coast of Kuwait. Attacks on tankers and other commercial vessels in the Gulf were increased by both sides during 1986, and Iran intensified its practice of intercepting merchant shipping and confiscating goods that it believed to be destined for Iraq.

The next important engagement, in terms of territory gained, did not occur until 1986. On 9 February Iran launched the Wal-Fajr (Dawn) 8 offensive—so called to commemorate the month of Ayatollah Khomeini's return to Iran in 1979 from exile in France. Iranian forces (reportedly comprising some 85,000 troops) crossed the Shatt al-Arab waterway and, on 11 February 1986, occupied the disused Iraqi port of Faw, and, according to Iran, about 800 sq km of the Faw peninsula. From this position—within sight of the Kuwaiti island of Bubiyan, commanding the Khor Abdullah channel between the Faw peninsula and the island—Iran threatened Iraq's only access to the Gulf and, if it could extend the offensive to the west, Iraq's Umm Qasr naval base. However, the marsh and then desert terrain to the west was not conducive to further Iranian gains, and the position on the Faw peninsula was defensible only with difficulty, given the problem of maintaining supply lines across the Shatt al-Arab. At the same time as the assault on Faw, an operation along the Faw–Basra road was intended to divert Iraqi forces. When Iraq launched a counter-offensive on Faw in mid-February, Iran opened up a second front in Iraqi Kurdistan, hundreds of miles to the north, with the Wal-Fajr 9 offensive. Despite heavy fighting, Iraq's counter-offensive made little progress and failed to dislodge an estimated 30,000 Iranian troops, now firmly entrenched in and around Faw. In Resolution 582, adopted at the end of February, the UN Security Council, while urging a cease-fire, for the first time cited Iraq as being responsible for starting the war.

In May 1986 Iraq made its first armed incursions into Iran since withdrawing its forces from Iranian territory in 1982. About 150 sq km of land, including the deserted town of Mehran (about 160 km east of Baghdad), were occupied. (Iran recaptured Mehran in July.) Also in May, in the first Iraqi air raid on Tehran since June 1985, Iran's second largest oil refinery was bombed, signalling a renewal of reciprocal attacks on urban and economic targets, which continued for the remainder of 1986 and into 1987. According to the *Washington Post* in December 1986, for the previous two years Iraq had received US intelligence assistance in targeting attacks on Iranian oil terminals and power plants. However, US intelligence sources were subsequently reported as asserting that both Iran and Iraq had been supplied with deliberately distorted or misleading information to assist the strategy of the Reagan Administration.

On 24 December 1986 Iran mounted an offensive (named Karbala-4, after the holy Shi'ite city in Iraq) in the region of Basra but failed to penetrate Iraqi defences on four islands in the Shatt al-Arab waterway. On 8 January 1987 a two-pronged attack (Karbala-5) was launched towards Basra. Iranian forces, attacking from the east, established a bridgehead inside Iraq, between the Shatt al-Arab, to the west, and the artificial Fish Lake to the east, and advanced gradually towards Basra, sustaining heavy casualties, while an assault from the south-east secured a group of islands in the Shatt al-Arab. Iran opened a second front, 400 km to the north, with the Karbala-6 offensive

on 13 January. By mid-February Iranian forces from the east had advanced to within about 10 km of Basra, but no further gains were made and the Karbala-5 offensive was officially terminated at the end of the month.

In November 1986 it emerged that the USA, despite its official discouragement of arms sales to Iran by other countries, had been conducting secret negotiations with the Islamic Republic since July 1985, and had made three shipments of weapons and spare parts (valued at an estimated US \$100m.) to Iran, through Israeli and Saudi Arabian intermediaries, in September 1985 and in July and October 1986. The shipments were allegedly in exchange for Iranian assistance in securing the release of US hostages who had been kidnapped by Shi'ite extremists in Lebanon, and an Iranian undertaking to abstain from involvement in international terrorism. The talks were reportedly conducted on the Iranian side by the Speaker of the Majlis, Hojatoleslam Ali Akbar Hashemi Rafsanjani, with Ayatollah Khomeini's consent but without the knowledge of other senior government figures, including the Prime Minister and the President.

THE IRAN–IRAQ WAR: 1987

Iran rejected the offer of a cease-fire and peace talks made by Saddam Hussain in January 1987, and in the following months demonstrated its ability to launch attacks from one end to the other of its 1,200-km frontier with Iraq. The Karbala-7 offensive, in March, penetrated north-eastern Iraqi territory to a depth of about 20 km in the Gerdmand mountains, near Rawanduz—itself only some 100 km from Iraq's largest oilfields at Kirkuk. On the southern front, in April Iran launched the Karbala-8 offensive from the salient 10 km east of Basra, which had been secured in Karbala-5. The Iranians claimed to have established a new front line about 1 km towards Basra, west of the artificial Twin Canals water barrier, although Iraq claimed that the attack had been repulsed. An almost simultaneous offensive, Karbala-9, was mounted in the central sector of the Iran–Iraq border, from near the Iranian town of Qasr-e-Shirin.

The war entered a potentially explosive new phase in 1987. Once more, the danger of an escalation of the conflict was focused on the shipping lanes of the Persian Gulf. During 1986 there had been some 100 attacks by Iran and Iraq on shipping in the Gulf. Iran had begun to use squads of high-speed patrol boats, crewed by Islamic Revolutionary Guards (*Pasdaran Inqilab*), stationed on islands in the Gulf, in attacks on commercial ships. In reprisal for Kuwait's support for Iraq, Iranian attacks were concentrated on Kuwaiti shipping and on neutral vessels and tankers carrying oil or other cargoes to and from Iraq via Kuwait. Between October 1986 and April 1987 15 ships bound to or from Kuwait were attacked by Iran in the Gulf, and several Kuwaiti cargoes were seized. Alarmed by the repeated attacks on its merchant ships and by the apparent indifference of the outside world to the war, Kuwait sought the protection of the leading powers for its shipping in the Gulf, and, by involving them more closely, hoped to persuade them of the urgent need for international co-operation in achieving a peaceful end to the conflict. The USSR and, subsequently, the USA were asked to re-register Kuwaiti ships under their flags, which they would then be obliged to defend if they came under attack. On 24 March, the day after the USA had made its navy available to escort Kuwaiti tankers, Iran threatened to halt the traffic in oil through the Gulf. In April the USSR allowed Kuwait to charter three Soviet tankers, and proposed international talks on the protection of commercial shipping in the Gulf. The USA rejected the Soviet proposal, but in May agreed to re-register 11 Kuwaiti tankers under the US flag and to increase its naval presence in the Gulf in order to protect them. This decision followed the apparently accidental attack in the Gulf by an Iraqi *Mirage* F-1 fighter plane on the *USS Stark* on 17 May, only hours after one of the Soviet tankers chartered by Kuwait had struck a mine while approaching a Kuwaiti port. Iraq desisted from attacks on tankers for the next five weeks. At the end of June, following a hiatus of five weeks, and one week after Iraq, Iran resumed its attacks on Gulf shipping using high-speed launches based on the islands of Minou, Farsi and Abu Musa. Iran made it clear that it considered the US naval presence in the Gulf to be provocative, and fears of a military confrontation grew.

The escalation of tension in the Gulf resulted in a rare display of unanimity in the UN Security Council, which adopted a 10-point resolution (No. 598) on 20 July 1987, urging an immediate cease-fire in the Iran–Iraq War; the withdrawal of all forces to internationally recognized boundaries; and the co-operation of Iran and Iraq in mediation efforts to achieve a peace settlement. Iraq said that it would abide by the resolution if Iran did so (Iraqi attacks on tanker traffic had been halted in mid-July). Iran criticized the resolution for failing to identify Iraq as the original aggressor in the war, and claimed that the belligerent US naval presence in the Gulf (which rose to a peak of 48 vessels in 1987) rendered it null and void, but failed to deliver an official, unequivocal response.

The *USS Bridgeton* and the *USS Gas Prince*, the first Kuwaiti tankers to be re-registered under the US flag, passed unharmed through the Strait of Hormuz with a US naval escort on 22 July 1987. However, on 24 July the *Bridgeton* struck a mine (probably Iranian) near the Iranian island of Farsi, and struggled to port in Kuwait. The US naval force in the Gulf was ill equipped to deal with mines, and US Government requests for mine-sweeping assistance were initially refused by its main NATO allies, who were anxious to avoid a confrontation with Iran. In August, however, the United Kingdom and France announced that they were to send minesweepers to the Gulf region; these were followed in September by minesweeping vessels from Belgium, the Netherlands and Italy. Iran was believed to have laid mines on the shipping routes to Kuwait, including the al-Ahmadi channel, the approach to Kuwait's main oil ports.

POLITICAL AND DIPLOMATIC DEVELOPMENTS: 1987–88

During 1987 the conviction grew among the international community that Iran was attempting to spread the Islamic Revolution through a network of agents operating in its diplomatic missions abroad and controlled by the Iranian Ministry of Intelligence and Internal Security. In March Tunisia broke off diplomatic relations with Iran, accusing it of fomenting Islamic fundamentalist opposition to the Government, and of recruiting Tunisians for terrorist operations abroad through its embassy in Tunis. Eight suspected terrorists (six of whom held Tunisian passports) were arrested in Paris in March. They were believed to be members of a network of 'sleeper' terrorist cells co-ordinated by Iran and established several years before. In June the French authorities sought to interview Wahid Gordji, who was officially listed as a translator at the Iranian embassy in Paris, in connection with a bombing campaign in the city in 1986. Although Gordji did not have diplomatic status the Iranians refused to give him up, and armed French police surrounded the embassy. The Iranian Government retaliated by throwing a cordon of armed Revolutionary Guards around the French embassy in Tehran. On 17 July France severed its diplomatic relations with Iran. The embassy siege was lifted at the end of November, when Gordji was permitted to leave France. Two days after his release two French hostages held by Iranian-backed groups in Lebanon were set free. The French Prime Minister, Jacques Chirac, denied that a ransom had been paid to the hostages' captors but admitted that negotiations were continuing between France and Iran over the repayment of the US $670m. balance on $1,000m. loaned by the Shah to France in 1978. It was also rumoured that France had agreed to supply arms to Iran in order to secure the hostages' release. France and Iran resumed diplomatic relations and exchanged ambassadors in June 1988.

In June 1987 Ayatollah Khomeini approved a proposal by Hashemi Rafsanjani, the Speaker of the Majlis, which was reluctantly supported by President Khamenei, to disband the IRP. In a letter to Khomeini, the two leaders stated that, the institutions of the Islamic Republic having been established, contrary to the IRP's intended function, 'party polarization under the present conditions may provide an excuse for discord and factionalism'.

On 31 July 1987 attention was diverted from the Gulf by the deaths in riots in Mecca of 402 people, including 275 Iranian pilgrims (the majority of them women) engaged on the *Hajj* (pilgrimage) to the city's Muslim shrines. The Saudi authorities maintained that most of the victims had been trampled to death when some 150,000 Iranians (who, in contravention of Saudi

laws governing the *Hajj*, had been demonstrating in support of Ayatollah Khomeini) went on the rampage, attacking Saudi security forces. The Iranians alleged that the Saudi police had opened fire on the pilgrims, and accused Saudi Arabia and the USA of planning the incident. A 'day of hatred' was proclaimed by the Government on 2 August, and Hashemi Rafsanjani promised vengeance.

In August 1987 Hojatoleslam Mehdi Hashemi, a close associate of Ayatollah Ali Hossain Montazeri (who had been elected as eventual successor to Ayatollah Khomeini by the Council of Experts in 1985), was tried by a specially-appointed Islamic court and convicted of murder, the kidnapping of a Syrian diplomat in Tehran, of forming a private army (with the aim of overthrowing the Government and installing a more rigorous Islamic regime), and of planning explosions in Mecca during the *Hajj*. It was Hashemi who, in an attempt to disrupt the planned sale of US arms to Iran, had revealed to a Lebanese magazine, *Ash-Shira'*, details of the secret visits of the then US National Security Adviser, Robert McFarlane, and Lt-Col Oliver North, a senior National Security Council adviser, to Tehran in May 1986. Hashemi was executed on 28 September 1987.

In April 1988, following further Iranian attacks on Saudi and other neutral shipping in the Gulf, Saudi Arabia severed its diplomatic relations with Iran. Iran had been insisting on sending as many as 150,000 pilgrims on the *Hajj* to Mecca in 1988 (the same number as in 1987), despite the events of July 1987 and the subsequent deterioration in bilateral relations. A meeting of the Organization of the Islamic Conference (OIC) in Amman had agreed a formula for 1988, whereby each Muslim nation would be permitted to send 1,000 pilgrims per 1m. citizens, giving Iran a quota of 45,000. Finally, Iran decided that it would send no pilgrims on the *Hajj* at all.

THE UN FAILS TO ENFORCE RESOLUTION 598

Frustrated by Iran's temporizing over a definitive response to UN Security Council Resolution 598, on 29 August 1987 Iraq (contrary to advice from Western governments) resumed attacks on Iranian oil installations and industrial targets, and on tankers in the Gulf transporting Iranian oil. Iran had exploited the 45-day lull in Iraqi attacks to raise its levels of oil production and exports. Resolution 598 made provision for unspecified sanctions in the event of the failure of either or both sides to comply with its terms for a cease-fire. However, the resumption of Iraqi attacks weakened the UN's position in its attempts to secure a cease-fire through diplomacy, and made it less likely that the USSR, if it would accept the principle at all, could be persuaded that the arms embargo proposed by the USA and the United Kingdom should apply only to Iran.

Iranian threats of reprisals against Saudi Arabia and Kuwait for their support of Iraq ceased to be purely rhetorical when Iran fired three *Silkworm* missiles into Kuwaiti territory at the beginning of September 1987 (and a further three before the end of the year). Kuwait expelled five Iranian diplomats on 5 September. The visit, in mid-September, of UN Secretary-General Javier Pérez de Cuéllar to Iran and Iraq was preceded by an intensification of Iraqi attacks on Iranian economic targets. In Tehran, Iranian leaders told Pérez de Cuéllar that they supported the provision in Resolution 598 for the setting up of an 'impartial body' to apportion responsibility for starting the war, but that Iraq's guilt in this matter had to be established before Iran would observe a cease-fire. For its part, Iraq was prepared to accept the ruling of a judicial body in determining responsibility for the war, but stated that a formal cease-fire, according to the terms of Resolution 598, should precede the establishment of such a body.

Signs of an apparent willingness on Iran's part to modify its stance on Resolution 598 forestalled attempts by the USA, the United Kingdom and France to promote their proposal of an arms embargo against Iran, and also pre-empted the adoption of diplomatic or other sanctions by the League of Arab States (the Arab League) at its meeting in Tunis on 20 September 1987. On 25 September Iran presented a plan to the UN Security Council whereby it would observe a *de facto* cease-fire while a UN-appointed commission of inquiry determined which side was responsible for starting the war. An official cease-fire would take effect when the commission had identified the aggressor (by implication, Iraq). Iraq rejected these proposals as being a deviation from the terms of Resolution 598.

By mid-October 1987 the number of tankers being employed by Iran to shuttle oil from Kharg Island to Sirri and Larak Islands had declined to an estimated 20 vessels, owing to damage sustained during Iraq's intensified campaign of attacks in the Gulf. On 19 October four US naval vessels destroyed Iran's Rostam and Rakhsh oil platforms, about 100 km east of Qatar, which were, the USA alleged, being used to launch military operations against shipping.

On 22 December 1987 the USSR proposed discussions within the UN Security Council to consider a mandatory ban on the sale of arms to Iran. According to the Soviet proposal, these talks would take place at the same time as discussions on the introduction of an international naval force in the Gulf, under UN control, which would replace the various national forces patrolling the region. Although all five permanent members of the Security Council subsequently agreed on the need for further measures to be taken to ensure the compliance of both combatants with Resolution 598, the USSR's insistence on the withdrawal of foreign navies and the deployment of a UN naval force in the Gulf as a complementary measure, and the USA's growing military involvement in the area during 1988 (see below), prevented the adoption of an arms embargo.

CEASE-FIRE AND POLITICAL UNCERTAINTY: 1988–89

During the first half of 1988 Iran suffered a series of military reverses in the war with Iraq, offsetting the gains that it had made during the previous few years. Meanwhile, divisions within the Government over the conduct of the war became more apparent, as Ayatollah Khomeini grew more frail and the political struggle for the succession intensified. However, the world was taken by surprise in July 1988 when, after 12 months of prevarication, Iran agreed, unconditionally, to accept Resolution 598 in all its parts.

In January 1988 Ayatollah Khomeini had intervened in a debate over the role of the government in an Islamic Republic to reject a narrow interpretation of its competence by President Khamenei, who had asserted that the government operated 'within the limits of Islamic law and Islamic principles'. Khomeini had replied that, on the contrary, the government was the primary instrument of Islamic rule and was competent to override certain aspects of Islam, even such practices as prayer (*salat*), fasting and the *Hajj* (three of the five 'pillars' of Islam), if it was in the interests of the state. In asserting the primacy of the government, Khomeini was believed to have strengthened the position of 'reformers', identified with Majlis Speaker Rafsanjani and Prime Minister Moussavi, who were attempting to enact legislation hitherto obstructed by the 'conservative' clerics on the Council of Guardians.

The elections to the third Majlis in April and May 1988 provided a further boost for the 'reformers'. The elections were the first not to be contested by the IRP, which had been dissolved in June 1987. Instead, all 1,600 candidates for the 270 seats in the Majlis were examined for eligibility by local committees and sought election as individuals. A record 16,988,799 people (68% of the electorate) voted in the first round of the elections on 8 April (when the majority of seats were contested), compared with 15.8m. in 1984 and 10.8m. in 1980. In June Hashemi Rafsanjani was re-elected as Speaker of the Majlis and Hossein Moussavi was overwhelmingly endorsed as Prime Minister. He presented a new Council of Ministers to the Majlis in July.

In January 1988 Iraq resumed the so-called 'tanker war'. During 1987, according to Lloyd's of London, Iran and Iraq had damaged 178 vessels in the Gulf (34 in December alone), compared with 80 during 1986. Although the US Navy continued to escort reflagged Kuwaiti vessels, traffic not under its protection, including Kuwaiti shipping, remained a target for Iranian attack. (By the time the cease-fire was proclaimed in July, a total of 546 vessels had been attacked since the 'tanker war' began in earnest in 1981.) At the end of February 1988 the so-called 'war of the cities' (which had not been pursued uninterruptedly since early 1987) was resumed when Iraq bombed a petroleum refinery on the outskirts of Tehran. Iran retaliated by bombing a petrochemicals plant in Basra. Thus began a

series of reciprocal attacks on civil and economic targets in the two countries which lasted for several months.

During 1987/88, for the first time in six years, owing to poor mobilization, disorganization and a shortage of volunteers, Iran was unable to launch a major winter offensive and began to lose ground to Iraqi advances along the length of the war front. In mid-April 1988 Iraqi forces regained control of the Faw peninsula, where the Iranians, who had been unable to make further gains since capturing the area in 1986, had scaled down their presence. Iran accused Kuwait of allowing Iraqi forces to use Bubiyan Island during the offensive. In March the Mujahidin Iranian National Liberation Army (NLA), supported by Iraq, undertook a major offensive for the first time since its creation in 1987, attacking Iranian units in Iran's south-western province of Khuzestan. In May Iraq recaptured the Shalamcheh area, south-east of Basra, driving Iranian forces across the Shatt al-Arab into Iran.

Identifying military inefficiency as the principal cause of these reverses, Ayatollah Khomeini appointed Hashemi Rafsanjani as acting Commander-in-Chief of the Armed Forces on 2 June 1988 and gave him the task of unifying the command structure and improving co-ordination between the regular armed forces, the Revolutionary Guards Corps (*Pasdaran*) (with its own land, naval and air forces) and the Mobilization (*Basij*) Volunteers Corps. At the beginning of July Rafsanjani announced the creation of a general command headquarters to rationalize the disjointed military command structure, but a merger of the army and the Revolutionary Guards was ruled out. The changes came too late to prevent further Iranian defeats. Having won back more territory from the Iranian army in the north of Iraq near Sulaimaniya in mid-June 1988, at the end of the month Iraq recaptured Majnoun Island and the surrounding area (the site of one of the world's biggest oilfields) in the al-Hawizah marshes, on the southern front.

In the Gulf, fears of a serious military confrontation between Iran and the USA were realized on 18 April 1988, when the US navy destroyed two Iranian oil platforms (Sassan and Nasr) in the southern Gulf, and six Iranian military vessels (a guided-missile boat, three speedboats and two frigates) were either sunk or badly damaged, in retaliation for damage allegedly inflicted on a US frigate by an Iranian mine on 14 April. On 3 July the *USS Vincennes*, the US navy's most sophisticated guided-missile destroyer, which had only recently been deployed in the Gulf to counter the threat to shipping of Iran's *Silkworm* missiles (the USA believed these were soon to become operational from a permanent site near the Strait of Hormuz), mistakenly shot down an Iran Air Airbus A300B over the Strait of Hormuz, having, according to official statements, assumed it to be an attacking F-14 fighter-bomber; all 290 passengers and crew were killed.

Iranian forces were expelled from more Iraqi territory in Kurdistan during June and July 1988. Iraqi troops forced Iranian units back over the international border in the central sector of the war front, crossing into Iranian territory on 13 July for the first time since 1986, and capturing the Iranian border town of Dehloran. Meanwhile, the last pockets of Iranian occupation in southern Iraq were cleared by Iraqi troops. On 18 July Iran officially announced its unconditional acceptance of Resolution 598. The first clause of the Resolution required the combatants to withdraw to international borders and to observe a cease-fire. Iraqi troops advanced further into Iran before retiring behind the border on 24 July. On the other hand, the NLA, over which Iraq claimed to have no control, launched a three-day offensive on 25 July, penetrating as far as 150 km into Iranian territory before being forced to withdraw. Iraq professed to have no designs on Iranian territory, but was possibly using the NLA as a proxy to prevent the Iranian forces from regrouping during a cease-fire which might prove to be only temporary. The implementation of a cease-fire was delayed by Iran's refusal to accede to an Iraqi demand for direct peace talks, under UN auspices, to commence prior to a cessation of hostilities. Iran protested that Resolution 598 did not require this. However, Iraq withdrew its demand and a cease-fire finally came into force on 20 August, monitored by a specially-created UN observer force of 350 officers, the UN Iran-Iraq Military Observer Group (UNIIMOG).

UN-sponsored negotiations between Iran and Iraq for a comprehensive peace settlement began at foreign ministerial level in Geneva, Switzerland, on 25 August 1988. One of the most contentious issues to be decided at these talks was the status of the 1975 Algiers Agreement between Iran and Iraq, which Iran insisted should be the basis for negotiations but which Iraq rejected. According to the terms of the Algiers Agreement, which defined the southern border between Iran and Iraq as running along the deepest channel of the Shatt al-Arab waterway (the Thalweg line), the two countries exercised joint sovereignty over the waterway. However, President Saddam Hussain of Iraq publicly tore up the agreement (to which he had been a signatory) immediately prior to the Iraqi invasion of Iran in 1980, demanding full Iraqi sovereignty over the waterway, which Iraq had held under previous agreements in 1847, 1913 and 1937. The matter of determining responsibility for starting the war was another potential obstacle to the negotiation of a lasting peace. It was generally accepted that Iraq initiated the conflict by invading Iran on 22 September 1980. Iraq, however, maintained that the war began on 4 September with Iranian shelling of Iraqi border posts. Resolution 598 provided for the establishment of an impartial body to apportion responsibility for the war. Finally, Iraq rejected Iranian demands for the payment of reparations, for which Resolution 598 did not provide.

The peace negotiations soon became deadlocked in disputes concerning sovereignty over the Shatt al-Arab and the right of navigation in the waterway and the Gulf, the exchange of prisoners of war, and the withdrawal of troops to within international borders. By August 1989 progress in the negotiations, at least as far as the border issue was concerned, had been insignificant, although some prisoner exchanges had taken place. In November, in an attempt to unblock the negotiations, Iran proposed an immediate exchange of prisoners of war, accompanied by the withdrawal of troops to within international borders. By the end of the year, however, the cease-fire remained the only element of Resolution 598 to have been successfully implemented.

THE RUSHDIE AFFAIR

On 14 February 1989 Ayatollah Khomeini issued a religious edict *(fatwa)*, pronouncing a sentence of death on a British writer, Salman Rushdie, and his publishers, and exhorting all Muslims to carry out the sentence. Khomeini's edict followed demonstrations in India and Pakistan in protest at the imminent publication in the USA of Rushdie's novel *The Satanic Verses*, the content of which was considered to be blasphemous by some Muslims. (Rushdie, born a Muslim himself, was therefore guilty of apostasy, an offence punishable by death under *Shari'a* law.) The novel had first been published in the United Kingdom in September 1988. The *fatwa* led to a sharp deterioration in relations between Iran and the United Kingdom and other Western countries. On 20 February Khomeini's sentence on Rushdie was condemned at a meeting of ministers responsible for foreign affairs of the 12 member states of the European Community (EC, now European Union—EU). Senior-level diplomatic contacts between the member states and Iran were suspended, while the United Kingdom announced the withdrawal of its diplomatic representatives and personnel in Tehran. Iran, in turn, announced the withdrawal of all diplomatic representatives and staff in EC member countries, and on 7 March severed diplomatic relations with the United Kingdom.

While the significance of the Rushdie affair was initially defined in terms of its effect on Iran's foreign relations, it soon became apparent that the issue was being used tactically by vying factions within the Iranian leadership. In a speech on 22 February 1989 Khomeini referred explicitly to a division in the Iranian leadership (between 'liberals' who sought Western participation in Iran's post-war reconstruction, and 'conservatives' who opposed Western involvement) in terms which implied that *The Satanic Verses* was the culmination of a Western conspiracy against Islam, and declared that he would never allow the 'liberal' faction to prevail.

By late March 1989 it was clear that Khomeini's intervention had decisively strengthened the hand of the 'conservatives'. In early April Khomeini's designated successor, Ayatollah Montazeri, perceived as a 'liberal', resigned. It was reported that, in the absence of any individual with sufficient authority to assume

the role, the Council of Experts had established a five-member leadership council to replace Montazeri as Khomeini's successor. On 24 April a 20-member council was appointed by Ayatollah Khomeini to draft amendments to the Iranian Constitution.

IRAN AFTER KHOMEINI

Ayatollah Khomeini died on 3 June 1989. In an emergency session on 4 June the Council of Experts elected President Khamenei to succeed Ayatollah Khomeini as Iran's spiritual leader, and on 5 June Prime Minister Hossein Moussavi declared his support, and that of all government institutions, for Khamenei. On 8 June Hashemi Rafsanjani reiterated his intention to stand as a candidate at the forthcoming presidential election, and on 12 June he was re-elected for a further one-year term as Speaker of the Majlis.

Despite the apparent intensification in the struggle for power within the Iranian leadership in the months preceding Ayatollah Khomeini's long-anticipated death, both 'conservatives' and 'liberals' gave their support to the candidacy of Hashemi Rafsanjani for the Presidency. The presidential election, held on 28 July 1989, was contested by only Rafsanjani and Abbas Sheibani, a former minister who was widely regarded as a 'token' candidate. According to official figures, Rafsanjani received some 15.5m. (95.9%) of a total 16.2m. votes cast. At the same time 95% of voters approved 45 proposed amendments to the Constitution, the most important of which were the elevation of the President to the Government's Chief Executive and the abolition of the post of Prime Minister. Rafsanjani was sworn in as President on 17 August. The new Council of Ministers was regarded as a balanced coalition of 'conservatives', 'liberals' and technocrats, and its endorsement by the Majlis was viewed as a mandate for Rafsanjani to conduct a more conciliatory foreign policy towards the West (in particular with regard to the Western hostages held captive by pro-Iranian Shi'ite groups in Lebanon) and to introduce economic reforms.

While the amendments to the Constitution increased the power of the presidency, it was anticipated that Rafsanjani's leadership would be challenged by several factions, including Ahmad Khomeini, son of the late Ayatollah Khomeini, and by the Minister of the Interior, Ali Akbar Mohtashami, and the Minister of Intelligence, Muhammad Muhammadi Reyshahri, both of whom were said to be advocates of a doctrine of 'permanent revolution' and to accept international terrorism as a means to achieve this aim. Both Mohtashami and Reyshahri were excluded from the new Council of Ministers.

Western support was regarded as vital to Iran's economic reconstruction by Rafsanjani and his supporters within the Iranian leadership, but was regarded as anathema by his opponents, who feared that it would lead to the erosion of Islamic values and the betrayal of the Revolution. Rafsanjani's fundamental problem on assuming the presidency was to find a way of securing Western support without alienating the 'conservative' faction within the leadership, which remained too powerful to be directly confronted. The urgency of the need for economic reform was demonstrated by increased incidents of popular protest against food shortages and high prices in early 1990. In May of that year an 'open letter' was addressed to Rafsanjani by 90 prominent clerics, professionals and retired soldiers associated with Nehzat-e Azadi-ye Iran (Liberation Movement of Iran), which was legal but did not enjoy official approval. The widespread arrests that followed the publication of the 'open letter', which criticized government policies, complained of massive corruption and regretted Iran's international isolation, appeared to indicate that Rafsanjani was unable to control his 'conservative' opponents. Divisions within ruling circles were exemplified by the dispute between Rafsanjani and his opponents over whether to accept Western aid following an earthquake in Gilan and Zanjan provinces in June, in which some 40,000 people died. After initial hesitation, in what was regarded as an important victory for Rafsanjani, Western aid was accepted.

FOREIGN RELATIONS

Although the death sentence on Salman Rushdie remained in force, the tension created by its initial pronouncement in February 1989 lessened somewhat in the ensuing months. In March EC ministers of foreign affairs agreed that member states should be allowed to reinstall their ambassadors in Tehran. There was evidence, too, of an improvement in relations between Iran and the communist bloc. In late June Rafsanjani visited the USSR, where he and the Soviet leader, Mikhail Gorbachev, signed a 'declaration on the principles of relations' between Iran and the USSR. These relations were strained in January 1990, however, when Iranian politicians voiced support for the Muslim Azerbaijani revolt against the Soviet central Government in the Nakhichevan enclave, on the Iranian border.

In July 1989 the USA unexpectedly offered to pay compensation direct to the families of the 290 passengers and crew of the Iran Air Airbus mistakenly shot down by the *USS Vincennes* a year earlier. However, the Iranian Government insisted that the compensation should be distributed through its agencies, rather than privately, and took the matter to the ICJ. The fragility of Iran's relations with the USA was underlined in early August when, in response to the abduction by Israeli forces of the Lebanese Shi'a Muslim leader Sheikh Abdul Karim Obeid, a US hostage in Lebanon, Lt-Col William Higgins, was executed by his captors, who threatened the execution of more hostages if Sheikh Obeid was not released. While Iran denied any involvement in the death of Lt-Col Higgins, it was widely suspected of complicity. Whatever its role, the USA immediately engaged in urgent negotiations with Iranian leaders in order to prevent further killings. In November 1989 the USA agreed to release US $567m. of the total of $810m. of Iranian assets that had been seized 10 years previously, at the time of the siege of the US embassy in Tehran, in order to secure US bank claims on Iran. In April 1990, following the release of two US citizens who had been held hostage by pro-Iranian groups in Lebanon, the USA thanked both the Syrian and the Iranian Governments for their role in securing the hostages' release. In May the USA and Iran concluded a 'small claims agreement', whereby US claimants were to be repaid for losses incurred during the Iranian Revolution in 1979. Moreover, in June 1990 Iran agreed to pay the US company Amoco $600m. in compensation for US oil operations expropriated during the Revolution.

Relations between Iran and the United Kingdom fluctuated during the first half of 1990. In February the United Kingdom expelled nine Iranian diplomats for reasons of national security, and, as a retaliatory gesture, Iran closed the office of the British Broadcasting Corporation in Tehran. In the same month, however, President Rafsanjani described the *fatwa* against Rushdie as an exclusively Islamic issue (implying that it ought not to interfere with the re-establishment of normal relations between Iran and the United Kingdom), while trade between the two countries was reported to be increasing. In May it was reported that the United Kingdom was involved in indirect contacts with Iran concerning four British nationals held hostage by pro-Iranian groups in Lebanon, and the United Kingdom announced that it was prepared to resume direct talks with the Iranian Government. In June, however, Ayatollah Khamenei declared that the *fatwa* could never be repealed.

Iran's position of strict neutrality during the Kuwait conflict (see below) brought rapid dividends. On 27 September 1990 Iran and the United Kingdom resumed diplomatic relations after Iran had assured the United Kingdom of its respect for international law and of its commitment to achieving the release of Western hostages held in Lebanon. The United Kingdom assured Iran of its respect for Islam, and stated that it understood the offence that Rushdie had caused to Muslims. In October the EC revoked its ban on senior-level diplomatic contacts with Iran.

In May 1990, meanwhile, during a meeting with EC officials in Dublin, Ireland, an Iranian delegation reiterated Iran's pledge to work towards securing the release of Western hostages in Lebanon. A diplomatic initiative by the Irish Government was believed to have brought about the release, in August, of an Irish citizen held hostage for four years by a pro-Iranian group in Lebanon.

IRAQ CONCEDES IRAN'S PEACE TERMS

In early 1990 Iran and Iraq agreed to resume negotiations in the USSR, at the invitation of the Soviet Ministry of Foreign Affairs. In July the Iraqi and Iranian Ministers of Foreign Affairs conferred at the UN in Geneva. It was the first such direct meeting between them since the cease-fire in the war had

taken effect, and had been facilitated by an exchange of letters between Presidents Saddam Hussain and Rafsanjani in May. However, this breakthrough in the peace process was quickly overtaken by the consequences of Iraq's invasion and annexation of Kuwait in August 1990.

On 16 August 1990 Saddam Hussain abruptly sought an immediate, formal peace with Iran by accepting all the claims that Iran had pursued since the declaration of a cease-fire, including the reinstatement of the Algiers Agreement of 1975 dividing the Shatt al-Arab. While these concessions were transparently dictated by expediency (on 17 August Iraq began to redeploy in Kuwait troops hitherto positioned on its border with Iran) and thus left the conflicts underlying the Iran–Iraq War unresolved, they were welcomed by Iran—which none the less insisted that the issue of peace with Iraq was separate from that of Iraq's occupation of Kuwait. Exchanges of an estimated 80,000 prisoners of war commenced on 17 August, and on 18 August Iraq began to withdraw troops from the central border areas of Ilam, Meymak, Mehran and Naft Shahr. On 11 September Iran and Iraq re-established diplomatic relations.

The withdrawal of all armed forces to the internationally recognized boundaries was verified and confirmed as complete on 20 February 1991 by UNIIMOG, whose mandate was terminated on 28 February by the UN Security Council. Iran and Iraq subsequently initiated a 'confidence-building' process of reducing the levels of troops and military equipment in the border areas. Prisoner exchanges had continued until 16 January 1991, when the multinational force commenced military operations to expel Iraqi armed forces from Kuwait. At this time Iran still held 30,000 Iraqi prisoners of war. Preliminary negotiations on the full implementation of Resolution 598 were also curtailed.

The publication in August 1991 of the report of a UN delegation sent to Iran—in accordance with the terms of Resolution 598—to assess the level of human and material damage caused by the war with Iraq seemed to indicate that the UN was once again considering the need for a comprehensive peace settlement. The Iranian Government released its own assessment of the damage caused by the war: it estimated that Iran had experienced direct damage amounting to IR 30,811,000m.; that 50 towns and 4,000 villages were destroyed or badly damaged; and that 14,000 civilians were killed and 1.25m. people displaced.

IRAN AND THE CONFLICT OVER KUWAIT

Iran condemned Iraq's invasion of Kuwait in August 1990 and offered to defend other Gulf states from Iraqi aggression, but it welcomed Iraq's offer of a formal settlement of the Iran–Iraq War on Iran's terms (see above). While Iran stated that it would observe the economic sanctions imposed on Iraq by the UN, Iraq was believed to have tried to persuade Iran to trade oil for food. However, the Iranian Government adhered to its pledge to implement economic sanctions for the duration of the conflict over Kuwait, sending only supplies of food and medicine to Iraq on a humanitarian basis.

As the deployment of a multinational force (assembled in accordance with Article 51 of the UN Charter) for the defence of Saudi Arabia gathered pace, Iran urged the simultaneous and unconditional withdrawal of Western—above all of US—armed forces from the Gulf region, and of Iraqi armed forces from Kuwait. In September 1990 Ayatollah Khamenei almost endorsed the demands of 'conservatives', such as Hojatoleslam Ali Akbar Mohtashemi, for Iran to ally itself with Iraq in a *jihad* (holy war) against Western forces in the Gulf. President Rafsanjani's position was that the presence of these forces was tolerable on condition that they withdrew as soon as the conflict in Kuwait had been resolved.

Following the outbreak of military hostilities between Iraq and the multinational force in January 1991, Iran attempted, unsuccessfully, to intercede. After having consulted with Algeria, Yemen, France, the USSR and the Non-aligned Movement, Iran urged an 'Islamic solution' to the conflict. On 4 February President Rafsanjani announced that the terms of an Iranian peace proposal had been conveyed to Saddam Hussain during the visit to Tehran, on 1–3 February, of Iraq's Deputy Prime Minister, Dr Sa'adoun Hammadi; and claimed that the terms of the proposal were consistent with resolutions adopted by the UN Security Council. An immediate cease-fire was to be followed by the simultaneous and complete withdrawal of Iraqi armed forces from Kuwait, and of all foreign forces from the Gulf region. In deference to Iraq's insistence on the 'linkage' of the conflict in Kuwait with other conflicts in the Middle East (in particular the continuing Israeli occupation of the West Bank and Gaza Strip), Iran also urged the immediate cessation of new Israeli settlements in the Occupied Territories.

While the Iranian peace proposal was welcomed by the USSR, it was rejected by the USA, and on 8 February 1991, in a letter to President Rafsanjani, Saddam Hussain dismissed it, stating that Iraq had no intention of withdrawing from Kuwait and accusing the USA of seeking to dominate the Middle East by destroying Iraq. There was no clear expression of support for the Iranian peace proposal at a closed session of the Non-aligned Movement, held in Belgrade, Yugoslavia, on 11–12 February, and thereafter Soviet diplomacy came to the fore in attempting to find peace terms which might avert a ground war. Iran claimed some of the credit for the concessions offered in an Iraqi peace proposal on 15 February, and urged the multinational force not to initiate hostilities on the ground until the limits of Iraq's flexibility had been determined. However, the countries contributing to the multinational force were unwilling, by this stage, to allow Iraq the opportunity to procrastinate.

As the air bombardment of Iraq and occupied Kuwait continued, Iran accused the multinational force of exceeding the terms of resolutions adopted by the UN Security Council by seeking to destroy Iraq's military and industrial facilities. However, when, in late January 1991, more than 100 Iraqi fighter aircraft landed in Iran without having sought permission to do so, Iran lodged a protest with Iraq and impounded both the aircraft and their pilots for the duration of the conflict.

Relations between Iran and Iraq deteriorated after the conclusion of hostilities between Iraq and the multinational force. In response to the suppression, by Iraqi armed forces loyal to President Saddam Hussain, of the Shi'a-led rebellion in southern and central Iraq, Iran declared its commitment to the territorial integrity of Iraq but demanded the resignation of Saddam Hussain and protested at the damage inflicted by Iraqi armed forces on Shi'a shrines at Najaf, Karbala and Samarra. Iraq accused Iran of providing material and human support for the southern and central rebellions, citing the involvement of the Tehran-based Supreme Council of the Islamic Revolution in Iraq. In a clear indication of deteriorating relations, Iraq later resumed support for the military activities of the largest Iranian dissident groups, the Mujahidin-e-Khalq and the Kurdish Democratic Party (KDP). Iraq's suppression of the internal rebellions led to a mass flight of Iraqi Kurds and Shi'a Muslims across the Iranian border. By May 1991 more than 1m. Iraqi Kurds had fled to Iran, while the number of Shi'a refugees in Iran was estimated at 65,000.

Iran supported the Western initiative to establish 'safe havens' for Iraqi Kurds in northern Iraq, and urged, unsuccessfully, similar support for Iraqi refugees in Iran. Throughout June and July 1991 Iran accused the Iraqi armed forces of harassing Iraqi Shi'a Muslims who had fled into the marshes of southern Iraq after the defeat of the southern rebellion in March. There were conflicting reports regarding the accuracy of these allegations and of the number—estimated by Iran at 600,000—of Shi'a Muslims who had sought refuge in the marshes.

DOMESTIC REFORM UNDER RAFSANJANI

The onset of the Gulf crisis in August 1990 led to further friction between the rival factions in the Iranian leadership, but President Rafsanjani gradually asserted his authority and began the long process of seeking to reduce the power of the 'conservatives'. At times his relationship with Ayatollah Khamenei became tense, especially with regard to foreign policy issues. However, in October they formed an alliance to prevent the election of many powerful 'conservatives' to the 83-seat Council of Experts, which selects Iran's supreme leader and interprets the Constitution. Hojatoleslam Ali Akbar Mohtashemi and Ayatollah Khalkhali were among those rejected as candidates by Khamenei, on the grounds that their expertise in the Koran was inadequate. In December the Majlis enacted

legislation to allow defendants legal representation, in an apparent move towards the less rigorous application of Islamic law.

In April 1991 it was announced that Iran's internal security services—the police, the gendarmerie and the Islamic *Komitehs*—were to be merged. The *Komitehs* had hitherto acted as the chief enforcers of 'Islamic behaviour' within post-revolutionary Iranian society. In the same month the release of a British businessman who had been imprisoned without trial since 1985 for alleged espionage was regarded as a further sign of Rafsanjani's ascendancy. In May 1991 Amnesty International was allowed access to Iran for the first time since the Revolution.

Disturbances and demonstrations in Tehran and other parts of the country in August 1991 indicated significant levels of popular discontent. In April and May 1992 further demonstrations occurred, most notably in Tehran and Mashad. Eight protesters were executed by the authorities. An important factor in the unrest was municipal action in many cities against squatter settlements.

Elections to the fourth Majlis in April and May 1992 seemed to provide Rafsanjani with the opportunity further to shift the balance of power against the 'conservatives'. An estimated 70% of the deputies elected to the new Majlis were supporters of the President. The incoming deputies appeared to be more highly educated, younger and more technocratic in orientation than their predecessors. Rafsanjani installed a new Speaker of the Majlis, Ali Akbar Nateq Nouri, who replaced the 'conservative' Mahdi Karrubi. However, it subsequently became clear that assessments predicting the support of the majority of the new deputies for Rafsanjani's policies were incorrect.

The new Government indicated that it wished to proceed rapidly with measures to end all subsidies and the system of multiple foreign exchange rates; and to allow full foreign ownership of companies. In fact, the pace of economic reform in the months following the election to the fourth Majlis remained cautious, and Rafsanjani remained constrained not least by the fact that economic reform was lowering the standard of living of the traditional constituency of the Islamic regime, the urban lower classes. The middle classes, supposedly one of the engines of reform, remained deeply distrustful of the regime. Rafsanjani quickly discovered, too, that the nominally 'reformist' deputies in the new Majlis were far from uncritical in their support for his policies.

The extent to which Rafsanjani had lost popular support became clear when he stood for re-election to the presidency on 11 June 1993. Competing against three supposedly 'token' candidates, Rafsanjani received 63.2% of the vote in a low electoral turn-out of 56%. His nearest rival, former Minister of Labour, Ahmed Tavakkoli, received 24% of the vote, a performance widely attributed to his stringent criticisms of state corruption, social injustice and economic mismanagement.

During 1994 there were numerous signals that the problems encountered by Rafsanjani in implementing his reform programme were emboldening 'conservative' forces, encouraged by Ayatollah Khamenei, to challenge the President more directly. In February there was an attempt on his life during a speech he made at Khomeini's tomb. Responsibility for the attack was later claimed by the self-styled 'Free Officers of the Revolutionary Guards'. Later in the month the President was obliged to replace the Minister of Culture and Islamic Guidance after Ayatollah Khamenei had approved the appointment of the incumbent minister, Ali Larijani, to replace the President's brother, Muhammad Hashemi, as director-general of the national broadcasting authority. For several months prior to his dismissal Muhammad Hashemi Rafsanjani had been criticized by 'conservatives' within the Majlis for mismanagement and for encouraging immoral broadcasts. While President Rafsanjani denied that the dismissal of his brother reflected on him, it was perhaps significant that, shortly afterwards, he announced that he would not seek a constitutional amendment which would allow him to serve a third term as President. Opponents of the President in the Majlis also sought to modify economic reforms proposed by the Government. In May the Government indicated that it would proceed more cautiously with a plan to reduce economic subsidies applied to basic commodities. (Muhammad Hashemi Rafsanjani was appointed Vice-President in charge of Executive Affairs and War Reconstruction in August 1995.)

The atmosphere of political malaise was further deepened in June 1994 by the bombing of the Imam Reza shrine in Mashad, which left at least 24 dead. The Government blamed the Mujahidin-e-Khalq; others speculated that it might be the work of militant members of Iran's Sunni minority, angered by the destruction of a Sunni mosque earlier in the year. A crisis threatened in the following month when, in the space of a few days, two Iranian Christian leaders were assassinated in Tehran and bombs wreaked havoc against Jewish targets in London, United Kingdom, and Buenos Aires, Argentina.

In August 1995 members of the special commission for monitoring political parties were reported to have stated that political parties, associations and groups were free to conduct political activities in Iran on condition that they honoured the country's Constitution. At the same time, however, it was reported that Nehzat-e Azadi-ye Iran (Liberation Movement of Iran) had been refused permission formally to register as a political party, despite its hitherto quasi-legal status. Earlier in the month representatives of Nehzat-e Azadi had criticized new legislation granting the 12-member Council of Guardians the power to approve election candidates.

Elections to the fifth Majlis in March and April 1996 provided another important gauge of the shifting balance of power between 'liberals' and 'conservatives' in Iranian politics. The 'liberals' were grouped around a political faction named the Servants of Iran's Construction, which enjoyed the tacit support of President Rafsanjani. Its 'conservative' counterpart was the Society of Combatant Clergy, of which the unofficial patron was Ayatollah Khamenei. While a total of 10 political groups were acknowledged to have presented candidates for election, official disapproval of such groups was reflected in the authorities' refusal to publish the political affiliations of successful candidates. According to unofficial sources, however, the Society of Combatant Clergy was expected to enjoy the support of 110–120 deputies in the new Majlis, and the Servants of Iran's Construction that of 90–100.

FOREIGN RELATIONS UNDER RAFSANJANI

Efforts at domestic reform under Rafsanjani were accompanied by periodic diplomatic initiatives by Iran, aimed at securing its reintegration into the international community. The greatest single obstacle to improved relations with Western countries was initially Iran's perceived complicity in the holding of Western hostages in Lebanon by groups linked to the pro-Iranian Hezbollah. Between August and December 1991, with Iran, Syria, Israel and the UN diplomatically active, all remaining British and US hostages were released. While the aim of the captors was to trade the release of such hostages for the release of Shi'a hostages held by Israel, it was decided ultimately to release them unconditionally. The last remaining Western hostages were freed in June 1992.

The release of US hostages, accompanied by some progress at the US-Iran Claims Tribunal in The Hague, Netherlands, temporarily removed some of the tension between the USA and Iran. In September 1990 the USA paid Iran US $200m. for armaments not delivered after the Revolution of 1979. In December 1991 a further $278m. was paid by the USA. In March 1992 the USA was ordered to compensate Iran for property frozen in the USA after 1979.

Relations between the USA and Iran deteriorated after President Bill Clinton took office in the USA in January 1993. Throughout the year the Clinton Administration pressed initially reluctant Western allies to reduce levels of economic assistance to Iran and sought to block Iranian efforts to reschedule its international debts. In May 1994 US pressure was evident when it emerged that no new loans would be made to Iran by the World Bank in the foreseeable future. In June President Rafsanjani stated at a press conference that Iran sought a gesture of goodwill, such as the release of frozen assets, from the USA as a prelude to improved relations. In July the bomb attacks against Jewish targets in London and Buenos Aires prompted the USA to accuse Iran—which it alleged was responsible for the attacks—of seeking to disrupt the Middle East peace process. In August, however, the Argentinian authorities decided that there was insufficient evidence to pursue charges against four Iranians for whose arrest international warrants had earlier been issued. (A former Iranian intelligence agent alleged in July 2002 that Iranian agents had plotted and carried out the bombing in Buenos Aires, with the backing of the Iranian Government.)

In early 1995 the USA, the United Kingdom and Israel were reported to be alarmed at the possibility that Iran might be able to manufacture nuclear weapons within a few years. This was at the time of a final preparatory UN session before a conference on the extension of the Treaty on the Non-Proliferation of Nuclear Weapons (the Non-Proliferation Treaty—NPT) took place; Iran was reported to be seeking a more effective effort from the five principal nuclear powers to disarm further, and insisting that Israel should also sign the NPT. (Israel had previously refused to do so because it perceived itself to be potentially at risk of nuclear attack by Syria, Iraq and Iran.) According to some observers, Iran's aim was to pressure Western governments into offering it assistance with its civilian nuclear programme. The head of the Atomic Energy Organization of Iran subsequently suggested that Iran would remain a party to the NPT whether Israel signed it or not. The International Atomic Energy Agency stated that it had found no evidence to suggest that Iran was seeking to develop nuclear weapons. In early 1995 Russia was reported to be determined to sell at least one 1,000-MW nuclear reactor to Iran in accordance with an agreement concluded despite the objections of the USA. Japan's decision, in February, to postpone the extension of a US $450m. loan to Iran to finance the Godar-e-Landar dam was reported to be the result of US diplomatic pressure, in particular the disclosure to the Japanese authorities of US intelligence reports about unspecified Iranian activities. In March the US company Conoco withdrew from a contract to develop Iranian oil fields after the USA announced that President Clinton would shortly issue an executive order prohibiting US companies from such activities.

On 30 April 1995 US efforts to isolate Iran internationally culminated in the announcement of a complete ban on trade with Iran within 30 days: all US companies and their foreign subsidiaries would be prevented from investing in Iran, and from undertaking any trade with it. There was little international support for such an embargo, and without the support of Iran's European trading partners and of Japan it was far from clear how the embargo would damage Iran's long-term economic interests. Furthermore, the USA subsequently conceded that US oil companies active in the Caucasus and in Central Asia would be allowed to participate in exchange deals with Iran in order to facilitate the marketing of petroleum from former Soviet states. In the immediate aftermath of its announcement, however, the value of the Iranian rial declined by about one-third. In an interview broadcast by US cable television in early July, President Rafsanjani denied US allegations that Iran sponsored terrorism and was seeking to develop nuclear weapons, or that Iran was offering any material assistance to Palestinian groups opposed to the Middle East peace process.

In late 1995, in response to the lack of international support—except that of Israel—for the ban on trade with Iran, the US Congress drafted legislation aimed at pressurizing other countries into observing it. The US Administration, however, opposed initial attempts by the US Congress to force the USA's trading partners to impose trade sanctions on Iran, and Japan and the EU threatened to refer the issue to the World Trade Organization if such legislation were to be adopted. In March 1996 the USA and Israel accused Iran of being an active supporter of the Palestinian Islamist group Hamas, which had claimed responsibility for a wave of suicide bombings in Israel. Iran denied any involvement in the bombing campaign. Moreover, the US Government publicly stated that it was investigating allegations of Iranian involvement in the June 1996 bomb attack on US military personnel at al-Khobar, near Dhahran, in Saudi Arabia.

In June 1996 the US House of Representatives approved legislation seeking to penalize companies operating in US markets that were investing US $40m. or more in Iran's oil and gas industry. The sanctions received presidential assent despite sustained protests from Japan and the EU. The investment 'ceiling' was lowered to $20m. in August 1997. Like the trade embargo imposed in 1995, however, these so-called secondary sanctions were effectively disregarded by the international community.

Despite US pressure, and in spite of the unresolved issue of the *fatwa* seeking the death of Salman Rushdie, the EU persisted with a policy of 'critical dialogue' with Iran. However, in March 1996 it threatened to reconsider this policy following alleged remarks by President Rafsanjani welcoming the assassination of the Israeli Prime Minister, Itzhak Rabin. In the same month the German Government announced that a warrant had been issued for the arrest of the Iranian Minister of Information, Ali Falahian, in connection with the murders of four prominent members of the dissident Democratic Party of Iranian Kurdistan in Berlin in 1992. 'Critical dialogue' was suspended in April 1997, after a German court ruled that the Iranian authorities had ordered the dissidents' assassination: testimonies at the trial directly implicated senior members of the Iranian political and religious establishment in the murders, and, moreover, alleged that Falahian had attempted to influence the outcome of the case. (The court found two defendants— an Iranian and a Lebanese national—guilty of the murders, sentencing them to life imprisonment, and two others—both Lebanese nationals—of having been accessories to the killings.) Germany announced the withdrawal of its ambassador to Tehran and expelled four Iranian diplomats, and other EU members similarly withdrew their representatives. Iran retaliated by threatening to bring lawsuits against 24 German companies allegedly involved in supplying chemical weapons to Iraq during the Iran–Iraq War.

During the conflict over Kuwait in 1990–91 and its aftermath, Iran sought to normalize its relations with Egypt, Tunisia, Jordan and the Gulf states, and to reassert itself as a regional power. In March 1991 it re-established diplomatic relations with Saudi Arabia, and about 115,000 Iranian pilgrims subsequently participated in that year's *Hajj*. Thereafter, however, relations were characterized by mistrust.

In August 1991 Iran and Iraq met directly for talks on a comprehensive settlement to the 1980–88 war. A UN commission had formally blamed Iraq for starting the Iran–Iraq War, and Iran expected a proposed UN conference to award it US $100,000m. in reparations. In April 1992 Iran launched air-strikes against Mujahidin-e-Khalq camps in Iraq, which protested to the UN Security Council. The treatment by the Iraqi Government of its southern Shi'a population continued to obstruct relations between Iran and Iraq. In February 1995 and again in May Iran denied Iraqi allegations that armed groups under Iranian control had been responsible for attacks inside Iraqi territory on Iraqi armed forces as well as a base of the Mujahidin-e-Khalq. In May there was evidence, in the form of preparations for a visit to Baghdad of the Iranian Minister of Foreign Affairs, that Iran was seeking an improvement in its relations with Iraq, possibly so that the two countries could co-operate to counter US hostility. In August, however, on the anniversary of the end of the Iran–Iraq War, the Iraqi President made an uncompromising speech in which he criticized Iran for continuing to detain Iraqi prisoners of war, for refusing to release Iraqi aircraft impounded in January 1991, and for rejecting Iraqi efforts to secure peace.

Iran reacted negatively to efforts based on the Damascus Declaration of March 1991 to create a regional security structure in the Gulf from which it was itself excluded. While opposing the defence agreements which the Gulf states subsequently negotiated with the USA, Iran focused its diplomatic efforts on improving its relations with them. Significant progress in that sphere was thwarted by a dispute between Iran and the United Arab Emirates (UAE) over the islands of Abu Musa after March 1992, when Iran occupied those parts of the Abu Musa islands and the Greater and Lesser Tunbs that had remained under the control of the Emirate of Sharjah since the original occupation in 1971. In September 1992 the Arab League expressed its support for the UAE in the dispute over the islands, and at the end of the month negotiations between Iran and the UAE collapsed. In September 1993 Iran refused to accept any pre-conditions for discussions with the UAE on the dispute. In December 1994 the UAE announced its intention to refer the dispute to the ICJ. Iran and the UAE held direct talks on the issue for the first time in three years in November 1995, but again no progress was made.

A further source of tension between Iran and the members of the Co-operation Council for the Arab States of the Gulf (or Gulf Co-operation Council—GCC) states arose in June 1996, when the GCC accused Iran of plotting to overthrow the Government of Bahrain. The allegations, which were strongly denied by Iran, prompted a downgrading of diplomatic relations between Iran and Bahrain.

The dramatic developments in the USSR after August 1991 opened up a new arena for Iranian diplomacy in Central Asia, as Iran, Saudi Arabia and Turkey vied for influence in the newly-independent states of the region. Iran sought to strengthen its position in Central Asia through bilateral agreements and institutions such as the Tehran-based Economic Co-operation Organization (ECO). These new alliances gave rise to renewed concern in the West at the extent of Iranian political, economic and religious influence. In June 1994, under UN auspices, Iran attempted to mediate a cease-fire in the civil war which had erupted in Tajikistan in 1992. In September 1994 the Tajik Government and its opponents signed a cease-fire agreement in Tehran. In July 1995 Iran sponsored further talks between the Tajik Government and its opponents, which resulted in an extension of the cease-fire agreement.

During 1996 Iran became increasingly interested in events in Afghanistan, owing to the military advance there of the Sunni fundamentalist Taliban guerrilla fighters. Following the Taliban capture of the Afghan capital, Kabul, in September, Iran accused the group of being a proxy for US, Saudi and Pakistani interests in the country. The Iranian Government refused to recognize the Taliban-sponsored authorities in Kabul, and continued to express support for ousted President Rabbani. In early June 1997, amid accusations of espionage activities, the Taliban authorities in the Afghan capital closed the Iranian embassy and requested the departure from Afghanistan of all Iranian diplomats. In retaliation, Iran ordered the halt of all trade (including goods in transit) across its land border to Afghanistan, prompting Taliban accusations that Iran had perpetrated 'a violation of international protocols'.

In April–May 1991 President Rafsanjani made an official visit to Turkey—the first such visit by an Iranian Head of State since 1975—where he publicly stated his agreement with Turkey's President Turgut Özal that a Kurdish state should not be established in northern Iraq. In early 1992 Turkey alleged that Iran was lending support to guerrillas of the Kurdistan Workers' Party (Partiya Karkeren Kurdistan—PKK, now Congress for Freedom and Democracy in Kurdistan—KADEK) engaged in hostilities with Turkish armed forces in north-east Turkey. Despite a further deterioration in Iran's relations with Turkey, in October the Turkish Prime Minister, Süleyman Demirel, made a visit to Tehran, as a result of which it was agreed to increase economic and political co-operation. In December 1993 Iran's First Vice-President, Hassan Habibi, visited Turkey, where he signed a bilateral agreement on security co-operation. In March 1995 Iran criticized a military operation undertaken by the Turkish armed forces against PKK fighters in northern Iraq, fearing that the hostilities might spread to Iran. In April 1996 new tensions arose in relations with Turkey after four Iranian diplomats were arrested there for alleged espionage; retaliatory expulsions of Turkish diplomats by Iran ensued. Iran was reported to be increasingly anxious at growing military co-operation between Turkey and Israel. In June the rise to power of a governing coalition in Turkey led by the Islamist Welfare Party facilitated closer relations between Turkey and Iran. However, Iranian influence was cited as one of the main reasons for the sustained political offensive by the Turkish military to bring down the coalition, which duly collapsed in June 1997. In the same month Iran became a founder member of the İstanbul-based Developing Eight (D-8) group of Islamic countries. Meanwhile, in February the Iranian ambassador to Turkey provoked a diplomatic crisis by advocating the introduction of *Shari'a* law in Turkey. Criticism of the actions of the Turkish military by an Iranian consul-general later in that month resulted in both men being asked to leave the country. Iran responded by expelling two Turkish diplomats. However, both countries immediately undertook initiatives to restore relations, and in March it was agreed, during a visit to Turkey by Iran's Minister of Foreign Affairs, that all bilateral agreements were to be pursued. Ambassadors were exchanged in early 1998.

In July 1995 Iran was reported to have organized a month-long extension of a cease-fire between rival Kurdish groups in northern Iraq, prompting Iraq to denounce Iranian interference in its internal affairs. In September 1996 Iran appealed for international assistance to provide emergency aid to as many as 500,000 Kurdish refugees, who had fled towards the Iranian border in response to inter-Kurdish hostilities around the towns of Arbil and As-Sulaimaniya in the Kurdish 'safe haven' in northern Iraq. Supporting the Patriotic Union of Kurdistan (PUK) in these hostilities, Iran apparently aimed to defeat US allies in Iraqi Kurdistan and assert its own influence.

ELECTION OF KHATAMI

The months following the 1996 Majlis elections were something of an interregnum, as 'liberals' and 'conservatives' manoeuvred in anticipation of the presidential elections scheduled for May 1997 and it became clear that the Constitution would not be amended to allow Rafsanjani to seek re-election for a third term. In March 1997 Rafsanjani was appointed Chairman of the Council to Determine the Expediency of the Islamic Order (which arbitrates in disputes between the Majlis and the Council of Guardians) for a further five-year term, indicating that he would continue to play an influential role in political life upon the expiry of his presidential mandate. (Rafsanjani was reappointed as head of the Expediency Council in March 2002.) In May the Council of Guardians approved four candidates for the presidential election (a further 234 were rejected). The selected candidates were Ali Akbar Nateq Nouri (Speaker of the Majlis); Sayed Muhammad Khatami (a presidential adviser and former Minister of Culture and Islamic Guidance); Muhammad Muhammadi Reyshahri (previously Minister of Intelligence and Internal Security, Prosecutor-General and, of late, Khamenei's representative in *Hajj* and pilgrimage affairs); and Sayed Reza Zavarei (hitherto vice-president of the judiciary and a member of the Council of Guardians). Despite early expectations that Nateq Nouri would secure an easy victory, Khatami emerged as a strong contender in the days prior to the election, which took place on 23 May. Regarded as a 'liberal', Khatami—supported by the Servants of Iran's Construction, as well as by intellectuals, women's and youth groups, and by the business classes—took some 69.1% of the total votes cast, ahead of Nateq Nouri with 24.9%. The rate of participation by voters was in excess of 88%. (Nouri was re-elected Speaker of the Majlis at the beginning of June.)

Khatami was sworn in by Khamenei on 3 August 1997, and took the presidential oath of office before the Majlis on the following day. The new President stated that it would be the responsibility of his administration to create a safe forum for free speech, within the framework of regulations defined by Islam and the Constitution, and to promote 'easy and transparent' relations between the people and the organs of state. Khatami emphasized his commitment to fostering sustained and balanced growth in the political, economic, cultural and educational spheres, and to the freedom of the individual and respect for the rights of the nation, in the context of the rule of law. In foreign affairs, the President undertook to promote the principle of mutual respect, but pledged that Iran would resist any power seeking to subjugate Iranian sovereignty. Despite some concern that 'conservatives' in the Majlis might oppose some of the more pro-reform members of Khatami's first Council of Ministers, which was presented for approval in mid-August, all of the nominees were endorsed by the assembly after several days' debate. Notable among the 'moderate' appointees were Ata'ollah Mohajerani (a former Vice-President) as Minister of Culture and Islamic Guidance, and Abdollah Nuri as Minister of the Interior (a post he had previously held in 1989–1993). Kamal Kharrazi (hitherto Iran's ambassador to the UN) replaced the long-serving Ali Akbar Velayati as Minister of Foreign Affairs, while Qorbanali Dorri Najafabadi became Minister of Information. Upon taking office, Khatami had reappointed Hassan Habibi as First Vice-President. Six further Vice-Presidents were named later in the month, among them Muhammad Hashemi Rafsanjani, who retained the post of Vice-President in charge of Executive Affairs; Ma'sumeh Ebtekar, as Vice-President and Head of the Organization for the Protection of the Environment, was the first woman to be appointed to a government post of such seniority since the Islamic Revolution. In mid-October Khatami named former Prime Minister Hossein Moussavi as his senior adviser. In the following month the President appointed a new Committee for Ensuring and Supervising the Implementation of the Constitution.

INTERNAL POLITICAL RIVALRIES

Although Khatami pledged his allegiance to Khamenei as Iran's spiritual leader, the new President's assumption of office revived long-standing rivalries among the senior clergy. The focus of opposition to Khamenei was seemingly Ayatollah Montazeri (Khomeini's designated successor prior to March 1989), who began openly to question Khamenei's authority and to demand that Khatami be allowed to govern without interference. In mid-November 1997 police used tear-gas to disperse a violent demonstration in Qom by supporters of Khamenei, who had gathered to denounce Montazeri and one of his allies, Ayatollah Azari Qumi. Demonstrations in support of Khamenei persisted in Qom, Tehran and elsewhere for several days, until Khamenei urged an end to the protests; none the less, he demanded that Montazeri be tried for treason, and that all others who questioned his authority be prosecuted in accordance with the law. In mid-December the General Secretary of Nehzat-e Azadi, Ibrahim Yazdi, who had reportedly met with Montazeri shortly before the latter had publicly criticized Khamenei, was detained for almost two weeks, on charges of desecrating religious sanctities, after he had signed an open letter to Khatami urging that Montazeri's rights be respected.

During the first months of his presidency, in spite of his relative lack of experience in government, Khatami was judged to have strengthened his position, and that of his supporters, mainly through the successful conduct of foreign policy (see below); and in January 1998 the Iranian Union of Journalists was sufficiently emboldened to express rare public criticism of the powerful Head of the Judiciary, Ayatollah Muhammad Yazdi (an influential member of the Council to Determine the Expediency of the Islamic Order, appointed by, and responsible only to, Khamenei), whom it accused of seeking to obstruct the freedom of the press. In April the Mayor of Tehran, Gholamhossein Karbaschi, became the focus of political rivalry when he was arrested on charges of fraud and mismanagement. Karbaschi was a popular national figure and a prominent supporter of President Khatami, and on the day of his arrest the Council of Ministers issued a public statement criticizing the decision to detain him. Later in the month students demonstrating in support of Karbaschi were involved in violent clashes with the police. The political nature of the case was further underlined in May, when it was announced that the Servants of Iran's Construction had been authorized by the Ministry of the Interior to form a political party of the same name and that Karbaschi would be the party's Secretary-General.

Karbaschi's trial, broadcast in full on Iranian television, commenced in early June 1998 and achieved unprecedented publicity. Any concerns that an unwarranted level of attention was being directed at a simple case of corruption in local government were dispelled later that month by the impeachment, by 'conservative' deputies in the Majlis, of the Minister of the Interior, Abdollah Nuri, who had expressed his personal support for Karbaschi and had expressed criticism of Yazdi for allegedly persecuting Karbaschi and his aides. Nuri was duly dismissed from the interior portfolio, the Majlis having upheld a motion expressing 'no confidence' in him. However, Khatami promptly demonstrated his full support for Nuri by appointing him Vice-President in charge of Development and Social Affairs, an appointment which allowed him to retain a position in the Council of Ministers, beyond the scrutiny of the Majlis. In July the Majlis approved the appointment of Khatami's former Vice-President in charge of Legal and Parliamentary Affairs, Sayed Abdolvahed Musavi-Lari (perceived as a 'moderate'), as Minister of the Interior. Later in the month Karbaschi was sentenced to five years' imprisonment and 60 lashes. He was also fined and banned from holding public office for 20 years. Following an appeal, in late December the duration of the custodial sentence was reduced to two years; the punishment of 60 lashes, suspended at the time of sentencing, was commuted to a fine of IR 10m. (in addition to one of IR 1,000m. imposed in July), and the term of prohibition from holding public office was reduced to 10 years. A further appeal failed to overturn the conviction, and Karbaschi began his custodial term in May 1999. (He was released in late January 2000, shortly before the legislative elections, having been pardoned by President Khatami.)

Several months of factional tensions preceded the next major test of strength between 'conservatives' and 'liberals', the elections to the Council of Experts (the body responsible for the appointment of the country's spiritual leader), held on 23 October 1998. The 'conservatives' retained control of the Council, but, to many observers, the low turn-out at the polls significantly undermined the legitimacy of their victory. Leaders of the 'conservatives' none the less hailed the election results as a sign of public devotion to religious values. More than 60% of the seats in the 86 member body went to the radical right wing, some 30% to 'conservative' candidates, while 'centrists' secured about 10%. This outcome had been widely predicted, as the Council of Guardians (responsible for scrutinizing candidates), which was firmly in the hands of 'conservative' elements, had approved only 161 of 400 candidates, of whom 130 were declared 'conservatives'; all were clerics. Although the 'conservatives' had done their best to mobilize voters, it appeared that public disillusion with the electoral process led to a poor level of participation. The number of voters was estimated at between 15m. and 18m., about 40% of all eligible voters. (In the 1997 presidential elections 29m. had voted.) None the less, the figures apparently confirmed that the 'conservatives' retained a real social base, estimated at around 30% of the population.

During the campaign President Khatami himself had little room for manoeuvre. He criticized the election authorities for not allowing a larger number of competent figures to stand, but joined the 'conservatives' in urging the population to vote. The elections represented the culmination of a 'conservative' offensive against the 'reformist' coalition. The 'leftist' wing of this coalition refused to give its support to any candidates after its own list was rejected by the election authorities, while the centre, although many of its candidates were also refused, none the less persisted with the remainder and succeeded in establishing for the first time a minority opposition group in the Assembly. The day after the election results were announced the Ministry of the Interior, which remained in the hands of the 'reformists', declared that the first local council elections were to be held early in 1999, thus immediately precipitating another round of factional struggles.

In the final weeks of 1998 the murders of a number of political dissidents engendered an atmosphere of terror among Iran's intelligentsia. The first, and most prominent, victim was Dariush Foruhar, who was killed with his wife at their home in Tehran. Foruhar had founded the Iranian People's Party, and had for some time also edited a newsletter that was critical of the regime. In subsequent weeks three more dissidents were kidnapped and murdered: all three were writers and campaigners against censorship, who were attempting to revive the secular Writers' Association. The murders prompted outcry both within Iran and abroad, and it was immediately rumoured—and widely believed—that a radical right-wing group, possibly with links to elements within the State, was responsible. President Khatami and members of his Cabinet denounced the crimes, and Ayatollah Khamenei also condemned the killings and urged the intelligence service to arrest and punish the culprits.

President Khatami and his supporters made another significant advance after their victory in the local council elections on 26 February 1999. The 'conservatives' had again tried to preclude a large victory for the 'reformers' by vetting candidates (through the Council of Guardians) ahead of the poll, and had disqualified many contenders allegedly for rejecting the doctrine of *velayat-i faqih* (i.e. that ultimate political authority should rest with Iran's spiritual leader). None the less, the elections themselves were generally accepted to have been among the most transparent in the country's history. Three tendencies competed for votes, the 'left-wing' pro-Khatami Participation Front, the 'centrist' pro-Rafsanjani Servants of Construction Party, and the 'conservative' Green Coalition. The Participation Front and the Servants of Construction campaigned on a 'reformist' platform, and presented candidates in many areas. However, owing to their rudimentary organization, all three tendencies managed to field candidates in only about 25 major cities. The rest of the constituencies, some 700 smaller towns and 33,000 villages, were mostly controlled by independents,

who were motivated more by local concerns than by issues of national politics. In Tehran and the larger cities the victory of the Participation Front and the Servants of Construction was decisive. In the capital they won all 15 seats, thus ensuring that the next mayor of Tehran would also be a 'reformist'. In Esfahan and Shiraz they also won substantial majorities. Even in Mashad, a 'conservative' stronghold, 'reformers' secured five of 11 council seats, with a further two going to independents. Women did well in the elections. The most prominent woman elected was Jamileh Kadivar, sister of the 'reformist' thinker Mohsen Kadivar and the wife of the pro-Khatami Minister of Culture and Islamic Guidance, Ata'ollah Mohajerani. Jamileh Kadivar polled third in Tehran, with 370,000 out of 1.4m. votes. Although numerically still small (some 5,000 female candidates were among a total of 300,000 contenders, winning 300 of 197,000 seats), women's electoral successes, and the proportion of the vote that they received, represented a significant step forward in their participation in the political process.

Iran's 'conservatives' immediately responded to the success of the 'reformists' with renewed efforts to use the institutions that they still controlled, particularly the judiciary, to restrict the freedom of action of the 'reformers' and the press. In the immediate aftermath of the elections the political philosopher Mohsen Kadivar was arrested. The main focus of Kadivar's thought and published work was that the doctrine of *velayat-i faqih*, a key ideological tenet of the Islamic Republic, was an innovation in Islamic thought. In April Kadivar was ordered to be detained for 18 months by the Special Clerical Court on charges of spreading fabrications and inciting public unrest, although his books remained freely available. In this action against Kadivar, the 'conservatives' apparently hoped to limit the influence of those offering legitimacy to popular demands for more say in political and social affairs. The tactic failed, however, as Kadivar was widely represented as a martyr and—even more significantly—hundreds of otherwise 'conservative' clerics in the holy city of Qom parted ways with the establishment and signed petitions demanding Kadivar's release, insisting that he had done no more than exercise the traditional right of a learned theologian to interpret religion. (Kadivar was released from prison in July 2000, although he was expected to be indicted on further 'yet unknown' political charges.)

The second focus for the 'conservatives' was the press, most notably the 'reformist' women's daily *Zan*, run by Faezeh Hashemi, daughter of former president Hashemi Rafsanjani. *Zan* was accused of anti-revolutionary activity for publishing a Nowrooz (new year) message from the widow of the deposed Shah, Farah Diba, and ordered to cease publication immediately. These actions, against Kadivar and *Zan*, were apparently part of a co-ordinated right-wing strategy to reduce the influence of the 'reformists' prior to the crucial Majlis elections scheduled for early 2000.

In April 1999 the 'conservatives', while still attempting (with eventual success) to have five leading pro-reform city councillors (among them former Minister of the Interior Abdollah Nuri) in Tehran removed from office on technicalities, turned their attention to the Minister of Culture and Islamic Guidance. Mohajerani, staunchly pro-Khatami and a leading member of the reform movement, had for the past 18 months been providing political and financial support to help build up an independent press. As a result, the number of publications increased rapidly, newspaper readership grew by several millions, and the press became an important arena for the 'reformers' in their efforts against the 'conservatives' and 'hardliners'. In an attempt to check the ideological advances of the 'reformers', a group of 'conservative' Majlis deputies tabled a motion to impeach Mohajerani, on the grounds that his 'liberal' strategy was undermining religious and revolutionary values. In the parliamentary debate on the impeachment, at the beginning of May, Mohajerani was accused of being un-Islamic, anti-revolutionary, immoral, unwise, corrupt, politically naive and deviant. In his defence, Mohajerani elaborated the ideas that had become the hallmarks of the 'reform' movement: tolerance, the rule of law, freedom, constitutionalism and civil society, often quoting classical Persian poetry and verses from the Koran. In the final vote a large number of independent deputies joined with the 'reformers' and the impeachment motion was defeated by 135 votes to 128.

The arrest, revealed in June 1999, of 13 Iranian Jews in Shiraz and Esfahan, on charges of spying for Israel and the USA, was widely interpreted as an attempt by 'conservatives' to undermine President Khatami's policy of *détente* with the West. Meanwhile, 'conservatives' and 'reformers' also appeared to be vying for control of the Ministry of Information. In mid-June a former deputy minister, Said Emami, committed suicide while in detention; he and three other intelligence officers had earlier been arrested on charges of arranging the murders of political dissidents in late 1998 (see above). It was believed that a group had existed within the ministry for the purpose of the systematic elimination of opponents of the regime, although it was not certain who may have given this group its orders. None the less, the 'reformers' seized this issue as an opportunity to wrest control of the Ministry of Information from the 'conservatives', demanding that the ministry be restructured and that radical right-wingers be purged from it. The 'conservatives', greatly embarrassed by such revelations, tried to distance themselves from Emami, claiming he was an Israeli spy, but the independent press continued to demand explanations.

In early July 1999 one of the most serious challenges to the regime in many years erupted on the streets of Tehran. The crisis began when the 'conservative'-dominated Majlis approved legislation aimed at curbing press freedom. The new press law was an integral part of efforts by 'conservatives' to ensure their success in the forthcoming Majlis elections. The judiciary, equally 'conservative'-controlled, immediately seized the opportunity to ban the publication of *Salam*, Iran's oldest pro-reform newspaper, on 7 July. The same night hundreds of Tehran university students held a demonstration in support of the suppressed daily. The response to this relatively minor disturbance followed swiftly, as early the next morning right-wing vigilantes of the Ansar-e Hezbollah, with police assistance, forcibly entered halls of residence. Their assaults on the students left several hundred injured and at least one student dead; about 200 arrests were made. In subsequent days thousands of students gathered in Tehran, and unrest spread to other cities. Student leaders made speeches demanding radical change; there were repeated clashes with riot police, and there was open criticism of Ayatollah Khamenei. Supporters of President Khatami came to the defence of the students, and Tehran university chancellors resigned in protest at the police violence. Khamenei also distanced himself from the attack on the students, and the Supreme Council for National Security ordered the dismissal of two senior police-officers.

The student movement is regarded as an important element of the pro-Khatami coalition, with several effective networks that are mostly controlled by 'moderate' Islamists. In the course of the demonstrations, however, leftist and secular elements emerged more clearly, and the split between the 'moderate' and 'radical' wings of the student movement became more apparent. Khatami appealed for restraint, and the unrest subsided when the students dispersed for the summer vacation. However, it was announced in September 1999 that four students had been sentenced to death for their part in the July riots, although the death sentences were commuted to 15 years' imprisonment in April 2000. In mid-August 1999, meanwhile, Ayatollah Sayed Mahmoud Hashemi Shahrudi, considered a 'modernist' but none the less 'conservative', assumed the post of Head of the Judiciary, in succession to Ayatollah Yazdi, who was immediately appointed to the Council of Guardians.

In early September 1999 the 'conservatives' intensified their campaign against pro-reform elements to coincide with the official announcement of the next legislative elections by the Ministry of the Interior. One victim of the campaign was the 'liberal' newspaper, *Neshat*, which was closed down on the orders of the 'conservative'-controlled press court. *Neshat* had published an open letter to Khamenei urging him to transfer his support from the 'conservatives' to the 'reformists' and had also questioned the legitimacy of capital punishment in an Islamic country. Published by associates of the 'liberal' Islamic philosopher, Abd al-Karim Sorush, *Neshat* enjoyed the third largest circulation in the country. The press court found the newspaper guilty of insulting Islam and the person of Ayatollah Khamenei. Iran's Minister of Culture and Islamic Guidance challenged the legality of the court's ruling, while warning the press not to give the 'conservatives' any pretext for action. The

hopes of 'reformers' that the appointment of Ayatollah Hashemi Shahrudi as Head of the Judiciary might lead the courts to adopt a less partisan approach were thus disappointed, as they had been by the death sentences passed on the students. Meanwhile, 'conservative' deputies introduced legislation into the Majlis seeking to give the Council of Guardians extensive powers to vet election candidates in advance of the parliamentary elections scheduled for February 2000.

As the campaign for the legislative elections intensified, the judiciary became the focus of the rivalry between 'conservatives' and 'reformers'. The 'reformers' criticized Ayatollah Hashemi Shahrudi's predecessor, Muhammad Yazdi, claiming that he had given too much power to the clerical and revolutionary courts, had undermined the judicial process by combining the role of prosecutor and judge, and had encouraged political appointments among judges. During his first weeks in office Hashemi Shahrudi initiated a process of consultation with independent lawyers and dismissed several 'hardliners' among his senior staff. The pro-reform press welcomed Shahrudi's declared objectives of gradually changing the administrative structure and of conducting a review of legal procedures. At the same time, however, it expressed doubts as to whether he would be able to implement reforms without external support or a political reshuffle of his staff. Meanwhile, the 'conservative'-dominated Majlis began studying draft legislation designed to give the press court the power to discount jury verdicts and to conduct summary trials. Pro-'conservative' judges made their position clear in late September 1999 when the press court sentenced the publisher of *Neshat* to two-and-a-half years in prison and ordered the newspaper's indefinite suspension. With regard to the forthcoming legislative elections, the strategy of the 'conservatives' was, broadly, to use the courts to restrain the press and to weaken public enthusiasm for reform, in preparation for a low-profile election in which they hoped to minimize their losses.

In October 1999 the 'conservatives' reinforced their effort to prevent a landslide victory for 'reformers' in the forthcoming elections by attempting, via the judiciary, to bring about the downfall of former Minister of the Interior Abdollah Nuri, a leading pro-reform figure associated with the Servants of Construction. Nuri was indicted by the Special Clerical Court on charges that he had insulted religious sanctities, attempted to establish relations with the USA, encouraged the recognition of Israel, campaigned for the 'liberal' Nehzat-e Azadi, and supported Grand Ayatollah Montazeri, Iran's most senior dissident cleric. The 'conservatives' further accused Nuri of using his position as managing editor of the popular pro-reform newspaper, *Khordad*, to undermine Islamic and revolutionary values, and demanded that he change the newspaper's editorial board in order to avoid standing trial. Nuri responded by refusing to recognize the Court, stating that charges brought against *Khordad* should be heard by the press court in the presence of a jury. In late November the Special Clerical Court sentenced Nuri to a term of five years' imprisonment, having found him guilty of a number of charges—among them insulting religious beliefs, deviating from the teachings of Ayatollah Khomeini, undermining public confidence and working against the Islamic Republic. Nuri was imprisoned immediately, thus being denied the usual 10-day 'grace' period in which to appeal. (However, Nuri had already stated that he would not launch an appeal as he did not recognize the Special Clerical Court.) The verdict, regarded as a victory by 'conservatives', was unanimously condemned by 'reformers', and President Khatami expressed his regret at the Court's decision. An appeal lodged with the Supreme Court was rejected in January 2000, on the grounds that the Court had no constitutional authority to overturn a verdict of the Special Clerical Court.

In December 1999 the registration of candidates for the forthcoming legislative elections commenced. The decision of the former President, Ali Akbar Hashemi Rafsanjani, to participate aroused alarm in 'reformist' circles and prompted an alliance of 12 'conservative' factions to place Rafsanjani at the head of their list of 160 candidates. Rafsanjani based his decision to stand for election on the hope that he would be able to consolidate 'centrist' tendencies and contain the rivalry between 'reformers' and 'conservatives'. However, 'reformers' claimed that he would split the pro-reform vote. Both moderate 'conservatives', including those associated with the Servants of Construction, and the right-wing press expressed enthusiastic support for Rafsanjani's candidacy.

In January 2000 the Council of Guardians began the task of determining the eligibility of the more than 6,000 candidates who had registered to participate in the elections. Early in the month 30 prominent 'reformers' had sent an open letter to President Khatami, in which they alleged that the Council sought to debar candidates who were not associated with the 'conservative' establishment. The letter reflected a widespread belief that the 'conservatives' intended to use the official vetting process as a last resort to prevent an overwhelming pro-Khatami victory at the elections. For its part, the Council of Guardians denied any partiality and declared that it would not submit to an orchestrated campaign to discredit its decisions, stating, further, that its only concern was to uphold the rule of law. Towards the end of 1999 the Majlis had ratified an amendment to the electoral law that strengthened the Council's ability to direct the electoral process. However, the amendment also introduced a new requirement that the Council should inform disqualified candidates in writing of the reasons for their rejection and institute a process of appeal.

In an open letter, the imprisoned former Minister of the Interior, Abdollah Nuri, who had been registered as an election candidate by his lawyers, urged the judiciary to quash his sentence so that he could participate. Meanwhile, 'reformers' intensified their campaign to discredit Rafsanjani. In a discussion of a scandal that implicated agents from the Ministry of Information in the murder of dissidents, two pro-reform newspapers, *Sobh Emruz* and *Fath*, implied that Rafsanjani must have had some knowledge of the inner workings of the ministry during his eight years in office and demanded a clarification.

During January 2000 the Council of Guardians disqualified dozens of 'reformers' from participating in the elections. From a total of 6,459 registered candidates, 401 (5.8%) were disqualified on the alleged grounds that they were disloyal to Islam, to Iran's Constitution or to the country's spiritual leader. The Council appeared to target the most controversial candidates, while it endorsed the participation of those it regarded as more 'centrist'. President Khatami undertook a tour of the country in order to raise support for the elections. He warned that if the poll was not seen to be conducted fairly, then the relationship between the State and the people would be damaged. The elections were also anticipated by the publication, in three pro-reform newspapers, of an interview between the dissident Grand Ayatollah Montazeri and the Tehran correspondents of Reuters news agency and a British newspaper, *The Guardian*. Montazeri called for the powers of Iran's supreme leader, Ayatollah Khamenei, to be curbed, and stated that greater respect should be shown for people's right to determine their own destiny. He also described the Council of Guardians' disqualification of election candidates as unconstitutional.

Legislative voting, in which an estimated 80% of Iran's 38.7m.-strong electorate participated, proceeded in a calm atmosphere on 18 February 2000. Some 5,000 candidates contested the 290 seats in the Majlis. In Tehran, where voting is regarded as the most accurate indicator of national trends, nine joint candidates of the two major pro-reform parties—the 'left-wing' Participation Front and the more 'centrist' Servants of Construction—secured the 25% of votes necessary to secure election. The Participation Front was the clear overall winner, its exclusive candidates faring much better than those of the Servants of Construction. Rafsanjani, who was the leading candidate of both the Servants of Construction and the 'conservatives', fared badly. Muhammad Reza Khatami, brother of President Khatami and the Participation Front's most prestigious candidate (as well as its Secretary-General), polled first position among the Tehran candidates, and his success was regarded as a renewal of the popular mandate for the President's 'reformist' programme. The 'conservatives', meanwhile, suffered a devastating defeat in the capital: not one of their candidates was elected. In Mashad, Iran's second largest city, 'reformist' candidates gained all five seats, as they did in Esfahan. They also achieved decisive victories in Shiraz and Tabriz. There was a marked increase in the proportion of Majlis seats won by women; by contrast, the number of clerics in the new assembly declined. For seats where the result was

inconclusive in the first round of voting supplementary elections were held in May 2000.

In the aftermath of the elections fears were expressed that right-wing elements might resort to violence, and rumours circulated of a possible *coup d'état* by units of the Revolutionary Guards. In an apparent effort to demonstrate that the State would not tolerate acts of provocation, 20 police-officers (including the former Tehran chief of police, Brig.-Gen. Farhad Nazari) were arraigned on charges of involvement in the assaults on students that had triggered the unrest of July 1999. (Nazari and 17 co-defendants were acquitted in July 2000, while two police-officers received custodial sentences.) The judiciary continued its campaign against the press, which 'conservatives' held responsible for their electoral defeat. Many journalists were imprisoned and several newspapers closed down. In mid-March 2000 Sayed Hajjarian, a prominent 'reformer' and one of President Khatami's leading political advisers, was shot and seriously injured by an attacker who appeared to have links with the security forces. A former deputy intelligence minister and a member of Tehran's city council, Hajjarian was also manager of the outspoken daily newspaper *Sobh Emruz*. He had contributed to the development of Khatami's ideas about Islamic democracy and had become a particular focus of resentment among right-wing elements, who accused him of waging a campaign of psychological warfare against them. The assassination attempt prompted 'reformers' to urge that control of the security forces be transferred from Ayatollah Khamenei to the President, so that they could be purged of radical and maverick elements. In mid-May five men (including alleged religious activists and members of the Revolutionary Guards) were found guilty of having carried out Hajjarian's attempted assassination and sentenced to prison terms ranging from three to 15 years; three others were acquitted.

In the immediate aftermath of the legislative elections in February 2000 tensions had arisen regarding the future of Rafsanjani, who, with fewer votes than any of the other candidates elected outright in Tehran, had barely achieved election to the Majlis. After complaints about electoral malpractice, the Council of Guardians ordered that almost one-third of the votes cast in Tehran should be re-counted. In May the Council invalidated 726,000 votes cast in the capital and rearranged the order of the successful candidates. Rafsanjani, who was believed to have been in 30th place after the preliminary results were announced, was now ranked 20th in Tehran, while three 'reformers' were deprived of their seats. The veracity of the revised count was challenged both by the public and by 'reformist' politicians, who argued that Rafsanjani's unpopularity among young voters and other key sections of the electorate meant that he was unlikely to have achieved such a position. Rafsanjani himself, publicly humiliated by the apparent machinations of the Council of Guardians, resigned his seat, thus relinquishing his ambition to become the new Speaker of the Majlis, a powerful position which the 'conservatives' were expected to use to obstruct reform. Nevertheless, Rafsanjani retained a power base as Chairman of the Council to Determine the Expediency of the Islamic Order.

The first session of the sixth Majlis began on 27 May 2000. It was apparent that divisions existed among 'reformers' with regard to issues such as the election of a new Speaker and new legislation governing the press. Leaders of the 'reformists' clearly intended to proceed cautiously, with the Participation Front accepting the election of the Servants of Construction's candidate, Ayatollah Mahdi Karrubi, as Speaker.

During June 2000 it was reported that elements within the judiciary continued to attempt to obstruct the 'liberal' cause through, among other measures, the suppression of newspapers associated with it. (Much of the 'reformist' press had been closed down in April.) In June the 'reformist' daily, *Bayan*, became the 20th newspaper to be closed down. Early in the month the election of Muhammad Reza Khatami and Behzad Nabavi as, respectively, First and Second Deputy Speaker of the Majlis had represented a considerable victory for the 'reformist' tendency in Iranian politics. It was estimated by this time that 'reformist' or 'liberal' deputies in the new assembly numbered some 200, with the remaining 90 seats occupied by 'conservatives'. (Each group included deputies who were nominally independent of any factional allegiance.) The Majlis had reportedly begun to draft amendments to new press legislation that would make the judicial suppression of newspapers more difficult.

The State Plan and Budget Organization was merged with the State Administrative and Employment Office in June 2000. Muhammad Reza Aref was made responsible for the resultant Organization of Administration and Planning within the Council of Ministers, while Nasrollah Jahangard was appointed as his temporary successor as Minister of Posts, Telegraphs and Telephones. Jahangard's nomination was, however, rejected by the Majlis in October. Also in June, meanwhile, Muhammad Ali Najafi and Muhammad Baqerian were appointed as Advisers to the President with the rank of Vice-President.

On 1 July 2000, following a trial in camera that had begun in May, the Shiraz Revolutionary Court passed its initial sentences on the 13 Iranian Jews accused of spying for Israel. Eight Muslims were also tried by the Court. None of the defendants received a death sentence, but 10 of the Jews were given terms of imprisonment ranging from four to 13 years (the latter in two cases). The remaining three Jews, already released on bail, were acquitted. Two Iranian Muslims accused of espionage were given two-year prison sentences. That no capital sentences were passed on the defendants was regarded as a significant victory for their defence lawyers, and was interpreted by some as a sign that Iran had heeded international criticism. Israel had denied that it had any connection with the alleged spies, and several Western governments had expressed concern over the affair. The case had attracted an intense degree of outside interest, and there were fears that the 'conservatives' who dominate the judiciary might use the episode to undermine President Khatami's standing abroad. In the event, Western governments did not react sharply to the sentences, especially since they were subject to appeal. The appeals court announced its verdict on 21 September. All the Jews had their sentences reduced (after they were acquitted of one charge of belonging to an illegal organization); the two highest were cut by six and four years respectively, while the others were lessened by two or four years. The two Muslims were still awaiting the results of their appeal. Although Israeli and US officials expressed disappointment that the Jews had not been released on appeal, other Western governments accepted the reduced sentences. It was reported in February 2001 that the Supreme Court had rejected further appeals against the Jews' prison terms. However, one of the Jews was released in early March, having already served two years in detention; a second was freed in January 2002.

In early August 2000 Iran's supreme leader, Ayatollah Khamenei, acted to block the amendments proposed within the Majlis to legislation governing the press. He did so on the grounds that the envisaged reforms would endanger state security, and his intervention appeared to sanction an even more rigorous campaign against the press than was already being pursued by the judiciary, thus prompting strong criticism from international press organizations. In the same month a report in a Saudi Arabian pan-Arab daily newspaper, *Asharq al-Awsat*, indicated that Iran's Head of the Judiciary, Ayatollah Hashemi Shahrudi, had been designated by the Iranian Council of Experts as deputy to and successor of Khamenei.

In October 2000 it was reported that Ata'ollah Mohajerani, the 'liberal' Minister of Culture and Islamic Guidance (who had narrowly survived an impeachment motion in 1999) had tendered his resignation. However, President Khatami apparently delayed official acceptance of his resignation until mid-December, when Mohajerani was redesignated Chairman of the Organization for the Dialogue of Civilizations. Ahmad Masjed Jame'i, reputed to be more 'conservative' than Mohajerani, was confirmed as the new Minister of Culture and Islamic Guidance in mid-January 2001, when the Majlis endorsed this and other recent ministerial nominations. One of the new appointments, the Minister of Roads and Transport, Rahman Dadman, was killed in an aircraft accident in May. Meanwhile, in December 2000 it was announced that the Ministries of Agriculture and of Construction Jihad had been merged to create a new Ministry of Agricultural Jihad, while those of Industries and of Mines and Metals had been transformed into a Ministry of Industries and Mines.

By late 2000 the main battleground in the continuing struggle between 'conservatives' and 'reformers' remained the courts. Although in September 1999 the new judiciary chief, Ayatollah Hashemi Shahrudi, had been appointed with a brief to reform the institution, very little change had taken place and the courts continued to constitute a potent weapon in the hands of the 'conservatives'. Having closed at least 30 pro-reform publications since April 2000 and prosecuted a number of prominent journalists, by November the courts were occupied with a succession of cases relating to a conference, sponsored by the German Green Party's Heinrich Böll Foundation, which had been held in Berlin in April to discuss Iran's political future. Among the defendants in the trial, which opened in Tehran on 2 November, were a number of prominent 'reformers'. They included the politician Jamileh Kadivar, two of Iran's best known 'liberal' feminists—the publisher Shahla Lahiji and the lawyer Mehrangiz Kar—the veteran opposition figure Ezatollah Sahabi and the outspoken journalist Akbar Ganji, who also faced a range of charges in the press court arising from his assertions about official complicity in the murders of dissident writers and intellectuals in 1998. The charges against most of the defendants were of undermining state security and propagandizing against the Islamic system. The Berlin conference had been disrupted by Iranian opposition elements in exile, and those before the Iranian courts were accused largely on the basis of guilt by association, although also on account of statements they had made on issues such as female *hejab* (the veil).

Towards the end of 2000 President Khatami appeared increasingly embattled, and speculation began to mount as to whether he would stand in the presidential election scheduled for June 2001. He was apparently opposed to standing again if his role was to be reduced to that of a 'front' for an unreformed regime dominated by 'ultra-conservatives'. On 26 November 2000 Khatami admitted publicly that the presidency lacked the requisite powers to safeguard the Constitution. Meanwhile, the courts continued to be used against the proponents of change, and the 'reformist' majority in the Majlis was again frustrated in its attempts to resist the closure of the pro-reform press when, in early November, the Council of Guardians again rejected a bill that would have closed the legal loophole under which newspapers were being closed down. In that month the Majlis announced that by-elections would be held concurrently with the presidential election for 18 seats where the results of earlier voting had been annulled. The Council of Guardians, in mid-December, declared the date of the presidential election to be 8 June 2001.

On 23 December 2000 the trial began before a military tribunal in Tehran of those accused of the murders of four dissident writers and intellectuals in 1998. A group of 18 defendants, some of them senior intelligence officers, were charged with ordering or participating in the murders. Public interest in the case was profound. Only a few weeks previously the journalist Akbar Ganji had at his own trial repeated in open court accusations that the former information minister, Ali Falahian, had ordered the murders with the blessing of senior hard-line clerics. Ganji also claimed that there had been at least 80 such murders during the previous decade and that the then President, Hashemi Rafsanjani, had known and approved of them. The trial was held in camera, with only the defendants and their lawyers present, the victims' families having boycotted the proceedings. The verdict was announced on 27 January 2001. Three of the accused—intelligence agents who admitted to having physically carried out the killings—were condemned to death; five others were sentenced to life imprisonment, some of them several times over; seven accomplices received prison terms of up to 10 years; and three of the defendants were acquitted. Full details of the trial proceedings were not released, although it appears that only three of the accused had denied the charges against them and that at least two, in mitigation of their own role, implicated the former information minister, Qorbanali Dorri Najafabadi, who had resigned under pressure from President Khatami shortly after the scandal broke in early 1999. (However, charges against Najafabadi in relation to the case were abandoned in December 2000.) Although the sentences were correct in terms of Iranian law, Iran's largest 'reformist' faction, the Participation Front, denounced the outcome of the trial, saying that it left too many questions unanswered. The victims' families also rejected the court's decision, asserting that the proceedings had been designed mainly to conceal the extent of the murders and the true burden of responsibility. In mid-August 2001 the Supreme Court ordered a retrial of the 15 agents who had been convicted in January.

Meanwhile, in the case of the 17 'reformists' prosecuted for attending the Berlin conference, severe sentences had been handed down by the Tehran Revolutionary Court on 13 January 2001. With the exception of a dissident cleric tried separately by the Special Clerical Court and reportedly sentenced to death, the most harshly punished was Akbar Ganji, who was sentenced to 10 years' imprisonment followed by five years' internal exile, having been convicted of charges of harming national security, possessing secret documents, committing offences against leading Iranian officials, and of propagandizing against the Islamic regime. A translator at the German embassy in Tehran received a custodial sentence of 10 years, and an interpreter at the conference one of nine years; the two feminist activists, Shahla Lahiji and Mehrangiz Kar, each received four years. Jamileh Kadivar, however, was among six defendants to be acquitted. Appeals were immediately lodged by all those convicted.

The pro-reform movement was united in seeing the sentences against the Berlin conference participants as another politically motivated blow at a delicate moment when President Khatami was still undecided as to whether, and if so on what terms, to seek re-election in June 2001. By early March the 'conservatives' had still not agreed on a candidate, nor had Khatami come to a decision, but the judiciary was continuing its campaign against the 'reformers'. On 4 March, following trial proceedings initiated in January, Tehran's Civil Service Court found Mustafa Tajzadeh, Deputy Minister of the Interior and a 'reformist' selected by Khatami to supervise the forthcoming presidential elections, guilty of complicity in electoral fraud during the previous year's elections to the Majlis. Tajzadeh was sentenced to one year in gaol; he was barred from monitoring elections for six years and from holding a government post for 39 months. (Tajzadeh was also accused of incitement to violence during four days of clashes between pro-reform students and 'conservative' students and security forces in Khorramabad in August 2000.) The 'reformist' Governor of Tehran, Ayatollah Azarmi, was given an 18-month custodial sentence on a similar fraud charge, and a distinguished journalist, Masoud Behnoud, was sentenced to 19 months' imprisonment for spreading lies and insulting Islam. In fact, more than two dozen prominent 'reformist' journalists, politicians and even Majlis deputies, were brought to trial during a two-week period in February 2001. In that month divisions also emerged between uncompromising 'ultra-conservative' clerics and students and less radical 'conservatives' who supported Ayatollah Khamenei.

There was a new wave of arrests in April 2001. On 7 April 42 prominent 'liberals', mostly members of the proscribed Nehzat-e Azadi, were arrested on charges of conspiracy to overthrow the Islamic regime. They included relatives and close associates of the movement's founder, Mehdi Bazargan (Iran's first Prime Minister after the Revolution), among them his nephew, his son-in-law and two members of his former government. The arrests prompted 150 Majlis deputies to sign an angry letter to the Head of the Judiciary, Ayatollah Hashemi Shahrudi, challenging the legality of the action. One of the most outspoken deputies, Mohsen Armin, declared that the campaign of arrests was designed to convince President Khatami that his standing for re-election would be futile. Khatami himself expressed regret over the arrests and press closures, but he still did not announce whether he would be standing in the June election. Pressure on the President to declare his candidacy—from all the major 'reformist' groupings and a large majority of deputies—was steadily mounting, since to decline would be to accept that the reform process had lost all hope of advance.

On 15 May 2001 an appeals court in Tehran cleared Akbar Ganji of all but one of the charges of which he had been found guilty in January. Ganji was convicted only of having propagandized against the State, and his prison sentence was thus reduced to one of six months. Ganji was released from gaol on 16 May; however, in mid-July he was found guilty of having threatened national security and was sentenced to six years' imprisonment. In the same month Mustafa Tajzadeh was acquitted of vote-rigging charges. A ban on some 40 pro-reform publications was also revoked.

The deadline for the registration of presidential candidates was 6 May 2001. Only two days before this deadline President Khatami, clearly under severe stress, finally declared himself as a candidate for the Islamic Republic's eighth presidential election. His aides stated that two weeks earlier he had decided not to run but had been swayed by pressure from his supporters. Although Khatami may have been hoping to wring a deal out of the 'conservatives' in return for continuing to confer legitimacy on the system, Ayatollah Khamenei, Iran's supreme leader, remained aloof from endorsing Khatami's candidacy. A total of 814 people put themselves forward as presidential candidates, including 45 women, although in mid-May the Council of Guardians reduced this number to a shortlist of 10. The 'conservatives' failed to agree on a single candidate, although several independent 'conservatives' were running for election. The most prominent 'conservative' candidates were former Minister of Information Ali Falahian and Ahmed Tavakkoli, an economist and former Minister of Labour (who had stood against Rafsanjani in 1993); also standing was the Minister of Defence and Logistics, Ali Shamkhani, who claimed to be a 'balancing force' in Iranian politics. The right wing, whose strength had stabilized over the past four years at around 20%–25% of the electorate, and knowing that its candidates would be overwhelmingly defeated at the polls by Khatami, instead began to present the argument that if the President was returned with a reduced majority, this would be evidence of the failure of his reform project.

KHATAMI RE-ELECTED

Khatami was indeed returned to office on 8 June 2001 with around 21.7m. votes, exceeding the record 20m. votes he had received in 1997 and thus becoming the first Iranian President to win more votes for his second term than for his first. This was significant because the 'conservatives' were thus unable to argue that the 'reform' movement had lost its legitimacy. It was also an important achievement because of a degree of disillusionment and impatience that had emerged among those who had voted for Khatami in 1997, and because of voter apathy induced by the certainty of his victory and discontent over the economic situation. The incumbent President had faced nine opponents, all of whom were 'conservatives' but none of whom had received the official endorsement of the 'conservative' hierarchy—which did not wish to be identified with a humiliating defeat. The election, therefore, had rather the character of a referendum on the reform programme. Khatami's closest rival, Ahmed Tavakkoli, only received about 15.6% of the total votes cast. Electoral turn-out, at some 67% of eligible voters, was numerically lower—by about 1m. votes—than it had been in 1997, and was lower still when seen as a proportion of the electorate because a further 5m. young voters had been added to the electoral register since then. Khatami's share of the total vote increased from 69% in 1997 to about 76.9%, but as a proportion of the total electorate it remained almost exactly the same, at 51.5%.

Khatami's election in 1997 had, to some extent, been seen as the result of a protest vote against the system. This time, however, the voting was interpreted as a positive expression of support for the President personally, and for his reform programme. This endorsement gave Khatami the strength to return to the struggle with the 'conservatives', but also put him under greater pressure from his own constituency to achieve certain concrete goals. In his message to the nation after his victory, Khatami spoke of the establishment and consolidation of the democratic system, of freedom of speech, and even of protest within the framework of the law. There were initial signs following Khatami's victory that the 'conservative' camp was beginning to disintegrate, with moderate 'conservatives' moving towards the political centre and the 'hard core' finding itself increasingly isolated. In late June 2001 'reformists' were encouraged by the announcement that Ayatollah Khamenei had approved the holding of a parliamentary inquiry into the financial affairs and alleged partiality of the 'conservative'-controlled state broadcasting monopoly.

However, it swiftly became apparent that the 'ultra-conservatives' were unwilling to cede control of the Council of Guardians to 'reformist' supporters of Khatami. The President was due to be sworn in for his second term of office by Ayatollah Khamenei on 5 August 2001, but the ceremony was postponed after the 'reformist' Majlis refused to approve two of the judiciary's 'conservative' nominations to the Council of Guardians. Khamenei requested that the dispute be resolved by the Council to Determine the Expediency of the Islamic Order. This decision was strongly opposed by 'reformists', since the Council (chaired by former President Rafsanjani) is dominated by 'conservatives'. However, it was announced on 7 August that the Majlis had finally endorsed the two candidates, following a ruling that candidates did not require the support of a majority of deputies in order to be elected to the Council of Guardians. Khatami was duly sworn in as President on 8 August. He presented his 20-member Council of Ministers to the Majlis on 12 August, in which the key portfolios remained unchanged and only five new ministers were appointed. One notable appointment was that of Tahmasb Mazaheri as the new Minister of Economic Affairs and Finance. The President's failure to implement a more radical ministerial reshuffle led to speculation that 'reformist' deputies might prevent parliamentary approval of the list. However, the Majlis endorsed the new Council of Ministers on 22 August. Also in that month Muhammad Reza Aref, previously head of the Organization of Administration and Planning, became Iran's First Vice-President, replacing Hassan Habibi who had resigned in early July.

FOREIGN RELATIONS UNDER KHATAMI

The success of President Khatami's 'reformist' project depends on ending Iran's isolation—both political and economic—by seeking an improvement in relations with the West. Any such improvement will be determined by the course of Iran's relations with the USA. This key area of foreign policy is also most likely to provoke conflict between opposed factions within the Iranian leadership. In August 1997 President Khatami identified Iran's need for 'an active and fresh presence' in the sphere of foreign relations. The US Department of State greeted the announcement of a new Iranian Council of Ministers in that month with a statement of its willingness to engage in dialogue, provided that Iran would discuss the issues of nuclear weapons, 'terrorism' and the Middle East peace process. This was tantamount to setting impossible conditions for dialogue: Iran's definition of 'terrorism', for instance, was substantially different to that of the USA; and Iran had long regarded the Middle East peace process as dead. In mid-1997 official US attitudes towards Iran continued to be dominated by concern about the country's weapons programmes. In June, during a tour of the Gulf states, the US Secretary of Defense, William Cohen, repeatedly claimed that such programmes posed a threat to Iran's weaker neighbours. Later in the month, the commander of US forces in the Gulf warned that Iran was still seeking to develop nuclear weapons and that it might be closer to achieving this goal than had previously been thought. In July the announcement that Russia was to assist Iran to complete the nuclear power plant at Bushehr prompted the USA to reiterate its concern that Iran might attempt to exploit civilian nuclear technology for the development of nuclear weapons. In September the US Vice-President announced that US and Russian investigators had concluded that Iran was engaged in a 'vigorous effort' to obtain technology for the manufacture of nuclear weapons and ballistic missiles capable of transporting them. (Earlier in September the Russian authorities had stated that they would be willing to allow the USA to monitor the Bushehr nuclear plant.) In October China announced an end to the sale of nuclear technology, as well as of conventional weaponry, to Iran. In November Iran became a signatory to the International Chemical Weapons Convention; under its terms, which prohibit the production and possession of chemical weapons, Iran became subject to mandatory international inspections. Earlier in the month the USA had reportedly purchased fighter aircraft from Moldova in order to prevent their sale to Iran.

As a result of a visit to Tehran at the end of November 1998 by Russia's minister responsible for nuclear power, Yevgenii Adamov, it became all the more evident that Russia intended to finish building the nuclear power plant at Bushehr. Despite unrelenting pressure from the USA and Israel to withdraw from the project, Russia was determined to continue with its programme of nuclear co-operation with Iran. In Tehran Adamov signed an agreement with Muhammad Aghazadeh,

head of the Atomic Energy Organization of Iran, committing Russia to complete the installation of the first reactor at Bushehr and to conduct a feasibility study for the construction of three additional units at the site. Although Iran has signed and ratified the NPT and gives the IAEA full access to Bushehr, the USA and Israel repeatedly alleged that the reactor could give Iran the technology it needs to develop nuclear weapons. Adamov, however, reiterated assurances that Bushehr could not be used for military purposes. In December 2000 Russia agreed to resume military co-operation with Iran, a decision which angered US officials. During an official visit to Russia by President Khatami in March 2001, his Russian counterpart, Vladimir Putin, emphasized that Russia would only export weapons to Iran to be used for defensive purposes. As part of a bilateral security and co-operation agreement, it was also confirmed that Russia would assist Iran with the completion of the Bushehr power plant. In May Russia agreed to the sale of advanced ship-borne cruise missiles to Iran. A military co-operation accord—reportedly amounting to annual sales to Iran of Russian weaponry worth some US \$300m.—was signed by the two sides in October.

Khatami's election had inevitably aroused widespread speculation in Western media regarding the prospects for an improvement in relations with the USA and other Western countries. However the Clinton Administration might feel disposed towards a new Iranian President with exemplary democratic credentials, who had clearly revealed his 'reformist' instincts, the secondary sanctions act, sponsored by US Senators Alfonse D'Amato and Edward Kennedy, and approved by the US Congress in mid-1996 (also known as the Iran-Libya Sanctions Act—ILSA) remained an obstacle to any *rapprochement*; however, the sanctions act was being increasingly undermined by commercial and geopolitical realities: European companies, and their governments, were simply not prepared to forgo opportunities in the development of the energy resources of the newly independent states of Central Asia for the sake of US foreign policy aims. In July 1997 the Clinton Administration raised no formal objection to a project to construct a 2,000-mile pipeline to carry gas from Central Asia to Turkey and, thence, to Europe, despite the fact that the pipeline would cross some 788 miles of Iranian territory. The US dilemma regarding sanctions was to become more acute as the year progressed. At the end of July it became clear that the French energy company, Total, was determined, in partnership with Gazprom of Russia and Petronas of Malaysia, to proceed with a US \$2,000m. investment in Iran's South Pars gas field. US Senator D'Amato immediately urged the US Government to impose sanctions on Total. However, such a move would risk provoking a 'trade war' with the EU, damaging relations with Russia, and thus further complicating other areas of US foreign policy—the question of Iraq's compliance with UN Security Council resolutions, for instance—where European and Russian co-operation was essential. US commercial interests were also at stake. At the same time, the US Administration was conscious that revoking objections to investments in the Iranian gas industry could precipitate the collapse of its aim, in the longer term, to direct the flow of energy from the Caspian Basin via Turkey rather than Iran. In October the USA was reported to be seeking an agreement with the EU whereby it would suspend the implementation of sanctions in return for increased European pressure on Iran to curb its alleged involvement in terrorism.

Any failure by the USA to impose sanctions could be claimed as a 'victory' by the Iranian authorities. In combination with other factors, ILSA began to have the perverse effect of isolating the USA rather than Iran. This was nowhere more apparent than at the eighth summit meeting of the OIC, held in Tehran in early December 1997: the attendance of the leaders of many of the USA's erstwhile 'moderate' Arab allies appeared to undermine the USA's credibility in the region, primarily owing to its failure to promote any progress in the Middle East peace process. The presence of so many Arab leaders at the meeting was in stark contrast to the US-sponsored Middle East and North Africa economic conference in Doha, Qatar, the previous month. Both Ayatollah Khamenei and President Khatami addressed the inaugural session of the OIC summit meeting, in dramatically differing tones. While Khamenei lambasted the pernicious, corrupting influence of the West, on which he fixed the blame for the 'calamitous condition' of the Islamic world, Khatami spoke of the accomplishments of Western civilization and their potential role in the development of the Islamic world. Later in December, at a press conference in Tehran, President Khatami expressed his hope for a 'thoughtful dialogue' with the 'great American people'. Such a gesture, unprecedented in the recent history of relations between the two states, appeared to perturb the US authorities, triggering in some official quarters the stock reaction that Iran remained a sponsor of terrorism, a manufacturer of weapons of mass destruction and a potential saboteur of the Middle East peace process. However, the response of President Clinton was unexpectedly warm, expressing a cautious willingness to discuss relevant issues.

In late April 1998 the US Department of State identified Iran as the most active state sponsor of terrorism, alleging that during the past year Iranian agents had perpetrated at least 13 assassinations and noting the continued support of the Iranian Government for 'extremist' groups such as Hezbollah and Hamas. On 19 June, however, the USA demonstrated readiness to improve relations with Iran, when, in a speech in New York, US Secretary of State Madeleine Albright indicated US willingness to grant Iran a role in regional security provided that it abided by 'international standards of behaviour'.

The election of President Khatami and the appointment, in August 1997, of a new Minister of Foreign Affairs apparently led to a relaxation of tensions in EU–Iranian relations (see above), and in November a compromise arrangement was finally reached allowing the return to Iran of all ambassadors from EU countries. The EU's policy of 'critical dialogue' remained in suspension, however, and the new Iranian regime initially appeared either unwilling or unable to make the compromises which might facilitate a resolution of the Rushdie affair. In late September 1998, however, following intensive negotiations between the British Secretary of State for Foreign and Commonwealth Affairs, Robin Cook, and the Iranian Minister of Foreign Affairs, Kamal Kharrazi, it was announced that the British Government had secured oral assurances from the Iranian Government that it would not support the bounty on Rushdie's head, although the 1989 *fatwa* could not be formally revoked. In January 1998 Germany's troubled relations with Iran were further complicated when an Iranian court sentenced to death a German businessman whom it had found guilty of illicit sexual relations with a Muslim woman. (However, the Supreme Court overruled the verdict in February 1999, and in a retrial in October the defendant was convicted and fined in respect of a lesser offence.) In late February 1998 the EU revoked its ban on high-level ministerial contacts between member states and Iran, stating that it wished to encourage moderate political forces in the Islamic Republic. Shortly afterwards, in March, the Italian Minister of Foreign Affairs, Lamberto Dini, visited Tehran, where he asserted that Iran was not engaged in terrorist activities and that its weapons programmes posed no threat. Italian commentators suggested that Dini's remarks might have been aimed partly at furthering Italy's commercial interests. The Rushdie affair and ILSA notwithstanding, European companies were actively pursuing opportunities in the energy industries of the Caspian Basin and in Iran.

The 'active and fresh presence' in the sphere of foreign relations to which President Khatami referred in August 1997 had, by mid-1998, yielded results in the field of Iranian–Arab relations. To the declared openness of the new Iranian regime, there now corresponded a growing perception, even among those Arab states most closely aligned with the USA, that the obstructed Middle East peace process was nurturing a popular backlash which improved relations with the Islamic Republic might help to forestall. Syria was reported to have played an important background role in effecting this *rapprochement*, exploiting the shared suspicion in the Arab world of closer relations between Turkey and Israel.

In late 1998 Iran played an active role in reducing tensions between Turkey and Syria over alleged Syrian support for Kurdish rebels. Kharrazi visited Damascus and Ankara in October for talks with his Syrian and Turkish counterparts and with the President of each country. These efforts were interpreted as an indication of a new feeling of confidence in Tehran following improvements in its relations with Europe,

particularly the United Kingdom, and also resulting from its prominent role within the OIC.

The OIC Conference held in Tehran in December 1997 illustrated how far the Arab position had shifted towards Iran. Saudi Arabia, long the target of Iranian criticism for the style of its guardianship of the holy cities of Mecca and Medina and its dependence on the USA for its security, was represented at the OIC summit meeting by Crown Prince Abdullah ibn Abd al-Aziz as-Sa'ud and by its Minister of Foreign Affairs. Their attendance was considered to represent a significant further stage in the process of reconciliation, which had begun with the visit of a Saudi Arabian ministerial delegation to Iran in July, and culminated, in February 1998, in an official visit by former Iranian President Hashemi Rafsanjani to Saudi Arabia. This was the first visit by an Iranian leader of such seniority since the 1979 Revolution, and its aims transcended the largely symbolic nature of earlier contacts to address pressing economic issues. Iran was reported to be seeking Saudi Arabian support for a reallocation of OPEC production quotas; it also sought to persuade Saudi Arabia to take fuller advantage of Iranian infrastructure to transport its exports to Central Asia; and to make greater use of surplus Iranian labour. Iran was also expected to raise the issue of a regional security alliance incorporating all of the states bordering the Gulf. In May 1998 Iran and Saudi Arabia concluded a comprehensive co-operation agreement, the scope of which extended from key economic areas to culture and sports.

In May 1999 President Khatami embarked on a tour of Arab capitals, visiting first Syria, where he reaffirmed the alliance with President Hafiz al-Assad. The Iranian President then proceeded to Saudi Arabia, on a visit that marked the culmination of the steady improvement in relations between these two countries. Discussions during Khatami's five-day visit included Gulf security, efforts to bring about higher oil prices, the situation in Iraq, and the development of a common approach to regional issues. The Saudi authorities, encouraged by the partial *détente* between Iran and the USA, showed themselves to be particularly keen to co-operate with Khatami. Furthermore, the signing of a Saudi-Iranian security agreement was announced in April 2001.

There were, however, fewer signs of improvement in Iran's relations with the UAE, which had deteriorated further in 1996 after Iran opened an airport on Abu Musa in March and a power station on Greater Tunb in April. In January and February 1997 the UAE protested that Iran was repeatedly violating its territorial waters. Talks held in March were inconclusive, and in June the UAE protested to Iran and the UN about Iran's construction of a pier on Greater Tunb. Following a meeting with the UAE's Minister of Foreign Affairs during the OIC summit in December, President Khatami emphasized his willingness to discuss bilateral issues directly with President Zayed bin Sultan an-Nahyan of the UAE. Although the latter was said to be cautious about Iran's attempts at *rapprochement*, in January 1998 authorities in the UAE and Iran stated that the UAE was willing to enter into negotiations. None the less, both countries continued to assert their sovereignty over the three disputed islands (see above). In March Iran pre-empted an expected demand by the GCC member states that it should resolve its dispute with the UAE as a condition for a general improvement in relations by organizing a conference in Tehran for its own diplomatic representatives to those countries. At the conference, the Iranian Minister of Foreign Affairs reportedly emphasized the importance that Iran attached to its relations with the GCC states, while making no mention of the dispute with the UAE. Kharrazi's address was also reported to contain implicit criticism of the GCC's support for the US military presence in the Gulf region. Observers noted the relative isolation of the UAE in its dispute with Iran. Oman and Qatar had maintained good relations with Iran, while Iran's relations with Saudi Arabia, Kuwait and Bahrain continued to improve.

The apparent *rapprochement* between Iran and Saudi Arabia during 1999 caused a bitter crisis within the GCC. In June a meeting of GCC ministers responsible for foreign affairs was unable to agree a common stand on the UAE's dispute with Iran over the three Gulf islands. The result of the GCC meeting was interpreted in Tehran as evidence of Saudi Arabia's desire to pursue closer relations with Iran.

Since the election of President Khatami in 1997 there have also been signs of an improvement in relations with Iraq. In September of that year Iraq opened its border with Iran in order to allow Iranian pilgrims access to its Shi'ite shrines for the first time in 17 years. At the end of the month, however, Iranian aircraft violated the air exclusion zone over southern Iraq in order to bomb two bases of the Mujahidin-e-Khalq in that country (prompting Iraqi aircraft also to enter the zone). The Iraqi Vice-President, Taha Yassin Ramadan, attending the December OIC conference, was the most senior Iraqi official to visit Iran since 1979. Following the summit, President Khatami expressed the hope that problems between the two countries could be resolved 'through negotiation and understanding'. In April 1998 Iran was reported to have released more than 5,000 Iraqi prisoners of war in recent weeks, while Iraq had released 319 Iranian prisoners of war. In mid-October 2000 Kamal Kharrazi became the first Iranian Minister of Foreign Affairs to visit Iraq for a decade. The two countries agreed to reactivate a 1975 border and security agreement that had been in abeyance since 1980. However, there were unconfirmed reports in that month that Iran's Supreme Council for National Security was to suspend all high-level contacts with the Iraqi Government, following a series of mortar attacks on targets in Tehran apparently perpetrated by the Mujahidin-e-Khalq. Similar attacks continued during 2001, however, and tensions between the two sides escalated in mid-April when Iran launched a heavy missile attack against Iraqi military bases used by the Mujahidin. Despite a protest lodged with the UN by Iraq in June 2002, stating that Iran was continuing to violate agreements reached at the end of the Iran–Iraq War, a general thaw in bilateral relations was evident.

A major priority of Iran's economic policy under President Khatami is the increased development of its reserves of natural gas, and it is also seeking to exploit its potential as a principal transit point for the export of hydrocarbons from the Central Asian republics of the former USSR. These two factors have, moreover, hindered US-led attempts to isolate Iran by means of economic sanctions (see above). In December 1997 a pipeline was inaugurated to transport natural gas from Turkmenistan to northern Iran; it was anticipated that the project would subsequently be extended to Turkey and, ultimately, to western Europe. (Russia had hitherto controlled all export outlets for energy from Turkmenistan, Kazakhstan and Azerbaijan.) In May 1998 Iran issued an international tender for the construction of a pipeline to carry oil from the Caspian Basin to Tehran, the first stage of a project which aims, eventually, to transport oil to Iran's Kharg terminal in the Gulf. In early August 2001, with relations between Iran and Azerbaijan already tense owing to their dispute over a contested section of the Caspian Basin, Iran denied accusations by Azeri officials that Iranian military aircraft had violated Azeri airspace.

In September 1997 the Taliban leadership in Afghanistan accused Iran of providing military assistance to its opponents and threatened retaliatory action. In late 1997 it was reported that, since the election of President Khatami, Iran had begun to participate in meetings at the UN with (among others) US officials in an attempt to identify ways of ending the Afghan civil war. Iran's principal concerns with regard to Afghanistan have been to contain any instability resulting from the conflict there, and to remove the strain placed on its domestic resources by the presence of large numbers of Afghan refugees. Eleven Iranian diplomats and more than 30 other Iranian nationals were among those allegedly captured by Taliban forces during a renewed offensive in Afghanistan in August 1998. This development prompted warnings from the Iranian leadership that retaliatory action would be undertaken if the hostages were not released unharmed. In early September, following Taliban denials that they were holding the diplomats hostage, the Iranian Government organized large-scale military exercises (involving some 70,000 troops) near the border with Afghanistan. Tensions continued to escalate in mid-September, following the discovery, in Afghanistan, of the bodies of several of the missing diplomats, and the situation was exacerbated by further territorial gains made by Taliban forces and reports that thousands of Afghanistan's Shi'a Muslim population were being murdered as a result. Relations remained tense in late September, as the number of Iranian troops in the border region was increased to some 250,000 and Ayatollah Khamenei announced that the country's armed forces should be placed on full alert. Overt military conflict with Afghanistan was averted, although Iran maintained some 200,000 troops on the border. Iran's relations with Pakistan, however, were adversely affected by the Afghan crisis. The Iranian Ministry of Foreign Affairs took the view that although the Taliban had some social base, the fundamentalists would not have advanced so successfully without logistical support from Pakistan and without Saudi finance, and that Iran's regional interests had been ignored. Iran continued to hope for the emergence of a regime in Afghanistan that would not, in Iran's view, be subservient to foreign powers, particularly Pakistan.

In the second half of 1999 there were new indications of a possible resumption of relations between Iran and the USA. In August the Iranian Deputy Minister of Foreign Affairs, Mohsen Aminzadeh, stated that Iranian policy towards the USA had changed and that there should be more debate on the state of bilateral relations. He was reported to favour Iran's approaching the USA from a position of strength in order to gain as many concessions as possible, particularly with regard to Azerbaijani oil contracts and the lifting of economic sanctions. Although Aminzadeh later complained that his remarks had been quoted out of context, and that he had also criticized US policy, his views were none the less regarded as an accurate reflection of official policy. On 19 March 2000 US Secretary of State Madeleine Albright delivered a well-publicized address in which she announced an end to import restrictions on Iranian carpets and foodstuffs; she also acknowledged Iran's importance, the failure of US policy towards the country and the prospects for improved future relations. Besides praising Iranian 'reformers', Albright came close to apologizing for the role the USA had played in the overthrow of Muhammad Musaddiq in 1953 and for its support of Iraq in the Iran–Iraq War.

However, any improvements in US-Iranian relations again faltered when, in June 2001, 14 men were indicted *in absentia* by the US Government, having been charged with involvement in the bombing at al-Khobar, Saudi Arabia, in 1996. The accused men—13 Saudis and one Lebanese—included the leader of Saudi Hezbollah and prominent members of Hezbollah's military wing. Announcing the list, US Attorney-General John Ashcroft, alleged that members of the Iranian Government 'inspired, supported and supervised' Saudi Hezbollah, and that the terrorists 'reported surveillance activities to Iranian officials'. However, the list was noteworthy for its omission of any Iranian names. This was a considerable climb-down for the US Federal Bureau of Investigation (FBI) whose outgoing Director, Louis Freeh, had for years insisted that the organization possessed enough information to indict senior members of Iran's intelligence services, and even its spiritual leader, Ayatollah Khamenei. Freeh held the Administration of President Bill Clinton, whose term of office had ended in January 2001, responsible for having slowed down the investigation in the interests of *rapprochement* with Iran, although US government representatives maintained that Freeh had never possessed the conclusive proof necessary to bring charges against Iranian officials.

Although Iranian officials welcomed early indications that the new Administration of President George W. Bush, inaugurated in January 2001, was reviewing US policy on sanctions, in early August the USA confirmed that ILSA was to be extended for a further five years. (The legislation incorporated an option for President Bush to review the sanctions in 2003.) In July 2001 the USA had, for the second time since May, blocked Iran's bid to enter negotiations regarding membership of the World Trade Organization; an Iranian application was again vetoed by the USA in February 2002.

In the immediate aftermath of the devastating suicide attacks on New York and Washington, DC, on 11 September 2001, there was considerable speculation among Western observers as to Iran's likely response to US prosecution of a campaign against the al-Qa'ida (Base) organization of its chief suspect, Osama bin Laden, the Saudi-born fundamentalist dissident based in Afghanistan. President Khatami was swift to offer his 'deep sympathy. . .to the American nation,' asserting that terrorism was 'condemned' and urging the international community to take 'effective measures against it'. In a letter to the UN Secretary-General, Khatami stated that he regarded the UN as the most appropriate mechanism to achieve the eradication of terrorism, while Minister of Foreign Affairs Kamal Kharrazi indicated that Iran supported 'a UN-led retaliatory move and fight against terrorism'. Ayatollah Khamenei, for his part, remained initially silent on the issue. When he did comment, almost a week after the attacks, he condemned the atrocities in the strongest terms but cautioned against a military offensive against Afghanistan which might result in the deaths of innocent civilians and create a new refugee exodus, asserting that Iran would similarly condemn any 'catastrophe' brought about in Afghanistan by US-led conflict; he warned furthermore, that the USA's problems would multiply if the country sought to establish a presence in Pakistan and send troops into Afghanistan. Khamenei's views were echoed in Iran's 'conservative' press. While it was considered by many that some form of co-operation against bin Laden, and potentially his Taliban hosts, could be advantageous to both Iran and the USA, influential forces within both the Iranian and US regimes remained implacably opposed to such an expedient. By late September indications that the USA was seeking to establish a channel of communication with the authorities in Tehran were apparently confirmed when it was announced that the British Secretary of State for Foreign and Commonwealth Affairs, Jack Straw, was to bring forward an official visit to Iran which had been planned for November. However, Iran emphasized that it would not lend military assistance to the US-led campaign against Afghanistan, and both 'liberals' and 'conservatives' in the Iranian regime strongly condemned the commencement of hostilities in early October.

In January 2000 Kamal Kharrazi made a two-day visit to London, United Kingdom, in a further attempt to normalize relations between the two countries. 'Reformers' in the Iranian foreign ministry hoped in particular to foster improved trade relations with the United Kingdom, and a final communiqué referred to forthcoming discussions on the promotion of British investment in Iran. Co-operation was also to be sought on the prevention of drugs-trafficking and in coping with the large number of refugees in Iran. A visit to Iran by the British Secretary of State for Foreign and Commonwealth Affairs, Robin Cook, scheduled for May, was delayed until July and was again postponed in late June, shortly before the anticipated delivery of sentences in the Shiraz espionage trial. British officials none the less denied that these and subsequent cancellations were linked to events in Iran. A visit to Iran by Cook's successor, Jack Straw, which had been scheduled for November 2001, was brought forward to late September following the terrorist attacks on the USA in that month (see above).

In July 2000 President Khatami became the first Iranian leader for more than 30 years to make an official visit to Germany. The visit was marked by widespread protests by Iranian dissidents resident there, and by a correspondingly firm response by the German police force to protect Khatami from his opponents. In January 2001 Iran and Italy signed an agreement to co-operate in fighting organized crime; it was the first such accord to be signed between Iran and a Western government.

Meanwhile, in June 2000 President Khatami made a state visit to the People's Republic of China. A communiqué issued at the conclusion of his visit affirmed the satisfactory nature of relations between Iran and China. Both countries undertook to strengthen co-operation in trade and economic affairs and to engage in a dialogue with regard to social and cultural issues. In September Iran and Algeria agreed to resume diplomatic relations; Algeria had severed links in 1993, accusing the Iranian Government of sponsoring armed Islamist groups in their conflict with the Algerian military regime. The Turkish Minister of Foreign Affairs, İsmail Cem, made an official visit to Iran in February 2001, during which he offered assurances to Iranian officials that Turkey's military alliance with Israel was not directed against Iran.

KHATAMI'S SECOND TERM: TENSIONS WITHIN THE ISLAMIC REGIME—REPERCUSSIONS OF THE 'WAR AGAINST TERROR'

As soon as the US-led military offensive against Afghanistan began in October 2001, and before its extent or repercussions were clear, Iran issued a statement declaring that the air-strikes

were unacceptable, that innocent civilians would inevitably be victims, and that the military campaign was being carried out in defiance of world opinion, especially that of the Muslim world. Iran also reminded the USA to respect Iranian airspace and its territorial integrity. The Minister of Defence and Logistics, Rear-Adm. Ali Shamkhani, had earlier warned that Iran would confront any intrusions onto its territory. This was in contrast to Iran's position during the Gulf war 10 years previously, when Iran had ignored occasional sorties through its airspace by the US-led multinational force to launch attacks on Iraq.

Amid the general preoccupation with events in Afghanistan, the struggle between Iran's 'reformists' and 'conservatives' continued. In the latter part of 2001 the main focus of this conflict was, once again, the judiciary. On 10 October President Khatami issued a formal constitutional warning to the Head of the Judiciary, Ayatollah Hashemi Shahrudi, with regard to the prosecution of pro-reform Majlis deputies despite their parliamentary immunity under the terms of the Constitution. At least two deputies, including Fatima Haqiqatjou, a 'reformist', had been given prison sentences for remarks made during a session of the Majlis, although they had not yet actually been imprisoned. Haqiqatjou had been sentenced in August to 22 months' imprisonment for her remarks concerning the arrest of a journalist, Fariba Daoudi-Mohajer, six months previously. She was found guilty of misinterpreting the words of Ayatollah Khomeini and insulting members of the Council of Guardians. Unusually, Khatami's letter was published in the 'reformist' press, with the apparent aim of maximizing pressure on the judiciary. However, far from obliging Shahrudi to back down, it received a sharp response from the judiciary head and his associates. With the deadlock still firm, the 'reformists' began to call for a referendum on the issue, in the hope that they could mobilize their greater popular support.

By the end of 2001 the number of deputies facing charges for their speeches in the Majlis had reached 60. All had been summoned to court, and on 26 December Hossein Loqmanian, a 'reformist' deputy, was the first actually to be gaoled, after he was given a 10-month sentence (this a reduced sentence from an original one of 13 months) for attacking the judiciary—in particular over the issue of its closure of several pro-reform publications—in a speech to the assembly. (On the same day the gaol term imposed on Haqiqatjou was reduced by an appeals court to one of 17 months.) In a heated debate in the Majlis, some deputies appealed to Ayatollah Khamenei to intervene, while others denounced Loqmanian's imprisonment as a virtual *coup d'état* and demanded a referendum on the future of the judiciary. However, the Head of the Judiciary, Ayatollah Hashemi Shahrudi, made a conciliatory move by proposing a meeting between himself, President Khatami and the Speaker of the Majlis, Hojatoleslam Mahdi Karrubi, to resolve the contentious issue of constitutional immunity. Equally conciliatory was the decision on 29 December by the Court of Appeal in Tehran to reduce dramatically the prison sentences given to five Iranians convicted for their participation in the Berlin conference in 2000 (see above). The four-year gaol terms of feminist activists Mehrangiz Kar and Shahla Lahiji were converted to fines. On 15 January 2002 Majlis Speaker Karrubi made a dramatic intervention when he forced the release of Hossein Loqmanian by walking out of parliament and essentially going on strike until Khamenei was obliged to intervene and pardon the imprisoned deputy: Loqmanian was duly released. Meanwhile, in that month two trials were instigated by the judiciary: one involved some 15 opposition activists (mostly academics and writers) accused of anti-State activities and of seeking to foment student unrest; the other involved legal proceedings against at least 10 people (including state officials) accused of economic corruption.

The internal power struggle was undoubtedly affected by the international crisis over Afghanistan, with some 'reformists' hoping that the conflict there might help to open the way for a dialogue with the US Administration, although Ayatollah Khamenei continued to denounce the USA in the strongest terms. Iran's long border with Afghanistan and its influence over the Western-backed opposition forces, known collectively as the United National Islamic Front for the Salvation of Afghanistan, or the Northern Alliance, especially the Shi'ite Hizb-i Wahdat, gave it key influence in the Afghan situation. The latter part of 2001 saw a series of visits to Iran by foreign dignitaries, among them several European ministers of foreign affairs and the UN Special Representative of the Secretary-General for Afghanistan, Lakhdar Brahimi, for discussions concerning the composition of a future Afghan government.

Iran had a number of concerns relating to the outcome of the Afghan campaign. Already host to an estimated 2.3m. Afghans, it feared an influx of thousands of new refugees. In the latter part of September 2001, as the USA began preparations for military action against al-Qa'ida and its Taliban hosts, Iran moved to stem the refugee tide by closing its eastern border with Afghanistan and sending a large contingent of troops there. In the following month, however, when the US-led military action began, Iran reportedly agreed to the establishment of eight refugee camps within its borders to provide shelter for some 250,000 Afghan refugees. In early 2002 the Iranian authorities and the office of the UN High Commissioner for Refugees (UNHCR) were co-operating in establishing registration centres for refugees wishing to return to Afghanistan. A programme for voluntary returns under UNHCR auspices was inaugurated by the Iranian and Afghan authorities in early April, although UNHCR put the number of what it termed 'spontaneous' repatriations prior to that date at 57,000. Some 400,000 refugees were expected to have returned from Iran to Afghanistan by the end of 2002.

The Iranian leadership was also suspicious of the potential installation of another hostile, US-engineered regime in Kabul (a role once played by the Taliban), and was anxious about the instability that might result from a long and inconclusive conflict. Some 'reformers' insisted that talking to all parties in the conflict, including the USA, was essential to securing Iran's national interests and a favourable formula for Afghanistan's future. Iran was already involved in the long-standing 'Six plus Two' group which brought together under UN auspices Afghanistan's neighbours with Russia and the USA. Iran continued to assert that the UN should play a pivotal role in the construction of a post-war government in Afghanistan, and pressed this view on Lakhdar Brahimi during his talks in Tehran.

Any hopes entertained by 'reformists' in Tehran and 'doves' in Washington that the Afghan crisis might lead to a *rapprochement* between the two countries were frustrated by US President George W. Bush's annual State of the Union address on 29 January 2002, in which he linked Iran with Iraq and the Democratic People's Republic of Korea (North Korea) in what he termed an 'axis of evil'. In the days following the address, Bush's senior aides repeated and expanded the charges against Iran. The US Administration's charges against Iran included involvement in the *Karine A* affair (the seizure by Israeli naval forces in the Red Sea earlier in the month of a freighter alleged to be carrying some 50 metric tons of Iranian-supplied weaponry destined for Palestinians in the Gaza Strip); continued support for the Lebanese Hezbollah and the militant Palestinian groups Hamas and Islamic Jihad; undermining US influence by arming and encouraging local leaders, particularly the warlord Ismail Khan, in western Afghanistan, allowing al-Qa'ida and Taliban fugitives to flee across the border and find sanctuary in Iran; and sustained efforts to acquire nuclear technology and weapons of mass destruction. Iran's riposte was strong: officials questioned why the Palestinians should not seek arms when the Israelis were demolishing their infrastructure and homes with fighter aircraft and missiles; why Israel's nuclear status should be unchallenged when its facilities were, in Iran's view, acquired by highly dubious means and had never been opened to inspection, and when Israel had failed to join the NPT; and why Iran should not take steps to secure its interests in the border regions of Afghanistan, a highly unstable country which has posed a continuing threat to its security. Tehran was particularly aggrieved as even the Bush Administration conceded that Iran had played a constructive role at the conference held during late November and early December 2001 in Bonn, Germany, that had led to the formation of a new interim Afghan administration under Hamid Karzai (Iran had pledged more than US \$500m. to Kabul), and at the fund-raising conference in Tokyo, Japan.

The immediate impact of the US-led military campaign in Afghanistan was to force a closing of ranks across the Iranian political spectrum, as opposing sides united in condemnation of

what they deemed to be US hostility and threats. However, the internal conflict continued. In particular, the 'reformists' complained that Said Emami's parallel intelligence apparatus had been revived (see above). The rallies that took place in Tehran and elsewhere on 11 February 2002 to mark the anniversary of the 1979 Revolution were larger than usual, and popular and political discourse was dominated by the possibility that the Bush Administration's veiled threats against Iran might crystallize into military action, with US forces even targeting the nuclear reactor at Bushehr.

To offset apparent US hostility, Tehran placed renewed emphasis on developing its relations with the EU. European diplomats credited Iran with persuading Ismail Khan, the pre-Taliban Governor of Herat, now reinstated, to support the administration under Hamid Karzai. EU governments refused to fall into line with Washington's stance towards Iran, and the 'institutional dialogue' between Iran and the EU was pursued with a session in Madrid, Spain, on 4–5 February 2002. However, a setback occurred within days, when Iran formally rejected the United Kingdom's nomination of David Reddaway as its new ambassador to Tehran, accusing him of being an agent of the British intelligence service. (The status of Iran's ambassador to Britain was subsequently downgraded to that of chargé d'affaires.) None the less, European states continued to negotiate closer trade and political relations with Iran. In mid-June EU ministers of foreign affairs, meeting in Luxembourg, agreed to initiate negotiations with Iran regarding a trade and co-operation agreement later in 2002, provided that the accord be linked with consideration of political issues, such as human rights and terrorism; the talks were expected to begin in late October. Meanwhile, it was announced in late September that Iran had accepted the United Kingdom's nomination of Richard Dalton (then British ambassador to Libya) as its ambassador to Tehran; he was to take up the post in January 2003.

Iran did, however, take discreet steps aimed at defusing some of the US allegations against the Islamic regime. To counter accusations that al-Qa'ida and Taliban fugitives had found sanctuary in Iran, the authorities made it known in mid-February 2002 that 150 people had been arrested after leaving Afghanistan and crossing illegally into Iran from Pakistan. Most of them were women and children with only 30–40 males of fighting age, these mainly of Arab origin. They were described as sympathizers rather than members of either group, and were handed over to their own embassies for repatriation. Earlier in February Iran also closed down the offices of Gulbuddin Hekmatyar, the *mujahidin* commander who had been involved in the destruction of Kabul in the early 1990s and who had, from his base in north Tehran, directed a barrage of hostile rhetoric towards the USA and the Karzai administration in Afghanistan. At the same time as these conciliatory gestures, Iran made it clear in public declarations that it intended to continue the pursuit of what it considered to be its legitimate national interests in Afghanistan. On 13 August 2002 President Khatami became the first Iranian Head of State to visit Afghanistan for 40 years. Meanwhile, it was reported that Iran had, in June, extradited 16 Saudi citizens believed to be al-Qa'ida militants who had fled the conflict in Afghanistan.

Disagreements persisted both between 'reformists' and 'conservatives' and within both camps over how to respond to the perceived US threat. It was widely believed that the USA was intent on attacking Iraq in order to remove Saddam Hussein from power, and that it would then turn its attention to Iran. In mid-March 2002 Senator Joseph Biden, Jr, Chairman of the US Senate Foreign Relations Committee, made an offer to Iranian legislators to enter into a dialogue aimed at overcoming bilateral tensions. A number of Majlis deputies gave the overture a cautious welcome, and a spokesperson for President Khatami also welcomed the proposal but stated that it was a matter for the deputies themselves. However, Ayatollah Khamenei spoke out against any negotiations with the USA, and within the broad pro-reform movement there were also dissenting voices, notably that of Ali Akbar Mohtashemi, a leading figure in the Society of Combatant Clergy who was alleged to have long-standing connections with the Lebanese Hezbollah. However, Biden himself raised sensitive issues such as Iranian support for Hezbollah, weapons of mass destruction and Iran's opposition to the recently proposed Saudi peace initiative for Israel and the

Palestinian territories, and although a handful of 'reformists' within Iran still favoured talks with the USA, it became clear that the broad Tehran establishment did not.

As 2002 progressed, the perception among Iranians across the political spectrum was increasingly one of threat posed from abroad. US armed forces and their allies had taken over Afghanistan; a similar move against Iraq was apparently only being delayed by the tense situation in Israel and the Palestinian territories; while the pro-Israeli lobby in the USA was constantly campaigning against Iran. A further source of external pressure was added in April when a summit of the five littoral states failed to resolve the legal status of the Caspian Sea. Tehran interpreted the position adopted by Russia and Azerbaijan as reflecting the US desire to step up pressure on Iran, with the implicit threat of outside military intervention in the Caspian region. Iran argued that the Caspian Sea and its resources should preferably be regarded as common property or, failing that, be shared equally among the five littoral states. However, only Turkmenistan shared this view. Russia, Azerbaijan and Kazakhstan believed that ownership of the Caspian should be allocated in proportion to each country's shoreline, which would give Iran just 13%. Iran also feared that the USA might be attempting to reignite its dispute with the UAE over the islands of Abu Musa and the Greater and Lesser Tunbs.

The appropriate response to the US position remained a highly controversial issue within Iran, and in April 2002 the Deputy Foreign Minister for Education and Research, Sadegh Kharrazi, was forced to resign amid rumours of contacts with US officials. In other respects, there were brief signs of a lessening of internal tension. In late April the leader of Nehzat-e Azadi-ye Iran, Ibrahim Yazdi, was allowed to return to Iran and remain at liberty, although a warrant for his arrest remained outstanding. In November 2001 more than 30 members of the proscribed movement had been put on trial, having been charged with acting against national security and plotting to overthrow the Islamic regime. Custodial sentences of up to 10 years were handed down to the activists by the Revolutionary Court in late July 2002 and Nehzat-e Azadi was officially banned. Meanwhile, on 22 April the UN Commission on Human Rights narrowly voted to reject a draft resolution that included Iran among a group of countries criticized for human rights violations. In mid-April the death of the veteran 'liberal', Yadullah Sahabi, produced many statements of respect from 'conservatives', including a warm homily from Ayatollah Khamenei.

Nevertheless, there was a renewed clamp-down on the pro-reform movement by the judiciary in May 2002, with the closure ordered in that month of two 'liberal' newspapers. Moreover, the debate surrounding the future of relations with the USA continued acrimoniously, and in late May the Tehran judiciary issued a warning to newspapers that the publication of any material favouring the idea of negotiations with US officials would be deemed a criminal offence. President Khatami, in an address to the Majlis, also asked 'reformist' deputies not to

attempt to hold talks with US officials. Shortly beforehand the US Department of State had once again designated Iran as the world's 'most active' sponsor of terrorism, and US Secretary of Defense Donald Rumsfeld persistently maintained that he had information that Iran was sheltering al-Qa'ida fighters who had fled Afghanistan, although he declined to publish this evidence. Washington also reiterated its claims that Iran was building nuclear missiles with Russian assistance.

During mid-2002 US President Bush again sought to persuade his Russian counterpart, Vladimir Putin, to cease the transfer of Russian nuclear knowledge and technology to Iran by ending its involvement with the power plant at Bushehr. In late July Russian officials angered the US Administration by signing a draft development and co-operation accord with Iran, which was reported to include the construction of three more nuclear reactors at the Bushehr plant. Iran did, nevertheless, accept an offer of humanitarian aid from the USA following a major earthquake in the north-west of the country in late June 2002. However, the deterioration in Iranian–US relations was evident when, towards the end of July, President Khatami openly condemned US plans to use military force to bring about 'regime change' in Iraq, warning that such action posed a serious risk to regional stability. It was reported at the end of the month that Iran had placed its armed forces and Revolutionary Guards on alert in preparation for any US military action.

The crack-down against Iranian 'liberals' appeared to be intensified in July 2002. The authorities declared a ban on any rallies and protests organized to commemorate the third anniversary of the violent clashes that had occurred between students and the security forces in 1999. However, several hundred protesters were reported to have defied the ban in Tehran, resulting in sporadic clashes between protesters demanding political reform on the one side and security forces and 'right-wing' elements on the other. A prominent 'reformist' cleric in Esfahan, Ayatollah Jalaleddin Taheri, announced his resignation the following day, launching a strong attack against the 'conservative' religious establishment, citing its poor management of the country, corruption, and its failure to meet the expectations of the people. On 17 July 2002, during its annual conference, the 'left-wing' Participation Front threatened to withdraw its co-operation with the Government and Majlis if 'hardliners' continued to block social and political reforms. In late July Mohsen Mirdamadi, a Majlis deputy and publisher of the Participation Front's *Norouz*, Iran's main pro-reform newspaper, was given a six-month gaol term for propagandizing against the Islamic regime; Mirdamadi was also fined and banned from involvement in press activities for four years, and his publication was closed down for six months. More than 30 other 'reformists' were also imprisoned during that month.

On 12 June 2002 Mahdi Karrubi was re-elected as Speaker of the Majlis for another 12 months. Behzad Nabavi became the First Deputy Speaker of the assembly, replacing Muhammad Reza Khatami, who assumed Nabavi's previous role as Second Deputy Speaker.

Economy

ALAN J. DAY

Traditionally an agricultural country, Iran has benefited from the exploitation of its large oil and gas reserves, exports of which have been its major source of revenue since the Second World War. Under successive five-year plans since 1947, oil revenues have been used to finance balanced economic development, including non-oil industrialization and the maintenance of a substantial agricultural sector. The Islamic Revolution of 1979 represented a major watershed, not only politically but also economically. The new regime declared its determination to end Iran's large degree of dependence on the West, the resultant dislocation being compounded by the 1980–88 war with Iraq. Since that conflict, efforts to resume broad economic development and diversification have been hindered by volatile world oil prices, by internal structural weaknesses and rampant

inflation, and by persistent political tensions with the West, especially the USA. Although the oil sector has accounted for a diminishing share of gross domestic product (GDP) in recent years, the Government remains heavily dependent on oil revenues in its quest to improve the living standards of Iran's large population.

At the census of November 1966 the population of Iran was recorded as 25,788,722. Of this total, about 9.8m. were urban residents. The November 1976 census enumerated a total population of 33,708,744, and the October 1986 census recorded 49,445,010 inhabitants (including 2.6m. refugees), of whom 26,844,561 resided in urban areas, an increase of 70% since 1976. In early 1992 the Statistical Centre of Iran reported that the population had increased by almost 40% since 1979, to more than 58m. The rate of growth in urban areas was twice that recorded in rural areas. The population of Tehran was reported to have more than doubled since the late 1970s, exceeding 10m. According to the 1996 census, the population of Iran (in October of that year) was 60,055,488, of whom 61.3% were urban dwellers. Iran's average annual population growth rate decreased from 2.5% during 1986–92 to 1.5% during 1992–97. The population increased at an average annual rate of 1.6% in 1990–2000. The population was officially estimated at 64,528,162 at mid-2001. It was estimated that by 2025 some three-quarters of Iran's population would be living in cities. Much of the Iranian population is concentrated in the fertile northern areas of the country, while the central desert lands are sparsely populated.

Major refugee influxes in the 1980s included the arrival of up to 3m. Afghans and over 1m. Iraqi Kurds and Shi'as. According to the office of the UN High Commissioner for Refugees, Iran's registered refugee population at the end of 2000 numbered 1,868,000, of whom 1,482,000 were from Afghanistan and 386,000 were from Iraq. A further influx from Afghanistan in late 2001, as a result of the US-led military intervention (see History), boosted the number of registered Afghan refugees in Iran to some 2,350,000, with several hundred thousand remaining unregistered. However, the fall of the Taliban regime in Kabul in December resulted in the drafting of a UN programme of assisted repatriation of Afghanis from Iran.

Government officials have cited Iran's expanding population as a major constraint on economic development. In July 1992 the head of the Population and Family Planning Department of the Ministry of Health stated that if the population continued to grow at a rapid rate, 600,000 new jobs would have to be created each year, and 40,000 classrooms and 500,000 houses constructed. The country's farmers would not be able to meet the demand for food and half the population would face starvation. Unemployment in 1991 was officially estimated at about 11% of the labour force, although other sources had suggested as recently as the previous year that the rate of unemployment might in fact be as high as 20%. Only 2.2m. new jobs were created between 1980 and 1990: an inadequate total, in view of the rising demand for employment. According to official sources, unemployment at the end of the 1996/97 Iranian year (running from 21 March to 20 March) had fallen to 9.1%, compared with 10.0% a year earlier. According to preliminary data for 1997–98, however, unemployment increased to 13.1% in that year. The size of the nomadic population, estimated at 248,463 in October 1986, has declined dramatically since the 1940s (it was estimated to be 641,937 at the 1966 census), as a result of government settlement programmes.

In 1978, the last year of the Shah's reign, per caput income was calculated at about US $2,500, up from about $200 in 1963. During the period of the Fourth Development Plan (1968–73), Iran's gross national product (GNP) rose at an annual average of 11.2% in real terms. Over the period of the 1973–78 Plan, GNP rose in real terms from $17,000m. to $55,300m. The growth rate of GNP, which was as much as 41% in 1974/75, slowed to about 17% in the following year, owing to declining revenues from petroleum (which provided about 40% of the total GNP). In real terms, GDP was estimated to have grown by as little as 2.6% in 1975/76. In 1976/77 GDP grew at over 14% in real terms, but during 1977 the economy showed signs of further deceleration. Total GDP for 1977/78 was estimated at $56,500m., representing growth in real terms of about 10% over the previous year.

The revolutionary Government that followed the Shah's downfall reassessed nearly all of Iran's economic and social strategies. The new leaders announced that priority would be given to low growth rates, a concentration on small-scale projects in industry, emphasis on traditional agriculture and stringent control of petroleum exports. Three years after the Revolution, however, Iran's economy was in deep crisis. The war with Iraq, loss of forecast petroleum revenues in mid-1980 as the world went into economic recession, and the failure of public utilities (mainly electricity) were among the problems advanced to account for a deteriorating economic situation. The war had indeed taken its toll of physical damage to infrastructure in the south. However, political conflicts and confusion over the management of the economy aggravated these problems and resulted in contradictions in policy and economic mismanagement.

In early 1981 President Bani-Sadr reported that agricultural output remained static, industrial production had declined dramatically and even the minimum petroleum output that Iran required for national survival was not being attained. The disappointing performance of the major economic sectors had resulted in declines in real GDP of 13% in 1979/80 and 10% in 1980/81, and in a further fall in 1981/82. At the same time, Ayatollah Khomeini warned Iranians that there would be 10 years of austerity ahead before the country became productive enough to fulfil its needs from domestic sources.

Some real growth in the economy did take place as a result of developments in the construction sector and some expansion in industrial output. However, as both were at low base levels, real gains were small. In reality it was the petroleum sector which was responsible for the improvement in the country's economic prospects in 1982 and 1983. An increase in sales of crude petroleum during 1982, by means of discounts and special incentives to purchasers, resulted in rising revenues, which, in turn, stimulated economic activity. The Iranian economy remained petroleum-based, and the pattern of growth reflected the performance of that sector. The oil sector fared badly in 1984, with production down by 13% in a deteriorating market oversupplied with oil and subject to falling world prices. Production costs have always been higher for Iran than for its regional competitors, and the situation was aggravated by the escalation of the conflict with Iraq, with the consequent rise in the costs of insurance, storage and transport. As a result of the continuing decline in international prices for crude petroleum, government income was seriously reduced during 1986, and income from oil exports totalled US $6,600m. in 1986/87, according to OPEC. This downward trend was halted in early 1987, when the volume of exports of oil increased and prices rose. In 1987/88 the value of oil exports was estimated at $8,000m.–$9,000m., with a further $1,100m. in earnings from rising non-oil exports.

From September 1980 until the August 1988 cease-fire, the war with Iraq dominated all economic and political life in Iran. War needs dictated planning priorities, distorting the economy and forcing long-term objectives to be sacrificed to expediency. It has been estimated that annual expenditure of foreign exchange on the war was US $5,000m.–$9,000m. After the announcement of the cease-fire, attempts were made to assess the extent of the damage inflicted on the Iranian economy during the war and widely diverging figures were quoted for the cost of reconstruction. The cost of repairing industrial plant alone was estimated at $40,000m. Positive leadership often appeared to be lacking, resulting in the inability or unwillingness to resolve fundamental issues of principle. One crucial issue affecting the economy after the Revolution was disagreement over the degree of government involvement in business. After 1981 the Government appeared to favour an increase in state control, particularly the nationalization of foreign trade. However, 'conservative' religious leaders, businessmen, the Council of Guardians (which ensures that legislation conforms with Islamic precepts) and many members of the Majlis (Consultative Assembly) maintained that the Government should play a minimal role. Although new appointments to the Council of Ministers and the changing character of the Majlis strengthened those elements in government favouring more control of the economy by the state (in particular more land reform, nationalization of trade and the spread of collective organization among the industrial work-force), the 'conservative' elements in government (in particular the Council of Guardians) succeeded in delaying radical reform. In a vigorous press campaign at the end of 1985 the radicals alleged that the courts were overturning revolutionary measures and allowing expropriated industries to be returned to their former owners. In January 1988 Ayatollah Khomeini decreed that government policies could overrule Islamic law where this was in the interest of the state. In the following month a 13-member Council to Determine the Expediency of the Islamic Order was appointed to settle disputes by majority vote whenever the Majlis and the Council of Guardians could not agree on the direction of policy. However, despite the strength of the radicals in the third Majlis, the Committee proceeded cautiously, seeking to maintain a consensus between 'conservatives' and radicals.

In the agricultural sector, the problem of rights of ownership has affected about 1.2m. ha, or one-quarter of Iran's prime cultivable land, since the Revolution, and government plans for land reform were consistently obstructed by the Council of Guardians, making long-term planning difficult. As a result, the technocrats in government have concentrated on industry and other areas of the economy where quick results were easier to obtain. In February 1989 the Minister of Oil, Gholamreza Aqazadeh, announced the end of a six-month debate concerning the future structure of the Iranian economy. The Council of Ministers had decided, he reported, to approve a limited number of foreign loans for infrastructural schemes, and to encourage private enterprise. In May the Minister of Planning and Budget, Massoud Roghani Zanjani, outlined the Government's plans for the economy over the next five years, confirming that they included 'privatization' of non-strategic state-owned industries. It was also revealed that Ayatollah Khomeini had approved foreign borrowing to finance major projects if it did not result in political dependence. Foreign-financed projects should lead to savings in convertible currency or generate new revenue in convertible currency. These objectives were enshrined in a new Five-Year Development Plan, which ran from March 1990. The new Plan, together with the announcement of the annual budget in that month, strengthened economic activity, resulting in increased imports of raw materials, equipment and spares.

As a consequence of Iraq's invasion of Kuwait in August 1990, Iran's economic prospects briefly improved. According to official sources, earnings from exports of petroleum rose to US $18,400m. in 1990–91 as a result of an increase in volume and price triggered by the conflict over Kuwait. With his leadership strengthened, President Rafsanjani took advantage of extra oil revenues to accelerate the implementation of economic reforms which resulted in the rapid dismantling of the state-controlled economy created during the years of war with Iraq. The private sector expanded and came to play a significant role in trade and investment. Imports by the private sector rose, non-petroleum exports doubled and there was considerable investment in housing construction and industry after the deregulation of price and trade controls. However, his reforms to revive the economy caused widespread hardship and contributed to the riots and urban unrest in mid-1992. Moreover, the economy remained excessively dependent on oil, while bureaucratic inefficiency and a serious shortage of skilled workers and managers continued to obstruct the realization of optimistic aims.

At the start of his second term of office in August 1993, President Rafsanjani vowed to proceed with economic reforms so that Iran would no longer be dependent on other countries for their markets and products. He claimed that during his first term of office (1989–93) the old state economy had been transformed, production had increased and unemployment had fallen from 16% to 10%–11%. Outlining his policies for the next four years to the Majlis, Rafsanjani declared that his Government would not embark on adventures abroad but would concentrate on reforming and rebuilding the economy. He stressed that costly state subsidies had to be reduced, but promised that this would be done gradually so as not to disrupt people's lives. In the Majlis and in the press, however, there was strong criticism of the Government for mishandling the economy and allowing the country to accumulate more than US $20,000m. in external debts, mainly as a result of falling oil revenues.

In response to these criticisms, in August 1993 Bank Markazi (central bank) relaxed some import restrictions to ease pressures on industry and consumers. However, Rafsanjani rejected calls in the Majlis to postpone the second Five-Year Plan until 1996 because of the economic crisis. The President presented the plan document to the Majlis on 21 December and sought approval for higher spending based on increased domestic revenues. The day before Ayatollah Khamenei had announced new guide-lines for economic and social planning, urging a reduction in the country's dependence on foreign finance and special efforts to settle outstanding obligations. He also urged caution in privatizing state enterprises and emphasized that privatization should promote economic development and conform with the Constitution of the Islamic Republic. He stressed that social equity should be central to the Government's development policy. Deprived regions should receive more attention and development policies should benefit those who had worked hard

for the Revolution. Priority should be given to promoting domestic production, particularly agriculture, in order to satisfy people's basic needs. Imports of consumer goods should be reduced and non-oil exports increased. Corruption should be eliminated and waste and extravagance discouraged. At the same time, Khamenei gave his support to the President and attempted to underplay the scale of the country's economic problems.

In early January 1994 Rafsanjani declared that the Iranian economy was no longer totally dependent on oil revenues and could survive even if oil exports were completely cut off; falling oil prices would not hurt Iran as much as other oil exporters. He pointed to Iran's success in increasing its non-oil exports, which he estimated would earn US $5,000m. in 1993/94, nearly one-third of total hard currency revenues. In contrast, Mohammad Reza Bahonar, a member of the Majlis economy and finance committee, argued that Iran must free itself from its dependence on oil revenues during the next few years because low oil prices and a rapidly growing population had resulted in a fall in per caput oil income to about $15 a month. Rafsanjani also repeated accusations made by other Iranian officials that the 30% fall in oil prices during 1993 had been orchestrated by hostile countries, principally the USA, because they were alarmed by Iran's economic recovery. Later in the year Khamenei accused Saudi Arabia of helping 'international thieves' to keep oil prices low. In March 1994 the Majlis reduced projected revenue and expenditure before approving the Government's 1994/95 budget because of concern over low oil prices and the high level of foreign debt. Announcing the decision, Ali Akbar Nateq Nouri, the Speaker of the Majlis, stated that economic reforms, including the reduction of subsidies, should be slowed down to protect the vulnerable strata of society. Yet despite opposition from within the Majlis, in April Rafsanjani renewed his attack on some state subsidies which he stated cost the country $15,000m. every year. He declared that energy subsidies alone cost $11,000m. per year, more than projected oil revenues for 1994/95. He argued that subsidies for agriculture and for assisting the families of those killed during the Revolution and the war with Iraq were justified, whereas bread subsidies for the general population and energy subsidies were unjust and should be eliminated. This programme was a matter of urgency because subsidies were preventing the country's economic recovery. After the failure of an attempt within the Majlis in May to remove control over price-setting from the Government, Rafsanjani appeared to compromise and promised that subsidy reforms would be introduced gradually. Nothing would be done until the new Five-Year Development Plan was ready because subsidy cuts directly affected the people's standard of living and could cause resentment against the Government. By the end of 1994 Bank Markazi had successfully rescheduled almost $10,000m. in short-term foreign debts into medium-term obligations. By the early months of 1995 official and private reschedulings were reported to have reached $14,000m., marking the end of the immediate debt crisis which had destroyed the country's creditworthiness. Most of the rescheduling agreements provided Iran with a two-year grace period, with repayments deferred until 1996. Nevertheless, Iran faced an annual foreign debt-servicing burden of between $4,000m. and $5,000m. until the end of the century, which could only aggravate the side-effects of the Government's reform programme. Despite opposition from the USA, Switzerland and Germany began once again to offer insurance cover for exports to Iran in the early part of 1995. However, poor relations with the West continued to accentuate Iran's economic difficulties. In May 1995 the USA imposed a near-total trade embargo on Iran, with the aim of crippling the country's economy, and urged other Western nations to follow its example. The embargo affected primarily the oil industry. US oil companies had purchased nearly a quarter of Iran's crude oil output in 1994. However, in June 1995 oil traders reported that Iran appeared to have experienced no difficulty finding alternative markets for the oil previously sold to US companies.

At the sectoral level, agriculture finally appeared to have experienced a revival by the mid-1990s after decades of decline, achieving higher farm output and greater efficiency. The Ministry of Agriculture even predicted that Iran would become a net exporter of foodstuffs by the turn of the century. Moreover, the gap between farmers' income and that of average city-dwellers closed considerably. Industry has proved more difficult to reform, with low rates of capacity utilization persisting in some branches, especially the state-owned heavy industries. The restructuring of ailing industries has experienced problems, but the Government remains committed to removing most state subsidies. Privatization plans were delayed in mid-1994, when the Majlis approved legislation giving certain groups privileged access to shares in companies being sold off. Nevertheless, in early 1995 the Minister of Industries declared that by 2000 only 10% of Iranian industry would be state-owned, compared with 45% in 1990, and that ultimately only very large industries would remain under state control. Plans to attract foreign investment in Iranian industry met with little success despite amendments to the foreign investment law. In his new year message on 21 March 1995, President Rafsanjani promised that Iran would become self-sufficient by the turn of the century and would not have to depend on foreign assistance to run the economy. He stated that reconstruction would be accelerated under the second Five-Year Plan, ending in March 2000, because the country was now less reliant on imported materials.

For ordinary Iranians rapid price rises resulting, in part, from cuts in state subsidies have been the main concern. As the Government has attempted to restructure the economy, life for the average Iranian has become harder, provoking widespread dissatisfaction. At the beginning of April 1995 the first mass protests against the Government's economic policies erupted as rioting took place in the working-class suburb of Eslamshahr, close to Tehran. Demands for better water supplies escalated into a wider protest against the doubling of fuel prices introduced in March as part of the new Five-Year Plan. Less than a year before, President Rafsanjani had promised that cuts in fuel subsidies would be introduced gradually. The police quickly restored order, but the demonstrations were regarded by some observers as a warning to the Government that there could be further trouble if economic conditions continued to deteriorate.

In December 1995 the World Bank released an economic memorandum on Iran in which it concluded that substantial progress had been made in macroeconomic stabilization and in implementing structural reforms over the past six years and pointed to a dramatic improvement in social indicators since the mid-1980s. However, both the World Bank and the IMF advised the Government that it would achieve a higher rate of economic growth and more success in reducing inflation if it adopted more ambitious stabilization and structural reform policies, given the extent of macroeconomic imbalances, distortions in resource allocation, and the external environment. They urged the Government to speed up the programme of economic reforms, and to improve resource mobilization and the quality of management. In discussions with the IMF, Bank Markazi officials emphasized that they were giving top priority to repaying the country's foreign debts on time, reducing inflation and strengthening the bank's external reserves. However, they insisted that the objectives of the second Five-Year Plan could be achieved by following a gradualist approach to stabilization and structural reform.

In January 1996, during the approach to legislative elections, a group of senior officials, including the Governor of Bank Markazi, Mohsen Nourbakhsh, and the Mayor of Tehran, Gholamhossein Karbaschi, all close allies of President Rafsanjani, issued a statement urging voters to support the President's tough economic policies. They argued that the main threat facing the country was not from external pressures, but from internal economic problems. Iranians should direct their efforts towards strengthening the country's economic policies and social structures. Economic issues dominated campaigning prior to the first round of voting on 8 March, with the pro-Rafsanjani modernizers of the newly-formed Servants of Iran's Construction challenging the 'conservative' Society of Combatant Clergy, which had used its predominance in the previous Majlis to slow down the President's economic reform programme. After the first round of voting both groups claimed victory, although some Iranian newspapers proclaimed that candidates of the Servants of Iran's Construction would dominate the new Majlis. Following the second round of voting, in April, it emerged that the Society of Combatant Clergy had lost overall control but remained the largest single group.

On the eve of the second round of voting in the legislative elections, Bank Markazi declared that the economy had improved significantly as a result of the Government's successful strategy to restore financial credibility. The Government's budget proposals for 1996/97 foresaw high expenditure of hard currency, but central bank officials stressed that the country would still meet all of its debt repayments.

At the beginning of August 1996 the US Administration ceded to pressure from the Republican-dominated US Congress and President Bill Clinton signed legislation (commonly known as the Iran-Libya Sanctions Act—ILSA) imposing penalties on non-US companies investing in oil and gas projects in Iran (see Petroleum, below). He described Iran as one of the most dangerous supporters of terrorism in the world. The US trade embargo imposed in June 1995 had had little effect on Iranian oil exports, and most observers maintained that the new sanctions were unlikely to damage the country's export capacity. Despite US pressure and the threat of legislation imposing a secondary boycott on Iran, several European oil companies continued with their investment programmes in the oil and gas sectors during the first half of 1996 and agreements on a number of important new finance lines were reached with European and Japanese banks. However, some analysts argued that the effect of the new sanctions would be indirect and psychological, and might undermine business confidence and make it more difficult for the Government to carry out its economic reforms. In April 1997, moreover, all governments of the European Union (EU) except Greece suspended 'critical dialogue' with Iran after a German court implicated the Iranian leadership in the assassination of Iranian Kurdish dissidents in Berlin in 1992.

Between the Majlis elections in early 1996 and the presidential elections in mid-1997 there were few new economic policy initiatives, and the Government concentrated on restoring economic confidence in Iran and ensuring repayments of the country's foreign debt. Higher oil prices during most of 1996 and the early months of 1997 enabled Bank Markazi to meet annual foreign debt repayments of some US $5,000m., and allowed a modest increase in the value of imports which had been reduced since 1994.

The IMF acknowledged Iran's achievements in curbing inflation (by nearly 50% in 1996/97), reducing the external debt and meeting foreign debt payments, and registering GDP growth of 4.7% in 1996/97 (against an average of 3.8% per year over the previous four years), with growth in the non-oil sector increasing to 5.3%. Nevertheless, the Fund warned that the reimposition of strict foreign-exchange controls in 1995, while reducing inflation, had damaged non-oil exports. It also warned that the slow pace of economic restructuring meant that large sectors of the economy continued to be dependent on state subsidies, with subsequent market distortion and inefficiency.

The victory of the pro-reform Sayed Muhammad Khatami in the May 1997 presidential election heralded a more determined pursuit of economic restructuring, deregulation and liberalization. Improved relations with the EU persuaded the latter's ministers responsible for foreign affairs in February 1998 to rescind the ban on ministerial contacts with Iran, although there was no resumption of the previous 'critical dialogue' between the two sides. In the following month the Iranian Government announced that almost all aspects of oil and gas development would be made available to foreign investors, including onshore projects, which had been excluded from the previous opening to foreign investors in 1988. In the same month Khatami advocated a fundamental reform of Iran's economy, citing major income disparities, a preference for speculation over production, and over-dependence on oil exports as the key weaknesses. However, options for reform were reduced by a sharp fall in world oil prices from late 1997, which necessitated at least two revisions of the 1998/99 budget, as originally presented, to account for expectations of much lower oil revenue.

The further opening of the oil and gas industry to foreign investment was expedited by a US decision in mid-May 1998 not to seek to apply the 1996 ILSA 'secondary' sanctions act against the EU and some other states in respect of investment in Iran. A list of 42 projects for which foreign tenders were invited was officially published at a London conference in early July; it was forecast that total investment of some US $8,000m. would be attracted from European and other sources (although not from US companies, which remained prohibited from investing in Iran under the sanctions act).

With the economy so dependent on unpredictable oil revenue, the downturn in prices in 1998 and early 1999 had a severe effect on Iran. Although GDP had expanded by 5% in 1996/97 and by 3.2% in 1997/98, growth in 1998/99 was officially put at only 1.6% and the trade balance and the current account went into deficit. However, sharply rising oil prices from April 1999 brought an economic upturn, featuring GDP growth of 2.5% in 1999/2000 and 4.5% in 2000/01, in which year record oil revenue underpinned a return to trade and current-account surpluses. Official statistics for 2000/01 also showed the rates of inflation (12.6%) and unemployment (12.7%) to be at their lowest levels for some years. The new Five-Year Plan beginning in March 2000 (see Budget, Investment and Finance) reaffirmed the Khatami Government's commitment to privatization and liberalization, while the victory of the 'reformists' in the February 2000 Majlis elections strengthened the prospects not only of domestic economic reform but also of the rebuilding of links with the West. Although US sanctions on participation in the Iranian oil industry were renewed in March 2000, trade restrictions were relaxed for a number of non-oil items, amid rising expectations of an eventual normalization of US-Iranian economic relations. The US oil industry sanctions were again renewed in March 2001, but became increasingly difficult to justify on political grounds after President Khatami's re-election in June. While the powerful pro-Israeli lobby in the US Congress urged the renewal of ILSA for five years on expiry of the current legislation in August 2001, the Bush Administration argued for a shortened renewal period of two years. The US sanctions were extended for five years in early August, but with the option of a presidential review in 2003.

President Khatami began his second term of office in August 2001 by appointing a new Minister of Economic Affairs and Finance, Tahmasb Mazaheri, reputed to be more in favour of liberalization and privatization than his predecessor. The Government had the advantage of a continued strong inflow of oil export earnings: despite the global economic downturn caused by the September suicide attacks in the USA, rising tensions in the Middle East and cuts in OPEC production kept oil prices high. Against this background, Iranian petroleum revenues remained buoyant, supplemented by growing non-oil exports, and were the main factor boosting real GDP growth to 5.9% in the 2001/02 financial year, during which inflation increased slightly, to 14%, and the official rate of unemployment rose to 15% (and unofficially to as much as 25%). The Khatami Government was therefore able to project further GDP growth of 5.5%–6% in 2002/03 as well as strong trade and current-account surpluses, while inflation was expected to remain at 14% and official unemployment at 15%. In its budget for 2002/03 the Government also took the significant step of introducing a unified quasi-market exchange rate for the rial against the US dollar, thus ending the effective subsidizing of imports of basic commodities. However, this success for the 'reformers' was offset by the refusal of the 'conservative' Council of Guardians in December 2001 to endorse government legislation aimed at encouraging foreign investment by guaranteeing the repatriation of profits (although a modified law was approved in mid-2002—see Budget, Investment and Finance).

In late June 2002 north-western Iran was hit by a serious earthquake, resulting in the deaths of about 230 people and the destruction of at least 100 villages. The disaster led to renewed calls for the Government to construct more housing for Iran's rapidly growing population. Later in the year it was announced that the World Bank was to assist the Ministry of Housing and Urban Development with a large-scale project involving the construction of affordable housing for low- and middle-income families.

AGRICULTURE AND FISHING

Of a total surface area of 165m. ha, the 1988 agricultural census reported, there were 56m. ha of cultivable farm land, of which 16.8m. ha were actually being cultivated. Cultivated land has since risen to 18.5m. ha., of which about one-half is dry-farmed, while rain-fed agriculture is important in the western provinces of Kermanshah, Kurdistan and Azerbaijan. Irrigated areas are fed from modern water-storage systems or from the ancient

system of *qanat* (underground water channels), although these have fallen into disrepair in recent years. In 1986 Iran had 17 operational dams which provided irrigation for 871,200 ha of land. By 1996 a further 49 dams were under construction, the aim being to increase utilization of water resources from 70,000m. cu m to 110,000m. cu m by 2000.

The traditional dominance of agriculture was eroded by post-1945 oil and gas exploitation, which became the country's major source of export revenues as population growth obliged Iran to become a net importer of foodstuffs. The agricultural sector has nevertheless usually been the largest contributor to GDP, its share falling only slightly in the 1990s, from 23.9% in 1992/93 to 20.2% in 1996/97, when it was narrowly overtaken by the industrial sector; agriculture contributed an estimated 12.8% of GDP in 2000/01. An objective of the Second Five-Year Development Plan (SFYDP) was to encourage food self-sufficiency and transform Iran into a net exporter of agricultural produce. However, the latter aim remained unfulfilled half-way through the plan period, the value of agricultural exports decreasing to just US $5m. in 1995/96, after increasing dramatically to $90m. in 1994/95. The chief factors limiting the size of agricultural production are: inadequate communications, which limits access to markets; poor seeds, implements and techniques of cultivation; scarcity of water and under-capitalization, chiefly the result of the low incomes of peasant households. About four-fifths of all farms have an area of less than 11 ha. Iran was self-sufficient in foodstuffs until the late 1960s but then began importing vast quantities, owing to the failure of agricultural output to keep pace with increasing domestic consumption and the failure of the Government to produce a sound agricultural policy. Natural disasters have also taken their toll. Early in 1992 nearly 5% of cultivated land, mostly in the north of the country, was damaged by floods.

A large variety of crops are cultivated in the diverse climatic regions of Iran. Grains are the chief crops, including wheat (the major staple), barley and rice. According to the 1988 agricultural census, the area sown to wheat rose to 5.3m. ha during the previous six years, while the average yield per hectare reached 1,082 kg. Under the First Five-Year Development Plan (FFYDP—introduced in January 1990), it was aimed to increase wheat production to 11m. metric tons per year by 1995. In 1991 Iran's Deputy Minister of Agriculture declared that wheat yields would rise significantly, from 1.96 tons per hectare to 3.2 tons per hectare, through the expansion of irrigation; and that by 1993 wheat production would reach 12.5m. tons, making self-sufficiency possible. However, the use of scarce water resources for the cultivation of cereals rather than of crops that would give higher yields has been questioned. Moreover, given the current trend away from wheat cultivation to more profitable cash crops, expectations regarding the achievement of self-sufficiency appear to be misplaced. According to FAO, Iranian production rose from a low of 5.79m. tons in the drought year 1989 to 7m. tons in 1990. Production was estimated at 8.9m. tons in 1991. The 1992 wheat harvest totalled 10.2m. tons, 17% more than forecast in the Plan. The Ministry of Agriculture stated that production would meet 80% of domestic requirements and that 2.5m. tons only would be imported. Under the SFYDP, which began in March 1995, annual wheat production was projected to rise by 40% to 14m. tons. According to official sources, wheat production in 1996/97 decreased to 10.0m. tons from an area of 6.3m. ha. Output remained at this level in 1997/98, but recovered to 11.9m. tons in 1998/99. Barley production reached 2.6m. tons in 1989, while the yield per hectare was 1,040 kg; production was estimated at 3.6m. tons in 1991, but fell to 2.5m. tons in 1997/98 from an area of 1.5m. ha. Output in 1998/99 was 3.3m. tons. In 1988 rice production rose to more than 1.5m. tons, although the yield per hectare improved only slightly, to 2,700 kg. After falling to 1.2m. tons in 1989, rice production rose to 1.7m. tons in 1990, declining, however, to 1.4m. tons in 1991. Production rose again, to 2.4m. tons, in 1992, falling to 2.3m. tons in 1993 but thereafter rising steadily to 2.7m. tons in 1996/97, from an area of 600,000 ha. Output was 2.4m. tons, from 563,000 ha, in 1997/98. Some farmers are reported to have shifted from grain cultivation to more profitable poultry farming and in the early 1990s, as milk prices rose, to dairy farming and commercial milk production. Between 1982 and 1988 the area sown with sugar beet declined by 65,000 ha, to 131,890 ha, but annual production remained steady at 3.4m. tons. Production was estimated at 3.4m. tons again in 1989. In 1991/92 sugar beet production rose to 5m. tons, 1.4m. tons more than in the previous year, according to the Ministry of Agriculture. Sugar beet provides 50% of Iran's sugar requirements. Production of sugar beet reached 5.5m. tons in 1995/96 (from 203,000 ha), but fell sharply in 1996/97, to 3.7m. tons from a much reduced area of 149,000 ha, before recovering to 4.8 m. tons (191,000 ha) in 1997/98. Output of cotton was 523,000 tons in 1995/96 and increased to 598,000 tons in 1996/97, from an area of 320,000 ha. in the latter year, but declined to 451,000 tons (238,000 ha) in 1997/98. Output of potatoes declined from 2.3m. tons in 1987 to an estimated 1.4m. tons in 1989, while the planted area remained almost the same, at 77,000 ha but increased sharply, reaching 3.3m. tons in 1996/97, from an area of 158,000 ha. Also of commercial importance is production of green tea (309,000 tons in 1997/98), oil seeds (267,000 tons), tobacco (24,000 tons), onions (1.2m. tons), dates (860,000 tons) and pistachio nuts (112,000 tons). Iran's status as the world's largest producer and exporter of pistachio nuts was jeopardized in September 1997 by an EU prohibition of imports from Iran after toxic substances had been found in some consignments. However, the ban was revoked in December after the Iranian industry (employing some 300,000 people) had given quality assurances. Iranian exports of pistachio nuts to EU countries declined to 40,000 tons in 1997 (from 84,000 tons in 1996).

Despite the early social and political benefits of land reform, which the Shah had vigorously pursued in the 1960s and 1970s, agriculture in general suffered under the Shah, to the point where it became one of the principal issues raised against him by his opponents. Typical of the Shah's grandiose projects were four joint ventures set up with foreign companies in 1970 on over 60,000 ha of land in Khuzestan, in the south-west, involving the removal of some 6,500 peasant families. Despite massive injections of funds, these projects began to collapse within a few years owing to inadequate planning, a lack of skilled manpower and delays in irrigation schemes. By the time of the Revolution the projects were in the process of being wound up.

Having made such an issue of agriculture in the political battle against the Shah, the victorious revolutionaries made its revival one of their priorities. Self-sufficiency in foodstuffs, above all else, became central to their economic philosophy, but the authorities have acknowledged that, unlike the former regime, they do not have the money to extend the cultivated area through building dams and irrigation schemes. Instead of spending capital, the Government has emphasized the intensification of agriculture, i.e. the improvement of farming on existing lands. To this end, the Government increased support prices for grains and other crops. The biggest subsidies have gone to wheat, the country's most important crop. The Government increased its support to IR 53 (US $0.74) per kg, compared with the pre-Revolution price of IR 18 per kg. Since March 1983 the Government has been providing further subsidies in kind as well as giving tax exemption for 10 years to all farmers who follow official guide-lines. For each metric ton of wheat produced, the Government offers 100 kg of fertilizer, four kg of cube sugar, and one kg of tea. Farmers have also been told that they can pay for a tractor at cost price in wheat delivered to the local grains and cereals organization. Subsidies, though less generous, have been introduced for rice and other grains. However, many farmers can sell their wheat on the unofficial market for as much as IR 60–IR 70 ($0.65–$0.75). It has been estimated that the government agencies purchase less than 15% of Iran's total wheat production. Towards the end of 1991 the Government announced that it had purchased 1.82m. tons of wheat in the current farming year, and declared its intention to purchase 20% more wheat from farmers the following season in order to encourage the cultivation of the crop after the high production and modest prices of the previous season. In early 1994 President Rafsanjani stated that the $350m. spent on subsidizing the agricultural sector were justified and should be maintained. Rural projects, such as the building of schools, mosques, public baths, silos, roads and irrigation networks and the extension of electricity to villages, were undertaken by the Ministry of Construction Jihad, which combined the roles of three agencies of the Shah's 'White Revolution', the Literacy, Health and Agric-

ultural Extension corps. It was constituted as a Ministry at the end of 1983, and in July 1984 announced a plan to commit 1m. ha to dry farming. Delays in implementing these projects have added to rural insecurity and are an additional cause of rural-to-urban migration.

The Ministry of Construction Jihad and the Ministry of Agriculture were known to hold conflicting views on almost every aspect of policy, with the Ministry of Construction Jihad strongly in favour of more extensive land reform. Proposals for the merger of the two Ministries in 1987 encountered resistance inside both organizations. While the Ministry of Agriculture favoured an essentially advisory and technical role in the agricultural sector, the Jihad promoted the creation of collective farming organizations and a reduction in the role of the private landowner. Although the Jihad had achieved spectacular success in some villages, fears were expressed that an extension of its authority could impede production, with ideological factors taking precedence over sound farm management. The merger of the two ministries finally proceeded at the end of 2000.

Short-term credit to farmers has been greatly increased. In the last year of the old regime the Agricultural Bank lent some US $600m.; in 1982/83 it lent $11,900m., and in 1983/84 $2,300m. In spite of expanded credit facilities, farmers have been reluctant to start long-term, high-value cultivation of perennial crops. Instead, they have put their effort into annual crops that yield a quick return, particularly wheat. Moreover, the impact has been uneven, with big changes in the centre of the country, around Tehran, but in other areas, those disrupted by the war and those where tribe–state relations are bad, the villages have hardly been touched by the new policies. More than a decade after the Revolution Iran was no more self-sufficient than it was in the latter days of the Shah's rule. In spite of successes claimed in increasing agricultural output, US Department of Agriculture estimates revealed that Iranian imports of foodstuffs reached $3,670m. in 1984 and were only modestly reduced in 1985. Agricultural imports reached $1,900m. in 1987/88, according to the Minister of Agriculture. The allocation for agricultural imports in 1988/89 was $2,000m. In the Iranian year 1990/91 the value of food imports through government agencies was $5,300m. (Imports by the private sector are not officially recorded.) Imports of wheat were estimated at 4.5m. metric tons, those of rice at 800,000 tons and those of coarse grains at 1.3m. tons. According to the International Grains Council, wheat imports reached 5m. tons in 1995/96, and an estimated 7m. tons in 1996/97 (making Iran the world's largest wheat importer). Imports declined to 3.8m. tons in 1997/98 and to 2.5m.–3m. tons in 1998/99.

Problems of land ownership and uncertainty about the Government's land reform policies have added to the difficulties affecting the agricultural sector. After the fall of the Shah, when the authority of the central Government was weak, land seizures began in many villages. The most dramatic examples occurred in Turkoman and Kurdish areas, where concentrations of large absentee land-holdings were especially pronounced, but other areas were also affected. In some cases the Government did not intervene but, where it did, it tended to oppose land seizures. The events were accompanied by mass migration from the countryside to the cities—nearly 1.5m. rural dwellers migrated to Tehran alone during the first year of the Revolution. The regime recognized the economic disaster that this migration threatened. Nearly one-quarter of the most fertile farm land awaits settlement of ownership claims between big landlords and the farmers who have taken over their lands. The redistribution of these lands is decreed by the Revolution but, according to the rules of Islam, property is sacred and the right to it absolute. The issue has been complicated by the radical element in the Government which advocates the appropriation of more land by the state. A land reform programme, prepared by the Ministry of Agriculture, was submitted to the Revolutionary Council at the end of 1979. The programme planned to limit the size of holdings to three times the average in an area. The large landowners were accused of influencing the clergy to oppose the new measures, but the necessary legislation was eventually introduced. It was approved by the Majlis in 1981, but was later rejected by the Council of Guardians as un-Islamic. The form of the land reform bill was then altered considerably. Land was to be confiscated only from former enemies of the Revolution and only if it was barren or uncultivated. After many months before the Majlis and deep controversy over the acceptability of the law in the light of Islamic principles, the bill was again rejected by the Council of Guardians. A compromise law, giving farmers, peasants and squatters rights to land (amounting to some 800,000 ha) settled by them after the Revolution, but allowing big landlords who avoided the redistribution of land to retain their estates, was approved by the Majlis in May 1985, though it was not ratified by the Council of Guardians. The law would affect about 630,000 ha of farmland belonging to some 5,300 landlords who fled the country or whose lands were appropriated. Some 800,000 ha of land, confiscated from officers and others linked with the Shah's regime, have been redistributed since the Revolution. (More than 50% of this land is uncultivable or grazing land, but 200,000 ha of cultivable land have been given to poor or landless peasants.) For more than two decades the authorities have been trying to reconcile Islamic principles with revolutionary goals and expectations, while a comprehensive settlement of the land ownership reform question is still awaited.

In early 1990 changes in government policy on the utilization of agricultural land were announced. Instead of granting confiscated and unused land to small farmers, henceforth official teams (consisting of seven members) were to grant land in blocks to groups of investors, in order to ensure its rapid development. Consequently, some 200,000 ha of land have been leased to farmers for temporary cultivation, and it is aimed to lease a further 250,000 ha under the new terms.

The war with Iraq imposed numerous constraints on agriculture. Between 1980 and 1982 10% of agricultural land fell under Iraqi occupation; a disproportionate number of volunteers for the war effort were drawn from the villages; and the heavy financial burden of the war imposed limits on spending. Since the end of the war, despite drought in the western rain-fed areas and the earthquake of 1990, which destroyed irrigation works, orchards and farms in the fertile north-western provinces of Gilan and Zanjan, the Ministry of Agriculture claimed to have succeeded in reviving the agricultural sector after three decades of decline. The Ministry reported that an annual growth in farm output of 6% had been achieved under the 1990–94 FFYDP, wheat output had doubled to 11m. metric tons, sugar plants were now working at full capacity, agriculture had been made more viable by reducing subsidies to farmers on products such as fertilizers and pesticides, and water reservoirs had been expanded. Under the new Plan which began in March 1995, the Ministry of Agriculture projected annual growth of 5%. It was planned to build some 20 dams during the term of SFYDP and to increase water utilization by cutting losses in irrigation canals. Subsidies on pesticides were to be phased out within three years and those on fertilizers within five years. Increased mechanization was identified as a key priority, especially in rice farming. As the average Iranian farm is small (only 5.3 ha), farmers must pool their land for successful mechanization. The Minister of Agriculture stated that the Majlis had approved the necessary legislation. Co-operatives were being encouraged and would be supplied with machinery and a guarantee that the Government would buy 70% of their production. The new Plan aimed at the expansion of food processing industries with investment mainly from the private sector, which has shown particular interest in processing plants for vegetables and fruits and dairy products. The Minister of Agriculture stated that he welcomed foreign investment in agriculture and expected that most of it would be directed towards food processing industries. A US $47m. baby-food factory was set up in 1994 by Nestlé of Switzerland as a joint venture with a local firm. Special efforts were being made to improve the processing and packaging of fruit for export to markets in the Gulf and Europe and this sector was scheduled for rapid growth. The Minister forecast self-sufficiency in sugar, fodder crops, tea, meat and dairy products by 2000. Some imports would be necessary, especially of vegetable oil, of which about 85% of requirements is imported; however, a major effort was to be made to expand olive cultivation. The Minister of Agriculture also maintained that the gap between rural and urban incomes had narrowed and that within the next five years no village would be without proper roads, electricity or health facilities.

Notwithstanding the aim of self-sufficiency in certain crops and products, production of wheat fell to 10m. metric tons in both the 1996/97 and 1997/98 seasons (from 11m. tons in 1994/95), while barley and rice production also declined, to 2.5m. tons and 2.4m. tons respectively in 1997/98. In mid-1999 agricultural output suffered from the worst drought for 30 years, resulting in the destruction of 25% of the grain crop; subsequent heavy rain and floods in the north and west did further damage to crops, with the result that Iran imported a record 6m. tons of wheat in 1999/2000, twice as much as in 1998/99. Also imported in 1999 were 800,000 tons of rice, 780,000 tons of raw vegetable oil and 880,000 tons of white and raw sugar. An emergency US $183m. aid package for farmers affected by adverse weather was introduced in May 2000, when state banks were instructed to give farmers a two-year deferral period on the repayment of loans. Iran expected to produce 6.4m. tons of wheat and to import 4.8m. tons of wheat in 2001/02. Imports of rice were expected to amount to 720,000 tons in that year, and imports of vegetable oil and oilseeds to 650,000 tons. In February 2000 President Khatami inaugurated a $100m. cane sugar plant in Shushtar with an annual capacity of 100,000 tons, forming part of the Haft Tappeh sugar cane development complex of seven refineries with a total annual capacity of 700,000 tons. Iran imported 400,000 tons of sugar in 2001/02, less than half as much as in the previous year.

The principal products of the nomad sector of Iranian agriculture are livestock products—dairy produce, wool, hair and hides. According to the 1988 agricultural census, nomads' herds included 40.7m. sheep and lambs, of which more than one-third were in the provinces of Khorassan and east and west Azerbaijan. About 40% of sheep and goats are raised by semi-nomadic tribal herdsmen. Production is limited by the prevalence of animal pests and the apparently inevitable poor productivity of pastoral stock breeding compared with its domestic counterpart. However, account must be taken of the fact that most of the land grazed by the nomads' herds is land which could not be made economically viable in any other way. During the reign of Reza Shah (1925–41) the Iranian Government tried to enforce settlement on the nomads but the tribes rebelled. Since the early 1960s government 'encouragement' and economic pressures have resulted in significant settlement. By contrast, the Revolutionary Government accepts the tribes as part of the social structure and is providing the nomads with support to expand meat production. Local output of red meat increased from 560,000 metric tons in 1989/90 to 680,000 tons in 1994/95.

About 11.5% of Iran is under forest or woodland, including the Caspian area—the main source of commercial timber—and the Zagros mountains. Forestry in an economic sense is a recent activity and it is only since the nationalization of forest land in 1963 that effective attempts have been made, under the Forestry Commission, at protection, conservation and reafforestation. Total roundwood output in 2000 was estimated at 1.1m. cu m.

Although Iran has direct access to both the Caspian Sea and the Gulf, fishing remains poorly developed in both areas. The Caspian fisheries are chiefly noted for the production of caviar, mostly for export. During the 1990s prices fell by about one-third due to an increase in smuggling through Russia. In August 1993 Iran, Russia, Azerbaijan, Kazakhstan and Turkmenistan agreed to establish a cartel to regulate international prices of caviar, to co-ordinate exports and to protect stocks of sturgeon. Pollution and the steadily falling water-level of the Caspian Sea are two serious problems being tackled under a Soviet-Iranian agreement signed in 1973. One survey estimated that, if fully developed, Iran's southern fisheries could earn as much as US $200m. annually, chiefly from high-grade shrimps and prawns. At the end of 1982 a $1,300m. five-year plan for the development of the fishing industry was announced. The first phase of a giant fishing port at Javad al-A'emeh, in Hormozgan province, was completed in June 1986, at a cost of $3m. Under a $20m. protocol signed in August 1987, Iran agreed to buy 36 trawlers from the People's Republic of China, 18 of which were to be assembled in Iran from Chinese parts. China was also to assist in the construction of factories producing canned fish at three Iranian ports. Government expenditure of $4,520m. on the sector was planned over the period 1990–95; projects included the construction of 13 new fishing ports along the Gulf and the Sea of Oman, and the purchase or charter of fishing vessels. In May 1993 a new fishing port, which was to be equipped with cold storage facilities, opened on Hormuz Island. At the end of November 1993 a $1.4m. fish canning plant was opened in the Qeshm Island free zone, with a daily capacity of 40,000 cans. As a result of pollution caused by the war in the Gulf in 1991, Iran's shrimp catch was reported to have fallen by almost two-thirds, to 4,000 metric tons, in the Iranian year 1370 (1991/92).

The total Iranian fish catch rose from 327,727 metric tons in the year 1991/92 to 400,020 tons in 1996/97, but in 1997/98 fell to 385,200 tons, of which 244,000 tons came from the Gulf and the Oman Sea, 76,200 tons from the Caspian Sea and 65,000 tons from inland waters. The Government remained committed to increasing the annual catch to at least 700,000 tons, principally by the development of fisheries in the southern waters. In 1999/2000 Iran exported 80 tons of caviar worth US $32m., benefiting from a doubling of the international market price attributed to a decline in Russian production.

PETROLEUM

The major economic activity in Iran is the petroleum industry. According to official figures, Iran's proven oil reserves at the end of 2001 were 89,700m. barrels, representing about 9% of world reserves and 13.1% of those in the Middle East, and were expected to last for 64.7 years at current production rates.

The history of commercial exploitation dates back to 1901, when William Knox D'Arcy was granted a 60-year monopoly of the right to explore for and exploit petroleum in Iran, with the exception of the five northern provinces, which fell within the sphere of Russian influence. Petroleum was eventually discovered in commercial quantities at Masjid-i-Sulaiman in 1908 and the Anglo-Persian Oil Co was formed in 1909. The Company was renamed Anglo-Iranian in 1935. A long series of disputes between the Iranian Government and Anglo-Iranian ended with the nationalization of the petroleum industry by Iran in 1951 and the replacement in 1954 of Anglo-Iranian by what became known as the Consortium until it was dissolved in March 1979. The Consortium was an amalgam of interests (British Petroleum 40%; Royal Dutch Shell 14%; Gulf Oil, Socony, Mobil, Exxon, Standard Oil of California and Texaco each with 7%; Compagnie Française des Pétroles 6%; and a group of independents under the umbrella of the Iricon Agency 5%), formed to extract petroleum in the area of the old Anglo-Iranian concession as redefined in 1933. The Consortium's concession was to have lasted until 1979, with the possibility of a series of extensions under modified conditions for a further 15 years. Ownership of petroleum deposits throughout Iran and the right to exploit them, or to make arrangements for their exploitation, was vested in the National Iranian Oil Co (NIOC), an Iranian state enterprise. In July 2001 the Council of Ministers approved the creation of a Supreme Energy Council (SEC), which would have strategic oversight of energy projects.

Until 1973 Iran had a leasing agreement with the Consortium, but the Iranian Government then insisted that the companies should either continue under existing arrangements until 1979 and then become ordinary 'arm's-length buyers', or else negotiate an entirely new 'agency' agreement immediately. The Consortium opted for the latter plan, and on 31 July 1973 a contract was signed in Tehran under which NIOC formally took over ownership and control of the petroleum industry in the Consortium area, while the Consortium was to set up a new operating company, Oil Service Co of Iran, which would act as production contractor for NIOC. In return, the western companies were granted a 20-year supply of crude petroleum as privileged buyers, which they would take in proportion to their shareholding in the Consortium.

Strikes at the petroleum installations, halting petroleum exports, constituted one of the difficulties that forced the Shah to leave Iran in January 1979. Iran did not restore supplies to the rest of the world until 5 March 1979. The first shipments were sold on the spot market, fetching prices as high as US $20 per barrel, but NIOC announced that this was a temporary measure. Within a matter of weeks, three dozen long-term contracts were signed with international companies for the supply of Iranian petroleum.

NIOC cancelled the 1973 agreement to market Iranian petroleum through the Consortium, and since 5 March 1979 has sold petroleum directly to individual companies and countries. After initial resistance, the former members of the Consortium accepted the new arrangement and signed new nine-month supply agreements effective from 1 April. The role of the Consortium effectively came to an end on 1 July 1981, when Kala Ltd, a subsidiary of NIOC which had been established to undertake purchasing and service functions for Iran's petroleum industry, replaced the Iranian Oil Service Co (IROS), one of the subsidiaries of the Consortium.

The period April 1980 to June 1981 was very poor for Iran's petroleum industry. The country was in a continuous state of political turmoil, which spilled over into the hydrocarbons industry. Stoppages, strikes, go-slows and sabotage seriously hindered production. The loss of foreign personnel for oilfield maintenance on the onshore fields was compounded by the sanctions imposed in May 1980 by the European Community (EC—now EU) in support of the USA over the US hostages in Iran. The EC's action prevented Iran from purchasing some of the sophisticated spares and components required for repairs and maintenance. Iran's response, however, deprived the country of some petroleum customers, since it suspended supplies to any country supporting the sanctions.

The Iraqi attack on Iran across the Shatt al-Arab waterway in September 1980, and the consequent expanded and prolonged hostilities, further weakened the industry. Iraqi shelling of the 628,000 barrels per day (b/d) Abadan refinery put the plant out of action. Sporadic attacks on shipping in the Gulf caused some disruption, but the movement of ultra-large cargo carriers and other vessels was virtually uninterrupted until May 1984, when Iraq began to concentrate its attacks on ships using Iran's main terminal for crude oil exports, at Kharg Island, and on the terminal itself. Only part of the terminal's export capacity was damaged, and, with an installed capacity of 6.5m. b/d, the loss of an estimated 2.5m. b/d capacity still enabled the terminal to deal effectively with Iran's levels of export in early 1983, which remained well below pre-Revolution figures. During periods of concerted Iraqi action in the Gulf, there were massive increases in insurance charges for tankers, followed by sharp falls during periods of relative military inactivity. Iraqi raids disrupted the product lines extending from Bandar Mahshahr along the length of the country, and delayed construction of the giant petrochemical complex at Bandar Khomeini, a joint Iranian-Japanese project (see Manufacturing and Industry, below).

From the depressed levels of early 1982, Iran's output of petroleum rose significantly during the first half of 1983: in January oil rationing for domestic consumers was ended. Domestic consumption in mid-1982 was believed to be between 600,000 b/d and 700,000 b/d, of which some 300,000 b/d was being refined outside Iran, leaving exports at between 1.6m. b/d and 1.7m. b/d. In the second half of 1983 output dropped to 2.6m. b/d, compared with an OPEC production quota of 2.4m. b/d, under which exports of 1.7m. b/d were possible, after domestic consumption. Petroleum exports in June 1984 rose to 1.4m. b/d after falling below 1m. b/d in May, following Iraqi attacks on tankers in the Gulf. Japanese companies, the principal customers for Iranian crude oil, lifted more than 400,000 b/d in early 1984. Between May and July Japan banned its tankers from Kharg Island, and Iran offered lower prices to certain customers to bolster sales in the absence of its largest customer.

In 1982/83, with its oil priced at US $34 per barrel, Iran's export earnings reached $23,000m.; in 1983/84, when Iran's oil was priced at $28 per barrel, earnings totalled $21,500m., about $4,000m. more than the OPEC quota (which was reduced by 100,000 b/d, to 2.3m. b/d, in October 1984) would have allowed. Iran responded to the need to increase earnings by breaking OPEC production limits (Iran repeatedly pressed for an increase in its OPEC production quota, until the crisis of 1985–86, when prices fell precipitously in a glutted market—see below) and by energetic price-cutting policies, actions which offended its OPEC partners. It was reliably reported that Iran priced its crude petroleum in 1984 considerably below the official market level of $29 per barrel, as it was known to have done with the previous official price of $34. Some liftings were reportedly offered at approximately $26.50 per barrel in September and October 1984. Special insurance rates were made available to offset Iraqi threats to tanker traffic in the Gulf, and extended credit was also reportedly used as an incentive. Some customers, in particular Japan, began to turn to Saudi Arabia and Kuwait for their oil, as the risk of attacks on tankers and, commensurately, the rate of insurance were lower.

In 1985, despite its stated wish to abide by OPEC's official pricing structure, Iran continued to offer discounts on its oil, below official OPEC prices, to attract customers otherwise deterred by risks to shipping in the Gulf from Iraqi air attacks and by the increased rates of insurance charged on vessels using the Kharg Island oil terminal. In January Iran brought its prices into line with those of OPEC by raising the price of its light crude oil by US $1.11 to $29.10 per barrel. In February, when OPEC prices were reduced, Iran cut the price of its light crude by $1.05 to $28.05 per barrel. By mid-1985, however, Iran was again offering discounts on its oil. Despite efforts to remain competitive (which included rebate incentives, discounts and the shuttling of oil from Kharg Island by tanker to a safer lifting point, see below), Iran's revenue from oil exports (of 1.68m. b/d) fell to $17,000m. in 1984/85, 15% less than had been predicted. The Government blamed the war with Iraq and the OPEC decision to reduce its prices by $1.00 per barrel.

The Ministry of Oil argued publicly against the use of barter deals to stimulate oil exports while the Ministry of Foreign Affairs adopted barter and bilateral agreements as one of the main features of Iran's foreign policy. New barter deals were agreed in 1985 but their profitability was low and often fell short of the country's real needs; bartering returned to favour, however, with the appointment of a new Council of Ministers in January 1986.

A suggested long-term solution to the threat to oil exports, posed by Iraqi attacks on Kharg Island, was the construction of a new oil terminal, either at the end of a pipeline outside the Gulf area, or at Sirri Island, close to the mouth of the Gulf, 450 km south-east of Kharg Island, safer from Iraqi attack. An immediate and cheaper alternative, more a short-term solution to the problem of Iraqi air raids on Kharg, involved the establishment of a tanker shuttle service between Kharg and a makeshift floating oil terminal at Sirri Island, using tankers anchored off shore, where the oil was stored and reloaded. The Sirri facility began operating in March 1985 and proved its worth between August 1985 and January 1986, when Iraq launched a series of some 60 attacks against the Kharg Island terminal (which was still responsible for more than 80% of Iran's oil exports).

Average oil production in Iran at the end of 1985 was between 2.2m. b/d and 2.5m. b/d, while exports averaged about 1.6m. b/d. The rate of export fell from about 1.5m. b/d in January 1986 to 1.2m. b/d in February. At the end of January Iran offered to halve its oil production, and in February pressed OPEC to suspend oil exports for two weeks in an attempt to force prices up again. It was perhaps no coincidence that Iran's most vehement advocacy of production discipline within OPEC occurred at a time when the depredations of war prevented it from producing and exporting sufficient oil in excess of its OPEC quota to obviate the effects of falling prices. In fact, it could barely meet its quota in early 1986. In July prices fell below US $10 per barrel (following six months of unrestrained production by OPEC in pursuit of a 'fair' market share), and in August OPEC members, at Iran's suggestion, agreed to cut output for two months from 1 September—effectively reverting to the production quotas imposed in October 1984, giving Iran a quota of 2.3m. b/d. Although Iraq refused to participate in the agreement, considering its quota of less than 1.5m. b/d to be too low, and demanding one commensurate with its production capacity or, at least, the equal of Iran's, Iran averred that military action in the Gulf would effectively restrain Iraqi oil production.

In October 1986, when the price of oil had risen to about US $15 per barrel, OPEC members agreed to increase collective production by some 200,000 b/d. In December all OPEC members (with the exception of Iraq, which, once more, since it was not expected to comply, received a notional quota) accepted a 7.25% reduction in their output, effective for the first half of 1987. It was hoped that this measure would enable the organization to support a fixed price of $18 per barrel, effective from 1 February, replacing the policy of pricing according to spot market rates, which prevailed in 1986. The reduction gave Iran a production quota of 2.26m. b/d, compared with 2.32m. b/d in November 1986–January 1987. Iran's average output of crude oil was estimated by OPEC to be 2.04m. b/d in 1986,

compared with 2.19m. b/d in 1985, well below its OPEC quota. Production fluctuated during the first half of 1987 between 1.7m. b/d in February and 2.6m. b/d in June.

The OPEC production programme succeeded in sustaining the price of its oil at US $18 per barrel during the first half of 1987, and during the month of July prices on the spot market rose above $20 per barrel, in response to alarm over the growing threat to oil supplies posed by developments in the Iran–Iraq War. In June OPEC members agreed to retain the $18 per barrel benchmark, but to increase their collective production by 800,000 b/d during the second half of the year to 16.6m. b/d (including a notional quota for Iraq). Iran's quota was raised to 2.37m. b/d, an increase of 111,000 b/d. In August, however, output averaged 2.8m. b/d, according to oil industry sources, despite having counselled restraint at the June meeting. Iran had, since 1985, urged a return to a price of $28 per barrel, as OPEC's ultimate goal, in tandem with lower production—obviously with regard to its own difficulties in sustaining production levels.

At the OPEC meeting in December 1987 Iran demanded an increase in the central reference price of at least US $2 per barrel and output reductions by members, and refused to participate in a new agreement that awarded Iraq the same quota as that given to Iran. It was finally agreed to retain the $18 per barrel reference price and the ceiling of 16.6m. b/d (15.06m. b/d excluding Iraq) on collective production for a further six months from 1 January 1988. Prices remained well below the OPEC reference level during the first half of 1988, owing to member states' flouting of their quotas, but in May OPEC decided to retain the 16.6m. b/d ceiling and the $18 reference price for a further six months. In August, when the cease-fire in the Iran–Iraq War took effect, Iran was producing at its quota level of about 2.37m. b/d, although, owing to Iraqi attacks on oil installations (including the first for five months on Larak Island in May), it had rarely been able to produce so much during the preceding six months. While Iranian representatives at OPEC meetings strongly urged reductions in output, to defend the $18 benchmark, Iran was allegedly so desperate for oil revenue that it was selling oil at less than $10 per barrel.

At a meeting of OPEC's Long-Term Strategy Committee in November 1988 (at which Iran reluctantly adopted a more flexible approach to Iraq's demand for quota parity), member states agreed a production ceiling of 18.5m. b/d for the first half of 1989. By December it was apparent that world demand for oil had surged, and prices strengthened to a level close to the US $18 per barrel reference price which remained in force. According to oil industry sources, Iranian production averaged 2.27m. b/d in 1988, while OPEC's provisional estimate of Iranian petroleum revenues in that year was $8,170m. In early 1989 the agreement signed in November 1988 was undermined when Kuwait rejected the quota assigned to it within the 18.5m. b/d ceiling. By the time that the next full OPEC meeting was held, at the beginning of June 1989, prices had weakened considerably. To take account of the increased volume of Kuwaiti production, which OPEC member states regarded as inevitable, the production ceiling was raised by only 1m. b/d, to 19.5m. b/d, thus reducing the extra volume to which other members were entitled.

At the Long-Term Strategy Committee meeting (subsequently redesignated a full-scale quota and pricing meeting) in June 1989, Iran demanded a redistribution of OPEC quotas, to favour Kuwait, the United Arab Emirates (UAE), Ecuador and Gabon, within a ceiling of 21.5m. b/d. In the event, a ceiling of 20.5m. b/d was set; Kuwait duly rejected its quota of 1.149m. b/d for the final quarter of 1989, and overproduction continued to such an extent that by the end of 1989 total OPEC output had reached almost 24m. b/d. According to oil industry sources, Iranian production averaged 2.87m. b/d during 1989, while Iran's petroleum revenues were estimated at US $13,600m. At the next full OPEC meeting, held in November 1989, the production ceiling was raised to 22m. b/d, although most members regarded this as inadequate, since the *de facto* level of production was already 24m. b/d.

In early 1989 the Ministry of Oil issued a number of contracts for the construction and repair of offshore oil platforms destroyed during the Iran–Iraq War as part of a major expansion programme valued at US $2,000m. Offshore production had totalled some 500,000 b/d before the war, but by 1986 it was estimated that production had fallen to 250,000 b/d. Offshore production may have fallen to 50,000 b/d by the end of the war. In April 1988 US warships severely damaged Salman, one of three rigs 150 km west of Sirri Island, feeding the Lavan Island terminals, and installations in the Nasr oilfield off Sirri. Rigs in the Reshadat and Risala'at oilfields, and the Raksh and Rostan platforms, had been destroyed by US attacks in April and October 1987.

In June 1990 there were reports that Iran had agreed to pay the US oil company Amoco US $600m. in compensation for operations which had been expropriated during the Revolution. This was the first major settlement of US corporate oil claims totalling $1,800m., and was regarded as a step towards the restoration of oil trade between Iran and the USA. In December it was announced that a US company, Atlantic Richfield, had secured compensation of $9m. from Iran for its share in the former international oil Consortium; this represented the last in a series of settlements (totalling $320m.) made by Iran to US members of the former Consortium. At the end of 1990 the USA eased the three-year ban on purchases of Iranian crude, but Iran objected to the US Administration's stipulation that all payments had to be made into a security account in The Hague, Netherlands, for use by the special US-Iran Claims Tribunal. However, in early 1991 Iran approved two sales to US companies, Coastal Corpn and Mobil Corpn. Coastal Corpn, Chevron and Amerada Hess purchased shipments of Iranian oil for the US market in 1991. Mobil and other US oil firms also purchased Iranian crude petroleum, but for delivery outside of the USA. In August 1992 Atlantic Richfield and Sun Oil agreed to accept $130m. each in compensation for their share in the joint venture, Lavan Petroleum Company, nationalized after the Revolution. Two other US shareholders, Murphy and Union, settled in 1986.

By mid-July 1990 oil prices had fallen as low as US $14.40 per barrel, and both Iran and Iraq were demanding that a minimum reference price of $25 per barrel be fixed at the full OPEC meeting scheduled for the end of July. At the meeting, however, a minimum reference price of $21 per barrel was set, within a 22.5m. b/d ceiling. Nevertheless, the agreement apparently indicated a new political alliance between Iran, Iraq and Saudi Arabia, and its immediate effect was to raise prices.

Iraq's invasion and annexation of Kuwait in August 1990 gave rise to a further, dramatic rise in the price of crude petroleum. It also created serious divisions within OPEC. Iran criticized those member states, principally Saudi Arabia, which, in the aftermath of the Iraqi invasion, sought to raise OPEC production in order to compensate for the loss of Iraqi and Kuwaiti supplies, due to the economic sanctions imposed by the UN. At an emergency OPEC meeting convened in late August and attended by the oil ministers of all member states except Iraq and Libya, a draft agreement was signed which effectively allowed for a suspension of the production quotas agreed in July. Iran refused to support the agreement, however, and proposed that oil companies and industrialized countries release petroleum stocks in order to relieve pressure on prices, which had risen above $30 per barrel during August. However, it appeared likely in late August that production quotas would be ignored until a resolution of the Gulf conflict made it possible to convene an OPEC meeting in which all 13 members could participate.

In October 1990 the Iranian Ministry of Oil announced that, since August, output of crude oil had been averaging 3.2m. b/d, slightly above the OPEC quota of 3.14m. b/d. It was further reported that exports of crude oil to Japan had trebled and that exports to the Republic of Korea and the Philippines had also increased. Sales to Asian countries accounted for nearly 60% of total oil exports. For the first time, contracts in convertible currency were signed with several eastern European countries that had previously bought oil from Iran through clearing accounts linked to reciprocal purchases of goods. In addition, in late 1990 and early 1991 revenue from oil exports increased by between US $700m. and $800m. per month, as a result of the rise in prices for oil (precipitated by the crisis in the Gulf region).

Iran's production of crude petroleum in 1991 reportedly averaged 3,238m. b/d, with exports averaging 2.41m. b/d, of which 2.35m. b/d were from onshore fields and 65,000 b/d from offshore fields. Iran's production capacity was estimated to have in-

creased from 3.5m. b/d in 1991 to almost 4m. b/d in 1992. On 20 January 1992 the Ministry of Oil announced that it was reducing petroleum production by 50,000 b/d in an attempt to increase the international price of crude petroleum. In March the Ministry stated that, as of 1 March, oil production had been reduced to 3.184m. b/d in line with new OPEC quota allocations.

According to the Minister of Oil, Gholamreza Aqazadeh, oil production was officially raised to 3.5m. b/d–3.6m. b/d from 23 September 1992, following divisions within OPEC over production policy. In mid-October oil production was temporarily raised to 4m. b/d to demonstrate Iran's improved capacity and to establish Iran's position as OPEC's biggest producer after Saudi Arabia, and to support its claims for a larger share of OPEC's market. The well-publicized increase in output, 3.6m. b/d from onshore fields and 400,000 b/d from offshore fields, was maintained for a week. Normal production in previous months had averaged about 3.5m. b/d, with about 1m. b/d designated for domestic consumption. Officials stated that production capacity would be raised to 4.5m. b/d in March 1993—equivalent to about 50% of Saudi Arabia's capacity—although actual production would be in line with OPEC quotas. Analysts argued that export capacity would be limited to about 2.5m. b/d until work on the reconstruction of the Kharg Island terminal was completed in 1994. In December 1992 the Minister of Oil announced that crude oil production would average 3.5m. b/d from 1 December 1992 to 31 March 1993, representing a cut-back of 400,000 b/d from the November level of 3.9m. b/d. In March 1993 the Minister of Oil announced that output had been cut to 3.34m. b/d on 1 March in line with OPEC's new quota, but explained that the reduction would be compensated for by higher prices. About 2.4m. b/d would be available for export. A Plan and Budget Organization report released in April 1993 revealed that oil exports during the first nine months of 1992/93 averaged 2.386m. b/d, 448,000 b/d less than the budget level and 265,000 b/d less than the Ministry of Oil's export timetable. Observers estimated oil revenues for the Iranian year ending 20 March 1993 at US $14,500m., $2,000m. below the budget projection.

Following the OPEC meeting in Geneva, Switzerland, in September 1993 the Minister of Oil announced that from 1 October Iran's quota would be 3.6m. b/d, 240,000 b/d more than the previous level, allowing exports to rise to 2.6m. b/d. However, international traders stated that actual exports had averaged 2.7m. b/d in 1993, with production estimated at some 200,000 b/d more than Iran's earlier OPEC quota of 3.34m. b/d. Aqazadeh reiterated previous claims that output was scheduled to rise to 4.6m. b/d in 1994, with a further rise to 5.5m. b/d–6m. b/d by 2000 (i.e. to the level of production before the Revolution). He also stated that Iran planned to produce an average of 4.5m. b/d during the SFYDP, due to begin in March 1994. In January 1994 Mostafa Khoee, Managing Director of the Iranian Offshore Oil Co, stated that crude capacity was 4.2m. b/d; 3.8m. b/d on shore and 400,000 b/d off shore. He did not indicate whether these figures were sustainable. Actual output during 1993 averaged 3.6m. b/d. Defending his record as Minister of Oil before the Majlis in August 1993, Aqazadeh stated that during the first 52 months of the FFYDP, oil revenues totalled US $61,720m., slightly higher than the Plan's target. Early in 1994 Aqazadeh announced that 9,530m. barrels of oil, worth $45,000m. had been discovered during the term of the FFYDP. In early 1995 NIOC announced the discovery of a new oilfield named Shur, south of Gachsaran in Khuzestan province, with recoverable reserves estimated at 100m. barrels. Production was 10,000 b/d and output was due to rise to 30,000 b/d when two more wells came on stream.

Independent observers stated that Iran had been producing crude at or near 3.6m. b/d from early 1993, and that at the end of 1994 sustained production capacity was at least 3.8m. b/d and perhaps 3.9m. b/d. In May 1995 NIOC ordered a 500,000 b/d increase in oil production for one week. NIOC officials stated that by boosting production Iran was demonstrating its potential following the US embargo on direct oil purchases (see below) and proving that it could produce well above its OPEC quota of 3.6m. b/d. Nevertheless, speculation remained that, owing to shortages of equipment and technical problems, Iran would not be able to maintain higher production trends. It was reported that considerable drilling of new wells and recovery work on its existing fields was necessary to achieve its crude capacity expansion plans.

Amid renewed interest from international oil companies in Iran's offshore fields in the Gulf, in March 1994 the Minister of Oil confirmed that talks were being held with several US companies and that Conoco of Houston had submitted a proposal to develop the offshore Sirri E crude oilfield. An agreement between Conoco and NIOC to develop the Sirri A and E offshore fields, which have combined reserves estimated at nearly 500m. barrels, was finally concluded at the beginning of March 1995. The US $600m. scheme was to have been financed through a buy-back agreement. However, on 14 March the US Administration announced that President Clinton would shortly issue an executive order banning US companies from developing Iran's oil. Conoco subsequently announced that it was withdrawing from the agreement, the first oilfield development scheme awarded to a foreign company since 1979. The intervention by the US Administration was part of an intensive campaign aimed at isolating and crippling Iran economically. President Clinton's executive order of 8 May 1995, formally imposing an economic embargo against Iran, prevented US oil companies from work in developing Iran's oil and gas resources for the foreseeable future. Some observers argued that by granting the contract to Conoco, rather than to French companies, Iran was making a political gesture to the USA. President Rafsanjani confirmed this in a US television interview on 15 May. However, Conoco also had advantages over other companies in that it was already operating in the region and would have been able to take associated gas from Sirri for use in its operations in Dubai. In May the Ministry of Oil announced that it was negotiating with Total of France and the Royal Dutch Shell Group to develop the Sirri oilfields. In July 1995 NIOC announced that the contract had been awarded to Total, which had been involved in three years of negotiations for work in Iran (see also below). Earlier, on 16 March, the Ministry of Oil had announced that a Dutch-German consortium, John Brown Engineers and Constructors and Ingenieurbetrieb Anlagenbau (IAB) Leipzig, had agreed to renovate the offshore Abuzar oilfield. The Minister of Oil declared that Iran did not need US companies and that Europe welcomed oil co-operation with Iran. The Abuzar project involved the reconstruction of the war-damaged platform in the northern Gulf and expansion of capacity to 150,000 b/d–200,000 b/d.

In February 1996, when the French Minister of Transport visited Tehran, President Rafsanjani told him that Iran appreciated France's principled stand against a trade and investment ban on Iran. Earlier, in December 1995 the US Senate had approved legislation for a secondary economic boycott of Iran (and Libya), and in early August 1996, under pressure from the Republican-dominated Congress, US President Clinton finally endorsed ILSA, penalizing non-US companies that invested US $40m. ($20m. from August 1997) or more in oil and gas projects in those countries. Contracts already signed were exempt from the new legislation. The USA's attempt to extend its domestic legislation abroad was strongly criticized by the EU and Russia. Iran stated that it did not believe that European companies would be deterred by the new legislation, pointing out that existing US sanctions had harmed US companies which had lost business to their European competitors. Independent observers argued that the US trade embargo imposed in June 1995 had not damaged Iran's oil exports, and that even a total freeze on foreign investment in the Iranian oil industry would not reduce Iran's export capacity until beyond 2000. They predicted that Iran's main trading partners were unlikely to take any action that would make it more difficult for Iran to repay its substantial foreign debts.

In August 1996 Total announced that Petronas of Malaysia had agreed to purchase a 30% stake in its development of the Sirri A and E offshore fields and that the partnership deal had been approved by the Iranian authorities. The Sirri A field began producing in October 1998, and the Sirri E in February 1999. NIOC plans to increase total offshore output to 1.1m. b/d by 2005, and has sought foreign partners to develop other fields on similar terms to the Sirri agreement with Total. In March 1999 Elf Aquitaine of France and Italy's Agip signed a US $1,000m. buy-back deal to upgrade and develop the Doroud offshore field, with the aim of increasing output from 90,000 b/d

to 220,000 b/d. In the following month it was announced that a Franco-Canadian consortium (comprising Elf Petroleum Iran and Bow Valley Energy) had been awarded the contract for developing the Balal offshore field. The project was expected to cost $300m., and crude output was planned at 40,000 b/d from 2001.

At the end of 1998 NIOC awarded a US $19m. contract to the British LASMO and the Royal Dutch Shell Group to explore for oil in the Caspian Sea (the first upstream contract since the 1979 revolution). For NIOC, the deal was the first exploration contract awarded from a list of nearly 50 projects (including 20 exploration permits) offered to foreign investors on a buy-back basis in 1998. In June 1999 NIOC invited bids for seven oil and gas exploration projects off shore in the Gulf and on the mainland, the Government's aim being to increase Iran's overall sustainable crude output capacity to above 4m. b/d by 2002. In November 1999 NIOC signed an $850m. buy-back agreement with Royal Dutch Shell for the repair and expansion of the offshore Soroush and Nowruz oilfields west of Kharg Island, the objectives being that Soroush would achieve production of 100,000 b/d by late 2001 and Nowruz 90,000 b/d by late 2003. The US Department of State said that this deal would be investigated to establish whether it involved sanctionable activity under ILSA, but industry sources expressed confidence that no action would be taken against Royal Dutch Shell. It was announced in June 2001 that the Abu Dhabi-based National Petroleum Construction Company (NPCC) had won the major contract for the construction of full production facilities at the Soroush and Nowruz oilfields.

Average Iranian oil production in 1996 was 3.66m. b/d, compared with 3.57m. b/d in 1995. The dramatic decrease in world oil prices from late 1997, to below early 1973 levels in real terms, prompted OPEC to decree that its members should reduce production from 1 April 1998 in an effort to boost prices. Iran's allotted cut was 140,000 b/d, so that its quota became 3.942m. b/d. This action failed to bring about the desired effect; OPEC thus implemented further cuts on 1 July, whereby Iran agreed to reduce its output by 300,000 b/d (although Iran maintained that its reduction should be taken from a baseline of 3.9m. b/d, rather than 3.6m. b/d, which had the effect of undermining the OPEC deal). However, in March 1999, as OPEC agreed a new round of output reductions, Iran accepted that the benchmark for its future production cuts would be 3.6m. b/d. Under this arrangement Iran agreed to reduce its output by 7.3%, to 3.359m. b/d. In September it was agreed that, despite the sharp rise in world oil prices, the reduced quotas would be retained; in fact, Iranian daily oil production in 1999 and early 2000 was somewhat above its OPEC quota. When in March 2000 OPEC responded to what was seen as a dangerously high world oil price of around US $30 per barrel by increasing aggregate production quotas by 1.7m. b/d from 1 April, only Iran declined to accept the Saudi-proposed plan, on the grounds that OPEC was buckling to US pressure for lower oil prices. However, in June Iran agreed to a further increase in OPEC output targets, the new Iranian quota being 3.727m. b/d from 1 July; a further increase, to 3.844m. b/d from 1 October, was agreed in September. From the beginning of November 2000 Iran's OPEC quota was further raised to 3.917m. b/d, as OPEC continued to respond to upward price pressures in world oil markets. Actual Iranian oil output levels in the second half of 2000 were close to or slightly below the country's agreed OPEC quota levels. As market conditions eased in the first half of 2001 OPEC production allocations were again reduced in order to maintain a firm price 'floor'. Iran accepted a quota of 3.698m. b/d from the beginning of February, reduced to 3.552m. b/d from 1 April, to 3.406m. b/d from 1 September and to 3.186m. b/d from 1 January 2002. Actual Iranian oil output levels in 2001 were reliably reported to have been consistently above the OPEC quota, averaging some 3.8m. b/d, although in August the Government denied Western reports that output had hit 4.1m. b/d. In the first half of 2002 Iran acted to reduce its oil production to around 3.3m. b/d, still considerably in excess of its official OPEC quota.

Having risen by 27%, to US $19,300m., in the 1996/97 financial year, the Government's oil and gas revenues fell to $15,471m. in 1997/98 and to $9,933m. in 1998/99. As a result of sharply rising world oil prices from mid-1999, export revenues increased to $17,089m. in 1999/2000 and to a record high of $24,226m. in 2000/01. In 2001/02 they were estimated to have decreased again, to $20,500m., while industry forecasts for 2002/03 anticipated that they would fall to $16,400m.

In September 1999 NIOC announced the discovery of the biggest new oilfield for 30 years, at Azadegan in south-western Iran, which was subsequently estimated to contain recoverable reserves of 5,000m.–6,000m. barrels. In February 2001, moreover, NIOC reported the discovery of a large new offshore oilfield, named Dasht-e Abadan and located in shallow waters near the port of Abadan, which was believed to be comparable in size to Azadegan. Iranian planners, therefore, began to upgrade their assessments of Iran's total recoverable oil reserves to reflect additional resources in newly discovered fields, together with increases in the production potential of existing fields attainable through the introduction of improved technology. Some NIOC officials expected the estimate of total recoverable reserves to reach 130,000m. barrels in due course. Against this background, a long-established policy of restricting the growth of output capacity (in conformity with a political agenda that had favoured tight production controls in order to maximize price levels) was replaced by a programme to add about 1m. b/d of new net output capacity every five years until 2020. Under this programme, requiring estimated investment in excess of US $30,000m., capacity would approach 5m. b/d in 2005, eventually rising to nearly 8m. b/d (well above its pre-1979 level) by 2020. At the same time Iran continued to subscribe to decisions on OPEC production quotas intended to support oil prices, although without observing them to the letter.

In May 2000 the Norwegian Norex Group began negotiations with European and two US oil companies (Arco and Mobil) on selling data from its 'Persian Carpet 2000' seismic survey of some 110,000 sq km of Iranian territory hitherto unexplored for hydrocarbons, which was said to be the biggest such project anywhere in the world. The US interest reflected the companies' hope that the US prohibition on private investment in the Iranian oil industry would eventually be revoked, following the relaxation of US restrictions on the importation of non-oil items in March 2000.

As part of a streamlining of NIOC, in late 1999 NIOC International was created to take control of the state company's crude oil, oil products and shipping operations. The reorganization was understood to reflect the Government's desire to accelerate the decentralization and privatization of the hydrocarbons industry. Pedec (Petroleum Engineering and Development Co), the NIOC subsidiary in charge of negotiating buy-back contracts for oil development outside the South Pars zone and the Caspian Sea, came under strong pressure in 2000 to revise the terms of such contracts. According to critics in the Majlis, the existing buy-back formula (dating from 1995) required Iran to bear all the risks, while providing no incentive for developers to maximize production. Pedec subsequently sought to incorporate performance guarantees into new buy-back contracts, thereby exposing itself to criticism from foreign oil companies, whose principal complaint was that it was unrealistic to expect them to acquiesce in a system of rewards and penalties while production operations were in the hands of NIOC (which was required by Iranian law to be the operator of oilfield developments).

Plans to privatize the National Iranian Drilling Co (NIDC) were halted by the Ministry of Oil in October 2000, following a strike and other protest action by NIDC employees, who alleged that the company was being offered at less than its true value and that certain oil officials would make large windfall profits if the sale was allowed to proceed on this basis. However, plans to privatize the oil industry's shipping company, National Iranian Tanker Co (NITC), proceeded normally in 2000. Shares in NITC were to be transferred to the Social Welfare Organization, which is responsible for the management of pension funds. In late January 2001 the Majlis formally blocked the NIDC privatization and opened an inquiry into the valuations of more than 20 other subsidiary oil businesses scheduled to be privatized by 2005.

At the end of June 2001, following lengthy negotiations, NIOC and Ente Nazionale Idrocarburi (ENI) of Italy signed a buy-back contract worth an estimated US $1,000m. to develop the Darkhovin oilfield in the province of Khuzestan. In early July NIOC also signed a preliminary agreement with a Japanese-led consortium to conduct a joint evaluation of the Azadegan oilfield, for which the consortium hoped to conclude a $4,500m. buy-back arrangement providing for eventual production of 800,000 b/d. Other major oil buy-back agreements under negotiation in mid-2002 included a $3,000m. plan to increase output from the Bangestan field from 250,000 b/d to 600,000 b/d (submitted by BP, ENI, Royal Dutch Shell and TotalFinalElf), as well as a project for increasing production from the Cheshmeh Khosh onshore field from 30,000 b/d to 80,000 b/d (submitted by Cepsa of Spain). However, the foreign oil companies involved were reported to be increasingly doubtful about the commercial attractiveness of such deals under the terms prescribed, particularly the short contract periods and NIOC's insistence that developers would be penalized if a field failed to reach its production target. On the Iranian side, growing criticism of buy-back arrangements focused on the scope they gave for corruption and on their perceived insufficient return for Iran.

Nevertheless, in May 2002 NIOC signed a US $585m. buy-back contract with Jersey-registered Petro Iran under which production from the offshore Foroozan and Esfandiar oilfields would be increased from 40,000 b/d to 110,000 b/d within three years. At the end of May, moreover, Sheer Energy of Canada signed an $88m. buy-back agreement with NIOC under which it would increase output from the Masjid-e-Sulayman (MIS) onshore field in Khuzestan province from 5,000 b/d to 25,000 b/d. Sheer Energy subsequently insisted that it remained committed to the MIS project, notwithstanding US congressional calls for ILSA sanctions to be imposed on the company.

External Oil Participation

Iran seeks to establish a presence in the hydrocarbons industries of neighbouring countries but has been hampered by US opposition to any such role, particularly to the routing of pipelines from the Caspian Sea and the Central Asian republics through Iranian territory. Since the dissolution of the USSR, moreover, difficult territorial issues have arisen regarding rights to the extensive Caspian Sea oil reserves, with Iran basing itself on treaties of 1921 and 1940 to contend that all five Caspian littoral states (Iran, Azerbaijan, Russia, Kazakhstan and Turkmenistan) must approve jointly any offshore oil exploitation and that any unilateral activity is illegal.

In November 1994 Iran took a 5% share in an international consortium formed to develop three oilfields in the Republic of Azerbaijan. The consortium is led by BP and includes Norwegian, US, Saudi Arabian, Turkish and Russian companies. Iran was brought into the US $7,000m. scheme by the Azeri state oil company (SOCAR), which was unable to contribute its portion of the financing and agreed to give Iran a quarter of its 20% share in return for some $350m. to help Azerbaijan finance energy projects. Iran has encouraged states in the Caspian Sea basin to export their oil through its territory, and in September of that year the consortium had indicated that it hoped to use Iranian facilities to export some of its initial output from the offshore oilfields in the Caspian Sea. Iran offered to help the consortium export up to 260,000 b/d of Azeri oil through oil-swap deals. Azeri oil would be delivered to Iran for use in its northern refineries and an equivalent amount of Iranian crude would be delivered to the consortium's customers from the Gulf. Iran also sought to promote the use of an Iranian route for an export pipeline, connecting, eventually, with a Turkish terminal on the Mediterranean coast. However, the Azeri decision to bring Iran into the consortium was strongly opposed by the USA, and in March 1995 the consortium vetoed Iranian participation. In April it was disclosed that, under US pressure, Azerbaijan had withdrawn its offer to Iran, whose 5% share had been transferred to the Exxon Corpn of the USA.

In May 1995 the President of Azerbaijan stated that he wished to avoid any further deterioration in relations with Iran and that the construction of an export pipeline through Turkey, via Iran, had not been ruled out. When imposing an oil and trade embargo on Iran in early May, President Clinton exempted from the embargo US companies wishing to conclude swap deals of the kind described above with Iran, in order to supply crude oil from their operations in Azerbaijan, Kazakhstan and Turkmenistan to outside markets. However, Iran warned that it might reject such deals involving US companies in Azerbaijan unless the USA abandoned its opposition to Iranian participation in the consortium developing the Azeri oilfields. Iranian officials stated that it was unfair of the consortium to reject Iran's participation and at the same time expect Iranian help in exporting Azeri oil. An official at the Ministry of Oil was reported to have stated that Iran still considered its agreement with Azerbaijan to be valid, arguing that the consortium was dependent on Iran to export its oil, the first shipments of which were due in 1995. Alternative export routes through Georgia, Armenia and Russia presented serious political and economic problems. Nevertheless, in June the Chairman of US McDermott International stated that the consortium was not considering proposals for pipelines through Iran, but that agreement was close to build two pipelines, one through Russia and the other through Georgia. In January 1996 there were reports that the National Iranian Drilling Co and SOCAR had agreed in principle to establish a joint-venture drilling company to explore for oil in the Iranian sector of the Caspian Sea. In May Oil Industries Engineering & Construction, partly owned by NIOC, agreed to take a 10% stake in Azerbaijan's Shakh-Deniz oilfield in the Caspian Sea, which is being developed by a consortium comprising SOCAR, BP, Statoil of Norway and TPAO of Turkey. The field is estimated to contain some 1,800m. barrels of oil, light oil condensates and gas, and the total cost of development is estimated at about US $4,000m. Azerbaijan was reported to have offered Iran a share in the Shakh-Deniz field after withdrawing its earlier offer of a share in Azerbaijan International Operating Consortium (see above). After some seven months of negotiations, Iran and Kazakhstan signed an oil swap agreement in May 1996. The agreement was regarded as a breakthrough for Iran's economic and political ambitions in the Central Asian region. Swap deals with Iran involving US oil companies operating in the area of the former USSR were exempted from the US trade and investment embargo imposed on Iran by the Clinton Administration.

However, the agreement with Kazakhstan was not implemented until January 1997, partly because both countries wished to circumvent possible difficulties caused by US sanctions. The contract lasts 10 years, with average deliveries scheduled to rise from 40,000 b/d during the first two years to 120,000 b/d by the sixth year. Crude from Kazakhstan's Tengiz oil field will be delivered to the Iranian port of Neka on the Caspian Sea and an equivalent amount of Iranian crude will be lifted at Iran's Gulf terminal at Kharg Island. The Kazakh crude involved in the swap deal will come from supplies owned by the Kazakh Government, not from the US companies Mobil and Chevron which are partners in the development of the Tengiz oilfield. The first deliveries of Kazakh crude to northern Iran took place in January 1997, but problems arose because of the oil's inferior quality and it was not until May that the first reciprocal lifting of Iranian crude from the Gulf began. In December 1996 Iran and Russia announced that they had formed a joint company to explore for oil under the Caspian Sea. In May 1997 it was reported that Oil Industries Engineering and Construction had obtained a 10% stake in the Lenkoran-Talyush Deniz offshore oilfield in Azerbaijan being developed by Elf-Aquitaine and Total of France, Deminex of Germany, Agip of Italy and Azerbaijan's SOCAR.

The construction of a 325-km oil pipeline from the Iranian Caspian Sea port of Neka to Tehran—a US $360m. contract for which had been won by the state-owned Iran Power Plant Projects Management Company (MAPNA) in December 1998—encountered delays when MAPNA and an associated Chinese consortium failed to raise the necessary finance in late 1999, following which the China National Petroleum Corpn withdrew in June 2000. The Iranian Government nevertheless continued to promote the pipeline, envisaging that up to 370,000 b/d of oil from Kazakhstan and Turkmenistan would be carried to refineries in northern Iran and equivalent quantities of 'swap' crude provided at Gulf terminals to customers of the two Central Asian states. The first stage of the pipeline was completed in January 2001, when Kazakhstan and Turkmenistan began to supply oil at the rate of 50,000 b/d. Iran also initiated talks on a longer 1,500-km pipeline linking onshore oilfields in Kazakhstan and Turkmenistan with the Iranian pipeline network, claiming that it could be completed within three years at half the cost of the US-sponsored plan, provisionally agreed in November 1999,

for a pipeline to carry Central Asian and Caspian Sea oil from Baku (Azerbaijan) to Ceyhan (Turkey), thus bypassing Iran.

In May 2000 the Majlis authorized NIOC to seek foreign investment partners in developing the oil and gas resources of the Caspian Sea, on the basis of Iran's contention that the sea should be divided into equal sectors between the five littoral states. In March 2002 the Iranian Minister of Oil asserted that Iran would begin exploiting its sector within a short time and would not permit any other party to engage in oil exploration in that area. A meeting of the five countries in May ended without agreement on a delimitation treaty.

Refineries and Facilities

The loss of the Abadan refinery, destroyed in the early stages of the war with Iraq, with a production capacity that had reached 628,000 b/d, affected the already difficult situation in Iran for oil products. Iran has traditionally imported some refined products, such as kerosene in winter, and has had shortages in the middle distillates range (diesel oil, kerosene and heating oil). The loss of Abadan denied Iran the flexibility of changing product volumes to meet market or seasonal variations of demand. Abadan was a highly sophisticated and flexible refinery, capable of substantial product conversion. It was also one of the main sources of aviation fuel and gasoline. With the Abadan refinery destroyed, Iran's refining capacity stood at 555,000 b/d in 1980; this had risen to 574,000 b/d by mid-1985, produced at Esfahan (200,000 b/d), Tehran (254,000 b/d), Tabriz (80,000 b/d) and Shiraz (40,000 b/d). However, Iran succeeded in raising its refinery output to levels far above rated capacity. Refinery output was 642,000 b/d in 1983/84 and 685,310 b/d in 1984/85, and at the end of 1985 the refineries were reported to be operating at 31% above design capacity, giving a total output of 728,000 b/d. The refineries at Esfahan (its capacity increased to 380,000 b/d by 1986) and Shiraz were said to be producing at 50% and 35% above their respective capacities. However, Iraqi air attacks were believed to have reduced capacity to about 500,000 b/d by 1988, resulting in the reimposition of petrol rationing and the need to import some petroleum products.

Following the 1988 cease-fire, the Government started to rebuild its oil facilities. The Abadan oil refinery is symbolic of this reconstruction, and the first phase was completed in April 1989, allowing production of 130,000 b/d. The second phase was completed in April 1991, bringing the plant's capacity to 250,000 b/d. In early 1996 the refinery was reported to be operating at 300,000 b/d, about one-half of its pre-war capacity. In March 1996 the refinery began producing jet fuel, with a daily output of 1.33m. litres, saving Iran an estimated US $200,000 per day in hard currency previously spent on imports. The reconstruction of the Abadan refinery brought the total output of domestic refineries to about 800,000 b/d. It was reported in May 1999 that the National Iranian Oil Refining and Distribution Company (NIORDC) had invited bids for a US $300m. upgrading of the main Abadan refinery.

In April 1993 President Rafsanjani stated that imports of petroleum products amounting to 300,000 b/d were a wasteful expenditure, costing up to $1,800m. per year. The Minister of Oil told a press conference held in April 1993 that Iran's refining capacity would reach 1,285m. b/d in early 1994, and could be raised to 1.6m. b/d in emergencies. He stated that 1993 was the last year in which refined products would have to be imported. In May 1995, however, the Ministry of Oil projected that oil product imports would average 70,000 b/d during 1995/96 and that they had been as high as 100,000 b/d during the winter months.

In September 1989 it was announced that the reconstruction of the Tabriz and Esfahan oil refineries was complete and that they were supplying almost 50% of Iran's domestic oil requirements. Expansion work at the Tehran and Kermanshah refineries was also reported to be progressing. Bids for a continuous catalytic reforming unit for the Tehran refinery commenced in April 1992. In September 1994 a new furnace was commissioned at the Shiraz oil refinery which, together with other work, raised capacity there from 45,000 b/d to 55,000 b/d. In early 1995 it was reported that the Tabriz and Tehran refineries together could process more than 300,000 b/d, and the Esfahan refinery 300,000 b/d. The construction of new refineries at Bandar Abbas, Bandar Taheri and Arak, and the expansion of the Esfahan refinery, were designated priority projects by NIOC, but the programme experienced considerable delays. The contract for the 150,000-b/d Arak refinery was awarded to an Italian-Japanese consortium in May 1989. The US $1,100m. refinery was inaugurated by President Rafsanjani in September 1993, and in April 1994 it was reported to be producing 165,000 b/d, 10% more than its nominal capacity. Construction of the export refinery at Bandar Abbas should have been completed in 1993, but financial problems delayed work on the project. The contract had originally been awarded to Snamprogetti of Italy and Chiyoda Corpn of Japan, but when the partnership had financing problems NIOC handed over the project to local contractors working under the supervision of Snamprogetti and Chiyoda. The plant has a crude refining capacity of 232,000 b/d, and can process 12,000 b/d of condensates from the nearby Sarkhun fields. In March 1994 the Director-General of the National Iranian Tanker Co announced that six 80,000-ton tankers would be purchased in order to supply the Bandar Abbas refinery. A $10m. jetty, near Bandar Abbas port, for handling tankers bringing crude oil from the Kharg Island terminal to the Bandar Abbas refinery, was due to open in March 1996. The Bandar Abbas refinery received its first cargo of crude oil in May 1997 and was officially opened on 26 July. NIOC received bids in November 1998 for the construction of a 35,000-b/d condensates refining facility at the Bandar Abbas refinery. The scheme is a reduced version of a 70,000–80,000 b/d condensates refinery originally planned at Bandar Taheri. The facility was resited and retendered in 1995, but NIOC decided to reduce its capacity in 1997 and integrate it into Bandar Abbas. A new isomax unit came on stream at Bandar Abbas in February 1999. In March 1995 the Minister of Oil stated that Iran planned to increase refinery capacity from 1.1m. b/d to 1.7m. b/d by 2000. In October 1996 the oil ministry announced that the country's refinery capacity had reached 1.24m. b/d. In June 1995 it was reported that the Daewoo Corpn of South Korea was to build five 300,000-dwt oil tankers for the National Iranian Tanker Co, to be delivered in 1996. A $490m. loan had been arranged from a banking consortium led by South Korean institutions.

With the increase in domestic refinery capacity, petrol rationing was ended in February 1991. Three years after the end of the war with Iraq NIOC's inability to meet growing domestic demand for petroleum products provoked strong criticism. Iran continued to experience fuel shortages during the winter months of most years because of insufficient refinery capacity and transportation problems. In January 1994 the Minister of Oil stated that there was a stockpile of some 1,700m. litres of fuel, and thus no serious shortages were envisaged that year. Iran also expected to resume oil supplies to the Sasolburg refinery in South Africa, in which NIOC has had a 17.5% share since 1970. Until 1979, when oil supplies were suspended, Iran was supplying 70% of the refinery's crude oil under a 20-year agreement. NIOC has retained its shareholding despite the suspension in oil supplies. Negotiations between Iran and South Africa began early in 1994 for South African refineries to resume purchases of Iranian crude after the multi-racial elections in April. Iran was South Africa's major supplier of crude until 1979. During a visit to Tehran in April 1996 South Africa's Minister of Foreign Affairs stated that an agreement negotiated in 1995 for storage facilities for Iranian crude at Saldanha Bay, near Cape Town (to improve Iranian access to African, and possibly transatlantic, markets) was pending resolution of technical problems unrelated to politics. He reaffirmed that, despite US pressure, South Africa would continue to co-operate with Iran in oil, gas and mining. Since the end of apartheid Iran has supplied almost three-quarters of South Africa's crude oil imports. When President Rafsanjani visited South Africa in September 1996 he advocated greater co-operation between the two countries' oil industries, but indicated that Iran would not be making use of the Saldanha Bay facility immediately because it had insufficient supplies of crude petroleum available.

As of January 2002 Iran possessed nine operational refineries (Abadan, Esfahan, Tehran, Bandar Abbas, Arak, Tabriz, Shiraz, Kermanshah and Lavan) with an aggregate capacity of 1.5m. b/d, the Government's aim being to boost refining capacity to 2m. b/d during the TFYDP (to 2005). New refineries planned for the early 21st century include a 225,000 b/d plant at Shah

Bahar, a 120,000 b/d unit on Qeshm Island and one in the Sarakhs special zone on the north-eastern border with Turkmenistan. In June 2001 a contract was awarded for upgrading work at the Tehran and Tabriz refineries to enable them to process crude petroleum supplied by neighbouring Caspian countries via a new pipeline (see External Oil Participation, above).

The country's 6,000-km internal pipeline network currently handles 1.3m. b/d of crude and oil products for domestic use. A pipeline is being constructed between the Tehran refinery and Tabriz, and another line is to be built from the new Bandar Abbas refinery to cities such as Rafsanjan, Kerman and Yazd. In early 1988 the Government revived the Moharram pipeline project, which had been abandoned in mid-1986. However, only one of two planned 320-km export pipelines—running from the Gurreh pumping station on the mainland, just north of the main Kharg Island export terminal, to export facilities at Taheri, near the central Gulf—was to be built. The project was intended to provide a safer alternative to the Kharg terminal.

NATURAL GAS

With proven reserves of 23,000,000m. cu m (at the end of 2001), Iran is the world's second richest country in natural gas resources after Russia, with some 15% of the global total and 44% of the Middle East regional total. Major new discoveries of gas deposits have been made in the last two decades, notably the South Pars offshore field, which is an extension of Qatar's North Field—officially the largest natural gas reserve in the world. As a result of such discoveries, exploitation of gas reserves has become a key government objective on a par with the development of more immediately profitable oil reserves, although attracting the necessary investment finance has proved to be problematic. While production is principally intended to meet domestic demand, in January 2002 the first exports of Iranian gas since the 1979 Islamic Revolution, to Turkey, boosted confidence that the resource would become a major export earner in the 21st century. Production of natural gas (excluding flared or recycled gas) in 2000 was estimated at 60,200m. cu m, the bulk of which was consumed domestically in line with the Government's policy of substituting gas for petroleum production for the purposes of home consumption. Natural gas currently accounts for about 40% of total domestic energy consumption.

The latest estimates put reserves in the South Pars field at around 8,000,000m. cu m of gas, of which a large proportion is recoverable at an eventual projected rate of up to 225m. cu m a day, and at 17,000m. barrels of condensate. Development of the field has become Iran's largest energy project, having attracted some US $20,000m. in investment by the end of 2001, and has so far been planned to take place in 12 phases. Eventually allocated to Petropars (60% owned by NIOC) and to the Petroleum Development and Engineering Co (Pedec, an NIOC affiliate), phase one is scheduled for completion by the end of 2002, although it is reported to be running several months behind schedule; it will result in daily production of 25m. cu m of gas and 40,000 b/d of condensate. Phases two and three have been allocated to TotalFinaElf of France in association with Hyundai of South Korea, and are expected to produce around 50m. cu m. of gas a day and 80,000 b/d of condensate. In April 2002 the first delivery of 300,000 barrels of condensate from South Pars phase two and three treatment centres was exported to the UAE. Phases four and five, each projected to cost $2,000m., are being handled by ENI of Italy in association with Petropars and are scheduled to come on line in 2004–05. Phases six, seven and eight, intended to result in combined production of 75m. cu m of gas a day and 120,000 b/d of condensate, are being handled by Petropars in a 20% association with Enterprise Oil of the United Kingdom, although the acquisition of Enterprise by Royal Dutch Shell in May 2002 raised a question-mark over its continued participation. By mid-2002 several international bidders had been short-listed for phases nine, 10, 11 and 12, although the award of contracts for the projected $4,000m. further development was being delayed by uncertainty over the terms of buy-back clauses.

In April 1993 preliminary discussions began between the National Iranian Gas Co and a number of foreign companies on the development of the offshore Pars field, often referred to as

North Pars, as distinct from South Pars. Plans to develop the field, based on exports of LNG, were first discussed in the 1970s, but were abandoned after the Revolution in 1979. Under the revised scheme, gas would be treated for domestic use only. In January 1994 there were reports that negotiations were under way with Royal Dutch Shell for an agreement on engineering studies for the North Pars field. Shell appeared to be insisting on equity participation in the project, but foreign ownership of national hydrocarbon resources is not permitted under Iran's Constitution. However, in March it was reported that the Majlis had authorized NIOC to raise up to US $3,500m. in foreign finance on a buy-back basis in order to develop oil- and gasfields together with two refineries. There was speculation that this decision might lead to a compromise with Shell over financing arrangements for the North Pars field. In November the Minister of Oil stated that negotiations between NIOC and Royal Dutch Shell about developing the North Pars gasfield were continuing, but that there were differences between the rate of return requested by Shell and that which Iran had agreed to give. The Minister said that Shell was considering exporting gas from the field to Pakistan. Shell officials confirmed that differences over the level of remuneration remained, but that negotiations were continuing because both sides were keen to reach an agreement.

In early 1994 the Minister of Oil announced the discovery of a new offshore gasfield 50 km west of the South Pars field and 180 km south-east of Bushehr, estimated to contain 566,000m. cu m of gas and 1,000m. barrels of condensate. In February 1995 Iran and Oman reportedly agreed on the joint development of the Hengam-Khasib gasfield near the Iranian island of Hengam in the Strait of Hormuz. The field has reserves of 28,300m. cu m and could, according to NIOC, be brought into production within three years. Negotiations between the two countries were concluded in January 1997, and Iran was expected to tender the development of the field under a buy-back deal at a later date.

In April 2000 the discovery was announced by the Ministry of Oil of the country's biggest onshore sweet gasfield to date, called Tabnak and situated in the Gavband region north of Bushehr. Estimated to contain 445,000m. cu m of gas not needing to be refined, as well as 240m. barrels of liquid gas, the field is expected to yield revenue of US $16,500m. over 30 years and to be brought into production in 2003.

At the core of domestic gas distribution is the projected US $4,000m. Iranian gas trunkline (IGAT) pipeline network, which is also intended to become a major conduit for gas exports, drawing in particular on output from South Pars. The completed IGAT-1 and IGAT-2 pipelines run respectively from Ahwaz to Astara in the north and from Nan-Kangan on the southern coast to Qazvin in the north, with a possible extension to Tabriz in the north-west. Under construction in 2002, IGAT-3 will run from the southern coast to Tehran, while IGAT-4 was under evaluation as the gas pipeline link between the southern port of Bandar Abbas and the industrial centre of Esfahan in central Iran. In June 2002 it was disclosed that Mitsui of Japan was negotiating to provide finance for the proposed 500-km IGAT-5 trunkline to carry South Pars gas for reinjection into the Aghajari oilfield.

Following the disintegration of the USSR, Iran sought to establish economic agreements with the newly-independent former Soviet republics. In February 1992 the Iranian Minister of Oil announced details of an agreement, signed in January, to supply gas to the Ukraine via Azerbaijan. Some 3,000m. cu m of gas were to be supplied during 1992 through the existing IGAT-1 pipeline. Over the four years covered by the agreement gas exports were to total 75,000m. cu m. In February 1993 Iran and Ukraine agreed to build a gas pipeline from Iran to Ukraine through Azerbaijan and Russia, with a capacity of 25,000m. cu m per year. In March 1993 it was reported that the gas project had failed to gain formal consent from Russia. In November 1992 an agreement was signed with Azerbaijan for Iran to supply 300m. cu m of gas per year in exchange for 100,000 tons of gasoil. Gas was to be supplied through the IGAT-1 trunkline. Gasoil from Azerbaijan would supply Iran's north-western provinces to make up for shortages in domestic distribution. In August 1994 an agreement was announced on the supply of Iranian gas to the Azeri republic of Nakhichevan and to Georgia. The gas

exports would reportedly be taken from the IGAT-1 trunkline during off-peak months, as most of the throughput supplies Iranian domestic users. Georgia would be supplied with 5m. cu m per day, starting in 1994, using an existing pipeline through the Republic of Azerbaijan; and an 80-km pipeline was to be built to Nakhichevan to carry 1m. cu m of gas. Also in August 1994 Iran and Turkmenistan agreed to co-operate in the construction of a gas pipeline to Europe, a project expected to cost US $7,000m. The pipeline would be 4,000 km long, with some 1,450 km passing through Iran. The cost of the Iranian section was estimated at $3,500m., but no details were given about how the scheme would be financed. Iran would earn transit fees for Turkmen gas passing through the pipeline. According to the Ministry of Oil, the pipeline would carry up to 15,000m. cu m of gas per year in the first phase, with throughput eventually almost doubling to 28,000m. cu m. The proposed pipeline provoked opposition from the USA, which urged Turkmenistan to seek alternative routes. In September 1995 it was announced that Iran and Turkmenistan had agreed on a $190m. project to build a 200-km gas pipeline across their common border, through which up to 10,000m. cu m per year would be pumped from Turkmenistan's Korpedzhe gasfield to Kurt-Kui in Iran. Gas began flowing through the pipeline in December 1997 at a rate of 10m. cu m per day, which was set to increase to 26m. cu m a day in late 2000.

In January 1994 officials of the Iranian Institute for Political and International Studies announced that they had proposed a major gas pipeline loop system around Iran from which spurs could be constructed to India, the Central Asian republics, Turkey and, eventually, Europe via Turkey. They had named it PEACE (Pipeline Extending from Asian Countries to Europe). More than one-half of the loop was already in existence. One of the officials commented that LNG schemes were not economical while oil prices remained below US $20 per barrel. In spite of the resumption of gas exports, the use of gas is still being encouraged for domestic purposes, in order to save oil and to reduce pollution. More than 13,000 km of gas distribution lines have been built in cities since 1979, but implementation of the residential gas programme has been delayed by a shortage of regulators. The SFYDP, which began in March 1995, proposed greater domestic use of gas resources in order to allow more oil to be exported.

In October 1990 NIOC announced a joint study with Gaz de France to assess the cost of transporting natural gas to France and other European countries. In April 1993 it was reported that Ruhrgas of Germany, Austria's ONV and Enagas of Spain would take part in the consortium with Gaz de France. If the plans proceed, central and eastern European countries could be supplied first by pipeline, but for western Europe it remained unclear whether transport by pipeline or ship would be preferred. In November 1993 Iran and India signed a memorandum of understanding regarding a gas pipeline from Bandar Abbas to the Indian state of Gujarat. During a visit to New Delhi in April 1995 by President Rafsanjani, India and Iran agreed on wide-ranging co-operation in the oil and gas sectors, which included the completion, in 1995, of the feasibility study for a 2,200-km gas pipeline from southern Iran to the west coast of India with a capacity of 50m. cu m a day, a project estimated to cost US $5,000m. Iran was said to favour a route through Pakistan, but India preferred an underwater route off the Pakistan coast. Subsequent talks on the proposal failed to make much progress because of financial and political obstacles. In March 2000, however, the Gas Authority of India confirmed that it was engaged in fresh discussions with NIOC on a deepwater pipeline that would not involve Pakistan, and in February 2001 Iran and India reportedly reached agreement regarding construction of the deep-water pipeline.

In September 1994 Iran agreed to participate in a US $3,200m. project, initiated by the UAE-based Crescent Petroleum Co, to build a 1,600-km pipeline to carry gas from Qatar to Pakistan. Under the agreement Iran would allow the pipeline to go through Iranian coastal waters and have the option of using the line for its own gas exports, but would have no financial involvement. The pipeline was to have a capacity of 45m. cu m a day by 1999, and its capacity could be doubled by increasing the number of compressors in the line. Discussions have been taking place between Iran and Pakistan for some time about a possible overland gas pipeline linking the two countries, and in January 1995 Iran and Pakistan were said to have reached an agreement to set up a consortium to build a gas pipeline from Bandar Asaluyeh to Karachi. As a number of US companies are involved in the Qatar gas line, the future of Iranian participation may be questioned as a result of the US trade embargo on Iran introduced in May 1995. In February 1996 the National Iranian Gas Co announced that, following completion of a feasibility study, construction work would begin on a joint natural gas pipeline with Pakistan, with a capacity of about 45m. cu m per day and costing $2,000m. In mid-1999 the main contractor, BHP Petroleum of Australia, confirmed that it had put the project on hold because of promising gas finds in Pakistan itself, although Pakistani officials continued to express interest in the pipeline.

In mid-November 1994 a team from ENI of Italy had visited Tehran for talks on participation in gas, pipeline and energy projects in Iran, Central Asia and the Caucasus. ENI stated that it wished to participate in the proposed US $7,000m. gas pipeline project from Turkmenistan to Europe via Iran and Turkey and had discussed Iran's own gas export pipeline scheme to Europe.

In August 1996 Iran signed an agreement worth US $20,000m. to supply gas to Turkey over a 22-year period. The contract was worded so that the Turkish state oil company, BOTAŞ, would not incur US sanctions for its involvement in the project. Nevertheless, several members of the US Congress condemned the accord and demanded sanctions against BOTAŞ. US officials visited Ankara but failed to persuade the Turkish Government to withdraw from the project: they insisted that the agreement was a necessary element of their plans to diversify the country's energy sources. The project involves the construction of a pipeline, 1,420-km long, from Tabriz in Iran to Erzurum in Turkey, an extension of the Turkish section of the pipeline from Erzurum to Ankara being planned at a later stage. Each country is responsible for financing the section of the pipeline in its own territory. Under the original schedule the pipeline was to have been completed by 1999, with initial deliveries of gas rising from 3,000m. cu m per day to 10,000m. cu m per day in 2005. However, after each side had accused the other of not being ready with their section of the pipeline and successive revised target dates had not been met, deliveries eventually started in January 2002 and were the first Iranian gas exports since before the Revolution.

At the end of December 1996 Iran's Minister of Oil signed a memorandum of understanding with the Turkish oil minister and the Deputy Prime Minister of Turkmenistan for the delivery of Turkmen gas to Turkey via the Iranian pipeline system after the completion of the Turkish-Iranian gas pipeline. At the end of July 1997 the US Administration announced that it would not oppose the construction of a US $1,600m. pipeline to carry natural gas from land-locked Turkmenistan to Turkey across a 788-km stretch of northern Iran because the project did not technically violate the 1996 secondary sanctions law. It was reported that Iran had agreed to finance and build the section of the pipeline passing through its territory. Turkey signed an agreement in May 1997 to purchase Turkmen gas, and US officials maintained that the agreement would ensure Turkey's reliance on Turkmen rather than Iranian gas. However, an oil industry source stated that under the agreement Turkmen gas would be pumped into the Iranian pipeline system and that Iran would send an equivalent amount of gas to Turkey.

OTHER MINERALS

According to the latest official statistics available, there are 2,704 producing mines in Iran, breaking down as follows by type of activity: gravel and sand 1,223, rubble stone 335, decorative stones 305, gypsum 206, limestone 164, silica 71, salt 62, coal 61, kaolin and fireclay 60, barite (barytes) 24, sodium sulphate 23, iron ore 20, magnesite 19, ores slag 18, other 113. The total value of non-hydrocarbon mineral production in 1995/96 was IR 1,936,000m.

Deposits of lead-zinc ore are mined at Bafq near Yazd, at Khomeini, west of Esfahan, and at Ravanj, near Qom, with a combined potential of 600 metric tons of concentrates daily, though current plans for development are limited to Bafq. In June 1992 a German-Canadian consortium won a US $250m.

contract to build a zinc plant in Zanjan province. However, the facility was eventually built by local firms and opened in April 1997. The plant has a capacity of 7,000 tons of zinc sheets per year, and there are plans to double output. Iran Zinc Mines Development Co issued a tender in February 1999 for the construction, with 49% foreign participation, of a zinc ingot plant, with an annual production capacity of 100,000 tons, to be located in Zanjan province, intended to meet a national annual production target of 400,000 tons by 2010. Iran's largest lead mine is at Nakhlak, near Esfahan. In 1995/96 the value of Iran's lead and zinc output was IR 92,000m.

Chromium from the Elburz mountains and near Bandar Abbas, red oxide from Hormuz in the Persian Gulf and turquoise from Nishapur are all produced for export. Sulphur and salt are produced on the coast of the Gulf, near Bandar Abbas, and Iran exported 105,000 metric tons in the year 1985/86. Iran is also the second largest exporter of strontium, after Mexico, and during the second half of 1985/86 and the first half of 1986/87 exported 25,000 tons, valued at US $2.9m. Strontium reserves are estimated at 1.1m. tons. In 1986 Iran's phosphate resources were calculated at 220m. tons. Annual imports of phosphate fertilizers total 1m. tons, worth $300m., so a major portion of domestic demand would be met by developing the country's phosphate reserves. In July 1992 it was announced that the country's largest phosphate deposit, with reserves of 400m. tons, had been discovered in Charam in the southern province of Yasuj.

The major iron ore deposits are in Kerman province in south-east Iran, in particular at Bafq, where proven reserves total 911m. metric tons of ore, and at Chadormelo mine, in Yazd province, which has proven reserves of 500m. tons. In February 1992 it was reported that Bafq was producing 4m. tons per year. In December 1991 a Japanese consortium signed a contract to build an ore concentrator at Chadormelo, with a projected annual production rate of 5m. tons, to supply the Mobarakeh steel complex at Esfahan. In late 1991 the Ministry of Mines and Metals invited bids to expand the existing Chogart iron ore complex near Yazd. After lengthy negotiations the US $100m. contract was eventually offered to a European consortium led by Voest Alpine of Austria in October 1994. The consortium was to supply two concentrators, each with an annual capacity of 1.6m. tons and would also carry out engineering work, supervision of erection and the commissioning of the facility. Output at the mine was scheduled to rise from 3m. tons to 6m. tons per year. The ore from Bafq was to be carried 540 km by a specially developed railway to the $4,700m. Mobarakeh steel plant. The Gol-e-Gohar iron ore mining complex in Kerman province, originally planned before the Revolution, was officially opened in March 1994 by President Rafsanjani. Production at the $114m. complex began in December 1993. Output of 2.5m. tons of concentrate will be used to supply the Mobarakeh steel plant at Esfahan. Production will eventually be expanded to 5m. tons per year. Total output from Iran's 20 iron-ore mines was valued at IR 231,000m. in 1995/96.

Coal reserves are estimated at 6,000m. metric tons, of which about one-third are capable of exploitation. The main mines are around Kerman and in Mazandaran, Semnan and Tabas. An 85-km railway is being built from Kerman, the major mining area, to supply coal shale to the Zarand refinery. The Shahroud mines in Semnan supply 15% of the requirements of the Esfahan steel mill. In 1987/88 Iran produced 95,706 tons of melted cast iron and 1,471,699 tons of steel. Coal production in 1985 recovered to the pre-Revolutionary level of 900,000 tons per year, but remained insufficient for domestic consumption, requiring imports of around 400,000 tons per year. Production declined to 722,000 tons in 1986, but rose to 791,000 tons in 1987. Production from Iran's 61 coal mines was worth IR 358,000m. in 1995/96, making it the largest non-oil mining sector by value. Coal production in 2000 was estimated at 1.4m. tons and domestic consumption at 2.2m. tons. In January 2002 plans were confirmed under which the Tabas coal mine would become Iran's first mechanized underground mine, with annual output of 1.5m. tons of coking coal that would be used by steel plants in Esfahan currently dependent on imported supplies.

Deposits of copper ore have been found in Azerbaijan province, Kerman and in the Yazd and Anarak areas. A number of very important deposits have been discovered since 1967 in the

Kerman area, the most important being at Sar Cheshmeh. The reserves at Sar Cheshmeh are estimated at 1,200m. metric tons (the second largest deposit in the world), including perhaps 600m. tons of 1.12% copper content, with another 600m. tons of lower grade beneath. The project includes the construction of road and rail links to connect the mine with Bandar Abbas 400 km away on the Gulf, a training school, and a new town for the families of the work-force. The construction of a large smelter/refinery and associated rolling mill and two continuous casting mills was halted during the Revolution. The mine was officially opened in May 1982. Initially the plant operated at substantially below its capacity of 158,000 tons of refined copper per year but, since production began in mid-1984, output rose to 40,000 tons in 1985/86, and to 50,000 tons in 1986/87. Following the opening of new units in February 1989, output increased to 100,000 tons per year by mid-1992. Techpro Mining and Metallurgy of the United Kingdom was appointed as general consultant by the National Iranian Copper Industries Co (NICICO) to advise on expanding production at Sar Cheshmeh. By 1994 Sar Cheshmeh had a capacity of 120,000 tons per year and there were plans eventually to expand it to 200,000 tons. A molybdenum production unit started operating at the Sar Cheshmeh copper refinery in June 1983. A copper extrusion plant was installed at the Shahid Bahonar copper complex, in Kerman, in 1987. Output of copper and copper alloy semi-finished products—tube, sheet, bar and rods from the plant, which opened in 1989, has risen from less than 10,000 tons per year to 18,000 tons per year. The plant was expected to have reached full capacity of 55,000 tons in 1996. A substantial proportion of the output is exported, mainly to Japan and other countries in the Far East. In 1986/87 28,000 tons of copper and molybdenum from Sar Cheshmeh were exported in the form of copper wire and molybdenum, and a further 6,000 tons of blister copper. A much smaller copper mine at Minakhan, developed in association with Japanese interests, has been brought under complete Iranian ownership. In September 1994 work began on a US $106m. copper smelter at Khatounabad, about 40 km west of the main Sar Cheshmeh mine and complex. The smelter, which will have a capacity of 80,000 tons, will use ore from the undeveloped Meidouk mines nearby, and ore from Sungun in East Azerbaijan and Ahar mines will also be used. Output will supply the Sar Cheshmeh complex and nearby downstream facilities. The project is a joint venture between NICICO and National Non-Ferrous Metals Co of China. Originally it had been projected to cost $300m., but in order to save hard currency about 40% of the work will be done with domestic resources. According to the Minister of Mines and Metals, national copper production increased from 74,000 tons to 100,000 tons in 1994/95, while copper ore output was valued at IR 269,000m. in 1995/96. In 1996 NICICO projected that copper production in 1996/97 would reach 150,000 tons, with capacity increasing to 250,000 tons within a few years. Some 30,000 tons of copper were to be exported in 1996/97. To augment production capacity, NICICO purchased an 80,000 tons-per-year smelter from the People's Republic of China which was expected to start production by 2000. Some parts of NICICO's operations had already been privatized and the company prepared to be floated on the Tehran stock market during 1997.

In March 1976 it was announced that important uranium deposits had been found in Iran's northern and western regions, and in 1978 agreements were signed with West German and French companies to carry out surveys. The scope and pace of exploration were reduced after the Revolution, but deposits of more than 5,000 metric tons of uranium ore were discovered in the Saghand region of Yazd in central Iran in 1984 and there were plans to develop the site. Long-term plans, proposed during the reign of the Shah, for a network of 20 nuclear power stations were abandoned because the project was too expensive, too dependent on Western technology and unnecessary in view of the availability of cheap natural gas.

In 1988 construction work began on a gold-processing plant at Muteh, near Esfahan, using ore from a deposit estimated at 1.2m. metric tons, which, it was hoped, would yield 5 tons of gold. In April 1999 the South African-based Anglo-American Corporation signed a memorandum of understanding with the state General Iranian Mining Company (GIMCO) for the development of the Zarshuran gold mine, near Orumiyeh in north-western Iran, which was reported to require investment of at least US $300m.

Two rich mineral deposits were discovered in the northern provinces of Gilan and Mazandaran in the first half of 1985: one consisted of an estimated 51,000 metric tons of mica, and the other of 20m. tons of silica. Further discoveries of reserves of silica, limestone, granite and iron, totalling an estimated 194m. tons, were made in Gilan during the last quarter of 1985. Proven reserves of bauxite at Jafarm are estimated at 22m. tons, with an average purity of 48%. In June 1995 President Rafsanjani inaugurated work on a 20,000-tons-per-year pilot alumina extraction plant being constructed at Azarshahr, in eastern Azerbaijan province. The plant was due to be completed in two years, extracting alumina from the nepheline-syenite mines of Kolebar and Sarab which have estimated deposits of 30,000m. tons. The state-owned Iran Aluminium Co (Iralco) subsequently established an aluminium smelter at Arak with output capacity of 120,000 tons per year and another at Bandar Abbas with a potential capacity of 110,000 tons per year. In November 2001 Iralco awarded a US $200m. contract to a Chinese company for the construction of a second aluminium smelter at Arak with a capacity of 110,000 tons per year, as part of the Government's objective of increasing aluminium production to 1m. tons per year by 2009.

Iran's exports of non-hydrocarbon minerals in 1985/86, mainly copper, coal, chromite and metal concentrates, were valued at US $70m., and the total was increased to $85m. in 1986/87: of the 50m. metric tons of minerals extracted in that year, 230,000 tons were exported. Mineral exports reached 486,413 tons in 1987/88, worth $90.2m., although total mineral extraction from Iran's active mines declined to 45m. tons. During the five years to March 1993 it was planned to spend some $5,000m. in order to increase the mining sector's share of GDP from 1% to 5%. This represented the fulfilment of one of the Iranian Government's stated aims: the development of the country's non-hydrocarbon raw materials to supply the demands of the country's expanding metal manufacturing facilities. In April 1994 the Minister of Mines and Metals announced that exports of metal concentrates and minerals had earned $1,400m. during the three years to March 1994. At the beginning of 1995 the minister stated that, following extensive privatization in recent years, the ministry retained control over only three to four big mines that required heavy investment. The non-oil mining sector's share of GDP remained consistently at 0.5% during 1992–98. The value of exports of minerals and metals increased by nearly 50% by 1997/98, to $374m., and rose further, to $460m., in 1998/99.

At a mining conference held in Tehran in October 1999 international investors were offered mining and metals projects worth more than US $10,000m.; the Minister of Mines and Metals further announced that the Government also wished to sell off 60 state-owned mines and six incomplete state projects. In March 2000 excavation began at the Venarej manganese deposits south-west of Qom, where reserves of 6m. metric tons were expected to yield annual production of 100,000 tons of high-grade ore.

MANUFACTURING AND INDUSTRY

After the 1979 Revolution no clear policy was formulated for the industrial sector. Of the modern manufacturing plants that were established under the Shah's regime, those which remained in production (estimated at only 20% of the total by value of output) encountered serious difficulties. Raw materials were in short supply, as were spare parts and other inputs. In March 1981 President Bani-Sadr estimated that in the period March 1979–March 1980 industrial and related output declined by 34% and was still falling, possibly at an even faster rate. In 1982 some reports indicated that increased reserves of foreign exchange and larger imports of raw materials had allowed production in many factories to be expanded. They also noted that factories producing goods for the war effort were working overtime, with Iranian engineers and technicians learning to repair, adapt and make items that had formerly been imported. Nevertheless, officials admitted that only a small number of factories were properly operational. Many factories were operating at only 30% capacity in the late 1980s, although considerable improvement has been reported in state-owned industrial producers since 1990.

After the end of the war with Iraq the FFYDP placed emphasis on the development of heavy industry, and this sector was given priority access to reserves of foreign exchange. In spite of debate about the privatization of Iranian industry, until 1991 almost all industrial projects were state-sponsored. However, in February 1991 the Minister of Economic Affairs and Finance announced that 400 state-controlled light industrial companies would be sold during the next three years as part of the Government's plans for privatization. It was also announced that heavy industry, previously monopolized by the state, would be opened to private investment. In May 1991 the Minister of Industries announced that the National Iranian Industries Organization (NIIO) was to offer shares to the value of IR 100,000m. in its companies for acquisition by the public during 1991–92. In April the Ministry of Oil invited the private sector to invest in petrochemical projects and gave an assurance that other sectors of the oil industry would be made accessible to private investors. In addition, foreign companies are now able to invest in heavy industries. There was speculation that the Government would face criticism—on purely political grounds—for opening the door to foreign capital even though the Constitution does not forbid foreign investment or ownership. In July 1992 there were reports that the International Finance Corporation (IFC) was entering the private-sector market in Iran with possible equity participation or finance for two large industrial projects. The IFC's involvement followed the return to Iran of the World Bank. Privatization of state industries appears to have made only slow progress. In March 1994 Massoud Roghani Zanjani of the Plan and Budget Organization stated that privatization through the Tehran Stock Exchange had not proved satisfactory. The Government planned to sell factories by auction or negotiation in order to accelerate the privatization process. In August 1993 shares were offered on the stock exchange in Iran Khodro, the country's largest car assembly plant. The plant was nationalized after the Revolution. Some 33% of the shares were reserved for workers, with employees at the plant offered preferential terms.

Privatization plans received a set-back in mid-1994, when the Majlis approved legislation giving selected groups, such as former prisoners of war, the war disabled, the families of those killed in the war with Iraq and members of the paramilitary *basij*, privileged access to shares. The priority goal of the privatization process was to achieve a more equitable distribution of wealth, and the new legislation required proceeds from share sales to be devoted to the country's underdeveloped regions. The aims conflicted with those of the Industrial Development and Renovation Organization (IDRO) and the NIIO, the two state organizations involved in the privatization programme, which hoped to use the sales to raise revenues, to develop the capital market and to raise the standard of industrial management. IDRO officials admitted that the new legislation had made privatization more difficult and had slowed down the process. However, they expressed the hope that the involvement of new, less affluent groups of shareholders would inject new vigour into the privatization process. In the three years to March 1994, out of a total of 130 companies scheduled for privatization, IDRO had sold 50 factories through the Tehran Stock Exchange and in bilateral deals, raising IR 240,000m. (US $140m.). Of the 80 remaining companies, which had an aggregate turnover of $1,000m., 10 car makers accounted for over one-half of the annual turnover. In early 1995 the Minister of Industries forecast that only 10% of Iranian industry would be state-owned by 2000, compared with 45% in 1990. Only very large industries would ultimately remain under state control. Early in 1997 it was reported that the Government was still committed to the sale of 57% of all IDRO's assets. The privatization programme had been relatively slow in 1992–96, raising only $200m., but sales rose sharply in 1996/97 when IDRO raised an estimated $260m. State-owned vehicle companies, which have undergone considerable restructuring, were expected to be targeted for privatization in 1997/98, when IDRO hoped to raise $260m. from sales of its assets. Nevertheless, it is likely to be many years before Iranian industry shifts from predominantly state to largely private ownership. More than one-half of the country's annual budget expenditure is devoted to supporting loss-making state industries and banks.

In September 1994 the Majlis approved legislation merging the Ministry of Heavy Industries with the Ministry of Industry, but rejected a proposal to include the Ministry of Metals and Minerals in the merger on the grounds that a special ministry was necessary to develop minerals as a major export item. The plan to merge the three ministries had been proposed in the Majlis three years previously, but was opposed by the Government. Both the Ministry of Industries and the Ministry of Mines and Metals (which finally merged at the end of 2000) have emphasized the need to encourage training in modern management and the establishment of research and development departments. Co-operation is also being encouraged between industry and the country's universities. The Minister of Industries claimed that Iran can design in many fields and has a domestic engineering capability. In addition to the private companies that have grown up around the Esfahan steel complex (see below), innovation has been notable in the car industry. An affiliate of IDRO, Sazeh Gostar Co, has redesigned and re-engineered the Renault 5 car, which used to be assembled from imported kits, and the first completely Iranian-made model was expected to be manufactured by early 1996 and on sale at half the price of its nearest equivalent. Some predict a transformation of the Iranian car industry in the coming years as more local design, engineering and manufacture develop. The country's own design and engineering capacity is being utilized increasingly through the greater involvement of local contractors in building industrial plants, reducing costs and leading to savings in hard currency.

A new strategic plan for industry was incorporated into the SFYDP, which began in March 1995; the emphasis was on the themes of restructuring, good administration, privatization, mobilizing domestic expertise and manufacturing capacity, selective foreign investment, and developing exports. It is hoped that industrial exports will eventually earn between US $2,000m. and $4,000m. annually, with food manufacturing industries registering the greatest expansion in export earnings. At present it is steel, copper and aluminium which earn the major share of export earnings. In July 1996 the Minister of Industries stated that the Government was ensuring that the industrial sector received allocations of foreign exchange to pay for vital inputs, and that some $640m. had been allocated to fund imports for the industrial sector during 1996/97. The minister also proposed new legislation to establish a clearer framework to encourage greater private investment in the industrial sector. In November 1996, in his budget speech to the Majlis, President Rafsanjani commented on the success of the industrial sector in recent years and claimed that the value of industrial exports had increased from $150m. in 1989/90 to a projected $1,500m. in 1996/97.

Steel, petrochemicals and copper remain the country's three basic industries. Other important branches are automobile manufacture (many assembled from kits, under licence from Western and Japanese manufactures, such as Nissan), which has expanded rapidly in recent years, machine tools, construction materials, pharmaceuticals, textiles and food processing. With the exception of one major petrochemical plant and a number of textile and construction materials ventures, all these industries were nationalized after the Revolution. Annual cement production doubled between 1976 and 1986, reaching 13m. metric tons in the latter year. Output declined to 12.5m. tons in 1988. In early 1989 a foreign-exchange allocation of US $40m. was announced to equip a cement works. Two plants have been built in Kurdistan and Hormuzgan, and a 2,300-tons-per-day plant at Orumiyah commenced operations in 1989. In 1990 the Ministry of Industries announced plans to increase the total national output of cement to 33m. tons per year by the late 1990s. Some 27 new cement works were to be built, at a cost of $800m., in the five years to 1995. In 1990 the annual capacity of the existing 15 cement plants was 17m. tons, but only 12m. tons per year was being produced, owing to shortages of foreign exchange and electricity. Production in 1992/93 was estimated at 16m. tons, and annual domestic demand at 20m. tons. In November 1992 the Ministry of Industries stated that 19 cement plants, costing $555m., were under construction and another 31 'in-principle' agreements had been signed. During 1993 the

IFC was involved in negotiations concerning investment in or lending to at least four cement schemes and was negotiating with several European equipment suppliers as potential investors. In January 1995 it was reported that 20 new cement plants would start production within two years, raising national output to 25m. tons and allowing substantial exports. Officials stated that some 40 cement companies were producing 13.7m. tons per year. In August 1994 the Minister of Industries had stated that cement plants with a combined capacity of more than 9m. tons per year would be built during the SFYDP period, raising national capacity to 26m. tons. He also stated that the cement industry was the only sector that did not require state subsidies, but was paying the equivalent of $130m. a year to the Organization for the Protection of Consumers and Producers. By early 2002 Iran had 35 cement factories producing a total of 30m. tons a year, making it the largest cement producer in the Middle East and a net exporter, albeit at a low volume of about 1.5m. tons a year. With local demand for cement rising steadily due to population growth and other factors, the Government aimed to double production to 60m. tons per year by 2021.

In early 1995 the Chamber of Commerce and Industry reported that Iran's textile mills were operating at an average of 56% of capacity, owing to shortages of foreign exchange and raw material. In the Iranian year ending 20 March 1995 just over 24m. sq m of textiles were produced. At the beginning of 1996 the Ministry of Industries announced that output from local sugar plants had reached just under 1m. metric tons per year and would be sufficient to meet domestic demand within 10 years. Annual consumption of sugar was projected to rise to 2m. tons by 1998. In March 1996 the Minister of Industries stated that 80,000 passenger cars had been manufactured locally in 1995/96, and that the industry had been allowed additional hard currency for imports in order to expand production capacity to 135,000 in 1996/97. The launch of the Samand 'national car' in 2001 confirmed Iran Khodro Co (IKCO) as the leading Iranian and regional car manufacturer, producing some 350,000 passenger cars per year. In May 2002 IKCO announced plans to increase its output of cars to 500,000 within two years and to expand into neighbouring markets, in continued partnerships with DaimlerChrysler of Germany and Peugeot Citroën of France.

In March 2001 Qazvin Glass Co (Iran's largest glass manufacturer, with a turnover of IR 215,000m. in 2000) announced a joint venture with the British company Pilkington Glass whereby Pilkington would acquire an unspecified 'major equity interest' in Qazvin in return for funding the construction of a new float glass plant with an annual capacity of 180,000 metric tons. The deal was said to represent the first significant foreign joint venture since the 1979 Revolution.

Electricity generation was severely restricted by Iraqi attacks on power stations during the Iran–Iraq War, reducing viable capacity from 8,000 MW to 5,000 MW, according to one estimate. In December 1988 the Minister of Energy stated that the generating capacity of the national grid was deficient by 2,500 MW, owing to war damage, lack of fuel and inadequate rainfall. It was reported that electricity demand increased from 2,876 MW to 7,850 MW between 1979 and 1989. The Government planned to increase generation by 1,000 MW annually during the period 1989–94, and allocated US $7,500m. to this end. In 1989 $1,200m. in foreign exchange was set aside for the reactivation of dormant contracts and for the completion of repairs to damaged power stations. Installed capacity was reported to be 14,630 MW in 1990. In September 1994 the Minister of Energy stated that the national electricity network generated 73,400m. kWh of electricity in 1993/94, 11% more than in the previous year. Some 86.5% of electricity was produced by thermal power plants and the rest by hydroelectric stations.

In June 1991 Kraftwerk Union AG of Germany was awarded a $1,450m. contract to construct a 2,080-MW combined-cycle plant south of Tehran, the largest single power contract to be awarded since the Revolution. The company had earlier won a $700m. contract to construct a smaller plant in Guilan. In January 1992 a Canadian-European consortium won a $770m. contract to build a 1,100-MW gas/oil-fired-power station at Arak, to be completed in 1996. Work was due to start in late 1992, but more than a year after the contract was awarded implementation of the project was still being delayed because of financing

problems. In early 1992 it was also reported that repairs to the country's biggest power plant at Neka on the Caspian Sea, damaged during the war with Iraq, had been completed. In November 1992 it was reported that Bharat Heavy Electricals of India had been selected to build a 1,000-MW thermal power station in Kerman. Some of the major hydroelectric power schemes require large amounts of foreign exchange, and it was unclear whether the development programme would remain on schedule. In May 1992 a consortium led by Asea Brown Boveri (ABB) was awarded a $1,250m. contract to build a 3,000-MW hydroelectric dam on the Karun river, designated as Karun-3, but in June 1994 the Ministry of Energy cancelled the contract and awarded it to a local company, Sabir, a subsidiary of the Ministry of Energy, claiming that this would halve the cost of the project. ABB had encountered difficulties arranging finance for the project. Construction work, to be carried out in two stages, began in early 1995. In May 1993 Japan's Overseas Economic Co-operation Fund disbursed the first tranche ($458m.) of a $1,450m. untied concessional loan for the Godar-e-Landar hydroelectric dam on the Karun river, 160 km north of Ahwaz, in Khuzestan, previously known as Karun-4. The dam, which was to be operational by 2001, will have a capacity of 1,000 MW and a further 1,000 MW will be added in the second phase. Preconstruction work started in 1992, and work on the first stage eventually began in November 1994. Japan was originally due to have disbursed the second tranche of $602m. in May 1994, but came under pressure from the USA not to make the loan. In April 1995 a $463m. contract for civil works at the dam was awarded to Daelim Industrial Co of South Korea, which has taken charge of the project. In January 1996 there was an unconfirmed report that the Japanese Government had decided to continue its freeze on loans to Iran, in particular the second tranche of the loan package for the Godar-e-Landar dam, until March 1997 in order to avoid antagonizing the USA. In March 1993 the World Bank approved a loan of $165m. to upgrade the country's power plants and distribution network, including the conversion of the Qom power station to combined cycle. The conversion would double the plant's capacity, to 600 MW. In April 1994 the contract for the conversion work was awarded to ABB. The plant was expected to go into operation in late 1996. The World Bank loan also covered the cost of constructing 400-kV sub-stations and transmission lines to strengthen the country's north–south connection. Subsidiaries of ABB received three equipment supply orders in mid-1995 worth nearly $40m., and in early 1996 the company's Swedish subsidiary was awarded a $60m. contract to supply instrument transformers and to help set up local support facilities for the state-owned Iran Electric Organization. In April Tavanir invited prequalification bids for the construction of a 650-MW steam power plant in East Azerbaijan province, the first big power project for some years. Most other power generation work was linked to hydroelectricity projects and the Bushehr nuclear facility. In that month the official Iranian news agency stated that a $46m. power plant had been built on the disputed Gulf island of Greater Tunb. In March 1995 the Ministry of Energy awarded a contract to Monenco AGRA of Canada to prepare a master-plan for the development of the electricity sector. The plan would assist the Ministry in preparing a comprehensive strategy, including the evaluation of energy resources, pricing strategies, environmental impact assessments and recommendations for training, research and development. The project was also included in the World Bank loan.

In October 1994 the Ministry of Energy awarded a US $700m. contract to build a dam on the Karkheh river in Khuzestan to the Islamic Revolutionary Guards, in line with the Government's new policy of involving more local organizations and companies in construction to reduce costs. The Karkheh dam would generate 400 MW of electricity and irrigate 220,000 ha in Khuzestan province. As part of an agreement signed in May 1995 the People's Republic of China was to co-operate in the building of the combined cycle power plant at Arak, and to take part in the construction of the Karun-3 and Karkheh dams. In mid-2001 detailed plans were in place for a project to export water from the Karkheh dam (which opened in April) via a pipeline to Kuwait, where it would be sold for less than the cost of desalinated water. The project, drawn up by a consortium of European and Gulf investors for implementation on a 'build, operate, transfer' (BOT) basis, envisaged a throughput of up to 200m. gallons daily for a concession term of 30 years, beginning in 2005. The proposed pipeline would include a submarine section, thus avoiding the territory of Iraq.

The Ministry of Energy stated in April 1995 that Godar-e-Landar and Karun were among 30 large dams under construction. Two of these dams, Shahid Abbaspur and Barun, were due to be completed by March 1996, while a number of others, including Tanguyeh in Kerman, Alavian and Nahand in Khorassan, Raysar-Delvari in Bushehr and Salman Farsi, Kavar and Hanna in Fars, were to be completed later. The Ministry also reported that two large tunnels, Kuhrang and Gavmishan, were being completed to take water from the Karun river in Khuzestan to the Zayandehrud river in Esfahan. In May 1996 the Iran Water and Power Resources Development Co, an affiliate of the Ministry of Energy, invited international power generation companies to submit prequalification bids for the construction of four hydroelectric power plants: a 1-GW plant in Gotvand and a 750-MW plant on the Karun dam (Karun-4), both in Khuzestan, a 320-MW plant in Hini and a 250-MW plant in Sazbon, both in Ilam province. Companies submitting bids would also be required to arrange financing for the projects. In September 1992 it was announced that the Government planned to extend the privatization programme to electricity generation plants, most of which would be run as independent companies, with 51% of shares being transferred to the staff. A decade later, however, the state-controlled Tavanir organization continued to run the power sector, including not only power generation but also the transmission networks.

By early 2002 Iran had an installed generating capacity of about 31,500 MW, with another 5,000 MW coming from private generators; about 80% of capacity was fired by natural gas, the remainder being hydroelectric- or oil-fired. With demand for electricity growing by about 8% annually, it was planned to increase the capacity of the national network to 40,000 MW by 2005 and to 96,000 MW by 2022. Power plants currently under construction, and due for completion in 2002–03, will add about 13,000 MW to the national grid. Some 8,000 MW of this will come from hydroelectric dams (although the proportion of hydro-electricity will fall in subsequent years). The balance of 5,000 MW under construction comes from gas-fuelled plants and from combined-cycle facilities. An agreement worth about $1,000m. was signed in May 1999 between state-owned Mapna and Ansaldo Energia of Italy for the supply of 30 gas turbines (with an aggregate capacity of 4,700 MW) for power plants in the south of Iran.

Iran currently has five small nuclear reactors, one in Tehran and four in Esfahan, all officially for non-military purposes (Iran is a party to the Treaty on the Non-Proliferation of Nuclear Weapons or Non-Proliferation Treaty—NPT) and intended to free up hydrocarbon resources for export. Since the Revolution, however, the US Government has strenuously opposed the development of nuclear capability by Iran, arguing that it has ample hydrocarbon reserves for power generation and that nuclear reactors could be used for military purposes.

Iran's nuclear programme dates from the signature in May 1987 of a co-operation agreement with Argentina, the details of which were not disclosed but were thought to include an Argentine letter of intent to supply a US $5.5m. reactor core and enriched uranium for a nuclear research centre to be established in Tehran University. West Germany's Kraftwerk Union AG began building a 2,400-MW twin reactor nuclear plant at Bushehr before the 1979 Revolution; about 80% of the work on the plant had been completed by the time of the outbreak of the Iran–Iraq War in 1980. After several Iraqi air attacks on the plant, however, the company withdrew its staff in 1987. The West German Government refused to issue export licences for machinery and equipment until a peace agreement had been signed between Iran and Iraq. More than $3,700m. has already been spent on the plant. Iran wishes to complete at least one of the 1,200-MW reactors and has estimated the cost of this at about $1,000m. Independent sources, however, have argued that the true cost is more likely to be $3,000m. and have advised against proceeding. The Ministry of Energy does not have responsibility for the Bushehr nuclear facility, and a decision to complete what could be one of Iran's largest power plants could divert scarce financial resources from other parts of the country's

ambitious energy programme. Iran is believed to have received technical advice and training for its atomic engineers from Pakistan. In November 1989 the head of the Atomic Energy Organization of Iran (AEOI) announced that work on the Bushehr nuclear power plant had recommenced, and it is thought that vital equipment, placed in storage during the Iran–Iraq War, has been reinstalled. In January 1992 there were reports that Brazil had offered to resell to Iran equipment purchased from the former West Germany for the construction of its third nuclear plant, which had been delayed as a result of financial problems. Such equipment could be used in the construction of the Bushehr plant. On 15 February 1993, during a tour of the facility, President Rafsanjani stated that the Bushehr plant would be completed, whatever the cost. In August 1992 the AEOI announced that it had filed international suits against Siemens of Germany (Kraftwerk Union AG's parent company), for breaking the contract to complete the Bushehr reactor. Kraftwerk Union maintained that it was unable to do so because of a German government ban on the export of sensitive equipment. For some years negotiations with Indian, Russian and other suppliers ended in failure because of opposition from the USA. However, in December 1993 the Russian ambassador to Iran stated that Russia had agreed in principle to complete the Bushehr plant and to build a conventional power plant at Bushehr. A spokesman for Siemens stated that the main building at Bushehr would not be suitable for a Russian-designed reactor, and there was speculation that Iran may be planning to use some of the facilities at Bushehr to reduce the cost of the Russian reactor. In 1993 Iran signed an agreement with the People's Republic of China for at least one 300-MW nuclear reactor, and, despite pressure from the USA, China has indicated that it plans to proceed with the agreement.

Teams from the International Atomic Energy Agency (IAEA) visited nuclear sites in Iran in February 1992 and November 1993, reporting that they had found no evidence that Iran was developing nuclear weapons. In January 1995 Russia signed a US $800m. contract to build a 1,000-MW pressurized light-water-cooled VVER-100 reactor at Bushehr on the base of the reactor left unfinished by Siemens. Russia was also believed to have options on building three other reactors. The USA reiterated its opposition to any nuclear co-operation with Iran by Russia, asserting that the deal would help Iran accelerate a secret programme to develop nuclear weapons. However, Russian officials expressed their determination to proceed with the deal and to sell nuclear reactors to Iran, and denied that work on the Bushehr project was in any way connected with the development of nuclear weapons. In March the head of the AEOI stated that some 200 Russian and 500 Iranian experts and technicians were co-operating on the construction of the Bushehr reactor. In June 1996 the Russian Government indicated that it would invest $60m. in the Bushehr project during 1996. A Russian intelligence agency issued a report in early 1995 supporting the IAEA's assessment that there was no evidence of a military nuclear programme in Iran. In April 1995 China also rejected US appeals not to sell nuclear reactors to Iran, and Chinese officials maintained that negotiations with Iran to supply two 300-MW nuclear reactors did not pose a threat to the NPT. The USA stated that nuclear co-operation and the transfer of technology to Iran was dangerous as it was open to abuse. Iran appears to be aiming at a nuclear programme of 3,000 MW–5,000 MW, compared with the Shah's ambitious programme of 24,000 MW. The AEOI argues that it needs to familiarize itself with nuclear technology in order to carry out medical and other civilian research and to place greater reliance on renewable sources of energy so that its hydrocarbon resources are available for export. In June 1995 President Rafsanjani opened the first section of a nuclear research centre in East Azerbaijan province to enable experiments on the preservation of fresh fruit and vegetables by irradiation.

At a nuclear safety summit meeting held in Moscow in April 1996 the Russian Minister of Nuclear Energy refused to discuss the Bushehr reactor, but insisted that the facility would use too little nuclear material to allow Iran to develop nuclear weapons. He added that IAEA officials had visited the plant and that Russia was adhering to the NPT. The USA continued to oppose the involvement of Russian companies in the project. In July 1997 the announcement that Russia was to assist Iran to complete the nuclear power plant at Bushehr prompted the USA to reiterate its concern that Iran might seek to exploit civilian nuclear technology for the development of nuclear weapons. In September the Russian authorities stated that they would be willing to allow the USA to monitor the Bushehr nuclear plant. In the same month Israel was reported to be attempting to persuade the Clinton Administration to impose sanctions on Russian organizations and companies involved in supplying missile technology to Iran. In October China announced an end to the sale of nuclear technology, as well as of conventional weaponry, to Iran. After allegations by both the USA and Israel that Iran had a secret nuclear plant at Neka, on the Caspian Sea coast, the IAEA stated in April 1996 that it had inspected all suspected nuclear sites in Iran and it had not discovered any nuclear facilities at Neka. Russia's commitment to completing the Bushehr reactor was reaffirmed by President Putin during talks with the Iranian President in Moscow in March 2001, following which Russia sought to reassure the USA that the plant would not be a source of nuclear proliferation. Completion of the reactor was scheduled for March 2004, before which date the Iranian Government would decide whether to purchase a second Russian-built reactor at Bushehr.

A 5-kV solar power plant, built by the AEOI, opened in Ardakan, near Tehran, in November 1993, following the allocation of new funds to research into solar energy during the SFYDP. In May 1994 President Rafsanjani stated that there should be greater investment in new sources of energy in order to reduce dependence on oil. Iran's first wind-powered electricity plant is being constructed at Manjil, in the north-west of the country. In January 1996 President Rafsanjani, on a visit to a facility run by the AEOI to carry out nuclear, solar, tidal, geothermal and wind energy research, stated that Iran would continue with research on fusion and other alternative energy sources despite opposition from the USA. Iranian radio reported that the AEOI had set up four solar and wind-powered generating plants. In February 1996 it was announced that Iran, together with Russia, China and India, had agreed to establish the Asiatic Fund for Thermonuclear Research to explore the possibility of harnessing thermonuclear power for commercial purposes.

Steel

Post-Revolutionary government policies, like those of the Shah, have been directed towards achieving self-sufficiency in steel production and ending dependence on imports. In 1980 steel accounted for almost one-sixth of total imports. Consumption was estimated at 6m. metric tons per year in mid-1981 and was expected to rise to 10m. tons by 1983. Domestic production and development plans were severely affected by the 1979 Revolution and the subsequent war with Iraq. By early 1983 output had been raised to 58,000 tons per month, equivalent to about 700,000 tons per year, produced by an old-fashioned coal-fired steel mill which was built by the USSR in Esfahan (formerly known as the Aryameh Steel Mill), where installed capacity before the Revolution was claimed to be 1.1m. tons per year. Built under a US $286m. credit arrangement concluded with the USSR in 1965, the mill came into operation in March 1973. Subsequently, however, the mill has been beset by technical and production problems. For some time output was running at about 50% of its design capacity of 1.9m. tons per year. Agreements with the former USSR to expand the obsolete facility appear to have been abandoned and in January 1992 Danieli of Italy won a $600m. contract to expand steel-making and rolling capacity at the plant. In October 1994 it was reported that the plant was producing at 2m. tons per year, slightly above design capacity, and was no longer receiving state subsidies. A $470m. expansion plan was under way to raise output to 2.4m. tons per year in 1997. In December 1994 Danieli was reported to have renegotiated its contract at the plant and was to expand capacity at the existing Esfahan Steel Co complex to 3.2m. tons per year by adding a line for nearly 800,000 tons of flat products. Negotiations were also reported with a number of European firms for a complete change of instrumentation at the complex. Management of the plant was reported to have improved greatly, although it still suffered from overmanning despite a reduction of the work-force by one-third to 19,000. Further cuts were to be made to reduce the work-force to 12,000 by 1998. The Esfahan

mill has become a centre for new technological developments in steel. At the end of 1994 Esfahan Steel Co's Managing Director, Ahmad Sadeqi, claimed to have developed a commercially viable new direct-reduction process in steel manufacture at a pilot plant in Esfahan which is being patented under the name of Tahre Qaem. Sadeqi has stated that he plans to convert the Esfahan steel mill from the coke-burning technology introduced by the former USSR to direct reduction, using natural gas. The cost of the new technology is projected at one-half of that of the Midrex direct-reduction modules installed at Mobarakeh. A private firm, one of 30 companies set up by former managers and employees at the Esfahan Steel Co to provide services ranging from transport to engineering, has commissioned a ferrosilicon pilot plant with a capacity of 3,000 tons per year, which is now supplying about one-third of the steel plant's requirements for ferrosilicon. A 30,000-tons-per-year ferro-manganese plant at the Esfahan industrial estate was due to be completed in 1995. The plant was to supply both the Esfahan and Mobarakeh steel complexes. Hylsa of Mexico has a contract at Iran's second largest production facility, the Ahwaz steel plant, to expand the unit's capacity to 1.1m. tons per year and, eventually, to 1.7m. tons per year. The National Iranian Steel Co (NISCO) reported that the plant produced 805,000 tons of steel in 1992/93, an increase of 54% over the previous year. In December 1993 it was reported that production at the plant had improved and that it was now producing quality steel for export. In December 1994 Danieli had reportedly been contracted to carry out work worth $100m. to improve flexibility in semi-finished products at Ahwaz, but some uncertainty was expressed over whether the project would proceed. In June Kudremukh Iron Ore Co of India signed an agreement with the NISCO to provide technical services for the Ahwaz steel plant. By 1996 the Ahwaz complex was producing 1.5m. tons annually. Furnace capacity was being increased by 3.2m. tons per year and there were plans for a new sheet mill with a capacity of 3.8m. tons per year. Another direct-reduction plant with a capacity of 700,000 tons per year using the new Iranian technology developed at Esfahan was planned to begin production in 1998. The Ahwaz Steel Company is to set up a $400m. turnkey flat products steel mill with a production capacity of 700,000 tons of wide plates per year, rising to 1.05m. tons per year. International steel manufacturers bidding for the project (bids were opened in March 1999) include Danieli and Japan's Nippon Steel. In September 1991 President Rafsanjani opened the first stage of the Mobarakeh steel mill in Esfahan, one of the most modern steel mills in the world. However, the plant was reported to have encountered problems achieving the target annual production capacity of 2.4m. tons, and in 1995 annual production capacity was only 1.6m. tons. NISCO planned to expand capacity to 3.2m. tons per year by March 1998. Actual production capacity in 2001 was 2.85m. tons per year. In June 2001 contracts were awarded for upgrading and expansion work to increase annual capacity at Mobarakeh to 4.1m. tons in 2003. In June 1989 the construction of a $192m. steel-rolling complex at Miyaneh, in East Azerbaijan province, was announced. In February 1992 a Japanese-Italian consortium won a $550m. contract to build a steel plant near Yazd, which was inaugurated by President Rafsanjani in June 1997. In March 1993 it was announced that Italy's Simimpianti had won a $112m. contract to supply equipment, supervision, expertise and training for a specialized steel mill near Mashad which will have an annual capacity of 250,000 tons. In late 1994 Danieli of Italy was awarded a contract to build the steel-rolling mill at Miyaneh and a second new mill at Neishabur in Khorassan province. The Miyaneh mill was to have a capacity of 350,000 tons and would process slabs imported from the former Soviet republics on the western side of the Caspian Sea. The $160m. Neishabur complex would have an initial capacity of 600,000 tons per year with production rising to 1.8m. tons. In mid-1996 it was reported that NISCO had secured a $561m. loan from Japanese and European banks to finance the renovation and upgrading of steel plants at Ahwaz, Khorassan and Miyaneh to be carried out by Danieli of Italy. NISCO was also engaged in negotiations with foreign companies for the construction of an integrated steel mill at Hormuzgan, in the Bandar Abbas special economic zone near the Strait of Hormuz, and an associated pelletizing plant at Sirjan in Kerman province. Financial difficulties may delay these projects until state insurance agencies resume cover for Iran. Hormuzgan is also the site of a ferro-alloy plant built with Chinese assistance. The $39m. plant became operational in early 1995, producing 15,000 tons per year of ferro-chrome and 20,000 tons per year of ferro-manganese. Some 5,000 tons were exported to Japan in April 1995 and the plant is expected to earn some $10m. per year in export sales. Between 1981 and 1986 Iranian steel production officially totalled 5.3m. tons, of which 1.2m. tons were produced in 1986. According to the Ministry of Mines and Metals, Iran's steel production in 1988/89 totalled 1.4m. tons and rose to 3.8m. tons in 1992/93. Output for 1993/94 was projected at 4.5m. tons The Ministry of Mines and Metals had earlier forecast an expansion in output to 5.5m. tons per year by March 1994, when the first Five-Year Plan ended. Actual output was well below target even according to the Ministry's own figures. As part of its plan to increase production, Japan's Nippon Steel Co was awarded a $1.8m. contract in May 1993 to improve the management of NISCO. According to the Ministry of Mines and Metals, steel output rose to 4.6m. tons in 1994/95. According to NISCO, steel output would reach 6m. tons in 1996/97. In 1996 NISCO announced a development plan to expand steel production capacity by 1m. tons per year until 2006, when total capacity was projected to reach 17.5m. tons per year. In October 1992 the International Institute of Iron and Steel was reported to have accepted Iran as a full member, as its raw steel production exceeded 2m. tons per year. For many years Iran has been a major purchaser of steel on the world market, and imports, principally from Spain and Japan, have averaged 2m.–5m. tons per year. Domestic consumption of steel was estimated at 3.5m. tons per year in early 1989, and was projected to rise to 7m. tons annually as post-war reconstruction got under way. Total steel exports for 1994 were estimated at 1.5m. tons. Despite its emergence as a steel exporter, Iran was still importing a roughly equivalent amount of steel at the end of the 1990s. Raw steel production in 1998/99 was 5.7m. tons. Bids were received in March 2002 for the contract to build the proposed new integrated steel mill at Hormuzgan, while the contract for the Sirjan pelletizing plant was retendered following a government decision to impose stricter guidelines on foreign bids. However, uncertainty about the future of new steel projects deepened because of intense competition in the international steel market and also because of rumoured financial difficulties at NISCO.

Petrochemicals

The Shah had planned a huge petrochemical sector that would not only meet local demand but also provide US $2,000m. worth of exports by 1983. Development of the industry was paralysed after the Revolution. However, in 1983 the Ministry of Oil announced that it would place greater emphasis on further development and expansion of the petrochemicals industry. Several new plants were to be built with the aim of making Iran not only self-sufficient but also an exporter of surplus nitrogenous fertilizer, plastics and other products. Iran intended to become a leading world producer of petrochemicals during the 1990s. At that time the sector comprised the following major ventures: the Iran Fertilizer Co, the Razi Chemical Co (formerly Shahpour), the Abadan Petrochemical Co, the Kharg Chemical Co, the Iran Carbon Co, the Iran Nippon Chemical Co, Aliaf Co and Polyacryl Corpn. All these companies were nationalized in 1979 and were administered by the National Petrochemical Co (NPC) under the Ministry of Oil.

Under the Shah the cornerstone of the petrochemical industry was the Iran-Japan petrochemical complex at Bandar Khomeini, which had a planned capacity of 300,000 metric tons per year of olefins and aromatics. This began in 1973 as a joint venture shared equally between the NIOC and a Mitsui-led consortium, the Iran Chemical Development Co (ICDC). It was originally projected to cost US $300m., but this estimate had increased to $3,000m. by 1979. The immense 13-unit complex was 85% finished at the time of the Revolution. Work was resumed briefly in the summer of 1980, but was halted again after Iraqi bombers attacked the plant several times in late September and early October. Disputes between the NPC and its Japanese partners were numerous. In mid-1984 Iran suspended a $10.8m. interest payment on a loan because the Japanese consortium, concerned with safety in the war zone, had withdrawn its technicians from

the site. After renewed Iraqi bombings in September 1984, the ICDC again withdrew all of its technicians. In February 1986 Iran decided to end all repayments on credits and loans received from Japan. In the late 1980s Mitsui estimated that it would cost at least $2,000m. to complete the scheme, taking into account extensive war damage and the fact that some of the original units were obsolete. Iran disputed these estimates. The Japanese consortium expressed its desire to withdraw from the scheme, but Iran stated that it wished to complete the project and claimed that the Japanese estimates were pessimistic and that the cost would be about $1,000m. In November 1989, after prolonged negotiations, the Japanese consortium agreed to dissolve the $4,500m. partnership for the complex, and in February 1990, as part of the agreement, it paid the Iranian Government $910m. Dutch and German companies were contracted to help the NPC to reconstruct some of the complex's 13 units. In November the Daelim Industrial Co, a South Korean venture, secured a $150m. contract to reconstruct the olefins plant. In April 1994 the head of the NPC stated that test production would start that month on the second phase of the complex which would treble annual production capacity to 3m. tons. Three-quarters of the plant's output had been sold in advance to German, French and Finnish companies to help finance its construction. The complex is the country's biggest petrochemical plant. Its second phase opened in August and in September the head of the NPC stated that 500,000 tons of liquefied petroleum gas would be exported to South Korea in 1995. This represented part of the $900m. of the plant's production which had been sold in advance to fund construction. Under the SFYDP, which began in March 1995, the annual capacity of the olefin unit of the complex was to be doubled. In November 1994 it was announced that the port of Bandar Khomeini and the nearby petrochemical complexes, the Bandar Khomeini complex and the Razi fertilizer complex, would be declared a protected industrial zone in early 1995. Free-zone regulations would apply to the region in order to promote joint ventures and attract foreign investment in petrochemicals. The NPC was trying to interest private investors in the construction of a methyl tertiary butyl ether (MTBE) plant at the Bandar Khomeini complex. In March the official news agency reported that the polyvinyl chloride unit at the complex had started production with an annual capacity of 175,000 tons. The aromatics unit was due to open later in 1995. In May 1996 the NPC announced plans to build a paraxylene plant with an annual capacity of 150,000 tons at the Bandar Khomeini petrochemical plant. In mid-1999 NPC was finalizing tender documents for an olefins plant, to be sited in the Bandar Khomeini special zone. The facility is scheduled to produce annually 700,000 tons of polyethylene, 300,000 tons of polypropylene and 105,000 tons of propylene.

The expanded Shiraz petrochemical complex, located next to a smaller 20-year-old unit at Marvdasht, 50 km from the city, was opened in February 1986. The plant's daily output has been increased nearly 10-fold to produce 1,200 metric tons of ammonia, 1,500 tons of urea, 100 tons of nitric acid and 750 tons of ammonium nitrate. The initial capacity of the Shiraz plant was 500,000 tons per year, rising to 850,000 tons in 1987. A chloro-alkali unit with a capacity of 60,000 tons per year was completed in February 1989 at Shiraz, and the Shiraz methanol plant commenced production in May 1990. Contracts worth US $33m. were awarded to expand a dense soda ash plant and the ammonia plant. In September 1993 NPC officials reported that the Razi fertilizer complex near Bandar Khomeini was operating at only three-quarters of its planned capacity of 2m. tons per year. In October 1994 it was announced that the war-damaged sulphuric acid unit at the Razi complex had resumed production at 1,320 tons per day. As part of the NPC's ambitious petrochemicals expansion programme, a $2,200m. complex has been constructed at Arak using feedstocks from the Esfahan refinery and the new Arak refinery. The first phase of the complex was opened in July 1993, and planned output is 550,000 tons of products per year. Another project was the petrochemicals complex at Esfahan to produce benzine and toluene as well as polyethylene, polystyrene and polyols. In April 1994 it was reported that the Ministry of Heavy Industry had taken over responsibility for a $1,900m. olefins petrochemical complex at Esfahan from the NPC. The project would be financed by a buy-back arrangement. In October 1993 it was announced that the benzine plant would start production in March 1994 with an annual capacity of 50,000 tons. Japan's Kawasaki Corpn and MW Kellog Co of the USA have built a petrochemical complex in Khorassan in the north-east of the country. Work on the plant, which is designed to produce 330,000 tons annually of ammonia and 495,000 tons annually of urea, began in 1988 and production was scheduled to start in March 1995. A $1,000m. petrochemical complex was also being built at Tabriz, near to the Tabriz refinery, and was due to become operational in March 1995. A $80m. private sector petrochemical plant was also to be built at Tabriz, producing 50,000 tons of polypropylene, half of which would be exported. In October 1993 two German companies, Lurgi and BASF, were awarded the contract to set up and equip the plant for Polynar, a subsidiary of Narhan, a private consulting firm involved in local petrochemical and oil industries. The financial package was to be concluded in 1994 and construction was due to be completed in three years. Polynar was given the concession in 1992 by the NPC as part of its programme to encourage more private sector investment in petrochemicals. The Tabriz plant is reported to be one of nine petrochemical projects handed over to the private sector, including a 660,000-tons-per-year methanol plant and a 500,000-tons-per-year MTBE facility. In September 1994 the head of the NPC stated that as part of the state company's privatization programme, production units were being leased to the newly-established Petrochemical Investment Co as an intermediate step towards their flotation on the stock market; no further details were given. In October the NPC approached Lurgi of Germany to carry out basic engineering for a major new methanol plant on Kharg Island, with construction, undertaken by local firms, beginning in 1995. The complex would use gases from a petrochemical plant on the island and when operational would produce 660,000 tons of methanol and 50,000 tons of acetic acid annually. Some two-thirds of the methanol output would be destined for export, with the balance fed to the new MTBE plant to be built at Bandar Khomeini (see above). In February 1996 it was reported that Belleli of Italy had been awarded a $7.5m. contract to supply two 250-ton petrochemical reactors early in 1997 for use in the methanol plant on Kharg Island. This plant is one of five petrochemical projects to be given priority during the second Five-Year Plan which began in March 1995. The other projects include the expansion of the olefins unit at Bandar Khomeini, an MTBE plant in the south to manufacture additives for 500,000 tons of unleaded gasoline per year, and two plastics plants. The five projects are estimated to require government investment of $1,800m.

The total import bill for petrochemicals was US $1,500m. in 1987. During the 1990s Iran sought to satisfy internal demand and have a surplus output to export a range of products. Output has risen steadily since the end of the war with Iraq, reaching 2.1m. metric tons in 1989/90 and more than 3.5m. tons in 1990/91. Output in 1991/92 totalled 4.3m. tons, according to the NPC, and 970,000 tons of petrochemicals were exported, worth $100m. About 5.4m. tons of petrochemicals were produced in 1992/93. In February 1994 the head of the NPC stated that annual production had reached 5.5m. tons, well below the target figure of 9m. tons planned for March 1994. However, in January 1995 he claimed that petrochemical output had increased by almost 40% in 1994, to 7.5m. tons, and would rise to 9m. tons in 1995 and to 14.5m. tons by 2000. There were conflicting figures from other sources. In March the Minister of Oil claimed that Iran's annual output of petrochemical products was 9m. tons and would rise to 15.5m. tons by 2000. In late September 1994 the Minister of Economy and Finance claimed that annual production of petrochemicals had increased 20-fold since 1989, to about 8m. tons per year. The NPC reported that output in 1995/96 rose by 1.2m. tons to 8.6m. tons, and that 2.4m. tons were exported. Other sources claimed that production at the end of 1996 was around 10m. tons per year and that annual capacity would be increased to 15.5m. tons by 2000, with a higher proportion of output destined for export. The NPC predicted that petrochemical production would reach 11.8m. tons in 1998/99, compared with 10.8m. tons in the previous year. In August 1993 the head of the NPC urged the Majlis to approve new incentives to encourage private and foreign investment in petrochemical projects during the term of the SFYDP. He

reported that 14 projects which commenced under the Plan ending in March 1994 had been delayed because of the shortage of funds. Foreign finance and expertise were urgently needed if the petrochemical sector was to be developed successfully over the next five years. The NPC was seeking approval from the Majlis to guarantee foreign loans and secure concessionary domestic credit for private projects from March 1994. In October 1994 the head of the NPC stated that no private local or foreign investors had expressed interest in petrochemical ventures. He was reported to have asked the Majlis to allow foreign investors to take 100% ownership in projects instead of the 49% currently permitted. In 1996 officials reported increased interest in the petrochemicals sector from private investors. In 1992 around 1.5m. tons of petrochemicals were exported, earning $150m. Nevertheless, the head of the NPC stated in September 1993 that Iran was still spending $3,000m. each year on petrochemical imports. The NPC stated that annual production in 1993/94 was worth $1,000m. and was expected to rise to $1,800m. in 1994/95. Petrochemical exports were estimated to have earned $200m. in 1993/94, and according to the NPC earned $408m. in 1995/96. Exports in 1996/97 were $506m., and increased to $560m. in 1997/98. In the first half of 1998/99 exports were $265m. According to the NPC, more than 650,000 tons of sulphur, from total production of 880,000 tons, was exported in the Iranian year ending 20 March 1994, making Iran the sixth biggest sulphur exporter in that period. The NPC stated in January 1995 that Iran was meeting 85% of its petrochemical needs from domestic production.

The NPC's five-phase strategic development plan (originally announced in 1997 and revised subsequently) envisages total output of petrochemicals rising to 50m. metric tons per year by 2015 (compared with output of 14m. tons in 2001). The plan involves investment of US $20,600m. (phases three to five being open to foreign investors on a buy-back basis). The first two phases are in progress. Phase three (comprising four large complexes to be sited at a new special zone at Bandar Asaluyeh and one at Bandar Khomeini special zone, with a projected combined annual capacity of more than 6.7m. tons) is on course to be completed by 2005. Government predictions were that Iran's share of world petrochemicals production would quintuple, to 2%, by 2005 and that the value of exports would rise from $500m. in 1999 to $2,000m in 2005. Between mid-2000 and the end of the Iranian financial year in March 2001, petrochemicals development contracts worth more than $2,000m. were awarded by the NPC and its affiliates. European and Japanese contractors had little difficulty in raising project finance from banks in their home countries (or insurance cover from state export credit guarantors), and it was anticipated that contract awards would continue to be made on this scale for some time. Many of the new projects were located in the Bandar Asaluyeh special economic zone, which receives its feedstock supplies from the South Pars gasfield.

TRANSPORT AND COMMUNICATIONS

The threat of a US naval embargo in the Gulf at the time of the hostage crisis in 1980 focused attention on land supply lines through the USSR and Turkey and air routes from Pakistan. A protocol with the USSR, including arrangements for land supply lines across the border, was approved by the Islamic Revolutionary Council in May 1980. After the Revolution, however, there was little investment in the transport and communications sector, and in many areas the low level of maintenance of roads and railways resulted in reduced efficiency of existing routes. Conflicts of interest over resource allocation affected the planning of new roads, and there was pressure to give priority to improving transport in rural areas. Ministry officials criticized the annual allocation of US $150m. for road construction as inadequate. They argued that two-thirds of the $30,000m. spent on transporting goods within the country was wasted because of inadequate transport facilities and poor co-ordination. This situation appeared to be changing, however, and in 1990 the Ministry of Roads and Transport announced that expenditure on the transport system during the term of the FFYDP would total some $16,000m., including $4,300m. in convertible currency. In August 1993 it was reported that the Government planned to denationalize a wide range of transport activities and that a detailed plan would be completed by the Ministry of

Roads and Transport early in 1994. The involvement of the private sector in the country's transportation system has been encouraged by the Government since 1991, and a number of projects have been offered to the private sector. These include the new Tehran international airport, the motorway from Tehran to the Caspian Sea, and a railway line from Mashad to Bafq. The Supreme Administrative Council wants to reduce state expenditure on transport in the future by involving the private and co-operative sectors in developing and maintaining all parts of the transport network. In December 1992 the Ministry of Roads and Transport stated that more than 1,400 km of roads had been repaired since March and that another 11,000 km were under construction. In November 1993 there were reports that the Ministry of Roads and Transport had approved the $800m. motorway from Tehran to Chalus on the Caspian Sea and that the private sector had been invited to participate in its construction.

The State Railways Organization is extending and upgrading the country's 6,000-km rail network with the assistance of several international firms. The major improvement since the Revolution has been the opening of the final section of electrified track on the 146-km link between Tabriz and Djulfa, used to bring imports from the former USSR. Priority was given to completing a 730-km line connecting Bandar Abbas to Bafq and the national network, and to constructing a 560-km line from Kerman to Zahedan, providing a link with Pakistan. In August 1992 Iran and Pakistan agreed to establish a joint venture to lay track between Bafq and Bandar Abbas. In September 1992 Pakistan Railways engineers were due to visit Tehran in order to discuss the rehabilitation of the 540-km Kerman–Zahedan and the 500-km Kerman–Bandar Abbas lines. The 112-km line from Bandar Khomeini to Ahwaz was to be double-tracked, in order to reduce congestion at the port, and long-term projects included double-tracking the line from Tehran to Ahwaz and the construction of new lines. The first phase of construction of a 175-km line from Mashad to Sarakhs by the Engineering Corps of the Islamic Revolutionary Guards Corps began in May 1992. Since the disintegration of the USSR the line now forms part of a plan to link the rail systems of the independent former Soviet Central Asian republics to the Iranian national network and the Gulf, thus establishing Iran as the gateway to Central Asia. In March 1995 President Rafsanjani opened the 730-km Bafq–Bandar Abbas railway at a ceremony attended by the Presidents of Turkmenistan, Kyrgyzstan, Armenia and Afghanistan. The new rail link, which cost nearly US $900m. and took 13 years to build, links Iran's main port, Bandar Abbas, with the national network, which in turn connects with the Turkish railway system. In the north-west the national network runs to the Azerbaijan border, and in the north-east local contractors are completing a 140-km link to the Turkmen border at Sarakhs. At the opening ceremony President Rafsanjani stated that the new rail link was important for the former Soviet republics of Central Asia and the Caucasus, providing them with the option of another link to the world. He invited Arab Gulf states to use the line for access to areas north of Iran. In April 1995 it was reported that the Indian Railway Construction Co (Ircon) might participate in building a 780-km rail link between Mashad and Bafq. The scheme would cost $400m. and would provide direct access from Bandar Abbas to the Turkmen border at Sarakhs. Ircon was asked to submit offers for track and signalling work for sections of the Kerman–Zahedan railway link, and was awarded a $25m. contract to install signalling equipment on the Ahvaz–Bandar Khomeini line. The 110-km line from Ahvaz to Khorramshahr reopened in July 1989. Under the FFYDP $6,800m. was allocated to the State Railways Organization. It was aimed to increase annual transport capacity to 10m. passengers and 25m. metric tons of freight. About 1,000 km of new track were to be completed by 1995, and 1,750 km of existing track were to be renovated during the same period. In February 1994 the deputy director of the State Railways Organization stated that the railways carried 9m. passengers a year and 19m. tons of freight. During preliminary discussions about the SFYDP the Minister of Roads and Transport stated that the allocation to railways should be doubled, to $17,700m. It was reported in May 1999 that European railway equipment manufacturers were trying to organize $500m. of finance for construction of a high-speed railway line between Qom and

Esfahan. The 250-km line is part of the 400-km Tehran–Esfahan scheme started some years ago and completed up to Qom. In May 1996 a 300-km railway line was opened linking the Iranian national network with that of the former USSR and allowing Turkmenistan access to Iran's Gulf ports. As part of an accord signed in February 1996, France is to assist in the construction of an express rail link between Tehran and Esfahan. Passenger trains were scheduled to begin operating between the Iranian, Turkish and Syrian capitals in early 2001 (the Tehran–İstanbul service having been suspended for eight years).

An underground railway project for Tehran began in the late 1970s, but work stopped for some 10 years after the Revolution. Construction began again in the late 1980s, but negotiations with foreign suppliers were not completed because of financing problems. Only a few contracts were awarded, including a US $52m. deal for a maintenance workshop with HMT International of India. However, in May 1995 the Tehran Urban and Suburban Railway Co signed the last of three contracts with Chinese companies to supply equipment for two underground railway lines, including rolling stock, locomotives, and signalling equipment, and for a rapid transit line west of the capital. Together the contracts are worth $573m. Some 80% of the civil engineering work on the two underground lines had already been completed. One 32-km line will link north and south Tehran, and a second 20-km line will run east–west across the city. The original plan envisaged five lines, but officials indicated that a decision on the remaining three lines would only be taken if the first phase of the project proved successful. The third contract was for an electrified railway from Tehran to the western suburb of Karaj. There was some criticism that Chinese companies had been awarded the work. According to some experts, the People's Republic of China is inexperienced in such projects and has awarded its own underground railway schemes to European companies. Financial reasons appear to have determined the choice of Chinese companies as Tehran encountered financial difficulties in its discussions with European contractors. In March 1996 it was reported that the Tehran Urban and Suburban Railway Co had arranged for two letters of credit, worth $230m., to be opened in favour of the Chinese companies providing equipment for the Tehran underground railway system, with a third, worth $4,270m., to be opened in the Iranian year beginning 21 March 1996. The three Chinese companies involved in the project are China North Industries Corpn, China National Technology Import and Export and China International Trust and Investment Corpn. It was reported in December 1998 that China had started shipping underground railway trains ordered by Iran, under a $138m. contract to supply 217 trains by early 2001. The 31-km Tehran–Karaj suburban line was inaugurated in February 1999, with phased sections of the urban lines due to enter service from the end of the year.

In the ports sector a decision was taken in September 1981 to complete work on a major extension of Bandar Abbas, a project designed before the Revolution but scaled down after the fall of the Shah. Because of war damage at the traditional seaports of Bandar Khomeini and Khorramshahr, Iran became heavily dependent on Bandar Abbas for its sea-borne imports. A new port, Bandar Shahid Rajai, was inaugurated in 1983, handling 9m. metric tons of the total of 12m. tons of cargo passing through Iran's Persian Gulf ports every year. Work on the port development at Bandar Abbas began in February 1985. However, only two of the original three phases of the project have been completed. There are plans to build a new jetty at the port for mineral exports, at a cost of US $770m. The jetty will have a handling capacity of 10m. tons per year. Two new ports at Chah Bahar (the first called Shahid Beheshti, costing $37m.) were opened in February 1984 and September 1988, respectively, while Bushehr port is being expanded. The Ganaveh oil export port, with an export capacity of 2m. b/d, was opened in August 1988. Before the cease-fire in the Iran–Iraq War was announced, in preparation for a possible international economic embargo and closure of the Gulf to shipping, Iran made arrangements to use ports and oil refineries in neighbouring countries. Agreements were signed with Pakistan, Turkey and the USSR. Pakistan agreed in October 1987 to permit Iran's use of Karachi and Qasim ports to import up to 2m. tons of goods. In August 1992 it was announced that the port of

Khorramshahr, destroyed in the Iran–Iraq War, had been reopened to freight traffic. In November 1994 it was reported that four new jetties were to be built at Bandar Anzali port on the Caspian Sea as part of a $2.2m. expansion project. The tonnage of goods handled by the port increased by almost one-third in 1994 compared with the previous year. In January 1996 Iran was said to be building a harbour on the disputed Gulf island of Abu Musa, with the first of two port jetties expected to be operational in March. In 2000 40% of Iran's exports by value were transported by sea, compared with 46% by truck, 13% by air and 1% by train.

One of Iran's major transport projects is the construction of the Imam Khomeini international airport south-west of Tehran. When the first phase was completed in 1997 the airport was reportedly capable of handling 12m. passengers per year, and it will eventually have a capacity of 30m. passengers per year. It was hoped that the new airport would replace Mehrabad Airport for all international flights and would be linked to Tehran by a special underground railway system. In July 1992 it was announced that some US $800m. in foreign credits had been allocated towards the cost of completing Imam Khomeini International Airport, and another $350m. to other airports. Some IR 30,000m. was spent on airport modernization during 1991/92. Abadan airport reopened in 1991 and started handling international traffic in January 1994. The Civil Aviation Organization announced in early 1995 that 56 airports would be built under the SFYDP and another 43 airport projects undertaken in subsequent years. In December 1995 Aéroports de Paris won the design contract for the terminal at Imam Khomeini international airport, and in February 1996 an agreement was signed under the terms of which France would assist in establishing repair facilities and other services at the new international airport. In March it was reported that in order to improve the country's air transport the Supreme Economic Council had allocated $164m. for 10 radar units, $17m. for compass units and additional sums for new equipment for the control towers of Tehran and Shiraz airports and to pay for the leasing of 10 passenger aircraft. In recent years the national carrier, Iran Air, which uses Boeing and Airbus aircraft, has experienced problems obtaining more aircraft from the USA and Europe owing to economic sanctions. Although Iran took delivery of two Airbus passenger jets in 1994/95, restrictions on further purchases from the West prompted it to charter Russian aircraft to meet the shortfall in capacity. Iran also entered into a joint venture with the Ukrainian aircraft manufacturer Antonov for the construction at Esfahan of up to 10 An-140 passenger jets per year, with production scheduled to begin in 1999. It was announced in May 1999 that Iran Air (with a current fleet of 32 aircraft) had received government approval to buy four Airbus aircraft. This would raise the airline's Airbus fleet to 11, suggesting that the Iranian aviation industry is planning a long-term shift away from reliance on US suppliers to their European counterparts. The Airbuses are expected to be delivered by 2004. Iran Air stated in mid-2002 that it was negotiating the eventual purchase of 10 more Airbus jets. The airline's Managing Director said in 2000 that its state subsidies had ended at the start of the 2000/01 financial year, leaving it wholly reliant on income from its commercial operations. According to figures published by the International Air Transport Association, Iran Air carried 1,040,142 international and 5,914,130 domestic passengers in 2001. In December of that year the Government decided to sell 46% of Iran Air to the private sector as the first step towards disposing of 49% of the national carrier with the aim of financing the purchase of new aircraft.

FOREIGN TRADE AND BALANCE OF PAYMENTS

Iran's exports of crude petroleum or petroleum products account for the major part of the country's export revenue. After the 1979 Revolution the Government declared that it would pursue an increase in trade with Islamic and developing countries. New trading patterns have emerged, but Iran remains heavily dependent on the advanced industrial economies because of its oil and gas output.

For several years following the Revolution, government policy concerning foreign trade favoured forms of trade other than cash payments. Straight barter—a direct exchange of goods for oil—was rare; much more common were the counter-trade

triangle and the clearing account. During the early part of 1985, however, the Government urged foreign suppliers to take payment for goods in crude oil in order to maintain oil exports at a time of weak demand, and to conserve reserves of foreign exchange. The shift in policy caused argument within the establishment. The Ministry of Oil would have preferred to sell petroleum for cash, as it foresaw an improvement in the market. In the second half of April, partly owing to barter deals, oil exports reached a post-revolutionary peak of more than 2.3m. b/d and the practice of barter trading lost some of its appeal. From May customers for bartered oil were required to refine it in their own countries and to supply it to their domestic markets alone. By 1991 existing barter arrangements, mainly with eastern European countries, were being progressively terminated in favour of cash transactions.

The post-Revolution Government declared itself in favour of the nationalization of foreign trade, and progress was made towards its achievement. Nearly all foreign trade was channelled through government-controlled purchasing and distribution companies (PDCs), of which 13 were established during the 1980s for chemicals, electrical appliances, electronic and surgical instruments, food processing, a variety of light industrial products, machinery and spare parts, metals, plastics materials, textiles, tools and hardware, and wood and paper. Their main aim was to exercise strict controls over prices and import levels. In spite of the nationalization measures, the Government found it difficult, in practice, to exercise proper control over all aspects of imports and distribution. Consequently, by 1991 the PDCs were being progressively dissolved, and efforts were under way to simplify regulations and to eliminate bureaucratic obstacles to international trade. The PDCs were officially abolished in August 1991. Part of the responsibility for foreign trade lay with the Ministry of Commerce and part with Bank Markazi (the central bank), which exerted considerable control over foreign trade through constraints on letters of credit and the issue of regulations. However, in April 1995 President Rafsanjani confirmed that the Ministry of Commerce now had sole responsibility for trade policy.

Despite the enactment of US legislation in 1996 seeking to penalize non-US firms investing in Iran's oil and gas industry, independent analysts argued that the country's oil export capacity was unlikely to be affected (see above). Non-oil exports earned US $4,825m. in 1994/95, but their value fell sharply, to $3,200m., in 1995/96 after strict foreign-exchange restrictions were imposed in May 1995, requiring exporters to repatriate all their earnings at the official exchange rate of $1 = IR 3,000 (see Investment and Finance). However, a senior official of the central bank claimed that exporters had tended to under-report their earnings since the introduction of the new restrictions and argued that the main reason why earnings had fallen was the Government's ban on exports of manufactured goods, such as steel and petrochemicals, and of certain agricultural products in short supply. The ban on industrial exports may have cost the Government $500m. in foreign-exchange earnings, but it was claimed that the restrictions had helped to control inflation.

A trade surplus of US $6,818m. was recorded in 1994/95 (after deficits in the two previous years) on the strength of exports valued at $19,435m. (of which $14,604m. was from oil and gas) and imports down to $12,617m. In 1995/96 the surplus was somewhat lower, at $5,586m., from exports of $18,360m. ($15,103m. from oil and gas) and imports of $12,774m. In 1996/97 the surplus recovered to a record $7,523m. from exports of $22,496m. ($19,271m. from oil and gas) and imports of $14,973m. In 1997/98 a reduced trade surplus, of $4,258m., was recorded as a result of exports valued at $18,381m. ($15,471m. from oil and gas) and imports of $14,123m. In 1998/99 imports grew to $14,286m., but exports declined to $13,118m. (including $9,933m. from oil and gas), producing a trade deficit of $1,168m., which contributed to a current-account deficit of $2,140m. Official figures for 1999/2000 showed that Iran's visible trade was in surplus by $7,597m., with exports valued at $21,030m. (including $17,089m. from oil and gas) and import spending of $13,433m. After taking account of invisibles (principally a $1,241m. deficit on services), there was an overall current-account surplus of $6,589m. Statistics for the 2000/01 financial year showed that the visible trade surplus had almost doubled, to $13,138m., from exports of $28,345m. (including $24,226m. from oil and gas) and imports of $15,207m. The overall current-account surplus was $12,645m. In the first three quarters of the 2001/02 financial year imports increased by nearly 20%, compared with the same period in 2000/01, so that the total for the full year was likely to exceed the $16,000m. import ceiling decreed by the Government, although the trade balance and current account were expected to continue in healthy surplus.

In 1995/96 Japan remained substantially Iran's largest customer, taking 15.1% of exports by value, followed by Italy (8.6%), the United Kingdom (7.8%) and South Korea (6.0%). In the same year, Germany remained Iran's most important source of imports with 14.4% of the total, followed by Japan (7.2%), Belgium (5.4%), Argentina (4.4%), Italy (4.3%), Switzerland (4.1%) and the United Kingdom (4.1%). Japanese imports from Iran decreased from US $3,835.4m. in 1996 to $2,787.3m. in 1997, while the value of exports rose from $844m. to $882m. over the period. However, Italy replaced Japan as Iran's second largest supplier in 1998/99, exporting goods and services worth $1,188m. (compared with $1,005m. for Japan). By 1998 the United Kingdom had become Iran's largest customer, taking 16.8% of exports by value, followed by Japan (15.7%), Italy (8.6%), the UAE (6.7%), Greece (5.0%) and South Korea (4.9%). In 2000/01 Germany remained the principal supplier of goods to Iran, accounting for 10.5% of imports by value, followed by the UAE (8.0%) and Russia (6.4%). In that year Japan took 16.5% of exports by value, compared to the United Kingdom's 15.3%. Iranian-British trade relations were boosted by the conclusion in March 2002 of an agreement resolving a long-standing dispute over pre-Revolution debts owed by Iran to the United Kingdom's Export Credits Guarantee Department (ECGD). Although Iran agreed to pay only a small symbolic portion of more than £100m. claimed by the ECGD, the agreement was expected to lead to the normalization of ECGD medium-term cover for trade with Iran.

In July 1993 Bank Markazi relaxed restrictions on imports of primary raw materials and spare parts, and at the same time restrictions were tightened on cheap consumer imports through the country's free zones. These measures were designed to assist local industry, following complaints from industrialists. However, the Governor of the central bank urged industrialists to restrict their cash imports to the most urgent commodities and to use medium-term rather than short-term credit facilities. The new measures were welcomed by industrialists, but they also increased the demand for foreign exchange—resulting in a fall in the rial's free-market value. In October the Majlis reportedly authorized the Government to increase customs tariffs to help protect local industry from cheap imports. The 95% devaluation of the rial in March 1993 effectively cut import duties. The import tax on primary raw materials for industry, together with machinery and spare parts that could not be manufactured locally, was not to be raised. It was expected to take some months to prepare the necessary export-import legislation. In March 1994 the Government made the Ministry of Commerce responsible for the administration of export-import regulations. In October the Ministry of Commerce imposed restrictions on exports of raw materials in order to counteract shortages in supplies to domestic factories and shops. The new policy began with a temporary ban on food exports, but also affected a wide range of raw materials including petrochemicals and steel and was predicted to slow down the high rate of growth of non-oil export earnings. The new regulations required the internal market to be saturated with a particular raw material before an export licence could be issued for it. The restrictions were extended to cover the Iranian year beginning 21 March 1995. In May strict foreign-exchange restrictions were imposed, requiring exporters to repatriate all their earnings at the official exchange rate of US $1 = IR 3,000 (see Budget, Investment and Finance).

In 1996 Iran applied to join the World Trade Organization (WTO), but the application was blocked by the USA. There were also differences within the Iranian leadership over the application. President Rafsanjani and his supporters were keen to promote the liberalization of trade and therefore favoured membership, but they were opposed by 'conservative' clergy and traditional merchants who feared that their control over the country's trade would be weakened. In May 2001, after the Majlis had (in the context of a wider debate) voted in favour of ratifying an international convention on the enforcement of arbitration awards, Egypt asked the WTO General Council to reconsider Iran's application for WTO membership, in abeyance since 1996. While immediate acceptance of the application was vetoed by the USA (but not opposed by any other country in the 140-member council), it was agreed that the matter should be reviewed in July 2001. However, the USA continued to veto Iran's admission to the WTO, most recently in February 2002.

After lengthy preliminary contracts, the EU Council of Ministers decided in June 2002 to open formal trade negotiations with Iran, in the expectation that 'the deepening of economic and commercial relations between the EU and Iran should be matched by similar progress in all other aspects of the EU's relations with this country'. The US Administration responded that it expected any economic incentives for Iran to be closely linked to improvements in the areas of concern to the USA, such as Iran's alleged quest for weapons of mass destruction and its human rights observance, and would assess any deals between European firms and Iran in terms of US sanctions law.

Since the late 1980s Qeshm and Kish Islands in the Gulf have been developed as free-trade and industrial zones. Kish Island was designated a free zone before the Revolution. The port of Chahbahar has also been designated a free zone and is being promoted as the gateway to the former Soviet republics of Central Asia. In addition, there are three special free trade zones for transit trade in Sirjan, Sarakhs and Bandar Enzeli. After a prolonged debate and amendments demanded by the Council of Guardians, the legislation confirming the special status of the free zones was ratified in September 1993, but it was another year before basic regulations governing investment in the free zones was completed. The free zones are intended to act as centres of production, export and tourism attracting foreign investment and promoting non-oil exports. They are exempt from most restrictions in force on the mainland. All foreign investments in these zones are guaranteed, profits can be repatriated and disputes taken to international arbitration. Foreign ownership is allowed up to 100%. Foreign banks and foreign credit institutions are also allowed to set up branches in the free zones where the exchange rate will be determined by the free market. In 1993, however, there was criticism that the free zones were using their special status to import some US $1,500m. of finished consumer products into Iran every year. In July business people and government agencies were banned from purchasing individual travellers' rights to bring in goods from the free zones to form large-scale commercial import operations. In November the amount of goods travellers were permitted to bring into Iran from the free zones was reduced from $700 to $200 from Kish and $80 from Qeshm. In December President Rafsanjani was reported to have dismissed the heads of the country's free zones, and there was speculation that this action was taken because of their opposition to these new restrictions. According to the General Secretary of the High Council of Free-Trade Zones, Morteza Alviri, in a statement at the beginning of 1995, Qeshm had attracted most attention from potential investors because it offers discounted natural gas to energy-intensive industries. Negotiations were under way with the Ministry of Oil so that the free zone could offer gas at prices competitive with other free zones in the Gulf region. In early February 1995 the High Council approved a proposal by the Daewoo Corpn of South Korea to build a petrochemical plant on Qeshm, and Sun-Lin of Singapore signed a memorandum of understanding for a 180,000-b/d oil refinery there. Kobe Steel of Japan was negotiating to set up a hot-briquetted iron plant, and INDCONS of India proposed building a $350m. fertilizer plant to produce urea and ammonia. Alviri admitted that infrastructure was still inadequate at Qeshm, but stated that an international airport would be opened later in 1995. In March 1996 the head of the Qeshm Free Zone Authority reported that the free zone had attracted $4,000m. from 541 investors and that many projects had been carried out, including the construction of a ferro-manganese plant and an aluminium smelter. The island's population was reported to have increased by 40%, to 75,000, in recent years and was expected to exceed 400,000 within 10 years.

In April 1996 the Majlis approved legislation to relax foreign-exchange rules in the free-trade zones. Under the new rules, exchange dealings are allowed at a free-market rate and branches of foreign banks in the zone are placed under international regulations. The new legislation also permitted the free transfer of hard currency from the free-trade zones abroad and into Iran. Transfers into the zones from the rest of the country remain strictly controlled by the state. Later in the year the Majlis amended the legislation at the insistence of the Council of Guardians so that the established IR 3,000 = US $1 export rate would apply to the free zones. Legislation was enacted in 1999 to allow private financial institutions to set up operations in Iran's free zones and to permit foreign banks and insurance companies to hold 100% stakes (rather than the 49% ceiling) in free-zone companies. In August 2000 Bank Markazi invited applications for licences from insurance companies, which were required to have a minimum capital of IR 15,000m. for insurance business (IR 85,000m. for reinsurance business) if they intended to base their operations in a free zone, or of IR 300m. if the business was to be a representative office of a foreign firm. In the following month foreign banks and credit institutions were invited to apply to operate in the free zones, the minimum capital requirements being $10m. for banks and $5m. for non-banking credit institutions. After 10 applicants were reported in October to have withdrawn, HSBC was named in February 2001 as one of the current applicants for a free-zone licence.

BUDGET, INVESTMENT AND FINANCE

The five-year development planning concept was introduced in 1947 by the Shah's regime, whose fifth and last plan ended in March 1978. A projected sixth plan remained unpublished at the time of the 1979 Revolution. What became known as the First Five-Year Development Plan (FFYDP) of the new Islamic Republic, drafted in 1981–82, was scheduled to begin in March 1983 but was deferred owing to the demands of the 1980–88 war with Iraq. The FFYDP was eventually introduced in January 1990, its primary objective being 'to remove the legacy of the economic burdens brought about by the Iraqi invasion of Iran'. It envisaged an annual growth rate of 8%, the creation of some 2m. new jobs, the rehabilitation and expansion of the industry, and greater decentralization and private-sector participation.

Despite various inhibiting factors, including rapid population increase and endemic inflation, the FFYDP was hailed as a success by the Government. In a review of the plan published in September 1994, Bank Markazi recorded that US $110,000m., mostly generated from oil revenues, had been disbursed among the various development sectors, compared with $128,000m. originally envisaged. The FFYDP's major achievements reportedly included the transfer of a number of public-sector industries to the private sector; average annual GDP growth of 7.3%; an increase of per caput GDP from IR 197,000 to IR 246,000; yearly rises in private and public consumption of 7.7% and 5.5% respectively; and annual growth of 5.6% in agriculture, 15% in the industrial sector, 18.9% in water, gas and electricity, and 11.9% in the transport sector. However, following rapid expansion in the five plan years, buoyed by an increase in world oil prices and the temporary lifting of OPEC quotas (resulting from Iraq's invasion of Kuwait), decreasing oil prices in 1992 and a consequent decline in imports by the Government resulted in a deceleration of economic growth. Additionally, macroeconomic imbalances emerged, including a deteriorating balance of payments and an increase in external debt arrears, while government investment continued to outpace private investment, at 14.1% and 8% respectively.

The SFYDP took into account the achievements and failures of the FFYDP with a specific objective to complete unfinished infrastructure and development projects. Covering the period March 1995 to 2000, the SFYDP envisaged an average annual GDP growth rate of 5.1% over the five years (including 1.6% for the oil sector, 4.3% for agriculture, 5.9% for industry and mining, and 3.1% for the services sector), an average annual inflation rate of 12.4% and the creation of a further 2m. new jobs. Imports were projected to increase at an average annual rate of 4.3%, oil exports at 3.4% per year and non-oil exports at 8.4% per year. Development and administrative expenditure was projected to total US $135,500m. over the plan period, deriving principally from anticipated oil revenues of $86,500m. (later revised down to $64,000m.) and tax revenues of $40,400m. The key SFYDP

objectives and policies in the external sphere were that the foreign-exchange system should be based on a managed unified floating exchange rate consistent with maintaining convertibility of the rial for current international payments; and that the level of customs tariffs should take account of the need to protect domestic producers and consumers and to maintain comparative advantage for Iranian goods in international markets. In the fiscal sector, plan objectives included increasing the share of direct taxes (excluding wage taxes) in total tax revenue; channelling oil revenue to development expenditure; and undertaking a tax system reform. In the agricultural sector, the maintenance of sustained growth was to be combined with the aim of reducing subsidies and making them more transparent in the budget. In the social sphere, the SFYDP gave special attention to the role of mothers 'in the shaping of society and its human resources', establishing as a national priority the eradication of illiteracy among young mothers.

The Third Five-Year Development Plan (TFYDP), as tabled in August 1999 and beginning in March 2000, set an ambitious target of 6% annual GDP growth over the period of the plan, while annual inflation would be kept to no more than 16% and unemployment reduced to 10%. Aiming at the total restructuring of the economy, particularly through privatization of major industries such as communications, postal services, railways and tobacco, the TFYDP was based on an assumed oil price of US $12.50 per barrel and projected hard-currency requirements of $112,400m. over the five-year period, of which about one-half would come from oil and gas export revenues.

As part of the envisaged new economic regime under the TFYDP, the Government in November 1999 drew up legislation on the attraction and protection of foreign investment, specifying that to qualify for protection projects must contribute to increasing non-oil exports, fill production gaps, promote the exploitation of mineral resources, improve market competition and raise the quality of goods and services. Foreign investment in oil and mining enterprises was limited to 49%, but other qualifying ventures would be open to 80% foreign participation. It was stated that both these ceilings could be raised in special circumstances as determined by the Government, while ceilings for foreign participation were revoked entirely for BOT or buy-back joint ventures. However, although the Majlis approved the legislation in May 2001, it was rejected the following month by the 'conservative' Council of Guardians, as was a heavily amended law in December. The new foreign investment law was finally passed by the Council to Determine the Expediency of the Islamic Order at the end of May 2002; it included the provision that investors would not be able to acquire more than a 25% market share in any one sector and no more than 35% in individual industries. Moreover, government approval was given to the first foreign take-over of an Iranian company in March 2002, when the Henkel chemical products group of Germany was allowed to purchase a 60% stake in the Pakvash detergents company for some US $18m.

Following the 1979 Revolution, successive budgets were dominated by the requirements of the 1980–88 conflict with Iraq. The budget for 1990/91, approved by the Majlis in March 1990, projected overall expenditure of US $79,900m. and revenue of $57,300m., leaving a deficit of $22,600m. An additional $21,000m. was to be invested by state enterprises. Major projects were allocated $5,400m. in foreign credits. In July 1990 the Majlis authorized an amendment to the annual budget, whereby the allocations for disaster relief and post-war reconstruction were doubled; in addition, it approved a $300m. emergency fund for provinces devastated by the earthquake of 21 June 1990; the cost of damage to the provinces of Gilan and Zanjan was believed to exceed $7,000m. In March 1991 the World Bank approved an emergency loan of $250m. for reconstruction projects to repair damage caused by the earthquake. A supplementary budget was introduced in November 1990 to cover the remaining five months of the year; the revised estimates assumed higher revenues than had previously been forecast. Total government revenue in the period March–September 1990 was reported to have amounted to $37,700m., and expenditure to $46,400m., leaving a deficit of $8,700m. Oil and gas revenues over the same period were estimated at $8,000m. With oil and gas revenues expected to rise (owing to increases in both prices and output), the 1991/92 budget forecast total government revenue of IR 7,300,000m. and expenditure of IR 8,640,000m. (an increase of 54% compared with 1990/91), leaving a deficit of IR 1,340,000m. A further budget of IR 11,440,000m. was agreed for state-owned companies, bringing overall planned expenditure in the general budget for 1991/92 to IR 20,080,000m. The budget in convertible currency, set at $24,000m., was the highest ever introduced. In January 1992 the Majlis approved the budget law for 1992/93 despite criticism by deputies of its inflationary aspects. The general budget remained at the level requested by the Government, IR 28,800,000m., but within it the Government budget was increased from around IR 10,000,000m. to IR 12,400,000m. Deficit financing remained unchanged at IR 623,000m. The Majlis increased the proportion of revenues from taxation in order to reduce dependence on oil revenues. In addition it reduced the proportion of current spending (i.e. that on education, health and social security) and increased that of development expenditure to one-third of the total. In October 1992 the Minister of Economy and Finance forecast that the budget deficit for 1992/93 would amount to $10,570m. The Government's budget proposals for 1993/94 finally received approval by the Majlis in February 1993. The general budget was set at IR 54,400,000m. and the Government's budget at IR 25,400,000m. Efforts by the Majlis to reduce expenditure by 10% appeared to have been unsuccessful. The Government set aside $3,800m. at the existing official exchange rate of about $1 = IR 70 in order to subsidize essential imports and prices. Subsidies included $1,200m. for oil product imports, the same amount for basic food items, $452m. for medicine and baby food, $80m. for Iranian students abroad and $850m. for defence. The Majlis authorized NIOC to use up to $2,600m. in foreign finance in order to build and expand the Bandar Abbas oil refinery and its lubricants unit, and for five offshore oil fields in the Gulf.

The Majlis, concerned about low oil prices and debt repayment problems, secured cuts in both projected expenditure and revenue before the Government's budget for the year beginning March 1994 was approved. Projected revenue was reduced by 10% and expenditure by 7%–13% in various sectors. Revenue was projected at IR 30,700,000m. (US $17,700m.), including oil revenues of $10,150m. The overall budget was set at IR 69,800,000m. ($36,900m.), of which government expenditure accounted for IR 32,300,000m. ($18,500m.), with the balance to state banks and companies. Despite the reductions secured by the Majlis, the overall budget was still substantially higher than the level approved for the year 1993/94. The Government's proposal to reduce subsidies on fuel prices in order to raise revenues was rejected by the Majlis.

In December 1994 President Rafsanjani presented the draft budget for the year commencing 21 March 1995 to the Majlis. On the basis of higher oil revenues the President requested approval for spending of IR 95,300,000m. (US $54,500m.), 37% higher than the 1994/95 level. In March 1995 the Majlis approved a nominally balanced budget that was slightly higher than the draft proposal, at IR 96,100,000m. ($54,900m.). However, it imposed new controls on the Government instead of granting its request to be allowed greater flexibility. Oil revenues for 1995/96 were projected at $13,500m., based on a crude oil price of $17 a barrel. Some IR 2,180,000m. ($1,240m.) was allocated for defence, and $1,750m. for essential imports, including medicine and powdered milk for babies. A further $1,100m. in foreign exchange was allocated to the Ministry of Oil, but with the requirement that spending must be justified on a monthly basis. No new state firms could be established, and existing ones were required to make their accounts available at the request of the Majlis. State enterprises were also forbidden to purchase goods abroad if equivalents were available locally.

In January 1996 the Majlis approved the budget for the year beginning 21 March 1996 after making only minor amendments. The budget proposed total expenditure of IR 55,780,000m. (US $31,870m.), of which $16,000m. was to be provided by oil revenues, based on an oil price of $15.5 per barrel. The contribution of earnings from oil to total revenue was forecast to fall by 9% compared with the year beginning 21 March 1995— one of the lowest contributions since the Revolution. The budget made no reference to non-oil exports, which declined sharply in 1995/96. Total expenditure was forecast at IR 137,120,000m.

($78,370m. at the official exchange rate), about $400m. less than the original draft had requested. About 60% of total expenditure was to be allocated to subsidize loss-making state industries and banks. State subsidies for basic food items were increased by $212m. to $1,460m. in hard currency allocations. A further $388m. was allocated for subsidies for medicine and powdered milk. The Government was also required, under the new budget legislation, to reduce the country's debt by $1,640m. in 1996/97. The allocation to the Ministry of Defence was increased slightly, from $1,250m. to $1,260m., although it was reported that the total defence budget had been increased by almost one-third to $3,310m. The Majlis also approved a special fund of some $20m. to counter a proposal before the US Congress to establish a covert action fund to destabilize the Iranian Government. Iran had threatened to begin proceedings against the USA at the International Court of Justice if the US Congress approved the proposal. In April 1996 the Government announced that it was committed to higher expenditure of hard currency in 1996/97 and that it had allocated $19,000m. to finance imports of basic goods and machinery and to service debts. Non-oil revenues were projected at a conservative $3,000m. Officials of Bank Markazi insisted that higher targeted expenditure would not affect the country's ability to service its external debts.

In November 1996 President Rafsanjani presented the draft budget for the year beginning 21 March 1997 to the Majlis. He emphasized that his Government remained committed to strict controls over spending but would maintain its efforts to protect low-income groups. Overall budget expenditure was set at IR 188,149,000m., which analysts believed to be about 10% higher, in real terms, than the level set in 1996/97. Some IR 117,960,000m. was allocated for state-owned industries and IR 81,287,000m. for the general government budget. IR 29,100,000m. of the general government budget was allocated to development projects including the oil sector, water and electricity. Of the general budget revenue projected at IR 75,909,000m., IR 30,713,000m. was to come from oil revenues and IR 18,727,000m. from taxation. Oil revenues were projected on the basis of an average export price for Iranian oil of US $17.50 per barrel.

As tabled in late November 1997, the first version of the 1998/99 budget was based on the Government's assumption of an average oil price of US $17.50 per barrel and provided for a balance between expenditure and income at IR 233,700,000m. However, sharply falling world prices from late 1997 necessitated two successive revisions of the budget, the first in 1998 based on a $16 per barrel price assumption and the second in April on $12 per barrel. It was officially stated that the latest version was a 'temporary' budget that would be amended again if oil prices increased later in the year. However, a further decrease in the Gulf crude price to less than $10 per barrel by mid-1998 again undermined the feasibility of the final 1998/99 budget—the out-turn being a sixfold increase in the budget deficit, to IR 17,700,000m.

In January 1999 the Majlis approved a nominally balanced IR 276,000,000m. budget for the year beginning 21 March 1999. About 60% of that amount was to support loss-making state industries and banks, with the balance making up the Government's spending budget for the ministries. Revenue from crude oil exports was projected at US $10,600m. (based on a price of $11.80 per barrel). The budget projected increased tax revenue, and reduced energy subsidies resulting in price rises of up to 75% for some grades of petrol and other products. To offset an anticipated budget deficit, the Government in August launched an issue of state bonds (called 'national participation certificates') aimed at raising some $665m. at the official exchange rate. However, the marked rise in world oil prices, particularly during the last 1999/2000 quarter, resulted in an actual budget surplus equivalent to 1% of GDP (against a deficit of 7% of GDP in the previous year).

The general budget for the year beginning 21 March 2000, as finally approved by the outgoing Majlis on 12 March, totalled IR 360,000,000m., representing a 30% increase over 1999/2000. The projection for oil income was US $13,500m., based on a price of $15.80 per barrel. The Majlis set a ceiling of 10% on domestic energy price increases, well below the 20%–28% originally proposed by the Government. A contingency fund was created in 2000 to hold 'surplus' oil revenue received as a result of higher than budgeted world oil prices. In October of that year (when surplus oil revenue of at least $8,000m. was being predicted for 2000/01) the Majlis approved a government proposal that about one-half of the predicted surplus should be used to increase expenditure above the level originally budgeted, while the balance should be held in reserve in a 'stabilization fund' to offset the effects of future downward movements in oil markets. According to Bank Markazi, allocations of $1,000m. for hard-currency loans to the Iranian private sector, and of $500m. for credits to foreign buyers of Iranian goods, were in place in early 2001, although no disbursements had so far been made.

The budget for 2001/02 was finalized in February 2001, after the Council to Determine the Expediency of the Islamic Order had reviewed the Council of Guardians' objections to certain measures approved by the Majlis. In particular, the Expediency Council upheld a provision authorizing state agencies to raise up to US $1,500m. of overseas financing for development projects, which was deemed un-Islamic by the Council of Guardians because it would involve interest payments on foreign loans (interest—or *riba*—being contrary to *Shari'a* law). The total budget for 2001/02 was IR 455,107,000m., with 50.6% of budgeted revenue being derived from oil (which the budget assumed would sell for an average of $20 per barrel in 2001/02). Spending on subsidies on foodstuffs was to rise by 20%, while subsidies to loss-making state industries would amount to IR 230,000,000m. in 2001/02. Defence spending was increased by 22%, and spending on national security by 40%. Expenditure on job creation measures in 2001/02 would nearly double, to IR 4,700,000m.

The Government's budget for the 2002/03 financial year starting on 21 March incorporated for the first time a unified exchange rate for the rial, set at US $1 = IR 7,900 (i.e. close to the current free-market rate). Described by observers as one of the most significant reforms since President Khatami took office in 1997, the introduction of a single parity meant the effective abolition of the US $1 = IR 1,750 rate hitherto used to subsidize state imports of basic commodities (see below) and was expected to produce greater transparency in government finances and to remove a major source of racketeering. The budget provided for total expenditure of IR 663,700m., the nominal increase of 45.6% on the previous year being attributable in part to the new accounting method. No breakdown was given of expenditure (except that the equivalent of $4,800m. had been set aside for state subsidies), nor of revenue sources, although government officials said that the budget was close to being balanced and was based on a conservative assumption of an average oil price of $18 per barrel throughout the year.

Inflation has become a persistent problem for the economy. Import controls have tended to increase inflation in a situation of growing shortages, and especially in view of a policy favouring wage increases for the lower paid without increases in productivity. The annual rate of inflation officially fell from 32.5% in 1980/81 to 17% in 1983/84, and in May 1985 the central bank reported that wholesale prices had risen by only 7.6% in the Iranian year 1984/85. IMF figures suggest that inflation for the year ended September 1984 was approximately 13%–14%. In October 1985 the Government continued to maintain that inflation was falling, and that the annual rate was a mere 5.5%. In the first half of 1987, when the annual rate of inflation was unofficially estimated at 30%–50%, the Government appeared indirectly to admit the seriousness of the problem by announcing that, henceforth, the prices of 22 basic commodities would be controlled in order to check inflation. In an interview in November 1991 the Governor of Bank Markazi stated that inflation was running at 15%. Given the reconstruction and development programmes and the adjustment of a war-stricken economy that were taking place, he regarded the level of inflation as a matter of minor concern. According to the central bank, the rate of inflation rose to 22% in 1993/94 when the rial was devalued and oil prices fell sharply. A year of 'monetary discipline' was declared in 1994/95, and it was predicted that a tight monetary policy would reduce inflation to less than 20%. The Majlis was reported to have imposed a 15% ceiling on the growth of liquidity in 1994/95 in order to control inflation, while the rates charged by state banks on loans to various sectors were to remain

unchanged. In October 1994 President Rafsanjani announced an anti-profiteering campaign after a surge in inflation to about 40%. In its first phase price controls were applied to government-controlled goods, such as sugar, flour, primary dairy products, red meat, washing powder, domestically-produced paper and tyres, fodder, chemical fertilizers and ironware. There were temporary shortages as traders withheld goods, but the Government subsequently saturated the market with emergency imports sold through co-operatives and state stores in order to undermine the merchants. The Government also announced that in 1995 it was opening a chain of 1,000 publicly-owned stores selling goods at low prices, a move aimed at breaking the hold of the bazaar merchants. The campaign against inflation was reinforced in January of that year when the list of goods subject to price controls was extended. Since the beginning of 1995 price controls have been applied to hundreds of items, including cars, household appliances, medicines, cigarettes, foodstuffs, construction materials and beverages. Some 1,000 centres were set up across the country in order to investigate public complaints and to prosecute offenders. There were official raids on some warehouses where merchants were hoarding goods. According to the central bank, the annual rate of inflation rose to a record 58.8% in April/May 1995, following a substantial decline in the value of the rial which forced the Government to fix the exchange rate at $1 = IR 3,000 and to impose strict hard-currency controls in May. Prices of many goods were reported to have fallen in the second half of June. At the beginning of 1996 the Ministry of Justice announced that some 280,000 rulings had been issued by the special courts to enforce state prices since they were established in October 1994; and that fines totalling IR 32,000m. ($11m.) had been imposed. Potatoes were added to the list of goods subject to price controls after their price doubled at the end of 1995. The special courts were criticized in the media, however: it was claimed that they were not effective and that the anti-inflation measures had merely created a thriving black market. After rising to 49.4% in 1995/96, the annual inflation rate was halved to 23.3% in 1996/97 and then further reduced to 17.3% in 1997/98. However, owing to renewed inflationary pressures, the annual rate rose to 21% in 1998/99 and to 23% in 1999/2000. The target set in the TFYDP, which began in March 2000, was annual inflation of no more than 16%. Official figures for 2000/01 estimated annual inflation of 12.6% in 2000/01 and 14% in 2001/02.

The state continues to offer a wide range of subsidies on basic foodstuffs. In an interview in November 1991 the Minister of Economic Affairs and Finance stated that the Government would continue to subsidize essential goods, notably foodstuffs (such as bread, rice, cooking oil and sugar) and medicines, until 1994. Other subsidies would gradually be reduced. Figures produced by the Consumer and Producer Protection Organization indicated that prices of local goods were rising much faster than claimed by the central bank. Rising prices in the extensive 'black' market in goods are not taken into account in official price indices, while rents in the housing market have increased substantially in urban areas throughout the country. At the beginning of his second term of office in August 1993, President Rafsanjani warned the country to expect a gradual reduction of some state subsidies and the elimination of others, particularly those on fuel and electricity. He stated that subsidies were wasting public funds, distorting the economy and preventing the growth of a healthy private sector. Furthermore, he believed that the system of subsidies was unjust. The rich were the main beneficiaries because of their high level of consumption. The result was that the majority of Iranians were in effect subsidizing the living standards of the richest 10% of the population. Some subsidies had been removed during 1992/93, but a comprehensive programme to phase them out was incorporated into the draft SFYDP. These proposals met with strong opposition in the Majlis, largely because of the political risks involved. In February 1994 the Majlis rejected proposed price increases for petroleum products and domestic gas supplies. Nevertheless, the President renewed his attack on subsidies in April, stating that energy subsidies alone cost the Government US $11,000m. per year, which was more than projected oil revenues for 1994/95. Rafsanjani estimated that the total cost of subsidies was $15,000m. per year. He acknowledged that some subsidies were justified; these included the $360m. for agriculture, and $230m.

for assistance to families of those killed in the Revolution and the Iran–Iraq War. However, he condemned bread and energy subsidies as unjust because the rich benefited most from them. In April some deputies proposed legislation to cancel all price rises announced since 21 March and to transfer price-setting powers from the Supreme Economic Council, which is headed by the President, to the Majlis. Since February 1994 the Supreme Economic Council had authorized increases in telephone charges, postal rates and domestic air fares, while there were also increases in inter-city bus and train fares. The motion was postponed indefinitely as other deputies supported the Government, but at the end of May Rafsanjani announced that the Government would act cautiously on subsidies and indicated that those on bread and fuel would not be removed during the next five years. However, in November, under pressure from the Government, the Majlis approved the doubling of fuel prices from March 1995 and annual increases of 20% until the end of the decade. In April 1996 domestic fuel prices were, none the less, increased by more than 20%. In December 1995 the IMF had recommended that domestic fuel prices should be increased in stages to international levels by 2000. In April 1997 domestic fuel prices were again substantially increased, but again the overall impact was negligible because of the effect of inflation. In April 1998 the IMF estimated that the 'implicit subsidies' arising from the underpricing of domestic petroleum products were equivalent to nearly 10% of GDP, the largest share being attributed to gas-oil, the domestic price of which was about one-fourteenth of the prevailing world price. Hard currency allocations for state subsidies on basic food items were increased by $212m. to $1,460m. in the 1996/97 budget, but were reduced slightly, to $1,420m., in the 1997/98 budget. Subsidies to cover the cost of medicines and other goods rose from $338m. in 1996/97 to a projected $500m. in 1997/98.

In June 1990, under pressure to reduce inflation, the Government enacted major reforms of the foreign-exchange market and import-export regulations. Foreign currency dealings outside authorized money-changing houses became illegal, and restrictions on importers and exporters were relaxed. A new rate for the rial against the US dollar was intended to encourage exports by giving industrialists access to hard currency for raw materials and machinery. In February 1993 the Minister of Economy and Finance announced that the Government would use a variety of financial instruments, including forward selling, to keep the rial stable after the planned currency devaluation on 21 March. Public sector demand for hard currency would be controlled in order to create a hard currency surplus to support the rial in the free market. The rial was declared fully convertible by the central bank on 13 April 1993. After devaluing the rial by more than 96% in April 1993, the central bank responded to downward market pressure by further devaluing its floating rate. The value of the rial fell to record lows from late 1993. After April 1994, when new restrictions were introduced requiring nearly all importers to use limited official supplies of hard currency earned from non-oil exports, the rial's value on the open market plunged dramatically. On 7 May 1994 the central bank introduced a new currency exchange rate, known as the import-against-export rate, which was applied to most imports. The rate announced on 7 May was US $1 = IR 2,585, compared with a floating rate of $1 = IR 1,748. The central bank stated that the new rate would be IR 50 below the open market rate which had fluctuated in the range IR 2,500–IR 2,800. The new rate effectively devalued the rial by 32%. A bank official stated that very limited funds had been allocated by the Government to some ministries for essential imports, such as machinery and medicine, but that most goods would have to be imported at the new rate.

Following his appointment as Governor of Bank Markazi in September 1994, Mohsen Nourbakhsh stated that he would work to introduce a single foreign-exchange rate and moved quickly to tighten supervision of hard currency transactions. At the beginning of October police arrested at least 30 money dealers operating in Tehran, but by January 1995 many were back in action using motorcycles to deliver foreign currency direct to their customers. By late January the free-market value of the rial had fallen to an all-time low of US $1 = IR 4,000. However, the rial recovered somewhat when the central bank announced that it was easing some import restrictions so that exporters would be able to use half of their hard currency earnings to purchase goods from abroad; and increasing the supply of gold coins sought by investors. The Governor of Bank Markazi informed the Majlis that the fall in the value of the rial was due to a lack of investment opportunities, which encouraged the public to engage in speculative activities. New export-import regulations became effective from 4 February 1995. Exporters were once again permitted to sell up to one-half of their hard currency earnings to importers, on condition that they repatriated the other half of their earnings from abroad. There had been speculation that much of Iran's hard currency earnings from non-oil exports in 1993/94 had been kept abroad. In April 1995, in a move aimed at encouraging exporters to repatriate their hard currency earnings, the central bank effectively devalued the rial by 43%. The export exchange rate was altered from $1 = IR 2,340 to $1 = IR 4,123 in late April. The official floating rate of $1 = IR 1,750 continued to apply for essential imports. The value of the rial against the US dollar fell sharply in April and May, with the biggest losses occurring after President Clinton announced a trade embargo on Iran. The rial fell to $1 = IR 6,300 in early May, losing about one-third of its value in only two weeks. President Rafsanjani blamed 'speculators and profiteers' for the sharp fall in the rial and threatened resolute action against them. There was further criticism of the central bank, which was accused in the local press of having lost control over the foreign-exchange market. On 17 May the Government revalued the rial and imposed strict foreign exchange controls. The new regulations, which took effect on 21 May, set a fixed rate of $1 = IR 3,000. This was initially valid until March 1996, but was subsequently extended. All other rates were eliminated except the official rate of $1 = IR 1,750, used for imports of essential commodities. All hard currency transactions had to be carried out through state banks—an allocation system was to be introduced giving priority to imports of raw materials and spare parts for industry—and exporters had to repatriate all their hard currency earnings from abroad. A new government crack-down on illegal exchange dealers was reported to have begun. However, there was speculation that the Government would not be able to maintain the new fixed rate for more than two months. Some observers argued that the new regulations requiring exporters to repatriate all their hard currency earnings within six months could damage non-oil exports, but central bank officials claimed that non-oil exports would become more competitive. In late 1995 the IMF, as part of its economic programme for Iran, recommended that the unification of exchange rates should take place by 21 March 1996, with market-related management of rates to continue after unification. However, Bank Markazi indicated that it preferred to continue with a more gradualist approach, with currency reforms proceeding in sequence and the stringent foreign-exchange restrictions imposed in May 1995 to be dismantled last of all. The central bank's Deputy Governor stated that the Government would continue its campaign against the currency black market and smuggling for the foreseeable future; and insisted that the Government's intervention in the foreign currency market in May 1995 and the stabilization of the rial had had a positive effect on inflation. Early in 1997 the Governor of Bank Markazi indicated that the exchange rate system was unlikely to be unified until mid-1999. He also acknowledged that reimposing strict exchange controls had resulted in some negative effects, notably the reappearance of an active parallel currency market. By the end of the 1996/97 financial year, according to the IMF, the rial had appreciated by about 80% in real terms against the official 'export' rate of $1 = IR 3,000, although this appreciation was partly offset by the effective depreciation of the weighted average exchange rate resulting from the shifting of transaction from the more-appreciated 'floating' rate to the 'export' rate. Accordingly, on a weighted average basis, the real effective appreciation amounted to only about 16% in 1996/97 (for current account transactions). Although Bank Markazi stated in October 1998 that the rial would be subject to fixed exchange rates until at least March 2000 (the end of the SFYDP), in June 1999 a new official floating rate close to the black market rate (of about $1 = IR 9,400) was introduced for most imports. By the end of 2000 the black market rate had fallen below IR 8,000 per dollar, to reach virtual parity with the official floating rate.

Following the June 1979 nationalization of banking and insurance, in 1980 the Government announced the establishment of an Islamic banking system, which officially came into force on 21 March 1984. Interest on loans (*riba*, which is prohibited under Islamic law) was replaced by a commission—4% per year, compared with the traditional 14%—and interest on deposits was replaced with profits—estimated at a minimum 7%–8.5% per year. The banks would become temporary shareholders in major industrial enterprises to which they lent money. On 21 March 1985 all bank loans and advances were Islamized.

In March 1980 the 22 small commercial banks were merged into two major new institutions, Bank Tejarat and Bank Mellat. Other large institutions in the Iranian commercial banking system are: Bank Keshavarzi, Bank Melli Iran, Bank Refah Kargaran, Bank Saderat Iran, Bank Sepah, the Islamic Economy Organization, Bank Sanat va Madan and the Export Development Bank of Iran.

In 1992 rumours that state banks might be privatized were strongly denied by the central bank. Nevertheless, in recent years the state banks have been encouraged to operate on more commercial lines, and competition between them for customers is now intense. In May 1994 the Council of Ministers authorized the establishment of private savings and loan associations, described by the Governor of Bank Markazi as 'non-banking credit associations', which would be allowed to take deposits and make loans, but would not be permitted to offer current accounts. He stated that the aim of these associations was to encourage savings by providing a range of institutions able to take deposits. It was not clear whether the interest-free Islamic banking law would be applied to the new associations.

In September 1998 the Majlis approved legislation allowing co-operatives to set up banks, potentially opening the way for a competitive commercial banking system. In May 2000 the Governor of Bank Markazi stated that radical reforms were imminent in the banking system, potentially involving the licensing of co-operative and other private onshore banks and the merger of some state banks to enable them to compete. Under the reforms, moreover, it was envisaged that the market would be allowed to determine interest rates. Bank Markazi subsequently received more than 20 applications for private banking licences, two of which, Bank Eqtesad-e Novin and Parsian Bank, were granted licences in September 2001. The Governor of the central bank had said in February 2001 that he foresaw private ownership of half of Iranian onshore banking assets in the long term. The total assets of Iran's established state banks amounted to some US $30,000m. in 2000.

No official information regarding Iran's reserves of foreign exchange was released between 1982 and 1994. In 1982 reserves were recorded at US $5,700m. (excluding gold), representing less than 50% of the level prevailing before the Revolution. In March 1984 the Majlis approved legislation preventing the Government from spending more than it earned. As a result, drawings on foreign reserves were believed to have been limited in 1984 and 1985. About $3,000m. was withdrawn by the Government during 1986, when the price of oil collapsed, but there followed a steady improvement in reserve holdings. In mid-1988 Iran's foreign-exchange reserves were estimated at $6,000m.–$7,000m. (including gold holdings) compared with $3,000m.–$4,000m. in mid-1986. In June 1991 the Bank for International Settlements (BIS) reported that the value of Iranian assets had fallen by 25% during the previous 12 months, to $5,019m., while during the same period the extent of Iran's liabilities had risen to $3,784m. The BIS reported that liabilities to commercial banks in countries of the Organisation for Economic Development and Co-operation (OECD) were at an all-time high of $9,105m. in March 1993, when Iranian deposits with the same banks were estimated at $5,935m. By the final quarter of 1993 the BIS reported that liabilities to foreign banks and other financial institutions were $8,553m., with Iran's assets standing at $5,561m. In the second half of 1994 the BIS reported that Iranian deposits in commercial banks in OECD countries rose by about $1,000m. to $6,492m., and in December 1994 they had returned to the same level as in early 1991. Sources in Tehran reported that the central bank intended to add another $1,000m.–$2,000m. to reserves in 1995, raising the total to about $8,000m., the highest level since the mid-1980s. This increase in reserves was being achieved by reducing expenditure and imports, and was an attempt by Iran to improve its international creditworthiness and to guarantee the repayment of foreign debts due in 1996. According to the BIS, Iran's liabilities to commercial banks in OECD countries rose by $1,700m., to $9,910m., in the third quarter of 1994. In the third quarter of 1995 Iranian deposits in commercial banks in OECD countries rose by $458m., to the record level of $8,398m., according to the BIS. Iran's liabilities to these banks rose by $290m. to $11,660m. According to Bank Markazi, net repayment of foreign debt resulted in a $2,115m. decrease in exchange reserves in the first half of the 1997/98 financial year; no figure for the remaining reserves was given, but Western estimates put them at $5,000m.–$6,000m. at the end of the year. The Bank's Governor stressed that reserves were not allowed to drop below six months' import cover and that all foreign obligations would continue to be met on time. The BIS assessed that Iran's deposits in commercial banks in OECD countries had fallen to $7,457m. by September 1997, against total liabilities of $8,613m. Iran reportedly depleted its foreign-exchange reserves by $533m. in the second quarter of 1998 to compensate for falling oil revenues. The reduction followed drawdowns totalling $3,705m. in the previous 12 months. Foreign-exchange reserves had fallen from $10,917m. in March 1997 to $6,750m. in March 1998, according to the BIS. According to Bank Markazi estimates, reserves in March 1999 stood at $6,500m., while BIS estimates put the level at $8,100m. in December 1999.

The World Bank, reporting on Iran for the first time since 1979, stated that Iran's total external debt had risen to just over US $9,000m. by December 1990, of which one-fifth consisted of long-term commitments. Figures from the BIS and OECD indicated that Iran's external debt rose from $5,560m. in December 1989 to $6,469m. in June 1990, and to $10,000m. by the end of that year. According to the BIS, external debts rose rapidly in 1991, reaching an estimated $13,653m. by December. By June 1992 they had increased to about $15,000m. A lower figure of $11,500m. was reported by the World Bank for December 1991. The World Bank estimate showed a $2,500m. increase compared to December 1990, and a $5,000m. increase compared to December 1989. According to the World Bank, $8,775m. of the total external debt consisted of short-term debts and $2,775m. of long-term debts. However, in February 1993 the Chairman of the Majlis Plan and Budget Committee declared that Iran had accumulated about $30,000m. in short-term external debts by March 1992—the first official acknowledgement of the country's high external indebtedness. He reported that $18,000m. had been added to the external debt since 1989. The World Bank reported a lower estimate of $14,166m. in December 1992, of which $11,102m. consisted of short-term debts. The Bank estimated that the total cost of debt-servicing was $810m. The BIS estimated Iran's total external debt at $16,107m. in mid-1993, consisting of $8,826m. in external bank claims and $7,281m. of non-bank credits.

By the end of the 1993/94 Iranian year, Iran's total external debt had reached US $23,000m., of which $17,600m. was in the form of short-term credits accumulated during the early years of President Rafsanjani's first term of office, when government spending was at a high level. From mid-1992 Iran experienced problems paying its external debts as oil revenues declined. During 1993 Western creditors became increasingly concerned about arrears on repayments, which are believed to have risen as high as $10,000m. until the massive reschedulings of 1994 (see below). In early 1993 a series of rescheduling agreements were concluded regarding letters of credit payments not covered by export guarantee organizations. In April 1993 German, French and Japanese banks holding more than $2,000m. in Iranian letters of credit agreed to defer payment for one year to allow Iran time to bring its short-term debt repayments back on schedule. Belgian creditors followed, and by the end of the year agreement had been reached to reschedule debts totalling $3,000m. In November Iran's total payment arrears were estimated to have reached at least $7,000m. Early in 1994 it was rumoured that Iran was exploring the possibility of bilateral government-to-government deals with Germany and France in order to avoid a rescheduling by the 'Paris Club' of official creditors, the implications of which would be politically unacceptable to the Iranian Government. Despite opposition from the USA, agreements of bilateral rescheduling were concluded with several European creditors and with Japan during the first half of 1994. In February Germany agreed to restructure about $2,400m. of short-term debts into medium-term debt. Similar agreements followed with Japan, Austria, Switzerland, Denmark, Spain, Belgium, Italy and France. The package included a two-year grace period, with payments spread over four years starting in 1996. The agreements reached with Italy and France in June 1994 brought the amount of debt rescheduled to about $8,000m. A central bank official stated in May that the refinancing deals had been arranged so that annual repayments beginning in 1996 would not exceed 25% of projected government revenue. In September 1994 Bank Markazi reported that it had signed 75 agreements with various creditors to reschedule arrears. It estimated Iran's total foreign debt at $18,000m.–$20,000m. and described the 21% ratio of foreign debt to GDP as relatively low when compared with similar economies. In the second half of 1994 rescheduling agreements were signed with Finland, with German creditors without state insurance cover—raising German debt reschedulings to more than $3,000m.—and with Swiss creditors without state insurance cover. After some technical and political problems with the rescheduling of debts to Italian creditors, for which an in-principle agreement had been reached in July 1994, a rescheduling package for $1,000m. owed to official creditors was finalized in early 1995 and another agreement for $400m. for private Italian creditors was due to be signed in March.

At the end of December 1995 creditor nations which had rescheduled some US $14,000m. of Iran's foreign debt since 1993 received their first payment of principal. In February 1996 Bank Markazi reported that the total principal foreign debt stood at $23,412m. on 22 September 1995. Of this, $20,145m. was classified as long- and medium-term debt and $3,267m. as short-term debt. Bank Markazi's figures indicated that total debt stocks, including principal and interest obligations, were $30,600m. In April 1996 Bank Markazi reported that repayments of rescheduled short-term debt and medium-term obligations had totalled $5,660m. in the year ending 20 March 1996, a substantially higher amount than the central bank's earlier projection of $4,300m. and than an independent estimate of $4,800m. Announcing a rise in hard currency spending in April, the central bank insisted that the country's ability to service its external debts would not be affected, and independent observers appeared confident that Iran would repay its debts on time in order to try to regain its international creditworthiness.

In 1996 the Governor of Bank Markazi stated that Iran had repaid US $15,400m. of debt between March 1992 and March 1996 ($6,800m. of rescheduled debt and $8,600m. of non-rescheduled debt) and that the remaining debt would be paid off in five years. Further progress was achieved in 1996/97 in reducing the outstanding stock of external debt and improving its maturity structure. Total outstanding external debt declined from $21,900m. in March 1996 to $16,800m. by March 1997, of which about $12,000m. was medium- and long-term debt (down from $16,000m. at the end of 1994/95.) Concurrently, the outstanding short-term debt dropped substantially, to $4,800m. by March 1997, and external arrears were virtually eliminated. By March 1998 total external debt had been further reduced to $11,700m., of which $5,300m. consisted of rescheduled debts. From mid-1998 Iran experienced serious liquidity shortages, owing to the slump in oil prices and corresponding decline in revenues, its debt stock having reached $11,949m. in September ($8,391m. in medium- and long-term exposure and $3,558m. in short-term obligations). Further debt refinancing facilities worth a total of $2,000m.–$3,000m. (in particular with German and Italian creditors) were reported to have been concluded by April 1999. Iran's total external debt was estimated by the World Bank as $10,357m. at the end of 1999, falling to $7,953m. at the end of 2000. By early 2002 the country's external debt had been reduced to $7,000m., a level considered manageable even during a period of low oil prices.

Early in 1994 the USA succeeded in its campaign to stop further World Bank loans to Iran, and in April the Bank's lending programme was frozen at US $850m. A $150m. loan proposal to develop livestock and arable land and a $125m. proposal to develop basic education were shelved indefinitely. Earlier, in September 1993, Iran had been told to seek alternative sources of funding for two proposals for gas flaring reduction and rail and ports rehabilitation because the Bank considered them to be controversial. However, in December 1996 the Bank agreed to extend a 25-year credit facility worth $600m. to Iran to fund infrastructure and health projects. Moreover, a resumption of full participation in the World Bank appeared more feasible as US-Iranian relations began to thaw in the first half of 1998. In April the Governor of Bank Markazi led an Iranian delegation to the spring meeting of the Bank and the IMF in Washington, DC, reportedly with the aim of securing support to rescind the 1994 ban. In 1996 Iran stated that it would take legal action to secure the release of Iranian assets that remain frozen in the USA. The Iranian Government claimed that these assets total $12,000m., but independent sources suggest that they are probably between $3,500m. and $5,000m.

After two postponements because of US opposition, the World Bank in May 2000 resumed lending to Iran by approving two infrastructure loans totalling US $230m., for a sewerage works and a primary health care project. World Bank officials stressed that under the institution's charter only economic considerations should be taken into account in lending decisions.

It was reported in late May 2002 that BNP Paribas of France and Commerzbank of Germany had been appointed as joint lead arrangers for Iran's first foreign-currency-denominated sovereign bond to be issued since 1979, thereby signalling the country's return to international capital markets. The Eurobonds, valued at €500m., were issued in early July 2002.

ECONOMIC PROSPECTS

The sharp rise in world oil prices from mid-1999 proved to be a boon for the finances of the Iranian Government, enabling it to embark upon the TFYDP from March 2000 in a buoyant economic atmosphere and with some confidence that resources would be available for the plan's ambitious objectives. Major new oil and gas discoveries, as well as the long-delayed start of gas exports, have given additional confidence to Iranian policymakers. The oil price recovery has also stimulated strong development in the private manufacturing and retail sectors, in contrast to the general stagnation and inefficiency of non-oil state enterprises. The victory of the 'reformists' in the February 2000 parliamentary elections strengthened the Government of President Khatami in its declared policy of liberalizing economic structures, notably by proceeding with plans to privatize some 2,000 enterprises in the inefficient state sector. However, vested interests and 'conservative' political forces have continued to obstruct the implementation of such plans, including the Government's attempt to make foreign investment in Iran more attractive and secure.

The dominance of the state-owned oil and gas sectors means that the private sector still accounts for only about 20% of the economy, a proportion that is likely to increase only slowly despite the Government's commitment to privatization. Various forms of subsidy continue to absorb more than 50% of current budget expenditure, highlighting the persistence of underlying structural problems in the economy. Iran also has a rapidly growing population with limited employment prospects and high levels of poverty, especially in rural areas.

The re-election of President Khatami in June 2001 sent the clearest possible signal to his 'conservative' opponents that popular opinion was in favour of reform, and that the Government was mandated to press for early implementation of its plans. The same signal went out to the international community, including in particular the USA, where the long-term status of trade sanctions against Iran remains uncertain, despite their renewal in August of that year. A key factor in Iran's economic prospects is whether it will be able to gain full readmittance to the international trading community, which will depend in large part on the outcome of the political contest in Tehran.

Statistical Survey

The Iranian year runs from 21 March to 20 March.

Source (except where otherwise stated): Statistical Centre of Iran, POB 14155-6133, Dr Fatemi Ave, Tehran 14144;
tel. (21) 8965061; fax (21) 8963451; e-mail sci@sci.or.ir; internet www.sci.or.ir;
Bank Markazi Jomhouri Islami Iran (Central Bank), POB 15875-7177, 144 Mirdamad Blvd, Tehran;
tel. (21) 3110231; fax (21) 3115674; e-mail g.secdept@cbi.ir; internet www.cbi.ir.

Area and Population

AREA, POPULATION AND DENSITY

Area (sq km)	1,648,195*
Population (census results)†	
1 October 1991	55,837,163
25 October 1996	
Males	30,515,159
Females	29,540,329
Total	60,055,488
Population (official estimate at mid-year)	
1999	62,736,002
2000	63,663,942
2001	64,528,162
Density (per sq km) at mid-2001	39.2

* 636,372 sq miles.
† Excluding adjustment for underenumeration.

PROVINCES (mid-2001)*

Province (Ostan)	Area (sq km)†	Population (estimates)	Provincial capital
Tehran (Teheran). . .	19,196	11,450,574	Tehran (Teheran)
Markazi (Central) . .	29,406	1,286,549	Arak
Gilan	14,106	2,295,726	Rasht
Mazandaran . . .	23,833	2,718,129	Sari
Azarbayejan-e-Sharqi			
(East Azerbaijan) .	45,481	3,368,610	Tabriz
Azarbayejan-e-Gharbi			
(West Azerbaijan) . .	37,463	2,723,170	Orumiyeh
Bakhtaran (Kermanshah)	24,641	1,929,858	Bakhtaran
Khuzestan . . .	63,213	4,366,057	Ahwaz
Fars	121,825	4,079,207	Shiraz
Kerman	181,714	2,174,278	Kerman
Khorasan . . .	302,966	6,081,991	Mashad
Esfahan	107,027	4,238,903	Esfahan
Sistan and Baluchestan	178,431	2,018,178	Zahedan
Kordestan (Kurdistan) .	28,817	1,465,205	Sanandaj
Hamadan . . .	19,547	1,710,412	Hamadan
Chaharmahal and			
Bakhtiari . . .	16,201	786,787	Shahr-e-Kord
Lorestan	28,392	1,656,952	Khorramabad
Ilam	20,150	539,200	Ilam
Kohgiluyeh and			
Boyerahmad . .	15,563	610,290	Yasuj
Bushehr	23,168	787,677	Bushehr
Zanjan	21,841	930,776	Zanjan
Semnan	96,816	551,986	Semnan
Yazd.	73,467	823,787	Yazd
Hormozgan . . .	71,193	1,204,388	Bandar-e-Abbas
Ardabil	17,881	1,197,364	Ardabil
Qom	11,237	950,066	Qom
Qazvin	15,491	1,046,606	Qazvin
Golestan	20,893	1,532,436	Gorgan
Total	1,629,959	64,528,162	—

* On 1 January 1997 the legislature approved a law creating a new province, Qazvin (with its capital in the city of Qazvin), by dividing the existing province of Zanjan. In June 1997 the Council of Ministers approved draft legislation to establish another new province, Golestan (with its capital in the city of Gorgan), by dividing the existing province of Mazandaran.
† Excluding inland water (totalling 18,236 sq km).

PRINCIPAL TOWNS (population at 1996 census)

Tehran (Teheran, the capital) .	6,758,845	Rasht	417,748
		Hamadan . . .	401,281
Mashad (Meshed) .	1,887,405	Kerman	384,991
Esfahan (Isfahan) .	1,266,072	Arak	380,755
Tabriz	1,191,043	Ardabil (Ardebil). .	340,386
Shiraz	1,053,025	Yazd	326,776
Karaj	940,968*	Qazvin	291,117
Ahwaz	804,980	Zanjan	286,295
Qom	777,677	Sanandaj . . .	277,808
Bakhtaran		Bandar-e-Abbas . .	273,578
(Kermanshah) .	692,986	Khorramabad . .	272,815
Orumiyeh . . .	435,200	Eslamshahr	
Zahedan. . . .	419,518	(Islam Shahr) . .	265,450

* Including towns of Rajayishahr and Mehrshahr. Estimated population of Mehrshahr at 1 October 1994 was 413,299 (Source: UN, *Demographic Yearbook*).

BIRTHS AND DEATHS (UN estimates, annual averages)

	1985–90	1990–95	1995–2000
Birth rate (per 1,000) . . .	40.1	31.4	23.5
Death rate (per 1,000) . . .	8.2	6.4	5.3

Source: UN, *World Population Prospects: The 2000 Revision*.

Expectation of life (WHO estimates, years at birth, 2000): Males 68.1; Females 69.9 (Source: WHO, *World Health Report*).

1999: Registered live births 1,177,557 (birth rate 18.8 per 1,000); Registered deaths 374,838 (death rate 6.0 per 1,000) (Source: UN, *Population and Vital Statistics Report*).

Note: Registration is incomplete.

Marriages: 531,490 in 1998; 611,073 in 1999; 646,498 in 2000.

ECONOMICALLY ACTIVE POPULATION
(persons aged 6 years and over, 1996 census)

	Males	Females	Total
Agriculture, hunting and forestry .	3,024,380	294,156	3,318,536
Fishing	38,418	309	38,727
Mining and quarrying . . .	115,185	4,699	119,884
Manufacturing	1,968,806	583,156	2,551,962
Electricity, gas and water supply .	145,239	5,392	150,631
Construction.	1,634,682	15,799	1,650,481
Wholesale and retail trade; repair of motor vehicles, motorcycles and personal and household goods	1,804,143	38,146	1,842,289
Hotels and restaurants . .	82,293	2,485	84,778
Transport, storage and communications	955,271	17,541	972,792
Financial intermediation . .	139,286	13,586	152,872
Real estate, renting and business activities	137,039	12,051	149,090
Public administration and defence; compulsory social security	1,519,449	98,651	1,618,100
Education	581,597	459,459	1,041,056
Health and social work . .	184,242	118,897	303,139
Other community, social and personal service activities . .	183,246	41,159	224,405
Private households with employed persons	57,037	4,933	61,970

— continued	Males	Females	Total
Extra-territorial organizations and bodies	660	220	880
Central departments and offices	30,389	2,563	32,952
Activities not adequately defined	204,808	52,220	257,028
Total employed	12,806,170	1,765,402	14,571,572

Unemployed ('000 persons, 1996 census): 1,455 (males 1,183; females 272).

1997/98 ('000 persons): Total employed 14,803; Unemployed 2,037; Total labour force 16,840.

1998/99 ('000 persons): Total employed 14,897; Unemployed 2,415; Total labour force 17,312.

Health and Welfare

KEY INDICATORS

Fertility (births per woman, 2000)	3.0
Under 5 mortality rate (per 1,000 live births, 2000)	44
HIV/AIDS (% of persons aged 15–49, 2001)	<0.10
Physicians (per 1,000 head, 1996)	0.85
Hospital beds (per 1,000 head, 1996)	1.6
Health expenditure (1998): US $ per head (PPP)	397
% of GDP	5.7
public (% of total)	48.6
Access to water (% of persons, 2000)	95
Access to sanitation (% of persons, 2000)	81
Human Development Index (2000): ranking	98
value	0.721

For sources and definitions, see explanatory note on p. vi.

Agriculture

PRINCIPAL CROPS ('000 metric tons)

	1998	1999	2000
Wheat	11,955	8,673	7,000*
Rice (paddy)	2,771	2,348	2,300*
Barley	3,301	1,999	1,200*
Maize	941	1,156	700*
Potatoes	3,340	3,433	3,100†
Sugar cane	1,970	2,236	2,050*
Sugar beet	4,987	5,548	4,750*
Dry beans	183	183	175†
Chick-peas	249	165	160†
Lentils	95	63	60†
Almonds	112	96	90†
Walnuts	146	143	140†
Pistachios	314	131	120†
Soybeans (Soya beans)	138	140*	140*
Sunflower seed	53	45*	40*
Cottonseed*	250	265	290
Tomatoes	3,204	3,490	3,200†
Pumpkins, squash and gourds	662	500†	450†
Cucumbers and gherkins	1,302	1,367	1,400*
Dry onions	1,210	1,677	1,500†
Other vegetables†	2,309	2,061	1,860
Oranges	1,749	1,866	1,700†
Tangerines, mandarins, clementines and satsumas	727	760	700†
Lemons and limes	891	972	900†
Other citrus fruits	155	157	153
Apples	1,944	2,137	2,000†
Pears	187	162	155†
Apricots	243	241	230†
Peaches and nectarines	267	318	280†
Plums	118	133	130†
Grapes	2,315	2,342	2,200†
Watermelons	2,473	2,179	2,299*
Cantaloupes and other melons	1,168	1,055	1,100*
Figs	79	70	68†
Dates	918	908	900†
Cotton (lint)*	139	145	150
Tea (made)	60	80*	60†

* Unofficial figure(s).   † FAO estimate(s).

Source: FAO.

LIVESTOCK ('000 head, year ending September)

	1998	1999	2000*
Horses*	130	120	150
Mules	137†	173†	175
Asses	1,400†	1,554†	1,600
Cattle	8,785	8,047	7,500
Buffaloes	474	474	450
Camels	143	145*	145
Sheep	53,245	53,900	53,500
Goats	25,757	25,757	25,500
Chickens (million)*	230	220	210

* FAO estimate(s).   † Unofficial figure.

Source: FAO.

LIVESTOCK PRODUCTS ('000 metric tons)

	1998	1999	2000
Beef and veal	315	295	250*
Buffalo meat	10.7	10.7	10.5
Mutton and lamb	309	293	285*
Goat meat	109	104	103*
Chicken meat	696	725	685*
Turkey meat	15.6	15.0	15.0
Other meat	10.6	10.5	10.5
Cows' milk	4,095	4,403	4,100*
Buffaloes' milk	169.0	176.3	160.0*
Sheep's milk	463	549	540*
Goats' milk	398	396	390*
Cheese	199.2	212.9	202.8
Butter and ghee	128.0	139.4	130.8
Hen eggs	498	538	500*
Honey	24.6	24.5	24.5*
Wool (greasy)	62.7	73.9	73.9*
Cattle hides	45.4	42.5	36
Sheepskins	57.9	54.9	53.4
Goatskins	19.5	18.6	18.4

* FAO estimate.

Source: FAO.

Forestry

ROUNDWOOD REMOVALS ('000 cubic metres, excl. bark)

	1998	1999	2000
Sawlogs, veneer logs and logs for sleepers	341	310	319
Pulpwood	448	394	488
Other industrial wood	270	256	253
Fuel wood	227	189	54
Total	1,286	1,149	1,114

Source: FAO.

SAWNWOOD PRODUCTION
('000 cubic metres, incl. railway sleepers)

	1998	1999	2000
Total (all broadleaved)	129	96	106

Source: FAO.

Fishing

('000 metric tons, live weight)

	1997	1998	1999
Capture	342.3	367.2	387.2
Silver carp	15.8	11.6	14.4
Other cyprinids . . .	12.9	19.6	10.8
Caspian shads	60.4	85.0	95.0
Clupeoids	10.0	9.7	13.0
Skipjack tuna	6.0	6.7	16.6
Longtail tuna	20.1	19.7	23.5
Yellowfin tuna	21.3	21.5	26.9
Aquaculture	30.3	33.2	31.8
Common carp	16.3	16.4	13.8
Total catch	**372.6**	**400.4**	**419.0**

Source: FAO, *Yearbook of Fishery Statistics.*

Production of caviar (metric tons, year ending 20 March): 281 in 1988/89; 310 in 1989/90; 233 in 1990/91.

Mining

CRUDE PETROLEUM

('000 barrels per day, year ending 20 March)

	1998/99	1999/2000	2000/01
Total production	3,666	3,373	3,762

NATURAL GAS (million cu metres, year ending 20 March)*

	1997/98	1998/99	1999/2000†
Consumption (domestic)‡ . .	47,600	51,500	58,700
Flared	11,500	11,100	10,800
Regional uses and wastes . .	10,400	9,900	10,500
Total production	**69,500**	**72,500**	**80,000**

* Excluding gas injected into oil wells.
† Estimates.
‡ Includes gas for household, commercial, industrial, generator and refinery consumption.

Source: IMF, *Islamic Republic of Iran: Statistical Appendix* (September 2000).

OTHER MINERALS

('000 metric tons, unless otherwise indicated, year ending 20 March)

	1998/99	1999/2000	2000/01*
Iron ore: gross weight . . .	10,536	10,776	11,000
metal content* . . .	5,200	5,300	5,400
Copper concentrates† . . .	128	131	120
Bauxite	336	912	400
Lead concentrates†	11	11*	15
Zinc concentrates*†	80	80	85
Manganese ore‡	101.4	104.1	105.0
Chromium concentrates§ . . .	313.9	311.2	310.0
Molybdenum concentrates (metric tons)*†	1,400	1,600	1,600
Silver (metric tons)†	19	21	22
Gold (kilograms)†	856	930	950
Bentonite	83.3	65.0	70.0
Kaolin	582.5	837.3	800.0
Other clays*	450	400	450
Magnesite	109.6	141.1	141.0
Fluorspar (Fluorite)	25.9	18.4	20.0
Feldspar	185.7	239.8	240.0
Barite (Barytes)	187.7	183.9	185.0
Salt (unrefined)	1,912	1,600	1,600
Gypsum (crude)	11,843	10,834	11,000
Pumice and related materials* .	150	150	150
Mica (metric tons)	1,084	1,425	2,000
Talc	27	25*	25
Turquoise (kilograms) . . .	6,000	20,000*	20,000

* Estimated production.
† Figures refer to the metal content of ores and concentrates.
‡ Figures refer to gross weight. The estimated metal content (in '000 metric tons) was: 30.5 in 1998/99; 32.0 in 1999/2000; 32.0 in 2000/01.
§ Figures refer to gross weight. The estimated chromic oxide content (in '000 metric tons) was: 138 in 1998/99; 137 in 1999/2000; 137 in 2000/01.

Source: US Geological Survey.

Hard coal (provisional figure, '000 metric tons, year ending 20 March): 1,169 in 1998/99 (Source: UN, *Industrial Commodity Statistics Yearbook*).

Industry

PETROLEUM PRODUCTS

('000 metric tons, year ending 20 March)

	1996/97	1997/98	1998/99
Liquefied petroleum gas* . .	3,750	3,730	3,920
Naphtha	692	679	1,871*
Motor spirit (petrol) . . .	7,643	7,893	9,025*
Aviation gasoline . . .	78	99	96*
Kerosene*	4,655	4,700	4,750
White spirit*	300	320	320
Jet fuel*	1,300	1,325	1,350
Gas-diesel (distillate fuel) oil . .	15,500	16,000	16,850
Residual fuel oils* . . .	18,500	19,000	19,500
Lubricating oils*	650	675	695
Petroleum bitumen (asphalt)* . .	2,806	2,839	2,841

* Provisional or estimated figures.

Source: UN, *Industrial Commodity Statistics Yearbook.*

OTHER PRODUCTS (year ending 20 March)

	1996/97	1997/98	1998/99
Refined sugar ('000 metric tons)* .	832	1,055	1,050
Cigarettes (million)* .	11,860	10,304	14,335
Paints ('000 metric tons)*.	33	39	41
Cement ('000 metric tons)†	17,703	18,349	20,049
Refrigerators ('000)*	756	702	1,104
Telephone sets ('000)*	224	248	318
Radios and recorders ('000)	56	76	127
Television receivers ('000)*	453	751	769
Footwear (million pairs)*.	28.3	27.3	22.4
Carpets and rugs ('000 sq m)*.	59,487	84,457	85,163

* Figures refer to production in manufacturing establishments with 10 workers or more.
† Figures refer to production in large-scale manufacturing establishments with 50 workers or more.

Source: UN, *Industrial Commodity Statistics Yearbook*.

Production of Electricity (million kWh, year ending 20 March): *Ministry of Energy:* 80,044 in 1995/96; 85,825 in 1996/97; 92,310 in 1997/98; 97,863 in 1998/99; 107,148 in 1999/2000; 115,156 in 2000/01. *Private Sector:* 4,925 in 1995/96; 5,026 in 1996/97; 5,434 in 1997/98; 5,550 in 1998/99; 5,389 in 1999/2000; 5,624 (provisional) in 2000/01.

Finance

CURRENCY AND EXCHANGE RATES

Monetary Units
100 dinars = 1 Iranian rial (IR).

Sterling, Dollar and Euro Equivalents (31 May 2002)
£1 sterling = 11,623.6 rials;
US $1 = 7,925.0 rials;
€1 = 7,439.2 rials;
100,000 Iranian rials = £8.603 = $12.618 = €13.442.

Average Exchange Rate (rials per US $)
1999   1,752.93
2000   1,764.43
2001   1,753.56

Note: In March 1993 the former multiple exchange rate system was unified, and since then the exchange rate of the rial has been market-determined. The foregoing information on average exchange rates refers to the base rate, applicable to receipts from exports of petroleum and gas, payments for imports of essential goods and services, debt-servicing costs and imports related to large national projects. There was also an export rate, set at a mid-point of US $1 = 3,007.5 rials in May 1995, which applied to receipts from non-petroleum exports and to all other official current account transactions not effected at the base rate. In addition, a market rate was determined by transactions on the Tehran Stock Exchange: at 31 January 2002 it was US $1 = 7,924 rials. The weighted average of all exchange rates (rials per US $, year ending 20 December) was: 3,206 in 1997/98; 4,172 in 1998/99; 5,731 in 1999/2000. A new unified exchange rate, based on the market rate, took effect from 21 March 2002.

BUDGET ('000 million rials, year ending 20 March)*

Revenue	1999/2000	2000/01	2001/02†
Oil and gas revenues. .	44,487	59,448	68,653
Non-oil revenues. .	59,404	61,673	88,833
Taxation . .	38,757	33,298	45,389
Income and wealth taxes .	15,432	18,129	25,416
Corporate taxes . .	10,049	11,295	15,766
Public corporations .	4,944	4,899	7,266
Private corporations .	5,105	6,396	8,500
Taxes on wages and salaries	2,469	3,413	5,000
Taxes on other income .	2,914	3,421	4,650
Import taxes . .	5,806	7,948	11,276
Customs duties . .	3,046	4,158	7,150
Order registration fees .	2,532	3,480	3,700
Taxes on consumpton and sales	16,367	5,765	5,899
Non-tax revenues . .	9,072	11,895	20,727
Services and sales of goods	4,982	6,615	9,270
Other revenues‡ . .	4,090	5,279	11,457
Special revenues . .	11,575	16,481	22,717
Total . . .	103,891	121,122	157,486

Expenditure§	1998/99	1999/2000	2000/2001†
General services . .	6,469	8,457	12,047
National defence. .	8,144	9,472	17,390
Social services . .	31,150	37,558	45,733
Education . .	16,344	19,656	24,031
Health and nutrition .	3,694	4,007	5,004
Social security and welfare .	6,686	8,464	10,195
Other social services .	4,426	5,431	6,503
Economic services . .	13,921	20,359	14,210
Agriculture . .	1,592	2,104	2,515
Water resources . .	1,444	2,407	3,914
Petroleum, fuel and power .	6,803	10,470	707
Transport and communication .	3,157	4,300	4,601
Other economic services .	927	1,078	2,473
Other expenditure‡ . .	11,259	17,084	21,856
Sub-total . . .	70,943	92,929	111,236
Current . .	53,518	67,987	84,866
Capital . .	17,425	24,942	26,370
Foreign exchange obligations .	5,077	1,993	—
Special expenditures . .	8,931	11,575	16,481
Total . . .	84,951	106,497	127,717

2001/02 (approved budget, '000 million rials): Total expenditure and net lending 141,155 (current expenditure 104,538).

* Figures refer to the consolidated accounts of the central Government, comprising the General Budget, the operations of the Social Security Organization and special (extrabudgetary) revenue and expenditure.
† Forecasts.
‡ Including operations of the Organization for Protection of Consumers and Producers, a central government unit with its own budget.
§ Excluding lending minus repayments ('000 million rials): –187 in 1998/99.

INTERNATIONAL RESERVES (US $ million at 31 December)*

	1993	1994	1995
Gold (national valuation). .	229	242	252
IMF special drawing rights . .	144	143	134
Total . . .	373	385	386

* Excluding reserves of foreign exchange, for which no figures are available since 1982 (when the value of reserves was US $5,287m.).

IMF special drawing rights (US $ million at 31 December): 345 in 1996; 330 in 1997; 2 in 1998; 139 in 1999; 349 in 2000; 336 in 2001.

Source: IMF, *International Financial Statistics*.

MONEY SUPPLY ('000 million rials at 20 December)

	1999	2000	2001
Currency outside banks . .	16,652	20,020	21,840
Non-financial public enterprises' deposits at Central Bank .	5,304	7,859	4,552
Demand deposits at commercial banks. .	59,996	74,291	99,275
Total money . . .	81,952	102,170	125,667

Source: IMF, *International Financial Statistics*.

COST OF LIVING (Consumer Price Index in urban areas, year ending 20 March; base: 1997/98 = 100)

	1998/99	1999/2000	2000/01
Food, beverages and tobacco . .	124.5	152.7	166.3
Clothing. . .	105.3	112.1	121.8
Housing, fuel and light . .	120.8	143.4	169.8
All items (incl. others) . .	118.1	141.8	159.7

NATIONAL ACCOUNTS
('000 million rials at current prices, year ending 20 March)
National Income and Product

	1998/99	1999/2000*	2000/01*
Domestic factor incomes† . . .	236,575.5	330,803.5	463,081.5
Consumption of fixed capital . .	80,070.7	94,083.1	116,193.0
Gross domestic product (GDP) at factor cost	316,646.2	424,886.6	579,274.5
Indirect taxes . . . . .} *Less* Subsidies . . . . .}	438.1	1,480.8	2,775.8
GDP in purchasers' values . .	317,084.3	426,367.4	582,050.3
Factor income from abroad . .} *Less* Factor income paid abroad .}	580.7	56.4	−2,764.9
Gross national product (GNP) .	317,665.0	426,423.8	579,285.4
Less Consumption of fixed capital .	80,070.7	94,083.1	116,193.0
National income in market prices	237,594.3	332,340.7	463,092.4

* Provisional figures.
† Compensation of employees and the operating surplus of enterprises.

Expenditure on the Gross Domestic Product

	1998/99	1999/2000	2000/01*
Government final consumption expenditure . . .	50,460.6	65,412.4	83,795.0
Private final consumption expenditure . . .	180,345.1	225,100.0	263,936.4
Increase in stocks . . .	1,894.7	−10,299.9	−17,268.3
Gross fixed capital formation . .	96,298.5	121,287.0	157,555.6
Statistical discrepancy . .	−6,225.0		
Total domestic expenditure .	322,773.9	401,499.5	488,018.7
Exports of goods and services .	44,884.7	89,193.8	188,897.1
Less Imports of goods and services	50,574.3	64,326.0	94,865.5
GDP in purchasers' values . .	317,084.3	426,367.3	582,050.3
GDP at constant 1990/91 prices†	45,222.7	48,483.0	52,875.6

* Provisional figures.
† Including adjustment for changes in terms of trade ('000 million rials): −2,407.6 in 1998/99; −601.8 in 1999/2000; 811.3 in 2000/01.

Gross Domestic Product by Economic Activity

	1998/99	1999/2000*	2000/01*
Agriculture, hunting, forestry and fishing	52,501.4	60,407.2	74,725.5
Mining and quarrying† . .	1,914.0	2,577.4	3,412.4
Manufacturing† . . .	72,532.6	122,049.0	204,003.5
Electricity, gas and water. .	3,509.8	4,250.9	4,969.2
Construction. . . .	12,262.7	16,815.0	20,009.9
Trade, restaurants and hotels. .	55,041.8	67,939.3	83,916.1
Transport, storage and communications . .	25,033.4	29,768.8	36,249.0
Financial and monetary institutions . . .	4,790.6	7,027.7	10,206.9
Real estate, specialized and professional services . .	44,881.6	55,928.2	68,321.5
Government services . . .	39,876.3	51,588.7	66,045.6
Other services . . .	8,407.8	11,751.6	13,784.7
Sub-total . . .	320,752.0	430,103.8	585,644.3
Less Imputed bank service charge .	4,105.6	5,217.2	6,370.2
GDP at basic prices . .	316,646.4	424,886.6	579,274.5
Indirect taxes (net) . . .	438.1	1,480.8	2,775.8
GDP in purchasers' values . .	317,084.5	426,367.4	582,050.3

* Provisional figures.
† Refining of petroleum is included in mining and excluded from manufacturing.

BALANCE OF PAYMENTS (US $ million, year ending 20 March)

	1998/99	1999/2000	2000/01*
Exports of goods f.o.b. . . .	13,118	21,030	28,345
Petroleum and gas . . .	9,933	17,089	24,226
Non-petroleum and gas exports .	3,185	3,941	4,119
Imports of goods f.o.b. . .	−14,286	−13,433	−15,207
Trade balance . . .	−1,168	7,597	13,138
Exports of services . . .	1,793	1,215	1,383
Imports of services . . .	−2,761	−2,456	−2,297
Balance on goods and services	−2,136	6,356	12,224
Other income received . . .	230	181	404
Other income paid . . .	−731	−473	−604
Balance on goods, services and income	−2,637	6,064	12,024
Unrequited transfers (net) . .	497	525	621
Current balance . . .	−2,140	6,589	12,645
Long-term capital (net) . . .	−1	−3,342	−2,612
Short-term capital (net) . . .	2,271	−2,552	−7,579
Net errors and omissions . . .	−1,702	1,150	−1,517
Overall balance . . .	−1,572	1,845	937

* Provisional figures.

External Trade

PRINCIPAL COMMODITIES (US $ million, year ending 20 March)

Imports c.i.f. (distribution by SITC)*	1998/99	1999/2000	2000/01
Food and live animals . . .	1,583	1,953	1,977
Cereals and cereal preparations .	878	1,319	1,390
Crude materials (inedible) except fuels . . .	596	648	707
Animal and vegetable oils and fats	654	516	417
Vegetable oils and fats . .	633	499	408
Chemicals	1,774	1,894	2,027
Chemical elements and compounds	458	470	460
Plastic, cellulose and artificial resins	413	391	428
Basic manufactures . . .	2,520	2,213	3,185
Iron and steel	1,287	1,173	1,819
Machinery and transport equipment	6,348	4,785	5,172
Non-electric machinery . . .	3,501	3,021	2,976
Electrical machinery, apparatus, etc.	1,521	961	1,085
Transport equipment. . .	1,326	803	1,111
Miscellaneous manufactured articles	538	305	447
Total (incl. others) . . .	14,323	12,683	14,347

* Including registration fee, but excluding defence-related imports.

Exports f.o.b.*	1998/99	1999/2000	2000/01†
Agricultural and traditional goods.	1,412.3	1,478.0	1,466
Carpets	570.1	691.2	620
Fruit and nuts (fresh and dried) .	591.9	517.3	504
Pistachios . . .	416.0	315.1	n.a.
Industrial manufactures . .	1,588.2	1,847.7	2,259
Chemical products . . .	139.7	83.3	110
Iron and steel . . .	138.6	219.4	301
Hydrocarbons (gas) . . .	183.4	150.7	194
Total	3,013.3	3,361.9	4,119

* Excluding exports of petroleum and gas (US $ million): 9,933 in 1998/99; 17,089 in 1999/2000; 24,226 in 2000/01.
† Figures are rounded.

PRINCIPAL TRADING PARTNERS
(US $ million, year ending 20 March)

Imports c.i.f.	1998/99	1999/2000	2000/01
Argentina	632	131	304
Australia	358	298	403
Austria	267	304	277
Belgium	899	597	426
Brazil	472	681	538
Canada	311	531	477
China, People's Republic	655	613	565
France	556	685	617
Germany	1,660	1,382	1,504
India	204	199	254
Indonesia	139	111	156
Italy	1,188	901	856
Japan	1,005	590	684
Kazakhstan	87	132	345
Korea, Republic	687	708	737
Netherlands	362	213	270
Russia	549	532	920
Singapore	106	100	155
Spain	410	341	343
Sweden	148	120	310
Switzerland	326	336	327
Thailand	162	214	228
Turkey	272	228	233
United Arab Emirates	759	769	1,154
United Kingdom	574	439	510
Total (incl. others)	14,323	12,683	14,347

Exports f.o.b.	1997/98	1998/99	1999/2000*
Azerbaijan	213.4	132.6	n.a.
Belgium	236.0	176.6	115
Brazil	351.7	81.1	n.a.
China, People's Republic	543.4	350.3	771
France	683.9	444.5	576
Germany	427.5	434.2	472
Greece	988.9	651.2	810
Hong Kong	248.5	n.a.	n.a.
India	530.9	364.6	718
Italy	1,630.9	1,122.3	1,500
Japan	2,787.3	2,060.2	3,479
Korea, Republic	1,280.2	648.0	1,349
Russia	250.0	111.2	n.a.
Singapore	694.5	513.8	858
Spain	633.7	431.3	n.a.
Sweden	220.1	173.0	n.a.
Taiwan	376.1	308.8	n.a.
Thailand	252.1	n.a.	n.a.
Turkey	545.9	497.1	723
United Arab Emirates	775.4	885.3	1,584
United Kingdom	3,037.2	2,204.0	3,238
Total (incl. others)	18,380.8	13,118.0	21,030

* Figures are rounded.

Transport

RAILWAYS (traffic)

	1998	1999	2000
Passenger-km (million)	5,631	6,451	7,128
Freight ton-km (million)	12,638	14,082	14,179

ROAD TRAFFIC (estimates, motor vehicles in use)

	1994	1995	1996
Passenger cars	1,636,000	1,714,000	1,793,000
Buses and coaches	n.a.	n.a.	55,457
Lorries and vans	626,000	657,000	180,154
Motorcycles and mopeds	2,262,000	2,380,500	2,565,585

1997: Buses and coaches 54,108; Lorries and vans 177,774.
1998: Buses and coaches 52,075; Lorries and vans 178,040.
Source: International Road Federation, *World Road Statistics*.

SHIPPING
Merchant Fleet (registered at 31 December)

	1999	2000	2001
Number of vessels	380	395	389
Displacement ('000 grt)	3,546.2	4,234.4	3,943.6

Source: Lloyd's Register-Fairplay, *World Fleet Statistics*.

International Sea-borne Freight Traffic
('000 metric tons)

	1994	1995	1996
Goods loaded	128,026	132,677	140,581
Crude petroleum and petroleum products	123,457	127,143	134,615
Goods unloaded	20,692	22,604	27,816
Petroleum products	6,949	7,240	7,855

CIVIL AVIATION (traffic on scheduled services)

	1996	1997	1998
Kilometres flown (million)	50	70	68
Passengers carried ('000)	7,610	9,804	9,303
Passenger-km (million)	6,634	8,963	8,539
Total ton-km (million)	708	901	856

Source: UN, *Statistical Yearbook*.

Tourism

FOREIGN TOURIST ARRIVALS

Country of nationality	1997	1998	1999
Afghanistan	69,728	125,189	146,322
Armenia	17,793	11,758	13,743
Azerbaijan	264,564	383,123	447,797
Bahrain	14,918	14,322	16,740
Kuwait	17,191	26,472	30,941
Pakistan	111,556	115,431	134,917
Russia	34,296	10,191	11,911
Saudi Arabia	16,770	21,093	24,654
Turkey	70,108	160,959	188,130
Total (incl. others)	739,711	1,007,597	1,320,690*

* Including 147,000 of unspecified nationality.
Source: World Tourism Organization, *Yearbook of Tourism Statistics*.
2000: Total arrivals 1,341,762.

Tourism receipts (US $ million): 351 in 1997; 464 in 1998; 586 in 1999; 671 in 2000.

Communications Media

	1999	2000	2001
Television receivers ('000 in use) .	10,300	10,400	n.a.
Telephones ('000 main lines in use)	8,371.2	9,486.3	10,005.5
Mobile cellular telephones ('000 subscribers)	490.5	962.6	1,484.8
Personal computers ('000 in use)	3,500	n.a.	4,500
Internet users ('000) . . .	100	250	402
Book production*:			
Titles	20,642	23,305	n.a.
Copies ('000)	105,687	117,785	n.a.

Radio receivers ('000 in use): 17,000 in 1997.

Facsimile machines (number in use)†: 30,000 in 1994.

Daily newspapers (1996): (number) 32; average circulation 1,651,000.

Periodicals (number): 623 in 1995.

* Including pamphlets.

† Twelve months ending March following the year stated.

Sources: mostly International Telecommunication Union; UNESCO, *Statistical Yearbook*; UN, *Statistical Yearbook*.

Education

(2000/01)

	Insti-tutions	Teachers	Students		
			Males	Females	Total
Pre-primary . .	7,382	97,529	142,538	144,365	286,903
Primary . . .	69,149	314,654	4,175,849	3,792,588	7,968,437
Secondary:					
General* . . .	42,079	337,912	4,814,139	4,276,799	9,090,938
Teacher-training .	82	1,018	7,757	6,584	14,321
Higher . . .	n.a.	n.a.	828,404	744,918	1,573,322

* Including evening classes.

Adult literacy rate (UNESCO estimates): 76.3% (males 83.2%; females 69.3%) in 2000 (Source: UNDP, *Human Development Report*).

Directory

The Constitution

A draft constitution for the Islamic Republic of Iran was published on 18 June 1979. It was submitted to a 'Council of Experts', elected by popular vote on 3 August 1979, to debate the various clauses and to propose amendments. The amended Constitution was approved by a referendum on 2–3 December 1979. A further 45 amendments to the Constitution were approved by a referendum on 28 July 1989.

The Constitution states that the form of government of Iran is that of an Islamic Republic, and that the spirituality and ethics of Islam are to be the basis for political, social and economic relations. Persians, Turks, Kurds, Arabs, Balochis, Turkomans and others will enjoy completely equal rights.

The Constitution provides for a President to act as chief executive. The President is elected by universal adult suffrage for a term of four years. Legislative power is held by the Majlis (Islamic Consultative Assembly), with 290 members (effective from the 2000 election) who are similarly elected for a four-year term. Provision is made for the representation of Zoroastrians, Jews and Christians.

All legislation passed by the Islamic Consultative Assembly must be sent to the Council for the Protection of the Constitution (Article 94), which will ensure that it is in accordance with the Constitution and Islamic legislation. The Council for the Protection of the Constitution consists of six religious lawyers appointed by the Faqih (see below) and six lawyers appointed by the High Council of the Judiciary and approved by the Islamic Consultative Assembly. Articles 19–42 deal with the basic rights of individuals, and provide for equality of men and women before the law and for equal human, political, economic, social and cultural rights for both sexes.

The press is free, except in matters that are contrary to public morality or insult religious belief. The formation of religious, political and professional parties, associations and societies is free, provided they do not negate the principles of independence, freedom, sovereignty and national unity, or the basis of Islam.

The Constitution provides for a Wali Faqih (religious leader) who, in the absence of the Imam Mehdi (the hidden Twelfth Imam), carries the burden of leadership. The amendments to the Constitution that were approved in July 1989 increased the powers of the Presidency by abolishing the post of Prime Minister, formerly the Chief Executive of the Government.

The Government

WALI FAQIH (RELIGIOUS LEADER)

Ayatollah SAYED ALI KHAMENEI.

HEAD OF STATE

President: Hojatoleslam Dr SAYED MUHAMMAD KHATAMI (assumed office 3 August 1997; re-elected 8 June 2001).

First Vice-President: MOHAMMAD REZA AREF.

Vice-President in charge of Legal and Parliamentary Affairs: Hojatoleslam MOHAMMAD ALI ABTAHI.

Vice-President and Head of the Iranian Atomic Energy Organization: GHOLAMREZA AGHAZADEH.

Vice-President and Head of the Organization for the Protection of the Environment: MASUMEH EBTEKAR.

Vice-President and Head of the Physical Education Organization: MOHSEN MEHRALIZADEH.

Advisers to the President with the rank of Vice-President: MUHAMMAD BAQERIAN, MUHAMMAD ALI NAJAFI.

COUNCIL OF MINISTERS
(September 2002)

Minister of Foreign Affairs: KAMAL KHARRAZI.

Minister of Education: MORTEZA HAJI.

Minister of Culture and Islamic Guidance: AHMAD MASJED JAME'I.

Minister of Information: Hojatoleslam ALI YUNESI.

Minister of Commerce: MUHAMMAD SHARI'ATMADARI.

Minister of Health: MASSOUD PEZESHKIAN.

Minister of Posts, Telegraphs and Telephones: AHMAD MO'TAMEDI.

Minister of Justice: Hojatoleslam MUHAMMAD ISMAÏL SHOUSHTARI.

Minister of Defence and Logistics: Rear-Adm. ALI SHAMKHANI.

Minister of Roads and Transport: AHMAD KHORRAM.

Minister of Science, Research and Technology: MOSTAFA MO'IN.

Minister of Industries and Mines: ESHAQ JAHANGIRI.

Minister of Labour and Social Affairs: SAFDAR HOSSEINI.

Minister of the Interior: Hojatoleslam SAYED ABDOLVAHED MUSAVI-LARI.

Minister of Agricultural Jihad: MAHMUD HOJJATI.

Minister of Housing and Urban Development: ALI ABD AL-ALIZADEH.

Minister of Energy: HABIBOLLAH BITARAF.

Minister of Oil: BIJAN NAMDAR ZANGENEH.

Minister of Economic Affairs and Finance: TAHMASB MAZAHERI.

Minister of Co-operatives: ALI SOUFI.

MINISTRIES

Office of the President: Palestine Ave, Azerbaijan Intersection, Tehran; e-mail khatami@president.ir; internet www.president.ir.

Ministry of Agricultural Jihad: 20 Malaei Ave, Vali-e-Asr Sq., Tehran; tel. (21) 8895354; fax (21) 8904357; e-mail webinfo@asid.moa.or.ir; internet www.moa.or.ir.

Ministry of Commerce: Vali-e-Asr Ave, Tehran; tel. (21) 8893620; fax (2) 896504; e-mail irantradepoint@irtp.com; internet www.irtp.com.

Ministry of Co-operatives: 16 Bozorgmehr St, Vali-e-Asr Ave, Tehran 14169; tel. (21) 6400938; fax (21) 6498440; e-mail international_affairs@icm.gov.ir.

Ministry of Culture and Islamic Guidance: Baharestan Sq., Tehran; tel. (21) 32411; fax (21) 3117535; e-mail ershad@neda.net; internet www.farhang.gov.ir.

Ministry of Defence and Logistics: Shahid Yousuf Kaboli St, Sayed Khandan Area, Tehran; tel. (21) 21401; fax (21) 864008; e-mail vds@isiran.com.

Ministry of Economic Affairs and Finance: Sour Israfil St, Babe Homayoon Ave, Tehran; tel. (21) 3251; fax (21) 390528.

Ministry of Education: Si-e-Tir St, Emam Khomeini Sq., Tehran; tel. (21) 32421; fax (21) 675503.

Ministry of Energy: North Palestine St, Tehran; tel. (21) 890001; fax (21) 8801995; e-mail webmaster@moe.or.ir; internet www.moe.or.ir.

Ministry of Foreign Affairs: Shahid Abd al-Hamid Mesri St, Ferdowsi Ave, Tehran; tel. (21) 3211; fax (21) 3212763; e-mail matbuat@mfa.gov.ir; internet www.mfa.gov.ir.

Ministry of Health and Medical Education: POB 15655-415, 371 Dr Shariati Ave, Averezi Station, Tehran 16139; tel. (21) 767631; fax (21) 7676733; e-mail webmaster@hbi.dmr.or.ir; internet www.hbi.dmr.or.ir.

Ministry of Housing and Urban Development: Shahid Khoddami St, Vanak Sq., Tehran; tel. (21) 877711; fax (21) 8776634; e-mail hud@icic.gov.ir.

Ministry of Industries and Mines: POB 1416, Somayeh St, Tehran 15996; tel. (21) 8807026; fax (21) 8807031; e-mail minister@mim.gov.ir; internet www.mim.gov.ir.

Ministry of Information: POB 16765-1947, Tehran; tel. (21) 233031; fax (21) 23305.

Ministry of the Interior: Jahad Sq., Fatemi St, Tehran; tel. (21) 61311; fax (21) 650912.

Ministry of Justice: Panzdah-e-Khordad Sq., Tehran; tel. (21) 8191; fax (21) 3113143.

Ministry of Labour and Social Affairs: Azadi Ave, Tehran; tel. (21) 930050; fax (21) 931066.

Ministry of Oil: Hafez St, Taleghani Ave, Tehran; tel. (21) 6152738; fax (21) 6152823; e-mail webmaster@nioc.org; internet www.nioc.org.

Ministry of Posts, Telegraphs and Telephones: POB 11365-931, Dr Shariati Ave, Tehran 16314; tel. (21) 864796; fax (21) 866023; e-mail webmaster@195.146.32.12; internet www.iranpac.net.ir.

Ministry of Roads and Transport: 49 Taleghani Ave, Spahbod Gharani St, Tehran; tel. (21) 6460583; fax (21) 6407991.

Ministry of Science, Research and Technology: POB 15875-4375, Central Bldg, Ostad Nejatollahi Ave, Tehran; tel. (21) 8891065; fax (21) 8827234; e-mail oise@msrt.gov.ir.

President and Legislature

PRESIDENT

Election, 8 June 2001

Candidates	Votes	%
Sayed Muhammad Khatami	21,656,476	76.9
Ahmed Tavakkoli	4,387,112	15.6
Ali Shamkhani	737,051	2.6
Abdollah Jasbi	259,759	0.9
Mahmoud Kashani	237,660	0.8
Hassan Ghafuri-Fard	129,155	0.5
Mansur Razavi	114,616	0.4
Shahabeddin Sadr	60,546	0.2
Ali Falahian	55,225	0.2
Moustafa Hashemi-Taba	27,949	0.1
Invalid votes	493,740	1.8
Total	28,159,289	100.0

MAJLIS-E-SHURA E ISLAMI—ISLAMIC CONSULTATIVE ASSEMBLY

A first round of voting in elections to the sixth Majlis took place on 18 February 2000; and a second, for 66 undecided seats, on 5 May. Successful candidates in both rounds of voting were, for the most

part, associated with either the 'conservative' tendency or its 'reformist' counterpart that are generally held to characterize Iranian political life. However, a significant number of independent candidates, who might ally themselves with either of the two principal tendencies, also contested the elections successfully. The sixth Majlis was notable as the first in which 'reformist' or 'liberal' candidates were estimated to have gained a working majority.

Speaker: Hojatoleslam MAHDI KARRUBI.

First Deputy Speaker: BEHZAD NABAVI.

Second Deputy Speaker: MUHAMMAD REZA KHATAMI.

SHURA-YE ALI-YE AMNIYYAT-E MELLI—SUPREME COUNCIL FOR NATIONAL SECURITY

Formed in July 1989 to co-ordinate defence and national security policies, the political programme and intelligence reports, and social, cultural and economic activities related to defence and security. The Council is chaired by the President and includes two representatives of the Wali Faqih, the Head of the Judiciary, the Speaker of the Majlis, the Chief of Staff, the General Command of the Armed Forces, the Minister of Foreign Affairs, the Minister of the Interior, the Minister of Information and the Head of the Plan and Budget Organization.

MAJLIS-E KHOBREGAN—COUNCIL OF EXPERTS

Elections were held on 10 December 1982 to appoint a Council of Experts which was to choose an eventual successor to the Wali Faqih (then Ayatollah Khomeini) after his death. The Constitution provides for a three- or five-man body to assume the leadership of the country if there is no recognized successor on the death of the Wali Faqih. The Council comprises 86 clerics. Elections to a third term of the Council were held on 23 October 1998.

Speaker: Ayatollah ALI MESHKINI.

First Deputy Speaker: Hojatoleslam ALI AKBAR HASHEMI RAFSANJANI.

Second Deputy Speaker: Ayatollah IBRAHIM AMINI NAJAFABADI.

Secretaries: Hojatoleslam HASSAN TAHERI-KHORRAMABADI, Ayatollah QORBANALI DORRI NAJAFABADI.

SHURA-E-NIGAHBAN—COUNCIL OF GUARDIANS

The Council of Guardians, composed of six qualified Muslim jurists appointed by Ayatollah Khomeini and six lay Muslim lawyers, appointed by the Majlis from among candidates nominated by the Head of the Judiciary, was established in 1980 to supervise elections and to examine legislation adopted by the Majlis, ensuring that it accords with the Constitution and with Islamic precepts.

Chairman: Ayatollah AHMAD JANNATI.

SHURA-YE TASHKHIS-E MASLAHAT-E NEZAM— COUNCIL TO DETERMINE THE EXPEDIENCY OF THE ISLAMIC ORDER

Formed in February 1988, by order of Ayatollah Khomeini, to arbitrate on legal and theological questions in legislation passed by the Majlis, in the event of a dispute between the latter and the supervisory Council of Guardians. Its permanent members, defined in March 1997, are Heads of the Legislative, Judiciary and Executive Powers, the jurist members of the Council of Guardians and the Minister or head of organization concerned with the pertinent arbitration. Four new members were appointed to the Expediency Council in March 2002, when Rafsanjani was reappointed as Chairman.

Chairman: Hojatoleslam ALI AKBAR HASHEMI RAFSANJANI.

HEY'AT-E PEYGIRI-YE QANUN ASASI VA NEZARAT BAR AN—COMMITTEE FOR ENSURING AND SUPERVISING THE IMPLEMENTATION OF THE CONSTITUTION

Formed by President Khatami in November 1997; members are appointed for a four-year term.

Members: Dr GUDARZ EFTEKHAR-JAHROMI; MUHAMMAD ISMAIL SHOUSHTARI; Sayed ABDOLVAHED MUSAVI-LARI; Dr HOSSEIN MEHRPUR; Dr MUHAMMAD HOSSEIN HASHEMI.

Political Organizations

Numerous political organizations were registered in the late 1990s, following the election of President Khatami, among them several political tendencies that had formed within the Majlis. The following organizations appeared to have achieved considerable success at elections to the sixth Majlis in early 2000:

Chekad-e Azadandishan (Freethinkers' Front).

Hezb-e E'tedal va Towse'eh (Moderation and Development Party).

Hezb-e Hambastegi-ye Iran-e Islami (Islamic Iran Solidarity Party).

Hezb-e Kargozaran-e Sazandegi (Servants of Construction Party): Sec.-Gen. GHOLAMHOSSEIN KARBASCHI.

Jam'iyat-e Isargaran (Society of Self-sacrificing Devotees).

Jebbeh-ye Masharekat-e Iran-e Islami (Islamic Iran Participation Front): Leader (vacant).

Majma'-e Niruha-ye Khat-e Imam (Assembly of the Followers of the Imam's Line).

Most of the following organizations are opposed to the Iranian Government:

Ansar-e Hezbollah: f. 1995; youth movement; seeks to gain access to the political process for religious militants.

Democratic Party of Iranian Kurdistan: POB 102, Paris 75623, France; e-mail pdkiran@club-internet.fr; internet www.pdk -iran.org; f. 1945; seeks autonomy for Kurdish area; mem. of the National Council of Resistance; 54,000 mems; Sec.-Gen. MUSTAPHA HASSANZADEH.

Fedayin-e-Khalq (Warriors of the People): urban Marxist guerrillas; Spokesman FARRAKH NEGAHDAR.

Fraksion-e Hezbollah: f. 1996 by deputies in the Majlis who had contested the 1996 legislative elections as a loose coalition known as the Society of Combatant Clergy; Leader ALI AKBAR HOSSAINI.

Hezb-e-Komunist Iran (Communist Party of Iran): e-mail cpi@ cpiran.org; internet www.cpiran.org; f. 1979 by dissident mems of Tudeh Party; Sec.-Gen. 'AZARYUN'.

Komala: e-mail komala@cpiran.org; internet www.cpiran.org/En/ Komala; f. 1969; Kurdish wing of the Communist Party of Iran; Marxist-Leninist; First Sec. IBRAHIM ALIZADEH.

Mujahidin-e-Khalq (Holy Warriors of the People): Islamic guerrilla group; since June 1987 comprising the National Liberation Army; mem. of the National Council of Resistance; Leaders MASSOUD RAJAVI and MARYAM RAJAVI (in Baghdad, 1986–).

National Democratic Front: e-mail ndfi@azadi-iran.org; internet www.azadi-iran.org; f. March 1979; Leader HEDAYATOLLAH MATINE-DAFTARI (in Paris, January 1982–).

National Front (Union of National Front Forces): comprises Iran Nationalist Party, Iranian Party, and Society of Iranian Students; Leader Dr KARIM SANJABI (in Paris, August 1978–).

Nehzat-e Azadi-ye Iran (Liberation Movement of Iran): e-mail mizan@nehzateazadi.org; internet www.nehzateazadi.org; f. 1961; emphasis on basic human rights as defined by Islam; Gen. Sec. Dr IBRAHIM YAZDI; Principal Officers Prof. SAHABI, S. SADR, Dr SADR, Eng. SABAGHIAN, Eng. TAVASSOLI.

Pan-Iranist Party: extreme right-wing; calls for a Greater Persia; Leader Dr MOHSEN PEZESHKPOUR.

Sazmane Peykar dar Rahe Azadieh Tabaqe Kargar (Organization Struggling for the Freedom of the Working Class): Marxist Leninist.

Tudeh Party (Communist): e-mail mardom@tudehpartyiran.org; internet www.tudehpartyiran.org; f. 1941; declared illegal 1949; came into open 1979, banned again April 1983; First Sec. Cen. Cttee ALI KHAVARI.

The **National Council of Resistance (NCR)** was formed in Paris in October 1981 by former President ABOLHASAN BANI-SADR and the Council's current leader, MASSOUD RAJAVI, the leader of the Mujahidin-e-Khalq in Iran. In 1984 the Council comprised 15 opposition groups, operating either clandestinely in Iran or from exile abroad. Bani-Sadr left the Council in 1984 because of his objection to Rajavi's growing links with the Iraqi Government. The French Government asked Rajavi to leave Paris in June 1986 and he is now based in Baghdad, Iraq. On 20 June 1987 Rajavi, Secretary of the NCR, announced the formation of a National Liberation Army (10,000–15,000-strong) as the military wing of the Mujahidin-e-Khalq. There is also a National Movement of Iranian Resistance, based in Paris. Dissident members of the Tudeh Party founded the Democratic Party of the Iranian People in Paris in February 1988. A new pro-reform party, **Will of the Iranian Nation** (Leader HAKIMI POUR), was founded in February 2001.

Diplomatic Representation

EMBASSIES IN IRAN

Afghanistan: Dr Beheshti Ave, Corner of 4th St, Pakistan St, Tehran; tel. (21) 8735600; Ambassador: AHMAD MOSHAHED.

Albania: Tehran; Ambassador: GILANI SHEHU.

Algeria: Tehran; Ambassador: ABD AL-QADER HAJJAR.

Angola: Tehran; Ambassador: MANUEL BERNARDO DE SOUSA.

Argentina: POB 15875-4335, 3rd and 4th Floor, 7 Argentina Sq., Tehran; tel. (21) 8718294; fax (21) 8712583; e-mail alvarez951@ yahoo.com; Chargé d'affaires: ERNESTO CARLOS ALVAREZ.

Armenia: 1 Ostad Shahriar St, Razi St, Jomhouri Islami Ave, Tehran 11337; tel. (21) 674833; fax (21) 670657; e-mail armemb iran@www.dci.co.ir; Ambassador: YAHAN BAIBOURDIAN.

Australia: POB 15875-4334, No. 13, 23rd St, Khaled al-Islambuli Ave, Tehran 15138; tel. (21) 8724456; fax (21) 8720484; e-mail dfat -tehran@dfat.gov.au; internet www.iran.embassy.gov.au; Ambassador: JEREMY R. NEWMAN.

Austria: 3rd Floor, 78 Argentine Sq., Tehran; tel. (21) 8710753; fax (21) 8710778; e-mail teheran-ob@bmaa.gov.at; Ambassador: Dr MICHAEL STIGELBAUER.

Azerbaijan: 10 Malek St, Dr Shariati Ave, Tehran; tel. (21) 2280063; fax (21) 2284929; e-mail azaremb @www.dci.co.ir; Ambassador: ABBASALI K. HASANOV.

Bahrain: 248 Africa Ave, Cnr of Zoubin Alley, Tehran; tel. (21) 8773383; fax (21) 8779112; e-mail bahmanama@neda.net; internet www.inet.com; Ambassador: KAMAL SALEH AS-SALEH.

Bangladesh: POB 11365-3711, Gandhi Ave, 5th St, Building No. 14, Tehran; tel. (21) 8772979; fax (21) 8778295; e-mail banglaemb@ irtp.com; Ambassador: ABDOLLAH AL-HASSAN.

Belarus: No. 18, Ghem-Magham Farahani Ave, 6th St, Ground Floor, Tehran; tel. (21) 8731601.

Belgium: POB 11365-115, 3 Babak Alley, Shabdiz St, Shahid Fayyaz Bakhsh Ave, Tehran 19659; tel. (21) 2009507; e-mail teheran@diplobel.org; Ambassador: GUILLAUME METTEN.

Bosnia and Herzegovina: No. 485, Aban Alley, 4th St, Iran Zamin Ave, Shahrak-e-Ghods, Tehran; tel. (21) 8092728; Ambassador: IBRAHIM IFDIĆ.

Brazil: Vanak Sq., 58 Vanak St, Tehran 19918-44959; tel. (21) 8035175; fax (21) 8083348; e-mail emb_brazil@yahoo.com; Ambassador: CESARIO MELANTONIO NETO.

Brunei: POB 19395-6671, 318 Vahid Dastgerdi Ave, Vali-e-Asr Ave, Tehran 19687; tel. (21) 8781979; e-mail bneiran@yahoo.com.

Bulgaria: POB 11365-7451, Vali-e-Asr Ave, Dr Abbaspour Ave, Nezami-e-Ganjavi St, No. 82, Tehran; tel. (21) 8775662; e-mail bulgr.tehr@neda.net; Ambassador: DUBROV GEORGIEV.

Burkina Faso: 25 Western Taban St, Africa Ave, Tehran; tel. (21) 2225292.

Canada: POB 11365-4647, 57 Shahid Sarafraz St, Ostad Motahhari Ave; tel. (21) 8732623; fax 8733202; e-mail teran@dfait-maeci.gc.ca; Ambassador: PHILIP M. KINNON.

Chad: Tehran.

Chile: Tehran; Ambassador: JUAN GABRIEL VALDES.

China, People's Republic: 13 Narenjestan 7th, Pasdaran Ave, Tehran; tel. (21) 8031240; e-mail emchnir@neda.net; Ambassador: SUN BIGAN.

Colombia: 5 Faryar St, Hedayat St, Darrous, Tehran; tel. (21) 2541981; e-mail emteh@apadana.com; Ambassador: RAFAEL CANAL SANDOVAL.

Congo, Democratic Republic: Tehran; tel. (21) 222190; Chargé d'affaires: N'DJATE ESELE SASA.

Côte d'Ivoire: Tehran; Ambassador: TIETI ROCH D'ASSOMTION.

Croatia: No. 25, 1st Behestan, Pasdaran St, Tehran; tel. (21) 2589923; fax (21) 2549199; e-mail croatia@istn.irost.com; Chargé d'affaires a.i.: TOLUŠIĆ MIJO.

Cuba: 10 Taban Alley, Naft-e-Jonobi, Mirdamad, Tehran; tel. (21) 2257809; e-mail embacub.iran@apadana.com; Ambassador: JOSÉ RAMÓN RODRIGUES.

Cyprus: 55 Shahid Sartip Reza Saeidi, Farmanieh Ave, Tehran; tel. (21) 2299795; fax (21) 2299794; Ambassador: STAVROS LOIZIDES.

Czech Republic: POB 11365-4457, Mirza-ye Shirazi Ave, Ali Mirza Hassani St, No. 15, Tehran; tel. (21) 8716720; fax (21) 8717858; e-mail teheran@embassy.mzv.cz; Chargé d'affaires a.i.: MARTIN KLEP-ETKO.

Denmark: POB 19395-5358, 18 Dashti Ave, Tehran 19148; tel. (21) 2601363; fax (21) 2030007; e-mail thramb@um.dk; internet www.inet.uni2.dk/home/ambadane.teheran; Ambassador: JØRGEN REIMERS.

Ethiopia: 38 Darabad Ave, Tehran; tel. (21) 2289338; Ambassador: MOHAMMED HASAN KAHIM.

Finland: Cnr of Nilou St, Vanak Sq., Vali-e-Asr Ave, Tehran; tel. (21) 8889151; fax (21) 2210948; e-mail finlandiran@hotmail.com; Ambassador: YRJÖ KARINEN.

France: 85 Neauphle-le-Château Ave, Tehran; tel. (21) 6706018; e-mail ambafrance.teheran@kanoon.net; Ambassador: FRANÇOIS NIC-OULLAUD.

Gambia: Tehran; Ambassador: OMAR JAH.

Georgia: POB 19575-379, Elahiyeh, Tehran; tel. (21) 2211470; fax (21) 2206848; e-mail georgia@apadana.com; Ambassador: JEMSHID GIUNASHVILI.

Germany: POB 11365-179, 320–324 Ferdowsi Ave, Tehran; tel. (21) 3114111; fax (21) 3119883; e-mail fmst@tehe.auswaertiges-amt.de; internet www.apadana.com/germ-emb-ir; Ambassador: Dr RÜDIGER REYELS.

Ghana: Tehran; Ambassador: Mr AL-HASSAN.

Greece: POB 11365-8151, Africa Ave, Esfandiar St, No. 43, Tehran 19686; tel. (21) 2050533; fax (21) 8087431; Ambassador: DIMITRI TSI-KOURIS.

Guinea: POB 11365-4716, Dr Shariati Ave, Malek St, No. 10, Tehran; tel. (21) 7535744; fax (21) 7535743; e-mail ambaguinee_thr@hotmail.com; Ambassador: ALPHA IBRAHIMA SOW.

Holy See: Apostolic Nunciature, POB 11365-178, Razi Ave, No. 97, Neauphle-le-Château Ave, Tehran; tel. (21) 6403574; fax (21) 6419442; e-mail apnun-thr@ravan.com; Apostolic Nuncio: Most Rev. ANGELO MOTTOLA, Titular Archbishop of Cercina.

Hungary: POB 6363-19395, Darrous, Hedayat Sq, Shadloo St, No. 15, Tehran; tel. (21) 2550460; fax (21) 2550503; e-mail huembthr@neda.net; Ambassador: Dr ISTVÁN VÁSÁRY.

India: POB 15875-4118, 46 Mir-Emad St, Cnr of 9th St, Dr Beheshti Ave, Tehran; tel. (21) 8755103; fax (21) 8755973; e-mail emteh@dpimail.net; internet www.indianembassy-tehran.com; Ambassador: S. K. ARORA.

Indonesia: POB 11365-4564, Ghaem Magham Farahani Ave, No. 210, Tehran; tel. (21) 8716865; Ambassador: BAMBANG SUDARSONO.

Iraq: Karamian Alley, No. 17, Pol-e-Roomi, Dr Shariati Ave, Tehran; tel. (21) 2218386; Chargé d'affaires: ABD AS-SATTAR AR-RAWI.

Ireland: Razan Shomali St, No. 8, Mirdamad Ave, Tehran; tel. (21) 2222731; fax (21) 2286933; e-mail irelembteh@padisar.net; Ambassador: THOMAS O. BOLSTER.

Italy: POB 11365-7863, 81 Neauphle-le-Château Ave, Tehran; tel. (21) 6726955; fax (21) 6726961; e-mail itaembtehe@kanoon.net; Ambassador: RICCARDO SESSA.

Japan: POB 11365-814, Bucharest Ave, Corner of 5th St, Tehran; tel. (21) 8713396; Ambassador: TAKEKAZU KAWAMURA.

Jordan: Mahestan St, Tehran; tel. (21) 8082466; fax (21) 8090734; e-mail jordanembteh@neda.net; Ambassador: Dr BASSAM ALI AL-OMOUSH.

Kazakhstan: Darrus, Hedayat St, Masjed Alley, No. 4, Tehran; tel. (21) 2565933; fax (21) 2546400; e-mail kazembir@apadana.com; Ambassador: TULEGEN ZHUKEYEV.

Kenya: 60 Hormoz Satari St, Africa Ave, Tehran; tel. (21) 2270795; fax (21) 2270160; e-mail kenemteh@irtp.com; Ambassador: HASSAN MUHAMMAD SALEH BAQA.

Korea, Democratic People's Republic: 349 Vahid Dastjerdi Ave, Africa Ave, Tehran; tel. (21) 2223341; Ambassador: KIM JONG NAM.

Korea, Republic: No. 37, Ahmad Ghasir Ave, Tehran; tel. (21) 8731389; fax (21) 8737917; e-mail korth@dpi.net.ir; Ambassador: LI SUNG-CHOOL.

Kuwait: No. 323/2, Vahid Dastjerdi Ave, Tehran; tel. (21) 8785997; Ambassador: AHMAD AZ-ZAFIRI.

Kyrgyzstan: POB 19579-3511, Bldg 12, 5th Naranjestan Alley, Pasdaran St; tel. (21) 2830354; fax (21) 2281720; e-mail krembiri@kanoon.net; Ambassador: MEDET SADYRKULOV.

Laos: Tehran; Ambassador: CHANPHENG SIHAPHOM.

Lebanon: No. 31, Shahid Kalantari St, Ghantari Ave, Tehran; tel. (21) 8908451; fax (21) 8907345; Ambassador: ADNAN MANSOUR.

Libya: Ostad Motahari Ave, No. 163, Tehran; tel. (21) 8742572; Ambassador: ALI MARIA.

Macedonia, former Yugoslav republic: Tehran; Chargé d'affaires: SOUFESKI CHOUTKO.

Malaysia: 72 Fereshteh Ave, Tehran; tel. (21) 2009275; fax (21) 2009143; e-mail mwtehran@neda.net; Ambassador: MEZLAN MOHAMMAD.

Mexico: POB 15875-4636, No. 41, Golfam St, Africa Ave, Tehran; tel. (21) 2057586; fax (21) 2225375; e-mail embamex@apadana.com; Ambassador: ANTONIO DUEÑAS PULIDO.

Mongolia: Tehran; Ambassador: L. KHASHOAT.

Morocco: Tehran; tel. (21) 2059707; fax (21) 2051872; e-mail ambas.du.maroc@tavana.net; Ambassador: JAMAL EDDINE GHAZI.

Mozambique: Tehran; Ambassador: MURADE ISAC MIGUIGY MURARGY.

Myanmar: Tehran; Ambassador: U SAW HLAING.

Namibia: Tehran; Ambassador: MWAILEPENI T. P. SHITILIFA.

Nepal: Tehran; Ambassador: Gen. ARJUN NARSING RONA.

Netherlands: POB 11365-138, Darrous, Shahrzad Blvd, Kamasaie St, 1st East Lane, No. 33, Tehran 19498; tel. (21) 2567005; fax (21) 2566990; e-mail nlambiran@dpi.net.ir; Ambassador: R. A. MOLLINGER.

New Zealand: POB 15875-4313, 34 North Golestan Complex, Cnr of 2nd Park Alley and Sosan St, Aghdasiyeh St, Niavaran, Tehran; tel. (21) 2800289; fax (21) 2831673; e-mail <newzealand@mavara.com; Ambassador: NIELS HOLM.

Niger: Tehran.

Nigeria: No. 11, 31st St, Shahid Khalid Islambuli Ave, Tehran; tel. (21) 8774936; e-mail ngrembtehran@yahoo.com; Ambassador: ADO SANUSI.

Norway: POB 19395-5398, Lavasani Ave 201, Tehran; tel. (21) 2291333; fax (21) 2292776; e-mail emb.tehran@mfa.no; Ambassador: SVEIN AASS.

Oman: No. 12, Tandis Alley, Africa Ave, Tehran; tel. (21) 2056831; Chargé d'affaires a.i.: RASHID BIN MUBARAK BIN RASHID AL-ODWALI.

Pakistan: Dr Fatemi Ave, Jamshidabad Shomali, Mashal St, No. 1, Tehran; tel. (21) 934332; e-mail pareptehran@yahoo.com; Ambassador: JAVID HUSSEIN.

Peru: Tehran; Ambassador LUIS HERNÁNDEZ ORTIZ.

Philippines: POB 19395-4797, No. 13, Mahyar St, Africa Ave, Tehran; tel. (21) 2047802; fax (21) 2046239; e-mail tehranpe@dfa.gov.ph; Ambassador ERNESTO V. LLAMAS.

Poland: Africa Ave, Piruz St, No. 1/3, Tehran; tel. (21) 8787262; e-mail ambrpri@sokhan.net; Ambassador: WITOLD WASZCZYKOWSKI.

Portugal: No. 13, Rouzbeh Alley, Darrous, Hedayat St, Tehran; tel. (21) 2543237; fax (21) 2552668; e-mail portugal@sr.co.ir; Ambassador: Dr JOSÉ MANUEL DA COSTA ARSÉNIO.

Qatar: POB 11365-5631, Africa Ave, Golazin Ave, Parke Davar, No. 4, Tehran; tel. (21) 2051255; fax (21) 2056023; Ambassador: ALI ABDULLAH ZAID AL-MAHMOOD.

Romania: Fakhrabad Ave 12, Baharestan Ave, Tehran; tel. (21) 7539041; fax (21) 7535291; e-mail ambrotehran@sokhan.net; Ambassador: NICOLAE STAN.

Russia: 39 Neauphle-le-Château Ave, Tehran; tel. (21) 6701161; e-mail russembassy@apadana.com; Ambassador: ALEKSANDR MARYASOV.

Saudi Arabia: No. 1, Niloufar, Boustan, Pasdaran Ave, Tehran; tel. (21) 2050081; fax (21) 2050083; Ambassador: JAMIL BIN ABDULLAH AL-JISHI.

Senegal: No. 7, Piroze Sharghi St, Africa Ave, Tehran; tel. (21) 8783596.

Sierra Leone: No. 10, Malek St, Off Dr Shariati Ave, Tehran; tel. (21) 7502819.

Slovakia: POB 11365-4451, No. 24, Babak Markazi St, Africa Ave, Tehran; tel. (21) 2271058; fax (21) 2271057; Ambassador: VLADIMIR LOMEN.

Slovenia: Narenjestan 8th Alley, Pasdaran Ave, Tehran; tel. (21) 2802223; fax (21) 2282131; e-mail vte@mzz-dkp.sigov.si.

Somalia: 20 Sohail St, Dr Shariati Ave, Tehran; tel. (21) 8796509.

South Africa: POB 11365-7476, 5 Yekta St, Vali-e-Asr Ave, Tehran; tel. (21) 2702866; fax (21) 2716191; e-mail saemb@neda.net; Ambassador: MZOLISI MABUDE.

Spain: 76 Sarv St, Africa Ave, Tehran; tel. (21) 8714575; fax (21) 8724581; e-mail embespir@mail.mac.cs; Ambassador: LEOPOLDO STAMPA PIÑEIRO.

Sri Lanka: 28 Golazin St, Africa Ave, Tehran; tel. (21) 2052688; fax (21) 2052149; e-mail emblanka@afranet.com; Chargé d'affaires a.i.: MOONA SINGHE.

Sudan: No. 39, Babak B'ahrami Alley, Zafar St, Africa Ave, Tehran; tel. (21) 8781183; fax (21) 295008; Ambassador: HAMED ALI MOHAMMAD AT-TINAY.

Sweden: POB 19575-458, 2 Nastaran St, Pasdaran Ave, Tehran; tel. (21) 2296802; fax (21) 2296451; e-mail ambassaden.teheran@foreign.ministry.se; Ambassador: STEEN HOHWÜ-CHRISTENSEN.

Switzerland: POB 19395-4683, 13/1 Boustan Ave, Elahieh, 19649 Tehran; tel. (21) 2008333; fax 2006002; e-mail vertretung@teh.rep.admin.ch; Ambassador: TIM GULDIMANN.

Syria: 19 Iraj St, Africa Ave, Tehran; tel. (21) 2052780; e-mail syrambir@www.dci.co.ir; Ambassador: Dr TURKI MUHAMMAD SAQR.

Tajikistan: Tehran; Ambassador: RAMAZAN MIRZOYEV.

Tanzania: Tehran.

Thailand: POB 11495-111, Baharestan Ave, Parc Amin ed-Doleh, No. 4, Tehran; tel. (21) 7531433; fax (21) 7532022; e-mail thairan@bkk2000.org; Ambassador: MAHADI WIMANA.

Tunisia: No. 12, Shahid Dr Lavasani, Tehran; tel. (21) 2704161; Ambassador: MOLADI AS-SAKERI.

Turkey: Ferdowsi Ave, No. 337, Tehran; tel. (21) 3925619; fax (21) 3117928; e-mail tctahranbe@parsonline.net; Ambassador: SELAHATTIN ALPAR.

Turkmenistan: No. 39, 5th Golestan St, Pasdaran Ave, Tehran; tel. (21) 2542178; Ambassador: MURAT NAZAROV.

Ukraine: 101 Vanak Sq., Tehran 487; tel. (21) 8005650; fax (21) 8007130; e-mail embukraine@afranet.com; Ambassador: VADIM PRIMACHENKO.

United Arab Emirates: POB 19395-4616, No. 355, Vahid Dastjerdi Ave, Vali-e-Asr Ave, Tehran; tel. (21) 8781333; fax (21) 8884250; e-mail uae_emb_thr@universalmail.com; Ambassador: AHMAD MUHAMMAD BORHEIMAH.

United Kingdom: POB 11365-4474, 143 Ferdowsi Ave, Tehran 11344; tel. (21) 6705011; fax (21) 6708021; e-mail britemb@neda.net; Ambassador: RICHARD DALTON (from Jan. 2003).

Uruguay: 45 Shabnam Alley, Atefi Shargi St, Africa Ave, Tehran; tel. (21) 2052030; e-mail uruter@chapar.net; Ambassador: JOSÉ LOUISE.

Uzbekistan: No. 6, Nastaran Alley, Boostan St, Pasdaran Ave; tel. (21) 2299158; Ambassador: ILHAM AKRAMOV.

Venezuela: POB 15875-4354, No. 26, Tandis St, Africa Ave, Tehran; tel. (21) 8715185; fax (21) 2053677; e-mail embeveneziran@chapar.net; Ambassador: VALDMAR RODRÍGUEZ.

Viet Nam: 155 Feresteh St, Vali-e-Asr Ave, Tehran; tel. (21) 2949247; fax (21) 2047350; e-mail sqvn.iran@mail.dci.co.ir; Ambassador: NGO VAN QUANG.

Yemen: No. 17, Giti Blvd, Golestan Blvd, Africa Ave, Tehran; tel. (21) 2048619; e-mail yem.emb.ir@neda.net; Ambassador: ABDOLQAVI AR-RYANI.

Yugoslavia: POB 11365-118, Vali-e-Asr Ave, Fereshteh Ave, Bossni Alley, No. 12, 19659 Tehran; tel. (21) 2044126; fax (21) 2044978; e-mail yuembth1@neda.net; Chargé d'affaires: VLADIMIR KEREĆKI.

Judicial System

In August 1982 the Supreme Court revoked all laws dating from the previous regime which did not conform with Islam; in October all courts set up prior to the Islamic Revolution were abolished. In June 1987 Ayatollah Khomeini ordered the creation of clerical courts to try members of the clergy opposed to government policy. A new system of *qisas* (retribution) was established, placing the emphasis on swift justice. Islamic codes of correction were introduced in 1983, including the dismembering of a hand for theft, flogging for fornication and violations of the strict code of dress for women, and stoning for adultery. In 1984 there was a total of 2,200 judges. The Supreme Court has 16 branches.

Head of the Judiciary: Ayatollah SAYED MAHMOUD HASHEMI SHAHRUDI.

SUPREME COURT

Chief Justice: Hojatoleslam MUHAMMAD MUHAMMADI GUILANI.
Prosecutor-General: Hojatoleslam MORTEZA MOQTADAI.

Religion

According to the 1979 Constitution, the official religion is Islam of the Ja'fari sect (Shi'ite), but other Islamic sects, including Zeydi, Hanafi, Maleki, Shafe'i and Hanbali, are valid and will be respected. Zoroastrians, Jews and Christians will be recognized as official religious minorities. According to the 1996 census, there were 59,788,791 Muslims, 78,745 Christians (mainly Armenian), 27,920 Zoroastrians and 12,737 Jews in Iran.

ISLAM

The great majority of the Iranian people are Shi'a Muslims, but there is a minority of Sunni Muslims. Persians and Azerbaijanis are mainly Shi'i, while the other ethnic groups are mainly Sunni.

CHRISTIANITY

The Roman Catholic Church

At 31 December 2000 there were an estimated 25,000 adherents in Iran, comprising 10,000 of the Armenian Rite, 10,000 of the Latin Rite and 5,000 of the Chaldean Rite.

Armenian Rite

Bishop of Esfahan: NECHAN KARAKEHEYAN, Armenian Catholic Bishopric, POB 11365-445, Khiaban Ghazzali 22, Tehran; tel. (21) 6707204; fax (21) 8715191.

Chaldean Rite

Archbishop of Ahwaz: HANNA ZORA, Archbishop's House, POB 61956, Naderi St, Ahwaz; tel. (61) 224980.

Archbishop of Tehran: RAMZI GARMOU, Archevêché, Enghelab St, Sayyed Abbas Mousavi Ave 91, Tehran 15819; tel. (21) 8823549; fax (21) 8308714.

Archbishop of Urmia (Rezayeh) and Bishop of Salmas (Shahpour): THOMAS MERAM, Khalifagari Kaldani Katholiq, POB 338, Orumiyeh 57135; tel. (441) 222739; fax (441) 236031; e-mail catholic@mail.dci.co.ir.

Latin Rite

Archbishop of Esfahan: IGNAZIO BEDINI, Consolata Church, POB 11365-445, 75 Neauphle-le-Château Ave, Tehran; tel. (21) 6703210; fax (21) 6724947; e-mail ispahan.latinorum@ravan.com.

The Anglican Communion

Anglicans in Iran are adherents of the Episcopal Church in Jerusalem and the Middle East, formally inaugurated in January 1976.

Bishop in Iran and President of the Episcopal Church in Jerusalem and the Middle East: Rt Rev. IRAJ KALIMI MOTTAHEDEH, St Luke's Church, POB 81465-135, Abbas-abad Rd, Esfahan; tel. (31) 2331435; fax (31) 2334675; e-mail bishraj@chavoosh.com; diocese founded 1912.

Presbyterian Church

Synod of the Evangelical (Presbyterian) Church in Iran: Assyrian Evangelical Church, Khiaban-i Hanifnejad, Khiaban-i Aramanch, Tehran; Moderator Rev. ADEL NAKHOSTEEN.

ZOROASTRIANS

There are almost 28,000 Zoroastrians, a remnant of a once widespread sect. Their religious leader is MOUBAD.

OTHER COMMUNITIES

Communities of Armenians, and somewhat smaller numbers of Jews, Assyrians, Greek Orthodox Christians, Uniates and Latin Christians are also found as officially recognized faiths. The Bahá'í faith, which originated in Iran, has about 300,000 Iranian adherents, although at least 10,000 are believed to have fled since 1979 in order to escape persecution. The Government banned all Bahá'í institutions in August 1983.

The Press

Tehran dominates the media, as many of the daily papers are published there, and the bi-weekly, weekly and less frequent publications in the provinces generally depend on the major metropolitan dailies as a source of news. A press law announced in August 1979 required all newspapers and magazines to be licensed and imposed penalties of imprisonment for insulting senior religious figures. Offences against the Act will be tried in the criminal courts. Under the Constitution the press is free, except in matters that are contrary to public morality, insult religious belief or slander the honour and reputation of individuals. Since the late 1990s the press has been the target of an intense judicial campaign to curb its freedoms.

PRINCIPAL DAILIES

Abrar (Rightly Guided): 26 Shahid Denesh Kian Alley, Below Zartasht St, Vali-e-Asr Ave, Tehran; tel. (21) 8848270; fax (21) 8849200; f. 1985 after closure of *Azadegan* by order of the Prosecutor-General; morning; Farsi; circ. 75,000.

Aftab-e-Yazd (Sun of Yazd): POB 13145-1134, Tehran; tel. (21) 6495833; fax (21) 6495835; e-mail info@aftabnews.com; internet www.aftabnews.com; f. 2000; pro-reform; Chief Editor MOJTABA VAHEDI; circ. 100,000.

Alik: POB 11365-953, Jomhouri Islami Ave, Alik Alley, Tehran 11357; tel. (21) 676671; f. 1931; afternoon; political and literary; Armenian; Propr A. AJEMIAN; circ. 3,400.

Bahari Iran: Khayaban Khayham, Shiraz; tel. (71) 33738.

Entekhab: 12 Noorbakhsh Ave, Vali-e-Asr Ave, Tehran; tel. (21) 8893954; fax (21) 8893951; e-mail public-relations@entekhab-daily.com; internet www.entekhab-daily.com.

Ettela'at (Information): Ettela'at Bldg, Mirdamad Ave, South Naft St, Tehran 15499; tel. (21) 29999; fax (21) 2258022; e-mail ettelaat@ettelaat.com; internet www.ettelaat.com; f. 1925; evening; Farsi; political and literary; operates under the direct supervision of Wilayat-e-Faqih (religious jurisprudence); Editor SAYED MAHMOUD DO'AYI; circ. 500,000.

Fath: POB 19395-7475, Tehran; pro-reform; Man. Dir YADOLLAH ESLAMI. (Publication suspended in 2000.)

Hayat-e No (New Life): 50 North Sohrvardi Ave, Tehran; tel. (21) 8747437; fax (21) 8766373; internet www.aria.ws/hayateno; f. 2000; pro-reform; Man. Dir SAYED HADI KHAMENEI.

Iran News: POB 15115-658, 41 Lida St, Vali-e-Asr Ave, North of Vanak Sq., Tehran 19697; tel. (21) 8880231; fax (21) 8786475; e-mail ininfo@iran-news.com; internet www.iran-news.com; f. 1994; English; Man. Dir MUHAMMAD SOLTANIFAR.

Kayhan (Universe): POB 11365-9631, Ferdowsi Ave, Tehran 11444; tel. (21) 3110251; fax (21) 3111120; e-mail kayhan@ofogh.net; internet www.kayhannews.com; f. 1941; evening; Farsi; political; also publishes *Kayhan International* (f. 1959; daily; English; Editor HAMID NAJAFI), *Kayhan Arabic* (f. 1980; daily; Arabic), *Kayhan Persian* (f. 1942; daily; Persian), *Kayhan Havaie* (f. 1950; weekly for Iranians abroad; Farsi), *Zan-e-Ruz* (Woman Today; f. 1964; weekly; Farsi), *Kayhan Varzeshi* (World of Sport; f. 1955; weekly; Farsi), *Kayhan Bacheha* (Children's World; f. 1956; weekly; Farsi), *Kayhan Farhangi* (World of Culture; f. 1984; monthly; Farsi); owned and managed by Mostazafin Foundation from October 1979 until 1 January 1987, when it was placed under the direct supervision of Wilayat-e-Faqih (religious jurisprudence); Chief Editor HOSSEIN SHARIATMADARI; circ. 350,000.

Khorassan: Mashad; Head Office: Khorassan Daily Newspapers, 14 Zohre St, Mobarezan Ave, Tehran; f. 1948; Propr MUHAMMAD SADEGH TEHERANIAN; circ. 40,000.

Khordad: Tehran; pro-reform. (Publication suspended in 1999.)

Neshat: Tehran; pro-reform; Man. Dir MASHALLAH SHAMSOLVAEZIN. (Publication suspended in 1999.)

Rahnejat: Darvazeh Dowlat, Esfahan; political and social; Propr N. RAHNEJAT.

Ressallat (The Message): POB 11365-777, 53 Ostad Nejatollahi Ave, Tehran; tel. (21) 8902642; fax (21) 8900587; e-mail info@resalat-news.com; internet www.resalat-news.com; f. 1985; organ of right-wing group of the same name; political, economic, social; Propr Ressallat Foundation; Man. Dir SAYED MORTEZA NABAVI; circ. 100,000.

Salam: 2 Shahid Reza Nayebi Alley, South Felestin St, Tehran; tel. (21) 6495831; fax (21) 6495835; f. 1991; Farsi; political, cultural, economic, social; Editor MUHAMMAD MUSAVI KHOIENI. (Closure ordered July 1999.)

Sobh Emruz: Tehran; pro-reform; Man. SAYED HAJJARIAN. (Publication suspended in 2000.)

Tehran Times: 32 Bimeh Alley, Ostad Nejatollahi Ave, Tehran 15998; tel. (21) 8810293; fax (21) 8808214; e-mail webmaster@tehrantimes.com; internet www.tehrantimes.com; f. 1979; independent; English; Man. Dir ABBAS SALIMI NAMIN.

PRINCIPAL PERIODICALS

Acta Medica Iranica: Bldg No. 8, Faculty of Medicine, Tehran Medical Sciences Univ., Poursina St, Tehran 14174; tel. and fax (21) 8962510; e-mail acta@sina.tums.ac.ir; internet www.tums.ac.ir; f. 1960; quarterly; English; Editors-in-Chief A. R. DEHPOUR, M. SAMINI; circ. 2,000.

Akhbar-e-Pezeshki: 86 Ghaem Magham Farahani Ave, Tehran; weekly; medical; Propr Dr T. FORUZIN.

Ashur: Ostad Motahhari Ave, 11-21 Kuhe Nour Ave, Tehran; tel. (21) 622117; f. 1969; Assyrian; monthly; Founder and Editor Dr W. BET-MANSOUR; circ. 8,000.

Auditor: 77 Ferdowsi Ave North, Tehran; quarterly; financial and managerial studies.

Ayandeh: POB 19575-583, Niyavaran, Tehran; tel. (21) 283254; fax (21) 6406426; monthly; Iranian literary, historical and book review journal; Editor Prof. IRAJ AFSHAR.

Bulletin of the National Film Archive of Iran: POB 5158, Baharestan Sq., Tehran 11365; tel. 311242; f. 1989; English periodical; Editor M. H. KHOSHNEVIS.

Daneshmand (The Knowledgeable): POB 15875-3646, Tehran; tel. (21) 8883148; f. 1963; monthly; scientific and technical magazine; Editor-in-Chief A. R. KARAMI.

Daneshkadeh Pezeshki: Faculty of Medicine, Tehran Medical Sciences University; tel. (21) 6112743; fax (21) 6404377; f. 1947; 10 a year; medical magazine; Propr Dr HASSAN AREFI; circ. 1,500.

Donaye Varzesh: Khayyam Ave, Ettela'at Bldg, Tehran; tel. (21) 3281; fax (21) 3115530; weekly; sport; Editor G. H. SHABANI; circ. 200,000.

The Echo of Iran: POB 14155-1168, 4 Hourtab Alley, Hafez Ave, Tehran; tel. (21) 6468114; fax (21) 6464790; e-mail support@echoiran.com; internet www.echoiran.com; f. 1952; monthly; English; news, politics and economics; Editor J. BEHROUZ.

Echo of Islam: POB 14155-3899, Tehran; tel. (21) 8897663; fax (21) 8902725; e-mail echoofislam@itf.org.ir; internet www.itf.org.ir; monthly; English; published by the Islamic Thought Foundation; Man. Dir ALI AKBAR ZIAIE; Editor-in-Chief HAMID TEHRANI.

Economic Echo: POB 14155-1168, 4 Hourtab Alley, Hafez Ave, Tehran; tel. (21) 6468114; fax (21) 6464790; e-mail support@echoiran.com; internet www.echoiran.com; f. 1998; English.

Ettela'at Elmi: 11 Khayyam Ave, Tehran; tel. (21) 3281; fax (21) 3115530; f. 1985; fortnightly; sciences; Editor Mrs GHASEMI; circ. 75,000.

Ettela'at Haftegi: 11 Khayyam Ave, Tehran; tel. (21) 311238; fax (21) 3115530; f. 1941; general weekly; Editor F. JAVADI; circ. 150,000.

Ettela'at Javanan: POB 15499-51199, Ettela'at Bldg, Mirdamad Ave, South Naft St, Tehran; tel. (21) 29999; fax (21) 2258022; f. 1966; weekly; youth; Editor M. J. RAFIZADEH; circ. 120,000.

Farhang-e-Iran Zamin: POB 19575-583, Niyavaran, Tehran; tel. (21) 283254; annual; Iranian studies; Editor Prof. IRAJ AFSHAR.

Film International, Iranian Film Quarterly: POB 11365-875, Tehran; tel. (21) 6709373; fax (21) 6719971; e-mail filmmag@apadana.com; f. 1993; quarterly; English; Editor HOUSHANG GOLMAKANI; circ 20,000.

Iran Tribune: POB 111244, Tehran; monthly; internet www.irantribune.com.

Iran Who's Who: POB 14155, 4 Hourtab Alley, Hafez Ave, Tehran; tel. (21) 6468114; fax (21) 6464790; e-mail support@echoiran.com; internet www.echoiran.com; annual; English; Editor KARAN BEHROUZ.

Iranian Cinema: POB 5158, Baharestan Sq., Tehran 11365; tel. 311242; f. 1985; annual; English; Editor B. REYPOUR.

JIDA: POB 14185-518, Tehran; tel. (21) 8269591; fax 8269592; e-mail ida.dental@yahoo.com; internet www.geocities.com/ida_dental; f. 1963; four a year; journal of the Iranian Dental Association; Editor-in-Chief Dr ALI KOWSARI.

Kayhan Bacheha (Children's World): Shahid Shahsheragi Ave, Tehran; tel. (21) 310251; f. 1956; weekly; Editor AMIR HOSSEIN FARDI; circ. 150,000.

Kayhan Varzeshi (World of Sport): Ferdowsi Ave, Tehran; tel. (21) 310251; f. 1955; weekly; Dir MAHMAD MONSETI; circ. 125,000.

Mahjubah: Tehran; tel. (21) 8000067; fax (21) 8001453; e-mail tjamshid@chamran.ut.ac.ir; Islamic family magazine; published by the Islamic Thought Foundation.

Music Iran: 1029 Amiriye Ave, Tehran; f. 1951; monthly; Editor BAHMAN HIRBOD; circ. 7,000.

Negin: Vali-e-Asr Ave, Adl St 52, Tehran; monthly; scientific and literary; Propr and Dir M. ENAYAT.

Salamate Fekr: M.20, Kharg St, Tehran; tel. (21) 223034; f. 1958; monthly; organ of the Mental Health Soc.; Editors Prof. E. TCHEHRAZI, ALI REZA SHAFAI.

Soroush: POB 15875-1163, Soroush Bldg, Motahhari Ave, Mofatteh Crossroads, Tehran; tel. and fax (21) 8847602; e-mail webmaster@soroushpress.com; internet www.soroushpress.com; f. 1972; one weekly magazine; four monthly magazines, one for women, two for adolescents and one for children; one quarterly review of philosophy; all in Farsi; Editor-in-Chief ALI AKBAR ASHARI.

Zan-e-Ruz (Woman Today): Ferdowsi Ave, Tehran; tel. (21) 3911570; fax (21) 3911569; e-mail kayhan@istn.irost.com; internet www.irost.com/kayhan; f. 1964; weekly; women's; circ. over 60,000. (Closure ordered April 1999.)

PRESS ASSOCIATION

Association of Iranian Journalists: No. 87, 7th Alley, Shahid Kabkanian St, Keshavarz Blvd, Tehran; tel. (21) 8954796; fax (21) 8963539; e-mail secretary@aoij.org; internet www.aoij.org.

NEWS AGENCIES

Islamic Republic News Agency (IRNA): POB 764, 873 Vali-e-Asr Ave, Tehran; tel. (21) 8902050; fax (21) 8905068; e-mail irna@irna.com; internet www.irna.com; f. 1936; Man. Dir Dr ABDOLLAH NASSERI TAHERI.

Foreign Bureaux

Agence France-Presse (AFP): POB 15115-513, Office 207, 8 Vanak Ave, Vanak Sq., Tehran 19919; tel. (21) 8777509; fax (21) 8886289; Correspondent CHRISTOPHE DE ROQUEFEUIL.

Agenzia Nazionale Stampa Associata (ANSA) (Italy): Tehran; tel. (21) 276930; Chief of Bureau LUCIANO CAUSA.

Informatsionnoye Telegrafnoye Agentstvo Rossii—Telegrafnoye Agentstvo Suverennykh Stran (ITAR—TASS) (Russia): Kehyaban Hamid, Kouche Masoud 73, Tehran.

Kyodo Tsushin (Japan): No. 23, First Floor, Couche Kargozar, Couche Sharsaz Ave, Zafar, Tehran; tel. (21) 220448; Correspondent MASARU IMAI.

Reuters (UK): POB 15875-1193, Tehran; tel. (21) 847700.

Xinhua (New China) News Agency (People's Republic of China): Tehran; tel. (21) 241852; Correspondent CHEN MING.

Publishers

Amir Kabir Book Publishing and Distribution Co: POB 11365-4191, Jomhouri Islami Ave, Esteghlal Sq, Tehran; tel. (21) 6463487; fax (21) 390752; f. 1948; historical, social, literary and children's books; Dir H. ANWARY.

Avayenoor Publications: 31 Roshan Alley, Vali-e-Asr Ave, Tehran; tel. (21) 8899001; fax (21) 8907452; e-mail info@avayenoor.com; internet www.avayenoor.com; f. 1988; sociology, politics and economics; Editor-in-Chief Sayed MOHAMMAD MIRHOSSEINI.

Ebn-e-Sina: Meydane 25 Shahrivar, Tehran; f. 1957; educational publishers and booksellers; Dir EBRAHIM RAMAZANI.

Echo Publishers & Printers: POB 14155-1168, 4 Hourtab Alley, Hafez Ave, Tehran; tel. (21) 6468114; fax (21) 6464790; e-mail support@echoiran.com; internet www.echoiran.com; politics, economics and current affairs.

Eghbal Printing & Publishing Organization: 15 Booshehr St, Dr Shariati Ave, Tehran; tel. (21) 768113; f. 1903; Man. Dir DJAVAD EGHBAL.

Iran Chap Co: Mirdamad Ave, South Naft St, Tehran; tel. (21) 29999; fax (21) 2258022; e-mail iranchap@hotmail.com; f. 1966; newspapers, books, magazines, book binding, colour printing and engraving; Man. Dir M. DOAEI.

Iran Exports Publication Co Ltd: POB 14335-746, 27 Eftekhar St, Vali-e-Asr Ave, Tehran 15956; tel. (21) 8801800; fax (21) 8900547; f. 1987; business and trade.

Ketab Sara: Tehran; Chair. SADEGH SAMII.

Khayyam: Jomhouri Islami Ave, Tehran; Dir MUHAMMAD ALI TARAGHI.

Majlis Press: Ketab-Khane Majlis-e-Showray-e Eslami No. 1 and the Documentation Centre, POB 11365-866, Baharestan Sq., Tehran; tel. (21) 3130919; fax (21) 3124339; e-mail frelations@majlis lib.com; internet www.majlislib.org; f. 1923; Ketab-Khane Majlis-e-Showray-e Eslami No. 2, Imam Khomeini Ave, Tehran 13174; tel. (21) 6135335; fax (21) 3124339; f. 1950; library, museum and documentation centre of the Islamic Consultative Assembly; arts, humanities, social sciences, politics, Iranian and Islamic studies; Dir SAYED MUHAMMAD ALI AHMADI ABHARI.

Sahab Geographic and Drafting Institute: POB 11365-617, 30 Somayeh St, Hoquqi Crossroads, Dr Ali Shariati Ave, Tehran 16517; tel. (21) 7535907; fax (21) 7535876; maps, atlases, and books on geography, science, history and Islamic art; Man. Dir MUHAMMAD REZA SAHAB.

Scientific and Cultural Publications Co: Ministry of Science, Research and Technology, 64th St, Sayyed Jamal-ed-Din Asad Abadi Ave, Tehran; tel. (21) 8048037; f. 1974; Iranian and Islamic studies and scientific and cultural books; Pres. SAYED JAVAD AZHARS.

Soroush Press: POB 15875-1163, Soroush Bldg, Motahhari Ave, Mofatteh Crossroads, Tehran; tel. and fax (21) 8847602; e-mail webmaster@soroushpress.com; internet www.soroushpress.com; part of Soroush Publication Group, the publications dept of Islamic Republic of Iran Broadcasting; Man. Dir ALI AKBAR ASHARI.

Tehran University Press: 16 Kargar Shomali Ave, Tehran; tel. (21) 8012076; fax (21) 8012077; f. 1944; university textbooks; Man. Dir Dr M. SHEKARCI.

Broadcasting and Communications

TELECOMMUNICATIONS

Telecommunications Co of Iran (TCI): POB 3316–17, Dr Ali Shariati Ave, Tehran; tel. (21) 8429595; fax (21) 8405055; Chair. and Man. Dir Dr ALIREZA BAHRAMPOUR.

BROADCASTING

Islamic Republic of Iran Broadcasting (IRIB): POB 19395-3333, Vali-e-Asr Ave, Jame Jam St, Tehran; tel. (21) 21961; fax (21) 2045056; e-mail webmaster@irib.com; internet www.irib.com; semi-autonomous authority, affiliated with the Ministry of Culture and Islamic Guidance; non-commercial; operates five national television and three national radio channels, as well as local provincial radio stations throughout the country; Dir-Gen. Dr ALI LARIJANI.

Radio

Radio Network 1 (Voice of the Islamic Republic of Iran): there are three national radio channels: Radio Networks 1 and 2 and Radio Quran, which broadcasts recitals of the Quran (Koran) and other programmes related to it; covers whole of Iran and reaches whole of Europe, the Central Asian republics of the CIS, whole of Asia, Africa and part of USA; medium-wave regional broadcasts in local languages; Arabic, Armenian, Assyrian, Azerbaijani, Balochi, Bandari, Dari, Farsi, Kurdish, Mazandarani, Pashtu, Turkoman, Turkish and Urdu; external broadcasts in English, French, German, Spanish, Turkish, Arabic, Kurdish, Urdu, Pashtu, Armenian, Bengali, Russian and special overseas programme in Farsi; Hebrew service introduced in 2002; 53 transmitters.

Television

Television (Vision of the Islamic Republic of Iran): 625-line, System B; Secam colour; two production centres in Tehran producing for two networks and 28 local TV stations.

Finance

(cap. = capital; res = reserves; dep. = deposits;
brs = branches; m. = million; amounts in rials)

BANKING

Banks were nationalized in June 1979 and a revised commercial banking system was introduced consisting of nine banks (subsequently expanded to 10). Three banks were reorganized, two (Bank Tejarat and Bank Mellat) resulted from mergers of 22 existing small banks, three specialize in industry and agriculture and one, the Islamic Bank (now Islamic Economy Organization), set up in May 1979, was exempt from nationalization. The tenth bank, the Export Development Bank, specializes in the promotion of exports. A change-over to an Islamic banking system, with interest (forbidden under Islamic law) being replaced by a 4% commission on loans, began on 21 March 1984. All short- and medium-term private deposits and all bank loans and advances are subject to Islamic rules. A partial liberalization of the banking sector is planned by the Khatami administration, and the establishment of the first private banks was authorized in late 2001.

Although the number of foreign banks operating in Iran has fallen dramatically since the Revolution, some 30 are still represented.

Central Bank

Bank Markazi Jomhouri Islami Iran (Central Bank): POB 15875-7177, 144 Mirdamad Blvd, Tehran; tel. (21) 3110231; fax (21) 3115674; e-mail g.secdept@cbi.ir; internet www.cbi.ir; f. 1960; Bank Markazi Iran until Dec. 1983; issuing bank, government banking; cap. 350,000m., res 360,832m., dep. 106,239,671m. (March 2001); Gov. Dr MOHSEN NOURBAKHSH.

Commercial Banks

Bank Eqtesad-e Novin (Modern Economic Bank): Tehran; private bank; granted operating licence in 2001; Pres. FARID ZIAOLMOLKI.

Bank Keshavarzi (Agricultural Bank): POB 14155-6395, 129 Patrice Lumumba Ave, Jalal al-Ahmad Expressway, Tehran 14454; tel. (21) 8250135; fax (21) 8262313; e-mail info@agri-bank.com; internet www.agri-bank.com; f. 1979 by merger; state-owned; cap. 752,792m., res 2,860m., dep. 6,701,052m. (March 2000); Chair. and Man. Dir Dr JALAL RASOULOF; 1,700 brs.

Bank Mellat (Nation's Bank): Head Office Bldg, 327 Taleghani Ave, Cnr Forsat St, Tehran 15817; tel. (21) 82961; fax (21) 82962700; e-mail mellat@mellatbank.com; f. 1980 by merger of 10 fmr private banks; state-owned; cap. 1,239,000m., res 42,823m., dep. 38,285,211m. (March 2001); Chair. and Man. Dir S. MANOUCHEHRI; 1,949 brs in Iran, 6 abroad.

Bank Melli Iran (The National Bank of Iran): POB 11365-171, Ferdowsi Ave, Tehran; tel. (21) 3231; fax (21) 3912813; e-mail inter@bankmelli-iran.com; internet www.bankmelli-iran.com; f. 1928, present name since 1943; state-owned; cap. 2,260,000m., res 52,775m., dep. 84,612,092m. (March 2001); Chair. and Man. Dir VALIOLLAH SEIF; 2,998 brs in Iran, 21 abroad.

Bank Refah Kargaran (Workers' Welfare Bank): POB 15815/1866, 40 Mollasadra Ave, Northern Shiraz St, Tehran 19917; tel. (21) 8042926; fax (21) 8041394; e-mail info@bank-refah.com; internet www.bank-refah.com; f. 1960; state-owned; cap. 95,000m., res 50,359m., dep. 6,937,916m. (March 2001); Chair. and Man. Dir Dr PAHVIZ AHMADI; 461 brs.

Bank Saderat Iran (The Export Bank of Iran): POB 15745-631, Bank Saderat Tower, 43 Somayeh Ave, Tehran; tel. (21) 8306091; fax (21) 8839539; internet www.bank-saderat-iran.com; f. 1952; state-owned; cap. 948,000m., res 28,784m., dep. 41,322,059m. (March

2000); Chair. and Man. Dir AHMAD HATAMI YAZD; 3,254 brs in Iran, 24 abroad.

Bank Sepah: POB 9569, Imam Khomeini Sq., Tehran 11364; tel. (21) 3111091; fax (21) 2255267; e-mail info@banksepah.com; internet www.banksepah.com; f. 1925; nationalized in June 1979; cap. 1,052,000m., total assets 31,748,706m. (Dec. 2001); Chair. and Man. Dir Dr ALIREZA SHIRANI; 1,629 brs in Iran, 4 abroad.

Bank Tejarat (Commercial Bank): POB 11365-5416, 130 Taleghani Ave, Nejatoullahie, Tehran 15994; tel. (21) 8901257; fax (21) 8828215; e-mail webmaster@tejarat-bank.com; internet www .tejarat-bank.com; f. 1979 by merger of 12 banks; state-owned; cap. 1,231,120m., res 60,364m., dep. 33,061,406m. (March 2001); Chair. and Pres. SAYED ALI MILANI; 2,056 brs in Iran, 3 abroad.

Islamic Economy Organization (formerly Islamic Bank of Iran): Ferdowsi Ave, Tehran; f. 1980; cap. 2,000m.; provides interest-free loans and investment in small industry.

Parsian Bank: Tehran; private bank; granted operating licence in 2001; Pres. BAHRAM FATHALI.

Development Banks

Bank Sanat va Madan (Bank of Industry and Mine): POB 15875-4459, 593 Hafiz Ave, Tehran; tel. (21) 8903271; fax (21) 8899294; e-mail webmaster@iran-bim.com; internet www.iran-bim.com; f. 1979 as merger of the following: Industrial Credit Bank (ICB), Industrial and Mining Development Bank of Iran (IMDBI), Development and Investment Bank of Iran (DIBI), Iranian Bankers Investment Company (IBICO); cap. 1,613,000m., res 64,000m., total assets 5,264,000m. (2000); Chair. and Man. Dir ABDORAHMAN NADIMI BOU-SHEHRI.

Export Development Bank of Iran: POB 15875-5964, 2 Gandhi Ave, Tehran 15167; tel. (21) 8725140; fax (21) 8716979; e-mail kohzadi@edbi-iran.com; internet www.edbi-iran.com; f. 1991; cap. 1,120,000m., res 17,420m., dep. 368,103m. (August 2001); Chair. and Man. Dir Dr NOWROOZ KOHZADI; 26 brs.

Housing Bank

Bank Maskan (Housing Bank): POB 11365-5699, 247 Ferdowsi Ave, Tehran; tel. (21) 675021; fax (21) 673262; f. 1980; state-owned; cap. 140,000m., dep. 7,996,390m., total assets 9,838,667m. (March 2000); provides mortgage and housing finance; 630 brs; Chair. and Man. Dir AHMAD FARSHCHIAN.

Regulatory Authority

Supreme Council of Banks: Tehran; comprises two bankers and five ministerial appointees; regulates internal affairs of all Iranian banks; Chair. Dr HOSSEIN NEMAZI.

STOCK EXCHANGE

Tehran Stock Exchange: 228 Hafez Ave, Tehran 11389; tel. (21) 6708385; fax (21) 6710111; e-mail int.dept@tse.or.ir; internet www.tse.or.ir; f. 1966; Sec.-Gen. SAYED AHMAD MIR MOTAHARI.

INSURANCE

The nationalization of insurance companies was announced in June 1979.

Bimeh Alborz (Alborz Insurance Co): POB 4489-15875, Alborz Bldg, 234 Sepahboad Garani Ave, Tehran; tel. (21) 8903201; fax (21) 8803771; f. 1959; state-owned insurance company; all types of insurance; Man. Dir ALI FATHALI.

Bimeh Asia (Asia Insurance Co): POB 15815-1885, Asia Insurance Bldg, 297-299 Taleghani Ave, Tehran; f. 1959; tel. (21) 8800951; fax (21) 8898113; all types of insurance; Man. Dir MASOUM ZAMIRI; 6 brs.

Bimeh Dana (Dana Insurance Co): 25 Fifteenth Ave, Gandi St, Tehran 15178; tel. (21) 8770971; fax 8770812; f. 1988; life, personal accident and health insurance; Chair. and Man. Dir Dr ALI FARHANDI.

Bimeh Iran (Iran Insurance Co): POB 14155-6363, Dr Fatemi Ave, No. 107, Tehran; tel. (21) 6704346; fax (21) 6712646; e-mail info@bimeh-iran.com; internet www.bimeh-iran.com; f. 1935; all types of insurance; Chair. and Man. Dir ALI MOUSA REZA.

Bimeh Markazi Iran (Central Insurance of Iran): POB 19395-5588, 72 Africa Ave, Tehran 19157; tel. (21) 2050001; fax (21) 2054099; e-mail cent-ir@kanoon.net; f. 1971; supervises the insurance market and tariffs for new types of insurance cover; the sole state reinsurer for domestic insurance companies, which are obliged to reinsure 50% of their direct business in life insurance and 25% of business in non-life insurance with Bimeh Markazi Iran; Pres. ABDOLNASSER HEMMATI.

Trade and Industry

CHAMBER OF COMMERCE

Iran Chamber of Commerce, Industries and Mines: 254 Taleghani Ave, Tehran; tel. (21) 8846031; fax (21) 8825111; e-mail info@ iccim.org; internet www.iccim.org; supervises the affiliated 32 Chambers in the provinces; Pres. ALI NAGHI KHAMOUSHI.

INDUSTRIAL AND TRADE ASSOCIATIONS

National Iranian Industries Organization (NIIO): POB 14155-3579, 133 Dr Fatemi Ave, Tehran; tel. (21) 656031-40; fax (21) 658070; f. 1979; owns 400 factories in Iran.

National Iranian Industries Organization Export Co (NECO): POB 14335-589, No. 8, 2nd St, Ahmad Ghasir Ave, Tehran 15944; tel. (21) 8733564; fax (21) 8732586.

STATE HYDROCARBONS COMPANIES

Iranian Offshore Oil Co (IOOC): POB 15875-4546, 339 Dr Beheshti Ave, Tehran; tel. (21) 8714102; fax (21) 8717420; wholly owned subsidiary of NIOC; f. 1980; development, exploitation and production of crude petroleum, natural gas and other hydrocarbons in all offshore areas of Iran in the Persian (Arabian) Gulf and the Caspian Sea; Chair. M. AGAZADEH; Dir S. A. JALILIAN.

National Iranian Gas Co (NIGC): Man. Dir MUHAMMAD MUHAM-MADNEZHAD.

National Iranian Oil Co (NIOC): POB 1863, Taleghani Ave, Tehran; tel. (21) 6151; internet www.nioc.org; state organization controlling all 'upstream' activities in the petroleum and natural gas industries; incorporated April 1951 on nationalization of petroleum industry to engage in all phases of petroleum operations; in February 1979 it was announced that, in future, Iran would sell petroleum direct to the petroleum companies, and in September 1979 the Ministry of Oil assumed control of the National Iranian Oil Company; Chair. of Board BIJAN NAMDAR ZANGENEH (Minister of Oil); Man. Dir SAYED MAHDI MIR MOEZI.

National Iranian Oil Refining and Distribution Co (NIORDC): POB 15815-3499, NIORDC Bldg, 140 Ostad Nejatollahi Ave, Tehran 15989; tel. (21) 8801001; fax (21) 6152142; f. 1992 to assume responsibility for refining, pipeline distribution, engineering, construction and research in the petroleum industry from NIOC; Chair. and Man. Dir GHOLAMREZA AQAZADEH.

CO-OPERATIVES

Central Organization for Co-operatives of Iran: Ministry of Co-operatives, 16 Bozorgmehr St, Vali-e-Asr Ave, Tehran 14169; tel. (21) 6400938; fax (21) 6417041; e-mail min-coops@www.dci.co.ir; f. 1993; 15m. mems in 55,000 co-operative societies.

Central Organization for Rural Co-operatives of Iran (CORC): Vali-e-Asr Ave, Tehran 15948; e-mail smmirm@yahoo.com; internet www.ircorc.org; f. 1963; educational, technical, commercial and credit assistance to rural co-operative societies and unions; Chair. and Man. Dir SAYED MUHAMMAD MIRMUHAMMADI.

MAJOR COMPANIES

Behran Oil Co: POB 15815-1633, No. 2/1, 21 St, Khaled Eslamboli Ave, Tehran; tel. (21) 8712907; fax (21) 8723205; f. 1962; manufacturer of engine and industrial lubricants, anti-freeze and paraffin wax; Chair. A. PANAHI; 580 employees.

Behshahr Industrial Co: No. 56/2, 13th Alley, Mirza-e-Shirazi Ave, Tehran 15857; tel. (21) 8300167; fax (21) 8823373; e-mail behshahr.1@neda.net; internet www.behshahrind.com; f. 1951; manufacturer of cooking oil; share cap. 96,000m. rials; Chair. EBRAHIM BAHADORANI; 1,300 employees.

Chemi Darou Industrial Co: POB 16765-1189, Abali Rd, Km 3, Tehran; tel. (21) 7330291; fax (21) 7336458; e-mail info@ chemidaro.com; internet www.chemidaro.com; f. 1964; publicly-owned; manufacturer of pharmaceuticals and chemicals; Man. Dir Dr ASEF YAGHOUBI.

Darou Pakhsh PLC: POB 11365-7388, Km 18 Karaj Freeway, Daroupakhsh St, Tehran; tel. (21) 6026476; fax (21) 6026475; e-mail dpakhsh@irnet.net.ir; f. 1956; share cap. 40m. rials (Mar. 1997); manufacturer of human and veterinary pharmaceuticals; Chair. and Man. Dir MAHMOUD N. ARAB; 2,000 employees.

Iran Electronics Industries (IEI): POB 19575/365, Tehran; tel. (21) 2549057; fax (21) 2548065; e-mail marketing@ieicorp.com; internet www.ieicorp.com; f. 1973; Man. Dir MAHMOUD JARRAHI; 5,000 employees.

Iran Khodro PLC: POB 11365-7313, Km 14 Karaj Rd, Tehran; tel. (21) 9142718; fax (21) 6012202; e-mail ikco-webmaster@ikco.com; internet www.irkhodro.com; f. 1962; publicly-owned; manufacturer of cars, pick-ups, ambulance minibuses and buses; share cap. 684,000m. rials (Mar. 1999); Pres. MANOOCHEHR GHARAVI; 11,000 employees.

Iran Tractor Manufacturing Co (Sherkat-e Teraktor Sazi-e Iran): No. 14, 17th St, Mirzay-e Shirazi Ave, Tehran; tel. (21) 8833391; fax (21) 8844567; e-mail info@itm.co.ir; internet www.itm.co.ir; f. 1968;

publicly-owned; manufacturer of tractors; cap. 75,000m. rials (Mar. 2000); Chair. A. SHAREATI; 2,321 employees.

Iran Vanet (Sherkat-e Iran Vanet): POB 11365-645, Km 21 Karaj Old Rd, Tehran; tel. (21) 6028010; fax (21) 6028718; f. 1964; publicly-owned; manufacturer of pick-up trucks; Chair. H. SHEIKHOLESAMI; 950 employees.

Kaf Joint Stock Co: POB 15815/3478, No. 13, 9th St, Khaled Eslamboli Ave, Tehran 15134; tel. (21) 8716300; fax (21) 8710913; f. 1928; manufacturer of personal products, including skin lotions and creams, shampoos and bath oils; Man. Dir EBRAHIM KHODA-BAKHSD.

Kashi & Ceramic Alvand: mining and minerals; cap. US $72m. (Sept. 1998).

Lastik-e Kerman: rubber and plastics; cap. US $70m. (Sept. 1998).

Lavazem Khanegi Pars: manufactures; cap. US $113m. (Sept. 1998).

Margarine MFG Co: POB 15815-3555, Shahd Bldg, Ferdowsi Sq., Tehran 15999-43161; tel. (21) 8809098; fax (21) 8809268; e-mail margarine@neda.net; f. 1952; manufacturer of margarine, edible vegetable oils and fats; share cap. 63,089m. rials; CEO MOHSEN ASGARI AZAD.

Motogen MFG Co: Motogen Bldg, 253 Ostad Motahhari St, Tehran 15868; tel. (21) 8739425; fax (21) 8730844; e-mail info@motogen.com; internet www.motogen.com; f. 1973; manufacturer of industrial and household electrical motors; Chair. REZA DANESH FAHIM; 1,200 employees.

Paksan: chemicals and petrochemicals; cap. US $75m. (Sept. 1998).

Pars Electric MFG Co: Km 11, Jadeh Makhsous Karadj, Tehran; tel. (21) 4905113; fax (21) 4905091; e-mail info@parselectric.com; internet www.parselectric.com; f. 1962; publicly-owned; manufacturer of radio cassette recorders, television receivers, etc.; share cap. 150,000m. rials (Mar. 1999); Man. Dir EHSAN KHATAMI; 1,200 employees.

Polyacryl Iran Corpn: f. 1974; manufacturer of polyester and acrylic products; cap. US $171m. (Sept. 1998).

Saipa Corpn: POB 13445/554, Km 15 Karaj Special Rd, Tehran; tel. (21) 6026550; fax (21) 6026563; e-mail saipacorp@hotmail.com; manufacturer of motor vehicles; cap. US $299m. (Sept. 1998); Pres. S. EBRAHIMI; 5,000 employees.

Sanati Khavar: automotives; cap. US $121m. (Sept. 1998).

Sanati Minoo (Khoramdareh) PLC: POB 15875-611, 55 Ghanbar Zadeh Ave, Dr Beheshti Ave, Tehran; tel. (21) 8766654; fax (21) 8766122; manufacturer of caramels, cakes, confectionery, etc.; Man. Dir. MUHAMMAD-TAGHI KAZEMI-MOJARAD.

Sanaye Mess Bahonar: manufactures; cap. US $65m. (Sept. 1998).

Sarmayeh Gozari-e Alborz PLC: POB 41-4775/14155, Tehran 15986; tel. (21) 2222759; fax (21) 2272508; f. 1966; finance/investment; share cap. 756,000m. rials (Aug. 2001); CEO Dr MAJID JAM-SHIDI.

Sarmayeh Gozari-e Ghadir: finance/investment; cap. US $360m. (Sept. 1998).

Sarmayeh Gozari-e Mellat (Mellat Investment Corpn) PLC: 8 Rooz Alley, Tavanir St, Vali-e-Asr Ave, Tehran 14348; tel. (21) 8880797; fax (2) 8770621; e-mail irmic@iranfair.com; internet www.irmic.com; f. 1991; publicly-owned; investment, international trade; share cap. 235,000m. rials (Sept. 1999); Chair. A. AFKHAMI; 45 employees.

Sarmayeh Gozari-e Melli Iran (Public Joint-Stock Co): POB 41-4775/14155, Tehran 15986; tel. (21) 8903293; fax (21) 8902796; e-mail sama@isiran.com; f. 1975; publicly-owned; finance/investment; share cap. 272,000m. rials (Aug. 2001); Chair. A. A. AFKHAMI.

Sarmayeh Gozari-e Petrochimie: finance/investment; cap. US $76m. (Sept. 1998).

Sarmayeh Gozari-e Rena: finance/investment; cap. US $105m. (Sept. 1998).

Sarmayeh Gozari-e Sepah: finance/investment; cap. US $98m. (Sept. 1998).

Siman Fars & Khozestan: mining and minerals; cap. US $138m. (Sept. 1998).

Tolid Mavvad Avallieh Alyaf: chemicals and petrochemicals; cap. US $76m. (Sept. 1998).

Towse'e Sanayeh Behshahr: finance/investment; cap. US $330m. (Sept. 1998).

Transport

RAILWAYS

Iranian Islamic Republic Railways: POB 13185-1498, Shahid Kalantari Bldg, Railway Sq., Tehran 13165; tel. (21) 5641600; fax (21) 5650532; e-mail info@irirw.com; internet www.irirw.com; f. 1934; affiliated with Ministry of Roads and Transport; Pres. Deputy Minister of Roads and Transport; Pres. MOHAMMAD SAID NEJAD.

In 1999 the Iranian railway system comprised 6,300 km of standard 1,435 mm gauge, 146 km of electrified lines, and 94 km of wide 1,676 mm gauge. The railway network was estimated to comprise 6,668 km of mainline track in 2000. The system includes the following main routes:

Trans-Iranian Railway runs 1,392 km from Bandar Turkman on the Caspian Sea in the north, through Tehran, and south to Bandar Imam Khomeini on the Persian (Arabian) Gulf.

Southern Line links Tehran to Khorramshahr via Qom, Arak, Dorood, Andimeshk and Ahwaz; 937 km.

Northern Line links Tehran to Gorgan via Garmsar, Firooz Kooh and Sari; 499 km.

Tehran–Kerman Line via Kashan, Yazd and Zarand; 1,106 km.

Tehran–Tabriz Line linking with the Azerbaijan Railway; 736 km.

Tabriz–Djulfa Electric Line: 146 km.

Garmsar–Meshed Line connects Tehran with Meshed via Semnan, Damghan, Shahrud and Nishabur; 812 km. A line is under construction to link Meshed with Sarakhs on the Turkmen border. A 768-km line linking Meshed with Bafq is also under construction.

Qom–Zahedan Line when completed will be an intercontinental line linking Europe and Turkey, through Iran, with India. Zahedan is situated 91.7 km west of the Baluchistan frontier, and is the end of the Pakistani broad gauge railway. The section at present links Qom to Kerman via Kashan, Sistan, Yazd, Bafq and Zarand; 1,005 km. A branch line from Sistan was opened in 1971 via Esfahan to the steel mill at Zarrin Shahr; 112 km. A broad-gauge (1,976-mm) track connects Zahedan and Mirjaveh, on the border with Pakistan; 94 km.

Zahedan–Quetta (Pakistan) Line: 685 km; not linked to national network.

Ahwaz–Bandar Khomeini Line connects Bandar Khomeini with the Trans-Iranian railway at Ahwaz; this line is due to be double-tracked; 112 km.

Azerbaijan Railway extends from Tabriz to Djulfa (146.5 km), meeting the Caucasian railways at the Azerbaijani frontier. Electrification works for this section have been completed and the electrified line was opened in April 1982. A standard gauge railway line (139 km) extends from Tabriz (via Sharaf–Khaneh) to the Turkish frontier at Razi.

Bandar Abbas–Bafq: construction of a 730-km double-track line to link Bandar Abbas and Bafq commenced in 1982. The first phase, linking Bafq to Sirjan (260 km), was opened in May 1990, and the second phase was opened in March 1995. The line provides access to the copper mines at Sarcheshmeh and the iron ore mines at Gole-Gohar.

Bafq–Chadormalou: a 130-km line connecting Bafq to the Chadormalou iron-ore mines is under construction.

Chadormalou–Tabas: a 220-km line is under construction.

A passenger service running from Dushanbe (Tajikistan) to Tehran, via Uzbekistan and Turkmenistan, was scheduled to begin in 2001.

Underground Railway

In May 1995 the Tehran Urban and Suburban Railway Co concluded agreements with three Chinese companies for the completion of the Tehran underground railway, on which work had originally commenced in 1977. It was reported that about 80% of the work on two lines (one, 34 km in length, running north to south, and a second, 20 km in length, running east to west) had been completed. A 31-km suburban line, linking Tehran with the satellite city of Karaj, was inaugurated in February 1999, while phased sections of the urban lines were to enter service from the end of that year.

Tehran Urban and Suburban Railway Co (Metro): POB 4661, 37 Mir Emad St, Tehran 15878; tel. (21) 8740110; fax (21) 8740114; e-mail info@tehranmetro.com; Chair. and Man. Dir MOHSEN HASHEMI.

ROADS

In 1998 there were an estimated 167,157 km of roads, including 890 km of motorways, 24,940 km of highways, main or national roads and 68,238 km of secondary or regional roads; about 56% of the road network was paved. There is a paved highway (A1, 2,089 km) from Bazargan on the Turkish border to the Afghanistan border. The A2 highway runs 2,473 km from the Iraqi border to Mir Javeh on the Pakistan border.

Ministry of Roads and Transport: (see Ministries, above).

INLAND WATERWAYS

Principal waterways:

Lake Rezaiyeh (Lake Urmia): 80 km west of Tabriz in North-West Iran; and Karun river flowing south through the oilfields into the Shatt al-Arab, thence to the head of the Persian Gulf near Abadan.

Lake Rezaiyeh: From Sharafkhaneh to Golmankhaneh there is a twice-weekly service of tugs and barges for transport of passengers and goods.

Karun River: Regular cargo service is operated by the Mesopotamia-Iran Corpn Ltd. Iranian firms also operate daily motor-boat services for passengers and goods.

SHIPPING

Persian (Arabian) Gulf: The main oil terminal is at Kharg Island. The principal commercial non-oil ports are Bandar Shahid Rajai (which was officially inaugurated in 1983 and handles 9m. of the 12m. tons of cargo passing annually through Iran's Gulf ports), Bandar Khomeini, Bushehr, Bandar Abbas and Chah Bahar. A project to develop Bandar Abbas port, which predates the Islamic Revolution and was originally to cost IR 1,900,000m., is now in progress. Khorramshahr, Iran's biggest port, was disabled in the war with Iraq, and Bushehr and Bandar Khomeini also sustained war damage, which has restricted their use. In August 1988 the Iranian news agency (IRNA) announced that Iran was to spend US $200m. on the construction of six 'multi-purpose' ports on the Arabian and Caspian Seas, while ports which had been damaged in the war were to be repaired.

Caspian Sea: Principal ports Bandar Anzali (formerly Bandar Pahlavi) and Bandar Nowshahr.

Ports and Shipping Organization: 751 Enghelab Ave, Tehran; tel. (21) 8809280; fax (21) 8804100; affiliated with Ministry of Roads and Transport; Man. Dir MOKHTAR KALANTARY.

Principal Shipping Companies

Iran Marine Services Co: Iran Marine Services Bldg, 151 Mirdamad Blvd, Tehran 19116; tel. (21) 2222249; fax (21) 2276203; e-mail imsco@neda.net; Chair. and Man. Dir ALIREZA HAJI BABAEI.

Irano–Hind Shipping Co: POB 15875-4647, 18 Sedaghat St, Vali-e-Asr Ave, Tehran; tel. (21) 2058095; fax (21) 2057739; joint venture between the Islamic Republic of Iran and the Shipping Corpn of India; Chair. AHAD MUHAMMADI.

Islamic Republic of Iran Shipping Lines (IRISL): POB 15875-4646, 675 North East Corner of Vali-e-Asr Sq., Tehran; tel. (21) 8893801; fax (21) 889413; e-mail e-it@irisl.net; internet www.irisl.net; f. 1967; liner services between the Persian (Arabian) Gulf and Europe, the Far East and South America and between the Caspian Sea and Central Asia; Chair. and Man. Dir Eng. ALI ASHRAF AFKHAMI.

National Iranian Tanker Co (NITC): POB 19395-4834, 67–68 Atefis St, Africa Ave, Tehran; tel. (21) 2229093; fax (21) 2228065; Chair. and Man. Dir MUHAMMAD SOURI.

CIVIL AVIATION

The two main international airports are Mehrabad (Tehran) and Abadan. An international airport was opened at Esfahan in July 1984 and the first international flight took place in March 1986. Work on a new international airport, 40 km south of Tehran, abandoned in 1979, resumed in the mid-1980s, and work on three others, at Tabas, Ardebil and Ilam was under way in mid-1990. The airports at Urumiyeh, Ahwaz, Bakhtaran, Sanandaz, Abadan, Hamadan and Shiraz were to be modernized and smaller ones constructed at Lar, Lamard, Rajsanjan, Barm, Kashan, Maragheh, Khoy, Sirjan and Abadeh. In early 1995 the Economic Co-operation Organization (ECO) agreed to establish a regional airline (Eco Air), based in Tehran. Construction of the Imam Khomeini International Airport in Tehran, anticipated to be one of the largest airports in the world, began in the late 1990s. The first phase of the project was completed in early 2001, and the airport was expected to be fully operational by mid-2002.

Civil Aviation Organization (CAO): Tehran; affiliated with Ministry of Roads and Transport; Head ASGHAR KETABCHI.

Iran Air (Airline of the Islamic Republic of Iran): POB 13185-755, Iran Air Bldg, Mehrabad Airport, Tehran; tel. (21) 9116689; fax (21) 6003248; internet www.iranair.co.ir; f. 1962; serves the Middle East and Persian (Arabian) Gulf area, Europe, Asia and the Far East; scheduled for part-privatization; Chair. and Man. Dir DAVOOD KESHAVARZIAN.

Iran Air Tours: 191 Motahhari Ave, Dr Moffateh Rd, Tehran 15879; tel. (21) 8758390; fax (21) 8755884; e-mail info@iranairtours.com; internet www.iranairtours.com; f. 1992; serves Middle East; Chair. MAHDI SADEGHI.

Iran Aseman Airlines: POB 141748, Mehrabad Airport, Tehran 13145-1476; tel. (21) 6484198; fax (21) 6404318; internet www.iran-aseman-airlines.com; f. 1980 as result of merger of Air Taxi Co (f. 1958), Pars Air (f. 1969), Air Service Co (f. 1962) and Hoor Asseman; domestic routes and charter services; Man. Dir ALI ABED-ZADEH.

Kish Air: POB 19395-4639, 215 Africa Ave, Tehran 19697; tel. (21) 4665639; fax (21) 4665221; f. 1991 under the auspices of the Kish Development Organization; serves Persian Gulf area, Frankfurt, London and Paris; Pres. Capt. YADOLLAH KHALILI.

Mahan Air: POB 14515-411, Mahan Tower, 21 Azadegan St, Tehran; tel. (21) 4076081; fax (21) 4070404; e-mail airmahan@peyam.net; internet www.mahanairlines.com; f. 1991; domestic routes and charter services between Europe and the Middle East; Man. Dir HAMID ARABNEJAD.

Saha Airline: POB 13445-956, Karadj Old Rd, Tehran 13873; tel. (21) 6696200; fax (21) 6698016; f. 1990; operates passenger and cargo charter domestic flights and services to Europe, Asia and Africa; Man. Dir Capt. A. SAEDI.

Tourism

Tourism was adversely affected by political upheaval following the Revolution. Iran's chief attraction for tourists is its wealth of historical sites, notably Esfahan, Rasht, Tabriz, Susa and Persepolis. Some 1,341,762 international tourist arrivals were recorded in 2000, compared with 326,048 in 1994. Receipts from tourism in 2000 totalled US $671m. Tourism centres are currently administered by the State, through the Ministry of Culture and Islamic Guidance, although in late 1997 the ministry indicated its intention to transfer all tourism affairs to the private sector.

Iran National Tourist Organization (INTO): Tehran; internet www.iran-tourism.com; f. 1979; affiliated with Ministry of Culture and Islamic Guidance; Man. Dir ABDOLLAH HOSSEINI.

Iran Touring and Tourism Organization (ITTO): info@itto.org; internet www.itto.org.

Defence

Budgeted defence expenditure (2001): 15,900,000m. rials (US $9,100m.).

Chairman of the Supreme Defence Council: Ayatollah SAYED ALI KHAMENEI.

Chief of Staff of the Armed Forces and Commander of the Gendarmerie: Brig.-Gen. ALI SHAHBAZI.

Commander of the Army: Maj.-Gen. MUHAMMAD SALAMI.

Commander of the Air Force: Gen. SHAHRAM ROSTAMI (acting).

Commander of the Navy: Rear-Adm. ABBAS MOHTAJ.

Chief of Staff of the Revolutionary Guards Corps (Pasdaran Inquilab): ALI-REZA AFSHAR.

Commander of the Islamic Revolutionary Guards Corps: Lt-Gen. SAYED YANYA RAHIM-SAFAVI.

Commander of Basij (Mobilization) War Volunteers Corps: Brig.-Gen. MUHAMMAD HEJAZI.

Military service: 21 months.

Total armed forces: In August 2001 it was estimated that Iran's armed forces totalled 513,000 men (excluding 350,000 reserves): army 325,000 men; navy 18,000; air force an estimated 45,000; Revolutionary Guard Corps (*Pasdaran Inqilab*, which has its own land, navy and marine units) some 125,000.

Education

PRIMARY AND SECONDARY EDUCATION

Primary education, beginning at age six and lasting for five years, is compulsory for all children and is provided free of charge. Secondary education may last for a further seven years, divided into two cycles; one of three, and another of four, years. In 1996 the total enrolment at primary and secondary schools was equivalent to 86% of the school-age population (90% of boys; 83% of girls), compared with 63% in 1980 (75% of boys; 50% of girls). In 1996 primary enrolment included 90% of children in the relevant age-group (91% of boys; 88% of girls). According to the Government, 24,000 schools were built between the 1979 Revolution and 1984.

HIGHER EDUCATION

Iran has 37 universities of various types, including 16 in Tehran. Universities were closed by the government in 1980 but have been reopened gradually since 1983. According to official sources, some 737,073 students were enrolled at Iran's public colleges and universities in the 2000/01 academic year, in addition to the 836,249 students enrolled at the Islamic Azad University. Apart from Tehran, there are universities in Bakhtaran, Esfahan, Hamadan, Tabriz, Ahwaz, Babolsar, Meshed, Kermanshah, Rasht, Shiraz, Zahedan, Kerman, Shahrekord, Urmia and Yazd. There are *c.* 50 colleges of higher education, *c.* 40 technological institutes, *c.* 20 teacher training colleges, several colleges of advanced technology, and colleges of agriculture in Hamadan, Zanjan, Sari and Abadan. Vocational training schools also exist in Tehran, Ahwaz, Meshed, Shiraz and other cities. Budgetary expenditure on education by the central Government in the financial year 2000/2001 was IR 24,031,000m. (equivalent to 18.8% of total spending).

Bibliography

GENERAL

Afshar, Haleh. *Islam and Feminism: An Iranian Case Study.* London, Macmillan, 1998.

Amirahmadi, Hooshang, and Entessar, Nader. *Iran and the Arab World.* Basingstoke, Macmillan, 1993.

Cambridge History of Iran (8 Vols). Cambridge University Press, reissued edn, 1993.

De Planhol, X. *Recherches sur la Géographie humaine de l'Iran Septentrional.* Paris, 1964.

Ehteshami, Anoushiravan, and Hinnebusch, Raymond. *Syria and Iran: Middle Powers in a Penetrated Regional System.* London/New York, Routledge, 1997.

Elwell-Sutton, L. P. *Modern Iran.* London, 1941.

   A Guide to Iranian Area Study. Ann Arbor, 1952.

   Persian Oil: A Study in Power Politics. London, 1955.

Eskelund, Karl. *Behind the Peacock Throne.* New York, Alvin Redman, 1965.

Frye, Richard N. *Persia.* London, Allen and Unwin, 3rd edn, 1969.

Haeri, Shahla. *Law of Desire: temporary marriage in Iran.* London, I. B. Tauris, 1990.

Huot, Jean Louis. *Persia,* Vol. I. London, Muller, 1966.

Iran Research Group (Ed.). *Who's Who in Iran.* Wisbech, Menas Associates, 1990.

Keddie, Nikki R. *Historical Obstacles to Agrarian Change in Iran.* Claremont, 1960.

   Iran. Religion, Politics and Society. London, Frank Cass, 1980.

   (Ed. with Gasiorowski, Mark). *Neither East nor West: Iran, the Soviet Union and the United States.* New Haven, CT, Yale University Press, 1990.

Khomeini, Ayatollah Ruhollah. *A Clarification of Questions.* Boulder, CT, Westview Press, 1985.

Lambton, A. K. S. *Landlord and Peasant in Persia.* New York, 1953.

   Islamic Society in Persia. London, 1954.

   A Persian Vocabulary. Cambridge, 1961.

   The Persian Land Reform 1962–66. Oxford, Clarendon Press, 1969.

Marlowe, John. *Iran, a Short Political Guide.* London and New York, Pall Mall Press, 1963.

Mehdevi, A. S. *Persian Adventure.* New York, 1954.

   Persia Revisited. London, 1965.

Millspaugh, A. C. *Americans in Persia.* Washington, DC, 1946.

Mohammadi, Ali, and Ehteshami, Anoushiravan (Eds). *Iran and Eurasia.* Ithaca Press, 2000.

Motter, T. H. Vail. *The Persian Corridor and Aid to Russia.* Washington, DC, 1952.

Ramazani, Rouhollah K. *The Persian Gulf: Iran's Role.* Charlottesville, VA, University Press of Virginia, 1972.

Sabahi, Hushang. *British Policy in Persia 1918–1925.* London, Frank Cass, 1990.

Sanghvi, Ramesh. *Aryamehr: The Shah of Iran.* London, Macmillan, 1968.

Savory, Roger. *Iran under the Safavids.* Cambridge University Press, 1980.

Sciolino, Elaine. *Persian Mirrors: The Elusive Face of Iran.* New York, Free Press, 2000.

Shah of Iran. *Mission for My Country.* London, Hutchinson, 1961.

Shearman, I. *Land and People of Iran.* London, 1962.

Sirdar, Ikbal Ali Shah. *Persia of the Persians.* London, 1929.

Stark, Freya. *The Valleys of the Assassins.* London, 1934.

   East is West. London, 1945.

al-Suwaidi, Jamal S. (Ed.). *Iran and the Gulf: A Search for Stability.* Abu Dhabi, Emirates Centre for Strategic Studies and Research, 1996. (Distrib. I. B. Tauris, London).

Wickens, G. M., and Savory, R. M. *Persia in Islamic Times, a practical bibliography of its history, culture and language.* Montreal, Institute of Islamic Studies, McGill University, 1964.

Wilber, Donald N. *Iran: Past and Present: from Monarchy to Islamic Republic.* Princeton University Press, 1955, 9th edn 1982.

   Iran: Oasis of Stability in the Middle East. New York, Foreign Political Association, Inc., 1959.

Wright, Robin B. *The Last Great Revolution: Turmoil and Transformation in Iran.* New York, Alfred A. Knopf, 2000.

Zabih, Sepehr. *The Communist Movement in Iran.* University of California Press, 1967.

CIVILIZATION AND LITERATURE

Arberry, A. J. (Ed.). *The Legacy of Persia.* London and New York, 1953.

   Shiraz: The Persian City of Saints and Poets. Univ. of Oklahoma Press, 1960.

   Tales from the Masnavi. London, 1961.

   More Tales from the Masnavi. London, 1963.

Barth, F. *Nomads of South Persia.* London, 1961.

Bausani, A. *Der Perser: von den Anfängen bis zur Gegenwart.* Stuttgart, Kohlhammer, 1965.

Browne, E. G. *A Literary History of Persia.* 4 vols, Cambridge, 1928.

Colledge, M. A. R. *The Parthians.* London, Thames and Hudson, 1968.

Culican, William. *The Medes and the Persians.* 1965.

Duchesne-Guillemin, Jacques. *The Hymns of Zarathustra* (trans. with commentary). Beacon, L. R., Boston, MA, 1963.

Ekhtiar, Maryam. *Modern Science, Education and Reform in Qajar Iran.* Richmond, Curzon Press, 1999.

Ferrier, R. W. *A Journey to Persia: Jean Chardin's portrait of a seventeenth-century empire.* London, I. B. Tauris, 1996.

Ghirshman, R. *L'Iran: des Origines à Islam.* Paris, 1951. (trans. as *Iran from the Earliest Times to the Islamic Conquest.* London, 1954).

   Arts of Ancient Persia from the Origins to Alexander the Great. London, 1963.

   Iran. New York, 1964.

Herzfeld, E. *Iran in the Ancient East.* Oxford, 1941.

Hovannisian, Richard, and Sabagh, Georges. *The Persian Presence in the Islamic World.* Cambridge University Press, 1999.

Levy, Reuben. *The Persian Language.* New York, 1952.

   Persian Literature. 1928.

Lockhart, L. *Famous Cities of Iran.* London, 1939.

   The Fall of the Safavi Dynasty and the Afghan Occupation of Persia. Cambridge University Press, 1958.

Melville, Charles (Ed.). *Safavid Persia.* 1996.

Milani, Farzaneh. *Veils and Words: The Emerging Voices of Iranian Women Writers.* London, I. B. Tauris, 1990.

Minoui, Delphine (Ed.). *Jeunesse d'Iran: Les voix du changement.* Paris, Autrement, 2001.

Monteil, V. *Les Tribus du Fars et la sédentarisation des nomades.* Paris and The Hague, Mouton, 1966.

Olmstead, A. T. *History of the Persian Empire, Achaemenid Period.* Chicago, 1948.

Pope, Arthur. *Survey of Persian Art from Prehistoric Times to the Present.* Vols 1–6. Oxford University Press, 1938–58.

Rice, Cyprian. *The Persian Sufis.* London, Allen and Unwin, 1964.

Ross, Sir Denison. *Eastern Art and Literature.* London, 1928.

   The Persians. London, 1931.

Sansarian, Eliz. *Religious Minorities in Iran.* Cambridge University Press, 2000.

Storey, C. A. *Persian Literature.* London, 1927.

Sykes, Sir Percy. *Persia.* Oxford, 1922.

A History of Persia (2 vols; 3rd edition, with supplementary essays). London, 1930.

Tapper, Richard, and Thompson, Jon. *The Nomadic Peoples of Iran.* London, Azimuth Editions, 2002.

Teague-Jones, Reginald. *Adventures in Persia.* London, Gollancz, 1990.

Widengren. *Die Religionen Irans.* Stuttgart, Kohlhammer, 1965.

Wiesehofer, Josef. *Ancient Persia.* London, I. B. Tauris, 2001.

Wulfe, H. E. *The Traditional Crafts of Persia.* Cambridge, MA, M.I.T. Press, 1966.

RECENT HISTORY

Abrahamian, Errand. *Tortured Confessions: Prisons and Public Recantations in Modern Iran.* University of California Press, 1999.

Afkham, Mahnaz, and Friedl, Erika (Eds). *In the Eye of the Storm: Women in Post-Revolutionary Iran.* London, I. B. Tauris, 1998.

Akhavi, Shahrough. *Religion and Politics in Contemporary Iran.* State University of New York Press, 1980.

Alikhani, Hossein. *Sanctioning Iran: Anatomy of a Failed Policy.* London, I. B. Tauris, 2000.

Amirahmadi, Hooshang, and Entessar, Nader. *Reconstruction and Regional Diplomacy in the Persian Gulf.* London, Routledge, 1992.

Amirsadeghi, Hossein. *Twentieth Century Iran.* London, Heinemann, 1977.

Ansari, Ali M. *Iran, Islam and Democracy: The Politics of Managing Change.* Washington, DC, Brookings Institution Press, 2001.

Assadollah, Alam. *The Shah and I: The Confidential Diaries of Iran's Royal Court, 1969–77.* London, I. B. Tauris, 1991.

Azimi, Fakhreddin. *Iran: The Crisis of Democracy 1941–1953.* London, I. B. Tauris, 1990.

Bakhash, Shaul. *The Reign of the Ayatollahs.* London, I. B. Tauris, 1984.

Balta, Paul. *Iran–Irak: une guerre de 5,000 ans.* Paris, Editions Anthropos, 1987.

Banani, Amin. *The Modernization of Iran, 1921–1924.* Stanford, 1961.

Bani-Sadr, Abol-Hassan. *My Turn to Speak: Iran, the revolution and secret deals with the US.* New York, Brassey's, 1991.

Behrouz, Maziar. *Rebels with a Cause: the Failure of the Left in Iran.* London and New York, I. B. Tauris, 2000.

Benard, Cheryl, and Zalmay, Khalilzad. *The Government of God: Iran's Islamic Republic.* New York, Columbia University Press, 1984.

Bill, James A. *The Lion and the Eagle: the Tragedy of American-Iranian Relations.* New Haven, CT, Yale University Press, 1988.

Brumberg, Daniel. *Reinventing Khomeini: The Struggle for Reform in Iran.* University of Chicago Press, 2001.

Bullard, Render. *Letters from Tehran: a British ambassador in World War II Persia.* London, I. B. Tauris, 1991.

Bunya, Ali Akbar. *A Political and Diplomatic History of Persia.* Tehran, 1955.

Byman, Daniel L., Chubin, Shamran, Ehteshami, Anoushiravan, and Green, Jerrold. *Iran's Security Policy in the Post-Revolutionary Era.* Santa Monica, CA, RAND, 2001.

Chaqueri, Cosroe. *Origins of Social Democracy in Modern Iran.* University of Washington Press, 2001.

Chubin, Shahram, and Tripp, Charles. *Iran and Iraq at War.* London, I. B. Tauris, 1988.

Chubin, Shahram, and Zabih, Sepehr. *The Foreign Relations of Iran: A Developing State in the Zone of a Great-Power Conflict.* University of California Press, 1975.

Cordesman, Anthony H. *The Iran–Iraq War and Western Security 1984–87.* London, Jane's Publishing Company, 1987.

Cottam, Richard W. *Nationalism in Iran.* Pittsburgh University Press, 1964.

Iran and the United States: a cold war case study. University of Pittsburgh Press, 1988.

Cronin, Stephanie. *The Army and the Creation of the Pahlavi State in Iran 1910–1926.* London and New York, I. B. Tauris, 1997.

Delannoy, Christian. *Savak.* Paris, Editions Stock, 1991.

Ehteshami, Anoushiravan. *After Khomeini: The Iranian Second Republic.* London/New York, Routledge, 1995.

Esposito, John L., and Ramazani, R. K. *Iran at the Crossroads.* Basingstoke, Palgrave, 2001.

Farsoon, Samih K., and Mashayekhi, Mehrdad. *Iran: Political Culture in the Islamic Republic.* London, Routledge, 1993.

Fischer, M. J. *Iran: From Religious Dispute to Revolution.* Harvard University Press, 1980.

Goode, James F. *The United States and Iran, 1946–51: The Diplomacy of Neglect.* New York, St. Martin's Press, 1989.

Halliday, Fred. *Iran: Dictatorship and Development.* London, 1978.

Hamzavi, A. H. K. *Persia and the Powers: An Account of Diplomatic Relations, 1941–46.* London, 1946.

Harvey, Desmond. *The Priest and the King: An Eyewitness Account of the Iranian Revolution.* London, I. B. Tauris, 1999.

Heikal, Muhammad. *The Return of the Ayatollah.* London, André Deutsch, 1981.

Herzig, Edmund. *Iran and the Former Soviet South.* London, Chatham House, 1996.

Hiro, Dilip. *Iran under the Ayatollahs.* London, Routledge and Kegan Paul, 1984.

The Longest War: The Iran–Iraq Military Conflict. London, Grafton, 1989.

Neighbours, Not Friends: Iraq and Iran after the Gulf Wars. London, Routledge, 2001.

Hoveyda, Ferydoun. *The Fall of the Shah.* London, Weidenfeld and Nicolson, 1979.

Humphreys, Eileen. *The Royal Road: a popular history of Iran.* London, Scorpion, 1991.

Huyser, Gen. Robert E. *Mission to Tehran.* London, André Deutsch, 1986.

Ismael, Tareq Y. *Iran and Iraq: Roots of Conflict.* Syracuse University Press, 1983.

Issawi, Charles. *The Economic History of Iran, 1800–1919.* University of Chicago Press, 1972.

Kapuściński, Ryszard. *Shah of Shahs.* San Diego, Harcourt Brace Jovanovich, 1985.

Katouzian, Homa. *State and Society in Iran: the Eclipse of the Qajars and the Emergence of the Pahlavis.* London and New York, I. B. Tauris, 2000.

Musaddiq and the Struggle for Power in Iran. London, I. B. Tauris, 2000.

Katzman, Kenneth. *The Warriors of Islam: Iran's Revolutionary Guard.* Boulder, CO, and Oxford, Westview Press, 1994.

Keddie, Nikki. *Roots of Revolution.* Yale University Press, 1982.

Khomeini, Ayatollah Ruhollah. *Islam and Revolution: Writings and Declarations of Imam Khomeini,* trans. and ed. by Hamid Algar. Berkeley, CA, Mizan Press, 1982.

Laing, Margaret. *The Shah.* London, Sidgwick and Jackson, 1977.

Lenczowski, George. *Russia and the West in Iran.* Cornell University Press, 1949.

Lenczowsci, G. (Ed.). *Iran under the Pahlavis.* Stanford, Hoover Institution Press, 1978.

Martin, Vanessa. *Creating an Islamic State: Khomeini and the Making of a New Iran.* London and New York, I. B. Tauris, 2000.

Menashri, David. *Post-Revolutionary Politics in Iran: Religion, Society, Power.* London, Frank Cass, 2001.

Milani, Abbas. *The Persian Sphinx: Amir Abbas Hoveyda and the Riddle of the Iranian Revolution.* London, I. B Tauris, 2000.

Moin, Baqer. *Khomeini: Life of the Ayatollah.* London and New York, I. B. Tauris, 1999.

Mojtahed-Zadeh, Pirouz. *Security and Territoriality in the Persian Gulf: A Maritime Political Geography.* Richmond, Curzon, 1999.

Mottahedeh, Roy. *The Mantle of the Prophet: Religion and Politics in Iran.* London, Chatto and Windus, 1985.

Nakhai, M. *L'Evolution Politique de l'Iran.* Brussels, 1938.

Naraghi, Ehsan. *Des Palais du Chah aux prisons de la révolution.* Paris, Editions Balland, 1993.

Omid, Homa. *Islam and the Post-Revolutionary State in Iran.* London, Macmillan, 1993.

Paidar, Parvin. *Women and the Political Process in Twentieth-Century Iran.* Cambridge University Press, 1995.

Parsa, Misagh. *Social Origins of the Iranian Revolution.* New Brunswick, New Jersey and London, Rutgers University Press, 1989.

Parsons, Sir Anthony. *The Pride and the Fall: Iran 1974–79.* London, Jonathan Cape, 1984.

Pelletiere, Stephen. *The Iran–Iraq War: chaos in a vacuum.* London and New York, Praeger Publishers, Inc., 1992.

Rahnema, Ali, and Nomani, Farhad. *The Sewlar Miracle: religion, politics and economic policy in Iran.* London, Zed Books, 1990.

Rahnema, Saeed, and Bedad, Sohrab (Eds). *Iran After the Revolution: Crisis of an Islamic State.* London, I. B. Tauris, 1995.

Rajaee, Farhang (Ed.). *The Iran–Iraq War: The Politics of Aggression.* Gainsville, University Press of Florida, 1994.

Ramazani, Rouhollah K. *The Foreign Policy of Iran 1500–1941.* University Press of Virginia, 1966.

Rezun, Miron (Ed.). *Iran at the Crossroads: global relations in a turbulent decade.* Oxford, Westview Press, 1990.

Roosevelt, Kermit. *Countercoup: the Struggle for the Control of Iran.* McGraw-Hill, 1980.

Sick, Gary. *All Fall Down: America's Tragic Encounter with Iran.* New York, Random House, 1985.

   October Surprise. New York, Random House, 1991.

Stempel, John D. *Inside the Iranian Revolution.* Indiana University Press, 1982.

Steppat, Fritz. *Iran zwischen den Grossmächten, 1941–48.* Oberursel, 1948.

Taheri, Amir. *The Spirit of Allah: Khomeini and the Iranian Revolution.* London, Hutchinson, 1985.

Upton, Joseph M. *The History of Modern Iran: An Interpretation.* Harvard University Press, 1960.

Villiers, Gerard de. *The Imperial Shah: An Informal Biography.* London, Weidenfeld and Nicolson, 1977.

Wroe, Ann. *Lives, Lies and the Iran-Contra Affair.* London, I. B. Tauris, 1991.

Zonis, Marrin. *Majestic Failure: The Fall of the Shah.* University of Chicago Press, 1991.

ECONOMY AND PETROLEUM

Alizadeh, Parvin. (Ed.) *The Economy of Iran: The Dilemmas of an Islamic State.* London, I. B. Tauris, 2001.

Amid, Mohammad Javad. *Poverty, Agriculture and Reform in Iran.* London, Routledge, 1990.

Amuzegar, Jahangir. *An Economic Profile.* Middle East Institute, 1977.

   The Dynamics of the Iranian Revolution. SUNY Press, 1991

   Iran's Economy under the Islamic Republic. London, I. B. Tauris, 1993.

Baldwin, George B. *Planning and Development in Iran.* Baltimore, Johns Hopkins Press, 1967.

Bharier, Julian. *Economic Development in Iran 1900–1970.* London, Oxford University Press, 1971.

Elm, Mostafa. *Oil, Power and Principle: Iran's oil nationalization and its aftermath.* Syracuse, Syracuse University Press, 1992.

Ghosh, Sunil Kanti. *The Anglo–Iranian Oil Dispute.* Calcutta, 1960.

Gupta, Raj Narain. *Iran: An Economic Study.* New Delhi, 1947.

Heiss, Mary Ann. *Empire and Nationhood: The United States, Great Britain and Iranian Oil, 1950–1954.* New York, Columbia University Press, 1998.

Mason, F. C. *Iran: Economic and Commercial Conditions in Iran.* London, HMSO, 1957.

Mofid, Kamran. *The Economic Consequences of the Gulf War.* London, Routledge, 1990.

Nahai, L., and Kibell, C. L. *The Petroleum Industry of Iran.* Washington, US Department of the Interior, Bureau of Mines, 1963.

Nirumand, Bahman. *Persien, Modell eines Entwicklungslande, oder Die Diktatur der freien Welt.* Reinbek-bei-Hamburg, Rowohlt-Verlag, 1967.

Shakoori, Ali. *The State and Rural Development in Post-Revolutionary Iran.* New York, St Martins Press, 2001.

Sotoudeh, H. *L'Evolution Economique de l'Iran et ses Problèmes.* Paris, 1957.

IRAQ

Physical and Social Geography

W. B. FISHER

Iraq is bounded on the north by Turkey, on the east by Iran, on the south by Kuwait and the Persian Gulf, on the south-west by Saudi Arabia and Jordan, and on the north-west by Syria. The actual frontier lines present one or two unusual features. In the first place, there exists between Iraq, Kuwait, and Saudi Arabia a 'neutral zone', rhomboidal in shape, which was devised to facilitate the migrations of pastoral nomads, who cover great distances each year in search of pasture for their animals and who move regularly between several countries. Hence the stabilization or closing of a frontier could be for them a matter of life and death. Secondly, the frontier with Iran in its extreme southern portion, below Basra, follows the course of the Shatt al-Arab waterway (the confluence of the Tigris and Euphrates), which flows into the Persian (Arabian) Gulf, but from 1936 until March 1975 the frontier was at the left (east) bank, placing the whole of the river within Iraq. This situation had become increasingly unacceptable to Iran, and under the Algiers Agreement of March 1975 the border was restored to the Thalweg Line in the middle of the deepest shipping channel in the Shatt al-Arab estuary. The dispute over the precise position of this border was one of the causes of the war with Iran which began in 1980. Thirdly, the inclusion of the northern province of Mosul within Iraq was agreed only in 1926. Because of its petroleum deposits, this territory was in dispute between Turkey, Syria and Iraq. Again, the presence of large numbers of migratory nomads, journeying each season between Iran, Turkey, Syria and Iraq, was a further complicating factor. In March 1984 a treaty was signed by Jordan and Iraq which finally demarcated the border between the two countries and under which Iraq ceded some 50 sq km to Jordan.

PHYSICAL FEATURES

The old name of Iraq (Mesopotamia = land between the rivers) indicates the main physical aspect of the country—the presence of the two river valleys of the Tigris and Euphrates, which merge in their lower courses. On the eastern side of this double valley the Zagros Mountains appear as an abrupt wall, overhanging the riverine lowlands, particularly in the south, below Baghdad. North of the latitude of Baghdad the rise to the mountains is more gradual, with several intervening hill ranges, such as the Jebel Hamrin. These ranges are fairly low and narrow at first, with separating lowlands, but towards the main Zagros topography becomes more imposing, and summits over 3,000 m in height occur. This region, lying north and east of Baghdad, is the ancient land of Assyria; nowadays the higher hill ranges lying in the extreme east are known as Iraqi Kurdistan, since many Kurdish tribes inhabit them.

On the western side of the river valley the land rises gradually to form the plateau which continues into Syria, Jordan, and Saudi Arabia, and its maximum height in Iraq is about 1,000 m. In places it is possible to trace a cliff formation, where a more resistant bed of rock stands out prominently, and from this the name of the country is said to be derived (Iraq = cliff). There is no sharp geographical break between Iraq and its western neighbours comparable with that between Iraq and Iran; the frontier lines are artificial.

THE RIVERS

The Tigris, 1,850 km (1,150 miles) in length, rises in Turkey, and is joined by numerous and often large tributaries both in Turkey and Iraq. The Euphrates, 2,350 km in length, also rises in Turkey and flows first through Syria and then Iraq, joining the Tigris in its lower course at Qurnah, to form the stream known as the Shatt al-Arab (or Arvand river, as it is called by the Iranians), which is 185 km in length. Unlike the Tigris, the Euphrates receives no tributaries during its passage of Iraq.

Above the region of Baghdad both rivers flow in well-defined channels, with retaining valley walls. Below Baghdad, however, the vestiges of a retaining valley disappear, and the rivers meander over a vast open plain with only a slight drop in level—in places merely 1.5 m or 2 m in 100 km. Here the rivers are raised on great levees, or banks of silt and mud (which they themselves have laid down), and now lie several feet above the level of the surrounding plain. One remarkable feature is the change in relative level of the two river beds—water can be led from one to the other according to the actual district, and this possibility, utilized by irrigation engineers for many centuries, still remains the basic principle of present-day development. Old river channels, fully or partially abandoned by the river, are also a feature of the Mesopotamian lowland, associated with wide areas of swamp, lakes, and sandbars. The Tigris, though narrower than the Euphrates, is swifter, and carries far more water.

As the sources of both rivers lie in the mountains of Turkey, the current is very fast, and upstream navigation is difficult in the middle and upper reaches. In spring, following the melting of snows in Asia Minor, both rivers begin to rise, reaching a maximum in April (Tigris) and May (Euphrates). During the season floods of 3.6 m to 6.0 m occur, and 10 m is known—this in a region where the land may fall only 4 m or less in level over 100 km. Immense areas are regularly inundated, levees often collapse, and villages and roads, where these exist, must be built on high embankments. The Tigris is particularly liable to sudden flooding, and can rise at the rate of one foot per hour. In lower Iraq wide expanses are inundated every year. Construction of the Wadi Tharthar control scheme has, however, greatly reduced the incidence of severe flooding, particularly along the Tigris, and continued expansion of irrigation schemes (which has been a feature of Iraq since the late 1960s) is having a further effect.

Roads were formerly difficult to maintain because of floods, and the rail system was of different gauges. New standard-gauge rail links have now been constructed: north–south from Mosul to Basra via Baghdad; various cross-country lines; and an extension along the Euphrates valley towards north-eastern Syria.

Because of the former difficulties in communication, many communities of differing cultures and ways of life have persisted. Minority groups have thus been a feature in Iraq.

CLIMATE AND ECONOMIC ACTIVITY

The summers are overwhelmingly hot, with shade temperatures of over 43°C. Winters may be surprisingly cold: frost, though very rare in the south, can be severe in the north. Sudden hot spells during winter are another feature in the centre and south of Iraq. Rainfall is scanty over all of the country, except for the north-east (Assyria), where annual falls of 400 mm–600 mm occur—enough to grow crops without irrigation. Elsewhere farming is entirely dependent upon irrigation from river water. The great extent of standing water in many parts of Iraq leads to an unduly high air humidity, which explains the notorious reputation of the Mesopotamian summer.

The unusual physical conditions outlined present a number of obstacles to human activity. The flood waters are rather less 'manageable' than in Egypt, for example, and there is less of the regular deposition of thick, rich silt that is such a feature of the Nile. The effects of this are strikingly visible in the relatively small extent of land actually cultivated—at most, only one-sixth of the potentially cultivable territory and 3% of the total area of the country. Because of the easy availability of agricultural land, wasteful, 'extensive' farming methods are often followed, giving a low yield. On the whole, Iraq is under-populated, and could support larger numbers of inhabitants.

The unusual physical conditions have greatly restricted movement and the development of communications of all kinds. In the upper reaches of the rivers, boat journeys can only be made downstream, while nearer the sea the rivers are wider and slower but often very shallow. Roads and railways are difficult to maintain because of the floods.

THE PEOPLE

In the marshes of the extreme south there are a number of boat-and raft-based Arab communities. Other important minorities live in, or close to, the hill country of the north: the Kurds, who number an estimated 3.5m. and migrate extensively into Syria, Turkey and Iran (see History); the Yazidis of the Jebel Sinjar; the Assyrian Christians (the name refers to their geographical location, and has no historical connection); and various communities of Uniate and Orthodox Christians. In addition, there were important groups of Jews—more than in most other Muslim countries—though, since the establishment of the State of Israel, much emigration has taken place. It should be noted that while the majority of the Muslims follow Shi'a rites, the wealthier Muslims have tended to be of Sunni adherence.

Ethnically, the position is very complicated. The northern and eastern hill districts contain many racial elements—Turki, Persian, and proto-Nordic, with Armenoid strains predominating. The pastoral nomads of western Iraq are, as might be expected, of fairly unmixed Mediterranean ancestry, like the nomads of Syria, Jordan, and Saudi Arabia; but the population of the riverine districts of Iraq displays a mixture of Armenoid and Mediterranean elements. North of the Baghdad district the Armenoid strain is dominant, but to the south, it is less important, though still present.

Arabic is the official and most widely used language, Kurdish and dialects of Turkish are current in the north, whilst variants of Persian are spoken by tribes in the east. An estimate, probably over-generous to the Arabic speakers, puts the relative proportions at: Arabic 79%, Kurdish 16%, Persian 3%, and Turkish 2% of the total population.

History

Revised for this edition by RICHARD I. LAWLESS

EARLY HISTORY

By the advent of Islam in the seventh century AD Iraq had already experienced more than 3,500 years of civilization. The Sumerians were, in turn, succeeded by the Elamites, the Amorites, the Mittani, the Hittites, and the Assyrians, until in 612 BC the subject peoples rose and sacked Nineveh. Iraq then became the centre of a neo-Babylonian state, which, under Nebuchadnezzar (604–538 BC), included much of the Fertile Crescent (from the Euphrates to the Nile Valley), but soon fell to the Persians, who seized Babylon in 539–538 BC.

Iraq then became a province of the Achaemenid Empire until the military successes of Alexander the Great in 334–327 BC. After about 100 years of Seleucid rule Iraq became a frontier province of the Parthian Empire against the might of Rome. Between AD 113 and 117 Trajan conquered much of Iraq but his successor Hadrian withdrew. Roman reoccupation later took place. Parthian rule eventually gave way before the emergence of the Sasanid regime in the second century AD. Frontier wars with Rome broke out from time to time, but by the seventh century both Persia and Byzantium were exhausted, and the way was open to conquest from the south.

THE RISE OF ISLAM

The spectacular birth and growth of Islam in the first quarter of the seventh century set the Arabs on the path of conquest outside Arabia. In 637, at the battle of Jalula, the Arabs virtually ended Sasanid power in Iraq. There immediately followed a period of struggle between Ali, the son-in-law of the Prophet, and Mu'awiya, who had been governor of Syria. Ali fell in battle, however, in 661, making way for the Umaiyad dynasty, under Syrian hegemony, until 750. A movement arose known as the Shi'atu Ali (i.e. the party of Ali) and most new converts gave their allegiance to the Shi'a, partly as an expression of their social and political grievance against the established order. In 750 Umaiyad rule was replaced by that of the Abbasid dynasty, with Iraq becoming the dominant and most prosperous part of the empire. The second Abbasid, al-Mansour (754–775), quickly abandoned the Shi'ite extremists who had brought the Abbasids to power. Abbasid power waned, and Baghdad fell under the rule of the Shi'ite Buwaihids from the middle of the 10th to the middle of the 11th century, when effective power passed to the Seljuq Turks, although the Abbasid Caliph was, in name, the head of state.

MONGOL INVASIONS

In 1253 Hulagu, a grandson of Chinghiz (Jenghiz) Khan, moved westward in force, captured Baghdad in 1258 and thus made an end of the Abbasid Caliphate. Now subordinate to the Mongol Khan of Persia, Iraq became a mere frontier province. After the death of the Mongol Khan Abu Sa'id in 1335, Iraq passed to the Jala'irids who ruled until the early years of the 15th century. Iraq then passed successively under the power of two rival Turkoman confederations (the Black Sheep and the White Sheep) until, in the years 1499–1508, the White Sheep regime was destroyed by the Safavid Ismail, who made himself Shah of Persia. The Sunni Ottoman Turks considered the Shi'ite Ismail to be a threat, and the Sultan Suleyman, in the course of his campaign against Persia, conquered Baghdad in 1534–35.

OTTOMAN IRAQ

Although Persian control was restored for a brief period between 1623 and 1638, Iraq was to remain, at least nominally, under Turkish control until the First World War. A series of Mamluk pashas in the 18th century engaged in wars with Persia, and towards the end of the century had to contend with Kurdish insurrection in the north and raids by Wahhabi tribesmen from the south. In the early 19th century the Ottoman Sultan decided to regain direct possession of Iraq and end the Mamluk system. Sultan Mahmoud II sent Ali Ridha Pasha to perform this task in 1831. A severe outbreak of plague hampered the Mamluks, Da'ud Pasha was deposed, and the Mamluk regiments were exterminated.

WESTERN INFLUENCE

Although some of the European nations had long been in contact with Iraq through their commercial interests in the Persian (Arabian) Gulf, Western influences were slow to penetrate the province. By 1800 there was a British Resident at Basra and two years later a British Consulate at Baghdad. France also maintained agents in these cities. French and Italian religious orders had settlements in the land. It was not, however, until after 1831 that signs of more rapid European penetration became visible, such as steamboats on the rivers of Iraq in 1836, telegraph lines from 1861 and a number of proposals for railways, none of which was to materialize for a long time to come. The Ottoman Government did much in the period between 1831 and 1850 to impose direct control over Kurdistan and the mountainous areas close to the Persian border, but the introduction of reforms was not, in fact, begun until 1869, when Midhat Pasha arrived at Baghdad. Although much of his work, performed in the brief space of three years, proved to be superficial and ill-considered, achievements, however imperfect, such as a newspaper, military factories, a hospital, an alms-house, schools, a tramway, conscription for the army, municipal and administrative councils, comparative security on the main routes and a reasoned policy of settling tribes on the land did bear solid witness to the vigour of his rule. After his departure in 1872, reform and European influence continued to advance, although slowly. Postal services were much developed, a railway from Baghdad to Samarra was completed in 1914 (part of the projected *Baghdad-bahn* which betokened the rapid growth of German interest in the Ottoman Empire) and the important Hindiya Barrage on the Euphrates was rebuilt between 1910 and 1913. The measures of reform and improvement introduced between 1831 and 1914 must indeed be judged as belated and inadequate—the Iraq of 1900 differed little from that of 1500— yet a process of fundamental change had begun.

In November 1914 Britain and the Ottoman Empire were at war. British troops occupied the Shatt al-Arab region and, through the necessity of war, transformed Basra into an efficient and well-equipped port. A premature advance on Baghdad in 1915 ended in the retreat of the British forces to Kut, their prolonged defence of that town and, when all attempts to relieve it had failed, the capitulation to the Ottomans in April 1916. A new offensive launched from Basra in the autumn of that year brought about the capture of Baghdad in March 1917. Kirkuk was taken in 1918, but, before the Allies could seize Mosul, the Ottoman Government sought and obtained an armistice in October. For two years, until the winter of 1920, the Commander-in-Chief of the British Forces, acting through a civil commissioner, continued to be responsible for the administration of Iraq from Basra to Mosul, all the apparatus of a modern system of rule being created at Baghdad—e.g. departments of land, posts and telegraphs, agriculture, irrigation, police, customs, finance, etc. The new regime was Christian, foreign and strange; resented by reason of its very efficiency, feared and distrusted no less by those whose loyalties were Muslim and Ottoman than by important elements who desired self-determination for Iraq.

The last phase of Ottoman domination in Iraq, especially during the years after the Young Turk Revolution in 1908, had witnessed a marked growth of Arab nationalist sentiment. Local circles in Iraq now made contact with the Ottoman Decentralization Party at Cairo, Egypt, founded in 1912, and with the Young Arab Society, which moved from Paris to Beirut in 1913. Basra, in particular, became a centre of Arab aspirations and took the lead in demanding from İstanbul a measure of autonomy for Iraq. A secret organization, al-'Ahd (the Covenant), included a number of Iraqi officers serving in the Ottoman armies. The prospect of independence which the Allies held out to the Arabs in the course of the war strengthened and extended the nationalist movement. In April 1920 Britain received from the conference at San Remo a mandate for Iraq. This news was soon followed by a serious insurrection amongst the tribesmen of the south. The revolt, caused partly by instinctive dislike of foreign rule but also by vigorous nationalist propaganda, was not wholly suppressed until early in the next year. In October 1920 military rule was formally terminated in Iraq. An Arab Council of State, advised by British officials and responsible for the administration, now came into being and in March 1921 the Amir Faisal ibn Hussain agreed to rule as King at Baghdad. His ceremonial accession took place on 23 August 1921.

The Najdi (Saudi Arabian) frontier with Iraq was defined in the Treaty of Mohammara in May 1922. Saudi concern over loss of traditional grazing rights resulted in further talks between Ibn Saud and the British Civil Commissioner in Iraq, and a Neutral Zone of 7,000 sq km was established adjacent to the western tip of the Kuwait frontier. No military or permanent buildings were to be erected in the zone and the nomads of both countries were to have unimpeded access to its pastures and wells. A further agreement concerning the administration of this zone was signed between Iraq and Saudi Arabia in May 1938.

MODERN IRAQ

Despite the opposition of the more extreme nationalists, an Anglo-Iraqi Treaty was signed on 10 October 1922. It embodied the provisions of the mandate, safeguarded the judicial rights of foreigners and guaranteed the special interests of Britain in Iraq. An electoral law facilitated the choice of a constituent assembly, which met in March 1924 and, despite strong opposition by the nationalists, ratified the treaty with Britain. It accepted, too, an organic law declaring Iraq to be a sovereign state with a constitutional hereditary monarchy and a representative system of government. In 1925 the League of Nations

recommended that the *wilaya* (administrative district) of Mosul, to which the Turks had laid claim, be incorporated into the new kingdom, a decision finally implemented in the treaty of July 1926 between the interested parties: Britain, Turkey and Iraq. By 1926 a fully constituted parliament was in session at Baghdad and all the ministries, as well as most of the larger departments of the administration, were in effective control. In 1930 a new treaty was signed with Britain, which established between the two countries a close alliance for a period of 25 years and granted Britain the use of airbases at Shuaiba and Habbaniya. On 3 October 1932 Iraq entered the League of Nations as an independent power, the mandate being now terminated.

Numerous difficulties confronted the Kingdom in the period after 1932: for example the animosities between the Sunni Muslims and the powerful Shi'ite tribes on the Euphrates, which tended to divide and embitter political life; the problem of relations with the Kurds, some of whom wanted a separate Kurdish state, and with other minorities like the Assyrians; the complicated task of reform in land tenure and of improvement in agriculture, irrigation, flood control, public services and communications. During these years the Government was little more than a façade of democratic forms concealing faction and intrigue. The realities of the political scene were an often ill-informed and xenophobic press; 'parties' better described as cliques gathered around prominent personalities; a small ruling class of tribal sheikhs; landowners; and the intelligentsia— lawyers, students, journalists, doctors, ex-officers—frequently torn by sharp rivalries. It is not surprising, therefore, that the first years of full independence made rather halting progress towards efficient rule. The dangerous nature of domestic tensions was demonstrated by the Assyrian massacre of 1933 perpetrated by troops of the Iraqi army. Political intrigue from Baghdad was partly responsible for the outbreak of tribal revolt along the Euphrates in 1935–36. The army crushed the insurrection without much difficulty and then, under the leadership of General Bakr Sidqi, and in alliance with disappointed politicians and reformist elements, brought about a *coup d'état* in October 1936. The new regime failed to fulfil its assurances of reform; its policies alienated the tribal chieftains and gave rise to serious tensions even within the armed forces, tensions which led to the assassination of Bakr Sidqi in August 1937.

Of vast importance for Iraq was the rapid development of the petroleum industry during these years. Concessions were granted in 1925, 1932 and 1938 to the Iraq, Mosul and Basra Petroleum Cos. Oil had been discovered in the Kirkuk area in 1927 and by the end of 1934 the Iraq Petroleum Co (IPC) was exporting crude oil through two pipelines, one leading to Tripoli and the other to Haifa. Exploitation of the Mosul and Basra fields did not begin on a commercial scale until after the Second World War.

In 1937 Iraq joined Turkey, Persia and Afghanistan in the Sa'dabad Pact, which arranged for consultation in all disputes that might affect the common interests of the four states. A treaty signed with Persia in July 1937 and ratified in the following year provided for the specific acceptance of the boundary between the two countries as it had been defined in 1914. Relations with Britain deteriorated in the period after 1937, mainly because of the growth of anti-Zionist feeling and of resentment at British policy in Palestine. German influence increased very much at this time in Iraq, especially among those political and military circles associated with the army group later to be known as the Golden Square. Iraq severed its diplomatic connections with Germany at the beginning of the Second World War, but in 1941 the army commanders carried out a new *coup d'état*, establishing, under the nominal leadership of Rashid 'Ali al-Gaylani, a regime which announced its non-belligerent intentions. A disagreement over the passage of British troops through Iraq left no doubt of the pro-German sympathies of the Gaylani Government and led to hostilities that ended with the allied occupation of Basra and Baghdad in May 1941. Thereafter, Iraq co-operated with the Allies and declared war on the Axis powers in 1943.

Iraq, during the years after the Second World War, was to experience much internal tension and unrest. Negotiations with Britain led to the signing, at Portsmouth in January 1948, of a new Anglo-Iraqi agreement designed to replace that of 1930 and incorporating substantial concessions, among them the British evacuation of the airbases at Shuaiba and Habbaniya and the creation of a joint board for the co-ordination of all matters relating to mutual defence. The animosities arising from the situation in Palestine provoked riots at Baghdad directed against the new agreement with Britain, which were sufficiently disturbing to oblige the Iraqi Government to repudiate the Portsmouth settlement.

ARAB–ISRAELI WAR, 1948

With anti-Jewish and anti-Western feeling so intense, it was inevitable that troops should be sent from Iraq to the Arab–Israeli war which began on 15 May 1948. The Iraqi troops shared in the hostilities for a period of just over two months, their participation terminating in a truce operative from 18 July. Their final withdrawal from Palestine did not commence, however, until April 1949. Subsequently, there was a considerable emigration of Jews from Iraq to Israel, especially in the years 1951–52.

The expense of the war against Israel, together with bad harvests and the general indigence of the people, created serious tensions resulting in rioting at Baghdad in November 1952 and the imposition of martial law until October 1953. None the less, there were some favourable prospects for the future—notably a large expansion of the oil industry. New pipelines were built to Tripoli in 1949 and to Banias in Syria in 1952; the oilfields of Mosul and Basra were producing significant amounts of crude petroleum by 1951–52. A National Development Board was created in 1950 and became later, in 1953, a national ministry. An agreement of February 1952 allowed the Iraqi Government 50% of the oil companies' profits before deductions for foreign taxes. Abundant resources were thus available for development projects of national benefit (e.g. the flood control and irrigation works opened in April 1956 on the Tigris at Samarra and on the Euphrates at Ramadi).

THE BAGHDAD PACT

Iraq, in the field of foreign relations, was confronted during these years with a choice between the Western powers, eager to establish in the Middle East an organized pattern of defence, and the USSR, entering at this time into a diplomatic propaganda and economic drive to increase its influence in the Arab lands. In February 1955 Iraq made an alliance with Turkey for mutual co-operation and defence. Britain acceded to this pact in the following April, agreeing also to end the Anglo-Iraqi agreement of 1930 and to surrender its air bases at Shuaiba and Habbaniya. With the adherence of Pakistan in September and of Iran in October 1955, the so-called Baghdad Pact was completed: a defensive cordon now existed along the southern fringe of the USSR.

CONSEQUENCES OF THE SUEZ CRISIS

The outbreak of hostilities between Israel and Egypt on 29 October 1956, and the armed intervention of British and French forces against Egypt (31 October–6 November) led to a delicate situation in Iraq, where strong elements were still opposed to all connections with the Western Powers. Iraq, indeed, broke off diplomatic relations with France on 9 November and announced that, for the immediate future at least, it could give no assurance of taking part in further sessions of the Council of the Baghdad Pact, if delegates from Britain were present.

The equivocal attitude of the Baghdad Government during the Suez crisis had provoked unrest in Iraq. Disturbances at Najaf and Mosul resulted in some loss of life. Student demonstrations against the Anglo-French intervention in Egypt and the Israeli campaign in Sinai led the Iraqi Government to close colleges and schools. Martial law, imposed on 31 October 1956, was not raised until 27 May 1957.

The tension born of the Suez crisis persisted for some time to come. President Dwight D. Eisenhower of the USA, concerned over the flow of Soviet arms to Syria and Egypt, sought permission from Congress to deploy US armed forces to defend nations exposed to danger from countries under the influence of international communism. He also secured authorization to disburse economic and military aid to the Middle East states prepared to co-operate with the West. This programme became known as the 'Eisenhower Doctrine'.

RELATIONS WITH SYRIA AND JORDAN

At the time of the Suez crisis there had been sharp tension between Iraq and Syria. Pumping-stations located inside Syria and belonging to the IPC were sabotaged in November 1956. Iraq consequently suffered a large financial loss through the interruption in the flow of oil to the Mediterranean coast. Not until March 1957 did Syria allow the IPC to begin the repair of the pipelines.

Since the Suez crisis of 1956 troops of Iraq and Syria had been stationed in Jordan as a precaution against an Israeli advance to the east. Iraq, in December 1956, announced that its troops would be withdrawn; the Syrian forces, however, still remained in Jordan. The fear that Syria might intervene in favour of the elements in Jordan opposed to King Hussein brought about further recriminations between Baghdad and Damascus. The danger of an acute crisis receded in April 1957, when the USA declared that the independence of Jordan was a matter of vital concern and underlined this statement by sending its Sixth Fleet to the eastern Mediterranean. In February 1958 King Faisal of Iraq and King Hussein of Jordan joined together in an abortive Arab Federation.

OVERTHROW OF THE MONARCHY

King Faisal II, together with the Crown Prince of Iraq and Gen. Nouri as-Said, were killed in the course of a *coup d'état* begun on 14 July 1958 by units of the Iraqi army. Iraq was now to become a republic. Power was placed in the hands of a Council of Sovereignty exercising presidential authority, and of a Cabinet led by Brig. Abd al-Karim Kassem, with the rank of Prime Minister.

A power struggle developed between the two main architects of the July *coup d'état*—Brig. (later Gen.) Kassem, the Prime Minister, and Col (later Field-Marshal) Abd as-Salam Muhammad Aref, the Deputy Prime Minister and Minister of the Interior. Col Aref was associated with the influential Baath Party and had shown himself to be a supporter of union between Iraq and the United Arab Republic (UAR—the union of Egypt and Syria). In September 1958 he was dismissed from his offices and, in November, was tried on a charge of plotting against the interests of Iraq. As reconstituted in February 1959 the new regime was more hostile to the UAR and inclined to favour a form of independent nationalism with left-wing tendencies.

Gen. Kassem announced the withdrawal of Iraq from the Baghdad Pact on 24 March 1959. Since the revolution of July 1958 Iraq's adherence to the Pact had been little more than nominal. One result of this withdrawal was the termination of the special agreement existing between Britain and Iraq since 1955 under the first article of the Baghdad Pact. On 31 March it was made known that the British Royal Air Force contingent at Habbaniya would be recalled.

PROBLEMS OF THE KASSEM REGIME

Earlier in 1959 the communist elements in Iraq had been refused representation in the Government. The communists operated through a number of professional organizations and also through the so-called People's Resistance Force. Communist elements had infiltrated into the armed forces of Iraq and into the civil service. Gen. Kassem now began to introduce measures to limit communist influence inside the Government and the administration of the country. In July 1959 fighting occurred at Kirkuk between the Kurds (supported by the People's Resistance Force) and the Turkomans, with the result that Kassem disbanded the People's Resistance Force. More important for the Government at Baghdad was the fact that, in March 1961, a considerable section of the Kurdish population in northern Iraq rose in rebellion under Mustafa Barzani, the President of the Kurdistan Democratic Party (KDP)—a party established in 1958 after the return of Barzani from an exile occasioned by an earlier unsuccessful revolt in 1946. The refusal of the central regime at Baghdad to grant the reiterated Kurdish demands for autonomous status had contributed greatly to bringing about the new insurrection. Mustafa Barzani in March 1961 proclaimed an independent Kurdish state. By September 1961 the rebels controlled some 250 miles of mountainous territory along the Iraq–Turkey and Iraq–Iran frontiers, from Zakho in the west to Sulaimaniya in the east. The Kurds were able to consolidate their hold over much of northern Iraq during the course of 1962. The Kurds used guerrilla tactics with much success to isolate and deprive the government garrisons in the north of supplies. By December 1963 Kurdish forces had advanced south towards the Khanaqin area and the main road linking Iraq with Iran. The government troops found themselves in fact confined to the larger towns such as Kirkuk, Sulaimaniya and Khanaqin. Negotiations for peace began near Sulaimaniya in January 1964 and led to a cease-fire on 10 February. The national claims of the Kurds were to be recognized in a new provisional constitution for Iraq. Moreover, a general amnesty would be granted by the Iraqi Government. The Kurdish tribes, however, refused to lay aside their arms until their political demands had been given practical effect. Despite the negotiation of this settlement it soon emerged that no final solution of the Kurdish problem was apparent.

FALL OF KASSEM

A military coup executed in Baghdad on 8 February 1963 overthrew the regime of Gen. Kassem, the General himself being captured and shot. The coup arose out of an alliance between nationalist army officers and the Baath Party. Col Aref was now raised to the office of President and a new Cabinet was created under Brig. Ahmad al-Bakr. The Baath Party, founded in 1941 (in Syria) and dedicated to the ideas of Arab unity, socialism and freedom, drew its main support from military elements, intellectuals and the middle classes. It was, however, divided in Iraq into a pro-Egyptian wing advocating union with the UAR and a more independent wing disinclined to accept authoritarian control from Egypt. The coup of February 1963 was followed by the arrest of pro-Kassem and communist elements, by mass trials and a number of executions, by confiscations of property and by a purge of the officer corps and of the civil service.

A number of efforts were made, during the years 1963–65, to further the cause of Arab unification, but agreements made between Syria and Iraq, and between Egypt, Syria and Iraq, had little practical effect.

MANOEUVRES OF THE BAATH PARTY

These same years saw in Iraq itself a conflict for control between the extremist and the more moderate Baath elements. At the end of September 1963 the extremists dominated the Baath Regional Council in Iraq. An international Baath conference held at Damascus in October 1963 strengthened the position of the extremists through its support of a federal union between Syria and Iraq and its approval of more radical social and economic policies. A further Baathist conference at Baghdad in November 1963 enabled the moderates to elect a new Baath Regional Council in Iraq with their own adherents in control. At this juncture the extremists attempted a *coup d'état*, in the course of which air force elements attacked the Presidential Palace and the Ministry of Defence.

On 18 November 1963 President Aref assumed full powers in Iraq, with the support of the armed forces, and a new Revolutionary Command was established at Baghdad. Sporadic fighting occurred between government troops and the pro-Baathist National Guard. A main factor in the sudden fall of the Baathists was the attitude of the professional officer class. Officers with communist, Kassemite or pro-Nasser sympathies, or with no strong political views, or of Kurdish origin, had all been removed from important commands and offices. The privileged position of the National Guard caused further resentment in the army. The protracted operations against the Kurds, the known dissensions within the Baathist ranks in Iraq and the intervention of Baath politicians from abroad in Iraqi affairs also contributed to discredit the extreme elements amongst the Baathists. On 20 November 1963 a new Cabinet was formed at Baghdad, consisting of officers, moderate Baathists, independents and non-party experts.

THE ARAB SOCIALIST UNION

On 14 July 1964 President Aref announced that all political parties would be merged in a new organization known as the 'Iraqi Arab Socialist Union'. At the same time it was revealed that all banks and insurance companies, together with 32 important industrial concerns, would undergo nationalization.

In July 1965 a number of pro-Nasser ministers resigned. At the beginning of September a new administration was installed with Brig. Aref Abd ar-Razzaq as Prime Minister. Abd ar-Razzaq, reputed to be pro-Nasser in his sympathies, attempted to seize full power in Iraq, but his attempted *coup d'état* failed and on 16 September he himself, together with some of his supporters, found refuge in Cairo. On 13 April 1966 President Abd as-Salam Aref was killed in a helicopter crash. His brother, Maj.-Gen. Abd ar-Rahman Aref, succeeded him as President with the approval of the Cabinet and of the National Defence Council. In late June Abd ar-Razzaq led a second abortive coup, which was foiled by the prompt action of President Aref.

KURDISH NATIONALISM

The war against the Kurds, halted only for a short while by the cease-fire of February 1964, dragged out its inconclusive course during 1964–66. Some of the fighting in December 1965 occurred close to the Iraq–Iran border, leading to a number of frontier violations which exacerbated tensions between the two states during the first half of 1966. In June 1966 Dr Abd al-Rahman al-Bazzaz, Iraq's Prime Minister since September 1965, formulated new proposals for a settlement of the conflict with the Kurds. Kurdish nationalism and language would receive legal recognition; the administration was to be decentralized, allowing the Kurds to run educational, health and municipal affairs in their own districts; the Kurds would have proportional representation in parliament and in the Cabinet and the various state services; the Kurdish armed forces (some 15,000 strong) were to be dissolved. Mustafa Barzani, the Kurdish leader, declared himself to be well disposed towards these proposals.

This entente was implemented only to a limited extent. The Cabinet formed in May 1967 contained Kurdish elements, and President Aref, after a visit to the north in late 1967, reaffirmed his intention to make available to the Kurds appointments of ministerial rank, to help with the rehabilitation of the war-affected areas in Kurdistan, and to work towards effective co-operation with the Kurds in the government of Iraq. This state of quiescence was, however, broken in the first half of 1968 by reports of dissension amongst the Kurds themselves, with open violence between the adherents of Mustafa Barzani and the supporters of Jalal Talabani, who had co-operated with the Government.

OIL DISPUTES AND THE JUNE WAR

Although the winter of 1966–67 brought an improvement in relations with Iran, it also witnessed a dispute between Syria and the IPC over alleged losses of revenue on oil from Iraq passing through Syria by pipeline. The flow of oil was halted for a time, and settlement was not reached until well into 1967.

When the Arab–Israeli war was renewed in June 1967, the movement of Iraqi oil was again affected. Problems connected with its production and export constituted a major preoccupation of the Baghdad Government during the period immediately following the war. Iraq had at the outset severed diplomatic relations with the USA and Britain after Arab charges that the two states had aided Israel in the war, and it also banned the export of oil to them. When, at the end of June, supplies of Iraqi oil began to be moved once more from the pipeline terminals on the Mediterranean, this embargo remained. In August Iraq, Syria and Lebanon resolved to allow the export of Iraqi oil to most of the countries of Europe, the United Kingdom being still subject, however, to the embargo.

Relations with the West improved slightly during the autumn and winter of 1967. The remaining oil embargoes were gradually removed, and in December Gen. Sabri led a military delegation to Paris. This was followed by President Aref's official visit to France in February 1968, and in April France agreed to supply Iraq with 54 *Mirage* aircraft over the period 1969–73. In May diplomatic relations with the United Kingdom were resumed.

THE 1968 COUP AND ITS AFTERMATH

Throughout the first half of 1968 the regime conspicuously lacked popular support, being commonly thought to be both corrupt and inefficient, and the sudden bloodless *coup d'état* of 17 July did not surprise many observers. Gen. Ahmad Hassan al-Bakr, a former Prime Minister, became President; the deposed

President Aref went into exile and his Prime Minister, Taher Yahya, was imprisoned on corruption charges. A new Government was soon dismissed by the President, who accused it of 'reactionary tendencies'. He then appointed himself Prime Minister and Commander-in-Chief of the Armed Forces.

During the second half of 1968 the internal political situation deteriorated steadily. By November there were frequent reports of a purge directed against opponents of the new regime, and freedom of verbal political comment seemed to have disappeared. A former Minister of Foreign Affairs, Dr Nasser al-Hani, was found murdered, and a distinguished former Prime Minister, Dr al-Bazzaz, and other members of former governments were arrested as 'counter-revolutionary leaders'; most were later sentenced to long terms of imprisonment. Open hostilities with the Kurds erupted in October 1968 for the first time since the June 1966 cease-fire, and continued on an extensive scale throughout the winter. Efforts by the Iraqi army and air force to enforce the writ of the Baghdad Government had little success; the regime claimed that the rebels were receiving aid from Iran and Israel. Fighting continued unabated through 1969, the Kurds demanding autonomy within the state and asking for UN mediation.

SETTLEMENT WITH THE KURDS

The most important event of 1970 was the settlement with the Kurds when, in March, a 15-article peace plan was announced by the Revolutionary Command Council (RCC) and the Kurdish leaders. The plan conceded that the Kurds should participate fully in government; that Kurdish officials should be appointed in areas inhabited by a Kurdish majority; that Kurdish should be the official language, along with Arabic, in Kurdish areas; that development of Kurdish areas should be implemented; and that the Provisional Constitution should be amended to incorporate the rights of the Kurds.

The agreement was generally accepted by the Kurdish community, and fighting ceased immediately. The war had been very expensive for Iraq and it had seriously delayed the national development programme. The Kurdish settlement, although not entirely satisfactory, did introduce an element of stability into life in Iraq and allowed a number of reforms to be initiated. In October 1970 the state of emergency, in operation almost continuously since July 1958, was lifted. Many political detainees, including former ministers, were released. Censorship of mail was abolished at the end of the year, having lasted for over 13 years, and a month later the censorship of foreign correspondents' cables was brought to an end after a similar period.

Kurdish unity was boosted in February 1971 by the decision of the Kurdish Revolutionary Party (KRP) to merge with the KDP, led by Masoud Barzani, and in July 1971 a new Provisional Constitution was announced which embodied many of the points contained in the 1970 settlement. The Kurds were directed by the Supreme Committee for Kurdish Affairs to surrender their arms by August 1971.

Evidence of unrest, however, was growing both in Kurdistan and in the Government itself. In July 1971 an attempted coup by army and air force officers was put down by the Government but dissatisfaction continued to be reported. The Kurds were beginning to show discontent with the delays in implementing the 1970 agreement. Their demand for participation in the RCC was refused and in September 1971 an attempt was made on Barzani's life.

THE CONTINUING KURDISH PROBLEM

During 1972, possibly because of increasing preoccupation with foreign affairs, dissension within the Government was less evident. Clashes with the Kurds, however, became more frequent and there was another plot to assassinate Barzani in July. The Baath Party's deteriorating relations with the Kurds brought a threat from the KDP to renew the civil war. One of the main Kurdish grievances was that the census agreed upon in 1970 had still not taken place. The two sides met to discuss their differences, the Kurdish side pointing to the unfulfilled provisions of the 1970 agreement and the Baath reiterating the various development projects carried out in Kurdish areas. In December 1972 divisions arose in the Kurdish ranks when it

was reported that a breakaway party was to be established in opposition to Barzani's party.

FOREIGN RELATIONS 1968–71

The more radical section of the Arab world had initially viewed the July 1968 coup with disfavour and the new regime was at pains to prove itself as militant an exponent of Arab nationalism as its predecessor. The regime gradually became an accepted member of the nationalist group, but there was some Arab criticism of its policies, notably the public hangings and their effect on world opinion.

Iraq adopted an uncompromising attitude to the Palestinian problem. All peace proposals—US, Egyptian and Jordanian—were rejected. In theory, total support was given to the Palestine liberation movement. However, despite a threat to the Jordanian Government at the beginning of September 1970 to intervene in Jordan on behalf of the Palestinian guerrillas, the Iraqi forces stationed there did not take part in the fighting. In January 1971 most of Iraq's 20,000 troops withdrew from both Jordan and Syria. In March it was reported in Cairo that Iraq's monthly contribution to the Palestine Liberation Army (PLA) had ceased. Iraq's attitude to Middle East peace proposals provoked a rift with Egypt even before President Nasser's death, and Iraq's contempt for the proposed Egypt-Libya-Syria federation, as well as for any negotiated settlement with Israel, preserved its isolation from Egypt and almost all the other Arab states. In July 1971 there were signs that Iraq wished to effect a degree of reconciliation, offering to co-operate again with the Arab states if they abandoned attempts to negotiate with Israel, but the renewal of hostilities between the Jordanian Government and the guerrillas prompted a deterioration in relations with Jordan. Iraq closed the border, demanded Jordan's expulsion from the League of Arab States (the Arab League) and proscribed its participation in the Eighth International Baghdad Fair.

Meanwhile, relations with Iran remained hostile. Iraq frequently accused the Iranian Government of assisting the Kurdish rebellion and in April 1969 the Shatt al-Arab waterway again caused a minor confrontation. Iraq had benefited from a 1937 treaty which gave it control of the waterway. Iran attempted to force a renegotiation of the treaty by illegally sending through vessels flying the Iranian flag. Being unwilling (or politically unable) to yield any of its sovereignty, and unable to challenge Iran militarily, Iraq was obliged to accept this situation. Iraq proposed referring the dispute to the International Court of Justice (ICJ) in The Hague, Netherlands, but Iran rejected the suggestion. Sporadic border skirmishes between the two sides' forces continued, and both Iran and Iraq accused each other of attempting to foment coups. Not surprisingly, the two countries were also divided on policy towards the Gulf states. Iraq severed diplomatic relations with Iran (and the United Kingdom) after Iran's seizure of the Tunb Islands in the Persian Gulf in November 1971.

Relations with the Western world, and the USA in particular, remained poor, and several people were arrested or expelled in late 1968, after having been accused of spying for the USA. Meanwhile, cordial relations with the Soviet Union remained the major factor influencing Iraq's foreign policy, particularly since the USSR was supplying the major portion of Iraq's military equipment.

THE PROBLEM OF OIL

In June 1972 Iraq nationalized the IPC's interests, and agreement on outstanding points of dispute was finally reached on 28 February 1973. The company agreed to settle Iraqi claims for retrospective royalties by paying £141m., and to waive its objections to Law No. 80 under which the North Rumaila fields were seized in 1961. The Government agreed to deliver a total of 15m. metric tons of crude petroleum from Kirkuk, to be loaded at Eastern Mediterranean ports, to the companies as compensation. The Mosul Petroleum Co agreed to relinquish all its assets without compensation, and the Basrah Petroleum Co—the only one of the group to remain operational in Iraq—undertook to increase output from 32m. tons in 1972 to 80m. tons in 1976. This agreement was regarded on the whole as a victory for the Iraqi Government, although the companies were by no means financially disadvantaged by it.

With the IPC dispute settled, Iraq showed its unwillingness to continue indefinitely with exporting oil on a barter basis to the Eastern bloc countries. The Government emphasized that it would press for a cash basis to future agreements.

FOREIGN RELATIONS 1972–73

The nationalization of the IPC brought expressions of approval from a number of countries, including Arab states and the USSR. The 15-year friendship treaty with the USSR, signed in March 1972, was ratified in July, and Iraq's relations with the Eastern bloc remained cordial. Despite this, the Government was well aware of the dangers of too close and too exclusive a relationship with the Soviet bloc. France was specifically identified as the Western country most favoured by the Arabs, and the President's fourth anniversary speech in July revealed that Iraq would not be unwilling to initiate friendly relations with Western countries. Although diplomatic relations with the USA remained severed, the USA established an 'interests section' in Baghdad.

CONSTITUTIONAL CHANGE

In July 1973 an abortive coup took place, led by the security chief, Nazim Kazzar, in which the Minister of Defence, Gen. Hammad Shehab, was killed. There was some speculation that the coup had been attempted by a civilian faction within the Baath Party in an attempt to eliminate President Bakr and the military faction. Consequences of the attempted coup included an amendment to the Constitution giving more power to the President, and the formation of a National Front between the Baath Party and the Iraqi Communist Party (ICP).

CLIMAX AND END OF KURDISH WAR

According to the agreement made between the Iraqi Government and the Kurds in March 1970, the deadline for implementation of the agreement was 11 March 1974. An uneasy peace between the Kurds and the Iraqis existed between those two dates. On expiry of the deadline, Saddam Hussain Takriti, the Vice-President of the RCC and the 'strong man' of the regime, announced the granting of autonomy to the Kurds. Barzani and his KDP felt that the Iraqi offer did not fulfil their demands for full government representation, which included membership of the RCC. A minority of Kurds, who belonged to Abd as-Satter Sharif's KRP welcomed the proposals, however. Barzani and his militia, the *peshmerga* ('those who confront death'), began armed resistance in north Iraq. In April 1974 the Iraqi Government replaced five Kurdish ministers known to support Barzani by five other Kurds who supported the government plan for giving the Kurds a measure of autonomy. Later in April the Iraqi Government appointed a Kurd, Taha Mohi ed-Din Marouf, as Vice-President of Iraq, but since he had long been a supporter of the Baghdad Government, it seemed unlikely that this would mollify the Kurds of the KDP.

By August 1974 the Kurdish war had reached a new level of intensity. The Government in Baghdad was directing large military resources against the *peshmerga*, and was deploying tanks, field guns and bombers. About 130,000 Kurds, mainly women, children and old men, took refuge in Iran. The *peshmerga* were able to continue their resistance in Iraq only with the help of arms and other supplies from Iran. When, therefore, an agreement to end their border dispute was signed by Iraq and Iran at the meeting of the Organization of the Petroleum Exporting Countries (OPEC) in Algiers on 6 March 1975, both countries also agreed to end 'infiltrations of a subversive character' and the Kurdish rebellion collapsed. Barzani felt that he could not continue his struggle without Iran's aid, and fled to Tehran. A cease-fire was arranged on 13 March and a series of amnesties granted to Kurds who had fled to Iran encouraged most of them to return to Iraq. By February 1976, however, it was reported that the KDP was secretly reorganizing inside Iraqi Kurdistan and preparing to resume its struggle. In March there were reports of clashes between Kurds and Iraqi security forces in the Rawanduz area, after Iraqi attempts to clear the frontier area with Iran and resettle Kurds in less sensitive areas of Iraq. A new political organization, the National Union of Kurdistan (NUK), was also established in Damascus quite separately from the KDP, which, in the opinion of the NUK,

had become discredited. Renewed Kurdish activity occurred in 1976 but was not serious enough to weaken the Iraqi claim that the Kurdish problem had been solved. Reconstruction and school-building was certainly undertaken in Kurdish areas in 1977, and in April 1977 the Iraqi authorities allowed 40,000 Kurds who had been compulsorily settled in the south in 1975 to return to their homes in the north. It was also decided in April 1977 by the Executive Council of the Kurdish Autonomous Region that Kurdish should become the official language to be used in all communications and by all government departments in the Kurdish Autonomous Region which had no connection with the central Government.

FOREIGN AFFAIRS 1973–76

At the outbreak of the October 1973 war between the Arabs and Israel, Iraq sent considerable land forces to the Syrian front and took advantage of Iran's offer to resume diplomatic relations. The Iraqi Government, however, had taken offence at President Anwar Sadat's failure to consult Iraq prior to the offensive, and, therefore, Iraqi forces were withdrawn from Syria as soon as the cease-fire entered effect, and Iraq boycotted the Arab League summit meeting in Algiers in November.

Relations deteriorated with Iran in the early months of 1974, when frontier fighting broke out; it was only after the appointment of a UN mediator in March that 'normal' relations on the frontier were restored, and they worsened again in August in spite of talks in İstanbul, Turkey, between Iraqi and Iranian diplomats. There were further border clashes in December 1974, and secret talks in İstanbul between the Iraqi and Iranian Ministers of Foreign Affairs in January 1975 failed to prevent the outbreak of fresh clashes in February. It was therefore something of a surprise when, at the OPEC meeting at Algiers in March 1975, it was announced that Saddam Hussain, Vice-President of the RCC, and the Shah of Iran had signed an agreement that 'completely eliminated the conflict between the two brotherly countries'. This agreement also ended the Kurdish war (see above), and was embodied in a treaty signed between the two countries in June 1975. The frontiers were defined on the basis of the Protocol of Constantinople of 1913 and the verbal agreement on frontiers of 1914. The Shatt al-Arab frontier was defined according to the Thalweg Line, which runs down the middle of the deepest shipping channel.

THE BAATH PARTY AND RELATIONS WITH SYRIA

Iraq was one of the many Arab states that were severely critical of the second interim disengagement agreement signed between Egypt and Israel in September 1975. Iraqi reaction to the agreement was similar to that of Syria, but this condemnation was perhaps the only issue upon which the two countries agreed between 1975 and 1978. Rivalry between the two wings of the Baath party in Baghdad and Damascus, and a dispute over the sharing of the water from the Euphrates, were just two areas of contention. In February 1976 Iraq was reported to be diverting much of its oil from pipelines to the Mediterranean to terminals near Basra, thus depriving Syria of valuable pipeline revenues. Iraq was also very critical of Syria's intervention in Lebanon. In addition, Syrian agents were blamed for violence which took place in the Shi'a holy cities of Najaf and Karbala in February 1977. Relations with Syria deteriorated even further in late 1977, and Iraq became somewhat isolated after President Sadat of Egypt's peace initiative in visiting Jerusalem in November 1977. At the Tripoli Conference, summoned by the states opposed to President Sadat's approach, Iraq advocated a specific rejection of UN Security Council Resolution 242 (see Documents on Palestine, p. 57). The stand taken by the other participants—Syria, Libya, the People's Democratic Republic of Yemen (PDRY), Algeria and the Palestine Liberation Organization (PLO)—was considered too moderate by Iraq, which abandoned the conference. Iraq subsequently boycotted the Algiers conference of 'rejectionist' states in February 1978, hoping, unsuccessfully, to form its own 'steadfastness and liberation front' at a Baghdad conference.

NEW ALIGNMENTS

Iraq opposed the Camp David agreements made between Egypt and Israel in September 1978, but, continuing its policy of boycott, it did not attend the Damascus Arab League summit which immediately followed the Camp David agreements. In October, however, President Hafiz al-Assad of Syria visited Baghdad and, as a result, Iraq and Syria signed a charter outlining plans for political and economic union between the two countries. Old rivalries and animosities were set aside in an effort to form a political and military power which would constitute a sizeable counterweight to Egypt in Middle Eastern affairs. In November Iraq successfully convened a pan-Arab summit which threatened sanctions against Egypt if a peace treaty with Israel should be signed, and in March 1979, when the peace treaty became a fact, Baghdad was the venue for the meeting of the Arab ministers of foreign and economic affairs which resolved to put into practice the threats made to Egypt in the previous November.

The plans for complete political and economic union of Iraq and Syria were pursued with enthusiasm but little real practical application by both countries until July 1979. On 16 July 1979 Saddam Hussain replaced Ahmad Hassan al-Bakr as President of Iraq and Chairman of the RCC. A few days later, an attempted coup was reported, and several members of the RCC were sentenced to death for their alleged part in the plot. Saddam Hussain believed Syria to be implicated, in spite of Syrian denials, and the newly-formed alliance foundered. Another aspect of this political unrest in Iraq was the dissolution of the alliance between the Baath Party and the ICP. In the summer of 1978 21 army personnel were executed for conducting political activity in the armed forces. Relations with the communists continued to deteriorate; they withdrew from the National Progressive Front in March 1979, and in early 1980 President Saddam Hussain referred to them in a speech as 'a rotten, atheistic, yellow storm which has plagued Iraq'. This led to a decrease in dependence on the USSR and to tentative moves to improve relations with the West. Saddam Hussain joined in the general Arab condemnation of the Soviet invasion of Afghanistan at the end of 1979.

In February 1980 President Saddam Hussain announced his 'National Charter', which reaffirmed the principles of non-alignment, rejecting 'the existence of foreign armies, military forces, troops and bases in the Arab Homeland', and made a plea for Arab solidarity. With President Sadat of Egypt compromised by his *rapprochement* with Israel, Saddam Hussain saw himself in a position of virtual pre-eminence in the Arab world and, with the Non-aligned Summit due to take place in Baghdad in 1982, he would be in a position to present himself as the responsible leader of the non-aligned world.

Domestically, Saddam Hussain was engaged in restoring parliamentary government to Iraq. The intention had been announced some years earlier, but on 16 March 1980 laws were adopted for the election of an Iraqi National Assembly of 250 deputies for a four-year session, and also for a Legislative Council for the Autonomous Region of Kurdistan, consisting of 50 members elected for a three-year term. Elections took place on 20 June 1980, with deputies elected by a direct, free and secret ballot. The first session of the National Assembly opened on 30 June, and one of the deputy premiers, Naim Haddad, was elected Chairman and Speaker. Elections to a 50-member Kurdish Legislative Council took place in September 1980.

WAR WITH IRAN

Although the 1975 peace agreement with Iran had virtually ended the Kurdish rebellion, Iraq was dissatisfied and wanted a return to the Shatt al-Arab boundary whereby it controlled the whole waterway, and also the withdrawal of Iranian forces from Abu Musa and Tunb Islands, which Iran had occupied in 1971. Conflict also became evident after the Iranian Revolution over Arab demands for autonomy in Iran's Khuzestan (termed 'Arabistan' by Arabs), which Iran accused Iraq of encouraging. In addition, Iraq's Sunni leadership was suspicious of Shi'ite Iran and fearful that the Islamic Revolution in Iran might spread to its own Shi'ites, who are in the majority in Iraq. Border fighting between Iran and Iraq occurred frequently as 1980 progressed, and open warfare began on 22 September when Iraqi forces advanced into Iran along a 480-km front. Iran had ignored Iraqi diplomatic efforts demanding the withdrawal of Iranian forces from Zain ul-Qos on the border. Iraq maintained that this territory should have been returned by Iran

under the 1975 agreement. Iraq therefore abrogated the Shatt al-Arab agreement on 16 September.

Most commentators agree that Saddam Hussain's real intention when he invaded Iran was to topple the Islamic revolutionary regime. Resistance was fiercer than he expected, however, and stalemate was soon reached along the invasion front, while various international peace missions sought in vain for a solution. In the spring of 1982 Iranian forces launched successful counter-offensives, one in the region of Dezful in March, and another in April which resulted in the recapture of Khorramshahr by the Iranians in May.

By late June 1982 Saddam Hussain had to acknowledge that the invasion of Iran had been a failure, and he arranged for the complete withdrawal of Iraqi troops from Iranian territory. In July the Iranian army crossed into Iraq, giving rise to the heaviest fighting of the war thus far.

INTERNAL OPPOSITION TO SADDAM HUSSAIN

As well as the deteriorating military situation, Saddam Hussain was confronted by a number of other threats to his position from within Iraq. The 'Iraqi Front of Revolutionary, Islamic and National Forces', consisting of Kurds, exiled Shi'ites and disaffected Baath party members, formed in 1981 with the backing of Syria—whose President Assad was as anxious as Ayatollah Khomeini in Iran to see the downfall of Saddam Hussain, his Baathist rival. In northern Iraq, Kurdish rebels were becoming active again and there existed the possibility that Iraq's majority Shi'ite community (55% of the population) would turn against the Sunnis (the sect of the Iraqi leadership). However, the bulk of Iraq's Shi'ites seemed to distrust the harsh fundamentalism of Khomeini's Iran. Against this background, Saddam Hussain was re-elected Chairman of the RCC and regional secretary of the Arab Baath Socialist Party, and in July 1982, having purged his administration, was apparently more firmly in control than ever.

In November 1982 new opposition arose from the Supreme Council of Iraqi Opposition Groups, under the leadership of an exiled Shi'ite leader, Hojatoleslam Muhammad Baqir Hakim, in Tehran. However, as the war with Iran degenerated into a conflict of attrition after the first Iranian advance into Iraq, the severe burden that it placed upon the country's economy emerged as the most critical concern for Saddam Hussain in 1983. Petroleum revenues had been slashed by almost 75% following the destruction of Iraq's Gulf terminals, the closure of the pipeline across hostile Syria and the decline in oil prices. Iraq was searching for ways to avoid defaulting on payments for foreign construction contracts and was already borrowing money from friendly Gulf states.

In October 1983 there were rumours of an attempted coup in Baghdad, led by the recently dismissed head of intelligence, Barzan at-Takriti (the President's half-brother), and a number of senior army officers who were later reported to have been executed.

An abiding problem for Iraqi governments has been the question of Kurdish autonomy within Iraq. The drain on military and financial resources resulting from efforts to contain Kurdish secessionist forces was of particular significance at this time, since costly equipment and manpower was being diverted from critical areas in the war with Iran. Unable to fight wars on two fronts, Saddam Hussain sought an accommodation with the Kurds. A series of talks with Jalal Talabani, leader of the Patriotic Union of Kurdistan (PUK) and of an estimated 40,000 Kurdish soldiers, began in December 1983, after a cease-fire was agreed. The PUK demanded the release of 49 Kurdish political prisoners, the return of 8,000 Kurdish families, moved from Kurdistan to southern Iraq, and the extension of the Kurdish autonomous area to include the oil town of Kirkuk. The talks could have provided only a partial solution, as they did not include the KDP, which sought to further the cause of Kurdish autonomy by siding with Iran (and which was antipathetic towards the PUK). Thoughts of a government of national unity, including the PUK and the ICP, were short-lived. Saddam Hussain's attitude changed, possibly prompted by the greater international support for Iraq which was forthcoming in the first half of 1984, and the talks broke down in May. The dialogue between the two sides was resumed and continued sporadically, with Saddam Hussain trying to persuade the PUK to join the National Progressive Front. To win its support, Saddam Hussain would have had to make major concessions to the PUK, such as granting Kurdish control of Kirkuk province, where Iraq's main oilfields are situated, and giving the Kurds a sizeable fixed share of national oil revenues, and this he was unlikely to do. Negotiations on Kurdish autonomy collapsed again in January 1985 and fighting broke out in Kurdistan between PUK guerrillas and government troops after a 14-month cease-fire. The PUK blamed the Government's continued persecution and execution of Kurds; its refusal to include consideration of the one-third of Kurdistan containing the Kirkuk oilfields in autonomy talks; and an agreement with Turkey to act jointly to quell Kurdish resistance, which had been made in October 1984. The PUK then rejected the offer of an amnesty for Saddam Hussain's political opponents at home and abroad in February, and fighting continued.

THE IRAN–IRAQ WAR, OCTOBER 1983–DECEMBER 1984

Beginning in October 1983, Iran launched a series of attacks across its northern border with Iraq. About 700 sq km of Iraqi territory were gained, threatening the last outlet for Iraqi exports of petroleum through the Kirkuk pipeline. Iraq intensified its missile attacks and bombing raids against Iranian towns and petroleum installations. During the autumn of 1983 Iraq took delivery of five French-built *Super Etendard* fighter aircraft. With these, and with the *Exocet* missiles already in its possession, Iraq threatened to destroy Iran's petroleum export industry, centred on the Kharg Island oil terminal in the Gulf. (In fact, Iraq did not use the *Super Etendards* and *Exocet* missiles in tandem until the end of March 1984 in the Gulf.) Iran responded by promising to make the Gulf impassable to all traffic (including exports of one-sixth of the West's petroleum requirements) by blocking the Strait of Hormuz, if Iraqi military action made it impossible for Iran to export its own petroleum by that route.

Despite approaches from the UN and various governments (Egypt, Saudi Arabia and Syria among them), Iran refused to negotiate with Iraq and was adamant that nothing less than the removal of the regime of Saddam Hussain, the withdrawal of Iraqi troops from Iranian territory and the agreement to pay reparations for war damages could bring hostilities to an end.

In August 1982 Iraq declared a maritime exclusion zone in the Gulf, extending from the Khor Abdullah channel, at the mouth of the Shatt al-Arab waterway, to a point south of the Iranian port of Bushehr. This zone included the Kharg Island oil terminal. Iraq carried out sporadic attacks on shipping (not only tankers) making for Kharg or returning from it, or fired indiscriminately on ships well outside the zone. The aim was to make the export of petroleum from Iran as difficult and expensive as possible and, by the threat of military action, to deter shipping from using Iranian ports, thus starving Iran of vital oil revenues. These tactics succeeded to a limited extent. Rates of insurance for shipping using the Gulf rose dramatically, and Japan, the largest customer for Iranian oil, briefly ordered its tankers not to use Iranian ports in mid-1984. Iraq refrained, however, from implementing its threat to attack Kharg Island itself and tankers loading there until May 1984. When the attack came, it was not immediately followed up, and the sequence of isolated attacks of limited effectiveness seemed to be continuing. The dangers of the war's spreading to other Gulf states were shown when Iran retaliated by attacking Saudi Arabian and Kuwaiti tankers, and tankers using oil terminals belonging to those countries. During 1984 the conviction grew that neither Iran nor Iraq possessed the capability to give effect to its worst threats.

Iraq certainly had no shortage of financial and military supporters. Egypt is estimated to have supplied military equipment and spare parts worth more than US $2,000m.; according to *The Washington Post*, the People's Republic of China sold arms to Iraq worth $3,100m. between 1981 and 1985 (compared with sales to Iran, over the same period, worth $575m.); Brazil and Chile sold weapons to Iraq; the USSR (previously officially neutral in the war) increased its aid, following a *rapprochement* with Iraq in March 1984, and had already sold SS-12 missiles to Iraq; and the USA supplied helicopters and other heavy military equipment, though it remained officially neutral. (Both the USA and the USSR also sold arms to Iran.) Saudi Arabia and Kuwait supported Iraq with loans and the revenue from sales of up to 310,000 barrels per day (b/d) of petroleum (250,000 b/d from the neutral zone and the remainder from Saudi Arabia), sold on Iraq's behalf.

In February 1984 Iran launched an offensive in the marshlands around Majnoon Island, the site of rich oilfields in southern Iraq, near the confluence of the Tigris and Euphrates rivers. Iraq failed to regain control of this territory, and was condemned for using mustard gas in the fighting. Iraq subsequently established extensive and formidable defences, including a system of dams and embankments, along the southern front, near Basra, in anticipation of a possibly decisive offensive by Iran, which massed some 500,000 men there.

In 1984 the balance of military power moved in Iraq's favour, and the USA and the USSR, both officially neutral in the war with Iran, provided aid. The USSR increased its military aid following a *rapprochement* in March between the two Governments, precipitated by Iran's anti-Soviet stance, and was responsible for supplying an estimated two-thirds of Iraq's total armaments and much of its ammunition. At the end of 1987 it was estimated that the USSR had supplied Iraq with military aid worth US $10,000m. since lifting a ban on arms sales in 1982. The USA assisted Iraq with the financing of crucial oil export pipeline projects and with an increasing allocation of commodity credits. Iraq and the USA re-established full diplomatic relations in November 1984, more than 17 years after they had been broken off by Iraq following the Arab–Israeli war of 1967.

Iraq had a substantial advantage in the strength of its air force. At the end of 1984 Iraq had 580 combat aircraft and 130 armed helicopters, while Iran had 110 combat aircraft, only 50 to 60 of which were thought to be operational. On the ground, Iraq's tank force was superior in numbers and sophistication.

THE IRAN–IRAQ WAR, 1985–86

A resumption in December 1984 of Iraqi attacks on shipping in the Gulf, in particular on oil tankers using the terminal at Kharg Island caused a sharp increase in hull insurance rates. Iran's oil exports fell to a record low level in January 1985 as a result of Iraqi action but, after another lull in military activity, in a pattern which became familiar during the next four years, insurance rates were reduced and custom returned. Attacks on shipping continued but Iraq failed decisively to exploit its superiority in the air. The Kharg Island oil terminal remained operational and largely undamaged for much of 1985 and Iran was quite successful in circumventing Iraqi attempts to debilitate its oil export industry. It consistently offered oil at discount and rebate deals to attract customers deterred by the high cost of war insurance, and in February established a makeshift floating export terminal at Sirri Island, militarily a much less exposed location (journeys to which commanded lower rates of insurance), 800 km (500 miles) south-east of Kharg, from where it received its oil by tanker shuttle.

In March Iran committed an estimated 50,000 troops to an offensive on the southern front in the region of the Hawizah marshes, east of the Tigris. Iranian forces succeeded in crossing the Tigris and for a time closed the main road connecting Baghdad and Basra before being repulsed. Iraq was again accused of using chemical weapons during this engagement.

In June 1984 the UN engineered the suspension by Iran and Iraq of attacks on civilian targets. However, in March 1985, with the war on the ground at a stalemate, Iraq resorted to air raids on Iranian towns and declared Iranian airspace a war zone. Saddam Hussain's stated intention was to carry the war to every part of Iran until Ayatollah Khomeini should decide to come to the negotiating table. The first Iraqi air raid on Tehran in four years took place in March. Although Iraq initially identified its targets as industrial, government and military installations only, thousands of civilians inevitably were killed as Iraqi aircraft attacked more than 30 Iranian towns with bombs, missiles and shellfire. Iran retaliated with shelling and air raids of its own on Iraqi economic, industrial and civilian targets, and with ground-based missile attacks on Baghdad itself. In this instance, Iraq was taking full advantage of its military superiority. In March King Hussein of Jordan and President Mubarak of Egypt unexpectedly visited Baghdad to show their support for Saddam Hussain, despite the fact that full diplomatic relations had not existed between Egypt and Iraq since Egypt's signing of the peace treaty with Israel in 1979.

The UN Secretary-General, Javier Pérez de Cuéllar, visited both Tehran and Baghdad in April to try to establish a basis for peace negotiations. Iraq made it clear that it was interested only in a permanent cease-fire and immediate peace negotiations; while Iran, though placing less official emphasis on the removal of Saddam Hussain's regime as a pre-condition of peace, accepted that, if he acquiesced in the other conditions, including the payment of reparations calculated by Iran at US $350,000m. in March 1985, he would fall anyway.

Twice during 1985 (in April and June) President Saddam Hussain ordered a suspension of air raids on Iranian cities, as an inducement to Iran to begin peace negotiations. On both occasions Iran ignored the gesture and Iraqi air raids were resumed.

In response to a joint Irano-Libyan strategic alliance which was becoming more open in character, Iraq withdrew its diplomatic mission from Tripoli in June 1985 and asked the Libyans to withdraw theirs from Baghdad. Iraq had severed its diplomatic links with Libya in late 1980, accusing Col Qaddafi of assisting Iran in the war, but limited diplomatic contact was restored and Libya was said to have had diplomatic representatives in Baghdad since 1984.

Until mid-1985 Iraq had failed to launch attacks against the main Iranian oil export terminal on Kharg Island of sufficient frequency or intensity seriously to threaten the continuation of oil exports. In August, however, Iraq made the first of a concentrated series of raids on Kharg, causing a reduction in Iranian oil exports from 1.2m. b/d–1.5m. b/d, in the months leading up to the raids, to less than 1m. b/d in September. Exports from Kharg were temporarily halted during the latter half of September. During October–December the raids became progressively less frequent and less damaging in their effect, and, by dint of rapid repairs and the taking up of Kharg's ample spare capacity, the Iranian Ministry of Oil was able to claim in October, with little exaggeration, that exports of oil had risen to 1.7m. b/d. Between August and the end of 1985 some 60 attacks on Kharg Island were reported. Despite Iran's earlier success in minimizing the effect of Iraqi raids and in developing alternative means of exporting oil (such as the floating terminal at Sirri Island), by the end of 1985 exports from Kharg had reportedly been reduced to a trickle compared with its 6.5m. b d capacity, and Iraq had turned its attention to the tankers shuttling oil to Sirri Island for transhipment.

In February 1986 Iraq announced an expansion of the area of the Gulf from which it would try to exclude Iranian shipping. Previously confined to the waters around Iran's Gulf ports, the area was broadened to include the coast of Kuwait. Attacks on tankers and other commercial vessels in the Gulf were intensified by both sides during 1986, and they totalled 105 during the year. In the first half of 1986 Iraq continued to attack Kharg Island and tankers shuttling oil to Sirri Island, and in August an Iraqi raid demonstrated that the Sirri export facility itself was vulnerable to attack, bringing about an immediate doubling of insurance rates for vessels travelling there. Iran was forced to transfer more of its oil export operations to the remoter floating terminal at Larak Island, at the mouth of the Gulf, but this, too, proved accessible to Iraqi aircraft, employing mid-air refuelling facilities, and was itself attacked in November. Loading berths, refining facilities, and several tankers docked at Iran's Lavan Island oil terminal, were destroyed or badly damaged by an Iraqi raid in September 1986.

In the land war, the next important engagements, in terms of land gained, occurred in 1986, when, on 9 February, Iran launched the Wal-Fajr (Dawn) 8 offensive. Some 85,000 Iranian troops (leaving about 400,000 uncommitted on the southern front) crossed the Shatt al-Arab waterway and, on 11 February, occupied the disused Iraqi oil port of Faw, on the Persian Gulf, and, according to Iran, about 800 sq km of the Faw peninsula. From this position, within sight of the Kuwaiti island of Bubiyan, commanding the Khor Abdullah channel between the Faw peninsula and the island, Iran threatened Iraq's only access to the Gulf and, if it could extend the offensive to the north-west, Iraq's Umm Qasr naval base. However, the marsh and then desert terrain to the west was not conducive to further

Iranian gains, and the position on the Faw peninsula was defensible only with difficulty, given the problem of maintaining supply lines across the Shatt al-Arab. At the same time as the attack upon Faw, Iran began a complementary operation along the Faw–Basra road to divert Iraqi forces. When Iraq launched a counter-offensive on Faw in mid-February, Iran opened up a second front in Iraqi Kurdistan, hundreds of miles to the north, with the Wal-Fajr 9 offensive. Iranian forces drove Iraqi and counter-revolutionary Iranian Kurds out of some 40 villages in the area of Sulaimaniya.

At the end of February 1986 the UN Security Council, while urging for a cease-fire, effectively accused Iraq of starting the war. Despite heavy fighting, Iraq failed to dislodge an estimated 30,000 Iranian troops from in and around Faw. The proximity of Kuwaiti territory to the hostilities notwithstanding, Iran promised not to involve Kuwait in the war, provided that it did not allow Iraq the use of its territory (part of which, Bubiyan Island, is claimed by Iraq) for military purposes.

The Faw offensive prompted a change in tactics by Iraq. In May 1986 Iraq made its first armed incursions into Iran since withdrawing its forces from Iranian territory in 1982. An area of about 150 sq km of Iranian land was occupied, including the deserted town of Mehran (about 160 km east of Baghdad), but Iran recaptured the town in July and forced the Iraqis back across the border. Also in May, Iraqi aircraft raided Tehran for the first time since June 1985, signalling a new wave of reciprocal attacks on urban and industrial targets in Iran and Iraq that continued for the remainder of 1986. For perhaps the first time during the war, Iraq took full advantage of its aerial superiority to damage Iran's industry and to limit its oil production, with numerous attacks on oil installations and tankers shuttling oil to floating terminals near the mouth of the Gulf.

In July the ruling Arab Baath Socialist Party held an extraordinary regional conference, the first since June 1982. Three new members were elected to the party's Regional Command, increasing its number to 17. Naim Haddad, who had been a member of the Regional Command and of the ruling RCC since their formation in 1968, was not re-elected to the Regional Command and was subsequently removed from the RCC, on which he was replaced by Sa'adoun Hammadi, the Chairman, or Speaker, of the National Assembly. These changes effectively strengthened Saddam Hussain's position as leader of the party.

A meeting between the Ministers of Foreign Affairs of Iraq and Syria, scheduled for June 1986, which was heralded as the beginning of a reconciliation between the two countries, was cancelled at the last minute by President Assad of Syria. However, rumours of a *rapprochement* were revived by reports that President Hussain and President Assad had met in secret in Jordan in April 1987. Ministers from both countries met on several occasions in the ensuing weeks, and the reopening of the oil pipeline from Haditha, in Iraq, to the Syrian port of Banias, was discussed. There were, however, no public statements from either side to confirm the improvement in relations.

THE IRAN–IRAQ WAR, 1987

From mid-1986 onwards, Iran was reported to be reinforcing its army at numerous points along the Iraqi border. When an Iranian offensive (Karbala-4: after the holy Shi'ite city in Iraq) was launched on 24 December, it came, as anticipated, in the region of Basra, but failed to penetrate Iraqi defences on four islands in the Shatt al-Arab waterway. On 8 January 1987 a two-pronged attack (Karbala-5) was launched towards Basra. Iranian forces, attacking from the east, established a bridgehead inside Iraq, between the Shatt al-Arab, to the west, and the artificial water barrier, Fish Lake, to the east, and slowly advanced towards Basra, sustaining heavy casualties; while an assault from the south-east secured a group of islands in the Shatt al-Arab. (On 13 January Iran mounted the Karbala-6 offensive in north-east Iraq.) By mid-February Iranian forces from the east had advanced to within about 10 km of Basra but no further gains were made and the Karbala-5 offensive was officially terminated at the end of the month.

In January 1987, at the height of the Karbala-5 offensive, President Hussain of Iraq offered Iran a cease-fire and peace negotiations. Iran rejected the offer, and in the following months demonstrated its ability to launch attacks at several points from one end to the other of the 1,200-km war front. The Karbala-7 offensive, in March, penetrated north-eastern Iraqi territory to a depth of about 20 km in the Gerdmand heights, near Rawanduz, only some 100 km from Iraq's largest oilfields, at Kirkuk. In April, on the southern front, Iran launched the Karbala-8 offensive from the salient, 10 km east of Basra, which had been secured in Karbala-5. The Iranians claimed that the attack established a new front line about 1 km nearer Basra, west of the artificial Twin Canals water barrier, though Iraq claimed that it had been repulsed. At the same time, another offensive, Karbala-9, was mounted in the central sector of the war front, from near the Iranian border town of Qasr-e-Shirin.

Iraq announced a two-week moratorium on its bombing of Iranian towns and cities on 18 February 1987, which Iran agreed to observe in respect of its artillery and missile bombardment of Iraqi cities. In April, following new Iranian attacks east of Basra, and well after the initially stipulated two-week period had expired, Iraq said that it was no longer bound by the unofficial agreement. However, Iraqi air raids did not resume in earnest until May.

Iraq continued to attack tankers shuttling Iranian oil from Kharg Island to the floating terminals at Sirri and Larak islands during the first half of 1986. However, an apparently accidental attack in the Gulf by an Iraqi *Mirage* F-1 fighter plane on the frigate USS *Stark*, part of the US naval force, which had been deployed in the Gulf to protect shipping, created a crisis in Iraqi–US relations. The fighter fired two *Exocet* missiles at the *Stark*, only one of which exploded, killing 37 US sailors. Iraq apologized for the 'error' and desisted from attacks on tankers for the next five weeks. Although it is plausible that the attack was the result of error and inexperience on the part of the Iraqi pilot, Iraq had recently had occasion to record its displeasure at US policy regarding the war. In November 1986 it had emerged that the USA, contrary to its official policy of neutrality, and of discouraging sales of arms to Iran by other countries, had made three shipments of weapons and military spare parts to the Islamic Republic since September 1985. Then, in December, it was reported in *The Washington Post* that the USA had been supplying Iraq with detailed intelligence information for at least two years, to assist it in the war with Iran. In particular, the USA's Central Intelligence Agency (CIA) was said to have provided satellite reconnaissance data, to assist Iraq in its raids on Iranian oil installations and power plants. One month later, US intelligence sources revealed that the USA had, in fact, provided both Iran and Iraq with deliberately misleading or inaccurate information. The explanation of the apparent contradictions in US policy seemed to be that the USA had been trying to engineer a stalemate in the Iran–Iraq War, to prevent either side from gaining a decisive advantage. Iraq subsequently attributed the loss of the disused oil port of Faw in February 1986 to false intelligence reports supplied by the USA.

Tension in the Gulf escalated in May 1987 after the USA's decision to accede to a request from Kuwait for 11 Kuwaiti tankers to be re-registered under the US flag, entitling them to US naval protection. Apart from the financial aid it gave Iraq, Kuwait was a transit point for goods (including military equipment) destined for Iraq, and for exports of oil sold on Iraq's behalf. Iran warned Kuwait on several occasions of the dire consequences of its continued support for Iraq, and between October 1986 and April 1987 15 ships bound to or from Kuwait were attacked in the Gulf by Iran, and several Kuwaiti cargoes were seized. After the USA made its navy available to escort reregistered Kuwaiti tankers through the Gulf, Iran announced that it would not hesitate to sink US warships if provoked.

The possibility of a confrontation between the USA and Iran resulted in a rare display of unanimity in the UN Security Council, which, on 20 July 1987, adopted a resolution (No. 598) urging an immediate cease-fire in the Iran–Iraq War; the withdrawal of all forces to internationally recognized boundaries; and the co-operation of Iran and Iraq in mediation efforts to achieve a peace settlement. Iraq agreed to abide by the terms of the resolution if Iran did so. Iran said that the Resolution was 'unjust', and criticized it for failing to identify Iraq as the original aggressor in the war. Moreover, it maintained that the belligerent US naval presence in the Gulf, effectively in support of Iraq, rendered the Resolution null and void. However, by mid-September Iran had still not delivered an unequivocal response to the Resolution. Iraq, meanwhile, had halted its attacks on tankers in the Gulf in mid-July and Iran had exploited the lull by raising the level of its oil production and exports.

THE UN FAILS TO ENFORCE RESOLUTION 598

Contrary to advice from Western governments, Iraq resumed attacks on Iranian oil installations and industrial targets, and on tankers in the Gulf transporting Iranian oil, on 29 August 1987. Resolution 598 made provision for unspecified sanctions in the event of the failure of either or both sides to comply with its terms. However, the resumption of Iraqi attacks weakened the UN's position in its attempts to secure a cease-fire through diplomacy, and made it less likely that the USSR could be persuaded to agree to the imposition of an arms embargo, whether against Iran alone or against both protagonists.

During the remainder of the year the UN Secretary-General, Javier Pérez de Cuéllar, sought a cease-fire formula which would be acceptable to Iran. His visit to the Gulf region, for talks in Iran and Iraq, between 11 and 15 September 1987, was preceded by an intensification of Iraqi attacks on Iranian economic targets. In Tehran, Iranian leaders told Pérez de Cuéllar that they supported the provision in Resolution 598 for the establishment of an 'impartial body' to apportion responsibility for starting the war, but that Iraq's guilt in this matter had to be established before Iran would observe a cease-fire. For its part, Iraq was prepared to accept the ruling of a judicial body in determining responsibility for the war but refused to countenance any deviation from the original terms of Resolution 598, which stated that a formal cease-fire should precede the establishment of such a body.

Signs of an apparent willingness on Iran's part to modify its stand on Resolution 598 forestalled attempts by the USA, the United Kingdom and France to promote their proposal of an arms embargo against Iran, and also pre-empted the adoption of diplomatic or other sanctions by the Arab League, at its meeting in Tunis on 20 September 1987. An extraordinary session of the Arab League in Amman, Jordan, from 8–11 November, produced a final communiqué which unanimously condemned Iran for prolonging the war with Iraq and for its occupation of Arab (i.e. Iraqi) territory, and urged Iran to implement Resolution 598 without pre-conditions.

Following the summit meeting in Amman, the Iraqi Government, in common with a number of other Arab countries, re-established diplomatic relations with Egypt. During the summit, a meeting had taken place between Saddam Hussain and President Assad, reviving speculation of a *rapprochement* between Iraq and Syria, which had supported Iran in war. President Assad, however, obstructed the League's adoption of an Iraqi proposal that member states should sever their diplomatic links with Iran, and Syria subsequently averred that its good relations with Iran were unimpaired.

On 3 November 1987 the Iranian Deputy Minister of Foreign Affairs, Muhammad Javad Larijani, stated that Iran would observe a cease-fire if the UN Security Council were to identify Iraq as the aggressor in the Iran–Iraq War. The USA and the United Kingdom interpreted this announcement as a device to forestall a change in Soviet policy on the question of an arms embargo. The USSR had persistently refused to consider an embargo, and argued that Iran should be allowed more time in which to accept Resolution 598. At the beginning of December, during further discussions with Pérez de Cuéllar in New York, Larijani made the additional condition that Iraq should agree to pay war reparations prior to the introduction of a cease-fire, and cited Iraqi intransigence and the presence of US ships in the Gulf as the principal obstacles to peace.

On 22 December the USSR itself proposed discussions within the Security Council to consider a mandatory prohibition on the sale of arms to Iran, which would take place at the same time as discussions on the introduction of an international naval force in the Gulf, under the control of the UN, to replace the various national forces patrolling the region. Although all the five permanent members of the Security Council subsequently agreed on the need for further measures to be taken to ensure the compliance of both combatants with Resolution 598, the USSR's insistence on the withdrawal of foreign navies followed by the deployment of a UN naval force in the Gulf, and the

USA's growing military involvement in the area during 1988, prevented the adoption of an arms embargo.

CEASE-FIRE IN THE IRAN–IRAQ WAR

During the first half of 1988 Iraq regained much of the territory which it had lost to Iran in previous years, taking advantage of Iranian military inefficiency and the confused aims of a divided Iranian leadership. However, the world was taken by surprise in July 1988 when, after 12 months of prevarication, Iran agreed, unconditionally, to accept Resolution 598.

In January 1988 Iran and Iraq rebuffed a Syrian initiative to engineer a diplomatic end to the war by opening a dialogue between Iran and the Gulf states. After a lull of 10 days, Iraq resumed the so-called 'tanker war', accusing Syria of violating Arab solidarity against Iran. During 1987, according to Lloyd's of London, Iranian and Iraqi attacks had damaged 178 vessels in the Gulf (including 34 in December alone), compared with 80 during 1986. (When a cease-fire was proclaimed in July, a total of 546 vessels had been hit since 1981, when the 'tanker war' began in earnest.)

At the end of February 1988 Iraq resumed the 'war of the cities' (which, apart from sporadic attacks, had been halted in early 1987), signalling the beginning of a series of reciprocal raids on civil and economic targets in the two countries which lasted for several months.

During 1987/88, for the first time in six years, owing to poor mobilization, disorganization and a shortage of volunteers, Iran was unable to launch a major winter offensive and began to lose ground to Iraqi advances along the length of the war front. However, this was not before Kurdish guerrillas, in February 1988, had advanced into government-controlled territory in Iraqi Kurdistan, where Iranian forces, with Kurdish assistance, had established bridgeheads, particularly in the Mawat region, along the Iranian border. The Kurdish part in these operations represented the largest Kurdish offensive since 1974/75, uniting forces from the KDP and the PUK, which, in November 1986, had agreed to co-ordinate their military and political activities and were in the process of forming a coalition of Kurdish nationalist groups (see below). In March 1988, in a retaliatory attack against the captured town of Halabja, Iraq is believed to have used chemical weapons, killing 4,000 Kurdish civilians. (In July Iraq admitted its use of chemical weapons during the war. A UN report compiled in April had concluded that there were victims of chemical weapons on both sides; a team of UN experts reported in August that Iraq had used mustard gas against Iranian civilians.)

After the success of the Iranian-Kurdish offensive, the following months witnessed a catalogue of Iraqi victories over Iranian forces. In March 1988 the National Liberation Army (NLA), the military wing of the Iranian resistance group, Mujahidin-e-Khalq, supported by Iraq, undertook a major offensive for the first time since its creation in 1987, attacking Iranian units in Iran's south-western province of Khuzestan. In mid-April Iraqi forces regained control of the Faw peninsula, where the Iranians, who had been unable to strike out to make further territorial gains since capturing the area in 1986, had scaled down their presence. (Iran accused Kuwait of allowing Iraqi forces to use the nearby Bubiyan Island during the Faw offensive.) Then, in May, Iraq recaptured the Shalamcheh area, south-east of Basra, driving the Iranians back across the Shatt al-Arab.

A radical military reorganization by Iran, undertaken in June and July 1988, failed to reverse the tide of defeat. Having won back more territory in the north of Iraq, near Sulaimaniya, in mid-June, Iraq recaptured Majnoon Island and the surrounding area in the al-Hawizah marshes (the site of one of the world's biggest oilfields), on the southern front, at the end of the month. Also at the end of June, and in July, Iraq expelled Iranian forces from Iraqi territory in Kurdistan, recapturing the border town of Mawat and key mountain areas to the north-east of Halabja. On 13 July, in the central sector of the front, Iraqi forces crossed into Iranian territory for the first time since 1986, and captured the Iranian border town of Dehloran. The last pockets of Iranian occupation in southern Iraq were cleared by Iraqi troops in mid-July and, on 18 July, Iran officially announced its unconditional acceptance of Resolution 598. Iraqi troops in the central sector advanced further into Iran before retiring behind the border on

24 July. However, the NLA, over which Iraq claimed to have no control, launched a three-day offensive on 25 July, penetrating as far as 150 km into Iranian territory, before being forced to withdraw. Iraq professed to have no designs on Iranian territory but it was suggested that the NLA was being used as a proxy by Iraq to prevent Iranian forces from reorganizing during a cease-fire which might prove to be only temporary. At the beginning of August, owing to uncertainty over the war, Iraq's general elections, which had been scheduled to take place at the end of the month, were postponed for six months.

The implementation of a cease-fire was delayed by an Iraqi demand for the initiation of direct peace talks with Iran, under UN auspices, prior to a cessation of hostilities. Iran protested that Resolution 598 did not require this. However, on 6 August 1988 Iraq withdrew its insistence on the necessity for direct talks to take place before a cease-fire and, on the following day, Iran agreed to direct talks following the end of hostilities. Accordingly, a cease-fire finally came into force on 20 August, monitored by a specially-created UN observer force of 350 officers, the UN Iran-Iraq Military Observer Group (UNIIMOG).

PEACE TALKS

Negotiations between Iran and Iraq for a comprehensive peace settlement, based on the full implementation of Resolution 598, began at foreign ministerial level in Geneva on 25 August 1988, under the aegis of the UN. With the question of the location of frontiers a matter of dispute, the requirement in Clause One of Resolution 598 for military forces to retire behind internationally recognized borders was causing problems before the talks began, and, once started, they soon reached stalemate. Iran insisted that the Algiers Agreement of 1975 between the two countries should be the basis for negotiations. According to the terms of the Algiers Agreement, which defined the southern border between Iran and Iraq as running along the deepest channel of the Shatt al-Arab waterway (the Thalweg Line), the two countries exercise joint sovereignty over the waterway. However, President Hussain of Iraq, who had been a signatory to the agreement, publicly rejected it immediately prior to the Iraqi invasion of Iran in 1980, claiming that it had been made under duress, and demanded full Iraqi sovereignty over the Shatt al-Arab, which Iraq held under previous agreements in 1847, 1913 and 1937. Iraq also claimed the right of navigation through the Shatt al-Arab and the Gulf during the cease-fire, unhindered by Iranian vessels. When Iran claimed to have stopped and searched an Iraqi cargo vessel which was making its way through the Strait of Hormuz into the Gulf on 20 August 1988, Iraq (though it denied the Iranian claim) threatened to resume hostilities if Iraqi vessels were harassed in this way. It also insisted that an agreement for the dredging of the Shatt al-Arab and the removal of sunken ships be finalized before the discussion of final (mainly Iraqi) troop withdrawals and the exchange of prisoners of war could proceed. Iran claimed that it was, technically, still at war with Iraq and was, therefore, entitled, under international law, to search Iraqi and other vessels for war supplies, for as long as Iraqi troops were in occupation of Iranian territory (an estimated 1,500 sq km, according to Iran).

These disputes, largely concerning issues for which there was no provision in Resolution 598, delayed the implementation of the Resolution beyond the introduction of a cease-fire. Clause Three, for example, urged the repatriation of prisoners of war. By mid-1988 the International Committee of the Red Cross (ICRC) had registered 50,182 Iraqi prisoners of war held in Iran, and 19,284 Iranians held in Iraq, although the actual figures were thought to be higher, as the Red Cross had not been allowed access to all prisoners. In November Iran and Iraq agreed to exchange all sick and wounded prisoners of war. The first exchanges took place in the same month, but the arrangements collapsed shortly afterwards, following a dispute over the number of prisoners involved. Resolution 598 also provided for the creation of an impartial judicial body to determine where the responsibility for starting the war lay. It was generally accepted that Iraq had initiated the conflict by invading Iran on 22 September 1980. Iraq, however, maintained that the war began on 4 September with Iranian shelling of Iraqi border posts. The negotiations for a comprehensive peace settlement remained deadlocked for two years.

On 16 August 1990 President Hussain of Iraq abruptly sought an immediate, formal peace with Iran (for full details, see chapter on Iran, History) by accepting almost all of the claims that Iran had pursued since the declaration of a cease-fire in the war in August 1988. On 10 September 1990 Iran and Iraq formally agreed to resume diplomatic relations.

IRAQI SUPPRESSION OF THE KURDS

Since 1987, when the Iranian military threat began to wane, Iraq had concentrated more resources in the north of the country to deal with the Kurdish separatist movement, which claimed to control a 'liberated zone' of 10,000 sq km. It had intensified its 'scorched earth' policy, which is believed first to have been employed in Kurdistan in 1975 when, following the suppression of a Kurdish guerrilla campaign, 800 Kurdish villages along the border with Iran were razed to create a 'security belt', and Kurds were resettled inside Kurdistan or deported to the south of Iraq. The systematic depopulation of Kurdish areas, achieved by the destruction of Kurdish villages and the resettlement elsewhere in the country of those inhabitants who were not driven into more remote mountain areas, or into neighbouring Iran, was intensified in early 1988, in response to Kurdish support for new Iranian offensives in Iraqi Kurdistan. It was estimated at this time that, with the destruction of some 1,000 villages during the previous year, only about 1,000 of the 4,000 Kurdish villages which had existed before were still standing, and more than one-third of the area of Iraqi Kurdistan was completely depopulated.

In May 1988 the two principal Kurdish dissident groups, the KDP and the PUK, announced the formation of a coalition of six organizations, which would continue the struggle for Kurdish self-determination and co-operate militarily with Iran. Apart from the KDP and the PUK, the new front consisted of the Socialist Party of Kurdistan (SPK), the People's Democratic Party of Kurdistan (PDPK), the United Socialist Party of Kurdistan (USPK), and the predominantly Kurdish ICP.

The introduction of a cease-fire in the Iran–Iraq War in August 1988 allowed Iraq to divert more troops and equipment to Kurdistan, apparently in an attempt to effect a final military solution to the problem of the Kurdish separatist movement. At the end of August an estimated 60,000–70,000 Iraqi troops launched a new offensive to conquer guerrilla bases near the borders with Iran and Turkey, bombarding villages, allegedly using chemical weapons, and forcing thousands of Kurdish civilians and fighters (*peshmerga*) to escape into Iran and Turkey. By mid-September more than 100,000 Kurdish refugees were believed to have fled across the border into Turkey, while Iraqi Kurds seeking refuge in Iran joined an estimated 100,000 others from their country, some 40,000 of whom had escaped from Halabja, after the chemical attack on the city in March. The death toll from the new offensive was estimated at 15,000 in early September.

On 26 August 1988 the UN Security Council adopted a resolution (No. 620) unanimously condemning the use of chemical weapons in the Iran–Iraq War. However, Iraq was not censured by name and continued to deny that it was using chemical weapons against the Kurds, despite what the USA, in September, called 'compelling evidence' to the contrary. On 9 September the US Senate voted to impose economic sanctions against Iraq, which, if they were legally adopted, would halt US credits and exports of US goods worth $800m., prohibit US imports of Iraqi oil, and require US representatives on international financial bodies to vote against all loans and aid to Iraq. Reacting to the vote of the US Senate, an estimated 150,000 Iraqis took part, in Baghdad, in a massive anti-US demonstration.

On 6 September 1988, with its army effectively in control of the border with Turkey, the Iraqi Government offered a full amnesty to all Iraqi Kurds inside and outside the country (excluding only Jalal Talabani, the leader of the PUK), inviting those Kurds abroad to return within 30 days and promising to release all Kurds held on political grounds. The offer was generally dismissed by Kurds as a propaganda ploy, although the Government subsequently claimed that more than 60,000 Kurdish refugees had taken advantage of the amnesty to return to Iraq.

On 17 September 1988 the Government began to evacuate inhabitants of the Kurdish Autonomous Region to the interior of Iraq, as the first step towards the creation of a 30 km-wide uninhabited 'security zone' along the whole of Iraq's border with Iran and Turkey. In June 1989 Kurdish opposition groups appealed for international assistance to halt the evacuations, claiming that they were, in fact, forcible deportations of Kurds to areas more susceptible to government control, and that many of the evacuees (reported to number 300,000 by August 1989) did not reside in the border strip which was to be incorporated into the 'security zone', but in other areas of the Kurdish Autonomous Region. However, the Iraqi Government apparently remained impervious to international criticism of the 'evacuation' programme.

PROPOSED POLITICAL REFORMS

While the cease-fire in the Iran–Iraq War in August 1988, which was precipitated by Iraqi military successes, strengthened Saddam Hussain's position, it also allowed domestic conflicts to find expression again. Hussain's regime is widely regarded as one of the most autocratic in the Arab world, and in February 1989 there were reports of a further attempt by senior army officers to stage a coup. In November 1988 Saddam Hussain announced a programme of political reforms, including the introduction of a multi-party political system, and in January 1989 he declared that a committee was to be established to draft a new constitution. These developments were regarded as attempts to retain the loyalty of Iraq's Shi'ite community, which sought the liberalization of Iraqi society as a reward for its role in the war against Iran.

In April 1989 elections were held to the 250-member National Assembly for the third time since its creation in 1980. The 250 seats were reportedly contested by 911 candidates, one-quarter of whom were members of the Baath Party. The remaining candidates were reported to be either independent or members of the National Progressive Front. It was estimated that 75% of Iraq's electorate (totalling about 8m.) voted in the elections, and that more than 50% of the newly-elected deputies were members of the Baath Party. A new draft Constitution was completed in January 1990, and approved by the National Assembly in July, when its provisions were published in the Iraqi press. It allowed for a multi-party political system, and there was speculation that defunct political parties, such as the National Democratic Party (NDP), would be permitted to re-form and participate in future elections. Under the terms of the draft Constitution, a Consultative Assembly was to be established. This, together with the National Assembly, was to assume the duties of the RCC, which was to be abolished after a presidential election (to be held within two months of the draft Constitution's approval by the National Assembly) had taken place. Following its approval by the National Assembly, the draft Constitution was to be subjected to a popular referendum before ratification by the President.

FOREIGN RELATIONS

From late 1989 there was increased concern in Western countries about the scale of a military expansion programme apparently under way in Iraq; about the involvement of Western companies in the programme; and about covert attempts by Iraq to obtain advanced military technology from the West. International attention focused on Iraq in September 1989, following an explosion at an Iraqi defence industry complex which was thought to be a major installation in a missile development programme.

In March 1990 Iraq's conviction for espionage, and subsequent execution, of an Iranian-born UK journalist, Farzad Bazoft, provoked international outrage and damaged relations with the United Kingdom. The incident emphasized the sensitivity of the Iraqi Government to the question of its military capabilities: in his defence, Bazoft claimed that, as a *bona fide* journalist, he had been investigating the explosion at the Iraqi defence industry complex in September 1989. At the end of March 1990 the British Government claimed to have thwarted attempts by Iraq to import prohibited military devices from the United Kingdom, and in April it alleged that steel tubes which Iraq had ordered from a British company were to be used to construct a 'supergun'.

In April 1990 the US President, George Bush, also urged Iraq to abandon production of chemical weapons, and in June the US media alleged that France had helped to extend the range, and improve the accuracy, of Iraqi missiles. At the end of July the US Congress voted to impose sanctions on Iraq, which formally prohibited sales of weapons and military technology to Iraq.

As its relations with the West deteriorated, Iraq's reputation in the Arab world improved. The outrage that was provoked by Iraq's execution of Farzad Bazoft, together with more general criticisms in Western media of its human rights record, elicited expressions of support for Iraq from the Arab League and from individual Arab states. In April 1990, after Saddam Hussain had referred to Iraq's chemical weapons as a deterrent against a nuclear attack by Israel, there were further expressions of support, even from Iraq's staunchest Arab rival, Syria, for Iraq's right to defend itself.

IRAQ'S INVASION OF KUWAIT

Prior to a meeting of the OPEC ministerial council in Geneva on 25 July 1990, Iraq had implied that it might take military action against countries which continued to flout their oil production quotas. It had also accused Kuwait of violating the Iraqi border in order to steal Iraqi oil resources worth US $2,400m., and suggested that Iraq's debt to Kuwait, accumulated largely during the Iran–Iraq War, should be waived. On the eve of the OPEC meeting in Geneva, Iraq stationed two armoured divisions (about 30,000 troops) on its border with Kuwait.

The Iraqi threat and military mobilization led to a sharp increase in regional tension. Before the OPEC meeting in Geneva on 25 July 1990, President Mubarak of Egypt and Chedli Klibi, the Secretary-General of the Arab League, travelled to Baghdad in an attempt to calm the situation. The USA, meanwhile, placed on alert its naval forces stationed in Bahrain. At the conclusion of the OPEC meeting, however, the threat of Iraqi military action appeared to recede: both Kuwait and the United Arab Emirates (UAE) agreed to reduce their petroleum production, while OPEC agreed to raise its 'benchmark' price of crude petroleum from US $18 to $21 per barrel.

Direct negotiations between Iraq and Kuwait commenced in Saudi Arabia at the end of July 1990, with the aim of resolving disputes over territory, oil pricing and Iraq's debt to Kuwait. Kuwait was expected to accede to Iraqi demands for early negotiations to draft a border demarcation treaty, and Iraq was expected to emphasize a claim to the strategic islands of Bubiyan and Warbah, situated at the mouth of the Shatt al-Arab. (After Kuwait obtained independence in 1961—it had formerly been under the protection of the United Kingdom—Iraq claimed sovereignty over the country. Kuwait was placed under the protection of British troops, who were later withdrawn and replaced by Arab League forces. On 4 October 1963 the Iraqi Government formally recognized Kuwait's complete independence and sovereignty within its present borders.) On 1 August, however, the talks collapsed, and on 2 August Iraq invaded Kuwait, taking control of the country and establishing a (short-lived) Provisional Free Government.

There was no evidence at all to support Iraq's claim that its forces had entered Kuwait at the invitation of insurgents who had overthrown the Kuwaiti Government. The invasion appeared more likely to have been motivated by Iraq's financial difficulties in the aftermath of the Iran–Iraq War in addition to strategic interests—Iraq had long sought the direct access to the Persian Gulf which it gained by occupying Kuwait.

The immediate response, on 2 August 1990, of the UN Security Council to the invasion of Kuwait was to convene and to adopt unanimously a resolution (No. 660), which condemned the Iraqi invasion of Kuwait; demanded the immediate and unconditional withdrawal of Iraqi forces from Kuwait; and appealed for a negotiated settlement of the conflict. On 6 August the UN Security Council convened again and adopted a further resolution (No. 661), which imposed mandatory economic sanctions on Iraq and on occupied Kuwait, affecting all commodities with the exception of medical supplies and foodstuffs 'in humanitarian circumstances'.

As early as 3 August 1990 it was feared that the economic sanctions being imposed on Iraq and Kuwait would be superseded by international military conflict. On 3 August Iraqi troops began to deploy along Kuwait's border with Saudi Arabia, and the USA and the United Kingdom announced that they were sending naval vessels to the Gulf. On 7 August, at the request of King Fahd of Saudi Arabia, the USA dispatched combat troops and aircraft to Saudi Arabia, in order to secure the country's border with Kuwait against a possible attack by Iraq. US troops began to occupy positions in Saudi Arabia on 9 August, one day after Iraq announced its formal annexation of Kuwait. On the same day, the UN Security Council convened and adopted a unanimous resolution (No. 662), which declared the annexation of Kuwait to be null and void, and urged all states and institutions not to recognize it.

The dispatch of US troops signified the beginning of 'Operation Desert Shield' for the defence of Saudi Arabia, in accordance with Article 51 of the UN Charter. By the end of January 1991 some 30 countries had contributed ground troops, aircraft and warships to the multinational force in Saudi Arabia and the Gulf region. By far the biggest contributor was the USA, which, it was estimated, had deployed some 500,000 military personnel. Arab countries participating in the multinational force were Egypt, Syria, Morocco and the members of the Co-operation Council for the Arab States of the Gulf (Gulf Co-operation Council—GCC)—Bahrain, Kuwait, Oman, Qatar, Saudi Arabia and the UAE. It was estimated that Iraq had deployed some 555,000 troops in Kuwait and southern Iraq by the end of January 1991.

Iraq's invasion and annexation of Kuwait altered the pattern of relations prevailing in the Arab world. In the immediate aftermath of the invasion, individual Arab states condemned Iraq's action, and on 3 August 1990 a hastily-convened meeting of the Arab League in Cairo agreed a resolution (endorsed by 14 of the 21 member states and opposed by Iraq, Jordan, Mauritania, Sudan, Yemen and the PLO) which condemned the invasion of Kuwait and demanded the immediate and unconditional withdrawal of Iraqi forces. At a summit meeting of Arab League Heads of State, held in Cairo on 10 August, the demand for Iraq to withdraw from Kuwait was reiterated, and 12 of the 20 members participating in the meeting voted to send an Arab deterrent force to the Gulf in support of the US-led effort to deter potential aggression against Saudi Arabia.

As the crisis in the Gulf developed, Western diplomacy strove to maintain Iraq's isolation. The invasion of Kuwait had provoked widespread popular support for Iraq, notably in Jordan, where there was a huge Palestinian population, and also in the Maghreb states. Although conducted with the approval of the UN, in pursuit of aims formulated in specific UN resolutions, and with the active support of Egypt, Syria, Morocco and the Gulf states, both 'Operation Desert Shield' and its successor, 'Operation Desert Storm', were widely perceived, in parts of the Arab world, to be US-led campaigns to secure US interests in the Gulf region.

On 12 August 1990 Saddam Hussain proposed an initiative for the resolution of the conflict in the Gulf, linking Iraq's occupation of Kuwait with other conflicts in the Middle East, in particular the continuing Israeli occupation of the West Bank of Jordan and the Gaza Strip, and the Palestinian question. This was the first explicit example of so-called 'linkage' in diplomatic efforts to resolve the crisis in the Gulf. Practically, 'linkage' would have amounted to the trading of an Iraqi withdrawal from Kuwait for, at least, the convening of an international conference on the Palestinian issue, and it was repeatedly rejected by the USA, which considered that 'linkage' would reward Iraq's aggression and enhance the country's reputation in the Arab world.

The authority for the deployment of a multinational force for the defence of Saudi Arabia was contained in Article 51 of the UN Charter, which affirms 'the inherent right of individual or collective self-defence if an armed attack occurs against a member of the United Nations, until the Security Council has taken measures necessary to maintain international peace and security'. The UN Security Council warned, however, that its authorization would be necessary for the use of force to implement the economic sanctions imposed on Iraq and Kuwait. Article 42 of the UN Charter provided for the taking of 'such action by air, sea or land forces as may be necessary to maintain international peace and security', including the use of a blockade. In order to clarify the Charter's provisions, the USA drafted a resolution which would allow the UN to use legitimately the force necessary to maintain a blockade against Iraq. On 25 August 1990 the UN Security Council adopted a resolution (No. 665) which requested, with immediate effect, member states deploying maritime forces in the area to use 'such measures commensurate to the specific circumstances as may be necessary under the authority of the Security Council to halt all inward and outward maritime shipping in order to inspect and verify the cargoes and destinations' and ensure the implementation of the mandatory economic sanctions against Iraq and Kuwait. The resolution also invited all states to co-operate, by political and diplomatic means, to ensure compliance with sanctions.

Successive diplomatic efforts to achieve a peaceful solution to the crisis in the Gulf—undertaken, at different times, by the UN and by numerous individual countries—between August 1990 and mid-January 1991 foundered, virtually without exception, on Iraq's steadfast refusal to withdraw its forces from Kuwait. Diplomacy was initially complicated by the treatment of Western citizens residing in Iraq and Kuwait. On 9 August 1990 Iraq closed its borders to foreigners, and on 13 August all US and British nationals in Kuwait were ordered to assemble at hotels prior to their removal to Iraq. Iraq subsequently announced that Westerners would be housed near military locations in order to deter an attack on Iraq by the multinational force in Saudi Arabia. On 28 August, however, Iraq announced that all foreign women and children were free to leave Iraq and Kuwait, extending this permission to all foreigners on 6 December.

On 29 November 1990 the UN Security Council convened and adopted a resolution (No. 678), drafted by the USA, which, with reference to its previous resolutions regarding Iraq's occupation of Kuwait, authorized 'all member states co-operating with the Government of Kuwait, unless Iraq on or before 15 January 1991, fully implements...the foregoing resolutions, to use all necessary means to uphold and implement Security Council Resolution 660 and all subsequent relevant resolutions and to restore international peace and security in the area'. Iraq denounced Resolution 678, the first UN resolution since 1950 which authorized the use of force, as a threat, and reiterated its demand for the UN Security Council to address equally all the problems of the Middle East.

'Operation Desert Storm'—in effect, war with Iraq—in pursuance of the liberation of Kuwait, as demanded by UN Resolution 660, commenced on the night of 16–17 January 1991. It was preceded by intense diplomatic activity to achieve a peaceful solution to the crisis in the Gulf, in particular a visit, on 10 January, by the UN Secretary-General, Javier Pérez de Cuéllar, to Baghdad for talks with Saddam Hussain. The failure of this mission was widely regarded as signalling the inevitability of military conflict. On 14 January Iraq's National Assembly approved a resolution which afforded the President all constitutional powers to respond to any 'US-led' attack.

The declared aim of the multinational force in Saudi Arabia, in the initial phase of 'Operation Desert Storm', was to gain air superiority, and then air supremacy, over Iraqi forces, in order to facilitate air attacks on Iraqi military and industrial installations. Hostilities commenced with air raids on Baghdad, and by late February 1991 a total of 91,000 attacking air missions were reported to have been flown over Iraq and Kuwait by the multinational air forces.

The multinational force claimed air supremacy over Iraq and Kuwait on 30 January 1991, and air attacks were refocused on the fortified positions of Iraqi ground troops in Kuwait, in preparation for a ground offensive. During the initial phase of the air campaign, the Iraqi air force appeared to have offered surprisingly little resistance. Indeed, by 8 February it was reported that more than 100 Iraqi fighter aircraft had sought refuge in Iran, and the apparent good faith of Iran's reaffirmation of its neutrality in the conflict prompted speculation that they had been directed there deliberately in an attempt to prevent the total destruction of the Iraqi air force.

Iraq's most serious response to the military campaign waged against it was attacks with *Scud* missiles on Israel. While these were of little military significance, they threatened to provoke Israeli retaliation against Iraq and the consequent disintegration of the multinational force, since it would have been politi-cally impossible for any Arab state to fight alongside Israel against Iraq. US diplomacy, together with the installation in Israel of advanced US air defence systems, averted the threat of Israeli retaliation for the attacks by the missiles, 37 of which had been launched by late February 1991. In addition, Iraq launched 35 *Scud* missiles against Saudi Arabia.

On 6 February 1991 Iraq formally severed diplomatic relations with the USA, the United Kingdom, France, Italy, Egypt and Saudi Arabia. Between August 1990 and January 1991 many foreign embassies in Baghdad had closed, and most countries had withdrawn their diplomatic staff before the outbreak of hostilities in the Gulf.

On 15 February 1991 the Iraqi Government abruptly expressed its willingness to 'deal with' the UN Security Council resolutions pertaining to its occupation of Kuwait. However, its offer to do so was conditional upon the fulfilment of a long list of requirements (including an assurance that the as-Sabah family would not be restored to power in Kuwait) and was accordingly unacceptable to the countries contributing to the multinational force. The offer to 'deal with' the UN resolutions was nevertheless thought to indicate a new flexibility on the part of the Iraqi leadership.

Soviet diplomacy came to the fore in seeking to persuade Iraq to alter its offer to withdraw from Kuwait into one which the multinational force could accept. On 21 February 1991 Iraq agreed to an eight-point Soviet peace plan which stipulated that: Iraq should make a full and unconditional withdrawal from Kuwait; the withdrawal was to begin on the second day of a cease-fire; the withdrawal should take place within a fixed time-frame; after two-thirds of Iraq's forces had withdrawn from Kuwait, the UN-sponsored economic sanctions were to be repealed; the relevant UN Security Council resolutions should be waived following Iraq's withdrawal; all prisoners of war were to be released following a cease-fire; the withdrawal was to be monitored by observers from neutral countries following a cease-fire; other details were to be discussed at a later stage.

The eight-point Soviet peace plan remained unacceptable to the multinational force, not least because it stipulated that a cease-fire should take effect before Iraq began to withdraw from Kuwait. On 22 February 1991, in response, the USA, representing the multinational force, demanded that Iraq commence a large-scale withdrawal of its forces from Kuwait by noon (US Eastern Standard Time) on 23 February, and that the withdrawal should be completed within one week. In response to this ultimatum, the USSR proposed a further plan for peace, this time containing six points—subsequently formally approved by Iraq—in a final attempt to avert a ground war in Kuwait and Iraq. However, once again the plan was rejected by the multinational force because it did not amount to the unconditional withdrawal of Iraqi forces from Kuwait which UN Security Council Resolution 660 demanded.

During the night of 23–24 February 1991 the multinational force launched a ground offensive for the liberation of Kuwait. Iraqi troops defending Kuwait's border with Saudi Arabia were quickly defeated, offering little resistance to the multinational force. A flanking movement, far to the west, by French units and elements of the 101st US Airborne Division succeeded in severing the main road west from Basra, while the road leading north from Basra was breached by repeated bombing. Divisions of Iraq's élite Republican Guards in the Kuwait area were thus isolated to the south of the Tigris and Euphrates rivers and prevented from retreating towards Baghdad. On 28 February 1991 President Bush announced that the war to liberate Kuwait had been won, and he declared a cease-fire. Iraq had agreed to renounce its claim to Kuwait, and to release all prisoners of war. It also indicated that it would comply with the remaining relevant UN Security Council resolutions. On 3 March Iraq accepted the cease-fire terms that had been dictated, at a meeting with Iraqi military commanders, by the commander of the multinational force, Gen. Norman Schwarzkopf of the US army.

On 3 April 1991 the UN Security Council adopted a resolution (No. 687) which stipulated the terms for a full cease-fire in the Gulf. These terms were accepted on 5 April by Iraq's RCC, and on the following day by the National Assembly. A separate UN Security Council resolution (No. 689), adopted on 9 April, created a demilitarized zone between Iraq and Kuwait, to be monitored by military personnel from the five permanent members of the UN Security Council.

INTERNAL REVOLT

Following the rout of the Iraqi army by the UN-sponsored multinational force in February 1991, armed rebellion broke out among the largely Shi'ite population of southern Iraq and among the Iraqi Kurds in the Kurdish northern provinces of the country. In the south the town of Basra was the centre of the rebellion. On 4 March it was reported that supporters of the Tehran-based Supreme Council for the Islamic Revolution in Iraq (SCIRI) had gained control of the towns of Basra, Amarah, Samawah and Nasiriyah. At a conference of Iraqi groups opposed to the Government of Saddam Hussain, in Beirut on 11–13 March, it was claimed that, despite the prominent role of SCIRI, the uprising in the south was secular and was not an attempt to establish an Iranian-style Islamic republic in Iraq. Already, on 5 March, the assessment of US intelligence sources, that the southern rebellion lacked sufficient organization to succeed, appeared to be corroborated: armed forces loyal to the Government were reported to be regaining control of the cities which had fallen to the rebels. On the same day it was announced that Ali Hassan al-Majid had been appointed Minister of the Interior, with express instructions to suppress the southern rebellion; and on the following day the Government announced financial bonuses for certain elements of the armed forces, in order to stem disaffection. Crucially, there was no military intervention by the multinational force in support of the rebellion. In this respect there appeared to have been a fundamental shift in the policy of the US Government: claiming that actively to support the southern rebellion would constitute unjustified interference in Iraq's internal affairs, its principal aim now seemed to be to prevent the disintegration of Iraq, rather than to oust Saddam Hussain from power. By contrast, at the conference of Iraqi opposition groups held in Beirut in mid-March, it was agreed to seek the overthrow of Saddam Hussain; the abolition of the Arab Baath Socialist Party; and the establishment of a democratic system of government in Iraq.

By mid-March 1991 armed forces loyal to the Government had effectively crushed the rebellion in the south, but their deployment there had allowed a simultaneous revolt by Kurdish guerrilla groups in the Kurdish northern provinces of Iraq to gather momentum. In late March it was reported that Kurdish rebels had gained control of Kirkuk and of important oil installations to the west of the city, and in early April Kurdish leaders claimed that as many as 100,000 guerrillas were involved in hostilities against government forces. The various Kurdish factions appeared to have achieved greater unity of purpose through their alliance, in May 1988, in the Kurdistan Iraqi Front (KIF). Rather than seeking the creation of an independent Kurdish state (which would not be tolerated by the Turkish and Iranian Governments), the KIF claimed that the objective of the northern insurrection was the full implementation of the 15-article peace plan which had been concluded between Kurdish leaders and the Iraqi Government in 1970. At the same time, however, the KIF invited the leaders of other Iraqi groups opposed to the Government to join it in the newly captured areas of northern Iraq in order to establish a unified anti-government movement.

Lacking military support from the multinational force—which was denied to them for the same reasons that it had been denied to the southern insurgents—the Kurdish guerrillas were unable to resist the onslaught of the Iraqi armed forces, which were redeployed northwards as soon as they had crushed the uprising in southern Iraq. By early April 1991 government forces had recaptured Kirkuk, Arbil, Dohok and Zakho. Some 50,000 Kurds were reported to have been killed in the hostilities and, fearing genocide, an estimated 1m.–2m. Kurds fled before the Iraqi army across the northern mountains into Turkey and Iran. On 5 April, as Saddam Hussain offered an amnesty to all Kurds with the exception of 'criminal elements', the UN Security Council adopted a resolution (No. 688) which condemned 'the repression of the Iraqi civilian population in many parts of Iraq' and demanded that the Iraqi Government permit the immediate access of international humanitarian organizations to persons in need of assistance. As relief operations were subsequently mounted, the means were sought whereby the Kurdish refugees

could return to Iraq without fear of a renewed onslaught by the Iraqi armed forces.

As the 'Kurdish crisis' had developed, France, the United Kingdom and the USA had all committed troops to maintain a 'safe haven' for the Kurds in northern Iraq. On 8 April 1991 a proposal by the British Prime Minister, John Major, that a UN-supervised enclave should be created in northern Iraq, for the protection of the Kurdish population, was approved by the leaders of the member states of the EC (European Community, now European Union—EU). The US Government withheld its formal approval of the proposal, but on 10 April it warned Iraq that any interference in relief operations north of latitude 36°N would prompt military retaliation. The UN response to the proposal to create Kurdish 'safe havens' under its auspices also remained cautious. On 17 April the UN Secretary-General, Javier Pérez de Cuéllar, warned that the Iraqi Government's permission would have to be obtained before foreign troops were deployed in northern Iraq, and that the UN Security Council would need to approve the policing of the Kurdish enclave by a UN-backed force. Nevertheless, in late April UN relief agencies reported that Kurdish refugees were returning to Iraq in large numbers.

In mid-May 1991 the UN reported that progress had been achieved in the implementation of Security Council Resolution 688, and the Secretary-General announced that the UN was negotiating with the Iraqi Government over the deployment of a 'UN police force' to safeguard the Kurdish enclave. By mid-June UN agencies and other non-governmental organizations were reported to have assumed responsibility for the provision of essential services in the Kurdish enclave, and the transition from military to UN-backed security was under way.

As international diplomacy sought to create secure conditions for Iraqi Kurds within Iraq, the leaders of Kurdish groups began negotiations with the Iraqi Government on the future status of Iraqi Kurds. In late April 1991 the leader of the PUK, Jalal Talabani, announced that President Saddam Hussain had agreed in principle to implement the provisions of the Kurdish peace plan of 1970. By mid-June, however, negotiations with the Iraqi Government were reported to be in deadlock over the question of the frontiers of the Kurdish Autonomous Area, and at the end of August leaders of Kurdish groups announced their decision to suspend further negotiations with the Iraqi Government until various issues relating to an autonomy agreement had been clarified. Renewed clashes between government forces and Kurdish guerrillas in northern Iraq in September were succeeded, in late October, by the Iraqi Government's withdrawal of all services from Iraqi Kurdistan, effectively subjecting it to an economic blockade.

In the absence of a negotiated autonomy agreement with the Iraqi Government, the KIF organized elections to a 105-member Iraqi Kurdistan National Assembly, and for a paramount Kurdish leader. The result of the elections to the Assembly, held on 19 May 1992 and in which virtually the whole of the estimated 1.1m.-strong electorate participated, was that the KDP and the PUK were entitled to an almost equal number of seats. None of the smaller Kurdish parties achieved representation and the KDP and the PUK subsequently agreed to share equally the seats in the new Assembly. The election for an overall Kurdish leader was inconclusive, Masoud Barzani, the leader of the KDP, receiving 47.5% of the votes cast; and Jalal Talabani, the leader of the PUK, 44.9%. A run-off election was to be held at a future date. In December a member of the Kurdish Cabinet, elected by the Iraqi Kurdistan National Assembly in July 1992, appealed for increased Western aid for the Kurdish-controlled area of northern Iraq, and criticized the UN for its use of Saddam Hussain's regime as an intermediary in the provision of humanitarian relief. At the end of the year it was announced that relief supplies entering the Kurdish-controlled north from Turkey or central Iraq would be protected by UN forces in order to prevent the recurrence of acts of sabotage allegedly perpetrated by agents of Saddam Hussain's regime. The Iraqi Government was reported to have agreed, in principle, to allow UN forces to escort food convoys into Kurdish-controlled areas.

DEVELOPMENTS IN THE KURDISH ENCLAVE

In March 1993 the Kurdish Cabinet elected in July 1992 was dismissed by the Iraqi Kurdistan National Assembly for its failure to deal effectively with the crisis in the region. A new Cabinet was appointed at the end of April. In late December armed conflict was reported to have taken place between fighters of the PUK and the Islamic League of Kurdistan (ILK, also known as the Islamic Movement of Iraqi Kurdistan—IMIK). The two parties were reported to have signed a peace agreement in February 1994 following mediation by the Iraqi National Congress (INC). More serious armed conflict, between fighters belonging to the PUK and the KDP, was reported in May to have led to the division of the northern Kurdish-controlled enclave into two zones. The two parties were reported to have concluded a peace agreement in early June, but fighting broke out again in August. In late November the PUK and the KDP were reported to have concluded another peace agreement, which provided for a census of the region and for the holding of elections in May 1995. In November 1994 it was also reported that the Kurdish Prime Minister had tendered the resignation of the Kurdish Cabinet to the Iraqi Kurdistan National Assembly but had been urged to continue in office in an interim capacity. A further outbreak of fighting in late December was succeeded by another short-lived peace agreement. In early January 1995 fighting erupted again, prompting Saddam Hussain to offer, on 16 January, to mediate in the dispute, and the United Kingdom to warn that the conflict might provide Iraq with a pretext to reassert control over the north. Both sides denied responsibility for a car bomb which exploded in Zakho in late February, resulting in 80 deaths. In March Turkey mounted a major operation to destroy bases of the Kurdistan Workers' Party (Partiya Karkeren Kurdistan—PKK) in the Kurdish enclave, deploying some 35,000 troops across the border. By early May, after appeals from the USA and the EU, Turkey had withdrawn its troops, but 30,000 Turkish troops were again briefly deployed across the border in July. In June the IMIK withdrew from the INC, accusing its leadership of incompetence and corruption. There was renewed fighting between PUK and KDP forces in July, prompting attempts at mediation by the USA and Iran. In the opinion of the USA, inter-Kurdish hostilities strengthened the Iraqi regime, but it was strongly opposed to Iranian mediation, fearing that this would allow Iran to exert greater influence in the Kurdish enclave. As a result of the resumption of fighting between Kurdish factions, elections to the Iraqi Kurdistan National Assembly were abandoned and the existing council extended its mandate for another year.

After delegations from Amnesty International had visited the Kurdish enclave during the first half of 1995, the organization reported widespread human rights abuses and urged the Kurdish leadership to end arbitrary arrests, torture and deliberate and arbitrary killings. According to information received by UNHCR staff, conditions in the enclave were worsening owing to the continuing insecurity, with serious shortages of medicine and inadequate relief supplies to the poorest families.

US-sponsored peace negotiations near Dublin, Ireland, in September 1995 made little progress. The PUK and KDP failed to agree on a common approach to the PKK, whose forces had clashed with the KDP in the Kurdish enclave; to the demilitarization of the enclave's capital, Arbil; or to the sharing of income from customs duties levied on traffic crossing the border from Turkey. Another cease-fire was, however, agreed and despite some clashes between PUK and KDP forces there was no resumption of widespread fighting. The PKK was reported to have taken advantage of the instability in the enclave to strengthen its bases there. In September, Kusrat Rasoul Ali, the Kurdish Prime Minister, survived a bomb attack in Arbil. The PUK accused the KDP of being responsible for the attack, but the KDP denied any involvement in it. In November an official from the US Department of State visited the enclave and held talks with leaders of the two principal Kurdish factions in an attempt to broker a peace agreement and to counter Iranian efforts to mediate between the warring factions. Both the USA and Turkey expressed concern at reports that the 5,000-strong Badr brigade, part of the armed wing of the pro-Iranian SCIRI, had begun to deploy inside the Kurdish enclave in November. Turkey continued to support the KDP in its efforts to expel PKK fighters from the enclave, and there were reports of fierce clashes between KDP and PKK forces. Turkish support for the KDP was believed to have encouraged the PUK to turn to Iran for support.

In February 1996 Turkey and NATO agreed to continue 'Operation Provide Comfort' under which US, British and French aircraft based in Turkey enforce the Iraqi air exclusion zone north of latitude 36°N in order to protect the Kurdish enclave. However, the operation became increasingly controversial in Turkey because of the existence of PKK bases in the enclave from which attacks were launched into Turkish territory, and the Turkish Prime Minister promised the Turkish National Assembly that the arrangement would not continue beyond June 1996. In that month the Turkish parliament extended the operation's mandate for one month and at the end of July the National Assembly agreed to a further prolongation until the end of 1996. Early in 1996 Jalal Talabani, the leader of the PUK, offered to take part in direct or indirect talks with the KDP about a peace settlement, and to participate in new elections to the Iraqi Kurdistan National Assembly. However, he criticized the KDP for controlling some 70% of the region's revenue and for not spending these funds fairly. Control over customs duties has been a major source of discord between the two rival groups. The KDP controls the lucrative customs duties levied on vehicles crossing the Turkish border, and while it claims to use these revenues to finance its organization and military forces, it has been alleged that some of the money is embezzled by party officials. Although the PUK levies similar duties on cross-border trade with Iran, this route is much less profitable. In February there were signs that the KDP and the PKK might settle their differences after Abdullah Öcalan, the PKK leader, met a delegation from the KDP and agreed to participate in further negotiations in the near future.

At the end of April Masoud Barzani and a KDP delegation visited Damascus for talks with the Syrian leadership concerning the situation in the enclave and in Iraq as a whole. There were reports of renewed shelling of villages in the enclave by Baghdad and by Turkey. In May the PUK and KDP held separate talks with Robert Deutsch of the US Department of State but failed to reach an agreement. Nevertheless at the end of the month the PUK announced that it had agreed with the KDP to extend the mandate of the Iraqi Kurdistan National Assembly for another year and that the Assembly, in which each party holds 50 seats, should seek to resolve the differences between the rival groups. Both parties agreed to examine ways of enlarging the Assembly to include members from other political groups, and independent deputies.

In the early months of 1996 a series of clandestine meetings were reported to have been held between the KDP and representatives of Saddam Hussain's administration following a visit to the enclave by Mukarem Talabani, a Kurdish official in the Baghdad Government, whose attempts to mediate between the KDP and PUK were intended to increase Baghdad's influence in the Kurdish-controlled area. Following further discussions between KDP representatives and Saddam Hussain's son, Qusay, Iraqi government experts were permitted to enter KDP-controlled areas to examine the oil pipeline from Iraq to Turkey to be used for oil exports under the 'oil-for-food' accord (see below). In late July Iranian troops were reported to have entered the enclave in pursuit of Kurdish Democratic Party of Iran (KDPI) guerrillas who had retreated to an area held by the KDP. There was some speculation that, following the KDP's refusal to grant permission to Iranian agents to continue the pursuit, the Iranian authorities had colluded in the organization of a PUK attack against KDP positions in the region. US officials, who had persisted with efforts to reconcile the two rival Kurdish factions, held private talks in London with representatives of the PUK and KDP at the end of August to discuss a new cease-fire and the creation of an observer system to monitor it. However, the talks were abandoned after Iraqi security forces invaded the enclave on 31 August, seized the administrative centre, Arbil, and advanced towards Sulaimaniya. Deputy Prime Minister Tareq Aziz announced that military action to curb Iranian activity in the enclave—in support of the PUK—had been authorized only after a formal request for military assistance had been made by the KDP. The Iraqi assault, involving some 40,000 troops with tanks and artillery, amounted to Baghdad's largest offensive since 1991. PUK spokesmen claimed the Iraqi air force had also attacked their forces, close to Arbil, thereby flouting observance of the air exclusion zone. Jalal Talabani warned that the PUK would seek

Iranian support if Iraqi forces threatened Sulaimaniya and the Western allies did not intervene. (US military forces in the region were ordered to adopt an increased state of alert.) The Turkish foreign minister warned Iraq to withdraw its forces immediately from the Kurdish enclave and also insisted that any military co-operation between Iran and the PUK must end. On 2 September there were unconfirmed reports that Iraqi forces were withdrawing from Arbil, entrusting the city to KDP control. In early September, having failed to secure the support of other Gulf War coalition partners for allied military intervention to force an Iraqi withdrawal from the enclave (largely as a result of international uncertainty regarding the extent to which such an undertaking could be justified by the terms of those UN resolutions which had prescribed the end of the Gulf War), US forces launched a series of air missile attacks (operation 'Desert Strike') against Iraqi military installations in southern Iraq. However, despite both sides' use of powerful rhetoric, and a unilateral US declaration of an expansion of the air exclusion zone north to the 33rd parallel, continuing lack of international support for the US initiative (only the United Kingdom fully endorsed the action) discouraged the US Government from engaging in more direct military confrontation. Domestic media coverage of the KDP's Government-backed capture (from the PUK) of Sulaimaniya, some days later (see below), suggested that the Iraqi Government had inflicted a severe diplomatic humiliation on the USA.

Renewed fighting was reported between PUK and KDP forces around Arbil and on 9 September 1996 the PUK-controlled city of Sulaimaniya fell to KDP forces resulting in the flight to the Iranian border of thousands of refugees. Within days some 20,000 Kurds had crossed the border into Iran, and Iranian officials expressed concern that tens of thousands more were waiting to enter the country. Following the fall of Sulaimaniya Saddam Hussain announced that amnesty was to be extended to all Kurdish opponents who had occupied the northern 'safe havens', while declaring the restoration of trade links with the northern regions and the reassertion of Iraqi sovereignty over the Kurdish Autonomous Regions. Suggestions that Kurds who had co-operated with humanitarian agencies and non-governmental organizations would be exempt from the amnesty prompted fears for the safety of such individuals, and US and EU missions prepared to evacuate some 8,000 Kurdish employees from the region. Such a large-scale evacuation would inevitably result in the collapse of the assistance programmes established in the region over the previous five years. After the public execution of nearly one hundred members of the INC by the Iraqi army during their assault on Arbil, most of the Iraqi opposition groups based in Iraqi Kurdistan fled the region. Many observers were convinced that a major objective of Iraqi intervention in the north was the elimination of the INC.

After the capture of Sulaimaniya, the PUK leader, Jalal Talabani, pledged to continue fighting, declaring that the struggle was no longer between Kurdish factions but between the Kurds and those who had sided with the enemy of the Kurdish people. Talabani also condemned the USA and its allies for failing to honour their stated commitment to protect the Kurdish population. In late September the KDP announced that it was to lead a 16-member coalition government for the Kurdish Autonomous Regions, also comprising members of other regional ethnic groupings (but excluding the PUK). In mid-October, however, the PUK regained much of the territory they had lost in September, including Sulaimaniya. Their forces also advanced on Arbil but did not attack the city for fear of provoking renewed intervention by Baghdad. However, PUK forces took control of the Dukan dam and power station which supplies both Arbil and Sulaimaniya with water and electricity. At the end of October the US Assistant Secretary of State, Robert Pelletreau, announced that a truce had been negotiated between the two rival factions, following US mediation of a meeting in Ankara, Turkey. Both the PUK and the KDP agreed to work towards a permanent cease-fire, to avoid enlisting the help of external forces, and to accept the organization and deployment of a peace monitoring body. The agreement also proposed that all customs duties and other taxes collected should be accounted for and shared in order to benefit all the people of the region. The US brokered a new round of peace talks in November at which both factions agreed to attempt to resolve their political

differences and to co-operate in re-establishing a regional administration. Nevertheless, as a technical delegation attempted to delineate the cease-fire line, each side accused the other of violating the peace. At the same time the KDP was reportedly attempting to improve its relations with Iran while the PUK was believed to be communicating privately with Baghdad. In December the Iranian authorities reported that many of the 70,000 Iraqi Kurds who had fled to Iran during fighting in August and September had started to return to their homes. In the same month the US began to evacuate 5,000 Iraqi Kurds employed by American relief organizations in the enclave who were to be granted political asylum in the USA. It was feared that their departure would impede food distribution procedures established under the terms of UN Resolution 968 (see below). Other aid agencies reported that many of their Kurdish staff were also demanding to be evacuated, fearing reprisals by Baghdad. Early in 1997 relief agencies still operating in the enclave claimed that more than 70,000 Iraqi Kurds, including women and children, had been forcibly displaced since the cease-fire; both the PUK and the KDP were accused of intimidating and persecuting rival supporters living in their territory, although both factions rejected such allegations. Relief agencies also stated that tens of thousands of refugees remained destitute, while uncertainty about future Western funding of aid programmes continued.

In April 1997 David Welch, the acting US Assistant Secretary of State for Near Eastern Affairs, held talks with Barzani and Talabani, both of whom reaffirmed their commitment to the reconciliation process begun in November 1996. President Clinton later announced that further talks between the rival factions had been arranged to consolidate the cease-fire and to encourage the KDP and PUK to resolve their political differences. Also in April a Peace Monitoring Force (PMF), with US political, financial and logistical support, began deployment in the region to demarcate the cease-fire boundary and to monitor the truce between the KDP and the PUK. In May President Clinton reported that the PMF had already resolved several violations of the terms of the cease-fire, but that security in the enclave remained tenuous. Nevertheless, he stated that progress had been made, especially in securing the release of prisoners held by both factions, and that both the KDP and the PUK were participating in a joint Higher Co-ordination Committee in an attempt to improve the provision of basic services such as electricity and health care.

At the end of December 1996 'Operation Provide Comfort' was terminated at Turkey's request and was replaced by a new surveillance system whereby air cover alone was to be provided by Turkey, the USA and Britain. France refused to participate in this new operation, which was inaugurated on 1 January 1997, since it did not include the provision of humanitarian aid. At the end of 1996 Turkish forces resumed artillery and air attacks on PKK bases in northern Iraq, which were immediately denounced by the Iraqi Government. In mid-May 1997 an estimated 25,000—50,000 Turkish troops, with support from tanks and fighter aircraft, crossed into northern Iraq to launch another attack on PKK bases there. Turkish sources claimed that more than 900 rebels were killed, a figure rejected as a gross exaggeration by pro-PKK sources. Fighting was also reported between KDP and PKK forces in Arbil. A KDP spokesman claimed that PKK activities threatened peace and security in the city and hampered relief work by the UN and other aid agencies. During the fighting between the KDP and the PUK in August and September 1996 the PKK was reported to have increased its influence in the mountainous region along the Turkish border. Turkey claimed that its latest incursion into northern Iraq was undertaken in order to help the KDP regain control of the border areas.

As a result of the Turkish incursion, which was fiercely condemned by the Iraqi Government, the Baghdad authorities postponed a planned military campaign against the PUK which aimed to recapture the Dukan dam. The Iraqi Government had accused the PUK of cutting off the water supply to the provinces of Kirkuk and Ba'qubah and of depriving large areas of agricultural land in the Tigris basin of water for irrigation. A new round of peace talks between the PUK and the KDP, sponsored by the USA, the United Kingdom and Turkey, which began in Ankara on the same day as the Turkish incursion, promptly collapsed. Further talks between the two factions in July failed to produce an agreement. Although Turkey had withdrawn most of its troops from northern Iraq, it launched a new military campaign against the PKK at the end of September 1997, and there were reports that Turkish forces, comprising 8,000–15,000 troops with armoured vehicles and air support, had penetrated Iraqi territory. It appeared that the Turkish strategy of using a client militia in a war against the PKK had failed, forcing Ankara to provide direct support to the KDP. The PUK, on the other hand, lent military support to the PKK in its battle with the KDP, increasing instability in the enclave. Fighting erupted between KDP and PUK forces in October, in violation of the cease-fire agreement concluded in 1996. The PUK reportedly achieved some success in its attempt to secure control over the lucrative north–south supply route, but in November the KDP, supported by Turkish forces, launched a successful counter-attack, thereby regaining control of the route. In January 1998 the PUK leader, Jalal Talabani, proposed peace and reconcilia-tion and the establishment of a transitional government, in which both the PUK and the KDP would be represented, to assume sole responsibility for customs duties on cross-border trade. Following its recent military success against the PUK, however, the KDP leadership did not respond. Iran continued to offer some support to the PUK, but appeared unwilling to become more directly involved in the Kurdish enclave. There were reports that delegations from both Kurdish factions had been invited for talks in Baghdad in November 1997. However, Saddam Hussain's aim of eventually re-establishing Baghdad's control over the northern region could only be encouraged by continued in-fighting between the Kurdish factions.

By mid-1998 the fragile cease-fire between the PUK and the KDP appeared to be holding, and, after a number of meetings between representatives of the two factions, agreement was reached on an exchange of prisoners and on the establishment of a joint committee to promote co-operation in public health, education and energy. Meanwhile, the issue of KDP control over customs duties on cross-border trade from Turkey, which had thwarted previous attempts to reconcile the rival factions, remained unresolved. Nevertheless, the two factions continued to hold regular meetings, and both parties pledged to co-operate to secure a permanent settlement with Baghdad that would provide for Kurdish autonomy. In May the KDP leader stated that all Kurdish factions were prepared to make peace with the Government in Baghdad, on condition that Baghdad agreed to devolve power to a regional Kurdish government and grant it jurisdiction over the oil-rich Kirkuk district. Earlier, the Deputy Prime Minister, Tareq Aziz, had asserted that Baghdad had maintained regular contact with both the KDP and PUK for several years. In June the PUK leader admitted that he had met with the head of Iraqi intelligence services, Rafa at-Tikriti. The Iraqi authorities remained firmly opposed to allowing Kur-dish control over Kirkuk, and preferred to maintain separate contacts with the two main factions in the hope of undermining their tentative alliance.

In September 1998 the USA brokered a peace agreement between the PUK and KDP; the accord, signed in Washington, DC, provided for new elections in 1999, a unified regional administration, the sharing of local revenues, an end to hostili-ties and interfactional fighting, and co-operation in imple-menting the oil-for-food programme to benefit the Kurdish population. By late 1999, although the cease-fire remained in place and the two factions had suspended their press campaigns against one another, little progress had been made in imple-menting the Washington accord and differences remained on fundamental issues such as the formation of a new government and the division of financial resources. Representatives of both factions attended a meeting of 11 Iraqi opposition groups held in London, United Kingdom, at the beginning of April (see below), but it appeared unlikely that either the KDP or the PUK would be willing to see other opposition groups based in Kurdish territory, and both the KDP and PUK continued their dialogue with Baghdad. New elections to the Iraqi Kurdistan National Assembly, provided for in the Washington accord, failed to take place as scheduled in July 1999 despite a visit to the area by US State Department officials. Later in the year reports suggested some improvement in relations between the KDP and the PUK, and both groups sent delegations to an Iraqi opposition conference which met in New York in October. Speculation that the arrival in the enclave of several thousand PKK fighters from south-eastern Turkey would undermine the *rapprochement* between the two main Kurdish parties proved unfounded, and there were no signs of a renewed alliance between the PUK and the PKK against the more powerful KDP. Nevertheless, there was still no progress towards establishing an effective and united Kurdish administration in the northern region, a development Iran, Turkey and Syria continued to oppose. In December 1999 the KDP announced the composition of a new 25-member Kurdish coalition administration (com-prising the KDP, the Iraqi Communist Party, the Assyrian Movement, the Independent Workers' Party of Kurdistan, the Islamic Union and independents) for the areas under its control (principally the departments of Irbil and D'hok). In early Feb-ruary 2000 a group of US State Department officials headed by Philo Dibble, director of the Iraq/Iran section, visited the enclave for talks with Kurdish leaders on reconciliation. The State Department spokesman reported that the Kurdish leaders had agreed to work as quickly as possible towards the implementa-tion of the 1998 Washington agreement. On a visit to Turkey in July, PUK leader Jalal Talabani claimed that Baghdad had moved some 50,000 troops to the border of the Kurdish-con-trolled areas, a claim supported by the London-based daily *Al-Hayat*, which reported that in June Saddam Hussain's son, Qusay, had inspected units of the Republican Guard stationed on the border—possibly as a prelude to another Iraqi incursion into the enclave if there was a further deterioration in relations between the two rival Kurdish factions. A PUK delegation visited Washington at the end of June to express its concerns, and was apparently reassured by US officials that the USA would continue to protect the Kurdish enclave. There were reports that tensions between the PUK and KDP had increased in recent months. Implementation of the 1998 Washington peace agreement between the rival factions continued to make little progress. Prospects for holding the long-delayed elections to the Iraqi Kurdistan National Assembly appeared remote, and there was still no agreement on sharing local revenues. Each faction accused the other of preparing to renew hostilities.

In early December 2000 two Iraqi battalions and an infantry division invaded the enclave, advancing some 5 km into KDP-controlled territory where they were reported to have deployed close to the town of Baidrah, near D'hok, before withdrawing from Kurdish-controlled areas two days later. There were no reports of clashes with KDP forces, but a spokesman for the group declared that it would respond fully to any further incur-sions by the Iraqi army. After the latest threat from Baghdad, the leaders of the two rival Kurdish factions held talks in January 2001 at which they agreed to continue the negotiations, but their relations remained characterized by deep mistrust. In recent months the PUK had been receiving weapons and other assistance from Turkey, regarded as the main power broker in the Kurdish-controlled areas, in return for its help in controlling the PKK.

Most of the 908 refugees aboard the *East-Sea*, which ran aground on the Mediterranean coast of France in February 2001, were Iraqi Kurds from the Mosul region, where the Iraqi authorities were continuing an Arabization policy. Many of the refugees interviewed claimed that they had fled from Iraq to escape persecution for their attachment to the Kurdish cause. They confirmed what they alleged was the existence of an organized network of agents in Iraq and Turkey who smuggled people to Europe, charging up to US $2,500 for each adult. According to Ahmed Bamarni, the PUK representative in France, those parts of northern Iraq controlled by Baghdad were being subjected to a policy of 'ethnic cleansing', with Kurds being deported to the southern provinces of Iraq or forced to take refuge in the Kurdish enclave. In these conditions many Kurds believed that their only option was to emigrate to western Europe. The KDP representative in France, Saywan Barzani, stated that the Turkish authorities knew of these movements but chose not to intervene. He insisted that it was in the interest of both Baghdad and Ankara to see Kurds emigrate. According to French sources, some 108,000 Kurds had fled from areas controlled by Baghdad to the Kurdish enclave between 1993 and 2000, and an unknown number had been deported to the southern provinces of Iraq. Less than 20% of Kirkuk's population was now Kurdish, compared(with more than 48% in 1957.

In April 2001, in an address to the Iraqi National Assembly, Saddam Hussain urged Iraqi Kurds to embrace their role as a part of 'the Arab nation', and in July he was reported to have invited Kurdish representatives to take part in an 'open dialogue' with Baghdad over the future of the three Kurdish-controlled regions. There were reports in the KDP-sponsored media that the party was considering the Iraqi leader's invitation, but the PUK reminded its supporters of Baghdad's long-standing hostility towards the Kurdish cause, and the party's official newspaper reiterated claims that the Iraqi Government was engaged in a programme of 'ethnic cleansing' to Arabize areas under its control with large Kurdish populations, such as the provinces of Mosul and Kirkuk. During September there were renewed reports that the Iraqi Government was reinforcing its military presence on the borders of the Kurdish enclave, although it was unclear whether the redeployments represented an offensive or defensive initiative, given the US Administration's clear indication that the removal of the incumbent Iraqi administration would constitute a key component of its post-11 September 'anti-terror' campaign (see below). The reinforcement of Iraqi troops in the border regions lent fresh impetus to negotiations between the two principal Kurdish factions, who promptly agreed to co-ordinate any armed response to a new Iraqi attack and to allow civilians displaced during fighting between the two groups in the 1990s to return to their homes. Moreover, in September the KDP was reported to have provided some military and financial support for a PUK assault on positions held by Jund al-Islam (a new militant Islamist faction of the Islamic Unity Movement of Kurdistan allegedly funded and trained by Osama bin Laden's al-Qa'ida terrorist group) in Halabja, near the border with Iran. In November the KDP was reported to have sent a delegation to Baghdad for talks with Saddam Hussain during which Barzani was believed to have reaffirmed his commitment to the 'federal status' of the Kurdish areas. In December spokesmen for both the KDP and the PUK, allegedly fearful that the progress towards autonomy that had been achieved might be lost if they were compelled to join a US-led campaign to overthrow Saddam Hussain, urged the US Government not to extend its armed anti-terrorism campaign to Iraq, but rather to allow the Iraqi peoples to determine their own fate. In April 2002 US military sources reported that the Iraqi Government had moved more anti-aircraft batteries beyond the boundary of the northern 'no-fly' zone and that Iraqi tanks would be capable of reaching Arbil and Sulaimaniya within one hour. Meanwhile, significant progress was believed to have been made during renewed discussions between Barzani and Talibani conducted in Germany, where the agenda included proposals for reuniting their two administrations and holding new elections in the Kurdish enclave. In August it was reported that representatives of the two parties had agreed to the inauguration of a transitional joint parliamentary session (with representation based on the results of the May 1992 elections) before the end of the year. An agreement to this effect was signed on 8 September. Both factions continued to maintain contacts with Baghdad.

OTHER POST-WAR DEVELOPMENTS

By mid-August 1991, despite the failure of his Kuwaiti adventure and the outbreak of internal revolts in its aftermath, the overthrow of President Saddam Hussain, which had been widely predicted during the crisis in the Gulf, seemed unlikely in the short term. Indeed, it was arguable that his position was more secure than it had been at the time of the invasion of Kuwait: opponents of the Government in the south of the country had been ruthlessly suppressed; a negotiated settlement of the Kurdish question was under discussion; and, in the wake of several alleged attempts to mount a military *coup d'état*, the Government appeared to have strengthened its control of the army, which remained the key to its survival in power. A reshuffle of the Council of Ministers in March 1991 had placed the President's closest supporters and members of his family in the most important positions of government and additional governmental adjustments later in the year, and in February and August 1992, furthered this process. Above all, it emerged that the US

Government was not willing actively to seek Saddam Hussain's overthrow at the expense of the integrity of Iraq.

The survival of the Iraqi Government in the long term depended on three factors: its continued control of the armed forces; the length of time and the stringency with which economic sanctions would continue to be applied against Iraq; and the degree to which popular disaffection, created by the economic sanctions, could be appeased by the granting of limited political reform.

In September 1991 the Government introduced legislation providing for the establishment of a multi-party political system, in accordance with the draft of the new permanent Constitution. New political parties were to be subject to stringent controls, however, and later in the month the President stated that the Baath Party would retain its leading role in Iraqi political life. In early September the Baath Party held its 10th Congress—the first such Congress since 1982—at which Saddam Hussain was re-elected Secretary-General of the party's powerful regional command.

Iraq's post-war relations with the international community have been dominated by conflicts over the way in which the Iraqi regime has apparently sought to circumvent demands by the UN—as stipulated by UN Security Council Resolution 687—that it should disclose the full extent of its programmes to develop chemical weapons, nuclear weapons and missiles, and should eliminate its weapons of mass destruction. One consequence of the conflicts over Iraqi compliance with Resolution 687 was that there was no easing of the economic sanctions that were first imposed on Iraq on 6 August 1990, under the terms of UN Security Council Resolution 661.

In May 1991 the UN Security Council decided to establish a compensation fund for victims of Iraqi aggression (both governments and individuals), to be financed by a levy (subsequently fixed at 30%) on Iraqi petroleum revenues. In August the UN Security Council adopted a resolution (No. 706, subsequently approved in Resolution 712 in September) proposing that Iraq should be allowed to sell petroleum worth up to US $1,600m. over a six-month period, the revenue from which would be paid into an escrow account controlled by the UN. Part of the sum thus realized was to be made available to Iraq for the purchase of food, medicines and supplies for essential civilian needs.

Iraq rejected the terms proposed by the UN for the resumption of exports of petroleum, and in February 1992 withdrew from further negotiations on the issue. In April the UN reiterated its demand that Iraq should comply with the terms of Security Council Resolutions 706 and 712 before resuming petroleum exports. In late June a further session of negotiations between Iraq and the UN on the resumption of petroleum exports ended indecisively. On 2 October the UN Security Council adopted a resolution (No. 778) permitting it to confiscate up to US $500m.-worth of oil-related Iraqi assets in order to place further pressure on Iraq to accept the UN's terms for renewed exports of petroleum. In late October the UN commission responsible for the supervision of the destruction of Iraqi weapons proposed a relaxation of the embargo on sales of Iraqi oil in return for increased co-operation by Iraq with the UN. However, this suggestion did not gain the support of Western governments or of Iraqi opposition movements, and in late November the UN Security Council refused a request by an Iraqi delegation to repeal the economic sanctions in force against Iraq.

In January 1993 a 52-member team of UN weapons inspectors arrived in Iraq, the Government having revoked a prohibition on all UN flights into the country, in response to renewed air attacks by Western forces (see below). In early July, however, another team of UN weapons inspectors departed abruptly from Baghdad after the Government had refused to allow them to station surveillance equipment at missile-testing locations. Iraq continued to refuse the terms of UN Security Council Resolution 715, which governed the long-term monitoring of its weapons programmes. In early July a further session of negotiations between Iraq and the UN on the resumption of petroleum exports ended inconclusively, and later in the month the UN Security Council renewed the economic sanctions in force against Iraq. At the beginning of September Iraq's Deputy Prime Minister, Tareq Aziz, met the UN Secretary-General to discuss the resumption of Iraqi petroleum sales and the lifting of the economic sanctions. The UN was reportedly anxious to raise funds from such sales in order to finance its own operations in Iraq. The talks were inconclusive, however, and at the end of September the economic sanctions in force against Iraq were renewed. In early October the Government agreed to UN demands that it should release details of its weapons suppliers. In the absence of any progress on the issue of UN Security Council Resolution 715, however, economic sanctions were extended for a further 60 days in late November. Shortly after their renewal, the Iraqi Government was reported to have agreed to the provisions for weapons-monitoring contained in Resolution 715, and the UN to have begun plans for their implementation. However, it was clear by the end of December that neither the UN Security Council nor the US Government would be willing to allow even a partial easing of sanctions until Iraq had demonstrated its commitment to the dismantling of its weapons systems for a period of at least six months. Moreover, the US Government insisted that Iraq must first also comply with all other relevant UN resolutions, recognize the newly-demarcated border with Kuwait and cease the repression of its Kurdish and southern Shi'ite communities. In September hundreds of inhabitants of Iraq's southern marshlands were reported to have been killed by government forces using chemical weapons; and in November the UN accused the Government of indiscriminate attacks on civilians in that area.

From March 1994 the Iraqi Government engaged in a campaign of diplomacy to obtain the lifting of economic sanctions, and in mid-July evidence emerged of a division within the UN Security Council regarding their continuation. Russia, France and China were all reported to be in favour of acknowledging Iraq's increased co-operation with UN agencies. In September, however, the Security Council extended the sanctions for a further period of 60 days. Russia and France had proposed that the Security Council should draw up a timetable for the ending of sanctions, but had not obtained the agreement of other permanent members of the Council.

On 6 October 1994 the leader of the UN Special Commission on Iraq (UNSCOM—responsible for inspecting the country's weapons) announced that a system for monitoring Iraqi defence industries was ready to begin operating. On the same day, however, there was a large movement of Iraqi forces towards the border with Kuwait, apparently to draw attention to Iraq's demands for swift action to ease the sanctions. In response, Kuwait deployed most of its army to protect its side of the border on 9 October, and the USA sent reinforcements to Kuwait and other parts of the Gulf region to support the 12,000 US troops already stationed there. On 10 October Iraq announced that it would withdraw its troops northward from their positions near the Kuwaiti border. On 15 October the Security Council adopted a resolution (No. 949) demanding that the withdrawal of all Iraqi forces recently transferred to southern Iraq be completed immediately; and stipulating that Iraq must not 'utilize its military or any other forces in a hostile or provocative manner to threaten its neighbours or the UN operations in Iraq'.

On 10 November 1994 the Iraqi National Assembly voted to recognize Kuwait within the borders defined by the UN in April 1992 and May 1993. Nevertheless, on 14 November the UN Security Council renewed the economic sanctions in force against Iraq for a further 60 days. Russia, China and France were all reportedly in favour of responding to Iraq's recognition of Kuwait with an easing of the sanctions. In a statement issued on 16 November, however, the Security Council welcomed Iraq's recognition of Kuwait, but emphasized that it must comply with all the relevant UN resolutions before any such relaxation could occur.

In mid-December 1994 the Iraqi Deputy Prime Minister visited Moscow, Russia, for talks with the Russian Minister of Foreign Affairs, Andrei Kozyrev. Following the talks, Kozyrev stated that the UN Security Council should adopt a more flexible attitude towards Iraq in respect of economic sanctions. On 20 December the Security Council met to study a report by the head of UNSCOM, in which he expressed his confidence that Iraq no longer had any nuclear, chemical or ballistic weapons. Russia, France, China and Spain were all reported to have urged the Security Council to acknowledge Iraq's co-operation with the UN's weapons inspectorate. The USA and the United Kingdom, however, expressed concern at Iraq's past failures to co-operate.

On 7 January 1995 the UN Secretary-General offered to resume dialogue with Iraq on a partial lifting of the economic sanctions. On 12 January the UN Security Council renewed the sanctions in force against Iraq for a further 60 days. Both the US and the UK Governments had again reportedly insisted that Iraq should comply with all the relevant UN resolutions before sanctions were eased, prompting Iraq to accuse them of unfairness and illegality. France and Russia were reported to have argued within the Security Council for a partial lifting of sanctions, provided that Iraq co-operated fully with the UN weapons-monitoring programme. The division between the members of the Security Council regarding the easing of sanctions had intensified as a result of France's announcement, on 6 January, that it was to establish an interests section at the Romanian embassy in Baghdad.

UN sanctions against Iraq were again renewed for 60 days on 13 March 1995. In April the Iraqi Government rejected as a violation of its sovereignty a revised UN proposal (Resolution 986) for the partial resumption of exports of Iraqi petroleum. Iraqi attempts to secure an end to the sanctions had suffered a serious reversal in February when, following a visit to Baghdad in the same month, the head of UNSCOM announced that the Iraqi authorities had failed satisfactorily to account for a substantial amount of material used in the manufacture of biological weapons, known to have been imported by Iraq in 1988. Further concerns regarding the use of these stockpiles were expressed by the Commission in April, May and June. However, expectations of a prompt easing of sanctions were renewed in early July, following the Iraqi Government's acknowledgement of the past existence of a biological weapons development programme for offensive as well as research purposes. Notwithstanding this admission, on 11 July the UN Security Council voted to extend sanctions against Iraq for a further 60 days, prompting the Iraqi Minister of Foreign Affairs, Muhammad Saeed as-Sahaf, to insist that the Special Commission should complete its report and promote an end to the sanctions by the end of August if it wished to avoid the complete cessation of co-operation from the Iraqi authorities. By mid-August, however, the Iraqi Government had adopted a more conciliatory stance towards the Commission, and it was reported that crucial new information regarding Iraq's military programme had been made available to its officers. This change in attitude and the sudden appearance of new information appeared to be related to the defection of Hussain Kamel al-Majid (see below), a former Iraqi Minister of Industry and Military Production, and consequent Iraqi fears that he might divulge information to the UN and hamper efforts to obtain the lifting of sanctions. Rolf Ekeus, the head of UNSCOM, stated that preliminary work on the new data appeared to show that Iraq had developed a more extensive weapons programme than had so far been discovered, and that it had been concealing a significant biological weapons programme. In September it was reported that illegal shipments of oil from Iraq were continuing, even though the US Navy had increased its efforts to enforce the UN blockade. (Since October 1994 14 cargoes had been confiscated by the US Navy.) In October 1995 UNSCOM reported that its work was far from over and that Iraq had concealed evidence of biological weapons development, chemical missile flight tests and work on missiles with nuclear capability. As a result, areas of investigation that had been closed would have to be reopened. At the end of November the head of the Commission told a press conference that Iraq had not been co-operating fully in its investigations and that it was still trying to mislead UN inspection teams. In December Jordan intercepted missile parts and toxic chemicals destined for Iraq.

Meanwhile, on 26 August 1992 the Governments of the USA, the United Kingdom, France and Russia had announced their decision to establish a zone in southern Iraq, south of latitude 32°N, from which all flights by Iraqi fixed-wing and rotary-wing aircraft were to be excluded. Although the air exclusion zone was not formally established by a UN Security Council resolution, the UN Secretary-General subsequently indicated his own support for the measure and stated that it enjoyed that of the Security Council. The exclusion zone was established in response to renewed attacks by Iraqi government forces on southern Iraqi Shi'ite communities and on the inhabitants of the marshlands of southern Iraq. In April 1992 Saddam Hussain had ordered the evacuation of the marshlands and the resettlement of their inhabitants; and in June Iraqi armed forces were reported to have encircled the areas and to have intensified their attacks on the communities there. The Iraqi Government reacted with predictable anger to the establishment of the air exclusion zone, but it was reported in early September to have withdrawn all flights over the area. However, large numbers of troops remained there and continued to attack the civilian population. Other Arab governments, notably those of Algeria, Jordan, Sudan, Syria and Yemen, also condemned the establishment of the air exclusion zone as a step towards the disintegration of Iraq, which, as a result of the other, UN-authorized exclusion zone north of latitude 36°N (see above), was now effectively divided into three parts.

In late December 1992 a US combat aircraft shot down an Iraqi fighter aircraft which had allegedly entered the southern air exclusion zone; and on 6 January 1993 the USA, with the support of the British and French Governments, demanded that Iraq should withdraw anti-aircraft missile batteries from within the zone. Iraq was reported to have complied with this demand, but subsequent Iraqi military operations inside Kuwaiti territory, to recover military equipment, provoked air attacks by Western forces on targets in southern Iraq on 13 January. A ban which the Iraqi Government had imposed on UN flights into the country was cited as a further justification for the attacks. Further air raids by Western forces on targets in northern and southern Iraq took place in late January. In late May, in response to the deployment of Iraqi armed forces close to the UN-authorized exclusion zone north of latitude 36°N, the USA warned Iraq that it might suffer military reprisals in the event of any incursion into the Kurdish-held north. In late June the USA launched an attack against intelligence headquarters in Baghdad, in retaliation for Iraq's role in an alleged conspiracy to assassinate former US President Bush in Kuwait in April 1993. Iraq made a formal protest to the UN Security Council over the attack, which provoked widespread international condemnation, not least because it was regarded by many observers as an attempt by the Clinton administration to increase its domestic popularity. In early July Iraqi armed forces were reported to have renewed the Government's offensive against the inhabitants of the marshlands of southern Iraq, and the London-based INC urged the UN Security Council to send emergency supplies of food and medicine to the communities there. In late July the Food and Agriculture Organization (FAO) of the UN warned that pre-famine conditions existed in much of Iraq and appealed for the economic sanctions in force against the country to be either alleviated or lifted. In late August it was reported that the Government had drained some 70% of the southern marshlands and that some 3,000 of their inhabitants had fled to Iran. In December 1995 SCIRI reported that Iraqi armed forces were continuing their offensive against the civilian population in the southern marshlands, but claimed that its own forces were carrying out regular attacks against Iraqi military positions in the south. In January 1996 it was reported that the exodus of refugees from the southern marshlands was continuing, with an estimated 60,000–70,000 people living in camps in south-western Iran and many more in other parts of the country. In addition it was estimated that some 200,000 people in southern Iraq had been internally displaced, having fled to other parts of the country.

ECONOMIC CRISIS, MILITARY INSTABILITY AND CONFLICTS WITHIN HUSSAIN'S REGIME

By October 1994 the living standards of large sections of the Iraqi population had reportedly been reduced to subsistence level. The Iraqi Government appeared increasingly desperate to maintain order in the face of this economic crisis. In May 1994 Saddam Hussain himself had assumed the post of Prime Minister in a reshuffle of the Council of Ministers in which the Ministers of Finance and Agriculture were dismissed. In June, and again in September, harsh new punishments for those convicted of theft were announced by the RCC. Also in September a substantial reduction in the daily ration of some staple food items was announced. In December another Minister of Agriculture was dismissed, and subsequent reports claimed that

he had been imprisoned on charges relating to the neglect of his duties. (The agriculture portfolio was allocated to Khalid Abd al-Munim Rashid in April 1995.)

Dissatisfaction within the armed forces resurfaced in early 1995. An unsuccessful coup attempt in January prompted a comprehensive reorganization of military ranks, including the (unconfirmed) dismissal of 68 air force officers. In March another coup attempt, organized by the former head of Iraqi military intelligence during the 1990–91 hostilities in the Gulf, and supported by Kurdish insurgents in the north and Shi'ite rebels in the south, was also thwarted. Further reorganization of military personnel resulted in the appointment of a new Chief of the General Staff in April 1995. The scale of disruption within the armed forces provoked widespread anxiety among the civilian population, and civil disturbances began to escalate (particularly in Anbar province), leading to the replacement of the Minister of the Interior in May. Regional reports of a substantial insurrection by the armed forces at the Abu Ghraid army base, near Baghdad, in mid-June were strenuously denied by the Iraqi Government. However, there was mounting evidence to suggest that an uprising had been organized by members of the Sunni Dulaimi clan (many of whom had been killed in continuing disturbances in Ramadi, the capital of Anbar province), with the support of the élite 14 July battalion of the Iraqi army. While unconfirmed reports suggested that those responsible for the rebellion had been immediately and severely punished (many by execution), the loss of the support of the previously loyal Dulaimi clan was widely interpreted as the beginning of the disintegration of Saddam Hussain's traditional support base of powerful Sunni Muslim clans.

A minor reorganization of portfolios in the Council of Ministers was effected in late June 1995, and in July a new Minister of Defence and a new Chief of the General Staff were appointed in an attempt to consolidate support for the President. However, in early August further significant divisions within Saddam Hussain's power base became apparent following the defection to Jordan of two sons-in-law of the President, Lt-Gen. Hussain Kamel al-Majid and his brother Col Saddam Kamel, together with their wives. Both were senior figures in the regime. Hussain Kamel had been Minister of Industry and Military Production, responsible for Iraq's weapons development programme, and Saddam Kamel the head of the Presidential Guard, responsible for presidential security. It was rumoured that they had become alarmed at the increasing concentration of power in the hands of Saddam Hussain's two sons, Uday and Qusay, and that they feared for their lives. The two men were immediately granted political asylum by King Hussein of Jordan. From Amman, Hussain Kamel urged the Iraqi army to overthrow Saddam Hussain's regime, and Iraqi opposition groups to unite and form a government-in-exile. There was speculation that he himself was regarded as a possible successor to Saddam Hussain. Hussain Kamel also met Rolf Ekeus, the head of UNSCOM, and was believed to have provided further information on Iraq's weapons development programmes. Iraq condemned both men as traitors and a wave of arrests and executions followed their defection as Saddam Hussain ordered a purge of senior army officers and government officials who had been close to the two brothers.

In a move widely interpreted as an attempt to re-establish domestic and international recognition of Saddam Hussain's mandate, a meeting of the RCC was convened on 7 September 1995 and an interim amendment to the Constitution was approved whereby the elected Chairman of the RCC would automatically assume the Presidency of the Republic, subject to the approval of the National Assembly and endorsement by national plebiscite. Saddam Hussain's candidature was duly approved by the National Assembly on 10 September. The meticulously organized referendum took place on 15 October and a 99.96%-endorsement of the President's continuance in office for a seven-year renewable term was recorded. An official turn-out of 99.47% of the estimated 8.4m. electorate was reported to have voted. This unprecedented level of support provoked widespread incredulity throughout the international community. At the end of October Hussain promised further elections and 'more democratization' and emphasized the leading role of Baath Party in achieving political pluralism. Some observers argued that as a result of the conflict within his immediate family and the defections of Hussain and Saddam Kamel, Saddam Hussain might use the Baath Party structures, his original power base, to bolster his position. The Iraqi leader appeared to have curbed the power of his son Uday at least temporarily. The Deputy Prime Minister Tareq Aziz implied in October that Uday had no official political role. There were further changes in the Council of Ministers at the end of the year, with new appointments made to the portfolios of education, agriculture, irrigation and finance.

In February 1996 the two defectors, Hussain and Saddam Kamel, returned to Baghdad, having been granted a pardon by Saddam Hussain. Immediately after their return to Iraq the two men (who were promptly divorced from their wives) were assassinated. Unconfirmed reports suggested that their father, Kamel Hassan al-Majid, and a number of their children were also killed in the attack, allegedly perpetrated by men under the command of Saddam Hussain's son, Uday. Their assassination led to international condemnation and was followed by reports of armed clashes among rival clans in Baghdad, and in the Ajwa region of Tikrit. In December Uday sustained serious injuries after surviving an attempted assassination in Baghdad. Both the Dulaimi tribe and the Shi'a group, Ad-Da'wa al-Islamiya, claimed responsibility for the attack, but there was considerable speculation that the attack had been perpetrated in retaliation for the murders of Hussain and Saddam Kamel. At the end of March another high-level defection had occurred when Lt-Gen. Nizar Kharaji, Chief of Staff of the Iraqi Army during the Gulf War, fled to Amman, Jordan, where he joined the Iraqi National Accord (INA—see below). In June reports emerged of a new coup plot involving senior officers of the Republican Guard and close associates of Saddam Hussain from Tikrit. More than 100 officers, including two army commanders, were arrested and subsequently executed. Mounting opposition to the President from within the armed forces was widely considered to have prompted his decision to transfer responsibility for the national military intelligence department from the Ministry of Defence, and to create new paramilitary units entrusted with the protection of his own family.

Elections to 220 of the 250 seats in the National Assembly were held in March 1996. Predictably, all 160 candidates from the ruling Baath Party gained seats, with the remaining 60 seats being won by so-called independent candidates. According to official sources, 93.5% of the approximately 8m.-strong electorate participated in the poll. Iraqi opposition groups derided the regime's claim to have introduced greater democracy and denounced the elections as a farce. Elections to local councils were conducted in May. The new councils were to be responsible not only for municipal services, but also for food rationing. In December Latif Jasim was relieved of the Labour and Social Affairs portfolio in order to devote himself to Baath Party activities; he was succeeded by Abd al-Hamid Aziz Muhammad Salih as-Sayigh.

In May 1996 government forces were reported to have launched a major offensive against the Shi'a opposition and tribes in the Basra Governorate and further fighting in the southern marshlands was reported in September. At the end of the year there were armed clashes between the security forces and the Shi'a opposition throughout the southern regions as the Government attempted to eliminate popular unrest in that part of the country. Early in 1997, the US-based Human Rights Watch condemned the fiercely repressive activities of Iraqi Government forces in the southern marshlands during 1996 and also claimed that Saddam Hussain's regime was continuing to engage in severe abuses of human rights against the Iraqi people. Saddam Hussain's absence from celebrations organized to mark his 60th birthday, at the end of April 1997, prompted speculation that security concerns surrounding the President had intensified severely since the assassination attempt on his son, Uday. In June it was reported that a senior air force commander, Maj.-Gen. Izz ad-Dulaimi, had been assassinated in Baghdad. In mid-1997 a number of changes were made to senior military posts, including, most notably, the reported replacement of Qusay Hussain by one of the President's nephews, Kemal Mustafa at-Tikriti, as Commander of the Republican Guard, in August. (Qusay's removal was somewhat unexpected since his political profile appeared to have been enhanced since the attempt on his brother's life, and some commentators

had described his recent status as being akin to 'heir apparent'.) New appointments were also made to head the national intelligence directorate (where a new anti-corruption campaign for the ranks of the Baath Party and the armed forces was to be formulated) and to a number of provincial governorships in the central and southern regions. Ali Hassan al-Majid, a former member of the RCC and a cousin of the President, was appointed Military Governor of the southern provinces of Basra and Nasiriya. Al-Majid had gained a reputation for his uncompromising response to insurrection during the Kurdish uprisings of the late 1980s, and reports soon emerged of a fresh campaign of subjugation in the southern marshlands.

Towards the end of 1997 reports began to emerge of renewed efforts by Saddam Hussain to impose his authority on the nation. A number of senior military officers and Baath Party members (several of them relatives or known associates of Maj.-Gen. Wafiq as-Samarrai, a former head of military intelligence who had fled Iraq some three years previously to join the opposition INC, and had successfully sought political asylum in the United Kingdom) were executed, as were an estimated 800 prisoners suspected of belonging to opposition organizations. Many mid-level and senior Baath Party officials were also replaced in a political purge that was thought to have been organized in order to dilute the influence of increasingly powerful provincial party groups.

Iraqi opposition groups, however, remained weak and divided. One of the founding members of the INA, Gen. Tawfiq al-Yasiri, resigned in February 1998, accusing the organization's leadership of misappropriating funds. In early 1998 one of the leaders of the rival, London-based INC, Ahmad Chalabi, visited Washington, DC, to lobby support from the US Congress. Chalabi claimed that Iraq was ripe for a broad-based revolt, and urged the US Government to transform the existing air exclusion zones in the north and south of the country into total exclusion zones for the Baghdad authorities, from which an INC provisional government could operate, protected from Saddam Hussain's military forces. Although certain Republican politicians in Washington were sympathetic to Chalabi's request, the US Administration remained cautious about encouraging civil war in Iraq and questioned the INC's ability to topple the Iraqi leader. Later in the year, however, the US Administration announced that 73 exiled opposition groups would benefit from US support. Assistant Secretary of State Martin Indyk further stated that although he did not believe that the opposition groups were capable of ousting Saddam Hussain, they warranted assistance because they represented an alternative vision for Iraq to Saddam Hussain that was 'democratic in its aspirations'. After it was revealed that the USA had given some $21m. directly to Ahmad Chalabi, other groups protested that they had not been consulted. In October the US Congress overwhelmingly approved the Iraq Liberation Act, which allows the President to provide up to $97m. in military assistance to the exiled opposition groups. While Congress appeared convinced that direct attempts to destabilize Saddam Hussain's regime by means of some sort of military offensive organized by the Iraqi opposition were the only way forward, the Clinton administration, and particularly the State Department, remained sceptical that a reinvigorated opposition could bring down the Iraqi leader, given the infighting that was endemic within and between the different groups, as well as the high level of corruption. Muhammad Baqir al-Hakim, the leader of the Shi'ite opposition SCIRI, refused to involve his group in any US-sponsored plan to overthrow Saddam Hussain. In January 1999 the USA selected seven opposition groups that it judged worthy of receiving US assistance, but also widened its contacts to include other groups and individuals. At the beginning of April 11 opposition groups gathered in London, United Kingdom, where they pledged to relaunch and reform the moribund INC and to prepare by July a plan of campaign against Saddam Hussain's regime. Although the two main Kurdish factions, the KDP and the PUK, as well as the INA, attended the meeting, SCIRI and the ICP did not participate. The US special representative for transition in Iraq, Frank Ricciardone, and the Vice-Chairman of the US Senate Intelligence Committee, Senator Bob Kerry, also attended. Two new organizations were created at the meeting: a collegiate leadership of seven members (six members were nominated, with the remaining place reserved for a representative of SCIRI), and a five-member committee charged with contacting all opposition groups in preparation for a meeting in July, intended to be a sort of constituent assembly of a united opposition. Ahmad Chalabi was removed from his post as president of the INC, and Salah esh-Sheikhli of the INA was named as the new spokesman for the organization. Indyk described the London meeting as an important step towards the downfall of Saddam Hussain's regime, but most observers were far from optimistic that the opposition groups would be able to put aside their differences. The fact that little progress had been made in implementing the accord between the two Kurdish factions (see above) did not augur well for the success of a much larger coalition of groups. A US official was reported as stating inform- ally that the Clinton administration was unlikely to release the bulk of the \$97m. in military assistance until the opposition agreed on a viable strategy. At the end of May the US Secretary of State, Madeleine Albright, met the new interim leadership of the INC and six other opponents of Saddam Hussain. At the same time the State Department announced that a plan to provide the opposition in exile with equipment and training to set up a headquarters, publicize its cause and prepare for running the country had been prepared and would shortly be submitted to Congress. In mid-June Bruce Riedel, senior director of Near East and South Asian Affairs at the National Security Council, told journalists that the USA would continue to encourage a change of leadership in Baghdad and would work towards that goal with the Iraqi opposition in exile. However, Riedel made no reference to American military assistance to the Iraqi opposition in exile, but appealed directly to the Iraqi army to overthrow Saddam Hussain. In September Secretary of State Albright received an Iraqi opposition delegation including the INC, and in October the USA organized and funded a conference of the INC in New York at which a new leadership was installed. In late October Thomas Pickering, Under Secretary for Political Affairs at the State Department, declared that the USA could see no alternative to the revival and reunification of the INC. However, some commentators argued that despite pressure from Congress for more substan- tive assistance to the INC, the Clinton administration still had serious doubts about the organization's ability to bring about political change in Iraq and was unlikely to provide any substan- tive material support. The unity of the revived INC remained fragile and SCIRI, one of the few opposition groups with a significant fighting force inside Iraq, still refused to join the organization. In November a spokesman for SCIRI stated that his group was not convinced that the USA was strongly com- mitted to the Iraqi opposition and maintained that the INC's reputation in Iraq had been seriously undermined by its close links with Washington.

SCIRI, financed and equipped by Iran, continued its high profile attacks on key symbols of Saddam Hussain's regime. The Shi'ite opposition group appeared to have carried out a rocket attack on the Military Intelligence Directorate in Baghdad in March 2000, and in early May it claimed responsi- bility for a rocket attack on the presidential palace in Baghdad as a result of which a number of Republican Guards were killed. It was reported that Saddam Hussain had been due to meet his two sons at the palace at that time. Meanwhile the ICP, with its base in the Kurdish enclave, nevertheless remained active in the centre and south of the country, and periodic attacks on the security forces and members of the Baath party in these areas were attributed to its militants. In an interview with *Ash-Sharq al-Awsat* in May, the Speaker of the National Assembly, Sa'adoun Hammadi, declared that some opposition groups now in exile would be allowed to return to Iraq and under proposed new legislation whereby they could apply to form political par- ties. The new proposals embraced all 'nationalist' forces, but reaffirmed the dominant role of the ruling Baath Party which alone would be allowed to campaign among members of the army and security forces. There seemed little likelihood of any opposition group taking up the offer. In December the outgoing Clinton Administration approved a US \$12m. programme to help the INC to re-establish a base in the Kurdish enclave, from which it was expected to launch clandestine operations into Iraqi Government-controlled areas to distribute humanitarian relief and engage in propaganda. However, the extent to which

the USA would be willing to assist and protect the opposition remained unclear. Although some senior US Republicans had called for the USA to recognize a provisional government of Iraq headed by the INC, Colin Powell, Secretary of State in the new Administration of George W. Bush, was reported to have expressed serious reservations about the effectiveness of the Iraqi opposition and was therefore unlikely to support the plan. In January 2002 the US Department of State suspended funding to the INC after an audit revealed 'weaknesses' in accounting for US financial assistance to the movement. Although funding was subsequently restored, the episode revealed a significant lack of confidence in an organization regarded by some US officials as a crucial element in plans to overthrow Saddam Hussain. In March the State Department announced a donation of \$5m. to the Middle East Institute in Washington, DC, to finance a meeting of Iraqi opposition interests.

The annual report of the UN special rapporteur on Iraq, Max Van der Stoel, presented to the UN Commission on Human Rights in Geneva in April 1998, was once again highly critical of the Iraqi regime's record on human rights. The report stated that at least 1,500 people had been executed during 1997, mainly for political reasons, and that most of that number were killed as part of the 'prison cleansing' operation conducted in November and December. Iraqi officials dismissed the report as 'a mere repetition of the same allegations and false accusations'. (A separate report published in March claimed that some 16,000 instances of forced disappearance had been registered in Iraq during the previous 10 years—the highest number in the world.) Also in April the Iran-based SCIRI claimed that a renewed offensive against the Shi'a opposition in the southern regions had resulted in the execution of some 60 Shi'ites during March. Van der Stoel later denounced the assassinations of two senior Shi'a religious leaders, Ayatollah Murtada al-Burujirdi and Grand Ayatollah Mirza Ali al-Gharawi, in April and June re- spectively. Van der Stoel reported that both men had been harassed and warned by the Iraqi authorities to cease organizing prayer meetings, and expressed fears that the murders were part of a systematic attack on the independent leadership of Iraq's Shi'a Muslims. Although Ayatollah al-Gharawi had never been involved in political activity, there had been reports that the Iraqi Government wished to replace him as *Marja* (a senior spiritual leader of Shi'a Muslims) by another candidate whom many leading Shi'a religious scholars believed was unqualified for the position. Van der Stoel stated that the Iraqi authorities failed to investigate either murder thoroughly. The Iraqi Gov- ernment, however, denied any involvement in the killings, attri- buting them instead to 'malicious foreign-based elements'. Some observers argued that there may have been a link between the attempted assassination of Izzat Ibrahim ad-Duri, Vice- President of the RCC, during a visit to the holy city of Karbala in October 1998, and the murders of the two Shi'a clerics. Towards the end of 1998 there were several reports alleging that the security forces had undertaken new campaigns in the southern provinces involving attacks on villages, mass arrests and executions. The appointment of Saddam Hussain's cousin, Ali Hassan al-Majid, as military commander of the southern provinces, was interpreted as evidence of the regime's determin- ation to eliminate unrest in the region. In a new report sub- mitted by Van der Stoel in November, the special rapporteur asserted that human rights violations continued to be perpe- trated by the Government of Iraq, and that the information he had received presented 'an alarming picture of one of the most repressive regimes in the world since the end of the Second World War'. Van der Stoel reported that he had received allega- tions that mass executions continued in Abu Ghrayb prison, where he believed that more than 170 detainees from the southern and north-central areas of Iraq had been executed between December 1997 and July 1998. He further stated that inhuman and degrading punishments remained in force, and that, despite the regime's denials, he had evidence that these continued to be imposed sometimes without due process of law and by persons who held no judicial or similar authority. In addition to cases of torture, Van der Stoel continued to receive lists of persons arbitrarily arrested and detained in extremely harsh conditions without specific charges or trial, lists of cases of disappearances, as well as lists of families forced on ethnic grounds to leave their homes. As part of a long-running policy of 'Arabization' of the oil-rich Kirkuk region, Van der Stoel asserted that some 150,000 people of Kurdish origin had been evicted from their homes, and that evictions were occurring on a daily basis. The report stated that more than 200,000 people had been internally displaced in the rest of the country, mainly in the southern provinces. Van der Stoel identified the plight of displaced persons, many of whom were women and children, as one of the most pressing humanitarian concerns in Iraq. Despite the expanded oil-for-food programme, available resources were not being channelled adequately to those in the southern provinces who were in the greatest need. It was Van der Stoel's assessment that the situation with regard to food and health remained 'precarious', and that the primary responsibility for the suffering of the Iraqi people lay with the Government in Baghdad.

In February 1999 Ayatollah as-Sadr was assassinated in the holy city of Najaf, the third senior Shi'a cleric to be murdered in less than a year. In his last sermon, a week before his death, as-Sadr had called on the authorities to release immediately an estimated 100 Shi'a clerics who had been arbitrarily arrested. The Iraqi Government again denied any involvement in the murder, and swiftly suppressed widespread riots among Shi'ites throughout the southern provinces, as well as in at least one major suburb of Baghdad, which erupted following as-Sadr's murder. In April the Iraqi authorities announced that four men had been executed for the murder of the Ayatollah. While most sources maintained that as-Sadr had been murdered by government agents, others claimed that he may have been killed by other Shi'a who regarded him as a 'puppet' of the regime. There were reports of continuing unrest among Shi'a in the southern provinces. In June it was reported that Saddam Hussain had dismissed Ali Hassan al-Majid as military commander of the southern region and replaced him with Gen. Ayad Fitayeh ar-Rawi, a former commander of the Republican Guard. Al-Majid is believed to have quarrelled with Saddam Hussain's son, Qusay, over how to deal with unrest in the south and some sources claimed that Qusay had demanded al-Majid's removal from office. However, by the end of the year al-Majid appeared to have been reinstated in his former post. Reports in early 2000 suggested that unrest in the southern provinces had diminished and that the Government was no longer on the defensive in this region. Some Shi'a leaders continued to face intimidation, even murder, while others were offered 'pardons' if they co-operated with Saddam Hussain's regime.

In May 1998 the Minister of Labour and Social Affairs, Abd al-Hamid Aziz Muhammad Salih as-Sayigh, was dismissed after stating that Iraq's prisons were grossly over-populated. He was replaced in July with Saadi Tuma-Abbas, who had been Minister of Defence at the time of the Gulf War. Salih as-Sayigh (who was himself imprisoned following his dismissal) was reported to have fallen victim to Saddam Hussain's elder son, Uday, who, having been disregarded as a political force as a result of the serious injuries sustained in the attempt on his life in December 1996, now appeared to have recovered sufficiently to pursue his ambitions, although the extent of his political influence remained unclear. Uday was also believed to have been responsible for the dismissal of Nouri Faisal ash-Shaher as governor of Baghdad. Also in May 1998 the opposition claimed that 22 officers of the Republican Guard and the Special Republican Guard had been executed for plotting a coup, and their bodies publicly displayed in Baghdad. However, the Iraqi Government insisted that the men were executed after having been found guilty of corruption and bribery. In June Jordanian newspapers reported that Saddam Hussain's daughter, Rana, was seeking to gain control of a bank account in Amman that had been opened by her late husband, Saddam Kamel, after his defection. The report provided the first firm evidence that the Iraqi authorities were trying to recover some of the tens of millions of dollars believed to have been taken out of the country by Saddam and Hussain Kamel (see above).

Saddam Hussain's half-brother, Barzan at-Tikriti, who had spent several years in Geneva as Iraq's envoy to the UN, was due to return to Baghdad in October 1998 but appeared reluctant to do so, and opposition sources claimed that members of his family had been placed under house arrest to induce him to return. The main reason put forward for Barzan's reluctance to return to Baghdad was his strained relations with his nephew, Saddam

Hussain's son Uday, whose brief marriage to Barzan's daughter had failed and who had apparently been involved in 1993 in the shooting of one of Barzan's brothers and the imprisonment of another. In late January 1999 rumours surfaced that the authorities had in the previous month successfully foiled a coup attempt by officers of the third army corps. Some sources claimed that the coup was to have been launched to coincide with 'Operation Desert Fox' (see below) but was uncovered just before the air-strikes began. At the same time SCIRI reported that Lt-Gen. Kamil Sachit al-Janabi, deputy commander in the southern provinces, had been executed, along with eight others, for conspiring against the regime. In the early months of 1999 there were unconfirmed reports of more purges within the armed forces, involving the arrest and execution of hundreds of officers. Saddam Hussain's son Qusay was also reported to have been accorded further 'special security' powers to interrogate senior figures within the regime suspected of being disloyal. Among those he was claimed to have summoned was Barzan at-Tikriti, who had eventually returned to Baghdad but whose loyalty was again questioned after one of his aides defected to the opposition. An unconfirmed report claimed that in late May violent clashes broke out between units of the Republican Guard based at the Suwayrah barracks south of Baghdad in which a number of soldiers and officers were killed. After the alleged incident there were reports that security had been tightened in and around the capital indicating that the regime may have regarded the clashes between Republican Guard units as an attempted *coup d'état*. Later in the year there were reports in the Arabic press that Qusay had been appointed deputy commander of the Iraqi army and commander of the northern military region, while one of the newspapers claimed that Saddam Hussain had also decided to make his younger son heir apparent. Some sources argued that Qusay's elevation was in response to continued unrest within the armed forces and the attempted assassination, in early September, of the Vice-President, Taha Yassin Ramadan, near Tikrit, possibly by Iraqi soldiers. Qusay has extensive experience of Kurdish affairs and his appointment to the northern region would allow him to exploit tensions between the two main Kurdish factions (the KDP and the PUK) and thus undermine the fragile cease-fire in the Kurdish enclave to the advantage of the Government. Early in 2000 the London-based *Al-Hayat* newspaper reported that Qusay had assumed the task of improving the efficiency of the general security services following the removal and execution of the head of the Mukhabarat, Rafi Dahham al-Tikriti, a development that was interpreted by some as an attempt by Qusay to establish his own power base. It was claimed that Qusay's promotion had antagonized important members of Saddam Hussain's immediate and extended family, notably his elder son, Uday, who had not abandoned his own political ambitions, the al-Majid clan, who in the past had been responsible for ensuring the loyalty of the armed forces, and the Ibrahim branch, especially its senior member, Barzan al-Tikriti. In September there were reports that Barzan had defected to the UAE because of tensions with both Qusay and his elder brother. Official sources in Baghdad strongly denied these reports and insisted that Barzan was merely on a private visit to Switzerland. Nevertheless, it was rumoured that Barzan had met Sheikh Zayed, the President of the UAE, who was also visiting Geneva at this time, and that his request for asylum had been refused. In November the opposition claimed that Barzan had been placed under house arrest after his office at the ministry of foreign affairs, where he is a special adviser to the President, had been closed. Later Barzan was reported to have been interrogated by the Deputy Prime Minister, Tareq Aziz, and Saddam Hussain's private secretary, Abd Hamid Hamud, about his movements when he was abroad earlier in the year. Early in 2000 speculation about Qusay's elevation was fuelled by an unconfirmed report in *Al-Watan al-Arabi*, published in Paris, that Saddam Hussain had called a meeting of senior members of his extended family at which he had declared his younger son to be his official successor. Subsequent reports appeared to confirm the news of Qusay's nomination as Saddam Hussain's heir apparent.

Elections to the National Assembly were held in March 2000 in which, according to official results, all 165 candidates from the ruling Baath Party were elected; the remaining 55 elective seats were secured by independent candidates, while a further

30 independents were nominated by the Government to fill the 30 seats reserved for representatives of the Kurdish areas of the north, where the Iraqi authorities stated it was impossible to organize elections since the region remained 'occupied' by the USA. To little surprise, Saddam Hussain's elder son, Uday, standing for the first time, won the highest number of votes cast for a single candidate. At the first session of the new parliament in early April, Sa'adoun Hammadi was unanimously re-elected Speaker. There had been some speculation that Uday would be elected to that post; however, according to reports in the London-based Arabic press, after 'a verbal altercation' between Uday, Hammadi and RCC Vice-President Izzat Ibrahim, during which Uday accused Hammadi of being too old to carry out the duties of Speaker, Saddam Hussain intervened and insisted that Hammadi be re-elected. Reports in June that Uday had refused to attend new parliamentary sessions were interpreted by some observers as evidence that his differences with Hammadi had not been resolved. Others, however, claimed that Uday's absence resulted from an unsuccessful operation which had left him immobile. Uday did not appear at the National Assembly until December, and in his first address was highly critical of several ministries. However, it was his attack on the Ministry of Awqaf (Religious Endowments) and Religious Affairs that attracted most attention: he accused the ministry of 'sectarian discrimination' for failing to build enough mosques in Shi'ite Muslim areas. For a leading member of Iraq's Sunni-dominated élite to refer publicly to such a sensitive issue was unprecedented. The fact that most of the official media avoided any reference to this part of this address suggested that his comments were not authorized by Saddam Hussain. Some observers claimed that Uday was trying to 'reinvent' himself as the people's champion. Others interpreted his latest outburst as a further attempt to provoke a confrontation with his younger brother, since Uday remained bitterly resentful of Qusay's rapid elevation within the Iraqi regime.

Meanwhile, in May 2000 Abd al-Jabbar Tawfiq Muhammad was removed from his post as Minister of Higher Education and Scientific Research by presidential decree; his responsibilities were assumed by the Minister of Education, Fahd Salim ash-Shokrah. In late June it was announced that Shabib Lazim al-Malki would retire as Minister of Justice in July and be replaced by Mundhir Ibrahim ash-Shawi. In early August Abd at-Tawab Mullah Howeich, the Minister for Military Industrialization, was promoted to become the fourth Deputy Prime Minister.

In June 2000 *Al-Hayat* reported that some 20 members of the security forces had been killed after fighting flared up with tribes hostile to the regime in the agricultural areas between Najaf and Diwaniyah, south of Baghdad. According to the report the Iraqi authorities had accused the tribes of using revenues from the sale of rice to the Gulf states to purchase weapons which they used to attack security posts and party headquarters. The military commander of the Central Euphrates had been ordered to quell down the unrest. A report in *Al-Arab al-Youm* in July claiming that 81 senior officials from the Baath Party's 'Iraqi Command' had been dismissed was strongly denied by the Iraqi authorities. However, some observers considered that the report could have some substance because of a proclamation by Saddam Hussain, broadcast by Iraqi television, that the four Baath Party regional commands established in late 1998, just before Operation Desert Fox, had been suspended with immediate effect. Although the Iraqi leader claimed that the commands were no longer needed because 'the result of the battle is in Iraq's favour', their suspension was probably aimed at removing any potential for the emergence of rival power centres.

In early September 2000 a report appeared in *Ash-Sharq al-Awsat* stating that Saddam Hussain was suffering from lymphatic cancer and was being treated by a team of European doctors in Baghdad, where he was preparing to undergo chemotherapy. Iraqi officials rejected the report out of hand, insisting that Saddam Hussain continued to enjoy good health. Arabic news sources later reported that the President's younger son, Qusay, had been appointed head of a family council established to govern Iraq should Saddam Hussain die or become incapacitated. Rumours of Saddam Hussain's declining health persisted, and there were reports that he had suffered a stroke after reviewing a military parade at the end of December. Most such rumours emanated from the Iraqi opposition and could not be substantiated.

In mid-April 2001 the Deputy Prime Minister, Tareq Aziz, was named acting Minister of Foreign Affairs, replacing Muhammad Saeed as-Sahaf who became Minister of Culture and Information. Humam Abd-al-Khaliq Abd al-Ghafur was transferred from the latter post to that of Minister of Higher Education and Scientific Research, while Naji Sabri Ahmad al-Hadithi, formerly Iraq's ambassador to Austria, was appointed to the new post of Minister of State for Foreign Affairs; he was formally named Minister of Foreign Affairs in August. No official explanation was given for the portfolio changes, although as-Sahaf was believed to have been transferred because of his poor performance at a summit meeting of Arab leaders, convened in Amman in March, when Iraq failed to secure unanimous support for the immediate lifting of UN sanctions. In mid-May, at its 12th Regional Congress, Saddam Hussain was re-elected Secretary-General of the Baath Party, while Qusay was appointed to the party's Iraqi Command for the first time, and was subsequently awarded a deputy command post in its powerful military branch. Qusay's elevation was widely interpreted as further confirmation that he was being groomed to succeed his father. Izzat Ibrahim, Vice-President of the RCC, remained the party's Deputy Secretary-General while Vice-President Taha Yassin Ramadan, Deputy Prime Minister Tareq Aziz and Ali Hassan al-Majid all retained their party posts. In late May the Minister of Irrigation, Mahmoud Diyab al-Ahmad, was appointed acting Minister of the Interior, in place of Muhammad Ziman Abd ar-Razzaq, while Muhammad Hamzah az-Zubaydi was removed from the office of Deputy Prime Minister. Presidential decrees issued in early and late July respectively elevated the Head of the Presidential Office, Ahmad Hussain Khudayyir, and the Minister of State for Military Industrialization, Abd at-Tawab Mullah Howeich, to the rank of Deputy Prime Minister. Qusay swiftly began to remove from office those senior officers whom he believed were not in favour of his rapid elevation through the military high command, replacing them with his own loyal supporters. Meanwhile, Izzat Ibrahim was given the task of mobilizing support for Qusay among Baath Party members. A report published in the British press in July in which it was claimed that Saddam Hussain's elder son, Uday, had converted to Shi'ism in an attempt to win popularity among the country's Shi'a majority was strongly denied in his newspaper, *Babil*.

The sudden death of Grand Ayatollah Sayed Hussain Bahr al-'Ulum in late June 2001 and his hasty burial the same day aroused suspicions among some commentators that he had not died of natural causes. Three other senior Shi'a religious leaders (Ayatollahs al-Burujirdi, al-Gharawi and as-Sadr) had been murdered in 1998 and 1999 (see above). Shortly before his death Bahr al-'Ulum, a member of one of the most prominent families of clerics in Iraq, had refused a request by the television channel owned by Uday Hussain to express his approval at the appointment of Qusay Hussain to the regional leadership of the Baath Party, asserting that every year his calls to the government for the release of the many religious scholars held in detention had been ignored. Conveniently ignoring his own sons' misdemeanours, Saddam Hussain was reported to have rebuked senior officials at a government meeting in August, alleging that their children were abusing their privileged position. One of the first to be made an example of was Tareq Aziz's son, Ziyad, who was sentenced to 20 years' imprisonment for taking 'commissions' on contracts made with foreign companies.

As speculation mounted that Iraq would become a target in the USA's 'war against terror' (arising from the 11 September suicide attacks against New York and Washington, DC), unconfirmed reports emerged that the Iraqi regime had begun arming tribes loyal to Saddam Hussain, in the hope that they might suppress any attempted insurrection in the provinces in the event of a US-led ground attack. The Government had also given instructions for fuel-tanks and storage facilities to be built, specifically for the use of those units of the Republican Guard on whose loyalty the regime believed it could count. In February 2002, as the Bush Administration reiterated its determination to secure the downfall of Saddam Hussain's regime, Baghdad made further preparations for a possible US-led attack, reinforcing military units deployed along the borders of the Kurdish enclave, transferring documents and sensitive equipment to secret locations and organizing the mobilization of numerous military and paramilitary groups.

Several days of festivities were held to mark Saddam Hussain's 65th birthday on 28 April 2002 (although some sources insisted that he was only 63 years old) at which the Iraqi leader made a rare public appearance to greet Iraqi children at one of the presidential palaces.

CONCLUSION OF AGREEMENT ON PETROLEUM SALES

In January 1996 Iraq indicated that it was willing to 'enter into a dialogue' on an oil-for-food agreement with the UN, provided that no conditions were attached to it. Iraq had originally rejected UN Security Council Resolution 986 of April 1995 (see above), arguing that the terms were a violation of its sovereignty. Under the conditions of the resolution, Iraq had to accept UN monitoring of the distribution of humanitarian supplies and to agree to the supply of specified amounts of food and medicine to the Kurdish-controlled enclave in the north. On several occasions the Iraqi Government had indicated that it wished to renegotiate the terms of the resolution, but the UN Security Council had refused and insisted that Iraq must accept the conditions as set out in the original offer. The Security Council agreed that the UN Secretary-General should begin new talks with Iraq on the implementation of Resolution 986, and a first round commenced in early February 1996. By the end of April UN and Iraqi negotiators had held three rounds of talks, but no agreement had been reached on a draft memorandum of understanding. It was reported that agreement could have been reached, but that the USA and the United Kingdom had insisted on certain changes to the original terms of Resolution 986, including a demand that Iraq should play no part in the supply and distribution of supplies to the Kurdish governorates. Despite these problems, Iraq proceeded in early March to sign a protocol with Turkey on resuming oil exports through the two pipelines from the Kirkuk oilfields to the Turkish ports of Ceyhan and Yumurtalık on the Mediterranean. A fourth round of talks between the UN and Iraq began in early May, but in the middle of the month the two sides remained divided over the conditions which should govern limited sales of Iraqi petroleum. On 20 May, however, Iraq accepted the UN terms. The memorandum of agreement, which had to be renewed every six months, detailed stringent conditions for the sale of up to US $4,000m.-worth of Iraqi oil a year in order to purchase food and medicine, and to finance UN operations in Iraq. The agreement stipulated that 30% of the revenues obtained would be used to pay war reparations, and that a further 13%–15% would be spent on aid to the Kurdish provinces. Independent inspection agents would be appointed by the UN to verify the arrival of humanitarian supplies in Iraq and their equitable distribution. The UN would take direct charge of the distribution of supplies in the Kurdish-held areas. Dr al-Anbari, Iraq's chief negotiator at the UN, hoped that the agreement would be the first step leading to the gradual lifting of the embargo, but this appeared unlikely. There was, however, general acknowledgement that the agreement represented the biggest change in Iraq's relations with the international community since the war with the multinational force in 1991.

In March 1996 UN sanctions against Iraq were renewed for a further 60 days. The head of UNSCOM, Rolf Ekeus, reported to the Security Council that Iraq had not yet surrendered certain proscribed weapons or related materials and he expressed concern that Iraq might still be engaged in the development of prohibited weapons systems. He feared that Iraq was concealing as many as 16 surface-to-surface missiles armed with biological warheads from UN inspectors. On 27 March, in response to these fears, the Security Council unanimously approved Resolution 1051, which provided for the establishment of an elaborate system to monitor the export of any material and equipment to Iraq that could be used in the production of weapons of mass destruction, to come into force as soon as trade sanctions were lifted.

Confrontations between UN inspectors and Iraqi officials continued. In March 1996, for example, inspectors were prevented from entering and searching sites on five occasions. In June, during a visit to Baghdad, Ekeus signed an agreement with Tareq Aziz whereby Iraq promised to grant UN inspectors immediate access to sites provided they fully respected Iraq's concerns over sovereignty when visiting those sites deemed to be 'sensitive'. Yet, despite this, in late July a team of UN inspectors was barred from entering a 'sensitive site' and was forced to suspend its operations.

In late July 1996 Iraq's chief negotiator at the UN stated that Iraq's amended food distribution plan had been approved by the UN Secretary-General and that Iraq hoped that the agreement would now be swiftly implemented. On 31 July, however, it was announced that the USA, at a meeting of the UN Security Council sanctions committee, had withheld its approval of the amended food distribution plan as it required further details of monitoring procedures. Final approval of the sanctions committee (including that of the USA) for the implementation of Resolution 986 was granted on 8 August, and it was announced that the means of monitoring exports of Iraqi petroleum and the purchase and distribution of humanitarian goods inside Iraq were in the process of being established. In mid-September, however, the implementation of Resolution 986 was postponed indefinitely, following the deployment of Iraqi armed forces (in alliance with the forces of the KDP) inside the Kurdish 'safe haven' in northern Iraq. In response, the USA launched missile attacks on targets in southern Iraq. The threat of further retaliatory US attacks on Iraqi targets receded on 13 September, when Iraq announced that it would cease targeting allied aircraft enforcing the air exclusion zones. There was, in any case, little support among the international community for the escalation of retaliatory action which the USA appeared, initially, to wish to pursue. The US Government, nevertheless, continued to reinforce its military capabilities in the Gulf region. At the end of October Italy followed France in opening an interests section in a diplomatic mission in Baghdad, and in December Spain announced that it was sending a permanent diplomatic representative to its Baghdad embassy. Other Western countries were expected to begin to re-establish diplomatic relations with Iraq (suspended in 1991) following the implementation of the oil-for-food agreement.

At the beginning of December 1996 the UN Secretary-General issued a memorandum of understanding finally implementing Resolution 986, Iraq having accepted all the conditions stipulated by the UN. Petroleum began to flow through the pipeline to Turkey on 10 December. Revenues from the sale of Iraqi oil were to be deposited in a special account at the Banque Nationale de Paris in New York which was to issue letters of credit for all supplies of food and medicine ordered by the Iraqi authorities, and funds would only be released when the goods had been inspected and verified by UN monitors on the Iraqi border. UN teams had the right to visit all humanitarian supply centres in Iraq without prior warning, and 151 UN monitors were to supervise the actual distribution of humanitarian supplies. However, international agencies expressed doubts that the funds made available for humanitarian relief under the terms of the agreement would be sufficient to alleviate the high levels of malnutrition and disease among the Iraqi population. Part of Iraq's oil revenue was to be allocated to the UN Compensation Commission (UNCC), which had been unable to settle the majority of Gulf War compensation claims because of inadequate funds. The first shipments of food and humanitarian supplies purchased under the new agreement reached Iraq in late March 1997.

Following approval of the oil-for-food agreement, a new dispute arose between UNSCOM and the Iraqi authorities. Ekeus reported that Iraqi officials had refused UN inspectors permission to remove *Scud* missile components for examination abroad. At the end of December 1996 all UN sanctions against Iraq were renewed for a further 60 days. At the beginning of April 1997 Iraq violated the southern air exclusion zone in order to fly pilgrims to Jeddah, Saudi Arabia, and at the end of the month, ignoring US warnings, Iraqi helicopters collected returning pilgrims from the Saudi border. Both President Clinton and the US Secretary of Defense, William Cohen, issued renewed warnings to the Iraqi Government that it should not challenge international restrictions on the use of its airspace, but no retaliatory measures were undertaken. In its six-monthly report, presented to the UN Security Council on 18 April, UNSCOM stated that it was still not satisfied that Iraq had disclosed full details of its past nuclear, biological and chemical weapons programme and warned that there could be 'political consequences' if Iraq continued to undermine the Commission's activities. These claims were rejected by the Iraqi Deputy Prime Minister, Tareq Aziz, in a letter to the Chairman of the Security Council. In May Iraq again accused the USA of disrupting the delivery of food and medicine purchased under UN Resolution 986 by delaying its approval of contracts without satisfactory reason.

Reporting to the US Congress in May 1997 on efforts to secure Iraq's compliance with UN resolutions, President Clinton reaffirmed that Saddam Hussain remained a serious threat to the Iraqi people and to regional peace and stability. He declared that the USA would not relax its sanctions until the Iraqi authorities complied with all of their obligations under UN resolutions. The US President stated that the northern and southern air exclusion zones would be maintained and emphasized the scale of US forces in the region. He criticized the Iraqi leadership for refusing to co-operate fully with UN weapons inspectors and condemned Iraqi efforts to impose new restrictions on UN officials responsible for monitoring the distribution of humanitarian supplies to the Iraqi people. He stated that his administration would continue to support the various Iraqi opposition groups and non-governmental organizations monitoring the human rights situation in Iraq. At the beginning of June the UN Security Council unanimously approved the extension of the oil-for-food agreement for a further six months, despite complaints from both the USA and Iraq. The Security Council indicated that it would consider extending the programme for a third six-month period if there were no major problems during the second stage, but rejected Iraq's request to increase the amount of oil that it was permitted to sell under the agreement. In response to demands from the USA and the United Kingdom for more information on the distribution of humanitarian supplies, the UN Secretary-General, Kofi Annan, dispatched his Under-Secretary-General for Humanitarian Affairs, Yasushi Akashi, to Iraq to investigate these concerns. Akashi confirmed that almost all of the UN World Food Programme (WFP) observers were in place and had been given access to all parts of the country, but had discovered no evidence of discrimination in the distribution of supplies. Akashi's report also drew attention to certain administrative and financial deficiencies in the UN's implementation of the oil-for-food agreement which continued to result in serious delays in the processing and distribution of humanitarian supplies. However, later in June Iraq suspended oil exports under the agreement, and on 18 June the Minister of Oil, Amir Muhammad Rashid, stated that exports would resume following UN approval of a new distribution plan proposed by the Iraqi authorities.

The Iraqi authorities continued to complain about the large number of contracts, especially for medical and water-treatment equipment, that had either been rejected or delayed by the UN Security Council sanctions committee, and to accuse the USA of obstructing humanitarian efforts. The Iraqi authorities drew attention to the contrast between the slow pace of progress of the work of the sanctions committee and the speed at which the UNCC had moved to deal with claims for compensation arising from Iraq's invasion of Kuwait. US officials, however, insisted that the Iraqi Government was deliberately abusing its humanitarian imports facility to obtain goods that could be used for other purposes. Iraq and the UN agreed a new distribution plan in early August 1997, incorporating improvements designed to accelerate the approval process, and Iraqi oil exports resumed on 14 August. In order to enable Iraq to meet its revenue target for the first three months of the second phase of the oil-for-food agreement, in September the UN Security Council extended the deadline to the beginning of October. By the end of August, 672 contracts had been approved by the sanctions committee, 20 rejected and 83 withheld. The UN renewed the agreement for a third six-month period on 4 December and agreed to consider changes to the procedures and value of oil exports during that period. This move failed to satisfy Iraq, and oil exports were immediately suspended. In early January 1998 revisions proposed by Iraq to a new plan for the distribution of food and medicine during the third phase were approved by the UN Secretary-General, and by mid-January Iraqi oil exports had resumed.

Following a visit to Iraq in January 1998, the UN Secretary-General, Kofi Annan, recommended an increase in the value of oil exports allocated to Iraq under the oil-for-food agreement, and on 20 February the UN Security Council agreed Resolution 1153, which more than doubled, to US $5,200m., the level of six-monthly revenue permitted to the Iraqi Government. Iraq was to be entitled to spend up to $3,550m. every six months on humanitarian imports, the definition of which was broadened to include investment in infrastructure projects such as repairs to oil production facilities and power generators. The remaining $1,650m. was to be used to pay war reparations and the cost of UN operations in Iraq. Some aspects of the new arrangement provoked criticism from Baghdad. The Iraqi authorities were particularly insistent that all additional revenues should be allocated to humanitarian imports. They also stated that they would not recognize any agreements concluded between the UN and the Kurds without consultation with Iraq, and would refuse to be dictated to by the UN on decisions relating to infrastructure projects. Despite its acceptance of the original oil-for-food agreement, the Iraqi Government had always been concerned that the deal would delay the full lifting of sanctions. The Iraqi authorities complained that the new arrangement implied a permanence to the agreement, and that it further violated Iraq's sovereignty. In addition, Iraq's ambassador to the UN, Nizar Hamdoon, stated that until vital rehabilitation of the oil sector was completed, Iraq could export no more than $4,000m. of oil every six months. A UN technical team visited Iraq in mid-March and reported that six-monthly exports worth only $3,000m. were currently possible and that this level of production could only be maintained if Iraq was permitted to import essential spare parts. As a result, the UN Secretary-General asked the Security Council to allocate $300m. for repairs to oil production facilities and requested that the value of Iraqi oil exports under the revised agreement be reduced to $4,000m. every six months. Iraq was required to submit a new aid distribution programme before the revised agreement could take effect. The new plan was submitted in early May and approved by the UN Secretary-General at the end of the month. It provided for oil sales of $4,500m. over the following six months, of which $3,100m. was to be allocated for humanitarian supplies and emergency infrastructure repairs, while the remainder would finance war reparations.

UN Security Council Resolution 1175, approved unanimously in mid-June 1998, stated that the new distribution plan would remain in effect, subject to constant review and amended as necessary. Iraq was permitted to import spare parts to the value of US $300m. in order to increase its oil production. The list of spare parts was to be approved by the sanctions committee, and not by UN overseers as Iraq had requested. Despite an increase in oil exports under phase four of the oil-for-food programme, the sharp fall in international petroleum prices meant that only some $3,000m. in revenues was generated. The fourth phase of the programme ended in late November, and there was a smooth transition to phase five, effective to May 1999. In late 1998 the UN co-ordinator of the oil-for-food programme, Denis Halliday, resigned, declaring that UN sanctions had served to strengthen Saddam Hussain's regime while causing poverty and disastrous social problems for the Iraqi people. He later wrote of what he termed a climate of despair, anger and frustration in Iraq, and warned that sanctions were fostering fanaticism. Halliday argued that while Saddam Hussain's regime was perceived in the West as 'extremist', there were many Iraqis who were critical of any attempt to reach a compromise with the UN, and that within the ruling Baath Party there were those who wanted Iraq to cease all co-operation with the UN and call on solidarity with Arab and Islamic states to secure food, medicines and other basic commodities. In late May 1999 the oil-for-food programme was extended for a sixth phase, to 20 November. In mid-May the Iraqi Minister of Health criticized the programme, claiming that although supply contracts had been signed, no new medical supplies had arrived in the country since the fifth phase began. At the same time the Iraqi Government again accused the USA and the United Kingdom of blocking contracts for spare parts that were essential for upgrading the country's oil facilities.

In March 1998 the US Department of State welcomed efforts by Iraq's neighbours, particularly Iran, to curtail the illegal export of crude oil and petroleum products by Saddam Hussain's regime. The scale of the smuggling, mainly through Iran, Turkey and the Gulf, was difficult to quantify, but US officials estimated that during February Iraq had been illegally transporting 100,000 b/d, providing the regime with annual revenues of some US $700m. which, it was believed, would be devoted to the security services and to the purchase of luxury goods for the political élite. In May the US Administration reported that oil-smuggling had increased once again, especially through Iran's territorial waters, a route that has proved difficult for the Multilateral Interdiction Force to police.

Following a number of incidents during June 1997 in which UNSCOM inspectors were further obstructed by Iraqi officials, on 21 June the UN Security Council unanimously adopted Resolution 1115, condemning the Iraqi authorities for repeatedly refusing to allow inspection teams access to sites and indicating that further sanctions might be imposed on Iraq if the authorities failed to co-operate with UNSCOM. A decision on the imposition of further sanctions was postponed until October. In July Rolf Ekeus, who had headed UNSCOM for six years, resigned and was replaced by an Australian diplomat, Richard Butler. During a visit to Baghdad, undertaken soon after his appointment, Butler noted a new spirit of co-operation with the Iraqi authorities, but in the weeks that followed UN operations appeared to be systematically frustrated by Iraqi officials. In October Butler presented his report of UNSCOM's operations during the previous five months to the UN Security Council. Despite noting significant progress in determining the scale of Iraq's chemical weapons programme, the report was essentially highly critical of the authorities in Baghdad, emphasizing a persistent lack of co-operation from the Iraqi Government. Subsequently, within the UN Security Council, the USA and the United Kingdom proposed a resolution to prohibit Iraqi officials considered to be responsible for obstructing weapons inspectors from leaving the country. France and Russia objected to the draft resolution but approved a revised version to impose a travel ban on Iraqi officials in April 1998, should non-co-operation with UNSCOM continue. At the same time sanctions against Iraq were renewed for a further 60 days.

In late October 1997 the RCC criticized the high proportion of UNSCOM personnel supplied by the USA, claiming that they were predisposed to resist the ending of sanctions. Iraq demanded that all such personnel should leave the country by 5 November. This deadline was extended by one week, however, in order to allow a UN mission to travel to Baghdad in an attempt to resolve the dispute. Negotiations proved unsuccessful, and therefore the UN Security Council unanimously adopted a resolution (No. 1137) that immediately activated the travel ban proposed earlier. The resolution also stipulated that Iraq should retract its decision to expel US personnel and stated that further Iraqi intransigence regarding weapons inspections would result in the suspension of the 60-day sanctions review until April 1998 and, furthermore, possibly provoke military action. Nevertheless, Iraq refused to rescind its decision and US weapons inspectors were forced to leave the country on 13 November. In response to the escalating crisis, both the USA and the United Kingdom ordered military reinforcements into the region, with both Kuwait and Bahrain reluctantly allowing warplanes to be deployed on their territory. Tensions appeared to ease on 19 November, after the Iraqi Deputy Prime Minister, Tareq Aziz, met the Russian Minister of Foreign Affairs, Yevgenii Primakov, who affirmed that Russia would continue to urge an end to economic sanctions, provided that Iraq complied with Resolution 1137. Following this assurance, UNSCOM weapons inspectors were permitted to return to Iraq on 21 November. Renewed Iraqi co-operation with UNSCOM was short-lived, however: shortly after the inspectors' return, Iraqi officials refused to allow UNSCOM the unconditional access that it sought to areas designated as presidential palaces. In mid-December Richard Butler, accompanied by commissioners from the United Kingdom, France and Russia, held talks in Baghdad with Tareq Aziz. Although Aziz expressed satisfaction at the presence of representatives of countries other than the USA, no progress was achieved. In response to the impasse, the US Secretary of Defense, William Cohen, reiterated the threat of military action in order to force Saddam Hussain to capitulate to UN demands, a move which was condemned by Russia. On

12 January 1998 Iraq prohibited inspections by a former US marine officer, Scott Ritter, claiming that he was spying for the CIA. On 19 January Richard Butler returned to Iraq, where he agreed to Russian requests to introduce outside experts into technical talks regarding the weapons inspections, scheduled to commence in February, thereby diluting the presence of US personnel. In spite of this concession, Iraq maintained a policy of non-co-operation with UNSCOM. In response, the US Secretary of State, Madeleine Albright, warned that the time for diplomacy was fast expiring and embarked on an intensive diplomatic mission in Europe and the Middle East in order to secure support for possible military action against Iraq. Albright subsequently announced that Egypt, Jordan, Kuwait, Bahrain, Saudi Arabia and Israel were prepared for a military response. France, the People's Republic of China and Russia opposed the use of force. The apparently increased likelihood of air-strikes against Iraq prompted Russia's Deputy Minister of Foreign Affairs, Viktor Posuvalyuk, to hold extensive talks with Iraqi officials in Baghdad in late January and early February. The USA did not consider that Russia had achieved a breakthrough, and began to make preparations to evacuate 450 UN staff to secure hotels. However, the Russian President, Boris Yeltsin, maintained that progress was indeed being made and threatened that Russia would veto any Security Council resolutions authorizing military attacks on Iraq. The extent of Russian opposition to military force became evident on 4 February, after Yeltsin warned that US military strikes could have serious international repercussions. Indeed, and despite Albright's earlier claims, it became apparent that there was little support among the Gulf states for military action. Only Kuwait announced its approval for the use of force if diplomatic efforts should fail, while Saudi Arabia and Bahrain refused to authorize military attacks from their territories. Meanwhile, senior representatives from the Arab League, Russia, Turkey and France met on 3 February, in Baghdad, in an attempt to defuse the crisis. In mid-February the five permanent members of the UN Security Council approved a compromise formula whereby a special group of diplomats, appointed by the UN Secretary-General in consultation with experts from UNSCOM and the International Atomic Energy Agency (IAEA), would be allowed unconditional and unrestricted access to presidential palaces. A visit to Baghdad by Kofi Annan on 22 February resulted in agreement on a memorandum of understanding between the UN and Iraq, which narrowly averted the immediate threat of military action. Under the terms of the memorandum, signed on 23 February, the Iraqi Government (which reiterated its acceptance of all relevant UN resolutions) agreed to grant UNSCOM immediate, unconditional and unrestricted access to all sites, while UNSCOM agreed to respect the legitimate concerns of Iraq relating to national security, sovereignty and dignity. A Special Group to inspect the eight presidential sites was to be created, comprising senior diplomats and experts from UNSCOM, and headed by a Commissioner appointed by the UN Secretary-General. The special group was to operate under the established procedures of UNSCOM, and specific detailed procedures which were to be developed given the special nature of the presidential sites. Noting the progress already achieved by UNSCOM and the need to intensify efforts to complete its mandate, the UN and the Iraqi Government agreed to improve co-operation, and efficiency, effectiveness and transparency of work. Finally, the memorandum noted that the ending of sanctions was of paramount importance to the people and Government of Iraq, and the Secretary-General undertook to bring this matter to the full attention of members of the UN Security Council.

Iraq's Deputy Prime Minister, Tareq Aziz, who signed the memorandum on behalf of the Iraqi Government, asserted that Iraq had achieved 'excellent political gains for the present and for the future and practical gains related to the lifting of sanctions'. Kofi Annan was careful to highlight the role played by the USA in securing the agreement, stating that 'diplomacy backed up by force' had facilitated the negotiating process. There was general agreement that Saddam Hussain had improved his position domestically and in the Arab world by confronting the USA. Iraq also viewed the personal involvement of the UN Secretary-General as an important achievement, hoping that he would use his influence to effect an early end to the regime's international isolation. On the other hand, Iraq had been forced to make some concessions, notably to allow UNSCOM access to all suspect areas, including presidential sites. However, it was clear that the establishment of the special group to inspect the presidential sites would complicate the work of UNSCOM and the organization of unannounced visits to these sites. The Secretary-General had also declined to place a six-month time limit on UNSCOM's work, as requested by Iraq, insisting that sanctions would only be revoked when UNSCOM confirmed that all of Iraq's alleged nuclear, chemical and biological weapons and facilities had been destroyed. According to some observers, Saddam Hussain's decision to accept the compromise agreement brokered by Kofi Annan was strongly influenced by his reluctance to see the key pillars of his regime, the Republican Guard and the Presidential Guard, become the target of US and British air-strikes. Despite the apparent breakthrough, both the USA and the United Kingdom remained cautious, and urged the UN Security Council to adopt a resolution advocating the use of force should Iraq breach the agreement. On 2 March 1998 the UN Security Council unanimously approved a resolution warning of extreme consequences, but not immediate use of force, if the agreement was reneged upon by Iraq. UNSCOM inspection teams returned to Iraq on 5 March, and, after a meeting with Tareq Aziz on 23 March, Richard Butler reported that his teams had been allowed access to many 'sensitive' sites. In early March Kofi Annan appointed the Indian diplomatist Prakash Shah to be the UN Secretary-General's special representative to Iraq. The special group, led by Jayantha Dhanapala of Sri Lanka, who had been appointed chief UN disarmament officer in February, completed a first round of inspections of presidential sites in late March and early April, finding most of the buildings virtually empty. On 3 April Dhanapala stated that the group had been 'able to fulfil their mandated task'. In contrast, Charles Duelfer, the deputy head of UNSCOM, reported that Iraqi officials had informed him that inspections of presidential sites would not be permitted indefinitely and concluded that the fundamental problem of continuing access had been postponed rather than solved. The US press accused some senior UN officials close to the Secretary-General of supporting Iraqi complaints against UNSCOM inspectors, and advocated an end to sanctions and weapons inspections. In his six-monthly report to the UN Security Council in April, Richard Butler stated that virtually no progress in verifying disarmament had been made since October 1997 because of the recent crisis, for which he held Iraq responsible, and he insisted that the destruction of Iraq's chemical and biological weapons was far from complete. Butler criticized Iraq's policy of 'disarmament by declaration', and stated that verification was essential to establish the credibility of these claims. The Iraqi authorities continued to maintain that they had destroyed all weapons of mass destruction and requested the complete and comprehensive ending of sanctions. On 27 April the Security Council, having examined Butler's latest report, voted not to review the sanctions regime against Iraq. Russia, however, did prepare a draft resolution urging an end to UN inspections into Iraq's nuclear weapons programme. The IAEA had recently reported that it had no evidence of a covert Iraqi nuclear weapons programme, and that the authorities in Baghdad had answered all relevant questions on the subject satisfactorily. Despite French and Chinese support for the resolution, opposition from the United Kingdom and the USA forestalled further discussion of the draft document. Meanwhile, Iraqi officials continued to complain that, despite the increased involvement of some Russian and French diplomats in UNSCOM, the weapons inspectorate was still dominated by specialists from the United Kingdom and the USA.

In late June 1998 Richard Butler reported to the UN Security Council that traces of a lethal chemical agent known as VX had been discovered following US laboratory tests on remnants of missile warheads recovered from an Iraqi weapons destruction pit. Despite claims by a former head of Iraqi military intelligence (currently resident in the United Kingdom—see above) that VX had been employed in Iraq's war with Iran, the Iraqi Government stressed that the chemical had never been used as a weapon. In response to Iraqi demands that the tests should be repeated at neutral locations, in early July the UN agreed to re-examine fragments of the warheads at laboratories in France and Switzerland. However, the results of these tests were inconclusive. On 2 August Butler visited Baghdad for talks with Iraqi officials which it was hoped would expedite completion of the arms inspection programme. Negotiations collapsed two days later, however, after Tareq Aziz rejected Butler's proposal for further inspections. Furthermore, Aziz urged the UNSCOM Chairman to report to the UN Security Council that Iraq had eliminated its weapons of mass destruction, a request that Butler claimed he could not fulfil, owing to lack of evidence. Consequently, the Iraqi Council of Ministers suspended arms inspections on 5 August and Saddam Hussain presented new terms and conditions for the inspections to resume, including the establishment of a new executive bureau to oversee UNSCOM's operations and the transfer of UNSCOM headquarters from New York to Vienna. Resumption of arms inspections was authorized by the UN on 18 August, but the Iraqi authorities continued to insist that co-operation with the inspection teams would be withheld. On 14 September the Iraqi Government announced that it was suspending all co-operation with UNSCOM indefinitely, unless the UN Security Council revoked a decision, taken on 9 August, to suspend the periodic review of the maintenance of sanctions against Iraq. In late October, in an attempt to persuade Iraq to resume co-operation with UNSCOM, the Security Council agreed to a comprehensive review of the sanctions regime, to be conducted by the UN Secretary-General. A balance sheet was to be compiled of work completed hitherto by the weapons inspectors, and on that basis a list of requirements would be prepared that Iraq would be required to fulfil for the oil embargo to be revoked, together with a 'reasonable timescale' for the inspections work to be completed. Iraq, however, rejected the proposal, insisting that the review should lead automatically to the ending of sanctions, and proceeded to ban all UNSCOM inspections of new or existing sites. Iraq's stance was condemned by the Security Council, and the USA and the United Kingdom stated that they were prepared to undertake military action against Iraq if necessary. In November, as the US and British forces were about to launch air-strikes, Saddam Hussain relented and allowed UNSCOM inspectors to resume their investigations. Although the USA and United Kingdom had called off their air-strikes, they warned Iraq that if it interfered with UNSCOM's work in the future, there would be an immediate military response.

'OPERATION DESERT FOX'

Only a few weeks after the return of the UN weapons inspectors a new crisis erupted. In mid-December 1998 Richard Butler submitted a new report to the UN Security Council that was critical of Iraq's attitude towards UNSCOM. On 16 December, as the Security Council considered Butler's report, the USA and United Kingdom launched an intensive bombing campaign against Iraq over four consecutive nights, involving 'cruise' missiles, fighter aircraft and heavy bombers. The stated aim of the campaign was to diminish and degrade Saddam Hussain's ability to use and deploy weapons of mass destruction. The air attacks targeted Iraq's air-defence system, sites such as missiles factories, and repair sites alleged to be connected with weapons of mass destruction (but not sites where it was believed chemical and biological agents were being stored), together with command centres such as the headquarters of the Republican Guard, the Special Republican Guard and the intelligence services. The Iraqi Government remained defiant and claimed that the bombing had caused heavy civilian casualties. Both China and Russia immediately condemned the attacks. Russia temporarily withdrew its ambassadors from Washington, DC, and London, and the Duma urged the Russian Government to end sanctions against Iraq. Criticism was also voiced, albeit less vehemently, by France, while Germany expressed support for the air-strikes. Across the Arab and Islamic world numerous popular demonstrations condemned the bombings and expressed support for Iraq. Seeking to capitalize on this popular sympathy, Saddam Hussain condemned Arab leaders, especially those allied to the USA, and called on the people to rise up and overthrow their governments.

A number of analysts were critical of the role played by Richard Butler, arguing that in his report, which provided the pretext for the air-strikes, he chose to emphasize several relatively minor difficulties with the Iraqi authorities rather than mention the large number of inspections that had taken place without incident in less than a month. While few observers doubted that Saddam Hussain was determined to rebuild a part of his military capability, they pointed out that of the four dossiers on disarmament, three—those relating to nuclear weapons, missiles and chemical weapons—were either complete or nearing completion. A US official was reported to have admitted that Butler had discussed the content of his report with senior members of the Clinton administration before producing the final draft, and former UNSCOM inspector Scott Ritter insisted that Butler had been in regular contact with members of the US National Security Council. This led some commentators to assert that the White House had influenced the tone of Butler's report. Although the use of military force against Iraq was seen as a long-established element in US strategy of political and military primacy in the Middle East and in the Gulf, several observers argued that the actual timing of US-British air-strikes may well have been determined by political considerations in Washington, DC—where President Clinton was, notably, threatened with impeachment over the Lewinsky affair. Others maintained that military action was inevitable given the time and effort that the USA had expended on denouncing the menace posed by Saddam Hussain's regime, and that the timing of the air-strikes was of secondary importance.

At the end of the bombing campaign the US Department of Defense claimed that the air-strikes had set back Iraq's chemical and biological weapons programme by a year. However, independent observers challenged these claims, pointing out that the Iraqi authorities had probably moved vital weapons material to more remote sites before the bombing campaign began and that only empty buildings would have been destroyed. Despite targeting the regime's power structure, there was little evidence that Saddam Hussain's authority had been weakened. On the contrary, surveillance cameras installed by UNSCOM as part of its long-term monitoring programme were no longer functioning; Iraq proclaimed that UNSCOM's disarmament work, undertaken over seven years, risked being written off. The attacks failed to bring about a revolt within the Iraqi armed forces, and there was no proof that they had achieved their stated objective of degrading the regime's ability to produce weapons of mass destruction. The bombings underscored and deepened divisions within the UN Security Council regarding policy towards Iraq, and some commentators argued that the UN itself had been discredited. A number of analysts considered that the air-strikes had better served the long-term strategic objectives of Saddam Hussain's regime than those of the USA and its British ally.

In an address on 19 December 1998 announcing the end of 'Operation Desert Fox', President Clinton outlined the main elements of future US strategy towards Iraq. Both the USA and United Kingdom would maintain a substantial military force in the Gulf, ready to carry out new strikes if necessary. Sanctions, which he described as 'the most extensive in the history of the UN', would be maintained. Inspectors from UNSCOM and the IAEA would resume their work, on condition that the Iraqi authorities demonstrated their preparedness to co-operate; if not, force would be used to eliminate all efforts by Iraq to resume a programme to develop weapons of mass destruction. Finally, the USA would seek the overthrow of Saddam Hussain. France, Russia and China all criticized this pledge to seek the removal of Saddam Hussain, which—although supported by the British Government—caused considerable disquiet within the international community. In mid-January 1999 France suggested an alternative approach, proposing that the oil embargo should be revoked and UNSCOM replaced by a new organization which would concentrate its efforts on ensuring that Iraq was prevented from acquiring any new weapons of mass destruction, rather than seeking to trace and document past development programmes. Although the French proposals received broad support from the UN Secretary-General and from Russia, they were opposed by the USA, which claimed that to end the oil embargo would merely strengthen Saddam Hussain's regime. The USA did, however, propose raising the existing limit on Iraqi oil sales under the terms of the oil-for-food programme in order to address the humanitarian needs of the Iraqi people. Iraq, for its part, insisted that all sanctions must be ended and that under no circumstances would it contemplate the return

of UNSCOM. Also in January the Iraqi parliament voted to renounce all commitments made to the UN Security Council, including Iraqi recognition of the Iraq–Kuwait border.

In late January 1999 *The Washington Post* reported that it had been informed by US officials that the USA had been monitoring coded radio communications of Saddam Hussain's personal security forces, using equipment secretly installed by UNSCOM weapons inspectors. It was stated that UNSCOM had quickly concluded that the Iraqi authorities did not intend to co-operate and were determined to hide evidence of their weapons programmes from the UN inspection teams. As Saddam Hussain's personal security forces were charged with facilitating inspections, UNSCOM had found it necessary to penetrate their operations, thus providing an opportunity for the USA to gather intelligence about other aspects of the security forces' operations. Scott Ritter, who had resigned from UNSCOM in August 1998, further claimed that the USA had later decided to install its own permanent surveillance equipment in sensitive sites, giving the US formidable intelligence capabilities within Iraq. Ritter, a controversial figure, had earlier admitted to having co-operated with Mossad, the Israeli intelligence service, in his efforts to expose Iraq's weapons programmes. In late March 1999 the British Broadcasting Corporation claimed in a televised documentary that, in its efforts to uncover Iraq's weapons programmes, UNSCOM had developed close links with the CIA and other Western intelligence services, using their expertise and personnel to penetrate Iraqi security services, but that the organization had increasingly been used as a 'cover', by the CIA in particular, to conduct intelligence operations in Iraq. These operations had provided vital intelligence used to select targets during 'Operation Desert Fox'. It was also claimed that Richard Butler had lost control over UNSCOM's intelligence operations, some of which were carried out without his consent. The documentary concluded that the CIA had virtually taken over UNSCOM, seriously undermining the organization's credibility. Iraq had for some time accused UNSCOM inspectors of acting as agents for Western intelligence services, and these latest allegations strengthened calls within the UN Security Council for UNSCOM's mandate to be terminated and a new system of monitoring introduced. Some commentators had long maintained that since the USA had no intention of agreeing to the ending of sanctions against Iraq while Saddam Hussain remained in power, it had always regarded UNSCOM as merely a useful means of gathering intelligence.

By mid-January 1999 Iraq had aimed, but not fired, missiles at US and British aircraft patrolling the northern and southern air exclusion zones on several occasions, and for the first time in six years Iraqi jets had made sorties into these zones. Iraq declared that it would confront any infringement of its airspace and continue to challenge allied aircraft monitoring these zones. During the early months of 1999 US and British forces continued to attack military targets in both zones, extending the range of targets from surface-to-air missile batteries to their command and control infrastructure, and began attacking some oil-related installations. Iraq insisted that the bombing of military installations had resulted in civilian casualties. In March China urged the USA and the United Kingdom to end their air-strikes against Iraq, and together with Russia continued to maintain that the 'no-fly' zones were illegal because they had not been authorized by the UN. In April Russia strongly criticized the bombing of Iraqi oil installations. By mid-1999 US and British aircraft were reported to have made more than 200 multi-missile air-strikes against Iraq since the end of 'Operation Desert Fox', with only a temporary pause in bombing raids in and around the northern 'no-fly' zone during the second half of March (during the military preparations for NATO air-strikes against Yugoslavia). It was estimated that some 55 Iraqis had been killed, and more than 160 injured, in these attacks.

Meanwhile, the UN Security Council had the difficult task of trying to establish a new policy towards Iraq. In an effort to formulate a basis for a new approach to Iraq following the December 1998 bombing campaign, the UN established three panels—to consider the question of Iraq's weapons of mass destruction, to examine the issue of Kuwaiti prisoners of war, and to review the humanitarian situation—which reported in March 1999. The panel on weapons took an uncompromising stance: it concluded that outstanding issues remained in almost every weapons category, notably those relating to Iraq's biological weapons programme, and urged a reinforced continuous monitoring and verification system that would be both comprehensive and intrusive, requiring full and free access to all suspect sites. Only minor concessions were made to the Russian and Chinese panel members, who had sought a more conciliatory approach. The panel investigating the fate of Kuwaiti prisoners of war and property looted in 1991 reported that Iraq had not yet supplied adequate information to the UN. The humanitarian panel, in contrast, adopted a more conciliatory position: its report stated that Iraq had fallen from relative affluence to massive poverty since 1991, with infant mortality and chronic malnutrition particularly serious problems. It recommended that Iraq should be permitted to export as much oil as it could to finance goods under the oil-for-food programme, and that production-sharing agreements with foreign companies should be allowed in order to increase output. Foreign companies might also be allowed to invest in other Iraqi export sectors. It also recommended that the UN sanctions committee allow Iraq freely to import food, medicines, agricultural equipment and basic educational supplies, but insisted that all future revenues from oil exports should continue to be deposited in UN accounts, and that foreign companies operating in Iraq should be monitored closely by the UN sanctions committee. The proposals suggested a radical revision of the UN sanctions regime. Iraq immediately issued a memorandum denouncing the proposals of all three panels, declaring that they merely re-presented old conclusions and provided a pretext for continued aggression by Iraq's enemies. *Ath-Thawra*, the organ of the Baath Party, stated that the Iraqi Government would continue to reject the proposals unless wide-ranging sanctions were lifted.

In mid-April 1999 the United Kingdom and the Netherlands presented a proposal to the UN Security Council whereby UNSCOM would be replaced by a new and expanded weapons inspections body, to be known as the UN Commission for Investigation, Inspection and Monitoring. Iraq would be required to grant the new commission's inspection teams immediate, unconditional and unrestricted access to all areas, facilities, equipment, records and means of transportation. In return, the existing US $5,250m. limit on the amount of oil that Iraq was permitted to sell under the oil-for-food agreement would be abolished, and the plan recommended that the UN Secretary-General establish a committee to recommend ways of increasing Iraq's oil production. There were also provisions temporarily to reduce Iraq's contributions to the fund for victims of the Iraqi invasion of Kuwait. This initiative was an attempt to find a compromise that would be acceptable to all of the permanent members of the UN Security Council. Whereas France, Russia and China favoured a significant relaxation in sanctions, the USA insisted on maintaining a resolute stance towards Iraq. In June the United Kingdom and the Netherlands revised their proposal, recommending that foreign companies should be allowed to invest in the Iraqi oil industry if the Iraqi Government co-operated with the proposed new weapons inspection organization, and that if co-operation continued the UN Security Council should suspend sanctions on all Iraqi exports. This decision would be reconsidered every four months, and a new system of financial controls would be establish to prevent Iraq spending any of its export earnings on prohibited weapons. Sanctions would only be lifted when the new inspection organization was satisfied that Iraq had complied with all of its disarmament obligations. The USA offered qualified support for the revised proposal, but there were indications that it had serious doubts about the effectiveness of arms inspections and was totally opposed to any lifting of UN controls on Iraqi export earnings. Some observers suspected that the USA would never agree to the lifting of sanctions while Saddam Hussain remained in power. Iraq predictably rejected the draft resolution, stating that as it had complied with all obligations under UN resolutions sanctions should be lifted immediately. Russia, China and France also rejected the UK/Dutch proposal. Russia, for its part presented its own draft resolution. It proposed that sanctions on civilian goods and the air and sea embargo should be lifted 100 days after Iraq began co-operation with the new weapons inspection organization, which, under the Russian plan, would be made up of civil servants and not arms inspectors. The situation would then be reviewed on a monthly basis and

sanctions reimposed if the UN reported that Iraq was failing to co-operate. The Russian proposal also provided for a relaxation in UN control over Iraqi export earnings and for foreign companies to be allowed to invest in the Iraqi oil industry. At a meeting held in New York in September between the Russian and Iraqi foreign ministers, Igor Ivanov promised that Russia would continue to work for the earliest repeal of sanctions. France also prepared a draft resolution which, like the Russian plan, proposed suspending sanctions once a new arms inspection organization had begun operations and called for UN control over Iraqi export earnings to be lifted. Meanwhile, US/UK airstrikes, mainly directed at Iraqi air defences in the northern and southern 'no-fly' zones, continued during the second half of 1999.

After months of stalemate a new resolution on Iraq (No. 1284) was eventually adopted by the UN Security Council in mid-December 1999. The resolution was prepared principally by the United Kingdom and was based on the earlier UK/Dutch draft proposal. It did not secure unanimous support in the Security Council and three permanent members, Russia, China and France, remained critical and abstained from the vote. Under the terms of the new resolution UNSCOM is replaced by the UN Monitoring, Verification and Inspection Commission (UNMOVIC)—made up of personnel drawn from 'the broadest possible geographical base'. The new Commission's staff, moreover, will be 'international civil servants' accountable to the UN Secretariat and not military or intelligence personnel temporarily seconded as in the case of UNSCOM. UNMOVIC is charged with putting in place a reinforced system of ongoing monitoring and verification and identifying additional sites to be included within the arms inspection programme. If Iraq co-operates fully with UNMOVIC for a period of four months, sanctions on trade, excluding military and related imports, will be suspended, and the suspension extended subject to a satisfactory review at regular intervals by the UN Security Council. Once trade sanctions have been suspended, the resolution provides for new financial arrangements to be put in place to ensure that Iraq does not acquire prohibited items. With immediate effect, the limit on Iraqi oil exports is removed (in practice Iraqi oil production is already near full capacity and massive investment is needed from foreign companies to increase production) and Iraq may now spend a proportion of its oil revenues on locally produced goods rather than solely on imports. A group of experts was to report on the state of Iraq's oil industry, provide advice on boosting production and export capacity and on the involvement of foreign oil companies in the sector. Responsibility for the approval of contracts for spare parts for the oil industry, which previously lay with the UN sanctions committee, was transferred to another group of experts who were instructed to expedite applications. Lists of imported humanitarian items are to be drawn up that will no longer require approval from the sanctions committee. The committee was also instructed to speed up approval of other contracts for humanitarian imports. Iraq is still liable for the full costs of UNMOVIC although the allocation of 30% of revenue from the oil-for-food programme destined for the UNCC was suspended for six months. Despite a number of concessions to Iraq, notably on the composition of UNMOVIC, and some changes to the humanitarian relief programme, the resolution was regarded as a reiteration of the hard-line position long advocated by the USA and the United Kingdom and their determination to continue the arms inspection programme before considering the suspension of sanctions. One source described the resolution as 'a combination of compromise and ambiguity' that was sufficient to ensure its adoption but which left many important issues unresolved. The state-controlled Iraqi press condemned the resolution, reiterated Iraq's determination not to allow the return of UN weapons inspectors, and demanded that sanctions should be lifted immediately and without conditions. *Babel*, the newspaper owned by Saddam Hussain's elder son Uday, protested that the resolution aimed to convert Iraq into a colony governed from outside using Iraqi funds, and also expressed its frustration with Russia, France and China for failing to prevent its adoption. By mid-2000 Iraq showed no signs of compromising. Indeed in July the Vice-President informed the local press that Iraq had rejected Resolution 1284 completely and also any attempt to negotiate or amend it.

In late January 2000, after much negotiation and some delay, the UN Security Council unanimously agreed to the appointment of Hans Blix of Sweden, the recently retired director of the IAEA, as executive director of UNMOVIC. As head of the IAEA Blix had been criticized by the USA for not taking a tougher stance in his dealings with Iraq—IAEA inspections were less intrusive than those of UNSCOM—and for suggesting that UNSCOM should move on from investigating Iraq's past weapons programmes and concentrate on monitoring the current situation. A team of IAEA inspectors, led by an Egyptian national, carried out routine checks on nuclear facilities in Iraq in late January—the first such visit since 1998—and commented with satisfaction on Iraqi co-operation. Meanwhile, *The New York Times* claimed that satellite photographs and US intelligence reports had shown that Iraq had succeeded in rebuilding military and industrial sites damaged during Operation Desert Fox. It reported that the Clinton Administration was concerned that as a result of the absence of UN weapons inspectors Iraq was continuing its pursuit of biological and chemical weapons.

At the beginning of February 2000 the ICRC released a damning report on the effect of sanctions on Iraq. It stated that the oil-for-food programme had failed to halt the collapse of the country's health system and the deterioration of water supplies; and highlighted the plight of children, noting that infant mortality had trebled since 1990. In mid-February the head of the oil-for-food programme in Baghdad, Hans von Sponeck, and Jutta Burghardt, head of WFP in Iraq, resigned in protest at what they considered the disastrous effects of UN sanctions on the most vulnerable in Iraqi society and at the inadequacy of the UN's humanitarian programme. Von Sponeck, in particular, like his predecessor, Denis Halliday, had become increasingly outspoken about the damage caused by sanctions to the fabric of Iraqi society. In response to the resignations the US State Department, which had regarded von Sponeck as too sympathetic to Iraq, declared that concern should focus on the Iraqi Government's refusal to spend hard currency for the welfare of the Iraqi people.

The team of UN-appointed oil experts (see above) which visited Iraq in January 2000 subsequently reported that Iraq would prefer short-term technical service contracts in the oil industry rather than significant long-term investment or production-sharing agreements under the UN oil-for-food programme. On 31 March the UN Security Council agreed unanimously to double to US $1,200m. the amount that Iraq may spend each year on spare parts and equipment for the oil industry. The Security Council also approved measures to accelerate procedures for the approval by the UN sanctions committee of contracts under the oil-for-food programme. To this end, four lists of goods had been drawn up that were subject to accelerated procedures for approval and covered food, educational supplies, pharmaceuticals and basic medical equipment and standard agricultural equipment and supplies. On taking up his appointment as head of UNMOVIC in March, Hans Blix declared his determination to insist on unrestricted access for his inspectors to sites in Iraq, but also stressed that UNMOVIC's role was not to humiliate Iraq. He stated that no member of UNMOVIC would be permitted to share any intelligence information about Iraq's armaments programmes obtained during their work, or communicate such information to any national government. Some former members of UNSCOM would work for UNMOVIC, allowing it to take advantage of their experience and also providing continuity. Significantly, Blix admitted that in his opinion UNMOVIC would be unable to verify with certainty that all Iraq's nuclear, biological and chemical weapons programmes had been dismantled, and suggested that the Security Council must determine what it regarded as an acceptable goal for which to aim. Interviewed in late May, former UNSCOM head Richard Butler reaffirmed his conviction that Saddam Hussain remained a real threat to regional and international order and asserted that the Iraqi leader had used the absence of weapons inspectors over the past 18 months to restock his weapons arsenal. He claimed to have evidence that Baghdad was attempting to procure missile manufacturing equipment from the West, was restocking chemical and biological agents, and could soon have nuclear weapons.

SANCTIONS ERODED

In early April 2000 a small private aircraft carrying a party of anti-sanctions campaigners, led by an Italian member of the European Parliament, Vittorio Sgarbi, flew via Jordan to Baghdad, thus deliberately flouting the UN embargo on flights to Iraq as a protest against UN sanctions. Also in April Tony Hall, on a mission to assess the impact of a decade of sanctions, became the first US congressman to visit Iraq since 1990; he expressed his deep concern about the extent of the suffering inflicted on ordinary Iraqis. Earlier in the year 70 members of the US Congress had written to President Clinton urging him to separate broad economic sanctions from the military embargo against Iraq. However, although the anti-sanctions movement was gaining strength in the USA, in the run-up to presidential elections no major political figure was prepared to challenge existing policy on sanctions or to make Iraq an election issue. In late April the Iraqi Minister of Foreign Affairs, Muhammad Saeed as-Sahaf, insisted in a letter to the UN Secretary-General that continued US air-strikes against Iraq targeted not only defence systems but also civilians, and demanded compensation for loss of life and damage to property resulting from the bombing. Iraq claimed that 16 civilians had been killed in three separate US attacks in the 'no-fly' zones in early April. France, which remained strongly critical of the unilaterally declared 'no-fly' zones, expressed profound unease at these attacks. In August Baghdad claimed that 315 people had been killed and 900 injured by Allied air-strikes on its northern and southern regions since the end of Operation Desert Fox. US sources later stated that on average allied air attacks in the 'no-fly' zones occurred seven or eight days every month.

At the beginning of June 2000 the Security Council approved an extension of the oil-for-food programme for a further six months (the eighth phase). In late June an Iraqi citizen, Fuad Hussain Haider, shot dead two FAO employees, and injured a further seven, after entering the organization's headquarters in the suburbs of Baghdad. Haider then held some 40 UN staff hostage before surrendering to the security forces. He stated that he had wanted to protest at the impact of UN sanctions on the Iraqi people. In early July the USA alleged that Iraq had carried out several tests of short-range missiles. Although these are permitted under UN Resolution 687 of April 1991, the USA insisted that the tests proved Iraq remained a threat that must be contained. Later that month the Iraqi Minister of the Interior wrote to the UN Secretary-General accusing the USA and the United Kingdom of blocking 30 contracts for sanitary equipment, worth US $107m., submitted by Iraq under the oil-for-food programme.

In early August 2000 Hugo Chávez Frías, President of Venezuela, in his capacity as Chairman of the OPEC Conference, visited Baghdad, where he was warmly greeted by the Iraqi leadership. Chávez was the first head of state to visit Iraq since the 1990–91 Gulf conflict. During the visit he invited Saddam Hussain to attend OPEC's summit meeting in Caracas the following month. Although Chávez travelled overland to Baghdad from Iran to avoid breaking the UN air embargo, his visit was strongly criticized by the US Administration, which had earlier tried to persuade him to cancel the trip. Shortly afterwards President Abdurrahman Wahid of Indonesia joined Chávez in voicing opposition to sanctions and announced his intention of visiting Baghdad in the coming months. Speaking at the beginning of August, on the 10th anniversary of Iraq's invasion of Kuwait, the French Minister of Foreign Affairs, Hubert Védrine, described sanctions against Iraq as 'cruel, ineffective and dangerous' and warned that their continuation threatened Iraq's social cohesion and regional stability. In mid-August the USA and the United Kingdom resumed air-strikes against Iraq after an interval of several weeks. The British Ministry of Defence insisted that its forces had been compelled to respond after Iraqi air defence units had fired at allied aircraft patrolling the southern 'no-fly' zone. The Iraqi state-controlled media later alleged that US and British combat aircraft had attacked civilian targets near the town of Samawa. Earlier in the month a spokesman for the US Department of State had stated that the USA hoped in time to bring Saddam Hussain to an international criminal court to face charges of war crimes resulting from the Iran–Iraq War of 1980–88 and the 1990 invasion of Kuwait. At this time Thomas Pickering,

Under Secretary for Political Affairs at the US State Department, stated that sanctions were criticized unfairly, based on insufficient information, and repeated that Saddam Hussain was using the misery of his people to persuade the world to remove the sanctions.

In mid August 2000 the Minister of Transport and Communications, Ahmad Murtada Ahmad Khalil, officially reopened the newly refurbished Saddam International Airport on the outskirts of Baghdad, a move interpreted as a symbolic challenge to the UN sanctions regime. In September flights arrived from both Russia and France. A flight carrying Russian oil experts to Baghdad was approved in advance by the UN sanctions committee, which accepted that it was a humanitarian mission, but the French Government insisted that a flight from Paris to Baghdad carrying doctors, athletes and artists was humanitarian and therefore did not require clearance from the Committee. The flights reignited the debate on UN sanctions against Iraq, and served to underline the very evident divisions within the UN Security Council regarding policy towards Baghdad. The USA and United Kingdom accused France of violating sanctions, reiterating their position that sanctions included an air embargo and that all requests for flights into Iraq had to be presented to the UN Security Council sanctions committee. Shortly afterwards Jordan became the first Arab country to send a flight to Iraq carrying a Government delegation. At the beginning of October it was reported that the Iraqi Minister of Transport and Communications had announced that scheduled flights between Russia and Baghdad would begin in two weeks, and that permission was being sought from Tehran to use Iranian airspace. The Russian state carrier, Aeroflot, stated that it had signed a memorandum with Iraqi Airways to restore a regular air link with Iraq but that no date had been set for the service to commence. By the end of October it was reported that there were almost daily flights into Saddam International Airport from European and Arab countries. In early November Iraqi Airways resumed regular domestic flights passing through the northern and southern 'no-fly' zones. Its aircraft had been grounded since the imposition of sanctions 10 years earlier. The USA and United Kingdom stated that they did not object to these civilian flights within Iraqi territory, and that the 'no-fly' zones were imposed to monitor military activity. At this time it was also reported that Jordan had stopped monitoring goods destined for Iraq passing through the port of Aqaba. In August rail links had been resumed between Iraq and Syria.

Russia stepped up its campaign for an end to the sanctions against Iraq in September 2000, claiming that it had lost US $30,000m. in business since the imposition of the embargo. The Russian Minister of Foreign Affairs, Igor Ivanov, complained in a letter to the UN Secretary-General that his Government was coming under increasing domestic pressure on this subject. Tareq Aziz stated that the Russian letter demonstrated that Iraq's trading partners were becoming increasingly impatient with the embargo. In late September the UN Security Council agreed to uphold a claim for damages against Iraq by the Kuwait Petroleum Company (KPC) for US $15,900m., the largest claim to come before the UNCC hitherto, but agreed to reduce the amount of Iraq's oil revenues levied for the UN Gulf War Compensation Fund from 30% to 25%. Both Russia and France had opposed the size of the award, and Russia had proposed that Iraq's contribution to the compensation fund should be reduced to 20%. However, after the USA and United Kingdom conceded a reduction in Iraq's contribution to 25%, Russia and France agreed to vote in favour of upholding the claim. At the same time the permanent members of the Security Council pledged to review Iraq's contribution, which could be further reduced in the event of a fall in oil prices. Some $260,000m. in claims have been made against Iraq but not yet settled. A report in the British press highlighted the fact that the UNCC does not permit Iraq to hire legal staff to defend itself against the claims, that Iraq has no right of appeal against decisions of the commission, and is obliged to pay $50m. every year to finance the commission's operations. The report pointed out that the damages awarded to KPC were more than double the amount that Iraq's oil-for-food programme had provided for humanitarian goods in 1996–99, and that Iraq was being forced to pay endless reparations to former enemies—some of which were already extremely wealthy.

In October 2000 a Western press report claimed that Iraq was earning US $2,000m. annually from oil-smuggling and that the proceeds were spent on weapons and luxuries for the Iraqi leadership, making a mockery of the UN embargo and undermining claims by the regime that sanctions are responsible for widespread public hardship and malnutrition. It was alleged that about one-third of the smuggled oil products—mainly fuel oil—went by road to central and northern Iran, but that the bulk of the oil was carried in small tankers, owned by companies based mainly in the UAE, from the Iraqi ports of Fao and Umm Qasr through Iranian coastal waters to Arab Gulf ports where the authorities chose to ignore the traffic. (Later estimates put the revenues from oil smuggling at more than $650m., but suggested that with the addition of illegal surcharges on oil exports and humanitarian imports—see below—Baghdad was receiving some $2,000m. each year in revenues that were outside UN control.) Furthermore, a press report in early November claimed that a number of leading US oil service companies were discreetly doing business worth millions of dollars with Iraq by submitting their contracts to the UN via European subsidiaries.

In November 2000 the UN confirmed that Iraq was preparing to export crude oil to Syria, a development easily interpreted by analysts as another challenge by Baghdad to the sanctions regime. This involved reopening the Kirkuk to Banias pipeline, closed since 1982. Under the proposed arrangement Syria would buy oil from Iraq at a discount for use in its own refineries, exporting an equivalent amount of its own oil to Mediterranean markets. Under the terms of UN resolutions, Iraqi exports of oil to Syria would require UN approval because the oil-for-food programme allows Iraq to export oil through only two designated border points—Zakho on the border with Turkey and Mina al-Bakr, Iraq's offshore Gulf oil terminal. Both the USA and United Kingdom were reported to have put pressure on the Syrian authorities to come to an understanding with the UN before reopening the pipeline; nevertheless, exports were believed to have begun during November without an arrangement having been reached.

Iraq's State Oil Marketing Organization informed its customers at the end of November 2000 that they risked losing their contracts unless they paid a surcharge of 50 US cents per barrel into an escrow account outside the UN oil-for-food programme. A few days earlier the UN had rejected Iraq's oil price formula for December after Baghdad had proposed a lower-than-market price for December sales so that the proposed surcharge would not make Iraqi oil uncompetitive against similar Russian crudes. With international support for sanctions waning, tight demand on world oil markets and an effective political interregnum in Washington following the US presidential election, some sources saw the surcharge as Baghdad's boldest step in its efforts to evade UN controls and secure direct access to Iraq's oil revenues. Others suspected that the Iraqi Government had imposed the surcharge to put pressure on the UN to allocate part of export revenues to local oil industry expenses at a time when the oil-for-food programme once again came up for review by the Security Council. Shortly afterwards the Security Council agreed to extend the oil-for-food programme for a further six months—the ninth phase—and agreed to allow Iraq to use up to US $525m. of its revenues to pay the local costs of maintaining the oil industry. Although Baghdad indicated that the crisis had been defused, it did not immediately resume official oil exports, which had been suspended since the beginning of the month after the UN refused to agree to the Iraqi surcharge. Moreover, there were reports that Iraq was continuing to insist that its customers pay the surcharge (now reduced to 40 cents per barrel). The major international companies refused to pay the surcharge, but unconfirmed reports suggested that lesser-known companies had agreed to pay. In November Iraq had insisted that the UN allow its customers to pay for its crude oil in euros rather than dollars, in protest at the US Administration's tough stance on sanctions. By the early part of 2001 there were indications that the majority of companies purchasing Iraq oil were paying a surcharge of between 25 and 40 cents per barrel, which over a year would amount to between $90m. and $140m. Furthermore, it was reported that for several months Iraq had imposed and collected a 10% surcharge on every contract for humanitarian imports such as food and medicines, which in the course of a year would produce revenues of $500m.

A year after the adoption of Resolution 1284 Iraq continued to oppose the resumption of UN arms inspections. However, the US Administration, anxious to avoid a confrontation with Iraq during a presidential election year, had done nothing to press for the return of UN arms inspectors (who by this time had been kept out of Iraq for two years). At the summit meeting of the Organization of the Islamic Conference (OIC) in Doha, Qatar, in November the UN Secretary-General, Kofi Annan, called for a 'dialogue without preconditions' with the Iraqi leadership. Annan subsequently suggested that if the existing sanctions regime was not achieving its objective it should be revised to offer more incentives and less punishment. In mid-January 2001, on the 10th anniversary of the outbreak of hostilities in the Gulf War, Saddam Hussain delivered a defiant speech declaring that Iraq would emerge victorious over the USA.

The details of the ninth phase of the oil-for-food programme were finalized in early 2001. In a letter addressed to the Iraqi authorities in mid-February, the UN Secretary-General urged them to provide more food for the civilian population, and in particular to allocate a greater part of their oil revenues to improving the health of children suffering from malnutrition. This was the third time in a month that the UN had appealed to the Iraqi Government to work to improve the nutritional levels of the population. Sources close to the UN revealed that the proportion of Iraq's budget devoted to the humanitarian programme had been declining steadily as part of a deliberate strategy aimed at tightening control over the civilian population. Meanwhile, the USA continued to block contracts presented by Iraq to the UN for approval. The total value of contracts awaiting approval had risen to over US $3,000m., comprising $2,700m. for humanitarian goods and $435m. for spare parts for the petroleum industry. The Iraqi people, the sources insisted, were caught between, on one side, the failures of the Baghdad Government and, on the other, US efforts to ensure that Iraq did not reconstruct its military infrastructure.

NEW ALLIED AIR-STRIKES AGAINST BAGHDAD

On 16 February 2001 US and British fighter aircraft attacked five ground-to-air missile bases and anti-aircraft batteries on the outskirts of Baghdad for the first time since Operation Desert Fox in December 1998. Defence officials of both the USA and United Kingdom stated that the operation had been essential because of an intensification of Iraqi attacks against US and British aircraft patrolling the 'no-fly' zones: they reported that more Iraqi missiles had been fired at allied aircraft in January 2001 than during the whole of the previous year. All allied aircraft were reported to have returned safely after the operation, and defence officials insisted that missiles had struck only designated military targets. The Iraqi authorities, however, claimed that the attacks had resulted in a number of civilian casualties. The USA and United Kingdom did not rule out further air-strikes to ensure the safety of their aircraft patrolling the 'no-fly' zones. Iraq vowed to defend its airspace and territory by all means possible. Saddam Hussain immediately met with his military commanders to consider possible Iraqi retaliation in the event of further attacks. Two days later thousands of Iraqis took part in demonstrations in Baghdad organized by the ruling Baath Party to protest against the allied attacks during which US and Israeli flags were burnt. The allied operation was interpreted as an indication that the new US President, George W. Bush, was determined to take a tougher stance on Iraq than had been adopted during the last months of the Clinton Administration. After his nomination as Secretary of State in the new Bush Administration Colin Powell (who had been Chairman of the US Joint Chiefs of Staff at the time of the Gulf conflict) asserted that Saddam Hussain's regime was a menace to Iraq's neighbours and to its own people, while the new Vice-President, Dick Cheney, and Secretary of Defense, Donald Rumsfeld, were also known to support an uncompromising stance against Iraq. Some commentators believed that the sharp increase in Iraqi attacks on allied aircraft during January was part of a strategy on the part of Saddam Hussain strategy of testing the new Bush Administration.

The allied air attacks met with strong criticism across the international community, and there were renewed calls for an urgent review of UN sanctions against Iraq. The three other permanent members of the Security Council—Russia, the People's Republic of China and France—all expressed their deep disquiet. A spokesman for the French Ministry of Foreign Affairs stated that the attacks only served to increase tension between Iraq and the international community and made it more difficult to secure Iraqi acceptance of Resolution 1284. Shortly afterwards the French foreign minister declared that Iraqis were being held hostage by UN sanctions. Turkey also condemned the attacks, while the Government of Turkey sought to emphasize that none of the allied aircraft taking part in the operation had flown from Turkish military bases. In the United Kingdom a number of the governing Labour Party's members of parliament expressed their opposition to the attacks and drew attention to the resulting civilian casualties. Across the Arab world there was outrage at news of the attacks, which were strongly condemned by the Arab League. Pro-Iraqi demonstrations were held in Egypt, Syria and Jordan. Baghdad was swift to capitalize on international disquiet, urging the UN Secretary-General to condemn the attacks.

International reaction to the latest air-strikes served to highlight the fact that the USA and United Kingdom were increasingly isolated in their hard-line approach to Iraq. Just before the first meeting between President George W. Bush and Prime Minister Tony Blair in Washington in late February, it was announced that the USA and United Kingdom proposed to reassess the use of sanctions. Instead of the blanket sanctions currently in place, they suggested that sanctions might be applied more selectively—through so-called 'smart' sanctions—focusing on those restrictions that have helped to contain Iraq while relaxing those in other areas so as to alleviate the hardships suffered by the Iraqi people. Commercial pressures from a growing number of countries wishing to resume trade with Iraq, the increasingly vocal humanitarian campaign, and the Baghdad regime's propaganda success in blaming sanctions for all the ills of the Iraqi people, were among the factors which had come together to put pressure on the USA and United Kingdom to rethink the sanctions regime. A week after the allied air-strikes against military installations near Baghdad, US fighter jets on a routine patrol over the northern 'no-fly' zone retaliated when Iraqi anti-aircraft batteries near Mosul opened fire on them. At the end of February UN Secretary-General Kofi Annan held talks with Iraq's Minister of Foreign Affairs, Muhammad Saeed as-Sahaf, the first meeting at this level for two years. As-Sahaf reiterated Iraq's refusal to consider the return of UN weapons inspectors even if sanctions were lifted; he demanded that Israel's nuclear arsenal be subject to control, and rejected new ideas from the Bush Administration on reforming the sanctions regime. Reporting to the Security Council shortly afterwards, Annan none the less stated that Iraq was looking for a negotiated solution to its problems with the UN, and that further discussions would take place.

Meanwhile, the German intelligence service stated that it had information that Iraq would be able to threaten its neighbours with nuclear weapons within three years. It also claimed that since the suspension of UN arms inspections in December 1998 the number of plants manufacturing chemicals had been greatly expanded, and that 20 were directly linked to arms production; German agents believed that Baghdad was preparing to resume the manufacture of biological weapons. In early March 2001 the British Broadcasting Corporation televised a documentary claiming that before the 1991 Gulf conflict Iraq had set up two groups, each using different methods, to develop nuclear weapons, and that after the war UNSCOM had failed to detect and destroy one of these, known as Group 4—a major weapons design group which continued to operate under the direct supervision of Saddam Hussain. The detailed investigative report, based on information supplied by an Iraqi nuclear scientist now living in exile in the West, produced what was claimed to be evidence that Group 4 was working on a nuclear device similar to the one used by the USA at Hiroshima at the end of the Second World War, that it had acquired highly enriched uranium from South Africa, and had conducted a secret underground nuclear test in September 1989. Interviewed on the programme, Hans Blix, the executive director of UNMOVIC, confirmed that the IAEA knew nothing about the existence of Group 4 but was sceptical that Iraq could have carried out a full nuclear test. In 1998 the IAEA had reported that it had no evidence of a covert nuclear weapons programme in Iraq. The documentary concluded that repeated warnings by highly-placed Iraqi defectors about Saddam Hussain's nuclear weapons programme had been ignored, and expressed concern that with sanctions crumbling nuclear components might be being smuggled into the country once again. However, at a conference in Cambridge, United Kingdom, in the same month on policy alternatives to sanctions on Iraq, Dr Hussain Shahristani, former chief scientific adviser to the Iraqi energy programme until 1979, insisted that Iraq's nuclear capacity had been largely destroyed. At the same time Shahristani emphasized that UNSCOM had failed to uncover the full extent of Iraq's biological and chemical weapons capabilities, and that there was evidence from inside Iraq that these programmes had been resumed.

In late March 2001 *The Washington Post* published outlines of the Bush Administration's plan to replace the current sanctions regime. The plan proposed posting UN monitors on Iraq's borders and at key foreign airports to prevent the Iraqi Government importing military goods; allowing Iraq to sell oil at discounted prices to neighbouring states, in order to persuade these to co-operate and to compensate them for losses incurred by ending the extensive smuggling trade; and for the UN to establish a list of oil companies authorized to purchase Iraqi oil so as to eliminate those intermediaries suspected of making illegal payments to the Iraqi regime. The new proposals are reported to have been welcomed by crucial members of the Security Council, notably France and Russia, but analysts pointed to the formidable practical difficulties of monitoring Iraq's long and porous borders, and of sustaining the new sanctions regime over the long-term until Baghdad agreed to accept Resolution 1284 and the return of UN weapons inspectors. Reports from Washington also indicated 'fundamental' differences between the US Departments of State and of Defense on policy towards Iraq, with the latter taking a much harder line—namely seeking the overthrow of Saddam Hussain's regime. None the less, sources within the US political establishment predicted that Secretary of State Colin Powell's views on Iraq would prevail within the new Administration. On a visit to the European Parliament in Brussels, Belgium, in late February, Powell had acknowledged the need to reform current sanctions against Iraq to concentrate on military aspects and alleviate their impact on the civilian population. He discussed the new US proposals on Iraq with the French Minister of Foreign Affairs, Hubert Védrine, on the latter's visit to Washington in late March. The issue of Iraq had proved an important point of friction between France and the Clinton Administration. In early April the World Health Organization (WHO) confirmed that, together with the Iraqi authorities, it was planning to examine links between the use of depleted uranium (as a weapons component) and illnesses affecting the Iraqi population following the 1991 Gulf War; a team of WHO experts was due to visit Iraq in late August.

Vice-President Taha Yassin Ramadan visited Russia in April 2001, at the head of a delegation which included the Ministers of Trade and Oil. He held talks with President Vladimir Putin and other senior Russian officials. Ramadan was the most senior Iraqi official to visit Russia since the Gulf War. He received assurances from Russian officials that Moscow would continue its efforts to help secure an end to UN sanctions against Iraq, but was reported to have failed to persuade Russia to withdraw unilaterally from the sanctions regime. During the visit the two countries signed agreements on the supply of Russian equipment for the Iraqi oil and gas industry and on joint geological work in Iraq.

At the end of April 2001 British police announced that they were investigating allegations of war crimes by Saddam Hussain related to the case of the 4,500 British nationals taken hostage in Iraq and Kuwait at the beginning of the 1990–91 Gulf War. Indict, a British-based human rights organization, had gathered evidence relating to Saddam Hussain and vice-premier Tareq Aziz, which it had passed to the British Attorney-General who had asked the police authorities to investigate.

US Secretary of State Colin Powell stated in early May 2001 that the USA wished to continue isolating the regimes in Iraq and Iran, and that as far as Iraq was concerned he was confident that US proposals for reforming the UN sanctions regime were gaining support. In late May the United Kingdom submitted a draft resolution on Iraq to the UN Security Council under the

terms of which sanctions would be refocused to improve the flow of civilian goods while strengthening controls on the sale of military goods and on oil-smuggling. Although the resolution on the introduction of so-called 'smart' sanctions received strong backing from the USA, it had not secured support from other permanent members of the Security Council by early June when the ninth phase of the oil-for-food programme came to an end. Consequently, it was decided to extend the ninth phase until 3 July, in order to give Security Council members more time to discuss the draft resolution. In response, Iraq announced that it was suspending UN-authorized oil exports and would only resume sales under the oil-for-food programme when the proposals to alter existing sanctions had been defeated. At the end of June Russia rejected the draft resolution, declaring that the proposed changes to the sanctions regime would not avert a humanitarian catastrophe in Iraq and would devastate the country's economy. Russia proceeded to introduce its own resolution, proposing a reworking of Resolution 1284 to permit a suspension of sanctions if Iraq agreed to allow the return UN weapons inspectors. After this resolution was rejected by other members of the Security Council Russia threatened to use its veto to block the British resolution. The United Kingdom thus decided on 3 July to withdraw its own draft resolution, and the Security Council voted unanimously to extend the oil-for-food programme for a further five months. Earlier the USA, United Kingdom, France and the People's Republic of China had agreed a compromise list of products that Iraq was forbidden to import under the proposed new sanctions regime. The USA had agreed to 'unblock' Chinese sales contracts to the value of US $90m. that it had been holding up at the UN sanctions committee, and in return China had accepted the revised list. Saddam Hussain thanked Russia for its opposition to the 'evil colonialist project' of 'smart' sanctions. At the same time the Russian legislature voted almost unanimously in favour of a motion supporting the ending of sanctions against Iraq, and called on the Russian Government to use its veto in the UN Security Council to avert any attempt to strengthen existing sanctions which it held responsible for the suffering of the Iraqi people. Despite their set-back, the United Kingdom and the USA insisted that they would not abandon their plans to introduce 'smart' sanctions and the United Kingdom stated that it would continue to try to persuade Russia to accept the proposals. However, Iraq's neighbours, Jordan, Syria and Turkey, whose co-operation was essential for the successful implementation of the new sanctions regime, refused to support the proposals (see below). On 9 July the Iraqi Government accepted the five-month extension of the oil-for-food programme, and the next day resumed oil exports from both of its UN-authorized loading outlets. In August the Iraqi Minister of Oil was reported to have stated that the majority of contracts for the rehabilitation of the country's oil industry would be awarded to Russian firms. In contrast, the French Government's support for the proposals for a revised sanctions regime was the subject of severe criticism in Baghdad.

In late June 2001 two Iraqi diplomats at Iraq's mission to the UN in New York, Muhammad al-Humaimidi (the deputy head of the mission) and Fela Hesan ar-Rubaie, were reported to have applied for asylum in the USA. Both had been due to return to Iraq the following month.

On 20 June 2001 Baghdad announced that 23 Iraqi civilians had been killed and 11 wounded in an air-strike by US-British allied forces in northern Iraq. It was claimed that the victims had been playing football near the village of Tel-Afr within the northern exclusion zone. The US and British authorities denied responsibility for the attack. In late July the US Department of Defense reported that Iraq had launched a ground-to-air missile at a US plane on a surveillance mission in Kuwaiti airspace, but that it had failed to hit its target. Air-strikes by British and US military aircraft were launched against Iraqi air-defence installations in the northern and southern air exclusion zones during August–October 2001, and in early September 2002, after incidents in which aircraft from both countries had been tracked and targeted from ground positions in both regions.

Initially Iraq refused to condemn the suicide attacks of 11 September 2001 on New York and Washington, DC, although Deputy Prime Minister Tareq Aziz expressed sympathy for the families of the victims. There was immediate speculation surrounding possible Iraqi links with Osama bin Laden's al-

Qa'ida network (held responsible for the attacks), and also suggestions that Iraq might become a target for US military retaliation, although it was widely argued that there was little evidence of significant Iraqi involvement with the activities of radical Islamist militants. However, in October the Minister of the Interior of the Czech Republic appeared to confirm reports that Muhammad Atta, one of the hijackers of the passenger aircraft that were used in the attacks on 11 September, and the presumed leader of the terrorist cell that mounted the assault, had met a senior member of the Iraqi intelligence service in Prague earlier in 2001. The Iraqi agent, who had been consul and second secretary at the Iraqi embassy in the Czech capital, had been expelled shortly after the meeting with Atta for activities described as incompatible with his diplomatic status. The Iraqi authorities denied that there had been any contact between the two men. The CIA appeared not to attach particular importance to these contacts, and subsequent articles published in the Czech press cast doubt on the veracity of the previous reports concerning the alleged meeting.

However, Saddam Hussain's Government continued to represent a significant obstacle to US ambitions to rehabilitate so-called 'rogue' states, and this was felt acutely in the aftermath of the September attacks. Commentators identified two distinct groups within the Bush Administration, each advocating a different approach to the problem posed by Iraq. The first group, prominent among them Deputy Secretary of Defense Paul Wolfowitz and National Security Adviser Condoleezza Rice, favoured removing Saddam Hussain and his regime by force, using US air power to support a ground offensive by Iraqi opposition forces reinforced with a limited US military presence. They insisted that even without evidence of Iraqi involvement in the 11 September attacks, Iraq's refusal to allow UN weapons inspections for three years had potentially allowed the resumption of nuclear, chemical and biological weapons development programmes which would ultimately be used against Western targets. The second group, led by US Secretary of State Colin Powell, argued that attempting to remove Saddam Hussain by force carried too many risks. They did not believe that the Iraqi opposition could mount a successful ground attack and that the deployment of US military units would involve high casualties. Moreover, they argued that even if the military campaign were successful, it would merely serve to exacerbate anti-US feeling in the Arab world and probably alienate the USA's allies in the region. Instead of a military option, they recommended a diplomatic approach to isolate Iraq and force Saddam Hussain to allow the return of UN weapons inspectors as the best guarantee of identifying and eliminating weapons of mass destruction. While there was widespread consensus that Saddam Hussain would almost certainly have used the absence of UN weapons inspectors to resume weapons development programmes, most of the limited evidence for this came from Iraqi opposition sources. With regard to Iraq's conventional weapons, in January 2002 a senior member of the Washington Institute for Near East Policy expressed the opinion that most of the military hardware was old and that, with the exception of air-defence systems, the regime had been unable to procure much new ordnance for more than a decade.

At the end of November 2001 the UN Security Council was unanimous in approving Resolution 1382, whereby the oil-for-food programme was extended for a further six months and a new arrangement for the import of goods into Iraq was to be negotiated by 1 June 2002. There was some speculation that these proposals had originally been put forward to counter mounting international criticism of the humanitarian impact of the sanctions on the Iraqi people. However, it was suggested that after 11 September the USA no longer felt compelled to address these concerns. At the beginning of December the Iraqi Government formally accepted the extension of the oil-for-food programme, but also declared its intention to reject the application of the 'goods review list' attached to the resolution. Baghdad continued to oppose any return of UN weapons inspectors to the country and to deny that it possessed weapons of mass destruction.

Following the swift victory of US-led forces against the Taliban regime in Afghanistan in late 2001, demands within the US political establishment for a similar campaign in Iraq increased. By the end of the year statements made by senior US

officials appeared to suggest that if Iraq did not agree to the prompt return of UN weapons inspectors, the Bush Administration was prepared to resort to military action. Indeed, the US media appeared to be under the impression that a military attack on Iraq was imminent. In his State of the Union address at the end of January 2002 President Bush maintained that the 'war against terror' alone was insufficient to satisfy the security needs of US citizens and that Iraq, together with Iran and the Democratic People's Republic of Korea (North Korea), continued to comprise an 'axis of evil' of rogue states threatening nuclear devastation that needed to be confronted. Moreover, the US President claimed that Iraq in particular continued to flaunt both its hostility towards the USA and its support for terrorism. Shortly afterwards US Secretary of State Colin Powell assured the USA's allies that they would be consulted before the US Government embarked on any military adventure in Iraq, but insisted that 'all options were open', including unilateral action by the USA. At this time there was speculation that Powell had been forced to adopt a tougher stance with regard to Iraq or risk becoming marginalized on the issue. The threat of possible US military action against Iraq aroused grave concern in Europe, Russia and the Arab world. The UN Secretary-General declared that although there was no indication that Iraq was willing to accept the return of UN weapons inspectors, he did not believe that military action was advisable at this time and that such action would only exacerbate tensions in the region. President Putin of Russia reiterated his country's opposition to all military action against Iraq in the context of the 'war' against terrorism, pointing out that Iraq was not one of the countries whose nationals had fought alongside the Taliban or helped to finance them. He acknowledged that Iraq posed a regional security problem and stated that Russia was actively engaged in discussions with Baghdad to find a solution. However, during a visit to Moscow by Tareq Aziz in January 2002 the Russian Government appeared to have made no progress in persuading Iraq to allow the return of weapons inspectors. Many believed that Russian concerns for the future of Iraq were conditioned by fears that highly lucrative oil contracts would be granted to Western rather than Russian companies in the event of Saddam Hussain's overthrow. The question of a possible US offensive against Iraq dominated discussions among EU and OIC ministers of foreign affairs meeting in İstanbul in mid-February, and although most delegates avoided voicing any direct criticism of the USA, the Bush Administration's attitude towards Iraq caused considerable disquiet, especially among Muslim states. Within the EU only the British Government expressed support for possible US military intervention in Iraq. During a visit by Tareq Aziz to Beijing, People's Republic of China, at the end of January 2002, the Chinese Government made known its opposition to an extension of the 'war against terror', but the Chinese Vice-President expressed the hope that Iraq would co-operate with the UN to avoid further complications. In early February Saddam Hussain contacted the UN Secretary-General with proposals for new discussions 'without preconditions', agreeing to allow the UN special rapporteur on the situation of human rights in Iraq, Andreas Mavrommatis, to lead a fact-finding mission to Iraq. However, the Secretary-General made it clear that he was only prepared to resume dialogue on condition that Baghdad accepted the return of UN weapons inspectors. At the end of February the director of the UN oil-for-food programme, Benon V. Sevan, presented a report to the Security Council in which he expressed the opinion that, despite its many difficulties, the programme had significantly improved the living conditions of Iraq's civilian population and was continuing to do so. However, Sevan also pointed to a deepening financial crisis within the programme, owing in part to a substantial decline in Iraq's oil revenues in recent months. He also expressed particular concern about the large number of contracts blocked at the UN Security Council sanctions committee—some 2,089 contracts, worth an estimated US $5,320m.—and emphasized the urgent need to revise the working practices of the committee. Furthermore, it was considered essential to safeguard the humanitarian dimension of the programme, which had become increasingly politicized. In early March US officials informed the UN that evidence from intelligence satellites demonstrated that a large number of trucks imported by the Iraqi authorities, ostensibly for the distribution of humanitarian supplies, had been converted into mobile missile launchers, in breach of UN sanctions regulations. Meanwhile, UN Secretary-General Kofi Annan met the Iraqi Minister of Foreign Affairs in New York, USA, the first such contact between Iraq and the UN at this level for many months. According to Annan the discussions were 'frank and useful', and the Iraqi delegation described them as 'constructive and positive'. The Secretary-General had been given a clear mandate from all five permanent members of the UN Security Council to demand the unconditional return of UN weapons inspectors to Iraq. During the discussions the Iraqi delegation was reported to have sought assurances that UN inspectors would not provide the US Government with military intelligence. Hans Blix, the head of UNMOVIC, who participated in the talks, evidently reassured the Iraqi delegation about 'the impartiality of the inspectors and the transparency of their work'. Towards the end of March the Iraqi authorities presented to the UN Secretary-General a list of some 20 questions to which answers were required before, they asserted, any decision on the return of UN weapons inspectors could be made. Diplomatic sources in New York indicated that while some of the questions were regarded as essentially technical, others were clearly political and certain further to complicate the issue.

During a tour of the Middle East in early March 2002 US Vice-President Dick Cheney attempted to re-emphasize the threat considered to be posed by a new Iraqi weapons development programme, but Arab leaders reiterated their opposition to a US military campaign in Iraq, arguing that the USA should prioritize a resolution to the conflict between Israel and the Palestinians. At the end of March President Bush announced that the USA had no immediate plans to attack Iraq and would continue to consult with its allies on the matter. During a meeting with President Bush in Crawford, Texas, in early April British Prime Minister Tony Blair endorsed the President's contention that the international community could not afford to ignore the continuing problem posed by Iraq, and invoked once again the possibility of military action against Baghdad if Saddam Hussain did not agree to the return of UN weapons inspectors with unrestricted access. In the United Kingdom some 120 parliamentary members of Blair's own party expressed their opposition to military action against Iraq.

In early April 2002, in response to Israel's uncompromising military intervention in Palestinian-controlled areas of the West Bank, Saddam Hussain announced that he was suspending Iraqi oil exports for 30 days, or until Israeli forces withdrew from Palestinian areas. World prices for oil rose sharply as a result of Iraq's decision. At the end of April, as Saddam Hussain celebrated his 65th birthday, US sources reported that President Bush had conceded that a change of regime in Iraq could not be achieved by a military coup or by arming internal opposition forces, but, rather, would require a massive deployment of US forces.

UN AGREES NEW SANCTIONS REGIME

In mid-May 2002 the UN Security Council unanimously approved a new resolution (No. 1409), revising the UN sanctions regime with regard to Iraq. A new goods review list, agreed after negotiations between Russia and the USA, was to enter into force on 30 May 2002. All humanitarian products not included on the list were henceforth to be freely sold to Iraq after perfunctory checks, while the sale of goods deemed to have potential dual military and civilian uses, included on the new review list, was to be subject to the approval of both UNMOVIC and the IAEA. The goods review list was to be regularly assessed by the UN Security Council, and the embargo on all arms exports to Iraq was to remain in place. It was believed that Russia and China had been prevailed upon to support the changes after the USA pledged to 'unblock' major contracts that they had signed with Iraq. The reforms were widely considered to represent the most sweeping overhaul of the oil-for-food programme since its introduction. Iraq's prompt acceptance of the new terms led to speculation that Baghdad was increasingly anxious not to antagonize the international community or provide the USA with further cause for a military offensive. Although Iraq resumed oil exports under the oil-for-food programme in early May, the UN Office for the Iraq Programme reported that funds were only available for the most urgent humanitarian products. After further talks with the UN Secre-

tary-General, at the beginning of May, on the issue of redeploying UNMOVIC inspectors in Iraq, the Iraqi Minister of Foreign Affairs described the discussions as constructive and indicated that they would continue at a later date. Reports suggested that the talks had focused on the technical aspects of returning weapons inspectors to Iraq, giving the UN some grounds for optimism.

In an interview televised by the US NBC television network in mid-May 2002, US Vice-President Dick Cheney expressed the opinion that even if an agreement were reached between Iraq and the UN on the return of weapons inspectors, it was highly unlikely that they would be given the necessary rights of access to prove that Saddam Hussain was not developing advanced weapons programmes. Cheney reiterated official US claims to have evidence that the Iraqi leader had been developing chemical and biological weapons and was attempting to establish a nuclear capacity. On a visit to Germany at the end of the month President Bush insisted that there was no concrete plan for military intervention in Iraq, and at the same time the US media reported that enthusiasm for such an attack was beginning to wane in US military circles.

By August 2002 the Iraqi Government had made a number of well-publicized offers to resume negotiations with the UN on the return of weapons inspectors to Iraq. However, these were largely dismissed by US and British officials as cosmetic delaying exercises, and there was considerable speculation that these Iraqi overtures were designed to capitalize on mounting international opposition to foreign military intervention in Iraq. The announcement, in mid-August, that Iraq had concluded a huge trade agreement with Russia, under the terms of the UN oil-for-food programme, worth some US $25,000m., seemed likely further to undermine US efforts to gain support for a military offensive in Iraq from the international community at large. None the less, the USA continued to give strong signals of its intention to intervene to bring about 'regime change' in Baghdad, pursuing attempts to secure a UN Security Council resolution that would authorize military action against Iraq, and greeted with scepticism both the Iraqi Government's indication, on 16 September, of its willingness to readmit weapons inspectors without precondition and the agreement subsequently reached with UNMOVIC and IAEA representatives for the resumption of inspections.

RELATIONS WITH NEIGHBOURING STATES

Since the end of the conflict in the Gulf in 1990–91 Jordan had continued to distance itself from Saddam Hussain's regime and on a number of occasions King Hussein spoke publicly of the need for political change in Iraq. However, the defections of Saddam Hussain's sons-in-law in August 1995 marked a sharp deterioration in relations between the two countries. Jordan immediately granted the two men political asylum and shortly after their defection King Hussein praised Hussain Kamel as a great patriot and strongly criticized the Iraqi leader, accusing him of planning a new invasion of Kuwait and of Saudi Arabia's oil-rich eastern province. The King also referred at length to the period when Iraq was under Hashemite rule and to the brief union between Jordan and Iraq, although he denied that he was seeking to revive a Hashemite claim to Iraq. Iraq's response to King Hussein's remarks was muted and despite their political differences economic co-operation between the two countries continued. Iraq remained Jordan's principal supplier of oil, and Jordan remained Iraq's most important link with the international community. King Hussein acknowledged that it would be difficult to sever all economic links with Iraq and refused a request by the USA to increase the pressure on Saddam Hussain by closing Jordan's border with Iraq, although border controls were tightened. In October King Hussein renewed his criticism of the Iraqi regime, denouncing the presidential elections there as a farce. He also made contact with Iraqi opposition groups based in London, United Kingdom, and promoted the idea of a congress in Amman to bring the different factions together in order to discuss political change in Iraq. However, the Iraqi opposition groups vociferously objected to the King's suggestion of a federal approach to Iraq's political future on the grounds that it might lead to the fragmentation of the country. In April 1996 Jordan gave permission for the stationing of US fighter aircraft at an air force base at Azraq to assist in the enforcement of the air exclusion zone in southern Iraq. Diplomatic sources in Washington, DC, reiterated that the USA had promised military support for Jordan in the event of an attack by Iraq. However, the Jordanian Government insisted that it would not permit the country to be used as a base for attacks against Iraq. Nevertheless, King Hussein had met with Iraqi opposition leaders in London in March and allowed the INA to open an office in Amman. At the end of June it was reported that US, British, Saudi Arabian and Jordanian intelligence officers had met in Saudi Arabia in January and that they had agreed that Amman would become the centre of operations for the Iraqi opposition. They agreed to support the INA, which had been established in 1990 with funding from Saudi Arabia. The INA claims to have contacts with high-ranking officers in the Iraqi armed forces and favours a decisive *coup d'état* that would depose Saddam Hussain but leave the country intact. It was also reported that US President Clinton had authorized a grant of some £6m. to finance the INA's operations in Amman, which include radio broadcasts to most parts of Iraq. Additional funds were to be provided by Saudi Arabia, Kuwait and several other Arab countries. Speaking in Washington, DC, in June, the Jordanian Minister of Information stated that Jordan preferred to support the INA because its rival, the INC, had no credibility in either Iraq or Jordan. (The INC, an umbrella organization of some 30 groups, which is based in Kurdish-controlled northern Iraq, has been paralysed by internal dissent.) In May 1996 relations with Iraq deteriorated further after the murder of a Jordanian student in Baghdad, the fifth Jordanian student to have been killed in Iraq since the beginning of the year. With growing concern for Jordanian nationals living in Iraq, the Jordanian Prime Minister informed the Iraqi authorities that he held them responsible for the safety of all Jordanians living in Iraq and recalled Jordan's ambassador from Baghdad for consultations.

Some observers regarded Jordan's dramatic break with Saddam Hussain and its *rapprochement* with Saudi Arabia and the Gulf states as part of a plan carefully orchestrated by the USA to redraw the political map of the region with the aim of further isolating Iraq, politically and economically. In April 1996, when it was revealed that Turkey had signed a secret military agreement with Israel earlier in the year, some analysts argued that a new strategic partnership was emerging in the region, bringing together the USA, Israel, Turkey and Jordan in a military union designed essentially to protect Israeli and US interests and to isolate those states opposed to them. Both the Egyptian and Syrian Governments expressed disquiet at Jordan's new policy towards Iraq, fearing that they were being excluded from plans for Iraq's future after the fall of Saddam Hussain. Syria condemned the defector, Hussain Kamel, and stated its commitment to preserving Iraq's territorial integrity, and its opposition to foreign interference in the country's internal affairs. These sentiments were appreciated in Iraq and the Iraqi Minister of Foreign Affairs stated that Iraq was willing to build new relations with any Arab country. However, in view of the long-standing differences between the two regimes, any significant improvement in relations appeared unlikely. Indeed, in April Syria hosted a congress of Iraqi opposition groups, including SCIRI, the PUK and the newly formed Hizb al-Watan, or Homeland Party. Nevertheless, it was alleged that Saddam Hussain had conducted a clandestine meeting with the Syrian President, Hafiz al-Assad, on the Syrian-Iraqi border in early May to discuss common issues including Turkey's military agreement with Israel, although some sources maintained that the meeting was only attended by their representatives.

In October 1995 Sheikh Zayed, the President of the UAE, appealed for the lifting of the UN-imposed sanctions on Iraq and for reconciliation between Iraq and the Gulf states. His remarks were criticized by Saudi Arabia and Kuwait, which, together with Bahrain, continued to express extreme disapproval of Saddam Hussain's regime. Oman and Qatar, however, like the UAE, have pursued more conciliatory policies towards Iraq. In March 1995 the Iraqi Minister of Foreign Affairs had visited Doha for talks with his Qatari counterpart, after which the Qatari Government expressed surprise that economic sanctions on Iraq had not been lifted. The Kuwait National Committee for Missing People and Prisoners of War claimed in 1994 that 625 Kuwaiti nationals were still in detention, or missing, in Iraq, and the fate of missing persons remains a major obstacle to any future normalization of relations between the two countries. Since mid-1996 Iraqi and Kuwaiti officials have held meetings in the mutual border area to discuss the fate of those not accounted for. The meetings have been conducted in closed sessions under the auspices of the ICRC, and have been attended by international observers. Although the Iraqi Government stated that it was holding no Kuwaiti prisoners of war, in late 1997 Kuwait claimed to be in possession of documentation, given to the ICRC by Iraq, relating to 126 Kuwaiti prisoners of war. In July 1998 delegations from both countries met in Geneva for 'highly confidential' discussions on this issue. Iraq was the only state not invited to the emergency summit meeting of Arab League member states in Cairo, Egypt, at the end of June, because of what President Mubarak of Egypt referred to as 'continuing sensitivities'. However, the final communiqué of the meeting urged all Arabs to oppose any policy that affected the territorial integrity of Iraq. In September US missile attacks against targets in southern Iraq were condemned by several Arab states, including Jordan and Saudi Arabia, both of which refused to allow their air bases to be used for new US air-strikes against Iraq. Kuwait, however, reluctantly endorsed the US attacks and allowed the reinforcement of US military forces stationed in the emirate. At the GCC's annual summit meeting in Qatar in December, the UAE again requested reconciliation with Iraq, but this initiative was rejected by the other member states. The summit also condemned Iraq's failure to implement all UN resolutions pertaining to the Gulf War, indicating that any normalization of relations between Iraq and the Gulf states would be dependent on Baghdad fulfilling the terms of those resolutions. The UAE, meanwhile, continued to send food and medical supplies to Iraq.

At the end of 1996 Jordan attempted to improve relations with Iraq by sending a ministerial delegation to Baghdad, the first high-level meeting between officials of the two countries since August 1995. King Hussein reportedly had been opposed to any relaxation of sanctions against Saddam Hussain's regime until Iraq's acceptance of Resolution 986. The Iraqi foreign and trade ministers held talks with the Jordanian Prime Minister in Amman in December at which Jordanian industrialists were informed that they would be given preference when Iraq began placing orders for the supply of basic goods. Nevertheless, the INA was permitted to maintain its office in Amman, despite reports that it had been infiltrated by Iraqi agents. The Jordanian Government repeatedly asserted that Jordan would not be used as a base for armed operations against the Iraqi regime. Suggestions of improved relations between Syria and Iraq emerged in May 1997, when an economic delegation from Syria which included the Chairman of the Federation of Syrian Chambers of Commerce and six other Syrian businessmen met the Iraqi Minister of Trade, Muhammad Mahdi Salih, in Baghdad to discuss possible Syrian exports to Iraq following the implementation of the oil-for-food agreement. On 2 June, as discussions on bilateral trade agreements proceeded, border crossings between the two countries, which had remained closed for 18 years, were reopened. Contracts worth US $20m. (for Syrian exports of food and medicines to Iraq) were signed during the visit. An Iraqi delegation led by the head of the Baghdad Chamber of Commerce and Industry visited Damascus in June. The import of goods to Iraq through Syrian ports and the reopening of the oil pipeline from Iraq to the Mediterranean through Syria, which has been closed since 1982, were discussed and agreement was reached to open three border posts. The Iraqi Minister of Foreign Affairs, Muhammad Saeed as-Sahaf, was keen to portray these contacts as a major diplomatic breakthrough, whereas Syrian officials were more cautious and emphasized the fact that the economic links proposed were in accordance with UN resolutions. Syria's willingness to improve its relations with Iraq appeared to be strongly influenced by its concerns about Turkey's military co-operation with Israel, and Turkey's recent military operations in northern Iraq. In June Iraq closed down Voice of Arab Syria, a radio station established in the late 1970s in Baghdad, which had been broadcasting attacks on the Assad regime, and the following month the Syrian Government curtailed the operations of Radio Voice of Iraq, a radio station which had been broadcasting anti-Iraqi propaganda since 1980. In August the Syrian Chamber of Commerce obtained a contract for exports to Iraq worth $13m., and further economic co-operation between the two countries was encouraged by UN approval of a new border crossing at al-Walid. Despite considerable progress in re-establishing economic links, at the end of September Muhammad Saeed as-Sahaf voiced frustration at the slow pace of *rapprochement* with Syria. However, at the end of the year, as tension between Iraq and the USA mounted, the Iraqi Deputy Prime Minister, Tareq Aziz, was received in Damascus by the Syrian Minister of Foreign Affairs, Farouk ash-Shara, the first public meeting between senior ministers of the two countries for 17 years. After the meeting there were reports that ash-Shara travelled to Riyadh with a communication from President Assad to King Fahd, detailing proposals for reintegrating Iraq into the Arab 'fold'. It was also claimed that Iraq was prepared to make a goodwill concession to Kuwait by providing information on alleged Kuwaiti prisoners of war held in Iraq. Tareq Aziz was also officially received in Cairo, and, although he did not meet President Mubarak, his visits to Syria and Egypt were viewed in some quarters as a significant diplomatic victory for Saddam Hussain's regime. In early February 1998, when the USA sought renewed regional support for air-strikes against Iraq, Syria strongly opposed such action. President Assad received as-Sahaf in Damascus on 10 February, the first time that he had met publicly with a senior Iraqi official since the early 1980s. In March Iyad ash-Shatti, the Syrian Minister of Health, became the first Syrian minister to visit Baghdad for almost 20 years. Kuwait, however, remained firmly opposed to any rehabilitation of Iraq under Saddam Hussain, and a meeting of the GCC in Kuwait in late December 1997 demanded that Iraq comply with all UN Security Council resolutions 'without selection' and blamed the Iraqi leader for the continued suffering of the Iraqi people. Earlier in the year pressure from the Kuwaiti Government had frustrated efforts by Baghdad to re-establish links with Lebanon. In February 1998 Kuwait was the only Arab state that publicly supported US demands for new air-strikes against Iraq. In March Kuwait's First Deputy Prime Minister and Minister of Foreign Affairs, Sheikh Sabah al-Ahmad al-Jaber as-Sabah, stated that normalization of relations with Iraq would be possible only when Baghdad had formally apologized for the invasion of Kuwait, implemented all relevant UN resolutions and released all Kuwaiti prisoners of war. Saudi Arabia did not publicly support US recommendations for the use of force against Iraq in February 1998 but some analysts speculated that the USA would have been permitted to launch military strikes from Saudi bases if diplomatic efforts had failed to defuse the crisis. Although anxious to see Iraq's territorial integrity maintained, Saudi Arabia has continued to resist Iraq's reintegration into the Arab world.

In Jordan, meanwhile, Abd al-Karim al-Kabariti, a vociferous critic of Iraq, was replaced as Prime Minister in March 1997 by Abd as-Salam al-Majali, who attempted to improve relations with Iraq, ordering the closure, in July, of an INC-controlled radio station established in 1996. In December the execution in Baghdad of four young Jordanians, convicted by Iraqi courts of smuggling activities, was denounced by King Hussein as a 'heinous crime', and prompted widespread outrage in Jordan. The Jordanian Government expelled almost one-half of the total number of Iraqi diplomatic staff in Amman and recalled its chargé d'affaires from Baghdad. In an attempt to defuse the situation, Iraq commuted the death sentence imposed on a fifth Jordanian convicted of a similar charge, and promised the release of other Jordanians in Iraqi prisons. Iraq's deputy ambassador to Jordan, Hikmat al-Hajou, his wife and a prominent Iraqi businessman were among the casualties of a multiple murder in Amman in January 1998, prompting speculation that Iraqi Government agents had been involved in the incident; the murders threatened to exacerbate tensions between the two countries. However, following the arrests of several Jordanians on charges connected to the murders, the Jordanian Minister of the Interior, Nadhir Rashid, insisted that the attack had not been politically motivated and had no connection with neighbouring countries. During the crisis over UNSCOM inspections in February, the Jordanian authorities urged Iraq to comply with UN resolutions regarding weapons inspections but also stated that they would not allow Jordanian territory or airspace to be used in an attack on Iraq. Widespread popular

support for Iraq prevailed throughout the crisis, although the Jordanian Government prohibited pro-Iraqi demonstrations. Following the death of King Hussein of Jordan in February 1999, his successor, King Abdullah, made efforts to improve bilateral relations and publicly expressed his concern for the plight of the Iraqi people. There was speculation that Jordan might close the offices of the INA in Amman and ban an Iraqi opposition radio station from broadcasting from the kingdom in the hope that Iraq would not exploit the uncertain political situation in Jordan by fomenting unrest. In January 2000 the two countries renewed their annual trade and oil protocols. Under the new oil agreement half of the crude oil and derivatives supplied to Jordan by Iraq will be free of charge, while the annual trade protocol was increased in value from US $200m. to $300m., a move welcomed by Jordanian businessmen. Some sources argued that as the first priority of Jordan's new ruler was the country's troubled economy, he had been persuaded to avoid taking a political stand against Saddam Hussain's regime and to work towards strengthening trade relations. In mid-July Vice-President Ramadan visited Amman, where he held talks with King Abdullah and Abd ar-Raouf ar-Rawabdeh, a supporter of closer ties with Iraq, who had been appointed Jordan's Prime Minister in March 1999. In late September 2000 Jordan became the first Arab country to send a flight to Baghdad carrying a government delegation; the airliner carried a group of Jordanian MPs as well as doctors and medical supplies. The Jordanian Government insisted that in its view UN resolutions allowed civilian flights in and out of Baghdad. However, while Jordanian calls for an end to the UN embargo became more vocal, the Government emphasized that Jordan would continue to abide by sanctions so long as they existed. Nevertheless, it was reported that Jordan had withdrawn its monitors from the port of Aqaba, where they had been responsible for checking goods destined for Iraq. In December, however, Royal Jordanian Airlines announced that it was suspending regular flights to Iraq and that as a result of pressure from the UN Security Council sanctions committee it was carrying out only occasional humanitarian flights.

In June 1998 Egypt's Minister of Supply and Trade, Ahmad Gueily, became the first senior Egyptian official to visit Baghdad since 1991. He took part in talks regarding the sale of Egyptian food products to Iraq under the terms of the oil-for-food programme. Iraq made some efforts to improve relations with Egypt during the year, but with limited success. The two countries are traditional rivals within the Arab world, and Egypt's tentative moves towards dialogue with Iraq were interpreted by some analysts as merely a means of pressurizing the USA to advance the Arab-Israeli peace process. Iraq's relations with its Arab neighbours deteriorated sharply at the end of the year in the wake of 'Operation Desert Fox'. While there were popular demonstrations across the Arab world in support of Iraq, Saddam Hussain denounced those Arab leaders closely allied with the USA, and urged their people to rise up against them. Iraq's demands to be included in preliminary discussions in advance of the Arab League meeting in Cairo in late January 1999 were rejected. In the same month demands by the Iraqi National Assembly for the restoration of lands lost to Kuwait as a result of the UN border demarcation of 1993–94 caused particular unease. Commercial relations between Iraq and Syria continued to develop, and in late May 1999 the Iraqi Minister of Transport and Communications stated that talks were being held with Syria to restore railway links closed for some 20 years. However, little progress was recorded in improving relations at a political level. In July Saddam Hussain condemned Saudi Arabia and Kuwait for allowing US and British fighter aircraft to use their air bases for the surveillance of the southern 'no-fly' zone and described both countries as 'accomplices to US aggression'.

Iraq's strong support for Serbia during the Kosovo crisis was in sharp contrast to the position adopted in most of the Arab world, where solidarity was expressed for the ethnic Albanian inhabitants of the province. Nevertheless, in September 1999, for the first time since the 1990–91 Gulf Crisis, the Arab League invited Iraq to chair a meeting of foreign ministers in Cairo at which the atmosphere was described as 'positive'. However, a meeting of GCC foreign ministers that month blamed the Iraqi Government for the suffering of the Iraqi people and urged Iraq to comply with all UN resolutions and demonstrate its peaceful intentions towards its neighbours. In November the GCC again urged Iraq to comply with all UN resolutions, but US efforts to persuade the Gulf states to support the exiled Iraqi opposition proved unsuccessful. In April 2000 the UAE and Bahrain re-opened their embassies in Baghdad for the first time since Iraq's invasion of Kuwait, leaving only Saudi Arabia and Kuwait among the six GCC member states without diplomatic representation in Iraq. At a meeting of the Damascus Declaration group (the GCC states, together with Egypt and Syria) in June, Egypt's Minister of Foreign Affairs, Amr Moussa, declared that it was no longer possible to continue the embargo against Iraq 'without any light at the end of the tunnel'. While deploring the suffering of the Iraqi people, Egyptian officials had previously emphasized the need for Baghdad to observe all pertinent sanctions. The death in June of Syria's President Hafiz al-Assad removed one of Saddam Hussain's principal adversaries from the Middle East political scene, and the Iraqi Minister of Foreign Affairs, Muhammad Saeed as-Sahaf, was swift to visit Damascus for talks with Assad's second son and successor, Bashar.

A new committee to investigate the fate of Iraqi soldiers registered as missing in action in Kuwait held its inaugural meeting in June 2000, attended by the Iraq's Minister of Foreign Affairs. Iraq claimed that 1,150 of its soldiers had been registered as missing in action after Iraqi forces were driven out of Kuwait in 1991, and demanded that Kuwait free them or release their bodies. Sheikh Sabah al-Ahmad al-Jaber as-Salem, Kuwait's Deputy Prime Minister and Minister of Foreign Affairs, insisted that no Iraqi soldiers were being held in Kuwait and repeated his Government's demand that all property stolen by Iraqi forces during the occupation should be returned. During a speech in mid-August Saddam Hussain again fiercely denounced the leaders of Saudi Arabia and Kuwait; his comments were reinforced by Vice-President Taha Yassin Ramadan, who criticized both countries for supporting US aggression by providing bases for US and British military aircraft. At the same time Ramadan accused Saudi Arabia, Kuwait and the Arab League of complicity in Iraq's suffering through their failure to denounce UN sanctions. In September Iraq accused Kuwait of 'stealing' its oil by carrying out drilling in a field on the border between the two countries. Kuwait strongly denied the allegation, offering to allow independent experts to analyse production at the field. Iraq repeatedly stated that it was ready to take all measures to stop the drilling, but later insisted that this did not include military action against Kuwait. Kuwait responded to reports that Iraqi forces had entered the demilitarized zone between the two countries by strengthening its security forces along the border. At the same time Baghdad accused Saudi Arabia of appropriating oil that it was transporting to customers under the UN oil-for-food programme, of breaking OPEC quotas, and of deliberately inflicting suffering on the Iraqi people. Following these allegations several Iraqi jets penetrated Saudi airspace. In late September the UN Security Council agreed to uphold the KPC's US $15,900m. damages claim against Iraq— the largest claim hitherto to come before the UNCC (see above). At the beginning of October Kuwait announced that it was deploying extra police along the border with Iraq to prevent any attempt by several hundred stateless tribesmen (*bidoon*), who claimed the right to Kuwaiti citizenship, from crossing from the Iraqi side of the demilitarized zone. A spokesman of the US Department of State stated that this appeared to be the latest in a series of propaganda ploys by Iraq, and some analysts suggested that Saddam Hussain was trying to exploit this issue to engage in a policy of brinkmanship with Kuwait. In mid-October, however, when a Saudi Arabian Airlines passenger aircraft was hijacked by Saudi dissidents to Baghdad, the Iraqi authorities quickly negotiated the release of the passengers (among them a member of the Saudi royal family) and crew, who reported that they had been extremely well treated by their Iraqi hosts.

Later in October 2000, despite the objections of Saudi Arabia and Kuwait, Saddam Hussain was invited to join other Arab leaders at an emergency summit meeting of the Arab League in Cairo, convened in response to the escalating violence between the Palestinians and the Israeli security forces. The Iraqi President chose not to attend personally but sent senior officials. Although Baghdad subsequently criticized the sum-

mit's stance as 'weak and suspect', the invitation in itself was described by one analyst as 'the single most important Iraqi foreign policy gain in a decade'. At this time Saddam Hussain announced that volunteers would be trained in Baghdad to fight alongside the Palestinians. In late November a member of Qatar's ruling family, Sheikh Hamad bin Ali ath-Thani, flew to Baghdad in his own Boeing 747 which he presented to Saddam Hussain as a gift; the Qatari Minister of Foreign Affairs, Sheikh Hamad bin Jasim bin Jaber ath-Thani, also visited Iraq in late 2000. In November Damascus agreed to the reopening of the Kirkuk–Banias oil pipeline, closed since 1982, allowing Iraq to export crude oil to Syria outside the control of the oil-for-food programme. Observers noted a significant increase in Syria's exports of crude oil, indicating that it might be substituting Iraqi imports for domestic use. The Iraqi Government insisted that its oil exports to Syria were a gift, and some analysts argued that through the reopening of this conduit Iraq was seeking political rather than financial gains. Furthermore, rail links between the two countries had been resumed (the Baghdad–Aleppo line) in August after an interval of some 20 years; an Iraqi interests section was opened in Damascus together with an Iraqi Airlines office; and Syria was reported to have lifted restrictions on its citizens travelling to Iraq. Although the Iraqi media continued to condemn Saudi Arabia and Kuwait for allowing US and British air-strikes against Iraq from their territories, the GCC at its December meeting refrained for the first time since the Gulf crisis from condemning the Iraqi Government or blaming it for the suffering of the Iraqi people. The summit's final communiqué called on Iraq to engage in a 'comprehensive dialogue' with the UN to secure an end to sanctions, and pledged support for any humanitarian effort to ease the suffering of the Iraqi people.

By the end of 2000 the apparent collapse of the US-sponsored Middle East peace process, renewed violence between Israel and the Palestinians and rising anti-US sentiment in the Arab world had all helped to accelerate Iraq's rehabilitation in the region. Although Saddam Hussain had not left Iraq since 1990, nor met with another Arab leader, in mid-January 2001 Vice-President Taha Yassin Ramadan flew to Egypt for talks with President Mubarak, the highest level contact between the two countries since the Gulf crisis. The visit, during which the two countries signed a free trade agreement, was interpreted by some as a prelude to the restoration of full diplomatic relations. The allied air-strikes against Baghdad in February (see above) provoked outrage across the Arab world, and there were pro-Iraqi demonstrations in Egypt, Syria and Jordan. President Mubarak of Egypt went so far as to declare that Saddam Hussain was no longer a threat to the international community. Nevertheless, when Arab League foreign ministers met in Amman in late March, the question of Iraq continued to prove divisive, and the summit was unable to find a formula to satisfy both Iraq on the one hand and Kuwait and Saudi Arabia on the other. Iraq demanded that the Arab League support its demands for the lifting of sanctions, an end to US-British patrols over the northern and southern air exclusion zones, and the resumption of commercial air services with Iraq; Kuwait, supported by Saudi Arabia, insisted that Iraq must agree to certain conditions before the League could support an end to sanctions. In early June Saudi Arabia confiscated an oil pipeline running from Iraq to the Red Sea, stating that the action had been taken in response to repeated cross-border raids by Iraq in recent months. The 1,100-km pipeline had only been in full operation from September 1989 to August 1990. Egypt's former Minister of Foreign Affairs, Amr Moussa, now Secretary-General of the Arab League, began intensive contacts with Iraqi and Saudi authorities to ease tensions with regard to this issue. In early July Saudi Arabia's ambassador to the UN complained to the Security Council that an Iraqi group had crossed the border on 11 June and had only withdrawn after being fired on by Saudi border guards. Saudi Arabia demanded that Iraq cease such border violations, which it claimed sought to undermine security and stability in the area.

In June 2001 Jordan and Syria, which maintained crucial economic links with Baghdad, refused to support British and US proposals for the imposition of a so-called 'smart' sanctions regime on Iraq. Syria was particularly dismissive of the proposals (although in May 2002 it voted, in its capacity as a non-permanent member of the UN Security Council, in favour of a reform of the UN sanctions regime), and continued to deny that it was importing Iraqi crude petroleum (although oil industry experts claimed Syria was receiving some 180,000 b/d which it was using for domestic consumption, thereby enabling the export of a larger share of its own oil production). During a three-day visit to Baghdad in August 2001 the Syrian Prime Minister, Dr Muhammad Mustafa Mero, signed a number of economic co-operation agreements. The Jordanian and Syrian Governments also expressed strong opposition to military intervention in Iraq as part of the US-led international 'coalition against terrorism' in the aftermath of the 11 September suicide attacks on the US mainland. Egypt also declared itself unwilling to support such an offensive on an Arab country. In October Saddam Hussain was highly critical of the Gulf states for their refusal to denounce what he described as US aggression and terrorism around the world. In the same month, however, Iraq appointed its first ambassador to Bahrain since the 1990–91 Gulf War.

Meanwhile, border tensions with Kuwait continued. In September two Iraqis who had crossed into Kuwait were arrested and accused of being engaged in espionage activities, while Iraq accused Kuwait of over-exploiting an oilfield situated on the border between the two countries. In November Kuwait made a formal complaint to the UN when machine guns and mortars were fired from Iraq into the Kuwaiti side of the demilitarized zone. In early January 2002, however, amid growing speculation that Iraq would soon be targeted in the US 'war against terror', Saddam Hussain appealed to Arab states to put aside their differences and present united opposition to any such initiative. In mid-January the Secretary-General of the Arab League, Amr Moussa, made a short visit to Baghdad—the first visit to Iraq by the head of that organization since the 1990–91 Gulf conflict—where he held talks with Saddam Hussain and senior Iraqi government officials. The discussions were reported to have focused on the possibility of Iraqi reconciliation with Kuwait and Saudi Arabia—the only Arab nations not to have restored diplomatic relations with Baghdad after 1991—and on ways of strengthening ties between Arab states in preparation for the forthcoming summit meeting of Arab League Heads of State. An Iraqi official subsequently announced that his Government would now be willing to allow an official Kuwaiti delegation to visit Iraq in order to verify Iraqi Government claims that no Kuwaiti prisoners captured during the Gulf War were being held there—Kuwaiti Government claims to the contrary had remained a key obstacle to the normalization of relations between the two countries. At a summit meeting held in Beirut, Lebanon, in late March 2002, Arab leaders reiterated their opposition to any US-led military intervention in Iraq. The head of the Iraqi delegation, RCC Vice-President Izzat Ibrahim, thanked delegates for opposing US threats against Iraq, and declared Iraq to be particularly grateful for Saudi Arabian support. He also announced that Iraq would henceforth agree to respect the sovereignty of Kuwait, and guarantee its independence, stability and security within its internationally recognized borders. The other Arab states expressed the hope that Iraq and Kuwait would now begin to co-operate to resolve the outstanding issues between them. The summit's final declaration included assurances that there would be no repeat of Iraq's 1990 annexation of Kuwait, and urged Iraq and Kuwait to end their use of propaganda against each other. Further declarations issued during the summit meeting included demands for international recognition of the independence, sovereignty and security of Iraq and respect for its territorial integrity. Moreover, Arab leaders expressed their opposition to any aggression or threat of aggression against Arab states in general, and against Iraq in particular, stating that such action would be regarded as an attack on the security of all Arab nations. In May 2002 Iraq informed the UN that it intended to return to Kuwait the national archives and official documents it had removed during the 1990–91 occupation.

Iraq's relations with Turkey deteriorated in early 1995. In March Turkish armed forces mounted a major operation to destroy PKK bases in the Kurdish enclave in northern Iraq (see above), and although the troops were withdrawn in May a smaller force crossed the border again in July. These actions, and statements by the Turkish President, Süleyman Demirel,

revived fears of a Turkish claim to the former Ottoman province of Mosul. In a number of interviews with the Turkish media in May, Demirel stated that the alignment of the border with Iraq was wrong and that certain adjustments were needed to improve Turkey's security. He also pointed out that that the province of Mosul was still Ottoman territory when the Turkish Republic was founded in 1923 and had not become part of Iraq until 1929. Although Turkish officials emphasized that only minor border changes were being suggested, the President's comments were denounced by Iraq. However, the appointment of a new Turkish Government under Prime Minister Necmettin Erbakan was followed by an improvement in relations between Iraq and Turkey, and in mid-August 1996 the two countries signed a 'mutual understanding' memorandum which provided for improved political and economic links, increased trade and the construction of a gas pipeline. Under the agreement Turkey indicated that it hoped to supply all of Iraq's food imports and to receive payment in Iraqi oil. Turkey insisted that the oil-for-food agreement had been signed within the framework of UN Resolution 986. However, some analysts observed that the memorandum was politically inspired and unlikely to have any tangible results. At the end of August, Turkey condemned Iraq's invasion of the Kurdish enclave but did not endorse US missile attacks against Iraq in early September. Turkey did announce, however, that it was establishing a security zone in northern Iraq (just south of the border) which would be patrolled by Turkish army units, and launched new attacks against PKK bases in the Kurdish enclave. Iran, Egypt, Jordan and Syria demanded that Turkey cease actions which threatened the territorial integrity of Iraq. In May 1997 a major new Turkish assault on PKK bases in northern Iraq was condemned by Iraq and several other Arab countries, notably Syria. Before the invasion, Turkey had accused both Syria and Iran of mobilizing troops along the border with northern Iraq and providing support for the PKK. Cautious moves by Syria to improve relations with Iraq (see above) were attributed, in part, to growing concern in Damascus over Turkish actions in northern Iraq and to Turkey's 1996 military co-operation agreement with Israel. The UN Secretary-General, Kofi Annan, demanded the withdrawal of Turkish troops from the area and declared that UN relief operations, as well as food supplies to the Kurdish enclave, could be jeopardized by the invasion. The USA, however, anxious to 'disengage' from northern Iraq, appeared to support the Turkish intervention. Despite Turkey's military operations in northern Iraq, economic links between the two countries showed some improvement. In July Turkey revoked its ban on border trade with Iraq and in September an official of the Turkish Ministry of Foreign Affairs visited Baghdad to discuss economic co-operation. During the visit agreement was reached on increasing the number of Turkish diplomats in Baghdad and on the transfer of Turkish prisoners held in Iraq to prisons in Turkey. At the end of September, however, Turkish forces again invaded northern Iraq, and although the campaign was smaller in scale than that of May, Turkish troops were reported to have penetrated much deeper into Iraqi territory. Iraq protested to the UN, portraying the Turkish invasion as part of a US-Zionist campaign aimed at 'the Arab nations'. Although its aims in northern Iraq appeared to be limited to the removal of PKK bases there, Syria and the Kurdish groups insisted that Turkey still had designs on Mosul and Kirkuk. In May 1998 the Iraqi Minister of Foreign Affairs repeated claims that Turkey was violating international law by building several dams on the Euphrates and Tigris rivers without consultation with other riparian nations.

In February 1999 Tareq Aziz visited Ankara for talks with the new Turkish Prime Minister, Bülent Ecevit. None the less, Iraq's efforts to improve relations with Turkey appeared to make little progress, as the Turkish military had made it clear to Ecevit that it would not accept any change to the existing policy of allowing the USA and United Kingdom to use Turkish air bases to patrol the northern 'no-fly' zone. In early July Iraq condemned a new invasion by Turkish forces into northern Iraq in an operation against PKK bases there. Some 15,000 Turkish troops, supported by helicopters and fighter aircraft, were reported to have taken part in the operation. In April 2000 Turkish troops again crossed the border into northern Iraq to attack PKK bases in the Kurdish enclave. Despite tensions over Turkey's involvement in the Kurdish-controlled areas of northern Iraq, its refusal to enter into talks with Baghdad and Damascus about sharing waters from the Tigris-Euphrates system and a compensation claim for US $1,250m. for the closure of the Kirkuk–Ceyhan oil pipeline as a result of the 1990–91 Gulf crisis, the Turkish Government appointed an ambassador to Baghdad in January 2001—thus restoring diplomatic relations to the pre-1990 level. Turkey expressed disapproval of the US-British air-strikes against Baghdad in February 2001, and emphasized that none of the aircraft taking part in the raid had flown from Turkish airbases. The Turkish Government was unconvinced by British and US proposals in mid-2001 for the imposition of a so-called 'smart' sanctions regime on Iraq, and later in the year expressed strong opposition to any US-led military intervention in Iraq as part of the US Government's 'war against terror' in the aftermath of the 11 September attacks on the US mainland. On a visit to Ankara in early December US Secretary of State Colin Powell assured the Turkish Government that the USA had no immediate plans for a military offensive in Iraq. During a meeting with President George W. Bush in Washington, DC, in January 2002 the Turkish Prime Minister described a US-led military adventure in Iraq as a potential disaster that would threaten the stability of the region. In the following weeks, as the Bush Administration reiterated its determination to achieve 'regime change' in Baghdad and confirmed that it was considering all options for achieving this, Ecevit wrote to the Iraqi leader urging him to allow the return of UN weapons inspectors. Although he received no reply from Baghdad, Ecevit later stated that he had discussed the matter with the Iraqi Minister of Foreign Affairs during his visit to İstanbul for an EU-OIC summit in mid-February 2002 and had detected some flexibility in Iraq's position. It was widely believed that the Turkish leadership feared that US military intervention in Iraq and the removal of Saddam Hussain might lead to the emergence of a federative republic in Iraq and greater autonomy for the country's Kurdish minority, or even the dismantling of Iraq and the creation of an independent Kurdish state, developments that would have serious implications for Turkey's own Kurdish population.

Iraq has expressed disquiet at Iran's growing involvement in the conflict between Kurdish factions in the Kurdish enclave (see above). Disputes over the question of prisoners of war from the 1980–88 Iran–Iraq War, and each country's support for the other's opponents, have prevented any significant improvement in relations. Early in 1996 Iraq urged Iran to adopt an 'objective and serious approach' to their relations, based on respect for each country's sovereignty and non-interference in each other's internal affairs. Later in 1996 there were unconfirmed reports of Iranian military intervention in northern Iraq, where the Iranian Government had developed a range of activities, including the supply of humanitarian relief. One of the justifications given by Iraqi officials for Iraq's intervention in the Kurdish enclave in August was the need to address Iran's growing influence there. In November Saddam Hussain sent an envoy to Tehran to inform the Iranian leadership that he wished to achieve good relations with Iran and to engage in discussions concerning regional issues, as well as the release of prisoners of war. After the visit, Iran released more than 700 Iraqi prisoners of war and indicated that it was willing to discuss the release of other prisoners in order to foster improved relations. According to Iraqi sources, more than 18,000 Iraqi prisoners of the Iran–Iraq War are still being held in Iran. Several visits were undertaken at ministerial level during 1997, and in August Saddam Hussain offered to allow Iranian pilgrims to visit Shi'a holy shrines in Iraq. The Ministers of Foreign Affairs of the two countries held talks at the UN in New York in late September, but the Iraqi foreign minister stated that further gestures of reconciliation from Tehran, in particular the return of Iraqi fighter aircraft that had landed in Iran at the beginning of the 1990–91 Gulf War, were necessary if relations were to improve. A few days later Iranian military aircraft attacked bases of an Iranian opposition group, the Mujahidin-e-Khalq, near Baghdad. In December 1997 Iraqi Vice-President Taha Yassin Ramadan held talks with the new Iranian President, Sayed Muhammad Khatami, at a summit meeting of the OIC in Tehran. Iran was opposed to US demands for renewed air-strikes against Iraq in February 1998, but in March US officials

welcomed Iranian efforts to curtail the illegal export of Iraqi oil through Iranian territorial waters. In early April it was reported that some 1,500 Iraqi and 89 Iranian prisoners of the 1980–88 war had been exchanged by the two sides as part of an arrangement to release 5,592 Iraqi and 250 Iranian prisoners of war. In May 1998 the two countries embarked on an unprecedented joint operation to locate the remains of soldiers killed in the Iran–Iraq War.

There was considerable disquiet in Baghdad at the beginning of 1998 when Iran successfully tested medium-range missiles. Indeed, a number of analysts argued that Iraq's determination to resume its weapons programmes was motivated more by fears that a number of its neighbours were acquiring or expanding their arsenal of weapons of mass destruction rather than by a desire to threaten neighbouring states. Relations with Iran became tenser still after the murders in southern Iraq in the first half of 1998 of two senior Shi'a clerics, both Iranians. Iraqi opposition sources claimed that the Iraqi Government was responsible for the killings, and while Iran avoided directly accusing Iraq of responsibility, it urged the Iraqi authorities to make every effort to protect Shi'a religious leaders in Iraq. Later in the year Tareq Aziz asserted that despite Iraqi efforts to improve relations, Iran had not 'fully responded' to these initiatives. Further tension arose in early 1999 when the Mujahidin-e-Khalq assassinated the Iranian deputy chief of staff. Iraq, for its part, accused the Iranian-backed Shi'a opposition group, SCIRI, of fomenting violent demonstrations in the southern city of Basra. In mid-April both countries deployed troops along the border and a further deterioration in relations was only avoided through the exchange of bodies of soldiers killed during the Iran-Iraq War. In February and March 2000 the Mujahidin-e-Khalq launched new attacks against what it claimed were military and official targets in Tehran. However, the Iranian authorities claimed that the attacks had been carried out in residential areas and had caused civilian casualties. Several days after the second attack mortar fire in a residential area in Baghdad was reported to have killed five people and injured 38. Iraq accused agents of the Iranian regime of carrying out this attack and the funeral of those killed developed into a protest against Iran, the first since the end of the Iran–Iraq War. Earlier in March a US initiative to improve relations with Iran had aroused concern in Iraq. The official daily newspaper, *Ath-Thawra*, expressed fears that a future *rapprochement* between Iran and the USA might create a front hostile to Iraq. In early April the Iraqi media claimed that two bases of the Mujahidin-e-Khalq had been attacked by a group that had crossed the border from Iran. Iran's decision to seize several ships smuggling oil from Iraq through Iranian territorial waters at this time may have been intended to warn Iraq to cease its support for the Mujahidin-e-Khalq. In May the Mujahidin-e-Khalq claimed responsibility for mortar attacks on police headquarters in Tehran and Kermanshah and on a Revolutionary Guard base in Tehran. At the end of May Iran allowed Iraq to resume oil-smuggling through Iranian territorial waters, even though the USA claimed that some of the revenues from illegal oil exports were used by Baghdad to fund the Mujahidin-e-Khalq. In October a three-day visit to Baghdad by Iran's Minister of Foreign Affairs, Kamal Kharrazi, prompted reports that the two countries were prepared to enter into a comprehensive security arrangement under which they would cease to support the activities of SCIRI and the Mujahidin-e-Khalq respectively. A verbal agreement on this subject had been reached at a meeting between the Iraqi Vice-President, Taha Yassin Ramadan, and Iran's President, Muhammad Khatami, at the OPEC summit in Caracas, Venezuela, at the end of September. However, at the end of January 2001 Iran claimed that a series of explosions near the Iranian Revolutionary Guards complex north of Tehran had been perpetrated by the Mujahidin-e-Khalq, and Ali Shamkhani, the Iranian Minister of Defence and Logistics, stated that Iran could not rely on promises made by the Iraqi Government. In mid-April the Mujahidin-e-Khalq claimed that one of its members, together with several Iraqi civilians, had been killed during Iranian missile attacks on Mujahidin bases near Basra and Faeza, in southern Iraq and Achraf east of Baghdad. At the end of January 2002, under threat of possible US military intervention as part of the US-led 'war against terror', Iraq made new diplomatic overtures to

Iran, announcing that commercial flights would be resumed between the two countries.

According to the ICRC, some 2,000 Iraqi prisoners of war were released by Iran in early April 2000, the largest such repatriation since 1998, in what was described by Iran as a gesture to improve relations. The head of the Iraqi war victims'

committee claimed that Iran was still holding 13,000 Iraqi prisoners, but denied that Iraq held any Iranian prisoners. Iran, however, insisted that Iraq still held 2,806 Iranian prisoners. Iran agreed to release another 700 Iraqi prisoners of war in early 2001.

Economy

Revised for this edition by RICHARD I. LAWLESS

INTRODUCTION

Having begun to recover from the effects of the 1980–88 conflict with Iran, the Iraqi economy entered a new period of trauma in August 1990, as a result of the UN sanctions that were imposed because of Iraq's invasion of Kuwait. It then suffered substantial material damage in the war with the US-led multi-national force in early 1991; a UN report suggested that aerial bombardment had reduced Iraq to a 'pre-industrial' state in the immediate aftermath of the 1991 hostilities. Although the authorities succeeded in restoring a measure of basic infrastructural viability by early 1992, having given priority to the rapid rebuilding of key installations and facilities, there was no prospect of a full normalization of economic life while Iraq remained subject to UN trade sanctions. Having relied on petroleum for 98% of export earnings over the previous decade, the country suffered a massive loss of revenue when it was excluded from the world oil market in 1990. In September 1993 Iraq's Minister of Trade estimated that three years of sanctions had cost the country US $60,000m. in lost oil revenues. By 1994 the living standards of large sections of the Iraqi population had been reduced to subsistence level by the prolongation of conditions of acute economic hardship. According to unofficial Western estimates, the annual rate of decline in Iraq's gross domestic product (GDP) was about 10% in 1994 and 1995 and 15% in 1996, suggesting a GDP of $11,500m. at the end of that year. In March 1996 the head of the UN Special Commission on Iraq (UNSCOM) estimated that the country was losing about $15,000m. of revenue per year as a result of trade sanctions. In the previous month Iraq had opened negotiations with the UN with a view to agreeing terms for the export of a limited volume of oil to finance a UN-supervised humanitarian programme (centred on the import and distribution of medical and food supplies). UN trade sanctions would be subject to temporary modification while the proposed scheme was operating. Especially given the unacceptability to Iraq of plans, promoted within the UN Security Council by the USA and United Kingdom, for the introduction of what were termed 'smart' sanctions, no date for the full lifting of sanctions could be foreseen in mid-2002.

The earlier war with Iran had itself severely affected Iraq's economic development, which had been steadily gaining momentum since 1977, forcing expenditure on former priority areas, such as water and electricity, to be reduced, with funds being transferred to defence. Towards the end of that conflict, the Government initiated, in March 1987, an economic reform programme which was supposed to reduce the extent of state control over industry, this having previously been an article of faith of the Baath Socialist Party regime which came to power in 1968. Many state organizations were abolished, and others sold to the private sector, the emphasis being placed on securing greater efficiency in the industrial and agricultural sectors and on the performance of workers and management, rather than on the state bureaucracy. More liberal import regulations—including the use of 'offshore' foreign currency funds—were introduced to enable private companies to become more involved in foreign trade.

Emerging from the hostilities of 1980–88, Iraq was generally considered to have strong development prospects, despite its continuing allocation of huge sums to military expenditure. Unlike other Arab states in the region, Iraq had the advantage of a relatively large population (16,335,199 at the census of October 1987), giving it the labour force necessary for industrial development. It also placed considerable emphasis on education

and the creation of a skilled work-force. Moreover, Iraq continued to have an extensive and productive agricultural sector, assisted by substantial investment funds, ample supplies of irrigation water and availability of fertile land. However, by the late 1980s agriculture had become overshadowed by large-scale production of petroleum and natural gas. Both the 1970–75 and the 1976–80 development plans had given priority to the petroleum and industrial sectors, the aim being not only to maximize earnings from exports of oil and gas, but also to diversify into other industrial exports. These objectives were maintained in the 1981–85 development plan, but this was abandoned amid the exigencies of the 1980–88 war with Iran, after which planning was conducted on an annual basis. The country's increasing industrialization was reflected in the population distribution: according to World Bank estimates, 71% of the population were classed as urban at mid-1990, compared with 51% in 1965 and 64% in 1977, when only 30% of the labour force were employed in agriculture, compared with 53% in 1960. Nevertheless, the industrial sector remained totally dominated by oil and gas production, which accounted for more than 99% of export earnings in 1989.

Lack of reliable official data has prevented the World Bank from publishing recent statistics for Iraq's overall national output and income. According to the Statistical Office of Iraq, GDP at factor cost increased from ID 1,139m. in 1970 to ID 15,647m. in 1980, while GDP per caput rose from ID 120 to ID 1,181 over the same period. The Iran–Iraq War resulted in a decline in GDP to ID 11,215m. in 1981, and in GDP per caput to ID 820, but thereafter GDP rose steadily, to ID 15,551m. in 1987 and to ID 20,811m. in 1989, while GDP per caput recovered to ID 1,186 by 1989, just above the pre-war level. The effect of the 1980–88 war was particularly apparent in the decline in oil export revenues, from ID 7,718.4m. in 1980 to ID 5,982.4m. in 1982, although by 1988 revenue from this source had recovered to ID 7,223.9m. National income increased from ID 10,589m. (ID 826 per caput) in 1979 to ID 17,290m. (ID 986 per caput) in 1989. According to Iraqi officials, overall GDP in dinar terms rose by 16% in 1989, compared with 1988 (and per-caput GDP by 20%) and by 78% during 1979–89 (in which period national income grew by 63%), despite the adverse effects of the Iran–Iraq War. According to Western estimates, the real growth in GDP in 1989 was 6.5%, following zero growth in 1988, an increase of 7.7% in 1987, an actual decline of 2.9% in 1986, an increase of 3.2% in 1985 and an increase of 15.7% in 1984.

Iraq's development plans were, however, seriously compromised by a continuing shortage of foreign exchange (reserves were estimated at between zero and US $2,000m. in 1987) and the accumulation of massive foreign debts during the 1980–88 war. Estimated at more than $50,000m. at the end of 1986, Iraq's total foreign debt was thought to have increased to about $65,000m. by mid-1990, including some $30,000m. in the form of loans from neighbouring Gulf states, about $13,000m. in civil debt guaranteed by export credit agencies and a further $6,000m. owed to Western companies and not covered by export credit guarantees; some $3,000m. per year was required to service the Western portion of the debt. In the late 1980s Iraq successfully negotiated a number of debt-rescheduling agreements, enabling it to proceed with major development projects in the petroleum, industrial and water-management sectors, with foreign contractors accepting deferred payment terms or using credit lines to finance contracts. Nevertheless, Iraq's international financial standing continued to be eroded by the decline in international petroleum prices in 1989 and early 1990, which, in turn, explained the country's fierce criticism of Kuwait and other Gulf states within the Organization of the Petroleum Exporting Countries (OPEC) for exceeding production quotas agreed by the organization (see Petroleum and Natural Gas, below). Against this background, Iraq's invasion of Kuwait in August 1990 had a powerful economic motivation, although in the event it was to lead to economic catastrophe.

SANCTIONS AND OIL-FOR-FOOD

The mandatory economic sanctions that were imposed on Iraq (and Iraqi-controlled Kuwait) by the UN Security Council on 6 August 1990 included bans on the purchase or transhipment of Iraqi oil and other commodities and on the sale or supply of all goods and products to Iraq (with possible humanitarian exceptions for medical supplies and foodstuffs). Also prescribed were an interdiction of new investment in Iraq and Kuwait and the 'freezing' of Iraqi and Kuwaiti assets abroad. Adopted unanimously and applied by virtually the whole international community, these sanctions were tightened on 25 September to include interdiction of air traffic and obligatory detention of Iraqi-registered ships violating the trade embargo. Their effect was to place the Iraqi economy in almost total isolation, except that the land route from Jordan remained open for certain supplies. Particularly damaging for Iraq was the abrupt cessation of its oil and gas exports, including those via pipelines through Saudi Arabia and Turkey, which were closed. With its prime source of revenue thus interrupted, the Government responded by introducing rationing for basic food items and by taking various emergency measures to promote economic self-sufficiency. It also sought to counter the damaging effects of the flight from Iraq and Kuwait of hundreds of thousands of foreign workers, mostly from other Arab countries and the Indian subcontinent. Moreover, under Law 57 of 1990, announced on 18 September but backdated to 8 August, the Government declared Iraq's non-recognition of all seizures of Iraqi assets and decreed the seizure of the assets of all countries and organizations which 'issued arbitrary decisions' against Iraq. As part of this strategy, Iraq suspended debt repayments to the USA and other members of the anti-Iraq coalition.

Western reports indicated that, despite some shortages and steeply rising prices, the Iraqi economy continued to function on an emergency basis in the latter months of 1990. The situation changed dramatically, however, during the active hostilities of January–February 1991, particularly as a result of the massive allied bombing campaign against both military and strategic economic targets. According to an official UN report compiled in mid-March 1991, the conflict 'wrought near-apocalyptic results on the economic infrastructure', destroying or damaging most modern means of life support and relegating Iraq for some time to come to a 'pre-industrial age but with all the disabilities of post-industrial dependency on an intensive use of energy and technology'. The report detailed the effects of the war in the various economic sectors (see separate sections, below) and warned, in particular, of the danger of famine and epidemics spreading because of the collapse of water-distribution and sewerage systems. Of various forecasts made of the potential cost of repairing the war damage, US officials estimated in April that some US $30,000m. would be required for the reconstruction of roads, power plants and oil installations. Other Western estimates assessed the total cost of the conflict to Iraq at some $50,000m. as at mid-May 1991, including the loss of 50% of GDP since August 1990 as well as war damage. The Iraqi Government, in April 1991, estimated the cost of reconstruction at $25,800m., excluding repairs in the private sector and damage to the military and nuclear industries.

The maintenance of most UN sanctions after the cease-fire agreement of 3 March 1991 (except those on food and medical supplies), meant that the Iraqi Government was obliged to begin its reconstruction efforts within those constraints, involving the continued non-availability of crucial oil revenues. An emergency six-month reconstruction budget, announced on 2 May, incorporated a reduction of state expenditure in 1991 to the equivalent of US $44,760m. (from the original total of $47,080m.) but still assumed a partial resumption of oil revenues in the second half of the year. As a result of the consequential Iraqi campaigning for the removal of the UN embargo, the sanctions committee

agreed on 9 May to a partial 'unfreezing' of Iraqi assets abroad, officially estimated at $4,000m., so that Iraq could pay for essential civilian items. However, Iraqi requests for the repeal of the oil export embargo were complicated by the UN Security Council's decision, on 20 May, to establish a Geneva-based Compensation Commission (UNCC) to administer a fund for victims of Iraq's aggression (governments, corporations and individuals), to be financed by a percentage levy on Iraqi oil revenues. With Western estimates valuing the possible extent of claims for damages at between $50,000m. and $100,000m., Iraq appealed for a five-year moratorium on payments from the fund and also urged that the country be permitted to export at least $1,000m.-worth of oil in 1991 to pay for urgently needed imports. It also opposed, as unrealistic, the level of 'up to 30%' which the Security Council eventually set for the UNCC's fund level, on the proposal of the UN Secretary-General.

In support of its requests to the UN for more lenient treatment, the Iraqi Government, on 29 April 1991, took the unprecedented step of submitting a report on its external debt position. This showed that at the end of 1990 outstanding debts totalled US $43,320m., excluding interest already due (of some $32,350m.) and what Iraq termed 'grants' from other Gulf states (estimated at between $30,000m. and $40,000m.). The report calculated that a total of $75,450m. would be required to service the debt in the 1991–95 period (during which 97% of the outstanding amount fell due) and that the foreign currency requirement for imports, development and reconstruction would total $140,000m. Export earnings over this period were forecast at $65,455m., on the assumption of progress to approaching pre-war oil export levels by 1993, so that an overall external deficit of $150,000m. was expected to accumulate by 1995. Western analysts noted that these calculations were based on the conservative assumption of a constant nominal price for crude petroleum of $16 per barrel. They nevertheless agreed that, if any substantial proportion of Iraqi oil revenues was diverted to war reparations in this period, an even greater deficit would accumulate and that the other commitment categories would not be fulfilled as specified.

In the event, Iraqi resistance to full observance of the UN cease-fire resolution terms meant that the UN embargo was still in force in mid-2002. Moreover, UN Security Council Resolutions 706 and 712 of 16 August and 19 September 1991 respectively, authorizing Iraq to export oil to the value of US $1,600m. to pay for emergency food and medical imports, were not immediately utilized by Iraq, which claimed that the stringent terms attached thereto amounted to an infringement of the country's sovereignty. The Security Council's decision was prompted by an FAO study of Iraq, warning that a 'widespread and acute food supply crisis' threatened 'massive starvation throughout the country', and describing the effects of the economic blockade as 'alarming'. Iraq's rejection of Resolutions 706 and 712 was reaffirmed in February 1994 by a government spokesman, who said that no oil would be sold on terms which constituted 'a flagrant violation of Iraq's sovereignty'. UN Security Council Resolution 986 of 14 April 1995 extended a revised offer to Iraq to permit the supervised export of petroleum to the value of $2,000m. over a period of 180 days, with the possibility of further 180-day renewals thereafter. Revised monitoring arrangements would allow limited use of Iraq's Gulf export facilities (rather than requiring all the petroleum to be piped via Turkey), while the UN would be more flexible than previously proposed in its monitoring of the distribution of the humanitarian supplies to be purchased with 50% of the permitted petroleum export income. Some 30% of the revenue would be allocated to war reparations, and most of the remaining 20% to UN relief work in northern Iraq. Initially Iraq rejected the scheme, objecting in particular to the use of petroleum income to fund relief work in the predominantly Kurdish north, a proposal which the Government interpreted as 'part of a UN plan to dissect Iraqi sovereignty and establish secession in the north'.

Countries which 'unfroze' part of the Iraqi assets under their jurisdiction included the United Kingdom (in November 1991) and Italy (in January 1992). Such relaxations enabled Iraq to import some urgently-needed items, although the country relied mainly on overland supplies, in breach of UN sanctions. According to a US report of January 1992, substantial 'seepage' through the sanctions net had resulted in Iraq being able to import goods worth some US $2,000m. since the end of the war, representing about 25% of the pre-crisis level.

During the first half of 1993 it was clear that Iraq's economic position was rapidly deteriorating; hyperinflation in the market prices of most goods, including basic foodstuffs, was accompanied by a collapse in the value of the currency and sharp rises in unemployment and destitution. Even in the central regions, where the Government was most concerned to underpin minimum living standards, growing numbers of people lacked the means to supplement the official ration of subsidized staple foods. Increases in this ration entitlement in early 1993 raised its estimated calorific value to about two-thirds of the minimum subsistence level defined by UN humanitarian agencies. The Government claimed in March 1993 that nearly 234,000 people, including 83,000 children under the age of five, had died 'as a result of sanctions' between August 1990 and January 1993, over which period the provision of basic health care had been compromised by an 85% shortfall in medical supplies. A report by the UN Children's Fund (UNICEF) estimated that Iraq's infant mortality rate had tripled over this period. Subsequent reports from UN agencies re-emphasized the human costs of the situation. FAO and the World Food Programme (WFP) issued a statement on 26 May 1994 describing present-day Iraq as a country crippled by 'massive deprivation, chronic hunger, endemic under-nutrition for the vast majority of the population, collapse of personal incomes and rapidly increasing numbers of destitute people'. In September WFP announced a six-month emergency programme to supply over 100,000 metric tons of food aid to 1.3m. people in Iraq at a cost of US $33.6m. In May 1995 the UN agencies monitoring Iraq's economic crisis estimated that about 4m. Iraqis currently depended on the basic state food ration, that at least 1m. of these experienced chronic hunger, and that about 23% of children under the age of five were suffering from malnutrition. A $183.3m. UN aid programme for Iraqi civilians was proposed for the 12 months to March 1996 to alleviate hunger, to support health, water, sanitation and educational projects and to resettle displaced families. By October 1995, however, less than $40m. had been pledged to this relief programme by donors.

By the end of May 1994 (two months before its scheduled closing date for claims) the UNCC had received claims totalling US $81,000m. (including $15,000m. claimed by the Kuwait Government). The UNCC's resources at this time totalled about $43m., derived from 'frozen' Iraqi assets and voluntary contributions by Saudi Arabia and the USA. These resources were expected to be significantly depleted by payments to priority claimants, namely individuals who had been severely injured and families of those who had been killed. The first awards in this category (to 670 persons from 16 countries) were approved on 26 May and totalled $2.7m.

It was estimated that funds held in the escrow account established under Security Council Resolution 778 (see 'Finance and Banking', below) might be sufficient to meet an estimated US $150m. in claims by workers forced to leave Kuwait as a result of the invasion, and might also cover the slightly lower estimate for aggregate claims by individuals who had suffered personal losses of up to $100,000, including loss of earnings or assets held in Kuwait. However, the claims which made up the greater part of the total—those submitted by governments and businesses and by individuals with losses exceeding $100,000—stood no chance of even partial settlement while the intended funding mechanism remained inoperable for want of any Iraqi oil revenues to appropriate.

In early April 1996 WFP made an urgent appeal to donor countries for US $162m. of emergency food supplies for Iraq. On 20 May, at the conclusion of four rounds of talks over a period of four months, the Iraqi Government signed a memorandum of understanding accepting the terms of UN Security Council Resolution 986 of April 1995. Having taken this step, Iraq was required to agree a detailed implementation plan with the UN Security Council's sanctions committee. The UN subsequently came under pressure from the USA to establish strong supervisory mechanisms at every stage of the proposed export, import and distribution activities. The USA was particularly concerned to ensure that the UN applied a very narrow definition of humanitarian supplies in order to prevent the import of items that could be diverted to other uses.

An implementation plan was eventually approved by the sanctions committee in early August 1996, and it was expected that all the required procedures and personnel would be established by mid-September. However, the new crisis in US–Iraqi relations at the start of September 1996 (see History) caused a temporary suspension of UN preparatory work within Iraq, and it was not until late November that arrangements to monitor oil sales under the terms of Resolution 986 were completed. Production of oil for export under UN supervision began on 10 December 1996. The export of oil to the value of some US $2,000m. was to be permitted over a period of 180 days, and all proceeds were to be paid into a special UN escrow account in New York. Of the $2,000m., $20m. was allocated for the operation of the escrow account, $44.32m. for UN operational and administrative costs, $15m. for UNSCOM (tasked with verifying compliance with cease-fire conditions) and $600m. for the UNCC's fund for war reparations. This left $1,320.68m. available for spending on humanitarian supplies, of which $260m. was assigned for the UN co-ordinated relief programme in Kurdish-controlled areas of Iraq and $1,060.68m. for supplies to the remainder of Iraq. Some 61% of total humanitarian spending was allocated for imports of foodstuffs, 16% for medicines and 8% for soaps and detergents. Priority imports for the electricity, agricultural and educational sectors accounted for 11% of authorized humanitarian spending, compared with 3% for water and sanitation services and 1% for health infrastructure and nutrition. By mid-March 1997 the UN had approved a total of 39 oil export contracts and had received $719m. of deposits in the relevant escrow account, of which $473m. had been allocated to humanitarian supplies. The UNCC used its first allowance of oil export revenues to pay a total of $144m. to 57,636 claimants from 63 countries on 1 March 1997. The first shipment of humanitarian goods arrived in Iraq on 25 March, by which time more than 100 international inspectors had been appointed to monitor the distribution process. In May 1997 the Iraqi Government accused the USA of seeking to 'delay and disrupt' deliveries of humanitarian supplies, including medicines and ambulances, by challenging the validity of many of the import contracts submitted by Iraq for UN approval. It was subsequently stated that more than 40 'medical contracts' (including an order for agricultural pesticides) were being delayed by the UN Security Council's sanctions committee in response to US insistence.

By the end of May 1997, shortly before the expiry of the first 180-day 'oil-for-food' arrangement, the UN had processed approximately US $2,110m.-worth of oil export contracts, had received nearly $1,750m. in oil sales revenues and had issued a total of $466m. of bank credits to pay for humanitarian supplies. The renewal of the arrangement for a further 180 days was unanimously approved by the UN Security Council on 5 June. However, Iraq suspended its UN-supervised oil exports at the start of the renewal period in protest at the slow rate of delivery of humanitarian supplies under existing arrangements. The Government intended to maintain the suspension until a more satisfactory distribution plan was implemented. Cumulative food deliveries to Iraq under Resolution 986 amounted to around 1m. metric tons by early July. In that month Iraq submitted a new distribution plan, and, following UN approval, it recommenced exports of petroleum in mid-August.

The oil-for-food arrangement was renewed in December 1997; it was revised in February 1998 after the UN Security Council approved a plan to increase Iraq's export entitlement to US $5,200m., of which $3,550m. was to be spent on humanitarian goods and $1,650m. was to finance reparations and UN operations. Exports were expected to increase following agreement on a new distribution programme between Iraq and the UN, which was duly approved at the end of May. The programme did not cover Iraq's full export entitlement, owing to Iraqi claims that it could not fulfil the quota unless essential repairs to oil installations were made. The distribution plan provided for oil exports of up to $4,500m. over six months, if oil production facilities were upgraded; of this amount, $3,100m. would be used to purchase humanitarian goods. In mid-June the UN Security Council unanimously approved a resolution allowing Iraq to purchase equipment to the value of $300m. for its oil industry. In early July the Iraqi Minister of Oil announced that 40 contracts for oil equipment worth $50m. had been awarded.

Despite an increase in oil exports under phase four of the oil-for-food programme, the sharp fall in the price of oil meant that only some $3,000m. in revenues was generated. The fourth phase of the programme ended in late November 1998, and phase five ran to May 1999. In late May the oil-for-food programme was extended for a further six months. In October the UN Security Council unanimously adopted a resolution permitting Iraq to sell oil to the value of $3,040m., in addition to the quota agreed in May, with the intention of compensating for a shortfall in oil revenues in the two previous sale periods. However, Iraq's request to spend a further $300m. on equipment for the oil industry was not granted. In late November Iraq temporarily suspended oil exports, having rejected a proposal by the Security Council that the sixth phase should be extended for a further two weeks, pending revision of the programme's terms of reference; the suspension briefly caused world prices to rise to their highest levels since 1990. In December the Security Council voted unanimously to extend the oil-for-food programme for a further six months. In March 2000, in response to a report in which Kofi Annan recommended that Iraq be allowed to purchase increased quantities of parts and equipment to offset permanent damage to its oil industry, the UN Security Council unanimously approved a resolution permitting Iraq to make such purchases to the value of $600m. over six months. The oil-for-food programme was extended for its eighth phase in June.

As world oil prices declined (when compared with very high levels earlier in the year) towards the end of 2000, a dispute between Iraq and the UN in early November arising from Iraq's demand that it would henceforth require payment for petroleum exports under the oil-for-food programme in euros, rather than in US dollars, had little sustained effect on markets. Neither did Iraq's effective suspension of exports for much of the first half of December, as a consequence of a new confrontation with the UN over pricing: Iraq was seeking a lower price for its oil sales under the oil-for-food programme, to enable it to levy a surcharge on purchases that would be paid into an Iraqi-controlled account. By the early part of 2001 there were indications that the majority of companies purchasing Iraq oil were paying a surcharge of between 25 and 40 US cents per barrel, which, over the course of a year, would represent between US $90m. and $140m. outside the authority of the oil-for-food programme. Meanwhile, the Security Council agreed to extend the oil-for-food programme for a further six months and agreed to allow Iraq to use up to $525m. of its revenues to pay the local costs of maintaining the oil industry.

The new US Administration of George W. Bush, which took office in January 2001, swiftly made clear its intention to influence a reform of the sanctions regime and the oil-for-food programme—the terms of which were being bypassed with considerable success by Iraq and an increasing number of international partners. From the late 1990s the smuggling of oil out of Iraq increased dramatically. In addition to oil illegally exported to Syria and Turkey, it was estimated that a further 100,000 barrels per day (b/d) of oil were being shipped illegally into the Gulf via the Shatt al-Arab waterway. Through such unauthorized exports, it was estimated that the Iraqi Government was able to procure some US $1,000m. annually beyond the control of the UN. However, such revenues were clearly not reaching the Iraqi people in terms of improved health and nutritional provision, just as humanitarian relief operations under the existing sanctions regime were failing the Iraqi civilian population. The 'smart' sanctions initiative, as promoted within the UN Security Council by the USA and United Kingdom, was designed to remove most restrictions on the flow of food and other consumer goods while strengthening controls on the sale of military goods and on oil-smuggling. However, a British-drafted resolution for the introduction of 'smart' sanctions failed to secure support from the People's Republic of China, France and Russia (the other permanent members of the Security Council) by the time of the expiry of the ninth phase of the oil-for-food programme in early June. The ninth phase was thus extended until 3 July, pending further discussion of the issue. In protest at the proposed changes to the sanctions regime, Iraq announced that it was suspending oil exports under the UN programme. Eventually, the British draft resolution was withdrawn, and it was agreed in early July to

extend the oil-for-food programme for a further five months. Agreement had in the mean time been reached by the permanent members of the Security Council (except Russia) on a compromise list of products that Iraq was forbidden to import under an eventual new sanctions regime; in order to secure China's acceptance of the list, the USA had agreed to withdraw its block on some $90m. in Chinese contracts, including a major telecommunications project, that it had been delaying at the UN Security Council's sanctions committee. On 10 July Iraq resumed oil exports from both of its UN-authorized outlets. The USA and United Kingdom made clear their intention to continue to promote the 'smart' sanctions initiative. On 29 November 2001 the oil-for-food programme was renewed for a further six months, to 30 May 2002 (the 11th phase). However, the UN Security Council was to draw up a new 'goods review list' of items deemed to have potential dual military and civilian uses and, if agreement could be reached (notably between the USA and Russia) by the beginning of the 12th phase of the programme, Iraq would be able to import humanitarian goods not included on the list without recourse to scrutiny by the sanctions committee from 1 June. In mid-May, after intensive negotiations between the USA and Russia, the UN Security Council unanimously approved Resolution 1409 establishing the 12th phase of the programme (to expire on 25 November 2002) and revising the UN sanctions regime to allow Iraq to import all humanitarian goods not included on the new goods review list with only minimal checks. Goods featured on the list were only to be sold to Iraq after contracts had been screened and approved by the UN Monitoring, Verification and Inspection Commission (UNMOVIC) and the International Atomic Energy Agency (IAEA). The list was to be reviewed regularly by the Security Council. The embargo on all arms sales to Iraq remained in place.

Exports under the oil-for-food programme increased from 120m. barrels in phase one (December 1996–June 1997) to almost 390m. barrels during phase six (June–November 1999), falling to 293m. barrels under the ninth phase, before rising again, to slightly more than 300m. barrels under the 10th phase (July–November 2001), only to decline again, to some 226m. barrels, under the 11th phase (December 2001–May 2002). Revenues increased from US $2,150m. under the first phase to $9,564m. during the eighth phase (June–November 2000) following a significant increase in world prices for petroleum from the second half of 1999, but dwindled thereafter (to $5,638m. under the ninth phase, $5,350m. under the 10th phase and $4,589m. under the 11th phase) as a result of a slump in world oil prices and Iraq's suspension of petroleum exports for five weeks beginning in early June 2001. The decline in petroleum exports during the 11th phase was initially attributed to the impact of oil surcharges introduced by the Iraqi Government at the end of 2000 (and paid directly to the Iraqi regime in contravention of UN sanctions) and to UN efforts to combat this development with a policy of retroactive pricing of Iraqi crude petroleum. However, the Iraqi Oil Marketing Co continued to impose surcharges of 25–30 cents per barrel on official exports of crude petroleum (although the surcharge was reduced to 15 cents in June 2002), and it was noted that the bulk of these exports were contracted by small 'shell' companies registered in 'third' countries, such as Liechtenstein, which would then sell the petroleum on, at a profit, to the major international oil companies. Before the surcharge system was introduced, the major international companies purchased petroleum direct from Iraq through term contracts. By early February 2002 only 30m. of the 181m. barrels of crude petroleum contracted thus far in the 11th phase of the programme had been purchased by recognized international companies. In response to Israel's uncompromising military intervention in Palestinian-controlled areas of the West Bank in early 2002, in early April Iraq announced that it was suspending petroleum exports for one month, or until Israel withdrew its forces from Palestinian areas. Exports under the oil-for-food programme resumed on 9 May 2002.

In October 2001 the UN Office of the Iraq Programme alleged that Iraq had exported additional crude petroleum, valued at some US $10m., by topping up officially approved shipments after UN inspectors had completed their checks. Iraq denied the allegation but the UN proposed a tightening of loading procedures at the officially designated export terminals. Furthermore, industry sources estimated that some 410,000 b/d of total oil production of 2.31m. b/d in January 2002 was being exported illegally (180,000 b/d to Syria; 110,000 b/d to Jordan; 80,000 b/d to Turkey; and 40,000 b/d to the Gulf region). Taking into account crude petroleum used in domestic refining, these estimates suggested that illicit exports were equivalent to more than one-quarter of the total amount of petroleum exported under the oil-for-food programme. Both official and independent smuggling networks were believed to be supplying crude petroleum and petroleum products. The UN, meanwhile, was reluctant to censure the alleged recipient countries owing to wider political considerations in the region. The UN Office of the Iraq Programme also expressed concern about the continuing number of contracts (particularly those for humanitarian purposes) under the oil-for-food programme stalled by the UN Security Council's sanctions committee owing to administrative difficulties or because of suspicions that the goods requested might be used for military purposes; at mid-May 2002 contracts to the value of $5,170m. were described as 'on hold' (equivalent to almost 18% of the total value of applications considered by the sanctions committee). During December 1996–December 2001 more than one-half of contracts submitted for the electricity sector remained on hold, together with a high proportion of contracts for telecommunications, water and sanitation. In contrast, virtually all contracts relating to the Kurdish autonomous regions had been approved and processed. In an assessment of the situation published on 28 September 2001 by the UN Secretary-General, it was conceded that lower-than-projected oil revenues, the erratic way contracts were submitted by Iraq and delays in approving and processing some contracts by the sanctions committee had resulted in some sectors being fully funded according to the agreed distribution plan, while other sectors—particularly agriculture, education, electricity, health and water—had experienced shortages and delays. Although it was hoped that approval of Resolution 1409 would allow many contracts currently on hold to be reassessed promptly by the sanctions committee, it was suggested that, because of a shortage of available funds, the Iraqi authorities might not be in a position to pay for the released goods, so that (at least in the short term) ordinary Iraqis were unlikely to benefit from the latest changes to the sanctions regime.

According to estimated national accounts statistics compiled by the UN Economic and Social Commission for Western Asia (ESCWA) in 2000, Iraq's GDP was some ID 3,890,629m. in 1997, ID 4,738,786m. in 1998 and ID 5,591,768m. in 1999. Real GDP growth was estimated at 25% for 1997, 15% for 1998 and 8% for 1999. Estimates of real GDP growth per head were 28% for 1997, 12% for 1998 and 5% for 1999. In terms of US dollars, GDP was $3,461m. ($163 per head) in 1997, $3,949.0m. ($181 per head) in 1998, and $4,142.1m. ($184 per head) in 1999.

The UNCC had received about US $400m. of oil export revenues by late April 1997, enabling it to settle many of the individual and small claims and to make plans for substantial payments in the second half of the year (although the disbursement schedule had to be modified because of Iraq's suspension of oil exports in June 1997). Meanwhile, the UNCC was beginning its evaluation of the corporate claims (numbering more than 6,000) which accounted for the bulk of the reparations being sought from Iraq. (In June 2002 it was reported that some 185 international companies had withdrawn claims amounting to $2,900m. during the previous four years in the hope that this would improve their chances of securing future business with the Iraqi regime after the eventual lifting of UN sanctions.) About one-half of the claims were by bodies in Kuwait, including the Kuwait Oil Company, whose entitlement in respect of the cost of extinguishing oilfield fires started by Iraqi troops was provisionally assessed by the UNCC at $613m. (plus interest). The home countries of non-Kuwaiti corporate claimants included the United Kingdom (451 claimants), Egypt (450), Germany (314) and the USA (152).

At the end of September 2000 the UN Security Council approved the payment to Kuwait of US $15,900m. in compensation for lost production and sales of petroleum as a result of the 1990–91 occupation. However, it was agreed at the same time to reduce the levy on Iraq's petroleum revenues destined for reparations under the oil-for-food programme from 30% to 25% (see History).

A survey carried out in April 1997 by WFP, UNICEF and the Iraqi Ministry of Health found that 27% of Iraq's child population of five years of age and less were affected by chronic malnutrition. In September the Minister of Health, Umeed Madhat Mubarak, claimed that sanctions had dramatically increased the mortality rate of Iraqi citizens: the rate for children under five years of age had increased from an annual average of 506 per month in the pre-war years to an annual average of 6,500 per month following the imposition of sanctions. Likewise, the death rate of those over five years of age had increased from a yearly average of 1,600 per month before the sanctions to 8,000 per month in the period after their implementation. Upon his resignation in September 1998, the first co-ordinator of the UN oil-for-food programme estimated that 4,000–5,000 Iraqi children were dying each month as a result of contaminated water supplies, poor sanitation, malnutrition and inadequate health facilities. His successor resigned in February 2000, as did the head of WFP operations in Iraq, in protest at what they considered to be the unacceptable consequences of the sanctions regime and the inadequacy of the humanitarian programme to meet the basic requirements of the Iraqi people. In August 1999 a report by UNICEF claimed that infant mortality rates in areas under Iraqi government control had more than doubled since the imposition of economic sanctions in 1990. UNICEF claimed that in some parts of Iraq that were outside government control infant mortality rates had fallen. (Iraqi claims that the increases were the result of the sanctions regime were countered by the US Administration, which accused the Iraqi authorities of inadequate ordering and distribution of supplies.) A report issued by the International Committee of the Red Cross in February 2000 stated that infant mortality had risen threefold since the imposition of sanctions in 1990, and that the death rate among children under five years of age was at least five times greater than the level prior to the Gulf crisis; a report published in the United Kingdom in the medical journal *The Lancet* in May 2000 similarly attributed a more than doubling of child mortality rates since the imposition of sanctions to malnutrition, to shortages of power and water in hospitals, and to increases in the incidence of communicable diseases.

In early 2001 the UN Secretary-General urged the Iraqi authorities to provide more food for the civilian population, and in particular to allocate a greater part of their oil revenues to improving the health of children suffering from malnutrition.

AGRICULTURE AND FOOD

Despite the increasing dominance of oil and gas production, the Government continued, through the 1980s, to allocate substantial resources to the development of agriculture, with the aim of achieving food self-sufficiency and even surpluses for export. At the same time, state control of the agricultural sector was steadily relaxed in favour of allowing a greater role for private initiative and for private-sector investment from both Iraqi and other Arab sources. The total area under cultivation rose from 3.2m. ha in 1984 to about 3.7m. ha. in 1989, it being estimated that a further 20% increase was required to achieve self-sufficiency. Like the rest of the economy, however, agriculture suffered major disruption in the Gulf crisis and hostilities of 1990–91, one consequence of which was a return to state control and direction.

Until the 1958 revolution, agricultural improvement was often inhibited by the need for adequate land reform. In October 1958 the incoming Government announced a new and more radical land reform project. This provided for the break-up of large estates whose owners were to be compelled to forfeit their 'excess' land to the Government, which would redistribute the land to new peasant owners. Landowners losing land were to be compensated in state bonds (in 1969 all the state's liabilities to recompense land-owners were cancelled). It was hoped that the reform would take only five years to complete, but the application of the law was initially mismanaged: expropriation of land was administered much faster than its redistribution. By the end of 1972 some 4.73m. dunums (1 dunum = 0.25 ha approx.) had been requisitioned from landlords and allocated to 100,646 families. By 1988, more than 300,000 families had received 10.8m. dunums. The Government has been promoting the growth of co-operatives and collective farms since 1967. By the end of 1987 there were 857 agricultural co-operatives, with a total of 376,329 members. In 1984 there were 23 state farms, covering 188,000 ha. By 2000 the percentage of the labour force engaged in agriculture had decreased to 10.1%, compared with 50% in 1965 and 53% in 1960.

Government awareness that the rate of progress in the agricultural sector had been disappointing encouraged measures to be taken to allow greater private involvement in agriculture. By 1986 the land area occupied by state farms had fallen to only 52,925 ha, and by 1988 more than 220,000 ha had been leased—a total investment estimated at ID 72m.—as a result of the 1983 law enabling local and other Arab companies or individuals to lease land at nominal rates. Other incentives included encouragement for agriculturists and graduates working for the Ministry of Agriculture and Agrarian Reform to take up farming, and there was a more liberal attitude towards profit-making. Farmers could now bypass the state marketing system and sell direct, either to public wholesale markets or to private shops licensed for wholesale trade. Higher procurement prices were now paid by the state. These concessions were intended to ease supply difficulties, and to encourage local farmers.

In May 1987 there was belated recognition of criticism voiced in 1982, at the Baath Party regional congress, that state intervention had often proved more of a hindrance than a help to small farms, and that state and collective farms were frequently unprofitable. It was announced that all state farms (including six dairy farms) were for sale or lease to local or Arab investors or companies, provided that the land continued to be used for agriculture. In July 1987 the Ministry of Agriculture and Agrarian Reform was reorganized, and in September the ministry was merged with the Ministry of Irrigation to become the Ministry of Agriculture and Irrigation.

A wide variety of crops is grown but the most important are barley and wheat. Production estimates vary considerably. In the case of wheat, annual output fluctuated around 950,000 metric tons in the 1980s, although drought severely affected the 1984 crop, which slumped to 471,000 tons. A good crop is dependent on favourable rains, and in 2000, according to FAO estimates only 384,000 tons of wheat was produced, while barley production was estimated at 226,000 tons, compared with 743,000 tons in 1987.

Other crops grown include rice, vegetables, maize and millet, sugar cane and beet, oil seeds, pulses, dates and other fruits (the main fruit being melon), fodder, tobacco and cotton. Drought caused production to fall in 1984, but output recovered after 1986. In 2000 Iraq produced an estimated 130,000 metric tons of paddy rice and 53,000 tons of maize, compared with 196,000 tons and 61,000 tons respectively in 1987. Total vegetable output (including cabbages, spinach, carrots, tomatoes, okra, beans, cauliflowers and potatoes), which had been about 3m. tons per year in 1982 and 1983, fell to an estimated 1.8m. tons in 1984. In 2000 production of vegetables was estimated at 1.9m. tons, compared with 3.3m. tons in 1990. Following several years of drought, it was reported in mid-2001 that good rains had increased Iraq's agricultural productive capacity.

Production of dates, the country's main export after petroleum, was also affected by drought. During 1983–88 production of dates averaged about 350,000 metric tons per year. Iraq had about 29m. date palms in 1987, compared with 25m. in 1985. In 1986/87 some 150,000 tons were exported to Japan, France, Canada, India and to Arab and Asian countries. Exports rose to 163,000 tons in 1988/89, and to 373,000 tons (worth US $75m.) in 1989/90. Dates are not only a lucrative export, but are also being put to industrial use. Several years ago the former Ministry of Industry and Minerals started a major programme to produce sugar, dry sugar alcohol, vinegar and concentrated protein from dates. Such factories together with the private sector, will use up to 100,000 tons of dates per year when operating at full capacity. As part of the Government's programme for economic reform, a new mixed-sector company, the Iraqi Date Processing and Marketing Company (IDPMC), was established to replace the Iraqi Dates Commission, which was formerly responsible for production and marketing. Deliveries to the IDPMC in the 1990/91 season were estimated at 350,000 tons. Production of dates was estimated at 400,000 tons in 2000, compared with

630,000 tons in 1998. Output averaged an estimated 602,000 tons per year in 1990–2000.

The livestock and poultry sector was developed in the 1980s with the assistance of Dutch, British, West German and Hungarian companies. Iraq's annual output of eggs was 1,274m. in 1988, almost enough to meet local demand which is estimated at about 1,350m. eggs per year. White meat production amounted to 199,000 metric tons in 1988. A significant decline in livestock products was witnessed in the mid-1990s, owing to reduced production of animal feed. A report compiled by UN and US sources stated that domestic production of meat, milk and eggs during 1993–96 was less than 50% of levels of output recorded in 1990. According to estimates published by FAO, Iraq produced 127,000 tons of meat in 2000 (of which 557,000 tons of poultry meat), 557,000 tons of milk and 14,000 tons of eggs.

Provision has also been made to develop a fishing industry and the private sector has been encouraged to establish fish farms on many of the lakes and reservoirs which have been created by the construction of new dams. In 2000 catches of freshwater fish were estimated at 9,700 metric tons, while the marine fish catch was estimated at 13,500 tons.

Aid to farmers is channelled through the Agricultural Co-operative Bank, which loaned ID 570m. over the period 1980–87 and increased its lending after the cease-fire in the Iran–Iraq War. To encourage farmers to use its services, the bank offers a low interest rate and has raised its maximum credit limit.

The country's food import bill, which reached US $3,100m. in 1984, declined to $2,712m. in 1986, and remained at a similar level thereafter. The USA was formerly a major agricultural supplier, retaining a large share of the market under a credit programme. The European Community (EC, now European Union—EU) supplied some $345m. worth of farm products in 1986, equivalent to a 12.7% market share, compared with 16% in 1984. Canada and Australia were long-term wheat suppliers. Cuba was a long-standing sugar supplier and Thailand supplied rice.

Following the implementation of UN economic sanctions against Iraq in August 1990, the Government announced the introduction, from 1 September, of rationing for flour, tea, sugar and rice; other items, such as cooking-oil, children's milk and salt, were later added to the list. The Government also steadily raised the official purchase prices for important crops, with the aim of encouraging greater production, and initiated an urgent programme to increase the cultivated area, especially in northern Iraq. From October it became compulsory for cereal farmers to deliver their output to state collection centres within two weeks of harvesting. The Government also took emergency powers to confiscate land from farmers who failed to fulfil production quotas, and from November it introduced the death penalty for hoarding of cereals. According to Iraqi officials, the 1990 cereal harvest was the best for several years, including nearly 1.2m. metric tons of wheat (an increase of 75% compared with 1989), more than 1.8m. tons of barley and 500,000 tons of rice. These figures were, however, questioned by US government officials, who estimated that Iraq would need to import some 1.75m. tons of grain in 1991 to feed its population.

The combined effect of rationing, increased local production, use of reserves and imports through Jordan was to prevent the development of serious food shortages in Iraq until the outbreak of actual hostilities in January 1991, although prices rose steeply. Thereafter, the devastation resulting from allied bombing seriously disrupted not only agricultural production but also food distribution, and food stocks declined to a record low in the war's immediate aftermath. On 23 March the UN Security Council's sanctions committee eased restrictions on food exports to Iraq, following which several countries agreed in principle to resume supplies. However, the continuing UN embargo on Iraqi petroleum exports rendered payment for imported food problematical, even though the UN committee decided, on 9 May, to 'unfreeze' sufficient Iraqi assets to pay for emergency food and medical supplies (see Sanctions and Oil-for-Food, above).

As part of its post-war reconstruction plans, the Government launched a national agricultural campaign on 12 April 1991, involving new incentives for farmers, priority allocation of fuel and machinery, and the creation of a special ministerial committee to supervise the 1991 harvest and to maintain the state's monopoly of food sales. The emergency six-month reconstruction budget, announced on 2 May, included provision for substantial state subsidies on cereal production in order to reduce consumer prices.

An FAO report of August 1991 found that Iraq would have to spend about US $500m. to restore the country's agricultural output. FAO estimated the 1991 grain harvest at only 1.25m. metric tons, about one-third of the 1990 yield, while other crops, as well as the livestock and poultry sectors, had been devastated by the war. Prospects of speedy recovery were regarded as bleak, given that seed stocks were deficient and much of the sector's machinery and irrigation system was out of commission. The Iraqi Minister of Agriculture, speaking in May 1992, estimated that 50% of the country's cereal and seed stocks had been destroyed during the 1991 war, as had 95% of the breeding stock of the poultry and livestock industry. Efforts by the Government to import food supplies included the signing of agreements with Thailand (for rice), Malaysia (for palm oil), Sri Lanka (for tea), France and Australia (for wheat) and Morocco (for various items).

In July 1993 FAO estimated that Iraq's food import requirement for the coming year would amount to 5.4m. metric tons, valued at US $2,500m. FAO experts said that the threat of famine was exacerbated by the prolonged deadlock over utilization of the emergency petroleum export quota authorized by the UN Security Council on humanitarian grounds in summer 1991. Western observers had earlier reported that the Government had started using gold reserves to fund essential food imports in the latter part of 1992, having virtually exhausted its hard-currency resources.

The execution, in July 1992, of 42 merchants accused of 'profiteering' served only to intensify the problem of persistent food price inflation, as a consequent drop in the volume of trade with Jordan added further scarcity value to items in short supply. The market prices of such staple items as wheat flour reached up to 500 times their mid-1990 levels at some points during the first half of 1993, while the estimated ratio of the average urban wage to the average market price of a typical family's food requirements widened from about 1:3 to 1:9 between April and July 1993.

Following increases in January and April 1993, the monthly ration of state-subsidized foodstuffs comprised 9 kg of flour, 2.25 kg of rice, 1.75 kg of cooking-oil and 1.5 kg of sugar. The Government implicitly acknowledged the seriousness of the food supply situation when it distributed an extra month's rations (in September 1992), brought forward a scheduled distribution date (in February 1993) and announced a supplementary Ramadan distribution of one chicken per family (in March 1993). So-called 'economic crime squads' were established in March 1993 to enforce harsh laws against overcharging for price-controlled basic foods.

Efficient administration of the rationing system was reported throughout most of Iraq, with the main exceptions in government-controlled Kurdish areas to the south of the Kurdish-controlled 'safe havens'. The availability of subsidized supplies in these areas was assessed to represent no more than 10% of the ration entitlement. There were also reports of some supply shortfalls in southern cities, attributed by Shi'a spokesmen to a government policy of moving food-processing operations and storage facilities out of the southern exclusion zone.

The prices of a wide range of food items outside the rationing system, including meat, eggs and dairy produce, exceeded the budget of the average Iraqi worker in mid-1993. Government efforts to stimulate domestic food production included price incentives for farmers to sell staple crops through state marketing channels, coupled with penalties for such offences as failing to harvest crops.

There were reports in May 1993 that Kurdish farmers were being harassed by troops based in Iraqi-controlled cities south of the Kurds' northern 'safe haven', but it was not clear whether there was any systematic government campaign to commandeer local agricultural production. Within the Kurdish-controlled 'safe haven', there was a heavy dependence on international relief supplies in mid-1993, when early efforts to rebuild local agriculture were being hampered by shortages of fertilizer and other inputs. Agricultural rehabilitation projects and the provi-

sion of food supplements remained high on the UN's list of aid priorities for the 'safe haven' in 1994.

Against a background of worsening hyperinflation, the Iraqi Government ordered the official rations of rice, cooking-oil and tea (but not flour or sugar) to be increased by up to one-third from February 1994. However, supplies of food to supplement the still-meagre ration were priced even further beyond the reach of most wage-earners, as the depreciation of the Iraqi dinar accelerated in subsequent months. By mid-May the average monthly salary of a schoolteacher would buy about 800 g of meat, or 21 eggs or 70 cl of cooking-oil, at current market prices. It was not unusual for middle-class households to sell or barter valuable possessions in order to buy food, while Iraq's crime rate (once very low by regional standards) increased dramatically as theft became a major problem.

In early May 1994 the Government announced that the theft of goods worth more than ID 5,000 (about US $12 at the prevailing unofficial exchange rate) would henceforth be punishable by the amputation of a hand, while in early June branches of the Baath Party were empowered to incarcerate shopkeepers or traders who violated official price guide-lines. The Minister of Agriculture was dismissed on 25 May for having 'failed to check the rise in food prices', and on 22 June the Government banned the import of many foodstuffs, including canned meat, fish, eggs, potatoes, spaghetti and chicken, in order to conserve foreign exchange. Traders who failed to clear their shelves of banned goods within two months would be subject to 'stringent penalties'. The Iraqi business community was urged to make voluntary financial contributions to the Government (repayable after the lifting of UN sanctions) to finance government food imports. Public-sector wages, pensions and allowances were increased from July, bringing little real benefit against a background of spiralling price inflation. In September the Government reduced the monthly ration of basic foodstuffs to 6 kg of flour, 1.25 kg of rice, 750 g of sugar and 625 g of cooking-oil, prompting a wave of panic buying which caused the market prices of many commodities to double in a matter of days. Public-sector incomes were again increased by amounts which barely kept pace with inflation. By early November rice was selling for ID 350 per kg and flour for ID 450 per kg in the shops, while the average civil service salary was ID 2,500 per month. By the end of January 1995, when the average civil service salary was ID 3,000 per month, meat was selling for around ID 1,150 per kg, while the price of one litre of imported vegetable oil had reached a similar level. Six months later an average civil service salary of ID 3,500 per month was sufficient to buy 38 eggs at prevailing market prices. Subsequent pay rises of 70% for military personnel and 50% for civil servants were expected to fuel a further round of price inflation. According to UN estimates, average shop prices of essential commodities stood at 850 times their July 1990 level in July 1995.

In October 1995 the Government announced increases in the monthly rations of flour (from 6 kg to 7 kg) and vegetable oil (from 625 g to 750 g), giving no explanation for the availability of additional supplies at this time. Estimates published by FAO in April 1996 gave Iraq's 1994/95 cereal production total as 2.2m. metric tons (20% less than in 1993/94 and 25% below the average for the previous five years). The cost of Iraq's basic food import requirements in 1995/96 was estimated by FAO at US $2,700m. Iraq's estimated wheat imports totalled 933,000 tons in 1993/94 and around 1m. tons in 1994/95, compared with an annual average of 3.1m. tons in the four years preceding the imposition of UN trade sanctions. The severity of Iraq's food supply crisis was believed to be the main motivating factor behind the Government's January 1996 decision to seek an early agreement on limited oil exports. Food prices within Iraq became subject to violent fluctuation during the first half of 1996 as traders responded to every reported development in the negotiations taking place at UN headquarters in New York.

The arrival in March 1997 of Iraq's first food imports under the long-delayed oil-for-food scheme had a dramatic effect on local market prices, causing immediate reductions of up to 45% for eggs and 33% for flour and meat. In April the Government increased the monthly flour ration to 9 kg, while in May the rice ration was raised to 2 kg and the cooking-oil ration to 1 kg. In July the monthly rice ration was further increased to 2.5 kg and the ration of pulses was doubled from 500 g to 1 kg. Other ration entitlements in July included 2 kg of sugar, 150 g of tea, 250 g of soap, 350 g of detergent and 150 g of table salt. It was reported in mid-1997 that Iraqi cereal growers had been guaranteed 'above-market' crop prices by the Government in order to protect them from the impact of resumed food imports.

In May 1998 the Government reduced the monthly ration of basic foodstuffs, citing slow distribution of aid under the oil-for-food agreement as the reason for the cuts. The new rations included 100 g of tea, 625 g of cooking-oil and 150 g of pulses.

A survey of Iraqi agricultural output over the period 1990–96 (based on US and UN estimates) indicated a decrease in yields of poultry and livestock products to less than one-half of the 1990 level, from 1993 onwards. This was due to a lack of local and imported animal feed, coupled with reductions in local output of animal feed as greater priority was given to crops for human consumption. Recent poor cereal crops (see above) were attributed in part to a lack of pesticides which had caused yields to decline at a rate faster than that by which farmers had increased the areas planted. However, total grain production in 1996 was estimated to have recovered to 3.0m. metric tons following a good harvest, before declining to 2.3m. tons in 1997. Grain production totalled an estimated 2.5m. tons in 1998, but fell to only 795,000 tons in 2000. Within the Kurdish-controlled areas of Iraq, grain production exceeded local consumption by an estimated 100,000 tons per year from 1994 onwards, and in 1996 the Baghdad authorities agreed to supply electricity, fuel and rice to these areas in exchange for Kurdish farmers' surplus grain. In 2000 Iraq produced an estimated 865,000 tons of tomatoes (up from 722,000 tons in 1990) following a policy decision to devote irrigated land primarily to vegetable production. By 2000, however, output was just 500,000 tons. Production of potatoes reached 420,000 tons in 1998 (compared with 167,000 tons in 1991), although output in 2000 fell to an estimated 150,000 tons. Average annual production of dates, more than ever an important staple, was substantially higher than in the 1980s (see above). Barley, previously regarded as an animal feed, was used as a supplementary ingredient in bread-making as supplies of wheat-flour diminished during the first half of the 1990s. In 1996 the average daily caloric intake of Iraqis was thought to be about 30% below its 1990 level. According to international aid organizations, at least 2.15m. Iraqis were receiving less than 50% of their calorific requirement in 1996. According to a report by the UN Secretary-General, published on 19 November 2001, the large number of contracts for agricultural inputs submitted by the Iraqi Government under the oil-for-food programme but placed 'on hold' by the sanctions committee of the UN Security Council was adversely affecting all parts of the agricultural sector. For example, it was reported that some 15,000 ha of citrus orchards had been invaded by whitefly, and, because contracts for pesticides and agricultural sprayers remained stalled at the UN, diseases associated with the pest had spread to vegetables (especially cucumbers and tomatoes) resulting in a sharp decline in yields.

RIVER CONTROL AND IRRIGATION

River control policy in Iraq has three main objectives: the provision of water for irrigation, the prevention of devastating floods, and the creation of hydroelectric power. An extensive dam-building programme has been instituted on the River Tigris and its tributaries in northern Iraq, with the aim of using stored water to irrigate land which has traditionally been rain-fed. However, such installations were among those which suffered serious damage and dislocation in the 1991 Gulf hostilities.

When operational, the main systems providing flow irrigation are based in the Euphrates (serving nearly 3m. dunums), the Tigris (1.7m. dunums), the Diyalah river and the Lesser Zab river. Pumps are used extensively along both the Euphrates and the Tigris. A series of dams, barrages or reservoirs (at Samarra, Dokan, Derbendi Khan, and Habbaniya) provide security against flood dangers. When the waters of the Euphrates and Tigris are fully utilized through dams and reservoirs, the area of cultivated land in Iraq will be almost doubled.

After delays during the Iran–Iraq War, the Government evinced renewed determination to proceed with its programme of water control and storage. In the summer of 1984 the Government was able to release stored water to farmers, to offset the low levels of the Euphrates. It was hoped that the completion

of the Mosul (on the Tigris) and Haditha (on the Euphrates) dams (renamed the Saddam and Qadisiya dams) would ease concern over Syrian and Turkish dam-building plans for the upper reaches of the Tigris and Euphrates, which were expected to reduce the flow of water significantly. The Qadisiya dam and its associated 600-MW hydroelectric power plant were opened in 1986. By 1990, however, the distribution of these water resources had become a fundamental issue in Iraq's relations with Syria and Turkey, following Turkey's diversion of the Euphrates in order to fill the reservoir of its new Atatürk dam. Discussions between Iraq, Syria and Turkey, held in June 1990, failed to resolve the issue, and Iraq subsequently announced that future water shortages might create the need for water rationing. In early 1993 Turkey appointed a German-led consortium to implement a major hydroelectric project at Birecik on the Euphrates. Iraq, which had condemned this project as an infringement of its water rights under international law, announced its intention to take legal action against the contractors.

In September 1986 a US $1,485m. contract to build the Bekme dam, in the north-east, 40 km from the Iranian border, on the Greater Zab, a tributary of the Tigris, was awarded to a joint venture of Turkey's Enka and Yugoslavia's Hidrogradnja companies. Work on the dam commenced in 1987, and the first phase of the diversion of the Greater Zab had been completed by June 1990. In November 1990 the Bekme dam was renamed 'Al-Faris' (Knight), an appellation which the Iraqi media often used for Saddam Hussain. Another Yugoslav company, Energoprojekt, was chosen to design dams at Badush, also on the Tigris, and at Mandawa, on the Greater Zab. There are also plans to construct dams at Taqtaq, Dujala and Farha. River control projects are also under way at Hindiya, Kifl-Shinafiya and Baghdadi.

In December 1983 the 87,500-ha first stage of the massive Kirkuk irrigation project (now renamed Saddam) was opened. More than 300,000 ha will eventually be irrigated at a cost of more than ID 1,000m. Contracts have been awarded to Chinese and South Korean companies to work on the North Jazira irrigation project, which will be fed with water stored by the Saddam dam; and to local and international companies for work on the East Jazira irrigation project, involving the installation of irrigation networks on more than 70,000 ha of rain-fed land near Mosul. These projects are part of an ID 820m.-scheme to irrigate 250,000 ha of the Jazira plain. South of Baghdad, completed land reclamation schemes include Lower Khalis, Diwaniya-Dalmaj, Ishaqi, Dujaila and much of Abu Ghraib. The massive Dujaila project is intended to produce about 22% of Iraq's output of crop and animal products. Consultants have designed irrigation schemes for Kifl-Shinafiya, East Gharraf, Saba Nissan, New Rumaitha, Zubair, Bastora, Greater Musayyib and Makhmour. The project's main outfall canal, completed in December 1992, is known as the 'third river'. It runs for 565 km from Mahmudiya, south of Baghdad, to Qurnah, north of Basra, and carries saline water (flushed away from 1.5m. ha of reclaimed land) to an outlet on the Gulf.

A 120-km 'fourth river', designed to irrigate an area of 250,000 ha, and the 140 km Qadisiya canal, branching off from the Euphrates and designed to irrigate an area of 125,000 ha, were under construction in early 1993. Political opponents of the Iraqi Government claimed that this major programme of irrigation works, together with a number of drainage schemes in the southern marshes in 1992/93, was partly aimed at Shi'ite dissidents living in the area. However, the Government was able to provide numerous economic justifications for its policy (including, on the issue of marsh drainage, the fact that the area contained large untapped petroleum reserves).

Since 60% of Iraq's land area has no access to the major river irrigation schemes, a programme of well-drilling has been initiated under the direction of the State Co for Water Wells Drilling (SCWWD). In November 1990 the SCWWD announced that it had drilled 1,615 wells and supplied 1,159 pumps since its creation in 1987.

In the war with the multinational force in 1991, several dams were hit in the bombing campaign, but the wholesale dislocation of the country's river control and irrigation systems was mainly attributable to the multinational force's destruction of Iraq's power supply network. Restoration of such installations to proper functioning became a major priority of the Government's post-war reconstruction programme, as did restoration of drinking water supplies and sewerage systems in Baghdad and other major cities. Many of the failures of urban sewerage systems in 1992/93 were attributed to shortages of imported spare parts for pump motors. The UN Development Programme (UNDP), which had a US $4m. budget for projects in Iraq, announced in June 1994 that $1m. had been allocated for the rehabilitation of two major sewage plants in Baghdad and $1m. for the repair of water treatment plants in southern population centres. Serious sewerage breakdowns and contamination of water supplies continued to be reported in Iraqi towns and cities in 1998. In mid-1998 the British Department for International Development announced that it was financing a $3.2m. project to improve water and sanitation.

In May 2000 the Government announced that the third phase of the 'Loyalty to the Leader' drinking water project had been completed at a cost of ID 13,283m. The project will supply the city of Basra and the area surrounding it with an additional 105m. gallons of drinking water. In June 2001 it was reported that the Syrian General Company for Irrigation and Water was nearing agreement with the Iraqi Government on a contract for the construction of a 19.2-km tunnel to transport water from the Euphrates to irrigate agricultural land in the Mosul region. By the end of 2001 there were few signs of improvement in domestic water supply according to the report of the UN Secretary-General to the Security Council. For households in rural areas, it was estimated, only 32 litres of water were available per person per day.

PETROLEUM AND NATURAL GAS

Following the nationalization of the hydrocarbons sector in the early 1970s, Iraq rapidly increased its output of crude petroleum, becoming, by 1979, the world's second largest exporter, after Saudi Arabia. Production in 1979 totalled 170.6m. metric tons (compared with 83.5m. tons in 1971, the last full year before nationalization, and 47.5m. tons in 1960). Exports in 1979 and 1980 averaged 3.3m. b/d, producing revenues of US $21,300m. and $26,300m. respectively. However, because of the outbreak of the Iran–Iraq War in September 1980, output sharply declined in 1981 and exports fell to 800,000 b/d by 1982 (worth $10,000m.), before rising to 1.4m. b/d in 1986, although lower world petroleum prices reduced revenues in that year to $7,000m. The end of the war with Iran in 1988 facilitated further recovery in production, from 127.4m. tons (2.6m. b/d) in 1988 to 138.6m. tons (2.8m. b/d) in 1989, earning export revenues of some $13,000m. and $12,000m. respectively. In the first half of 1990 production was averaging about 3.1m. b/d (almost back to the pre-1980 level) and 1990 export earnings from this source were expected to total $15,400m. However, Iraq's petroleum exports were then brought to a virtual halt by the UN embargo, imposed as a consequence of its invasion of Kuwait, and in the Gulf hostilities of early 1991 the massive damage sustained by Iraqi oil installations brought production to a standstill.

Iraq's petroleum industry has been highly dependent on pipelines carrying Iraqi oil through neighbouring territories or to the Gulf coast. In 1980 these were the 'strategic' reversible-flow pipeline (with a capacity of 1m. b/d) from Rumaila to Haditha and Kirkuk which links oilfields in the north and south of Iraq; a pipeline running for 980 km (609 miles) from Kirkuk, through Turkey, to Dörtyol, on the Mediterranean coast in the Gulf of İskenderun; another from Haditha, via Syria, to the port of Tripoli, in Lebanon and Banias, in Syria; and lines running from the southern oilfields near Basra to the offshore Gulf export terminals of Mina al-Bakr and Khor al-Amaya, with capacities of 2.7m. b/d and 1.8m. b/d, respectively, which were exporting up to 2.9m. b/d before the Iran–Iraq War.

Following Iranian air raids on key installations in the early stages of the war, however, exports soon ceased from Iraq's offshore oil terminals in the Gulf, and production declined to 900,000 b/d in 1981. Refineries, pipelines, pumping stations and petrochemical plants were all damaged. Exports of petroleum were, at first, diverted to Mediterranean ports via Iraq's reversible pipeline pumping network, but these were then brought to a halt by an explosion on the line through Turkey, reportedly

the work of Kurdish guerrillas, and by Iranian bombing of the K-1 pumping station at the Kirkuk oilfield in the north.

By December 1980 petroleum exports through the Mediterranean ports had resumed but total exports consisted only of petroleum being pumped through the pipeline across Turkey at a rate of around 650,000 b/d, supplemented by 60,000 b/d–80,000 b/d transported by road to Jordan. Not all of this was for worldwide exports, however, since Turkey was taking 250,000 b/d as its entitlement under the pipeline transit agreement. Preference for sales was given to countries that were major customers for Iraqi petroleum before the war and had suffered most from the cessation of petroleum exports in the fourth quarter of 1980. These included Japan and France.

Pumping through the Banias pipeline resumed in early December 1981, despite tense political relations between Iraq and Syria and the Iraqi decision of April 1976 to suspend deliveries through the pipeline because of a dispute over transit fees and other political issues. The long period of disuse limited the throughput to 350,000 b/d, compared with the full capacity of 1.4m. b/d, and pumping soon halted, not to be resumed until the end of February 1982. On 10 April 1982, however, Syria closed the pipeline, depriving Iraq of a possible US $17m. per day in revenues and leaving the Turkish pipeline as Iraq's only outlet for petroleum exports. The loss of the Gulf terminals and the vulnerability of the Turkish and Syrian pipelines forced Iraq to consider alternative pipelines.

To complement the pipeline through Turkey, which was pumping about 1m. b/d by mid-1987, the Government decided to build new export pipelines across Turkey (to run parallel to the existing line), Saudi Arabia and Jordan. In September 1984 a US $507m. order to build the first (640 km) phase of the Saudi Arabian project (IPSA-1)—to link Iraq's southern oilfields with Saudi Arabia's east-west Petroline to the terminal at Yanbu—was awarded to an Italian consortium, led by Saipem and including France's Spie-Capag. The French and Italian Governments provided credit to support the project, and the contractors agreed to accept Iraqi petroleum in part-payment. The spur line began pumping in September 1985. Although Japanese and Indian customers were secured, throughput was limited to 350,000 b/d–400,000 b/d by the Saudi Arabian Government. In March 1987, however, Saudi Arabia agreed to allow Iraq to export petroleum through its terminal at Yanbu at the spur line's full capacity of 500,000 b/d, on condition that it charged OPEC's official prices for crude. The second phase (IPSA-2), for which a contract was awarded in September 1987 to a consortium led by Italian and Japanese companies, envisaged an independent 970-km Iraqi pipeline (with a capacity of 1.15m. b/d) across Saudi Arabia, parallel to the Saudi line, to a new export terminal on the Red Sea coast, near Yanbu, providing a total throughput via Saudi Arabia of 1.65m. b/d.

A consortium of Italian and Turkish companies began work in February 1986 on the second 980-km trans-Turkey line, parallel to the existing line from Kirkuk to the Mediterranean port of Yumurtalık in Turkey. With a capacity of 500,000 b/d, this boosted total possible exports through Turkey to 1.5m. b/d, when it became operational at the end of July 1987, and there were plans to double the capacity of this line. Plans for an oil pipeline to Aqaba, in Jordan, were suspended in 1984, as Iraq could secure no guarantee of compensation from the US Bechtel Corpn, the project's managing contractor, for loss of earnings in the event of Israeli sabotage of the pipeline, which would have terminated near the Israeli border. In April 1987 Turkey and Iraq agreed plans to construct a third trans-Turkey pipeline, with a capacity of 70,000 b/d, from oilfields at Ain Zalah, near Mosul, to the Batman oil refinery in Turkey, a distance of 240 km. With its promised new export capacity, Iraq now had less need for the reopening of the pipeline across Syria, despite speculation in 1987 of a possible reconciliation with Damascus. Repair work started in March 1989, and by July tankers were lifting 200,000 b/d from the Mina al-Bakr terminal. Iraq also exported between 100,000 b/d and 250,000 b/d of refined petroleum products by road through Jordan and Turkey. In 1986 Saudi Arabia and Kuwait, through the Arabian Oil Co which operates in the Neutral Zone, renewed an agreement whereby they sold as much as 310,000 b/d (250,000 b/d from the Zone and the remainder from Saudi Arabia), with the proceeds going to Iraq to compensate it for lost export capacity. This agreement was terminated at the end of 1988.

When war broke out with Iran in September 1980, many major oil and gas development projects were in progress. War damage was not as extensive as was originally believed, although the Basra petroleum refinery, with a capacity of 140,000 b/d, was bombed early in the war. Repair work began in 1988, and by mid-1989 the refinery was again producing oil products for export. Iraq was already short of refining capacity, so the damage to the Basra refinery had a severe impact on the domestic supply of petroleum products. The country was left with the 70,000 b/d Dawra refining facility, near Baghdad, which also came under attack, and some 100,000 b/d topping capacity at a number of other locations. At 1 January 1981 refinery capacity stood at 118,000 b/d. The 150,000 b/d north Baiji refinery (Baiji II), built by Chiyoda of Japan, was opened in 1983, complementing the 71,000 b/d Czechoslovak-built refinery (Baiji I) already in operation. In the first quarter of 1987 the Baiji lubricating oil refinery, built by Technip of France, began operations. During its first year of operations, about 70,000 metric tons were expected to be available for export, rising subsequently to 200,000 tons per year. Plans were also announced to quadruple refining capacity. In mid-1988 international companies submitted offers to construct a 140,000 b/d refinery south of Baghdad.

Before the outbreak of war in 1980, the West German-US consortium of Thyssen Rheinstahl Technik and C. E. Lummus completed a petrochemicals complex at Khor az-Zubair, near Basra. The plant sustained minor damage during the war, but recommissioning began in 1988, and by 1989 some units had resumed operations. The complex was intended to produce 150,000 metric tons per year of low- and high-density polyethylene and PVC, and 40,000 tons per year of caustic soda, using 90m. cu ft per day of natural gas as feedstock. The Government also approved plans for a second petrochemicals complex about 60 km south of Baghdad, near the planned new refinery.

Other projects in the Basra area include a gas liquefaction and treatment plant at Zubair, which was constructed by a French company, Technip, under a US $239m. 'turnkey' contract, awarded in March 1980. The recommissioning of this plant began in 1989, with the intention that it would use as feedstock 6,000m. cu m of associated gas from the Rumaila oilfields to produce 4m. metric tons of propane and butane and 1.5m. tons per year of condensate. The plant is part of the southern gas project, which entails gathering and compression facilities that will be capable of handling 16,000m. cu m of gas per year from the Rumaila oilfields. Part of the project, a southern gas-gathering complex with the capacity to process and export as much as 4m. tons of associated gas annually, commenced operations in July 1990. A similar scheme exists in the north. Both are part of a government programme to increase its use of gas as an energy resource.

Total gas reserves, three-quarters of which are associated with oil, were estimated at 3,110,000m. cu m at the end of 2001. Gas production rose from 5,900m. cu m in 1966 to 20,160m. cu m in 1979, but declined, owing to the war with Iran, to 5,290m. cu m in 1984. By 1986 output had recovered to 8,270m. cu m, and in 1989 it totalled 10,680m. cu m. Whereas 80% of gas production was flared in 1979, projects to make wider use of gas, particularly in industry, resulted in a decline in this proportion to 40% by 1989. Gas exports also increased, from 8.3% of production in 1986 to some 30% in 1989. Shortly before the onset of the August 1990 Gulf crisis, Petrobrás of Brazil shipped Iraq's first export cargo of liquefied petroleum gas (LPG).

In 1986 a Soviet contractor, Tsvetmetpromexport (TSMPE), was awarded a US $154m.-contract to construct the first section, 345 km in length, of the trans-Iraq dry gas pipeline. This section runs from Nasiriya, in the south, to Baghdad, and was initially to carry 4.2m. cu m of gas per day. By 2002 Iraq was believed to be producing some 300m. cu m of gas per month, entirely for domestic use. However, in August 2000 the Iraqi Ministry of Oil announced that it was negotiating a major gas export project with Turkey, with the aim of establishing itself as a major exporter to southern Europe after UN sanctions are lifted. The project envisaged exporting some 10,000m. cu m of gas annually from five non-associated gasfields in northern Iraq where

reserves were estimated at 275,000m. cu m. Little progress had been made on the project by mid-2001, and Turkish officials emphasized that the project would not proceed until the end of the UN sanctions regime.

In the late 1970s and early 1980s the Iraq National Oil Co (INOC), then the supreme state body exercising control over the hydrocarbons sector, pursued a programme of further exploration for oil and gas reserves. Five major fields were identified in 1981 for future development—Majnoon, Nahr-Umr, Halfaya, East Baghdad and West Qurnah. These fields are likely to increase production capacity by some 2m. b/d. Exploitation of the East Baghdad field (with estimated reserves of 5,000m. barrels) began at the end of 1984, with the award of a US $60m. contract to establish a plant to process and degas an initial 30,000 b/d to Italy's Snamprogetti and its British affiliate. Production began in April 1989, and capacity was to be eventually increased to 150,000 b/d. The main contractor at West Qurnah was Technoexport of the USSR, with TPL of Italy. The Soviet company also undertook development work at the North Rumaila field, which was producing at a rate of 500,000 b/d in 1987, compared with potential capacity of 800,000 b/d. Development of Halfaya and Nahr-Umr was delayed by the war with Iran. In the north, exploitation of the Sfaya oilfield is under way. In 1988 experimental production started at Nasiriya, Gharraf, Subba, Balad and West Tikrit. Contracts were awarded in 1988 to Technip, of France, and Mannesmann, of West Germany, to develop the Khabbaz and Saddam oilfields to produce 30,000 b/d and 45,000 b/d respectively; both came into production in 1990. The recapture from Iran of Majnoon Island and the surrounding area of the al-Hawizah marshes, in June 1988, restored to Iraq oilfields containing reserves estimated at 30,000m. barrels. Plans for a second reversible-flow pipeline, parallel to the first, 670 km in length, linking new oilfields in the south with northern petroleum installations, and capable of pumping 900,000 b/d, were announced in April 1988. Plans for a $500m. oil-products storage complex at Khor az-Zubair were also announced.

INOC's activities extended beyond exploration for, and production of, crude petroleum. In 1972 it established an autonomous company to be responsible for the operation and management of a tanker fleet. In May 1987, however, INOC and the Ministry of Oil were merged as part of a programme to reorganize the oil industry and make it more efficient. At the same time, a number of state organizations, hitherto responsible for, among other functions, oil-refining, distribution and industrial training, under the auspices of INOC, were removed from INOC control and converted into separate national companies, responsible to the ministry.

Iraq is one of the founder members of OPEC. It was not required to make a reduction in its output in October 1984, when OPEC cut production by 1.5m. b/d in order to prevent a further decrease in prices on the world market, which was oversupplied with oil. With new export outlets becoming available, Iraq frequently lobbied for an increase in its OPEC production quota, while consistently exceeding its allocation. During 1986 oil prices continued to decline, falling below US $10 per barrel in July. When, in August, OPEC decided to reduce production to a maximum 16.7m. b/d for two months from 1 September, effectively reverting to the quota restrictions imposed in October 1984, in order to raise petroleum prices, Iraq declined to be a party to the decision, demanding at least parity with Iran, and continued to produce as much as it could to finance its war effort. The proposal for a reduction in output was made by Iran, whose Minister of Oil said that Iran would 'act in a way to prevent Iraq getting its desired quota'. Iraq then opted out of a succession of OPEC production agreements, between October 1986 and May 1988 (although it was allocated notional quotas in each), and stated that it would continue to do so while its quota allocations were lower than those allotted to Iran, and failed to take account of Iraq's increased export capacity. For the second half of 1987 a ceiling of 16.6m. b/d was placed on OPEC production, including a notional quota for Iraq of 1.54m. b/d, compared with actual export capacity of about 2.7m. b/d in August, and the 2.37m. b/d allocated to Iran. A reference price for OPEC petroleum of $18 per barrel had been in force since February 1987. At OPEC's meeting in December 1987 Iraq declined to participate in the agreement covering production in the first half of 1988, whereby the ceiling on collective output and Iraq's notional quota were unchanged.

The cease-fire in the Iran–Iraq War prompted preliminary efforts by OPEC to accommodate Iraq in future production agreements by raising its quota to take account of increased export capacity, even though Iran had clearly stated that it would not participate in an agreement which awarded Iraq quota parity with itself. In late 1988 OPEC granted Iraq parity with Iran and set its production quota at 2.64m. b/d. Iraqi production had reached 2.8m. b/d in November 1987, and was subject to government reviews during 1988, when output was maintained at about 2.6m. b/d. By the end of 1988 production had risen to about 2.7m. b/d, and exports were running at about 2.3m. b/d. On 1 January 1989 Iraq temporarily reduced production to match its quota, halting the bulk of its crude petroleum exports by road to Jordan and Turkey. In mid-1989 Iraq's quota was raised to 2.783m. b/d, still maintaining parity with Iran, and average output in 1989 amounted to some 2.8m. b/d.

In view of the need to reconstruct its economy, Iraq sought, following the cease-fire in the Iran–Iraq War, to maximize its oil revenues and to raise the OPEC minimum reference price. At the OPEC meeting held in June 1989, Kuwait claimed a quota of 1.35m. b/d, rather than the 1.12m. b/d which would have been allocated to it under a simple pro-rata distribution of the 20m. b/d ceiling which the majority of members judged to be reasonable in order to stabilize prices. Since Kuwaiti overproduction was now regarded as inevitable (it had already been overproducing by some 800,000 b/d–900,000 b/d in May and June), the new production ceiling was raised by only 1m. b/d, to 19.5m. b/d. In September a new ceiling of 20.5m. b/d was fixed, but Kuwait rejected its quota of 1.149m. b/d for the final quarter of 1989. Overproduction continued, and by the end of 1989 total OPEC output had reached almost 24m. b/d, with a consequential depressive effect on world petroleum prices.

At the next OPEC meeting, held in November 1989, the production ceiling was raised to 22m. b/d, although the *de facto* level of production was already 24m. b/d. Quotas were redistributed, with Kuwait being allocated 6.82% of total output, compared with 5.61% previously. Owing to optimistic estimates of demand, and closer adherence to quotas by member states, prices rose following the November meeting, reaching their highest level for two years in January 1990. By May, however, quotas were again largely being ignored, and prices had slumped. Iraq's crude petroleum production at this time was estimated at about 3.14m. b/d—approximately its quota level.

By May 1990 overproduction had continued to such an extent that increasing numbers of tankers were being chartered for floating storage. At a meeting of OPEC's ministerial monitoring committee, held on 2 May, it was agreed to reduce production by 1.445m. b/d from an average level of 23.5m. b/d. However, the effect of this on prices was negligible. In June 1990 an Iraqi Deputy Prime Minister, Dr Sa'adoun Hammadi, condemned Kuwait and the UAE for producing above their quota levels, and stated that there should be no further review of quotas until a 'fair' price for crude petroleum—US $25 per barrel—had been achieved. Kuwaiti overproduction was regarded as an attempt to wreck efforts within OPEC to raise the minimum reference price above $18 per barrel, and Iraq claimed to be losing $1,000m. annually for every reduction of $1 per barrel in the price of petroleum. In July President Saddam Hussain blamed overproduction for low petroleum prices, and warned of action against those states—Kuwait and the UAE—which persistently flouted their quotas. He claimed that the decline in the price of petroleum in the first half of 1990 had cost Iraq $14,000m. Iraq subsequently accused Kuwait of violating the Iraqi border in order to acquire resources worth more than $2,400m. from Iraq's section of the Rumaila oilfields.

At the full OPEC meeting held in Geneva in late July 1990, Iraq sought to raise the minimum reference price for crude petroleum to US $25 per barrel. Although the agreement that was achieved at the meeting raised the reference price to only $21 per barrel until the end of 1990, and fixed the production ceiling at 22.5m. b/d, it was regarded as OPEC's most serious attempt to address the problem of overproduction for many years. However, the markets were thrown into turmoil by Iraq's invasion and annexation of Kuwait at the beginning of August

1990 and by the consequential imposition of mandatory UN sanctions on all trade with Iraq and Iraqi-controlled territory. By late August, prices had risen as high as $30 per barrel, and an emergency OPEC meeting was held in an attempt to restore stability to the market. At the meeting, which was attended by the oil ministers of all OPEC member states except Libya and Iraq, a draft agreement to suspend the production quotas that had been agreed in July (and thus compensate for the loss of Iraqi and Kuwaiti production) was endorsed by all member states attending except Iran.

In the context of the UN embargo and the closure of its pipeline outlets through Saudi Arabia and Turkey, Iraq reduced its production to less than 400,000 b/d in the latter months of 1990, sufficient to supply its domestic refining capacity. Although consumer prices increased sharply, a move by the Minister of Oil to introduce petrol rationing on 19 October was countermanded by the Revolutionary Command Council 10 days later (and the Minister was dismissed). The situation deteriorated rapidly with the onset of hostilities in January 1991, when the allied bombing campaign resulted in the destruction of most of Iraq's oil and gas installations, both 'upstream' and 'downstream'. By mid-February petrol was officially rationed (but virtually unobtainable), as were heating-oil and gas. A UN report, compiled in March, estimated that restoration of 25% of pre-war refinery capacity—the minimum needed for survival—would take from four to 13 months. Some refineries resumed limited production in April–May, enabling the Government to end petrol rationing on 28 April and to reduce consumer prices, but government claims that oil exports of 1.5m. b/d could be resumed in July 1991 (if UN sanctions were repealed), rising to 2m. b/d in 1992, were not put to the test, because the UN embargo remained in place. In its emergency six-month reconstruction budget, announced on 2 May, the Government identified the restoration of oil production, refining and pipeline facilities as a central priority. The appointment of a new Minister of Oil on 27 May confirmed the dominance over the hydrocarbons sector of the Ministry of Industry, Minerals and Military Industrialization.

By mid 1992 Iraq appeared to have made substantial progress in restoring its production, refining and storage capacity, in accordance with the priorities laid down in the reconstruction plan. Annual average oil production (including natural gas liquids) rose from 235,000 b/d in 1991 to 480,000 b/d in 1992 (compared with average production of 2.01m. b/d in 1990 and a production level of over 3m. b/d before the August 1990 invasion of Kuwait). Output averaged 495,500 b/d in 1993 and 601,700 b/d in 1994. In the first half of 1992, Iraq claimed that it had restored its output capacity to 3m. b/d, although the non-availability of export markets (and Iraq's refusal to utilize the UN concession of limited, authorized exports to pay for emergency imports) precluded an early attempt to bring the bulk of this capacity back on stream. Iraq's refining capacity, which had been around 700,000 b/d before the 1990–91 Gulf conflict, was seriously damaged during the hostilities and repairs were hindered by UN sanctions. However, by the end of 2001 capacity was estimated at 644,000 b/d from 10 refineries of which the most important were Baiji North, Basra and Dawra.

In April 1993 the head of oil operations in the south of the country announced that available productive capacity in this region amounted to 1.8m. b/d (compared with production of 2.25m. b/d from the southern fields in August 1990), and that facilities were in place to export up to 800,000 b/d via the Mina al-Bakr terminal and 1m. b/d via the strategic pipeline to the north. Mina al-Bakr was Iraq's preferred export point for UN-authorized petroleum exports, whereas the sanctions administrators proposed that any shipments should be made via Turkey to facilitate strict monitoring. The Turkish authorities also declared their anxiety about possible corrosion problems associated with a prolonged pipeline shut-down. Technical arrangements for repairing and flushing Iraq's Turkish pipeline were agreed in principle between the two Governments in the first half of 1994, with Turkey proposing to use the resulting outflow of trapped petroleum on its domestic market and to arrange for 30% of the payment due to Iraq to be deposited in the UNCC's fund for victims of Iraq's aggression, while the remaining 70% would be used to finance Iraqi imports of essential foodstuffs and medical supplies. It was estimated that 12m. barrels of petroleum (of which 3.8m. barrels were already owned by Turkey) would be discharged in the course of the proposed maintenance operation. Iraq made it clear that the scheme (for which Turkey was hoping to obtain early UN clearance) could not proceed if the UN sought to attach the same conditions that had caused Iraq to reject UN Security Council Resolutions 706 and 712.

In March 1995 Iraq's Minister of Oil stated that the country was currently producing petroleum at the rate of 700,000 b/d but could raise output to 2m. b/d 'within a few weeks' of the lifting of UN trade sanctions. He estimated that it would take 14 months to achieve an output level of 3.5m. b/d and four to five years to bring capacity up to 4.5m. b/d. A full-scale resumption of Iraq's oil development programme (including the opening of hitherto undeveloped oilfields) would, he said, require investment totalling around US $30,000m. over a period of five to eight years. French and Russian oil companies were widely reported to have reached preliminary agreements with Iraq in 1993/94 to develop key oilfields after the lifting of UN sanctions, while companies from several other countries (including Italy and Brazil) had held discussions on aspects of Iraq's oil development plans. Delegates from 29 countries attended a two-day seminar on future oil and gas markets, held in Baghdad in March 1995. Many of the claims made by Iraqi officials during the Baghdad seminar were challenged in the following month at the annual conference of the London-based Centre for Global Energy Studies (CGES), whose executive director estimated that it could take Iraq up to three years after the lifting of the export embargo to increase its production capacity to 3.2m b/d, and rather longer to bring export capacity fully into line with production capacity. The CGES estimated that Iraq would need to spend up to $6,000m. on essential repairs and reconstruction in the oil sector. The CGES conference was attended by a representative of the British-based opposition Iraqi National Congress, who stated that foreign oil companies currently negotiating with Iraq should not expect any 'post-Saddam democratic government' to honour oil agreements drawn up in the present circumstances.

Although the resumption of its own petroleum exports remained in abeyance, Iraq continued to attend OPEC meetings to express formal opposition to pricing and production decisions adopted by the other member countries from 1991 to mid-1993. At the end of 1992 the Iraqi Minister of Oil accused OPEC of failing to uphold 'the interests of producing countries'. In June 1993 the Deputy Prime Minister, Tareq Aziz, indicated that Iraq's eventual return to the oil export market would be geared to the country's revenue needs, and that the Government would be prepared to see prices fall to US $5 per barrel if necessary, 'since now we get nothing'. He pointed out that the UN had defined the proposed emergency export quota in cash terms, setting no limit on the volume of petroleum that could be exported to generate income of $1,600m. By early 1994 Iraqi ministers and officials had moderated their criticism of OPEC, and appeared to be laying the foundations for a reasoned claim for a high OPEC quota allocation at such time as Iraq was able to rejoin the export market. At the end of 1994 Iraq's formal claim within OPEC was for quota parity with Iran when exports resumed.

In March 1996 Iraq and Turkey held technical talks on the reopening of pipelines to handle part of the limited oil exports for which Iraq was currently seeking UN approval. A Turkish company was mandated to repair any pipeline damage, although this work would not start until all negotiations with the UN had been satisfactorily concluded. The effective capacity of the Kirkuk to Yumurtalık pipeline was expected to be in the range of 300,000 b/d to 500,000 b/d in the initial stages because of the settling of trapped oil and the loss of an important pumping station in northern Iraq (destroyed by bombing during the Gulf War). In the south, Iraq claimed to have an initial 1.2m. b/d of export capacity available at its Gulf terminal of Mina al-Bakr, which was said to be ready to handle tankers of up to 350,000 dwt. Both the safety of the port approaches and the adequacy of the loading facilities were, however, called into question by Western oil analysts. Iraq's estimated oil output in the first half of 1996 was between 550,000 b/d and 700,000 b/d, of which up to 80,000 b/d was exported to Jordan and the balance consumed within Iraq. At prevailing prices, Iraq expected to have to

increase its production by between 700,000 b/d and 800,000 b/d to take full advantage of the formula set out in UN Security Council Resolution 986 (which provided for export revenue of up to US $2,000m. over a period of 180 days). In June 1996 an OPEC ministerial meeting agreed that Iraq's OPEC production quota (currently a nominal 400,000 b/d) should be raised to 1.2m. b/d in the second half of 1996 in anticipation of an early agreement between Iraq and the UN on implementation of Resolution 986. The subsequent delay in implementation of Resolution 986 until December meant that Iraq's average 1996 oil output was, at an estimated 590,000 b/d, only 50,000 b/d higher than the average for 1995. The greater part of the petroleum exported under UN supervision in the first half of 1997 was pumped via Yumurtalık, with the balance shipped from Mina al-Bakr. The largest single export contract concluded at the end of 1996 was for the supply of 75,000 b/d to the Turkish refiner Tupras throughout the 180 days of the initial export period authorized by the UN Security Council. It later emerged that Iraq was seeking to divide its export allocation among a large number of different buyers requiring delivery of limited volumes over short periods. In addition to contract sales, the UN authorized some spot-market transactions in February 1997 to maintain oil earnings at target levels. In June 1998 production resumed at three southern oilfields after a suspension of some 20 years.

In 1998 Iraqi oil production averaged some 2.2m. b/d (compared with 630,000 b/d in 1996). Following the February 1998 revision of the terms of the UN oil-for-food arrangement, whereby the value of Iraqi oil exports permitted by the UN was to be increased from US $2,000m. to $5,200m. in a six-month period, production increased significantly, and exports were officially estimated to be averaging 1.6m.–1.7m. b/d by mid-June, although UN officials calculated that exports peaked at 2.4m. b/d in the final two weeks of June. It was expected that exports would approach a sustainable 2.6m. b/d by early 1999, following UN approval, announced in June 1998, of an Iraqi request to spend $300m. on the purchase of vital new equipment to upgrade and overhaul oil-production facilities. Without the necessary renovation, it was estimated, Iraq would be able to fulfil only $4,000m. of its new six-monthly export quota. In November the UN Security Council renewed the oil-for-food agreement, allowing Iraq to sell $5,200m.-worth of petroleum over the six-month period beginning on 26 November. Owing to low world prices for oil and infrastructural inadequacy, however, it appeared unlikely that Iraq would sell more than $3,000m.-worth of oil during the period.

In May 1999 the oil-for-food programme was extended for a sixth phase, to 20 November. At the end of May Iraq forecast that its crude oil production would rise to 3m. b/d by the end of 1999, and by a further 500,000 b/d in 2000. In October the UN Security Council unanimously adopted a resolution (No. 1242) that permitted Iraq to sell US $3,040m.-worth of petroleum, in addition to the quota agreed in May. The increase was intended to compensate for a shortfall in oil revenues in the two previous six-month sale periods. However, Iraq's request to spend a further $300m. on equipment for the oil industry was not granted. On 21 November the Government rejected a proposal by the UN Security Council that the oil-for-food programme should be extended until 4 December pending the revision of the programme's terms of reference. On the following day Iraq temporarily suspended its exports of petroleum, causing world prices to rise to their highest levels since 1990. On 10 December the Security Council voted unanimously to extend the oil-for-food programme for a further six months.

In February 2000 it was reported that the Government intended to export no more than US $5,260m.-worth of oil in the current phase of the oil-for-food programme, even though UN Resolution 1248, adopted in December 1999, had removed all restrictions on the value of oil exports. In March the Security Council voted unanimously in favour of increasing to $1,200m. the sum Iraq was allowed to spend annually on the rehabilitation of oil industry facilities. In May it was reported that the greater availability of spare parts had increased the likelihood of Iraq's attaining its oil production target of 3m. b/d. The oil-for-food programme was further extended in June and December, and again in July and December 2001 and May 2002. Oil production averaged 2.62m. b/d in 2000 and 2.41m. b/d in

2001. In response to the efforts of the United Kingdom and the USA to change the sanctions regime by introducing the so-called 'smart' sanctions, Baghdad suspended its oil exports for almost the entire month of June 2001, but other OPEC producers were quick to compensate for the shortfall in supply. Nevertheless, the volatility of Iraqi exports under the oil-for-food programme posed a serious threat to market stability. In January 2002 international oil industry sources estimated production at 2.31m. b/d, of which 410,000 b/d, it was believed, were being exported illegally (see Sanctions and Oil-for-Food, above). Following Israel's uncompromising military intervention in Palestinian-controlled areas of the West Bank in March 2002, Iraq attempted to rally support for a new Arab oil embargo to put pressure on Israel and the USA, and in April announced that it was immediately suspending oil exports for 30 days, or until Israel withdrew its forces from the Palestinian areas. Despite Baghdad's unilateral moratorium, Iraqi oil exports to Jordan and Syria continued. Exports under the oil-for-food programme resumed in May.

The technical and infrastructural problems affecting the oil sector were highlighted in the report of a UN-appointed group of oil experts who visited Iraq's oilfields in March 2001. It was noted that the high levels of oil production achieved during the sixth and seventh phases of the oil-for-food programme had only been realized by inflicting long-term damage on oil-bearing structures, with increased ancillary damage to surface facilities operating beyond their recommended maintenance periods. It was estimated that production at the Kirkuk field could decline by 50% in 2002, to 500,000 b/d, and that the South Rumaila field had lost 150,000 b/d of production capacity during 2000. The experts concluded that without immediate action total export capacity could be reduced to 1.4m.–1.5m. b/d. New producing fields were urgently needed to stabilize current production levels, and the Government was planning 380 new wells to increase production capacity in the longterm. The report urged the sanctions committee of the UN Security Council to release equipment for the oil sector without delay, and recommended that the UN provide a regular monthly cash component in local currency to be spent on installation and maintenance of equipment and staff training, accompanied by careful monitoring of this expenditure and site visits by UN officials.

In March 1997 Iraq signed an agreement with Russia (ratified by the Iraqi National Assembly in the following month) for the future development of the West Qurnah oilfield in southern Iraq. A consortium of Russian companies was to take a 75% interest (Lukoil 52.5%, RVO Zarubezhneft 11.25% and VO Mashinoimport 11.25%) and Iraq a 25% interest in a 23-year contract to develop 600,000 b/d of production capacity and associated infrastructure after the lifting of UN sanctions against Iraq. In June the Chinese National Petroleum Corporation signed an agreement to develop 90,000 b/d of capacity in the Adhab oilfield after the lifting of sanctions. A consortium of Turkish companies reached a preliminary agreement with Iraq in May, envisaging the development of a major gas export project after the ending of sanctions (see above). In March 1998 the French petroleum company, Total, announced that it was negotiating an agreement to develop the Bin Umar oilfield (with an estimated production capacity of 450,000 b/d), whilst Ranger Oil, the Canadian group, confirmed that it was in the process of securing a US $250m. field-development contract and exploration block in the Western Desert. In June an Indian joint venture between the Oil and Natural Gas Corporation and Reliance Petroleum secured a deal to develop the Tuba oilfield. In July 2000 Iraq announced that it would no longer conclude production-sharing agreements with international oil companies. Instead, these were to be replaced by production contracts similar to 'buy-back' contracts offered by neighbouring Iran. In early 2002 the Iraqi Ministry of Oil announced proven oil reserves of 113,000m. barrels, a figure supported by international oil industry sources. Probable reserves were estimated at a further 220,000m. barrels, 70% of which could become viable in the future given the finance, technical skills and equipment needed for development. Iraq has continued to sign memoranda of understanding with a number of foreign companies to provide the financial investment to open up new fields, but these agreements cannot be implemented until sanctions are lifted.

INDUSTRY

Until the 1970s Iraq had few large industries apart from petroleum. In greater Baghdad the larger enterprises were concerned with electricity and water supply and the building materials industry. In addition, there was a large number of smaller-unit industries concerned with food- and drinks-processing (date-packing, breweries, etc.), cigarette-making, textiles, chemicals, furniture, shoe-making, jewellery and various metal manufactures.

However, greater priority was subsequently given to industrial developments, as the Government sought to reduce Iraq's dependence on the petroleum industry. Between 1970 and 1986 more than ID 14,000m. was invested in the industrial sector, and Iraq developed a number of major industrial plants. An iron and steel works at Khor az-Zubair, built by Creusot-Loire of France, began operations in 1978 and was expected to have eventual maximum annual output of 1.2m. metric tons of sponge iron and 400,000 tons of steel. Plans for a second iron and steel works were announced at the beginning of 1988. Khor az-Zubair was also the site of a major petrochemicals complex (see Petroleum and Natural Gas, above).

Iraq's mineral resources, apart from hydrocarbons, include sulphur and phosphate rock. Mining for sulphur at Mishraq, near Mosul, began in 1972. The mining complex, including a sulphuric acid plant, had a design capacity of 1.25m. metric tons per year. However, a record 1.4m. tons were produced in 1989, of which 1.2m. tons were for export, compared with 950,000 tons and 750,000 tons, respectively, in 1988. A new sulphur recovery and sulphuric acid plant, built by Japanese contractors, used Mishraq sulphur. Production began in 1988 and raised exports of sulphur by more than 50%, from their former level of 500,000 tons per year. Some 500,000 tons of sulphur were sent for sulphuric acid production at the phosphate processing plant at al-Qaim, but it was hoped that sulphur exports would be maintained by increasing the rate of sulphur recovery (from 90%) during hydrocarbons processing. In 1988 proven reserves of sulphur stood at 515m. tons, the largest in the world, according to the Iraqi Government.

Phosphate rock reserves, mostly in the Akashat area, and in the Marbat region, north-west of Baghdad, were estimated at 10,000m. metric tons in 1988. The phosphate fertilizer plant at al-Qaim was built by Sybetra of Belgium, which also installed the phosphate mine in Akashat. The mine, with reserves estimated at 3,500m. tons, opened in 1981 and was intended to produce 3.4m. tons per year of phosphate rock for the al-Qaim plant, which received the first loads from the mine by rail in 1982. Iraq achieved self-sufficiency in fertilizers, producing slightly more than 1.2m. tons in 1989. Of this amount, some 766,000 tons were exported. The al-Qaim plant began production in 1984, with the expectation that it would export 75% of its output. A US $400m. programme to double production at al-Qaim was initiated in 1989. Daily production of 1,000 tons of ammonia and 1,700 tons of urea also commenced at a fourth nitrogenous fertilizer factory at Baiji. One of the contractors, the M. W. Kellogg Co, was appointed in 1988 to attempt to double capacity at the Baiji plant. There were also plans to build a new ammonia/urea factory at al-Qaim, and work to expand capacity at the Basra fertilizer plant commenced in early 1990.

Other major state-owned industrial enterprises included a textile factory at Mosul, producing calico from local cotton; three sugar refineries, at Karbala, Sulaimaniya and Mosul, with another four planned; a tractor assembly plant which produced 2,500 tractors in 1975; a paperboard factory at Basra, a synthetic fibres complex, at Hindiya; and a number of flour mills. Shoe and cigarette factories served the domestic market. Other developments in the manufacturing sector included factories to produce pharmaceuticals, electrical goods, telephone cables and plastics, together with additional food-processing plants. In 1984 Iraq's annual capacity for cement production was 11m. metric tons; this was expected to reach 20m. tons when the country's newest cement works were operating at full capacity. Two cement works, a plant at al-Qaim with a capacity of 1m. tons per year, and another at Sinjar, in Nineveh Governorate, with a capacity of 2m. tons, were built by Uzinexportimport of Romania. Exports of 1m. tons of cement to Egypt began in 1986. Production of cement reached 13m. tons in 1989, when 5.4m.

tons were exported, mainly to other Arab countries. Brick production in 1984 reached 1,607m. units, rising to 1,773m. in 1986. Much of the output was used to build homes. Up to 4m. homes were expected to be built in the years 1981–2000. According to official development plans, the local construction industry was also to be supplied by three new factories—a steel foundry, a central moulds factory and a steel formworks—built on at-Taji industrial estate. Trucks and buses designed by the Swedish firm Saab-Scania were assembled under licence in Iskandariya from 1973.

The USSR assisted with the construction of 11 factories, including a steel mill and an electrical equipment factory at Baghdad, a drug factory at Samarra and a tractor plant at Musayib. A large share of industrial development took place in co-operation with Eastern bloc countries and several agreements were signed, including one at the end of 1984 with Bulgaria's Bulgartabac to extend the northern tobacco industry. Other projects included the establishment of an electronics industry, by Thomson CSF of France.

Local industry came under increasing scrutiny during 1987 and 1988 and a wide improvement was sought both in the quantity and the quality of production, while particular emphasis was placed on import substitution by local production and on producing surpluses for export. Priority continued to be given to meeting local demands for raw materials, spare parts, new machinery and equipment. There was also official recognition of private and mixed-sector companies' ability to meet vital consumer needs more effectively than the State.

In July 1988, following a number of earlier attempts to reorganize the government departments responsible for industry in Iraq, responsibility for all civilian and military industry was placed under the control of a single Ministry of Industry, Minerals and Military Industrialization. This was to run large-scale and strategic industries such as power-generation, minerals and petrochemicals, and military industrial production, through the Military Industries Commission which was attached to it. Some state factories producing light industrial goods were auctioned off to private companies, or to newly established mixed-sector firms. In August 1988 the new Ministry announced that it was to sell 47 factories to the private sector by the end of the year. Iraq allocated the equivalent of US $11,500m. to investment in development projects in fiscal 1988, some 42% of which was to be devoted to industrial and agricultural schemes. Some 229 light industrial schemes (involving investment of ID 234m.) were listed in the Five-Year (1986–90) Industrial Development Plan and were also open to private and Arab investment. In April 1988, the Arab Investment Law No. 46 was passed, offering Arab investors tax exemptions and profit remittances.

Industrial production was valued at a record US $8,500m. in 1987, owing (according to government sources) to optimum use of production facilities and greater use of local, rather than imported, raw materials, which was estimated to have saved $130m. By 1987 the proportion of the labour force employed in industry was just over 21%. The foreign labour force was reduced by one-third during 1987, saving an additional $50m., according to government announcements. Some 218 development projects worth a total of ID 2,496m. ($8,051m.) were completed in 1987, according to the Ministry of Planning, including 50 agricultural schemes (worth $2,319m.) and 33 industrial schemes ($1,574m.). During 1989 the Ministry of Industry, Minerals and Military Industrialization emerged as the leading client for new business. Danieli of Italy was awarded a contract to construct a special steel factory at Taji, and a rolling mill for flat steel products at Khor az-Zubair. Contracts for new pipe factories were awarded to companies from Italy and the Federal Republic of Germany. The Ministry's Technical Corpn for Special Projects also assumed responsibility for the new petrochemicals complex and for the new central oil refinery in mid-1989. The Ministry also announced plans in 1989 to manufacture cars, tractors, trucks and buses. A licensing agreement for the production of cars was signed with General Motors of the USA, and an agreement for the production of trucks and buses was concluded with Mercedes-Benz of Germany.

Investment in the power-generation sector, which was severely disrupted during the early years of the Iran–Iraq War, was also given a high priority by the Government. In 1981 a

large number of contracts—worth more than US $2,000m.—were awarded for additional generation and transmission facilities (including a 600-MW power station at Haditha), as well as for the expansion and renovation of local and national networks, and the supply of emergency back-up systems. From 1982, contracts for 400-kV 'supergrid' and 132-kV transmission lines and substations were awarded to South Korean, French, Italian, Yugoslav and Japanese companies. The first of three 1,200-MW thermal power stations planned during the early 1980s was to be built at al-Musayyib, under a $730m. contract awarded to the Hyundai Engineering and Construction Co of South Korea. The second, at Yousufia, on the Euphrates, comprising six 200-MW units, was to be built by the USSR's Technopromexport under the terms of a Soviet-Iraq agreement covering the period 1986–90, which also provided for co-operation on an 800-MW power plant in Mosul; and a 300-MW–400-MW hydroelectric plant and dam, costing $200m., in Baghdadi, on the Euphrates. The USSR also helped to build an 840-MW thermal power plant in Nasiriya; a 400-MW hydroelectric plant in Dukan; and a 200-MW thermal power plant in Najibiya. A West German consultant, Fichtner, was chosen to design the third 1,200-MW power station, the al-Anbar plant, which was to be built near Ramadi, on the Euphrates. Italy's GIE completed an expansion of Baghdad's Dawra power station, and was appointed in 1989 to add two 350-MW units to al-Musayyib power station. Another new plant, the 1,400-MW oil-fired power station at ash-Shamal, on the Tigris, was being designed by Energoprojekt of Yugoslavia, and four 350-MW turbine generators were to be supplied by Northern Engineering Industries of the United Kingdom.

In 1987 six new hydroelectric plants, one power station and 18 transformer units began operating, raising Iraq's generating capacity by 6%, to 8,538 MW. By mid-1990 capacity had reached 9,000 MW and was expected to double by the end of the century. However, it was estimated that demand for power would increase fourfold by 2000. By 1990 about 95% of the population had access to electricity, with millions connected to the network since the rural supply scheme began in 1975. Consumption was 1,450 kWh per head in 1987, compared with 1,344 kWh per head in 1986. The connection with the Turkish grid was also completed, and wider inter-Arab power connections were the subject of further discussion. Iraq was expected to be the first exporter of electricity in the Middle East.

Iraq's experimental 70-MW Osirak nuclear reactor was destroyed by an Israeli air force bombing attack in June 1981. In 1990, according to official sources, Iraq had only one nuclear reactor: the 5-MW reactor at Temmuz, supplied by the USSR in the 1960s. Nevertheless, the USA and allied governments remained convinced that Iraq was pursuing a large-scale nuclear development programme with the aim of producing nuclear weapons. During the 1991 hostilities, it was reported that Iraqi nuclear installations had been bombed to destruction. However, the issue resurfaced in the post-war period, when it was believed that Iraq's nuclear potential had partially survived, although the Government continued to insist that only civilian nuclear research was being conducted.

The UN embargo that was imposed on Iraq in August 1990 resulted in the suspension of most industrial development projects involving foreign co-operation. The industrial sector was also adversely affected by the loss of technicians from Western countries. The outbreak of actual hostilities in January 1991 led to massive destruction of Iraq's heavy industrial capacity and infrastructure, including as much as 90% of its electricity generating and transmission facilities as well as oil refineries, oil export terminals, petrochemical plants, iron and steel foundries, engineering factories, and phosphate and cement plants. The light industrial sector, which normally supplied the domestic market, was also badly disrupted by the general infrastructural collapse, chronic shortages of fuel and power, and destruction of communications. By early 1992, however, the Government claimed that 75% of the national power grid had been restored.

The director-general of one of Iraq's main power stations stated in early June 1997 that the national electricity-generating system was currently operating at less than 50% of capacity because of a lack of spare parts. He added that the US $36m. allocated (but not yet disbursed) for the purchase of parts under the prevailing 180-day oil export agreement with the UN would meet 'only 4% of the needs of the power grid'. In

1998 it was announced that Baghdad had been suffering power cuts for five–six hours daily, whilst rural areas had been known to lack electricity for 14–16 hours daily. In his report to the Security Council in October 2001, the UN Secretary-General stated that despite significant investment in the power sector, by August 2001 the power deficit in Iraq had reached 2,800 MW during the hours of peak consumption. Hydroelectric power's generating capacity, in particular, had fallen from 2,500 MW to just 434 MW, and, because of widespread drought over several years, this source of supply had become unreliable. It was noted that the release of relevant contracts currently described as 'on hold' by the UN Security Council's sanctions committee, could reduce the deficit to 1,500 MW during peak hours by 2003 and 1,000 MW by 2006, taking into account the growth in consumer demand.

A major priority in the Government's six-month emergency reconstruction budget, announced on 2 May 1991, was the restoration of sufficient industrial production to ensure self-sufficiency in certain basic areas. Sectors that were identified for special attention included drugs manufacturing, geological surveys and mining, phosphate, fertilizer and sulphur production, and electricity generation and transmission. Priority repairs were also to be undertaken to factories making electrical fittings, bricks, cigarettes and textiles. According to the minister responsible, the rebuilding of civilian industry would have priority over military production (which had traditionally absorbed a large, albeit undisclosed, proportion of resources); however, Western reports of urgent Iraqi moves to re-establish its armaments production capacity (to as much as 87% of the pre-war level by September 1992) cast doubt on this stated policy. Also in May 1991 the Government approved the replacement of Arab Investment Law No. 46 of 1988 by new rules that were designed to encourage greater Arab investment in the private and mixed industrial sectors by granting Arab nationals the right to implement industrial projects and offering them tax and other incentives. Moreover, in August 1991 Law 115 of 1982 was replaced by Law 25 of 1991, which aimed to accelerate industrial development in the private and mixed sectors through the provision of state assistance to selected projects. Strategic and export-orientated industries using local raw materials were to be targeted under the new policy, which specified that a project must involve the use of plant worth at least ID 100,000.

In April 1993 the Iraqi Minister of Labour stated that the prolonged UN embargo was causing many factories to close or to shed labour, with the result that 'for the first time in Iraq's modern history we have registered a large number of unemployed people'. In September the Ministry of Industry and Minerals (which had reverted to its former name in 1991), which was responsible for thousands of state enterprises in areas other than oil production and arms manufacture, was authorized to incorporate these enterprises as limited companies and to offer up to 75% of their shares for sale on the Baghdad stock exchange. Companies which passed into majority private ownership would enjoy tax exemptions for 10 years. About 150m. shares in four of the largest companies—producing textiles, bricks and cement—were offered for sale later in the year, but the level of public indifference to this exercise was such that less than 1m. shares were bought. In the case of a major cement company, the reported take-up was 40,000 shares, each priced at ID 125, out of 75m. shares offered. By mid-1995, however, the Baghdad stock exchange was reported to be trading as many as 6m. shares per week, mainly in companies still under formation. Within the state-controlled armaments industry, import-substitution achievements announced in 1995 included the local manufacture of electrical production-line equipment for use in a 'major steel project'.

COMMUNICATIONS

Iraq has international airports at Baghdad and Basra, built in the 1980s, and smaller civilian airports at Haditha, Kirkuk and Mosul. Under the terms of UN sanctions imposed against Iraq during 1990, all international civilian flights were prohibited from entering or leaving Iraqi airspace, although the specific references of UN resolutions dealing with this were dismissed as ambiguous and disputed by some foreign countries. In August 2000 Saddam International Airport at Baghdad was reopened after undergoing refurbishment, a move widely interpreted as

a symbolic challenge to the UN sanctions regime. Shortly afterwards France and Russia, together with a number of Arab countries, resumed commercial flights to Baghdad, and by October it was reported that there were almost daily services into Baghdad from some European and Arab destinations, despite US and British insistence that the air embargo was a crucial component of the sanctions regime and that all requests for air transit to Iraq had to receive prior approval from the UN Security Council's sanctions committee. In early November Iraqi Airways, whose aircraft had been grounded since the imposition of sanctions, resumed regular services on domestic routes, passing through the northern and southern air exclusion zones imposed by the victorious multinational force in 1991. However, the USA and the United Kingdom raised few objections to civilian flights within Iraqi territory, as the 'no-fly' zones had been established primarily to prevent renewed military activity in these regions.

Iraq is virtually landlocked, and its main port at Basra (on the Shatt al-Arab waterway) was effectively disabled during the Iran–Iraq War. Before the outbreak of hostilities with Iran two new ports were developed, at Umm Qasr and Khor az-Zubair (the latter linked to Umm Qasr and the Gulf via a 40-km ship canal). Post-war modernization and expansion of Umm Qasr was a transport priority, and new berths and a new terminal were constructed. In November 1993 ships unloaded at Umm Qasr for the first time since 1990. (Before 1990 the Jordanian port of Aqaba had been a major entrepôt for Iraqi imports.) In 1997 Umm Qasr became the major entry point for humanitarian supplies delivered under the UN oil-for-food programme, but only some of the berths were of use owing to the limited draught of many and the dangerous wrecks submerged in others. In his report to the Security Council in October 2001, the UN Secretary-General noted that there had been some improvement in container operations at Umm Qasr, but warned that constant dredging was required to keep the port operational; he also urged the sanctions committee of the UN Security Council to release contracts currently 'on hold' for the necessary equipment, including new dredgers, service boats and tugboats, for the maintenance of port access channels and other services.

The railway network depends on three major lines, Baghdad–Basra–Umm Qasr, Baghdad–Mosul–Tel Kotchek and Baghdad–Kirkuk–Arbil. A 273-km line linking Kirkuk, Baiji and Haditha (built by South Korean firms) and a 550-km line connecting Baghdad to Hasaibah on the Syrian border (built by a Brazilian construction company) were both opened in 1986. Before Iraq's illegal annexation of Kuwait in 1990 (and the consequent imposition of UN sanctions), ambitious plans were under way to expand and modernize the railway system; these included the construction of high-speed links and a Baghdad 'loop' line. After a decade of sanctions the railway infrastructure was in considerable disrepair, with services infrequent and unreliable. In August 2000 services between the northern city of Mosul and Aleppo in Syria resumed after an interval of 20 years. In July 2001 it was announced that a weekly rail link with south-east Turkey, via Syria, had also been restored.

Before 1991 considerable emphasis had been put on road construction; good progress was made on a number of international expressways designed to link Iraq to the Mediterranean and the Gulf states, and several urban motorways were built in Baghdad. A fast road link between Baghdad and the Turkish border was also planned. During the Iran–Iraq War many roads in the eastern part of the country (towards the Iranian border) were upgraded for military purposes. However, numerous roads and bridges were destroyed during Operation Desert Storm in 1991, and in the immediate aftermath of the war the only viable surface transport link to the outside world was the route through Amman in Jordan to the port of Aqaba. Repair work to the country's 39,000-km road network and bridges was given priority in the post-war period, and considerable progress was made, but road transport, essential for the distribution of humanitarian supplies, continued to be affected by the shortage of trucks and spare parts for motor vehicles.

Prior to the 1990–91 Gulf conflict, Iraq had been modernizing its telecommunications systems, introducing crossbar telephone switching, a telex system, a microwave link between major cities and an earth satellite connection for international communications. Colossal damage was inflicted on the internal and external telephone networks during Operation Desert Storm; almost 50% of the country's telephone lines were destroyed during the hostilities, and efforts to repair the system were undermined by renewed allied air-strikes in December 1998. By 2000 it was reported that some 70% of the value of all Iraqi contracts for telecommunications equipment submitted under the oil-for-food programme had been blocked by the UN Security Council's sanctions committee. As a result of the severe shortage of spare parts for repair and maintenance, only a small fraction of the telephone system was operational.

FINANCE AND BANKING

Owing to Iraq's inability to export large quantities of petroleum during the early years of the Iran–Iraq War, the reduction of petroleum prices, the heavy cost of the conflict (estimated at US $600m.–$1,000m. per month at the beginning of 1986) and the additional burden of funding economic development, the country's official reserves of foreign exchange had declined to below $5,000m. by mid-1983. This was to be compared with the pre-war estimate of $35,000m. Little new information has become available since, and 1989 estimates were between zero and $2,000m. To minimize the continuing annual deficits on the current account of the balance of payments (an estimated $1,571m. in 1986), the Iraqi Government imposed stringent controls on foreign currency payments and imports. In the absence of Iraqi statistics, Western sources estimated, before the 1990–91 Gulf crisis, that the current-account deficit would be about $1,500m. in 1990, declining to $200m. per year by 1992 and then going into increasing surplus in the mid-1990s. However, the combined effects of the UN embargo, the 'freezing' of Iraqi assets abroad, the physical destruction of the 1991 war and the post-war requirement on Iraq to pay reparations served to reduce Iraq's national finances to a state of total disarray (see Sanctions and Oil-for-Food, above).

In comparison with other Arab countries, Iraq has few banks and all are state-controlled, although in May 1991 the Government adopted an amendment to the banking laws, enabling the creation of private banks, provided that they undertook to operate under the supervision of the Central Bank. The Central Bank of Iraq, founded in 1947 as a successor to the National Bank of Iraq, was one of the first Arab monetary authorities.

For many years, the only commercial bank was Rafidain Bank, which was founded in 1941. Rafidain was long considered the biggest Arab commercial bank in terms of deposits and gross assets. In 1996 its total assets reached ID 221,132m. Rafidain had 152 local branches and nine branches abroad. Rafidain was also permitted to take part in the Arab and international markets for syndicated loans and bonds. It was a shareholder in several European-Arab consortia banks, such as the Paris-based Union de Banques Arabes et Françaises, and development agencies. It was also one of the seven shareholders in Gulf International Bank, established in Bahrain in 1977 as a regional commercial bank. At the end of 1981 Rafidain established a joint venture bank with Banco do Brasil. Its capital was set at US $17.5m. In 1987 Rafidain's capital was doubled to ID 100m. in the first stage of a programme to upgrade and expand the banking system. In May 1988 the Government announced that a second commercial bank, Rashid Bank, would be established, with capital of ID 100m., to compete with Rafidain Bank. Competition was also to be encouraged in the insurance sector. The three companies in this sector were all absorbed into the Ministry of Finance, as were the country's three specialist banks. The ministry encouraged them to expand, and the banks were given administrative and financial autonomy, bound only by the Government's fiscal policy.

The country's oldest specialized bank was the Agricultural Co-operative Bank, established in 1936, which provided medium- and long-term credits to farmers and agricultural development organizations. After 1981, when a record ID 186m. was loaned, lending levels fell as a consequence of the war. In 1987 the bank loaned a total of ID 25.4m., compared with ID 43.2m. in 1986. Total lending by the bank over the period 1980–87 amounted to ID 570m. The Industrial Bank, established in 1940, provided short-, medium- and long-term loans to public and private industrial companies. Between 1980 and 1987 the bank extended ID 52m. in loans and credits. During 1987 total loans amounted to ID 1.5m., compared with ID 14.9m. in 1982. The

bank held shares worth US $62.9m. in 14 mixed-sector joint-stock companies and was instructed to become more involved in offering finance to both local and Arab investors, as private and mixed-sector companies were encouraged to play a wider role in the development of the economy. The Real Estate Bank, founded in 1949, provided credits for housing, construction and tourism. Lending over the period 1980–87 totalled ID 2,770m., although annual levels declined after the 1982 peak of ID 750.5m. In mid-1988 the bank's capital was raised by ID 50m., to ID 800m. to enable it to play a wider role in encouraging people to build their own houses. A government decree of June 1991 established a new state-owned Socialist Bank, with an initial capital of ID 500m., its principal stated role being to make interest-free loans to civil servants and decorated veterans of the war with Iran.

Iraq was also a major aid donor before the Iran–Iraq War, being the third biggest among Arab states, after Saudi Arabia and Kuwait. In 1979, according to figures published by the Organisation for Economic Co-operation and Development, its disbursements totalled US $861.5m., representing about 3% of gross national product (GNP) at that time. Most of this was channelled through the Iraqi Fund for External Development which had a capital of $677m. In mid-1979 Iraq decided to compensate poorer customers for its petroleum for any future petroleum price increases by granting them long-term interest-free loans. Under this system, 12 developing countries received over $200m. in the second half of 1979.

Donations of aid had resumed by 1990, and in June Iraq announced that it would grant Jordan US $50m. (for 1990) and the Palestine Liberation Organization $25m. In September 1990 the Iraqi Government offered to supply free petroleum to developing countries, but this was widely seen as a public relations exercise, intended to undermine international support for the UN embargo that had been imposed on Iraq in the previous month because of its invasion of Kuwait.

An amendment to Law 64 of 1976, introduced in May 1991, authorized the operation of private banks and thus ended the state monopoly of banking dating from 1964. Applications were subsequently lodged by four prospective new banks, namely the Alitimad Bank, the Baghdad Bank, the Iraqi Commercial Bank and the Private Bank. The step was intended to encourage a wider private-sector role in the economy, in accordance with the Government's post-1989 liberalization policy. However, observers commented that the authorization of private banks was unlikely to affect the banking system substantially until the Central Bank relaxed its tight control of monetary policy. A stock exchange was established in Baghdad in March 1992.

Having acted as the Iraqi Government's main means of paying external debts before the country was isolated from the international financial system, Rafidain Bank was exposed to numerous claims from overseas creditors after 1990. However, a creditors' meeting held in London in April 1993 was informed by British liquidation experts that liquidation of Rafidain's international operations would yield only a minimal recovery, as these operations currently showed a net deficiency of funds totalling £5,560m. (US $8,800m.).

UN Security Council Resolution 778 of 2 October 1992 authorized the impounding of oil-related Iraqi assets ('frozen' in overseas accounts since August 1990) for the purpose of funding UN programmes connected with the Gulf crisis and its aftermath, including humanitarian relief operations, administration of war victims' compensation claims and inspection and destruction of Iraqi weapons. Assets so impounded were to be transferred to a UN escrow account in New York, disbursements from which would be refundable to Iraq if the Iraqi Government agreed to sell petroleum under UN supervision. Notwithstanding an Iraqi Government threat to take legal action against foreign banks transferring funds to the escrow account, a total of US $101.5m. had been so transferred by 30 April 1993. In response to a UN appeal for further transfers to meet ongoing programme costs, the US Government said that it was prepared to authorize the transfer of $200m. of the $637.4m. of impounded Iraqi assets within its jurisdiction, provided that transfers of US-based funds never exceeded 50% of total transfers. Among other overseas fund holders, the Bank of Tokyo said that assets totalling $44.88m. could not be transferred in view of third-party rights over them, while Tunisia indicated that $15.8m. in locally-held assets had been used to offset outstanding Iraqi debts to Tunisia.

Total Iraqi assets held in UK banks fell from about US $1,100m. at the time of the invasion of Kuwait to $748m. at the beginning of 1995, as a result of the release of funds to pay debts owed to British companies and to finance exports of food and medicines to Iraq. In March 1995 the Iraqi Ministry of Finance claimed that seven predominantly Arab countries owed Iraq a total of $1,282m. in loans, payments for oil, profits withheld by Arab companies and assets belonging to Iraqi banks. Saudi Arabia was said to owe 35% of the total, Syria 28%, Bahrain 20%, Kuwait 10% and Somalia 5%, with the UAE and Egypt responsible for the remainder.

The black-market value of the Iraqi dinar, already worth only a fraction of the official exchange rate of US $1 = ID 0.31, was further depressed by the UN Security Council's October 1992 decision on external asset transfers. Punctuated by occasional extreme fluctuations (e.g. from $1 = ID 23 in February 1993 to $1 = ID 95 in April 1993), the underlying decline of the currency continued during the first half of 1993, taking the average market rate to around $1 = ID 65 during July.

In early May 1993 the Iraqi Government announced a six-day deadline for the exchange of old-style Swiss-printed 25-dinar notes for locally-printed equivalents, introduced after the 1990–91 Gulf crisis. The old-style notes were not exchangeable outside the country, and the border with Jordan, where speculators and currency traders held notes with an estimated market value of US $200m., was closed during the exchange period. Within Iraq, this exercise highlighted the problematical status of the Kurdish-controlled area in the north, which was effectively deprived of the exchange facility yet unable to relinquish its formal currency link with Baghdad. It led to a marked rise in Kurdish use of the Turkish lira as a preferred medium of exchange within the 'safe haven', this arrangement being presented as a strictly practical (i.e. politically neutral) matter.

Western observers had difficulty in discerning a clear-cut economic motive for the May 1993 currency initiative. It was readily accepted in Iraqi government circles that the post-war reconstruction drive had been accompanied by rapid growth in the money supply, making price inflation and currency depreciation inevitable while the external position continued to deteriorate. Moreover, the Government had virtually institutionalized the unofficial currency trade by itself relying on the black market to supply part of its hard currency requirement (estimated at US $90m. per month in the first half of 1993) to maintain the food rationing system.

The unofficial exchange rate fell below US $1 = ID 100 for the first time on 26 October 1993. The Government responded to this development by halting its own purchases of dollars on the black market. At the beginning of December, when the unofficial rate had fallen below $1 = ID 150, the Government authorized its ministries to deal in hard currency with the private sector. At the beginning of January 1994 Iraqis were permitted to deal legally in foreign exchange and to open foreign cash accounts in domestic banks, while 28 firms were licensed by the Central Bank to buy and sell foreign currency at rates determined by 'daily supply and demand'. On 5 February, after the unofficial exchange rate had fallen below $1 = ID 200, state banks were authorized to buy and sell hard currency outside the official rate of $1 = ID 0.31. As Iraq's chronic economic crisis intensified, the rate of currency depreciation accelerated, taking the unofficial rate per dollar to around ID 250 in March, ID 300 in April, ID 400 in mid-May and ID 500 by the beginning of June. The Central Bank, which had previously issued no currency notes above 25 dinars, announced the launch of a 50-dinar note in March and a 100-dinar note in May. During January 1995, when the Central Bank issued a 250-dinar note for the first time, the unofficial exchange rate declined from $1 = ID 665 to $1 = ID 750, while the authorized dealing rate was devalued from $1 = ID 550 to $1 = ID 600. The unofficial exchange rate reached 1,000 dinars to the dollar for the first time in March, after which the value of the currency depreciated further to 1,300 dinars per dollar by late June and 1,450 dinars per dollar by mid-July. In May the Government announced an issue of five-year bonds paying interest of 20% per year (more than the prevailing bank deposit rates but far less than the rate of inflation). The annual interest rate for two-year deposits at

state-owned commercial banks was raised from 15% to 18% in June.

The unofficial exchange rate slumped from 2,000 dinars per US dollar in September 1995 to 2,600 dinars per dollar in October 1995. The Government had in September lifted an import ban on 232 types of foreign goods (imposed in 1993 for exchange-control reasons). In mid-December, when the unofficial rate was around 2,550 dinars per dollar, the Government devalued its authorized dealing rate from $1 = ID 600 to $1 = ID 1,000, stating that it was determined 'not to allow the exchange rate to suffer any further setbacks'. In January 1996 the Government halted the printing of new banknotes; raised petrol prices by 600% and doubled the fees for official building permits; and further relaxed the exchange-control and currency trading regulations. Having depreciated below the level of $1 = ID 3,000 for the first time in early January the unofficial exchange rate recovered to $1 = ID 1,500 towards the end of the month following Iraq's decision to open talks on UN Security Council Resolution 986. As the talks proceeded the dinar's free-market value moved above the authorized dealing rate of 1,000 dinars per dollar. In mid-June the unofficial exchange rate stood at 900 dinars to the dollar, having touched a high point of 580 dinars per dollar in February. During the second half of 1996 the rate decreased to a low point of 1,780 dinars per dollar in November, before recovering to 600 dinars per dollar in mid-December after the delayed implementation of Resolution 986. From October 1996 state banks were authorized to exchange dinars for hard currency needed for any legitimate purpose, whereas previously they had sold hard currency only to licensed importers, students studying abroad and Iraqis receiving medical treatment abroad. In January 1997 it was reported that the Central Bank was applying 'strict monetary policies' in order to support the exchange rate of the dinar. The unofficial exchange rate fluctuated mainly within the range 1,000 to 1,200 dinars per dollar during the first half of 1997. At September 1998 the unofficial rate was $1 = ID 1,600. The unofficial rate in June 1999 was $1 = ID 1,800; it remained at this level in September 2000, and had reverted to $1 = ID 1,600 in March 2001.

FOREIGN TRADE

Exports of petroleum have been, by far, Iraq's most important source of revenue, providing more than 95% of the country's earnings of foreign exchange. Receipts from these exports rose sharply in the mid- and late 1970s, partly because of higher production, but mainly because of the rise in prices. By 1979, Iraq's petroleum exports were earning three times as much as in 1974, and by 1980 these exports were worth US $26,278m. However, owing to Iraq's inability to export sufficient petroleum, because of the war with Iran, and because of the fall in world prices, exports fell to $9,198m. in 1981. Revenues from oil exports were in the range $9,000m.–$11,000m. per year in 1982–85, and declined to an estimated $6,813m. in 1986. The higher oil prices recorded in the first half of 1987 were believed to have brought about a revival in the value of petroleum sales to more than $11,000m. in 1987, to about $13,000m. in 1988 and to about $12,000m. in 1989. While earnings declined in 1981 and 1982, Iraq continued to spend, importing goods worth more than $18,000m. in 1981 and $19,000m. in 1982, before imposing a sharp decrease in the level of imports, to about $12,000m. per year in 1983, 1984 and 1985. Imports were reduced to between $8,000m. and $9,000m. per year in 1986 and 1987 (though Western analysts estimate that they reached $9,700m. in 1987), and to $7,146m. in 1988. In 1989, according to Western calculations, total exports were worth $12,080m., while imports rose to $10,290m.

Although several countries exported a diminishing number of goods to Iraq during the second half of the 1980s, imports from Western countries generally rose during 1988 and 1989. The value of Japanese exports rose to US $406m. in 1988 and to $490m. in 1989, compared with $391m. in 1987. French exports were worth $445m. in 1988 and $478m. in 1989, compared with $391m. in 1987, while the value of the United Kingdom's exports rose from $445m. in 1987 to $720m. per year in both 1988 and 1989. The value of West German exports rose from $457m. in 1987 to $884m. in 1988 and to $1,168m. in 1989. The value of imports from Italy declined to $174m. in 1988, compared with $225m. in 1987, but rose to $372m. in 1989, while that of imports from Brazil fell to $228m. in 1988, compared with $305m. in 1987. The value of imports from the USSR declined from $511m. in 1987 to $509m. in 1988 and to $405m. in 1989. In 1988 the USA supplanted Turkey as Iraq's leading trading partner, exporting $1,156m. worth of goods (mainly agricultural products), compared with $683m. in 1987. US exports to Iraq were valued at $1,173m. in 1989. Like the United Kingdom, the USA extended a credit line to Iraq in 1988 in order to guarantee the volume of its exports. The value of Turkish exports to Iraq increased from $945m. in 1987 to $986m. in 1988, but fell to $445m. in 1989.

The value of Iraq's exports to the USA, at US $2,408m., more than quadrupled in 1989, compared with 1987, as a result of Iraq's decision to market its crude petroleum more attractively in the USA. Another leading importer of Iraqi petroleum was the USSR, the value of whose total imports from Iraq rose from $1,243m. in 1987 to $1,585m. in 1988, but declined to $1,549m. in 1989. The value of Turkish imports from Iraq was $1,650m. in 1989, compared with $1,154m. in 1987, while the value of Italian imports declined from $1,214m. in 1987 to $996m. in 1988 and to $674m. in 1989.

In the first half of 1990 there were increased efforts by Iraq's trading partners to prevent exports of industrial goods that might possibly serve as components for missiles and atomic weapons. In March the United Kingdom and the USA claimed to have frustrated Iraqi attempts to import nuclear detonators, and in April two UK companies were prevented from exporting to Iraq steel cylinders which were later proved to be components for a planned 'supergun'. The USA has also claimed that Iraq planned to use loans made improperly by the Atlanta (USA) branch of Italy's Banca Nazionale del Lavoro to acquire military technology. In February 1995 a US company which had illegally supplied artillery fuses to Iraq in 1990 was fined US $500,000 by a US court and was ordered to dissolve itself.

The imposition of the UN trade embargo on Iraq in August 1990 and the subsequent Gulf hostilities brought about the total disruption of Iraq's external trade, subsequently prolonged by disagreements between the Iraqi Government and UN sanctions administrators (see Sanctions and Oil-for-Food, above). The IMF estimated the value of Iraq's total imports in 1992 as ID 78.2m., compared with ID 118.9m. in 1991 and ID 2,042.4m. in 1990. The estimated 1992 total was equivalent to about US $250m. at the official exchange rate, but only a fraction of this at prevailing black-market rates. Unofficial estimates of Iraq's external trade in 1994 suggested that import spending had totalled $2,000m., while exports had earned $500m. The volume of basic commodities imported via the Jordanian port of Aqaba in the first quarter of 1995 totalled 233,800 tons (of which nearly two-thirds was wheat). The embargo on Iraqi oil exports from the Gulf was closely monitored by naval patrols acting on behalf of the UN, which occasionally reported instances of vessels attempting to use false Iranian documentation as a cover for shipments of Iraqi oil. By the end of April 1996 UN naval patrols had boarded about 10,000 vessels in all, of which 76 had come under suspicion of breaking the trade embargo.

According to figures published by the IMF, the USA was Iraq's principal trading partner in 2000, with crude oil imports from Iraq (under oil-for-food) valued at US $5,800m., representing 46.2% of the total value of Iraq's exports. Italy took 12.2% of Iraqi exports, followed by France (9.6%), Spain (8.6%) and Japan (4.6%). France and Australia together accounted for 44.5% of all exports to Iraq, followed by China (5.8%) Russia (5.8%) and Germany (5.4%). By the end of 2001, Russian companies were reported to have emerged as the major purchasers of Iraqi crude petroleum, and were believed to have secured an important share of contracts for humanitarian aid. In November Iraq renewed its oil agreement with Jordan; exports of crude petroleum to that country were expected to increase by 10% during 2002. In the same month the Turkish Minister of Foreign Affairs stated that Turkey's trade with Iraq was increasing rapidly and was expected to reach $1,000m. by the end of the year. Iraq has signed free-trade agreements with Egypt, the UAE, Tunisia and Syria. In June 2001, furthermore, following a meeting in Baghdad of the Council of Arab Economic Unity, plans were advanced for a quadripartite free-trade zone encom-

passing Egypt, Iraq, Libya and Syria, in the context of a long-standing commitment to establish a regional common market under the auspices of the Council. Some 50 countries took part in the Baghdad Trade Fair in November. In July Iraq signed an agreement with India to increase trade in a wide range of commodities, most notably petroleum. In mid-August 2002 it was reported that Iraq had concluded a huge trade agreement with Russia, within the terms of the oil-for-food programme, thought to be worth some $25,000m.

DEVELOPMENT AND PLANNING

At the beginning of the 1980s Iraq did not need to seek external loans, economic development having been funded mainly from the State's petroleum revenues. The sustained rise in petroleum prices gave Iraq a major opportunity to increase its development spending. Despite the high costs incurred by the war with Iran, the 1982 expenditure programme allocated an estimated ID 7,000m. to the ordinary budget and ID 7,000m. to investment spending. The import programme was allocated ID 5,000m. Iraq was unable to maintain the early momentum of its development programme, however, because of falling petroleum revenues and the high cost of the Iran–Iraq War. No detailed budget figures were disclosed from 1982 to 1989, and the 1981–85 Development Plan had to be abandoned, although longer-term plans were published for specific sectors.

In the Government's published budget for 1990, expenditure was forecast at ID 24,400m. The new 'consolidated general budget' reportedly projected a deficit of ID 6,600m., compared with a deficit of ID 7,200m. in 1989. The budget proposals also incorporated a total investment allocation of ID 5,600m., of which industry was to receive ID 2,965m. Because of the Gulf crisis, no details were disclosed of the 1991 budget until it was substantially revised to take account of damage sustained in the hostilities. A six-month emergency reconstruction budget, announced on 2 May 1991, reduced planned expenditure in the general consolidated budget to ID 13,876m. (from the original total of ID 14,596m.) and cut the investment budget to ID 1,660m. (from ID 2,340m.). It was stated that non-essential development projects had been postponed until 1992, and available resources diverted to the reconstruction effort. Nevertheless, over the five-year period 1991–95, it was envisaged that ID 28,700m. would be spent on development projects, of which the foreign currency component would be some US $56,000m.

In the 1980s Iraq attracted substantial foreign investment for its development projects, notably from West European countries, Japan and the USSR. In 1984 the USSR pledged US $2,000m. in long-term credits for Iraq, which also obtained lines of credit or other credit facilities from the United Kingdom, the USA and the Federal Republic of Germany (the latter two agreeing in 1987–88 to restore export credit guarantees which had earlier been withdrawn when Iraq defaulted on debt repayments). Nevertheless, as a result of persistent repayment problems, much of the credit—and the goodwill—had again ceased by the end of the decade, despite the conclusion of various inter-governmental refinancing agreements. By mid-1990 the claims on Iraq of banks reporting to the Bank for International Settlements were calculated as totalling $7,690m. worldwide, while national credit guarantee agencies with major exposure to outstanding Iraqi debts were headed by Coface of France (some $3,200m.) and included those of Japan and Italy (each some $3,000m.) and of Germany ($2,000m.).

On a multilateral basis, loans worth more than US $250m. were agreed with the Islamic Development Bank to fund imports and hospital work. The Arab Monetary Fund also loaned money ($523m. between 1983 and mid-1989) to support Iraq's balance of payments. Loans to support a coldstore project, telecommunications, an earthquake warning system, agricultural and industrial development and the upgrading and extension of power-generation units were made by the AFESD. Iraq secured two Euroloans of $500m., in 1983 and 1985, to finance foreign trade and development projects, but was forced to reschedule payments due on them, owing to a shortage of foreign exchange.

Against this background, there was considerable doubt regarding continued foreign investment in Iraqi development projects even before the onset of the Gulf crisis in August 1990 brought about the suspension of virtually all such co-operation and of Iraqi repayments on outstanding debts. In September

1990 Iraq's total foreign debt was estimated at US $65,000m., a total which the Iraqi Government itself appeared to revise upwards in a post-war submission to the UN in April 1991 (see Sanctions and Oil-for-Food, above).

Statistical Survey

Source (unless otherwise indicated): Central Statistical Organization, Ministry of Planning, Karradat Mariam, ash-Shawaf Sq., Baghdad; tel. (1) 537-0071.

Area and Population

AREA, POPULATION AND DENSITY*

Area (sq km)	438,317†
Population (census results)	
17 October 1987	16,335,199
17 October 1997	
Males	10,940,764
Females	11,077,219
Total	22,017,983
Density (per sq km) in October 1997	50.2

* No account has been taken of the reduction in the area of Iraq as a result of the adjustment to the border with Kuwait that came into force on 15 January 1993.

† 169,235 sq miles. This figure includes 924 sq km (357 sq miles) of territorial waters but excludes the Neutral Zone, of which Iraq's share is 3,522 sq km (1,360 sq miles). The Zone lies between Iraq and Saudi Arabia, and is administered jointly by the two countries. Nomads move freely through it but there are no permanent inhabitants.

GOVERNORATES (population at 1987 census)

	Area* (sq km)	Popu- lation	Density (per sq km)
Nineveh	37,698	1,479,430	39.2
Salah ad-Din	29,004	726,138	25.0
At-Ta'meem	10,391	601,219	57.9
Diala	19,292	961,073	49.8
Baghdad	5,159	3,841,268	744.6
Al-Anbar	137,723	820,690	6.0
Babylon	5,258	1,109,574	211.0
Karbala	5,034	469,282	93.2
An-Najaf	27,844	590,078	21.2
Al-Qadisiya	8,507	559,805	65.8
Al-Muthanna	51,029	315,816	6.2
Thi-Qar	13,626	921,066	67.6
Wasit	17,308	564,670	32.6
Maysan	14,103	487,448	34.6
Al-Basrah (Basra) . . .	19,070	872,176	45.7
Autonomous Regions:			
D'hok	6,120	293,304	47.9
Irbil (Arbil)	14,471	770,439	53.2
As-Sulaimaniya (Sulaimaniya) .	15,756	951,723	60.4
Total	437,393	16,335,199	37.3

* Excluding territorial waters (924 sq km).

PRINCIPAL TOWNS (estimated population 1970)

Baghdad (capital) .	1,984,142	Al-Hillah (Hilla) .	.	103,544
Al-Basrah (Basra) .	333,684	As-Sulaimaniya		
Al-Mawsil (Mosul) .	310,313	(Sulaimaniya)	.	103,091
Kirkuk . . .	191,294	Irbil (Arbil) .	.	101,779
An-Najaf . .	147,855			

Mid-2000 (UN estimate, incl. suburbs): Mosul 1,131,000.
Mid-2001 (UN estimate, incl. suburbs): Baghdad 4,958,000.

Source: UN, *World Urbanization Prospects: The 2001 Revision.*

BIRTHS AND DEATHS (UN estimates, annual averages)

	1985–90	1990–95	1995–2000
Birth rate (per 1,000) . . .	40.3	38.4	36.5
Death rate (per 1,000) . . .	7.2	10.4	9.9

Source: UN, *World Population Prospects: The 2000 Revision.*

Expectation of life (WHO estimates, years at birth, 2000): Males 61.7; Females 64.7 (Source: WHO, *World Health Report*).

Registered live births (1992) 502,415 (birth rate 27.4 per 1,000); Registered deaths (1990) 76,683 (death rate 4.4 per 1,000). Note: Registration is incomplete.

ECONOMICALLY ACTIVE POPULATION*
(persons aged 7 years and over, 1987 census)

	Males	Females	Total
Agriculture, forestry and fishing .	422,265	70,741	493,006
Mining and quarrying . . .	40,439	4,698	45,137
Manufacturing	228,242	38,719	266,961
Electricity, gas and water. .	31,786	4,450	36,236
Construction	332,645	8,541	341,186
Trade, restaurants and hotels. .	191,116	24,489	215,605
Transport, storage and communications . . .	212,116	12,155	224,271
Financing, insurance, real estate and business services . .	16,204	10,811	27,015
Community, social and personal services . . .	1,721,748	233,068	1,954,816
Activities not adequately defined .	146,616	18,232	167,848
Total labour force	3,346,177	425,904	3,772,081

* Figures exclude persons seeking work for the first time, totalling 184,264 (males 149,938, females 34,326), but include other unemployed persons.
Source: ILO, *Yearbook of Labour Statistics.*

Mid-2000 (estimates in '000): Agriculture, etc. 641; Total 6,339 (Source: FAO).

Health and Welfare

KEY INDICATORS

Fertility (births per woman, 2000)	5.0
Under-5 mortality rate (per 1,000 live births, 2000) . .	130
HIV/AIDS (% of persons aged 15–49, 2001) . . .	<0.10
Physicians (per 1,000 head, 1998)	0.55
Hospital beds (per 1,000 head, 1998)	1.45
Health expenditure (1998): US $ per head (PPP) . .	209
% of GDP	4.2
public (% of total) . . .	59.1
Access to water (% of persons, 2000) . . .	85
Access to sanitation (% of persons, 2000) . . .	79
Human Development Index (1999): value	0.567*

* Based on incomplete information.

For sources and definitions, see explanatory note on p. vi.

Agriculture

PRINCIPAL CROPS ('000 metric tons)

	1998	1999	2000
Wheat	1,130†	1,050†	550*
Rice (paddy)	300†	180*	130*
Barley	859†	500*	430*
Maize	133†	112*	53*
Potatoes*	420	365	150
Dry broad beans* . .	19	17	10
Sunflower seed† . . .	70	66	66
Sesame seed† . . .	14	14	8
Olives*	14	12	10
Cabbages*	21	16	12
Tomatoes*	865	650	500
Cauliflower*	34	25	19
Pumpkins, etc.* . . .	62	46	35
Cucumbers and gherkins* .	344	260	215
Aubergines (Eggplants)* . .	155	115	85
Chillies and peppers (green)* . .	32	24	18
Onions (dry)*	74	55	40
Carrots*	11	8	6
Other vegetables* . . .	740	547	403
Watermelons* . . .	455	400	380
Melons*	226	210	195
Grapes*	305	290	265
Dates	630*	438†	400*
Sugar cane*	71	68	65
Apples*	86	80	75
Peaches and nectarines* . .	26	25	20
Plums*	31	30	27
Oranges*	316	300	270
Tangerines, etc.* . . .	43	39	37
Lemons and limes* . .	16	15	14
Apricots*	32	30	27
Other fruits and berries* . .	94	84	73
Tobacco (leaves)* . . .	3	2	2
Cotton (lint)	9	9	6

* FAO estimate(s).   † Unofficial figure(s).

Source: FAO.

LIVESTOCK (estimates, '000 head, year ending September)

	1998	1999	2000*
Horses	48	46	47
Mules	13	11	11
Asses	385	375	380
Cattle	1,320	1,325	1,350
Buffaloes	64	64	65
Camels	8	8	8
Sheep	6,700	6,750	6,780
Goats	1,500	1,550	1,600
Poultry	13,000	22,000	23,000

* FAO estimates.

Source: FAO.

LIVESTOCK PRODUCTS ('000 metric tons)

	1998	1999	2000
Beef and veal*	45	45	45
Buffalo meat*	2	2	2
Mutton and lamb . . .	20	20	20
Goat meat*	8	8	8
Poultry meat*	44	49	50
Cows' milk*	315	317	319
Buffalo milk*	26	26	27
Sheep's milk	156	157	156
Goats' milk	53	54	54
Cheese	30	30	31
Butter	8	8	8
Hen eggs*	1	9	14
Wool (greasy)* . . .	13	13	13
Cattle and buffalo hides . .	5	5	5
Sheepskins	4	4	4
Goatskins	2	2	2

* FAO estimates.

Source: FAO.

Forestry

ROUNDWOOD REMOVALS ('000 cubic metres, excl. bark)

	1996	1997	1998
Sawlogs, veneer logs and logs for sleepers	20	20	25
Other industrial wood . . .	30	30	34
Fuel wood	49	111	118
Total	99	161	177

1999–2000: Annual removals as in 1998 (FAO estimates).

Source: FAO.

SAWNWOOD PRODUCTION ('000 cu m, incl. railway sleepers)

	1996	1997	1998
Total (all broadleaved) . . .	8	8	12

1999–2000: Annual production as in 1998 (FAO estimates).

Source: FAO.

Fishing

(FAO estimates, '000 metric tons, live weight)

	1997	1998	1999
Capture	31.3	22.6	24.6
Common carp	4.2	2.3	2.2
Other cyprinids . . .	4.8	1.7	5.7
Other freshwater fishes .	11.6	5.1	3.6
Marine fishes . .	10.8	13.5	13.1
Aquaculture (Common carp) .	3.4	0.6	2.2
Total catch	34.7	23.2	26.8

Source: FAO, *Yearbook of Fishery Statistics.*

Mining

(estimates, '000 metric tons, unless otherwise indicated)

	1998	1999	2000
Crude petroleum ('000 barrels)	750*	915*	930
Natural gas (million cu m) . .	6,000	7,000	7,500
Native sulphur	250	250	225
Natural phosphates† . . .	1,000	1,100	1,000
Salt (unrefined)	250	300	300
Gypsum (crude)	450	n.a.	n.a.

* Reported figure.
† Gross weight. The estimated phosphoric acid content was 30%.

Source: US Geological Survey.

Industry

SELECTED PRODUCTS
(estimates, '000 metric tons, unless otherwise indicated)

	1996	1997	1998
Naphtha	482	489	505
Motor spirit (petrol)	2,927	2,968	3,066
Kerosene	977	991	1,023
Jet fuel	541	549	567
Gas-diesel (distillate fuel) oil	6,608	6,701	6,921
Residual fuel oils	7,495	7,601	7,850
Lubricating oils	220	223	230
Paraffin wax	86	87	90
Petroleum bitumen (asphalt)	451	457	472
Liquefied petroleum gas:			
from natural gas plants	1,590	1,620	1,650
from petroleum refineries	600	610	610
Cement*	1,600	1,700	2,000
Electric energy (million kWh)	29,050	29,561	30,346

* Data from the US Geological Survey.
Cigarettes: 5,794 million in 1992.
Footwear (excluding rubber): 4,087,000 pairs in 1992.
Source: UN, *Industrial Commodity Statistics Yearbook*.

1999: Cement ('000 metric tons) 2,000*; Electric energy (million kWh) 28,800 (net)†.

* Source: US Geological Survey (estimate).
† Source: US Energy Information Administration.

Finance

CURRENCY AND EXCHANGE RATES

Monetary Units
1,000 fils = 20 dirhams = 1 Iraqi dinar (ID).

Sterling, Dollar and Euro Equivalents (31 May 2002)
£1 sterling = 455.93 fils;
US $1 = 310.86 fils;
€1 = 291.80 fils;
100 Iraqi dinars = £219.33 = $321.69 = €342.70.

Exchange Rate
From February 1973 to October 1982 the Iraqi dinar was valued at US $3.3862. Since October 1982 it has been valued at $3.2169. The dinar's average value in 1982 was $3.3513. The aforementioned data refer to the official exchange rate. There is, in addition, a special rate for exports and also a free-market rate. The unofficial exchange rate was $1 – 1,900 dinars in March 2002.

BUDGET ESTIMATES (ID million)

Revenue	1981	1982
Ordinary	5,025.0	8,740.0
Economic development plan	6,742.8	7,700.0
Autonomous government agencies	7,667.8	n.a.
Total	19,434.9	n.a.

Petroleum revenues (estimates, US $ million): 9,198 in 1981; 10,250 in 1982; 9,650 in 1983; 10,000 in 1984; 11,900 in 1985; 6,813 in 1986; 11,300 in 1987.

Expenditure	1981	1982
Ordinary	5,025.0	8,740.0
Economic development plan	6,742.0	7,700.0
Autonomous government agencies	7,982.4	n.a.
Total	19,750.2	n.a.

1991 (ID million): General consolidated state budget expenditure 13,876; Investment budget expenditure 1,660.

INTERNATIONAL RESERVES (US $ million at 31 December)

	1975	1976	1977
Gold	168.0	166.7	176.1
IMF special drawing rights	26.9	32.5	41.5
Reserve position in IMF	31.9	31.7	33.4
Foreign exchange	2,500.5	4,369.8	6,744.7
Total	2,727.3	4,600.7	6,995.7

IMF special drawing rights (US $ million at 31 December): 132.3 in 1981; 81.9 in 1982; 9.0 in 1983; 0.1 in 1984; 7.2 in 1987.
Reserve position in IMF (US $ million at 31 December): 130.3 in 1981; 123.5 in 1982.
Note: No figures for gold or foreign exchange have been available since 1977.
Source: IMF, *International Financial Statistics*.

COST OF LIVING (Consumer Price Index; base: 1990 = 100)

	1991*
Food	363.9
Fuel and light	135.4
Clothing	251.1
Rent	107.0
All items (incl. others)	286.5

* May to December only.
Source: ILO, *Yearbook of Labour Statistics*.

NATIONAL ACCOUNTS (UN estimates, ID million at current prices)
National Income and Product

	1997	1998	1999
Compensation of employees	1,375,121	1,674,787	1,976,037
Operating surplus	2,250,234	2,740,763	3,234,182
Domestic factor incomes	3,625,355	4,415,550	5,210,219
Consumption of fixed capital	394,464	480,426	566,896
Gross domestic product (GDP) at factor cost	4,019,819	4,895,976	5,777,115
Indirect taxes	63,041	76,852	90,705
Less Subsidies	192,231	234,042	276,052
GDP in purchasers' values	3,890,629	4,738,786	5,591,768

Source: UN, Economic and Social Commission for Western Asia, *National Accounts Studies of the ESCWA Region* (2000).

Expenditure on the Gross Domestic Product

	1997	1998	1999
Government final consumption expenditure	754,429	845,432	954,275
Private final consumption expenditure	2,948,725	3,563,417	4,175,437
Increase in stocks	−35,053	−19,129	−12,144
Gross fixed capital formation	262,740	398,560	511,801
Total domestic expenditure	3,930,841	4,788,280	5,629,369
Exports of goods and services	408,281	548,090	752,336
Less Imports of goods and services	448,493	597,584	789,937
GDP in purchasers' values	3,890,629	4,738,786	5,591,768
GDP at constant 1995 prices	2,874,396	3,305,556	3,570,000

Source: UN, Economic and Social Commission for Western Asia, *National Accounts Studies of the ESCWA Region* (2000).

Gross Domestic Product by Economic Activity

	1997	1998	1999
Agriculture, hunting, forestry and fishing	1,288,408	1,520,236	1,671,103
Mining and quarrying }	219,181	324,882	429,180
Manufacturing			
Electricity, gas and water.	13,649	20,396	26,105
Construction.	68,691	104,203	135,717
Trade, restaurants and hotels	983,907	1,200,120	1,402,469
Transport, storage and communications	721,414	837,382	940,650
Finance, insurance and real estate*	334,554	424,240	566,095
Government, community, social and personal services†	361,081	428,618	573,640
Sub-total	3,990,885	4,860,077	5,744,949
Less Imputed bank service charge	100,256	121,291	153,191
GDP in purchasers' values	3,890,629	4,738,786	5,591,768

* Including imputed rents of owner-occupied dwellings.

† Including private non-profit services to households, domestic services of households and import duties.

Source: UN, Economic and Social Commission for Western Asia, *National Accounts Studies of the ESCWA Region* (2000).

External Trade

PRINCIPAL COMMODITIES (ID million)

Imports c.i.f.	1976	1977*	1978
Food and live animals	159.6	154.0	134.5
Cereals and cereal preparations	70.0	79.9	74.9
Sugar, sugar preparations and honey.	37.2	24.1	10.2
Crude materials (inedible) except fuels	33.7	20.5	25.1
Chemicals	58.5	47.4	58.7
Basic manufactures	293.3	236.7	285.2
Textile yarn, fabrics, etc.	44.3	69.4	72.7
Iron and steel	127.5	44.3	73.2
Machinery and transport equipment	557.4	625.8	667.4
Non-electric machinery	285.4	352.5	368.1
Electrical machinery, apparatus, etc.	106.9	120.2	160.5
Transport equipment.	165.2	153.1	138.8
Miscellaneous manufactured articles	33.2	49.4	51.7
Total (incl. others)	1,150.9	1,151.3	1,244.1

* Figures are provisional. Revised total is ID 1,323.2 million.

Total imports (official estimates, ID million): 1,738.9 in 1979; 2,208.1 in 1980; 2,333.8 in 1981.

Total imports (IMF estimates, ID million): 6,013.0 in 1981; 6,309.0 in 1982; 3,086.2 in 1983; 3,032.4 in 1984; 3,285.7 in 1985; 2,773.0 in 1986; 2,268.7 in 1987; 2,888.8 in 1988; 3,077.1 in 1989; 2,028.5 in 1990; 131.5 in 1991; 187.3 in 1992; 165.6 in 1993; 155.0 in 1994; 206.9 in 1995; 176.7 in 1996; 354.4 in 1997; 562.1 in 1998; 640.2 in 1999; 910.5 in 2000; 1,042.9 in 2001 (Source: IMF, *International Financial Statistics*).

Total exports (ID million): 5,614.6 (crude petroleum 5,571.9) in 1977; 6,422.7 (crude petroleum 6,360.5) in 1978; 12,522.0 (crude petroleum 12,480.0) in 1979.

Exports of crude petroleum (estimates, ID million): 15,321.3 in 1980; 6,089.6 in 1981; 5,982.4 in 1982; 5,954.8 in 1983; 6,937.0 in 1984; 8,142.5 in 1985; 5,126.2 in 1986; 6,988.9 in 1987; 7,245.8 in 1988.

Source: IMF, *International Financial Statistics*.

Exports of crude petroleum under UN-administered oil-for-food programme (six-month phases, unless otherwise indicated, beginning December 1996, US $ million): first 2,150; second 2,125; third 2,085; fourth 3,027; fifth 3,947; sixth* 7,402; seventh 8,302†; eighth 9,564; ninth (seven months to the end of June 2001) 5,638; 10th (five months beginning July 2001) 5,350; 11th 4,589.

* Iraq was permitted to export additional petroleum to the value of US $3,000m. under the sixth phase.

† UN Security Council Resolution 1284, adopted in December 1999, removed restrictions on the amount of petroleum that Iraq was permitted to export under the oil-for-food programme.

Source: UN Office of the Iraq Programme.

PRINCIPAL TRADING PARTNERS (US $ million)

Imports c.i.f.	1988	1989	1990
Australia	153.4	196.2	108.7
Austria	n.a.	1.1	50.9
Belgium-Luxembourg	57.6	68.2	68.3
Brazil	346.0	416.4	139.5
Canada	169.9	225.1	150.4
China, People's Republic	99.2	148.0	157.9
France	278.0	410.4	278.3
Germany	322.3	459.6	389.4
India	32.3	65.2	57.5
Indonesia	38.9	122.7	104.9
Ireland	150.4	144.9	31.6
Italy	129.6	285.1	194.0
Japan	533.0	621.1	397.2
Jordan	164.3	210.0	220.3
Korea, Republic	98.5	123.9	149.4
Netherlands.	111.6	102.6	93.8
Romania	113.3	91.1	30.1
Saudi Arabia	37.2	96.5	62.5
Spain	43.4	129.0	40.5
Sri Lanka	50.1	33.5	52.3
Sweden.	63.0	40.6	64.8
Switzerland	65.7	94.4	126.6
Thailand	22.3	59.2	68.9
Turkey	874.7	408.9	196.0
USSR	70.7	75.7	77.9
United Kingdom	394.6	448.5	322.1
USA	979.3	1,001.7	658.4
Yugoslavia	154.5	182.0	123.1
Total (incl. others)	5,960.0	6,956.2	4,833.9

Exports f.o.b.	1988	1989	1990*
Belgium-Luxembourg	147.5	249.6	n.a.
Brazil	1,002.8	1,197.2	n.a.
France	517.4	623.9	0.8
Germany	122.0	76.9	1.7
Greece	192.5	189.4	0.3
India	293.0	438.8	14.7
Italy	687.1	549.7	10.6
Japan	712.1	117.1	0.1
Jordan	28.4	25.2	101.6
Netherlands.	152.9	532.3	0.2
Portugal.	120.8	125.8	n.a.
Spain	370.0	575.7	0.7
Turkey	1,052.6	1,331.0	83.5
USSR	835.7	1,331.7	8.9
United Kingdom	293.1	167.0	4.4
USA	1,458.9	2,290.8	0.2
Yugoslavia	425.4	342.0	10.4
Total (incl. others)	10,268.3	12,333.7	392.0

* Excluding exports of most petroleum products.

Source: UN, *International Trade Statistics Yearbook*.

Transport

RAILWAYS (traffic)

	1995*	1996†	1997†
Passenger-km (million)	2,198	1,169	1,169
Freight ton-km (million)	1,120	931	956

* Source: UN, *Statistical Yearbook*.

† Source: Railway Gazette International, *Railway Directory*.

ROAD TRAFFIC (estimates, '000 motor vehicles in use)

	1995	1996
Passenger cars	770.1	773.0
Buses and coaches	50.9	51.4
Lorries and vans	269.9	272.5
Road tractors	37.2	37.2

Source: IRF, *World Road Statistics*.

SHIPPING

Merchant Fleet (registered at 31 December)

	1999	2000	2001
Number of vessels	98	99	91
Total displacement ('000 grt) .	510.6	511.0	240.6

Source: Lloyd's Register-Fairplay, *World Fleet Statistics*.

CIVIL AVIATION (revenue traffic on scheduled services)

	1991	1992	1994*
Kilometres flown (million) . .	0	0	0
Passengers carried ('000) . .	28	53	31
Passenger-km (million) . . .	17	35	20
Freight ton-km (million) . . .	0	3	2

* Figures for 1993 unavailable.

Source: UN, *Statistical Yearbook*.

Tourism

ARRIVALS AT FRONTIERS OF VISITORS FROM ABROAD*

Country of nationality	1998	1999	2000
Afghanistan	392	250	1,041
India	1,523	4,893	3,092
Iran	35,234	20,849	69,155
Lebanon	2,536	780	8
Pakistan	2,833	2,063	2,985
Total (incl. others) . . .	44,885	30,328	78,457

* Including same-day visitors.

Source: World Tourism Organization, *Yearbook of Tourism Statistics*.

Tourism receipts (US $ million): 13 in 1998.

Communications Media

	1997	1998	1999
Radio receivers ('000 in use) . .	4,850	n.a.	n.a.
Television receivers ('000 in use) .	1,750	n.a.	n.a.
Telephones ('000 main lines in use)	651	650	675*

* Estimate.

Daily newspapers (1996): number 4; average circulation 407,000.

Sources: UNESCO, *Statistical Yearbook*; International Telecommunication Union.

Education

(1995/96)

	Insti-tutions	Teachers	Students		
			Males	Females	Total
Pre-primary . . .	571	4,841	43,889	41,135	85,024
Primary . . .	8,145	145,455	1,602,071	1,301,852	2,903,923
Secondary:					
General . . .	n.a.	52,393	631,457	406,025	1,037,482
Teacher training .	n.a.	1,392	9,414	14,120	23,534
Vocational . .	n.a.	8,511	81,917	17,488	99,405

Source: UNESCO, *Statistical Yearbook*.

Adult literacy rate (UNESCO estimates): 55.9% in 2000. (Source: UNDP, *Human Development Report*).

Directory

The Constitution

The following are the principal features of the Provisional Constitution, issued on 22 September 1968:

The Iraqi Republic is a popular democratic and sovereign state. Islam is the state religion.

The political economy of the State is founded on socialism.

The State will protect liberty of religion, freedom of speech and opinion. Public meetings are permitted under the law. All discrimination based on race, religion or language is forbidden. There shall be freedom of the Press, and the right to form societies and trade unions in conformity with the law is guaranteed.

The Iraqi people is composed of two main nationalities: Arabs and Kurds. The Constitution confirms the nationalistic rights of the Kurdish people and the legitimate rights of all other minorities within the framework of Iraqi unity.

The highest authority in the country is the Council of Command of the Revolution (or Revolutionary Command Council—RCC), which will promulgate laws until the election of a National Assembly. The Council exercises its prerogatives and powers by a two-thirds' majority.

Two amendments to the Constitution were announced in November 1969. The President, already Chief of State and Head of the Government, also became the official Supreme Commander of the Armed Forces and President of the RCC. Membership of the latter body was to increase from five to a larger number at the President's discretion.

Earlier, a Presidential decree replaced the 14 local government districts by 16 governorates, each headed by a governor with wide powers. In April 1976 Tikrit (Salah ad-Din) and Karbala became separate governorates, bringing the number of governorates to 18, although three of these are designated Autonomous Regions.

The 15-article statement which aimed to end the Kurdish war was issued on 11 March 1970. In accordance with this statement, a form of autonomy was offered to the Kurds in March 1974, but some of the Kurds rejected the offer and fresh fighting broke out. The new Provisional Constitution was announced in July 1970. Two amendments were introduced in 1973 and 1974, the 1974 amendment stating that 'the area whose majority of population is Kurdish shall enjoy autonomy in accordance with what is defined by the Law'.

The President and Vice-President are elected by a two-thirds' majority of the Council. The President, Vice-President and members of the Council will be responsible to the Council. Vice-Presidents and Ministers will be responsible to the President.

Details of a new, permanent Constitution were announced in March 1989. The principal innovations proposed in the permanent Constitution, which was approved by the National Assembly in July 1990, were the abolition of the RCC, following a presidential election, and the assumption of its duties by a 50-member Consultative Assembly and the existing National Assembly; and the incorporation of the freedom to form political parties. The new, permanent Constitution is to be submitted to a popular referendum for approval.

In September 1995 an interim constitutional amendment was endorsed by the RCC whereby the elected Chairman of the RCC will assume the Presidency of the Republic subject to the approval of the National Assembly and endorsement by national referendum.

In July 1973 President Bakr announced a National Charter as a first step towards establishing the Progressive National Front. A National Assembly and People's Councils are features of the Charter. A law to create a 250-member National Assembly and a 50-member Kurdish Legislative Council was adopted on 16 March 1980, and the two Assemblies were elected in June and September 1980 respectively.

The Government

HEAD OF STATE

President of the Republic and President of the Revolutionary Command Council (RCC): SADDAM HUSSAIN (assumed power 16 July 1979; confirmed in office by national referendum 15 October 1995).

Vice-Presidents: TAHA YASSIN RAMADAN, TAHA MOHI ED-DIN MARUF.

Vice-President of the RCC: IZZAT IBRAHIM.

COUNCIL OF MINISTERS
(September 2002)

Prime Minister: SADDAM HUSSAIN.

Deputy Prime Minister: TAREQ AZIZ.

Deputy Prime Minister and Minister of Finance: HIKMAT MIZBAN IBRAHIM.

Deputy Prime Minister and Head of the Presidential Office: AHMAD HUSSAIN KHUDAYYIR.

Deputy Prime Minister and Minister of State for Military Industrialization: ABD AT-TAWAB MULLAH HOWEICH.

Minister of Trade: MUHAMMAD MAHDI SALIH.

Minister of Justice: MUNDHIR IBRAHIM ASH-SHAWI.

Minister of Defence: Gen. SULTAN HASHIM AHMAD.

Minister of Oil: Gen. AMIR MUHAMMAD RASHID.

Minister of Health: UMEED MADHAT MUBARAK.

Minister of Labour and Social Affairs: Gen. SAADI TUMA ABBAS.

Minister of Irrigation and acting Minister of the Interior: MAHMOUD DIYAB AL-AHMAD.

Minister of Agriculture: ABDULLAH HAMEED MAHMOUD SALEH.

Minister of Transport and Communications: Dr AHMAD MURTADA AHMAD KHALIL.

Minister of Industry and Minerals: MUYASSAR RAJA SHALAH.

Minister of Higher Education and Scientific Research: HUMAM ABD AL-KHALIQ ABD AL-GHAFUR.

Minister of Education: FAHD SALIM ASH-SHAKRAH.

Minister of Awqaf (Religious Endowments) and Religious Affairs: Dr ABD AL-MUNIM AHMAD SALIH.

Minister of Information and Culture: MUHAMMAD SAEED AS-SAHAF.

Minister of Housing and Construction: MAAN ABDULLAH SARSAM.

Minister of Foreign Affairs: Dr NAJI SABRI.

Minister of State for Military Affairs: Gen. ABD AL-JABBAR KHALIL ASH-SHANSHAL.

Ministers of State: ARSHAD MUHAMMAD AHMAD MUHAMMAD AZ-ZIBARI, ABD AL-WAHHAB UMAR MIRZA AL-ATRUSHI, SAMAL MAJID FARAJ.

President of the Planning Committee: HASSAN ABD AL-MONIM AL-KHATAB.

Director of the State Electricity Organization: FAISAL SAIIDAN.

MINISTRIES

Office of the President: Presidential Palace, Karradat Mariam, Baghdad; e-mail press@uruklink.net; internet www.uruklink.net.

Ministry of Agriculture: Khulafa St, Khullani Sq., Baghdad; tel. (1) 887-3251.

Ministry of Awqaf (Religious Endowments) and Religious Affairs: North Gate, St opposite College of Engineering, Baghdad; tel. (1) 888-9561.

Ministry of Defence: North Gate, Baghdad; tel. (1) 888-9071.

Ministry of Education: POB 258, Baghdad; tel. (1) 886-0000.

Ministry of Finance: Khulafa St, Nr ar-Russafi Sq., Baghdad; tel. (1) 887-4871.

Ministry of Foreign Affairs: Opposite State Org. for Roads and Bridges, Karradat Mariam, Baghdad; tel. (1) 537-0091; e-mail foreign@uruklink.net; internet www.uruklink.net/mofa.

Ministry of Health: Khulafa St, Khullani Sq., Baghdad; tel. (1) 887-1881; e-mail health@uruklink.net; internet www.uruklink .net/health.

Ministry of Industry and Minerals: Nidhal St, Nr Sa'adoun Petrol Station, Baghdad; tel. (1) 887-2006.

Ministry of Information and Culture: Nr an-Nusoor Sq., fmrly Qasr as-Salaam Bldg, Baghdad; tel. (1) 551-4333; internet www .uruklink.net/iraqinfo.

Ministry of Oil: POB 19244, Zayouna, Baghdad; tel. (1) 817-7000; fax (1) 886-9432; e-mail oil@uruklink.net.

Ministry of Planning: POB 8001, Karradat Mariam, ash-Shawaf Sq., Baghdad; tel. and fax (1) 885-3653; e-mail plan@uruklink.net.

Ministry of Trade: Khulafa St, Khullani Sq., Baghdad; tel. (1) 887-2682.

Ministry of Transport and Communications: Nr Martyr's Monument, Karradat Dakhil, Baghdad; tel. (1) 776-6041.

Legislature

NATIONAL ASSEMBLY

Speaker: Dr SA'ADOUN HAMMADI.

Elections to the 220 elective seats of the fifth National Assembly took place on 27 March 2000. According to official results, candidates of the ruling Baath Party successfully contested 165 of the Assembly's seats, while independent candidates were returned to the remaining 55 elective seats. The remaining 30 seats of the Assembly that are reserved for representatives of the Kurdish Autonomous Regions were filled by government-appointed independents.

Kurdish Autonomous Regions

The efforts of successive Iraqi administrations to address the grievances and aspirations of the Kurdish population by conferring limited autonomy on the Kurdish-inhabited regions began to be formalized in 1970 (under the terms of a 15-article accord providing for the creation of a unified autonomous area comprising the administrative departments of As-Sulaimaniya, D'hok and Irbil (Arbil), and the Kurdish sector of the city of Kirkuk, and the establishment of a 50-member Kurdish Legislative Council), but have consistently fallen short of the, often disparate, demands and expectations of various Iraqi Kurd political parties and interest groups. Following the recapture of Kuwait from Iraqi forces by a multinational military coalition, in early 1991, a designated 'safe haven' north of latitude 36°N (encompassing much of the Kurdish territories) was imposed by the coalition partners. Renewed negotiations between the Iraqi Government (under Saddam Hussain) and Kurdish groups stalled over the status of Kirkuk, and in October 1991 the central Government withdrew all services from the region, effectively severing all economic and administrative support. In May 1992 the Kurdish Iraqi Front (KIF), an alliance of several Kurdish factions—including the two largest, the Patriotic Union of Kurdistan (PUK) and the Kurdistan Democratic Party (KDP)—established in 1988, organized elections to a new 105-member Iraqi Kurdistan National Assembly (see below). The results of a poll to select a Kurdish leader, conducted at the same time, were deemed inconclusive. Bitter factional disputes, including armed conflict between elements of the KDP and the PUK, subsequently led to the effective disintegration of the KIF, and thwarted attempts to consolidate Kurdish regional autonomy. In September 1996 the Iraqi Government announced the restoration of full Iraqi sovereignty over the Kurdish areas, but the KDP, which, under Masoud Barzani, had established the predominant influence in the region, announced the composition of a coalition administration for the territories (excluding the PUK, with which it was still in open conflict), to be based in Irbil, later in the same month. In September 1998 the USA brokered a formal peace agreement between representatives of the PUK and the KDP in Washington, DC, which provided for a unified regional administration, the sharing of local revenues and co-operation in implementing the UN-sponsored 'oil-for-food' programme. Fresh legislative elections, scheduled to take place in 1999 under the terms of the Washington agreement, were subsequently postponed. In December 1999 the KDP, still led by Barzani, announced the composition of a new 25-member coalition administration (comprising the KDP, the Iraqi Communist Party, the Assyrian Movement, the Independent Workers' Party of Kurdistan, the Islamic Union and independents—internet www.krg.org/about/cabinet.asp) for the areas under its control (principally the departments of Irbil and D'hok). Municipal elections (to select 571 officials) were conducted in the KDP-administered region in May 2001; according to official KDP sources, KDP candidates received 81% of votes cast, and the rate of voter participation was recorded at 79%. Negotiations between representatives of the KDP and PUK for the full implementation of the Washington accord were progressing in 2002, and were expected to result in the resumption of a transitional joint session of the Iraqi Kurdistan National Assembly before the end of the year (see below).

IRAQI KURDISTAN NATIONAL ASSEMBLY

In May 1992, negotiations with the Iraqi Government over the full implementation of the 1970 accord on Kurdish regional autonomy having stalled, the KIF organized elections to a 105-member Iraqi Kurdistan National Assembly, in which almost the entire electorate of 1.1m. participated, unilaterally. The KDP and the PUK were the only parties to achieve representation in the new Assembly and subsequently agreed to share seats equally (50 seats each—five having been reserved for two Assyrian Christian parties). The subsequent disintegration of the KIF and prolonged armed conflict between elements of the KDP and the PUK prevented the Assembly from becoming properly instituted, although the KDP attempted to incorporate the legislature into the administration of the territories under its control in the late 1990s and early 2000s, retaining the name of the Assembly and continuing to appoint officials (Jawhar N. Salem and Farsat A. Abdullah were serving as President and Secretary, respectively, in August 2002). Relations between the KDP and the PUK were generally improved following the Washington agreement of September 1998, and in August 2002 it was reported that representatives of the two parties had agreed to the inauguration of a transitional joint parliamentary session (with representation based on the results of the May 1992 elections) before the end of the year: an agreement to this effect was signed on 8 September.

Political Organizations

National Progressive Front: Baghdad; f. July 1973, when Arab Baath Socialist Party and Iraqi Communist Party signed a joint manifesto agreeing to establish a comprehensive progressive national and nationalistic front. In 1975 representatives of Kurdish parties and organizations and other national and independent forces joined the Front; the Iraqi Communist Party left the National Progressive Front in mid-March 1979; Sec.-Gen. NAIM HADDAD (Baath).

> **Arab Baath Socialist Party:** POB 6012, al-Mansour, Baghdad; revolutionary Arab socialist movement founded in Damascus in 1947; has ruled Iraq since July 1968, and between July 1973 and March 1979 in alliance with the Iraqi Communist Party in the National Progressive Front; founder MICHEL AFLAQ; Regional Command Sec.-Gen. SADDAM HUSSAIN; Deputy Regional Command Sec.-Gen. IZZAT IBRAHIM; 18-mem. Regional Command; approx. 100,000 mems.

> **Kurdistan Revolutionary Party:** f. 1972; succeeded Democratic Kurdistan Party; admitted to National Progressive Front 1974; Sec.-Gen. ABD AS-SATTAR TAHER SHAREF.

There are several illegal opposition groups, including:

Ad-Da'wa al-Islamiya (Voice of Islam): f. 1968; based in Tehran; mem. of the Supreme Council of the Islamic Revolution in Iraq (see below); guerrilla group; Leader Sheikh AL-ASSEFIE.

Iraqi Communist Party: Baghdad; f. 1934; became legally recognized in July 1973 on formation of National Progressive Front; left National Progressive Front March 1979; proscribed as a result of its support for Iran during the Iran–Iraq War; First Sec. AZIZ MUHAMMAD.

Umma (Nation) Party: f. 1982; opposes Saddam Hussain's regime; Leader SAAD SALEH JABR.

Principal Kurdish Parties

Kurdistan Democratic Party (KDP): European Office (Germany), 10749 Berlin, POB 301516; tel. (30) 79743741; fax (30) 79743746; e-mail kdpeurope@t-online.de; internet www.kdp.pp.se; f. 1946; seeks to protect Kurdish rights and promote Kurdish culture and interests through regional political and legislative autonomy, as part of a federative republic; Pres. MASOUD BARZANI; Vice-Pres. ALI ABDULLAH.

Patriotic Union of Kurdistan (PUK): European Office (Germany), 10502 Berlin, POB 210213; tel. (30) 34097850; fax (30) 34097849; e-mail pukoffice@pukq.de; internet www.puk.org; f. 1975; seeks to protect and promote Kurdish rights and interests through self-determination; Pres. JALAL TALABANI.

There is also a breakaway element of the Arab Baath Socialist Party represented on the Iraqi National Joint Action Cttee (see below); the Democratic Gathering (Leader SALEH DOUBLAH); the Iraqi Socialist Party (ISP; Leader Gen. HASSAN AN-NAQUIB); the Socialist Party of Kurdistan (SPK; f. 1975; Leader RASSOUL MARMAND); the Kurdistan Toilers' Party (KTP; f. 1985; Leader QADIR AZIZ), a breakaway faction of the SPK; the United Socialist Party of Kurdistan (USPK; Leader MAHMOUD OSMAN), a breakaway group from the PUK; the Kurdistan People's Democratic Party (KPDP; Leader SAMI ABD AR-RAHMAN); the Kurdish Workers' Party (PKK); the Islamic League of Kurdistan (ILK, also known as the Islamic Movement of Iraqi Kurdistan (IMIK)); the Islamic Union; the Islamic Unity Movement of Kurdistan (IUMK); Jund al-Islam (a militant Islamist faction of

the IUMK; f. 2001; Leader ABU ABDULLAH ASH-SHAFTI); Ansar al-Islam (f. 2002 by merger of Islah group and Jund al-Islam; Leader Mullah KREKAR); the Kurdish Hezbollah (Party of God; f. 1985; Leader Sheikh MUHAMMAD KHALED), a breakaway group from the KDP and a member of the Supreme Council of the Islamic Revolution in Iraq (SCIRI), which is based in Tehran under the leadership of the exiled Iraqi Shi'ite leader, Hojatoleslam MUHAMMAD BAQIR AL-HAKIM, and has a military wing, the Badr Brigade; the Iraqi National Accord (INA; Leader SALAH ESH-SHEIKHLI); the Constitutional Monarchy Movement (based in the United Kingdom), which supports the claim to the Iraqi throne of Sharif ALI BIN AL-HUSSAIN, cousin to the late King FAISAL II; the Bet-Nahrain Democratic Party, which is seeking the creation of an autonomous state for Assyrians in Bet-Nahrain; and Hizb al-Watan, or Homeland Party (Leader MISHAAN AL-JUBOURI).

Various alliances of political and religious groups have been formed to oppose the regime of Saddam Hussain in recent years. They include the Kurdistan Iraqi Front (KIF; f. 1988), an alliance of the KDP, the PUK, the SPK, the KPDP and other, smaller Kurdish groups, which subsequently disintegrated; the Iraqi National Joint Action Cttee, formed in Damascus in 1990 and grouping together the SCIRI, the four principal Kurdish parties belonging to the KIF, Ad-Da'wa al-Islamiya, the Movement of the Iraqi Mujahidin (based in Tehran; Leaders Hojatoleslam MUHAMMAD BAQIR AL-HAKIM and SAID MUHAMMAD AL-HAIDARI), the Islamic Movement in Iraq (Shi'ite group based in Tehran; Leader Sheikh MUHAMMAD MAHDI AL-KALISI), Jund al-Imam (Imam Soldiers; Shi'ite; Leader ABU ZAID), the Islamic Action Organization (based in Tehran; Leader Sheikh TAQI MODARESSI), the Islamic Alliance (based in Saudi Arabia; Sunni; Leader ABU YASSER AL-ALOUSI), the Independent Group, the Iraqi Socialist Party, the Arab Socialist Movement, the Nasserite Unionist Gathering and the National Reconciliation Group. In September 1992 the KPDP, the SPK and the Kurdish Democratic Independence Party were reported to have merged to form the Kurdistan Unity Party (KUP).

The Iraqi National Congress (INC), based in London, United Kingdom, has sought to unite the various factions of the opposition. At a conference held in London in April 1999 a new collegiate leadership, under SALAH ESH-SHEIKHLI of the INA, was appointed. In November some 300 delegates to a national assembly, held in New York, USA, elected a 65-member central council and a new, seven-member collegiate leadership (AYAD ALLAWI, INA; RIYAD AL-YAWAR, independent; Sharif ALI BIN AL-HUSSAIN, Constitutional Monarchy Movement; AHMAD CHALABI, independent; Sheikh MUHAMMAD MUHAMMAD ALI, independent; LATIF RASHID, PUK; HOSHYAR AZ-ZIBARI, KDP). Several leading members of the INC, including AHMAD CHALABI, have relocated to the USA.

Diplomatic Representation

EMBASSIES IN IRAQ

Algeria: 13/14/613 Hay ad-Daoudi, Baghdad; tel. (1) 543-4137; fax (1) 542-5829; Chargé d'affaires: MONCEF BENHADDID.

Armenia: 929/7/27 Hay Babel, Baghdad; tel. (1) 718-9853; fax (1) 718-9853; Chargé d'affaires: MOURAD MKHITARIAN.

Bahrain: 41/6/605, Hay al-Mutanabi, Baghdad; tel. (1) 541-0841 fax (1) 541-2027; Chargé d'affaires: HASSAN AL-ANSARI.

Bangladesh: 6/14/929 Hay Babel, Baghdad; tel. (1) 719-0068; fax (1) 718-6045; Ambassador: MUHAMMAD FAZLUR RAHMA.

Belarus: 47/5/929 Hay Babel, Baghdad; tel. and fax (1) 719-5565; Chargé d'affaires: IGOR SYRETS.

Bulgaria: 12/25/624 al-Ameriya, Baghdad; tel. (1) 556-8197; fax (1) 556-4182; Chargé d'affaires: VENELIN LAZAROV.

Chad: 12/32/611 Hay ad-Daoudi, Baghdad; tel. (1) 542-3588; fax (1) 541-3449; Ambassador: OUSMAN KALIBOU BELLA.

China, People's Republic: POB 15097, 624 New Embassy Area, Hitteen Quarter, Baghdad; tel. (1) 556-7880; fax (1) 556-7879; Ambassador: ZHANG WEIQIU.

Cuba: 8/29/923 Hay Babel, Baghdad; tel. (1) 717-0899; fax (1) 718-0701; Ambassador: HÉCTOR ESTRADA ACOSTA.

Czech Republic: 37/11/601 al-Mansour, Baghdad; tel. (1) 541-7136; fax (1) 543-0275; Chargé d'affaires: MIROSLAV BELICA.

Djibouti: 21/8/605 Hay al-Mutanabi, Baghdad; tel. (1) 541-3805; fax (1) 542-5002; Ambassador: IDRISS AHMAD CHIRWA.

Egypt: 53A/11/601 al-Mansour, Baghdad; tel. (1) 543-0572; fax (1) 542-5839; e-mail egypt@uruklink.net; Chargé d'affaires: MAHMOUD SHERIF RIHAN.

Germany: 40/2/929 Hay Babel, Baghdad; tel. (1) 719-2039; Chargé d'affaires a.i.: CLAUDE ROBERT ELLNER.

Greece: 63/13/913 Hay Babel, Baghdad; tel. (1) 718-2433; fax (1) 781-8729; Chargé d'affaires: KONSTANTINOS BIKAS.

Holy See: Apostolic Nuncio: Most Rev. FERNANDO FILONI, Titular Archbishop of Volturno (Resident in Amman, Jordan).

Hungary: 43/4/609 al-Mansour, Hay al-Mutanabi, Baghdad; tel. (1) 543-2956; Chargé d'affaires: ERNO JUHASZ.

India: 6/25/306 Hay al-Maghrib, Baghdad; tel. (1) 422-2014; fax (1) 422-9549; Ambassador: R. DAYAKAR.

Indonesia: POB 420, 906/02/77 Hay al-Wahda, Baghdad; tel. (1) 719-8677; fax (1) 719-8680; e-mail kombgd@warkaa.net; Ambassador: DACHLAN ABDUL HAMIED.

Iran: 35/19/222 Hay as-Salehiya, Baghdad; tel. (1) 885-3714; fax (1) 884-3033; Ambassador: ALI REZA HAQIQIAN.

Japan: 50/21/929 Hay Babel, Baghdad; tel. (1) 776-6791; Chargé d'affaires: MASAHI KONO.

Jordan: 145/49/617 Hay al-Andalus, Baghdad; tel. (1) 541-2892; fax (1) 541-2009; e-mail jordan@uruklink.net; Ambassador: HMROUD AL-QATARNAH.

Libya: 21/11/601 al-Mansour, Hay al-Amerat, Baghdad; tel. (1) 541-8590; fax (1) 541-7398; Head of the Libyan People's Bureau: IBRAHIM MUHAMMAD ABU KHAZA.

Malaysia: POB 1275, 17/22/915 Jadiriyah, Hay al-Jamiyah, Baghdad; tel. (1) 776-6388; fax (1) 717-3619; e-mail mwiraq@ur uklink.net; Ambassador: ABDUL LATIF BIN AWANG.

Morocco: POB 6039, 27/11/601 al-Mansour, Baghdad; tel. (1) 542-1779; fax (1) 542-3030; Ambassador: MUHAMMAD AURAGH.

Nigeria: 43/11/601 al-Mansour, Baghdad; tel. (1) 419-915-1750; fax (1) 543-4513; Ambassador: IBRAHIM MOHAMMED.

Oman: 2/5/613 Hay al-Andalus, Baghdad; tel. (1) 451-8198; fax (1) 541-3617; Chargé d'affaires: AMIR BIN HAMID AL-HAJRI.

Pakistan: 14/7/609 al-Mansour, Baghdad; tel. (1) 542-5343; fax (1) 542-8707; Ambassador: MANZAR SHAFIQ.

Philippines: 4/22/915 al-Jadriyah, Hay al-Jamiyah, Baghdad; tel. (1) 776-2696; fax 719-3228; e-mail bipe@uruklink.net; Ambassador: RONALDO B. PARUNGAO.

Poland: 22–24/60/904 Hay al-Wihda, Baghdad; tel. (1) 719-0297; fax (1) 719-0296; Ambassador: ROMAN TCHALACZKIEWICZ.

Qatar: 114/15/611 Hay ad-Daoudi, Baghdad; tel. (1) 542-1954; fax (1) 542-9056; Chargé d'affaires: HAMAD BIN MUHAMMAD BIN MUBARAK AL-KHALIFA.

Romania: 4/31/929 Hay Babel, Baghdad; tel. (1) 776-2860; fax (1) 776-7553; Chargé d'affaires: EMILIAN ION.

Russia: 4/5/605 Hay al-Mutanabi, Baghdad; tel. (1) 541-4749; fax (1) 543-4462; Ambassador: ALEKSANDR P. CHEVIN.

Slovakia: 94/28/923 Hay Babel, Baghdad; tel. (1) 776-7367; fax (1) 776-7368; Chargé d'affaires a.i.: JOZEF MARÉFKA.

Somalia: 609/10/10 al-Mansour, Baghdad; tel. (1) 541-0088; fax (1) 541-6697; Ambassador: ISSA ALI MOHAMMED.

Spain: 1/3/609 al-Mansour, Baghdad; tel. (1) 542-4827; Chargé d'affaires: FERNANDO VALDERRAMA.

Sri Lanka: 20–21/34/611 Hay al-Andalus, al-Mansour, Baghdad; tel. (1) 543-9986; fax (1) 543-9965; Ambassador: MOHAMED MOHIDEEN AMANUL FARUK.

Sudan: 32/1/609 al-Mansour, Baghdad; tel. (1) 542-7982; fax (1) 542-5287; e-mail sudan@uruklink.net; Ambassador: BUSHRA ESH-SHEIKH DAFALLA.

Thailand: POB 6062,18/18/601, al-Mansour, Baghdad; tel. (1) 541-8798; fax (1) 541-2618; Ambassador: TAWATCHAI PIYARAT.

Tunisia: 1/49/617 Hay al-Andalus, Baghdad; tel. (1) 542-0602; fax (1) 542-8585; Ambassador: HADI BEN NASR.

Turkey: 7/1/301 al-Waziriyah, Baghdad; tel. (1) 422-0022; fax (1) 422-8353; Ambassador: MEHMET AKAT.

Ukraine: 20/1/609 al-Mansour, Baghdad; tel. and fax (1) 542-6677; Chargé d'affaires: VALENTIN NOVYKOV.

United Arab Emirates: 81/34/611 Hay al-Andalus (ad-Daoudi), Baghdad; tel. (1) 543-9174; fax (1) 543-9093; Chargé d'affaires: AHMAD ABDULLAH BIN SAYEED.

Venezuela: 5/79/611 Hay ad-Daoudi, Baghdad; tel. and fax (1) 541-6133; e-mail evenik@uruklink.net; Ambassador: JORGE RONDON UZCATEGUI.

Viet Nam: 71/34 Hay al-Andalus, Baghdad; tel. and fax (1) 541-1388; e-mail vietnam@uruklink.net; Ambassador: NGUYEN VAN LINH.

Yemen: 4/36/904 Hay al-Wahada, Baghdad; tel. (1) 718-6682; fax (1) 717-2318; Ambassador: ABD AL-MALIK SAID ABDO.

Yugoslavia: 16/35/923 Hay Babel, Baghdad; tel. (1) 776-7887; fax (1) 717-1069; e-mail embyugag@uruklink.net; Ambassador: ENES KARABEGOVIĆ.

Note: France, Italy and Switzerland maintain interest sections or liaison offices in Baghdad; US interests are represented by the embassy of Poland.

Judicial System

Courts in Iraq consist of the following: The Court of Cassation, Courts of Appeal, First Instance Courts, Peace Courts, Courts of Sessions, *Shari'a* Courts and Penal Courts.

The Court of Cassation: This is the highest judicial bench of all the Civil Courts; it sits in Baghdad, and consists of the President and a number of vice-presidents and not fewer than 15 permanent judges, delegated judges and reporters as necessity requires. There are four bodies in the Court of Cassation, these are: (*a*) the General body, (*b*) Civil and Commercial body, (*c*) Personal Status body, (*d*) the Penal body.

Courts of Appeal: The country is divided into five Districts of Appeal: Baghdad, Mosul, Basra, Hilla, and Kirkuk, each with its Court of Appeal consisting of a president, vice-presidents and not fewer than three members, who consider the objections against the decisions issued by the First Instance Courts of first grade.

Courts of First Instance: These courts are of two kinds: Limited and Unlimited in jurisdiction.

Limited Courts deal with Civil and Commercial suits, the value of which is 500 Iraqi dinars and less; and suits, the value of which cannot be defined, and which are subject to fixed fees. Limited Courts consider these suits in the final stage and they are subject to Cassation.

Unlimited Courts consider the Civil and Commercial suits irrespective of their value, and suits the value of which exceeds 500 Iraqi dinars with first grade subject to appeal.

First Instance Courts consist of one judge in the centre of each *Liwa*, some *Qadhas* and *Nahiyas*, as the Minister of Justice judges necessary.

Courts of Sessions: There is in every District of Appeal a Court of Sessions which consists of three judges under the presidency of the President of the Court of Appeal or one of his vice-presidents. It considers the penal suits prescribed by Penal Proceedings Law and other laws. More than one Court of Sessions may be established in one District of Appeal by notification issued by the Minister of Justice mentioning therein its headquarters, jurisdiction and the manner of its establishment.

Shari'a Courts: A *Shari'a* Court is established wherever there is a First Instance Court; the Muslim judge of the First Instance Court may be a *Qadhi* to the *Shari'a* Court if a special *Qadhi* has not been appointed thereto. The *Shari'a* Court considers matters of personal status and religious matters in accordance with the provisions of the law supplement to the Civil and Commercial Proceedings Law.

Penal Courts: A Penal Court of first grade is established in every First Instance Court. The judge of the First Instance Court is considered as penal judge unless a special judge is appointed thereto. More than one Penal Court may be established to consider the suits prescribed by the Penal Proceedings Law and other laws.

One or more Investigation Court may be established in the centre of each *Liwa* and a judge is appointed thereto. They may be established in the centres of *Qadhas* and *Nahiyas* by order of the Minister of Justice. The judge carries out the investigation in accordance with the provisions of Penal Proceedings Law and the other laws.

There is in every First Instance Court a department for the execution of judgments presided over by the Judge of First Instance if a special president is not appointed thereto. It carries out its duties in accordance with the provisions of Execution Law.

Religion

ISLAM

About 95% of the population are Muslims, more than 50% of whom are Shi'ite. The Arabs of northern Iraq, the Bedouins, the Kurds, the Turkomans and some of the inhabitants of Baghdad and Basra are mainly of the Sunni sect, while the remaining Arabs south of the Diyali belong to the Shi'i sect.

CHRISTIANITY

There are Christian communities in all the principal towns of Iraq, but their principal villages lie mostly in the Mosul district. The Christians of Iraq comprise three groups: (*a*) the free Churches, including the Nestorian, Gregorian and Syrian Orthodox; (*b*) the churches known as Uniate, since they are in union with the Roman Catholic Church, including the Armenian Uniates, Syrian Uniates and Chaldeans; (*c*) mixed bodies of Protestant converts, New Chaldeans and Orthodox Armenians.

The Assyrian Church

Assyrian Christians, an ancient sect having sympathies with Nestorian beliefs, were forced to leave their mountainous homeland in northern Kurdistan in the early part of the 20th century. The estimated 550,000 members of the Apostolic Catholic Assyrian Church of the East are now exiles, mainly in Iraq, Syria, Lebanon and the USA. Their leader is the Catholicos Patriarch, His Holiness MAR DINKHA IV.

The Orthodox Churches

Armenian Apostolic Church: Archbishop AVAK ASADOURIAN, Primate of the Armenian Diocese of Iraq, POB 2280, Younis as-Saba'awi Sq., Baghdad; tel. (1) 815-1853; fax (1) 815-1857; 10 churches (four in Baghdad); 18,000 adherents, mainly in Baghdad.

Syrian Orthodox Church: about 12,000 adherents in Iraq.

The Greek Orthodox Church is also represented in Iraq.

The Roman Catholic Church

Armenian Rite

At 31 December 2000 the archdiocese of Baghdad contained an estimated 2,000 adherents.

Archbishop of Baghdad: (vacant), 27/903 Archevêché Arménien Catholique, Karrada Sharkiya, POB 2344, Baghdad; tel. (1) 719-1827.

Chaldean Rite

Iraq comprises the patriarchate of Babylon, five archdioceses (including the patriarchal see of Baghdad) and five dioceses (all of which are suffragan to the patriarchate). Altogether, the Patriarch has jurisdiction over 21 archdioceses and dioceses in Iraq, Egypt, Iran, Lebanon, Syria, Turkey and the USA, and the Patriarchal Vicariate of Jerusalem. At 31 December 2000 there were an estimated 220,573 Chaldean Catholics in Iraq (including 155,000 in the archdiocese of Baghdad).

Patriarch of Babylon of the Chaldeans: His Beatitude RAPHAËL I BIDAWID, POB 6112, Patriarcat Chaldéen Catholique, Baghdad; tel. (1) 887-9604; fax (1) 884-9967.

Archbishop of Arbil: Most Rev. YACOUB DENHA SCHER, Archevêché Catholique Chaldéen, Ainkawa, Arbil; tel. (665) 27463.

Archbishop of Baghdad: the Patriarch of Babylon (see above).

Archbishop of Basra: Most Rev. DJIBRAIL KASSAB, Archevêché Chaldéen, POB 217, Ashar-Basra; tel. (40) 210323.

Archbishop of Kirkuk: Most Rev. ANDRÉ SANA, Archevêché Chaldéen, POB 490, Kirkuk; tel. (50) 213978.

Archbishop of Mosul: Most Rev. PAULOS FARAJ RAHHO, Archevêché Chaldéen, POB 757, Mayassa, Mosul; tel. (60) 762022; fax (60) 772460.

Latin Rite

The archdiocese of Baghdad, directly responsible to the Holy See, contained an estimated 2,500 adherents at 31 December 2000.

Archbishop of Baghdad: Most Rev. JEAN BENJAMIN SLEIMAN, Archevêché Latin, Hay al-Wahda—Mahallat 904, rue 8, Imm. 44, POB 35130, 12906 Baghdad; tel. (1) 719-9537; fax (1) 717-2471.

Melkite Rite

The Greek-Melkite Patriarch of Antioch (GRÉGOIRE III LAHAM) is resident in Damascus, Syria.

Patriarchal Exarchate of Iraq: Asfar St, Karrada Sharkiya, Baghdad; tel. (1) 719-1082; 600 adherents (31 December 1995); Exarch Patriarchal: GEORGES EL-MURR.

Syrian Rite

Iraq comprises two archdioceses and the Patriarchal Exarchate of Basra; there were an estimated 55,700 adherents at 31 December 2000.

Archbishop of Baghdad: Most Rev. ATHANASE MATTI SHABA MATOKA, Archevêché Syrien Catholique, 1/2/903 Baghdad; tel. (1) 719-1850; fax (1) 719-0168.

Archbishop of Mosul: Most Rev. BASILE GEORGES CASMOUSSA, Archevêché Syrien Catholique, Hosh al-Khan, Mosul; tel. (60) 762160; fax (60) 771439.

The Anglican Communion

Within the Episcopal Church in Jerusalem and the Middle East, Iraq forms part of the diocese of Cyprus and the Gulf. Expatriate congregations in Iraq meet at St George's Church, Baghdad (Hon. Sec. GRAHAM SPURGEON). The Bishop in Cyprus and the Gulf is resident in Cyprus.

JUDAISM

Unofficial estimates assess the present size of the Jewish community at 2,500, almost all residing in Baghdad.

OTHERS

About 30,000 Yazidis and a smaller number of Turkomans, Sabians and Shebeks reside in Iraq.

Sabian Community: Nasiriyah; 20,000 adherents; Mandeans, mostly in Nasiriyah; Head Sheikh DAKHIL.

Yazidis: Ainsifni; 30,000 adherents; Leader TASHIN BAIK.

The Press

DAILIES

Al-Baath ar-Riyadhi: Baghdad; sports; Propr and Editor UDAY SADDAM HUSSAIN.

Babil (Babylon): Baghdad; internet www.iraq2000.com/babil; f. 1991; Propr and Editor UDAY SADDAM HUSSAIN.

Baghdad Observer: POB 624, Karantina, Baghdad; tel. (1) 416-9341; f. 1967; English; state-sponsored; Editor-in-Chief NAJI AL-HADITHI; circ. 22,000.

Al-Iraq: POB 5717, Baghdad; internet www.uruklink.net/al-iraq; f. 1976; Kurdish; formerly *Al-Ta'akhi*; organ of the National Progressive Front; Editor-in-Chief SALAHUDIN SAEED; circ. 30,000.

Al-Jumhuriya (The Republic): POB 491, Waziriya, Baghdad; internet www.uruklink.net/jumhuriya; f. 1963, refounded 1967; Arabic; Editor-in-Chief SAMI MAHDI; circ. 150,000.

Al-Qadisiya: Baghdad; internet www.uruklink.net/qadissiya; organ of the army.

Ar-Riyadhi (Sportsman): POB 58, Jadid Hassan Pasha, Baghdad; internet www.iraq2000.com/alryadhi; f. 1971; Arabic; published by Ministry of Youth; circ. 30,000.

Tariq ash-Sha'ab (People's Path): as-Sa'adoun St, Baghdad; Arabic; organ of the Iraqi Communist Party; Editor ABD AR-RAZZAK AS-SAFI.

Ath-Thawra (Revolution): POB 2009, Aqaba bin Nafi's Sq., Baghdad; tel. (1) 719-6161; internet www.uruklink.net/thawra; f. 1968; Arabic; organ of Baath Party; Editor-in-Chief HAMEED SAEED; circ. 250,000.

WEEKLIES

Alif Baa (Alphabet): Ministry of Information and Culture, Baghdad; tel. (1) 886-2948; fax (1) 538-1296; internet www.uruklink.net/alef-ba; Arabic and English; Editor-in-Chief AMIR AL-HILOU; circ. 33,000.

Al-Idaa'a wal-Television (Radio and Television): Iraqi Broadcasting and Television Establishment, Karradat Mariam, Baghdad; tel. (1) 537-1161; radio and television programmes and articles; Arabic; Editor-in-Chief KAMIL HAMDI ASH-SHARQI; circ. 40,000.

Majallati: Children's Culture House, POB 8041, Baghdad; Arabic; children's newspaper; Editor-in-Chief RAAD BENDER; circ. 35,000.

Ar-Rased (The Observer): Baghdad; Arabic; general.

Sabaa Nisan: Baghdad; f. 1976; Arabic; organ of the General Union of the Youth of Iraq.

Sawt al-Fallah (Voice of the Peasant): Karradat Mariam, Baghdad; f. 1968; Arabic; organ of the General Union of Farmers Societies; circ. 40,000.

Waee ul-Ummal (The Workers' Consciousness): Headquarters of General Federation of Trade Unions in Iraq, POB 2307, Gialani St, Senak, Baghdad; Arabic; Iraq Trades Union organ; Chief Editor KHALID MAHMOUD HUSSEIN; circ. 25,000.

PERIODICALS

Afaq Arabiya (Arab Horizons): POB 2009, Aqaba bin Nafi's Sq., Baghdad; monthly; Arabic; literary and political; Editor-in-Chief Dr MOHSIN J. AL-MUSAWI.

Al-Aqlam (Pens): POB 4032, Adamiya, Baghdad; tel. (1) 443-3644; f. 1964; publ. by the Ministry of Culture and Information; monthly; Arabic; literary; Editor-in-Chief Dr ALI J. AL-ALLAQ; circ. 7,000.

Bagdad: Dar al-Ma'mun for Translation and Publishing, POB 24015, Karradat Mariam, Baghdad; tel. (1) 538-3171; fortnightly; French; cultural and political.

Al-Funoon al-Ida'iya (Fields of Broadcasting): Cultural Affairs House, Karradat Mariam, Baghdad; quarterly; Arabic; supervised by Broadcasting and TV Training Institute; engineering and technical; Chief Editor MUHAMMAD AL-JAZA'RI.

Gilgamesh: Dar al-Ma'mun for Translation and Publishing, POB 24015, Karradat Mariam, Baghdad; tel. (1) 538-3171; quarterly; English; cultural.

Hurras al-Watan: Baghdad; Arabic.

L'Iraq Aujourd'hui: POB 2009, Aqaba bin Nafi's Sq., Baghdad; f. 1976; bi-monthly; French; cultural and political; Editor NADJI AL-HADITHI; circ. 12,000.

Iraq Oil News: POB 6178, al-Mansour, Baghdad; tel. (1) 541-0031; f. 1973; monthly; English; publ. by the Information and Public Relations Div. of the Ministry of Oil.

The Journal of the Faculty of Medicine: College of Medicine, University of Baghdad, Jadiriya, Baghdad; tel. (1) 93091; f. 1935; quarterly; Arabic and English; medical and technical; Editor Prof. YOUSUF D. AN-NAAMAN.

Al-Maarif an-Naftiah: Oil Institute, POB 4836, Waziriya, Baghdad; f. 2001; monthly; Arabic; Editor-in-Chief SHARIF MUTSIN AL-HADITHI.

Majallat al-Majma' al-'Ilmi al-'Iraqi (Journal of the Academy of Sciences): POB 4023, Waziriya, Baghdad; tel. (1) 422-1733; fax (1) 425-4523; f. 1950; quarterly; Arabic; scholarly magazine on Arabic Islamic culture; Editor-in-Chief Dr NAJIH M. K. AR-RAWI.

Majallat ath-Thawra az-Ziraia (Magazine of Iraq Agriculture): Baghdad; quarterly; Arabic; agricultural; published by the Ministry of Agriculture.

Al-Maskukat (Coins): Dept of Antiquities and Heritage, Karkh, Salihiya St, Baghdad; tel. (1) 884-0875; f. 1969; annually; numismatics; Chair. of Ed. Board RABI' AL-QAISI.

Al-Masrah wal-Cinema: Iraqi Broadcasting, Television and Cinema Establishment, Salihiya St, Baghdad; monthly; Arabic; artistic, theatrical and cinema.

Al-Mawrid: POB 2009, Aqaba bin Nafi's Sq., Baghdad; f. 1971; monthly; Arabic; cultural.

Al-Mu'allem al-Jadid: Ministry of Education, al-Imam al-A'dham St, A'dhamaiya, Nr Antar Sq., Baghdad; tel. (1) 422-2594. 1935; quarterly; Arabic; educational, social, and general; Editor-in-Chief KHALIL I. HAMASH; circ. 190,000.

Sawt at-Talaba (The Voice of Students): al-Maghreb St, Waziriya, Baghdad; internet www.iraq2000.com/talaba; f. 1968; monthly; Arabic; organ of National Union of Iraqi Students; circ. 25,000.

As-Sina'a (Industry): POB 5665, Baghdad; every 2 months; Arabic and English; publ. by Ministry of Industry and Minerals; Editor-in-Chief ABD AL-QADER ABD AL-LATIF; circ. 16,000.

Sumer: Dept of Antiquities and Heritage, Karkh, Salihiya St, Baghdad; tel. (1) 884-0875; f. 1945; annually; archaeological, historical journal; Chair. of Ed. Board RABI' AL-QAISI.

Ath-Thaquafa (Culture): Place at-Tahrir, Baghdad; f. 1970; monthly; Arabic; cultural; Editor-in-Chief SALAH KHALIS; circ. 5,000.

Ath-Thaquafa al-Jadida (The New Culture): Baghdad; f. 1969; monthly; pro-Communist; Editor-in-Chief SAFA AL-HAFIZ; circ. 3,000.

At-Turath ash-Sha'abi (Popular Heritage): POB 2009, Aqaba bin Nafi's Sq., Baghdad; monthly; Arabic; specializes in Iraqi and Arabic folklore; Editor-in-Chief LUTFI AL-KHOURI; circ. 15,000.

Al-Waqai al-Iraqiya (Official Gazette of Republic of Iraq): Ministry of Justice, Baghdad; f. 1922; Arabic and English weekly editions; circ. Arabic 4,000, English 400; Dir HASHIM N. JAAFER.

PRESS ORGANIZATIONS

The General Federation of Journalists: POB 6017, Baghdad; tel. (1) 541-3993.

Iraqi Journalists' Union: POB 14101, Baghdad; tel. (1) 537-0762.

NEWS AGENCIES

Iraqi News Agency (INA): POB 3084, 28 Nissan Complex—Baghdad, Sadoun; tel. (1) 8863024.; e-mail ina@uruklink.net; internet www.uruklink.net/iraqnews; f. 1959; Dir-Gen. UDAI EL-TAIE.

Foreign Bureaux

Agence France-Presse (AFP): POB 190, Apt 761-91-97, Baghdad; tel. (1) 551-4333; Correspondent FAROUQ CHOUKRI.

Agenzia Nazionale Stampa Associata (ANSA) (Italy): POB 5602, Baghdad; tel. (1) 776-2558; Correspondent SALAH H. NASRAWI.

Associated Press (AP) (USA): Hay al-Khadra 629, Zuqaq No. 23, Baghdad; tel. (1) 555-9041; Correspondent SALAH H. NASRAWI.

Deutsche Presse-Agentur (dpa) (Germany): POB 5699, Baghdad; Correspondent NAJHAT KOTANI.

Informatsionnoye Telegrafnoye Agentstvo Rossii—Telegrafnoye Agentstvo Suverennykh Stran (ITAR—TASS) (Russia): 67 Street 52, Alwiya, Baghdad; Correspondent ANDREI OSTALSKY.

Reuters (UK): House No. 8, Zuqaq 75, Mahalla 903, Hay al-Karada, Baghdad; tel. (1) 719-1843; Correspondent SUBHY HADDAD.

Xinhua (New China) News Agency (People's Republic of China): al-Mansour, Adrus District, 611 Small District, 5 Lane No. 8, Baghdad; tel. (1) 541-8904; Correspondent ZHU SHAOHUA.

Publishers

National House for Publishing, Distribution and Advertising: Ministry of Culture and Information, POB 624, al-Jumhuriyah St, Baghdad; tel. (1) 425-1846. 1972; publishes books on politics, economics, education, agriculture, sociology, commerce and science in Arabic and other Middle Eastern languages; sole importer and distributor of newspapers, magazines, periodicals and books; controls all advertising activities, inside Iraq as well as outside; Dir-Gen. M. A. ASKAR.

Afaq Arabiya Publishing House: POB 4032, Adamiya, Baghdad; tel. (1) 443-6044; fax (1) 444-8760; publisher of literary monthlies, *Al-Aqlam* and *Afaq Arabiya*, periodicals, *Foreign Culture, Art, Folklore,* and cultural books; Chair. Dr MOHSIN AL-MUSAWI.

Dar al-Ma'mun for Translation and Publishing: POB 24015, Karradat Mariam, Baghdad; tel. (1) 538-3171; publisher of newspapers and magazines including: the *Baghdad Observer* (daily newspaper), *Bagdad* (monthly magazine), *Gilgamesh* (quarterly magazine).

Al-Hurriyah Printing Establishment: Karantina, Sarrafia, Baghdad; tel. (1) 69721; f. 1970; largest printing and publishing establishment in Iraq; state-owned; controls *Al-Jumhuriyah* (see below).

Al-Jamaheer Press House: POB 491, Sarrafia, Baghdad; tel. (1) 416-9341; fax (1) 416-1875; f. 1963; publisher of a number of newspapers and magazines, *Al-Jumhuriyah, Baghdad Observer, Alif Baa, Yord Weekly;* Pres. SAAD QASSEM HAMMOUDI.

Al-Ma'arif Ltd: Mutanabi St, Baghdad; f. 1929; publishes periodicals and books in Arabic, Kurdish, Turkish, French and English.

Al-Muthanna Library: Mutanabi St, Baghdad; f. 1936; booksellers and publishers of books in Arabic and oriental languages; Man. ANAS K. AR-RAJAB.

An-Nahdah: Mutanabi St, Baghdad; politics, Arab affairs.

Kurdish Culture Publishing House: Baghdad; f. 1976; attached to the Ministry of Information and Culture.

Ath-Thawra Printing and Publishing House: POB 2009, Aqaba bin Nafi's Sq., Baghdad; tel. (1) 719-6161; f. 1970; state-owned; Chair. TAREQ AZIZ.

Thnayan Printing House: Baghdad.

Broadcasting and Communications

TELECOMMUNICATIONS

Iraqi Telecommunications and Posts: POB 2450, Karrada Dakhil, Baghdad; tel. (1) 718-0400; fax (1) 718-2125; Dir-Gen. Eng. MEZHER M. HASAN.

BROADCASTING

State Enterprise for Communications and Post: f. 1987 from State Org. for Post, Telegraph and Telephones, and its subsidiaries.

State Organization for Broadcasting and Television: Broadcasting and Television Bldg, Salihiya, Karkh, Baghdad; tel. (1) 537-1161.

Iraqi Broadcasting and Television Establishment: Salihiya, Baghdad; tel. (1) 884-4412; fax (1) 541-0480; f. 1936; radio broadcasts began 1936; home service broadcasts in Arabic, Kurdish, Syriac and Turkoman; foreign service in French, German, English, Russian, Azeri, Hebrew and Spanish; Dir-Gen. SABAH YASEEN.

Radio

Idaa'a Baghdad (Radio Baghdad): f. 1936; 22 hours daily.

Idaa'a Sawt al-Jamahir: f. 1970; 24 hours.

Other stations include **Idaa'a al-Kurdia, Idaa'a al-Farisiya** (Persian).

Radio Iraq International: POB 8145, Baghdad.

Television

Baghdad Television: Ministry of Information and Culture, Iraqi Broadcasting and Television Establishment, Salihiya, Karkh, Baghdad; tel. (1) 537-1151; f. 1956; government station operating daily on two channels for 9 hours and 8 hours respectively; Dir-Gen. Dr MAJID AHMAD AS-SAMARRIE.

Kirkuk Television: f. 1967; government station; 6 hours daily.

Mosul Television: f. 1968; government station; 6 hours daily.

Basra Television: f. 1968; government station; 6 hours daily.

Missan Television: f. 1974; government station; 6 hours daily.

Kurdish Television: f. 1974; government station; 8 hours daily.

There are 18 other TV stations operating in the Iraqi provinces.

Finance

(cap. = capital; dep. = deposits; res = reserves;
brs = branches; m. = million; amounts in Iraqi dinars)

All banks and insurance companies, including all foreign companies, were nationalized in July 1964. The assets of foreign companies were taken over by the State. In May 1991 the Government announced its decision to end the State's monopoly in banking, and by mid-1992 three private banks had commenced operations.

BANKING
Central Bank

Central Bank of Iraq: POB 64, Rashid St, Baghdad; tel. (1) 816-5171; fax (1) 816-6321; e-mail cbi@uruklink.net; f. 1947 as National Bank of Iraq; name changed as above 1956; has the sole right of note issue; cap. and res 125m. (Sept. 1988); Gov. ISSAM RASHID HOWEICH; brs in Mosul and Basra.

Nationalized Commercial Banks

Rafidain Bank: New Banks St, Baghdad; tel. (1) 415-8001; f. 1941; state-owned; cap. 2,000m., res 1,702.3m., dep. 453,678m., total assets 503,145.1m. (Dec. 1998); Pres. DHIA HABIB AL-KHAYYOON; 152 brs in Iraq, 9 brs abroad.

Rashid Bank: BOP 7177, Haifa St, Baghdad; tel. (1) 885-3411; f. 1988; state-owned; cap. 1,000m., res 1.5m., dep. 236.1m. (1999); Chair. and Gen. Man. FAIQ M. AL-OBAIDY; 133 brs.

Private Commercial Banks

Bank of Baghdad: POB 3192 Alwiya, Al-Karada St, Baghdad; tel. (1) 717-5007; fax (1) 717-5006; e-mail bankdad@uruklink.net; f. 1992; cap. 1,750m.; Chair. MUNIB K. AS-SIKOUTI.

Commercial Bank of Iraq SA: POB 5639, 13/14/904 Al-Wahda St, Baghdad; tel. (1) 707-0049, fax (1) 718-4312; e-mail commerce@uruklink.net; f. 1992; cap. 1,800m.; Chair. MUHAMMAD H. DRAGH.

Specialized Banks

Al-Ahli Bank for Agricultural Investment and Financing: Al-Huria Sq., Al-Ahh, Baghdad.

Agricultural Co-operative Bank of Iraq: POB 2421, Rashid St, Baghdad; tel. (1) 886-4768; fax (1) 886-5047; f. 1936; state-owned; cap. 295.7m., res 14m., dep. 10.5m., total assets 351.6m. (Dec. 1988); Dir-Gen. HDIYA H. AL-KHAYOUN; 32 brs.

Industrial Bank of Iraq: POB 5825, as-Sinak, Baghdad; tel. (1) 887-2181; fax (1) 888-3047; f. 1940; state-owned; cap. 59.7m., dep. 77.9m. (Dec. 1988); Dir-Gen. BASSIMA ABD AL-HADDI ADH-DHAHIR; 5 brs.

Investment Bank of Iraq: POB 3724, 102/91/24 Hay as-Sadoon, Alwiya, Baghdad; tel. (1) 718-4624; fax (1) 719-8505; f. 1993; cap. 300m., res 39.2m. (Dec. 1998); Chair. THAMIR R. SHAIKHLY; Man. Dir MOWAFAQ HASAN MAHMOOD.

Iraqi Islamic Bank SA: POB 940, Al-Kahiay, Bab Al-Muathem, Baghdad; tel. (1) 414-0694.

Iraqi Middle East Investment Bank: POB 10379, Bldg 65, Hay Babel, 929 Arasat al-Hindiya, Baghdad; tel. (1) 717-3745; f. 1993; cap., res and dep. 3,254.8m. (1998).

Real Estate Bank of Iraq: POB 8118, 29/222 Haifa St, Baghdad; tel. (1) 885-3212; fax (1) 884-0980; f. 1949; state-owned; gives loans to assist the building industry; cap. 800m., res 11m., total assets 2,593.6m. (Dec. 1988); acquired the Co-operative Bank in 1970; Dir-Gen. ABD AR-RAZZAQ AZIZ; 18 brs.

INSURANCE

Iraq Life Insurance Co: POB 989, Aqaba bin Nafi's Sq., Khalid bin al-Waleed St, Baghdad; tel. (1) 719-2184; fax (1) 719-2606; f. 1959; state-owned; Chair. and Gen. Man. WALID SALIH ABD AL-WAHAB.

Iraq Reinsurance Co: POB 297, Aqaba bin Nafi's Sq., Khalid bin al-Waleed St, Baghdad; tel. (1) 719-5131; fax (1) 791497; f. 1960; state-owned; transacts reinsurance business on the international market; total assets 93.2m. (1985); Chair. and Gen. Man. K. M. AL-MUDARIES.

National Insurance Co: POB 248, National Insurance Co Bldg, Al-Khullani St, Baghdad; tel. (1) 885-3026; fax (1) 886-1486; f. 1950; cap. 20m.; all types of general and life insurance, reinsurance and investment; Chair. and Gen. Man. MUHAMMAD HUSSAIN JAAFAR ABBAS.

STOCK EXCHANGE

Capital Market Authority: Baghdad; Chair. MUHAMMAD HASSAN FAG EN-NOUR.

Trade and Industry

CHAMBERS OF COMMERCE

Federation of Iraqi Chambers of Commerce: Mustansir St, Baghdad; tel. (1) 886-1811; fax (1) 886-0283; f. 1969; all Iraqi Chambers of Commerce are affiliated to the Federation; Chair. ZUHAIR A. AL-YOUNIS; Sec.-Gen. FALIH A. AS-SALEH.

INDUSTRIAL AND TRADE ASSOCIATIONS

In 1987 and 1988, as part of a programme of economic and administrative reform, to increase efficiency and productivity in industry and agriculture, many of the state organizations previously responsible for various industries were abolished or merged, and new state enterprises or mixed-sector national companies were established to replace them.

Military Industries Commission (MIC): Baghdad; attached to the Ministry of Defence; Chair. ABD AT-TAWAB MULLAH HOWEICH (Minister of State for Military Industrialization).

State enterprises include the following:

Iraqi State Enterprise for Cement: f. 1987 by merger of central and southern state cement enterprises.

National Co for Chemical and Plastics Industries: Dir-Gen. RAJA BAYYATI.

The Rafidain Co for Building Dams: f. 1987 to replace the State Org. for Dams.

State Enterprise for Battery Manufacture: f. 1987; Dir-Gen. ADEL ABBOUD.

State Enterprise for Construction Industries: f. 1987 by merger of state orgs for gypsum, asbestos, and the plastic and concrete industries.

State Enterprise for Cotton Industries: f. 1988 by merger of State Org. for Cotton Textiles and Knitting, and the Mosul State Org. for Textiles.

State Enterprise for Drinks and Mineral Water: f. 1987 by merger of enterprises responsible for soft and alcoholic drinks.

State Enterprise for the Fertilizer Industries: f. by merger of Basra-based and central fertilizer enterprises.

State Enterprise for Import and Export: f. 1987 to replace the five state organizations responsible to the Ministry of Trade for productive commodities, consumer commodities, grain and food products, exports and imports.

State Enterprise for Leather Industries: f. 1987; Dir-Gen. MUHAMMAD ABD AL-MAJID.

State Enterprise for Sugar Beet: f. 1987 by merger of sugar enterprises in Mosul and Sulaimaniya.

State Enterprise for Textiles: f. 1987 to replace the enterprise for textiles in Baghdad, and the enterprise for plastic sacks in Tikrit.

State Enterprise for Tobacco and Cigarettes.

State Enterprise for Woollen Industries: f. by merger of state orgs for textiles and woollen textiles and Arbil-based enterprise for woollen textiles and women's clothing.

AGRICULTURAL ORGANIZATIONS

The following bodies are responsible to the Ministry of Agriculture:

State Agricultural Enterprise in Dujaila.

State Enterprise for Agricultural Supplies: Dir-Gen. MUHAMMAD KHAIRI.

State Enterprise for Developing Animal Wealth.

State Enterprise for Fodder.

State Enterprise for Grain Trading and Processing: Dir-Gen. ZUHAIR ABD AR-RAHMAN.

State Enterprise for Poultry (Central and Southern Areas).

State Enterprise for Poultry (Northern Area).

State Enterprise for Sea Fisheries: POB 260, Basra; Baghdad office: POB 3296, Baghdad; tel. (1) 92023; fleet of 3 fish factory ships, 2 fish carriers, 1 fishing boat.

PEASANT SOCIETIES

General Federation of Peasant Societies: Baghdad; f. 1959; has 734 affiliated Peasant Societies.

EMPLOYERS' ORGANIZATION

Iraqi Federation of Industries: Iraqi Federation of Industries Bldg, al-Khullani Sq., Baghdad; f. 1956; 6,000 mems; Pres. HATAM ABD AR-RASHID.

PETROLEUM AND GAS

Ministry of Oil: POB 19244, Zayouna, Baghdad; tel. (1) 817-7000; fax (1) 886-9432; e-mail oil@uruklink.net; merged with INOC in 1987; affiliated cos: Oil Marketing Co, Oil Projects Co, Midland Refineries Co, Oil Exploration Co, Oil Products Distribution Co, Gas Filling Co, Petroleum Pipelines Co, Iraqi Drilling Co, South Oil Co, South Refineries Co, North Oil Co, North Refineries Co, North Gas Co, South Gas Co, Iraqi Oil Tankers Co, Research and Development Centre; Minister of Oil Gen. AMIR MUHAMMAD RASHID.

Iraq National Oil Co (INOC): POB 476, al-Khullani Sq., Baghdad; tel. (1) 887-1115. in 1964 to operate the petroleum industry at home and abroad; when Iraq nationalized its petroleum industry, structural changes took place in INOC, and it became solely responsible for exploration, production, transportation and marketing of Iraqi crude petroleum and petroleum products. INOC was merged with the Ministry of Oil in 1987, and the functions of some of the organizations under its control were transferred to newly-created ministerial departments or to companies responsible to the ministry.

UTILITIES
Electricity

State Enterprise for Generation and Transmission of Electricity: f. 1987 from State Org. for Major Electrical Projects; Dir SALAH YUSUF KUZAYR.

TRADE UNIONS

General Federation of Trade Unions of Iraq (GFTU): POB 3049, Tahrir Sq., Rashid St, Baghdad; tel. (1) 887-0810; fax (1) 886-3820; f. 1959; incorporates six vocational trade unions and 18 local trade union federations in the governorates of Iraq; the number of workers in industry is 536,245, in agriculture 150,967 (excluding peasants) and in other services 476,621 (1986); GFTU is a member of the International Confederation of Arab Trade Unions and of the World Federation of Trade Unions; Pres. FADHIL MAHMOUD GHAREB.

Union of Teachers: Al-Mansour, Baghdad; Pres. Dr ISSA SALMAN HAMID.

Union of Palestinian Workers in Iraq: Baghdad; Sec.-Gen. SAMI ASH-SHAWISH.

There are also unions of doctors, pharmacologists, jurists, artists, and a General Federation of Iraqi Women (Chair. MANAL YOUNIS).

Transport

RAILWAYS

Iraq's railway lines extend over some 2,339 km. A line covers the length of the country, from Rabia, on the Syrian border, via Mosul, to Baghdad (534 km), and from Baghdad to Basra and Umm Qasr (608 km), on the Persian (Arabian) Gulf. A 404-km line links Baghdad, via Radi and Haditha to Husaibah, near the Iraqi–Syrian frontier. Baghdad is linked with Arbil via Khanaqin and Kirkuk, and a 252-km line (designed to serve industrial projects along its route) runs from Kirkuk via Baiji to Haditha. A 638-km line runs from Baghdad, via al-Qaim (on the Syrian border), to Akashat (with a 150-km line linking the Akashat phosphate mines and the fertilizer complex at al-Qaim). As well as the internal service, there is a regular international service between Baghdad and Istanbul, Turkey. Passenger rail services between Mosul and Aleppo, Syria, resumed in August 2000 after an interruption of almost 20 years. It was reported in mid-2001 that international contractors were submitting bids to revise and develop earlier plans for a 'loop' railway project for Baghdad.

State Enterprise for Iraqi Railways: Baghdad Central Station Bldg, Damascus Sq., Baghdad; tel. (1) 543-4404; fax (1) 884-0480; fmrly the Iraqi Republic Railways, under the supervision of State Org. for Iraqi Railways; re-formed as a State Enterprise in 1987, under the Ministry of Transport and Communications; Dir-Gen. GHASSAN ABD AR-RAZAQ AL-ANI.

New Railways Implementation Authority: POB 17040, al-Hurriya, Baghdad; tel. (1) 537-0021; responsible for development of railway network; Sec.-Gen. R. A. AL-UMARI.

ROADS

At the end of 1999, according to estimates by the International Road Federation, Iraq's road network extended over 45,550 km, of which approximately 38,400 km were paved.

The most important roads are: Baghdad–Mosul–Tel Kotchuk (Syrian border), 521 km; Baghdad–Kirkuk–Arbil–Mosul-Zakho (border with Turkey), 544 km; Kirkuk–As-Sulaimaniya, 160 km; Baghdad–Hilla–Diwaniya–Nasiriya–Basra, 586 km; Baghdad-Kut-Nasirya, 186 km; Baghdad–Ramadi–Rurba (border with Syria),

555 km; Baghdad–Kut–Umara–Basra–Safwan (border with Kuwait), 660 km; Baghdad–Baqaba–Kanikien (border with Iran). Most sections of the six-lane 1,264-km international Express Highway, linking Safwan (on the Kuwaiti border) with the Jordanian and Syrian borders, had been completed by June 1990. Studies have been completed for a second, 525-km Express Highway, linking Baghdad and Zakho on the Turkish border. A complex network of roads was constructed behind the war front with Iran in order to facilitate the movement of troops and supplies during the 1980–88 conflict.

Iraqi Land Transport Co: Baghdad; f. 1988 to replace State Organization for Land Transport; fleet of more than 1,000 large trucks; Dir Gen. AYSAR AS-SAFI.

Joint Land Transport Co: Baghdad; joint venture between Iraq and Jordan; operates a fleet of some 750 trucks.

State Enterprise for Implementation of Expressways: f. 1987; Dir-Gen. FAIZ MUHAMMAD SAID.

State Enterprise for Passenger Transport: Dir-Gen. THABIT MAHMUD GHARIB.

State Enterprise for Roads and Bridges: POB 917, Karradat Mariam, Karkh, Baghdad; tel. (1) 32141; responsible for road and bridge construction projects under the Ministry of Housing and Construction.

SHIPPING

The ports of Basra and Umm Qasr are usually the commercial gateway of Iraq. They are connected by various ocean routes with all parts of the world, and constitute the natural distributing centre for overseas supplies. The Iraqi State Enterprise for Maritime Transport maintains a regular service between Basra, the Gulf and north European ports. There is also a port at Khor az-Zubair, which came into use during 1979.

At Basra there is accommodation for 12 vessels at the Maqal Wharves and accommodation for seven vessels at the buoys. There is one silo berth and two berths for petroleum products at Muftia and one berth for fertilizer products at Abu Flus. There is room for eight vessels at Umm Qasr. There are deep-water tanker terminals at Khor al-Amaya and Faw for three and four vessels respectively. The latter port, however, was abandoned during the early part of the Iran–Iraq War.

For the inland waterways, which are now under the control of the General Establishment for Iraqi Ports, there are 1,036 registered river craft, 48 motor vessels and 105 motor boats.

General Establishment for Iraqi Ports: Maqal, Basra; tel. (40) 413211; f. 1987, when State Org. for Iraqi Ports was abolished; Dir-Gen. ABD AR-RAZZAQ ABD AL-WAHAB.

State Enterprise for Iraqi Water Transport: POB 23016, Airport St, al-Furat Quarter, Baghdad; f. 1987 when State Org. for Iraqi Water Transport was abolished; responsible for the planning, supervision and control of six nat. water transportation enterprises, incl.:

State Enterprise for Maritime Transport (Iraqi Line): POB 13038, al-Jadiriya al-Hurriya Ave, Baghdad; tel. (1) 776-3201; Basra office: 14 July St, POB 766, Basra; tel. 210206; f. 1952; Dir-Gen. JABER Q. HASSAN; Operations Man. M. A. ALI.

Shipping Company

Arab Bridge Maritime Navigation Co: Aqaba, Jordan; tel. (03) 316307; fax (03) 316313; f. 1987; joint venture by Egypt, Iraq and Jordan to improve economic co-operation; an expansion of the company that established a ferry link between the ports of Aqaba, Jordan, and Nuweibeh, Egypt, in 1985; cap. US $6m.; Chair. NABEEH AL-ABWAH.

CIVIL AVIATION

There are international airports near Baghdad, at Bamerni, and at Basra. Baghdad's Saddam International Airport reopened after postwar refurbishment in August 2000. However, international air links have been virtually halted by the UN embargo imposed in 1990. Internal flights, connecting Baghdad to Basra and Mosul, recommenced in November of that year. Civilian, as well as military, airports sustained heavy damage during the war with the multinational force in 1991.

National Co for Civil Aviation Services: al-Mansour, Baghdad; tel. (1) 551-9443; f. 1987 following the abolition of the State Organization for Civil Aviation; responsible for the provision of aircraft, and for airport and passenger services.

Iraqi Airways Co: Saddam International Airport, Baghdad; tel. (1) 887-2400; fax (1) 887-5808; f. 1948; Dir-Gen. AYAD ABD AL-KARIM HAMAM.

Tourism

In 2000 an estimated 78,457 tourists visited Iraq. Tourist receipts in 1998 were estimated at US $13m.

Iraq Tourism Board: Baghdad; e-mail iraqmail@uruklink.net; internet www.uruklink.net/tourism.

Defence

Defence Expenditure (2001): Estimated at US $1,400m.

Military service: 18 months–2 years.

Total armed forces (August 2001): Estimated at 424,000 (mostly conscripts): army 375,000 (incl. 100,000 recalled reserves); air force 30,000; navy 2,000; air defence command 17,000. Additionally, 42,000–44,000 in paramilitary forces; 650,000 reserves.

Commander-in-Chief of the Armed Forces: SADDAM HUSSAIN.

Chief of the General Staff: Gen. ABD AL-WAHHAB CHANNAN AR-RABBAT.

Commander of the Popular Army: TAHA YASSIN RAMADAN.

Commander of the Air Force: Lt-Gen. MUZAHIM SA'AB HASSAN.

Commander of the Air Defence Command: Lt-Gen. SHAHIN YASIN MUHAMMAD.

Commander of the Republican Guard: Maj.-Gen. KEMAL MUSTAFA AT-TIKRITI.

Education

After the establishment of the Republic in 1958, there was a marked expansion in education at all levels. Spending on education increased substantially after that time, reaching ID 211m. in the 1980 budget. During the mid-1970s free education was established at all stages from pre-primary to higher and private education was abolished; all existing private schools were transformed into state schools. Pre-school education was also expanding, although it had yet to reach more than a small proportion of children in this age-group. Primary education, lasting six years, was officially compulsory, and there were plans to extend full-time education to nine years as soon as possible. However, military conflict and economic sanctions during the 1980s and 1990s undermined much of the progress made in education during the previous two decades. Primary enrolment of children aged six to 11 reached 99% in 1980, but by 1995 enrolment included just 76% of students in the relevant age-group. At present, secondary education, which is expanding rapidly, is available for six years (two three-year cycles). In 1992 enrolment at secondary schools included 37% of students in the relevant age-group. A US $22m. a literacy campaign began during the 1978/79 academic year. There are 47 teacher-training institutes, 19 technical institutes and eight universities. In the 1991/92 academic year 46,250 students were reported to have enrolled in courses of higher education. Science, medical and engineering faculties of the universities have undergone considerable expansion, although technical training is less developed. Two branches of Baghdad University at Basra and Mosul became independent universities in 1967. The universities are situated in Baghdad, Basra, Mosul, Salah ad-Din (in Arbil), al-Mustansiriya (in Baghdad) and Tikrit. Preliminary designs of two new universities at Salah ad-Din and ar-Rashid have been completed, and in February 1988 plans were announced for a further four to be established in Tikrit, al-Kufa, Ramadi (in al-Anbar governorate) and Diwaniya (in al-Qadisiya governorate).

Bibliography

GENERAL

Al-Khalil, Samir. *The Monument: Art, Vulgarity and Responsibility in Iraq.* London, André Deutsch, 1991.

Litvak, Meir. *Shi'i Scholars of Nineteenth-Century Iraq: The Ulama of Najaf and Karbala.* Cambridge University Press, 1998.

Lloyd, Seton, F. H. *Iraq*: Oxford Pamphlet. Bombay, 1943.

   Twin Rivers: A Brief History of Iraq from the Earliest Times to the Present Day. Oxford, 1943.

   Foundations in the Dust. Oxford, 1949.

Longrigg, S. H., and Stoakes, F. *Iraq.* London, Ernest Benn, 1958.

Nakash, Yitzhak. *The Shi'is of Iraq.* Princeton, Princeton University Press, 1995.

Salter, Lord, assisted by Payton, S. W. *The Development of Iraq: A Plan of Action.* Baghdad, 1955.

Stark, Freya. *Baghdad Sketches.* London, John Murray, 1937.

Stewart, Desmond, and Haylock, John. *New Babylon: a Portrait of Iraq.* London, Collins, 1956.

RECENT HISTORY

Ali, Omar. *Crisis in The Arab Gulf: an independent Iraqi view.* London, The European Group, 1994.

Amnesty International. *Iraq: Victims of Systematic Repression.* London, 1999.

Anderson, Ewan W., and Rashidian, Khalil. *Iraq and the Continuing Middle East Crisis.* London, Printer Publishers, 1991.

Arburish, Said. *Saddam Hussein: the Politics of Revenge.* London, Bloomsbury, 2000.

Arnove, Anthony (Ed.). *Iraq Under Siege: The Deadly Impact of Sanctions and War.* London, Pluto Press, 2000.

Baram, Amatzia. *Culture, History and Ideology in the Formation of Baathist Iraq, 1968–89.* Basingstoke, Macmillan, 1991.

   Building towards Crisis: Saddam Hosayn's strategy for survival. Washington Institute for Near East Policy, 1998.

Batatu, Hanna. *The Old Social Classes and the Revolutionary Movements of Iraq.* Princeton University Press, 1978.

Bengio, Ofra. *Saddam's World: political discourse in Iraq.* Oxford, Oxford University Press, 1998.

Bennis, Phyllis, and Moushabeck, Michael (Eds). *Beyond the Storm: A Gulf Crisis Reader.* Edinburgh, Canongate Press, 1992.

Bséréni, Alice. *Chroniques de Baghdad 1997–99: la guerre qui n'avoue pas son nom.* Paris, L'Harmattan, 2000.

Butler, Richard. *Saddam Defiant: The Threat of Weapons of Mass Destruction, and the Growing Crisis of Global Security.* London, Weidenfeld & Nicolson, 2000.

Chubin, Shahram, and Tripp, Charles. *Iran and Iraq at War.* London, I. B. Tauris, 1988.

Cockburn, Andrew, and Cockburn, Patrick. *Out of the Ashes: the Resurrection of Saddam Hussein.* New York, HarperCollins, 1999.

   Saddam Hussein: An American Obsession. London, Verso, 2002.

Cordesman, Anthony H. *The Iran-Iraq War and Western Security 1984–87.* London, Jane's Publishing Company, 1987.

Cortright, David, Millar, Alistair, and Lopez, George A. (contributing Ed. Gerber, Linda). *Smart Sanctions: Restructuring UN Policy in Iraq.* Policy Brief Series, Notre Dame and Goshen, IN, Joan B. Kroc Institute for International Peace Studies and Fourth Freedom Forum, 2001.

Dann, Uriel. *Iraq under Qassem: A Political History 1958–63.* New York, Praeger, 1969.

Darwish, Adel, and Alexander, Gregory. *Unholy Babylon: the secret history of Saddam's war.* London, Gollancz, 1991.

Dauphin, Jacques. *Incertain Irak: Tableau d'un royaume avant la tempête.* Paris, Geuthner, 1993.

Farouk-Sluglett, Marion, and Sluglett, Peter. *Iraq since 1958: from Revolution to Dictatorship.* London, I. B. Tauris, revised edn, 2001.

Gallman, W. J. *Iraq under General Nuri.* Johns Hopkins Press, 1964.

Gittings, John (Ed.). *Beyond the Gulf War: The Middle East and the New World Order.* London, Catholic Institute for International Relations, 1991.

Graham-Brown, Sarah. *Sanctioning Saddam: The Politics of Intervention in Iraq.* Reading, Ithaca Press, 1999.

Haj, Samira. *The Making of Iraq, 1900–1963: Capital, Power and Ideology.* State University of New York Press, 1997.

Heikal, Mohammed. *Illusions of Triumph: An Arab View of the Gulf War.* London, HarperCollins, 1992.

Henderson, Simon. *Instant Empire: Saddam's Ambition for Iraq.* San Francisco, Mercury House, 1991.

Hiro, Dilip. *The Longest War: The Iran–Iraq Military Conflict.* London, Grafton, 1989.

   Desert Shield to Desert Storm: The Second Gulf War. London, Routledge, 1992.

   Neighbours, Not Friends: Iraq and Iran after the Gulf Wars. London, Routledge, 2001.

Iraq: A decade of devastation. Middle East Report no. 215. Vol. 30, no. 2. Summer 2000.

Ismael, Tareq Y. *Iran and Iraq: Roots of Conflict.* Syracuse, New York, Syracuse University Press, 1983.

Karsh, Efraim, and Ravtsi, Inari. *Saddam Hussein: A Political Biography.* London, Brasseys (UK), 1992.

Kent, Marian. *Oil and Empire: British Policy and Mesopotamian Oil, 1900–1920*. London, Macmillan, 1976.

Khadduri, Majid. *Independent Iraq 1932–58, A Study of Iraqi Politics*. 2nd edition, Oxford University Press, 1960.

Republican Iraq: *A study in Iraqi Politics since the Revolution of 1958*. Oxford University Press, 1970.

Socialist Iraq: *A Study in Iraqi Politics since 1968*. Washington, DC, The Middle East Institute, 1978.

and Ghareeb, Edmund. *War in the Gulf 1990–91*. New York, Oxford University Press, 1997.

Kienle, Eberhard. *Ba'th versus Ba'th: The Conflict between Iraq and Syria*. London, I. B. Tauris, 1990.

Korn, David A. *Human Rights in Iraq*. New Haven, CT, Yale University Press, 1990.

Leigh, David. *Betrayed*. London, Bloomsbury, 1993.

Longrigg, S. H. *Four Centuries of Modern Iraq*. Oxford, 1925.

Iraq 1900–1950: A Political, Social and Economic History. London, 1953.

Lowther, William. *Arms and the Man: Dr Gerald Bull, Iraq and the Supergun*. London, Macmillan, 1991.

MacArthur, Brian (Ed.). *Despatches from the Gulf War*. London, Bloomsbury, 1991.

MacKey, Sandra. *The Reckoning: Iraq and the Legacy of Saddam Hussein*. New York, W. W. Norton & Co, 2002.

Makiya, Kanan. *Republic of Fear: the politics of modern Iraq*, 2nd edition. Berkeley, University of California Press, 1998.

Marayati, Abid A. al-. *A Diplomatic History of Modern Iraq*. New York, Speller, 1961.

Mark, Phoebe. *The History of Modern Iraq*. London, Longman, 1983.

Mosallam, Mosallam Ali. *The Iraqi Invasion of Kuwait: Saddam Hussein, his State and International Politics*. London, I. B. Tauris, 1996.

Pelletiere, Stephen. *Iraq and the international oil system: why America went to war in the Gulf*. Westport, CT, and London, Praeger, 2001.

Penrose, Edith and E. F. *Iraq: International Relations and National Development*. Benn, Tonbridge, 1978.

Radi, Nuha ar-. *Baghdad Diaries*. London, Saqi Books, 1998.

Rahman, H. *The Making of the Gulf War: origins of Kuwait's long-standing territorial dispute with Iraq*. Ithaca Press, 1997.

Ritter, Scott. *Endgame: Solving the Iraq Problem—Once and For All*. New York, Simon & Schuster, 1999.

Salih, Khalid. *State-Making, Nation-Building and the Military: Iraq 1941–1958*. Göteborg University Press, 1996.

El-Sayed El-Shazly, Nadia. *The Gulf Tanker War: Iran and Iraq's Maritime Swordplay*. New York, St Martin's Press, 1998.

Schofield, R. *Kuwait and Iraq: Historical Claims and Territorial Disputes*. 2nd edition, London, Royal Institute of International Affairs, 1993.

Simpson, John. *From the House of War*. London, Hutchinson, 1991.

Sweeney, John. *Trading with the Enemy*. London, Pan Macmillan, 1993.

Timmerman, Kenneth R. *The Death Lobby*. London, Fourth Estate, 1992.

Tripp, Charles. *A History of Iraq*. Cambridge University Press, 2000.

Weller, Marc. *The Control and Monitoring of Iraqi Weaponry*. Cambridge University Press, 1995.

MINORITIES

Arfa, Hassan. *The Kurds*. Oxford, Oxford University Press, 1966.

Badger, G. P. *The Nestorians and their Rituals*. 2 vols, London, 1888.

Blunt, A. T. N. *Bedouin Tribes of the Euphrates*. 2 vols, London, 1879.

Cook, Helena. *The Safe Haven in Northern Iraq: International Responsibility for Iraqi Kurdistan*. Kurdistan Human Rights Project, 1995.

Damluji, S. *The Yezidis*. Baghdad, 1948 (in Arabic).

Drower, E. S. *Peacock Angel (Being some account of Votaries of a Secret Cult and their Sanctuaries)*. London, 1941.

The Mandeans of Iraq and Iran. Oxford, 1937.

Field, H. *Arabs of Central Iraq: Their History, Ethnology, and Physical Characters*. Chicago, 1935.

The Anthropology of Iraq. 4 vols, 1940, 1949, 1951, 1952, Chicago (first 2 vols), Cambridge, MA (last 2 vols).

Fuccaro, Nelida. *The other Kurds: Yazidis in colonial Iraq*. London and New York, I. B. Tauris, 1999.

Gat, Moshe. *The Jewish Exodus from Iraq 1948–1951*. London and Portland, OR, Frank Cass, 1997.

Kinnane, Dirk. *The Kurdish Problem*. Oxford, 1964.

The Kurds and Kurdistan. Oxford, 1965.

Luke, Sir H. C. *Mosul and its Minorities*. London, 1925.

McDowall, David. *A Modern History of the Kurds*. London, I. B. Tauris, 1995.

O'Ballance, Edgar. *The Kurdish Revolt 1961–1970*. London, Faber and Faber, 1974.

Randall, Johnathan. *After Such Knowledge What Forgiveness?* New York, Farrar, Straus and Giroux Inc, 1997.

Salim, S. M. *Marsh Dwellers of the Euphrates Delta*. New York, 1961.

Short, Martin, and McDermott, Anthony. *The Kurds*. London, Minority Rights Group, 1975.

Thesiger, Wilfred. *The Marsh Arabs*. London, 1964.

Van Bruinessen, Martin. *Agha, Sheikh and State. The Social and Political Structures of Kurdistan*. London, Zed Books, 1992.

ISRAEL

Physical and Social Geography

W. B. FISHER

The pre-1967 frontiers of Israel are defined by armistice agreements signed with neighbouring Arab states, and represent the stabilization of a military front as it existed in late 1948 and early 1949. These boundaries are thus, in many respects, fortuitous, and have little geographical basis. Indeed, prior to 1918, the whole area which is now partitioned between Syria, Israel, the Palestinian Autonomous Areas and Jordan formed part of the Ottoman Empire, and was spoken of as 'Syria'. Then, after 1918, came the establishment of the territories of Lebanon, Syria, Palestine and Transjordan—with the frontier between the last two lying, for the most part, along the Jordan river.

The present state of Israel is bounded on the north by Lebanon, on the north-east by Syria, on the east by Jordan and the Palestinian Autonomous Area in the West Bank, and on the south and south-west by the Gulf of Aqaba and the Sinai Desert, occupied in 1967 and returned in April 1982 to Egyptian sovereignty. The so-called 'Gaza Strip', a small piece of territory some 40 km long, formed part of Palestine but was, under the Armistice Agreement of February 1949, then left in Egyptian control. Since May 1994 the Gaza Strip has been under the limited jurisdiction of the Palestinian (National) Authority (PA) and will eventually—it is envisaged—form part of a single Palestinian entity, together with the Palestinian Autonomous Area in the West Bank. The territories which were occupied after the war of June 1967 are not recognized as forming part of the State of Israel, although it seems unlikely that Israel will reverse its annexation of the Old City of Jerusalem. The geographical descriptions of these territories are, therefore, given in the supplementary section at the end of the chapter.

Owing to the nature of the frontiers, which partition natural geographical units, it is more convenient to discuss the geography of Israel partly in association with that of its neighbour, Jordan. The Jordan Valley itself is dealt with in the chapter on Jordan, but the uplands of Samaria-Judaea, from Jenin to Hebron, and including Jerusalem, which form a single unit, will be discussed below, though parts of this territory lie outside the frontiers of Israel.

PHYSICAL FEATURES

The physical geography of Israel is surprisingly complex and, though the area of the state is small, a considerable number of regions are easily distinguished. In the extreme north the hills of the Lebanon range continue without break, though of lower altitude, to form the uplands of Galilee, where the maximum height is just over 1,200 m. The Galilee hills fall away steeply on three sides: on the east to the well-defined Jordan Valley (see Jordan), on the west to a narrow coastal plain, and on the south at the Vale of Esdraelon or 'Emek Yezreel'. This latter is a rather irregular trough formed by subsidence along faults, with a flat floor and steep sides, and it runs inland from the Mediterranean south-eastwards to reach the Jordan Valley. At its western end the vale opens into the wide Bay of Acre, 25 km–30 km in breadth, but it narrows inland to only a few km before opening out once again where it joins the Jordan Valley. This lowland area has a very fertile soil and an annual rainfall of 400 mm, which is sufficient, with limited irrigation, for agriculture. Formerly highly malarial and largely uncultivated, the vale is now very productive. For centuries it has been a corridor of major importance linking the Mediterranean coast and Egypt with the interior of south-west Asia, and has thus been a passageway for ethnic, cultural and military invasions.

South of Esdraelon there is an upland plateau extending for about 150 km. This is a broad upfold of rock, consisting mainly of limestone and reaching 900 m in altitude. In the north, where there is a moderate rainfall, the plateau has been eroded into valleys, some of which are fertile, though less so than those of Esdraelon or Galilee. This district, centred on Jenin and Nablus,

is the ancient country of Samaria, until 1967 part of Jordan. Further south rainfall is reduced and erosion is far less prominent; hence this second region, Judaea proper, stands out as a more strongly defined ridge, with far fewer streams and a barer open landscape of a more arid and dusty character. Jerusalem, Bethlehem and Hebron are the main towns. Towards the southeast rainfall becomes scarce and the Wilderness of Judaea, an area of semi-desert, unfolds. In the extreme south the height of the plateau begins to decline, passing finally into a second plateau only 300 m–450 m above sea-level, but broader, and broken by occasional ranges of hills that reach 900 m in height. This is the Negev, a territory comprising nearly one-half of the total area of Israel, and bounded on the east by the lower Jordan Valley and on the west by the Sinai Desert. Agriculture, entirely dependent on irrigation, is carried on in a few places in the north, but for the most part the Negev consists of steppe or semi-desert. Irrigation schemes have been developed in those areas where soils are productive.

Between the uplands of Samaria-Judaea and the Mediterranean Sea there occurs a low-lying coastal plain that stretches southwards from Haifa as far as the Egyptian frontier at Gaza. In the north the plain is closely hemmed in by the spur of Mount Carmel (550 m), which almost reaches the sea; but the plain soon opens out to form a fertile lowland—the Plain of Sharon. Still further south the plain becomes broader again, but with a more arid climate and a sandier soil—this is the ancient Philistia. Ultimately the plain becomes quite arid, with loose sand dunes, and it merges into the Sinai Desert.

One other area remains to be mentioned—the Shephelah, which is a shallow upland basin lying in the foothills of the Judaean plateau, just east of the Plain of Sharon. This region, distinguished by a fertile soil and moister climate, is heavily cultivated, chiefly in cereals.

CLIMATE

Climatically Israel has the typical 'Mediterranean' cycle of hot, dry summers, when the temperature reaches 32°C–38°C, and mild, rainy winters. Altitude has a considerable effect, in that although snow may fall on the hills, it is not frequent on the lowlands. Several inches of snow may fall in Jerusalem in winter, whereas Upper Galilee may receive several feet. The valleys, especially Esdraelon and adjacent parts of the upper Jordan, lying below sea-level, can become extremely hot (more than 40°C) and very humid.

Rainfall varies greatly from one part of Israel to another. Parts of Galilee receive over 1,000 mm annually, but the amount decreases rapidly southwards, until in the Negev and Plain of Gaza, it is 250 mm or less. This is because the prevailing southwesterly winds blow off the sea to reach the north of Israel, but further south they come from Egypt, with only a short sea track, and therefore lack moisture.

RACE AND LANGUAGE

Discussion of the racial affinities of the Jewish people has continued for many years, but there has been little agreement on the subject. One view is that the Jewish people, whatever their origin, have now taken on many of the characteristics of the peoples among whom they have lived since the Dispersal— e.g. the Jews of Germany were often quite similar in anthropological character to the Germans; the Jews of Iraq resembled the Arabs; and the Jews of Ethiopia had black skin. Upholders of such a view would largely deny the separateness of ethnic qualities amongst the Jews. On the other hand, it has been suggested that the Jews are really a particular and somewhat individual intermixture of racial strains that are found over wider areas of the Middle East: a special genetic 'mix' with ingredients by no means restricted to the Jews themselves. The correctness of either viewpoint is largely a matter of personal interpretation.

Under British mandatory rule there were three official languages in Palestine—Arabic, spoken by a majority of the inhabitants (all Arabs and a few Jews); Hebrew, the ancient language of the Jews; and English. This last was considered to be standard if doubt arose as to the meaning of translation from the other two. Since the establishment of the State of Israel the relative importance of the languages has changed. Hebrew is now dominant, Arabic has greatly declined following the flight of Arab refugees, and English is also less important, though it remains the first foreign language of many Israelis.

Hebrew, widely current in biblical days, was largely eclipsed after the dispersal of Jewish people by the Romans, and until fairly recently its use was largely restricted to scholarship, serious literature and religious observance. Most Jews of Eastern and Southern Europe did not employ Hebrew as their everyday speech, but spoke either Yiddish or Ladino, the former being a Jewish-German dialect current in East and Central Europe, and the latter a form of Spanish. Immigrants into Israel since 1890, however, have been encouraged to use Hebrew in normal everyday speech, and Hebrew is now the living tongue of most Israeli Jews. The revival has been a potent agent in the unification of the Israeli Jewish people since, in addition to the two widely different forms of speech, Yiddish and Ladino, most Jewish immigrants spoke yet another language according to their country of origin, and the census of 1931 recorded more than 60 such languages in common usage within Palestine. Now, as the proportion of native-born Israelis increases, Hebrew is dominant, and the use of other languages is diminishing.

It is only by a revival of Hebrew that the Jewish community has found a reasonable *modus vivendi*—yet this step was not easy, for some devout Jews opposed the use of Hebrew for secular speech. Furthermore, there was controversy as to the way Hebrew should be pronounced, although the Sephardic pronunciation was finally adopted.

History

TOM LITTLE

Revised for this edition by Nur Masalha

For most Jews, the creation of the State of Israel in 1948 was the fulfilment of Biblical prophecy; to some, in this more secular age, it is a state justifiably won by political skill and force of arms in a world that denied them one for nearly 2,000 years; but, however regarded, it is seen as the fulfilment of Jewish history.

Although clearly a more ancient people from east of the Euphrates, the Jews trace their descent from Abraham, the first of the Patriarchs, who departed from Ur, the centre of the ancient Chaldean civilization, about 2,000 years BC. Oral tradition, as recorded in the Old Testament, states that he was instructed by God to leave Chaldea with his family and proceed to Canaan (Phoenicia), or Palestine, the land of the Philistines, where he would father a great nation which would play an important part in human history. The authors of the Old Testament were primarily concerned to establish the descent of the Jewish people from Abraham under the guidance of God but, in so doing, they preserved the ancient history of the Jews which archaeology has tended to confirm within a debatable chronology.

Abraham's nomad family eventually reached Canaan and grazed their flocks there for a time before crossing Sinai to the richer pastures of Egypt. They remained in Egypt for about 400 years and multiplied greatly, but their separateness in race, religion and customs at last excited the fears of the pharaohs, who enslaved them. Moses, who had escaped this slavery because he was brought up as an Egyptian, fled with the Jews from the country (c. 1200 BC) and gave them his law (the Torah), proclaiming the absolute oneness of God and establishing the disciplines for worship. They wandered for some decades in the wilderness before reaching the Jordan river. Moses' successor, Joshua, led some of the families (or tribes) across the Jordan and conquered Canaan. It was a stormy occupation of constant conflict with the indigenous peoples until the warrior Saul triumphed and became the first 'king'. His successor, David, completed the subjugation of the Israelites' enemies and briefly united all the tribes. King Solomon, his son, raised the country to its peak and built the Temple of Jerusalem which came to be recognized as the temple of all the Jews and the focal point of worship. His magnificence burdened the people, and this and his tolerance of the worship of idols provoked a successful revolt of the 10 northern tribes under Jereboam who established Israel as his own kingdom. This division into two parts, Israel and Judah (which contained Jerusalem), was disastrous, for Israel was soon overcome by the Assyrians and its people were taken into captivity and lost to history. About 100 years later Judah fell victim to the Babylonians and its people were also taken captive, but their community endured to become an important element in the future of Judaism. The Babylonians destroyed Solomon's temple.

When the Persian leader Cyrus conquered Babylon he gave the Jews permission to return to Jerusalem, as some did. There they set about rebuilding the Temple, which was completed about 500 BC, and in 200 years of relative tranquillity their religion was consolidated by a series of great teachers. Palestine, in turn, was conquered by Alexander the Great, becoming (together with the Jews) part of his empire; but Alexander was tolerant, as were his successors in Egypt, the Ptolemies, and consequently Alexandria became the centre of a learned school of Hellenic Judaism.

This tolerant policy was reversed under the Roman Empire, which succeeded the Ptolemies. The Jews rebelled against the oppressive Roman rule and Nero sent his greatest general, Vespasian, and his son, Titus, to suppress them. The conquest was completed by Titus; Jerusalem and the second temple were destroyed (c. AD 70), and the Diaspora which began with the Assyrian conquest of Israel was complete. A small community of Jews remained in Jerusalem and the surrounding countryside, and devoted themselves to their religion, producing their version of the Talmud, the repository of Judaic history, learning and interpretation which, with the Torah and the Old Testament became the essence of the faith. However, it was the version of the Talmud produced by the Babylonian scholars which became the accepted document.

Scattered across the world, throughout Arabia, Asia as far as China, North Africa and Europe as far as Poland and Russia, Jewish communities continued to exist, sometimes powerful, often persecuted, but united by religion and certain central themes: their belief in the oneness of God, His promise to Abraham, the promise of the 'return', and the Temple as the temple of all Jews. The duration of Jewish occupation of Palestine was relatively short and for even less of that time did they hold or rule it all, but the scattered communities continued to look towards Jerusalem.

THE ZIONIST MOVEMENT

In the late 19th century there were affluent and even powerful groups of Jews in Europe, but the people as a whole were usually treated as second-class citizens in the countries where they lived. The large, pious and orthodox groups in Eastern Europe, in particular, were subject intermittently to persecution, and in 1881 there was a series of pogroms in Russia which stirred the conscience of world Jewry into forming plans for their escape. For the Eastern Jews there could be only one destination: Palestine. The pogroms led directly to the formation in Russia of a movement called the Lovers of Zion (Hovevei Zion), and within that movement another was formed, called the Bilu, by a large community of young Jews in the Kharkov region. In 1882 a Bilu group in Constantinople issued a manifesto demanding a home in Palestine. They proposed that they should beg it from the Sultan of Turkey, in whose empire Palestine lay.

The word Zionism was coined by a Russian about a decade later as a spiritual-humanitarian concept but Theodor Herzl, who became the leader of the movement, defined its aim specifically at the Basle Congress of 1897 (see Documents on Palestine, p. 50): 'Zionism', he said, 'strives to create for the Jewish people a home in Palestine secured by public law.' He wrote in his journal after the congress: 'At Basle I founded the Jewish State. . .perhaps in five years, and certainly fifty, everyone will know it.' Herzl is recognized as the founder of political Zionism.

Herzl was concerned essentially with the creation of a safe refuge for the suffering communities of Eastern Europe and thought that their migration and settlement could and should be financed by prosperous Jews. When he failed to get help from the Sultan he considered other possible 'homes' as far apart as Uganda and Latin America, but even safe places could never have the same appeal to orthodox Jews as Palestine, sanctioned in their scriptures and 'promised' to them by God. Some of the Jews of Russia and Poland escaped persecution to make their own way to Palestine and became the earliest immigrant communities there.

When the Turkish Empire was destroyed by Allied forces in the 1914–18 (First World) War, new possibilities of securing a 'home' or state in Palestine opened up before the Zionists. During 1915–16 Sir Mark Sykes for Britain and M. Charles Georges-Picot for France had, in fact, drafted an agreement (see Documents on Palestine, p. 50) in which, while undertaking 'to recognize and protect an independent Arab State or Confederation of Arab States', the two powers in effect carved the Middle East into their respective spheres of influence and authority pending the time of its liberation from Turkey. Influential Zionists, notably Dr Chaim Weizmann, saw their opportunity to press Britain for a commitment to provide a home for the Jews in Palestine and secured the help of Judge Louis Brandeis, a leading US Zionist and principal adviser to President Woodrow Wilson, in bringing the USA into the war on the side of the Allies in April 1917. The outcome was the Balfour Declaration (see Documents on Palestine, p. 51) which was contained in a letter from Arthur James Balfour to Lord Rothschild on behalf of the Zionist Federation, dated 2 November 1917. It stated:

'His Majesty's Government view with favour the establishment in Palestine of a national home for the Jewish people, and will use their best endeavours to facilitate the achievement of this object, it being clearly understood that nothing shall be done which may prejudice the existing civil and religious rights of existing non-Jewish communities in Palestine, or the rights and political status of Jews in other countries.'

The San Remo Conference decided on 24 April 1920 to give the Mandate under the newly formed League of Nations to Britain (the terms of which were approved by the USA, which was not a member of the League, before they were finally agreed by the League Council on 24 July 1922). The terms (see Documents on Palestine, p. 53) included a restatement of the Balfour Declaration and provided that 'an appropriate Jewish agency' should be established to advise and co-operate with the Palestine Administration in matters affecting the Jewish national home and to take part in the development of the country. This gave the Zionist Organization a special position because the Mandate stipulated that it should be recognized as such an agency if the mandatory authority thought it appropriate. Britain took over the Mandate in September 1923.

THE MANDATE

Herzl's first aim had thereby been achieved: the national home of the Jewish people had been 'secured by public law'; but major obstacles were still to be overcome before the home, or state, became a reality. When the Mandate was granted, the Arabs constituted 92% of the population and owned 98% of the land

in Palestine, and it could clearly not be a home unless the demography and land ownership were changed in favour of the Jews. It was to these ends that the Zionist movement now directed itself, but Britain had different views concerning what was meant by 'favouring' the establishment of the home, both in the matter of boundaries and immigration, even while it remained sympathetic to the enterprise. This was important, for although nominally under the supervision of the Mandates Commission of the League, Britain was able to run Palestine very much as a Crown Colony and administered it through the Colonial Office.

The World Zionist Organization had presented a memorandum to the Paris Peace Conference in 1919 setting forth its territorial concept of the home, as follows:

The whole of Palestine, southern Lebanon, including the towns of Tyre and Sidon, the headwaters of the Jordan river on Mount Hermon and the southern portion of the Litani river; the Golan Heights in Syria, including the town of Quneitra, the Yarmouk river and al-Himmeh hot springs; the whole of the Jordan valley, the Dead Sea, and the eastern highlands up to the outskirts of Amman, thence in a southerly direction along the Hedjaz railway to the Gulf of Aqaba; in Egypt, from el-Arish, on the Mediterranean coast, in a straight line in a southerly direction to Sharm esh-Sheikh on the Gulf of Aqaba.

The League of Nations and the Peace Settlement did not accept these boundaries but the Mandate given to Britain included Transjordan, the territory east of the river and beyond Amman. Britain allotted Transjordan as an Emirate to Emir Abdullah in 1921 and with the grant of full independence in 1946 it became a kingdom.

The Arabs bitterly opposed the Balfour Declaration and Jewish immigration, and advocated the prohibition of land sales to Jews. Britain would neither accede to their demands nor to Jewish claims to a majority in Palestine. There were intermittent outbreaks of Arab violence, notably in 1922 and 1929, which brought the Arabs into conflict with the mandatory government. Four British Commissions of Inquiry were established and two White Papers were issued (see Documents on Palestine, pp. 53–54) on the situation before 1936, none of which envisaged a Jewish majority. In 1936 there was an effective six-month general strike of the Arab population followed by a large-scale rebellion which lasted until the outbreak of the Second World War, and in 1939 another Commission issued the third White Paper (see Documents on Palestine, p. 55) which stated that Britain would not continue to develop the Jewish national home beyond the point already reached and proposed that 75,000 more Jews should be admitted over five years after which time Jewish immigration would cease. Finally, it proposed that self-governing institutions should be established at the end of the five years. This would have preserved the Arab majority in the country and its legislature.

THE BILTMORE PROGRAMME AND AFTER

International opinion at that time was conditioned by the horrifying Nazi policy of exterminating Jews—a practice which was to reach even more frightful proportions after the outbreak of war. Zionists and Jews generally regarded the White Paper as a betrayal of the terms of the Mandate. During a visit to New York in 1942 by David Ben-Gurion, Chairman of the Jewish Agency Executive, an Extraordinary Zionist Conference was held at the Biltmore Hotel, which utterly rejected the White Paper and reformulated Zionist policy. The declaration of the conference (see Documents on Palestine, p. 56), issued on 11 May 1942, concluded as follows:

The conference urges that the gates of Palestine be opened; that the Jewish Agency be vested with control of immigration into Palestine and with the necessary authority for upbuilding the country, including the development of its unoccupied and uncultivated lands; and that Palestine be established as a Jewish Commonwealth integrated into the new structure of the democratic world.

This policy brought the Jews into direct conflict with the Palestine Government before the war was over. Those in Europe who escaped the Nazi holocaust were herded into refugee camps and some, with organized Zionist help, tried to reach Palestine, but the British authorities, in accordance with the 1939 policy, attempted to prevent their entry.

The British failed, however. The Jewish population which had been 56,000 at the time of the Mandate was 608,000 in 1946 and was estimated to be 650,000 on the eve of the creation of Israel, or about two-fifths of the entire population. Furthermore, the Jewish Agency had formed its own military organizations, the Haganah, and its units of shock troops, the Palmach, which were strengthened by those Jews who had fought on the side of the British during the war, and supported by two smaller extremist groups, the Irgun Zvaei Leumi and the Stern Gang. Towards the end of the war they embarked on a policy of violence designed to impose the Biltmore programme. They successfully made the Mandate unworkable and Britain referred it to the United Nations (which had replaced the League) on 2 April 1947.

The UN General Assembly sent a Special Commission (UNSCOP) to Palestine to report on the situation, and its report, issued on 31 August 1947, proposed two plans: a majority plan for the partition of Palestine into two states, one Jewish and one Arab, with economic union; and a minority plan for a federal state. The Assembly adopted the majority plan (see Documents on Palestine, p. 56) on 29 November by 33 votes for and 13 against, with 10 abstentions. The plan divided Palestine into six principal parts, three of which, comprising 56% of the total area, were reserved for the Jewish state, and three (with the enclave of Jaffa), comprising 43% of the area, for the Arab state. It provided that Jerusalem would be an international zone administered by the UN as the holy city for Jews, Muslims and Christians. The Arabs refused to accept this decision and, in the subsequent disorders, about 1,700 people were killed. In April 1948 the Jewish forces launched a full-scale attack and, by the time the Mandate was terminated on 14 May, 400,000 Arabs had evacuated their homes to become refugees in neighbouring Arab countries.

THE STATE ESTABLISHED

The Mandate was relinquished by Britain at 6 p.m. Washington time; at 6.01 p.m. the State of Israel was officially declared by the Jewish authorities in Palestine; at 6.11 p.m. the USA accorded it recognition and immediately afterwards the USSR did likewise. Thus Israel came into existence only one year later than Herzl's 50-year diary prophecy. The Arab states belatedly came to the help of the Palestinian Arabs, but their attempt to overthrow the new state failed and Israel was left in possession of more territory than had been allotted to it under the UN partition plan, including new (non-Arab) Jerusalem. Israel rejected the proposed internationalization of the city, for the Jews considered the return to Jerusalem to be central to their divine legacy.

A provisional government was formed in Tel-Aviv the day before the Mandate ended, with Ben-Gurion as Prime Minister and other members of the Jewish Agency Executive in leading ministerial posts. The Constitution and electoral laws had already been prepared and the first general elections were held in January 1949 for a single-chamber Knesset (or Parliament) elected by proportional representation. This enabled several parties to gain representation, with Ben-Gurion's Labour Party (Mapai) usually in the majority but never predominant. As a result, government has usually been conducted by uneasy coalitions.

After the war another 400,000 Arabs fled from the additional territory conquered by Israel and in the course of another year about 300,000 more left the impoverished Arab West Bank for Transjordan. (In 1950 Abdullah held a referendum in which the West Bank Arabs agreed to be part of his kingdom which then became known as Jordan.) The Israeli Government maintained the mandatory military control, established in the earlier unrest, over those Arab populations which remained within its territory but allowed 'co-operative' Arabs to be elected to the Knesset; four were elected to the first Parliament.

A gigantic programme of immigration was launched immediately after the Provisional Government took over and within three years the Jewish population was doubled. This result, unparalleled in history, was assisted by Iraq which expelled the larger part of its age-old Jewish communities. The 1961 census recorded Israel's population at 2,260,700, of whom 230,000 were Arabs. The two-millionth Jew arrived in May 1962 and the

three-millionth early in 1972. A massive plan for land development to provide for the immigrants was executed concomitantly with the early immigration programme; the Jewish National Fund took over 3m. dunums of former Arab land and used heavy mechanical equipment to bring it rapidly back into production. This was made possible by the massive support from abroad which came in the form of private gifts from world Jewry, state loans and aid, and private Jewish investments. The USA was both privately and publicly the major contributor, but following negotiations conducted between the Conference on Jewish Material Claims and the Israeli and West German authorities at The Hague (the Netherlands) in 1952, the Federal Republic of Germany agreed to pay reparations for Nazi crimes. These payments amounted to £216m. in Deutsche Marks before they were concluded in 1966. One effect of this influx of unearned money from all sources was to cause serious inflation, which was still a problem in the 1990s (see Economy).

Israel was admitted to the UN, albeit on conditions concerning Jerusalem and refugees which were contrary to its overall policy and were never fulfilled. Its relations with the Arab states were governed by a series of armistice agreements reached in Rhodes in 1949 which, in effect, established an uneasy truce without an Arab commitment to permanent peace. The Arabs continued to insist that the creation of Israel was a usurpation of Arab territory and rights and a denial of UN principles. Defence policy therefore dominated Israel's political thinking and firmly established the principle that it would remain militarily superior to any combination of Arab states. In the early 1950s, however, it was the Palestinian refugees who caused intermittent frontier trouble, mainly from Syria and Jordan, but to some extent from the Gaza Strip which, since the 1948 war, had been administered by Egypt.

Whenever one of the frontiers became too troublesome, Israel mounted a retaliatory raid *pour décourager les autres*. Acting on the principle that Nasser's Egypt was the only serious danger, Ben-Gurion ordered a raid which, on 28 February 1955, annihilated the small Egyptian garrison at Gaza and the reinforcements travelling by road to its support. The result was contrary to Ben-Gurion's intention: Nasser determined to secure adequate military strength and to that end entered into the 'Czech' arms agreement in August, by which he bartered cotton and took credits from the USSR for substantial quantities of arms and aircraft which began to arrive promptly. The threat to Israel was therefore increased.

SUEZ

On 26 July 1956 Nasser nationalized the Suez Canal Co of which Britain and France were the principal shareholders (see the chapter on Egypt) and the two European powers prepared to retake control of it. Neither could expect any support from the two 'superpowers', or from world opinion in general, for open invasion, but in October Ben-Gurion entered into a secret pact with them by which Israel would invade Sinai and thus justify Britain and France intervening to keep the combatants apart. Israel invaded on 29 October and rapidly advanced towards the Canal. The following day Britain and France issued their ultimatum that both sides should withdraw to 20 miles from the Canal. Israel, which had by this time taken almost all of the Sinai, including the Gaza Strip and Sharm esh-Sheikh at the entrance to the Gulf of Aqaba, readily agreed to comply with the ultimatum, but Egypt refused on the grounds that it was being asked to withdraw from its own territory.

The Anglo-French force thereupon invaded the Port Said area and advanced some miles along the Suez Canal. There it was halted by Sir Anthony Eden, the British Prime Minister, in face of the forthright condemnation of the UN and financial sanctions threatened by the USA; a decision which the French Prime Minister, Guy Mollet, reluctantly accepted. Both countries had withdrawn their troops by the end of 1956. This was a severe blow to Ben-Gurion, who had counted on holding at least a security buffer zone on a line from el-Arish, on the Mediterranean coast, to Sharm esh-Sheikh (the Zionist 1919 frontier proposal). Therefore Israel delayed its final withdrawal from Egypt until January 1957, and from the Gaza Strip until March, when a UN Emergency Force was safely established on the Sinai frontier and at Sharm esh-Sheikh.

A development of great consequence to Israel at this time was the increasing involvement of the Soviet Union in the Middle East, especially in Egypt. The USSR took no less than 50% of Egyptian exports in 1957, and in 1958 agreed to finance and direct the building of the huge High Dam at Aswan. In keeping with this policy, the Soviet Union adopted a strongly pro-Arab and anti-Israeli line and steadily rearmed Nasser's forces.

Ben-Gurion resigned, to pursue non-political ambitions, in June 1963 and was succeeded by Levi Eshkol, the Minister of Finance, who had been a minister continuously since joining the Provisional Government from the Jewish Agency in 1948. He was politically inclined to a more conciliatory policy which he hoped would in time erode Arab enmity. This was opposed by many in the ruling hierarchy, notably the veteran Ben-Gurion and Gen. Moshe Dayan, who had commanded the Israeli forces in their brilliant victory of 1956.

There was a notable increase in Arab guerrilla activity across the frontiers with Egypt, Jordan and Syria in the mid-1960s. The Palestinians formed a guerrilla organization called Fatah, for which the Syrian Prime Minister publicly declared his support in 1966. Mutual accusations of frontier violations followed, and President Nasser warned that he would have to activate the Egypt-Syrian Joint Defence Agreement if Israel's 'aggression' did not cease. In May 1967 King Hussein brought Jordan into the agreement and in that same month Nasser received information, which later proved to be unfounded, that Israeli troops were massing on the Syrian frontier. In response Nasser ordered the withdrawal of the UN Emergency Force from the Gaza Strip, the Sinai Desert and Sharm esh-Sheikh. U Thant, the Secretary-General of the UN, immediately complied, and Nasser then imposed a total blockade on Israeli shipping in the Straits of Tiran, although Israel had always made it plain that this would be considered a *casus belli*.

U Thant flew to Cairo on 22 May 1967 but, by that time, Nasser had already strengthened his forces in the Sinai and summoned his reserves. Israel, Jordan and Syria had also mobilized. Israel formed a national government, introducing to the Cabinet one representative of each of the three opposition parties. Gen. Moshe Dayan, the leader of the 1956 Sinai campaign, was appointed Minister of Defence.

THE JUNE WAR

Israel made its pre-emptive strike in the early hours of 5 June 1967 when its armoured forces moved into Sinai. Israeli planes attacked 25 airfields in Egypt, Jordan, Syria and Iraq, destroying large numbers of aircraft on the ground and disabling the runways, thus effectively depriving the Egyptian and Jordanian ground forces of air cover. There were some fierce armoured battles in the Sinai but Israeli forces were in position along the Suez Canal on 8 June: they took Sharm esh-Sheikh without armed opposition. On the eastern front, they reached the Jordan river on 7 June and entered and conquered Old (Arab) Jerusalem on the same day. Their main forces destroyed, President Nasser and King Hussein accepted a cease-fire on 8 June. Israel then turned its attention to the Syrian fortifications on the Golan Heights from which Israeli settlements were being shelled. In a brilliant but costly action, armour and infantry captured the heights. Syria accepted a cease-fire on 9 June but Israel ignored it until 10 June, by which time its troops were in possession of Quneitra, on the road to Damascus. The 'Six-Day War', as it became known, was over; Israel had achieved a victory more sweeping even than that of 1956.

Israel had recovered Jerusalem and access to the Western Wall of the Temples of Solomon and Herod, which were the most sacred places of worship for all Jews but to which they had been denied access since the partition of the city between the Arabs and Israel in 1948. Israel immediately tore down the barriers, reunited the city, brought the administration of Arab Jerusalem under its existing city administration, and effectively annexed it. The UN General Assembly passed a resolution on 4 July 1967 (which Israel disregarded), urging the Israeli authorities to rescind all the measures taken and to desist from any further action that would change the status of the holy city. Israel asserted from the outset that it would not countenance the return of Old Jerusalem to Arab possession in any peace settlement.

The UN and the world powers busied themselves with the peace process. On 29 August 1967 the heads of the Arab states began a summit conference in Khartoum at which they decided to seek a political settlement but not to make peace with or recognize Israel, nor to negotiate directly with it, and meanwhile 'to adopt necessary measures to strengthen military preparation to face all eventualities'. On 22 November, after many attempts, the UN Security Council agreed to Resolution 242, which stated that the establishment of a just and lasting peace in the Middle East should include the application of the following principles:

(i) withdrawal of Israeli armed forces from territories occupied in the recent conflict; and (ii) termination of all claims or states of belligerency and respect for and acknowledgement of the sovereignty, territorial integrity, and political independence of every State in the area, and their right to live in peace within secure and recognized boundaries free from threats or acts of force. The Council affirmed also the necessity for (a) guaranteeing freedom of navigation through international waterways in the area, and (b) achieving a just settlement of the refugee problem.

The UN Secretary-General designated Ambassador Gunnar Jarring of Sweden as Special Representative to assist the process of finding a peaceful settlement on this basis.

The essential ambiguity of the Resolution was contained in the phrase 'withdrawal...from territories occupied...' (which in the French translation became 'les territoires'), and the Israeli Government contended that it meant an agreed withdrawal from some occupied territories 'to secure and recognized boundaries'. This was, in Israel's view, precluded by the Arab states' Khartoum Resolution and their insistence that Resolution 242 meant total withdrawal from the territories occupied in 1967. Furthermore, Israel insisted that it would only negotiate withdrawal directly with Egypt and the Arab states as part of a peace settlement and that the function of Jarring was to bring this about and not to initiate proposals of his own for a settlement.

UNEASY SECURITY

Meanwhile, Israel based its policy on retention of the Occupied Territories as warranty for its security. The 1967 defeat had severely damaged the USSR's prestige in the Arab world, and to repair its position it began immediately to restore the Egyptian armed forces, including the air force. In that year French President Charles de Gaulle imposed an arms embargo on Israel and refused to deliver 50 supersonic *Mirage* IV fighters which Israel had ordered and paid for. Israel therefore turned to the USA, arguing that the balance of military power must, for its security, be maintained in its favour. This point was conceded by the USA in 1968 with a contract to deliver 50 *Phantom* jet fighter-bombers, which brought Cairo within range and were more powerful than any MiG aircraft in Egypt.

Using powerful artillery installed by the USSR west of the Canal, Nasser began in 1968 a 'war of attrition' in order to force Israel to accept his terms. Relatively heavy casualties were inflicted on the Israeli troops, notably in July and October, and throughout the period Israel retaliated with air and artillery attacks which forced Egypt to evacuate the Canal zone towns. Suez and its oil refineries were destroyed. The zone remained unsettled until 1970.

Israel's Prime Minister, Levi Eshkol, died on 26 February 1969, and was succeeded in the following month by Mrs Golda Meir, who had been Minister for Foreign Affairs from 1956 to 1966.

President Nixon, who had taken office in the USA, supported an initiative by his Secretary of State, William Rogers, 'to encourage the parties to stop shooting and start talking'. This was announced on 25 June 1970, and was unfavourably received in the Arab world. Nasser flew to Moscow with a proposal to accept it on condition that Russia supplied SAM-III missiles capable of destroying low-flying aircraft. He returned to Cairo and stunned Egypt and the Arab world with an unconditional acceptance of the Rogers plan and its related Canal zone 90-day cease-fire. King Hussein immediately associated Jordan with Nasser's acceptance. Israel accepted the Rogers plan on 7 August, but immediately complained that Egypt had broken the cease-fire agreement by moving SAM-III missile sites into the 30-mile wide 'standstill' area along the canal.

President Nasser died suddenly on 28 September 1970, but President Sadat, who succeeded him, sustained his policy. Although he only agreed to extend the cease-fire for another 90 days, it continued indefinitely. The US effort was directed towards securing an interim agreement by which Israel would withdraw from the Suez Canal and allow it to be reopened. However, Israel, again on the basic principle of its security, would only consider a limited withdrawal and would not agree that Egyptian troops should cross the Canal, terms which Egypt refused. US–Israeli relations, vital to Israel, were uneasy during most of 1971 while the Department of State pressed the Israeli Government to concede unacceptable terms of withdrawal from the Canal. President Sadat gave the end of the year as a deadline for 'peace or war', but before the year was over Mrs Golda Meir secured a commitment to Israeli security from President Nixon firmer than any obtained in the past; the Rogers plan was thereby abandoned, but 1972 began without the threatened outbreak of war with Egypt. Instead, there was a series of terrorist acts by various Palestinian groups, which in turn provoked punitive raids by Israeli forces.

The stated objective of Israeli raids on Syria and Lebanon was to compel both countries to prevent the Palestinian resistance groups from mounting raids from within their borders, whether against Israel or in other countries. This objective seemed most successfully achieved in Lebanon on 10 April 1973 by a daring commando raid into the heart of Beirut, where the raiders killed three resistance leaders, while other commando units attacked two refugee camps outside the city and destroyed the head-quarters of the Popular Democratic Front for the Liberation of Palestine, killing one of its leaders. The Israeli authorities were able to make a number of arrests in the Occupied Territories from information gained in this raid.

THE OCCUPIED TERRITORIES

About 380,000 Arabs fled from the West Bank to Jordan, but nearly one million remained under Israeli occupation; of these, the 70,000 in East (Arab) Jerusalem, which was annexed, were treated as Israeli citizens and the remainder brought under military administration. This was of necessity strict for the first three years because of help given to Palestinian guerrillas by the Arabs in the Occupied Territories and, in some instances, in Israel proper. The Gaza Strip was by far the most troublesome and it was not until the end of 1971 that Israeli security operations, including the clearance of one large refugee camp which had proved particularly difficult, brought the area under control. It was announced in March 1973 that the strip would be incorporated into Israel, that Jewish settlement there would continue and that Arab inhabitants could circulate freely in Israel during the day. Higher living standards enjoyed by the Arabs under occupation, 60,000 of whom found work in Israel itself, the inevitable growth of collaboration with the Israeli authorities and, finally, the disarray in which the Palestinian movement found itself by late 1970, rendered the security problem inside the country minimal during 1971. In March 1972 the Israeli military authorities successfully held elections for the mayors and municipalities in the main Arab towns, despite guerrilla threats of reprisals against any Arabs taking part.

Government policy was officially that in a peace settlement substantial territories would be returned to the Arabs, but there was no clear consensus in the Government or the country as to what they would amount to, except to the extent that Israel should have 'secure frontiers'. However, statements by ministers emphasized that in addition to East Jerusalem and the Gaza Strip, which had been effectively annexed, the Golan Heights of occupied Syria and parts of the Jordanian West Bank would not be returned. There was also increasing evidence on the ground. An extensive building programme to house immigrants was rapidly being executed in and around Jerusalem; 42 settlements had been established by January 1973 although, according to Israeli figures, only 3,150 Israeli civilians had been allowed to take up permanent residence in the areas.

Israel radio announced on 18 August 1973 that another 35 settlements would be built in the Occupied Territories, bringing the total to 77. The Jewish National Fund and the Israeli Lands Administration had between them acquired 15,000 acres (6,070 ha) of Arab land and the army was in occupation of another 20,000 acres (8,100 ha). A plan advanced by Deputy Prime Minister Yigal Allon, although not publicly approved by the Government, seemed to be in the process of *de facto* execution. He proposed that a chain of Israeli settlements should be established along the Jordan river (which was effectively being done), a second chain along the Samarian hills on the West Bank, and a third along the road from Jerusalem to Jericho, in order to establish Israel's security. The rest of the West Bank and the main towns, except Jericho, would then be returned to Jordan.

The virtue of the Allon plan for most Israelis was that it would absorb few Arabs, for the core of the dispute within Israel remained the question of demographic balance between Arabs and Jews which would be changed in the Arabs' favour by the absorption of territory in which many of them were resident. For that reason, the Government refused the request, submitted by the newly-elected mayors of the Arab towns on the West Bank, that those Arabs who had fled the area after the 1967 war should be allowed to return. To restore the population balance the Jewish Agency, which was responsible for organizing immigration, concentrated upon Jews in the USSR, who were the largest reservoir of would-be immigrants. The USSR began to relax its stringent opposition to Jewish emigration in 1971, with the result that thousands of Soviet Jews began to arrive in Israel.

THE YOM KIPPUR WAR

Although the Arab world had been urging Sadat to attack Israel, it was firmly believed that Egypt was afraid to go to war again and that the Bar-Lev defences along the eastern bank of the Suez Canal could not be overcome. In fact Sadat was working steadily towards war, against the advice of his Soviet ally. He secured the financial support of King Faisal of Saudi Arabia to buy arms for hard currency, the agreement of Syria's President Hafiz al-Assad to a limited war for the recovery of territories lost in 1967, made his peace with King Hussein of Jordan and finally secured the arms required from the USSR.

At 2 p.m. on 6 October 1973—the most important religious festival in Israel, Yom Kippur (the Day of Atonement)—the Egyptians launched their attack, demolishing the supposedly impregnable sand banks of the Bar-Lev line with powerful water-jets, throwing pontoon bridges across the Suez Canal and breaking into Sinai. By midnight that day, the Egyptians had 500 tanks and missiles across the Canal and destroyed 100 Israeli tanks. Almost simultaneously the Syrian armed forces had broken through the Israeli lines on the Golan Heights.

Israel began the rapid mobilization of its reserve forces, the highly trained and numerically most important part of its defensive system, but before they could play an effective part Egyptian armed forces had occupied the east bank of the Canal to a depth of several miles and by the third day were advancing to the strategic Mitla pass in Sinai. The Syrian forces had by that time reached a point five miles from the Israeli frontier in Golan.

While fierce tank battles, said to be bigger than any in the Second World War, raged in Sinai, Israel halted the Syrian forces on its vulnerable northern frontier and counter-attacked successfully, driving them in a fighting retreat back over the 1967 cease-fire lines to within 20 miles of Damascus, where its forces were halted on the Syrian second line of defence. The Egyptian forces held their positions in Sinai but did not reach the Mitla pass.

The Egyptian High Command blundered on the twelfth day when it allowed a small Israeli commando force to cross to the west bank of the Suez Canal near Deversoir at the northern end of the Great Bitter Lake. The Israeli force was able to reinforce the bridgehead with a force strong enough to swing southwards to Suez and endanger the Egyptian Third Army on the east bank. Losses were very heavy on both sides.

After three UN Security Council resolutions, a precarious cease-fire came into effect on 25 October 1973, but even this was honoured more in the breach than the observance until the end of the year. The US Secretary of State, Dr Henry Kissinger, did much to maintain a peace-making momentum by touring the Arab countries to secure negotiations for a permanent settlement in Geneva on 18 December, and in November Israel had accepted 'in principle' the terms of an agreement Dr Kissinger had reached with President Sadat for the 'scrupulous' observance of the cease-fire.

Talks were soon adjourned to an unspecified date in order to allow time for the Israeli general elections, which had been postponed from 30 October to 31 December 1973 because of the war. Kissinger returned to the Middle East in January 1974 and after days of intensive diplomatic activity, shuttling back and forth between Israel and Egypt, he secured the agreement of both countries to a disengagement of their forces which was signed on 18 January (see Documents on Palestine, p. 61). Israel agreed to withdraw its troops in Sinai to a line approximately 20 miles from the Suez Canal and Egypt to reduce its forces on the east bank. There was to be a neutral buffer zone between the two armies manned by troops of the UN Emergency Force.

Agreement for the disengagement of forces on the northern front was not signed until 31 May 1974 (see Documents on Palestine, p. 61) and then only after further shuttle diplomacy by Dr Kissinger. Israel and Syria agreed to withdraw their troops to lines on each side of the 1967 cease-fire line, and the ruined town of Quneitra, capital of the Golan Heights, was handed back to Syria.

Two important factors weakened Israel's position. In the last days of the war the Arab oil-producing states banned the supply of oil to the USA and the Netherlands, and reduced supplies to Western Europe. (Britain and France were exempted but, in fact, were unable to obtain their full supplies.) This, combined with steep increases in oil prices which caused serious balance-of-payments problems for the European countries—although this had nothing to do with the war—led the EC to issue a joint declaration in the Arab favour. Even more damaging to Israel was the confrontation which almost developed between the USSR and the USA when they both began delivering heavy supplies of war equipment to the Arabs and Israel respectively. Dr Kissinger emphasized to Israel that the USA would continue to support Israel, but only within the limits imposed by *détente* with the USSR. President Nixon went on a peace-making mission to the Middle East in June 1974, and shortly afterwards Israel's Minister of Finance, Shimon Peres, visited Washington. The outcome was the conversion of a $500m. loan into a gift and an undertaking to supply a powerful fleet of fighter aircraft to ensure Israel's security.

THE AFTERMATH

The war had a profoundly disturbing effect on Israeli public opinion. The country had never suffered such losses before: nearly 3,000 dead and missing. The ease with which the Egyptian forces had crossed the Canal and overrun the Bar-Lev line and the firmness with which the Syrian forces held the second line of defence 20 miles from Damascus were not offset in Israeli eyes by the fact that Israeli troops had broken through and recrossed the Canal and had made territorial gains in Syria. The public's confidence in the overwhelming superiority of their own army and air force was severely shaken, with the result that a sharp division of opinion occurred between those who thought the war emphasized the need to keep defensible frontiers at all costs and those, less numerous, who viewed it as an argument for a more diligent search for a permanent peace. There was widespread dissatisfaction with the Government and a public debate ensued over the failure to anticipate the outbreak of war and the breakdown of military intelligence. There were mutual recriminations among the generals and the Minister of Defence Moshe Dayan's popularity in the country slumped. General Ariel Sharon, whose forces had made the breakthrough and Canal crossing in Egypt, resigned from the army to join the right-wing Likud party.

The elections of December 1973 reflected this confusion. The Labour Alignment, led by the United Workers' Party (Mapam), emerged as the strongest party, with 51 seats. Likud, the main opposition, made substantial gains and won 39 seats. Mrs Golda Meir reformed her coalition but resigned in April 1974, when the report on the 1973 war was published. She was succeeded in June by Gen. Itzhak Rabin, whose Cabinet contained neither Moshe Dayan nor Abba Eban, who had been Minister of Foreign Affairs since 1966. General Rabin and his Minister of Foreign Affairs, Yigal Allon, were both willing to make territorial sacrifices to achieve a settlement with the Arabs, and in September 1975 Israel and Egypt signed a second disengagement agreement, whereby Israeli forces withdrew from some territory in the Sinai peninsula.

Meanwhile, the Palestine Liberation Organization (PLO) had achieved recognition by the Arabs as 'sole representative of the Palestinian people' at the Rabat summit of November 1974, but Rabin asserted Israeli policy, which he was to maintain throughout his premiership, of refusing to recognize a PLO delegation at any renewed Geneva peace talks.

Rabin was never able to command the support that he needed as Prime Minister. Moreover, Israel's economic difficulties cost Rabin considerable popularity, and it seemed that the austerity measures that he was forced to introduce to combat inflation were hugely unpopular, discouraged immigration, and made little visible progress towards a sounder economy.

In December 1976 the National Religious Party (NRP) abstained in a 'confidence' vote in the Knesset arising from charges that the Sabbath had been desecrated at a ceremony marking the arrival of three US aircraft. Rabin subsequently dismissed two NRP ministers from the Cabinet, and the consequent withdrawal of NRP support left the Government in a minority in the Knesset, thus precipitating Rabin's resignation. After continuing in a caretaker capacity until the election of May 1977, in April of that year Rabin resigned as leader of the Labour Party. On 10 April the Labour Party selected Shimon Peres as its new leader (Peres having been narrowly defeated by Rabin in the February poll for the party leadership).

ISRAEL UNDER BEGIN

When the elections for the ninth Knesset took place on 17 May 1977, the result was a surprise victory for the Likud party, under Menachem Begin, who won 43 of the 120 seats—the largest single total. The Likud victory removed the Labour Party from the predominant position it had held in Israel since 1949. With the support of the NRP, Agudat Israel (the Union of Israel) and Ariel Sharon's Realization of Zion (Shlomzion), Begin was able to form a Government on 19 June 1977, and his position was strengthened in October when the Democratic Movement for Change (DMC) joined the Likud coalition. In September 1978, however, the DMC split into two factions, with seven Knesset members leaving Begin's coalition because they felt that his plans for building further Israeli settlements on the West Bank were endangering prospects for peace.

A permanent peace settlement suddenly seemed possible when President Sadat of Egypt visited Jerusalem in November 1977 and addressed the Knesset. Talks between Sadat and Begin continued, and finally an unexpected breakthrough occurred in September 1978 after talks at Camp David, USA, under the guidance of President Carter, when Begin and Sadat signed two agreements. The first was a 'framework for peace in the Middle East' (see Documents on Palestine, p. 63) and the second was a 'framework for the conclusion of a peace treaty between Egypt and Israel'. The first agreement provided for a five-year transitional period during which the inhabitants of the Israeli-occupied West Bank and Gaza would obtain full autonomy and self-government, and the second agreement provided for the signing of a peace treaty between Egypt and Israel, which was finally signed on 27 March 1979. The treaty provided for a phased withdrawal from Sinai which was successfully completed on 25 April 1982. Diplomatic relations between Israel and Egypt were established on 26 January 1980.

Proposals for Palestinian autonomy provided for negotiations to be completed by 26 May 1980. However, that date passed without agreement. It became clear during the talks that Egypt and the Palestinians were considering 'autonomy' in terms of an independent Palestinian state, whereas Israel envisaged only some form of administrative self-government for the Palestinian Arabs in the West Bank. The announcement of new Israeli settlements in the West Bank, and a Knesset bill making East Jerusalem an integral part of the Jewish capital, gave Arabs little ground for hope that a Palestinian state would ever emerge from the negotiations, though both Israel and Egypt maintained their adherence to the 'Camp David process'.

BEGIN'S PROBLEMS

After becoming Prime Minister, Begin had to contend with two opposed factions in his Cabinet. Ariel Sharon, then Minister of Agriculture and the Minister responsible for Settlements, was a supporter of the Gush Emunim movement, which endeavoured to push the maximum number of Israeli settlements into the

West Bank as quickly as possible. As the deadline for the autonomy talks (26 May 1980) approached, plans for more settlements were announced. Begin prevaricated on the subject of the settlements, but more often than not he supported them. The uncertainty of his exact position on many policy matters led to tensions in the Cabinet. Begin's health was also a cause for concern at times. In October 1979 Moshe Dayan resigned as Minister of Foreign Affairs, because he considered the Israeli Government's stand on Palestinian autonomy to be too intransigent, and at the end of May 1980 Ezer Weizman resigned as Minister of Defence, ostensibly because of reductions in planned expenditure on defence, although his dissatisfaction with the settlements position and with the autonomy talks was well known. In the consequent Cabinet reshuffle Begin assumed the defence portfolio himself, after his proposal to appoint the Minister of Foreign Affairs, Itzhak Shamir, as Minister of Defence had encountered opposition.

Begin's biggest problem, however, was the state of the Israeli economy. Rampant inflation demanded austerity measures, and the Minister of Finance, Yigael Hurwitz, resigned in early January 1981 when the Knesset voted to award pay increases to teachers. Hurwitz withdrew his Rafi Party, with three Knesset members, from the Likud coalition and the Government could no longer command a majority. General elections were then planned for 30 June. It was thought in early 1981 that Begin was certain to be defeated in the forthcoming elections, but his position grew stronger as they approached. The tax-cutting policies of the new Minister of Finance, Yoram Aridor, proved popular, as did Begin's support for the Christians in Lebanon, in their struggle with the Syrians (who had stationed SAM missiles on Lebanese soil).

A SECOND TERM FOR BEGIN

Although the election results were close, Begin was able to present a new coalition to the Knesset in early August 1981. This was possible only by making an agreement with the religious parties, in particular Agudat Israel, by which numerous undertakings on religious observance, affecting most aspects of everyday life, were guaranteed. Although these measures were welcomed by zealots, more secular elements in Israeli society found them unpalatable.

Begin's majority was precarious, and it is remarkable that his Government survived as long as it did. In December he formally annexed the strategically important Golan Heights, a step which pleased right-wing political elements in Israel, but which angered the USA sufficiently to cause it to suspend the strategic co-operation agreement which it had signed with Israel less than one month previously.

As the time for withdrawal from Sinai drew nearer, there was increasing pressure from settlers in Sinai (particularly Yamit) to remain there. Squatters from the extreme right-wing Tehiya party adopted a belligerent stance, but they were eventually removed and the withdrawal took place as planned on 25 April 1982.

ADVANCE INTO LEBANON

During 1982 and the first half of 1983, Arab disturbances on the West Bank became more severe, and there were even Jewish demonstrations against Israel's settlement of the area. The number of Jewish settlements in the West Bank increased to more than 100 in 1983, and more land was expropriated. The event which provoked another major Middle East crisis, however, was Israel's 'Operation Peace for Galilee', an armed incursion into Lebanon which was launched on 6 June 1982 and intended as a brief and limited campaign. By the end of June, however, Israeli forces had advanced across Lebanon and surrounded West Beirut, where 6,000 PLO fighters had become trapped. Israel's action met with almost world-wide disapproval, and the support of the USA became questionable after Secretary of State Haig's resignation at the end of June, and his replacement by George Shultz. Israel declared a cease-fire and demanded that the Palestinians lay down their heavy arms and leave Lebanon.

Intensive diplomatic efforts, hampered by repeated outbreaks of fighting, were made between June and August to find an acceptable basis for the supervised withdrawal of the trapped Palestinian and Syrian forces. With the help of a US envoy,

Philip Habib, their evacuation began on 21 August and was completed by 1 September (estimates put the number of evacuees at 14,500–15,000).

Israeli forces remained in effective control of Beirut, although, under the terms of the evacuation agreement, an international peace-keeping force (predominantly comprising US, French and Italian troops) was stationed in various parts of the city until early September 1982. Despite US protests, Israeli forces moved into West Beirut again on 15 September, taking up positions around Palestinian refugee camps located in the Muslim sectors. On 17 September reports began to emerge of a massacre committed in the Sabra and Chatila camps by armed men who were ostensibly seeking PLO guerrillas. The identity of the killers was uncertain but evidence suggested their being Christian Phalangist militiamen, whose entry into the camps had been facilitated by Israeli troops. Israel rejected the Arab world's charge of responsibility for the massacre, but on 28 September the Government initiated a full judicial inquiry, led by the Chief Justice of the Supreme Court, Itzhak Kahan. Published on 8 February 1983, the report of the inquiry placed actual responsibility for the massacre on Lebanese Phalangists, but concluded that Israel's political and military leaders bore indirect responsibility for the tragic events by failing properly to supervise the militiamen in the area. Begin was censured merely for showing indifference to reports reaching him of Phalangists entering the camps. As recommended by the inquiry, Ariel Sharon resigned as Minister of Defence (though he remained in the Government as Minister without Portfolio), to be replaced by the Ambassador to the USA, Moshe Arens.

Direct talks between Israel and Lebanon for the withdrawal of foreign forces began on 28 December. Progress was slow but a 12-article agreement, formulated by US Secretary of State Shultz and declaring the end of hostilities, was finally signed on 17 May 1983. Syria rejected the agreement and its forces held their positions in the Beka'a valley, raising the possibility of open war with Israel, which, in turn, refused to withdraw while the Syrians remained. On the same day that Israel signed its agreement with Lebanon, it concluded another secret one with the USA which recognized Israel's right, despite the accord with Lebanon, to retaliate against terrorist attacks in Lebanon and to delay its withdrawal, beyond the date agreed in that accord (three months from the date of signing), if Syrian and PLO forces remained there. In July Israel, with its casualties from guerrilla attacks increasing, decided to redeploy its forces south of Beirut along the Awali river.

BEGIN'S RESIGNATION

Support for Begin's Government had been sustained throughout the early weeks of 'Operation Peace for Galilee' but, as the planned, limited incursion developed into a costly occupation, opposition to government policy increased, not only among the Israeli public but also in the army.

By the summer of 1983, Israel was sliding into an economic crisis and the involvement in Lebanon had become an expensive stalemate. The Government's prestige had been severely undermined by the Beirut massacres and by a capitulation to wage demands by doctors, whose four-month strike for higher pay had taken medical services to the brink of collapse. Begin, distressed by the death of his wife in November and by the events in Lebanon, announced his resignation as Prime Minister and leader of the Likud bloc on 30 August. Itzhak Shamir, the Minister of Foreign Affairs since 1980, was elected leader of Likud on 2 September 1983. Begin withheld his formal resignation until 15 September, while a period of political wrangling ensued to find a viable coalition government. Although Labour was the largest single party in the Knesset, Shamir was asked to form a government on 21 September, his Likud grouping having a theoretical majority of seven seats with the support of minority religious parties. Shamir pronounced his commitment to the Israeli presence in Lebanon, to the continuation of the West Bank settlement programme and to tackling the country's economic problems.

During the second half of 1983 a severe monetary crisis contributed to the declining popularity of the Government. The lack of a co-ordinated approach to the crisis led to the resignation, in October, of the Minister of Finance, Yoram Aridor, whose policies, diluted by the Cabinet, failed to prevent inflation from soaring. The rigorously applied austerity measures of Aridor's successor, Yigal Cohen-Orgad, however, threatened to alienate elements of Shamir's fragile coalition, prompting concerns over the effects of cuts in social services and increases in food prices, and provoking growing labour unrest. A plan virtually to 'freeze' the programme of creating Jewish settlements on Israeli-occupied territory in the West Bank and Gaza Strip, in order to save government funds, generated further uproar at the beginning of 1984. Although the rate of settlement had slowed down owing to Israel's economic recession, the number of settlements established since 1967 had risen to 129 (114 in the West Bank) by March 1985, and the number of Israeli settlers to 46,000 (42,500 in the West Bank). By that month, Israel had direct control of more than 50% of the 490,000 ha of land in the West Bank. The depth of feeling on the issue was illustrated by the exposure in April 1984 of a Jewish anti-Palestinian terrorist organization operating in the West Bank, some of whose members were active in Gush Emunim.

THE 1984 GENERAL ELECTION

Inflation continued to rise sharply in 1984 and in January the Government narrowly survived a vote of 'no confidence' in the Knesset. Its position was further weakened by the resignation from the Cabinet (and the loss of the guaranteed vote) of the Minister without Portfolio, Mordechai Ben-Porat, one week later. Finally, in March, the Government failed by 61 votes to 58 to prevent the passage of a bill, sponsored by the Labour Party, proposing the dissolution of the Knesset prior to a general election. The general election was set for 23 July.

The election campaign was conducted against a background of strikes, as the state of the economy continued to deteriorate. The overall rate of inflation passed 400% in July and it was apparent that the most important issue for voters was the economy. Bans which had been imposed by the parliamentary election committee on the ultra-right-wing Kach and the left-wing Progressive List for Peace parties, preventing them from contesting the election, were overturned by the Supreme Court so that 27 parties (including 16 new groupings, mostly splinter groups from existing parties) were expected to compete for seats on 23 July.

Although an opinion poll conducted three weeks before the election indicated a clear Labour lead, the election produced no conclusive result. The Labour Alignment won 44 seats in the Knesset (an insufficient number to enable it to form Israel's first single-party government), while Likud gained 41. The balance of power lay, once again, with the minority parties which won the remaining 35 seats in the 120-seat assembly. When what was required was the swift establishment of a new government to deal with the deteriorating economy, both Labour and Likud were embroiled in negotiations to win the support of the minority parties for a viable coalition administration. These talks provided no clear majority in the Knesset for either side, and it became increasingly likely that a government of national unity, comprising both Labour and Likud, presented the only resolution to the political impasse, short of calling a second election. President Herzog nominated the Labour leader, Shimon Peres, as Prime Minister-designate on 5 August and invited him to form a coalition government. The 11th Knesset was inaugurated on 13 August in an atmosphere of great uncertainty as to whether Labour and Likud could bridge the political gap between them in order to form a national government.

THE ISRAELI OCCUPATION OF SOUTHERN LEBANON

The withdrawal in September 1983 of Israeli forces in Lebanon to the Awali river, south of Beirut, produced a *de facto* partition of the country. Israeli troops (reduced to some 10,000 by the end of 1983) faced about 50,000 Syrian troops and 2,000–4,000 Palestinian guerrillas entrenched in the Beka'a valley to the north. The 2,500 men of Maj. Sa'ad Haddad's Israeli-controlled southern Lebanese militia, the so-called 'South Lebanon Army' (SLA), were employed to police the occupied area, with the Israeli troops, and to combat guerrilla attacks on the occupying forces. Israel also armed other, independent, militias (including Shi'ite Muslim groups) so that they could control their own areas of influence. Despite these measures and, perhaps, partly because of them, Israeli soldiers continued to be the target of

guerrilla attacks (the Israeli death toll in the 'Peace for Galilee' operation approached 600 by July 1984). Although, after the withdrawal to the Awali river, the Israeli air force and navy were involved in attacks on Syrian targets in north Lebanon and against the PLO in the port of Tripoli (in November and December 1983), there were no serious land-based exchanges between Israeli and Syrian forces in Lebanon during the first half of 1984. Some isolated Israeli shelling of Palestinian positions in the Beka'a took place in retaliation against the activities of Palestinian guerrilla squads which infiltrated the Israeli-occupied areas to make their attacks.

Major Sa'ad Haddad died in December 1983 and Maj.-Gen. Antoine Lahad replaced him as leader of the SLA in March 1984. In the same month, under the influence of Syria, President Gemayel abrogated the 17 May agreement with Israel. Although the agreement had effectively been a 'dead-letter' for some time, the rising cost of involvement in Lebanon and the unpopularity of that policy at home disposed Israel at least to consider withdrawing. It was clear, however, that, much as Israel would prefer to spare the expense of occupation and the lives of its people by leaving the policing of southern Lebanon to Maj.-Gen. Lahad's and other militias, it would not withdraw either until it felt secure within its existing boundaries against terrorist attacks launched from Lebanese territory, or until it was politically impossible for it to remain. The official policy of the Shamir Government was that Syrian withdrawal from Lebanon was a precondition of Israeli withdrawal. Shimon Peres, the Labour Party leader, had pledged to adopt a more flexible pragmatic approach to negotiations on an Israeli withdrawal if he came to power. However, Labour's failure to win an overall majority in the election, and the likely formation of a government of national unity with Likud, meant that Labour might have to make compromises, over controversial issues, in the very policies which distinguished it from Likud.

THE GOVERNMENT OF NATIONAL UNITY

Six weeks of negotiation were required before Peres and Itzhak Shamir could agree on the composition and policy of a coalition government. The new Government, whose component parties accounted for 97 of the 120 Knesset seats, was formed on 13 September 1984. It contained representatives of the two major party groupings (Labour and Likud), four religious parties (the NRP, Shas, Agudat Israel and Morasha) and the Shinui, Yahad and Ometz parties. Under the terms of the coalition agreement, Shimon Peres was to hold the premiership for the first 25 months of the government, while Itzhak Shamir served as Deputy Prime Minister and Minister of Foreign Affairs, after which time they were to exchange their respective posts for a further period of 25 months. Within the Cabinet of 25 ministers, an 'inner Cabinet' of 10 (including five members each from Labour and Likud) was formed.

ISRAEL'S WITHDRAWAL FROM LEBANON

The Government of national unity pledged itself to withdrawing the Israel Defence Forces (IDF) from Lebanon, and to improving the economy. Any withdrawal agreement with Lebanon was not to be without conditions, however. To ensure the security of its northern border, ideally, Israel sought Syrian commitments not to redeploy its forces in areas evacuated by the IDF; to prevent the infiltration of PLO terrorists into the south of Lebanon; to grant freedom of operation to the SLA; and to allow the UN Interim Force in Lebanon (UNIFIL) to deploy north of the SLA area up to Syrian lines in the Beka'a valley. Lebanon, for its part, demanded $10,000m. in reparations, and the unconditional withdrawal of the IDF. More realistically, Israel dropped its demand for simultaneous Syrian withdrawal, provided satisfactory military arrangements could be made, and Syria approved a series of UN-sponsored talks between Lebanese and Israeli army representatives, to agree the terms of withdrawal. Talks began in an-Naqoura (Lebanon) in November 1984 but repeatedly foundered on the question of which forces should replace the IDF, to prevent intercommunal fighting. The Lebanese, influenced by Syria, wanted UNIFIL to police the Israel–Lebanon border (as it had been mandated to do in 1978), and the Lebanese army to deploy north of the Litani river, between UNIFIL and the Syrian forces. Israel was not convinced of the competence of the Lebanese army, and wanted UNIFIL held 30 of the 60 seats, was dissolved (for further details, see the chapter on Jordan).

King Hussein's action appeared finally to end hopes that the Shultz Plan could be implemented and to damage the prospects of a victory for Shimon Peres' Labour Alignment in the Israeli general election, which was scheduled to take place in November 1988. The peace plans of both Shultz and Peres had relied on the Palestinians being represented at negotiations in a joint Jordanian-Palestinian delegation (the so-called 'Jordanian option'). Without the participation of Jordan, which had voluntarily withdrawn from the West Bank and renounced any pretension to represent the Palestinians, the PLO could make a stronger claim to be the sole legitimate representative of the Palestinian people. The Israeli Government, however, was united in refusing to negotiate with the PLO. The possibility did exist, though, that the PLO might make the sort of concessions that would persuade Israel to reconsider its position. The severance of Jordanian links with the West Bank provoked a heated debate within the PLO on the issues of recognizing Israel's right to exist, declaring an independent Palestinian state in the West Bank and proclaiming a Palestinian government-in-exile. To have done so would, by implication, have been to place the emphasis of the Palestinian independence movement on a diplomatic and political search for a solution, rather than on armed struggle. Israel's Prime Minister Shamir, however, immediately announced that he would use an 'iron fist' to prevent the creation of such a government or state. The Labour Party of Shimon Peres, on the other hand, bereft of the 'Jordanian option', offered to talk to 'any Palestinians' who renounced the use of violence and recognized the Jewish State.

NEW INITIATIVES BY THE PLO

In continuation of the spirit expressed at the June 1988 Arab summit, the Palestine National Council met in Algiers in November and the PLO declared an independent Palestinian state (notionally on the West Bank) and endorsed UN Security Council Resolution 242, thereby implicitly granting recognition to Israel. A month later, Yasser Arafat stated explicitly in Stockholm that 'the Palestine National Council accepted two states, a Palestinian state and a Jewish state, Israel'. Later in December, Arafat presented a three-point peace initiative to the UN General Assembly in Geneva. He proposed the convening of a UN-sponsored international conference, the creation of a UN force to supervise Israeli withdrawal from the Occupied Territories, and the implementation of a comprehensive settlement based on UN Security Council Resolutions 242 and 338. Although the USA refused to accept the PLO proposals (alleging ambiguities), the explicit rejection of violence encouraged the US Government to open a dialogue with the PLO, implying a change in the direction of US-Israeli policy over Palestine. The United Kingdom and the USSR, among other countries, urged Israel to make a positive response to the PLO's new position.

ISRAELI PEACE PLANS

External initiatives appeared to have little impact on the daily operations of the *intifada* and by the time of the Israeli general election on 1 November 1988, it had claimed the lives of an estimated 300 Palestinians and six Israelis. The election once again produced a result whereby neither Likud (which won 40 of the 120 seats in the Knesset) nor Labour (with 39 seats) secured enough seats to be able to form a coalition with groups of smaller parties. The religious parties won 18 seats, gaining potential significance in the formation of a government either by Likud or Labour. After two changes of direction, Peres and the Labour Party eventually agreed to the formation in December of another government of national unity under the Likud leader, Itzhak Shamir, with Peres as Deputy Prime Minister and Minister of Finance. The protracted wrangling over forming a coalition had diverted attention from the PLO's peace initiative, and in the coalition accord no mention was made of an international peace settlement, nor were any new proposals advanced for solving the Arab–Israeli problem.

When municipal elections took place at the end of February 1989, Likud made sweeping gains, obtaining control of six of the 10 largest cities and also of many middle-sized towns. Likud regarded these election results as a vindication of their bitter opposition to the PLO. Shamir continued to maintain that the

PLO remained a terrorist organization and presented his own four-point proposals for peace when he visited Washington in April. The proposals comprised: (i) reaffirmation by Egypt, Israel and the USA of their dedication to the 1978 Camp David accords; (ii) abandonment by Arab states of their hostility towards Israel; (iii) efforts to solve the Arab refugee problem; (iv) free democratic elections in the West Bank and Gaza to elect delegates who could negotiate self-rule under Israeli authority, but only if the violence ceased. A 20-point programme, developed from these proposals, was endorsed by both the Cabinet and the Knesset in May. Although Palestinian activists dismissed these proposals as unacceptable (because direct negotiations with the PLO were excluded), many observers felt that they offered a chance for talks to begin.

After a meeting of the Likud Central Committee on 5 July 1989, however, Shamir agreed to attach stringent conditions to the Government's peace initiative. He stated that Israel would never allow the establishment of a Palestinian state on the West Bank nor negotiate peace with the PLO, nor would it end Jewish settlements in the territories. This tougher approach threatened to cause the dissolution of the coalition with Labour; however, the threat was averted when the Cabinet reaffirmed the original peace initiative on 23 July.

The USA was, by now, exerting pressure on the PLO to consider the Israeli plan for elections in the West Bank and Gaza, but in August 1989 Yasser Abd ar-Rabbuh, a senior PLO spokesman, declared that 'the PLO does not consider, in any way, that elections can establish the basis for a political settlement'. In mid-September President Mubarak of Egypt invited Israeli clarification on 10 points connected with Shamir's election plans and also offered to convene an Israeli-Palestinian meeting to discuss election details. Mubarak's 10-point plan was accepted by the Labour Party members of the 'inner' Cabinet, but was vetoed in early October by the Likud ministers who did not want any direct contact with a Palestinian delegation. In early November the 'inner' Cabinet provisionally accepted a five-point initiative proposed by the US Secretary of State, James Baker, regarding a preliminary Israeli-Palestinian meeting to discuss the holding of elections in the West Bank and Gaza Strip, on condition that Israel would not be required to negotiate directly with a Palestinian delegation, and that the talks would be concerned only with Israel's election proposals. However, the PLO continued to demand a direct role in talks with Israel.

At the end of July 1989 Israeli agents abducted Sheikh Obeid, a leading Shi'a Muslim, from a village in southern Lebanon, with the aim of securing the release of three Israeli soldiers held by Hezbollah. Col William Higgins, a US hostage held by Hezbollah, was murdered in retaliation. World attention was then focused on the position of all Middle East hostages, and it seemed at first that some agreement leading to their release was imminent. However, no final solution to the problem was immediately forthcoming.

In January 1990 the dismissal from the Government of Ezer Weizman, the Labour Minister of Science and Technology, for unauthorized contact with the PLO, endangered the fragile Likud-Labour coalition. The Labour Party claimed that, under the coalition agreement, Prime Minister Shamir was not allowed to dismiss Labour ministers. A compromise was eventually reached, whereby Weizman resigned from the 'inner' Cabinet (recently expanded to 12 members), but retained the science and technology portfolio. The coalition was further undermined on 28 January when five disaffected members of the Knesset, led by Itzhak Modai, the Minister of Economic Affairs, split from the Likud to form an independent party, the Movement for the Advancement of the Zionist Idea (MAZI).

In February 1990 Ariel Sharon launched a campaign for the premiership after resigning the post of Minister of Trade and Industry in protest at Shamir's peace policy and the Government's failure to suppress the *intifada*. One obstacle to the progress of the peace negotiations was the question of whether residents of East Jerusalem should be allowed to participate in proposed elections in the Occupied Territories. On 28 February the USA suggested a compromise solution, which would allow East Jerusalem residents with second homes in the West Bank and some deported activists to stand in the elections. The USA attempted to apply further pressure to Israel to accelerate the pace of the peace process at the beginning of March, when President Bush opposed the grant to Israel of a $400m. loan for the housing of Soviet immigrants, since Israel would give no assurances that the housing in question would not be in the Occupied Territories, including East Jerusalem.

LIKUD-LABOUR COALITION COLLAPSES

On 11 March 1990 Shimon Peres and five Labour colleagues withdrew from a cabinet meeting in protest at further delays to a proposed vote on US plans for talks between an Israeli and a Palestinian delegation. Two days later Prime Minister Shamir dismissed Peres, the Labour leader and Minister of Finance, from the Government, prompting the resignation of all the Labour ministers. On 15 March a vote of 'no confidence' was upheld against Prime Minister Shamir, the first such vote against an Israeli Government to have succeeded. Shamir was left in charge of a transitional administration, since he had managed to ensure he would retain the premiership by preventing the vote of 'no confidence' from being brought forward to when the Labour ministers remained in office (all resignations and dismissals take 48 hours to come into effect). On 20 March President Herzog invited Peres to form a new coalition government after he had received assurances of the support of five members of the Knesset belonging to Agudat Israel. A two-month period of political wrangling ensued, however, during which both Likud and Labour tried to establish a viable coalition government by soliciting the support of the minor religious parties.

The concessions extracted by the minor religious parties during the period of political manoeuvring aroused growing public resentment that became manifest in a demonstration by some 100,000 people in Jerusalem on 8 April 1990. The demands for electoral reform subsequently led to a ruling by the Supreme Court requiring all political parties to publish the details of coalition agreements before a government could be formed. By the end of April Peres acknowledged failure in his own attempts to form a new government. President Herzog accordingly invited Shamir to form a new administration. Although initially given 21 days to accomplish the task, this period was later extended by Herzog as it emerged that the announcement of a new Likud-led coalition was being delayed by arguments with potential coalition partners over cabinet posts. The political wrangling in Israel took place against a backdrop of ongoing unrest and violence. In mid-April riots engulfed parts of the Christian quarter of Jerusalem's Old City when 150 Orthodox Jewish settlers occupied the St John's Hospice, a Greek patriarchate building. Palestinian anger was fuelled by revelations that Israel's Ministry of Housing had financed the occupation. Tensions were exacerbated on 19 May when seven Palestinian workers were murdered in Rishon LeZiyyon by an Israeli civilian gunman. Reports that the killer was mentally unstable and politically unaffiliated failed to prevent three days of sustained demonstrations in the Occupied Territories, resulting in the deaths of 21 Palestinians. At the end of the month gunmen of the Palestine Liberation Front (PLF) were intercepted by Israeli forces as they attempted a sea-borne raid south of Tel-Aviv. The aim of the abortive raid was unclear, but the US Government immediately urged Yasser Arafat to issue a condemnation of the group. When he failed to do so in terms satisfactory to Washington, the US Department of State declared that it was suspending dialogue with the PLO. On 31 May the USA also vetoed a UN Security Council resolution urging the dispatch of international observers to the Territories.

THE RIGHT RETURNS TO POWER

On 8 June 1990 Itzhak Shamir announced the formation of a new Government, following the signing of a coalition agreement which gave him the support of 62 of the 120 members of the Knesset. A policy document underlined the uncompromising character of the new partnership. In it Shamir emphasized the right of Jews to settle in all parts of Greater Israel; his opposition to the creation of an independent Palestinian state; and his refusal to negotiate with the PLO, indeed with any Palestinians other than those resident in the Occupied Territories (excluding East Jerusalem). On 11 June in the Knesset the new Government won a vote of confidence by 62 votes to 57 with one abstention. The Government thus empowered was a narrow,

right-wing coalition of Likud and five small parties (the MAZI, the NRP, Shas and the Tzomet and Tehiya parties), together with three independent members of the Knesset. Ariel Sharon was appointed Minister of Housing in the new Government, Moshe Arens Minister of Defence, and David Levy Minister of Foreign Affairs.

On 18 June Prime Minister Shamir invited President Assad of Syria to visit Israel for peace negotiations, and on 22 June Jean-Claude Aimé, a special envoy of the UN Secretary-General, visited Israel to discuss issues related to the Occupied Territories. Shamir was believed to be seeking to appease the USA after US Secretary of State, James Baker, had expressed impatience at the lack of progress in the peace process. However, on 27 June Shamir wrote to US President Bush rejecting the principal elements of US proposals for direct talks between Israeli and Palestinian delegations.

Controversy surrounding the settlement of Soviet Jewish immigrants in the Occupied Territories intensified in June 1990 when Moshe Arens, the Minister of Defence, ordered the creation of a civil guard in the West Bank in order to protect Jewish settlers. The huge influx of immigrants from the USSR (250,000 were expected to arrive in 1990 and 1m. by 1992, increasing Israel's population by one-fifth) gave rise to fears of the further erosion of Arab rights. On 16 June the EC criticized Israel for failing to respect the human rights of Palestinians in the Territories. Israel rejected the criticism, however, and on 18 July refused to sanction the establishment of an EC consulate in East Jerusalem.

Israel's relations with African countries, the USSR and other eastern European countries improved significantly in late 1989 and 1990. In September 1989 Hungary became the first country of the Eastern bloc to restore diplomatic relations (severed in 1967) with Israel. In January 1990 the USSR upgraded its diplomatic links with both Israel and the PLO, while Israeli and East German officials held secret talks on establishing diplomatic relations. In February Israel restored diplomatic relations with Poland and Czechoslovakia, and with Bulgaria in May. The Greek Government also formally recognized Israel in May 1990, the last member state of the EC to do so, following an Israeli High Court ruling that the settlers who had occupied the St John's Hospice in Jerusalem should evacuate the building (see above).

ISRAEL AND THE CONFLICT OVER KUWAIT

Iraq's invasion and annexation of Kuwait in August 1990 led to improved relations between Israel and the USA, because it was vital, if a broad coalition of Western and Arab powers opposed to Iraq was to be maintained, that Israel did not become actively involved in the new conflict. On 12 August President Saddam Hussain of Iraq offered to withdraw his forces from Kuwait if Israel would withdraw from the Occupied Territories. Israel firmly rejected any analogy between the occupation of Kuwait and its presence in the Territories. As a crisis developed in the Gulf region, there was support for Iraq both from Palestinians resident in the Occupied Territories and from the PLO. The PLO's support for Iraq led left left-wing Israeli groups to cancel scheduled meetings with PLO representatives and other Palestinian leaders.

The improvement taking place in US-Israeli relations was seriously jeopardized in October 1990, when Israeli police shot and killed some 17 Palestinians on the Temple Mount in Jerusalem, after they had clashed with Jewish worshippers there. The killings provoked international outrage and sustained the arguments of those who sought to link Iraq's occupation of Kuwait with the Israeli presence in the Occupied Territories in any solution to the Gulf crisis. There was intense pressure on the UN to respond to this outrage, since it was with UN authority that a multinational force had been deployed in Saudi Arabia for the protection of the Kingdom. To many Arabs, the disparity between the vigour with which the UN was seeking to implement successive resolutions pertaining to the occupation of Kuwait and its long-standing impotence with regard to successive resolutions pertaining to the Occupied Territories was now more conspicuous than before.

The UN Security Council voted to send a mission to the Occupied Territories to investigate the Temple Mount killings, but the Israeli Cabinet announced that it would not co-operate with any such delegation. In early November 1990 the UN Secretary-General asked the Security Council to request the convening of an unprecedented international conference, with the aim of forcing Israel to accept that Palestinians in the Territories were protected by the provisions of the Fourth Geneva Convention (concerning the protection of civilians during wartime). On 13 November the Israeli Government announced that it would permit a UN emissary to visit Israel to discuss the situation in the Occupied Territories.

In mid-December 1990 the USA resisted attempts by the UN Security Council to draft a resolution advocating the convening of a Middle East peace conference and an increased UN presence in the Occupied Territories. The USA feared that the holding of a peace conference, at this time, could be construed as a concession to Saddam Hussain's concept of 'linkage'. Meanwhile, Shamir visited the USA to confer with President Bush. He was reported to have sought, and received, assurances from Bush that any diplomatic solution to the crisis in the Gulf would protect Israeli interests. Nevertheless, only days later, the USA proposed a UN Security Council resolution condemning Israel's reinstatement of a policy of deporting Palestinians, in response to violence in the Territories, as a violation of the Fourth Geneva Convention. The USA also supported further criticism by the UN of Israel's treatment of Palestinians in the West Bank and Gaza and supported a separate UN appeal for an 'active negotiating process' in the Middle East 'at an appropriate time'. However, in view of the Gulf crisis, the USA did not believe that such a time had arrived.

Attacks on Israel by Iraqi *Scud* missiles, beginning on 18 January 1991, created the most serious threat to the integrity of the multinational force which had commenced hostilities against Iraq on 16–17 January. It was widely expected that Israel would retaliate immediately, so risking the withdrawal of Arab countries from the multinational force. While Egypt implied that it would accept a measured degree of retaliation, Syria stated bluntly that it would change sides in response to any Israeli attacks on Iraq which violated Jordanian airspace. Graver still was the possibility of Iranian involvement on the side of Iraq in response to Israeli military action. US diplomacy, supported by the installation in Israel of advanced US air defence systems, succeeded in averting an immediate Israeli military response, although Israel vowed that it would, ultimately, retaliate for the attacks. By late February Iraq had launched 39 *Scud* missiles against Israel, killing two people and injuring more than 200.

Wider strategic considerations apart, a policy of restraint appeared to be in Israel's best interest. The Iraqi missile attacks, together with fears that similar attacks using chemical warheads might be launched, provoked a rare, open outburst of international sympathy for Israel. They also strengthened the Israeli case for rejecting any 'linkage' between the occupation of Kuwait and the Occupied Territories, and undermined the PLO's claim to be the only credible interlocutor in a future dialogue with the Israeli Government. In response to the widespread support, expressed by ordinary Palestinians and in official PLO policy, for Saddam Hussain, the attitude of the Israeli Government hardened. Its new mood was symbolized by the appointment by Shamir, in February 1991, of Gen. Rechavam Ze'evi, the leader of the Moledet (Homeland) party, as Minister without Portfolio and a member of the policy-making 'inner Cabinet'. The appointment was strongly opposed by some cabinet members, as Ze'evi was known to advocate a policy of 'transfer' (i.e. the forcible, mass deportation of Palestinians) as a solution to the Arab–Israeli conflict. In early February Shamir again rejected proposals for convening an international conference on the Palestinian issue, and promoted his own peace plan, formulated in 1989 (see above), as the only starting-point for any peace dialogue involving the Israeli Government.

RENEWED ATTEMPTS TO CONVENE A PEACE CONFERENCE

For Israel the defeat of Iraq by the multinational force in February 1991 had ambiguous implications, since it left President Saddam Hussain in power—Israel had openly urged his removal—as a potential threat to Israel's security. Israel's greatest gain from the conflict over Kuwait had been the renewed goodwill of the USA: in late February the US Secretary

of State, James Baker, signed a guarantee for a US loan to Israel of US \$400m. for the housing of immigrants. (Baker had previously refused to sign the guarantee, owing to his concern that the funds would be used to establish immigrant communities in the Occupied Territories.) However, it was clear that the USA would seek to use its increased influence in the Middle East to achieve a resolution of the Arab–Israeli conflict, and that the USA's continued extension of goodwill and financial aid would require concessions by the Shamir Government.

At the beginning of March 1991 US President George Bush stated that a settlement of the Arab–Israeli conflict was one of the principal aims of US foreign policy, and in mid-March James Baker made his first visit, as US Secretary of State, to Israel, where he sought to initiate a 'confidence-building' process between Israelis and Arabs, as a preparatory step towards peace negotiations. The visit to Israel was followed by one to Syria for discussions with President Assad. The USA's efforts to initiate peace talks intensified in the first half of April, when the US Secretary of State returned to the Middle East, visiting Israel, Egypt and Syria, in order to promote the idea of a regional peace conference. The proposal gained only limited support. While the Israeli Government tentatively endorsed the idea of a regional conference—comprising an initial, symbolic session, to be followed by direct talks with Arab states and a joint Jordanian-Palestinian delegation—its continued refusal to negotiate with any Palestinian delegation which comprised either residents of East Jerusalem or PLO members appeared to present an insurmountable obstacle to any further progress towards an Arab–Israeli settlement. Syria, Egypt and the PLO, meanwhile, rejected the proposed regional conference outright, favouring instead an international conference endorsed by the UN and with full PLO participation.

After James Baker had again failed, following further talks with Shamir in mid-April 1991, to extract any flexibility from the Israeli Government, the question of a settlement to the Arab–Israeli conflict appeared as intractable as it had before Iraq's recent invasion of Kuwait. It was generally accepted that Shamir would seek to prevaricate to a degree which would allow him to continue to enjoy both the goodwill—and financial aid— of the USA and the support of the extreme right-wing elements of his coalition Government, which remained firmly opposed to peace negotiations. The continued settlement of Soviet Jewish immigrants to Israel in the Occupied Territories became increasingly controversial. Visiting the USA in late April 1991, the Israeli Minister of Housing and Construction, Ariel Sharon (with whom the settlement policy was most closely identified), was rebuffed when he sought meetings with senior US officials. The US Secretary of State described the settlement of the immigrants in the Territories as the biggest obstacle to the convening of a Middle East peace conference.

On 18 July 1991, in a remarkable volte-face, President Assad of Syria agreed for the first time, following a meeting with Baker, to participate in direct negotiations with Israel at a regional conference, for which the terms of reference would be a comprehensive peace settlement based on UN Security Council Resolutions 242 (see Documents on Palestine, p. 57) and 338 (ibid., p. 61). By agreeing to participate in a peace conference on the USA's terms, Syria decisively increased the intense diplomatic pressure on Israel to do likewise: the US initiative already enjoyed the express support of the G-7 group of industrialized countries, the USSR, the UN Security Council and the EC; and, following Syria's concession, Egypt and Jordan indicated that they would also be willing to participate in direct discussions with Israel.

On closer examination, however, substantive progress towards a resolution of the Arab–Israeli conflict appeared illusory. The publicly-stated positions of the Israeli and Syrian Governments remained as far apart as ever. Each claimed, towards the end of July 1991, to have received confidential (and incompatible) assurances from the USA: Israel with regard to the composition of a Jordanian-Palestinian delegation to the peace conference; and Syria with regard to the return of the Israeli-occupied Golan Heights. For its part, the US Government insisted that there were no preconditions for attending the peace conference, and that, with regard to the composition of the Jordanian-Palestinian delegation, only members of the PLO were excluded.

On 31 July 1991, at the conclusion of a summit meeting between Presidents George Bush and Mikhail Gorbachev, the USA and the USSR announced their intention to act as joint chairmen of a Middle East peace conference which they had scheduled—without having received the prior, formal consent of the Israeli Government—to take place in October of that year, and which representatives of the UN and the EC would attend in the capacity of observers. On 4 August 1991 the Israeli Cabinet formally agreed to attend a peace conference on the terms proposed by the USA and the USSR.

OTHER POST-WAR DEVELOPMENTS

The signing, in May 1991, by Syria and Lebanon of a treaty of 'fraternity, co-operation and co-ordination' was immediately denounced by Israel as a further step towards the formal transformation of Lebanon into a Syrian protectorate. The signing of the treaty appeared to reduce the likelihood that, in response to the deployment of the Lebanese army in southern Lebanon, Israel would comply with UN Security Council Resolution 425 (adopted in March 1978) and withdraw its forces from its self-declared 'security zone'. As the Lebanese army began to deploy east of the coastal town of Sidon in July 1991, Israel continued to launch attacks on Palestinian and Hezbollah militia units which, it claimed, the Lebanese army (which it regarded as little more than a Syrian proxy force) was unable to suppress. A serious escalation of the conflict endemic to southern Lebanon occurred in February 1992, when Israeli armed forces advanced beyond Israel's 'security zone' to attack alleged positions of Hezbollah; and again in May, when the Israeli air force attacked Hezbollah villages to the north and west of the 'security zone', in response to attacks by Hezbollah units on positions occupied by the South Lebanon Army.

In August 1991 Israel claimed that one of a number of conditions to which the USA had agreed in return for Israel's participation in the regional peace conference scheduled for October was the re-establishment of full diplomatic relations with the USSR. Soviet promotion of the USA's proposed regional peace conference had already led to closer contacts between Israel and the USSR. In April 1991 Shamir met the Soviet Prime Minister, Valentin Pavlov, in London; and in May the Soviet Minister of Foreign Affairs, Aleksandr Bessmertnykh, made a visit to Israel, where he met the Israeli Prime Minister and the Minister of Foreign Affairs, David Levy. Full diplomatic relations with the USSR—superseded by the establishment of relations with some of the newly-independent, former Soviet republics—were formally re-established, after an interval of 24 years, in November; and in January 1992 Israel established diplomatic relations with the People's Republic of China for the first time.

DEADLOCKED NEGOTIATIONS

By March 1992, following an initial, 'symbolic' session of the conference, held in Madrid, Spain, in October 1991, four sessions of negotiations between Israeli, Syrian, Lebanese and Palestinian-Jordanian delegations had been held, but little progress had been achieved with regard to substantive issues, in particular the question of transitional Palestinian autonomy in the West Bank and Gaza Strip, pending discussions on the 'final status' of those territories. Rather, these bilateral talks had become deadlocked over procedural issues. Israeli delegations, wary of making any gesture which might be construed as recognition of Palestinian independence, consistently questioned the status of the Palestinian-Jordanian delegation and the right of the Palestinian component to participate separately in negotiations; while Israel's refusal to halt the construction of new settlements in the Occupied Territories posed a constant threat to the faltering peace process and further damaged its relations with the USA. In February 1992, immediately prior to the fourth session of the peace talks, the US Secretary of State, James Baker, demanded a complete halt to Israeli settlement in the Territories as a condition for the granting of US $10,000m. in US-guaranteed loans for the housing of Jewish immigrants from the former USSR.

While the Israeli Government's refusal to 'freeze' the construction of new settlements was regarded as provocative by all the other parties to the peace conference, and by the US Government, the right-wing minority members of Israel's governing coalition, which opposed any Israeli participation in the peace conference at all, threatened to withdraw from the coalition if funds were not made available for the settlement programme. In December 1991 the Government's majority in the 120-seat Knesset was reduced when the Minister of Agriculture, Rafael Eitan (a member of the right-wing, nationalist Tzomet Party), resigned his portfolio in protest at the Prime Minister's opposition to electoral reform; and in mid-January 1992 the majority was lost entirely when two other right-wing, nationalist political parties, Moledet and Tehiya (which together held five seats in the Knesset) withdrew from the coalition. Their withdrawal was a deliberate attempt to obstruct the third session of the Middle East peace conference in Moscow, Russia, where delegates had begun to address the granting of transitional autonomy to Palestinians in the Occupied Territories. A general election was subsequently scheduled to be held in June 1992, and Itzhak Shamir remained the head of a transitional, minority government.

In late February 1992 Shamir was re-elected as leader of the Likud party. At the same time, Itzhak Rabin, a former Israeli Prime Minister, was elected Chairman of the Labour Party, replacing Shimon Peres. Rabin's election was regarded as having significantly improved Labour's prospects at the forthcoming general election, since, while he favoured the continuation of peace negotiations, he also enjoyed more popular confidence than Peres with regard to issues affecting Israel's security.

A fifth round of bilateral negotiations, between Israeli, Syrian, Lebanese and Palestinian-Jordanian delegations, was held in Washington, USA, at the end of April 1992. In this session procedural issues were resolved, and, in its talks with the Palestinian component of the Palestinian-Jordanian delegation, the Israeli delegation presented proposals for the holding of municipal elections in the West Bank and Gaza; and for the transfer of control of health amenities there to Palestinian authorities. The Palestinian delegation, for its part, did not reject the proposals outright, although they fell far short of Palestinians' ambition for full legislative control of the Occupied Territories. No progress was made in the meetings between Israeli and Syrian delegations to discuss Israel's continued occupation of the Golan Heights.

In May 1992 the first multilateral negotiations between the parties to the Middle East peace conference commenced; however, the sessions were boycotted by Syria and Lebanon, which considered them futile until progress had been made in the bilateral negotiations. Various combinations of delegations attended meetings convened to discuss regional economic co-operation and arms control, the question of Palestinian refugees, water resources, and environmental issues. Israel boycotted the discussions on Palestinian refugees and regional economic development after the USA approved Palestinian proposals to allow exiles (i.e. non-residents of the Occupied Territories) to be included in the participating Palestinian delegations. The session of talks on Palestinian refugees became especially controversial after both components of the Palestinian-Jordanian delegation asserted the right of Palestinian refugees to return to the Occupied Territories, in accordance with UN General Assembly Resolution 194 of 1948. However, the US Government subsequently indicated that the terms of reference for the peace conference were UN Security Council Resolutions 242 and 338 only.

A NEW LABOUR COALITION

In the general election held on 23 June 1992, the Labour Party won 44 seats in the Knesset and Likud 32. Meretz—an alliance of Ratz (Civil Rights and Peace Movement), Shinui and the United Workers' Party which had won 12 seats in the Knesset—confirmed its willingness to form a coalition government with the Labour Party on 24 June. However, even with the support of the two Arab parties—the Arab Democratic Party and Hadash—which together held five seats, such a coalition would have enjoyed a majority of only two votes over the so-called 'right bloc' (Likud, Tzomet, Moledet and Tehiya) and the religious parties which had allied themselves with Likud in the previous Knesset. Formally invited to form a government on 28 June, the Labour leader, Itzhak Rabin, was accordingly obliged to solicit support among certain religious parties. On 13 July Rabin presented a new government for approval by the Knesset. The new coalition, an alliance of Labour, Meretz and the ultra-orthodox Jewish party, Shas, had a total of 62 seats in the 120-seat Knesset; and also enjoyed the unspoken support of five deputies from the two Arab parties.

Immediately after the election the Labour Party had re-affirmed its commitment to granting Palestinian autonomy within nine months, while maintaining Israel's control of defence and security measures in the Occupied Territories, and its responsibility for existing settlements there. It also expressed its desire for improved relations with the USA. However, it remained unclear precisely what Labour's policy would be with regard to the occupied Golan Heights and occupied areas of southern Lebanon. As it strove to form a coalition that included right-wing religious parties, Labour became of necessity less outspoken in its commitment to some of its stated aims, giving rise to fears that improved relations with the USA might ultimately force Palestinians to accept limited autonomy entirely on Israel's terms.

A sixth round of bilateral negotiations between Israeli, Syrian, Lebanese and Palestinian-Jordanian delegations, the first since the new Israeli Government had taken office, commenced in Washington in late August 1992. Again, little progress was achieved on substantive issues. The Israeli delegation and the Palestinian component of the Palestinian-Jordanian delegation, for instance, were unable to agree terms for negotiating an initial, five-year period of Palestinian autonomy in the West Bank and Gaza Strip prior to a permanent settlement. Talks between the Israeli and the Syrian delegations remained dead-locked over the issue of the Golan Heights, and in private delegates reportedly admitted that they were likely to remain so without the eventual diplomatic intervention of the USA.

In early October 1992, in a clear gesture of support for the new Israeli Government, the USA granted Israel the US \$10,000m. in US-guaranteed loans for the housing of immi-grants that it had previously withheld, owing to Israel's settle-ment programme in the Occupied Territories. In late October a seventh round of bilateral negotiations between the parties to the Middle East peace conference commenced in Washington. The discussions were adjourned, pending the conclusion of the US presidential election, but resumed in early November. No tangible progress was achieved, however. Multilateral discus-sions on the issue of refugees took place in Ottawa, Canada, on 11–12 November. In spite of the hopes that had been expressed for the prospects of the peace process since the election of the Labour-led Israeli Government, October and November were marked by violent clashes between Palestinians and the Israeli security forces in the Occupied Territories. At the end of Nov-ember it was reported that, since 1987, 959 Palestinians, 543 alleged Palestinian 'collaborators' and 103 Israelis had died in the Palestinian *intifada*.

DEPORTATIONS STALL TALKS

In early December 1992 an eighth round of bilateral negotiations between Israeli and Arab delegations commenced in Wash-ington. However, the talks were quickly overtaken by events in the Occupied Territories, which led to the withdrawal of the Arab delegations. On 16 December, in response to the deaths in the Territories of five members of the Israeli security forces, and to the abduction and murder by the Islamic Resistance Movement (Hamas) of an Israeli border policeman, the Israeli Cabinet ordered the deportation to Lebanon of more than 400 alleged Palestinian supporters of Hamas. Owing to the Lebanese Government's refusal to co-operate in this action, the deportees were stranded in the territory between Israel's southern Leb-anese 'security zone' and Lebanon proper.

The deportations provoked international outrage, and intense diplomatic pressure was placed on Israel to revoke the expulsion order. On 18 December the UN Security Council unanimously approved a resolution (No. 799) condemning the deportations and demanding the return of the deportees to Israel. At the end of December, however, the Israeli Government asserted that only 10 of the deportees had been unjustifiably expelled and could return to Israel. The remainder would continue in exile. The future of the Middle East peace process, meanwhile, remained in doubt. The Palestinian delegation to the eighth round of bilateral negotiations had indicated that it would not resume talks until all of the deportees had been allowed to

return to Israel, and the PLO formally expressed the same position in mid-January 1993. At the beginning of February the Israeli Government reportedly indicated its willingness to allow some 100 of the deportees to return, but insisted that the remainder should serve a period of exile lasting at least until the end of 1993. On 5 February the ninth round of bilateral negotiations was formally suspended, but later in the month the UN Security Council was reported to have welcomed the Israeli Government's decision to permit 100 of the deportees to return to Israel, and to be ready to take no further action over the issue. Palestinians party to the peace negotiations, however, insisted that UN Security Council Resolution 799 should be implemented in full before they would resume discussions. In late February the US Secretary of State, Warren Christopher, made a tour of the Middle East, visiting Syria, Saudi Arabia, Kuwait, Lebanon and Israel, in an attempt to revive the peace process.

During March 1993 the number of violent confrontations between Palestinians and the Israeli security forces in the Occupied Territories (especially in the Gaza Strip) increased to such an extent that, at the end of the month, the Israeli Cabinet responded by sealing off the West Bank and Gaza indefinitely. Also, in late March the Knesset elected Ezer Weizman, leader of the Yahad political party, to replace Chaim Herzog as Presi-dent of Israel in May 1993; and Binyamin Netanyahu was elected leader of the opposition Likud in place of Itzhak Shamir. Ezer Weizman formally assumed the presidency in mid-May. At the end of the month a minor reshuffle of the Cabinet averted the defection of the ultra-orthodox Jewish party, Shas, from the governing coalition.

Meanwhile, on 27 April 1993 the ninth round of bilateral negotiations in the Middle East peace process, which had been formally suspended in February, resumed in Washington. The Palestinian delegation had reportedly only agreed to attend this round of talks following pressure from Arab governments, and after Israel had agreed to allow Faisal Husseini, the nominal leader of the delegation, to participate. Israel had previously refused to grant this concession because Husseini was a resident of East Jerusalem, the status of which Israel regards as distinct from that of the West Bank, the Gaza Strip and the Golan Heights. Israel was also reported to have undertaken no longer to resort to punitive deportations, and, with the USA, to have reaffirmed its commitment to UN Security Council Resolutions 242 and 338 as the terms of reference for the peace process. However, as previously, the talks achieved no progress on sub-stantive issues. In particular, Israel and the Palestinian delega-tion were reported to have failed to agree on a statement of principles regarding Palestinian self-rule in the Occupied Territories. A tenth round of bilateral negotiations, held in Washington on 15 June–1 July, concluded in deadlock, having achieved no progress on a statement of principles concerning Palestinian self-rule, which was now regarded as the key ele-ment in the Middle East peace process. However, it was reported that a committee had been established in an attempt to facilitate progress on this issue.

UNEXPECTED BREAKTHROUGH IN THE PEACE PROCESS

In late July 1993 Israeli armed forces mounted the most inten-sive air and artillery attacks on targets in Lebanon since 'Oper-ation Peace for Galilee' in 1982. The offensive ('Operation Accountability') was mounted in retaliation for attacks by Hez-bollah fighters on settlements in northern Israel, and provoked widespread international criticism for the high number of civi-lian casualties that it caused and for the perceived threat it posed to the Middle East peace process. At the eleventh round of bilateral negotiations, however, which commenced in Wash-ington on 31 August 1993, a major, unexpected breakthrough was achieved between Israel and the Palestinian delegation, which culminated in the signing, on 13 September, by Israel and the PLO, of a declaration of principles on Palestinian self-rule in the Occupied Territories. The agreement, which entailed mutual recognition by Israel and the PLO, had been elaborated during a series of secret negotiations mediated by Norwegian diplomacy (and was therefore commonly known as the Oslo accords). The Declaration of Principles established a detailed timetable for Israel's disengagement from the Occupied Territories and stipulated that a permanent settlement of the Palestinian question should be in place by December 1998. From 13 October 1993 Palestinian authorities were to assume responsibility for education and culture, health, social welfare, direct taxation and tourism in the Gaza Strip and the Jericho area of the West Bank, and a transitional period of Palestinian self-rule was to begin on 13 December. (For full details of the Declaration of Principles on Palestinian Self-Rule, see Documents on Palestine, p. 72.)

REACTION TO THE DECLARATION OF PRINCIPLES

While it was welcomed as a major breakthrough in the Middle East peace process, the Declaration of Principles was nevertheless regarded as only a tentative first step towards the resolution of the region's conflicts. Although the Israeli Prime Minister was able to obtain the ratification of the Declaration of Principles, and of Israel's recognition of the PLO, by the Knesset on 23 September 1993, there was widespread opposition to it from right-wing Israeli political groups. By the same token, the conclusion of the agreement aggravated divisions within the PLO and the wider Palestinian liberation movement. Within the PLO some senior officials, hitherto loyal to Yasser Arafat's leadership, now declared their opposition to him, while dissident groups, such as the Democratic Front for the Liberation of Palestine (DFLP), Hamas and Islamic Jihad denounced the Declaration of Principles as treason. Most observers regarded the future success of the agreement between Israel and the PLO as dependent on the ability of the mainstream PLO to gain popular support for it from Palestinians residing in the West Bank and Gaza. Reaction to the Declaration of Principles by other Arab governments engaged in peace negotiations with Israel was mixed. King Hussein welcomed the accord and Jordan immediately agreed an agenda for direct talks with Israel, which was also ratified by the Knesset on 23 September. Lebanon, however, feared that the divisions that the Declaration of Principles had provoked among Palestinians might lead to renewed conflict in Lebanon. It remained unclear, too, whether Syria—which neither condemned nor welcomed the agreement—would continue to support those Palestinian groups opposed to the PLO's position.

In mid-September 1993 the resignation of Aryeh Der'i as Minister of the Interior, following allegations of corruption, provoked the resignation of other Shas ministers from the Cabinet, thus reducing the governing coalition to an alliance between the Labour Party and Meretz (and the Government's majority in the Knesset to only two). In mid-March 1994, however, the Labour Party and Shas were reported to have concluded a new coalition agreement.

BEGINNING OF PALESTINIAN SELF-RULE

On 6 October 1993 Itzhak Rabin and Yasser Arafat held their first meeting in the context of the Declaration of Principles in Cairo, Egypt, where they agreed to begin talks on the implementation of the accord, and to establish general liaison, technical, economic and regional co-operation committees. On 13 October the PLO-Israeli joint liaison committee met for the first time, with delegations headed, respectively, by Mahmud Abbas and Shimon Peres, the Israeli Minister of Foreign Affairs. The committee was to meet frequently to monitor the implementation of the Declaration of Principles. The technical committee also held three meetings during October in the Egyptian coastal resort of Taba. Its task was to establish the precise details of Israel's military withdrawal from the Gaza Strip and Jericho, scheduled, under the terms of the accord, to take place between 13 December 1993 and 13 April 1994. At the October 1993 meetings, progress was apparently made on the creation of a Palestinian police force, although the issue of security measures to protect Israeli settlers in the Gaza Strip remained unresolved. Israel also reportedly agreed to the gradual release of some of the Palestinian prisoners that it held. Also in early October the Palestinian Central Council (a body of the PLO) formally approved the Declaration of Principles by a large majority. The joint PLO-Israel technical committee met on several occasions during November, but by the end of the month it appeared unlikely to have made sufficient progress for Israel's military withdrawal from the Gaza Strip and from Jericho to begin by 13 December. In particular, it was proving difficult to reach

agreement on three issues: arrangements for border security; the delineation of the Jericho (Ariha) area; and the release of Palestinian prisoners.

At the beginning of October 1993 talks had taken place in Washington, DC, between Crown Prince Hassan of Jordan and Shimon Peres. Despite reports of subsequent secret negotiations, King Hussein of Jordan insisted, during visits to Egypt and Syria in November, that Jordan would not conclude a separate peace agreement with Israel.

As had been feared, it proved impossible satisfactorily to negotiate the details of Israel's military withdrawal from the Gaza Strip and Jericho by 13 December 1993. This failure cast doubt on the whole of the September agreement between Israel and the PLO. The main cause of the failure remained the issue of security arrangements for border crossings between the Gaza Strip and Jericho and Jordan and Egypt. The PLO continued to insist that the border crossings should come under full, exclusive Palestinian control. Israel, however, opposed this claim since to grant it would imply at least a partial recognition of something resembling Palestinian sovereignty.

Following meetings in Damascus between the US Secretary of State, Warren Christopher, and Syria's President Assad and Minister of Foreign Affairs in early December 1993, Syria announced its willingness to resume bilateral negotiations with Israel in early 1994. Syrian Jews wishing to leave Syria were also to be granted exit visas. In early January, before a meeting between US President Clinton and President Assad took place, Israel appeared to indicate, tentatively, that it might be prepared to execute a full withdrawal from the Golan Heights in return for a comprehensive peace agreement with Syria. On 17 January it was reported that the Government would put the issue to a referendum before making such a withdrawal, apparently in an attempt to deflect in advance any pressure for a swift move towards a peace agreement with Syria that might emerge at the forthcoming summit meeting between the US and Syrian Presidents. There was likely to be far less support in the Knesset for a peace agreement with Syria—in particular, for concessions regarding the Golan Heights—than there had been for an agreement with the PLO. Bilateral negotiations between Israeli and Syrian delegations resumed in Washington on 24 January after a four-month hiatus.

On 9 February 1994 Israel and the PLO appeared to achieve a breakthrough in their stalled negotiations when they signed an agreement to share control of the two future international border crossings. It was reported that security arrangements for Jewish settlers in the Gaza Strip had also been decided: three access routes to Jewish settlements there were to remain under Israeli control. However, the boundaries of the Jericho enclave remained undefined. Further talks began on 14 February to address the implementation of the first stage of Palestinian autonomy in the Gaza Strip and the Jericho area; the size, structure and jurisdiction of a future Palestinian police force; control of sea and air space; and the delineation of the Jericho enclave.

In late February 1994 the PLO, together with the other Arab parties, withdrew from the peace process with Israel, following the murder, by a right-wing Jewish extremist, of some 30 Muslim worshippers in a mosque in Hebron (Al-Khalil) on the West Bank. Discussions between the PLO and Israel resumed at the end of March, when the two sides signed an agreement on security in Hebron and the whole of the Occupied Territories. Israel agreed, among other things, to allow a team of international observers to monitor efforts to restore stability in Hebron. Earlier in the month the UN Security Council had adopted a resolution (No. 904) condemning the killings there, prompting Syria, Jordan and Lebanon to agree to resume talks with Israel in April.

In late April 1994 Israel and the PLO signed an agreement concerning economic relations between Israel and the autonomous Palestinian entity during the five-year period leading to self-rule. At the end of the month it was reported that the US Secretary of State, Warren Christopher, had submitted to President Assad of Syria Israel's proposals regarding a withdrawal from the occupied Golan Heights in exchange for a full peace agreement with Syria.

On 4 May 1994 in Cairo (Egypt), Israel and the PLO signed an agreement detailing arrangements for Palestinian self-rule in Gaza and Jericho (see Documents on Palestine, p. 76). The agreement provided for Israel's military withdrawal from Gaza and Jericho and the deployment there of a 9,000-strong Palestinian police force. A nominated Palestinian (National) Authority (PA) was to assume the responsibilities of the Israeli military administration in Gaza and Jericho, although Israeli authorities were to retain control in matters of external security and foreign affairs. Elections for a Palestinian Council, which, under the terms of the Declaration of Principles, were to have taken place in Gaza and the West Bank in July, were now postponed until October. Israel's military withdrawal from Gaza and Jericho was completed on 13 May, and on 17 May the PLO formally assumed control of the Israeli civil administration's departments there. On 18 May Yasser Arafat held talks with Israel's Minister of Foreign Affairs, Shimon Peres, regarding future negotiations on the extension of Palestinian self-rule in the West Bank. On 26–28 May the PA held its inaugural meeting in Tunis, setting out a political programme and distributing ministerial portfolios. It had originally been Arafat's intention to appoint 24 members to the PA (12 from within the Occupied Territories and 12 from the Palestinian diaspora). In the event, some of his appointees refused to serve on the PA—reflecting the extent of divisions within the mainstream Palestinian movement regarding the terms of the peace with Israel—and only 20 members assembled in Tunis. The PA held its first meeting in Gaza in late June.

On 1 July 1994 Arafat returned to Gaza City, a homecoming that had far more symbolic than practical significance. Negotiations with Israel continued on the extension of Palestinian authority, the redeployment of Israeli armed forces in the West Bank and on the holding of Palestinian elections. In late July Israel and Jordan signed a joint declaration that formally ended the state of war between them and further defined the arrangements for future bilateral discussions. In late August Israel and the PLO signed an agreement which extended the authority of the PA to include education, health, tourism, social welfare and taxation. In September the PA was said to have approved plans for elections to be held in Gaza and the West Bank within three months. However, the size of the future Palestinian legislature remained unclear. The PLO reportedly wished to elect a 100-member council, while Israel insisted on no more than 25 members.

IMPROVED RELATIONS WITH THE ARAB WORLD

At the beginning of September 1994 Morocco became the second Arab state to establish diplomatic relations with Israel, albeit at a low level. Tunisia did likewise on the following day. On 8 September Itzhak Rabin announced the details of a plan for a partial withdrawal of Israeli armed forces from the occupied Golan Heights, after which a three-year trial period of Israeli-Syrian 'normalization' would ensue. The proposals were rejected by President Assad, although he did state his willingness to work towards peace with Israel. Israel also enjoyed rapidly improving relations with Jordan. King Hussein met with Rabin in Aqaba at the end of September to draft a timetable for a full Israeli-Jordanian peace treaty. This was achieved in late October when the two countries signed a formal peace agreement, fixing their borders and providing for normal relations. The treaty was criticized by the Syrian Government, which had long opposed such bilateral initiatives. Despite the belief in the Arab world that Jordan's move to normalize relations with Israel had been overly hasty, there were continuing signs of a less antagonistic attitude towards the Jewish State. On 29 September the six member states of the Co-operation Council for the Arab States of the Gulf (Gulf Co-operation Council—GCC) announced their decision to lift the subsidiary elements of the Arab economic boycott of Israel. At the end of October US President Clinton visited Damascus in an attempt to break the deadlock in Israeli-Syrian negotiations. In December there were reports of high-level military contacts between the two countries. In February 1995 Israel completed its withdrawal from a small area of Jordanian territory it had occupied since the war of June 1967.

NEW CRISIS IN NEGOTIATIONS

A conference of international donors, sponsored by the World Bank, in Paris, France, on 8–9 September 1994, collapsed almost immediately owing to an Israeli–Palestinian dispute over Palestinian investment plans to fund projects in East Jerusalem. Israel regarded such plans as compromising negotiations on the final status of Jerusalem which, under the terms of the Declaration of Principles, were not due to begin before May 1996. On 13 September 1994 Yasser Arafat and the Israeli Minister of Foreign Affairs met in Oslo, Norway, and negotiated a 15-point agreement whose aim was to accelerate economic aid to the PA. The issue of economic aid was to assume increasing importance during late 1994 and early 1995, as Arafat's leadership of the PA and, indeed, the authority of the entire 'moderate' Palestinian movement became ever more crisis-stricken as a result of what its opponents viewed as its increasingly conspicuous injustices. Mainstream Palestinians argued that it was impossible for the newly-formed Palestinian police force to keep the peace in the volatile Gaza Strip without increased economic aid. The failure of the Palestinian authorities to guarantee security in the areas over which they now had partial control provided Israel with an excuse not to allow them to extend their jurisdiction in the West Bank, even though Israeli armed forces had also been unable to guarantee secure conditions in the Gaza Strip. On 25 September 1994 Arafat and Rabin met at the Erez crossing point between Gaza and Israel to discuss the future Palestinian elections. It was agreed to meet again in October to negotiate a compromise on the size of the Palestinian Council, Israel having rejected Arafat's proposal to hold the elections on 1 November as unrealistic. At the same time, Arafat agreed to 'take all measures' to prevent attacks on Israeli targets by opponents of the Oslo accords.

One reason for the growing crisis in negotiations between Israel and the Palestinians was the revival of the controversial issue of Jewish settlements in the West Bank. On 26 September 1994 Rabin approved a plan to construct some 1,000 new housing units at a Jewish settlement some 3 km inside the West Bank in an apparent reversal of the 'freeze' he had imposed on new construction in 1992 in return for US loan guarantees. The PLO claimed that this decision contravened both the letter and the spirit of the Declaration of Principles. (It was later reported that the number of Jewish settlers in the West Bank had increased by 10% during 1994.)

ISLAMIST ATTACKS THREATEN PEACE PROCESS

The Islamist organizations remained the most militant opponents of the Oslo accords and in the autumn of 1994 both Hamas and Islamic Jihad escalated their campaigns of violence. On 9 October Hamas claimed responsibility for an attack in Jerusalem, in which an Israeli soldier and a Palestinian died. On the same day another Israeli soldier was kidnapped near Tel-Aviv by Hamas fighters, who subsequently demanded the release from Israeli jails of their leader, Sheikh Ahmad Yassin, and other Palestinian prisoners in exchange for his life. Despite Palestinian action to detain some 300 Hamas members in the Gaza Strip, the kidnapped soldier was killed in the West Bank on 14 October during an abortive rescue attempt by the IDF. On 19 October an attack by a Hamas suicide bomber in Tel-Aviv, in which 22 people died, prompted Israel to close its borders with the West Bank and Gaza for an indefinite period.

On 2 November 1994 a member of Islamic Jihad was killed in a car bomb attack in Gaza. Many Palestinians blamed the attack on the Israeli security forces. On 11 November three Israeli soldiers were killed in a suicide bombing by Islamic Jihad near a Jewish settlement in the Gaza Strip. Inevitably the arrest by the PA of Hamas and Islamic Jihad cadres increased tensions between the opposing factions, which erupted into violence on 18 November when Palestinian security forces opened fire on Islamist demonstrators in the centre of Gaza. Twelve Palestinians were reportedly killed in the incident and the subsequent violence that broke out throughout the Gaza Strip. The shootings appeared to confirm the perception of opponents of the peace process that the PA and its security forces were fast becoming a proxy of the State of Israel. The EU responded to the crisis by stating that it would expedite US $125m. in loans and guarantees promised earlier in the month. For its part, the Palestinian opposition denied that the clashes had arisen as a result of economic factors, attributing the disturbances instead to the perceived intrinsic deficiencies of the Declaration of Principles. Further violence in the Gaza

Strip on 19 November resulted in the deaths of two Palestinians and an Israeli soldier, prompting a UN official to claim that aid programmes to the PA were failing and that the situation in Gaza had deteriorated since the start of the Oslo process. It became clear in December that Israel's security concerns would continue to delay the redeployment of its armed forces in the West Bank and the holding of Palestinian elections, since Rabin stated that the elections would either have to take place in the continued presence of Israeli armed forces, or be postponed for a year.

Perhaps the most serious blow yet to the peace negotiations between Israel and the PLO was the suicide bombing at Beit Lid in Israel on 22 January 1995, in which 21 people—mostly Israeli soldiers—died and more than 60 were injured. Islamic Jihad claimed responsibility for the attack, which resulted in the Israeli Cabinet again sealing Israel's borders with the Occupied Territories, and postponing the planned release of some 5,500 Palestinian prisoners. Opinion polls published in Israel on 27 January revealed that the majority of Israeli citizens now opposed the peace process; while the majority of Palestinians favoured further suicide attacks against Israeli targets. The polls also revealed a drastic decline in support for the Israeli Labour Party. The leader of Likud, Binyamin Netanyahu, responding to public opinion, made an electoral promise to end the peace negotiations, take tougher measures against suspected terrorists and abandon the promised return of more land occupied in 1967.

At the beginning of February 1995 an emergency meeting of the leaders of Egypt, Israel, Jordan and the PLO was held in Cairo: the meeting's final communiqué condemned acts of terror and violence; and expressed support for the Oslo accords and the wider peace process. On 12 February US President Clinton held a meeting with the Israeli and the Egyptian Ministers of Foreign Affairs and the Palestinian (PA) Minister of Planning and Economic Co-operation, Nabil Shaath, in Washington, DC. Shimon Peres, the Israeli Minister of Foreign Affairs, reportedly stated after the meeting that any further expansion of Palestinian self-rule in the West Bank was conditional upon real progress by the PA in suppressing terrorism. In early March Yasser Arafat and Shimon Peres met in Gaza for talks, after which it was announced that 1 July 1995 had been adopted as the date by which an agreement on the expansion of Palestinian self-rule in the West Bank should be concluded.

CABINET RESHUFFLES

On 21 February 1995 Rabin appointed ministers, in an acting capacity, to two portfolios which had been reserved for the Shas religious party. (Shas had announced at the beginning of the month that, owing to its fears regarding Jewish security and the peace process, it would not rejoin the coalition Government.) The Likud party appeared to suffer a serious division in the same month, when one of its most prominent members, the former Minister of Foreign Affairs, David Levy, announced that he was forming a new party to contest the legislative elections scheduled for 1996. The division was reportedly the result of Levy's opposition to new selection procedures for general election candidates which Likud had formally adopted on 5 June. Levy's new, anonymous political movement (later identified as Gesher) was formally inaugurated on 18 June, although Levy himself remained a member of Likud.

ISRAEL–SYRIA TALKS RESUME

In mid-March 1995 it was announced that Israel and Syria had agreed to resume peace negotiations, which had been suspended since February 1994. The resumption of talks would initially involve the Israeli and Syrian ambassadors to the USA, meeting, at Syria's insistence, in the presence of US officials. At a later stage it was planned to introduce to the negotiations military technicians and, ultimately, the Syrian and Israeli Chiefs of Staff. Speculation that a breakthrough might shortly be achieved was subdued, however, in late April, when the Syrian Vice-President made it clear that Syria had no intention of renouncing its demand that Israel should withdraw from the Golan Heights to the border pertaining before the June 1967 war. Nevertheless, on 24 May Syria and Israel concluded a 'framework understanding on security arrangements' which was intended to facilitate negotiations on security issues. At the end

of the month Shimon Peres stated that Israel had proposed that its forces should withdraw from the Golan Heights over a four-year period. Syria, however, had insisted that the withdrawal should be effected over 18 months. Peace talks between Israel and Syria resumed in late December 1995 in Maryland, USA, and a second round of US-mediated talks took place there in early January 1996.

VIOLENCE PRECEDES AGREEMENT

In early April 1995 two suicide bomb attacks in the Gaza Strip killed seven Israeli soldiers and wounded more than 50 people. Hamas and Islamic Jihad subsequently claimed responsibility for the attacks, in the aftermath of which the Palestinian police force reportedly arrested as many as 300 members of the two groups. The following day the PA announced that the Palestinian police force would disarm all members of 'rejectionist' groups opposed to the Oslo accords. On 18 April PA officials met representatives of Islamic Jihad and Hamas and demanded that the two groups should terminate all of their armed operations against Israeli targets in and from the autonomous areas. The representatives were reported to be willing to agree to a limited cease-fire, provided that the PA released members of the two organizations held in detention, did not disarm the groups, and undertook not to allow Israeli armed forces to carry out operations against them. Attention once again shifted to the issue of settlements, when in late April it was announced that the Israeli Government had approved a plan to take possession of some 54 ha of mainly Arab-owned land in two sections of East Jerusalem for the construction of Jewish neighbourhoods and facilities. An emergency meeting of the Arab League condemned Israel's decision to expropriate the land. The UN Security Council subsequently prepared a resolution which demanded that the decision be rescinded; however, the USA exercised its veto to prevent its adoption. On 22 May 1995, however, the Israeli Government announced that the plan had been suspended after Hadash and the Democratic Arab Party drafted a 'no-confidence' motion in response, which Likud was likely to have supported. (The Democratic Arab Party subsequently forced a confidence vote in the Knesset which the Government won.)

Despite intensive negotiations, it proved impossible to conclude an agreement on the expansion of Palestinian self-rule in the West Bank by the target date of 1 July 1995. The principal obstacles to an accord were the question of precisely to where Israeli troops in the West Bank would redeploy; and the exact nature of security arrangements to be made for about 130,000 Jewish settlers who were to remain there.

On 21 August 1995 a suicide bombing of a bus in Jerusalem killed six people. Hamas claimed responsibility for the attack, which raised the number of deaths in bombings over the previous 16 months to 77 and inevitably provoked further demands from those Israeli elements opposed to the Declaration of Principles that the talks should be suspended. Some opponents of the peace process argued that there was now little point in proceeding with interim agreements, and that 'final status' negotiations between Israel and the Palestinians should begin immediately. This was the general consensus of the nationalist right wing and derived from a belief that the less land that was under Palestinian control at the time of 'final status' talks, the weaker the PA's bargaining position would be over such crucial issues as settlement and Jerusalem.

It was not until 28 September 1995 that the Israeli-Palestinian Interim Agreement on the West Bank and the Gaza Strip was finally signed by Israel and the PLO (see Documents on Palestine, p. 80). Its main provisions were the withdrawal of Israeli armed forces from a further six West Bank towns— Nablus (Nabulus), Ramallah (Ram Allah), Jenin (Janin), Tulkaram (Tulkarm), Kakilya (Qalqilya) and Bethlehem (Beit Lahm)—and a partial redeployment away from the town of Hebron; Palestinian legislative elections to an 82-member Palestinian Council, and for a Palestinian Executive President; and the release, in three phases, of Palestinian prisoners detained by Israel. There were many criticisms of the new agreement, many of which focused on the sheer complexity–and corresponding ambiguity–of the 400-page document. It was inevitable, too, that the Interim Agreement would raise further, serious doubts about precisely what kind of entity the PA might be at the conclusion of 'final status' negotiations, given Israel's clear desire to maintain jurisdiction over the West Bank settlements. Opposition Palestinian groups condemned the accord as inadequate, while Israeli hardliners denounced it for having granted too many concessions to the Palestinians. In mid-October, meanwhile, Israeli armed forces launched an intensive military operation in southern Lebanon after a bomb attack by Hezbollah had caused the deaths of six Israeli soldiers.

RABIN'S ASSASSINATION AND ITS AFTERMATH

The peace process was once again jeopardized on 4 November 1995 when the Israeli Prime Minister was assassinated while leaving a peace rally in Tel-Aviv. His assassin, Yigal Amir, was a young religious nationalist who opposed the peace process, and in particular Israeli withdrawal from the West Bank. While it was apparently an independent act, the assassination seemed certain further to marginalize those on the extreme right wing of Israeli politics who had advocated violence as a means of halting the implementation of the Oslo accords. The assassination also provoked criticism of Likud which, it was widely felt, had not sufficiently distanced itself from such extremist elements. Following the assassination, Shimon Peres, hitherto the Minister of Foreign Affairs, became acting Prime Minister. On 15 November, with the agreement of the opposition Likud, Peres was invited to form a new government. On 21 November the leaders of the outgoing coalition parties—Labour, Meretz and Yi'ud—signed a new coalition agreement, and Peres announced a new Cabinet, which was formally approved by the Knesset on the following day.

In spite of Rabin's assassination, Israeli armed forces completed their withdrawal from the West Bank town of Jenin on 13 November 1995, and during December they withdrew from Tulkarm, Nablus, Qalqilya, Bethlehem and Ramallah. With regard to Hebron, Israel and the PA signed an agreement transferring jurisdiction in some 17 areas of civilian affairs from Israel to the PA. In early December Shimon Peres and Yasser Arafat held talks at the Erez border point between Israel and the Gaza Strip, at which Peres confirmed that Israel would release some 1,000 Palestinian prisoners before the Palestinian legislative and presidential elections scheduled for January 1996. In February 1996 Peres announced that elections to the Knesset and—for the first time—the direct election of the Prime Minister, would take place as soon as electoral legislation allowed—in late May.

RELATIONS WITH JORDAN

On 10 January 1996 King Hussein of Jordan began a public visit to Tel-Aviv, during the course of which Israel and Jordan signed a number of agreements relating to the normalization of economic and cultural relations. These included a transport agreement dealing with road links between Israel, Jordan and the Palestinian Autonomous Areas and providing for an air link between Israel and Jordan. However, the attempted assassination of Hamas leader Khalid Meshaal by Israeli Mossad agents in Amman, Jordan, in late September 1997 provoked a flurry of diplomatic activity to preserve cordial relations between Israel and Jordan (see below).

SUICIDE BOMB ATTACKS RESUME

Palestinian legislative and presidential elections were held in late January 1996, leading in principle to the final stage of the peace process, when Palestinian and Israeli negotiators would address such issues as Jerusalem, the rights of Palestinian refugees, the status of Jewish settlements in the Palestinian Autonomous Areas and the extent of that autonomy. In late February and early March, however, suicide bombings in Jerusalem, Ashkelon and Tel-Aviv caused the deaths of more than 50 Israelis and led to a further suspension of the peace process. Following the attacks in Jerusalem and Ashkelon, Israel ordered the indefinite closure of the West Bank and Gaza and demanded that the Palestinian authorities suppress the activities of Hamas and Islamic Jihad in the areas under their control. It was unclear, however, whether either of these groups was responsible for the bomb attacks. A hitherto unknown group, the 'Yahya Ayyash Units', claimed responsibility for the first attacks on 25 February, apparently to avenge the assassination—

allegedly by Israeli agents—of a leading member (Yahya Ayyash) of Hamas in January 1996. Yasser Arafat, now the elected Palestinian President, condemned the bombings and in late February more than 200 Hamas activists were reportedly detained by the Palestinian security forces.

The two suicide bomb attacks carried out at the beginning of March 1996 (for which the 'Yahya Ayyash Units' again claimed responsibility) led Israel to impose even more stringent security measures and to assert the right of its armed forces to enter the areas under Palestinian jurisdiction when its security was at stake. The Palestinian authorities were reported to have held emergency talks with the leadership of Hamas and Islamic Jihad and to have outlawed their armed wings and other, unspecified Palestinian paramilitary groups.

The suicide bombings also affected the talks taking place between Israeli and Syrian negotiators in the USA. Following the second attacks in March 1996 the Israeli team returned to Israel. On 18 March Peres revealed that peace negotiations with Syria had effectively been suspended because Syria had refused to condemn the violence in precisely the way the USA had requested; and to give an assurance that it would not sponsor terrorist activities. Syria claimed that it did condemn terrorism in all forms, but drew a distinction between terrorism and legitimate resistance against occupation.

'OPERATION GRAPES OF WRATH'

Syria and Lebanon both declined an invitation to attend a summit meeting, held in the Egyptian town of Sharm esh-Sheikh on 13 March 1996, at which representatives of 27 countries expressed their support for the Middle East peace process and pledged to redouble their efforts to combat terrorism. On 10 April Israel launched a 16-day bombing operation ('Grapes of Wrath') to destroy Hezbollah bases in southern Lebanon, resulting in the displacement of some 400,000 civilians (see the chapter on Lebanon). The military campaign ended suddenly after Israeli shells hit a UN base at Qana and killed more than 100 Lebanese civilians sheltering there. On 27 April a partial cease-fire was agreed between the two sides, stipulating that neither side should target civilians. An international monitoring committee (the Israel-Lebanon Monitoring Group—ILMG), consisting of French, Israeli, Syrian, Lebanese and US officials, was established in order to oversee adherence to the terms of the cease-fire. The Israeli authorities insisted that the Qana shelling had been an accident, and on 14 June 1997 Israel rejected a UN resolution proposing that it should pay a total of US \$1.7m. in compensation for the victims of the incident.

In early April 1996 Israel and Turkey signed a number of military co-operation agreements, one of which provided for the establishment of a joint organization for research and strategy. Syria condemned the agreement as a threat to its own security and to that of all Arab and Islamic countries.

Israel welcomed the decision of the Palestine National Council in late April 1996 to amend the Palestinian National Charter, or PLO Covenant (the constitution of the Palestinian resistance movement), thereby removing all clauses demanding the destruction of Israel. The Israeli Government had demanded that the Covenant be amended by 7 May 1996 as a precondition for its participation in the final stage of peace negotiations with the PLO.

LIKUD RETURNS TO POWER

In the months following the assassination of Itzhak Rabin, the victory of the Labour Party and its leader, Shimon Peres, in the legislative and prime ministerial elections scheduled for 29 May 1996 was widely regarded as inevitable. Most significantly the US Administration appeared to exclude the possibility of any other outcome, even though the suicide bombings during February and March led to increased public support for Likud and other right-wing political groups. In the event, no party gained an outright majority of the 120 seats in the new Knesset, but the Likud leader, Binyamin Netanyahu, gained a marginal and unexpected victory over Shimon Peres in the direct election of the Prime Minister. Prior to the legislative election a formal alliance between Likud, the Tzomet party and Gesher had been announced. The success of the religious parties, Shas and the NRP—even though they probably gained seats at the expense of the Likud-led alliance—was the key factor in determining that the new Government would be formed by Likud. A reported 79.7% of the 3.9m.-strong Israeli electorate participated in the elections.

The election of a Likud-led Government appeared to have grave implications for the future of the Israeli-Palestinian peace negotiations since, during the election campaign, the Likud alliance had explicitly stated that it would never agree to the establishment of a Palestinian state and even seemed to indicate that it was prepared to renege on some aspects of agreements which Israel had already concluded with the Palestinians. On 31 May 1996 the Palestinian Council of Ministers (formed after the Palestinian legislative elections in January) and the Executive Committee of the PLO held a joint meeting in Gaza and urged the incoming Israeli Government to implement all previous accords and to commence the final stage of the peace talks.

Prime Minister Netanyahu commenced negotiations to form a cabinet on 2 June 1996, and on 16 and 17 June signed a series of agreements between the Likud alliance and Shas, the NRP, Israel B'Aliyah, United Torah Judaism and the Third Way to form a coalition which would command the support of 66 deputies in the 120-member Knesset. In addition, Moledet agreed to support the Government, but did not formally enter the coalition. On 18 June the new Government received the approval of the Knesset. Its statement of policy excluded the possibility of granting Palestinian statehood or, with regard to Syria, of relinquishing *de facto* sovereignty of the occupied Golan Heights.

On 21–23 June 1996, in response to Likud's electoral victory, a summit meeting of the leaders of all Arab countries (with the exception of Iraq) was convened in Cairo. The meeting's final communiqué reiterated Israel's withdrawal from all occupied territories (including East Jerusalem) as a basic requirement for a comprehensive Middle East peace settlement. In July the intransigent character of the new Israeli Government was enhanced by the incorporation into the Cabinet of Ariel Sharon—who had played a leading role in the creation and expansion of controversial Jewish settlements in the West Bank—although his appointment as Minister of Infrastructure was made only after the Minister of Foreign Affairs had forced it by threatening to resign, thus endangering Likud's alliance with Gesher.

IDF-PA CLASHES THREATEN PEACE PROCESS

By late August 1996 Palestinian frustration at what were regarded as deliberate attempts by the new Israeli Government to slow down the peace process was increasingly evident. In June it was reported that Prime Minister Netanyahu had postponed further discussion of the withdrawal of Israeli armed forces from the West Bank town of Hebron—where they remained in order to provide security for some 400 Jewish settlers. An agreement for their withdrawal by 20 March 1996 had been concluded with the Palestinian authorities, but had been suspended by Shimon Peres following the suicide bomb attacks in February and March. Furthermore, Netanyahu had refused to meet Yasser Arafat and had stated he would never do so. As a sign of their growing dissatisfaction with the new Likud-led Government, the PA organized a short general strike at the end of the month. The strike was held in particular protest at the refusal of the Israeli authorities to allow Palestinian Muslims to participate in Friday prayers at the al-Aqsa Mosque in Jerusalem and also at a government decision to expand existing Jewish settlements in the West Bank. In response to US pressure, Netanyahu and Arafat met, for the first time, at the Erez crossing point between Israel and Gaza, on 4 September. At a press conference following the meeting, they confirmed their commitment to the implementation of the Interim Agreement.

In mid-September 1996, at a meeting of the Arab League member states, the Syrian Minister of Foreign Affairs stated that the Arab states represented there had agreed in future to link relations with Israel to progress made in the peace process. Shortly afterwards it was announced that the Israeli Ministry of Defence had approved plans to construct some 1,800 new homes at existing Jewish settlements in the West Bank.

On 25 September 1996 violent confrontations began between Palestinian security forces, Palestinian civilians and the Israeli armed forces; at least 50 Palestinians and 18 Israelis were killed and hundreds wounded. The West Bank town of Ramallah

was the initial point of confrontation, and the direct cause of the disturbances was attributed to the decision of the Israeli Government to open the north end of the Hasmonean tunnel which ran beneath the al-Aqsa Mosque in East Jerusalem. Most observers, however, viewed the violence as the inevitable culmination of Palestinian anger at the Israeli Government's failure to implement agreements it had signed with the PA. There was speculation that the violence, the most serious in the West Bank and Gaza since 1967, marked the beginning of a new Palestinian *intifada* and signalled the end of the peace process. The Israeli military authorities declared a state of emergency in the Gaza Strip and the West Bank, and threatened military intervention to suppress the disturbances. A special session of the UN Security Council was convened, and intense international diplomacy led to the holding of a crisis summit meeting in Washington, DC, hosted by US President Bill Clinton and attended by Binyamin Netanyahu, Yasser Arafat and King Hussein of Jordan. The meeting reportedly achieved nothing, but on 6 October it was announced that, following further US mediation, Israel had agreed to resume negotiations on the partial withdrawal of its armed forces from Hebron. On 7 October, at the opening of the winter session of the Knesset, Netanyahu stated that once the question of the redeployment from Hebron had been settled, Israel would reopen its borders with the West Bank and Gaza—which had remained closed since February 1996—and move quickly towards seeking a final settlement with the Palestinians.

HEBRON AGREEMENTS

In mid-January 1997 Israel and the PA finally concluded an agreement on the withdrawal of Israeli armed forces from Hebron. The principal terms of the US-brokered agreement were that Israeli forces should withdraw from 80% of the town of Hebron within ten days, and that the first of three subsequent withdrawals from the West Bank should take place six weeks after the signing of the agreement, and the remaining two by August 1998. With regard to security arrangements for Jewish settlers in central Hebron, Palestinian police patrols would be armed only with pistols in areas close to the Jewish enclaves, while joint Israeli-Palestinian patrols would secure the heights above the enclaves. The 'final status' negotiations on borders, the Jerusalem issue, Jewish settlements and Palestinian refugees— arguably the most intractable elements of the entire Arab–Israeli dispute—were to commence within two months of the signing of the agreement on Hebron. As guarantor of the agreements, the USA undertook to obtain the release of some Palestinian prisoners, and to ensure that Israel continued to engage in negotiations for a Palestinian airport in the Gaza Strip and for safe passage for Palestinians between the West Bank and Gaza. The USA also sought to ensure that the Palestinians would continue to combat terrorism, complete the revision of the PLO Covenant and consider Israeli requests to extradite Palestinians suspected of involvement in attacks in Israel.

HAR HOMA

The conclusion of the agreement on the withdrawal of Israeli armed forces from Hebron marked the first significant progress in the peace process since Netanyahu's election as Prime Minister. However, renewed hopes for the future of the process appeared to be short-lived. The Israeli decision of February 1997 to proceed with the construction of 6,500 housing units at Har Homa in East Jerusalem attracted international criticism, but two UN Security Council resolutions, submitted during March, urging Israel to reconsider such plans were vetoed by the USA. The first veto was issued at a time of increasing tension between Israel and the PA after a unilateral decision was made by Israel to redeploy its troops from only 9% of the West Bank; Arafat rejected the proposal. Anti-Israeli sentiments intensified throughout the Arab world, but the Arab cause continued to be undermined by violent atrocities, including the massacre by a Jordanian soldier of seven Israeli schoolgirls in Nayarayim, an enclave between Israel and Jordan, on 13 March. On 14 March King Hussein visited the families of the deceased to express his condolences. Israeli intransigence over Har Homa prompted the Palestinians to abandon the 'final status' talks, scheduled to begin on 17 March, and on the following day construction at the site began. Riots erupted immediately, reaching a climax on 21 March when a bomb, planted by Hamas, exploded in a Tel-Aviv café, killing four and wounding more than 60 people. Netanyahu accused Arafat of extending an invitation to Islamist activists to resume terrorist attacks, and the Israeli Cabinet immediately ordered a general closure of the West Bank and Gaza. At the end of the month the League of Arab States voted to resume their economic boycott of Israel, suspend moves to establish diplomatic relations with that country, and withdraw from multilateral peace talks. (Jordan, the PA and Egypt were excluded from the legislation owing to their binding bilateral agreements with Israel.) On 1 April it was reported that two suicide bombers had killed themselves in an attempted attack on two buses containing schoolchildren travelling from Jewish settlements in the Gaza Strip. Despite the claims of an anonymous caller that the bombers were members of Hamas, both Hamas and Islamic Jihad denied responsibility for the attack, and the PA claimed that one of the alleged bombers had been, in fact, the victim of an Israeli grenade attack. Meanwhile, in New York, Arab states continued to petition the UN General Assembly to appeal for a halt to the Har Homa development. On 7 April Netanyahu met President Clinton in Washington and insisted that he would not 'freeze' construction. Riots erupted in Hebron the following day after a Palestinian was allegedly murdered by Jewish settlers. Three people died and more than 100 were wounded in the clashes. Demonstrations eventually subsided at the end of April, when the West Bank and Gaza were reopened.

The intensity of Palestinian opposition to the construction of Jewish settlements became increasingly apparent when, at the beginning of May 1997, the Palestinian Minister of Justice, Furayh Abu Middayn, announced that the PA would sentence to death any Palestinian who was found to have sold land to Jews. This proclamation provoked a spate of unlawful killings: within one month three Arab land dealers were reportedly executed by a newly established vigilante group called 'The Guardians of the Holy Land'. The extent of renewed Israeli–Palestinian hostility was also made evident during May when the USA's chief Middle East negotiator, Dennis Ross, returned to the USA following a nine-day mediation initiative in the region, having failed to secure any hope of a resumption of peace talks.

Both the Har Homa construction and the limited redeployment of the West Bank supported by the Israeli Government were regarded by many as a vitiation of the 1993 Declaration of Principles. The agreement was further undermined in May 1997 when the Minister of National Infrastructure, Ariel Sharon, proposed to deny Palestinians the right to drill for water and suggested that Israel should assume authority for one-half of the water resources on the West Bank. Hopes for the future resumption of the Oslo peace process were further frustrated when the Israeli daily newspaper, *Ha'aretz*, reported the results of a US study which claimed that more than 25% of Jewish settlers' homes in the West Bank and Gaza were uninhabited (although Israeli statisticians insisted that only 12% of the settlements were unoccupied). The same newspaper later reported that Netanyahu's original plan, evolved within the framework of the Oslo accords, to relinquish an eventual 90% of the West Bank had been revised in a new proposal—the so-called 'Allon plus' plan—to a 40% redeployment.

In mid-June 1997 the US House of Representatives voted in favour of recognizing Jerusalem as the undivided capital of Israel and of transferring the US embassy there, from Tel-Aviv. President Clinton was reported to have strongly disapproved of the vote and of its possible implications for the peace process. The decision coincided with violent clashes between Palestinian civilians and Israeli troops in both Gaza and Hebron: within one week more than 150 Palestinians were reportedly shot and wounded. Yasser Arafat, fearing Israeli reoccupation of Hebron (where the fighting reached a climax at the end of June), assigned 200 police officers to patrol the streets. Although the police presence appeared to be largely successful in Hebron, four police officers were arrested by Israeli police outside Nablus on suspicion of conspiring to attack Israeli targets. At the same time the Palestinian police force announced the discovery of large stocks of ammunition in Beit Sahur on the West Bank, alleged to belong to Hamas.

JERUSALEM BOMBS THWART HOPES FOR RENEWED TALKS

At the beginning of July 1997 a series of meetings were held between the US Under-Secretary of State for Political Affairs, Thomas Pickering, and Israeli and Palestinian officials, with the aim of resuming negotiations between Israel and the PA. On 28 July both sides announced that peace talks were to be resumed in early August. However on 30 July, the eve of a planned visit to Israel by Dennis Ross, two Hamas suicide bombers killed 14 civilians and wounded more than 150 others at a Jewish market in Jerusalem. The event effectively paralysed the peace process: Ross cancelled his visit and Israel immediately halted payment of tax revenues to the PA and closed the Gaza Strip and the West Bank. The sanctions provoked furious protest from Palestinians, as well as widespread international condemnation. Nevertheless, Binyamin Netanyahu insisted that restrictions would remain until the PA demonstrated a commitment to combat terrorism. On 18 August 30% of some US $50m. in tax revenue owed to the Palestinians was released by the Israeli Government. Rather than condemning Palestinian political organizations, Arafat convened a two-day forum in August during which he publicly embraced Hamas leaders and urged them, together with Islamic Jihad, to unite with the Palestinian people against Israeli policies. On 26 August Hamas rejected a request from Palestinian leaders to suspend their attacks. Nevertheless, Israel relaxed its closure of the Palestinian areas on 1 September. Sanctions were reinforced on 4 September, however, after a triple suicide bombing took place in West Jerusalem, killing eight people (five Israelis and the bombers), and wounding more than 150 others. The bombing, followed one day later by the death of 12 Israeli commandos in Lebanon (see below), prompted warnings from the Israeli Security Cabinet that possible military attacks on Palestinian and Arab territories might be launched. The security crisis cast doubt on the viability of a planned visit by Madeleine Albright, US Secretary of State, to the Middle East in mid-September, in order to discuss substantive political issues. However, Albright's tour of the region, undertaken during 10–15 September, was positively received, and renewed diplomatic activity resulted, in early October, in the first direct discussions between Netanyahu and Arafat for eight months.

ISRAELI CASUALTIES IN LEBANON

The deterioration in relations between Israel and the PA coincided with renewed hostilities in the north of the country, after Hezbollah launched their first major rocket attack for 16 months on civilians in the Israeli town of Kiryat Shmona in early August 1997. The barrage, in retaliation for attacks by Israeli commandos in which five Hezbollah members were killed, prompted further air-strikes against targets in southern Lebanon. Violence escalated and on 18 August the Israeli military proxy, the South Lebanon Army (SLA) shelled the Lebanese port of Sidon, killing at least six and wounding more than 30 civilians. Israeli denials of responsibility, claiming that the attack was the sole initiative of the SLA, were rejected by Hezbollah. The international monitoring committee convened in mid-August in response to the escalating violence but failed to achieve a reconciliation. Indeed, any hopes for an immediate restoration of peace were shattered when, on 5 September, 12 Israeli marines, who were alleged to be planning to assassinate Shi'ite leaders, were killed in the village of Insariyeh, south of Sidon. The Israeli commandos were reportedly killed by the joint forces of Hezbollah, Amal, and Lebanese soldiers. The death toll, the highest since 1985 when troops receded to the buffer zone, was expected to have grave implications for regional security.

NETANYAHU'S DOMESTIC PROBLEMS

In addition to the escalating security crisis in the region, Netanyahu also faced increasing domestic difficulty in April 1997, after police recommended that he be charged with fraud and breach of trust following his appointment in January 1997 of an undistinguished lawyer, Roni Bar-On, as Attorney-General. Bar-On resigned within 12 hours of his appointment after it was alleged that his promotion had been made in order to facilitate a plea bargain for Aryeh Der'i, leader of the orthodox

Shas party, who was facing separate corruption charges. There were suggestions that in return for Bar-On's appointment, Der'i had pledged Shas party support for the Cabinet's decision regarding the withdrawal from Hebron. In early May Aryeh Der'i was indicted for obstruction of justice but Elyaqim Rubenstein, Bar-On's successor, ruled that, owing to lack of evidence, charges would not be brought against Netanyahu. Despite Netanyahu's acquittal, there were strong demands for his resignation, and his credibility was further undermined by the resignations of the Finance Minister, Dan Meridor, and the Minister of Communications, Limor Livnat, who, although retaining her ministerial position, resigned from her post as Cabinet Spokeswoman. (On 9 July Michael Eitan was approved as Minister of Science, following the resignation of Binyamin Begin, and Yaacov Ne'eman was appointed Minister of Finance.) The extent of Netanyahu's declining popularity was made apparent on 21 July, when the Government was defeated by five votes in a motion of 'no confidence'. The Government survived, however, since legislation demands that an absolute majority of 61, which was not achieved, is required before change can be implemented.

In June Ehud Barak, a former cabinet minister and chief of staff of the army, won the Labour Party leadership election (to replace Shimon Peres), with 51% of the votes.

FLUCTUATING RELATIONS WITH JORDAN

On 25 September 1997 two Israeli Mossad agents, travelling on forged Canadian passports, were detained in the Jordanian capital, Amman, in connection with the attempted assassination, by poisoning, of the local Hamas chief, Khalid Meshaal. The two agents were apprehended by bodyguards at the scene of the incident, immediately after the attack. In response to the incident, which caused severe embarrassment to the Israeli Government, Canada withdrew its ambassador to Tel-Aviv, while King Hussein of Jordan threatened to try the arrested men for murder and to sever diplomatic relations with Israel unless the Israeli authorities promptly supplied an antidote for the potentially lethal chemical agent used in the attack. The antidote was duly dispatched by Israel, and in late September frantic diplomatic efforts were undertaken to preserve cordial relations between the two countries. In early October the release from Israeli prisons of dozens of Arab detainees, including Sheikh Ahmad Yassin, a founder of Hamas, was thought to have been negotiated with the Jordanian authorities in exchange for the return of the two Mossad agents. Yassin's return to Gaza on 6 October prompted scenes of popular jubilation, and proved a further embarrassment for Netanyahu, who had persistently exhorted the PA to distance itself from the Hamas leadership. The bungled Mossad attempt and its aftermath reportedly led to strong criticism of Netanyahu from certain members of his Cabinet. The report of a Government-appointed commission of investigation into the incident was published in February 1998 and was highly critical of the planning and execution of the 'mission', though not of the wider strategy. The head of Mossad, Maj.-Gen. Danny Yatom, resigned as a result of the report, and was replaced, in March, by Ephraim Halevy, a former diplomat. A series of high-level ministerial meetings between Jordanian and Israeli delegations (including direct contacts between Netanyahu and Crown Prince Hassan) were conducted in early March, resulting in renewed commitments to co-operate in the fields of bilateral trade, water and electricity resources and tourism. Netanyahu described the thaw in relations between the two sides as 'a new beginning'.

INTERNAL PROBLEMS

An attempt by Netanyahu to consolidate his leadership of Likud at a party conference convened in November 1997 prompted a crisis within both the party and the governing coalition, after the conference endorsed a proposal to reform the electoral system. According to the proposed reform, Likud candidates standing for election to the Knesset would henceforth be selected by the party's 2,700-strong Central Committee (dominated by Netanyahu's supporters) rather than the 200,000 registered members of the party. However, following numerous press reports that Likud party opponents and coalition party members alike were considering the creation of new parties in an attempt to arrest this consolidation of Netanyahu's support (at the

expense of the democratic process), Netanyahu retracted the plan, stating that the reform issue would be the subject of a future referendum. Meanwhile in November, at a meeting of some 200,000 Israelis to commemorate the second anniversary of the assassination of Itzhak Rabin, the Labour leader, Ehud Barak, pledged to continue Rabin's pursuit of a Middle East peace settlement.

REDEPLOYMENT PROPOSALS

Bilateral negotiations between Israeli and PA representatives resumed in early November 1997. Israel offered to decelerate its construction of Jewish settlements in return for Palestinian approval of a plan to delay further redeployments of Israeli troops from the West Bank. At the same time, the Israeli Government announced plans to build 900 new housing units in the area. The virtual stalemate in the peace process prompted several Arab states to boycott the Middle East and North Africa economic conference, held in Doha, Qatar, on 16–18 November. Separate peace talks, involving Madeleine Albright, Netanyahu and Arafat in mid-November, were inconclusive. Albright urged Israel to present plans for a significant withdrawal from the West Bank in the near future. On 30 November the Israeli Cabinet agreed in principle to a partial withdrawal from the West Bank, but specified neither its timing nor its scale; implementation would be dependent on the PA meeting its security commitments. The withdrawal proposals also affirmed Israel's right to continue 'reinforcement of settlements in Judaea and Samaria'. In addition to the agreement, the Cabinet undertook to create a team of ministers to decide which areas of the West Bank would be permanently retained by Israel, before the implementation of the second redeployment. Such a unilateralist initiative directly contravened the Oslo accords, which stated that the final settlement agreement was to be negotiated with the PA. A subsequent statement issued by Likud mayors in the West Bank settlements expressed support for the principle of 'separation' in Judaea, Samaria and Gaza. The statement not only bolstered Netanyahu's argument with nationalist hardliners in the Knesset (Likud municipal chiefs represented some 80% of Jewish settlers in the West Bank) but also marked a significant departure for Likud, which had previously adhered very firmly to the belief that all of historic Palestine was an indivisible part of the Jewish State. However, the Palestinians and much of the international community deemed the proposal to be an unacceptable departure from the Oslo and Hebron protocols. The Labour leader, Ehud Barak, dismissed the Government's proposals as 'irrelevant' and the US Government also signalled that the latest initiative was inadequate.

INDUSTRIAL UNREST, 1997

Meanwhile, the stringent fiscal and economic policies being pursued by the Minister of Finance, Yaacov Ne'emen, were increasingly bringing the Government into confrontation with the Histadrut (Israel's General Federation of Labour). Since his appointment, Ne'emen had promoted a campaign of privatization and public-spending cuts, measures which were welcomed by the business community but mistrusted by the Histadrut, which drew attention to rising unemployment and the threat of deteriorating social services. Of particular concern to the unions was speculation that Ne'emen was planning to revise the terms of new pensions legislation, endorsed by the previous administration, which he considered to be 'excessively generous'. Tensions were exacerbated in early December 1997 following Ne'emen's comparison of the critics who were seeking to undermine his monetary policy to the Palestinian suicide bombers who had frustrated recent peace initiatives. Despite issuing an apology for the ill-advised comparison, Ne'emen's confrontational style appeared to provide the final provocation for the organization, by union officials, of a general strike on 3 December. The industrial action, which was thought to involve some 700,000 mainly public sector employees, resulted in the closure of government offices, banks, schools and the Tel-Aviv Stock Exchange, and the suspension of many public transport facilities. Employees returned to work on 7 December following assurances from Ne'emen that the fundamental principles of the pensions reform proposal would be adhered to by the Likud-led coalition.

THE COALITION WEAKENED

Evidence of further divisions within the coalition emerged at the end of December 1997, prior to the 1998 budget vote, effectively a demonstration of confidence in the Prime Minister. In order to muster the necessary support, Netanyahu granted concessions to various parties, in particular to right-wing members of the coalition, to whom he offered increased funding for construction on the West Bank and for Orthodox schools. Opposition parties claimed that the Prime Minister had bribed coalition members in order to remain in power. David Levy, the leader of Gesher, also denounced the budget, claiming it to be an infringement of social principles; and on 4 January 1998 Levy resigned and Gesher withdrew from the Government, attributing the departure to dissatisfaction with the budget and with the slow rate of progress in the peace talks. The withdrawal of Gesher left Netanyahu with a majority of 61–59, and prompted speculation about the Government's imminent collapse. However, on the following day the budget was approved by a 58–52 majority. Later in the same month the Deputy Prime Minister and Minister of Education, Culture and Sport, Zevulun Hammer (the leader of the NRP), died. His cabinet responsibilities were assumed by Itzhak Levi, the NRP Minister of Transport and Energy. Levi was confirmed as Minister of Education and Culture, and of Religious Affairs (as well as the new NRP leader) in February; he was replaced as Minister of Transport and Energy by Shaul Yahalom, also of the NRP. Plans to form a government of national unity for a period of six months, proposed by Shimon Peres, were rejected after the former Labour leader failed to secure sufficient support from party members. In October Ariel Sharon was appointed Minister of Foreign Affairs, and was to retain his duties as Minister of National Infrastructure for a further three months. Sharon's promotion was widely regarded as an attempt by Netanyahu to secure the support of settler groups and right-wing nationalists, since he was known to be opposed to redeployment from a further 13% of the West Bank.

REJECTION OF US REDEPLOYMENT PROPOSALS

The departure of David Levy from the Cabinet reinforced a perceived shift to the right in the balance of power in the Israeli Government, and increased US concerns over the future of the peace process. A visit to Israel and the Palestinian areas undertaken by Dennis Ross on 6–9 January 1998 failed to ease relations between the Israelis and the Palestinians sufficiently to prepare for negotiations on further Israeli redeployment. Indeed, ignoring the exhortations of the US Secretary of State to suspend all construction activities in the West Bank and Gaza, the Israeli Government announced expansion plans for two West Bank settlements during Ross's visit. Netanyahu responded to criticism of these decisions by asserting that Israel was not bound to cease settlement activity by the terms of the Oslo accords. In January President Clinton invited Netanyahu and Arafat to attend separate meetings in Washington, DC, on 20 and 22 of the month respectively. Prior to discussions with the President and the Secretary of State, Netanyahu attended a series of high-profile meetings with pro-Israeli opponents of the Clinton Administration. During the discussions with President Clinton, Netanyahu reportedly rejected a US proposal for a phased second redeployment from the West Bank involving 10%–15% of the territory (a proposal which Arafat was reported to have reluctantly agreed to, despite initial indications that the PA would not contemplate acceptance of redeployment from less than 30% of the land), in return for the Palestinians' further revision of the Palestinian National Charter and fulfilment of Israeli security requirements.

Netanyahu was insistent that any second stage of redeployment would have to involve less than 10% of the territory. The Israeli Prime Minister's departure from the USA coincided with the announcement in Israel of the finalization of a US $1,400m. loan agreement with the US Government and the delivery, from the USA, of two highly advanced combat aircraft, purchased under favourable terms. By late January 1998 it was reported that direct contacts between the Palestinian delegation and the Israeli Prime Minister had been broken off. In late March the Israeli Cabinet rejected a new US proposal, delivered in Jerusalem by Dennis Ross, for an Israeli withdrawal from slightly more than 13% of West Bank territory, prompting US Secretary of State Albright to state that the peace process was on the verge of collapse and that the USA was considering ending its involvement as a mediator. It was increasingly apparent that even if agreement could be reached between the Palestinians and the Israelis on the scale of a proposed second redeployment from the West Bank, the issue of whether the withdrawal should take place prior to the commencement of 'final status' talks remained far more contentious.

WEIZMAN RE-ELECTED PRESIDENT

On 4 March 1998 the Knesset re-elected Ezer Weizman as President for a further five-year term, by 63 votes to 49. Weizman defeated Shaul Amor, a Likud member of the Knesset whose candidacy had been sponsored by Prime Minister Netanyahu.

PROPOSED WITHDRAWAL FROM LEBANON

In late 1997 and early 1998 Israel's Minister of Defence, Itzhak Mordechai, indicated that Israel would be prepared to withdraw from Lebanon, in accordance with UN Security Council Resolution 425 (of March 1978), but with the stipulation that Lebanon provide guarantees of the security of Israel's northern border. On 1 April 1998 the Israeli Security Cabinet voted to adopt Resolution 425, on this condition. However, Lebanon emphasized that the resolution demanded an unconditional withdrawal, and stated that neither would it be able to guarantee Israel's immunity from attack, nor would it be prepared to deploy the Lebanese army in southern Lebanon for this purpose; furthermore, Lebanon could not support the continued presence there of the SLA (whose integration with the Lebanese army was sought by the Israelis). Concern was also expressed that a unilateral withdrawal from Lebanon in the absence of a comprehensive Middle East peace settlement might foment regional instability. Israel's demand that Hezbollah be disarmed prior to any Israeli withdrawal was, moreover, unacceptable not only to Lebanon but also to Syria, which regarded its support for the resistance in southern Lebanon as essential leverage in its efforts to secure a parallel Israeli withdrawal from the Golan Heights.

INCREASED EU INVOLVEMENT

In early 1998 the European Commission published a detailed report on EU policies towards the Middle East, urging the adoption of a higher profile in the peace process. The report was highly critical of Israeli policies towards the PA, and made particular reference to 'obstacles to trade and economic activity' being responsible for economic deterioration in Palestinian areas. In February the President of the European Commission, Jacques Santer, visited the Middle East and questioned Israel's obstructionism towards economic development in the West Bank and Gaza, and, in particular, its blocking of a free-trade agreement between the EU and the PA. Although Santer ruled out the imposition of any form of EU sanctions against Israel, this concession did little to allay Likud's traditional suspicions of Europe. In March the British Secretary of State for Foreign and Commonwealth Affairs, Robin Cook, visited Israel and the Palestinian territories, representing the UK presidency of the EU. A proposed visit by Cook to the site of the Har Homa settlement in the company of Faisal Husseini, the PA Minister with Responsibility for Jerusalem Affairs, was declared 'unacceptable' by Netanyahu. Cook eventually agreed to be escorted to Har Homa by Israel's Cabinet Secretary, David Naveh, a compromise that satisfied neither the Israelis nor the Palestinians. Cook subsequently travelled to East Jerusalem where he met Husseini and laid a wreath to commemorate the Palestinian victims of the 1948 massacre at Deir Yassin. Netanyahu responded by cancelling a planned dinner engagement with Cook and cutting short another scheduled meeting to a symbolic 15 minutes. Relations between Europe and Israel deteriorated further in June 1998 after the Commission instructed Israel not to award 'made in Israel' certificates to goods originating from Israeli settlements in the Occupied Territories, as these were not entitled to receive the tax exemptions intended for goods produced in the State of Israel. The Commission also instructed Israeli exporters to desist from claiming that goods made by Palestinians in the West Bank and Gaza originated in

Israel. In late June EU foreign ministers met in Luxembourg and urged Israel to provide 'clarification' of its application of the EU's 'rules of origin' regulations. During a visit to the Middle East in April 1998, the British Prime Minister, Tony Blair, invited Netanyahu and Arafat to attend talks in London, scheduled for the following month, in an attempt to break the deadlock over redeployment.

LIMITED POPULARITY SUSTAINED AND REDEPLOYMENT TALKS REACTIVATED

Netanyahu's rejectionist position with regard to redeployment was unpopular with centrists within the governing coalition, as well as with broad sections of the Israeli public. However, threats made by Itzhak Mordechai to resign as Minister of Defence over the lack of movement on the redeployment issue were not carried out as Netanyahu maintained his lead in the opinion polls. The Israeli premier's buoyancy was aided by ongoing disarray within the Labour Party. Barak's decision to court the right-wing vote had caused dismay and disaffection among many party members, and support for the party consequently declined. In May he made a highly controversial visit to two ultra-nationalist settlements, once considered hostile territory for Labour officials, where he pledged strong support for the settlement movement. Following the tour his chief aide, Tsali Reshef, resigned citing a lack of ideological disparity between the Likud and Labour leaders.

At the beginning of May 1998 Israeli and Palestinian leaders met US Secretary of State, Madeleine Albright, for separate talks, held in London, aimed at reactivating negotiations concerning redeployment. The discussions ended inconclusively but with a further invitation for Israeli and Palestinian delegations to visit Washington in mid-May for another round of talks with President Clinton and US officials. Once again, these talks concluded with no obvious sign of progress but not before Netanyahu had again demonstrated to the Clinton Administration the depth of support in the US Congress for his own Government and its uncompromising security agenda.

RENEWED FRICTION IN JERUSALEM

Developments in Jerusalem also served to sustain frictions between the US and Israeli Governments: at the end of May 1998 a Jewish settler organization began constructing a new religious complex on disputed land in the Muslim quarter of East Jerusalem's Old City. (The site had previously been occupied by a Palestinian charitable organization, but dwellings were demolished by the Jerusalem municipality on the grounds that they had been built illegally.) According to press reports, the head of the group had met with Netanyahu, Ariel Sharon and Israel's police chief, Yehuda Wilk, prior to commencement of the building work, prompting speculation that there had been high-level government collusion with the settler operation. Peace groups promptly condemned the settler activity and a protest march to the site by Palestinian parliamentarians erupted into violence, with several of the politicians sustaining injuries. Building work was suspended in June after a restraining order was obtained from the Antiquities Authority on the grounds that the Old City walls were being damaged. The settlers agreed to abandon the construction, on condition that they would be able to submit a tender to build a religious school and 12 apartments after the Antiquities Authority had surveyed the site. In the mean time it was agreed that the settlers would guard the site during excavation work. James Rubin, spokesman for Madeleine Albright, denounced the settlers and their supporters for undermining the creation of an environment necessary for any Israeli-Palestinian reconciliation. In mid-June Jerusalem once again became a focus of international concern after Netanyahu won cabinet approval for a draft plan to widen the municipal boundaries of Jerusalem to encompass suburbs lying to the west of the city and also part of the West Bank. The Prime Minister attempted to avert criticism of the proposals by describing them as being aimed principally at rationalizing service provision and tax efficiency; nevertheless, he conceded that his strategic goal was to guarantee 'an absolute Jewish majority of at least 70%' in the city. The PA complained that the proposals would alter the demography of the city by increasing the Jewish population by 30,000, and also expressed fears that the plan was the precursor to the eventual extension

of city boundaries to incorporate such large urban settlements as Ma'aleh Edomin (an eventuality that would effectively split the West Bank in two). A decision by the Jerusalem and Ma'aleh Edomin municipalities to create a joint industrial zone in a strategic location between the borders of their jurisdictions had already heightened suspicions of Israel's long-term intentions.

BREAKTHROUGH ON REDEPLOYMENT?

By mid-1998 US exasperation with Israeli procrastination and intransigence had become increasingly apparent. Speaking at a news conference with the Egyptian Minister of Foreign Affairs on 10 July, Madeleine Albright stated that the existing stalemate 'couldn't go on indefinitely'. Three days later James Rubin blamed Israel for sustaining the impasse and urged the Israeli Government to work with the Palestinians, who according to Rubin were willing to reactivate discussions. On 19 July Israeli negotiators met their Palestinian counterparts directly for the first substantive talks in many months. After three days, however, Arafat withdrew his team, accusing the Israeli side of creating 'obscure formulations' on the US initiative. According to Israeli press reports the Palestinians had been angered by an Israeli proposition that 3% of the 13.1% of the West Bank territory subject to discussion under the US proposals should be transformed into a 'nature reserve' on which both Palestinian and Israeli construction would be prohibited. In late July a prominent Likud Knesset member and former intelligence chief, Gideon Ezra, exacerbated existing tensions by stating on Israeli television that Netanyahu wanted the 'final status' negotiations to continue for a minimum of 15 years in order to test Palestinian goodwill. Speculation that an unexpected breakthrough had been achieved on the issue of redeployment emerged in late September following renewed contacts between the Israeli and Palestinian leaders at a US-mediated meeting in Washington, DC. The adoption of a more conciliatory stance by both sides in early October encouraged hopes for significant progress at a new round of talks convened in mid-October at the Wye Plantation in Maryland (see below), near Washington, DC.

NO PROGRESS ON THE SYRIA TRACK

The possibility of a resumption of peace negotiations between Israel and Syria emerged after it was reported that the two countries had agreed to a French initiative to resume dialogue, based on an Israeli acceptance of the 'land-for-peace' formula and Syrian acceptance of Israel's security needs. However, prior to a visit to Paris by Syria's President Assad in mid-July 1998, Netanyahu apparently retracted his decision to accept the French initiative, reportedly owing to opposition from coalition partners. Later in July the Knesset gave preliminary approval to a bill which would require a majority vote in the Knesset and a referendum to be held prior to allowing an Israeli withdrawal from either the Golan Heights or Jerusalem. The legislation, which was fiercely denounced in Syria, was finally passed in January 1999.

Syria, Iran, Iraq and Egypt were among a number of Middle Eastern states to react angrily to joint military exercises, codenamed 'Reliant Mermaid', conducted by Israeli, Turkish and US forces in the Mediterranean in January 1998.

THE WYE RIVER MEMORANDUM

The Wye Plantation talks began on 15 October 1998, following a ceremonial meeting at the White House between President Clinton, Yasser Arafat and Binyamin Netanyahu. US negotiators at the intensive nine-day talks included Secretary of State Albright, Special Envoy Ross and the Director of the US Central Intelligence Agency (CIA), George Tenet; President Clinton spent an estimated 70 hours in discussions. President Mubarak of Egypt and King Hussein of Jordan were kept informed of progress in the discussions, the latter playing a significant role as mediator. On 23 October Arafat and Netanyahu signed the Wye River Memorandum (see Documents on Palestine, p. 86) in the presence of President Clinton and King Hussein. In essence, the Memorandum outlined a three-month timetable for the implementation of earlier agreements, notably the Interim Agreement of 28 September 1995 and the Hebron Protocol of 15 January 1997. The signing of the agreement ended a 19-month deadlock in the Israeli-Palestinian track of the peace process, and was achieved in spite of a grenade attack carried out by Hamas on 19 October 1998 in Beersheba, in which at least 60 people were injured. Under the terms of the agreement (based on a 'land-for-security' exchange), Israel agreed to redeploy its troops from 13.1% of the West Bank (in three stages), while the Palestinians agreed to intensify measures to guarantee Israel's security by eradicating terrorist activity and revising the Palestinian National Charter. Both sides also agreed to the immediate resumption of 'final status' talks (originally scheduled to have begun in May 1996), with the aim of concluding a permanent agreement by 4 May 1999, and made commitments to refrain from taking any unilateral actions that would alter the status of the West Bank or Gaza.

REACTION TO THE MEMORANDUM

On Netanyahu's return to Israel on 25 October 1998, Jewish settlers organized demonstrations in the West Bank to protest against the signing of the Wye Memorandum. In an attempt to reassure settler groups, the Israeli Prime Minister announced plans to proceed with settlement expansion, declaring on 26 October that Israel's commitments under the terms of the Wye Memorandum did not preclude the construction of new settlements or the confiscation of Palestinian land. At the end of October Netanyahu approved the construction of some 1,025 new housing units at the Har Homa settlement in East Jerusalem. In the days following the Wye agreement the PA appeared to be taking immediate action to meet its obligations on security issues, provoking occasional riots and prompting accusations of human rights abuses in the West Bank and Gaza. However, on 27 October Netanyahu postponed cabinet and Knesset ratification of the Memorandum, claiming that the Palestinians were already failing to meet their obligations. On 11 November, following considerable US pressure, the Israeli Cabinet finally reconvened and approved the Memorandum by a majority of eight votes to four (with several abstentions). Four previous scheduled meetings had been postponed owing to a suicide bombing by Islamic Jihad in central Jerusalem on 6 November and Israeli fears of further terrorist attacks. Netanyahu angered the Palestinian authorities by attaching a number of conditions to Israel's approval of the Memorandum (primarily the annulment of those clauses in the Palestinian National Charter concerning Israel's destruction), and by threatening effective Israeli annexation of areas of the West Bank if Palestinian statehood were to be declared unilaterally on 4 May 1999 (see below).

IMPLEMENTATION OF THE FIRST STAGE OF WYE

On 17 November 1998 the Israeli Knesset ratified the Wye Memorandum by 75 votes to 19. Three days later the Israeli Government implemented the first stage of renewed redeployment from the West Bank, also releasing 250 Palestinian prisoners and signing a protocol allowing for the inauguration of an international airport at Gaza.

DISSOLUTION OF THE KNESSET

During December 1998 it became increasingly evident that divisions within Netanyahu's party and coalition over implementation of the Wye Memorandum were making effective government untenable. Attempts to rescue the coalition by offering to reappoint David Levy to the Government were frustrated when the Gesher leader refused the terms proposed by Netanyahu. Moreover, on 16 December Yaacov Ne'eman, the Minister of Finance, announced his resignation, stating that the coalition was no longer functioning. On 21 December Netanyahu was forced to support an opposition motion demanding the dissolution of the Knesset and the organization of early elections to the legislature and premiership in the spring of 1999. A general election was subsequently scheduled for 17 May.

SUSPENSION OF PEACE PROCESS

There was considerable unrest in the West Bank and Gaza prior to a visit by President Clinton in mid-December 1998. Palestinians demonstrated in support of almost 700 prisoners who began a nine-day hunger strike to protest against Israel's failure to honour commitments agreed at the Wye Plantation to release Palestinians detained on political (rather than criminal)

charges. On 14 December Clinton attended a meeting of the PLO's Palestine National Council (PNC), at which the removal from the Palestinian National Charter of all clauses seeking Israel's destruction was reaffirmed. The US President also attended the formal inauguration of the new airport at Gaza. At a meeting between Clinton, Arafat and Netanyahu at the Erez check-point, Netanyahu reiterated accusations that the Palestinians had not adequately addressed their security commitments and announced that he would not release Palestinian prisoners considered to have 'blood on their hands'. Netanyahu also demanded that Arafat renounce his intention to declare Palestinian statehood in May 1999. Arafat, for his part, conveyed his own security concerns and reasserted demands for a 'freeze' on the construction of Jewish settlements in disputed territory. Following the meeting Netanyahu announced that the second phase of Israeli troop deployment envisaged by the Wye Memorandum, scheduled for 18 December, would not be undertaken. On 20 December the Knesset voted to suspend implementation of the Memorandum. In late December Hamas leader Sheikh Ahmad Yassin was released from house arrest in Gaza. Yassin had been detained as part of a high-profile initiative by the PA security forces to subdue Hamas activists following a failed suicide bomb attack on settler schoolchildren in late October.

SETTLEMENT PROGRAMME CONTINUES

Within three weeks of the signing of the Wye Memorandum, in mid-November 1998 the Minister of Foreign Affairs, Ariel Sharon, had publicly called upon settler groups to 'grab' as much West Bank land as possible to prevent it from remaining in Arab hands. In mid-1999 it was estimated that since the Wye agreement, Israel had established 17 new 'hilltop' settlements in the West Bank, all located close to areas specified for transfer to the PA under the terms of the accord.

ELECTION CAMPAIGN

Following the vote to dissolve the Knesset (see above), Israeli politicians embarked upon an election campaign that further undermined the country's political stability, prompting the emergence of several new political parties and a realignment of political allegiances. The disintegration of Likud continued, as Netanyahu's leadership was challenged by senior party members, including Binyamin Begin, the son of Menachem Begin, who left Likud to form his own right-wing party (New Herut). On 23 January 1999 Netanyahu dismissed the Minister of Defence, Itzhak Mordechai, after the latter had discussed the formation of a new centrist party with the former Army Chief of Staff, Amnon Lipkin-Shahak, and the former Likud Minister of Finance, Dan Meridor; they were subsequently joined by the outgoing mayor of Tel-Aviv, Roni Milo, another of Netanyahu's former allies. (Mordechai had been highly critical of Netanyahu's inability to negotiate with the Palestinians.) On 26 January Mordechai became leader of the new Centre Party, which hoped to attract the support of moderate, centrist and secular Israelis. Mordechai also joined Ehud Barak, Binyamin Begin, Azmi Bishara (an Arab Israeli) and Rabbi Israel Bagad in the contest for the premiership. Meanwhile, on 27 January Netanyahu appointed Moshe Arens as Minister of Defence. On 23 February Meir Shitrit, Likud's Knesset leader, became Minister of Finance. A further humiliation for Netanyahu was the decision of his former foreign minister, Gesher leader David Levy, to enter into an alliance with the Labour leader, Ehud Barak. By the end of March a record 33 parties had registered with Israel's Central Election Committee.

DEATH OF KING HUSSEIN OF JORDAN

Following the death of King Hussein of Jordan on 7 February 1999, Israeli flags were flown at half-mast and newspapers carried portraits of the King, together with eulogizing obituaries. Netanyahu attended King Hussein's funeral in Amman, although Hussein, who was a personal friend of Itzhak Rabin, was never on good terms with Netanyahu, believing him to have undermined the peace process. King Hussein was genuinely popular in Israel and there was a feeling of apprehension among Israelis about the future direction of Jordan under its new King, Abdullah II. Nevertheless, Moshe Arens stated that he expected there to be 'continuity' in Israel's relations with Jordan. A bilateral agreement signed in December 1998 had, for the first time, allowed foreign airlines en route to Jordan to travel through Israeli airspace. However, during 1999 an ongoing dispute over Israel's proposals to reduce, by 40%, its supply of water to Jordan (in contravention of the terms of the 1994 peace treaty) in order to compensate for a shortage of rainfall in Israel contributed to a slight deterioration in relations.

RELATIONS WITH WESTERN STATES

In early 1999 relations between the Israeli Government and the USA also continued to deteriorate. In early January it was reported that US Secretary of State Albright had signalled her disinclination to meet Ariel Sharon during a visit to the USA, owing to US frustration with Israel's suspension of the peace process. Moreover, the Clinton Administration threatened to withhold US $1,200m. pledged to Israel to cover the cost of its redeployment in the West Bank (in accordance with a bilateral accord signed shortly after the Wye Memorandum, while speculating that it might soon award $400m. in aid to the PA. The US authorities urged Israel to reactivate the peace process by complying with the terms of the Wye agreement. Clinton further angered Israelis by refusing, for several months, to hold a private meeting with Netanyahu, while agreeing to meet Arafat at the White House on 23 March to discuss Arafat's threatened unilateral declaration of Palestinian statehood on 4 May. (The declaration was postponed on 29 April, following intense international pressure.)

Meanwhile, relations between Israel and the EU deteriorated once again, largely as a result of EU annoyance over Likud's settlement expansion programme, which the EU deemed to be illegal, and owing to continuing disagreement over the status of Jerusalem. In mid-March 1999 the EU strongly condemned official Israeli instructions to foreign delegations not to visit Orient House, the PLO's *de facto* headquarters in Jerusalem. Earlier in the month the German Government, which was responsible for the EU presidency at that time, made official representations to Sharon, insisting that the EU regarded Jerusalem as a *corpus separatum* in accordance with the terms of UN Resolution 181 (1947), and was therefore outside Israeli sovereignty. The EU communication provoked a condemnatory response from the Israeli Government, and in mid-March a cabinet resolution reaffirmed Israel's sovereignty over a 'united Jerusalem', while Sharon declared the UN resolution to be 'null and void'.

PROTEST BY ULTRA-ORTHODOX JEWS

On 14 February 1999 some 200,000 ultra-Orthodox Jews staged a mass prayer meeting in front of the Supreme Court in Jerusalem, in protest against recent rulings by the judiciary which, they claimed, amounted to religious persecution. It was claimed that the influence of Orthodoxy in many areas of civil law, including those governing marriage and exemption from military service would be severely undermined by the pronouncements. Earlier in the month the spiritual leader of the ultra-Orthodox Shas party, Rabbi Ovadia Yosef, had been fiercely critical of Aharon Barak, the President of the Supreme Court. Secular Jews held a counter-demonstration in Jerusalem on the same day.

CONVICTION OF DER'I

In March 1999 the Shas party leader, Aryeh Der'i (a close associate of Prime Minister Netanyahu and an invaluable ally in the Likud-led coalition), was found guilty of bribery, fraud and breach of public trust by the Jerusalem District Court (see above). Der'i immediately announced his intention to appeal to the Supreme Court against the verdict. Although on 15 April he was sentenced to four years' imprisonment and asked to pay a 250,000-shekel fine, the District Court ruled that Der'i's sentence would be suspended until after the outcome of his appeal, thus enabling the Shas leader to campaign for the 17 May general election. In mid-June, however, Der'i resigned as Chairman of Shas.

NEW LABOUR COALITION

By mid-May 1999 Ehud Barak and Binyamin Netanyahu were the only remaining candidates for the premiership, four nomin-

ated contestants having withdrawn their candidacy. Following a decision by Itzhak Mordechai to transfer his support to Barak, who in late March had established the 'One Israel' movement (including Gesher and the moderate Meimad party), victory for the Labour leader appeared to be assured. On 17 May Ehud Barak was elected Prime Minister with 56.08% of the votes cast, compared with 43.92% for Netanyahu. In the elections to the Israeli Knesset, Barak's One Israel grouping secured 26 seats, while Likud's strength declined from 32 seats to 19. Shas, meanwhile, increased its representation from 10 to 17 seats. The newly-elected Knesset contained an unprecedented 15 factions. Some 78.8% of Israel's 4.3m.-strong electorate were reported to have participated in the elections.

In an unexpected move, Netanyahu conceded defeat less than 40 minutes after the close of voting, when exit polls indicated a sizeable defeat for the Likud leader. Netanyahu subsequently resigned from both the Knesset and the Likud leadership. In late May 1999 Ariel Sharon (whose indictment on charges relating to bribery, witness-tampering and obstruction of justice had been recommended by an Israeli police spokesman in April) became Chairman of the Likud party; Sharon's position was confirmed following a party ballot on 3 September.

The election campaign had been bitter and divisive. Most observers believed that the election was lost by Netanyahu and Likud, rather than won by the One Israel movement. Netanyahu had become increasingly unpopular and had disappointed significant sections of his traditional support base, particularly right-wing nationalists and settler groups. Furthermore, many in Israel's business community attributed responsibility for the economic recession on his 'freezing' of the peace process and his monetarist policies.

Despite having gained no overall majority in the Knesset, Ehud Barak had, by Israeli standards, received a clear mandate to form a broad coalition government that would attempt to restart the stalled Middle East peace process, tackle the secular–religious rift in Israeli society and seek to improve Israel's economy. The Prime Minister-Elect was, however, careful not to commit himself to more than a pledge to seek a formula for regional peace. In his victory speech of 18 May 1999, Barak stated that he would observe four 'security red lines' concerning the Palestinian track: Jerusalem would remain under Israeli sovereignty; there would be no return to the pre-1967 borders; most West Bank settlers would stay in settlements under Israeli sovereignty (although in early June Barak pledged to establish no new settlements); and no 'foreign armies' would be based west of the Jordan river. The last stage of the Oslo process, the 'final status' talks, were expected to begin shortly after the formation of a new Israeli government.

On 6 July 1999, after making full use of the 45 interim days allowed by law and following complex negotiations, Barak presented his Cabinet to the Knesset. He had formed a broad-based coalition, with the Centre Party, Shas, Meretz, Israel B'Aliyah and the NRP taking ministerial positions (talks with Likud having collapsed). Although largely honouring his election pledges, all indications were that the new Prime Minister intended to maintain firm control of his ministries: the most influential posts were reserved for himself (Barak was also appointed Minister of Defence) and for loyalists such as David Levy of Gesher, who became Minister of Foreign Affairs. Itzhak Mordechai was made one of three Deputy Prime Ministers (the others being David Levy and Binyamin Ben-Eliezer of One Israel) and was awarded the transport portfolio. In early August legislation to expand the Israeli Cabinet from 18 to 23 ministers was adopted, despite opposition from Barak's own Minister of Justice, Yossi Beilin, and from the new Knesset Speaker, Avraham Burg. Despite the formation of a fairly broad coalition, Barak received criticism from women's groups and Arab Israelis, who claimed that they were under-represented. The new Cabinet included only two women and no Arab Israelis (although on 5 August there was a minor reshuffle in which Nawaf Masalha was named as Deputy Foreign Minister). Barak's coalition could expect to receive the support of a vast majority in the Knesset: not only from its 75 represented members, but also from an additional 10 members representing Arab parties. (In an overtly conciliatory gesture, in July 1999 the Speaker of the Palestinian Legislative Council (PLC), Ahmad Quray, was invited by Avraham Burg to address the Knesset— the first visit to the Israeli parliament by a leading Palestinian official.)

GROWING DEMANDS FOR A WITHDRAWAL FROM LEBANON

Israel's costly occupation of southern Lebanon grew increasingly unpopular during early 1999. (Some 23 Israeli soldiers had been killed in Israel's 'security zone' during 1998.) On the night of 22–23 February three Israeli army officers were killed during fighting with Hezbollah guerrillas inside the zone. On 28 February Brig.-Gen. Erez Gerstein, the commander of the Israeli army's liaison unit with the SLA, was killed (together with three other Israelis) by a Hezbollah roadside bomb in the 'security zone': Gerstein was the most senior Israeli officer to be killed in Lebanon since the 1982 occupation. This loss was a particular blow to the morale of the Israeli army, which responded by launching its heaviest air bombardments against Lebanon since the 1996 'Grapes of Wrath' operation, and the two sides teetered on the brink of another major conflict. However, Israel's Minister of Defence, Moshe Arens, stated that Israel had no intention of escalating the conflict as long as the Syrians refrained from encouraging Hezbollah rocket attacks on northern Israel. Meanwhile, on 18 February it was reported that Israeli forces had annexed the village of Arnoun, located just outside the 'security zone'. Arnoun was subsequently 'liberated' from Israeli control by Lebanese students, although in mid-April Israel reportedly reannexed the village.

In mid-April 1999 Arens announced that 80% of Israel's army posts in southern Lebanon had been transferred to the SLA, thus enabling additional Israeli troops to withdraw from their 'security zone'. In mid-May senior Israeli commanders in southern Lebanon for the first time urged an immediate withdrawal. Meanwhile, the new Israeli Prime Minister-Elect, Ehud Barak, was reminded of his campaign pledge that, if elected, he would remove the IDF from Lebanon by June 2000. In early June 1999 the SLA completed a unilateral withdrawal from the Jezzine enclave, north of the 'security zone'. However, in late June Barak was reportedly angered when the outgoing Netanyahu Administration launched a massive series of air attacks on Lebanon, destroying Beirut's main power station and other infrastructure. The raids, undertaken in response to Hezbollah rocket attacks on northern Israel, were reported to be the largest carried out by Israel since 1996. On 15 July Barak announced that he would propose to his Cabinet a unilateral withdrawal from Lebanon if no peace accord had been reached (in the context of an agreement with Syria over the Golan Heights) within one year.

NEGOTIATIONS ON THE SYRIAN AND PALESTINIAN TRACKS

When Ehud Barak won the Israeli elections in May 1999, he and President Assad of Syria exchanged words of mutual esteem unprecedented for an Israeli and a Syrian leader. Speaking at the inauguration of the new Israeli Cabinet on 6 July, Barak promised to negotiate a bilateral peace with Syria, based on UN Resolutions 242 and 338. Observers interpreted this as a signal to Damascus of his intention to return most of the occupied Golan Heights in exchange for peace and normalized relations. Shortly afterwards Barak began a series of summit meetings with Arab and European leaders, starting with President Mubarak of Egypt on 9 July and culminating with direct discussions with President Clinton in mid-July. The USA, Syria and Israel were all encouraged by renewed prospects for a breakthrough in Israeli-Syrian relations leading to a resumption of peace talks. On 20 July Syria ordered a 'cease-fire' with Israel: however, serious difficulties were yet to be resolved, especially regarding a suitable starting point for renewed negotiations.

Meanwhile, the first direct talks between Yasser Arafat and Prime Minister Barak were held at the Erez check-point in Gaza on 11 July 1999, during which both sides reaffirmed their commitment to peace. By late July, however, relations had deteriorated somewhat, after Barak expressed the desire to combine the Israeli land withdrawals agreed under the terms of the Wye Memorandum with 'final status' negotiations. The Palestinians were angered by this proposed delay in implementing the Wye deal. Talks reached a further crisis in early August when the Palestinian negotiators walked out of discussions after Barak had accused them of refusing to compromise. However, in mid-August negotiations were resumed, after Israel agreed to withdraw its demand to postpone further land withdrawals.

IMPLEMENTING THE SHARM ESH-SHEIKH AGREEMENT

A revised Wye Memorandum was signed by Yasser Arafat and Ehud Barak in Sharm esh-Sheikh, Egypt, on 4 September 1999, in the presence of US Secretary of State Madeleine Albright, President Mubarak of Egypt and King Abdullah of Jordan. The Sharm esh-Sheikh Memorandum (or Wye Two—see Documents on Palestine, p. 88) was ratified by the Israeli Cabinet on 5 September and by the Knesset on 8 September, by 54 votes to 23 (with two abstentions). Most requirements of the new agreement reproduced those of the original Wye Memorandum. Provisions for interim issues such as further redeployments, security, safe passages, the seaport at Gaza and joint committees remained essentially the same, except for new target dates. However, Wye Two decreased to 350 the number of Palestinian prisoners that Israel was required to release (see below). The revised memorandum repeated the call for the swift resumption of accelerated 'final status' negotiations, but, unlike the original Wye agreement, called on Israel and the PA to conclude a Framework Agreement on Permanent Status issues (or FAPS) by 13 February 2000 and a comprehensive 'final status' agreement by 13 September 2000. The explosion of car bombs in Haifa and Tiberias on 5 September 1999, killing the three Arab bombers, failed to derail the implementation of the Sharm esh-Sheikh Memorandum. Following the signing of the agreement, Israel and the PA generally fulfilled their outstanding obligations, although frequently behind schedule. The major difficulty was the implementation of the second stage of further redeployments, scheduled for 15 November, which Israel postponed after Arafat disputed the areas that were to be turned over to the PA. The amount of land slated for transfer to full and partial PA control was the same under Wye Two as under the original Wye agreement; however, the transfer was to take place in three stages instead of two. Neither document included a map detailing the areas to be transferred by Israel (Area C) to complete (Area A) and partial/civilian (Area B) Palestinian control. Nevertheless, the Palestinians were given informal assurances that the transfer of land would, in the first redeployment, take place mainly in the northern part of the West Bank, the second in the Ramallah area, and the third around Hebron. Israel was late in carrying out the first stage of the Sharm esh-Sheikh redeployment. It turned over maps to the PA on 9 September 1999 and carried out the transfer of 7% of the West Bank from Area C to Area B on 10 September. However, the numerous pockets of land to come under PA control were sparsely populated, and no IDF forces or check-points were moved. On 20 September Israel announced the approval of some 14 military orders to seal off large areas of West Bank agricultural land belonging to about 79 Palestinian villages. The area affected was greater than the 7% of land recently transferred to PA partial control.

On 25 October 1999 a southern 'safe passage' for Palestinians travelling between Gaza and Hebron was finally opened, under the terms of the Wye Memorandum. On 15 November an additional 3% of the West Bank was supposed to be transferred from Area C to Area B, with an additional 2% moving from B to A. The third phase of redeployment was scheduled, on 20 January 2000, to see the transfer of an additional 1% of the territory from C to A status, while 5.1% was expected to be shifted from B to A status. On 11 November Israel presented the PA with the maps for the second stage of redeployment, but Arafat rejected them, stating that the areas proposed were too sparsely populated and did not link existing areas of PA control. According to press reports, the maps placed the 3% of land to be transferred to Area B in the Judean desert and classified it as a 'nature reserve'. The other 2% to be transferred to Area A was near Jenin, in the north of the West Bank. After three days of talks, held on 12–14 November, failed to produce a compromise, Israel postponed the second stage of redeployment.

Barak opposed placing any territorial constraints on the well-being of Jewish settlements in the West Bank, at least at this stage. Nevertheless, the anticipated redeployments around

Jenin and Nablus were expected to have minimal impact on settlements. With few exceptions, Jewish settlements in the affected areas would be connected by bypass roads, either existing or planned, to maintain transport routes to Israel. In total 12 new bypass roads were at various stages of planning and construction, although work on the US $70m. programme was impeded by the USA's refusal to supply the $1,200m. aid package promised as part of the understandings reached at Wye Plantation. (The US aid was 'frozen' when the peace process stalled in late 1998, and Congress had recently rejected an opportunity to advance the money.) In addition to settlements, new Israeli military camps were being established throughout the West Bank, particularly next to isolated Jewish settlements, thereby separating them from PA-controlled territory. According to the Israeli Chief of Staff, the cost of these military redeployments, estimated at $300m., would arrive as US aid.

LITTLE PROGRESS IN 'FINAL STATUS' NEGOTIATIONS

In mid-September 1999 focus shifted to 'final status' discussions between Israel and the PA. A symbolic opening ceremony was held at the Erez crossing on 13 September, the sixth anniversary of the Declaration of Principles of 1993. A few days later it was reported that Barak and Arafat had held a secret meeting to discuss an agenda for the talks. Arafat appointed his negotiating team quickly, but despite the Israeli premier's own insistence on accelerated talks, it was not until late October that Barak nominated the Israeli ambassador to Jordan, Oded Eran, to head Israel's 'final status' team. Meanwhile, in mid-September Israel signed an agreement with the USA to purchase 50 F-16 fighter aircraft.

During the autumn of 1999 the Israeli Prime Minister came under severe domestic criticism from left-wing groups, as well as from Palestinians, over his Government's apparent intention to continued to approve the expansion of Jewish settlements in the West Bank. While the Erez ceremony was taking place, Barak convened his ministerial committee on Jerusalem and vowed to consolidate Israeli sovereignty over the city 'especially in this year of intensive discussions on the permanent status agreement'. On 14 September Barak toured Ma'aleh Edomin, the largest Jewish settlement in the West Bank, and promised to expand the settlement so that it would remain 'forever part of Israel'. The issue of the 42 'outpost settlements' that had been set up in the West Bank under the previous Likud Government distracted attention from the 'final status' talks. On 10 October the Israeli Cabinet gave Barak the authority to decide the fate of the 'outposts'. On 12 October he ruled that 15 of the 42 outposts had been built illegally and should be removed. However, after discussions with the Settlers' Council, Barak agreed to remove only 10 and partially to disassemble two. In reality, this decision was symbolic: by 9 November settlers had left 11 of the 12 'outposts' voluntarily. In the end 30 new 'outposts' were validated by the Labour-led Government. Furthermore, on 11 October Barak approved the construction of 2,600 new Jewish housing units in the West Bank, near Jerusalem—roughly the number averaged each year under Netanyahu.

On 1 November 1999 US President Clinton held talks with Barak and Arafat in Oslo, during two days of ceremonies to commemorate the fourth anniversary of Itzhak Rabin's assassination. The talks sought to determine the best way to approach the 'final status' negotiations: whether they should deal with issues individually, with different committees for each, or whether they should discuss all issues simultaneously. Barak offered a third option of dividing the issues into two groups: 'possible' and 'difficult'. Israel and the PA would then work on reaching an agreement on all 'possible' issues by 13 September 2000, with the understanding that any 'difficult' issues that could not be resolved by September could be deferred indefinitely by mutual agreement. The Israeli Prime Minister explained that he saw the 'final status' issues in three categories: those, such as Jerusalem, that were non-negotiable; those that were vital but negotiable; and those on which there could be flexibility. He suggested that the USA convene a Camp David-style summit in January 2000. President Clinton agreed in principle, provided the two sides were near agreement, and promised to arrange regular visits to the region by US Special Envoy Dennis Ross and at least one by Secretary of State Albright before 2000.

Negotiations between Israel and the PA on 'final status' issues commenced on 8 November 1999 in the West Bank city of Ramallah. The first meeting was convened despite the explosion of three pipe bombs in the Israeli town of Netanya on 7 November, in which at least 33 people were injured. (Although no group claimed responsibility for the attack, it followed an alleged warning by the military wing of Hamas of an escalation of violence in protest at Israeli settlement policies.) The two negotiating teams, led by Oded Eran on the Israeli side and Yasser Abd ar-Rabbuh for the PA, agreed to meet two or three times a week, alternating between Jerusalem and Ramallah, and decided to deal with 'final status' issues as a 'package' rather than to form separate committees. The teams met again in mid-November, but no progress was reported. Indeed, the regular meetings being held to negotiate a FAPS by the deadline of 13 February 2000 never appeared to move beyond discussing procedural issues and presenting maximalist opening positions. Moreover, interim talks (led by Oded Eran and, for the Palestinians, Saeb Erakat) were deadlocked over the implementation of the second stage of redeployment. In late November and early December 1999 Israel approved two plans to expand Jewish settlements in the West Bank, which convinced the PA that Israel was not negotiating in good faith. By the end of November interim talks had reached an impasse, with the PA demanding accommodation on the issues of further redeployment and settlements and Israel refusing to reconsider the redeployment maps and claiming that it was obliged to pursue the previous Government's settlement programme.

To maintain the momentum on the FAPS talks, Dennis Ross arrived in Jerusalem on 16 November 1999; he refused to intervene in the dispute over redeployment, however, and attention shifted to plans for a regional tour by Madeleine Albright in early December. On 3 December Arafat announced that the 'final status' talks were deadlocked and accused Israel of using negotiations as a cover for settlement expansion. On 6 December, the day before Albright arrived in Israel, the PA suspended 'final status' meetings, saying it would no longer discuss anything with Israel except settlements. On 8 December Albright presented Arafat and Barak with a suggested timeline: by 10 January 2000 Israel and the PA would complete a draft FAPS that would facilitate a Camp David-style summit in the USA at some time before the 13 February deadline; soon afterwards, Arafat would meet with President Clinton in Washington, DC; on 15 January Ross would return to the region to oversee intensive FAPS talks, and Albright would follow in late January to ascertain whether enough progress on the draft document had been made for a successful summit to be held.

When, in early December 1999, the resumption of talks between Israel and Syria was announced, Barak and Clinton immediately sought to reassure Arafat that the resumption of the Syrian track would not affect progress on the Palestinian one. Albright's visit was sufficient for the PA to resume 'final status' meetings on 19 December, but since the US Secretary of State refused to intervene on the issues of redeployment and settlement expansion, no substantive progress was made. On 21 December Barak and Arafat held private discussions in Ramallah to revitalize the peace talks (their first ever meeting on Palestinian territory), after which they announced their intention to resolve quickly the two most important outstanding interim obligations: the second stage of redeployment and final prisoner releases. At the same time Eran and Abd ar-Rabbuh began holding almost daily meetings to complete a draft FAPS by the target date of 10 January 2000.

The second stage of West Bank redeployment was implemented on 6–7 January 2000, when Israel transferred 2% of jointly-controlled Area B to PA-controlled Area A and 3% of Israeli-controlled Area C to Area B, evacuating six IDF posts. The transfer of territory was low-key, mainly because of the disconnected assortment of villages, enclaves and a desert area categorized as 'nature reserves'. By mid-February Area A represented 12.1% of the West Bank, Area B 26.9% and Area C 61%. On 16 January Israel postponed the implementation of the third stage of redeployment, planned for 20 January, on the pretext that Barak would not have a chance to review the redeployment maps until he returned from his negotiation round with Syria. Meanwhile, on 17 January as many as 20 people were wounded in a bomb explosion at Hadera, northern Israel, which appeared to have been perpetrated by Palestinian militants. Although the 10 January deadline passed without a draft FAPS, the USA was sufficiently satisfied with both sides' efforts to host a meeting in Washington, DC, on 20 January, at which Arafat, Clinton, and Albright discussed delays on the Palestinian track, and the USA urged the PA to push forward with the FAPS talks and continue to aim for the 13 February deadline.

On 22 January 2000 Israel and the PA announced plans to hold intensive 'final status' negotiations, working simultaneously on issues such as Jerusalem, refugees, borders and settlements, but warned that talks could miss the 13 February deadline. On 26 January Oded Eran and Yasser Abd ar-Rabbuh opened a 10-day session of meetings. To close the gaps on both interim and 'final status' issues, which were stalling because of the new delay in further redeployment, Arafat and Barak met at the Erez check-point on 3 February; they failed, however, to make any progress. The PA, warning of a crisis, angrily reported that Barak had asked Arafat to delay the FAPS deadline by six months and to postpone the deadline for a permanent agreement until mid-June 2001. Israel dismissed the idea of a crisis, stating that 13 February 2000 had never been a firm deadline. The USA was forced to intervene. On 5 February Ross and the newly-installed US ambassador to Israel, Martin Indyk, met with Oded Eran and Saeb Erakat to try to solve the redeployment issue. Talks were unsuccessful, however, and Ross returned to Washington. On 6 February, the seventh day of the 10-day FAPS talks, the PA suspended discussions and cancelled a planned meeting between Arafat and Barak. The Palestinians said they would not resume negotiations until they had received acceptable answers to three questions: first, given that the 13 February deadline was impossible, did Israel want to eliminate the FAPS and go straight into talks on a full 'final status' agreement or did it seek to extend the FAPS deadline?; second, would Israel allow the PA to take part in drawing up the maps of the third stage of the second redeployment and of the third redeployment?; third, when did Israel plan to carry out the third redeployment? There was no official response from Israel.

The general optimism generated after September 1999 by the fulfilment of some of the interim obligations outlined in the Sharm esh-Sheikh Memorandum had evaporated by early 2000. Indeed, the 'final status' talks between Israel and the PA appeared to be heading towards a stalemate. However, on 19 March the Israeli Cabinet approved the transfer of a further 6.1% of the West Bank. The redeployment took place two days later. Meanwhile, on 8 March a landmark ruling by Israel's Supreme Court made it illegal for the Government to allocate state-owned land for the exclusive purpose of constructing Jewish settlements, stating that it must not discriminate on the basis of religion, nationality or ethnicity. The ruling paved the way for Israeli Arabs to buy land for the first time.

On 30 April 2000 a third round of 'final status' negotiations opened at the Red Sea port of Eilat. However, Palestinian negotiators began by denouncing Barak's latest 'violation of existing agreements', in protest at a decision by Israel's Ministry of Construction and Housing to put out to tender 174 new housing units in Ma'aleh Edomin. On 3 May US Special Envoy Ross joined the Eilat talks in an attempt to prevent the 'final status' negotiations from unravelling. Two days later Israeli chief negotiator Eran presented Barak's envisaged outline of a future Palestinian state: it showed a canton in Gaza and three smaller ones in the 'north', 'south' and 'centre' of the West Bank. Together these areas comprised 66% of the West Bank, with perhaps a further 14% to be added after a 'trial period' of a few years. The three areas in the West Bank were not contiguous but would be connected by a nexus of 'safe passages', including a single access road from Ramallah to the Jordanian border via Jericho. In return, Israel would annex 20% of the West Bank, including the main settlement blocs and two lateral land corridors connecting these to the Jordan Valley. The percentage to be annexed did not include Jerusalem, which was to remain 'united' under Israel's 'sovereignty'. Barak's vision of a truncated Palestinian state saw neither East Jerusalem as its capital nor the return of refugees to their homes and villages; the PA negotiators rejected the Israeli maps as 'utterly unacceptable'. On 7 May Barak and Arafat held a crisis meeting in Ramallah, during which Barak laid before Arafat the proposal of transferring to full PA control three Arab villages bordering Jerusalem

(Abu Dis, al-Azariyya and As-Sawahra), on condition that the third West Bank redeployment (scheduled to be implemented in June 2000) was suspended until after a 'permanent status' agreement had been reached. By this stage Israel and the PA had conceded that the 13 May deadline for reaching a FAPS was unachievable.

THE PRISONERS ISSUE AND THE 'DAY OF RAGE'

The future of the Palestinian political prisoners detained by Israel has always been central to any progress on the Israeli-Palestinian track. On 6 September 1999 the Israeli Supreme Court ruled that the use of 'physical force' by Shin Bet during the interrogation of suspects was illegal. The judgment invalidated a 1987 decision that allowed the use of 'moderate physical pressure' against those accused of plotting terrorist attacks against Israel; it was praised by human rights groups, although some members of the Cabinet claimed it would hinder the prevention of terrorism. By mid-November several Knesset members had drafted bills that, if approved, would allow the use of 'physical means in interrogation', effectively providing a legal basis for torture. On 9 February 2000 details of a report outlining Shin Bet's methods of interrogation during the Palestinian *intifada* (compiled by the State Comptroller in 1995) was finally made public. The report acknowledged the 'systematic torture' of Palestinian detainees (particularly in the Gaza Strip), which had far exceeded the guide-lines regarding 'moderate physical pressure'.

At the time of the negotiation of the Sharm esh-Sheikh Memorandum, Israel had not released 500 of the Palestinian prisoners whom it had agreed to free under the original Wye Memorandum. Wye Two reduced this number to 350 prisoners, who were freed by mid-October 1999, plus an undetermined number to be released at the beginning of the Muslim fasting month of Ramadan, around 9 December. (On 9 September Israel had released some 200 Palestinian prisoners; a further 151 were freed on 15 October.) On 12 December Israel announced that it would not release the prisoners until Barak returned from Washington, DC. On 29 December, following the recent meeting between Barak and Arafat, Israel freed 26 'security' prisoners, half of whom had only a few months left to serve. The PA, which expected to receive something closer to 150 prisoners, protested, claiming that Israel was not serious about implementing the Sharm esh-Sheikh agreement. As a compromise, Israel released another seven prisoners (all from East Jerusalem) on 30 December, although it refused to free prisoners deemed to have 'Jewish blood on their hands', as well as those affiliated with militant groups such as Hamas and Islamic Jihad. A further 15 Palestinian prisoners were released on 19–20 March 2000 and on 19 June three 'security' prisoners were freed as a 'goodwill' gesture.

On 1 May 2000 a hunger-strike was declared by 650–1,000 of the estimated 1,650 Palestinian political inmates held in Israeli gaols. The prisoners' cause commanded widespread support in the West Bank and Gaza, where Palestinian frustration at Israel's refusal to release more prisoners under the terms of the peace process and at the current impasse in the talks precipitated widespread unrest. Full-scale (and initially peaceful) demonstrations in support of the prisoners' action began on 10 May. However, the violence escalated dramatically on 15 May—the 52nd anniversary of the declaration of the State of Israel. On what was declared by Palestinians to be a 'day of rage', violent clashes erupted in the West Bank, with Israeli troops and Palestinian police fighting fierce gun battles in the worst manifestation of Palestinian anger since the violence that had followed the reopening of the Hasmonean tunnel four years previously. According to Palestinian sources, by 18 May, when the protests subsided, some seven Palestinians (including two policemen) had been killed and at least 1,000 protesters injured; nine Israeli troops were also hurt in the shooting and many civilians were wounded.

The 'day of rage' and the violent clashes came shortly after the expiry of another peace process deadline (13 May 2000), when Israeli and Palestinian negotiators were to have unveiled a framework for a final settlement. The clashes eclipsed a decision by the Israeli Cabinet on 15 May to transfer the three Palestinian villages of Abu Dis, al-Azariyya and as-Sawahra to full PA control. The decision was apparently aimed at mollifying

Palestinian anger, but the 'goodwill' gesture immediately incurred the wrath of the Israeli political right. It also put Barak's coalition Government at risk. On 15 May the Israeli Knesset approved the transfer, by 56 votes to 48, with one abstention. Following the vote, the NRP (one of two coalition parties that had voted against the move) announced that it was leaving the Government. Religious, right-wing and Russian immigrant parties in Israel regarded the decision to transfer the three villages to PA control as evidence that Barak intended to give up part of East Jerusalem to the Palestinians. On 15 May Jewish settler groups responded with a large demonstration in Jerusalem. On 17 May the Knesset approved in preliminary reading a Likud Knesset member's bill to limit changes in Jerusalem's municipal boundaries and to ban the transfer of powers within them to a foreign element, which many of Barak's coalition partners had supported.

At the same time the Israeli Government accused PA leader Yasser Arafat of stoking protests to force concessions on territory before the September 2000 deadline for a final peace agreement. Barak demanded that the PA take effective measures to end Palestinian unrest. On 21 May, after an Israeli child was seriously wounded in a petrol bomb attack near Jericho, Barak ordered his negotiators to return from 'secret' talks with the PA in Stockholm, Sweden, and also took the unusual step of banning Israelis and foreign tourists from Palestinian-controlled areas. He informed the Cabinet that the transfer of the three villages near Jerusalem was on hold until Arafat acted to curb the unrest. The PA responded by claiming that the Israeli army had provoked the protesters. On 21 May, Fatah, the leading political faction in the West Bank and Gaza, called for five days of peaceful protests on behalf of Palestinian prisoners in Israeli gaols. In early June US pressure seemed to have helped to persuade Barak to resume the peace talks, especially after the PA carried out a number of arbitrary arrests against those who had led many of the confrontations with the Israeli army. Arafat urged Palestinians that public demonstrations and rallies in solidarity with hunger-striking prisoners must be modified. However, the divisions between the two sides remained wide and, again, no substantive progress was reported. All the indications were that Barak would not deviate from the 'red lines' heralded following his election victory in mid-1999.

FAILURE OF THE CAMP DAVID SUMMIT

On 28 June 2000 US Secretary of State Madeleine Albright travelled to the region to meet Barak and Arafat, in an effort to arrange a summit meeting in the USA before the crucial 13 September deadline. On 5 July Clinton invited both the Israelis and Palestinians to the presidential retreat of Camp David (the site of the 1978 Israeli-Egyptian peace agreement). On 10 July Barak's coalition was shattered as three right-wing parties left the Government, fearing that the Prime Minister would concede too much to Arafat at the negotiating table. Barak narrowly survived a 'no confidence' motion in the Knesset on the eve of his departure for Camp David. On 11 July Clinton launched the summit, and on the following day Barak and Arafat held a bilateral meeting without US mediation. With a news black-out effectively in force, there were few details as to the progress of the talks. The US Administration described the discussions as 'tense', and press reports indicated that differences remained very wide on the major issues of Jerusalem, Palestinian refugees, borders and Jewish settlements. On 13 July Arafat threatened to walk out of the talks in anger at US bridging proposals that Palestinian officials regarded as too close to the Israeli position. However, Clinton withdrew the proposals and a crisis was averted. On 17 July US officials stated that talks had been intensified, while Clinton was scheduled to depart for a summit meeting of the G-8 group of industrialized nations in Okinawa, Japan, on 19 July. In the event, Clinton delayed his trip by one day to continue round-the-clock efforts to broker a peace agreement. On 19 July, after another collapse of the talks was narrowly avoided, Barak and Arafat agreed to remain at Camp David with their negotiating teams while President Clinton flew to Japan.

Upon his early return from the G-8 summit, on 23 July 2000, President Clinton renewed efforts to reinvigorate the talks at Camp David. However, his attempts to persuade Israel and the PA to sign an agreement collapsed on 25 July when negotiators failed to reach a compromise regarding the future status of Jerusalem. The Israelis and Palestinians had reportedly made progress in several areas: they had come to a broad agreement on the borders of a future Palestinian state, incorporating the Gaza Strip and at least 90% of the West Bank. The most densely populated Jewish settlements, with about 80% of the Jewish settlers of the West Bank, would be annexed to Israel, perhaps in return for territory within Israel itself. Less progress had been made on the issue of refugees. Israeli proposals apparently involved a refusal to accept any Israeli responsibility for the creation of this problem, but to accept the right of return for 5,000 Palestinians annually over a 20-year period. The fate of Jerusalem, however, had continued to present an obstacle to progress. Towards the end of the summit Israel had offered the PA municipal autonomy over certain parts of East Jerusalem and access to Islamic holy sites in the Old City, although Israel would retain full sovereignty. The issue of sovereignty, particularly over the holy sites, remained intractable; Arafat had insisted that the Palestinians must retain sovereignty over Islamic holy sites, in particular the Dome of the Rock and the al-Aqsa Mosque, and maintained that East Jerusalem should be the capital of a Palestinian state. The failure of the Camp David summit seriously damaged Clinton's hopes of reaching an historic accord before the expiry of his presidential term in November 2000. The US President convinced Barak and Arafat to approve a final statement committing both sides to continue the pursuit of a 'final status' agreement and to avoid 'unilateral actions'—thereby implying Arafat's threat to declare a state on or soon after 13 September. Nevertheless, the agreement not to abandon the peace process could not obscure the huge divide between the two sides, particularly over the fate of Jerusalem. The collapse of the Camp David talks also led to fears of renewed violence in the West Bank and Gaza. On 26 July Arafat and Barak returned to the Middle East—the Palestinian leader to a hero's welcome for refusing to yield on the issue of Palestinian claims to Jerusalem, and his Israeli counterpart to criticism from both left- and right-wing parties.

At the end of July 2000 President Clinton angered the Palestinians when he announced that the USA was to consider the relocation of its embassy from Tel-Aviv to Jerusalem, apparently in response to PA intransigence regarding the city. None the less, Israeli and Palestinian negotiators resumed discussions in an attempt to reactivate the peace process. There was even talk of convening a second summit meeting at Camp David in the autumn, despite clashes that occurred between Muslims and Jews in Jerusalem during early August, when Jewish extremists attempted to storm the al-Aqsa Mosque. On 17 August Israel's acting Minister of Foreign Affairs, Shlomo Ben-Ami, held his first discussions with Palestinian officials and US Special Envoy Dennis Ross. At that time the PA faced growing international pressure to postpone a unilateral declaration of independence on 13 September. (Shortly before that date the Palestinian legislature voted to delay such a declaration for an indefinite period.) Ben-Ami reportedly declared that the Palestinians must soften their position before a new summit could be convened. Ben-Ami also held talks with President Mubarak in Alexandria, Egypt, on 24 August; however, no agreement was reached between the two sides regarding the future status of Jerusalem. It was reported in mid-August that Barak had for the first time hinted at offering the Palestinians statehood in order to prevent a dangerous conflict in the region. During that month the Israeli security services had detained some 23 suspected Palestinian militants after uncovering a number of 'terrorist squads', one of which was said to be linked to the Saudi-born militant Islamist, Osama bin Laden.

WITHDRAWAL FROM LEBANON

In late 1999 and early 2000, following the resumption of Israeli-Syrian peace talks, armed resistance by Hezbollah against the Israeli occupation of southern Lebanon escalated dramatically, with Israeli retaliation being targeted at Lebanese civilian infrastructure. On 19 October 1999 the London-based newspaper *The Independent* reported that a Tel-Aviv court had ruled that Israel must release 19 Lebanese prisoners who had been held under 'administrative detention' for up to 12 years. The men had completed their sentences, on charges of belonging to illegal organizations, but had subsequently been detained without charge; Israel appeared to be using them in order to secure the release of one of its pilots, Ron Arad, who had been missing since 1986. On 12 April 2000 the Israeli Supreme Court ruled that Israel had no right to hold Lebanese prisoners as 'bargaining chips' and ordered their immediate release. Accordingly, 13 of the men were released by Israel on 19 April, although Prime Minister Barak subsequently demanded new legislation to allow the Government to detain 'illegal fighters' as a means of bargaining.

In mid-December 1999 Israel apologized for an attack in which some 18 Lebanese schoolchildren were injured. In late December Israel and Syria reportedly reached an 'understanding in principle' to limit the fighting in southern Lebanon; the 'cease-fire' did not last, however: on 30 January 2000 a senior SLA commander became the first Israeli soldier to be killed there for five months, as the result of a Hezbollah bomb. At the end of January the deaths of another three of its soldiers led Israel to declare that peace talks with Syria would not resume until Syria took action to restrain Hezbollah. On 7–8 February 2000, after attacks by Hezbollah escalated, Israel undertook a massive series of air-strikes on Lebanese infrastructure, including three major power stations. Israel subsequently declared a 'military state of emergency' along its northern border. Shortly afterwards Lebanese President Emile Lahoud and President Mubarak of Egypt met in Beirut and issued a firm statement condemning the Israeli raids and supporting Hezbollah's resistance against the occupation of the border zone. The Israelis were incensed by Mubarak's endorsement of Hezbollah. There were fears that Israel and Lebanon were once again on the brink of a major conflict. Following the killing of three Israeli soldiers by Hezbollah on 16 February, the Israeli Security Cabinet approved wide powers for the Prime Minister to order immediate retaliatory bombing raids into Lebanon, without consultation from the 'inner' Cabinet.

None the less, on 5 March 2000 the Israeli Cabinet unanimously endorsed the proposed withdrawal from southern Lebanon by 7 July. Lebanese Prime Minister Selim al-Hoss welcomed the proposed departure, while stressing his preference for it to be part of a wider deal involving Syria. He also demanded that Israeli forces should withdraw from an area at the foot of Mount Hermon (on the Syrian border), known as Shebaa Farms, without which action it would be difficult for Israel to claim that it had honoured UN Resolution 425 on ending Israel's illegal occupation of southern Lebanon. The Syrian Minister of Foreign Affairs, Farouk ash-Shara', went further by stating that it would be 'suicide' for Israel to pull out of southern Lebanon without first concluding an agreement with Syria. Damascus's main concern was that a unilateral withdrawal from Lebanon was aimed at strengthening Israel's ability to retain the Golan Heights, or at least to force concessions out of Syria in exchange for returning the territory.

The UN, formally notified in mid-April 2000 of Israel's intended withdrawal from southern Lebanon, in compliance with Resolutions 425 and 426, had requested that Israel disarm the SLA as a condition for strengthening UN forces there. However, on 15 May Israeli deputy defence minister Ephraim Sneh announced that Israel would leave the SLA a 'farewell gift' of arms and equipment, heightening fears of further bloodshed after withdrawal. Moreover, neither Lebanon nor Syria was willing to guarantee that Hezbollah would cease its operations in southern Lebanon in the event of an Israeli withdrawal. Sneh warned that Israel would respond with force to any attacks on its territory from Lebanon and would not hesitate to attack Syrian targets inside Lebanon. On 21 May Hezbollah fighters used mortars and machine guns against Israeli posts near the Golan Heights.

Meanwhile, there were reports of mass defections from the SLA. On 23 May 2000, as the proxy force fled in disarray, Israel's Security Cabinet voted to accelerate the withdrawal of all its remaining troops from Lebanon. Government sources stated that the pull-out would be effected within days, thus advancing the deadline for withdrawal by five weeks. Five Lebanese civilians were killed by shelling, as Israeli forces attempted to push back Shi'ite Muslins and Hezbollah guerrillas who were approaching the international border, and more than 100 SLA militiamen surrendered *en masse* as hopes of an orderly departure collapsed. On the same day Hezbollah moved into

villages abandoned by the SLA, taking control of one-third of the territory previously occupied by Israel and its allies and slicing the 'security zone' into two. The central sector of the zone disintegrated as the SLA fighters sought refuge in Israel or handed themselves over to Hezbollah or the Lebanese army. Meanwhile, the notorious al-Khiam jail in the 'security zone' was stormed by Lebanese villagers, and the prison's 144 inmates, some of whom had been detained since the late 1980s, were freed, after its pro-Israeli militia guards fled. Thus Hezbollah secured complete access to the Israeli frontier.

Israel's occupation of south Lebanon formally ended on 24 May 2000, when an Israeli army major walked back across the frontier. A few hours later the last Israeli posts were evacuated. Barak made a public statement officially ordering his army home and appealing to 'all powers in Lebanon to behave with restraint and responsibility'. The refugee influx into northern Israel reached several thousands as SLA members, fearing arrest and imprisonment for collaborating with a foreign occupier, streamed with their families towards the Israeli border. The SLA abandoned its tanks and other heavy equipment, while the regular Lebanese army had not advanced from the edge of the zone, nor had the troops of UNIFIL moved into the vacuum.

Thus Barak failed to achieve his aim of an orderly withdrawal, over several weeks, to be completed by 7 July 2000, with an expanded UN peace-keeping force taking control of border areas. On 23 May he wrote to the UN Secretary-General and world leaders, accusing Syria of trying to sabotage the Israeli departure from Lebanon. In the event, Israeli soldiers were driven out of Lebanon within 24 hours, in what was regarded as a humiliating rush for the border. A refugee influx had taken the Israeli Government by surprise, as had the rapid arrival in southern Lebanon of Hezbollah—well before Israel had time to complete its electrified border fence and other defences.

The withdrawal marked a change of strategy on the part of Israel, and most Israelis, considering that the cost of the occupation outweighed the benefits, were relieved to see their army leave southern Lebanon. Some 900 Israelis had died there since 1978. Hezbollah had lost 1,276 fighters since it began resistance operations in 1982, while many more Palestinians, Lebanese civilians and others also lost their lives in the conflict. Nevertheless, the success of Hezbollah was expected to strengthen the conviction among Palestinians in the Occupied Territories that resistance was the only option that produced results. Meanwhile, it was unclear in mid-2000 whether Israel's war in southern Lebanon was completely ended. Hezbollah had always maintained that it would not lay down arms until Israel had also withdrawn from Shebaa Farms. The guerrilla leaders also demanded a halt to Israeli violations of Lebanese airspace and territorial waters, and the release of the 19 remaining Lebanese prisoners held by Israel.

In mid-May 2000 the UN had some 4,515 troops in south Lebanon. On 23 May the Security Council endorsed a report by Secretary-General Kofi Annan on arrangements for the monitoring of Israel's withdrawal from Lebanon; *inter alia*, UNIFIL would be increased in strength to about 5,600 personnel with immediate effect, with an increase to some 7,935 personnel following confirmation of the withdrawal. Meanwhile, Israel and Lebanon (and also Syria) were required to provide assurances that their full co-operation would be given in the implementation of the Secretary-General's recommendations. Among the technical requirements was the need to identify a line to be adopted conforming to Lebanon's internationally recognized boundaries, for the purpose of confirming compliance with Resolution 425. In mid-June the UN Security Council formally confirmed that Israel had completed its withdrawal from Lebanon in compliance with UN Resolution 425. UNIFIL's mandate was extended for a six-month period at the end of July (by which time UN personnel were patrolling the area vacated by Israeli forces, monitoring the line of withdrawal and providing humanitarian assistance), and was renewed every six months thereafter. Now operating with the status of a UN observer mission, UNIFIL numbered 3,426 troops at the end of July 2002. The size of the mission was expected to be reduced to 2,000 by the end of the year.

The al-Aqsa *intifada*, which began in late September 2000, resulted in a renewed campaign by Hezbollah against Israel's armed forces. On 7 October three Israeli soldiers were kidnapped on the border with Lebanon by members of Hezbollah, which demanded the release of Palestinian prisoners held in Israeli gaols. One week later an Israeli army reservist was also captured by Hezbollah. Tensions escalated at the end of November when an Israeli soldier was killed by a Hezbollah bomb in Shebaa Farms; Israel responded by launching air raids on suspected Hezbollah targets. In mid-February 2001 an Israeli soldier was killed by a Hezbollah missile attack near Shebaa Farms.

NO PROGRESS ON THE ISRAELI-SYRIAN TRACK—DEATH OF PRESIDENT ASSAD

By the autumn of 1999 the Israeli and Syrian authorities were still unable to agree on the basis for a resumption of bilateral peace talks. Syria asserted that in August 1995 Itzhak Rabin had made an unpublicized commitment on a full Israeli withdrawal from the Golan Heights to the 4 June 1967 lines, to be implemented within the context of a comprehensive peace package; Israel, however, denied this. President Assad, who disliked ambiguities, wanted Barak to endorse such a commitment before negotiations resumed. Barak refused to do so and responded by stating that he wanted to hear from Syria on a host of other issues, including Lebanon, security arrangements, terrorism, and water sharing, before he would say how far he was prepared to withdraw. The USA supported the Israeli position, although with some ambiguity. On 7 December 1999 Secretary of State Albright held three hours of talks with President Assad in Damascus. The following day President Clinton announced that Syrian-Israeli negotiations were to be resumed from the point at which they had stalled in March 1996. The President's statement did not, however, give any details as to what the two sides had actually agreed when the talks ended. The Knesset subsequently approved the decision to resume talks (by 47 votes to 31), while Barak reasserted that any agreement concluded with Syria would be put to a national referendum.

On 15 December 1999 peace talks between Israel and Syria were inaugurated by President Bill Clinton in Washington, DC. At the welcoming ceremony, while Barak and Clinton spoke optimistically of the possibility of reaching an accord, the Syrian Minister of Foreign Affairs, Farouk ash-Shara', welcomed the talks but listed Syria's grievances; he also refused to shake hands with Barak. The remainder of the two-day talks were spent discussing procedural matters and confidence-building measures. Clinton and Secretary of State Albright met with Barak and ash-Shara' both together and separately, but Barak and ash-Shara' did not meet alone. The two agreed to hold their first round of intensive negotiations on 3–10 January 2000 in Shepherdstown, West Virginia, and conceded to a US request that the State Department handle all briefings so as to avoid leaks and unproductive statements. In late December 1999 Israel and Syria reportedly agreed an informal 'cease-fire' to curb the escalating hostilities in southern Lebanon.

The first day of the Shepherdstown negotiations, which opened as scheduled on 3 January 2000, involved meetings held separately by Clinton and Albright with Barak and ash-Shara' (in the course of which Barak handed Clinton a request for US $17,000m. in military aid). Talks focused on Israel's demand that security issues be addressed first, and on Syria's demand that the extent of an Israeli withdrawal be the principal item on the agenda. US officials convinced the two sides to set up four technical committees to discuss simultaneously the issues of borders, security, normalization of relations and water sharing. On 5 January the security and normalization committees began meeting, and US negotiators held separate, informal meetings with both sides on borders and water. On the fourth day of talks, however, Syria complained that Israel was refusing to convene the border and water committees and so withdrew from the normalization and security talks. Clinton flew to Shepherdstown and held six hours of talks with Barak and ash-Shara' but could not break the impasse.

On 10 January 2000 the Israelis and Syrians left Shepherdstown without having reached agreement. The talks were expected to be resumed in the USA on 19 January; however, on 16 January ash-Shara' informed Albright that Syria could not participate in further negotiations unless withdrawal was the principal issue for discussion. On the following day the second

round of talks was postponed indefinitely. On 19 January ash-Shara' stated that Syria would not return to the talks until Israel gave a written commitment to withdraw to the 1967 borders. Barak responded, on 23 January, that he would allow no such undertaking. The Israeli-Syrian negotiations had stalled specifically over a piece of land at the foot of the Golan Heights, on the shores of Lake Tiberias (the Sea of Galilee). Various proposals were offered by the USA, including a 'draft working document' which was presented to both sides as the basis for a framework agreement, but Israel was reluctant to consider them without a signal from Damascus that such a deal would guarantee peace between the two countries. Israel also demanded the personal involvement of President Assad in the peace process. In the face of US and Israeli pressure, the Syrian President apparently felt that his only course of action was to stand firm on the question of the Golan Heights. Assad offered Israel 'full peace for full withdrawal', emphasizing that a normalization of relations could take place only once Israel had committed itself to a full withdrawal from the Golan Heights and southern Lebanon. Meanwhile, there was growing public opposition within Israel to a possible return of the Golan Heights to Syria. In early January a demonstration was held in Tel-Aviv by at least 10,000 Israelis opposed to any withdrawal from the Golan Heights, while both Israel B'Aliyah and the NRP threatened to leave Barak's coalition in any such event.

On 20 March 2000 it was announced that Clinton and Assad were to meet on 26 March in Geneva, Switzerland, the venue of their summit six years earlier. Assad arrived with a large delegation for what he anticipated would be an historic meeting to get the peace process back on track, apparently assuming that Clinton would bring an assurance from Barak that he was at last ready to recognize the 4 June 1967 line as the border between the two countries. However, Barak's maximum requirements, as presented by the US President were of Israeli control of all the waters—not only of Lake Tiberias itself, but of the upper Jordan river and other tributaries flowing into the lake from the Golan Heights. The Syrian leader stated in response that he was not asking for anything more than Syria had held before the 1967 war and refused to modify his demands for a full, unconditional Israeli withdrawal to those borders. The failure of the summit, which appeared to damage Assad's hitherto cordial relationship with the US President, plunged regional peacemaking initiatives into confusion. On 11 April 2000 Clinton and Barak met in Washington, DC, where they appeared to agree that Israeli-Syrian peace efforts had reached deadlock, with the two sides' positions on the issue of border demarcation being deemed irreconcilable.

The death of President Hafiz al-Assad, on 10 June 2000, threw the Middle East peace process into further confusion. On 13 June six Arab members of the Knesset joined world leaders at Assad's funeral in Damascus, despite the absence of diplomatic relations between Israel and Syria. (The Israeli Government emphasized that the Knesset members were attending in a private capacity.) After Assad's death Barak adopted a conciliatory tone, expressing sympathy for the Syrian people and issuing a veiled invitation to resume the peace talks. However, the Israeli Government avoided any specific expression of regret about the passing of Israel's long-time opponent. On 10 July Assad's second son, Bashar, was approved as the new Syrian President at a national referendum. Bashar al-Assad pledged to pursue his father's aims of achieving a just and comprehensive peace in the Middle East. However, since Bashar was expected to require some time to consolidate his position within Syria, the Israeli-Syrian track of the peace process remained on hold, at least in the short term.

RELATIONS WITH OTHER STATES

During a meeting between the Israeli Minister for Regional Co-operation, Shimon Peres, and the President of Algeria, Abdelaziz Bouteflika, in Mallorca, Spain, on 22 October 1999, it was reported that Israel had offered technical assistance to Algeria in the fields of agriculture and high-technology; the offer was said to have angered some officials at the Israeli Ministry of Foreign Affairs. In mid-March 2000 it was announced that Israel would provide Algeria with technical and military help for the construction of a counter-terrorism unit; Algerian officials, however, denied the reports. Meanwhile, on 28 October 1999

Mauritania became the third member of the Arab League (after Egypt and Jordan) to establish full diplomatic relations with Israel, provoking protests in several Arab countries. On 12 January 2000 the Israeli Minister of Foreign Affairs, David Levy, undertook a four-day visit to Morocco, during which he held discussions with King Muhammad VI and other leading officials. It was announced during the visit that Israel and Morocco had agreed in principle to upgrade diplomatic relations to ambassadorial level, and to allow the Israeli national airline El Al to fly directly to Morocco. However, following a meeting of Arab leaders in Cairo on 21–22 October, Morocco announced that it had severed diplomatic relations with Israel, in protest at recent Israeli actions against Palestinians in the West Bank and Gaza (see below). Tunisia also decided to close its liaison office in Tel-Aviv and the Israeli interests office in Tunis.

Meanwhile, in late October 1999 Ehud Barak became the first Israeli Prime Minister to visit Turkey. During the visit Israel proposed to sell more military equipment to Turkey and to upgrade its tanks and aircraft. The Turkish leadership, for its part, was reported to have offered to mediate in negotiations between Israel and Syria. A major defence pact, worth some US $1,000m., was announced between Israel and Turkey in mid-June 2000. King Abdullah of Jordan made his first visit to Israel in late April of that year; the bilateral talks reportedly focused on water management.

President Jiang Zemin of the People's Republic of China met with Barak and other Israeli officials in mid-April 2000. However, his visit to Israel was overshadowed by US anger over a recent offer by Israel to sell military technology worth US $250m. to the Chinese Government, which resulted in threats, in June, by the US Congress to reduce military aid to Israel. The Israeli authorities, however, refused to cancel the contract until 12 July (the second day of the Camp David summit), by which time it had become clear to Barak that Israel could not afford to lose the US aid. In May Sri Lanka resumed diplomatic relations with Israel, after a 20-year break.

DOMESTIC TROUBLES

In mid-September 1999 former Prime Minister Binyamin Netanyahu and his wife, Sara, were questioned by police following allegations, published in the daily *Yediot Aharonoth* newspaper, that they had charged extensive private work on their residence to the Prime Minister's office while Netanyahu held the premiership. Further allegations of the misuse of public funds emerged, and on 20 October police reportedly seized several official gifts from Netanyahu's home and offices. The Netanyahus were also accused of having sought to pervert the course of justice. On 28 March 2000 the police recommended that Binyamin Netanyahu should stand trial on charges of bribery, fraud, breach of trust and obstruction of justice, while his wife should face charges of fraud and theft.

On 27 September 1999 Eliyahu Yishai, the Minister of Labour and Social Affairs, replaced Aryeh Der'i as Chairman of the ultra-orthodox Shas. In late September the Shas and Likud parties announced that they were to co-ordinate their policies on issues of national importance; however, Shas denied rumours that the party was about to join the opposition. (An ongoing dispute between Shas and the Government over the allocation of funds for Shas's education proposals regularly threatened Barak's new coalition.)

In early January 2000 a series of scandalous revelations about corruption in high office reached a new height in Israel with the disclosure that the President, Ezer Weizman, had been the recipient of regular cash payments, totalling almost US $450,000, from a wealthy French business executive, Edouard Saroussi. Weizman had received the payments between 1988 and 1993, while serving as a member of the Knesset (when, as a public official, he was obliged to declare any additional income). The President denied any misconduct and rejected calls for his resignation, insisting that the payments were a legitimate gift from a personal friend who had received no favours in return. However, it was alleged subsequently that Weizman and Saroussi had been jointly involved in lucrative arms deals in Latin America during the 1980s. On 20 January 2000 the Attorney-General Elyaqim Rubenstein, ordered that a criminal investigation be instituted into the President's financial affairs. However, in early April the police announced that

no prosecution would be brought against Weizman, owing to a lack of evidence. On 9 April Weizman informed Israelis that he would retire before the expiry of his second term of office in 2003, citing ill health. However, having failed to be completely exonerated by the police investigation, the President declared on 28 May that he would resign on 10 July. On 29 May the Labour Party nominated Shimon Peres as its presidential candidate, while Likud chose the little-known Moshe Katsav.

Following accusations by the State Comptroller that the One Israel campaign for the 1999 election had been assisted by foreign donations, on 27 January 2000 the Attorney-General ordered a criminal inquiry into the financing of One Israel and several other parties—Likud, the Centre Party, Israel B'Aitainu and United Torah Judaism—amid allegations that they had contravened legislation regarding party funding. A fine of 13.5m. new shekels was imposed on Barak's One Israel, although the Prime Minister himself disclaimed any responsibility for the origin of party funds.

On 8 March 2000 the Deputy Prime Minister and Minister of Transport, Itzhak Mordechai, took a leave of absence from the Government pending a police investigation into allegations of sexual harassment made by a female ministry employee. Although Mordechai vigorously denied the claims, in late May he was arraigned on charges of sexual harassment relating to three women. Mordechai subsequently resigned as leader of the Centre Party, and on 28 May the Minister of Tourism, Amnon Lipkin-Shahak, assumed the party chairmanship. In late March 2001 Mordechai was found guilty of committing indecent assault against two of the women, and in May he received an 18-month suspended sentence. Mordechai's prison sentence was upheld by a court of appeal in late November.

In mid-June 2000 Barak's Government nearly collapsed under the impact of a major crisis involving Shas, One Israel's largest coalition partner. Barak narrowly survived the crisis, but was left with an unstable Government that could sabotage his efforts to make peace with the Palestinians. After 10 days of political chaos, the four Shas ministers withdrew their resignations, after Barak capitulated to virtually all of the party's demands: extra cash injections for its religious schools, the legalization of its private radio network, and a greater say for the party in the peace process. The return of Shas to the Government came with a heavy trade-off: the departure of the liberal and secular Meretz party, which has been the greatest proponent of peace with the Palestinians, as the Minister of Industry and Trade, Ran Cohen, and the Minister of Education, Yossi Sarid, both resigned.

On 9 July 2000, the eve of Barak's departure for Camp David, the three right-wing and religious parties in his coalition carried out their threat to leave the Government in protest at Barak's readiness to concede Israeli territory to the PA. The resignation of six of his Cabinet ministers (from Shas, the NRP and Israel B'Aliyah—including the Minister of the Interior and leader of Israel B'Aliyah, Natan Sharansky) left Barak preparing to leave for a crucial summit meeting on the peace process with a seriously weakened Government. Moreover, Barak's Minister of Foreign Affairs, David Levy, refused to attend the Camp David talks, owing to disagreements regarding the peace process. After narrowly surviving a vote of 'no confidence' brought to the Knesset by the Likud party, the Prime Minister pledged to pursue his policy regarding peace with the Palestinians. On 30 July, however, the domestic situation worsened when Levy stated that he would resign unless Barak agreed to invite Likud to join his coalition.

In the presidential election held on 31 July 2000 the little-known Moshe Katsav, of Likud, unexpectedly defeated Barak's nominee, former Prime Minister Shimon Peres, by 63 votes to 57 in a second round of Knesset voting (neither candidate having secured an outright majority in the first). Katsav was duly sworn in as the eighth President of Israel on 1 August, to serve an exceptional seven-year term. Only hours after the election, Barak survived another 'no confidence' motion in the Knesset, thus managing to prevent early parliamentary elections. Nevertheless, on 2 August it appeared as if early elections might be inevitable, when Levy carried out his recent threat and resigned as Minister of Foreign Affairs, in protest at recent concessions made to the Palestinians. On the same day, the Prime Minister lost a vote giving preliminary approval for new elections. A minor reshuffle of the Cabinet was effected on 6 August, with

certain ministers being allocated additional portfolios, following
the departure of the right-wing and religious parties. On 10
August the Minister of Public Security, Shlomo Ben-Ami, was
also appointed acting Minister of Foreign Affairs. (He was
confirmed in this post in early November.) After almost one
month of violent protests by Palestinians in the West Bank
and Gaza (see below), in late October Barak held intensive
negotiations with Ariel Sharon of Likud, with a view to forming
a 'national unity' government prior to the reconvening of the
Knesset.

On 3 July 2000 a bill to exempt 30,000 students at Orthodox
seminaries from compulsory military service was given its first
reading by the Knesset. The bill had the overwhelming support
of the religious parties, including Shas, which threatened to
withdraw its vital support from Barak's coalition if the legislation did not go through. It had aroused widespread and bitter
opposition among secular Israelis, however, and about 100,000
people signed a petition against the proposal, regarding it as a
betrayal of one of Barak's election promises. It also antagonized
members of Barak's One Israel party, nine of whom voted
against the legislation. On 12 July the former leader of Shas,
Aryeh Der'i, was sentenced to three years' imprisonment, having
been found guilty of bribery and fraud charges; he began his
sentence in early September.

THE AL-AQSA UPRISING

The fall-out from the Camp David summit of July 2000 formed
the background to a new uprising by Palestinians in the West
Bank and Gaza Strip, which swiftly became known as the al-
Aqsa *intifada*. The uprising began in late September and was
to dominate the next two years. After the Camp David talks,
the USA and Israel presented a united front, portraying the
Palestinian leader, Yasser Arafat, as responsible for the failure
of the talks to produce a 'final status' agreement because of his
refusal to consider Ehud Barak's 'generous offer' to share East
Jerusalem, and urging other governments, particularly those of
EU and Arab states, to press the PA to make concessions over
Jerusalem. The failure of the Camp David summit created a
sense of foreboding about the future of the entire Middle East
peace process, and intensified Palestinian disillusionment with
the USA's role in the process, adding to the tensions between
Israelis and Palestinians that had already erupted into violence
during the 52nd anniversary of the founding of the State of
Israel in May. The al-Aqsa *intifada* showed all too clearly that
the gulf between Israel and the Palestinians was at least as
wide as it ever had been. Despite the general perception that
Barak had pursued conciliatory policies at Camp David, during
the tenure of his Government Israel failed to reach a single
agreement with the PA over any of the major contentious issues,
such as the question of Palestinian refugees, Jewish settlements
in the Occupied Territories, the status of Jerusalem, or even
the permanent borders between Israel and the Palestinian
enclaves. Moreover, while no further redeployment of Israeli
troops was implemented, there was a substantial increase in
the number of Jewish settlers living in the West Bank.

In August and September 2000 several incidents took place,
reflecting and adding to the increasing levels of civil unrest in
the Palestinian territories and Israel itself. On 12 September
Israel announced the arrest of 41 Arab Israeli citizens from the
town of Umm al-Fahm and of four West Bank Palestinians on
suspicion of forming an illegal organization, arms-trafficking
and plotting attacks on Israeli police-officers and soldiers. Three
days later 70,000 Arab Israelis staged a rally at Umm al-Fahm,
in support of Palestinian sovereignty over East Jerusalem. In
the Galilee region 1,000 Arab Israelis from the village of Ein
Mahel went on strike on 25 September to protest against the
Government's seizure of 1,800 dunums of their land for the
expansion of Jewish Upper Nazareth. In two separate incidents
in the West Bank, on 16 August and 6 September, Israeli
security forces had killed a 73-year-old man and beaten three
Palestinian labourers. On 19 August Jewish settlers attacked
Palestinians at Netzarim Junction in the Gaza Strip, while on
13 September Palestinians stoned settlers' cars and, later in the
month, detonated three roadside bombs against Jewish targets.

As tensions grew in the region, Prime Minister Barak continued his efforts to forge a coalition government, making offers
to almost every political party in the country. Barak's troubles

were exacerbated when the Israeli Attorney-General announced
on 27 September 2000 that he was dismissing the bribery and
corruption case against former Likud Prime Minister Binyamin
Netanyahu, owing to a lack of evidence, thereby clearing Netanyahu's way for a political comeback, should new elections be
called. On the same day, as renewed Israeli-Palestinian peace
talks were taking place in Virginia, USA, involving PA negotiators Saeb Erakat and Muhammad Dahlan, and Israeli Minister
of Public Security and acting Minister of Foreign Affairs, Shlomo
Ben-Ami, Israeli police in Jerusalem informed Muslim officials
there of a request from the Likud leader, Ariel Sharon, to visit
the Temple Mount/Haram ash-Sharif compound in Jerusalem's
Old City (site of the Dome of the Rock and the al-Aqsa Mosque)
on 28 September. Sharon apparently sought to demonstrate
Israeli 'sovereignty' over the holy sites. His request, however,
coming on the day that Netanyahu's corruption case was dismissed, was apparently intended to direct attention away from
his Likud rival. Muslim officials warned the police that the visit
would be viewed as a political provocation by the Palestinians
and could spark violence. Also informed of the impending visit,
the PA negotiating team in Virginia urged the USA to intercede
and press Barak and Ben-Ami not to authorize the visit. Barak
and Ben-Ami declined to intervene. The US Middle East Co-
ordinator, Dennis Ross, counselled against the visit.

Just after dawn on 28 September 2000, Ariel Sharon led a
group of Likud Knesset members into the Haram ash-Sharif
compound, under heavy police escort. Sharon attempted to enter
the Marwani Mosque (which some Jews consider to be the site
of Solomon's stables) but his way was barred by some 200
Palestinians, including several Israeli Arab parliamentarians.
After Sharon and his entourage left, Palestinians scuffled with
and threw stones at the estimated 1,000 Israeli riot police
deployed around the al-Aqsa compound. The police fired rubber
bullets and tear gas at the Palestinian protestors, injuring 24,
including three Israeli Arab Knesset members and the PA's
Minister of Jerusalem Affairs, Faisal Husseini. As word of
the incident travelled, rioting by Palestinians quickly spread
throughout East Jerusalem and to Ramallah in the West Bank.
Meanwhile, the Israeli-Palestinian talks in the USA had already
ended without progress. Anticipating more demonstrations on
29 September, when, it being a Friday, Muslims would engage
in prayers at the al-Aqsa Mosque, the Israeli Government
deployed some 2,000 riot police at the site. When Palestinians
emerging from prayers threw stones at them, Israeli police-
officers stormed the mosque compound, shooting live ammunition and rubber bullets. Four Palestinians were killed and more
than 200 wounded in the violence. Meanwhile, Palestinians in
Bethlehem and Hebron engaged in clashes with the Israeli
army. In Qalqilya, also in the West Bank, a member of the
Palestinian security forces on a joint patrol shot dead an Israeli
soldier, hastening the deterioration of Israeli-PA security co-
ordination. Barak phoned Arafat on 30 September to warn
him that further violence would not be tolerated and publicly
accusing the PA of 'spreading violence for political gains'.

The al-Aqsa *intifada* rapidly escalated into the most sustained
revolt by Palestinians in the West Bank and Gaza since their
first uprising of 1987–1993. PA officials blamed Barak for sanctioning Sharon's tour of the Muslim holy sites, and accused him
of colluding with Likud (who opposed the Oslo peace process).
Among Palestinians the perception was that the outbreak and
impetus of the *intifada* were largely spontaneous, driven more
by the enormous frustration of their people than by any strategic
decision by Arafat or the Palestinian leadership. Besides
Sharon's visit, other causes of the Palestinian anger were the
killing of seven Palestinians by Israeli border police at the
Haram ash-Sharif on 29 September 2000 and, on the next day,
the death (television footage of which was broadcast world-wide)
of a 12-year-old boy who was apparently hit by Israeli gunfire
at the Netzarim junction in Gaza. On 30 September the Arab
Monitoring Committee, an informal umbrella that represents
Israel's more than 1m. Palestinian citizens, called a general
strike in protest at the deaths of the seven Palestinians at the
al-Aqsa Mosque compound the day before. However, the fuel
that powered the al-Aqsa *intifada* was widely seen as being
Palestinian frustration at the lack of any improvement in their
situation despite the seven-year-old Oslo peace process. Palestinians initially seemed to be united by what was effectively a

national consensus that the terms and structures of the Oslo process must be overhauled, that a new basis for Israeli-Palestinian negotiations should be set, and that this must rely on international legitimacy and previous pertinent UN resolutions.

One determinant factor in the outbreak of the uprising was the massive growth of Jewish settlements in the Occupied Territories. Although Sharon's 'demonstration of Jewish sovereignty' over the Muslim holy places in Jerusalem was the catalyst for the renewed *intifada*, it was Israel's ongoing settlement policy that had apparently fostered the tensions that erupted into violence. There had been a 52% growth in settlement construction in Gaza and the West Bank since the Oslo accords were signed in September 1993, including 17% growth (2,830 units) during the tenure of Barak's Government. The expansion had swelled the Jewish settler population in the West Bank and Gaza from 115,000 in 1993 to some 200,000 by the end of 2000 (excluding the 180,000 settlers who live in East Jerusalem). The Jewish settlers reside in 145 official settlements and 55 unofficial 'outposts', scattered throughout the West Bank and Gaza and connected by a web of bypass roads. During the Oslo process the new Jewish settlements blocked any contiguous and urban development for and between the 700 Palestinian localities in the Occupied Territories.

For the Barak Government, however, the Palestinians' resort to mass protest and uprising was merely the first stage of a Palestinian war of independence—orchestrated by Arafat—whose ultimate objective was a declaration of Palestinian statehood with Jerusalem as its capital. It appeared to be this conviction that conditioned and explained Israel's severe response to the al-Aqsa *intifada*. As the crisis escalated, Barak issued a series of statements accusing the PA leadership of unleashing the violence and making no effort to restrain protesters. Under real domestic pressure after the collapse of his coalition and the erosion of his parliamentary majority, Barak offered no reply to right-wing critics who blamed the Palestinians' renewed uprising on the Government's 'excessively conciliatory' policies. From the outset a defiant Sharon refused to accept blame for igniting the al-Aqsa *intifada*, while Barak, focusing on Arafat in person, carefully avoided any reference to Sharon's role in provoking the bloodshed and seemed intent on avoiding any verbal duel with the Likud leader. While Jewish settlers railed against the Government for failing to end the Palestinian revolt, Barak was making efforts—in the brief period left before the reconvening of the Knesset, which threatened a vote of 'no confidence' that could bring down his Government—to forge an alliance with Sharon. This took the form of inviting Sharon and other opposition leaders to join a 'national emergency' coalition, and a tacit understanding that Barak would henceforth co-ordinate policy with the opposition, in return for which the right-wing majority in the Knesset would refrain from toppling his Government. The first month of the al-Aqsa *intifada* witnessed armed Palestinian attacks on Jewish settlements throughout the Occupied Territories and heavy Israeli military strikes against Palestinian targets. Following the eruption of the *intifada*, the settlements and the network of roads linking them effectively became Israel's new military borders, not only separating the Gaza Strip from the West Bank and closing both territories from East Jerusalem, but also separating Palestinian cities from each other.

Another marked change in the latest Israeli–Palestinian crisis was the unprecedented severity of the Israeli response: the crack-down by Israel's armed and security forces was more severe than the 'iron fist' policies of the late 1980s and early 1990s. To quell the Palestinian protests, the Israeli military deployed tanks, helicopter gunships, gunboats and missiles to launch strikes against PA installations and raze apartment blocks of those believed to be perpetrators of violence. The difference between the advanced weaponry and planned precision of the Israeli army and the more disorganized reaction of the Palestinians was reflected in the assessments of casualties. According to the Palestine Red Crescent Society (PCRS), by the end of November 2000 250 Palestinians had been killed and 9,640 wounded by Israeli armed forces and Jewish settlers. The Israeli death toll was 33, with 230 wounded. Among the Israeli dead were 13 Arab Israelis who were shot dead by Israeli police during a protest against their Government's actions.

THE SHARM ESH-SHEIKH SUMMIT

During the first few days of the al-Aqsa *intifada*, the international community (led by the EU, Russia, the USA and Egypt) engaged in telephone diplomacy to urge Israel and the PA to calm the situation, but otherwise seemed to be waiting for the USA to take the lead. For its part, the US Administration refused to blame Israel, but called on both sides, and sometimes on Arafat alone, to halt the violence. On 3 October 2000 the EU issued a statement condemning Israel's 'excessive use of force,' but the USA, and to a lesser extent the United Kingdom, mobilized to block the adoption by the UN of any resolution sanctioning Israel. On the previous day, when it became clear that the uprising would continue, US Secretary of State Madeleine Albright arranged for Arafat and Barak to meet with her in Paris, France, on 4 October, and for the three to proceed to Sharm esh-Sheikh to meet with President Mubarak of Egypt the following day. The situation continued to deteriorate, with Israel beginning to fire anti-tank weapons and using tanks and helicopter gunships against Palestinians. On 4 October Albright and the CIA Director, George Tenet, met with Arafat and Barak in Paris as planned. UN Secretary-General Kofi Annan and French President Jacques Chirac attended some of the meetings, and both also met separately with Arafat and Barak. After 12 hours of heated talks, the sides reached a 'tentative' arrangement under which Barak agreed to withdraw Israeli troops to their positions held before 28 September and Arafat agreed to try to curb Palestinian protests. The USA had hoped that the Israeli and Palestinian leaders would sign a cease-fire/security co-operation agreement, but Arafat refused to do so unless the text also provided for an international inquiry into the violence, a demand rejected by Barak. Barak and Albright proposed as an alternative that Israel and the PA each investigate the actions of their own forces, with the CIA acting as arbitrator; Arafat rejected this as inadequate. Afterwards Albright and Arafat left for Sharm esh-Sheikh for further talks with Mubarak, but Barak returned to Israel, stating that there was no point in meeting with the Egyptian President.

As a result of the Paris arrangements, Israeli–Palestinian clashes abated slightly. On 7 October 2000, however, Palestinian crowds sacked Joseph's Tomb in Nablus (a shrine of religious significance to both Jews and Muslims). In retaliation, armed Jewish settlers across the West Bank attacked Palestinian motorists and an historic mosque in Tiberias was vandalized. The Israeli authorities also ordered the closure of the Palestinian airport at Gaza. Also on 7 October Barak called up IDF reserves and issued a 48-hour deadline for the PA to halt the violence; he also threatened to implement a 'sanctions package' that would include sealing off the West Bank and Gaza and suspending monetary transfers owed to the PA. While US President Bill Clinton was closely monitoring the deteriorating situation, the USA's ambassador to the UN, Richard Holbrooke, tried unsuccessfully to block a UN Security Council resolution (No. 1322) condemning the 'provocation carried out' on 28 September and the 'excessive use of force' employed by the Israeli security forces against Palestinian demonstrators. (In the event, the USA abstained in the vote on the resolution.) Following further attempts by international diplomats to defuse the situation, Barak extended his 48-hour deadline indefinitely on 9 October, in the interest of possible mediation, even though the clashes continued unabated in the West Bank and Gaza. At this time the Israeli army extended the closure of the Palestinian territories for an indefinite period, cancelled all permits for Palestinians working in Israel, and began a full-scale campaign of razing any Palestinian private property that could be used to 'provide cover' for Palestinian stone-throwers or gunmen. Barak and his deputy defence minister, Ephraim Sneh, were also reported to have prepared a detailed 'disengagement plan' (presented to the Knesset Foreign Affairs and Defence Committee on 11 October but not released publicly) to be implemented if the peace process collapsed entirely or if the PA issued a unilateral declaration of statehood. The proposals reportedly delineated Israel's permanent borders and detailed the separation of Israeli and Palestinian infrastructures and economies. The 'disengagement' included the annexation of Jewish settlements to Israel.

On 16–17 October 2000 an emergency summit meeting between Barak and Arafat was convened by US President Clinton and hosted by President Mubarak at Sharm esh-Sheikh.

The summit was the outcome of intense international diplomacy and was precipitated by the significant escalation of force used by Israel against Palestinian targets following the killing of two Israeli army reservists by a Palestinian mob in Ramallah on 12 October. In immediate response to that attack, Israeli armed forces launched rocket attacks from both air and sea on PA police and administrative headquarters in Ramallah and Gaza (targeting the headquarters of Arafat's Fatah movement), Nablus, Hebron, Jericho and other Palestinian cities, leaving millions of dollars' worth of damage to property and at least 45 Palestinians injured. On the same day about 60 Hamas and Islamic Jihad militants were either released or escaped from PA gaols in Gaza and Nablus. Barak demanded subsequently that Arafat rearrest the militants. The Israelis deployed tanks on all access roads to and around PA cities, thereby sealing off the Palestinian-controlled Area A. To obstruct further movement, the Israeli army also began digging trenches and installing barricades at intersections between Israeli- and PA-controlled areas. At the time of the assault UN Special Co-ordinator for the Middle East peace process, Terje Roed-Larsen, was in session with Arafat, at the PA President's Gaza residence, in an attempt to broker a cease-fire. Over the next three days a procession of diplomats (including UN Secretary-General Kofi Annan, the High Representative for the Common Foreign and Security Policy of the EU, Javier Solana, and the British Secretary of State for Foreign and Commonwealth Affairs, Robin Cook—and by telephone Egyptian President Hosni Mubarak and Jordan's King Abdullah) prevailed on Arafat to impose some semblance of calm on his people. It was left to President Clinton to plead with Barak to consider a resumption of peace negotiations with Arafat, the man Barak held responsible for the violence in the Palestinian territories. The Palestinian leader, meanwhile, appeared to have only marginal control over the development of the al-Aqsa *intifada*.

With the violence escalating and the number of Palestinian deaths and casualties rising, Mubarak called on Arafat, Barak and Clinton to hold talks in Sharm esh-Sheikh. After the intervention of UN Secretary-General Annan, Arafat and Barak reluctantly agreed to meet with Clinton, Mubarak, King Abdullah of Jordan and Javier Solana on 16 October 2000. After more than 24 hours of nearly continuous talks, Clinton announced that Israel and the PA had agreed a fragile accord 'to issue public statements unequivocally calling for an end of violence', to take steps to eliminate points of friction, to set up an inquiry into the causes of the clashes, and to explore the possibility of resuming talks. After much wrangling, the sides had agreed as a compromise that a committee charged with investigating the causes of the recent violence would be appointed by President Clinton in consultation with Israel, the PA and the UN; it would be led by an American but would include international members. In fulfilment of the agreement reached at Sharm esh-Sheikh, Arafat and Barak both issued vague statements on 18 October calling for individuals to do their utmost to avoid inciting violence. On the same day Israel lifted the internal closure of the West Bank and Gaza, withdrew tanks from Nablus, and reopened the borders with Egypt and Gaza airport. The PA, for its part, had reportedly rearrested all Hamas and Islamic Jihad members released since late September, plus others including Hamas spokesman Abd al-Aziz ar-Rantisi. Palestinian and Israel security officials also met to discuss how to reduce tensions. Despite these steps, the clashes escalated on 19 October, when a fierce gun battle erupted near Nablus, pitting Israeli soldiers and settlers against Palestinian police-officers and civilians. Israeli soldiers had escorted a group of 40 settlers on a 'hike' near Askar al-Balad refugee camp. On 19–20 October the Israelis shelled areas around Nablus and Ramallah, killing 10 Palestinians and wounding 400.

The Sharm esh-Sheikh agreement was greeted with extreme scepticism by many Palestinians, who saw it as a bid to stifle their uprising against the Israeli occupation and contain its regional fall-out, the better to enable Israel to impose its political terms. The Sharm esh-Sheikh 'compromise' was rejected publicly at a Fatah-led march in Ramallah on 17 October 2000 and in a statement issued by the Palestinian National and Islamic Forces (PNIF), an umbrella movement made up of all the major Palestinian factions. Both Palestinian statements described the summit as a failure that did not meet the minimum expectations of Palestinians and called for a continuation of the 'people's peaceful uprising until sovereignty and independence are achieved'. Shortly after the Sharm esh-Sheikh statement, Jewish settlers shot dead a Palestinian near Nablus in the West Bank, while Palestinians opened fire on the Jewish settlement of Gilo in East Jerusalem. During 21–22 October there was an escalation of Israeli strikes on Palestinian targets in the West Bank and Gaza, where gun battles raged. On 20 October Barak vowed to call an official halt to the peace process if complete calm was not restored by the close of an emergency session of the Arab League to be held on 21–22 October in Cairo. However, clashes continued and on the same day Barak formally suspended the peace process. He reimposed the internal closure, shut crossings into Egypt and Jordan, closed Gaza airport again, and resumed military strikes on Palestinian residential areas, including Beit Jala and Beit Sahur. On 23 October the Israeli premier also opened talks with Sharon on forming a government of 'national unity'. On 26 October the Israeli army blocked the main north–south road in Gaza, effectively dividing it in half. Palestinians responded by stepping up their use of roadside bombs against the Israeli army and settler convoys.

On 29 October 2000 the Israeli Chief of Staff of the Armed Forces, Lt-Gen. Shaul Mofaz, announced that the army would henceforth initiate attacks against specific Palestinian targets, especially senior Fatah leaders, whom it held responsible for perpetrating violence against Israelis. This change of strategy did not appear to be related to a particular Palestinian act, although it did occur the day before the Knesset reconvened and followed a new campaign of violence by Palestinian militant groups opposed to the Oslo accords. On the same day the ultra-orthodox Shas signed an agreement with Barak to provide him with a one-month 'safety net' against early elections, promising to vote as a bloc with Labour-One Israel on any 'no-confidence' motion. However, Barak was still unable to reach a deal on forming a unity government with Sharon, who insisted on having the power to veto all decisions relating to national security as part of a coalition deal. On 30 October Israeli strikes by helicopter gunships against bases of the Tanzim (Fatah's military wing) further escalated after the death of a Jewish settler and two Israeli guards in East Jerusalem. Mofaz stated that Israel would send Israeli commandos into Area A to track down Palestinian gunmen who were firing on Israeli troops.

On 1 November 2000 Barak granted a request by the Minister of Regional Co-operation, Shimon Peres, to go to Gaza to meet with Arafat. Barak announced on 2 November that the sides had agreed a fragile 'cease-fire' in an attempt to implement the Sharm esh-Sheikh provisions. However, on the same day two Islamic Jihad militants detonated a car bomb in West Jerusalem, killing two Israelis and wounding at least nine. Nevertheless, it appeared that the Palestinian police were making greater efforts to deter stone-throwers, and Arafat denounced unequivocally the bombing. US President Clinton, while anxious to restore the Oslo peace process, continued to blame Arafat publicly, claiming later in the month that Arafat could 'dramatically reduce the level of violence' if he chose to do so. Meanwhile, on 5 November the White House announced that Israel and the PA had agreed to travel to Washington DC for separate meetings with Clinton—Arafat on 9 November and Barak on 12 November. The US State Department was reportedly planning to suggest that the two sides accept a territorial settlement that would temporarily set aside the issues of Jerusalem and refugees.

On 7 November 2000 the White House named the US-led investigative committee mandated at the Sharm esh-Sheikh summit to investigate the causes of the Israeli–Palestinian clashes. The panel was to be chaired by former US senator George Mitchell—who had previously won respect for his mediating role in Northern Ireland—and was to be composed of five members, including former Turkish President Süleyman Demirel, Norwegian Minister of Foreign Affairs Thorbjørn Jagland, former US Senator Warren Rudman, and the High Representative for the Common and Security Foreign Policy of the EU, Javier Solana. The 'Sharm esh-Sheikh Fact-Finding Committee' (or 'Mitchell Committee') would operate under UN auspices. Palestinians had sought such an investigation, but Israeli leaders objected—asserting that the committee could not operate fairly until the violence had ended. Israel also remained strongly opposed to the notion, again supported by the Palestinians, of an international observer force in the Gaza Strip and West Bank. The Mitchell Committee began its investigations into the clashes in early December.

On 9 November 2000, just before Arafat's meeting with President Clinton, Israeli forces killed a senior Fatah commander, Hussein Abayyat in Beit Sahur, tracking him by helicopter and shelling his car. Abayyat was the first victim of Israel's new policy of singling out for assassination leading Palestinian figures alleged to be orchestrators of 'terrorist' actions. The new type of killings, which Israeli officials described as 'initiated attacks', claimed the lives of at least 10 local Palestinian leaders between early November and the end of December. (On 13 February 2001 the Israeli army assassinated Lt-Col. Massoud Ayad, of Arafat's élite presidential guard—known as Force 17—thereby striking at the heart of Arafat's administration.) Although international opprobrium was mounting with regard to Israel's effective state-approved policy of assassination, the US Administration refused to condemn the policy but merely stated that neither Israel nor the PA had fulfilled the obligations agreed at Sharm esh-Sheikh in October. Arafat and Clinton held their meeting on 7 November 2000, but left without expressing optimism. Some unconfirmed reports claimed that Clinton had presented Arafat with an updated draft of the Camp David understandings, including bridging proposals for Jerusalem based on the idea of 'vertical sovereignty' but barring Israeli excavations. Arafat, meanwhile, sought US support in his appeal to the UN for an international peace-keeping force in the West Bank and Gaza. Barak met Clinton on 12 November and complained that the PA was trying to internationalize the conflict by involving the UN. He also urged the US President to move ahead with plans to upgrade the US-Israeli strategic relationship and to submit to the US Congress a request for supplemental aid to Israel. As Israeli–Palestinian clashes continued, by mid-November Israeli armed forces had tripled the number of troops in the West Bank and Gaza, reinforcing the economic blockade on Area A, and had secured control over movement along all major roads. The Israeli authorities also halted the payment of tax transfers owed to the PA.

The al-Aqsa *intifada* and Israel's subsequent crack-down on Palestinian demonstrators reverberated internationally. The UN, the EU and several Arab states all condemned Israel's 'excessive use of force'. Anti-Israeli demonstrations were held in many Arab and European capitals. The impact of the uprising on Palestinians living in other Arab countries was much in evidence: Palestinian refugees notably led mass protests in the Jordanian capital, Amman, Damascus in Syria, and throughout Lebanon. Egypt too was rocked by the largest and fiercest protests against Israel since the early 1970s. On 24 October 2000 some 25,000 Palestinians and Jordanians staged a massive 'march of return' on the Allenby Bridge in Jordan, leaving over 100 wounded in clashes with the Jordanian army.

ARAB LEAGUE SUMMIT IN CAIRO

The regional impact of these protests came on 21–22 October 2000 with the convening, in Cairo, of the first Arab League summit in four years (and the first for over a decade to include Iraq), followed by the Organization of the Islamic Conference (OIC) summit on 12–14 November in Doha, Qatar. Although decisions were meagre in terms of action, the two summits were significant in three ways. First, they affirmed that there would be no comprehensive peace with Israel without the restoration of full Palestinian sovereignty over East Jerusalem—a clear rebuttal of Israeli and US designs for the city as presented at Camp David. Second, they offered practical and financial support to the Palestinian uprising, a token signal at least that its cessation required tangible political gains for the Palestinians. Finally, they demonstrated that the Palestinian question remained the key to Israel's integration and acceptance in the Arab world. In the first two months of the al-Aqsa *intifada* four Arab countries—Tunisia, Oman, Morocco and Qatar—terminated whatever diplomatic relations they had with Israel, and Egypt recalled its ambassador from Tel-Aviv for the first time in 18 years.

The Cairo summit, on 21–22 October 2000, confirmed the deep rift that existed between the aspirations of the Arab people and the priorities of their leaders, above all the reluctance of the latter to defy the USA. The massive demonstrations that had been held in the Arab world since the start of the *intifada* had demanded tangible Arab action: severing ties with Israel and halting normalization; using oil and other sanctions to counter America's backing for Israel; opening borders for guerrilla action; or even bringing the Arab armies themselves into the equation. The Cairo summit stopped short of meeting the most modest of these demands, the closure of diplomatic missions. Instead, it called a halt to the establishment of new ties with Israel. Jordan and Egypt were therefore absolved of any commitment to break off diplomatic ties with Israel, which, they argued, they were bound by treaty to maintain, and were useful as a means of pressure. Nevertheless, the summit served as a warning that such action might ensue if Israeli forces continued their actions against the Palestinians. After Israeli military strikes on Fatah targets in Gaza on 20 November, Egypt decided to recall to Cairo its long-serving ambassador to Israel, Muhammad Abd al-Aziz Bassiouni. The only practical measure agreed at the Cairo summit was to establish a US \$1,000m. fund to support the *intifada*.

Barak waited no more than an hour after the publication of the Arab League's final communiqué before calling what he termed a 'time-out' on the Israeli-Palestinian track of the Middle East peace process. With all other channels blocked, Barak determined to form a 'national emergency' cabinet with the participation of Ariel Sharon's right-wing Likud. During November and December 2000 Barak repeatedly met with Sharon to discuss coalition terms, but Sharon again demanded a veto over any moves to revive peace talks with the Palestinians. There were reports at the end of November 2000 that the PA had rejected Barak's suggestion of a partial peace plan whereby Israel would effect further troop redeployments from the West Bank in exchange for a postponement of discussions relating to the remaining 'final status' issues.

NEW PREMIERSHIP ELECTION

On 28 November 2000 Ehud Barak unexpectedly announced that he would resign in order to seek early re-election to the premiership in 60 days. The Israeli Prime Minister stated that he wanted a fresh mandate to tackle the country's 'emergency situation', but that he wanted to prevent Israel from holding elections for both the premiership and the Knesset at a time of fragile national security. With a beleaguered and paralysed administration, Barak had few alternatives open to him: more than 70 members of the 120-member legislature were already committed to vote for the dissolution of the Knesset and early elections that would effectively end his term of office. Rather than succumb to a humiliating defeat, Barak hit back at his opponents with a defiant speech. However, the fact remained that less than 18 months after an unprecedented election victory, the increasingly discredited Prime Minister found himself with his coalition in tatters and a Knesset dominated by the opposition. Barak's supporters laid the blame for this outcome largely on Israel's so-called 'two-ballots' system (introduced in 1996) that provides for separate votes for Prime Minister and Knesset and which is seen as having eroded the power of the major parties and made the formation of a ruling coalition even more dependent on the minor parties. The dissent that would culminate in the defection of three right-wing factions from the coalition was exacerbated by Barak's personal shortcomings, his perceived self-confidence and disdain even for ministers of his own Labour Party. Yet it was Barak's failure to make good on his pledges to bring peace and domestic reform to Israel that was his undoing. Despite Barak having campaigned on a platform that also emphasized social concern and the need for domestic renewal, social and welfare services remained chronically under-funded. Moreover, his manner of negotiating with the Palestinians and Syria was considered to be brusque and domineering. Nevertheless, in his short tenure, he made one significant achievement. By allowing the question of Jerusalem to be introduced into negotiations with the PA, Barak had broken the taboo which had previously prevented any discussion of one the most crucial issues of the Middle East peace process and one that must be resolved if there is ever to be a viable peace in the region.

Barak formally resigned as Prime Minister on 9 December 2000, and a prime ministerial election was set for 6 February

2001. The Labour Party swiftly chose Barak, who remained the acting premier, as its candidate. On 19 December 2000 former Likud leader Binyamin Netanyahu withdrew from the contest. Netanyahu had urged the Knesset either to amend electoral legislation that prevents non-members from standing for election, or to vote for the assembly's dissolution; however, the Knesset voted against its own dissolution and thus avoided a general election being held prior to the end of its term in May 2001. Barak's main challenger from the other side of the political spectrum was the hardline Likud leader, Ariel Sharon.

Meanwhile, on 19 December 2000 Israeli and Palestinian officials met in Washington to try to resume peace talks. However, many observers saw this meeting as little more than a ploy on the part of Barak, possibly in co-ordination with the Clinton Administration, to enable Barak to be re-elected. In mid-December five Palestinian police-officers were killed by Israeli security forces during a gun battle in the Gaza Strip. On 23 December President Clinton submitted his latest proposals for resolving the Palestinian–Israeli conflict. Presented verbatim to the Israeli and PA negotiators, Clinton proposed that the Palestinians should have a 'non-militarized' state covering 95% of an (undefined) West Bank and all of Gaza. The PA should also receive 3% of land from within Israel's 1967 borders to compensate for the 5% of the West Bank that Clinton believed Israel needed in order to annex the three Jewish settlements of Ma'aleh Edomin, Ariel and Gush Etzion. In East Jerusalem, the Palestinians would have sovereignty over all Arab neighbourhoods while Israel would extend its sovereignty over the 11 Jewish settlements built within Jerusalem's annexed and enlarged city boundaries since 1967. The Old City of Jerusalem would be divided ethnically, with the Palestinians having sovereignty over the Muslim and Christian areas and Israel gaining sovereignty over the Jewish quarter, the Western Wall and the access road through the Armenian Quarter. (In effect Israel would have to hand over 85% of East Jerusalem.) Under the US proposals, Palestinian refugees would not have the right to return to their homes in Israel. Arafat was reported to have insisted on the right of return for Palestinian refugees, and both Israel and the PA sought clarifications on the proposals from the White House. The peace talks stalled in late December 2000 after two Israelis were killed in bomb explosions in Tel-Aviv and the Gaza Strip. On the last day of 2000 two particularly significant killings took place. During a day of widespread violence in which six Palestinians (including two children) were killed by Israeli gunfire, the Israeli army mounted a carefully-planned operation in Tulkarm to 'liquidate' Dr Thabet Thabet, a high-ranking Fatah official in the West Bank and a senior official at the PA's Ministry of Health. Also on 31 December Palestinian assailants in the West Bank killed Binyamin Zeev Kahane, leader of the extremist anti-Palestinian settler group, Kahane Chai, along with his wife. Kahane was the son of the late Meir Kahane, himself an extremist setter leader, murdered by an Egyptian-born US citizen in New York in November 1990.

With Bill Clinton's presidential term coming to an end in the USA, on 5 January 2001 two authoritative Israeli opinion polls signalled a potentially devastating defeat for incumbent Prime Minister Barak. No sooner had Clinton bidden farewell to his various partners in the Oslo peace process than Arafat dispatched his senior negotiators to Taba, Egypt, to meet their Israeli counterparts in the hope of reaching an accord. The latest round of 'intensive talks', which began on 21 January but broke down without agreement six days later, evolved out of a CIA-drafted security plan presented to the two sides in Cairo on 10 January. For both Arafat and Barak the reason for seeking some semblance of calm in the West Bank and Gaza was the growing realization that Ariel Sharon was almost certainly going to be Israel's next Prime Minister. The prospect of a Sharon victory had shaken the Palestinian leadership out of any pretence of not interfering in the Israeli election campaign. Most international observers commented that by electing Sharon the Israeli public would be demonstrating its resolve to reject the peace process altogether. Indeed, the majority of Israelis believed that Barak had been 'too generous' in offering territorial concessions to the PA.

SHARON'S GOVERNMENT OF 'NATIONAL UNITY'

Israel's decisive shift to the right ensured that Ariel Sharon won the prime ministerial election of 6 February 2001 with a 25% margin of victory over Ehud Barak: Sharon won 62.4% of the total votes cast. The rate of voter participation was estimated at 62.3%. (Arab parties in Israel—who had contributed significantly to Barak's election victory in 1999—urged their supporters to either boycott or abstain from the poll.) Sharon had railed against Barak for being 'soft', and it is beyond doubt that he owed his landslide election victory to his belligerent oratory and hardline military reputation: his election campaign slogan was 'Let the IDF win'. Sharon immediately set about constructing a government of 'national unity', but his Likud party could provide no more than 19 Knesset votes, clearly short of the majority the Prime Minister-elect needed to control the 120-member legislature. Barak, meanwhile, resigned the party leadership.

Labour's Central Committee voted on 26 February 2001 to enter into a coalition with Likud. Sharon's 26-member Government, which was dominated by Labour, Likud and Shas, but also included representatives from right-wing and religious parties, was presented for Knesset approval on 6 March and approved the following day. Many Israelis expressed reservations about the new Government, and Sharon's reputation as a hardline politician was reinforced by his choice of Labour's Binyamin Ben-Eliezer as Minister of Defence (Ben-Eliezer represented the right of the Labour Party) and of Rechavam Ze'evi of the extreme right-wing Haichud Haleumi as Minister of Tourism. The key post of Minister of the Interior was given to the leader of the more pragmatic ultra-orthodox Shas party, Eliyahu Yishai, while Sharon himself was to hold the Immigrant Absorption portfolio. Four deputy prime ministers were appointed. Possibly the most notable appointment was that of Labour's elder statesman and former Prime Minister, Shimon Peres, as Deputy Prime Minister and Minister of Foreign Affairs. Although an alliance with Labour was expected to give Sharon greater stability in the fractured Knesset which he inherited, and given the volatile situation in the region, many observers forecast that Sharon's new administration would have a short life span. Less than 48 hours after Sharon's election victory, a car bomb had exploded in an ultra-orthodox Jewish neighbourhood in Jerusalem, with two militant Palestinian groups, the Popular Resistance Forces and the Victims of Sabra and Chatila, claiming responsibility. In the weeks following the election Hamas stepped up its campaign of attacks against Israeli targets.

Sharon has been one of the most enthusiastic exponents of Israel's 'colonization' of the West Bank and Gaza, and especially of East Jerusalem. Under the new Government Israel continued the building of Jewish settlements in the Occupied Territories— a policy widely seen as constituting one of the principal reasons for the lack of progress in the search for peace. It was difficult, therefore, to see how Sharon would be able to succeed where previous right-wing premiers like Shamir and Netanyahu had failed, and where even Labour's Barak and his 'far-reaching concessions' to the Palestinians had been unable to secure peace. Sharon stated categorically that he would not discuss the future of Jerusalem or cede control over any part of the city to the PA. He also maintained that every Jewish settler would remain in place and that no Palestinian refugees would be granted the right of return. Sharon stated that what had been offered by his predecessor was no longer on the table, and that peace talks would not be resumed from where they stalled in January 2001. It was hard at this time to see how the Israeli–Palestinian conflict could become anything other than a long war of attrition, combining both civilian protests and increasingly guerrilla-type forms of armed struggle. It was also difficult to imagine any Israeli response other than a massive show of military might. The PA leadership was particularly apprehensive about the new Israeli Cabinet headed by Sharon. In mid-April came the announcement that the Israeli Government was tendering 708 new housing units in the West Bank settlements of Ma'aleh Edomin and Alfie Menashie, an especially provocative move given that there are an estimated 1,610 units currently vacant in Ma'aleh Edomin and about 20,000 vacant throughout the Occupied Territories.

Under President George W. Bush, a new US policy towards the Middle East began to emerge. Ominously for the Palestinians, the new Bush Administration appeared to endorse Sharon's stance, and was content to disengage itself from close involvement in Middle East diplomacy and to ignore Clinton's peace proposals for the region. Sharon had always been uneasy about US involvement in the Israeli-Palestinian conflict. As soon as Bush entered the White House it became apparent that he was giving priority to the issue of Iraq and was shunning active involvement in Arab-Israeli negotiations, effectively relegating peace-making initiatives to the side-lines. The key figure in the new US Administration, as far as both Sharon and Peres were concerned, was the new Secretary of State, Gen. Colin Powell, who has reiterated the USA's resolve to protect Israel's security. The US Department of State redefined the terms of reference by saying that the USA would engage in 'negotiations' and 'movement' towards peace rather than the peace process itself.

During his first tour of the Middle East at the end of February 2001 US Secretary of State Colin Powell was given a polite but cool reception in five of the six Arab capitals he visited. In order to meet Powell, Arafat travelled to Ramallah for the first time since the *intifada* erupted in late September 2000. However, the PA was displeased by the Secretary of State's demand for a halt to the violence and for a lifting of Israel's blockade on the Palestinian territories, without calling for an end to the Israeli occupation. During their joint press conference Arafat challenged both the Bush Administration and Israel by insisting that talks should resume from where they were suspended in January 2001. According to the Palestinians, the first two Bush initiatives destroyed the continuity of the peace process and represented a US capitulation to Israel, whose new Prime Minister had similarly declared recent exchanges in the peace process to be 'null and void'. In late February Powell had met the outgoing Israeli Prime Minister, Ehud Barak, as well as Prime Minister-elect Sharon. Powell assured Sharon that Washington's support for Israel remained firm, and joined his call for an end to violence; however, the US Secretary of State urged Sharon to lift the siege on the Palestinian self-rule areas and to transfer more than US $50m. in tax rebates to the PA in order to pay the salaries of civil servants and police. Sharon refused the demands until Palestinians ceased their attacks against Israelis.

Prime Minister Sharon made it clear that he would not meet with Arafat during a trip to Washington DC, on 19–20 March 2001, when he held talks with US President Bush. Sharon also unveiled Israel's new military policy in the Occupied Territories, which consisted of three 3.5 m.-deep trenches built in the road linking Ramallah to 33 Palestinian villages in its northern West Bank hinterland, as well as the presence of Israeli tanks along Ramallah's main road to Jerusalem. The blockade effectively imprisoned 50,000 Palestinians within Ramallah and 165,000 others in its hinterland. The 'suffocating siege' was imposed following Israeli army intelligence that a Palestinian militant group in Ramallah was about to perpetrate a string of bomb blasts in Jerusalem. Similar Israeli tactics had been employed around Jericho and other Gazan and West Bank towns. Israeli helicopter gunships attacked Palestinian military installations in Ramallah and Gaza on 28 March, in retaliation for the deaths of two Israeli schoolchildren and a Jewish settler's baby. Meanwhile, Israel continued its assassination of suspected Palestinian militant leaders. These included an Islamic Jihad activist, Iyad Hardan, in Jenin on 4 April and a Hamas military leader, Muhammad Yassin Nasser, in Gaza on 14 April. On 8 April there was an ambush by Israeli soldiers on PA Preventive Security Force chief Muhammad Dahlan and other PA security heads at the Erez check-point, following a meeting with their Israeli counterparts in Tel-Aviv. Dahlan said he would not engage in further security co-operation until an apology or explanation was forthcoming from the Israeli authorities.

On 15 April 2001 Israeli helicopter gunships bombed a Syrian radar station 35 km east of Beirut near the mountain town of Dahr al-Baydar, killing at least one Syrian soldier and wounding several others. The Israeli assault, the first against Syrian targets since 1996, was ostensibly in retaliation for the killing by Hezbollah of an Israeli soldier in Shebaa Farms on 14 April 2001. The UN Secretary-General's personal representative in Lebanon, Steffan de Mistura, described the Israeli attack as a clear infringement of UN Security Council Resolution 425 requiring Israel to withdraw its forces from Lebanon. Israel carried out a further air attack on a Syrian radar station south of Baalbek on 2 July.

On 17 April 2001 Israeli tanks and bulldozers forced their way 1 km into Beit Hanun, thus occupying a small town in the Gaza Strip under full PA control. Israeli helicopters and gunboats also pitched rockets at Palestinian residential and security installations in Gaza City, Deir al-Balah and Rafah, while its army mounted blockades across Gaza's main lateral roads, effectively slicing the Strip into three: south, north and middle enclaves. Although Israeli army officials had announced their intention to maintain their presence in Beit Hanun for months, by the early hours of 18 April the picture had changed. Under heavy pressure from the US Administration, Israeli forces abruptly withdrew from the town. The *casus belli* had been a mortar attack on Sderot, an Israeli town some 5 km north of Gaza. The US pressure on Israel was rather less predictable. It came as something of a surprise when the USA, in the person of Secretary of State Colin Powell, criticized Israel's 'reoccupation' of part of Gaza as 'excessive and disproportionate'. This statement was accompanied by a call to the Israeli Prime Minister to pull his forces back. Sharon promptly obliged. As for Washington's intervention, the signal was not easy to read. Doubtless growing unease at the Israeli escalation, particularly after its attack on Syrian targets in Lebanon, was compounded by Sharon's abrupt dismissal of an Egyptian-Jordanian peace initiative, drawn up soon after the heads of state of both countries had visited the US capital. However, by declaring the reoccupation of PA-controlled territory to be out of bounds, in effect the USA appeared to be affirming that whatever else Israel did in response to the *intifada* was permissible.

Israel's encroachments into territories that it had transferred to PA control failed to quell the Palestinian *intifada*. Clashes continued in both Gaza and the West Bank during and after the Israeli reoccupation of Beit Hanun. In mid-April 2001 there were tentative telephone contacts between Sharon and Arafat, a meeting between Arafat and the Israeli leader's son, and even an attempt to bring about the resumption of bilateral security co-operation. Israeli and PA security officials held talks on 20 April 2001. However, the last initiative was abruptly curtailed when Israeli forces opened fire on the Palestinian delegation as it was returning home.

In mid-April 2001 the so-called 'Egyptian-Jordanian initiative' for halting the violence in Israel and the Palestinian territories and restarting peace negotiations between Israel and the PA was revived. The plan set out to revive the Oslo process, using as a reference the fragile accord reached at Sharm esh-Sheikh in October 2000 and providing for the resumption of 'final status' negotiations after the two sides had taken steps to 'end confrontation' and had restored the situation on the ground to the *status quo ante* (i.e. how it had been prior to the outbreak of the al-Aqsa *intifada*). In addition, it envisaged various confidence-building measures, including the resumption of security co-operation and a suspension of Jewish settlement expansion in the West Bank and Gaza. The Israeli Government initially rejected the plan, but decided that it would be more beneficial to adopt a position of conditional endorsement, contingent on suitable amendments being made. Sharon side-stepped the initiative; having originally dismissed it as a Palestinian ruse to get Israel to negotiate 'under fire'. However, on 25 April 2001 he changed tack, describing it as 'important' but requiring 'some changes and improvement'. The Israeli Government now sought to amend the initiative's core demands that negotiations be resumed from the point at which they left off at Taba in January and that they be accompanied by a total and complete 'freeze' on all settlement activities, including those in East Jerusalem. Sharon then dispatched his Deputy Prime Minister and Minister of Foreign Affairs, Shimon Peres, to Cairo and Amman on 29 April, and subsequently to Washington to explain Israel's position. The Israeli premier also repeated that 'there must be a complete halt to violence on the ground' before any diplomatic plan could take off, a position shared at this time by the US Administration. The revival of the Egyptian-Jordanian proposals, or Taba plan, was bound up with the US's belated intervention of 18 April to demand that Israeli troops withdraw from Beit Hanun. It gave renewed hope to supporters of the Oslo process within the PA leadership. Diplomatic optimism was bolstered by the active interest in the peace plan shown by the EU, the UN and Russia.

In mid-May 2001 Israelis marked the 53rd anniversary of the founding of the State of Israel in subdued mood. On 18 May Israel unleashed its F-16 fighter aircraft against security compounds in the West Bank towns of Nablus and Ramallah, killing several Palestinians. The offensive was launched hours after a suicide bombing carried out by Hamas in Netanya killed five Israelis. The Israeli action marked the first use of US-made fighter jets against Palestinians in the West Bank and Gaza since Israel occupied these territories in 1967. Earlier, on 14 May 2001, Israeli troops had killed five Palestinian police-officers in the West Bank, later admitting that the deaths were accidental. Foreign affairs ministers of the Arab League states held an emergency meeting in Cairo on 19 May, at which they announced an end to 'political' contacts with Israel. The OIC did likewise later in May.

On 20 May 2001 the Report of the Sharm esh-Sheikh Fact-Finding Committee (the 'Mitchell Report') was officially released (see Documents on Palestine, p. 90). The report failed to appor-tion blame for the recent Israeli–Palestinian violence; it described Sharon's visit to the Temple Mount/Haram ash-Sharif compound in late September 2000 as 'poorly timed' and 'provoca-tive', but declared that this had not caused the violence. The Mitchell Committee also failed to accept that the PA leadership had orchestrated Palestinian violence following the failed Camp David talks, called for a 'freeze' on Jewish settlement expansion in the West Bank and Gaza, and also demanded an end to the economic blockade on the Palestinian areas. However, the report demanded a greater effort by Palestinian leaders to prevent 'terrorist' attacks on Israeli targets.

On 1 June 2001 20 Israelis were killed and scores wounded in a Palestinian suicide bombing at a beach-front disco in Tel-Aviv. (In mid-June another Israeli died as a result of injuries sustained in the attack.) The dramatic escalation of Israeli–Palestinian violence compelled the USA to increase its involvement in the conflict, attempting to broker a new round of talks from late May. On 5 June CIA Director George Tenet arrived in Israel, taking the Bush Administration a step further towards re-engagement in Arab-Israeli affairs. Tenet sought to consolidate the fragile cease-fire he had earlier helped to negot-iate between Israel and the PA, and to implement the recommen-dations contained in the Mitchell Report. The Mitchell recommendations mapped out steps towards restoring the polit-ical process, ending the eight-month crisis and introducing confidence-building measures, including a 'freeze' on Israeli settlement building. Tenet's efforts at consolidating the cease-fire were part of wider US efforts aimed at reviving President Clinton's policy of engagement, which the incoming Bush Admi-nistration had initially derided. As the crisis between Israel and the Palestinians deepened, President Bush appointed a special envoy to the Middle East, William Burns, as a belated successor to Clinton's Middle East Co-ordinator, Dennis Ross. Both Burns and Tenet were aiming to bring about a 'cooling-off' period of six weeks, in the hope that this would recreate the conditions for a political dialogue between the two sides. By 12 June Tenet had persuaded Israel and the PA to agree the terms of an 'outline cease-fire deal'. However, despite the formal cease-fire negotiated by Tenet, violence between Israelis and Palestin-ians continued and the CIA-led talks were suspended.

Despite having begun to implement the cease-fire require-ments to withdraw tanks from PA-controlled areas and to ease the economic blockade, on 14 June 2001 Israel was reported to be 'reassessing' the cease-fire following the killing by Palestinian gunmen of two Jewish settlers in the West Bank on 18 June. Arafat, meanwhile, asserted that any extended cease-fire should form part of a comprehensive peace plan, including a 'freeze' on the settlement-building programme and the resumption of peace negotiations. On 22 June two Israeli soldiers were killed in a suicide bomb attack in the Gaza Strip. Sharon held talks with President Bush on 26 June in Washington. It was reported that the US President had refused to endorse Sharon's demand for 10 days of 'total calm' before Israel would begin implementing the US peace plan. On the following day Secretary of State

Colin Powell undertook a two-day visit to the Middle East region to discuss the US peace proposals with Israeli, Palestinian and Egyptian leaders. Powell reportedly agreed with the Israeli Prime Minister the details of a timetable for implementing the cease-fire. However, the PA rejected the terms, claiming that they were weighted in Israel's favour.

By late June and early July 2001 the Israeli Cabinet was evidently in turmoil. On 26 June the Government was placed under severe strain over a Labour-proposed plan to dismantle 15 Jewish 'settlement outposts' recently set up in the Palestinian enclaves. On 5 July the Hebrew daily *Ma'ariv* revealed that the Cabinet was deeply divided over the issue of whether to launch a massive strike aimed at toppling PA President Arafat. Appar-ently the option was put on hold, although Sharon was in favour of removing Arafat if there were further Palestinian suicide bombings in Israel. Two extreme right-wing ministers, Rechavam Ze'evi and Avigdor Lieberman, pushing for the adop-tion of a harder line against Arafat, threatened to boycott cabinet meetings over its failure to agree a military strike against Arafat. However, any attempt to assassinate Arafat was certain to provoke outrage both among Palestinians and the international community, and would lead inevitably to the rise of militant Islamist groups such as Hamas. Earlier, on 4 July, Israel's 'inner' Security Cabinet had voted to step-up its policy of assassinating suspected Palestinian militants. Some extreme right-wing members wanted to go further, urging a formal end to the cease-fire agreement and massive strikes against PA infrastructure. Israel's policy of 'extra-judicial' killing, which had begun in November and was in defiance of international opinion, had provoked an outcry from human rights groups. UN Secretary-General Kofi Annan called on Israel to halt its practice of 'targeted assassinations' and urged both sides to implement the recommendations contained in the Mit-chell Report.

The cycle of revenge attacks between Israelis and Palestinians continued throughout July 2001, and it appeared unlikely that Tenet's 'cease-fire' would hold. The international community was highly critical of Israel for carrying out the demolition of a number of 'illegal' Palestinian homes in East Jerusalem and the Gaza Strip. On 13 July Israeli armed forces shelled the West Bank town of Nablus, killing a senior Palestinian police-officer, in retaliation for an attack on Jewish settlers there. The next day Shimon Peres and Arafat held talks in Cairo, with mediation by President Mubarak of Egypt, in an effort to bring the violence to an end. However, on 17 July Israel sent extra troops and tanks into West Bank flashpoints such as Bethlehem and Hebron, leading to fears of a renewed crisis in the region. The Israeli Government insisted, however, that it did not intend to retake Palestinian territory that had been returned to PA control since 1994. In mid-July 2001 the US Administration for the first time signalled that it would approve the deployment of international monitors to assist in the implementation of the Mitchell recommendations, which the Israeli Government continued to resist. At the end of the month Israel launched an air-strike on the offices of Hamas in Nablus, killing at least eight Palestinians, among them two senior Hamas members accused of involvement in the Tel-Aviv night-club bombing in June. The Israeli attack was strongly condemned by the US Government and other world leaders. However, Sharon vowed to continue Israel's policy of 'pinpoint liquidations' or 'targeted killings'. On 6 August Israel published a 'most wanted' list of seven Palestinians whom it held responsible for 'terrorist' attacks against Israelis. Three days later a suicide bomber killed at least 15 Israelis at a restaurant in Jerusalem, leading the Israeli Government, on 10 August, to seize control of Orient House, the *de facto* headquarters of the PA in East Jerusalem, as a 'temporary measure'. In the second half of August Israeli armed forces on several occasions entered Palestinian-controlled towns in the West Bank, including Jenin, Hebron and Beit Jala, claiming that Palestinians in those areas were shooting at Jewish targets. Israeli tanks also entered a refugee camp in Gaza. Tensions increased on 27 August when the leader of the Popular Front for the Liberation of Palestine (PFLP), Abu Ali Moustafa, was killed by Israeli security forces at the PFLP headquarters in Ramallah.

Meanwhile, in late July 2001 the UN declared that it would allow Israeli and Lebanese officials to view a censored copy of a video-cassette made by a UN peace-keeper in Lebanon, which Israel believed would give vital information relating to the three Israeli soldiers abducted by Hezbollah in October 2000. The UN had previously denied the existence of the tape. However, Israeli military officials admitted at the end of October 2001 that the soldiers were 'almost certainly' dead.

The election for the Labour Party leadership proved inconclusive in early September 2001, when one of the two candidates, the Minister of Defence, Binyamin Ben-Eliezer, alleged that Knesset Speaker Avraham Burg (who had won a narrow victory) had engaged in vote-rigging. Ben-Eliezer initiated legal proceedings against the outcome of the ballot, and following a second election on 27 December was named as the new Labour leader (having received 51.2% of the votes cast). At the end of September a report released by the State Comptroller raised doubts about the legality of certain donations made to Ariel Sharon and his campaign team in the approach to the premiership election. In early October the Attorney-General ordered a criminal investigation into the alleged violation of campaign funding regulations; the Prime Minister and his son, Omri (who had managed Sharon's campaign), were both questioned by police. In mid-November Sharon was obliged to repay what had been found to be an illegal donation received by his campaign team.

In mid-October 2001 the right-wing Haichud Haleumi-Israel B'Aitainu bloc withdrew from Sharon's coalition, in protest at the Government's decision to withdraw Israeli troops from the West Bank town of Hebron and proposals to ease the blockade on the Palestinian territories; the bloc's representatives, the Minister of National Infrastructure, Avigdor Lieberman, and the Minister of Tourism, Rechavam Ze'evi, both resigned from the Cabinet. Two days later (when the ministers' resignations were due to take effect), Ze'evi was assassinated at a hotel in East Jerusalem by a militant of the PFLP, which claimed that the killing was in revenge for the recent assassination of its leader. Ze'evi was the first Israeli cabinet minister to be killed by an Arab militant. Following his assassination, the Haichud Haleumi-Israel B'Aitainu bloc remained in the Government, with Lieberman retaining his post and Binyamin Elon subsequently being named as Minister of Tourism.

The Knesset voted, on 7 November 2001, to revoke the parliamentary immunity of its most prominent Arab Israeli member, Azmi Bishara, in order that Bishara could answer charges of supporting terrorism against Israel and of undermining the Jewish State. The action of the legislature followed comments made by Bishara in support of the Lebanese resistance organization, Hezbollah, and after he had assisted a group of Arab Israelis to visit their families in Syria. Trial proceedings against Bishara began on 10 December.

CONTINUED ESCALATION OF ISRAELI–PALESTINIAN HOSTILITIES

The second half of 2001 was marked by a continued and steady escalation of Israeli–Palestinian hostilities. The dynamics of the situation on the ground were altered after the massive suicide attacks on the World Trade Center in New York and the Pentagon in Washington, DC, on 11 September, in which some 3,000 people were killed. Furthermore, US President George W. Bush's subsequent launch of a 'war on terror' against the militant Islamist al-Qa'ida group believed to have perpetrated the attacks appeared to encourage Ariel Sharon to step up the Israeli army's assaults on Palestinian targets and ultimately to reoccupy six major West Bank cities. The two recent assassinations—of Abu Ali Moustafa, Secretary-General of the PFLP (and the most senior Palestinian figure to be targeted by Israel since the start of the al-Aqsa intifada), and of Israel's right-wing Minister of Tourism, Rechavam Ze'evi, by the PFLP—further escalated the spiral of violence. By the time of the first anniversary of the eruption of the intifada, at least 600 Palestinians and more than 160 Israelis had died as a result of the conflict. In late September, meanwhile, Shimon Peres held talks with Yasser Arafat in the Gaza Strip, at which the two sides agreed to reactivate the cease-fire provisions brokered by CIA Director Tenet in June, and to implement the recommendations of the Mitchell Committee.

Although Arafat immediately denounced Ze'evi's murder, ordering Palestinian security forces to arrest the perpetrators and reportedly outlawing the armed wing of the PFLP, on 17 October 2001 Sharon issued an ultimatum to the PA leader that he arrest and extradite Ze'evi's assassins and other PFLP leaders or face a response more severe than any in recent history. (The Secretary-General of the PFLP, Ahmad Saadat, was detained by Palestinian security forces on 15 January 2002, and three men alleged to have been responsible for the minister's murder were arrested on 21 February.) Israel was swift to equate the 11 September attacks on the USA with 'violence' emanating from the Palestinian territories (and by implication Arafat with al-Qa'ida leader Osama bin Laden), apparently so as to justify harsher military actions against the Palestinians. The USA, on the other hand, was eager for Israel to resume talks with the PA and for the two sides to implement previous cease-fire agreements that would facilitate US coalition-building for the war being waged against Islamist militants in Afghanistan. In the hope of invigorating the cease-fire and as a public relations move designed to help US coalition-building, US Secretary of Defense Donald Rumsfeld toured the Middle East in early October, and President Bush declared on 2 October that the creation of a Palestinian state 'has always been a part of our vision, so long as the right of Israel to exist is respected'. Although this marked the first explicit support for statehood by a Republican administration, the US State Department denied any shift in official policy. Bush reiterated his support for a Palestinian state through negotiations on 11 October. Sharon was reportedly angered, not only by the statement but also because Rumsfeld had not come to Israel during his regional consultations on the US campaign against 'terror'. The USA, after 11 September, did not back Israel's demand for the extradition of Ze'evi's killers. Together with the EU and Russia, the USA continued to press both Israel and the PA to adhere to the cease-fire arrangement of 29 August, which had been mediated by the High Representative for the Common and Security Foreign Policy of the EU, Javier Solana, although no new political initiatives were offered and no progress was made.

Sharon, rejecting personal appeals by President Bush and US Secretary of State Colin Powell to resume talks with the PA, on 18 October 2001 suspended all contacts with the PA, and gave the Israeli army authorization to step up its policy of 'initiated attacks' against Palestinians deemed to be involved in 'terrorist' actions, threatening to wage a war against Arafat. Some right-wing members of the Knesset went even further, calling for the expulsion of Arafat from the West Bank and Gaza. Within hours of Ze'evi's assassination, the Israeli army deployed helicopter gunships over Palestinian cities and moved troops into the outer fringes of Jenin (Area A territory). On 18 October Israeli forces reoccupied Jenin, Nablus and Ramallah; Bethlehem and Beit Jala were taken by Israel on 19 October, and Qalqilya and Tulkarm on the following day. On 22 October the USA condemned the reoccupation of West Bank cities and towns in Area A as 'unacceptable' and demanded Israel's immediate withdrawal. Israel was forced to withdraw from the West Bank cities, but its army continued to occupy sectors controlled by the PA and to assassinate senior members of Hamas. With no new political initiatives on offer and no diplomatic progress in sight, Israeli–Palestinian clashes continued throughout November and December.

In late November 2001 the USA sent to the region its two special envoys to the Middle East, William Burns and Anthony Zinni (the former had been named Assistant Secretary of State for Near Eastern Affairs in May, while Zinni's appointment had been made earlier in November), in an attempt to broker a new cease-fire. However, hopes for a breakthrough were dimmed when Israel announced that it had appointed an uncompromising former army general, Meir Dagan, as its chief negotiator in talks with US and PA representatives. In early December the Israeli–Palestinian crisis witnessed a considerable escalation: in a single weekend (1–2 December) some 25 Israelis were killed, and scores wounded, in suicide bombings perpetrated by Palestinian extremists in Haifa and Jerusalem, in retaliation for the killing of a leading Hamas official. Sharon cut short his official visit to the USA and on his return to Israel convened an emergency Cabinet meeting, at which it was decided to formally declare the PA as an 'entity that supports terrorism'. (Labour ministers did not attend the vote.) Israel also launched heavy military strikes against Palestinian security targets in the Occupied Territories; two of Arafat's helicopters were destroyed in an Israeli raid on 3 December. The PA was reported to have arrested at least 100 Hamas and Islamic Jihad members in the aftermath of the weekend attacks; however the US Government urged Arafat to do more to end the violence. Although Israeli military action continued, especially in the Gaza Strip, senior Israeli and Palestinian security officials resumed talks a few days later. Israel escalated its military operations in the Territories in mid-December after 10 Israelis had died in a bomb attack near a Jewish settlement in the West Bank. The Government responded to a televised address by Arafat on 16 December, in which he ordered militant groups to end their armed campaign against Israelis and pledged to arrest the perpetrators of the violence, by demanding 'concrete action' from the PA. On 20 December Israeli armed forces staged a 'tactical' withdrawal from areas around Nablus and Ramallah to permit Arafat's security forces to arrest wanted Palestinian militants. However, Arafat remained confined to his headquarters in Ramallah after Israel imposed a travel ban on the Palestinian leader.

THE KARINE-A AFFAIR

On 3 January 2002 Israeli naval commandos in the Red Sea captured a freighter, the *Karine-A*, which Israel claimed was carrying some 50 metric tons of heavy weaponry destined for the PA. Among the arms seized were rockets and missiles that, according to the Israelis, could have reached Ben-Gurion International Airport and major Israeli cities from PA-controlled territory in the West Bank. Israeli leaders claimed that the smuggling operation had been initiated by the PA and had been carried out with Arafat's consent. They also accused Iran of involvement in the supply of the weapons to the PA. Both the PA and Iran denied any involvement in the shipment; however, Arafat did order an internal inquiry into the affair. The US Administration, meanwhile, adopted Israel's position regarding the affair, concluding that senior members of the PA had been involved in organizing the operation; US officials claimed that the arms were designed to 'promote terror', although Secretary of State Powell stated that he had no evidence linking the shipment of arms to Arafat himself. The US State Department also maintained that it had 'convincing evidence' proving that Iran and Hezbollah were linked to the smuggling attempt.

Shortly after the *Karine-A* affair, following a three-week period of relative calm, on 9 January 2002 four Israeli soldiers were killed by Hamas gunmen at an army outpost in the Gaza Strip. Israel retaliated with force, bulldozing more than 50 buildings in the Rafah refugee camp (where the Hamas gunmen had lived) and even destroying the runway at Gaza airport on 11 January. On 14 January Israeli forces assassinated a leader of Fatah's military wing, the al-Aqsa Martyrs Brigades, provoking retaliatory attacks by that organization in Hadera and Jerusalem in which six Israelis died. Israeli forces proceeded to tighten the blockade around Arafat's Ramallah offices, and on 21 January seized control of the West Bank town of Tulkarm. On 27 January it was reported that a suicide bombing had for the first time been carried out by a Palestinian woman, apparently on behalf of the al-Aqsa Martyrs Brigades. Two days later Sharon approved a security plan involving the physical 'separation' of Jerusalem from the West Bank in order to prevent attacks by Palestinian Islamist groups on Israeli territory.

In early February 2002 Sharon reportedly rejected new proposals for a peace settlement drafted by Shimon Peres and PLC Speaker Ahmad Quray; the proposals were said to include the immediate recognition of a limited Palestinian 'state'. Meanwhile, it appeared that Palestinian militants were increasingly targeting their attacks against the Israeli military and Jewish settlers in the Occupied Territories. On 10 February Israel announced that Hamas had for the first time launched rudimentary, short-range *Qassam-2* missiles into Israeli territory from the Gaza Strip. On 19 February six Israeli soldiers died in a Palestinian assault on their check-point near Ramallah—this was the most serious attack on Israeli military forces since the start of the al-Aqsa *intifada*. The Israeli–Palestinian violence escalated significantly at this time, with the death toll rising on both sides as Israeli forces responded to Palestinian armed attacks on Israelis by launching heavy air-strikes against Ramallah and Gaza. In a televised address on 21 February Prime Minister Sharon declared that his Government planned the immediate establishment of 'buffer zones' between Israel and

the Palestinian self-rule areas. Nevertheless, CIA-brokered talks resumed between Israeli and PA security officials in late February. At the end of the month fierce gun battles erupted when Israeli forces occupied two refugee camps at Nablus and Jenin in order to search for Palestinian militants.

THE RAMALLAH INCURSION OF MARCH 2002

Throughout early 2002 Israeli–Palestinian hostilities continued to escalate. The scale of Israeli attacks on Palestinian towns and refugee camps in the West Bank and Gaza was 'disproportionate and often reckless', according to an Amnesty International report. Amnesty estimated that in the six weeks from 1 March to mid-April more that 600 Palestinians had been killed and over 3,000 wounded by Israeli soldiers. By mid-March 2002 at least 1,065 Palestinians and 344 Israelis had been killed since the al-Aqsa *intifada* began in September 2000. During 2–3 March some 21 Israelis were killed in gun attacks in Gaza and the West Bank and a suicide bombing in Jerusalem; the attacks provoked a strong Israeli military response. Following a continuation of the cycle of fatal revenge attacks between Palestinian extremists and Israeli forces, a major escalation of hostilities occurred on the night of 11 March, when the Israeli army entered Ramallah, the Palestinians' commercial and political centre in the West Bank, in what Israel said was part of a general sweep for militants who had led the uprising against Israeli occupation since September 2000. This massive incursion, which involved up to 150 tanks, was part of Israel's biggest military offensive in the West Bank and Gaza Strip since the invasion of these territories in 1967. The Israeli incursion, which also involved the occupation of the Jabalya refugee camp in Gaza, took place against the backdrop of the largely unsuccessful mediation efforts by US special envoy Anthony Zinni, who had arrived in Israel on 14 March—his third trip to the region since November 2001—to seek implementation of the US-brokered truce-to-talks plan and a cease-fire under the terms of the Mitchell Committee. Zinni's visit followed the adoption by the UN Security Council, meeting on 12 March 2002, of Resolution 1397 (see Documents on Palestine, p. 98), which for the first time affirmed the idea of a Palestinian state. The resolution, the first on the Middle East to be drafted by the USA for some 25 years, asserted the UN's 'vision of a region where two States, Israel and Palestine, live side by side within secure and recognized borders'.

The Ramallah incursion resulted in huge damage to Palestinian infrastructure, estimated by PA officials at tens of millions of US dollars. Some 12 Palestinians were also killed during the assault on Ramallah. On 14–15 March 2002 dozens of Israeli tanks left Ramallah, ending a brief reoccupation of PA President Arafat's power base. Arafat, however, denounced the withdrawal as a trick, stating that the tanks remained outside the city. The Israeli army, meanwhile, declared that its forces had left positions in two other West Bank cities (Tulkarm and Qalqilya) but that they remained in Area A territory on the outskirts of four cities: Bethlehem, Nablus, Jenin and Hebron. The Israeli army also formed a cordon around Ramallah.

In the aftermath of the Ramallah incursion the chief representative for the International Committee of the Red Cross (ICRC) in Israel and the Palestinian areas, René Kosirnik, lambasted the Israeli army's behaviour towards Palestinian medical teams in the Occupied Territories. He said on 18 March that the army had 'wantonly and crudely trampled' all over the protocols of the Fourth Geneva Convention (relating to civilians in time of war). Kosirnik mentioned the four doctors, medical personnel and Palestinian ambulance drivers who had been killed by Israeli military fire in recent weeks, and stated that he was yet to receive any proof of Israeli claims that ambulances of the PCRS were being used to smuggle armed activists.

As Zinni pressed ahead with truce talks between Israel and the PA, the US Administration called for a complete withdrawal of all Israeli forces from PA-administered areas, stating that this would create a better environment for Zinni to try to broker a truce. The envoy held talks in Tel-Aviv on 15 March 2002 with the Israeli Minister of Defence, Binyamin Ben-Eliezer. However, Arafat urged the USA to put more pressure on Israel to help Zinni secure a cease-fire, while both Israel and the USA continued to repeat their demand that Arafat do more to rein in Palestinian militants and halt attacks on Israelis.

On 19 March 2002 Anthony Zinni and the other three members of the 'Quartet' of international envoys—UN Special Co-ordinator for the Middle East peace process, Terje Roed-Larsen, EU special envoy Miguel Moratinos, and Russian envoy Andrei Vodobin—met with the Israeli Minister of Foreign Affairs, Shimon Peres, and his ministry's Director-General, Avi Gil, to exchange views on how to advance a cease-fire and resume political negotiations. Initially, Zinni aimed for a cease-fire declaration on 20 March, after he had convened the joint Israeli-Palestinian security committee for discussions on how to move into the 'Tenet work plan' (the security plan prepared the previous year by CIA Director George Tenet), but he was unable to reach a co-ordinated statement acceptable to Sharon and Arafat. On the same day a suicide bomber from Islamic Jihad killed at least seven Israelis on a bus in northern Israel.

The joint Israeli-Palestinian security committee met on 20 and 21 March 2002, with Zinni in attendance; however, both meetings ended without agreement. Taking part in the meetings for the Israeli side were the chief of Shin Bet, Avi Dichter, and the IDF's Chief of Planning, Maj.-Gen. Giora Eiland. Representing the Palestinians were Jibril Rajoub (the Palestinians' security chief in the West Bank) and his Gaza counterpart, Muhammad Dahlan. There were differences of opinion between the two sides as to the length of time allocated to the Tenet work plan before the diplomatic process could resume. There was also disagreement over the arrest of Palestinian militants wanted by Israel. The Israeli Government demanded the arrest of those involved in past attacks against Israelis, but the Palestinians said that they would only detain those who were plotting future attacks. There was no agreement on a cease-fire because the Israelis sought to separate the security issues from the rest of the conditions laid out in the Tenet cease-fire plan. Moreover, the Palestinians continued to demand that Israel pull back its troops to their positions as at 28 September 2000, and lift all the sieges and remove all check-points from around Palestinian towns and villages, and that international observers be positioned in the Occupied Territories. Spokespeople for the PA stated that, despite the difficulties posed by the Tenet plan, they would do what was required, but only if they could show the Palestinian public that there would be an immediate result in the form of significant abatements of the sieges and closures, and only if the security arrangements and calm would lead to a resumption of the political negotiations. For its part, the Israeli Government wanted the Palestinians first to take a series of steps against militant groups, such as ordering arrests, dismantling the militias and collecting weapons. The PA remained opposed to Sharon's 'selective reading' of the Tenet plan, claiming that the Israeli premier disregarded the commitments required of Israel in the plan. However, while the PA did not believe that Sharon was genuinely interested in resuming peace negotiations, or even implementing the Mitchell plan (which required a complete 'freeze' on Jewish settlement activity), they began to explain to mainstream Fatah activists and the Palestinian public that Sharon had to be put to the test, and that if a cease-fire were achieved they would expose his lack of willingness to advance the political negotiations.

In mid-March 2002 US Vice-President Dick Cheney embarked on a 10-day trip to the Middle East, including a visit to Israel on 18–19 March. Cheney's visit to the region was designed to build support for a possible widening of the USA's 'war on terror' to include Iraq. Yet Arab leaders apparently told the Vice-President that there was little appetite for a strike on Iraq while the Israeli–Palestinian violence raged. Cheney refused to meet with Arafat, but hinted that such a meeting could take place in the near future if Arafat implemented the Tenet recommendations. The US Department of State increased the pressure on Arafat to act to stem the violence, demanding that he personally make a public statement in both English and Arabic condemning suicide bombings. (The State Department had, meanwhile, decided to designate the al-Aqsa Martyrs Brigades, which claimed responsibility for suicide bombings in Israel in late March, a 'terrorist organization', making it illegal to provide it with funds and requiring banks to freeze its assets.)

Amid ongoing Israeli–Palestinian violence and continued Palestinian suicide attacks inside Israel, public opinion polls conducted in Israel in late March 2002 showed a sharp decline in the popularity of Ariel Sharon, with 60% of Israelis polled

expressing their dissatisfaction with his premiership. This reflected Sharon's political dilemma in Israel, where he had been under intense pressure from the Likud party and the Israeli right wing in general to take tougher actions against the Palestinians. On the other hand, there was also a growing number of Israeli army reservists who were refusing to serve in the Occupied Territories.

THE SAUDI PEACE PLAN AND THE BEIRUT SUMMIT

Parallel to the intense mediation activity conducted by Anthony Zinni were preparations for the summit meeting of the Arab League Council, to be held in the Lebanese capital on 27–28 March 2002. Israel, however, refused to allow the PA President to attend the Arab summit. It had restricted Arafat's freedom of movement for months, and Sharon offered to lift the ban to enable Arafat to attend the conference only if there was a total cease-fire. Sharon also indicated that Israel might not let Arafat return if Palestinian attacks were launched against Israelis while he was in Beirut. While the Bush Administration applied some pressure on Israel to allow Arafat to attend the summit, at the same time it maintained strong pressure on Arafat to make more effort to suppress Palestinian militants. A principal consideration of the Beirut summit was a recent Saudi peace initiative, put forward in early March by Crown Prince Abdullah, which had prompted a flurry of consultations in the Arab world. The Saudi proposals (see Arab–Israeli Relations 1967–2002, p. 32) essentially required a complete Israeli withdrawal from all Arab land occupied since 1967, a 'just solution' to the refugee issue, and the establishment of a 'viable Palestinian state' with East Jerusalem as its capital. In return, the Arab nations would recognize the State of Israel and normalize diplomatic relations. The final declaration of the Arab League summit endorsed the Saudi initiative, which also referred to the need to find a 'just solution' to the issue of Palestinian refugees.

The Saudi peace plan received support from the Palestinians, the EU, Egypt, Jordan and, most importantly, Syria and Lebanon. The USA quietly welcomed it. Although Israeli officials, especially Shimon Peres, had shown some interest in Crown Prince Abdullah's initiative, Sharon rejected any full withdrawal to the pre-1967 borders and tensions between Israel and the Palestinians remained extremely high.

'OPERATION DEFENSIVE SHIELD': FULL-SCALE INVASION OF WEST BANK POPULATION CENTRES

On 29 March 2002 Israel launched a large-scale offensive in the West Bank, in response to a series of suicide attacks by Palestinian militants and, more specifically, to a suicide bombing on 27 March that killed 29 Israelis who were celebrating the start of Passover in the coastal city of Netanya. This was the bloodiest attack since the start of the al-Aqsa *intifada*. Hamas claimed responsibility for the Netanya attack, declaring that it was intended to avenge previous Israeli killings and military raids on Palestinian targets. The stated goal of Israel's full-scale invasion of Palestinian cities in the West Bank was to wipe out militant networks and seize weapons. One of the main purposes behind the campaign appeared to be to destroy the Palestinian defence establishment and to transfer the handling of all security matters in the Palestinian territories to Israel. In other words, to turn Area A—territory under full PA control—into Area B, with Israeli control of security matters, while the PA maintained control of civilian concerns. Sharon was under intense pressure from right-wing members of his Cabinet to step up military action and oust Arafat. The Israelis held the PA responsible for the failure of Zinni's recent mission. Speaking after an emergency Cabinet meeting that lasted most of the night, Sharon declared that 'Arafat, who has established a coalition of terror against Israel, is an enemy and at this point he will be isolated'. The USA, for its part, condemned the Passover bombing and stated that it showed the need for Arafat to crack down on militants. Meanwhile, Arafat told his aides that he feared for his life since Sharon was showing signs that he wanted to harm him personally.

As 'Operation Defensive Shield' began, Israeli troops swept into Ramallah, forcing their way into Arafat's presidential compound and battling with Palestinian security forces around his headquarters there. As Israeli armoured vehicles enter the compound surrounding Arafat's offices, troops ran inside, prompting heavy shooting. The Israeli military action was the toughest against Arafat since the beginning of the al-Aqsa *intifada* and it posed the biggest threat to Arafat's grip on power since his return to the West Bank from exile in 1994. As Israeli forces entered the compound, the Palestinian leader took cover in a windowless office. With landlines blocked, Arafat was left with a mobile telephone as his only connection to the outside world. Although Israel's Minister of Defence, Binyamin Ben-Eliezer, asserted that Israel had no intention of harming Arafat personally, PA officials warned that Arafat's life was in danger. On the same day the UN Security Council adopted Resolution 1402, expressing 'grave concern' at the escalation of violence in Israel and the Palestinian self-rule areas.

On 30 March 2002 Israel began calling up thousands of army reservists and combat reserve units for a large-scale operation against the Palestinians. Israeli Army Radio reported that the mobilization would be the most significant call-up since just before the Gulf War in 1990, and indicated that a new military campaign might be widespread and protracted. On 4 April the Israeli Minister of Defence, Binyamin Ben-Eliezer, ordered the mobilization of some 31,000 reservists. The Minister of Public Security, Uzi Landau, instructed the Commissioner of Police, Shlomo Aharonishki, and the ministry's legal adviser to prepare the groundwork for using the military draft to induct conscripts into the police. Landau stated he had decided to initiate a law that would enable the police to draft conscripts 'because of the deterioration in the security situation and the tremendous burden on the police from a lack of resources and manpower'.

On 1 April 2002 Israeli tanks entered the town of Beitunya, near Ramallah, surrounding the Preventive Security compound of West Bank security chief Jibril Rajoub and causing widespread damage to the complex. The Preventive Security apparatus had been the strongest and most prominent of all PA forces on the West Bank. Israeli tanks also entered the Palestinian town of Beit Jala, adjacent to Bethlehem, and Bethlehem itself, stopping some 500 yards from the Church of the Nativity (believed by Christians to be the birthplace of Jesus Christ). Earlier, dozens of Israeli tanks had rolled into the West Bank town of Qalqilya. Sharon announced that the operation would continue for weeks, if not longer. He also called on all Israelis to unite behind the Government since he expected mounting international pressure over the military operation. Yet the full-scale Israeli invasion of Palestinian cities achieved no immediate success in reducing suicide attacks. Several hours later a suicide bomber blew herself up in a Jerusalem supermarket, killing two Israelis and wounding at least 20. World leaders expressed alarm at the rapidly deteriorating situation in the region, with Russia criticizing Israel's measures to 'isolate' Arafat. US Secretary of State Powell told reporters at a press briefing that he had received a commitment from Sharon that the operation would not bring any harm to Arafat himself. The EU reaffirmed that Arafat remained a legitimate authority and its interlocutor for peace. The Palestinian President himself responded defiantly, declaring that Palestinians would not surrender or give up their struggle for an independent state. Hours earlier, Arafat had offered an immediate cease-fire, but this was swiftly dismissed by Israel. Fighting between Palestinian security forces and Israeli troops erupted as an armoured bulldozer punched a hole in the outer wall of Arafat's compound and tanks fired shells at his office building.

The Israeli offensive, which came a day after Arab leaders meeting in the Lebanese capital had endorsed the Saudi peace plan, sparked off Arab and international protests. Mass demonstrations in Damascus, Cairo, Amman and Beirut took place from 30 March 2002 onwards to denounce Israel's assault on Yasser Arafat. Emotions ran high throughout the Arab world as television stations broadcast images of Israeli troops and tanks fighting with Palestinian security forces in Ramallah, resulting in the deaths of five Palestinians and an Israeli soldier. Meanwhile, in early April Hezbollah guerrillas in Lebanon opened fire with mortars and rockets on an Israeli army post in a disputed border area, prompting Israeli air-strikes on positions in southern Lebanon and raising the prospect of a new front being opened. (Tensions on the Israel–Lebanon border continued during the following month.) Arab leaders accused Israel of trying to wreck their collective call for peace made at

Beirut. Egyptian President Hosni Mubarak sent a message to US President Bush calling for immediate US intervention, while Qatar called for an emergency UN Security Council session to discuss the violence. Russia and France were also critical of the Israeli operation.

The attack in Netanya represented the 'strategic attack' that led the Sharon Government to another turning-point in its relationship with the PA. Sharon now sought to expel Arafat from the area, publicly suggesting on 2 April 2002 that he should be sent into exile. However, although US Secretary of State Colin Powell stated that Israel had the right to 'self-defence', US officials urged Israel to show restraint and the Bush Administration effectively imposed on Sharon three restrictions: 'no' to expelling Arafat, 'no' to bringing down the PA, and 'no' to reconquering PA-administered territories.

Meanwhile, Israeli forces clamped down on Palestinians in Ramallah, searching for gunmen and imposing a curfew. An estimated 11 Palestinians were killed during Israel's invasion of Ramallah; two Israeli soldiers also died. The military announced that it had arrested a total of 145 suspected Palestinian militants during the two-day operation, including more than 60 who were detained in Arafat's presidential compound; however, Arafat's aides claimed that most of those captured in his headquarters were civilians. As the stand-off continued, Sharon came under increasing pressure to pull Israeli troops out of Arafat's headquarters. Israeli troops, however, appeared to be preparing for a long stay at the hilltop compound in Ramallah. Tanks and armoured personnel carriers formed barriers in an ever-widening radius in the streets outside the compound. The army began digging trenches across some streets and building earthen barricades on others.

On 2 April 2002 Israel widened its offensive by seizing more towns and cities in the West Bank. On the same day Prime Minister Ariel Sharon convened his 'inner' Security Cabinet to approve the next stage of 'Operation Defensive Shield'. The next day some 300–400 Israeli tanks moved into the West Bank's largest city, Nablus, and encircled three adjacent refugee camps amid heavy fighting with Palestinian militiamen. By 3 April Israel had taken control of several key cities and towns in the West Bank, stating that it was acting to eliminate the Palestinian 'terrorist infrastructure'. Only two major West Bank towns—Hebron and Jericho—were still under Palestinian control. In the eight major Palestinian cities and towns under full Israeli control—Ramallah, Nablus, Qalqilya, Jenin, Salfit, Tulkarm, Bethlehem and Beit Jala—tanks patrolled streets, enforcing strict curfews that confined hundreds of thousands of Palestinians to their homes. Israeli troops had also laid siege to Jenin's refugee camp, battling with Palestinians who barricaded entrances and fought back with bombs and guns. Soldiers also encircled about 200 Palestinians—among them militiamen (reportedly from Hamas, Islamic Jihad and the Tanzim), policemen, officials, clerics and church workers—in the Church of the Nativity in Bethlehem: on 2 April armed Palestinians had forced their way into the shrine while fleeing Israeli forces during prolonged gun battles (in which four Palestinian militants were killed) near the church and adjacent Manger Square. Colin Powell urged Israel to end the campaign quickly, but suggested that the USA would not insist on an immediate Israeli withdrawal.

Under pressure from its own citizens and from elsewhere in the Arab world to sever ties completely with Israel, Egypt took a more limited step on 3 April 2002, announcing that it would suspend all diplomatic contacts with Israel except those that 'serve the Palestinian cause'. On the same day the crisis in the Middle East was also the subject of an open debate at the UN Security Council. Delegates from more than 50 countries spoke at the session, during which the Palestinians pushed for a new UN resolution calling on Israel to pull its tanks and troops out of West Bank cities immediately. Virtually every speaker expressed concern over the Israeli offensive and called on it to withdraw from the Palestinian self-rule areas. Some nations also demanded an end to Palestinian suicide attacks. On 4 April the UN adopted a resolution (No. 1403) calling for both sides 'to move immediately to a meaningful cease-fire' and for 'the withdrawal of Israeli troops from Palestinian cities, including Ramallah'. The USA supported the resolution, but subsequently stated that Israel was not required to act until the PA agreed to a cease-fire. On 3 April Israel's Ambassador to the UN, Yehuda Lancry, declared that any new resolution must be balanced with a demand for Palestinians to end suicide attacks.

Meanwhile, Arab leaders, with considerable support from the EU, were demanding that US President Bush force Israeli Prime Minister Sharon to withdraw Israeli troops from Palestinian-held areas. Declaring US mediation thus far to be a failure, the EU called on 4 April for a broad alliance of nations, including the USA, to take over peacemaking responsibilities in the Middle East. However, Secretary of State Colin Powell rejected European criticism and any suggestion that the US Administration should step down as the primary mediator in the region. Powell added that he might intervene personally with Israeli and Arab leaders to prevent a further escalation of the violence. Responding to a proposal by the President of the European Commission, Romano Prodi, for an international conference to mediate a cease-fire and peace accord between Israel and the PA, Powell was reported to have stated that the primary aim should first to be to reduce the levels of terrorism and violence in the region. Under intense international and European pressure to end the escalating violence, President Bush announced that he was sending Powell to the Middle East the following week. Bush urged Israel to halt its incursions in the West Bank, but he also urged the Palestinians to stop suicide bomb attacks. Powell indicated that he intended to step up his efforts to enable a Palestinian state to emerge quickly, once negotiations resumed. He also announced that he would meet with his EU counterparts and with the Russian Minister of Foreign Affairs, Igor Ivanov, in Madrid, Spain (which had assumed the EU presidency), the following week and that he was considering the possibility of a meeting with Israeli and Arab leaders during his trip to Europe.

While US special envoy Anthony Zinni was still in the Middle East striving to implement the truce plan brokered by George Tenet in June 2001, on 4 April 2002 a high-level EU mission arrived in the region to attempt to mediate a cease-fire. The European mission (which was led by the EU's High Representative for the Common Foreign and Security Policy, Javier Solana, and Spain's Minister of Foreign Affairs, Josep Piqué i Camps) was intended to increase pressure on all sides to comply with the terms of UN Resolution 1397. However, Sharon's spokesman, Raanan Gissin, stated that the delegation would not be allowed to meet with Yasser Arafat, who was besieged by Israeli troops at his headquarters in Ramallah. The two EU envoys held talks with Israel's Minister of Foreign Affairs, Shimon Peres, but ended their mission after failing to secure a cease-fire or a meeting with Arafat. The same day President Bush called on Israel to stop its military incursions and to begin withdrawing from PA-controlled cities 'without delay'. However, Bush was also critical of Arafat, asserting that 'the situation in which he finds himself today is largely of his own making'. Israel, meanwhile, maintained its large-scale offensive in the West Bank during the first week of April, despite international demands to withdraw from the territory. Sharon only pledged to try to 'expedite' the operation, without announcing a deadline for a withdrawal.

In early April 2002 Ariel Sharon strengthened his coalition Government by bringing into the Israeli Cabinet two ministers from the NRP (including the recently elected NRP leader, Efraim Eitam) as well as David Levy of Gesher.

THE JENIN CONTROVERSY

The heaviest fighting between the Israeli army and Palestinian militias took place in the Jenin refugee camp, the home of some 13,000 Palestinian refugees. Dozens of Israeli tanks had entered Jenin and surrounded the adjacent refugee camp early on 3 April 2002. Helicopters and tanks fired machine guns at Palestinians, who hurled grenades and fired on the Israeli troops with assault rifles. Initially Israeli commandos moved from house to house, under covering fire from the helicopters and tanks. The fighting in Jenin was the fiercest aspect of 'Operation Defensive Shield'. The army encountered stiff resistance from Palestinian fighters holed up in the refugee camp. The Palestinian militiamen in the camp said they believed that this was their last stand against the Israeli military, judging by the tough army sweeps through other West Bank towns. They had prepared large numbers of home-made bombs for the Israeli raid on Jenin, the

seventh since the start of the al-Aqsa *intifada* in September 2000. Palestinians charged that innocent civilians were bearing the brunt of the Israeli assault. On 9 April 2002 13 Israeli army reservists were killed after entering a booby-trapped building in the refugee camp.

Many of the camp's inhabitants had fled during the fighting, especially those whose homes were at its centre, which came under the heaviest assault from Israeli tanks and helicopters. However, Palestinian militiamen in the camp had reportedly vowed to continue the struggle. Palestinians estimated the number of dead at the Jenin camp at more than 100 people, although an independent count was not possible because Israel had barred journalists and medical personnel from the area, declaring it to be a 'closed military zone'. The Association for Civil Rights in Israel reported that dozens of bodies were piled in the streets of the camp and residents were prevented from obtaining food and water. In a complaint to the Ministry of Defence, the Israeli organization alleged that the military had committed serious human rights violations in the camp, including the demolition of homes with residents still inside. On 9 April 2002 Palestinian medical workers confirmed that at least 124 Palestinians had been killed in the Israeli campaign, but the Palestinian death toll was expected to rise.

The fighting in the Jenin camp ended on 11 April 2002. On the following day, with the camp still closed to outsiders, Israelis and Palestinians traded bitter accusations over the number and nature of the casualties. Israel suggested that many of the dead were armed fighters; however, although Palestinian residents of the camp acknowledged that militiamen were among the fatalities, they insisted that large numbers of civilians were also killed. The Israeli army would not confirm Palestinian allegations that dozens of bodies had been removed in military trucks, or whether burials had taken place. On 12 April Israel's Supreme Court ordered that the bodies of dead Palestinians should not be removed, pending an appeal issued by Israeli Arab members of the Knesset. Humanitarian aid groups, including the ICRC and the PCRS, complained that they had been denied permission to enter the camp. However, on 14 April the High Court ruled that the bodies could be removed, and humanitarian organizations were allowed into Jenin on 15 April. Meanwhile, the ICRC accused Israel of 'humiliating' its Palestinian medical staff in the Occupied Territories by firing at their vehicles or making them wait at check-points for long periods of time.

Since early April 2002 the Palestinians have embraced the Jenin refugee camp as a symbol of wider resistance to the Israeli occupation. In the Gaza Strip hundreds of people demonstrated in sympathy with the Palestinian militiamen who died in fighting in the camp. Jenin also became a bitter symbol for the Israelis. Several suicide bombers who carried out attacks in Israel had lived in the camp, and subduing Jenin had a heavy cost: the assault on Jenin was the single deadliest incident involving Israeli forces since the eruption of the al-Aqsa *intifada*. By the end of the offensive as many as 23 Israeli soldiers had been killed in Jenin's refugee camp.

The Palestinians, who contended that there had been a 'massacre' in the refugee camp at Jenin, pushed for UN intervention, possibly through peace-keepers or observers, to end the 18-month conflict. Meanwhile, Arab and Muslim states asked the UN Human Rights Commission to condemn Israel for 'mass killings', demanding that the Jewish State end its military offensive in the Palestinian self-rule areas. On 15 April 2002 the Human Rights Commission voted by 40 votes to five (with seven abstentions) to express its 'grave concern' over the Israeli incursion, which it said included 'acts of mass killings perpetrated by the Israeli occupying authorities against the Palestinian people'. Also on 15 April Marwan Barghouthi, the West Bank Fatah leader who had turned the mainstream Tanzim from a civil guard into a major militia, was detained by an Israeli army operation in Ramallah. (Trial proceedings began on 5 September against Barghouthi; among the charges against him was one of heading the al-Aqsa Martyrs Brigades.) The following day Israel reopened Ketziot, a detention camp in the southern Israeli Negev desert, in order to hold some of the 4,000 Palestinians it had rounded up during 'Operation Defensive Shield'. (Ketziot had held prisoners detained during the first Palestinian uprising of 1987–93.)

Meanwhile, on 9 April 2002 the USA made fresh demands for an Israeli withdrawal from PA-controlled areas, while Sharon vowed that the fight would continue until the Palestinian militias were crushed. Under intense pressure from President Bush, and with the impending arrival of US Secretary of State Powell, on that day the Israeli army began withdrawing from Qalqilya and Tulkarm, but defied its closest political ally and main financial benefactor with raids on more Palestinian towns. On 11 April Powell arrived in Israel on a mission to forge a cease-fire. On his arrival, Powell stated that Israel should find a way to make a deal with Yasser Arafat. The Israelis responded by handing the USA documents purportedly showing that Arafat had authorized payments in recent months to militants wanted by Israel. The Palestinian Minister of Information and Culture, Yasser Abd ar-Rabbuh, replied that the documents were part of a campaign being waged by Israel to discredit the PA. Powell met with both Sharon and Arafat and also visited Syria and Lebanon, discussing Sharon's idea of convening a regional conference on the Middle East. However, Powell's visit failed to secure a cease-fire; Sharon refused to promise a timetable for the withdrawal of Israeli troops from the West Bank, and Powell could not secure an unconditional pledge from Arafat to rein in Palestinian militants. Sharon indicated his desire for a regional conference that would include heads of states but exclude Arafat.

On 12 April 2002 UN Secretary-General Kofi Annan asked the Security Council to consider calling for an international force in the Middle East to curb the ongoing violence between Israelis and Palestinians. This followed the deaths of some 14 Israelis in a bus bombing in Haifa and an attack perpetrated in Jerusalem by the al-Aqsa Martyrs Brigades in that week. In New York, the UN Security Council met in emergency session to hear the Under-Secretary-General for Political Affairs, Kieran Prendergast, discuss Annan's proposal. However, Annan's spokesman, Fred Eckhard, stated that deploying such a force would require both a Security Council resolution and the approval of Israel and the PA. The Palestinian observer to the UN, Nasser al-Kidwa, said he hoped that the Council would quickly accept the idea of an international force, but Israel's UN spokesman, Ariel Milo, replied that Israel would object to the request.

By mid-April 2002 events at the Jenin refugee camp had become the centre of a heated dispute. The UN Security Council voted unanimously to back a fact-finding mission to establish what had happened during the Israeli military assault on the Jenin camp. On 23 April, the day after Secretary-General Annan's appointment of the high-level team headed by former Finnish President Martti Ahtisaari, the Israelis demanded that a retired US general be made a full member of the panel. While the Palestinians welcomed the appointment of the three-member team, the Israelis complained that its members had not been chosen in co-ordination with Israel and challenged both the impartiality and military expertise of the team. In late April Israeli officials accused the UN of conducting a 'smear campaign' against Israel, as the Israeli Cabinet further delayed the arrival of the mission. Finally, on 30 April Israel announced that it would not co-operate with the UN inquiry into the events at Jenin—defying a call by Annan to allow his fact-finding team to begin work immediately. The team was disbanded by Annan on 1 May.

ENDING THE SIEGES OF THE CHURCH OF THE NATIVITY AND ARAFAT'S COMPOUND

By 23 April 2002 Israeli forces had pulled back from most West Bank cities, but still surrounded Yasser Arafat's presidential compound in Ramallah and the Church of the Nativity in Bethlehem. Arafat met with UN envoy William Burns in his besieged office to discuss the stand-offs; until they were resolved, there was little hope for an Israeli-Palestinian cease-fire. Israel stated that it would end the blockade in Bethlehem only after the Palestinian gunmen barricaded in the church surrendered. In Ramallah, Israel demanded that Arafat hand over five men suspected of involvement in the assassination of Rechavam Ze'evi, as well as the alleged mastermind behind the shipment of weapons to the PA aboard the *Karine-A*. Despite initially refusing, Arafat now took pre-emptive legal action by putting the suspected assassins of Ze'evi on trial in a makeshift court using Palestinian policemen in the Ramallah compound as

judges. On 25 April the court imposed gaol terms (of between one and 18 years) on four men for involvement in Ze'evi's murder. On 28 April the Israeli Cabinet approved a US proposal (by a vote of 17–8) aimed at ending the month-old siege of Arafat's compound. The US plan called for US and British personnel to guard six Palestinians wanted by Israel and, in turn, on 2 May Arafat was allowed to leave his compound and to move freely throughout the Palestinian areas of the West Bank and Gaza Strip.

With US and EU mediation, an accord to end the siege of the Church of the Nativity was eventually devised. Arafat agreed that the 13 'most dangerous' Palestinians wanted by Israel would go to Europe, and 26 other Palestinian militants would be sent into 'exile' in Gaza, despite strong Fatah and Hamas criticism of the arrangement. On 1 May 2002 six Palestinians (the four men convicted of involvement in Ze'evi's assassination, PFLP leader Ahmad Saadat and a Palestinian accused of involvement in the *Karine-A* affair) were moved from the Ramallah compound to a Jericho prison. Finally, on 12 May the remaining 13 Palestinian militants were flown under international guard to Cyprus, pending their dispersal to permanent exile in Europe.

LIKUD'S REJECTION OF A PALESTINIAN STATE

On 12 May 2002 the Likud party's Central Committee adopted a resolution categorically rejecting the creation of a Palestinian state in the West Bank and Gaza. At a heated meeting in Tel-Aviv, Ariel Sharon and his rival, former Prime Minister Binyamin Netanyahu, clashed over whether the party should vote on the resolution. A proposal by Sharon to postpone the vote was defeated in a secret ballot by 669 to 465 votes. Sharon argued that it would precipitate international pressure on Israel and tie his hands diplomatically. Sharon had recently admitted that a Palestinian state was inevitable, but favoured offering the Palestinians about 40% of the West Bank—in sections to be divided by Jewish settlements. After Binyamin Netanyahu criticized Sharon's idea of a regional peace summit, Sharon reminded party members that a Likud-led Government had already participated in a regional peace conference—in Madrid in 1991—and that Netanyahu had been part of that Israeli delegation. Netanyahu had earlier addressed the Central Committee, calling for Arafat to be exiled from the Palestinian territories. The former party leader stated that he supported an entity that allowed the Palestinians to govern themselves, but opposed granting them all of the rights emanating from statehood—such as maintaining an army and acquiring weapons—because such a state would threaten Israel.

In a poll conducted by the Dahaf Institute and published in *Yediot Aharonoth* in mid-May 2002, 63% of Israelis stated that they would support the creation of a Palestinian state provided that it was accompanied by a peace agreement with the Palestinians. However, just hours after the Likud resolution, the Israeli human rights group B'Tselem published a report showing that about 40% of the West Bank was under the management of Israeli local authorities. Most Jewish settlements had grandiose expansion plans on paper, incorporating land many times the present size of the enclaves. Since Israel took over the West Bank from Jordan in 1967, successive Israeli governments had dotted the territory with 123 settlements housing 198,000 Israelis along the main north–south highway and encircling Palestinian towns and cities. (In mid-March 2002 an Israeli peace movement claimed that 34 new settlements had been built thus far in 2002.)

Since mid-May 2002 Sharon had been urging the USA to replace Arafat and the PA with an interim Palestinian administration that would, over a one-year period, implement wide-ranging reforms as a precondition for peace talks with the Palestinians. In a meeting with US President George W. Bush in Washington, Sharon proposed that Arafat be sidelined and given a symbolic position devoid of authority. President Bush apparently rebuffed Sharon's proposal, asserting that Israel would have to find a way to keep working with the Palestinians' elected leader.

SHARON'S DISMISSAL OF CABINET MINISTERS

On 20 May 2002 Ariel Sharon ordered the removal from the Cabinet of members of the ultra-Orthodox Shas party, setting off a political crisis that threatened the survival of his broadly-based coalition. Sharon also dismissed deputy ministers from another ultra-Orthodox party, United Torah Judaism, effectively expelling the two parties from his Government. Shas headed the Ministries of Health, of Labour and Social Affairs, of the Interior and of Religious Affairs. The decision to remove the ministers came after the two parties failed to support the Government on an emergency economic package presented to the Knesset. However, the dismissals were not to take effect for 48 hours, leaving time for last-minute bargaining. Expelling the two parties would have erased Sharon's huge parliamentary majority and if both parties left the coalition, Sharon would command exactly one-half of the 120 seats in parliament and could be vulnerable to a 'no-confidence' motion that would topple his Government and force early elections. Absence of a clear majority would put Sharon at the mercy of opposing forces among his remaining coalition members—Labour, which favoured some concessions to the Palestinians in order to achieve peace, and the NRP, which represents the interests of Jewish settlers in the West Bank and Gaza Strip.

Shas and United Torah Judaism were vehemently opposed to the Government's economic austerity measures, which would have cut benefits for the lowest echelons of Israeli society. Israel's economy was in crisis partly because of the world economic downturn and partly as result of the effects of almost 20 months of conflict with the Palestinians. However, the emergency economic programme was defeated in the Knesset by 47 to 44 votes. Within an hour of the vote, Sharon's office released a statement announcing that he had dismissed the four Shas ministers and five deputy ministers from Shas and United Torah Judaism. A fifth Shas minister, who was not a member of parliament, declared that he would resign in solidarity with his party colleagues. On 21 May 2002 the Chairman of Shas, Eliyahu Yishai, announced that he was open to negotiating a new economic plan that would allow his party to remain in Sharon's coalition. However, Sharon did not relinquish his demand that Shas must support his emergency economic programme. In a letter to Shas's spiritual leader, Rabbi Ovadia Yosef, Sharon wrote that Shas would have to support the economic plan in its second and third readings in the Knesset and respect government decisions which it had ignored in recent months if it wanted its ministers to resume their positions in the Cabinet. On 22 May Sharon won a budget vote in the Knesset (with Shas and United Torah Judaism abstaining), but the victory left his coalition stripped of its clear majority and vulnerable to collapse as the dismissals of ministers and deputy ministers from the two Orthodox Jewish parties entered effect. Sharon's Government thus commanded only 60 of the 120 seats in parliament, losing its absolute majority. The Minister of Finance, Silvan Shalom, stated that the crisis had stabilized the Government by demonstrating that Sharon would not tolerate Cabinet rebellions. However, Sharon and his right-wing Likud party clearly became more vulnerable to threats from the Labour Party to take its 23 parliamentary votes into opposition, where it could push for early elections. According to Israeli media reports, Sharon was seeking a pledge from Labour not to leave the coalition for at least a year since elections were in any case due in the autumn of 2003. At the end of May 2002 the Labour and Likud parties were still working on a deal to keep their shaky alliance intact for another year. In the event, however, Shas was brought back into the Cabinet on 3 June and Sharon retained his solid majority.

SECURITY ISSUES

In the aftermath of the Israeli army's incursions into Palestinian cities in April 2002 Israel remained highly vulnerable to Palestinian suicide bombings. The Palestinian leadership denounced individual attacks, but the largely paralysed administration did not appear to be in a position to halt the practice. In the spring and early summer of 2002 Israel began enforcing new restrictions in the West Bank, requiring Palestinians to obtain permits to move from town to town, and putting up fences and digging trenches to block those trying to pass military checkpoints. Following a new wave of suicide bombings, the Israeli military accelerated the construction of barriers on the outskirts of Palestinian towns and the Israeli Cabinet authorized the construction of a security fence of thick coils of wire around East Jerusalem. Construction of the fence began in mid-June.

In late May 2002 Israel launched a new satellite into space: the *Ofek-5* gave Israel an extended capacity to monitor military developments in the region and also demonstrated its advanced missile ability. Israeli television announced that *Ofek-5* would concentrate its high-resolution cameras on Iran, Iraq and Syria. The *Shavit* missile used to launch the satellite is related to the long-range *Jericho* surface-to-surface missile, which foreign experts were quoted as saying was capable of carrying nuclear warheads.

At the end of May 2002 President Bush decided to send to the region first William Burns, the Assistant Secretary of State for the Near East, then CIA Director George Tenet. Burns would seek the views of Egyptian, Israeli, Palestinian, Jordanian, Saudi Arabian, Syrian and Lebanese officials, while Tenet intended to focus on 'revamping security arrangements' in the West Bank and Gaza. The US Administration had already offered a broad outline of what it intended to see eventually come out of peace talks between Israel and the PA: security for Israel against suicide attacks and a 'provisional' Palestinian state on 40% of the West Bank. The concept was similar to the one raised by Shimon Peres—the declaration of a 'provisional' Palestinian state first, and then negotiations over borders, Jerusalem, Jewish settlements and Palestinian refugees—which the Israeli Minister of Foreign Affairs had apparently raised with the US National Security Adviser, Condoleezza Rice. However, the Bush Administration was still reluctant to table a US plan with specific deadlines.

Meanwhile, in response to a Palestinian suicide bombing on 5 June 2002 close to Israel's border with the West Bank, in which as many as 17 Israelis (most of them soldiers) were killed, Israeli troops again moved into Ramallah, stating that they would remain there for a 'limited time'. On 10 June Israeli forces pulled out of the city, lifting their latest blockade on Arafat's office, as US Secretary of State Powell raised the idea of a 'provisional' Palestinian state. The previous day Arafat had announced a new, streamlined Palestinian Cabinet.

'OPERATION DETERMINED PATH': REOCCUPATION OF WEST BANK CITIES

The cycle of revenge attacks escalated again in June 2002. In late June, after two recent suicide bombings in Jerusalem had killed at least 26 Israelis, the Israeli army began to reoccupy large sections of the West Bank, keeping at least 600,000 Palestinians under effective house arrest with round-the-clock curfews and largely barring the media from covering its manoeuvres. The new operation, code-named 'Operation Determined Path' and which had begun on 19 June, was met with minimal Palestinian resistance and limited international criticism, and troops moved steadily into the Palestinian areas. The one exception was Qalqilya, where two Israeli soldiers were killed in a gun battle as soldiers entered the town. On 23 June, Israeli tanks again surrounded the PA President and his aides in his compound. However, the lack of prolonged resistance and extensive aerial bombardments, as well as daily pictures of devastation, had muted European criticism of this Israeli campaign. Israeli troops were enforcing more stringent curfews in terms of both extent and duration. Israeli troops imposed round-the-clock curfews on the six Palestinian cities and towns they now controlled—Bethlehem, Nablus, Jenin, Tulkarm, Qalqilya and Ramallah. (Typically, the curfew was lifted for about three hours every third day, during which residents were allowed to stock up on food.) Palestinians declared that Israel's goal was clear: to destroy the PA and replace it with Israeli rule, as was the case before the two sides signed the breakthrough Oslo agreement in 1993.

As Israeli forces clamped down harder on Palestinians in the West Bank, Sharon pledged to extend his military offensive to the Gaza Strip. On 24 June 2002 six Palestinians were killed (including at least one senior Hamas leader) in an Israeli missile attack at Rafah in the Gaza Strip. The latest reoccupation came as President Bush delivered a long-awaited Middle East policy address.

BUSH'S PLAN FOR THE MIDDLE EAST

On 24 June 2002 US President George W. Bush, in his long-awaited speech on the Middle East, set out his proposals for peace in the region. President Bush called on the Palestinians to elect a 'new and different Palestinian leadership' and to adopt a new constitution with a fully empowered parliament, local government and an independent judiciary. The USA and its allies would help to organize multi-party local elections by the end of the year, with national elections to follow. Bush added that Palestinians should implement financial reforms, including the introduction of independent auditing to ensure 'honest enterprise'. In turn, the USA would increase the levels of humanitarian aid provided to the PA. After these steps were taken, Palestinians would be able to count on US support for a 'provisional state of Palestine', whose final borders, capital and other aspects of sovereignty would be negotiated between Israel and the PA. The President's plan envisaged a peace settlement within three years. Bush called on Israel to withdraw its forces to positions it had held in the West Bank on 28 September 2000 and to stop building Jewish settlements in the West Bank and Gaza. Ultimately, Israel should agree to pull back to the borders it had held before the 1967 war. President Bush also called on Israel to restore freedom of movement in the Palestinian areas so that civilians could resume work and normal life. Questions about the status of Jerusalem and the right of Palestinian refugees to return home were to be left to negotiation between the two sides. The US President added that the Arab world should build closer diplomatic and commercial ties with Israel, leading to a 'full normalization of relations between Israel and the entire Arab world'. It should also stop the flow of money, supplies and recruits to 'terror groups' such as Hamas, Islamic Jihad and Hezbollah, which sought the destruction of Israel.

While the speech was being delivered, Israeli forces took control of the West Bank city of Hebron, where three Palestinian policemen were killed. Israeli officials, meanwhile, praised Bush's speech (which had avoided any reference to the ongoing reoccupation of the West Bank), but rejected the concept of a 'provisional Palestinian state'. PA officials, for their part, insisted that Bush's call for the PA to replace Arafat was unacceptable. Moreover, even before the presidential address, the US proposal for a 'provisional Palestinian state' had received a cool response in the Middle East. Sharon had contended it was not the time for any sort of Palestinian state, while the Palestinian Minister of Information, Yasser Abd ar-Rabbuh, had stated that the US Administration must put pressure on Israel to pull back its forces from Palestinian cities before any peace initiative was agreed.

FURTHER POLITICAL AND MILITARY DEVELOPMENTS

At the end of June 2002 Israeli forces began the removal of a small number of settler 'outposts' deemed to be illegal. Meanwhile, there were reports that a senior commander of Hamas' military wing had been killed by Israeli troops in Nablus; Israel alleged that he was a prominent bomb-maker, who had been responsible for attacks such as the Passover bombing in Netanya. In early July almost all of the West Bank was again reoccupied, after Israel had called up further army reservists. Israel claimed at this time that the offensive to arrest or kill Palestinian militants was having considerable success. On 7 July the Israeli Cabinet agreed to support an amendment to the Israeli Lands Law that would ban Arab Israelis from living in new homes built on Israeli state land; the bill awaited the approval of the Knesset. In early July senior-level talks were resumed between Israel and the PA, while the Quartet group (comprising the USA, Russia, the UN and the EU) held discussions in London, in a bid to reactivate the Oslo peace process. On 9 July a new Israeli army Chief of Staff, Lt-Gen. Moshe Ya'alon, was named as a replacement to Shaul Mofaz.

Violence again appeared to be on the increase when several Israelis died in an attack on a bus near a Jewish settlement in the West Bank on 16 July 2002, for which three Palestinian militant groups all claimed responsibility. The increased vio-

lence came as new peace talks were convened by the Quartet group. Israel responded to the renewed Palestinian assaults by shooting dead a suspected militant and by 'freezing' plans to ease some of the restrictions imposed on Palestinians living in the Territories. Shortly afterwards Israeli forces in Nablus refugee camp detained up to 21 male relatives of two suspected Palestinian militants and announced plans to deport some of them to the Gaza Strip. The announcement attracted strong criticism from human rights organizations; however, in early September the Israeli Supreme Court ruled that the expulsion of militants' relatives was legitimate. Meanwhile, tensions increased between Israelis and Palestinians on 23 July, when an Israeli air-strike on a residential building in Gaza City resulted in the deaths of up to 15 Palestinians (including several children). The Israeli raid had achieved its aim of assassinating a leader of Hamas' military wing. However, the civilian deaths were condemned by both the PA and the international community, leading Israeli officials to express 'regret' at the loss of civilian lives. Following international (and especially US) pressure, Israel moved to ease the restrictions in the West Bank and Gaza, and Sharon pledged to release some of the tax revenues owed to the PA. The Gaza air-strike precipitated a new round of violence, however, with four Jewish settlers being killed near Hebron on 26 July. Israel responded by ordering tanks into the Gaza Strip. However, on 31 July at least seven Israelis were killed in a suicide bomb attack at the Hebrew University in Jerusalem; Hamas claimed responsibility for the blast. On 29 July one of the Ministers without Portfolio, David Levy of Gesher, resigned from Sharon's coalition, owing to disagreement over the Prime Minister's style of government.

There were at least 15 further Israeli fatalities in early August 2002 as a result of attacks by militant Palestinians. The Israeli Government responded by ordering a total ban on freedom of movement for Palestinians in most West Bank cities. The UN again called on Israel to withdraw immediately from PA-controlled territory, referring to the serious humanitarian situation there. On 5 August the Israeli Minister of Defence, Binyamin Ben-Eliezer, held discussions with the PA Minister of the Interior, Abd ar-Razzak Yahya, in an attempt to calm the situation. The PA accused Israel of reneging on a recent pledge to pull its troops out of PA-administered towns and villages. The focus of much of Israel's military campaign during late August was the Gaza Strip, where a number of leading militants and civilians were killed. On 18 August Israel and the PA agreed to implement a security plan (termed the 'Gaza, Bethlehem First' plan) whereby Israel would withdraw from the Gaza Strip and Bethlehem in return for Palestinian security guarantees and a crack-down on militants. Israel began to withdraw its forces from Bethlehem on the following day; however, violence continued throughout the Territories and further talks were cancelled. Following further Palestinian civilian deaths, in early September 2002 Israel announced that it would launch an inquiry into the circumstances of the deaths. On 9 September a landmark decision by the Israeli Ministry of the Interior revoked the citizenship of an Arab Israeli who was accused of assisting Palestinian militants in plotting suicide attacks against Israelis. The situation deteriorated further in mid-September, with two suicide bombings in Um al-Fahm and Tel-Aviv. Israeli forces entered Arafat's Ramallah compound once again on 19 September, and began the systematic destruction of buildings there, in a stated attempt to force the surrender of some 20 Palestinian militants believed by the Israeli authorities to be sheltering there. Israel asserted that Arafat, who was sheltering in the only building that remained standing within two days of the reoccupation, was not a target, but that a decision had been taken to 'isolate' the PA leader following the suicide attacks. Nevertheless, following considerable pressure from the US Administration, Israel agreed to withdraw its forces from the presidential compound on 29 September.

Economy

Revised for this edition by ALAN J. DAY

INTRODUCTION

The total area of the State of Israel, within its 1949 armistice frontiers, amounts to 20,700 sq km, as compared with the 27,090 sq km area of Palestine under the British mandate. At the census of 4 June 1983 the population of Israel (including East Jerusalem and the Golan Heights) was 4,037,620, of whom 3,349,997 (83%) were Jews. In addition, there were about 1m. persons in other areas which were brought under Israeli administration as a result of the 1967 war, and after the Sinai peninsula was evacuated at the end of April 1982. According to official figures, by 31 December 2001 the (*de jure*) population of Israel was estimated to have increased to 6.5m., of whom 77.3% were Jews, 15.4% Muslims, 2.1% Christians, 1.6% Druze and 3.6% of no recorded affiliation.

The population density of Israel was 184 per sq km at the June 1983 census and 296.6 per sq km at mid-2001. The population is heavily concentrated in the coastal strip, with about three-quarters of Jewish inhabitants and nearly two-thirds of the non-Jewish population located between Ashkelon and Naharia. The main reason for the growth of the population has been Jewish immigration, accounting for 58% of the yearly increase between 1948 and 1977. On 31 December 1996, 38.4% of the Jewish population had been born abroad. These included 1,202,200 born in Europe and America, 327,100 in Africa and 249,900 in Asia. Of the 2,858,200 Israeli-born Jews, 1,198,400 were second-generation Israelis. Immigration up to 1948 totalled 482,857 persons, of whom nearly 90% came from Europe and America. The biggest wave of immigrants arrived within six years of the founding of the new state. These were refugees from war-torn Europe, followed by Jews emigrating from the Arab states. Large numbers have come from North Africa as a result of political developments there, and during 1955–64 more than 200,000 emigrated from Africa into Israel. Although immigration from Eastern Europe resumed in 1956, the overall number of arrivals declined in the 1960s, falling to 14,469 in 1967. The 1967 war sparked renewed immigration, with some 300,000 arriving in the period up to the 1974 war, 70% of these from the USA and Europe. After the Yom Kippur war, immigration declined again, falling from 54,886 in 1973 to 12,599 in 1981; a rise to 19,981 in 1984 was attributable to the arrival of 7,800 Ethiopian Jews (Falashas). In 1988 new immigrants (13,034) were actually outnumbered by Israelis emigrating from the country (18,900). However, in 1989 the collapse of communism in Eastern Europe resulted in a renewed surge of immigration, mainly from the USSR (especially the Russian Federation), to total 199,516 people in 1990. Thereafter immigrant numbers decreased, while remaining relatively high at 70,919 in 1996 and 66,221 in 1997. A new upward trend was registered in 1999, to 76,766, representing a 35% increase over the 1998 level, before the numbers decreased to 60,192 in 2000 and 43,580 in 2001.

Israel has been able to build a modern developed economy, making significant progress in the 1980s and 1990s as the proportion of gross domestic product (GDP) allocated to defence expenditure fell from a high of over 40% in 1973 to 21.2% in 1985 and progressively to 8.9% in 1999. However, renewed Palestinian insurrection in the Occupied Territories from September 2000 resulted in an increase in the proportion to 12% in that year, and to an estimated 15% in 2001. Israel has been assisted both by continuing substantial levels of official US military assistance and other aid and by large financial donations from US and other Jewish communities abroad, the latter being estimated at more than US $100,000m. since the foundation of the state and being used in particular to assist the absorption of Jewish immigrants to Israel. Also beneficial was the introduction in February 1980 of the shekel as the official currency unit in succession to the previous Israeli pound (or lira), after a period of rapid currency depreciation and rampant inflation. This step was followed by the start of an assault on the socialist structures and institutions that had dominated the economy since the state's foundation and by moves to eradicate the parallel black economy, so that Israel would become better placed to compete with other world markets.

In 1995 Israel's GDP, measured at constant prices, increased by 7.1%, compared with average annual growth of about 6% during the previous five years. The business sector recorded real growth of 8.3% in 1995, compared with an average annual rate of growth of 7% in 1990–94. Private consumption, in real terms, increased by 7.2% in 1995. Relatively high growth was recorded in the consumption of durable goods. Consumption per head, which reflects the standard of living, increased by 4.6% in 1995, compared with an increase of 6.3% in 1994. The decline in per caput growth in private consumption was accompanied by an upturn in the rate of private savings, following a continued fall in private savings during 1992–94. As the economy grew at an accelerated rate, the number of persons in employment increased by some 5.4%. Some 80% of this increase was accounted for by the business sector.

In 1995 consumer prices increased at an average annual rate of 10.0%, compared with an increase of 12.3% in 1994. The wholesale price index of industrial output rose by some 10% during 1995, a rate of increase similar to that recorded in 1994. The expansion of almost all economic sectors continued in 1995. The output of the construction sector increased by some 12% in real terms, mainly because of expanded public residential construction. The output of the industrial sectors—accounting for approximately one-third of total business production—grew, in real terms, by 8%. Industrial exports, however, increased at a lower rate of about 6% in real terms, and this erosion of profitability was attributed to the continued appreciation in the value of Israel's currency, the shekel, in 1995. Output in the trade and services sectors increased, in real terms, by some 8%, while output in the public and community services sectors grew by some 4%, in real terms, in 1995.

In 1996 Israel's GDP growth, in real terms, slowed to 4.6%, equivalent to a rise of 1.7% per head (compared with an increase of 4.2% per head in 1995). Business sector production increased by 5.2% in 1996, compared with 8.9% growth in the previous year. In the first half of 1996 the consumer price index increased by 15.4% (in annual, seasonally-adjusted terms) but it slowed in the last six months, resulting in an average annual increase of 11.3%. In 1996 the inflationary trend was accordingly uneven: its rapid acceleration in the first six months caused the Bank of Israel to adopt a restrictive monetary policy and to raise its interest rates on sources. Consequently, inflation decreased in the second half of 1996 to an annual average of 6.2%. In 1996 high rates of interest, compared with overseas rates, contributed to an inflow of foreign capital. In relation to a 'basket' of five major foreign currencies, the shekel depreciated by a mere 1.6%—in contrast to the rate of increase of consumer prices.

In 1997 Israel's GDP increased, in real terms, by only 2.9%. As the country's population increased by more than 2%, real GDP per head rose by only 0.1% during the year. Business sector production declined by 1.5% in 1997, compared with growth of 1.5% in 1996. The inflation rate in 1997 declined to 7%, from 10.6% in 1996.

The inflation rate increased to 8.6% in 1998, owing to a sharp depreciation in the value of the currency in the second half of the year, as the Central Bank cut base lending rates in response to the economic crises in the Far East and Russia. GDP growth slowed further, to only 2% in 1998, so that real GDP per head actually fell by 0.4%. During 1990–2000 consumer prices rose by an average annual rate of 9.5%. However, tight monetary policy and falling house prices reduced the inflation rate to 5.2% in 1999 and to 1.1% in 2000. GDP growth edged up in 1999 to 3.0% but GDP per head again declined, by 0.2%, to stand at

NIS 66,935 (US $16,837). Some progress was made with the privatization and liberalization programme of the centre-right Netanyahu Government (elected in 1996); but the economic slowdown inhibited any substantial restructuring, as the authorities gave priority to curbing inflation and achieving macroeconomic stability.

Recovery from recession began in 2000 under the new Barak Government (elected in mid-1999), and was assisted by the new impetus in the Middle East peace process. The first three quarters of 2000 were characterized by rapid economic growth, led by exports which rose by 19.9% in volume terms. However, an economic slowdown was reported in the fourth quarter, largely as a result of the renewed Palestinian uprising. The rate of GDP growth for the year as a whole was nevertheless 6.9%, while GDP per capita was US $17,500, an increase of 3.4% after two years of negative growth. Israel's GDP increased, in real terms, by an average of 5.1% annually in 1990–2000. Business sector growth accelerated to 7.4% in 2000 (from 2.0% in 1999), reflecting a rise in the output of high technology industries, although growth rates in the traditional manufacturing and construction industries remained low. Private consumption, in real terms, rose by 5.4% (2.8% per capita) resulting from the 17.5% increase in the purchase of consumer durables, which was affected by the increase in real wages and wealth derived from stock market activity. The low rate of inflation in 2000 was mainly attributable to the significant appreciation of the shekel, brought about by an unexpected surge in foreign direct investment.

The worsening Israeli–Palestinian conflict and the September suicide attacks on the USA aggravated Israel's economic downturn in 2001, when a 50% slump in tourist arrivals contributed to a contraction in GDP—the first since 1953—of 0.6%, to NIS 465,200m., equivalent to US $110,600m. at the market exchange rate and $123,400m. on an international purchasing-power parity basis (PPP). Reduced government revenues and increased military and security spending produced a widening budget deficit in 2001, in which year GDP per capita fell to $17,190 at market rates and to $19,330 at PPP. The inflation rate rose slightly, to 1.1%, in 2001, although it remained well below the 4.4% annual average for the five-year period 1997–2001.

Faced with increasingly bitter hostilities in 2002 and resultant extra demands on the defence budget, the Government took politically controversial steps to curb other categories of state expenditure and to raise more revenue by taxation (see Budget, Investment and Finance, below). The contraction in GDP continued in the first half of 2002, at an anticipated annual rate of 1.4%

In 2001 the Israeli civilian labour force averaged 2,499,000, or 54.3% of the population aged 15 years and over. The growth in the labour force from 735,800 in 1960 was attributable chiefly to the rise in total population, since the participation rate declined slightly. Having risen to a record level of 11.2% in 1992, the unemployment rate fell steadily thereafter to 6.6% in 1996, before rising to 7.5% in 1997, 8.6% in 1998 and 8.9% in 1999. Unemployment decreased slightly, to 8.8%, in 2000, but increased again, to 9.3%, in 2001. Seasonally-adjusted unemployment had risen to 10.6% by May 2002.

In 2001 the distribution of employment by economic activity was as follows: industry (comprising manufacturing, mining and industry) 17.3%; wholesale and retail trade and repairs 13.2%; education 12.3%; real estate, rental and business activities 12.3%; health and social work 9.9%, transport, storage and communications 6.6%; public administration and defence (including compulsory social security) 5.7%; construction 5.2%; other community, social and personal services 4.7%; hotels and restaurants 4.2%; financial intermediation 3.3%; agriculture (including hunting, forestry and fishing) 2.0%; domestic work 1.5%; electricity, gas and water supply 0.8%.

AGRICULTURE

The agricultural sector is relatively small, accounting for about 3% of GDP in 2000 and employing 2.0% of the employed labour force in 2001. In spite of this, Israeli agriculture has attracted a great deal of international attention and, more than any other sector of the economy, has been the focus of ideological pressure. For centuries, Jews in the Diaspora were barred from owning land and the Zionist movement therefore saw land settlement as one of the chief objectives of Jewish colonization. Since the establishment of the State of Israel, government agricultural policy has centred chiefly on the attainment of self-sufficiency in foodstuffs, in view of military considerations and Israel's possible isolation from its chief foreign food supplies; on the saving of foreign exchange through import substitution and the promotion of agricultural exports; and on the absorption of the large numbers of immigrants into the agricultural sector. In line with these objectives, the promotion of mixed farming and of co-operative farming settlements has also been an important element in government policy. Although the increase in agricultural production (which rose by an annual average of 0.05% during 1985–96) has resulted in Israel becoming largely self-sufficient in foodstuffs—it is seriously deficient only in grains, oils and fats—and important savings have been made in foreign exchange, government intervention in the agricultural sector has been criticized as having resulted in a misallocation of resources and having reduced efficiency in the sector.

Cultivation has undergone a profound transformation and from an extensive, primitive and mainly dry-farming structure it has developed into a modern intensive irrigated husbandry. A special feature of Israel's agriculture is its co-operative settlements, which have been developed to meet the special needs and challenges encountered by a farming community new both to its surroundings and its profession. While there are a number of different forms of co-operative settlements, all are derived from two basic types: the *moshav* and the *kibbutz*. The *moshav* is a co-operative smallholders' village. Individual farms in any one village are of equal size and every farmer works his own land to the best of his ability. He is responsible for his own farm, but his economic and social security is guaranteed by the co-operative structure of the village, which handles the marketing of his produce, purchases his farm and household equipment, and provides him with credit and many other services. On 31 December 1998 a total of 194,600 people inhabited 454 *moshavim* and collective *moshavim* (3.3% of the total population).

The *kibbutz* is a unique form of collective settlement developed in Israel. It is based on common ownership of resources and on the pooling of labour, income and expenditure. Every member is expected to work to the best of his or her ability; he or she is paid no wages but is supplied by the *kibbutz* with all necessary goods and services. The *kibbutz* is based on voluntary action and mutual liability, on equal rights for all members, and assumes for them full material responsibility. On 31 December 1998 a total of 267 *kibbutzim* were inhabited by 115,500 people (1.9% of the total population). The large co-operatives are heavily subsidized, although the introduction of structural reforms in the agricultural sector (which included the abolition of production quotas for major categories) opened the market to wider competition from individual units which receive fewer subsidies.

During the years following the establishment of the State of Israel a large-scale expansion of the area under cultivation took place. This was caused by the heavy influx of immigrants and the recultivation and rehabilitation of land from which Arabs had been forced to flee. The cultivated area increased from 1,650,000 dunums (1 dunum = 1,000 sq m) in the 1948/49 agricultural year to 4,110,000 dunums in 1958/59 and to 4,402,000 dunums in 1978/79. The cultivated area in 2000 totalled 4,236,000 dunums, including 1,866,000 dunums of irrigated crops.

Without taking into consideration the cost or availability of irrigation water, it is estimated that the land potential ultimately available for farming under irrigation is 5.3m. dunums, while an estimated 4.1m. dunums are potentially available for dry farming. There are also 8.5m. dunums available for natural pasture and 0.9m. dunums for afforestation.

The main factor limiting agricultural development is not land, but the availability of water. Further development of the sector will involve intensifying the yield of existing land and the reuse of treated wastewater to preserve freshwater essential for household consumption. Consumption of water reached 1,924m. cu m in 2000, of which 59.1% was attributable to agriculture, 34.4% to domestic households and 6.4% to industry. The state-owned Mekorot Water Co, which supplied 66% of Israel's fresh water in 2000, spent approximately NIS 2,300m. on capital investment between 1992 and 1997. Moreover, the Government established a special Water Administration, headed by a Water Commissioner who has statutory powers to control and regulate both the supply and the consumption of water.

The Water Administration has been charged, among other tasks, with the implementation of the national water project. The purpose of this project is to convey a substantial part of the waters of the Jordan river and of other water sources from the north to southern Judaea and the Negev, to store excess supplies of water from winter to summer and from periods of heavy rainfall to periods of drought, and to serve as a regulator between the various regional water supply systems. Essential to the national water project is the main conduit from Lake Tiberias to Rosh Haayin (near Tel-Aviv), known as the National Water Carrier, which has an annual capacity of 320m. cu m. Two other large schemes, also in operation, are the Western Galilee–Kishon and the Yarkon–Negev projects. As reported in January 1999, Israel and Jordan are to proceed (in accordance with the provisions of the 1994 peace treaty) with a project to build a US $150m. desalination plant in the Jordan Valley, in order to produce 50m. cu m of water per year. A new working structure is proposed to examine the feasibility of the Dead Sea–Red Sea canal project, which envisages the production of 851m. cu m of water per year, at an estimated cost of $4,500m.

The Government confirmed in January 2000 that tenders would be invited from the private sector later in the year for a new desalination plant on a 'build-operate-transfer' (BOT) basis, probably to be located at Ashkelon on the southern coast and with a capacity of between 50m. and 100m. cu m per year. The first ever BOT project initiated in Israel, the plant would be the first of a possible series of coastal desalination units located adjacent to existing power stations, intended to provide a long-term national solution to water shortage problems which were being aggravated by the deterioration of natural sources due to over-use and pollution. Government officials noted the dramatic fall in the cost of producing consumable water by desalination, from US $5.50 per cu m in the late 1970s to $0.55 per cu m by 2000.

In 2000 agricultural production was valued at NIS 13,998.1m. (compared with NIS 13,099.3m. in 1999), with value by activity being as follows: citrus and other fruits NIS 2,951.0m. (21.1%); poultry 2,675.1m. (19.1%); vegetables, potatoes and melons 2,482.7m. (17.7%); cattle 2,401.2m. (17.1%); field crops 965.2m. (6.9%); flowers and garden plants 791.6m. (5.7%); miscellaneous 1,731.3 m. (12.4%). In 2000 production of cows' milk was 1,149m. litres (compared with 1,157m. litres in 1999); egg production was 1,570m. (1,640m. in 1999) and output of poultry meat increased to 406,200 metric tons (from 260,000 tons in 1999). Potato production reached 349,600 tons in 2000 (compared with 363,500 tons in 1999); avocado production was 73,300 tons (55,900 tons in 1999); and wheat production rose sharply, to 94,000 tons (from 29,000 tons in 1999). Output in 2000 also included over 1,201,100 tons of vegetables, 751,600 tons of citrus fruit, 97,500 tons of beef and 38,600 tons of fish.

Severe drought conditions caused the Government to declare an official drought emergency in April 1999 and to impose a 40% reduction in water allocation to farmers. Cereal production in 1999 fell to 159,000 metric tons (from 175,000 tons in 1998), although cereal imports remained stable at 2.6m. tons. In mid-1999 it was reported that 98% of Israel's wheat crop had been destroyed owing to drought, and that 150,000 extra tons were to be imported from the USA. In early 2001 farmers were forced to destroy several thousand tons of harvested agricultural produce destined for European and US markets because of a severe shortage of manpower (as a result of the Israeli–Palestinian conflict).

Cultivation of citrus fruit is one of the oldest and most important agricultural activities, and produces the main export crop. In 1996 Israel exported 341,535 metric tons of citrus fruit, valued at US $170m., which declined to 338,600 tons (valued at $166m.) in 1997. Total area under cultivation in 2000 was about 235,000 dunums. The Citrus Marketing and Control Board supervises all aspects of the growing and marketing of the fruit, particularly exports. The principal markets for citrus exports are the United Kingdom, Germany and France.

Increasing emphasis is being placed on the cultivation of floral plants. About 90% of production is usually exported to the European Union (EU). In 1997 Israel exported 1,475.7m. flowers and ornamental branches (mainly roses, carnations and gypsophila), earning US $198.1m., compared with $196.6m. in 1997. The state-owned Flower Marketing Board is increasing the number of its packing-houses, and is investing heavily in modern equipment. In 1995 11,298 dunums were under glasshouse cultivation. Agricultural exports totalled $702.1m. in 2000 (compared with $782.3m. in 1999), representing 2.3% of total merchandise exports. The export of exotic fruits, winter vegetables and flowers has increased significantly in recent years.

MINERALS

The Petroleum Law of 1952 regulates the conditions for the granting of licences for petroleum prospecting, divides the country into petroleum districts and fixes a basic royalty of 12.5%. Petroleum was discovered in 1955 at the Heletz-Bror field on the coastal plain, and later at Kokhav, Brur and Negba, but these finds were not of the order to permit commercial production. From the time of the 1967 war to the 1975 Disengagement Agreement with Egypt, Israel was able to exploit the petroleum resources of the occupied Sinai and, during 1978–79, those of the Suez Gulf (Alma fields), from which a quarter of Israeli requirements were produced until the area was returned to Egypt in 1979. In July 1988 the Israeli Government awarded an offshore oil-prospecting concession of 7,000 sq km, about 16 km from Israel's southern Mediterranean coast, to a consortium of local and foreign companies headed by the late Dr Armand Hammer, Chairman of Occidental Petroleum Inc. The consortium, Negev Joint Venture, invested US $25.5m. in test drilling over a three-year period from late 1988, although without substantive results. Givot Olam Oil Exploration Company reported in February 1999 the discovery of potential oil reserves in central Israel and is to fund the $4m. drilling cost through a rights issue. In November BG International of the United Kingdom announced an oil strike off the southern Israeli coast, where significant gas discoveries were being made (see below) and where possible oil reserves underneath gas deposits were estimated by Israeli officials at up to 5,000m. barrels. However, there appeared to be little immediate prospect of significantly increasing Israel's current crude output of less than 500 b/d from proven reserves of only 3.9m. barrels.

Recent offshore exploration for natural gas has been much more promising. For some years output of natural gas had been confined to small fields in the Dead Sea area, transported through a 29-km pipeline to the Dead Sea potash works at Sodom and through a 49-km line to towns in the Negev and to the Oron phosphate plant. In late 1999 and early 2000, however, both the US-Israeli Yam Thetis consortium and BG International announced significant discoveries in the Med Yavne offshore concession 20 km off Ashkelon, where proven reserves of 40,000m cu m were claimed by Yam Thetis for its Noah and Mary fields, while BG International stated that test drilling in its Or-1 well indicated reserves of 3,000m. cu m. The two groups declared their intention to co-operate in exploiting the reserves, with the aim of supplying a new gas transmission network planned by the state-owned Israel Electric Corporation Ltd (IEC). In May 2000 letters of intent were received from four approved bidders for the IEC's US $300m. BOT project, envisaging that 2,000m. cu m per year of gas would be delivered to the three principal IEC power stations (currently oil-fired) beginning in 2003 and later to smaller stations and industrial users.

The possibility of Israel's natural gas requirements being supplied by a 'peace pipeline' from Egypt's offshore and Nile Delta fields has been under discussion for a decade. The talks stalled in 1996 but were revived in 1999 and resulted, in December, in Egyptian agreement in principle that the pipeline should be built. The Israeli Government's approach remained cautious, to allow time for evaluation of the recent gas finds in Israeli offshore waters in order to establish whether they could meet future domestic requirements (given the Government's decision, on cost and environmental grounds, that natural gas should become the country's principal energy source in the 21st century). Nevertheless, in June 2000 the Israeli-Egyptian consortium East Mediterranean Gas (EMG) began talks with the IEC on the EMG's proposal for an underwater pipeline with a daily capacity of 1,500m. cu m, which would carry gas from Egypt to the Israeli port of Haifa (with exits at other coastal Israeli power stations) and would eventually be extended to Turkey. Also under consideration is an alternative proposal for an overland gas pipeline from Egypt running across Sinai to the Gaza Strip and Israel. Gas industry specialists have expressed confidence that, given the anticipated rapid growth in Israeli demand for gas, a pipeline from Egypt would be commercially viable even though substantial gas production from Israeli offshore fields was likely.

Pending significant production from recent gas discoveries, Israel is forced to import more than 90% of its energy requirements. Imports of petroleum and petroleum products, which rose in value from US $210.6m. in 1973 to $597m. in the following year and to $775m. in 1978, reached about $2,000m. in 1980 and cost $2,259.9m., at current prices, in 1997. In the same year petroleum constituted 7.8% of all goods imports (or 20% of the trade deficit). Israel currently imports most of its crude oil requirements of some 48m. barrels per year under long-term contracts with Egypt (which provides about 25% of the total), Mexico (35%) and Norway (10%), and buys the remainder on the 'spot' market. Most imported crude oil is refined at the Haifa oil refinery, which has a capacity of more than 6m. tons per year.

Israel continues to meet 25% of its energy requirements with imported coal, of which 10.8m. metric tons were imported in 1998 (compared with 9.4m. tons in 1997). About one-half of all coal imports come from South Africa, with which Israel signed new contracts in the second half of 1999 to take advantage of attractive price levels. Completion of Israel's fourth coal-fired power station, at Ashkelon, was scheduled for 2001, as a result of which coal imports were expected to rise to 12m. tons a year.

The Dead Sea, which contains potash, bromides, magnesium and other salts in high concentration, is the country's chief source of mineral wealth. The potash works on the southern shore of the Dead Sea are owned by Dead Sea Works Ltd. The works are linked by road to Beersheba, from where a railway runs northward. Phosphates are mined at Oron in the Negev, and in the Arava. A total of 2.45m. metric tons of phosphate rock was produced in 1996. In the same year Israel produced 12,243 tons of sodium hydrochlorate, 40,892 tons of caustic soda, 34,630 tons of chlorine, 8,324 tons of paraffin, and 2,939 tons of potassium carbonate.

Gold in potentially commercial quantities was discovered near the Negev copper mines in 1988, and further exploration is under way.

INDUSTRY, MANUFACTURING AND CONSTRUCTION

Israel's industry was originally developed to supply such basic commodities as soap, vegetable oil and margarine, bread, ice, farm implements, printing and electricity. It used raw materials available locally to produce citrus juices and other citrus by-products, canned fruit and vegetables, cement, glass and bricks. In order to save foreign exchange, imports of manufactured goods were curtailed, thus giving local industry the opportunity of adding local labour value to semi-manufactures imported from abroad.

Although most of Israel's industrial production is still for domestic consumption, industrial exports (including diamonds) constituted 95% of total exports by value in 2000. In this area also, there has been a very rapid expansion as a result of tax and investment incentives from the Government. The value of Israeli industrial exports, only US $18m. in 1950, had risen to $780m. by 1971, and by 2000 had reached $21,004.6m. (excluding diamonds).

Israel's most important industrial export product is cut and polished diamonds, most of the expertise for the finishing of which was supplied by immigrants from Belgium and the Netherlands. In 2000 Israel exported US $9,661.8m.-worth of cut diamonds (compared with $6,441.5m.-worth supplied in 1999), while importing uncut diamonds worth $6,746.3m. It therefore continued to be one of the world's largest traders, second only to Belgium in processing diamonds, with approximately three-quarters of the international market in medium-sized stones, Israel's speciality.

The 28% increase in industrial exports in 2000 over the same period in 1999 reflected a process of structural change from traditional to advanced industrial exports since 1995. Industries with technological strengths exported 35% of their gross sales in 2000, in comparison with 28% in 1995. Exports grew substantially in the field of electronic components, reaching US $1,900m. (reflecting the effect of the start of production, in accordance with its full potential, at the new Intel plant at Kiryat Gat), while exports of electronic communications equipment increased to $2,800m.

Israel's high-technology electronics industry specializes in equipment for military and communications purposes and more recently in computer and internet software in Israel's so-called 'Silicon Wadi'. The value of exports from this sector and of metal products and machinery rose from US $12.8m. in 1970 to $5,606.1m. in 1997. Computer software exports were worth $1,500m. in 1998, representing a 275% increase over 1997, when such exports had slumped because of the Asian economic crisis. The rapid advance of Israel's information technology (IT) sector, which included the start-up of some 100 new companies each year in the late 1990s, has attracted substantial investment by US corporations, estimated at more than $14,000m. by 2000. The biggest US acquisitions to date have been Intel's $1,600m. buy-out of DSPC Communications in 1999 and Lucent Technologies' $4,500m. purchase of Chromatis networks in 2000. However, the recession which began in late 2000, the economic uncertainty arising from the renewed Palestinian uprising and the events of September 2001 in the USA resulted in the virtual cessation of new foreign investment in Israel's IT sector.

Once the leading sector in Israel, construction, with affiliated industries (cement, wood, glass and ceramics), now accounts for about 7% of gross national product (GNP), the decrease from 30% in 1950 being attributed to falling immigration levels. According to official estimates, during 2001 there were 7.8m. sq m of building area completed and 7.2m. sq m on which building was started. Housing starts in 2000 numbered 45,700 and houses completed 42,700 (as against corresponding figures of 38,459 and 45,423 in 1999).

In 2001 there were 14,061 construction establishments, which engaged a total of 350,600 employees. Of these establishments, 441 engaged between 100 and 300 persons, and 140 more than 300 persons. In the latter category 116,800 were employed. On the other hand, 5,903 establishments engaged four or fewer persons, and 3,140 between five and nine persons. In 2001 13,624 establishments belonged to the private sector, 422 to the Histadrut (the General Federation of Labour) and 15 to the public sector (most of which were government companies). The main branches of these establishments were: metal products; wood and its products; clothing and made-up textiles; food, beverages and tobacco. In view of the heavy power needs of irrigation and water installations, agriculture and industry are large-scale consumers of electricity. Almost all electric power is provided by the state-owned IEC, although the 1996 Electricity Industry Law granted separate licences for generation, distribution and transmission to private power producers to sell up to 20% of Israel's electricity through the IEC's network. In 1997 the Government announced plans to establish a natural gas infrastructure in Israel: at the first stage the IEC would purchase natural gas to be used in its existing power stations. In 1999 the IEC commenced a project to build new gas turbines in order to generate an additional 740 MW capacity by 2005. Total installed generating capacity at the end of 2000 was 9,129 MW. Generation during 2000 totalled 42,912 kWh (compared with 39,180m. kWh in 1999). Out of total sales of electricity of 39,317m. kWh in 2000, commerce accounted for 12,692m. kWh, household consumption 11,899m. kWh, manufacturing industry 10,801m. kWh, water pumping 2,319m. kWh and agriculture 1,607m. kWh.

TRANSPORT AND COMMUNICATIONS

Since 1949 Israel has operated its own international air carrier—El Al Israel Airlines Ltd. Regular scheduled services to Europe, the USA, Canada, Cyprus, and to parts of Africa and Asia are maintained. In June 1997 the Government announced plans to privatize the airline by the end of 1998, with 10% of El Al's shares being offered to employees and the remainder sold to the public. However, opposition to privatization from staff unions, the Government's reluctance to push through the measure, and the significant cuts in the airline's activities (which have included removing aircraft from the fleet and stopping flights to about 10 of the 15 destinations served), meant that 'preparations' to privatize the airline were still in progress in 2002. It was reported in July 2002 that the Government had agreed to float an initial 49% of El Al on the Tel-Aviv Stock Exchange in early 2003. In 1976 a new private company— CAL, specializing in cargo air transportation to Europe—was constituted. In April 2000 the Government approved funding arrangements to enable the Airports Authority to complete a third terminal at Ben-Gurion International Airport near Tel-Aviv, at a total cost of US \$558m., and to enable the airport to handle 12m. passengers a year. Also planned is a direct rail link from the airport to Tel-Aviv city centre. There were 28,980 commercial aircraft landings in Israel in 2001, carrying 8.0m. passengers and 296,055 metric tons of freight.

Israel's merchant navy has been undergoing contraction, while the passenger fleet has been practically abolished. The number of vessels under the Israeli flag at 31 December 2001 totalled 48, with an aggregate displacement of 611,396 grt (compared with 100 vessels and 2,463,000 tons in 1980). Israel Shipyards Ltd, at Haifa, can build ships with a capacity of as much as 10,000 dwt. In the north, the port of Haifa and its Kishon harbour extension provide Israel's main port facilities. The south is served by the port at the head of the Gulf of Aqaba, and mainly by the deep-water port of Hayovel at Ashdod, some 50 km south of Tel-Aviv. In June 2000 the Ports and Railways Authority received five bids for a proposed US \$500m. upgrade of Hayovel port, involving new cargo and container quays, a breakwater extension and hinterland development. Major improvements to passenger facilities at Haifa port are also planned. The amount of cargo loaded at seaports in 2001 totalled 13.3m. metric tons, while the amount unloaded was 29.7m. tons (excluding petroleum).

Israeli railways operate some 684 km of main lines and 260 km of branch lines. The service extends from Nahariya, north of Haifa to Jerusalem and Tel-Aviv and then southwards through Beersheba. In 1965 it reached Dimona and in 1970 the phosphate works at Oron. Traction is wholly by diesel locomotives. In 2001 traffic comprised 15.1m. passengers and 8.1m. tons of freight. In April 1996 a state-owned company was established to plan and promote the construction of a mass transportation system in Tel-Aviv, including a light railway. In December 1999 the Jerusalem municipal authorities invited bids for the construction and operation of a 14-km light railway in the city on a 30-year BOT basis.

Roads are the chief means of transport. In 2001 there were 16,563 km of paved roads, of which 9,508 km were urban, 5,523 km were non-urban and 1,532 km were access roads. In 1998 the local Derech Eretz consortium obtained the BOT contract for the construction of the US \$1,250m. north–south Cross-Israel Highway as Israel's first toll road, on which work began in mid-2000. Travelling Israel's existing roads at the end of 2001 were 1,460,851 private vehicles, 11,897 buses and coaches, and 326,428 lorries and vans. The first privatized bus lines came into operation in 1997, and in March 2000 the Ministry of Transport invited bids from private operators for 120 urban and district routes currently run by the Egged Transport Co-operative, as the first stage of a nine-year privatization programme covering half of Egged's 1,400 routes.

At the end of 2000 97% of Israeli households had at least one direct telephone line. Three cellular telephone networks, Pelephone Communications Ltd, Cellcom Israel and Partner Communications Co Ltd, with a combined subscription rate of approximately 2.5m., were in operation. Bezeq Israel Telecom, the state-owned telecommunications company which has a monopoly over the domestic market, providing 3m. direct exchange lines, is scheduled to be part-privatized.

TOURISM

The decline in the number of tourists entering Israel from 1973 (a slowdown had already been recorded in the second half of 1972) continued in 1975; 1976 witnessed a recovery, and the number of tourists rose thereafter, reaching 1,175,800 in 1980. Then, in 1981, a slight decline, to 1,137,055, was recorded, and in 1982 the industry slumped by 12%, with only 997,510 tourists

entering Israel. The war in Lebanon, labour disputes at El Al and less favourable exchange rates for tourists were responsible for the situation. These reasons also contributed to the number of Israeli tourists leaving the country; in 1982 they totalled about 600,000, spending some US \$600m. abroad. Nevertheless, 1984 witnessed a recovery, when 1,260,000 tourists visited the country, and income from tourism doubled in the six years up to 1984, reaching \$1,000m. per year. In 1985 a total of 1,264,367 tourists visited Israel. In 1986 the total declined by 13%, to 1,101,481, and revenue from tourism fell by \$107m. In 1987 the number of tourists rose by 25%, to 1,378,742, and revenue increased to a record \$1,635m. In 1988, however, the number of tourists declined to 1,169,582, mainly as a result of continued unrest in the Occupied Territories. In 1989 the number of tourists recovered slightly, to reach 1,176,500, with revenue totalling \$1,467.7m. This increase continued throughout the first half of 1990. However, following Iraq's invasion of Kuwait in August 1990 and the ensuing crisis in the Persian (Arabian) Gulf region, the number of tourist arrivals fell sharply in that year, to 1,131,700. Revenue amounted to \$1,381.7m.

Tourism revived again in 1992, when 1,509,520 tourist arrivals were recorded and revenue from tourism amounted to US \$1,891m. In 1995 tourist arrivals totalled 2,215,552, an increase of 20% on the previous year's figure. Total revenue from tourism amounted to \$2,784m. in that year. In 1996 tourism declined once again, however, with approximately 2,100,552 tourist arrivals generating revenues of \$2,955m. This trend continued in 1997 and 1998, in which arrivals dipped to 2.01m. and 1.94m. respectively. Tourism revenues also fell, to \$2,813m. in 1997 and \$2,637m. in 1998. In 1999, however, tourist numbers recovered sharply, to 2.31m., generating revenue of \$3,971m. The Israeli tourist industry was boosted by preparations for the millennium celebrations, many of which were focused upon Israel.

Although tourist arrivals and revenue from tourism continued to expand strongly in the first three quarters of 2000, the second Palestinian uprising from September 2000 produced a dramatic slump in the fourth quarter, with the result that arrivals for the year as a whole were only 4% up on 1999, at 2.42m., yielding revenue of US \$3,859m. In 2001 the negative effect on tourism of the ongoing regional conflict was aggravated by the September suicide attacks in the USA, resulting in a 50% drop in tourist arrivals (1.20m.) compared with 2000 and a corresponding drop in revenue, to \$2,460m. The slump continued in the first half of 2002, when arrivals were about 40% lower than in the same period of 2001.

Overall administration of Israeli tourism is sponsored by the Ministry of Tourism, which maintains 20 offices abroad. It is also in charge of regulating tourist services in Israel, including arrangement of 'package' tours and the provision of multilingual guides. In 1976 the Ministry promoted the inauguration of charter flights from the USA and Europe to Israel. At the end of 2001 Israel had 339 hotels with 46,658 rooms, some 50% more than in 1990.

BUDGET, INVESTMENT AND FINANCE

In 1996, as in previous years, there was a substantial deficit in the operations of the state budget. Total revenue (including borrowings from the National Insurance Institute) in 1996 was NIS 116,648m. This amount excludes grants received from abroad (NIS 12,985m.) and proceeds from the sale of government assets (NIS 349m.). Total expenditure (including repayments to the National Insurance Institute) in the same year was NIS 141,099m. This excludes net lending operations of the Government (NIS 807m.).

In the first four months of 1996 the Bank of Israel's reduced interest rates on monetary tenders stabilized to a nominal annual average of 13.9% (an effective rate of 14.9%). Between May and July, however, the Central Bank raised its lending rate to 17% (an effective rate of 18.5%) on an annual basis. In the last months of 1996 this was reduced by a cumulative 1.8%, and in March 1997 the rate returned to 13.9%. In mid-June, after the resignation of the Minister of Finance, Dan Meridor, an additional reduction of 1% in the interest rate was announced. However, in August the Central Bank announced that the rate would be increased to 13.4% in order to curb rising inflation. After various adjustments, the rate was reduced in May 1998 to 11.6%, its lowest level for four years. The success of the anti-inflation strategy by late 1999 enabled further reductions to be made, taking the rate down to 9.3% in April 2000. A series of small further reductions brought the rate down to 6% by July 2001 and to 3.8% by the end of 2001. However, deteriorating economic conditions obliged the Central Bank to increase the interest rate to 4.4% in March 2002 and to 4.6% in the following month.

State budget revenue in 1997 totalled NIS 134,000m. (with foreign grants providing a further NIS 10,390m.), while total expenditure was NIS 153,801m. State budget revenue in 1998 was set at NIS 165,058m. and expenditure at NIS 173,341m., but the out-turn was a deficit of NIS 12,200m. (equivalent to 2.4% of GDP), which was financed mostly from domestic public borrowing. The approved budget for 1999 set both total revenue and total expenditure at NIS 214,975m., but the out-turn was a deficit equivalent to 2.25% of GDP (which would have been 3.25% but for the start of economic recovery and higher tax receipts in the second half of the year). As approved by the Knesset in December 1999, the 2000 budget provided for expenditure of NIS 227,400m. and a deficit of NIS 10,400m., envisaging that government expenditure as a proportion of GDP would fall from 46.3% in 1999 to 45.5% and government debt from 107% to 105% of GDP. The Government declared its intention to amend the Deficit Reduction Law 'to create a new and binding trajectory in which the total government deficit (not including allocation of credit) shall not exceed 2.5% of GDP in 2000 and shall decline by no less than 0.25% year-on-year in 2001–02'.

The total government deficit in 2000 (excluding net allocation of credit) was NIS 2,800m. (0.6% of GDP); this resulted from three quarters in which there was a surplus and a final quarter in which there was a large deficit as a result of security-related events. The deficit for 2000 was lower than the target set in the budget Deficit Reduction Law by 3% of GDP (i.e. NIS 13,000m.) and also 2.8% of GDP lower than the deficit in 1999. Budget revenue totalled NIS 177,269m., while total expenditure was NIS 178,367m. The state budget for 2001, approved by the Knesset in March of that year, provided for expenditure of NIS 245,813m. and a deficit of NIS 8,400m., equivalent to 1.75% of GDP. However, the need for increased spending on security provisions, in the face of Palestinian insurrection, and the first fall in overall GDP since 1953 (of 0.6%) resulted in the actual 2001 budget deficit rising to NIS 21,300m., representing 4.6% of GDP.

In light of the continuing Israeli–Palestinian conflict and the world economic downturn caused by the September 2001 suicide attacks in the USA, the Government was forced to revise the GDP growth forecast that underpinned its 2002 budget proposals from 4% to 2% and to revise its original spending plans. As adopted by the Knesset in February 2002 after acrimonious debate, the budget provided for expenditure of NIS 248,000m. and a deficit equivalent to 3% of GDP. However, further fiscal deterioration and continuing contraction in overall GDP forced the Government to introduce a controversial economic austerity package which, as finally adopted by the Knesset in May 2002, included cuts in social welfare and other spending totalling NIS 6,000m. as well as tax increases of NIS 3,000m., including the raising of value-added tax (VAT) from 17% to 18%. The revised target was a budget deficit in 2002 of 3.9% of GDP, to be followed by a deficit of 3.5% of GDP in 2003. It quickly became apparent, however, that without further corrective measures the 2002 budget deficit would rise to about 6% of GDP, partly as the result of an anticipated further contraction of about 1.4% in overall GDP.

Between 1986 and 1996 the Israeli Government sold part or all of its shareholding in 79 companies. In 1996 revenue from privatization was equivalent to US $109.3m. In 1997 a total of $2,463m. was generated from privatization; this amount included $2,156m. from sales in the banking sector and $193.94m. from the sale of Israel Chemicals. In 1998 proceeds from privatization totalled $1,128m. In 2000 total government holdings continued to decline; privatization proceeds totalled $682m., which included the sale of the Government's remaining stake in Bank Hapoalim. The offering, which was 1.7 times over-subscribed, raised $580m. In May 2001 the new Sharon Government announced the start of its privatization programme by inviting tenders for its controlling stake in Bank Leumi.

During 1996 the stock market remained relatively stable and experienced a reduction in the volume of activity. High interest rates in local currency, large withdrawals from provident funds, and increased activity from non-resident investors made a significant impact on the capital market. Issues of capital on the Tel-Aviv Stock Exchange during 1996 totalled more than NIS 758m. During 1996 the general share index decreased in real terms. The multi-sided index declined by 8.5%. In terms of December 1996 prices, average daily trade in that year was NIS 108m., having decreased by 16.9% from the NIS 130m. recorded in 1995. At the end of 1996 the current market value of shares and negotiable securities was NIS 117,000m. at current prices. By the end of 1997 the current market value was NIS 163,810m. at current prices. According to Bank of Israel data, foreign financial investment in Israeli securities listed on the Stock Exchange and abroad dropped to US $525m. in 1998 from $1,900m. in 1997. However, the Bank of Israel reported a steady increase in overall foreign investment from $694m. in 1994 (after the Oslo Agreement was signed) to $3,276m. in 1997, $5,300m. in 1998 and $7,500m. in 1999.

In 2000 overall foreign investment increased to US $11,400m. Direct foreign investment increased steadily, notably in the high technology industry, during the first three quarters of the year ($600m. in the first quarter, $1,700m. in the second and $1,800m. in the third) before decreasing (to $900m.) in the final quarter; the $5,000m. total compared to an average of $2,200m. during 1997–99. However, for the period January to April 2001 foreign financial investment in Israeli negotiable securities plunged by 92% over the corresponding period in 2000, following the downturn on the Tel-Aviv and US stock exchanges. In 2001 as a whole, foreign investment slumped to $4,000m.

In April 1998 foreign-exchange restrictions were removed in order to increase competition in the financial services sector and encourage foreign investment in Israel's economy. The Stock Exchange index increased by 62.5% in 1999, total market capitalization at the end of the year being the equivalent of $59,762m. and remaining at the same level at the end of 2000. In June 2000 the Stock Exchange announced that 23 of its listed 681 companies were included in the newly launched FTSE All-World Index, the constituents of which include stocks from 49 exchanges worldwide. The Israeli Securities Authority adopted a dual listing regulation, allowing for securities that are traded on the US stock exchanges to trade on the Tel-Aviv exchange without additional regulatory requirements.

Israel possesses a highly developed banking system, consisting of a central bank (the Bank of Israel), 14 commercial banks, five mortgage banks, and other financial institutions. Nevertheless, three bank-groups—the Bank Leumi group, Bank Hapoalim and Bank Discount—hold 92% of the total assets of the banking system. Their subsidiaries are represented all over the world and enjoy a growing reputation; due to devaluation their share in the consolidated balance sheet is increasing markedly. Long-term credits are granted by mortgage banks, the Israel Agricultural Bank, the Industrial Development Bank and the Maritime Bank. At the end of 2000 the amount of outstanding credit allocated by the banks to the public stood at NIS 353,647m.

The function of the central bank is to issue currency (and commemorative coins), to accept deposits from banking institutions and extend temporary advances to the Government, to act as the Government's sole fiscal and banking agent and to manage the public debt. Its governor supervises the liquidity position of the commercial banks and regulates the volume of bank advances. Central recommendations to reform and restructure the banking system, including the appointment of independent governors to hold the Government's shares in banks, and the sale of its interests and shares in banks, have been adopted. Since October 1997 some US $2,156m. has been raised in privatization revenue from share sales in Bank Hapoalim (worth $1,434m.), United Mizrahi Bank ($131m.), Bank Leumi ($407m.) and Israel Discount Bank ($184m.). The sale of Bank Hapoalim—Israel's largest bank—in mid-2000 represented the first significant privatization undertaken by the Barak Government.

The severe recession in 2001, the worsening security situation and the crises affecting capital markets both in Israel and abroad had a deleterious effect on the performance of Israel's banking system. The net income of the five major banking groups contracted significantly, from NIS 3,800m. in 2000 to NIS 1,900m. in 2001, while the return on capital was also halved, from 11.8% to 5.9%. Nevertheless, the total assets of the commercial banks rose by 8% in 2001, standing at NIS 663,000m. at the end of the year.

FOREIGN TRADE AND BALANCE OF PAYMENTS

Israel's balance-of-payments deficit on trade in goods and services stood at US $10,185m. in 1996, declining to $8,490m. in 1997. The value of exports of goods and services in 1997 amounted to $30,320m., compared with $28,800m. in 1996, while the value of imports amounted to $38,810m., compared with $38,984m. in 1996. Israel's deficit on merchandise trade, which relates to goods only, amounted to US $5,848m. in 1997, compared with the record deficit of $7,646m. incurred in 1996.

In 1997 net transfer payments, most of which consisted of US aid, were worth US $6,267m., compared with $6,370m. in 1996. They covered 73.8% of the deficit on goods and services in 1997, compared with 62.5% in 1996. Israel recorded a deficit on the current account of the balance of payments (goods, services, income and transfers) in each of the years 1990–97. The deficit increased from $6,205m. in 1995 to a record $6,646m. in 1996 (owing to an increase in the net trade and services deficit, despite the growth in exports of goods and services for the fourth consecutive year), but was reduced to $5,014m. in 1997. Israel's foreign currency reserves, held by the Bank of Israel, stood at $20,600m. at the end of 1997, compared with $11,800m. at the end of 1996. At the end of 1999 they totalled $22,515m., while Israel's foreign assets totalled $52,170m., compared to $43,024 at the end of 1998.

The value of Israel's merchandise exports increased from US $22,974m. in 1998 to $25,577m. in 1999. Meanwhile, imports of goods (valued f.o.b.) increased from $26,315m. in 1998 to $30,041m. in 1999. In that year the trade deficit was $4,464m. and the current-account deficit $3,277m., although the overall balance of payments showed a surplus of $9m. In 2000 the trade deficit fell to $3,089m., from imports of $34,036m. and exports of $30,947m. The current account deficit decreased to $1,974m., following a sharp increase in exports of services to $15,181m., resulting from the contribution of start-up companies. As a result of economic recession, merchandise imports fell in 2001 to $30,942m. and exports to $27,678m., giving a trade deficit of $3,264m. and a current-account deficit of $1,852m. Foreign reserves stood at $24,300m. in May 2002.

The focus of Israel's foreign trade is mainly the European Union (EU, formerly European Community—EC) and North America. An Israeli-EC Chamber of Commerce was founded in June 1986. Duties on goods imported from the EC and the USA were reduced by an average of 60% on 1 January 1987, under the terms of separate bilateral trade agreements. In October 1988 the European Parliament approved three trade protocols, giving Israel privileged access to EC markets, having withheld its approval in March and July and delayed further votes, in protest against Israel's treatment of Palestinians during the *intifada* in the Occupied Territories. The Israeli Government, in an attempt to placate the EC, had undertaken to allow Palestinian farmers in the West Bank to export their produce directly to the EC, unimpeded by the occupation authorities. In July 1995 Israel concluded a free-trade agreement with the EU regarding financial services, government procurement, co-operation in research and development, additional agricultural products and an improvement in Israel's access to European markets in the high technology sector. An association agreement between the EU and Israel entered into force on 1 June 2000.

ECONOMIC PROSPECTS

Israel's short- and medium-term economic prospects clearly depend on whether a solution can be found to the conflict with the Palestinians, and whether peace can be restored to a region traumatized by an increasingly bloody and bitter struggle since September 2000 and by the consequent disruption to the Israeli economy. Aggravated by the September 2001 attacks in the USA, the recession that developed in that year appeared set to deepen in 2002, with Israel's important tourism and high-technology sectors being particularly badly hit by the international economic downturn. Owing to a fall-off in state revenues and the need for additional security expenditure, the Government's economic austerity package adopted in May 2002 was considered unlikely to achieve the revised target of a 3.9% budget deficit for that year. Without further corrective measures, the deficit was set to rise to around 6% in 2002, well above the notional ceiling prescribed by law.

In the absence of a peace settlement with the Palestinians, economic conditions were likely to remain unfavourable in 2003, aggravated by a continuing need for additional expenditure on security. Without a return to conditions of economic growth, bringing the budget deficit under control will require the Government to take difficult decisions on a further retrenchment in spending, despite the prospect of a general election in 2003.

Statistical Survey

Source: Central Bureau of Statistics, POB 13015, Hakirya, Romema, Jerusalem 91130; tel. 2-6592037; fax 2-6521340; e-mail yael@cbs.gov.il; internet www.cbs.gov.il.

Area and Population

AREA, POPULATION AND DENSITY

Area (sq km)	
Land	21,671
Inland water	474
Total	22,145*
Population (*de jure*; census results)†	
4 June 1983	4,037,620
4 November 1995	
Males	2,738,175
Females	2,810,348
Total	5,548,523
Population (*de jure*; official estimates at mid-year)†	
2000	6,282,300
2001	6,433,500
2002	6,568,500
Density (per sq km) at mid-2002† . . .	296.6

* 8,550 sq miles. Area includes East Jerusalem, annexed by Israel in June 1967, and the Golan sub-district (1,154 sq km), annexed by Israel in December 1981.
† Including the population of East Jerusalem and Israeli residents in certain other areas under Israeli military occupation since June 1967. Beginning in 1981, figures also include non-Jews in the Golan sub-district, an Israeli-occupied area of Syrian territory. Census results exclude adjustment for underenumeration.

POPULATION BY RELIGION (31 December 2001)

	Number	%
Jews	5,025,000	77.25
Muslims	1,004,600	15.44
Christians	138,500	2.13
Druze	106,300	1.63
Unclassified	230,900	3.55
Total*	6,505,200	100.00

* Excluding Lebanese not classified by religion (3,600 at 31 December 2001).
30 June 2002: Jews (number) 5,322,400.

DISTRICTS (31 December 2001)

	Area (sq km)*	Population†	Density (per sq km)
Jerusalem‡	652	777,400	1,192.3
Northern§	4,478	1,105,500	246.9
Haifa	863	830,200	962.0
Central	1,276	1,502,100	1,177.2
Tel-Aviv	171	1,160,700	6,787.7
Southern	14,231	924,600	65.0
Total	21,671	6,300,500	290.7

* Excluding lakes, with a total area of 474 sq km.
† Excluding Israelis residing in Jewish localities in the West Bank and Gaza Strip, totalling 208,300.
‡ Including East Jerusalem, annexed by Israel in June 1967.
§ Including the Golan sub-district (area 1,154 sq km, population 35,400 at 31 December 2001), annexed by Israel in December 1981.

PRINCIPAL TOWNS (estimated population at 31 December 2001)

Jerusalem (capital) .	670,000*	Petach-Tikva . . .	170,700
Tel-Aviv—Jaffa .	358,800	Holon	166,200
Haifa . .	272,200	Netanya . . .	163,700
Rishon LeZiyyon .	207,900	Bene Beraq . .	139,000
Ashdod . .	181,100	Bat Yam . .	135,500
Beersheba . .	177,900	Ramat Gan . .	127,400

* Including East Jerusalem, annexed in June 1967.

BIRTHS, MARRIAGES AND DEATHS*

	Registered live births		Registered marriages		Registered deaths	
	Number	Rate (per 1,000)	Number	Rate (per 1,000)	Number	Rate (per 1,000)
1994 . .	114,543	21.2	36,035	6.7	33,535	6.2
1995 . .	116,886	21.1	35,990	6.5	35,348	6.4
1996 . .	121,333	21.3	36,081	6.3	34,647	6.1
1997 . .	124,478	21.4	37,611	6.5	36,106	6.2
1998 . .	130,080	21.8	40,137	6.7	36,953	6.2
1999 . .	131,936	21.5	40,236	6.6	37,247	6.1
2000 . .	136,390	21.7	38,894	6.4	37,618	6.0
2001† .	136,638	21.2	n.a.	n.a.	37,146	5.8

* Including East Jerusalem.
† Provisional figures.

Expectation of life (WHO estimates, years at birth, 2000): Males 76.6; Females 80.6 (Source: WHO, *World Health Report*).

IMMIGRATION*

	1999	2000	2001
Immigrants:			
on immigrant visas . . .	70,586	55,736	39,571
on tourist visas† . . .	6,104	4,428	3,974
Potential immigrants:			
on potential immigrant visas .	18	12	6
on tourist visas† . . .	58	16	29
Total	76,766	60,192	43,580

* Excluding immigrating citizens (3,226 in 1999; 3,372 in 2000; 2,930 in 2001) and Israeli residents returning from abroad.
† Figures refer to tourists who changed their status to immigrants or potential immigrants.

ECONOMICALLY ACTIVE POPULATION (sample surveys, '000 persons aged 15 years and over, excluding armed forces)*

	1999	2000	2001
Agriculture, hunting, forestry and fishing	49.6	47.9	45.1
Industry†	389.9	396.6	392.7
Electricity, gas and water supply	19.2	19.3	18.8
Construction	120.3	116.4	117.0
Wholesale and retail trade; repair of motor vehicles, motorcycles and personal and household goods	281.6	295.6	299.1
Hotels and restaurants	90.2	101.7	95.9
Transport, storage and communications	135.4	144.9	149.9
Financial intermediation	73.7	73.2	75.2
Real estate, renting and business activities	224.7	258.7	277.8
Public administration and defence; compulsory social security	116.3	119.9	129.0
Education	267.9	272.4	279.5
Health and social work	211.3	213.6	225.0
Other community, social and personal service activities	99.9	106.4	107.2
Private households with employed persons	40.1	34.7	34.9
Extra-territorial organizations and bodies	1.9	1.3	1.6
Not classifiable by economic activity	14.6	18.5	16.2
Total employed	2,136.7	2,221.3	2,264.9
Unemployed	208.5	213.8	234.0
Total labour force	2,345.3	2,435.1	2,499.0
Males	1,285.1	1,323.4	1,357.0
Females	1,060.2	1,111.6	1,142.0

* Figures are estimated independently, so the totals may not be the sum of the component parts.

† Comprising mining and quarrying, and manufacturing.

Source: partly ILO, *Yearbook of Labour Statistics*.

Health and Welfare

KEY INDICATORS

Fertility (births per woman, 2000)	2.8
Under-5 mortality rate (per 1,000 live births, 2000)	6
HIV/AIDS (% of persons aged 15–49, 2001)	0.10
Physicians (per 1,000 head, 1998)	3.85
Hospital beds (per 1,000 head, 1995)	5.98
Health expenditure (1998): US $ per head (PPP)	1,607
% of GDP	8.8
public (% of total)	66.8
Human Development Index (2000): ranking	22
value	0.896

For sources and definitions, see explanatory note on p. vi.

Agriculture

PRINCIPAL CROPS ('000 metric tons)

	1998	1999	2000
Wheat	155	29	94
Maize	73.5*	82.2*	85.0†
Potatoes	346.5	363.5	349.6
Olives	32.0	23.2	56.0
Cottonseed	81.3	39.6	26.9
Cabbages	55.4	48.7	50.0†
Lettuce	40.3	37.3	38.6
Tomatoes	493.1	574.6	465.4
Pumpkins, squash and gourds	35.3	28.7	28.7†
Cucumbers	115.5	108.3	108.3†
Aubergines (Eggplants)	53.9	61.0	61.0†
Chillies and green peppers	95.5	102.3	90.9
Dry onions	80.6	92.6	112.6
Carrots	87.8	65.0	70.1
Other vegetables	180.3	172.3	175.5
Watermelons	333.8	375.0	400.0†
Cantaloupes and other melons	80.8	71.7	71.7†
Bananas	108.6	117.8	135.6
Oranges	312.9	203.5	247.6
Tangerines, mandarins, clementines and satsumas	177.6	127.6	156.5
Grapefruit	377.5	372.2	347.5
Apples	102.9	127.5	109.3
Peaches	47.1	45.8	54.4
Grapes	88.6	85.0	87.2
Avocados	65.7	55.9	73.3
Other fruits and berries	173.6	165.3	189.5
Cotton (lint)	50.3	24.8	16.0

* Unofficial figure.   † FAO estimate.

Source: FAO.

LIVESTOCK ('000 head, year ending September)

	1998	1999	2000
Cattle	388	395	400*
Pigs*	163	150	150
Sheep	350	350	380
Goats	74	75	75
Chickens	25,340	27,340	28,000*
Geese*	1,400	1,400	1,400
Turkeys	4,430	4,900	5,000*
Ducks	200	200*	200*

* FAO estimate(s).

Source: FAO.

LIVESTOCK PRODUCTS ('000 metric tons)

	1998	1999	2000
Beef and veal	43.8	46.4	51.6
Mutton and lamb*	5.4	5.4	5.4
Pig meat	12.1	8.7	10.0
Chicken meat*	175	189	201
Goose meat†	5.1	5.1	5.1
Turkey meat*	89	86	90
Cows' milk	1,197.1	1,194.0	1,185.2
Sheep's milk	18.5	18.5	19.4
Goats' milk	14.0	14.5	11.3
Cheese	95.1	96.7	99.6
Butter	8.2	7.9	7.4
Hen eggs	86.8	91.8	87.9
Honey	2.5	3.0	2.6
Cattle hides†	4.6	4.7	4.7

* Unofficial figures.   FAO estimates.

Source: FAO.

Forestry

ROUNDWOOD REMOVALS ('000 cubic metres, excl. bark)

	1997	1998	1999
Sawlogs, veneer logs and logs for sleepers*	40	36	36
Pulpwood*	35	32	32
Other industrial wood*	35	32	32
Fuel wood*	14	13	13
Total	124	113	113

* FAO estimates.

2000: Production as in 1999 (FAO estimates).

Source: FAO.

Fishing

('000 metric tons, live weight)

	1997	1998	1999
Capture	5,204	6,300	5,884
Carps, barbels, etc.	696	1,396	1,302
Aquaculture	18,264	18,556	18,777
Common carp	7,684	7,172	7,062
Tilapias	6,007	6,696	6,410
Gilthead seabream	1,326	1,643	2,210
Flathead grey mullet	1,562	1,476	1,542
Total catch	23,468	24,856	24,661

Note: Figures exclude crocodiles and alligators, recorded by number rather than weight. The number of American alligators caught was: 210 in 1997; 401 in 1998; 425 in 1999.

Source: FAO, *Yearbook of Fishery Statistics*.

Mining

('000 metric tons, unless otherwise indicated)

	1998	1999*	2000*
Crude petroleum ('000 barrels)	38.9	31.6	31.6
Natural gas (million cu m)*	11.4	10.0	9.3
Kaolin	27.0	27.3	26.7
Phosphate rock†	4,067	4,128	4,110
Potash salts‡	1,668	1,702	1,710
Salt (unrefined)	874	883	863
Gypsum (crude)	56.0	50.0	45.8

* Estimated production.
† Figures refer to beneficiated production. The phosphoric acid content (in '000 metric tons) was: 1,288 in 1998; 1,310 in 1999; 1,300 in 2000.
‡ Figures refer to K₂O content.

Source: US Geological Survey.

Industry

SELECTED PRODUCTS
('000 metric tons, unless otherwise indicated)

	1992	1993	1994
Refined vegetable oils (metric tons)	56,463	57,558	45,447
Margarine	35.1	33.8	24.7
Wine ('000 litres)	12,373	12,733	n.a.
Beer ('000 litres)	51,078	58,681	50,750
Cigarettes (metric tons)	5,742	5,525	5,638
Newsprint (metric tons)	0	247	0
Writing and printing paper (metric tons)	66,334	65,426	65,790
Other paper (metric tons)	32,368	30,446	28,985
Cardboard (metric tons)	92,072	95,108	103,142
Rubber tyres ('000)	892	854	966
Ammonia (metric tons)	41,072	n.a.	n.a.
Ammonium sulphate (metric tons)	12,444	n.a.	n.a.
Sulphuric acid	138	n.a.	n.a.
Chlorine (metric tons)	33,912	35,241	37,555
Caustic soda (metric tons)	29,459	29,851	32,765
Polyethylene (metric tons)	128,739	144,147	126,979
Paints (metric tons)	58,963	57,429	53,260
Cement	3,960	4,536	4,800
Commercial vehicles (number)	852	836	1,260
Electricity (million kWh)	24,731	26,042	28,327

1996 ('000 metric tons, unless otherwise indicated): Margarine 35; Cigarettes (metric tons) 4,793; Chlorine 35; Caustic soda 41; Paints 58.0 (Source: UN, *Industrial Commodity Statistics Yearbook*).
1997: Rubber tyres ('000) 792; Cement ('000 metric tons) 5,916.
1999: Writing and printing paper (metric tons) 95,000 (Source: UN, *Industrial Commodity Statistics Yearbook*).
2000: Commercial vehicles (number) 373 (Source: International Road Federation, *World Road Statistics*); Electricity (million kWh) 42,912 (Source: UN, *Monthly Bulletin of Statistics*).

Finance

CURRENCY AND EXCHANGE RATES

Monetary Units

100 agorot (singular: agora) = 1 new sheqel (plural: sheqalim) or shekel (NIS).

Sterling, Dollar and Euro Equivalents (31 May 2002)
£1 sterling = NIS 7.210;
US $1 = NIS 4.916;
€1 = NIS 4.615;
NIS 100 = £13.87 = $20.34 = €21.67.

Average Exchange Rate (NIS per US $)
1999   4.1397
2000   4.0773
2001   4.2057

STATE BUDGET (NIS million)

Revenue*	1998	1999†	2000†
Tax revenue‡	114,560	126,460	132,870
Taxes on income and profits	54,207	59,681	61,780
Companies	12,817	13,100	14,000
Individuals	41,390	45,200	47,780
Taxes on property	2,847	3,240	3,760
Taxes on goods and services	56,162	60,609	65,410
Value-added tax	39,962	42,170	46,320
Excises	6,960	7,360	8,440
Fuel	5,238	5,650	6,570
Purchase tax	8,069	8,610	9,310
Non-tax revenue	27,698	31,798	32,907
Interest	2,823	3,540	3,490
Loans from National Insurance Institute	5,550	6,320	5,490
Fees, royalties, pension provisions, etc.	11,176	12,571	13,223
Revenue for revenue-dependent expenditure	7,146	8,167	9,654
Total	142,258	158,258	165,777

Expenditure§	1998	1999†	2000†
General administration . . .	10,467	10,466	11,748
Defence	37,909	36,426	39,138
Public order	4,229	5,265	5,893
Education	23,769	26,258	28,013
Health	14,951	15,031	16,088
Labour and welfare . . .	19,144	21,008	22,834
Other social services . . .	11,595	14,188	15,039
Housing	7,985	10,186	10,799
Economic services . . .	9,860	12,115	12,826
Manufacturing . . .	3,329	4,039	3,926
Unallocable and other functions .	26,019	32,657	31,781
Interest	24,424	23,836	26,339
General transfers . . .	4,510	4,577	4,294
Reserves‖	—	7,417	4,449
Sub-total	157,943	173,414	183,360
Adjustment	5,582	4,642	5,567
Total	163,525	178,056	188,927
Current‖	156,438	161,761	174,772
Capital	7,087	9,164	9,743

* Excluding proceeds from sale of assets (NIS million): 5,094 in 1998; 4,590 (forecast) in 1999; 3,500 (forecast) in 2000. Also excluded are grants received from abroad (NIS million): 12,572 in 1998; 11,808 (forecast) in 1999; 12,260 (forecast) in 2000.

† Figures are forecasts.

‡ Excluding fees, classified as non-tax revenue.

§ Expenditure includes repayments to the National Insurance Institute (NIS million): 4,323 in 1998; 4,741 (forecast) in 1999; 5,095 (forecast) in 2000. It excludes the central Government's lending minus repayments (NIS million): −909 (forecast) in 1998; 97 (forecast) in 1999.

‖ Net transfers to reserves are included in current expenditure.

IMF, *Israel: Selected Issues and Statistical Appendix* (April 2000).

2001 (draft budget, NIS million): Total revenue 245,813; Total expenditure 245,813. Source: Ministry of Finance.

2002 (draft budget, NIS million): Total expenditure 248,000.

CENTRAL BANK RESERVES (US $ million at 31 December)

	1999	2000	2001
Gold*	0.0	0.0	0.0
IMF special drawing rights . .	0.2	1.1	1.7
Reserve position in IMF . . .	89.9	117.1	197.8
Foreign exchange	22,514.8	23,163.0	23,179.1
Total	22,604.9	23,281.2	23,378.6

* Valued at SDR 35 per troy ounce.

Source: IMF, *International Financial Statistics.*

MONEY SUPPLY (NIS million at 31 December)

	1999	2000	2001
Currency outside banks . . .	12,178	12,347	14,580
Demand deposits at deposit money banks	17,933	18,537	23,053
Total money (incl. others) . .	30,263	31,030	37,796

Source: IMF, *International Financial Statistics.*

COST OF LIVING

(Consumer Price Index, annual averages; base: 1990 = 100)

	1998	1999	2000
Food (incl. beverages) . . .	203.9	218.1	223.2
Electricity, gas and other fuels .	213.6	228.0	242.1
Clothing (incl. footwear) . . .	150.2	150.4	150.2
Rent	361.0	370.4	362.4
All items (incl. others) . . .	233.7	245.8	248.6

Source: ILO, *Yearbook of Labour Statistics.*

NATIONAL ACCOUNTS (NIS million at current prices)

National Income and Product (provisional)

	1995	1996	1997
Compensation of employees . .	144,182	168,356	189,741
Operating surplus	47,106	52,746	55,532
Domestic factor incomes . .	191,288	221,102	245,273
Consumption of fixed capital . .	37,049	42,892	49,073
Gross domestic product at factor cost	228,337	263,994	292,547*
Indirect taxes	52,396	61,274	67,866
Less Subsidies	4,817	4,687	4,743
GDP in purchasers' values .	275,917	320,581	355,670
Factor income received from abroad	4,696	5,330	6,498
Less Factor income paid abroad .	13,687	16,112	18,639
Gross national product . .	266,926	309,799	343,529
Less Consumption of fixed capital .	37,049	42,892	49,073
National income in market prices	229,877	266,907	294,456
Other current transfers received from abroad	21,885	25,260	27,914
Less Other current transfers paid abroad	756	890	939
National disposable income .	251,005	291,277	321,431

* Including statistical discrepancy.

Source: UN, *National Accounts Statistics.*

Expenditure on the Gross Domestic Product

	1999	2000	2001
Government final consumption expenditure	122,274	129,379	137,293
Private final consumption expenditure	240,503	259,424	271,737
Increase in stocks	5,293	5,397	9,761
Gross fixed capital formation .	92,556	92,657	87,239
Total domestic expenditure* .	442,793	469,812	n.a.
Exports of goods and services .	151,485	184,492	163,032
Less Imports of goods and services	189,257	211,256	n.a.
GDP in purchasers' values .	405,021	443,048	481,385
GDP at constant 1995 prices .	307,324	328,669	n.a.

* Including statistical discrepancy.

Source: IMF, *International Financial Statistics.*

Net Domestic Product by Economic Activity (at factor cost)

	1995	1996	1997
Agriculture, hunting, forestry and fishing	4,619	4,792	4,971
Manufacturing, mining and quarrying	36,539	41,491	47,280
Electricity, gas and water . .	2,229	2,344	2,557
Construction	16,416	19,124	20,607
Wholesale and retail trade, restaurants and hotels . .	23,373	26,632	28,862
Transport, storage and communications	14,670	15,201	15,709
Finance, insurance, real estate and business services . . .	51,736	63,859	71,687
Government services	48,360	55,927	61,159
Other community, social and personal services . . .	6,210	7,168	8,176
Statistical discrepancy . . .	363	295	189
Sub-total	204,335	236,833	261,197
Less Imputed bank service charge	8,757	10,520	11,285
Other adjustments (incl. errors and omissions)	−4,291	−5,211	−6,433
Total	191,289	221,102	243,479

Source: UN, *National Accounts Statistics.*

BALANCE OF PAYMENTS (US $ million)

	1999	2000	2001
Exports of goods f.o.b. . . .	25,577	30,947	27,678
Imports of goods f.o.b. . . .	−30,041	−34,036	−30,942
Trade balance	−4,464	−3,089	−3,264
Exports of services . . .	11,447	15,181	11,991
Imports of services . . .	−10,708	−12,529	−12,563
Balance on goods and services	−3,726	−437	−3,836
Other income received . . .	2,553	3,353	3,545
Other income paid . . .	−8,420	−11,360	−7,959
Balance on goods, services and income	−9,592	−8,443	−8,251
Current transfers received . .	7,125	7,483	7,531
Current transfers paid . . .	−809	−1,015	−1,132
Current balance	−3,277	−1,974	−1,852
Capital account (net) . . .	569	455	681
Direct investment abroad . .	−933	−2,859	−1,135
Direct investment from abroad .	2,873	4,524	3,224
Portfolio investment assets . .	−830	−2,139	−1,199
Portfolio investment liabilities .	1,499	4,361	656
Other investment assets . .	−3,948	−2,854	−2,850
Other investment liabilities . .	3,379	1,950	1,194
Net errors and omissions . .	677	−1,591	1,477
Overall balance	9	−128	196

Source: IMF, *International Financial Statistics*.

External Trade

PRINCIPAL COMMODITIES (US $ million)*

Imports c.i.f.†	1999	2000	2001
Food and live animals . . .	1,526.9	1,534.2	1,543.8
Mineral fuels, lubricants, etc. .	1,818.1	3,247.7	2,717.9
Petroleum, petroleum products, etc.	1,807.9	3,219.0	2,702.0
Chemicals and related products	2,888.1	3,230.5	3,169.0
Basic manufactures . . .	9,542.5	10,682.2	9,227.6
Non-metallic mineral manufactures	6,250.8	7,229.4	6,056.0
Machinery and transport equipment	10,969.2	12,431.3	11,931.4
General industrial machinery, equipment and parts . .	1,178.2	1,178.2	1,126.2
Office machines and automatic data-processing machines . .	1,421.4	1,716.9	1,410.4
Telecommunications and sound equipment	1,452.8	1,667.0	1,431.6
Other electrical machinery, apparatus, etc. . . .	2,304.5	3,599.7	3,373.0
Road vehicles and parts‡ . .	1,845.7	2,315.8	2,171.9
Other transport equipment and parts‡	1,149.0	493.6	1,038.7
Miscellaneous manufactured articles	2,988.8	3,217.9	3,224.7
Total (incl. others) . . .	31,090.0	35,749.5	33,303.2

Exports f.o.b.	1999	2000	2001
Chemicals and related products	3,534.2	4,042.5	4,159.4
Organic chemicals	904.0	999.4	990.7
Basic manufactures . . .	9,375.6	11,365.9	10,513.4
Non-metallic mineral manufactures	7,853.7	9,727.5	8,857.9
Machinery and transport equipment	7,608.1	11,133.3	9,986.9
Telecommunications and sound equipment.	3,038.7	4,256.3	3,610.7
Other electrical machinery, apparatus, etc. . . .	1,554.3	3,556.0	3,192.8
Road vehicles and other transport equipment and parts‡ . .	908.9	982.5	1,025.0
Miscellaneous manufactured articles	2,889.1	3,174.8	2,948.6
Professional, scientific and controlling instruments, etc. .	718.8	934.7	921.2
Total (incl. others)	25,016.6	31,403.8	29,060.9

* The data exclude trade with the West Bank and the Gaza Strip. Including such transactions, the value of total trade (in US $ million) was: Imports c.i.f. (excl. military goods) 31,389.3 in 1999; 36,029.9 in 2000; 33,642.8 in 2001; Exports f.o.b. 27,505.3 in 1999; 32,938.6 in 2000; 30,408.5 in 2001.
† Figures exclude military goods. After deducting net returned imports, the value of total imports (in US $ million), excluding trade with the West Bank and the Gaza Strip, was: 33,165.5 in 1999; 31,404.2 in 2000; 35,464.8 in 2001 (Source: IMF, *International Financial Statistics*).
‡ Data on parts exclude tyres, engines and electrical parts.

PRINCIPAL TRADING PARTNERS (US $ million)*

Imports (excl. military goods) c.i.f.	1999	2000	2001
Belgium-Luxembourg . . .	3,527.5	3,565.2	2,655.0
China, People's Republic . . .	400.3	602.3	737.3
France	1,221.2	1,157.6	1,254.0
Germany	2,524.0	2,673.2	2,614.8
Hong Kong	635.0	898.3	805.6
India	455.0	534.8	429.5
Italy	1,657.1	1,720.7	1,651.3
Japan	1,097.0	1,186.7	1,011.8
Korea, Republic	473.8	650.0	523.7
Netherlands	1,193.6	1,436.7	1,353.7
Russia	302.4	472.6	507.1
South Africa	275.7	287.1	345.9
Spain	579.8	685.3	673.6
Sweden	342.5	411.1	422.0
Switzerland-Liechtenstein . .	1,730.2	1,918.3	1,774.7
Taiwan	406.9	570.8	430.4
Turkey	557.1	586.5	683.3
United Kingdom	2,334.3	2,714.6	2,208.5
USA	6,317.0	6,645.5	6,704.6
Total (incl. others) . . .	31,090.0	35,749.5	33,303.2

Exports	1999	2000	2001
Australia	279.5	226.5	235.6
Belgium-Luxembourg . . .	1,380.9	1,877.5	1,573.9
Brazil	241.2	320.0	392.1
China, People's Republic . . .	n.a.	261.6	349.6
France	682.4	747.4	712.7
Germany	1,161.5	1,521.4	1,288.1
Hong Kong	1,052.1	1,383.7	1,254.4
India	536.3	557.0	473.5
Italy	719.3	803.6	766.3
Japan	838.5	838.7	800.4
Korea, Republic	n.a.	396.2	322.4
Malaysia	n.a.	732.4	615.9
Netherlands	975.3	898.7	829.6
Philippines	n.a.	386.5	245.6
Singapore	239.5	327.3	261.9
Spain	431.0	436.1	506.5
Switzerland-Liechtenstein . .	358.5	501.6	343.4
Taiwan	n.a.	407.5	330.5
Thailand	n.a.	341.4	330.8
Turkey	338.3	434.4	316.5
United Kingdom	1,346.2	1,358.4	1,219.5
USA	8,750.0	11,733.6	11,111.9
Total (incl. others)	25,016.6	31,403.7	29,060.9

* Imports by country of purchase; exports by country of destination. The totals exclude trade with the West Bank and the Gaza Strip (US $ million): Imports c.i.f. 300 in 1999; 308 in 2000; 238 in 2001; Exports f.o.b. 1,712 in 1999; 1,631 in 2000; 1,163 in 2001.

Transport

RAILWAYS (traffic)

	1999	2000	2001
Freight ton-km (million) . . .	1,128	1,173	1,098
Passenger-km (million) . . .	529	781	961

ROAD TRAFFIC (motor vehicles in use at 31 December)

	1999	2000	2001
Private passenger cars . . .	1,316,765	1,396,947	1,460,851
Taxis	13,836	14,806	15,163
Minibuses	16,240	16,476	16,752
Buses and coaches . . .	11,303	11,849	11,897
Lorries, vans and road tractors	292,038	309,987	326,428
Special service vehicles . .	3,932	3,993	4,068
Motorcycles and mopeds . .	75,643	77,472	79,736

SHIPPING
Merchant Fleet (registered at 31 December)

	1999	2000	2001
Number of vessels	52	49	48
Displacement ('000 grt) . . .	728.4	611.7	611.4

Source: Lloyd's Register of Shipping, *World Fleet Statistics.*

International Sea-borne Freight Traffic ('000 metric tons)

	1999	2000	2001
Goods loaded	12,875	13,866	13,287
Goods unloaded*	28,750	29,197	29,695

* Including traffic between Israeli ports.

CIVIL AVIATION (traffic on scheduled services)

	1996	1997	1998
Kilometres flown (million) . .	74	75	79
Passengers carried ('000) . .	3,695	3,754	3,699
Passenger-km (million) . . .	11,793	11,776	12,418
Total ton-km (million) . . .	2,179	2,195	2,241

Source: UN, *Statistical Yearbook.*

Tourism

TOURIST ARRIVALS ('000)*

Country of residence	1999	2000	2001†
Canada	51.4	55.0	34.2
France	194.9	202.4	129.3
Germany	181.0	176.0	65.5
Italy	146.7	171.4	25.0
Jordan	59.8	77.9	24.6
Netherlands	90.4	91.3	43.3
Russia	55.4	35.9	55.8
Spain	35.1	65.6	11.8
Ukraine	27.9	38.0	33.5
United Kingdom	195.5	201.2	140.2
USA	515.2	488.5	266.2
Total (incl. others)	2,312.3	2,416.8	1,195.7

* Excluding arrivals of Israeli nationals residing abroad.
† Provisional figures.

Tourism receipts (US $ million): 3,971 in 1999; 3,859 in 2000; 2,460 in 2001.

Communications Media

	1999	2000	2001
Television receivers ('000 in use)	2,000	2,100	n.a.
Telephones ('000 main lines in use)	2,877	3,021	3,100
Mobile cellular telephones ('000 subscribers)	2,880	4,400	5,260
Personal computers ('000 in use)	1,360	1,590	1,600
Internet users ('000)	800	1,270	1,500

Radio receivers (1997): 3,070,000 in use.

Facsimile machines (1995): 140,000 in use.

Book production (1992): 2,310 titles (excluding government publications) and 9,368,000 copies.

Daily newspapers (1996): 34 titles (estimated circulation 1,650,000 copies).

Non-daily newspapers (1988): 80 titles.

Other periodicals (1985): 807 titles.

Sources: International Telecommunication Union; UNESCO, *Statistical Yearbook*; UN, *Statistical Yearbook*.

Education

(2001/02, unless otherwise indicated)

	Schools	Pupils	Teachers
Jewish			
Kindergarten	n.a.	295,000	n.a.
Primary schools	1,770	552,762	44,106†
Intermediate schools	502	191,927	25,635*
Secondary schools	1,064	284,549	37,922*
Vocational schools . . .	104	119,395	n.a.
Agricultural schools . . .	2	3,321	n.a.
Teacher training colleges . . .	46	30,761	n.a.
Others (handicapped) . . .	188	9,517	4,300‡
Arab			
Kindergarten	n.a.	70,000	n.a.
Primary schools	393	195,733	9,830†
Intermediate schools	112	52,338	4,398*
Secondary schools	159	54,876	4,413*
Vocational schools . . .	16	16,017	n.a.
Agricultural schools . . .	—	557	n.a.
Teacher training colleges . . .	3	3,061	n.a.
Others (handicapped) . . .	40	2,161	604‡

* 1999/2000 figures.   † 1997/98 figures.   ‡ 1996/97 figures.

Adult literacy rate (UNESCO estimates): 94.6% (males 96.8%; females 92.4%) in 2000 (Source: UN Development Programme, *Human Development Report*).

Directory

The Constitution

There is no written constitution. In June 1950 the Knesset voted to adopt a state constitution by evolution over an unspecified period. A number of laws, including the Law of Return (1950), the Nationality Law (1952), the State President (Tenure) Law (1952), the Education Law (1953) and the 'Yad-va-Shem' Memorial Law (1953), are considered as incorporated into the state Constitution. Other constitutional laws are: The Law and Administration Ordinance (1948), the Knesset Election Law (1951), the Law of Equal Rights for Women (1951), the Judges Act (1953), the National Service and National Insurance Acts (1953), and the Basic Law (The Knesset) (1958). The provisions of constitutional legislation that affect the main organs of government are summarized below:

THE PRESIDENT

The President is elected by the Knesset for a maximum of two five-year terms.*

Ten or more Knesset members may propose a candidate for the Presidency.

Voting will be by secret ballot.

The President may not leave the country without the consent of the Government.

The President may resign by submitting his resignation in writing to the Speaker.

The President may be relieved of his duties by the Knesset for misdemeanour.

The Knesset is entitled to decide by a two-thirds majority that the President is too incapacitated owing to ill health to fulfil his duties permanently.

The Speaker of the Knesset will act for the President when the President leaves the country, or when he cannot perform his duties owing to ill health.

* Moshe Katsav was elected to the presidency on 31 July 2000 for a seven-year term of office.

THE KNESSET

The Knesset is the parliament of the state. There are 120 members.

It is elected by general, national, direct, equal, secret and proportional elections.

Every Israeli national of 18 years or over shall have the right to vote in elections to the Knesset unless a court has deprived him of that right by virtue of any law.

Every Israeli national of 21 and over shall have the right to be elected to the Knesset unless a court has deprived him of that right by virtue of any law.

The following shall not be candidates: the President of the State; the two Chief Rabbis; a judge (shofet) in office; a judge (dayan) of a religious court; the State Comptroller; the Chief of the General Staff of the Defence Army of Israel; rabbis and ministers of other religions in office; senior state employees and senior army officers of such ranks and in such functions as shall be determined by law.

The term of office of the Knesset shall be four years.

The elections to the Knesset shall take place on the third Tuesday of the month of Marcheshvan in the year in which the tenure of the outgoing Knesset ends.

Election day shall be a day of rest, but transport and other public services shall function normally.

Results of the elections shall be published within 14 days.

The Knesset shall elect from among its members a Chairman and Vice-Chairman.

The Knesset shall elect from among its members permanent committees, and may elect committees for specific matters.

The Knesset may appoint commissions of inquiry to investigate matters designated by the Knesset.

The Knesset shall hold two sessions a year; one of them shall open within four weeks after the Feast of the Tabernacles, the other within four weeks after Independence Day; the aggregate duration of the two sessions shall not be less than eight months.

The outgoing Knesset shall continue to hold office until the convening of the incoming Knesset.

The members of the Knesset shall receive a remuneration as provided by law.

THE GOVERNMENT

The Government shall tender its resignation to the President immediately after his election, but shall continue with its duties until the formation of a new government. After consultation with representatives of the parties in the Knesset, the President shall charge one of the members with the formation of a government. The Government shall be composed of a Prime Minister (directly elected from May 1996, but from 2003 to revert to the previous system of election on a party basis) and a number of ministers from among the Knesset members or from outside the Knesset. After it has been chosen, the Government shall appear before the Knesset and shall be considered as formed after having received a vote of confidence. Within seven days of receiving a vote of confidence, the Prime Minister and the other ministers shall swear allegiance to the State of Israel and its Laws and undertake to carry out the decisions of the Knesset.

The Government

HEAD OF STATE

President: MOSHE KATSAV (took office 1 August 2000).

THE CABINET
(September 2002)

A coalition of Likud, Labour, Shas, Israel B'Aliyah, the Centre Party, Am Ehad and the National Religious Party (NRP).

Prime Minister and Minister of Immigrant Absorption, of National Infrastructure and of Tourism: ARIEL SHARON (Likud).

Deputy Prime Minister and Minister of Foreign Affairs: SHIMON PERES (Labour).

Deputy Prime Minister and Minister of Finance: SILVAN SHALOM (Likud).

Deputy Prime Minister and Minister of Construction and Housing: NATAN SHARANSKY (Israel B'Aliyah).

Deputy Prime Minister and Minister of the Interior: ELIYAHU YISHAI (Shas).

Minister of Defence: BINYAMIN BEN-ELIEZER (Labour).

Minister of Labour and Social Affairs: SHLOMO BENIZRI (Shas).

Minister of Health: NISSIM DAHAN (Shas).

Minister of the Environment: TZACHI HANEGBI (Likud).

Minister of Industry and Trade: DALIA ITZIK (Labour).

Minister of Education: LIMOR LIVNAT (Likud).

Minister of Regional Co-operation: RONI MILO (Centre Party).

Minister of Public Security: UZI LANDAU (Likud).

Minister of Religious Affairs: ASHER OHANA (Shas).

Minister of Communications: REUVEN RIVLIN (Likud).

Minister of Justice: MEIR SHEETRIT (Likud).

Minister of Agriculture and Rural Development: SHALOM SIMHON (Labour).

Minister of Transport: EPHRAIM SNEH (Labour).

Minister of Science, Culture and Sport: MATAN VILNAI (Labour).

Minister without Portfolio, responsible for Social Affairs Co-ordination: SHMUEL AVITAL (Am Ehad).

Minister without Portfolio, responsible for Government-Knesset Liaison: DAN NAVEH (Likud).

Ministers without Portfolio: RA'ANAN COHEN (Labour), TZIPI LIVNI (Likud), DAN MERIDOR (Centre Party), EFRAIM EITAM (NRP), ITZHAK LEVY (NRP), ELIYAHU SUISSA (Shas).

MINISTRIES

Office of the Prime Minister: POB 187, 3 Rehov Kaplan, Kiryat Ben-Gurion, Jerusalem 91919; tel. 2-6705511; fax 2-6512631; e-mail webmaster@pmo.gov.il; internet www.pmo.gov.il.

Ministry of Agriculture and Rural Development: POB 30, 14 Arnia St, Hakirya, Tel-Aviv 50200; tel. 3-9485561; fax 3-9485870; e-mail webmaster@moag.gov.il; internet www.moag.gov.il.

Ministry of Communications: 23 Jaffa St, Jerusalem 91999; tel. 2-6706320; fax 2-6706372; internet www.moc.gov.il.

Ministry of Construction and Housing: POB 18110, Kiryat Hamemshala (East), Jerusalem 91180; tel. 2-5847654; fax 2-5847250; e-mail webmaster@moch.gov.il; internet www.moch.gov.il.

Ministry of Defence: Kaplan St, Hakirya, Tel-Aviv 67659; tel. 3-5692010; fax 3-6916940; e-mail public@mod.gov.il; internet www.mod.gov.il.

Ministry of Education: POB 292, 34 Shivtei Israel St, Jerusalem 91911; tel. 2-5602222; fax 2-5602752; e-mail info@education.gov.il; internet www.education.gov.il.

Ministry of the Environment: POB 34033, 5 Kanfei Nesharim St, Givat Shaul, Jerusalem 95464; tel. 2-6553745; fax 2-6553752; e-mail ori@sviva.gov.il; internet www.sviva.gov.il.

Ministry of Finance: POB 13191, 1 Rehov Kaplan, Kiryat Ben-Gurion, Jerusalem 91008; tel. 2-5317111; fax 2-5637891; e-mail webmaster@mof.gov.il; internet www.mof.gov.il.

Ministry of Foreign Affairs: Hakirya, Romema, Jerusalem 91950; tel. 2-5303111; fax 2-5303367; e-mail ask@israel-info.gov.il; internet www.mfa.gov.il.

Ministry of Health: POB 1176, 2 Ben-Tabai St, Jerusalem 91010; tel. 2-6705705; fax 2-6796267; e-mail yonit.mor@moh.health.gov.il; internet www.health.gov.il.

Ministry of Immigrant Absorption: POB 13061, 13 Rehov Kaplan, Kiryat Ben-Gurion, Jerusalem 91006; tel. 2-6752696; fax 2-5618138; e-mail info@moia.gov.il; internet www.moia.gov.il.

Ministry of Industry and Trade: POB 299, 30 Rehov Agron, Jerusalem 94190; tel. 2-6220661; fax 2-6222412; e-mail dover@moit.gov.il; internet www.tamas.gov.il.

Ministry of the Interior: POB 6158, 2 Rehov Kaplan, Kiryat Ben-Gurion, Jerusalem 91008; tel. 2-6701411; fax 2-6701628; e-mail pniot@moin.gov.il; internet www.moin.gov.il.

Ministry of Justice: POB 1087, 29 Rehov Salahadin, Jerusalem 91010; tel. 2-6466666; fax 2-6287757; e-mail pniot@justice.gov.il; internet www.justice.gov.il.

Ministry of Labour and Social Affairs: POB 915, 2 Rehov Kaplan, Kiryat Ben-Gurion, Jerusalem 91008; tel. 2-6752311; fax 2-6752803; e-mail sar@molsa.gov.il.

Ministry of National Infrastructure: Ala Bldg, 216 Jaffa St, Jerusalem; e-mail pniot@mmi.gov.il; internet www.mni.gov.il; also responsible for **Israel Lands Administration:** POB 2600, 6 Shamai St, Jerusalem 94631; tel. 2-6208422; fax 2-6234960; e-mail pniot@mmi.gov.il; internet www.mmi.gov.il.

Ministry of Public Security: POB 18182, Bldg 3, Kiryat Hamemshala (East), Jerusalem 91181; tel. 2-5308003; fax 2-5847872; e-mail mops@netvision.net.il.

Ministry of Regional Co-operation: 8 Shaul Hamelech Blvd, Tel-Aviv 64733; tel. 3-6086111; fax 3-6086126; e-mail m_r_c@netvision.net.il; internet www.mrc.gov.il.

Ministry of Religious Affairs: POB 13059, 7 Kanfei Nesharim St, Jerusalem 95464; tel. 2-5311182; fax 2-6513679; e-mail dover@religions.gov.il; internet www.religions.gov.il.

Ministry of Science, Culture and Sport: POB 49100, Kiryat Hamemshala, Hamizrachit, Bldg 3, Jerusalem 91490; tel. 2-5411100; fax 2-5811613; e-mail nps@most.gov.il; internet www.most.gov.il.

Ministry of Tourism: POB 1018, 24 Rehov King George, Jerusalem 91009; tel. 2-6754811; fax 2-6253407; e-mail pniot@tourism.gov.il; internet www.tourism.gov.il.

Ministry of Transport: Klal Bldg, 97 Jaffa St, Jerusalem 91000; tel. 2-6228211; fax 2-6228693; e-mail pniot@mot.gov.il; internet www.mot.gov.il.

Legislature

KNESSET

Speaker: AVRAHAM BURG.

General Election, 17 May 1999

Party	Valid votes cast	% of valid votes	Seats
Israel Ahat (One Israel) .	670,484	20.3	26
Likud	468,103	14.1	19
Shas	430,676	13.0	17
Meretz-Democratic Israel	253,525	7.7	10
Israel B'Aliyah . .	171,705	5.2	6
Shinui	167,748	5.1	6
Centre Party . . .	165,622	5.0	6
National Religious Party .	140,307	4.2	5
United Torah Judaism .	125,741	3.8	5
United Arab List . .	114,810	3.5	5
Haichud Haleumi (National Unity)	100,181	3.0	4
Hadash	87,022	2.6	3
Israel B'Aitainu (Israel Is Our Home) . . .	86,153	2.6	4
Balad (National Democratic Alliance) . . .	66,103	2.0	2
Am Ehad (One Nation) . .	64,143	1.9	2
Others*	197,093	6.0	—
Total	**3,309,416†**	**100.0**	**120**

* Including Penina Rosenblum (1.4%), Koah Lagimlaim (Power for Pensioners—1.1%), Mifleget Aleh Yarok (Green Leaf Party—1.0%), Third Way (0.8%), Ha Yerukim (Green Party—0.4%), Tiqva (Hope—0.2%), Casino Party (0.2%), Lev-Olim (Immigrants for Israel—0.2%), Negev Party (0.1%), Tzomet—Movement for Renewed Zionism (0.1%).
† Excluding 64,332 invalid votes.

According to Israel's General Election Committee, 78.7% of the 4.3m.-strong electorate participated in the legislative elections held on 17 May 1999. Voting to select the leader of the government took place at the same time as elections to the Knesset (the position of Prime Minister having become elective in 1996). Following the resignation of Ehud Barak on 10 December 2000, a special election for Prime Minister was held on 6 February 2001—the first time that a premiership election had been held separately from legislative elections. Ariel Sharon, leader of Likud, secured 62.38% (1,698,077) of the valid votes cast, defeating the incumbent Prime Minister and leader of the Labour Party and its Israel Ahat (One Israel) alliance, Ehud Barak, who received 37.62% (1,023,944). The rate of voter participation was reported to be 62.3%.

Political Organizations

Agudat Israel: POB 513, Jerusalem; tel. 2-385251; fax 2-385145; orthodox Jewish party; stands for strict observance of Jewish religious law; Leaders AVRAHAM SHAPIRO, MENACHEM PORUSH.

Agudat Israel World Organization (AIWO): POB 326, Hacherut Sq., Jerusalem 91002; tel. 2-5384357; fax 2-5383634; f. 1912 at Congress of Orthodox Jewry, Kattowitz, Germany (now Katowice, Poland), to help solve the problems facing Jewish people worldwide; more than 500,000 mems in 25 countries; Chair. Rabbi J. M. ABRA-MOWITZ (Jerusalem); Secs Rabbi MOSHE GEWIRTZ, Rabbi CHAIM WEIN-STOCK.

Am Ehad (One Nation): Workers' and pensioners' party affiliated to Histadrut trade union federation; Leader AMIR PERETZ.

Balad (National Democratic Alliance): f. 1999; united Arab party; Leader AZMI BISHARA.

Centre Party: f. 1999; centrist electoral list, formed as an alternative to Likud and the Israel Labour Party; concerned primarily with the peace process and relations between religious and secular Jews; Leader DAN MERIDOR.

Council for Peace and Security: f. 1988 by four retd Israeli generals: Maj.-Gen. AHARON YARIV, Maj.-Gen. ORI ORR, Brig.-Gen. YORAM AGMON and Brig.-Gen. EPHRAIM SNEH; MOSHE AMIRAV of Shinui a founder mem.; aims: an Israeli withdrawal from the Occupied Territories in return for a peace treaty with the Arab nations.

Degel Hatora: 103 Rehov Beit Vegan, Jerusalem; tel. 2-6438106; fax 2-6418967; f. 1988 as breakaway from Agudat Israel; orthodox Western Jews; Chair. AVRAHAM RAVITZ.

Democratic Arab Party (DAP): Nazareth; tel. 6-6560937; fax 6-6560938; e-mail dap@g-ol.com; f. 1988; aims: to unify Arab political forces so as to influence Palestinian and Israeli policy; international recognition of the Palestinian people's right to self-determination; the withdrawal of Israel from all territories occupied in 1967, including East Jerusalem; the DAP also aims to achieve full civil equality between Arab and Jewish citizens of Israel, to eliminate discrimination and improve the social, economic and political conditions of the Arab minority in Israel; contested the 1999 elections as part of the coalition of the United Arab List; Dir MUHAMMAD DARAWSHE.

Gesher (Bridge): internet www.gesher.org.il; f. 1996; Leader DAVID LEVY.

Gush Emunim (Bloc of the Faithful): f. 1967; engaged in unauthorized establishment of Jewish settlements in the Occupied Territories; Leader Rabbi MOSHE LEVINGER.

Hadash (Democratic Front for Peace and Equality—Communist Party of Israel): 5 Hess St, Tel-Aviv; tel. 3-6293944; fax 3-6297263; e-mail maki@maki.org.il; internet www.maki.org.il; descended from the Socialist Workers' Party of Palestine (f. 1919); renamed Communist Party of Palestine 1921, Communist Party of Israel (Maki) 1948; pro-Soviet anti-Zionist group formed New Communist Party of Israel (Rakah) 1965; Jewish Arab membership; aims for a socialist system in Israel, a lasting peace between Israel and the Arab countries and the Palestinian Arab people, favours full implementation of UN Security Council Resolutions 242 and 338, Israeli withdrawal from all Arab territories occupied since 1967, formation of a Palestinian Arab state in the West Bank and Gaza Strip (with East Jerusalem as its capital), recognition of national rights of State of Israel and Palestinian people, democratic rights and defence of working class interests, and demands an end to discrimination against Arab minority in Israel and against oriental Jewish communities; Sec. (Hadash) ODDE BSHARAT; Gen. Sec. (Communist Party) MUHAMMAD NAFAH.

Haichud Haleumi (National Unity): f. 1999; right-wing coalition comprising Herut, Moledet and Tekuma parties; in February 2000 Herut withdrew from the coalition, which subsequently merged with Israel B'Aitainu; Leader (vacant).

Herut (Freedom): f. 1948, reconstituted 1998; right-wing nationalist party; opposed to further Israeli withdrawal from the Occupied Territories; Leader ZE'EV BINYAMIN (BENNY) BEGIN.

Israel B'Aitainu (Israel Is Our Home): f. 1999; right-wing immigrant party, formed as a rival to Israel B'Aliyah; Leader AVIGDOR LIEBERMAN.

Israel B'Aliyah: f. 1995; campaigns for immigrants' rights; Leader NATAN SHARANSKY.

Israel Labour Party: POB 62033, Tel-Aviv 61620; tel. 3-6899444; fax 3-6899420; e-mail avoda@inter.net.il; f. 1968 as a merger of the three Labour groups, Mapai, Rafi and Achdut Ha'avoda; a Zionist democratic socialist party; Chair. BINYAMIN BEN-ELIEZER; Sec.-Gen. RA'ANAN COHEN.

Kahane Chai (Kahane Lives): 111 Agripas St, Jerusalem; tel. 2-231081; f. 1977 as 'Kach' (Thus); right-wing religious nationalist party; advocates creation of a Torah state and expulsion of all Arabs from Israel and the annexation of the Occupied Territories; Leader (vacant).

Likud (Consolidation): 38 Rehov King George, Tel-Aviv 61231; tel. 3-5630666; fax 3-5282901; internet www.likud.org.il; f. September 1973; fmrly a parliamentary bloc of Herut (Freedom; f. 1948; Leader ITZHAK SHAMIR; Sec.-Gen. MOSHE ARENS), the Liberal Party of Israel (f. 1961; Chair. AVRAHAM SHARIR), Laam (For the Nation) (f. 1976; fmrly led by YIGAEL HURWITZ, who left the coalition to form his own party, Ometz, before the 1984 general election), Ahdut (a one-man faction, HILLEL SEIDEL), Tami (f. 1981; represents the interests of Sephardic Jews; Leader AHARON UZAN), which joined Likud in June 1987, and an independent faction (f. 1990; Leader ITZHAK MODAI), which formed the nucleus of a new Party for the Advancement of the Zionist Idea; Herut and the Liberal Party formally merged in August 1988 to form the Likud-National Liberal Movement; aims: territorial integrity (advocates retention of all the territory of post-1922 mandatory Palestine); absorption of newcomers; a social order based on freedom and justice, elimination of poverty and want; development of an economy that will ensure a decent standard of living; improvement of the environment and the quality of life; Leader of Likud ARIEL SHARON.

Meimad: internet www.meimad.org.il; moderate Jewish party; Leader Rabbi MICHAEL MELCHIOR.

Meretz (Vitality): Tel-Aviv; tel. 3-6360111; fax 3-5375107; e-mail information@meretz.org.il; internet www.meretz.org.il; an alliance of Ratz, Shinui and the United Workers' Party; stands for civil rights, electoral reform, welfarism, Palestinian self-determination, separation of religion from the state and a halt to settlement in the Occupied Territories; Leader YOSSI SARID.

Moledet (Homeland): 14 Rehov Yehuda Halevi, Tel-Aviv; tel. 3-654580; internet www.moledet.org.il; f. 1988; right-wing nationalist party; aims: the expulsion ('transfer') of the 1.5m. Palestinians living in the West Bank and Gaza Strip; united with Tehiya—Zionist Revival Movement in June 1994 as the Moledet—the Eretz Israel Faithful and the Tehiya; Leader Rabbi BINYAMIN (BENNY) ELON.

Movement for the Advancement of the Zionist Idea (MAZI): f. 1990 as breakaway group of Likud; Leader ITZHAK MODAI.

National Religious Party (NRP): Jerusalem; tel. 2-377277; fax 2-377757; f. 1902; as the Mizrachi Organization within the Zionist Movement; present name adopted in 1956; stands for strict adherence to Jewish religion and tradition, and strives to achieve the application of religious precepts of Judaism in everyday life; it is also endeavouring to establish a Constitution for Israel based on Jewish religious law (the Torah); 126,000 mems; Leader EFRAIM EITAM; Sec.-Gen. ZEVULUN ORLEV.

New Liberal Party: Tel-Aviv; f. 1987 as a merger of three groups: Shinui-Movement for Change (f. 1974 and restored 1978, when Democratic Movement for Change split into two parties; centrist; Leader AMNON RUBINSTEIN), the Centre Liberal Party (f. 1986 by members of the Liberal Party of Israel; Leader ITZHAK BERMAN), and the Independent Liberal Party (f. 1965 by seven Liberal Party of Israel Knesset mems, after the formation of the Herut Movement and Liberal Party of Israel bloc; 20,000 mems; Chair. MOSHE KOL; Gen. Sec. NISSIM ELIAD); Leaders AMNON RUBINSTEIN, ITZHAK BERMAN and MOSHE KOL.

Poale Agudat Israel: f. 1924; working-class Orthodox Judaist party; Leader Dr KALMAN KAHANE.

Political Zionist Opposition (Ometz): f. 1982; one-man party, YIGAEL HURWITZ.

Progressive List for Peace: 5 Simtat Lane, Nes Tziona, Tel-Aviv; tel. 3-662457; fax 3-659474; f. 1984; Jewish-Arab; advocates recognition of the PLO and the establishment of a Palestinian state in the West Bank and Gaza Strip; Leader MUHAMMAD MI'ARI.

Ratz (Civil Rights and Peace Movement): 21 Tchernihovsky St, Tel-Aviv 63291; tel. 3-5254847; fax 3-5255008; f. 1973; concerned with human and civil rights, opposes discrimination on basis of religion, gender or ethnic identification and advocates a peace settlement with the Arab countries and the Palestinians; Leader Mrs SHULAMIT ALONI.

Shahar (Dawn): f. 2002; left-wing movement which seeks to guarantee the 'Jewish and democratic existence of Israel, based on peace and social justice'; Founder YOSSI BEILIN.

Shas (Sephardic Torah Guardians): Beit Abodi, Rehov Hahida, Bene Beraq; tel. 3-579776; f. 1984 by splinter groups from Agudat

Israel; ultra-orthodox Jewish party; Spiritual Leader Rabbi OVADIA YOSEF; Leader ELIYAHU YISHAI.

Shinui (Change): POB 20533, 100 Ha' Hashmonaim St, Tel-Aviv 67133; tel. 3-5620118; fax 3-5620139; e-mail shinui@shinui.org.il; internet www.shinui.org.il; f. 1974 as a new liberal party; combines an anti-religious coercion policy with a free-market economic philosophy; Leaders JOSEPH (TOMMY) LAPID, AVRAHAM PORAZ.

Third Way: f. 1995; opposed to any transfer of the Golan Heights to Syria; Leader AVIGDOR KAHALANI.

Tiqva (Hope): f. 1999; campaigns for rights of new immigrants from former USSR; Leader ALEX TENCHER.

Tzomet (Crossroads): 22 Rehov Huberman, Tel-Aviv; tel. 3-204444; f. 1988; right-wing nationalist party; breakaway group from Tehiya party; Leader RAFAEL EITAN.

United Arab List: Arab party affiliated to Labour Party.

United Torah Judaism: electoral list of four minor ultra-orthodox parties (Moria, Degel Hatora, Poale Agudat Israel, Agudat Israel) formed, prior to 1992 election, to overcome the increase in election threshold from 1% to 1.5% and help to counter the rising influence of the secular Russian vote; contested 1999 election comprised of Degel Hatora and Agudat Israel.

United Workers' Party (Mapam): POB 1777, 2 Homa U'Migdal St, Tel-Aviv; tel. 3-6360111; fax 3-5375107; f. 1948; left-wing socialist-Zionist Jewish-Arab party; grouped in Labour-Mapam Alignment with Israel Labour Party from January 1969 until Sept. 1984 when it withdrew in protest over Labour's formation of a Government with Likud; member of the Socialist International; 77,000 mems; Chair. CHANAN EREZ; Sec.-Gen. VICTOR BLIT.

Yahad (Together): f. 1984; advocates a peace settlement with the Arab peoples and the Palestinians; joined the Labour Party parliamentary bloc in January 1987.

Yi'ud: f. 1994; breakaway group from the Tzomet Party.

Other parties that contested the 1999 general election included Atid (Future; Leader RONI MILO), Casino Party (Leader EZRA TISSUNA), Organization for Democratic Action, Ale-Yarok (Green Leaf Party), Ha Yerukim (Green Party; Leader DEDI ZUCKER), Ihud Aravi (Arab Unity), Koah Lagimlaim (Power for Pensioners; Leader GIDEON BEN-ISRAEL), Lev-Olim (Immigrants for Israel), Men's Family Rights, Moreshet Avot (Tradition of the Fathers), Natural Law Party, New Arab Party (Leader MAKRAM HURI MAHUL), Penina Rosenblum, Progressive Centre Party (for Romanian immigrants), Tekuma (Revival; Leaders URI ARIEL, NATAN NATHANSON, BENI KATZOVER).

Diplomatic Representation

EMBASSIES IN ISRAEL

Argentina: Apt 3, Medinat Hayeudim 85, Herzliya Business Park, Herzliya; tel. 9-9702743; fax 9-9702748; e-mail embarg@netvision .net.il; Ambassador: GREGORIO JOSÉ DUPONT.

Australia: Beit Europa, 4th Floor, 37 Shaul Hamelech Blvd, Tel-Aviv 64928; tel. 3-6950451; fax 3-6968404; Ambassador: ROSS BURNS.

Austria: Beit Crystal, 12 Hahilazon, Ramat-Gan, Tel-Aviv 52522; tel. 3-6120924; fax 3-7510716; e-mail autambta@netvision.net.il; Ambassador: Dr WOLFGANG PAUL.

Belarus: 2 Rehov Kaufman, Tel-Aviv 68012; tel. 3-5102236; fax 3-5102235; Ambassador: MIKHAIL FARFEL.

Belgium: 12 Hahilazon, Ramat-Gan, Tel-Aviv 52522; tel. 3-6138130; fax 3-6138160; e-mail telaviv@diplobel.org; Ambassador: WILFRIED GEENS.

Bolivia: Toyota Bldg, 65 Rehov Yigal Alon, 13A/2, Tel-Aviv 67443; tel. 3-5621992; fax 3-5621990; e-mail embolivia-telaviv@emb.co.il; Ambassador: Dr VÍCTOR TORRES ACHA.

Brazil: 2 Rehov Kaplan, Beit Yachin, 8th Floor, Tel-Aviv 64734; tel. 3-6919292; fax 3-6916060; Ambassador: JOSÉ NOGUEIRA FILHO.

Bulgaria: 4th Floor, 21 Leonardo da Vinci St, Tel-Aviv 64733; tel. 3-6961361; fax 3-6961430; e-mail bgemtlv@hotmail.com; Ambassador: Prof. TSANKO YABLANSKI.

Cameroon: Tel-Aviv; tel. 3-5298401; fax 3-5298249; Chargé d'affaires a.i.: HENRI ETOUNDI ESSOMBA.

Canada: 3 Nirim St, Tel-Aviv; tel. 3-6363300; fax 3-6363385; Ambassador: MICHAEL D. BELL.

Chile: 4 Rehov Kaufman, Tel-Aviv 68012; tel. 3-5102751; fax 3-5100102; e-mail echileil@inter.net.il; Ambassador: SALLY BENDERSKY SCHACHNER.

China, People's Republic: Tel-Aviv; Ambassador: PAN ZHALIN.

Colombia: 52 Rehov Pinkas, Apt 26, Tel-Aviv 62261; tel. 3-5461717; fax 3-5461404; e-mail emcolis@netvision.net.il; Ambassador: DAVID DE LA ROSA PEREZ.

Congo, Democratic Republic: Apt 5, 60 Hei Be'Iyar, Kikar Hamedina, Tel-Aviv 62198; tel. 3-452681; Ambassador: Gen. ELUKI MONGA AUNDU.

Costa Rica: 13 Rehov Diskin, Apt 1, Kiryat Wolfson, Jerusalem 92473; tel. 2-5666197; fax 2-5632591; e-mail emcri@netmedia .net.il; Ambassador: RODRIGO X. CARRERAS.

Côte d'Ivoire: South Africa Bldg, 25 Bezalel St, Ramat-Gan, Tel-Aviv 52521; tel. 3-6126677; fax 3-6126688; e-mail ambacita@ netvision.net.il; Ambassador: LÉON H. KACOU ADOM.

Cyprus: 14th Floor, Top Tower, Dizengoff Centre, 50 Dizengoff St, Tel-Aviv 64322; tel. 3-5250212; fax 3-6290535; e-mail cyprus@ netvision.net.il.

Czech Republic: POB 16361, 23 Rehov Zeitlin, Tel-Aviv 61664; tel. 3-6918282; fax 3-6918286; e-mail telaviv@embassy.mzv.cz; internet www.mfa.cz/telaviv; Ambassador DANIEL KUMERMANN.

Denmark: POB 21080, 23 Rehov Bnei Moshe, Tel-Aviv 61210; tel. 3-5442144; fax 3-5465502; e-mail tlvamb@um.dk; internet www.dk -embassy.org.il; Ambassador: HANS MICHAEL KOFOED-HANSEN.

Dominican Republic: 19 Soutine St, Tel-Aviv 64684; tel. 3-5277073; fax 3-5277074; e-mail embajdom@netvision.net.il; Ambassador: Dr MANUEL MORALES-LAMA.

Ecuador: Asia House, 4 Rehov Weizman, Tel-Aviv 64239; tel. 3-6958764; fax 3-6913604; e-mail mecuaisr@infolink.net.il; Ambassador: LEONARDO RUILOVA.

Egypt: 54 Rehov Bazel, Tel-Aviv 62744; tel. 3-5464151; fax 3-5441615; e-mail egypem.ta@zahav.net.il; Chargé d'affaires Dr IHAB ESH-SHARIF (Ambassador withdrawn in Nov. 2000).

El Salvador: POB 4005, Jerusalem 91039; tel. 2-6728411; fax 2-6733641; e-mail embasal@inter.net.il; internet www.el-salvador .org.il; Ambassador: ERNESTO ARRIETA PERALTA.

Ethiopia: 48 Darech Petach Tikva, Tel-Aviv 66184; tel. 3-6397831; fax 3-6397837; e-mail ethembis@netvision.net.il; Ambassador: FIT ZEWDIE OTTORO.

Finland: POB 39666, 40 Einstein St, Tel-Aviv 69101; tel. 3-7440303; fax 3-7440314; e-mail sanomat.tel@formin.fi; Ambassador: PASI PATOKALLIO.

France: 112 Tayelet Herbert Samuel, Tel-Aviv 63572; tel. 3-5208300; fax 3-5208342; e-mail diplomatie@ambafrance-il.org; internet www.ambafrance-il.org; Ambassador: JACQUES HUNTZINGER.

Germany: POB 16038, 19th Floor, 3 Rehov Daniel Frisch, Tel-Aviv 61160; tel 3-6931313; fax 3-6969217; e-mail ger_emb@netvision .net.il; internet www.germanemb.org.il; Ambassador: RUDOLF DRESSLER.

Greece: 3 Daniel Frisch St, Tel-Aviv 64731; tel. 3-6953060; fax 3-6951329; e-mail gremil@netvision.net.il; Ambassador: Dr SOTIRIOS VAROUXAKIS.

Guatemala: Ackerstein Bldg, 103 Medinat Hayeudim, Herzliya Pituach, Herzliya B. 46130; tel. 9-9577335; fax 9-9518506; Ambassador: MARCO TULIO ZÚÑIGA.

Haiti: Tel-Aviv 64336; tel. 3-280285; Ambassador: FRANCK M. JOSEPH.

Holy See: POB 19199, Jerusalem 91191; tel. 2-6282298; fax 2-6281880; e-mail vatge@netvision.net.il; Apostolic Nuncio: Mgr PIETRO SAMBI, Titular Archbishop of Belcastro.

Honduras: Zohar Tal 1, Herziya Pituach, Tel-Aviv 46741; tel. 9-9577686; fax 9-9577457; e-mail honduras@netvision.net.il; Ambassador: FRANCISCO ZEPEDA ANDINO.

Hungary: 18 Rehov Pinkas, Tel-Aviv 62661; tel. 3-5466860; fax 3-5468968; Ambassador: Dr JÁNOS HÓVÁRI.

India: 4 Rehov Kaufman, Tel-Aviv; tel. 3-5101431; fax 3-5101434; e-mail indemtel@indembassy.co.il; Ambassador: R. S. JASSAL.

Ireland: 17th Floor, The Tower, 3 Daniel Frisch St, Tel-Aviv 64731; tel. 3-6964166; Ambassador: PATRICK HENNESSY.

Italy: Asia House, 4 Rehov Weizman, Tel-Aviv 64239; tel. 3-6964223; fax 3-6918428; e-mail italemb@netvision.net.il; internet www .italian-embassy-israel.org; Ambassador: GIAN PAOLO CAVARAI.

Japan: Asia House, 4 Rehov Weizman, Tel-Aviv 64239; tel. 3-6957292; fax 3-6910516; Ambassador: HIROSHI SHIGETA.

Jordan: 14 Abba Hillel, Ramat-Gan, Tel-Aviv 52506; tel. 3-7517722; fax 3-7517712; e-mail jordan1@barak.net.il; Chargé d'affaires a.i.: Dr MAZEN TAL.

Kazakhstan: 185 Rehov Hayarkon, Tel-Aviv 63453; tel. 3-5236776; fax 3-5239045; e-mail embacy@internet-zahav.net; Ambassador: BYRGANYM AITIMOVA.

Korea, Republic: 38 Sderot Chen, Tel-Aviv 64166; tel. 3-6963244; fax 3-6963243; Ambassador: LEE CHANG-HO.

Latvia: 9 Marmorek St, Tel-Aviv 64254; tel. 3-6869544; fax 3-6869543; e-mail latvembi@netvision.net.il; Ambassador: JĀNIS LOVNIKS.

Liberia: 6 Shimon Frug, Ramat-Gan, Tel-Aviv 524282; tel. 3-728525; Ambassador: Maj. SAMUEL B. PEARSON, Jr.

Lithuania: 14th Floor, Top Tower, Dizengoff Centre, Tel-Aviv 64332; tel. 3-5288514; fax 3-5257265; e-mail lrambizr@netvision .net.il; Ambassador: ALFONSAS EIDINTAS.

Mauritania: Tel-Aviv; Ambassador: AHMAD OULD TEGUEDDI.

Mexico: 25 Hamered St, 5th Floor, Trade Tower, Tel-Aviv 68125; tel. 3-5163938; fax 3-5163711; e-mail embamex@netvision.net.il; Ambassador: ANDRES VALENCIA BENAVIDE.

Myanmar: 26 Rehov Hayarkon, Tel-Aviv 68011; tel. 3-5170760; fax 3-5171440; e-mail teltaman@classnet.co.il; Ambassador: U TIN WIN.

Netherlands: Asia House, 4 Rehov Weizman, Tel-Aviv 64239; tel. 3-6910036; fax 3-6910071; e-mail tel-cdp@minbuza.nl; Ambassador: H. R. R. V. FROGER.

Nigeria: POB 3339, 34 Gordon St, Tel-Aviv 61030; tel. 3-5222144; fax 3-5237886; Ambassador: E. EGBARA.

Norway: POB 17575, 40 Einstein St, Tel-Aviv 69101; tel. 3-7441490; fax 3-7441498; e-mail norambta@netvision.net.il; Ambassador: MONA JUUL.

Panama: 10 Rehov Hei Be'Iyar, Kikar Hamedina, Tel-Aviv 62998; tel. 3-6960849; fax 3-6910045; Ambassador: Prof. PAULINO C. ROMERO.

Peru: 37 Rehov Hamarganit, Shikun Vatikin, Ramat-Gan, Tel-Aviv 52584; tel. 3-6135591; fax 3-7512286; e-mail emperu@netvision .net.il; Ambassador: NICOLAS RONCAGLIOLO.

Philippines: POB 50085, 13th Floor, Textile Centre Bldg, 2 Rehov Kaufman, Tel-Aviv 68012; tel. 3-5175263; fax 3-5102229; e-mail filembis@netvision.net.il; Ambassador: ROSALINDA DE PERIO-SANTOS.

Poland: 16 Soutine St, Tel-Aviv 64684; tel. 3-5240186; fax 3-5237806; e-mail embpol@netvision.net.il; Ambassador: MACIEJ KOZŁOWSKI.

Portugal: 4 Daniel Frisch St, Tel-Aviv 64731; tel. 3-6956373; fax 3-6956366; e-mail eptel@netvision.net.il; Ambassador: ANTÓNIO TÂNGER CORRÊA.

Romania: 24 Rehov Adam Hacohen, Tel-Aviv 64585; tel. 3-5230066; fax 3-5247379; e-mail ambtaviv@zahav.net.il; Ambassador: VALERIA MARIANA STOICA.

Russia: 120 Rehov Hayarkon, Tel-Aviv 63573; tel. 3-5226736; fax 3-5226713; e-mail amb_ru@mail.netvision.net.il; internet www .israel.mid.ru; Ambassador: MIKHAIL BOGDANOV.

Slovakia: POB 6459, 37 Jabotinsky St, Tel-Aviv 61064; tel. 3-5440066; fax 3-5449144; Ambassador Dr MAROŠ ŠEFČOVIĆ.

Slovenia: Tel-Aviv; Ambassador: PETER TOS.

South Africa: POB 7138, 16th Floor, Top Tower, 50 Dizengoff St, Tel-Aviv 61071; tel. 3-5252566; fax 3-5252530; e-mail saemtel@ isdn.net.il; internet www.safis.co.il; Ambassador: JOHANN MARX.

Spain: Dubnov Tower, 3 Rehov Daniel Frisch, 16th Floor, Tel-Aviv 64731; tel. 3-6965218; fax 3-6965217; Ambassador: FERMÍN ZELADA JURADO.

Sweden: Asia House, 4 Rehov Weizman, Tel-Aviv 64239; tel. 3-6958111; fax 3-6958116; e-mail swembtlv@trendline.co.il; internet www.swedishembassy.co.il; Ambassador: ANDERS LIDÉN.

Switzerland: 228 Rehov Hayarkon, Tel-Aviv 63405; tel. 3-5464455; fax 3-5464408; e-mail vertretung@tel.rep.admin.ch; internet www.eda.admin.ch/telaviv; Ambassador: ERNST ITEN.

Thailand: Tel-Aviv; Ambassador: DOMEDEJ BUNNAG.

Turkey: 202 Rehov Hayarkon, Tel-Aviv 63405; tel. 3-5241101; fax 3-5241390; e-mail turqua2@netvision.net.il; internet www.turkish embassy-telaviv.org; Ambassador: FERIDUN SINIRLIOGLU.

Ukraine: 50 Yirmiyagu, Tel-Aviv 62594; tel. 3-6040242; fax 3-6042512; e-mail embukr@netvision.net.il; internet www.ukraine -embassy.co.il; Ambassador: (vacant).

United Kingdom: 192 Rehov Hayarkon, Tel-Aviv 63405; tel. 3-7251222; fax 3-5243313; e-mail webmaster.telaviv@fco.gov.uk; internet www.britemb.org.il; Ambassador: SHERARD COWPER-COLES.

USA: POB 26180, 1 Ben Yahuda St, Tel-Aviv; tel. 3-5103822; fax 3-5103828; e-mail webmaster@usembassy-israel.org.il; internet usembassy-israel.org.il; Ambassador: DANIEL C. KURTZER.

Uruguay: Tel-Aviv 62261; tel. 3-440411; Ambassador: JOSÉ LUÍS POMBO.

Venezuela: Textile Center, 2 Rehov Kaufman, 16th Floor, Tel-Aviv 61500; tel. 3-5176287; fax 3-5176210; Chargé d'affaires: JORGE MENDEZ MONTILLA.

Yugoslavia: Iderot Shaul Hamelech 8, Tel-Aviv 64733; tel. 3-6938412; fax 3-6938411; Chargé d'affaires a.i.: MIRKO STEFANOVIĆ.

The Jewish Agency for Israel

POB 92, Jerusalem 91000; tel. 2-6202222; fax 2-6202303; e-mail elibir@jazo.org.il; internet www.jafi.org.il.

Organization: The governing bodies are the Assembly which determines basic policy, the Board of Governors which sets policy for the Agency between Assembly meetings and the Executive responsible for the day-to-day running of the Agency.

Chairman of Executive: SALLAI MERIDOR.

Chairman of Board of Governors: ALEX GRASS.

Director-General: AHARON ABRAMOWITZ.

Secretary-General: ILAN RUBIN.

Functions: According to the Agreement of 1971, the Jewish Agency undertakes the immigration and absorption of immigrants in Israel, including absorption in agricultural settlement and immigrant housing; social welfare and health services in connection with immigrants; education, youth care and training; neighbourhood rehabilitation through project renewal.

Budget (2000): US $376m.

Judicial System

The law of Israel is composed of the enactments of the Knesset and, to a lesser extent, of the acts, orders-in-council and ordinances that remain from the period of the British Mandate in Palestine (1922–48). The pre-1948 law has largely been replaced, amended or reorganized, in the interests of codification, by Israeli legislation. This legislation generally follows a pattern which is very similar to that operating in England and the USA.

Attorney-General: ELYAQIM RUBENSTEIN.

CIVIL COURTS

The Supreme Court: Sha'arei Mishpat St, Kiryat David Ben-Gurion, Jerusalem 91950; tel. 2-6759666; fax 2-6759648; e-mail marcia@supreme.court.gov.il; internet www.court.gov.il. This is the highest judicial authority in the state. It has jurisdiction as an Appellate Court over appeals from the District Courts in all matters, both civil and criminal (sitting as a Court of Civil Appeal or as a Court of Criminal Appeal). In addition it is a Court of First Instance (sitting as the High Court of Justice) in actions against governmental authorities, and in matters in which it considers it necessary to grant relief in the interests of justice and which are not within the jurisdiction of any other court or tribunal. The High Court's exclusive power to issue orders in the nature of *habeas corpus, mandamus,* prohibition and *certiorari* enables the court to review the legality of and redress grievances against acts of administrative authorities of all kinds and religious tribunals.

President of the Supreme Court: AHARON BARAK.

Deputy President of the Supreme Court: SHLOMO LEVIN.

Justices of the Supreme Court: DORIT BEINISCH, JACOB TÜRKEL, MISHAEL CHESHIN, TOVA STRASBERG-COHEN, THEODORE OR, ELIYAHU MAZZA, ITZHAK ENGLARD, DALIA DORNER, ELIEZER RIVLIN, EDMOND E. LEVY, AYALA PROCACCIA, MIRIAM NAOR (acting).

Registrars: Judge MICHAL AGMON; Attorney HAGIT MACK-KALMANO-WITCH.

The District Courts: There are five District Courts (Jerusalem, Tel-Aviv, Haifa, Beersheba, Nazareth). They have residual jurisdiction as Courts of First Instance over all civil and criminal matters not within the jurisdiction of a Magistrates' Court, all matters not within the exclusive jurisdiction of any other tribunal, and matters within the concurrent jurisdiction of any other tribunal so long as such tribunal does not deal with them. In addition, the District Courts have appellate jurisdiction over appeals from judgments and decisions of Magistrates' Courts and judgments of Municipal Courts and various administrative tribunals.

Magistrates' Courts: There are 29 Magistrates' Courts, having criminal jurisdiction to try contraventions, misdemeanours and certain felonies, and civil jurisdiction to try actions concerning possession or use of immovable property, or the partition thereof whatever may be the value of the subject matter of the action, and other civil claims not exceeding one million shekels.

Labour Courts: Established in 1969. Regional Labour Courts in Jerusalem, Tel-Aviv, Haifa, Beersheba and Nazareth, composed of judges and representatives of the public. A National Labour Court in Jerusalem. The Courts have jurisdiction over all matters arising out of the relationship between employer and employee or parties to a collective labour agreement, and matters concerning the National Insurance Law and the Labour Law and Rules.

RELIGIOUS COURTS

The Religious Courts are the courts of the recognized religious communities. They have jurisdiction over certain defined matters of personal status concerning members of their respective communities. Where any action of personal status involves persons of different religious communities the President of the Supreme Court decides which Court will decide the matter. Whenever a question arises as to whether or not a case is one of personal status within the exclusive jurisdiction of a Religious Court, the matter must be referred to a Special Tribunal composed of two Justices of the Supreme Court and the President of the highest court of the religious community concerned in Israel. The judgments of the Religious Courts are executed by the process and offices of the Civil Courts. Neither these Courts nor the Civil Courts have jurisdiction to dissolve the marriage of a foreign subject.

Jewish Rabbinical Courts: These Courts have exclusive jurisdiction over matters of marriage and divorce of Jews in Israel who are Israeli citizens or residents. In all other matters of personal status they have concurrent jurisdiction with the District Courts.

Muslim Religious Courts: These Courts have exclusive jurisdiction over matters of marriage and divorce of Muslims who are not foreigners, or who are foreigners subject by their national law to the jurisdiction of Muslim Religious Courts in such matters. In all other matters of personal status they have concurrent jurisdiction with the District Courts.

Christian Religious Courts: The Courts of the recognized Christian communities have exclusive jurisdiction over matters of marriage and divorce of members of their communities who are not foreigners. In all other matters of personal status they have concurrent jurisdiction with the District Courts.

Druze Courts: These Courts, established in 1963, have exclusive jurisdiction over matters of marriage and divorce of Druze in Israel, who are Israeli citizens or residents, and concurrent jurisdiction with the District Courts over all other matters of personal status of Druze.

Religion

JUDAISM

Judaism, the religion of the Jews, is the faith of the majority of Israel's inhabitants. On 31 December 2001 Judaism's adherents totalled 5,025,000, equivalent to 77.25% of the country's population. Its basis is a belief in an ethical monotheism.

There are two main Jewish communities: the Ashkenazim and the Sephardim. The former are the Jews from Eastern, Central, or Northern Europe, while the latter originate from the Balkan countries, North Africa and the Middle East.

There is also a community of about 10,000 Falashas (Ethiopian Jews) who have been airlifted to Israel at various times since the fall of Emperor Haile Selassie in 1974.

The supreme religious authority is vested in the Chief Rabbinate, which consists of the Ashkenazi and Sephardi Chief Rabbis and the Supreme Rabbinical Council. It makes decisions on interpretation of the Jewish law, and supervises the Rabbinical Courts. There are 8 regional Rabbinical Courts, and a Rabbinical Court of Appeal presided over by the two Chief Rabbis.

According to the Rabbinical Courts Jurisdiction Law of 1953, marriage and divorce among Jews in Israel are exclusively within the jurisdiction of the Rabbinical Courts. Provided that all the parties concerned agree, other matters of personal status can also be decided by the Rabbinical Courts.

There are 195 Religious Councils, which maintain religious services and supply religious needs, and about 405 religious committees with similar functions in smaller settlements. Their expenses are borne jointly by the state and the local authorities. The Religious Councils are under the administrative control of the Ministry of Religious Affairs. In all matters of religion, the Religious Councils are subject to the authority of the Chief Rabbinate. There are 365 officially appointed rabbis. The total number of synagogues is about 7,000, most of which are organized within the framework of the Union of Israel Synagogues.

Head of the Ashkenazi Community: The Chief Rabbi ISRAEL MEIR LAU.

Head of the Sephardic Community: Jerusalem; tel. 2-244785; The Chief Rabbi ELIYAHU BAKSHI-DORON.

Two Jewish sects still loyal to their distinctive customs are:

The Karaites, a sect which recognizes only the Jewish written law and not the oral law of the Mishna and Talmud. The community of about 12,000, many of whom live in or near Ramla, has been augmented by immigration from Egypt.

The Samaritans, an ancient sect mentioned in 2 Kings xvii, 24. They recognize only the Torah. The community in Israel numbers about 500; about one-half of this number live in Holon, where a Samaritan synagogue has been built, and the remainder, including the High Priest, live in Nablus, near Mt Gerazim, which is sacred to the Samaritans.

ISLAM

The Muslims in Israel are mainly Sunnis, and are divided among the four rites of the Sunni sect of Islam: the Shafe'i, the Hanbali,

the Hanafi and the Maliki. Before June 1967 they numbered approx. 175,000; in 1971, approx. 343,900. On 31 December 2001 the total Muslim population of Israel was 1,004,600.

Mufti of Jerusalem: POB 19859, Jerusalem; tel. 2-283528; Sheikh ABD AL-QADIR ABIDIN (also Chair. Supreme Muslim Council for Jerusalem). The Palestinian National Authority also claims the right to appoint the Mufti of Jerusalem and has named Sheikh AKRAM SA'ID SABRI as its choice.

There was also a total of 106,300 Druzes in Israel at 31 December 2001.

CHRISTIANITY

The total Christian population of Israel (including East Jerusalem) at 31 December 2001 was 138,500.

United Christian Council in Israel: POB 116, Jerusalem 91000; tel. 2-6714351; fax 2-6721349; e-mail kopp@galanet.net; f. 1956; 28 mems (churches and other bodies); Chair. CHARLES KOPP.

The Roman Catholic Church

Armenian Rite

The Armenian Catholic Patriarch of Cilicia is resident in Beirut, Lebanon.

Patriarchal Exarchate of Jerusalem: POB 19546, Via Dolorosa 36, Jerusalem 91190; tel. 2-6284262; fax 2-6272123; f. 1885; about 425 adherents (2000); Exarch Patriarchal GEORGES KHAZZOUM.

Chaldean Rite

The Chaldean Patriarch of Babylon is resident in Baghdad, Iraq.

Patriarchal Exarchate of Jerusalem: Chaldean Patriarchal Vicariate, POB 20108, 7 Chaldean St, Saad and Said Quarter, Jerusalem 91200; tel. 2-6284519; fax 2-6274614; Exarch Patriarchal Mgr PAUL COLLIN.

Latin Rite

The Patriarchate of Jerusalem covers Palestine, Jordan and Cyprus. At 31 December 2000 there were an estimated 77,000 adherents.

Bishops' Conference: Conférence des Evêques Latins dans les Régions Arabes, Notre Dame of Jerusalem Center, POB 20531, Jerusalem 91204; tel. 2-6288554; fax 2-6288555; e-mail evcat@palnet.com; f. 1967; Pres. His Beatitude MICHEL SABBAH; Patriarch of Jerusalem.

Patriarchate of Jerusalem: Patriarcat Latin, POB 14152, Jerusalem 91141; tel. 2-6282323; fax 2-6271652; e-mail latinpat@actcom.co.il; internet www.lpj.org; Patriarch: His Beatitude MICHEL SABBAH; Vicar-General for Jerusalem: KAMAL HANNA BATHISH (Titular Bishop of Jericho); Vicar-General for Israel: GIACINTO-BOULOS MARCUZZO (Titular Bishop of Emmaus Nicopolis), Vicariat Patriarcal Latin, Street 6191/3, Nazareth 16100; tel. 4-6554075; fax 4-6452416; e-mail latinpat@rannet.com.

Maronite Rite

The Maronite community, under the jurisdiction of the Maronite Patriarch of Antioch (resident in Lebanon), has about 7,000 members.

Patriarchal Exarchate of Jerusalem: Maronite Patriarchal Exarchate, POB 14219, 25 Maronite Convent St, Jaffa Gate, Jerusalem 91141; tel. 2-6282158; fax 2-6272821; about 504 adherents (2000); Exarch Patriarchal Mgr PAUL NABIL SAYAH (also the Archbishop of Haifa and the Holy Land).

Melkite Rite

The Greek-Melkite Patriarch of Antioch and all the East, of Alexandria and of Jerusalem (GRÉGOIRE III LAHAM) is resident in Damascus, Syria.

Patriarchal Vicariate of Jerusalem: Patriarcat Grec-Melkite Catholique, POB 14130, Porte de Jaffa, Jerusalem 91141; tel. 2-6271968; fax 2-6286652; e-mail gcpjer@p-ol.com; about 3,300 adherents (2000); Protosyncellus Archim. MTANIOS HADDAD (resident in Rome).

Archbishop of Akka (Acre): Most Rev. PIERRE MOUALLEM, Archevêché Grec-Catholique, POB 279, 33 Hagefen St, 31002 Haifa; tel. 4-8523114; fax 4-8520798; 65,200 adherents at 31 December 2001.

Syrian Rite

The Syrian Catholic Patriarch of Antioch is resident in Beirut, Lebanon.

Patriarchal Exarchate of Jerusalem: Vicariat Patriarcal Syrien Catholique, POB 19787, 6 Chaldean St, Jerusalem 91191; tel. 2-6282657; fax 2-6284217; e-mail stjossc@l-ol.com; about 10,298 adherents (Dec. 2000); Exarch Patriarchal Mgr GRÉGOIRE PIERRE MELKI.

The Armenian Apostolic (Orthodox) Church

Patriarch of Jerusalem: TORKOM MANOOGIAN, St James's Cathedral, Jerusalem; tel. 2-6264853; fax 2-6264862.

The Greek Orthodox Church

The Patriarchate of Jerusalem contains an estimated 260,000 adherents in Israel, the Occupied Territories, Jordan, Kuwait, the United Arab Emirates and Saudi Arabia.

Patriarch of Jerusalem: IRINEOS I, POB 19632-633, Greek Orthodox Patriarchate St, Old City, Jerusalem; tel. 2-6271657; fax 2-6282048.

The Anglican Communion

Episcopal Church in Jerusalem and the Middle East: POB 19122, St George's Cathedral Close, Jerusalem; tel. 2-6271670; fax 2-6273847; e-mail ediosces@netvision.net.il; Bishop The Rt. Rev. RIAH ABU AL-ASSAL.

Other Christian Churches

Other denominations include the Coptic Orthodox Church (700 members), the Russian Orthodox Church, the Ethiopian Orthodox Church, the Romanian Orthodox Church, the Baptist Church, the Lutheran Church and the Church of Scotland.

The Press

Tel-Aviv is the main publishing centre. Largely for economic reasons, no local press has developed away from the main cities; hence all papers regard themselves as national. Friday editions, issued on Sabbath eve, are increased to as much as twice the normal size by special weekend supplements, and experience a considerable rise in circulation. No newspapers appear on Saturday.

Most of the daily papers are in Hebrew, and others appear in Arabic, English, French, Polish, Yiddish, Hungarian, Russian and German. The total daily circulation is 500,000–600,000 copies, or 21 papers per hundred people, although most citizens read more than one daily paper.

Most Hebrew morning dailies have strong political or religious affiliations. *Hatzofeh*, for example, is affiliated to the National Religious Party. Most newspapers depend on subsidies from political parties, religious organizations or public funds. The limiting effect on freedom of commentary entailed by this party press system has provoked repeated criticism. There are around 400 other newspapers and magazines including some 50 weekly and 150 fortnightly; over 250 of them are in Hebrew, the remainder in 11 other languages.

The most influential and respected daily, for both quality of news coverage and commentary, is *Ha'aretz*. This is the most widely read of the morning papers, exceeded only by the popular afternoon press, *Ma'ariv* and *Yedioth Aharonoth*. The *Jerusalem Post* gives detailed and sound news coverage in English.

The Israeli Press Council (Chair. ITZHAK ZAMIR), established in 1963, deals with matters of common interest to the Press such as drafting the code of professional ethics which is binding on all journalists.

The Daily Newspaper Publishers' Association represents publishers in negotiations with official and public bodies, negotiates contracts with employees and purchases and distributes newsprint.

DAILIES

Al Anba (The News): Jerusalem Publications Ltd, POB 428, 37 Hillel St, Jerusalem; f. 1968; circ. 10,000.

Globes: POB 5126, Rishon le Zion 75150; tel. 3-9538888; fax 3-9525971; e-mail mailbox@globes.co.il; internet www.globes.co.il; f. 1983; evening; Hebrew; business, economics; CEO AMI EVEN; Editor-in-Chief HAGGAI GOLAN; circ. 40,000.

Ha'aretz (The Land): POB 233, 21 Salman Schocken St, Tel-Aviv 61001; tel. 3-5121110; fax 3-6815859; e-mail iht@haaretz.co.il; internet www.haaretz.co.il; f. 1918; morning; Hebrew; liberal, independent; Editor HANOCH MARMARI; circ. 65,000 (weekdays), 75,000 (weekends).

Hadashot (The News): 108 Igal Alon St, Tel-Aviv; 3-5120555; fax 3-5623084; late morning; Hebrew.

Hamodia (The Informer): POB 1306, Yehuda Hamackabbi 3, Jerusalem; tel. 2-5389255; fax 2-539108; e-mail moll@hamodia-mod.co.il; morning; Hebrew; also publishes weekly English-language edition; organ of Agudat Israel; Editors M. A. DRUCK, H. M. KNOPF; circ. 25,000.

Hatzofeh (The Watchman): POB 2045, 66 Hamasger St, Tel-Aviv; tel. 3-5622951; fax 3-5621502; e-mail hazofe@zahav.net.il; internet www.hazofe.co.il; f. 1938; morning; Hebrew; organ of the National Religious Party; Editor GONEN GINAT; circ. 60,000.

Israel Nachrichten (News of Israel): POB 35248, 49 Tschlenow St, Tel-Aviv 66048; tel. 3-5372059; fax 3-6877142; f. 1974; morning; German; Editor ALICE SCHWARZ-GARDOS; circ. 20,000.

Al-Itihad (Unity): POB 104, Haifa; tel. 4-511296; fax 4-511297; f. 1944; Arabic; organ of Hadash; Editor AHMAD SA'AD; circ. 60,000.

The Jerusalem Post: POB 81, Romema, Jerusalem 91000; tel. 2-5315666; fax 2-5389527; e-mail jpedt@jpost.co.il; internet www.jpost.com; f. 1932; morning; English; independent; Pres. PAUL STASZEWSKI; Editor CARL SCHRAG; circ. 30,000 (weekdays), 50,000 (weekend edition); there is also a weekly international edition, circ. 70,000, and a weekly French-language edition, circ. 7,500.

Le Journal d'Israël: Tel-Aviv; tel. 3-33188; f. 1971; French; independent; Chief Editor J. RABIN; circ. 10,000; also overseas weekly selection; circ. 15,000.

Letzte Nyess (Late News): Tel-Aviv; tel. 3-35815; f. 1949; morning; Yiddish; Editor S. HIMMELFARB; circ. 23,000.

Ma'ariv (Evening Prayer): 2 Carlebach St, Tel-Aviv 61200; tel. 3-5632111; fax 3-5610614; f. 1948; mid-morning; Hebrew; independent; published by Modiin Publishing House; Editor OFER NIMRODI; circ. 160,000 (weekdays), 270,000 (weekends).

Mabat: 8 Toshia St, Tel-Aviv 67218; tel. 3-5627711; fax 3-5627719; f. 1971; morning; Hebrew; economic and social; Editor S. YARKONI; circ. 7,000.

Nasha Strana (Our Country): 52 Harakeret St, Tel-Aviv 67770; tel. 3-370011; fax 3-5371921; f. 1970; morning; Russian; Editor S. HIMMELFARB; circ. 35,000.

Al-Quds (Jerusalem): POB 19788, Jerusalem; tel. 2-6272663; fax 2-6272657; e-mail info@alquds.com; internet www.alquds.com; f. 1968; Arabic; Founder and Publr MAHMOUD ABU ZALAF; Gen. Man. Dr MARWAN ABU ZALAF; circ. 55,000.

Ash Shaab (The People): POB 19154, Jerusalem; tel. 2-289881.

Shearim (The Gates): POB 11044, 64 Frishman St, Tel-Aviv; tel. 3-242126; organ of the Poale Agudat Israel Party.

Uj Kelet: 49 Tchlenor St, Tel-Aviv; tel. 3-5371395; fax 3-377142; f. 1918; morning; Hungarian; independent; Editor D. DRORY; circ. 20,000.

Viata Noastra: 49 Tchlenor St, Tel-Aviv 61351; tel. 3-5372059; fax 3-6877142; e-mail erancourt@shani.co.il; f. 1950; morning; Romanian; Editor GEORGE EDRI; circ. 30,000.

Yated Ne'eman: POB 328, Bnei Brak; tel. 3-6170800; fax 3-6170801; e-mail let-edit@yatedneman.co.il; f. 1986; morning; religious; Editors Y. ROTH and N.GROSSMAN; circ. 25,000.

Yedioth Aharonoth (The Latest News): 2 Yehuda and Noah Mozes St, Tel-Aviv 61000; tel. 3-6972222; fax 3-6953950; f. 1939; evening; Hebrew; independent; Editor-in-Chief MOSHE VARDI; circ. 300,000, Friday 600,000.

WEEKLIES AND FORTNIGHTLIES

Aurora: Aurora Ltd, POB 18066, Tel-Aviv 61180; tel. 3-5625216; fax 3-5625082; e-mail aurora@aurora-israel.co.il; internet www.aurora-israel.co.il; f. 1963; weekly; Spanish; for Spanish-speakers in Israel and abroad; Pres. ARIE AVIDOR; circ. 20,000.

Bama'alah: 120 Kibbutz Gabuyot St, Tel-Aviv; tel. 3-6814488; fax 3-6816852; Hebrew; journal of the young Histadrut Movement; Editor ODED BAR-MEIR.

Bamahane (In the Camp): Military POB 1013, Tel-Aviv; f. 1948; military, illustrated weekly of the Israel Armed Forces; Hebrew; Editor-in-Chief YOSSEF ESHKOL; circ. 70,000.

Ethgar (The Challenge): 75 Einstein St, Tel-Aviv; twice weekly; Hebrew; Editor NATHAN YALIN-MOR.

Al Fajr (The Dawn): POB 19315, Jerusalem; tel. 2-271649; fax 2-273521; f. 1980; weekly; Editor-in-Chief MANNA SINIORA.

Glasul Populurui: Tel-Aviv; weekly of the Communist Party of Israel; Romanian; Editor MEIR SEMO.

Harefuah (Medicine): POB 3566, 35 Jabotinsky St, Ramat-Gan 52136; tel. 3-6100444; fax 3-5751616; f. 1920; fortnightly journal of the Israeli Medical Association; Hebrew with English summaries; an English publication, IMAJ, has also been published since 1999; Editor Y. SHOENFELD; circ. 16,000.

Hotam: Al-Hamishmar House, Choma U'Migdal St, Tel-Aviv; Hebrew.

Al-Hurriya (Freedom): 38 King George St, Tel-Aviv; Arabic weekly of the Herut Party.

Illustrirte WeltWoch: Tel-Aviv; f. 1956; weekly; Yiddish; Editor M. KARPINOVITZ.

Information Week: POB 1161, 13 Yad Harutzim St, Tel-Aviv 61116; tel. 3-6385858; fax 3-6889207; e-mail world@pc.co.il; internet www.people-and-computers.co.il; weekly; Man. Dirs DAHLIA PELED, PELI PELED; Editor-in Chief PELI PELED.

The Israeli Tourist Guide Magazine: Tourist Guide Communications Ltd, POB 53333, Tel-Aviv 61533; tel. 3-5168282; fax 3-5168284; e-mail ishchori@touristguide.co.il; internet www.touristguide.co.il; f. 1994; weekly; Publisher and Editor ILAN SHCHORI; circ. 10,000.

Jerusalem Post International Edition: POB 81, Romema, Jerusalem 91000; tel. 2-5315666; fax 2-5389527; e-mail jpedt@jpost.co.il; internet www.jpost.co.il; f. 1959; weekly; English; overseas edition of the *Jerusalem Post* (q.v.); circ. 70,000 to 106 countries.

Jerusalem Report: POB 1805, Jerusalem 91017; tel. 2-5315440; fax 2-5379489; e-mail jrep@jreport.co.il; internet www.jrep.com; f. 1990; bi-weekly; English; Publr and Editor DAVID HOROVITZ; published by *Jerusalem Report Publications*; circ. 65,000 worldwide.

The Jerusalem Times: POB 20185, Jerusalem; tel. 2-6264883; fax 2-6264975; e-mail tjt@jerusalem-times.net; f. 1994; weekly; English; Editor HANNA SINIORA.

Kol Ha'am (Voice of the People): Tel-Aviv; f. 1947; Hebrew; organ of the Communist Party of Israel; Editor B. BALTI.

Laisha (For Women): POB 28122, 35 Bnei Brak St, Tel-Aviv 67132; tel. 3-6386969; fax 3-6386933; f. 1946; Hebrew; women's magazine; Editor MIRIAM NOFECH-MOSES; circ. 150,000.

Ma'ariv Lanoar: POB 20020, 2 Carlebach St, Tel-Aviv 67132; tel. 3-5632525; fax 3-5632030; e-mail maariv_lanoar@maariv.co.il; f. 1957; weekly for teenagers; Hebrew; Editor DANA BEN-NAFTALI; circ. 100,000.

MB (Mitteilungsblatt): POB 1480, Tel-Aviv 61014; tel. 3-5164461; fax 3-5164435; f. 1932; German monthly journal of the Irgun Olei Merkas Europa (The Association of Immigrants from Central Europe); Editor Prof. PAUL ALSBERG.

Otiot: Jerusalem; tel. 2-895097; fax 2-895196; f. 1987; weekly for children; English; Editor URI AUERBACH.

People and Computers: POB 11616, 13 Yad Harutzim St, Tel-Aviv 61116; tel. 3-6385888; fax 3-6889207; e-mail world@enet.co.il; internet www.enet.co.il; f. 1981; weekly; Hebrew; information technology; CEOs PELI PELED, DAHLIA PELED; circ. 15,000.

Reshumot: Ministry of Justice, POB 1087, 29 Rehov Salahadin, Jerusalem 91010; f. 1948; Hebrew, Arabic and English; official government gazette.

Sada at-Tarbia (The Echo of Education): published by the Histadrut and Teachers' Association, POB 2306, Rehovot; f. 1952; fortnightly; Arabic; educational; Editor TUVIA SHAMOSH.

As-Sinnarah: Nazareth; internet www.asennara.com; twice weekly; for Christian and Muslim Arabs in the region; Arabic; Editor-in-Chief LUFTI MASH'UR.

OTHER PERIODICALS

Adi 'Or: Miller Freeman (Israel) Ltd, POB 3441, Silver Bldg, 7 Abba Hillel St, Ramat-Gan, Tel-Aviv 52133; tel. 3-5750196; fax 3-5754829; e-mail millisra@trendline.co.il; f. 1990; quarterly; jewellery; Publr CHAIM EVEN-ZOHAR.

Ariel: the Israel Review of Arts and Letters: Cultural and Scientific Relations Division, Ministry of Foreign Affairs, Jerusalem; Distributor: Youval Tal Ltd, POB 2160, Jerusalem 91021; tel. 2-6248897; fax 2-6245434; e-mail magariel@netvision.net.il; internet www .israel-mfa.gov.il; Editorial Office: 214 Jaffa Road, Jerusalem 94383; tel. 2-6432147; fax 2-6437502; f. 1962; quarterly review of all aspects of culture in Israel; regular edns in English, Spanish, French, German, Arabic and Russian; occasional edns in other languages; Editor ASHER WEILL; circ. 30,000.

Asakim Vekalkala (Business and Economics): POB 20027, 84 Ha' Hashmonaim St, Tel-Aviv 61200; tel. 3-5631010; fax 3-5619025; monthly; Hebrew; Editor ZVI AMIT.

Bitaon Heyl Ha'avir (Israel Air Force Magazine): Military POB 01560, Zahal; tel. 3-5694153; fax 3-5695806; e-mail iaf@inter.net.il; internet www.iaf.org.il; f. 1948; bi-monthly; Hebrew; Dep. Editor U. ETSION; Editor-in-Chief MERAV HALPERIN; circ. 30,000.

Al-Bushra (Good News): POB 6228, Haifa 31061; tel. 4-8385002; fax 4-8371612; f. 1935; monthly; Arabic; organ of the Ahmadiyya movement; Editor MUSA ASA'AD O'DEH.

Business Diary: Haifa; f. 1947; weekly; English, Hebrew; shipping movements, import licences, stock exchange listings, business failures, etc.; Editor G. ALON.

Challenge: POB 41199, Jaffa 61411; tel. 3-6839145; fax 3-6839148; e-mail oda@netvision.net.il; internet www.hanitzotz.com/challenge/; f. 1989; magazine on the Israeli–Palestinian conflict, published by Hanitzotz Publishing House; bi-monthly; English; Editor-in-Chief RONI BEN EFRAT; Editor LIZ LEYH LEVAC; circ. 3,000.

Christian News from Israel: 30 Jaffa Rd, Jerusalem; f. 1949; half-yearly; English, French, Spanish; issued by the Ministry of Religious Affairs; Editor SHALOM BEN-ZAKKAI; circ. 10,000.

Divrei Haknesset: c/o The Knesset, Jerusalem; f. 1949; Hebrew; records of the proceedings of the Knesset; published by the Government Printer, Jerusalem; Editor DVORA AVIVI (acting); circ. 350.

Eastern Mediterranean Tourism and Travel: Israel Travel News Ltd, POB 3251, Tel-Aviv 61032; tel. 3-5251646; fax 3-5251605; f. 1979; monthly; English; circ. 19,515.

The Easy Way to do Business with Israel: POB 20027, Tel-Aviv; tel. 3-5612444; fax 3-5612614; published by Federation of Israeli Chambers of Commerce; Editor Y. SHOSTAK.

Eitanim (Popular Medicine): POB 16250, Merkez Kupat Holim, Tel-Aviv 62098; f. 1948; Hebrew; monthly; circ. 20,000.

Folk un Zion: POB 7053, Tel-Aviv 61070; tel. 3-5423317; f. 1950; bi-monthly; current events relating to Israel and World Jewry; Editor MOSHE KALCHHEIM; circ. 3,000.

Frei Israel: POB 8512, Tel-Aviv; progressive monthly; published by Asscn for Popular Culture; Yiddish.

Hamizrah Hehadash (The New East): Israel Oriental Society, The Hebrew University, Mount Scopus, Jerusalem 91905; tel. 2-5883633; e-mail ios49@hotmail.com; f. 1949; annual of the Israel Oriental Society; Middle Eastern, Asian and African Affairs; Hebrew with English summary; Editors HAIM GERBER, ELIE PODEH; circ. 1,500–2,000.

Hamionai (The Hotelier): Tel-Aviv; f. 1962; monthly of the Israel Hotel Asscn; Hebrew and English; Editor Z. PELTZ.

Hapraklit (Law): POB 14152, 8 Wilson St, Tel-Aviv 61141; tel. 3-5614695; fax 3-561476; f. 1943; quarterly; Hebrew; published by the Israel Bar Asscn; Editor-in-Chief A. POLONSKI; Editor ARNAN GAVRIELI; circ. 7,000.

Hassadeh: POB 40044, 8 Shaul Hamelech Blvd, Tel-Aviv 61400; tel. 3-6929018; fax 3-6929979; f. 1920; monthly; review of Israeli agriculture; English and Hebrew; Publr GUY KING; Editor NAAMA DOTAN; circ. 13,000.

Hed Hagan: 8 Ben Saruk St, Tel-Aviv 62969; tel. 3-6922958; f. 1935; quarterly; Hebrew; educational; Editor MIRIAM SNAPIR; circ. 9,000.

Hed Hahinukh: 8 Ben Saruk St, Tel-Aviv 62969; tel. 3-5432911; fax 3-5432928; f. 1926; monthly; Hebrew; educational; published by the Israeli Teachers' Union; Editor DALIA LACHMAN; circ. 40,000.

Historia: POB 4179, Jerusalem 91041; tel. 2-5637171; fax 2-5662135; e-mail shazar@shazar.org.il; f. 1998; Hebrew, with English summaries; general history; published by the Historical Society of Israel; Editors STEVEN ASCHHEIM, MICHAEL HEYD, RANON KATZOFF, SHULAMIT SHAHAR.

Internet World (Israel): POB 1161, 13 Yad Harutzim St, Tel-Aviv 61116; tel. 3-6385858; fax 3-6889207; e-mail benrun@netvision .net.il; internet www.people-and-computers.co.il; 24 a year; computers and information technology; Man. Dirs DAHLIA PELED, PELI PELED; Editor-in-Chief PELI PELED.

Israel Agritechnology Focus: 8 Twersky St, Tel-Aviv 61574; tel. 3-5628511; fax 3-5628512; f. 1993; quarterly; farming technology, agricultural company and investment news; Editor NICKY BLACKMAN.

Israel Economist: 6 Hazanowitz St, Jerusalem; tel. 2-234131; fax 2-246569; f. 1945; monthly; English; independent; political and economic; Editor BEN MOLLOV; Publisher ISRAEL KELMAN; also publishes *Keeping Posted* (diplomatic magazine), *Mazel and Brucha* (jewellers' magazine); annuals: *Travel Agents' Manual, Electronics, International Conventions in Israel, Arkia, In Flight,* various hotel magazines.

Israel Environment Bulletin: Ministry of the Environment, POB 34033, 5 Kanfei Nesharim St, Jerusalem 95464; tel. 2-6553777; fax 2-6535937; internet www.environment.gov.il; f. 1973; Editor SHOSHANA GABBAY; circ. 3,500.

Israel Exploration Journal: POB 7041, 5 Avida St, Jerusalem 91070; tel. 2-6257991; fax 2-6247772; e-mail ies@vms.huji.ac.il; internet www.hum.huji.ac.il/ies; f. 1950; bi-annual; English; general and biblical archaeology, ancient history and historical geography of Israel and the Holy Land; Editors S. ACHITUV, MIRIAM TADMOR; circ. 2,500.

Israel Export: POB 57500, 8 Twersky St, Tel-Aviv 61574; tel. and fax 3-5628512; f. 1993; annual; Editor NAOYA NAKAMURA.

Israel Export News: Tel-Aviv; tel. 3-5142947; f. 1949; bi-monthly; English; commercial and economic; published by Israel Export Institute; Dir of Media Dept DANI BLOCH.

Israel Journal of Chemistry: POB 35409, Jerusalem 91352; tel. 2-6522226; fax 2-6522277; e-mail laserpages@netmedia.net.il; internet www.sciencefromisrael.com; f. 1951; quarterly; published by Laser Pages Publishing Ltd; Editor Prof. H. LEVANON.

Israel Journal of Earth Sciences: POB 35409, Jerusalem 91352; tel. 2-6522226; fax. 2-6522277; e-mail laserpages@netmedia.net.il; internet www.sciencefromisrael.com; f. 1951; quarterly; published by Laser Pages Publishing Ltd; Editors Prof. ALAN MATTHEWS, Dr AHUUA ALMOGI.

Israel Journal of Mathematics: POB 39099, Jerusalem 91390; tel. 2-6586660; fax 2-5633370; e-mail magnes@vms.huji.ac.il; f. 1951; monthly, four vols of three issues per year; published by Magnes Press; Editor Prof. G. KALAI.

Israel Journal of Medical Sciences: Jerusalem; tel. 2-5817727; fax 2-5815722; f. 1965; monthly; Editor-in-Chief Prof. MOSHE PRYWES; circ. 5,500.

Israel Journal of Plant Sciences: POB 35409, Jerusalem 91352; tel. 2-6522226; fax. 2-6522277; e-mail laserpages@netmedia.net.il; internet www.sciencefromisrael.com; f. 1951 as *Israel Journal of Botany*; quarterly; published by Laser Pages Publishing Ltd; Editor Prof. A. M. MAYER.

Israel Journal of Psychiatry and Related Sciences: Gefen Publishing House Ltd, POB 36004, Jerusalem 91360; tel. 2-5380247; fax 2-5388423; e-mail info@gefenpublishing.com; internet www.gefenbooks.com; f. 1963; quarterly; Editor-in-Chief Dr DAVID GREENBERG.

Israel Journal of Veterinary Medicine: POB 3076, Rishon Le-Zion 75130; tel. 9-7419929; fax 9-7431778; e-mail ivma@internet-zahav.net; internet www.isrvma.org; f. 1943; formerly *Refuah Veterinarith*; quarterly of the Israel Veterinary Medical Asscn; Editors G. SIMON, I. GLAS.

Israel Journal of Zoology: POB 35409, Jerusalem 91352; tel. 2-6522226; fax 2-6522277; e-mail laserpages@netmedia.net.il; internet www.sciencefromisrael.com; f. 1951; quarterly; published by Laser Pages Publishing Ltd; Editors Prof. ALAN DEGEN, Prof. MICHA ILAN, Prof. ORA MANHEIM.

Israel Law Review: Faculty of Law, The Hebrew University of Jerusalem, Mount Scopus, Jerusalem 91905; tel. 2-5882520; fax 2-5882565; e-mail msilr@mscc.huji.ac.il; f. 1965; quarterly; published by the Israel Law Review Association.

Israel Press Service: POB 33188, Jerusalem 91330; tel. 2-6419783; fax 2-6439377; e-mail junes@netvision.net.il; f. 1956; English; Zionist; Editor JUNE SPITZER.

Israel-South Africa Trade Journal: Tel-Aviv; f. 1973; bi-monthly; English; commercial and economic; published by Israel Publications Corpn Ltd; Man. Dir Z. PELTZ.

Israels Aussenhandel: Tel-Aviv; tel. 3-5280215; f. 1967; monthly; German; commercial; published by Israel Periodicals Co Ltd; Editor PELTZ NOEMI; Man. Dir ZALMAN PELTZ.

Al-Jadid (The New): POB 104, Haifa; f. 1951; literary monthly; Arabic; Editor SALEM JUBRAN; circ. 5,000.

Journal d'Analyse Mathématique: f. 1955; 2 vols per year; published by Magnes Press; Editor Prof. L. ZALCMAN.

Kibbutz Trends: Yad Tabenkin, Ramat Efal 52960; tel. 3-5301217; fax 3-5346376; e-mail yadtab@inter.net.il; f. 1991; bi-annual; English language journal on kibbutz; Editors IDIT PAZ, NEIL HARRIS, ROCHELLE MASS; circ. 1,500.

Leshonenu: Academy of the Hebrew Language, POB 3449, Jerusalem 91034; tel. 2-6493555; fax 2-5617065; e-mail acad2u@vms.huji.ac.il; internet www.hebrew-academy.huji.ac.il; f. 1929; 4 a year; for the study of the Hebrew language and cognate subjects; Editor M. BAR-ASHER.

Leshonenu La'am: Academy of the Hebrew Language, POB 3449, Jerusalem 91034; tel. 2-6493555; fax 2-5617065; e-mail acad2u@vms.huji.ac.il; internet www.hebrew-academy.huji.ac.il; f. 1945; 4 a year; popular Hebrew philology; Editors C. E. COHEN, D. TALSHIR, Y. OFER.

Lilac: Nazareth; internet www.lilac-m.com; f. 2000; monthly; Arabic; Israel's first magazine for Arab women.

Ma'arachot (Campaigns): POB 7026, Hakirya, 3 Albert Mendler St, Tel-Aviv 61070; tel. 3-5694345; fax 3-5694343; f. 1939; military and political bi-monthly; Hebrew; periodical of Israel Defence Force; Editors HAGGAI GOLAN, EFI MELZER; circ. 20,000.

Magallati (My Magazine): POB 28049, Tel-Aviv; tel. 3-371438; f. 1960; monthly children's magazine; circ. 3,000.

Melaha Vetaassiya (Trade and Industry): Tel-Aviv; f. 1969; bi-monthly review of the Union of Artisans and Small Manufacturers of Israel; Hebrew; Man. Dir Z. PELTZ; circ. 8,500.

M'Lakha V'ta Asiya (Israel Industry): POB 11587, 40 Rembrandt St, Tel-Aviv; monthly; published by Israel Publications Corporation Ltd; circ. 8,500.

Moznaim (Balance): POB 7098, Tel-Aviv; tel. 3-6953256; fax 3-6919681; f. 1929; monthly; Hebrew; literature and culture; Editors ASHER REICH, AZRIEL KAUFMAN; circ. 2,500.

Na'amat: 93 Arlozorof St, Tel-Aviv 62098; tel. 3-6921111; fax 3-6912725; monthly; published by Histadrut; trade union issues.

Nekuda: Hebrew; organ of the Jewish settlers of the West Bank and Gaza Strip.

New Outlook: 9 Gordon St, Tel-Aviv 63458; tel. 3-5236496; fax 3-5232252; f. 1957; bi-monthly; Israeli and Middle Eastern Affairs; dedicated to the quest for Arab-Israeli peace; Editor-in-Chief CHAIM SHUR; Senior Editor DAN LEON; circ. 10,000.

News from Within: POB 31417, Jerusalem; tel. 2-6241159; fax 2-6253151; e-mail nfw@alt-info.org; internet www.alternativenews.org; monthly; joint Israeli-Palestinian publication; political, economic, social and cultural; publ. by the Alternative Information Centre.

OTOT: 10 Beit Shamai, Tel-Aviv; tel. 3-5615310; fax 3-5615281; e-mail igud@inter.net.il; f. 1975; monthly; Hebrew; advertising, marketing and communications; Editor-in-Chief YAIR FELDMANN; Editor RAYA RUBIN; circ. 4,000.

PC Magazine (Israel): PC Media, POB 11438, 13 Yad Harutzim St, Tel-Aviv 61114; tel. 3-6385810; fax 3-6889207; e-mail editor@pc.co.il; f. 1992; monthly; Hebrew; information on personal computers; Man. Dirs DAHLIA PELED, YEHUDA ELYADA; Editor-in-Chief YEHUDA ELYADA; circ. 13,500.

Proche-Orient Chrétien: POB 19079, Jerusalem 91190; tel. 2-6283285; fax 2-6280764; e-mail poc@steanne.org; f. 1951; quarterly on churches and religion in the Middle East; circ. 1,000.

Publish Israel: Tel-Aviv; tel. 3-5622744; fax 3-5621808; e-mail olamot@inter.net.il; f. 1998; six times a year; magazine for printers and publishers; Gen. Man. DAN SHEKEL; circ. 12,000.

The Sea: POB 33706, Hane'emanim 8, Haifa; tel. 4-529818; every six months; published by Israel Maritime League; review of marine problems; Pres. M. POMROCK; Chief Editor M. LITOVSKI; circ. 5,000.

Shituf (Co-operation): POB 7151, 24 Ha'arba St, Tel-Aviv; f. 1948; bi-monthly; Hebrew; economic, social and co-operative problems in Israel; published by the Central Union of Industrial, Transport and Service Co-operative Societies; Editor L. LOSH; circ. 12,000.

Shivuk (Marketing): POB 20027, Tel-Aviv 61200; tel. 3-5631010; fax 3-5612614; monthly; Hebrew; publ. by Federation of Israeli Chambers of Commerce; Editor SARA LIPKIN.

Sinai: POB 642, Jerusalem 91006; tel. 2-6526231; fax 2-6526968; f. 1937; Hebrew; Torah science and literature; Editor Rabbi YOSEF MOVSHOVITZ.

As-Sindibad: POB 28049, Tel-Aviv; tel. 3-371438; f. 1970; children's monthly; Arabic; Man. JOSEPH ELIAHOU; Editor WALID HUSSEIN; circ. 8,000.

Terra Santa: POB 14038, Jaffa Gate, Jerusalem 91140; tel. 2-6272692; fax 2-6286417; e-mail cicts@netmedia.net.il; f. 1921; every two months; published by the Custody of the Holy Land (the official custodians of the Holy Shrines); Italian, Spanish, French, English and Arabic editions published in Jerusalem, by the Franciscan Printing Press, German edition in Munich, Maltese edition in Valletta.

WIZO Review: Women's International Zionist Organization, 38 Sderot David Hamelech Blvd, Tel-Aviv 64237; tel. 3-6923805; fax 3-6923801; e-mail wreview@wizo.org; internet www.wizo.org; f. 1947; English edition (quarterly), Spanish and German editions (two a year); Editor HILLEL SCHENKER; circ. 20,000.

World Fellowship of the Israel Medical Asscn (Mif'al Haverut Hutz): POB 3604, 2 Twin Towers, 35 Jabotinsky St, Ramat Gan 52136; tel. 3-6100424; fax 3-6133274; e-mail ingrid@ima.org.il; internet www.ima.org.il/wf; quarterly; English.

The Youth Times: POB 54065, Jerusalem; tel. 2-2343428; fax 2-2343430; e-mail pyalara@pyalara.org; internet www.pyalara.org; f. 1998; monthly; Arabic and English; Editor-in-Chief HANIA BITAR.

Zion: POB 4179, Jerusalem 91041; tel. 2-5637171; fax 2-5662135; e-mail shazar@shazar.org.il; f. 1935; quarterly; published by the Historical Society of Israel; Hebrew, with English summaries; research in Jewish history; Editors I. ETKES, A. OPPENHEIMER, Y. KAPLAN; circ. 1,000.

Zraim: POB 40027, 7 Dubnov St, Tel-Aviv; tel. 3-691745; fax 3-6953199; f. 1953; Hebrew; journal of the Bnei Akiva (Youth of Tora Va-avoda) Movement; Editor URI AUERBACH.

Zrakor: Haifa; f. 1947; monthly; Hebrew; news digest, trade, finance, economics, shipping; Editor G. ALON.

PRESS ASSOCIATIONS

Daily Newspaper Publishers' Asscn of Israel: POB 51202, 74 Petach Tikva Rd, Tel-Aviv 61200; fax 3-5617938; safeguards professional interests and maintains standards, supplies newsprint to dailies; negotiates with trade unions, etc.; mems all daily papers; affiliated to International Federation of Newspaper Publishers; Pres. SHABTAI HIMMELFARB; Gen. Sec. BETZALEL EYAL.

Foreign Press Asscn: Beit Sokolov, 4 Kaplan St, Tel-Aviv; tel. 3-6916143; fax 3-6961548; e-mail fpa@netvision.net.il; Chair. DAN PERRY.

Israel Association of the Periodical Press (IAPP): 93 Arlozorof St, Tel-Aviv 62098; tel. 3-6921238; fax 3-6960155; e-mail lavied@arg.huji.ac.il; Chair. DAVID LAVIE.

Israel Press Asscn: Sokolov House, 4 Kaplan St, Tel-Aviv.

NEWS AGENCIES

ITIM—The Israeli News Agency: 10 Tiomkin St, Tel-Aviv; tel. 3-5601011; fax 3-5605190; e-mail noy@itim.co.il; internet www.itim.co.il; f. 1950; Editor-in-Chief HAIM NOY.

Jewish Telegraphic Agency (JTA): Israel Bureau, Jerusalem Post Bldg, Romema, Jerusalem 91000; tel. 2-610579; fax 2-536635; Dir DAVID LANDAU.

Palestine Press Service: Salah ad-Din St, East Jerusalem; Proprs IBRAHIM QARA'EEN, Mrs RAYMONDA TAWIL; only Arab news agency in the Occupied Territories.

Foreign Bureaux

Agence France-Presse: POB 1507, 206 Jaffa Rd, Jerusalem 91014; tel. 2-5373243; fax 2-5373873; e-mail afpjer@netvision.net.il; Correspondent LUC DE BAROCHEZ.

Agencia EFE (Spain): POB 37190, 18 Hilel St, Jerusalem 91371; tel. 2-6242038; fax 2-6242056; e-mail postigocarmen@hotmail.com; Correspondent CARMEN POSTIGO.

Agenzia Nazionale Stampa Associata (ANSA) (Italy): 30 Dizengoff St, Tel-Aviv 64332; tel. 3-6299319; fax 3-5250302; Bureau Chief SANDRO PARONE; 9 Lloyd George St, Jerusalem 93110; Correspondent GIORGIO RACCAH.

Associated Press (AP) (USA): POB 13172, 206 Jaffa Rd, Jerusalem 91131; tel. 2-5385577; fax 2-5376083; Chief of Bureau DAN PERRY.

Deutsche Presse-Agentur (dpa) (Germany): 30 Ibn Gvirol St, Tel-Aviv 64078; tel. 3-6959007; fax 3-6969594; e-mail dpatlv@trendline.co.il; Correspondents Dr HEINZ-RUDOLF OTHMERDING, JEFF ABRAMOVITZ.

Jiji Tsushin-Sha (Japan): 9 Schmuel Hanagld, Jerusalem 94592; tel. 2-232553; fax 2-232402; Correspondent HIROKAZU OIKAWA.

Kyodo News Service (Japan): Tel-Aviv; tel. 3-6958185; fax 3-6917478; Correspondent HAJIME OZAKI.

Reuters (UK): 38 Hamasger St, Tel-Aviv 67211; tel. 3-5372211; fax 3-5372045; Jerusalem Capital Studios (JCS) 206 Jaffa Rd, Jerusalem 91131; tel. 2-5370502; fax 2-5374241; Chief of Bureau PAUL HOLMES.

United Press International (UPI) (USA): 138 Petach Tikva Rd, Tel-Aviv; Bureau Man. BROOKE W. KROEGER; Bureau Man. in Jerusalem LOUIS TOSCANO.

Informatsionnoye Telegrafnoye Agentstvo Rossii—Telegrafnoye Agentstvo Suverennykh Stran (ITAR—TASS) (Russia) is also represented.

Publishers

Achiasaf Ltd: POB 8414, Netanya 42504, tel. 9-8851390; fax 9-8851391; e-mail achiasaf@netvision.net.il; f. 1933; general; Man. Dir MATAN ACHIASAF.

Am Oved Publishers Ltd: POB 470, 22 Mazeh St, Tel-Aviv 61003; tel. 3-6291526; fax 3-6298911; e-mail info@am-oved.co.il; internet www.am-oved.co.il; f. 1942; fiction, non-fiction, reference books, school and university textbooks, children's books, poetry, classics, science fiction; Man. Dir YARON SADAN.

'Amihai' Publishing House Ltd: POB 8448, 19 Yad Harutzim St, Netanya Darom 42505; tel. 9-8859099; fax 9-8853464; e-mail oron@idc.ac.il; f. 1948; fiction, general science, linguistics, languages, arts; Dir YITZHAK ORON.

Arabic Publishing House: 93 Arlozorof St, Tel-Aviv; tel. 3-6921674; f. 1960; established by the Histadrut; periodicals and books; Gen. Man. GASSAN MUKLASHI.

Ariel Publishing House: POB 3328, Jerusalem 91033; tel. 2-6434540; fax 2-6436164; e-mail elysch@netvision.net.il; f. 1976; history, archaeology, religion, geography, folklore; CEO ELY SCHILLER.

Astrolog Publishing House: POB 11231, Hod Hasharon 45111; tel. 9-7412044; fax 9-7442714; e-mail sarabm@netvision.net.il; f. 1994; general non-fiction, religion, alternative medicine; Man. Dir SARA BEN-MORDECHAI.

Bitan Publishers A. S. Media International Ltd: POB 3068, Ramat-Hasharon 47130; tel. 3-6040089; fax 3-5404792; f. 1965; aeronautics, biography, child development, fiction, educational, literature and literary criticism, mysteries, leisure, travel, women's studies, self-help books; Man. A. BITAN.

Carta, The Israel Map and Publishing Co Ltd: POB 2500, 18 Ha'uman St, Industrial Area, Talpiot, Jerusalem 91024; tel. 2-6783355; fax 2-6782373; e-mail cartaben@netvision.net.il; internet www.holyland-jerusalem.com; f. 1958; the principal cartographic publisher; Pres. and CEO SHAY HAUSMAN.

Dvir Publishing Co Ltd: POB 22383, 32 Schocken St, Tel-Aviv; tel. 3-6812244; fax 3-6826138; e-mail info@zmora.co.il; internet www.zmora.co.il; f. 1924; literature, science, art, education; Publr OHAD ZMORA.

Rodney Franklin Agency: POB 37727, 53 Mazeh St, Tel-Aviv 65789; tel. 3-5600724; fax 3-5600479; e-mail rodneyf@netvision.net.il; f. 1974; exclusive representative of various British, other European, US and Canadian publishers; Dir RODNEY FRANKLIN.

Gefen Publishing House Ltd: POB 36004, 6 Hatzvi St, Jerusalem 91360; tel. 2-5380247; fax 2-5388423; e-mail info@gefenpublishing.com; internet www.israelbooks.com; f. 1981; the largest publisher of English-language books; also publishes wide range of fiction and non-fiction; CEOs ILAN GREENFIELD, DROR GREENFIELD.

Globes Publishers: POB 18041, 127 Igal Alon St, Tel-Aviv 67443; tel. 3-6979797; fax 3-6910334; internet www.globes.co.il.

Gvanim: POB 11138, 29 Bar-Kochba St, Tel-Aviv 61111; tel. 3-5281044; fax 3-5283648; e-mail traklinm@zahav.net.il; f. 1992; poetry, belles lettres, fiction; Man. Dir MARITZA ROSMAN.

Hakibbutz Hameuchad Publishing House Ltd: POB 1432, Bnei Brak, Tel-Aviv 51114; tel. 3-5785810; fax 3-5785811; e-mail bruria@kibutz-poalim.co.il; f. 1940; general; Dir UZI SHAVIT.

Hanitzotz A-Sharara Publishing House: POB 41199, Jaffa 61411; tel. 3-6839145; fax 3-6839148; e-mail oda@netvision.net.il; internet www.hanitzotz.com; 'progressive' booklets and publications in Arabic, Hebrew and English.

Hed Arzi (Ma'ariv) Publishing Ltd: 3A Yoni Netanyahu St, Or-Yehuda, Tel-Aviv 60376; tel. 3-5383333; fax 3-6343205; e-mail shimoni@hed-arzi.co.il; f. 1954 as Sifriat-Ma'ariv Ltd; later known as Ma'ariv Book Guild Ltd; general; Man. Dir and Editor-in-Chief ITZIK GLIK.

Hod-Ami—Computer Books Ltd: POB 6108, Herzliya 46160; tel. 9-9564716; fax 9-9571582; e-mail info@hod-ami.co.il; internet www.hod-ami.co.il; f. 1984; computer science; CEO ITZHAK AMIHUD.

Intermedia Publishing Enterprises Ltd (IPE): POB 2121, 23 Hataas St, Kefar-Sava 44641; tel. 9-5608501; fax 9-5608513; e-mail freed@inter.net.il; f. 1993; business, education, English as a second language, journalism, health, nutrition, mathematics, medicine, philosophy, self-help; Man. Dir ARIE FRIED.

Israeli Music Publications Ltd: POB 7681, Jerusalem 94188; tel. 2-6251370; fax 2-6241378; e-mail khanukaev@pop.isracom.net.il; f. 1949; books on music, dance and musical works; Dir of Music Publications SERGEI KHANUKAEV.

Jerusalem Center for Public Affairs: 13 Tel Hai St, Jerusalem 92107; tel. 2-5619281; fax 2-5619112; e-mail jcenter@jcpa.org; internet www.jcpa.org; f. 1976; Jewish political tradition; publishes the Jewish Political Studies Review.

The Jerusalem Publishing House Ltd: POB 7147, 39 Tchernechovski St, Jerusalem 91071; tel. 2-5636511; fax 2-5634266; e-mail jphgagi@netvision.net.il; f. 1967; biblical research, history, encyclopedias, archaeology, arts of the Holy Land, cookbooks, guidebooks, economics, politics; Dir SHLOMO S. GAFNI; Man. Editor RACHEL GILON.

The Jewish Agency—Department of Jewish Zionist Education: POB 10615, Jerusalem 91104; tel. 2-6202629; fax 2-6204122; e-mail bookshop@jazo.org.il; f. 1945; education, Jewish philosophy, studies in the Bible, children's books published in Hebrew, English, French, Spanish, German, Swedish and Portuguese, Hebrew teaching material.

Jewish History Publications (Israel 1961) Ltd: POB 1232, 29 Jabotinsky St, Jerusalem 92141; tel. 2-5632310; f. 1961; encyclopedias, World History of the Jewish People series; Chair. ALEXANDER PELI.

Karni Publishers Ltd: 32 Zalman Schocken St, Tel-Aviv 66556; tel. 3-6812244; fax 3-6826138; e-mail info@zmora.co.il; internet www.zmora.co.il; f. 1951; biography, fiction, poetry, children's and educational books; Publr OHAD ZMORA.

Keter Publishing House Ltd: POB 7145, Givat Shaul B, Jerusalem 91071; tel. 2-6557822; fax 2-6536811; e-mail info@keter-books.co.il; internet www.keter-books.co.il; f. 1959; original and translated works of fiction, encyclopedias, non-fiction, guidebooks and children's books; publishing imprints: Israel Program for Scientific Translations, Keter Books, Domino, Encyclopedia Judaica; Man. Dir YIPHTACH DEKEL.

Kinneret Publishing House: 14 Habanai St, Holon 58850; tel. 3-5582252; fax 3-5582255; e-mail kinbooks@netvision.net.il; f. 1980;

child development and care, cookery, dance, educational, humour, non-fiction, music, home-care, psychology, psychiatry, travel; Man. Dir YORAM ROS.

Kiryat Sefer: Tel-Aviv 65812; tel. 3-5660188; fax 3-5100227; f. 1933; concordances, dictionaries, textbooks, maps, scientific books; Dir AVRAHAM SIVAN.

Laser Pages Publishing Ltd: POB 35409, Merkaz Sapir 6/36, Givat Shaul, Jerusalem 91352; tel. 2-6522226; fax 2-6522277; e-mail laserpages@netmedia.net.il; internet www.sciencefromisrael .com; scientific journals.

LB Publishing Co: POB 32056, Jerusalem 91000; tel. and fax 2-5664637; f. 1993; history, regional issues, religion; Pres. LILI BREZINER.

Magnes Press: The Hebrew University, POB 39099, Jerusalem 91390; tel. 2-6586656; fax 2-5633370; e-mail magnes@vms.huji.ac.il; f. 1929; biblical studies, Judaica, and all academic fields; Dir DAN BENOVICI.

MAP-Mapping and Publishing Ltd (Tel-Aviv Books): POB 56024, 17 Tchernikhovski St, Tel-Aviv 61560; tel. 3-6210500; fax 3-5257725; e-mail info@mapa.co.il; internet www.mapa.co.il; f. 1985; maps, atlases, travel guides, textbooks and reference books; Man. Dir DANI TRACZ; Editor-in-Chief MOULI MELTZER.

Rubin Mass Ltd: POB 990, 7 Ha-Ayin-Het St, Jerusalem 91009; tel. 2-6277863; fax 2-6277864; e-mail rmass@inter.net.il; internet www.id-knowledge.com/mas; f. 1927; Hebraica, Judaica, export of all Israeli books and periodicals; Dir OREN MASS.

Ministry of Defence Publishing House: 107 Ha' Hashmonaim St, Tel-Aviv 67133; tel. 3-5655900; fax 3-5655994; e-mail publish@ attmail.com; internet www.modpublishing.co.il; f. 1939; military literature, Judaism, history and geography of Israel; Dir JOSEPH PERLOVITZ.

M. Mizrachi Publishing House Ltd: 106 Allenby St, Tel-Aviv 65815; tel. 3-5601579; fax 3-5660274; f. 1960; children's books, fiction, history, medicine, science; Dirs MEIR MIZRACHI, ISRAEL MIZRACHI.

Mosad Harav Kook: POB 642, 1 Maimon St, Jerusalem 91006; tel. 2-6526231; fax 2-6526968; f. 1937; editions of classical works, Torah and Jewish studies; Dir Rabbi YOSEF MOVSHOVITZ.

Otsar Hamoreh: c/o Israel Teachers' Union, 8 Ben Saruk, Tel-Aviv 62969; tel. 3-6922983; fax 3-6922988; f. 1951; educational; Man. Dir JOSEPH SALOMAN.

PC Media: POB 11438, 13 Yad Harutzim St, Tel-Aviv 61114; tel. 3-6385810; fax 3-6889207; e-mail pcmedia@pc.co.il; internet www.zdnet.co.il; information technology; Man. Dir DAHLIA PELED.

Alexander Peli Jerusalem Publishing Co Ltd: POB 1232, 29 Jabotinsky St, Jerusalem 92141; tel. 2-5632310; f. 1961; encyclopedias, Judaica, history, the arts, educational material; Chair. ALEXANDER PELI.

Schocken Publishing House Ltd: POB 2316, 24 Nathan Yelin Mor St, Tel-Aviv 67015; tel. 3 5610130; fax 3-5622668; internet www.schocken.co.il; f. 1938; general; Dir Mrs RACHELI EDELMAN.

Shalem Press: 22A Hatzfira St, Jerusalem 93102; tel. 2-5662202; e-mail shalem@shalem.org.il; internet www.shalem.org.il; f. 1994; economics, political science, history, philosophy, cultural issues.

Shikmona Publishing Co Ltd: POB 7145, Givat Shaul B, Jerusalem 91071; tel. 2-6557822; fax 2-6536811; e-mail info@keter-books .co.il; internet www.keter-books.co.il; f. 1965; Zionism, archaeology, art, guidebooks, fiction and non-fiction; Man. Dir YIPHTACH DEKEL.

Sifriat Poalim: POB 1432, Bnei Brak, Tel-Aviv 51114; tel. 3-5785810; fax 3-5785811; e-mail avram@kibutz-poalim.co.il; internet www.dbook.co.il/images/poalim/default.html; f. 1939; general literature; Gen. Man. AVRAM KANTOR.

Sinai Publishing: 72 Allenby St, Tel-Aviv 65812; tel. 3-5163672; fax 3-5176783; f. 1853; Hebrew books and religious articles; Dir MOSHE SCHLESINGER.

Steinhart-Katzir: POB 8333, Netanya 42505; tel. 9-8854770; fax 9-8854771; e-mail mail@haolam.co.il; internet www.haolam.co.il; f. 1991; travel; Man. Dir OHAD SHARAV.

Tcehrikover Publishers Ltd: 12 Hasharon St, Tel-Aviv 66185; tel. 3-6870621; fax 3-6874729; e-mail barkay@inter.net.il; education, psychology, economics, psychiatry, literature, literary criticism, essays, history geography, criminology, art, languages, management; Man. Editor S. TCHERIKOVER.

Yachdav United Publishers Co Ltd: POB 20123, 29 Carlebach St, Tel-Aviv 67132; tel. 3-5614121; fax 3-5611996; e-mail info@tbpai.co.il; f. 1960; educational; Chair. EPHRAIM BEN-DOR; Exec. Dir AMNON BEN-SHMUEL.

Yavneh Publishing House Ltd: 4 Mazeh St, Tel-Aviv 65213; tel. 3-6297856; fax 3-6293638; e-mail publishing@yavneh.co.il; f. 1932; general; Dir NIRA PREISKEL.

Yeda Lakol Publications Ltd: POB 1232, 29 Jabotinsky St, Jerusalem 92141; tel. 2-5632310; f. 1961; encyclopedias, Judaica, the arts, educational material, children's books; Chair. ALEXANDER PELI.

Yedioth Ahronoth Books: POB 37744, 3 Mikunis St, Tel-Aviv 61376; tel. 3-6888466; fax 3-5377820; e-mail books@yedioth.co.il; f. 1952; non-fiction, politics, Jewish religion, health, music, dance, fiction, education; Man. Dir DOV EICHENWALD; Editor-in-Chief ALIZA ZIGLER.

S. Zack and Co: 2 King George St, Jerusalem 94229; tel. 2-6257819; fax 2-6252493; e-mail zackpublishers@bezeqint.net; f. c. 1930; fiction, science, philosophy, Judaism, children's books, educational and reference books, dictionaries; Dir MICHAEL ZACK.

PUBLISHERS' ASSOCIATION

The Book Publishers' Association of Israel: POB 20123, 29 Carlebach St, Tel-Aviv 67132; tel. 3-5614121; fax 3-5611996; e-mail info@tbpai.co.il; internet www.tbpai.co.il; f. 1939; mems: 84 publishing firms; Chair. SHAI HAUSMAN; Man. Dir AMNON BEN-SHMUEL.

Broadcasting and Communications

TELECOMMUNICATIONS

Barak I.T.C.: Cibel Industrial Park, 15 Hamelacha St, Rosh Ha'ayin 48091; tel 3-9001900; fax 3-9001800; internet www.barak-online .net; f. 1998; Chair. MAIR LAISER; Pres. and CEO AVI PATIR.

Bezeq—The Israel Telecommunication Corpn Ltd: POB 1088, 15 Hazvi St, Jerusalem 91010; tel. 2-5395503; fax 2-5000410; e-mail bzq.spk@attmail.com; internet www.bezeq.co.il; 54.6% state-owned; scheduled for full privatization in 2002; launched own cellular network, Pelephone Communications Ltd, in 1986; total assets US $4,837m. (Dec. 1997); Chair. ISRAEL TAPOOHI; Pres. and CEO AMI EREL.

Pelephone Communications Ltd: 33 Hagvura St, Givatayim, Tel-Aviv 53483; tel. 3-5728881; fax 3-5728111; internet www .pelephone.co.il; Pres. and CEO YIGAL BAR-YOUSSEF.

Cellcom Israel: POB 3164, 3 Hagalim Blvd, Herzlia Pituach, Herzlia B, Netanya 46131; tel. 9-9599599; fax 9-9599700; internet www.cellcom.co.il; f. 1994; mobile telecommunications operator; Chair. S. PIOTRKOWSKY; Pres. and CEO JACOB PERRY.

ECI Telecom Ltd: POB 3038, 30 Hasivim St, Petach Tikva, Tel-Aviv 49133; tel. 3-9266555; fax 3-9266500; internet www.ecitele .com; Chair. JONATHON B. KOLBER; Pres. and Gen. Man. DAVID RUBNER.

Partner Communications Co Ltd: POB 435, Rosh Ha'ayin, Tel-Aviv 48103; tel. 3-9054888; fax 3-9054999; mobile telecommunications operator; f. 1998 when obtained licence to operate Israel's first GSM system; CEO AMIKAM COHEN; Man. Dir E. COHEN.

Vocal Tec: Tel-Aviv; Gen. Man. DORON SINGER.

BROADCASTING

Radio

Israel Broadcasting Authority (IBA) (Radio): POB 28080, Jerusalem 91280; tel. 2-240124; fax 2-257034; internet www.iba.org.il; f. 1948; state-owned station in Jerusalem with additional studios in Tel-Aviv and Haifa. IBA broadcasts six programmes for local and overseas listeners on medium, shortwave and VHF/FM in 16 languages; Hebrew, Arabic, English, Yiddish, Ladino, Romanian, Hungarian, Moghrabi, Persian, French, Russian, Bucharian, Georgian, Portuguese, Spanish and Amharic; Chair. MICHA YINON; Dir-Gen. URI PORAT; Dir of Radio (vacant); Dir External Services VICTOR GRAJEWSKY.

Galei Zahal: MPOB 01005, Zahal; tel. 3-5126666; fax 3-5126760; e-mail galatz@glz.co.il; internet www.glz.co.il; f. 1950; Israeli Defence Force broadcasting station, Tel-Aviv, with studios in Jerusalem; broadcasts news, current affairs, music and cultural programmes on medium-wave and FM stereo, 24-hour in Hebrew; Dir ISACK TUNIK.

Kol Israel (The Voice of Israel): POB 1082, 21 Heleni Hamalka, Jerusalem 91010; tel. 2-6248715; fax 2-5383173; internet www .artificia.com/html/news.cgi; broadcasts music, news, and multilingual programmes for immigrants in Hebrew, Arabic, French and English on medium wave and FM stereo; Dir and Prog. Dir AMNON NADAV.

Television

Israel Broadcasting Authority (IBA): POB 7139, Jerusalem 91071; tel. 2-5301333; fax 2-292944; internet www.iba.org.il; broadcasts began in 1968; station in Jerusalem with additional studios in Tel-Aviv; one colour network (VHF with UHF available in all areas); one satellite channel; broadcasts in Hebrew, Arabic and English; Dir-Gen URI PORAT; Dir of Television YAIR STERN; Dir of Engineering RAFI YEOSHUA.

The Council of Cable TV and Satellite Broadcasting: 23 Jaffa Rd, Jerusalem 91999; tel. 2-6702210; fax 2-6702273; e-mail inbard @moc.gov.il; Chair. Dorit Inbar.

Israel Educational Television: Ministry of Education, 14 Klausner St, Tel-Aviv; tel. 3-6415270; fax 3-6427091; f. 1966 by Hanadiv (Rothschild Memorial Group) as Instructional Television Trust; began transmission in 1966; school programmes form an integral part of the syllabus in a wide range of subjects; also adult education; Gen. Man. Ahuva Fainmesse; Dir of Engineering S. Kasif.

Second Channel TV and Radio Administration: 3 Kanfi Nesharim St, POB 34112, Jerusalem 95464; tel. 2-6556222; fax 2-6556287; e-mail channel2@netvision.net.il; f. 1991; Chair. Prof. Gideon Doron; Man. Dir Nachman Shai.

In 1986 the Government approved the establishment of a commercial radio and television network to be run in competition with the state system.

Finance

(cap. = capital; dep. = deposits; m. = million; res = reserves; brs = branches; amounts in shekels)

BANKING

During 1991–98 the Government raised some US $3,995m. through privatization and the issuance of shares and convertible securities in the banking sector.

Central Bank

Bank of Israel: POB 780, Bank of Israel Bldg, Kiryat Ben-Gurion, Jerusalem 91007; tel. 2-6552211; fax 2-6528805; e-mail webmaster@ bankisrael.gov.il; internet www.bankisrael.gov.il; f. 1954 as the Central Bank of the State of Israel; cap. 60m., res −14,552m., dep. 103,269m. (Dec. 2000); Gov. David Klein; 2 brs.

Principal Israeli Banks

Arab-Israel Bank Ltd: POB 27, Nesher 20300; tel. 4-8308222; fax 4-8308250; internet www.bank-aravi-israeli.co.il; total assets 3,198.4m., dep. 2,873.4m. (Dec. 1999); subsidiary of Bank Leumi le-Israel BM; Chair. D. Efrima; Gen. Man. Y. Azrad.

Bank Hapoalim: POB 27, 50 Rothschild Blvd, Tel-Aviv 66883; tel. 3-5673333; fax 3-5607028; e-mail international@bnhp.co.il; internet www.bankhapoalim.co.il; f. 1921 as the Workers' Bank, name changed as above 1961; American-Israel Bank merged into the above 1999; privatized in June 2000; total assets 240,250m., dep. 205,729m. (Dec. 2001); Chair. Shlomo Nehama; 364 brs in Israel and abroad.

Bank of Jerusalem Ltd: POB 2255, 2 Herbert Samuel St, Jerusalem 91022; tel. 2-6706211; fax 2-6246793; e-mail webmaster@bank jerusalem.co.il; internet www.bankjerusalem.co.il; private bank; total assets 6,057m., dep. 5,463m. (Dec. 2001); Chair. David Blumberg; Man. Dir and Gen. Man. David Baruch.

Bank Leumi le-Israel BM: POB 2, 24–32 Yehuda Halevi St, Tel-Aviv 65546; tel. 3-5148111; fax 3-5661872; internet www.bankleumi .com; f. 1902 as Anglo-Palestine Co; renamed Anglo-Palestine Bank 1930; reincorporated as above 1951; 41.73% state-owned; total assets 234,261m., dep. 204,589m. (Dec. 2001); Chair. Eitan Raff; Pres., CEO and Gen. Man. Galia Maor; 229 brs in Israel and abroad.

Euro-Trade Bank Ltd: POB 37318, 2 Yavne St, Tel-Aviv 61372; tel. 3-6216806; fax 3-6209062; e-mail info@eurotrade.co.il; internet www.eurotrade.co.il; f. 1953; renamed Israel Building Bank Ltd 1978; name changed as above 1993; total assets 261,274m., dep. 208,932m. (Dec. 2000); Chair. of Bd Zelekha Shlomo; Man. Dir Joseph Pinchasof.

First International Bank of Israel Ltd: POB 29036, Shalom Mayer Tower, 9 Ahad Ha'am St, Tel-Aviv 62251; tel. 3-5196111; fax 3-5100316; e-mail yuval@fibimail.co.il; internet www.fibi.co.il; f. 1972 as a result of a merger between Foreign Trade Bank Ltd and Export Bank Ltd; total assets 64,996m., cap. 3,142m., dep. 57,223m. (June 2001); Chair. Shlomo Piotrkowsky; Man. Dir and CEO David Granot; 90 brs.

Industrial Development Bank of Israel Ltd: POB 33580, Asia House, 4 Weizman St, Tel-Aviv 61334; tel. 3-6972727; fax 3-6972893; internet www.idbi.co.il; f. 1957; 61% state-owned; total assets 12,839.4m., dep. 11,599.6m. (Dec. 2000); Chair. Shlomo Borochev; Gen. Man. Yehoshua Ichilov.

Investec Bank (Israel) Ltd: POB 677, 38 Rothschild Blvd, Tel-Aviv 61006; tel. 3-5645645; fax 3-5645210; e-mail irroni@igb.co.il; internet www.investec.co.il; f. 1934 as Palestine Credit Utility Bank Ltd, renamed Israel General Bank Ltd 1964; ownership transferred

to Investec Bank Ltd (South Africa) in 1996; name changed to Investec Clali Bank Ltd 1999, and as above 2001; total assets 5,856.7m., dep. 5,278.8m. (Dec. 1999); Chair. Hugh Sydney Herman; Man. Dir and CEO Jonathon Irroni; 3 brs.

Israel Continental Bank Ltd: POB 37406, 65 Rothschild Blvd, Tel-Aviv 61373; tel. 3-5641616; fax 3-6200399; f. 1974; capital held jointly by Bank Hapoalim BM (63.3%) and Bank für Gemeinwirtschaft AG (36.7%); total assets 1,982.8m., dep. 1,671.7m. (Dec. 2001); Chair. Amiram Sivan; Man. Dir P. Horev; 3 brs.

Israel Discount Bank Ltd: 27 Yehuda Halevi St, Tel-Aviv 65136; tel. 3-5145555; fax 3-5145346; e-mail contact@discountbank.net; internet www.discountbank.net; f. 1935; 57.09% state-owned; cap. 98m., dep. 116,844m. (March 2002); Chair. Arie Mientkavich; some 139 brs in Israel and abroad.

Leumi Industrial Development Bank Ltd: POB 2, 13 Ahad Haam St, Tel-Aviv 61000; tel. 3-5149951; fax 3-5149897; e-mail michaelz@bll.co.il; f. 1944; subsidiary of Bank Leumi le-Israel BM; cap. and res 100.1m. (Dec. 2001); Chair. B. Naveh; Gen. Man. Michael Ziv.

Maritime Bank of Israel Ltd: POB 29373, 35 Ahad Ha'am St, Tel-Aviv 61293; tel. 3-5642222; fax 3-5642323; e-mail sap_mat@ netvision.net.il; internet www.sapanut.co.il; f. 1962; total assets 1,257.1m., cap. 6.0m., res 237.4m., dep. 883.0m. (Dec. 2001). Chair. Shimon Topor; CEO and Gen. Man. David Levinson.

Mercantile Discount Bank Ltd: POB 1292, 103 Allenby Rd, Tel-Aviv 61012; tel. 3-7105550; fax 3-7105532; e-mail fec@mdb.co.il; internet www.mercantile.co.il; f. as Barclays Discount Bank Ltd in 1971 by Barclays Bank International Ltd and Israel Discount Bank Ltd to incorporate Israel brs of Barclays; Israel Discount Bank Ltd became the sole owner in February 1993; name changed as above April 1993; absorbed Mercantile Bank of Israel Ltd in 1997; total assets 13,734m., cap. 48m., dep. 12,539m. (Dec. 2000); Chair. of Bd Arie Mientkavich; Gen. Man. Prof. Shalom Josef Hochman; 67 brs.

Union Bank of Israel Ltd: POB 2428, 6–8 Ahuzat Bayit St, Tel-Aviv 65143; tel. 3-5191111; fax 3-5191274; internet www.unionbank .co.il; f. 1951; 18.4% state-owned; total assets 22,100m., dep. 19,411m. (Dec. 2001); Chair. Z. Abeles; CEO and Gen. Man. B. Oshman; 28 brs.

United Mizrahi Bank Ltd: POB 309, Tel-Aviv 61002; tel. 3-5679433; fax 3-5679121; e-mail umb_ifts@mizrahi.co.il; internet www.mizrahi.co.il; f. 1923 as Mizrahi Bank Ltd; 1969 absorbed Hapoel Hamizrahi Bank Ltd and name changed as above; absorbed Finance and Trade Bank Ltd in 1990; 1.23% state-owned; total assets 68,760m., dep. 62,842m. (Dec. 2000); Pres. and CEO Victor Medina; 101 brs.

Mortgage Banks

Discount Mortgage Bank Ltd: POB 2844, 16–18 Simtat Beit Hashoeva, Tel-Aviv 61027; tel. 3-5643311; fax 3-5661704; f. 1959; subsidiary of Israel Discount Bank Ltd; cap. p.u. 1.3m., res 463.6m. (Dec. 1997); Chair. Arie Mientkavich; Man. M. Eldar.

First International Mortgage Bank Ltd.: 39 Montefiore St, Tel-Aviv 65201; tel. 3-5643311; fax 3-5643321; f. 1922 as the Mortgage and Savings Bank, name changed as above 1996; subsidiary of First International Bank of Israel Ltd; cap. and res 334m. (Dec. 1996); Chair. Shlomo Piotrkowsky; Man. Dir P. Hamo; 50 brs.

Leumi Mortgage Bank Ltd: POB 69, 31–37 Montefiore St, Tel-Aviv 65201; tel. 3-5648444; fax 3-5648334; f. 1921 as General Mortgage Bank Ltd; subsidiary of Bank Leumi le-Israel BM; total assets 26,155m., dep. 23,830m. (Dec. 2000); Chair. A. Zeldman; Gen. Man. R. Zabag; 9 brs.

Mishkan-Hapoalim Mortgage Bank Ltd: POB 1610, 2 Ibn Gvirol St, Tel-Aviv 61015; tel. 3-6970505; fax 3-6961379; f. 1950; subsidiary of Bank Hapoalim BM; total assets 8,289m., dep. 10,268.3m. (Dec. 1993); Chair. M. Olenik; Man. Dir A. Kroizer; 131 brs.

Tefahot, Israel Mortgage Bank Ltd: POB 93, 9 Heleni Hamalka St, Jerusalem 91902; tel. 2-6755222; fax 2-6755344; f. 1945; subsidiary of United Mizrahi Bank Ltd; total assets 27,442m., cap. and res 1,446m. (Dec. 2000); Chair. Reuven Adler; Man. Dir Chaim Freilichman; 50 brs.

STOCK EXCHANGE

The Tel-Aviv Stock Exchange: 54 Ahad Ha'am St, Tel-Aviv 65202; tel. 3-5677411; fax 3-5105379; e-mail spokesperson@tase .co.il; internet www.tase.co.il; f. 1953; Chair. Prof. Yair E. Orgler; Gen. Man. Saul Bronfeld.

INSURANCE

The Israel Insurance Asscn lists 15 member companies; a selection of these are listed below, as are some non-members.

Ararat Insurance Co Ltd: Ararat House, 13 Montefiore St, Tel-Aviv 65164; tel. 3-640888; f. 1949; Co-Chair. Aharon Dovrat, Philip Zuckerman; Gen. Man. Pinchas Cohen.

Aryeh Insurance Co of Israel Ltd: 9 Ahad Ha'am St, Tel-Aviv 65251; tel. 3-5141777; fax 3-5179339; e-mail rubens@aryeh-ins.co.il; f. 1948; Pres. Ruben Sharoni; Chair. Avigdor Kaplan.

Clal Insurance Co Ltd: POB 326, 46 Petach Tikva Rd, Tel-Aviv 66184; tel. 3-6387777; fax 3-6387676; e-mail avigdork@clal-ins.co.il; f. 1962; Pres. and CEO Avigdor Kaplan; Man. Dir Rimon Ben-Shaoul.

Eliahu Insurance Co Ltd: 2 Ibn Gvirol St, Tel-Aviv 64077; tel. 3-6920911; fax 3-6956995; e-mail ofer@eliahu.com; Chair. Ofer Eliahu.

Hassneh Insurance Co of Israel Ltd: POB 805, 115 Allenby St, Tel-Aviv 61007; tel. 3-5649111; f. 1924; Man. Dir M. Michael Miller.

Israel Phoenix Assurance Co Ltd: 30 Levontin St, Tel-Aviv 61020; tel. 3-7141111; fax 3-5666902; e-mail vardab@phoenix.co.il; internet www.phoenix.co.il; f. 1949; CEO Bar-Kochva Ben-Gera; Chair. of Bd Joseph D. Hackmey.

Menorah Insurance Co Ltd: Menorah House, 15 Allenby St, Tel-Aviv 65786; tel. 3-7107777; fax 3-7107402; e-mail anat-by@bezeqint.net; f. 1935; Chair. Menachem Gurewitz; Gen. Man. Shabtai Engel.

Migdal Insurance Co Ltd: POB 37633, 26 Sa'adiya Ga'on St, Tel-Aviv 67135; tel. 3-5637637; fax 3-5610220; e-mail sarav@migdal -group.co.il; internet www.migdal.co.il; part of Bank Leumi Group; f. 1934; Chair. Aharon Fogel; CEO Izzy Cohen.

Palglass Palestine Plate Glass Insurance Co Ltd: Tel-Aviv 65541; f. 1934; Gen. Man. Akiva Zalzman.

Sahar-Zion Insurance Co Ltd: 3 Abba Hillel St, Ramat-Gan, Tel-Aviv; tel. 3-7547777; fax 3-7547800; e-mail mukya@sahar-zion.co.il; f. 1949; Chair. Gideon Hamburger.

Samson Insurance Co Ltd: POB 33678, Avgad Bldg, 5 Jabotinsky St, Ramat-Gan, Tel-Aviv 52520; tel. 3-7521616; fax 3-7516644; f. 1933; Chair. E. Ben-Amram; Gen. Man. Giora Sagi.

Sela Insurance Co Ltd: Tel-Aviv; tel. 3-61028; f. 1938; Man. Dir E. Shani.

Shiloah Insurance Co Ltd: 3 Abba-Hillel St, Ramat-Gan, Tel-Aviv 52118; tel. 3-7547777; fax 3-7545100; e-mail y_hamburger@harel -hamishmar.co.il; f. 1933; Chair. Yair Hamburger; Gen. Man. Dr S. Bamirah.

Trade and Industry

CHAMBERS OF COMMERCE

Federation of Bi-National Chambers of Commerce and Industry with and in Israel: POB 50196, 29 Hamered St, Tel-Aviv 61500; tel. 3-5173261; fax 3-5173283; federates: Israel-British Chamber of Commerce; Australia-Israel Chamber of Commerce; Chamber of Commerce and Industry Israel-Asia; Chamber of Commerce Israel-Belgique-Luxembourg; Canada-Israel Chamber of Commerce and Industry; Israel-Denmark Chamber of Commerce; Chambre de Commerce Israel-France; Chamber of Commerce and Industry Israel-Germany; Camera di Commercio Israeli-Italia; Israel-Japan Chamber of Commerce; Israel-Latin America, Spain and Portugal Chamber of Commerce; Netherlands-Israel Chamber of Commerce; Israel-Greece Chamber of Commerce; Israel-Bulgaria Chamber of Commerce; Israel-Ireland Chamber of Commerce; Handelskammer Israel-Schweiz; Israel-South Africa Chamber of Commerce; Israel-Sweden Chamber of Commerce; Israel-Hungary Chamber of Commerce; Israel-Romania Chamber of Commerce; Israel-Russia Chamber of Commerce; Israel-Poland Chamber of Commerce; Israel-Austria Chamber of Commerce; Israel-Ukraine Chamber of Commerce; Israel-Africa Chamber of Commerce; Israel-Jordan Chamber of Commerce; Israel-Egypt Chamber of Commerce; Israel-Morocco Chamber of Commerce; Israel-Moldova Chamber of Commerce; Israel-Norway Chamber of Commerce; Israel-Slovakia Chamber of Commerce; Israel-Portugal Chamber of Commerce; Israel-Finland Chamber of Commerce; Israel-Kazakhstan Chamber of Commerce; Israel-Turkey Chamber of Commerce; Israel-Thailand Chamber of Commerce; Chair. G. Propper.

Federation of Israeli Chambers of Commerce: POB 20027, 84 Ha 'Hashmonaim St, Tel-Aviv 67011; tel. 3-5631010; fax 3-5619025; e-mail chamber@tlv-chamber.org.il; internet www.tlv-chamber .org.il; co-ordinates the Tel-Aviv, Jerusalem, Haifa and Beersheba Chambers of Commerce; Pres. Dan Gillerman.

Haifa Chamber of Commerce and Industry (Haifa and District): POB 33176, 53 Haatzmaut Rd, Haifa 31331; tel. 4-8626364; fax 4-8645428; e-mail main@haifachamber.org.il; internet www.haifa chamber.com; f. 1921; 700 mems; Pres. E. Melamud; S. Gantz; Man. Dir D. Marom.

Israel-British Chamber of Commerce: POB 50321, 29 Hamered St, Tel-Aviv 61502; tel. 3-5109424; fax 3-5109540; e-mail isrbrit@ netvision.net.il; f. 1951; 350 mems; Chair. Amnon Dotan; Exec. Dir Felix Kipper.

Jerusalem Chamber of Commerce: POB 2083, Jerusalem 91020; tel. 2-6254333; fax 2-6254335; e-mail jerccom@inter.net.il; internet www.jerccom.co.il; f. 1908; c. 300 mems; Pres. Shmulik Semmel.

Tel-Aviv-Jaffa Chamber of Commerce: POB 20027, 84 Ha 'Hashmonaim St, Tel-Aviv 61200; tel. 3-5631010; fax 3-5619025; e-mail chamber@chamber.org.il; internet www.chamber.org.il; f. 1919; 2,500 mems; Pres. Dan Gillerman.

INDUSTRIAL AND TRADE ASSOCIATIONS

Agricultural Export Co (AGREXCO): Tel-Aviv; state-owned agricultural marketing organization; Dir-Gen. Amotz Amiad.

The Agricultural Union: Tel-Aviv; consists of more than 50 agricultural settlements and is connected with marketing and supplying organizations, and Bahan Ltd, controllers and auditors.

The Centre for International Agricultural Development Cooperation (CINADCO): POB 30, Beit Dagan 50200; tel. 3-9485776; fax 3-9485761; e-mail cinadco@moag.gov.il; shares agricultural experience through the integration of research and project development; runs specialized training courses, advisory missions and feasibility projects in Israel and abroad; Dir Zvi Herman.

Citrus Marketing Board: POB 80, Beit Dagan 50250; tel. 3-9683811; fax 3-9683838; e-mail cmbi@netvision.net.il; internet www.online.co.il/cmbi; f. 1942; the central co-ordinating body of citrus growers and exporters in Israel; represents the citrus industry in international organizations; licenses private exporters; controls the quality of fruit; has responsibility for Jaffa trademarks; mounts advertising and promotion campaigns for Jaffa citrus fruit worldwide; carries out research and development of new varieties of citrus fruit, and 'environmentally friendly' fruit; Chair. D. Kritchman; Gen. Man. M. Davidson.

Farmers' Union of Israel: POB 209, 8 Kaplan St, Tel-Aviv; tel. 3-69502227; fax 3-6918228; f. 1913; membership of 7,000 independent farmers, citrus and winegrape growers; Pres. Pesach Grupper; Dir-Gen. Shlomo Reisman.

Flower Board of Israel: 2 Kaplan St, Tel-Aviv 64734; e-mail fbi@fbi.org.il; internet www.fbi.org.il.

Fruit Board of Israel: POB 20117, 119 Rehov Ha 'Hashmonaim, Tel-Aviv 61200; tel. 3-5632929; fax 3-5614672; e-mail fruits@ fruit.org.il; internet www.fruit.org.il; Dir-Gen. Dany Bruner.

General Asscn of Merchants in Israel: Tel-Aviv; the organization of retail traders; has a membership of 30,000 in 60 brs.

Israel Cotton Production and Marketing Board Ltd: POB 384, Herzlia B 46103; tel. 9-9509491; fax 9-9509159.

Israel Diamond Exchange Ltd: POB 3222, Ramat-Gan, Tel-Aviv; tel. 3-5760211; fax 3-5750652; e-mail judi@isde.co.il; f. 1937; production, export, import and finance facilities; net exports (2000) US \$5,322m.; Pres. Shmuel Schnitzer.

Israel Export Institute: POB 50084, 29 Hamered St, Tel-Aviv 68125; tel. 3-5142830; fax 3-5142902; e-mail library@export.gov.il; internet www.export.gov.il; Dir-Gen. Israel Shotland.

Israel Journalists' Asscn: 4 Kaplan St, Tel-Aviv 64734; tel. 3-6956141; Man. Dir Tuvia Saar.

Kibbutz Industries' Asscn: 8 Rehov Shaul Hamelech, Tel-Aviv 64733; tel. 3-6955413; fax 3-6951464; e-mail kiakia@netvision.co.il; liaison office for marketing and export of the goods produced by Israel's kibbutzim; Pres. Giora Masad.

Manufacturers' Asscn of Israel: POB 50022, Industry House, 29 Hamered St, Tel-Aviv 61500; tel. 3-5198787; fax 3-5162026; e-mail gendiv@industry.org.il; internet www.industry.org.il; 1,700 mem. enterprises employing nearly 85% of industrial workers in Israel; Pres. Oded Tyrah.

National Federation of Israeli Journalists: POB 7009, 4 Kaplan St, Tel-Aviv 64734; tel. 3-6956141; fax 3-6951438.

UTILITIES

The Israel Electric Corporation Ltd and the **Mekorot (Israel National Water Co)** are two of Israel's largest state-owned companies, with total assets valued at US \$10,832m. and US \$1,978m., respectively, at the end of 1997.

Israel Electric Corporation Ltd (IEC): POB 8810, 2 Ha 'Haganah St, Haifa 31086; tel. 4-8548148; fax 4-8538149; internet www.israel -electric.co.il; Chair. Gad Ya'acobi.

Mekorot (Israel National Water Co): 9 Lincoln St Development, Tel-Aviv 61201; tel. 3-6230806; fax 3-6230598; e-mail akanarek@ mekorot.co.il; internet www.mekorot.co.il.

MAJOR COMPANIES

Elbit Systems Ltd: POB 539, Advanced Technical Centre, Haifa 31053; tel. 4-8315315; fax 4-8550002; e-mail elbit-systems@elbit .co.il; internet www.elbit.co.il; producers of computers and defence electronics; subsidiary of ELRON Electronic Industries; sales US $415m., profits US $29m. (1998); Chair. EMMANUEL GILL; Pres. and CEO JOSEPH ACKERMAN.

Elscint Ltd: POB 550, Advance Technologies Center, Haifa 31004; tel. 4-8310310; fax 4-525608; f. 1969; designers and mfrs of electronic medical diagnostic equipment (body and brain scanners), nuclear medicine cameras and processors, whole body computerized tomographers, magnetic resonance imagers (MRI) and ultrasound scanners; Pres. JONATHAN ADERETH; 1,970 employees.

Israel Aircraft Industries Ltd (IAI): Ben-Gurion International Airport, Tel-Aviv 70100; tel. 3-9353111; fax 3-9358278; e-mail corpmkg@hdq.iai.co.il; internet www.iai.co.il; f. 1953; 100% state-owned; sales US $2,089m. (2001); designers and mfrs of military and civil aerospace; Chair. Maj.-Gen. ORI ORR; Pres. and CEO MOSHE KERET; 14,500 employees.

Israel Chemicals Ltd: POB 20245, Tel-Aviv 61202; tel. 3-6844401; fax 3-6844428; internet www.israelchemicals.co.il; f. 1968; 49% state-owned; total assets US $2,940.4m. (Dec. 2001); Chair. YOSSI ROSEN; Pres. and CEO AKIVA MOZES.

Koor Industries Ltd: Platinum House, 21 Ha'arba'ah St, Tel-Aviv 64739; tel. 3-6238333; fax 3-6238334; e-mail info@koor.com; internet www.koor.com; Israel's leading investment holding company; investments in telecommunications, defence electronics, agrochemicals and venture capital; Vice-Chair. and CEO JONATHAN KOLBER; Pres. DANNY BIRAN; 31,000 employees (June 1988).

Polgat Industries: 3 Arie Shenkar St, Herzliya 46725; tel. 9-9585885; fax 9-9213566; mfrs of textiles; Chair. ISRAEL POLLACK.

Scitex Corporation Ltd: POB 330, Herzliya 46103; tel. 9-9597222; fax 9-9502922; f. 1968; mfr of computerized imaging equipment for the publishing industry; sales US $640m.; Chair. DOV TADMOR; Pres. and CEO YOAV Z. CHELOUCHE.

Soltam Ltd: Haifa; mfr of artillery; Man. Dir ELAZAR BARAK.

Tadiran Israel Electronics Industries Ltd: Givat Shmuel; Israel's leading mfr of civil and military electronics; subsidiary of Koor Industries Ltd.

The Histadrut

Histadrut (General Federation of Labour in Israel): 93 Arlozorof St, Tel-Aviv 62098; tel 3-6921513; fax 3-6921512; e-mail histint@netvision.net.il; f. 1920.

The General Federation of Labour in Israel, the Histadrut, is the largest labour organization in Israel. It strives to ensure the social security, welfare and rights of workers, and to assist in their professional advancement, while endeavouring to reduce the divisions in Israeli society. Membership of the Histadrut is voluntary, and open to all men and women of 18 years of age and above who live on the earnings of their own labour without exploiting the work of others. These include the self-employed and professionals, as well as housewives, students, pensioners and the unemployed. Workers' interests are protected through a number of occupational and professional unions affiliated to the Histadrut (see below). The organization operates courses for trade unionists and new immigrants, as well as apprenticeship classes. It maintains an Institute for Social and Economic Issues and the International Institute, one of the largest centres of leadership training in Israel, for students from Africa, Asia, Latin America and Eastern Europe, which includes the Levinson Centre for Adult Education and the Jewish-Arab Institute for Regional Co-operation. Attached to the Histadrut is Na'amat, a women's organization which promotes changes in legislation, operates a network of legal service bureaux and vocational training courses, and runs counselling centres for the treatment and prevention of domestic violence.

Chair.: AMIR PERETZ.

Secretary-General: HAIM RAMON.

ORGANIZATION

In 1989 the Histadrut had a membership of 1,630,000. In addition some 110,000 young people under 18 years of age belong to the Organization of Working and Student Youth, a direct affiliate of the Histadrut.

All members take part in elections to the Histadrut Convention (Veida), which elects the General Council (Moetsa) and the Executive Committee (Vaad Hapoel). The latter elects the 41-member Executive Bureau (Vaada Merakezet), which is responsible for day-to-day implementation of policy. The Executive Committee also elects the Secretary-General, who acts as its chairman as well as head of the organization as a whole and chairman of the Executive Bureau. Nearly all political parties are represented on the Histadrut Executive Committee.

The Executive Committee has the following departments: Trade Union, Organization and Labour Councils, Education and Culture,

Social Security, Industrial Democracy, Students, Youth and Sports, Consumer Protection, Administration, Finance and International.

TRADE UNION ACTIVITIES

Collective agreements with employers fix wage scales, which are linked with the retail price index; provide for social benefits, including paid sick leave and employers' contributions to sick and pension and provident funds; and regulate dismissals. Dismissal compensation is regulated by law. The Histadrut actively promotes productivity through labour management boards and the National Productivity Institute, and supports incentive pay schemes.

There are unions for the following groups: clerical workers, building workers, teachers, engineers, agricultural workers, technicians, textile workers, printing workers, diamond workers, metal workers, food and bakery workers, wood workers, government employees, seamen, nurses, civilian employees of the armed forces, actors, musicians and variety artists, social workers, watchmen, cinema technicians, institutional and school staffs, pharmacy employees, medical laboratory workers, X-ray technicians, physiotherapists, social scientists, microbiologists, psychologists, salaried lawyers, pharmacists, physicians, occupational therapists, truck and taxi drivers, hotel and restaurant workers, workers in Histadrut-owned industry, garment, shoe and leather workers, plastic and rubber workers, editors of periodicals, painters and sculptors and industrial workers.

Histadrut Trade Union Department: Dir SHLOMO SHANI.

ECONOMIC ACTIVITIES AND SOCIAL SERVICES

These include Hevrat Haovdim (employing 260,000 workers in 1983), Kupat Holim (the Sick Fund, covering almost 77% of Israel's population), seven pension funds, and Na'amat (see above).

Other Trade Unions

General Federation of West Bank Trade Unions: Sec.-Gen. SHAHER SAAD.

Histadrut Haovdim Haleumit (National Labour Federation): 23 Sprintzak St, Tel-Aviv 64738; tel. 3-6958351; fax 3-6961753; e-mail nol@netvision.net.il; f. 1934; 220,000 mems; CEO ITZHAK RUSSO.

Histadrut Hapoel Hamizrahi (National Religious Workers' Party): 166 Ibn Gvirol St, Tel-Aviv 62023; tel. 3-5442151; fax 3-5468942; 150,000 mems in 85 settlements and 15 kibbutzim; Sec.-Gen. ELIEZER ABTABI.

Histadrut Poale Agudat Israel (Agudat Israel Workers' Organization): POB 11044, 64 Frishman St, Tel-Aviv; tel. 3-5242126; fax 3-5230689; has 33,000 members in 16 settlements and 8 educational insts.

Transport

RAILWAYS

Freight traffic consists mainly of grain, phosphates, potash, containers, petroleum and building materials. Rail service serves Haifa and Ashdod ports on the Mediterranean Sea, while a combined rail-road service extends to Eilat port on the Red Sea. Passenger services operate between the main towns: Nahariya, Haifa, Tel-Aviv and Jerusalem. In 1988 the National Ports Authority assumed responsibility for the rail system, creating the Ports and Railways Authority. It was decided in 1996 that Israel Railways should become a separate state concern, although this has not yet occurred. Bids to construct the first line of a US $1,400m. light railway network in Jerusalem (to be launched in 2004) were expected in 2000.

Israel Railways (IR): POB 18085, Central Station, Tel-Aviv 61180; tel. 3-6937401; fax 3-6937480; internet www.israrail.org.il; in 2001 the total length of railway line was 684 km; Dir-Gen. AMOS UZANI; Gen. Man. EHUD HADAR.

Underground Railway

Haifa Underground Funicular Railway: 122 Hanassi Ave, Haifa 34633; tel. 4-8376861; fax 4-8376875; e-mail funicular@netvision.net.il; opened 1959; 2 km in operation; Man. AVI TELLEM.

ROADS

In 2001 there were 16,563 km of paved roads, of which 9,508 km were urban roads, 5,523 km were non-urban roads and 1,532 km were access roads.

Ministry of Transport: Public Works Dept, Klal Bldg, 97 Jaffa St, Jerusalem 91000; tel. 2-6228211; fax 2-6228693; e-mail pniot@mot.gov.il; internet www.mot.gov.il.

SHIPPING

At 31 December 2001 Israel's merchant fleet consisted of 48 vessels amounting to 611,396 grt.

Haifa and Ashdod are the main ports in Israel. The former is a natural harbour, enclosed by two main breakwaters and dredged to 45 ft below mean sea-level. In 1965 the deep water port was completed at Ashdod which had a capacity of about 8.6m. tons in 1988.

The port of Eilat is Israel's gateway to the Red Sea. It is a natural harbour, operated from a wharf. Another port, to the south of the original one, started operating in 1965.

Israel Ports and Railways Authority (PRA): POB 20121, 74 Menachem Begin Rd, Tel-Aviv 61201; tel. 3-5657000; fax 3-5617142; e-mail dovf@israports.org.il; internet www.israports.org.il; f. 1961; to plan, build, develop, maintain and operate Israel's commercial ports and Israel Railways. A contract to expand Ashdod port was awarded in mid-2000, involving 1,900 m of new cargo and container quays, a breakwater extension and hinterland development; the first ship was scheduled to be handled at the new facilities in 2004. A proposed extension to Haifa port was also under way. Cargo traffic in 2001 amounted to 32m. tons; Chair. GAD YAACOBI; Dir-Gen. AMOS RON.

Ofer (Ships Holding) Ltd: POB 1755, 2 Hanamal St, Haifa 31016; tel. 4-8610610; fax 4-8675666; e-mail ops@oferb.co.il; runs cargo and container services; operates some 18 vessels; Chair. Y. OFER; Man. Dir E. ANGEL.

ZIM Israel Navigation Co Ltd: POB 1723, 7–9 Pal-Yam Ave, Haifa 31000; tel. 4-8652111; fax 4-8652956; e-mail zimpress@zim.co.il; internet www.zim.co.il; f. 1945; international integrated transportation system providing door-to-door services to the Mediterranean, Northern Europe, North, South and Central America, East, South and West Africa, the Far East and Australia; operates about 80 vessels; total cargo carried: 1,333,581 TEUs in 2001; Chair. U. ANGEL; Pres. and CEO Dr YORAM SEBBA.

CIVIL AVIATION

Israel Airports Authority: Ben-Gurion International Airport, Tel-Aviv; tel. 3-9710101; fax 3-9712436; internet www.ben-gurion -airport.co.il; Chair. TSVI SHALOM; Dir-Gen. GABRIEL OFFIR.

El Al Israel Airlines Ltd: POB 41, Ben-Gurion International Airport, Tel-Aviv 70100; tel. 3-9716111; fax 3-9716040; internet www.elal.com; f. 1948; 100% state-owned, but scheduled for privatization; total assets US $980m. (Dec. 1997); daily services to most capitals of Europe; over 20 flights weekly to New York; services to the USA, Canada, China, Egypt, India, Kenya, South Africa, Thailand and Turkey; scheduled for privatization; Chair. MICHAEL LEVY; Pres. AMOS SHAPIRA.

Arkia Israeli Airlines Ltd: POB 39301, Dov Airport, Tel-Aviv 61392; tel. 3-6902222; fax 3-6991512; e-mail income@arkia.co.il; internet www.arkia.co.il; f. 1980 through merger of Kanaf-Arkia Airlines and Aviation Services; scheduled passenger services linking Tel-Aviv, Jerusalem, Haifa, Eilat, Rosh Pina, Kiryat Shmona and Yotveta; charter services to European destinations; Chair. YIGAL ARNON; Pres. and CEO Prof. ISRAEL BOROVICH.

Tourism

In 2001 some 1,195,700 tourists visited Israel. Tourist receipts in that year totalled US $2,460m.

Ministry of Tourism: POB 1018, 24 Rehov King George, Jerusalem 91009; tel. 2-6754811; fax 2-6253407; e-mail pniot@ tourism.gov.il; internet www.tourism.gov.il; Dir-Gen. DAVID LITVAK.

Defence

The General Staff: This consists of the Chiefs of the General Staff, Personnel, Technology and Logistics, Intelligence, Operations, and Plans and Policy Branches of the Defence Forces, the Commanders-in-Chief of the Air Force and the Navy, and the officers commanding the four Territorial Commands (Northern, Central, Southern and Home Front). It is headed by the Chief of Staff of the Armed Forces.

Chief of Staff of the Armed Forces: Lt-Gen. MOSHE YA'ALON.

Commander of Army Headquarters: Maj.-Gen. YIFTAH RON TAL.

Commander-in-Chief of the Air Force: Maj.-Gen. DAN HALOUTZ.

Commander-in-Chief of the Navy: Rear-Admiral YEDIDIA YA'ARI.

Defence Budget Forecast (2001): 37,400m. shekels.

Military Service (Jewish and Druze population only; Christians and Arabs may volunteer): Officers are conscripted for regular service of 48 months, men 36 months, women 21 months. Annual training as reservists thereafter, to age 41 for men (54 for some specialists), 24 (or marriage) for women.

Total Armed Forces (August 2001): an estimated 163,500; including 107,500 conscripts; this can be raised to 588,500 by mobilizing the 425,000 reservists within 48–72 hours; army 120,000 (85,000 conscripts); navy an estimated 6,500 (2,500 conscripts); air force 37,000 (20,000 conscripts).

Paramilitary Forces (August 2001): an estimated 8,050.

Education

The present-day school system is based on the Compulsory Education Law (1949), the State Education Law (1953), the School Inspection Law (1969) and on certain provisions of the 1933 Education Ordinance dating back to the British Mandatory Administration. The first of these introduced free compulsory primary education for all children aged between five and 13 (one year kindergarten, eight years' elementary schooling). This law was extended, with the school reform of 1968, to include the ninth and tenth grades. In the 1979/ 80 school year free, but not compulsory, education was extended up to and including the 12th grade. Further legislation was passed in 1999 allowing for the introduction of free education for pre-primary children.

The State Education Law abolished the old complicated Trend Education System, and vested the responsibility for education in the Government, thus providing a unified state-controlled elementary school system. The law does, however, recognize two main forms of Primary Education—(a) State Education; (b) Recognized Non-State Education. State Education may be sub-divided into two distinct categories of schools—State Schools and State Religious Schools where the language of instruction is Hebrew, and State Schools where the language of instruction is Arabic. Schools and kindergartens of the state system are in the joint ownership of the state and the local authorities, while the recognized non-state institutions are essentially privately-owned and mainly religious, although they are subsidized and supervised by the state and the local authorities.

The largest 'recognized' school system is the Agudat Israel Schools (ultra-orthodox religious). The others are mainly Christian denominational schools.

State Primary Education is financed by a partnership of the central government and the local authorities. Since 1953 the salaries of all teachers of State Schools have been paid by the central government, while the cost of maintenance and of maintenance services, and the provision of new buildings and equipment have been the responsibility of the local authorities. The state does not impose an education tax but local authorities may, with the Ministry's approval, levy a rate on parents for special services. In 2000 budgetary expenditure on education by the central Government was forecast at NIS 28,013m. (14.8% of total spending).

The state provides schools in which the language of instruction is either Hebrew or Arabic according to the language spoken by the majority of the local population. Nevertheless, some Arab children attend Jewish secondary, vocational, agricultural and teacher-training colleges. In the Jewish sector there is a distinct line of division between the secular State Schools and the religious State Schools, which are established on the demand of parents in any locality, provided that a certain minimum number of pupils have first been enrolled. In the Arab Schools all instruction is in Arabic, and there is a special Department for Arabic Education in the Ministry of Education. The administration of Arab education is in the process of being decentralized. Some 90% of Arab children attend school regularly.

The Compulsory Education Law and the institutions it established for absorbing weak students have cancelled the need for special systems for working youth. The law provides special education for emotionally or physically handicapped children, as well as for those children who are culturally deprived.

Post-Primary Education is free, lasts for six years (four of which are compulsory), and is divided into an intermediate and a higher level. The intermediate level provides general education and the higher level is roughly divided into academic; technical and vocational; and agricultural. The last two categories also have pre-academic streams lasting from one to two years and receive all the benefits of the regular post-primary schools. The pupils graduating from academic high school receive either a school leaving certificate or *bagrut* (matriculation). The *bagrut* certificate entitles the pupil to enter university, although the university is not obliged to accept him or her.

The frameworks offered by vocational and technical schools can be divided into three types: practical-technical; general-technical; and secondary-technical. All three types are of three or four years' duration, depending on whether they are run under the Reform or under the old system. Very few of the practical-technical schools still offer a two-year course, i.e. a total of 11 years' schooling. The practical-technical schools train their pupils mainly for a profession and the ratio between general studies and vocational-technical studies is 40 : 60. The general-technical schools award a school leaving certificate to those pupils who complete the course successfully. This entitles them to continue their studies in the third level of education after some complementary examinations, either for one additional year to obtain a technician's certificate (Techna'i), or for two additional years to obtain the certificate of a practical engineer (Handessa'i). The ratio between general studies and vocational studies in these schools is 50 : 50. All graduates of the secondary-technical schools may sit for the *bagrut* examinations. Even without achieving the *bagrut* certificate the pupils may continue their studies in the short-cycle post-secondary schools, described above, without further examination and obtain the technician or practical engineer certificate. The ratio between general studies and technical-vocational studies in these schools is 60 : 40. Those who graduate and complete their matriculation (*bagrut*) examinations are eligible for admission to any Israeli university.

Agricultural post-primary courses are of either three or four years' duration (again depending on the Reform) and some schools offer an additional year or year-and-a-half (13th and 14th grade) leading to a practical engineer certificate. The holders of this certificate are eligible, without further examinations, for study in agricultural engineering or general agricultural higher studies in the Technion (the Israel Institute of Technology) at Haifa or the Faculty of Agriculture at the Hebrew University of Jerusalem. Unlike pupils at vocational-technical post-primary schools, all those completing agricultural courses may sit for the *bagrut* examinations. In general,

agricultural post-primary schools are boarding schools although some, mainly those of the kibbutz and the moshav movements, are regional day schools.

Adult Education. There is an extensive adult education programme. Programmes extend from literacy courses through primary and secondary level studies up to second-chance university facilities. There are post-army preparatory courses for entry into university. High school courses may be completed in the army and in 1976 the Everyman's University was founded, based on the British model of Open University.

Teacher Training. Almost all kindergarten and primary school teachers are trained in three to three-and-a-half year courses at post-secondary teacher training institutions (Mossadot Le-Hakhsharat Morim Ve Gananot). The Ministry's policy is to have only three-year teacher training colleges and to extend the training period to four years for a B.Ed. degree. Government regulations require that teachers for grades seven to 10 have a BA and a university teaching certificate, while for grades 11 and 12 they are required to have a master's degree and a university teaching certificate. The *bagrut* certificate and a passing grade in the psychometric examination are required for admittance to the above teacher training institutions. In some of the teacher training schools there are special courses for instruction in Arabic education, in addition to separate Arab teacher training schools.

Occupied Territories

THE GOLAN HEIGHTS

Location, Climate

The Golan Heights, a mountainous plateau which formed most of Syria's Quneitra Province (1,710 sq km) and parts of Dera'a Province, was occupied by Israel after the 1967 Arab–Israeli War. Following the Disengagement Agreement of 1974, Israel continued to occupy some 70% of the territory (1,176 sq km), valued for its strategic position and abundant water resources (the headwaters of the Jordan river have their source on the slopes of Mount Hermon). The average height of the Golan is approximately 1,200 m above sea-level in the northern region and about 300 m above sea-level in the southern region, near Lake Tiberias (the Sea of Galilee). Rainfall ranges from about 1,000 mm per year in the north to less than 600 mm per year in the southern region.

Administration

Prior to the Israeli occupation, the Golan Heights were incorporated by Syria into a provincial administration of which the city of Quneitra, with a population at the time of 27,378, was capital. The disengagement agreement that was mediated by US Secretary of State Henry Kissinger in 1974 (after the 1973 Arab–Israeli War) provided for the withdrawal of Israeli forces from Quneitra. Before they withdrew, however, Israeli army engineers destroyed the city. In December 1981 the Israeli Knesset enacted the Golan Annexation Law, whereby Israeli civilian legislation was extended to the territory of Golan, now under the administrative jurisdiction of the Commissioner for the Northern District of Israel. The Arab-Druze community of the Golan immediately responded by declaring a strike and appealed to the UN Secretary-General to force Israel to rescind the annexation decision. At the seventh round of multilateral talks between Israel and Arab delegations in Washington, DC, USA, in August 1992, the Israeli Government of Itzhak Rabin for the first time accepted that UN Security Council Resolution 242, adopted in 1967, applied to the Golan Heights. In January 1999 the Knesset passed legislation which stated that any transfer of land under Israeli sovereignty (referring to the Golan Heights and East Jerusalem) was conditional on the approval of at least 61 of the 120 Knesset members and of the Israeli electorate in a subsequent national referendum. Following the election of Ehud Barak as Israel's Prime Minister in May 1999, peace negotiations between Israel and Syria were resumed in mid-December. However, in January 2000 the talks were postponed indefinitely after Syria demanded a written commitment from Israel to withdraw from the Golan Heights. In July 2001 Israel's recently elected premier, Ariel Sharon, stated that he would be prepared to resume peace talks with Syria; however, Sharon also declared that the Israeli occupation of the Golan was 'irreversible'. The withdrawal of Israel from the disputed territory is one of Syria's primary objectives in any future peace agreement with Israel. Peace negotiations between Israel and Syria had not resumed by mid-2002.

Demography and Economic Affairs

As a consequence of the Israeli occupation, an estimated 93% of the ethnically diverse Syrian population of 147,613, distributed across

163 villages and towns and 108 individual farms, was expelled. The majority were Arab Sunni Muslims, but the population also included Alawite and Druze minorities and some Circassians, Turcomen, Armenians and Kurds. Approximately 9,000 Palestinian refugees from the 1948 Arab–Israeli War also inhabited the area. At the time of the occupation, the Golan was a predominantly agricultural province, 64% of the labour force being employed in agriculture. Only one-fifth of the population resided in the administrative centres. By 1991 the Golan Heights had a Jewish population of about 12,000 living in 21 Jewish settlements (four new settlements had been created by the end of 1992), and a predominantly Druze population of some 16,000 living in the only six remaining villages, of which Majd ash-Shams is by far the largest. According to official figures, at the end of 2001 the Golan Heights had a total population of 35,400 (including 15,100 Jews, 17,700 Druze and 1,800 Muslims). The Golan Heights have remained largely an agricultural area, and although many Druze now work in Israeli industry in Eilat, Tel-Aviv and Jerusalem, the indigenous economy relies almost solely on the cultivation of apples, for which the area is famous. The apple orchards benefit from a unique combination of fertile soils, abundance of water and a conducive climate.

EAST JERUSALEM

Location

Greater Jerusalem includes Israeli West Jerusalem (99% Jewish), the Old City and Mount of Olives, East Jerusalem (the Palestinian residential and commercial centre), Arab villages declared to be part of Jerusalem by Israel in 1967 and Jewish neighbourhoods constructed since 1967, either on land expropriated from Arab villages or in areas requisitioned as 'government land'. Although the area of the Greater Jerusalem district is 627 sq km, the Old City of Jerusalem covers just 1 sq km.

Administration

Until the 1967 Arab–Israeli War, Jerusalem had been divided into the new city of West Jerusalem—captured by Jewish forces in 1948—and the old city, East Jerusalem, which was part of Jordan. Israel's victory in 1967, however, reunited the city under Israeli control. Two weeks after the fighting had ended, on 28 June, Israeli law was applied to East Jerusalem and the municipal boundaries were extended by 45 km (28 miles). Jerusalem had effectively been annexed. Israeli officials, however, still refer to the 'reunification' of Jerusalem.

Demography and Economic Affairs

In June 1993 the Deputy Mayor of Jerusalem, Avraham Kahila, declared that the city now had 'a majority of Jews', based on population forecasts which estimated the Jewish population at 158,000 and the Arab population at 155,000. For the Israeli administration this signified the achievement of a long-term objective. Immediately prior to the June 1967 Arab–Israeli War, East Jerusalem and its Arab environs had an Arab population of approximately 70,000, and a small Jewish population in the old Jewish quarter of the city. By contrast, Israeli West Jerusalem had a Jewish population of 196,000. As a result of this imbalance, in the Greater Jerusalem district as a whole the Jewish population was in the majority even prior to the occupation of the whole city in 1967. Israeli policy following the occupation of East Jerusalem and the West Bank consisted of encircling the eastern sector of the city with Jewish settlements. In contrast to the more politically sensitive siting of Jewish settlements in the old Arab quarter of Jerusalem, the Government of Itzhak Rabin concentrated on the outer circle of settlement building. Official statistics for the end of 1998 reported that Greater Jerusalem had a total population of 633,700, of whom 433,600 (68%) were Jews. At the end of 2001 the city's population was 670,000. The Jerusalem Institute for Israel Studies estimates that the Arab population of Greater Jerusalem is increasing at a rate three times greater than the Jewish population.

The Old City, within the walls of which are found the ancient quarters of the Jews, Christians, Muslims and Armenians, has a population of approximately 25,500 Arabs and 2,600 Jews. In addition, there are some 600 recent Jewish settlers in the Arab quarter.

Many imaginative plans have been submitted with the aim of finding a solution to the problem of sharing Jerusalem between Arabs and Jews, including the proposal that the city be placed under international trusteeship, under UN auspices. However, to make the implementation of such plans an administrative as well as a political quagmire, the Israeli administration, after occupying the whole city in June 1967, began creating 'facts on the ground'. Immediately following the occupation, all electricity, water and telephone grids in West Jerusalem were extended to the east. Roads were widened and cleared, and the Arab population immediately in front of the 'Wailing Wall' was forcibly evicted. Arabs living in East Jerusalem became 'permanent residents' and could apply for Israeli citizenship if they wished (in contrast to Arabs in the West Bank and Gaza Strip). However, few chose to do so. None the less, issued with identity cards (excluding the estimated 25,000 Arabs from the West Bank and Gaza living illegally in the city), the Arab residents were taxed by the Israeli authorities, and their businesses and banks became subject to Israeli laws and business regulations. Now controlling approximately one-half of all land in East Jerusalem and the surrounding Palestinian villages (previously communally, or privately, owned by Palestinians), the Israeli authorities allowed Arabs to construct buildings on only 10%–15% of the land in the city; and East Jerusalem's commercial district has been limited to three streets.

Since the 1993 signing of the Declaration of Principles on Palestinian Self-Rule, the future status of Jerusalem and the continuing expansion of Jewish settlements in East Jerusalem have emerged as two of the most crucial issues affecting the peace process. In May 1999 the Israeli Government announced its refusal to grant Israeli citizenship to several hundred Arabs living in East Jerusalem, regardless of their compliance with the conditions stipulated under the Citizenship Law. In October, however, Israel ended its policy of revoking the right of Palestinians to reside in Jerusalem if they had spent more than seven years outside the city. Moreover, the Israeli Government announced in March 2000 that Palestinian residents of Jerusalem who had had their identity cards revoked could apply for their restoration.

At the Camp David talks held between Israel and the Palestinian (National) Authority (PA) in July 2000, the issue of who would have sovereignty over East Jerusalem in a future 'permanent status' agreement proved to be the principal obstacle to the achievement of a peace deal. It was reported in late July that the Israeli Government had offered the PA municipal autonomy over certain areas of East Jerusalem (including access to the Islamic holy sites), although sovereignty would remain in Israeli hands; the proposals were rejected by Yasser Arafat. In late September 2000 the holy sites of East Jerusalem were the initial focal point of a renewed uprising by Palestinians against the Israeli authorities, which became known as the al-Aqsa *intifada* and which continued into mid-2002. The prospects for an imminent resumption of Israeli-Palestinian discussions with a view to resolving the Jerusalem issue appeared unlikely at that time.

Bibliography

GENERAL

Arian, Asher. *Security Threatened: Surveying Israeli Opinion on Peace and War.* Cambridge University Press, 1996.

Avnery, Uri. *Israel without Zionists.* London, Collier-Macmillan, 1969.

Black, Ian, and Morris, Benny. *Israel's Secret Wars: History of Israel's Intelligence Services.* New York, Grove Weidenfeld, 1992.

Burr, Gerald. *Behind the Star: inside Israel today.* London, Constable, 1990.

Cohen, Mark R., and Udovitch, Abraham L. *Jews among Arabs: Contacts and Boundaries.* Princeton, The Darwin Press, 1994.

Eban, Abba. *Personal Witness: Israel through my eyes.* London, Jonathan Cape, 1993.

Ellis, Mark H. *Beyond Innocence and Redemption: Confronting the Holocaust and Israeli Power.* San Francisco, Harper and Row, 1990.

Ezrahi, Yaron. *Rubber Bullets: Power and Conscience in Modern Israel.* New York, Farrar Strauss Giroux, 1997.

Glueck, Nelson. *The River Jordan.* Philadelphia, 1946.

Rivers in the Desert: A History of the Negev. London, 1959.

Hersh, Seymour. *The Samson Option: Israel, America and the Bomb.* London, Faber and Faber, 1991.

Koestler, Arthur. *The Thirteenth Tribe.* London, Random House, 1976.

Kohn, Hans. *Nationalism and Imperialism in the Hither East.* London, 1932.

Landau, David (Ed.). *Battling for Peace.* London, Weidenfeld and Nicolson, 1995.

Marmorstein, Emile. *Heaven at Bay: The Jewish Kulturkampf in the Holy Land.* Oxford University Press, 1969.

Masalha, Nur. *Imperial Israel and the Palestinians: The Politics of Expansion.* London, Pluto Press, 2000.

Orni, E., and Efrat, E. *The Geography of Israel.* New York, Darey, 1965.

Parfitt, Tudor (Ed.). *Israel and Ishmael: Studies in Muslim–Jewish Relations.* Richmond, Curzon Press, 1999.

Parkes, J. W. *The Emergence of the Jewish Problem, 1878–1939.* Oxford, 1946.

A History of Palestine from AD 135 to Modern Times. London, Gollancz, 1949.

End of Exile. New York, 1954.

Whose Land? A History of the Peoples of Palestine. Harmondsworth, Pelican, 1970.

Patai, R. *Israel Between East and West.* Philadelphia, 1953.

Culture and Conflict. New York, 1962.

Raviv, Dan, and Melman, Yossi. *Every Spy a Prince: the complete history of Israel's intelligence community.* Boston, Houghton Mifflin, 1990.

Safran, Alexandre. *Israël et ses racines.* 2001.

Schwarz, Tanya. *Ethiopian Jewish Immigrants in Israel.* Richmond, Curzon Press, 1999.

Shapiro, Harry L. *The Jewish People: a biological history.* UNESCO, 1960.

Summerfield, Daniel. *From Falashas to Ethiopian Jews.* Richmond, Curzon Press, 1999.

Tuchman, Barbara W. *Bible and Sword.* London, Redman, 1957; New York, Minerva, 1968.

Weingrod, Alex. *Reluctant Pioneers, Village Development in Israel.* New York, Cornell University Press, 1966.

Winter, Dave, and Matthews, John (Eds). *Israel Handbook with the Palestinian Authority Areas.* Bath, Footprint Handbook, 1998.

Zander, Walter. *Israel and the Holy Places of Christendom.* Weidenfeld and Nicolson, 1972.

RECENT HISTORY

Allon, Yigal. *The Making of Israel's Army.* London, Vallentine, Mitchell, 1970.

Aruri, Naseer. *The Obstruction of Peace: the US, Israel and the Palestinians.* Monroe, Maine, Common Courage Press, 1995.

Auld, Sylvia, and Prof. Hillenbrand, Robert (Eds). *Ottoman Jerusalem: The Living City 1517–1917.* London, Altajir World of Islam, 2001.

Barbour, Nevill. *Nisi Dominus: a survey of the Palestine Controversy.* London, Harrap, 1946, reprinted by the Institute for Palestine Studies, Beirut, 1969.

Ben-Zvi, Abraham. *The United States and Israel: the limits of the special relationship.* New York, Columbia University Press, 1993.

Bentwich, Norman and Helen. *Mandate Memories, 1918–1948.* London, Hogarth Press, 1965.

Berger, Earl. *The Covenant and the Sword, Arab-Israeli Relations 1948–56*. Toronto, University of Toronto Press, 1965.

Bermant, Chaim. *Israel*. London, Thames and Hudson, 1967.

Bethell, Nicholas. *The Palestine Triangle: the Struggle Between the British, the Jews and the Arabs, 1935–48*. London, André Deutsch, 1979.

Bishara, Marwan. *Palestine/Israel: Peace or Apartheid. Prospects for Resolving the Conflict*. London, Zed Books, 2001.

Cattan, Henry. *Palestine, the Arabs and Israel*. London, Longmans Green, 1969.

The Palestine Question*. London, Croom Helm; New York, Methuen, 1987.

Cohen, Avner. *Israel and the Bomb*. New York, Columbia University Press, 1998.

Cohen, Michael J. *Palestine, Retreat from the Mandate: The Making of British Policy*. London, Elek, 1978.

Crossman, R. H. S. *Palestine Mission*. London, 1947.

Draper, T. *Israel and World Politics: Roots of the Third Arab–Israeli War*. London, Secker and Warburg, 1968.

Enderlin, Charles. *Le rêve brisé, histoire de l'échec du processus de paix au Proche-Orient, 1995–2002*. Paris, Editions Fayard, 2002.

Esco Foundation for Palestine. *Palestine: A Study of Jewish, Arab and British Policies*. 2 vols, New Haven, 1947.

Eshed, Haggai. *Reuven Shiloah: The Man Behind the Mossad*. London, Frank Cass, 1997.

Farsoun, Samir K., and Zacharia, Christina E. *Palestine and the Palestinians*. London, Harper Collins, 1997.

Finkelstein, Norman G. *Image and Reality of the Israel–Palestine Conflict*. London and New York, Verso, 1995.

Frankel, Glenn. *Beyond the Promised Land: Jews and Arabs on a hard road to a new Israel*. New York, Simon and Schuster, 1995.

Fraser, T. G. *The Arab–Israeli Conflict*. London, Macmillan, 1995.

Gabbay, Rony E. *A Political Study of the Arab–Jewish Conflict, the Arab Refugee Problem*. Geneva and Paris, 1959.

Green, Stephen. *Taking Sides: America and Israel in the Middle East, 1948–1967*. London, Faber and Faber, 1984.

Living by the Sword: America and Israel in the Middle East, 1968–1987*. London, Faber and Faber, 1988.

Grossman, David. *The Yellow Wind*. London, Jonathan Cape, 1988.

Heller, Joseph. *The Stern Gang: ideology, politics and terror 1940–49*. London, Frank Cass, 1995.

Howard, M., and Hunter, R. *Israel and the Arab World*. Beirut, Institute for Palestine Studies.

Jansen, Michael. *The Battle of Beirut*. London, Zed Press, 1982.

Jiryis, Sabri. *The Arabs in Israel*. Beirut, Institute for Palestine Studies, 1968.

Kader, Razzak Abdel. *The Arab–Jewish Conflict*. 1961.

Karsh, Efraim. *Peace in the Middle East: the challenge for Israel*. London, Frank Cass, 1994.

(Ed.) *Israel: The First Hundred Years, Vol. 1. Israel's Transition from Community to State*. London, Frank Cass, 2000.

(Ed.) *Israel: The First Hundred Years, Vol. 2. From War to Peace?* London, Frank Cass, 2000.

(Ed.) *Israel: The First Hundred Years, Vol. 3. Israeli Politics and Society since 1948. Problems of Collective Identity*. London, Frank Cass, 2001.

Katz, Samuel M. *Guards without Frontiers: Israel's war against terrorism*. London, Arms and Armour Press, 1990.

Kaye, Dalia Dassa. *Beyond the Handshake: Multilateral Co-operation in the Arab-Israeli Peace Process, 1991–96*. New York, Columbia University Press, 2001.

Khalidi, Walid. *From Haven to Conquest: Readings in Zionism and the Palestine Problem until 1948*. Beirut, Institute for Palestine Studies, 1971.

Kimche, Jon. *Palestine or Israel*. London, Secker & Warburg, 1973.

Kimche, Jon and David. *Both Sides of the Hill: Britain and the Palestine War*. London, Secker and Warburg, 1960.

Koestler, Arthur. *Promise and Fulfilment: Palestine, 1917–1949*. London, 1949.

Thieves in the Night*. New York and London, 1946.

La Guardia, Anton. *Holy Land, Unholy War. Israelis and Palestinians*. London, John Murray, 2001.

Landau, Jacob M. *The Arabs in Israel*. London, Oxford University Press, 1969.

Laqueur, Walter. *The Road to War, 1967*. London, Weidenfeld and Nicolson, 1968.

The Israel-Arab Reader*. London, Weidenfeld and Nicolson, 1969.

Lazin, A., and Mahler, G. S. *Israel in the Nineties: Development and Conflict*. University Press of Florida, 1996.

Levran, Aharon. *Israeli Strategy after Desert Storm: lessons of the second Gulf war*. London, Frank Cass, 1997.

Lilienthal, Alfred M. *The Other Side of the Coin: An American Perspective of the Arab–Israeli Conflict*. New York, 1965.

Lorch, N. *The Edge of the Sword: Israel's War of Independence 1947–49*. New York, Putnam, 1961.

Lucas, Noah. *The Modern History of Israel*. London, Weidenfeld and Nicolson, 1974–75.

McDowall, David. *Palestine and Israel: the uprising and beyond*. London, I. B. Tauris, 1989.

Marlowe, John. *The Seat of Pilate, An Account of the Palestine Mandate*. London, Cresset, 1959; Philadelphia, Dufour, 1958.

O'Ballance, E. *The Arab–Israeli War*. New York, Praeger, 1957.

The Third Arab–Israeli War*. London, Faber & Faber, 1972.

Oren, Michael B. *Six Days of War: June 1967 and the Making of the Modern Middle East*. Oxford University Press, 2002.

Oz, Amos. *In the Land of Israel*. London, Chatto and Windus, 1983.

Peretz, Don. *Israel and the Palestine Arabs*. Washington, The Middle East Institute, 1958.

Intifada*. Oxford, Westview Press, 1990.

Perlmutter, Amos. *Military and Politics in Israel, 1948–1967*. 2nd edn. London, Frank Cass, 1977.

Politics and the Military in Israel, 1967–1976*. London, Frank Cass, 1977.

Rabin, Yitzhak. *The Rabin Memoirs*. London, Weidenfeld and Nicolson, 1979.

Reiter, Yitzhak. *Islamic Endowments in Jerusalem under the British Mandate*. London, Frank Cass, 1997.

Rizk, Edward. *The Palestine Question, Seminar of Arab Jurists on Palestine, Algiers, 1967*. Beirut, Institute for Palestine Studies, 1968.

Rodinson, Maxime. *Israel and the Arabs*. Harmondsworth, Penguin Books, 1968; New York, Pantheon, 1969.

Rothstein, Robert L., Ma'oz, Moshe, Shikaki, Khalil (Eds). *The Israeli-Palestinian Peace Process: Oslo and the Lessons of Failure*. Sussex Academic Press, 2002.

Rouleau, Eric, and Held, Jean-Francis. *Israël et les Arabes*. Paris, Editions du Seuil, 1967.

Royal Institute of International Affairs. *Great Britain and Palestine 1915–45*. London, 1946.

Sachar, Howard M. *A History of Israel: Vol. I: From the Rise of Zionism to Our Time; Vol. II: From the Aftermath of the Yom Kippur War*. Corby, Oxford University Press, 1987.

Savir, Uri. *The Process: 1,100 Days that Changed the Middle East*. London, Random House, 1998.

Schiff, Ze'ev, and Ya'ari Ehud. *Israel's Lebanon War*. New York, Simon and Schuster, 1984.

Intifada: the Palestinian uprising—Israel's third front*. London, Simon and Shuster, 1990.

Schindler, Colin. *Ploughshares into Swords?: Israelis and Jews in the Shadow of the Intifada*. London, I. B. Tauris, 1992.

Israel, Likud and the Zionist Dream: Power, Politics, and Ideology from Begin to Netanyahu*. London, I. B. Tauris, 1995.

Segev, Tom. *One Palestine, Complete: Jews and Arabs Under the British Mandate*. New York, Metropolitan Books/Henry Holt & Co, 2000.

Seikaly, May. *Haifa: Transformation of an Arab Society, 1918–1939*. London, I B. Tauris, 2001.

Shahak, Israel. *Open Secrets: Israeli Foreign and Nuclear Policies*. London, Pluto Press, 1997.

Sharabi, Hisham B. *Palestine and Israel: The Lethal Dilemma*. New York, Van Nostrand Reinhold, 1969.

Shipler, David K. *Arab and Jew: Wounded Spirits in a Promised Land*. London, Bloomsbury, 1987.

Stendel, Ori. *The Arabs in Israel*. Sussex Academic Press, 1996.

Sykes, Christopher. *Crossroads to Israel*. London, Collins, 1965.

Timerman, Jacob. *The Longest War*. London, Chatto and Windus, 1982.

Weizman, Ezer. *The Battle for Peace*. New York, Bantam Books, 1981.

Wolf, Aaron T. *Hydropolitics Along the Jordan River: Scarce Water and its Impact on the Arab–Israeli Conflict*. Tokyo, United Nations Press, 1996.

Yaniv, Avner. *Dilemmas of Security—Politics, Strategy and the Israeli Experience in Lebanon*. Oxford, Oxford University Press, 1987.

THE STATE

Al-Haj, Majid, and Rosenfeld, Henry. *Arab Local Government in Israel*. Boulder, CO, San Francisco, CA, and London, Westview Press, 1990.

Avi-hai, Avraham. *Ben Gurion, State Builder*. Israel Universities Press, 1974.

Badi, Joseph. *Fundamental Laws of the State of Israel*. New York, 1961.

Bar-Zohar, Michael. *Ben-Gurion: A Biography*. London, Weidenfeld and Nicolson, 1978.

Baruth, K. H. *The Physical Planning of Israel*. London, 1949.

Ben Gurion, D. *Rebirth and Destiny of Israel*. New York, 1954.

Israel: A Personal History. London, New English Library, 1972.

Bentwich, Norman. *Fulfilment in the Promised Land 1917–37*. London, 1938.

Judea Lives Again. London, 1944.

Israel Resurgent. Ernest Benn, 1960.

The New-old Land of Israel. Allen and Unwin, 1960.

Israel, Two Fateful Years 1967–69. London, Elek, 1970.

Brecher, Michael. *The Foreign Policy System of Israel*. London, Oxford University Press, 1972.

Comay, Joan, and Pearlman, Moshe. *Israel*. New York, 1965.

Crossman, R. H. S. *A Nation Reborn*. London, Hamish Hamilton, 1960.

Davis, Moshe (Ed.). *Israel: Its Role in Civilisation* New York, 1956.

Davis, Uri. *Israel: An Apartheid State*. London, Zed Press, 1987.

Dayan, Shmuel. *The Promised Land*. London, 1961.

De Gaury, Gerald. *The New State of Israel*. New York, 1952.

Eban, Abba. *The Voice of Israel*. New York, Horizon Press, 1957.

The Story of Modern Israel. London, Weidenfeld and Nicolson, 1973.

Edelman, Maurice. *Ben Gurion, a Political Biography*. London, Hodder and Stoughton, 1964.

Frankel, William. *Israel Observed: An Anatomy of the State*. London, Thames and Hudson, 1980.

Hazony, Yoram. *The Jewish State: The Struggle for Israel's Soul*. New York, Basic Books, 2000.

Hollis, Rosemary. *Israel on the Brink of Decision: division, unity and cross-currents in the Israeli body politic*. London, Research Institute for the Study of Conflict and Terrorism, 1990.

Janowsky, Oscar I. *Foundations of Israel: Emergence of a Welfare State*. Princeton, Anvil Nostrand Co, 1959.

Kraines, O. *Government and Politics in Israel*. London, Allen and Unwin, 1961.

Likhovski, Eliahu S. *Israel's Parliament: The Law of the Knesset*. Oxford, Clarendon Press, 1971.

Medding, Peter. *Mapai in Israel: Political Organisation and Government in a New Society*. London, Cambridge University Press, 1972.

Meir, Golda. *This is our Strength*. New York, 1963.

Merhav, Peretz. *The Israeli Left: History, Problems, Documents*. Tantivy Press, 1981.

Nusseibeh, Sari, and Heller, Mark A. *No Trumpets, No Drums: A Two-State Settlement of the Israeli–Palestinian Conflict*. London, I. B. Tauris, 1992.

Perlmutter, Amos. *The Times and Life of Menachem Begin*. New York, Doubleday, 1987.

Preuss, W. *Co-operation in Israel and the World*. Jerusalem, 1960.

Sachar, Howard M. *The Peoples of Israel*. New York, 1962.

Safran, Nadav. *The United States and Israel*. Harvard University Press, 1963.

Samuel, The Hon. Edwin. *Problems of Government in the State of Israel*. Jerusalem, 1956.

Segre, V. D. *Israel: A Society in Transition*. London, Oxford University Press, 1971.

Shatil, J. *L'Économie Collective du Kibboutz Israélien*. Paris, Les Editions de Minuit, 1960.

Teveth, Shabtai. *Ben-Gurion*. Boston, Houghton Mifflin, 1987.

ZIONISM

Avishai, Bernard. *The Tragedy of Zionism*. Farrar Strauss Giroux, 1986.

Bein, Alex. *Theodor Herzl*. London, East and West Library, 1957.

Cohen, Israel. *A Short History of Zionism*. London, Frederick Muller, 1951.

Dieckhoff, Alain. *Les Espaces d'Israël*. Paris, Fondation pour les études de la défense nationale, 1987.

Engle, Anita. *The Nili Spies*. London, Frank Cass, 1997.

Fisch, Harold. *The Zionist Revolution: A New Perspective*. London, Weidenfeld and Nicolson, 1978.

Frankl, Oscar Benjamin. *Theodor Herzl: The Jew and Man*. New York, 1949.

Huneidi, Sahar. *A Broken Trust: Herbert Samuel, Zionism and the Palestinians*. London, I. B. Tauris, 2001.

Laqueur, Walter. *A History of Zionism*. London, Weidenfeld and Nicolson, 1972.

Lowenthal, Marvin (Ed. and trans.). *Diaries of Theodor Herzl*. New York, Grosset and Dunlap, 1965.

O'Brien, Conor Cruise. *The Siege: The Saga of Israel and Zionism*. London, Weidenfeld and Nicolson, 1986.

Prior, Michael. *Zionism and the State of Israel: A Moral Inquiry*. London, Routledge, 1999.

Rose, Norman. *Chaim Weizmann*. London, Weidenfeld and Nicolson, 1987.

Rubinstein, Amnon. *From Herzl to Rabin: The changing image of Zionism*. New York, Holmes and Meier, 2001.

Schama, Simon. *Two Rothschilds and the Land of Israel*. London, Collins, 1978.

Schechtman, J. *Rebel and Statesman: the Jabotinsky Story*. New York, Thomas Yoseloff, 1956.

Sober, Moshe. *Beyond the Jewish State: confessions of a former Zionist*. Toronto, Summerhill Press, 1990.

Sokolow, Nahum. *History of Zionism*. 2 vols, London, Longmans, 1919; New York, Ktav, 1969.

Stein, Leonard, and Yogev, Gedilia (Eds). *The Letters and Papers of Chaim Weizmann; Volume I 1885–1902*. Oxford University Press, 1968.

Vital, David. *The Origins of Zionism*. Oxford University Press, 1975, re-issued 1980.

Zionism: The Formative Years. Oxford University Press, 1981.

Weisgal, Meyer, and Carmichael, Joel. *Chaim Weizmann—a Biography by Several Hands*. London, Weidenfeld and Nicolson, 1962.

Weizmann, Dr Chaim. *The Jewish People and Palestine*. London, 1939.

Trial and Error: the Autobiography of Chaim Weizmann. London, Hamish Hamilton, 1949; New York, Schocken, 1966.

ECONOMY

Aharoni, Yair. *The Israeli Economy: Dreams and Realities*. London, Routledge, 1991.

Haidar, Aziz. *On The Margins: The Arab Population in the Israeli Economy*. Hurst and Co, 1997.

OFFICIAL PUBLICATIONS

Report of the Palestine Royal Commission, 1937. Cmd 5479, London.

Report of the Palestine Partition Commission, 1938. Cmd 5854, London.

Statement of Policy by His Majesty's Government in the United Kingdom. Cmd 3692, London, 1930; Cmd 5893, London, 1938; Cmd 6019, London, 1939; Cmd 6180, London, 1940.

Government Survey of Palestine. 2 vols, 1945–46, Jerusalem. Supplement, July 1947, Jerusalem.

Report of the Anglo-American Committee of Enquiry. Lausanne, 1946.

Report to the United Nations General Assembly by the UN Special Committee on Palestine. Geneva, 1947.

Report of the UN Economic Survey Mission for the Middle East. December 1949, United Nations, Lake Success, NY; HM Stationery Office.

Annual Yearbook of the Government of Israel.

Jewish Agency for Palestine. Documents Submitted to General Assembly of UN, relating to the National Home, 1947.

The Jewish Plan for Palestine. Jerusalem, 1947.

Statistical Survey of the Middle East. 1944.

Statistical Abstract of Israel. Central Bureau of Statistics, annual.

OCCUPIED TERRITORIES

Armstrong, Karen. *A History of Jerusalem: One City, Three Faiths*. London, HarperCollins, 1997.

Cattan, Henry. *Jerusalem*. London, Saqi Books, 2000.

Dumper, Michael. *The Politics of Jerusalem since 1967*. New York, Columbia University Press, 1997.

El-Assal, Riah Abu (Bishop of Jerusalem). *Caught In Between: The Extraordinary Story of an Arab Palestinian Christian Israeli.* London, SPCK, 1999.

Friedland, Roger, and Hecht, Richard. *To Rule Jerusalem.* Cambridge University Press, 1997.

Humphries, Hugh. *In the beginning—Jerusalem: Israeli or Palestinian owned? How to occupy and dominate a city: a lay guide.* Glasgow, Scottish Friends of Palestine, 1997.

Klein, Menachem. *Jerusalem: The Contested City.* London, C. Hurst & Co, 2001.

Kollek, Teddy, and Pearlman, Moshe. *Jerusalem, Sacred City of Mankind.* London, Weidenfeld and Nicolson, 1968.

Wasserstein, Bernard. *Divided Jerusalem: The Struggle for the Holy City.* London, Profile, 2001.

JORDAN

Physical and Social Geography

W. B. FISHER

The Hashemite Kingdom of Jordan (previously Transjordan) came officially into existence under its present name in 1947 and was enlarged in 1950 to include the districts of Samaria and part of Judaea that had previously formed part of Arab Palestine. The country is bounded on the north by Syria, on the north-east by Iraq, on the east and south by Saudi Arabia, and on the west by Israel and the Palestinian Autonomous Areas. The total area of Jordan is 97,740 sq km (37,738 sq miles). The territory west of the Jordan river (the West Bank)—some 5,633 sq km (2,175 sq miles)—was occupied by Israel in June 1967, but since May 1994 the Palestinian (National) Authority (PA) has assumed jurisdiction for civil affairs in some areas. According to official estimates for December 2001, the population of the East Bank (area 89,342 sq km—34,495 sq miles) was 5,182,000, compared with 2,100,019 at the census of November 1979. In June 2002 there were 1,679,623 Palestinian refugees registered with the United Nations Relief and Works Agency (UNRWA) in Jordan, and a further 626,532 in the West Bank.

PHYSICAL FEATURES

The greater part of the State of Jordan consists of a plateau lying some 700 m–1,000 m above sea-level, which forms the north-western corner of the great plateau of Arabia (see the chapter on Saudi Arabia). There are no natural topographical frontiers between Jordan and its neighbours Syria, Iraq and Saudi Arabia, and the plateau continues unbroken into all three countries, with the artificial frontier boundaries drawn as straight lines between defined points. Along its western edge, facing the Jordan Valley, the plateau is uptilted to give a line of hills that rise 300 m–700 m above plateau-level. An old river course, the Wadi Sirhan, now almost dry with only occasional wells, fractures the plateau surface on the south-east and continues into Saudi Arabia.

The Jordanian plateau consists of a core or table of ancient rocks, covered by layers of newer rock (chiefly limestone) lying almost horizontally. In a few places (e.g. on the southern edge of the Jordan Valley) these old rocks are exposed at the surface. On its western side the plateau has been fractured and dislocated by the development of strongly marked tear faults that run from the Red Sea via the Gulf of Aqaba northwards to Lebanon and Syria. The narrow zone between the faults has sunk, to give the well-known Jordan rift valley, which is bordered both on the east and west by steep-sided walls, especially in the south near the Dead Sea, where the drop is often precipitous. The valley has a maximum width of 22 km and is now thought to have been produced by lateral shearing of two continental plates that on the east have been displaced by about 80 km.

The floor of the Jordan Valley varies considerably in level. At its northern end it is just above sea-level; the surface of Lake Tiberias (the Sea of Galilee) is 209 m below sea-level, with the deepest part of the lake over 200 m lower still. The greatest depth of the valley is at the Dead Sea (surface 400 m below sea-level, maximum depth 396 m).

Dislocation of the rock strata in the region of the Jordan Valley has had two further effects: firstly, earth tremors are still frequent along the valley; and secondly, considerable quantities of lava have welled up, forming enormous sheets that cover wide expanses of territory in the State of Jordan and southern Syria, and produce a desolate, forbidding landscape. One small lava flow, by forming a natural dam across the Jordan Valley, has impounded the waters to form Lake Tiberias.

The Jordan river rises just inside the frontiers of Syria and Lebanon—a recurrent source of dispute between the two countries and Israel. The river is 251 km (156 miles) long, and after first flowing for 96 km in Israel, it lies within Jordanian territory for the remaining 152 km. Its main tributary, the Yarmouk, is

40 km long, and close to its junction with the Jordan forms the boundary between the State of Jordan, Israel and Syria. A few kilometres from its source, the Jordan river used to open into Lake Huleh, a shallow, marsh-fringed expanse of water which was previously a breeding ground of malaria, but which has now been drained. Lake Tiberias, also, like the former Huleh, in Israel, covers an area of 316 sq km and measures 22 km from north to south, and 26 km from east to west. River water outflowing from the lake is used for the generation of hydroelectricity.

The river then flows through the barren, inhospitable country of its middle and lower valley, very little of which is actually, or potentially, cultivable, and finally enters the Dead Sea. This lake is 65 km long and 16 km wide. Owing to the very high air temperatures at most seasons of the year, evaporation from the lake is intense, and has been estimated as equivalent to 8.5m. metric tons of water per day. At the surface the Dead Sea water contains about 250g of dissolved salts per litre, and at a depth of 110 m the water is chemically saturated (i.e. holds its maximum possible content). Magnesium chloride is the most abundant mineral, with sodium chloride next in importance; but commercial interest centres on the less abundant potash and bromide salts.

Climatically, Jordan shows close affinity to its neighbours. Summers are hot, especially on the plateau and in the Jordan Valley, where temperatures of up to 49°C have been recorded. Winters are fairly cold, and on the plateau frost and some snow are usual, though not in the lower Jordan Valley. The significant element of the climate of Jordan is rainfall. In the higher parts (i.e. the uplands of Samaria and Judaea and the hills overlooking the eastern Jordan Valley) 380 mm–630 mm of rainfall occur, enough for agriculture; but elsewhere as little as 200 mm or less may fall, and pastoral nomadism is the only possible way of life. Only about 25% of the total area of Jordan is sufficiently humid for cultivation.

Hence the main features of economic life in Jordan are subsistence agriculture of a marginal kind, carried on in Judaea-Samaria and on the north-eastern edge of the plateau, close to Amman, with migratory herding of animals—sheep, goats, cattle and camels—over the remaining and by far the larger portion of the country. As a result, the natural wealth of Jordan is small, and tribal ways of life exist in parts. Before the June 1967 war tourism (with which must be included religious pilgrimage, mainly to the holy Christian places of Jerusalem) had developed into a very important industry but was then seriously jeopardized by the Israeli occupation of the West Bank territory and annexation of Jerusalem. However, the civil war in Lebanon and the reopening of the Suez Canal (which greatly affects the Jordanian port of Aqaba) were very favourable factors. The war between Iran and Iraq also had a very beneficial effect at first, since Aqaba, with the denial of Gulf ports to Iraq, became a major supply base. Iraq was Jordan's most important export market between 1980 and 1983 but the cost of continuing the war later severely curtailed the purchase by Iraq of goods from Jordan. By the time of Iraq's invasion of Kuwait in August 1990, Iraq had again become Jordan's principal trading partner; and the economic sanctions imposed on Iraq as a consequence of its invasion of Kuwait had a disastrous effect on the Jordanian economy (see Economy). More recently, with international sanctions still in force against Iraq, Jordan has effectively been that country's UN-endorsed economic conduit to the world, and important parts of Jordan's industry, banking and transport sectors are heavily dependent upon trade with Iraq

RACE, LANGUAGE AND RELIGION

A division must be drawn between the Jordanians living east of the Jordan river who, in the main, are ethnically similar to the desert populations of Syria and Saudi Arabia, and the Arabs of the Jordan Valley and Samaria-Judaea. These latter are slightly taller, more heavily built, and have a broader head-form. Some authorities suggest that they are descendants of the Canaanites, who may have originated far to the north-east, in the Zagros area. An Iranian racial affinity is thus implied— but this must be of very ancient date, as the Arabs west of the Jordan Valley have been settled in their present home for many thousands of years. Besides the two groups of Arabs, there are also small colonies of Circassians from the Caucasus of Russia, who settled in Jordan as refugees during the 19th and 20th centuries AD.

Arabic is spoken everywhere, except in a few Circassian villages.

Over 90% of the population are Sunni Muslims, and King Abdullah can trace unbroken descent from the Prophet Muhammad. There is a Christian minority, as well as smaller numbers of Shi'a Muslims.

History

Revised for this edition by NUR MASALHA

Jordan, as an independent state, is a 20th-century development. Before then it was seldom more than a rugged and backward appendage to more powerful kingdoms and empires, and indeed never existed alone. In biblical times the area was covered roughly by Gilead, Ammon, Moab and Edom, and the western portions formed for a time part of the Kingdom of Israel. During the sixth century BC the Arabian tribe of the Nabateans established their capital at Petra in the south and continued to preserve their independence when, during the fourth and third centuries, the northern half was incorporated into the Seleucid province of Syria. It was under Seleucid rule that cities such as Philadelphia (the Biblical Rabbath Ammon and the modern Amman) and Gerasa (now Jerash) rose to prominence. During the first century BC the Nabateans extended their rule over the greater part of present-day Jordan and Syria; they then began to recede before the advance of Rome, and in AD 105–6 Petra was incorporated into the Roman Empire. The lands east of the Jordan shared in a brief blaze of glory under the Palmyrene sovereigns Odenathus (Udaynath) and Zenobia (az-Zabba') in the middle of the third century AD, and during the fifth and sixth centuries formed part of the dominions of the Christian Ghassanid dynasty, vassals of the Byzantine Empire. Finally, after 50 years of anarchy in which Byzantine, Persian and local rulers intervened, Transjordania was conquered by the Arabs and absorbed into the Islamic empire.

For centuries nothing more was heard of the country; it formed normally a part of Syria, and as such was generally governed from Egypt. From the beginning of the 16th century it was included in the Ottoman *vilayet* (administrative district) of Damascus, and remained in a condition of stagnation until the outbreak of the First World War in 1914. European travellers and explorers of the 19th century rediscovered the beauties of Petra and Gerasa, but otherwise the desert tribes were left undisturbed. Even the course of the war in its early stages gave little hint of the upheaval that was to take place in Jordan's fortunes. The area was included in the zone of influence allocated to Britain under the Sykes-Picot agreement of May 1916 (see Documents on Palestine, p. 50), and Zionists held that it also came within the area designated as a Jewish National Home in the promise contained in the Balfour Declaration of November 1917 (see Documents on Palestine, p. 51). Apart from these somewhat remote political events the tide of war did not reach Jordanian territory until the capture of Aqaba by the Arab armies under Faisal, the third son of King Hussein of the Hedjaz, in July 1917. A year later, in September 1918, they shared in the final push north by capturing Amman and Deraa.

The end of the war thus found a large area, which included almost the whole of present-day Jordan, in Arab hands under the leadership of Faisal. To begin with, the territory to the east of the Jordan river was not looked on as a separate unit. Faisal, with the assistance of British officers and Iraqi nationalists, established an autonomous government in Damascus, a step encouraged by the Anglo-French Declaration of 7 November 1918, favouring the establishment of indigenous governments in Syria and Iraq. Arab demands, however, as expressed by Faisal at the Paris Peace Conference in January 1919, went a good deal further in claiming independence throughout the Arab world. This represented a challenge to both French and Zionist claims in the Near East, and when, in March 1920, the General Syrian Congress in Damascus declared the independence of Syria and Iraq, with Faisal and Abdullah, Hussein's second son, as kings, the decisions were denounced by France and Britain. In the following month the San Remo Conference awarded the Palestine Mandate to Britain, and thus separated it effectively from Syria proper, which fell within the French share. Faisal was forced out of Damascus by the French in July and left the country.

THE KINGDOM OF TRANSJORDAN

The position of Transjordania was not altogether clear under the new dispensation. After the withdrawal of Faisal the British High Commissioner informed a meeting of notables at es-Salt that the British Government favoured self-government for the territory with British advisers. In December 1920 the provisional frontiers of the Mandates were extended eastwards by Anglo-French agreement so as to include Transjordania within the Palestine Mandate, and therefore presumably within the provisions regarding the establishment of a Jewish National Home. Yet another twist of policy came as the result of a conference in Cairo in March 1921 attended by Winston Churchill, the new British Colonial Secretary, Abdullah, T. E. Lawrence and Sir Herbert Samuel, High Commissioner for Palestine. At this meeting it was recommended that Faisal should be proclaimed King of Iraq, while Abdullah was persuaded to stand down in his favour by the promise of an Arab administration in Transjordania. He had in fact been in effective control in Amman since his arrival the previous winter to organize an uprising against the French in Syria. This project he now abandoned, and in April 1921 he was officially recognized as *de facto* ruler of Transjordan. The final draft of the Palestine Mandate confirmed by the Council of the League of Nations in July 1922 contained a clause giving the Mandatory Power considerable latitude in the administration of the territory east of the Jordan (see Documents on Palestine, p. 53). On the basis of this clause, a memorandum was approved in the following September, expressly excluding Transjordan from the clauses relating to the establishment of the Jewish National Home, and, although many Zionists continued to press for the reversal of this policy, the country thenceforth remained, in practice, separate from Palestine proper.

Like much of the post-war boundary delineation, the borders of the new state were somewhat arbitrary. Although they lay mainly in desert areas, they frequently cut across tribal areas and grazing grounds, with small respect for tradition. Of the 300,000–400,000 inhabitants, only about one-fifth were town-dwellers, and these confined to four small cities ranging in population from 10,000 to 30,000. Nevertheless, Transjordan's early years were destined to be comparatively peaceful. On 15 May 1923 Britain formally recognized Transjordan as an independent constitutional state under the rule of the Amir Abdullah with British tutelage, and with the aid of a British subsidy it was possible to make some slow progress towards development and modernization. A small but efficient armed force, the Arab Legion, was built up under the guidance of Peake Pasha and later Glubb Pasha; this force distinguished itself particularly during the Iraqi rebellion of May 1941. It also played a significant role in the fighting with Israel during 1948.

Other British advisers assisted in the development of health services and schools.

The Amir Abdullah very nearly became involved in the fall of his father, King Hussein, in 1924. It was in Amman on 5 March 1924, that the latter was proclaimed Caliph, and during the subsequent fighting with Ibn Sa'ud Wahhabi troops penetrated into Transjordanian territory. They subsequently withdrew to the south, and in June 1925, after the abdication of Hussein's eldest son, Ali, Abdullah formally incorporated Ma'an and Aqaba within his dominions. The move was not disputed by the new ruler of the Hedjaz and Najd, and thereafter the southern frontier of Transjordan remained unaltered.

INDEPENDENCE

In February 1928 a treaty was signed with Great Britain granting a still larger measure of independence, though reserving for the advice of a British Resident such matters as financial policy and foreign relations. The same treaty provided for a Constitution, and this was duly promulgated in April 1928, the first Legislative Council meeting one year later. In January 1934 a supplementary agreement was added permitting Transjordan to appoint consular representatives in Arab countries, and in May 1939 Britain agreed to the conversion of the Legislative Council into a regular Cabinet with ministers in charge of specified departments. The outbreak of war delayed further advances towards independence, but this was finally achieved, in name at least, by the Treaty of London of 22 March 1946. On 25 May 1946 Abdullah was proclaimed king and a new Constitution replaced that of 1928.

Transjordan was not slow in taking its place in the community of nations. In 1947 King Abdullah signed treaties with Turkey and Iraq and applied for membership of the United Nations (UN); this last, however, was thwarted by the Soviet veto and by lack of US recognition of Transjordan's status as an independent nation. In March 1948 Britain agreed to the signing of a new treaty in which virtually the only restrictive clauses related to military and defence matters. Britain was to have certain peacetime military privileges, including the maintenance of airfields and communications, transit facilities and co-ordination of training methods. It was also to provide economic and social aid.

Transjordan had not, however, waited for independence before making its weight felt in Arab affairs in the Middle East. It had not been very active before the war, its first appearance on the international scene being in May 1939, when Transjordanian delegates were invited to the Round Table Conference on Palestine in London. Transjordan took part in the preliminary discussions during 1943 and 1944 that finally led to the formation of the League of Arab States (the Arab League) in March 1945, and was one of the original members of that League. During the years immediately following it seemed possible that political and dynastic differences would be forgotten in this common effort for unity. Under the stresses and strains of 1948, however, the old contradictions began to reappear. Abdullah had long favoured the project of a 'Greater Syria', that is, the union of Transjordan, Syria and Palestine, as a step towards the final unification of the Fertile Crescent by the inclusion of Iraq. This was favoured on dynastic grounds by various parties in Iraq, and also by some elements in Syria and Palestine. On the other hand, it met with violent opposition from many Syrian nationalists, from the rulers of Egypt and Saudi Arabia—neither of whom were disposed to favour any strengthening of the Hashemite house—and of course from Zionists and the French. It is in the light of these conflicts of interest that developments subsequent to the establishment of the State of Israel must be considered.

FORMATION OF ISRAEL

On 14–15 May 1948 British troops were withdrawn to the port of Haifa as a preliminary to the final evacuation of Palestine, the State of Israel was proclaimed, and Arab armies entered the former Palestinian territory from all sides. Only those from Transjordan played any significant part in the fighting, and by the time that major hostilities ceased in July they had succeeded in occupying a considerable area. The suspicion now inevitably arose that Abdullah was prepared to accept a *fait accompli* and to negotiate with the Israeli authorities for a formal recognition

of the existing military boundaries. Moreover, whereas the other Arab countries refused to accept any other move that implied a tacit recognition of the status quo—such as the resettlement of refugees—Transjordan seemed to be following a different line. In September 1948 an Arab government was formed at Gaza under Egyptian tutelage, and this was answered from the Transjordanian side by the proclamation in December at Jericho of Abdullah as King of All Palestine. In the following April the country's name was changed to Jordan and three Palestinians were included in the Cabinet. In the mean time, armistices were being signed by all the Arab countries, including Jordan, and on 31 January 1949 Jordan was finally recognized by the USA.

On the three major problems confronting the Arab states in their dispute with Israel, Jordan continued to differ more or less openly with its colleagues. It refused to agree to the internationalization of Jerusalem, it initiated plans for the resettlement of the Arab refugees, and it showed a disposition to accept as permanent the armistice frontiers. In April 1950, after rumours of negotiations between Jordan and Israel, the Arab League Council in Cairo succeeded in securing Jordan's adherence to resolutions forbidding negotiations with Israel or annexation of Palestinian territory. Nevertheless, in the same month elections were held in Jordan and Arab Palestine, the results of which encouraged Abdullah formally to annex the latter territory on 24 April 1950. This step was immediately recognized by Britain.

At the meeting of the Arab League that followed, Egypt led the opposition to Jordan, which drew support, however, from Iraq. The decisions reached by the Council were inconclusive, but thereafter Jordan began to deviate from Arab League policy. Jordan signed a four-point agreement with the USA in March 1951. Although at the same time there was constant friction between Jordan and Israel, the unified opposition of the Arab states to the new Jewish state seemed to have ended, and inter-Arab differences were gaining the upper hand.

ABDULLAH ASSASSINATED

On 20 July 1951 King Abdullah was assassinated in Jerusalem. Evidence which emerged at the trial of those implicated in the plot revealed that the murder had been partly motivated by opposition to Adbullah's Greater Syria policy, and it was significant that Egypt refused to extradite some of those convicted. Nevertheless, the stability of the young Jordanian state revealed itself in the calm in which the King's eldest son Talal succeeded to the throne, and the peaceful elections held shortly afterwards. In January 1952 a new Constitution was promulgated. Even more significant, perhaps, was the dignity with which, only one year after his accession, King Talal, whose mental condition had long been a cause for anxiety, abdicated in favour of his son, Hussein—still a minor. In foreign policy Talal had shown some signs of rejecting his father's ideas in favour of a *rapprochement* with Syria and Egypt, one example being Jordan's signature of the Arab Collective Security Pact which it had failed to join in the summer of 1950.

This policy was continued during the reign of his son, King Hussein, notably by the conclusion of an economic and financial agreement with Syria in February 1953, and a joint scheme for the construction of a dam across the Yarmouk river to supply irrigation and hydroelectric power. One problem which became pressing in 1954 was the elaborate US-sponsored scheme for the sharing of the Jordan waters between Jordan, Iraq, Syria and Israel, which could make no progress in the absence of political agreement.

During December 1954 a financial aid agreement was signed with the United Kingdom, and the opportunity was taken to discuss the revision of the Anglo-Jordanian Treaty of 1948. Agreement over this was not possible owing to British insistence that any new pact should fit into a general Middle East defence system. In May 1955 Premier Abu'l-Huda was replaced by Sa'id al-Mufti, while an exchange of state visits with King Sa'ud hinted at a *rapprochement* with Saudi Arabia. Nevertheless, in November Jordan declared its unwillingness to adhere either to the Egyptian-Syrian-Saudi Arabian bloc or to the Baghdad Pact.

DISMISSAL OF GLUBB PASHA

On 15 December 1955, following a visit to General Sir G. Templer, Chief of the Imperial General Staff, Sa'id al-Mufti resigned and was replaced by Hazza al-Majali, known to be in favour of the Baghdad Pact. The following day there were violent demonstrations in Amman, and on 20 December Ibrahim Hashim became Prime Minister, to be succeeded on 9 January 1956 by Samir Rifai. In February the new Prime Minister visited Syria, Lebanon, Iraq, Egypt and Saudi Arabia, and shortly after his return, on 2 March, King Hussein announced the dismissal of Glubb Pasha, Commander-in-Chief of the Jordanian armed forces, replacing him with Maj.-Gen. Radi Annab. The Egyptian-Syrian-Saudi Arabian bloc at this juncture offered to replace the British financial subsidy to Jordan; but the latter was not in fact withdrawn, and King Hussein and the Jordanian Government evidently felt that they had moved far enough in one direction, and committed themselves to a policy of strict neutrality. In April, however, the King and the Prime Minister paid a visit to the Syrian President in Damascus, and in May Maj.-Gen. Annab was replaced by his deputy, Lt-Col Ali Abu Nuwar, generally regarded as the leader of the movement to eliminate foreign influence from the Jordanian army and government. This coincided with the reappointment of Sa'id al-Mufti as Prime Minister. During the same period discussions culminated in agreements for military co-operation between Jordan and Syria, Lebanon and Egypt, and in July Jordan and Syria formed an economic union. At the beginning of the same month al-Mufti was replaced by Ibrahim Hashim.

RELATIONS WITH ISRAEL AND WITH THE OTHER ARAB STATES

Meanwhile, relations with Israel, including the problem of the Arab refugees, the use of Jordan waters, the definition of the frontier, and the status of Jerusalem, continued to provide a cause for anxiety. Tension between Jordan and Israel was further increased after the Israeli, British and French military action in Egypt. A new Cabinet, headed by Sulayman Nabulsi, had taken office in October, and new elections were followed by the opening of negotiations for the abrogation of the Anglo-Jordanian Treaty of 1948, and the substitution of financial aid from the Arab countries, notably Saudi Arabia, Egypt and Syria. Owing to subsequent political developments, however, the shares due from Egypt and Syria were not paid. On 13 March 1957 an Anglo-Jordanian agreement was signed abrogating the 1948 treaty, and by 2 July the last British troops had left. In the mean time, Nabulsi's evident leanings towards the Soviet connection, clashing with the recently enunciated Eisenhower doctrine in the USA, led to his breach with King Hussein and his resignation on 10 April, to be succeeded by Ibrahim Hashim. All political parties were suppressed, and plans to establish diplomatic relations with the USSR were dropped. Gen. Ali Abu Nuwar was removed from the post of Commander-in-Chief, and the USA announced its determination to preserve Jordan's independence—a policy underlined by a major air-lift of arms to Amman in September in response to Syria's alignment with the USSR. In May Syrian troops serving under the joint Syro-Egypto-Jordanian command were withdrawn from Jordanian territory at Jordan's request, and in June there was a partial rupture of diplomatic relations with Egypt.

On 14 February 1958 the merger of the kingdoms of Iraq and Jordan in a federal union to be called the Arab Federation was proclaimed in Amman by King Faisal of Iraq and King Hussein. This new federation proved abortive. Samir Rifai became Prime Minister of Jordan in May, on the resignation of Ibrahim Hashim who took up the appointment of vice-premier in the short-lived Arab Federation.

British troops were flown to Amman from Cyprus on 17 July 1958, in response to an appeal by King Hussein. They had all been withdrawn by the beginning of November—under UN auspices—and in the two years that followed Jordan enjoyed a period of comparative peace. Hazza al-Majali succeeded Rifai as Prime Minister on 6 May 1959. Firm measures were taken against communism and subversive activities and collaboration with the West was, if anything, encouraged by the country's isolation between Iraq, Israel and the two halves of the United Arab Republic (UAR). American loans continued to arrive at the rate of about US $50m. per year, and there was also technical aid from Britain, West Germany and other countries. An important development was the official opening of the port of Aqaba on the Red Sea.

Relations with Jordan's Arab neighbours continued to be uneasy, although diplomatic relations with the UAR, broken off in July 1958, were resumed in August 1959. Incidents on the Syrian border were almost as frequent as those on the Israeli border, and there were no signs of a *rapprochement* with Iraq. In January 1960 both the King and the Prime Minister condemned the Arab leaders' approach to the Palestine problem, and in February Jordanian citizenship was offered to all Arab refugees who applied for it. There was little change in the general position that Jordan wished for formal recognition of its absorption of the Palestinian territory west of the Jordan, while the UAR and other Arab countries favoured the establishment of an independent Palestine Arab government.

On 29 August 1960 the Jordanian Prime Minister, Hazza al-Majali, was assassinated; he was succeeded by several prime ministers during the next five years. In April 1965 a constitutional uncertainty was resolved, with the nomination of the King's brother Hassan as Crown Prince; the King's own children were thus excluded from the succession to the throne, at this time.

Meanwhile, in September 1963 the creation of a unified 'Palestinian entity' was approved by the Council of the Arab League, despite opposition from the Jordanian Government, which regarded the proposal as a threat to Jordan's sovereignty over the West Bank. The first congress of Palestinian Arab groups was held in the Jordanian sector of Jerusalem in May–June 1964, when the participants unanimously agreed to form the Palestine Liberation Organization (PLO) as 'the only legitimate spokesman for all matters concerning the Palestinian people'. The PLO was to be financed by the Arab League and was to recruit military units, from among refugees, to constitute a Palestine Liberation Army (PLA). From the outset, King Hussein refused to allow the PLA to train forces in Jordan or the PLO to levy taxes from Palestinian refugees in his country.

WAR WITH ISRAEL

During the latter part of 1966 Jordan's deteriorating foreign relations were exacerbated by the widening breach with Syria. Charges and counter-charges of plots to subvert each other's governments were made, and while the UAR and the USSR supported Syria, Jordan looked to Saudi Arabia and the USA for backing. This situation made it increasingly difficult for Jordan's relations with Israel to be regularized. During 1965–66 the principal guerrilla organization to emerge from the PLO, Fatah (the Palestine National Liberation Movement), unleashed a series of terrorist attacks against Israel, usually across the Jordanian border, which, in turn, provoked violent reprisal attacks by Israeli forces. In July 1966 Jordan suspended support for the PLO, accusing its Secretary, Ahmad Shukairi, of pro-communist activity. While Jordan introduced conscription and Saudi Arabia promised military aid, Syria and the PLO appealed to Jordanians to revolt against King Hussein. Negotiations to implement the resolution of the Supreme Council for Arab Defence that Iraqi and Saudi troops should be sent to Jordan, to assist in its defence, collapsed in December. This was followed by clashes on the Jordanian–Syrian frontier, by PLO-sponsored bomb outrages in Jordan (resulting in the closure of the PLO headquarters in Jerusalem), and by worsening relations between Jordan and the UAR and a ban by the latter on aircraft carrying British and US armaments to Jordan. In retaliation, Jordan withdrew recognition of the Sallal regime in Yemen, and boycotted the next meeting of the Arab Defence Council. On 5 March Wasfi at-Tal resigned and was succeeded by Hussein bin Nasser at the head of an interim government.

As the prospect of war with Israel drew nearer, King Hussein composed his differences with Egypt, and personally flew to Cairo to sign a defence agreement. Jordanian troops, together with those of the UAR, Iraq and Saudi Arabia, went into action immediately on the outbreak of hostilities in June 1967. By the end of the Six-Day War, however, all Jordanian territory west of the Jordan river had been occupied by Israeli troops, and a steady stream of West Bank Jordanians began to cross the river to the East Bank. These estimated 150,000–250,000 persons swelled Jordan's refugee population and presented the Government with intractable social and economic problems.

In August 1967 King Hussein formed a nine-man Consultative Council, composed of former premiers and politicians of varying sympathies, to meet weekly and to participate in the 'responsibility of power'. Later a Senate was formed, consisting of 15 representatives from the inhabitants of the West Bank area and 15 from eastern Jordan. Several changes of government took place and the King took over personal command of the country's armed forces.

Meanwhile, the uneasy situation along the frontier with Israel persisted, aggravated by the deteriorating economic situation in Jordan. Reprisal actions by Israel, after numerous commando raids directed against its authority in Jerusalem and the West Bank and operating from Jordanian territory, provoked Jordan to appeal for UN intervention. In June 1969 Israeli commandos blew up the diversion system of the Ghor Canal, Jordan's principal irrigation project.

THE GUERRILLA CHALLENGE

The instability in Amman after the Six-Day War was reflected in the short life of Jordanian cabinets—it became rare for one to remain unchanged for more than three months. A careful balance had to be struck between the Palestinians and the King's traditional supporters. Thus, in the new Cabinet announced after the June 1970 crisis (see below), Palestinians were given more of the key ministries, including the interior portfolio. Abd al-Munem Rifai, Jordan's senior diplomat, became Prime Minister for the second time.

The main factor in Jordan's internal politics between June 1967 and 1971 was the rivalry between the Government and Palestinian guerrilla organizations, principally Fatah, which from 1968 was led by Yasser Arafat, the Chairman of the PLO. These organizations gradually assumed effective control of the refugee camps and commanded widespread support amongst the Palestinian majority of Jordan's population. They also received armaments and training assistance from other Arab countries, particularly Syria, and finance from the oil-rich states bordering the Persian (Arabian) Gulf. The *fedayeen* ('martyrs') movement virtually became a state within a state. Its leaders stated that they 'have no wish to interfere in the internal affairs of Jordan provided it does not place any obstacles in the way of our struggle to liberate Palestine'. In practice, however, its popularity and influence represented a challenge to the Government, whilst its actions attracted Israeli reprisals that did serious damage to the East Bank, now the only fertile part of Jordan, and generally reduced the possibilities of a peace settlement on which Jordan's long-term future depended.

A major confrontation between the two forces occurred in November 1968, after massive demonstrations in Amman on the anniversary of the Balfour Declaration. Extensive street fighting broke out between guerrillas and the army, and for a short period a civil war seemed possible, but both sides soon backed down. Similar confrontations followed in February and June 1970, and on both occasions the Government was forced to yield to Palestinian pressures. King Hussein and Arafat (whose own position was threatened by the rise of small extremist groups in Jordan) concluded an agreement redefining their respective spheres of influence. The guerrillas appeared to have granted little or nothing, but Hussein was forced to dismiss his Commander-in-Chief and a cabinet minister, both relatives. These were regarded as the leaders of the anti-*fedayeen* faction, which remained strong amongst the Bedouin sheikhs. Despite the accord, the tension between the Government and the guerrillas continued, aggravated by opposition to the Government's concessions from intransigent army officers.

A new and dangerous stage in relations between the two sides in Jordan was reached in July 1970 with the acceptance by the Government of the US peace proposals for the Middle East. The guerrilla groups, with few exceptions, rejected these, and, as the cease-fire between the UAR and Israel came into operation on 7 August, it was clear that the Jordanian Government was preparing for a full-scale confrontation with them.

CIVIL WAR

Bitter fighting between government and guerrilla forces broke out at the end of August 1970. This escalated into full civil war in the latter half of September, with thousands of deaths and injuries. On 16 September a military Cabinet was formed under Brig. Muhammad Daoud—in any case martial law had been in force since the end of the June 1967 war—and immediately

Field Marshal Habis Majali replaced as Commander-in-Chief Lt-Gen. Mashour Haditha, who had been sympathetic to the commandos and had tried to restrain their severest opponents in the army.

In the fighting that followed, the guerrillas claimed full control in the north, aided by Syrian forces and, it was later revealed, three battalions of the PLA sent back by President Nasser from the Suez front. The Arab states generally appealed for an end to the fighting. Libya threatened to intervene and later broke off diplomatic relations, while Kuwait stopped its aid to the Government; however, the Iraqi troops stationed on the eastern front against Israel notably failed to intervene. On the government side talks were held with the USA about direct military assistance. In the event such a dangerous widening of the Palestinian confrontation was avoided by the scale of the casualties in Jordan and by the diplomacy of Arab heads of state (reinforced by President Nasser's reported threat to intervene on the guerrillas' behalf) who prevailed upon King Hussein and Yasser Arafat to sign an agreement in Cairo on 27 September 1970, ending the war. The previous day a civilian Cabinet had been restored under Ahmad Toukan. Five military members were retained.

A definitive accord, very favourable to the liberation organizations, was signed by Hussein and Arafat on 13 October 1970 in Amman, but this proved to be simply the beginning of a phase of sporadic warfare between the two parties, punctuated by new agreements, during which the commandos were gradually forced out of Amman and driven from their positions in the north back towards the Syrian frontier. At the end of October a new Government, still containing three army officers, was formed under Wasfi at-Tal. By January 1971 army moves against the Palestine guerrillas had become much more blatant, and the UAR, Syria and Algeria all issued strong protests at the Jordanian Government's attempt to 'liquidate' the liberation movements. All but two brigades of Iraqi troops were, however, withdrawn from Jordan.

By April 1971 the Jordanian Government seemed strong enough to set a deadline for the guerrillas' withdrawal of their remaining men and heavy armaments from the capital. On 13 July a major government attack began on the guerrillas entrenched in the Jerash-Ajloun area, which lasted four days. The Government claimed that all the bases had been destroyed and that 2,300 of 2,500 guerrillas in them had been captured. Most of the Palestinians taken prisoner by the Jordanian authorities were released a few days later.

The 'solution' (in King Hussein's word) of the guerrilla 'problem' provoked strong reaction from other Arab governments. Iraq and Syria closed their borders with Jordan; Algeria suspended diplomatic relations; and Egypt, Libya, Sudan and both Yemens voiced public criticism. Relations with Syria deteriorated fastest of all, but normal trading and diplomatic relations were restored by February 1972.

Meanwhile, Saudi Arabia had been attempting to bring together guerrilla leaders and Jordanian Government representatives to work out a new version of the Cairo and Amman agreements. Meetings in Jeddah were fruitless, however, and the Palestinians responded in their own way to the events of July. Three unsuccessful attempts were made in September to hijack Jordanian airliners. Then, on 28 September 1971, Wasfi at-Tal, the Prime Minister and Minister of Defence, was assassinated by members of a Palestinian guerrilla group, the Black September organization, and other assassination attempts were made.

HUSSEIN'S ANSWER

Throughout the period since the liquidation of the guerrillas in July 1971, Hussein had been seeking to strengthen his political position. In August he announced the creation of a tribal council—a body of sheikhs or other notables, appointed by him and chaired by the Crown Prince—which was to deal with the affairs of tribal areas. A month later the formation of the Jordanian National Union was announced. This (renamed the Arab National Union in March 1972) was to be Jordan's only legal political organization. It was not a party in the usual sense; proponents of 'imported ideologies' were debarred from membership; the King became president, and the Crown Prince vice-president, and appointed the 36 members of the Supreme Executive Committee.

However, the King's boldest political move, and an obvious attempt to regain his standing in the eyes of Palestinians, was his unfolding of plans for a United Arab Kingdom in March 1972. This kingdom was to federate a Jordanian region, with Amman as its capital and also federal capital, and a Palestinian region, with Jerusalem as its capital. Each region was to be virtually autonomous, though the King would rule both and there would be a federal Council of Ministers.

Outside Jordan there was almost universal criticism of this plan from interested parties—Israel, the Palestinian organizations and Egypt, which in the following month broke off diplomatic relations. Jordan's isolation in the Arab world had never been more complete. Throughout the rest of 1972 and the first half of 1973, however, Hussein continued to adhere to his original plans for a United Arab Kingdom, while insisting that peace with Israel could be arrived at only within the framework of UN Security Council Resolution 242 (see Documents on Palestine, p. 57). He strongly denied suggestions from other Arab states that he was considering signing a separate peace treaty with Israel.

The internal security of Jordan was threatened in November 1972 when an attempted military coup in Amman by Maj. Rafeh Hindawi was thwarted. In February 1973 Abu Daoud, one of the leaders of Fatah, and 16 other guerrillas were arrested on charges of infiltrating into Jordan for the purpose of subversive activities. The latter affair took place while King Hussein was on a visit to the USA requesting defence and financial aid. On his return he commuted the death sentences passed on the guerrillas by a Jordanian military court and previously confirmed by himself, to life imprisonment. In May 1973 Hussein's Prime Minister, Ahmad Lauzi, resigned for health reasons and a new Government under Zaid ar-Rifai, who was known as an opponent of the Palestinian guerrillas, was formed.

In September 1973 Hussein attended a 'reconciliation summit' with Presidents Sadat of Egypt and Assad of Syria. This was Jordan's first official contact with the two states since they had broken off diplomatic relations, and they were restored after the summit. The meeting was condemned by Fatah, Libya and Iraq, but Jordan regained some stature in the Arab world after Hussein's general amnesty for all political prisoners; among those released was Abu Daoud.

During the 1973 October War with Israel Jordan sent troops to support Syria on the Golan Heights but was otherwise not actively involved, and did not open a third front against Israel as in the 1967 war. Jordan was represented at the Geneva talks in December 1973.

In April 1974 Hussein announced that the Arab National Union, which was then the sole political organization in Jordan, was to be reorganized with an executive and council of reduced numbers.

During most of 1974 King Hussein's policy towards the PLO and the status of the West Bank was somewhat ambiguous. He continued to try to preserve the West Bank as part of his kingdom despite strong pressure from other Arab states and the increasing influence of the PLO. In September after a meeting between Egypt, Syria and the PLO expressing support for the PLO as the 'only legitimate representative of the Palestinian people', Jordan refused to participate in further Middle East peace talks. However, in October at the Arab Summit Conference at Rabat (see Documents on Palestine, p. 62), representatives of 20 Arab Heads of State unanimously recognized the PLO as the sole legitimate representative of the Palestinians, and its right to establish a national authority over any liberated Palestinian territory. Effectively ceding Jordan's claim to represent the Palestinians and reincorporate the West Bank, when recaptured, into the Hashemite kingdom, Hussein reluctantly assented to the resolution. Hussein declared that Jordan would continue to strive for the liberation of the West Bank and recognize the full rights of citizenship of Palestinians in Jordan. The prospect of a separate, independently-ruled Palestinian state was strongly condemned by Israel.

JORDAN AFTER THE RABAT SUMMIT

Following the Rabat Conference Hussein was given more extensive powers in revisions to the Jordanian Constitution approved by the National Assembly in November 1974. He was allowed to rule without the National Assembly for one year, and to reorganize his kingdom in order to lessen the numbers of Palestinians in the executive and legislative branches of government, his 1972 plan for a United Arab Kingdom now being wholly defunct. The National Assembly was dissolved and a new Government formed in November, with Zaid ar-Rifai remaining Prime Minister. Palestinian representation was decreased, and the question of citizenship of the estimated 800,000 Palestinians on the East Bank became contentious. Elections in Jordan were postponed in March 1975 and when the National Assembly was briefly reconvened in February 1976 a constitutional amendment was enacted to suspend elections indefinitely.

The success of the PLO at the Rabat Conference had, despite internal feuds, considerably strengthened its position. This stance was consolidated in November when the UN acknowledged the PLO as the sole legitimate representative of the Palestinians by an overwhelming majority, and also granted it observer status.

One of the most notable results of the Rabat Summit Conference, and of Hussein's virtual abandonment of his claim to the West Bank, was an improvement in relations with the Arab world, especially Syria. During 1975 various links with Syria were forged and strengthened. Early in the year Hussein visited Damascus, and President Assad visited Jordan in June. A supreme joint committee was set up to co-ordinate military and political planning, with the two countries' Prime Ministers as chairmen. In August a Supreme Command Council, headed by the King and President Assad, was formed to direct military and political action against Israel, and in December 1976 it was announced that a form of political union was to be elaborated.

This close relationship, however, was jeopardized by President Sadat's visit to Israel in November 1977, and subsequently threatened by Syria's proposed *rapprochement* with Iraq. Jordan, unlike Syria, was anxious not to condemn Sadat's peace initiative, but did not want to destroy its growing relationship with Syria. King Hussein, therefore, remained uncommitted and tried to act as a conciliator between Egypt on the one hand and the 'rejectionist' states (Algeria, Libya, Iraq, Syria and the People's Democratic Republic of Yemen—PDRY) on the other. Jordan, however, emphatically rejected Israel's peace proposals which were put forward by Prime Minister Begin in December 1977, and maintained its policy of demanding an Israeli withdrawal from Gaza and the West Bank, including East Jerusalem, leaving no Jewish settlements. Jordan also wanted the creation of a Palestinian homeland; the nature of that territory's link with Jordan was to be decided by a referendum.

It was these factors which helped to determine Jordan's attitude to the Camp David agreements (see Documents on Palestine, p. 63) in September 1978 and the subsequent peace treaty between Egypt and Israel (see Documents on Palestine, p. 65) in March 1979. Jordan refused to be drawn into the Camp David talks by the USA, and joined the other Arab states at the Baghdad Arab summit in drawing up a list of sanctions against Egypt.

Immediately prior to the signing of the peace treaty, Jordan showed its commitment to the PLO by welcoming Yasser Arafat on an official visit, and after the treaty was signed Jordan was the first Arab country still having diplomatic relations with Egypt to sever them. In subsequent months, however, Jordan's hostility to Egypt subsided, and was replaced by the souring of relations with Syria. In spite of Jordanian denials, Syria was convinced that the Muslim Brotherhood (allowed limited freedom in Jordan) was fostering treachery inside Syria. Syria also disapproved of Jordan's support for Iraq in the Iran–Iraq War. These factors led to a build-up of Syrian and Jordanian troops on the frontier in December 1980, and to mediation between the two sides by Saudi Arabia. Relations did not improve in February 1981 when the Jordanian chargé d'affaires in Beirut was abducted (allegedly by Syrians), and Jordan responded by abrogating a six-year economic and customs agreement with Syria.

Throughout 1981 Jordan continued with its policy of supporting Iraq, and in January 1982 King Hussein announced that he was prepared to take charge of a special 'Yarmouk Force' of Jordanians to give military help to Iraq. In April, however, as Iraq's position in the war with Iran grew weaker,

Hussein tried, unsuccessfully, to encourage a negotiated settlement between Iran and Iraq (by 1984, however, Hussein was, once more, offering military assistance to Iraq). He also supported a revival of Saudi Arabia's Fahd plan for a resolution of the Arab–Israeli question. After the Israeli invasion of Lebanon in June 1982, Hussein found himself a key part of US President Ronald Reagan's peace plan involving the creation of an autonomous Palestinian authority on the West Bank in association with Jordan (see Documents on Palestine, p. 68). Hussein discussed the matter in Washington, DC, in December, and in January 1983 held talks with the PLO leader, Yasser Arafat, in Amman.

Opinion within Jordan was very sceptical of the supposed advantages that would accrue to Jordan if Hussein associated himself too deeply with President Reagan's peace plan. As well as a military threat from Syria, there was the possibility of the withdrawal of aid from other Arab countries. Talks between Hussein and Arafat again took place in early April 1983, however, when Arafat stressed his commitment to the plan which had been agreed at the Arab summit held in Fez, Morocco, in September 1982 (see Documents on Palestine, p. 68). By the middle of April the Reagan peace plan seemed dead, when Arafat rejected the draft agreement which Hussein had prepared. In the weeks that followed, Hussein still claimed to support the Reagan plan. Much of his time, however, was spent in taking steps to control emigration of Palestinians from the West Bank in Jordan.

In domestic affairs, Hussein had dissolved the House of Representatives in 1974, but in April 1978 he formed a 60-member National Consultative Council (NCC) appointed by royal decree. The third term of the NCC began on 20 April 1982. In December 1979 Sharif Abd al-Hamid Sharaf replaced Mudar Badran as Prime Minister. Sharaf died of a heart attack on 3 July 1980, and was replaced as Prime Minister by the former Minister of Agriculture, Qassim ar-Rimawi. In August, however, a new Government under former Prime Minister Mudar Badran was introduced.

THE RECALL OF THE NATIONAL ASSEMBLY

Despite the failure to agree a formula for the creation of a Palestinian state on the West Bank with Yasser Arafat, Jordan gave diplomatic support to Arafat when a Syrian-backed revolt against his leadership of Fatah, the major guerrilla group within the PLO, erupted in Lebanon in May 1983. During the last three months of 1983 Jordanian diplomats in several European countries and targets in Amman came under attack from terrorists thought to be members of a radical Arab group, based in Syria, which was angered by Jordan's call for Egypt to be readmitted to the community of Arab states, by its backing for Arafat and by the prospect of a revival of President Reagan's peace plan.

With a view to recovering something from the West Bank before Jewish settlement there produced a *de facto* extension of Israel, King Hussein dissolved the National Consultative Council on 5 January 1984 and reconvened the National Assembly, which had been suspended in 1974, for its first session since 1967. At the same time, he embarked upon a series of talks with Yasser Arafat regarding the Palestinian question, which sought to consolidate their good relations and to establish a moderate core of opinion as a counter-weight to the intransigent Syrian, Libyan and extremist PLO position, that a solution could only be achieved by armed struggle. Hussein, moreover, was mindful of the fact that some 60% of his subjects were Palestinians. By recalling the National Assembly, Hussein seemed, effectively, to be creating the kind of Palestinian forum which was detailed in the Reagan plan. This was not, as it turned out, a prelude to a concerted move by Hussein and Arafat towards establishing a Palestinian state on the West Bank. The National Assembly provided a focus for a debate which revealed strong opposition among Jordanian Palestinians to the Reagan plan. As the talks between Hussein and Arafat progressed, they were at pains to stress that they stood by the resolution of the Rabat Summit Conference in 1974, which recognized the PLO as the sole legitimate representative of the Palestinian people.

Israel allowed the surviving West Bank deputies to attend the reconvened House of Representatives (the Lower House), which unanimously approved constitutional amendments en-

abling elections to the House to be held in the East Bank alone but giving itself the right to elect deputies from the West Bank, without whom the House would have been inquorate. The first elections in Jordan for 17 years, and the first in which women were allowed to vote, took place on 12 March 1984 (although political parties were still banned). The House of Representatives had already, in January, elected seven deputies from the West Bank by majority vote to fill the places of members who had died since 1974, increasing the membership of the House to 52. The 12 March 1984 elections filled the remaining 8 seats from the East Bank. Any thought that Hussein, in reviving the National Assembly, might, in the absence of agreement with the PLO on the Reagan plan, seek a mandate from the West Bank deputies to begin talks with Israel on Palestinian autonomy, was set further aside by the election of three Muslim fundamentalists and an Arab nationalist in the eight East Bank by-elections. The extent of the opposition to a solution based on the Reagan plan was apparent.

The nucleus of a moderate body of Arab opinion on the Palestinian question did, none the less, give the impression of being formed around Jordan and Yasser Arafat, with likely support to come from Saudi Arabia, Egypt and the Gulf states. The opposition to these developments of other Arab groups was reaffirmed when the Jordanian embassy in Tripoli, Libya, was burnt down in February 1984. Jordan responded by severing diplomatic relations with Libya. Sporadic attacks on Jordanian diplomats, principally in Europe, continued throughout 1984 and 1985, for which responsibility was claimed by various extremist Arab groups including Islamic Jihad and the re-emergent Black September organization, which was formed after the expulsion of the PLO from Jordan in September 1970. Jordan suspected Syria and Libya of being behind these attacks.

In January 1984 the Jordanian Cabinet resigned, and a new one, containing a higher proportion of Palestinians and with Ahmad Ubeidat as Prime Minister, took office.

RELATIONS WITH THE 'SUPERPOWERS'

At the beginning of 1984 the US Government tried to renew its efforts to gain congressional approval for a US $220m. plan to supply Jordan with arms and equipment for an 8,000-strong Jordanian strike force. King Hussein tried to distance Jordan from any interest or involvement in the creation of such a force, and the plans were abandoned by the Reagan Administration in June.

Hussein, frustrated by the unwillingness of the USA to use its influence with Israel to 'freeze' Jewish settlement of the West Bank and unable to buy arms from the USA, began to look to the USSR for diplomatic backing in solving the problem of Palestinian autonomy and for armaments with which to defend his country. In January 1985 Jordan purchased an air defence system from the USSR, having already made an agreement to buy French anti-aircraft missiles in September 1984. The need to re-equip the Jordanian air force was acute: in 1984 the Jordanians possessed only about 100 effective fighter aircraft, compared with the 630 and 600 aircraft, respectively, of Israel and Syria, according to 1982/83 figures.

Although US President Reagan was advocating the sale of arms worth US $500m.–$750m. to Jordan in 1985, there was still considerable opposition to the proposal, and he was advised not to put it before Congress and risk a Senate veto. Instead, on 12 June, King Hussein was offered extra economic aid of $250m., to be spread over 1985 and 1986, by Secretary of State Shultz, as a token of US support for his efforts to achieve a peace settlement between the Arabs and Israel. Jordan received US aid of $136m. in 1984, and the level of aid in 1985 and 1986 had originally been set at $111.7m. and $117m. respectively. The Senate authorized the aid but spread it over 27 months, not 15, as the Reagan Administration had requested.

JOINT JORDANIAN-PALESTINIAN PEACE PROPOSALS

In September 1984, to the anger of radical Arab states, Jordan decided to re-establish diplomatic relations with Egypt, five years after breaking them off in protest at the Egypt-Israel peace treaty of 1979. Hussein rejected the Israeli offer of direct negotiations, excluding the PLO, in October, calling instead for a conference of all the concerned parties in the Middle East, including, on an equal footing with nation states in the region, the PLO. He required Israel to accept the principle of 'land for peace'. Negotiations, according to Hussein, should proceed on the basis of UN Security Council Resolution 242 of November 1967. This last point was the impediment to Jordanian and PLO agreement to a programme for peace talks. Resolution 242 had not been acceptable to the PLO as it referred to the Palestinian Arabs as refugees, implicitly denying the existence of a Palestinian nation and Palestinians' right to self-determination, and recognized Israel's right to exist. The Palestine National Council (PNC), which finally convened in Amman in November 1984, replied non-committally to King Hussein's offer of a joint Jordanian-Palestinian peace initiative, without explicit rejection or acceptance of the principles embodied in Resolution 242, and referred the proposal to the PLO Executive Committee for examination.

On 23 February 1985, in Amman, King Hussein and Yasser Arafat announced the terms of a joint Jordanian-Palestinian agreement on the framework for a peace settlement in the Middle East, which the two leaders had finalized on 11 February. It held that peace talks should take the form of an international conference including the five permanent members of the UN Security Council and all parties to the conflict, including the PLO, representing the Palestinian people in a joint Jordanian-Palestinian delegation. The Palestinian people would in future exercise their right to self-determination in the context of a proposed confederated state of Jordan and Palestine. The Jordanian Government claimed that the agreement was based on a number of UN resolutions and not solely Resolution 242, though the published text of the accord (see Documents on Palestine, p. 69) gave land in exchange for peace, a central tenet of that resolution, as its first principle. The PLO Executive Committee, in approving the terms of the accord (providing that they received full Arab support) on 20 February, complicated the position by stressing that the joint position stemmed, in fact, from a rejection of Camp David, the Reagan plan and Resolution 242 as well. According to King Hussein, Arafat subsequently accepted Resolution 242 as the basis for future peace negotiations, but made no public declaration of acceptance. Argument over the implications of the agreement persisted, and the PLO adopted a new position on the status of the Palestinian representation at future peace talks, which, it said, should be within a united Arab, not merely a Jordanian-Palestinian, delegation. Syria, Libya and the rebel PLO factions predictably rejected the Amman agreement.

In March 1985 President Mubarak of Egypt called for talks between Egypt, the USA and a joint Jordanian-Palestinian delegation. The PLO Executive Committee rejected the proposal as it deviated from the accord with Jordan. Israel rejected the idea of preliminary talks and any suggestion that the USA might negotiate with the PLO, as it had always refused to do unless the PLO renounced terrorism and accepted Israel's right to exist. In May King Hussein, still averring that the PLO accepted UN Security Council Resolutions 242 and 338 as the basis for negotiations, put forward a four-stage plan in Washington, DC. Under the terms of the plan, the USA would first meet a Jordanian-Palestinian delegation, not including PLO representatives. Arafat would then be prepared to make a formal declaration of the PLO's readiness to recognize and negotiate with Israel if the USA publicly stated its support for Palestinian self-determination within the context of a Jordanian-Palestinian confederation, as proposed in the 11 February agreement between King Hussein and Arafat. The USA would then hold a second meeting with a Jordanian-Palestinian delegation, including PLO representatives, at which the terms of the third and fourth stages of the plan, an international conference under the auspices of the five permanent members of the UN Security Council, leading to direct negotiations between Israel and a Jordanian-Palestinian delegation, would be discussed. Israel rejected the plan and the call for an international peace conference, and instead proposed enlisting the support of the permanent members of the Security Council for direct talks between Israel and a joint Jordanian-Palestinian delegation including 'authentic Palestinian representatives' from the Occupied Territories who were not members of the PLO or the PNC. In July Israel rejected a list of seven Palestinians, five of whom were members of the PLO loyal to Arafat or had links with

the PNC, whom King Hussein had presented to the USA as candidates for inclusion in a joint Jordanian-Palestinian delegation to hold preliminary talks with the USA. The Israeli Prime Minister, Shimon Peres, later conceded that two of the seven fulfilled his requirements.

The Prime Minister, Ahmad Ubeidat, resigned in April 1985. On 5 April a new Cabinet was sworn in under the premiership of Zaid ar-Rifai, who had served as Prime Minister during the 1970s.

THE COLLAPSE OF THE JORDANIAN-PALESTINIAN PEACE INITIATIVE

King Hussein and Yasser Arafat continued to seek Arab support for their peace initiative, but an extraordinary meeting of the Arab states in Casablanca, in August 1985 (which was boycotted by Syria, Libya, Lebanon, the PDRY and Algeria), merely noted the existence of the Jordanian-Palestinian agreement and reaffirmed Arab allegiance to the Fez plan of September 1982.

Further progress was then hampered by a series of attacks carried out by militant Palestinian organizations. In September three Israelis were murdered in Larnaca, Cyprus; Israel blamed the PLO's élite Force 17 and retaliated by bombing the PLO's headquarters in Tunis on 1 October. Later in October an Italian cruise ship, the *Achille Lauro*, was hijacked in the eastern Mediterranean by members of the Palestine Liberation Front (the faction of that name led by Muhammad 'Abu' Abbas, nominally loyal to Arafat), who killed an elderly American Jewish passenger.

King Hussein was under increasing pressure to advance the peace process, if necessary without the participation of the PLO. In September President Reagan revived a plan to sell US arms worth US $1,900m. to Jordan. The proposal was approved by Congress on the condition that Jordan entered into direct talks with Israel before 1 March 1986. However, a *rapprochement* developed between Jordan and Syria, which made such a development even more unlikely. In February 1986 the Reagan Administration indefinitely postponed its proposed arms sale to Jordan (worth $1,500m., with the withdrawal of *Hawk* missiles from the package) when it became clear that it would not be approved by the Senate. King Hussein said that he would look instead to European countries and the USSR for arms supplies.

Relations between Jordan and Syria had been poor since 1979, when Syria had accused Jordan of harbouring anti-Syrian groups. Their policies also diverged in respect of the Iran–Iraq War, in which Syria supported Iran, and Jordan Iraq. In November 1985 King Hussein admitted that Jordan had, unwittingly, been a base for the Sunni fundamentalist Muslim Brotherhood in its attempts to overthrow Syria's President Assad, but stated that members of the group would no longer receive shelter there. The Prime Ministers of the two countries met in Damascus in November and agreed on the need for 'joint Arab action' to achieve peace in the Middle East. At previous talks in Saudi Arabia in October, Jordan and Syria had rejected 'partial and unilateral' solutions and affirmed their adherence to the Fez plan, omitting all mention of the Jordanian-Palestinian peace initiative. President Assad and King Hussein confirmed the improved state of Syrian-Jordanian relations when they met in Damascus in December.

By pursuing a reconciliation with Syria, which was opposed to Yasser Arafat's leadership of the PLO, King Hussein may have hoped to exert pressure on Arafat to take the initiative in the peace process and finally signal PLO acceptance of Resolution 242. Arafat was also under pressure from King Hussein and President Mubarak to promote the PLO's credibility as a prospective partner in peace talks by renouncing terrorism. He responded to their appeals in November 1985, in Cairo, by effectively reiterating a PLO decision of 1974 to confine military operations to the Occupied Territories and Israel. Any credence that this declaration may have won was immediately dispelled by Arafat's aides, who repudiated it. Then, in December, the PLO Executive Committee reiterated its opposition to Resolution 242.

Shimon Peres, although still opposed to the idea of preliminary negotiations excluding Israel, intimated in a speech at the UN in October 1985 that he would not rule out the possibility of an international conference on the Palestinian question. Rumours of a secret meeting between King Hussein and Prime

Minister Peres were followed at the end of October by the disclosure to the Israeli press of a document, drawn up by the Israeli Prime Minister's office, which purported to summarize the state of negotiations between Israel and Jordan. The document suggested the establishment of an interim Israeli-Jordanian condominium of the West Bank, granting a form of Palestinian autonomy, and recorded mutual agreement on the need for an international forum for peace talks. Israel would consent to the participation of the USSR in such a forum (on the condition that it re-established diplomatic relations with Israel), and of Syria, but not of the PLO, on whose involvement King Hussein still insisted.

Given Yasser Arafat's persistent refusal to accept UN Security Council Resolutions 242 and 338 as the basis for peace talks, the demise of the Jordanian-Palestinian peace initiative had been forecast for some time. On 19 February 1986 King Hussein publicly severed political links with the PLO 'until such time as their word becomes their bond, characterized by commitment, credibility and constancy'. Arafat was ordered to close his main PLO offices in Jordan by 1 April, and a number of Fatah officials, loyal to Arafat, were expelled. King Hussein made efforts to strengthen Jordanian influence and create a Palestinian constituency in the Occupied Territories, independent of Arafat's PLO, including: the passing of a draft law by the House of Representatives in March 1986, increasing the number of seats in the House from 60 to 142 (71 seats each for the East and West Bank), thereby providing for greater West Bank Palestinian representation in the House; and the introduction, in August 1986, with Israeli support, of a US $1,300m. five-year development plan for the West Bank and Gaza.

This last measure provoked strong criticism from Yasser Arafat and from West Bank Palestinians, who claimed that it represented a normalization of relations between Jordan and Israel. There was considerable support for Arafat among Palestinians in Jordan and in the West Bank, and this was consolidated after he re-established himself at the head of a reunified PLO at the PNC session in Algiers in April 1987 (when the Jordan-PLO accord of 1985 was formally abrogated). As criticism of King Hussein mounted in Jordan and the West Bank, the authorities responded by imposing new security measures, arresting dissidents (in particular members of the fundamentalist Muslim Brotherhood and the banned Jordanian Communist Party), tightening press censorship and 'blacklisting' journalists deemed to be too critical of the Government.

After the termination of political co-ordination with the PLO, Jordan continued to reject Israeli requests for direct peace talks which excluded a form of PLO representation. However, Jordan's subsequent efforts to strengthen its influence in the Israeli-occupied territories and to foster a Palestinian constituency there which was independent of the PLO, complemented Israeli measures to grant limited autonomy to Palestinians in the West Bank, by appointing Arab mayors instead of Israeli military administrators in four towns. In May 1987, after a number of secret meetings with King Hussein, Peres (who was now the Israeli Minister of Foreign Affairs) claimed to have made significant progress on the critical issue of Palestinian representation at a peace conference, and to have the consent of Egypt, Jordan and the USA for convening an international conference, including the five members of the UN Security Council and a delegation of Palestinians (presumably not PLO members) who 'reject terrorism and violence' and accept UN Resolutions 242 and 338 as the basis for negotiations. King Hussein continued publicly to insist on the need for PLO representation, but he appeared to have accepted (contrary to his long-standing official policy) that the conference would have no power to impose a peace settlement, and would be only a preliminary to direct talks between the main protagonists in the Middle East conflict. However, the prospect of an international peace conference remained academic for as long as there was no majority in the Israeli Cabinet in favour of Peres' plan and, therefore, for as long as the Israeli coalition Government of National Unity remained in power. The Prime Minister, Itzhak Shamir, was opposed, in principle, to such a conference, which would negotiate on the basis of 'land for peace'. He reiterated his alternative proposal to Peres' plan, namely, direct regional talks involving Israel, Egypt, Jordan, Palestinian representatives and the USA.

ARAB LEAGUE SUMMIT IN AMMAN

During 1987 King Hussein pursued his efforts, begun in 1986, to reconcile Syria and Iraq, with the wider aim of securing Arab unity. He was instrumental in arranging the first full summit meeting of the Arab League (excluding Egyptian representation) for eight years, which took place in Amman in November, principally to discuss the Iran–Iraq War. In September Jordan had restored diplomatic relations with Libya, which had modified its support for Iran and now urged a cease-fire. The Arab summit meeting unanimously adopted a resolution of solidarity with Iraq, which condemned Iran for its occupation of Arab territory and for prolonging the war (although Syria obstructed the adoption of diplomatic or other sanctions). King Hussein's appeal for Egypt to be restored to membership of the League was successfully resisted by Syria and Libya, but nine Arab states re-established diplomatic relations with Egypt soon after the summit, and these were followed by Tunisia in January 1988 and by the PDRY in February. President Saddam Hussain of Iraq and President Assad of Syria held two sessions of talks at the summit, and the resumption of co-operation between Jordan and the PLO was announced.

THE PALESTINIAN UPRISING AND THE SHULTZ PLAN

In December 1987 Palestinians began a violent uprising (*intifada*) against Israeli occupation of the West Bank and Gaza Strip. Despite intensive and often brutal security measures, Israel was unable to suppress the revolt. Public demonstrations in Jordan in support of the *intifada* were muted, owing mainly to security precautions taken by the authorities to prevent unrest. In April the Palestinian extremist group, Black September, claimed responsibility for a series of bomb attacks in Amman, which, it said, were directed against the 'client Zionist regime in Jordan'.

The intensity of the *intifada*, the world-wide condemnation of Israeli security tactics, and revulsion at the degrading conditions in which many Palestinians were forced to live in the Occupied Territories, alerted the international community to the need for a revival of efforts to secure an Arab-Israeli peace agreement. At the end of February 1988 the US Secretary of State, George Shultz, embarked on a tour of Middle East capitals, in an attempt to elicit support for a new peace initiative. The so-called 'Shultz plan' proposed the convening of an international peace conference, involving all parties to the Arab–Israeli conflict and the five members of the UN Security Council, with the Palestinians represented in a joint Jordanian-Palestinian delegation, excluding the PLO. This conference would have no power to impose a settlement and would act only as a consultative forum prior to and during subsequent direct talks between Israel and each of its Arab neighbours, and between Israel and a joint Jordanian-Palestinian delegation. The latter talks would determine the details of a three-year transitional period of autonomy for the 1.5m. Palestinians in the Occupied Territories, leading (before the start of the transitional period) to negotiations to determine the final status of government in the Territories. (For full details of the Shultz plan, see Documents on Palestine, p. 69.)

The plan's refusal to contemplate the participation of the PLO, the Palestinians' right to self-determination, and the establishment of an independent Palestinian state in the West Bank (i.e. the principles of the Fez plan formulated in 1982), made it impossible for the Arab nations to accept. Jordan, which had initially welcomed a renewal of the USA's commitment to peace in the Middle East, became disillusioned by its failure to apply persuasive pressure on Israel's Prime Minister, Itzhak Shamir, to modify his opposition to the Shultz plan. King Hussein pronounced himself sceptical that Israel would withdraw militarily from the West Bank prior to the transitional autonomy period, as the plan would require it to do, and reiterated his opposition, in accordance with Arab summit resolutions, to 'partial or interim solutions'. He welcomed US acceptance, on 1 March 1988, of the concept of the Palestinians' 'legitimate rights', although he asked the USA to clarify its definition of those 'rights'. However, given the resumption of Jordanian political co-operation with the PLO, the enhanced status conferred on the organization by the *intifada*, and the potentially threatening reaction of Palestinians in Jordan, King Hussein was effectively constrained from supporting the Shultz plan.

An extraordinary summit meeting of the Arab League was held in Algiers in June 1988 to discuss the continuing *intifada* and the Arab–Israeli conflict in general. Addressing the summit, King Hussein gave his unconditional support to the *intifada* and disclaimed any ambition to restore Jordanian rule in the West Bank. He insisted that the PLO must represent the Palestinians at any future peace conference, and repeatedly stressed the PLO's status as 'the sole legitimate representative of the Palestinian people'. The Shultz plan, he claimed, had been launched only because the *intifada* had taken on the appearance of a Palestinian war against Israel. The final communiqué of the summit, which hailed the 'heroic' Palestinian uprising, effectively rejected the Shultz plan by endorsing the Palestinians' right to self-determination and the establishment of an independent Palestinian state in the West Bank, and insisting on PLO participation in future peace talks.

JORDAN SEVERS ITS LINKS WITH THE WEST BANK

The effect of the *intifada* had been to increase international support for Palestinian national rights, to heighten Palestinian aspirations to statehood and to reinforce support for the PLO as the Palestinians' representative in achieving it. From King Hussein's point of view, the *intifada* had created a new set of conditions in which Jordan could no longer realistically present itself as an alternative to the PLO. The King's subsequent actions were entirely consistent with his acknowledgement of the new realities, as expressed at the Algiers summit, yet they were still greeted with surprise.

On 28 July 1988 Jordan cancelled its US $1,300m.-development plan for the West Bank, which had been opposed by the PLO since its launch in 1986 and had remained substantially underfunded. Then, two days later, King Hussein severed Jordan's legal and administrative links with the West Bank, dissolving the lower house of the Jordanian Parliament (the House of Representatives), where Palestinian representatives for the West Bank occupied 30 of the 60 seats. The King explained that his actions were taken in accordance with the PLO's wishes and with the resolutions of the Rabat and Fez Arab summits in 1974 and 1982, and the positions adopted at the recent Algiers summit, which recognized the PLO as 'the sole legitimate representative of the Palestinian people'.

The extent to which Jordan was actually disengaging from the West Bank was uncertain and it appeared that King Hussein was leaving the way open for the future resumption of political co-ordination between Jordan and the PLO. For example, King Hussein stopped short of formally and irrevocably repealing the 'union agreement' of 1950 (Jordan's annexation of the West Bank) uniting the East and West Banks of the Jordan river. Moreover, the notion that, by dissolving the House of Representatives and dismantling Jordanian civil institutions, the King was actually transferring administrative responsibility for the West Bank to the PLO was not persuasive: the Jordanian legislature had exercised little or no practical influence over the territory's affairs since the Israeli occupation began in 1967, and Israel soon introduced measures to restrict the activities of Palestinian institutions, in order to prevent the PLO from filling the administrative vacuum left by the dismissal of about 20,000 Jordanian teachers and civil servants who had continued to run public services in the West Bank after 1967. It was suggested that, in giving responsibility for the Palestinians in the West Bank and for furthering the peace process to the PLO, King Hussein foresaw the inevitable failure of the PLO to finance and administer public services, and a political and diplomatic impasse that would demonstrate to Palestinians the necessity of Jordanian involvement if their hopes for self-government were to be realized. For its part, the PLO leadership complained that it had not been consulted prior to the announcement of the removal of Jordanian links, but the move was generally welcomed by the 850,000 Palestinians in the West Bank. According to the Jordanian Government, Palestinians residing there were no longer considered to be Jordanian citizens; they were still entitled to hold a Jordanian passport, but this would, in future, only have the status of a 'travel document'.

Jordan's withdrawal from the West Bank appeared finally to make the Shultz plan redundant and to damage the prospects

of a victory for Shimon Peres' Labour Party in the Israeli general election, which was scheduled to take place in November 1988. The peace plans of both Shultz and Peres had relied on the Palestinians' being represented at negotiations by a joint Jordanian-Palestinian delegation. Deprived of the so-called 'Jordanian option', the Israeli Labour Party signalled its willingness to negotiate with 'any Palestinians' who renounced the use of violence and recognized Israel's right to exist.

On 15 November 1988 the PNC proclaimed the establishment of an independent State of Palestine and, for the first time, endorsed UN Security Council Resolution 242 as a basis for a Middle East peace settlement, thus implicitly recognizing Israel. Jordan and 60 other countries recognized the new state. In December Yasser Arafat addressed a special session of the UN General Assembly in Geneva, where he renounced violence on behalf of the PLO. Subsequently, the USA opened a dialogue with the PLO, and it appeared that Israel too would have to negotiate directly with the PLO if it sought a solution to the Palestinian question.

In December 1988 Marwan al-Qassim was appointed Minister of Foreign Affairs, replacing Taher al-Masri, who had been the principal opponent of King Hussein's decision to withdraw from the West Bank and also of the severe economic measures which the Prime Minister, Zaid ar-Rifai, had introduced. In April 1989 rioting erupted in several cities in southern Jordan, spreading rapidly to areas near Amman, after the Government had imposed significant price rises on basic goods and services. The riots led to the resignation of the Prime Minister and his Cabinet. On 24 April Field Marshal Sharif Zaid ibn Shaker, who had been Commander-in-Chief of the Jordanian armed forces between 1976 and 1988, was appointed Prime Minister, at the head of a new 24-member Cabinet. While King Hussein refused to make any concessions regarding the price increases (which had been approved by the IMF), he announced that a general election would be held for the first time since 1967.

TOWARDS DEMOCRACY

A general election to the 80-seat House of Representatives took place on 8 November 1989 and was contested by 647 candidates, mostly independents, as the ban on political parties (in force since 1963) remained. However, the Muslim Brotherhood was able to present candidates for election, owing to its legal status as a charity rather than a political party. At the election, in which 63% of the electorate voted, the Muslim Brotherhood won 20 seats, while independent Islamists (who supported the Muslim Brotherhood) won a further 14 seats. Palestinian or Arab nationalists won an estimated seven seats and 'leftist' candidates won four. The remainder were won by candidates who were broadly considered to be pro-Government. The strength of support for the opposition candidates was regarded as surprising, especially since a disproportionately large number of seats had been assigned to rural areas, from which the Government had traditionally drawn most support.

On 4 December 1989 Mudar Badran was appointed Prime Minister by King Hussein. (Badran had served as Prime Minister twice previously, during 1976–79 and 1980–84.) The Muslim Brotherhood declined participation in Badran's Cabinet after its demand for the education portfolio was rejected. Included in the new Cabinet, however, were three independent Muslim deputies and three 'leftists', all of whom were regarded as members of the opposition. The Government received a vote of confidence from the House of Representatives on 1 January 1990. The Prime Minister affirmed continuing support for prevailing austerity measures, and at the end of January announced the abolition of the 1954 anti-communism law.

Following the 1989 election, King Hussein, under increasing pressure to initiate constitutional reform, promised to allow political parties more freedom and to tighten controls on corruption. In April 1990 he appointed a 60-member Royal Commission to draft a National Charter that would regulate political life in Jordan. A former Prime Minister, Ahmad Ubeidat, was appointed to chair the commission, whose members included figures from Jordan's various political and religious groupings, including left-wingers and religious fundamentalists, and whose influence in all areas of public life became increasingly evident during the course of the year. In October 1990 a National Islamic Bloc was formed by more than one-half of the deputies in the

House of Representatives. In a cabinet reshuffle in January 1991 Taher al-Masri, a leading Palestinian, was appointed Minister of Foreign Affairs (a post that he had held during 1984–88), in succession to Marwan al-Qassim. Four members of the Muslim Brotherhood were given portfolios in the new Cabinet.

On 9 June 1991 the National Charter was endorsed by the King and leading political figures. Among other things, the Charter revoked the ban on Jordanian political parties (which had been imposed since 1963) in return for their allegiance to the monarchy. On 19 June the King accepted the resignation of the Government headed by Mudar Badran and appointed a new Cabinet, with Taher al-Masri, the erstwhile Minister of Foreign Affairs, as Prime Minister. Taher al-Masri was Jordan's first Palestinian-born Prime Minister and, in spite of his support for Saddam Hussain during the 1990–91 Gulf crisis, was known for his liberal, pro-Western views. Badran's resignation was attributed to the King's disapproval of his sympathy for the Muslim Brotherhood, which had urged that *Shari'a* (Islamic) law should govern the new National Charter and whose members were again excluded from the Cabinet. The new Government obtained a parliamentary vote of confidence on 18 July.

On 7 July 1991 the King issued a decree repealing the provisions of martial law which had been in force since 1967, reportedly at the request of the new Prime Minister, who sought to continue the progress towards greater political freedom and democracy.

ARAB LEAGUE SUMMIT IN BAGHDAD

An emergency summit meeting of the Arab League was held in Baghdad on 28–30 May 1990. Convened under pressure from Jordan and the Palestinians to discuss the 'threat to pan-Arab security' that was presented by the mass emigration of Soviet Jews to Israel, the meeting was boycotted by President Assad of Syria, a long-term adversary of Iraq's President Saddam Hussain, and by four other Arab heads of state. In October 1989 King Hussein had warned against further Jewish colonization of the Occupied Territories, claiming that Israel was seeking to settle the Soviet immigrants there, thus causing more Palestinians to flee to Jordan and effectively transforming it into a surrogate Palestinian state. The *intifada* had already resulted in a net movement of Palestinians into Jordan. King Hussein urged other Arab nations to provide economic and military assistance to Jordan, declaring that mass Jewish immigration into Israel and the Territories posed a threat to Jordan which it could not afford to confront alone. Israel had selected Jordan as 'the point through which to penetrate. . .the Arab Nation', he declared. The PLO leader, Yasser Arafat, urged other Arab states, in vain, to impose economic sanctions on countries involved in the transfer of Jews to Arab lands. Saddam Hussain, supported by King Hussein (who rejected the more moderate stance of both Egypt and Saudi Arabia), vehemently denounced Israel and threatened to use weapons of mass destruction against it. In the summit's final communiqué, Arab leaders criticized US economic and military assistance to Israel and reaffirmed their commitment to the defence of Jordanian sovereignty and national security. The question of financial aid for Jordan would be a matter for bilateral negotiations. An Iraqi promise of US $50m. on 1 June was followed by further promises of aid from Saudi Arabia ($100m.) and from Kuwait and the UAE ($200m.).

JORDAN'S POSITION IN THE GULF CRISIS

Even before the Iraqi invasion of Kuwait on 2 August 1990, Jordan's economy was in severe difficulties; the country's foreign debt of US $800m. was equivalent to one-quarter of annual gross domestic product (GDP). Of all the Arab states affected, Jordan was probably the nation which was most likely to suffer from the effects of the conflict and the imposition of economic sanctions against Iraq, as stipulated by UN Security Council Resolution 661 of 6 August 1990. The loss of remittances from thousands of Jordanian workers who returned, destitute, from Iraq and Kuwait; the increased cost of importing petroleum products (almost all of Jordan's oil had been imported from Iraq); the threatened loss of as much as one-quarter of the country's exports and its transit trade with Iraq and Kuwait; the sudden decline in activity at the Red Sea port of Aqaba, as

a result of the naval blockade and increases in insurance rates for shipping in the war zone; the enormous cost of humanitarian aid to refugees fleeing the conflict through its territory: all these were potentially disastrous for Jordan, which was embroiled in events beyond its control.

Following Iraq's invasion of Kuwait, the Palestinians and the PLO supported Saddam Hussain. Officially Jordan, in its own interests, remained neutral in the conflict. King Hussein 'regretted', but did not condemn, the action of Saddam Hussain in invading Kuwait, and Jordanian public opinion was solidly pro-Iraq for the duration of the crisis. Arab League ministers, attending a meeting of the Organization of the Islamic Conference (OIC) in Cairo on 3 August 1990, issued a statement, opposed by Jordan, condemning the invasion and demanding Iraq's immediate and unconditional withdrawal. At the emergency summit meeting of the Arab League, held in Cairo on 10 August, Jordan abstained in a vote to denounce the annexation of Kuwait and to advocate the deployment of a pan-Arab force to defend Saudi Arabia and neighbouring states from invasion by Iraqi armed forces. King Hussein welcomed Saddam Hussain's proposal, on 12 August, to link Iraq's occupation of Kuwait with the continued Israeli occupations, and he held talks with the Iraqi leader in Baghdad on the following day. Another Arab League meeting in Cairo (30–31 August) was boycotted by Jordan and other Arab nations which supported Iraq. King Hussein persistently argued in favour of an Arab solution to the crisis and opposed the deployment of a multinational armed force in the Gulf region.

In the West, which had always regarded King Hussein as one of its chief allies in the region, there was much criticism of the King's pro-Iraq stance, though this was tempered with acknowledgement of the extremely difficult position in which he found himself. Talks in the USA between the King and President Bush, at Kennebunkport on 16 August, resulted in promises of US financial assistance in return for Jordanian observance of the economic embargo imposed on Iraq. A report by a UN envoy in October 1990 estimated that the crisis would cost Jordan some 30% of its GDP in 1990 and as much as 50% in 1991.

Following the Iraqi invasion of Kuwait, Jordan was overwhelmed by an influx of refugees, who included thousands of migrant workers from Egypt and the Indian sub-continent, fleeing the conflict. The congestion was such that Jordan was forced temporarily to close its border with Iraq in late August 1990, in an attempt to cope with the accumulation of refugees who could not immediately be transported to Aqaba port or airlifted to their countries of origin. On 3 September Jordan issued an urgent appeal for international aid, partially to offset the costs of caring for the refugees. By October some 800,000 refugees had passed through the country, at a cost of some US $40m. to the Jordanian authorities.

In mid-September 1990 two of King Hussein's former Palestinian opponents, George Habash of the Popular Front for the Liberation of Palestine (PFLP) and Naif Hawatmeh of the Democratic Front for the Liberation of Palestine (DFLP), who had been expelled during the civil war in 1970, were allowed to return to Amman for a pro-Iraqi conference of 'Arab Popular Forces'. The two Damascus-based leaders were received by the King in a display of unity and reconciliation fostered by the Gulf crisis. The conference, which was opened by the Speaker of the Jordanian House of Representatives (although not attended by the King), heard severe criticisms of governments opposed to Saddam Hussain and ended with pledges to wage a *jihad* against foreign forces in the Gulf region if Iraq were attacked. This led to a denunciation of King Hussein by the Saudi Arabian ambassador in Washington, DC, and Saudi Arabia subsequently expelled Jordanian diplomats and many Jordanian immigrant workers. It also halted oil supplies to the kingdom, claiming that Jordan had not paid for earlier deliveries.

King Hussein invested considerable personal effort in the search for a peaceful solution to the crisis, visiting London, Paris and Washington. In late August 1990 he arrived in Libya at the start of a peace mission among Arab leaders. He continued to advocate an Arab solution to the crisis and, in a televised message to the US Congress and people on 23 September, he urged the immediate withdrawal of the multinational force from the Gulf region. Speaking at the World Climate Conference in Geneva on 6 November, the King warned of the potentially disastrous environmental consequences of war in the Gulf region (a fear which was subsequently realized when Iraq released oil into the waters of the Gulf and ignited Kuwait's oil installations).

Following talks in Baghdad with Saddam Hussain on 4 December 1990, the King proposed a peace plan linking the Iraqi–Kuwait dispute and the Arab–Israeli conflict. He urged the convening of a Middle East peace conference, and that all Arab leaders should join in a dialogue on the crisis, to take place simultaneously with the talks between the USA and Iraq, which had been proposed by President Bush at the end of November.

THE 1991 GULF WAR

The King's diplomatic efforts continued into 1991, when he embarked, in January, on a fresh tour of European capitals in a final attempt to avert war in the Gulf region. Diplomatic ties with Iran, severed in 1981 after the start of the Iran–Iraq War, were resumed in mid-January 1991, and Jordan was later reported to be supporting Iranian proposals to end the crisis. On 10 January Jordan had closed its ar-Ruweishid border post, on the frontier with Iraq, to all except Jordanian refugees. As war became imminent, Jordan feared a further influx of refugees from Iraq and Kuwait, and claimed that it had still not received UN aid promised for the August 1990 exodus. However, after receiving assurances of UN assistance with the cost of caring for the refugees, the border was reopened on 18 January.

Following the outbreak of hostilities between Iraq and a US-led multinational force on 16 January 1991, the Jordanian Government condemned the bombardment of Iraq as a 'brutal onslaught against an Arab and Muslim nation'. Large-scale anti-Western and anti-Israeli demonstrations occurred throughout Jordan, where overwhelming popular support for Iraq was expressed. Sentiments were further aroused when air attacks on goods vehicles (including tanker-trucks carrying oil) on the Baghdad–ar-Ruweishid highway in late January killed at least six Jordanian civilians. Jordan had been entirely dependent on Iraqi oil since Saudi Arabian supplies were suspended in September 1990. Now these consignments were halted, and Jordan, which introduced petrol-rationing in February, was obliged to obtain more expensive supplies from Syria and Yemen. Oil imports from Iraq were eventually resumed in April 1991.

In a televised address in February 1991, King Hussein paid tribute to the people and armed forces of Iraq, describing them as victims of this 'savage and large-scale war' and claiming that the war was directed against all Arabs and Muslims. The speech was condemned by the US Administration, which accused Jordan of abandoning its neutrality and threatened to review its economic aid. In March the US Congress approved legislation cancelling a US $57m. aid programme. The law was signed by President Bush in April. However, the effects were offset, to some extent, by the announcement of a $450m. Japanese concessionary loan. As the multinational force launched a ground offensive to liberate Kuwait on 24 February, Prime Minister Badran announced that the conflict had at that point cost Jordan some $8,000m.

Fears that Iraq would provoke Israel into entering the conflict, thus making Jordan part of the combat zone, were not realized, owing to the Israeli decision not to retaliate in response to the *Scud* missile attacks launched by Iraq against its territory. At the end of December 1990, Jordan had deployed 80,000 troops in defensive positions facing Israel. King Hussein declared, in mid-January 1991, that Jordan would defend its territory and air space against any incursions. In early February a Jordanian air force officer and a truck-driver were executed, having been convicted by a military court of spying for Israel.

On 1 March 1991, following the liberation of Kuwait and the end of hostilities between Iraq and the multinational force, King Hussein, in a televised address to the nation, advocated regional reconciliation. In late March he travelled to Damascus for talks with President Assad, and subsequently sought to improve relations with the West, visiting President Mitterrand in Paris later that month.

THE MIDDLE EAST PEACE PROCESS 1991–94

US Secretary of State James Baker visited Jordan on 20–21 July 1991, when King Hussein announced his intention to accept an invitation to Jordan to attend a Middle East peace conference sponsored by the USA and the USSR. It was hoped that the conference would be attended by delegations from Israel, Egypt, Syria and Lebanon, and by a joint Jordanian-Palestinian delegation; and that it would thus become the first occasion when Israel, the Palestinians and the Arab nations would participate in direct negotiations. The Jordanian House of Representatives opposed the plan, however, demanding Israeli withdrawal from the Occupied Territories and East Jerusalem as a precondition for Jordan's attendance, and rejecting Israel's insistence that neither Palestinians from East Jerusalem nor overt supporters of the PLO should be allowed to attend. James Baker visited Amman again in September and October for further rounds of pre-conference diplomacy, and on 12 October King Hussein announced that a Jordanian delegation would attend the conference, in spite of intense opposition from the Muslim Brotherhood and leftist political groupings. He stated that he had received assurances from the USA that it would do its utmost to ensure that a transitional period of Palestinian 'autonomy' in the Occupied Territories would be negotiated within one year of the opening of the conference; and that he had considered abdicating over the Arab–Israeli confrontation, but believed that attending the discussions would increase international pressure on Israel to withdraw from the Territories. The Central Council of the PLO, meeting in Tunis on 16–17 October, approved the formation of a joint Jordanian-Palestinian delegation, a decision strongly criticized by the leader of the PFLP, George Habash.

The opening session of the historic Middle East peace conference, convened within the framework of UN Security Council Resolutions 242 and 338, and chaired by President Bush of the USA and the Soviet President, Mikhail Gorbachev, was held in Madrid, Spain, during 30 October–1 November 1991. The joint Jordanian-Palestinian delegation was led by Kamel Abu Jaber, a US-educated professor of political science, who had been appointed Jordan's Minister of Foreign Affairs following the resignation, on 3 October, of Dr Abdullah an-Nusur and two other ministers opposed to Jordan's participation. The delegation included diplomats, civil servants and academics. In his speech, calling for the withdrawal of Israeli forces from all occupied lands, Abu Jaber stated that King Hussein would have preferred a separate Palestinian delegation but 'we have no objection to providing an umbrella for our Palestinian brethren. . .the Palestinian people must be allowed to exercise their right of self-determination in their ancestral homeland'. 'Let me speak plainly', he added, 'Jordan has never been Palestine and will not be so.'

Subsequent negotiations in Washington, DC, and Moscow between the Israeli and the joint Jordanian-Palestinian delegations remained deadlocked, with regard to substantive issues. However, secret talks between the PLO and the Israeli Government in Norway, which had begun early in 1993, led to an agreement, on 19 August, on a Declaration of Principles which involved a degree of Palestinian self government in the Occupied Territories. The Declaration of Principles, (see Documents on Palestine, p. 72) was signed in Washington on 13 September 1993. News of the agreement apparently came as a surprise to King Hussein, who had not been informed that negotiations were taking place in Oslo and the agreement reportedly caused grave embarrassment to the Palestinian negotiators in Washington. Despite the King's initial irritation at the Israeli-PLO accord, which presented a socio-economic as well as a political challenge for Jordan, he quickly accepted the Declaration of Principles. On 14 September Jordan and Israel concluded a 'common agenda' for subsequent bilateral negotiations, which aimed to achieve 'a just, lasting and comprehensive peace' between the Arab states, the Palestinians and Israel. Jordan and Israel agreed to respect each other's security and to discuss future co-operation on territorial and economic issues. The signing of the agenda was publicized as being the first agreement between an Arab state and Israel since the peace accord between Egypt and Israel in 1979; King Hussein, however, stressed that it was not a peace agreement but an outline of topics to be discussed at future talks. Much of the agenda had already been agreed in 1992 but an official signing was delayed because of Palestinian objections.

Within Jordan, news of the signing of the Declaration of Principles was greeted with considerable cynicism. Opposition appeared to be strongest in the vast Palestinian refugee camp at Baqa'a, and most Islamist and leftist politicians condemned the Israeli-PLO accord. The agreement initiated a sometimes acrimonious debate on the vexed question of Palestinian identity and the future of Palestinians in Jordan. Since October 1993 Jordan had become increasingly frustrated with the PLO over its failure to implement agreements on closer co-operation. In particular, Jordan was concerned that the PLO Chairman, Yasser Arafat, appeared to be unwilling to sign a draft economic agreement that had been drawn up earlier in the year. At the beginning of 1994 King Hussein publicly criticized Arafat because Jordan had not been continuously advised about the progress of talks between the PLO and Israel concerning the implementation of Palestinian self-rule in Gaza and Jericho and economic co-operation. He requested that Arafat stop making references to a future Jordanian-Palestinian confederation because this was an issue on which no decision had yet been made.

Following the King's criticisms, a PLO delegation led by Farouk Kaddoumi, the head of the PLO's political department, visited Amman and an agreement on economic co-operation, covering tourism, agriculture, infrastructure, investment promotion and private sector co-operation, was signed on 7 January 1994. Just over a week later, Jordan and the PLO drew up a draft accord on security and the exchange of intelligence information. Jordan was particularly concerned about who would control the bridges across the Jordan river after the establishment of Palestinian autonomy. At a meeting of the Higher Jordanian-Palestinian Committee in February it was agreed that a number of joint committees, originally set up in 1993 to discuss relations between Jordan and the Occupied Territories during the period of transitional Palestinian self-rule, would be reconvened. Jordanian experts were reported to be present as observers at talks between the PLO and Israel in Paris on economic and monetary questions. Yet in spite of a personal visit to Amman by Arafat to brief King Hussein on the Cairo talks with Israel, relations between Jordan and the PLO remained strained. At the end of March King Hussein blamed the PLO for mishandling the negotiations leading up to UN Security Council Resolution 904 which had allowed the USA to abstain on the paragraph in the preamble concerning Jerusalem. The King argued that the US vote could have been avoided if the PLO had consulted Jordan. There was a relatively subdued reaction from the Jordanian Government to the Cairo Agreement signed by Israel and the PLO (see Documents on Palestine, p. 76) on 4 May 1994. Arafat visited Amman on 5 May to brief King Hussein on the Cairo agreement but the King remained disillusioned by Arafat's failure to liaise with Jordan in the peace process.

Following a secret meeting in November 1993 between King Hussein and Shimon Peres, the Israeli Minister of Foreign Affairs, there was optimism in Israeli government circles that Jordan would soon sign a formal peace agreement with Israel. These hopes were dashed in late January 1994 when King Hussein insisted that the key issues which lay behind the Arab–Israeli conflict must be discussed before any accord could be signed, and that it was unacceptable to leave negotiations until after the signing. Jordan, together with Syria and Lebanon, withdrew temporarily from the current round of bilateral talks with Israel in Washington immediately after the Hebron massacre in February, although the gesture appeared to be largely symbolic and aimed at appeasing public anger at the incident. The King firmly rejected calls made by Islamist deputies for Jordan to withdraw permanently from the peace talks.

The National Assembly requested that the Government link Jordan's resumption of peace negotiations with new arrangements for inspecting ships with cargo bound for Iraq through Aqaba port. There had been growing criticism of the policy of intercepting and searching ships bound for Aqaba in the Tiran Straits by a multinational inspection force led by the US navy. The system of inspection, introduced in August 1991 in order to verify compliance with international sanctions against Iraq, resulted in long delays and loss of revenue to the Jordanian

authorities. When the USA failed to respond to Jordanian requests for new arrangements, this was interpreted in Amman as a means of putting pressure on Jordan to finalize a peace agreement with Israel. In late March 1994 King Hussein announced that Jordan would not resume peace negotiations with Israel unless the naval blockade of Aqaba was lifted. However, it was not until the end of April that the USA accepted a Jordanian proposal for a new land-based system of inspection. Prime Minister Majali told the press on 25 April that his Government was now willing to sign agreements on all individual items on the Jordan-Israel agenda and to participate in all multilateral talks in the hope that the discussions would lead eventually to a peace treaty.

THE PEACE TREATY WITH ISRAEL

In May–June 1994 the peace process received a new impetus, after King Hussein unexpectedly decided to proceed unilaterally with talks with Israel. After secret talks between the King and the Israeli Prime Minister, Itzhak Rabin, in London, United Kingdom, at the end of May, negotiations resumed at a meeting of the Jordanian-Israeli-US Trilateral Commission, held on 6–7 June in Washington, DC. At the meeting Jordan and Israel agreed to hold future bilateral talks in their countries, and to establish joint sub-commissions on boundary demarcation, security, and water and environmental issues. These sub-commissions began work on 18–19 July, at a meeting on the Jordanian–Israeli border.

At a ceremony at the White House on 25 July 1994 King Hussein and the Prime Minister of Israel, Itzhak Rabin, signed the 'Washington Declaration' ending the state of war which had existed between Jordan and Israel since 1948. After years of secret meetings, it was the first time that King Hussein had publicly met an Israeli Prime Minister. The declaration stopped short of a full peace treaty, but US Secretary of State Warren Christopher stated that he expected it to speed the process for a formal peace agreement 'within a matter of months'.

In Jordan opposition to the Declaration was limited, and there were no large-scale protests. Islamists declared 'a day of sadness and mourning' and at a modest protest meeting at the central mosque in Amman, Bahjat Abu-Gharbiah, head of the Arab-Jordanian Popular Committee Against Normalization, told the demonstrators that the peace was 'an attempt to consolidate the hegemony of the Zionist entity through normalization that allows its cancerous spread until the shores of the Arabian Gulf'. From Gaza, PLO Chairman Arafat sent his congratulations to the Israeli and Jordanian leaders on the declaration and expressed the hope that Syria and Lebanon would also make peace with Israel. However, Palestinian leaders were angered by a statement in the Declaration endorsing the special role of King Hussein as guardian of the Muslim holy places in Jerusalem. They argued that it undermined the Palestinian claim to sovereignty over Jerusalem, and that it contradicted the Israeli-PLO Declaration of Principles, which stated that the final status of Jerusalem would be determined by negotiation between Israel and the PLO. The Syrian press criticized the Washington Declaration, arguing that separate peace deals weakened the Arab cause. Nevertheless, President Assad appeared to be privately reconciled to the negotiations.

Bilateral talks between Jordanian and Israeli delegations continued in August and September 1994. In mid-October, despite reports that problems remained over border demarcation and water resource allocation, the Israeli Prime Minister, Itzhak Rabin, visited Amman, and agreement was reached on a final peace treaty between the two countries. On 26 October the Treaty was formally signed at a ceremony held on the Jordanian–Israeli border, Jordan thus becoming only the second Arab state (after Egypt) to conclude a peace treaty with Israel. The Peace Treaty included agreements on border demarcation, security, water allocation and the restoration of bilateral economic relations. King Hussein's role as guardian of the Muslim shrines in Jerusalem was also reaffirmed. The Treaty was adopted by both houses of the Jordanian National Assembly, and ratified by King Hussein on 9 November. As agreed in the Treaty, full diplomatic relations between Jordan and Israel were established in late November (although ambassadors were not exchanged until April 1995). Also in November the Jordanian–Israeli border was opened to citizens of the two countries, and Israeli troops began withdrawing from some 340 sq km of land occupied since the 1967 war.

Within Jordan little effort had been made to prepare public opinion for the peace agreement. Following an Islamist-led demonstration against the treaty in Amman by some 5,000 people, the Government banned all public meetings. The Islamic Action Front (IAF) and its allies continued to oppose the treaty and began a campaign in the National Assembly against the normalization of relations with Israel. They attempted to prevent the repeal of legislation limiting relations with Israel, including a law (adopted in 1973) prohibiting land sales to Israelis, a 1958 law imposing a total economic boycott of Israel, and legislation from 1953 outlawing trade between the two states. Rumours that Israeli citizens had already bought land in certain parts of Jordan were strongly denied by the Minister of Justice.

Initially, the Peace Treaty did little to improve relations with the Palestinian leadership. The reaffirmation of King Hussein's special role as guardian of the Muslim holy places in East Jerusalem was criticized by the PLO leadership. In September 1994 the Palestinian (National) Authority (PA) had claimed responsibility for all Islamic institutions in East Jerusalem, the West Bank and Gaza Strip. In response, Jordan had agreed to relinquish its rights over sites in the West Bank and Gaza, but it refused to renounce its guardianship over the holy shrines of East Jerusalem. A compromise was reached on the issue in late January 1995, when a bilateral accord was signed. The Palestinians agreed to recognize the Jordanian-Israeli Peace Treaty, thus implying *de facto* recognition of Jordanian rights over the Jerusalem shrines, at least until the city came under Palestinian sovereignty. In return, Jordan reaffirmed its support for Palestinian autonomy and for the future creation of a Palestinian state, with East Jerusalem as its capital. The accord also covered economic, cultural and administrative affairs, and included an agreement to use the Jordanian currency in Palestinian territories. The timing of the agreement prompted observers to argue that Arafat was seeking better relations with Jordan, because of Israel's increasingly intransigent approach to the Palestinian question, and in response to growing pressure from Islamist groups violently opposed to the PLO-Israel accords.

POLITICAL REFORM AND MULTI-PARTY ELECTIONS

On 6 October 1991 an alliance of 49 deputies in the House of Representatives, from the Muslim Brotherhood (MB), the 'constitutional bloc', the 'Democratic Alliance', and some independent Islamist deputies, signed a petition in protest at the terms of Jordan's participation in the Middle East peace conference. They urged the resignation of the Government, and on 16 November Taher al-Masri resigned as Prime Minister, having lost the confidence of the House. The King appointed his cousin, Sharif Zaid ibn Shaker, who had led a transitional government in 1989, as Prime Minister, and a new, broader-based government received a vote of confidence on 16 December. The Muslim Brotherhood was again excluded from the Cabinet and 18 of its members voted against the new Government in the confidence motion.

In June 1992 an extraordinary session of the House of Representatives was convened in order to debate new laws regarding political parties and the press. In early July the House adopted new legislation whereby, subject to certain conditions, political parties were formally legalized, in preparation for the country's first multi-party elections since 1956, which were to be held before November 1993. The new legislation was approved by royal decree at the end of August, and by March 1993 nine political parties had received the Government's formal approval of their activities.

In May 1993 King Hussein appointed a new Cabinet, in which Dr Abd as-Salam al-Majali, the leader of the Jordanian delegation to the Middle East peace conference, replaced Sharif Zaid ibn Shaker as Prime Minister. The new Government was regarded as a transitional administration, pending the country's first multi-party election.

At the beginning of August 1993 King Hussein unexpectedly dissolved the House of Representatives, provoking criticism from some politicians who had expected the House to debate proposed changes to the country's electoral law. Changes in voting procedures at the general election, which was scheduled to be held on 8 November, were subsequently announced by the King in mid-August. Voters were to be allowed to cast one vote only, rather than a number equal to that of the number of candidates contesting a given constituency, as before.

After the announcement of the Israeli-PLO accord in September 1993, King Hussein appeared to be unsure whether or not to proceed with the elections, fearing that they might be dominated by the debate about the peace process. Eventually the King decided to hold the elections as planned on 8 November 1993. The election campaign went smoothly and peacefully. Some 820,000 Jordanians (52% of eligible voters and 68% of registered voters) cast ballots at one of the 2,906 polling stations in the 20 electoral districts. However, the independent New Jordan Research Centre estimated that 70% of Jordanians of Palestinian origin abstained, apparently due to the fact that they felt excluded from the political system and also that the prevailing system of electoral districts favoured areas dominated by East Bankers.

In all, some 534 candidates contested the election and one-half of the 20 registered political parties fielded candidates. The majority of candidates, however, stood as independents. The political parties, which had been legal for less than a year, had little time to organize and amass public support. Domestic issues, such as unemployment, were the main issues in the electoral campaign, with traditionalist candidates focusing on local issues and promising to improve the provision of public services in their constituencies. Of the 80 deputies returned, 45 were independents. With the traditions of tribalism deeply rooted in the customs of the country, they won largely because of their tribal affiliations and personal influence.

The Islamic Action Front (IAF), an alliance between the Muslim Brotherhood and other Islamist groups, won 16 seats, the largest number of any political party, but six fewer than in the 1989 elections. This reversal was largely thought to result from the new electoral law which embodied the 'one man, one vote' principle. Indeed, the new law was widely interpreted as an attempt to weaken the IAF. Others felt that the Islamists had misjudged the mood of the country and had not devoted enough attention in their campaign to basic issues related to the impact of the economic recession on the lives of ordinary Jordanians. Of the other political parties, leftists and Arab nationalists won eight seats while five conservative and right-of-centre parties claimed a total of 14 seats. Only 14 of the 80 new deputies were of Palestinian origin. Among the new deputies was the first woman to be elected to the Assembly, Toujan al-Faisal, who won one of the seats reserved for the Circassian minority.

Soon after the election a number of political groupings were formed in addition to the IAF. The Progressive Democratic Coalition, consisting of liberal deputies and leftist and Arab nationalists, claimed the support of 22 deputies; the National Action Front (NAF) and the Jordan Action Front (JAF), both groupings of conservative parties and their allies, claimed 18 and 9 seats respectively. However, the IAF remained the largest single political organization in the country. Some deputies saw the emergence of parliamentary blocs as the first step in a move towards the formation of larger political parties.

Taher al-Masri, widely regarded as the most influential Palestinian in Jordanian politics and a former Prime Minister, was elected Speaker of the National Assembly on 23 November 1993. Al-Masri won an overwhelming victory against his rival, an IAF deputy. Dr Abd as-Salam al-Majali remained Prime Minister and although he made few significant changes to his Cabinet, there was some surprise that, for the first time, the Cabinet did not include any parliamentary deputies. His new Government won a vote of confidence on 8 December after a prolonged debate during which the Prime Minister was criticized for changes to the country's electoral law and for not making an independent statement of government policy but simply adopting the King's speech from the throne at the opening of Parliament.

In another cautious move towards democratization, in March 1994 the National Assembly approved legislation to allow municipal elections in Greater Amman, home to some two-fifths of the country's population. The Government, no doubt concerned about the strength of Palestinian and Islamist opposition in the capital, had originally proposed that only one-half of the municipal council should be elected, but this was increased to two-thirds by the National Assembly. The remaining one-third of the council, together with the mayor, were to continue to be appointed by the Government.

In early June 1994 Prime Minister al-Majali announced a major cabinet reshuffle. There were no changes in the key portfolios of finance, the interior and information, but 18 new appointments were made to the 31-member Cabinet. Among the new ministers were deputies from the three main political groupings in the lower house, the NAF, the Jordanian National Alliance and the Progressive Democratic Coalition, but none were selected from the biggest parliamentary faction, the IAF. However, one well-known Islamic activist, Abd al-Baki Jammu, was included in the new Government.

In early January 1995 there was a further extensive reorganization of the Government, following the dismissal of al-Majali as Prime Minister. He was replaced by Sharif Zaid ibn Shaker, who had served as Prime Minister in 1989 and 1991–93, and was a close ally and a cousin of the King. Only seven ministers from the previous administration retained their portfolios in the new Government. Among the new ministers were Basel Jardaneh, as Minister of Finance, and Abd al-Karim al-Kabariti, as Minister of Foreign Affairs. At the same time, Taher al-Masri resigned as Speaker of the House of Representatives, and was replaced by Saed Hayel as-Srour, who represented one of the northern Bedouin constituencies. The new Government easily won a vote of confidence in January 1995.

Two new political blocs emerged in the National Assembly in early 1995. The Independent National Action Front (INAF), with 17 deputies, was formed by a merger of the NAF and the bloc of independent deputies in the Assembly. The former Speaker of the National Assembly, Taher al-Masri, formed a second new grouping of some 15 liberal and independent Islamist deputies. In early June the authorities arrested six members of an illegal Islamist organization, the Islamic Renewal Group, believed to be active among Jordanians who had returned from Kuwait after the Iraqi invasion of 1990, and claimed to have found weapons and explosives that were to be used in attacks against US interests in Jordan. Early in 1996 the Prime Minister admitted that there had been 36 attempted terrorist attacks in the previous six months aimed at destabilizing the country. In municipal elections held nationwide for the first time in July 1995 Islamist and left-wing groups failed to gain significant popular support, most elected candidates being largely pro-government or independent. The IAF alleged that its poor performance was due to a low level of voter participation, and to government harassment of its members during the campaign. In November King Hussein warned that the country's professional organizations, several of which strongly opposed the normalization of relations with Israel, were becoming too involved in national politics and that this was against the interest of their members. In December Leith Shbeilat, head of the Jordan Engineers' Association and an outspoken Islamist critic of the regime, was arrested and later jailed for three years, a move regarded by some observers as an attempt to intimidate supporters of the 'anti-normalization' movement.

KABARITI APPOINTED PRIME MINISTER

At the beginning of February 1996 King Hussein appointed the Minister of Foreign Affairs, Abd al-Karim al-Kabariti, as Prime Minister. The King was believed to have clashed with Kabariti's predecessor, Sharif Zaid ibn Shaker, on the pace of normalization with Israel and the severing of ties with Iraq. Kabariti's appointment was followed by the most radical reshuffle of the Government for many years. He appointed a new Cabinet in which the majority of ministers took office for the first time. Twenty-two of the 31 members, including the Minister of the Interior, were deputies in the House of Representatives, strengthening the new administration's democratic credentials. Negotiations between the new Prime Minister and the IAF leadership failed to achieve agreement, and there was some criticism among Islamist deputies who argued that their leaders should have adopted a more positive stance towards entering government. The King hoped that the new Government would work towards 'full and comprehensive change'. In early March Kabariti's new

administration easily won a vote of confidence in the House of Representatives, gaining the approval of deputies for its domestic policy. The Prime Minister emphasized the need to promote pluralism and democracy, safeguard public freedoms, and respect human rights. Kabariti announced his commitment to the independence of the judiciary and the media, to increasing public access to information and, eventually, to the abolition of the Ministry of Information. He also outlined plans to reform the Ministry of the Interior and the system of government appointments in order to combat nepotism and corruption, which had become an important political issue in recent years. Kabariti retained the foreign affairs portfolio and was known to be a strong supporter of the King's new policy on Iraq and of strengthening ties with Israel, policies that were likely to prove more controversial than his domestic programme.

The popularity of Kabariti's Government in the House of Representatives and, indeed, in Jordan as a whole was short-lived. In mid-August 1996 fierce rioting erupted in the south of the country after the Government more than doubled the price of bread. The price rise was part of an IMF-sponsored economic plan to remove the agricultural subsidies that stabilized food prices and thus help reduce the budget deficit in order to meet IMF fiscal targets. About one-third of Jordan's population were believed to be living below the poverty line, and many people feared that the rise in the price of bread, the country's staple food, would lead to increases in the prices of all foodstuffs. The rioting quickly spread to other parts of the country, including the poor suburbs of Amman. King Hussein vowed to employ stern measures to suppress the demonstrations and told the Western media that he believed that the ringleaders had been 'educated in Iraq'. He suspended the legislature and deployed élite units of the army to re-establish control in Karak, the scene of the most severe rioting. The army quickly regained control over the town, which was placed under curfew, and some 190 people were reportedly arrested. After peace was restored, the King visited different parts of the country to meet with civil and tribal leaders in a reconciliation attempt. The curfews were soon lifted, and by November all those arrested during the protests had been released and charges against them dropped. Price increases, however, were not revoked. The IAF (which had earlier protested vigorously at the price increases), together with a number of smaller opposition parties, urged Kabariti to resign, blaming his Government for the rioting. Several observers argued that, although the demonstrations had been triggered primarily by the Government's austerity programme, the deeply unpopular peace treaty with Israel and the King's dramatic break with Iraq had also contributed to growing popular discontent. In an attempt to calm political tensions, the IAF had cancelled a mass demonstration against the economic austerity measures, scheduled for 23 August, and withdrew its demand for the Prime Minister's resignation. In response, King Hussein emphasized that the rioters were not members of the IAF. In November the King ordered the release of Leith Shbeilat, who had served only six months of his three-year sentence. In January 1997 the shura council of the Muslim Brotherhood, the dominant group within the IAF, voted against the party's joining a future government because this would imply recognition of Israel. However, moderates in the IAF opposed the decision, maintaining that it condemned the party to a relatively ineffective role in politics and could lose them electoral support.

King Hussein did not hold his Prime Minister responsible for the August riots, and Kabariti quickly attempted to restore his reputation. It therefore came as a surprise when the King dismissed Kabariti on 19 March 1997 and again appointed Abd as-Salam al-Majali to the premiership. There were reports that the King and Kabariti had disagreed over issues relating to the peace process and relations with Israel, as well as rumours of enmity between Kabariti and Crown Prince Hassan. King Hussein's public criticism of the outgoing Prime Minister suggested that he was unlikely to appoint Kabariti to head a future government. The new Prime Minister, a veteran and trusted politician who had been head of government when Jordan signed the peace treaty with Israel in October 1994, appointed a 23-member Cabinet consisting mainly of technocrats; he retained five ministers from the previous administration, including Dr Abdullah an-Nusur, an East Banker, promoted to Deputy Prime Minister, and Dr Jawad al-Anani, a Palestinian and former

Minister of Labour and Industry, also became a Deputy Prime Minister, with special responsibility for development matters. In his letter of appointment to al-Majali, King Hussein gave priority to internal affairs. The new Government's primary task was to supervise the forthcoming legislative elections. In preparation for the elections, the National Assembly voted to continue the 'one man, one vote' system adopted for the 1993 elections, rather than return to the previous multi-vote system. The King also urged the Government to eliminate corruption in public office, to alleviate unemployment and to modify the education system to the needs of society.

In May 1997, following increasing media criticism of a number of government policies, several amendments were made to legislation governing the press, prompting strong protests from editors, journalists, professional associations and opposition groups. The amendments included a considerable increase in the minimum capital that weekly journals were required to raise as a precondition for publishing, an extension of the range of prohibited subjects to include the armed forces and the security services, and a substantial rise in the fines that could be levied for contravening press legislation. Opposition activists feared that these measures represented the return of closer state control over the press. Also in May nine centre parties, including Pledge and the Jordan National Party, announced that they had united to form the National Constitutional Party (NCP), which became the country's largest political grouping. The formation of the NCP, together with the establishment in 1996 of the Unionist Arab Democratic Party (a coalition of three leftist parties), reduced the total number of political parties from 24 to 14. A further political grouping subsequently emerged; the progressive alliance included a number of eminent political figures (among them two former prime ministers, Ahmad Ubeidat and Taher al-Masri, and a former parliamentary speaker, Sulayman Arar). In June King Hussein appointed his close associate and adviser, Zaid ar-Rifai, as Speaker of the Senate.

THE 1997 ELECTIONS AND 1998 GOVERNMENT

In July 1997 the Muslim Brotherhood declared that it would boycott the forthcoming parliamentary elections, which, King Hussein had announced, were to proceed in November, as scheduled. This decision, which was opposed by some prominent members of the movement, appeared to reflect growing disillusionment with the role of the National Assembly, which was perceived to have little or no influence over important political and economic decisions in the country. After intensive discussions, the IAF endorsed the Muslim Brotherhood's decision by a large majority. In the two months prior to the elections, discussions between the Government and the opposition parties failed to achieve any significant progress. The IAF, together with nine smaller leftist and nationalist parties, had, in particular, demanded changes in the electoral legislation, arguing that the existing 'one man, one vote' system favoured candidates with strong tribal affiliations over those representing 'ideological' parties; however, King Hussein and al-Majali refused to make any concessions. In September the Government suspended some 13 weekly newspapers for three months (effectively during the electoral period) for failing to comply with the amendments to the press regulations that had been introduced in May.

The elections on 4 November 1997, which were boycotted by many parties, professional associations and respected political figures, attracted little popular enthusiasm. An estimated 55% of the registered electorate participated, with a voter turn-out of only 26% in parts of Amman. There were widespread allegations of electoral malpractice, and in a number of regions the security forces were obliged to intervene to suppress clashes between rival candidates and their supporters. Deputies with tribal affiliations dominated the new parliament. Only 26 deputies who served in the outgoing parliament were re-elected, and many leading political figures, such as Taher al-Masri and Abd al-Karim al-Kabariti, were absent from the new legislature. The NCP, which some sections of the press referred to as the 'party of the regime', presented 11 candidates but won only two seats. Although some opponents of the Government were represented in the new Assembly, including Islamist politicians Abdullah Akaileh and Muhammad Azaydeh (who contested the election in defiance of the IAF boycott), government claims of a significant

opposition presence appeared to be greatly exaggerated. Saed Hayel as-Srour was re-elected Speaker of the House of Representatives. Among the new members appointed by King Hussein to the 40-member Senate was Kabariti (a move which was viewed as marking his political rehabilitation). Zaid ar-Rifai was retained as Speaker of the Senate. Political figures critical of the Government were completely absent from the upper house. King Hussein also confirmed the appointment of al-Majali to the office of Prime Minister.

Elections to the IAF's ruling body, the 120-member Shura Council, took place in December 1997. Despite the victory of the hardliners who ensured that the party boycotted the parliamentary elections in November, moderates and centrists succeeded in maintaining their dominant position on the Council, indicating that the party would avoid outright confrontation with the Government. In January 1998 the High Court ruled that the amendments to the press laws introduced in May 1997 were unconstitutional and that actions taken by the Government under the amendments were thus invalid. The authorities reluctantly agreed to accept the ruling, and several newspapers that had been banned resumed publishing in March. The country's Chief Justice, Farouq al-Kailani, claimed that, owing to his role in the High Court ruling on the press legislation, the Government had forced him to resign.

During the increase in tension between the USA and Iraq in early 1998 (see below) there was widespread support among Jordanians for Iraq and, to a certain extent, for the Iraqi leader, Saddam Hussain. The authorities, however, decided to ban all pro-Iraqi demonstrations and urged the press to adopt the official government policy on the situation. When a grouping of Islamists, leftists and nationalists opposed to US policy in the Middle East attempted to hold a large rally in Amman in mid-February, the police quickly dispersed the meeting, and a number of leading government opponents were assaulted during the disturbances. Later in February there were violent clashes in the southern town of Ma'an when members of the security forces intervened to prevent a pro-Iraqi demonstration; the security forces subsequently denied responsibility for the death of one of the demonstrators. The Minister of the Interior, Nadhir Rashid, claimed that the riots in Ma'an had been instigated by the outspoken Islamist, Leith Shbeilat, who had addressed a meeting in the town that day, and stated that he would be put on trial for his involvement in the disturbances. Supporters of Shbeilat, however, insisted that he had left Ma'an before the violence erupted and was arrested on his return to Amman. Shbeilat was sentenced to nine months' imprisonment, but King Hussein ordered his release later in the year. Although order was quickly restored, the situation in Ma'an remained tense for some days after the protests, and the authorities imposed a curfew on the town for almost a week. Many arrests were made and some of those detained were not released until the beginning of April. After his release from prison, Shbeilat called openly for the establishment of a constitutional monarchy that would place limits on the King's powers to dissolve the National Assembly and to appoint and dismiss members of the Government.

In early 1998 al-Majali announced a cabinet reorganization, in which five new ministers were appointed, notably Dr Bassam al-Umush, a member of the Muslim Brotherhood who had been suspended from the movement in 1997. The other new ministers had served with al-Majali when he was premier in the early 1990s. Rashid, who had been criticized for the suppression of the pro-Iraqi demonstrations by the security forces, retained his portfolio, but Samir Mutawi was replaced as Minister of State for Information and his responsibilities assigned to one of the two Deputy Prime Ministers, Abdullah an-Nusuf. Dr Fayez at-Tarawneh, hitherto the Minister of Foreign Affairs, became Chief of the Royal Court, traditionally a move towards the premiership, with Jawad al-Anani assuming the foreign affairs portfolio.

In July 1998 severe water shortages and a deterioration in the quality of existing water supplies in Amman caused public discontent, prompting the resignation of the Minister of Water and Irrigation, Mundhir Haddadin. In August King Hussein (who was undergoing medical treatment in the USA) appointed Fayez at-Tarawneh to the office of Prime Minister, replacing Abd as-Salam al-Majali. Al-Majali's removal was largely attributed to the criticism that the Government had attracted over the continuing water crisis in Amman. Later in August a new Cabinet, which included 10 new ministers, was installed; al-Anani replaced at-Tarawneh as Chief of the Royal Court. In December Abd al-Hadi al-Majali was appointed as Speaker of the House of Representatives.

In the months following his appointment as Prime Minister, at-Tarawneh made efforts to establish a dialogue with the opposition but failed to make any significant progress on key issues relating to foreign affairs or greater democratization at home. Meanwhile, the authorities moved quickly to control protests organized in opposition to the Wye Memorandum signed by Israel and the PA in October 1998 (see the chapter on Israel and Documents on Palestine, p. 86), while public demonstrations against the US and British air-strikes carried out against Iraq in December (see the chapter on Iraq) were also restricted by the security forces. Despite the new Prime Minister's declared commitment to eradicate corruption in public office, those cases that were referred to court appeared to disappear without trace. In November the Minister of Administrative Development, Bassam al-Umush, accused the Government of lacking the will to implement urgently-needed administrative reforms, rendering his ministry powerless to execute the tasks assigned to it. Despite such outspoken criticism, al-Umush retained his post, although his outburst provoked little evidence of government action regarding public sector reforms. The Government also encountered criticism from Jordan's business community; whereas the Jordanian authorities enthusiastically promoted membership of the World Trade Organization and Jordan's association with the EU, the Amman Chamber of Industry favoured prioritizing the further development of existing bilateral agreements with several Arab states.

DEATH OF KING HUSSEIN

In July 1998 King Hussein began to undergo treatment in the USA for lymphatic cancer. In August he issued a royal decree which transferred responsibility for certain executive duties, including the appointment of ministers, to his brother, Crown Prince Hassan. On King Hussein's return to Jordan on 19 January 1999, amid considerable public celebration and government assurances that his health had been restored, the King prompted renewed speculation about the royal succession by appointing Crown Prince Hassan as his 'deputy' (a position believed to involve limited authority). On 24 January King Hussein issued a royal decree naming his eldest son, Abdullah, as Crown Prince of Jordan. It was reported that a letter had been conveyed from King Hussein to Crown Prince Hassan, who had been regent since 1965, in which the King had expressed his dissatisfaction with his brother's handling of Jordanian affairs during his six-month absence, in particular his attempts to interfere in military affairs. King Hussein had also accused his brother's supporters of slandering his immediate family, prompting speculation that serious divisions had emerged within the royal family. Many Jordanians were surprised by the harsh tone of Hussein's criticism, since Hassan had always been outwardly loyal to his brother and had been one of his most trusted advisers. Concern was also expressed at the notion of rivalries within the royal family at a time when a united front was considered vital to the country's stability. Meanwhile, some sections of the US press suggested that the Clinton Administration had encouraged the replacement of Hassan as Crown Prince, owing to his perceived hostility towards Palestinian negotiators and alleged willingness to ally himself with the extremist Muslim Brotherhood.

On 26 January 1999 King Hussein left Jordan for emergency treatment in the USA, following a rapid deterioration in his health. However, King Hussein returned to Amman on 5 February, and was pronounced dead on 7 February. The Jordanian public had been given little accurate information about the King's condition by the official media, and were genuinely shocked by the news of his death. Hussein had been the Middle East's longest-serving ruler, controlling the fortunes of Jordan for the greater part of its modern history, during which time the country was transformed from an essentially artificial creation with few resources into a modern state. The funeral of King Hussein, held in Amman on 8 February, was attended by more than 50 heads of state or government, including US

President Clinton, the Israeli Prime Minister, Binyamin Netanyahu, and Syria's President Assad.

A few hours after King Hussein's death, on 7 February 1999 the newly-appointed Crown Prince was sworn in as King Abdullah ibn al-Hussein of Jordan. After formal education in the United Kingdom and the USA, Abdullah had embarked on a distinguished military career, becoming Commander of Special Forces with the rank of major-general. Before Abdullah's designation as Crown Prince, many Jordanians expected that he would eventually take over as Commander-in-Chief of the armed forces. Abdullah is reported to have good relations with younger members of the ruling families of the Gulf states, as well as useful contacts within the US political establishment. His wife, Rania Yassin, is a Palestinian, whose family originates from the West Bank, although English, rather than Arabic, is Abdullah's mother tongue. However, although King Abdullah's many connections were seen as advantageous, some commentators expressed concern that the new monarch lacked political experience at a time when Jordan faced serious problems both at home and abroad. Soon after his father's death, the new King made a televised address to the nation, appealing for Jordanian unity and pledging to continue his father's policies. He subsequently named his half-brother, and the youngest son of King Hussein, Prince Hamzeh ibn al-Hussein, as the new Crown Prince of Jordan (apparently in accordance with the wishes of the late King).

KING ABDULLAH TAKES CONTROL

Before the official 40-day period of mourning for King Hussein had ended, the new King made a number of key changes at the Royal Palace and in the military high command and also appointed a new Government. In late February 1999 four senior army officers, who were believed to have pledged their loyalty to Prince Hassan shortly before King Hussein's death, were removed from their posts. In mid-March Prince Hassan was appointed to head the Higher Council of Science and Technology, while King Hussein's widow, Queen Noor, became head of the new King Hussein Foundation. While these appointments helped to preserve their elevated status, it was clear that henceforth both were expected to confine their activities to these well-defined roles, and had been excluded from positions of power. On 21 March King Abdullah issued a royal decree naming his wife, Rania, as the Queen of Jordan. The new Queen quickly established a role for herself through her involvement in social development issues. Also in March Jawad al-Anani, Chief of the Royal Court and a close associate of Prince Hassan, was replaced by former Prime Minister Abd al-Karim al-Kabariti, while Adnan Abu Odeh, an aide to King Hussein for many years, returned to the Palace as an adviser. Later in the year King Abdullah appointed his half-brother, Prince Ali, the son of King Hussein and his third wife, Queen Alia, to head a special force responsible for protecting the King.

On 4 March 1999 King Abdullah appointed a new 24-member Cabinet, with Abd ar-Raouf ar-Rawabdeh replacing Fayez at-Tarawneh as Prime Minister. The former Deputy Prime Minister and mayor of Amman was widely considered to be an experienced politician capable of implementing an effective reform programme. Ar-Rawabdeh's Cabinet contained eight ministers from the outgoing administration, including the three key portfolios of the interior, finance and foreign affairs. However, several ministers regarded as loyal to Prince Hassan were replaced, although the respected Minister of Finance, Michel Marto, also a protégé of Prince Hassan, retained his post. In his letter of appointment to the new Prime Minister, King Abdullah prescribed 'fundamental reforms', including the strengthening of the rule of law and further democratization; he also called on ar-Rawabdeh to address the serious problems of poverty and unemployment in Jordan. In his policy statement to the National Assembly, ar-Rawabdeh acknowledged that Jordan had entered a period of recession, and stated that his aim was to accelerate the implementation of economic reforms and to eradicate corrupt practices; however, no details explaining how this was to be achieved were revealed. Nevertheless, the Government won a strong vote of confidence from the National Assembly on 8 April. Those who did vote against the Government were left-wing and Islamist deputies, who criticized the new administration for having failed to make provision for political reform in its publicized programme, in particular with regard to the electoral and press laws. However, opposition groups were willing to express cautious loyalty to the new King. The Muslim Brotherhood immediately sought an audience with King Abdullah, stressing the organization's strong links with the monarchy while continuing to press for changes to the electoral law. The Muslim Brotherhood also called for an open dialogue with the Government, and its political wing, the IAF, indicated that it would participate in municipal elections scheduled for July 1999 (despite having boycotted the 1997 parliamentary elections). However, the IAF did not join the Popular Participation Bloc, a new grouping of 13 leftist, Baathist and pan-Arab parties formed in mid-May 1999 to contest the municipal elections, owing to a lack of agreement over the quotas of candidates to be fielded by each party.

In early April 1999 all censorship of Arab and foreign newspapers and magazines was removed, as was censorship of imported audio and video cassettes. In mid-March King Abdullah had met with members of the Jordan Press Association, and Prime Minister ar-Rawabdeh had encouraged members to put forward proposals regarding amendments to the controversial Press and Publications Law, in order to ease certain restrictions on journalists. Amendments to the Law were approved by the National Assembly in September, although critics remained dissatisfied. Meanwhile, in late March King Abdullah released almost 500 prisoners (including some 20 members of the banned at-Tahrir party) as part of a recent amnesty law, while the Government also ended the security surveillance imposed on the outspoken Islamist, Leith Shbeilat (see above). However, accusations of human rights abuses in Jordan continued in 1999. In its annual report, released in April, the Arab Human Rights Organization in Jordan criticized the Government for a 'considerable increase' in human rights violations, including the arrest of journalists and harsh treatment of prisoners held in detention centres. Moreover, a report by Amnesty International, published in June, alleged numerous cases of torture in Jordanian prisons. The Government refused to respond to the report. Shortly afterwards, Petra, the official news agency in Jordan, and two leading semi-official Arabic dailies accused sections of the independent press of disloyalty to their country, while in late July a journalist from *Al-Masa'iyah* was arrested and charged with having links with 'foreign powers'.

In early July 1999 the Minister of Youth and Sports, Muhammad Kheir Mamsar, announced his resignation following controversy over the 9th Pan-Arab Games, which were to be held in Jordan in August. (The announcement followed Mamsar's insistence that Kuwait should not boycott the event, as it was threatening to do, owing to the participation of Iraqi athletes.) On 14–15 July municipal elections were conducted throughout Jordan; despite some violence being reported between supporters of rival tribal candidates, in which two people died, in general the elections were judged to have been relatively free and fair. The overall level of voter participation was reported at 60%, with turn-out particularly low in urban areas. The final results indicated that independent and tribal candidates had gained the most seats in the elections, while Islamists too were successful in their traditional urban strongholds of Zarqa, Irbid, Rusayfa and Tafilah. The IAF also won five of the 20 elected seats on the Great Amman Municipality, and at the national level 70 of its 100 candidates were successful. The local elections marked the return of the IAF to the formal political process. Later in 1999 the Prime Minister agreed to consider changes to the electoral system which had been proposed by the Muslim Brotherhood. The Muslim Brotherhood, together with several other opposition groups which had sought electoral reforms before the 1997 poll, suggested increasing the number of seats in the House of Representatives from 80 to 120. The country would be divided into 80 electoral districts and voters would each cast two votes, one for their chosen candidate and the second for a political party list. Those parties securing the highest share of the vote would be allocated the additional 40 seats. Some political groupings, however, were unhappy with these proposals, fearing that they would result in the Islamists re-establishing their dominant position in the lower house. On 18 July 1999 King Abdullah issued a royal decree appointing Lt-Gen. Muhammad Yousuf al-Malkawi as Chairman of the

Joint Chiefs of Staff, replacing Field Marshal Abd al-Hafez Mar'i al-Ka'ahinah, who became the King's own military adviser.

Relations between the Jordanian Government and the Muslim Brotherhood were strained at the end of August 1999, when the security forces closed down the Amman offices of the Palestinian Islamist movement, Hamas, following claims by the Ministry of the Interior that the offices were being used for illegal political activities by non-Jordanian groups. The authorities alleged that Hamas had organized military camps and created weapons dumps across the country. The home of Khalid Meshaal, head of Hamas's political bureau, was also raided, while some 15 Hamas officials were detained and arrest warrants were issued for a further five of the group's leaders. In late September three of the five (including Meshaal and the Hamas spokesman, Ibrahim Ghosheh) were arrested by Jordanian security forces on their return to Amman from Iran, on charges of involvement in illicit political activities and the illegal possession of firearms. One of the men, a Yemeni national, faced immediate deportation. More serious charges relating to the possession of weapons for illegal use and the planning of military operations—which could carry the death penalty—were brought against Meshaal and Ghosheh in early October. In early November another senior Hamas representative was arrested, amid reports that the organization had rejected an offer by the Government to release the detained activists, provided that they agreed to cease all political activity and that their leaders left the country. However, later in the month the Jordanian authorities released some 24 Hamas officials, including four leaders who were immediately expelled to Qatar; this occurred despite attempts by the Muslim Brotherhood—which enjoys close relations with Hamas—to resolve the crisis through negotiation.

On 1 September 1999 a government reorganization was effected; Prime Minister ar-Rawabdeh brought two new ministers into the Cabinet, including Sa'id Shuqum as the Minister of Youth and Sports. In mid-September the Government agreed in principle to some of the opposition's demands regarding changes in the electoral law (see above); these included the division of Jordan into 80 electoral districts and an increase in the number of seats in the lower house to 120. It was announced in late October that a new 'centrist green' party, the New Generations Party, had been licensed by the authorities. On 28 December the Minister of Transport, Nasser Lozi, tendered his resignation and was replaced temporarily by Jamal as-Sarayreh, the Minister of Post and Telecommunications. Seven new ministers were appointed in a cabinet reshuffle on 15 January 2000, which resulted in a Government dominated by technocrats and supporters of Prime Minister ar-Rawabdeh; the premier charged his three deputy prime ministers with ensuring better co-operation and co-ordination between ministries. Meanwhile, in mid-January Abd al-Karim al-Kabariti resigned as Chief of the Royal Court less than a year after his appointment and was replaced by former Prime Minister Fayez at-Tarawneh (who had held the same post during 1998). Although citing unspecified 'political and personal reasons', Kabariti—seen as the most prominent of the 'liberal reformists' among Jordan's political élite—was reported to have been frustrated by repeated clashes with ar-Rawabdeh and by the resistance mounted by the traditionalist 'old guard' to his efforts to promote a 'reformist' agenda. Liberal reformists, who sought to introduce greater freedom, to reduce official bureaucracy (in order to promote investment), and to promote political equality for Jordan's Palestinian population, saw the departure of Kabariti as a major defeat, especially as there had been widespread speculation that King Abdullah would replace ar-Rawabdeh given his failure to address the urgent economic crisis. Some observers argued that the conflict between the liberal reformists and the 'old guard' had become the major feature of political life during the first year of the King's reign.

In mid-December 1999 16 suspected terrorists (including Jordanians, an Iraqi and an Algerian) were arrested on charges of plotting attacks against US and Israeli tourist targets in Jordan. The detainees, who were alleged to belong to the al-Qa'ida (Base) organization—linked to the Saudi-born militant Islamist Osama bin Laden—were brought to trial before a military court in Amman in late April 2000; a further 12 members of al-Qa'ida were to be tried *in absentia*. In mid-September six of the militants were sentenced to death, having been convicted of the manufacture of explosives, membership of an illegal organization and fraud; 16 were sentenced to terms of imprisonment ranging from seven years to life, while the remaining six were acquitted. Another large group of Islamist militants from the northern town of Irbid was arrested later in December 1999. Opposition circles argued that the authorities' clamp-down on Islamist groups supporting an armed struggle against Israel was serving the interests of the USA and Israel rather than that of Jordan. In mid-July 2000 another group of suspected militant Islamists was detained by the authorities, on suspicion of plotting sabotage in the country; the arrests were believed to be linked to a recent warning that the US embassy in Amman was about to be targeted by Islamist fundamentalists. Four of the defendants were sentenced to death in September.

In mid-January 2000 the four Hamas leaders who had, in November, been expelled to Qatar—among them Khalid Meshaal and Ibrahim Ghosheh—filed an appeal with the Higher Court of Justice, on the grounds that their expulsion was unconstitutional. The appeal was rejected in late June, however. It was reported in late January 2000 that the Jordanian Government had rejected an offer by Meshaal for Hamas to enter into a dialogue with the authorities. At the same time Ghosheh strongly criticized the Muslim Brotherhood for failing to support them during the crisis and for abandoning the campaign to 'liberate Palestine' (although Hamas's spiritual leader, Sheikh Ahmad Yassin, praised the role played by the Muslim Brotherhood). Some sources claimed that one of the Government's objectives in taking action against Hamas was to cause a rift between the Palestinian resistance movement and the Muslim Brotherhood. Ghosheh provoked considerable controversy in mid-June 2001 when he returned to Amman, claiming that he was doing so with the backing of the Hamas leadership. However, he was forbidden by the Jordanian authorities to enter the country. The situation was resolved later in the month when Ghosheh travelled to the Thai capital, Bangkok. At the end of June Jordan's Ministry of Information announced that Ghosheh would be permitted to enter the country, after he agreed to cease his activities on behalf of Hamas.

Meanwhile, during January 2000 there were further indications that Jordan's political establishment had entered a period of instability, following allegations of corruption made against Prime Minister ar-Rawabdeh. Only days before the cabinet reshuffle (see above), ar-Rawabdeh and his son Issam were accused publicly by an independent parliamentary deputy of having demanded a JD 15m. (US \$20m.) bribe from an Arab Gulf investor, in return for securing official approval to build a planned tourism complex in Jordan. In mid-February the parliamentary committee charged with examining the allegations—the first time that a Jordanian premier had been subject to a public investigation on corruption charges—cleared both the Prime Minister and his son of any misdemeanour, owing to a lack of evidence, and Issam ar-Rawabdeh subsequently filed a libel suit against the deputy. On 24 February Dr Rima Khalaf al-Hunaidi resigned as Deputy Prime Minister and Minister of Planning, following alleged differences with the Prime Minister over the implementation of economic reforms. The Minister of Industry and Trade, Dr Muhammad al-Halaiqa, took on the planning portfolio in an acting capacity, while on 1 May Taleb ar-Rifai was named as the new Minister of Planning.

Despite strong backing from King Abdullah and Queen Rania, as well as the Chief Islamic Justice, Sheikh Izzedin al-Khatib at-Tamimi, government efforts to repeal an article in the penal code relating to so-called 'honour killings' were twice rejected by the House of Representatives with a large majority, in late 1999 and early 2000. The Government wished to abolish Article 340, which protects those found guilty of murdering female relatives in the name of 'family honour', and to impose tough punishment for such crimes. Opponents in the lower house argued that such changes would encourage adultery and accelerate the decline in the country's moral values that, they considered, had taken place as a result of the normalization of relations with Israel. The response of the lower house demonstrated the difficulties faced by the Government in trying to legislate on sensitive social issues, especially those relating to the position of women in society. On 14 February 2000 some 6,000 protesters marched to the National Assembly building and then to the Prime Minister's office demanding that parliament

revoke the article related to 'honour killings'. It was the largest public demonstration in Amman for some years and was led by King Abdullah's half-brother, Prince Ali, and the King's cousin and adviser on tribal affairs, Prince Ghazi bin Muhammad. A few days later an opposition newspaper reported that Prince Ali had publicly accused the Prime Minister of not giving his full backing to the legislation and of trying to obstruct the King's efforts to introduce reform and liberalization. (This was believed to be the first time that a member of the royal family had openly criticized ar-Rawabdeh.) The Governor of Amman subsequently rejected a request from the Muslim Brotherhood to hold a counter-demonstration, and the Secretary-General of the IAF urged the Government to hold a national referendum before taking any action on the issue. Meanwhile, majorities in both houses of parliament voted against an anti-corruption bill under which public servants would be required to disclose all of their assets before taking office. In late February a majority of deputies in the House of Representatives submitted a petition to the Speaker, Abd al-Hadi al-Majali, demanding the implementation of *Shari'a* law, stating that only Islamic law could prevent corruption and nepotism and solve the current economic crisis. In response, al-Majali declared that several parliamentary committees would have to identify those laws which needed amending in order to bring them into line with *Shari'a* law, effectively ensuring that no action was taken in the short-term. Some observers interpreted the petition as a response to the Government's efforts to introduce new legislation on 'honour killings', amid widespread alarm in conservative circles at the threat of 'moral degradation' as Jordan becomes more closely integrated into the global economy. Others, however, suspected that the Government might be using the petition as a warning to its Western allies that without further economic assistance, conservative and Islamist forces could pose a threat to the regime.

In early April 2000 a political adviser to the King, Adnan Abu Odeh, surprised many by resigning his post, citing the widespread controversy caused by his plans to reform legislation concerning Jordanians of Palestinian origin. He was replaced by Samir ar-Rifa'i, who was to remain the Secretary-General of the Royal Court, in early August. Meanwhile, in mid-April 2000 a significant number of deputies in the House of Representatives, including senior figures such as Speaker al-Majali and the Chairman of the Economic and Finance Committee, Ali Abu ar-Ragheb, called on King Abdullah to dismiss the Government for failing to introduce political and economic reforms and for violating public freedoms. They also urged the King to form a 'parliamentary government' composed of deputies. At the same time opposition parties accused the Government of employing excessive force to quell dissent. King Abdullah responded by expressing his confidence in premier ar-Rawabdeh.

Nevertheless, on 18 June 2000 King Abdullah dismissed the conservative ar-Rawabdeh after 15 months in office and named Ali Abu ar-Ragheb as Jordan's new Prime Minister. Ar-Ragheb, a liberal independent deputy and former Minister of Industry and Trade, was a prominent member of the Consultative Economic Council established by the King to increase government initiatives regarding development. On 19 June ar-Ragheb appointed a new 29-member Cabinet, which was reported to include nine Palestinian ministers and three with 'Islamist leanings'. However, several ministers remained from the previous administration, including the Minister of Foreign Affairs, Abd al-Ilah al-Khatib, and the Minister of Finance, Dr Michel Marto. Among the objectives for the new Government, as outlined by King Abdullah, were to ensure national unity through the principle of equal opportunities for all Jordanian citizens, both East Bankers and Palestinians; to end nepotism in public office; and to draft modern electoral legislation to pave the way for completely free parliamentary elections scheduled for late 2001. He also placed great emphasis on accelerating the implementation of IMF-sponsored economic reforms. Meanwhile, the IAF decided, in late June 2000, to 'freeze' the membership of one of its leading members, Abd ar-Rahim al-Akour, after he joined the Government as the Minister of Municipal, Rural and Environmental Affairs. In mid-July the new ar-Ragheb Government won an overwhelming vote of confidence in the National Assembly. It was announced in late August that King Abdullah had ordered the establishment of a royal committee, to be headed by the Prime Minister, which would be charged with carrying out a 'drastic review' of Jordan's judicial system. At the end of September former Prime Ministers Taher al-Masri and Ahmad Ubeidat founded a new political bloc, the Arab Democratic Front, which declared as one of its principal aims the development of the country's 'civil society institutions'. Al-Majali was re-elected Speaker of the House of Representatives in late November.

RELATIONS WITH THE USA

On 20 June 1991 the US House of Representatives voted to withhold US $27m. in military aid, pending assurances that 'the Government of Jordan has taken steps to advance the peace process in the Middle East'. However, the US Department of State indicated that the Bush Administration opposed legislation to prohibit the sending of US aid to Jordan. In October, following Jordan's acceptance of an invitation to attend the opening session of the Middle East peace conference in Madrid (see above), President Bush announced the USA's intention to resume military aid to Jordan.

In June 1992 the USA postponed a joint military exercise with Jordan in order to express its disapproval of the assistance that Jordan was allegedly providing to Iraq to enable it to circumvent the UN trade embargo. The USA subsequently proposed that UN observers should be dispatched to Jordan in order to suppress the smuggling of goods to Iraq. Jordan rejected the proposal outright as an infringement of its sovereignty. In late August both the Jordanian Government and the House of Representatives condemned Western plans to establish an air exclusion zone in southern Iraq. In January 1993 King Hussein strongly criticized renewed air attacks on targets in Iraq by Western air forces, but he emphasized that Jordan would remain on friendly terms with the USA under the newly-elected Clinton Administration. In June King Hussein visited the USA, where he held talks for the first time with President Clinton. Although bilateral relations were described as good, the USA was reported to be continuing to withhold financial aid in retaliation for Jordan's alleged assistance to Iraq during the 1991 Gulf War. Prior to his visit to the USA, King Hussein had stated publicly that he did not support the Iraqi leadership or its policies. At the end of July the USA reportedly informed Jordan that it must make payments to the UN's Compensation Fund for Kuwait if it continued to receive deliveries of petroleum from Iraq. In mid-September, however, President Clinton announced that some US $30m. in economic and military aid to Jordan was to be released, in recognition of the country's enforcement of sanctions against Iraq and of its role in the Middle East peace process.

As part of his plans to improve relations with the USA, King Hussein visited Washington, DC, in late January 1994 where he met President Clinton and the Secretary of State, Warren Christopher. Their talks centred on the Arab-Israeli peace process and future US arms sales to Jordan. During the visit the King stated publicly that he would be willing to meet Itzhak Rabin, the Israeli Prime Minister. In March, however, new tensions emerged with the USA over Jerusalem and over the US-led naval blockade of Jordan's only port at Aqaba. After the adoption of Resolution 904 by the UN Security Council on 18 March 1994, Jordan protested strongly about the US position on the status of Jerusalem. The USA had abstained on two paragraphs in the preamble, in which East Jerusalem was referred to as part of the Occupied Territories. Jordan was worried about the legal and political implications of what appeared to be an important change in US policy towards Jerusalem. However, most of King Hussein's fury over this reversal was directed towards PLO Chairman Yasser Arafat, who was accused of mishandling the negotiations which preceded the adoption of the Resolution by failing to consult with Jordan on its wording.

In an address to the Jordanian National Assembly on 26 October 1994, President Clinton pledged to cancel Jordan's official debts to the USA, totalling US $702m., apparently as a reward for signing the peace treaty with Israel. Although some $220m. of debt was written off during the fiscal year 1994, the new Republican-dominated US Congress was inclined to be less generous in 1995. President Clinton had requested the cancellation of $270m.-worth of debt in the fiscal year 1995, but the US House of Representatives only agreed to write off $50m.

During a visit to Jordan in March 1995, US Vice-President Al Gore pledged that Clinton's original promise would be honoured. However, King Hussein was forced to visit the USA the following month in an attempt to persuade Congress to permit the debt-cancellation plan to proceed. In September an agreement was finally signed by the USA and Jordan, cancelling $420m. of Jordan's outstanding debt. In August 1995, as King Hussein broke openly with Iraq (see below), President Clinton immediately promised to support Jordan if any threat was made to its security. Joint manoeuvres were held between US and Jordanian armed forces, although Jordan maintained that these had been arranged some time before. Nevertheless, efforts by the USA to persuade Jordan to sever all of its economic links with Iraq were rejected. In January 1996 the US Secretary of Defense announced that the USA would supply Jordan with 12 F-16A and four F-16B fighter aircraft, and in late February President Clinton authorized the supply of military equipment worth $100m. as a grant to Jordan. After King Hussein visited Washington, DC, in March, the USA announced that bilateral military co-operation would be expanded, a move interpreted by some as a warning to other states in the region not to attempt to destabilize Jordan. In April 34 US F-15 and F-16 fighter aircraft were stationed in Jordan for an indefinite period in order to undertake flights over southern Iraq.

Some observers interpreted Jordan's *rapprochement* with Saudi Arabia and the Gulf states and the break with Iraq as part of a plan orchestrated by the USA to redraw the political map of the region, with the aim of further isolating Iraq, politically and economically, and linking the Jordanian economy more closely with that of Israel. In April 1996, when it was revealed that Turkey had signed a secret military agreement with Israel in February, some analysts argued that a new strategic partnership was emerging to replace the long-promised Middle East peace accords, bringing together the USA, Israel, Turkey and Jordan in a military alliance designed to protect Israeli and US interests in the region and to isolate those states opposed to them. In May US and Jordanian forces carried out joint military exercises in the south of the kingdom.

In June 1996 King Hussein was the first Arab leader to visit Washington, DC, after the right-wing Likud victory in the Israeli elections. Discussions focused on the Middle East peace process and on Jordan's strategic relationship with the USA. Soon after the King's visit another series of joint military manoeuvres was carried out in southern Jordan, and at the end of the month the Chairman of the US Joint Chiefs of Staff, Gen. John Shalikashvili, visited Jordan to strengthen the military relationship between the two countries. In October, after violent clashes between Israelis and Palestinians following Israel's decision to open a tunnel in Jerusalem close to Muslim holy places (see below), President Clinton invited King Hussein, Yasser Arafat, and the new Israeli Prime Minister, Binyamin Netanyahu, to Washington in order to reduce tensions. Little progress was made at their meeting, although it was agreed that direct talks would be resumed between Israel and the PA on the redeployment of Israeli troops in Hebron.

In November 1996 President Clinton announced that Jordan was being granted special military status, thus making the kingdom eligible for increases in US military aid. In December Jordan received the first US $100m. instalment of a $300m.-package of military equipment as part of a US commitment to help modernize the Jordanian armed forces. In early March 1997, when the USA vetoed a UN Security Council resolution criticizing Israel's plans to build a new housing complex on the outskirts of Arab East Jerusalem, King Hussein claimed that the veto had damaged the credibility of the USA as an honest broker in the Middle East. Nevertheless, joint exercises between Jordanian and US forces continued, and the first group of F-16 fighter aircraft, pledged under the rearmament agreement of late 1996, arrived in December 1997, with the rest of the aircraft scheduled for delivery in early 1998. In September 1997 the US Secretary of State, Madeleine Albright, met King Hussein for discussions in Amman, as part of her first visit to the Middle East since taking office. The talks in Jordan were very cordial; however, Albright's visit to the region failed to resolve the deadlock in the Middle East peace process. In October the US Government accorded Irbid in northern Jordan, where there were a number of Jordanian-Israeli joint ventures, the status of 'qualifying industrial zone', thereby allowing all goods exported from it duty-free access to the US market. In November Jordan dispatched a high-level delegation, headed by Jawad al-Anani, to the US-sponsored Middle East and North Africa economic conference in Doha, Qatar, while both Egypt and Saudi Arabia boycotted the meeting, owing to Israeli participation. Despite the close alliance with the US Government and the suppression of pro-Iraqi demonstrations during the increased tension between the USA and Iraq in early 1998, Jordan indicated that it would not allow its territory or airspace to be used for an attack on Iraq. During his visit to Washington in March King Hussein was said to have requested that the US Government increase aid to Jordan and exert pressure on Israel to make concessions over the West Bank. There was a limited response from US officials to the King's suggestion that Jordan assist in the organization of discussions between the Governments of the USA and Iraq. A senior Jordanian naval officer was present at a joint exercise between the naval forces of the USA, Israel and Turkey (the first time that the three countries had co-operated in a military exercise).

In July 1998 King Hussein arrived in the USA for further cancer treatment and remained there for almost six months. The King's mediation at the US-brokered peace summit which took place between Israel and the Palestinians at the Wye Plantation, Maryland, in October was crucial to the signing of the Wye Memorandum (see the chapter on Israel and Documents on Palestine, p. 86). In December, after renewed US and British air-strikes against Iraq, the Jordanian authorities allowed pro-Iraqi protests by the public, but ensured that they were contained and policed.

On 8 May 1999 the new King of Jordan, Abdullah, began a three-week tour of the USA and several European capitals. Prior to the visit, King Abdullah had announced that, in anticipation of a summit of G-8 leaders, due to be held in Germany in June, he would be seeking US support for an agreement by Western countries to write off as much as 50% of Jordan's debt. He achieved some success when, on 20 May (two days after an interview with President Clinton) the 'Paris Club' of international official creditors agreed to reschedule some US $800m. of Jordan's debt, in the context of its economic reform programme. In late June the G-8 summit leaders recommended a more active programme of debt relief and debt-swap arrangements between Jordan and individual Western creditors. However, there were no indications that the G-8 countries would consider writing off a significant proportion of Jordan's debts. King Abdullah made another successful visit to the USA in October, despite continuing differences between the two countries over Iraq. In early July 2000 Abdullah again visited the USA for talks with President Clinton and senior US officials regarding bilateral trade and the Middle East peace process. Jordan and the USA signed a free-trade agreement during a visit by the King to Washington, DC, in late October (see below).

RELATIONS WITH ARAB STATES

Since the end of the 1990–91 Gulf War, Jordan has continued to distance itself from Saddam Hussain's regime in Iraq and has tried to improve relations with the Gulf states. In 1992 King Hussein spoke publicly of the need for change in Iraq, but denied that he had discussed ways of removing the Iraqi leader with the US CIA. Jordan protested at the harassment of Iraqi refugees in Jordan by the Iraqi secret service and at the execution of Jordanian merchants in Iraq accused of economic crimes. Jordan welcomed Iraq's decision, in November 1994, to recognize the sovereignty and territorial integrity of Kuwait. However, Jordan continued to favour the international rehabilitation of Iraq, including the relaxation of UN sanctions. In June 1995 King Hussein was openly critical of US policy towards Iraq. After a visit to Amman later that month by Viktor Possovalyuk, the Russian Deputy Minister of Foreign Affairs, both Jordan and Russia agreed to co-operate to end UN sanctions against Iraq.

At the end of November 1993 King Hussein made his first official visit to Egypt since the Gulf crisis. Relations with Egypt had slowly improved after diplomatic efforts by the King, who made an unofficial visit to Cairo in October 1992 to offer condolences just after the city suffered a serious earthquake. During a visit to Amman by the Egyptian Minister of Foreign Affairs in October 1993 it was agreed to reconvene the Higher Jordanian-

Egyptian Joint Committee which had not met since the Gulf crisis. In January 1995 President Mubarak of Egypt made his first official visit to Jordan since the Iraqi invasion of Kuwait, and in February Jordan, together with representatives of the PLO and Israel, attended a summit meeting in Cairo, in an attempt to avert a breakdown in the peace process. In March the Higher Jordanian-Egyptian Joint Committee convened in Cairo, where it was agreed to co-ordinate the activities of the two countries' respective interior ministries, a decision apparently aimed at increasing co-operation against the threat of Islamist extremism.

Following visits by Crown Prince Hassan to Doha in late 1993 and by Sheikh Hamad bin Jaber ath-Thani, the Qatari Minister of Foreign Affairs, to Amman at the beginning of 1994, normal relations between Jordan and Qatar were restored after being strained by Jordan's support for Iraq in the Gulf War. In March 1994 King Hussein made his first visit to Doha since the Gulf crisis. However, the normalization of relations with Qatar did not include the resumption of financial aid to Jordan from the emirate. King Hussein also visited Oman, where discussions included the efforts by both countries to mediate between the two factions in Yemen, but visits to Bahrain and the UAE were cancelled. In November a three-year programme of bilateral co-operation in education, science and culture was agreed with Qatar, and in January 1995 King Hussein made a private visit to Oman for talks with Sultan Qaboos. There were also signs of some improvement in relations with Bahrain and the UAE. After the coup in Qatar in June 1995 in which Sheikh Hamad bin Khalifa ath-Thani deposed his father, King Hussein offered his congratulations to the new Amir, who had been largely responsible for the policy of improving relations with Jordan. During the second half of 1995 relations with Yemen were also strengthened.

In 1994–95 there was some improvement in relations with Kuwait, which had been severely strained since the Iraqi invasion of Kuwait in 1990. A senior Jordanian diplomat visited Kuwait in September 1994, and it was later announced that the Jordanian embassy in Kuwait would reopen and that Kuwait had agreed to allow several thousand Jordanians who had been expelled in 1991 to return. Nevertheless, relations remained difficult.

In late 1994 there appeared to be signs of a tentative *rapprochement* with Saudi Arabia, despite the personal animosity believed to exist between King Fahd and King Hussein (thought to be due to the long rivalry between the Hashemites and the House of Sa'ud) and the serious rift in relations caused by the Gulf crisis. In September co-operation on border issues resumed. A ban on granting residence permits to the dependants of all Jordanians and Palestinians working in Saudi Arabia, which had been imposed since the Gulf crisis, was partly revoked in March 1995, when residence permits were granted to the families of those Jordanians employed in 'vital positions'. The refusal of King Fahd to meet King Hussein in that month, while the Jordanian monarch was performing the *umra* (minor pilgrimage), was defused by the Jordanian leadership, anxious not to escalate tensions with its powerful neighbour. After a visit to Riyadh by the Jordanian Minister of Foreign Affairs in July there were signs that Saudi Arabia was ready to restore diplomatic representation with Jordan to ambassadorial level.

BREAKDOWN IN RELATIONS WITH IRAQ

In early August 1995 King Hussein granted political asylum to Hussain Kamel al-Majid, his brother Saddam Kamel and their wives after they fled from Baghdad to Amman. Hussain and Saddam Kamel had been senior figures in the Iraqi regime and were married to daughters of Saddam Hussain, the Iraqi President. Their defection marked a sharp deterioration in relations between Jordan and Iraq. At a press conference shortly after arriving in Jordan, Hussain Kamel appealed for the removal of Saddam Hussain and spoke of his hopes of leading an Iraqi opposition movement to rescue Iraqis from their worsening plight. Later that month King Hussein delivered a speech in which he praised Hussain Kamel as a great patriot and strongly criticized the Iraqi leader, although he stopped short of seeking the fall of the Iraqi regime. He also denied speculation, especially rife in the Egyptian and Syrian press, that he was seeking to revive Hashemite claims to Iraq. In response, Iraq denounced

Hussain Kamel as a traitor and a US agent, but carefully avoided attacks on King Hussein. Despite the political rupture, economic co-operation continued, with Iraq remaining Jordan's main source of oil supplies. Jordan continued to provide Iraq with a vitally important link with the outside world. In October King Hussein renewed his attack on the Iraqi regime, denouncing the presidential elections there as a farce. He also established contact with Iraqi opposition groups in London, United Kingdom, and promoted the idea of holding a congress in Amman to bring the different factions together in order to discuss political change in Iraq. However, the proposed congress drew criticism, especially from Syria, and the idea was abandoned. The King was also criticized for appearing to favour a federal approach to Iraq's political future as this might have threatened the country's unity. In any case, his support for Hussain Kamel was short-lived. It quickly became clear that Kamel had few supporters in Iraq, while his appeals to the Iraqi opposition-in-exile were firmly rejected. By the end of 1995 his presence in Jordan had become something of an embarrassment. When Hussain Kamel and his brother decided to return to Iraq in February 1996, after hearing that they had been pardoned, rumours circulated that the Jordanian authorities may have encouraged them in their decision. Nevertheless, the brutal murder of the two men by order of Saddam Hussain only days after their return was strongly condemned by Jordan.

In April 1996, after US aircraft were stationed at Azraq to enforce the air exclusion zone in southern Iraq, the Jordanian Government insisted that it would not permit the country to be used as a base for attacks against Iraq. Nevertheless, King Hussein met with Iraqi opposition leaders in London, United Kingdom, in March and gave permission for the Iraqi National Accord (INA) to open an office in Amman. In March there was another high-level defection from Iraq when Gen. Nizar Kazraji, a former Chief of Staff of the Iraqi army, arrived in Jordan and associated himself with the INA. In late March, amid speculation that Iraqi agents operating in Jordan might be seeking to target Jordanians, the first expulsion of an Iraqi diplomat from Jordan occurred, although no explanation for it was made public. In retaliation, Iraq expelled a Jordanian diplomat. At the end of June it was reported that US, British, Saudi Arabian and Jordanian intelligence officers meeting in Saudi Arabia in January had agreed that Amman should become the centre of operations for the Iraqi opposition. They had agreed to support the INA, which claimed to be in contact with high-ranking officers in the Iraqi armed forces, and which favoured a swift *coup d'état* that would remove Saddam Hussain from power but leave the country intact. There were also reports that US President Clinton had authorized a grant of some US $6m. to finance the INA's operations in Amman, with additional funds being provided by Saudi Arabia, Kuwait and several other Arab countries. Speaking in Washington, DC, in June, the Jordanian Minister of Information stated that Jordan preferred to support the INA because its rival, the Iraqi National Congress (INC), had no credibility in either Iraq or Jordan.

Relations with Iraq improved slightly in December 1996, when the Iraqi Ministers of Trade and Foreign Affairs held talks in Amman with senior Jordanian officials, marking a resumption in high-level contacts between the two countries. King Hussein had reportedly been opposed to any relaxation of sanctions against Saddam Hussain's regime, but, after Baghdad accepted UN Security Council Resolution 986 allowing Iraq to sell limited quantities of oil in order to purchase food and medicine, he was willing to adopt a less confrontational stance to protect Jordan's economic interests. In addition, the invasion of Iraqi Kurdistan by Saddam Hussain's forces in August 1996, and the destruction of the Iraqi opposition based there, may have convinced the King that an early removal of the Iraqi leader was extremely unlikely. The Jordanian Government deliberately refrained from commenting on the Iraqi invasion, but voiced concern over the US missile attacks against Iraq. The Jordanian National Assembly, in contrast, strongly condemned the American action. The Iraqi National Accord (INA) was allowed to keep its office in Amman, despite reports that the group had been infiltrated by Iraqi agents, but Jordan repeatedly asserted that it would not be used as a base for operations against the Iraqi regime.

In December 1997 bilateral relations once again became strained, after the Iraqi authorities executed four Jordanian nationals who had been convicted of smuggling offences. King Hussein condemned the executions, expelled a number of Iraqi diplomats from Amman, and recalled the Jordanian chargé d'affaires from Baghdad. In an attempt to improve relations, Iraq announced that it would commute the death sentence of a fifth Jordanian convicted of smuggling and release a number of Jordanians held in Iraqi prisons. The killing of Iraq's chargé d'affaires in Amman in January 1998 prompted rumours that Iraqi government agents may have been responsible. In May, however, the Jordanian Minister of the Interior announced that a number of Jordanian nationals had been arrested in connection with the killing, which, he insisted, had not been politically motivated and did not involve 'neighbouring countries'. During the Gulf crisis in early 1998 there was widespread popular support for Iraq in Jordan, but the authorities banned pro-Iraqi demonstrations. Despite Jordan's close alliance with the US Government, however, the authorities again indicated that they would not allow Jordanian territory or airspace to be used for air-strikes against Iraq, but they urged the Iraqi Government to comply with all UN resolutions and allow UN weapons inspectors access to all suspect sites. Jordanian support for the Arab League's efforts to resolve the crisis by diplomatic means contributed to an improvement in relations with some other Arab states, notably Egypt. Although relations with Iraq remained uneasy, economic co-operation continued, and in February 1998 the two countries renewed the 1991 oil agreement. Most ordinary Jordanians remained strongly pro-Iraqi and, although they were strictly controlled by the Jordanian authorities, public demonstrations were allowed in protest at US and British air-strikes against Iraq in December 1998. The Jordanian Government also strongly condemned the attacks. At the end of December an emergency meeting of the Arab Parliamentary Union was held in Amman at which Crown Prince Hassan, acting as regent in the absence of King Hussein, called for the lifting of sanctions against Iraq. However, comments made by Hassan regarding the need for greater democracy in Iraq, and his demands for the release of all Kuwaiti prisoners of war held there angered the Iraqi delegation. In early 1999 the Jordanian National Assembly voted to end the embargo imposed on Iraq by the UN.

Following King Hussein's death in early February 1999, King Abdullah made efforts to improve bilateral relations with Iraq and publicly expressed his concern for the plight of the Iraqi people. There was speculation that Jordan might close the offices of the INA in Amman and prevent an Iraqi opposition radio station from broadcasting from the kingdom in the hope that Baghdad would not exploit the uncertain political situation in Jordan by fomenting unrest. In late January 2000 the two countries renewed their annual trade protocol. Under the new oil agreement one-half of the crude oil and derivatives supplied to Jordan by Iraq would be free of charge, while the annual trade protocol (in place since 1990) was increased in value from US $200m. to $300m. Some sources argued that since the priority of Jordan's new ruler was the country's troubled economy, he had been persuaded to avoid taking a political stand against Saddam Hussain's regime and to work towards strengthening economic relations. Nevertheless, political differences remained and in June Amman condemned the execution by Iraq of a Jordanian national accused of spying for the US CIA. However, some progress was apparently made in improving relations during a visit to Amman in mid-July by Iraqi Vice-President Taha Yassin Ramadan, who held talks with King Abdullah and his new Prime Minister, Ali Abu ar-Ragheb, a strong advocate of closer links with Iraq. In early November ar-Ragheb undertook an official visit to Iraq—the first by a Jordanian premier since 1991—and the two countries agreed to increase the value of their trade agreement from US $300m. in 2000 to $450m. in 2001.

RELATIONS WITH OTHER ARAB STATES

Jordan's new policy on Iraq was welcomed by Saudi Arabia and relations between the two countries continued to improve. Shortly after Hussain Kamel's defection (see above), the Jordanian Minister of Foreign Affairs was invited to visit Riyadh where he was received by King Fahd. Full diplomatic relations were restored with the appointment of a new Saudi ambassador to Amman in November 1995. In January 1996 the Saudi Minister of Foreign Affairs visited Jordan, the first visit by a senior member of the Saudi regime since the 1990–91 Gulf crisis, and offered to resume supplies of some 40,000 b/d of crude oil (cut off in September 1990) to Jordan. Relations with Bahrain, which, like Saudi Arabia, had taken a hard line on relations with Jordan since 1990, also improved after Jordan's political rupture with Iraq. In November 1995 two high-level Jordanian delegations visited Manama and there was speculation that Jordanian assistance in Bahrain's internal security was one of the main topics of discussion. In early 1996 Jordan's new Prime Minister reaffirmed the country's support for the Bahrain Government and did not exclude the dispatching of Jordanian troops to assist its security forces. During the second half of 1995 relations with Qatar and Oman were further strengthened. King Hussein visited Doha and Muscat in August, and in September the new Amir of Qatar visited Amman. Jordan's efforts to improve its relations with the Gulf states were rewarded when the GCC countries agreed to take part in an economic summit meeting held in Amman in October. However, relations with Kuwait remained uneasy. The Jordanian Minister of Foreign Affairs met his Kuwaiti counterpart in Cairo in September 1995, but was told that it was still too early for normal diplomacy between the two countries to resume. In December, however, the Kuwaiti Minister of Foreign Affairs urged the resumption of diplomatic relations with Jordan following the political break with Iraq and the improvement in Jordan's relations with other Gulf states. In a public disagreement, the Kuwaiti Prime Minister opposed the move, arguing that public opinion in Kuwait was still against normalization. In order to resolve their differences, telephone and postal links were restored, but Jordan was informed that the re-establishment of diplomatic relations would require the agreement of the Kuwaiti Government, its people and its press.

Jordan's policy towards Iraq caused disquiet in Egypt and Syria, which feared that it could lead to a new, US-backed strategic reorientation in the region. The Egyptian and Syrian press accused King Hussein of pursuing his own ambitions in Iraq. The King had talks with Egypt's President Mubarak in Washington, DC, at the end of September 1995 during the signing of the Israeli-Palestinian Interim Agreement on the West Bank and Gaza Strip (see Documents on Palestine, p. 80), and in late December President Mubarak visited Amman. At the end of this visit the two leaders issued a joint statement in which they emphasized the need to ensure the unity of Iraq and to allow the Iraqi people to decide their own future. Nevertheless, while King Hussein appeared to have gone some way towards reassuring the Egyptian President, bilateral relations remained uneasy owing to Egypt's sensitivities about its regional status. In contrast, Syria's attitude provoked strong criticism from Jordan, and resulted in a further deterioration in relations which had been poor since Jordan signed a separate peace agreement with Israel. At the end of June 1996 President Mubarak attempted to mediate between King Hussein and Syria's President Assad during the emergency Arab League summit meeting in Cairo. Jordan had accused Syria of sponsoring terrorist organizations in order to destabilize the kingdom, while Syria had denounced Jordan for working with Israel and Turkey to undermine President Assad's regime. Jordanian officials claimed that some progress had been made during the talks, and further contacts between the two leaders in July indicated an improvement in bilateral relations.

After the right-wing Likud victory in the Israeli elections, King Hussein urged other Arab leaders not to judge the new Prime Minister, Binyamin Netanyahu, until his policies concerning the peace process were announced. In order to review the new situation, King Hussein held talks with President Mubarak of Egypt and the Palestinian leader, Yasser Arafat, in Aqaba in early June 1996, but was not invited to the mini-summit between the leaders of Egypt, Syria and Saudi Arabia in Damascus. At the full Arab League summit in Cairo during 21–23 June, King Hussein joined other moderate Arab leaders to ensure that the final communiqué to be adopted was more restrained than many had predicted.

During the second half of 1997 there were indications that King Hussein wished to achieve an improvement in relations with Syria. Speaking at Irbid, in northern Jordan, the King praised President Assad, but also urged the Syrian Government to reciprocate by ceasing to support some Jordanian opposition parties and professional associations. For their part, the Jordanian authorities ordered the head of the Syrian branch of the Muslim Brotherhood's information office in Amman to leave the country. However, by the end of 1998 bilateral relations had deteriorated once again. In October Mustafa Tlass, the Syrian Minister of Defence, claimed that Jordan was 'Judaizing' its people, and accused the authorities there of having refused to allow army units from Saudi Arabia to assist Syria during the Arab–Israeli War of 1973 (see above). Nevertheless, on the death of King Hussein in early February 1999, the Syrian Government immediately announced three days of official mourning and President Assad attended the King's funeral at the head of a high-level Syrian delegation. Some commentators suggested that Assad's presence there marked a clear indication to the new King that Damascus wished to improve relations with its southern neighbour and that closer links with Syria might offer an alternative to Jordan's current reliance on good relations with Israel and the USA. In late April King Abdullah made his first official visit to Syria.

Further evidence of an improvement in bilateral relations emerged when, in early May 1999, it was announced that Syria would supply Jordan with water, in order to ease Jordan's drought over the summer months. Syria began to supply the water in mid-May and was to continue for four months. In late June Jordan refused to participate in joint Turkish-Israeli naval exercises, scheduled for the following month; in 1998 similar exercises had created a diplomatic crisis with Syria. Jordan and Syria also agreed to proceed with the long-standing Yarmouk dam project, and to seek financing jointly. In late July 1999, following the election of a new Israeli Prime Minister (see below) Abdullah made an unannounced visit to Syria, amid Jordanian concerns that any peace agreement concluded by Israel and Syria could damage the Palestinians' position and effectively isolate them in future peace negotiations. In early August the joint Jordanian-Syrian Higher Committee began talks in Amman—the first time in almost 10 years that a senior Syrian delegation had visited the Jordanian capital. The meeting resulted in a bilateral agreement which officials hoped might double the volume of trade between the two countries. Later in the month Syria agreed to allow the free circulation of Jordanian newspapers and publications, ending a 10-year ban.

In mid-September 1999 King Abdullah made an official visit to Lebanon—the first by a Jordanian monarch since 1965—where he held discussions with senior Lebanese officials regarding the Middle East peace process, as well as other bilateral issues (notably the planned free-trade agreement). Jordanian officials advocated greater economic integration between Jordan, Lebanon and Syria, especially to secure greater benefits from their relations with the EU. The early results of this initiative, however, were modest. Nevertheless, the improvement in Jordan's relations with Syria and Lebanon was thought to have been viewed with displeasure in Cairo. After peace talks between Syria and Israel resumed in December 1999, King Abdullah urged the Israeli premier, Ehud Barak, to make concessions in order to advance the negotiations. In June 2000 the King attended the funeral of President Assad in Damascus, where he had talks with the son and designated successor of the late President, Bashar, with whom he is reported to have established good relations. Syria confirmed in late November that it had upgraded its diplomatic representation in Amman to ambassadorial status, and the Syrian state airline resumed regular flights to Jordan's capital after a break of more than 20 years. Moreover, the Syrian leadership announced in January 2001 that all Jordanian prisoners held in Syria would soon be released.

The normalization of relations with Saudi Arabia was sealed in mid-August 1996 by a visit by King Hussein and a senior delegation to Riyadh, where the Jordanian monarch held his first talks with King Fahd since the 1990–91 Gulf crisis. Their discussions covered issues including the Middle East peace process and co-operation against terrorism. Both leaders agreed to strengthen bilateral relations, and agreements were concluded on the employment of Jordanians in Saudi Arabia and on resuming Jordanian agricultural exports to the kingdom. In

July 1996 a meeting of the Jordanian-Qatari Higher Committee, attended by the foreign ministers of the two countries, and visits by other senior officials indicated a further consolidation of relations between Jordan and Qatar. In December King Hussein made his first visit to the United Arab Emirates since the Gulf crisis and held talks with the UAE President, Sheikh Zayed bin Sultan an-Nahyan. Relations with Kuwait remained problematic, and a dispute over Jordanian prisoners held in Kuwait since the Iraqi invasion threatened to destroy the limited progress that had been made to reconcile the two countries. In January 1997 the Jordanian press reported that Jordanian prisoners in Kuwait were being ill-treated, and journalists criticized their own Government for not taking action. Tension mounted after official exchanges on the issue, but the crisis was defused when the Amir of Kuwait included 10 Jordanians in a group of prisoners released to mark the Id al-Fitr celebrations in the following month. In June the Kuwaiti Minister of Foreign Affairs declared that Kuwait was prepared to normalize relations with Jordan, Sudan and Yemen, the three Arab states which it had accused of supporting Iraq during the Gulf crisis. In the following month the Kuwaiti Government indicated that it favoured a faster normalization of relations with Jordan, but emphasized that the Jordanian press would have to modify its strongly critical attitude towards Kuwait. Relations with Saudi Arabia continued to improve, with a visit by the Saudi Arabian Minister of Foreign Affairs to Amman in June, while good relations with the other Gulf states, especially Oman and Qatar, were consolidated. A high-level Jordanian delegation attended the Middle East and North Africa economic conference in Doha, the Qatari capital, in November, and Jordan benefited from increased economic co-operation with Qatar.

The Saudi Arabian Minister of Defence visited Amman in January 1999 to deliver a message of congratulations from King Fahd to Prince Abdullah on his designation as Crown Prince. At the beginning of March Jordan's embassy in Kuwait was reopened, following the restoration of full diplomatic relations between the two countries (which had been severed after Iraq's 1990 invasion of Kuwait), and later Kuwait began issuing visas to Jordanians. On his accession, Jordan's new King, Abdullah, immediately made efforts to strengthen relations with the Arab world and during the first year of his reign travelled extensively in the region. His first major foreign visit was to Egypt for talks with President Mubarak in mid-March. During April Abdullah visited Saudi Arabia, Libya, Morocco, the UAE and Kuwait. During three days of talks with King Fahd on 5–7 April, Abdullah was reported to have called for greater economic co-operation between Jordan and Saudi Arabia, and for both countries to adopt a unified approach to peace talks with Israel. King Abdullah held further talks with King Fahd in late December when he visited Saudi Arabia for the lesser pilgrimage. In early September 1999 King Abdullah and Queen Rania had received a warm welcome during a visit to Kuwait, which was seen as confirming the *rapprochement* between the two countries. Kuwait announced subsequently that it would lift a nine-year ban on the sale of Jordanian newspapers, and in mid-October restored its ambassador to Amman (the post having been vacant since 1990). In early 2000 it was announced that the Amir of Kuwait planned to make his first visit to Jordan since the 1990–91 Gulf crisis. In April 2000 Sheikh Zayed bin Sultan an-Nahyan of Abu Dhabi made a grant of US \$200m. to support the Jordanian economy.

RELATIONS WITH ISRAEL AND THE PA

In May 1995 the Government banned a conference (organized by the IAF) to oppose the normalization of relations with Israel, claiming that it posed a threat to national security and to Jordan's image. In June Israel began to pipe 30m. cu m of drinking water per year from Lake Tiberias (the Sea of Galilee) to Jordan as agreed in the 1994 peace treaty. The project aimed to help Jordan overcome a growing shortage of drinking water and was promoted by the Jordanian authorities as one of the dividends of the peace process. However, there was some embarrassment when Israel indicated that the flow of water to Jordan could not be guaranteed in the event of shortages in Israel owing to drought. Opposition within many sections of Jordanian society to the peace treaty with Israel continued. In July 1995, under the terms of the peace treaty, Jordan finally annulled

laws banning Jordanians from having contact with, doing business with or selling land to Israelis, but only after several weeks of angry debate in the House of Representatives. After the assassination of the Israeli Prime Minister, Itzhak Rabin, in early November, King Hussein made his first visit to Jerusalem since 1967 in order to attend the funeral, at which he delivered an emotional oration. Clearly shocked by Rabin's murder, the King emphasized the need to continue the peace process. In December Jordan expelled an Iranian diplomat, amid speculation that he may have been involved in planning an attack on Israeli tourists visiting the country. In order to strengthen bilateral relations, Shimon Peres, the new Israeli Prime Minister, visited Jordan in December, and King Hussein made a state visit to Israel in January 1996. A transport agreement was signed in January establishing direct road and air links between the two countries. The King and senior government officials condemned the spate of suicide bomb attacks which were carried out in Israel during February and repeatedly criticized the actions of Hamas militants. (Claims by some Palestinian sources that the attacks might have been organized from Jordanian territory were immediately rejected by Jordan's Minister of Information.) King Hussein attended the anti-terrorism summit meeting in Sharm esh-Sheikh, Egypt, in March, which was held in response to the suicide bombings, and it was subsequently reported that the Jordanian authorities had adopted a tough line with Hamas representatives and had carried out new arrests of Hamas sympathizers.

Relations with Palestinian President Yasser Arafat continued to improve during 1995. Arafat received a warm reception when he visited Amman in May, and King Hussein used the opportunity to express his firm support for the Palestinian leader, who was under pressure from his opponents because of serious setbacks to the peace accord with Israel, and to reject claims that he was forming an alliance with Hamas. At the beginning of June the Jordanian authorities expelled two members of Hamas' political bureau who had been based in Jordan. The Jordanian Government welcomed the Israeli-Palestinian Interim Agreement on the West Bank and the Gaza Strip (see p. 80) signed in Washington, DC, on 28 September. Conscious of the tensions that had arisen between Jordan and the PLO during earlier discussions between the Palestinians and Israel, Arafat visited Amman to inform the Jordanian leadership about the main provisions of the new accord and thanked King Hussein for his support during the long negotiations.

After the surprise victory of Likud in the Israeli elections of May 1996, and the creation of a new right-wing Israeli Government, King Hussein declared that the implications of this did not worry him. He was the only Arab leader to have met Netanyahu when he led the Israeli opposition and had maintained contacts with the Likud leader for some two years. An Israeli source indicated that the new Prime Minister expected the process of normalization with Jordan to continue, and revealed that Dore Gold, Netanyahu's political adviser, had visited Amman several times in recent months in order to assure King Hussein that the new Likud Government would seek to promote Jordan's role in the West Bank. Other analysts also argued that Netanyahu's victory had revived talk of the so-called 'Jordanian option', provoking fears among Palestinians that Israel would encourage Jordan to share in the administration of the West Bank, leaving the PA in full control of only the Gaza Strip. King Hussein's optimism about the new Israeli administration soon transformed into despair and frustration at the intransigence of Netanyahu's Government with regard to the peace process. The Israeli Government did not inform Jordan in advance about its decision in September to reopen an ancient tunnel in East Jerusalem, which resulted in violent clashes between the Israeli security services and Palestinian demonstrators. King Hussein tried to defuse the crisis by requesting an international inquiry to examine whether the opening of the tunnel had damaged nearby Muslim religious sites and urged Israel to resume peace talks with the PA. After his discussions with Netanyahu in Washington, DC, in October, the King attempted to persuade the Israeli Prime Minister to adopt a more constructive position on the redeployment of Israeli forces on the West Bank, set out in the Declaration of Principles but not yet implemented. As the peace process appeared to be expiring, protests against the normalization of relations with

Israel intensified and succeeded in delaying the opening of the first Israeli trade fair in Amman by several weeks. The eventual opening of the fair, in January 1997, was attended by a demonstration organized by a 'national committee' consisting of political parties and trade unions, in which more than 2,500 Jordanians participated. In that month King Hussein intervened to support US efforts to secure an agreement between Israel and the PA on the issue of redeployment outlined in the Declaration of Principles. The King apparently persuaded Yasser Arafat to compromise on the timing of the second redeployment of Israeli forces from rural areas in the West Bank in order not to jeopardize the deal already made on Hebron. Israel's rapid redeployment of most of its forces from Hebron was welcomed by the Jordanian Government, and the release of three Jordanian prisoners held in Israel also helped to reduce tensions. At the end of February Prime Minister Netanyahu visited Amman to discuss bilateral relations, but his decision to continue with the construction of a large new Jewish settlement at Jabal Abu Ghunaim (Har Homa) on the outskirts of Jerusalem, plunged bilateral relations into a new crisis: the completed Har Homa project would result in Arab East Jerusalem becoming virtually surrounded by Jewish settlements, thereby prejudicing the future status of the city which was due to be discussed during 'final status' negotiations between Israel and the PA. After the visit, in an exchange of letters, King Hussein stated that Netanyahu's policies threatened to destroy the peace process and could lead to violence. Shortly afterwards Crown Prince Hassan cancelled a visit to Israel where he had been due to attend a ceremony in memory of Itzhak Rabin. On 13 March, two days after the publication of the King's outspoken letter, a Jordanian soldier opened fire on a party of Israeli schoolgirls at Nayarayim, on the border with Jordan, killing seven of the girls and wounding six others. King Hussein, who cut short a visit to Spain to return to Amman, and Crown Prince Hassan immediately expressed their sorrow and distress at the killings and promised a full investigation. Three days after the attack the King, together with Prime Minister Netanyahu, visited the relatives of the deceased to offer their condolences. Some Israelis argued that King Hussein's letter had provoked the massacre of the schoolgirls, an allegation strongly denied by the King. The perpetrator of the attack, Ahmad ad-Daqamseh, went on trial at the end of May and his case was taken up by those Jordanians opposed to the normalization of relations with Israel. A military court later sentenced ad-Daqamseh to 25 years' imprisonment.

Despite the increasing strain on bilateral relations, an agreement was reached in May 1997 on the transfer of drinking water from Israel to Jordan (under the provisions of the 1994 peace treaty), following talks between King Hussein and Netanyahu in Aqaba. At the end of August the two countries signed an accord to divert international flights from the airport serving Israel's Red Sea resort at Eilat, which is heavily congested, to nearby Aqaba airport in Jordan. In July Israel's Chief of Staff, Lt-Gen. Amnon Lipkin-Shahak, visited Jordan, the first official visit by the head of Israel's armed forces to an Arab country. The two countries were reported to have extended their co-operation in the fields of security and intelligence. However, the attempted assassination of Khalid Meshaal, the head of the political bureau of Hamas, in Amman in late September by agents of the Israeli secret service, Mossad, created further bilateral tensions. The attack was apparently ordered by the Israeli Prime Minister and was only agreed to reluctantly by Mossad leaders. King Hussein demanded and secured the release of Sheikh Ahmad Yassin, the spiritual leader of Hamas, and a number of other Palestinians who had been imprisoned in Israel, in exchange for the return of the two Mossad agents. King Hussein reportedly threatened to suspend diplomatic relations if the Israeli authorities failed to meet his demands. Following the attack on Meshaal, there were few high-level political contacts between Jordan and Israel for some months, although economic co-operation continued. After the resignation of the Mossad chief, Danny Yatom, in February 1998 and his replacement by Ephraim Halevy, who had been closely involved in the negotiations leading to the 1994 peace treaty, bilateral relations improved. In early March 1998 Ariel Sharon, the Israeli Minister of National Infrastructure, and the senior Israeli responsible for relations with Jordan, visited Amman,

followed by the Israeli Minister of Trade and Industry. Also in March a high-level Jordanian delegation, led by Crown Prince Hassan, visited Israel to hold talks with Netanyahu and the Israeli Minister of Defence, Itzhak Mordechai. Shortly afterwards, however, Ariel Sharon angered the Jordanian authorities by stating, in an Israeli news broadcast, that Israel was still determined to kill Khalid Meshaal. Abdullah an-Nusur, then the acting premier, condemned the statement and reminded Israel that Meshaal was a Jordanian national. Sharon subsequently wrote to Crown Prince Hassan, claiming that his comments had been misinterpreted and insisting that he respected Jordan's sovereignty. There was further embarrassment for the Jordanian authorities when Israeli radio reported that King Hussein had donated US $1m. to the families of the Israeli schoolgirls killed by a Jordanian soldier in March 1997 (see above). (In view of the strong opposition in Jordan to the normalization of relations with Israel, King Hussein had requested that no publicity should be given to the donation.)

In October 1998, while undergoing treatment for cancer in the USA, King Hussein attended the US-sponsored peace talks between Israel and the PA at Wye Plantation, Maryland. His participation was crucial in securing the two sides' agreement to the Wye Memorandum (see the chapter on Israel and Documents on Palestine, p. 86). Following the signing of the Memorandum, Prime Minister at-Tarawneh warned Hamas activists in Jordan not to resort to violence in an attempt to undermine the agreement. On the death of King Hussein in early February 1999 numerous tributes were paid to the late monarch by prominent Israeli politicians and statesmen. President Weizman, who referred to the King as one of the great leaders of the 20th century, led a large Israeli delegation, including Prime Minister Netanyahu, to Hussein's funeral.

Jordan's new ruler, King Abdullah, immediately assured Israel that he was committed to continuing his father's support for the Middle East peace process. Although little immediate progress was made in strengthening relations between the two countries, regular contacts between senior officials continued. The Israeli Government's decision in early 1999 to seek to reduce trade barriers between Jordan and both Israel and the Palestinian Autonomous Areas appeared to have been prompted by concern over stability in the Hashemite kingdom following the death of King Hussein. In late February Netanyahu's first official visit to Amman to meet the new King was largely overshadowed by comments made by the Israeli Prime Minister a few days earlier expressing the belief that Jordan might be about to strengthen its links with Iraq at the expense of a greater normalization of relations with Israel. In mid-March bilateral relations were further strained when Israel indicated that it would only be able to supply Jordan with some 60% of water supplies agreed under the 1994 peace treaty, as it was experiencing its own drought. King Abdullah and ar-Rawabdeh, anxious to avoid a water crisis like that experienced during 1998, were uncompromising in their opposition to this announcement, and in mid-April 1999 Israel agreed to supply Jordan with its full share of water. In mid-July King Abdullah held talks with the new Israeli Prime Minister, Ehud Barak, reportedly concerning ways to revive the peace process. As bilateral relations showed signs of improvement, in August the new Israeli Minister of Foreign Affairs, David Levy, made his first visit to Jordan since his appointment, and there were talks between Jordanian ministers and their Israeli counterparts on advancing co-operation in the fields of transport, tourism and telecommunications as proposed under the terms of the 1994 peace treaty.

King Abdullah welcomed the unexpected reactivation of the stalled Wye Memorandum following the signing of the Sharm esh-Sheikh Memorandum (Wye Two accords—see the chapter on Israel and Documents on Palestine, p. 88) by Yasser Arafat and Ehud Barak in Egypt on 4 September 1999. However, relations became strained in October when a Jordanian parliamentary delegation visiting the West Bank town of Hebron received verbal abuse from right-wing Israeli settlers and Israeli soldiers failed to intervene. The incident was aggravated by Israel's initial reluctance to issue an apology, as demanded by the Jordanian Government. Meanwhile, the anti-normalization campaign in Jordan continued, although it was weakened by internal divisions. In mid-February 2000 King Abdullah postponed a scheduled visit to Israel; Jordanian officials stated that the King sought greater progress in the Middle East peace process prior to holding talks with the Israeli Prime Minister, but the principal reason for the postponement appeared to be Israel's recent launching of air-strikes against infrastructural targets in Lebanon, an action which King Abdullah strongly condemned. The King did not make his first visit to Israel until April of that year, when he held brief discussions with Ehud Barak at Eilat, in an attempt to revive the peace process and to resolve bilateral issues, especially regarding water management.

As the Jordanian leadership became increasingly critical of the Netanyahu Government, its relations with the PA improved. At his meeting with Yasser Arafat in Aqaba in June 1996, King Hussein emphasized that under no circumstances would Jordan seek to replace the Palestinian leadership in negotiations with Israel over the 'final status' of the West Bank. When King Hussein visited Washington, DC, in the same month, the Jordanian Minister of Information stressed that Jordan's role was to assist Israeli-Palestinian discussions and not to supplant the PA. Arafat visited Amman at the end of December when the Jordanian leadership reiterated its full support for Palestinian independence. In November the two sides had reached agreement over the controversial issue of responsibility for the holy sites in East Jerusalem. It was agreed that Jordan would retain formal jurisdiction over the sites until the 'final status' talks between Israel and the Palestinians had been successfully completed. The management of the sites, however, would be transferred from Jordan's Ministry of Awqaf and Islamic Affairs to the PA.

The eighth conference of the OIC, which took place in Tehran in December 1997, unanimously recognized Jordan's role in preserving Jerusalem's Muslim identity. Also in December Prime Minister al-Majali held discussions with PA President Arafat in the West Bank town of Ramallah; the Jordanian Government angered the Israeli authorities by suggesting that Jewish West Jerusalem, as well as occupied Arab East Jerusalem, should be discussed during 'final status' negotiations between Israel and the PA. On the occasion of his visit to Israel in March 1998 Crown Prince Hassan also met Arafat, although the meeting was viewed as one of courtesy rather than an opportunity for substantive talks. Following King Hussein's death in February 1999, King Abdullah appeared content to leave the issue of Jerusalem's future status to PA negotiators rather than to emphasize the special role of the Hashemites in the city. Indeed, some commentators argued that the new King did not share his father's preoccupation with the West Bank and East Jerusalem and preferred to focus on Jordan's role within the global economy. The Jordanian Government's crackdown on the Palestinian Islamist Hamas in late August (see above) was interpreted as a move to support the PA in its talks with Israel concerning a reactivation of the peace process. Jordan was also reported to be involved in moves to bring about reconciliation between Yasser Arafat and PLO dissidents based in Damascus, notably the DFLP. Despite pressure from Israel and the USA, King Abdullah refused to discuss the issue of confederation until the Palestinians had achieved statehood and future relations with Jordan could be negotiated between their respective governments.

The sensitive issue of Jordan's Palestinian population came to the fore in late 1999 as Israel and the PA agreed to resume 'final status' negotiations. In early October King Abdullah visited the country's largest Palestinian refugee camp at Baqa'a, where he pledged to cement national unity and equality among all Jordanians. Prior to the Camp David summit held between Israel and the PA in July 2000, Jordan's new Prime Minister, Ali Abu ar-Ragheb, informed the National Assembly that his Government would refuse to absorb any more refugees or immigrants and would support the right of return for Palestinian refugees. (Ar-Ragheb's statement apparently came after suggestions that Jordan might be a suitable home for those Palestinian refugees currently residing in Lebanon.)

IMPACT OF THE AL-AQSA UPRISING ON THE JORDANIAN-ISRAELI TRACK

The official Jordanian position with regard to the collapse of the Israeli-Palestinian peace process following the eruption of the al-Aqsa *intifada* by Palestinians in September 2000 was

that Jordan would better serve the Palestinians by maintaining diplomatic relations with Israel, although as a symbolic protest Jordan decided on 7 October not to dispatch its newly appointed ambassador to Israel. The Jordanian Government generally distanced itself from the Israeli–Palestinian conflict to the extent possible; however, at US President Clinton's request and Egyptian President Mubarak's invitation, King Abdullah participated in the talks held between Ehud Barak and Yasser Arafat at Sharm esh-Sheikh on 16–17 October. In the weeks between the failure of the Camp David talks and the outbreak of the *intifada*, King Abdullah met with Barak three times, and reiterated the fact that Jordan would not accept Israeli or international sovereignty over the Islamic holy sites in East Jerusalem. The only other diplomatic incident occurred on 8 September, when Jordan's Minister of Education met with PA officials in East Jerusalem without first clearing the visit with Israel. The Israeli Government claimed the visit 'undermined Israeli sovereignty and violated accepted norms between Israel and Jordan', but the incident did not have any lasting consequences. One explanation for Jordan's initially low profile with regard to the crisis in the West Bank and Gaza was its eagerness to conclude a free-trade agreement with the USA before President Clinton's departure from office at the beginning of 2001. The final round of negotiations relating to the treaty opened on 12 September, and the final text, which was to be submitted to the US Congress for approval, was signed by Abdullah and Clinton on 24 October. Under the free-trade agreement Jordan and the USA are to phase out all customs duties over a 10-year period. On the same day as the accord was signed, Jordanian security forces used considerable violence to suppress a long-planned march by the country's professional associations in support of Palestinian refugees. Even before the outbreak of the al-Aqsa *intifada*, anti-Israeli and anti-normalization demonstrations had been common in Jordan, led by both the trade unions and the Muslim Brotherhood. Moreover, many Jordanians had reportedly been angered by King Abdullah's decision to proceed with the signing of a trade agreement with the USA at all.

Popular Jordanian outrage in support of the Palestinians was expressed in sharp contrast with the country's official position. Jordan is home to the single largest Palestinian refugee population, estimated at 1,679,623 at mid-2002. Immediately following the violent events in East Jerusalem on 28–29 September 2000, anti-Israeli protests erupted across the kingdom. On 3 and 4 October stone-throwing demonstrators attempted to march on the Israeli embassy in Amman. The Government deployed tanks around the embassy and sent in riot police, who clashed with demonstrators, injuring at least 60. Tensions culminated on 6 October with an 'anti-normalization' rally in the capital which was attended by 30,000 Palestinian East Bankers and Jordanians—the largest demonstration in Jordan since the Gulf War of 1991. Jordanian police, fearing that the crowd would again march on the Israeli embassy, fired tear gas to disperse them. In Amman's Baqa'a refugee camp, police opened fire with live ammunition on 2,000 Palestinians, killing one and injuring 50. On the same day King Abdullah banned public demonstrations and several protesters were arrested. However, following Israel's shelling of Palestinian targets in the West Bank and Gaza on 12 October 2000, the Jordanian Government permitted a rally in Amman, sponsored by the opposition parties, which was attended by 8,000 people. The 24 October marches in support of the right of return for Palestinian refugees turned into a demonstration in support of the Palestinian uprising and against the King's signing of the US trade agreement. Tens of thousands of Jordanians participated in the rally, after which groups marched towards the border with the West Bank. Jordanian riot police and security forces, with helicopter support, confronted the marchers near the Allenby Bridge on the Jordan river, forcing them back with water cannons, batons and tear gas, and injuring hundreds. On 26 October the Government released about half of the 300 protesters arrested during various demonstrations. More peaceful demonstrations were later held in Wahdat on 9 November and in Amman on 10 November.

On 19 November 2000 the Israeli Vice-Consul, Yoram Havivian, was injured when a gunman fired on his car in Amman, reawakening fear that the uprising in the Occupied Territories might spread to Jordan. Two previously unknown groups, the

Jordanian Islamic Resistance Movement for Struggle and the Group of the Holy Warrior Ahmad ad-Daqamsah (named after the Jordanian soldier who had killed seven Israeli schoolgirls three years earlier), claimed responsibility for the attack. As the Jordanian Government became increasingly nervous at the prospect of the al-Aqsa *intifada* spilling over into Jordan, Jordanian officials confirmed that the kingdom was working hard with Egypt and the PA to find a formula 'for ending the bloodshed' in the West Bank and Gaza Strip. The Jordanian Government was also eager for the unrest in the Occupied Territories to end for economic reasons. There was, for example, a major drop in tourism, Jordan's second largest source of foreign currency, after the outbreak of the al-Aqsa *intifada*. Officials estimated that 40% of bookings were cancelled, and many hotels that were normally full during the winter season reported low occupancy. Critics of the Government blamed the subsequent downturn on the fact that it had previously promoted Jordan as a tourist destination in conjunction with Israel, rather than on its own merit or as a 'package' with Lebanon and Syria.

Other than the economic losses blamed on the violence in the West Bank and Gaza, the Government had other worries that were heightened by the al-Aqsa *intifada*. The banning of all public demonstrations failed to solve the country's 'security problem'. Widespread calls for the closure of the Israeli embassy and the severing of all ties with Israel continued to be declared at rallies held behind closed doors. The impact of two shooting incidents against Israeli diplomats, a second attack having occurred on 5 December 2000, prompted the Israeli embassy to send families of its staff back to Israel, and drew applause from the popular anti-Israeli camp. Although the authorities did not arrest anyone involved, the Government condemned the incidents as 'aggression against Jordanian security' and warned that those responsible would be punished. Further pressure was brought to bear on the Government on 13 December when 14 deputies in the House of Representatives tabled a motion for an open debate to review Jordan's peace treaty with Israel. Their principal motive appeared to be to use the issue as a campaign platform for re-election amid the substantial increase in anti-Israeli and anti-US sentiments. The anti-normalization campaign led by the powerful professional syndicates was certainly strengthened by the unrest. In November 2000 the syndicates finally published their black-list of Jordanian 'normalizers' with Israel, apparently sensing that the Government would not make good its pre-uprising warnings to take legal action against them for 'infringing civil liberties' of individuals. Meanwhile, there were protests in Ma'an in southern Jordan—a city with few Palestinians but which has in recent years been at the forefront of protests against price increases of basic commodities—demanding the release of local people detained in connection with earlier anti-Israeli demonstrations. Hundreds of protesters, grouped in what they called the Islamic and Popular Forces in Ma'an, began an indefinite sit-in on 10 December, also calling for the severing of ties with Israel and for serious government action to combat corruption and nepotism. On 24 December King Abdullah made uncompromising comments about 'national unity' to the armed forces and Public Security Department, warning that he and his military would crush any attempt to destabilize the country's social fabric.

The traditional political antagonism between the Government and the country's powerful professional syndicates, which represent some 130,000 members, moved towards a climax on 27 January 2001, when the authorities broke into the homes of prominent members of the associations' joint Anti-Normalization Committee before dawn and arrested seven of them, including the Islamist President of the Committee and Secretary-General of the Jordan Engineers' Association, Ali Abu as-Sukkar. (However, all the trade unionists were released on bail, pending trial, at the end of February.) The syndicates' committee had directly challenged the Government by proceeding, on 22 January, with the publication of a list of 68 companies, two private schools, a hotel and various businessmen, artists and journalists alleged to have links with Israel. The syndicates had delayed the publication for two years to avoid confrontation with the Government, which had threatened to take legal action. On 24 January the Minister of the Interior, Dr Awad Khleifat, summoned the heads of the 13 trade unions and warned that the authorities were about to act. The confrontation also opened

the debate about the political role of the syndicates. Jordan's 80-seat House of Representatives demanded a special session on 4 February to debate the possibility of introducing legislation to curb significantly the syndicates' political activity. The lower house is dominated by tribal and pro-establishment figures, and the majority of deputies joined forces with the Government against the unions. Earlier, Prime Minister Ali Abu ar-Ragheb had decided to delay drafting a new election law, even though parliamentary polls were due to be held in November of that year. Officials indicated at this time that there would be no significant change to the current voting system or the configuration of constituency boundaries—which serves in effect to under-represent Jordanians of Palestinian origin, who are concentrated in and around Amman—until their long-term fate is determined in negotiations with Israel.

ARAB LEAGUE SUMMIT IN AMMAN

In late February 2001 King Abdullah met US Secretary of State Colin Powell in Amman and urged him to press for an end to Israel's closure of the Palestinian enclaves, to resume Washington's central role in the peace process and lift all US sanctions on Iraq. Increasing Jordanian involvement in the Palestinian–Israeli crisis was reflected in the hosting of the Arab League summit in Amman on 27–28 March. The Palestinian issue has almost always been the *raison d'être* of Arab summits, and was again to head the agenda when the members of the Arab League convened in the Jordanian capital. The Amman summit had taken place mainly because of popular Arab outrage at the events in the Palestinian territories and Iraq. The overall aim of the summit was to re-establish greater co-ordination between the Arab states and to express solidarity with the Palestinian cause. The fact that the summit met at all amounted to a victory for the majority of Arab states which sought unity and reconciliation: it was the first annual gathering since the Arab world was divided by Iraq's invasion of Kuwait in August 1990. It was also significant that the venue was Amman because the late King Hussein had strongly opposed the US-led military assault on Iraq, favouring instead an Arab diplomatic solution to the Gulf crisis. (In mid-February 2001 Jordan again condemned the air-strikes launched on Baghdad by US and British air forces.) Jordan, Egypt and Syria assumed responsibility for arranging the conference, and their leaders toured the region in order to secure a consensus on a 24-item agenda. Jordan's Minister of Foreign Affairs, Abd al-Ilah al-Khatib, stated that the summit's work would focus on the Arab-Israeli peace process, economic co-operation, and the modernization of the Arab League. In the event, however, the discussions were dominated by reconciliation efforts.

Although approaches to Israel among the Arab states differed, Jordan remained committed to the Oslo peace process. Confirming the US $1,000m. fund established by the Arab 'emergency' summit in Cairo of October 2000 in support of the *intifada*, the Amman summit agreed to transfer $40m. per month to the PA. Specific funds would be remitted for health programmes and welfare payments to the families of those killed and wounded during the al-Aqsa *intifada*. The Islamic Development Bank, responsible for the disbursement of the funds claimed to have delivered $23m. of the $1,000m. to authorities in the West Bank and Gaza, while Palestinians put the total at a mere $3m. Meanwhile, according to the UN, the Palestinian economy had sustained losses of $1,150m. Although the Arab states were more politically united than they were a year earlier, Arab leaders failed to come up with a policy to meet the very serious challenges they faced from Israel and the USA. The Amman gathering, however, did achieve a general consensus on all the issues discussed, with the exception of Iraq. Like previous Arab summits, it was impeded by the contradiction between each government's perception of its own interests and that of its population.

Despite a long and impassioned speech against Israeli Prime Minister Ariel Sharon by Syria's President Bashar al-Assad, on the whole this was a low-key summit; Arab leaders focused on practical matters and attempted to achieve pragmatic consensus. If its rhetoric was to be believed, the Arab League summit effectively redrew the old fault lines between the Arab world and Israel. Although Jordan and Egypt, the two Arab countries that have signed peace treaties with Israel, would not implement a formal break in diplomatic relations, both countries refused to return their ambassadors to Tel-Aviv and declared that there would be no new diplomatic contacts or commercial deals with Israel until it ended its campaign of repression against the Palestinians. The Amman conference also reaffirmed political 'red lines' not to be crossed by external powers if they wanted good relations with the Arab states, which committed themselves to suspending relations with any country that transferred its embassy from Tel-Aviv to Jerusalem. In essence, the final communiqué of the summit, the so-called 'Amman Declaration', reiterated the need for Arab countries to present a united front and called once again for the withdrawal of Israeli armed forces from all occupied land.

At the end of March 2001 it was reported that Jordanian and Egyptian officials had submitted a series of proposals for achieving peace in the Middle East to the USA and European Union; there was hope at this time that a joint Egyptian-Jordanian peace initiative might enable Israel and the PA to resume peace negotiations. During a meeting with President George W. Bush in Washington, DC, on 10 April, King Abdullah sought to persuade the US President to assume a more active role in the search for a lasting peace between Israelis and Palestinians. However, in early August a militant Islamist group claimed responsibility for the murder of an Israeli businessman in Amman, again leading to fears that the unrest in Israel and the PA-controlled areas was spreading to Jordan.

LEGISLATIVE ELECTIONS POSTPONED UNTIL 2002

On 23 April 2001 King Abdullah exercised his constitutional right to extend the current term of the House of Representatives by two years. Parliamentary elections had been due to be held in November. However, observers noted that the ongoing Israeli–Palestinian conflict had significantly affected Jordan's already difficult economic and political situation, and that the King had acted in order to prevent a serious challenge to his Government being mounted by Islamist opposition parties which had declared their intention to participate fully in the forthcoming elections (having boycotted the 1997 poll) and which were highly critical of the Government's failure to take a firmer stance against Israel. In early May 2001 large-scale public protests were held in Amman to mark the 53rd anniversary of the foundation of the Israeli state. The demonstrations met with a forceful response from the Jordanian security forces. On 16 June King Abdullah ordered the dissolution of the House of Representatives (which had been sitting in extraordinary session since April) and carried out a reorganization of the ar-Ragheb Government. Eleven new ministers were appointed to the Cabinet, although the key ministerial portfolios remained unchanged. On the following day King Abdullah informed the Government that it had one month in which to formulate a new electoral law.

The new electoral legislation drafted by the Government was ratified by King Abdullah on 22 July 2001. The principal changes to the existing law were a reorganization of electoral boundaries (the number of constituencies was to rise from 21 to 44) in order to increase the number of seats in the House of Representatives from 80 to 104, and a reduction in the voting age from 19 to 18. Although the Muslim Brotherhood had pressed for an increase in the number of deputies sitting in the lower house, the failure of the Government to reintroduce a system of electoral lists (which had existed prior to 1997) resulted in a threat by the Muslim Brotherhood to boycott the legislative elections. Two days later it was announced that the November elections would be postponed, probably until late 2002. At the end of August 2001 legislation was enacted imposing a ban on public gatherings and demonstrations. On 23 November King Abdullah appointed a new 40-member Senate upon the expiry of its term.

JORDAN FEARS LOSING OIL SUPPLY FROM IRAQ

By mid-2001 Jordan, battered economically by almost 10 months of Israeli–Palestinian conflict, was braced for another blow to its economy. As the first likely economic casualty should the US-driven 'smart' sanctions against Iraq proceed, Jordan was confronted by the risk of losing its entire oil supply from Iraq, as well as its main export market in the region. Under the proposed new sanctions regime (then being debated by the UN Security Council), although civilian trade with Iraq would be

relaxed, border checks for military or dual-use goods would be tightened. This would place extra responsibility on Iraq's neighbours in general and on Jordan in particular, as the Iraqi President, Saddam Hussain, threatened to cease trading with any country that helped to implement the new sanctions regime. Jordan's oil agreement with Iraq (see above) accounts for about one-third of Jordan's exports, and thousands of Jordanians depend on it for their livelihood. According to a World Bank report, replacing the Iraqi oil at market rates would cost between US \$750m.–\$1,000m. a year. The Jordanian Government was reported to have publicly declared its opposition to 'smart' sanctions, while privately assuring Western governments that it would accept them. In contrast, Jordanian public opinion was solidly behind Iraq, and the local newspapers carried many reports of what the new sanctions would entail. The Government was likely to defy public opinion and fall into line with the West, not least because its trade agreement with the USA, signed in October 2000, was at this time awaiting congressional approval. The UN Security Council was holding talks with Jordanian officials about compensating it for any losses incurred as a result of 'smart' sanctions, should these be adopted. (See the chapter on Iraq for fuller details of the 'smart' sanctions initiative.) Meanwhile, in early June 2001 the state airline, Royal Jordanian, resumed scheduled flights to Iraq for the first time since 1990. Discussions were held between senior Jordanian and Iraqi officials during early 2002; in January the two countries renewed their oil protocol and also agreed to the creation of a free-trade zone.

King Abdullah was unequivocal in his condemnation of the September 2001 suicide attacks against New York and Washington, DC, for which the USA held Osama bin Laden's al-Qa'ida network principally responsible, swiftly affirming his country's preparedness to join the USA's proposed international 'coalition against terror'. However, he emphasized that the forging of any such alliance must be linked to a renewal of efforts to resolve the Israeli–Palestinian conflict. Jordan was, furthermore, anxious that any US-led military offensive against alleged terrorist targets must avoid attacks against Arab countries, notably Iraq. King Abdullah, who travelled to Washington in late September to sign the bilateral trade agreement, was the first Arab leader to meet the US President after the suicide attacks; during his visit the King also held talks with the US Secretary of State, Colin Powell. The bilateral trade accord was fully implemented in early December.

ECONOMIC REFORMS

On 25 October 2001 King Abdullah gave Prime Minister Ali Abu ar-Ragheb a three-week deadline to draw up an 'integrated socio-economic' plan to improve standards of living and alleviate unemployment. King Abdullah's instructions to Abu ar-Ragheb to improve Jordan's economic performance were designed to lend credibility to the King's promises to his subjects since he assumed the throne in February 1999—namely that their economic conditions would witness substantial improvements. In October 2001 the King announced that he expected the reform programme to be part of the country's fiscal budget for 2002. However, like all legislation issued since the dissolution of parliament in June 2001, the Jordanian budget would not be subject to parliamentary scrutiny. Responding to King Abdullah's demands, on 27 October ar-Ragheb made some cosmetic changes to the Cabinet, with five ministers leaving and three joining the Government, in what was the second reshuffle in four months. The Prime Minister retained several ministers for what were clearly tribal and political considerations, but introduced two younger men: these were the Minister of Planning, Dr Bassem Awadallah, and the Minister of Industry and Trade, Salah al-Bashir. This led a group of 16 opposition parties, on 29 October, to criticize the cabinet changes as falling below expectations. The changes included the abolition of the Ministries of Information and of Youth and Sports, which were to be replaced by independent higher councils. On 28 October ar-Ragheb flew to Tokyo, seeking Japanese help for his economic plans. Japan is Jordan's largest single donor, holding 20% (US \$1,800m. dollars) of the kingdom's \$7,000m. foreign debt. Three days later the Prime Minister returned to Amman with pledges from Japanese officials that they would use their influence with the 'Paris Club' to partially relieve or reschedule Jordan's debts at lower interest rates.

SECURITY TRIALS AND DISPATCH OF TROOPS TO AFGHANISTAN

In the aftermath of the 11 September 2001 attacks, the Jordanian authorities ushered in new restrictions on the press (with tougher penalties for those found guilty of 'publication crimes'), apparently as the Government's latest weapon in its struggle against political dissent. Moreover, by late 2001 security trials had become frequent in Jordan, all of which involved radical Islamists. Jordanian officials were quick to point out that the country had been 'struggling against terrorism' since the 1950s and that security trials were not new in Jordan. Over the years hundreds of political activists, often referred to as 'terrorists', had been in and out of prison, and in and out of military courts, on charges of seeking to topple the Hashemite regime, plotting 'terrorist activities' and 'destabilizing the security' of the country. In recent years the threat to the Hashemite regime has been perceived as stemming from radical and militant Islamism. In early October 2001 King Abdullah issued a royal decree amending Jordan's penal code in order to strengthen counter-terrorism measures. A number of security trials assumed a higher profile after the 11 September attacks. The retrial of Raed Hijazi, a Jordanian-US citizen of Palestinian origin, received the most attention in the press, mainly because he was charged with belonging to al-Qa'ida and was included by the US Federal Bureau of Investigation on a list of wanted 'terrorists'. Hijazi had already been sentenced to death *in absentia* by the State Security Court in 2000, in a case involving 28 Islamists accused of planning 'terrorist attacks' and of having links to al-Qa'ida (see above); he had been detained in 2001 in Syria and extradited to Jordan. (Under Jordanian law a person convicted *in absentia* must be retried on return to the country.) In early February 2002 Raed Hijazi was sentenced to death for his role in the terrorist plot, although he was cleared of involvement with al-Qa'ida. The second security trial was that of 12 Jordanians and an Egyptian accused of belonging to an illegal group dubbed al-Khalaya (the Cell) and possessing and manufacturing explosives for illegal use as well as conspiring to carry out 'terrorist attacks' in Jordan. The third security trial was of three alleged Islamists accused of possessing explosives and plotting 'terrorist activities' in the Occupied Territories from bases in Jordan. In late April, after five months of legal proceedings, the State Security Court convicted four members of the PA security forces (two *in absentia*) on weapons and explosives charges, sentencing them variously to prison terms of between seven and 15 years, with hard labour, but acquitting them of planning terrorist attacks against Israelis in the West Bank. A fifth defendant was acquitted of all charges.

Jordan moved swiftly to restrict manifestations of opposition to the US-led military campaign against suspected al-Qa'ida bases and the Sunni fundamentalist Taliban regime in Afghanistan from early October 2001. Jordan also went so far as to send troops on a 'humanitarian mission' to the war-ravaged city of Mazar-i-Sharif in northern Afghanistan. One of the most controversial of several 'temporary laws' introduced by the Government since the dissolution of the House of Representatives in June 2001 was the rapid amendment in mid-November of the Armed Forces Law, after the Government decided to contribute to peace-keeping forces in Afghanistan. The 1964 Law was amended to provide legal cover for the deployment of Jordanian troops abroad, thus frustrating opposition plans to file a suit against the Government for violating Article 3 of the Constitution, which prohibits placing the life of Jordanian citizens in danger. (Jordan had apparently been in violation of its Constitution since 1989, when it began sending troops abroad, with 22,000 troops serving in 16 countries as part of UN peace-keeping operations.) However, the decision to send Jordanian troops to Afghanistan was heavily criticized by opposition parties as offering 'unconditional support' for the US-led war in Afghanistan.

CABINET RESHUFFLE FOLLOWED BY RIOTS IN MA'AN

In mid-January 2002 Prime Minister ar-Ragheb again submitted the resignation of his Government, but was asked by King Abdullah to form a new administration capable of initiating economic and social reforms prior to parliamentary elections. On 14 January a new 27-member Cabinet was formed by ar-Ragheb, with seven ministers being appointed and six leaving the Government. However, the only significant changes were a new Minister of Foreign Affairs, Marwan al-Muasher, who had served as Jordan's ambassador to both the USA and Israel, and a new Minister of the Interior, Qaftan al-Majali, who had formerly been Secretary-General of the same ministry. The cabinet reshuffle came only one day after the Government adopted its annual budget of JD 2,350m. dinars (US $3,300m.) for the first time without parliamentary approval since the 1989 legislative elections. The change of Government was largely symbolic, and was apparently designed to show that the regime was serious about holding parliamentary elections in 2002, after postponing them indefinitely in November 2001. In his letter of appointment to Prime Minister ar-Ragheb, the King entrusted him with the 'task of undertaking preparations for elections to be held at their constitutional date', adding that he expected the polls to be held with a 'high sense of transparency and utmost integrity so that they yield good fruits of democracy'. The King, whose dissolution of parliament had been followed by a series of controversial and often restrictive 'provisional laws', stated that 'short-lived and unexpected circumstances have brought about the absence of parliamentary life in Jordan', clearly referring to the Palestinian *intifada*. Both the King and Prime Minister confirmed that elections were to be held later in the year. It was not clear, however, whether the biggest and most influential opposition party, the Muslim Brotherhood's Islamic Action Front, which led 25 other opposition groups, intended to abandon its boycott of the electoral process—undertaken in 1997 in protest against the 'temporary' elections law that the Islamists, as well other leftists and pan-Arab nationalists, saw as guaranteeing legislative seats for tribal and pro-establishment figures. Although the number of parliamentary seats was raised from 80 to 104, the distribution of seats maintained the same ratio despite demands to increase the number according to demography rather than geography. Islamist leaders asserted they would require a 'neutral government' to oversee free and fair elections if they were to abandon their boycott.

Unrest in the southern town of Ma'an was the first test of the new Government. On 21 January 2002 a large number of people took to the streets of Ma'an, in another expression of rage after a local youth, Sulayman Ahmad al-Fanatseh, died in police custody. There were allegations of police brutality, although the authorities insisted that the boy had died of natural causes. The riots and violent confrontations with the police lasted for two days and resulted in the death of a policeman who was shot by unknown gunmen. As many as 15 people were injured, half of them police-officers. Although the new Minister of the Interior denied reports that al-Fanatseh had been detained for political or religious reasons, Islamist activists accused the authorities of using the unrest as a pretext to detain local Islamists and further to harass and stifle the Islamist opposition. Despite its small population (25,000 predominantly tribal residents with historic links to nearby Saudi Arabia), Ma'an has for years been a centre of political activism notably against the economic policies of the Jordanian regime. The violent riots in January appeared to stem from issues of poverty and high unemployment. Following the unrest, the Government announced that two investigations had been launched to determine the causes of both the adolescent's death and the subsequent riots.

CORRUPTION CHARGES AGAINST LEADING ESTABLISHMENT FIGURES

In late January 2002, apparently under orders from the King himself, the Government took legal action to investigate alleged corruption and fraud involving several leading establishment figures who had allegedly embezzled large sums of money and forged documents over the past four years to obtain credit facilities without sufficient guarantees. The affair, dubbed the 'credit facilities case', emerged in late January when Majid Shumayla, general manager of Global Business, a company providing computers and information technology to various government institutions, fled the country with tens of million of US dollars obtained from several banks in unsecured loans.

Shumayla had allegedly given the banks forged documents from the state-controlled General Intelligence Department—one of his clients—in order to obtain the loans. Other figures named in the press included a close associate of King Abdullah, Senate member Samih al-Batikhi, a former army general who had until mid-2000 served as the head of the powerful General Intelligence Department; al-Batikhi's former deputy and a former agriculture minister; Nasser Masaadeh, Shumayla's business partner and the son of a former interior minister; and Ali Husari, Chairman of the Export and Finance Bank, a son-in-law of former Prime Minister Sharif Zaid bin Shaker. In mid-February 2002 the Government referred the case to the State Security Court, and Samih al-Batikhi was arrested in mid-March. Despite the military prosecution's strict ban on coverage of the investigation, newspapers—apparently with clearance from the Government—published the full names of more than 100 individuals and firms being investigated, whose assets were put under 'precautionary seizure' and who were banned from travel. Investigations continued into one of Jordan's largest fraud cases.

WIDESPREAD PROTESTS AGAINST US AND ISRAELI POLICIES

In March 2002 the bloodiest violence yet in the almost 18-month-long Israeli–Palestinian confrontation sparked a new round of demonstrations and mass street protests in Jordan. Many mosques across the kingdom held prayers for Palestinians in the West Bank and Gaza, and Muslim preachers called for donations of blood to the wounded. The Jordanian authorities were swift to block opposition-led protests and demonstrations, on the grounds that these had not been authorized in advance. The authorities cited concerns that demonstrations might be used by opposition parties to challenge official intolerance towards public displays of anti-Israeli and anti-US sentiments.

Jordanian officials repeatedly stated that they could not accept any new influx of Palestinian refugees from the West Bank. Plans were already in place to close border crossings across the Jordan river to prevent any new influx of refugees from the Palestinian enclaves. Since the outbreak of the al-Aqsa *intifada* in September 2000, Jordanian police had frequently clashed with Islamist groups that took to the streets after the Muslim Friday prayers to protest against Israeli policies. In 2000 and 2001 Jordan had imposed tough laws banning demonstrations after public sympathy with the Palestinian uprising produced the largest street protests in Jordan in more than a decade. Yet on rare occasions the Government disregarded the demonstrations or allowed them to proceed in a gesture to public opinion. In March 2002, however, the authorities announced that organizers of demonstrations must apply for permits. On 9 March anti-riot police intervened to disperse a sit-in of solidarity with the Palestinian people and with Iraq outside the Iraqi embassy in Amman. However, the Muslim Brotherhood did manage to hold a march of 3,000 people on 8 March in the Baqa'a and Amman New Camp (Wihdat) Palestinian refugee camps and near the University of Jordan in Amman.

Public anger within Jordan was further fuelled by Israel's reoccupation of Palestinian-controlled population centres in the West Bank from late March 2002, provoking mass street protests in Jordanian cities, with many unlicensed rallies often ending after considerable use of force by Jordanian riot police, who resorted to tear gas, water cannons and beatings. On 29 March Jordanian riot police fired tear gas to control hundreds of stone-throwing Palestinians at an anti-Israeli march at the Amman New Camp which had erupted into violence. On 30 March, in the Palestinian refugee camp of Baqa'a, which is home to 120,000 refugees, thousands of youths and supporters of PA President Yasser Arafat, many carrying his picture, took to the streets inside the camp in a show of solidarity. The authorities had earlier deployed armoured troop carriers and positioned hundreds of riot police close to the major Palestinian refugee camps across the country. The clashes began when police blocked the path of Palestinians trying to march to a main street leading out of the Amman New Camp in an impoverished quarter of the city. Camp residents and disenchanted youths were venting their anger at the police for barring them from publicly displaying solidarity with their Palestinian kin on the other side of the Jordan river. Riot police and scores

of armoured vehicles dispersed several hundred worshippers after Friday prayers at a mosque close to the Israeli embassy in Amman, a scene of many past clashes. More than 1,000 students at the University of Jordan held a rally on 1 April, chanting pro-Palestinian slogans, burning Israeli flags and demanding that Jordan break off diplomatic ties with Israel. Riot police dispersed the students with tear gas and water cannons when they stormed the campus gates and tried to take their protest to the streets of the capital.

On the diplomatic front, on 30 March Jordan warned Israel not to harm Palestinian President Yasser Arafat, warning that its assault on his headquarters in Ramallah threatened to undermine the Israeli-Jordanian peace treaty. Jordanian officials stated that the Israeli military attack on Arafat's Ramallah headquarters was quickly pushing the region back to an 'atmosphere of war' that threatened to engulf the entire Middle East in more violence. The Jordanian news agency, Petra, reported that King Abdullah, one of the main Arab allies of the USA, had urged President George W. Bush to take urgent steps to force Israel to withdraw its troops from Ramallah and other Palestinian cities. Minister of Foreign Affairs Marwan al-Muasher added that Israel's offensive 'ran contrary to any spirit of peace that we are trying to promote in the region'. In early April there were reports that Jordan was considering expelling Israel's ambassador to Amman, David Dadon, in protest against Israeli attacks on the PA-controlled areas. Jordan (like Egypt) had recalled its ambassador to Tel-Aviv more than a year previously, in protest against Israeli policies in the Occupied Territories. Its embassy in Tel-Aviv was run by a chargé d'affaires as Amman delayed the dispatch of its designated ambassador, Abdullah al-Kurdi, in the early months of the Palestinian uprising. In early April al-Muasher summoned Dadon and warned him of unspecified consequences if Israeli troops did not immediately withdraw from the Palestinian territories and end the siege of Arafat's headquarters in Ramallah.

US Secretary of State Colin Powell made a brief visit to Amman on 11 April—the last stop in his Middle East peace mission before heading for Israel. Hundreds of Jordanians burned US and Israeli flags in Amman, protesting against Powell's visit. The growing popular pressure on the Jordanian Government to adopt a firm position and practical steps against Israel was apparently relayed to Powell by King Abdullah.

Calls for the Jordanian Government to sever diplomatic ties with Israel were thought unlikely to be heeded. The Government typically adopted a pragmatic approach, apparently hoping that the Israeli offensive would be short-lived and therefore that it would not have to act on its threats of severing diplomatic ties with Israel. However, when the Israeli offensive in the West Bank continued into its third week, and after international diplomatic efforts had failed to end the siege of Palestinian cities, Jordanian officials justified the Government's decision to maintain ties, asserting that it was aimed at keeping its 'channels open and to be able to deliver humanitarian assistance' to the Palestinians. Meanwhile, opposition parties and professional syndicates disregarded a government ban and planned a large demonstration near the Israeli embassy, in the affluent Rabiya area of Amman, for 12 April. To show his determination to stop such protests, Prime Minister Abu ar-Ragheb summoned opposition leaders to the Ministry of the Interior to warn them that the authorities were prepared to use all means at their disposal to prevent the rally from going ahead. King Abdullah, who had unexpectedly arrived at the meeting, was also reported to have warned the opposition parties that such a protest would 'destabilize national unity and security' and thus should not go ahead. As the opposition proceeded with its plans in defiance of the King, the authorities cordoned off the area within a 10 km radius of the planned venue, forcing the opposition to call off the rally in order to avoid a serious confrontation.

Thus, the Jordanian Government remained in a critical situation, between its dependence on its close relationship with Washington and its own public's anti-Israeli and anti-US sentiment. Undermining Israel's attempt to 'isolate' Arafat, Minister of Foreign Affairs Marwan al-Muasher met with the Palestinian leader at his Ramallah headquarters on 18 April 2002. On 19 May Prime Minister ar-Ragheb and al-Muasher met Arafat (who had finally been allowed to leave his compound at the beginning of the month) in Ramallah to discuss the stalled political process. Ar-Ragheb and al-Muasher also briefed Arafat on the outcome of talks which had taken place in Washington earlier in May between King Abdullah and US President Bush.

From mid-April 2002 the streets of Jordanian cities began to quieten as people returned to their daily lives, apparently unwilling to risk violent confrontation with the authorities or the disruption of their livelihoods. The streets around the Israeli embassy were cordoned off by barbed wire in late April, to deter would-be demonstrators from attempting to gather in the area after Friday prayers. Meanwhile, to silence domestic critics of its refusal to sever diplomatic ties with Israel, the Jordanian Government began to deliver humanitarian aid gathered in Jordan and in other Arab countries to the West Bank by truck and helicopters. King Abdullah announced that Jordan was opening up 'an air bridge' to the West Bank, and that aid for the Palestinians was pouring into his country from other Arab nations. Jordanian officials argued that had Jordan suspended ties with Israel, the Israelis would never have allowed it to distribute relief supplies to the Palestinians. Nor would the Israeli authorities have allowed a team from the Royal Medical Service of the Jordanian armed forces to set up makeshift field hospitals in Palestinian towns hardest hit by the Israeli offensive. The relief effort contributed to easing opposition to the Government's position. As the relief efforts continued, King Abdullah commenced a two-week trip to the USA on 1 May to lobby for US support to force the Palestinians and Israelis to return to negotiations.

JORDAN'S BUSINESS COMMUNITY AND CALLS FOR A BOYCOTT OF US PRODUCTS

As waves of condemnation of what was perceived as US support for Israeli aggression against the Palestinians swept across Jordan and the entire Arab world, the business community in Jordan appeared divided over the feasibility of a renewed call to boycott US products in protest against the Bush Administration's failure to act to halt the Israeli offensive in the Palestinian territories. The USA had been one of Jordan's major trade partners in the previous year, with bilateral trade amounting to some JD 444m. The US market was the largest consumer of Jordanian exports in 2001, purchasing goods worth JD 164m. These exports are mainly manufactured in one of Jordan's four Qualified Industrial Zones (QIZs): goods manufactured under a QIZ formula can access the US market quota free and duty free provided that a minimum 8% of their input is of Israeli origin. The USA was also the biggest exporter to the Kingdom, with goods to the value of JD 280m. sold to Amman in 2001. Jordan had also been one of the largest recipients of US Agency for International Development (USAID) funds over the past years. Apart from USAID and military assistance, Amman had benefited from an annual wheat donation programme worth several million dollars. While some Jordanian businessmen urged an immediate boycott of all items of US origin, others argued that such a drive should be well calculated and implemented within an Arab context in order to have a tangible effect on the US economy. In early April Jordan's Professional Associations' Council renewed the campaign it had launched soon after the outbreak of the *intifada* to boycott all US-made goods in protest against 'US bias towards Israel'. However, some Jordanian business executives conceded that the proposed sanctions would mean boycotting important goods, such as wheat and cigarettes, and would harm the national economy, while the fact that Jordan is a small market would mean that the impact of a boycott by Jordan alone would be minimal for the USA. Opponents of a boycott also considered that the Jordanian economy would suffer under a boycott of US goods since it would adversely affect Jordanian investors in US chains and importers of US goods

Jordan (like Egypt and Mauritania, both of which have relations with Israel) was absent from a session in late April 2002 of the Damascus-based Central Boycott Office of the Arab League. Arab officials failed to revive the moribund boycott of companies doing business with Israel but declared that the sanctions regime remained an important tool to deter Israeli military action against Palestinians.

STALLING ON PARLIAMENTARY ELECTIONS

On 30 May 2002 Prime Minister ar-Ragheb stated that his Government had finalized plans for 'free and transparent elections', but added that only King Abdullah had the constitutional right to call elections. The Jordanian Constitution gives the king the right to postpone elections indefinitely, but he also tends to rely on his government and advisors for recommendations prior to issuing decrees. Political critics, however, reacted by saying that the Prime Minister's remarks on the timetable for elections were aimed at 'silencing' their criticism over delays on calling elections, by linking their criticism of the Government with criticism of the King. The Prime Minister had recently said that an election date would be announced in July 2002, probably setting a date for November 2002. However, the Jordanian Government failed to make a clear commitment on this, with officials leaking information about 'other options'. These included another year's delay, recalling the House of Representatives which had been dissolved by the King a year previously, and even setting up an appointed 'consultative council', although the latter was ruled out by ar-Ragheb. Initially, when the Government decided to delay parliamentary elections, it cited 'procedural considerations', which it finally resolved. These procedures included a new and controversial provisional elections law that increased the number of seats in the lower house from 80 to 104, and the issuing of magnetic identify cards to every Jordanian citizen. The Government failed to provide justification for the continued delay, as stipulated by the Constitution. 'Extraordinary circumstances,' mainly 'regional tensions' such as the Palestinian *intifada* and Israel's onslaught on the West Bank, as well as President Bush's threat to attack Iraq, were the reasons cited by Jordanian officials for failing to hold parliamentary elections in November 2001. The authorities also sought to avoid issues embraced by the opposition, such as the revocation of the 1994 Jordanian-Israeli peace treaty and the censure of US policy on Iraq, from becoming the main focus of a general election campaign.

Moreover, since the dissolution of the Jordanian parliament a year previously there had been an increasing tendency on the part of Government to clamp down on criticism and opposition activities. Since then the Government had enacted more than 80 'temporary laws', including the threat of prison terms for journalists and individuals who criticized official policies, and a public assembly law that banned unauthorized public demonstrations. Earlier, on 16 May 2002, the State Security Court imposed on Toujan al-Faisal, once Jordan's only female legislator, an 18-month gaol sentence after finding her guilty on four charges of seditious libel 'deemed harmful to the dignity of the state'. The court also punished al-Faisal for having criticized Prime Minister ar-Ragheb via the Qatar-based television station Al-Jazeera as well as for distributing via the internet a letter to King Abdullah criticizing government policies. Al-Faisal—who was prosecuted under a 'provisional law' that not only barred criticism of officials, but also prevented defendants from appealing against a verdict in the State Security Court if the prison sentence imposed was shorter than three years—was the first women to be jailed for political reasons. However, al-Faisal was subsequently pardoned by King Abdullah. Although the President of the Jordanian Bar Association contested the Government's 'provisional laws' again in the Higher Court of Justice as unconstitutional, the Court has yet to issue its verdict on the issue.

In early July 2002 there were reports that some 10 Jordanians had been arrested in Amman, on suspicion of plotting to launch terrorist attacks on US and Israeli targets in the country. At the end of the month King Abdullah again urged the US Administration to show restraint towards Iraq, especially in the absence of any resolution of the Israeli–Palestinian conflict. (The King had, earlier in July, warned that Jordan would not allow its territory to be used by US troops to launch a military attack against Iraq.) In early August Jordan's relations with Qatar deteriorated after the Jordanian authorities announced a ban on broadcasts in Jordan by the Al-Jazeera television station, following criticism of the Government's foreign policy. The Jordanian authorities responded by summoning the Qatari ambassador and later withdrawing its ambassador to Qatar. In mid-August King Abdullah announced that legislative elections would be postponed until 2003, owing to the continuing instability in the region.

In late August 2002 Jordan and Syria signed an agreement under which Syria was to provide Jordan with water, in order to ease Jordan's problem of water shortages.

Economy

ALAN J. DAY

Having twice been completely disrupted by war between the Arab states and Israel (first in 1948, and then in 1967), Jordan's economy was again severely affected by a regional conflict during the Gulf crisis and hostilities of 1990–91. This latest dislocation of established patterns of trade, aid and labour migration had a negative short-term impact on the vulnerable Jordanian economy, but failed to produce the sustained downturn that was widely predicted at the height of the crisis. By 1992 a strong recovery was under way, and it was clear that the restored Kuwaiti Government's expulsion of large numbers of Palestinians in 1991 had (because these 'returnees' were relatively affluent) provided Jordan with a timely economic stimulus. For its part, the Jordanian Government had, by adhering closely to IMF-approved economic policies, exerted a strong stabilizing influence throughout the crisis and its aftermath. From September 1993 onwards, Jordan's planners had to modify all medium- and long-term forecasts to take account of the implications of the PLO-Israel peace agreement. A further radical reappraisal was prompted by the Jordan-Israel peace treaty of October 1994, the potential economic consequences of which were a major topic of discussion in Jordan in 1995. However, initiatives to strengthen regional economic co-operation were generally scaled down in 1996 and 1997, following the re-emergence of regional political tensions. By 1998 it was widely acknowledged that Jordan had derived only limited economic benefit from the peace process. Although its macroeconomic position remained strong, initial government claims of high economic growth in 1996–98 were revised sharply downwards in 1999, during which growth of 3.1% was achieved. A government campaign to attract new foreign investment to Jordan was compromised by the sharp deterioration in the regional security situation after September 2000. Nevertheless, healthy economic growth of around 4% was achieved in both 2000 and 2001.

In the 1948–49 Arab–Israeli War, Jordan acquired some 5,600 sq km of new territory—the large salient that juts out into Israel west of the Jordan river—and the country's population increased more than threefold. Before the war broke out, the population was perhaps 400,000. The number of those living on the West Bank of the Jordan river in the territory acquired in 1948 was well over 800,000. This territory was occupied by Israel in 1967, and perhaps 350,000 of the inhabitants fled to non-occupied Jordan. Jordan's 1979 census gave a total population for the East Bank of 2,100,019, which implied an annual growth rate between 1961 and 1979 of 4.8%. Natural increase accounted for 3.8% and immigration for 1.0%. The rate of growth in the mid-1980s was estimated at 4%. The population of the East Bank was officially estimated to have risen to 2,796,100 by the end of 1986, and to 3.9m. by 1992, the annual rate of increase in 1980–90 being 3.7%, compared with 4.3% in 1965–80. According to World Bank estimates, in 1990–2000 the annual rate of population growth was 4.4%. The population of the East Bank was officially estimated to be 5,182,000 at the end of 2001. Of the present population, some 34% reside in the capital Amman, while the cities of Irbid and Zarqa are also home to large numbers of Jordanians. The World Bank assessed the urban population proportion as 74% in 2000, compared with 61% in 1990. As a result of these levels of population increase in the major towns, water shortages are becoming one of the most severe of the country's economic problems. The absorption of the refugees of 1948 and of 1967 caused problems which were accentuated by ethnic, cultural and religious differences. Jordanians before 1948 were mainly Bedouin and mostly engaged in pastoral, and even nomadic, activities. They therefore had little in common with the Palestinians, many of whom established themselves in Jordan as traders and professional men. In June 2002 there were 1,679,623 Palestinian refugees registered with the United Nations Relief and Works Agency (UNRWA) in Jordan, and a further 626,532 in the West Bank. The vast majority of the country's inhabitants are Sunni Muslims, but about 6% are Christians, mostly Greek Orthodox. Jordan's December 1994 census enumerated a population of 4,139,458 in the East Bank area. The authorities did not release statistics on the number of Palestinians within this total, stating that it would not be in the national interest to do so. The categories listed in the published census results were 'Jordanians' (92.4%), 'Gulf returnees' (5.2%) and 'foreigners' (2.4%). The average rate of population growth between 1952 and 1994 was 4.7% per annum.

The loss of the West Bank of Jordan to Israel in the summer of 1967 created a whole series of new economic difficulties. The result was the loss not only of some efficiently farmed agricultural land, but also of a large part of the important and growing tourist industry, and the large sums in foreign exchange received from the people who annually visited the old city of Jerusalem and Bethlehem. Some of the immediate problems caused by the war of 1967 were met by aid from Arab countries, but Jordan's economic future, in the long term, obviously depended on the evolution of the Arab–Israeli dispute and of regional relations generally.

During 1979 and the early part of 1980, Jordan moved closer to Iraq in both political and economic terms. The war between Iran and Iraq, which began in September 1980, further strengthened this alliance, notably by increasing trade for Iraq through Aqaba. Towards the end of 1980, Iraq and Jordan signed agreements to confirm their closer economic links, which were strengthened by various trade and aid protocols in 1981, in which year Jordanian exports to Iraq increased to US $186.8m. (compared with $42.3m. in 1979). Owing to war-induced cutbacks in Iraq, Jordanian exports declined to $180m. in 1982 and to $72.9m. in 1983. At Jordan's proposal, an oil-for-goods barter system was instituted. This facilitated a rise in Jordanian exports to $176.5m. in 1984 and, after a further downturn in 1986–87 (owing to lower world oil prices and the continuing Iran–Iraq War), a further rise, to $216m., in 1989.

Jordan, its economy underpinned by foreign aid and by remittances from Jordanian workers abroad, enjoyed sustained economic growth from the mid-1970s into the early 1980s, although difficulties were encountered thereafter. Between 1974 and 1984 it had one of the highest growth rates in the world, with the East Bank region's GDP expanding, in real terms, at an average annual rate of more than 8%. In spite of the problems brought about by the conflicts with Israel and the uncertainty caused by the Iran–Iraq War, real GDP increased by 17.6% in 1980 and by 9.8% in 1981, but the growth rate slowed to 5.6% in 1982, 2.5% in 1983 and 0.8% in 1984. A major cause of this deceleration was the non-receipt of three-quarters of the special development aid of US $1,250m. per year that was promised to Jordan at the 1978 Baghdad Arab Summit Conference, which had condemned the Camp David accords between Israel and Egypt: of the seven Arab states party to the pledge, only Saudi Arabia honoured its commitments to Jordan in full. In consequence, the targets of Jordan's 1981–85 Development Plan were not attained, while in 1981 Jordan recorded its first current-account deficit for five years and continued to record deficits in 1982–85. These shortfalls, combined with Jordan's customary trade deficit (generally in excess of $2,000m. per year during the 1980s), obliged the Government to obtain new foreign development loans, which, in turn, assisted a partial recovery of GDP growth to 2.7% in 1985, 2.4% in 1986 and 1.9% in 1987.

Meanwhile, the annual rate of inflation had fallen steadily, from 12% in 1981 to 0% in 1986, but then rose steeply to 14% in 1988, in which year the national budget deficit increased to 24% of GDP. Moreover, the current-account balance, having recorded a small surplus in 1986, showed deficits of 7% and 6% of GDP in 1987 and 1988 respectively. Against this background, the Government submitted to the disciplines of the IMF in mid-1989, agreeing to a five-year structural adjustment programme aiming, by 1993, to bring inflation down to 7%, to reduce the budget deficit to 5% of GDP and to eliminate the current account deficit (see Budget, Investment and Finance, below).

Immediate slippage on these targets included, in 1989, a rise of inflation to 25% and a budget deficit still around 20% of GDP, compared with the IMF target of 12.4%. Nevertheless, the current account recorded a surplus of US $335m. in 1989 and the Government was able to conclude interim debt-rescheduling agreements with its major foreign creditors. Jordan's foreign debt remained high, at $8,400m. in early 1990, but by then the Government believed that economic prospects had improved; inflation was running at only 8%, the budget deficit was on course to fall and substantial GDP growth was expected. Moreover, exports, particularly of vegetables, were buoyant, while remittances and foreign aid were expected to exceed budgeted figures. This relatively hopeful scenario was, however, changed dramatically by the onset of the new Gulf crisis in August 1990.

AFTERMATH OF THE 1990–91 GULF CRISIS

At the time of Iraq's occupation of Kuwait, in August 1990, Iraq was Jordan's principal trading partner, taking at least 23% of Jordan's exports and supplying more than 80% of Jordan's petroleum. Total adherence by Jordan to the UN sanctions against Iraq, imposed by Security Council Resolution 661, therefore threatened the whole basis of Jordan's already troubled economy. On 25 August the Jordanian Ministry of Transport issued a circular stating that Jordan adhered to UN Security Council Resolution 661, but Jordan continued to import oil from Iraq by road tanker. Indeed, following the cessation of Saudi Arabian oil deliveries in late September, Jordanian imports from Iraq increased, until the outbreak of hostilities in the Gulf, in mid-January 1991, forced Jordan to find alternative suppliers and also to introduce petrol rationing (see Mining, Minerals and Energy, below).

Loss of trade with Iraq was not the only problem facing Jordan's economy as a result of the Gulf crisis. Remittances from Jordanians working in the Gulf states (estimated at JD 470m. in 1989) dwindled to almost nothing as activity in Kuwait slowed or ceased, and business in the other Gulf states became affected. Moreover, many of these Jordanians returned to Jordan, as did thousands of Palestinians with Jordanian passports, raising the level of unemployment to 30%, increasing the population by 10% and putting an additional strain on health and education budgets. A further problem was the passage of thousands of migrants through Jordan, many of them attempting to return to the Indian sub-continent and South-East Asia. According to Jordanian officials, about 470,000 foreigners fled to Jordan in the five weeks following the Iraqi invasion of Kuwait. Many of these, particularly non-Arab Asians, remained stranded in overcrowded camps on the Iraqi–Jordanian border, suffering severe privations, while awaiting repatriation. Conditions improved in early September, as new camps were established and chartered aircraft carried some of the refugees to their countries of origin.

Official Jordanian statistics showed that other negative effects of the crisis included a rise in inflation to more than 16% in 1990 as a whole and a nominal GDP growth rate of only 1.1%, which, according to the IMF, amounted to a fall in real terms of 7.9%, while gross national product (GNP) fell by 4% in nominal terms and by 17% in dollar terms. According to a survey published by the UN Children's Fund (UNICEF) in March 1991, nearly one-third of the Jordanian population were living in poverty (defined as a family income of less than JD 86 per month), compared with 20% before the crisis. Because of the crisis, disbursements to Jordan, under the IMF stand-by facility and under an associated US $150m. World Bank structural loan, were suspended from September 1990. Subsequent negotiations resulted in a new agreement with the IMF in October 1991, through which Jordan was to undertake a

seven-year economic reform programme (1992–98) and as part of which the 1992 budget envisaged a reduced deficit and GDP growth of 3% compared with 1% in 1991 (see Budget, Investment and Finance, below).

Having weathered the 1990/91 crisis and its immediate aftermath with the help of external emergency aid, Jordan experienced an unexpectedly strong recovery in 1992, prompting a radical reappraisal of the medium-term economic outlook. The effective fiscal deficit, estimated to have equalled 14% of GDP in 1991, was cut to about 6% of GDP in 1991 (when domestic revenue exceeded current expenditure for the first time in Jordan's history), while GDP increased by 10.1% in real terms in 1992, as against 1.6% in 1991. The return of some 300,000 Palestinians, expelled by Kuwait in 1991, brought new capital resources into Jordan and helped to boost construction activity to 220% of its 1990 level by 1992, with consequential growth in many related areas of the economy. As UN sanctions against Iraq continued into a third year, it was clear that Jordan's external trading position had not been undermined to the extent that many 'worst-case scenarios' had predicted.

While acknowledging in mid-1993 that serious structural problems remained, including an external debt burden equivalent to 140% of GDP (down from 200% of GDP in the late 1980s) and an unemployment rate of around 25%, Jordanian ministers and business leaders were generally optimistic about the prospects for continued progress in meeting IMF economic targets. The IMF subsequently extended substantial new assistance to support the process of structural reform, while Jordan's main creditors arranged a major debt rescheduling package. In addition, a new Five-Year Economic and Social Development Plan, drafted for the period 1993–97, provided for a major extension of the private sector through the privatization of state enterprises, objectives which were redefined under a further Five-Year Plan for 1999–2003 and in a Plan for Social and Economic Transformation published in November 2001 (see Budget, Investment and Finance, below).

The World Bank estimated Jordan's gross national Product (GNP) in 2000 at US $8,360m. on a conventional exchange-rate basis, or $19,310m. using the World Bank's purchasing-power parity (PPP) index (USA = 100); GNP per caput was $1,710 on the former basis and $3,950 on the latter. Gross domestic product (GDP) in 2000 was estimated at $8,340m. on the conventional basis (and GDP per caput at $1,668), and at $19,380m. at PPP (and GDP per caput at $3,876). Jordanian figures gave nominal GDP in 2001 as JD 6,259m. and GDP per caput as JD 1,208, compared with JD 5,912m. and JD 1,173, respectively, in 2000.

According to World Bank figures, real GDP grew by an average annual rate of 7.6% in 1990–95 and by 3.0% in 1995–2000. The rate of growth was 3.1% in 1999 and 4.0% in 2000, although GDP per caput was static in 1999 and grew by only 1% in 2000. Despite the worsening regional crisis and the international economic downturn after the 11 September 2001 suicide attacks on the USA, GDP growth of 4.2% was recorded in 2001, in which year GDP per caput increased by about 3%. Unemployment was officially given as having averaged 13.4% in 1999, 13.7% in 2000 and 14.7% in 2001, but was unofficially estimated to be twice as high, with as much as 30% of the population living on or below the poverty line. Since the mid-1993 revision of government planning targets (which coincided with increased concern that privatization progress was too slow) some state assets have been sold and other projects have progressed, although there is still a considerable lobby against the foreign ownership of Jordanian industries. The accession of King Abdullah in February 1999 gave new impetus to economic reform, as did Jordan's admittance to membership of the World Trade Organization (WTO) in April 2000. Moreover, the appointment in June of a new Government under the premiership of Ali Abu ar-Ragheb, who came from a strong private-sector background, indicated that the country's pro-reform 'camp' had gained the ascendancy over entrenched conservative forces. The economic ministerial team remained in place in a major reshuffle carried out in January 2002 following adoption of the 2002 budget, which provided for a reduction in the fiscal deficit and aimed to combat unemployment and poverty. The Government also remained committed to co-operation with the International Monetary Fund (IMF) to bring about structural economic reform, including further privatization of state-owned industries.

THE REGIONAL PEACE PROCESS

A wide-ranging economic co-operation agreement between Jordan and the PLO was signed in Amman on 7 January 1994 to provide a framework for future approaches to specific issues 'as the peace process progresses'. It was agreed in principle that trade, investment, industry, agriculture, energy, water, electricity, telecommunications and private-sector enterprises were all fields of activity in which Jordan might be expected to co-operate closely with a developing PLO administration. It was predicted that Jordan could develop new trade flows of the order of US $250m.–$500m. per year if Israel relinquished its dominant role in the Palestinian market.

On an issue of immediate concern to Jordan, the agreement in principle confirmed the Jordanian dinar as legal tender in the West Bank, gave the Central Bank of Jordan (CBJ) supervisory powers over Jordanian banks operating in the West Bank, and set up a joint Jordan-PLO committee to co-ordinate financial policy in the Occupied Territories.

A follow-up meeting in May 1994 re-examined the outlook for Jordanian-Palestinian co-operation in the light of a recently signed Israeli-Palestinian economic agreement, which gave the Palestinian economy a measure of independence from Israel. The latter agreement's provision for the creation of a Palestine Monetary Authority (PMA) had raised many questions in Jordan about the PMA's role and intended relationship with the CBJ. Jordan maintained that CBJ supervision of banking in the Occupied Territories was essential as long as the Jordanian currency was in use, in order to preserve control over the expansion of credit and ensure proper regulation of the money supply in Jordan. However, economists at the Palestinian Economic Council for Development and Reconstruction (PECDAR) insisted that the PMA must assume a genuinely influential position within the regulatory process, and that key issues of bank licensing, currency management and payments administration should be examined in great detail before any binding agreements were concluded. Other topics discussed at this inconclusive meeting included trade, tariffs, tourism, transit rights and private Jordanian investment in the Occupied Territories.

In January 1995 a Jordanian-Palestinian co-operation protocol was signed under which agreements were to be drawn up in areas of economic policy, trade, finance, banking, education, cultural affairs, transport, telecommunications, information and administration. Under the protocol the Palestinian (National) Authority (PA) undertook to accept the Jordanian dinar as legal tender in all official and private dealings and to use it 'to the fullest degree possible, pending the issue of the new Palestinian currency'. Neither Jordan nor the PA would 'under any circumstances enforce any sudden unilateral monetary policy that would undermine the monetary stability and the economic security of either country'.

In March 1995 the PMA and the CBJ completed guide-lines for an agreement on banking supervision in the West Bank and the Palestinian self-rule areas. Drawn up in consultation with the IMF, the guide-lines confirmed the CBJ's predominant supervisory role in the self-rule areas until such time as the PMA developed its own expertise, while in the West Bank the CBJ's role would become liable to review in the context of any future Israeli-Palestinian agreement on a transfer of power. By the end of May 1995 seven Jordanian banks were operating a total of 32 branches in Gaza and the West Bank and others were in the process of establishing a presence. The level of direct local lending was as yet relatively low, partly because it was difficult for banks to organize loan security in the absence of a land registry and an established judicial framework, and it remained common practice for Palestinians with access to collateral in Jordan to obtain loans from bank branches within Jordan.

In May 1995, as 'a first step towards a free-trade agreement', a detailed Palestinian-Jordanian trade accord was signed after three months of talks in which officials were obliged to heed the terms of an Israeli-Palestinian accord of April 1994 limiting the number of products the Palestinians could import from Jordan. The May 1995 accord covered trade in about 50 products,

including cement, steel and electrical products. The Palestinians were permitted to export 25 categories of product to Jordan free of customs duties and import fees and another 25 free of customs duties only, all the products being ultimately subject to Jordan's sales tax. About 50 Jordanian product categories were exempted from Palestinian customs duties but were subject to the levies payable on locally produced products. In the first two months after the signing of the accord, Palestinian-Jordanian trade was worth about US $8m. In June 1995 Jordan and the PA signed an agreement guaranteeing freedom of movement by land and air for nationals and vehicles from both sides (although in practice control over the border between Jordan and the West Bank remained in Israel's hands at this time).

The Jordan-Israel peace treaty signed on 26 October 1994 included a number of economic provisions. Each country recognized the other's 'rightful allocation' of water resources from the Jordan and Yarmouk rivers and the Araba groundwater source and agreed to co-operate in the management and development of existing and potential water resources. Economic relations were to be normalized by removing discriminatory barriers and ending economic boycotts, and talks 'aimed at establishing a free-trade area' were to be organized at an early date. There was to be free cross-border movement of nationals and vehicles, and talks were to be held about the building of a highway between Egypt, Jordan and Israel near Eilat. Arrangements on freedom of navigation and access to seaports were to be normalized, a civil aviation agreement was to be drawn up, and an international air corridor was to be negotiated. Both countries would work for the creation of a Jordan Valley development master plan. Talks would be held on the joint development of the towns of Aqaba and Eilat, including the interconnection of their electricity grids. Co-operation agreements would be drawn up covering tourism, posts and telecommunications, environmental issues, energy, health and agriculture.

Agreements on border crossings, tourism and security were initialled in February 1995 and agreements on agriculture, energy and the environment in May. Topics covered by the draft energy agreement included the transit of neighbouring states' oil and gas, trade in oil and gas products, and exchange of information on oil exploration. Negotiations on trade were deadlocked in mid-1995 because Jordan and Israel disagreed over the wording of a preferential trade agreement. Israel favoured an agreement incorporating a stated goal of free trade within 12 years, whereas Jordan did not at this point wish to commit itself to a specific timetable for achieving free trade, preferring to defer a decision until a preferential trading system had been in operation for three years.

An annex to the October 1994 treaty specified that Jordan should receive 215m. cu m of water per year from resources currently controlled by Israel and outlined means of achieving this aim. A joint Jordan-Israel water committee began to meet weekly from November of that year, when it agreed to prioritize the building of a 3.3-km pipeline to transfer up to 30m. cu m of water per year from Lake Tiberias (the Sea of Galilee) in Israel to the King Abdullah canal in Jordan. The newly completed pipeline was brought into operation on 20 June 1995. It was agreed in February 1995 to initiate a feasibility study for a dam on the Yarmouk river which would restrict the annual flow of water to Israel from this source to 25m. cu m, leaving the remainder available to Jordan. Also under consideration was a scheme to build a storage facility and conveyer system at the confluence of the Yarmouk and Jordan rivers. In 1996 Israel delivered a total of 31.5m. cu m of water (1.5% of Israel's water supply) to Jordan. A commitment to build a desalination plant to the west of Lake Tiberias to treat salty spring water remained unfulfilled in mid-2000 because of difficulties in drawing up an agreement on the division of financial contributions and operational responsibilities. Under an interim arrangement introduced in May 1997, Israel began pumping fresh water to Jordan in lieu of the projected supply from the delayed desalination plant. In early September 2002 the two countries signed a preliminary agreement to construct a pipeline in order to transport water from the Gulf of Aqaba to the Dead Sea.

Israel and Jordan signed a transport agreement on 16 January 1996 which included provisions for the direct transfer of goods from Jordan to the Palestinian territories and for Palestinian access to the port of Aqaba. Agreements relating to the normalization of other aspects of Jordanian-Israeli economic relations (including definition of the maritime boundary at the Gulf of Aqaba) were signed on 18 January. Commercial air services between Jordan and Israel began in April, as did tourist bus services, with public bus services starting up in the following month and road haulage of goods in late June. In 1996 Israel exported US $12.25m. worth of goods to Jordan and imported $7.75m. worth of goods from Jordan. Israeli and Jordanian ministers met in June 1997 to discuss border-crossing problems and other obstacles to trade. In September, in a measure which was designed to reduce non-tariff barriers between the two countries, Israel announced a doubling of its quota of cement imports from Jordan, to 30,000 metric tons per year.

At further high-level meetings in March 1998 Jordan and Israel agreed to expand co-operation in the development of water resources and storage facilities in the Jordan Valley, to accelerate plans for the inter-connection of the electricity grid between Aqaba and Eilat, and to develop joint solar and wind energy projects. The two sides also agreed to examine joint tourism projects in the Wadi Araba and Umm Qais regions, and the feasibility of a canal between the Red and Dead Seas. Bilateral trade between Jordan and Israel in 1997 was valued at US $31m. by Jordan, and at $32.5m. by Israel. In 1998 bilateral trade was estimated at $40m. and the value of joint ventures at $300m.

Following a US $11m. expansion, the four-lane Sheikh Hussein Bridge crossing between Jordan and Israel, 50 km south of Lake Tiberias, officially opened in August 1999, and in the following month Jordan and Israel undertook to revive plans for a joint airport at Aqaba. In December Israel proposed a major $1,000m. cross-border development project to link Aqaba with the Israeli resort of Eilat and to use a former mined area and adjoining waters for construction of conference and entertainment facilities and several floating hotels. In May 2000 Israel agreed to implement the 1996 agreement to allow direct transport of goods between Jordan and the Palestinian self-rule areas, ending the 'back-to-back' system requiring goods to be transferred from Jordanian to Palestinian lorries at border points, and vice versa for goods moving in the other direction. The new arrangements required lorries travelling to the West Bank and the Gaza Strip to return to Jordan within 14 and 20 hours respectively. The imposition of stringent Israeli controls on the borders of the Palestinian self-rule areas after September 2000 hampered the flow of exports from Jordan. The Jordan Cement Factories Company (JCFC) diversified into new export markets in the Red Sea region in 2001, in order to offset the increasing difficulty of supplying its Palestinian markets. A new four-lane bridge and 8-km feeder road connecting Jordan to the West Bank was opened to traffic in May 2001. Financed by a Japanese government grant, the bridge (replacing a single-lane crossing point) had a capacity of 12,000 vehicles per day. However, as the security situation in the West Bank deteriorated in 2001–02, the new link was frequently closed by reoccupying Israeli forces.

AGRICULTURE

The loss of the relatively fertile West Bank in the 1967 war, and subsequent events on the East Bank, caused major disruption to the agricultural sector, which was compounded by severe drought conditions from 1974 to late 1979. In the 1980s, however, major investment in irrigation, particularly in the Jordan Valley, began to show results, and agricultural output increased by an average of 6% per year in 1980–88, owing mainly to the rapid expansion in the output of vegetables and of dairy and poultry products, much of it exported. Whereas the 1981–85 Five-Year Plan had originally envisaged a decline in agriculture's share of GDP from 8.5% to 7.2%, non-attainment of industrial growth targets in that period, combined with greater emphasis on agricultural expansion in the 1986–90 Plan, in fact resulted in agriculture's retaining an average 10% share of GDP through the 1980s, although the proportion later fell to 8% in 1990, and to less than 7% in 1991 and 1992. Under the 1986–90 Plan, increases in the output of cereals, red meat and dairy produce were the major targets, and spending on agricultural projects was estimated at JD 337m. (about 10% of total investment), supplemented by JD 130m. for dam construction and JD 105m. for irrigation. A specific objective was to reduce the

share of food imports (mainly cereals) in domestic consumption, which in the late 1970s had risen to 66% and in the late 1980s remained above 50%. In the 1980s migration away from the agricultural sector reduced its importance as an employer within the economy: in the late 1970s approximately 18% of the labour force were employed in agriculture, but by the late 1980s the proportion had declined to 10%. Just over 4% of the labour force were employed in the sector in 2001, while agricultural output (including hunting, forestry and fishing) contributed only 2.2% of Jordan's GDP in 2000 (compared with 8% in 1980). According to the World Bank, during 1990–2000 agricultural GDP decreased by an annual average of 2.0%.

A contrast can be drawn between the rain-fed upland zone (comprising about 90% of the cultivable land) and the irrigated Jordan Valley, which, since 1973, has been subject to its own development plan. As a result of irrigation and the production of high-value crops, the productivity of the Jordan Valley is far higher than that of the uplands, where cultivation is concentrated mainly on wheat and barley. Before the Jordan Valley Development Plan, only about 10% of the country's land was considered suitable for cultivation because of the low rainfall and vast areas of desert or semi-desert. The Jordan Valley, with its more favourable sub-tropical climate and available water, has been intensively exploited by small farmers who, using plasticulture and drip irrigation, obtained huge increases in production (particularly of fruit and vegetables). The development of irrigation in the Jordan Valley began in 1958, and between then and 1963 work on the East Ghor canal, carrying water from the Yarmouk river and running parallel to the Jordan, added about 120,000 ha to the country's irrigated area. The installations were severely damaged by Israeli bombardment in 1967 and repairs were not carried out until after the 1970–71 civil war. Stage I of the Jordan Valley Development Plan, funded by a great variety of foreign aid bodies, finished at the end of 1979. Irrigation projects centred mainly on the extension of the East Ghor canal and the Zarqa river complex. The King Talal dam was constructed between 1972 and 1978, the East Ghor canal extended between 1975 and 1978, and the Zarqa Triangle Irrigation Project finished in 1978. Other irrigation works include the Hisban Kafrein project, constructed between 1976 and 1978, and the North-East Ghor complex. Many of the irrigation projects undertaken in the second stage of the Plan have been completed or are under implementation. Projects under way include the construction of the Wadi al-Arab dam, the raising of the King Talal dam, the extension of the 98-km East Ghor main canal, and the irrigation of 4,700 ha in the Southern Ghor (see below). The Jordan Valley Development scheme is, however, more than just a complex of irrigation projects, and includes the development of transport links, grading, packing and marketing centres, the development of schools and health centres, and also a housing programme. The use of plastic tunnels, greenhouses and drip-irrigation has greatly expanded within the valley and by 1978 6,000 dunums (1 dunum = 1,000 sq m) had plastic tunnels and 741 dunums had greenhouses. Most of the JD 42m. allocated to agricultural development in the 1976–80 Five-Year Plan was to be used for development of the valley. As well as irrigation, crop-raising has also been improved by the introduction of special strains of seed, inorganic fertilizers and mechanization.

Attempts to alleviate the critical problems of water supply, highlighted by severe drought in 1984 (the worst for 37 years), have been given high priority by the Government. In 1983 work started on the US $50m. project to raise the height of the King Talal dam by 16 m to 108 m. This has increased the capacity of the dam to 85m.–90m. cu m and, in addition to the construction of a 2.5-MW hydroelectric power station, has enabled 8,200 ha to be irrigated. Following the discovery of a major artesian well, estimated to be capable of producing 75m. cu m of water per year, at al-Muhaibeh in the north during 1982, an 11.6-km canal was rapidly constructed to take the water to join the East Ghor canal at Adasiya. This was opened in March 1983 at a cost of JD 3m. South Korea's Hanbo Corpn, who built this canal, also constructed a dam of 20m. cu m capacity in the Wadi al-Arab as part of the Wadi al-Arab irrigation project, which began in early 1986 to increase the irrigated area between Wadi al-Arab, the Yarmouk river and the Jordan Valley by 2,800 ha.

The Water Authority of Jordan was established in 1984, and JD 521.7m. of the 1981–85 Development Plan budget was allocated to increase the irrigated area by 180,000 dunums. One of the major schemes for the 1980s was to have been the construction of the Maqarin dam and an associated hydroelectric power station on the Yarmouk river. However, plans for the dam were deferred. Under the 1986–90 Plan, an additional 114,000 dunums (11,400 ha) were to be brought under irrigation in the Jordan Valley, the Southern Ghor and the Wadi al-Arab. The Maqarin dam project was revived in 1988 as the al-Wahdeh ('Unity') dam and hydroelectric power station scheme, a joint Jordanian-Syrian venture to build a dam 100 m high on the Yarmouk river, to store 225m. cu m of water for drinking, irrigation and electricity generation. Plans were finalized in September 1988, but concern was subsequently expressed that, whereas the cost of building the dam was to be borne exclusively by Jordan, water stored therein was to be used to irrigate both Jordanian and Syrian land and 78% of the electricity to be generated by the dam was to be taken by Syria (see below).

Programmes initiated in 1991 included the North Ghor Conversion Project, involving the conversion of 7,300 ha in the Jordan Valley from surface to pressurized irrigation (with a consequential 20% water saving) at an estimated cost of US $25m.–$30m., of which 80% was to be provided by Japan. Final preparations were under way in 1993 to implement a programme to raise the storage capacity of the Kafrein dam on the Jordan river, from 4.3m. cu m to 7.5m. cu m, and to construct new dams at Walah, Mujib, Karameh and Tannour. The overall goal of this programme was to create a total of 115m. cu m of additional storage capacity by 1996, at an estimated cost of over $200m. The Kafrein dam project, and an associated scheme to reduce leakage from irrigation canals, was expected to bring an additional 1,830 ha of land into cultivation. In early 1992 a series of contracts for water projects included the Marhib wells scheme, involving the pumping of water from the wells to the existing Marhib and Awaja reservoirs and to a projected new reservoir at Berain. There was a further project to research water-harvesting at Muwaqar, east of Amman.

Describing the water supply outlook in early 1993, the Secretary-General of the Water Authority of Jordan said that 60% of current supply came from groundwater reserves, mainly in the desert areas in the east of the country; that farmers currently used two-thirds of Jordan's total water supply; and that the total supply was expected to increase from 550m. cu m per year to 700m. cu m per year during the decade 1990–2000, over which period the underlying level of annual demand was expected to rise from 900m. cu m to 1,600m. cu m, necessitating increasingly harsh restrictions on water use (already rationed for up to seven months of the year). He added that there was considerable scope for improving the efficiency of water use in the agricultural sector (e.g. by discouraging diversification into water-intensive crops like bananas, which currently provided farmers with higher profit margins than crops requiring far less irrigation).

Details of Jordan's water development strategy to the year 2011, published by the Government in November 1997, listed 61 projects, involving total investment of some US $5,000m. The strategy was based on a projected growth in water consumption from 1,450m. cu m in 1995 to 1,720m. cu m in 2010, of which agriculture would account for a constant share of 1,088m. cu m. A figure of $5,000m. would need to be invested in new projects to relieve the water deficit which was estimated to rise from 501m. cu m in 1995, to 559m. cu m. by 2000 and 620m. cu m by 2010. New projects cover the entire water chain. The Southern Ghors integrated project is the largest scheme to improve water collection, costing $139m.; the three-dam project (Mujib, Tannour and Walah) and the weir diversion at Mujib will provide water for Dead Sea industrial and tourist projects and irrigation in the southern Jordan Valley. The management of Greater Amman's water and wastewater networks (which cater for over 35% of Jordan's population) was contracted out to the private sector in April 1999.

The projected Jordanian-Syrian al-Wahdeh dam on the Yarmouk river came nearer to fruition in May 2000 when pre-qualification bids were submitted for the US $220m. construction contracts, about half of the required funding having been pledged by the Islamic Development Bank and Gulf aid donors. Tendering international companies were required to work in partnership with Jordanian and Syrian contractors so that they obtained about 50% of contract values. Further delays ensued as the al-Wahdeh specifications were revised because of a decline in the Yarmouk's flow; however, the project was again put out for tender in April 2002. In the same month, after a decade of deliberations on the project, a shortlist of five groups was drawn up for the $625m. contract to build a 325-km pipeline to bring 100m. cu m of high quality water per year to Amman from some 65 wells to be sunk into the Disi aquifer in the south of the country. The main contract for the Disi project, which the Government hoped would solve most of Jordan's domestic water supply shortages, was expected to be awarded in October 2002. Other major water development projects being actively pursued at mid-2002 included the rehabilitation of the Amman water supply network, to reduce the estimated 50% loss of production currently being suffered; a $150m. wastewater treatment plant at Kherbet as-Samra, capable of supplying 270,000 cu m of water per day; and a $70m. desalination scheme to purify brackish water from the Hisban aquifer close to Amman. All the active projects involved private-sector participation. The Government also drew up plans to combat the illegal tapping of underground water reservoirs, which was believed to deprive the network of up to 250m. cu m a year. Official figures gave available water resources at the end of 2001 as around 1,000m. cu m a year, leaving an annual water deficit of about 220m. cu m, which was predicted to reach 250m. cu m by 2010. In advancing expensive schemes for new water development, Jordanian planners have been encouraged by an authoritative calculation that the cost of new desalinated water would be one-thousandth of the cost to the consumer of the imported bottled water currently bought by Jordanians in large quantities.

Cereals, fruit and vegetables are the mainstays of Jordan's agriculture. Production levels vary widely, depending on the prevailing weather conditions. For example, after 1974 (a record year) yields of wheat and barley (which is used as animal fodder) were severely reduced, owing to drought, so that by 1979, despite similar areas being under cultivation, wheat production on the East Bank fell to what was then a record low of only 16,500 metric tons. As a result of the rains in November 1979, there was a great increase in the cultivated area and, following the excellent harvest produced in 1980, the Government banned imports of wheat, barley and lentils, and paid farmers almost double the normal price for imports. Field crop production rose appreciably from 32,400 tons in 1979 to 204,000 tons in 1980. In January 1980 the King Talal dam was full for the first time since its completion in 1978. In addition, the heavy rainfall also replenished depleting groundwater resources. Towards the end of 1980 grain storage was also greatly improved with the opening of new silos at Aqaba, with a storage capacity of 50,000 tons. However, the 1981 harvest was 60% down on that of 1980, with a wheat production of 50,600 tons and barley, 19,200 tons. The 1982 harvest was generally worse, and production in subsequent years continued to fluctuate as conditions alternated between rainfall and drought. Following favourable winter rains, annual production of wheat reached 80,000 tons in 1987/88 and in 1988/89. Although this was a relatively high yield, compared with the all-time low of less than 10,000 tons in 1983/84, it was still less than one-quarter of Jordan's annual requirement of 450,000 tons, which by 1990 had risen to 500,000 tons. The barley crop reached 40,000 tons in 1988/89, compared with an all-time low of 3,500 tons in 1983/84. Jordan continued to rely heavily on imports of food, which cost about US $400m. per year. Wheat consumption reached 627,000 metric tons in 1993 (50% higher than in 1988), owing partly to the increase in population after the Kuwait crisis and partly to Jordan's low bread prices.

The loss of the West Bank had a serious effect on cereal production, but its effect on fruit and vegetable cultivation was disastrous, removing some 80% of the fruit-growing area and 45% of the area under vegetables, and depriving Jordan of an important and expanding source of some of its major export commodities. Production of fruit and vegetables on the East Bank fluctuated widely in the 1970s, partly because of the weather and partly as a result of political instability. However, the general trend recently has been for increases in fruit and vegetable production, particularly in citrus fruits, tomatoes, melons and cucumbers. Between 1973 and 1986, overall vegetable production increased by 149%, fruit production by 546% and field crops by 88%, according to the US Agency for International Development (USAID). Under the 1986–90 Plan, up to 200,000 dunums (20,000 ha) of government land in southern and eastern Jordan were to be cultivated for the first time to produce cereals, forage and red meat, while output of fruit was set to increase as areas planted since 1979 began to produce. Increases in fruit and vegetable production, however, were not matched by a corresponding development in the areas of sales and marketing. The country was also faced with the problem of excessive production of tomatoes, cucumbers and aubergines, which cost the Ministry of Agriculture substantial sums each year in support for growers who could not sell their produce. In early 1985 the Ministry introduced an optional cropping system for irrigated vegetable growing. Under the system, farmers could be fined if they exceeded their allocation of tomato production, and the maximum production of tomatoes for 1985 was fixed at 242,000 metric tons, 158,000 tons less than production in 1984. Emphasis has been placed on the growing of other crops and Jordan is now self-sufficient in potatoes and 80% self-sufficient in onions. The establishment of a government-owned public marketing organization (the Agricultural Marketing and Processing Co) to handle agricultural produce, which had been decided on in March 1983, was achieved in 1984.

Production of fruit and vegetables increased in the late 1980s, as did exports, especially after the devaluation of the currency in 1988. Moreover, the signature of the Iran-Iraq cease-fire agreement of August 1988 led to a rapid expansion of deliveries to Iraq, Kuwait and other Gulf markets. A record 522,000 metric tons of vegetables were exported in the 1989/90 season, and a further record of 650,000 tons had been anticipated in 1990/91, before trade was disrupted by the latest Gulf crisis in August 1990. The value of vegetable exports in 1991 was JD 43.5m., compared with JD 36.8m. in 1990 and JD 27.9m. in 1989.

In a crisis-induced move to increase domestic agricultural production, the Government decided in November 1990 to offer unused state-owned land for lease at a rent of JD 1 per dunum. Another measure affecting farmers was the enactment, in December 1990, of a law specifying that women could inherit only half as much land as their brothers could, rather than an equal share. The Government explained that equal shares for women, which had been guaranteed under legislation dating from the Ottoman period, was contrary to Islamic law.

The Jordanian Minister of Agriculture stated in January 1993 that dependence on uncertain rainfall patterns had helped to engender a 'low-risk' approach to farming, and that higher levels of productivity could be achieved if Jordan improved its standards of resource management. Endorsing the findings of a policy study drawn up with FAO assistance, he accepted that there had been excessive state regulation of agriculture in the past, and that farmers' interests would be better served if the Government devoted itself more to broad policy-making and co-ordination. He advocated a further shift from cereals into the growing of 'off-season' vegetables for export; criticized the spread of restrictive trade policies in many export markets; and proposed an expansion of local food-processing capacity to provide new market outlets for farmers, particularly those producing highly perishable commodities.

The aggregate value of agricultural output rose from JD 213.3m. in 1995 to JD 232.9m. in 1996, and to JD 250.5m. in 1997. Among field crops, production of wheat increased to 58,500 metric tons in 1995 but fell to 42,700 tons in 1996, while barley production fell to 29,200 tons in 1996 (from 31,700 tons in 1995). Of the vegetable crops, production of tomatoes fell sharply from 439,700 tons in 1995 to 291,300 tons in 1996, whereas output of melons, potatoes and cucumbers remained relatively stable in 1996, at 106,400, 95,200 and 74,200 tons respectively. In the tree fruits' category, citrus fruits remained the most important, with production of 133,100 tons in 1996, followed by olives, at 88,600 tons. Under the livestock heading, output of eggs totalled 726m. in 1996 (compared with 871m. in 1994 and 715m. in 1995); milk production increased to 165,100 tons (from 147,000 tons in 1995); and poultry-meat output fell to 100,000 tons (from 107,000 tons in 1995). The value of Jordan's exports of agricultural produce (including oil and fats) rose from JD 224.5m. in 1996 to JD 268.0m. in 1997, with live animals and vegetables forming the two largest categories. Imports of agricultural produce (including oil and fats) were

valued at JD 636.3m. in 1997, significantly less than the 1996 value of JD 759.6m.

Land under permanent crops was only about 1% of the country's total area in 1998 (compared with 0.4% in 1980), of which 18% was irrigated (compared with 11% in 1980). The cultivated area devoted to field crops rose to 1.7m. dunums in 1998 (from 1.3m. dunums in 1990) and the area bearing trees to 846,500 dunums in 1998 (from 545,500 dunums in 1990). In 1999 the worst drought for decades resulted in the lowest cereal harvest since records began. According to official figures, the production of wheat fell to 9,300 metric tons and that of barley to 4,900 tons, sufficient to meet less than 1% of domestic consumption (instead of the normal 10%) and creating a need for cereal imports of some 2m. tons in the 1999/2000 marketing year. Production of citrus fruits and olives also fell sharply, to 85,600 tons and 38,300 tons respectively, although output of other fruits and of most vegetables, meat, milk and eggs were not seriously affected, and in some cases increased compared with 1998 figures.

Official figures gave agricultural production in 2000 as follows: wheat 25,000 metric tons, barley 12,000 tons, maize 19,000 tons, tobacco 2,700 tons, lentils 1,100 tons, clover 61,900 tons, tomatoes 354,300 tons, melons 69,000 tons, cucumbers 135,600 tons, potatoes 97,100 tons, cauliflowers and cabbages 38,300 tons, eggplants (aubergines) 35,700 tons, courgettes 49,500 tons, citrus fruits 124,700 tons, olives 134,300 tons, apples 37,500 tons, bananas 20,800 tons, grapes 23,900 tons, peaches 6,900 tons, milk 204,600 tons, poultry meat 118,500 tons, red meat 15,100 tons, eggs 752m.

MINING, MINERALS AND ENERGY

In a country short of natural resources, Jordan's mineral wealth lies predominantly in its phosphate reserves, which are estimated at more than 2,000m. metric tons, providing the country with its main export commodity and accounting for 24.5% of export value in 1987. The proportion was 40% in 1983 but later returns were affected by the low world price for phosphates. Jordan is the fifth largest producer of phosphate rock, after the USA, the (combined) countries of the former USSR, Morocco and the People's Republic of China, and the third largest exporter, after Morocco and the USA. The mining and marketing of phosphate is handled by the Jordan Phosphate Mines Company Ltd (JPMC). The expansion of the phosphate industry has been a major element in successive Development Plans. Quantities of uranium and vanadium are now known to be mixed in with the phosphate reserves. There are also known to be deposits of good-quality copper ore at Wadi al-Arab. Other minerals include gypsum, manganese ore, abundant quantities of glass sand and the clays and feldspar required for manufacturing ceramics. Foreign investors have been found to finance the establishment of companies to produce ceramics and sheet glass and also to exploit potash deposits in the Dead Sea.

The Arab Potash Company Ltd (APC), formed in 1956 as one of the earliest Arab joint ventures, is 52.8% owned by the Jordanian Government. The company was reconstituted in 1983 and produced 486,868 tons of potash in 1984, its first full year of operation, selling 450,000 tons, worth US $36.4m. In 1990 the APC recorded its first profit (of JD 39.6m.) since it began commercial operations in 1983. In 1996 the annual capacity of the APC's Ghor as-Safi extraction plant on the Dead Sea totalled 1.8m. tons, comprising 1.4m. tons of hot leach capacity and 400,000 tons of cold crystallization capacity. It was planned to add a further 200,000 tons of cold crystallization capacity by 1999. In 1996 the APC made a net profit of JD 34.2m. on sales of JD 131.3m. Production in that year totalled 1.76m. tons. The company's main markets in 1996 were India (27.5% of sales); the European Union (19.7%); the Republic of Korea (9.3%); and Malaysia (9%). In 1998 the APC reported a net profit of JD 24.1m. (42.4% more than in 1997) on sales of JD 119m. and production of 1.5m. tons. In 1999 the APC declared a profit of JD 31.6m. from production of 1.8m. tons and sales of 1.7m. tons, which included $185m. in exports. Total potash output in 2000 was 1.94m. tons. Having included the APC on a list of state enterprises to be privatized, in June 2002 the Government initiated the sale of a 26% stake in the company; expected to bring in JD 83m., the sale would result in the APC being owned as to 67.2% by private interests.

The Jordan Safi Salt Co (Jossco, set up in 1996 by Jordan Dead Sea Industries Co, an APC subsidiary) started production in mid-1997 with a capacity of 1.2m. metric tons of industrial salt and 45,000 tons of table salt per year. It was the largest salt producer in the Middle East, with exports of around 550,000 tons in 2000. Qatar Vinyl Company was due to begin imports of 250,000 tons per year of industrial salt from Jossco in November 2001, under a five-year contract signed in 2000.

In 1999 APC started a four-stage expansion project to increase its basic potash production capacity to 2.4m. tons per year by 2004, with stronger foreign participation in its activities. A new 100,000-tons-per-year industrial potash plant began production in early 1999, preceding the commission of a new granular potash plant. Other projects include Jordan Bromine, a 50-50 joint venture with Albermarle Holdings of the USA, to establish a US $120m. plant at the Dead Sea (the world's richest bromine lake) to produce bromine-based products. Another joint venture was finalized in June with Finland's Kemira Agro for a $100m. facility to produce 150,000 tons per year of potassium nitrate and 75,000 tons per year of dicalcium phosphate at Aqaba. APC's subsidiary, Jordan Magnesia Co, has signed an $80m. contract with a Canadian-Turkish joint venture for 'turnkey' construction of a magnesium oxide plant at Numeira. The APC holds a 20% interest in a joint-venture project set up in 1993 in partnership with a Japanese consortium (60%) and the JPMC (20%). The production capacity of the Nippon Jordan Fertilizer Co plant at Aqaba is 300,000 tons of compound fertilizers and ammonium phosphates per year.

Rich beds of phosphates exist at Rusaifa, a few km north-east of Amman, and, from 1963 onwards, were exploited by a local company financed partly by the Government. Other deposits in the Wadi Hasa area, south of Amman, have been developed by US and Italian interests, and phosphates are also produced at Wadi al-Abyad. For many years production was centred on these three sites. However, in mid-1985 the JPMC was forced to close its Rusaifa mine because of falling demand for low-grade phosphate. In the longer term, the industry will focus on a major new, low-cost, mine at Shidiya, near Ma'an, in the south-east, which the JPMC is developing in two stages. The Shidiya mine has proven phosphate reserves of 1,200m. metric tons, and started production in the second half of 1988.

In 1968 the country's total production of natural phosphates was 1,162,000 metric tons, more than five times the production in 1956. By 1976 annual production exceeded 1.76m. tons. Export earnings from phosphates, constant in 1974 and 1975 at JD 19.5m., declined to JD 19.2m. in 1976. This was due to a fall in the international price of phosphate rock and prompted Jordan in 1976 to join with Morocco, Tunisia and Senegal in an association of phosphate exporters. In 1985, when the Rusaifa mine was closed, output totalled 5.92m. tons. At the beginning of 1986 the JPMC secured a 10-year contract with Thailand to supply 650,000 tons of phosphates per year. Phosphates output rose to 6.25m. tons (exports 5.2m. tons) in 1986 and 6.7m. tons (exports 5.7m. tons) in 1987. Production in 1988 was 6.5m. tons (exports 5.5m. tons). Revenue from exports of phosphates amounted to US $262m. in 1988, compared with $176m. in 1986. In 1989 the JPMC exported 6.4m. tons of phosphates and reported profits of JD 107.2m., but in 1990 exports decreased to 4.9m. tons and profits to JD 41.4m. (compared with a target of JD 108m.). While the Gulf crisis contributed to this decline in 1990, its major cause was a sharp fall in demand in Eastern Europe, exports to which were only 580,000 tons, compared with 2m. tons in 1989. By 1992 the JPMC's phosphate exports amounted to only 4.26m. tons (out of its total production of 5.2m. tons), although the company's share of the shrinking world market was, at 15.2%, slightly higher than before. The value of exports in 1992 was JD 206.1m. ($300m.), while the JPMC's net profit was JD 16.1m. In 1993 the JPMC recorded a loss of JD 20m., but was able to achieve a profit of JD 2.3m. in 1994 after reducing stock levels and introducing cost-cutting measures. In 1995 the company made a profit of JD 4.1m. on sales of JD 237m. Its largest phosphate export markets in 1995 were India (1.2m. tons), Indonesia (543,000 tons) and the Netherlands (448,000 tons). In 1996 the JPMC made a net profit of JD 15.8m. on sales of JD 254m. In April 1997 JPMC shareholders approved a plan to raise $100m. through the international capital markets in order to finance part of the cost

of a $250m. expansion programme at the Shidiya mine. In 1998 the JPMC reported a net profit of JD 5.1m. on total sales of JD 255m., compared with a net profit of JD 4.1m. on total sales of JD 245m. in 1997. The increase in sales came despite the downturn in the Asian economies, and the largest market was India, taking 33% of exports. The JPMC produced 5.82m. tons of rock phosphate (of which 3.74m. tons were exported) in 1998. In 1999 output rose to just over 6m. tons, but the JPMC recorded a net loss of JD 21.7m. The JPMC's annual loss increased to JD 127.9m. in 2000, in which year phosphate production fell to 5.51m. tons.

A major restructuring programme, under which up to 1,500 of the JPMC's 6,500 personnel were offered early retirement, resulted in the company recording a profit of JD 2.1m. in 2001. In February 2001 the JPMC announced that its accumulated debts (totalling JD 350m.) were to be significantly reduced through the conversion into shares of a government loan, worth JD 104.3m, taken out at the time of its purchase of Jordan Fertilizer Industries Company in 1986 (see below). In June 2001 the Government announced a target date of late 2002 for the privatization of the JPMC, a development that was welcomed by local financial analysts who had strongly criticized the company's management practices in recent years. A 50% limit on foreign ownership of Jordanian mining companies was removed in February 2001.

Allied industries form an important part of Jordan's industrial development programme. A US $400m. phosphate fertilizer plant south of Aqaba began production in June 1982. The 1981–85 Five-Year Plan allocated JD 15m. to the development of the plant. It was designed to produce 750,000 metric tons of diammonium phosphate and 105,000 tons of phosphoric acid per year, but has failed to produce to more than 65% of its phosphoric acid capacity. The original project, which was managed by the Jordan Fertilizer Industries Company (JFIC), cost $410m. and included an aluminium fluoride plant with an annual capacity of 12,000 tons, which entered production in mid-1984. The JFIC made a JD 12.9m. loss in 1984, its first full year of trading, owing to a slump in world fertilizer prices; production reached 568,968 tons, of which 524,900 tons were sold. However, in 1986 the JPMC bought the JFIC (which had accumulated losses of JD 40.3m. by the end of 1985) for JD 60m. A loss of JD 1.3m. at the Aqaba plant in 1992 was attributed by the JPMC partly to depressed world prices (blamed on dumping by US and Russian producers), and partly to the plant's high staffing level. The JPMC's plans for future 'downstream' development centred on joint ventures with foreign partners who would provide investment funds and guarantee long-term export markets. The Indo-Jordan Chemicals Co (a joint venture with India's Southern Petrochemical Industries Co and Saudi Arabia's Arab Investment Co) opened a 224,000-tons-per-year phosphoric acid plant at Shidiya in 1997. Jordan's total production of fertilizers in 2000 was 619,500 tons.

Jordan is almost wholly dependent on imports of crude petroleum for its energy needs. Its main sources, before the onset of the Gulf crisis in August 1990, were Iraq and Saudi Arabia, the former having replaced the latter as Jordan's main supplier in the late 1980s. In November 1984 a Ministry of Energy and Mineral Resources was created, and in the following month the Government announced a plan to double investment in oil exploration, following oil strikes in the Azraq area on the border with Iraq and Saudi Arabia, and to reduce oil consumption by cutting oil subsidies and by increasing the prices of electricity and petroleum-based products. However, no commercial oil discoveries were made in the late 1980s, while production from the Azraq area declined to 315 barrels per day (b/d) in 1988 and to only 40 b/d by mid-1990. Over this period the cost of imported oil declined in relative terms, owing to reductions in world prices and to the availability of Iraqi oil at preferential prices. Jordan's proven reserves of crude petroleum at end-2000 totalled only 890,000 barrels.

Output of petroleum products from Jordan's only oil refinery, at Zarqa, increased steadily from 445,800 metric tons in 1970 to 748,000 tons in 1974, and to 1,114,600 tons in 1976. Production capacity was scheduled to reach 3.5m. tons per year by the end of 1979. This would have been more than sufficient to satisfy Jordan's domestic requirements. In 1980 the refinery, in fact, produced only 1,760,000 tons, but by 1982 it had an output capacity of 3m. tons per year (60,000 b/d). Between 1982 and 1984, maximum daily throughput was raised to 12,300 tons (about 86,000 b/d), an annual capacity of about 4.3m. tons. In 1985, when the refinery's capacity was raised to 5m. tons (100,000 b/d), output rose to 2.6m. tons, compared with 2.3m. tons in 1984. Of this total, 1.8m. tons came from Saudi Arabia and 698,600 tons from Iraq. In addition, 10,000 tons of liquefied petroleum gas (LPG) and 395,000 tons of fuel oil were imported from Iraq for domestic needs. Under an agreement designed to relieve pressure on reserves of foreign exchange, Jordan imported from Iraq, in payment for goods, about one-sixth of its crude oil requirements in 1984 and 395,000 tons of fuel oil in 1985. Imports of crude petroleum amounted to 2.5m. tons, averaging 48,743 b/d, in 1988. Of this, 33,415 b/d was imported from Iraq and 15,000 b/d from Saudi Arabia.

In an attempt to reduce petroleum imports, attention has been given to the possibility of exploiting the estimated 40,000m. metric tons of shale oil deposits (containing about 4,000m. tons of oil) in southern Jordan. In the early 1980s Technopromexport of the USSR carried out an oil-shale survey at Lajjoun, but no production resulted from this exercise. In 2001 a Canadian company, Suncor, was finalizing plans to develop the Lajjoun deposits using a distillation process. In its first phase (with an estimated cost of US $400m.) the proposed Suncor project would have an initial production capacity of 17,000 barrels of oil per day, with the potential for expansion to 210,000 b/d. A separate project to develop shale oil resources at Sultaneh was outlined by the Ministry of Energy and Mineral Resources in November 2000, when companies were invited to submit 'build, own, operate' plans for a power plant with between 100 MW and 300 MW of generating capacity, to be fired by a direct combustion process incorporating fluid-bed technology. The Government's target date for bringing this type of power plant into operation is 2007. The deferment, in 1985, of plans to construct a pipeline to convey crude petroleum from Iraq to Aqaba contributed to the decision to renew an agreement to receive Saudi Arabian crude petroleum, via the Trans-Arabian Pipeline (Tapline), at the Zarqa refinery. Originally constructed in the 1940s as the principal means of exporting Saudi oil to the West via Jordan and the port of Haifa, the Tapline had been diverted to Sidon, Lebanon, following the creation of Israel in 1948, but had been used exclusively to transport oil to Jordan after the closure of the Lebanese section in 1983. At the outbreak of the Gulf crisis in August 1990, Jordan was importing more than 80% of its oil requirements from Iraq, with almost all the remainder coming from Saudi Arabia. When Jordan, in late August, announced its acceptance of the UN trade embargo on Iraq, Saudi Arabia pledged itself to supply at least half of Jordan's oil needs through Tapline. However, Jordan's reluctance to apply the UN embargo resulted in Saudi Arabia's suspension of all oil supplies to Jordan in late September (the official reason given was non-payment of outstanding oil bills of US $46m.). Jordan accordingly became entirely dependent on Iraqi supplies by road tanker, which rose to some 60,000 b/d by mid-January 1991. The start of hostilities then resulted in the virtual cessation of such supplies, obliging Jordan to impose petrol rationing and to conclude emergency agreements to import oil from Yemen and Syria (at a higher price than the preferential rate charged by Iraq). In April 1991 it was announced that Iraqi supplies to Jordan would be resumed, but the after-effects of the war in Iraq inhibited normal trade for some time. Official Jordanian figures, issued in April 1991, showed that Iraq had supplied 86% (2.3m. metric tons) of Jordan's oil imports in 1990, and Saudi Arabia 13.2%, and that the Zarqa refinery had processed 2.7m. tons in the year, an increase of 11% over the 1989 level. (See Foreign Trade and Balance of Payments, below, for the subsequent development of Iraqi-Jordanian oil trade.)

In March 1995 the Government approved the establishment of a National Petroleum Company (NPC) to be owned by the Jordan Investment Corpn (JIC). The JIC would contribute JD 2m. of working capital, while the new company would take over ownership of JD 18m. worth of oil and gas exploration and production equipment from the National Resources Authority. Half of the Government's US $10m. per year revenues from the ar-Risha gasfield (see below) would be used to fund the new company's initial activities. The company would function as an independent entity, with no government involvement in day-to-

day management, and would be free to co-operate with foreign oil companies. State investment in hydrocarbon exploration in Jordan in the period 1980 to 1994 had amounted to $300m. In March 1996 two US companies, Andarko Petroleum Corpn and Trans Global Resources, signed agreements to explore for oil and gas in Jordan. In February 1997 another US company, Union Texas Petroleum, reached an agreement with Andarko to take a 50% interest in Andarko's 4.2m. acre Safawi exploration block in north-eastern Jordan. In August 2000 five hitherto unallocated exploration blocks were made available to bidders on improved production-sharing terms (allowing cost recovery from 70% of initial production, with the Government having a half-share in the remaining 30% of initial production and in the full amount of subsequent production). In October 2000 Star Petroleum (United Kingdom) and Black Rock Petroleum (Australia) jointly acquired exploration rights in northern Jordan, while Dauntless Oil (Canada) acquired rights in the south of the country.

Proposals were announced in the first half of 1995 to develop a 250,000-b/d export refinery at Aqaba, to be located in a free zone and financed and operated by foreign investors, with the Government receiving a royalty on exported oil and a discount on prices of any refined products supplied to Jordan. Following the withdrawal of a US company which had signed a preliminary agreement in 1996, new bids were invited in 1997 for a modified scheme with 210,000 b/d of capacity, to be developed on a 'build-own-operate' basis. The Jordan Petroleum Refining Company (JPRC), whose monopoly rights to supply refined products within Jordan were valid until 2008, announced in 1997 that it planned to upgrade and expand its Zarqa refinery. It was estimated that an investment of $500m. would be required to diversify the refinery's product range and increase its total capacity to 140,000 b/d by 2002. In August 1999 the NPC was divided into two separate entities, the Petra Drilling Company being established as a commercial enterprise which would be privatized to take better advantage of local and regional contract opportunities, while the NPC would concentrate on gas production and exploration.

The discovery of reserves of natural gas at locations around ar-Risha in north-east Jordan in 1987 and 1988 encouraged speculation that the deposits would be sufficient to satisfy a significant proportion of Jordan's future energy requirements. By 1989 gas from the new discoveries was fuelling a 60-MW electricity generating plant at ar-Risha, which is connected to the main grid by a 220-km high-voltage transmission line. Total generating capacity at the ar-Risha plant (which uses diesel as its secondary fuel) was doubled to 120 MW in 1993–94. About 10%–13% of Jordan's national electricity supply was generated at ar-Risha in the late 1990s. The results of a review of the ar-Risha gasfield completed in April 2000 were generally disappointing, effectively ending hopes of a major increase in domestic gas production in the short term. Nevertheless, the NPC expressed confidence in the field's potential and in March 2002 entered into a joint venture with Golden Spike of Indonesia for the further exploration of the southern part of ar-Risha. Jordan's end-2001 reserves of natural gas totalled 6,400m. cu m. Gas production in 2000 was around 306m. cu m (all of which was utilized for electricity generation).

In early June 2001 Jordan concluded an agreement with Egypt for the supply of Egyptian gas via a proposed high-capacity export pipeline, which Egypt hoped to extend in subsequent years to supply gas to Syria, Lebanon, Cyprus and Turkey. It was envisaged that sales of Egyptian gas to Jordan would begin in 2003 at an initial rate of 1,100m. cu m per year. In the longer term, it was envisaged that the pipeline would carry 10,000m. cu m of gas a year from Egypt, to be used by Jordan to develop new industrial capacity in the north of the country. Its short-term priorities were to convert the main Jordanian power station at Aqaba to enable it to use Egyptian gas; to convert the diesel-fuelled Rehab power plant to combined-cycle technology; to secure the implementation of an independent power project (see below) which had been delayed pending a decision on the supply of gas; and to develop local gas distribution pipelines to serve these and other facilities.

A link between the Egyptian and Jordanian electricity grids (the first phase of a regional inter-connection project supported by the Arab Fund for Economic and Social Development) was completed in March 1999, at a cost to Jordan of $80m. A link between the Jordanian and Syrian grids was inaugurated in March 2001. In September 1996 the Jordan Electricity Authority was superseded by the state-owned National Electric Power Company (NEPCO). In January 1999 NEPCO was divided into three separate companies (for generation, transmission and distribution) under the 1996 Electricity Law, which also provided for an industry regulatory body and for the encouragement of private-sector participation in future power generation projects. The name NEPCO was retained by the transmission company, which was to remain in state ownership, whereas the generating company (Central Electricity Generating Co—CEGCO) and the distribution company (Electricity Distribution Co—EDCO) were both included in privatization plans announced by the Government in 2000. In that year Jordan's total installed generating capacity was 1,530 MW and its total output of electricity was 7,210m. kWh. The three largest power stations were at Aqaba (650 MW), Zarqa (397 MW) and Rehab (160 MW). A contract to install 100 MW of additional generating capacity at the Rehab plant was awarded in June 2001. The Belgian company Tractebel began negotiations with the Jordanian Government in November 1999 for a 'build-operate-transfer' (BOT) agreement to establish an independent private-sector power station at Kherbet as-Samra, near Amman. It was hoped that the announcement in May 2001 of a project to import gas from Egypt (see above) would enable the Kherbet as-Samra project to be finalized. Its planned generating capacity of between 300 MW and 450 MW was expected to be needed by 2004 if electricity demand grew at the forecast rate of 6.4% per year.

MANUFACTURING AND INDUSTRY

Manufacturing industry, which is almost entirely of recent origin, is concentrated around Amman (following the loss of the Nablus industrial centre on the West Bank in 1967). During the 1976–80 Plan period it experienced an average growth rate of 13.6% per annum, which was only one-half of the planned rate. Moreover, the targets of the 1981–85 Plan period, during which manufacturing and mining were, together, expected to achieve an annual growth rate of 17.8%, fell even further short of being achieved. By 2000, according to World Bank estimates, industry (including mining, manufacturing, construction and power) contributed 25% of GDP. During 1990–2000 industrial GDP rose by an average annual rate of 4.7%. The GDP of the manufacturing sector increased by an annual average of 5.4% over the same period. Industrial investment in 1993 totalled JD 271m., up from JD 161m. in 1992, and remained buoyant in the first half of 1994, helping to allay Jordanian concern about the possible diversion of new investment to the West Bank and Gaza. The majority of factories produce food products, clothing or consumer goods but the major industrial income derives from the three heavier industries—phosphate extraction, cement manufacture and petroleum refining.

Cement production reached 964,300 metric tons in 1981. Within the 1981–85 Plan, 37% of the money allocated to mining and manufacturing was set aside for four cement projects, including the construction of a cement works in the south, at Rashidiya. The existing plant at Fuheis, near Amman, owned by the Jordan Cement Factories Company (JCFC), has undergone an expansion, bringing its capacity up to 4.2m. tons per year. By the end of 1983 the first production line at the South Cement Company (SCC) works at Rashidiya was completed, and the second line was finished in the autumn of 1984, giving a total plant capacity of 2m. tons per year. The production of cement, having declined to 793,400 tons in 1982, rose in each of the subsequent three years, reaching 2,023,000 tons in 1985. Local demand rose by 5% in 1987, to 1.6m. tons. In 1987 and 1988 Egypt agreed to buy 750,000 tons of cement annually from Jordan. Total exports, which reached 800,000 tons in 1987, increased to 1m. tons in 1988. The struggling SCC merged with the JCFC in September 1985. The discovery in the Tafila area of gypsum reserves totalling an estimated 1.5m. tons, sufficient to satisfy demand for 10 years, was announced in March 1985. In 1990 the JCFC achieved record exports of 1.4m. tons of cement and clinker, and also sold 1.5m. tons of cement in the domestic market.

Construction was the fastest growing sector of the economy in 1993, when its share of GDP reached 8.3% (up from 7.6% in 1991). Stimulated mainly by the influx of 'returnees' from Kuwait, new building projects totalled 5.9m. sq m in 1992, as against 4.4m. sq m in 1991 and 2.7m. sq m in 1990. In 1994 domestic demand for cement declined, but a 19% increase in cement exports (to 887,000 metric tons, shipped mainly to Saudi Arabia and Yemen) enabled the JCFC to maintain total production at the 1993 level of 3.4m. tons. JCFC production in 1995 was 3.1m. tons. RMC Jordan (a wholly-owned subsidiary of the British company RMC) opened its first plant in 1996. Situated near Amman, the plant had a capacity of 100 cu m of ready-mixed concrete per hour. In October 1996 the state-owned Jordan Investment Corpn (JIC), which held 49.5% of the shares in the JCFC, invited bids for 22% of JCFC shares. A total of 16 international cement companies submitted bids, but none was accepted. The JCFC had made a net profit of JD 9.8m. on sales of JD 104.3m. in 1995. In April 1997 the Government approved an increase in Jordan's basic cement price (held at JD 44 per ton since 1992) to JD 48 per ton. In June 1997 the JIC indicated its intention to make a 50% increase (from 22% to 33% of JCFC shares) in the number of shares to be offered when it next invited bids from interested companies. In November 1998 the Government sold a 33% stake in the company, valued at US $101m., to the Lafarge Group (of France), which subsequently increased its holding to 40%. A group of Arab investors acquired an 8.5% stake in February 1999. The fall in pre-tax profits from JD 11.7m. in 1997 to JD 9.1m. in 1998 was attributed to a decline in exports due to Israeli impediments, since local sales rose by 3% to JD 81.3m. Output of cement fell sharply in 1998 to 2,650,300 tons (from 3,250,500 tons in 1997), but recovered slightly to 2,687,000 tons in 1999, for which the JCFC posted profits 73% up at JD 15.8m. In February 2000 the company launched a systems upgrading programme to prepare for the ending of its monopoly on the manufacture and sale of cement. In 2000 Jordan produced 2.64m. tons of cement and 2.4m. tons of clinker and exported cement to the value of JD 16.3m. The JCFC, which had established an export flow of 1,000 tons per day to the West Bank and Gaza, stated in early 2001 that Israeli restrictions on access to PA-controlled areas had cost it an estimated JD 300,000 per month in lost sales since the end of September 2000.

In 1981 construction began on the 225-ha Sahab industrial estate, 18 km south-east of Amman, which is being built at a cost of JD 18m. The first phase of the estate, covering 85 ha, was opened at the end of 1982, and will include 15 ready-built factories and 15 other factories that are being built by the companies which are to use them. Work on the second phase of the Sahab industrial estate began in 1985. Nevertheless, the main focus of the 1981–85 and 1986–90 Plans appeared to be decentralization, putting emphasis on locating industries in geographically underdeveloped areas, especially the Soputj. An example of this is the Encouragement of Investment Law, which was enacted in February 1984. This divides the country into the following three zones: (a) Amman and its suburbs; (b) the other major cities; and (c) the remainder of the country. The Government hopes to encourage dispersal of investment by regulating the amount of assets required by companies setting up in each zone, with the minimum requirement of fixed assets for zone (a) being almost three times that for zone (c). The 1981–85 Plan, with a centrepiece in the construction of the US $1,000m. Yarmouk University (which received its first students in 1985), concentrated on manpower, technology transfer and regional development. Export industries were also to be promoted. The industrial plans for the region around Irbid (where an industrial estate is to be built at a cost of $20m.) and the Ma'an-Aqaba area will form magnets for attracting benefits away from the industrial core of Amman. However, plans to build an iron and steel plant at Irbid were postponed in November 1990. The Middle East Complex for Engineering, Electronics and Heavy Industry—a conglomerate formed in 1994 through the merger of three companies with manufacturing and trading interests in electrical equipment, household goods and related products and components—announced in late 1996 that it had reached an agreement for the local assembly of four-wheel-drive vehicles supplied in kit form by Ssangyong Motor Company of South Korea. Output of Musso and Korando models was planned to rise from 1,000 units per year in 1997 to more than 4,000 units per year from 2000. In October 2000 Ole Automotive Trading signed an agreement with Land Rover to import 5,000 Defender models per year from the United Kingdom as completely knocked-down kits for assembly in Jordan.

In an effort to boost Jordan's role as an entrepôt, a free-trade zone was introduced at Aqaba in 1976, and a second free-trade zone was opened at Zarqa in February 1983. The amount of goods that passed through these zones totalled 350,000 metric tons in 1984. In March 1985 it was announced that two more duty-free zones would be established, at Queen Alia international airport and at the port of Aqaba. There is another free-trade zone at Ramtha, on the Syrian border, while an industrial free zone was planned for the Shidiya phosphates-producing area (see above). All the zones are operated by the Free Zones Corpn under the aegis of the Ministry of Finance. In 1995, when 668,000 tons of goods passed through the zones, the Corporation made a profit of JD 4.7m. In May 1997 the Government agreed that the Aqaba region should be converted into a fully fledged free zone offering special incentives for the development of manufacturing and service industries in addition to the existing free-trade facilities. After a study conducted for the Aqaba Regional Authority had, in May 1999, affirmed the feasibility of a project to transform the Aqaba region into a free-trade zone, a ministerial task force was established in June 2000 to bring the zone into operation in 2001. The zone's Chief Commissioner (Jordan's Minister of Transport) announced in September 2000 that he expected the sectoral distribution of new investment in the zone to be 50% tourism, 30% services, 13% heavy industry and 7% light industry. The 375-sq km Aqaba Special Economic Zone (ASEZ) became operational in February 2001 and was formally inaugurated in May, including within its boundary a population of 70,000, an established sea port and airport installations, Jordan's largest power station and some of the country's principal mineral-processing facilities. Over 100 registration applications (half of them for new projects) were submitted by businesses in the first week of ASEZ operations. A Qualifying Industrial Zone (QIZ—see below) was to be built within the ASEZ, with completion of the first QIZ facilities scheduled for 2002.

QIZ terms were first designated in November 1997. Companies qualifying for QIZ status are required to have a Jordanian and Israeli manufacturer, each contributing a minimum of 20% of total production costs; alternatively Jordanian and Israeli manufacturers must contribute specified proportions of the content of goods produced, in order to qualify for duty and quota-free access to US markets. Jordan's Century Investments Group (CIG) has eight joint ventures in operation and others under development in the Al-Hassan Industrial Estate. CIG was reported to be developing its own estate (having applied to the World Bank for a possible US $10m. loan) and to be planning a $100m. QIZ fund to acquire under-performing US companies in order to transfer their manufacturing capabilities to Jordan and take advantage of the QIZ lower production costs. The success of the QIZ concept has encouraged other investors. For example, in May 2000 the Hong Kong-based Boscan International Company launched the $100m. first phase of 'Cyber City', a multi-purpose industrial and technology zone using 4 sq km of land adjacent to the Jordan University for Science and Technology, which would enjoy both QIZ and free zone status. Also announced in mid-2000 was the Mushatta International Complex, to be created on land close to Amman's international airport, while the Hashemite University north-east of Amman was working with US interests to set up a 150-ha QIZ estate. The Jordan Gateway Projects Company (a joint venture with Israeli interests) qualified as a QIZ in April 1999 to develop a new estate on both the Jordanian and Israeli-occupied banks of the Jordan river. Other QIZ ventures include the Al-Kerak and Al-Hassan industrial estates, both under the aegis of the Jordan Industrial Estates Corporation, while a Karachi-based textiles firm, A. Majeed & Sons, in late 1999 became the first company to obtain QIZ status for the manufacture of ready-made garments in Jordan for supply to the US retail chain Walmart. Jordanian exports to the USA (valued at JD 45.4m. in 2000) were expected to triple in 2001, with virtually all the growth coming from QIZ activities.

By mid-1998 a number of major state-owned enterprises had been designated for complete or partial privatization. The partial sell-off of the JCFC followed, whilst restructuring of the water and electricity industries was instituted to bring in private investment. Partial privatization of the postal service was also mooted. In July 1999 bids were received for Jordan's first independent private power station (see Mining, Minerals and Energy, above). The private management and expansion of Aqaba Railways Corporation and the construction of a new Light Rail System were also pursued (see Transport and Communications, below). However, delays resulted from uncertainty over the Government's precise intentions as to desired post-privatization arrangements, on which conflicting statements were made by officials. There was also opposition to the disposals within some of the enterprises concerned, backed by a sizeable contingent of parliamentary deputies, who feared that privatized companies would be acquired by wealthy and well-connected businessmen rather than a wider share-owning public. Another concern was that strategic Jordanian industries would pass into foreign ownership.

In August 1999 the JIC completed the sale of its minority stakes in a number of state companies, as part of its strategy of disposing of its holdings in long-established public concerns and concentrating on new projects. In the following month 9m. shares in the state-owned Housing Bank were sold for JD 21.5m. to the Social Security Corpn, the country's largest savings fund, with assets of JD 1,200m. In January 2000, moreover, the sale of a 40% stake in the Jordan Telecommunications Company (JTC) to France Télécom was completed, while plans for the partial privatization and restructuring of Royal Jordanian Airline moved forward later in the year (see Transport and Communications, below). In May the House of Representatives approved a new privatization law giving the Government the option of retaining a 'golden share' in any privatized entity. At the end of 2000 the JIC stated that it had earned a total of JD 110m. from sales of shares since 1993. It still held shares in 33 companies listed on the Amman Stock Exchange and planned to sell its shareholdings in 10 listed companies during 2001. Further privatization of state assets was foreshadowed in the Plan for Social and Economic Transformation launched in November 2001 (see Budget, Investment and Finance, below).

TRANSPORT AND COMMUNICATIONS

The transport sector has contributed around 15% of Jordan's GDP since the early 1970s, and provided direct or indirect employment for some 20% of the private-sector work-force in the 1990s.

Jordan's only seaport is situated at Aqaba on the country's 20-km Red Sea coastline. Cargo-handling facilities expanded rapidly during the 1980s, an important factor being the re-routing through Aqaba of much Iraqi trade when the Iran–Iraq War of 1980–88 severely dislocated trade through Iraq's own Gulf outlets. In 1989 Aqaba handled 2,446 vessels and 18.7m. metric tons of cargo, of which 8.7m. tons were Jordanian exports and 2.5m. tons were Jordanian imports. In mid-1990 the port had more than 20 berths, one container terminal, two 40-ton gantry cranes and 299,000 sq m of storage facilities. A new industrial jetty was under construction at the port of Aqaba in the late 1990s.

Aqaba's transit trade was severely affected by the imposition of UN sanctions against Iraq from August 1990. According to the Jordan Shipping Agents Association, the cumulative loss of transport revenues (including government port fees) amounted to US $570m. by the end of 1992. The total cargo loaded at Aqaba in 1992 was 13.4m. metric tons, of which only 2.1m. tons was transit cargo (mainly Iraqi government imports of basic foods). Iraqi exports via Aqaba, which had amounted to about 1.15m. tons per year before the imposition of sanctions, ceased entirely. The estimated reduction in Aqaba's Iraq-bound imports as a result of sanctions was about 3.5m. tons per year, while up to 2.85m. tons of transit cargo for countries other than Iraq were being re-routed to non-Jordanian ports by shippers who did not wish to suffer the delays and inconveniences of UN monitoring of Aqaba-bound cargoes. For the same reason, some shippers were also routing part of Jordan's own import trade via Mediterranean ports in Syria and Lebanon. Although the number of ships calling at Aqaba in 1992 was, at 2,430, only 16 fewer than in 1989, the proportion of cargo vessels in the total fell from 64% in 1989 to 52% in 1992, while the number of shipping lines calling regularly at Aqaba fell from 41 to 26.

The US-led naval patrol responsible for enforcing the UN monitoring of shipping at Aqaba was discontinued in late April 1994 in favour of land-based inspections by agents of Lloyd's Register of Shipping. The change occurred after repeated and vigorous protests to the US Government by King Hussein, citing estimates that diversions and delays caused by the naval blockade had cost the port about US $440m. in lost revenue in 1993. A US spokesman acknowledged in April 1994 that only six of the 460 ships turned away from Aqaba by the naval patrol had been carrying embargoed goods, while the remainder had merely lacked correct documentation. Between 1993 and 1994 Aqaba's annual trade volume declined from 11.63m. metric tons to 10.47m. tons, leaving about 50% of the port's capacity unused in the latter year. There was an 11% increase in the tonnage of cargo passing through Aqaba in 1995. From June 1996 the port authorities implemented cuts of 20% to 25% in overall handling fees; an additional 5% reduction in port fees on goods in transit; a 50% cut in fees for any cargoes transhipped from Aqaba to Eilat; and (by arrangement with Egypt's Suez Canal Authority) discounts on Suez Canal tolls of 20% for Aqaba-bound container vessels and 10% for Aqaba-bound bulk-cargo vessels. In 1996 the volume of cargo passing through Aqaba increased from 11.8m. tons to 12.2m. tons. The number of containers handled rose from 55,783 in 1995 to 75,333 in 1996. Design work was under way in 1997 for an expansion of port capacity (to include a new 400-m industrial wharf for vessels of up to 50,000 tons) to keep pace with the planned growth of Jordan's mineral exports. In mid-1997 the port authorities announced new cuts in Aqaba's handling fees, designed, in part, to stimulate the growth of transit trade. In late 1999 Jordan and Iraq agreed to seek to restore Aqaba's former role as a major entry point for goods destined for Iraq. In 2001 Aqaba was used by 2,673 vessels and handled a total cargo volume of 13.04m. tons.

A ferry service between Aqaba and the Egyptian port of Nuweibeh, opened in 1985, is one of the main low-cost passenger links between North Africa and the Gulf region (and as such carried most of the Egyptian workers who left Kuwait and Iraq in August 1990). In 1992 this service carried a total of 1.2m. passengers (many of them en route to Saudi Arabia), and its operator (the Arab Bridge Maritime Company) made a record profit of US $9m.

The Jordanian section of the narrow-gauge Hedjaz railway runs from the Syrian border, via Amman and Ma'an, to the Saudi border. A 115-km link to a phosphate export terminal at Aqaba was added in the 1970s. A further 68 km of track, including a 48-km link to the Shidiya phosphate mines, was to be added in the mid-1990s. Freight (mainly phosphates) accounts for virtually all of Jordan's current rail traffic, but future diversification into passenger services has not been ruled out. Plans to build a 1,000-km standard-gauge railway from Aqaba to Baghdad were approved in principle in 1989 but shelved in the following year when Iraq's development plans were overtaken by political events. An express rail link between Amman and the Syrian capital, Damascus (using a section of the Hedjaz railway), was launched in August 1999. Proposals to build a 41.7-km light rail link between Amman and Zarqa were drawn up in 1996 with a view to seeking foreign investment in a 'build-own-operate' or 'build-operate-transfer' project. The Ministry of Transport invited bids in 1999 for the operating concession and the construction (at an estimated cost of JD 28m.) of an electrified light rail system to carry 140,000 passengers per day between Amman and Zarqa. The Aqaba Railway Corpn (ARC, established in 1972 to manage the rail transport of rock phosphate and related products) made a net loss of JD 11.6m. in 1995, and carried accumulated losses of US $98.7m. in 1998. In August 1999 the Government signed a 25-year management and operation agreement for ARC with a US-led consortium which undertook to invest $130m. to connect the existing railway network with JPMC's Shidiya mine, situated near the Saudi Arabian border.

The Jordanian road system includes a number of major national and international transit routes, among which the main north–south desert highway from Amman to Aqaba had, by 1993, been upgraded along all but 71 km of its 330-km length. Improvements to the dilapidated section of the highway, between Ras an-Naqb and Wadi Yutm in a mountainous area in the south, were scheduled for completion by the end of 1996. Even after the suspension of much of Iraq's trade through Aqaba, an estimated 300,000 trucks were using the port in 1991, due in part to the fact that all of Jordan's potash exports, and about half of its phosphate exports, are transported to Aqaba by road. Around 22,000 Turkish trucks used Jordan as a freight transit route in 1992, while Jordan's own sizeable haulage fleet was increasingly active on routes to North Africa, Turkey and Eastern Europe to replace export business lost through the UN embargo on Iraq and a decline in some Jordanian markets in other Gulf states. The Iraqi-Jordanian Land Transport Company, operating exclusively between these two countries, cut its fleet from 900 to 336 trucks in 1992. In 1997 the Government announced plans to privatize the Public Transportation Corpn (responsible for bus services in Amman). However, following accumulated monthly losses, accountants were appointed to liquidate PTC in October 1998. Private companies will take over the operation of its bus routes in Amman.

The national airline, Royal Jordanian, operates passenger and freight services from Queen Alia international airport at Zizya, 40 km south of Amman. It carried 44,520 metric tons of freight in 1992 (compared with a peak of 55,170 tons in 1990 and a decline to 41,637 tons in 1991 as a result of the Gulf crisis). Passenger numbers in 1992 totalled 1,109,000, compared with 798,000 in 1991 and a recent peak of 1,226,800 in 1988. The airline's operating profit reached a 5-year peak of JD 37.9m. in 1992, but its (unpublished) net profit position was believed to reflect an annual debt service requirement of around US $40m. (which would have been even greater had the airline not cancelled an option on four additional European Airbus aircraft in 1991). Plans to privatize Royal Jordanian, first put forward in 1987, had still to be finalized in 1993, when a consultants' report recommended a major increase in capital to resolve cash-flow problems. Revenue in 1994 totalled around $400m. following a 3.9% increase in passenger numbers (to 1.22m.) and a 1.3% increase in freight (to 55,000 tons), but operating profits fell by 36% to JD 26.63m. In early 1995 the airline raised about $30m. through sales of shares in its hotel and duty-free shopping interests. The airline signed agreements in 1998 with two consortia to advise on its restructuring and privatization. Royal Jordanian subsequently presented a financial restructuring package to the Government and cleared some of its debts to local banks, while in mid-2000 bids were being considered or anticipated for 100% acquisitions by private investors of six separate companies formed from operations previously conducted by the airline, including duty-free shopping, catering, training and simulation, engine overhaul and aircraft maintenance. The duty-free business was sold in July 2000, the training and simulation business in January 2001, and 80% of the catering business in May. However, private/foreign participation in the core transportation activities of Royal Jordanian (through the sale of a 26%–49%-interest in the airline) remained to be arranged in mid-2001, the Government having reportedly rejected offers from two foreign airlines on the grounds that they were too low. Royal Jordanian's employee numbers were reduced from the equivalent of 337 per aircraft in 1999 to 200 per aircraft in 2001, in order to bring them closer to current international norms. In 1999 the airline carried 1.25m. passengers and 56,050 tons of freight. Some 1.28m. passengers were carried by Royal Jordanian in 2000. It was announced in mid-2000 that Jordan's first privately-owned airline, Jordan Aviation (JATE), would inaugurate its first flights in October of that year. Focusing primarily on charter operations to Red Sea tourist resorts, JATE aimed to operate six aircraft and employ 120 staff within two years.

A telecommunications law enacted in August 1995 provided for the licensing of private-sector competitors to the state-owned Jordan Telecommunications Corporation. During 1996 private companies were granted licences to develop new mobile communications, data communications and public payphone systems, although the state enterprise remained the sole provider of basic fixed-line services. With effect from January 1997 the Telecommunications Corporation was restructured as the Jordan Telecommunications Company (JTC), with a share capital of JD 250m., and advisers were appointed to organize the proposed sale of part of the company's equity to the private sector. In January 2000 Jordan signed an agreement under which a consortium led by France Télécom obtained a 40% stake in the JTC for $508m., with a further 8% being acquired by the Social Security Corporation for $102m. and 1% being allocated to the JTC staff fund, so that the Government retained a 51% majority stake. The JTC currently had 560,000 subscribers, with a further 70,000 due to be added in 2000. Its monopoly on fixed-line services was due to expire at the end of 2004.

There was controversy over the award of Jordan's second mobile cellular telephone network licence, with the private operator, Fastlink (then owned by Motorola), whose monopoly expired in October 1998, arguing that the second licence should be put out to tender. However, the second licence was awarded in 1998 to JTC, whose subsidiary MobileCom launched its service in competition with Fastlink in September 2000. Industry analysts subsequently published estimates suggesting that the Government had foregone potential revenue of US $150m. by not putting the second licence out to tender. In mid-2001 Fastlink (91.6% of whose shares were now owned by the Egyptian company, Orascom Telecom) had around 550,000 subscribers and was developing capacity to expand this to 750,000, while MobileCom had over 100,000 subscribers. The rapid growth of demand was attributable in part to an intensification of price competition in 2001. In February 2002 the arrangement of a JD 60m. loan to MobileCom to finance the expansion of the mobile network was said to be the largest loan by local banks to date for a private-sector project in Jordan.

Jordan made rapid progress in the late 1990s as a regional centre for information technology (IT) and computer software innovation, attracting substantial US and other Arab investment in the sector. Particular importance was attached to the IT sector by King Abdullah, who in February 2000 secured the agreement of Microsoft to a 'co-operation framework' under which the US giant would assist with the building of IT infrastructure and skills in Jordan. A USAID-financed study presented to King Abdullah in November 1999 had suggested that with appropriate attention to infrastructure and training Jordan could generate 30,000 IT jobs and US $500m. annually from IT exports by 2004. In September 2000 the Ministry of Education introduced a three-year programme to equip all Jordan's state schools with computer laboratories and to provide teachers with access to soft loans to purchase personal computers. JTC introduced a high-speed data network in December and reduced its charges to internet service providers, data network providers and dial-up internet users. In January 2001 JTC purchased Jordan's largest established internet service provider, Global One Communications, in order to become the market leader in the direct public provision of internet services. Orascom Telecom, the Egyptian majority shareholder in Fastlink, sited its regional technical centre in Amman, and in June 2001 indicated its readiness (subject to the negotiation of a satisfactory agreement with Jordanian telecommunications regulators) to establish a call centre in Aqaba to serve all 19 of its affiliated companies in the Middle East and North Africa. The Jordanian Government announced in May 2001 that it was planning to create a National Frequency Register and to reconstitute the kingdom's Telecommunications Regulatory Commission as a fully independent body with an expanded remit (to include radio and television broadcasting).

TOURISM

Before 1967 net earnings from the tourist trade and income from private donations constituted the only important invisible export from Jordan. After 1967 income from tourism and private transfers fell dramatically. In 1974, however, the Jordanian Government decided to allow its visitors to cross over the West Bank and the number of tourists arriving in the country that year rose by 79% on the 1973 total to reach 554,913, nearly regaining the 1966 level of 617,000, while income from tourism exceeded it, reaching JD 17.3m., compared with JD 11.3m. Tourism continued to expand during the 1970s and 1980s, reaching 2,677,021 in 1985. Earnings from tourism reached a record JD 310m. (US $546m.) in 1989, when the number of European long-stay visitors totalled 130,000. In 1990 the Gulf crisis effectively ended all tourism from September onwards, while a slow recovery in the latter part of the following year

took total European arrivals to 57,000 in 1991. In 1992, when European arrivals rose to 121,000, a strong revival of tourism (at least among non-Arab visitors) generated estimated net receipts of around $300m.

Strong overseas marketing campaigns by the Government, private-sector tour operators and Royal Jordanian Airline produced significant increases in tourism from 1993 to 1996, but from 1997 the number of visitors began to decline, reportedly owing to fears concerning militant Islamism and rising Israeli–Palestinian tensions. A main aim of government tourism development policy for the 1990s was to provide a varied range of attractions in different parts of the country, while taking steps to prevent over-development of Jordan's world heritage site at Petra. In 1994 a total of 696,760 visitors generated an estimated JD 443m. of tourism revenue, representing increases of 12% in visitor numbers and 13.6% in revenue compared with 1993. Moves towards a regional peace settlement greatly enhanced Jordan's appeal to overseas tourists, while the opening of the border with Israel prompted a significant influx of Israeli tourists from late 1994 onwards. Income from tourism in 1995 was estimated as JD 568m. (US $800m.). At the end of the year 23 new hotels were under construction and many more were planned. Total visitor numbers in 1995 exceeded 1m., of whom 400,000 were classed as leisure and culture tourists. An estimated 100,000 Israelis visited Jordan in 1995, while tourist arrivals from Japan and Korea began to feature significantly in the tourism statistics for the first time. The re-emergence of regional political tensions in 1996 led to a significant decline in visitor numbers, with some hotels reporting occupancy rates as low as 10% at some points in that year. The number of European and US visitors totalled 444,600 in 1996, declining to 429,700 in 1997 and showing little sign of recovering in 1998. Nevertheless, the Ministry of Tourism and Antiquities pursued an expansion of tourist facilities, including hotels, on the basis of a $44m. development programme announced in May 1997. In November, moreover, the Government announced the establishment of a new Jordan Tourism Board (JTB) as a public-private venture to promote Jordan as a tourist destination. Major new private tourism projects initiated in 1998 included a 6,000-bed hotel complex at Aqaba, at a projected cost of $452m., and a 540-sq km national park, which was part of an overall $44m. World Bank-financed project to develop Jordan's main tourist areas in Aqaba, Petra and Wadi Rum. According to the Ministry of Tourism and Antiquities, in 1998 receipts from tourism increased to some US $852.6m. The Jordan Valley Authority (JVA) is putting in the infrastructure for the development of the Dead Sea coast as a major tourist resort based on curative tourism, for which it has drawn up a 25-year master-plan confining hotel development to specified zones. Three large hotels were under construction in 1999, in addition to the new 230-room Mövenpick Hotel, which opened in March of that year.

Tourist arrivals in 1999 totalled 1,357,822 (up from 1,256,428 in 1998), the sector generating revenue of an estimated JD 564m. and contributing 10.5% of GDP. The Nabataean site of Petra, Jordan's most popular tourist site, attracted over 420,000 visitors in 1999 (more than double the number in 1994), having 24 hotels with a total of 3,100 beds. In 2000 tourist arrivals were some 10% up on 1999 figures until the deterioration in Israeli–Palestinian relations from September, following which a significant fall in bookings resulted in the year's revenue from tourism falling to some JD 512m. There were 1,426,879 tourist arrivals in 2000. The sector remained depressed in 2001, in which year tourist arrivals numbered 1,477,697, but revenue decreased again, to an estimated JD 496m.

In June 2000 the Jordan Projects for Tourism and Development Co (JPTD) acquired a 2.7m. sq m site from the Aqaba Regional Authority (ARA) for a US $300m. tourist development project, while ARA itself invited private investors to bid for a range of new projects, including a dolphin park, an underwater observatory, a water theme park and a five-star hotel. In May 2001 work began on JPTD's Tala Bay Resort project in the Aqaba special economic zone (SEZ), involving the building of three four-star hotels as the first stage of converting some 10 km of Red Sea coastline into the 'Jordanian riviera'.

BUDGET, INVESTMENT AND FINANCE

Jordan's first Five-Year Development Plan, for 1962–67, aimed to invest JD 137m. in the economy, to raise GDP to JD 144m. This plan, however, was superseded by a Seven-Year Plan that was due to run from 1964 to 1970. In its turn, this was disrupted and abandoned after the loss of the West Bank in 1967, and a new Three-Year Plan, covering the period 1973–75, was introduced, with a total proposed expenditure of JD 179m. The three largest items of expenditure were transport, housing and government buildings, and mining and industry. The 1976–80 Plan, which followed the 1973–75 Plan, envisaged total expenditure of JD 756m., with the public and private sectors contributing in equal proportions. The Government felt that the Jordanian economy was too heavily biased towards the services sector, and one of the chief aims of the plan was the development of the commodity-producing sector and its increased contribution to GDP. In the event, although GDP failed to rise at the planned rate of 11.9% per annum, by 1980 it had risen by a substantial 62% compared with its 1976 value.

During the 1976–80 Plan period, the growth of agriculture was below target, but the 1981–85 Five-Year Plan still set goals. Agriculture was planned to have an annual growth rate of 7.5%, mining and manufacturing 17.8%, electricity and water supply 18.9% and construction 12.6%. These compare with an annual industrial growth rate of 13.6% during the 1976–80 Plan. In contrast, investment during the period 1976–80 overshot planned levels by 150%, largely owing to high levels of private investment. The initial planned investment for the 1981–85 Plan was JD 2,800m. (US $8,446m.). Industry was to account for 21%, water and irrigation 18%, transport 18% and housing 11%. By October 1981, however, Iraq had promised financial support of JD 500m., and this led to an increase in the planned level of investment to JD 3,300m., of which JD 1,162m. was to be from overseas assistance. Over the period there was planned to be an annual growth rate in GDP of 10.4%, compared with the 8.5% rate of the 1976–80 Plan. However, the targets of the 1981–85 Plan were not met.

Under the 1986–90 Plan, expenditure was set at JD 3,115m. (US $9,727m.), 52% of which was allocated to projects in the public sector and 48% to the private sector. Of total expenditure, 33% was to be provided by foreign borrowing. The Plan aimed for real economic growth of 5% per year and, with 39% of total investment to be allocated to the services sector (compared with less than 30% in the previous Plan), it was hoped that as many as 100,000 jobs would be created during its term. Agriculture was allocated 10% of total investment, compared with 5% and 7% in the previous two Plans, and agricultural production was expected to increase at an annual rate of 7%–8%. The phosphate industry was to be expanded with development plans focusing on the Shidiya phosphate deposits (see Mining, Minerals and Energy), while potash mining and other important export industries were also to be developed with the aim of increasing the value of exports by an annual rate of 8.3%. At the same time, it was planned to reduce the annual growth of imports to 2.8% for goods and 3.6% for services. These measures were intended to reduce the deficit on the current account of the balance of payments—one of the Plan's key objectives. However, major slippages on the Plan's targets were compounded towards the end of its term by the onset of the 1990–91 Gulf crisis. According to World Bank figures, Jordan's GDP increased, in real terms, by an annual average of 4.2% in 1980–88, in which period agricultural output increased by 6% per year, industry by 3.6% and services by 4.4%.

A Five-Year Development Plan for the Occupied Territories (1986–90) was launched in November 1986. With total required investment of JD 461.5m. (US $1,292.3m.) for projects in the West Bank and the Gaza Strip, the aim of the plan was to enable the 1.3m. Palestinians living in these areas to achieve a greater degree of economic independence; creating 20,000 jobs, constructing 8,500 homes and limiting the movement to Israel and, more especially, to Jordan (where immigrants might contribute to social, economic and political problems) of Palestinians deprived of work and opportunities. (About 850,000 West Bank Palestinians are entitled to Jordanian citizenship.) About 654,000 residents of the Occupied Territories left or were forced to leave between 1967 and 1984 (most of them to Jordan), and more than 100,000 Arab workers from the Territories, about

one-third of the labour force, work in Israel. Israel took measures to facilitate the implementation of the Plan, such as the appointment in September 1986 of Arab mayors in four West Bank towns, and agreeing to the opening of four branches of the Cairo-Amman Bank, which were to provide the main channel for the transfer of funds to development projects. The Plan had singularly failed to attract sufficient investment from abroad and appeared to be struggling for financial viability when, on 28 July 1988, it was abandoned by King Hussein on political grounds (see History). On 31 July King Hussein severed Jordan's legal and administrative links with the West Bank. The practical effects of this were that 5,300 teachers and civil servants, and other government workers employed by Jordan in the West Bank before the Israeli occupation in 1967, and fully paid by Jordan, were retired on full pension; subsidies from the Jordanian Government, including salaries, to some 10,000 teachers and 5,000 civil servants, employed since 1967, were removed (although most of these received a salary from Israel and only a monthly bonus from Jordan). An additional 2,000 employees, working in departments of religious affairs and Islamic law, were to continue to be employed in order to preserve an Islamic cultural identity in the area. It was estimated that the removal of subsidies would save Jordan $60m. per year. The PLO undertook to compensate all former Jordanian employees for the loss of their jobs but, owing to the restrictions imposed by Israel on the movement of funds into the Occupied Territories, this promise has proved difficult to honour.

Following the 1990–91 Gulf crisis, Jordan's 1991 budget estimates included an allocation of JD 230.2m. for capital expenditure, as well as an emergency budget of JD 120m., intended to assist the recovery of important economic sectors such as industry, transport, agriculture and tourism. Substantial additional aid commitments from external sources made it possible to implement this emergency budget, but the Government came under domestic criticism for using the extra aid to reduce the budget and external deficits, as required by the IMF, rather than to compensate the sectors that had been damaged during the recent crisis.

In conjunction with IMF-decreed structural adjustment, the Government in 1993 introduced a further Five-Year Economic and Social Development Plan, covering the period to 1997. Allotting a major role to the private sector through the disposal of stakes in government-owned concerns, the plan also aimed to encourage export-oriented investment and production; to stabilize the exchange rate of the dinar; to increase Jordan's foreign currency reserves to at least three months' export cover; to shift revenue generation from income to consumption, while eliminating taxation on investments and savings; to remove market distortions arising from price-fixing agreements and monopolies; to reduce and restructure subsidies; to dismantle trade and investment barriers; and to alleviate the associated problems of poverty and unemployment. Following the completion of the 1993–97 Plan period, the Government drafted a rolling National Economic and Development Strategy, capable of being adjusted on a year-by-year basis.

In 1997 the Government collaborated with the World Bank to establish a two-phase programme to improve living conditions for the poor and to create jobs for impoverished Jordanians and for skilled middle class workers. The first stage included the enlargement of the National Aid Fund (NAF), which provides direct financial aid to the poor; expansion of basic infrastructure; provision of credit for small enterprises through private and commercial banks; development of private work placement agencies; and the establishment of training for former armed services and civil services personnel for future employment in the private sector. In January 1999 the Government announced plans for the introduction of a national health service, scheduled for completion in 2010.

A Five-Year Plan for the period 1999–2003 envisages average annual economic growth of 5%, export growth of 8% and import reduction of 6% per year, the creation of 250,000 new jobs and reduction of the unemployment rate to 10% by 2003. Specific economic and social reform objectives under the plan were drawn up at a symposium of government and business leaders chaired by King Abdullah in November 1999, and focused on encouraging greater co-operation between the public and private sectors. Recommendations from the meeting included the continuation of the privatization programme, more administrative and financial reforms to encourage private sector development and investment, and a revision of educational policies. At the beginning of 2000 the King appointed a 20-member Economic Consultative Council to supervise implementation of the plan and related measures. The King convened a further symposium (or National Economic Forum), attended by 300 representatives of public and private sector bodies, in March–April 2001. Having discussed strategies to stimulate economic development and promote social justice, the symposium recommended the establishment of task forces on agriculture, education, financial reform, administrative reform and investment policy.

Jordan's persistent financial problems in the 1980s had culminated in a budget deficit of 24% of GDP in 1988, but thereafter, in accordance with IMF prescriptions, efforts were made to improve matters. Budget proposals for 1989 envisaged total expenditure of JD 1,035.0m. (a reduction of 16% compared with the budget for 1988, due mainly to the decline in the value of the dinar), incorporating development spending of JD 346.5m., compared with JD 451.5m. in 1988, a reduction of 23%. The budget deficit was originally projected at JD 122.3m., but the Government subsequently introduced measures to reduce the budget deficit by 4.5% of GDP in 1989. Budget estimates for 1990 envisaged expenditure at JD 1,105.8m. and revenue at JD 906.7m., resulting in a deficit of JD 199.1m. Capital and development expenditure was reduced to only JD 253.3m., compared with JD 346.5m. in 1989. Projected current expenditure was subsequently reduced by JD 15.1m., before the budget proposals received legislative approval. A further revision in the course of 1990 reduced total budgeted expenditure to JD 1,033.7m. and increased forecast revenues to JD 938.7m. resulting in a deficit of JD 182.4m. after loan repayments of JD 87.4m. up to August 1990. The 1991 budget, as adopted by the House of Representatives, envisaged total expenditure of JD 1,109.2m. and loan repayments of JD 135.2m., compared with revenues of JD 902.5m., resulting in a projected deficit of JD 341.9m. It was noted, however, that the expenditure total excluded certain debit items (notably oil subsidies), which, if included, would produce a deficit of at least 16% of GDP. The Government also presented a separate emergency budget of JD 120m., intended to assist the economy to overcome the effects of the Gulf crisis, its implementation being dependent on receipts of special aid (see below).

The 1992 budget proposals reflected the terms of the October 1991 IMF agreement; government subsidies being cut by 30%, and new consumption taxes imposed, in order to reduce the deficit to JD 107m. In the event, there was an overall budget surplus of JD 149m. in 1992 (due mainly to additional revenue from 'returnees'), total domestic revenue (JD 1,098m.) being higher than current expenditure (JD 932m.) for the first time in Jordan's history. The 1993 budget envisaged an excess of domestic revenue over current expenditure of JD 87m. and an overall budget deficit of JD 55m. Despite the achievement of a budget surplus in 1992, the effective fiscal deficit for the year (as cited in discussions with international financial institutions) was put at about 6% of GDP. Total GDP was JD 3,189m. (US $4,600m.) in 1992, up 10.1% in real terms on 1991 after allowing for inflation of 3%. Pledges of $380m. in aid to close Jordan's 1993 financing gap were made by international donors at a meeting organized by the World Bank in January 1993.

Of the structural reform measures proposed in the 1993 budget, price increases on selected oil products (including fuel for electricity generation and aviation fuel supplied to Royal Jordanian Airline) were implemented in June. However, a new sales tax, which should have superseded existing consumption taxes in May 1993, was deferred following strong protests from private businesses which claimed that they would be subject to an unfair burden, notwithstanding the Government's intention to raise only an extra JD 30m. per year, as against JD 100m. when the sales tax was first proposed. In the event, the Government amended the scope of the consumption tax system to raise an additional JD 3.5m., a step that was accepted by the IMF as 'a temporary alternative'.

The 'London Club' of commercial creditors signed a debt rescheduling agreement in December 1993 covering US $740m. in principal and $150m. in interest owed by the Jordan Govern-

ment to more than 80 lenders. The details of the agreement had been negotiated in July of that year.

The 1994 budget provided for revenue of JD 1,488m. (including domestic revenue of JD 1,311m.) and expenditure of JD 1,488m. (JD 1,124m. on current account and JD 364m. on capital account). Excluded from the budget were an unspecified amount of military spending, to be met by 'friendly Arab states', and the cost of servicing Jordan's foreign debt, which would have to be covered by fresh domestic and foreign borrowing to raise some JD 300m. In addition to the normal budget, the Government drew up an emergency budget providing for JD 66m. of development expenditure if sufficient foreign grants and/or soft loans could be raised. The controversial sales tax, after being strongly attacked during parliamentary debates, was finally approved on 14 May 1994 and took effect at the beginning of July.

The parliamentary passage of the sales tax legislation paved the way for the IMF Executive Board to announce on 25 May 1994 its formal approval of a three-year Extended Fund Facility (EFF) to support the next stage of the Government's structural adjustment programme. Worth SDR 127.8m. (US $178.9m.), the EFF would be used to further a programme whose main 1994 objectives were stated as real GDP growth of 5.5%, an annual inflation rate held at 5%, a reduction of the current-account deficit to 9.7% of GDP (compared with 12.5% in 1993), and an increase in the Central Bank's foreign exchange reserves to $665m. or the equivalent of 2.4 months' import cover. The aim of fiscal policy should be 'to enhance efficiency and revenue-elasticity' through tax reform. Areas of structural change which the Government should address more convincingly included the formulation of action plans for the agriculture and water sectors. The IMF said that the Government's on-target achievements in 1993 had included real growth of 5.8% of GDP, an inflation rate of 4.8% and a fiscal deficit of 6.4% of GDP.

The IMF agreement paved the way for successful negotiations with the 'Paris Club' of official creditors, culminating in an agreement on 29 June 1994 to reschedule US $1,215m. of debt payments over 20 years, including 10 years' grace. Jordan's Prime Minister described the terms as very favourable and designed to alleviate pressure on the Jordanian economy during the EFF period. World Bank statistics for 1992 gave Jordan's total debt as $6,914m., of which $3,454m. (including $2,704m. in concessionary loans) was owed to official bilateral creditors. Prior to the IMF and 'Paris Club' announcements, the Government had, on 18 May, obtained $200m. of aid from the Jordan consultative group of donors to finance the 1994 balance-of-payments deficit.

The IMF augmented Jordan's EFF allocation by SDR 25m. (about US $37m.) in September 1994 and by a further SDR 36.5m. (about $54m.) in February 1995. A favourable IMF review of the economy in June 1995 showed that Jordan was on course to achieve 6.2% economic growth in 1995, with inflation of less than 4% and a current-account deficit equal to 5% of GDP, bettering its planning targets in each case. In 1994 the real GDP growth rate had been 5.7% (virtually unchanged from 1993) and the end-1994 foreign debt (totalling $5,644m.) had been equivalent to 91.8% of GDP, compared with a debt to GDP ratio of 109% at the end of 1993. Net foreign reserves in the banking system totalled $2,430m. at end-1994, compared with $2,280m. at end-1993.

In July 1994, when Jordan and Israel first committed themselves to an early peace agreement, the World Bank advocated substantial foreign debt relief for Jordan to strengthen its economic position during the early stages of the peace, thereby reinforcing popular support for the peace process and providing a more attractive climate for foreign investment. While early Jordanian hopes of a major debt forgiveness initiative worth up to US $3,300m. proved to be groundless, some further relief was secured through bilateral agreements with various creditor countries.

The full writing-off of some US $700m. of debts owed to the USA was approved by the US Congress in July 1995. As most of these debts had already been rescheduled through the 'Paris Club', Jordan did not gain an immediate cash-flow benefit from this development. The United Kingdom agreed in July 1994 to convert $92m. of loans into grants to support Jordan's peace initiatives. In mid-1995 Jordan's outstanding debts to the

United Kingdom totalled \$531m., of which \$348m. had been rescheduled (including \$267m. rescheduled under the terms of the June 1994 'Paris Club' agreement). Germany agreed in November 1994 to restructure \$101.3m. of Jordanian debt under the 'Paris Club' agreement and to cancel \$32.9m. of debt, half of this through a debt-equity swap to provide investment funds for environmental projects. In August 1994 France cancelled \$4.6m. of Jordanian debts and provided a \$5.6m. line of credit for Franco-Jordanian joint ventures. In October France agreed to reschedule \$200m. of Jordanian debt under the 'Paris Club' agreement and to finalize a debt-equity swap programme worth \$100m. Jordan's total debt to France (excluding outstanding aircraft leasing payments) totalled around \$600m. in 1994. Jordan's largest bilateral creditor, Japan, was owed around \$1,800m. at the end of 1994. In mid-1995 Jordan requested \$500m. of balance-of-payments support loans for 1995/96 and an increase in Japanese grant aid to \$50m. per year from 1996. In October 1995 Japan extended a \$135m. balance-of-payments support loan to Jordan. In the same month the World Bank made an \$80m. economic reform and development loan, while a further \$20m. was loaned by France. In December 1995 Japan signed agreements to loan \$80m. to Jordan in support of its economic reform programme and to reschedule \$101m. of government debt and \$51m. of commercial debt, bringing the total amount of Jordanian debt rescheduled by Japan since 1989 to \$400m.

Jordan's 1995 budget provided for expenditure totalling JD 1,674m. (JD 1,231m. on current account and JD 443m. on capital account). Debt servicing of JD 300m. was not included in this total. The budgeted revenue totalled JD 1,624m., including domestic revenue of JD 1,400m. A supplement to the main budget provided for JD 390m. of spending on development projects, dependent on the availability of international assistance. The 1996 budget provided for total spending of JD 1,798m. (of which JD 1,328m. was recurrent expenditure and JD 470m. was capital expenditure) and total revenue of JD 1,635m. (of which JD 1,575m. was classed as local revenue and JD 60m. as repaid loans), leaving a deficit of JD 163m. to be covered by foreign grants and loans.

In February 1996 the IMF approved a Jordanian request for new credits totalling SDR 200.8m. (about US \$195m.) to support the Government's economic and structural reform programme over the period 1996 to 1998. This new EFF arrangement replaced the previous arrangement approved in 1994, which the IMF regarded as broadly successful. The Government's economic targets for the period to 1998 included average GDP growth of at least 6% per annum (with an initial target of 6.5% growth in 1996); achievement of low inflation rates similar to those in industrialized countries (with an initial target of less than 3.5% inflation in 1996); a reduction in the balance-of-payments deficit on the current account to less than 3% of GDP (with a 1996 target of less than 4% of GDP); the accumulation of sufficient gross official reserves to cover about three months' expenditure on imports; and the reduction of the budget deficit to no more than 2.5% of GDP by 1998 (compared with 4.8% of GDP in 1995 and a target level of 3.8% for 1996). The IMF recommended that maintenance of a tight monetary policy should be combined with the use of 'flexible interest rates geared to maintaining the relative attractiveness of dinar-denominated assets'. The ongoing process of structural reform was to include further reductions in public subsidies, including in 1996 the subsidies on water charges, wheat prices and animal feed prices. A wide-ranging privatization programme was to be introduced, with five major sales of government shareholdings planned for 1996. The top rate of customs levy on all imports except cars, alcohol and tobacco was to be cut to 30% by 1998. (From the beginning of 1996 the maximum levy on goods other than cars, alcohol and tobacco, inclusive of any fees and taxes imposed in addition to customs duty, was reduced to 50%, with many categories of goods becoming subject to a ceiling of 40%.)

A 1996 IMF report on Jordan's economic strategy included an overview of the main fiscal trends in recent years. From the mid-1970s to 1988, about 12% of GDP had been made up of grants from oil-producing countries, while an average 10% of GDP was devoted to servicing foreign debts and a further 10% to military spending. Over the period 1976 to 1994, deficit budgeting had inhibited economic growth by an estimated 2%

per annum after allowing for foreign grants of budgetary aid (without which growth would have been inhibited by 5% per annum). Between 1988 and 1994, the Government had cut the budget deficit from about 18% of GDP to less than 6% of GDP through a 65% cut-back in expenditure and a 35% increase in revenue (notably from postal and telecommunication services). Public-sector employment had risen by 15% between 1991 and 1994, while the public-sector wage bill increased by 40% in real terms and accounted for about 25% of total budget expenditure in 1994. However, overall government spending was equal to only 35% of GDP in 1994, compared with 47% of GDP in 1989. The report concluded that the Government's 'remarkable fiscal adjustment in recent years' had greatly improved the kingdom's investment climate and growth prospects.

Jordan's 1997 budget provided for total spending of JD 1,753m. and total revenue of JD 1,651m., leaving a surplus of JD 102m. In February 1997 the IMF increased the total amount of credit available to Jordan under the current (1996–98) extended fund facility by SDR 37.2m. to SDR 238m. (US \$330.5m.). In 1996 the 'Paris Club' had agreed to reschedule \$308m. of Jordanian official debt (\$250m. of principal and \$58m. of interest) falling due between July 1996 and May 1997. Repayment over 15 years would begin in June 1999. In 1997 the 'Paris Club' agreed to reschedule \$450m. of Jordanian debt falling due between June 1997 and September 1999. The repayment period would be 22 years (with 10 years' grace) for bilateral debt and 20 years (with 5 years' grace) for export credits. In September 1997 the USA agreed to cancel Jordan's remaining US debt of \$63.4m., following two earlier agreements under which \$1,100m. had been cancelled. Jordan's total foreign debt at the end of 1997 was \$6,469.7m. (81.7% of GDP), of which about \$4,000m. was owed to bilateral creditors. A rescheduling agreement, signed with Germany in March 1998, provided for the cancellation of about \$22m. if Jordan spent half of that amount on poverty-alleviating or environmental projects. The 1998 budget provided for expenditure of JD 1,950m. and a net deficit (after aid receipts) of only JD 37m., but the out-turn was a deficit of 6% of GDP. In April of that year, Jordan's official foreign-currency reserves stood at JD 1,110.9m., equivalent to 4.8 months' export cover.

In April 1999 the IMF approved loans totalling SDR 161.98m. (US \$220m.) to support the Government's economic and structural reform programme for 1999–2001. The loans were divided between a Compensatory and Contingency Financing Facility (CCFF) of SDR 34.1m. (\$46m.) to offset a shortfall in exports, and a new EFF credit of SDR 127.88m. (\$162m.). The new EFF programme targeted GDP growth of 2% in 1999, rising to 2.5% in 2001 and 3.5% in 2002, and a strengthening of reserves to \$1,191m. by the end of 1999 and \$1,691m. by 2001. The dinar would continue to be pegged to the US dollar at its current rate (709–711 fils). The IMF recommended a faster pace of structural reform in 1999, and identified as major targets the reform of the tax system and the introduction of a new banking law to improve regulation and supervision and establish a deposit insurance scheme. In May 1999 the 'Paris Club' agreed to reschedule \$800m. of Jordan's debt service payments due between March 1999 and April 2002, to support the economic reform programme agreed with the IMF. The repayment period would be 20 years. Further disbursements of the EFF credit were made by the IMF in July 2000 and August 2001, and were completed in April 2002 with the release of the final SDR 60.89m. (\$77m.).

Jordan's 1999 budget provided for total spending of JD 2,160m., 5% higher than the revised 1998 figure. Most of the increase was to come in the capital expenditure budget, which was expected to reach JD 477m. Current spending was expected to rise by only 3.8%. Total revenues, including aid, were forecast at JD 1,925m., 9% higher than the revised 1998 figure. The projected JD 435m. budget deficit would be part-financed by aid. Partly because of an increase in sales tax from 10% to 13%, the out-turn for 1999 was a deficit of 3.5% of GDP, which was regarded as satisfactory progress compared with the 1998 out-turn. At the end of 1999 Jordan's total external debt stood at JD 5,186m. (US \$7,409m.), equivalent to 96.4% of GDP (compared with \$7,066m. at the end of 1998). As approved by the House of Representatives in January, the budget for 2000 originally provided for a deficit of 7% of GDP on projected expenditure of JD 2,210m., despite a 25% reduction in capital spending. In March 2000 the Government imposed a freeze on public-sector job creation for the rest of the year, the share of state expenditure currently absorbed by civil service salaries being estimated at about 40%, amid evidence of pervasive over-staffing and nepotism in the state bureaucracy. The out-turn was a budget deficit contained to 4.7% of GDP.

The 2001 budget, providing for expenditure of JD 2,300m., incorporated a projected deficit of JD 380m. before foreign aid. As originally drafted, the budget included capital spending totalling JD 470m., while the original revenue projections included up to JD 80m. from planned increases in oil product prices in 2001. Implementation of these price increases was, however, 'postponed' after they were opposed by parliamentary deputies, who recommended that the Government should instead make an equivalent downward adjustment in its capital spending plans. The out-turn was a satisfactory reduction in the budget deficit to 3.7% of GDP, achieved by expenditure restraint to offset revenue shortfalls in the second half of the year. The shortfalls resulted from 'teething' problems with the extension of the sales tax to the retail sector, disappointing revenues from phosphate and potash exports and a decline in tourism (see Tourism, above). The lower fiscal deficit helped to reduce net public debt from 96% to 94% of GDP by the end of 2001, when the Central Bank's net usable reserves stood at $2,600m., equivalent to seven months' import cover.

The 2002 budget provided for expenditure of JD 2,350m. and incorporated measures to reduce unemployment and poverty levels, while at the same time aiming for a further reduction in the fiscal deficit. However, the simultaneous launching of the four-year Plan for Economic Transformation (PSET), envisaging expenditure of JD 250m.–275m. a year in the period 2002–05, was expected by the IMF to result in a small increase in the budget deficit in 2002, to 4.1% of GDP, although net public debt was projected to fall to 88% of GDP. As announced by King Abdullah in November 2001, the PSET aimed to accelerate and deepen the pace of structural reform, while simultaneously fostering human resource development to promote private investment and employment generation. The Government stated that outlays under the PSET would be financed through additional grants and a limited use of future privatization proceeds and that as from 2003 it would be fully integrated into the regular state budget.

After delivering a generally favourable report on Jordan's economic performance in the face of difficult circumstances, the IMF on 3 July 2002 approved a new two-year stand-by credit of SDR 85.28m. (about US $113m.) to support the Government's programme. As part of the agreement, the Government pledged the immediate reduction of state subsidies on basic commodities, including fuel oil, gas and flour. It was anticipated that the new IMF credit would enable the Government to reschedule current debts of $3,800m. to the Paris Club. Jordan's total foreign debt at that time stood at some $7,000m., which was costing over $800m. a year to service.

Jordan's banking sector grew with the economy, but recent changes in the country's economic fortunes have enforced a new caution. The number of institutions grew nearly threefold to 36 between 1973 and 1983. In January 1984 the Central Bank announced measures to 'Jordanize' foreign banks operating in Amman. They were given three (later extended to five) years to comply with regulations requiring that 51% of their equity be held by Jordanian nationals. The only foreign bank to respond was the Arab Land Bank. However, in April 1985, the new Government of Prime Minister Zaid ar-Rifai abandoned the regulation, though this did not affect another requirement for all banks to raise their capital from JD 3m. to JD 5m. in line with local commercial banks. ('Jordanization' would have taken the capital of foreign banks above the new minimum requirement.) In July Said Nabulsi resigned as Governor of the Central Bank of Jordan, a decision thought to have been influenced by the Government's rejection of his measures to 'Jordanize' foreign banks. The Chase Manhattan Bank decided to withdraw from Jordan in 1986, rather than comply with the direction to increase its capital. In February 1984 new Central Bank regulations stated that all banks must invest at least 4% of their total deposits either in government bonds or in government-guaranteed public corporation bonds, together with a further

4% in treasury bills. In addition, banks must now also invest at least 15%, but not more than 75%, of paid-up capital and domestic reserves in public shares. In July 1990 the financially-troubled Petra Bank went into liquidation, as did the Syrian-Jordanian Bank in May 1991, only 12 years after its creation as a joint venture of the Damascus and Amman Governments.

In January 1986 the Government lifted most of the restrictions preventing non-Jordanian Arabs from investing in the Jordanian economy. The only restriction to remain in force was that permitting a 49% maximum shareholding for non-Jordanian Arabs in retail trade, banking, finance and insurance companies. The change of policy was seen as an attempt to attract private capital to Jordan to offset the decline in Arab aid.

In December 1984 insurance companies were instructed to raise their capital to JD 600,000 by the end of 1986 or to merge with other companies. The regulation affected nine of the country's 21 insurance companies. Two mergers, between the Arab Belgium Insurance Company and the United Insurance Co, and the National Insurance Company and Al-Ahlia (Jordan) Insurance Company took place between October 1985 and August 1986. Six new insurance companies were established between 1996 and 1999. As a result, extreme levels of competitiveness on pricing exist in the sector, and tighter regulations (including the establishment of an independent Insurance Regulatory Commission) were due to be introduced in 1999.

In August 1991 the Central Bank imposed new credit ceilings in accordance with the IMF-decreed reforms. These included a 9% per annum limit on the increase in commercial credit and a specification that, in extending credit, commercial banks should not exceed 10 times their capital and reserves, or 90% of total customer deposits. In May 1993 an overall ceiling of JD 400m. was imposed on the growth of bank credit in the current year. This followed a surge in lending as banks sought to make profitable use of the strong inflow of deposits from 'returnees' over the previous two years. By the beginning of July the 1993 loan total already exceeded JD 300m. The Central Bank had earlier imposed restrictions on bank lending to finance customers' share purchases following signs that the Amman stock market was overheating in mid-June 1993 (when daily trading volumes of JD 16m. were recorded, compared with the normal average of JD 4m.).

At the beginning of 1993 the Central Bank ordered commercial banks to increase their bad debt provisions on around JD 2,200m. of outstanding loans. This move (which occurred at a time when bank profits were at record levels) effectively paved the way for the writing off of nearly JD 400m. of bad debts dating from the late 1980s. The banks had until 1995 to bring their loan cover up to new minimum levels. In January 1995 the Central Bank set an end-1996 deadline for 16 small banks to increase their capital to JD 20m. (US $28m.), making it clear that it would prefer banks to achieve this through mergers rather than increases in individual capital. At the same time Jordanian banks were warned that a July 1993 law limiting loans to 70% of total deposits was to be more strictly enforced than hitherto.

At the end of June 1997 the authorities abolished exchange-control restrictions, allowing free movement of currency for the first time in Jordan, this step being followed in early July by Central Bank action to reduce interest rates for the first time since 1989. However, bank lending rates remained high, at 13%–14%, contributing to the continuation of sluggish growth in 1998–99 and leading to criticism of the banks for their reluctance to reduce rates; meanwhile, there was a steady decline in deposit rates in 1998–99, to around 6%. At the end of 1999 the banking sector held some JD 8,000m. in deposits. In January 2000 the Central Bank lowered its mandatory reserves requirement for bank savings and deposits from 14% to 12% with effect from 1 March on balances outstanding at end-February. Most banks responded by reducing their prime lending rates to 10.5%–11.5% in line with the Central Bank's objective. In July the Central Bank further lowered its mandatory reserves requirement to 10% with effect from 1 August on balances outstanding at end-July. A government proposal to cut the rate of taxation on banks from 35% to 25% was rejected by the Jordanian House of Representatives in June 2001.

A new investment law introduced at the end of 1995 permitted foreign investors to buy shares on the Amman stock market without applying for government permission. A limit of 50% was set on the proportion of an existing listed company's shares that could be owned by foreign interests. In the case of companies whose shares were being publicly floated for the first time, foreign buyers could purchase holdings of up to 100% with the government's permission (which was required for any bid for foreign ownership of more than 50% of a newly floated company's shares). The minimum level for foreign investment through the stock market was reduced from JD 5,000 to JD 1,000. The minimum level for direct foreign investment in Jordan was set at JD 50,000. A limit of 25% was imposed on foreign participation in local printing and publishing companies (previously prohibited under Jordanian law). In mid-1997 the Higher Council for Investment recommended that the 50% ceiling on foreign ownership of shares be abolished in selected sectors, including banking and insurance. The proposal was made in order to encourage sustained foreign interest after the Government abolished a 15% tax on capitalized reserves in May 1997. The 1997 Securities Law divided stock exchange activity between three bodies: the Jordan Securities Commission (an independent regulatory body); the Depository & Transfer Centre to settle and clear stock; and the privately-run Amman Stock Exchange (ASE), which replaced the Amman Financial Market in March 1999. Net foreign investment in the market reached US $174.9m. (from $80.4m. in 1997) and non-Jordanian ownership stood at 44% (from 38% in 1997). Turnover on the market rose by 32% in 1998, to $653m., and total market capitalization at the end of 1998 was $5,842m. In 1999, however, ASE turnover fell by 16% to $549m., and a 1.6% fall in the ASE index resulted in total market capitalization declining to $5,780m. at the end of 1999. Negative factors included the damage to Jordan's manufacturing industry caused by the continuing UN embargo against Iraq and high domestic interest rates. A report on Jordan's financial markets, submitted to King Abdullah in October 2000, made 28 recommendations for a 'thorough overhaul' of laws, institutions and procedures. In 2000 the ASE suffered further falls in turnover (to $472m.) and market capitalization (to $4,950m.). There was a net outflow of $16.6m. of foreign funds in that year (compared with a net inflow of $21.8m. in 1999), leaving foreign shareholders with 41% of the market. The head of the ASE called on the Government to support the exchange by making greater use of it in privatization exercises.

In July 1998 the inaugural meeting was held of the Jordan Investment Trust (Jordinvest), which had been established by the Kuwait-based Gulfinvest International investment holding company to provide investment and financial services to local and foreign investors in the Jordanian economy. With initial paid-up capital of some US $22m. (including $5m. raised through a public share offering), Jordinvest was to specialize in recapitalizations and mergers of local banks and companies. Having posted after-tax income of JD 1.1m. in 1999, Jordinvest in May 2000 launched the country's first open-ended investment fund, which would invest at least 50% of its resources in Jordan (and a maximum of 25% in any one foreign country) and would target local institutions seeking to diversify their portfolios. In 2001 the ASE share index rose by 30%, buoyed in part by a strong financial performance by the banking sector.

FOREIGN TRADE AND BALANCE OF PAYMENTS

For many years phosphates have dominated Jordan's exports but, despite increasing in overall value, they fell in relative importance, accounting for only 22.6% of total export earnings in 1981 and 1982, compared with 43.6% in 1979. The proportion rose to 32.2% in 1983 (though this was principally due to a 40% fall in total export earnings), but fell to 26.6% (JD 69.6m.) in 1984 and 25.9% (JD 66.1m.) in 1985. It rose again to 28.7% (JD 64.8m.) in 1986 but fell to 24.5% (JD 61m.) in 1987. Phosphates and potash together accounted for 38.5% (JD 146.9m.) of the value of total exports in 1988 and 35.2% (JD 224.9) in 1989. In 1992 phosphates valued at JD 206.1m. (24.9% of total exports), and potash valued at JD 95.3m. (11.5% of exports), together accounted for 36.4% of Jordan's export earnings. The overall contribution of mineral resources to exports in 1992 was estimated to exceed 60% after taking account of processed derivatives (fertilizers and fertilizer inputs). Jordan's exports of phosphoric acid and other derivatives were forecast to increase substantially after the mid-1990s, when joint ventures with

several Asian importers were scheduled to come into production. Cement, tomatoes, vegetables and fruit are other important exports.

Saudi Arabia was Jordan's principal supplier between 1979 and 1985. Saudi Arabia's share of imports rose to a peak of 20.4% in 1982, when it sold goods to Jordan worth JD 233.5m. The proportion declined to 5.8% in 1986, when sales to Jordan were valued at JD 49.7m. and the USA became Jordan's principal supplier, though its share of total imports in that year declined from 11.9% (JD 128m.) in 1985 to 8.9% (JD 75.5m.). The USA's share rose to 10.2% (JD 93.4m.) in 1987, but Iraq became Jordan's leading supplier with 10.9% (JD 99.4m.) of total imports. Other leading suppliers are, traditionally, Germany, Italy, Japan and the United Kingdom. Iraq overtook Saudi Arabia as the largest purchaser of Jordan's exports in 1980, when it accounted for 23.6% of the total. Iraq's share rose to 26% (valued at JD 63.5m.) in 1981 and declined slightly to 25.2% (worth JD 66.6m.) in 1982. Jordan's exports to Iraq slumped to only 16% (JD 26m.) of the total in 1983, and Saudi Arabia once more became the principal customer for Jordanian exports, though only for one year, as Iraq accounted for 26% (JD 67.8m.) of Jordanian imports in 1984 and 25.8% (JD 65.9m.) in 1985. Iraq's share declined to 18.8% in 1986 and rose to 24.1% in 1987. Iraq, Saudi Arabia (with 10.5% of the total) and India (8.9%) were by far the most important purchasers of Jordanian exports in that year. In 2001 Iraq was again the principal destination for Jordanian exports (with 22.1% of the total); the USA and India received 12.2% and 10.7% respectively.

Iraq's position as Jordan's main trading partner made it inevitable that the UN sanctions against trade with Iraq, imposed after Iraq's occupation of Kuwait in August 1990, would be fulfilled only with reluctance by Jordan. In 1989 Jordan exported approximately JD 147.9m. worth of goods to Iraq (about 23% of its total commodity exports), while imports from Iraq totalled approximately JD 221.8m. (mainly petroleum). More than 80% of Jordan's petroleum is normally imported from Iraq. By the end of August 1990 transit trade with Iraq through the port of Aqaba had virtually ceased (see Transport and Communications, above), and the outbreak of hostilities in January 1991 resulted in the virtual cessation of Iraqi oil deliveries. Following the end of hostilities, Iraq declared in April that it wished to resume normal trade with Jordan, which it proposed to make its main channel to the outside world. However, while some Jordanian food exports resumed to Iraq, a restoration of full bilateral trading links depended on the repeal of the UN embargo.

In mid-1993 Jordan's full oil import requirement was supplied by road from Iraq under a bilateral arrangement (then in its third year) which was deemed by Jordan to fall outside UN sanctions because it involved no financial transfers. Just over half of the supply was free of charge, while the remainder (valued at US $16 per barrel, inclusive of transport) was counted as a repayment of Iraqi debt to Jordan. The agreement, which was understood to cover 55,000 b/d of crude oil in 1993, was informally monitored by UN sanctions administrators but did not have the formal approval of the UN sanctions committee. Following widespread reports in early 1993 that there was a growing barter element (mainly involving the supply of Jordanian food to Iraq) in this trade, the US Government began to exert pressure on Jordan to contribute 30% of the value of its oil imports to the UN-administered compensation fund for claims arising out of the Iraqi invasion of Kuwait. (This was the percentage levy that the UN intended to impose on UN-supervised oil exports from Iraq under a scheme which Iraq had so far declined to implement.) Iraq continued to supply all of Jordan's oil imports in 1994 and 1995, and it was announced in April 1995 that Jordan and Iraq planned to build a 590-km. pipeline to supply up to 70,000 b/d of Iraqi crude to Jordan's Zarqa refinery by about 1998 (although Jordan would not begin to operate the proposed pipeline while Iraq remained subject to UN sanctions). Import costs via such a pipeline were expected to be at least 50% less than the current trucking cost of $10 per metric ton. In January 1996 the Government announced its intention to reduce Jordan's annual exports to Iraq (latterly worth $400m.) to $200m. 'in the interests of reinforcing Jordan's foreign currency reserves'. Jordan's total exports to Iraq from

1989 to 1995 were estimated to be worth JD 1,525m. ($2,170m.), comprising mainly foodstuffs and detergents.

Jordan's traditionally large trade deficit is offset, somewhat variably, by expatriate remittances, re-exports, international aid and tourism. In 1985 import duties were raised by between 11% and 50% in an effort to cut the import bill by US $30m. Exports declined by 2.2% in 1985 to JD 255.3m., and imports rose by 0.3%, to JD 1,074.4m., giving a visible trade deficit of JD 819.1m. In 1986 exports declined by 11.6% to JD 225.6m., and imports declined by 20.9% to JD 850.2m., a deficit of JD 624.6m. In 1987 the trade deficit narrowed to JD 596.9m. (exports JD 315.7m., imports JD 912.6m.), but in 1988 it widened again, to JD 638.5m. (exports JD 381.5m., imports JD 1,020m.). In 1989 a rise in exports of phosphates and chemicals was largely responsible for narrowing the trade deficit to JD 576.5m. (exports JD 637.6m., imports JD 1,214.2m.). Devaluations of the Jordanian dinar in 1988–89 made the country's exports more competitive and restricted Jordanian consumers' ability to buy imported goods. From a deficit of JD 1,008.6m. in 1990, the visible trade balance improved slightly to a deficit of JD 994.1m. in 1991, when exports totalled JD 770.7m. and imports JD 1,764.8m. In 1992 imports rose sharply to JD 2,291m. ($3,363.2m.), mainly because of additional demand generated by 'returnees' from Kuwait, leaving a visible trade deficit of JD 1,461.7m. ($2,144m.) after taking account of exports worth JD 829.3m. ($1,217.4m.). In 1993 the visible trade deficit reached JD 1,593m. (imports totalling JD 2,234m. while exports totalled JD 641m.).

Jordan's balance of payments showed a current-account deficit of JD 148.2m. in 1990, a surplus of JD 269m. in 1991 and a deficit of JD 520m. in 1992. The main factor in the 1991 surplus was a sharp dip in outgoings on the invisibles account, while the main factor in the 1992 deficit was the steep rise in spending on visible imports (see above). External debt was reduced to US $6,600m. by the end of 1992, when the country's foreign exchange reserves exceeded $800m.

In 1994 import spending totalled US $3,543m. (3.9% less than in 1993) and export earnings totalled $1,437m. (14.7% more than in 1993), leaving a visible trade deficit of $2,106m. Customs tariffs, whose weighted average rate had already been cut from 35% to 21% in two years as part of the Government's economic restructuring programme, were further adjusted in May 1995 to eliminate or reduce the import duties on many industrial raw materials and intermediate products, although at the same time many agricultural products became subject to higher duties. In 1995 Jordan recorded a visible trade deficit of $1,518.2m. and an overall current-account deficit of $258.6m. (compared with a current-account deficit of $550m. in 1994). In mid-1996 the Ministry of Supply, which for the previous 22 years had acted as the monopoly importer of basic foodstuffs, with responsibility for controlling the retail prices of 25 food items, announced plans to open the import trade in rice and sugar to the private sector as the first stage in the phasing-out of its monopoly. The ministry was responsible for JD 320m. of food imports in 1995.

The trade deficit widened to JD 1,753m. in 1996 (from imports of JD 3,041.6m. and exports of JD 1,288.2m.), contributing to a current-account deficit of JD 157.4m. and an overall balance-of-payments deficit of JD 248.3m. In 1997 exports of JD 1,301.4m. and imports of JD 2,906.5m. produced a trade deficit of JD 1,605.1m., although the current account showed a small surplus of JD 20.8m. and the overall balance of payments a surplus of JD 193.9m. The current account remained in narrow surplus of JD 15.5m. in 1998, when the trade deficit was JD 1,434.5m. (from imports of JD 2,712.4m. and exports of JD 1,277.9m.), but the overall balance of payments showed a deficit of JD 84.1m. In 1999 the overall balance showed a surplus of JD 441.3m. and the current account a surplus of JD 287.1m., owing in part to a narrowing of the trade deficit to JD 1,323.7m. (from imports of JD 2,622.5m. and exports of JD 1,298.8m.). In April 2000 Jordan's foreign exchange reserves stood at US $2,700m., providing 8.5 months of import cover, which was double the end-1998 level and six times the end-1995 level. In February 2001 foreign exchange reserves totalled $2,791m. (representing 8.1 months of import cover). In 2000 Jordan's merchandise trade was in deficit by JD 1,898.6m. (imports JD 3,245.2m., exports JD 1,346.6m.), while the current account

of the balance of payments (including public grants) was in surplus by JD 15.5m. In 2001, despite regional instability and the world economic downturn after 11 September, Jordan's exports increased to JD 1,625.7m. by value; imports increased at a lower rate, to JD 3,407.3m., so that the trade deficit fell to JD 1,781.6m., while the current-account surplus rose to JD 20.8m.

An important source of foreign exchange in recent years has been remittances from Jordanians working abroad. In 1979 these totalled JD 180.4m. (including transfers through the banking system but not those through 'black market' money changers or by hand, which, it is estimated, would increase the total by at least 50%) and by 1981 had risen to US $987m. In real terms the income from foreign remittances fell in 1982, but rose by 5% (JD 20m.) to JD 402m. ($1,040m.) in 1983. In 1984 remittances from the 340,000 Jordanians working abroad were worth JD 475m. ($1,228m.). However, the world oil glut and a fall in oil prices adversely affected the economies of oil-producing countries in the Middle East, in particular the Gulf states where 85% of expatriate Jordanian workers are employed, and this, in turn, affected the level of remittances. These fell, accordingly, by 17%, to JD 403.5m. ($1,204m.) in 1985. Although they recovered to JD 414.5m. ($1,243.5m.) in 1986, they declined to JD 317.7m. ($953.1m.) in 1987. The decline in Gulf economies also added to the number of the unemployed as workers returned from abroad.

Remittances rose to JD 335.7m. in 1988, and to an estimated JD 470m. in 1989. Statistics issued by the Central Bank in May 1993 gave remittances in the years 1990, 1991 and 1992 as JD 331.8m., JD 306.3m. and JD 573.1m. respectively. The 1992 total was believed to include a large element of deferred transfers by workers who had returned to Jordan from Kuwait in 1991. Total remittances rose to JD 720.7m. in 1993, JD 763.7m. in 1994, JD 871.7m. in 1995, JD 1,024.0m. in 1996 and JD 1,031.7m. in 1997. The steady growth reflected the reopening of job opportunities for Jordanian nationals in the oil-rich Gulf states; in June 1998 the Government gave initial approval to the establishment of Jordan's first private employment agency, specializing in placing applicants in the Gulf. Remittances fell back to JD 947.0m. in 1998, but recovered to JD 1,180m. in 1999, JD 1,308m. in 2000 and JD 1,426m. in 2001. New employment opportunities became available in Kuwait from 2001 following the restoration of a labour agreement between Jordan and Kuwait.

In January 1997 Jordan and Iraq signed a protocol covering their bilateral trade in the coming year. Iraqi petroleum supplies to Jordan were to total 25m. barrels of crude oil and 7m. barrels of refined products, the agreed value of these supplies being US $611.2m. Within this total, $300m. represented oil supplied free of charge, $225m. represented payment for Jordanian goods and services to be supplied to Iraq, and the remaining $56.2m. represented a partial repayment of Iraq's accumulated debt to Jordan. In addition to the goods supplied under the terms of the bilateral protocol, Jordanian exports to Iraq in 1997 included humanitarian supplies within the framework of the UN 'oil-for-food' programme which came into operation in December 1996. In the first 180-day phase of the UN programme, Jordanian firms obtained UN approval for an estimated $146m. worth of humanitarian exports to Iraq. A Jordan-Iraq trade protocol for 1998 provided for the supply of 4.8m. metric tons of Iraqi petroleum and petroleum products (an increase of 12% compared with 1997), in exchange for Jordanian goods valued at $255m. In July 1998 Jordan and Iraq agreed to resume talks on the feasibility of a 750-km oil pipeline from Haditha in Iraq to the Zarqa refinery and Aqaba in Jordan, to transport supplies currently moved to Jordan by road (at a cost of $80m. per year), and to provide Iraq with a Red Sea outlet for its crude oil. In December 2001 the Jordanian Government invited bids for the contract to build a 250,000 b/d pipeline on a BOT basis, the estimated cost of $365m. to be shared by Jordan and Iraq.

Jordan and Iraq reviewed their trade protocol for 1999, to provide for the supply of 4.8m. tons of Iraqi crude oil (50% provided free), in exchange for Jordanian goods valued at US $200m. The trade protocol was reduced in value in line with the decline (at that time) in world oil prices. In 2000 Jordan's trade protocol with Iraq was worth $300m. There was an upward revision of the value of oil supplied by Iraq (reflecting the current upturn in world market prices), although Jordan's internal oil product prices for end users were held unchanged (necessitating cut-backs in other areas of government spending). By mid-2000 the cumulative value of Jordan's exports to Iraq under the UN 'oil-for-food' programme totalled $850m., including $204m. for the first half of 2000. From November 2000 Jordan was due to begin importing sulphur from Iraq in accordance with plans to expand the range of Jordanian imports covered by the trade protocol. It was envisaged that the Aqaba fertilizer plant of the Jordan Phosphate Mines Company might eventually obtain all its sulphur imports (up to 750,000 tons per year) from Iraq at a favourable price (initially $32 per ton, compared with current Saudi Arabian and UAE prices of $47 per ton). The 2001 Iraq-Jordan trade protocol was worth $450m. Iraq undertook to supply Jordan with 5m. tons of crude oil and products at a maximum price of $20.90 per barrel for the 50% of supplies that were not provided free. Government plans to increase oil product prices for Jordanian end users in 2001 were postponed after meeting strong opposition in the Jordanian parliament.

In 1997 Jordan's exports to Egypt were valued at only US $20.3m., and its imports at $36m. In mid-1998 the two countries signed an agreement providing for the establishment of a free-trade zone by the year 2005 (a 25% reduction in taxes and customs duties taking effect in January 1999, to be followed by a 15% reduction for three years and a 10% reduction over a further three years). In 1998 Jordan's exports to the USA were valued at $353m. ($402m. in 1997) and its imports at $17m. ($26m. in 1997). Jordan signed two economic agreements with the USA in March 1999. The first designated the Jordan Gateway as a QIZ (see Manufacturing and Industry, above) and the second established a Trade and Investment Framework Agreement (TIFA). A free-trade agreement between Jordan and the USA was initialled in Washington in October 2000. Jordan and Algeria ratified a 1997 trade agreement in 1999 exempting each other's agricultural and industrial products from customs duties.

In May 1991 Jordan signed its fourth financial co-operation protocol with the European Community (now European Union—EU), which undertook to provide a total of ECU 126m. in development grants and loans over a five-year period from November 1991. Under the three previous protocols, covering the period 1977–91, Jordan had received a total of ECU 203m. In April 1997, following two years of negotiation, Jordanian and EU representatives initialled an association agreement providing for the progressive liberalization of trading arrangements over a 12-year period. The agreement was eventually ratified by the Jordanian parliament in September 1999 and came into effect on 1 January 2000. EU aid equivalent to US $133m. in 2000 brought the funds allocated to Jordan since the launching in 1995 of the Euro-Med Partnership (MEDA) programme to $498.8m. Two €40m. tranches of direct budgetary assistance to Jordan (agreed in April 2000 to support the Government's structural reform programme) were disbursed in August 2000 and January 2001.

Lengthy negotiations on Jordan's application for membership of the WTO covered in particular Jordan's import duty regime and aspects of Jordanian copyright and patents law that were not consistent with prevailing international standards. The negotiations were successfully concluded in December 1999, and Jordan was formally admitted as the 136th member of the WTO on 11 April 2000, having reduced its maximum rate of customs duty from 35% to 30% on 1 March (in accordance with WTO requirements). In December 2001 a free-trade agreement with the USA entered into force, providing for the elimination of all bilateral tariff and other trade restrictions over a 10-year period.

ECONOMIC PROSPECTS

The IMF's mid-2002 assessment of Jordan's recent economic performance found that it was generally exceeding expectations and showing resilience in the face of ongoing regional conflict and the negative economic effects of the September 2001 attacks on the USA. Jordan's macroeconomic performance was expected to strengthen further with healthy export-led GDP growth in 2002–2003 and with a fiscal position in line with deficit level undertakings given to the Fund. Although unemployment is expected to remain a serious problem given the country's population structure and the rapid expansion of the working-age population, the Government's renewed commitment to privatization of the still-extensive state sector, the obligations of WTO membership, recent legislation to liberalize and regulate the financial sector, and an easing of monetary policy by the Central Bank from late 1999 are seen as factors boosting the confidence and opportunities of the private sector and foreign investors, as well as providing a stimulus to further improvement of the country's export performance. Expectations of medium-term growth are based in part on projected inflows of new investment in tourism and information technology and on the take-up of QIZ facilities allowing duty-free and quota-free access to the US market.

Statistical Survey

Source: Department of Statistics, POB 2015, Amman; tel. (6) 5300700; fax (6) 5300710; e-mail stat@dos.gov.jo; internet www.dos.gov.jo.

Area and Population

AREA, POPULATION AND DENSITY (East Bank only)

Area (sq km)	89,342*
Population (census results)	
10–11 November 1979	2,100,019
10 December 1994	
Males	2,160,725
Females	1,978,733
Total	4,139,458
Population (official estimates at 31 December)	
1999	4,900,000
2000	5,039,000
2001	5,182,000
Density (per sq km) at 31 December 2001 . . .	58.0

* 34,495 sq miles.

GOVERNORATES

(East Bank only; estimated population at 31 December 2001)

	Area (sq km)	Population	Density (per sq km)
Amman	8,231	1,971,750	239.6
Irbid	1,621	924,470	570.3
Zarqa	4,080	815,130	199.8
Balqa	1,076	339,940	315.9
Mafraq	26,435	238,890	9.0
Karak	3,217	208,315	64.8
Jarash	402	152,350	379.0
Madaba	2,008	132,140	65.8
Ajloun	412	115,040	279.2
Aqaba	6,583	101,050	15.4
Ma'an	33,163	104,160	3.1
Tafilah	2,114	78,765	37.3
Total	89,342	5,182,000	58.0

PRINCIPAL TOWNS (including suburbs)

Population at 31 December 2001: Amman (capital) 1,766,155; Zarqa 447,122; Irbid 257,795; Russeifa 227,544.

BIRTHS, MARRIAGES AND DEATHS (East Bank only)*

	Registered live births		Registered marriages		Registered deaths	
	Number	Rate (per 1,000)	Number	Rate (per 1,000)	Number	Rate (per 1,000)
1993 . .	134,489	n.a.	40,391	n.a.	11,915	n.a.
1994 . .	140,444	34.5	36,132	8.9	12,290	3.0
1995 . .	141,319	33.5	35,501	8.4	13,018	3.1
1996 . .	142,404	32.6	34,425	7.9	13,302	3.0
1997 . .	130,633	28.4	37,278	8.1	13,190	2.9
1998 . .	133,714	28.1	39,376	8.3	13,552	2.8
1999 . .	135,300†	28.0	39,443†	8.2	13,900†	2.9
2000 . .	143,800†	28.0	45,600†	9.0	14,600†	5.0

* Data are tabulated by year of registration rather than by year of occurrence. Registration of births and marriages is reported to be complete, but death registration is incomplete. Figures exclude foreigners, but include registered Palestinian refugees.
† Figures are rounded.

Expectation of life (years at birth, 2000): Males 68.6; Females 71.0.

ECONOMICALLY ACTIVE POPULATION (Jordanians only)

	1990	1991	1992
Agriculture	38,266	40,848	44,400
Mining and manufacturing . .	53,468	56,856	61,800
Electricity and water . . .	6,815	7,176	6,600
Construction	51,895	54,096	60,000
Trade	52,944	56,856	63,000
Transport and communications .	44,557	48,576	52,200
Financial and insurance services .	16,774	17,664	19,800
Social and administrative services	259,478	269,928	292,200
Total employed	524,197	552,000	600,000
Unemployed	106,000	128,000	106,000
Total civilian labour force .	630,197	680,000	706,000

Source: Ministry of Labour, *Annual Report*.

2001 (% of total): Agriculture 4.1; Mining and quarrying 1.5; Manufacturing 12.1; Electricity, gas and water supply 1.5; Construction 6.8; Wholesale and retail trade 18.0; Hotels and restaurants 2.5; Transport, storage and communications 10.0; Financial intermediation 2.1; Real estate, renting and business activities 3.7; Public administration 15.9; Education 11.4; Health and social work 4.5; Other community activities 5.5; Private households with employed persons 0.3; Extra-territorial organizations and bodies 0.2.

Health and Welfare

KEY INDICATORS

Fertility (births per woman, 2000)	4.5
Under-5 mortality rate (per 1,000 live births, 2000) . . .	34
HIV/AIDS (% of persons aged 15–49, 2001)	<0.10
Physicians (per 1,000 head, 1997)	1.66
Hospital beds (per 1,000 head, 1997)	1.8
Health expenditure (1998): US $ per head (PPP) . . .	348
% of GDP	8.5
Public (% of total) . . .	62.1
Access to water (% of persons, 2000)	96
Access to sanitation (% of persons, 2000)	99
Human Development Index (2000): Ranking . . .	99
Value . . .	0.717

For sources and definitions, see explanatory note on p. vi.

Agriculture

PRINCIPAL CROPS (East Bank only; '000 metric tons)

	1998	1999	2000
Wheat	36	9	25
Barley	27	5	12
Potatoes	88	96	97
Olives	138	38	134
Cabbages	15	35	12
Tomatoes	300	293	354
Cauliflowers	48	49	26
Pumpkins, squash and gourds	37	36	49
Cucumbers and gherkins	90	66	133
Eggplants (Aubergines)	53	44	36
Green peppers	24	23	22
Onions (dry)	21	28	47
Green beans	18	11	14
Other vegetables	104	95	78
Watermelons	90	121	35
Melons	17	21	34
Grapes	18	18	24
Apples	39	31	37
Oranges	38	19	40
Tangerines, mandarins, clementines and satsumas	73	33	50
Lemons and limes	43	24	29
Bananas	24	24†	21
Other fruits and berries	48	18	35
Tobacco (leaves)	2	1	3

* Unofficial figure.   † FAO estimate.

Source: FAO.

LIVESTOCK (East Bank only; '000 head, year ending September)

	1998	1999	2000
Horses*	4	4	4
Mules*	3	3	3
Asses*	18	18	18
Cattle	61	65	65
Camels*	18	18	18
Sheep	1,581	1,934	1,896
Goats	631	641	640
Chickens	22,000	23,000	23,500

* FAO estimate(s).

Source: FAO.

LIVESTOCK PRODUCTS (East Bank only; '000 metric tons)

	1998	1999	2000
Beef and veal	3	4	3
Mutton and lamb	15	13	9
Goat meat	4	3	2
Poultry meat	93	111	119
Cows' milk	123	141	162
Sheeps' milk	31	20	31
Goats' milk	16	12	11
Cheese	4	2	4
Hen eggs	51	48	46
Greasy wool	4	4	2
Sheepskins	102	113	94

Source: FAO.

Forestry

ROUNDWOOD REMOVALS
(estimates, '000 cubic metres, excluding bark)

	1995	1996	1997
Industrial wood	4	8	1
Fuel wood	6	6	7
Total	10	14	8

1998–2000: Annual production as in 1997 (FAO estimates).

Source: FAO, *Yearbook of Forest Products*.

Fishing

(metric tons, live weight)

	1997	1998	1999
Capture	450	470	510
Freshwater fishes	350	350	350
Tunas	n.a.	70	96
Other marine fishes	100	3	7
Aquaculture	200	293	515
Freshwater fishes	200	293	515
Total catch	650	763	1,025

Source: FAO, *Yearbook of Fishery Statistics*.

Mining

('000 metric tons)

	1998	1999*	2000*
Crude petroleum	202	196	194
Phosphate rock	5,925	6,014	5,458
Potash salts†	916	1,080	1,160
Salt (unrefined)	263	279	311

* Estimates.

† Figures refer to the K₂O content.

Source: US Geological Survey.

Industry

SELECTED PRODUCTS ('000 barrels, unless otherwise indicated)

	1998	1999	2000
Liquefied petroleum gas	1,660	1,505	1,684
Motor spirit (petrol)	5,429	4,685	4,957
Kerosene	1,517	1,382	1,991
Jet fuels	245	1,722	1,950
Distillate fuel oils	6,882	8,222	10,001
Residual fuel oils	7,105	0	0
Other refinery products	783	830	688
Phosphate fertilizers ('000 metric tons)	579.8	613.8	409.1
Cement ('000 metric tons)	2,652	2,687	2,640
Electricity (million kWh)	6,336	6,456	7,056

2001: Cement ('000 metric tons) 3,180; Electricity (million kWh) 7,200.

Nitrogenous fertilizers (metric tons, (a)*): 121,000 in 1996.

Potassic fertilizers (metric tons, (b)*): 987 in 1997.

Cigarettes (million): 2,652 in 1996.

* Production in terms of (a) nitrogen; (b) potassic acid.

Source: US Geological Survey; UN, *Monthly Bulletin of Statistics*.

Finance

CURRENCY AND EXCHANGE RATES

Monetary Units
1,000 fils = 1 Jordanian dinar (JD).

Sterling, Dollar and Euro Equivalents (31 May 2002)
£1 sterling = JD 1.0399;
US $1 = 709.0 fils;
€1 = 665.5 fils;
JD 100 = £96.16 = $141.04 = €150.25.

Exchange Rate
An official mid-point rate of US $1 = 709 fils (JD1 = $1.4104) has been maintained since October 1995.

BUDGET (East Bank only; JD million)*

Revenue†	1999	2000	2001‡
Taxation	884.2	961.9	1,020.0
Taxes on income and profits .	152.8	161.0	195.0
Corporations. . . .	94.2	97.3	129.5
Individuals . . .	35.7	37.9	39.4
Taxes on domestic transactions	435.0	520.2	566.5
General sales tax . .	372.5	464.5	515.0
Taxes on foreign trade . . .	279.3	264.7	240.0
Customs duties . . .	274.0	260.5	235.5
Other revenue	701.1	598.8	618.1
Licences	24.9	37.4	33.0
Fees	172.4	200.1	215.0
Interest and profits . . .	197.4	140.7	145.0
Total	1,585.3	1,560.7	1,638.1

Expenditure§	1999	2000	2001‡
Wages and salaries . . .	343.4	366.0	380.3
Purchases of goods and services	72.6	72.2	81.7
Interest payments . . .	278.1	293.1	275.0
Food subsidies	15.0	—	—
Other transfers	376.7	408.4	452.5
Pensions	238.5	268.6	292.7
Decentralized agencies . .	66.8	67.2	77.4
University and municipalities	43.0	43.0	48.0
Defence and security . . .	512.1	531.2	537.2
Total	1,942.1	2,006.7	2,112.4
Current	1,643.1	1,718.3	1,786.9
Capital‖	299.0	288.4	325.5

* Figures represent a consolidation of the Current, Capital and Development Plan Budgets of the central Government. The data exclude the operations of the Health Security Fund and of other government agencies with individual budgets.
† Excluding foreign grants received (JD million): 198.5 in 1999; 240.2 in 2000; 247.0 in 2001.
‡ Preliminary figures.
§ Excluding lending minus repayments (JD million): 65.3 in 1999; –2.0 in 2000; –36.9 in 2001.
‖ Includes overdue settlements and arrears on public sector.

Source: Central Bank of Jordan.

INTERNATIONAL RESERVES (US $ million at 31 December)

	1999	2000	2001
Gold*	120.0	99.1	112.2
IMF special drawing rights . .	0.3	0.6	1.2
Foreign exchange	2,628.8	3,330.6	3,061.0
Total	2,749.1	3,430.3	3,174.4

* National valuation.
Source: IMF, *International Financial Statistics.*

MONEY SUPPLY (JD million at 31 December)

	1999	2000	2001
Currency outside banks . .	1,106.6	1,239.9	1,202.4
Demand deposits at commercial banks	658.0	774.2	888.4
Total money (incl. others) . .	1,766.1	2,017.4	2,094.8

Source: IMF, *International Financial Statistics.*

COST OF LIVING (Consumer Price Index; base: 1997 = 100)

	1999	2000	2001
Food (incl. beverages) . .	103.1	102.4	102.7
Clothing (incl. footwear) . .	109.3	110.0	111.3
Housing	102.6	104.0	105.9
Other goods and services . .	104.7	107.6	112.7
All items	103.7	104.4	106.3

Source: Central Bank of Jordan.

NATIONAL ACCOUNTS (East Bank only; JD million at current prices)
Expenditure on the Gross Domestic Product

	1998	1999	2000
Government final consumption expenditure	1,367.0	1,386.7	1,421.6
Private final consumption expenditure	4,110.7	4,166.3	4,856.1
Increase in stocks . . .	35.6	–106.6	64.0
Gross fixed capital formation . .	1,189.8	1,353.5	1,263.2
Total domestic expenditure .	6,703.1	6,799.9	7,604.9
Exports of goods and services .	2,515.7	2,505.4	2,507.0
Less Imports of goods and services	3,608.7	3,537.9	4,109.5
GDP in purchasers' values .	5,610.1	5,767.4	6,002.4
GDP at constant 1994 prices .	5,027.4	5,181.5	5,399.8

Gross Domestic Product by Economic Activity

	1996	1997	1998*
Agriculture, hunting, forestry and fishing	158.6	148.3	144.8
Mining and quarrying . . .	153.7	169.9	170.4
Manufacturing	570.0	621.6	742.0
Electricity and water	104.4	117.8	121.2
Construction	254.8	240.5	214.6
Wholesale and retail trade, restaurants and hotels . .	425.9	510.6	532.4
Transport, storage and communications . . .	642.7	672.7	717.1
Finance, insurance, real estate and business services . .	882.2	918.5	979.1
Government services . . .	827.4	896.2	943.2
Other community, social and personal services . . .	144.4	178.3	200.3
Private non-profit services to households	51.5	52.9	56.1
Domestic services of households	5.3	5.2	6.6
Sub-total	4,220.9	4,532.5	4,827.8
Less Imputed bank service charge	77.3	80.9	107.5
GDP at factor cost . . .	4,143.6	4,451.6	4,720.3
Indirect taxes, *less* subsidies . .	768.7	686.2	889.6
GDP in purchasers' values .	4,912.3	5,137.8	5,609.9

*Preliminary figures.

BALANCE OF PAYMENTS (US $ million)

	1997	1998	1999
Exports of goods f.o.b. . . .	1,835.5	1,802.4	1,831.9
Imports of goods f.o.b. . . .	–3,648.5	–3,403.9	–3,292.0
Trade balance	–1,813.0	–1,601.6	–1,460.1
Exports of services . . .	1,736.8	1,825.1	1,701.7
Imports of services	–1,537.2	–1,783.8	–1,698.0
Balance on goods and services	–1,613.4	–1,560.2	–1,456.4
Other income received . .	248.2	306.9	301.1
Other income paid	–457.0	–445.0	–455.6
Balance on goods, services and income	–1,822.1	–1,698.3	–1,610.9
Current transfers received . .	2,096.1	1,984.3	2,321.3
Current transfers paid . . .	–244.6	–271.9	–305.5
Current balance	29.3	14.1	404.9
Capital account (net) . . .	163.8	81.1	90.3
Direct investment abroad . . .	—	—	–4.5
Direct investment from abroad .	360.9	310.0	158.0
Other investment assets . .	16.4	–80.3	–73.5
Other investment liabilities . .	–135.0	–407.1	353.9
Net errors and omissions . . .	–160.8	–454.0	–10.2
Overall balance	274.6	–536.1	972.9

Source: IMF, *International Financial Statistics.*

External Trade

PRINCIPAL COMMODITIES (distribution by SITC, JD '000)

Imports c.i.f.	1999	2000	2001
Food and live animals . . .	484,133	529,895	524,323
Crude materials (inedible) except fuels	84,384	103,790	106,101
Mineral fuels, lubricants, etc. .	319,046	508,811	495,376
Crude petroleum . . .	220,479	373,131	385,871
Chemicals	334,216	349,603	379,414
Basic manufactures . .	391,234	493,722	666,575
Machinery and transport equipment	724,876	931,114	938,668
Miscellaneous manufactured articles	180,649	180,806	204,985
Total (incl. others) . . .	2,635,207	3,259,404	3,453,729

Exports f.o.b.	1999	2000	2001
Natural calcium phosphates . .	115,165	90,864	90,485
Natural potassic salts, crude . .	125,956	138,061	138,334
Chemicals	352,528	347,161	345,135
Fertilizers	78,224	59,768	61,099
Vegetables, fruit and nuts . .	78,191	71,849	94,393
Basic manufactures . . .	108,650	113,619	168,795
Machinery and transport equipment	68,025	69,253	122,826
Miscellaneous manufactured articles	77,569	131,497	264,262
Total (incl. others) . . .	1,051,353	1,080,817	1,352,371

Source: Central Bank of Jordan.

PRINCIPAL TRADING PARTNERS
(countries of consignment, JD million)

Imports c.i.f.	1999	2000	2001
Argentina	49.2	69.7	73.0
Australia	39.6	46.6	52.9
Belgium-Luxembourg . .	30.2	39.3	30.5
China, People's Republic . .	83.7	125.6	168.6
Egypt	29.2	30.9	36.6
France	102.3	124.0	131.8
Germany	256.1	375.2	317.1
India	42.3	45.6	52.1
Indonesia	30.0	42.1	42.3
Iraq	296.0	483.9	485.6
Italy	108.5	118.7	114.0
Japan	166.2	127.8	124.1
Korea, Republic . . .	114.6	116.7	99.6
Lebanon	27.6	31.5	n.a.
Malaysia	34.3	37.0	34.1
Netherlands	52.7	52.5	47.8
Russia	51.3	42.5	n.a.
Saudi Arabia . . .	107.2	106.2	111.0
Spain	31.8	31.9	60.0
Sweden	24.5	56.6	n.a.
Switzerland	39.3	40.1	n.a.
Syria	31.8	47.1	n.a.
Turkey	54.9	64.3	86.4
United Arab Emirates . .	26.1	34.9	41.7
United Kingdom . . .	124.3	148.3	124.3
USA	259.7	322.0	280.7
Total (incl. others) . . .	2,635.2	3,259.4	3,453.7

Exports f.o.b.	1999	2000	2001
Bahrain	10.5	10.6	13.0
China, People's Republic . . .	33.0	29.5	n.a.
Egypt	15.4	16.9	14.9
India	180.5	172.2	145.3
Indonesia	18.5	20.0	21.0
Iraq	80.4	100.1	299.4
Italy	12.8	4.8	4.8
Japan	10.6	9.3	9.1
Kuwait	20.2	19.5	24.8
Lebanon	22.4	24.1	27.7
Malaysia	20.6	14.8	16.7
Netherlands	12.6	1.9	1.3
Pakistan	12.5	24.4	18.1
Qatar	15.7	15.2	17.8
Saudi Arabia . . .	99.6	92.0	95.6
Syria	16.5	25.6	n.a.
United Arab Emirates . .	61.7	47.6	58.9
United Kingdom . . .	8.1	8.0	14.8
USA	9.3	44.8	164.6
Total (incl. others)	1,051.4	1,080.8	1,352.4

Source: Central Bank of Jordan

Transport

RAILWAYS (traffic)

	1998	1999	2000
Passenger-km (million) . .	2.0	2.5	2.1
Freight ton-km (million) . .	596	585	348

ROAD TRAFFIC (motor vehicles in use at 31 December)

	1998	1999	2000
Passenger cars	191,940	203,503	245,357
Buses and coaches . . .	10,104	9,962	9,839
Lorries and vans	101,343	94,028	102,531
Motorcycles and mopeds . .	271	311	273

SHIPPING

Merchant Fleet (registered at 31 December)

	1999	2000	2001
Number of vessels . . .	10	9	10
Displacement (grt) . . .	42.1	41.8	42.1

Source: Lloyd's Register-Fairplay, *World Fleet Statistics.*

International Sea-borne Freight Traffic ('000 metric tons)

	1998	1999	2000
Goods loaded	7,310	7,480	7,193
Goods unloaded	5,334	5,374	5,360

Source: UN, *Monthly Bulletin of Statistics.*

CIVIL AVIATION (traffic on scheduled services)

	1996	1997	1998
Kilometres flown (million) . .	42	40	35
Passengers carried ('000) . .	1,299	1,353	1,187
Passenger-km (million) . .	4,750	4,900	4,065
Total ton-km (million) . .	731	721	596

Source: UN, *Statistical Yearbook.*

Passengers carried ('000): 1,187 in 1998; 1,252 in 1999; 1,282 in 2000.

Tourism

ARRIVALS BY NATIONALITY ('000)*

	1999	2000	2001
Egypt	270.4	215.0	325.1
Iraq	358.0	330.2	417.5
Israel	125.5	136.7	185.4
Kuwait	73.8	58.1	80.5
Saudi Arabia	609.2	471.1	602.7
Syria	939.3	898.6	1,127.2
Turkey	78.2	59.4	70.7
USA	100.5	99.2	59.1
Total (incl. others)	3,315.2	3,019.6	2,366.3

* Including pilgrims and excursionists (same-day visitors). The total number of tourist arrivals (in '000) was: 1,357.8 in 1999; 1,426.9 in 2000; 1,477.7 in 2001.

Source: partly World Tourism Organization, *Yearbook of Tourism Statistics*.

Tourism receipts (preliminary estimates, JD million): 564.1 in 1999; 512.4 in 2000; 496.1 in 2001. (Source: Central Bank of Jordan).

Communications Media

(East Bank only)

	1999	2000	2001
Television receivers ('000 in use)	540	560	n.a.
Telephones ('000 main lines in use)	565.3	620.0	660.0
Mobile cellular telephones ('000 subscribers)	118.4	388.9	745.5
Personal computers ('000 in use)	90	150	170
Internet users ('000)	120.0	127.3	212.0

Radio receivers ('000 in use): 1,660 in 1997.
Facsimile machines ('000 in use): 51.6 in 1998.
Book production (titles): 511 in 1996.
Daily newspapers (1996): 4 titles; (average circulation) 250,000 copies.
Non-daily newspapers (1996): 4 titles; (average circulation) 95,000 copies.

Sources: International Telecommunication Union; UNESCO, *Statistical Yearbook*.

Education

(East Bank, 2001, unless otherwise indicated)

	Schools	Teachers	Pupils
Pre-primary	1,165	3,878	83,777
Primary	2,708	50,562	1,173,314
Secondary: general	912	11,254	129,894
Secondary: vocational	214	3,026	43,861
Higher	22	6,036	153,965
of which universities*	n.a.	3,982	89,010

* 1996/97 figures.

Adult literacy rate (UNESCO estimates): 89.7% (males 95.1%; females 83.9%) in 2000 (Source: UNDP, *Human Development Report*).

Directory

The Constitution

The revised Constitution was approved by King Talal I on 1 January 1952.

The Hashemite Kingdom of Jordan is an independent, indivisible sovereign state. Its official religion is Islam; its official language Arabic.

RIGHTS OF THE INDIVIDUAL

There is to be no discrimination between Jordanians on account of race, religion or language. Work, education and equal opportunities shall be afforded to all as far as is possible. The freedom of the individual is guaranteed, as are his dwelling and property. No Jordanian shall be exiled. Labour shall be made compulsory only in a national emergency, or as a result of a conviction; conditions, hours worked and allowances are under the protection of the state.

The Press, and all opinions, are free, except under martial law. Societies can be formed, within the law. Schools may be established freely, but they must follow a recognized curriculum and educational policy. Elementary education is free and compulsory. All religions are tolerated. Every Jordanian is eligible for public office, and choices are to be made by merit only. Power belongs to the people.

THE LEGISLATIVE POWER

Legislative power is vested in the National Assembly and the King. The National Assembly consists of two houses: the Senate and the House of Representatives.

THE SENATE

The number of Senators is one-half of the number of members of the House of Representatives. Senators must be unrelated to the King, over 40, and are chosen from present and past Prime Ministers and Ministers, past Ambassadors or Ministers Plenipotentiary, past Presidents of the House of Representatives, past Presidents and members of the Court of Cassation and of the Civil and *Shari'a*

Courts of Appeal, retired officers of the rank of General and above, former members of the House of Representatives who have been elected twice to that House, etc. . . They may not hold public office. Senators are appointed for four years. They may be reappointed. The President of the Senate is appointed for two years.

THE HOUSE OF REPRESENTATIVES

The members of the House of Representatives are elected by secret ballot in a general direct election and retain their mandate for four years. General elections take place during the four months preceding the end of the term. The President of the House is elected by secret ballot each year by the Representatives. Representatives must be Jordanians of over 30, they must have a clean record, no active business interests, and are debarred from public office. Close relatives of the King are not eligible. If the House of Representatives is dissolved, the new House shall assemble in extraordinary session not more than four months after the date of dissolution. The new House cannot be dissolved for the same reason as the last.

GENERAL PROVISIONS FOR THE NATIONAL ASSEMBLY

The King summons the National Assembly to its ordinary session on 1 November each year. This date can be postponed by the King for two months, or he can dissolve the Assembly before the end of its three months' session. Alternatively, he can extend the session up to a total period of six months. Each session is opened by a speech from the throne.

Decisions in the House of Representatives and the Senate are made by a majority vote. The quorum is two-thirds of the total number of members in each House. When the voting concerns the Constitution, or confidence in the Council of Ministers, 'the votes shall be taken by calling the members by name in a loud voice'. Sessions are public, though secret sessions can be held at the request of the Government or of five members. Complete freedom of speech, within the rules of either House, is allowed.

The Prime Minister places proposals before the House of Representatives; if accepted there, they are referred to the Senate and finally sent to the King for confirmation. If one house rejects a law while the other accepts it, a joint session of the House of Representatives and the Senate is called, and a decision made by a two-thirds majority. If the King withholds his approval from a law, he returns it to the Assembly within six months with the reasons for his dissent; a joint session of the Houses then makes a decision, and if the law is accepted by this decision it is promulgated. The Budget is submitted to the National Assembly one month before the beginning of the financial year.

THE KING

The throne of the Hashemite Kingdom devolves by male descent in the dynasty of King Abdullah ibn al-Hussein. The King attains his majority on his eighteenth lunar year; if the throne is inherited by a minor, the powers of the King are exercised by a Regent or a Council of Regency. If the King, through illness or absence, cannot perform his duties, his powers are given to a Deputy, or to a Council of the Throne. This Deputy, or Council, may be appointed by Iradas (decrees) by the King, or, if he is incapable, by the Council of Ministers.

On his accession, the King takes the oath to respect and observe the provisions of the Constitution and to be loyal to the nation. As Head of State he is immune from all liability or responsibility. He approves laws and promulgates them. He declares war, concludes peace and signs treaties; treaties, however, must be approved by the National Assembly. The King is Commander-in-Chief of the navy, the army and the air force. He orders the holding of elections; convenes, inaugurates, adjourns and prorogues the House of Representatives. The Prime Minister is appointed by him, as are the President and members of the Senate. Military and civil ranks are also granted, or withdrawn, by the King. No death sentence is carried out until he has confirmed it.

MINISTERS

The Council of Ministers consists of the Prime Minister, President of the Council, and of his ministers. Ministers are forbidden to become members of any company, to receive a salary from any company, or to participate in any financial act of trade. The Council of Ministers is entrusted with the conduct of all affairs of state, internal and external.

The Council of Ministers is responsible to the House of Representatives for matters of general policy. Ministers may speak in either House, and, if they are members of one House, they may also vote in that House. Votes of confidence in the Council are cast in the House of Representatives, and decided by a two-thirds majority. If a vote of 'no confidence' is returned, the ministers are bound to resign. Every newly-formed Council of Ministers must present its programme to the House of Representatives and ask for a vote of confidence. The House of Representatives can impeach ministers, as it impeaches its own members.

AMENDMENTS

Two amendments were passed in November 1974 giving the King the right to dissolve the Senate or to take away membership from any of its members, and to postpone general elections for a period not to exceed a year, if there are circumstances in which the Council of Ministers feels that it is impossible to hold elections. A further amendment in February 1976 enabled the King to postpone elections indefinitely. In January 1984 two amendments were passed, allowing elections 'in any part of the country where it is possible to hold them' (effectively, only the East Bank) and empowering the National Assembly to elect deputies from the Israeli-held West Bank.

The Government

HEAD OF STATE

King ABDULLAH IBN AL-HUSSEIN (succeeded to the throne on 7 February 1999).

CABINET*
(September 2002)

Prime Minister and Minister of Defence: Eng. ALI ABU AR-RAGHEB.

Minister of the Interior: QAFTAN AL-MAJALI.

Minister of Justice and Minister of State for Legal Affairs: FARIS AN-NABULSI.

Minister of National Economy and Minister of State: Dr MUHAMMAD AL-HALAIQA.

Minister of Awqaf (Religious Endowments) and Islamic Affairs: Dr AHMAD HILAYEL.

Minister of Health: Dr FALEH AN-NASSER.

Minister of Foreign Affairs: MARWAN AL-MUASHER.

Minister of Tourism and Antiquities: Dr TALEB AR-RIFAI.

Minister of Finance: Dr MICHEL MARTO.

Minister of Labour: MUZAHIM AL-MUHAISIN.

Minister of Public Works and Housing: Eng. HOSNI ABU GHEIDA.

Minister of Energy and Mineral Resources: MUHAMMAD ALI AL-BATAYNEH.

Minister of Education: Dr KHALID TOUQAN.

Minister of Higher Education and Scientific Research: WALID AL-MAANI.

Minister of Municipal, Rural and Environmental Affairs: ABD AR-RAZZAQ TBEISHAT.

Minister of Culture: HAIDAR MAHMOUD.

Minister of Agriculture: Dr MAHMOUD AD-DUWEIRI.

Minister of Industry and Trade: SALAH AL-BASHIR.

Minister of Planning: Dr BASSEM AWADALLAH.

Minister of Water and Irrigation: Dr HAZEM AN-NASSER.

Minister of Social Development: TAMAM AL-GHOUL.

Minister of Information and Communications Technology: Dr FAWWAZ HATIM AZ-ZU'BI.

Minister of Transport: NADER AD-DAHABI.

Minister of State for Foreign Affairs: SHAHER BAK.

Minister of State for Cabinet Affairs: MOUSTAFA AL-QAISI.

Minister of State for Political Affairs and Information: MUHAMMAD AFFASH AL-ADWAN.

Minister of State for Administrative Development: Dr MUHAMMAD ATH-THNEIBAT.

* The Head of Intelligence and the Governor of the Central Bank also have full ministerial status.

MINISTRIES

Office of the Prime Minister: POB 80, Amman; tel. (6) 4641211; fax (6) 4642520; e-mail pmic@pm.gov.jo; internet www .pm.gov. jo.

Ministry of Agriculture: POB 2099, Amman; tel. (6) 5686151; fax (6) 5686310; e-mail agri@moa.gov.jo; internet www.moa.gov.jo.

Ministry of Awqaf (Religious Endowments) and Islamic Affairs: POB 659, Amman; tel. (6) 5666141; fax (6) 5602254.

Ministry of Culture: POB 6140, Amman; tel. (6) 5696218; fax (6) 5696598; e-mail info@culture.gov.jo; internet www.culture.gov.jo.

Ministry of Defence: POB 80, Amman; tel. (6) 4641211; fax (6) 4642520.

Ministry of Development Affairs: POB 1577, Amman; tel. (6) 4644361; fax (6) 4648825.

Ministry of Education: POB 1646, Amman 11118; tel. (6) 5607181; fax (6) 5666019; e-mail moe@amra.nic.gov.jo; internet www.moe .gov.jo.

Ministry of Energy and Mineral Resources: POB 2310, Amman; tel. (6) 5863326; fax (6) 5818336; e-mail memr@amra.nic .gov.jo; internet www.nic.gov.jo/memr/memr.html.

Ministry of Finance: POB 85, Amman 11118; tel. (6) 4636321; fax (6) 4643132; e-mail webmaster@mof.gov.jo; internet www.mof .gov.jo.

Ministry of Foreign Affairs: POB 35217, Amman 11180; tel. (6) 4644361; fax (6) 4648825.

Ministry of Health: POB 86, Amman; tel. (6) 5665131; fax (6) 5665232.

Ministry of Industry and Trade: POB 2019, Amman; tel. (6) 5607191; fax (6) 5603721; e-mail info@mit.gov.jo; internet www.mit .gov.jo.

Ministry of the Interior: POB 100, Amman; tel. (6) 4638849; fax (6) 5606908.

Ministry of Justice: POB 6040, Amman; tel. (6) 4653533; fax (6) 4643197; e-mail moj@amra.nic.gov.jo.

Ministry of Labour: POB 8160, Amman; tel. (6) 5607481; fax (6) 5667193; internet www.mol.gov.jo.

Ministry of Municipal, Rural and Environmental Affairs: POB 1799, Amman; tel. (6) 4641393; fax (6) 4640404.

Ministry of Planning: POB 555, Amman 11118; tel. (6) 4641460; fax (6) 4649341; e-mail mop@mop.gov.jo; internet www.mop.gov.jo.

Ministry of Information and Communications Technology: POB 9903, Amman 11191; tel. (6) 5859001; fax (6) 5825262; e-mail cio@mopc.gov.jo; internet www.mopc.gov.jo/moict.htm.

Ministry of Public Works and Housing: POB 1220, Amman; tel. (6) 5850470; fax (6) 5857590; e-mail mhpw@amra.nic.gov.jo.

Ministry of Social Development: POB 6720, Amman; tel. (6) 5931391; fax (6) 5673198; internet www.mosd.gov.jo.

Ministry of Tourism and Antiquities: POB 224, Amman 11118; tel. (6) 4642311; fax (6) 4648465; e-mail tourism@mota.gov.jo; internet www.mota.gov.jo.

Ministry of Transport: POB 35214, Amman; tel. (6) 5518111; fax (6) 5527233; e-mail mot1@go.com.jo.

Ministry of Water and Irrigation: POB 2412, Amman 5012; tel. (6) 5680100; fax (6) 5680075; e-mail info@mwi.gov.jo; internet www.mwi.gov.jo.

Legislature

MAJLIS AL-UMMA
(National Assembly)

Senate

Speaker: ZAID AR-RIFAI.

The Senate (House of Notables) consists of 40 members, appointed by the King. A new Senate was appointed by the King on 22 November 1997.

House of Representatives

Speaker: ABD AL-HADI AL-MAJALI.

General Election, 4 November 1997*

Party/Group	Seats
Pro-Government†	60
Independent nationalists and leftists	10
Independent Islamists	8
National Constitutional Party (NCP)	2
Total	80

* The 1997 general election was boycotted by all the principal opposition parties in Jordan, including the Islamic Action Front (which had emerged as the largest single party in the House of Representatives after the 1993 elections).

† Excluding NCP.

Note: On 22 July 2001 legislation was introduced whereby membership of the lower house was to be increased from 80 to 104, with effect from the next general election.

Political Organizations

Political parties were banned before the elections of July 1963. In September 1971 King Hussein announced the formation of a Jordanian National Union, which was the only legal political organization. Communists, Marxists and 'other advocates of imported ideologies' were ineligible for membership. In March 1972 the organization was renamed the Arab National Union. In April 1974 King Hussein dissolved the executive committee of the Arab National Union, and accepted the resignation of the Secretary-General. In February 1976 the Cabinet approved a law abolishing the Union. A royal commission was appointed in April 1990 to draft a National Charter, one feature of which was the legalization of political parties. In January 1991 King Hussein approved the National Charter, which was formally endorsed in June. In July 1992 the House of Representatives adopted draft legislation which formally permitted the establishment of political parties, subject to certain conditions. In the same month a joint session of the Senate and the House of Representatives was convened to debate amendments to the new legislation, proposed by the Senate. The organizations that achieved representation in the general election of November 1993 were: the Islamic Action Front (Sec.-Gen. Dr ABD AL-LATIF ARABIYAT; Dep. Sec.-Gen. HAMZEH MANSUR); al-Mustaqbal (Future) Party (Sec.-Gen. SULEIMAN ARAR); the Jordanian Arab Socialist Baath Party (Sec.-Gen. TAYSEER SALAMEH AL-HOMSI); al-Yakatha (Reawakening) Party; al-Ahd (Pledge) Party; the Jordan National Alliance; the Jordan People's Democratic Party (Leader TAYSIR AZ-ZABRI; Sec.-Gen. SALEM NAHHAS); the Jordan Social Democratic Party; and the Jordanian Arab Democratic Party. In May 1997 nine centre parties, including al-Ahd and the Jordan National Alliance, united to form the National Constitutional Party (NCP; Sec.-Gen. ABD AL-HADI AL-MAJALI), which became Jordan's largest political grouping. The formation of the NCP, together with the establishment in 1996 of the Unionist Arab Democratic Party (a coalition of three leftist parties), reduced the total number of political parties from 24 to 14. In July 1997 the establishment of a new Jordanian party, the Popular Democratic Pan-Arab Movement, was announced. In May 1999 the Popular Participation Bloc was established to contest the municipal elec-

tions, held in July; it was a new grouping of 13 leftist, Baathist and pan-Arab parties. The formation of two new political parties was announced in late 1999: the New Generations Party (centrist green party; Leader ZAHI KARIM) and the Jordanian Arab New Dawn Party. In September 2000 a new political grouping, the Arab Democratic Front (Founders AHMAD UBEIDAT, TAHER AL-MASRI), was established. Two new political organizations were granted licences in late 2001: the Jordanian People's Committees Movement (moderate; Sec.-Gen. KHALID SHUBAKI) and the Jordan Rafah (Welfare) Party (Leader MUHAMMAD RIJJAL SHUMALI). In July 2001 the moderate Muslim Centrist Party was formed by dissidents of the Muslim Brotherhood and the Islamic Action Front.

Diplomatic Representation

EMBASSIES IN JORDAN

Algeria: POB 830375, Amman 11183; tel. (6) 4641271; fax (6) 4647957; Ambassador: HAMID CHEBIRA.

Australia: POB 35201, Amman 11180; tel. (6) 5930246; fax (6) 5932160; e-mail ausemb@nets.com.jo; Ambassador: JOHN A. TILEMANN.

Austria: POB 830795, Amman 11183; tel. (6) 4644635; fax (6) 4612725; e-mail austemb@go.com.jo; Ambassador: Dr HEINRICH QUERNER.

Bahrain: POB 5220, Amman 11183; tel. (6) 5664148; fax (6) 5664190; Ambassador: MUHAMMAD SEIF JABER AL-MSALLAM.

Belgium: POB 942, Amman 11118; tel. (6) 5932683; fax (6) 5930487; e-mail belgica@nol.com.jo; Ambassador: MARC DO SCHOUTHEETE.

Bosnia and Herzegovina: POB 850836, Amman 11185; tel. (6) 5856921; fax (6) 5856923; e-mail bosnia@go.com.jo; Ambassador JASKO LUPI.

Brazil: POB 5497, Amman 11183; tel. (6) 4642183; fax (6) 4641328; e-mail jorbrem@go.com.jo; Ambassador: SERGIO HENRIQUE NABUCO DE CASTRO.

Brunei: POB 851752, Amman 11185; tel. (6) 5928021; fax (6) 5928024; e-mail bruneijo@go.com.jo; Ambassador: Pehin Dato HJ HUSSAIN BIN AHMAD.

Bulgaria: POB 950578, Amman 11195; tel. (6) 5529391; fax (6) 5539393; Chargé d'affaires: NIKOLAY NIKOLOV.

Canada: POB 815403, Amman 11180; tel. (6) 5666124; fax (6) 5689227; Ambassador: RODERICK BELL.

Chile: POB 830663, 28 Hussein Abu Ragheb St, Abdoun, Amman 11183; tel. (6) 5923360; fax (6) 5924263; e-mail echilejo@go.com.jo; Ambassador: ALFREDO TAPIA.

China, People's Republic: POB 7365, Amman 11118; tel. (6) 5516136; fax (6) 5518713; Ambassador: CHEN YONGLONG.

Czech Republic: POB 2213, Amman 11181; tel. (6) 5927051; fax (6) 5927053; e-mail amman@embassy.mzv.cz; internet www.mzv.cz/amman; Chargé d'affaires LUBOR STEHLIK (designate).

Denmark: POB 222, 24 Sharif Abd-al Hamid Sharaf St, Shmeisani, Amman 11118; tel. (6) 5604644; fax (6) 5604664; e-mail dancons@kawar.com.jo; Ambassador OLE WØHLERS OLSEN.

Egypt: POB 35178, Amman 11180; tel. (6) 5605175; fax (6) 5604082; Ambassador: MUHAMMAD HIJAZI.

France: POB 5348, Amman 11183; tel. (6) 4641273; fax (6) 4659606; e-mail ambafr@joinnet.com.jo; internet www.ambafrance.org.jo; Ambassador: BERNARD EMIÉ.

Germany: POB 183, Benghazi St, Jabal Amman 11118; tel. (6) 5930351; fax (6) 5932887; e-mail germaemb@go.com.jo; Ambassador: Dr MARTIN SCHNELLER.

Greece: POB 35069, Amman 11180; tel. (6) 5672331; fax (6) 5696591; e-mail greekemb@nol.com.jo; Ambassador: CONSTANTIN KARABETSIS.

Holy See: POB 142916, Amman 11814; tel. (6) 5929934; fax (6) 5929931; e-mail nuntius@nol.com.jo; Apostolic Nuncio: Most Rev. FERNANDO FILONI, Titular Archbishop of Volturno.

Hungary: POB 3441, Amman 11181; tel. (6) 5925614; fax (6) 5930836; e-mail huembamm@nol.com.jo; Ambassador: BALAZS BOKOR.

India: POB 2168, Amman 11181; tel. (6) 4622098; fax (6) 4659540; e-mail indembjo@firstnet.com.jo; Ambassador: M. VENKATRAMAN.

Indonesia: POB 811784, South Um-Uthaina, 6th Circle, Amman 11181; tel. (6) 5538911; fax (6) 5528380; e-mail amman96@go.com.jo; Ambassador: EDHIMURTI SUNOKO.

Iran: POB 173, Amman 11118; tel. (6) 4641281; fax (6) 4641383; e-mail emb@go.com.jo; Ambassador: NOSRATOLLAH TAJIK.

Iraq: POB 2025, 1st Circle, Jabal Amman; tel. (6) 4623175; fax (6) 4619172; Ambassador: Dr SABAH YASEEN ALI.

Israel: POB 950866, Amman 11195; tel. (6) 5524680; fax (6) 5524689; e-mail isrem@go.com.jo; Ambassador: DAVID DADON.

Italy: POB 9800, Jabal Luweibdeh, Amman 11191; tel. (6) 4638185; fax (6) 4659730; e-mail italemb1@go.com.jo; internet www .italembamman.org; Ambassador: STEFANO JEDRKIEWICZ.

Japan: POB 2835, Amman 11181; tel. (6) 5932005; fax (6) 5931006; e-mail mail@embjapan.org.jo; Ambassador: SHINTARO SASAKI.

Korea, Democratic People's Republic: Amman; tel. (6) 5666349; Ambassador: (vacant).

Korea, Republic: POB 3060, Amman 11181; tel. (6) 5930745; fax (6) 5930280; e-mail skorea@go.com.jo; Ambassador: KIM KYUNG-KEUN.

Kuwait: POB 2107, Jabal Amman; tel. (6) 5675135; fax (6) 5699217; Ambassador FAYSAL AL-MESHA'AN.

Lebanon: POB 811779, Amman 11181; tel. and fax (6) 5929111; Ambassador: ADIB ALAM ED-DIN.

Morocco: POB 2175, Amman 11183; tel. (6) 5921771; fax (6) 5926069; Ambassador: MOULAY MEHDI ALAOUI.

Netherlands: POB 94136, Amman 11194; tel. (6) 5930581; fax (6) 5930214; e-mail nlgovamm@index.com.jo; Ambassador: Mrs M. DE KWAASTENIET.

Norway: POB 830510, Amman 11183; tel. (6) 5931646; fax (6) 5931650; e-mail emb.amman@mfa.no; Ambassador SVERRE STUB.

Oman: POB 20192, Amman 11110; tel. (6) 5686155; fax (6) 5689404; Ambassador: HAMAD BIN HILAL AL-MA'MARI.

Pakistan: POB 1232, Amman 11118; tel. (6) 4622787; fax (6) 4611633; e-mail pakembjo@go.com.jo; Ambassador: TARIQ FATEMI.

Poland: POB 42050, Amman 11194; tel. (6) 5512593; fax (6) 5512595; e-mail polemb@nol.com.jo; Chargé d'affaires: MARIUSZ WOŹ-NIAK.

Qatar: POB 5098, Amman 11183; tel. (6) 5607311; fax (6) 5607350; e-mail qeamman@jonet.com; Ambassador: Sheikh ABD AR-RAHMAN BIN JASSIM BIN MUHAMMAD ATH-THANI.

Romania: POB 2869, 33 Madina Munawwara St, Amman; tel. (6) 5813423; fax (6) 5812521; e-mail romania@accessme.com; Ambassador: VASILE SOFINETI.

Russia: POB 2187, Amman 11181; tel. (6) 4641158; fax (6) 4647448; e-mail russjo@nets.com.jo; Ambassador: IVANOV GALITSIM.

Saudi Arabia: POB 2132, 5th Circle, Jabal Amman; tel. (6) 5924154; fax (6) 5921154; Ambassador ABD AR-RAHMAN N. AL-OHALY.

South Africa: POB 851508, Sweifieh 11185, Amman; tel. (6) 5921194; fax (6) 5920080; e-mail saembjor@index.com.jo; Ambassador: Dr VINCENT T. ZULU.

Spain: Zahran St, POB 454, Amman 11118; tel. (6) 4614166; fax (6) 4614173; e-mail embespjo@mail.mae.es; Ambassador: ANTONIO LÓPEZ MARTÍNEZ.

Sri Lanka: POB 830731, Amman 11183; tel. (6) 5820611; fax (6) 5820615; e-mail lankaemb@go.com.jo; Ambassador: KATHAN MARI-MUTTU.

Sudan: Jabal Amman; tel. (6) 5624145; Ambassador: AHMAD DIAB.

Sweden: POB 830536, 4th Circle, Amman 11183; tel. (6) 5931177; fax (6) 5930179; e-mail info@swe-embamman.org; internet www.swe-embamman.org; Ambassador: KLAS GIEROW.

Switzerland: POB 5341, Amman 11183; tel. (6) 5931416; fax (6) 5930685; e-mail vertretung@amm.rep.admin.ch; Ambassador: ROLF BODENMÜLLER.

Syria: POB 1733, Amman 11118; tel. (6) 4641935; fax (6) 4651945; Ambassador: ABD AL-FATTAH AMMOURAH.

Tunisia: POB 17185, Amman 11195; tel. (6) 5674307; fax (6) 5605790; Ambassador: HABIB KAABACHI.

Turkey: POB 2062, Amman 11181; tel. (6) 4641251; fax (6) 4612353; e-mail tcammanbe@index.com.jo; Ambassador: ERCAN OZER.

United Arab Emirates: POB 2623, Amman 11181; tel. (6) 5934780; fax (6) 5932666; Ambassador: RAHMA HUSSAIN R. AZ-ZA'ABI.

United Kingdom: POB 87, Abdoun Amman 11118; tel. (6) 5923100; fax (6) 5923759; e-mail info@britain.org.jo; internet www.britain .org.jo; Ambassador: CHRISTOPHER PRENTICE.

USA: POB 354, Amman 11118; tel. (6) 5920101; fax (6) 5920163; e-mail administration@usembassy-amman.org.jo; Ambassador: EDWARD WILLIAM GNEHM, Jr.

Yemen: POB 3085, Amman 11181; tel. (6) 5923771; fax (6) 5923773; Ambassador: Dr IBRAHIM S. AL-ADOOF.

Yugoslavia: POB 5227, Amman 11183; tel. (6) 4647593; fax (6) 4647605; e-mail yugoembjo@nets.com.jo; Ambassador: RADONJA RADOVIĆ.

Judicial System

With the exception of matters of purely personal nature concerning members of non-Muslim communities, the law of Jordan was based on Islamic Law for both civil and criminal matters. During the days of the Ottoman Empire, certain aspects of Continental law, especially French commercial law and civil and criminal procedure, were introduced. Due to British occupation of Palestine and Transjordan from 1917 to 1948, the Palestine territory has adopted, either by statute or case law, much of the English common law. Since the annexation of the non-occupied part of Palestine and the formation of the Hashemite Kingdom of Jordan, there has been a continuous effort to unify the law.

Court of Cassation. The Court of Cassation consists of seven judges, who sit in full panel for exceptionally important cases. In most appeals, however, only five members sit to hear the case. All cases involving amounts of more than JD 100 may be reviewed by this Court, as well as cases involving lesser amounts and cases which cannot be monetarily valued. However, for the latter types of cases, review is available only by leave of the Court of Appeal, or, upon refusal by the Court of Appeal, by leave of the President of the Court of Cassation. In addition to these functions as final and Supreme Court of Appeal, the Court of Cassation also sits as High Court of Justice to hear applications in the nature of habeas corpus, mandamus and certiorari dealing with complaints of a citizen against abuse of governmental authority.

Courts of Appeal. There are two Courts of Appeal, each of which is composed of three judges, whether for hearing of appeals or for dealing with Magistrates Courts' judgments in chambers. Jurisdiction of the two Courts is geographical, with the Court for the Western Region (which has not sat since June 1967) sitting in Jerusalem and the Court for the Eastern Region sitting in Amman. The regions are separated by the Jordan river. Appellate review of the Courts of Appeal extends to judgments rendered in the Courts of First Instance, the Magistrates' Courts, and Religious Courts.

Courts of First Instance. The Courts of First Instance are courts of general jurisdiction in all matters civil and criminal except those specifically allocated to the Magistrates' Courts. Three judges sit in all felony trials, while only two judges sit for misdemeanour and civil cases. Each of the seven Courts of First Instance also exercises appellate jurisdiction in cases involving judgments of less than JD 20 and fines of less than JD 10, rendered by the Magistrates' Courts.

Magistrates' Courts. There are 14 Magistrates' Courts, which exercise jurisdiction in civil cases involving no more than JD 250 and in criminal cases involving maximum fines of JD 100 or maximum imprisonment of one year.

Religious Courts. There are two types of religious court: The *Shari'a* Courts (Muslims): and the Ecclesiastical Courts (Eastern Orthodox, Greek Melkite, Roman Catholic and Protestant). Jurisdiction extends to personal (family) matters, such as marriage, divorce, alimony, inheritance, guardianship, wills, interdiction and, for the Muslim community, the constitution of Waqfs (Religious Endowments). When a dispute involves persons of different religious communities, the Civil Courts have jurisdiction in the matter unless the parties agree to submit to the jurisdiction of one or the other of the Religious Courts involved.

Each *Shari'a* (Muslim) Court consists of one judge (*Qadi*), while most of the Ecclesiastical (Christian) Courts are normally composed of three judges, who are usually clerics. *Shari'a* Courts apply the doctrines of Islamic Law, based on the Koran and the *Hadith* (Precepts of Muhammad), while the Ecclesiastical Courts base their law on various aspects of Canon Law. In the event of conflict between any two Religious Courts or between a Religious Court and a Civil Court, a Special Tribunal of three judges is appointed by the President of the Court of Cassation, to decide which court shall have jurisdiction. Upon the advice of experts on the law of the various communities, this Special Tribunal decides on the venue for the case at hand.

Religion

Over 80% of the population are Sunni Muslims, and the King can trace unbroken descent from the Prophet Muhammad. There is a Christian minority, living mainly in the towns, and there are smaller numbers of non-Sunni Muslims.

ISLAM

Chief Justice and President of the Supreme Muslim Secular Council: Sheikh IZZEDIN AL-KHATIB AT-TAMIMI.

Director of Shari'a Courts: Sheikh SUBHI AL-MUWQQAT.

Mufti of the Hashemite Kingdom of Jordan: Sheikh MUHAMMAD ABDO HASHEM.

CHRISTIANITY
The Roman Catholic Church

Latin Rite

Jordan forms part of the Patriarchate of Jerusalem (see the chapter on Israel).

Vicar-General for Transjordan: Mgr SELIM SAYEGH (Titular Bishop of Aquae in Proconsulari), Latin Vicariate, POB 851379, Sweifieh, Amman 11185; tel. (6) 5929546; fax (6) 5920548; e-mail proffice@joinnet.com.jo.

Melkite Rite

The Greek-Melkite archdiocese of Petra (Wadi Musa) and Philadelphia (Amman) contained 31,300 adherents at 31 December 2000.

Archbishop of Petra and Philadelphia: Most Rev. GEORGES EL-MURR, Archevêché Grec-Melkite Catholique, POB 2435, Jabal Amman 11181; tel. (6) 4624757; fax (6) 4628560.

Syrian Rite

The Syrian Catholic Patriarch of Antioch is resident in Beirut, Lebanon.

Patriarchal Exarchate of Jerusalem: Mont Achrafieh, POB 510393, Rue Barto, Amman; e-mail stjossc@p-ol.com; Exarch Patriarchal Mgr GRÉGOIRE PIERRE MELKI.

The Anglican Communion

Within the Episcopal Church in Jerusalem and the Middle East, Jordan forms part of the diocese of Jerusalem. The President Bishop of the Church is the Bishop in Jerusalem (see the chapter on Israel).

Assistant Bishop in Amman: Rt Rev. Elia Khoury, POB 598, Amman.

Other Christian Churches

The Coptic Orthodox Church, the Greek Orthodox Church (Patriarchate of Jerusalem) and the Evangelical Lutheran Church in Jordan are also active.

The Press

Jordan Press Association (JPA): Amman; Pres. RAKAN AL-MAJALI; Vice-Pres. TARIQ MUMANI; Sec.-Gen. NIDAL MANSUR.

DAILIES

Al-Akhbar (News): POB 62420, Amman; f. 1976; Arabic; publ. by the Arab Press Co; Editor RACAN EL-MAJALI; circ. 15,000.

Arab Daily: Amman; f. 1999; English.

Al-Aswaq (Markets): POB 11117, Queen Rania St, Amman 11123; tel. (6) 5157690, fax (6) 5154390; e-mail alaswaq@nets.com.jo; f. 1992; Arabic; business; Man. Editor YAHYA MAHMOUD; Editor-in-Chief MUSTAFA ABU LIBDEH; circ. 40,000.

Ad-Dustour (The Constitution): POB 591, Amman 11118; tel. (6) 5664153; fax (6) 5667170; e-mail dustour@go.com.jo; internet www.addustour.com; f. 1967; Arabic; publ. by the Jordan Press and Publishing Co; owns commercial printing facilities; Chair. KAMEL ASH-SHERIF; Editor Dr NABIL ASH-SHARIF; Man. Dir SAIF ASH-SHARIF; circ. 70,000.

The Jordan Times: POB 6710, Amman 11118; tel. (6) 5696331; fax (6) 5696183; e-mail jotimes@jpf.com.jo; internet www.jordantimes.com; f. 1975; English; publ. by Jordan Press Foundation; Chief Editor ABDULLAH HASANAT; circ. 10,000.

Al-Mithaq (The Covenant): Amman; f. 1993; Arabic.

Ar-Rai (Opinion): POB 6710, Queen Rania St, Amman 11118; tel. (6) 5667171; fax (6) 5676581; e-mail alrai@jpf.com.jo; internet www .alrai.com; f. 1971; morning; Arabic; independent; publ. by Jordan Press Foundation; Chair. AHMAD ABD AL-FATTAH; Editor-in-Chief GEORGE HAWATMEH; circ. 100,000.

Sawt ash-Shaab (Voice of the People): POB 3037, Amman; tel. (6) 5667101; fax (6) 5667993; f. 1983; Arabic; Editor-in-Chief: HASHEM KHAISAT; circ. 30,000.

WEEKLIES

Al-Ahali (The People): POB 9966, Amman; tel. (6) 691452; fax (6) 5686857; e-mail ahali@go.com.jo; internet www.hashd_ahalia.org; f. 1990; Arabic; publ. by the Jordan People's Democratic Party; Editor-in-Chief SALEM NAHHAS; circ. 5,000.

Akhbar al-Usbou (News of the Week): POB 605, Amman; tel. (6) 5677881; fax (6) 5677882; f. 1959; Arabic; economic, social, political; Chief Editor and Publr ABD AL-HAFIZ MUHAMMAD; circ. 50,000.

Al-Liwa' (The Standard): POB 3067, 2nd Circle, Jabal Amman 11181; tel. (6) 5642770; fax (6) 5656324; e-mail info@al-liwa.com; internet www.al-liwa.com; f. 1972; Arabic; Editor-in-Chief HASSAN AT-TAL; circ. 15,000.

Al-Majd (The Glory): POB 926856, Amman 11190; tel. (6) 5530553; fax (6) 5530352; f. 1994; Arabic; political; Editor FAHD AR-RIMAWI; circ. 8,000.

As-Sabah (The Morning): POB 2396, Amman; Arabic; circ. 6,000.

Shihan: POB 96-654, Amman; tel. (6) 5603585; fax (6) 5696183; e-mail shihan@go.com.jo; internet www.access2arabia.com/shihan; Arabic; Editor-in-Chief JIHAD MONANI; circ. 60,000.

The Star: POB 591, University St, Amman 11118; tel. (6) 5664153; fax (6) 5667170; e-mail star@addustour.com.jo; internet www.star.arabia.com; f. 1966 as The Jerusalem Star; resumed publication in Jordan in 1990; English and French; political, economic and cultural; publ. by the Jordan Press and Publishing Co; Publr and Editor-in-Chief OSAMA ASH-SHERIF; circ. 12,000.

PERIODICALS

Arabia Online: POB 91128, Amman 11191; tel. (6) 5154238; fax (6) 5154239; e-mail info@arabia.com; internet www.arabia.com; f. 1995; monthly; Arabic; information technology; Editor-in-Chief KHALDOON TABAZA.

Al-Ghad al-Iqtisadi: Media Services International, POB 9313, Amman 11191; tel. (6) 5645380; fax (6) 5648298; fortnightly; English; economic; Chief Editor RIAD AL-KHOURI.

Huda El-Islam (The Right Way of Islam): POB 659, Amman; tel. (6) 5666141; f. 1956; monthly; Arabic; scientific and literary; published by the Ministry of Awqaf and Islamic Affairs; Editor Dr AHMAD MUHAMMAD HULAYYEL.

Jordan: POB 224, Amman; f. 1969; published quarterly by Jordan Information Bureau, Washington; circ. 100,000.

Jordan Today: Media Services International, POB 9313, Amman 11191; tel. (6) 652380; fax (6) 648298; e-mail star@arabia.com; internet www.corp.arabia.com/JordanToday; f. 1995; monthly; English; tourism, culture and entertainment; Editor-in-Chief ZEID NASSER.

Military Magazine: Army Headquarters, Amman; f. 1955; quarterly; dealing with military and literary subjects; published by Armed Forces.

Royal Wings: POB 302, Amman; tel. (6) 5672872; fax (6) 5672527; bi-monthly; Arabic and English; magazine for Royal Jordanian Airline; circ. 40,000.

Shari'a: POB 585, Amman; f. 1959; fortnightly; Islamic affairs; published by Shari'a College; circ. 5,000.

World Travel Gazette (WTG): POB 658, Amman; tel. (6) 5665091; fax (6) 5667933; Arabic.

NEWS AGENCIES

Jordan News Agency (PETRA): POB 6845, Amman; tel. (6) 5644455; e-mail petra@petranews.gov.jo; internet www.petra.gov.jo; f. 1965; government-controlled; Dir-Gen. ABDULLAH AL-UTUM.

Foreign News Bureaux

Agence France-Presse (AFP): POB 3340, Amman 11181; tel. (6) 4642976; fax (6) 4654680; e-mail afp@globalone.com.jo; Bureau Man. Mrs RANDA HABIB.

Agenzia Nazionale Stampa Associata (ANSA) (Italy): POB 35111, Amman; tel. (6) 5644092.

Associated Press (AP) (USA): POB 35111, Amman 11180; tel. (6) 4614660; fax (6) 4614661; e-mail jhalaby@ap.org; Correspondent JAMAL HALABY.

Deutsche Presse Agentur (dpa) (Germany): POB 35111, Amman; tel. (6) 5623907.

Reuters (UK): POB 667, Amman; tel. (6) 5623776; fax (6) 5619231; Bureau Chief JACK REDDEN.

Central News Agency (Taiwan), Iraqi News Agency, Kuwait News Agency (KUNA), Middle East News Agency (Egypt), Qatar News Agency, Saudi Press Agency and UPI (USA) also maintain bureaux in Amman.

Publishers

Alfaris Publishing and Distribution Co: POB 9157, Amman 11191; tel. (6) 5605432; fax (6) 5685501; e-mail mkayyali@nets .com.jo; Dir MAHER SAID KAYYALI.

Aram Studies Publishing and Distribution House: POB 997, Amman 11941; tel. (6) 835015; fax (6) 835079; art, finance, health, management, science, business; Gen. Dir SALEH ABOUSBA.

Jordan Book Centre Co Ltd: POB 301, Al-Jubeiha, Amman 11941; tel. (6) 5151882; fax (6) 5152016; e-mail jbc@go.com.jo; f. 1982; fiction, business, economics, computer science, medicine, engineering, general non-fiction; Man. Dir J. J. SHARBAIN.

Jordan Distribution Agency Co Ltd: POB 375, Amman 11118; tel. (6) 4630191; fax (6) 4635152; e-mail jda@go.com.jo; internet www.jda-jo.com; f. 1951; history; Chair. and Gen. Man. RAJA ELISSA; Dir NADIA ELISSA.

Jordan House for Publication: POB 1121, Basman St, Amman; tel. (6) 24224; fax (6) 51062; f. 1952; medicine, nursing, dentistry; Man. Dir MURSI EL-ASHKAR.

Jordan Press and Publishing Co Ltd: POB 591, Amman 11118; tel. (6) 5664153; fax (6) 5667170; e-mail dustour@go.com.jo; f. 1967 by *Al-Manar* and *Falastin* dailies; publishes *Ad-Dustour* (daily), *Ad-Dustour Sport* (weekly) and *The Star* (English weekly); Chair. KAMEL ASH-SHARIF; Dir-Gen. SEIF ASH-SHERIF.

Jordan Press Foundation: POB 6710, Amman 11118; tel. (6) 5667171; fax (6) 5661242; e-mail alrai@jpf.com.jo; internet www .alrai.com.jo; f. 1971; publishes *Ar-Rai* (daily), the *Jordan Times* (daily) and *Hatem* (monthly for children); Chair. AHMAD ABD AL-FATAH; Gen. Dir NADER HORANI.

El-Nafa'es: POB 211511, Al-Abdali, Amman 11121; tel. (6) 5693940; fax (6) 5693941; e-mail alnafaes@hotmail.com; f. 1990; education, Islamic; CEO SUFYAN OMAR AL-ASHQR.

At-Tanwir al-Ilmi (Scientific Enlightenment Publishing House): POB 4237, Al-Mahatta, Amman 11131; tel. and fax (6) 4899619; e-mail taisir@yahoo.com; education,engineering, philosophy, science, sociology; Owner DR TAISIR SUBHI MAHMOUD.

Other publishers in Amman include: Dairat al-Ihsaat al-Amman, George N. Kawar, Al-Matbaat al-Hashmiya and The National Press.

Broadcasting and Communications

TELECOMMUNICATIONS

Telecommunications Regulatory Commission (TRC): POB 850967, Amman 11185; tel. (6) 5862020; fax (6) 5863641; e-mail webmaster@trc.gov.jo; internet www.trc.gov.jo; f. 1995; Dir-Gen. MAMOUN BALQAR.

Jordan Mobile Telephone Services Company (JMTS—Fastlink): POB 940821, 8th Circle, King Abdullah II St, Amman 11194; tel. (6) 5828100; fax (6) 5828200; e-mail info@fastlink.com.jo; internet www.jmts-fastlink.com; f. 1994; private co; since 1995 operates Jordan's first mobile telecommunications network; Pres. and CEO MICHAEL DAGHER.

Jordan Telecom: POB 1689, Amman 11118; tel. (6) 4606666; fax (6) 4649882; e-mail info@jtc.com.jo; internet www.jordantelecom.jo; f. 1971; formerly Jordan Telecommunications Corpn and then Jordan Telecommunications Co; 60% govt-owned; 40% privately-owned; Chair. SHABIB AMMARI; Man. Dir WALID DWEIK.

MobileCom: POB 851114, Amman 11185; internet www.mobile com.jo; f. 1999; launched cellular telecommunications service in 2000; subsidiary of Jordan Telecom.

BROADCASTING

Radio and Television

Jordan Radio and Television Corporation (JRTV): POB 1041, Amman; tel. (6) 773111; fax (6) 751503; e-mail general@jrtv .gov.jo; internet www.jrtv.com; f. 1968; government TV station broadcasts for 90 hours weekly in Arabic and English; in colour; advertising accepted; Dir-Gen. IHSAN RAMZI SHIKIM; Dir of Television NASSER JUDEH; Dir of Radio HASHIM KHURAYSAT.

Finance

(cap. = capital; dep. = deposits; m. = million; res = reserves; brs = branches; JD = Jordanian dinars)

BANKING

Central Bank

Central Bank of Jordan: POB 37, King Hussein St, Amman 11118; tel. (6) 4630301; fax (6) 4638889; e-mail redp@cbj.gov.jo; internet www.cbj.gov.jo; f. 1964; cap. JD 18m., res JD 59.3m., dep. JD 2,868.1m. (Dec. 2001); Gov. and Chair. Dr UMMAYA TOUKAN; Dep. Govs Dr AHMAD MOUSTAFA, SALEH AT-TAYEH.

National Banks

Arab Bank PLC: POB 950545, Shmeisani, Amman 11195; tel. (6) 5607231; fax (6) 5606793; e-mail international@arabbank.com.jo; internet www.arabbank.com; f. 1930; cap. JD 146.9m., res

JD 2,161.8m., dep. JD 19,010.2m. (Dec. 2001); CEO and Dep. Chair. ABD AL-MAJID SHOMAN; Dep. Chair. and Pres. KHALID SHOMAN; 92 brs in Jordan, 87 brs abroad.

Bank of Jordan PLC: POB 2140, Shmeisani, Amman 11181; tel. (6) 5696277; fax (6) 5696291; e-mail boj@bankofjordan.com.jo; internet www.bankofjordan.com; f. 1960; cap. JD 21m., res JD 14.1m., dep. JD 553.8m. (Dec. 1999); Chair. TAWFIK SHAKER FAKHOURI; Gen. Man. MUHAMMAD JOMAH ALQASSIM; 64 brs.

Cairo Amman Bank: POB 950661, Cairo Amman Bank Bldg, Wadi Saqra St, Amman 11195; tel. (6) 4616910; fax (6) 4642883; e-mail cainfo@ca-bank.com.jo; internet www.ca-bank.com; f. 1960; cap. JD 20m., res JD 32.5m., dep. JD 754.0m. (Dec. 2001); Chair. KHALED AL-MASRI; Gen. Man. YAZID AL-MUFTI; 50 brs in Jordan, 19 brs in the Palestinian self-rule areas.

Export and Finance Bank: POB 941283, Issam Ajlouni St, Amman 11194; tel. (6) 5694250; fax (6) 5692062; e-mail info@efbank .com.jo; internet www.efbank.com.jo; f. 1995; cap. JD 25.3m., res JD 3.7m., dep. JD 132.7m. (Dec. 2001); Chair. and CEO MUHAMMAD ALI AL-HUSRY; Gen. Man. HAKOUB BANNAYAN (acting).

Jordan Gulf Bank: POB 9989, Shmeisani-Al Burj Area, Amman 11191; tel. (6) 5603931; fax (6) 5664110; e-mail jgb@jgbank.com.jo; internet www.jgbank.com.jo; f. 1977; cap JD 33m., res JD –0.1m., dep. JD 253.8m. (Dec. 1999); Chair. NABEEL YOUSUF BARAKAT; Gen. Man. FAYEZ ABU AL-ENEIN; 33 brs.

Jordan Islamic Bank for Finance and Investment: POB 926225, Shmeisani, Amman 11190; tel. (6) 5677377; fax (6) 5666326; e-mail jib@islamicbank.com.jo; internet www.jordan islamicbank.com; f. 1978; cap. JD 38.5m., res JD 11.8m., dep. JD 151.2m. (Dec. 2001); Chair. MAHMOUD J. HASSOUBEH; Vice-Chair. and Gen. Man. MUSA ABD AL-AZIZ SHIHADEH; 54 brs.

Jordan Kuwait Bank: POB 9776, Amman 11191; tel. (6) 5688814; fax (6) 5687452; e-mail webmaster@jkbank.com.jo; internet www.jordan-kuwait-bank.com; f. 1976; cap. JD 35.3m., res JD 23.3m., dep. JD 583.9m. (Dec. 2001); Chair. and CEO ABD AL-KARIM AL-KABARITI; Gen. Man. MUHAMMAD YASSER AL-ASMAR; 19 brs.

Jordan National Bank PLC: POB 3103, Queen Noor St, Shmeisani, Amman 11181; tel. (6) 5622283; fax (6) 5622281; e-mail info@jnb.com.jo; internet www.ahli.com; f. 1955; cap. JD 42m., res JD 24.4m., dep. JD 1,085.6m. (Dec. 2000); Chair., CEO and Gen. Man. Dr RAJAI MOUASHER; CEO and Man. Dir WASEF AZAR; 55 brs in Jordan, 10 brs abroad.

Middle East Investment Bank: POB 560, 30 Prince Shaker bin Zeid St, Shmeisani, Amman 11118; tel. (6) 5695470; fax (6) 5693410; e-mail meibsg@meib.com; internet www.meib.com; f. 1981; cap. JD 15.9m., res JD 0.8m., dep. JD 36.0m. (Dec. 2001); Chair. MUHAMMAD ALI MANGO; Gen. Man. FADI JABRY; 16 brs.

Foreign Banks

ANZ Grindlays Bank: POB 9997, Shmeisani, Amman 11191; tel. (6) 5607201; fax (6) 5679115; e-mail zahranm@anz.com; internet www.anz.com; cap. JD 13m., dep. JD 244m., total assets JD 274m. (Dec. 1999); Gen. Man. DIVED MANSON; 8 brs.

Arab Banking Corpn: POB 926691, ABC Bldg, Al-Malekah Noor St, Shmeisani, Amman 11190; tel. (6) 5664183; fax (6) 5686291; e-mail info@arabbanking.com.jo; internet www.arabbanking.com.jo; f. 1990; cap. JD 20m., res JD 4.0m., dep. JD 234.0m., total assets JD 310.5m. (Dec. 2001); Chair. GHAZI M. ABD AL-JAWAD; Dep. CEO Dr ZIAD FARIZ; 16 brs.

Citibank NA (USA): POB 5055, Prince Muhammad St, Jabal Amman 11183; tel. (6) 4644065; fax (6) 4658693; internet www .citibank.com/jordan; f. 1974; cap. JD 5m., dep. JD 56.2m., total assets JD 75.4m. (Dec. 1992); Chair. and CEO JOHN S. REED; Gen. Man. SUHEIR AL-ALI; 3 brs.

Egyptian Arab Land Bank: POB 6729, Queen Noor St, Amman 11118; tel. (6) 5650180; fax (6) 5677574; e-mail ealb@arakari.com.jo; internet www.arakari.com.jo; f. 1976; wholly-owned by Government of Egypt; cap. JD 10m., dep. JD 103.3m., res JD 5.5m., total assets JD 136.1m. (Dec. 1997); Chair. ALAA AL-OUSSIYA; Gen. Man. SAMIR MAHDI; 19 brs in Jordan, 32 brs abroad.

HSBC Bank Middle East (United Kingdom): POB 925286, Khalid Bin Walid St, Jebel Hussein, Amman 11110; tel. (6) 5607471; fax (6) 5682047; f. 1889; cap. JD 5m., dep. JD 150m., total assets JD 169m. (Dec. 1994); Chair. Sir JOHN BOND; Gen. Man. ROBERT JAMES BRAY; 4 brs.

Islamic International Arab Bank: POB 925802, Amman 11190; tel. (6) 5694901; fax (6) 5694914; f. 1997; cap. JD 40m; Chair. ABD AL-HAMID SHOMAN; Gen. Man. JAMEEL AD-DASOQI; 9 brs.

Rafidain Bank (Iraq): POB 1194, Amman 11118; tel. (6) 4624365; fax (6) 4658698; f. 1941; cap. JD 5m., res JD 2.1m., dep. JD 31.4m. (Dec. 1992); Pres. and Chair. DHIA HABEEB AL-KHAYOON; Regional Man. MUHSEN ABD AL-HASSAN; 4 brs.

Bank Al-Mashrek (Lebanon) also has a branch in Amman.

Specialized Credit Institutions

Agricultural Credit Corporation: POB 77, Amman; tel. (6) 5661105; fax (6) 5698365; e-mail agri-cc@nets.com.jo; f. 1959; cap. JD 24m., res JD 12.4m., total assets JD 125.1m. (Dec. 2000); Chair. Mahmoud Duwayri; Dir-Gen. Nimer an-Nabulsi; 20 brs.

Arab Jordan Investment Bank: POB 8797, Arab Jordan Investment Bank Bldg, Shmeisani Commercial Area, Amman 11121; tel. (6) 5607126; fax (6) 5681482; e-mail info@ajib.com; internet www.ajib.com; f. 1978; cap. JD 20m., res JD 13.7m., dep. JD 248.4m. (Dec. 2001); Chair. and CEO Abd al-Kader al-Qadi; 15 brs in Jordan, 1 br abroad.

Cities and Villages Development Bank: POB 1572, Amman 11118; tel. (6) 5668151; fax (6) 5668153; e-mail cvdb100 @hotmail.com; f. 1979; cap. JD 25m., res JD 14.5m., total assets JD 66.5m. (Dec. 1998); Gen. Man. Dr Ibrahim an-Nsour; 4 brs.

Housing Bank for Trade and Finance: POB 7693, Parliament St, Amman 11118; tel. (6) 5667126; fax (6) 5678121; e-mail quality@hbtf.com.jo; internet www.the-housingbank.com.jo; f. 1973; cap. JD 100m., res JD 149.1m., dep. JD 1,365.3m. (Dec. 2001); Chair. Zuhair Khouri; Gen. Man. Abd al-Qader Dweik; 97 brs.

Industrial Development Bank: POB 1982, Zahran St, Amman 11118; tel. (6) 4642216; fax (6) 4647821; e-mail idb@indevbank .com.jo; internet www.indevbank.com.jo; f. 1965; cap. JD 24m., res JD 21.8m., dep. JD 44.7m. (Dec. 2000); Chair. Mofleh Akel; Gen. Man. Marwan Awad; 3 brs.

Jordan Co-operative Organization: POB 1343, Amman; tel. (6) 5665171; f. 1968; cap. JD 5.2m., dep. JD 11.5m., res JD 6.8m. (Nov. 1992); Chair. and Dir-Gen. Jamal al-Bedour.

Jordan Investment and Finance Bank (JIFBANK): POB 950601, Issam Ajlouni St, Shmeisani, Amman 11195; tel. (6) 5665145; fax (6) 5681410; e-mail souha@jifbank.com; internet www.jifbank.com; f. 1982 as Jordan Investment and Finance Corpn, name changed 1989; cap. JD 20m., res JD 5.9m., dep. JD 303.9m. (Dec. 2000); Chair. Nizar Jardaneh; Man. Dir Basil Jardaneh; 5 brs.

Jordan Investment Board (JIB): POB 893, Amman 11821; tel. (6) 5608400; fax (6) 5608416; e-mail info@jib.com; internet www .jordaninvestment.com; Dir-Gen. Reem Badran.

Jordan Investment Corporation (JIC): Amman; state-owned; Dir-Gen. (vacant).

Social Security Corporation: POB 926031, Amman 11110; tel. (6) 4643000; fax (6) 4610014; f. 1978; Dir-Gen. Dr Safwan Toqan.

Union Bank for Savings and Investment: POB 35104, Prince Shaker Bin Zeid St, Shmeisani, Amman 11180; tel. (6) 5607011; fax (6) 5666149; e-mail info@unionbankjo.com; internet www.union bankjo.com; f. 1978 as Arab Finance Corpn, named changed 1991; cap. JD 20m., res 9.4m., dep. 269.4m. (Dec. 2001); Chair. and Gen. Man. Isam as-Salfiti; Dep. Gen. Man. Ammar Hadaddin; 14 brs.

STOCK EXCHANGE

Amman Stock Exchange (ASE): POB 212466, Arjan, nr Ministry of the Interior, Amman 11121; tel. (6) 5664109; fax (6) 5664071; e-mail exchange@go.com.jo; internet www.ase.com.jo; f. 1978 as Amman Financial Market; name changed March 1999; Chair. Dr Abd ar-Rahman Toukan; Exec. Man. Jalil Tarif.

INSURANCE

Jordan Insurance Co Ltd: POB 279, Company's Bldg, 3rd Circle, Jabal Amman, Amman; tel. (6) 4634161; fax (6) 4637905; e-mail jicjo@go.com.jo; f. 1951; cap. JD 9.9m.; Chair. Khaldun Abu Hassan; 7 brs (3 in Saudi Arabia, 3 in the United Arab Emirates, 1 in Lebanon).

Middle East Insurance Co Ltd: POB 1802, Al Kindy St, Um Uthaina 5th Circle, Jabal Amman, Amman; tel. (6) 5527100; fax (6) 5527801; e-mail meico@go.com.jo; internet www.meico.com.jo; f. 1963; cap. US $5.0m.; Chair. Samir Kawar; 1 br. in Saudi Arabia.

National Ahlia Insurance Co: POB 6156-2938, Sayed Qotub St, Shmeisani, Amman 11118; tel. (6) 5671169; fax (6) 5684900; e-mail natinsur@go.com.jo; internet www.nationalahlia.com; f. 1965; cap. JD 2m.; Chair. Mustafa Abu-Goura; Gen. Man. Ghaleb Abu-Goura.

United Insurance Co Ltd: POB 7521, United Insurance Bldg, King Hussein St, Amman; tel. (6) 4648513; fax (6) 4629417; e-mail uic@united.com.jo; internet www.1stjordan.net/united-insurance; f. 1972; all types of insurance; cap. JD 2m.; Gen. Man. Taisir Mashal.

There are 17 local and one foreign insurance company operating in Jordan.

Trade and Industry

DEVELOPMENT ORGANIZATIONS

Amman Development Corporation: POB 926621, Amman; tel. (6) 5629471; f. 1979; development of services in the Amman munici-pality by constructing and running real estate; industrial and other complexes; Dir Gen. Sami ar-Rashid.

Jordan Valley Authority (JVA): POB 2769, Amman; tel. (6) 5689400; fax (6) 5689916; e-mail jvadewan2@mwi.gov.jo; f. 1977 as a governmental organization responsible for the integrated social and economic development of the Jordan Valley. Projects in Stage I of the Jordan Valley Development Plan were completed in 1979. In 1988 the JVA was incorporated into the Ministry of Water and Irrigation. By late 2000 completed infrastructure projects included 2,205 km of roads, 2,223 housing units, 90 schools, 15 health centres, 16 local government buildings, 4 marketing centres, 2 tomato paste factories, 1 cold storage facility and several workshops. Electricity is now provided to all towns and villages in the valley from the national network and potable water is supplied to them from tube wells. Many of the Stage II irrigation projects are now completed. These include the construction of the King Talal, Wadi Arab, Kafrein and Karamah dams; the extension of the King Abdullah Canal to total 110.5 km in length; the construction of major municipal water projects in Amman and Irbid; the construction and conversion of a surface irrigation system into a pressurized pipe system covering an irrigated area of 25,000 ha; the development of groundwater resources and subsurface drainage systems. Projects under way include the construction of the Al-Wehdeh, Tanour and Wala dams, as well as the Mujeb dam and diversion weir. Future developments in tourist and industrial infrastructure will include the development of the Dead Sea East shore, Christ's baptism site on the Jordan river, and industrial free zones; Sec.-Gen. Avedis Serpekian.

CHAMBERS OF COMMERCE AND INDUSTRY

Amman Chamber of Commerce: POB 1800, Amman 11118; tel. (6) 5666151; e-mail aci@amra.nic.gov.jo; f. 1923; Pres. Haider Murad; Sec.-Gen. Muhammad al-Muhtasseb.

Amman Chamber of Industry: POB 1800, Amman; tel. (6) 5643001; fax (6) 5647852; e-mail aci@aci.org.jo; internet www .aci.org.jo; f. 1962; 7,500 industrial companies registered (1999); Pres. Khaldun Abu Hassan; Dir.-Gen. Dr Muhammad Smadi.

Federation of the Jordanian Chambers of Commerce: POB 7029, Amman 11118; e-mail fjcc@nets.com.jo; internet www.fjcc.com; tel. (6) 5665492; fax (6) 5685997; f. 1955; Chair. Haidar Murad; Sec.-Gen. Amin Husseini.

Professional Associations Council (PAC): Professional Associations Complex, Amman; Pres. Hashim Gharaibeh.

UTILITIES

Electricity

Jordanian Electric Power Company (JEPCO): POB 618, Amman 11118; tel. (6) 4636381; fax (6) 4648482; e-mail jepco@go .com.jo; privately-owned; Chair. Issam Bdeir; Gen. Man. Eng. Marwan Bushnaq.

Central Electricity Generating Company (CEGCO): POB 3148, Amman 11181; tel. (6) 5865171; fax (6) 5820975; internet www .cegco.com.jo; electricity generation; govt-owned; scheduled for privatization; Chair. Eng. Ali Y. Ensour.

Electricity Distribution Company (EDCO): POB 2310, Orthodox St, 7th Circle, Jabal Amman; tel. (6) 5858615; fax (6) 5818336; e-mail info@nepco.com.jo; internet www.edco.com.jo; electricity distribution; govt-owned; scheduled for privatization.

National Electric Power Company (NEPCO): POB 2310, Amman 11118; tel. (6) 5858615; fax (6) 5818336; e-mail info@nepco .com.jo; internet www.nepco.com.jo; f. 1996; formerly Jordan Electricity Authority; electricity transmission; govt-owned; scheduled for privatization; Man. Dir Eng. Muhammad Azzam.

Water

Water Authority of Jordan (WAJ): Amman.

MAJOR COMPANIES

Adnan Sha'lan & Co: POB 1428, King Hussein St, Amman 11118; tel. (6) 4621122; fax (6) 4626946; f. 1953; manufacturers of paints, glues, refrigerators, gas cookers, dairy products and cosmetics; sales US $10m. (1982); cap. US $3m.; Chair. Adnan Sha'lan; Man. Dir Fawez Sha'lan; 400 employees.

Agricultural Marketing and Processing Co of Jordan: POB 7314, 38 Muhammad Ali-Janah St, Amman; tel. (6) 819161; fax (6) 819164; f. 1984; govt-owned; Chair. Dr Abd al-Hadi Alaween; Gen. Man. Saleh ar-Refai.

Arab Centre for Pharmaceuticals and Chemicals (ACPC): POB 607, Wadi es-Seer, Amman 11810; tel. (6) 5818567; fax (6) 5827282; e-mail gman@acpc.com.jo; internet www.acpc.com.jo; f. 1984; manufacturers of pharmaceuticals and chemicals; cap. JD 5m. (1998); Man. Dir Awni al-Bashir; 280 employees.

Arab Investment and International Trade Co Ltd: POB 94, Sehab Old Rd, ar-Raqim, Amman; tel. (6) 4163008; fax (6) 4161504; e-mail aiit@go.com.jo; f. 1978; manufacturers of toiletries; sales JD 3.6m. (1998); cap. p.u. JD 5m. (1999); Chair. ABD AL-MALIK SAID; Gen. Man. Eng. MUHAMMAD S. ABU SALAH; 170 employees.

Arab Pharmaceutical Manufacturing Co Ltd: POB 1695, Amman; tel. (6) 5685121; fax (6) 5685131; f. 1964; manufacturers of pharmaceuticals; sales JD 30m. (1999); cap. p.u. JD 18m.; Chair. ANIS MOASHER; Man. Dir ISSAM SAKET; 850 employees.

Arab Potash Co Ltd (APC): POB 1470, Amman 11118; tel. (6) 5666165; fax (6) 5674416; e-mail info@arabpotash.com; internet www.arabpotash.com; f. 1956; production of potash, with a by-product of salt; production 1.8m. tons, sales 1.7m. tons (1999); 53% state-owned; Chair. SULEIMAN HAFEZ; Gen. Man. ISSA AYYOUB; 2,316 employees.

Elba House Co WLL: POB 3449, Amman 11181; tel. (6) 5342600; fax (6) 5342603; f. 1976; manufacturers of prefabricated buildings, caravans, steel structures, vehicle bodies and construction plant; Pres. and Dir-Gen. USAMA MUSA KHOURY; Chair. ZUHAIR MUSA KHOURY; 800 employees.

General Investment Co Ltd: POB 312, Abujaber Bldg, Prince Muhammad St, Amman 11118; tel. (6) 4625161; fax (6) 4657679; e-mail gic@go.com.jo; internet www.gicjo.com; f. 1986 by merger of Jordan Brewery Co Ltd (f. 1955) and its subsidiary the General Investment Co Ltd; producers of beer, non-alcoholic malt beverages, soft drinks and alcohol for medical purposes; investment and real estate brokers; sales US $12m. (2001); cap. US $14m. (2002); Chair. FARHAN ABUJABER; Gen. Man. MARWAN ABUJABER.

Industrial, Commercial and Agricultural Co Ltd (ICA): POB 6066, Amman 11118; tel. 3741945; fax 3741198; e-mail ica-sales@ica-jo.com; internet www.ica-jo.com; f. 1961; industrial, commercial and agricultural investment; operates factories producing (under licence) soap, detergents, toiletries, paints, biscuits, ice-cream and containers; sales JD 21.5m.; cap. p.u. JD 9m. (1999); Chair. and Man. Dir MUHAMMAD A. ABU HASSAN; 550 employees.

International Contracting and Investment Co: POB 19170, Amman; tel. (6) 5666133; f. 1977; building, civil construction, etc.; sales JD 10m. (1982); cap. p.u. JD 4m.; Chair. FAKHRY ABU SHAKRA; Vice-Pres. HASSAN SHIHABI; 176 employees.

Jordan Cement Factories Co Ltd: POB 610, Amman 11118; tel. (6) 4729901; fax (6) 4729921; e-mail cement@go.com.jo; f. 1951; merged with South Cement Co Sept. 1985; annual production at two works 3.1m. tons (1995); partially privatized in 1998; Chair. HAMDI M. S TABBA'A; Gen. Man. SAMIR BERAKDAR; 2,330 employees.

Jordan Petroleum Refinery Co: POB 1079, Amman 11118; tel. (6) 4657600; fax (6) 4657934; e-mail addewan@jopetrol.com.jo; f. 1956; petroleum refining and distribution of refined petroleum products (lube oil blending and canning; fmr of LPG cylinders); production 3.6m. tons, sales 4.5m. tons (JD 618.7m.), profits JD 6.0m. ($8.5m.) (2001); Chair. ABD AL-HAMID SHOMAN; Dir-Gen. MUHAMMAD SAFADI (acting); Refinery Man. ADNAN BUSHNAQ; 3,278 employees.

Jordan Phosphate Mines Co Ltd (JPMC): POB 30, Amman 11118; tel. (6) 5607141; fax (6) 5682290; e-mail jpmc@nets.com.jo; internet www.jpmc-jordan.com; f. 1930; engaged in production and export of rock phosphate; absorbed Jordan Fertilizer Industries Co; three mines in operation; production 6m. tons (1999); exports 3.7m. tons (1998); Chair. Dr HANNA ODEH; Gen. Man. SAMEH MADANI.

Jordan Plastics Co: POB 2394, Amman; tel. (6) 4205144; fax (6) 4203570; manufacturers of plastics (household goods); Chair. TAWFIQ G. ABUEITA; Man. Dir ISSAM E. ABUEITA.

Jordan Tobacco and Cigarettes Co Ltd: POB 59, Ras El-Ain St, Amman 11118; tel. (6) 4388112; fax (6) 4389123; e-mail hkhayyat @yahoo.com; f. 1931; manufacturers of cigarettes; tobacco growers; Chair. Dr M. ABU HAMMOUR; Gen. Man. HAITHAM KHAYYAT; 316 employees.

Metal Industries Co Ltd (Metalco): POB 134, Amman Industrial Estate, Amman 11814; tel. (6) 4023015; fax (6) 4023621; e-mail info@metalco.com; internet www.metalco.com; f. 1976; manufacturers of steel panel radiators and boilers; sales US $2.5m. (1995); cap. p.u. US $1.5m.; Chair. Eng. M. A. JARDANEH; Gen. Man. LUAY M. JARDANEH.

TRADE UNIONS

The General Federation of Jordanian Trade Unions: POB 1065, Amman; tel. (6) 5675533; f. 1954; 33,000 mems; member of Arab Trade Unions Confederation; Chair. KHALIL ABU KHURMAH; Gen. Sec. ABD AL-HALIM KHADDAM.

There are also a number of independent unions, including:

Drivers' Union: POB 846, Amman; tel. (6) 4765637; fax (6) 4765829; Sec.-Gen. MAHMOUD ABD AL-HADI HAMMAD.

Jordan Engineers' Association (JEA): POB 940188, Shmeisani, Amman; tel. (6) 5607616; fax (6) 5676933; e-mail info@jea.org.jo;

internet www.jea.org.jo; f. 1958; Pres. AZZAM HUNEIDI; Sec.-Gen. ALI ABU AS-SUKKAR.

Union of Petroleum Workers and Employees: POB 1346, Amman; Sec.-Gen. BRAHIM HADI.

Transport

RAILWAYS

Aqaba Railways Corporation (ARC): POB 50, Ma'an; tel. (3) 2132114; fax (3) 2131861; e-mail arc@go.com.jo; f. 1975; length of track 292 km (1,050-mm gauge); scheduled for privatization; Dir-Gen. ABDULLAH KHAWALDIH.

Formerly a division of the Hedjaz–Jordan Railway (see below), the Aqaba Railway was established as a separate entity in 1972; it retains close links with the Hedjaz but there is no regular through traffic between Aqaba and Amman. It comprises the 169-km line south of Menzil (leased from the Hedjaz–Jordan Railway) and the 115-km extension to Aqaba, opened in October 1975, which serves phosphate mines at el-Hasa and Wadi el-Abyad.

Hedjaz–Jordan Railway: POB 4448, Amman; tel. (6) 4895414; fax (6) 4894117; e-mail hji@nets.com.jo; f. 1902; administered by the Ministry of Transport; length of track 496 km (1,050-mm gauge); Chair. NADER DAHABI; Dir-Gen. A. ABULAL-FEILAT.

This was formerly a section of the Hedjaz Railway (Damascus to Medina) for Muslim pilgrims to Medina and Mecca. It crosses the Syrian border and enters Jordanian territory south of Dera'a, and runs for approximately 366 km to Naqb Ishtar, passing through Zarqa, Amman, Qatrana and Ma'an. Some 844 km of the line, from Ma'an to Medina in Saudi Arabia, were abandoned for more than 60 years. Reconstruction of the Medina line, begun in 1965, was scheduled to be completed in 1971 at a cost of £15m., divided equally between Jordan, Saudi Arabia and Syria. However, the reconstruction work was suspended at the request of the Arab states concerned, pending further studies on costs. The line between Ma'an and Saudi Arabia (114 km) is now completed, as well as 15 km in Saudi Arabia as far as Halet Ammar Station. A new 115-km extension to Aqaba (owned by the Aqaba Railway Corporation (see above) was opened in 1975. In 1987 a study conducted by Dorsch Consult (Federal Republic of Germany) into the feasibility of reconstructing the Hedjaz Railway to high international specifications to connect Saudi Arabia, Jordan and Syria concluded that the reopening of the Hedjaz line would be viable only if it were to be connected with European rail networks. In August 1999 an express rail link between Amman and the Syrian capital, Damascus, was inaugurated.

ROADS

Amman is linked by road with all parts of the kingdom and with neighbouring countries. All cities and most towns are connected by a two-lane paved road system. In addition, several thousand km of tracks make all villages accessible to motor transport. In 2000 the total road network of the East Bank of Jordan was an estimated 7,245 km: 2,911 km of main roads, 2,059 km of secondary roads (both types asphalted) and 2,275 km of other roads.

Joint Land Transport Co: Amman; joint venture of Govts of Jordan and Iraq; operates about 750 trucks.

Jordanian-Syrian Land Transport Co: POB 20686, Amman; tel. (6) 5661134; fax (6) 5669645; internet www.josyco@joinnet.com.jo; f. 1976; transports goods between ports in Jordan and Syria; Chair. and Gen. Man. HAMDI AL-HABASHNEH.

SHIPPING

The port of Aqaba is Jordan's only outlet to the sea and has more than 20 modern and specialized berths, and one container terminal (540 m in length). The port has 299,000 sq m of storage area, and is used for Jordan's international trade and regional transit trade (mainly with Iraq). There is a ferry link between Aqaba and the Egyptian port of Nuweibeh.

Jordanian Ports Corporation (JPC): POB 115, Aqaba 77110; tel. (3) 2014031; fax (3) 2016204; e-mail ports@amra.nic.gov.jo; Dir-Gen. Eng. ABDULLAH ABU ALIM.

Amman Shipping & Trading Co: POB 213083, 5th Floor, Al-Aqqad Trading Centre, Gardens St; tel. (6) 5514620; fax (6) 5532324.

Arab Bridge Maritime Co: Aqaba; f. 1987; joint venture by Egypt, Iraq and Jordan to improve economic co-operation; an extension of the company that established a ferry link between Aqaba and the Egyptian port of Nuweibeh in 1985; Chair. Eng. MUHAMMAD N. ALKOUSI; Dir Capt. BASSAM AL-KINJI.

Arrow Trans Shipping SA: POB 213083, 5th Floor, Aqad Complex Bldg, Wasfi at-Tal St, Amman 11121; tel. (6) 5512621; fax (6) 5532324; e-mail arrow@albitar.com; f. 1990; Gen. Man. MARWAN JAMAL ED-DIN BITAR.

Assaf Shipping Co SA: POB 2637, Irbid 21110; tel. (2) 7279117; fax (2) 7261329; e-mail reefer_assaf@yahoo.com.

Tawfiq Gargour & Fils: POB 419, 4th Floor, Da'ssan Commercial Centre, Wasfi at-Tal St, Amman; tel. (6) 5524142; fax (6) 5530512; e-mail tgf@tgf.com.jo; f. 1928; shipping agents and owners; Chair. JOHN GARGOUR; Man. Dir NADIM GARGOUR.

Hijazi & Ghosheh Co: POB 183292, Amman; tel. (6) 4886166; fax (6) 4886211.

International Ship Management Co Ltd (ISM): POB 941430, 2nd Floor, Noor Centre, Islam Abad St, Ar-Rabeiah, Amman 11194; tel. (6) 5512607; fax (6) 5532083; e-mail ism@go.com.jo; Gen. Man. MOUSTAFA MASSAD.

Jordan National Shipping Lines Co Ltd: POB 5406, Nasir Ben Jameel St, Wadi Saqra, Amman 11183; tel. (6) 5511500; fax (6) 5515119; e-mail jnl@go.com.jo; internet www.jnsl-jo.com; POB 557, Aqaba; tel. (3) 2018739; fax (3) 318738; 75% govt-owned; service from Antwerp, Bremen and Tilbury to Aqaba; daily passenger ferry service to Egypt; land transportation to destinations in Iraq and elsewhere in the region; Chair. MUHAMMAD SMADI; Gen. Man. Eng. AKEF ABU TAYEH.

Amin Kawar & Sons Co W.L.L.: POB 222, 24 Abd al-Hamid Sharaf St, Shmeisani, Amman 11118; tel. (6) 5603703; fax (6) 5672170; e-mail kawar@kawar.com.jo; internet www.kawar.com.jo; chartering, forwarding and shipping line agents; Chair. TAWFIQ A. KAWAR; CEO RUDAIN T. KAWAR; Gen. Man. GHASSOUB F. KAWAR.

Al-Mansour Marine Transportation and Trading Co: POB 960359, Amman; tel. (6) 697958; fax (6) 702352.

Orient Shipping Co Ltd: POB 207, Amman 11118; tel. (6) 5641695; fax (6) 5651567.

Petra Navigation and International Trading Co Ltd: POB 8362, White Star Bldg, King Hussein St, Amman 11121; tel. (6) 5607021; fax (6) 5601362; e-mail petra@armoush.com.jo; general cargo, ro/ro and passenger ferries; Chair. MAJED ARMOUSH.

Salam International Transport and Trading Co: King Hussein St, Abdali, Amman 11121; tel. (6) 5607021.

Syrian-Jordanian Shipping Co: POB 148, rue Port Said, Latakia, Syria; tel. (41) 471635; fax (41) 470250; Chair. OSMAN LEBBADI.

PIPELINES

Two oil pipelines cross Jordan. The former Iraq Petroleum Co pipeline, carrying petroleum from the oilfields in Iraq to Haifa, has not operated since 1967. The 1,717-km (1,067-mile) pipeline, known as the Trans-Arabian Pipeline (Tapline), carries petroleum from the oilfields of Dhahran in Saudi Arabia to Sidon on the Mediterranean seaboard in Lebanon. Tapline traverses Jordan for a distance of 177 km (110 miles) and has frequently been cut by hostile action. Tapline stopped pumping to Syria and Lebanon at the end of 1983, when it was first due to close. It was later scheduled to close in 1985, but in September 1984 Jordan renewed an agreement to receive Saudi Arabian crude oil through Tapline. The agreement can be cancelled by either party at two years' notice.

CIVIL AVIATION

There are international airports at Amman and Aqaba. The Queen Alia International Airport at Zizya, 40 km south of Amman, was opened in 1983.

Jordan Civil Aviation Authority (JCAA): POB 7547, Amman; tel. (6) 4891401; fax (6) 4892065; e-mail info@jcaa.gov.jo; internet www.jcaa.gov.jo; f. 1950; Dir-Gen. Capt. JIHAD IRSHAID.

Royal Jordanian Airline: Head Office: POB 302, Housing Bank Commercial Centre, Shmeisani, Amman 11118; tel. (6) 5607300; fax (6) 5672527; e-mail rj@go.com.jo; internet www.rjair.com; f. 1963; partial privatization in Feb. 2001; scheduled and charter services to Middle East, North Africa, Europe, USA and Far East; Chair. WALID ASFOUR; Pres. and CEO SAMER MAJALI.

Arab Wings Co Ltd: POB 341018, Amman 11134; tel. (6) 4893901; fax (6) 4893158; e-mail info@arabwings.com.jo; internet www.arabwings.com.jo; f. 1975; subsidiary of Royal Jordanian; executive jet charter service, air ambulances, priority cargo; Man. Dir AHED QUNTAR.

Royal Wings Co Ltd: POB 314018, Amman 11134; tel. (6) 4875206; fax (6) 4875656; e-mail info@royalwings.com.jo; internet www.royalwings.com.jo; f. 1996; subsidiary of Royal Jordanian; operates scheduled and charter regional and domestic services; Man. Dir AHED QUNTAR.

Tourism

The ancient cities of Jerash and Petra, and Jordan's proximity to biblical sites, have encouraged tourism. The development of Jordan's Dead Sea coast is currently under way; owing to the Sea's mineral-rich waters, the growth of curative tourism is anticipated. The Red Sea port of Aqaba is also undergoing a major programme of development, with a view to becoming a centre for diving holidays. In 2001 Jordan received some 2.4m. visitors (including pilgrims and excursionists). Income from tourism in that year was estimated at JD \$496m.

Ministry of Tourism and Antiquities: POB 224, Amman 11118; tel. (6) 4642311; fax (6) 4648465; e-mail tourism@mota.gov.jo; internet www.mota.gov.jo; f. 1952; Minister of Tourism and Antiquities Dr TALEB AR-RIFAI; Sec.-Gen. SULTAN ABU JABER.

Jordan Tourism Board: POB 830688, Amman 11183; tel. (6) 5678294; fax (6) 5678295; f. 1997; e-mail jtb@nets.com.jo; internet www.see-jordan.com; Man. Dir MARWAN KHOURY.

Defence

Commander-in-Chief of the Armed Forces: Maj.-Gen. FATHI ABU TALIB.

Assistant Commander-in-Chief of the Armed Forces: Brig. TAYSEER ZAROUR.

Chairman of Joint Chiefs of Staff: Gen. MUHAMMAD YOUSUF AL-MALKAWI.

Commander of the Royal Jordanian Air Force: Lt-Gen. IHSAN HAMID SHURDUM.

Chief of the General Staff: Lt-Gen. ABDEL HADI AL-MAJAH.

Defence Expenditure (2000): JD 370m.

Military Service: conscription, two years authorized.

Total Armed Forces (August 2001): 100,240: army 84,700; navy (estimated) 540; air force 15,000. Reserves 35,000 (army 30,000).

Paramilitary Forces: (estimated) 45,000 (10,000 Public Security Force, 35,000 Civil Militia).

Education

The Ministry of Education adopted the principle of decentralization from the beginning of 1980. It divided the East Bank into 18 districts, called Offices of Education, distributed over five Directorates of Education, each one run by a Director-General who is in charge of implementing educational policies and procedures in that area. The Ministry of Education's Central Office is still responsible for all major educational decisions related to planning curricula, projects and examinations.

Education in Jordan is provided by public and private sectors. In 1982/83, 70.6% of school enrolment was provided by the Ministry of Education, 1% by other governmental agencies (such as the Ministries of Defence, Health, Labour and Islamic Affairs), 9.9% by the private sector and 15.9% by UNRWA, which offers educational facilities and services for Palestinian refugees in collaboration with UNESCO. The University of Jordan, Yarmouk University and Mo'ata University provided 2.6% of total school enrolment.

Primary education is free and compulsory. It starts at the age of six years and lasts for 10 years. The preparatory cycle is followed by a two-year secondary cycle, which is divided into three types: general, vocational and comprehensive school. The Ministry of Education, in accordance with law No. 16 of 1964, provides textbooks free of charge for the compulsory cycle, and at cost price for the secondary cycle. At the end of the latter cycle, students who pass the General Secondary Examination are entitled to continue their higher education by enrolling either in the universities of Jordan (at Amman, Irbid and Mo'ata) or in Community Colleges—or in foreign universities and colleges. In 1986 Yarmouk University, at Irbid, was divided into two separate institutions to create the University of Science and Technology. An open university, Al-Quds University, opened in October 1988.

Community Colleges, of two-year post-secondary duration, include 12 colleges controlled by the Ministry, 22 colleges controlled by the private sector and supervised by the Ministry, and seven other colleges controlled by other governmental agencies such as the Ministries of Health and Social Development, the armed forces, the Department of Statistics and the Central Bank of Jordan. According to the Department of Statistics, some 24,657 students were enrolled at Community Colleges in 1998.

Education was allocated a total of JD 215m. (US \$620m.) under the 1986–90 Development Plan. Budgetary expenditure on education by the central Government in 1997 was JD 245.1m. (14.6% of total spending).

In 1989 a 10-year programme to reform the state education system was announced. The programme, which was to be implemented in three phases (1989–92, 1993–95 and 1996–98), aimed to revise curricula; to produce new textbooks and teaching aids; to train 4,000 new primary school teachers, 1,500 new secondary school teachers and 360 new school principals and supervisors; and to construct 420 schools.

According to the Department of Statistics, in 2001 there were 50,562 teachers and 1,173,314 pupils at the primary level. At the secondary level (including both general and vocational education) there were 14,280 teachers and 173,755 pupils. There were 6,036 teachers and 153,965 students in higher education in 2001, in which year there were 4,999 schools and 22 universities in Jordan.

Bibliography

Abdullah of Transjordan, King. *Memoirs,* trans. G. Khuri, ed. P. Graves. London and New York, 1950.

Abidi, A. H. H. *Jordan, a Political Study 1948–1957.* Delhi, Asia Publishing House, 1966.

Abu Nowar, Maan. *The Struggle for Independence 1939–1947. A History of the Hashemite Kingdom of Jordan.* Reading, Ithaca Press, 1999.

Boulby, Marion. *The Muslim Brotherhood and the Kings of Jordan 1945–1993.* Atlanta, GA, Scholars Press, 1999.

Day, Arthur. *East Bank, West Bank.* Council on Foreign Relations, 1986.

Dearden, Ann. *Jordan.* London, Hale, 1958.

Foreign Area Studies. *Jordan: A Country Study.* Washington, DC, American University, 1980.

Glubb, J. B. *The Story of the Arab Legion.* London, 1948.

A Soldier with the Arabs. Hodder and Stoughton, 1957.

Britain and the Arabs: A Study of Fifty Years 1908–1958. London, Hodder and Stoughton, 1959.

War in the Desert. London, 1960.

The Middle East Crisis—A Personal Interpretation. London 1967.

Syria, Lebanon, Jordan. London, 1967.

Peace in the Holy Land. London, 1971.

Goichon, A. M. *L'Eau: Problème Vital de la Région du Jourdain.* Brussels, Centre pour l'Etudes des Problèmes du Monde Musulmane Contemporain, 1964.

Jordanie réelle. Paris, Maisonneuve et Larose, 1972.

Gubser, Peter. *Jordan: Crossroads of Middle Eastern Events.* Boulder, Colorado, Westview Press, 1983.

Hussein, His Majesty King. *Uneasy Lies the Head.* London, 1962.

Ma guerre avec Israël. Paris, Albin Michel, 1968.

Mon métier de roi. Paris, Laffont, 1975.

International Bank for Reconstruction and Development. *The Economic Development of Jordan.* Baltimore, Johns Hopkins Press, 1957.

Jarvis, C. S. *Arab Command: the Biography of Lt-Col. F. W. Peake Pasha.* London, 1942.

Joffé, George (Ed.) *Jordan in Transition 1990–2000.* London, C. Hurst & Co, 2001.

Johnston, Charles. *The Brink of Jordan.* London, Hamish Hamilton, 1972.

Kohn, Hans. *Die staats- und verfassungsrechtliche Entwicklung des Emirats Transjordanien.* Tübingen, 1929.

Konikof, A. *Transjordan: An Economic Survey.* 2nd edn, Jerusalem, 1946.

Layne, Linda. *Home and Homeland: the dialogues of tribal and national identities in Jordan.* Chichester, Princeton University Press, 1994.

Lowi, Miriam R. *Water and Power: The Politics of a Scarce Resource in the Jordan River Basin.* Cambridge, Cambridge University Press, 1994.

Luke, Sir Harry C., and Keith-Roach, E. *The Handbook of Palestine and Transjordan.* London, 1934.

Lunt, James. *Hussein of Jordan.* London, Macmillan, 1989.

Lyautey, Pierre. *La Jordanie Nouvelle.* Paris, Juillard, 1966.

Marashdeh, Omar. *The Jordanian Economy.* Al-Jawal Corpn, 1996.

Mishal, Shaul. *West Bank/East Bank: The Palestinians in Jordan 1949–67.* New Haven, London, Yale University Press.

Moaddel, Mansoor. *Jordanian Exceptionalism.* Basingstoke, Palgrave, 2001.

Morris, James. *The Hashemite Kings.* London, Faber, 1959.

Patai, R. *The Kingdom of Jordan.* Princeton, 1958.

Peake, F. G. *History of Jordan and Its Tribes.* Univ. of Miami Press, 1958.

Phillips, Paul G. *The Hashemite Kingdom of Jordan: Prolegomena to a Technical Assistance Programme.* Chicago, 1954.

Piro, Timothy J. *The political economy of market reform in Jordan.* Lanham, MD, Rowan and Littlefield, 1998.

Rogan, Eugene L., and Tell, Tariq (Eds). *Village, Steppe and State: the social origins of modern Jordan.* London, British Academic Press, 1994.

Salibi, Kamal. *The Modern History of Jordan.* London, I. B. Tauris, 1999.

Sanger, Richard H. *Where the Jordan Flows.* Washington, DC, Middle East Institute, 1965.

Shipler, David K. *Arab and Jew: Wounded Spirits in a Promised Land.* London, Bloomsbury, 1987.

Shlaim, Avi. *Collusion Across the Jordan.* Oxford University Press, 1988.

Shwadran, B. *Jordan: A State of Tension.* New York, Council for Middle Eastern Affairs, 1959.

Smith, Sir G. A. *Historical Geography of the Holy Land.* 25th edn, London, 1931.

Snow, Peter. *Hussein: A Biography.* London, Barrie and Jenkins, 1972.

Sparrow, Gerald. *Hussein of Jordan (the authorized biography).* London, Harrap, 1961.

Modern Jordan. Allen and Unwin, 1961.

Toukan, Baha Uddin. *A Short History of Transjordan.* London, 1945.

US Government Printing Office. *Area Handbook for the Hashemite Kingdom of Jordan.* Washington, DC, 1970.

Vatikiotis, P. J. *Politics and the Military in Jordan 1921–57.* New York, Praeger, 1967.

Verdes, Jacques Mansour. *Pour les Fidayine.* Paris, 1969.

Wilson, Rodney (Ed.). *Politics and Economy in Jordan.* London, Routledge, 1991.

KUWAIT

Physical and Social Geography

Kuwait lies at the head of the Persian (Arabian) Gulf, bordering Iraq and Saudi Arabia. The area of the State of Kuwait is 17,818 sq km (6,880 sq miles), including the Kuwaiti share of the Neutral or Partitioned Zone (see below) but without taking into account the increase in territory resulting from the adjustment to the border with Iraq that came into effect in January 1993.

Although, for some time, the Gulf was thought to extend much further north, geological evidence suggests that the coastline has remained broadly at its present position, while the immense masses of silt brought down by the Tigris and Euphrates cause irregular downwarping at the head of the Gulf. Local variation in the coastline is therefore likely, with possible changes since ancient times. The development of Kuwait (which means 'little fortress') owed much to its zone of slightly higher, firmer ground (giving access from the Gulf inland to Iraq) and to its reasonably good and sheltered harbour, away from nearby sandbanks and coral reefs.

The territory of Kuwait is mainly flat desert with a few oases. An annual rainfall of 1 cm–37 cm falls almost entirely between November and April, and there is a spring 'flush' of grass. Summer shade temperature may reach 49°C (120°F), although in January, the coldest month, temperatures range between −2.8°C and 28.3°C (27°F–85°F), with a rare frost. There is little inland drinking water, and supplies are largely distilled from sea water, and brought by pipeline from the Shatt al-Arab waterway, which runs into the Gulf.

According to census results, the population of Kuwait increased from 206,473 in February 1957 to 1,357,952 by April 1980 and to 1,697,301 by April 1985. It was estimated that in 1991, following the war to end the Iraqi occupation, the population had declined to only 1.2m., mainly as a result of the departure of a large proportion of the former non-Kuwaiti residents, who had previously formed a majority of the inhabitants (see below). The census of April 1995 recorded a total population of 1,575,570, including 653,616 Kuwaiti nationals. By mid-2001 the population had increased to 2,274,980, according to official estimates. During 1963–70 the average annual increase in Kuwait's population was 10%, the highest growth rate recorded in any independent country. The average annual increase in 1970–80 was 6.3%, although in 1985–90 the rate of growth slowed to 4.0% per year, and the population actually declined by 4.8% per year during 1990–96. During 1980–99, according to the World Bank, the average annual rate of growth of the population had slowed to 1.8%, and the population was esti-mated to have declined by an annual average of 0.7% during 1990–2000.

Much of Kuwait's previous population growth had been the result of immigration, although the country also had one of the highest natural increase rates in the world. The birth rate for the Kuwaiti population alone exceeded 50 per 1,000 each year in 1973–76. Between 1957 and 1983 the non-Kuwaiti population grew from less than 93,000 (45% of the total) to about 870,000 (57.4%), most of them from other Arab states. At the 1995 census the non-Kuwaiti population, based on the definition of citizenship then in use, represented 58.5% of the total. In 2000 there were 41,843 recorded births and only 4,227 deaths. In 1995 females comprised only 42% of the country's population, including non-Kuwaitis.

According to the results of the 1995 census, Kuwait City, the capital and principal harbour, had a population of 28,747 (compared with 44,335 in 1985 and 60,525 in 1980), although the largest town was Salmiya, with 129,775 inhabitants. Other sizeable localities were Jaleeb ash-Shuyukh (population 102,169) and Hawalli (population 82,154).

Apart from the distinction between Kuwaiti citizens and immigrants, Kuwaiti nationals can be divided into six groups. These groups reflect the tribal origins of Kuwaiti society. The first tribe of settlers, the Anaiza (led by the Sabah family) and later settlers, including the Bahar, Hamad and Babtain families, originated in the Nejd (central Arabia). Another group, the Kenaat (including the Mutawa family and its offshoot, the Saleh), came to Kuwait from Iraq, and remain distinct from the Nejdi families. There are also a few large families of Persian (Iranian) origin, including the Behbanis. The remaining citizens may be described as 'new Kuwaitis'; a few are former Palestinians, although most are bedouin who have been granted second-class citizenship. The majority of the Kuwaitis (including the ruling family) are Sunni Muslims, but most of the Persian families belong to the Shi'a sect. They, together with other Persians, comprise an estimated 150,000 (or one-quarter) of all Kuwaiti citizens. About 30% of the total population are thought to be Shi'ites.

Immediately to the south of Kuwait, along the Gulf, is a Neutral or Partitioned Zone of 5,700 sq km, which is divided between Kuwait and Saudi Arabia. Each country administers its own half as an integral part of the state. However, the oil wealth of the whole Zone remains undivided, and production from the onshore concessions in the Neutral/Partitioned Zone is normally shared equally between the two states.

History

Revised for this edition by Kamil Mahdi

The establishment of the present city of Kuwait is usually dated from the beginning of the 18th century, when a number of families of the Anaiza tribe migrated from the interior to the Arabian shore of the Gulf. The foundation of the present Sabah ruling dynasty dates from about 1756, when the settlers of Kuwait took the protection of a sheikh against other tribal threats and in order to administer their affairs, provide them with security and represent them in their dealings with the Ottoman rulers of Iraq. The town prospered and in 1765 it was estimated to contain some 10,000 inhabitants possessing 800 vessels, engaged in trading, fishing and pearling.

Between 1775 and 1779, during the Persian occupation of Basra, the British East India Company moved the southern terminal of its overland mail route to Aleppo from Basra to Kuwait, and much of the trade of Basra was diverted to Kuwait.

Such a shift was repeated again in 1793 and in 1821–22, and many merchant families migrated from Basra to Kuwait. At around the same time Kuwait was repeatedly threatened by raids from the Wahhabis, puritanical Islamist tribesmen from central Arabia, and the need for protection led to closer contacts with the East India Company, which had a depot in the town. Conflict between British and Arab fleets over control of the sea trade caused a decline in prosperity during the early years of the 19th century, but trade later expanded again under British ascendancy. The growth of production in the region and the expansion of trade in the second half of the century brought renewed prosperity.

Although not under direct Turkish administration, the Sheikh of Kuwait recognized a general Ottoman suzerainty over the area by the payment of tribute and Sheikh Abdullah bin Sabah al-Jabir (1866–92) accepted the title of Qa'immaqam (district governor) under the Turkish Vali (Governor) of Basra in 1871. The reign of Sheikh Mubarak, from 1896 to 1915, was notable for the increase of British ascendancy in Kuwait. Mubarak 'the Great' feared that the Turks would bring Kuwait under direct administration, and in 1899, in return for British protection, he signed an agreement with the British not to cede, mortgage or otherwise dispose of parts of his territories to anyone except the British Government, nor to enter into any other relationship with a foreign government without British consent. In 1904 a British political agent was appointed, and in 1909 Great Britain and Turkey discussed proposals which, although never ratified because of the outbreak of the First World War, in practice secured the British protectorate status of Kuwait.

Nevertheless, Mubarak's second son, Sheikh Salim, who succeeded to the sheikhdom in 1917, supported the Turks in the First World War, thus incurring a blockade of Kuwait. Sheikh Salim was succeeded in 1921 by his nephew, Sheikh Ahmad al-Jabir. His rule witnessed the collapse of Gulf pearling income under the twin shocks of the rise of Japanese culture pearling and the Great Depression. Kuwait was able to adjust to those shocks by benefiting from the growth of Iraqi trade and through payments received for oil exploration. By 1937, Kuwait was a relatively prosperous mercantile community, with a population of about 75,000. There were strong civic demands for representation within Kuwait and, under King Ghazi, the newly-independent Iraq was seeking the port city's integration and the end of British protection for Kuwait. Some of these demands were echoed within Kuwait itself, particularly during the short-lived period of an elected representative assembly in the late 1930s.

The foundations of Kuwait's petroleum industry were laid during the 1930s. A joint concession was granted in 1934 to the Gulf Oil Corpn of the USA and the Anglo-Persian Oil Co of Great Britain, which formed the Kuwait Oil Co Ltd. Deep drilling started in 1936, and was just beginning to show promising results when the Second World War began in 1939. The oil wells were plugged in 1942 and drilling was suspended until the end of the war.

THE MODERN STATE

After the war the petroleum industry in Kuwait was revived on an extensive scale (see Economy), and within a few years the town of Kuwait had developed from a traditional dhow port to a thriving modern commercial city, supported by the revenues of the petroleum industry. In 1950 Sheikh Ahmad died and was succeeded by Sheikh Abdullah as-Salim, whose policies focused on the use of petroleum revenues to improve public welfare. In 1951 he inaugurated a programme of public works and educational and medical developments which transformed Kuwait into a country with a modern infrastructure and a high standard of living for the indigenous population. The relationship between the ruling as-Sabah family and the traditional merchant élite and general Kuwaiti population began to change. Instead of the original two-way dependence between the Amir and the merchant élite, with the Amir providing representation with powers outside the territory and a measure of internal security, in return for a limited ability to tax local merchant activity, the Amir now became the main economic provider for the population, including acting as benefactor of the merchant élite, in addition to holding a much wider political, security, administrative and judicial role. Consequently, the Amir came also to rely more on his family than on building alliances with the traditional merchant élite and with other sections of the population. Being a small, wealthy entity in a turbulent region, many Kuwaitis seem to recognize and accept their dependence upon the ruling family as the price of a privileged economic position. Thus, domestic opposition was muted, despite the increased education of the population.

Kuwait has gradually built up comprehensive welfare services, which are for the most part free of charge, at least to native Kuwaitis. Education is provided completely free of charge. The health service is largely free and considered to be of a very high standard. A heavily subsidized housing programme has provided accommodation for many residents who satisfy the country's generous criteria of 'poverty'. In addition, the state sector has virtually guaranteed well-paid employment and retirement pensions to Kuwaiti citizens, while making minimal tax demands upon them. Citizens were also given advantageous positions in business, and for several decades the scale of oil revenues enabled the Government to guarantee widespread benefits, including huge subsidies of water, electricity and consumer products, while the ruling as-Sabah family continued to enjoy its own special privileges.

The 1899 agreement, under which the United Kingdom assumed responsibility for the conduct of Kuwait's foreign policy, was terminated in 1961; Kuwait became a fully independent state on 19 June. The ruling Sheikh took the title of Amir, and Kuwait was admitted to the League of Arab States (Arab League).

Iraq, under the leadership of Gen. Abd al-Karim Kassem (1958–63), did not recognize Kuwait's independence and revived a long-standing claim to sovereignty over the territory. In response to a request from the Kuwaiti Amir for assistance, British troops landed in Kuwait in order to deter Iraq from taking military action in support of its claim. The Arab League met in July 1961 and agreed that an Arab League force should be provided to replace the British troops as a guarantor of Kuwait's independence. This force, composed of contingents from Saudi Arabia, Jordan, the United Arab Republic (UAR) and Sudan, arrived in Kuwait in September. The UAR contingent was withdrawn in December, and those of Jordan, Saudi Arabia and Sudan before the end of February 1963.

In December 1961, for the first time in Kuwait's history, an election was held to choose 20 members of the Constituent Assembly (the other members being ministers). This Assembly drafted a new Constitution under which a National Assembly (Majlis al-Umma) of 50 members was elected in January 1963, and the first session was held, with Sheikh Sabah as-Salim as-Sabah, brother of the Amir and heir apparent, as the Prime Minister of a new Council of Ministers.

In October 1963, with the Baath Party now in power, the Iraqi Government announced its decision to recognize Kuwait's complete independence, in an attempt to dispel the tense atmosphere between the two countries. Kuwait was thought to have made a substantial grant to Iraq at this juncture.

In January 1965 a constitutional crisis, reflecting the friction between the ruling house and the National Assembly, resulted in the formation of a strengthened Council of Ministers under the heir apparent, Sheikh Sabah as-Salim as-Sabah. On 24 November 1965 Sheikh Abdullah died and was succeeded by Sheikh Sabah. His post as Prime Minister was assumed by another member of the ruling family, Sheikh Jaber al-Ahmad, who became heir apparent in May 1966.

Kuwait adopted a neutral role in inter-Arab conflicts during 1966 and 1967. It declared its support for the Arab countries in the June 1967 war with Israel, and joined in the oil embargo imposed against the USA and the United Kingdom. The Government donated KD 25m. to the Arab war effort. At the Khartoum Conference in September 1967 Kuwait joined Saudi Arabia and Libya in offering financial aid to the UAR and Jordan, to help their economies to recover from the 1967 war.

In 1968 it was announced that the agreement of June 1961—whereby Britain had undertaken to give military assistance to Kuwait if asked to do so by its ruler—would terminate by 1971. This followed an earlier announcement that Britain would withdraw all troops from the Gulf region by the end of 1971.

Following the war of June 1967, Kuwait ceased to be a target of radical Arab criticism, largely because of its financial support for the countries affected by war, and for the Palestinian guerrilla movements. A factor in this assistance was the large Palestinian community, totalling more than 350,000, in Kuwait; many of the most able and educated Palestinians had made a career in the country. Financial aid to Jordan, on the other hand, was suspended in September 1970, following the armed conflict between the Jordanian Government and Palestinian guerrilla forces.

During the 1960s the Kuwaiti leadership's policies led to extensive redistribution of income, through the use of oil revenues in public expenditure and through the land compensation scheme. At the same time, however, there was popular discontent about corruption and inefficiency in public services and the manipulation of the press and the National Assembly.

In response to public opinion, the ruling family permitted the assembly elections of January 1971 to be held on the basis of a free vote, although women, illiterate males and all non-Kuwaitis were excluded. There was a lively election campaign, with 184 candidates contesting the 50 seats, despite the absence of political parties, which remained illegal. Several members and supporters of the Arab Nationalist Movement, founded in the 1950s by Dr George Habash (later leader of the Popular Front for the Liberation of Palestine), were elected. This radical group, led by Dr Ahmad al-Khatib, was generally regarded as the principal opposition to the Government.

After the 1971 elections the Crown Prince was reappointed Prime Minister and formed a new Council of Ministers. The representation of the ruling family was reduced from five to three and, for the first time, the Council of Ministers included two ministers drawn from the elected members of the National Assembly.

In August 1976 the Amir suspended the National Assembly on the grounds that, among other things, it had been delaying legislation. A committee was ordered to be formed to review the Constitution. The episode highlighted the strength of political patronage and the limitations of Kuwait's democracy. The Kuwaiti rulers were determined to insulate the state from the popular nationalist trend that was still thriving in the Arab region.

Sheikh Sabah died on 31 December 1977; he was succeeded by his cousin, Crown Prince Sheikh Jaber al-Ahmad as-Sabah. Sheikh Saad al-Abdullah as-Salim as-Sabah became Prime Minister as well as Crown Prince. Both the Amir and the Prime Minister publicly reaffirmed the Government's intention to reconvene the National Assembly and to restore democratic government by August 1980. In response to increasing public pressure, a 50-member committee was established in early 1980 to consider constitutional amendments and a revised form of legislature. Following its recommendations, an Amiri decree provided for the election of a new assembly before the end of February 1981. Despite the uncertainty generated by the Iran–Iraq War, the election campaign proceeded, with 448 candidates contesting the 50 seats. The franchise was limited to 90,000 'first-class' Kuwaiti citizens, and of these fewer than half (or about 3% of the population) registered to vote. A conservative assembly was returned, including 23 tribal leaders, sympathetic to the ruling sheikhs, and 13 young technocrats. The radical Arab nationalists, the fiercest opposition to the Government in the previous Assembly, failed to win any seats, while the Shi'a minority's representation was reduced to four seats. However, five Islamic fundamentalists of the Sunni sect were elected. The Crown Prince was subsequently reappointed Prime Minister and formed a new 15-member Council of Ministers in which the ruling family retained the major posts.

PETROLEUM AND EXTERNAL RELATIONS 1973–1981

Despite recognition by Iraq in 1963, Kuwait's borders, including those with Iraq, remained unsettled. Of all the Gulf states, Kuwait has been the most vulnerable to regional disruption. In March 1973 Iraqi troops and tanks occupied a Kuwaiti outpost at Samtah, on the border with Iraq. Iraq later withdrew its troops, but a source of potential dispute remained over Iraq's territorial claim on Bubiyan island and its desire to have secure access to the deep waters of the Gulf. Along with other Gulf states, Kuwait allocated larger sums for the expansion of its armed forces after 1973, and it established its own navy. Legislation to introduce conscription was approved in 1975, but it was generally accepted that Kuwait's security could not be guaranteed through its own armed strength.

During the Arab–Israeli war of October 1973 Kuwaiti forces stationed along the Suez Canal were involved in fighting, and Kuwait contributed considerable financial aid, totalling KD 100m., to other Arab states. While the war was still in progress, Kuwait called for a meeting of the Organization of Arab Petroleum Exporting Countries (OAPEC) to draw up a common Arab policy for the use of oil as a means to put pressure on Western countries, particularly the USA, to force an Israeli withdrawal from occupied Arab territory. Kuwait also joined other Gulf states in announcing a unilateral increase of 70% in the posted price of crude petroleum (the reference price used for tax and royalty purposes) from 1 November 1973. Earlier,

at the OAPEC meeting that took place in Kuwait, the organization's 10 member states decided to reduce petroleum production by at least 5% progressively each month. Kuwait also imposed a total embargo on petroleum shipments to the USA and, later, to the Netherlands.

In November oil ministers from the Arab states also agreed on an extra 5% reduction in output, which effectively led to an overall decrease in supply of 25% in January 1974, compared with the previous September's levels, to be followed by further reductions. Just before this, in December, the Gulf states belonging to the Organization of the Petroleum Exporting Countries (OPEC) had agreed on a further sharp increase in the posted price of oil, effective from 1 January 1974.

Kuwait played a leading part in all these moves and made considerable reductions in national oil output. Monthly production fell from 13.4m. metric tons in September 1973 to 9.8m. tons in November. There was later a reversal in this trend, and monthly output was more than 10m. tons in the first half of 1974.

Following the January conclusion of a disengagement agreement between Egypt and Israel and the consequent improvement in Arab relations with the USA, seven of the Arab oil-producing states (including Kuwait) agreed in March to lift the embargo on supplies to the USA. In July 1974 the Arab countries also lifted the oil embargo on the Netherlands. None the less, Kuwait's policy of conserving petroleum reserves, and the fall in the world demand, meant that production fell from a peak of 3.3m. barrels per day (b/d) in 1972 to an average of below 1m. b/d in 1981. Since then, OPEC agreements have imposed a maximum quota on every member country's production (see Economy).

At the Baghdad Arab summit in November 1978 Kuwait pressed for unanimity among the Arab nations in condemning the Egypt-Israeli peace agreement, and supported the use of sanctions against Egypt. The Kuwaiti ambassador was recalled from Cairo and all aid, except that for specific development projects, was withdrawn. Kuwait mediated successfully in the conflict between the Yemen Arab Republic and the People's Democratic Republic of Yemen in 1979, eventually bringing about a cease-fire, and was instrumental in resolving a political crisis in the United Arab Emirates (UAE) in the same year.

During the first two decades of Kuwait's independence, it sought to project a distinct foreign policy and attempted to enhance its security by broadening its international relations, including relations with the communist states, with non-aligned countries and across the Arab world. A new direction in Kuwaiti foreign policy was taken from May 1981, when Kuwait, with Saudi Arabia, the UAE, Qatar, Oman and Bahrain, founded the Co-operation Council for the Arab States of the Gulf (the Gulf Co-operation Council—GCC). By encouraging economic and social integration, it was hoped that the GCC would increase the security of the small oil-producing states of the Gulf. Subsequently the heads and key officials of the GCC states have met regularly, but the cement of the alliance has been the perceived common threats as well as the rulers' alliances with the USA and the United Kingdom. Only in recent years has a more positive regional integration agenda started to make slow progress, with the beginnings of co-ordination of trade policies and with the resolution of border disputes among the member states themselves. Steps towards establishing some internal consultation and representation mechanisms have also improved relations among the ruling families of the Gulf. Nevertheless, it has sometimes been discernible that the northern states of Kuwait and Bahrain are more closely aligned with Saudi Arabian policy than are the other Gulf states.

THE IRAN–IRAQ WAR

Kuwait's regional security position began to change with the sequence of events that began with the Iranian Revolution of 1979 and with the war between Iran and Iraq, which began in September 1980. In that war, Kuwait supported Iraq, granting access to its strategic ports, and, with Saudi Arabia, exporting up to 310,000 b/d (250,000 b/d from the Neutral Zone and the remainder from Saudi Arabia) on Iraq's behalf, and contributing to the substantial financial aid, which by the end of the war, in 1988, was thought to have reached US $40,000m. (donated by both Kuwait and Saudi Arabia, as well as other Gulf states, mainly the UAE). Relations with Iran were, however, maintained.

Events at the end of 1983 and in early 1984 increased concern for the country's security. The potential threat of a rising domestic religious opposition was coupled with the authorities' suspicion that a number of bomb attacks had been directed by Iran in retaliation for Kuwaiti support of Iraq in the Iran–Iraq War. As a result of the bombings, more than 600 Iranian workers were deported from Kuwait in early 1984.

In May 1984 two Kuwaiti and several Saudi Arabian tankers were bombed in a series of attacks by unidentified aircraft on shipping in the Gulf. Although both Iran and Iraq were known to have been firing at shipping, Iran was blamed for the attacks on Kuwaiti tankers. The bombings were seen as a warning to Kuwait to reduce its aid to Iraq and to put pressure on Iraq to desist from attacking tankers carrying Iranian oil. The GCC withdrew offers to mediate in the Iran–Iraq War and condemned Iran. Much concern arose as to whether the GCC countries could defend themselves unaided, and at the GCC summit conference in November the member states agreed to form a joint military force, capable of rapid deployment and aimed at combating any spread of the Iran–Iraq War.

Kuwait's attempts to mediate in the Iran–Iraq War in 1984 were hampered by Iran's increasing suspicion about the outcome of outstanding border disputes between Iraq and Kuwait. Iran believed that Kuwait was about to transfer three strategically important islands (Bubiyan, Warba and Failaka) to Iraq. In January 1985, however, Kuwait announced plans to build its own military bases on Bubiyan and Warba, and two months later Bubiyan was declared an out-of-bounds war zone. Kuwaiti forces were put on alert in February 1986, when Iranian forces crossed the Shatt al-Arab waterway and captured the Iraqi port of Faw, near Kuwait's north-eastern border. Iran pledged that Kuwait would not become embroiled in its war with Iraq provided that it maintained its military neutrality.

Between October 1986 and April 1987 Iranian forces attacked merchant ships sailing to or from Kuwait and seized cargoes, in reprisal for loading petroleum sold on Iraq's behalf and for the use of Kuwait's ports for Iraqi imports. In an attempt to deter Iranian attacks in the Gulf, Kuwait re-registered most of its fleet of oil tankers under the flags of the USA, Liberia, the USSR and the United Kingdom. Kuwait received help from the USA and Saudi Arabia in clearing mines from the channel leading to its main oil-loading facilities at Mina al-Ahmadi. Later, France, the United Kingdom and other European states also joined minesweeping operations.

Six Iranian diplomats were expelled from Kuwait in September 1987, following Iranian attacks on Kuwaiti installations. Kuwait's main offshore oil-loading terminal was closed between October and December, after an Iranian missile attack in which three workers were injured. A summit meeting of the GCC in December 1987 urged the UN Security Council to enforce its Resolution 598, which ordered a cease-fire to be observed in the Iran–Iraq War, and approved a pact to increase security co-operation between the member states.

Two Kuwaiti soldiers were wounded in March 1988, as Iranian and Kuwaiti armed forces clashed for the first time during the Iran–Iraq War when three Iranian gunboats attacked Bubiyan island, situated 25 km from the southern coast of Iraq. In the following month an Iranian missile landed at al-Wafra oilfield, 80 km south of Kuwait City. The launching of the missile was believed to represent an Iranian warning to Kuwait for allegedly permitting Iraqi armed forces to use Bubiyan island in an attempt to recapture the Iranian-occupied Faw peninsula.

The cease-fire in the Iran–Iraq War in August 1988 brought a revival of economic growth in Kuwait. Relations between Kuwait and Iran improved, and in April 1989 the Prime Minister, Saad al-Abdullah as-Salim as-Sabah, announced that relations with Iran were 'moving towards stability and normalization'. Co-operation with Iraq also appeared to increase.

INTERNAL UNREST AND THE SECOND SUSPENSION OF THE NATIONAL ASSEMBLY

In May 1985 an Iraqi member of the banned opposition ad-Dawa al-Islamiya (the Call of Islam) organization attempted to assassinate the Amir of Kuwait by driving a car bomb into a royal procession. As a result of the attack, the Government resolved to introduce appropriate legislation and temporarily to suspend the issue of entry visas and residence permits. In July the National Assembly unanimously approved legislation to impose the death penalty for terrorist acts resulting in loss of life, and the Government announced plans to establish popular security committees in all districts. In June 1986 four simultaneous explosions occurred at Kuwait's main oil export refinery at Mina al-Ahmadi. A hitherto unknown organization, the 'Arab Revolutionaries Group', later claimed responsibility for the attacks, which had been intended to force Kuwait to reduce its petroleum output.

In 1985 and 1986 almost 27,000 expatriates, many of whom were Iranian, were deported, and concern about Iranian influence over the Shi'ite minority (about 30% of the population) led to severe measures to curb political subversion. In June 1987 six Kuwaiti Shi'a Muslims were sentenced to death for their part in sabotaging oil installations and plotting against the Government. There were further explosions in May and July. In June 1989 a Kuwaiti court sentenced 22 people, accused of plotting to overthrow the royal family, to prison terms of up to 15 years.

The tension in and surrounding Kuwait was reflected in the general political atmosphere. Although the traditional Arab nationalist opposition was dealt a severe blow by the dissolution of the National Assembly in 1976, political demands came to be more explicitly expressed on the basis of religious and tribal alliances represented within the new National Assembly. In July 1986, following 15 months of increasing confrontation with the National Assembly, the Amir dissolved the Assembly for a second time and suspended relevant articles of the Constitution. A new Government, also with Crown Prince Sheikh Saad al-Abdullah as-Salim as-Sabah as Prime Minister, was appointed and given greater powers of censorship, including the right to close down newspapers for up to two years.

In December 1989 a number of former members of the National Assembly launched a campaign to restore the Assembly. In mid-January 1990 the Amir appealed for political dialogue, and in March the Prime Minister declared that he would welcome the restoration of an elected legislature. However, the Government was only prepared to permit a partly elected council with severely limited powers, which the opposition rejected and urged all parties to boycott. On 10 June 62% of the electorate voted at a general election for 50 members of this new and distinct National *Council*. The Council was to be an interim body and its members were to hold office for four years. It comprised 75 members, of whom 25 were appointed by the Amir.

Following the election, the Kuwaiti Government resigned. On 13 June 1990 the Amir reappointed the Crown Prince, Sheikh Saad al-Abdullah as-Salim as-Sabah, as Prime Minister and on 23 June a government reshuffle resulted in 10 new appointments to the Council of Ministers. Only three ministers not belonging to the as-Sabah family retained their posts, while the new members of the Council were technocrats with no previous experience of government. The Council was believed to have been reshuffled in an attempt to satisfy domestic demands for new government policies. However, the fact that the as-Sabah family retained the majority of important positions in the Government, and that restoration of the National Assembly did not seem a realistic prospect, undermined the attempt to placate critics of the Government. In late June it was announced that five ministers from the reshuffled Council of Ministers had been appointed by the Amir to the National Council, the first session of which was held on 9 July.

IRAQ'S INVASION OF KUWAIT: THE GULF CRISIS

In July 1990 President Saddam Hussain of Iraq publicly criticized unnamed states for exceeding the petroleum production quotas that had been established by OPEC in May in order to increase prices. He accused Kuwait of having 'stolen' US $2,400m.-worth of Iraqi oil reserves from a field that straddles the unsettled border. The Iraqi Minister of Foreign Affairs, Tareq Aziz, declared that Kuwait should not only cancel Iraq's war debt, but also compensate it for losses of revenue incurred during the war with Iran, and as a result of Kuwait's overproduction of oil, to which he attributed a decline in prices. Later in July Iraq began to deploy armed forces on the

Kuwait–Iraq border, immediately before a meeting of the OPEC ministerial council in Geneva, Switzerland. At the meeting the minimum reference price for petroleum was increased, as Iraq had demanded. On 31 July representatives of Kuwait and Iraq conferred in Jeddah, Saudi Arabia, in an attempt to resolve the dispute, but the negotiations collapsed. A number of differing accounts of Kuwait's willingness at the Jeddah meeting to compromise on Iraq's financial claims have been offered.

On 2 August 1990 Iraq invaded Kuwait with 100,000 troops. The Iraqi Government claimed that its forces entered Kuwait at the invitation of insurgents who had overthrown the Kuwaiti Government, but there was no evidence to verify this. The Amir and other members of the Government escaped to Saudi Arabia, along with many Kuwaiti citizens. The immediate response of the UN Security Council to the invasion of Kuwait was to adopt a series of resolutions which condemned the invasion, demanded the immediate and unconditional withdrawal of Iraqi forces from Kuwait, and appealed for a negotiated settlement of the conflict. A comprehensive economic blockade was also imposed on Iraq and Kuwait. Immediately after the invasion, the USA and the members of the European Community (EC, now European Union—EU) 'froze' all Kuwaiti assets to prevent an Iraqi-imposed regime from transferring them back to Kuwait.

On 7 August 1990, President George Bush of the USA ordered the deployment of US troops and aircraft in Saudi Arabia, with the declared aim of securing the country's borders with Kuwait in the event of an Iraqi attack. A number of European governments, together with some members of the Arab League, agreed to provide military support for the US forces. On 8 August the Iraqi Government announced the formal annexation of Kuwait, and at the end of the month most of Kuwait was officially declared to be the 19th governorate of Iraq, while a northern strip was incorporated into Basra governorate. Successive diplomatic efforts failed to achieve a peaceful solution to the crisis in the Gulf region. Attempts to pursue a diplomatic solution were complicated by the detention of Western citizens resident in Kuwait and Iraq. By early December, however, all hostages had been released.

Following the Iraqi invasion, there were widespread reports of looting in Kuwait City as Iraqi forces were searching for Kuwaiti resistance fighters and Westerners in hiding. Some installations were said to have been dismantled and removed to Iraq. By early October an estimated 430,000 Iraqi troops had been deployed in southern Iraq and Kuwait. Kuwait's population was estimated to have decreased from approximately 2m., prior to the invasion, to about 700,000, of whom Kuwaitis constituted an estimated 300,000 and Palestinians 200,000, while the remainder comprised other Arab expatriate workers and Asians.

In early October 1990 a conference was held in Jeddah, where the exiled Crown Prince and Prime Minister of Kuwait, Sheikh Saad al-Abdullah as-Salim as-Sabah, addressed approximately 1,000 Kuwaiti citizens, including 'opposition' members of the dissolved National Assembly. He agreed to establish committees to advise the Government on political, social and financial matters, and pledged that, after the liberation of Kuwait, the country's constitution and legislature would be restored, and that free elections would be held. This was seen as a necessary concession in order to maintain national unity, particularly given the emerging divide between Kuwait's wealthier citizens, most of whom were now living in exile, and those who remained in Kuwait.

In late November 1990 the UN Security Council adopted a resolution which authorized the use of 'all necessary means' to liberate Kuwait. Iraq was allowed until 15 January 1991 to begin to implement the 10 resolutions that had so far been adopted, including that stipulating unconditional withdrawal from Kuwait. Upon the expiry of this period, it was implied, military force would be employed against Iraq in order to remove its troops from Kuwait. In the interim, a massive build-up of around 600,000 US troops, along with further substantial forces from a coalition of over 30 states, was assembled in Saudi Arabia and in other parts of the region in preparation for a military campaign against Iraq. Unsuccessful diplomatic attempts were made to avert a military confrontation between the multinational and Iraqi forces. On 17 January 1991 the UN-backed, US-led multinational force launched its military campaign with an intensive aerial bombardment of Iraq, with the aim of disabling that country's economic and military infrastructure. Soviet attempts to mediate were deemed unacceptable by the USA and its allies, as they proposed that a cease-fire should be declared before Iraq began to withdraw from Kuwait. On 24 February the US-led ground forces entered Kuwait, encountering little effective Iraqi opposition. Within three days the Iraqi Government had agreed to accept all resolutions of the UN Security Council concerning Kuwait, and on 28 February the US Government announced a suspension of military operations, but not before Iraqi troops and fleeing civilians were bombarded by US aircraft at Mutla Ridge, north of Kuwait city, resulting in heavy casualties. In March the UN Security Council set out the terms for a permanent cease-fire. These included the release of all allied prisoners of war and of Kuwaitis who had been detained as potential hostages. They also required Iraq to repeal all laws and decrees concerning the annexation of Kuwait. Iraq promptly announced its compliance with these conditions. Another resolution, adopted in April, provided for the establishment of a demilitarized zone, supervised by the UN Iraq-Kuwait Observer Mission (UNIKOM), between the two countries. The UNIKOM mandate was subsequently renewed at six-monthly intervals.

POLITICAL DEVELOPMENTS AND HUMAN RIGHTS AFTER THE IRAQI WITHDRAWAL

In mid-January 1991 a conference in Jeddah was attended by members of the Kuwaiti Government-in-exile and opposition delegates. Islamic and Arab nationalist groups had collaborated in forming a 'National Constitutional Front' and demanded an immediate return of parliamentary and press freedom, while the more radical elements in the movement demanded the resignation of the as-Sabah family from all important positions in the Government, and the establishment of a constitutional monarchy. In February, despite the expression of discontent among the exiled Kuwaiti community, the Kuwaiti Government-in-exile excluded the possibility of early elections after Kuwait had been liberated, on the grounds that the need to rebuild and repopulate the country took precedence. The opposition parties were further frustrated by the stated aim of the UN resolutions to reinstate Kuwait's 'legitimate' Government prior to the invasion by Iraq, namely the as-Sabah family. In late February, the Amir decreed that martial law would be enforced in Kuwait for the subsequent three months. The decree was contested by some members of Kuwait's opposition-in-exile, who expressed the need for the legislature to reconvene before any such decision could be made. In early March the opposition groups in exile made public their intention to form a coalition against the Government of the as-Sabah family. In the same month, the Amir announced the formation of a committee to administer martial law and to supervise the state's security internally and abroad. The committee's domestic objectives were to identify people who had collaborated with Iraq, to prevent the formation of 'vigilante' groups, and to identify civilians brought by the Iraqi authorities to settle in the emirate. On 4 March the Prime Minister and other members of the exiled Government returned to Kuwait, followed by the Amir 10 days later. The country was in a condition of instability, largely because of the collapse of services owing to the emigration or exile of most of the non-national work-force. Bitter resentment was felt by Kuwaiti citizens against members of the Palestinian community who were suspected of having collaborated with Iraq; human rights groups documented the use of torture against suspected collaborators by the Kuwaiti security forces. Later in March the Government announced that elections would take place within six to 12 months, following the return of Kuwaiti exiles and the compilation of a new electoral roll. The Government also declared its intention to reduce the number of foreign workers in Kuwait. On 20 March the Council of Ministers resigned, apparently in response to public discontent at the Government's failure to restore supplies of electricity, water and food. On 20 April the formation of a new Council of Ministers by the Crown Prince was announced. Although several technocrats were appointed to important positions within the Council (mainly the economic portfolios), the major portfolios—foreign affairs, defence and the interior—were all retained by members of the as-Sabah family. Members of opposition groups immediately denounced the new Council of Ministers as 'unrepresentative'.

In May 1991 it was reported that 900 people were under investigation in connection with crimes committed during the Iraqi occupation. In late May a prominent British-based human rights organization, Amnesty International, alleged that trials were being conducted in Kuwait without the provision of adequate defence counsel, and that, in some cases, torture had been used in order to extract confessions from defendants. In the same month, the Prime Minister admitted that the abduction and torture of non-Kuwaiti nationals resident in Kuwait was taking place. He promised that the matter would be investigated.

In June 1991 the Amir formally decreed that elections to a new National Assembly would be held in October 1992, and he ordered the National Council (which had been established in June 1990) to reconvene on 9 July 1991 in order to prepare for the elections. However, the announcement failed to satisfy opposition groups, whose members continued to demand the immediate introduction of democracy into Kuwait, and an end to the dominance of the as-Sabah family.

It was reported in June 1991 that 29 of a total of 200 defendants in trials for alleged collaboration during the occupation of Kuwait had been sentenced to death. The sentences were condemned by international human rights organizations as having resulted from the abuse of the judicial system. On 26 June, however, the Government repealed martial law and quashed all of the death sentences that had been imposed in recent trials. Subsequent trials of those accused of collaboration were to be referred to civilian courts.

In July 1991 it was estimated that the Kuwaiti population had declined to about 600,000 since August 1990. The Palestinian population, which had totalled an estimated 400,000 prior to the Iraqi invasion, was estimated to have declined to 80,000. In August, large-scale expulsions of Palestinians continued with airlifts to Jordan. International human rights organizations produced a report critical of the continued deportation of non-Kuwaiti nationals, citing the 1949 Fourth Geneva Convention, which prohibits such action against civilians who are justified in fearing persecution for their political or religious beliefs.

The first half of 1992 was characterized by an unprecedented breakdown of law and order in Kuwait, with regular shootings and other incidents of violence. Many of these were directed against expatriate communities, especially Palestinians. There were widespread allegations that the Government was using the shootings, and the fear of further conflict with Iraq, as a pretext to restrict the press and opposition meetings.

In late June 1991, with British and US armed forces scheduled to leave Kuwait in July and September respectively, the Minister of Defence announced that an agreement had been reached for their replacement by a united Arab force, to comprise contingents from the GCC states, Egypt and Syria (relations with Egypt had been restored in 1987). In September, however, it was announced that US armed forces would remain in the country for several more months, owing to the slow progress made in rebuilding the Kuwaiti security forces. The Arab alliance of the six GCC states, Egypt and Syria, known as the Damascus Declaration, never materialized, and the USA continued to have the predominant direct military role in the region.

On 19 September 1991 the Kuwaiti Minister of Defence signed a 10-year defence pact with the USA. The agreement included provisions for the stockpiling of US military equipment in Kuwait, the use of Kuwaiti ports by US troops, and joint training exercises. The agreement was renewed for a further 10 years in early 2001, and Kuwait continued to spend considerable sums on facilities and infrastructure for US troops and pre-positioned equipment, in addition to an annual payment of US $35m. made in lieu of the cost of stationing US military personnel. US companies were awarded lucrative contracts to 'rebuild' Kuwait. The Amir made visits to Saudi Arabia, Oman, the UAE, Qatar, Egypt and Syria in order to discuss defence and economic co-operation. In October he visited the USA, the United Kingdom and France, where he expressed his gratitude for their military support. On 11 February 1992 Kuwait signed a defence pact (similar to that with the USA) with the United Kingdom. A defence pact with France was signed in August.

RELATIONS WITH IRAQ FOLLOWING THE GULF CRISIS

On 16 April 1992 the UN Iraq-Kuwait Boundary Demarcation Commission adjudged that the border should be set 570 m to the north of the then existing position. This had the effect of awarding part of the port of Umm Qasr and several of the Rumaila oilwells to Kuwait. The decision was controversial, and the first Demarcation Commission Chairman had earlier resigned in disagreement. It was also unprecedented in that the border settlement was imposed by the Security Council rather than agreed by the relevant parties. Iraq initially rejected the validity of this decision.

In August 1992, after the Iraqi Government had refused to allow inspections of weapons facilities by the UN (as stipulated by the 1991 cease-fire agreement), the US Government deployed missiles in Kuwait, and some 7,500 US troops participated in a military exercise in the emirate. At the end of the month, the UN Security Council adopted a resolution guaranteeing the new land frontier between Kuwait and Iraq. Demarcation was to take place before the end of the year, and the new border was to come into force on 15 January 1993. In the week leading up to this deadline, however, Iraqi forces made several incursions into disputed territory, during which they recovered armaments left behind at the end of the Gulf War. At the same time, as US aircraft led air attacks on Iraq, more than 1,000 US troops were dispatched to Kuwait. Following the deadline for enforcement of the border, Iraqi operatives began to dismantle installations on what was now Kuwaiti territory. Nevertheless, the US Government deployed further missiles in Kuwait, and in early February the UN Security Council agreed to strengthen UNIKOM by approving the dispatch of armed troops (in addition to the existing unarmed personnel in the force) to patrol the Kuwaiti border with Iraq. In the same month Kuwait and Russia signed a memorandum of understanding leading to a defence pact between the two countries.

In March 1993 the UN Iraq-Kuwait Boundary Demarcation Commission announced that it had completed demarcation of the maritime border between the two countries along the median line of the Khor Abdullah waterway. The UN demarcation placed access to Iraq's only deep water port at Umm Qasr inside Kuwaiti territorial waters. In May Kuwait announced that construction was to begin of a trench, to be protected by mines and a wall of sand, along the entire length of the land border. Allegations by Kuwait of Iraqi violations of the border intensified during the second half of 1993, and there were reports of exchanges of fire in the border region. In mid-November it was reported that some 300 Iraqi civilians had crossed the border in the Umm Qasr region to protest against the digging of the trench, while Iraqi troops were reported to have attacked a border post. These incursions coincided with the beginning of the evacuation, under UN supervision, of Iraqi nationals and property from the Kuwaiti side of the new border. In November a 775-strong armed UNIKOM reinforcement was deployed in northern Kuwait, with authorization (under specific circumstances) to use its weapons to assist the unarmed force already in the demilitarized zone. During the 1990s there were few incidents involving UNIKOM itself, although there were numerous minor confrontations on the heavily-reinforced Kuwaiti border, and in Gulf waters, between Kuwaiti troops and Iraqi refugees, potential migrants, smugglers and fishermen. In the spring of 2001, as the USA and the United Kingdom maintained air activity, including the bombardment of Iraqi targets, Iraq formally demanded that UNIKOM log aerial activity above the demilitarized zone. The UN response was that UNIKOM was not technically equipped for the task, thereby avoiding the question of the USA and the United Kingdom violating Iraqi airspace in flights from Kuwait or through Kuwaiti airspace.

In September 1994 the UN Security Council agreed what had become an almost routine extension of international sanctions against Iraq for a further period. On 6 October the head of the UN Special Commission (UNSCOM, responsible for the programme of weapons inspections) announced that a system for monitoring Iraqi defence industries was ready to begin operating. On the same day, however, there were reports of a large movement of Iraqi forces towards the border with Kuwait, apparently to draw attention to Iraq's demands for swift action to ease UN sanctions (not due to be considered by the Security Council until mid-November). Over the next few days the accumulation of Iraqi military units in the border area amounted to some 70,000 troops and 700 tanks. In response to the apparent threat, Kuwait dispatched some 20,000 troops to the border region. The USA sent reinforcements (including combat aircraft and warships) to Kuwait and other parts of the Gulf region, to support the 12,000 US troops already stationed there. France and the United Kingdom deployed naval vessels, and some 1,200 British troops were dispatched to support the US military presence. On 10 October, as the first unit of additional US forces arrived in Kuwait, Iraq announced that it would withdraw its troops northward from their positions near the Kuwaiti border. On 13 October, as a result of mediation by Russia, the Iraqi Government reportedly offered to comply with the Security Council's demands to recognize the UN-demarcated border with Kuwait and to acknowledge Kuwait's sovereignty. In return, the Russian Government agreed to urge the relaxation of the UN sanctions against Iraq. On 15 October the Security Council demanded that Iraq grant unconditional recognition to Kuwait and that all the Iraqi forces recently transferred to southern Iraq be redeployed to their original positions. Later in the month the USA (in a statement also signed by the United Kingdom and several GCC states) indicated that 'appropriate action' would be taken if Iraq deployed its forces south of latitude 32°N (the boundary of the southern air exclusion zone, unilaterally declared by the USA, the United Kingdom and, for a time, France in August 1992), and in late October 1994, during a visit to Kuwait, the US President, Bill Clinton, reiterated his country's commitment to the defence of Kuwait. On 10 November Iraq officially recognized Kuwait's sovereignty, territorial integrity and political independence, as well as its UN-defined borders. Although the declaration was welcomed by the Kuwaiti authorities, they continued to demand the release of all Kuwaiti citizens detained in Iraq and appealed for international sanctions against Iraq to be maintained until that country had complied with all pertinent UN resolutions. By the end of the year most of the US and British troops that had been rushed to the Gulf region in October had been withdrawn. Pre-positioned heavy equipment and aircraft remained in the region, together with the Western forces present prior to the October incident.

The UN Compensation Commission (UNCC), the Geneva-based body established to consider claims for compensation arising from the 1990–91 Gulf crisis, approved the first disbursements in May 1994. The rate of disbursements increased rapidly following the implementation in December 1996 of UN Security Council Resolution 986 (the 'oil-for-food' arrangement), and by mid-2001 about US $12,000m. had been paid, amounting to nearly as much as the total value of merchandise received by Iraq during the four-and-a-half years of the operation of the oil-for-food arrangement. Almost all individual claimants, both Kuwaitis and expatriates who had been living in Iraq and Kuwait at the time of the conflict, have been compensated, and major corporate payments commenced in late 2000. Earlier, in June 2000 a controversial Kuwaiti claim for $21,000m. to compensate for oil revenue lost as a result of the Iraqi occupation brought the issue of the major corporate claims to the fore. The UNCC initially postponed a decision, and Russia and France meanwhile urged a full review of the underlying principles and operations of the Commission. Russia also called for an immediate reduction of the proportion of Iraqi oil revenues deducted for the purposes of compensation from 30% to 20%. The claims, totalling more than $320,000m., plus interest, are likely to be a continuing source of tension and controversy in the region. In September 2000 the governing council of the UNCC (which is made up of the 15 member states of the Security Council) approved a reduced Kuwaiti oil claim of $15,900m., at the same time as the UN Security Council reduced the proportion of Iraqi oil revenues set aside for compensation purposes from 30% to 25%. An oil analyst writing in the specialist journal *Middle East Economic Survey* criticized the award as being exaggerated by $12,500m. In the summer of 2001 the UNCC began considering a Kuwait Investment Authority claim of $86,000m., mostly for assumed lost interest earnings. The scale of the claims, and the politicized nature of the process, threatened to impede a regional political settlement. In July 2002 the UNCC awarded some $490m. to corporate and individual

claimants in Kuwait, while a further $60m. was to be paid to the Kuwaiti Government.

The Kuwait National Committee for Missing People and Prisoners of War claimed in 1994 that 625 Kuwaiti residents, including more than 300 Kuwaiti nationals, were still in detention, or missing, in Iraq, and the fate of missing persons remains a major obstacle to any future normalization of relations between the two countries. From mid-1996 Iraqi and Kuwaiti officials held meetings in their mutual border area to discuss the fate of those not accounted for. The meetings were conducted in closed sessions under the auspices of the International Committee of the Red Cross (ICRC), and were attended by observers from the USA, the United Kingdom and France. Although Iraq has stated that it is not holding any Kuwaiti nationals, in late 1997 Kuwait claimed to be in possession of documentation, submitted to the ICRC by Iraq, relating to 126 Kuwaiti prisoners of war whose whereabouts remain unknown. The Iraqi authorities claim to have lost contact with the captives during the allied bombardment and the subsequent opposition uprising in Iraq in 1991. In July 1998 delegations from both countries met in Geneva for 'highly confidential' discussions on this issue. Iraq withdrew from a subsequent meeting scheduled for January 1999, following Kuwait's support for renewed US-British bombings of targets in Iraq in December 1998. The Iraqi Government has also demanded that the whereabouts of more than 1,000 Iraqi citizens, allegedly missing in Kuwait since 1991, should be included in any negotiations on this issue, and that representatives of states that have no missing persons should not take part in the negotiations.

During early 1997 several allegations of attacks on shipping were made by both countries, and in July Kuwaiti pressure resulted in Iraq's exclusion from the Pan-Arab Games, a measure of Iraqi isolation. Kuwait continued to urge the GCC states to maintain an uncompromising stance towards Iraq, and to continue fully to enforce UN sanctions imposed against Iraq. At a meeting of GCC foreign ministers in Riyadh, Saudi Arabia, in June 1998, extreme concern was expressed at a statement made by the Vice-Chairman of Iraq's Revolutionary Command Council dismissing the terms of the UN resolution which had demarcated the boundary between Iraq and Kuwait following the 1990–91 Gulf crisis. Similar concern was expressed by GCC foreign ministers in September 2000, in response to repeated Iraqi statements denouncing Kuwait and Saudi Arabia for permitting US and British aircraft to use their airspace and facilities to maintain attacks on Iraq. During the same period, Kuwaiti military units were active in intercepting small commercial vessels destined for and sailing from Iraqi ports.

However, during 1998 the Kuwaiti Government declared its support for a diplomatic solution to the rapid escalation of hostilities between the UNSCOM inspectors and the Iraqi authorities. Kuwait indicated that it would not be used as a base for a US-led attack on Iraq to enforce the UNSCOM mandate, but US and British air-strikes against strategic Iraqi installations were launched for this purpose from the Gulf in late 1998 with full logistical support from Kuwait. The USA has since maintained a strong military presence in Kuwait and other Gulf states, and projects have been undertaken to expand existing air bases and accommodate additional US military aircraft in Kuwait. Following the 11 September 2001 terrorist attacks on the US mainland, US military units in Kuwait were reinforced and the Kuwaiti Government intensified defence procurement negotiations with Western nations. The increase in world prices for petroleum after 1999 allowed for an increase in military expenditure, but the National Assembly continued to scrutinize military purchases carefully. During 2002 the Government was pursuing an expanded military programme of contracts and purchases thought to be worth some US $3,000m. and likely to include the purchase of air-defence systems, F-18 fighter aircraft and combat helicopters.

During the first half of 1998 there was a discernible shift in Kuwaiti foreign policy, with the First Deputy Prime Minister and Minister of Foreign Affairs declaring that Kuwait no longer opposed Iraqi participation in Arab summit meetings; in May the Kuwaiti Red Crescent offered to send humanitarian supplies to Iraq. Subsequently, the National Assembly hosted a seminar that discussed the future of Iraqi–Kuwaiti relations, with the participation of Iraqis who were not supporters of the present

Iraqi Government. While Kuwait's policy towards relations with the Iraqi Government had not changed, there was an implicit recognition that Kuwait could not rely alone and indefinitely upon the defence umbrella provided by the USA. The change in Kuwait's policy tone continued, with Minister of Foreign Affairs Sabah al-Ahmad al-Jaber as-Sabah declaring, at the Arab League summit conference in Amman, Jordan, in March 2001, that sanctions against Iraq should be revoked. This position was in line with sentiments in Arab countries at both the official and popular levels, but it did not satisfy the Iraqi Government, which wanted Arab countries to declare that they would break UN sanctions and prevent the USA from attacking Iraq from neighbouring territories. Iraq, which had since 1998 been emerging from its diplomatic isolation, failed to gain practical Arab League support for its position, while Kuwait averted being itself isolated. The new Kuwaiti position was usually prefaced with the stipulation that Iraq should comply with all pertinent UN resolutions, but the general perception that Iraq should be rehabilitated was gathering support in the Arab world, conditioned by heightened concerns about the humanitarian cost to Iraqi civilians of maintaining the sanctions regime, by mounting opposition to continuing US and British air-strikes inside Iraq (see below), and by renewed Arab unity in support of a renewed Palestinian *intifada* against Israeli occupation after September 2000.

British and US aircraft based in Kuwait, continued to mount bombing and reconnaissance missions over Iraq. On 16 February 2001 a US and British bombing raid on Baghdad prompted Iraq to threaten retaliation against Kuwait for permitting aircraft to use its facilities. Air-strikes by British and US military aircraft were launched against Iraqi air-defence installations in the northern and southern air exclusion zones during August–October 2001, and in early September 2002, after incidents in which aircraft from both countries had been tracked and targeted from ground positions in both regions. General opposition to the hosting of US and other Western forces in the region increased from the late 1990s; one way in which this opposition manifested itself was the perpetration of terrorist attacks of increasing violence against US targets both within the region and elsewhere in the world. In Kuwait itself, in November 2000 six Kuwaitis were arrested on suspicion of planning bombing attacks on US forces stationed in the country. In the aftermath of the September 2001 terrorist attacks on the US mainland some commentators attached considerable significance to the prominent positions occupied by Kuwaiti nationals in Osama bin Laden's al-Qa'ida terrorist network.

ELECTIONS AND POLITICAL LIFE AFTER 1991

In January 1992 the Government finally revoked its pre-publication censorship of written (but not broadcast) media. However, it retained the right to close publications responsible for 'objectionable' articles. The following month was the deadline for registration for the October elections to the National Assembly. Only 'first-class' Kuwaiti male citizens, who numbered about 81,400 (just under 15% of the adult population), were eligible to vote. The Minister of Justice and Legal Affairs excluded the possibility of foreign observers monitoring the elections. A total of 280 candidates, many of them affiliated to one of several quasi-political organizations, contested elections to the new National Assembly on 5 October 1992. Groups of women staged protests against their exclusion from the political process. Anti-Government candidates, in particular representatives of Islamic groups, secured 31 of the Assembly's 50 seats, and several of those elected had been members of the legislature dissolved in 1986. The Prime Minister submitted the resignation of his Government, and in the following week named a new administration. The revised Council of Ministers included six members of the new National Assembly. Among these was Ali Ahmad al-Baghli, the new Minister of Oil and a critic of the economic policy of the previous Government; members of the Assembly were also given responsibility for education, Islamic affairs and justice. The ruling family, however, retained control of the important defence, foreign affairs and interior portfolios.

In January 1993, in an attempt to curb financial corruption, the Assembly adopted a law that all state companies and investment organizations must produce accounts for the auditor-general, who must pass them on to a commission of members

of the Assembly. The law also provided for harsher penalties for those who misused public funds. In February a delegation of members of the Assembly travelled to London to investigate allegations that millions of dollars had been embezzled via the Kuwait Investment Office (KIO) in London. In March the Assembly voted to rescind a law of secrecy, which had been regarded as a legal mechanism to facilitate corruption. In the same month there were reports of criticism from members of the Assembly after the Government estimated defence spending for 1992/93 at US $6,200m. Moreover, in July a report of the National Assembly's finance and economy commission was highly critical of the Government's management of overseas investments and its failure to ensure the accountability of officials. In mid-August the Prime Minister submitted a proposal to the National Assembly, according to which future budgets would contain, for the first time, details of purchases of defence equipment. In January 1994 the National Assembly abrogated an earlier decree demanding that, in the case of legal proceedings, government ministers be tried by a special court. In the same month Sheikh Ali al-Khalifah as-Sabah, a former Minister of Finance and of Oil, and Abd al-Fattah al-Bader, a former chairman of the company, were among five people brought to trial in connection with alleged embezzlement from the Kuwait Oil Tanker Co; hearings were subsequently adjourned, and legal proceedings continued into 1996. Meanwhile, in November 1995 a criminal court had ruled that the trial of the former minister would be held in a special court for cases involving ministers, in spite of the National Assembly's earlier ruling. In July 1996 three of the four former executives to be tried by the criminal court were found guilty of corruption, and received prison sentences of between 15 and 40 years. In addition, they were ordered to repay the embezzled funds, together with fines totalling more than $100m. The fourth defendant, a British national, was acquitted. The charges against the former oil and finance minister were later withdrawn—it was ruled that the correct procedures had not been followed to bring the case to trial. In early August 1999 a senior official of the KIO, Sheikh Fahd Muhammad as-Sabah, was convicted *in absentia* by the High Court in London of a $460m. fraud against the KIO's Spanish subsidiary. Two other senior officials were also convicted. It was announced in 2000 that the KIO's head office would be transferred to Kuwait.

From 1993 Government attempts to pursue an agenda of economic reform encountered opposition in the National Assembly and within the ruling family, and were largely abandoned during periods in which strong prices for petroleum prevailed on world markets. During April 1994 the Government resigned, and a new administration was named. It was subsequently announced that the new Government would persevere with economic reforms, including privatization.

Relations between the Government and the National Assembly became increasingly strained during late 1994 and early 1995, not least because of the discord apparent between the Prime Minister, Crown Prince Sheikh Saad al-Abdullah as-Salim as-Sabah, and the then Speaker of the National Assembly, Ahmad Abd al-Aziz as-Saadun, who appealed for a government composed only of elected members. A potential constitutional crisis developed in early 1995 with regard to the interpretation of Article 71 of the Constitution. Article 71 regulates the Amir's power to rule by decree during parliamentary recesses or when the Assembly is dissolved for new elections: the National Assembly is obliged to endorse all such legislation when it reconvenes. The Assembly argued that the Article did not apply to the 1976–81 or 1986–92 periods, when the Assembly was closed unconstitutionally by the Amir. Following these periods, a political agreement was reached with the Amir, whereby the Assembly would review the Amiri decrees, rejecting, approving or amending the legislation accordingly. In February 1995, however, the Constitutional Court had overruled the National Assembly's rejection of a 1986 decree that allowed the Government to close down newspapers; in the following month the Government exercised its right to do so, temporarily suspending publication of a newspaper, *Al-Anbaa*. In April the Government referred Article 71 to the Constitutional Court for interpretation in the light of the ruling on press censorship. If the Court were to rule in the Government's favour, the authority of the Assembly would effectively be threatened, as the Amir could force through controversial legislation by dissolving and subsequently reconvening the Assembly. The Assembly protested by suspending consideration of more than 200 Amiri decrees until late May, when the Government withdrew its request for the interpretation of the Article.

In April 1995 the report of a parliamentary inquiry into state purchases of weapons alleged widespread waste and corruption in defence expenditure, and urged the Government to instigate judicial proceedings against those said to be involved. In the following month the report of the parliamentary commission of inquiry into the circumstances surrounding the 1990 invasion (established in December 1992) revealed profound negligence on the part of government and military officials, who had apparently ignored warnings of an imminent invasion. The report was critical of the flight of members of the royal family and the Council of Ministers immediately after the invasion, effectively depriving the country of political leadership and military organization.

In June 1995 the National Assembly approved legislation designed to increase the electorate by amending the 1959 nationality law to allow sons of naturalized Kuwaitis to vote. In July the Assembly approved a bill reducing the minimum period after which naturalized Kuwaitis become eligible to vote from 30 years to 20 years. In July 1996 the Ministry of the Interior announced that a recorded total electorate of 107,169 was enfranchised to vote in elections to the National Assembly, on 7 October 1996. Pro-Government candidates were the most successful at the elections, securing an estimated 19 of the 50 legislative seats. A number of small demonstrations, organized and attended by women in support of demands for female enfranchisement, were reported in the days preceding the poll. Following the elections, Sheikh Saad al-Abdullah as-Salim as-Sabah was reappointed Prime Minister. On 15 October, he announced the composition of the Council of Ministers, which included four new members. The new legislature convened on 20 October.

In June 1997 an assassination attempt was made on Abdullah an-Nibari, an opposition member of the National Assembly and a former Chairman of the Committee for the Protection of Public Funds. One of the five men charged in connection with the offence was discovered to be related to the Minister of Finance, Nasir ar-Rodhan. Answering suggestions that he should resign, ar-Rodhan insisted that he had possessed no knowledge of the attack and was therefore under no obligation to stand down. In November an incendiary bomb attack destroyed an-Nibari's office. There was widespread belief that a conspiracy linked to state corruption lay behind the attacks on an-Nibari, and these suspicions exacerbated tensions between the Government and the National Assembly. Later that month, ar-Rodhan was reported to have tendered his resignation, although the Prime Minister apparently asked him to remain in office.

Further tension between the Government and the National Assembly became apparent in early 1998, when a motion expressing 'no confidence' in the Minister of Information, Sa'ud Nasir as-Sabah, was brought before the legislature, following his decision to allow allegedly anti-Islamic publications to be displayed at the 1997 Kuwait Book Fair. On 15 March, however, two days before the vote was scheduled to take place in the National Assembly, the Council of Ministers resigned. The Crown Prince again formed a new Government. Sa'ud Nasir as-Sabah was transferred to the Ministry of Oil, while Nasir ar-Rodhan retained the post of Deputy Prime Minister and became Minister of State for Cabinet Affairs. The reshuffle apparently frustrated the opposition's desire to question certain ministers over their earlier decisions. Four new appointments were made, including Sheikh Ali Salim as-Sabah as Minister of Finance and Communications, bringing to six the number of members of the ruling family in the Council of Ministers. The sensitive portfolios of defence, foreign affairs and the interior were unchanged.

The National Assembly continued to monitor closely defence contracts, and other matters concerning public funds, including the alleged loss of KD 300m. as a result of speculation in stock options by the Public Institution for Social Security. In May 1998 the National Assembly approved a bill requiring public officials to declare their finances in order to aid transparency and to facilitate moves to counter corruption. In June 1998

there was evidence that the authorities were seeking to restrict further the freedom of the press. The Government brought legal proceedings for religious defamation against the independent *Al-Qabas* newspaper; the paper was closed for one week, and its Editor-in-Chief received a six-month prison sentence. In mid-June meetings involving the Speaker of the National Assembly, the Amir and the Government appeared to have averted an imminent confrontation over the cross-examination of the Interior Minister on matters relating to crime and the narcotics trade, although underlying problems remained unresolved.

The National Assembly had thus begun to assert its authority over a range of issues, and had claimed an increasing share of decision-making powers in areas previously considered the preserve of the ruling family (through the latter's dominance of the Government and through the ultimate constitutional authority of the Amir).

THE 1999 ELECTIONS AND POLITICAL DISCORD

The collapse in world petroleum prices during 1998 did not result in a radical alteration of economic policy, but it did reinvigorate the reform agenda. However, a lack of cohesion and of resolve within the ranks of the Government and the opposition once again reduced the likelihood of the introduction of any unpopular measures. In July the Government introduced amendments to legislation enacted in 1993 (and previously amended in 1995) regarding repayment of debts arising from the collapse of the Souk al-Manakh unofficial stock exchange in 1982. Many members of the National Assembly regarded new arrangements for the discharge of liabilities to be unduly favourable to debtors, many of whom were members of the ruling family, and boycotted an initial vote before reluctantly approving the amendments in early August 1998. Tensions between the Government and the National Assembly appeared to be the cause of the Amir's postponement of a scheduled visit to the USA. In early November the Council of Ministers accepted ar-Rodhan's resignation. Abd al-Aziz ad-Dakhil, hitherto Minister of Commerce and Industry, replaced ar-Rodhan in late December; Hisham al-Otaibi, formerly President of the Kuwait Stock Exchange, was appointed Minister of Commerce and Industry. In that month the Government formulated an economic reform plan in order to address the widening budget deficit. However, many of the economic reform proposals were eventually rejected by the National Assembly in February 1999. In March Kuwait, together with other OPEC members, agreed a further substantial reduction in petroleum production levels, and world petroleum prices made a rapid recovery which eased budgetary pressure in the short term; none the less, economic reform remained a long-term objective of the Government. Kuwait meanwhile came under increased pressure to allow international participation in the petroleum sector, and was willing to concede to international involvement in the provision of technical expertise, but not to foreign ownership of reserves. There is strong parliamentary opposition to foreign equity participation in the oil sector, which has been considered a matter of sovereignty since the nationalization of the petroleum industry in 1974. In early January 2001 the state-owned Kuwait Petroleum Corpn invited a number of foreign firms to submit proposals for the rehabilitation and development of five oilfields in the north of the country, close to the Iraqi border. Kuwait's eagerness to accelerate the exploitation of the northern fields has been sharply criticized by Iraq, whose Minister of Oil, Amir Muhammad Rashid, claimed in September 2000 that Kuwaiti activity was tantamount to transgression on Iraqi reserves. In Kuwait itself, controversy was provoked when the Government suddenly announced that agreement had been reached with the oil companies regarding development of the northern fields. National Assembly members demanded scrutiny of the agreement, and some alleged impropriety among the government officials responsible. The Government claimed that the agreement did not infringe the constitutional requirement of national ownership of oil resources, but it came under strong pressure to demonstrate that this was the case. The task of promoting the agreement was given to Dr Adil Khalid as-Sabih, the former Minister of Electricity and Water, who was appointed Minister of Oil in a February 2001 reshuffle of the Council of Ministers. As-Sabih attempted to address criticism of the Government by employing greater transparency in his dealings with the international oil companies and by attempting to attract smaller companies to compete in the bidding process, but suspicions within the National Assembly that the scheme was not in the country's best interests persisted. As-Sabih's difficulties were compounded by a fire in the northern Raudhatain oilfield in January 2002 which reduced Kuwait's total production capacity by some 600,000 b/d. The fire, which resulted in the deaths of a number of workers, focused renewed attention on the poor safety record of the Kuwaiti oil industry. Previous explosions in the major refineries at Mina al-Ahmadi and at Shuaiba had also caused a number of deaths and resulted in considerable damage. As-Sabih took responsibility for the Government's failure adequately to address safety concerns and resigned in February 2002, effectively suspending the Government's latest effort to involve foreign companies in the further development of the northern oilfields. The minister's resignation was accepted a few days later and the Minister of Information, Sheikh Ahmad al-Fahd al-Ahmad as-Sabah, was named as acting Minister of Oil. However, a political crisis ensued after it proved impossible to find a permanent replacement for Dr as-Sabih, and Sheikh Ahmad was asked to remain in charge of the oil portfolio until the general election (scheduled for mid-2003). Meanwhile, several members of the Majlis demanded the resignation of the entire Government, alleging that the explosion at Raudhatain was the result of state corruption and mismanagement. Industrial safety concerns resurfaced in 2002 following major outbreaks of fire at the Shuaiba refinery in February and at Kuwait International Airport in August. In early July the Minister of Finance, of Planning and Minister of State for Administrative Development, Dr Yousuf Hamad al-Ibrahim, narrowly survived a vote of 'no confidence' in the National Assembly, following a number of allegations of impropriety, including the mismanagement of public funds. The Government had threatened to resign if the vote had been successful.

In April 1999 further confrontation between the National Assembly and the Government, arising from widespread consternation among Islamist National Assembly members over errors that had appeared in copies of the Koran printed and distributed by the Ministry of Justice, Awqaf (Religious Endowments) and Islamic Affairs, prompted the Amir to dissolve the National Assembly. Legislative elections were conducted on 3 July, at which Government supporters retained only 12 of the 50 seats in the National Assembly (compared with 18 in 1996), behind Islamist candidates with 20 seats and liberals with 14 seats. Independent candidates secured the remaining four seats. The composition of a new Council of Ministers, selected and headed by the Crown Prince, was announced on 13 July. Members of the ruling family retained control of the most important portfolios (including Sheikh Sabah al-Ahmad al-Jaber as-Sabah who remained Deputy Prime Minister and Minister of Foreign Affairs), although a number of new, liberal members were also appointed (most notably to the finance portfolio), seemingly improving the chances of securing approval for the economic reform programme. Several portfolios were merged, and a new post of Minister of State for Foreign Affairs was created. Jasem al-Kharafi was elected as the new Speaker of the National Assembly on 17 July, replacing the more populist and confrontational Ahmad as-Saadun.

During the two-month legislative interval, the Government introduced substantial legislation by means of Amiri decrees that had subsequently to be approved by the new Assembly. Among the most significant decrees was one proposing the extension of the franchise and eligibility to seek public office to women. Some 60 decrees in total were issued, including legislation to accelerate privatization and to open up the economy to foreign investment. Other laws requiring National Assembly approval included those providing for reductions in subsidies and social spending, and measures to rationalize the labour market. The Government considered the new legislation to be crucial to the successful diversification of the economy, enhancement of the private sector and reform of the labour market. Liberal members of the Assembly objected to the decrees on constitutional grounds, while the measure on women's political participation was defeated by an alliance of conservatives and liberals in November 1999. The liberals subsequently introduced an identical bill of their own, but this in turn was defeated. Women activists continued to press for an end to the exclusion of women from the political process, and have raised the matter, without success, in the Constitutional Court. A gradual liberalization of attitudes towards traditional gender roles in Qatar and Bahrain, and the participation of women in the political processes of these two states (as well as in Oman) has highlighted the failure of Kuwait to modernize its institutions of state. Kuwaiti women have continued to organize themselves and to demand political rights, but the checks and balances inherent in the Kuwaiti system have, thus far, presented a considerable obstacle to the enfranchisement of women.

In late October 1999 riots broke out in a poor suburb of Kuwait after clashes between Egyptian and Bangladeshi workers. Security forces eventually dispersed the rioters; a number of arrests were made, and some Egyptian expatriates were deported from Kuwait. However, the Government played down the incident in an attempt to avoid damaging political consequences. Unrest was also reported in the mainly *bidoon* area of al-Jahra in July 2000. The *bidoon* are a community of more than 100,000 in Kuwait (with tens of thousands more who now live in Iraq); they are not known to have any nationality, and claim to be Kuwaiti. Although they are long-time residents of Kuwait and are well-integrated in Kuwaiti society, their claims are not recognized by the Kuwaiti authorities. The unrest was related to a law, approved in May, that would afford only a minority of *bidoon* the chance to acquire citizenship and its accompanying privileges. In the spring of 2001 about 1,000 *bidoon* were granted Kuwaiti citizenship, while protests continued from those whose claims were not recognized, with the protesters attempting to bring their case to international attention, thereby embarrassing the Kuwaiti Government.

In mid-January 2000, Alaa Hussein Ali, the leader of the provisional government installed by Iraq in August 1990, who had been in self-imposed exile (most recently in Norway) since 1991, returned to Kuwait in order to appeal against a death sentence pronounced in June 1993 for collaboration with Iraq in 1990–91. Giving evidence to the court in early March, the Minister of Information denied that he had, during a meeting with Hussein Ali, indicated the likelihood of a pardon or reduced sentence. In May it was announced that Hussein Ali's appeal had been unsuccessful, but, after a further challenge, in March 2001 the Court of Appeal commuted his sentence to one of life imprisonment. The continuing political importance of the Iraqi occupation experience and ongoing concern for the absent 'prisoners of war' should not be underestimated. Yet the results of an opinion poll conducted in 2001 revealed that Kuwaitis, like the citizens of other Gulf states, considered resolution of the Palestinian issue to be of paramount importance.

In March 2001 a prominent female journalist and Editor-in-Chief of *Al-Majaless* magazine, Hedaya Sultan as-Salem, was shot dead. *Al-Majaless* is one of Kuwait's oldest political publications and as-Salem was close to members of the ruling family. A police-officer was arrested, tried and then sentenced to death (subject to appeal) for her murder in February 2002.

In late January 2001 the Government submitted its resignation amid growing disagreements among its members, apparently stemming from rivalry between two branches of the ruling family—represented respectively by the Crown Prince and Prime Minister, Sheikh Saad al-Abdullah as-Salim as-Sabah, and the increasingly dominant First Deputy Prime Minister and Minister of Foreign Affairs, Sheikh Sabah al-Ahmad al-Jaber as-Sabah. After two weeks of discussions a new Council of Ministers was appointed in which both men retained their positions, but which appeared to reflect the growing ascendancy of Sheikh Sabah. Great uncertainty over the future political leadership of Kuwait resulted from the hospitalization of the Amir, in September, following a cerebral haemorrhage which incapacitated him until January 2002. The Amir's illness focused attention on a situation where the three most senior members of the ruling family are ageing and in various degrees of failing health. With the imminent passing of a generation that has dominated Kuwaiti politics through a turbulent period, there has been frank discussion of future possibilities for redefining the role of the ruling family and for restructuring its responsibilities, in particular, through the separation of the roles of the Crown Prince and the Prime Minister.

EXTERNAL RELATIONS 1993–2002

In mid-1993 it was announced that Kuwait was willing to restore relations with Arab states that had supported Iraq during the Gulf crisis, with the exception of Jordan and the leadership of the Palestine Liberation Organization (PLO). Despite the lack of progress towards a wider Gulf-Arab defence force, ministers responsible for defence in the GCC countries, meeting in Abu Dhabi (UAE) in November, agreed on the need to strengthen and extend the capabilities of the Peninsula Shield Force (the GCC's Saudi-based rapid deployment force). In the same month Kuwait signed a defence co-operation agreement with Russia, and in December the two countries participated in joint naval exercises in the Gulf. Relations between Kuwait and Jordan began to improve in early 1996, although in December 1995 Sheikh Sabah al-Ahmad al-Jaber as-Sabah, who favoured *rapprochement* with Jordan, had resigned as First Deputy Prime Minister and Minister of Foreign Affairs, in protest at the reluctance of the Crown Prince and the Prime Minister to seek a restoration of good relations (Sheikh Sabah subsequently withdrew his resignation). In 1997 and 1998, Kuwait pardoned and released Jordanians imprisoned in 1991 for collaboration with the Iraqi forces. Ministerial visits between Kuwait and Jordan were resumed in June 1998. In March 1999 the Jordanian embassy in Kuwait, which had been closed in 1990, was reopened. Later, Jordan's King Abdullah visited Kuwait; he returned for a second visit following the March 2001 Amman Arab League summit, which accorded him the task of trying to find common ground between Iraq and Kuwait.

Attempts to repair relations between the Palestinian leadership and the Kuwaiti Government were under way before the Palestinian uprising against Israeli occupation began in late September 2000, and a meeting between the President of the Palestinian (National) Authority, Yasser Arafat, and the Kuwaiti Minister of Foreign Affairs, Sheikh Sabah, had already taken place.

Following the Amir's attendance at the Organization of the Islamic Conference (OIC) summit meeting in Tehran in November 1997, several Iranian ministers visited Kuwait, and proposals for joint naval exercises with Iran were made, indicating a significant improvement in relations with that country. In July 2000, Kuwait and Saudi Arabia agreed the demarcation of their maritime borders, and Kuwait entered negotiations with Iran on delimiting their respective rights to the continental shelf. The talks had been convened following Kuwaiti and Saudi protests at Iran's decision to commence drilling for gas in a disputed offshore area; Iraq protested at its exclusion from the Kuwaiti-Iranian talks, on the grounds that it was a concerned party. Iran suspended drilling pending conclusion of the talks. Although no agreement had been reached by mid-2002, reports

that Iran was planning to export natural gas and water to Kuwait suggested that some progress had been made.

However, the developing relations with Iran, the Palestinians, and even Iraq, were profoundly affected by the political reverberations of the 11 September 2001 suicide attacks on New York and Washington, DC. The Kuwaiti Government expressed its readiness to take immediate action against individuals and groups suspected of involvement with those held responsible for the attacks. (The Kuwaiti-born spokesman for al-Qa'ida, Sulayman Abu Ghaith, was divested of his Kuwaiti citizenship forthwith.) In October the Government established a Supreme Council for Charity Work in order to expose charities being used to support al-Qa'ida or foster other proscribed activities; a number of branches of a Kuwaiti charitable organization were suspected by the US authorities of involvement in activities in support of militant Islamists. Six Kuwaitis were among those foreign nationals detained by US troops fighting Taliban and al-Qa'ida forces in Afghanistan in late 2001, and subsequently held without trial at the US military base at Guantánamo Bay, Cuba. Kuwait had expressed solidarity with the US Government and continued to facilitate the US military build-up in the region (US bases in Kuwait were used to provide logistical support to the campaign in Afghanistan during late 2001), but subsequent open discussion about the use of these bases for a possible new attack against Iraq, and a stream of prominent US government officials to Kuwait hoping to enlist full Kuwaiti participation in President Bush's declared 'war against terror', threatened to fuel opposition to a continued US presence in the region and exacerbate an increasingly tense political situation in Kuwait. One of Kuwait's most distinguished politicians, former GCC Secretary-General Abdullah Bishara, later conceded that, in his personal opinion, the Kuwaiti Government would be unable to prevent the US authorities from launching a military offensive against Iraq from bases in Kuwait, if they chose to do so.

At the Arab League summit held in Beirut, Lebanon, in late March 2002, Arab leaders reiterated their opposition to any US-led military intervention in Iraq. The head of the Iraqi delegation, Izzat Ibrahim ad-Dur, Vice-President of the Revolutionary Command Council, thanked delegates for opposing US threats against Iraq and announced that Iraq would henceforth agree to respect the sovereignty of Kuwait, and guarantee its independence, stability and security within its internationally recognized borders. The other Arab states expressed the hope that Iraq and Kuwait would now begin to co-operate to resolve the outstanding issues between them. The summit's final declaration included assurances that there would be no repeat of Iraq's 1990 annexation of Kuwait, and urged Iraq and Kuwait to end their use of propaganda against each other. In May Baghdad informed the UN that it intended to return to Kuwait the national archives and official documents removed during the 1990–91 Iraqi occupation.

Economy

ALAN J. DAY

(based on an original essay by P. T. H. UNWIN)
Revised for this edition by the Editorial staff

Kuwait is a relatively small, arid country with a severe climate. Fresh water is scarce, and agriculture limited. However, the discovery of extremely rich deposits of petroleum transformed the economy and gave the country a high level of material prosperity. Kuwait's population increased from approximately 200,000 in 1957 to 1,697,301 in 1985, of whom only 40% were Kuwaiti nationals; the remainder were non-Kuwaitis, mainly immigrant workers and their families. At mid-1990 the population was estimated to be 2,062,275, of whom 1,473,054 were non-Kuwaiti nationals (based on the definition of citizenship in

use in 1992). Twelve months later the estimated population had fallen to 1.2m., but census results for April 1995 recorded a total population of 1,575,570, of whom 653,616 were Kuwaiti nationals. By mid-2001 the population had increased to 2,274,980, according to official estimates. The population increase also intensified demands on the infrastructure of the country; for example, total potable water consumption in Kuwait increased from 255m. gallons in 1954 to 40,306m. gallons in 1987, and by 1999 had reached 84,070m. gallons. In August 1987 the Government initiated a five-year plan to reduce the number of expatriates in the Kuwaiti work-force. Taking advantage of the displacement caused by the Iraqi invasion, the Government subsequently announced its intention to restrict the level of non-Kuwaiti residents to less than 50% of the pre-crisis total. In pursuit of this policy, the Government attracted censure for its use of deportation and for its treatment of expatriate groups, especially Palestinians, within the country. In March 1994 it was officially reported that a total of 34,000 persons had been deported from Kuwait since June 1991.

Kuwait's level of gross national product (GNP) per head was the third highest in the world in 1980 and 1981, exceeded only by that of Qatar and the United Arab Emirates (UAE). According to estimates by the World Bank, Kuwait's GNP was US $33,150m. (equivalent to $24,160 per head) in 1980 and $30,600m. ($20,900 per head) in 1981 (at 1979–81 prices). Kuwait's GNP (at current prices), which had been KD 8,206.7m. in 1994, increased to KD 9,337.3m. in 1995 and KD 10,749.1m. in 1996. By 1997 Kuwait's GNP, according to the World Bank, was $35,152m., or $22,110 per head. Official estimates indicated that GNP increased by 10.5%—to KD 10,439m.—in 1999, by 25.0%—to KD 13,046m.—in 2000 (a year of very high petroleum revenues), and declined by 11.3%—to KD 11,577m. in 2001. Estimates of per-capita GNP were KD 4,591 in 1999, KD 5,855 in 2000 and KD 5,161 in 2001. Kuwait's gross domestic product (GDP) fluctuated over the period 1980–89, falling by an average of 0.7% per year. More severe contractions in 1990 and 1991 were brought about by the disruption of the Iraqi invasion. However, GDP has since recovered, rising to KD 9,060m. by 1997. The sharp decline in international petroleum prices in 1998 resulted in a decrease in GDP, to KD 7,742m., although GDP recovered to KD 8,884m. in 1999 and KD 10,991m. in 2000 (a nominal annual increase of 23.7%). In 2001 GDP declined to KD 10,057m. In real terms, GDP increased by 1.2% in 1997 and by 3.2% in 1998, only to decrease by 1.6% in 1999, before increasing again, by 3.9% in 2000, and finally decreasing again, by 1.0%, in 2001.

The immediate costs of the military operation to liberate Kuwait (about US $22,000m.) and of rebuilding the country's infrastructure (some $20,000m.) were, in large part, met by liquidating about one-half of Kuwait's overseas investment portfolio (including about one-half of the Reserve Fund for Future Generations—RFFG) and by external borrowing totalling $5,500m. In 1994 it was reported that the Kuwaiti economy had fully recovered from the effects of the Gulf crisis and rebuilding, and that the Government did not envisage further international borrowing. Economic growth in 1994 was primarily attributable to a recovery in the non-petroleum sector. However, Kuwait's contribution to the cost of the international military response to Iraqi troop movements in October 1994 increased spending obligations for 1994/95 by an estimated $500m. Earlier in the year the Government had announced its intention to eliminate the budget deficit by 2000. Proposals to reduce the deficit included an increase in customs fees, the imposition of a direct tax on commercial and industrial profits, the reform of the welfare system, the gradual withdrawal of subsidies on public services, the ending of protectionism, and the expansion of the privatization programme, although in 1998 the National Assembly failed to endorse a law for the privatization of the communications sector. Plans to continue the privatization programme through the divestment of public utilities remained under the consideration, as did proposals for a programme of economic reform designed to lower the level of state subsidies and to increase revenues. In 2000 the Government continued with its plans to further foreign investment in the economy, including the limited participation of foreign companies in the petroleum sector and the introduction of measures to allow foreign nationals to invest on the Kuwait stock exchange.

PETROLEUM

In 1938 the Kuwait Oil Co (KOC), operated jointly by the Anglo-Persian Oil Co (subsequently the British Petroleum Co PLC—BP) and the Gulf Oil Corpn, discovered a large oilfield at Burgan, about 40 km south of the town of Kuwait. The Second World War delayed development until 1945, and in 1948 6m. metric tons of crude petroleum were produced, although the main impetus to development was the Abadan affair in 1951, which effectively denied Iranian production to the rest of the world for

three years. By 1956 Kuwait's annual production had increased to 54m. tons, and was then the largest in the Middle East. Further fields were discovered, notably at Raudhatain, north of Kuwait, and annual production had reached over 148m. tons by 1972. To handle this vast production, a huge tanker port was constructed at Mina al-Ahmadi, not far from the Burgan field. From a terminal about 15 km off shore, the port can now handle the largest tankers. Kuwait was the first Arab petroleum-producing nation to achieve complete control of its own output, buying out Gulf Oil and BP in March 1975 for approximately £32m.

Kuwait was also the first state within the Organization of the Petroleum Exporting Countries (OPEC) to restrict petroleum production for reasons of conservation. Until December 1976, when Kuwait (together with 10 other OPEC countries) decided to raise petroleum prices by 10% (compared with a 5% increase by Saudi Arabia and the UAE), the country was generally regarded as moderate with regard to oil pricing. Subsequently Kuwait became increasingly 'hawkish', and during 1979 and 1980 the country was one of the first to set still higher prices every time that Saudi Arabia raised its prices in an attempt to achieve some kind of parity within OPEC.

After 1972 (when Kuwait's petroleum production reached 1,201.6m. barrels), output of petroleum fluctuated, rising from 760.8m. barrels in 1975 to 911.2m. barrels in 1979, accounting for 4.5% of the world's oil output, and falling to 607m. barrels in 1980, 3% of world oil output. The oil glut and the implementation of OPEC quota allocations led to lower prices and fluctuating production after 1982. In common with most OPEC members, Kuwait tended to exceed its petroleum production quota.

In August 1990 Kuwait's OPEC production quota was fixed at 1.5m. b/d, but, owing to the invasion by Iraq, output averaged 1.065m. b/d for that year. In the aftermath of the Gulf crisis, Kuwait argued persistently within OPEC for a rise in the production ceiling and an increase in the country's quota, in order to offset losses and to finance reconstruction.

Following the liberation of Kuwait from the Iraqi occupation in February 1991, it was estimated that some 800 of the country's 950 oil wells had been damaged, some 600 having been set alight by Iraqi troops shortly before their retreat. The rehabilitation of the petroleum sector became the Government's highest economic priority. By June 1991 about 140 of the burning wells had been 'capped', and by late July onshore production of crude petroleum had resumed at a level of 115,000 b/d, while offshore production from fields in the Neutral/Partitioned Zone was estimated at 70,000 b/d. Exports of petroleum had also resumed by late July.

By the end of 1991 total production had reached 500,000 b/d and was increasing at a monthly rate of 100,000 b/d. By mid-1992 production had exceeded 1m. b/d, and was projected to reach 1.5m. by 1993 and 2m. thereafter. In June 1993 a meeting of OPEC oil ministers was obliged to exempt Kuwait from an agreement on production quotas, effectively allowing Kuwait to increase production to 2m. b/d in the third quarter of that year. In September, at the following OPEC meeting, this allocation was confirmed for a further period of six months. Kuwait, however, rejected suggestions that it was seriously jeopardizing its reserves by forcing such a rapid rise in output. At the same time, the major work of repairing Kuwait's infrastructure had been completed. In 1997 current capacity was 2.4m. b/d and it was planned to increase capacity to 2.5m. b/d by 2000 and to 3.5m. b/d by 2005. In November 1997 Kuwait's OPEC quota increased to 2.19m. b/d although in March 1998, as a result of declining world prices, and in conjunction with other major petroleum producers, petroleum output was reduced by 125,000 b/d. Further cuts were made in July 1998, and in March 1999 Kuwait agreed to reduce production, in conjunction with other OPEC members, by 144,000 b/d, to 1,836,000 b/d, from 1 April. Petroleum prices improved dramatically in the second half of 1999, and at OPEC meetings in March 2000 and June 2000, Kuwait's production quota was increased to 1,980,000 b/d and 2,037,000 b/d, respectively. Petroleum prices continued to remain at a high level during 2000 and 2001, but entered a period of instability during the international crisis which followed the terrorist attacks in New York and Washington, DC (USA), in September of the latter year. Average production was

2.20m. b/d in 1999 and 2.17m. b/d in 2000. From 1 April 2001 Kuwait's OPEC production quota was set at 1.94m. b/d, and a reduction, to 1.86m. b/d, was agreed in late July, effective from 1 September. However, average production in 2001 exceeded OPEC quotas, at 2.14m. b/d. In December Kuwait agreed to a further reduction in its OPEC production quota, to 1.7m. b/d, effective from 1 January 2002. Reports of an explosion at oil-gathering facilities in Kuwait in February were initially expected to reduce production capacity, in the short term, by as much as 600,000 b/d.

At the end of 2001 Kuwait's proven recoverable reserves of petroleum were 96,500m. barrels, representing about 9.2% of world reserves. Income from Kuwait's petroleum sales has been channelled mainly to five areas: industrial diversification, the development of substantial social service provision, the creation of the RFFG, overseas investment, and aid to poorer countries through the Kuwait Fund for Arab Economic Development (KFAED).

The petroleum industry was reorganized in 1980, when the Kuwait Petroleum Corpn (KPC) was established to co-ordinate the four companies involved: the KOC, the Kuwait National Petroleum Co (KNPC), the Petrochemical Industries Co (PIC), and the Kuwait Oil Tanker Co (KOTC). This led to the centralization of oil sales and improved Kuwait's market competitiveness. In the early 1990s KPC was the twelfth largest petroleum company in the world. In addition to its oil refineries in Kuwait, it owns refineries abroad (in the Netherlands, Denmark and Italy). The sale of KPC stocks of oil was vital in supporting the Kuwaiti community in exile during the Iraqi occupation. In 1990/91 KPC's budgeted profits were KD 177.5m. Profits totalled KD 410m. in 1993/94 and increased to KD 729m. in 1994/95, largely owing to increased oil prices.

The KOC is currently developing capacity in the north and west of the country with the aim of increasing crude production capacity to 3.5m. b/d by 2005. The construction of gathering centres 27 and 28 in the Minagish and Umm Gudair fields, at a cost of nearly US $400m., was expected to raise the production capacity of the fields from 110,000 b/d to 500,000 b/d. Also, in July 1997, KOC awarded contracts for two enhanced oil recovery (EOR) projects at the Raudhatain field, costing an estimated $200m. each, which will increase production at the field by 250,000 b/d.

There are three oil refineries in Kuwait: one at Mina al-Ahmadi, built in 1946; one at Mina Abdullah, built in 1958; and one at Shuaiba, completed in 1969. Expansion of Mina al-Ahmadi was completed in 1986, and a programme of modernization at Mina Abdullah, costing US $2,100m., was completed in 1989. This project increased the refinery's capacity to 200,000 b/d, and raised total capacity in Kuwait to 670,000 b/d, mainly in high-quality products for export. Plans by KPC subsidiaries to expand and upgrade production prior to the Iraqi invasion were subsequently revised, but the Government remained committed to increasing Kuwait's petroleum assets as part of its reconstruction and development strategy. The Mina al-Ahmadi refinery had resumed operations by June 1991, but the Mina Abdullah and Shuaiba refineries were reported to be more seriously damaged. However, by early 1995 the refineries at Mina al-Ahmadi, Mina Abdullah and Shuaiba were producing at a rate of 400,000 b/d, 245,000 b/d and 155,000 b/d respectively. In 1996 the KNPC invited bids for work on a series of contracts to increase the capacity of steam systems at the three refineries, and awarded a contract for the design and construction of an acid gas removal plant at Mina al-Ahmadi. It is also pursuing an ongoing programme to upgrade and expand export facilities at Shuaiba and Mina al-Ahmadi. In June 2000, however, a fire at the Mina al-Ahmadi refinery, in which five people were killed and a further 50 injured, caused extensive damage. The total cost of the repair and upgrade project at Mina al-Ahmadi was estimated at $310m. in August 2001. Other effects of the fire were likely delays to projects related to the refineries, including the construction of a gas oil desulphurization plant and an oxygen enrichment plant, and the advancement of plans to construct a fourth refinery in southern Kuwait. At the end of 2001 total refining capacity had reached 720,000 b/d.

A further development in Kuwait's petroleum industry has been the expansion of downstream interests overseas. In 1981 the Kuwait Foreign Petroleum Exploration Co (KUFPEC) was established as a subsidiary of KPC. Later that year, it purchased a 22.5% interest in a 22,000-sq km concession in Morocco. KPC purchased the Santa Fe International Corpn (SFIC), allowing the country to secure wider rights and facilities in exploration, and to develop downstream facilities. Through KUFPEC and SFIC, Kuwait now has interests in concessions in Australia, China, Egypt, the North Sea and the USA.

Since 1981, Kuwait has been expanding facilities for the distribution, marketing and retail of its refined products. During the 1980s KPC acquired a network of petrol stations in Europe, which had been owned previously by Gulf Oil, Elf and Golden Eagle Petroleum. Kuwait Petroleum International (KPI), a subsidiary of KPC, was established at the end of 1983 to manage the newly-acquired distribution outlets. In 1986 KPC adopted a new trade name, Q8, for its petroleum products distributed in Europe, and by March 1987 KPI owned a total of 4,800 petrol stations in Europe. KPC's downstream overseas expansion programme continued during the Iraqi occupation. In 1991 an agreement was signed with KPC to provide Hungary with 17 Q8 petrol stations. This agreement was in accordance with KPC's plans to expand its East European and Far Eastern operations. By mid-2000 KPI owned a total of 6,500 petrol stations throughout Europe. Kuwait continued to pursue a policy of developing foreign refinery projects in the form of joint ventures, particularly in India, Pakistan and Thailand. In mid-1995 KPC and the Indian Oil Corpn agreed a joint venture to establish a refinery in the Indian state of Orissa, at a cost of US $2,600m. In July 1997 it was reported that a feasibility study for the project had been completed. The proposed refinery is expected to process about 184,000 b/d.

As part of the Government's economic reform programme, a parliamentary finance committee submitted a report on the proposed opening up of the petroleum extraction industry to international companies, known as Project Kuwait. However, a subsequent debate on the report in the National Assembly had to be postponed owing to the lack of a quorum.

NATURAL GAS

At the end of 2001 Kuwait's reserves of gas were estimated to be 1,490,000m. cu m (1.0% of world reserves). Gas production in 2001 totalled 9,500m. cu m (excluding flared and recycled gas). In November 1976 the Amir inaugurated the KOC's Gas Project. This involves the construction of extensive facilities to make use of the gas associated with the output of crude petroleum for the production of liquefied natural gas (LNG) and such derivatives as propane and butane. A three-train plant for the production of liquefied petroleum gas (LPG), together with a gas-gathering system (which came into operation in 1979), collects the gas, which is produced together with petroleum, at well-heads, removes LPG components and natural gasoline, then treats and distributes them to fuel users and to pressure-maintenance facilities.

The plant, built at a cost of over US $1,000m., has a capacity of 2.2m. metric tons of LPG per year (60% propane, 40% butane) at a crude oil production rate of 1.5m. b/d. It was originally designed to take crude oil production of 3m. b/d. However, Kuwait's production of gas is limited by the absence of any known reserves independent of petroleum. Owing to the association of gas with petroleum, much of the gas produced is flared to facilitate oil production, or reinjected, to maximize the production of petroleum by maintaining pressure in the reservoir. From the early 1980s the LPG plant was forced to operate substantially below capacity, exporting 1.05m. metric tons of products in 1982/83 (compared with 1.7m. tons per year previously).

Other projects which suffered as a result of decreased production of gas included the expansion of an ammonia and urea plant, where the annual capacity had been increased to about 900,000 metric tons of ammonia and various by-products. The lack of feedstock, however, meant that in early 1984 the plant was operating at about 50% of capacity, and certain lines had been suspended.

OTHER INDUSTRIES

Although oil-related activities still contribute the overwhelming proportion of Kuwait's total industrial output, the Government has tried to foster other industries in order to diversify the economy and to provide alternative sources of employment. Petroleum's share of GDP fell from almost 70% in 1980 to around 50% in 1983 and around 40% in 1993, and has since remained at roughly the same level. Between 1974 and 1984 the manufacturing sector in Kuwait registered an average annual rate of growth of 6.4%, although it subsequently suffered a decline as the downturn in the economy became more pronounced in the mid-1980s. In 2001 manufacturing (including petroleum refining) contributed an estimated 6.6% of Kuwait's GDP. The major branch of manufacturing has been the production of building materials and related projects such as aluminium extrusion. Fertilizer manufacturers have a substantial production capacity, mainly in the form of urea and ammonia products. The profitability of these products has, however, proved difficult to maintain because of technical problems and a weak market. The construction of a salt plant in Shuaiba, with a capacity of 150,000 metric tons, and a chlorine plant with an annual capacity of 27,000 tons, was approved in 1985. The expansion of Kuwait's petrochemicals industry gathered momentum in the mid-1990s, beginning with a US $2,000m. petrochemicals complex at Shuaiba, which commenced operations in mid-1997. The contract for the development of the complex was given to Equate, a joint venture between PIC and Union Carbide of the USA. The plant had an annual production capacity of 650,000 tons of ethylene, 450,000 tons of polyethylene and 350,000 tons of ethylene glycol. A $1,200m. project-financing agreement between a consortium of international, regional and local banks was signed in September 1996.

Unlike its neighbours, Kuwait has hesitated to undertake heavy industrial projects, fearing both for their viability and the excess of foreign labour which they involve. It has favoured, instead, joint projects with Bahrain, Saudi Arabia and other Gulf countries. At the end of 1982 a joint venture was established between PIC and the Tunisian state-owned Maghrebia Chemical Industries to build a 1,000-metric-tons-per-day diammonium phosphate fertilizer plant in Kuwait, at a cost of KD 16m. Towards the end of 1987, KPC also agreed to take a majority shareholding in Bahrain's ailing Iron and Steel Co (see chapter on Bahrain). In early 1989 PIC announced a joint venture, with Union Carbide, for the production of polypropylene. In July 1996 the local Kuwait Industries Co applied for a licence from the commerce and industry ministry to establish a 900,000 tons-per-year alumina factory to supply producers in the UAE and Bahrain. In the following November the finance ministry approved the business plan proposed by the US company, Raytheon Corpn, to build a 230,000 tons-per-year aluminium smelter with foreign and local partners. Both projects are estimated to cost about US $1,000m.

The construction industry is considerable, owing to the vast amount of infrastructural development since the early 1970s. During the 1970s major projects were carried out by foreign contractors, but in February 1981 the National Housing Authority (NHA) announced that 80% of future housing contracts would be awarded to local firms. Between 1974 and 1989 the NHA recorded 27,000 housing units built. In other sectors of construction, however, foreign companies continued to predominate. An indication of Kuwait's heavy reliance on foreign labour is the 2.4-km bridge from Subahiya to Bubiyan island, completed in 1982 by Chinese migrant workers. The economic recession of the mid-1980s damaged the construction industry considerably, and the collapse of petroleum prices in 1986 exacerbated the situation. In 1988, however, there was a distinct recovery, particularly in the private residential sector, where expansion was stimulated by the availability of cheap bank credits, as well as the completion of highway improvements in suburban Kuwait. In 1989 work began on the Amiri Diwan, a government facility which was to cost an estimated KD 65m.–80m. and was completed in 1992. In the aftermath of the Iraqi occupation, the Kuwaiti Government worked with the international construction companies with which it was familiar, in particular US companies, in order to rebuild Kuwait's infrastructure, and in the mid-1990s work that had been traditionally undertaken by the public sector was increasingly allocated to the private sector. In mid-1994 the Government approved the construction of three new cities, at Subahiya, Doha and Khiran, in order to alleviate the state's housing

shortage. The cities were to be built by private-sector companies, and were scheduled for completion in 1998. The biggest concentration of construction work currently in progress is at the new campus for Kuwait University at Shuwaikh, while the most advanced build-operate-transfer (BOT) project is the development of Kuwait City waterfront by Kuwait's National Real Estate Co (NREC). Designs for a prestigious new headquarters for the Kuwait Petroleum Co (KPC) are under consideration, and a number of new public buildings are at various stages of construction.

Many of the smaller industrial projects have been promoted by the Industrial Bank of Kuwait (IBK), founded in 1973, which is partially government-owned. By 1984, however, four leading commercial banks had combined with IBK to form a more specific concern, the Industrial Investment Company (IIC), to make new investments. During 1985 the Government took a further step in assisting local industry when it announced the introduction of protectionist trade measures for local industries which satisfy three criteria. Such industries should meet at least 40% of domestic requirements; should have a substantial added value and should contribute to national income; and the consumer should not be affected by any inflationary results of tariff protection.

In accordance with its aim of diversifying the economy, Kuwait has entered the international hotel industry at an accelerated rate. In 1988 Kuwait began to consolidate its assets by collecting them under one group, namely the Kuwait Hotels Co (KHC). The company was founded in 1962, soon after independence, and its main objectives were to assume control of all hotel management duties, and to take charge of all financial holdings. KHC was to concentrate initially on Kuwait and other Arab countries, before venturing into the wider international market. Substantial staff-training was a determining factor of the Government's aim to have all Kuwait-owned hotels managed by KHC.

In mid-1996 the NREC was appointed to manage Kuwait's first free-trade zone, to be established at the port of Shuwaikh. Activities will be limited to transhipment initially, but will be expanded later to include light manufacturing. The establishment of the free-trade zone was approved by the Government in May 1998.

PUBLIC UTILITIES AND TRANSPORT

All of the industrial developments referred to above, and the demographic growth associated with the necessary immigration, have required great increases in power generation. (The annual increase in power demand is estimated at some 7%.) The increasingly harsh economic climate led the Government to introduce higher electricity rates in April 1986. This was the first increase since 1966 and meant that consumers would pay 27% of actual power costs, compared with their previous payment of about 6%. By the end of 1987 the five power stations, at Shuwaikh, Shuaiba North, Shuaiba South, Doha East and Doha West, had a total installed capacity of 5,230 MW. A sixth power station, with an installed capacity of 2,511 MW, came into full production at az-Zour South in 1988. In mid-1990 the Ministry of Electricity and Water decided to provide desalination units for the Subahiya thermal power station. Two 6m.-gallons-per-day units are required for the 2,400-MW station. Subahiya's first unit began operation in 1992. Substantial damage to Kuwait's power stations was reported as a result of the Iraqi occupation; az-Zour South was the least damaged power station. By mid-1993 installed generating capacity remained 30% below the pre-invasion level of 7,100 MW, although Shuaiba North was the only station not to have resumed operations. In mid-1995 Cogelex Alsthom of France finalized a contract with the Ministry of Communications, Electricity and Water to supply and install an electricity substation at the Shuaiba petrochemical complex. Germany's AEG and Switzerland-based Asea Brown Boveri were contracted to supply and install a further three substations, representing the first phase of the expansion of Kuwait's grid following a series of contracts aimed primarily at repairing damage sustained during the Iraqi invasion. Installed capacity in Kuwait in 1996 totalled 6,898 MW. Plans to rebuild the Shuaiba North power station were abandoned in mid-1996, in favour of a proposal to construct a new 2,400-MW thermal power plant at az-Zour North. Tenders for construction of the plant were to be invited exclusively from US contractors. The project will also include a water desalination plant with a capacity of 48m. gallons per day. A new station is under construction at Subahiya; the station will increase Kuwait's total installed capacity to 9,280 MW and was due for completion by 1999. In 1999 the az-Zour power plant project was suspended, owing to budgetary restrictions, but in September 2001 the plan was re-approved, and the plant was scheduled to begin operation in 2006. Two further plants, totalling 1,000 MW in capacity, at Shuaiba and Subahiya, received approval at the same time.

Increased water demands have been met by the distillation plants at Shuwaikh, Shuaiba North, Shuaiba South, Doha East and Doha West, which, in 1986, gave Kuwait a total installed capacity of 35,286m. gallons per year. The rapid increase in water demand was reflected in the rise in average daily (potable) water consumption, from 3.8m. gallons in 1960, to 18.2m. gallons in 1970, 64.1m. gallons in 1980, 130.3m. gallons in 1990, and 230.3m. gallons in 1999. Traditionally, Kuwait had concentrated on distillation methods for obtaining fresh water, but at the end of 1984 the Doha reverse osmosis plant was inaugurated, with an annual capacity of 220m. gallons. The pumping of fresh water from underground aquifers declined from 700m. gallons in 1970 to 126m. gallons in 1980, and to 14m. gallons in 1990, and ceased in 1991, following damage caused by the Iraqi invasion which has yet to be repaired. The pumping of brackish water, however, increased from 11,319m. gallons in 1980 to 21,366m. gallons in 1989. By 1991, however, following the Iraqi invasion, production had decreased to 2,787m. gallons. By 1996 annual production had recovered to 22,010m. gallons. The fresh water and brackish water systems are piped through separate networks, and the latter is used primarily for blending with distilled water, for irrigation, watering livestock, construction and in the household. Oil released into the Persian (Arabian) Gulf by Iraq caused considerable damage to Kuwait's desalination facilities. In February 2001 an agreement was announced to build a privately-funded 540-km water pipeline from Iran's Karkheh dam to Kuwait. The pipeline would be laid across the Gulf and would supply up to 200m. gallons of water per day for Kuwaiti industrial and domestic use.

A new international airport was opened in 1980, and there is a national airline with an international service, Kuwait Airways Corpn (KAC). In 1990 KAC owned 19 aircraft, flying to 41 destinations. KAC lost two-thirds of its fleet during the Iraqi occupation, and six KAC airliners were held by Iran (until the end of July 1992), which demanded reparation for their upkeep. The airport infrastructure was also seriously damaged, but by 1993 the refurbished airport was operating normally. A major programme of aircraft replacement and fleet expansion began in 1992. By 1997 KAC owned 23 aircraft and served 47 destinations. KAC has been scheduled for privatization.

The Kuwait Oil Tanker Co (KOTC) was fully nationalized in 1979. The oil ministry then started to include the use of Kuwaiti tankers in the terms of sale of its crude petroleum. In early 1990 KOTC commissioned the Republic of Korea to supply a third 280,000-dwt very large crude carrier (VLCC) by 1992. Similarly, the company finalized a contract with Japan for the supply of two liquefied gas carriers, each with a capacity of 78,000 cu m, under a plan to enlarge its fleet of 28 oil tankers and 6 gas carriers, in order to enhance its position in the world tanker market. Kuwait's two main container ports are at Shuwaikh and Shuaiba. Despite the devastation caused by the Iraqi forces during their occupation of Kuwait, the Shuaiba port resumed operations in March 1991. The 1990–95 Ports Public Authority programme contained plans to expand both ports. In January 1997 KOTC awarded a US $610m. contract to South Korea's Hyundai Heavy Industries to build two 309,000-ton oil tankers. At the end of 2001 Kuwait's merchant fleet numbered 200 vessels, with a total displacement of 2,291,700 gross registered tons.

In recent years telecommunications have become increasingly important in Kuwait. At the end of 1997 Kuwait had 412,000 fixed telephone lines in use and some 210,000 subscribers to its mobile network. As part of its ongoing programme to upgrade the country's fixed line system, the communications ministry awarded a contract in July 1997 to Germany's Siemens to install 100,000 new telephone lines at five exchanges at Surra, Qurain, Sulaibikhat, Salwa and Old Salmiya. In 1998 plans were announced to privatize the state telecommunications sector which included the transformation of the Ministry of Communications into a Kuwaiti Communications Corpn. In May 2001 the Government commenced the sale of up to one-half of its 48% stake in the Mobile Telecommunications Co.

AGRICULTURE AND FISHERIES

Owing to the scarcity of water in Kuwait, little grain is produced, and, as a result, most of the country's food has to be imported. In 2001 agriculture and fishing contributed about 0.4% of Kuwait's GDP. The principal agricultural crops are tomatoes, potatoes, cucumbers and aubergines.

A five-year development plan for agriculture, initiated in 1982, was intended to increase the area under vegetables to 3,500 ha by 1986, raising overall vegetable production from 42,000 tons in 1981—supplying 24% of vegetable requirements—to 98,000 tons. Experiments with hydroponics gave Kuwait the confidence to set these optimistic targets, and the Public Authority for Agriculture and Fish Resources agreed to continue to subsidize agricultural products during 1986 and 1987. A considerable amount was also invested in the development of methods of using treated effluent for irrigation purposes.

The Government also encouraged animal husbandry, the main activity of the bedouin before the development of the oilfields. Subsidies were introduced in 1983 to assist farmers using artesian wells and greenhouses, and for the owners of small fishing boats. The Government also owned a 36-ha experimental farm. In the private sector the poultry and dairy industries expanded, as has the cultivation of dates, production of which totalled 7,000 tons in 1998. In 2000 milk production was estimated at 46,000 tons and there were an estimated 20,000 cattle, 450,000 sheep, 150,000 goats and 33m. poultry in Kuwait. Kuwait also invested in livestock overseas, but it still needed to import considerable numbers.

Fishing, particularly of prawns and shrimps, is also widely practised. Four fishing companies were amalgamated into Kuwait United Fisheries in 1972. A 20-year plan to develop the industry, at an estimated cost of US $1m., was announced in 1987, when local production was sufficient to satisfy only 25% of domestic demand. The total catch in 1999 was 6,535 tons, compared with 8,049 tons in 1998 and 8,080 tons in 1997.

FOREIGN TRADE AND BALANCE OF PAYMENTS

Kuwait's foreign trade is dominated by exports of crude petroleum and petroleum products, which generally account for over 90% of the value of export earnings each year. According to the IMF, total export earnings in 1990, the year of the Iraqi invasion, were reduced to KD 2,031.4m. (of which petroleum accounted for KD 1,842.0m.), from KD 3,378.0m. in 1989, and in 1991 the total slumped to KD 309.4m. Kuwait was liberated from Iraqi occupation at the end of February in that year, but the country's petroleum-production facilities were severely damaged, and it was not possible to resume exports at pre-war levels. In 1992, however, export revenue recovered to KD 1,931.1m., with the petroleum sector providing KD 1,824.9m. (94.5% of the total). By 1997 total export earnings had increased to KD 4,314.3m., of which petroleum accounted for KD 4,085.4m. (94.7% of the total). In 1998 export revenues decreased to KD 2,911.6m. (of which petroleum exports accounted for KD 2,581.8m., 88.7% of the total), as a result of the decline in international petroleum prices. As petroleum prices recovered, export revenues increased to KD 3,719.2m. in 1999, of which petroleum exports accounted for KD 3,356.5m. (90.2% of the total), and to KD 5,994.5m. in 2000 (petroleum accounting for KD 5,571.7m.—92.9% of the total).

The total value of imports reached KD 1,849.4m. in 1989. According to the IMF, Kuwait's imports fell to KD 1,145.7m. in 1990, but rose to KD 1,353.3m. in 1991 and to KD 2,129.2m. in 1992. The total value of imports increased further, to KD 2,501.6m. by 1997 and to KD 2,626.2m. in 1998, before declining slightly, to KD 2,318.3m. in 1999. The value of imports increased again, to KD 2,337.6m., in 2000. The most important commodity group in Kuwait's imports is usually machinery and transport equipment (which accounted for 39.7% of total imports in 1999), followed by basic manufactures (16.3% in 1999). In 1999 Kuwait's main source of imports was Japan, which supplied 12.8% of total imports. The USA, Germany, Saudi Arabia,

Italy and the United Kingdom are also important suppliers. Details concerning the destination of Kuwait's petroleum exports are not available for recent years. In 1999 the main customers for the country's non-petroleum exports (totalling KD 362.7m.) included Saudi Arabia (which took 11.5% of the total), the UAE (9.3%), India (8.6%) and Singapore (7.3%).

The current account surplus on the balance of payments was US $4,602m. in 1988, increasing to $9,136m. in 1989. The surplus declined to $3,886m. in 1990, when trade was disrupted by the Iraqi invasion and occupation. In 1991 Kuwait paid huge amounts to the countries that contributed to ending the occupation, resulting in a current deficit of $26,478m. By 1995 there was a surplus on the current account of $5,016m. which increased to $7,935m. by 1997. In 1998, however, largely owing to the decline in international petroleum prices, the surplus on the current account decreased to $2,215m. The current account surplus grew to $5,065m. in 1999 and to $14,669m. in 2000, largely owing to higher prices for petroleum, before declining again, to $8,566m., in 2001. In 1989 the trade surplus stood at $4,987m., but was reduced to $3,179m. in 1990. In 1991 Kuwait registered a visible trade deficit of $3,993m. By 1995 a trade surplus, of $5,579m., was recorded; the surplus increased to $6,997m. in 1996, before declining to $6,534m. in 1997 and to $1,903m. in 1998. Higher petroleum prices in 1999 and 2000 resulted in the trade surplus growing to $5,568m. and $13,027m., respectively. The trade surplus was $9,241m. in 2001.

BANKING AND FINANCE

In 1979 the Central Bank of Kuwait imposed tighter controls on the banking sector and demanded a significant reduction in overdrafts. Despite this, the banking sector continued to flourish in the early 1980s, with a 20% rise in total assets during 1982. However, the collapse of the Souk al-Manakh in 1982 (see below), the uncertainties caused by the Iran–Iraq War, and the problems associated with the falling price of oil led to severe difficulties for Kuwait's banking sector in the mid-1980s. In 1983 the banks' total assets rose by only 9.3%, and the decline in the commercial banking sector also led to the introduction of a two-tier exchange rate between April and August 1984. The foreign exchange market was effectively closed in June, when the Central Bank halted sales of US dollars, except for genuine commercial transactions.

In 1985 the banks faced a burgeoning debt crisis. Court cases involving bank debtors rose from 169 in 1981 to 437 in 1984, and in May 1985 bad debts held by commercial banks amounted to approximately KD 2,200m. (US $7,200m.). At the end of 1984 the Central Bank asked for full documentation on all commercial bank loans in excess of KD 250,000. By the end of 1985 its survey of the country's financial institutions revealed that, as of 11 September 1985, Kuwait's banks had gross claims against foreign banks totalling KD 1,534m. ($5,192m.), a sum which exceeded their corresponding obligations by KD 93m. The survey also revealed that Kuwait's banks had lent a total of KD 275.9m. to their own directors. At the end of 1985 three banks recorded zero net profits, and the National Bank of Kuwait (NBK—the country's largest bank) was the only bank to record an increase (of 11.1%) in net profits over the previous year's figure. The dissolution of the National Assembly was widely regarded as providing an opportunity for seeking a solution to the debt crisis, and a series of measures, approved by the Council of Ministers in August 1986, facilitated a 'rescue programme' whereby debtors should repay as much as they could afford, and the Government would pay the remainder of the debt. In 1989 the majority of the commercial banks in Kuwait remained dependent on this scheme for debt-restructuring. A range of other radical changes in the policy of the Central Bank were made between 1987 and 1989, promoting the further revival of the banking sector.

Following the Iraqi invasion of Kuwait, all Kuwaiti bank deposits were frozen, paralysing the operations of the country's banks. The Bank of England allowed individuals and organizations from Kuwait to operate in the United Kingdom, but all of the banks had to seek permission from the Bank of England to pay out Kuwait-controlled assets. The NBK was instrumental in efforts to resume operations. With the support of the Kuwait Investment Office (see Investment, below), it was able to free most of its blocked accounts, and to restore its liquidity position, by quickly selling US $2,000m. of its loan portfolio at little or no discount. The NBK played a central role in stabilizing the position of the other Kuwaiti banks. By early 1991 most Kuwaiti banks had resumed operations outside Kuwait and Iraq.

Following the liberation of Kuwait, the Kuwaiti banks resumed domestic operations, but NBK was the only bank able to participate in the reconstruction process. The Government encouraged rationalization and the merger of some of the numerous domestic banks. By mid-1996, however, little progress had been made in this direction. In March 1991 some branches of banks began to reopen, mainly to distribute the Government's cash grant to Kuwaiti citizens who had remained in the country during the occupation. Depositors were initially limited to cash withdrawals of US $14,000 per month until the end of June. By August all currency restrictions had been removed. In April 1991 an Amiri decree instructed the banks to cancel debts totalling $4,900m., and so cleared the debts of 180,000 people. As a result, many local bad debts that had been incurred in the stock market crisis of the mid-1980s were cancelled. On 20 May 1992 it was announced that the Government was to buy the entire domestic loan portfolio of the domestic banking system, covering credits to residents worth $20,400m. In the first half of 1993 there was intense debate between the Government and the National Assembly over the terms under which the loans should be repaid. As long as the issue remained unresolved, Kuwaiti banks were unwilling to approve loans, and investment outside the petroleum industry was very limited. In August 1993 the National Assembly approved legislation requiring debtors to register their preferred method of repayment by March 1994; debtors could either settle their accounts by September 1995 in exchange for debt forgiveness of up to 46%, or pay over a period of 12 years with no debt forgiveness. Even though the majority of debtors opted to repay their debts by September 1995, the rate of repayment was slow and the Government came under increasing pressure to extend the repayment period as any rapid liquidation of assets could undermine the economy. In June 1995 the Council of Ministers reviewed a draft law proposing significant amendments to the difficult debts law, which would allow debtors several more years in which to make their repayments. The National Assembly initially opposed the amendments, as it was feared that the extension of the terms of repayment would benefit politically powerful debtors, including members of the royal family, at the expense of the economy. In August, however, preliminary approval was granted to a bill which would ease repayment terms. Hopes for the success of the latest repayment programme were encouraged by the high proportion (77%) of obligations repaid on 6 April 1996, the first of five annual payment instalments.

In 2001 draft legislation was approved by the Council of Ministers which would allow foreign banks to open branches in Kuwait. The bill would require approval from the National Assembly. In the same year the Council of Ministers also approved bills that would permit foreign banks to own controlling interests in Kuwaiti financial institutions, and to reduce taxation on net profits paid by foreign companies operating in Kuwait from 55% to 25%. These proposed measures were part of the Government's programme of economic liberalization.

CAPITAL MARKET

A significant capital market has been developed in Kuwait through the activities of the leading investment companies and the IBK, and with the encouragement of the Government. An active bond market developed after 1973, mostly for international borrowers from the Third World and Eastern Europe. The Central Bank then closed the new issue market in November 1979 as part of its efforts to boost liquidity in Kuwait's money market, but by July 1981 the Kuwaiti dinar international bond market had reopened. Despite the issue of a number of new bonds, the market was to close again in September 1982. It reopened in June 1983 with a KD 5m. floating rate note bond for the United Bank of Kuwait's subsidiary, UBK Finance, and there followed a KD 14m. two-tranche bond offer for the Kuwait Foreign Trading Contracting and Investing Co in November. However, following the collapse of the stock market (see below), the bond market also lost its appeal, and in 1985 and 1986 only solitary domestic bonds were issued. In the last quarter of 1987 and the first quarter of 1988 the Government issued a series of bonds and treasury bills, in an attempt to finance the budget deficit. During 1987 the Central Bank's total assets fell by 31%, to KD 1,458.7m., mainly as a result of a decline in foreign deposits, which decreased by 44%, to KD 681.8m., by the end of the year.

In 1952 Kuwait had established what was, prior to the Iraqi invasion of August 1990, the world's twelfth largest stock exchange. The amount of capital holders seeking investment outlets in Kuwait, and the innate entrepreneurial spirit of locals, generally pushed the prices of shares far above their real value. In April 1978, in an attempt to stem this unhealthy trend, the Government sanctioned the reduction in nominal value of shares to one dinar, a move which resulted in a split of share values to 10%–13% of their current value, which broadened the base of the market.

Alongside the official market, an unofficial stock market, the Souk al-Manakh, also developed. After 1978 many Kuwaitis had invested in Iraq, and, as a result of the Iran–Iraq War, a severe cash-flow crisis emerged in Kuwait. In 1982 the liquidity shortage which this caused was particularly severe for the Souk al-Manakh. The unofficial market had been based on the use of post-dated cheques and the hope of continuously rising share prices. Then in September 1982 the system collapsed, as smaller creditors prematurely presented their post-dated cheques (perfectly legal under Kuwaiti law) at a time when many dealers were unable to pay. The collapse of the Souk al-Manakh initiated a major crisis in Kuwait's financial system, the impact of which lasted for several years.

Government measures to alleviate the crisis involved the immediate formation of the Kuwait Clearing Co, to register and process all cheques involved, and the establishment of a KD 500m. fund to protect, and pay, the smaller debtors whose investors were bankrupt. In August 1983 the Government urged the settlement of debts at the market price at the time of transaction, and set a maximum premium of 25% on post-dated cheques. Disagreement over the handling of the crisis led to the resignation of the Minister of Finance. In October the Government appointed an arbitration panel to revalue the debts of the 17 leading dealers in the Souk al-Manakh. These accounted for about $78,000m., or 82% of the estimated total of outstanding debts at the time of the crisis, and the dealers' assets were valued at between 20% and 30% of their liabilities. Since then, a new investment company has been established, with a capital of KD 300m. (in which the Government has a 40% share), to convert the debtors' non-liquid assets into payment for the creditors. In April 1984 the Council of Ministers announced further financial measures to resolve the crisis, including the division of assets into three categories. Bonds to repay creditors were issued in July, and, of the 254 people referred to the receivership, 88 were declared bankrupt, three restored their solvency and 163 reached agreements with their creditors.

In August 1984 the official stock exchange moved to new premises, and its permanent floor officially opened in April 1985. The Souk al-Manakh stock market was closed on 1 November 1984, and trading in shares was restricted to the official stock exchange and to a parallel market which it operated. To avoid a repetition of the Souk al-Manakh crisis, measures were introduced to limit the activities of brokers on the official market. Before being allowed on the floor, brokers had to pay a registration fee and provide a guarantee for KD 1m., while a percentage of brokers' commissions had to be paid to the exchange. By mid-January 1985 creditors who had been owed money by Souk al-Manakh defaulters had received cash and bonds totalling KD 759m., accounting for about three-quarters of the net debts. At the end of 1987, however, 17% of the debts resulting from the collapse of the Souk al-Manakh remained outstanding.

The Government bore the brunt of the crisis and was forced to inject large sums into the banking system to restore liquidity. At the end of November 1985, the Minister of Finance and Economy made the following recommendations: 33 companies should be dissolved; a number of the remaining 47 companies should be merged; from March 1986 the KIC was to purchase the companies that closed, on behalf of the Government; and companies registered in the Gulf that fell outside the jurisdiction of Kuwait were urged to comply with the Government's recommendations. These measures appeared to be necessary, owing to the fact that 24 of the 36 companies that had closed, and were under consideration for purchase by the Government, had incurred losses exceeding 50% of the paid-up capital invested in them. It was estimated that by mid-1986 this scheme had cost the Government approximately KD 121m. In May 1989 it was reported that stock market activity was disappointing, and measures to deregulate the stock market to some extent were to be introduced before the end of the year in the hope that a reduction in restrictions would encourage investors. Also in May it was announced that the Souk al-Manakh stock exchange was to be re-opened in June, to allow trading in companies that had failed to meet the minimum capital requirements of the official stock exchange.

In May 1988 the Government permitted citizens of all GCC member states to purchase shares on the Kuwait stock exchange. (Previously only Kuwaiti citizens had been permitted to do so.) Then, in 1992, the exchange was opened to international firms for the first time. In 1995 the exchange became the most active share market in the Arab world. Strong corporate earnings, excess liquidity and the privatization policy launched by the Kuwait Investment Authority (KIA) maintained the buoyancy of the stock market, and in June 1997 it was reported that the average market price of shares had increased by some 30% since the start of the year. The privatization programme began in mid-1994, and by early 1997 the KIA had sold KD 653m. worth of shares. In January 1997 it was announced that a further KD 1,000m. worth of shares were available for sale at current prices. By early 1999 the stock market was in decline as a result of the regional economic downturn, the absence of reforms to reduce the budget deficit and poor company results for 1998, and in November 1999 it reached its lowest level since 1996. In 1998 legislation was passed further rescheduling debts owed as a result of the collapse of the Souk al-Manakh in 1982 and in May 2000 a draft law was passed allowing foreign investment on the stock exchange, which, combined with the higher level of petroleum prices, was expected to lead to a recovery in share values; however, it was reported in early 2001 that they had continued to fall, reflecting a lack of confidence in the Government's economic reforms.

PUBLIC FINANCE

The cumulative costs of the Gulf conflict (1990–91) to the Kuwaiti Government inevitably increased its budget deficits. By the end of July 1991 the cost to Kuwait of paying the expenses of Kuwaitis living abroad during the Iraqi occupation, and of financing 'Operation Desert Storm', had increased to US $22,000m., which had been drawn from its reserves, with further expenditure expected. A further $6,000m.–$7,000m. was spent after liberation on stabilization measures, such as the cancellation of personal debts and cash grants to nationals who remained in Kuwait during the Iraqi occupation. The Kuwaiti Government stated that it had no intention of making large-scale sales of investments to create revenue, but it was nevertheless reported in mid-1993 that the value of Kuwait's overseas investments had more than halved in the previous three years (see also Investment). At the end of 1991 a $5,500m. international loan to Kuwait was announced, as well as export credit facilities worth the same amount with the USA, Japan, the UK, the Netherlands and France. Kuwait began repayments on the international loan in 1996. In 1994 the finance and economy committee of the National Assembly approved KD 3,500m. in extraordinary defence spending over the 12 years from 1992 to 2004. The budget for 1997/98 put expenditure at KD 4,378m. and revenues at KD 3,105m., although the deficit out-turn was far lower than predicted (at KD 370m.). Estimates for 1998/99 envisaged revenues of KD 2,444m., expenditure of KD 4,362m. and an increased budget deficit, as a result of the decline in international petroleum prices; the actual deficit for that year was KD 1,242m. Although a target of balancing the budget by 2000 had been announced in 1995, the draft budget for 1999/2000, with revenue of KD 2,224m. and expenditure of KD 4,295m., predicted an increased budget deficit of KD 2,071m. In early 1999 Government attempts to introduce a financial and economic reform package were rejected by the National Assembly, which requested more specific details of proposed measures to increase non-oil revenues. Petroleum prices had recovered by September 1999, however, and resulted in a budget surplus of KD 1,231m. The budget for 2000/01 predicted revenue of KD 4,965.4m. and expenditure of KD 3,188m. As the result of a planned change in the start of the fiscal year from 2001, the 2000/01 budget only covered a nine-month period, from 1 July 2000 to 31 March 2001. The budget for 2001/02 projected revenue of KD 3,832m. and expenditure of KD 5,274m.

INVESTMENT

Kuwait's main priority for spending its income from petroleum has been the development of its own economy and the provision, through the investment of surplus funds, of an income for its citizens in the future when the oil-wells have run dry. In the mid-1970s, in addition to the general reserve, the Government established a Reserve Fund for Future Generations (RFFG), to which at least 10% of total revenue must be added annually, by law, and which was not intended to be used until 2001. The value of the RFFG was estimated at KD 14,000m. before the world-wide collapse of prices on stock markets in October 1987.

Kuwait had a budget surplus for some years before 1973 and therefore developed an investment strategy considerably earlier than other petroleum-producing countries did. This strategy was implemented when Kuwait established the Kuwait Investment Office (KIO) in the 1950s, with the aim of providing for its future generations by investing part of the Government's share of profits from the country's petroleum industry. The KIO in London (which was formally merged with its parent, the KIA, in March 1993) handled much of the nation's investment in Europe and elsewhere. In 1979 the KIO also started to buy small interests in leading Japanese electronics companies. Many of Kuwait's investments are in the USA, and involve almost every one of the 500 leading US companies. Kuwait also has some major real estate projects there. Exceptions to Kuwait's traditional preference for small shares in foreign companies included its outright purchase of the St Martin's Property Corpn of the UK, and its purchase of substantial holdings in Daimler-Benz of Germany, the USA's Korf Industries and a Canadian copper-molybdenum mine.

Investment income from abroad increased to US $8,074m. in 1986, overtaking income from petroleum for the first time. In 1987 the KIO acquired further considerable shareholdings in Europe: in particular, it acquired a major stake in BP. However, in October 1988, after a report by the Monopolies and Mergers Commission in Britain, the KIO was forced to reduce its interest in BP from 21.68% to 9.9%. This disposal produced a profit of $700m. for the KIO, as the BP management raised its buy-back price for the shares in response to hostile bids from rival oil companies. (A further 3% stake in BP was sold by the KIA in May 1997 for about $2,000m.) By October 1987 the KIO had accumulated investments in Spain with a value of $2,400m., and, as a result of its acquisition of 37% of Torras Hostench, it established itself as a major force in Spain's chemicals industry; it also acquired 35% of Explosivos Rio Tinto (ERT) and further shares in several Spanish media groups.

In 1993 the dealings of the KIO were the subject of an inquiry by a commission comprising members of the new National Assembly. It was alleged that officials of the KIO had lost US $5,000m. in Spain since 1986, of which some $1,000m. had been embezzled through the collapsed Grupo Torras company. In mid-1993 it was reported that legal proceedings were being

prepared against former KIO officials in the United Kingdom and Spain. In July a report of the National Assembly's finance and economy commission was critical of the Government for failing to ensure the accountability of KIO officials. A series of legislative measures in 1993 attempted to ensure greater accountability from state investment organizations and to increase penalties for the misuse of public funds. In 1999 a court in the United Kingdom found three former senior managers of the KIO guilty, *in absentia*, of embezzling some $500m. from Grupo Torras.

Kuwaiti private investment is substantial. It is predominantly in real estate and high-yielding equities. Although this investment is concentrated in the USA, Europe and Japan, Kuwaitis have shown an interest in investment in other non-Arab countries in Asia, Africa and South America, as well as in the Arab world.

From August 1990 until July 1991, Kuwait's sole sources of income were earnings from its international financial investments and profits from Kuwait Petroleum International, which operates Kuwaiti petroleum companies in Europe and Asia. It was estimated that Kuwait's international investments in August 1990 were worth as much as US $100,000m., comprising the RFFG and the State General Reserve. The rate of return on these investments was estimated at 5% per year. Although the Kuwaiti Government refused to disclose any details concerning the sale of assets to fund its activities during the 1990–91 Gulf crisis, it was estimated in mid-1993 that the value of Kuwait's overseas investments had more than halved since August 1990. Following the liberation of Kuwait, the Government indicated that it did not envisage the sale of large-scale investments, especially of important strategic assets such as its interests in Daimler-Benz, Hoechst, Metallgesellschaft, Hogg Robinson, HSBC UK and BP. In mid-1994 Kuwait submitted a claim of almost $41,000m. to the UN Compensation Committee for losses incurred by the KIA during the Iraqi invasion. The claim was part of a total of $94,800m. worth of compensation claims made by Kuwait by the end of June 1994, with further submissions expected. Income from overseas investments increased by almost 30%, to $5,153m., in 1995.

After its own development, Kuwait's next priority is that of the rest of the Arab and Islamic world, and then of the Third World in general. It pioneered foreign aid in the Arab world, setting up the KFAED in 1961. Kuwait later raised the KFAED's capital considerably, and extended operations to Africa and Asia. Its capital in 1999 was KD 2,000m. The country also helped set up the Arab Fund for Economic and Social Development in Kuwait, and it is a member of various Arab, Islamic and OPEC aid organizations, notably the Islamic Development Bank, the Arab Bank for Economic Development in Africa (BADEA) and the OPEC Fund for International Development. It has also contributed to IMF and World Bank facilities.

Kuwait's total foreign aid, which was substantially more than that given on projected aid by the KFAED, ranged between about 8% and 15% of GNP during the second half of the 1970s. However, Kuwait's official contribution to development assistance declined over the period 1984–87, and Kuwaiti foreign aid further decreased in the post-liberation period of reconstruction. Overall, between 1962 and September 2002 it was estimated that the KFAED disbursed 623 loans, valued at KD 3,220m. Annual disbursements had increased from KD 69.7m. in 1987/88 to KD 157.5m. in 1999/2000.

Statistical Survey

Sources (unless otherwise stated): Economic Research Department, Central Bank of Kuwait, POB 526, 13006 Safat, Kuwait City; tel. 2403257; fax 2440887; e-mail cbk@cbk.gov.kw; internet www.cbk.gov.kw; Central Statistical Office, Ministry of Planning, POB 26188, 13122 Safat, Kuwait City; tel. 2454968; fax 2430464; e-mail salah@mop.gov.kw; internet www.mop.gov.kw.

Note: Unless otherwise indicated, data refer to the State of Kuwait as constituted at 1 August 1990, prior to the Iraqi invasion and annexation of the territory and its subsequent liberation. Furthermore, no account has been taken of the increase in the area of Kuwait as a result of the adjustment to the border with Iraq that came into force on 15 January 1993.

Area and Population

AREA, POPULATION AND DENSITY

Area (sq km) .	17,818*
Population (census results)†‡	
21 April 1985	1,697,301
20 April 1995	
Males	913,402
Females .	662,168
Total	1,575,570
Population (official estimates at mid-year)†	
1999	2,107,195
2000	2,189,668
2001	2,274,980
Density (per sq km) at mid-2001	127.7

* 6,880 sq miles.

† Figures include Kuwaiti nationals abroad. The total population at the 1995 census comprised 653,616 Kuwaiti nationals (326,301 males; 327,315 females) and 921,954 non-Kuwaitis (587,101 males; 334,853 females).

‡ Excluding adjustment for underenumeration.

GOVERNORATES (estimated population at mid-1998)

Governorate	Area (sq km)*	Popula-tion	Density (per sq km)	Capital
Capital . .	199.8	305,694	1,530.0	Kuwait City
Hawalli . .}	368.4 {	496,245 }	2,700.4 {	Hawalli
Farwaniya }		498,584 }		Farwaniya
Al-Jahra .	11,230.2	252,157	22.5	Jahra
Al-Ahmadi .	5,119.6	313,424	61.2	Ahmadi City
Total . .	**16,918.0**	**1,866,104**	**110.3**	

* Excluding the islands of Bubiyan and Warba (combined area 900 sq km).

Note: In November 1999 a sixth governorate, Great Mubarak, was created by dividing Hawalli.

PRINCIPAL TOWNS (population at 1995 census)

Kuwait City (capital) .	28,747	Subbah as-Salem . .	54,608
Salmiya . . .	129,775	Sulaibiah . . .	53,639
Jaleeb ash-Shuyukh .	102,169	Farwaniya . .	52,928
Hawalli . . .	82,154	Al-Kreen . . .	50,689
South Kheetan . .	62,241	Subahiya . . .	50,644

BIRTHS, MARRIAGES AND DEATHS

	Registered live births		Registered marriages		Registered deaths	
	Number	Rate (per 1,000)	Number	Rate (per 1,000)	Number	Rate (per 1,000)
1993 . .	37,379	25.6	10,077	6.9	3,441	2.4
1994 . .	38,868	24.0	9,550	5.9	3,464	2.1
1995 . .	41,169	22.8	9,515	5.3	3,781	2.1
1996 . .	44,620	23.6	9,022	4.8	3,812	2.0
1997 . .	42,817	21.6	9,610	4.9	4,017	2.0
1998 . .	41,424	20.4	10,335	5.1	4,216	2.1
1999 . .	41,135	19.5	10,847	5.1	4,187	2.0
2000 . .	41,843	19.1	10,785	4.9	4,227	1.9

Expectation of life (WHO estimates, years at birth, 2000): Males 74.2; Females 76.8 (Source: WHO, *World Health Report*).

ECONOMICALLY ACTIVE POPULATION
(persons aged 15 years and over, census of April 1995)*

	Kuwaitis	Non-Kuwaitis	Total
Agriculture, hunting and fishing .	216	15,140	15,356
Mining and quarrying . . .	7,168	8,306	15,474
Manufacturing	997	39,107	40,104
Electricity, gas and water . .	32	137	169
Construction	1,415	113,804	115,219
Trade, restaurants and hotels .	3,852	115,493	119,345
Transport, storage and communications . . .	4,865	20,637	25,502
Finance, insurance, real estate and business services . . .	4,139	53,077	57,216
Community, social and personal services	117,093	234,236	351,329
Activities not adequately defined	2,982	4,838	7,820
Total	**142,759**	**604,775**	**747,534**

* Figures exclude persons seeking work for the first time, totalling 14,086 (5,009 Kuwaitis; 9,077 non-Kuwaitis), but include other unemployed persons, totalling 15,919 (5,564 Kuwaitis; 10,355 non-Kuwaitis).

Mid-2000 (official estimates, persons aged 15 years and over): Total employed 1,197,887 (Kuwaitis 225,179; non-Kuwaitis 972,708); Unemployed 9,305 (Kuwaitis 2,351; non-Kuwaitis 6,954); *Total labour force* 1,207,192 (Kuwaitis 227,530; non-Kuwaitis 979,662).

Health and Welfare

KEY INDICATORS

Fertility (births per woman, 2000).	2.8
Under-5 mortality rate (per '000 live births, 2000) . .	10
HIV/AIDS (% of persons aged 15–49, 1994). . . .	0.12
Physicians (per 1,000 head, 1997)	1.9
Hospital beds (per 1,000 head, 1997)	2.76
Health expenditure (1998): US $ per head (PPP) . . .	536
% of GDP	4.0
public (% of total) . . .	87.1
Human Development Index (2000): ranking	45
value	0.813

For sources and definitions, see explanatory note on p. vi.

Agriculture

PRINCIPAL CROPS ('000 metric tons)

	1998	1999	2000
Potatoes.	21.9	24.4	28.6
Lettuce	4.3	4.7	5.4
Tomatoes	28.6	31.2	31.8
Cauliflower	3.9	4.1	4.2*
Pumpkins, squash and gourds .	4.9	3.5	4.9
Cucumber and gherkins . .	32.6	28.6	33.0
Aubergines (Eggplants) . .	9.5	11.5	12.0
Chillies and green peppers .	4.7	5.1	5.5
Other vegetables* . . .	30.1	30.2	31.4
Dates	6.5	7.9	8.6

* FAO estimate(s).

Source: FAO.

LIVESTOCK ('000 head, year ending September)

	1998	1999	2000*
Cattle	18	20*	20
Camels*	9	9	9
Sheep	421	445*	450
Goats	130	135*	150
Poultry	28,308	29,204	33,000

* FAO estimate(s).

Source: FAO.

LIVESTOCK PRODUCTS ('000 metric tons)

	1998	1999	2000
Beef and veal*	2.1	1.6	1.7
Mutton and lamb* . . .	37.9	37.8	32.3
Poultry meat	36.1	38.3	42.7
Cows' milk	32.0	33.7	41.4
Goats' milk	3.0	4.1	4.5
Poultry eggs	14.6	18.2	20.1
Sheepskins (fresh) . . .	13.4	13.4	13.3

* FAO estimates.

Source: FAO.

Fishing

(metric tons, live weight)

	1997	1998	1999
Capture	7,826	7,799	6,271
Hilsha shad	1,034	919	970
Groupers	241	264	237
Grunts and sweetlips .	163	174	245
Croakers and drums .	1,127	1,211	1,385
Yellowfin seabream . .	249	280	464
Mullets	693	1,137	1,054
Silver pomfret . . .	560	501	259
Indo-Pacific king mackerel .	206	166	211
Natantian decapods . .	2,066	1,598	720
Aquaculture	254*	250*	264
Total catch	8,080	8,049	6,535

* FAO estimate.

Source: FAO, *Yearbook of Fishery Statistics*.

Mining*

	1998	1999	2000
Crude petroleum ('000 metric tons)	102,471	93,532	99,087
Natural gas (million cubic feet)	391,334	358,176	380,587

* Including an equal share of production with Saudi Arabia from the Neutral/Partitioned Zone.

Industry

SELECTED PRODUCTS ('000 metric tons, unless otherwise stated)

	1998	1999	2000
Wheat flour	155	159	162
Sulphur (by-product)*† . . .	665	675	600
Chlorine.	19	18	15
Caustic soda (Sodium hydroxide) .	22	21	19
Nitrogenous fertilizers‡ . . .	361	331	288
Motor spirit (petrol) ('000 barrels)†§	17,520	17,000*	10,000*
Kerosene and jet fuels ('000 barrels)§	51,571	57,012	45,049
Gas-diesel (Distillate fuel) oils ('000 barrels)§	91,830	97,142	83,981
Residual fuel oils ('000 barrels)§	71,591	73,598	57,116
Petroleum bitumen (asphalt)*§	252	297	331
Liquefied petroleum gas§ . . .	3,124	3,228	2,997
Quicklime*†	40	40	40
Cement	2,310	947	n.a.
Electric energy (million kWh)§ .	29,988	31,576	32,323

* Provisional or estimated figure(s).

† Source: US Geological Survey.

‡ Production in terms of nitrogen.

§ Including an equal share of production with Saudi Arabia from the Neutral/Partitioned Zone.

Finance

CURRENCY AND EXCHANGE RATES

Monetary Units

1,000 fils = 10 dirhams = 1 Kuwaiti dinar (KD).

Sterling, Dollar and Euro Equivalents (31 May 2002)

£1 sterling = 446.26 fils;

US $1 = 304.26 fils;

€1 = 285.61 fils;

100 Kuwaiti dinars = £224.09 = $328.67 = €350.13.

Average Exchange Rate (US $ per KD)

1999   3.2850

2000   3.2600

2001   3.2620

GENERAL BUDGET (KD million, year ending 30 June)

Revenue	1999/2000*	2000/01*†	2001/02*‡
Tax revenue	98.8	72.9	110.4
International trade and transactions	75.9	58.6	81.4
Non-tax revenue	5,142.3	4,892.5	3,721.1
Oil revenue	4,794.4	4,528.0	3,236.3
Total operating revenue of government enterprises . .	270.3	222.1	337.0
Total	5,241.1	4,965.4	3,831.5

Expenditure	1998/99	1999/2000*	2000/01*†
Current expenditure . . .	2,692.8	2,773.2	2,248.8
Defence, security and justice .	887.9	921.2	733.7
Education	381.4	408.5	331.5
Health	265.7	257.2	203.0
Social and labour affairs . .	103.5	106.1	84.0
Electricity and water . . .	169.8	202.6	251.0
Communications . . .	74.5	65.0	52.5
Capital expenditure . . .	28.6	24.7	23.9
Development expenditure. . .	376.6	313.6	214.4
Public works . . .	73.2	76.0	66.9
Electricity and water . . .	238.7	187.5	103.3
Transfers to attached and public institutions	942.2	898.5	701.8
Total	**4,040.2**	**4,010.0**	**3,188.1**

* Approved budget figures.
† From 2001 the fiscal year was to end on 31 March, instead of 30 June. Consequently the budget for 2000/01 was for a nine-month period, from 1 July 2000 to 31 March 2001.
‡ Projections.
2001/02 (projection, KD million, year ending 31 March): Total expenditure 5,274.0.
2002/03 (projections, KD million, year ending 31 March): Total revenue 3,536 (oil revenue 2,984); Total expenditure 5,430.

INTERNATIONAL RESERVES (US $ million at 31 December)

	1999	2000	2001
Gold*	104.2	103.9	103.2
IMF special drawing rights . .	73.8	90.9	108.0
Reserve position in IMF . .	505.5	487.0	598.3
Foreign exchange . . .	4,244.4	6,504.4	9,191.1
Total	**4,927.9**	**7,186.3**	**10,000.6**

* National valuation of gold reserves (2,539,000 troy ounces in each year).
Source: IMF, *International Financial Statistics*.

MONEY SUPPLY (KD million at 31 December)

	1999	2000	2001
Currency outside banks . . .	442.9	416.6	401.2
Demand deposits at deposit money banks	928.5	1,051.1	1,240.2
Total money	**1,371.4**	**1,467.7**	**1,641.4**

Source: IMF, *International Financial Statistics*.

COST OF LIVING (Consumer Price Index; base: 1980 = 100)

	1999	2000	2001
Food	171.6	172.9	171.9
Beverages and tobacco . . .	299.9	305.8	311.8
Clothing and footwear . . .	263.7	259.4	268.7
Housing services	200.4	204.3	206.6
All items (incl. others) . .	205.5	209.2	211.7

NATIONAL ACCOUNTS (KD million at current prices)
Expenditure on the Gross Domestic Product

	1999	2000	2001
Government final consumption expenditure	2,463	2,485	2,646
Private final consumption expenditure	4,490	4,633	4,801
Increase in stocks . . . } Gross fixed capital formation . }	1,335	827	866
Total domestic expenditure .	**8,288**	**7,945**	**8,313**
Exports of goods and services . .	4,212	6,534	5,506
Less Imports of goods and services	3,616	3,488	3,762
GDP in purchasers' values . .	**8,884**	**10,991**	**10,057**

Source: IMF, *International Financial Statistics*.

Gross Domestic Product by Economic Activity

	1999*	2000†	2001†
Agriculture, hunting, forestry and fishing	39.2	41.1	38.9
Mining and quarrying . . .	3,328.6	5,543.1	4,587.2
Manufacturing	1,015.6	801.3	666.7
Electricity, gas and water. . .	−47.2	−101.9	−106.2
Construction.	239.6	242.5	245.3
Trade, restaurants and hotels. .	692.5	676.7	695.6
Transport, storage and communications	451.3	506.4	507.7
Finance, insurance, real estate and business services . .	1,247.8	1,326.8	1,364.3
Community, social and personal services	2,278.3	2,363.4	2,467.9
Sub-total	**9,245.7**	**11,399.4**	**10,467.4**
Import duties . . . . } *Less* Imputed bank service charges }	−361.7	−408.4	−410.4
GDP in purchasers' values . .	**8,884.0**	**10,991.0**	**10,057.0**

* Revised figures.   † Provisional figures.

BALANCE OF PAYMENTS (US $ million)

	1999	2000	2001
Exports of goods f.o.b. . . .	12,276	19,478	16,173
Imports of goods f.o.b. . . .	−6,708	−6,451	−6,932
Trade balance	**5,568**	**13,027**	**9,241**
Exports of services . . .	1,560	1,822	1,788
Imports of services . . .	−5,171	−4,923	−5,340
Balance on goods and services.	**1,958**	**9,926**	**5,689**
Other income received . . .	6,094	7,315	5,483
Other income paid . . .	−985	−616	−525
Balance on goods, services and income	**7,066**	**16,626**	**10,647**
Current transfers received . .	99	85	52
Current transfers paid . . .	−2,102	−2,041	−2,133
Current balance . . .	**5,062**	**14,670**	**8,566**
Capital account (net) . . .	703	2,217	2,933
Direct investment abroad . .	−23	303	−323
Direct investment from abroad .	72	16	−39
Portfolio investment assets . .	−2,638	−12,923	−7,375
Portfolio investment liabilities .	79	254	−78
Other investment assets . .	−3,512	−1,108	431
Other investment liabilities . .	315	150	1,347
Net errors and omissions . .	859	−1,311	−2,554
Overall balance . . .	**918**	**2,268**	**2,906**

Source: IMF, *International Financial Statistics*.

External Trade

PRINCIPAL COMMODITIES (distribution by SITC, KD million)

Imports c.i.f.	1997	1998	1999
Food and live animals	342.4	356.3	345.6
Vegetables and fruit	78.1	88.9	83.8
Chemicals and related products	209.2	203.5	201.0
Basic manufactures	503.0	480.6	378.2
Textile yarn, fabrics, etc.	80.0	75.0	63.2
Non-metallic mineral manufactures	93.5	92.8	80.2
Iron and steel	128.5	133.2	77.4
Machinery and transport equipment	964.7	1,081.9	920.4
Power-generating machinery and equipment, etc.	124.0	114.8	78.3
Machinery specialized for particular industries	109.0	104.1	107.6
General industrial machinery, equipment and parts	103.0	100.6	97.3
Telecommunications and sound equipment	69.4	78.8	85.5
Other electrical machinery, apparatus, etc.	107.7	96.2	91.0
Road vehicles and parts	384.7	421.0	372.6
Passenger motor cars (excl. buses)	244.4	254.8	223.6
Other transport equipment and parts	17.4	115.1	38.4
Miscellaneous manufactured articles	352.9	359.6	325.0
Clothing and accessories (excl. footwear)	106.0	113.4	100.3
Total (incl. others)	2,501.6	2,626.2	2,318.3

2000 (KD million): Food and live animals 349.0; Chemicals and related products 207.9; Basic manufactures 395.2; Machinery and transport equipment 820.1; Miscellaneous manufactured articles 304.3; Total (incl. others) 2,195.4.

Exports f.o.b.	1998	1999	2000
Mineral fuels, lubricants, etc.	2,598.0	3,356.8	5,581.3
Petroleum, petroleum products, etc.*	2,581.8	3,356.4	5,578.3
Chemicals and related products	180.2	213.7	255.0
Total (incl. others)*	2,911.6	3,702.8	5,962.7

2001 (KD million): Total imports c.i.f. 2,370.9; Total exports f.o.b. 4,948.4* (Petroleum, petroleum products, etc. 4,590.8*).

* Estimate(s) by the Central Bank of Kuwait.

PRINCIPAL TRADING PARTNERS (KD million)*

Imports c.i.f.	1998	1999	2000
Australia	58.4	74.6	64.9
Canada	42.4	47.6	52.6
China, People's Repub.	72.1	75.3	85.8
France (incl. Monaco)	97.4	86.1	70.8
Germany	183.1	178.3	178.4
India	91.8	86.8	82.8
Iran	22.1	31.5	35.3
Italy	151.9	135.2	117.1
Japan	356.8	296.7	214.1
Korea, Repub.	71.8	55.3	87.4
Malaysia	31.3	31.3	32.6
Netherlands	50.5	44.4	39.9
Saudi Arabia	163.2	143.6	154.4
South Africa	26.7	16.0	8.6
Spain	36.0	35.7	36.6
Switzerland-Liechtenstein	53.1	43.3	37.0
Taiwan	34.6	29.4	26.7
Thailand	29.2	29.9	27.4
Turkey	38.4	36.6	35.5
United Arab Emirates	56.5	73.2	79.5
United Kingdom	153.2	132.5	123.3
USA	404.9	284.8	239.3
Total (incl. others)	2,626.2	2,318.3	2,195.4

Exports f.o.b.†	1998	1999	2000
Bahrain	5.1	6.2	6.8
Belgium-Luxembourg	15.7	15.9	9.9
Canada	3.5	0.4	0.2
China, People's Repub.	15.9	15.8	23.3
Egypt	17.0	8.5	11.8
India	23.5	31.2	26.8
Indonesia	2.1	13.5	30.9
Iran	2.7	3.3	4.5
Italy	1.0	4.1	3.3
Japan	4.5	4.0	5.7
Jordan	6.4	7.6	7.7
Lebanon	3.6	4.5	5.1
Malaysia	4.1	3.1	2.9
Oman	4.3	6.1	5.4
Pakistan	13.6	14.7	18.4
Philippines	7.4	7.9	7.0
Qatar	5.4	5.2	7.5
Saudi Arabia	38.7	41.6	46.7
Singapore	39.4	26.3	8.0
Switzerland	2.3	4.6	0.1
Syria	6.3	6.0	8.0
Taiwan	5.8	4.2	4.3
Turkey	5.6	3.5	4.9
United Arab Emirates	30.6	33.9	27.7
USA	7.1	16.6	14.3
Total (incl. others)	329.8	362.7	386.6

* Imports by country of production; exports by country of last consignment.
† Excluding petroleum exports.

Transport

ROAD TRAFFIC (motor vehicles in use at 31 December)

	1995	1996	1997
Passenger cars	662,946	701,172	747,042
Buses and coaches	11,937	12,322	13,094
Goods vehicles	116,813	121,753	127,386

1999: Buses and coaches 12,775; Goods vehicles 97,706.
2000: Buses and coaches 10,974; Goods vehicles 80,378.

SHIPPING

Merchant Fleet (registered at 31 December)

	1999	2000	2001
Number of vessels	202	205	200
Displacement ('000 grt)	2,456.5	2,415.3	2,291.7

Source: Lloyd's Register-Fairplay, *World Fleet Statistics*.

International Sea-borne Freight Traffic ('000 metric tons)*

	1988	1989	1990
Goods loaded	61,778	69,097	51,400
Goods unloaded	7,123	7,015	4,522

* Including Kuwait's share of traffic in the Neutral/Partitioned Zone.

Source: UN, *Monthly Bulletin of Statistics.*

Goods loaded ('000 metric tons): 89,945 in 1997.

Goods unloaded ('000 metric tons): 746 in 1991 (July–December only); 2,537 in 1992; 4,228 in 1993; 5,120 in 1994; 5,854 in 1995; 6,497 in 1996; 6,049 in 1997.

CIVIL AVIATION (traffic on scheduled services)

	1996	1997	1998
Kilometres flown (million) . .	43	43	45
Passengers carried ('000) . .	2,133	2,114	2,190
Passenger-km (million) . .	6,073	5,997	6,207
Total ton-km (million) . .	929	912	932

Source: UN, *Statistical Yearbook.*

Tourism

VISITOR ARRIVALS BY COUNTRY OF ORIGIN
(incl. excursionists)

	1998	1999	2000
Bahrain	43,692	49,658	50,024
Bangladesh	76,934	79,731	54,466
Egypt	227,127	226,262	219,553
India	215,087	226,629	225,642
Iran	80,716	93,801	100,328
Lebanon	45,817	48,001	48,642
Pakistan	74,601	78,206	74,429
Philippines	38,696	37,357	43,310
Saudi Arabia	524,873	574,924	641,691
Sri Lanka	60,506	54,816	54,804
Syria	142,850	146,084	143,020
Total (incl. others) . . .	1,762,641	1,883,633	1,944,233

Tourism receipts (US $ million): 207 in 1998; 243 in 1999.

Source: World Tourism Organization, *Yearbook of Tourism Statistics.*

Communications Media

	1999	2000	2001
Television receivers ('000 in use)	910	930	n.a.
Telephones ('000 main lines in use)	455.6	467.1	472.4
Facsimile machines ('000 in use)	60	n.a.	n.a.
Mobile cellular telephones ('000 subscribers)	300.0	476.0	489.2
Personal computers ('000 in use)	230	250	260
Internet users ('000)	100	150	200

1992: Book titles published (government only) 196.
1996: Daily newspapers 8 (average circulation 635,000 copies); Non-daily newspapers 78.
1997: Radio receivers 1,175,000 in use.

Sources: UNESCO, *Statistical Yearbook*; UN, *Statistical Yearbook*; International Telecommunication Union.

Education

(state-controlled schools, 2000/01)

	Schools	Teachers	Students Males	Students Females	Students Total
Kindergarten . .	153	3,379	22,142	22,128	44,270
Primary . . .	184	8,151	48,796	49,322	98,118
Intermediate . .	165	9,073	47,955	47,509	95,464
Secondary . .	117	9,234	34,868	41,353	76,221
Religious institutes	7	351	n.a.	n.a.	2,454
Special training institutes . .	33	756	n.a.	n.a.	543

Private education (1996/97): 63 kindergarten schools (598 teachers, 12,172 students); 80 primary schools (2,341 teachers, 47,111 students); 82 intermediate schools (1,860 teachers, 36,254 students); 66 secondary schools (1,576 teachers, 20,932 students).

2000/01 (private education): 112 schools; 7,324 teachers; 128,204 students.

Adult literacy rate (UNESCO estimates): 82.0% (males 84.0%; females 79.7%) in 2000 (Source: UNDP, *Human Development Report*).

Directory

The Constitution

The principal provisions of the Constitution, promulgated on 16 November 1962, are set out below. On 29 August 1976 the Amir suspended four articles of the Constitution dealing with the National Assembly, the Majlis al-Umma. On 24 August 1980 the Amir issued a decree ordering the establishment of an elected legislature before the end of February 1981. The new Majlis was elected on 23 February 1981, and fresh legislative elections followed on 20 February 1985. The Majlis was dissolved by Amiri decree in July 1986, and some sections of the Constitution, including the stipulation that new elections should be held within two months of dissolving the legislature (see below), were suspended. A new Majlis was elected on 5 October 1992 and convened on 20 October.

SOVEREIGNTY

Kuwait is an independent sovereign Arab State; its sovereignty may not be surrendered, and no part of its territory may be relinquished. Offensive war is prohibited by the Constitution.

Succession as Amir is restricted to heirs of the late MUBARAK AS-SABAH, and an Heir Apparent must be appointed within one year of the accession of a new Amir.

EXECUTIVE AUTHORITY

Executive power is vested in the Amir, who exercises it through the Council of Ministers. The Amir will appoint the Prime Minister 'after the traditional consultations', and will appoint and dismiss ministers on the recommendation of the Prime Minister. Ministers need not be members of the Majlis al-Umma, although all ministers who are not members of parliament assume membership *ex officio* in the legislature for the duration of office. The Amir also formulates laws, which shall not be effective unless published in the *Official Gazette*. The Amir establishes public institutions. All decrees issued in these respects shall be conveyed to the Majlis. No law is issued unless it is approved by the Majlis.

LEGISLATURE

A National Assembly, the Majlis al-Umma, of 50 members will be elected for a four-year term by all natural-born Kuwaiti males over the age of 21 years, except servicemen and police, who may not vote. Candidates for election must possess the franchise, be over 30 years of age and literate. The Majlis will convene for at least eight months in any year, and new elections shall be held within two months of the last dissolution of the outgoing legislature.

Restrictions on the commercial activities of ministers include an injunction forbidding them to sell property to the Government.

The Amir may ask for reconsideration of a bill that has been approved by the Majlis and sent to him for ratification, but the bill would automatically become law if it were subsequently adopted by a two-thirds' majority at the next sitting, or by a simple majority at a subsequent sitting. The Amir may declare martial law, but only with the approval of the legislature.

The Majlis may adopt a vote of 'no confidence' in a minister, in which case the minister must resign. Such a vote is not permissible in the case of the Prime Minister, but the legislature may approach the Amir on the matter, and the Amir shall then either dismiss the Prime Minister or dissolve the Majlis.

CIVIL SERVICE

Entry to the civil service is confined to Kuwaiti citizens.

PUBLIC LIBERTIES

Kuwaitis are equal before the law in prestige, rights and duties. Individual freedom is guaranteed. No one shall be seized, arrested or exiled except within the rules of law.

No punishment shall be administered except for an act or abstaining from an act considered a crime in accordance with a law applicable at the time of committing it, and no penalty shall be imposed more severe than that which could have been imposed at the time of committing the crime.

Freedom of opinion is guaranteed to everyone, and each has the right to express himself through speech, writing or other means within the limits of the law.

The press is free within the limits of the law, and it should not be suppressed except in accordance with the dictates of law.

Freedom of performing religious rites is protected by the State according to prevailing customs, provided it does not violate the public order and morality.

Trade unions will be permitted and property must be respected. An owner is not banned from managing his property except within the boundaries of law. No property should be taken from anyone, except within the prerogatives of law, unless a just compensation be given.

Houses may not be entered, except in cases provided by law. Every Kuwaiti has freedom of movement and choice of place of residence within the State. This right shall not be controlled except in cases stipulated by law.

Every person has the right to education and freedom to choose his type of work. Freedom to form peaceful societies is guaranteed within the limits of law.

The Government

HEAD OF STATE

Amir of Kuwait: His Highness Sheikh JABER AL-AHMAD AS-SABAH (acceded 31 December 1977).

COUNCIL OF MINISTERS
(September 2002)

Crown Prince and Prime Minister: Sheikh SAAD AL-ABDULLAH AS-SALIM AS-SABAH.

First Deputy Prime Minister and Minister of Foreign Affairs: Sheikh SABAH AL-AHMAD AL-JABER AS-SABAH.

Deputy Prime Minister and Minister of Defence: Sheikh JABER MUBARAK AL-HAMAD AS-SABAH.

Deputy Prime Minister and Minister of the Interior: Sheikh MUHAMMAD KHALID AL-HAMAD AS-SABAH.

Deputy Prime Minister, Minister of State for Cabinet Affairs and for National Assembly Affairs: MUHAMMAD DHAIFALLAH SHARAR.

Minister of Communications: Sheikh AHMAD ABDULLAH AL-AHMAD AS-SABAH.

Minister of Justice and of Awqaf (Religious Endowments) and Islamic Affairs: AHMAD YA'QUB BAQIR AL-ABDULLAH.

Minister of Information and Acting Minister of Oil: Sheikh AHMAD AL-FAHD AL-AHMAD AS-SABAH.

Minister of State for Foreign Affairs: Sheikh MUHAMMAD SABAH AS-SALIM AS-SABAH.

Minister of Electricity and Water and Minister of Labour and Social Affairs: TALAL MUBARAK AL-AYYAR.

Minister of Commerce and Industry: SALEH ABD AR-REDA KHOR-SHED.

Minister of Public Works and Minister of State for Housing Affairs: FAHD DUWAYSAN AL-MAI'A.

Minister of Finance, of Planning and Minister of State for Administrative Development Affairs: Dr YOUSUF HAMAD AL-IBRAHIM.

Minister of Health: MUHAMMAD AHMAD AL-JARALLAH.

Minister of Education and Higher Education: Dr MUSAAD RASHID AL-HAROUN.

PROVINCIAL GOVERNORS

Al-Ahmadi: Sheikh ALI ABDULLAH AS-SALIM AS-SABAH.

Farwaniya: Dr IBRAHIM DUAIJ AL-IBRAHIM AS-SABAH.

Great Mubarak: MUBARAK HUMUD AL-JABER AS-SABAH.

Hawalli: IBRAHIM JASEM AL-MUDHAF.

Al-Jahra: ALI JABER AL-AHMAD AS-SABAH.

Kuwait (Capital): Dr DAUD MUSAED AS-SALIH.

MINISTRIES

Ministry of Awqaf (Religious Endowments) and Islamic Affairs: POB 13, 13001 Safat, Kuwait City; tel. 2466300; fax 2449943; internet www.awkaf.net.

Ministry of Commerce and Industry: POB 2944, 13030 Safat, Kuwait City; tel. 2463600; fax 2424411.

Ministry of Communications: POB 318, 13004 Safat, Kuwait City; tel. 4819033; fax 4847058; e-mail webmaster@moc.gulfsat.com; internet www.moc.gulfsat.com.

Ministry of Defence: POB 1170, 13012 Safat, Kuwait City; tel. 4819277; fax 4846059.

Ministry of Education: POB 7, 13001 Safat, Hilali St, Kuwait City; tel. 4836800; fax 2423676; e-mail webmaster@moe.edu.kw; internet www.moe.edu.kw.

Ministry of Electricity and Water: POB 12, 13001 Safat, Kuwait City; tel. 4896000; fax 4897484.

Ministry of Finance: POB 9, 13001 Safat, al-Morkab St, Ministries Complex, Kuwait City; tel. 2468200; fax 2404025; e-mail webmaster @mof.gov.kw; internet www.mof.gov.kw.

Ministry of Foreign Affairs: POB 3, 13001 Safat, Gulf St, Kuwait City; tel. 2425141; fax 2430559; e-mail info@mofa.org; internet www.mofa.gov.kw.

Ministry of Health: POB 5, 13001 Safat, Arabian Gulf St, Kuwait City; tel. 4877422; fax 4865414.

Ministry of Higher Education: POB 27130, 13132 Safat, Kuwait City; tel. 2401300; fax 2456319.

Ministry of Information: POB 193, 13002 Safat, as-Sour St, Kuwait City; tel. 2415300; fax 2419642; e-mail info@moinfo.gov.kw; internet www.moinfo.gov.kw.

Ministry of the Interior: POB 11, 13001 Safat, Kuwait City; tel. 2524199; fax 2561268.

Ministry of Justice: POB 6, 13001 Safat, al-Morkab St, Ministries Complex, Kuwait City; tel. 2467300; fax 2466957; e-mail qht@moj.gov.kw; internet www.moj.gov.kw.

Ministry of Labour and Social Affairs: POB 563, 13006 Safat, Kuwait City; tel. 2464500; fax 2419877.

Ministry of Oil: POB 5077, 13051 Safat, Fahd as-Salem St, Kuwait City; tel. 2415201; fax 2417088.

Ministry of Planning: POB 15, 13001 Safat, Kuwait City; tel. 2428100; fax 2414734; e-mail info@mop.gov.kw; internet www.mop .gov.kw.

Ministry of Public Works: POB 8, 13001 Safat, Kuwait City; tel. 5385520; fax 5380829.

Legislature

MAJLIS AL-UMMA
(National Assembly)

Speaker: JASEM AL-KHARAFI.

Elections to the 50-seat Majlis took place on 3 July 1999: 20 seats were secured by Islamist candidates, 14 were won by liberals, 12 by pro-Government candidates and four by independents.

Political Organizations

Political parties are not permitted in Kuwait. However, several quasi-political organizations are in existence. Among those that have been represented in the Majlis since 1992 are:

Constitutional Group: supported by merchants.

Islamic Constitutional Movement: Sunni Muslim; moderate.

Kuwait Democratic Forum: internet www.kuwaitdf.org/df; f. 1991; secular; liberal.

National Democratic Rally (NDR): f. 1997; secular; liberal; Sec.-Gen. Dr AHMAD BISHARA.

National Islamic Coalition: Shi'a Muslim.

Salafeen (Islamic Popular Movement): Sunni Muslim.

Diplomatic Representation

EMBASSIES IN KUWAIT

Afghanistan: POB 33186, Rawdah, Surra, Block 6, Surra St, House 16, Kuwait City; tel. 5329461; fax 5326274; e-mail afg_emb_kuw@hotmail.com; Chargé d'affaires: Dr Nasser Ahmad Noor.

Algeria: POB 578, 13006 Safat, Istiqlal St, Kuwait City; tel. 2519987; fax 2563052; Ambassador: Muhammad Buruba.

Argentina: POB 1125, 45712 Surra, Kuwait City; tel. 5323014; fax 5323053; e-mail embargkuwait@hotmail.com; Chargé d'affaires a.i. Armando Mauricio Becher.

Austria: POB 15013, Daiya, 35451 Kuwait City; tel. 2552532; fax 2563052; e-mail austremb@mail.qualitynet.net; Ambassador: Roland Hauser.

Bahrain: POB 196, 13002 Safat, Area 6, Surra Rd, Villa 35, Kuwait City; tel. 5318530; fax 5330882; e-mail 61116@kems.net; Ambassador: Abd ar-Rahman M. al-Fadhel.

Bangladesh: POB 22344, 13084 Safat, Khaldya, Block 6, Ali bin Abi Taleb St, House 361, Kuwait City; tel. 5316042; fax 5316041; e-mail bdoot@ncc.moc.kw; internet www.bdsociety.com/embassy; Ambassador: Aminul Hossain Sarker.

Belgium: POB 3280, 13033 Safat, Salmiya, Baghdad St, House 15, Kuwait City; tel. 5722014; fax 5748389; Ambassador: Philippe-Henri Arcq.

Bhutan: POB 1510, 13016 Safat, Jabriya, Block 9, St 20, Villa 7, Kuwait City; tel. 5331506; fax 5338959; e-mail bhutankuwait@hotmail.com; Ambassador: Tshering Wangdi.

Bosnia and Herzegovina: POB 6131, 32036 Hawalli, Kuwait City; tel. 5392637; fax 5392106; Ambassador: Edhem Pasić.

Brazil: POB 39761, 73058 Nuzha, Block 2, St 1, Jadah 1, Villa 8, Kuwait City; tel. 5328610; fax 5328613; e-mail brasemb @ncc.moc.kw; Ambassador: (vacant).

Bulgaria: POB 12090, 71651 Shamiya, Jabriya, Block 11, St 107, Kuwait City; tel. 5314459; fax 5321453; e-mail bgembkw@qualitynet.net; Ambassador: Angel N. Manchev.

Canada: POB 25281, 13113 Safat, Diiya, Block 4, 24 al-Motawakell St, Villa 24, Kuwait City; tel. 2563025; fax 2563023; e-mail kwait@dfait-maeci.gc.ca; Ambassador: Richard Mann.

China, People's Republic: POB 2346, 13024 Safat, Dasmah, Sheikh Ahmad al-Jaber Bldgs 4 & 5, Kuwait City; tel. 5333340; fax 5333341; Ambassador: Zeng Xuyong.

Czech Republic: POB 1151, 13012 Safat, Kuwait City; tel. 2529018; fax 2529021; e-mail kuwait@embassy.mzv; internet www.mzv.cz/kuwait; Chargé d'affaires a.i.: Dr Petr Korbel.

Egypt: POB 11252, 35153 Dasmah, Istiqlal St, Kuwait City; tel. 2519955; fax 2553877; Ambassador: Mahmoud Wajdi Abu Zeid.

Eritrea: POB 53016, 73015 Nuzha, Jabriya, Block 9, St 21, House 9, Kuwait City; tel. 5317426; fax 5317429; Ambassador: Mousa Yassien Sheikh ad-Din.

Ethiopia: POB 939, Surra, 45710 Safat, Kuwait City; tel. 5334276; fax 5331179; Ambassador: Razene Araya.

Finland: POB 26699, 13127 Safat, Surra, Block 4, St 1, Villa 8, Kuwait City; tel. 5312890; fax 5324198; Ambassador: Markku Nii-nioja.

France: POB 1037, 13011 Safat, Mansouriah, Block 1, St 13, No. 24, Kuwait City; tel. 2571061; fax 2571058; Ambassador: Patrice Paoli.

Germany: POB 805, 13009 Safat, Dahiya Abdullah as-Salem, Plot 1, St 14, Villa 13, Kuwait City; tel. 2520857; fax 2520763; e-mail 113061.3166@compuserve.com; Ambassador: Werner Krebs.

Greece: POB 23812, 13099 Safat, Khaldiya, Block 4, St 44, House 4, Kuwait City; tel. 4817101; fax 4817103; Ambassador: Rocanas Charalambos.

Hungary: POB 23955, 13100 Safat, Qortuba, Area 2, Al-Baha'a bin Zuheir St 776, Kuwait City; tel. 5323901; fax 5323904; e-mail huembkwi@q8online.com; Ambassador: Jenő Földesi.

India: POB 1450, 13015 Safat, 34 Istiqlal St, Kuwait City; tel. 2530600; fax 2525811; e-mail indemb@ncc.moc.kw; Ambassador: B. M. C. Myer.

Indonesia: POB 21560, 13076 Safat, Keifan, Block 5, As-Sebhani St, House 21, Kuwait City; tel. 4839927; fax 4819250; e-mail batik@ncc.moc.kw; Ambassador: D. Soesjono.

Iran: POB 4686, 13047 Safat, Daiyah, Embassies Area, Block B, Kuwait City; tel. 2560694; fax 2529868; Ambassador: Ali Jannati.

Italy: POB 4453, 13045 Safat, Shuwaikh 'B', Block 5, Villa 1, Kuwait City; tel. 4817400; fax 4817244; e-mail ambkuwa@ncc.moc.kw; Ambassador: Francesco Capece Galeota.

Japan: POB 2304, 13024 Safat, Jabriya, Area 9, Plot 496, Kuwait City; tel. 5312870; fax 5326168; Ambassador: Shigeru Tsumori.

Jordan: POB 15314, 35305 Diiya, Istiqlal St, Embassies Area, Kuwait City; tel. 2533500; Ambassador: Muhammad al-Quraan.

Korea, Republic: POB 20771, 13068 Safat, Rawda, Block 1, St 10, House 17, Kuwait City; tel. 2554206; fax 2526874; Ambassador: Choi Jo-Young.

Lebanon: POB 253, 13003 Safat, 31 Istiqlal St, Kuwait City; tel. 2562103; fax 2571682; Ambassador: Khaled al-Kilani.

Libya: POB 21460, 13075 Safat, 27 Istiqlal St, Kuwait City; tel. 2562103; fax 2571682; Chargé d'affaires: Idris Dahmani Bu Dib.

Malaysia: POB 4105, 13042 Safat, Surra Block 1, Tariq bin Ziad St, Villa 286, Kuwait City; tel. 5342091; fax 5341783; e-mail mwkuwait@qualitynet.net; Ambassador: Ismail bin Mustapha.

Morocco: POB 784, 13008 Safat, Jabriya, Block 12, Villa 24, St 101, Kuwait City; tel. 4813912; fax 4814156; Ambassador: Driss Kettani.

Netherlands: POB 21822, 13079 Safat, Jabriya, Area 9, St 1, Plot 40A, Kuwait City; tel. 5312650; fax 5326334; e-mail kwe@min buza.nl; Ambassador: Henk Revis.

Niger: POB 44451, 32059 Hawalli, Salwa, Block 12, St 6, Villa 183, Kuwait City; tel. 5652943; fax 5640478; Ambassador: Amadou Seyni.

Nigeria: POB 6432, 32039 Hawalli, Surra, Area 1, St 14, House 25, Kuwait City; tel. 5320794; fax 5320834; Ambassador: Muhammad Adamu Jumba.

Oman: POB 21975, 13080 Safat, Istiqlal St, Villa 3, Kuwait City; tel. 2561962; fax 2561963; Ambassador: Nasser bin Khalsan al-Kharossi.

Pakistan: POB 988, 13010 Safat, Jabriya, Plot 5, Block 11, Villa 7, Kuwait City; tel. 5327649; fax 5327648; Ambassador: Mushtaq Mehr.

Philippines: POB 26288, 13123 Safat, Jabriya, Police Station St, Area 10, House 363, Kuwait City; tel. 5329316; fax 5329319; e-mail phembkt@ncc.moc.kw; Ambassador: Sukarno D. Tanggol.

Poland: POB 5066, 13051 Safat, Jabriya, Plot 8, St 20, House 377, Kuwait City; tel. 5311571; fax 5311576; e-mail polamba@qualitynet.net; Ambassador: Wojciech Bożek.

Qatar: POB 1825, 13019 Safat, Diiyah, Istiqlal St, Kuwait City; tel. 2513606; fax 2513604; Ambassador: Muhammad Ali al-Ansari.

Romania: 13574 Khaitan, Kuwait City; tel. 4843419; fax 4848929; e-mail ambsaat@ncc.moc.kw; Ambassador: Patra Popescu.

Russia: POB 1765, 13018 Safat, Rawdah, Kuwait City; tel. 2560427; fax 2524969; Ambassador: Vladimir Shishov.

Saudi Arabia: POB 20498, 13065 Safat, Istiqlal St, Kuwait City; tel. 2400250; fax 2426541; Ambassador: Ahmad al-Hamad al-Yahya.

Senegal: POB 23892, 13099 Safat, Rawdah, Parcel 3, St 35, House 9, Kuwait City; tel. 2510823; fax 2542044; e-mail senegal_embassy@yahoo.com; Ambassador: Abdou Lahad Mbacke.

Somalia: POB 22766, 13088 Safat, Bayan, St 4, Block 4, Villa 4, Kuwait City; tel. 5394795; fax 5394829; e-mail som.emb@usa.net; Ambassador: Abdul Khadir Amin Abubaker.

South Africa: POB 2262, 40173 Mishref, Kuwait City; tel. 5617988; fax 5617917; e-mail saemb@southafrica.com; internet www.south africaq8.com; Chargé d'affaires: M. N. Slabber.

Spain: POB 22207, 13083 Safat, Surra, Block 3, St 14, Villa 19, Kuwait City; tel. 5325827; fax 5325826; Ambassador: José Luis Roselló.

Sri Lanka: POB 13212, 71952 Keifan, House 381, St 9, Block 5, Salwa; tel. 5612261; fax 5612264; e-mail lankemb@kuwait.net; Ambassador: Darsin Serasinghe.

Sweden: POB 21448, 13075 Safat, Faiha, Area 7, ash-Shahba St, Kuwait City; tel. 2523588; fax 2572157; Ambassador: Thomas Ganslandt.

Switzerland: POB 23954, 13100 Safat, Qortuba, Block 2, St 1, Villa 122, Kuwait City; tel. 5340175; fax 5340176; e-mail vertretung @kow.rep.admin.ch; Ambassador: Jean-Philippe Tissières.

Syria: POB 25600, 13116 Safat, Kuwait City; tel. 5396560; fax 5396509; Ambassador: Mustafa Haj Ali.

Thailand: POB 66647, 43757 Bayan, Surra, Area 3, Block 49, Ali bin Abi-Taleb St, Bldg No. 28, Kuwait City; tel. 5317531; fax 5317532; e-mail thaiemk@ncc.moc.kw; Ambassador: (vacant).

Tunisia: POB 5976, 13060 Safat, Nuzha, Plot 2, Nuzha St, Villa 45, Kuwait City; tel. 2542144; fax 2528995; e-mail tunemrku@ncc.moc.kw; Ambassador: Muhammad Saad.

Turkey: POB 20627, 13067 Safat, Block 16, Plot 10, Istiqlal St, Kuwait City; tel. 2531785; fax 2560653; e-mail trkemb@ncc.moc.kw; internet www.turkish-embassy.org.kw; Ambassador: Ahmet Ertay.

United Arab Emirates: POB 1828, 13019 Safat, Plot 70, Istiqlal St, Kuwait City; tel. 2528544; fax 2526382; Ambassador: Yousuf A. al-Ansari.

United Kingdom: POB 2, 13001 Safat, Arabian Gulf St, Kuwait City; tel. 2403336; fax 2426799; e-mail general@britishembassy-kuwait.org; internet www.britishembassy-kuwait.org; Ambassador: Richard Muir.

USA: POB 77, 13001 Safat, Bayan, Al-Masjeed Al-Aqsa St, Block 6, Plot 14, Kuwait City; tel. 5395307; fax 5380282; e-mail uskuwait@qualitynet.net; internet www.usembassy.gov.kw; Ambassador: RICHARD H. JONES.

Venezuela: POB 24440, 13105 Safat, Block 5, St 7, Area 356, Surra, Kuwait City; tel. 5324367; fax 5324368; Chargé d'affaires: ALBERTO ARMAS.

Yugoslavia: POB 20511, 13066 Safat, Jabriya, Block 7, St 12, Plot 382, Kuwait City; tel. 5327548; fax 5327568; e-mail yuembkuw@qualitynet.net; Ambassador: ZORAN VEJNOVIĆ.

Zimbabwe: POB 36484, 24755 Salmiya, Kuwait City; tel. 5621517; fax 5621491; e-mail ZimKuwait@hotmail.com; Ambassador: S. C. CHIKETA.

Judicial System

SPECIAL JUDICIARY

Constitutional Court: Comprises five judges. Interprets the provisions of the Constitution; considers disputes regarding the constitutionality of legislation, decrees and rules; has jurisdiction in challenges relating to the election of members, or eligibility for election, to the Majlis al-Umma.

ORDINARY JUDICIARY

Court of Cassation: Comprises five judges. Is competent to consider the legality of verdicts of the Court of Appeal and State Security Court. Chief Justice: MUHAMMAD YOUSUF AR-RIFA'I.

Court of Appeal: Comprises three judges. Considers verdicts of the Court of First Instance. Chief Justice: RASHED AL-HAMMAD.

Court of First Instance: Comprises the following divisions: Civil and Commercial (one judge), Personal Status Affairs (one judge), Lease (three judges), Labour (one judge), Crime (three judges), Administrative Disputes (three judges), Appeal (three judges), Challenged Misdemeanours (three judges). Chief Justice: MUHAMMAD AS-SAKHOBY.

Summary Courts: Each governorate has a Summary Court, comprising one or more divisions. The courts have jurisdiction in the following areas: Civil and Commercial, Urgent Cases, Lease, Misdemeanours. The verdict in each case is delivered by one judge.

There is also a **Traffic Court**, with one presiding judge.

Attorney-General: MUHAMMAD ABD AL-HAIH AL-BANNAIY.

Advocate-General: HAMED AL-UTHMAN.

Religion

ISLAM

The majority of Kuwaitis are Muslims of the Sunni or Shi'a sects. The Shi'ite community comprises about 30% of the total.

CHRISTIANITY
The Roman Catholic Church

Latin Rite

For ecclesiastical purposes, Kuwait forms an Apostolic Vicariate. At 31 December 2000 there were an estimated 153,000 adherents in the country.

Vicar Apostolic: Mgr FRANCIS ADEODATUS MICALLEF (Titular Bishop of Tinisa in Proconsulari), Bishop's House, POB 266, 13003 Safat, Kuwait City; tel. 2431561; fax 2409981.

Melkite Rite

The Greek-Melkite Patriarch of Antioch is resident in Damascus, Syria. The Patriarchal Exarchate of Kuwait had an estimated 700 adherents at 31 December 1999.

Exarch Patriarchal: Archimandrite BASILIOS KANAKRY, Vicariat Patriarcal Greek-Melkite, POB 1205, Salwa Block 12, St No. 6, House 58, 22013 Salmiya, Kuwait City; tel. 5652802.

Syrian Rite

The Syrian Catholic Patriarch of Antioch is resident in Beirut, Lebanon. The Patriarchal Exarchate of Basra and Kuwait, with an estimated 1,200 adherents at 31 December 2000, is based in Basra, Iraq.

The Anglican Communion

Within the Episcopal Church in Jerusalem and the Middle East, Kuwait forms part of the diocese of Cyprus and the Gulf. The Anglican congregation in Kuwait is entirely expatriate. The Bishop in Cyprus and the Gulf is resident in Cyprus, while the Archdeacon in the Gulf is resident in Qatar.

Other Christian Churches

National Evangelical Church in Kuwait: Rev. NABIL ATTALLAH, pastor of the Arabic-language congregation, Rev. JERRY A. ZANDSTRA, senior pastor of the English-speaking congregation, POB 80, 13001 Safat, Kuwait City; tel. 2407195; fax 2431087; e-mail elc@ncc.moc.kw; an independent Protestant Church founded by the Reformed Church in America; services in Arabic, English, Korean, Malayalam and other Indian languages; combined weekly congregation of some 20,000.

The Armenian, Greek, Coptic and Syrian Orthodox Churches are also represented in Kuwait.

The Press

Freedom of the press and publishing is guaranteed in the Constitution, although press censorship was in force between mid-1986 and early 1992 (when journalists adopted a voluntary code of practice); in February 1995 a ruling by the Constitutional Court effectively endorsed the Government's right to suspend publication of newspapers (see History). The Government provides financial support to newspapers and magazines. In 1999 there were eight daily and 20 weekly newspapers, and 196 periodicals.

DAILIES

Al-Anbaa (The News): POB 23915, 13100 Safat, Kuwait City; tel. 4831168; fax 4837914; f. 1976; Arabic; general; Editor-in-Chief BIBI KHALID AL-MARZOOQ; circ. 85,000.

Arab Times: POB 2270, 13023 Safat, Kuwait City; tel. 4813566; fax 4833628; f. 1977; English; political and financial; no Friday edition; Editor-in-Chief AHMAD ABD AL-AZIZ AL-JARALLAH; Man. Editor MISHAL AL-JARALLAH; circ. 41,922.

Kuwait Times: POB 1301, 13014 Safat, Kuwait City; tel. 4833199; fax 4835621; e-mail info@kuwaittimes.net; internet www.kuwait times.net; f. 1961; (weekend edition also published); English, Malayalam and Urdu; political; Owner and Editor-in-Chief YOUSUF ALYYAN; Gen. Man. BADRYA DARWISH; circ. 32,000.

Al-Qabas (Firebrand): POB 21800, 13078 Safat, Kuwait City; tel. 4812822; fax 4834355; e-mail alqabas@ncc.moc.kw; internet www.moc.kw/alqabas; f. 1972; Arabic; independent; Gen. Man. FOUZAN AL-FARES; Editor-in-Chief WALEED ABD AL-LATIF AN-NISF; circ. 60,000.

Ar-Ra'i al-'Aam (Public Opinion): POB 761, 13008 Safat, Kuwait City; tel. 4817777; fax 4838352; f. 1961; Arabic; political, social and cultural; Editor-in-Chief YOUSUF AL-JALAHMA; circ. 101,500.

As-Seyassah (Policy): POB 2270, Shuwaikh, Kuwait City; tel. 4816326; fax 4833628; e-mail alsyasah@qualitynet.net; f. 1965; Arabic; political and financial; Editor-in-Chief AHMAD ABD AL-AZIZ AL-JARALLAH; circ. 70,000.

Al-Watan (The Homeland): POB 1142, 13012 Safat, Kuwait City; tel. 4840950; fax 4818481; e-mail webmaster@alwatan.com.kw; internet www.alwatan.com.kw; f. 1962; Arabic; political; Editor-in-Chief MUHAMMAD ABD AL-QADER AL-JASEM; Gen. Man. YOUSUF BIN JASEM; circ. 91,726.

WEEKLIES AND PERIODICALS

Al-Balagh (Communiqué): POB 4558, 13046 Safat, Kuwait City; tel. 4818606; fax 4819008; f. 1969; weekly; Arabic; general, political and Islamic; Editor-in-Chief ABD AR-RAHMAN RASHID AL-WALAYATI; circ. 29,000.

Ad-Dakhiliya (The Interior): POB 71655, 12500 Shamiah, Kuwait City; tel. 2410091; fax 2410609; e-mail moipr@qualitynet.net; monthly; Arabic; official reports, transactions and proceedings; publ. by Public Relations Dept, Ministry of the Interior; Editor-in-Chief Lt-Col AHMED A. ASH-SHARQAWI.

Al-Hadaf (The Objective): POB 2270, 13023 Safat, Kuwait City; tel. 4813566; fax 4833628; f. 1964; weekly; Arabic; social and cultural; Editor-in-Chief AHMAD ABD AL-AZIZ AL-JARALLAH; circ. 268,904.

Hayatuna (Our Life): POB 26733, 13128 Safat, Kuwait City; tel. 2530120; fax 2530736; f. 1968; fortnightly; Arabic; medicine and hygiene; publ. by Al-Awadi Press Corpn; Editor-in-Chief ABD AR-RAHMAN AL-AWADI; circ. 6,000.

Al-Iqtisadi al-Kuwaiti (Kuwaiti Economist): POB 775, 13008 Safat, Kuwait City; tel. 805580; fax 2412927; e-mail kcci@kcci.org.kw; internet www.kcci.org.kw; f. 1960; monthly; Arabic; commerce, trade and economics; publ. by Kuwait Chamber of Commerce and Industry; Editor MAJED JAMAL AD-DIN; circ. 6,000.

Journal of the Gulf and Arabian Peninsula Studies: POB 17073, 72451 Khaldiya, Kuwait University, Kuwait City; tel. 4833215; fax 4833705; e-mail jotgaaps@kuc01.kuniv.edu.kw; f. 1974;

quarterly; Arabic; English; Editor-in-Chief Prof. AMAL YOUSUF AL-ADBAI AS-SABAH.

Al-Khaleej Business Magazine: POB 25725, 13118 Safat, Kuwait City; tel. 2433765; e-mail aljabriya@gulfweb.com; Editor-in-Chief AHMAD ISMAIL BEHBEHANI.

Kuwait al-Youm (Kuwait Today): POB 193, 13002 Safat, Kuwait City; tel. 4842167; fax 4831044; f. 1954; weekly; Arabic; statistics, Amiri decrees, laws, govt announcements, decisions, invitations for tenders, etc.; publ. by the Ministry of Information; circ. 5,000.

Al-Kuwaiti (The Kuwaiti): Information Dept, POB 9758, 61008 Ahmadi, Kuwait City; tel. 3989111; fax 3983661; e-mail kocinfo@kockw.com; f. 1961; monthly journal of the Kuwait Oil Co; Arabic; Editor-in-Chief ALI H. MURAD; circ. 6,500.

The Kuwaiti Digest: Information Dept, POB 9758, 61008 Ahmadi, Kuwait City; tel. 3980651; fax 3983661; e-mail kocinfo@kockw.com; f. 1972; quarterly journal of Kuwait Oil Co; English; Editor-in-Chief RA'AD SALEM AL-JANDAL; circ. 7,000.

Kuwait Medical Journal (KMJ): POB 1202, 13013 Safat, Kuwait City; tel. 5317972; fax 5312630; e-mail kmj@kma.org.kw; internet www.kma.org.kw/kmj; f. 1967; quarterly; English; case reports, articles, reviews; Editor-in-Chief Dr NAEL AN-NAQEEB; circ. 10,000.

Al-Majaless (Meetings): POB 5605, 13057 Safat, Kuwait City; tel. 4841178; fax 4847126; weekly; Arabic; current affairs; Editor-in-Chief (vacant); circ. 60,206.

Mejallat al-Kuwait (Kuwait Magazine): POB 193, 13002 Safat, Kuwait City; tel. 2415300; fax 2419642; f. 1961; monthly; Arabic; illustrated magazine; science, arts and literature; publ. by Ministry of Information.

Mirat al-Umma (Mirror of the Nation): POB 1142, 13012 Safat, Kuwait City; tel. 4837212; fax 4838671; weekly; Arabic; Editor-in-Chief MUHAMMAD AL-JASSEM; circ. 79,500.

An-Nahdha (The Renaissance): POB 695, 13007 Safat, Kuwait City; tel. 4813133; fax 4849298; f. 1967; weekly; Arabic; social and political; Editor-in-Chief THAMER AS-SALAH; circ. 170,000.

Osrati (My Family): POB 2995, 13030 Safat, Kuwait City; tel. 4813233; fax 4838933; f. 1978; weekly; Arabic; women's magazine; publ. by Fahad al-Marzouk Establishment; Editor GHANIMA F. AL-MARZOUK; circ. 10,500.

Sawt al-Khaleej (Voice of the Gulf): POB 659, Safat, Kuwait City; tel. 4815590; fax 4839261; f. 1962; politics and literature; Arabic; Editor-in-Chief CHRISTINE KHRAIBET; Owner BAKER ALI KHRAIBET; circ. 20,000.

At-Talia (The Ascendant): POB 1082, 13011 Safat, Kuwait City; tel. 4831200; fax 4840471; f. 1962; weekly; Arabic; politics and literature; Editor AHMAD YOUSUF AN-NAFISI; circ. 10,000.

Al-Yaqza (The Awakening): POB 6000, 13060 Safat, Kuwait City; tel. 4831318; fax 4840630; f. 1966; weekly; Arabic; political, economic, social and general; Editor-in-Chief AHMAD YOUSUF BEHBEHANI; circ. 91,340.

Az-Zamed: POB 42181, 13150 Safat, Kuwait City; tel. 4848279; fax 4819985; f. 1961; weekly; Arabic; political, social and cultural; Editor SHAWQI RAFA'E.

NEWS AGENCIES

Kuwait News Agency (KUNA): POB 24063, 13101 Safat, Kuwait City; tel. 4834546; fax 4813424; e-mail kuna@kuna.net.kw; internet www.kuna.net.kw; f. 1976; public corporate body; independent; also publishes research digests on topics of common and special interest; Chair. and Dir-Gen. MUHAMMAD AL-AJEERI.

Foreign Bureaux

Informatsionnoye Telegrafnoye Agentstvo Rossii—Telegrafnoye Agentstvo Suverennykh Stran (ITAR—TASS) (Russia): POB 1765, 13018 Safat, Kuwait City; tel. and fax 5639260; Correspondent CONSTANTINE MATHULSKI.

Middle East News Agency (MENA) (Egypt): POB 1927, Safat, Fahd as-Salem St, Kuwait City; Dir REDA SOLIMAN.

Reuters Middle East Ltd (UK): POB 5616, 13057 Safat, Mubarak al-Kabir St, Kuwait Stock Exchange Bldg, 4th Floor, Kuwait City; tel. 2431920; fax 2460340; internet www.reuters.com/gulf; Country Man. ISSAM MAKKI.

Xinhua (New China) News Agency (People's Republic of China): POB 22168, Safat, Sheikh Ahmad al-Jaber Bldg, 10 Dasman St, Kuwait City; tel. 4809423; fax 4809396; Correspondent HUANG JIANMING.

AFP (France), Agence Arabe Syrienne d'Information, Anatolian News Agency (Turkey), AP (USA), dpa (Germany), JANA (Libya), QNA (Qatar) and RIA—Novosti (Russia) are also represented.

PRESS ASSOCIATION

Kuwait Journalist Association: POB 5454, Safat, Kuwait City; tel. 4843351; fax 4842874; Chair. YOUSUF ALYYAN.

Publishers

Al-Abraj Translation and Publishing Co WLL: POB 26177, 13122 Safat, Kuwait City; tel. 2444665; fax 2436889; Man. Dir Dr TARIQ ABDULLAH.

Dar as-Seyassah Publishing, Printing and Distribution Co: POB 2270, 13023 Safat, Kuwait City; tel. 4813566; fax 4833628; internet www.contactkuwait.com/dar-alseyasa; publ. *Arab Times*, *As-Seyassah* and *Al-Hadaf*.

Gulf Centre Publishing and Publicity: POB 2722, 13028 Safat, Kuwait City; tel. 2402760; fax 2458833; Propr HAMZA ISMAIL ESSLAH.

Kuwait Publishing House: POB 29126, 13150 Safat, Kuwait City; tel. 2417810; Dir ESAM AS'AD ABU AL-FARAJ.

Kuwait United Advertising, Publishing and Distribution Co WLL: POB 29359, 13154 Safat, Kuwait City; tel. 4817747; fax 4817757.

At-Talia Printing and Publishing Co: POB 1082, Airport Rd, Shuwaikh, 13011 Safat, Kuwait City; tel. 4840470; fax 4815611; Man. AHMAD YOUSUF AN-NAFISI.

Government Publishing House

Ministry of Information: POB 193, 13002 Safat, as-Sour St, Kuwait City; tel. 2433038; fax 2434715; e-mail info@moinfo.gov.kw; internet www.moinfo.gov.kw.

Broadcasting and Communications

TELECOMMUNICATIONS

Plans to privatize the state telecommunications sector, and to reorganize the Ministry of Communications as a company, designated the Kuwaiti Communications Corporation, initiated in 1998, were completed by 2000, although their implementation was subject to political approval.

Mobile Telecommunications Co (MTC): POB 22244, 1308 Safat, Kuwait City; tel. 4842000; fax 4837755; e-mail mtcweb@mtc.com.kw; internet www.mtc.com.kw; f. 1983; Chair. and Man. Dir SALMAN YOUSUF AR-ROUMI.

National Mobile Telecommunications Co KSC (Wataniya Telecom): POB 613, 13007 Safat, Kuwait City; tel. 2435500; fax 2436600; f. 1998; internet www.wataniya.com; Chair. and Man. Dir SALAH FAHED AS-SULTAN; CEO and Gen. Man. DAVID MURRAY.

BROADCASTING
Radio

Radio of the State of Kuwait: POB 397, 13004 Safat, Kuwait City; tel. 2423774; fax 2456660; e-mail radiokuwait@radiokuwait.org; internet www.radiokuwait.org; f. 1951; broadcasts for 70 hours daily in Arabic, Farsi, English and Urdu, some in stereo; Dir of Radio Dr ABD AL-AZIZ ALI MANSOUR; Dir of Radio Programmes ABD AR-RAHMAN HADI.

Television

Kuwait Television: POB 193, 13002 Safat, Kuwait City; tel. 2413501; fax 2438403; internet www.moinfo.gov.kw/KTV/index.html; f. 1961 (transmission began privately in Kuwait in 1957); transmits in Arabic; colour television service began in 1973; has a total of five channels; Head of News Broadcasting MUHAMMAD AL-KAHTANI.

Plans were announced in early 1998 for the establishment of a private satellite broadcasting television channel, with administrative offices in Kuwait and transmission facilities in Dubai, United Arab Emirates.

Finance

(cap. = capital; res = reserves; dep. = deposits; m. = million; brs = branches; amounts in Kuwaiti dinars unless otherwise stated)

BANKING
Central Bank

Central Bank of Kuwait: POB 526, 13006 Safat, Abdullah as-Salem St, Kuwait City; tel. 2449200; fax 2464887; e-mail cbk@cbk.gov.kw; internet www.cbk.gov.kw; f. 1969; cap. 5m., res

230.2m., dep. 1,643.1m. (March 2001); Governor Sheikh SALEM ABD AL-AZIZ SA'UD AS-SABAH.

National Banks

Al-Ahli Bank of Kuwait KSC: POB 1387, 13014 Safat, Ahmad al-Jaber St, Safat Sq., Kuwait City; tel. 2400900; fax 2424557; e-mail headoffice@abkuwait.com; f. 1967; wholly owned by private Kuwaiti interests; cap. 87.9m., res 71.3m., dep. 999.7m. (Dec. 2001); Chair. MORAD YOUSUF BEHBEHANI; Gen. Man. and CEO ERVIN B. KNOX; 13 brs.

Bank of Bahrain and Kuwait: POB 24396, 13104 Safat, Ahmad al-Jaber St, Kuwait City; tel. 2417140; fax 2440937; e-mail bbk@batelco.com.bh; internet www.bbkonline.com; f. 1977; owned equally by the Govts of Bahrain and Kuwait; cap. BD56.9m., res BD34.2m., dep. BD896.3m. (Dec. 1999); Chair. HASSAN KHALIFA AL-JALAHMA; Gen. Man. and CEO MURAD ALI MURAD.

Bank of Kuwait and the Middle East KSC: POB 71, 13001 Safat, Joint Banking Centre, East Tower, Darwazat Abd ar-Razzak, Kuwait City; tel. 2459771; fax 2461430; e-mail bkmekw@qualitynet.net; internet www.bkme.com; f. 1971; 49% state-owned; cap. 70.4m., res 51.1m., dep. 855.2m. (Dec. 2000); Chair. MUSTAFA JASIM ASH-SHEMALI; Gen. Man. PHILIP ANTHONY HALPIN; 14 brs.

Burgan Bank SAK: POB 5389, 12170 Safat, Ahmad al-Jaber St, Kuwait City; tel. 2439000; fax 2461148; e-mail mainbr@burgan.com.kw; internet www.burgan.com; f. 1975; cap. 78.1m., res 100.6m., dep. 1,226.8m. (Dec. 2001); Chair. and Man. Dir ABD AL-AZIZ IBRAHIM AN-NABHAN; Chief Gen. Man. ROD GOOM; 15 brs.

Commercial Bank of Kuwait SAK: POB 2861, 13029 Safat, Mubarak al-Kabir St, Kuwait City; tel. 2411001; fax 2450150; e-mail cbkinq@banktijari.com; internet www.cbk.com; f. 1960 by Amiri decree; cap. 106.4m., res 120.9m., dep. 1,314.2m. (Dec. 2001); Chair. and Man. Dir Sheikh MUHAMMAD JARRAH AS-SABAH; Gen. Man. (acting) and CEO JAMAL AL-MUTAWA; 28 brs.

Gulf Bank KSC: POB 3200, 13032 Safat, Mubarak al-Kabir St, Kuwait City; tel. 2449501; fax 2445212; e-mail customerservice@gulfbank.com.kw; internet www.gulfbank.com.kw; f. 1960; cap. 82.1m., res 122.0m., dep. 1,611.5m. (Dec. 2001); Chair. and Man. Dir BASSAM Y. ALGHANIM; 26 brs.

Industrial Bank of Kuwait KSC: POB 3146, 13032 Safat, Joint Banking Centre, Commercial Area 9, Kuwait City; tel. 2457661; fax 2462057; e-mail em.ibk@ncc.moc.kw; internet www.ibkuwt.com; 31.4% state-owned; f. 1973; cap. 20.0m., res 105.4m., dep. 130.5m. (Dec. 2000); Chair. and Man. Dir SALEH MUHAMMAD AL-YOUSUF.

Kuwait Finance House KSC (KFH): POB 24989, 13110 Safat, Abdullah al-Mubarak St, Kuwait City; tel. 2445050; fax 2455135; e-mail kfh@kfh.com.kw; internet www.kfh.com; f. 1977; Islamic banking and investment company; 45% state-owned; cap. 65.0m., res 174.8m., dep. 1,857.1m. (Dec. 2001); Chair. and Man. Dir BADER ABD AL-MOHSEN AL-MUKHAISEEM; Gen. Man. JASSAR D. AL-JASSAR; 26 brs.

Kuwait Real Estate Bank KSC: POB 22822, 13089 Safat, West Tower—Joint Banking Centre, Darwazat Abd ar-Razzak, Kuwait City; tel. 2458177; fax 2462516; e-mail kreb@yahoo.com; internet www.akaribank.com; f. 1973; wholly owned by private Kuwaiti interests; cap. 43.5m., res 57.2m., dep. 471.1m. (Dec. 2001); Chair. ESSA MUHAMMAD AL-MAZIDI; Man. Dir WALID SALEH AL-QATTAN; 2 brs.

National Bank of Kuwait SAK (NBK): POB 95, 13001 Safat, Abdullah al-Ahmad St, Kuwait City; tel. 2422011; fax 2431888; e-mail webmaster@nbk.com; internet www.nbk.com; f. 1952; cap. 147.4m., res 231.4m., dep. 3,834.9m. (Dec. 2001); Chair. MUHAMMAD ABD AR-RAHMAN AL-BAHAR; CEO IBRAHIM S. DABDOUB; 41 brs in Kuwait, 14 abroad.

Savings and Credit Bank: POB 1454, 13015 Safat, ash-Shuhada St, Kuwait City; tel. 2411301; f. 1965; auth. cap. 2,500m.; Chair. and Gen. Man. Dr JASEM M. AD-DABBOUS.

INSURANCE

Al-Ahleia Insurance Co SAK: POB 1602, Ahmad al-Jaber St, 13017 Safat, Kuwait City; tel. 2448870; fax 2430308; f. 1962; all forms of insurance; cap. 11.7m.; Chair. and Man. Dir SULAYMAN HAMAD AD-DALALI; Gen. Man. TALAL SAKIR AL-QATAMI.

Al-Ittihad al-Watani Insurance Co for the Near East SAL: POB 781, 13008 Safat, Kuwait City; tel. 4843988; fax 4847244; Man. JOSEPH ZACCOUR.

Arab Commercial Enterprises WLL (Kuwait): POB 2474, 13025 Safat, Kuwait City; tel. 2425995; fax 2409450; e-mail acekwt@ace-ins.com; f. 1952.

Gulf Insurance Co KSC: POB 1040, 13011 Safat, Kuwait City; tel. 2423384; fax 2422320; f. 1962; cap. 11.3m.; all forms of insurance; Chair. FAISAL HAMAD AL-AYYAR.

Kuwait Insurance Co SAK (KIC): POB 769, 13008 Safat, Abdullah as-Salem St, Kuwait City; tel. 2420135; fax 2428530; e-

mail kins@ncc.moc.kw; f. 1960; cap. US $64.6m.; all life and non-life insurance; Chair. MUHAMMAD SALEH BEHBEHANI; Gen. Man. ALI HAMAD AL-BAHAR.

Kuwait Reinsurance Company: POB 21929, Munther Tower, Salhiya, 13080 Safat, Kuwait City; tel. 2432011; fax 2427823; e-mail kuwaitre@qualitynet.net; f. 1972; cap. 10.0m.; Gen. Man. AMIR AL-MUHANNA.

Kuwait Technical Insurance Office: POB 25349, 13114 Safat, Kuwait City; tel. 2413986; fax 2413986.

Mohd Saleh Behbehani & Co: POB 370, 13004 Safat, Kuwait City; tel. 2412085; fax 2412089.

New India Assurance Co: POB 370, 13004 Safat, Kuwait City; tel. 2412085; fax 2412089.

The Northern Insurance Co Ltd: POB 579, 13006 Safat, Kuwait City; tel. 2427930; fax 2462739.

The Oriental Insurance Co Ltd: POB 22431, 13085 Safat, Kuwait City; tel. 2424016; fax 2424017; Man. JUGAL KISHORE MADAAN.

Sumitomo Marine & Fire Insurance Co (Kuwait Agency): POB 3458, 13055 Safat, Kuwait City; tel. 2433087; fax 2430853.

Warba Insurance Co SAK: POB 24282, 13103 Safat, Kuwait City; tel. 2445140; fax 2466131; internet www.kuwait.net/~warba; f. 1976; Chair. ABDULLAH HASSAN JARALLAH; 1 br.

Some 20 Arab and other foreign insurance companies are active in Kuwait.

STOCK EXCHANGE

Kuwait Stock Exchange: POB 22235, 13083 Safat, Mubarak al-Kabir St, Kuwait City; tel. 2423130; fax 2429771; e-mail borse@qualitynet.net; internet www.kuwaitse.com; f. 1984; 88 companies and four mutual funds listed in January 2002; Dir-Gen. ABDULLAH AS-SEDERAWY.

Markets Association

Kuwait Financial Markets Association (KFMA): POB 25228, 13113 Safat, Kuwait City; internet www.kfma.org.kw; f. 1977; represents treasury, financial and capital markets and their members; Pres. THUNAYAN AL-GHANIM; Sec.-Gen. ZUHAIR AL-JUMA.

Trade and Industry

GOVERNMENT AGENCY

Kuwait Investment Authority (KIA): POB 64, 13001 Safat, Kuwait City, tel. 2439595; fax 2454059; e-mail webmaster@kia.gov.kw; internet www.kia.gov.kw; oversees the Kuwait Investment Office (London); responsible for the Kuwaiti General Reserve; Chair. Minister of Finance; Man. Dir SALEH MUBARAK AL-FALAH.

DEVELOPMENT ORGANIZATIONS

Arab Planning Institute (API): POB 5834, 13059 Safat, Kuwait City; tel. 4843130; fax 4842935; e-mail api@api.org.kw; f. 1966; 50 mems; publishes annual directory, *Journal of Development and Economic Policies* and proceedings of seminars and discussion group meetings, offers research, training programmes and advisory services; Dir ESSA ALGHAZALI.

Industrial Investments Company (IIC): POB 26019, 13121 Safat, Kuwait City; tel. 2429073; fax 2448850; f. 1983; invests directly in industry; partly owned by the Kuwait Investment Authority; privatization initiated in April 1996; Man. Dir TALEB A. ALI.

Kuwait Fund for Arab Economic Development (KFAED): POB 2921, 13030 Safat, cnr Mubarak al-Kabir St and al-Hilali St, Kuwait City; tel. 2468800; fax 2436289; e-mail info@kuwait-fund.org; internet www.kuwait-fund.org; f. 1961; cap. KD 2,000m.; state-owned; provides and administers financial and technical assistance to the countries of the developing world; Chair. Minister of Finance; Dir-Gen. BADER M. AL-HUMAIDHI.

Kuwait International Investment Co SAK (KIIC): POB 22792, 13088 Safat, as-Salhiya Commercial Complex, Kuwait City; tel. 2438273; fax 2454931; 30% state-owned; cap. p.u. 31.9m., total assets KD 146.9m. (1988); domestic real estate and share markets; Chair. and Man. Dir JASEM MUHAMMAD AL-BAHAR.

Kuwait Investment Co SAK (KIC): POB 1005, 13011 Safat, 5th Floor, al-Manakh Bldg, Mubarak al-Kabir St, Kuwait City; tel. 2438111; fax 2444896; e-mail info@kic.com.kw; f. 1981; 88% state-owned, 12% owned by private Kuwaiti interests; total resources KD 50.1m. (1996); international banking and investment; Chair. and Man. Dir BADER A. AR-RUSHAID AL-BADER.

Kuwait Planning Board: c/o Ministry of Planning, POB 21688, 13122 Safat, Kuwait City; tel. 2428200; fax 2414734; f. 1962; supervises long-term development plans; through its Central Statistical Office publishes information on Kuwait's economic activity; Dir-Gen. AHMAD ALI AD-DUAIJ.

National Industries Co SAK (NIC): POB 417, 13005 Safat, Kuwait City; tel. 4815466; fax 4839582; f. 1960; 22.7% owned by KIA; cap. p.u. KD 34.9m.; has controlling interest in various construction enterprises; privatization initiated in March 1995; Chair. and Man. Dir SAUD M. AL-OSMANI.

Shuaiba Area Authority SAA: POB 4690, 13047 Safat, Kuwait City; POB 10033, Shuaiba; tel. 3260903; f. 1964; an independent governmental authority to supervise and run the industrial area and Port of Shuaiba; has powers and duties to develop the area and its industries which include an oil refinery, cement factory, fishing plant, power stations and distillation plants, chemical fertilizer and petrochemical industries, sanitary ware factory, asbestos plant and sand lime bricks plant; Dir-Gen. SULAYMAN K. AL-HAMAD.

CHAMBER OF COMMERCE

Kuwait Chamber of Commerce and Industry: POB 775, 13008 Safat, Chamber's Bldg, ash-Shuhada St, Kuwait City; tel. 805580; fax 2404110; e-mail kcci@kcci.org.kw; internet www.kcci.org.kw; f. 1959; 50,000 mems; Chair. ABD AR-RAZZAK KHALID ZAID AL-KHALID; Dir-Gen. AHMAD RASHED AL-HAROUN.

STATE HYDROCARBONS COMPANIES

Kuwait Petroleum Corpn (KPC): POB 26565, 13126 Safat, as-Salhiya Commercial Complex, Fahed as-Salem St, Kuwait City; tel. 2455455; fax 2467159; e-mail webmaster@kpc.com.kw; internet www.kpc.com.kw; f. 1980; co-ordinating organization to manage the petroleum industry; controls Kuwait Aviation Fuelling Co (KAFCO), Kuwait Foreign Petroleum Exploration Co (KUFPEC), Kuwait National Petroleum Co (KNPC), Kuwait Oil Co (KOC), Kuwait Oil Tanker Co (KOTC), Kuwait Petroleum International Ltd (KPI), Petrochemical Industries Co (PIC), Santa Fe International Corpn (SFIC); Chair. Minister of Oil; Deputy Chair. and CEO NADER HAMAD SULTAN.

> **Kuwait Aviation Fuelling Co KSC:** POB 1654, 13017 Safat, Kuwait City; tel. 4330482; fax 4330475; Gen. Man. ABD AL-AZIZ AS-SERRI.

> **Kuwait Foreign Petroleum Exploration Co KSC (KUFPEC):** POB 5291, 13053 Safat, Kuwait City; tel. 2421677; fax 2420405; f. 1981; state-owned; overseas oil and gas exploration and development; Chair. and Man. Dir BADER AL-KHASHTI.

> **Kuwait National Petroleum Co KSC (KNPC):** POB 70, 13001 Safat, Ali as-Salem St, Kuwait City; tel. 2420121; fax 2433839; f. 1960; oil refining, production of liquefied petroleum gas, and domestic marketing and distribution of petroleum by-products; output of 855,000 b/d of refined petroleum in 1996/97; Chair. and Man. Dir HANI ABD AL-AZIZ HUSSEIN.

> **Kuwait Oil Co KSC (KOC):** POB 9758, 61008 Ahmadi; tel. 3989111; fax 3983661; e-mail kocinfo@kockw.com; internet www.kockw.com; f. 1934; state-owned; Chair. and Man. Dir AHMAD AL-ARBEED.

> **Kuwait Petroleum International Ltd (Q8) (KPI):** POB 1819, 13019 Safat, Chamber of Commerce and Industry Bldg, Al-Murgab, Mubarak al-Kabir St, Kuwait City; tel. 2404087; fax 2407523; internet www.q8.com; marketing division of KPC; controls 6,500 petrol retail stations in Europe, and European refineries with capacity of 235,000 b/d; Pres. KAMEL HARAMI.

UTILITIES

In 1998 there were plans to create regulatory bodies for each of Kuwait's utilities, with a view to facilitating their privatization.

Ministry of Electricity and Water: (see Ministries, above); provides subsidized services throughout Kuwait.

MAJOR COMPANIES

Aerated Concrete Industries Co KSC (ACICO): POB 24079, 13101 Safat, Kuwait City; tel. 2422100; fax 2422103; f. 1990; sales KD 5.0m. (1998); state-owned; production of concrete; Chair. and Man. Dir GHASSAN AL-KHALID.

Alghanim Industries: POB 24172, 13102 Safat, Kuwait City; tel. 4842988; fax 4847244; e-mail busidev@alghanim.com; internet www.alghanim.com; f. 1930; trading, contracting, manufacturing, shipping, travel and financial services; Chair. KUTAYBA YOUSUF ALGHANIM; Man. Dir C. BEN ROUSE; 4,000 employees.

Boubyan Petrochemical Co KSC: POB 2383, Safat, 13024 Kuwait City; tel. 2446686; fax 2414100; e-mail boubyan@boubyan.com; internet www.boubyan.com; f. 1995; cap. KD 40.0m. (2001); manufacture, import and distribution of petrochemical products; Chair. MARZOUK A. AL-GHANIM; Gen. Man. MUHAMMAD A. AL-BAHAR; 220 employees.

Contracting and Marine Services Co KSC: POB 22853, 13089 Safat, Kuwait City; tel. 2410270; fax 2442602; f. 1973; cap. KD 7.5m. (1997), sales KD 7.3m. (2000); marine construction works and services; Chair. and Man. Dir HISHAM SULAIMAN AL-OTAIBI.

Al-Fujaira Cement Industries Co: POB 23111, 13092 Safat, Kuwait City; tel. 2412815; fax 2418559; f. 1979; cap. KD 22.7m., sales KD 13.7m. (1998); cement production; Chair. Sheikh HAMAD BIN SAIF ASH-SHARQI; Gen. Man. NASER ALI KHAMAS; 240 employees.

Gulf Cable and Electrical Industries Co KSC: POB 1196, 13012 Safat, Kuwait City; tel. 4676546; fax 4675305; e-mail gceico@qualitynet.net; f. 1975; cap. KD 6.2m., sales KD 19.1m. (1999); manufacture of cables and electrical equipment; Chair. and Gen. Man. ABD AL-MOHSIN IBRAHIM AL-FARES; 296 employees.

Independent Petroleum Group SAK: POB 24027, 13101 Safat, Kuwait City; tel. 5312840; fax 5339858; e-mail general@ipg.com.kw; f. 1976; cap. KD 10.9m., sales KD 228.9m. (2000); industrial, commercial and consulting role in hydrocarbons industry; Chair. KHALAF AHMAD AL-KHALAF; Man. Dir WALID J. HADID.

Kuwait Aluminium Co KSC: POB 5335, 13054 Safat, ar-Rai Industrial Area, Plot 1636, St No. 13, Kuwait City; tel. 4734600; fax 4734419; e-mail kuwaital@kuwait.net; f. 1968; sales about KD 1.5m.; cap. p.u. KD 4m.; design, manufacture, erection and maintenance of aluminium and glass works for construction industry; Chair. NASSER NAKI; 190 employees.

Kuwait Cement Co KSC: POB 20581, 13066 Safat, Safat New Exhibition Bldg, 1st Floor, as-Sour St, Salhiya, Kuwait City; tel. 2401700; fax 2432956; e-mail alcement@kuwait-cement.com; internet www.kuwait-cement.com; f. 1968; 28% govt-owned; manufacture and marketing of cement; cap. KD 37.7m.; sales KD 17.4m. (2000); Chair. ABD AL-MOHSIN ABD AL-AZIZ AR-RASHID; Gen. Man. KHALED ABD AR-RAZZAK REZOOQI; 409 employees.

Kuwait Food Co (Americana) SAK: POB 5087, 13051 Safat, Safat Shuwaikh and Sabhan Industrial Area, Kuwait City; tel. 4815900; fax 4815914; e-mail headoffice@americanaf.com; internet www.americana-group.com; f. 1963; cap. KD 12.4m.; sales KD 126.2m. (1998); chain of restaurants, meat industry, bakery plant for oriental sweets and English cakes; Chair. NASSER MUHAMMAD ABD AL-MOHSIN AL-KHARAFI; Gen. Man. MOATAZ AL-ALFI; 10,498 employees.

Kuwait Metal Pipes Industries Co KSC: POB 3416, 13035 Safat, Kuwait City; tel. 4675622; fax 4675897; f. 1966; cap. KD 15.2m.; sales KD 8.9m. (1998); 16.6% govt-owned; manufacture of various pipes, tanks and coatings; cap. p.u. KD 15.2m.; Chair. AHMAD YOUSUF M. AR-ROUDAN; 250 employees.

Kuwait Portland Cement Co KSC: POB 42191, 70652 Shuwaikh, Kuwait City; tel. 4835615; fax 4846152; f. 1976; cap. KD 7.2m., sales KD 18.0m. (1998); imports, exports and trades in construction materials; Chair. ABED ALI BAHMAN; 122 employees.

Kuwait Prefabricated Building Co SAK: POB 5132, 13052 Safat, Kuwait City; tel. 4733055; fax 4749908; f. 1964; sales KD 2.1m. (1996); cap. p.u. KD 6.5m.; design and manufacture of pre-cast structures, pre-stressed hollowcore slabs, claddings, beams, welded wire mesh, terrazzo tiles, structural steel items; hot dip galvanization; Chair. and Man. Dir AHMAD MUHAMMAD SALEH AL-ADASANI; 375 employees.

Kuwait United Poultry KSC (KUPCO): POB 1236, 13013 Safat, Kuwait City; tel. 4818860; fax 4818864; f. 1974; cap. KD 11.5m., sales KD 7.6m. (1998); breeding and distribution of poultry and poultry products; Chair. AHMAD AS-SAID YACOUB AR-RIFA'AT; Gen. Man. MAHMOOD NASAR AN-NASAR; 660 employees.

Livestock Transport and Trading Co KSC: POB 23727, 13098 Safat, Kuwait City; tel. 2455700; fax 2402109; e-mail livestk@kltt.com.kw; f. 1973; cap. KD 21.7m., sales KD 36.2m. (1998); trade in livestock and livestock products; Chair. and Man. Dir FAISAL ABDULLAH AL-KHAZAM; 571 employees.

Packaging and Plastic Industries Co: POB 1148, 15462 Dasman, Kuwait City; tel. 2435841; fax 2435839; f. 1974; sales KD 6.5m. (2000); production of polypropylene woven bags for packaging fertilizers, polyethylene agricultural sheets, co-extruded flexible film packaging; Chair. Dr ABD AL-AZIZ SULTAN AL-ESSA; 200 employees.

United Fisheries of Kuwait KSC: POB 22044, 13081 Safat, Kuwait City; tel. 4833699; fax 4849612; e-mail ufk@unitedfisheries.com; internet www.ufkco.com; f. 1972; cap. KD 15.4m.; sales KD 10.9m. (1998); production, export and import of frozen fish and shrimps; Chair. GHASSAN AHMAD ABD AL-LATIF AS-SABAH; Man. ABD AR-RAZZAK AL-WAZZAN; 1,380 employees.

United Industries Co: POB 24821, 13119 Safat, Kuwait City; tel. 2423487; fax 2423486; e-mail uickwt@ncc.moc.kw; f. 1979; cap. 80.0m.; sales KD 30.8m. (1999); Chair and Man. Dir AMER THEYAB AT-TARNEEMI.

Kuwait Trade Union Federation (KTUF): POB 5185, 13052 Safat, Kuwait City; tel. 5616053; fax 5627159; e-mail ktuf@ kuwait2000.com; f. 1968; central authority to which all trade unions are affiliated.

KOC Workers Union: Kuwait City; f. 1964; Chair. HAMAD SAWYAN.

Federation of Petroleum and Petrochemical Workers: Kuwait City; f. 1965; Chair. JASEM ABD AL-WAHAB AT-TOURA.

Transport

RAILWAYS

There are no railways in Kuwait.

ROADS

Roads in the towns are metalled, and the most important are motorways or dual carriageways. There are metalled roads linking Kuwait City to Ahmadi, Mina al-Ahmadi and other centres of population in Kuwait, and to the Iraqi and Saudi Arabian borders, amounting to a total road network of 4,273 km in 1989 (280 km of motorways, 1,232 km of other major roads and 2,761 km of secondary roads). The total road network was estimated at 4,450 km in 1999.

Kuwait Public Transport Co SAK (KPTC): POB 375, 13004 Safat, Murghab, Safat Sq., Kuwait City; tel. 2469420; fax 2401265; e-mail info@kptc.com.kw; f. 1962; state-owned; provides internal bus service; regular service to Mecca, Saudi Arabia; Chair. and Man. Dir MAHMOUD A. AN-NOURI.

SHIPPING

Kuwait has three commercial seaports. The largest, Shuwaikh, situated about 3 km from Kuwait City, was built in 1960. By 1987 it comprised 21 deep-water berths, with a total length of 4 km, three shallow-water berths and three basins for small craft, each with a depth of 3.35 m. In 1988 3.6m. metric tons of cargo were imported and 133,185 tons were exported through the port. A total of 1,189 vessels passed through Shuwaikh in 1988.

Shuaiba Commercial Port, 56 km south of Kuwait City, was built in 1967 to facilitate the import of primary materials and heavy equipment, necessary for the construction of the Shuaiba Industrial Area. By 1987 the port comprised a total of 20 berths, plus two docks for small wooden boats. Four of the berths constitute a station for unloading containers. Shuaiba handled a total of 3,457,871 metric tons of dry cargo, barge cargo and containers in 1988.

Doha, the smallest port, was equipped in 1981 to receive small coastal ships carrying light goods between the Gulf states. It has 20 small berths, each 100 m long. Doha handled a total of 20,283 metric tons of dry cargo, barge cargo and containers in 1988.

The oil port at Mina al-Ahmadi, 40 km south of Kuwait City, is capable of handling the largest oil tankers afloat, and the loading of over 2m. barrels of oil per day. By 1987 the port comprised 12 tanker berths, one bitumen-carrier berth, two LPG export berths and bunkering facilities.

At 31 December 2001 Kuwait's merchant fleet numbered 200 vessels, with a total displacement of 2,291,672 grt.

Kuwait Ports Authority: POB 3874, 13039 Safat, Kuwait City; tel. 4812774; fax 4819714; f. 1977; Dir-Gen. ABD AR-RAHMAN AN-NAIBARI.

Principal Shipping Companies

Arab Maritime Petroleum Transport Co (AMPTC): POB 22525, 13086 Safat, OAPEC Bldg, Shuwaikh, Airport St, Kuwait City; tel. 4844500; fax 4842996; e-mail amptc@ncc.moc.kw; f. 1973; 7 tankers and 4 LPG carriers; sponsored by OAPEC and financed by Algeria, Bahrain, Egypt, Iraq, Kuwait, Libya, Qatar, Saudi Arabia and the UAE; Chair. Dr RAMADAN AS-SANUSSI BELHAG (Libya); Gen. Man. SULAYMAN I. AL-BASSAM.

Kuwait Maritime Transport Co KSC (KMTC): POB 25344, 13086 Safat, Nafisi and Khatrash Bldg, Jaber al-Mubarak St, Kuwait City; tel. 2449974; fax 2420513; f. 1981; Chair. FOUAD M. T. AL-GHANIM.

Kuwait Oil Tanker Co SAK (KOTC): POB 810, 13009 Safat, as-Salhiya Commercial Complex, Blocks 3, 5, 7 and 9, Kuwait City; tel. 2455455; fax 2445907; e-mail ysm@kotc.com.kw; internet www.kotc.com.kw; f. 1957; state-owned; operates 6 crude oil tankers, 16 product tankers and 6 LPG vessels; sole tanker agents for Mina al-Ahmadi, Shuaiba and Mina Abdullah and agents for other ports; LPG filling and distribution; Chair. and Man. Dir ABDULLAH HAMAD AR-ROUMI.

Kuwait Shipbuilding and Repairyard Co SAK (KSRC): POB 21998, 13080 Safat, Kuwait City; tel. 4830308; fax 4815947; e-mail mahmoud@ksrc.com.kw; internet www.ksrc.com.kw; ship repairs and engineering services, underwater services, maintenance of refi-

neries, power stations and storage tanks; maintains floating dock for vessels up to 35,000 dwt; synchrolift for vessels up to 5,000 dwt with transfer yard; seven repair jetties up to 550 m in length and floating workshop for vessels lying at anchor; Chair. and Man. MOUSA J. MARAFI; Commercial Man. MAHMOUD ASAD.

United Arab Shipping Co SAG (UASC): POB 3636, 13037 Safat, Shuwaikh, Airport Rd, Kuwait City; tel. 4843150; fax 4845388; e-mail gencom@uasc.com.kw; internet www.uasc.com.kw; f. 1976; national shipping company of six Arabian Gulf countries; services between Europe, Far East, Mediterranean ports, Japan and east coast of USA and South America, and ports of participant states on Persian (Arabian) Gulf and Red Sea; operates 24 container carriers and 27 general cargo vessels; subsidiary cos: Kuwait Shipping Agencies, Arab Transport Co (Aratrans), United Arab Chartering Ltd (United Kingdom), Middle East Container Repair Co (Dubai), Arabian Chemicals Carriers (Saudi Arabia), United Arab Agencies Inc. (USA) and United Arab Shipping Agencies Co (Saudi Arabia); Pres. and CEO ABDULLAH MAHDI AL-MAHDI.

CIVIL AVIATION

Kuwait International Airport opened in 1980, and is designed to receive up to 5.0m. passengers per year; in 2001 3.82m. arrivals and departures were recorded. The airport is undergoing a major programme of expansion, at a cost of some US $300m.

Directorate-General of Civil Aviation (DGCA): POB 17, 13001 Safat, Kuwait City; tel. 4335599; fax 4713504; e-mail isc@kuwait -airport.com.kw; internet www.kuwait-airport.com.kw; Pres. Sheikh JABER AL-MUBARAK AS-SABAH; Dir-Gen. YACOUB Y. AS-SAQER.

Kuwait Airways Corpn (KAC): POB 394, Kuwait International Airport, 13004 Safat, Kuwait City; tel. 4345555; fax 4314118; e-mail info@kuwait-airways.com; internet www.kuwait-airways.com; f. 1954; scheduled and charter passenger and cargo services to the Arabian peninsula, Asia, Africa, the USA and Europe; scheduled for privatization; Chair. and Man. Dir AHMAD FAISAL AZ-ZABIN.

Tourism

Attractions for visitors include the Kuwait Towers leisure and reservoir complex, the Entertainment City theme park, the Kuwait Zoological Garden in Omariya and the Khiran Resort tourist village near the border with Saudi Arabia, as well as extensive facilities for sailing and other water sports. In 1999 there were 20 hotels with a total of 3,222 beds for visitors.

Department of Tourism: Ministry of Information, POB 193, 13002 Safat, as-Sour St, Kuwait City; tel. 2463400; fax 2464460.

Touristic Enterprises Co (TEC): POB 23310, 13094 Safat, Kuwait City; tel. 5652775; fax 5657594; f. 1976; 92% state-owned; manages 23 tourist facilities; Chair. BADER AL-BAHAR; Vice-Chair. SHAKER AL-OTHMAN.

Defence

In August 2001 Kuwait's active armed forces numbered 15,500—a land army of 11,000 (including 1,600 foreign personnel), an air force of an estimated 2,500 and a navy of around 2,000—and there were reserve forces of 23,700. Paramilitary forces comprised a 5,000-strong national guard and a coastguard. There is a two-year period of compulsory military service (one year for university students). The defence budget for 2001 was estimated at KD 820m. Capital expenditure on defence procurement in 1992–2004 was to total some KD 3,500m.

A US force numbering 4,690 at August 2001 was stationed in Kuwait (2,600 army, 2,000 air force, 10 navy and 80 marines). The UN Iraq-Kuwait Observer Mission (UNIKOM) comprised 905 troops and 192 military observers at 31 January 2002.

Chief of Staff of Armed Forces: Gen. ALI AL-MOUMEN.

Education

In recent years a comprehensive system of kindergarten, primary, intermediate and secondary schools has been developed, and compulsory education for children between six and 14 years of age was introduced in 1966–67. However, many children spend two years prior to this in a kindergarten, and go on to complete their general education at the age of 18 years. It is government policy to provide free education to all Kuwaiti children from kindergarten stage to the University. In 2000/01 a total of 269,803 pupils attended 466 government schools (184 primary, 165 intermediate and 117 secondary). In that year a total of 128,204 pupils attended 112 private schools. Education was allocated KD 332m. in the Government's 2000/2001 budget, or 10.4% of total expenditure.

Primary education lasts four years, after which the pupils move on to an intermediate school for another four years. Secondary education, which is optional and lasts four more years, is given mainly in general schools. There are also commercial institutes, a Faculty of Technological Studies, a health institute, religious institutes (with intermediate and secondary stages) and 11 institutes for handicapped children. In 1996 enrolment at primary schools included 62% of children in the relevant age-group (males 62%; females 61%), while at secondary schools the rate included 61% of children in the relevant age-group (males 62%, females 61%).

Two-year courses at post-secondary teacher training institutes provide teachers for kindergartens and primary schools and the University provides for intermediate and secondary schools. The number of graduates is not enough to meet all the teaching staff requirements and so the Ministry of Education meets this shortage by recruiting teachers from other Arab countries.

Scholarships are granted to students to pursue courses which are not offered by Kuwait University. Such scholarships are mainly used to study in Egypt, Lebanon, the UK and the USA. There were also pupils from Arab, African and Asian states studying in Kuwait schools on Kuwait Government scholarships. Kuwait University has about 18,000 students, and also provides scholarships for a number of Arab, Asian and African students. In May 1996 the National Assembly approved a draft law to regulate students' behaviour, dress and activities, with regard to observance of the teachings of *Shari'a* (Islamic) law, and to eradicate coeducational classes at Kuwait University over a five-year period.

Between 1969 and 1985, 60,000 men and women graduated from the country's centres for illiteracy eradication and adult education, which in 1986 totalled 105, catering for 32,000 students.

Bibliography

Al-Dekhauel. Kuwait: *Oil, State and Political Legitimation*. London, Ithaca Press, 2000.

Al-Sabah, Y. S. F. *The Oil Economy of Kuwait*. Henley-on-Thames, Routledge and Kegan Paul, 1981.

Boutros-Ghali, Boutros (Ed.). *The United Nations and the Iraq–Kuwait Conflict, 1990–96* (UN Blue Books Series, V. 9). New York, United Nations Publications, 1996.

Chisholm, A. H. T. *The First Kuwait Oil Concession: A Record of the Negotiations 1911–1934*. London, Cass.

Cordesman, Anthony H. *Kuwait*. Boulder, CO, Westview Press, 1997.

Daniels, John. *Kuwait Journey*. Luton, White Crescent Press, 1972.

Dickson, H. R. P. *Kuwait and her Neighbours*. London, Allen and Unwin, 1956.

El Mallakh, Ragaei. *Economic Development and Regional Co-operation: Kuwait*. University of Chicago Press, 1968.

Finnie, David. *Shifting Lines in the Sand*. London, I. B. Tauris, 1992.

Gardiner, Stephen, and Cook, Ian. *Kuwait: The Making of a City*. London, Longman, 1983.

Government Printing Press. *Education and Development in Kuwait*. Kuwait.

Hakima, Abu A. M. *The Modern History of Kuwait: 1750–1966*. UK, The Westerham Press, 1983.

Hassan, Hamdi A. *The Iraqi Invasion of Kuwait: Religion, Identity and Otherness in the Analysis of War and Conflict*. London, Pluto Press, 1999.

Hay, Sir Rupert. *The Persian Gulf States*. Washington, DC, Middle East Institute, 1959.

International Bank for Reconstruction and Development. *The Economic Development of Kuwait*. Baltimore, Johns Hopkins Press, 1965.

Joyce, Miriam. *Kuwait, 1945–1996: An Anglo-American Perspective*. London, Frank Cass, 1999.

Khouja, M. W., and Sadler, P. G. *The Energy of Kuwait: Development and Role in International Finance*. London, Macmillan, 1978.

Kochwasser, Friedrich H. *Kuwait. Geschichte, Wesen und Funktion eines modernen Arabischen Staates*. Tübingen, Eldmann, 1961.

Kuwait Oil Co Ltd. *The Story of Kuwait*. London.

Mansfield, Peter. *Kuwait: Vanguard of the Gulf*. London, Hutchinson, 1990.

Marlowe, John. *The Persian Gulf in the 20th Century*. London, Cresset Press, 1962.

Mezerik, Avraham G. *The Kuwait–Iraq Dispute, 1961*. New York, 1961.

Ministry of Planning. *Kuwait in Figures: Twenty-Five Years of Independence*. Kuwait, Central Statistical Office, 1986.

Rahman, H. *The Making of the Gulf War*. Reading, Garnet, 1997.

Rush, Alan. *Al-Sabah History and Genealogy of Kuwait's Ruling Family 1752–1987*. London, Ithaca Press, 1987.

Saldanha, J. A. *The Persian Gulf: Administration Reports 1873–1957*. London, Archive Editions, 1986.

The Persian Gulf Precis 1903–1908. London, Archive Editions, 1986.

Sandwick, John A. *The Gulf Co-operation Council: Moderation and Stability in an Interdependent World*. London, Mansell Publishing Ltd.

Tetreault, Mary Ann. *Stories of Democracy: Politics and Society in Contemporary Kuwait*. New York, Columbia University Press, 2000.

Winstone, H. V. F., and Freeth, Zahra. *Kuwait: Prospect and Reality*. London, Allen and Unwin, 1972.

LEBANON

Physical and Social Geography

W. B. FISHER

The creation, after 1918, of the modern state of Lebanon, first under French mandatory rule and then as an independent territory, was designed to recognize the nationalist aspirations of a number of Christian groups that had lived for many centuries under Muslim rule along the coast of the eastern Mediterranean and in the hills immediately adjacent. At least as early as the 16th century AD there had been particularist Christian feeling that ultimately resulted in the granting of autonomy, though not independence, to Christians living in the territory of 'Mount Lebanon', which geographically was the hill region immediately inland and extending some 30 km–45 km north and south of Beirut. The territory of Mount Lebanon was later expanded, owing to French interest, into the much larger area of 'Greater Lebanon' with frontiers running along the crest of the Anti-Lebanon mountains, and reaching the sea some miles north of Tripoli to form the boundary with Syria. In the south there is a frontier with Israel, running inland from the promontory of Ras an-Naqoura to the head of the Jordan Valley. In drawing the frontiers so as to give a measure of geographical unity to the new state, which now occupies an area of 10,452 sq km (4,036 sq miles), large non-Christian elements of Muslims and Druzes were included, so that today the Christians of Lebanon form less than one-half of the total population.

PHYSICAL FEATURES

Structurally, Lebanon consists of an enormous simple upfold of rocks that runs parallel to the coast. There is, first, a very narrow and broken flat coastal strip—hardly a true plain—then the land rises steeply to a series of imposing crests and ridges. The highest crest of all is Qurnet as-Sauda, just over 3,000 m high, lying south-east of Tripoli; Mount Sannin, north-east of Beirut, is over 2,700 m high. A few miles east of the summits there is a precipitous drop along a sharp line to a broad, trough-like valley, known as the Beka'a (Biqa), about 16 km wide and some 110 km–130 km long. The eastern side of the Beka'a is formed by the Anti-Lebanon mountains, which rise to 2,800 m, and their southern continuation, the Hermon Range, of about the same height. The floor of the Beka'a valley, though much below the level of the surrounding mountain ranges, lies in places at 1,000 m above sea-level, with a low divide in the region of Ba'albek. Two rivers rise in the Beka'a—the Orontes, which flows northwards into Syria and the Gharb depression, ultimately reaching the Mediterranean through the Turkish territory of Antioch; and the Litani (Leontes) river. This latter river flows southwards, and then, at a short distance from the Israeli frontier, makes a sudden bend westwards and plunges through the Lebanon mountains by a deep gorge.

There exists in Lebanon an unusual feature of geological structure which is not present in either of the adjacent regions of Syria and Israel. This is the occurrence of a layer of non-porous rocks within the upfold forming the Lebanon mountains; and, because of this layer, water is forced to the surface in considerable quantities, producing large springs at the unusually high level of 1,200 m–1,500 m. Some of the springs have a flow of several thousand cu ft per second and emerge as small rivers; hence the western flanks of the Lebanon mountains, unlike those nearby in Syria and Israel, are relatively well watered and cultivation is possible up to a height of 1,200 m or 1,500 m.

With its great contrasts of relief, and the configuration of the main ranges, which lie across the path of the prevailing westerly winds, there is a wide variety in climatic conditions. The coastal lowlands are moderately hot in summer, and warm in winter, with complete absence of frost. But only 10 km or so away in the hills there is a heavy winter snowfall, and the higher hills

are covered from December to May, giving the unusual vista for the Middle East of snow-clad peaks. From this the name Lebanon (*laban*—Aramaic for 'white') is said to originate. The Beka'a has a moderately cold winter with some frost and snow, and a distinctly hot summer, as it is shut off from the tempering effect of the sea.

Rainfall is generally abundant but it decreases rapidly towards the east, so that the Beka'a and Anti-Lebanon are definitely drier than the west. On the coast, between 750 mm and 1,000 mm fall annually, with up to 1,250 mm in the mountains; but only 380 mm in the Beka'a. As almost all of this annual total falls between October and April (there are three months of complete aridity each summer), rain is extremely heavy while it lasts, and storms of surprising intensity sometimes occur. Another remarkable feature is the extremely high humidity of the coastal region during summer, when no rain falls.

ECONOMIC LIFE

The occurrence of high mountains near the sea, and the relatively abundant supplies of spring water, had a significant influence on economic development within Lebanon. Owing to the successive levels of terrain, an unusually wide range of crops can be grown, from bananas and pineapples on the hot, damp coastlands, olives, vines and figs on the lowest foothills, cereals, apricots and peaches on the middle slopes, to apples and potatoes on the highest levels. These last are the rarest crops and, with the growing market in the oilfield areas of Arabia and the Persian (Arabian) Gulf, they are sold for the highest price. Export of fruit is therefore important. In addition, abundant natural water led to the development of pinewoods and evergreen groves, which add greatly to the already considerable scenic beauty of the western hill country. Prior to the prolonged civil conflict in Lebanon (see History), there was an important tourist trade in the small hill villages, some of which have casinos, luxury hotels and cinemas. The greatest activity was during the summer months, when wealthy Middle Easterners and others arrived; but there was a smaller winter sports season, when skiing was pursued.

In addition, the geographical situation of Lebanon, as a 'façade' to the inland territories of Syria, Jordan, and even northern Iraq and southern Turkey, enabled the Lebanese ports to act as the commercial outlet for a very wide region. The importance of Beirut as a commercial centre was due in large part to the fact that Lebanon was a free market. More than one-half of the volume of Lebanon's former trade was transit traffic, and Lebanon used to handle most of the trade of Jordan. Byblos claims to be the oldest port in the world; Tyre and Sidon were for long world-famous, and the latter was reviving as the Mediterranean terminal of the Tapline (Trans-Arabian Pipeline) from Saudi Arabia until the Lebanese branch of the pipeline was closed at the end of 1983. Another ancient centre, Tripoli, was also a terminal of the pipeline from Iraq. Beirut is now, however, the leading town of the country, and contains more than one-half of the total population, including many displaced persons. Although local resources are not in general very great (there are no minerals or important raw materials in Lebanon), the city in normal times lived by commercial activity on a surprising scale, developed by the ingenuity and opportunism of its merchant class.

Beirut, of recent years, came to serve as a financial and holiday centre for the less attractive but oil-rich parts of the Middle East. Transfer of financial credit from the Middle East to Zürich, Paris, London, New York and Tokyo; a trade in gold and diamonds; and some connection with the narcotics trade of the Middle East—all these gave the city a very special function. Strenuous efforts began in 1977 to bring about reconstruction and redevelopment, assisted by loans from abroad. During 1980 a large contribution of 'front-line aid' was made by Arab League states, and this showed signs of producing significant economic recovery. However, the abrupt intensification of military activity in 1981–82, the effects of the subsequent Israeli invasion and the prolonged sectarian conflict negated these hopes. Production declined because of damage and disruption; the south was virtually disconnected from the remainder of the Lebanese state until Israeli forces withdrew to just inside the border in June 1985; such was the extent of factional division within the country that, in the early years of the recent civil conflict, the Government's authority was barely felt outside Beirut; by the late 1980s, if not before, even the capital had effectively lapsed into anarchy; the impossibility of controlling customs and tax collection caused a substantial reduction in government income. At least until the consequences of renewed violence between Israel and the Palestinians began to be felt in Lebanon, the economic situation appeared more favourable following the withdrawal of Israeli forces from southern Lebanon in May 2000. Moreover, in recent years some of the country's tourist trade has been revived.

RACE AND LANGUAGE

It is difficult to summarize the racial affinities of the Lebanese people. The western lowlands have an extremely mixed population possibly describable only as 'Levantine'. Basically Mediterranean, there are many other elements, including remarkably fair individuals—Arabs with blonde hair and grey eyes, who are possibly descendants of the Crusaders. The remaining parts of the country show a more decided tendency, with darker colouring and more pronounced facial features. In addition, small refugee groups, who came to the more inaccessible mountain zones in order to escape persecution, often have a different racial ancestry, so that parts of Lebanon form a mosaic of highly varying racial and cultural elements. Almost all Middle Eastern countries are represented racially within Lebanon.

Arabic is current throughout the whole country. French is probably still the leading European language in use in Lebanon, (although English is tending to replace it) and some of the higher schools and one university teach basically in this language. In addition, Aramaic is used by some religious sects, but only for ritual—there are no Aramaic speaking villages, unlike in Syria.

History

Revised for this edition by RICHARD I. LAWLESS

ANCIENT AND MEDIEVAL HISTORY

In the ancient world Lebanon was important for its pine, fir and cedarwood, much coveted by neighbouring powers, and during the long period of Egyptian, Assyrian, Persian and Seleucid rule the exploitation of the forests of Lebanon was normally a royal privilege. The area was also mined for its iron and copper in the time of the Ptolemies and the Romans. Gradually Lebanon came to have a distinct history of its own, for the mountainous character of the region prevented any complete subjugation to outside authority. It is probable that the Arab conquest of Syria did not include the 'Mountain', to which fled all those who were opposed to the Arab domination. The Caliph Mu'awiya (661–80) made some effort to assert a greater control, but the resistance of the native Aramaean Christians was reinforced by the arrival of the Mardaites from the fastnesses of the Taurus and the Amanus. These Christian nomads, led by Byzantine officers, made determined advances into Lebanon late in the seventh century, and seem to have united with the Maronite Christians who were later to become a Uniate Church of the Roman communion and to have a predominant role in the history of Lebanon. The Caliph Abd al-Malik (685–705) paid tribute to Byzantium in return for a withdrawal of most of the Mardaite forces; but it is clear that the 'Mountain' had begun to assume its historic function of providing a sure refuge for racial and religious minorities.

Lebanon maintained its Christian character until the ninth century when, among other elements, the Arab tribe of Tanukh established a principality in the region of al-Gharb, near Beirut, acting as a counterpoise to the Maronites of northern Lebanon and as a bulwark against Byzantine threats from the sea. Gradually, Islam and, more slowly still, the Arabic language penetrated the 'Mountain' where, however, Syriac lingered on in the Maronite districts until the 17th century (it is still spoken in three villages of the Anti-Lebanon). In the ninth and 10th centuries Muslim sects began to establish themselves in the 'Mountain' as, for example, the Shi'a, known in Lebanon under the name of Mitwali, and, in the 11th century, the Druze, which won a firm hold in southern Lebanon.

The Crusaders established in this area the County of Tripolis and the lordships of Gibelet and Batron, which enjoyed considerable support from the Christian population of northern Lebanon and were protected by a network of fortresses, the most famous being Hisn al-Akrad (Crac des Chevaliers). In the Mamluk period the rulers of Lebanon, by continued political manoeuvring, maintained for themselves a considerable degree of autonomy. The Tanukhid amirs, after a long period in which they had matched the Crusaders against the Islamic amirates, had eventually taken the Mamluk side. In northern Lebanon the Maronites, under their bishop, maintained contact with the Italian republics and also with the Roman Curia. Less fortunate were the Druzes and the Mitwali who, in the last years of the 13th century, took advantage of the Mamluk preoccupation with the Mongol threat from Persia and began a protracted revolt that led to widespread devastation in central Lebanon.

THE OTTOMAN PERIOD

In the 16th century the Turkoman family of Assaf and, after them, the Banu Saifa rose to prominence in the area from Beirut to the north of Tripoli; while in the south the Druze house of Ma'an supplanted the Tanukhid amirs. After the conquest of 1516–17 the Ottoman Sultan Selim I had confirmed the amirs of Lebanon in their privileges and had imposed only a small tribute; yet not infrequently there was open conflict with the Ottomans, as in 1584–85 when, after an attack on a convoy bearing the tribute from Egypt to Constantinople, the Sultan Murad III sent a punitive expedition to ravage the lands of the Banu Saifa and of the Druzes.

The power of the House of Ma'an now reached its zenith in the person of Fakhr ad-Din II (1586–1635), who by means of bribery, intrigue, foreign alliance and open force, set out to establish an independent power over the whole of Lebanon and parts of Palestine to the south. To this end he entered into close relations with the Grand Duke of Tuscany, negotiating in 1608 a commercial agreement that incorporated a secret military clause directed against the Sultan. In 1613 a naval and military expedition sent from the Porte (the Ottoman administration in Constantinople) compelled Fakhr ad-Din to seek refuge with his Tuscan ally. He returned in 1618, and within a few years had restored his power to become virtual ruler from Aleppo to the borders of Egypt. The Sultan, heavily engaged in repressing revolt in Anatolia, and in waging a long struggle with Persia, could do no more than recognize the *fait accompli*. Fakhr ad-Din embarked on an ambitious programme of development for Lebanon. He sought to equip a standing army with arms imported from Tuscany. Italian engineers and agricultural experts were employed to promote a better cultivation of the land and to increase production of silk and olives. The Christian peasantry were encouraged to move from northern to southern Lebanon. Beirut and Sidon flourished as a result of the favour he showed to commerce, and religious missions from Europe

(Capuchins, Jesuits, Carmelites) were allowed to settle throughout Syria—a development of great importance for France, which strove to assert a 'protectorate' over all the Catholic and other Christian elements in the Ottoman Empire. However, the ambitions of Fakhr ad-Din were doomed to failure, as by 1632 the Sultan Murad IV assumed effective control at Constantinople. The Pasha of Damascus, supported by a naval squadron, began a campaign to end the independent power of Lebanon, and in 1635 Fakhr ad-Din was executed at Constantinople.

In 1697 the Ma'an family became extinct and was succeeded by the House of Shihab, which maintained its predominance until 1840. In the course of the 18th century, the Shihab amirs gradually consolidated their position against the other factions of the 'Mountain' and for a while recovered control of Beirut. While normally the Shihab took care to remain on good terms with the Turkish pashas of Tripoli, Sidon and Damascus, the pashas themselves strove to exercise an indirect control by fomenting the family rivalries and religious differences that marked the course of Lebanese politics. With the advent of Bashir II (1788–1840) the House of Shihab attained the height of its influence. Not until the death of Ahmad Jazzar, Pasha of Acre (1804), was he free to develop his power, which he maintained by the traditional methods of setting one pasha against the other, and by bribing the officials of the Porte whenever it seemed expedient. In 1810 he helped the Ottomans to repel an invasion by the Wahhabi power of Arabia; but in 1831 he sided openly with Muhammad Ali of Egypt, when that ruler invaded Syria. Holding Lebanon as the vassal of Egypt, he was compelled, however, to apply to the 'Mountain' the unpopular policy imposed by Ibrahim Pasha, the son of Muhammad Ali, with the result that a revolt broke out, which, after the Egyptian withdrawal of 1840, led to his exile. The age of the Lebanese amirs was now at an end: the Ottomans assumed control of the 'Mountain', appointing two Kaimakams to rule there, one Druze and the other Maronite, under the supervision of the pashas of Sidon and Beirut.

The period of direct Ottoman rule saw the rapid growth between the Druzes and the Maronites of a mistrust already visible during the time of the Egyptian dominance, and now fostered by the Ottomans as the only means of maintaining their influence over Lebanon. As a result of social and economic discontent, due to the slow disintegration of the old feudal system, which had existed in Lebanon since the Middle Ages, the Maronite peasantry revolted in 1858 and destroyed the feudal privileges of the Maronite aristocracy, thus facilitating the creation of a system of independent smallholdings. The Druze aristocracy, fearing the consequences of a similar discontent among their own Maronite peasantry, made a series of attacks on the Maronites of northern Lebanon, who, owing to their own dissensions, could offer no effective resistance. The dubious attitude of the Turkish pashas, in the face of these massacres of 1860, led to French intervention, and in 1864 to the promulgation of an organic statute for Lebanon, which was now to become an autonomous province under a non-Lebanese Ottoman Christian governor, appointed by the Sultan and approved by the Great Powers. He was to be aided by an elected administrative council and a locally recruited police force. The statute also abolished legal feudalism in the area, thus consolidating the position won by the Maronite peasantry in 1858. The period from 1864 to 1914 was one of increasing prosperity, especially among the Christian elements, who also played an important role in the revival of Arab literature and Arab national feeling during the last years of the 19th century.

THE FRENCH MANDATE

Lebanon's privileged status ended when the Turks entered the First World War (1914–18); by 1918 the coastal areas of Lebanon were occupied by British and French forces. In September 1920 the French created the State of Greater Lebanon—which included not only the former autonomous province but also Tripoli, Sidon, Tyre and Beirut, some of which had in earlier times been under the control of the amirs of Lebanon. A Constitution, devised in 1926, proved unworkable and was suspended in 1932, from which time the President of the Republic carried on the administration. The President was, by convention, a Christian, while the Prime Minister was a Muslim, and both

worked towards the achievement of a careful balance between the various religious communities of the new state. Lebanon was not unaffected by the growth of the nationalist movement in Syria, some sections of which demanded the reduction of Lebanon to its pre-war limits and even the abolition of its existence as a separate state. These demands found some support amongst the Sunni Muslims of the areas added to Lebanon proper in 1920, with the result that the Syrian revolt of 1925–26 spread to parts of southern Lebanon. The Maronite Christians, on the whole, supported the idea of a separate Lebanon, but were not united in their attitude towards France on the one hand, and the Arab states on the other. The Franco-Lebanese Treaty of 1936 differed little from that which France negotiated at the same time with Syria, the chief difference being that the military convention gave France wider military powers in Lebanon than in Syria. A reformed Constitution was promulgated in 1937; but the French refusal to ratify the treaty in 1938, and the advent of the Second World War in 1939 prolonged a situation which, if outwardly calm, concealed a considerable discontent beneath the surface. In November 1941 the Free French Commander, General Catroux, formally proclaimed Lebanon a sovereign independent state. In September 1943 a new Parliament with a strong nationalist majority soon came into conflict with the French authorities over the transfer of the administrative services. When, in November 1943, the Lebanese Government approved legislation removing from the Constitution all provisions considered to be inconsistent with the independence of Lebanon, the French delegate-general arrested the President and suspended the Constitution. The other Arab states, together with the United Kingdom and the USA, supported the Lebanese demands, and in 1944 France began to transfer to Lebanese control all important public services, save for the Troupes spéciales (local units under French command), whose transfer the French authorities at first made conditional on the signing of a Franco-Lebanese Treaty. However, in 1945 the Troupes spéciales were handed over to Lebanon without such conditions, and an agreement between France and the Lebanese Government in 1946 provided for the withdrawal of French troops.

ECONOMIC DIFFICULTIES

Like the other Arab states, Lebanon was at war with the new State of Israel from May 1948; but negotiated an armistice in March 1949. Just as in Syria the failure of the Arab armies had led eventually to the *coup d'état* of March 1949, so in Lebanon the widespread disillusionment of Arab nationalist hopes prepared the ground for a conspiracy against the Government. This conspiracy was easily suppressed in June and its leader, Antun Sa'ade, was executed.

The Lebanese Government encountered considerable economic and financial difficulties after the 1939–45 war. When, in January 1948, France devalued the franc (to which both the Lebanese and the Syrian currencies were linked) Lebanon, economically weaker than Syria, felt obliged to sign a new agreement with France (February 1948). Syria refused to do so and began a long and complex dispute with Lebanon over the precise nature of the economic and financial arrangements which were to exist between the two states. In March 1950 the Lebanese Government refused a Syrian demand for full economic and financial union. The severance of economic relations which ensued did not end until the signing, in February 1952, of an agreement for the division of royalties owed from oil companies, and for the status, for customs purposes, of agricultural and industrial products passing between the two states.

In September 1952 Lebanon experienced a severe domestic crisis. Political and economic unrest brought about the fall of the Government and the resignation of President al-Khouri, who had held office since 1943. Charges of corruption were made against the President. During his long tenure of power al-Khouri had indeed used all his skills of political influence and manoeuvre in order to impose a real degree of unity on a state where the divergent interests of Maronites, Sunni and Shi'a Muslims, Druzes and other religious communities underlined the need for firm and coherent rule. To an even greater degree, however, the crisis was caused by economic problems. Lebanon had attained its independence in the period of war-time prosperity. The end of the war meant a progressive diminution of foreign expenditure in Lebanon, and the gradual disappearance of war shortages that had favoured Lebanese trade. The devaluation of the French franc, the unsuccessful war with Israel, and above all the economic rupture with Syria (the chief source of agricultural goods and principal customers for Lebanese industrial products) gave rise to further difficulties. By 1952 there was much discontent arising from the high cost of living and from considerable unemployment, and it was a loose coalition of all the elements of opposition, both political and economic, which brought about the fall of the al-Khouri regime.

CONSTITUTIONAL REFORM

Camille Chamoun became the new President of the republic. His administration, with the Amir Khalid Chehab as Prime Minister, pledged reforms including revision of the electoral and press laws, the enfranchisement of women and the reorganization of justice. Elections in July 1953 led to the formation of a 44-member chamber of deputies composed on a sectarian basis according to the electoral law of 1952.

Since the foundation of the republic, all seats in the Chamber of Deputies had been distributed among the various religious communities in proportion to their numerical strength. The chamber was thus intended as an institution reflecting the religious and social structure of the state, and was capable of harmonious function provided that the electoral system, which maintained a delicate balance between the communities, suffered no violent and prejudicial change. At the same time the Chamber contained a strong 'feudal' element—the tribal and religious leaders who, with their trusted retainers, formed powerful groups within the chamber and were often criticized as being 'anti-national' in their aims and methods. To end or at least weaken this 'feudalization' of Lebanese political life, without, however, impairing the equilibrium between the Muslim and Christian communities, had long been the purpose of those who advocated a reasonable and well-considered policy of reform. The law of 1952 created 33 electoral districts (during the previous life of the republic the number had been, as a rule, five) and allotted to 11 of them two seats, and to the remainder one seat each. Of the total of 44 seats, the Maronites were now to receive 13, the Sunni Muslims nine, the Shi'a Muslims eight, the Greek Orthodox Christians five, the Druzes three, the Greek-Melkite Catholics three, the Armenian Catholics two, and the other confessions (Protestant, Jewish, Nestorian, etc.) one seat.

FOREIGN RELATIONS 1953–56

In the period 1953–56 financial and economic relations with Syria remained on a provisional basis much the same as that which had prevailed since 1950, with earlier short-term arrangements being renewed as the need arose. Discussions with Syria in November 1953 over problems of currency, loan policy, banks and exchange difficulties made no effective progress. The Lebanese Government was more successful, however, in its efforts to promote internal development. It was announced in August 1955 that the World Bank had granted to Lebanon a loan of US $27m. for the Litani river scheme, which was expected to more than double the electric power available within the republic and also to irrigate a large area in the coastal region. A number of commercial treaties at this time bore witness to the growing penetration of the Eastern bloc into Arab lands.

THE EISENHOWER DOCTRINE

A state of emergency was declared in Lebanon during the Sinai-Suez crisis at the end of October 1956. The Chamber of Deputies announced its support for Egypt, but Lebanon did not break off diplomatic relations with the United Kingdom and France. In November there were disturbances, however, at Tripoli and Beirut against the attitude of the Government. The 'Eisenhower Doctrine', a new programme, announced in January 1957, of US economic and military aid intended as a means of ensuring an anti-Soviet front in the Middle East, evoked a favourable response in Lebanese official circles. Some of the political groups in Lebanon protested against this pro-Western alignment, asserting that it could not fail to isolate Lebanon from the other Arab states (which had declined to accept the terms of the Doctrine) and thus impair Arab solidarity. None the less, in

April the Government obtained from the Chamber of Deputies a vote expressing confidence in its policies. Military equipment granted under the Doctrine began to reach Beirut in June.

The problem of electoral reform had been under consideration in Lebanon during 1956. The main proposal now to be given effect was that the number of seats in the Chamber of Deputies should be raised from 44 to 66. As election time drew near in mid-1957, riots in Beirut compelled the Government to call out troops for the maintenance of order. According to reports at this time more than 100 communists were arrested for their part in the disturbances. The tense electoral campaign of June 1957 resulted in a marked triumph for the Government. Of the total of 66 seats, the Maronites now received 20, the Sunni Muslims 14, the Shi'a Muslims 12, the Greek Orthodox Christians seven, the Druzes four, the Greek-Melkite Catholics four, the Orthodox Armenians three, the Armenian Catholics one, and the other religious minorities also one seat.

It became clear that unrest, especially among those elements of the population that opposed the pro-Western policies of the Lebanese Government and favoured an alignment with Egypt and Syria, had not been quelled when several bombings and assassinations occurred in November 1957. The Government, in its desire to halt these subversive activities, now imposed a close control over all Palestinian refugees in Lebanon. Indeed, after renewed outbreaks of violence in December, the northern area of Lebanon was declared to be a military sector.

The Lebanese Government stated in March 1958 that it would not join the United Arab Republic (UAR) of Egypt and Syria; the Arab Federation of Iraq and Jordan, or indeed any association that might limit its own independence and sovereignty. Large sections of the Muslim population, both in the north (at Tripoli) and in the south (at Tyre and Sidon), were inclined to be pro-Arab rather than pro-Lebanese in sentiment—a mood greatly stimulated by the emergence of the new UAR and by the propaganda emitted from Cairo and Damascus for the return to Syria of those predominantly Muslim areas that had been joined to the old Lebanon under the French mandate. There was conflict, too, between those who, although reluctant to see Lebanon lose its separate political existence, were none the less strongly opposed to the pro-Western attitude of the Lebanese Government and those who, fearing the possible absorption of Lebanon into the framework of a larger Arab state, felt themselves bound to support fully the policies of the Beirut regime. The danger was real that these complex tensions might escalate in the form of a 'confessional' conflict between Muslims and Christians, in which, if not the continued independence, then at least the entire political orientation of Lebanon would be at stake.

THE CRISIS OF 1958

A reorganization of the Government, carried out in March 1958 and designed to remove those critical of the pro-Western policies of Lebanon who favoured closer co-operation with the UAR, brought no relief to the grave situation then developing. Serious disturbances, originating in Tripoli and the northern areas adjacent to the Syrian border, broke out in the second week of May and spread rapidly to Beirut and also to Tyre and Sidon in southern Lebanon. The Druze population in the south-east was also involved in the disorders, being sharply divided into pro- and anti-Government factions. Hostile demonstrations led to the destruction of the US information service centres at Tripoli and Beirut. At the request of the Lebanese Government, the USA agreed to dispatch in all haste supplies of arms and police equipment and decided at the same time to reinforce the US Sixth Fleet stationed in the Mediterranean. The USSR accused the USA of interference in Lebanese affairs and declared that Western intervention might have grave consequences. The Lebanese Government itself charged the UAR with interference in its internal affairs and appealed for redress to the Arab League—which, meeting at Benghazi in June, failed to agree on a course of action. The problem was brought before the UN, which resolved to send an observer corps to Lebanon.

The Lebanese Government was now, in fact, confronted with a widespread insurrection, in which the Muslim elements in the population were ranged against the Christian elements. The forces opposed to the existing regime controlled parts of Beirut, Tripoli and Sidon, as well as large areas in the north and the south of Lebanon. Attempts to negotiate a settlement led to no favourable result. The Prime Minister, Sami as-Sulh, gave an assurance that President Chamoun did not intend to ask for a constitutional amendment enabling him to seek re-election in September 1958, the date when his present tenure was due to end. To this assurance the leaders of the insurrection replied with a firm demand for the immediate resignation of the President, who made it clear, however, that he would not relinquish his office until September.

On 14 July 1958 (the date of the *coup d'état* which led to a change of regime in Iraq) President Chamoun requested the USA to send troops into Lebanon to maintain security and preserve Lebanese independence. About 10,000 US troops were dispatched to the Beirut area, and the USA warned that any action by forces under the control of the UAR against US troops in Lebanon might lead to serious consequences. The USSR and the People's Republic of China made strong protests against the US intervention and asked for the prompt withdrawal of the US forces from Lebanon. On 18 August the USA gave a written undertaking to withdraw its troops, either at the request of the Lebanese Government, or in the event of the UN's taking appropriate measures to ensure the integrity and peace of the country. The UN General Assembly thereupon adopted a resolution, framed by its Arab members, providing for the evacuation of US troops under the auspices of the UN and the Arab League.

PRESIDENT CHEHAB, 1958–64

Meanwhile, the Lebanese Chamber of Deputies had, on 31 July 1958, elected as the new President of the state Gen. Fouad Chehab, the Commander-in-Chief of the Lebanese army—a choice supported by members from both sides involved in the internal conflict. He assumed office on 23 September, in succession to President Chamoun, and at once invited Rashid Karami, the leader of the insurgents at Tripoli, to become Prime Minister. An agreement was made on 27 September to the effect that the US forces were to leave Lebanon by the end of October.

In October 1959 the Lebanese Cabinet was increased from four to eight members, so that greater representation might be given to the various political groups. The Chamber of Deputies approved in April 1960 an electoral reform bill, which imposed for the first time the principle of the secret ballot in Lebanese elections and also enlarged the Chamber itself from 66 to 99 deputies—a total figure that maintained the existing ratio (laid down in 1943) of six Christian to every five Muslim (including Druze) deputies in the Chamber. The Chamber was dissolved by President Chehab on 5 May 1960, the Government of Rashid Karami resigning nine days later. A general election was then held in four separate stages on 12, 19 and 26 June and 3 July. The election took place in an atmosphere of complete calm, strict security measures being enforced throughout the various stages of the electoral process. In the new Chamber of Deputies there were 30 Maronite Christians, 20 Sunni Muslims, 19 Shi'a Muslims, 11 Greek Orthodox Christians, six Greek-Melkite Catholics, six Druzes, four Armenian Orthodox Christians, one Armenian Catholic, one Protestant and one member representing other elements. A large number of the 'rebel' personalities prominent in the events of 1958 and hitherto not seated in the Chamber were now returned as members.

A new Government, under the leadership of Saeb Salam, took the oath of office on 2 August 1960. The Cabinet, which included several personalities active on one side or the other in the troubles of 1958, was prompt to reaffirm the traditional policies of non-expropriation, of minimal government intervention in private enterprise, of encouragement for private investment both foreign and domestic, and of currency convertibility. By 1960 Lebanon had recovered, in economic terms, almost completely from the disturbances in 1958.

CABINET REFORM

It had come to be felt, since August 1960, that the Lebanese Cabinet, 18 members strong, was too large for the maintenance of an efficient administration and so, on 22 May 1961, the Prime Minister established a new Cabinet consisting of eight ministers only. However, on 24 October, as the result of a dispute with some members of his Government (notably Kamal Joumblatt, the Druze leader, who was Minister of Works and Planning),

Salam resigned. Rashid Karami, a former Prime Minister, formed a new Government on 31 October.

Military elements, acting in conjunction with civilians described as supporters of the extremist Parti socialiste nationaliste, made an unsuccessful attempt, on 31 December 1961, to overthrow the Lebanese Government. The Parti socialiste nationaliste was in fact the old Parti populaire syrien, founded in the 1930s by Antoine Saadé with the aim of uniting several Arab states into a Greater Syria. Its current leader, Dr Abdallah Saadé, was now arrested and the party dissolved by the Lebanese Government on 1 January 1962. The Lebanese authorities took firm action against all the elements suspected of involvement in the revolt, and crushed it within a few days.

On 19 February 1964 the Cabinet led by Rashid Karami resigned, after President Chehab had signed a decree dissolving the Chamber of Deputies (elected in 1960) and ordering elections to be held on four successive Sundays from 5 April to 3 May 1964. A caretaker Cabinet was appointed to supervise the elections for the new Chamber of Deputies.

PRESIDENT HÉLOU

Gen. Chehab, whose six-year term of office as President of the republic was due to end in September 1964, rejected all appeals that he should submit himself as a candidate for a second time. Even when the Chamber of Deputies approved a motion in favour of an amendment to the Constitution which would enable him to stand for a further term of office, Gen. Chehab persisted in his refusal. On 18 August Charles Hélou, Minister of Education in the caretaker administration, succeeded Gen. Chehab as President, pledging himself to follow the policies and reforms introduced under his predecessor.

On 25 September 1964 Hussein Oweini, the head of the caretaker Cabinet, formed an administration at the request of President Hélou. The new administration aroused dissatisfaction, however, in the Chamber of Deputies, since, deriving from the Cabinet appointed originally to act as a caretaker during the period of the 1964 elections, it was in fact composed wholly of non-members of the Chamber. Oweini resigned on 13 November and, five days later, gathered together a new Cabinet which, save for himself and the Minister of Foreign Affairs, consisted of members drawn from the Chamber of Deputies and reflected in itself all the main trends of opinion within the Chamber.

FOREIGN RELATIONS

There was friction during the first months of 1965 between the Federal Republic of Germany and the Arab states because of the decision by Bonn to enter into formal diplomatic relations with Israel. Anti-German demonstrations occurred at Tripoli and Beirut, and on 13 May Lebanon severed diplomatic relations with West Germany. In May Lebanon signed an agreement on trade and technical co-operation with the European Economic Community (or European Community—EC). There was some friction between Israel and Lebanon over border incidents during the latter part of 1965. Members of the main Palestinian guerrilla organization, Fatah (the Palestine National Liberation Movement), made raids into Israel, provoking Israeli reprisals against the Lebanese village of Noule.

Meanwhile, on 20 July 1965 Prime Minister Oweini resigned. There had been much debate in the Chamber of Deputies about a proposed agreement to guarantee private US investment in Lebanon against expropriation, war or revolution—an agreement construed in some political circles as giving to the USA a possible excuse for intervention, at need, in Lebanese affairs. On 26 July Rashid Karami became the new Prime Minister, with a Cabinet of nine ministers, all chosen from outside the Chamber of Deputies.

FINANCIAL CRISIS

Rashid Karami modified his Cabinet in December 1965 and January 1966, these changes arising from difficulties which hindered the full implementation of an administrative and judicial reform programme, one of the main advocates of which was President Hélou. Between December 1965 and March 1966 an estimated 150 officials (including 100 civil servants) were compelled to withdraw from public life. This sustained attempt to curb corruption and the abuse of public office inevitably caused considerable tension. There was strong pressure in the Chamber of Deputies for a return to a Cabinet chosen mainly from the Chamber itself. This and other difficulties obliged Karami to offer his resignation to President Hélou, who appointed Dr Abdallah al-Yafi as the new Prime Minister. Dr al-Yafi assembled a 10-man Cabinet drawn entirely from the Chamber of Deputies with the exception of himself and Philippe Takla, the new Minister of Foreign Affairs. The constitution of the Cabinet represented a balance between the various religious interests and, from the point of view of politics, between the left-wing and right-wing elements in the Chamber.

In October 1966 the Intra Bank of Lebanon was compelled to suspend operations, owing to a series of withdrawals amounting to more than £L11m. in the preceding month. One result of that financial crisis was that the Government resolved to discourage the creation of new commercial banks, foreign or Lebanese, for a period of five years. Hitherto there had been an almost complete freedom to establish new banks in Lebanon and there had been a large expansion of the banking system based on the flow into Lebanon of vast oil revenues from Saudi Arabia and from the states of the Persian (Arabian) Gulf.

On 2 December 1966 Dr Abdallah al-Yafi offered the resignation of his Government to President Hélou. Rashid Karami formed a new administration on 7 December. It was composed of figures drawn from outside Parliament, six of whom held ministerial posts for the first time.

In June 1967 the Lebanese Government aligned itself with the Arab states then engaged in war against Israel. On 8 June the Government asked the ambassadors of the United Kingdom and the USA to leave Lebanon. However, the months following the war witnessed a gradual easing of tensions, and in September the Lebanese Cabinet agreed to reinstate its ambassadors in Washington and London.

POLITICAL INSTABILITY

Rashid Karami's Cabinet resigned from office in February 1968, whereupon President Hélou asked Dr Abdallah al-Yafi to form an interim administration, whose main task was to be the preparation and conduct of the general election in March 1968. The two most successful parties elected in the Chamber of Deputies were the Maronite-dominated Triple Alliance, of a right-wing leaning, and the Democratic Bloc, aligned further to the left. However, Dr al-Yafi's interim administration remained in office until October, when it was forced to resign, owing to bitter rivalry between the two main political groups, the 'Chamounists' and the 'Chehabists' (both named after former Presidents), disputes over sectional representation in the Cabinet, and the Government's inability to command a parliamentary majority. After a week of confusion, a new four-member Government was announced on 20 October, still headed by Dr al-Yafi.

THE GUERRILLAS AND ISRAEL

The first clash between Lebanese and Israeli forces on the border for over two years took place in May 1968. As the activities of the Palestinian guerrillas intensified, however, Lebanon became increasingly involved as a target for Israel's grievances against the Palestinians. On 26 December an Israeli airliner was machine-gunned by Arab guerrillas at Athens airport. Two days later, Israeli commandos raided Beirut airport and destroyed 13 aircraft, all belonging to Lebanese airlines. The Israeli Government stated that the raid should be regarded as a reprisal for the Athens attack, a warning to the Arab world not to make any repetition of it, and a further warning to Lebanon to police more effectively the activities of Palestinian *fedayin* (freedom fighters) in the country. The financial cost to Lebanon was relatively small, as most of the aircraft were insured abroad. The major after-effects of the raid were, firstly, the widespread criticism that it attracted even from countries normally favourable to Israel. Lebanon was viewed as a country which had taken little active part in the campaign against Israel, while the Palestinian *fedayin* within it were only enjoying the freedom available to them in Lebanon's open, tolerant society. The UN Security Council unanimously condemned Israel for the raid. The second effect was the fall of the Government on 7 January 1969, its alleged lack of preparedness for Israeli aggression dealing the final blow to a weak administra-

tion. On 20 January, after much political manoeuvring, a new Government was formed under Rashid Karami, who thus became Prime Minister for the seventh time.

This Government was immediately confronted with the basic problems underlying the Lebanese situation, foremost among these the Christian-Muslim balance. In theory, both religions were equally represented in Lebanon, but no census had been held since 1939 mainly because the authorities feared that the balance had shifted to a 60% Muslim predominance, which would seriously affect the political situation. (Indeed, according to 1983 estimates, the Muslim population of Lebanon, both Shi'a and Sunni, was 1.95m., while the combined Maronite and Greek Orthodox Christian communities numbered 1.15m.) The Christian community had a disproportionate share of the wealth and important positions, was generally conservative by Arab standards and took a moderate position on the Israel question. The less privileged Muslim majority was more in favour of both domestic reform (Lebanon had, for example, only the beginnings of a welfare state) and of a more militant position towards Israel. Early in 1969 numbers of Syrian guerrillas entered the country and spent as much time in action against the Lebanese army as against Israel. Unrest also appeared amongst the 260,000 Palestinian refugees in the Sidon camp; part of the frontier with Syria was eventually closed. Numerous strikes and demonstrations continued. The Karami Government felt unable to maintain the necessary coalition from the two communities and their various factions and resigned on 25 April. However, it continued to function as a caretaker administration as no stronger government could be formed.

In late 1969 a number of guerrilla groups were reported to have moved to new bases better sited for attacks on Israel, which continued to raid these bases in reprisal; the combination of these factors created some friction between the guerrillas and the Lebanese army. In October the army apparently attacked some of these camps in an attempt to restrict or direct their activities. This caused a political crisis in which the caretaker Government resigned, claiming that it had not authorized the army's actions, and the President and the armed forces administered the country directly. Radical elements and guerrillas took over Tripoli, the second largest city, for several days, and most of the Palestinian refugee camps were fully converted into military training and equipment centres. Militant support for the guerrillas was voiced throughout the Arab world, and there were threats of military intervention by Syria and Iraq.

On 2 November 1969 the Lebanese Commander-in-Chief and Yasser Arafat, the leader of Fatah, signed a cease-fire agreement in Cairo. This restricted the guerrillas' freedom of movement to certain areas; as further defined in January 1970, it also provided that camps had to be set up some distance from towns, that military training must cease in refugee camps, and that guerrillas must enter Israel before engaging in hostilities. The intention was not to impede guerrilla attacks, but to prevent innocent Lebanese from being injured, and their property from being damaged, by Israeli counter-attacks. The calmer atmosphere that followed the cease-fire enabled Karami to form another Cabinet towards the end of November. There was much concern about the weakness of the country's southern defences, and in January 1970 the new ministry felt strong enough to dismiss the Commander-in-Chief of the army, appointing instead Brig. Jean Njeim. In March there was a series of street battles in the Beirut area between the Palestinian guerrillas and militant right-wing Phalangist groups, but the Government and the army managed to avoid becoming involved. In May Israel launched a major air and ground attack on guerrilla positions in southern Lebanon, and occupied a substantial area for nearly two days. Syria sent air assistance for the small Lebanese air force.

POLITICAL CRISES

Sulayman Franjiya was elected President in August 1970, and a new Cabinet was formed by Saeb Salam. Some measures of political liberalization, such as the relaxation of media censorship and the removal of the ban on extremist parties, did little to curb domestic unrest. Strikes and demonstrations against unemployment and inflation, student disorders and fighting between Phalangists and the Parti populaire syrien continued throughout 1971. The parliamentary elections of April 1972 reflected a marked swing towards left-wing political groups.

The Palestinian guerrillas remained Lebanon's major problem. Their bases in the refugee camps became more important following the expulsion of the guerrillas from Jordan in July 1971, and guerrilla operations against Israel produced violent Israeli reprisals. The villages of southern Lebanon bore the brunt of Israeli raids, and their inhabitants secured a greater measure of Lebanese army control over guerrilla activities in March 1972. Arab terrorist actions still provoked Israeli reprisals against Lebanon, even when there was little connection between the terrorists and Israel's vulnerable northern neighbour. The killing of Israeli athletes at the Olympic Games in Munich, West Germany, in September 1972 led to Israeli ground and air attacks on guerrilla bases, in which the Lebanese army suffered a number of casualties. The Lebanese Government was unable to persuade the guerrillas to suspend their activities against Israel, and several clashes between the Lebanese army and the guerrillas occurred.

In February 1973 Israeli commandos attacked guerrilla training bases in refugee camps about 160 km north of the Lebanese frontier, and escaped virtually unopposed. A further Israeli raid, in which three guerrilla leaders were shot in their homes in the centre of Beirut, and an attempt to blow up oil storage tanks at the Zahrani terminal, attributed to Palestinian extremists, resulted in the fall of the Salam Government. Salam resigned, frustrated at the inability of the Lebanese armed forces to prevent an Israeli military action in the capital, and Dr Amin Hafez formed a new Government. Several members of the Salam Cabinet remained in office, the new Government including representatives of most of the major political and religious groups.

Tension between the Lebanese army and the guerrillas culminated in May 1973 in Lebanese ground and air attacks on the refugee camps. An invasion by guerrillas based in Syria was repulsed, and a cease-fire was brought about by the mediation of other Arab states. The guerrillas apparently agreed to stop their terrorist activities within Lebanon and to cease using the camps for training guerrillas.

The Hafez Government lasted only seven weeks. The Prime Minister resigned on 14 June 1973, unable to settle the Sunni Muslim claim for a greater share in the allocation of government posts, and it was not until 8 July that Taki ed-Din Solh was able to form a new administration. A moderate, Solh enjoyed the support of many Sunni factions, and his Cabinet included representatives of all the main religious blocs. Outside Parliament, however, violent disorders continued, with industrial disputes resulting in demonstrations and clashes with police.

The potential religious hostility within Lebanon, and the political implications of the division of government and administrative posts on a confessional basis, were again evidenced in February 1974. Civil service reforms, intended to overcome the sectarian nature of certain appointments, were opposed by Maronites who feared that they would lose posts traditionally reserved for their community. The liberal reformist Parti national libéral (PNL) threatened to withdraw its three cabinet members, and the proposed reforms were also condemned by the Phalange and the Bloc national. The Shi'a Muslims of southern Lebanon also made demands for increased representation and more investment and development in the south. The Shi'a leader, Imam Moussa as-Sadr, implied that he would organize his followers and arm them as protection against Israeli raids—as, indeed, he later did.

Although Lebanon was not directly involved in the October 1973 Arab–Israeli war, southern regions had continued to serve as a guerrilla base and to suffer Israeli reprisals. Southern villages were shelled intermittently, and small-scale raids across the border and acts of terrorism became commonplace.

In July 1974 there were clashes between Palestinians and Phalangists who continued to demand more government controls on guerrilla activities. Throughout 1974 and into 1975 Israeli shelling, air raids and incursions into Lebanon persisted, as did guerrilla attacks against the Israelis. Consequently the situation on the border remained tense. In September 1974, unable to curb internal sectarian violence by its ineffective ban on the possession of firearms, Taki ed-Din Solh's Cabinet resigned. In October a new Government was formed under

Rashid Solh, although violence continued, finally erupting in a bloody clash between troops and citizens of the port of Sidon. The Cabinet split over the granting of a Muslim demand to confer citizenship on long-time residents of the country. Letter-bomb and dynamite explosions and further border fighting between the Israelis and guerrilla groups were followed by further fierce conflict between the Phalangists and Palestinians, in which over 150 died. Much damage was caused in Beirut, and, after an agreement by Solh to normalize relations with the Palestinians and the fact that the security forces had not intervened in the fighting, the Phalangists appeared to be on the defensive.

CIVIL WAR

Intercommunal strife had never been far from the surface in Lebanon. In February 1975 a demonstration in Sidon by a group of Muslim fishermen, in protest at the granting of what they perceived to be unduly advantageous fishing rights to a Christian-owned company (chaired by former President Camille Chamoun), escalated into clashes with the Lebanese army. Tensions were heightened as the apparent intervention of Palestinian elements on the side of the Muslims convinced Christian groups, notably the Phalangists, that the Palestinians—whose presence in Lebanon was already making the country vulnerable to Israeli attack—were now interfering in internal Lebanese affairs. Following an incident in April 1975, when Palestinians made an attack on some Phalangists, the Phalangists killed the passengers of a bus, who were mainly Palestinians. Intercommunal fighting between Christians and Muslims quickly spread. At this point the official policy of Yasser Arafat's Palestine Liberation Organization (PLO) was to stand aloof from the conflict, and Arafat himself was, in fact, instrumental in securing some of the many cease-fires of subsequent months.

In May 1975, shortly after the fighting began, Rashid Solh resigned as Prime Minister, and was replaced by Rashid Karami, who continued as Prime Minister through an exceedingly turbulent period until December 1976. In September 1975 a national dialogue committee was formed, consisting of 20 members from all political and confessional groups, to try to restore 'normal life'—a task in which they were unsuccessful. By October there was evident dissatisfaction with President Franjiya and his inability to bring the fighting to an end, and it also became increasingly evident that, in spite of the official policy of the PLO not to interfere in the internal affairs of Lebanon, members of extremist Palestinian groups, particularly those of the 'rejectionist front', were being drawn into the fighting on the side of the Muslims. It was also, at this point, the official policy of the Lebanese army not to intervene, although, later, breakaway groups became involved in the fighting. By early 1976 the PLO was becoming increasingly embroiled in the conflict, and several Syrian-based units of the Palestine Liberation Army were fighting in Lebanon on the side of the Muslims. Under these increasingly ominous conditions the term of the Chamber of Deputies was extended by a year (later increased to two years) and the general elections scheduled for April 1976 were postponed for up to 26 months. In January 1978 the Chamber's term was extended until June 1980. In March 1979 the Chamber was renamed the National Assembly and in April 1980 its term was further extended to the middle of 1983.

A temporary cease-fire gave a brief respite in January 1976, but by March no agreement had been reached on political reforms, fighting had flared up again, and 70 deputies signed a petition seeking President Franjiya's resignation. Further weight was given to this request in April, when a parliamentary session took place and 90 deputies voted unanimously to amend Article 73 of the Constitution to allow presidential elections to be held up to six months before the expiry of the incumbent's term of office. Franjiya signed this amendment on 23 April, but, in spite of the election of his successor, refused to resign until the completion of his term of office in September 1976, when he was succeeded by Elias Sarkis, who had been Governor of the central bank.

INCREASED SYRIAN INTERVENTION

By May 1976 Syria was becoming increasingly involved in Lebanese affairs: it was estimated that about 40,000 Syrian-controlled troops were in Lebanon at this time. Yasser Arafat had ordered pro-Damascus Palestinian units to withdraw, and it now became clear that Arafat and the PLO had become entirely sympathetic to the Lebanese left wing. In early June Syria launched a full-scale invasion of Lebanon officially to end the civil war and restore peace, but unofficially, it became clear, to crush the Palestinians. The conflict threatened to assume an international dimension, and an emergency meeting of Arab foreign ministers was convened in Cairo under the sponsorship of the Arab League. It was agreed to send a joint Arab peace-keeping force to Lebanon, to be accompanied by a phased, but not complete, withdrawal of Syrian troops. The force was to include participants from Syria, Libya, Algeria, Sudan, Saudi Arabia and the PLO, under an Egyptian Commander-in-Chief, but by the end of June the 1,000-strong force was effectively made up of 500 Syrian troops and 500 Libyans. Meanwhile, fierce fighting broke out in the area of two Palestinian refugee camps, Tal az-Zaatar and Jisr al-Basha, and most of Beirut was without water or electricity. The Arab League took steps to hasten the arrival of further contingents of the peace-keeping force, but fighting continued unabated until October 1976, when Arab summit meetings in Riyadh and Cairo secured a lasting cease-fire. During the course of the fighting there had been more than 50 abortive cease-fires and an estimated 60,000 people had been killed and some 100,000 injured.

The Riyadh and Cairo summits arranged for a 30,000-strong, mainly-Syrian Arab Deterrent Force (ADF) to police Lebanon, and a four-party disengagement committee was established to attempt to implement the terms of the 1969 Cairo agreement between the Lebanese Government and the Palestinian guerrillas—considered to be one of the keys to an enduring peace. The committee began by restricting the level of heavy weapons allowed to the various factions, and then sought an agreement on the proportion of armed elements allowed in the Palestinian guerrilla camps. The Shtaura Agreement of July 1977 attempted to settle this problem by endeavouring to regulate the Palestinian base camps and to introduce a reconstituted Lebanese army into the border area.

In December 1976 President Sarkis appointed as Prime Minister Dr Selim al-Hoss, who formed a Cabinet of eight technocrats charged with rebuilding and reconstruction; the Government was granted the power to rule by decree for six months, subsequently extended. A Council for Development and Reconstruction was established, and this council took over the functions of the former Ministry of Planning. In January 1977 censorship was imposed on the press, initially on both Lebanese and foreign journalists, but restrictions on foreign dispatches were soon removed.

The Druze chief and leader of the Lebanese left, Kamal Joumblatt, was assassinated on 16 March 1977. Although his murder was followed by a wave of revenge killings, it did not lead to any renewed outbreak of major fighting. However, the southern area of Lebanon, between the Litani river and the Israeli border, became the scene of renewed fighting during 1977. This area was largely spared during the civil war, and fighting developed when the Palestinians moved to the hills of southern Lebanon after being subdued by the Syrians in the civil war. A war 'by proxy' developed, with Syria allied with the Palestinian guerrillas and Israel supporting the Lebanese Government. The Shtaura Agreement of July and a later cease-fire in September, arranged with the intervention of the USA, were ineffective.

The volatile situation flared up in March 1978 as a result of a raid by Fatah guerrillas into Israel on 11 March, when, in an attack on a bus near Tel-Aviv, more than 35 people were killed. In retaliation, and in order to prevent further raids, Israeli forces advanced into southern Lebanon three days later. On 19 March the UN Security Council adopted a Resolution (425) demanding that Israel cease its military action against Lebanese territorial integrity and withdraw its forces from Lebanese territory forthwith, and establishing a United Nations Interim Force in Lebanon (UNIFIL) to confirm the withdrawal and assist in the restoration of peace and of Lebanese government authority in the affected area. In May the Security Council endorsed a proposal to increase the eventual strength of UNIFIL from the 4,000 troops originally envisaged to 6,000. Israeli forces withdrew from southern Lebanon in June 1978, but relinquished

control in southern border areas not to UNIFIL but to a right-wing, mainly-Christian Lebanese militia under the command of Maj. Saad Haddad.

In July 1978 fighting erupted again in Beirut between the Syrian troops of the Arab deterrent force and right-wing Christian militias. A cease-fire was proclaimed in early October and the ministers responsible for foreign affairs of the states participating in the Arab deterrent force (Kuwait, Lebanon, Qatar, Saudi Arabia, Sudan, Syria and the United Arab Emirates—UAE) met at Beiteddin, near Beirut, and agreed on a declaration intended to bring peace to the area. It maintained that Lebanese central authority must be imposed, that armed militias must be curbed and that a truly national army must be formed.

LEBANON AFTER THE BEITEDDIN DECLARATION

The aims of the Beiteddin Declaration were not realized. In April 1979 Maj. Haddad proclaimed 'independent free Lebanon'—a slice of territory, covering about 1,800 sq km, next to the Israeli border. Encouraged and supplied by Israel, Haddad was able to maintain his 'independence'. In July 1980 the Phalangist Commander, Bachir Gemayel, consolidated his power by overcoming the militia of the PNL. This led to a strengthening of the Phalangist militia, with the result that Phalangist forces occupied the town of Zahle in the Beka'a valley. In April 1981 fighting developed between Syrian troops of the ADF and Christian militias in the Beirut area, and Syrian and Palestinian forces besieged Zahle. Syria maintained that Zahle and the Beka'a valley were essential for the security and defence of Syria against Israel, whereas the Phalangist forces sought the removal of Syrian forces from Lebanon.

During the remainder of April 1981 Israeli forces made frequent raids into southern Lebanon and Israeli aircraft strafed Palestinian guerrilla targets. When, at the beginning of May, two Syrian helicopters were destroyed by Israeli aircraft, Syria introduced surface-to-air missile (SAM) launchers into the Beka'a valley. Although it was thought that Israeli aircraft already had the capacity to withstand the outdated SAM missiles, the Israeli Prime Minister, Menachem Begin, adopted a very belligerent stance and threatened to destroy the missiles. An international crisis developed, but on 30 June Syrian forces ended the siege on Zahle, after mediation by the Saudi and Kuwaiti ambassadors to Lebanon. Regular troops of the Lebanese army then occupied positions in the town as the Phalangist militia withdrew. The US Middle East peace envoy, Philip Habib, was able to arrange a cease-fire which became effective on 24 July.

As during previous crises, the Lebanese Government, undermined by the divided interests imposed on its composition by the Constitution, was not able to exert its authority. In July 1979 Prime Minister al-Hoss introduced a Cabinet of 12 members, seven of whom were deputies, to replace the Government that had been in office since December 1976. In April 1980 the National Assembly voted to extend its term by three years, to 30 June 1983 (rather than by 18 months as the Government desired). President Sarkis tried to formulate a national accord. On 5 March 1980 he issued a 'message to the nation' which reiterated his policy for the future: the unity, independence and sovereignty of the whole territory; total opposition to mini-states and militias; allegiance to parliamentary democracy; acknowledgement that Lebanon was an Arab country; rejection of the Camp David agreements between Egypt and Israel; support for a future Palestinian state; co-operation with Syria; and support for UN resolutions concerning Lebanon.

On 7 June 1980 Dr al-Hoss offered his resignation, on the grounds that no progress had been made towards achieving accord on those principles. On 16 July Sarkis accepted al-Hoss's resignation; he appointed Taki ed-Din Solh as Prime Minister, but the latter soon resigned, unable to form a government. It was not until October that Chafic al-Wazzan was able to form a Cabinet.

ISRAEL'S 1982 INVASION OF LEBANON

The 1981 cease-fire lasted until the following spring, when fresh Israeli air raids, which provoked PLO shelling of northern Israel, culminated in a full-scale invasion of Lebanon by the Israeli army. On 6 June 1982 Israeli forces attacked on three fronts. While one column pursued the Syrian army, which was retreating up the Beka'a valley, the most serious fighting took place against PLO forces around Beaufort Castle and along the coast. The Israelis preceded their attacks with bombardments that devastated many Lebanese towns and villages. Parts of Tyre, Sidon, Damour and Nabatiyah were almost obliterated by Israeli bombing raids. Civilian casualties among both Lebanese and Palestinians were enormous—according to *The Times* of London's correspondent in Beirut, about 14,000 people, at least 80% of them civilians, were killed during the first fortnight of the war.

The confrontation between the Maronite Christians and the alliance of radical Arab nationalists and Palestinians, which had been at the heart of the civil war of 1975–76, survived the Israeli invasion. The militia of the National Movement, in particular the Sunni Murabitoun and the Shi'ite Amal, fought alongside the PLO in the south and later in Beirut. The Phalangists, however, welcomed the invasion, although they did not take part in the actual fighting. During Israel's siege of west Beirut, which lasted two months, the Phalangists and Maj. Saad Haddad's militiamen acted as auxiliaries for the Israelis. The Maronites also shared Israel's political aims, demanding the expulsion of the PLO from Lebanon and the removal of Syrian troops. During July and August 1982, while the Israelis kept up an almost continuous bombardment of west Beirut, negotiations took place between Americans, Israelis, Lebanese and Palestinians. The PLO commitment to withdrawal from the city, effected at the end of August, was negotiated by US diplomats through the mediation of former Lebanese Prime Minister Saeb Salam.

PRESIDENTIAL ELECTIONS

Bachir Gemayel, the younger son of Pierre Gemayel (the founder of the Phalangist Party and commander of the Lebanese Forces—LF—militia), had announced his presidential ambitions well in advance of the election. In peace-time there would have been no chance of his winning, but in the aftermath of the Israeli invasion he emerged as the obvious candidate. He was the strongest Maronite leader and the one most acceptable to the Israelis. Although Gemayel faced considerable opposition from the Muslim deputies, many of whom boycotted the voting, he succeeded in being elected on 23 August 1982. Three weeks later, before he had assumed power, he (with up to 60 others) was killed in a bomb explosion at the Phalangist Party headquarters. On the following day, 15 September, the Israeli army moved into Beirut, and on 16 September Phalangist militiamen, with the apparent collusion of the Israelis, entered the Palestinian refugee camps of Sabra and Chatila and began a massacre of their inhabitants.

A week after the assassination of Bachir Gemayel, his elder brother, Amin, was elected President. Amin was a Phalangist deputy with a reputation as a moderate, and his election was welcomed by many Muslims who hoped that he would be able to control the extremist elements inside the Phalangist Party. The problems confronting him were enormous. Lebanon was still occupied by two foreign armies and violence was continuing in many areas. After the Sabra/Chatila massacre the Israelis withdrew from Beirut—but only as far as the airport, just south of the city, from where they consolidated their hold on the southern half of the country. The north of Lebanon was still dominated by the Syrian army which refused to withdraw from the country until the Israelis did so. Towards the end of the year there was savage fighting between pro- and anti-Syrian forces in Tripoli, while in the Chouf area, where the Israelis were in control, there were frequent battles between Phalangists and Druze militiamen. The Government was in control of only a small area of central Lebanon, but even there it was often unable to assert authority.

TALKS BETWEEN ISRAEL AND LEBANON

After insistent pressure from the US Government, talks between the Israeli and Lebanese Governments finally commenced at the beginning of 1983. The Israelis eventually dropped their insistence that talks should take place in Jerusalem, and it was agreed that the two sides would meet alternately at Khalde in Lebanon and Kiryat Shmona in Israel. Israel's demands included security arrangements that would allow Israel to keep military bases inside Lebanon, a predominant role for Saad

Haddad in the reconstituted Lebanese army, and relations with Lebanon that stopped only just short of a formal peace treaty. All these demands were rejected by the Lebanese, and the USA also considered them to be excessive. On 22 February US President Ronald Reagan offered to guarantee the security of Israel's northern border once the army had withdrawn, but the proposal was rejected by the Israeli Government.

The negotiations remained stalled until the end of April 1983, when the US Secretary of State, George Shultz, made his first visit to the area. He was able to persuade the two sides to sign an agreement on 17 May, which provided for the withdrawal of Israeli forces from Lebanon. However, the Israeli Government announced that it would not be bound by the agreement unless Syria also agreed to withdraw its forces from the Beka'a valley. Shultz returned to the Middle East in July, but during a visit to Damascus he was unable to persuade President Assad to agree to a withdrawal. The Syrian Government declared that it would not accept an agreement which it believed was in the interest only of Israel and the USA; nor was it prepared to support President Gemayel's attempt to extend his control over the areas occupied by Syrian and Israeli forces. In July, as violence between Phalangist and Druze militias intensified in the Chouf, an opposition front was established to confront Gemayel. Calling itself the National Salvation Front, and relying entirely on Syrian support, it consisted of Walid Joumblatt, the Druze leader, former Prime Minister Rashid Karami and ex-President Sulayman Franjiya, one of the chief opponents of the Gemayel family.

ISRAELI REDEPLOYMENT

In July 1983 Israel, its casualties at the hands of the contending militias increasing, decided to redeploy its forces south of Beirut along the Awali river. The Israeli redeployment took place at the beginning of September, and by the end of the year the Israeli troop presence had been reduced from 30,000 to 10,000. However, owing to a lack of co-ordination between the Israeli and Lebanese armies in the handing over of military control of the vacated areas, a full-scale war erupted between the Druze and Christian militias in the Chouf mountains. In the southern, Israeli-occupied part of what had become, effectively, a partitioned country, Maj. Saad Haddad's 'South Lebanon Army' (SLA), armed and trained by Israel, was employed as a police force, intended progressively to assume the duties of the Israeli forces. (Haddad died in December 1983 and his successor, Maj.-Gen. Antoine Lahad, was appointed in March 1984.) Israeli personnel were a constant target of guerrilla attacks and, in order to reduce their exposure, as well as the burden of military supervision, the Israelis resorted to arming local militias, of whatever religious character, so that they could be responsible for the policing of their own areas. However, this effectively meant that arms provided by the Israelis were turned on them. Israel launched several punitive air raids against Palestinian positions in the Syrian-controlled Beka'a valley, in retaliation against the attacks of PLO guerrillas infiltrating from the north, and there were rumours that PLO fighters were returning to Beirut.

THE REVOLT AGAINST ARAFAT

From September 1983 the struggle for control of Fatah between the forces of its leader, Yasser Arafat (Chairman of the PLO), and those of the Syrian-backed rebels Abu Musa and Abu Saleh, which had begun in the Beka'a valley in May, was concentrated around Arafat's last stronghold, the northern Lebanese port of Tripoli. After months of bitter fighting, in which many Lebanese civilians, as well as Palestinian guerrillas, were killed or wounded, a truce was arranged through Saudi and Syrian mediation. This allowed Arafat and 4,000 of his supporters to leave Tripoli in December aboard five Greek-registered ships, under UN protection, bound for Algeria, Tunisia and the Yemen Arab Republic.

THE NATIONAL RECONCILIATION CONFERENCE

After the Israeli withdrawal, the 5,800-strong multinational force (comprising mainly French, Italian and US personnel), left to keep the peace between the various factions in Beirut, in the absence of an effective Lebanese army, was gradually drawn into the fighting. It came under attack from Muslim militiamen who were suspicious of its role in bolstering a Christian-led government, and of the presence off shore of massive, predominantly US, naval support. In the two most devastating incidents, 241 US and 58 French marines were killed in almost simultaneous suicide bombings, responsibility for which was claimed by two militant Shi'a groups, on 23 October 1983.

The inter-factional fighting in Beirut was punctuated by numerous short-lived cease-fires. The most successful of these began on 26 September 1983 and was accompanied by the resignation of Chafic al-Wazzan, who hoped to make way for a government of national unity. He was persuaded to remain in office, but these events were the prelude to a Conference of National Reconciliation, held in Geneva, Switzerland, from 31 October to 4 November. These talks were attended by most of the interested Lebanese parties, including the Shi'ite Amal militia, led by Nabih Berri, and the National Salvation Front, which had been proclaimed, with Syrian backing, in July by the Druze leader, Walid Joumblatt, in alliance with ex-President Franjiya, a pro-Syrian Maronite Christian, and former Prime Minister Rashid Karami, a Sunni Muslim. The conference effectively foundered on President Gemayel's refusal to do more than 'freeze' the 17 May agreement with Israel, rather than to abrogate the pact (as Syria wished) and risk losing US support for his Government. Broad agreement was reached, however, on the need for constitutional changes which would give Muslims representation in the Government commensurate with their majority status in the country.

In early February 1984, following abortive Saudi-mediated attempts to implement a comprehensive security agreement in Beirut, factional fighting developed with greater intensity than before, with the multinational force and the Lebanese army apparently powerless to prevent it. To the Muslim community, the reconstituted Lebanese army, armed and trained by the USA, appeared to be nothing more than an instrument to be used against them by the Christian President in co-operation with the Christian Phalangist militia. President Gemayel had refused to give the Amal leader, Nabih Berri, a post in the Cabinet, while Walid Joumblatt was openly committed to the President's removal. Muslim members of the army, unwilling to fight against their co-religionists, began to defect to the militias, while the Druze and Shi'ite forces co-operated in fighting the army. Chafic al-Wazzan (a Sunni Muslim) and the entire Cabinet tendered their resignation on 5 February. Shortly afterwards the USA, Italy and the United Kingdom decided to withdraw their peace-keeping troops from the multinational force. (The French troops were withdrawn in March.)

LEBANON ABROGATES THE 17 MAY AGREEMENT

By February 1984, Beirut was divided by the militias, east and west, along the so-called 'Green Line', into Christian- and Muslim-controlled sectors. On 16 February, with west Beirut in Shi'ite hands, the army sustaining defeats south of the capital, and his Government in effective control only of the eastern part of the city, Amin Gemayel offered, under the terms of a Saudi peace plan, to abrogate the 17 May agreement with Israel and to give greater government representation to Muslims; the President also proposed the formation of a 'national unity' government to institute the planned reforms of the Constitution. These proposals, which entailed the simultaneous withdrawal of all foreign forces from Lebanon and new security arrangements with Israel for southern Lebanon, proved to be unacceptable not only to Syria and to Gemayel's Muslim opponents, who largely took their lead from Syria (which equipped the Druze militia), but also to the Christian parties which were committed to the agreement with Israel as a means to preserve their dominance in Lebanese politics.

Finally, on 5 March 1984, bowing to Syria's influence in Lebanese affairs, President Gemayel abrogated the 17 May agreement in return for guarantees of internal security from Syrian President Assad. On the same day, Chafic al-Wazzan's Cabinet withdrew its resignation, and one week later the National Reconciliation Conference was reconvened in Lausanne, Switzerland. It failed to produce the results for which Syria had hoped. Moreover, it saw the beginning of the disintegration of the Lebanese National Salvation Front, as former President Franjiya vetoed Syrian plans for constitutional

changes in Lebanon involving the diminution of the powers of the President, by convention a Maronite Christian post. The Conference broke up, having agreed another cease-fire and recommended the formation of a 'national unity' government— though the composition of such a government was still undecided. (A movement replacing the National Salvation Front was announced in Damascus in March, including Walid Joumblatt, George Hawi, leader of the Parti communiste libanais, Assem Qansou, leader of the al-Baath party, Inaam Raad, leader of the Parti nationaliste syrien, and representatives of the Socialist Union and Arab Democratic parties, but not Nabih Berri of Amal.)

THE GOVERNMENT OF NATIONAL UNITY

At talks in Damascus in April 1984, President Assad of Syria approved plans for a Lebanese government of national unity, giving equal representation to Christians and Muslims, proposed to him by President Gemayel. Gemayel chose Rashid Karami, who had held the post on 10 previous occasions, as Prime Minister of the new Government, which was proclaimed on 30 April. Karami announced his principal aims as being the ending of the Israeli occupation of the south; the restoration of civil order; and the reformation of the Constitution to reflect the majority status of Lebanon's Muslims. On 30 April, without first consulting the appointees, Prime Minister Karami announced a 10-member Cabinet consisting of five leading members each from the Christian and Muslim communities. Nabih Berri, designated Minister of Water and Electrical Resources and of Justice, refused to participate in the Government unless some provision were made in it for dealing with the predominantly Shi'ite area of southern Lebanon occupied by the Israelis. A Ministry of State for Affairs of the South and Reconstruction was duly created, to which Nabih Berri was appointed on 7 May. The other appointees having accepted their posts, the Cabinet thus included the leaders of all Lebanon's main religious groups: only former President Franjiya, who was bitterly opposed to Pierre Gemayel and Camille Chamoun, both of whom were included in the Cabinet, refused to give his support to the Government. His son-in-law, Abdullah ar-Rassi, who had been made Minister of the Interior, boycotted Cabinet meetings in support of Franjiya's call for the dismissal of these two.

The new Government won the approval of the National Assembly in June 1984. Fighting in Beirut between Christian and Muslim militias had not ceased, however, and it was not until Syrian Vice-President Abd al-Halim Khaddam intervened to mediate between the two sides that a cease-fire took effect; this finally allowed the terms of a security plan, providing for the reorganization of the army and the disengagement of the rival militias, to be drawn up. An all-party Military Council, consisting of one member from each of the main religious groups, was established to supervise the reintegration of the 37,000-strong army and the disengagement of the militias. Brig.-Gen. Michel Awn (a Maronite Christian) was made Commander-in-Chief of the armed forces, with a Druze, Maj.-Gen. Nadim Hakim, as Chief of Staff. (Hakim died in a helicopter crash in August and was replaced by Maj.-Gen. Abu Dargham.) A new body, the Directorate of Internal Security, was placed under the control of a Shi'ite general, Uthman Uthman. Future appointments in the army would be distributed equally between Christians and Muslims.

The security plan was put into operation at the beginning of July 1984. Three army brigades began to take control of militia positions along the 'Green Line' and in the port and airport of Beirut. The militias had earlier removed their heavy weaponry from the area and there was virtually no opposition to the implementation of the plan, even from the Phalangist militia, which had bitterly opposed what it viewed as pro-Syrian, anti-Christian developments in Lebanese politics. The port and airport, closed since February, were reopened in mid-July, and more crossing points between the east and west of Beirut were also cleared.

However, Muslim and Druze dissatisfaction with the Government's lack of progress on constitutional reform, despite the Syrian influence on President Gemayel, led to sporadic fighting between rival Muslim and Christian militias and, occasionally, between Shi'a and Sunni Muslims belonging, respectively, to the Amal and Murabitoun militias. Troops of the Lebanese army failed to gain control of the city, although they reduced fighting along the 'Green Line'. President Gemayel's efforts to gain agreement on constitutional reform, already constrained by his fear of alienating his Christian supporters, were further handicapped by divisions within the Cabinet. Walid Joumblatt maintained a torrent of vituperation against Gemayel, and in September 1984 vetoed the extension of the security plan along the southern coastal road and into the Druze bastion of the Chouf mountains, as he regarded the Lebanese army as merely a tool of the Christian Phalangists.

In September 1984 Syrian mediation settled a feud in the northern port of Tripoli between the pro-Syrian Arab Democratic Party (known as the 'Red Knights') and the anti-Syrian, Sunni Muslim, Tawheed Islami (the Islamic Unification Movement), enabling a security plan to be implemented there.

In Beirut, sporadic violence continued and, at the end of October 1984, Walid Joumblatt (who was boycotting Cabinet meetings) and Nabih Berri threatened to resign from the Cabinet unless more progress was made on constitutional reform. A new security plan, effectively dictated by Syria, was introduced at the end of November. It was designed initially to put the whole of Beirut under the control of the Lebanese army, and then to extend the Government's authority north to Tripoli, south to Israeli-occupied territory and east to the Chouf mountains, demonstrating to the Israelis the ability of the Lebanese army to maintain security in the event of an Israeli withdrawal from the south of the country. Joumblatt's Druze militia repeatedly objected to the eastward deployment and obstructed the implementation of the plan. The army moved into Tripoli on 21 December, but a plan for the coastal areas to the north and south of Beirut was not agreed by all parties until 31 December. The army was deployed along the coast road to southern Lebanon in mid-January 1985.

ISRAEL'S WITHDRAWAL FROM LEBANON

With the cost of keeping a force in southern Lebanon proving a drain on a drastically weakened economy, and with its personnel increasingly the target of attacks by Lebanese resistance groups, Israel's Government of national unity, which was formed in September 1984, pledged itself to a withdrawal from Lebanon. Israel abandoned an unrealistic demand for a simultaneous withdrawal of Syrian forces from north-east Lebanon and, in November, entered into a series of talks at an-Naqoura, in southern Lebanon, with Lebanese government officials, who participated with Syrian approval. Israel's concern was that adequate security arrangements should be agreed to prevent the vacated areas from becoming bases for terrorist attacks on Israeli soldiers or territory, while the Lebanese Government wished to co-ordinate the withdrawal so as to prevent intercommunal fighting (such as occurred in the Chouf mountains in September 1983). The talks repeatedly foundered on the question of which forces should take the place of the Israeli Defence Forces (IDF). The Lebanese, influenced by Syria, wanted UNIFIL to police the border with Israel (as it had been mandated to do in 1978) and the Lebanese army to deploy north of the Litani river, between UNIFIL and the Syrian army. Israel did not consider the Lebanese army to be a credible security force, and wanted UNIFIL to deploy north of the Litani with the southern Lebanese border patrolled by the Israeli-backed SLA. In the absence of any agreement, Israel withdrew from talks, and on 14 January 1985 the Israeli Cabinet voted to take unilateral steps towards a complete withdrawal, which was to be effected in three phases. The first phase involved the evacuation of the IDF from the western occupied sector, covering about 500 sq km around Sidon, to the Litani river area, around Nabatiyah, and was implemented in February 1985. Israel was prepared to test the competence of the Lebanese army in handing over responsibility for security in the evacuated area to it, operating in tandem with UNIFIL. The Lebanese Government, however, rejected a peace-keeping role for the UN force, and the Lebanese army moved into Sidon in mid-February.

The second phase of the Israeli withdrawal, designed to evacuate the IDF from the occupied central and eastern sector, including the Beka'a valley, to redeploy around Hasbayyah, began on 3 March 1985 with no fixed deadline. The process was accelerated during April as the majority Shi'ite community of the south (which, antipathetic towards the PLO, had initially welcomed the IDF) now attacked it in retreat. This prompted the Israelis to pursue an 'Iron Fist' policy, attacking Shi'ite villages, killing many inhabitants and detaining hundreds of suspected guerrilla fighters. Instead of abating, the level of guerrilla activity against the IDF, orchestrated by the Shi'ite National Resistance Movement, intensified. After the evacuation of Tyre, the second phase of the Israeli withdrawal was completed on 29 April. The third and final phase, taking the IDF behind Israel's northern border and leaving a buffer zone between 10 km and 20 km wide along the border controlled by the SLA, was completed on 10 June, three months ahead of the original schedule. However, several hundred Israeli troops remained inside Lebanon to support the SLA, whose numbers had been depleted since the start of the withdrawal operation by desertion and defection to the southern Lebanese resistance movement. The role of the SLA was not recognized by the Lebanese Government, Syria or Lebanese Muslims, and friction between it and UNIFIL increased.

The Israeli invasion succeeded in that (at the cost of 654 Israeli lives) it temporarily removed the threat of attack by the PLO from within Lebanon (although internal divisions contributed equally to the diminution of PLO strength) and, by a coincidence of interest, the Shi'ites of southern Lebanon were unwilling to allow the PLO to re-establish a military power-base in the region. In the Shi'ites themselves, though, Israel created an enemy across its northern border which was more firmly entrenched and, potentially, more dangerous. In July 1985, less than one month after Israel completed its withdrawal from southern Lebanon, Syria withdrew 10,000–12,000 troops from the Beka'a valley, leaving some 25,000 in position.

CHRISTIAN REVOLT

After the initial euphoria of the Israeli departure from Sidon in February 1985, during the first phase of the IDF's withdrawal, fighting broke out between Christian Phalangists on one side and Druze and Shi'ite militias on the other, with the Lebanese army manifestly unable to keep the peace. In early March President Gemayel had approved a Syrian security plan which had the long-term aim of granting more political and constitutional power to Lebanon's Muslim majority, and which would immediately deprive Christian militias of revenues from illegal ports and the control of a key checkpoint on the road from Beirut to Tripoli. Samir Geagea, a commander in the LF militia, rebelled against what he viewed as a capitulation to Syrian and Muslim influence, and attracted substantial support from units of the LF in east Beirut and north of the capital. Geagea demanded the end of party control of the LF and the introduction of a collective leadership for the Phalange. He also requested a democratically elected council to be established in areas controlled by the LF, to decide on any political reforms. Geagea soon controlled most of the LF in east Beirut, and street battles were fought between pro- and anti-Gemayel Christian factions. At the same time, fighting was renewed between Christian and Muslim militias along the 'Green Line' dividing east and west Beirut. The split in the Christian militia and the partitionist sentiments implicit in Geagea's proposals raised the possibility of Syrian military intervention in Beirut, to bolster President Gemayel and prevent the first stage in what might prove to be the inexorable sectarian fragmentation of Lebanon (thus creating a threat to Syria's internal stability). However, Geagea's revolt ended, as suddenly as it had begun, on 9 May, when Elie Hobeika was elected Commander of the LF. He pronounced himself ready to open a dialogue with Druze and Shi'ite leaders, acknowledged the role of Syria in creating a stable Lebanon, and pledged to evacuate the LF from the last Christian enclave in southern Lebanon at Jezzine.

It was to Jezzine that at least 60,000 Christian refugees from Sidon had gone to escape the fighting around Sidon. At the end of March 1985, units of the rebel Christian militia had launched an offensive, allegedly with Israeli encouragement, against the Palestinian refugee camp of Ain el-Hilweh (to which PLO guerrillas had been returning) and Muslim militiamen and troops of the Lebanese army in Muslim suburbs of Sidon. The exodus of Christians from Sidon began when, at the end of April, prior to the evacuation of the IDF from Jezzine, the LF removed some 300 men from the area to reinforce Christian forces involved in battles with Muslim militias in Beirut, and the remaining

Christian militiamen retreated. The retiring IDF were followed into the buffer zone along the Lebanese border by 60,000 Christians from Jezzine.

On 10 April 1985 Prime Minister Rashid Karami, angered by the Government's inability to restore peace to Sidon and its failure to reinforce the beleaguered Lebanese army there, announced that he would boycott cabinet meetings until a cease-fire was agreed. Then, on 17 April, he announced, but was persuaded to withdraw, his resignation after west Beirut had been overwhelmed by fighting, instigated by the Shi'ite Amal militia and their Druze allies to crush the Sunni Murabitoun militia and its Palestinian allies, and to prevent the revival of a pro-Arafat PLO force in Beirut.

ATTEMPTED SYRIAN SUPPRESSION OF THE PLO IN BEIRUT

In May and June 1985, through its proxy, the Shi'ite Amal militia, and with the assistance of the largely Shi'ite Sixth Brigade of the Lebanese army, Syria renewed its attempt to prevent Yasser Arafat from re-establishing a power-base in Lebanon. Most of the estimated 5,000 PLO guerrillas who returned to Lebanon in anticipation of and after the Israeli withdrawal from the south were thought to be loyal to Yasser Arafat. The Palestinian refugee camps of Sabra, Chatila and Bourj el-Barajneh in Beirut were besieged by Amal guerrillas (without the assistance of the Druze militia, who helped the Palestinians to take in supplies and reinforcements), but they failed to gain control of the camps or to quell PLO resistance. Furthermore, Palestinians belonging to the Palestine National Salvation Front (PNSF) of pro-Syrian guerrilla organizations joined with Arafat supporters in resisting the Shi'ites, many of whom were among the 640 people killed in the fighting. An uneasy cease-fire was agreed in Damascus on 17 June between Amal and the pro-Syrian Palestinian element in the camps, but it subsequently collapsed repeatedly.

HIJACK CRISIS IN BEIRUT

On 14 June 1985 two Lebanese Shi'ite Muslims, reputedly members of Hezbollah (the Party of God), hijacked a TWA passenger aircraft, with 153 people on board, on a flight from Athens to Rome. After twice taking it to Beirut and Algiers, and releasing more than 100 hostages, the hijackers landed for the third time in Beirut on 16 June. On 17 June Nabih Berri, who was acting as spokesman for the hijackers, announced that the remaining 42 hostages, mostly Americans, had been taken to secret locations in Beirut, pending response to the hijackers' demand for the release of 766 Lebanese prisoners, mostly Shi'-ites, who were being held in Israeli prisons. Israel said that it would not release its prisoners unless asked to do so by the US Government. The USA declared that it would not use force to secure the release of the hostages, but threatened to impose sanctions against Lebanon. President Assad of Syria became involved in the negotiations for the release of the hostages (now reduced to 39 after further releases), through his links with Nabih Berri and Amal, and his influence was crucial in securing their freedom on 30 June.

ANOTHER SECURITY PLAN FOR BEIRUT

Weeks of fighting between Shi'ite, Sunni and Druze militias in west Beirut preceded another attempt by Syria to initiate the process of political reform. A security plan was introduced in July 1985, after 13 spiritual and temporal leaders of the Lebanese Muslim community had met for talks with Syrian leaders in Damascus. Under the terms of the plan, west Beirut was to be divided into five security zones, each controlled by its own security committee. The Muslim militias were asked to leave the streets and to close their offices. The plan was designed to lay the basis for its extension to Christian east Beirut, and for a renewal of inter-sectarian dialogue on political and constitutional reform, but its implementation was almost immediately disrupted by further fighting.

On 6 August 1985, in the central Lebanese town of Shtaura, representatives of most of the country's religious communities (but, crucially, no one of stature representing the Sunni population and no Maronite Christians) announced the formation of a pro-Syrian national unity front. It had first been proclaimed in July, after meetings between the Syrian Vice-President, Abd al-Halim Khaddam, the Druze leader, Walid Joumblatt, and the leader of Amal, Nabih Berri. The front was committed to ending the civil war and 'to the final liquidation of the sectarian regime' under disproportionate Maronite control.

Four weeks of intensive fighting between rival militias in Tripoli in September and October 1985 were interpreted as part of Syria's campaign to prevent the re-emergence in Lebanon of the pro-Arafat wing of the PLO. The pro-Arafat, Sunni Muslim Tawheed Islami and the pro-Syrian, Alawite, Arab Democratic Party fought for control of the city and its port, which was allegedly being used to distribute armaments and supplies to Arafat loyalists in other parts of the country. More than 500 people were killed and 500,000 were driven from their homes in Tripoli before a cease-fire was agreed in Damascus at the beginning of October, and the Syrian army moved into the city.

THE ABORTIVE NATIONAL AGREEMENT

A month of negotiations between the three main Lebanese militias (the Druze forces, Amal and the LF), beginning in October 1985, led to the preparation of a draft accord for a politico-military settlement of the civil war. Objections by the Christians to the curbing of presidential powers and a reduction in their political influence delayed approval of the accord, but on 28 December it was finally signed in Damascus by the three militia leaders (Joumblatt, Berri and Hobeika). It provided for an immediate cease-fire and for an end to the state of civil war within one year; the militias would be disarmed and disbanded, and responsibility for security would pass to a reconstituted and religiously integrated Lebanese army, supported by Syrian forces. The accord envisaged the immediate establishment of a national coalition government under a council of six ministers representing the main religious sects, for a transitional period of three years, after which the confessional system of power-sharing government would be abolished and a secular administration created. A new National Assembly would be elected within the three-year period to enact the necessary legislation. The number of deputies in the new assembly would be increased from 99 to 198, with the total divided equally between Christians and Muslims, and an upper house would be added to the legislature. For the period of transition, a Maronite would continue to hold the office of President, but some of his executive powers would pass to the Prime Minister. The agreement recognized Lebanon's community of interest with Syria and envisaged a 'strategic integration' of the two countries in the fields of military relations, foreign policy and security.

The agreement seemed to offer some hope for Lebanon, as it had been negotiated by the actual combatants in the civil war and not merely by politicians. However, the Shi'ite Hezbollah and the Sunni Murabitoun militias were not parties to the accord, the Christian community was divided over it, and it made no provision for dealing with the problem of Palestinian refugees. Muslim support for the agreement was not widespread. The Sunni community had been virtually ignored during negotiations, and under the agreement the Druzes (although Joumblatt had signed it) would be likely to lose their autonomy in the Chouf region. Only Amal appeared to be wholly in favour of the accord. President Gemayel, who had not been involved in drafting the agreement, refused to endorse it, and at the end of December 1985 clashes erupted in east Beirut between elements of the LF who supported the accord and those who resented the concessions that had been made on their behalf by Elie Hobeika. In January 1986 Hobeika was forced into exile; Samir Geagea, the LF's Chief of Staff, was elected Chairman of its Executive Committee on 24 January, and urged the renegotiation of the Damascus accord. This effectively ended all hope that the peace agreement with the Muslim militias could be implemented.

President Gemayel, who regained much support among the Christian community for his opposition to the Damascus accord, was blamed for its failure by Muslim leaders. By January 1986 the Cabinet had not met for five months, and Muslim ministers subsequently refused to have any dealings with the President. They rejected his request for the Damascus agreement to be referred to the National Assembly and persisted in attempts to engineer his downfall. Inter-sectarian clashes in Beirut resumed in earnest on 22 January.

THE RESURGENCE OF THE PLO CONTINUES

In southern Lebanon Israel was faced with the consequences of its invasion having failed. During 1986 rocket attacks on Israeli settlements in northern Israel were resumed by Palestinian guerrillas, who had been gradually returning to the refugee camps around Tyre and Sidon after the Israeli withdrawal in 1985, and had established a number of mobile bases in the south. Israel responded with air raids on Palestinian targets in southern Lebanon, mostly in the Syrian-occupied Beka'a valley, during 1986 and 1987. The Amal militia, while contributing to the southern Lebanese resistance movement within the Israeli-imposed security zone, north of the international border, was more concerned to liberate south Lebanon than to carry the struggle against Israel into Israel itself. It attempted, therefore, to keep PLO guerrillas and radical Lebanese groups as far away from the zone as possible, in order to prevent them from launching rocket and mortar attacks against Israeli territory or from infiltrating the zone and then Israel itself, which might provoke Israeli reprisals inside Lebanon. Amal's controlling influence in the south was coming under threat from the pro-Iranian Hezbollah, which was attracting increasing support. Hezbollah intensified resistance to the SLA, attacking its positions within the security zone along the border with Israel, and fired rockets into Israel itself. Despite the backing of Amal, the role of UNIFIL was cast into doubt by the increasing number of clashes between the peace-keeping force and the SLA and, in particular, Hezbollah, which viewed UNIFIL as an obstacle to the pursuit of war against Israel. In May it was reported that the Syrians, ignoring Israeli warnings, were constructing fortifications and tank and gun emplacements in the Lake Karoun area, in the southern Beka'a, immediately to the north of the SLA-patrolled security zone.

Fighting between Palestinian guerrillas and Shi'ite Amal militiamen for control of the refugee camps in the south of Beirut, which had continued sporadically ever since the nominal cease-fire of June 1985, erupted into major exchanges on 19 May 1986. The refugee camps of Sabra, Chatila and Bourj el-Barajneh were increasingly under the control of guerrillas loyal to Yasser Arafat, who were continuing to return to Lebanon. Sunni and Druze militias continued to lend discreet support to the Palestinians, and there was serious fighting in June between Sunni forces and the Syrian-backed Amal

THE SYRIAN ARMY'S RETURN TO BEIRUT

Leaders of the Muslim communities in Lebanon met Syrian government officials in Damascus, and agreed to impose a cease-fire around the Beirut refugee camps on 14 June 1986. The cease-fire, which succeeded in reducing the fighting to the level of sniper exchanges, proved to be the first element in a Syrian-sponsored peace plan for Muslim west Beirut. About 1,000 Lebanese troops were deployed in west Beirut at the end of June. The Amal, Druze and Sunni militias were ordered to close their offices and to remain off the streets. Crucial to their co-operation was the appearance in Beirut, for the first time since 1982, of uniformed Syrian soldiers (several hundred of them), supported by members of the Syrian *Muhabarat* (security service) under the command of Brig.-Gen. Ghazi Kena'an. The security plan was temporarily successful in its limited objective of curbing the activities of militias in west Beirut, but the plan (and Syria's active involvement in it) was strongly opposed in Christian east Beirut, and only in August, after lengthy negotiations with Amal and Hezbollah, was it tentatively extended to the predominantly Shi'ite southern suburbs, which contained the majority of the city's Palestinian refugees. The Syrian presence failed to end fighting across the 'Green Line', or to prevent a wave of car bombings and abductions of Westerners by extremist Islamist groups.

On 19 August 1986 the Prime Minister, Rashid Karami, urged the resumption of peace talks between the various Lebanese communities, and on 2 September, after a meeting of government ministers (excluding President Gemayel), a new truce (reportedly the 191st since the civil war broke out in April 1975) was agreed. At the same time, the drafting of a national charter, aiming to end the civil war and to reform the confessional system of political representation, was to be put in train.

THE WAR OF THE CAMPS

Resistance to the re-emergence of the pro-Arafat PLO in Lebanon spread from Beirut to the Palestinian refugee camps around Tyre and Sidon at the beginning of October 1986. Amal forces besieged Rashidiyah camp, to the south of Tyre, and the camps at Miyeh Miyeh and Ain el-Hilweh, outside Sidon, cutting off access to food and medical supplies. According to the Palestine Red Crescent relief organization, 1,924 Palestinians died in the Beirut camps between November 1986 and February 1987. In that month, after the plight of the Palestinians in Beirut, Tyre and Sidon had attracted worldwide sympathy, Amal agreed to allow supplies into Bourj el-Barajneh and to permit women from Rashidiyah to leave the camp to buy food. Syria reportedly asked Amal to abandon the siege of the camps but the respite for the inhabitants of Bourj el-Barajneh and Rashidiyah proved to be brief, and the siege of the other camps remained strictly in force.

PAX SYRIANA

In February 1987 fierce fighting occurred in west Beirut between Amal forces and an alliance of the Druze, Murabitoun and Communist Party militias. Muslim leaders appealed for Syria to intervene to restore order, and, with the consent of Karami, Berri and Joumblatt, about 4,000 Syrian troops were deployed in west Beirut on 22 February. The Syrian force (which was soon increased to some 7,500 troops) succeeded in enforcing a cease-fire in the central and northern districts of west Beirut, but, once again, its leaders hesitated to attempt to extend its control to the predominantly Shi'ite southern suburbs, which Syrian-backed Lebanese security forces had failed to secure in July 1986 when Syrian troops first re-entered Beirut. President Gemayel initially opposed the latest deployment of Syrian troops in Beirut as being 'unconstitutional', but in March 1987 he welcomed several clauses in a Syrian-sponsored agreement on political reform, which had been approved by Lebanese Muslim leaders and which would give Lebanon's Muslim majority a greater role in government and reduce the powers of the Christian President.

On 24 February 1987 Syrian troops moved into areas of west Beirut occupied by Hezbollah militiamen, killing 23 of them, but did not venture into the southern suburbs where Hezbollah had most influence. On the following day Syria claimed that all 75 militia offices in west Beirut had been closed. The remaining Hezbollah fighters there moved to the southern suburbs, while hundreds of Amal militiamen left Beirut to pursue the struggle against Israel in the south of Lebanon.

A Syrian-supervised cease-fire at all the embattled Palestinian refugee camps in Beirut began on 6 April 1987, and the siege of Chatila and Bourj el-Barajneh was suspended to allow supplies to be taken into the camps. The cease-fire accord was negotiated by representatives of Syria, Amal and the pro-Syrian PNSF, who had made common cause with pro-Arafat PLO members to defend the camps. However, in Sidon, outside effective Syrian jurisdiction, renewed fighting broke out between Amal and members of the PLO loyal to Yasser Arafat. Amal maintained that it would only agree fully to end the siege of the camps if Arafat loyalists withdrew from villages near Sidon that they had captured from Amal in October and November 1986. Some 150 Syrian troops were deployed around Sidon in mid-April.

On 1 June 1987 Prime Minister Karami was killed when a bomb exploded in the helicopter in which he was travelling. President Gemayel appointed the Minister of Labour, Education, and Fine Arts, Dr Selim al-Hoss, as acting Prime Minister. It was unclear who was responsible for Karami's assassination, though the Christian section of the divided Lebanese army and the Christian LF were considered by the Muslim community to be the leading suspects. Karami, a Sunni Muslim, had been a firm ally of Syria and had been instrumental in the deployment of Syrian troops in Beirut in February. On 5 June Hussain al-Hussaini, the Shi'ite President of the National Assembly, resigned, alleging that President Gemayel was trying to conceal the truth about the circumstances, and authors, of Karami's death. Muslim leaders demanded a full investigation into the assassination.

On 21 May 1987 the National Assembly had voted to abrogate the agreement, signed by Lebanon and Yasser Arafat (for the

PLO) in Cairo in 1969, which defined and regulated the PLO's activities and legitimized its presence in Lebanon. The annulment cancelled any theoretical right of the PLO to official Lebanese protection while it operated in Lebanon. In practice any such protection had long been withheld or had been impracticable. The abrogation of the Cairo accord was strongly suspected of being Syrian-inspired, coming, as it did, in the wake of the reunification of the PLO under Arafat's leadership at the 18th session of the Palestine National Council in Algiers in April, which had deprived the Syrian-sponsored PNSF of the support of the largest groups that had rebelled against Arafat in 1983. Although the divided Lebanese security forces were incapable of enforcing a withdrawal of PLO forces from Lebanon, in line with the abrogation of the Cairo accord, Syria, which had effectively assumed responsibility for security in Beirut, through its own forces and those of Amal was certainly in a position to attempt to do so. Such a policy would be merely a logical continuation of Syria's attempt to prevent the re-establishment of the PLO in Lebanon, and one which Syria could claim was sanctioned by the Lebanese National Assembly. (The Assembly also finally and formally cancelled the peace treaty of 17 May 1983 between Lebanon and Israel, abrogated by President Gemayel in March 1984 but on which the Assembly had never voted.)

Although the most intense fighting between Amal and PLO guerrillas had ended, and the removal of the blockade of the Palestinian refugee camps had been proclaimed in April 1987, the camps remained effectively under siege, apparently under the supervision of Syrian troops, and freedom of movement in and out of them was confined to women and children. On 11 September an agreement was announced between Amal (as part of the largely Muslim Unification and Liberation Front, which had been formed under Syrian auspices in July, and also included Walid Joumblatt's mainly Druze Parti socialiste progressiste—PSP) and the PLO in the camps, purportedly ending the 'war of the camps', in which more than 2,500 people had died. The accord provided for the ending of the siege of the camps and for the withdrawal of Palestinian fighters from strategic positions outside the Ain el-Hilweh refugee camp, east of Sidon. However, neither measure was implemented, and in October differences over the withdrawal of some 5,000–8,000 Palestinian guerrillas led to renewed fighting around the disputed positions to the east of Sidon. On 16 January 1988, avowedly as a gesture of support for the *intifada* (uprising) by Palestinians in the Israeli-occupied territories, which had begun in December 1987, Nabih Berri, the leader of Amal, announced the cessation of the siege of the Palestinian refugee camps in Beirut and southern Lebanon: Amal fighters and soldiers from the predominantly Shi'ite Sixth Brigade of the Lebanese army withdrew their positions around Bourj el-Barajneh and Chatila camps, to be replaced by Syrian troops, and the 14-month siege of Rashidiyah camp, near Tyre, was ended. However, pro-Arafat PLO guerrillas still refused to withdraw from their positions overlooking Ain el-Hilweh camp near Sidon, disrupting the withdrawal of Amal from around Rashidiyah.

AMAL AND HEZBOLLAH CLASH

In cynical terms, it was politically inexpedient for Syria to continue to employ its proxy, Amal, in its attempt to suppress the PLO in Lebanon, at a time when the Palestinian uprising in the Occupied Territories was attracting world-wide sympathy (particularly among Arabs) to the plight of the Palestinians. By suspending Amal's campaign against the pro-Arafat PLO, Nabih Berri's forces could be deployed against Hezbollah, whose ultimate aim was to establish an Islamic state in Lebanon on the Iranian model and whose strength was viewed by Syria as a threat to its own ambitions to control Lebanon. Amal's attacks were initially directed against Hezbollah bases in southern Lebanon, and clashes (the first military confrontation between the two groups) occurred at the end of March in the Nabatiyah area. On 9 April 1988 Amal claimed to have captured Hezbollah's last stronghold in the south, at Siddiqin, while Iranian Revolutionary Guards stationed at Sharqiyah and Jibshit had been ordered to leave the area.

In Beirut, Syria had demonstrated its opposition to hostage-taking by preventing a Kuwaiti Boeing 747, which had been hijacked by militant Islamists (alleged to be Lebanese), from

landing at the city's airport in early April 1988. On 5 May fighting broke out between the Amal and Hezbollah militias (the latter supported by Iranian Revolutionary Guards) in the southern suburbs of Beirut. Attempts to impose a cease-fire through Iranian and Syrian mediation failed, and Syrian troops became involved in the fighting on 13 May, when Hezbollah guerrillas, who had wrested control of about 90% of the southern suburbs from Amal, briefly advanced into a Syrian-controlled area of west Beirut. On 15 May Syrian troops encircled the southern suburbs, while intensive negotiations took place between Syria and Iran. On 27 May several hundred Syrian troops moved into the southern suburbs of Beirut to enforce a cease-fire agreement reached by Syria, Iran and their militia proxies on the previous day. When the Syrian deployment was complete, Amal and Hezbollah were to close down their military operations in all parts of the southern suburbs, except in areas adjoining the 'Green Line', where they would continue to be allowed to post their men. On 3 June, in accordance with the agreement, Nabih Berri announced the disbandment of the Amal militia in Beirut and the Beka'a valley (areas under Syrian control) and all other areas of the country except the south (which was not controlled by Syrian troops).

ARAFAT LOYALISTS DRIVEN OUT OF BEIRUT

At the end of April 1988, following a partial reconciliation between Yasser Arafat and President Assad of Syria, Arafat loyalists in the Palestinian refugee camps of Chatila and Bourj el-Barajneh attempted to drive out the fighters belonging to the Syrian-backed group, Fatah Intifada (Fatah Uprising) of Abu Musa. The Syrian troops who had surrounded the camps in April 1987 did not attempt to intervene in the fighting but, with Amal (Syria's other surrogate in Lebanon's factional conflict) otherwise occupied, they allowed reinforcements to reach the rebel Fatah group. On 27 June 1988 the Arafat loyalists in Chatila were overrun and surrendered to the forces of Abu Musa. The following day Syria granted 100 PLO guerrillas safe passage from Chatila to the Palestinian camp at Ain el-Hilweh, near Sidon, although their entry into the camp was allowed by the local Sunni Muslim militia (the Popular Liberation Army, led by Mustafa Saad) only after the personal intervention of the Libyan leader, Col Qaddafi. On 7 July Bourj el-Barajneh, Yasser Arafat's last stronghold in Beirut, was captured by the forces of Abu Musa, and 120 Arafat loyalists were evacuated to Ain el-Hilweh.

LEBANON FAILS TO ELECT A NEW PRESIDENT

President Gemayel's term of office was due to expire on 23 September 1988, and the National Assembly was required to elect a new President before that date. As the election approached, political manoeuvring began in an attempt to find a candidate for the post (under the confessional tradition a Maronite Christian) who would be acceptable to both Christians and Muslims. The question was complicated by divisions within the Maronite community and the unwillingness of most Christians to accept a candidate who was thought to represent Syrian interests. Discussions between Syria and the USA regarding a suitable candidate failed to produce a compromise choice.

By mid-August 1988 more than two dozen candidates for the presidency had declared themselves, but the three main contenders were: Gen. Michel Awn, the Commander-in-Chief of the Lebanese army; Raymond Eddé, the leader of the Maronite Bloc national libanais, who had been in exile in France since 1976; and former President Sulayman Franjiya. The latter did not announce his candidacy until 16 August 1988, two days before the date of the election, and the news immediately united President Gemayel and Samir Geagea, the commander of the LF, who opposed Franjiya's candidature on the grounds that he represented Syrian interests. (It was Franjiya who, as President, had invited Syria to intervene militarily in Lebanon to end the civil war in 1976.) President Gemayel and Geagea asserted that they would do everything legally in their power to prevent Franjiya from being elected. The reaction of Walid Joumblatt, the Druze leader, was to withdraw the presidential candidate of his own PSP and to support Franjiya's candidacy.

Votes for the presidency were to be cast in two ballots. To be elected, the successful candidate had to receive a majority vote of two-thirds of the members of the National Assembly in the first ballot and a simple majority in the second. In the event, only 38 members (10 of the 41 Christian deputies and 28 of the 35 Muslim deputies) attended the session on 18 August 1988 at the temporary parliamentary premises on the 'Green Line'; the session was thus declared to be inquorate, and the election was postponed.

On 2 September 1988 the acting Prime Minister, Dr Selim al-Hoss, withdrew the Government's resignation, which had been tendered by the late Rashid Karami in May 1987. President Gemayel claimed that al-Hoss's action was unconstitutional, insisting that his Government held office only in a caretaker capacity. Consultations between Syria and the USA resumed during September 1988 in an attempt to agree upon a compromise presidential candidate who might be acceptable to the majority in Lebanon. It was reported that they had agreed to support the candidacy of Mikhail ad-Daher, a parliamentary deputy, but Christian army and LF leaders repeated their rejection of any candidate imposed upon Lebanon by foreign powers. A second attempt at a presidential election was scheduled for 22 September but, again, the session of the National Assembly failed to achieve a quorum. Only 14 deputies gathered for the vote in the old parliament building in west Beirut. Christian deputies assembled, instead, at a villa in east Beirut to repeat their opposition to a Syrian-imposed presidential candidate (i.e. Mikhail ad-Daher) and to the siting of the venue for the election in Syrian-controlled, Muslim west Beirut.

President Gemayel's term of office expired at midnight on 22 September 1988, and, only minutes before, in accordance with his constitutional privilege, he appointed a six-member interim military Government, composed of three Christian and three Muslim officers, led by Gen. Awn, to rule until a new President was elected. His choice of a military government was made after Muslim politicians had refused to participate in an interim civilian government which was to be headed, contrary to the National Covenant of 1943 (which divided power between the Christian and Muslim communities), by a Maronite Prime Minister, Pierre Hélou, instead of by a Sunni Muslim. The three nominated Muslim officers refused to accept their posts in the interim military administration (which were assumed by the remaining Christian ministers on 4 October 1988), while the two Christian members of the Government of Dr Selim al-Hoss (Joseph Hashim and Victor Qasir) surrendered their posts in recognition of the authority of the interim military administration. Dr al-Hoss appointed a Greek Orthodox Christian, Abdullah ar-Rassi, as Deputy Prime Minister on 24 September.

Lebanon was plunged into a constitutional crisis, with two governments (one Christian, in east Beirut, and one predominantly Muslim, in west Beirut) claiming legitimacy. Syria, for its part, refused to recognize the interim military Government. Concern over the stability of Lebanon's central institutions increased in October 1988, when the National Assembly failed to elect a successor to Hussain al-Hussaini, the President of National Assembly, or to renew his one-year mandate. Meanwhile, each of the two governments claiming legitimacy warned the other not to encroach upon its jurisdiction. The authority of Gen. Awn's military administration was regarded as having been strengthened when Geagea's LF seized control of Gemayel's base in the Metn region, north of Beirut, in early October. Of Lebanon's central institutions, only the central bank remained intact, and it continued to make funds available to both governments for basic supplies of food and fuel.

In November 1988 Gen. Awn was dismissed as Commander-in-Chief of the army by Adel Osseiran, the Minister of Defence in the al-Hoss Government. However, since Awn retained the loyalty of large sections of the military, he remained its *de facto* leader. Fighting broke out in southern Beirut between rival Shi'a groups of the Syrian-supported Amal in that month, and between Amal and the Iranian-sponsored Hezbollah in January 1989. In the latter instance the two militias were reported to have agreed a cease-fire on 30 January. In February a major confrontation occurred between the LF and the Lebanese army, when Gen. Awn attempted to restore the Government's authority over the illegal, militia-controlled ports. While neither side achieved a decisive victory, the authority of the Lebanese army, which had been steadily eroded, was restored as a result of the clashes. The balance of power in Beirut was perceived as gradually altering, and there were hopes that the success of the Lebanese army in its encounters with the LF would lead to the reunification of Beirut.

AWN'S ATTEMPT TO EXPEL SYRIAN FORCES FROM LEBANON

In March 1989, however, the most violent clashes for two years erupted in Beirut between Christian and Muslim forces positioned on either side of the 'Green Line'. While the immediate cause of the fighting was the blockade of illegal ports in west and south Beirut by Christian forces, it was Gen. Awn's declared intention to take all measures for the immediate expulsion of Syrian forces from Lebanon. On 29 March a cease-fire, agreed in response to an appeal from a six-member Arab League committee on Lebanon, was declared. However, exchanges of artillery fire resumed within a matter of hours.

Throughout most of April 1989 Awn's forces and Syrian troops exchanged artillery fire on an almost daily basis, and by the end of the month almost 300 people had been killed. On 19 April, despite Awn's claim that he had a popular mandate to pursue the expulsion of Syrian forces from Lebanon, 23 Christian members of the National Assembly demanded an immediate cease-fire and appealed to the Arab League, the UN and the EC to intervene to end the fighting. In late April, following an emergency meeting of Arab League Ministers of Foreign Affairs, further proposals for a comprehensive peace plan were announced, recommending a cease-fire, under the supervision of an Arab cease-fire monitoring force. The cease-fire took effect on 28 April, but renewed exchanges of fire were reported on 30 April.

RENEWED DIPLOMATIC INITIATIVES AS THE CONFLICT ESCALATES

Renewed fighting between Christian and Muslim forces erupted at the beginning of May 1989, and on 3 May a delegation from the Arab League (consisting of the League's Assistant Secretary-General, Lakhdar al-Ibrahimi, and the Kuwaiti ambassador to Syria, Ahmed Abd al-Aziz Jassem) arrived in Beirut with the aim of enforcing the 28 April cease-fire and to arrange for the arrival of an Arab monitoring force. The delegation met the leaders of the rival Lebanese Governments, who had reportedly consented to the withdrawal of all land, sea and air blockades. Following a further outbreak of fighting, an urgent meeting was held between the Arab League delegation, the Syrian Government and the leaders of both Lebanese Governments. On 11 May it was announced that a further cease-fire had been agreed, but this collapsed on the same day.

At an emergency summit meeting of Arab leaders, held in Casablanca, Morocco, during 23–26 May 1989 (subsequently extended by two days in order to achieve a unified position on the Lebanese question), a tripartite Arab Committee, consisting of King Hassan of Morocco, King Fahd of Saudi Arabia and President Chadli of Algeria, was formed to supplement the efforts of the Arab League Committee on Lebanon. Its aims were: to implement a cease-fire agreement in Lebanon within six months; to install an Arab observer force to supervise the cease-fire; and to act as an intermediary between the conflicting forces in Lebanon in order to facilitate an agreement on the question of political reform and the election of a new President. However, many observers doubted that the newly-formed Committee, presided over by King Hassan, could achieve these aims, not least because there had been no indication at the Casablanca summit of any willingness on the part of either Syria or Iraq to resolve their conflicting interests in Lebanon. Since the cease-fire in the Iran–Iraq War of August 1988, the traditional enmity between Iraq and Syria (which had intensified as a result of Syria's support for Iran during the war) had increasingly found expression by proxy in the conflict within Lebanon. By mid-1989, as Gen. Awn pursued his campaign to expel Syrian forces from Lebanon, Iraq had become the principal supplier of weapons to the Lebanese army.

As in its attempt to persuade other Arab leaders to condemn Syria's role in Lebanon, Iraq was unsuccessful in its demand, made at the Casablanca summit, for the withdrawal of Syrian troops from Lebanon. Other Arab leaders, while reportedly willing to condemn Syria's 'negative' role in Lebanon in private, were believed to fear Iraqi ambitions and to have sought to maintain a balance between Iraq and Syria. Egypt, Iraq, Jordan and the PLO all supported a proposal for the withdrawal of Syrian troops from Lebanon and for their replacement by an Arab peace-keeping force, but the plan was abandoned, in response to Syrian opposition.

At the beginning of June 1989 the Tripartite Arab Committee on Lebanon issued a renewed appeal for a cease-fire, but further exchanges of artillery fire took place the following day. At the same time King Hassan, King Fahd and President Chadli were said to have instructed their Ministers of Foreign Affairs to begin the implementation of a 'plan of action' for Lebanon. On 10 June the three ministers travelled to Damascus, delivering to President Assad a letter from the Tripartite Arab Committee and receiving assurances from him of Syria's willingness to co-operate with the Committee. Lakhdar al-Ibrahimi also made further attempts to mediate between the opposed parties in Lebanon, holding talks with both President Assad and Gen. Awn. By mid-June, however, it had not been possible to reach an agreement regarding the composition of the proposed Arab cease-fire monitoring committee.

On 28 June 1989 the Tripartite Committee renewed its appeal for a cease-fire and announced details of its peace plan for Lebanon. The new plan proposed a cease-fire, the removal of blockades of Muslim and Christian ports in Lebanon and the opening of roads between east and west Beirut prior to a meeting of the Lebanese National Assembly in an unspecified foreign country. The last component of the new proposals was immediately rejected by Gen. Awn, however, on the grounds that such a meeting would 'contradict the principles of sovereignty and national unity'. Despite the appeal for a cease-fire, exchanges of artillery fire continued.

Evidence of Soviet support for the new peace plan emerged in early July 1989, when Aleksandr Bessmertnykh, the USSR's First Deputy Minister of Foreign Affairs, travelled to Damascus with a message to President Assad from President Mikhail Gorbachev, which reportedly appealed for an end to the fighting in Beirut. Iraq had previously responded to a similar communication by stating that it was prepared to halt all supplies of armaments to Gen. Awn's forces. However, while some observers optimistically attached their hopes for the salvation of Lebanon to the USSR, the extent of Soviet influence on Syria, as its principal supplier of arms, was limited. Despite the prolonged ferocity of the hostilities since March, it had long been inconceivable that either of the 'superpowers' would commit itself to the resolution of the Lebanese conflict. On 31 July the Tripartite Committee abruptly suspended its work and blamed Syrian intransigence for the lack of progress on the Lebanese question. The Committee issued a communiqué accusing Syria of having a concept of Lebanese sovereignty that was inconsistent with the independence of Lebanon.

By August 1989 more than 600 people had been killed since Gen. Awn had begun his attempt to expel Syrian forces from Lebanon. In mid-August France dispatched senior government envoys to Middle Eastern capitals in a new diplomatic initiative to halt the conflict. Since the escalation of hostilities in March France had evacuated badly-wounded victims from both Christian and Muslim communities and had urged its partners in the EC to join forces in an urgent humanitarian mission. Since a substantial number of Lebanese Christians enjoyed dual French-Lebanese nationality, the French Government was faced with increasing domestic pressure to send such a mission. However, the suspicions of Muslim Lebanese regarding France's true intentions, and its possible future extension of military support to Gen. Awn's forces, were only partially allayed by the French policy of providing aid to both Muslim and Christian communities. The new French diplomatic moves were made in response to a further, dramatic escalation of the fighting in Beirut. On 13 August Syrian forces made their first attempt for more than 14 years to penetrate Christian-held territory, launching an attack on the town of Souk el-Gharb. This assault, combined with increased artillery bombardments of east Beirut, was regarded as an attempt by Syria to compensate, by military means, for its increasing diplomatic isolation: at the end of July the Arab League had formally referred to Syria as the principal obstacle to a settlement in Lebanon, while the USA had condemned Syria's renewed use of heavy-calibre weapons in Beirut. Syria, however, claimed that Gen. Awn bore full responsibility

for the escalation of hostilities since he had earlier rejected an offer of a cease-fire by Lebanese militias allied to Syria.

The French diplomatic initiative was strongly condemned by the Iranian-backed Hezbollah militia, which described it as a French 'military adventure' to assist Gen. Awn. While France emphasized repeatedly that it was not considering any military intervention in Lebanon, the Beirut-based Revolutionary Justice Organization warned that such intervention by French forces (eight French naval vessels had been dispatched towards Lebanon by 22 August 1989, in anticipation of a renewed onslaught against Christian-held positions in Beirut) would rebound upon US hostages held in Beirut.

On 16 August 1989 the UN Secretary-General, Javier Pérez de Cuéllar, summoned an emergency meeting of the Security Council to discuss means of achieving a cease-fire in Lebanon. This meeting, convened under emergency powers of the Secretary-General which had been invoked on only two previous occasions, followed reports that both Syrian- and Iranian-backed militias in Beirut were preparing to join regular Syrian forces to defeat the Lebanese army.

In late August 1989 French diplomatic pressure was reported to have led to an offer by Gen. Awn to meet his Muslim rivals at a conference, with no reference to his previous condition that political reform in Lebanon could be discussed only after Syrian forces had withdrawn from the country. On 27 August a French peace plan for Lebanon was formally presented to Syria's Minister of Foreign Affairs, Farouk ash-Shara', by the Director-General of the French Ministry of Foreign Affairs, François Scheer. The plan proposed: a cease-fire; a halt to deliveries of armaments to either side involved in the conflict; the introduction of political reforms to end the predominance of the Christians in Lebanon; and the phased withdrawal of foreign forces from Lebanon, beginning with the withdrawal of Syrian forces from west Beirut. While there was no immediate official response to these proposals by Gen. Awn's Government, Christian Lebanese sources in Beirut dismissed the proposals as 'Syrian-inspired' and as seeking to distract the international community from the primary issue of ending the siege of east Beirut.

On 7 September 1989 the USA announced its decision to evacuate its ambassador to Cyprus and close its embassy in Beirut. The withdrawal of US diplomatic representation was regarded as signalling the failure of Gen. Awn's attempt to 'internationalize' the Lebanese conflict and to win Western support to expel Syrian forces.

On 18 September 1989 the Tripartite Arab Committee on Lebanon resumed its efforts to bring peace to Lebanon, following a meeting in Tripoli, Libya, at the beginning of September between President Assad and President Chadli, at which Assad agreed to have the Syrian presence in Lebanon debated. The Committee appealed for an 'immediate and comprehensive cease-fire'. A new peace plan was announced whereby a Lebanese security committee was to be established (under the auspices of the Assistant Secretary-General of the Arab League) to supervise the cease-fire. The new plan envisaged the removal of the Syrian naval blockade of Beirut's Christian enclave, while the committee would retain the right to inspect any ship reported to be carrying arms. At the same time, Beirut's international airport was to be reopened. Finally, the plan envisaged a meeting of the Lebanese National Assembly to discuss a 'charter of national reconciliation' drafted by the Tripartite Arab Committee. Members of the Assembly were to assemble on 30 September at a venue to be announced. Unlike the Committee's previous plan for peace in Lebanon, the new plan made no appeal for the withdrawal of Syrian troops, and was thus welcomed by the Syrian Government. Gen. Awn rejected the proposal for an exclusively Lebanese security committee, arguing that, since Syrian forces were directly involved in the conflict, Syria should be represented on any committee established to supervise a cease-fire. However, due to his diplomatic isolation (the charter was supported by the USA, the USSR, the United Kingdom, France and almost every Arab nation), Awn subsequently relented. The cease-fire accordingly took effect from 23 September.

THE TA'IF AGREEMENT

At the end of September the Lebanese National Assembly met in Ta'if, Saudi Arabia, to discuss the charter of national reconciliation. The session was attended by 31 Christian deputies and 31 Muslim deputies. (Of the 99 deputies elected in May 1972, only 73 still survived.) At a further meeting on 22 October 1989, the charter of national reconciliation was endorsed by 58 of the 62 deputies attending the session. Subsequent to its first being announced, the charter had been amended at informal sessions of the National Assembly. However, the section dealing with Syria's role in Lebanon was the result of a prior agreement between the Tripartite Committee and Syria, and Lebanese deputies were prohibited from altering it. With regard to political reform, the charter now provided for the transfer of executive power from the presidency to a cabinet, with portfolios divided equally among Christian and Muslim ministers. The appointment of the Prime Minister would remain the prerogative of the President, to be exercised in consultation with the members and President of the National Assembly. The charter further provided for an increase in the number of seats in the Assembly, from 99 to 108, to be divided equally among Christian and Muslim deputies. A further provision was the implementation of two security plans in Lebanon, one within six months and the other within 24 months. Following the endorsement of the charter, the election of a President and the formation of a new government, all Lebanese and non-Lebanese militias were to be disbanded within six months, while the internal security forces were to be strengthened. For a maximum period of two years the Syrian army would then assist the new government in implementing the security plan.

The endorsement of the charter of national reconciliation (the Ta'if agreement) by the National Assembly was immediately denounced by Gen. Awn as a betrayal of Lebanese sovereignty. Prior to their departure for Ta'if, Christian deputies to the Assembly had reportedly assured Gen. Awn that they would permit concessions on the question of political reform only in exchange for a full withdrawal of Syrian forces from Lebanon. While there was some support for Gen. Awn's position in east Beirut, the agreement had, to a large extent, been facilitated by the co-operation of Lebanon's Maronite leaders, most notably Georges Saadé, the leader of the Phalangist Party, who had played an important role in the Ta'if negotiations.

In an annex to the Ta'if agreement, the Tripartite Arab Committee on Lebanon had appealed to the National Assembly to meet in November 1989 to ratify the charter and to elect a new President. This session of the Assembly was duly held in the northern town of Qlaiaat on 5 November, when René Mouawad, a Maronite Christian deputy and a former Minister of Education and Arts, was elected as President. Deputies also unanimously endorsed the Ta'if agreement and re-elected Hussain al-Hussaini as President of the National Assembly. Prior to the meeting Gen. Awn had appealed to all Christian deputies to consult with him before attending. In response to the news that Muslim deputies had departed for Qlaiaat, Gen. Awn had announced the dissolution of the National Assembly. His reaction to the presidential election was to declare it unconstitutional, and the result null and void.

On 13 November 1989 President Mouawad invited Dr Selim al-Hoss to form a 'government of national reconciliation'. However, Maronite leaders were reluctant to participate in such an administration and thus openly oppose Gen. Awn. On 22 November, only 17 days after his election, President Mouawad was assassinated in a bomb explosion. Two days later, in the town of Shtaura, 52 deputies of the National Assembly convened and elected Elias Hrawi as the new President. At the same session, deputies voted to extend the Assembly's term of office until the end of 1994. A new Government was formed by Dr al-Hoss on 25 November.

Following a meeting of the new Cabinet on 28 November 1989, it was announced that Gen. Awn had again been dismissed as Commander-in-Chief of the Lebanese army, and that Gen. Emile Lahoud had been appointed in his place. It was feared that Syrian forces would now launch a major assault on Awn's stronghold in Baabda, east Beirut. Geagea announced that, in the event of such an assault, the LF would fight beside Gen. Awn. In December, in an attempt further to isolate Gen. Awn, the central bank halted all transfers of funds to areas of Beirut controlled by him, and the Ministry of Defence reportedly ceased paying the salaries of Awn's troops and officials.

On 31 January 1990 Gen. Awn ordered his forces to close all the barracks of the LF in east Beirut. There followed intense fighting between Awn's forces and the LF for control of the Christian enclave, precipitated by the refusal of Geagea to reject the Ta'if agreement, thus isolating Gen. Awn within the Christian community. Awn had accordingly declared the LF to be an ally of Syria. (Maronite leaders had sought to avoid open conflict with Gen. Awn by minimizing their approval of the Ta'if agreement, and on 29 January Georges Saadé, who had been appointed Minister of Posts and Telecommunications in November 1989, announced that he would not serve in the administration, thus damaging its credibility as a 'national unity' government.) By early March 1990 more than 800 people had been killed, and more than 2,500 wounded, in the inter-Christian fighting since 31 January. In March Gen. Awn declared a halt to the conflict between Christian factions, and expressed willingness to negotiate with his opponents, implying that he was willing to accept the Ta'if agreement in a modified form. Inter-Christian fighting, however, resumed later in the month. In April Geagea announced his recognition of the al-Hoss Government, formally accepting the Ta'if agreement, and in June Georges Saadé resumed his duties as Minister of Posts and Telecommunications.

In July 1990 fierce fighting erupted between Amal and Hezbollah in southern Lebanon. Clashes between the rival Shi'ite groups had occurred in March in southern Beirut, prompting the intervention of Syrian forces. At the beginning of August Israel warned that it would intervene if its interests were endangered by the hostilities.

Meanwhile, at the end of July 1990, the al-Hoss administration began an attempt to pressurize Gen. Awn into relinquishing his power base in east Beirut by seeking to prevent essential supplies from reaching his forces. In the last week of July Awn had conferred with the Assistant Secretary-General of the Arab League, Lakhdar al-Ibrahimi, but had rejected the suggestion—which had already been proposed in a diplomatic initiative pursued by the French Government and the Vatican in June—of joining the al-Hoss Government under the terms of the Ta'if agreement.

THE IMPLEMENTATION OF THE TA'IF AGREEMENT

The crisis in the Gulf region, which was precipitated by Iraq's invasion of Kuwait in August 1990, had serious repercussions for Lebanon. Iraq's Lebanese allies—Gen. Awn and the PLO—hoped that the Iraqi challenge to US and Saudi power would serve to weaken that power and subsequently undermine the regional and international consensus that supported the Ta'if agreement. The pro-Ta'if parties in Lebanon were apprehensive about the fate of the accord, in view of the crisis developing in the Gulf. In response, they succeeded, on 21 August, in convening a session of the National Assembly at which the Constitution was amended to incorporate the reforms agreed at Ta'if.

The reforms stipulated that new deputies (40 in all, taking account of the 32 vacant seats in the old assembly) were to be appointed, rather than elected, for one term, owing to the 'extraordinary situation' in the country. The powers of the National Assembly were increased to the point where it became virtually impossible to dissolve it. The term of office of the President of the National Assembly was increased from one to four years, and the holder of that office would in future play a role in appointing the Prime Minister. The President, meanwhile, was divested of his autonomous prerogatives. Presidential decisions now required the co-signature of the Prime Minister, except in two instances: the appointment of a Prime Minister, and when accepting the Government's resignation. Nominally the President continued to be Commander-in-Chief of the armed forces, but the army remained subject to the full authority of the Cabinet. In appointing a Prime Minister, the President could only follow the choice of deputies to the National Assembly. He no longer enjoyed the right to chair meetings of the Cabinet, to determine the agenda of such meetings or to vote at them.

With the stipulations of the Ta'if agreement incorporated into the Constitution, executive power was effectively transferred to the Lebanese Cabinet. The main beneficiary of the changes was the office of the Prime Minister, who became the head of the Government, speaking in its name, implementing its policies and co-ordinating the various ministries. In the event of a vacancy in the office of the President, the Cabinet, under the chairmanship of the Prime Minister, would assume the privileges and responsibilities of the presidency. The speed with which the National Assembly was convened on 21 August 1990 reflected an evolution in Syria's attitude towards the process of constitutional reform. Syria's renewed interest in the Ta'if agreement came in response to US assurances regarding Syria's continued dominance in Lebanon and US support to that end.

On 28 September 1990 units of the Lebanese army loyal to the al-Hoss Government imposed an economic blockade on the areas of Beirut controlled by Gen. Awn. The blockade, which enjoyed Syrian and US support, was designed to force Awn into either co-operating with the Government, or evacuating his base at the presidential palace at Baabda. On 13 October Syrian forces commenced a military assault against the presidential palace at Baabda and other strategic areas under Awn's control. In a clear breach of the 'Red Lines' agreement between Syria and Israel, which regulated the parameters within which each country could operate in Lebanon, the Syrian air force shelled the presidential palace. That Israel did not retaliate in response to such a breach of the agreement reflected the USA's support of the Syrian offensive. The Syrian military operation was the first of the repercussions of the Gulf crisis in Lebanon, where Syria had effectively been granted freedom of action as a reward for its participation in the US-led multinational force deployed in Saudi Arabia. Awn's forces were completely defeated, and the areas under his control overrun. During the fighting Awn had departed for the French embassy in Beirut, in order to negotiate a cease-fire. As soon as Baabda had fallen under Syrian control, he was advised to remain in the embassy for his own safety, and the French Government, considering his protection to be a matter of honour, offered him and his family political asylum. The Lebanese Government, however, refused to allow Awn to depart for France, seeking to place him on trial for embezzlement of funds and crimes against the state.

Following Awn's defeat, the Government began to implement a security plan for the Greater Beirut area. On 24 December 1990 a new Government of national reconciliation was formed under Omar Karami, hitherto the Minister of Education and Arts. It was the first Lebanese administration to be formed since the amendment of the Constitution in August 1990 and was intended to continue with the implementation of the Ta'if agreement, begun under the previous Government. The new Prime Minister enjoyed exclusive Syrian support. The 30-member Cabinet included various militia and party leaders as well as traditional political figures. Cabinet posts were divided equally between Muslims and Christians: six Sunni Muslims, six Maronite Christians, six Shi'a Muslims, three Druzes, four Greek Orthodox Christians, three Greek Catholics, one Armenian Catholic and one Armenian Orthodox Christian. The composition of the new Government attracted considerable criticism. Deputies in the National Assembly complained at their under-representation, while the Lebanese press questioned the appointment to the Cabinet of military leaders and the sons of prominent politicians. The Phalangist Party and the LF complained that the Government lacked 'national balance'. Druze representatives complained at the dilution of their influence, while Hezbollah, the Parti communiste libanais and the PNL were not represented in the Cabinet at all. The Government, meanwhile, adhered to the four-point programme which it had presented to the National Assembly, aiming to extend its authority over the whole of Lebanon; to disband the militias; to formalize Lebanon's 'special relations' with Syria; and to appoint deputies to the vacant seats in the Assembly and fill senior military and civilian posts.

On 6 February 1991 Lebanese army battalions were dispatched to the south of the country for the first time since the Israeli invasion of 1978. They were deployed in the wake of a serious escalation in Palestinian guerrilla operations in the south, and consequent Israeli retaliation, as a 'buffer' between the 6,000 Palestinian fighters in and around Sidon and units of the Israeli-backed SLA. However, the inadequacy of the army's capabilities in relation to the size of the area which it was meant to patrol meant that its deployment was largely symbolic. Its presence was nevertheless welcomed by the Shi'ite militia, Amal. The Iranian-backed Hezbollah reacted cautiously. Israel welcomed the deployment of the army in principle, but warned that swift and severe retaliation would ensue if it failed to suppress attacks against Israel.

On 28 March 1991 a full session of the Cabinet approved a plan to dissolve all Lebanese and non-Lebanese militias in the country and to appoint 40 new deputies to the National Assembly. All militias were to surrender their weapons and equipment to the Government during the period 28 March–30 April. Between the end of April and 20 June the army was to deploy in the region of Mount Lebanon, outside Greater Beirut, and to assume responsibility for the security of the rest of the country during 20 June–20 September. The new momentum in the Government's extension of its authority was a result of the defeat of Iraq by the multinational force in February. The USA, Saudi Arabia, Egypt and Syria, which had all contributed to the multinational force, were all also proponents of the Ta'if agreement. Ministers in the Government who had boycotted sessions of the Cabinet while awaiting the outcome of the Gulf War (Samir Geagea, Georges Saadé, Michel Sassine and Walid Joumblatt) now began to adjust their positions. On 7 March Joumblatt retracted his resignation (which he had presented in January), and by 20 March the LF representatives in the Government—Sassine and Saadé—had ended their boycott of the Cabinet sessions. Geagea refused to accept a post in the Cabinet, but nominated an adviser, Roger Deeb, in his place.

Not surprisingly, the larger militias viewed their own disbandment with little enthusiasm. The LF urged the creation of a national guard to assume responsibility for the security of certain regions, while the PSP argued that the militias should be incorporated into official military structures. Palestinian representatives, meanwhile, announced that they would not comply with the Government's decision, as the presence of Palestinian militias was a regional, rather than a domestic, issue. However, strong regional and international pressure ultimately compelled Lebanon's major militias to comply with the Government's order to disband, and army units were deployed in areas previously controlled by the LF and the PSP.

Apprehension remained, none the less, with regard to armed groups that had refused to disband. These included the 6,000-strong pro-Arafat PLO; the 2,000-strong Iranian Revolutionary Guards, stationed in and around the town of Ba'albek in the Beka'a valley; the 5,000-strong, Iranian-backed Hezbollah in the Beka'a valley and the south; and the 3,000-strong, Israeli-backed SLA. Arafat's Fatah group, based in Sidon, refused to disband, on the grounds that it did not constitute a militia, but, rather, a 'resistance movement' or, even, the regular Palestinian army. It accordingly refused to surrender its weapons, but indicated its willingness to come to an agreement with the Lebanese Government regarding their location and use. The Government, for its part, refused to negotiate an accord similar to the one signed in Cairo in 1969 and abrogated by the National Assembly in 1987. It also rejected the PLO's demands for its own embassy in Beirut; for a Palestinian brigade within the Lebanese army, with responsibility for the security of the Palestinian refugee camps; and for the right to launch attacks against Israel. After much pressure, however, the PLO finally declared that it would not impede the deployment of Lebanese troops in the south of the country.

The commander of the Iranian Revolutionary Guards, Hadi Rida Askari, insisted that they did not constitute a militia within Lebanon and that their withdrawal could take place only following a decision by the Iranian Government, made in consultation with Syria. Hezbollah, meanwhile, agreed to dismantle its military structure in Beirut, but insisted on maintaining armaments in the Beka'a valley and in southern Lebanon, in order to continue the struggle against Israel's occupation. The SLA rejected any suggestion that it would disarm or that Israel was ready to comply with the appeals of the Lebanese Government for the implementation of UN Security Council Resolution 425, which demanded the unconditional withdrawal of Israeli forces from Lebanon. Indeed, the fact that the Government had begun to disband Lebanese militias before their non-Lebanese counterparts aroused fears that its decision would be only partially applied and that the extension of its authority would encounter the perennial obstacle of the armed Palestinian presence in Lebanon, exacerbated by the presence of armed groups backed by Iran.

In accordance with the four-point political programme of the Government of national reconciliation, relations between Lebanon and Syria became closer, culminating in the signing, in May 1991, of a treaty of 'fraternity, co-operation and co-ordination'. The treaty was the natural outcome of the stipulations of the Ta'if agreement, establishing a formal structure for developing and implementing policies on a wide range of issues, and creating links between Lebanon and Syria in political, military, security and economic affairs. It received a mixed welcome, however. Georges Saadé and Roger Deeb abstained from voting at the Cabinet session at which the treaty was approved, and refused to join the official delegation which travelled to Damascus for its signing. The Maronite Patriarch, Nasrallah Sfeir, complained that such a treaty should not have been negotiated or signed before the Government had regained full sovereignty over the whole of Lebanon. He further warned that the treaty contravened the National Covenant of 1943.

The treaty declared that Syria and Lebanon had 'distinctive brotherly relations', based on their 'geographic propinquity, similar history, common belonging, shared destiny and common interests'. Moreover, it specified the executive mechanism by which these relations were to be managed and developed. Five joint councils were established, which were to meet regularly in order to develop and execute policies affecting Lebanon. The most important of these was the Higher Council, comprising the Presidents of Lebanon and Syria, their Prime Ministers, Deputy Prime Ministers and the presiding officers of their respective legislatures. The Higher Council assumed responsibility for the co-ordination and co-operation of the two states in political, economic, security, military and other spheres. Its decisions were to be binding, albeit within the constitutional and legal frameworks of both countries. Opponents of the treaty claimed that the joint councils constituted a violation of Lebanese sovereignty and amounted, in effect, to Syria's annexation of Lebanon. In view of Syria's military strength, they regarded the treaty as unbalanced, and predicted grave consequences for Lebanon's independence, its democratic practices and its traditional freedoms. They considered to be even more alarming the Syrian Government's refusal to formalize its recognition of Lebanese sovereignty through the establishment of diplomatic relations. The supporters of the treaty, however, argued that it did not affect Lebanese freedoms, and that close relations with Syria were necessary for Lebanon's stability and prosperity.

On 9 May 1991 the National Assembly approved an amendment to Lebanon's electoral law, allowing the exceptional appointment by the Cabinet of 40 deputies to the Assembly. The appointments were made to the 31 seats, which had become vacant since 1972, and to the nine new seats created in accordance with the Ta'if agreement. On 7 June 1991 the 40 deputies were selected (from a list of 384 candidates who had presented their credentials for office to the Ministry of the Interior) by the President, the Prime Minister and the President of the National Assembly, in close consultation with Syria. The term of office of the new assembly was to be four years. The appointed deputies were representative of the political and confessional breadth of the Cabinet. All except four (who represented the Phalangist Party and the LF) enjoyed close relations with Syria. Hezbollah and a new, popular 'Awnist' grouping remained unrepresented in the National Assembly.

Following the appointments to the National Assembly, the Government began to compile a list of militia members who would be enrolled into the state's security and administrative structures, and to establish a schedule and locations for their 'rehabilitation'. On 29 May 1991 the Government had decided that some 20,000 militia members would be incorporated into the state structures. The decision stipulated that equal numbers of Muslims and Christians would be assimilated, among them 6,500 members of the LF, 2,800 members of Amal and 2,800 members of the PSP. The remainder would be absorbed from other militias. All were to undergo retraining courses, lasting up to six months, before being assigned to employment in the service of the state.

In early June 1991 Israel launched its fiercest attacks on Palestinian bases in southern Lebanon since its invasion of the country in 1982. The attacks coincided with statements by Israeli officials that Israel had no intention of withdrawing from its self-declared 'security zone', nor of reducing its support for the SLA. The escalation of the fighting in the south appeared to serve the interests of both Israel and the Palestinians. It supported the Palestinians' assertion that they needed to retain their weapons in order to fight a war against Israel; and it allowed Israel to claim that its northern border remained insecure and that it needed to maintain an armed presence in southern Lebanon.

On 1 July 1991 the Lebanese army began to deploy in and around Sidon, encountering some armed resistance from pro-Arafat Palestinian guerrillas. On 4 July the Government and the PLO concluded an accord whereby the latter agreed to allow the army peacefully to impose the Government's authority in the area. The deployment of the army in southern Lebanon was subsequently reported to have proceeded according to plan, although its jurisdiction did not include the village of Jezzine, where, although the locality was technically outside Israel's buffer zone, units of the SLA occupied positions.

The release, in August 1991, of John McCarthy, a British citizen who had been held hostage in Lebanon by Islamic Jihad (a militant pro-Iranian guerrilla group) since 1986, signalled the beginning of intensive diplomatic efforts by the UN to achieve a comprehensive exchange of hostages who were being detained, respectively, by Israel and by various sectarian groups in Lebanon. By June 1992 the release of all of Western hostages in Lebanon had been secured.

In August 1991 the National Assembly approved a general amnesty for crimes committed during the civil war; several specified crimes committed during 1975–90 were not covered by the amnesty. Under the terms of a presidential pardon, Gen. Michel Awn was finally allowed to leave the French embassy compound (where he had been sheltering since his defeat in 1990) and depart for exile in France. A condition of the amnesty was that he remain in exile for at least five years and refrain from political activities during that time.

At the beginning of September 1991 Lebanon and Syria formally concluded a security agreement, as envisaged in the bilateral treaty of May 1991. The agreement permitted Lebanon and Syria to seek mutual military assistance in the event of a challenge to the stability of either country. In mid-October President Hrawi travelled to Damascus for the first session of the Lebanese-Syrian Higher Council, established by the May accord.

In early November 1991 Karami announced that the USA had requested Israel to cease military activity in southern Lebanon, since it jeopardized the newly-begun peace process. However, Israeli military activity intensified in late November, in response to alleged attacks by Hezbollah fighters. A further, more serious, escalation of the conflict in southern Lebanon was precipitated in February 1992 by the assassination, by the Israeli air force, of Sheikh Abbas Mussawi, the Secretary-General of Hezbollah. Retaliation by Hezbollah guerrillas prompted an incursion by Israeli armed forces beyond the buffer zone in order to attack alleged Hezbollah positions. Although the Lebanese army had begun to occupy positions in southern Lebanon that had been vacated by UNIFIL, Hezbollah had retained its freedom to conduct military operations, in an apparent reflection of Syria's belief that only by continued coercion would Israel withdraw from occupied Arab territories. In late March Syrian forces began to withdraw from Beirut, in preparation for their withdrawal to eastern Lebanon by September (in accordance with the Ta'if agreement).

During the early months of 1992 Lebanon's economic situation worsened dramatically, and the value of the Lebanese pound depreciated sharply; general strikes took place in April and May. There were widespread allegations of corruption and incompetence within the Government, and on 6 May Omar Karami and his Cabinet were forced to resign. Following discussions in Damascus between President Hrawi and Syrian leaders, Rashid Solh was appointed Prime Minister (a position he had held in 1974–75), and on 13 May his appointment was approved by 70 of the National Assembly's 108 deputies. A new Cabinet, announced on 16 May, included 15 members of its predecessor. It was regarded as insufficiently different in character from Karami's Government to modify the widespread perception of Lebanon as a Syrian protectorate, which many, including Karami, had blamed for the reluctance of Western countries to provide the country with significant economic assistance.

ELECTIONS TO THE NATIONAL ASSEMBLY

In addition to efforts to alleviate the economic crisis, a principal task of the Lebanese Government in mid-1992 was to prepare the country for its first legislative election since 1972. On 16 July the National Assembly approved a new electoral law whereby the number of seats in the Assembly was raised from 108 (as stipulated by the Ta'if agreement) to 128, to be divided equally between Christian and Muslim deputies. Voting was to take place in three phases: on 23 August in North Lebanon and the Beka'a area; on 30 August in Beirut and Mount Lebanon; and on 6 September in the South and in Nabatiyah. By mid-August it was clear that most Maronite Christian groups, in particular the Phalangist Party, would not present candidates. In July Syria had indicated that its troops would not withdraw to the Beka'a area until the process of constitutional reform was complete, in accordance with its interpretation of the Ta'if agreement. Christian groups maintained that a fair election could not take place until the Syrian armed forces had withdrawn. As the Lebanese Prime Minister and Cabinet had been chosen in close consultation with Syrian leaders, the Government continued to invoke the inability of the Lebanese army to guarantee the country's security in the absence of Syrian forces: the position of Christian ministers in the Cabinet thus appeared more compromised than ever.

The first round of the election to the National Assembly proceeded, as planned, on 23 August 1992. Voting in this round was to elect a total of 51 deputies—28 to represent North Lebanon and 23 the Beka'a area. A total of 273 candidates contested the first round, in which the participation of the estimated 900,000-strong electorate was described as high in Muslim districts and very low in Christian ones. There were widespread allegations of electoral malpractice both during and after the vote, prompting the resignation of the incumbent President of the National Assembly, Hussain al-Hussaini. All the candidates presented by the Iranian-backed Hezbollah, which contested the election as a political party, were elected. The religious denominations of the deputies elected to the National Assembly in the first round of voting were as follows: 16 Maronite Christians; 16 Sunni Muslims; 8 Shi'ite Muslims; 8 Greek Orthodox; 3 Greek Catholics; 2 Alawites; 1 Druze and 1 Armenian Orthodox.

The second round of voting in the election to the National Assembly—to elect 54 deputies to represent constituencies in the Beirut and Mount Lebanon areas—took place on 30 August 1992, characterized by the low participation of the electorate especially in Christian districts. As in the first round, there were widespread allegations of bribery and intimidation of the electorate. The religious denominations of the deputies elected to the National Assembly in the second round of voting were: 20 Maronite Christians; 8 Sunni Muslims; 6 Druze; 5 Shi'ite Muslims; 5 Greek Orthodox; 4 Armenian Orthodox; 1 Greek-Melkite Catholic; 1 Armenian Catholic; and 4 minority denominations.

The third round of voting, in constituencies in the South and in Nabatiyah, took place on 6 September 1992. The religious denominations of the deputies elected to the National Assembly in this round were as follows: 14 Shi'ite Muslims; 3 Sunni Muslims; 2 Maronite Christians; 2 Greek-Melkite Catholics; 1 Greek Orthodox; and 1 Druze. In October the Amal leader, Nabih Berri, was appointed President of the National Assembly.

LEBANON UNDER HARIRI

On 22 October 1992 Rafik Hariri was invited by President Hrawi to form a government. A new, 30-member Cabinet was appointed on 31 October. Hariri, a Lebanese-born Saudi Arabian entrepreneur, included many technocrats in his new Cabinet, and offices were not, as previously, distributed on an entirely confessional basis. His appointment was viewed as likely to restore some confidence in the country's economy and to facilitate its reconstruction. On 12 November the new Government secured a vote of confidence in the National Assembly.

On 16 December 1992, in response to the deaths in the Occupied Territories of five members of the Israeli security forces, and to the abduction and murder by the Islamic Resistance Movement (Hamas) of an Israeli border policeman, the Israeli Cabinet ordered the deportation to Lebanon of more than 400 alleged Palestinian supporters of Hamas. Owing to the Lebanese Government's refusal to co-operate in this action, the deportees were stranded in the territory between Israel's self-declared southern Lebanese security zone and Lebanon proper.

Serious escalations of the conflict in southern Lebanon between Hezbollah fighters, the SLA and Israeli armed forces occurred in October and November 1992, and fighting continued at a lower degree of intensity during the early months of 1993. In July the Government was reported to be attempting to curtail the activities of the Damascus-based Popular Front for the Liberation of Palestine—General Command (PFLP—GC), which had begun to mount guerrilla attacks on the positions of Israeli armed forces and Israeli-backed militias from southern Lebanon. On 25 July Israeli forces launched their heaviest artillery and air attacks on targets in southern Lebanon since 1982, with the declared aim of eradicating the threat posed by Hezbollah and Palestinian guerrillas and, moreover, of creating a flow of refugees so as to compel the Lebanese and Syrian authorities to take action to curb Hezbollah and the Palestinians. Syrian troops in Lebanon also reportedly came under fire. According to Lebanese figures, Israel's so-called 'Operation Accountability' displaced some 300,000 civilians towards the north and resulted in 128 (mainly civilian) deaths. What was termed a cease-fire 'understanding', brokered by the USA, entered into effect at the end of July 1993, ending the week-long Israeli campaign, but this proved short-lived, and mutual offensives continued in subsequent months. In August, meanwhile, apparently as part of the cease-fire understanding, units of the Lebanese army took up positions, assigned to UNIFIL since the late 1970s, near the Israeli security zone.

A sudden cessation of attacks by Hezbollah units on Israeli targets in January 1994, prior to a meeting between US President Bill Clinton and President Assad of Syria, was cited as evidence, by Israeli observers, of Syrian control of Hezbollah. Hezbollah resumed attacks on Israeli targets in February, giving rise to the usual pattern of Israeli reprisals against Hezbollah targets. In June Israeli forces mounted an air attack on an alleged Hezbollah training camp in the Beka'a valley, close to the Syrian border. In early August further attacks by Israeli armed forces against Hezbollah targets in southern Lebanon caused the death of eight civilians, for which Israel subsequently made a formal apology. Israel claimed that Hezbollah had been involved in the plotting of bomb attacks against Jewish targets in the United Kingdom and Argentina in July. An Israeli attack on the southern town of Nabatiyah on 19 October, in which seven civilians were killed, was unusual in that it was not a response to guerrilla activity in and around the security zone, but, rather, appeared to have been made in retaliation for operations by Hamas in Israel itself. Hezbollah responded with rocket attacks on targets in northern and western Israel. There was a further escalation of the southern conflict in December, during which some six Israeli soldiers and eight members of the SLA were reported to have been killed.

In February 1995 Israel imposed a blockade on southern Lebanese fishing ports, in retaliation for the imposition, by the Lebanese army, of stricter security controls between the security zone and sovereign Lebanese territory. These were enforced owing to the alleged involvement of Israeli agents in the planning of a car-bomb explosion in Beirut in December 1994. At the end of March 1995 the assassination of a Hezbollah leader by Israeli forces in southern Lebanon gave rise to fierce fighting between the two sides in the area east of Sidon, and to rocket attacks by Hezbollah on Israeli targets in Galilee. In late April a Hezbollah fighter carried out a suicide bomb attack on an Israeli military convoy inside the security zone in southern Lebanon, in which 11 Israeli soldiers were injured. On 8 July, in response to an attack three days earlier by Hezbollah guerrillas in which two Israeli soldiers were killed, Israeli armed forces reportedly attacked Nabatiyah with *fléchette* anti-personnel missiles—which were subject to an international ban; three children died in the attack. Hezbollah retaliated with rocket attacks on targets in northern Israel. Israeli armed forces launched air and artillery attacks against Hezbollah targets in August, which were reported to have resulted in heavy casualties.

In March 1994 the National Assembly approved legislation instituting the death penalty for what were termed 'politically-motivated' murders. Shortly afterwards the Phalangist LF was proscribed, on the grounds that the organization had promoted the establishment of a Christian enclave and, hence, the country's partition. In the following month the LF leader, Samir Geagea, was arrested; he and several of his associates were subsequently charged in connection with the murder, in October 1990, of Dany Chamoun, son of former President Camille Chamoun and the leader of the right-wing Maronite National Liberal Party, and with the bombing of a Maronite church outside Beirut in January 1994. In September it was reported that the LF had temporarily relieved Geagea of the organization's leadership, and that it had revoked Geagea's recognition of the Ta'if agreement; the LF command was also said to have countermanded Geagea's formal dissolution, in 1991, of the organization's militia status. In June 1995 Geagea and a co-defendant were convicted of instigating Chamoun's murder, and were (together with seven others convicted *in absentia*) sentenced to death; the sentences were immediately commuted to life imprisonment with hard labour. Hearings in connection with the Maronite church bombing had been postponed.

In December 1994 Hariri abruptly announced his resignation, a decision that was apparently a result of his frustration at perceived attempts within the National Assembly to obstruct Lebanon's economic reconstruction. Hariri withdrew his resignation on 6 December, but not before it had caused a dramatic decline in the value of the Lebanese pound and emphasized the fragility of the recovery process. In May 1995 Hariri again resigned as Prime Minister, but was subsequently persuaded by the President to remain in office and was reappointed on 21 May. It was reported that Hariri had resigned this time as a result of a dispute concerning the Constitution. Hariri had reportedly sought the amendment of the Constitution in order to allow President Hrawi to serve a second term of office, which Hariri believed was necessary to guarantee stability during the early phase of economic reconstruction. In October the Assembly voted to amend Article 49 of the Constitution, thereby extending Hrawi's mandate for a further three years.

In late February 1996 it was announced that elections to the National Assembly would be held in that September. On 29 February 1996 the Confédération Générale des Travailleurs du Liban (CGTL) organized a general strike in support of its demand for a 76%-increase in public-sector salaries and for a 100%-increase in the minimum wage. In response the Government placed the army in charge of national security for a three-month period and imposed a curfew in the principal cities and towns.

LEBANON AND THE PEACE PROCESS

The Government's decision to send a Lebanese delegation to the opening session of a Middle East peace conference, held in Madrid, Spain, in October 1991, and to participate in subsequent rounds of bilateral negotiations, was criticized in both governmental and non-governmental circles. Critics argued that, since the terms of reference for the conference were UN Security Council Resolutions 242 and 338 only, Lebanon's participation was tantamount to a repudiation of UN Security Council Resolution 425, which demanded a comprehensive withdrawal of all Israeli armed forces from southern Lebanon; and that the implementation of Resolution 425 would henceforth be linked to the implementation of other UN resolutions. They asserted, moreover, that Lebanon had nothing to discuss in bilateral negotiations with Israel, since its relations with that country were regulated by the Armistice agreement of 1949, which remained valid.

Before the opening session of the Middle East peace conference was convened, Lebanon sought assurances from the USA on the following issues: that the implementation of UN Resolution 425 would not be linked to the implementation of other UN resolutions; that the country would receive support for the establishment of an international fund for Lebanon; that restrictions imposed by the US Government on its citizens with regard to travelling and investing in Lebanon would be removed; that the US Consulate in Beirut would be reopened; that the Lebanese national carrier, Middle East Airlines, should be allowed to resume flights to New York; and that arms paid for by the Government during Amin Gemayel's presidency would be delivered by the USA, and US-based training programmes for Lebanese army officers would be resumed.

With regard to Resolution 425, Lebanese diplomacy was rewarded by a written US commitment to support its implementation in isolation from the wider Middle East peace process. On the other issues that Lebanon had raised, however, the USA remained non-committal, pending the release of all Western hostages being held in Lebanon. Some observers, too, regarded the US assurance on Resolution 425 to be unclear, since the US Government's letter of intent failed to distinguish between the nature of the Israeli and the Syrian armed presence in Lebanon. Another potential point of contention was the USA's demand that the activities of the Hezbollah militia in southern Lebanon should cease before the peace conference commenced, while the Government insisted that Hezbollah's resistance would continue until the Israeli armed forces had withdrawn from Lebanese territory.

Lebanon reacted cautiously to the Declaration of Principles on Palestinian Self-Rule in the Occupied Territories, signed by Israel and the PLO on 13 September 1993 (see Documents on Palestine, p. 72). Fears were expressed, for instance, that, if the Declaration of Principles were to provoke violent confrontations between rival Palestinian factions, most of the violence would be likely to occur in Lebanon, endangering the country's reconstruction. There was also concern about the ultimate fate of the estimated 350,000 Palestinian refugees residing in Lebanon.

In late February 1994 Lebanon, together with the other Arab parties, withdrew from the Middle East peace process, following the murder, by a right-wing Jewish extremist, of some 30 Muslim worshippers in a mosque in Hebron on the West Bank. Together with Syria and Jordan, Lebanon agreed to rejoin the peace process in March.

'OPERATION GRAPES OF WRATH'

On 11 April 1996 Israeli armed forces began an intense, sustained campaign of air and artillery attacks on what they claimed to be positions occupied by the Hezbollah militia. These included, for the first time since 1982, attacks on the southern suburbs of Beirut. The declared aim of the Israeli campaign (code-named 'Operation Grapes of Wrath') was to achieve the complete cessation of rocket attacks by Hezbollah on settlements in northern Israel. Immediately prior to the Israeli campaign such attacks had caused injuries to some 13 Israeli civilians. Hezbollah claimed, in turn, that the rocket attacks had been provoked by deliberate assaults on Lebanese civilians by Israeli armed forces or their proxies. (An important element of the 1993 cease-fire 'understanding' had been that Hezbollah and Israel had effectively largely confined their conflict to the region of the security zone by agreeing to halt unprovoked attacks on civilian targets.) As a result of the Israeli operation some 400,000 Lebanese were displaced northwards after the Israeli military authorities warned that they would be endangered by the attacks on Hezbollah targets in the south. However, not all of the Israeli air attacks targeted alleged Hezbollah positions: one was made on a power-station in Bselim, a village north of Beirut in the Maronite heartland of Lebanon where Hezbollah had never been established.

The Israeli campaign could be regarded as having been determined by the proximity of a general election in Israel and by the need of Israeli Prime Minister Shimon Peres to restore some of the confidence with the electorate which he had lost as a result of suicide bombings perpetrated earlier in 1996 by Hamas in Israel. It might also be interpreted as an attempt to pressurize Syria into exerting increased control over Hezbollah. On 18 April an Israeli attack on a UN base at Qana resulted in the deaths of more than 100 Lebanese refugees who had been sheltering there. The attack (in which four UNIFIL soldiers were also killed) led to an intensification of efforts to find a diplomatic solution to the conflict, especially by the USA—Secretary of State Warren Christopher was dispatched to the region—and France. A cease-fire 'understanding' between Israel and Hezbollah took effect on 27 April. As in 1993, this was effectively a compromise confining the conflict to the security zone in southern Lebanon, recognizing both Hezbollah's right to resist Israeli occupation and Israel's right to self-defence; the 'understanding' also envisaged the establishment of an Israel-Lebanon Monitoring Group (ILMG), comprising Israel, Lebanon, Syria, France and the USA, to supervise the cease-fire. According to the Israeli authorities, 'Operation Grapes of Wrath' resulted in no Israeli deaths, while 170–200 Lebanese civilians, in addition to some 50 fighters, were killed. For its part, Hezbollah claimed to have sustained minimal casualties, and its military capacity appeared largely undiminished. A UN report on the killing of Lebanese civilians at Qana, presented to the Security Council in May 1996, concluded that it was 'unlikely' that the shelling of the UNIFIL base had, as claimed by the Israelis, been accidental. The first meeting of the ILMG took place in July; the group was to be based in Cyprus, and would meet in an-Naqoura, near Lebanon's southern border. Prior to the meeting Israel and Hezbollah were reported to have exchanged prisoners and bodies of members of their armed forces for the first time since 1991.

ELECTIONS TO THE NATIONAL ASSEMBLY

In June 1996 the Cabinet approved a new electoral law in preparation for the legislative elections later in the year. Under the new legislation, the Beka'a valley was reunified as a single electoral area, having been divided into three areas for the 1992 legislative elections. In the forthcoming elections the 128 seats of the National Assembly would be divided among the country's five governorates as follows: Beirut, 19; the Beka'a valley, 23; the South and Nabatiyah, 23; the North, 28, and Mount Lebanon, 35.

In mid-July 1996 it was reported that Christian opposition leaders were urging Lebanon's Christian communities to participate in the forthcoming elections, and that there had been relatively few appeals for a boycott such as had occurred in 1992. However, leading Christians continued to criticize the new electoral legislation for its division of Mount Lebanon, where the Maronite community was concentrated, into five electoral constituencies (thereby effectively dividing the Maronite vote, to the advantage of other, i.e. Druze, communities).

In early August 1996 Lebanon's Constitutional Court decided that the amendments to the electoral law (which had been approved by the National Assembly in July) were unconstitutional. The National Assembly subsequently approved an amendment to the new electoral law which, while it retained the controversial division of Mount Lebanon governorate, stated that this was an exceptional measure to be employed solely for the 1996 election.

In the first round of voting in the legislative elections, which took place in Mount Lebanon governorate on 18 August 1996, supporters of the Hariri Government achieved a comprehensive victory, winning 32 of the 35 seats. Some 189 candidates were reported to have contested the seats and the participation of the electorate was said to have been relatively high—compared with that in the elections of 1992—at 45%. In the second round of voting, in the North on 25 August 1996, by contrast, opposition candidates reportedly enjoyed greater success. In the third round of voting, in Beirut governorate, on 1 September, candidates contesting the elections on the list headed by the Prime Minister secured 14 of the 19 seats. Hariri himself won a larger number of votes than any other candidate contesting the Beirut governorate. However, prominent opponents of the Government, such as former premier Dr Selim al-Hoss, also took seats in Beirut, where the participation of the electorate, at 30%, was relatively low. There was speculation that the marginalization of Hezbollah (through the creation of stronger links between Hariri and the President of the National Assembly and leader of Amal, Hezbollah's Shi'a rival, Nabih Berri) was taking place at Syria's insistence in order to appease Israel. In the fourth round of voting, in the South and Nabatiyah on 8 September, Hezbollah retained all four of its seats, having entered into an electoral alliance with Amal. The Amal-Hezbollah bloc, together with parties counted as their supporters, were reported to have won all of the 23 seats in the South. (In the previous rounds of voting Hezbollah had lost two of the eight seats it had held in the outgoing National Assembly.) Voter participation in the fourth round was an estimated 48%.

Prior to the fifth round of voting (in the Beka'a valley), it was reported that Syria had redeployed some 12,000 of its estimated 30,000 troops in Lebanon to the eastern part of the Beka'a valley. There was speculation that the redeployment had been made for fear of Israeli attacks. Under the terms of the Ta'if agreement the redeployment should have taken place before the legislative elections in 1992. In the final round of voting on

16 September 1996, the Amal-Hezbollah alliance won 22 of the governorate's 23 seats. The participation of voters, at 52%, was higher than in any of the previous rounds. This brought the average rate of voter participation in the five governorates to 45%, a marked improvement on the 32% average in 1992. (In May 1997 the Constitutional Court annulled the results of voting for four seats, having found evidence of electoral malpractice. By-elections took place in June, at which all but one of the deputies elected in 1996 were returned to office.)

Nabih Berri was re-elected President of the incoming National Assembly when it convened in October 1996. In late October Rafik Hariri was appointed for his third term as Prime Minister. Disputes reportedly ensued between the President, Prime Minister and President of the National Assembly regarding the composition of the Cabinet, and when this was named, in early November, following consultations with Syrian leaders, the distribution of portfolios among the various Lebanese interests remained largely unchanged. The new Government's statement of policy, as delivered to the National Assembly in that month, emphasized a continuation of economic recovery efforts, and made reference to controversial proposals to prohibit public demonstrations, and to close private radio and television stations. The partial implementation of this last measure had already provoked considerable controversy. In September the Government had announced a ban on political broadcasts by about 150 radio and 50 television stations, and ordered the closure of these stations by the end of November; licences to broadcast political items had been granted to only a small number of stations, most of which were owned by prominent political figures, including Hariri and Berri.

In December 1996 there was a spate of attacks against Syrians in Lebanon, including one in which a bus carrying Syrian workers was hit with machine-gun fire in a predominantly Christian area. Consequently, Syrian Vice-President Abd al-Halim Khaddam indirectly accused Christian opposition leaders, hostile to the incumbent Lebanese Government and to Syria's presence in Lebanon, of collaborating with Israel. In late November seven Christians were sentenced by a military court to up to 15 years' imprisonment, convicted of espionage on behalf of Israel.

INTERNAL AFFAIRS

A further death sentence (commuted to life imprisonment) was imposed on Samir Geagea in May 1996, following his conviction for ordering the assassination of another Maronite rival in 1990. In July 1996 he was acquitted of involvement in the Maronite church bombing of February 1994, although he received a 10-year prison sentence for attempting to recruit and arm militiamen after 1991 (when all militias had been banned). In August 1996 Geagea was further charged with orchestrating the death of Prime Minister Rashid Karami in 1987; his trial on this charge began in December 1997 and ended in June 1999 with another sentence of life imprisonment. Meanwhile, in May 1997 Geagea received yet another death sentence (which was again commuted to life imprisonment), having been convicted of an assassination attempt in 1991 against Michel Murr, who was at the time Minister of Defence.

In July 1997 Sheikh Sobhi Tufayli, Hezbollah Secretary-General in 1989–91, launched a campaign of civil disobedience (designated 'revolution of the hungry') in the Beka'a valley, in protest against the Government's perceived neglect of the region: Tufayli urged residents to withhold taxes and abstain from paying for utilities, in order to force the Government to reduce income taxes and increase development spending in the Beka'a. In November Tufayli instructed Beka'a residents to deny all ministers access to the region, prompting the Government to order the deployment of troops in the eastern Beka'a valley for a three-month period; it was also announced that residents who had joined the protests would be liable to prosecution by the Military Court. In December Tufayli announced an end to the blockade, after the Government announced new development projects for the Beka'a (although he subsequently threatened a resumption of the disobedience campaign if investment was not increased). In January 1998 Hezbollah announced the expulsion of Tufayli from the organization, although the former Secretary-General, who had been critical of Hezbollah's assimilation under its current Secretary-General, Sheikh Hasan Nasrallah, into 'mainstream' politics, maintained that he represented the 'true' spirit of Hezbollah. At the end of January at least eight people were killed as a result of a confrontation in Ba'albek involving Tufayli and his supporters and local Hezbollah officials, in which the army intervened. In February Tufayli and 19 of his associates were charged with offences including undermining national security, forming an armed group, and causing the deaths of three soldiers; Tufayli, who had evaded capture following the Ba'albek incident, was charged *in absentia*.

The issue of government restrictions on the broadcast media again provoked controversy in the second half of 1997. In September the authorities began to close down unlicensed broadcasters, and two people were killed when security forces opened fire on members of the fundamentalist Tawheed Islami group who were attempting to prevent the closure of a private station in Tripoli. In December the Minister of the Interior prohibited a televised broadcast, from France, by Gen. Michel Awn, on the grounds that such transmissions were undermining national security. (The private satellite company that was to have transmitted the interview was owned by the Minister's brother.) The ban provoked a violent demonstration in Beirut: a number of arrests were made, and it was subsequently announced that 10 people were to be tried by the Military Court for attacking the security forces, while civil charges were to be brought against a further 23 protesters who had defied a ban (imposed in 1993) on public demonstrations. Awn's interview was eventually broadcast in January 1998 by a private terrestrial channel. In that month the Government announced a ban on the broadcast of all news and political programmes by privately-owned satellite channels, after a company owned by prominent Maronite interests transmitted an interview with a National Assembly deputy who was an outspoken critic of the Government. It was stated that, henceforth, the stations in question (including a company owned by Hariri) would be authorized only to transmit news bulletins prepared by the state-controlled Télé-Liban.

EVENTS IN THE SOUTH

Despite the cease-fire 'understanding' of April 1996, clashes continued, and numerous complaints were made to the ILMG by both sides throughout 1996 and 1997. In mid-June 1997 Lebanon welcomed the adoption by the UN General Assembly of a resolution demanding that Israel should pay US $1.7m. in damages for the shelling of the UN base at Qana in April 1996. Tensions were exacerbated in mid-1997 after Hezbollah, which according to the ILMG, had not previously violated the agreement, launched a series of rocket attacks against Israeli targets. On 8 August it was reported that *Katyusha* rockets were aimed at the Israeli town of Kiryat Shmona in retaliation for Israeli attacks, which had caused the deaths of several Lebanese civilians, and an attack on 4 August in which five Hezbollah members were killed. Violence continued to escalate in mid-August, following the deaths of two civilians in a bomb explosion in Jezzine, an SLA stronghold north of the security zone. In reprisal, the SLA launched an artillery attack on Sidon, killing at least six civilians. Hezbollah in turn violated the cease-fire 'understanding' with rocket attacks into northern Israel, prompting the Israeli military to direct its most intensive airstrikes against presumed Hezbollah and PFLP—GC targets since 'Operation Grapes of Wrath' in April 1996. In late August 1997 four Amal fighters and four members of the Israeli security forces were killed following an ambush by the Israeli military on the edge of the occupied zone; this followed the death of an Amal commander by a car-bomb in central Beirut. In early September 12 members of an élite Israeli commando unit were killed (reportedly the highest Israeli death toll in a single operation since 1985) after Amal fighters and the Lebanese army foiled an operation, apparently against an Amal base, south of Sidon. Later in the month there was intense fighting within the security zone: among those killed was a son of the Hezbollah Secretary-General, Sheikh Hasan Nasrallah. Reciprocal attacks by Hezbollah and Israeli forces continued into October, with Israel additionally targeting PFLP—GC bases.

Meanwhile, the extent of Israeli casualties as a result of the occupation of southern Lebanon prompted a vocal campaign within Israel for a unilateral withdrawal from the security zone. At the beginning of April 1998 Israel's 'inner' Security Cabinet voted to adopt UN Security Council Resolution 425, but with the stipulation that Lebanon provide guarantees of the security of Israel's northern border. While welcoming the proposed departure from its territory, Lebanon emphasized that Resolution 425 demanded an unconditional withdrawal, and stated that neither would it be able to guarantee Israel's immunity from attack, nor would it be prepared to deploy the Lebanese army in southern Lebanon for this purpose; furthermore, Lebanon could not support the continued presence there of the SLA. Concern was also expressed that a unilateral withdrawal from Lebanon in the absence of a comprehensive Middle East peace settlement might foment regional instability. Israel's demand that Hezbollah be disarmed prior to any Israeli withdrawal was, moreover, unacceptable not only to Lebanon but also to Syria, which regarded its support for the resistance in southern Lebanon as essential leverage in its efforts to secure a parallel Israeli withdrawal from the Golan Heights.

Clashes persisted in southern Lebanon following Israel's 'adoption' of Resolution 425, amid continuing protests of violations of the April 1996 cease-fire 'understanding'. In mid-May 1998 at least 10 people were killed in an Israeli air raid on a Fatah training camp in the central Beka'a valley. At the end of the month, following a week of intense fighting in which five Hezbollah fighters and four SLA militiamen had died, two Israeli soldiers were killed in an ambush on their patrol. Another two Israeli soldiers were killed in late June. An exchange of bodies and prisoners of war proceeded none the less, under an arrangement brokered by the International Committee of the Red Cross: among the remains returned were those of an Israeli naval commander killed in the failed operation against Amal in September 1997, and those of the son of Sheikh Hasan Nasrallah. In late August 1998 at least nine Israelis were injured when rockets were fired into northern Israel, in retaliation for the death of an Amal commander near Tyre. The attack prompted the Israeli Cabinet to approve a proposal by the Minister of Internal Security that such operations would henceforth be countered with attacks against Lebanon's civilian infrastructure.

In July 1997 the US Secretary of State, Madeleine Albright, announced an end to her country's ban on travel to Lebanon, in response to a commitment by Hariri to increase co-operation in combating terrorism. (The USA had halted flights following the hijacking to Beirut of the TWA flight in 1985, and, in view of fears for the safety within Lebanon of US nationals, had announced in 1987 that US passports were invalid for travel to Lebanon.) In September Albright became the first US Secretary of State to visit Beirut since 1983. The Lebanese Prime Minister met with President Clinton and Albright in Washington, DC, in mid-June 1998; Hariri also held talks with the UN Secretary-General, Kofi Annan, in New York. The USA subsequently ended its ban on the sale of tickets to US citizens travelling to Lebanon, despite a rocket-grenade attack near the US embassy in Beirut, which the Lebanese authorities denounced as an attempt by Israeli sympathizers to undermine security in the capital.

MUNICIPAL ELECTIONS

Voting in Lebanon's first municipal elections since 1963 took place in four rounds, beginning on 24 May 1998. The elections had been due to take place in mid-1997, but were postponed after Hariri controversially withdrew draft legislation regulating the elections from parliamentary debate. At the first round (in Mount Lebanon governorate) Hezbollah won convincing victories in Beirut's southern suburbs, despite an attempt by Hariri and Berri to moderate the influence of the opposition by supporting joint lists of candidates; right-wing organizations opposed to the Government, including Dory Chamoun's PNL (which had boycotted the 1992 and 1996 elections), also took control of several councils. At the second round, in North Lebanon on 31 May 1998, efforts failed to achieve an inter-community balance in Tripoli, where a council comprising 23 Muslims and only one Christian was elected; elsewhere in the governorate there was notable success for candidates loyal to Samir Geagea. However, a joint list of candidates supported by Hariri and Berri (again in a stated attempt to reflect the sectarian balance) did win control of the Beirut council at the third round, on 7 June. Candidates endorsed by Hariri won seats in Sidon, while Berri's Amal gained overall control in

Tyre. The final round of voting (in the Beka'a valley) took place on 14 June, when Hezbollah candidates were largely defeated by their pro-Syrian secular rivals and by members of the governorate's leading families. Other than in Beirut, the rate of participation by voters at all stages was high (about 70%), and most political groups expressed satisfaction at the conduct and outcome of the polls.

THE ISSUE OF DECONFESSIONALIZATION

In March 1998 Hrawi presented legislation to the Cabinet that would enable marriages to be conducted by civil authorities. Supporters of the President's bill stated that this would facilitate inter-faith marriages and thus erode sectarian divisions. However, the legislation was strongly opposed not only by religious leaders (all marriages were hitherto regulated by the religious authorities), but also by the Prime Minister. After having failed to persuade government members to reject the legislation, Hariri refused to sign the bill, on the grounds that it would offend religious sensibilities and create divisions at a time when it was essential to preserve a consensus in order to facilitate the implementation of the Government's economic programme. The National Assembly President was reported to have lent his support to Hrawi's legislation after the latter sought the establishment of a parliamentary committee to consider the 'deconfessionalization' of public life—a process that, it was generally considered, would be to the advantage of the Shi'ite community.

Rafik Hariri's refusal to submit President Hrawi's proposal to the National Assembly was in itself regarded as exemplifying what many Lebanese now regarded as the need for a reform of the 'confessional' system on which Lebanese politics was based. It was increasingly recognized that, while this system had undoubtedly preserved civil peace since the conclusion of the Ta'if agreement, it had also fostered institutional paralysis and cronyism and thus hindered post-war recovery. Many thus believed that the power-sharing arrangement between the President, Prime Minister and President of the National Assembly could not endure into the next presidency.

ELECTION OF PRESIDENT LAHOUD

The issue of President Hrawi's succession dominated political debate as his mandate neared completion. Although he frequently emphasized his determination to relinquish the presidency upon the expiry of his term of office in November 1998, it was widely speculated that his mandate would again be extended. Meanwhile, the Commander-in-Chief of the armed forces, Gen. Emile Lahoud, was increasingly suggested as a suitable successor: it was widely believed that Lahoud's strong leadership and firm stance on corruption, in addition to his success in having reconstructed the army following the civil war, were the qualities required of the new President, in order to revive the process of political reform and economic regeneration. Moreover, despite Lahoud's reputation as a nationalist, by early October, when Hrawi and Assad met to discuss the succession, his candidacy had been fully endorsed by Syria, whose influence remained crucial in Lebanese matters of State. For Lahoud to be appointed, an exceptional amendment was necessary to Article 49 of the Constitution—which requires that senior civil servants, such as Lahoud, resign their post two years prior to seeking political office—and on 13 October the National Assembly was convened, whereupon it overwhelmingly endorsed the constitutional amendment bill. Lahoud was duly elected President on 15 October 1998, with the approval of all 118 National Assembly deputies present at the ballot (which was boycotted by the Druze leader, Walid Joumblatt, and his supporters). Lahoud took office on 24 November; in his inaugural speech to the Assembly, the new President identified law enforcement and the elimination of corruption in public life as priorities for his administration. At the end of the month it was announced that Hariri had unexpectedly declined an invitation from Lahoud to form a new government. Hitherto, it had been generally assumed that Hariri's continued premiership was essential to the process of economic reconstruction. Hariri attributed his effective resignation from the post that he had held since 1992 to what he regarded as a violation of constitutional procedures by Lahoud in appropriating powers not granted to the presidency by the Ta'if agreement: the accord specifies that

the appointment of a Prime Minister should be made following consultation with deputies, rather than directly by the President, and, while 83 deputies favoured Hariri's retention, 31 deputies had delegated their right to endorse the premier to Lahoud.

The election of Lahoud was widely believed to signal the beginning of a new era in which the President, rather than the Prime Minister, would play the central role in the political hierarchy and act as the principal channel of communication between the Lebanese establishment and the Syrian presidency.

FORMATION OF A NEW GOVERNMENT

Following consultations between President Lahoud and the National Assembly, at the beginning of December 1998 Dr Selim al-Hoss (who had headed four Governments during the civil war) was named as the new Prime Minister. A new, streamlined 16-member Cabinet was appointed, containing only two ministers from the previous administration, including, notably, Michel Murr, who retained the post of Deputy Prime Minister and Minister of the Interior (and was also awarded the municipal and rural affairs portfolio). The appointment of several 'reformists', together with the exclusion of representatives of the various 'confessional' blocs and former militia leaders was said to illustrate al-Hoss's declared commitment to a comprehensive programme of reconstruction under his leadership. (Hezbollah declined to participate in the new Government.) Al-Hoss presented his Government's programme—which emphasized reduction of the public debt, anti-corruption measures and economic liberalization, together with a review of legislation governing the broadcast media and accelerated electoral reform—to the National Assembly in December; the legislature approved a motion of confidence in the new administration shortly afterwards. Later in December the newly-promoted Gen. Michel Sulayman was appointed to succeed Lahoud as head of the armed forces. The incoming Government also revoked the five-year ban on the holding of public demonstrations.

One of the first acts of the al-Hoss Government was to implement an uncompromising initiative to eradicate state corruption and the inefficient use of public resources—which were estimated to have cost the State some US $4,500m. since 1990; the judiciary was granted powers to investigate a number of political scandals and bring both current and former high-ranking officials to trial. In early January 1999 19 senior civil servants and leading officials were removed from their posts at the initiative of the new Prime Minister and the recommendation of the Civil Service Council; four other officials also lost their jobs in the first stage of an ambitious project to reform a state bureaucracy which numbers more than 230,000. The majority of those dismissed owed their positions to either Hariri, former President Hrawi or former minister Walid Joumblatt, although it was Hariri's supporters who suffered most from the new reforms. For this reason, the former Prime Minister reacted furiously when the Government decided to liquidate his state telecommunications enterprise, Ogero.

In early May 1999 it was announced that eight people had been arrested and had reportedly admitted to plotting a series of bomb attacks against Syrian and Lebanese military sites. The saboteurs' arrests followed a grenade attack in Beirut on a hostel for Syrian migrant workers. The men, who were believed to have been protesting against the continued 'occupation' of Lebanon by Syrian forces, were also implicated in a similar attack on a Syrian military centre in Hadath in December 1998. In mid-May 1999 a senior Fatah official and his wife were killed by unidentified gunmen in Sidon; the attack was apparently perpetrated by members of the PLO opposed to Fatah's willingness to negotiate with Israel. A few days later, a car bomb exploded in southern Lebanon, seriously wounding another Fatah official; the incident led to fears of a renewed cycle of violence between rival Palestinian factions operating in Lebanon. In early June four judges, who were conducting the trial of two Palestinians in Sidon, were killed (and five bystanders wounded) when two men opened fire on the court room. The attack followed sporadic violence in the Sidon area, although most had involved rival Palestinian groups rather than state officials.

By mid-June 1999 many observers noted that what had effectively been a three-month 'truce' between the new administration and former Prime Minister Hariri appeared to have ended. The state-run National News Agency (NNA) published a strong verbal assault on Hariri, reportedly originating from anonymous 'ministerial sources', in which the former Prime Minister was accused of corruption, of seeking to undermine the Government in order to facilitate his return to power, and even of collusion with Israel. Al-Hoss, however, vehemently denied that his Government was responsible for the anti-Hariri statement, or, indeed, that it had any prior knowledge of it. Meanwhile, in mid-1999 concerns were expressed at the recent prosecution of several prominent journalists in Lebanon, leading to speculation that the trials had been politically motivated, and accusations that President Lahoud had, in fact, deliberately initiated a purge of journalists loyal to Hariri, thereby imposing new restrictions on the more outspoken elements of the media on the pretext of maintaining a strict level of law and order.

DEVELOPMENTS IN SOUTHERN LEBANON

In two separate incidents in November 1998, seven Israeli soldiers were killed as a result of attacks by Hezbollah on Israeli patrols in the occupied zone. There were further serious exchanges in late December, when 13 civilians were injured by Hezbollah rocket attacks in northern Israel, launched in reprisal for an Israeli air strike in southern Lebanon in which eight civilians were killed. (Israel subsequently issued a formal apology for the incident, and both assaults were condemned by the ILMG.) By the end of 1998, it was becoming increasingly clear that Israel was seeking a way out of its war in Lebanon. The Israeli army's annual report, issued in January 1999, claimed that the number of Hezbollah attacks against Israeli forces in southern Lebanon had risen from 715 in 1997 to around 1,200 in 1998, resulting in the deaths of some 23 soldiers in that year. In early January 1999 Israel's Security Cabinet voted to respond to future Hezbollah offensives by targeting infrastructure in central and northern Lebanon (thereby extending the conflict beyond suspected guerrilla bases in the south). At the end of the month it was reported that the Israeli Prime Minister, Binyamin Netanyahu, had confirmed remarks made by Itzhak Mordechai (recently dismissed as Israel's Minister of Defence) that the Israeli Government was involved in secret contacts with Lebanon. The Lebanese authorities, however, denied that any talks were in progress, while Netanyahu and his new defence minister, Moshe Arens, dismissed any likelihood of an imminent withdrawal. Since Netanyahu had lost his precarious parliamentary majority in December 1998 and an Israeli general election was scheduled for 17 May 1999, fears were expressed in Lebanon that Netanyahu, wishing to bolster his flagging popularity, might resort to a bombing campaign in Lebanon in order to force the Lebanese Government to restrict Hezbollah's operations. However, although Israel shelled several targets in the south during January, no major offensive was launched.

Hezbollah intensified its campaign of resistance in the months preceding the Israeli elections. In February 1999 it was reported that Israeli forces had responded by annexing the village of Arnoun, on the edge of the occupied zone. Hostilities escalated (in one incident three Israeli commandos were killed in exchanges with Hezbollah), and at the end of the month hundreds of Lebanese students stormed Arnoun in protest at the annexation, apparently forcing its release from Israeli control. In mid-April, however, Israeli forces reannexed the village. Meanwhile, at the end of February Brig.-Gen. Erez Gerstein, the commander of the Israeli army's liaison unit with the SLA, was killed (together with two other Israeli soldiers and a journalist) in an ambush by Hezbollah in the security zone: Gerstein was the most senior member of the Israeli command to be killed in Lebanon since the 1982 occupation. Israel, stunned by the attack, retaliated by launching intensive air attacks on selected Hezbollah targets, while warning of full-scale land, air and sea offensives across Lebanon. In April 1999 Moshe Arens announced that 80% of Israel's army posts in southern Lebanon had been transferred to the SLA and that further transfers were imminent, thus enabling additional Israeli troops to withdraw from the security zone. Nevertheless, there was a sharp escalation of fighting as the date of the Israeli elections approached. On 15 May, two days before the general election and coinciding with the 51st anniversary of Israel's foundation, Hezbollah attacked three outposts manned by SLA militiamen, successfully capturing one outpost at Beit Yahun, over which the guerrillas flew their own flag. An SLA commander was killed in the operation, and Israel responded by launching air-strikes and shelling several Hezbollah targets.

SLA WITHDRAWAL FROM JEZZINE

The incoming Israeli Prime Minister, Ehud Barak (who was elected on 17 May 1999), had made a pre-election pledge to effect an Israeli withdrawal from southern Lebanon by July 2000. After the victory of Barak's Labour-led One Israel coalition, Hezbollah began to concentrate its efforts on forcing Israel out of Lebanon and seeking to dismantle the demoralized SLA. On 31 May 1999 the SLA Commander, Gen. Antoine Lahad, announced that the SLA command had decided to withdraw unilaterally from the enclave of Jezzine, in the north-east of the occupied zone. The withdrawal of SLA forces began on 1 June and was reportedly completed by 3 June, when Lebanese internal security services officially took control of security in the town. (The Lebanese army refused to take control of Jezzine as this would effectively provide Israel with security guarantees in southern Lebanon prior to any comprehensive regional peace deal being concluded between Israel and Syria.) The Lebanese authorities claimed that the withdrawal from Jezzine was a victory for Lebanon's resistance movement led by Hezbollah, which had intensified its operations around the town in recent weeks. During the withdrawal, two SLA soldiers were killed, while some 100 SLA members reportedly surrendered to the Lebanese army. Clashes between Israeli forces and Hezbollah continued throughout the month. On the night of 24 June, as Barak was conducting delicate negotiations to form a new government, Netanyahu, who was still technically the Israeli Prime Minister, ordered a series of air-strikes against infrastructure targets in central and southern Lebanon—the heaviest aerial bombardment since 'Operation Grapes of Wrath' in 1996. Barak was reportedly not informed about the strikes, which destroyed two power plants in Beirut, a telecommunications centre and bridges connecting southern Lebanon with the rest of the country, killing at least eight civilians and injuring up to 70. The Israeli air-strikes followed a cross-border *Katyusha* rocket attack into the northern Israeli town of Kiryat Shmona (killing two civilians), which appeared to have been in response to an earlier Israeli attack in which some seven civilians were wounded. The Lebanese Prime Minister described the 24 June raids as a 'deliberate, barbaric' act; the air-strikes were also harshly condemned by the USA and by European Union (EU) leaders.

In June 1999 the outgoing Israeli Government boycotted a meeting of the ILMG, reportedly in protest against Hezbollah's non-compliance with the April 1996 'understanding'. However, the Israeli delegation agreed to resume the meetings in July. At the end of July the US-based Human Rights Watch published a report criticizing the mass expulsions of Lebanese civilians from their homes in the security zone, which had been carried out by Israel since 1985 (in violation of the Geneva Convention); the organization urged the new Israeli Government to allow the expellees to return home. Meanwhile, in June 1999 UNIFIL accused Hezbollah of encouraging attacks on UN positions near the occupied zone by using UNIFIL outposts to launch attacks on Israel and the SLA. In August a senior Hezbollah official was killed in a car bomb attack in Sidon; al-Hoss strongly condemned the killing and Hezbollah stated that it held Barak personally responsible, although Israel denied any responsibility for the death. Two Israeli soldiers were subsequently killed in retaliatory Hezbollah attacks, bringing the total killed thus far in 1999 to 13. Israel responded with raids on several villages outside the security zone.

With the formation of a new Israeli Government in early July 1999, a new mood of cautious optimism was noticeable in both Syria and Lebanon. Ehud Barak was widely considered to be much more likely than his predecessor to negotiate a peace agreement incorporating Israel's withdrawal from the Golan Heights and southern Lebanon. A period of intense diplomatic activity on all tracks of the Middle East peace process ensued, accompanied by a scaling down of Hezbollah's military operations (although its leaders urged a continuation of the armed struggle against Israeli occupying forces). Many Lebanese politicians and journalists remained sceptical about Barak's pledge to withdraw from southern Lebanon within one year of his election; in early July al-Hoss stated that Lebanon would wait to judge the new Prime Minister on his actions alone. On 4 September 1999 Barak and the President of the Palestinian (National) Authority (PA), Yasser Arafat, signed the Sharm esh-Sheikh Memorandum, popularly known as 'Wye Two' (see Documents on Palestine, p. 88), in Egypt: the agreement detailed a revised timetable for the outstanding provisions of the original Wye Memorandum (see the chapter on Israel and Documents on Palestine, p. 86), including the conclusion of 'final status' discussions within one year of the resumption of talks on these issues (to be initiated no later than 13 September). However, 'final status' negotiations between Israel and the PA finally commenced in early November 1999.

RELATIONS WITH OTHER STATES

In December 1998 Lebanon and Syria signed a bilateral trade agreement in preparation for their customs union that entered into effect on 1 January 1999. In September 1999 the recently-invested King Abdullah of Jordan visited Beirut—the first visit to the Lebanese capital by a Jordanian monarch since 1965. During his visit the King promoted trade between Jordan and Lebanon, as well as the idea of closer economic integration between Jordan, Syria and Lebanon, following his country's recent *rapprochement* with Damascus. The Lebanese Government reacted with caution to the resumption of peace negotiations between Syria and Israel in December 1999 (discussions having been suspended in February 1996). However, the talks were unproductive and were again broken off in January 2000. As preparations were under way for Israeli armed forces to depart from southern Lebanon, and after the withdrawal was carried out in May of that year, protests grew among the Lebanese opposition, particularly within the Maronite Christian community, regarding the continued presence of Syrian forces in Lebanon. In April the Syrian Government had denied that it would deploy troops in southern Lebanon following the Israeli withdrawal. Meanwhile, in February President Hosni Mubarak became the first Egyptian President to visit Lebanon. Following talks with President Lahoud in Beirut, the two leaders issued a joint statement of protest against recent Israeli air-strikes on Lebanese targets, and in support of Hezbollah's resistance to Israeli occupation.

In October 1999 a senior commander of the Palestinian Fatah movement received a death sentence *in absentia* from a military court in Beirut. Sultan Abu al-Aynayn had been found guilty of leading a militia and of encouraging anti-Government rebellion. However, al-Aynayn, a close ally of Yasser Arafat, claimed that his sentence was politically motivated; it was widely interpreted as evidence of a growing struggle between Arafat and the Lebanese and Syrian Governments for influence over Palestinian refugees in Lebanon. (In early December 2000, again *in absentia*, al-Aynayn was given a 15-year prison term by a military court, convicted of weapons-trafficking and of plotting terrorist actions in southern Lebanon.) Two other Fatah leaders in southern Lebanon were detained by the Lebanese military in November, on charges of murder and of plotting bomb attacks during the 1980s; five further officials of the organization were reportedly arrested in December 1999 and January 2000. At the end of December 1999 five Lebanese soldiers were killed in an ambush on their patrol near Tripoli in northern Lebanon. The perpetrators of the attack were believed to be members of an Egyptian-based Sunni Muslim fundamentalist group, Takfir wal Hijra, two of whom were about to be arrested for their alleged involvement in recent grenade attacks on Orthodox churches in the Tripoli area. The incident resulted in the largest Lebanese military operation for a decade, during which nine Lebanese soldiers and several Islamists, as well as at least two civilians, were killed; many arrests were made. In January 2000 the Government ordered a judicial enquiry into the recent upsurge in sectarian violence.

Lebanon's relations with Iran showed signs of improvement during 1999. In May Lebanon's Middle East Airlines (MEA) resumed flights between Beirut and the Iranian capital, Tehran, and in June Iran Air recommenced flights to Beirut (both airlines had suspended flights in 1979). Moreover, in June the Iranian Minister of Foreign Affairs, Kamal Kharrazi, led a high-level delegation to Beirut to discuss bilateral co-operation and recent regional developments; Kharrazi met President Lahoud, several senior Lebanese ministers and the Secretary-General of Hezbollah. At the same time, the President of the Lebanese National Assembly, Nabih Berri, visited Tehran, where he was elected deputy head of the newly-established parliamentary union of the Organization of the Islamic Conference.

PALESTINIAN REFUGEES IN LEBANON

In January 1999 the Lebanese authorities agreed to upgrade the status of travel documents issued to Palestinians residing in Lebanon, thereby allowing them to be treated as holders of Lebanese passports. However, as the prospect of Israel and the PA entering 'final status' peace negotiations increased in mid-1999, the issue of Palestinian refugees in Lebanon assumed particular importance. Prior to a tour of the region by the US Secretary of State, Madeleine Albright, in early September, Lebanese officials increasingly reiterated their rejection of the notion of permanent settlement of Palestinian refugees in Lebanon. (According to the United Nations Relief and Works Agency for Palestine Refugees in the Near East—UNRWA—at 31 December 2001 384,918 Palestinian refugees were registered in Lebanon). The Lebanese Government had been angered by an announcement made in July 1999 by the new Israeli Prime Minister, Ehud Barak, that the refugees would under no circumstances be permitted to return to Israel, and that 'a solution should be found in the countries where they are now living'. President Lahoud responded by demanding that any permanent peace agreement would have to guarantee the right of Palestinians to return home; he subsequently initiated legislation to prevent Palestinian refugees in Lebanon from being granted Lebanese citizenship.

ISRAELI WITHDRAWAL FROM LEBANON

In November 1999 it was announced that the Israeli army had begun preparations for a withdrawal from southern Lebanon, to be completed by July 2000. The Israeli Government issued an apology to the Lebanese authorities in December 1999, after an attack by its forces in which at least 15 Lebanese schoolchildren were injured. The incident came amid an escalation in Hezbollah operations following the announcement of a resumption of Israeli-Syrian peace negotiations. In order to facilitate progress in the talks, in December an 'understanding in principle' was reportedly reached between Israel and Syria to curb the fighting in southern Lebanon. However, in January 2000 the informal cease-fire ended when a senior SLA commander was killed; the deaths of three further Israeli soldiers at the end of the month led Israel to declare that peace talks with Syria could resume only if Syria took action to restrain Hezbollah. The conflict between Israeli forces and Hezbollah fighters intensified during February. By the middle of the month three Israeli soldiers had been killed in the security zone, and Israel announced that its Prime Minister would henceforth be empowered to order immediate retaliatory raids against Hezbollah without discussion with the 'inner' Security Cabinet. In February Israel had conducted a series of air raids against Hezbollah targets and Lebanese infrastructure (including three power stations outside Beirut). Further Israeli raids in March followed Hezbollah attacks on northern Israel.

Meanwhile, on 5 March 2000 the Israeli Cabinet voted unanimously to withdraw its forces from southern Lebanon by July, even if no peace agreement had been reached between Israel and Syria. In March Israeli forces attacked two Palestinian refugee camps to the east of Beirut, apparently in response to a recent resolution adopted by the Arab League warning that Palestinian militant groups might resume attacks on Israeli targets in the event of Israel's withdrawing from Lebanon without having negotiated the resettlement of Palestinian refugees currently residing in other Arab states. In April Israel released 13 Lebanese prisoners who had been held without trial for more than a decade as 'bargaining counters' for Israeli soldiers missing in Lebanon. On 17 April Israel gave the UN official notification that it intended to withdraw its forces from southern Lebanon 'in one phase' by 7 July, leading the Lebanese Prime Minister to talk of a 'resounding victory for Lebanon'. At the end of April the Lebanese Government stated for the first time that it would accept a UN peace-keeping force in southern

Lebanon after the Israeli withdrawal. In May there was a further escalation in the fighting between Israeli forces and Hezbollah; two senior SLA fighters were killed in the middle of the month. On 23 May Israel's Security Cabinet voted to accelerate the withdrawal of its remaining troops from Lebanon, after Hezbollah had taken control of about one-third of southern Lebanon following the evacuation by the SLA of outposts transferred to its control by the Israeli army. Both the Government of Israel and the UN had expected the withdrawal to take place on 1 June; however, amid considerable chaos, the rapid withdrawal of all Israeli forces from southern Lebanon was completed on 24 May, almost six weeks ahead of Barak's original deadline of July. As the withdrawal was taking place, on 23 May Lebanese citizens stormed the notorious al-Khiam prison in Israel's former 'security zone' and released around 144 Lebanese prisoners, several of whom had been detained there for many years. (For a more detailed account of the Israeli withdrawal, see the chapter on Israel.)

On 18 June 2000 the UN Security Council endorsed the verification of Secretary-General Kofi Annan that the Israeli withdrawal had been completed, although Hezbollah maintained that Israel was still required to depart from territory known as Shebaa Farms and to release all Lebanese prisoners. The disputed Shebaa Farms area is situated on the Israeli side of the line of withdrawal, as demarcated by the UN and known as the 'Blue Line'. Israel argues that the sovereignty of the area is an issue with Syria, not Lebanon, and insists on retaining control of Shebaa Farms until a peace settlement has been agreed with Damascus. Lebanon and Syria, however, maintain that Shebaa Farms is Lebanese territory. (The UN has maintained that Shebaa Farms is part of territory captured by Israel from Syria, and as such must be considered under the Israeli-Syrian track of the Middle East peace process.) At the end of July a limited contingent of UNIFIL troops began to redeploy close to the Lebanese border with Israel, to fill the vacuum created by the departure of Israeli forces. At the same time the UN Security Council voted to extend UNIFIL's mandate until the end of January 2001. In early August 2000 Lebanon's own army returned to southern Lebanon, with the exception of the border area: a Joint Security Force of some 1,000 Lebanese troops and Internal Security Forces were reported to have entered the territory on 9 August, with responsibility for the provision of general security. However, the area close to the Blue Line remained under the control of Hezbollah and there were numerous reports of stone-throwing by Lebanese at the heavily fortified Israeli outposts. Continuing tension had discouraged most of the civilian population from returning to the territory.

Meanwhile, in June 2000 the Lebanese authorities initiated military court proceedings (some *in absentia*) against more than 2,500 former SLA militiamen, on charges of having collaborated with Israel during its occupation of southern Lebanon. The trial attracted strong criticism from human rights organizations. Reports stated that 2,041 alleged collaborators had been convicted by early January 2001.

THE 2000 LEGISLATIVE ELECTIONS

Elections to the National Assembly took place in two rounds on 27 August (Mount Lebanon and North Lebanon) and 3 September 2000 (Beirut, the Beka'a valley, Nabatiyah and the South). For the first time since 1972 Lebanese citizens in the former Israeli-occupied zone of southern Lebanon participated in the poll. Voting patterns in the first round swiftly indicated a rejection of al-Hoss's premiership, as the Druze leader, Walid Joumblatt (one of former premier Rafiq Hariri's staunchest allies) secured an overwhelming victory in Mount Lebanon governorate. Furthermore, while Deputy Prime Minister Michel Murr retained his seat in the Maronite Northern Metn district, the election there of Pierre Gemayel, son of Amin Gemayel, was regarded as a considerable reverse for President Lahoud. Turnout by voters was estimated at 51% of the registered electorate. Once again the opposition Christian parties boycotted the election in order to highlight their hostility to Syria's dominant influence over Lebanese political life. At the second round of voting, with a period of political 'cohabitation' between Lahoud and Hariri already appearing likely, the former Prime Minister's Al-Karamah (Dignity) list proceeded to secure 18 of the 19

assembly seats in Beirut (the remaining seat being won by a Hezbollah candidate); al-Hoss lost his own seat in the legislature. In the south an alliance of Hezbollah and Amal candidates took all the governorate's 23 seats, while Hezbollah enjoyed similar successes in the Beka'a. Independent monitors reported numerous examples of voting irregularities during the elections. Shortly before voting in the first round began, Syria's new President, Bashar al-Assad, had visited Beirut for talks with key figures in Lebanese political affairs, indicating that the new Syrian leader was unlikely to alter his late father's role as power-broker in Lebanon. However, the decisive rejection of the Syrian-backed Government of al-Hoss prompted speculation that there might be some redefinition of Syrian influence in Lebanese politics. This was considered all the more probable given the electoral successes for Joumblatt, who appeared to make common cause with Maronite supporters of Amin Gemayel and the imprisoned Geagea in demanding the withdrawal of Syrian forces. Debate about Syria's role in Lebanon had become more intense later in September when thousands of Lebanese, many brandishing portraits of Geagea and Gen. Awn, greeted Cardinal Sfeir (head of the Maronite Church and leader of the anti-Syrian campaign) on his return from a visit to the USA. In response to this event, numerous Shi'ite and Sunni Muslim religious and political figures strongly defended the Syrian presence. The controversy deepened when, later in September, Maronite bishops issued a statement demanding the complete withdrawal of the Syrian army from Lebanon. Following the legislative elections several editorials in the Syrian state press declared that Damascus would not interfere in the choice of Lebanon's new prime minister.

Despite accusations that Rafik Hariri had spent some US $50m. on his election campaign (after the outgoing assembly had rejected legislation to impose limits on campaign funding), the decisive defeat of the al-Hoss administration was attributed primarily to its failure to address the country's economic problems during its two years in office. During the campaign Hariri and his allies were able to exploit widespread popular disillusionment with the previous Government's performance, even though the economic crisis it had to grapple with was largely the result of the over-ambitious development schemes introduced under Hariri's first administration (1992–1998). The election result was widely regarded as a defeat for President Lahoud. Before the vote the President had indicated both publicly and in private that he was opposed to Hariri's resuming the premiership. Moreover, as Lahoud was the principal channel through which Damascus exerted its political influence over Lebanon, his comments were also seen as representing Syria's position. The result of the vote, however, left President Lahoud with little alternative but to appoint Rafik Hariri as Lebanon's new Prime Minister. Unofficial reports stated that as many as 106 of the 128 deputies in the National Assembly had expressed their support for Hariri during private talks with the President. Nevertheless, in the new administration Hariri was not to enjoy the dominant position that he had during his previous terms of office. Before his appointment Hariri had reportedly come to an informal agreement with Lahoud under which Hariri would take charge of economic policy, while the President would control defence and security issues.

The composition of the newly expanded 30-member Cabinet, announced on 26 October 2000, reflected this power-sharing arrangement between the President and the Prime Minister, as well as the traditional practice of dividing portfolios among the main religious communities. Only four ministers remained from the previous Government. Hariri's appointments included Issam Fares as Deputy Prime Minister, Fouad Siniora as Minister of Finance, Bassel Fleihan as Minister of Economy and Trade, Samir Jisr as Minister of Justice, and Abd ar-Rahim Mrad as Minister of Education. The appointment of one of Hariri's allies to the justice portfolio and of his former justice minister, Bahij Tabara, as a Minister of State without portfolio was interpreted by some as an attempt to exonerate a number of the new Prime Minister's associates—notably the new Minister of Finance—who had been charged with corruption by the al-Hoss administration. Appointments made by President Lahoud included his son-in law, Elias Murr, who replaced his father, Michel Murr, as Minister of the Interior and of Municipal and Rural Affairs. The President also selected George Ephram as Minister of

Industry and Jean-Louis Kordahi as Minister of Telecommunications. Nabih Berri, the Shi'ite leader, who was re-elected
President of the National Assembly at the beginning of the new
session, nominated Muhammad Abd al-Hamid Baydoun (the
deputy leader of Amal) as Minister of Energy and Water, Ali
Ajaj Abdullah as Minister of Agriculture, Assad Dieb as Minister
of Social Affairs and Michel Moussa (a Christian deputy from
southern Lebanon) as Minister of the Environment. The Druze
leader, Walid Joumblatt, appointed Marwan Hamadeh as Minister of the Displaced, and Fouad Saad (a Maronite) as Minister
of State for Administrative Reform. Syria ensured that a number
of its loyal supporters remained in the Cabinet: Najib Miqati as
Minister of Public Works and Transport, Sulayman Franjiya as
Minister of Public Health, and Ali Kanso, leader of the Lebanese
branch of the Syrian Baath Party, as Minister of Labour. At
the last minute Hezbollah—which now has 12 deputies in the
Assembly as part of the Resistance and Development list—
declined to participate in the new Government, ending much
speculation that they would accept Cabinet posts. In early
November Hariri won a vote of 'no confidence', instigated by a
group of pro-Syrian deputies who had questioned his past criticism of Syria's continued military presence in Lebanon. Most of
the deputies who refused to support the vote were members of
Hezbollah. After the Israeli withdrawal from southern Lebanon
the movement had appeared uncertain about its future political
role in the country.

Soon after the new Lebanese Government was announced,
there were indications that, despite their power-sharing agreement, tensions between Prime Minister Hariri and President
Lahoud were re-emerging. At the end of 2000 Hariri claimed
that the security services, which are controlled by the President,
were tapping his telephone conversations with Nabih Berri.
Lahoud proceeded to call a meeting of the Higher Defence
Council, which normally meets only in time of a national emergency. There appeared to be no justification for convening the
Council, but as it is chaired by the President and not the Prime
Minister it enabled Lahoud to demonstrate his authority. In
January 2001, after Hariri reportedly invited the former Christian militia leader, Gen. Awn, to return to Lebanon from exile
in France and gave guarantees that he would not be arrested,
President Lahoud, acting through the security services, overruled the Prime Minister and insisted that Gen. Awn would be
put on trial if he returned. However, there were signs that
Prime Minister Hariri had secured support from both President
Lahoud and Nabih Berri for his ambitious programme of economic reforms (see Economy). The power-sharing agreement
between Hariri and Lahoud appeared to have been reaffirmed,
with the Prime Minister determining economic policy and the
President controlling security and foreign affairs. Observers
noted, for example, that the management of reductions in military spending had been left to the armed forces, which fell
firmly within Lahoud's political sphere. Hariri appeared to have
persuaded Berri to accept the need for public-sector cuts by
agreeing to support legislation that would replace the multi-
member, multi-constituency electoral system with a single electoral district. Such changes would strengthen Berri's control
over the National Assembly as the Shi'ites form the largest
single confessional group in the country. However, the proposed
changes met with strong protests from Christian and Druze
leaders and were unlikely to win parliamentary approval, given
the sensitivities aroused by any attempt to change the sectarian
balance within the Assembly.

In late February 2001 Prime Minister Hariri held talks
regarding Lebanon's growing debt crisis with World Bank and
EU officials in Paris. No formal agreement was reached; however, Hariri announced subsequently that his request for aid
totalling US $458m. (on condition that his Government imple-
ment necessary economic reforms) would be met by the international organizations. At the end of February a group of 101
Lebanese intellectuals, calling themselves the Democratic
Forum, issued a communiqué criticizing the authorities for their
failure to adopt a coherent policy over the disputed Shebaa
Farms (see above). The first municipal elections for almost 40
years were held in southern Lebanon in early September (the
region having been under Israeli occupation when the rest of
the country voted in 1998).

VIOLENCE ON SOUTHERN BORDER INCREASES

In late September 2000 the Middle East entered a period of
crisis, when Palestinians in the West Bank and Gaza resumed
their *intifada* against Israel. The uprising provided a pretext
for Hezbollah to step up its militant campaign against Israel.
The organization expressed strong support for the Palestinians,
urging them to continue their struggle against the Israeli state,
but its leadership refrained from offering direct military assistance to the Palestinians. Hezbollah launched a number of small-
scale attacks on Israeli positions in Shebaa Farms, and on 7
October Hezbollah militants captured three Israeli soldiers on
patrol there, demanding that Israel release dozens of Palestinian prisoners and 19 Lebanese being held in Israeli gaols. On
12 October UN Secretary-General Kofi Annan visited Beirut for
talks regarding the soldiers' release. In the following week,
however, Israel confirmed that a senior Israeli army reservist
had been kidnapped in Switzerland, apparently by Hezbollah
(who claimed that the officer was working for Israeli intelligence). During October Israel closed a section of its border with
Lebanon, amid fears of further abductions. It was unclear as to
whether the Syrian leadership was encouraging Hezbollah's
latest campaign against Israel, although some commentators
felt that Damascus was unlikely to support any activities that
might result in renewed Israeli attacks against Lebanon. There
were those who argued that since the death of President Hafiz
Assad and the Israeli withdrawal from southern Lebanon,
Syrian influence over Hezbollah had declined, and that Damascus might no longer be able to restrain Hezbollah fighters
from provoking Israel. Indeed, there was growing evidence that
Hezbollah was answerable primarily to its Lebanese constituency.

At the beginning of November 2000 the UN Secretary-
General, Kofi Annan, urged the Lebanese Government to take
effective military control of the whole of southern Lebanon and
deplored the fact that in practice Hezbollah still controlled the
Blue Line. Later that month the UN Security Council demanded
an end to the 'continuing dangerous violations' along the border,
citing in particular stone-throwing by Lebanese and Palestinians who were being transported to the border by Hezbollah in
order to protest against Israel. President Lahoud and the newly-
installed Lebanese Prime Minister, Rafik Hariri, rejected these
demands. (For a detailed account of the August–September
2000 legislative elections, see below). UNIFIL commanders met
on 21 November to draw up contingency plans that would reduce
the peace-keeping force from seven full-strength battalions to
two, and eventually to one 'truce supervision' battalion. The
threat of reducing the size of UNIFIL was seen as an attempt
by the UN to force the Lebanese army to deploy along the
southern border. However, Lebanon's position remained that it
would not deploy its forces along the border until Israel had
concluded peace agreements with both Lebanon and Syria. It
was assumed that Beirut, under pressure from Damascus, would
not extend its control over the border region until Israel returned
the Golan Heights to Syria. At this time the Israelis were
reported to be constructing a new concrete border fence. At the
end of November 2000 an Israeli soldier was killed and two
others wounded by an explosive device planted inside the disputed Shebaa Farms area; the operation was interpreted as a
signal from Hezbollah that it could strike at Israeli forces south
of the Blue Line and even within Israel itself. In retaliation
Israel used helicopter gunships to attack suspected Hezbollah
bases in southern Lebanon—the first Israeli air-strikes on Lebanon since the Israeli withdrawal in May. In December Israeli
troops opened fire on a group of Lebanese civilians who were
throwing stones at an Israeli border post, wounding five of them.
There were reports that since the Israeli withdrawal at least 12
demonstrators had been killed and 40 wounded during similar
incidents at three points along the Israeli-Lebanese border.
There were also exchanges of gunfire and mortar fire between
the two sides. Meanwhile, Austrian and German intermediaries
seeking the release of the Israeli soldiers captured by Hezbollah
in October reported that the three men were still alive, although
Hezbollah's Secretary-General refused to comment on the fate
of the soldiers. At the end of the year the SLA's radio station—
relocated inside Israel and renamed 'Voice of Experience from
the Mediterranean Basin'—resumed broadcasting, and verbally

attacked Syria's continuing military presence in Lebanon, and Iran for its support of Hezbollah.

In January 2001 the Lebanese Government ordered an investigation into claims that Israel had used weaponry with a depleted uranium (DU) component during its occupation of southern Lebanon. There were fears that the increased incidence of cancers among Lebanese civilians in areas targeted by Israeli air-strikes during 'Operation Grapes of Wrath' in 1996 might be related to the use of DU weaponry. The Lebanese administration was said to be considering the inclusion of DU pollution in a list of claims for compensation from Israel, as part of a reparations lawsuit that Lebanon had filed with the International Court of Justice at The Hague, Netherlands. However, the Israeli military denied the use of DU ammunition in Lebanon.

Also in January 2001, following complaints from the UN, Israel was reported to have stopped construction work on a section of its concrete security fence near the village of Ghajar (just north of the UN-delineated border and thus inside Lebanese territory). At the end of January the UN Security Council reiterated its demand that both Israel and Lebanon end the numerous violations of the Blue Line. The Security Council also voted for a further six-month extension of UNIFIL's mandate in Lebanon and announced that, as of July 2001, the operational strength of UNIFIL was to be reduced (see below). Meanwhile, at the end of January two PFLP—GC guerrillas were killed while attempting to infiltrate Shebaa Farms, this being the first operation by Palestinian guerrillas since the Israeli withdrawal from southern Lebanon. The operation was condemned by Prime Minister Hariri, who declared that Lebanon would not permit such activities and that Palestinians who wanted to fight against Israel should join the *intifada*. In February 2001, after the assassination of Massoud Ayyad, an officer in Arafat's presidential guard (Force 17), Israel claimed that Ayyad was an agent of Hezbollah, and accused Hezbollah of direct involvement in the violence in the West Bank and Gaza. Israeli sources alleged that Hezbollah was attempting to unite Palestinian groups 'under its umbrella', that the movement organized military training sessions in Lebanon and was trying to smuggle weapons into areas controlled by the PA. Hezbollah was accused of trying to enlist Palestinians into its ranks, and it was claimed that the organization was considering operations within the 'Green Line', that is, within Israel's pre-1967 borders. However, Sheikh Nasrallah strongly denied that his organization was involved in the Palestinian *intifada*, and several commentators argued that while Hezbollah was offering strong political support to the Palestinians, it was not in the movement's interest to become directly involved in the Israeli–Palestinian conflict. In February 2001 Hezbollah fighters killed an Israeli soldier in a missile attack against an Israeli army patrol in Shebaa Farms. Israel responded by shelling targets in southern Lebanon. The UN, France and the USA condemned the attack by Hezbollah, and the US Department of State urged the Lebanese Government to deploy its troops along the frontier with Israel. The attack proved particularly embarrassing for premier Hariri as it came the day after he had publicly assured President Chirac of France that there would be 'no provocation of Israel from our side because we seek security and peace'. Hariri had apparently failed to persuade the Hezbollah leadership to co-ordinate its operations with the state, although Sheikh Nasrallah informed the Lebanese press that his movement would try to co-operate with the Prime Minister, and stressed that Israel, and not Hariri, was Hezbollah's prime target. In February and March 2001 a number of clashes occurred between Hezbollah and UNIFIL units when Hezbollah fighters prevented the UN peacekeepers from establishing new positions in the border area. Increasingly frustrated at the problems which they faced in their role as peace-keepers, UNIFIL announced that it would reduce the size of its force from an estimated 5,700 troops to some 4,500 (the number of personnel deployed prior to the Israeli withdrawal), and rumours circulated in Beirut that the entire force might be withdrawn.

On assuming the Israeli premiership in early March 2001, the Likud leader Ariel Sharon declared that he wanted 'realistic political relations and a true peace' with Lebanon and Syria, based on formal peace treaties (as Israel had signed with Egypt and Jordan). In response to the formation of the Sharon Govern-

ment, Prime Minister Hariri declared that Lebanon and other Arab states wanted to make peace on condition that they regained the territories occupied by Israel in 1967, and on condition that the Israeli Government respected international laws, UN resolutions and human rights. Meanwhile, Hariri announced that he would wait and see what policies the Sharon Government adopted. However, the Lebanese press was less restrained and, reviving memories of the early 1980s, some newspapers declared that the return to power in Israel of the man whom they held responsible for the massacre of Palestinians in the Sabra and Chatila refugee camps in September 1982 (when Sharon was Israel's Minister of Defence) would again plunge the region into war. Soon after his election, Sharon claimed that Israel had discovered Hezbollah cells operating in the West Bank and Gaza that were supporting the Palestinian uprising, and alleged that Iran had supplied Hezbollah with new missiles capable of reaching urban centres in central Israel. He also threatened military action against Lebanon, insisting in mid-March 2001 that the diversion of water from the Hasbani river by Lebanese farmers threatened Israel's security. None of these claims was substantiated.

ISRAEL ATTACKS SYRIAN BASE IN LEBANON

In mid-April 2001, after a further attack by Hezbollah on Israeli military positions in Shebaa Farms in which an Israeli soldier was killed, Israel responded immediately by bombarding certain targets in southern Lebanon. Two days later the Israeli air force attacked and destroyed a Syrian radar station at Dahr al-Baydar, 45 km east of Beirut, killing at least one Syrian soldier, according to a statement from Damascus. (Earlier reports had indicated that two or three Syrian soldiers had been killed and four wounded.) Israel also placed its forces on alert along the frontier with Lebanon. An Israeli spokesman stated that the raid by his country's forces—the first military action by Israel against Syrian troops since 1996—was designed to send a clear message that the new Israeli Government headed by Ariel Sharon held Syria and Lebanon responsible for Hezbollah's actions, and that they would pay the price for the organization's 'anti-Israeli' activities. President Lahoud described the Israeli air-strike as a dangerous development which revealed once again the 'murderous methods' of Prime Minister Sharon and which could lead to a wider Middle Eastern conflict. Prime Minister Hariri warned of an Israeli plan to extend the 'zone of instability' in the region and called for action by the international community to contain this dangerous escalation of violence. Hezbollah, for its part, vowed to continue its resistance until the last inch of Lebanese territory had been liberated from Israeli occupation. The day after the attack by Hezbollah on Israeli positions in Shebaa Farms, the Lebanese daily, *Al-Mustuqbal*, which is owned by Hariri, asked whether it had been wise to carry out the operation with all its political, economic and social consequences, and questioned whether the timing of the attack was in the interest of Lebanon as a whole. Following Israel's attack on the Syrian radar station, Terje Roed-Larsen, UN Special Co-ordinator for the Middle East peace process, urged both Lebanon and Syria to do everything possible to calm the situation; Roed-Larsen was reported to have told the Syrian Minister of Foreign Affairs, Farouk ash-Shara', that if Lebanon did not deploy its army along the Blue Line, then countries currently contributing troops to UNIFIL would withdraw them. In late April the President of the National Assembly, Nabih Berri, and the Hezbollah Secretary-General, Sheikh Hasan Nasrallah, attended a conference hosted by Iran in support of the Islamic resistance to Israel, at which Sheikh Nasrallah promised that Hezbollah would continue its operations against the Jewish state.

Towards the end of April 2001, on a visit to Washington, DC, for talks with President George W. Bush, US Secretary of State Colin Powell and US National Security Adviser Condoleezza Rice, the Lebanese Prime Minister called on the Bush administration to play a more active role in advancing the Middle East peace process. Hariri also met the UN Secretary-General, Kofi Annan, during his visit to the USA. Both Powell and Annan are reported to have emphasized the importance of reducing the level of violence in the region before the international community could address questions of economic development. Hariri insisted, however, that the USA was not making the release of some US $20m. in economic aid to Lebanon conditional on the deployment of Lebanese armed forces along the southern border. Meanwhile, during talks with the Spanish Minister of Foreign Affairs, Josep Piqué i Camps, President Lahoud urged EU states to play a greater role in the peace process. At the end of April the French Foreign Minister, Hubert Védrine, visited Beirut and Damascus to explore the basis for restarting Middle East peace negotiations. In Beirut he was informed by President Lahoud that Lebanon would not deploy its troops in the south of the country because such an action would be interpreted as ratifying the frontier delimited by the UN—the Blue Line— which Lebanon contested and where a number of problems remained unresolved, notably the issue of Shebaa Farms. Lahoud again denounced the 'aggressive policy' of Israel's Prime Minister, Ariel Sharon, and invited the EU, and particularly France, to play an active role in saving the peace process. The Lebanese authorities also stressed that Hezbollah's activities against Israeli forces in Shebaa Farms area were 'legitimate'. Védrine regretted that almost a year after the withdrawal of Israeli forces from southern Lebanon, Israel and Lebanon were unable to settle their differences and stated that it was not in Lebanon's interest to use the dispute over Shebaa Farms to increase the already high level of tension with Israel.

In May 2001 President Lahoud made his first official visit to France since assuming office. His talks with President Jacques Chirac and Prime Minister Lionel Jospin covered bilateral relations, the Francophone summit planned for October in Beirut, and the current crisis in the Middle East. Lahoud called on the international community to revise their policies in order to force Israel to resume peace negotiations, and again urged the EU to play a more active role in reviving peace talks. President Chirac, for his part, stated that in order to prevent the escalating violence between Israel and the Palestinians from spreading to Lebanon, the Lebanese state must re-establish its authority in the south by deploying its troops in the border zone. President Lahoud insisted, however, that Lebanon had not deployed its troops in the liberated zone because for strategic and military reasons there was no question of the Israeli and Lebanese armies coming face-to-face while the two countries were still in a state of war. The Lebanese President stated that security in the interior of the liberated southern region was being maintained by Lebanon's army and the Internal Security Forces, but reiterated that Lebanon would not deploy its army along the Blue Line (to guarantee the security of northern Israel) until a peace settlement had been concluded. According to Lahoud, for there to be a peace settlement Israel must end its occupation of Shebaa Farms and the Syrian Golan Heights, recognize the right of return for Palestinians (under the terms of UN Security Council Resolution 194), and liberate all remaining Arab prisoners from Israeli gaols. The President stated that resistance would continue so long as an inch of Lebanese territory remained under Israeli occupation. At the beginning of June UNIFIL announced that it had already dismantled 152 of its positions in the former Israeli security zone and was planning to establish new ones along the actual border between Lebanon and Israel, in preparation for the final establishment of the international border. By the end of July the UNIFIL force was to be reduced to some 4,500 troops, with further reductions to 2,000 troops by July 2002. The Lebanese Government stated that it wished to see the peace-keeping force maintained at 4,500 troops, and criticized proposals by the UN Secretary-General to consider downgrading UNIFIL to the status of an observer mission.

At the end of June 2001 the UN revealed that it had in its possession a video-cassette which had reportedly been filmed by a member of the UNIFIL force 18 hours after the kidnapping of the three Israeli soldiers by Hezbollah in October 2000. The cassette was reported to show two UN vehicles—containing UN uniforms, arms and explosives—that were apparently used by Hezbollah in the abduction of the Israeli soldiers. Israeli television, which had obtained some pictures from the tape, demanded to know why UN officials had refused to hand over the video-cassette to the Israeli authorities as it could provide valuable evidence concerning the soldiers' kidnapping. There were reports that Israeli security forces suspected that UN peace-keepers had turned a blind eye to preparations for the Hezbollah operation and may even have witnessed the abductions. There was also speculation that the UN had refused to hand over the

cassette because it feared that any Israeli reprisals against the men pictured in the tape, who may or may not have been directly involved in the kidnapping, would compromise the organization's neutrality. The results of an internal UN investigation into the incident were published in early August 2001. The report concluded that UN officials were not guilty of any conspiracy or malice, but noted several 'lapses in judgment and failures in communication', which had prevented the existence of the video-cassette from coming to light more promptly after the abduction of the Israeli soldiers. Some months later reports indicated that the matter had been resolved and that Israeli officials, including a senior intelligence officer, had viewed the cassette together with two other tapes held by the UN also relating to the abduction of the three Israeli soldiers. At the beginning of November the IDF's chief rabbi declared that the three kidnapped soldiers were officially dead, an announcement dismissed by Hezbollah as an attempt to elicit information about the men.

At the beginning of July 2001 Israeli air forces attacked a Syrian radar station in Lebanon's Beka'a valley, in response to a Hezbollah operation in Shebaa Farms during which at least one Israeli soldier was wounded. Up to three Syrian soldiers and a Lebanese conscript were reportedly injured in the retaliatory attack. The Israeli administration stated that the Syrian authorities were preventing the deployment of the Lebanese army on the frontier and were allowing Hezbollah to rearm. The Arab League condemned the Israeli attack, while the US Department of State called on all parties to exercise maximum restraint. At the end of July the UN Security Council voted to extend UNIFIL's mandate in Lebanon until 31 January 2002. The UN also announced a reduction in the number of UNIFIL troops from 4,500 to 3,600 and the nominal downgrading of their peace-keeping mission to an 'observer mission'.

In mid-August 2001 tensions escalated again between Israeli forces and Hezbollah militants in the village of Ghajar, which straddles the Blue Line. However, during the following weeks the tensions were diffused by an increased number of patrols by UN peace-keeping forces in the area. In early October Hezbollah resumed its mortar attacks on Israeli positions in Shebaa Farms—the first for almost three months—to which Israeli forces responded, though no injuries were reported during the exchanges. Hezbollah announced that the attacks had been launched to show solidarity with the Palestinian *intifada*, but some observers contended that it was an act of defiance against the US 'war against terror' and a protest against the addition of Hezbollah to the US blacklist of terrorist organizations. Hezbollah mounted further attacks on Israeli positions in Shebaa Farms in late October. At the end of November the Israeli press reported that the Sharon Government had approached Hezbollah through an intermediary offering to end hostilities along the Blue Line, withdraw from Ghajar and Shebaa Farms and exchange prisoners, but that Hezbollah had rejected these overtures. Meanwhile, one Beirut newspaper reported tensions within Hezbollah between the pro-Iranian faction loyal to Ayatollah Khamenei, which was determined to continue military attacks against Israel, and the pro-Syrian faction, which urged greater restraint.

The withdrawal of troop detachments from Finland and Ireland at the end of October 2001 reduced the UNIFIL force to 3,494 military personnel. During a visit to UN headquarters in New York, the UNIFIL commander was reported to have advised against further reductions to the force, stating that they were already fully stretched. In early December the Israeli army provided UNIFIL with maps and documentation on minefields laid by Israeli forces during the occupation of south Lebanon and the suspected location of bombs and booby traps planted by Hezbollah and other organizations in the area. Some of this material had been handed over immediately after Israel's withdrawal from South Lebanon in May 2000, but UNIFIL stated that the vast amount of new material would be extremely useful to them. At the end of January 2002 the UN Security Council renewed UNIFIL's mandate for a further six months and reaffirmed its decision to reduce the force to 2000 by the end of the year, despite requests by the Lebanese Government that the force be maintained at its present level. Although there was some evidence that the Lebanese army and internal security forces were increasing their presence in the South, Lebanon still refused to deploy its forces along the Blue Line.

At the beginning of January 2002 Israel seized a freighter, the *Karine A*, in the Red Sea, carrying a cargo of arms that the Israelis claimed had been purchased by the PA from Iran using Hezbollah as an intermediary. The Palestinian leadership, Hezbollah and Iran denied any involvement in the affair. Independent sources suggested that PLO officials had probably been engaged in the arms trade and that Hezbollah and Iran may have been involved. In March Sheikh Nasrallah admitted that a number of Hezbollah members had been arrested by the Jordanian authorities earlier in the year while attempting to smuggle weapons from Jordan to Palestinian fighters in the West Bank. Addressing a rally in Beirut, Sheikh Nasrallah declared that Arab nations that were not prepared to smuggle arms to the Palestinians should not prohibit those groups who were willing to do so. Hezbollah also appeared to have allowed at least two Palestinian guerrillas to travel from Lebanon to carry out an ambush in northern Israel in which the guerrillas were killed along with several Israelis. From late 2001 Hezbollah had been markedly less hostile towards Yasser Arafat and the PA.

In late January 2002 Hezbollah began firing large-calibre anti-aircraft artillery across the border into Israel in retaliation for continued incursions by Israeli military aircraft into Lebanese airspace. In early March when Israel announced that it was reducing its 'reconnaissance' flights over Lebanon, Hezbollah described it as an 'Arab victory'. Meanwhile, Israel resumed construction work on a fence around the southern edge of Ghajar. In late March and early April, as Israeli forces began a major offensive in Palestinian-controlled territories in the West Bank, Hezbollah increased its cross-border attacks using anti-tank missiles and mortars, wounding several Israeli soldiers. The daily bombardment concentrated on Shebaa Farms, but Israeli sources indicated that attacks had also been carried out elsewhere along the border. The Hezbollah attacks were the most intensive since the Israeli withdrawal from southern Lebanon in May 2000. The Israeli army returned fire and, as a precautionary measure, the civilian population in some parts of northern Israel were ordered into shelters. Hezbollah declared that its cross-border attacks were being carried out not only to liberate occupied Lebanese territory but also 'in solidarity with the Palestinian people'. Reports also suggested that Hezbollah had given permission for militants from radical Palestinian groups to fire on Israeli settlements from inside Lebanon. Indeed some extremists within Hezbollah, such as the movement's southern commander, Sheikh Nabil Qaouk, called for a wider war against a weakened Israel 'to finish it off'. However, this did not appear to be a view shared by Hezbollah's senior leaders, and in a speech in April Sheikh Nasrallah insisted that there was no intention of opening up a 'second front' against Israel, a position repeated by Syria's ambassador to the UN and by the Iranian Minister of Foreign Affairs (see below).

LEBANON AND THE 'WAR AGAINST TERROR'

Most of Lebanon's political and religious leaders condemned the suicide attacks on New York and Washington on 11 September 2001, and Prime Minster Hariri stated that Lebanon would support US retaliation and would be ready to help 'if the evidence was clear'. Lebanon subsequently signed UN Security Council Resolution 1373, which was adopted to combat international terrorism. Some days after the attacks Hezbollah issued a statement in which it expressed regret at the killing of innocent people anywhere in the world but urged caution, arguing that the US Administration would use the resulting fear and panic to practice 'all manner of aggression and terrorism under the pretext of fighting aggression and terrorism'. The statement declared that the Lebanese had been the victims of repeated Zionist massacres which the US Administration had refused to condemn. Druze leader Walid Joumblatt, who had at first categorically condemned the 11 September attacks, later described Osama bin Laden (the presumed instigator of the attacks) as an 'invention' of US intelligence services and suggested that these agencies might have been involved in the attacks. In the wake of the suicide attacks the ninth Francophone summit, which was to have been held in Beirut on 16–19 October, was postponed. This was the first time that an Arab

capital had been selected as the venue for a Francophone summit, and, with delegates from 55 countries, it would have been the most important international event held in Beirut since the end of the civil war. Hezbollah denounced the subsequent US bombing campaign against Afghanistan, and its Secretary-General, Sheikh Hassan Nasrallah, declared that it was not permissible for any Islamic state, ruler or political organization to extend any assistance to the USA in its war against a Muslim country or group. He accused the USA of using the 11 September attacks as a pretext to wage war on its opponents and establish military bases around the world. Hezbollah did not appear on the first US list of terrorist groups associated with bin Laden whose assets were to be frozen. Asbat al-Ansar, with both Palestinian and Lebanese members based in the Ain el-Hilweh refugee camp in Sidon, was the only Lebanese group included on the list, which was published at the end of September. At a press conference Asbat al-Ansar's leadership immediately denied any links with bin Laden's al-Qa'ida (Base) organization. However, the USA subsequently included Hezbollah on an updated list of terrorist organizations along with Hamas, Islamic Jihad and the PFLP—GC. Sheikh Nasrallah asserted that the US Administration was acting under pressure from Israel, and accused the USA of waging war 'against every Muslim who refuses to bow to it'. A member of Hezbollah, Imad Mughniyah, was one of three Lebanese nationals included on a list issued by the US Federal Bureau of Investigation of its 22 'most wanted' terrorists. In early November the Lebanese Cabinet refused a US request to freeze Hezbollah's assets, stating that it was a resistance movement not a terrorist organization and arguing that resistance to Israel was legitimate so long as Israel occupied Arab lands. Shortly afterwards the US National Security Advisor, Condoleezza Rice, declared that Lebanon would not secure the international financial assistance it required for its economic recovery if it did not comply with the US Administration's demands. Towards the end of 2001 press reports, citing US and European intelligence sources, claimed that Hezbollah and al-Qa'ida were involved in the illegal trade in diamonds from rebel-held areas in Sierra Leone in West Africa. In December Condoleezza Rice urged Lebanon and Syria to dismantle Hezbollah's military wing, while the US ambassador to Beirut insisted that Hezbollah was an organization that carried out terrorist acts and was capable of staging them on a global scale. Sheikh Nasrallah demanded that the USA provide evidence of the organization's involvement in activities that were not linked to resistance. He also referred again to 'secret overtures' made by US representatives to Hezbollah following the 11 September attacks and repeated that they had been rejected. During a visit to Beirut in mid-December the US Assistant Secretary for Near Eastern Affairs, William Burns, stated that a report that included evidence of Hezbollah's terrorist activities was forthcoming but that the USA wished to handle this matter 'through practical and quiet dialogue' with the Lebanese authorities.

Hezbollah was not included on the EU's list of 'terrorist' groups and individuals, released at the end of December 2001: its omission appeared to have been the result of a late intervention by France. The United Kingdom for its part made a distinction between Hezbollah's domestic organization, which was deemed legitimate, and its external security organization, which was condemned as a terrorist group because of its attacks against Israeli interests abroad. On 17 June 2002, after negotiations lasting six years (which had been officially concluded in January), Lebanon signed a Euro-Mediterranean Association Agreement with the EU. Romano Prodi, the President of the European Commission, stated that by signing the agreement, which awaited ratification, Lebanon clearly indicated its commitment to the values shared by the EU on democracy, human rights, economic liberalization and regional security. The EU promised to support Lebanon's plans for economic liberalization and reform and to support Lebanon's application for membership of the World Trade Organization.

In early March 2002 Syria and Lebanon issued a joint communiqué, after a brief state visit to Beirut by Syrian President Bashar al-Assad, in response to the peace plan proposed by Crown Prince Abdullah of Saudi Arabia to end the Arab-Israeli conflict. While supporting the principle of an exchange of land for peace, the joint statement by Presidents al-Assad and

Lahoud drew attention to the right of return of Palestinian refugees—Lebanon in particular continued to reject the notion of the permanent settlement of some 200,000 Palestinian refugees in Lebanon—and the dismantling of Jewish settlements established in the Occupied Territories. This was Bashar al-Assad's first official visit to Lebanon since he assumed the Presidency and the first by a Syrian President to the presidential palace at Baabda. At the end of March the Beirut summit meeting of the Arab League Conference (the first to be held in Lebanon since 1956) which unanimously endorsed the Saudi peace plan. Arab leaders offered to normalize relations with Israel in return for an Israeli withdrawal from Arab territories occupied since 1967 (including the Syrian Golan Heights and Shebaa Farms), the establishment of a Palestinian state with East Jerusalem as its capital, and a 'just and negotiated solution' to the refugee problem. They also expressed their opposition to any US military attack against Iraq. Yasser Arafat (who was not permitted by the Israeli authorities to leave the West Bank), had been scheduled to address the summit by video link from his headquarters in Ramallah, but at the last minute the Lebanese authorities refused to allow the live transmission of his speech, causing the Palestinian and UAE delegations to threaten to leave the summit outright (they were prevailed on to stay by other participants). The Saudi delegation denounced the Lebanese action as 'inexplicable and unpardonable'. The Lebanese authorities gave few explanations apart from a concern that Israel might interfere with Arafat's address if it was transmitted live. Both Prime Minister Hariri and National Assembly Speaker Berri had boycotted the arrival ceremony after differences with President Lahoud over arrangements for meeting the arriving delegates. Addressing a crowd of some 200,000 people, Hezbollah's Secretary-General, Sheikh Nasrallah, condemned any normalization of relations with Israel. Earlier Hezbollah had rejected the Saudi peace plan and had called on the Arab leaders to send weapons to the Palestinians so that they could continue their resistance to Israeli aggression.

Israel's military offensive into Palestinian-controlled areas in the West Bank, from the end of March 2002, was condemned by all Lebanese political parties and all religious communities. Hezbollah stated that it could not ignore what was happening in the West Bank and that it was determined to continue the struggle for the liberation of those parts of Lebanon still occupied by Israel. Throughout the Israeli reoccupation of Palestinian-administered population centres in the West Bank, Hezbollah carried out almost daily attacks on Israeli positions in the border region. At the end of March 2002 demonstrations were held in Palestinian refugee camps across Lebanon, but security forces prevented the Palestinians from extending their protests to the surrounding streets. For the first time in many years the authorities allowed several hundred Palestinians of all ages to hold a demonstration in the heart of west Beirut to express support for Arafat, although the protest was closely monitored by the internal security forces. The next day a march was organized in Beirut when Lebanese protesters denounced Arab leaders as 'traitors to the Palestinian cause' and called on Presidents Lahoud and al-Assad to 'open the frontiers'.

In mid-April 2002 the US Secretary of State, Colin Powell, visited Beirut and Damascus as part of his Middle East mission. In both capitals he expressed concern that Hezbollah attacks along the border with Israel might lead to an extension of the conflict between Israel and the Palestinians, and called on countries with influence over Hezbollah to contain the group's military activities. Before his arrival in Beirut, thousands of angry demonstrators gathered along the route from the airport; protesters shouted slogans denouncing the USA and Israel and burnt US and Israeli flags. The demonstration was organized by Islamist parties, principally Hezbollah, left-wing parties and Palestinian movements. In their meetings with Powell President Lahoud and Prime Minister Hariri reiterated Lebanon's position, stating that respect for the Blue Line did not exclude 'resistance' operations by Hezbollah to liberate Shebaa Farms. Nabih Berri refused to take part in talks with Powell, and Hezbollah announced that despite US threats it would continue its operations in Shebaa Farms.

MOUNTING OPPOSITION TO SYRIAN PRESENCE

Pressure for Syria to withdraw its troops from Lebanon and to relinquish its dominant role in the country's internal affairs—which had been growing since the Israeli withdrawal from southern Lebanon in May 2000 and the death of Syria's President Hafiz Assad in June—continued to mount after the Lebanese elections. It was particularly significant that Walid Joumblatt, the Druze leader and a long-standing ally of Syria, in late 2000 joined the Christian opposition in demanding a 'reassessment' of Lebanon's relationship with Syria. Joumblatt's statement provoked disquiet in Damascus, where there were fears that the anti-Syrian movement in Lebanon might spread beyond the Maronite community and begin to acquire a wider nationalist dimension. Damascus responded by indicating that Joumblatt would no longer be given special treatment when he visited Syria, and when the Druze leader refused to withdraw his comments, Ali Kanso, the Minister of Labour and leader of the Lebanese branch of Syria's Baath Party, accused Joumblatt of treason. Meanwhile, in late November the Shi'ite leader and National Assembly President, Nabih Berri, provoked criticism from Damascus when, on a visit to Cardinal Sfeir, Berri announced that Syria would redeploy its troops from Lebanon 'in the near future'. Although Berri's meeting with the Cardinal had been made at Syria's request, Berri appeared to have exceeded his instructions by referring to the redeployment of Syrian troops. These developments were interpreted by some commentators as further evidence of divisions within the Syrian leadership over its policy on Lebanon. Syria's new President, Bashar al-Assad, had responded to mounting anti-Syrian feeling in Lebanon by seeking a *rapprochement* with the Maronite community, a policy which had been opposed by some of his advisers. In early December Syria began the release of Lebanese political prisoners held in its gaols, many of them supporters of Gen. Awn (for further details, see below). At the end of the year there were reports from Damascus that President Assad was examining proposals to pull back all Syrian troops currently in Lebanon to the Beka'a valley, but that he would only contemplate a complete withdrawal of Syrian forces within the context of a comprehensive Middle East peace settlement.

In the early part of 2001 the controversy about Syria's presence in Lebanon provoked inter-communal tensions, and even violence. In mid–March, on the 12th anniversary of Gen. Awn's attempt to expel Syrian forces from Lebanon, several thousand students staged protests at university campuses across Beirut, and the Lebanese army and security forces intervened to prevent the protesters from marching on a Syrian military position outside the capital. The debate became more acrimonious at the end of March when some 100,000 Lebanese Christians greeted Cardinal Sfeir on his return from the USA, where he had called for an end to Syrian tutelage. The crowds who lined the road from Beirut to Bkerke—the seat of the patriarch—again brandished portraits of Geagea, Bachir Gemayel and Gen. Awn. Strong criticism of Cardinal Sfeir from senior Sunni clerics, such as Sheikh Taha Sabounji of Tripoli, raised fears of renewed sectarian conflict within Lebanon. At the beginning of April former premier Selim al-Hoss established a National Action Front that called for an 'equitable relationship between the state of Lebanon and Syria to stop one from interfering in the domestic affairs of the other'. A few days later, when groups opposed to the Syrian military presence announced their intention to hold a popular demonstration in Beirut, the pro-Syrian camp declared that they would mount a counter-demonstration. As tensions mounted, the anti-Syrian camp decided to cancel their protest, while the Government imposed a ban on both demonstrations. Tensions appeared to subside temporarily, but not before several supporters of a militant pro-Syrian faction, the Ahbache, had demonstrated in west Beirut against the 'agents' who opposed Syria's involvement in Lebanon. On the previous day a parcel bomb had wounded three members of the family of PSP deputy Akram Chehayeb. The leader of the PSP, Walid Joumblatt, immediately declared that if the aim was to terrorize the Druze community, then such actions would achieve nothing, insisting that what was required was dialogue. Prime Minister Hariri admitted that the situation had become extremely dangerous and expressed his conviction that differences could only be resolved through dialogue. In a move to ease the tensions, in mid-April President Lahoud received Joumblatt—their first meeting for six months. Meanwhile, Sulayman Franjiya, the Minister of Public Health and a Christian with very close links with Syria, visited Cardinal Sfeir. The Cardinal adopted a more moderate tone, calling for 'narrow' but 'transparent' links with Damascus based on harmony and a sincere commitment to respect treaties. This message was repeated a day later when President Lahoud visited the Maronite patriarch on Easter Sunday. At the same time Cardinal Sfeir received an invitation from the Greek Catholic patriarch, whose seat is in Damascus, to visit Syria in May to take part in celebrations to greet the leader of the Roman Catholic Church, Pope John Paul II. However, in an interview with the French Catholic daily, *La Croix*, at the end of April, Cardinal Sfeir suggested that his forthcoming visit to Damascus might be exploited by Syria. During visits to Beirut and Damascus in late April, the French Minister of Foreign Affairs, Hubert Védrine, stated that he regarded the debate about the Syrian presence in Lebanon to be 'legitimate'. At the beginning of May Cardinal Sfeir announced that he would not visit Damascus to attend celebrations for Pope John Paul II owing to Lebanese public opinion.

SYRIAN WITHDRAWAL FROM BEIRUT FAILS TO EASE TENSIONS

In mid-June 2001 Syria began to withdraw its armed forces from Beirut and its southern and eastern suburbs, and from Mount Lebanon; many of the troops were redeployed in the Beka'a valley. Between 14–19 June an estimated 6,000–10,000 Syrian troops were withdrawn from more than 12 major bases and several smaller positions in and around the Lebanese capital, most of them in largely Christian areas and near government buildings (including the presidential palace at Baabda and the defence ministry in Yarza). The redeployment from Greater Beirut was believed by some to be intended to reduce pressure from Lebanese Christians for a full Syrian withdrawal from the country, and to demonstrate a return to Lebanese sovereignty in the capital. Other analysts, however, speculated that the movement of Syrian forces to the Beka'a valley demonstrated Syrian fears of a possible new confrontation with Israel. Cardinal Sfeir expressed his satisfaction at the redeployment, but noted that there was a long road to travel before relations between Lebanon and Syria could achieve a new 'equilibrium'. Walid Joumblatt stated that the redeployment was the first step in improving Lebanese-Syrian relations. However, some commentators saw the withdrawal as partial and merely symbolic—Syria retained 15 bases in strategic areas in Beirut, including the airport—and noted that Syria's intelligence services remained vigilant and omnipresent in Lebanon.

The Maronite patriarch, Cardinal Sfeir, visited the Chouf mountain region of Lebanon on 3–5 August 2001 to hold landmark discussions with Druze leader Walid Joumblatt, in order to demonstrate a new era of 'reconciliation' between their two communities. Joumblatt also visited several Christian towns in the south of Lebanon in the following week. However, two days after Sfeir's visit to the Chouf, the Lebanese army intelligence service (which is largely pro-Syrian) implemented a crackdown on Maronite Christians who were again vociferously demanding a complete Syrian withdrawal from Lebanon. According to Joumblatt, the authorities' action was largely due to Syria's dislike of the recent Maronite-Druze reconciliation. On 7 August as many as 250 Christians—most of whom were members of the prohibited LF or supporters of Gen. Awn's Free National Current (FNC) movement—were arrested on charges of involvement in 'illegal gatherings' and of seeking to destabilize and partition the country. Among those detained were Toufik Hindi, a senior official of the LF who was accused of conspiring with Israel against Lebanon and Syria, and Nadim Lteif, a retired army commander and leader of the FNC. It was unclear as to whether President Lahoud had ordered army intelligence officers to carry out the arrests, but reports stated that the Hariri Government had not been consulted; indeed, the Prime Minister was abroad when the crack-down began. Both Christian and Muslim deputies condemned the detentions as 'unconstitutional'. The mass arrest of Christian opposition activists led to clashes between the Lebanese police and protestors demonstrating against the growing influence of the military in the country. The authorities made further arrests, this time including activists of the PNL. Two leading Lebanese journalists

were also detained, on charges of having contacts with Israel. A few days after the crack-down, a military court began trial proceedings against more than 20 Christian activists who had taken part in the anti-Syrian protests. (A ruling by the Court of Cassation in early September meant that several of the detainees' cases were to be referred to civil courts.) By 20 August it was reported that the vast majority of those arrested for their role in the disturbances had been released or tried on more minor charges (leading to a maximum of 45 days' imprisonment). However, it was reported that those LF members accused of conspiracy with Israel remained in detention.

The political crisis facing Rafik Hariri increased during the latter part of August 2001. In mid-August the National Assembly passed legislation giving greater powers to President Lahoud. At the end of the month Hariri held talks with the President over the consequences of the recent security crackdown; the Prime Minister pledged to continue in office, despite being angered at the military's failure to consult him prior to its campaign of arrests. In early September Maronite bishops again issued a strong criticism of Syria's domination of Lebanese affairs. It was reported at this time that up to seven Syrians had been killed in Lebanon during the past month.

In October 2001 Karim Pakradoumi, former lawyer to LF leader Samir Geagea, won a decisive victory in elections for the leadership of the Phalange party, now only a shadow of its former strength. Since his return to Lebanon in 2000 former President Amin Gemayel, son of the Phalange's founder, Pierre Gemayel, had sought to take control of the party, promising to restore its influence, but in the end his supporters boycotted the leadership elections. In late November 2001 the internal security forces entered the Université Saint-Joseph in Beirut and dismantled a display set up by anti-Syrian students—which included Lebanese flags hung with black ribbons to symbolize Lebanon's loss of independence. They also prevented students from joining an anti-Syrian demonstration by mainly right-wing student groups at the Lebanese University campus. Although the State Prosecutor upheld the actions of the security forces, the Minister of the Interior condemned them and reprimanded three of its officers. In December, after months of wrangling within the ruling troika over appointments to the civil service, it was announced that agreement had been reached on some 171 posts, with 66 divided among Christian communities and the remainder allocated to Muslims. These appointments, especially senior posts such as directors-general of ministries, form an important part of the country's elaborate patronage system, and disputes over their distribution intensified as President, Prime Minister and National Assembly President each sought to use them to extend their authority and influence within the political system. Hariri was reported to have successfully placed his own supporters in a number of key posts, notably those of head of the Council for Development and Reconstruction and of Electricité du Liban. The remaining civil service appointments were finally agreed by late January 2002 when a new head of the National Security Fund was appointed.

At the end of January 2002 Elie Hobeika, former head of the LF, was killed when a car bomb exploded close to his home in a Beirut suburb. Hobeika's murder was the first high-profile political assassination for over a decade. Although Hobeika had many enemies, most Lebanese politicians, including government ministers, held Israel responsible for the assassination: many believed that it was a 'targeted killing' because Hobeika had agreed to testify against Israeli Prime Minister Ariel Sharon whose role in the 1982 Sabra and Chatila massacres (see above) was the subject of legal proceedings brought before a court in Brussels, Belgium, by several survivors of the massacres. (The complaint against Sharon was judged inadmissible by the Court of Appeal in Brussels at the end of June 2002.) Both Sharon and Israeli Minister Foreign of Foreign Affairs Shimon Peres dismissed accusations of any Israeli involvement in Hobeika's murder. As head of the LF's intelligence section in 1982, Hobeika was widely accused of 'overseeing' the massacres of Palestinians at Sabra and Chatila. He had later abandoned his Israeli patrons and made peace with Damascus. After the end of the civil war he served in three governments but lost his seat in the National Assembly at the 2000 elections. While Israeli agents remained the prime suspect for the killing, there were also suggestions that the assassination could have been the work of Palestinians or rival Christian groups, notably those linked to Samir Geagea. Israel strenuously denied any involvement in the assassination of Hobeika. In late January 2002 the LF held its first official meeting since being banned in 1994, in what the party asserted was the first step in relaunching the party and restoring its legal status.

At the end of February 2002 the trial began of Hassib Yunis, one of the journalists arrested in August 2001 (see above) for having contacts with Israel, went on trial and denied the charges against him. Meanwhile, three Lebanese Muslims were arrested and charged with recruiting on behalf of an Israeli espionage ring and selling information about Hezbollah activities in southern Lebanon and Lebanese and Syrian troop movements. Shortly afterwards a former senior Amal official was arrested on charges of spying for Israel. He was alleged to have been involved in a group that specialized in supplying information about the movements of senior members of Hezbollah.

Leaders of anti-Syrian factions, including the Maronite patriarch, broadly welcomed the official visit to Beirut by President Bashar al-Assad and his senior ministers in early March 2002 (see above). While pointing out that it was a useful 'first step', they continued to demand an end to Syria's dominant role in Lebanon's internal affairs. In April Syria announced that it was redeploying a further 20,000 troops based in Lebanon. It was expected that most of the units withdrawn from central Lebanon would be redeployed in the Beka'a valley with others returning to Syria. Some analysts interpreted the move as a sign that Syria was prepared to allow Lebanon greater autonomy in some areas while retaining tight control over security issues and foreign affairs. Others suggested that by concentrating its forces in the Beka'a valley Syria was adopting a more defensive position in case of an attack by Israel.

In late May 2002 Jihad Jibril, the head of the PFLP—GC's military operations and son of the group's leader, was killed by a car bomb in west Beirut. The Lebanese security forces attributed his murder to inter-Palestinian rivalries, while the PFLP—GC initially accused the Israeli secret service, Mossad, and then the Jordanian secret services. Israel categorically rejected any involvement in the incident, even though in recent months the PFLP—GC had been involved in a number of successful attacks across the Lebanese border into Israel and claimed to have been actively engaged in smuggling arms into the West Bank. There were also claims that Jibril's murder

might have been the work of right-wing Lebanese Christians who regarded the PFLP—GC as Syrian agents in Lebanon.

In August 2002 two people were killed and six others injured in the worst factional fighting at the Ain el-Hilweh Palestinian refugee camp for several years. Tensions escalated following the arrest of an Islamist militant the previous month (accused of killing three Lebanese army intelligence officers) by the Lebanese army aided by Fatah. Violent clashes between the Lebanese army and Palestinian militants occurred at the normally relatively calm al-Jalil refugee camp, near Ba'albek, in September, which left one soldier and three Palestinians dead and at least 11 others wounded. Lebanese soldiers had entered the camp in search of a wanted man and removed a cache of armaments from offices of the Fatah Revolutionary Council, an organization founded by the militant leader Abu Nidal, who was found dead in Baghdad, Iraq in August.

LEBANESE PRISONERS HELD IN SYRIA

In January 2001 the Lebanese Government set up a commission to examine the sensitive issue of Lebanese prisoners held in Syria. The commission was to be chaired by a minister and to include representatives of Lebanon's legal system, military intelligence, internal and national security. For two years, until the release of some 46 Lebanese and eight Palestinians by Syria in December 2000, the authorities in Beirut had denied that any Lebanese were imprisoned in Syria. Faced with official indifference, the families of the Lebanese citizens detained in Syria had set up a committee (Comité des familles de détenus libanais en Syrie) to campaign for their release. The committee reported that Syria had released 168 Lebanese prisoners in two groups since 1998 and estimated that some 263 Lebanese remained in Syrian gaols. The London-based human rights organization Amnesty International put the figure at 228. During the official visit of President Bashar al-Assad to France in late June 2001 the movement Solida (Soutien aux Libanais détenus arbitrairement) appealed to the Syrian President to stop the practice of forced disappearances from Lebanese territory and the secret detention of Lebanese nationals in Syria, and asked him to return the bodies of those detainees who had died in detention to their families or at least produce a list of those who had died. The French authorities were asked to take up the cause of Lebanese held arbitrarily in Syria and to make this a priority issue in bilateral relations with Damascus.

Economy

Revised for this edition by RICHARD I. LAWLESS

INTRODUCTION

Lebanon's role as the Middle East's leading centre for trade and financial services was destroyed by the civil war which erupted in 1975. Attempts to prepare plans for reconstruction were frustrated by recurring outbreaks of violence, culminating in the Israeli invasion of June 1982, which added a new dimension to the country's devastation. Lebanon's gross domestic product (GDP) expanded, in real terms, at an average annual rate of 6%–6.5% between 1964 and 1974. Average income per head in 1974 was estimated at US $1,300, one of the highest levels among developing countries at the time. With the outbreak of the civil war, however, real GDP declined sharply. Expressed in constant 1974 prices, it was estimated to have averaged £L4,800m. per year in 1975–81. The Israeli invasion caused a further sharp decline in GDP, which, again expressed in constant 1974 prices, was estimated at £L3,080m. in 1982. Despite the intervening years of turmoil, Lebanon's GDP, expressed in constant 1974 prices, was estimated to have recovered to £L8,600m. in 1987. However, although the banking sector actually thrived after 1975, the development of alternative Middle East banking and financial centres, particularly in the Persian (Arabian) Gulf region, made it unlikely that an unstable Lebanon would regain its position as the commercial centre of the Arab world. After Amin Gemayel became President in

September 1982 and formed a Cabinet comprising technical experts, it was hoped that the process of rehabilitating the country could begin in earnest. However, owing to the continued civil conflict and the unwillingness of potential aid donors to commit themselves before the restoration of stability, several such programmes were shelved. In the late 1980s, after years of relative resilience to political events, the deterioration of the political situation, combined with a high level of unemployment, major shifts in population, the breakdown of the infrastructure and the perpetual postponement of reconstruction and development projects, plunged the economy to new depths of depression, and it teetered on the verge of collapse. Those who could afford to leave the country made efforts to establish themselves abroad, often in Cyprus, the USA or Australia. For those with no escape route, however, the outlook was grim.

Hopes of an economic revival were raised when the civil war effectively ended in 1991. GDP for that year has been estimated at £L4,132,000m., measured at current prices, or £L3,720m. in constant 1974 prices, compared with an estimated £L1,973,000m. in 1990 (£L2,690m. in constant 1974 prices. In 1992, however, the Government of Omar Karami resigned, after it had failed to narrow the budget deficit and when, amid allegations of ministerial corruption, the value of the local currency collapsed, leading to a sharp rise in inflation. The legislative elections held in mid-1992 and the subsequent appointment of a billionaire entrepreneur, Rafik Hariri, as Prime Minister paved the way for a serious start to economic reconstruction, which was to be based on higher receipts of foreign aid. Until mid-1996 Lebanon experienced levels of annual growth averaging 6.5% in real terms, mainly as a result of high levels of government and private investment in the construction sector based on the expectation that the country would quickly regain is role as a regional tourism and leisure centre. The Israeli air and artillery attacks on Lebanon in April 1996 was one of the main factors that brought this phase to an end and, as inward private investment declined, the growth rate slowed. Lebanon's GDP grew at an estimated average annual rate of 4.8% in 1992–99. However, with the country in the throes of recession, GDP, in real terms, was estimated to have contracted by 1% in 1999 and by an estimated 0.5% in 2000. Independent analysts suggested some slow and uneven growth in 2001, especially towards the end of the year, but estimated GDP growth of less than 1%, which was less than the target of 3% set by the Government at the beginning of the year. Despite official growth estimates of 3%–5% in 2002 and 2003, respectively, independent sources projected that real GDP was unlikely to grow by more than 1.4% in 2002 and 2% in 2003. The absence of aggregated data on the economy continued to make it difficult to accurately determine growth trends.

Lebanon's economic life after the outbreak of the civil war in 1975 was intimately shaped by the violence, which included the Israeli invasions of the south in March 1978 and of the area up to and including Beirut in 1982. According to the Lebanese authorities, of a total of more than 100,000 people killed between 1975 and 1982, up to and including the Israeli invasion, 19,085 people were killed and 30,302 wounded between 4 June and 31 August 1982, and the Council for Development and Reconstruction (CDR—created in 1977 as the main co-ordinator of reconstruction efforts) estimated the cost of material damage at US $1,900m., with damage to housing alone of $670m.

In 1979 the CDR disclosed proposals for a five-year reconstruction programme that envisaged expenditure of £L22,000m. However, following the Israeli invasion, the CDR produced a revised, 10-year programme, covering the period 1982–91, with plans for estimated spending of £L68,000m. The CDR's proposals stressed that the private sector would continue to be the main generator of economic activity, and that credit programmes for the private sector would be strengthened. Of the total planned expenditure, one-quarter was to be raised locally, and the rest from Arab oil states, international lending agencies and foreign governments. As a result of fighting from September 1983, however, and the consequences of the Israeli invasion of the south, the cost of the 10-year plan had to be revised on more than one occasion: as the value of the Lebanese pound plummeted, and taking account of further damage, the figure was increased from £L62,200m. (US $13,000m.) in March 1983 to £L530,000m. ($33,000m.) at the beginning of 1985. In March 1983 the World Bank published its own report on Lebanon's reconstruction needs and also emphasized the need for a separate, $223.5m.-reconstruction project to cover urgent requirements, especially in Greater Beirut. In late 1991 a US engineering company, Bechtel, and a Lebanese consultancy, Dar al-Handasah, completed a government-commissioned plan for the country's emergency reconstruction needs. The $3,000m.-plan covered 133 projects, most of them for completion within three years. The emergency reconstruction plan, covering 1992 to 1995, formed part of a longer-term programme called Horizon 2000; it included road schemes, housing, sanitation and health-care projects. This originally envisaged public expenditure totalling $11,700m. (at constant prices of 1992). Of the total, $10,200m. was for physical infrastructure, $300m. for investments in institutions and planning and $1,200m. for grant and credit support for private sector enterprises. Horizon 2000 aims to double real GDP per caput in the 1995–2007 period.

Mobilizing resources for investment is one of the greatest challenges facing the Lebanese Government; flows of aid have been far smaller than the amounts pledged. The end of the civil war in early 1991 seemed likely to lead to an increase in foreign aid. In December of that year the World Bank sponsored a meeting of potential donors to Lebanon in Paris, at which the Lebanese Prime Minister, Omar Karami, reportedly requested US $4,450m. for urgent projects in the subsequent three to five

years. Following the meeting, it was confirmed that as much as $700m. in concessionary loans and grants had been pledged for the 1992–94 period, albeit mainly in earlier, bilateral meetings.

In late 1991 and early 1992 Lebanon secured a series of other aid commitments, although it was unclear whether these were included in the $700m. figure which had emerged after the Paris donors' meetings. In November 1991, for example, the Kuwait Fund for Arab Economic Development (KFAED) had granted a $36.2m.-loan for power projects, and in the following month the Arab Fund for Economic and Social Development (AFESD) issued a $73m.-loan, also for power schemes. In February 1992 it was announced that Italy had agreed to provide $460m. in loans and grants for electricity, water, telecommunications, refuse collection, health, agricultural and transport projects. Italy thus emerged as by far the biggest Western contributor to Lebanon's reconstruction.

Meanwhile, the Government's hopes that expatriate Lebanese might use some of their substantial funds to invest in their country's reconstruction appeared too optimistic. In 1991 the IMF estimated that $10,000m.–$15,000m. was held abroad by expatriates. Although there was a significant influx of private funds after the end of the fighting in 1991, these were mainly invested in property rather than in more directly productive areas.

After the civil war ended in 1991, the Italian company Emit began work on a US $30m. Italian Government-funded project to improve Beirut's water supply system, and in February 1992 French companies submitted offers for three French Government-funded contracts to repair and upgrade telecommunications and power installations. Local and international contracting firms were meanwhile preparing studies for a range of other schemes. There was a marked increase in the amount of foreign aid granted to Lebanon following the legislative elections, which took place in mid-1992, and the appointment of a new Government under Rafik Hariri. In March 1993 the World Bank agreed to grant the country $175m. for the reconstruction of its infrastructure. While this loan encouraged other lenders to grant aid, the World Bank made clear its concern at the Government's continued inability to bring state finances under control. In particular, the Bank was concerned at its failure to reduce the country's budget deficit. During 1993 and 1994 international confidence in Lebanon's new-found stability increased, and was reflected in a major influx of development aid from governments and lending agencies. During a visit to London in early 1994 Prime Minister Hariri said that the country had secured about $1,500m. in foreign funding and that a further $920m. was being negotiated. Private capital, mostly from expatriate Lebanese, had also begun to return on a large scale. Within one month of Hariri's appointment as Prime Minister and during the first nine months of 1993 aggregate bank deposits increased by a further $1,500m. In early 1995, however, according to the CDR, the total contribution of funds by donors to the Lebanese economic recovery programme amounted to $1,900m. Of this, $1,500m. was in loans and the remainder in grants, which meant that the CDR would be obliged to seek funds from other sources if it was to meet its financing needs. The European Union (EU), the World Bank, Saudi Arabia, Kuwait, the AFESD and Italy had provided most of the funds to date. In 1995 the World Bank, concerned about Lebanon's rapidly growing public debt, suggested that the Government should scale down its commitments under Horizon 2000, identify a core investment programme of no more than $3.5m. for the next two years and increase the role of the private sector in financing infrastructure, public health and education.

The Israeli attack on southern Lebanon and Beirut in April 1996 is estimated to have cost Lebanon some US $500m. in damage and disruption to business, and to have reduced economic growth by up to 2% of GDP. The instability caused by the bombing and by the election of a right-wing Government in Israel in May further depressed investor confidence.

After the cease-fire agreement between Hezbollah and Israel, Prime Minister Hariri sought to establish a consultative committee including the USA and EU member states to assist Lebanon's development. At the same time, he announced that his Government needed to raise US $5,000m. for reconstruction during the period 1997–2001, of which $270m. was to be spent on basic infrastructure; $216m. on social services including health, education and housing; $324m. on public services; $150m. on agriculture and industry; and $40m. on public facilities. This was the first indication that the Government acknowledged its inability to secure the scale of financing originally envisaged for Horizon 2000. The CDR reported that by April 1996 $2,700m. had been received from foreign donors; $2,303m. in loans, and the rest in grants. In December 1996, at the 'Friends of Lebanon' meeting held in Washington and attended by some 30 countries, as well as many international organizations, the Lebanese Government claimed to have received pledges of $3,200m. for the period to the end of 2001. However, the $1,800m. shortfall in donations, and the subsequent lack of detail concerning such projects raised doubts about the true extent of funding commitments made at the meeting. Moreover, the collapse of the Middle East peace process further jeopardized Lebanon's plans to re-establish Beirut as a regional services centre. None the less, institutions such as the Investment Development Authority of Lebanon (IDAL), established in 1994, began offering special incentives to foreign companies and wealthy expatriates to invest in southern Lebanon. Working in tandem with government plans to rebuild infrastructure, IDAL had offered four major investment licences by mid-2000, with several more being planned.

In late 1997 further doubt was cast on the viability of Lebanon's reconstruction programme when members of the Cabinet refused to endorse a proposal by the Prime Minister that petrol prices should be increased in order to raise $800m. in bonds on international markets to finance domestic social projects. This measure was part of an emergency plan proposed by Hariri to service Lebanon's foreign debt through revenue from taxes and price rises. Increasing concern had been expressed at the Government's financial management, in particular at its failure to reduce the huge, persistent budget deficit (see below). (Some 80% of government expenditure is absorbed by public-sector salaries and debt-servicing, while the collection of revenues is complicated by widespread tax evasion.) It was also noted that growth in Lebanon's GDP remained alarmingly low for a country engaged in infrastructural renewal (and considerably lower than the targeted annual average of 8% under Horizon 2000), and it remained uncertain to what extent the funding commitments that the Government claimed to have secured in December 1996 had been honoured. Public disquiet at the unavailability of funds for welfare spending may also have prompted Hariri's emergency proposals.

In an attempt to restructure Lebanon's public debt (equivalent to some 145% of GDP in early 2001) and thus reduce the cost of debt-servicing, some US $2,000m. was borrowed on international capital markets between mid-1998 and February 1999. The Government of Selim al-Hoss, which took office in December 1998, proposed further such borrowing in order to increase to about one-third the proportion of public debt denominated in foreign currency. Al-Hoss also pledged to implement administrative reforms, to reduce the burdensome public-sector payroll, counter corruption in public life and improve fiscal discipline. The elimination of monopolies was identified as a priority, and the private sector promoted as having a fundamental role in job creation: the telecommunications and electricity sectors were notable targets for deregulation, and a reorganization of the water supply network, delayed under the previous Government, was to proceed. The draft budget for 1999 envisaged a shortfall equivalent to 40% of expenditure (the 1998 target of 42% had been only marginally exceeded). In February 1999 the World Bank agreed to disburse some $600m. in concessionary loans over a three-year period for reconstruction projects and in budgetary support—an indication of the confidence of the international financial community in the new President, Gen. Emile Lahoud, and Prime Minister al-Hoss. In April 2000 the EU granted its first aid package to Lebanon (worth an estimated $47.9m.). Such loans, in addition to the willingness of the Lebanese to tolerate the austerity that economic adjustment will entail, will be essential to the restoration of international competitiveness and enhanced investment.

The withdrawal of Israeli troops from southern Lebanon in May 2000 renewed hopes that the intended reconstruction of the Lebanese economy (as mooted in 1991) could now begin in earnest. In late July the Government approached donor nations for more than US $6,500m. in aid for development projects.

Some $1,300m. of this aid was to go towards rehabilitating the damage caused to the economy during 22 years of Israeli occupation. The reincorporation of former Israeli-controlled areas in the south meant that Lebanon was once again—at least in principle—a fully integrated political and economic entity. By mid-2000 there were optimistic signs: new motorways were under construction in the north and south of the country; IDAL began attracting funds for development projects in southern Lebanon; many more franchise outlets for Western companies opened in the larger cities; cellular networks and other telecommunications systems seemed set to expand; inflation remained low; and a surplus was recorded on the balance of payments. However, plans to hold a conference of donor nations in October 2000 were postponed indefinitely. It was reported that the USA had indicated that it was unwilling to provide substantial aid until the Lebanese army, rather than Hezbollah, was in control of the southern border areas (see History).

Political weakness and divisions within the al-Hoss Government prevented his administration from carrying out many of its pledges on the economy. The Government failed to put in place key measures to boost state revenues—for example, it was unable to secure parliamentary support for the introduction of a value-added tax (VAT) and did little more than establish the principle of privatization (even though this was at the centre of its plan to reduce the size of the public debt), or to address the two main elements of government expenditure: debt-servicing and public-sector salaries. As a result the country was pushed further into recession. Rafik Hariri, who was appointed Prime Minister in October 2000, adopted a radically different approach to that of his predecessor; Hariri committed his administration to cut taxes, ease capital-spending controls and promote free trade, arguing that in the medium to long term such measures would lead to an increase in economic activity, higher revenues and greater economic stability. The basic outlines of Hariri's economic reform programme were set out in a 10-point plan. The Government quickly introduced an 'open skies' policy to encourage more foreign airlines to use Beirut's newly expanded international airport, proposed sweeping tariff cuts, pledged to cut private companies' contributions to the state social security system by up to 10%, and highlighted the importance of proceeding with the long-delayed privatization programme. It was hoped that privatization would reduce the burden of unprofitable state companies and generate revenues to help reduce public debt. While the local business community generally welcomed the new Government's strategy, some commentators expressed concern that its success appeared to depend on Lebanon re-establishing its role as the region's leading business and services centre. They emphasized the fact that Lebanon now had to compete with other countries in the Middle East that possessed well-developed business and tourist infrastructures, and to confront enduring negative images as a result of years of political instability and conflict.

In February 2001 the Cabinet approved the closure of the state television station, Télé-Liban SAL, initially for a three-month period, owing to the station's financial difficulties; the closure resulted in the loss of some 530 jobs. This represented the first large-scale redundancies among public-sector workers since the 1970s. In further moves to address the country's chronic debt problem, the Government also announced plans to restructure the national news agency, abolish sugar subsidies and privatize the state-owned Electricité du Liban (EDL) and Middle East Airlines (MEA). Prime Minister Hariri also stated that he wanted to see Ogero, the state-owned fixed line telephone operator, and EDL privatized before the end of 2001. In early March Hariri won support from the President of the National Assembly, Nabih Berri, for a sharp reduction in the number of civil servants and employees at the 64 commercial state companies. According to later statements, up to 4,000 public-sector workers could face redundancy. This issue is politically sensitive because posts in the public sector have traditionally been distributed proportionately between the country's main religious communities, providing an important source of patronage for community leaders. Some analysts predicted that the laying off of public-sector workers would only proceed slowly.

At a meeting in Paris at the end of February 2001 (subsequently known as the Paris I donor conference) the international financial community expressed support for the economic strategy of the Hariri Government. The meeting was organized at the initiative of French President Jacques Chirac and was attended by senior officials from the World Bank and the European Investment Bank, the President of the European Commission, Romano Prodi, the French Minister of Economy and Finance, together with premier Hariri and his ministers responsible for economy and finance. Some €500m. (US $458m.) was allocated to Lebanon unconditionally through the EU's MEDA programme: 30% as a gift and the remainder as long-term loans at preferential rates. In addition to the meeting in Paris, Hariri also made visits to Iran, Saudi Arabia and other Gulf states, and Japan, in an effort to secure investment or aid to help revive the Lebanese economy. Kuwait subsequently agreed to double its deposit in the Banque du Liban to $200m. and Saudi Arabia agreed to extend its deposit of $500m. at the central bank for a further three years. These funds were used to support the Lebanese pound. In the early months of 2002 several Gulf States announced loans on generous terms for infrastructure and development projects (see below) and at the beginning of July 2002, after a meeting in Paris between Prime Minister Hariri and President Chirac, France announced that a second meeting of the international financial community (known as the Paris II donor conference) would be held by the end of the year. Key issues to be addressed at the conference would be Lebanon's budget deficit and mounting public debt.

In early 2001 the UN's Inter-regional Crime and Justice Research Department claimed that corruption was endemic in Lebanon and that the Government was losing over US $1,000m. every year as a result of corruption in public administration. The report suggested that factors contributing to the widespread corruption were the effects of the long civil war, sectarianism, outside political interference, the low salaries of civil servants and the lack of an independent judiciary. The authorities were also criticized for not putting in place a clear strategy for combating corruption.

Despite strong opposition, Prime Minister Hariri proceeded with his economic reform programme, focussing on policies aimed at cutting expenditure by reducing the size of the public sector, increasing the proportion of the public debt held in foreign currency in order to reduce the burden of debt servicing, and raising revenues by introducing new taxes. In December 2001 after intense negotiations the National Assembly finally approved the law introducing VAT, the central feature of Hariri's fiscal reform programme, although its implementation was postponed until February 2002. Under the new legislation VAT was set at 10%, and an estimated 10,000 companies with a turnover of more than L£500,000m. were required to register. Items exempt from the new tax included fresh foods, medical supplies and services, books and newspapers, public transport, and banking and financial services. Despite some concerns that tax officials might have difficulties managing the complex new system, the Ministry of Finance estimated that the new tax would generate a further L£750,000m. a year in extra revenue. At the same time the Government made further tariff cuts and in February 2002 Hariri introduced legislation to remove import monopolies, a move that provoked strong opposition from those companies affected and their political allies. Lebanon signed a Euro-Mediterranean Association Agreement and an interim accord with the EU on 17 June (though negotiations were was officially concluded in January), a development which, it was hoped, would lead to EU aid and technical assistance and an increase in private foreign investment (see below). In contrast, the privatization programme (the revenues from which are earmarked to reduce public debt) made little progress notably in the case of EDL, MEA and the sale of two new cellular licences (see below).

POPULATION AND EMPLOYMENT

No proper census has been held in Lebanon since 1932, for fear of upsetting the delicate political balance between the various sects or confessions. Until 1991 all political and administrative offices were allocated on the basis of the 1932 census, which showed Christians in the majority by six to five over non-Christians. It has been widely recognized for many years, however, that Muslims account for about 60% of the total population. (In 1983 the combined Shi'a and Sunni Muslim population was estimated at 1.95m., while the combined Maronite and Greek Orthodox Christian communities were numbered at 1.15m.) The increase in the Muslim proportion occurred partly because of the higher ratio of Muslims in the Palestinian population in Lebanon and partly because Muslims tended to have a higher birth rate and to emigrate less than Christians. Demographic changes strained to the limit the delicate system of allocating offices on a sectarian basis which was adopted under the National Covenant of 1943. They were finally recognized in the Ta'if agreement of 1989, which stipulated, among other things, that Christians and Muslims should be represented by an equal number of deputies in the National Assembly.

The effects of the civil war on the size, composition and geographical distribution of Lebanon's population have been dramatic. From an estimated 3.1m. inhabitants in 1974 (which made Lebanon one of the most densely populated countries of the Middle East), the total is believed to have declined to 2.7m. in 1979, thereafter rising slightly, to reach about 2.9m. in 1990. By mid-2000, owing to the return of many Lebanese from exile, the population was estimated to have increased to almost 3.3m. According to Ministry of Health figures for 1996, 29.2% of the population were aged 14 or under, 63.8% 15–64 years, and 7% 65 years or over. The labour force was estimated at 1.4m. in 1997.

The total of those killed or disabled during 1975–76 was estimated by the Lebanese Chamber of Commerce, Industry and Agriculture at 30,000 (although other estimates were as high as 60,000), while thousands more were killed or wounded during the spring and autumn of 1978. By the Lebanese Government's reckoning, a further 19,085 people died as a result of the Israeli invasion of 1982. Each round of violence tended to trigger a fresh wave of population flow, whether within Lebanon, for example from the south into Beirut, or abroad. Those who went abroad often joined relatives or friends already there, for Lebanese emigration was considerable from the 1890s onwards, and by 1960 an estimated 2.5m. Lebanese, or people of Lebanese descent, were living outside the country. The biggest migrant community has traditionally been in the USA, and other favourite settling places were West Africa, Latin America and Australia. Remittances from Lebanese working abroad have traditionally been a staple source of national income. On average, the remittances from the 250,000–300,000 Lebanese workers abroad provided up to 35% of Lebanon's gross national product (GNP). However, returns slumped in 1983, according to US observers, as usual monthly remittances roughly halved, to US $75m.–$100m., reflecting the recession in the Gulf, where many Lebanese worked, caused by the world oil glut.

A study carried out at the American University of Beirut (AUB) showed the impact of the civil war and its aftermath on the labour force. It stated that in 1974 the non-agricultural labour force was 597,778, and had there been no civil war, the number would have reached 791,354 in 1979, instead of which it was only 426,239. The number of Lebanese working abroad in 1975 was 98,000, but by 1979 the number had risen to 210,000. Of these, 73,400 were in Saudi Arabia, 15,800 in Kuwait, and smaller numbers in other Arab states. Outside the Arab world, 17,300 were in West Africa, 27,000 in Europe, 17,000 in Latin America, 11,600 in North America and 14,000 in Australia. While Lebanon's recovery was hampered by the emigration of skilled labour, there was at the same time a pool of unemployed, estimated at more than 200,000 in 1979. The sectors in which there was the greatest contraction of the workforce between 1974 and 1979 were industry (from 138,359 to 86,941), construction (from 46,517 to 18,942) and transport and communications (from 47,113 to 25,256). Many of those not in regular employment were engaged in paramilitary activities, or were part of the thriving 'black' economy. The exodus of thousands of Palestinian and Syrian workers from Lebanon, as a result of the Israeli invasion, caused a shortage of skilled and unskilled labour. The construction industry, in particular, was seriously affected. In 1985 it was estimated that 28% of the active population (18–68 years old) were unemployed, whereas before the civil war the rate had been 5%. Unemployment was estimated at almost 50% in 1987 and at 35% in 1990. According to official estimates, unemployment declined from almost 50% in 1987, to 35% in 1990 and to 8.5% in 1997, although youth unemployment was reported to be much higher.

Many Syrians returned to Lebanon after the civil war, the majority to carry out menial labour, and their annual remittances to Syria have been estimated at some US $2,100m. However, with the downturn in the Lebanese economy, hostility towards these workers has grown and there has been concern among some Lebanese concerning proposals to grant them full citizenship. Syrian workers are generally not required to hold work permits, unlike other foreign nationals. According to Lebanon's Central Administration for Statistics, 71,732 work permits were issued in 1998: 22,183 to other Arabs, 39,145 to Asians (mostly Sri Lankans) and 10,134 to European, US and African nationals.

AGRICULTURE

Of the total area of the country, about 52% consists of mountain, swamp or desert, and a further 7% of forest. Only 23% of the area is cultivated, although a further 17% is considered cultivable. In late 1996, however, the Ministry of Agriculture warned that soil erosion and groundwater pollution had reached critical levels and that a reafforestation programme would be launched in order to prevent desertification. The coastal strip enjoys a Mediterranean climate and is exceedingly fertile, producing mainly olives, citrus fruits and bananas. Many of the steep valleys leading up from the coastal plain are carefully terraced and very productive in olives and soft fruit. In the Zahleh and Shtaura regions there are vineyards, while cotton and onions are grown in the hinterland of Tripoli. The main cereal-growing district is the Beka'a, the fertile valley between the Lebanon and the Anti-Lebanon ranges, to the north of which lies the source of the river Orontes. The Litani river also flows southwards through the Beka'a before turning west near Marjayoun to flow into the Mediterranean just north of Tyre. This valley is particularly fertile and cotton is now grown there with some success. Throughout the country the size of the average holding is extremely small and, even so, a small-holding, particularly in the mountains, may be broken up into several fragments some distance apart. The agricultural sector contributed over 9% of GDP between 1972 and 1974, but the proportion declined to about 8.5% during the civil war, when depopulation of the countryside occurred and both public and private investment in agriculture declined. The number of people employed in the agricultural sector fell from 147,724 in 1975 to an estimated 103,400, or 23% of the labour force, in 1985. In 2001 it was estimated that only 4% of the total labour force were employed in agriculture. The Hariri Government, which took office in 1992, was criticized for giving the agricultural sector a low priority in its investment plans, but by early 1997 the necessity of agricultural development had been recognized. Indeed, the Government encouraged commercial bank lending to the agricultural sector by subsidizing interest rates. The Ministry of Agriculture's budget was also increased so that it could finance more agricultural research and also supply farmers with basic needs. From October 1997 a list of prohibited agricultural imports was to be introduced to protect local producers. Cereals and products used by the food processing industry would be exempt. According to the World Bank, agriculture (including hunting, forestry and fishing) contributed an estimated 11.8% of GDP in 2000.

In early 1997 the CDR announced a number of projects, including the development of 5,600 ha of farmland by terracing hillslopes, building 300 km of roads in remote rural areas and assisting the Ministry of Agriculture with staff training, to be supported by a US $31m. grant from the World Bank.

Lebanon's wheat crop totalled an estimated 60,000 metric tons in 2000. Fruit-growing increased substantially from the early 1950s, but the rush to plant apple trees in the 1950s resulted in gluts, followed by reduced levels of output in the late 1960s. Production of apples was estimated at 120,000 tons in 2000, while production of grapes was estimated at 245,000 tons. Other significant crops include citrus fruits, tomatoes (of which an estimated 335,000 tons were produced in 2000), sugar beet (330,000 tons) and potatoes (270,000 tons), together with cucumbers, watermelons and olives. A small quantity of tobacco is also produced. The GDP of the agricultural sector was estimated to have increased by an average of 3.5% annually in 1992–99, although agricultural GDP declined by an estimated 1.2% in 1998 and by 0.7% in 1999. According to FAO data, agricultural production declined by 2.9% in 1999, but increased by 5.2% in 2000.

Agriculture was the sector worst affected by the Israeli attacks in April 1996, when the south and the western Beka'a valley experienced heavy bombardment. It was estimated that almost half of the 1996 tobacco crop was lost, together with 20% of the area's vegetable crop, and that citrus production had also been badly damaged. Losses to tobacco and vegetable crops were estimated at $26m. Further damage occurred during bombardments by Israeli forces in mid-2000.

The relative lack of security in Lebanon has allowed two crops to flourish: hemp (*Cannabis sativa*), the source of hashish; and the opium poppy (*Papaver somniferum*), the source of opium and its derivatives, heroin and morphine. Before the civil war, Lebanon's annual hashish production was estimated at 100 tons. Between 1987 and 1989 output averaged 700–900 tons, although production declined to 100 tons per year in 1990–91, owing to inclement weather. In 1988–91 annual opium production averaged 40 tons. More recently, the Government has tried to encourage farmers to substitute other crops for hemp and the opium poppy. As part of this programme, plans were announced in June 1996 to establish a crop substitution office for the north-eastern Ba'albek-Hermel region in the Beka'a valley. In late February 1997 the Government and the UN Development Programme (UNDP) reportedly signed an agreement to implement the second phase of the programme at a cost of US $12m. The Government and the UNDP were to contribute $4m. and $3.8m., respectively, while $2.2m. was to be invested by France, $595,000 by Italy and $690,000 by the EU.

In mid-2000 the UN Food and Agriculture Organization (FAO) criticized the Lebanese Government for 'unacceptable' neglect of the agricultural sector (which was allocated only US $11m., or 0.4%, of the 1999 budget). Private investment in the agricultural sector is also very limited. Meanwhile, the Middle East Intelligence Bulletin estimated that Lebanon exports US $200m.-worth of agricultural goods each year, but relies on imports for 75% of its food requirements, at an annual cost of some $1,500m. Lebanon faces stiff competition in export markets from heavily subsidized agricultural goods from the EU and other Middle Eastern countries. Severe lack of credit has, on occasion, forced small farmers to buy supplies at interest rates as high as 100% per year. Farmers have also protested against the alleged 'dumping' of cheaper Syrian produce on the fragile Lebanese market. To help counter the effects of such external competition, the UN's International Fund for Agricultural Development is funding a Smallholder Livestock Rehabilitation Project. It is hoped that this will ultimately make Lebanon 80% self-sufficient in milk. At the same time, the Ministry of Agriculture has announced the ambitious 'Plan 2000', which offers mechanisms for identifying constraints in the system, by means of an agricultural census. It has also suggested ways of increasing productivity, while protecting both consumers and the environment, by ensuring better animal health, protecting pastures, encouraging agronomic science and establishing fishery resources. In January 2002 the Kuwaiti Fund for Arab Economic Development agreed a loan of US $65m. to the CDR to finance the first phase of the Litani Project which will utilise water from the Litani River for agricultural and domestic purposes in the southern and eastern parts of the country. The project, which was originally conceived in the 1960s, will be carried out in two phases at a total cost of $456m. The Kuwaiti loan will be used to build three out of the planned 15 dams along the Litani River.

INDUSTRY

Until the time of the first sudden increase in petroleum prices, in 1973–74, the only minerals which were exploited in Lebanon were lignite and some iron ore, smelted in Beirut. There have been hopes of petroleum discoveries for a number of years but, so far, these hopes have been unfulfilled. Even so, Lebanon remains of considerable importance to the petroleum industry. Two of the world's most important oil pipelines cross the country, one from the Kirkuk oil wells in Iraq to Tripoli and the other from Saudi Arabia to Zahrani near Sidon. At each terminal there is an important petroleum refinery. Both the pipelines and the refineries have, however, been the subject of disputes.

Revenues from the Kirkuk–Tripoli pipeline, which was managed by the Iraq Petroleum Company (IPC), were reduced after both Iraq and Syria nationalized IPC assets in their countries on 1 June 1972. After the Iraqi Government and IPC had reached a settlement on the nationalization in 1973, a dispute over the ownership of the IPC refinery in Lebanon followed, as a result of which the Lebanese Government appropriated the refinery and agreed to compensate IPC. In April 1976, however, Iraq suspended pumping, choosing to direct its Kirkuk petroleum to the Persian (Arabian) Gulf instead. Lebanon was thus faced with a loss of around £L30m. per year in royalties as well as the loss of cheap petroleum. During the early part of 1977 the refinery at Tripoli was processing only 5,000 barrels per day (b/d), compared with an average of 36,000 b/d in 1975. By 1978, however, it was operating at around 75% of capacity on petroleum which reached Tripoli by sea or from nearby Zahrani. Iraq finally resumed pumping to Syria through the former IPC pipeline in early 1979, but the transfer of Kirkuk crude petroleum via Lebanon remained dependent on the conclusion of a new bilateral transit and supply agreement. It was reported in March 1981 that Iraq had agreed to start re-pumping after a break of five years. The initial rate of delivery was to be about 200,000 b/d, doubling after two months. Of this, 35,000 b/d were to be used domestically, with the remainder exported. At the time of the agreement, the Tripoli refinery was using 26,000 b/d of Saudi Arabian crude petroleum, which was pumped to Zahrani and then transported to Tripoli by tanker.

On 24 December 1981 Iraqi petroleum started to flow again, but within days the pipeline was damaged by a bomb blast, and in March 1982 it was blown up again. Politics intervened when, on 10 April, the trans-Syria pipeline was closed and Iraqi deliveries to Tripoli were suspended. The refinery subsequently processed Iraqi petroleum which had been transported via Turkey. The fighting between PLO loyalists and anti-Arafat factions in Tripoli in December 1983 caused damage to the refinery which was estimated at US $120m., while $60m.-worth of petroleum products were destroyed when 29 of the refinery's 36 major tanks, and 16 of its smaller tanks, were hit. The refinery began to receive shipments of Iraqi oil again in April 1984, when repairs were completed. In early 1991, after the completion of repairs and modifications, the Tripoli refinery resumed operations. Towards the end of 2000 Lebanon reached an agreement with Syria to repair the branch of the Kirkuk–Banias oil-pipeline linking it to Tripoli so that the refinery could receive Iraqi crude oil, to be supplied on concessionary terms. (Reports suggested that the Kirkuk–Banias pipeline was reopened in November 2000—see the chapter on Syria). There were also reports that Iraq had offered to finance repairs to the Tripoli refinery but that the Lebanese Government preferred to build a new refinery at Tripoli with an increased capacity of 150,000 b/d.

The Zahrani refinery was, until 1986, operated by the Mediterranean Refinery Co (Medreco), owned jointly by Caltex and Mobil. Mobil, Caltex's two parent firms (Texaco and Standard Oil of California) and Exxon also own the Trans-Arabian Pipeline Co (Tapline), which formerly operated the Saudi-Lebanese pipeline. Tapline suspended its pumping operations in early February 1975 because oil tankers found it cheaper to load petroleum directly from the Saudi terminal at Ras Tanura in the Gulf. This suspension cost Lebanon more than £L20m. in royalties. The company also demanded that the Lebanese Government pay for the higher cost of Saudi petroleum (previously supplied to the Zahrani refinery at a price of US $5 per barrel), claiming that it was owed $100m. in back payments. A settlement was reached in August 1975, and Tapline's operations recommenced in November 1976. One year later, the Saudi Government agreed to settle accumulated debts of $120m. However, Tapline only resumed full capacity when Iranian oil exports declined after the 1979 revolution.

In early August 1981 Tapline suspended all deliveries of crude petroleum to the Zahrani refinery because of non-payment of debts, but a few weeks later Saudi Arabia announced that it would pay most of Lebanon's petroleum bill. The Israeli invasion of Lebanon in 1982 presented further complications. The Zahrani refinery was out of action from June to November, after it had been bombed. Tapline's oil pipeline passed through Israeli-held territory, so Saudi crude petroleum was delivered by tanker. In February 1982 Tapline announced that it had lost some US $350m. on its Lebanese operations since 1975, and that it had decided to close the damaged pipeline, which, for political and security reasons, would not be repaired. In September 1983 Tapline gave 90 days' notice that it was to stop operating in Lebanon and Syria and in early 1984 the Government took control of Tapline's installations. In 1986 Medreco ceased operations and the Government took control of the Zahrani refinery. Plans to bring the refinery back into operation, announced in 1991, were abandoned amid talk of a proposed oil refinery in Syria that would supply Lebanon with petroleum products. In August 1998, however, a joint French-Iranian proposal that could reactivate the Tripoli refinery, out of service since 1993, was announced. Under the plan, the Iranian Government would finance a feasibility study, and, if rehabilitation was recommended, French contractors would undertake the work.

The civil war had a dramatic impact on Lebanese industry. Between 1975 and 1982, up to and including the Israeli invasion, some 400 industrial units were destroyed or seriously damaged, according to the CDR. During their invasion, Israeli forces were said to have destroyed 25 of the country's major industrial units and to have damaged many smaller enterprises. Damage to the textile industry was particularly severe. Before the invasion, fewer than 50% of the 1,200 textile factories which were operating before 1975 remained active, and during the invasion a further 70 enterprises were completely destroyed and more than 150 others damaged.

The Chouf war of autumn 1983 cost local industry an estimated £L10m. per day; 140 factories, employing 25,000 workers, in the Choueifat-Kfarchima district of southern Beirut were forced to close. The Israeli occupation of southern Lebanon also posed serious problems for industrialists, who had to compete with a large influx of Israeli goods entering the country. This not only meant that local goods were competing with cheaper Israeli items, but it also led to problems between Lebanon and its Arab neighbours, who suspected that Israeli goods were being exported to them via Lebanon and imposed an embargo on some Lebanese products. Other factors that hampered industrial development were the shortage of skilled workers (owing to emigration to the Gulf), ageing machinery, and the weak and damaged infrastructure.

Much of Lebanon's remaining industry is located in the Christian Zone, which until 1989 was relatively free of widespread violence. During the period 14 March–10 May 1989, however, 170 Lebanese factories were damaged in Gen. Awn's 'war of liberation' against Syria, 20 of them being completely destroyed. Factories sustained further damage during inter-Christian fighting in early 1990.

The civil conflict prevented any sustained revival of industry during the 1980s. The value of industrial exports in 1980 was 15% higher than in 1979, and in 1981 there was a further increase, of 25%, to £L2,290m. However, these increases were mainly due to the depreciation of the Lebanese pound. The major buyers of Lebanese industrial exports in 1981 were Iraq, Syria, Saudi Arabia and Jordan, which together accounted for 86% of all sales. The invasion of Lebanon by Israel in 1982 caused the value of industrial exports to decline to £L1,924m. in 1982 and to £L1,296.4m. in 1983. In 1984 their value fell to £L984m. Assisted by the rapid depreciation in the value of the Lebanese pound, the value of industrial exports subsequently increased sharply: to US $372m. in 1985, $438m. in 1986 and $690m. in 1987. In 1988, however, it amounted to only $274m., and in 1989—a year in which factories in east Beirut sustained particularly heavy damage—only $174m. The 1990 figure was $127m. With the end of the fighting in 1991, the value of industrial exports recovered to $206m.; the 1992 figure was $210m. The Israeli occupation of the south, the cumulative effect of years of violence, the recession in the Gulf, which was Lebanon's principal export market, and competition from cheap, smuggled goods, all contributed to the decline of industry. The new industrial zone around Sidon, which developed after 1976, was effectively throttled by the Israeli presence and the influx of subsidized Israeli goods. Lebanon's industrial sector was estimated to be operating at only 40% of capacity in early 1986, with textiles, leather goods and finished wood products accounting for the bulk of production, while the labour force employed in manufacturing industry had declined to an estimated 45,000 in 1985. The Hariri Government, which took office in 1992, was criticized both for giving the industrial sector a low priority in its investment plans and for implementing monetary policies which prevented the expansion of industrial production.

A survey carried out by the Ministry of Industry in 1998 reported that most of the 22,000 companies in the manufacturing sector remained small-scale operations (as was the case prior to the civil conflict), with over two-thirds employing less than five people and only 0.8% employing more than 50 people. Some 20% of the companies were involved in food processing, 16% in furniture and woodworking, 16% in metalwork and finishing, and 13% in clothing.

According to the World Bank, the industrial sector (including manufacturing, construction and power) contributed an estimated 20.8% of GDP in 2000. Manufacturing contributed an estimated 9.8% of GDP in 1999. The GDP of the industrial sector increased by an average of 1.7% per year in 1992–99, with growth in early years offset by a decline in industrial growth of 1.4% in 1999. Manufacturing GDP was estimated to have increased at an average annual rate of 1.9% in 1992–99; however, the sector's GDP declined by an estimated 0.9% in 1998 and 0.7% in 1999. In 1998 the value of industrial exports (of which food products were the most important) represented only 10% of the total value of imports. The Arab Gulf states purchased more than half of Lebanese industrial exports, and Europe 20%. While increases in customs tariffs have made raw material imports more expensive (so that it has become more difficult for manufacturers to compete in overseas markets), the resulting price rises for imported finished goods have made Lebanese manufactured goods more competitive in the domestic market.

Construction was the main sector fuelling economic recovery after the end of the civil war in 1990, as large amounts of public and private capital financed major infrastructure projects and numerous residential and commercial developments. The construction sector absorbed half of all private investment in 1992–1995, with most of it directed to small local companies. During that period construction contributed 10% of GDP. From 1996, however, investment fell sharply and the construction sector entered a period of decline. By 1999 apartments and offices valued at US $8,000m. remained unsold. Construction permits during the first 10 months of 2000 fell by nearly 18%, compared with the same period in 1999, while cement deliveries declined by nearly 12%. The area for which construction permits were issued rose by 1.9% in 2001 and cement deliveries by 3.5%, but the sector remained vulnerable to marked fluctuations from month to month. Solidère, the real estate company launched in 1994 by Rafik Hariri to redevelop Beirut's war-ravaged commercial centre, announced a 30% decease in profits in 1998 and for the first time failed to pay a dividend to shareholders, as the value of its shares on the Beirut Stock Exchange declined sharply. In mid-2000 Solidère again ruled out any dividend from its 1999 profits, which had fallen to just $3.7m., from $54.2m. in 1998. According to the Ministry of Industry 400 new factories, mainly in food processing, were established during the first nine months of 2001, creating some 3,000 new jobs. There was also a reported 4.5% increase in the import of industrial machinery during this period. However, the no information on the number of factory closures was produced while other data indicated a 55% decline in bank credit to the industrial sector and a 17% fall in capital investment in new ventures.

The lack of adequate sources of power hindered industrial development in the 1960s, but Lebanon gradually achieved the position of having excess capacity. In 1972 it began to supply power through a 100-kWh line to southern Syria, and in March 1976 the two countries agreed on the exchange of power through a similar line between Tripoli and Tartous. Work on implementing the power link-up project began in 1977 as part of moves to repair the country's badly damaged electricity network. A seven-year electrification scheme, costing some £L1,260m., was drafted, which was expected to be financed by the World Bank and the AFESD. An important feature of the plan was the upgrading of the Zouk power station, and in 1980 the European Investment Bank (EIB) lent around US $4.3m. for two 125-MW generators for the station. In early 1982 the state-owned EDL obtained a further loan of ECU 7m. to help to finance the expansion of the Zouk power station. Generating capacity in 1990 totalled 515 MW, with thermal stations accounting for 465 MW and hydroelectric plants for 50 MW. By comparison, a capacity of 1,200 MW was required to satisfy the peak level of 1991 demand. In early 1991 officials from EDL outlined plans for a series of projects to expand existing power facilities and establish new ones. The projects included the construction of a 200-MW gas turbine station in the Beka'a valley; the installation of a 200-MW gas turbine and a 100-MW steam turbine at Zahrani; the addition of a 150–180-MW steam turbine at the Zouk station; the installation of 100-MW and 150-MW steam turbines at the Jiyyeh power station; the construction of a 100-MW steam turbine at the Harisha power station; and the construction of a new power station, with a 250-MW steam turbine, at Batroun. According to EDL, Lebanon required an additional 2,400 MW of capacity in order to satisfy projected demand in the 1990s. Owing to the decline in the value of the local currency and the ending of subsidies on the prices of fuel oil and electricity to industry, raw materials and energy now cost more, and these higher costs will hamper any industrial recovery. In 1993 the Italian firm Ansaldo Energia, South Korea's Hyundai Corpn and two French firms, Bouygues and Clemessy, won contracts to repair and rehabilitate the electricity sector. The work was financed by the AFESD, the KFAED and the World Bank. Construction of two 450-MW combined-cycle power stations, one in the south, at Zahrani (near Sidon), the other in the north, at Beddawi (near Tripoli) was completed in 1998, although by mid-1999 both had a capacity of only 200 MW, largely owing to inadequate transmission. Another two 77-MW gas turbine stations were completed at Tyre and Ba'albek in June 1996. The Government has also begun a $300m. plan to expand and upgrade the electricity grid, including the construction of several substations linked to the four new power plants, in order to fulfil demand until 2005. By the beginning of 1997 international banks and financial institutions, including the EIB, had pledged some $184m. towards the cost of expanding the country's electricity grid. In early 1997 EDL launched a $100m. Eurobond to provide additional funds for the expansion programme.

Despite Israeli bombing in April 1996, which damaged two electricity transformer stations in Greater Beirut, electricity rationing was avoided and repairs were completed by July with French assistance, at an estimated cost of US $30m. Following the rehabilitation of many power stations, production by EDL increased by almost 50% in 1996, by 11.6% in 1997 and by 7.7% in 1998. Nevertheless, in early 1997 it was reported that 15% of all power generated was being lost, not only because equipment was out-dated, but also because of damage to the electricity network during the many years of civil conflict. Generating capacity in 1998 totalled 2,315 MW, with thermal stations accounting for 1,886 MW, hydraulic plants for 226 MW and gas turbines for 163 MW. Electricity production rose from 4,574m. kWh in 1994 to 9,030m. kWh in 1998. In June 1999 Israeli bombing again damaged Beirut's electricity infrastructure; attacks on two power stations at Bsalim and Jamhour resulted in damage worth an estimated $23m. Other power stations were damaged in Israeli raids carried out in February and May 2000, and the network was unable to satisfy peak demand during the summer months. By October, however, Egyptian technicians had repaired the Jamhour power station, and in November ABB High Voltage Technologies was awarded a $19.5m.-contract to repair damaged equipment and upgrade the Bsalim substation, a project being funded by the World Bank. Repairing the damage resulting from the Israeli air-strikes was a serious burden to EDL, which also faced the rising cost of fuel imports. During the first half of 2000 the company was unable to fund sufficient fuel imports to meet demand and as a result the country faced a growing number of power cuts. The Government had to intervene and is reported to have provided some £L177,000m. during the first seven months of 2000 to assist EDL. However, successive governments have failed to reform EDL. A parliamentary report in early 2001 stated that the company received revenues for only 55% of electricity output—30% of output was used by consumers who failed to pay and 15% of power was lost in transmission. EDL spent £L750,000m. annually on oil purchases alone, but received revenues from consumers of only £L600,000m. Higher tariffs and better collection rates are essential to make the company profitable, but would be extremely unpopular. In March 2001 it was announced that BNP Paribas of France had been appointed financial adviser to the Government for the privatization of EDL. During the first phase of a three-year plan, BNP Paribas will carry out a comprehensive privatization study and assist EDL in finding a strategic partner who will be required to take a 10%–15% stake in the company; it will also help the Government to formulate the legal and regulatory framework for the company's privatization. (The National Assembly passed a draft law to create such a framework in August 2002.) During the second stage the Government plans to sell a further stake in the company through the Beirut Stock Exchange, and the third stage will involve the complete privatization of EDL. The Government received criticism, however, because there was no international tender for the position of financial adviser. Moreover, serious doubts were raised as to whether anyone would be interested in investing in a company with such chronic problems and requiring urgent reforms. By mid-2002 little progress was made in finding a strategic partner, and an escalation in hostilities along the border with Israel was likely to further discourage foreign investors.

In 1998 it was reported that, in order to reduce the cost of fuel imports, the Government was considering a plan to convert the power stations at Beddawi and Zahrani to using natural gas, rather than fuel oil, for the generation of electricity. In December 2000 Lebanon reached an agreement with Egypt and Syria to build the first phase of an under-sea pipeline to transport Egyptian natural gas to Lebanon and eventually to Syria, Jordan and Turkey. The US $1,000m. pipeline will run from Arish in Egypt, under the Mediterranean Sea to Lebanon, and then overland to Syria, Jordan and Turkey.

EXTERNAL TRADE AND BALANCE OF PAYMENTS

Reflecting the post-war increase in reconstruction activity, the value of Lebanon's merchandise exports (valued f.o.b. at the official dollar rate) increased from US $455m. in 1990 to $546m. in 1991, while imports (valued f.o.b. at the customs dollar rate) rose from $2,528m. in 1990 to $3,748m. in 1991. The trade deficit thus increased from $2,073m. in 1990 to $3,202m. in 1991. Net transactions in services, other income and private unrequited transfers (including workers' remittances from abroad) produced a surplus of $303m. in 1991, resulting in a deficit on the current account of the balance of payments (excluding official transfers) of $2,899m. in that year. However, there was a surplus on the capital account (including net errors and omissions) of $3,973m. in 1991, leaving the overall balance in surplus by $1,074m. In 1992 there was a trade deficit of $3,185m. (exports $601m., imports $3,786m.) and a current-account deficit of $2,798m. The capital account was in surplus by $2,851m., resulting in an overall surplus of $53m. Meanwhile, the customs dollar rate, used to calculate to value of imports in terms of US currency, was adjusted in July 1992 to $1 = £L800 (having been $1 = £L200 since the beginning of the year). The new rate remained in operation until July 1995, although throughout this period the free market exchange rate was about £L1,700 per US dollar.

In 1995 the deficit in Lebanon's balance of trade increased to $5,770m. (exports $985m., imports $6,755m.) although the overall balance of payments recorded a surplus of $256m., owing to a surplus of $872m. on other current transactions and the inflow of $5,154m. in net capital receipts. In 1995 Lebanon's total export earnings included $161m. from re-exports (net of transit values). Of total domestic exports ($824m.) in that year, 28.7% were consigned to the United Arab Emirates (UAE), compared with 18% in 1994, while Italy and the USA were the principal suppliers of goods in 1995, accounting for 13% and 11%, respectively, of total imports (about $7,300m. on a c.i.f. basis). In July 1995 the use of differential exchange rates for valuing imports and exports was discontinued. Since that date the value of all external trade in US currency has been calculated on the basis of the official dollar rate (the previous month's average market rate).

From October 1997 the Government prohibited imports of certain foodstuffs in order to encourage local farmers and to reduce imports, which cost the country some $1,400m. annually. In 1997, overall, Lebanon recorded a surplus of $419.8m. on the balance of payments. In February 1998 it was reported that

Lebanon and Syria had agreed gradually to abolish customs tariffs, reducing them by 25% annually from 1999. In 1998 there was a trade deficit of $6,344m. (exports $716m., imports $7,060m.), and for the first time in several years overall balance of payments recorded a deficit of US $488m.

In 1999 the trade deficit declined to US $5,528m. (exports $677m, imports $62,07m.), but with net invisibles, transfers and capital flows of $6,249m. Lebanon recorded a surplus of $721m. on the balance of payments. The principal markets for Lebanese exports in 1999 were Saudi Arabia (10.5%), UAE (8.0%), France (7.7%) and the USA (6.2%). The principal suppliers of imports were Italy (10.9%), France (9.6%), Germany (8.9%) and the USA (8.1%). In 2000 the trade deficit remained virtually unchanged at $5,520m. (exports rose to $704m. and imports to $6,224m.). Exports accounted for only 11% of imports. Net transfers and capital flows, however, fell to $5,231m. (down 16% on 1999) giving a deficit of $288m on the balance of payments. According to Banque Audi, the principal markets for Lebanese exports in 2000 were Saudi Arabia (10.9%), the UAE, the USA, France, Syria and Kuwait. The principal suppliers of imports were Italy (10.9%), France, Germany, the USA, Switzerland and Syria. The principal exports in 2000 were food products, jewellery, chemical products, electrical equipment, metal manufactures and textiles. The principal imports in that year were food products, mineral products, electrical equipment, vehicles, chemical products and jewellery. In 2001 the trade deficit rose by 16% to $6,414m. (exports rose by 24% to $889m. and imports by 17% to $7,291m.). Exports accounted for only 12% of imports. The principal suppliers of imports were Italy 9.7%, France 8.8%, Germany 8.4% and USA 7.2%. Figures from the central bank indicated that non-trade inflows rose by only 0.7% to $5,268m. leaving a balance of payments deficit of $1,146m. As earnings from tourism increased during the year, analysts suggested that there had been a decline in net capital inflows.

During the 1990s trade barriers were steadily increased to boost government revenue and seek to halt the rising expenditure on imports. At the same time, however, the Government was negotiating trade agreements that committed Lebanon to reducing tariffs. Lebanon hoped to sign a full Association Agreement with the EU as part of a European initiative to establish a Euro-Mediterranean Economic Area, sought membership of the World Trade Organization (WTO), entered into a customs union with Syria and joined an Arab free-trade agreement. Soon after his appointment as Prime Minister in October 2000, Rafik Hariri announced an economic reform programme (see above) which included reducing tariff barriers and actively pursuing trade agreements with the EU, Arab states and the WTO. In November Hariri's Government reversed tariff increases imposed by the previous al-Hoss administration and proceeded to make sweeping cuts to the country's customs duties, abolishing some duties completely. Customs formalities at the main ports were to be streamlined and all non-tariff trade barriers removed as additional measures to promote free trade and an open economy. Further cuts were made to import tariff rates in early 2002 with the Government claiming that 70% of imports were currently subject to duties of 5% or less. Analysts were quick to point out that with customs duties accounting for some 40%–47% of government revenue in recent years, tariff cuts carried high risks and would certainly result in lower overall revenue. Figures for 2001 revealed that revenues from customs duties fell by 7% in that year.

After almost six years of negotiations Lebanon finally signed an association agreement with the EU in January 2002 as part of the EU's Euro-Mediterranean programme. The agreement has yet to be ratified by all 15 EU member states but a concurrently signed interim accord will allow some Lebanese products easier access to the EU before the ratification process is completed. Both parties agreed to eradicate all tariffs and quotas over a 12-year transitional period. It is hoped that the accord will encourage increased foreign investment in Lebanon.

In February 2002 Premier Hariri proposed terminating legal protection of import monopolies. Since 1967 local companies have been allowed to register as the sole legal importer of any foreign brand, and many used the privilege to overcharge for the product making many goods more expensive in Lebanon than elsewhere. To alleviate the impact of these reforms Hariri proposed that a 5% tax be added to new imports for a five-year period with the proceeds going to those companies that would loose their monopolies. Dismantling the system is essential if Lebanon is to succeed in its application for membership of the WTO. Although Hariri won support from President Lahoud and the National Assembly Speaker Nabih Berri, he was expected to face strong opposition from powerful importers and their political allies when the legislation comes before the National Assembly.

CURRENCY AND FINANCE

The importance of Beirut as the commercial and financial centre of the Middle East derived, in the 1950s and onwards, from the almost complete absence of restrictions on the free movement of goods and capital, and from the transference of the Middle Eastern headquarters of many foreign concerns from Cairo to Beirut after 1952. Moreover, large sums were earned in the Gulf by Arabs who sought to invest locally, especially in property, and for them Beirut was a convenient centre. Its dominance was further strengthened later by the massive increases in surplus oil revenue earned by the producing states, much of which was channelled through Lebanon.

The growing competitiveness of financial centres in Europe and the Gulf region had, even before the disruption caused by the civil conflict, led the Government to seek ways of enhancing Beirut's attractions as a banking centre. A banking free-zone law which took effect in April 1977, exempted non-residents' foreign currency accounts from taxes on interest earned, from payment of a deposit guarantee tax and from reserve requirements. Moreover, in June 1977 the Government decided to lift the moratorium on new bank licences, which had been imposed in the wake of the collapse of the Intra Bank in 1966. In 1977 a new specialized bank, the Banque de l'Habitat, was set up and in 1978 two new commercial banks, the International Commerce Bank and Universal Bank, were granted licences bringing the total number of banks operating in Lebanon to 81 as of mid-1979. In April 1980 the American Express International Banking Corpn became the first foreign bank to open a new branch in Beirut since 1975. In early 1983 the central bank raised the minimum capital requirement for new banks from £L50m. to £L75m., and that for new financial institutions from £L5m. to £L15m.—the third such increase since 1977.

Lebanon's banking system withstood the years of conflict surprisingly well, but by 1985 the strains were evident: non-performing loans accounted for 45% of banks' total loan portfolios, compared with 25% in 1984; costs were rising, while revenues were static or falling; and interest rates were extremely high, as a result of fierce competition in a depressed market. The number of banks operating in Lebanon rose to 88 in 1986. The balance sheet of Beirut's commercial banks for 1985 and 1986 looked impressive, but it had to be interpreted with care. Total assets/liabilities amounted to £L455,614m. in 1986, a rise of 181% compared with 1985 (during which a rise of 61.9%, compared with 1984, had been recorded). Loans to the private sector rose by 120.3%, and treasury bill holdings by 32.8%. Loans to non-resident banks rose by 446.4%, private-sector deposits by 184.2%, and liabilities to non-resident banks rose by 281.7% compared with 1985. Even more impressive apparent growth was recorded between the first quarter of 1986 and the first quarter of 1987. However, the rise in private-sector deposits was almost entirely attributable to the collapse in the value of the Lebanese pound, as almost all such deposits were in foreign currencies. The rise in loans to the private sector was more indicative of the high rate of inflation than of any general economic recovery. Loans to non-residents and non-resident banks had risen (hugely) because these advances were almost all in foreign currencies. The expansion in treasury bill holdings merely reflected the Government's increasing use of such bills to finance its growing deficits.

The remarkable resistance of the Lebanese pound to the pressures of the civil conflict was chiefly due to the absence of restrictions on withdrawals or foreign exchange transactions, to an increase in the supply of foreign currencies to finance the conflict, and to the pound's strong gold backing and the flow of remittances safeguarding the balance of payments. Shortly before the war, in October 1974, the pound had reached a record high value, standing at £L2.22 against the US dollar. It lost

just over 30% of this value during the war in 1975–76, but quickly recovered to £L3 after the cease-fire. Although the Lebanese pound declined in value in the two months following the beginning of the Israeli invasion in June 1982, from £L5.00 to the US dollar to £L5.20, it had strengthened to £L4.11 to the dollar by mid-November. Although officially valued at US $389.4m. in March 1982, the 9.22m. ounces of gold that were held by the central bank were worth some $4,000m. at mid-1987 market prices. In view of the legendary strength of the Lebanese pound, the rapid erosion of its value from late 1983 onwards was a considerable psychological blow. In July 1983 the exchange rate stood at $1 = £L4.15; by late June 1984 it had dropped below $1 = £L6, and by March 1985 it stood at $1 = £L20.00, at that time its lowest level ever. Excluding gold, Lebanon's official reserves declined from $1,903m. to $672m. in 1984. They recovered to $1,074m. at the end of 1985, owing to new import controls and a net inflow of capital, but fell to $488m. at the end of 1986, as imports began to rise again, and totalled only $368m. at the end of 1987. The appreciation of the Lebanese pound during much of 1988 prompted a recovery. By the end of 1988 reserves stood at $978m. They exceeded $1,000m. for most of the first three quarters of 1989, but by the end of the year they had declined to $938m. After further falls in the value of the Lebanese pound, the value of reserves was only $659.9m. by the end of 1990. During 1991 the stabilization of the exchange rate, the growth in exports and an influx of private funds from expatriate Lebanese combined to produce an increase in reserves to $1,276m. by the end of the year. At the end of November 1992 the value of reserves was $1,588m. During 1993 reserves continued to expand, to reach $1,900m. In April 1994 foreign reserves were $1,300m. but had increased again, to $5,932m. at the end of 1996, $5,976m. at the end of 1997, $6,556m. at the end of 1998 and $7,776m. at the end of 1999. The IMF estimated that foreign reserves had fallen to $4,966m. at the end of 2001.

By July 1986 the Lebanese pound had fallen to $1 = £L38, or by about 50% since the end of 1985. This included an official devaluation of the pound by 16.35% against the US dollar in March 1986. The exchange rate fell below $1 = £L100 for the first time in February 1987 and continued to fall, reaching $1 = £L455 at the end of 1987 and $1 = £L530 at the end of 1988, following the failure to elect a new President in September of that year. During much of 1989 the exchange rate was stable, at about $1 = £L510, despite the violence of Gen. Awn's 'war of liberation' against Syria. With Awn's acceptance of the Arab League peace plan in September, however, the pound strengthened, to $1 = £L460, and it appreciated further, to $1 = £L410, after the approval of the Ta'if agreement on 23 October and the election of President Mouawad. This was the highest level that the pound had reached since the spring of 1988. By mid-January 1990, following President Mouawad's assassination, the pound had declined again, to $1 = £L544. The continuing political deadlock between east and west Beirut; the inter-Christian fighting in east Beirut; and the impact of the crisis in the Gulf region from August all caused further deterioration in the value of the Lebanese pound. In September the average rate of exchange was $1 = £L1,080. Following the defeat of Gen. Awn in October, the reunification of Beirut and the disbandment of the militias, the Lebanese pound gained in strength. In January and February 1991 the exchange rate averaged $1 = £L1,000, but by the end of the year it had strengthened to about $1 = £L880. On 19 February 1992, however, the central bank resolved to cease its currency support operations, prompting a dramatic slide in the value of the Lebanese pound. By 5 May the exchange rate was $1 = £L1,600. The central bank claimed that it had withdrawn its support from the pound because the currency had become overvalued. It was widely believed, however, that the real reason was the central bank's concern over the Government's inability to reduce its deficit (see below). Rising tensions in the prelude to the legislative elections held in mid-1992, and the implications of the Maronite boycott of the elections, gave rise to a further decline in the value of the currency. On 21 July 1992 the exchange rate was $1 = £L2,050, and on 7 September it was almost $1 = £L2,800. Post-electoral stability and the establishment of the Government of Rafik Hariri caused the currency to strengthen, and in 1993 the exchange rate averaged $1 = £L1,741. In 1994 the average exchange rate appreciated to $1 = £L1,680. During the Israeli attacks on southern Lebanon and Beirut in April 1996 the exchange rate of the Lebanese pound to the US dollar remained stable, and moves by the central bank to support the national currency proved largely unnecessary. During 1996 the exchange rate averaged $1 = £L1,571, some 3% higher than the average of $1 = £L1,621 recorded in 1995. In early 1997 the central bank announced that it would intervene in the exchange rate only when there was a rise or fall of £L10 against the dollar. The Lebanese pound continued to appreciate against the US dollar in 1997, when an average rate of $1 = £L1,539.5—some 2% higher than the average for 1996—was recorded. The currency strengthened further in 1998, with the exchange rate moving from $1 = £L1,527.0 at the beginning of the year to $1 = £L1,508.0 at the end of December. Since September 1998 the Lebanese pound has remained within a trading zone of $1 = £L1,501–£L1,514, as decreed by the Banque du Liban, even though the al-Hoss administration had called for an easing of monetary policy. However, pressure on the Lebanese pound during 2000 prompted the central bank to intervene in order to hold the exchange rate at below $1 = £L1,514. Pressure continued during much of 2001 casting doubts on the central bank's ability to maintain the local currency within the authorized exchange rate band. Reports from the currency markets suggested that pressure had eased somewhat at the end of the year but resumed during the early part of 2002. One source estimated that the central bank had spent $400m. during the first three months of 2002 in order to maintain the Lebanese pound within the range $1=L£1,501—L£1,514.

Government budget deficits have risen in recent years (see Public Finance and Development, below). The 1987 deficit was projected at £L65,000m.; that for 1988 at £L60,300m.; that for 1989 at £L89,500m.; and that for 1990 at £L387,000m. The Government accordingly borrowed heavily from the central bank and the commercial banks. At the end of May 1984 the public debt amounted to £L35,529m. ($2,250m.). By the end of 1987 it had risen to £L194,100m., of which £L127,200m. represented outstanding treasury bills. At 31 October 1988 the debt totalled £L504,500m., but one year later it had risen to £L755,000m. By November 1990 it had reached £L1,442,000m., and by March 1992 it was reportedly £L2,800,000m. Net total debt at the end of 1993 reached £L4,993,900m. Debt-servicing became a heavy burden on state finances, with interest payments totalling £L784,000m. in 1993 and £L1,488,000m. in 1994. The public debt continued to increase, despite warnings from independent financial organizations, and reached £L16,238,700m. by the end of 1996, equivalent to about 79% of that year's GDP. By the end of 1997 Lebanon's net public debt had increased to £L22,094,400m., and by the end of 1998 it amounted to £L25,826,300m. During the first five months of 1999 the public debt increased by 4.9%, compared with an increase of 6.4% in the corresponding period of 1998. In April 1998 the Government converted part of the debt into foreign currency by borrowing on the Eurodollar market, in order to reduce debt-servicing obligations. Of total public debt at the end of December 1998, £L19,543,800m. (75.7%) was domestic debt. External debt increased from $1,304.6m. at the end of 1995 to $1,856.0m. at the end of 1996. It rose to $2,431.8m. at the end of 1997 and reached $4,166.1m. at the end of 1998. According to official figures, interest payments in 1995 totalled £L1,875,204m. (£L1,744,518m. on domestic debt and £L130,686m. on foreign debt), accounting for 32.0% of all government budgetary expenditure. The central bank reported that interest payments in 1996 totalled £L2,692,930m. (£L2,507,950m. on domestic debt and £L184,980m. on foreign debt), accounting for 37.2% of all budget spending. In 1997 interest payments increased to £L3,380,000m. (36.9% of total expenditure). In 1998 interest payments totalled £L3,214,000m. (41.1% of total expenditure). Almost all of Lebanon's domestic debt is in the form of treasury bills. During the early months of 1997 interest rates on treasury bills declined steadily and there was an increase in the proportion of longer-term bills, easing the pressure somewhat on repayments. The central bank was continuing to issue new treasury bills but was concentrating on those with longer maturities in order to restructure the domestic debt and make it more manageable. At the end of 1997 the share of long-term bonds in domestic debt had risen to 67%, compared with 54% at the

end of 1996; the share had increased to 78% at the end of 1998. In April 1998 the Treasury offered $1,000m. in three-year Eurobonds. Another issue—$100m. in 10-year bonds, issued on behalf of EDL—improved in value in May 2000.

By the end of October 2000 the Banque du Liban reported that public debt had risen by 17% since October 1999, to £L33,800,000m. (US $22,400m.), equivalent to 135% of GDP—the highest figure in the Middle East with the exception of Iraq—with both the local and foreign currency components experiencing growth. Net domestic debt rose to £L24,100,000m. by October 2000, compared with £L20,600,000m. in October 1999, with the foreign currency component rising from $5,500m. to $6,400m. over the same period (as the Government sold additional debt on the Eurobond market). By the end of 2000 the foreign currency component accounted for almost 29% of the total public debt. In its budget for 2000 the Government stated that it would continue to replace domestic debt with less expensive foreign debt, but indicated that it would not allow the foreign component to exceed one-third of the total debt. Interest payments on public-sector debt rose sharply in 1999 and 2000, becoming the major charge on government resources. Interest payments on public debt in 2000 were equivalent to 97% of total government revenue and 40% of total expenditure. Observers predicted that further growth in the public debt and rising interest payments would continue to put pressure on the balance of payments. Although the al-Hoss Government had earmarked privatization revenues to reduce government debt, the divestment of state enterprises made little progress despite the ambitious programme set out by the new Hariri administration. Debt stocks continued to rise as the Hariri Government borrowed heavily to fund the fiscal shortfall. Total public debt rose from L£33,800,000m. ($22,400m.) in October 2000, when it represented 135% of estimated GDP, to L£34,440,000m. ($26,160m.) by September 2001 when it represented 154% of estimated GDP. By the end of 2001 total net public debt had increased by 16% year-on-year and was equivalent to 165% of estimated GDP. Debt servicing costs rose by 3% year-on-year to L£4,312,000m. in 2001, which was equivalent to 48.6% of total spending (the largest single item of expenditure) and 93% of total revenue. Debt service expenditure in the 2002 budget was projected to rise by 4.7% to L£4,500,000m., equivalent to 47.7% of total expenditure. There has also been a sharp rise in the foreign component of the total debt stock, reflecting a change in debt management strategy with most new borrowing contracted in dollars through the sale of Eurobonds rather than in local currency in order to secure substantially lower coupon rates. The Ministry of Finance issued $3,100m. in Eurobonds in 2001 and has plans to sell $2,500m.–$3,000m. in Eurobonds during 2002. The majority of Eurobonds issued during 2001 were placed locally, mainly with local banks. In October 2000 the foreign component of the debt stock was $6,400m.(28.5% of total public-sector debt stock). By the end of September 2001 the proportion of public debt denominated in foreign currency had risen to 36%, exceeding the one-third limit decree in 2000. In April 2002 Standard and Poor announced that it had lowered its long-term ratings on Lebanon from B to B- reflecting mounting concern over levels of public debt and the Government's ability to implement its fiscal reform programme.

In October 1987, for the first time in Lebanese history, the commercial banks refused to co-operate with the monetary policies of the central bank (Banque du Liban). For the previous two years the central bank had tried to increase its control over the banking sector, in a vain attempt to halt the depreciation in the Lebanese pound. The commercial banks refused to continue to subscribe to treasury bills, which financed the majority of government spending, and initiated legal proceedings against the central bank, in respect of fines imposed on them in 1986 and 1987. The central bank was forced to concede, cancelling the fines and revoking some of its recently-promulgated measures.

In late 1988 rumours of a liquidity crisis caused a sudden withdrawal of deposits from Bank al-Mashrek, the banking arm of the partly state-owned Intra Investment Co. The bank's chairman, Roger Tamraz, was forced to resign and, amid controversy over Tamraz's role, the central bank agreed to underwrite only the claims of local non-institutional depositors. In early 1989 the Swiss and French banking authorities withdrew the licences of two of Bank al-Mashrek's affiliates, the Paris-based

Banque de Participations et de Placement (BPP) and the Lugano-based BPP, because of their failure to satisfy liquidity requirements. In both May and July 1989 France rescinded the licences of two Lebanese-controlled banks, United Bank Corpn and the Lebanese Arab Bank, respectively, in part due to over-lending to high-risk countries and creditors. The difficulties in France seriously undermined confidence in the entire Lebanese banking system, and in early August it was disclosed that more than US $200m. had been withdrawn from Lebanese banks, most of the funds having been transferred to France.

Currency speculation had become a major source of profit for commercial banks, especially the smaller ones, and the relative stability of the exchange rate in 1991 and early 1992 caused renewed problems in the banking sector. In 1991 some 20 of Beirut's 90 banks were reported to be in serious difficulty and late in the year four small banks ceased operations. In February 1992 the Banque Libano-Brésilienne and the Banque Tohme both closed, and in March the Globe Bank also ceased trading.

In late 1991 the central bank ordered commercial banks to increase their capital and reduce their 'hard' currency loan exposure by restricting lending to 55% of their 'hard' currency deposits by mid-September 1992. The banks were also instructed to make extra capital provisions for their head offices and for each branch. At the same time, the central bank informed commercial banks that they would soon be able to revalue their fixed assets. Their nominal value had remained constant for several years and had been rendered virtually meaningless by inflation. In 1991 the Lebanese Bankers' Association proposed a series of reforms, including new procedures for the liquidation and merging of banks. New banking and investment legislation required all Lebanese banks to meet the Bank for International Settlements' capital-asset ratio of 8% by February 1995.

In 1996 commercial banks announced record profits, in some cases 50% higher than in 1995, achieved largely through the purchase of treasury bills issued by the central bank. However, with Lebanon experiencing mounting public debt and decelerating economic growth (owing to low levels of investment), the central bank attempted to make the banks less dependent on treasury bills for their income and to encourage them to lend more. At 31 December 1998 the commercial banks had total deposits to the value of £L46,113,004m. held for customers, of which 34.5% were held in local currency. Loans to the private sector in local currency were worth only £L2,073,501m. or a mere 11.1% of all loans. Most lending was in foreign currency. In the first half of 1997 the Lebanese Banks' Association reduced the interest rate on the Lebanese pound from 24% to 16%, and the central bank abolished the regulation requiring banks to hold at least 40% of their local currency deposits in treasury bills. In April 1997 the central bank also attempted to reduce the high cost of credit by introducing a programme to subsidize short and medium-term loans by commercial banks to the private sector for productive projects. Independent financial analysts, however, argued that interest rates were still too high and doubts were expressed that banks would find new investment outlets. It was argued that Lebanon was unlikely to re-establish itself as a major financial centre while there were more than 70 commercial banks, since many of them are family-owned and previous government efforts to force them to merge have proved unsuccessful. It was reported that the country's leading 16 banks accounted for 84% of total assets in 1998. At the end of 1996 the Government introduced a regulation allowing banks to list up to 30% of their shares on the Beirut Stock Exchange but by mid-1997 only three banks had decided to do so. By the end of the 1990s the fact that Lebanese banks had subscribed to almost three-quarters of treasury bill debt denominated in both Lebanese pounds and foreign currency provoked unease at their high exposure to government debt. With falling interest rates on government treasury bills, the main commercial banks began to devote more attention to developing their retail banking services—introducing services such as internet banking—and by the end of 2000 the number of credit and debit cards issued by banks was reported to have increased significantly. In mid-2000 total assets of commercial banks amounted to £L64,100,000m. (US $42,500m.), about 13% higher than in mid-1999. The Lebanese banking system currently employs some 150,000 people. By early 2002 six Lebanese banks,

including Banque du Liban et d'Outre-Mer SAL (BLOM Bank)and Fransabank, had obtained licences to operate in Syrian free zones. For the moment their activities are to be limited to providing services to companies based in the free zones, but the banks hope eventually to be allowed to operate within the mainstream Syrian economy.

In April 2001 the National Assembly agreed to amend the banking secrecy law in response to international pressure on Lebanon to combat money laundering and to abide by international banking norms.

Long before the civil war, inflationary pressures had been one of Lebanon's most serious economic problems, and the conflict removed all vestiges of price restraint. The minimum monthly wage was increased to £L310 in 1977, then to £L415, and from that to £L525 in 1979, but this did little to relieve the chronic post-war hardship afflicting much of the population. In April 1982 the Cabinet approved a 17% pay rise for private and public sector workers. In 1983 the minimum wage was raised by 18.9% to £L1,100 per month, and by January 1987 it had been raised to £L3,200 per month. Inflation rose from about 20% in 1982 to an annual rate of 50% or more in early 1985. The 1986 figure was well over 100%, increasing to around 200% by the end of 1987 (with many basic consumer items registering a 300% increase), and the disastrous depreciation in the value of the Lebanese pound meant that the minimum monthly wage of £L4,300 was worth only US $15. Demonstrations against poverty and the continuing civil conflict became more frequent. Lebanon's reserves of foreign exchange declined to $300m. in August, but the Government was reluctant to reduce state subsidies on basic commodities (which cost about $100m. per year) for fear of provoking greater unrest. Despite substantial increases in the heavily subsidized domestic prices of petroleum products in June 1986 and January 1987, the IMF estimated that the cumulative deficit on the oil trade account would reach about £L17,000m. by the end of 1986, while the deficit for 1986 alone was expected to reach about £L4,000m. In September 1987 the government subsidy on petroleum was substantially reduced with the result that the price of petrol more than doubled. At the beginning of October the minimum monthly salary was raised to £L8,500 in order to compensate for the high rate of inflation, but in the same month the prices of bread and fuel were raised by 43% and 15%, respectively. Declines in standards of living prompted the Confédération Générale des Travailleurs du Liban (CGTL), the country's leading independent labour union, to call a five-day general strike in November, which was generally supported in an unprecedented display of national unity. During 1987, according to official estimates, the consumer price index rose by 420%.

In 1988–93 the value of the Lebanese pound continued to fall, giving rise to further price increases. In two months, from mid-February 1992, the value of the currency declined by 65%, causing the price of food and that of many other commodities to double. Strikes and street demonstrations followed, culminating in the resignation, in May, of Omar Karami's Government. During 1992 the inflation rate was estimated to have averaged 100%. In March 1991 the Government finally removed subsidies on bread and fuel, although, at the same time, it levied a tax of 18% on petrol. In August 1991 public-sector salaries were increased by 60% (the increase backdated to the beginning of the year) and in December they were increased again, by 120%. In the same month the remaining subsidies on wheat and flour were removed. Early in 1996 the CGTL requested a 76% increase in salaries and an increase in the minimum monthly wage from £L250,000 to £L500,000 but its demands were rejected by the Government. However, in May the Government did decree salary increases for workers in the private sector effective from the beginning of the year. The minimum monthly wage was increased to £L300,000, the wages of those earning over £L250,000 and £L800,000 were increased by 10%, and those earning over £L800,000 by 5%. The CGTL declared that the wage increases were too small, and private sector employers, who normally set their own wage levels, did not welcome government interference. In August 1999 fuel distributors threatened to take industrial action, after the Government raised the price of petrol over two successive weeks.

The stabilization of the exchange rate in 1992–93 resulted in lower inflation. In 1993 prices rose by about 10%. As of January

1994 the minimum monthly wage was increased to £L200,000, from £L118,000. According to the Beirut Chamber of Commerce, the annual rate of inflation averaged 6.8% in 1994, 9.4% in 1995 and 6.1% in 1996. In early 1997 the Government declared that, although it was determined to boost economic growth, it was also committed to maintaining annual inflation at less than 10%. The annual rate of inflation averaged 24.0% in 1990–98; however, the rate averaged only 2.1% in 1997. According to Banque Audi, by December 1998 the annual rate of inflation was 2.9%, and in 1999 the average annual rate fell to 2%. Inflation was expected to remain low in 2000. In July of that year the Ministry of Finance stated that the central bank's foreign reserves were at record levels. Ministry officials also mooted the possibility of reducing interest rates in order to end the country's recession, even if this risked shaking confidence in the currency, and announced plans to establish a debt-management team to examine foreign soft loans and grants, so as to draw on $1,000m. in hitherto unused loans.

The Beirut Stock Exchange reopened in September 1995 and trading began in January 1996 when three construction materials companies were listed. In 1997 the major real estate company, Solidère (see above), moved from the secondary market, increasing total capitalization from an estimated US $1,800m. to $2,600m. The addition of several banks brought the number of companies listed on the exchange to 12. However, interest in the bourse failed to develop and the number of companies listed remained low. Operating losses of $70,000 were reported in 1999, compared with a profit of $330,000 in 1998. Trading volumes in 1999 fell by 60%, compared with 1998, with turnover falling by 72.6% to $90.54m. The situation was aggravated by a dispute with Solidère—whose shares represent more than a third of all those traded—over transactions arranged by the real estate company outside the Beirut Stock Exchange. Average daily trading for most of 2000 was below $300,000. Hopes were expressed that the economic reform programme announced by Prime Minister Hariri at the end of 2000 would help to stimulate the market, with progress on privatization resulting in new listings. A decision in September 2000 by the Union of Arab Bourses—an organization bringing together stock markets across the Arab world—to move its headquarters from Cairo to Beirut was also expected to provide a boost to activity on the Beirut exchange.

TOURISM, TRANSPORT AND COMMUNICATIONS

Beirut's hotels, its port and airport, as well as Lebanon's largest non-government employer, MEA, were all severely affected by the civil conflict, which erupted just as tourism was beginning to recover from the effects of the October 1973 war. As the civil conflict progressed, the prosperous hotel district in the centre of Beirut became the scene of some of the fiercest fighting. According to the Lebanese Hotel Owners' Association, 145 hotels were damaged, incurring losses of some £L218m. In Beirut alone the number of hotels had fallen from 130 (with 10,486 beds) in 1975 to 44 (with 4,631 beds) by 1979. The contribution of tourism to GNP, which was 20% before 1975, declined to 7.4% in 1977. Visitors spent only 469,272 nights in Beirut in 1979, compared with 2,307,122 nights in 1974. In 1980 there was some improvement, with a 15% rise in the number of visitors to 135,548, who spent a total of 585,531 nights in Beirut. Overall occupancy was only 27%, however. The cost of damage sustained by Beirut's hotels during the Israeli invasion in 1982 was estimated at £L400m.

The National Council for Tourism in Lebanon (NCTL) undertook a massive promotional campaign through its nine offices in Europe, the USA and the Middle East, issuing a glossy monthly bulletin and preparing brochures, books and other materials. In the spring of 1983 the newly-formed National Council for External Economic Relations (NCEER) took over all the activities of the NCTL (until the disbandment of the NCEER in 1985). The Ministry of Tourism and the CDR drew up plans to rebuild the four international-class seaside hotels in Beirut at a cost of around US $100m. They also outlined schemes to clean up the beaches. Although the security problem made it difficult to move from area to area within Lebanon, inside those areas domestic tourism flourished during the years of the civil conflict. The Ministry of Tourism reported a significant rise in investment in hotel construction from the beginning of 1994 to

the middle of 1996, with total investment for that period reported at $325m. A number of leading pre-war hotels are to be refurbished and expanded, and new hotels built. The Phoenicia Intercontinental in Beirut, one of the city's major hotels, re-opened in early 2000. Although the number of tourists visiting Lebanon, mainly Lebanese living abroad, increased after the end of the civil war in 1990, by 1996 hoteliers still reported very low occupancy rates. The Israeli attacks on southern Lebanon and Beirut in April 1996 exacerbated the problem of diminished tourism levels, and a marketing campaign was launched by the Ministry of Trade and Industry in February 1997 to attract tourists from the Gulf states. Recent efforts to revive the tourist industry appear to have met with considerable success. Tourist arrivals increased by 22% in 1995, and by a further 3.5% in 1996. According to the Ministry of Tourism, the number of tourist arrivals (excluding Syrian nationals) in 1997 was 557,568, an increase of some 31.5%. Figures published by the World Tourism Organization show that the number of arrivals rose to 630,781 in 1998, 673,261 in 1999 and to 741,648 in 2000. Tourism receipts reached an estimated US $742m. in 2000, compared with $673m. in the previous year. Of total arrivals in 2000, 38.8% were from Arab countries (excluding Syria) and 30.9% were from Europe. The Lebanese Hotel Association estimated that by 1999 there were 12,000 hotel beds in the country, mainly in four- and five-star hotels. The 'open skies' policy announced by the Government in November 2000 (see below) and continued improvements in the country's tourist infrastructure were expected to boost the recovery of the tourist sector in the long term. Despite concerns that the regional impact of the Israel-Palestinian crisis would undermine the revival of Lebanese tourism, figures for 2001 suggested that visitor numbers (based on the number of arrivals at Beirut International Airport) rose by 6% compared with 2000 to 1,186,000 arrivals. The figures would have been higher but for the impact of the 11 September 2001 terrorist attacks on the USA, which led to a fall in the number of arrivals by some 14% in October and November of that year. However, tourism subsequently recovered and in late February 2002 the Ministry of Tourism estimated that there had been a 35% increase in tourist arrivals during the Id al-Adha festival. Local reports maintained that in the wake of the 11 September terrorist attacks, many Gulf Arabs preferred to spend their holidays in Lebanon rather than travel to Europe or the USA.

MEA suffered a loss of £L14m. in 1975, and of £L69.1m. in 1976. A recovery occurred in 1977, with profits reaching £L22m., but 1978 was again disappointing, with staff prevented by the fighting from reporting for duty and passenger traffic some 16% lower than had been expected. In 1979 MEA made a startling recovery, recording a profit of £L51.14m., its highest ever. However, the MEA Chairman, Asad Nasr, warned that inflation and increases in fuel prices meant the airline must expect narrower profit margins in the future. In 1980 profits slumped to £L9m., and in 1981 the airline's losses were £L88m. In October MEA increased its capital from £L100m. to £L150m. Shortly beforehand, plans had been announced to introduce new routes, including a service to New York. The Israeli invasion in 1982 plunged MEA into its worst-ever crisis. The airline was closed for 115 days, losing almost £L140m., and five aircraft were destroyed. The airline recorded a loss of £L187.5m. in 1982. The fighting in the Chouf in September 1983 led to the closure of Beirut airport. In that year MEA made a loss of about £L250m., and its problems continued in 1984. In that year Beirut airport was closed from February until July, during which time MEA lost US $250,000 per day. MEA's losses in 1985 amounted to £L454m., and they were expected to total £L50m. in 1986. In 1987 the airline's losses were £L452m., and in 1988 they totalled £L500m. In 1989 MEA was badly affected by a further, prolonged closure of Beirut airport during Gen. Awn's 'war of liberation' against the Syrian presence in Lebanon.

In 1987 MEA suffered from a dispute over the new, privately-developed Halat airport, sited in Christian-held territory to the north of Beirut and intended to enable Christians to travel to and from the country without having to enter Muslim-controlled west Beirut. The Government refused to recognize Halat as an international airport, and in January 1987 Christian LF militiamen closed Beirut airport by shellfire, in order to put pressure on the Government over the issue of Halat. One of

MEA's Boeing 707s was destroyed and the airline dispersed its fleet outside the country for fear of further losses. Beirut airport reopened in May, after the LF accepted assurances from the Minister of Transport that a newly established government commission, examining the feasibility of converting military airstrips to civilian use, would grant Halat airport official status. The destruction of the 707 in 1987 reduced MEA's active fleet to 11 aircraft. In addition, the company owns three Boeing 747s which, for several years, were leased to other airlines, generating annual revenues of about US $17m. In November 1989, however, the company decided to take the 747s back into service with MEA. One of the leased aircraft was returned in 1990, and another in 1991, when, the civil conflict apparently having concluded, MEA was achieving high occupancy rates for its services to and from Beirut. In 1991 the airport handled 825,000 passengers, compared with 638,000 in 1990. In early 1992 it was reported that MEA had leased two Airbus A310s from the Dutch airline KLM for three years. In 1992 MEA's losses amounted to $6m. MEA continued to renew its fleet and embarked on a programme to restructure the company in order to improve efficiency. Passenger numbers increased slightly in 1996 but the company recorded losses of $50m., two-thirds higher than the figure for 1995. At the end of 1996 it was reported that the central bank controlled a 90% stake in the company and in early 1997 it was announced that MEA had increased its capital by $47.4m.

MEA remains over-staffed and inefficient, has experienced a decline in passenger numbers and has been recording operational losses for several years. The company was bitterly opposed to the 'open skies' policy announced by the Hariri Government in November 2000, which will remove many restrictions in order to encourage more foreign airlines to use Beirut's newly-expanded international airport. MEA, which had previously enjoyed considerable protection from competition, claimed that it would lose its market share to lower-cost carriers and warned that it might be plunged into bankruptcy. In May 2001 the Cabinet announced plans to privatize the airline and lay off 1,200 workers, with a further 300 staff taking early retirement. The company currently employs around 4,300 people and costs the Government US $45m.–$50m. annually. The International Finance Corporation, the private-sector arm of the World Bank, is advising the Government on the privatization. The World Bank has provided a $60m. soft loan to pay for redundancies. Airline employees at Beirut International Airport staged a one-day strike in early May in protest against the Government's plans. By mid-2002 the airline continued to run at a loss and, despite rumours of interest from Air France, no foreign company had come forward as a strategic partner. Prospects for the company's successful privatization appeared bleak, particularly because of the impact of the September 11 terrorist attacks on the global airline industry.

There was an increase in airfreight, due to companies' reluctance to store goods in Lebanon, which in turn necessitated a faster turnaround that could be provided only by air. Lebanon's chief cargo-carrier, Trans-Mediterranean Airways (TMA), in operation since 1953, hoped to profit from this transport trend, although in 1982 the company made a loss of £L57m., of which £L50m. was attributable to the Israeli invasion. The airline was also badly affected by the discontinuation of its round-the-world service as a result of disputes over lost traffic rights in northern Europe, the USA and Japan. In 1983 TMA's losses totalled £L61m., and in May 1984 the company asked for immediate government financial assistance to assure its survival. In mid-1985 TMA suffered serious losses as a result of a three-week ban on its aircraft entering Saudi Arabian airspace. It failed to recapture the lost volume of freight when the ban was lifted, and was forced to request further financial help from the Government. Flights were suspended in July, when pilots organized a strike in protest at the company's failure to pay salaries. In August the airline was placed under government control. In July 1986 a majority stake in TMA was acquired by Jet Holdings, an east Beirut group headed by the financier Roger Tamraz. In December the airline resumed flights between Europe and the Middle and Far East. Following the collapse, in late 1988, of Roger Tamraz's business interests, the Lebanese central bank effectively took control of Jet Holdings and, through it, TMA. The move was resisted by Tamraz's partners in Jet Holdings,

and in early 1990 TMA's ownership was still disputed. In early 1991 it was reported that a committee, established by the Ministry of Transport to decide TMA's future, had estimated the company's debts at US $80m., while its assets amounted to only $45m. The committee proposed three options for TMA: a merger with MEA; the company's takeover by MEA; or a substantial grant of funds by the Government to enable the airline to resume operations in its own right. In March 1993 the 74% stake in TMA, formerly controlled by Roger Tamraz, was bought for $8m. by a holding company, the Lebanese Co for Aviation Investment (LCAI). The main shareholder in LCAI is Banque Libano-Française SAL. In approving the acquisition, the court handling the bankruptcy of the Tamraz-controlled Al-Mashrek Bank also waived TMA's $39m.-debt to the bank. TMA's fleet comprises seven Boeing 707s, one of which is on lease to Saudi Arabian Airlines and another to the Kuwait Airways Corpn. TMA continues to suffer from serious financial problems and this largely accounted for a decline in the volume of air cargo recorded in 1996 compared with 1995. In 1996 the company employed 450 workers. In May TMA announced that it had debts of $80m. and was unable to pay its employees.

In 1994 a joint venture, comprising the German company Hochtief and Athens-based Consolidated Contractors International Co, won an estimated US $490m.-contract to expand Beirut International Airport. By 2000 some 35 airlines were using the airport, where a $400m.-new terminal has been opened. By 1999 Beirut International Airport was handling some 2.11m passengers, compared with 1.67m in 1995 (but well below its capacity of 6m. passengers). Prime Minister Hariri claimed that his 'open skies' initiative announced in November 2000 would lead to a substantial increase in passenger numbers, enabling the airport the operate at almost full capacity. Some observers, however, felt that his predictions were over-optimistic.

During the early 1970s Beirut port suffered substantial congestion, owing, mainly, to the volume of goods bound for Saudi Arabia, Kuwait and Iraq, where petroleum revenues had boosted development expenditure. Shortly before the outbreak of the civil conflict in 1975, British consultants Peat, Marwick Mitchell & Co and consulting engineers Coode & Partners conducted a major study of Beirut and Tripoli ports and drafted a master plan. In 1977, the British consultants revised their forecasts to include reconstruction, and the CDR appointed a port committee in August 1977 to oversee the reconstruction and modernization process, the total cost of which was estimated at more than US $144m. Although work on the port continued, there were frequent disruptions, owing to the civil conflict.

With the reunification of Beirut after the siege of 1982, the reign of snipers and political factions at the port was ended for a while. A temporary strengthening of government authority began to ease the problem of illegal ports, of which at least 17 had begun operating as a result of the civil war. These ports imposed tariffs which were only a fraction of those payable at the official ports, and the official ports, for their part, were seriously affected by smuggling. Of particular significance was the appropriation by the Lebanese army, in March 1983, of the notorious fifth basin of Beirut port, which had been a valuable source of revenue for right-wing Lebanese militias for a number of years. According to some sources, it had accounted for 90% of the country's illegal trade. Import duties and airport and seaport charges, which had formerly accounted for more than 45% of government revenues, contributed less than 15% in 1983. Tripoli port remained under the control of pro-Syrian militias or was the scene of fierce fighting between rival groups, while Israeli forces continued to occupy the ports of Sidon and Tyre in the south. Fighting between rival militias intensified, however, and, after the withdrawal from Beirut of the multinational peace-keeping force in March 1984, the Government was unable to impose its authority over the operation of the ports. A brief expansion of government control took place during 1984, after the formation of an administration that was more representative of the country's diverse factions. This helped to increase customs' revenues from the ports, but the improvement was short-lived (see Public Finance and Development, below). In February 1989 Gen. Awn, the head of Lebanon's Christian Government, ousted the Lebanese Forces militia from the fifth basin of Beirut port and then, acting in the name of state legitimacy, moved to close illegal militia ports in the Muslim parts of the country, imposing an aerial and maritime blockade. Several weeks of bitter Christian–Muslim battles followed, and, during Gen. Awn's 'war of liberation' against Syrian forces, ports were a major target. The port of Tripoli made a significant recovery following the deployment there of Syrian troops at the end of 1985. After a two-year closure, Beirut port reopened on 15 March 1992, and in the first half of the year it handled 671 vessels and just over 1m. tons of cargo. This represented about one-quarter of pre-civil war traffic levels.

In late 1980 the CDR recommended to the Cabinet that the concession for a new port at Sidon should be granted to a Sidon businessman, Rafik Hariri. The CDR advised that Hariri should be granted the concession for 30 years, and that he should set up a joint company with the CDR, with capital of £L250m. It was a controversial decision, because the British consultants who had prepared the plans for Beirut port said that, in a politically unified Lebanon, only two ports, Beirut and Tripoli, were needed, and that if the South must have a port, then Tyre, further south, would be more suitable than Sidon. In 1985, however, Hariri's Paris-based company, Oger International, invited bids for the construction of the first phase of a new port at Sidon. The problem of illegal ports seemed, finally, to have been solved in May 1991, when, in an assertion of its authority, the new Government of national reconciliation disbanded the country's militias, and units of the Lebanese army were deployed in the ports. In May 1998 it was reported that bids were expected to be invited in the near future for the development of a new port in Sidon, requiring total projected investment of US $400m. The project, to be implemented in four stages, involved land reclamation, dredging and the construction of two breakwaters and two berths. By 1999 the estimated cost of the project had increased to $530m. (with infrastructure expected to cost $300m. and superstructure, to be carried out on a build-operate-transfer (BOT) basis, at $230m.).

In November 1993 Port Autonome de Marseille, of France, won a US $1m.-contract to advise on a scheme to redevelop Beirut port. Work began on the project in early 1997. Entrecanales of Spain secured a $102m.-contract to expand the four existing docks, to increase facilities for containers and to prepare a feasibility plan for a fifth dock. A loan worth $57m. was made by the EIB towards the cost of the project, which is also being financed by the private company managing the port, the Compagnie de Gestion et d'Exploitation du Port de Beyrouth (CGEPB). The work was scheduled for completion in 1999, when the port authority intended to spend some $40m. on new port equipment. The port's free-trade zone, closed since the mid-1970s, has reopened. The port handles some three-quarters of Lebanon's imports, but port traffic has declined since the mid-1990s as a result of the country's economic recession. The number of ships visiting Beirut port fell from 3,443 in 1995 to 2,812 in 1999, while the volume of freight handled also declined from 6,650m. tons in 1995 to 5,550m. tons in 1999. In 1998 the Government appointed the Dubai Ports Authority to run Beirut port under a 20-year contract in order to improve efficiency. In 1995 the port of Tripoli handled 938 vessels and 3,344,000 tons of freight, while Sidon handled 203 vessels and 306,000 tons of freight. The Minister of Transport announced in 1996 that these two ports would also be expanded.

In 1994 plans were announced for a US $500m.-scheme to rebuild Lebanon's coastal railway. The 170-km line links Tyre and Sidon in the south with Beirut and Tripoli in the north. The southern section of the line ceased operating in 1948, during the first Arab–Israeli War. Services on the section from Beirut to Tripoli stopped at the start of the Lebanese civil war. An east–west railway line from Beirut to the Syrian border also ceased operating during the civil war, but no plans have been announced for its reconstruction.

In July 1999 the CDR announced plans to invite bids for the first stage in the construction of a road linking Dbayeh, in north-east Beirut, to the northern suburb of Antélias. The cost of the initial project, which is being financed by the KFAED, is estimated at $25m. In August 2000 a new 8-km highway linking some 26 villages in the south of the country was inaugurated, demonstrating the infrastructural development that was taking place as a result of the end of Israeli occupation. In early 2001 the Saudi Development Fund agreed to provide US $45m. to fund improvements to part of the main Beirut–Damascus highway, and in March 2002 it agreed a loan of $30m. to finance construction of a road that would connect Tripoli with the Syrian border.

Meanwhile, in April 1983 the Ministry of Posts and Telecommunications confirmed that it intended to establish an autonomous body to administer the country's telephone and telecommunications services, as recommended by the World Bank. The deterioration of the telecommunications system during the civil war led many businesses to turn to private satellite communications systems. In early 1990 it was reported that 85 such systems were in use. In addition, international links were being maintained via cellular telephone systems operating through Cyprus, while private telephone systems were also in use for internal communications. In 1993 a major telecommunications rehabilitation project was launched, involving the replacement of existing exchanges and the installation of more than one million lines. As part of this project, Siemens of Germany won an estimated US $40m.-contract to install 420,000 new lines in and around Beirut, while the French company Alcatel began installing telephone exchanges with 270,000 new lines in the Beirut and Tripoli areas. Sweden's Ericsson was appointed to repair telephone switching systems in the south, the Beka'a valley and parts of Mount Lebanon. By early 1997 significant progress had been made but many lines were still not working and the Government estimated that an investment of some $500m. would be needed to repair and modernize the system. Nevertheless, in mid-1997 it was reported that the installation of some 250,000 new fixed telephone lines using local contractors to reduce the cost had begun. The use of mobile phones has increased, and Lebanon has the highest use of mobile phones per head of any Arab country. (In 2001 the International Telecommunication Union reported that 21% of Lebanese owned a mobile telephone, while some 52% of all telephones in the country were mobile.) In early 1997 two local companies, France-Télécom Mobile Liban (FTML) and Libancell, signed contracts with Ericsson of Sweden and Siemens of Germany respectively, to expand their network capacity. International consultants who were called in to advise the Government in subsequent negotiations recommended the introduction of licence agreements and suggested allowing an international operator to bid for a third cellular licence. In September 1998 the Ministry of Posts and Telecommunications invited tenders for the supply of a national network of 4,000 public telephones. In 2000 Cellis (FTML's cellular operator) and Libancell, with a total of 700,000 subscribers, proposed to replace their 10-year 'build-operate-transfer' (BOT) contract with a 20-year licence for which they would each pay $1,350m.; however, no agreement was reached due to differences within the al-Hoss administration. In mid-June 2001 the Hariri Government cancelled the BOT contracts of both FTML and Libancell, in order to prepare for the issue of two new 20-year GSM licences by the end of the year. However, the issue was delayed because of a dispute over the level of compensation owed to FTML and Libancell and the proportion of profits owed to the Government under the original contracts. In late April 2002 it was suggested, pending a full audit, that the Government could expect to pay the two companies a total of $322m. for terminating their licences. Cabinet ministers were divided over the proposed sale. Some favoured allowing FTML and Libancell to continue to operate the licences until new tenders were issued, while others demanded that the companies transfer their equipment to the telecommunications ministry immediately. The sharp downturn in the global telecommunications industry suggested that the sale might prove difficult and in August the Government agreed to postpone the sale of the licenses until January 2003. At the end of January 2001, meanwhile, the telecommunications minister announced that he would shortly be submitting a draft law to parliament including proposals for the establishment of a national regulator and the merger of the national fixed line operator, Ogero, with other state-owned providers in order to create a single operator, Liban Telecom, responsible for both local and international fixed lines. The new company would be granted a licence to become the third cellular operator. A stake of up to 35% in Liban Telecom would be sold to an international operator in 2001. In March it was announced that Ericsson of Sweden, together with Extreme Networks of the USA, would begin work on establishing a metropolitan area network for Ogero.

In July 1998 the CDR awarded a 12-year postal concession to two Canadian companies. As a result, a new operating company, to be called Liban Poste, was to provide the national postal service. The new company's seven-member board of directors, comprising three Canadians and four Lebanese, would be responsible for the management and upgrading of Lebanon's postal services.

PUBLIC FINANCE AND DEVELOPMENT

Poor budgetary predictions and persistent fiscal shortfalls have been a feature of the Lebanese economy in recent years. In addition, personal political considerations have often interfered with the normal budgetary process, which has served to undermine confidence in the economy. At the same time, successive governments have sought to revive the economy through budgetary measures.

The draft state budget for 1987 forecast total expenditure of £L27,250m., compared with £L17,937m. in 1986, an increase of 52%. In addition, there was a supplementary budget of £L42,000m., covering posts and telecommunications, the national lottery, and wheat, fuel and sugar subsidies. Moreover, the supplementary budget allocated £L20,000m. for the undersubscription of treasury bills. Revenue was expected to total £L4,250m., compared with £L12,712m. in the 1986 budget. In previous years, the Government's estimates of customs revenues had been wildly optimistic, given the authorities' continuing inability to wrest control of the ports from militias. The sharp fall in revenues projected in the draft 1987 budget indicated greater realism. The 1987 draft budget forecast a deficit of £L65,000m., about twice the actual shortfall during 1986.

In some years there was an alarming discrepancy between the budget proposals and the actual course of economic events, largely as a result of the political turbulence in the country. Thus, in 1986, the actual deficit was an estimated £L34,000m. (expenditure £L36,000m.; revenue £L2,000m.), compared with the £L5,225m. for which the budget had allowed. This was largely due to a huge shortfall in customs revenues. In more settled times, these would have been a major source of government revenue. From the mid-1970s, losses of revenue from taxation and customs duties, caused by the inability of the Government to impose taxes and the proliferation of illegal ports, deprived it of valuable income. As a result of stricter government control of the ports in 1983, customs revenues rose to £L1,280m. in that year, compared with only £L403m. in 1982. However, in 1984, when the Government might have expected to earn some £L3,000m. in customs duty, income from this source amounted to only £L452m., or nearly 65% less than in 1983. The Government introduced further measures to close illegal ports in October 1984, but parts of Beirut port were again under the control of the Christian militias by April 1985. In 1985 customs receipts totalled £L481m., compared with the budget projection of more than £L3,000m. (about 35% of total revenue).

The draft budget for 1989 was presented by the Cabinet of Prime Minister Dr Selim al-Hoss at the beginning of October 1988, despite the appointment of a military government by President Gemayel to administer the country during the transition from the end of his tenure until the election of a new President. Such was the political uncertainty during 1989, however, that the actual spending and revenue of the country's two governments probably bore only a slight resemblance to the al-Hoss draft budget. However, it forecast total expenditure during 1989 of £L219,500m. and total revenue of £L130,000m., leaving a deficit of £L89,500m. (the figures, were distorted by the huge depreciation in the value of the Lebanese pound). The allocation for servicing the national debt (£L194,100m. in January 1988)

was again the largest single item of expenditure, accounting for 32% (£L70,240m.) of the total. Debt service continued to be by far the biggest spending category in the budgets of the early 1990s. Actual revenues in 1993 totalled £L1,800,000m., which was 82% higher than in 1992. Customs duties accounted for £L662,000m. (twice the 1992 figure), while income tax receipts, at £L126,000m., were three times the level of the year before, underlining the success of the recently appointed Government of Rafik Hariri in establishing its authority.

Expenditure in the 1999 budget was projected at £L8,360,000m. and revenues at £L4,990,000m., giving a deficit of £L3,370,000m. Actual revenues amounted to £L4,868,000m., while expenditure rose slightly to £L8,454,000m., resulting in a deficit of £L3,586,000m. Projected expenditure in the 2000 budget was £L9,124,000m., with revenues at £L5,389,000m., giving a deficit of £L3,735,000m. In practice the deficit was £L5,900,000m., following a sharp increase in expenditure and a fall in revenues. The 2000 deficit was the largest ever recorded, equivalent to 56% of expenditure and almost 24% of GDP. There was speculation that the Hariri Government, which assumed office in October 2000, had held revenue over to the 2001 fiscal year and made allocations for 2001 expenditure in 2000, in order to show the outgoing al-Hoss administration's economic performance in a more unfavourable light. Interest payments on public debt in 2000 were equivalent to 97% of total government revenue and 40% of total expenditure. Before leaving office the al-Hoss Government approved the 2001 budget, which forecast expenditure of £L8,900,000m. and revenue at £L5,730,000m., giving a deficit of £L3,170,000m., equivalent to 35.6% of expenditure. The new Hariri Government produced its own budget for 2001 in January but it was not approved by the National Assembly until June. Revenues were projected to rise to L£4,900,000m., a 9.6% increase on 2000, with expenditure falling to L£9,975,000m., a 4% decrease on 2000, giving a target deficit of L£5,075,000m., down 13.5% on 2000 but equivalent to 50.9% of expenditure and 20.3% of GDP. Debt servicing was projected at L£4,300,000m., 43.1% of total expenditure. Official figures reveal that actual spending during 2001 fell by 16.4% compared with 2000 to L£8,878,000m. while revenues fell by 2.1% to L£4,650,000m., giving a total deficit of L£4,220,000m., (28% lower than 2000 and slightly below the projected figure). Nevertheless, the fiscal deficit was one of the largest in the world, equivalent to 17% of estimated GDP and 48% of expenditure. Debt servicing accounted for 93% of total revenue and almost half of all fiscal expenditure. Analysts suggested that the cuts in public spending achieved in 2001 would be difficult to sustain. However, the fall in customs revenue that resulted from cuts in customs duties was partly offset by a 5.5% increase in tax revenue. The draft budget for 2002, approved by the Cabinet in September 2001, projected revenues at L£5,650,000m. (US $3700m.), 15% higher than the target for 2001, and expenditure at L£9,430,000m., 5% lower than the target for 2001, giving a deficit of L£3,780,000m. (down 24.5% on the 2001 target and equivalent to 40.1% of expenditure). While sharp cuts in public spending were the main factor in reducing the budget deficit in 2001, in 2002 the emphasis was on a sharp increase in revenue to improve fiscal performance, notably revenues from VAT introduced from the beginning of February 2002 (see above). Debt service expenditure is projected at L£4,500,000m., an increase of 4.7% on 2001 and equivalent to 47.7% of total expenditure. Non-debt expenditure, however, is targeted to fall by 12% to L£4,930,000m. mainly as a result of a 30% reduction in capital spending. However, independent analysts maintained that these cuts would be difficult to achieve in practice. In the 2003 draft budget the Government proposed reducing expenditure by 10% and increasing revenue by 16%. Reducing the budget deficit was seen as essential to proving Lebanon's financial credibility before the Paris II donor conference, scheduled for late 2002.

Statistical Survey

Source (unless otherwise stated): Central Administration for Statistics, Beirut; internet www.cas.gov.lb; Direction Générale des Douanes, Beirut.

Area and Population

AREA, POPULATION AND DENSITY

Area (sq km)	10,452*
Population (official estimate)	
15 November 1970†	
Males	1,080,015
Females	1,046,310
Total	2,126,325
Population (UN estimates at mid-year)‡	
1999	3,438,000
2000	3,496,000
2001	3,556,000
Density (per sq km) at mid-2001	340.2

* 4,036 sq miles.
† Figures are based on the results of a sample survey, excluding Palestinian refugees in camps. The total of registered Palestinian refugees in Lebanon was 384,918 at 31 December 2001.
‡ Source: UN, *World Population Prospects: The 2000 Revision.*

PRINCIPAL TOWNS (estimated population in 1975)

Beirut (capital) 1,500,000; Tarabulus (Tripoli) 160,000; Zahleh 45,000; Saida (Sidon) 38,000; Sur (Tyre) 14,000.

BIRTHS AND DEATHS (UN estimates, annual averages)

	1985–90	1990–95	1995–2000
Birth rate (per 1,000) . .	27.9	25.6	20.3
Death rate (per 1,000) . .	7.8	6.8	5.4

Source: UN, *World Population Prospects: The 2000 Revision.*

2001 (official estimates, numbers registered): Live births 83,693; Marriages 32,225; Deaths 17,568.

Expectation of life (WHO estimates, years at birth, 2000): Males 69.1; Females 73.3 (Source: WHO, *World Health Report*).

EMPLOYMENT (ISIC Major Divisions)

	1975	1985*
Agriculture, hunting, forestry and fishing .	147,724	103,400
Manufacturing	139,471	45,000
Electricity, gas and water.	6,381	10,000
Construction.	47,356	25,000
Trade, restaurants and hotels. . . .	129,716	78,000
Transport, storage and communications . .	45,529	20,500
Other services	227,921	171,000
Total	744,098	452,900

* Estimates.

1997 (provisional estimates at mid-year): Total employed 1,246,000; Unemployed 116,000; Total labour force 1,362,000.

Source: National Employment Office.

Health and Welfare

KEY INDICATORS

Fertility (births per woman, 2000).	2.2
Under-5 mortality rate (per 1,000 live births, 2000). . .	32
HIV/AIDS (% of persons aged 15–49, 1994). . . .	0.09
Physicians (per 1,000 head, 1997)	2.10
Hospital beds (per 1,000 head, 1997)	2.7
Health expenditure (1998): US $ per head (PPP) . . .	594
% of GDP	11.6
public (% of total)	18.0
Access to water (% of persons, 2000)	100
Access to sanitation (% of persons, 2000)	99
Human Development Index (2000): ranking	75
value	0.755

For sources and definitions, see explanatory note on p. vi.

Agriculture

PRINCIPAL CROPS ('000 metric tons)

	1998	1999*	2000*
Wheat	59	58	60
Barley	29	28	29
Potatoes	264	250	270
Sugar beet	300	290	330
Almonds	39	31	35
Olives	100	95	105
Cabbages	81	75	83
Lettuce	81	75	82
Tomatoes	330	325	335
Cauliflower	41	40	42
Pumpkins, squash and gourds* .	39	39	39
Cucumbers and gherkins* . .	185	180	190
Aubergines (Eggplants)* . .	40	39	45
Dry onions	83	80	85
Garlic	48	45	49
Green beans	36	36	37
Green broad beans	22	22	23
Carrots	39	35	40
Other vegetables* . . .	103	103	104
Bananas	110	105	110
Oranges	155	155	165
Tangerines, mandarins, clementines and satsumas . .	35	35	35
Lemons and limes . . .	111	111	111
Grapefruit and pomelo . .	55	54	58
Apples	119	118	120
Pears	64	63	65
Apricots	62	62	65
Cherries.	87	87	87
Peaches and nectarines . . .	50	50	52
Plums	40	35	41
Grapes	247	245	245
Watermelons	130	130	135
Cantaloupes and other melons* .	35	35	35
Other fruits and berries* . . .	158	159	159

* FAO estimates.

Source: FAO.

LIVESTOCK ('000 head, year ending September)

	1998	1999	2000*
Horses*	6	6	6
Mules*	6	6	6
Asses*	25	25	25
Cattle	80	76	75
Pigs	60	62*	64
Sheep	350	378	380
Goats	450	436	445
Poultry	30,000	31,000*	32,000

* FAO estimate(s).

Source: FAO.

LIVESTOCK PRODUCTS ('000 metric tons)

	1998	1999	2000
Beef and veal	22.4	25.0	24.3
Mutton and lamb . . .	8.8	8.8	8.9
Goat meat	7.2	7.3	7.3
Pig meat	8.3	8.5	8.7
Poultry meat*	69.0	71.3	71.3
Cows' milk	200	201*	205*
Sheep's milk	33.7	33.8*	35.0*
Goats' milk	37.0	37.5*	39.0*
Cheese	21.0	21.1	21.6
Poultry eggs	44	42*	42*
Honey	1	1*	1*
Cattle hides	3.0	3.3	3.2
Sheepskins	1.2	1.2	1.2
Goatskins	1.2	1.2	1.2
Wool: greasy	1.5	1.6*	1.7*
scoured*	1.0	1.0	1.0

* FAO estimate(s).

Source: FAO.

Forestry

ROUNDWOOD REMOVALS ('000 cubic metres, excluding bark)

	1998	1999	2000
Industrial wood*	7	7	7
Fuel wood	83†	18	19
Total	90†	25	26

* Assumed unchanged since 1992 (FAO estimates).
† FAO estimate.

Source: FAO.

SAWNWOOD PRODUCTION
('000 cubic metres, including railway sleepers)

	1998	1999	2000
Total (all broadleaved)* . .	9	9	9

* Assumed unchanged since 1991 (FAO estimates).

Source: FAO.

Fishing

(metric tons, live weight)

	1997	1998	1999
Capture	3,655	3,520	3,560
Groupers and seabasses . .	150	250	250
Porgies and seabreams . .	350	400	450
Surmullets (Red mullets) . .	150	200	200
Barracudas	200	200	200
Mullets	300	300	300
Scorpionfishes	100	100	150
Carangids	350	400	350
Clupeoids	600	600	500
Tuna-like fishes . . .	700	400	400
Mackerel-like fishes . .	300	300	300
Marine crustaceans . .	150	50	125
Aquaculture	300	400	300
Rainbow trout	300	400	300
Total catch	3,955	3,920	3,860

Source: FAO, *Yearbook of Fishery Statistics*.

Mining

(estimates, '000 metric tons)

	1998	1999	2000
Salt (unrefined)	3.5	3.5	3.5

Source: US Geological Survey.

Industry

SELECTED PRODUCTS
('000 metric tons, unless otherwise indicated)

	1998	1999	2000
Olive oil*	5.6	6.3†	6.3‡
Sunflower seed oil* . . .	0.1	5.3	5.0
Raw sugar*	37†	40†	40‡
Wine*	18.6	18.8‡	18.8‡
Beer*	11.8	9.7	9.7
Plywood ('000 cubic metres)*‡ .	34	34	34
Paper*‡	42	42	42
Cement§	3,310	3,200	3,200‖

* Source: FAO.
† Unofficial figure.
‡ FAO estimate(s).
§ Source: US Geological Survey.
‖ Estimate.

Electric energy (provisional, million kWh): 7,467 in 2000.

Finance

CURRENCY AND EXCHANGE RATES

Monetary Units
100 piastres = 1 Lebanese pound (£L).

Sterling, Dollar and Euro Equivalents (31 May 2002)
£1 sterling = £L2,211.1;
US $1 = £L1,507.5;
€1 = £L1,415.1;
£L10,000 = £4.523 sterling = $6.633 = €7.067.

Average Exchange Rate (£L per US $)
1999   1,507.8
2000   1,507.5
2001   1,507.5

Note: The official exchange rate has been maintained at US $1 = £L1,507.5 since September 1999.

BUDGET (£L million)*

Revenue†	1996	1997	1998
Tax revenue	2,868,620	2,893,690	3,315,020
Taxes on income, profits and capital gains . . .	256,590	340,090	402,500
Taxes on property	322,490	376,780	373,110
Non-recurrent taxes on property	259,720	307,480	300,720
Domestic taxes on goods and services	139,070	244,590	372,240
Excises	29,330	24,740	170,320
Import duties	1,632,000	1,741,360	1,960,940
Other current revenue . .	665,050	859,520	1,125,850
Entrepreneurial and property income	272,150	265,760	486,010
Administrative fees and charges, non-industrial and incidental sales . . .	155,000	294,810	371,720
Total	3,533,670	3,753,200	4,440,870

Expenditure	1996	1997	1998
General public services . .	874,910	1,221,880	1,115,970
Defence	797,160	823,850	810,290
Public order and safety . .	348,730	320,490	318,160
Education	476,890	722,550	695,600
Health	167,350	221,560	220,830
Social security and welfare . .	596,390	752,430	536,430
Housing and community amenities	87,090	154,120	174,180
Recreational, cultural and religious affairs and services .	67,640	67,950	65,630
Economic affairs and services .	1,662,840	1,331,790	1,035,820
Fuel and energy . . .	122,540	2,150	1,980
Mining and mineral resources, manufacturing and construction	509,080	502,170	482,250
Transport and communications	582,190	493,080	303,200
Other purposes	2,653,000	4,111,370	3,412,560
Interest payments . . .	2,653,000	3,482,000	3,352,460
Total	7,732,000	9,728,000	8,385,460
Current	6,002,000	7,761,000	6,797,460
Capital	1,730,000	1,967,000	1,588,000

* Figures, which are rounded, represent the consolidated operations of the central Government's General Budget and the Council for Development and Reconstruction. The accounts of other central government units with individual budgets (including the general social security scheme) are excluded.

† Excluding grants received from abroad (£L million): 72,000 in 1997.

Source: IMF, *Government Finance Statistics Yearbook*.

1999 (£L million): Revenue 4,868,210; Expenditure 8,453,620.
2000 (£L million): Revenue 4,552,420; Expenditure 10,424,460.
2001 (estimates, £L million): Revenue 4,900,000; Expenditure 9,900,000.
2002 (estimates, £L million): Revenue 5,500,000; Expenditure 9,375,000.

Source: Ministry of Finance.

INTERNATIONAL RESERVES (US $ million at 31 December)

	1999	2000	2001
Gold*	2,678.0	2,524.6	2,561.1
IMF special drawing rights . .	22.5	23.7	24.3
Reserve position in IMF . .	25.8	24.5	23.7
Foreign exchange . . .	7,727.3	5,895.4	4,965.8
Total	10,453.6	8,468.3	7,574.9

* Valued at US $290.40 per troy ounce in 1999, at $273.75 per ounce in 2000 and at $277.70 per ounce in 2001.

Source: IMF, *International Financial Statistics*.

MONEY SUPPLY (£L '000 million at 31 December)

	1999	2000	2001
Currency outside banks . .	1,369.3	1,423.4	1,381.7
Demand deposits at commercial banks	845.8	862.2	889.6
Total money (incl. others) . .	2,260.8	2,389.3	2,365.3

Source: IMF, *International Financial Statistics*.

COST OF LIVING
(Consumer Price Index for Beirut; base: 1990 = 100)

	1995	1996	1997
Food and beverages . . .	349.6	379.3	377.1
Fuel and light	349.3	390.8	504.8
Clothing and footwear* . . .	259.0	261.0	261.4
Rent	8,944.7	9,190.9	9,252.3
All items (incl. others) . . .	412.7	438.1	447.1

* Including household linen.

Source: ILO, *Yearbook of Labour Statistics*.

NATIONAL ACCOUNTS
(UN estimates, £L '000 million at current prices)

Expenditure on the Gross Domestic Product

	1997	1998	1999
Government final consumption expenditure	2,544.7	2,594.3	2,581.3
Private final consumption expenditure	24,240.3	25,086.3	25,389.8
Increase in stocks . . . } Gross fixed capital formation . }	6,011.2	5,996.1	5,756.1
Total domestic expenditure	32,796.1	33,676.7	33,727.3
Exports of goods and services . .	1,632.3	1,829.5	1,993.4
Less Imports of goods and services	11,548.0	10,996.8	10,598.5
GDP in purchasers' values .	22,880.4	24,509.5	25,122.2
GDP at constant 1995 prices	19,230.3	19,807.2	20,005.2

Source: UN Economic and Social Commission for Western Asia, *National Accounts Studies of the ESCWA Region* (2000).

Gross Domestic Product by Economic Activity

	1997	1998	1999
Agriculture, hunting, forestry and fishing	2,522.8	2,601.5	2,612.9
Manufacturing	2,372.9	2,441.0	2,459.5
Electricity, gas and water . .	1,393.1	1,487.2	1,510.7
Construction	1,248.1	1,069.9	1,040.6
Trade, restaurants and hotels . .	6,528.4	6,757.4	6,679.1
Transport, storage and communications . . .	518.5	569.9	565.0
Finance, insurance, real estate and business services . .	4,323.3	5,360.7	5,972.9
Government services . . .	2,000.9	2,063.9	2,106.5
Other community, social and personal services . . .	1,972.5	2,158.1	2,175.0
GDP in purchasers' values .	22,880.4	24,509.5	25,122.2

Source: UN Economic and Social Commission for Western Asia, *National Accounts Studies of the ESCWA Region* (2000).

2000 (estimates, % of GDP): Agriculture 11.8, Industry 20.8, Services 67.4 (Source: World Bank).

BALANCE OF PAYMENTS (US $ million)

	1998	1999	2000
Exports of goods f.o.b. . . .	716	678	718
Imports of goods c.i.f. . . .	−7,060	−6,206	−6,228
Trade balance	−6,344	−5,528	−5,510
Services, income and current transfers (net)	481	−98	−120
Current balance	−5,863	−5,626	−5,630
Capital account (net) . . .	5,375	5,887	5,341
Overall balance	−487	261	−289

Source: Ministry of Economy and Trade.

External Trade

PRINCIPAL COMMODITIES (US $ million)*

Imports c.i.f.	1999	2000	2001
Live animals and animal products	349.8	336.1	359.4
Vegetable products	355.5	328.7	361.9
Prepared foodstuffs; beverages, spirits and vinegar; tobacco and manufactured substitutes	463.6	415.3	502.7
Mineral products	613.4	1,095.6	1,340.6
Products of chemical or allied industries	574.8	525.5	595.4
Plastics, rubber and articles thereof	230.6	222.0	257.8
Textiles and textile articles	386.2	352.0	464.7
Natural or cultured pearls, precious or semi-precious stones, precious metals and articles thereof; imitation jewellery; coin	461.7	423.3	363.9
Base metals and articles thereof	407.3	382.1	426.7
Machinery and mechanical appliances; electrical equipment; sound and television apparatus	910.2	800.4	999.0
Vehicles, aircraft, vessels and associated transport equipment	615.2	555.3	712.6
Total (incl. others)	6,206.5	6,227.9	7,291.1

Exports f.o.b.	1999	2000	2001
Vegetable products	52.3	48.5	49.8
Prepared foodstuffs; beverages, spirits and vinegar; tobacco and manufactured substitutes	74.0	72.5	99.7
Products of chemical or allied industries	84.9	88.4	88.1
Paper-making material; paper and paperboard and articles thereof	54.4	53.5	60.2
Textiles and textile articles	54.6	41.5	77.0
Natural or cultured pearls, precious or semi-precious stones, precious metals and articles thereof; imitation jewellery; coin	95.6	126.8	140.9
Base metals and articles thereof	78.6	63.1	65.2
Machinery and mechanical appliances; electrical equipment; sound and television apparatus	72.8	74.8	114.4
Total (incl. others)	676.8	714.3	889.3

* Figures are calculated on the basis of the official dollar rate, which is the previous month's average exchange rate of Lebanese pounds per US dollar.

Source: Ministry of Economy and Trade; Banque du Liban.

PRINCIPAL TRADING PARTNERS (US $ million)*

Imports c.i.f.	1999	2000	2001
Belgium	116.4	108.0	135.3
China, People's Republic	261.5	287.1	410.9
France	594.8	526.5	614.9
Germany	552.7	519.6	623.1
Greece	111.7	157.2	142.1
Ireland	89.9	n.a.	n.a.
Italy	679.0	679.9	708.4
Japan	259.0	210.9	235.4
Korea, Republic	n.a.	74.7	100.7
Netherlands	114.3	124.6	129.2
Russia	n.a.	215.2	409.3
Saudi Arabia	102.6	164.9	259.5
Spain	147.7	136.3	184.4
Switzerland	443.0	431.5	333.7
Syria	223.5	283.3	327.9
Taiwan	82.6	69.9	77.4
Turkey	163.9	138.5	237.2
Ukraine	108.9	88.4	125.8
United Kingdom	271.7	243.4	284.7
USA	500.9	457.4	515.0
Total (incl. others)	6,203.9	6,227.9	7,291.1

Exports f.o.b.	1999	2000	2001
Belgium	10.9	n.a.	n.a.
Cyprus	7.4	n.a.	n.a.
Egypt	15.3	22.4	23.9
France	52.1	30.1	38.2
Germany	24.5	17.7	17.2
India	14.7	13.9	14.2
Iraq	21.8	33.4	68.0
Italy	19.0	22.0	26.2
Jordan	27.0	31.2	30.7
Kuwait	30.4	26.3	27.8
Malta	6.8	11.0	20.3
Netherlands	15.3	13.6	15.7
Saudi Arabia	70.9	77.7	85.4
Spain	12.2	18.6	18.2
Switzerland	44.6	51.0	63.2
Syria	32.3	25.8	35.2
Turkey	14.4	23.2	24.8
United Arab Emirates	53.9	74.9	72.9
United Kingdom	24.3	11.0	14.3
USA	42.0	46.4	60.8
Total (incl. others)	676.8	714.2	889.3

* Imports by country of production; exports by country of last consignment.

Source: mainly Banque du Liban.

Transport

ROAD TRAFFIC (motor vehicles in use)

	1995	1996*	1997*
Passenger cars (incl. taxis)	1,197,521	1,217,000	1,299,398
Buses and coaches	5,514	5,640	6,833
Lorries and vans	79,222	81,000	85,242
Motorcycles and mopeds	53,317	54,450	61,471

* Estimates.

Source: International Road Federation, *World Road Statistics*.

SHIPPING

Merchant Fleet (registered at 31 December)

	1999	2000	2001
Number of vessels	106	105	99
Total displacement ('000 grt)	322.2	362.7	301.7

Source: Lloyd's Register-Fairplay, *World Fleet Statistics*.

International Sea-borne Freight Traffic ('000 metric tons)

	1988	1989	1990
Goods loaded	148	150	152
Goods unloaded	1,120	1,140	1,150

Source: UN, *Monthly Bulletin of Statistics*.

2001 ('000 metric tons, Beirut port only): Goods loaded 330; Goods unloaded 5,134.

CIVIL AVIATION (revenue traffic on scheduled services)

	1996	1997	1998
Kilometres flown (million)	19	21	20
Passengers carried ('000)	775	857	716
Passenger-km (million)	1,857	2,116	1,504
Total ton-km (million)	252	319	247

Source: UN, *Statistical Yearbook*.

Tourism

FOREIGN TOURIST ARRIVALS ('000)*

Country of nationality	1998	1999	2000
Australia	24.3	27.6	30.6
Canada	22.3	28.1	30.2
Egypt	39.2	34.4	35.7
France	58.5	67.0	64.8
Germany	27.1	30.0	35.4
Iran	6.0	14.0	23.2
Italy	14.7	15.8	14.7
Jordan	53.6	61.0	69.6
Kuwait	40.2	41.1	47.6
Saudi Arabia	71.1	82.6	98.3
Sri Lanka	16.6	10.3	16.5
United Kingdom	22.0	22.3	24.3
USA	31.4	40.4	43.3
Total (incl. others)	630.8	673.3	741.6

* Figures exclude arrivals of Syrian nationals, Palestinians and students.

Source: World Tourism Organization, *Yearbook of Tourism Statistics.*

Tourism receipts (US $ million): 1,221 in 1998; 673 in 1999; 742 in 2000 (Source: World Tourism Organization).

Communications Media

	1998	1999	2000
Television receivers ('000 in use)	1,120	1,150	1,170
Telephones ('000 main lines in use)	620.0	650.0	681.5
Mobile cellular telephones ('000 subscribers)	505.3	627.0	743.0
Personal computers ('000 in use)	125	150	175
Internet users ('000)	100	200	300

Personal computers ('000 in use): 200 in 2001.
Radio receivers ('000 in use): 2,850 in 1997.
Facsimile machines (number in use): 3,000 in 1992.
Daily newspapers (1996): 15 titles; average circulation (estimate, '000 copies) 435.
Non-daily newspapers (estimates, 1988): 15 titles; average circulation 240,000 copies.

Sources: UNESCO, *Statistical Yearbook*; UN, *Statistical Yearbook*; International Telecommunication Union.

Education

(1996/97, unless otherwise indicated)

	Institutions	Teachers	Students
Pre-primary	1,938	67,935†	164,397*
Primary	2,160		382,309*
Secondary:			
General	n.a.		292,002*
Vocational	275†	7,745	55,848*
Higher	n.a.	10,444‡	81,588‡

* Estimate.   † 1994 figure.   ‡ 1995/96 figure.

Sources: UNESCO, *Statistical Yearbook*; Banque du Liban, *Annual Report.*

Adult literacy rate (UNESCO estimates): 86.0% (males 92.1%; females 80.3%) in 2000 (Source: UNDP, *Human Development Report*).

Directory

The Constitution

The Constitution was promulgated on 23 May 1926 and amended by the Constitutional Laws of 1927, 1929, 1943, 1947 and 1990.

According to the Constitution, the Republic of Lebanon is an independent and sovereign state, and no part of the territory may be alienated or ceded. Lebanon has no state religion. Arabic is the official language. Beirut is the capital.

All Lebanese are equal in the eyes of the law. Personal freedom and freedom of the press are guaranteed and protected. The religious communities are entitled to maintain their own schools, on condition that they conform to the general requirements relating to public instruction, as defined by the state. Dwellings are inviolable; rights of ownership are protected by law. Every Lebanese citizen over 21 is an elector and qualifies for the franchise.

LEGISLATIVE POWER

Legislative power is exercised by one house, the National Assembly, with 108 seats (raised, without amendment of the Constitution, to 128 in 1992), which are divided equally between Christians and Muslims. Members of the National Assembly must be over 25 years of age, in possession of their full political and civil rights, and literate. They are considered representative of the whole nation, and are not bound to follow directives from their constituencies.

They can be suspended only by a two-thirds majority of their fellow-members. Secret ballot was introduced in a new election law of April 1960.

The National Assembly holds two sessions yearly, from the first Tuesday after 15 March to the end of May, and from the first Tuesday after 15 October to the end of the year. The normal term of the National Assembly is four years; general elections take place within 60 days before the end of this period. If the Assembly is dissolved before the end of its term, elections are held within three months of dissolution.

Voting in the Assembly is public—by acclamation, or by standing and sitting. A quorum of two-thirds and a majority vote is required for constitutional issues. The only exceptions to this occur when the Assembly becomes an electoral college, and chooses the President of the Republic, or Secretaries to the National Assembly, or when the President is accused of treason or of violating the Constitution. In such cases voting is secret, and a two-thirds majority is needed for a proposal to be adopted.

EXECUTIVE POWER

With the incorporation of the Ta'if agreement into the Lebanese Constitution in August 1990, executive power was effectively transferred from the presidency to the Cabinet. The President is elected for a term of six years and is not immediately re-eligible. He is responsible for the promulgation and execution of laws enacted

733

by the National Assembly, but all presidential decisions (with the exception of those to appoint a Prime Minister or to accept the resignation of a government) require the co-signature of the Prime Minister, who is head of the Government, implementing its policies and speaking in its name. The President must receive the approval of the Cabinet before dismissing a minister or ratifying an international treaty. The ministers and the Prime Minister are chosen by the President of the Republic in consultation with the members and President of the National Assembly. They are not necessarily members of the National Assembly, although they are responsible to it and have access to its debates. The President of the Republic must be a Maronite Christian, and the Prime Minister a Sunni Muslim; the choice of the other ministers must reflect the level of representation of the communities in the Assembly.

Note: In October 1998 the National Assembly endorsed an exceptional amendment to Article 49 of the Constitution to enable the election of Gen. Emile Lahoud, then Commander-in-Chief of the armed forces, as President of the Republic: the Constitution requires that senior state officials relinquish their responsibilities two years prior to seeking public office.

The Government

HEAD OF STATE

President: Gen. EMILE LAHOUD (inaugurated 24 November 1998).

CABINET
(September 2002)

Prime Minister: RAFIK HARIRI.

Deputy Prime Minister: ISSAM FARES.

Minister of Foreign Affairs and Emigrants: MAHMOUD HAMMOUD.

Minister of the Interior and Municipalities: ELIAS MURR.

Minister of National Defence: KHALIL HRAWI.

Minister of the Displaced: MARWAN HAMADEH.

Minister of Industry: GEORGE EPHRAM.

Minister of Energy and Water: MUHAMMAD ABD AL-HAMID BAYDOUN.

Minister of Public Health: SULAYMAN FRANJIYA.

Minister of Social Affairs: ASSAD DIEB.

Minister of Finance: FOUAD SINIORA.

Minister of Education and Higher Education: ABD AR-RAHIM MRAD.

Minister of the Environment: MICHEL MOUSSA.

Minister of Tourism: KARAM KARAM.

Minister of Public Works and Transport: NAJIB MIQATI.

Minister of Youth and Sports: SEBOUH HOFNANIAN.

Minister of Information: GHAZI ARIDI.

Minister of Economy and Trade: BASSEL FLEIHAN.

Minister of Justice: SAMIR JISR.

Minister of Labour: ALI KANSO.

Minister of Culture: GHASSAN SALAMEH.

Minister of Agriculture: ALI AJAJ ABDULLAH.

Minister of Telecommunications: JEAN-LOUIS KORDAHI.

Minister of State for Administrative Reform: FOUAD SAAD.

Ministers of State without portfolio: BAHIJ TABARA, PIERRE HELOU, TALAL ARSLAN, BESHARA MERHEJ, MICHEL PHARAOUN, NAZIH HABIB BAYDOUN.

MINISTRIES

Office of the President: Presidential Palace, Baabda, Beirut; tel. (5) 920900; fax (5) 922400; e-mail president_office@presidency.gov.lb; internet www.presidency.gov.lb.

Office of the President of the Council of Ministers: Grand Sérail, place Riad es-Solh, Beirut; tel. (1) 746800; fax (1) 865630.

Ministry of Agriculture: blvd Camille Chamoun, Beirut; tel. (1) 455631; fax (1) 455475; e-mail ministry@agriculture.gov.lb; internet www.agriculture.gov.lb.

Ministry of Culture: Beirut.

Ministry of the Displaced: Damour, Beirut; tel. (1) 325726; fax (1) 503040; e-mail mod@dm.net.lb.

Ministry of Economy and Trade: rue Artois, Hamra, Beirut; tel. (1) 340503; fax (1) 354640; e-mail postmaster@economy.gov.lb; internet www.economy.gov.lb.

Ministry of Education and Higher Education: Campus de l'Unesco, Beirut; tel. (1) 866430; fax (1) 645844.

Ministry of Energy and Water: Shiah, Beirut; tel. (1) 270256.

Ministry of the Environment: POB 70-1091, Antélias, Beirut; tel. (4) 522222; fax (4) 525080; e-mail webmaster@moe.gov.lb; internet www.moe.gov.lb.

Ministry of Finance: Immeuble MOF, place Riad es-Solh, Beirut; tel. (1) 981001; fax (1) 981059; e-mail infocenter@finance.gov.lb; internet www.finance.gov.lb.

Ministry of Foreign Affairs and Emigrants: rue Sursock, Achrafieh, Beirut; tel. (1) 333100; responsible for **General Directorate of Emigrants:** Beirut; e-mail info@emigrants.gov.lb; internet www.emigrants.gov.lb.

Ministry of Industry: rue Sami Solh, Beirut; tel. (1) 427042; fax (1) 427112; e-mail ministry@industry.gov.lb; internet www.industry.gov.lb.

Ministry of Information: rue Hamra, Beirut; tel. (1) 345800.

Ministry of the Interior and Municipalities: Grand Sérail, place Riad es-Solh, Beirut; tel. (1) 863910.

Ministry of Justice: rue Sami Solh, Beirut; tel. (1) 422953; e-mail justice@ministry.gov.lb; internet www.justice.gov.lb.

Ministry of Labour: Shiah, Beirut; tel. (1) 274140.

Ministry of National Defence: Yarze, Beirut; tel. (5) 452400; fax (5) 958757; e-mail ministry@leb-army.gov.lb.

Ministry of Public Health: place du Musée, Beirut; tel. (1) 645087; fax (1) 645062; e-mail mphealth@cyberia.net.lb; internet www.public-health.gov.lb.

Ministry of Public Works and Transport: Shiah, Beirut; tel. (1) 428980; internet www.public-works.gov.lb.

Ministry of State for Administrative Reform: Immeuble Starco, 5e étage, rue George Picot, Beirut; tel. (1) 371510; fax (1) 371599; e-mail newsletter@omsar.gov.lb; internet www.omsar.gov.lb.

Ministry of State for Affairs of the South and Reconstruction: Beirut.

Ministry of Telecommunications: rue Sami Solh, 3e étage, Beirut; tel. (1) 424400; fax (1) 888310; e-mail webmaster@mpt.gov.lb; internet www.mpt.gov.lb.

Ministry of Tourism: POB 11-5344, rue Banque du Liban 550, Beirut; tel. (1) 340940; fax (1) 340945; e-mail mot@lebanon-tourism.gov.lb; internet www.lebanon-tourism.gov.lb.

Ministry of Youth and Sports: Beirut.

Legislature

MAJLIS ALNWAB
(National Assembly)

The equal distribution of seats among Christians and Muslims is determined by law, and the Cabinet must reflect the level of representation achieved by the various religious denominations within that principal division. Deputies of the same religious denomination do not necessarily share the same political, or party allegiances. The distribution of seats is as follows: Maronite Catholics 34; Sunni Muslims 27; Shi'a Muslims 27; Greek Orthodox 14; Druzes 8; Greek-Melkite Catholics 8; Armenian Orthodox 5; Alawites 2; Armenian Catholics 1; Protestants 1; Others 1.

President: NABIH BERRI.

Vice-President: ELIE FERZLI.

General election, 27 August and 3 September 2000

Party list	Seats
Resistance and Development	23
Al-Karamah (Dignity)	18
Ba'albek-Hermel al-Ii'tilafiah (Ba'albek-Hermel Coalition)	9
Al-Jabhar an-Nidal al-Watani (National Defence Front)	8
Wahdal al-Jabal (Mountain Union)	7
Ii'tilafiah (Coalition)	6
Al-Karal (Decision)	6
Al-Kitla al-Chaabi—Elias Shaft (People's Front—Elias Shaft)	5
Al-Wifah al-Matni (Metn Accord)	5
Al-Karamah wah Tajdid (Dignity and Renewal)	5
Al-Karal al-Chaabi (Popular Decision)	3
Al-Wifac at-Tajdid (Reconciliation and Renewal)	3
Al-Irada al-Chaabia (Popular Will)	3
Al-Karamah al-Wataniyah (National Dignity)	2
At-Tawafoc al-Watani (National Understanding)	1
Al-Kitla al-Chaabi—Fouad el Turk (People's Front—Fouad el Turk)	1
Lubnan (Lebanon)	1
Al-Hurriya (Freedom)	1
Independents	20
Others	1
Total	**128**

Political Organizations

Amal (Hope): f. 1975; Shi'ite politico-military organization which in recent years has become more akin to a political party; Principal Controller of Command Council Sheikh MUHAMMAD MANDI SHAMS AD-DIN; Chair. SADR AD-DIN AS-SADR; Leader NABIH BERRI.

Armenian Revolutionary Federation (ARF): rue Spears, Beirut; f. 1890; principal Armenian party; also known as Tashnag Party, which was the dominant nationalist party in the independent Armenian Republic of Yerevan of 1917–21, prior to its becoming part of the USSR; socialist ideology; collective leadership.

Al-Baath: f. in Syria, 1940, by Michel Aflak; secular pro-Syrian party with policy of Arab union, branches in several Middle Eastern countries; Sec.-Gen. ABDULLAH AL-AMIN, Beirut.

Al-Baath: pro-Iraqi wing of Al-Baath party; Sec.-Gen. ABD AL-MAJID RAFEI.

Bloc national libanais: rue Pasteur, Gemmayze, Beirut; tel. (1) 584585; fax (1) 584591; f. 1943; right-wing Lebanese party with policy of power-sharing between Christians and Muslims and the exclusion of the military from politics; Pres. SÉLIM SALHAB; Sec.-Gen. JEAN HAWAT.

Hezbollah (Party of God): Beirut; e-mail hizbollahmedia@hizbollah.org; internet www.hizbollah.org; f. 1982 by Iranian Revolutionary Guards who were sent to Lebanon; militant Shi'ite faction which has become the leading organization of Lebanon's Shi'a community and a recognized political party; demands the withdrawal of Israeli forces from the occupied Shebaa Farms area of southern Lebanon and the release of all Lebanese prisoners from Israeli detention; Chair. MUHAMMAD RA'D; Spiritual leader MUHAMMAD HUSSEIN FADLALLAH; Leader and Sec.-Gen. Sheikh HASAN NASRALLAH.

Al-Katae'b (Phalanges Libanaises, Phalangist Party): POB 992, place Charles Hélou, Beirut; tel. (1) 584107; e-mail admin@kataeb.com; internet www.lebanese-kataeb.org; f. 1936 by the late PIERRE GEMAYEL; nationalist, reformist, democratic social party; largest Maronite party; 100,000 mems; announced merger with Parti national libéral, May 1979; Pres. MOUNIR EL-HAJJ; Sec.-Gen. JOSEPH ABOU KHALIL.

Lebanese Democratic Movement: Beirut; Pres. JACQUES TAMER; Sec.-Gen. NAJI HATAB.

An-Najjadé (The Helpers): c/o Sawt al-Uruba, POB 3537, Beirut; f. 1936; Arab socialist unionist party; 3,000 mems; Founder and Pres. ADNANE MOUSTAFA AL-HAKIM.

National Lebanese Front: Beirut; f. 1999; Pres. ERNEST KARAM.

Parti communiste libanais (Lebanese Communist Party): Beirut; e-mail info@communistparty-lb.org; internet www.communistparty-lb.org; f. 1924; officially dissolved 1948–71; Marxist, much support among intellectuals; Pres. MAURICE NOHRA; Sec.-Gen. FARUQ DAHRUJ.

Parti national libéral (PNL) (Al-Wataniyin al-Ahrar): POB 165576, rue du Liban, Beirut; tel. (1) 338000; fax (1) 200335; e-mail ahrar@ahrar.org.lb; internet www.ahrar.org.lb; f. 1958; liberal reformist secular party, although has traditionally had a predominantly Maronite Christian membership; Pres. DORY CHAMOUN.

Parti socialiste nationaliste syrien: internet www.ssnp.com; f. 1932, banned 1962–69; advocates a 'Greater Syria', composed of Lebanon, Syria, Iraq, Jordan, Palestine and Cyprus; Leader JIBRAN ARAIJI.

Parti socialiste progressiste (At-Takadumi al-Ishteraki—PSP): POB 2893, Moussaitbé, Beirut; tel. and fax (1) 301231; e-mail secretary@psp.org.lb; internet www.psp.org.lb; f. 1949; progressive party, advocates constitutional road to socialism and democracy; over 25,000 mems; mainly Druze support; Pres. WALID JOUMBLATT; Sec.-Gen. SHARIF FAYAD.

Al-Wa'ad (National Secular Democratic Party—Pledge): Beirut; f. after 1975–90 civil war by the late ELIE HOBEIKA; Leader (vacant).

Other parties include the **Independent Nasserite Movement** (Murabitoun; Sunni Muslim Militia; Leader IBRAHIM QULAYAT) and the **Lebanese Popular Congress** (Pres. KAMAL SHATILA). The **Nasserite Popular Organization** and the **Arab Socialist Union** merged in January 1987, retaining the name of the former (Sec.-Gen. MUSTAFA SAAD). The **Islamic Amal** is a breakaway group from Amal, based in Ba'albek (Leader HUSSEIN MOUSSAVI). **Islamic Jihad** (Islamic Holy War) is a pro-Iranian fundamentalist guerrilla group (Leader IMAAD MOUGNIEH). The **Popular Liberation Army** is a Sunni Muslim faction, active in the south of Lebanon (Leader MUSTAFA SAAD). **Tawheed Islami** (the Islamic Unification Movement; f. 1982; Sunni Muslim) and the **Arab Democratic Party** (or the Red Knights; Alawites; pro-Syrian; Leader ALI EID) are based in Tripoli.

Diplomatic Representation

EMBASSIES IN LEBANON

Algeria: POB 4794, face Hôtel Summerland, rue Jnah, Beirut; tel. (1) 826711; fax (1) 826712; Ambassador: AHMAD BOUTEHRI.

Argentina: Immeuble Khaled Daouk, 2e étage, Rue Melki/Omar Daouk, Centre Ville, Mina el Hosn, Beirut; tel. (1) 987900; fax (1) 987903; e-mail embarg@cyberia.net.lb; Ambassador: JOSÉ PEDRO PICO.

Armenia: POB 70607, rue Jasmin, Mtaileb, Beirut; tel. (4) 418860; fax (4) 402952; e-mail armenia@dm.net.lb; Ambassador: AREG HOVHANNISSIAN.

Australia: POB 11-1860, Farra Bldg, Bliss St, Ras Beirut; tel. (1) 374701; fax (1) 374709; e-mail austemle@cyberia.net.lb; internet www.lebanon.embassy.gov.au; Ambassador: STEPHANIE SHWABSKY.

Austria: Achrafieh, Beirut; tel. (1) 217360; fax (1) 217772; e-mail beirutob@bmaa.gv.at; Ambassador: Dr HELMUT FREUDENSCHUSS.

Bahrain: Sheikh Ahmed ath-Thani Bldg, Raoucheh, Beirut; tel. (1) 805495; Ambassador: MUHAMMAD BAHLOUL.

Belgium: Central District, Beirut; tel. (1) 976001; fax (1) 976007; e-mail beirut@diplobel.org; Ambassador: FRANÇOISE GUSTIN.

Bolivia: Dora, Beirut; tel. (1) 240711; fax (1) 240710; Chargé d'affaires a.i.: GEORGES NAGIB GHOSN.

Brazil: POB 166175, rue des Antonins, Baabda, Beirut; tel. (5) 921256; fax (5) 923001; Chargé d'affaires a.i.: RICARDO ALONSO BASTOS.

Bulgaria: POB 11-6544, Immeuble Hibri, rue de l'Australie 55, Raouche, Beirut; tel. (1) 861352; fax (1) 800265; e-mail bgemb_lb@hotmail.com; Ambassador: NIKOLAI ANDREEV.

Canada: POB 60163, 1e étage, Immeuble Coolrite, Autostrade Jal ed-Dib, Beirut; tel. (4) 713900; fax (4) 710595; e-mail berut@dfait-maeci.gc.ca; internet www.canada-lb.org; Ambassador: MICHEL DUVAL.

Chile: Beirut; tel. (4) 418670; fax (4) 418672; Ambassador: OVID HARASICH.

China, People's Republic: POB 11-8227, rue Nicolas Ibrahim Sursock 72, Mar Elias, Beirut; tel. (1) 850314; fax (1) 822492; e-mail emb.prc@dm.net.lb; Ambassador: LIU ZHENTANG.

Colombia: 5th Floor, Mazda Centre, Jal ed-Dib, Beirut; tel. (4) 712646; fax (4) 712656; e-mail colombia@cyberia.net.lb; Chargé d'affaires a.i.: ARMANDO ECHEVERRI JIMÉNEZ.

Cuba: Immeuble Ghazzal, rue Abd as-Sabbah, rue Sakiet el-Janzir/rue de Vienne, Beirut; tel. (1) 805025; fax (1) 810339; Ambassador: ENRIQUE ROMÁN HERNANDEZ.

Czech Republic: POB 40195, Baabda, Beirut; tel. (5) 468763; fax (5) 922120; e-mail czechemb@cyberia.net.lb; Ambassador: EVA FILIPIOVA.

Denmark: POB 11-5190, Immeuble 812 Tabaris, 3e étage, ave Charles Malek, Achrafieh, Beirut; tel. (1) 335828; fax (1) 335851; e-mail dk-emb@dm.net.lb; Ambassador: OLE WØHLERS OLSEN.

Egypt: rue Thomas Eddison, Beirut; tel. (1) 867917; fax (1) 863751; Ambassador: HATEM SEIF EL-NASR.

France: Résidence des Pins, Mar-Takla, Beirut; tel. (1) 420000; fax (1) 420007; e-mail ambafr@ciberia.net.lb; internet www.amba france-liban.org.lb; Ambassador: PHILIPPE LECOURTIER.

Gabon: Hadath, Beirut; tel. (5) 924875; fax (5) 924643; Ambassador: SIMON NTOUTOUME EMANE.

Germany: POB 11-2820, near Jesus and Mary High School, Rabieh/Mtaileb, Beirut; tel. (4) 914444; fax (4) 914450; e-mail germanemb@germanembassy.org.lb; internet www.germanembassy.org.lb; Ambassador: GISELA KAEMPFFE-SIKORA.

Greece: POB 16-6516, Immeuble Boukhater, rue des Ambassades, Naccache, Beirut; tel. (4) 521700; fax (4) 418772; Ambassador: GEORGES GABRIELIDES.

Holy See: POB 1061, Jounieh (Apostolic Nunciature); tel. (9) 903102; fax (9) 903763; e-mail naliban@opuslibani.org; Apostolic Nuncio: Most Rev. LUIGI GATTI, Titular Archbishop of Santa Giusta.

Hungary: POB 90618, Centre Massoud, Fanar, Beirut; tel. (1) 898840; fax (1) 873391; e-mail huembbej@inco.com.lb; Ambassador: PÁL JENÖ FÁBIÁN.

India: POB 113-5240, Immeuble Sahmarani, rue Kantari 31, Hamra, Beirut; tel. (1) 373539; fax (1) 373538; e-mail indembei@dm.net.lb; Ambassador: NANTU SARKAR.

Indonesia: Baabda, Beirut; tel. (5) 924682; fax (5) 924678; Ambassador: Maj. Gen. SYAN SOEMANEGARA.

Iran: Immeuble Sakina Mattar, Jnah, Beirut; tel. (1) 821224; fax (1) 821230; Chargé d'affaires a.i.: REZA GHOMI.

Italy: Immeuble Assicurazioni Generali, Beirut; tel. (1) 985200; fax (1) 985303; e-mail amb@ambitaliabeirut.org; internet www.ambital iabeirut.org; Ambassador: FRANCO MISTRETTA.

Japan: POB 11-3360, Army St, Zkak al-Blat, Serail Hill, Beirut; tel. (1) 985751; fax (1) 989754; e-mail japanemb@japanemb.org.lb; internet www.lb.emb-japan.go.jp; Ambassador: NAOTO AMAKI.

Jordan: POB 109, Baabda; tel. (5) 922500; fax (5) 922502; e-mail joremb@dm.net.lb; Ambassador: ANMAR AL-HMOUD.

Korea, Republic: Baabda, Beirut; tel. (5) 922151; fax (5) 922153; Ambassador: KI-HYUN LEE.

Kuwait: Rond-point du Stade, Bir Hassan, Beirut; tel. (1) 822515; fax (1) 840613; Ambassador: ALI SULEIMAN AS-SAEID.

Libya: Beirut; tel. (1) 806314; fax (1) 805349; Ambassador: (vacant).

Mexico: Beirut; tel. (4) 418870; fax (4) 418873; e-mail emba mex@dm.net.lb; internet www.embamex.org.lb; Ambassador. VICTOR MANUEL SOLANO MONTANO.

Morocco: Bir Hassan, Beirut; tel. (1) 859829; fax (1) 859839; e-mail sifmar@cyberia.net.lb; Ambassador: ABD AL-JALIL FENJIRO.

Netherlands: POB 167190, ABN AMRO Tower, 9e étage, ave Charles Malek, Achrafieh, Beirut; tel. (1) 204663; fax (1) 204664; e-mail nlgovbei@sodetel.net.lb; internet www.netherlandsembas sy.org.lb; Ambassador: JAN PIET KLEIWEG DE ZWAAN.

Norway: Immeuble Dimashki, rue Bliss, Ras Beirut, Beirut; tel. (1) 372977; fax (1) 372979; Ambassador: SVEIN SEVJE.

Pakistan: POB 135506, Immeuble Shell, 11e étage, Raoucheh, Beirut; tel. (1) 863041; fax (1) 864583; e-mail pakemblb@cyberia .net.lb; Ambassador: KHALID M. MIR.

Philippines: Raoucheh, Beirut; tel. (1) 791092; fax (1) 791095; Ambassador FORTUNATO OBLENA.

Poland: POB 40-215, Immeuble Khalifa, ave Président Sulayman Franjiya 52, Baabda, Beirut; tel. (5) 924881; fax (5) 924882; e-mail polamb@cyberia.net.lb; Chargé d'affaires: LIDIA MILKA WIECZORKIE-WICZ.

Qatar: POB 6717, Beirut; tel. (1) 865271; fax (1) 810460; Ambassador: ABDALLAH BIN MUHAMMAD AL-KHATER.

Romania: Route du Palais Presidentiel, Baabda, Beirut; tel. (5) 924848; fax (5) 924747; e-mail romembey@inco.com.lb; Chargé d'affaires a.i.: AUREL CALIN.

Russia: rue Mar Elias et-Tineh, Wata Mseitbeh, Beirut; tel. (1) 300041; fax (1) 303837; Ambassador: BORIS BOLOTINE.

Saudi Arabia: rue Bliss, Manara, Beirut; tel. (1) 860351; fax (1) 860411; Ambassador: FUAD BIN SADEK MUFTI.

Spain: POB 11-3039, Riad es-Solh, Beirut; tel. (5) 464120; fax (5) 464030; e-mail embspain@cyberia.net.lb; Ambassador: MIGUEL ANGEL CARRIEDO.

Sri Lanka: Baabda, Beirut; tel. (5) 924765; fax (5) 924768; Ambassador MUHAMMAD ISMAIL MUHSEN.

Sudan: Hamra, Beirut; tel. (1) 350057; fax (1) 353271; Ambassador: SAYED AHMAD AL-BAKHIT.

Switzerland: Beirut; tel. (1) 324129; fax (1) 324167; Ambassador: THOMAS LITSCHER.

Tunisia: Hazmieh, Mar-Takla, Beirut; tel. (5) 457431; fax (5) 950434; Ambassador: FETHI HOUIDI.

Turkey: POB 11-5031, zone II, rue 3, Rabieh, Beirut; tel. (4) 412080; fax (4) 407557; e-mail trbebeyr@intracom.net.lb; Ambassador: CELALETTIN KART.

Ukraine: POB 431, Jardin al-Bacha, Jisr al-Bacha, Sin el-Fil, Beirut; tel.(1) 510527; fax (1) 510531; e-mail ukrembassy@inco.c-om.lb; internet www.ukremblebanon.com; Ambassador: VALERII RYLACH.

United Arab Emirates: Immeuble Wafic Tanbara, Jnah, Beirut; tel. (1) 857000; fax (1) 857009; Ambassador: MUHAMMAD HAMAD OMRAN.

United Kingdom: POB 11-471, Embassies Complex, Army St, Zkak al-Blat, Serail Hill, Beirut; tel. (1) 990400; fax (1) 990420; e-mail britemb@cyberia.net.lb; internet www.britishembassy.org.lb; Ambassador: RICHARD KINCHEN.

USA: POB 70-840, Antélias, Aoucar, Beirut; tel. (4) 542600; fax (4) 544136; e-mail pas@inco.com.lb; internet www.usembassy.gov.lb; Ambassador: VINCENT M. BATTLE.

Uruguay: POB 2051, Centre Stella Marris, 7e étage, rue Banque du Liban, Jounieh; tel. (9) 636529; fax (9) 636531; e-mail uruliban@dm.net.lb; Ambassador: ALBERTO VOSS RUBIO.

Venezuela: POB 603, Immeuble Baezevale House, 5e étage, Zalka, Beirut; tel. (1) 888701; fax (1) 900757; e-mail embavene@dm.net.lb; Ambassador: EFRAIN SILVA.

Yemen: Bir Hassan, Beirut; tel. (1) 852688; fax (1) 821610; e-mail yemenembassy@yemenembassy-lebanon.org; internet www.yem enembassy-lebanon.org; Ambassador: AHMAD ABDULLAH AL-BASHA.

Note: Lebanon and Syria have very close relations but do not exchange formal ambassadors.

Judicial System

Law and justice in Lebanon are administered in accordance with the following codes, which are based upon modern theories of civil and criminal legislation:

Code de la Propriété (1930).
Code des Obligations et des Contrats (1932).
Code de Procédure Civile (1933).
Code Maritime (1947).
Code de Procédure Pénale (Code Ottoman Modifié).
Code Pénal (1943).
Code Pénal Militaire (1946).
Code d'Instruction Criminelle.

The following courts are now established:

(*a*) Fifty-six **'Single-Judge Courts'**, each consisting of a single judge, and dealing in the first instance with both civil and criminal cases; there are seventeen such courts at Beirut and seven at Tripoli.

(*b*) Eleven **Courts of Appeal**, each consisting of three judges, including a President and a Public Prosecutor, and dealing with civil and criminal cases; there are five such courts at Beirut.

(*c*) Four **Courts of Cassation**, three dealing with civil and commercial cases and the fourth with criminal cases. A Court of Cassation, to be properly constituted, must have at least three judges, one being the President and the other two Councillors. The First Court consists of the First President of the Court of Cassation, a President and two Councillors. The other two civil courts each consist of a President and three Councillors. If the Court of Cassation reverses the judgment of a lower court, it does not refer the case back but retries it itself.

First President of the Court of Cassation: MUNIR HONEIN.

(*d*) **The Council of State**, which deals with administrative cases. It consists of a President, Vice-President and four Councillors. A Commissioner represents the Government.

President of the Court of the Council of State: GHALEB GHANEM.

(*e*) **The Court of Justice**, which is a special court consisting of a President and four judges, deals with matters affecting the security of the State; there is no appeal against its verdicts.

In addition to the above, the Constitutional Court considers matters pertaining to the constitutionality of legislation. Military courts are competent to try crimes and misdemeanours involving the armed and security forces. Islamic (*Shari'a*), Christian and Jewish religious courts deal with affairs of personal status (marriage, death, inheritance, etc.).

Religion

Of all the regions of the Middle East, Lebanon probably presents the closest juxtaposition of sects and peoples within a small territory. Estimates for 1983 assessed the sizes of communities as: Shi'a Muslims 1.2m., Maronites 900,000, Sunni Muslims 750,000, Greek Orthodox 250,000, Druzes 250,000, Armenians 175,000. The Maronites, a uniate sect of the Roman Catholic Church, inhabited the old territory of Mount Lebanon, i.e. immediately east of Beirut. In the south, towards the Israeli frontier, Shi'a villages are most common, while between the Shi'a and the Maronites live the Druzes (divided between the Yazbakis and the Joumblatis). The Beka'a valley has many Greek Christians (both Roman Catholic and Orthodox), while the Tripoli area is mainly Sunni Muslim.

CHRISTIANITY
The Roman Catholic Church

Armenian Rite

Patriarchate of Cilicia: Patriarcat Arménien Catholique, rue de l'Hôpital Libanais, Jeitawi, 2400 Beirut; tel. (1) 585671; fax (1) 449160; e-mail patrarca@magnarama.com; f. 1742; established in Beirut since 1932; includes patriarchal diocese of Beirut, with an estimated 12,000 adherents (31 December 2000); Patriarch: Most Rev. NERSES BEDROS XIX TARMOUNI; Protosyncellus Rt Rev. VARTAN ACHKARIAN, Titulas Bishop of Tokat (Armenian Rite).

Chaldean Rite

Diocese of Beirut: Evêché Chaldéen de Beyrouth, POB 373, Hazmieh, Beirut; tel. (5) 459088; fax (5) 457731; e-mail chaldepiscopu s@hotmail.com; an estimated 12,500 adherents (31 December 2000); Bishop of Beirut MICHEL KASSARJI.

Latin Rite

Apostolic Vicariate of Beirut: Vicariat Apostolique, POB 11-4224, Beirut; tel. (9) 236101; fax (9) 236102; e-mail vicariatlat@hotmail.com; an estimated 20,000 adherents (31 December 2000); Vicar Apostolic PAUL DAHDAH, Titular Archbishop of Arae in Numidia.

Maronite Rite

Patriarchate of Antioch and all the East: Patriarcat Maronite, Bkerké; tel. (9) 915441; fax (9) 938844; e-mail jtawk@bkerke.org.lb; includes patriarchal dioceses of Jounieh, Sarba and Jobbé; Patriarch: Cardinal NASRALLAH PIERRE SFEIR. The Maronite Church in Lebanon comprises four archdioceses and six dioceses. At 31 December 2000 there were an estimated 1,373,587 adherents in the country.

> **Archbishop of Antélias:** Most Rev. JOSEPH MOHSEN BÉCHARA, Archevêché Maronite, POB 70400, Antélias; tel. (4) 410020; fax (4) 921313.

> **Archbishop of Beirut:** Most Rev. PAUL YOUSSEF MATAR, Archevêché Maronite, 10 rue Collège de la Sagesse, Beirut; tel. (1) 561980; fax (1) 561931; also representative of the Holy See for Roman Catholics of the Coptic Rite in Lebanon.

> **Archbishop of Tripoli:** Most Rev. YOUHANNA FOUAD EL-HAGE, Archevêché Maronite, POB 104, rue al-Moutran, Karm Sada, Tripoli; tel. (6) 624324; fax (6) 629393; e-mail rahmat@inco.com.lb.

> **Archbishop of Tyre:** Most Rev. MAROUN KHOURY SADER, Archevêché Maronite, Tyre; tel. (7) 740059; fax (7) 344891.

Melkite Rite

Patriarch of Antioch: The Patriarch of Antioch and all the East, of Alexandria and of Jerusalem, Most Rev. GRÉGOIRE III LAHAM, is resident in Damascus, Syria. The Melkite Church in Lebanon comprises seven archdioceses. At 31 December 2000 there were an estimated 381,250 adherents in the country.

> **Archbishop of Ba'albek:** Most Rev. CYRILLE SALIM BUSTROS, Archevêché Grec-Catholique, Ba'albek; tel. (8) 370200; fax (8) 373986.

> **Archbishop of Baniyas:** Most Rev. ANTOINE HAYEK, Archevêché de Panéas, Jdeidet Marjeyoun; tel. (3) 814487.

> **Archbishop of Beirut and Gibail:** JOSEPH KALLAS, Archevêché Grec-Melkite-Catholique, POB 901, rue de Damas, Beirut; tel. (1) 616104; fax (1) 616109; e-mail agmcb@terra.net.lb.

> **Archbishop of Sidon:** Most Rev. GEORGES KWAÏTER, Archevêché Grec-Melkite-Catholique, POB 247, rue el-Moutran, Sidon; tel. (7) 720100; fax (7) 722055; e-mail mkwaiter@inco.com.lb.

> **Archbishop of Tripoli:** Most Rev. GEORGE RIASHI, Archevêché Grec-Catholique, POB 72, Tripoli; tel. (6) 431602; fax (6) 441716.

> **Archbishop of Tyre:** Most Rev. JEAN ASSAAD HADDAD, Archevêché Grec-Melkite-Catholique, POB 257, Tyre; tel. (7) 740015; fax (7) 349180; e-mail eegc@inco.com.lb.

> **Archbishop of Zahleh and Furzol:** Most Rev. ANDRÉ HADDAD, Archevêché Grec-Melkite-Catholique, Saidat en-Najat, Zahleh; tel. (8) 820540; fax (8) 822406.

Syrian Rite

Patriarchate of Antioch: Patriarcat Syrien Catholique d'Antioche, rue de Damas, POB 116/5087, Beirut 1106-2010; tel. (1) 615892; fax (1) 616573; e-mail psc_lb@yahoo.com; jurisdiction over about 150,000 Syrian Catholics in the Middle East, including (at 31 December 2000) 20,000 in the diocese of Beirut; Patriarch: Most Rev. IGNACE PIERRE VIII ABDEL AHAD; Protosyncellus Mgr GEORGES MASRI.

The Anglican Communion

Within the Episcopal Church in Jerusalem and the Middle East, Lebanon forms part of the diocese of Jerusalem (see the chapter on Israel).

Other Christian Groups

Armenian Apostolic Orthodox: Armenian Catholicosate of Cilicia, POB 70317, Antélias, Beirut, Lebanon; tel. (4) 410001; fax (4) 419724; e-mail cathcil@inco.com.lb; internet www.cathcil.org; f. 1441 in Cilicia (now in Turkey), transferred to Antélias, Lebanon, 1930; Leader His Holiness ARAM I (KESHISHIAN), Catholicos of Cilicia; jurisdiction over an estimated 1m. adherents in Lebanon, Syria, Cyprus, Kuwait, Greece, Iran, the United Arab Emirates, the USA and Canada.

Greek Orthodox: Leader His Beatitude IGNATIUS IV, Patriarch of Antioch and all the East, Patriarcat Grec-Orthodoxe, POB 9, Damascus, Syria.

National Evangelical Synod of Syria and Lebanon: POB 70890, Antélias, Beirut; tel. (4) 525030; fax (4) 411184; e-mail nessl@minero.net; 80,000 adherents (2002); Gen. Sec. Rev. ADEEB AWAD.

Protestants: Leader Rev. Dr Salim Sahiouny, Pres. of Supreme Council of the Evangelical Community in Syria and Lebanon, POB 70/1065, rue Rabieh 34, Antélias; tel. (4) 525036; fax (4) 405490; e-mail suprcoun@minero.net.

Syrian Orthodox: Leader IGNATIUS ZAKKA I IWAS, Patriarch of Antioch and all the East, Patriarcat Syrien Orthodoxe, Bab Toma, POB 22260, Damascus, Syria; tel. 5432401; fax 5432400.

Union of the Armenian Evangelical Churches in the Near East: POB 11-377, Beirut; tel. (1) 565628; fax (1) 565629; e-mail uaecne@cyberia.net.lb; f. 1846 in Turkey; comprises about 30 Armenian Evangelical Churches in Syria, Lebanon, Egypt, Cyprus, Greece, Iran, Turkey and Australia; 7,500 mems (1990); Pres. Rev. MEGRDICH KARAGOEZIAN; Gen. Sec. SEBOUH TERZIAN.

ISLAM

Shi'a Muslims: Leader Imam SAYED MOUSSA AS-SADR (went missing during visit to Libya in August 1978), President of the Supreme Islamic Council of the Shi'a Community of Lebanon, Sheikh ABD AL-AMIR QABALAN (acting), Beirut.

Sunni Muslims: Leader SG Sheikh Dr MUHAMMAD RASHID QABBANI, Grand Mufti of Lebanon, Dar el-Fatwa, rue Ilewi Rushed, Beirut; tel. (1) 422340.

Druzes: Acting leader SG Sheikh BAHJAT GHEITH, Supreme Spiritual Leader of the Druze Community, Beirut; tel. (1) 341116.

Alawites: a schism of Shi'ite Islam; there are an estimated 50,000 Alawites in northern Lebanon, in and around Tripoli.

JUDAISM

Jews: Leader CHAHOUD CHREIM, Beirut.

The Press

DAILIES

Al-Ahrar: POB 165600, rue al-Jeitaoui al-Marsad, Beirut; tel. (1) 333899; published by Dar al-Bouhous.

Al-Amal (Hope): rue Libérateur, Beirut; tel. (1) 382992; f. 1939; Arabic; organ of the Phalangist Party; Chief Editor ELIAS RABABI; circ. 35,000.

Al-Anwar (Lights): c/o Dar Assayad, POB 11-1038, Hazmieh, Beirut; tel. (5) 456374; fax (5) 452700; e-mail info@alanwar.com; internet www.alanwar.com; f. 1959; Arabic; independent; supplement, Sunday, cultural and social; published by Dar Assayad SAL; Editors-in-Chief MICHEL RAAD, RAFIC KHOURY; circ. 25,000.

Ararat: Nor Hagin, Beirut; f. 1937; Armenian; Communist; Editor KRIKOR HAJENIAN; circ. 5,000.

Aztag: Beirut; tel. (1) 366607; f. 1927; Armenian; circ. 6,500.

Al-Bairaq (The Standard): rue Monot, Beirut; f. 1911; Arabic; published by Soc. Libanaise de Presse; Editor RAYMOND KAWASS; circ. 3,000.

Bairut: Beirut; f. 1952; Arabic.

Ach-Chaab (The People): POB 5140, Beirut; f. 1961; Arabic; Nationalist; Propr and Editor MUHAMMAD AMIN DUGHAN; circ. 7,000.

Ach-Chams (The Sun): Beirut; f. 1925; Arabic.

Ach-Charq (The East): POB 11-0838, rue Verdun, Riad es-Solh, Beirut; tel. (1) 810820; fax (1) 866105; e-mail info@elshark.com; f. 1926; Arabic; Editor AOUNI AL-KAAKI.

Daily Star: 6th Floor, Marine Tower, rue de la Sainte Famille, Achrafieh, Beirut; tel. (1) 587277; fax (1) 561333; e-mail webmaster@dailystar.com.lb; internet www.dailystar.com.lb; f. 1952; English; Publr and Editor-in-Chief JAMIL K. MROUE; circ. 10,550.

Ad-Diyar (The Homeland): an-Nahda Building, Yarze, Beirut; tel. (5) 923830; fax (5) 923773; e-mail aldiyar2002@yahoo.com; f. 1987; Arabic; Propr CHARLES AYYUB.

Ad-Dunya (The World): Beirut; f. 1943; Arabic; political; Chief Editor SULIMAN ABOU ZAID; circ. 25,000.

Al-Hakika (The Truth): Beirut; Arabic; published by Amal.

Al-Hayat (Life): POB 11–987, Immeuble Gargarian, rue Emil Eddé, Hamra, Beirut; tel. (1) 352674; fax (1) 866177; internet www.alhayat.com; f. 1946; Arabic; independent; circ. 196,800.

Al-Jarida (The (News) Paper): POB 220, place Tabaris, Beirut; f. 1953; Arabic; independent; Editor ABDULLA SKAFF; circ. 22,600.

Al-Jumhuriya (The Republic): Beirut; f. 1924; Arabic.

Journal al-Haddis: POB 300, Jounieh; f. 1927; Arabic; political; Owner GEORGES ARÈGE-SAADÉ.

Al-Khatib (The Speaker): rue Georges Picot, Beirut; Arabic.

Al-Kifah al-Arabi (The Arab Struggle): POB 5158–14, Immeuble Rouche-Shams, Beirut; f. 1974; Arabic; political, socialist, Pan-Arab; Publr and Chief Editor WALID HUSSEINI.

Lisan ul-Hal (The Organ): rue Châteaubriand, Beirut; f. 1877; Arabic; Editor GEBRAN HAYEK; circ. 33,000.

Al-Liwa' (The Standard): POB 11-2402, Beirut; tel. (1) 735749; fax (1) 735742; f. 1963; Arabic; Propr ABD AL-GHANI SALAM; Editor SALAH SALAM; circ. 26,000.

Al-Mustuqbal: Beirut; f. 1999; Owner RAFIK HARIRI; Editor FADHL SHALAQ; circ. 20,000.

An-Nahar (The Day): Immeuble Cooperative de Presse, rue Banque du Liban, Hamra, Beirut; tel. (1) 340960; fax (1) 344567; e-mail annahar@annahar.com.lb; internet www.annahar.com.lb; f. 1933; Arabic; independent; Pres. and Gen. Man. GEBRAN TUENI; Editor-in-Chief OUNSI EL-HAJJ; circ. 50,000.

An-Nass (The People): POB 4886, ave Fouad Chehab, Beirut; tel. (1) 308695; f. 1959; Arabic; Editor-in-Chief HASSAN YAGHI; circ. 22,000.

An-Nida (The Appeal): Beirut; f. 1959; Arabic; published by the Lebanese Communist Party; Editor KARIM MROUÉ; circ. 10,000.

Nida' al-Watan (Call of the Homeland): Beirut; f. 1937; Arabic.

An-Nidal (The Struggle): Beirut; f. 1939; Arabic.

L'Orient-Le Jour: POB 166495, rue Banque du Liban, Beirut; tel. (1) 340560; e-mail redaction@lorient-lejour.com.lb; internet www .lorient-lejour.com.lb; f. 1942; French; independent; Chair. MICHEL EDDÉ; Dir CAMILLE MENASSA; Editorial Dir AMINE ABOU-KHALED; Editor ISSA GORAÏEB; circ. 23,000.

Raqib al-Ahwal (The Observer): Beirut; f. 1937; Arabic; Editor SIMA'N FARAH SEIF.

Rayah (Banner): POB 4101, Beirut; Arabic.

Le Réveil: Beirut; tel. (1) 890700; f. 1977; French; Editor-in-Chief JEAN SHAMI; Dir RAYMOND DAOU; circ. 10,000.

Ar-Ruwwad: POB 2696, rue Mokhalsieh, Beirut; f. 1940; Arabic; Editor BESHARA MAROUN.

Sada Lubnan (Echo of Lebanon): Beirut; f. 1951; Arabic; Lebanese Pan-Arab; Editor MUHAMMAD BAALBAKI; circ. 25,000.

As-Safir: POB 113/5015, Immeuble as-Safir, rue Monimina, Hamra, Beirut 1103-2010; tel. (1) 350080; fax (1) 349431; e-mail co-ordinator @assafir.com; internet www.assafir.com; f. 1974; Arabic; political; Propr and Editor-in-Chief TALAL SALMAN; Gen. Man. YASSER NEHME; circ. 50,000.

Sawt al-Uruba (The Voice of Europe): POB 3537, Beirut; f. 1959; Arabic; organ of the An-Najjadé Party; Editor ADNANE AL-HAKIM.

Le Soir: POB 1470, rue de Syrie, Beirut; f. 1947; French; independent; Dir DIKRAN TOSBATH; Editor ANDRÉ KECATI; circ. 16,500.

Telegraf—Bairut: rue Béchara el-Khoury, Beirut; f. 1930; Arabic; political, economic and social; Editor TOUFIC ASSAD MATNI; circ. 15,500 (5,000 outside Lebanon).

Al-Yaum (Today): Beirut; f. 1937; Arabic; Editor WAFIC MUHAMMAD CHAKER AT-TIBY.

Az-Zamane: Beirut; f. 1947; Arabic.

Zartonk: POB 11-617, rue Nahr Ibrahim, Beirut; tel. and fax (1) 566709; e-mail zartonk@dm.net.lb; f. 1937; Armenian; official organ of Armenian Liberal Democratic Party; Man. Editor BAROUYR H. AGHBASHIAN.

WEEKLIES

Al-Alam al-Lubnani (The Lebanese World): POB 462, Beirut; f. 1964; Arabic, English, Spanish, French; politics, literature and social economy; Editor-in-Chief FAYEK KHOURY; Gen. Editor CHEIKH FADI GEMAYEL; circ. 45,000.

Achabaka (The Net): c/o Dar Assayad SAL, POB 11-1038, Hazmieh, Beirut; tel. (1) 456373; fax (5) 452700; f. 1956; Arabic; society and features; Founder SAID FREIHA; Editor GEORGE IBRAHIM EL-KHOURY; circ. 108,000.

Al-Ahad (Sunday): Beirut; Arabic; political; organ of Hezbollah; Editor RIAD TAHA; circ. 32,000.

Al-Akhbar (The News): Beirut; f. 1954; Arabic; published by the Lebanese Communist Party; circ. 21,000.

Al-Anwar Supplement: c/o Dar Assayad, POB 1038, Hazmieh, Beirut; cultural-social; every Sunday; supplement to daily *Al-Anwar*; Editor ISSAM FREIHA; circ. 90,000.

Argus: Bureau of Lebanese and Arab Documentation, POB 16–5403, Beirut; tel. (1) 219113; Arabic, French and English; economic bulletin; circ. 1,000.

Assayad (The Hunter): c/o Dar Assayad, POB 11-1038, Hazmieh, Beirut; tel. (5) 456373; fax (5) 452700; f. 1943; Arabic; political and social.

Le Commerce du Levant: Beirut; tel. (1) 297770; f. 1929; weekly and special issue quarterly; French; commercial and financial; publ. by Société de la Presse Economique; Pres. MAROUN AKL; circ. 15,000.

Dabbour: Place du Musée, Beirut; tel. (1) 616770; fax (1) 616771; e-mail addabbour@yahoo.com; internet www.addabbour.com; f. 1922; Arabic; Editor JOSEPH RICHARD MUKARZEL; circ. 12,000.

Ad-Dyar: Immeuble Bellevue, rue Verdun, Beirut; f. 1941; Arabic; political; circ. 46,000.

Al-Hadaf (The Target): Beirut; f. 1969; tel. (1) 420554; organ of Popular Front for the Liberation of Palestine (PFLP); Arabic; Editor-in-Chief SABER MOHI ED-DIN; circ. 40,000.

Al-Hawadess (Events): POB 1281, rue Clémenceau, Beirut; published from London (183–185 Askew Rd, W12 9AX); tel. (181) 740-4500; fax (181) 749-9781); f. 1911; Arabic; news; Editor-in-Chief MELHIM KAVAM; circ. 120,000.

Al-Hiwar (Dialogue): Beirut; f. 2000; Arabic; Chair. FOUAD MAKHZOUMI; Editor-in-Chief SAM MOUNASSA.

Al-Hurriya (Freedom): Beirut; f. 1960; Arabic; organ of the Democratic Front for the Liberation of Palestine; Editor DAOUD TALHAME; circ. 30,000.

Al-Iza'a (Broadcasting): POB 462, rue Selim Jazaerly, Beirut; f. 1938; Arabic; politics, art, literature and broadcasting; Editor FAYEK KHOURY; circ. 11,000.

Al-Jumhur (The Public): POB 1834, Moussaitbé, Beirut; f. 1936; Arabic; illustrated weekly news magazine; Editor FARID ABU SHAHLA; circ. 45,000, of which over 20,000 outside Lebanon.

Kul Shay' (Everything): POB 3250, rue Béchara el-Khoury, Beirut; Arabic.

Magazine: POB 1404, Immeuble Sayegh, rue Sursock, Beirut; tel. (1) 202070; fax (1) 202663; e-mail info@magazine.com.lb; internet www.magazine.com.lb; f. 1956; French; political, economic and social; published by Editions Orientales SAL; Pres. CHARLES ABOU ADAL; circ. 18,000.

Massis: c/o Patriarcat Arménien Catholique, rue de l'Hôpital Libanais Jeitawi, 2400 Beirut; Armenian; Catholic; Editor Fr ANTRANIK GRANIAN; circ. 2,500.

Al-Moharrir (The Liberator): Beirut; f. 1962; Arabic; circ. 87,000; Gen. Man. WALID ABOU ZAHR.

Monday Morning: POB 165612, Immeuble Dimitri Trad, rue Issa Maalouf, Sioufi, Beirut; tel. (1) 200961; fax (1) 334116; e-mail mondaymorning@mmorning.com; internet www.mmorning.com; f. 1972; news and current affairs; published by Dar Alf Leila wa Leila; circ. 11,000.

Al-Ousbou' al-Arabi (Arab Week): POB 1404, Immeuble Sayegh, rue Sursock, Beirut; tel. (1) 202070; fax (1) 202663; e-mail info@ arabweek.com.lb; internet www.arabweek.com.lb; f. 1959; Arabic; political and social; published by Editions Orientales SAL; Pres. CHARLES ABOU ADAL; circ. 88,407 (circulates throughout the Arab World).

Phoenix: POB 113222, Beirut; tel. (1) 346800; fax (1) 346359; for women; published by Al-Hasna.

Ar-Rassed: Beirut; Arabic; Editor GEORGE RAJJI.

Revue du Liban (Lebanon Review): POB 165612, rue Issa Maalouf, Beirut; tel. (1) 200961; fax (1) 334116; e-mail rdl@rdl.com.lb; internet www.rdl.com.lb; f. 1928; French; political, social, cultural; Publr MELHEM KARAM; Gen. Man. MICHEL MISK; circ. 22,000.

Sabah al-Khair (Good Morning): Beirut; Arabic; published by the Syrian Nationalist Party.

Samar: c/o Dar Assayad, POB 11-1038, Hazmieh, Beirut; tel. (5) 452700; fax (5) 452957; Arabic; for teenagers; published by Dar Assayad SAL.

Ash-Shira' (The Sail): POB 13-5250, Beirut; tel. (1) 70300; fax (1) 866050; Arabic; Editor HASSAN SABRA; circ. 40,000.

Travaux et Jours (Works and Days): Rectorat de l'Université Saint-Joseph, rue de Damas, Beirut; tel. (1) 611172; fax (1) 423369; e-mail travauxetjours@usj.edu.lb; internet www.usj.edu.lb; f. 1961; publ. weekly in spring and autumn; French; political, social and cultural; Editor MOUNIR CHAMOUN.

OTHER SELECTED PERIODICALS

Alam at-Tijarat (Business World): Immeuble Strand, rue Hamra, Beirut; f. 1965; monthly; commercial; Editor NADIM MAKDISI; international circ. 17,500.

Al Computer, Communications and Electronics: c/o Dar Assayad, POB 1038, Hazmieh, Beirut; tel. (5) 456374; fax (5) 452700; f. 1984; monthly; computer technology; published by Dar Assayad International; Chief Editor ANTOINE BOUTROS.

Arab Construction World: POB 13–5121, Chouran, Beirut 1102-2802; tel. (1) 352413; fax (1) 352419; e-mail acw@chatilapublishing .com.lb; internet www.chatilapublishing.com.lb; f. 1985; every two months; English and Arabic; published by Chatila Publishing House; Publr FATHI CHATILA; Editor-in-Chief RIYADH CHEHAB; circ. 10,353.

Arab Defense Journal: c/o Dar Assayad, POB 11-1038, Hazmieh, Beirut; tel. (5) 456373; fax (5) 452700; e-mail assayad@inco.com.lb;

f. 1976; monthly; military; published by Dar Assayad International; Chief Editor Gen. WADIH JUBRAN; circ. 24,325 (Jan.–June 1999).

Arab Economist: POB 11–6068, Beirut; monthly; published by Centre for Economic, Financial and Social Research and Documentation SAL; Chair. HEKMAT KASSIR.

Arab Water World: POB 13–5121, Chouran, Beirut 1102-2802; tel. (1) 352413; fax (1) 352419; e-mail aww@chatilapublishing.com.lb; internet www.chatilapublishing.com.lb; f. 1977; every two months; English and Arabic; published by Chatila Publishing House; Editor-in-Chief FATHI CHATILA; circ. 9,142.

The Arab World: POB 567, Jounieh; tel. and fax (9) 935096; f. 1985; 24 a year; published by Dar Naaman lith-Thaqafa; Editor NAJI NAAMAN.

Déco: POB 1404, Immeuble Sayegh, rue Sursock, Beirut; tel. (1) 202070; fax (1) 202663; e-mail info@decomag.com.lb; internet www.ediori.com.lb; f. 2000; quarterly; French; architecture and interior design; published by Editions Orientales SAL; Pres. CHARLES ABOU ADAL; circ. 14,000.

Fairuz Lebanon: c/o Dar Assayad, POB 11-1038, Hazmieh, Beirut; tel. (5) 456374; fax (5) 452700; f. 1982; monthly; Arabic; for women; also *Fairuz International*; published by Dar Assayad International; Chief Editor ELHAM FREIHA.

Fann at-Tasswir: POB 16-5947, Beirut; tel. (1) 498950; monthly; Arabic; photography.

Al Fares: c/o Dar Assayad, POB 11-1038, Hazmieh, Beirut; tel. (5) 456374; fax (5) 452700; f. 1991; monthly; Arabic; men's interest; published by Dar Assayad International; Chief Editor ELHAM FREIHA.

Al-Idari (The Manager): c/o Dar Assayad, POB 11-1038, Hamzieh, Beirut; tel. (5) 456374; fax (5) 452700; f. 1975; monthly; Arabic; business management, economics, finance and investment; published by Dar Assayad International; Pres. and Gen. Man. BASSAM FREIHA; Chief Editor HASSAN EL-KHOURY; circ. 31,867.

Al-Intilak (Outbreak): Al-Intilak Printing and Publishing House, POB 4958, Beirut; tel. (1) 302018; e-mail tonehnme@cyberia.net.lb; f. 1960; monthly; Arabic; literary; Chief Editor MICHEL NEHME.

Al-Jeel (The Generation): Beirut; monthly; Arabic; literary.

Al-Khalij Business Magazine: POB 13-5877, Beirut; tel. (1) 345568; fax (1) 602089; e-mail massaref@dm.net.lb; f. 1981; fmrly based in Kuwait; 6 a year; Arabic; Editor-in-Chief ZULFICAR KOBEISSI; circ. 16,325.

Lebanese and Arab Economy: POB 11-1801, Sanayeh, Beirut; tel. (1) 744160; fax (1) 353395; e-mail info@.ccib.org.lb; internet www.ccib.org.lb; f. 1951; monthly; Arabic, English and French; Publr Beirut Chamber of Commerce and Industry.

Majallat al-Iza'at al-Lubnaniat (Lebanese Broadcasting Magazine): c/o Radio Lebanon, rue des Arts et Métiers, Beirut; tel. (1) 863016; f. 1959; monthly; Arabic; broadcasting affairs.

Al-Mar'a: POB 1404, Immeuble Sayegh, rue Sursock, Beirut; tel. (1) 202070; fax (1) 202663; e-mail info@almara.com.lb; internet www.ediori.com.lb; f. 2000; monthly; Arabic; for women; published by Editions Orientales SAL; Pres. CHARLES ABOU ADAL; circ. 20,000.

Middle East Food: POB 13-5121, Chouran, Beirut 1102-2802; tel. (1) 352413; fax (1) 352419; e-mail mef@chatilapublishing.com.lb; internet www.chatilapublishing.com.lb; every two months; published by Chatila Publishing House; Editor-in-Chief SAAD CHEHAB; circ. 9,219.

Al-Mouktataf (The Selection): Beirut; monthly; Arabic; general.

Al-Mukhtar (Reader's Digest): Beirut; monthly; general interest.

Qitāboul A'lamil A'rabi (The Arab World Book): POB 567, Jounieh; tel. and fax (9) 935096; f. 1991; 6 a year; Arabic; published by Dar Naaman lith-Thaqafa; Editor NAJI NAAMAN.

Rijal al-Amal (Businessmen): Beirut; f. 1966; monthly; Arabic; business; Publr and Editor-in-Chief MAHIBA AL-MALKI; circ. 16,250.

Scoop: POB 55342, Beirut; tel. (1) 482185; fax (1) 490307; general interest; published by La Régie Libanaise de Publicité.

As-Sihāfa wal I'lām (Press and Information): POB 567, Jounieh; tel. and fax (9) 935096; f. 1987; 12 a year; Arabic; published by Dar Naaman lith-Thaqafa; Editor NAJI NAAMAN.

Siyassa was Strategia (Politics and Strategy): POB 567, Jounieh; tel. and fax (9) 935096; f. 1981; 36 a year; Arabic; published by Dar Naaman lith-Thaqafa; Editor NAJI NAAMAN.

Tabibok (Your Doctor): POB 90434, Beirut; tel. in Syria (963-11) 2212980; fax (963-11) 3738901; e-mail sskabbani@net.sy; f. 1956; monthly; Arabic; medical, social, scientific; Editor Dr SAMI KABBANI; circ. 90,000.

Takarir Wa Khalfiyat (Background Reports): c/o Dar Assayad, POB 11-1038, Hamzieh, Beirut; tel. (5) 456374; fax (5) 452700; f. 1976; tri-monthly; Arabic; political and economic bulletin; published by Dar Assayad SAL.

At-Tarik (The Road): Beirut; monthly; Arabic; cultural and theoretical; published by the Parti communiste libanais; circ. 5,000.

Welcome to Lebanon and the Middle East: Beirut; f. 1959; monthly; English; on entertainment, touring and travel; Editor SOUHAIL TOUFIK ABOU JAMRA; circ. 6,000.

NEWS AGENCIES

National News Agency (NNA): Hamra, Beirut; tel. (1) 342290; fax (1) 746031; e-mail nna-leb@nna-leb.gov.lb; internet www.nna-leb.gov.lb; state-owned; Dir KHALIL KHOURY.

Foreign Bureaux

Agence France-Presse (AFP): POB 11-1461, Immeuble Najjar, rue de Rome, Beirut; tel. (1) 347461; fax (1) 350318; e-mail afp_bey@inco.com.lb; internet www.afp.com; Dir PASCAL MALLET.

Agenzia Nazionale Stampa Associata (ANSA) (Italy): POB 113/6545, 2e étage, Immeuble Safieddine, rue Rashid Karame, Beirut; tel. (1) 787237; fax (1) 787236; e-mail ansa@sodetel.net.lb; Correspondent FURIO MORRONI.

Allgemeiner Deutscher Nachrichtendienst (ADN) (Germany): Beirut; Correspondent HARALD DITTMAR.

Associated Press (AP) (USA): POB 3780, Immeuble Shaker et Oueini, place Riad es-Solh, Beirut; tel. (1) 985190; fax (1) 985196; e-mail info@ap.org; internet www.ap.org; Correspondent SAM F. GHATTAS.

Kuwait News Agency (KUNA): Beirut; tel. (1) 354377; fax (1) 602088.

Kyodo Tsushin (Japan): POB 13-5060, Immeuble Makarem, rue Makdessi, Ras Beirut, Beirut; tel. (1) 863861; Correspondent IBRAHIM KHOURY.

Middle East News Agency (MENA) (Egypt): POB 2268, 72 rue al-Geish, Beirut.

Reuters (United Kingdom): POB 11-1006, Immeuble Hibat al-Maarad, place Riad es-Solh, Beirut; tel. (1) 983885; fax (1) 983889; e-mail samia.nakhoul@reuters.com; internet www.reuters.com; Bureau Chief SAMIA NAKHOUL.

Rossiiskoye Informatsionnoye Agentstvo—Novosti (RIA—Novosti) (Russia): POB 11-1086, Beirut; tel. (1) 300219; fax (1) 314168; e-mail novosti@cyberia.net.lb; Dir KONSTANTIN MAXIMOV.

United Press International (UPI) (USA): Hamra, Beirut; internet www.upi.com; Bureau Man. RIAD KAJ.

Xinhua (New China) News Agency (People's Republic of China): POB 114-5075, Beirut; tel. (1) 830359.

BTA (Bulgaria), INA (Iraq), JANA (Libya), Prensa Latina (Cuba) and Saudi Press Agency (SPA) are also represented in Lebanon.

PRESS ASSOCIATION

Lebanese Press Order: POB 3084, ave Saeb Salam, Beirut; tel. (1) 865519; fax (1) 865516; e-mail mail@pressorder.org; internet www.pressorder.org; f. 1911; 18 mems; Pres. MUHAMMAD AL-BAALBAKI; Vice-Pres. GEORGES SKAFF; Sec. MALEK MROUEH.

Publishers

Dar al-Adab: POB 11-4123, Beirut; tel. and fax (1) 861633; e-mail d_aladab@cyberia.net.lb; f. 1953; dictionaries, literary and general; Man. RANA IDRISS; Editor-in-Chief SAMAH IDRISS.

Arab Institute for Research and Publishing (Al-Mouasasah al-Arabiyah Lildirasat Walnashr): POB 11–5460, Tour Carlton, Saqiat el-Janzeer, Beirut; tel. and fax (1) 751438; e-mail mkayyali@joinnet.com.jo; f. 1969; Dir. MAHER KAYYALI; works in Arabic and English.

Arab Scientific Publishers BP: POB 13-5574, Immeuble Ein at-Tenah Reem, rue Sakiet al-Janzir, Beirut; tel. (1) 811385; fax (1) 860138; e-mail bchebaro@asp.com.lb; internet www.asp.com.lb; computer science, biological sciences, cookery, travel; Pres. BASSAM CHEBARO.

Dar Assayad Group (SAL and International): POB 11-1038, Hazmieh, Beirut; tel. (5) 456373; fax (5) 452700; e-mail assayad@inco.com.lb; internet www.interlink.com.lb/acce; f. 1943; Dar Assayad International founded in 1983; publishes in Arabic *Al-Anwar* (daily, plus weekly supplement), *Assayad* (weekly), *Achabaka* (weekly), *Background Reports* (three a month), *Arab Defense Journal* (monthly), *Fairuz Lebanon* (monthly, plus international monthly edition), *Al-Idari* (monthly), *Al Computer, Communications and Electronics* (monthly), *Al-Fares* (monthly); has offices and correspondents in Arab countries and most parts of the world; Chair. ISSAM FREIHA; Pres. and Man. Dir BASSAM FREIHA.

Chatila Publishing House: POB 13-5121, Chouran, Beirut 1102-2802; tel. (1) 352413; fax (1) 352419; e-mail info@chatilapublishing

.com; internet www.chatilapublishing.com; publishes *Arab Construction World* (every two months), *Arab Water World* (every two months), *Middle East Food* (every two months), *Middle East and World Food Directory* (bi-annual), *Middle East and World Water Directory* (bi-annual).

Edition Française pour le Monde Arabe (EDIFRAMO): POB 113-6140, Immeuble Elissar, rue Bliss, Beirut; tel. (1) 862437; Man. TAHSEEN S. KHAYAT.

Editions Orientales SAL: POB 1404, Immeuble Sayegh, rue Sursock, Beirut; tel. (1) 202070; fax (1) 202663; e-mail info@ediori.com.lb; internet www.ediori.com.lb; political and social newspapers and magazines; Pres. and Editor-in-Chief CHARLES ABOU ADAL.

Geoprojects SARL: POB 8375, Immeuble al-Wahad, rue Jeanne d'Arc, Beirut; tel. (1) 345460; fax (1) 79522107; f. 1978; regional issues, travel; Man. Dir TAHSEEN KHAYAT.

Dar el-Ilm Lilmalayin: POB 1085, Centre Metco, rue Mar Elias, Beirut; tel. (1) 306666; fax (1) 701657; e-mail malayin@cyberia.net.lb; internet www.malayin.com; f. 1945; dictionaries, encyclopaedias, reference books, textbooks, Islamic cultural books; CEO TAREF OSMAN.

Institute for Palestine Studies, Publishing and Research Organization (IPS): POB 11-7164, rue Anis Nsouli, off Verdun, Beirut; tel. and fax (1) 868387; e-mail ipsbrt@cyberia.net.lb; f. 1963; independent non-profit Arab research organization; to promote better understanding of the Palestine problem and the Arab–Israeli conflict; publishes books, reprints, research papers, etc.; Chair. Dr HISHAM NASHABE; Exec. Sec. Prof. WALID KHALIDI.

The International Documentary Center of Arab Manuscripts: POB 2668, Immeuble Hanna, Ras Beirut, Beirut; e-mail alafaq@cyberia.net.lb; f. 1965; publishes and reproduces ancient and rare Arabic texts; Propr ZOUHAIR BAALBAKI.

Dar al-Kashaf: POB 112091, rue Assad Malhamee, Beirut; tel. (1) 296805; f. 1930; publishers of *Al-Kashaf* (Arab Youth Magazine), maps, atlases and business books; printers and distributors; Propr M. A. FATHALLAH.

Khayat Book and Publishing Co SARL: 90–94 rue Bliss, Beirut; Middle East, Islam, history, medicine, social sciences, education, fiction; Man. Dir PAUL KHAYAT.

Dar al-Kitab al-Lubnani: Beirut; tel. (1) 861563; fax (1) 351433; f. 1929; Man. Dir HASSAN EZ-ZEIN.

Librairie du Liban Publishers: POB 11-9232, Beirut; tel. (9) 217944; fax (9) 217734; e-mail psayegh@librairie-du-liban.com.lb; internet www.librairie-du-liban.com.lb; f. 1944; publisher of children's books, dictionaries and reference books; distributor of books in English and French; Man. Dirs HABIB and PIERRE SAYEGH.

Dar al-Maaref Liban SARL: Beirut; tel. (1) 931243; f. 1959; children's books and textbooks in Arabic; Man. Dir Dr FOUAD IBRAHIM; Gen. Man. JOSEPH NACHOU.

Dar al-Machreq SARL: c/o Librairie orientale, POB 55206, Beirut; tel. (1) 202423; fax (1) 329348; e-mail machreq@cyberia.net.lb; internet www.darelmachreq.com; f. 1848; religion, art, Arabic and Islamic literature, history, languages, science, philosophy, school books, dictionaries and periodicals; Man. Dir CAMILLE HÉCHAIMÉ.

Dar Naamān lith-Thaqāfa: POB 567, Jounieh; tel. and fax (9) 935096; e-mail naamanculture@lynx.lb; f. 1979; publishes *Mawsou'atul 'Alamil 'Arabiyyil Mu'asser* (Encyclopaedia of Contemporary Arab World), *Mawsou'atul Waqa'e'il 'Arabiyya* (Encyclopaedia of Arab Events), *Qitāboul A'lamil A'rabi, Siyassa was Strategia, As-Sahafa wal I'lam* in Arabic and *The Arab World* in English; Propr NAJI NAAMAN; Exec. Man. MARCELLE AL-ASHKAR.

Dar an-Nahar SAL: POB 11-226, rue de Rome, Hamra, Beirut; f. 1967; tel. (1) 347176; fax (1) 738159; e-mail fadit@annahar.com.lb; a Pan-Arab publishing house; Pres. GHASSAN TUÉNI; Dir FADI TUÉNI.

Naufal Group SARL: POB 11-2161, Immeuble Naufal, rue Sourati, Beirut; tel. (1) 354898; fax (1) 354394; e-mail naufalgroup@terra.net.lb; f. 1970; subsidiary cos Macdonald Middle East Sarl, Les Editions Arabes; encyclopaedias, fiction, children's books, history, law and literature; Man. Dir TONY NAUFAL.

Publitec Publications: POB 166142, Beirut; tel. (1) 495401; fax (1) 493330; e-mail publitecpublications@hotmail.com; internet www.whoswhointhearabworld.info; f. 1965; publishes *Who's Who in Lebanon* and *Who's Who in the Arab World*; Pres. CHARLES GEDEON; Man. KRIKOR AYVAZIAN.

Dar ar-Raed al-Lubnani: POB 93, Immeuble Kamal al-Assad, Hazmieh, Sammouri, Beirut; tel. (5) 450757; f. 1971; CEO RAYED SAMMOURI.

Rihani Printing and Publishing House: Beirut; f. 1963; Propr ALBERT RIHANI; Man. DAOUD STEPHAN.

World Book Publishing: POB 11-3176, rue Emile Eddé, Beirut; tel. (1) 349370; fax (1) 351226; e-mail wbookpub@inco.com.lb; internet www.arabook.com; f. 1929; literature, education, philo-

sophy, poetry, Islam; Vice-Pres. TOUFIC EZ-ZEIN, RAFIC EZ-ZEIN; Dir-Gen. SAID MUHAMMAD EZ-ZEIN.

Broadcasting and Communications

TELECOMMUNICATIONS
Regulatory Authority

Direction Générale des Télécommunications pour l'Exploitation et la Maintenance: Ministry of Posts and Telecommunications (see above); Dir-Gen. ABDUL M. YOUSSEF.

Service Providers

France-Télécom Mobile Liban (FTML): POB 50257, Beirut; tel. (3) 391850; fax (3) 391859; internet www.ftml.com.lb; f. 1994; operates Cellis (see below); Chair. and Gen. Man. SALAH BOURAAD.

Cellis: Beirut; internet www.cellis.com.lb; f. 1995; provides mobile cellular telephone services.

LibanCell SAL: POB 136406, Immeuble LibanCell, ave Charles Hélou, Beirut; tel. (1) 566111; fax (1) 564184; e-mail info@libancell.com.lb; internet www.libancell.com.lb; provides mobile cellular telephone services; Chair. HUSSEIN RIFAI.

BROADCASTING
Radio

Radio Liban: rue Arts et Métiers, Beirut; part of the Ministry of Information; tel. (1) 346880; f. 1937; Dir-Gen. QASSEM HAGE ALI.

The Home Service broadcasts in Arabic on short wave, and the Foreign Service broadcasts in Portuguese, Armenian, Arabic, Spanish, French and English.

Television

Lebanese Broadcasting Corporation (LBC) Sat Ltd: POB 111, Zouk; tel. (9) 850850; fax (9) 850916; e-mail lbcsat@lbcsat.com.lb; internet www.lbcsat.com.lb; f. 1985 as Lebanese Broadcasting Corporation International SAL; name changed 1996; operates satellite channel on Arabsat 2A; programmes in Arabic, French and English; Chair. Sheikh PIERRE ED-DAHER.

Télé-Liban (TL) SAL: POB 11-5055, Hazmieh, 4848 Beirut; tel. and fax (1) 793000; fax (1) 950286; e-mail tl@tele-liban.com.lb; f. 1959; commercial service; programmes in Arabic, French and English on three channels; privatization pending in 2001; Chair. and Dir-Gen. IBRAHIM EL-KHOURY; Dep. Dir-Gen. MUHAMMAD S. KARIMEH.

Future Television: White House, rue Spears, Sanayeh, Beirut; tel. (1) 347121; fax (1) 602310; e-mail future@future.com.lb; internet www.future.com.lb; commercial; privately-owned; Owner RAFIK HARIRI; Gen. Man. NADIM AL-MONLA.

Al-Manar (Lighthouse): Beirut; f. 1991; television station owned by Lebanese Communication Group (LCG) and partly controlled by Hezbollah; operates satellite channel since May 2000; e-mail almanar@almanar.com.lb; Chair. of Bd NAYEF KRAYEM.

During 1996–98 the Government took measures to close down unlicensed private broadcasters, and to restrict the activities of those licensed to operate. In particular, the broadcasting of news and political programmes by private satellite television channels was banned.

Finance

(cap. = capital; dep. = deposits; res = reserves; m. = million; brs = branches; amounts in £L)

BANKING

Beirut was, for many years, the leading financial and commercial centre in the Middle East, but this role was destroyed by the civil conflict. To restore the city as a regional focus for investment banking is a key element of the Government's reconstruction plans.

Central Bank

Banque du Liban: POB 11-5544, rue Masraf Loubnane, Beirut; tel. (1) 750000; fax (1) 747600; e-mail bdlit@bdl.gov.lb; internet www.bdl.gov.lb; f. 1964 to take over the banking activities of the Banque de Syrie et du Liban in Lebanon; cap. and res £L911,900m., dep. £L9,341,400m. (Dec. 2000); Gov. RIAD SALAMEH; 9 brs.

Principal Commercial Banks

Allied Business Bank SAL: POB 113-7165, Allied House Bldg, ave Charles Malek, St Nicolas, Achrafieh, Beirut; tel. (1) 323116; fax (1) 200660; e-mail mailbox@abb.com.lb; internet www.abb.com.lb; f. 1962; cap. £L15,000m., res £L12,846m., dep. £L330,792m. (Dec.

2000); Chair. ABDULLAH S. ZAKHEM; Man. Dir HABIB F. ABU FADIL; 14 brs in Lebanon, 1 in Cyprus.

Al Mawarid Bank SAL: POB 113-6260, Immeuble Yared, 3e étage, rue Abd al-Aziz, Beirut; tel. (1) 350612; fax (1) 341340; e-mail mail@almawarid.com.lb; internet www.almawarid.com.lb; f. 1980; cap. £L12,500m., res £L4,545m., dep. £L398,993m. (Dec. 2000); Chair. and Gen. Man. SALIM KHEIREDDINE; 10 brs.

Bank of Beirut SAL: POB 11-7354, Bank of Beirut SAL Bldg, Foch St, Beirut Central District, Beirut; tel. (1) 985418; fax (1) 985327; e-mail executive@bankofbeirut.com.lb; internet www.bankofbeirut.com.lb; f. 1973; absorbed Transorient Bank 1999; merger with Beirut Riyad Bank pending; cap. £L52,338m., res £L107,208m., dep. £2,458,020m. (Dec. 2000); Chair. and Gen. Man. SALIM G. SFEIR; 32 brs.

Bank of Beirut and the Arab Countries SAL: POB 11-1536, Immeuble de la Banque, 250 rue Clémenceau, Riad es-Solh, Beirut 1107 2080; tel. (1) 366630; fax (1) 374299; e-mail marketing@bbac.com.lb; internet www.bbac.net; f. 1956; cap. £L72,000m., res £L54,142m., dep. £L2,092,817m. (Dec. 2000); Chair. and Gen. Man. GHASSAN T. ASSAF; 30 brs.

Bank of Kuwait and the Arab World SAL: POB 113-6248, Immeuble Belle Vue, Ain at-Tineh, Verdun, Beirut; tel. (1) 866305; fax (1) 865299; e-mail bkaw@sodetel.net.lb; f. 1959; cap. £L28,000m., res £L8,459m., dep. £L377,757m. (Dec. 2001); Chair. and Gen. Man. ABDUL RAZZAK ACHOUR; 13 brs.

Bank Al-Madina SAL: POB 113-7221, Immeuble Bank Al-Madina, rue Commodore, Hamra, Beirut; tel. (1) 351296; fax (1) 343762; e-mail intdep@bankal-madina.com; f. 1982; cap. £L45,540m., dep. £L226,084m. (Dec. 2000); Hon. Chair. and Gen. Man. Dr ADNAN ABOU AYYASH; Chair. and Gen. Man. Sheikh IBRAHIM ABOU AYYASH; 18 brs.

Banque Audi SAL: Banque Audi Plaza, Bab Idriss, POB 11-2560, Riad es-Solh, Beirut 1107 2808; tel. (1) 994000; fax (1) 990555; e-mail bkaudi@audi.com.lb; internet www.audi.com.lb; f. 1962; acquired Orient Credit Bank 1997 and Banque Nasr 1998; cap. £L37,799m., dep. £L5,844,321m. (Dec. 2001); Chair. and Gen. Man. RAYMOND W. AUDI; 65 brs.

Banque de la Beka'a SAL: POB 117, Centre Fakhoury, Zahleh, Beirut; tel. (8) 803217; fax (8) 429387; f. 1965; cap. £L2,000m., dep. £L112,650m. (Dec. 1996); Chair. and Gen. Man. CHAOUKI W. FAKHOURY.

Banque de Crédit National SAL: POB 110-204, Centre Gefinor, Bloc B, 15e étage, rue Clémenceau, Beirut; tel. (1) 752777; fax (1) 752555; e-mail bcnsafra@dm.net.lb; f. 1920; cap. £L11,000m., res £L2,443m., dep. £L17,809m. (Dec. 1998); Chair. and Gen. Man. EDMOND J. SAFRA.

Banque de l'Industrie et du Travail SAL: POB 11-3948, Riad es-Solh, Beirut 1107 2150; tel. (4) 712539; fax (4) 712538; e-mail international@bitbank.com.lb; internet www.bitbank.com.lb; f. 1960; cap. £L4,000m., res £L2,208m., dep. £L347,513m. (Dec. 2001); Chair. and Gen. Man. Sheikh FOUAD JAMIL EL-KHAZEN; Dir and Gen. Man. NABIL N. KHAIRALLAH; 12 brs.

Banque du Liban et d'Outre-Mer SAL (BLOM Bank): POB 11-1912, Immeuble BLOM Bank, rue Rachid Karameh, Verdun, Beirut 1107 2807; tel. (1) 743300; fax (1) 738946; e-mail blommail@blom.com.lb; internet www.blom.com.lb; f. 1951; cap. £L185,000m., res £L242,447m., dep. £L8,329,126m. (Dec. 2001); Chair. and Gen. Man. Dr NAAMAN AZHARI; Vice-Chair. and Gen. Man. SAMER AZHARI; 42 brs in Lebanon.

Banque Libano-Française SAL: POB 11-0808, Tour Liberty, rue de Rome, Beirut 1107-2804; tel. (1) 791332; fax (1) 340350; e-mail info@eblf.com; internet www.eblf.com; f. 1967; cap. £L100,000m., res £L175,992m., dep. £L4,371,259m. (Dec. 2001); Pres. and Chair. FARID RAPHAEL; 23 brs.

Banque de la Méditerranée SAL: POB 11-348, 482 rue Clémenceau, Beirut 2022 9302; tel. (1) 373937; fax (1) 362706; f. 1944; cap. £L530,000m., res £L33,259m., dep. £L5,077,238m. (Dec. 2000); Chair. and Gen. Man. Dr MUSTAFA H. RAZIAN; 25 brs.

Banque Misr-Liban SAL: POB 11-7, rue Riad es-Solh, Beirut; tel. (1) 980399; fax (1) 980604; e-mail mail@bml.com.lb; internet www.bml.com.lb; f. 1929; cap. £L27,000m., res £L19,961m., dep. £L608,124m. (Dec. 2001); Chair. Dr BAHAA ED-DIN HELMY; Gen. Man. MUHAMMAD ZAHRAN; 14 brs.

Banque Saradar SAL: POB 11-1121, Beirut 1107-2805; tel. (4) 416804; fax (4) 404490; e-mail saradar@saradar.com.lb; internet www.saradar.com.lb; f. 1948; cap. £L40,000m., res £L61,441m., dep. £L2,425,027m. (Dec. 2000); Chair. and Gen. Man. MARIO JOE SARADAR; 8 brs.

Beirut Riyad Bank SAL: POB 11-4668, Immeuble BRB, rue Riad es-Solh, Beirut 1107-2170; tel. (1) 980222; fax (1) 980358; e-mail beriba@cyberia.net.lb; internet www.brb.com.lb; f. 1958; merger with Bank of Beirut pending; cap. £L40,320m. (Dec. 2001); Chair.

and Gen. Man. ANWAR M. EL-KHALIL; Dep. Chair. and Gen. Man. SAMIR H. MANSOUR; 11 brs in Lebanon, 1 in UK.

BEMO (Banque Européenne pour le Moyen-Orient) SAL: POB 16-6353, Immeuble BEMO, place Sassine, Achrafieh, Beirut; tel. (1) 200505; fax (1) 602519; e-mail bemosal@dm.net.lb; internet www.bemo.com.lb; f. 1964; cap. £L44,247m., res £L7,624m., dep. £L558,312m. (Dec. 2000); Chair. HENRY Y. OBEGI; Gen. Man. RIAD B. OBEGI.

Byblos Bank SAL: POB 11-5605, ave Elias Sarkis, Achrafieh, Beirut; tel. (1) 335200; fax (1) 335540; e-mail byblosbk@byblosbank.com.lb; internet www.byblosbank.com.; f. 1959; merged with Banque Beyrouth pour le Commerce SAL 1997; acquired Byblos Bank Europe SA 1998 and Wedge Bank Middle East SAL 2001; cap. £L245,878m., res £L202,802m., dep. £L5,354,583m. (Dec. 2000); Chair. and Gen. Man. Dr FRANÇOIS SEMAAN BASSIL; 57 brs in Lebanon, 4 abroad.

Crédit Bancaire SAL: POB 16-5795, Immeuble Crédit Bancaire SAL, blvd Bachir Gemayel, Achrafieh, Beirut; tel. (1) 218183; fax (1) 200483; e-mail info@creditbancair.com.lb; internet www.creditbancaire.com.lb; f. 1981; cap. £L10,800m., res £L12,196m., dep. £L272,445m. (Dec. 2000); Chair. and Gen. Man. PAUL A. KEBBÉ; Man. Dir TAREK KHALIFEH; 9 brs.

Crédit Libanais SAL: POB 53492, Centre Sofil, ave Charles Malek, Beirut; tel. (1) 200028; fax (1) 602615; e-mail info@creditlibanais.com.lb; internet www.creditlibanais.com.lb; f. 1961; cap. £L80,000m., res £L147,204m., dep. £L2,694,740m. (Dec. 2001); Chair. and Gen. Man. Dr JOSEPH M. TORBEY; 47 brs.

Federal Bank of Lebanon SAL: POB 11-2209, Federal Bank Bldg, Dora Circle, Beirut; tel. (1) 269902; fax (1) 268711; e-mail fedliban@cyberia.net.lb; f. 1952; cap. £L10,063m., res £L10,986m., dep. £L80,837m. (Dec. 1998); Chair. and Gen. Man. AYOUB FARID MICHEL SAAB; Gen. Man. BECHARA CHAKIB MATTAR; 7 brs.

Fransabank SAL: POB 11-0393, Riad es-Solh, Beirut 1107 2803; tel. (1) 340180; fax (1) 354572; e-mail fsb@fransabank.com; internet www.fransabank.com; f. 1978 as merger of Banque Sabbag and Banque Française pour le Moyen Orient SAL; acquired Banque Tohmé SAL 1993, Universal Bank SAL 1999 and United Bank of Saudi and Lebanon SAL 2001; cap. £L216,000m., res £L76,940m., dep. £L3,818,477m. (Dec. 2001); Chair. ADNAN KASSAR; Vice-Chair. ADEL KASSAR; 48 brs.

Intercontinental Bank of Lebanon SAL: POB 11-5292, Ittihadiah Bldg, Charles Malek Ave, Beirut 1107-2190; tel. (1) 200350; fax (1) 204505; e-mail ibl@ibl.com.lb; f. 1961; cap. £L14,414m., res £L13,254m., dep. £L691,340m. (Dec. 2001); Chair. and Gen. Man. SELIM HABIB; 9 brs.

Jammal Trust Bank SAL: POB 11 5640, Immeuble Jammal, rue Verdun, Beirut; tel. (1) 805702; fax (1) 864170; e-mail info@jammalbank.com.lb; internet www.jammalbank.co.lb; f. 1963 as Investment Bank, SAL; cap. £L29,692m., res £L24,527m., dep. £L217,741m. (Dec. 2000); Pres., Chair. and Gen. Man. ALI ABDULLAH JAMMAL; 20 brs in Lebanon, 4 in Egypt.

Lebanese Canadian Bank: POB 11-2520, Immeuble Ghantous, blvd Dora, Riad es-Solh, Beirut 1107-2110; tel. (1) 250222; fax (1) 250777; e-mail lebcan@lebcanbank.com; internet www.lebcanbank.com; f. 1960; cap. £L14,000m., res £L11,196m., dep. £L684,790m. (Dec. 2000); Pres., Chair. and Gen. Man. GEORGES ZARD ABOU JAOUDÉ; 16 brs.

Lebanese Swiss Bank SAL: POB 11-9552, Immeuble Hoss, 6e étage, rue Emile Eddé, Hamra, Beirut; tel. (1) 354501; fax (1) 346242; e-mail lbs@t-net.com.lb; f. 1973; cap. £L24,000m., res £L8,289m., dep. £L326,889m. (Dec. 2000); Chair. and Gen. Man. Dr TANAL SABBAH; 7 brs.

Lebanon and Gulf Bank SAL: POB 113-6404, Immeuble Rinno, 585 rue de Lyon, Hamra, Beirut; tel. (1) 340190; fax (1) 743135; internet www.lgb@lgb.com.lb; f. 1963 as Banque de Crédit Agricole, name changed 1980; cap. £L30,000m., res £L5,842m., dep. £L832,068m. (Dec. 2000); Chair. and Gen. Man. ABD AL-HAFIZ MAHMOUD ITANI; 10 brs.

Middle East and North Africa Bank SAL: POB 14-5958, Beirut 1105 2080; tel. (1) 826740; fax (1) 841190; e-mail meabho@cyberia.net.lb; internet www.meabank.com; f. 1991; cap. £L24,000m., res £L978m., dep. £L296,791m. (Dec. 2000); Pres., Chair. and Gen. Man. HASSAN HEJEIJ; 4 brs.

National Bank of Kuwait (Lebanon) SAL: POB 11-5727, BAC Bldg, Sanayeh Sq., Justinien St, Riad es-Solh, Beirut 1107 2200; tel. (1) 741111; fax (1) 747866; e-mail info@nbk.com.lb; internet www.nbk.com.lb; f. 1963 as Rifbank, name changed 1996; cap. £L40,020m., res £L4,781m., dep. £L278,617m. (Dec. 2001); Chair. IBRAHIM DABDOUB; Gen. Man. HANY SHERIF; 9 brs.

Near East Commercial Bank SAL: POB 16-5766, 6e étage, Centre Sofil, ave Charles Malek, St Nicolas, Beirut; tel. and fax (1) 200331; e-mail necb@dm.net.lb; f. 1978; cap. £L11,500m., res £L991m., dep. £L180,919m. (Dec. 2001); Chair. and Gen. Man. PAUL CALAND; 5 brs.

North Africa Commercial Bank SAL: POB 11-9575, Centre Aresco, rue Justinian, Beirut; tel. (1) 346320; fax (1) 346322; e-mail nacb@sodetel.net.lb; f. 1973; cap. £L45,687m., dep. £L482,735m. (Dec. 2001); Pres. and Chair. ABOUBAKER ALI SHERIF; Gen. Man. HADI I. ENGIM; 2 brs.

Saudi Lebanese Bank SAL: POB 11-6765, Riad es-Solh, Beirut 1107 2220; tel. (1) 868987; fax (1) 790250; e-mail slbl@t-net.com.lb; f. 1979 as Lebanese Saudi Credit SAL, name changed as above 1981; cap. £L40,000m., res £L15,244m., dep. £L675,651m. (Dec. 1997); Chair. and Gen. Man. Dr MOUSTAFA RAZIAN; 6 brs.

Société Bancaire du Liban SAL: POB 165192, place Sassine, Achrafieh, Beirut 1100 2020; tel. (1) 204826; fax (1) 200455; e-mail sbl-dg@dm.net.lb; f. 1899; cap. £L11,344m., res £L3,229m., dep. £L119,572m. (Dec. 2001); Chair. ANDRE BOULOS; Vice-Chair. SOLLY LAWI; 4 brs.

Société Générale de Banque au Liban (SGBL): POB 11-2955, rond-point Salomé, Sin el-Fil, Beirut; tel. (1) 499813; fax (1) 502820; e-mail sgleb@socgen.com.lb; internet www.sgleb.com; f. 1953 as Société Générale Libano Européenne de Banque SAL (SGLEB); absorbed Inaash Bank SAL 2000; name changed as above 2001; cap. £L106,512m., res £L6,241m., dep. £L3,390,201m. (Dec. 2000); Pres., Chair. and Gen. Man. MAURICE SEHNAOUI; 43 brs in Lebanon.

Société Nouvelle de la Banque de Syrie et du Liban SAL (SNBSL): POB 11-957, rue Riad es-Solh, Beirut; tel. and fax (1) 405564; e-mail snbsl@snbsl.com.lb; f. 1963; cap. £L27,600m., res £L6,559m., dep. £L569,463m. (Dec. 2001); Chair. RAMSAY A. EL-KHOURY; Gen. Man. HABIB KAHAWATI; 17 brs.

Standard Chartered Bank SAL: POB 70216, Antélias, Beirut; tel. (4) 542474; fax (4) 542374; e-mail metro@metrob.com; internet www.standardchartered.com.lb; f. 1979; acquired Metropolitan Bank SAL 2000; cap. £L12,000m., res £L329m., dep. £L127,440m. (Dec. 2001); Chair. ZAHID RAHIM; Gen. Man. MICHELA CHERENHI; 5 brs.

Syrian Lebanese Commercial Bank SAL: POB 113-5127, Immeuble Cinéma Hamra, rue Hamra, Hamra, Beirut; tel. (1) 341262; fax (1) 341208; e-mail hamra@slcbk.com; f. 1974; cap. £L33,000m., res £L5,168m., dep. £L134,375m. (Dec. 2000); Pres., Chair. and Gen. Man. MAHMOUD NADIM MISKAL; 3 brs.

United Credit Bank SAL: POB 13-5086, Beirut; tel. (1) 792795; fax (1) 795094; f. 1982 as Commercial Facilities Bank SAL; name changed 1998; cap. £L14.3m., dep. £L29.6m. (Dec. 1999); Chair. and Gen. Man. Dr ADNAN M. ABOU AYYASH; 4 brs.

Development Bank

Audi Investment Bank SAL: POB 16-5110, Centre Sofil, ave Charles Malek, St Nicolas, Achrafieh, Beirut; tel. (1) 994000; fax (1) 990555; e-mail customerhelpline@audi.com.lb; internet www.audi.com.lb; f. 1974 as Investment and Finance Bank, present name since 1996; medium- and long-term loans, 100% from Lebanese sources; owned by Banque Audi SAL (99.3%); cap. £L25,075m., res £L9,846m., dep. £L802,127m. (Dec. 2000); Chair. and Gen. Man. RAYMOND WADIH AUDI.

Principal Foreign Banks

ABN AMRO Bank Lebanon (Netherlands): POB 113-5162, ABN AMRO Tower, ave Charles Malek, St Nicolas, Achrafieh, Beirut 1103-2807; tel. (1) 219200; fax (1) 217756; e-mail abn@abnamro.com.lb; internet www.abnamro.com.lb; f. 1954; cap. £L23,485m., res £L10,714m., dep. £L955,199m. (Dec. 2000); Man. Dir ELIA NAHAS; 6 brs.

Arab Bank plc (Jordan): POB 11-1015, rue Riad es-Solh, Beirut; tel. (1) 980246; fax (1) 980803; e-mail beirut@arabbank.com.lb; f. 1930; cap. £L31,700m., res £L31,100m.; dep. £L2,001,400m. (Dec. 2001); Exec. Vice-Pres. and Regional Man. Dr HISHAM BSAT.

Banque Nationale de Paris Intercontinentale SA (France): POB 11-1608, Tour el Ghazal/BNPI, ave Fouad Chehab, Beirut; tel. (1) 333717; fax (1) 200604; e-mail bnpi.liban@bnpi.com.lb; internet www.liban.bnpi.bnpgroup.com; f. 1944; total assets £L2,061,529m. (Dec. 2000); Pres. HENRI TYAN; Gen. Man. GUY LEPINARD.

Citibank NA (USA): POB 113-579, Centre Gefinor, Bloc E, rue Clémenceau, Beirut; tel. (1) 738400; fax (1) 738406; cap. £L7,943m., res £L738m., dep. £L171,860m. (Dec. 2000); CEO ELIA SAMAHA.

Habib Bank (Overseas) Ltd (Pakistan): POB 5616, Fadlallah Centre, 1st Floor, blvd esh-Shiah, Musharaffieh, Beirut; tel. (1) 558992; fax (1) 558995; e-mail habibbkbey@t-net.com.lb; Gen. Man. MUHAMMAD SHAHAB KHATTACK.

HSBC Bank Middle East (United Kingdom): POB 11-1380, HSBC Bldg, Minet el-Hosn, Riad es-Solh, Beirut 1107-2080; tel. (1) 377477; fax (1) 372362; internet www.hsbc.com; f. 1946; cap. £L10,750m. (Dec. 1999); CEO KEVIN SMORTHWAITE; 5 brs.

Jordan National Bank SA: POB 5186, Immeuble Diamond Tower, rue Verdun, Beirut; tel. (1) 797078; fax (1) 794955; e-mail jnbobs@netgate.com.lb; cap. £L7,961m., dep. £L121,964m. (Dec. 1997); Regional Gen. Man. RAFIC ARAMOUNI; 3 brs.

Saudi National Commercial Bank: POB 11-2355, Riad es-Solh, Beirut 1107 2160; tel. (1) 860863; fax (1) 867728; e-mail sncb@sncb.com.lb; cap. £L10,000m., res £L6,579m., dep. £L85,061m. (Dec. 2001); Gen. Man. HANI HOUSSAMI.

Numerous other foreign banks have representative offices in Beirut.

Banking Association

Association of Banks in Lebanon: POB 976, Association of Banks in Lebanon Bldg, Gouraud St, Saifi, Beirut; tel. (1) 970500; fax (1) 970501; e-mail abl@abl.org.lb; internet www.abl.org.lb; f. 1959; serves and promotes the interests of the banking community in Lebanon; mems: 66 banks and 9 banking rep. offices; Pres. Dr JOSEPH TORBEY; Gen. Sec. Dr MAKRAM SADER.

STOCK EXCHANGE

The Beirut Stock Exchange recommenced trading in January 1996.

Beirut Stock Exchange (BSE): POB 13-6690, Tour Soudat, 2e étage, rue Soudat, Hamra, Beirut; tel. (1) 786501; fax (1) 786499; e-mail bse@bse.com.lb; internet www.bse.com.lb; f. 1920; 10 cttee mems; Cttee Pres. Dr FADI KHALAF; Cttee VicePres. Dr GHALEB MAHMASANY.

INSURANCE

About 80 insurance companies were registered in Lebanon in the late 1990s, although less than one-half of these were operational. An insurance law enacted in mid-1999 will increase the required capital base for insurance firms and provide tax incentives for mergers within the sector.

Arabia Insurance Co SAL: POB 11-2172, Arabia House, rue de Phénicie, Beirut; tel. (1) 363610; fax (1) 365139; e-mail arabia@arabia-ins.com.lb; internet www.arabiainsurance.com; f. 1944; cap. £L51,000m.; Chair. Dr HISHAM BSAT; Gen. Man. FADY SHAMMAS; 20 brs.

Bankers Assurance SAL: POB 11-4293, Beirut; tel. (1) 200501; fax (1) 200544; e-mail mail@bankers.com.lb; internet www.bankers.com.lb; f. 1972; Chair. SABA NADER; Gen. Man. EUGÈNE NADER.

Commercial Insurance Co (Lebanon) SAL: POB 4351, Centre Starco, Beirut; tel. (1) 373070; fax (1) 373071; e-mail comins@commercialinsurance.com.lb; internet www.commercialinsurance.com.lb; POB 84, Jounieh; tel. (9) 211678; fax (9) 211686; f. 1962; Chair. MAX R. ZACCAR.

Compagnie Libanaise d'Assurances SAL: POB 3685, rue Riad es-Solh, Beirut; tel. (1) 868988; f. 1951; cap. £L3,000m. (1991); Chair. JEAN F. S. ABOUJAOUDÉ; Gen. Man. MAMDOUH RAHMOUN.

Al-Ittihad al-Watani: POB 1270, Immeuble Al-Ittihadia, ave Fouad Chehab, St Nicolas, Beirut; tel. (1) 330840; f. 1947; cap. £L30m.; Chair. JOE I. KAIROUZ; Exec. Dir TANNOUS FEGHALI.

Libano-Suisse Insurance Co SAL: POB 11-3821, Beirut 1107-2150; tel. (1) 374900; fax (1) 368724; e-mail insure@libano-suisse.com; internet www.libano-suisse.com.lb; f. 1959; cap. £L4,050m. (2000); Chair. MICHEL PIERRE PHARAON; Gen. Man. SAMIR NAHAS.

Al-Mashrek Insurance and Reinsurance SAL: POB 16-6154, Immeuble Al-Mashrek, 65 rue Aabrine, Beirut; tel. (1) 200541; fax (4) 418578; e-mail amirco@inco.com.lb; f. 1962; cap. £L5,000m., (1999); Chair. and Gen. Man. ABRAHAM MATOSSIAN.

'La Phénicienne' SAL: POB 11-5652, Immeuble Hanna Haddad, rue Amine Gemayel, Sioufi, Beirut; tel. (1) 425484; fax (1) 424532; f. 1964; Chair. and Gen. Man. TANNOUS C. FEGHALI.

Société Nationale d'Assurances SAL: POB 11-4805, Beirut; tel. (1) 956600; fax (1) 956624; f. 1963; Chair. ANTOINE WAKIM.

Trade and Industry

DEVELOPMENT ORGANIZATIONS

Council for Development and Reconstruction (CDR): POB 116-5351, Tallet es-Serail, Beirut; tel. (1) 643982; fax (1) 647947; e-mail general@cdr.gov.lb; internet www.cdr.gov.lb; f. 1977; an autonomous public institution reporting to the Cabinet, the CDR is charged with the co-ordination, planning and execution of Lebanon's public reconstruction programme; it plays a major role in attracting foreign funds; Pres. JAMAL ITANI; Sec.-Gen. GEORGE SAMAHA.

Investment Development Authority of Lebanon (IDAL): POB 113-7251, Cristal Bldg 1145, Hussein al-Adhab St, Nijmeh Sq., Beirut; tel. (1) 983306; fax (1) 983302; e-mail mail@idal.com.lb; internet www.idal.com.lb; f. 1994; state-owned; Chair. and Gen. Man. SAMIH BARBIR.

Société Libanaise pour le Développement et la Reconstruction de Beyrouth (SOLIDERE): POB 11-9493, 149 rue Saad

Zagholoul, Beirut; tel. (1) 980650; fax (1) 980662; e-mail solidere@solidere.com.lb; internet www.solidere.com.lb; f. 1994; real estate co responsible for reconstruction of Beirut Central District; Dir-Gen. MOUNIR DOUAIDY.

CHAMBERS OF COMMERCE AND INDUSTRY

International Chamber of Commerce in Lebanon: POB 11-1801, Immeuble Elias Abd-an Nour, Achrafieh, Beirut; tel. (1) 200437; fax (1) 321220; Chair. ADNAN KASSAR; Gen. Sec. LOUIS G. HOBEIKA.

Beirut Chamber of Commerce and Industry: POB 11-1801, rue Justinian, Sanayeh, Beirut; tel. (1) 744160; fax (1) 353395; e-mail info@ccib.org.lb; internet www.ccib.org.lb; f. 1898; 32,000 mems; Pres. ADNAN KASSAR; Dir-Gen. Dr WALID NAJA.

Tripoli Chamber of Commerce and Industry: POB 27, blvd Tripoli, Tripoli; tel. (6) 432790; Pres. HASSAN EL-MOUNLA.

Chamber of Commerce and Industry in Sidon and South Lebanon: POB 41, rue Maarouf Saad, Sidon; tel. (7) 720123; fax (7) 722986; e-mail chamber@ccias.org.lb; internet www.ccias.org.lb; f. 1933; Pres. MOHAMAD ZAATARI.

Zahleh Chamber of Commerce and Industry: POB 100, Zahleh; tel. (8) 802602; fax (8) 800050; f. 1939; 2,500 mems; Pres. EDMOND JREISSATI.

EMPLOYERS' ASSOCIATION

Association of Lebanese Industrialists: Chamber of Commerce and Industry Bldg, 5e étage, Sanayeh, Beirut; tel. (1) 350280; fax (1) 350282; e-mail ali@ali.org.lb; internet www.ali.org.lb; Pres. JACQUES J. SARRAF; Sec.-Gen. GHAZI F. YAHYA.

UTILITIES
Electricity

Electricité du Liban (EdL): POB 131, Immeuble de l'Electricité du Liban, 22 rue du Fleuve, Beirut; tel. (1) 442556; fax (1) 583084; f. 1954; state-owned; scheduled for privatization in 2003; Dir-Gen. KAMAL F. HAYEK.

Water

In the late 1990s the Government was in the process of establishing five new regional water authorities (in the governorates of the North, South, Beka'a, Beirut and Mount Lebanon), to replace the existing water authorities and committees. Under the re-organization the new authorities were to operate under the supervision of the Ministry of Energy and Water.

Beirut Water Supply Office: Beirut; Pres. LUCIEN MOBAYAD.

MAJOR COMPANIES

Arabian Construction Co SAL: POB 114-5175, Immeuble Shatila, 2e étage, rue Shubert, Ain at-Tineh, Verdun, Beirut; tel. (1) 861615; fax (1) 785623; e-mail accsal@destination.com.lb; f. 1971; construction of multi-storey buildings, hotels, houses, etc.; cap. US $1m.; Chair. GHASSAN ABDALLAH AL-MEREHBI; Vice-Chair. ANAS MIKATI; 1,500 employees.

Château Ksara SAL: Immeuble Nakhle Hanna, ave Charles Malek, POB 16-6184, Beirut; tel. (1) 200715; fax (1) 200716; e-mail info@ksara.com.lb; internet www.ksara.com.lb; f. 1857; wines and spirits (incl. Ksarak); Pres. ZAFER CHAOUI; Man. Dir CHARLES GHOSTINE; 75 employees.

Contracting and Trading Co (CAT) International Ltd: POB 11-1036, Immeuble CAT, rue al-Arz, Saifi, Beirut; tel. (1) 449910; fax (1) 442200; e-mail cat@cat.com.lb; internet www.cat.com.lb; f. 1942; civil, mechanical, electrical, pipeline and marine works contractors; sales US $21.1m.; total assets $34.9m. (2000); CEO SAMIR SAWAYA; 3,000 employees.

Filature Nationale de Coton SAL, Asseily & Cie: Immeuble Asseily, place Riad es-Solh, POB 11-4126, Beirut; tel. (1) 890610; production of textiles; Dir. G. ASSEILY.

Fonderies Ohannes H. Kassardjian SAL: POB 11-4150, Beirut; tel. (5) 462462; fax (5) 462948; e-mail okfond@cyberia.net.lb; f. 1939; production of brass and gun-metal valves and fittings for pipes, chromium-plated bathroom fittings and floor drains, cast iron valves, fittings for ductile iron pipes manhole covers and gratings, etc.; Pres. JOSEPH O. KASSARDJIAN; 300 employees.

Al-Hamra Engineering Co SARL: POB 11-6040, Modca Bldg, 7th Floor, Hamra St, Beirut; tel. and fax (1) 688747; e-mail hameng@bignet.com.lb; f. 1966; part of the Al-Hamra Group; civil, electrical and mechanical engineering; construction work on industrial projects, etc.; steel structures, offshore works; production and trading in building materials, etc.; sales US $300m. (1998); cap. $4.8m.; total assets $120m.; CEO HANNA AYOUB; Gen. Man. TONY HANANIA; 800 employees.

Industrial Development Co SARL (INDEVCO): POB 11-2354, Immeuble Frem, Tallat al-Ansafir, Ajaltoun, Beirut; tel. (9) 953600; fax (9) 953503; e-mail info@indevcogroup.com; f. 1963; mfrs of tissue and paperboard, kitchen cabinets and doors, carton boxes, consumer tissue products, diapers and disposable products; sales US $500m. (1995); Chair. GEORGES FREM; Man. Dir TONY FREM; 5,000 employees (Lebanon, Saudi Arabia, Arabian Gulf, Brazil and the USA).

Karoun Dairies SAL: Immeuble Baghdassarian, Cité Industrielle, Bauchrieh, POB 11-9150, Beirut; tel. (1) 497325; fax (1) 497080; e-mail dairies@karoun.com; internet www.karoun.com; f. 1931; dairy products; Chair. and Gen. Man. ARA BAGHDASSARIAN; 45 employees.

Lahoud Engineering Co Ltd: POB 55366, ave Charles de Gaulle, Sin el-Fil, Beirut; tel. (1) 513000; fax (1) 496540; f. 1972; construction of industrial plants; Man. Dir SAMIR LAHOUD.

Mothercat Ltd: POB 11–2036, Immeuble CAT, rue al-Arz, Saifi, Beirut; tel. (1) 449910; fax (1) 446931; f. 1994; civil, mechanical, electrical, pipeline, storage tanks and marine works contractors; sales US $40.0m. (2000); cap. US $7.5m.; total assets US $30.6m.; CEO SAMIR SAWAYA; 500 employees.

Société Nationale d'Entreprises: POB 11-7101, Beirut; tel. (1) 892805; fax (1) 892806; civil engineering including road construction and water contracting; Chair. JOSEPH KHOURY; 230 employees.

Zahrani Oil Installations: Beirut; tel. (1) 345702; oil refining; Gen. Man. G. A. AHMAD; 300 employees.

TRADE UNION FEDERATION

Confédération Générale des Travailleurs du Liban (CGTL): POB 4381, Beirut; f. 1958; 300,000 mems; only national labour centre in Lebanon and sole rep. of working classes; comprises 18 affiliated federations including all 150 unions in Lebanon; Chair. GHNEIM AZ-ZOGHBI; Pres. ELIAS ABU RIZQ.

Transport

RAILWAYS

Office des Chemins de Fer de l'Etat Libanais et du Transport en Commun: POB 109, Gare St Michel, Nahr, Beirut 55365; tel. (1) 442198; fax (1) 447007; since 1961 all railways in Lebanon have been state-owned. The original network of some 412 km no longer transports passengers. However, Lebanese authorities have planned a rail reconstruction project, costing US $40m.–$60m. Dir-Gen. JAMAL KRAYEM.

ROADS

At 31 December 1996 Lebanon had an estimated 6,350 km of roads, of which 2,170 km were highways, main or national roads and 1,370 km were secondary or regional roads. The total road network was estimated at 7,300 km in 1999. The two international motorways are the north–south coastal road and the road connecting Beirut with Damascus in Syria. Among the major roads are that crossing the Beka'a and continuing south to Bent-Jbail and the Shtaura–Ba'albek road. Hard-surfaced roads connect Jezzine with Moukhtara, Bzebdine with Metn, Meyroub with Afka and Tannourine. A road construction project, costing some US $100m., was planned for Beirut in the late 1990s. A new 8-km highway, linking around 26 villages in southern Lebanon, was inaugurated in August 2000.

SHIPPING

A two-phase programme to rehabilitate and expand the port of Beirut is currently under way. In the second phase, which commenced in early 1997, the construction of an industrial free zone, a fifth basin and a major container terminal are envisaged, at an estimated cost of US $1,000m. Tripoli, the northern Mediterranean terminus of the oil pipeline from Iraq (the other is Haifa, Israel—not in use since 1948), is also a busy port, with good equipment and facilities. Jounieh, north of Beirut, is Lebanon's third most important port. A new deep-water sea port is to be constructed south of Sidon. The reconstructed port of an-Naqoura, in the 'security zone' along the border with Israel, was inaugurated in June 1987.

Port Authorities

Gestion et Exploitation du Port de Beyrouth: POB 1490-1418, Beirut; tel. (1) 587063; fax (1) 582021; e-mail bey-port@cyberia.net.lb; Man. Dir ISSAM BEKDACH; Harbour Master MAROUN KHOURY.

Service d'Exploitation du Port de Tripoli: El Mina, Tripoli; tel. (6) 601225; fax (6) 220180; e-mail tport@terra.net.lb; f. 1959; Harbour Master MARWAN BAROUDI.

Principal Shipping Companies

Youssef A Abourahal and Hanna N Tabet: POB 11-5890, Immeuble Ghantous, autostrade Dora, Beirut; tel. (1) 263872.

Ets Paul Adem: Centre Moucarri, 6e étage, autostrade Dora, Beirut; tel. and fax (1) 582421.

Ademar Shipping Lines: POB 175-231, Beirut; tel. (1) 444100; fax (1) 444101.

Adriatica Levant Lines SARL: Immeuble Tanios Saba, rue Ibrahim Bacha, Medawar, Beirut; tel. (1) 580181.

Agence Générale Maritime (AGEMAR) SARL: POB 9255, Centre Burotec, 7e étage, rue Pasteur, Beirut; tel. (1) 583885; fax (1) 583884; Dirs S. MEDLEJ, N. MEDLEJ.

Kawar Amin & Sons: Beirut; tel. (1) 352525; fax (1) 353802; f. 1963; Chair. TAWFIQ KAWAR AMIN.

Arab Shipping and Chartering Co: POB 1084, Immeuble Ghandour, ave des Français, Beirut; tel. (1) 371044; fax (1) 373370; e-mail arabship@dm.net.lb; agents for China Ocean Shipping Co.

Associated Levant Lines SAL: POB 110371, Immeuble Mercedes, autostrade Dora, Beirut; tel. (1) 255366; fax (1) 255362; e-mail tgf-all@dm.net.lb; Dirs T. GARGOUR, N. GARGOUR, H. GARGOUR.

Wafic Begdache: Immeuble Wazi, 4e étage, rue Moussaitbé, Beirut; tel. (1) 319920; fax (1) 815002; e-mail mody@lebaneseshipping.com.

Bulk Traders International: POB 70-152, Centre St Elie, Bloc A, 6e étage, Antélias, Beirut; tel. (4) 410724; fax (4) 402842; e-mail bulk@cyberia.net.lb.

Continental Shipmanagement SARL: POB 901413, Centre Dora Moucarri, 8e étage, appt 804, Beirut; tel. (1) 583654; fax (1) 584440.

O. D. Debbas & Sons: Head Office: POB 166678, Immeuble Debbas, 530 blvd Corniche du Fleuve, Beirut; tel. (1) 585253; fax (1) 587135; e-mail oddebbas@oddebbas.com; f. 1892; Man. Dir OIDIH ELIE DEBBAS.

Dery Shipping Lines Ltd: POB 5720-113, Beirut; tel. (1) 862442; fax (1) 344146.

Diana K Shipping Co: POB 113-5125, Immeuble Ajouz, rue Kenedi, Ein Mreisseh, Beirut; tel. (1) 363314; fax (1) 369712; e-mail dianak@cyberia.net.lb; Marine Dept Man. Capt. AMIN HABBAL.

Fauzi Jemil Ghandour: POB 1084, Beirut; tel. (1) 373376; fax (1) 360048; e-mail alifgand@dm.net.lb; agents for Denizçlik Bankasi TAO (Denizvollari); Ecuadorian Line, Festival Shipping and Tourist Enterprises Ltd.

Gezairi Chartering and Shipping Co (GEZACHART): POB 11-1402, Immeuble Gezairi, place Gezairi, Ras Beirut; tel. (1) 783783; fax (1) 784784; e-mail gezachart@gezairi.com.; internet www.gezairi.com; ship management, chartering, brokerage.

Gulf Agency Co (Lebanon) Ltd: POB 4392, Beirut; tel. (1) 446086; fax (1) 446097; e-mail gacleltd@dm.net.lb; f. 1969; Gen. Man. SIMON G. BEJJANI.

Lebanese Navigators Co SARL: Beirut; tel. (1) 603335; fax (1) 603334.

Medawar Shipping Co SARL: POB 8962/11, Immeuble Kanafani, rue al-Arz, Saifi, Beirut; tel. (1) 447277; fax (1) 447662.

Mediterranean Feedering Co SARL: POB 70-1187, Immeuble Akak, autostrade Dbayeh, Beirut; tel. (1) 403056; fax (1) 406444; e-mail mfcbeirut@attmail.com; Man. Dir EMILE AKEF EL-KHOURY.

Orient Shipping and Trading Co SARL: POB 11-2561, Immeuble Moumneh, no 72, rue Ain al-Mraisseh 54, Beirut; tel. (1) 644252; fax (1) 602221; Dirs ELIE ZAROUBY, EMILE ZAROUBY.

Rassem Shipping Agency: POB 11-8460, Immeuble Agha, Raoucheh, Beirut; tel. (1) 866372; fax (1) 805593.

Riga Brothers: POB 17-5134, Immeuble Mitri Haddad, rue du Port, Beirut; tel. (1) 406882.

G. Sahyouni & Co SARL: POB 17-5452, Mar Mikhael, Beirut 1104 2040; tel. (1) 257046; fax (1) 241317; e-mail lloydsbey@inco.com.lb; f. 1989; agents for Baltic Control Lebanon Ltd., SARL, and Lloyds; Man. Dir. GEORGE SHYOUNI; Financial Man. HENRY CHIDIAC.

Sinno Trading and Navigation Agency: POB 113-6977, Immeuble Rebeiz, 4e étage, rue du Port, Beirut; tel. (1) 446698; fax (1) 446707; Chair. MUHIEDDINE F. SINNO; Man. Dir AHMED JABBOURY.

A Sleiman Co & Sons: Immeuble Saroulla, 3e étage, rue Hamra, Beirut; tel. (1) 354240; fax (1) 340262.

Union Shipping and Chartering Agency SAL: POB 2856, Immeuble Ghandour, ave des Français, Beirut; tel. (1) 373376; fax (1) 360048; e-mail unichart@dm.net.lb; agents for Croatia Line, Jadroslobodna, Jugo Oceania, Atlanska Plovidba, Jadroplov and Maruba S.C.A.

CIVIL AVIATION

Services from the country's principal airport, in Beirut, were subject to frequent disruptions after 1975; its location in predominantly Muslim west Beirut made it virtually inaccessible to non-Muslims. In 1986 a new airport, based on an existing military airfield, was opened at Halat, north of Beirut, by Christian concerns, but commer-

cial operations from the airport were not authorized by the Government. Services to and from Beirut by Middle East Airlines (MEA) were suspended, at the end of January 1987, after the Christian LF militia shelled the airport and threatened to attack MEA aircraft if services from their own airport, at Halat, did not receive official authorization. Beirut airport was reopened in May, after the LF accepted government assurances that Halat would receive the necessary authorization for civil use. However, the commission concluded that Halat did not possess the facilities to cater for international air traffic. Some 2.4m. passengers used Beirut International Airport in 2001. In late 2001 a major expansion project at the airport was completed, at an estimated cost of US $600m.; facilities included a new terminal building and two new runways, increasing handling capacity to 6m. passengers a year.

MEA (Middle East Airlines, Air Liban SAL): POB 206, Headquarters MEA, blvd de l'Aéroport, Beirut; tel. (1) 628888; fax (1) 629260; e-mail mea@mea.net.lb; internet www.mea.com.lb; f. 1945; took over Lebanese International Airways in 1969; privatization scheduled for 2002; regular services throughout Europe, the Middle East, North and West Africa, and the Far East; Chair. MUHAMMAD EL-HOUT; Commercial Man. NIZAR KHOURY.

Trans-Mediterranean Airways SAL (TMA): Beirut International Airport, POB 11–3018, Beirut; tel. (1) 629210; fax (1) 629219; e-mail cargo@tma.com.lb; internet www.tma.com.lb; f. 1953; scheduled services, charter activities and aircraft lease operations covering Europe, the Middle East, Africa and the Far East; also provides handling, storage and maintenance services; Chair. and Pres. FADI N. SAAB.

Tourism

Before the civil war, Lebanon was a major tourist centre, and its scenic beauty, sunny climate and historic sites attracted some 2m. visitors annually. In 1974 tourism contributed about 20% of the country's income. Since the end of the civil conflict, tourist facilities (in particular hotels) have begun to be reconstructed, and the Government has chosen to concentrate its efforts on the promotion of cultural as well as conference and exhibition-based tourism. In 1999 UNESCO declared Beirut as the Cultural Capital of the Arab World. Lebanon is also being promoted as an 'eco-tourism' destination. Excluding Syrian visitors, the annual total of tourist arrivals increased from 177,503 in 1992 to 741,648 in 2000. Tourism receipts reached an estimated US $1,221m. in 1998; however, receipts fell to $742m. in 2000. Of total arrivals in 2000, 38.8% were from Arab countries (excluding Syria) and 30.9% from Europe.

National Council of Tourism in Lebanon (NCTL): POB 11-5344, rue Banque du Liban 550, Beirut; tel. (1) 343196; fax (1) 343279; e-mail tourism@cyberia.net.lb; internet www.lebanon-tourism.gov.lb; government-sponsored autonomous organization responsible for the promotion of tourism; overseas offices in Paris (France) and Cairo (Egypt); Pres. FOUAD FAWAZ; Dir-Gen. NASSER SAFIEDDINE.

Defence

Commander-in-Chief of the Armed Forces: Gen. MICHEL SULAYMAN (Maronite Christian).

Chief of Staff of Armed Forces: Maj.-Gen. ABOU CHACRA (Druze).

Commander of the Air Force: Brig.-Gen. FAHIM AL-HAJJ.

Director-General of the Internal Security Forces: Brig.-Gen. MARWAN ZEIN (Shi'ite).

Defence Budget (2001): £L906,000m.

Total armed forces (August 2001): 71,830: army 70,000; air force 1,000; navy 830.

There is also an Internal Security Force of some 13,000 (under reorganization), attached to the Ministry of the Interior. The strengths of the principal sectarian militias (before they, with the exception of Hezbollah, began to disband in March 1991) were estimated as follows: Lebanese Forces (Christian) 18,500 regulars (16,500 reserves); Druze 8,500 regulars (6,500 reserves); Amal (Shi'ite) 10,200 regulars (4,800 reserves); Hezbollah (Shi'ite) 3,500 regulars (11,500 reserves). The Israeli-backed South Lebanon Army (SLA), patrolling the buffer zone along the border with Israel, numbered an estimated 2,500. In March 1978 a 6,000-strong UN Interim Force in Lebanon (UNIFIL) was deployed to try to keep the peace near the border with Israel; UNIFIL's strength was increased to 7,000 in February 1982. However, in May 2000 Israeli armed forces and the SLA withdrew from southern Lebanon. UNIFIL numbered 3,426 personnel in July 2002, assisted by some 50 military observers of the UN Truce Supervision Organization (UNTSO). An estimated 18,000 Syrian troops remained in Lebanon in August 2001. Syria redeployed an estimated 6,000–10,000 of its armed forces from Greater Beirut in mid-June 2001.

Education

Education is not compulsory. Primary education has been available free of charge in state schools since 1960, but private institutions still provide the main facilities for secondary and university education. Private schools enjoy almost complete autonomy, except for a certain number which receive government financial aid and are supervised by inspectors from the Ministry of Education and Higher Education.

Primary education begins at six years of age and lasts for five years. It is followed either by the four-year intermediate course or the three-year secondary course. The baccalaureate examination is taken in two parts at the end of the second and third years of secondary education, and a public examination is taken at the end of the intermediate course. Technical education is provided mainly at the National School of Arts and Crafts, which offers four-year courses in electronics, mechanics, architectural and industrial drawing, and other subjects. There are also public vocational schools providing courses for lower levels. In 1996 the total enrolment at primary and secondary schools was equivalent to 94% of all school-age children (93% of boys; 95% of girls); enrolment at secondary schools in that year was equivalent to 81% of the appropriate age-group (males 78%; females 84%).

Higher education is provided by 13 institutions, including six universities. Some 87,957 students were enrolled at Lebanese universities in the 1996/97 academic year. Teacher training is given at various levels. A three-year course which follows the intermediate course trains primary school teachers and another three-year course which follows the second part of the baccalaureate trains teachers for the intermediate school. Secondary school teachers are trained at the Higher Teachers' College at the Lebanese University. Two agricultural schools provide a three-year course for pupils holding the intermediate school degree. In 1998 Lebanon secured a loan of US $60m. from the World Bank, in order to restructure the country's system of technical and vocational education.

Lebanon has the highest literacy rate in the Arab world (see Statistical Survey). Expenditure on education by the central Government in 1998 was £L695,600m. (8.3% of total budgetary expenditure).

Bibliography

Abouchdid, E. E. *Thirty Years of Lebanon and Syria (1917–47)*. Beirut, 1948.

Agwani, M. S. (Ed.). *The Lebanese Crisis, 1958: a documentary study*. Asia Publishing House, 1965.

Ajami, Fouad. *The Vanished Imam: Musa al-Sadr and the Shi'a of Lebanon*. London, I. B. Tauris; New York, Cornell University Press, 1986.

The Beirut Massacre: the complete Kahan Commission Report. New York, Karz-Cohl, 1983.

Besoins et Possibilités de Développement du Liban. Étude Préliminaire, 2 Vols. Lebanese Ministry of Planning, Beirut, 1964.

Beydoun, Ahmad. *Le Liban. Itinéraires dans une guerre incivile*. Paris, Karthala and CERMOC, 1993.

Binder, Leonard (Ed.). *Politics in Lebanon*. New York, Wiley, 1966.

Bulloch, John. *Death of a Country: The Civil War in Lebanon*. London, Weidenfeld and Nicolson, 1977.

Final Conflict: The War in Lebanon. London, Century Publishing Co.

Burckhard, C. *Le Mandat Français en Syrie et au Liban*. Paris, 1925.

Catroux, G. *Dans la Bataille de Méditerranée*. Paris, Julliard, 1949.

Chamoun, C. *Les Mémoires de Camille Chamoun*. Beirut, 1949.

Dagher, Carole H. *Bring down the walls: Lebanon's post-war challenge*. New York, St Martin's Press, 1998.

El Khazen, Farid. *The Breakdown of the State in Lebanon, 1976–76*. Cambridge, MA, Harvard University Press, 2000.

Firro, Kais. *Inventing Lebanon: Nationalism and the State Under the Mandate*. London, I. B. Tauris, 2002.

Fisk, Robert. *Pity the Nation: Lebanon at War*. London, André Deutsch, 1990; revised edn. Oxford Paperbacks, 2001.

Gaunson, A. B. *The Anglo-French Clash in Lebanon and Syria, 1940–45*. London, Macmillan, 1987.

Ghattas, Emile. *The monetary system in the Lebanon*. New York 1961.

Giannou, Chris. *Besieged: a doctor's story of life and death in Beirut*. Toronto, Key Porter, 1990.

Gilmour, David. *Lebanon: the Fractured Country*. London, Martin Robertson, 1983.

Gilsenan, Michael. *Lords of the Lebanese Marches: Violence and Narrative in an Arab Society*. London, I. B. Tauris, 1998.

Glass, Charles. *Tribes with Flags: A Journey Curtailed*. London, Secker and Warburg, 1990.

Gulick, John. *Social Structure and Culture Change in a Lebanese Village*. New York, 1955.

Haddad, J. *Fifty Years of Modern Syria and Lebanon*. Beirut, 1950.

Halawi, Majed. *A Lebanon Defied: Mosa al-Sadr and the Shi'a community*. Oxford, Westview Press, 1993.

Harik, Iliya F. *Politics and Change in a Traditional Society—Lebanon 1711–1845*. Princeton University Press, 1968.

Hepburn, A. H. *Lebanon*. New York, 1966.

Himadeh, Raja S. *The Fiscal System of Lebanon*. Beirut, Khayat, 1961.

Hitti, Philip K. *Lebanon in History*. 3rd edn, London, Macmillan, 1967.

Hollis, Rosemary, and Shehadi, Nadim (Eds). *Lebanon on Hold: Implications for Middle East Peace*. London, Royal Institute for International Affairs, 1996.

Hourani, Albert K. *Syria and Lebanon*. London, 1946.

Hudson, Michael C. *The Precarious Republic: Political Modernization in the Lebanon*. New York, Random House, 1968.

Husayn, Abdul Rahim Abu. *The View from Istanbul: Ottoman Lebanon and the Druze Emirate*. London, I. B. Tauris, 2002.

Jaber, Hala. *Hezbollah*. London, Fourth Estate, 1997.

Johnson, Michael. *All Honourable Men: The Social Origins of War in Lebanon*. London, I. B. Tauris, 2001.

Kalawoun, Nasser M. *The Struggle for Lebanon. A Modern History of Lebanese-Egyptian Relations*. London, I. B. Tauris, 2000.

Kapeliouk, Amnon. *Sabra et Chatila: enquête sur un massacre*. Paris, Editions du Seuil.

Kassir, Samur. *La guerre du Liban. De la dissension nationale au conflit régional*. Paris, Karthala and CERMOC, 1994.

Khalaf, S. *Civil and Uncivil Violence: The Internationalization of Communal Conflict in Lebanon*. New York, NY, Columbia University Press, 2002.

Khater, Akram Fouad. *Inventing home: Emigration, Gender and the Middle Class in Lebanon 1870–1920*. Berkeley, CA, California University Press, 2001.

LaTeef, Nelda. *Women of Lebanon: Interviews with Champions for Peace*. Jefferson, North Carolina, McFarland and Co, 1997.

Lecerf, Marie-Ange. *Comprendre le Liban*. Paris, Karthala, 1988.

Longrigg, S. H. *Syria and Lebanon under French Mandate*. Oxford University Press, 1958.

Makdisi, Ussama. *The Culture of Sectarianism: Community, History and Violence in Nineteenth Century Ottoman Lebanon*. Berkeley, CA, University of California Press, 2000.

Mills, Arthur E. *Private Enterprise in Lebanon*. American University of Beirut, 1959.

O'Balance, Edgar. *Civil War in Lebanon, 1975–1992*. New York, St Martin's Press, 1998.

Picard, Elizabeth. *Lebanon: a Shattered Country*. New York and London, Holmes and Meier, 1996.

Qubain, Fahim I. *Crisis in Lebanon*. Washington, DC, Middle East Institute, 1961.

Randal, Jonathan. *The Tragedy of Lebanon*. London, Chatto and Windus, 1983.

Rondot, Pierre. *Les Institutions Politiques du Liban*. Paris, 1947.

Saad-Ghorayeb, Amal. *Hizbu'llah: Politics and Religion*. London, Pluto Press, 2001.

Saba, Elias S. *The Foreign Exchange Systems of Lebanon and Syria*. American University of Beirut, 1961.

Safa, Elie. *L'Emigration Libanaise*. Beirut, 1960.

Salem, Elie A. *Violence and Diplomacy in Lebanon*. London, I. B. Tauris, 1995.

Salibi, K. S. *The Modern History of Lebanon*. New York, Praeger, and London, Weidenfeld and Nicolson, 1964.

Cross Roads to Civil War: Lebanon 1958–76. New York, Caravan Books, 1976.

Sayigh, Y. A. *Entrepreneurs of Lebanon*. Cambridge, MA, 1962.

Soueid, Mahmoud. *Israël au Liban. La fin de 30 ans d'occupation?* Paris, Revue d'études Palestiniennes, 2000.

Stewart, Desmond. *Trouble in Beirut*. London, Wingate, 1959.

Suleiman, M. W. *Political Parties in Lebanon*. Ithaca, NY, Cornell University Press, 1967.

Sykes, John. *The Mountain Arabs*. London, Hutchinson, 1968.

Tibawi, A. L. *A Modern History of Greater Syria, including Lebanon and Palestine*. London, Macmillan, 1969.

Vallaud, Pierre. *Le Liban au Bout du Fusil*. Paris, Librairie Hachette, 1976.

Zamir, Meir. *The Foundation of Modern Lebanon*. London, Croom Helm, 1985.

Lebanon's Quest: The Road to Statehood 1926–1939. London, I. B. Tauris, 1998.

Ziadeh, Nicola. *Syria and Lebanon*. New York, Praeger, 1957.

Zisser, Eyal. *Lebanon: The Challenge of Independence*. London, I. B. Tauris, 2000.

LIBYA

(THE GREAT SOCIALIST PEOPLE'S LIBYAN ARAB JAMAHIRIYA)

Physical and Social Geography

W. B. FISHER

The Great Socialist People's Libyan Arab Jamahiriya (as Libya has been known since April 1986) is bounded on the north by the Mediterranean Sea, on the east by Egypt and Sudan, on the south and south-west by Chad and Niger, on the west by Algeria and on the north-west by Tunisia. The three component areas of Libya are: Tripolitania, in the west, with an area of 285,000 sq km (110,000 sq miles); Cyrenaica, in the east, which has an area of 905,000 sq km; and the Fezzan, in the south, with an area of 570,000 sq km—giving an approximate total for Libya of 1,760,000 sq km. The independence of Libya was proclaimed in December 1951; before that date, following conquest by the Italians, Tripolitania and Cyrenaica had been ruled by a British administration, at first military, then civil; and the Fezzan had been administered by France. The revolutionary Government which came to power in September 1969 renamed the three regions: Tripolitania became known as the Western provinces, Cyrenaica the Eastern provinces, and the Fezzan the Southern provinces.

The political and economic capital of Libya is Tripoli. However, as part of a radical government decentralization programme undertaken in September 1988, all but two of the secretariats of the General People's Committee (ministries) were relocated to other parts of the country.

PHYSICAL FEATURES

The whole of Libya may be said to form part of the vast plateau of North Africa, which extends from the Atlantic Ocean to the Red Sea; but there are certain minor geographical features which give individuality to the three component areas of Libya. Tripolitania consists of a series of regions at different levels, rising in the main towards the south, and thus broadly comparable with a flight of steps. In the extreme north, along the Mediterranean coast, there is a low-lying coastal plain called the Jefara. This is succeeded inland by a line of hills, or rather a scarp edge, that has several distinguishing local names, but is usually alluded to merely as the Jebel. Here and there in the Jebel occurs evidence of former volcanic activity—old craters, and sheets of lava. The Jefara and adjacent parts of the Jebel are by far the most important parts of Tripolitania, since they are better watered and contain most of the population, together with the capital town, Tripoli.

South of the Jebel there is an upland plateau—a dreary desert landscape of sand, scrub, and scattered irregular masses of stone. After several hundred kilometres the plateau gives place to a series of east–west running depressions, where artesian water, and hence oases, are found. These depressions make up the region of the Fezzan, which is merely a collection of oases on a fairly large scale, interspersed with areas of desert. In the extreme south the land rises considerably to form the mountains of the central Sahara, where some peaks reach 3,500 m in height.

Cyrenaica has a slightly different physical pattern. In the north, along the Mediterranean, there is an upland plateau that rises to 600 m in two very narrow steps, each only a few kilometres wide. This gives a bold, prominent coastline to much of Cyrenaica, and so there is a marked contrast with Tripolitania where the coast is low-lying, and in parts fringed by lagoons. The northern uplands of Cyrenaica are called the Jebel Akhdar (Green Mountain), and here, once again, are found the bulk of the population and the two main towns, Benghazi and Derna. On its western side the Jebel Akhdar drops fairly steeply to the shores of the Gulf of Sirte (Surt); but on the east it falls more gradually, and is traceable as a series of ridges, about 100 m in altitude, that extend as far as the Egyptian frontier. This eastern district, consisting of low ridges aligned parallel to the coast, is known as Marmarica, and its chief town is Tobruk.

South of the Jebel Akhdar, the land falls in elevation, producing an extensive lowland, which, except for its northern fringe, is mainly desert. Oases occur sporadically at Aujila (or Ojila), Jalo and Jaghbub in the north; and Jawf, Zighen and Kufra (the largest of all) in the south. These oases traditionally supported only a few thousand inhabitants and were less significant than those of the Fezzan, though some are now in petroleum-producing areas and, consequently, increasing in importance. In the same region, and becoming more widespread towards the east, is the Sand Sea—an expanse of fine, mobile sand, easily lifted by the wind into dunes that can sometimes reach about 100 m in height and more than 150 km in length. Finally, in the far south of Cyrenaica, lie the central Saharan mountains—the Tibesti Ranges, continuous with those to the south of the Fezzan.

The climate of Libya is characterized chiefly by its aridity and by its wide variation in temperatures. Lacking mountain barriers, the country is subject to the climatic influence of both the Sahara and the Mediterranean Sea, and, as a result, there can be abrupt transitions in climatic conditions. In winter it can be fairly raw and cold in the north, with sleet and even light snow on the hills. In summer it is extremely hot in the Jefara of Tripolitania, reaching temperatures of 40°C–45°C. In the southern deserts, conditions are hotter still; Gharian has recorded temperatures in excess of 49°C. Several feet of snow can also fall here in winter. Northern Cyrenaica has a markedly cooler summer of 27°C–32°C, but with high air humidity near the coast. A special feature is the *ghibli*—a hot, very dry wind from the south that can raise temperatures in the north by 15°C or even 20°C in a few hours, sometimes resulting in temperatures of 20°C or 25°C in January. This sand-laden, dry wind (which can cause considerable crop damage) may blow at any time of the year, but spring and autumn are the usual seasons.

The hills of Tripolitania and Cyrenaica annually receive as much as 400 mm–500 mm of rainfall, but in the remainder of the country the rainfall is usually 200 mm or less. Once every five or six years there is a pronounced drought, sometimes lasting for two successive seasons.

ECONOMIC LIFE

Such conditions imposed severe restriction on all forms of economic activity. Although petroleum was discovered in considerable quantities in Libya, physical and climatic conditions made exploitation difficult and, until the closure of the Suez Canal in 1967, the remote situation of the country, away from the currents of international trade, was a further handicap. However, production of crude petroleum increased rapidly and proximity to southern and central Europe presented a considerable advantage over the costly Suez passage that was reflected in the price. The introduction of petroleum revenues transformed the economic situation of Libya. Extensive development was undertaken, with the aim of improving housing, and the fostering of industries to produce consumer goods. Roads, electricity, improved water supplies, telecommunications links and reorganized town planning were all targeted by development initiatives, and the construction of a number of sizeable industrial plants was approved.

In the better-watered areas of the Jefara and, to a smaller extent, in northern Cyrenaica, barley, wheat, olives and Mediterranean fruit are cultivated.

The Fezzan and the smaller oases in Cyrenaica are almost rainless, and cultivation depends entirely upon irrigation from wells. Millet is the chief crop, and there are several million date palms, which provide the bulk of the food. Small quantities of vegetables and fruit—figs, pomegranates, squashes, artichokes and tubers—are produced from gardens. Along the northern coast, and especially on the lower slopes both of the Tripolitanian Jebel and the Jebel Akhdar, vines are grown, though less so than formerly because of the prohibition of wine-making since independence.

Over much of Libya, pastoral nomadism, based on the rearing of sheep and goats (and some cattle and camels), is the only possible activity. In Cyrenaica, nomads outnumbered the remainder of the population for many years, but in Tripolitania the main emphasis is on agriculture, although herding is still practised. Several industries have developed—petroleum refining, of course, plus some petrochemical activity, iron and steel production and some light industries. Overall, the scale of industrial activity is still small, but growing. Major efforts have been made to improve agriculture, with debatable success. One increasing difficulty is the exodus of rural workers to jobs in the developing towns, and foreign labour has had to be introduced on some rural development schemes. Another limitation is overuse of artesian water in the Jefara. In certain areas near the coast, the water-table has fallen by 3 m–5 m per year, resulting in invasion of the aquifers by seawater.

The population of Libya seems to have been Berber in origin, i.e. connected with many of the present-day inhabitants of Morocco, Algeria, and Tunisia. The establishment of Greek colonies, from about 650 BC onwards, seems to have had little ethnic effect on the population; but in the ninth and 10th centuries AD there were large-scale immigrations by Arabic-speaking tribes from the Najd of Arabia. This latter group, of relatively unmixed Mediterranean racial type, is now entirely dominant, ethnically speaking, especially in Cyrenaica, of which it has been said that no other part of the world (central Arabia alone excepted) is more thoroughly Arab.

A few Berber elements do, however, survive, mainly in the south and west of Libya; while the long-continued traffic in Negro slaves (which came to an end in the 1940s) has left a visible influence on peoples throughout Libya and especially in the south.

Arabic, introduced by the 10th century invaders, is the one official language of Libya, but a few Tamazight-speaking Berber villages remain.

History

Revised for this edition by RICHARD I. LAWLESS

PRE-ISLAMIC LIBYA

In earliest historical times two races inhabited Libya—the 'Libyans' and the 'Ethiopians'—the former, of Mediterranean stock, inhabited the coastal areas; the latter, of negroid and African stock, inhabited the interior. Phoenician sailors began to visit Libya in about 1000 BC to trade for gold and silver, ivory, apes and peacocks, and established the permanent colonies of Leptis, Uai'at (Tripoli) and Sabratha on the coast. A more famous Phoenician colony, Carthage, was established to the west of what is now called Libya, and by 517 BC had come to dominate the others. During the Punic wars between Rome and Carthage the Tripolitanian half of Libya fell under the control of the Numidians until Julius Caesar created the province of Africa Nova.

In about 600 BC the Greeks had colonized Cyrene, and raised it to be a powerful city. Cyrene later fell under the domination of Alexander the Great, came under the Ptolemies in about 322 BC and was bequeathed to Rome in 96 BC. Libya then enjoyed several centuries of prosperity under Roman rule, but, by the middle of the fourth century AD, decline had set in. In AD 431 the Vandals, under Genseric, conquered the country, but a hundred years later the Emperor Justinian's general Belisarius reconquered the country for the Byzantine Empire. Repeated rebellions by Berber tribes, however, soon reduced the country to anarchy.

ARAB INVASION

Arab invaders overran the country and captured Tripoli in 643. The majority of the invaders embraced Islam, but mainly in its schismatic forms as Kharijites, Ibadites and Shi'ites. Continual rebellion induced the Caliph of Baghdad, Haroun ar-Rashid, to appoint, in 800, Ibrahim ibn al-Aghlabid as governor, with his capital at Qairawan (now Kairouan, in Tunisia). This Aghlabid dynasty, virtually independent of the Abbasid caliphate of Baghdad, ended in the 10th century when a Shi'ite uprising founded the Shi'ite Fatimid Dynasty, which from Tunisia conquered Egypt, transferring the seat of government to Cairo in 972. Bulukkin ibn Ziri was made governor of Ifriqiya, and at the beginning of the 11th century the Zirid Amir returned to orthodox Sunnism and acknowledged the sovereignty of the Caliph of Baghdad.

The Fatimid Caliph of Baghdad reacted by invading Libya in 1049, and the next five centuries witnessed little but inter-tribal wars. By the 16th century the northern coast of Africa had become infested with the dens of pirates, and was attracting the crusading and imperialistic designs of Christian Spain. Ferdinand the Catholic sent an expedition which took Tripoli in 1510. The Muslim world had now become, under the Ottoman Turks, more united than it had been for 600 years, and Sinan Pasha was able to wrest Tripoli from the Knights Hospitallers of St John (to whom it had been confided by Charles V) in 1551. Ottoman rule was loose but oppressive. The professional soldiers, the Janissaries, became a power within the state, and the activities of the pirate corsairs, often with the blessing of the Ottoman pashas, attracted reprisals from the European naval powers.

In 1711 a local notable, Ahmad Karamanli, of Ottoman origin and an officer in the Janissaries, was proclaimed *dey*, (originally, deys were high officers of the Ottoman army of occupation) and eventually recognized as pasha. The Karamanli dynasty lasted until 1835. Piracy had again contributed much to its finance, and when European naval action suppressed piracy after the Napoleonic wars, the Karamanlis were ruined. In 1835, probably through fear of the extension of French power in Algiers and Tunis, the Sultan decided to reoccupy Libya and to bring it once more under the direct rule of the Porte (the Ottoman administration in Constantinople). The years that followed were marked by corruption, oppression and revolts, but also by the rise of the Sanusi religious brotherhood.

ITALO–TURKISH CONFLICTS

On 29 September 1911 Italy declared war on Turkey for reasons largely of national prestige. After a short bombardment, Italian troops landed at Tripoli on 3 October. Italy knew the Turks to be involved in the Balkans, and knew, through its commercial infiltration of Libya, their weakness in Africa. However, the attack on Libya was not the easy exercise Italy expected. The Turks withdrew inland but the Libyans organized themselves and joined the Turks, to whom the Porte sent assistance in the form of arms and of two senior officers, Ali Fethi Bey and Enver Pasha. The presence in the Italian army of Eritrean troops was a spur to the pride of the Libyans. In October and November a number of actions were fought around Tripoli in which the Italians had little success. A sea-borne Italian force then descended on Misurata and seized it, but could make no progress inland. At ar-Rumeila they suffered a considerable reverse. Turkey, however, defeated in the Balkan War, was anxious for peace, which was signed on 18 October 1912. One of the conditions of this peace was that the Libyans should be allowed 'administrative autonomy'. This was never realized.

Peace with Turkey did not, however, mean peace in Libya for the Italians. Although most of the Tripolitanians submitted and were disarmed within two years, the Sanusiya of Cyrenaica under Said Ahmad ash-Sharif, and their adherents in the Fezzan and Tripolitania, refused to yield. The Sanusiya maintained a forward post at Sirte (Surt) under Said Ahmad's brother, Said Safi ad-Din as-Sanusi. The extent of contact between the latter and Ramadan as-Sueihli of Misurata is not clear. Ramadan had been in the resistance to the Italians and two years later had appeared to be submissive. At all events, he found himself commanding Libyans in an action started by the Italians at al-Qaradabia in 1914, to push back Said Safi. Ramadan and his Misuratis changed sides in this action, to the discomfiture of the Italians. By the time that the First World War had started, the Italians held only the coastal towns of Tripoli, Benghazi, Derna and Tobruk, and a few coastal villages near Tripoli.

The First World War gave Turkey and its German allies the opportunity of fomenting trouble against Italy in Libya. Arms and munitions were sent by submarine. Nuri Pasha from Turkey and Abd ar-Rahman Azzam from Egypt joined Said Ahmad in Cyrenaica. Ramadan became head of a government at Misurata. The Sultan, to prevent quarrels, sent Osman Fu'ad, grandson of Sultan Mourad, as Amir, and Ishaq Pasha as commander-in-chief in Tripolitania. The strategic objective of these efforts was to engage Italian forces in Libya and British forces in the Western Desert. The climax of Nuri Pasha's efforts with the Sanusi was a disastrous action in the Western Desert against the British, as a result of which Said Ahmad handed over the leadership to Said Muhammad Idris. He was compelled to make the treaty of az-Zawiatna with the British and the Italians, who recognized him as Amir of the interior of Cyrenaica, provided that he desisted from attacks on the coastal towns and on Egypt.

The end of the war in 1918 left Italy weak and the Libyans, deserted by the Turks, weary. The Tripolitanians attempted to form a republic with headquarters at Gharian and with Azzam as adviser. The Italians made a truce with them at Suani ibn Adam, permitting a delegation to go to Rome, and entertaining the idea of 'administrative independence'. Ramadan visited Tripoli. In Cyrenaica, Said Muhammad Idris likewise attempted to come to terms; in 1921, at Sirte, the Tripolitanian leaders agreed with him to join forces to obtain Libya's rights and to pay homage to him as Amir of all Libya. Meanwhile the delegation to Rome had returned empty-handed and Ramadan had been slain in a tribal fight.

ITALIAN COLONIZATION

The advent of the Fascists to power in Italy (1922) coincided with the appointment in Tripoli of a vigorous governor, Count Volpi. Thereafter, it took until 1925 to occupy and pacify the province of Tripolitania and to disarm the population. In Cyrenaica, however, the ageing Said Omar al-Mukhtar, representing the Amir Muhammad Idris, whose health had collapsed, maintained the struggle. The Italians realized that the only effective policy was to deprive the Sanusiya of their bases, the oases of the south. Jaghbub was occupied in 1925, Zella, Ojila and Jalo in 1927. In 1928 Marshal Badoglio was appointed Governor-General and in 1929 he occupied Mizda in the Fezzan. Al-Mukhtar still resisted. The Italians removed the tribes of the Jebel Akhdar into concentration camps at al-Aqeila. In 1930 Rodolfo Graziani, an experienced Italian military commander, was dispatched to Cyrenaica, and a barbed-wire fence was erected along the frontier with Egypt. Finally, in 1931, isolated from all support, al-Mukhtar was surrounded, wounded, captured, and hanged.

Starting in the early 1920s, the Italians proceeded to colonize parts of Libya that they had occupied, and that geographical and ecological conditions rendered profitable for development. They enlarged and embellished the coastal towns and extended an excellent network of roads throughout the cultivable areas. They bored wells, planted trees, and stabilized sand-dunes. However, their civilizing policy was weighted heavily in favour of their own race. The object was clearly the settlement in Africa of as much as possible of Italy's surplus peasant population. The priority given to the progress of the Libyans was low. Primary education for the Libyans was encouraged, and schools provided for them, but the main medium of instruction was Italian. Very few Libyans were accepted into Italian secondary schools.

INDEPENDENCE

There followed the Second World War, and the occupation in 1942 of Cyrenaica and Tripolitania by a British military administration and of the Fezzan by French forces. Thereafter, until 1950, the country was administered with the greatest economy on a care and maintenance basis. Its final fate was long in doubt, until the UN decreed its independence by 1952. On 24 December 1951 Libya was declared an independent united kingdom with a federal constitution under King Idris, the former Amir Muhammad Idris, hero of the resistance.

According to the Constitution promulgated in October 1951, the State of Libya was a federal monarchy ruled by King Muhammad Idris al-Mahdi as-Sanusi and his heirs, and divided into the three provinces of Tripolitania, Cyrenaica and the Fezzan. The federal Government consisted of a bicameral legislature, i.e. a Chamber of Deputies, to which was responsible a Council of Ministers appointed by the King, and a Senate of 24 members (eight for each province). The King had the right to nominate 12 of the senators, to introduce and to veto legislation, and to dissolve the Lower House at his discretion. The Constitution also provided that provincial legislatures should be created for the subordinate provinces of the new realm.

On the attainment of full independence, serious political, financial and economic problems confronted Libya. Not the least of these was the task of fostering amongst the population a sense of national identity and unity. The loyalties of the people were still given to the village and the tribe, rather than to the new federal state.

These rivalries revealed themselves in the next two years. The Party of Independence, which supported the Constitution, won control in the February 1952 elections for the Federal Chamber of Deputies. The National Congress Party of Tripolitania, however, was opposed to the federal principle and advocated a unitary state, with elections based on proportional representation (which would have given Tripolitania the main voice). Disorders arising from this disagreement led to the outlawing of the Tripolitania party and the deportation of its leader, Bashir Bey as-Sa'adawi. A Legislative Council for Tripolitania was formed in 1952 but had to be dissolved in 1954 because of continued friction with the federal Government and the King.

FOREIGN RELATIONS IN THE 1950s

The first important development in the sphere of foreign relations was the admission of Libya to the League of Arab States (the Arab League) in March 1953. The second development reflected the economic difficulties of the new state and its close links with Western Europe. In July 1953 Libya concluded a 20-year treaty with the United Kingdom. In return for permission to maintain military bases in Libya, the United Kingdom undertook to grant the new state £1m. annually for economic development and a further annual sum of £2.75m. to offset budgetary deficits.

In September 1954 a similar agreement was signed with the USA. A number of air bases were granted to the USA in return for economic aid amounting to US $40m. over 20 years, an amount that was later substantially increased. Libya also consolidated relations with France, Italy and Egypt. The critical problem for Libya was to ensure that enough funds from abroad should be available to meet the normal expenses of the Government and to pay for much-needed improvements. At this time, its strategic position was all Libya had to sell, hence its involvement with the Western military alliance. The Libyan attitude to the communist world was much more reserved. Reliance on income from foreign military bases continued, therefore, to dominate foreign policy, and in the late 1950s and early 1960s Libya received subsidies and military assistance from both the United Kingdom and the USA in return for the use of military bases.

PETROLEUM DISCOVERIES

After 1955–56, when Libya granted concessions for oil exploration to several US companies, the search for petroleum resources became one of the main interests of the Libyan Government.

By the end of 1959 some 15 companies held petroleum concessions in Libya. An oilfield at Zelten in Cyrenaica was discovered in June 1959. By the end of the year, six productive wells had been found in Tripolitania, four in Cyrenaica and one in the Fezzan. By the beginning of July 1960 there were 35 petroleum wells in production, yielding some 93,000 barrels of petroleum per day. Petroleum production showed a tremendous increase in the 1962–66 period, with exports rising from 8m. metric tons in 1962 to more than 70m. tons in 1966.

A UNITARY REALM

A general election was held in Libya on 17 January 1960. Most of the 55 seats were contested, but there was no party system in operation. The election was fought mainly on a personal basis. Secret balloting, limited in earlier elections to the urban areas, was now extended to the rural districts. The Prime Minister, Abd al-Majid Koubar, and the other members of his Cabinet retained their seats.

Libya's increasing wealth was making the business of government more complex and several changes of administration ensued between 1960 and 1963. Finally, in March 1963, a new Cabinet was appointed under the premiership of Dr Mohi ed-Din Fekini.

Dr Fekini stated in April 1963 that his Government intended to introduce legislation designed to transform Libya from a federal into a unitary state—a change which would mean increased efficiency and considerable administrative economies. On 15 April Fekini presented a bill to the Chamber of Deputies containing a number of important reforms: (1) the franchise was to be granted to women; (2) Libya would have (as before) a bicameral parliamentary system, but henceforward the King was to nominate all the 24 members of the Senate (previously one-half were nominated and the other half were elected); (3) the Kingdom of Libya would cease to be a federal state comprising three provinces (Tripolitania, Cyrenaica and the Fezzan), becoming instead a unitary realm divided into 10 administrative areas; (4) the administrative councils established in each of the three provinces were to be abolished, the exercise of executive power residing now in the Council of Ministers. Libya became a unitary state by royal proclamation on 27 April 1963.

THE REALITY OF INDEPENDENCE

In the field of foreign relations, Libya was by now helped by the prospect of financial independence and was making its voice heard in international affairs, particularly in Africa. As a result of decisions taken at the Addis Ababa (Ethiopia) conference of African Heads of State in May 1963, Libya closed its air and sea ports to Portuguese and South African ships. The signing of pacts with Morocco (1962) and Algeria (1963) meant that Libya now had closer links with all the Maghreb countries. Libya was also showing signs of ending its dependence on the West. The 1955 agreement with France had allowed France to retain certain military facilities in Libya—notably in the field of communications—for the defence of French African territories, but Dr Fekini felt that, with the coming of independence to French African territories in the early 1960s, the matter should be reconsidered.

The question of foreign military bases in Libya now came to the fore. Dr Fekini resigned in January 1964 and the new Prime Minister was Mahmoud Muntasser, formerly Minister of Justice. The Government issued a statement on 23 February, stating that it did not propose to renew or extend its military agreements with the United Kingdom and the USA and that it supported the other Governments of the Arab world in the resistance to imperialism. Muntasser defined the aim of his Government as the termination of the existing agreements with the United Kingdom and the USA and the fixing of a date for the evacuation of the bases in Libya. The Chamber of Deputies then passed a resolution calling for the achievement of this aim and providing that, if negotiations were unsuccessful, the Chamber would pass legislation to abrogate the treaties and close the bases.

The Anglo-Libyan treaty of 1953 was due to expire in 1973. Under the treaty, the United Kingdom maintained a Royal Air Force staging post near Tobruk, an Air Force detachment at Idris airport in Tripoli and Army District Headquarters at Tripoli and Benghazi. The American-Libyan agreement of 1954 was to expire in 1971. The largest American airbase outside the USA was situated near Tripoli. Under the treaties, Libya had received large amounts of financial, economic and military aid from the USA and from the United Kingdom. Petroleum revenues had greatly reduced Libyan dependence on such aid. The United Kingdom withdrew the bulk of its forces in February and March 1966.

At elections for the Libyan Parliament, held in October 1964, in which women voted for the first time, moderate candidates won most of the 103 seats. King Idris dissolved the Parliament, however, on 13 February 1965, because of complaints about irregularities in the election procedure. The Prime Minister resigned, to be succeeded by Hussain Maziq, Minister for Foreign Affairs. A new election for Parliament was held on 8 May 1965, with over 200 candidates contesting the 91 seats and 16 members being returned unopposed.

The outbreak of the six-day Arab–Israeli war in June 1967 was followed by serious disturbances in Tripoli and Benghazi, in which port and oil workers and students, inflamed by Egyptian propaganda, played a prominent part. The British and US embassies were attacked and the Jewish minorities were subjected to violence and persecution that resulted in the emigration of most of them to Italy, Malta and elsewhere. The Prime Minister, Hussain Maziq, proved unable to control the situation and was dismissed by the King on 28 June. Firm measures by his successor, Abd al-Qadir Badri, brought a return to order but the antagonisms that he aroused forced him, in turn, to resign in October. He was succeeded as Prime Minister on 28 October by the Minister of Justice, Abd al-Hamid Bakkoush.

An immediate result of the June 1967 war was a decline of about 80% in the Libyan output of crude petroleum, owing to the boycott of oil supplies from Arab countries to the United Kingdom, the USA and the Federal Republic of Germany. There was a gradual return to full production in the months following the conflict, however, and the ban on the export of petroleum was lifted in September. The closure of the Suez Canal brought about a considerable increase in Libya's petroleum exports and general prosperity, although the Libyan Government agreed to make annual aid payments totalling £30m. to the United Arab Republic (UAR) and Jordan to alleviate the consequences of the war. Libya's petroleum output increased by about 50% in 1968 and the country became, after only seven and a half years, the second largest producer in the Arab world, with the great advantage, as a supplier to Europe, of being on the more convenient side of the Suez Canal.

Bakkoush initiated a programme of progressive change, seeking to modernize Libya's administration, reform the civil service and improve the educational system. He also sought to provide the armed forces with modern equipment, and, under a contract announced in April 1968, the purchase from a British firm of a surface-to-air missile defence system, costing £100m., was arranged. An agreement to buy British heavy arms followed, but in September 1968 Bakkoush was replaced as premier by Wanis al-Qaddafi, since the pace of Bakkoush's reforms had apparently alienated some conservative elements. Both Cabinets enjoyed close relationships with Western countries but played little part in Arab politics.

THE 1969 COUP

On 1 September 1969 a military coup was staged in Tripoli while the King was in Turkey for medical treatment. Within a few days the new regime gained complete control of the entire country. The coup was remarkable for the absence of opposition, relatively few arrests, virtually no fighting and no deaths at all being reported. A Revolution Command Council (RCC) took power and proclaimed the Libyan Arab Republic. The RCC initially remained anonymous but was soon revealed as a group of young army officers, the leader, Col Muammar al-Qaddafi, being only 27. The aged King Idris refused to abdicate but accepted exile in Egypt when it became obvious that the revolution had been completely accepted by his people. He remained there until his death, aged 93, in May 1983.

A provisional Constitution, announced in November, stated that supreme power would remain in the hands of the RCC, which appointed the Cabinet; there was no provision for a future general election or national assembly, and the royal ban on political parties was to continue. A largely civilian Cabinet was appointed, under close military supervision. The Ministers of Defence and of the Interior were accused of organizing an abortive counter-revolution in December, and were tried and sentenced in 1970. In January Col Qaddafi himself became Prime Minister and several of his colleagues also joined the Cabinet.

The principal force underlying the regime's policies was undoubtedly that of professed Arab nationalism. Internally, this led to the strict enforcement of the royal law requiring businesses operating in Libya to be controlled by Libyans— banks being particularly affected. The remaining British military establishment in Libya, requested to leave as soon as possible, was finally removed in March 1970, and the much larger US presence at Wheelus Field was removed in June. Most of the European and American specialists (managers, teachers, technicians and doctors), were replaced by Arabs, mainly from Egypt. English translations disappeared from street signs, official stationery and publications, and most hoardings, the use of Arabic alone being permitted; similarly, the Islamic prohibitions on alcoholic drinks and certain Western clothes were officially revived. In July 1970 the property of all Jews and Italians still living in Libya—some 25,000 people— was sequestered by the Government, and both communities were encouraged to leave without delay; some Jews were, however, offered compensation in government bonds. In the same month the three main petroleum marketing companies—Shell, Esso and an ENI subsidiary—had their distribution facilities nationalized.

Another anti-government plot was reported to have been crushed in July 1970. In the autumn two ministers resigned and there were signs of a power struggle developing within the RCC. The internal dissension apparently increased in the first part of 1970 over the proposed federation with the UAR, Syria and Sudan, and over Qaddafi's promises of a constitution and political institutions, including an elected President. A step towards introducing these was the announcement in June 1971 that an Arab Socialist Union (ASU) was to be created as the state's sole party.

FOREIGN POLICY AFTER THE COUP

The new regime almost immediately received enthusiastic recognition from the radical Arab countries and the USSR, and the rest of the world also granted recognition within a few days. As would be expected from the Arab nationalist inspiration behind the revolution, the monarchy's close ties with Western powers were abandoned in favour of close relations with the Arab world and Egypt in particular; this friendship became the basis of a triple alliance announced late in 1969, Sudan being the third member. The alliance was intended to develop both politically— as a strong bulwark against Israel and the West—and economically, in that the economies of the three countries complemented each other to a considerable extent. However, when a federation agreement was signed in April 1971, it was Syria that became the third member. Libya also adopted a militant position on the Palestine question, and this created some diplomatic problems regarding arms contracts, particularly with the United Kingdom.

Although in July 1970 the Libyan Government followed Egypt in accepting US proposals for a cease-fire with Israel, it continued its militant statements on the Middle East problem. Qaddafi rejected the UN Security Council resolution on which the US initiative was based. During the fighting between Palestinian guerrillas and the Jordanian army in September 1970, Libya redirected its financial aid from the Jordan Government to the guerrillas and severed diplomatic relations with King Hussein's government.

The coup appeared to have reoriented Libya away from the Maghreb; in the summer of 1970 Libya withdrew from the Maghreb Permanent Consultative Committee. Relations with Tunisia improved in the latter half of 1970, after initial concern in Tunis in 1969 at the radical leanings of the new regime, and Qaddafi headed a delegation to visit Tunisia in February 1971. Relations with Morocco were severed in July 1971, after the Libyan Government prematurely gave its support to an attempt to overthrow King Hassan, which failed within 24 hours.

There was little evidence of any closer relationship with the communist powers, although the People's Republic of China was recognized in June 1971 and the USSR was given due credit for its Middle East policies. However, communism was regarded in Libya as a 'foreign' ideology, antipathetic to more 'progressive' Arab socialism (as in Sudan). Hence, in July 1971, Qaddafi was ready to help President Nimeri of Sudan to regain power after a coup, led by communists, had ousted him. A British-operated scheduled flight from London, United Kingdom, to Khartoum was forced down over Libya and two leaders of the Sudanese coup, were taken from the plane and deported to Sudan, where they were promptly executed by the restored regime.

PETROLEUM POWER

In April 1971 the negotiations with the oil companies operating in Libya, which had begun soon after the 1969 coup, finally ended in a new five-year agreement raising the total posted price for Libyan crude petroleum to US \$3.447 per barrel. In the last stage of the negotiations, conducted in Tripoli, the Libyan Government also represented the interests of the Algerian, Iraqi and Saudi Arabian Governments. Threats of an embargo on the export of crude petroleum were used as a lever in the negotiations.

In 10 years Libya's position had changed from one of penury and dependence to one of power, based entirely on the country's ability to interrupt petroleum supplies. The pronouncements of Qaddafi were, therefore, by now of greater significance to the West. In July 1971 the Deputy Prime Minister, Maj. Abd as-Salam Jalloud, visited the Federal Republic of Germany, France and the United Kingdom: Federal Germany, which bought a particularly large proportion of its crude petroleum from Libya, needed to maintain good relations; France was anxious to discover the use to which Libya would put the *Mirage* jet-engined fighter aircraft that were being supplied under the 1970 agreement; the same anxiety was revealed in the United Kingdom over the supply of armaments, but none of these countries could afford to alienate Libya.

In December 1971, avowedly in retaliation for the United Kingdom's failure to prevent the Iranian occupation of the Tunb islands in the Gulf, Libya nationalized the assets of British Petroleum (BP). This began the process of nationalizing the foreign petroleum companies (described in more detail in Economy; see below).

Relations with the United Kingdom became very strained in the winter of 1971–72, not only because of the nationalization of BP but also because of Libyan intervention in the dispute with Malta over the British bases there. Libya had, for some time, been actively fostering relations with Malta, and talks on possible Libyan aid to Malta were held in August 1971. In January 1972 the British naval training mission was ordered to leave Libya, and in February the 1954 agreement with the USA was abrogated.

In domestic affairs, Qaddafi continued his attempts to run the legislature and the Government entirely in accordance with Islamic principles. At the end of March 1972 the ASU held its first national congress. At subsequent sessions, the ASU adopted resolutions to clarify its position and policies, and to abolish censorship of the press, while, at the same time, maintaining financial control of newspapers.

In July 1972 disagreement within the RCC led to Qaddafi's replacement as Prime Minister by Maj. Jalloud, who formed a new Cabinet in which all but two of the ministers were civilians.

ARAB UNITY

A recurrent feature of Qaddafi's foreign policy has been the announcement of proposals for the union of Libya with neighbouring states, and the subsequent collapse of such planned mergers. The Tripoli Charter of December 1969, establishing a revolutionary alliance of Libya, Egypt (then the UAR) and Sudan, was followed by gradual moves towards federation and the adhesion of Syria. Sudan withdrew, but in September 1971 referenda in Libya, Egypt and Syria approved the constitution of the Federation of Arab Republics, which officially came into existence on 1 January 1972, but which had few practical consequences.

The Federation was not Qaddafi's only attempt to export his ideals by means of merger. At the time of Malta's dispute with the United Kingdom over the use of bases, in 1971, he proposed a union of Malta with Libya, but was rebuffed. In December 1972, in a speech in the Tunisian capital, he proposed the union of Libya and Tunisia, much to the surprise of his audience, not least President Bourguiba, who immediately rejected the idea.

A merger of Libya and Egypt was agreed in principle in August 1972 but, as the date of implementation approached, certain difficulties became apparent. Qaddafi, who had recently launched his 'Cultural Revolution' of April 1973, was seen as a reactionary Muslim puritan in Egypt, and he was openly critical of Egyptian moral laxity. Egyptian suspicion of Libyan revolutionary enthusiasm, notwithstanding, the union came into effect on 1 September 1973, with the establishment, in theory, of unified political leadership and economic policy and a constituent assembly. The union soon fell apart, wrecked by Qaddafi's opposition to Egypt's conduct of the October 1973 Arab–Israeli war.

President Qaddafi's attitude towards the Palestine problem had long been a source of discord between Libya and other Arab states. He gave financial support to the Palestinian guerrillas, and a number of Libyan volunteers were sent to assist them, Qaddafi's objective being the complete destruction of Israel. He was extremely critical of what he saw as the lack of total commitment to the Palestinian cause on the part of Egypt and Syria, and frequently expressed the opinion that the Arab states could not, and did not deserve to, defeat Israel. He accused Egypt and Syria of being more interested in the recovery of territory lost in the 1967 war than in aiding the Palestinian resistance movement, which was being 'destroyed by the Arabs in co-operation with Israel'. Qaddafi was not informed of the Egyptian and Syrian plan to attack Israel in October 1973, was strongly critical of their battle plan, and refused to attend the Algiers meeting of Arab Heads of State after the war, declaring that it would only ratify Arab capitulation. Libya was nevertheless an enthusiastic proponent of the use of the Arab petroleum embargo against countries that were considered to be pro-Israel. During the war, Libya's participation had been limited to the supply of arms and equipment, and its conclusion seemed only to complete Qaddafi's disillusionment concerning the union with Egypt.

Presidents Qaddafi and Habib Bourguiba announced the union of Libya and Tunisia on 12 January 1974, following two days of talks. A referendum to approve the decision was to be held on 18 January, but was almost immediately postponed. The decision had been taken in the absence of the Tunisian Prime Minister, Hedi Nouira. When he returned to Tunisia, the pro-merger Minister of Foreign Affairs was dismissed, and Tunisia's attitude changed, to support the indefinite deferment of the union. Qaddafi's impetuous action aimed to produce a unified state, but Tunisia now treated the agreement as merely a declaration of principle, without any practical effect.

Qaddafi's enthusiasm for Arab unity continued unabated, but the failure of political mergers led him to propound a new course. His speeches attacked the Arab leaders who blocked unity and failed to 'liberate' Palestine, and he spoke of Libyan aid for revolution and the achievement of Arab union by popular pressure on the Governments of Tunisia, Egypt, Algeria and Morocco. Libya had, for some time, been providing money, arms and training for subversive or 'liberation' organizations operating in Ireland, Eritrea, the Philippines, Rhodesia (now Zimbabwe), Portuguese Guinea (now Guinea-Bissau), Morocco and Chad, as well as providing aid for sympathetic countries such as Pakistan, Uganda, Zambia, Togo and, after May 1973, Chad. Now it appeared that Libya was supporting subversion in Egypt and Sudan. Attempted coups in Egypt in April and Sudan in May 1974 were believed to have had Libyan support, and relations between Libya and other Arab states became increasingly hostile. Qaddafi's failed mergers and his interference in the internal affairs of other countries were believed to have been major factors in his withdrawal from an active political role in April 1974, when it was seen that he had failed in his policy of exporting the ideals of the Libyan 'Cultural Revolution'.

THE 'CULTURAL REVOLUTION'

President Qaddafi's somewhat idiosyncratic political and social philosophy first obtained full expression in a speech in April 1973, when he called for the immediate launching of a 'cultural revolution to destroy imported ideologies, whether they are eastern or western' and for the construction of a society based on the tenets of the Koran. The form that this revolution was to take was laid down in a five-point programme: 'people's committees' would be set up to carry out the revolution, the 'politically sick' would be purged, the revolutionary masses would be armed, a campaign would begin against bureaucracy and administrative abuses, while imported books that propagated communism, atheism or capitalism would be burned. The people's committees set about their task of supervising all aspects of social and economic life, criticizing and dismissing officials and business executives who failed to show the required revolutionary fervour, and destroying offensive books and magazines.

In May 1973 Qaddafi presented his 'third international theory', which was 'an alternative to capitalist materialism and communist atheism'. In effect, it appeared to be an appeal for a return to Islamic fundamentalism (an appeal subsequently echoed in other Middle Eastern countries), together with a rather confused combination of socialism and respect for private property, and much talk of tolerance and the rights of oppressed nationalities. While the 'Cultural Revolution' proceeded apace in Libya, Qaddafi seemed more concerned with foreign policy and his new-found role as a revolutionary philosopher, who had proposed a universally applicable theory to replace existing ideologies. Qaddafi concentrated on the formulation and propagation of his theory, and on his erratic, unsuccessful attempts to export the Libyan revolution by merger or by subversion, while the mundane details of administration were increasingly referred to Maj. Jalloud, the Prime Minister.

The return to the teachings of the Koran and the rejection of external influences took several forms, some of them petty, such as the insistence upon the use of Arabic in foreigners' passports, and some macabre, as in the revival of such features of Koranic law as the dismembering of thieves' hands. The theory was also invoked in the disputes with foreign oil companies in 1973 (dealt with in detail in the Economy section), presented as an expression of Libyan independence.

On 5 April 1974 it was announced that Qaddafi, while remaining Head of State and Commander-in-Chief, had been relieved of political, administrative and ceremonial duties, and was to devote himself to ideological and mass organization work. It appeared that, willingly or otherwise, Qaddafi had effectively been replaced by Prime Minister Jalloud. After a five-month withdrawal from active direction of the Government, Qaddafi re-emerged in the autumn of 1974 and it soon became apparent that he was more firmly in command than ever.

THE CREATION OF THE SOCIALIST PEOPLE'S LIBYAN ARAB JAMAHIRIYA

President Qaddafi's theories had, since 1973 (when he presented his third international theory), demonstrated a strong desire to foster 'people's assemblies' at all levels of Libyan life. Under a decree promulgated by the ruling RCC in November 1975, provision was made for the creation of a 618-member general national congress of the ASU, the country's only permitted political party. The congress, which held its first session in January 1976, comprised members of the RCC, leaders of existing 'people's congresses' and 'popular committees', and trade unions and professional organizations. Subsequently the General National Congress of the ASU became the General People's Congress (GPC), which first met in November 1976. Qaddafi announced plans for radical constitutional changes and these were endorsed by the GPC in March 1977. The official name of the country was changed to The Socialist People's Libyan Arab Jamahiriya, and power was vested in the people through the GPC and the groups represented in it. The RCC disappeared and a General Secretariat of the GPC, with Qaddafi as Secretary-General, was established. The Council of Ministers was replaced by the General People's Committee, with 26 members, each a secretary of a department. People's committees were set up at local level, ostensibly to give citizens control over their own affairs. In reality, their creation enabled Qaddafi to dispose of governors, ministers and local officials, some of whom were beginning to resist his more radical reforms. In March 1979 Qaddafi resigned from the post of Secretary-General of the General Secretariat of the GPC, so that he could devote more time to 'revolutionary work'. The General Secretariat was reorganized, as was the General People's Committee, which was reduced to 21 members.

In late 1979 Qaddafi urged Libyans living abroad to take over Libyan embassies; diplomats were ousted and 'people's bureaux' established in most Western countries. At the fifth meeting of the GPC, in January 1980, several government ministers were dismissed, notably the experienced Petroleum Secretary, 'Izz ad-Din Mabrouk, who was accused of inefficiency in nationalizing the petroleum industry. The sixth meeting of the GPC, in January 1981, reshuffled several ministerial appointments, discussed the 1981–85 economic plan, and made further proposals for transforming Libyan society along the lines described in Qaddafi's 'Green Book' (published in three volumes over the period 1976–79). The Ministry of Foreign Affairs was abolished and replaced by a Bureau of Foreign Liaison.

QADDAFI'S EXTERNAL INVOLVEMENTS

Relations with Egypt deteriorated after Qaddafi boycotted the Rabat summit meeting of Arab Heads of State in October 1974. Qaddafi was unhappy about the decision to recognize the Palestine Liberation Organization (PLO), under Yasser Arafat, as the sole legitimate representative of the Palestinians. He subsequently demonstrated support for the 'rejectionist front'— the wing of the Palestinian guerrilla movement that rejected the concept of a possible settlement of the Arab–Israeli conflict under terms acceptable to Arafat, Jordan and Egypt.

The war of words with Egypt continued in 1975, with articles in the Libyan press containing bitter personal attacks on President Sadat and with the Egyptian press accusing Qaddafi of preparing to mount an invasion of Egypt. A delegation from the National Assembly of the Federation of Arab Republics, which visited Tripoli and Cairo in May, was able to bring about a temporary reconciliation but, at the end of May, relations deteriorated again after reports that Libya was to allow the establishment of Soviet military bases on its territory in return for huge supplies of Soviet weapons. It later appeared that the arms deal did not include the establishment of Soviet military bases in Libya, and was, in fact, smaller than at first reported. Libya, in turn, condemned Egypt for signing the second interim disengagement agreement between Egypt and Israel in September 1975. Relations with Egypt did not improve in 1976 or 1977, and in July 1977 for a while, frontier clashes had the appearance of open war.

Relations with Egypt were not improved when, in November 1977, President Sadat of Egypt launched his peace initiative by visiting Israel. Qaddafi condemned Sadat's move and was a leading instigator of the Tripoli summit of 'rejectionist' states which formed a 'front of steadfastness and confrontation' against Israel in December 1977. Qaddafi remained strongly opposed to Sadat's peace initiative throughout 1978 and following the signing of the Egyptian-Israeli treaty in March 1979, Qaddafi withdrew from the Baghdad summit meeting of Arab states on the grounds that the sanctions being contemplated against Egypt were insufficiently far-reaching.

In early 1980 a serious rift developed between Qaddafi and Arafat who was accused of having abandoned the armed struggle in favour of a strategy of diplomacy and moderation. In January relations were formally broken with al-Fatah, the largest component organization of the PLO, and all aid was suspended, although Libya continued to support other wings of the movement. The Libyan authorities began to organize Palestinians in the country into 'people's congresses' to pursue war against Israel independently, and by May about 27 such groups were reported to have been set up. However, a summit meeting of the 'steadfastness front' in Tripoli in April seemed to restore a measure of solidarity, and the PLO representative returned to Tripoli in May.

Relations with the USA were erratic throughout 1979 and the first half of 1980. In early 1979 Qaddafi threatened to cut off petroleum exports unless US President Jimmy Carter lifted a ban on sales to Libya of agricultural and electronic equipment and transport aircraft. The sacking of the US embassy in Tripoli,

by mobs protesting at the presence in the USA of the exiled Shah of Iran, led to the withdrawal of the US ambassador in December 1979. In May 1980 Qaddafi announced that he was exacting compensation to the value of thousands of millions of dollars from the USA, the United Kingdom and Italy for damage sustained by Libya during the North African campaigns of the Second World War. These countries were threatened with a petroleum embargo and the withdrawal of Libyan assets from their banking systems if the demands were not met. In mid-1979 Libyan petroleum accounted for an estimated 600,000 of the 8m. barrels per day (b/d) that were being imported by the USA.

Although Qaddafi strenuously denied Libyan involvement, a guerrilla raid on the Tunisian mining town of Gafsa in early 1980, with the presumed intent to incite a popular rebellion, was attributed to Libya. France sent military aid to support the Tunisian Government against the potential Libyan threat, and in February the French embassy in Tripoli and consulate in Benghazi were burned as a demonstration of Libya's anger at this action. The incident prompted Qaddafi to pledge publicly his determination to counter French intervention in Africa by any means. In February 1982, however, relations between Libya and Tunisia improved when Qaddafi visited Tunisia and a co-operation agreement between the two countries was signed.

During the early months of 1981 there was a build-up of Soviet and East European military advisers in Libya, and in March 1983 it was announced that Qaddafi was to sign a treaty of friendship and co-operation with the USSR. The treaty was not expected, however, to contain military clauses that would commit the USSR to supporting Libya in the event of armed clashes. This increasing interest in the USSR closely paralleled worsening relations with the USA. The US embassy in Tripoli was closed in May 1981 and relations deteriorated further in August, when US aircraft shot down two Libyan aircraft that had intercepted them over the Gulf of Sirte, claimed by Libya as its territorial waters. In November 1981 President Ronald Reagan alleged that a Libyan 'hit-squad' had been sent to assassinate him.

In February 1983 relations with the USA deteriorated further with the discovery of an alleged Libyan coup plot against the Sudanese Government. US naval vessels moved into Libyan waters and four US surveillance aircraft were spotted over the Libyan–Sudanese border. The US Administration, however, denied that these events were anything more than routine military movements, and said that US troops were merely training Egyptian forces.

LIBYA'S INVOLVEMENT IN CHAD: 1973–88

For many years Libya had been supporting the Front de libération nationale du Tchad (FROLINAT) in its rebellion against the Chad Government. In 1973 Libya occupied the Aozou strip, a region of 114,000 sq km (reputed to contain valuable deposits of minerals) in the north of Chad, basing its action on an unratified treaty of 1935, whereby Italy and France altered the frontiers between their two colonies and, according to Libya, sovereignty over the strip passed to Italy and subsequently to Libya, when it achieved independence in 1951. Chad raised this grievance at the Organization of African Unity (OAU) conference in Gabon in July 1977, and an *ad hoc* committee of reconciliation was established to regulate affairs in the disputed area, but Libya consistently refused to attend its sessions. In March 1978 the FROLINAT rebels were achieving such success against the Chad army that Gen. Félix Malloum (the President of Chad) was forced to appeal to Libya to arrest the progress of the rebels. A cease-fire was arranged at reconciliation meetings, held in the Libyan towns of Sebha and Benghazi, at the end of March. Sporadic fighting continued, however, amid allegations that certain factions of FROLINAT were still receiving substantial Libyan support.

A series of military reverses resulted in the downfall of the Malloum Government in March 1979 and, following an initiative by Nigeria, a cease-fire was signed at Kano by the four opposing Chadian factions. With the prospect of a share in the government of Chad at last, the mainstream of FROLINAT and, earlier, certain splinter groups withdrew their support from Libya over its annexation of the Aozou strip. Although a signatory of the Kano agreement, Libya engaged in a series of retaliatory attacks deep inside the northern border in mid-April. In June a 2,500-strong Libyan army invaded northern Chad and was driven back after several days' fierce fighting by FROLINAT forces. Chad's new coalition Government, formed in late April, was dominated by former FROLINAT insurgents and excluded the extreme factions from the south. The secessionist movement that subsequently appeared in the south was soon known to be receiving considerable support from Libya, while Libyan military aid continued to be received by certain guerrilla groups in the north. Dissent by the south and external pressure led to the disintegration of the coalition Government, but a second attempt to implement a 'Government of National Unity' foundered as, parallel to the north-south conflict, the inter-Muslim conflict intensified between President Goukouni Oueddei and the Minister of Defence, Hissène Habré. By March 1980 the Chad capital, N'Djamena, was the site of a pitched battle between Habré's forces and the armies of the President and his allies. In May Libya responded to an appeal from President Goukouni (some of whose Muslim rivals had received Libyan backing a year earlier) for reinforcements to help in stemming the rapid advance of Habré's forces in the capital.

During the latter half of 1980 an increasing number of Libyan troops were engaged in Chad, eventually helping President Goukouni to overcome the forces of Hissène Habré in December. In January 1981 it was announced that Libya and Chad had resolved to work for 'complete unity'. This could have been interpreted either as an agreed merger or as an occupation that was imposed on Chad by Libya. Some Libyan units withdrew from Chad in May 1981, but others remained because of a supposed threat from Sudan, which distrusted Qaddafi's African intentions. Some observers considered that Qaddafi had plans for the creation of a vast 'Saharan Republic', comprising Libya, Niger, Chad, Algeria, Tunisia and Mauritania, but, if so, this plan received a set-back in October 1981, when President Goukouni of Chad requested the removal of some 10,000 Libyan troops from his country. They were subsequently replaced by an OAU peace-keeping force, although Libya maintained troops in the Aozou strip. Despite Libyan support, Goukouni was unable to keep control of Chad, and the capital, N'Djamena, was captured by Habré's forces in June 1982.

Qaddafi persistently denied the charge of interfering in Chad's internal affairs, but in June 1983 Libyan aircraft supported troops of ex-President Goukouni Oueddei in capturing the city of Faya-Largeau, in northern Chad, from Chadian government forces. Government troops repossessed the town at the end of July but, after prolonged bombing by Libyan aircraft, it again fell to the rebel forces in August. France responded to a request for aid from President Habré by deploying 3,000 troops in Chad from August, ostensibly in the role of military instructors, although they had orders to retaliate if fired upon. A defensive line across Chad at latitude 15° N, secured by French troops, caused a military stalemate, and serious fighting did not resume until after the collapse of peace negotiations in January 1984, when French troops extended the defensive line 100 km northwards to latitude 16° N. By April 1984 Libya was reported to have annexed the northern desert area of Chad and to have 6,000–7,000 troops in the region. The French force remained to the south, in the hope of a political solution. Libya, having made the Aozou strip secure, seemed to have achieved its main objective and to have abandoned all pretence of simply supporting the rebels. In May Qaddafi offered to withdraw Libyan troops from Chad if France would, in turn, withdraw its forces. In September, without consulting the Government of Chad, France and Libya reached an agreement providing for the evacuation of both countries' forces. In November it was reported that the joint withdrawal had been completed, although US and Chadian intelligence reports maintained that some 4,000–5,000 Libyan troops remained in northern Chad. In December 1984 President François Mitterrand of France declined to intervene to remove Libyan forces from Chad by force, except in the event of their moving south of latitude 16° N.

Libyan forces allegedly supported Goukouni's rebel army, when it ended a lull in the civil war in February 1986, by launching an offensive southwards, across latitude 16° N. France sent a small 'deterrent' force to support President Habré, and French fighter-bombers attacked the Libyan-built rebel airfield at Ouadi Doum. In October Libya transferred its support

from the Chadian rebels who were led by Goukouni to those led by Acheikh Ibn Oumar, the leader of the Conseil démocratique révolutionnaire (CDR), one of the factions in the loose coalition of Chadian opposition groups. The latter replaced Goukouni as the leader of the opposition coalition in November. Goukouni had been pursuing a conciliatory policy towards President Habré, and at the end of October he was reportedly wounded while resisting arrest in Tripoli. Goukouni's Forces armées populaires (FAP) declared allegiance to Habré's Government, in opposition to the Libyan presence in Chad. The FAP lost control of the oasis town of Zouar, in north-western Chad, in December, but recaptured it in early 1987, with the assistance of government troops, who had earlier occupied the Libyan garrison town of Fada, near latitude 16° N. At the end of March Libyan forces abandoned their last important base in Chad, at Faya-Largeau (after it had been rendered indefensible by the government troops' capture of the airbase at Ouadi Doum, 150 km to the north-west), and retreated towards Aozou. An estimated 4,000 Libyan soldiers were killed between January and the end of March, and Libya was forced to abandon Soviet-made aircraft, valued at US $500m., at Ouadi Doum. Libyan troops in Chad (whose involvement in the fighting Col Qaddafi publicly continued to deny) were supported by the Islamic Pan-African Legion, a force consisting of mercenaries and volunteers from many African countries, which was formed in Libya.

President Habré's forces advanced into the Aozou strip and captured the town of Aozou in a new offensive on 8 August 1987. France, which maintained a force of 2,400 troops to the south of latitude 16° N, refused to provide protective fighter aircraft, or to deploy troops north of that latitude, in support of the Chadian Government offensive, which it had counselled against. Libya responded to the loss of Aozou by bombing towns in northern Chad. Libyan counter-attacks on Aozou on 14 and 20 August were both repulsed, but on 28 August Libyan forces recaptured the town, and advanced on Ounianga-Kebir, 100 km south of the disputed strip. Chadian forces responded by capturing and destroying an airbase at Maaten as-Sarra, 100 km inside Libya (claimed to be a base for Libyan raids on Chad), on 6 September. France criticized the Chadian incursion into Libya, reiterating its opinion that the question of sovereignty over the Aozou strip should be determined by international arbitration. On 11 September Chad and Libya agreed to observe a cease-fire proposed by the OAU. Later in the month Col Qaddafi refused to attend a session in Lusaka, Zambia, of the six-nation *ad hoc* committee established by the OAU to consider the conflict in Chad. However, President Habré was present, and Libya was represented by the Secretary for Foreign Liaison, Jadallah Azouz at-Tali.

In November 1987 the UN General Assembly refused to debate the Aozou issue, concluding that its resolution was the responsibility of the OAU. The OAU *ad hoc* committee accordingly proposed a summit meeting of the Libyan and Chadian Heads of State, which, after several postponements, was finally scheduled for 24 May 1988. However, on the eve of the summit, it was announced that Col Qaddafi would not be attending, in protest at Chad's treatment of prisoners of war. Qaddafi had continued to state his terms for a peaceful settlement of the dispute as: the recognition of Libyan sovereignty over the Aozou strip; the withdrawal of 'foreign troops' from Chad; the conclusion of an armistice between President Habré and the opposition forces led by Goukouni; and the release of prisoners of war. On 25 May, however, in a speech delivered in Tripoli to celebrate the 25th anniversary of the foundation of the OAU, Col Qaddafi announced his willingness to recognize the Government of Hissène Habré. He also invited Habré and Goukouni to hold reconciliation talks in Libya and offered to provide financial aid for the reconstruction of bombed towns in northern Chad. In June Habré said that he was ready to re-establish diplomatic relations with Libya, which had been severed in 1982. The Ministers of Foreign Affairs of Libya and Chad held further talks in Gabon in July but, apart from reaching agreement, in principle, on the restoration of diplomatic links, no progress was made on the crucial issues of sovereignty over the Aozou strip, the return of Libyan prisoners of war and the future security of common borders.

On 3 October 1988 Libya and Chad announced the resumption of diplomatic relations and an undertaking to settle their differ-people were reported to have died in the raids, including many civilians, who were the inevitable victims of bombs and missiles that were directed against military or terrorist targets in largely civilian areas. On 16 April Libya fired two missiles at the Italian island of Lampedusa, the site of a US coastguard station.

The US raids were generally deplored as a new round in an escalation of violence in the Middle East, and an upsurge in terrorist activity in Europe and the Middle East was feared. However, there was little sympathy for Libya. Most other Arab countries confined themselves to verbal condemnation of the USA, and Libya was disappointed by the Soviet reaction, which was purely rhetorical. A meeting of the Arab League failed to take place after a disagreement over the agenda, which Qaddafi demanded should only include discussion of the US raid. Libya expelled about 250 foreign journalists at the end of April 1986, and in May, after the European Community (EC, now European Union—EU) had decided to limit the size of Libyan diplomatic and commercial delegations within the EC, to restrict the movement of Libyan diplomats, and to tighten immigration regulations against Libyans, Col Qaddafi ordered the expulsion from Libya of 36 diplomats representing seven West European countries.

In the weeks following the US raids, Col Qaddafi was only rarely seen in public. There were rumours that he had lost overall control of the Government to Maj. Jalloud, who, although he held no formal government post, was accepted to be Qaddafi's deputy and was head of Libya's revolutionary committees (popular organizations throughout the country, which exist independently of the government bureaucracy) and the revolutionary guard corps, which were entrusted with responsibility for preserving the integrity of the revolution. The US Government had hoped that the raids on Libya would destabilize the regime of Col Qaddafi and create the conditions in which opposition groups could stage a coup. However, as the year progressed, Qaddafi gradually emerged from his retreat and appeared to remain firmly in control of government. At the end of May 1986, the USSR promised to continue sales of military equipment to Libya, but urged the condemnation of terrorism.

Conflict with the USA erupted again in January 1989, when US aircraft shot down two Libyan fighter aircraft in 'self-defence' over international waters in the Mediterranean. The incident occurred at a time when the USA was becoming concerned that Libya was about to produce chemical weapons at a plant near Rabta, 60 km south of Tripoli. Qaddafi claimed that the plant was a pharmaceuticals factory, being built with West German and Japanese assistance.

MAGHREB UNITY

In March and June 1986, in an attempt to consolidate its good relations with Algeria, Libya proposed a union of the two countries. The proposal was submitted to President Chadli of Algeria by Col Qaddafi's deputy, Maj. Jalloud, in June 1987. At the end of Jalloud's visit to Algiers, the parties issued a joint communiqué stating that President Chadli and Col Qaddafi would meet to discuss the proposal, although Algeria, reacting unenthusiastically to Libya's approaches, emphasized the need for 'compatibilities' between the countries—apparently a reference to Algeria's concern over Libya's intervention in Chad and its policy towards Tunisia. Algeria subsequently suggested that a framework for a new Algerian-Libyan relationship (and, by definition, one not going as far as actual union) already existed in the Maghreb Fraternity and Co-operation Treaty of 1983, between Algeria, Mauritania and Tunisia. Later in June, at short notice, Col Qaddafi arrived in Algeria in an attempt to persuade President Chadli to accede to the union proposals. However, he succeeded only in achieving agreement on several minor co-operation issues.

Economic links between Libya and Algeria expanded, and in early October 1987 the two Governments agreed in principle on a treaty of political union. The accord was to be announced officially on 1 November, but, owing to political opposition in Algeria, the announcement was not made. Instead, the Algerian Government proposed that Libya should sign the Maghreb Fraternity and Co-operation Treaty. This eventuality was made more likely by the re-establishment of diplomatic relations (at consular level) between Libya and Tunisia at the end of December.

In February 1988 Col Qaddafi, President Chadli and President Ben Ali of Tunisia held discussions concerning a proposed regional political accord, following which the border between Libya and Tunisia was reopened.

An expansion of economic co-operation was treated as the first stage towards regional integration in other fields. In March 1988 Libya and Algeria signed two agreements relating to industrial development. The first was for a tripartite project to supply some 90,000m. cu m of Algerian natural gas to Libya, via a trans-Tunisian pipeline. The second provided for the construction of a combined aluminium and petroleum coke complex in Zuwarah, Libya, to generate electricity for both countries, and the establishment of a joint company to undertake petrochemical projects. In April Libya and Tunisia signed a co-operation pact encompassing political, economic, cultural and foreign relations. Few details were released, but plans included the construction of an oil pipeline between Libya and Tunisia. Qaddafi announced that, from the date of the pact, Tunisians would be given priority among foreign nationals seeking employment in Libya, while the border posts on the frontier with Tunisia would be dismantled and Libyans and Tunisians would be guaranteed freedom of movement in both directions.

The leaders of the five countries of the Maghreb (Algeria, Morocco, Tunisia, Libya and Mauritania) held a meeting in Algiers (the first of its kind since they achieved independence), after the Arab summit meeting there in June 1988, to discuss the prospects for 'a Maghreb without frontiers'. After the meeting, the participants issued a joint communiqué announcing the creation of a Maghreb commission, comprising a delegation from each of the five countries, to concentrate on the establishment of a semi-legislative, semi-consultative council which would co-ordinate legislation in the region and prepare joint economic projects. At the end of June, Algeria and Libya announced that they would each be holding a referendum on a proposed union of the two countries. The proposition to be considered by the peoples of Algeria and Libya, however, fell short of the total merger for which Col Qaddafi had hoped, and envisaged, instead, a federation of the two states, within a Great Arab Maghreb.

In July 1988 the Maghreb commission met for the first time, in Algiers, and announced the creation of five working parties to examine areas of regional integration (including education, finance, economy and regional security), which would report to the second meeting of the commission in October. In August President Ben Ali of Tunisia visited Libya, and he and Col Qaddafi signed a series of co-operation agreements and established a technical commission to examine means of accelerating co-operation and the merger process, as a prelude to the creation of the Great Arab Maghreb.

In February 1989, at a summit meeting in Morocco of North African Heads of State, the participants concluded a treaty proclaiming the formation of a Union of the Arab Maghreb (UMA), comprising Algeria, Libya, Mauritania, Morocco and Tunisia. The treaty envisaged the establishment of a council of Heads of State, regular meetings of Ministers of Foreign Affairs, and the eventual free movement of goods, services and capital throughout the countries of the region. At the second summit meeting of the UMA, held in Algiers in July 1990, it was decided that Libya would hold the annual presidency of the Union in 1991.

A third summit meeting of the UMA was held in Ras Lanouf, Libya, on 10 March 1991 and was opened by Col Qaddafi in his role as President of the organization for the first six months of that year. This was the first meeting of the UMA states since the invasion of Kuwait by Iraq in August 1990 and it reflected the difficulty they had encountered in maintaining a united response towards the conflict in the Gulf region. The final communiqué expressed 'deep pain over the tragic developments in the Gulf' and urged that the economic sanctions imposed on Iraq by the UN should be lifted. Agreement was reached on the establishment of a Maghreb Bank of Investment and Foreign Trade, and on co-operation in other fields. At a subsequent UMA summit meeting in Casablanca, Morocco, in September 1991 the forthcoming Middle East peace conference was discussed and the UN was urged to lift the economic sanctions that it had imposed on Libya.

GOVERNMENT CHANGES AND DOMESTIC REFORM

At its annual meeting in 1986, the GPC reduced the number of secretariats in the General People's Committee from 22 to 10. Several Committee posts were merged or abolished. Changes of personnel were also made in the composition of the General Secretariat of the GPC. The object of the changes was, apparently, greater administrative efficiency. The public service functions of the dismantled secretariats were, in future, to be handled by specially created national companies, such as already existed for the administration of the petroleum industry, the secretariat for which was among those to be abolished. The GPC also resolved to form 'suicide squads to strike at the enemy'. According to the human rights organization Amnesty International, Libya assassinated at least 25 of its political opponents abroad between 1980 and 1987. In March 1987 the GPC elected a new General People's Committee. Only three Secretaries were re-elected from the previous Committee, and only two of these retained their former posts.

Increasing dissatisfaction at home with political repression, a deteriorating economy and shortages of basic commodities, combined with opposition to the military involvement in Chad and pressure from abroad to improve the image of his Government and ease his political isolation, caused Col Qaddafi to embark on a series of liberalizing economic and political reforms during 1988. In foreign policy, Qaddafi openly admitted the error of his involvement in Chad and adopted a more pragmatic approach to his ambition of union within the Maghreb and to his relations with other Arab and African countries, eliminating barriers to trade and tourism with neighbouring countries and declaring his opposition to terrorism. At home, he accused Libya's revolutionary committees of murdering political opponents of his regime. In early March Qaddafi began to encourage the reopening of private businesses, in recognition of the failure of the state-sponsored supermarkets to satisfy the demand for even the most basic commodities, which had caused a thriving 'black market' to emerge. At the same time, all prisoners (including foreigners), except those convicted of violent crimes or of conspiring with foreign powers, were released; Libyan citizens were guaranteed freedom of travel abroad; and the revolutionary committees were deprived of their powers of arrest and imprisonment, which had often been indiscriminately and arbitrarily used. A new secretariat was formed in May for Jamahiri (Mass) Mobilization and Revolutionary Guidance, apparently to monitor and regulate the revolutionary committees. In June the GPC approved a charter of human rights, guaranteeing freedom of expression and condemning violence. In March the GPC had created a people's court and a people's prosecution bureau to replace the 'revolutionary courts'.

At the end of August 1988, Col Qaddafi announced the abolition of the army and the police force. The army was to be replaced by a force of Jamahiri Guards, comprising conscripts and members of the existing army and police force, which would be supervised by 'people's defence committees' located in strategic areas. The most obvious sign of the practical implementation of a new policy of government decentralization was the decision in September to relocate all but two of the secretariats of the General People's Committee (ministries) away from the capital, Tripoli, mostly to Sirte, 400 km east of Tripoli. Further reform was promised when, in January 1989, Qaddafi announced that all state institutions, including the state intelligence service and the official Libyan news agency, were to be abolished.

At the meeting of the 16th session of the GPC, held in Tripoli during 2–10 March 1990 to consider future government policy, Col Qaddafi strongly criticized corruption in government administration. The Secretary for Higher Education subsequently tendered his resignation, following criticism from delegates, and the Secretary for Transport also resigned, in protest at corruption and the exorbitant fares charged by the state-controlled Jerma Bus Company.

In October 1990 the GPC implemented the most extensive changes to the General People's Committee since March 1987. The appointment of the uncompromising Abu Zaid Omar Dorda as the new Secretary-General (Prime Minister) and of 11 new secretaries was approved, increasing the number of secretariats in the GPC from 19 to 22. The opposition NFSL claimed that several of those promoted had been involved in purges against

dissidents and had been expelled from European countries. The former Secretary-General, the moderate Umar Mustafa al-Muntasser, was appointed Secretary of a new combined Economic and Planning Secretariat. The new Strategic Industries Secretariat was to be headed by another moderate, Jadallah Azouz, who was replaced as Secretary for Foreign Liaison by Ibrahim Muhammad Bashari. The Secretariats for Electricity, Social Security and Youth and Sports, which had been abolished in 1986, were revived. The Secretariat for Jamahiri Mobilization and Revolutionary Guidance was abolished, and a new secretariat was created to promote co-operation with the UAM. At the same time, three of the five-member General Secretariat of the GPC were replaced, Abd ar-Raziq Sawsa becoming Secretary-General of the GPC in place of Dr Muftah al-Usta Omar.

DEVELOPMENTS IN EXTERNAL RELATIONS

Following his reconciliation with Yasser Arafat's wing of the PLO in March 1987, Col Qaddafi sponsored efforts to reunite the divided Palestinian movement prior to the 18th session of the Palestine National Council in Algiers in April, although this strained relations with Syria, which had supported the revolt against Arafat's leadership of the PLO in 1983. It appeared that, after years of relative political isolation, Qaddafi found it expedient to realign Libyan policy with that of the majority of Arab states. After the Palestinian uprising (*intifada*) in the Israeli Occupied Territories began in December 1987, Qaddafi intensified his efforts to reconcile the opposing factions within the PLO, and in June 1988, at the request of Yasser Arafat, he sent Libyan representatives to Lebanon to mediate between Palestinian guerrillas loyal to Arafat and members of the rebel Fatah, who were fighting for control of Beirut's Palestinian refugee camps. He subsequently intervened personally to persuade the Sunni Muslim militia in southern Lebanon to allow Arafat loyalists, who had been driven out of Beirut, to enter the Palestinian camp of Ain al-Hilweh, near Sidon. Yasser Arafat and representatives of the dissident, Syrian-backed PLO factions visited Tripoli in September 1988 to attend the anniversary celebrations of the Libyan revolution, and their presence gave rise to speculation of a reconciliation, engineered by Qaddafi. In June Qaddafi had attended an Arab summit meeting in Algiers (the first such summit that he had attended for 18 years), which had been arranged to discuss Arab support for the Palestinian uprising.

In May 1987 Australia ordered the closure of the Libyan people's bureau in Canberra, accusing Libya of trying to destabilize the South Pacific region. Libya had been providing paramilitary training to dissident groups in the French territory of New Caledonia and the Indonesian provinces of Irian Jaya and East Timor, and, according to the Australian Government, had been involved in subversive activities in Australia.

In September 1987 Libya re-established 'fraternal' links with Iraq, modifying its support for Iran in the Iran–Iraq War and urging the observance of a cease-fire. Later in the same month Jordan restored its diplomatic relations with Libya. However, Libyan support for Iran had not completely ceased. Col Qaddafi refused to attend the extraordinary summit meeting of the League of Arab States, which took place in Amman, Jordan, in November to discuss the war. His representative quickly dissociated Libya from an apparently unanimously supported resolution, which censured Iran for its occupation of Arab (i.e. Iraqi) territory and for failing to accept UN cease-fire proposals. Libya also dissented from the League's decision to remove the prohibition on diplomatic relations between member states and Egypt.

Libya attended an emergency summit meeting of the Arab League in Casablanca (Morocco) in May 1989, but not a meeting of the Ministers of Foreign Affairs of member states (held immediately prior to the summit meeting), at which Egypt was formally readmitted to the Arab League. Meetings between Col Qaddafi and President Hosni Mubarak of Egypt in October were thought to signal the countries' imminent reconciliation, but by mid-1991 Libya remained the only Arab state not to have restored full diplomatic relations with Egypt, following its diplomatic and economic isolation by Arab states in 1979. Meeting in Cairo in February 1990 for the fourth time since May 1989, Qaddafi and Mubarak agreed to strengthen financial and economic ties between Egypt and Libya.

In March 1990 both the USA and the Federal Republic of Germany claimed that Libya had commenced production of mustard gas at a plant near Rabta, 60 km south of Tripoli (see Conflict with the USA, above). When a fire broke out at the plant during the same month, Libya accused these countries, together with Israel, of involvement in sabotage. All three countries denied any involvement. The Federal German Government stated that it would take measures, in accordance with international law, to halt the production of chemical weapons at Rabta, while the US Government refused to discount future military action against the plant. In June the US Government alleged that the plant at Rabta had not been destroyed by fire, as Libya had claimed, and voiced suspicions that a second plant, for the production of chemical weapons, was under construction. In July the US Government claimed that members of a Muslim movement, which was trying to overthrow the Government of Trinidad and Tobago, had received training in Libya.

Libya's relations with France improved in April 1990, after the release of three Europeans who had been held hostage in Lebanon. The French Government formally thanked the Libyan Government for its role in obtaining their release. In March France had returned to Libya three *Mirage* jet fighter aircraft that it had impounded in 1986 after their delivery to France for repairs. However, the French Government denied that the return of the aircraft had played any part in securing the release of the hostages. However, in September, following an official investigation, France alleged that Col Qaddafi, together with President Assad of Syria and the leader of the Popular Front for the Liberation of Palestine, Ahmad Jibril, had been responsible for planning the bombing of a French passenger aircraft over the Sahara in September 1989.

In June 1991, following a secret visit to Tripoli by a member of the British Parliament, it was revealed that Col Qaddafi had offered £250,000 to a British police charity, together with a letter of regret for the death of a policewoman outside the Libyan people's bureau in London in 1984 (see Qaddafi's Attempts to Quell Opposition at Home and Abroad, above). The Member of Parliament was reported to have discussed with Col Qaddafi a series of proposals aimed at restoring diplomatic relations between the United Kingdom and Libya, which had been severed at the time of the incident. However, the proposal was rejected by the British Foreign and Commonwealth Office, which said that there could be no possibility of a resumption of relations until there was convincing evidence that the Libyans had renounced their support for groups engaged in international terrorism, including the Irish Republican Army (IRA). In addition, the United Kingdom emphasized that Libya should co-operate in bringing to justice those responsible for the murder of the policewoman.

Early in 1992 Col Qaddafi was reported to have given assurances, through intermediaries, that he would reveal to the British Government information about his dealings with the IRA, in return for improved relations with the United Kingdom. However, in an interview with a British newspaper in May 1992 he appeared to renege on this promise, claiming that he feared that the revelation of such information might be used to 'trick' him. He admitted that Libya had supplied the IRA with arms and explosives, but denied that IRA members had trained in Libya. All links with the IRA had now been severed, he maintained.

THE GULF CONFLICT 1990–91

Col Qaddafi attended the emergency summit meeting of the Arab League, held in Cairo on 10 August 1990 to discuss the Arab response to the invasion of Kuwait by Iraq. Subsequently, 12 Arab nations voted in favour of a motion condemning the invasion and advocating the deployment of a pan-Arab force for the defence of Saudi Arabia and other states from possible Iraqi aggression. Libya voted against the measure, and in September Libyan aircraft were reported to be transporting food supplies to Iraq in violation of UN Security Council Resolution 661 which imposed mandatory economic sanctions on Iraq. Libya also announced that its ports were at Iraq's disposal for the purpose of importing food supplies. Following the commencement, on 16 January 1991, by a multi-national armed force, of 'Operation Desert Storm' to secure the liberation of Kuwait, anti-war demonstrations occurred in Libya. The Saudi Arabian ambas-

sador in Tripoli urged Qaddafi to support the concerted action, but during February the Libyan Government offered to supply food, medicine and blankets to Iraq.

President Mubarak of Egypt was thought to have persuaded Col Qaddafi to exercise restraint during the war between Iraq and the multinational force, and relations between Egypt and Libya continued to improve in its aftermath. Talks were held on moves towards greater economic integration, and in March 1991 Col Qaddafi abolished immigration and customs controls for Egyptians travelling to Libya. However, the subsequent flood of visitors resulted in the reimposition of checkpoints. Col Qaddafi visited Cairo in early July 1991 for the ratification of 10 integration agreements, and on 6 August the Egyptian Government announced the opening of Egypt's border with Libya, removing all obstacles to travel and trade. A security agreement on border movements was signed on 23 August.

INAUGURATION OF THE GREAT MAN-MADE RIVER

The first phase of Libya's 'Great Man-made River' project (GMR), begun in 1984 and designed to carry water from Saharan wells through 2,400 miles of 13 ft-diameter pipes to the more populous coastal regions, and to provide irrigation for agriculture, was inaugurated by Col Qaddafi on 28 August 1991 in a ceremony near Benghazi, attended by several Arab and African leaders, PLO leader Yasser Arafat and the Secretary-General of the Arab League. Few Western leaders were present. The scheme, the largest irrigation project in the Middle East, will take 25 years to complete, at an estimated cost of US $25,000m. During his visit for the ceremony, President Mubarak of Egypt held further talks with Col Qaddafi on economic co-operation. Libya had offered to resettle up to 1m. Egyptian farmers on lands to be irrigated by the GMR project.

THE LOCKERBIE AFFAIR AND THE IMPOSITION OF UN ECONOMIC SANCTIONS

In December 1988 all 259 people aboard a Pan Am Boeing 747, en route to New York, died when the aircraft exploded over Lockerbie, Scotland. Eleven people in the village also died. The plane had been flying from Frankfurt-am-Main, Germany, where it was believed that a suitcase containing a bomb had been loaded on board. Investigations had revealed that this suitcase had arrived at Frankfurt on a flight from Malta, where an employee of Libyan Arab Airlines, Al-Amin Khalifa Fhimah, was stationed. On 13 November 1991 Scotland's Lord Advocate and the acting US Attorney-General issued international warrants for the arrest of Fhimah and the former security chief of the Libyan airline, Abd al-Baset al-Megrahi, accusing them of responsibility for the bombing of the Pan Am aircraft. Two days later the Libyan Secretariat for Foreign Affairs issued a statement denying any Libyan involvement in the bombing, condemning all forms of terrorism and urging the investigation of the charges by a neutral international body or the ICJ. A British demand for the extradition of the two men, presented by the Italian ambassador in Tripoli on 18 November, was refused, as was a repeated demand by the British and US authorities on 27 November.

A campaign was mounted by Libya among its Arab neighbours to enlist their support in countering the allegations, and it continued to resist pressure for the extradition of the two Lockerbie suspects and also for the arrest of four other Libyans sought by France in connection with the bombing of a French UTA DC-10 airliner over Niger in September 1989, in which 171 people had died. One of those accused over the latter incident, Abdallah Sannousi, was the brother-in-law of Col Qaddafi himself and deputy head of the Libyan intelligence services. On 5 December 1991 the Arab League Council, meeting in Cairo, expressed solidarity with Libya and urged the avoidance of sanctions. However, on 26 December US President George Bush extended economic sanctions, which the USA had imposed on Libya in January 1986, for a further year.

Meanwhile, Libya had announced that it would conduct its own inquiry into the Lockerbie allegations under the chairmanship of Judge Taher az-Zuai. He was reported to have stated, on 7 December 1991, that the two suspects had been detained and would stand trial in Libya. An offer by the Libyan Secretary for Foreign Liaison, Ibrahim Muhammad al-Bishari, to send

Libyan judges to London or Washington, DC, to discuss the case was rejected.

A unanimous resolution (no. 731) by the UN Security Council, adopted on 21 January 1992, demanded the extradition of the Lockerbie suspects to the USA or the United Kingdom as well as Libya's full co-operation with France's inquiry into the loss of its aircraft in Niger in 1989. Libya declined to extradite the men, but did offer to place them on trial in Libya. It also offered to allow French officials to interrogate the four men suspected of complicity in the Niger bombing. On 18 February al-Megrahi and Fhimah appeared in court in Tripoli, where the judge refused to allow their extradition, claiming that there were no grounds for it in international or criminal law. The Libyan response to Resolution 731 was rejected by the USA, the United Kingdom and France, which urged the UN to impose sanctions on Libya.

On 23 March Libya applied to the ICJ for an order confirming its right to refuse the extradition of the Lockerbie suspects by applying the terms of the 1971 Montreal Convention on airline terrorism. It was claimed that the convention allowed Libya the option of trying the suspects in its own courts, a view opposed by lawyers acting for the United Kingdom and the USA. A judgment was not expected for another two years but the ICJ nevertheless ruled, on 14 April, that it had no power to prevent the UN from enacting sanctions against Libya.

An offer in late March 1992 by Col Qaddafi to place the suspects under the jurisdiction of the Arab League was subsequently withdrawn. Intensive diplomacy by the League, spearheaded by President Mubarak of Egypt (who, at the request of the PLO, met Col Qaddafi in Tripoli on 12 April), came to nothing. On 31 March the UN Security Council adopted Resolution 748, imposing mandatory economic sanctions against Libya. From 15 April 1992 all civilian air links and arms trade with Libya were to be prohibited and its diplomatic representation reduced. An embargo on the sale of Libyan petroleum was not imposed. There was widespread hostility in the Arab world to the imposition of sanctions against a fellow Arab and Muslim state. The UN was accused of hypocrisy for not enforcing similar measures against Israel over its failure to comply with UN Security Council Resolution 242 (1967), which demanded Israeli withdrawal from the Occupied Territories. It was also feared that Islamist fundamentalists in countries such as Egypt, Algeria, Tunisia and Morocco might exploit the ensuing economic hardships for their own political ends.

In Libya itself demonstrators immediately took to the streets to condemn the West, and Col Qaddafi threatened to cut off oil supplies to, and withdraw all business from, those countries that complied with Resolution 748. Demonstrators besieged several Western embassies in Tripoli. The embassy of Venezuela (which had held the presidency of the Security Council when Resolution 748 was passed) was ransacked and burned. It was reported that exit visas had been refused to a number of foreign nationals, despite earlier assurances, and fears were expressed that Col Qaddafi might seek to use some of them as hostages. Speaking in Tripoli's Green Square on 4 April at a dawn rally to mark the end of the month of Ramadan, Col Qaddafi rejected Resolution 748 and sought to depict the situation as a new crusade against Islam by the Christian West. 'Muslims all over the world, the battle being waged by modern Western crusading forces, having ended against communism, is now being directed against Islam,' he declared.

UN sanctions took effect on 15 April 1992. The previous day Col Qaddafi had severed all international communications and travel links in a day of self-imposed isolation to mark the anniversary. Prior to the imposition of sanctions, Libya was reported to have been stockpiling food and medicines and to have transferred liquid capital from Europe to banking centres in the Gulf region and the Far East. Arab neighbours rallied to find new land and sea routes to circumvent the air embargo, and it was announced that a hydrofoil service from Malta to Tripoli would operate five times a week instead of weekly. The immediate effect of the sanctions was thus primarily psychological and it was thought that this would cause little more than inconvenience, rather than actual hardship, in the foreseeable future.

In May 1992, at Col Qaddafi's instigation, 1,500 people's congresses were convened in Libya and abroad, to enable ordi-

nary citizens to debate the fate of the two Lockerbie suspects and their response to the UN sanctions. Arab diplomats and the more pragmatic members of Qaddafi's circle had begun to urge a compromise, fearing that the imposition of further UN sanctions, particularly an embargo on sales of petroleum (Libya earns 95% of its income from such sales), would be disastrous. Observers concluded that Qaddafi was seeking to resolve his dilemma and save face by using the people's congresses as a means of distancing himself from any eventual 'surrender'. In late June the GPC announced its decision to allow the two Lockerbie suspects to stand trial abroad, provided the proceedings were 'fair and just'. It suggested that such a trial might take place under the auspices of either the Arab League or the UN. In August, at a meeting with Col Qaddafi, UN Under-Secretary-General Vladimir Petrovskii warned that if Libya continued to refuse to comply with Resolution 731, the UN might strengthen the sanctions already in force against it. On 12 August, however, the UN Security Council merely renewed the sanctions for a further 120 days.

In early January 1993 Libya closed all of its land borders for three days in protest at the UN's decision, taken in early December 1992, to renew the sanctions in force against Libya. In mid-February an article appeared in the US press that alleged that Libya was constructing an underground factory for the manufacture of chemical weapons at Tarhuna, west of Tripoli. In January Libya refused to a sign a UN convention banning chemical weapons, on the grounds that not all Middle Eastern and North African states were party to the convention.

During the approach to the UN Security Council's sanctions review in April 1993, Libya attempted to rally Arab support and announced in late March that it was tabling new proposals to try and break the deadlock. In the USA a group of senators, led by Edward Kennedy, urged the US Senate Foreign Relations Committee to seek the expansion of UN sanctions against Libya. At the same time, there were new allegations in the US press that Libya was building a second chemical weapons plant. Despite the USA's efforts to secure a tightening of the economic embargo, at its April meeting the Security Council did not modify the original sanctions which were retained for a further 120 days. Following the meeting, the USA stated that it would continue to consult its allies about tougher sanctions, including a possible ban on Libyan petroleum exports. However, the main European importers of Libyan crude petroleum, in particular Germany, Italy and Spain, remained firmly opposed to an oil embargo. In July the French Minister of Foreign Affairs, Alain Juppé, stated that France would demand tougher sanctions if Libya failed to comply with Resolution 731 before the next Security Council review in early August.

At its meeting on 13 August 1993 the Security Council decided to maintain existing sanctions. The USA, the United Kingdom and France, increasingly frustrated at Qaddafi's defiance, issued an ultimatum to Libya stating that if the two suspects were not surrendered for trial by 1 October 1993, they would propose a UN Security Council resolution imposing tougher sanctions, covering oil-related, financial and technical sectors. Libya rejected the deadline but repeated its offer to discuss holding the trial in a country other than the USA or the United Kingdom. In a television interview, Qaddafi claimed that 'all the sanctions in the world or even in the universe will never make Libya submit'.

As the 1 October 1993 deadline approached, pressure on Libya had mounted. US President Bill Clinton, in his first speech to the UN General Assembly, vowed to bring the perpetrators of the Lockerbie bombing to justice. When Libya failed to comply with Western demands, the USA, the United Kingdom and France introduced a draft resolution at the Security Council seeking to impose tighter sanctions. After further negotiations had failed to break the deadlock, the Security Council finally yielded to the demands of the USA, the United Kingdom and France. On 11 November UN Security Council Resolution 883 was adopted, imposing new sanctions against Libya. The resolution provided for the freezing of all Libyan assets abroad, with the exception of earnings from hydrocarbons exports, placed a ban on the sale to Libya of certain equipment for the 'downstream' oil and gas sectors and placed further restrictions on Libyan civil aviation, including the immediate closure of all Libyan Arab Airlines offices abroad. The new measures came into force on 1 December 1993. Resolution 883 stated that sanctions would be ended as soon as the two Libyans accused of responsibility for the Lockerbie bombing were handed over for trial in the United Kingdom or the USA and Libya co-operated fully with the French authorities investigating the bombing of the UTA airliner over Niger in 1989. It also made provision for the reimposition of sanctions within 90 days if Libya failed to comply with all the demands set out in Resolutions 731 and 748.

In response to Resolution 883, Qaddafi declared that he was prepared to destroy Libya's oilfields and ports as a gesture of defiance to the West. In a series of public speeches he urged the Libyan people to make sacrifices in the cause of national dignity and rejected all further negotiations with the UN and the Western powers on the Lockerbie affair. Through editorials in *Ash-Shams*, Qaddafi criticized his own foreign secretariat for urging the surrender of the two accused Libyans. This was interpreted as an attack on Omar al-Muntasser, the Libyan Secretary for Foreign Liaison and International Co-operation. Nevertheless, al-Muntasser retained his post in the reshuffle of the General People's Committee at the end of January 1994. When the GPC met in January 1994, the Lockerbie affair was high on the agenda, but the statement issued at the end of the session contained no hint that a compromise was possible and instead accused the USA of using sanctions to continue its policy of oppressing Libya and causing suffering to the Libyan people. In a speech in Misurata in February 1994 Qaddafi declared that the Lockerbie affair was closed, but two weeks later he proposed that the two accused men be tried by an Islamic court either in the USA, the United Kingdom or any other country, provided that the court officials were Muslims. The proposal was rejected by the British Foreign and Commonwealth Office. After the Secretary-General of the Arab League held talks in Tripoli at the end of February, JANA, the official Libyan press agency, accused the Arab League of submitting to US pressure over UN sanctions and declared that Libya wished to play no further part in the organization. In February 1994 President Clinton renewed US sanctions against Libya, originally imposed in 1986, and reaffirmed his determination to see the two Libyans accused of the Lockerbie bombing extradited to face trial. He described Libya as an exceptional threat to US national security and interests.

On 12 June 1994 the Ministers of Foreign Affairs of the OAU member states adopted a resolution urging the UN Security Council to revoke the sanctions that it had imposed on Libya. The following day a member of the Palestinian Fatah Revolutionary Council, who was on trial in Lebanon (accused of the assassination of a Jordanian diplomat), claimed that the Council had been responsible for the explosion that destroyed the aircraft over Lockerbie in December 1988. At various times since February 1992 various parties had alleged that Iranian, Syrian and Palestinian agents—sometimes separately, sometimes in collaboration—had been responsible for the explosion. Nevertheless, both the US and the British authorities remained convinced that there was still sufficient evidence to continue to seek the extradition of the two Libyan suspects who had been formally indicted for the offence in the USA and Scotland.

In mid-February 1995 the Government announced that it would not assume the chairmanship of the UMA, as it was due to do later in the year, because other UMA member states were enforcing the UN-imposed sanctions against Libya. In late March the US Secretary of State announced that the USA would seek to persuade the UN Security Council to apply a ban on Libyan sales of petroleum before its forthcoming review of the sanctions already in force. At the end of the month, however, the Security Council did no more than renew the existing sanctions, prompting the USA to announce that it would impose more stringent unilateral sanctions on Libya.

In April 1995 Col Qaddafi successfully defied UN sanctions by ordering a Libyan aircraft carrying 150 pilgrims to leave Tripoli for Jeddah in Saudi Arabia. His action came only hours after the UN had agreed to allow 6,000 Libyan pilgrims to visit Saudi Arabia for the annual *hajj* on 45 EgyptAir flights. The UN immediately condemned the Libyan action as a 'flagrant violation of the UN air embargo' and criticized Egypt and Saudi Arabia for their involvement. Both countries appeared to have had prior knowledge of the flight. However, the UN Security Council did not withdraw its permission for the EgyptAir flights. At the request of President Mubarak of Egypt, Col Qaddafi did not proceed with further Libyan flights to Saudi Arabia, but he claimed that the Libyan people had won a victory through their 'steadfastness and determination to die for the sacred right of the *hajj*'. Qaddafi himself declined to make the pilgrimage to Mecca.

In May 1995 Qaddafi adopted a new strategy over the extradition of the two Libyan Lockerbie suspects (see above) by insisting that the UN Security Council should first investigate the US bombing of Tripoli in 1986 and that Israel should first comply with some 40 UN resolutions. However, at the end of July 1995 the UN decided not to lift the sanctions in force against Libya, although it rejected persistent US demands for stronger sanctions, including an oil embargo. In November the USA again failed to convince its European allies to impose an embargo on Libyan petroleum, but despite appeals from Egypt and the Arab League for some relaxation in the sanctions, the existing embargo was once again renewed. The USA nevertheless continued its uncompromising stance towards Libya, and in December introduced domestic legislation to strengthen economic sanctions against both Libya and Iran, targeting in particular oil companies that invest in the two countries. In May 1996 it was reported that the EU Council of Ministers had protested against sanctions planned by the USA to penalize non-US companies investing in oil and gas projects and supplying refinery equipment to Libya. At the end of June Col Qaddafi once again flouted UN sanctions by flying to Cairo in order to attend the Arab summit meeting convened by President Mubarak following the victory of Likud leader Binyamin Netanyahu in the Israeli legislative elections. The summit meeting urged the UN to lift sanctions against Libya, and appealed to the United Kingdom and the USA to accept an Arab proposal that the two Libyan suspects in the Lockerbie affair should be given a neutral and fair trial in The Hague (rather than in the United Kingdom) but with Scottish judges in session and in accordance with Scottish law. Despite appeals by Russia, the People's Republic of China, Egypt, Indonesia and Botswana for sanctions to be revoked, and for the trial of the two Libyan suspects to be held in a third country, the UN renewed existing sanctions against Libya at the end of July 1996, and there seemed to be little prospect of them being lifted in the foreseeable future.

In October 1995 Libya withdrew its candidacy for a seat on the UN Security Council after the USA, the United Kingdom and France had organized a campaign to prevent its election. Libya relinquished its candidacy in favour of Egypt, stating that it did not wish to sit on the Council because the UN had become a tool of the USA. In November Libya was excluded from the summit meeting of Mediterranean countries in Barcelona, Spain, after strong pressure from the British Government. Later in that month a Libyan dissident, Ali Mehmed Abuzeid, a founder member of the NFSL, was killed in London amid reports that he had given information to the Italian police about arms smuggling to Libya. Although it was claimed that Abuzeid was the victim of a Libyan 'hit-squad', British intelligence sources dismissed the theory that the killing was political. Nevertheless, in December the British Government accused the senior Libyan diplomat in London of intimidating Libyan dissidents in exile there and expelled him. In retaliation, Libya immediately expelled a British diplomat.

At the beginning of 1996 there were acrimonious exchanges with the US authorities after Col Qaddafi appeared to support the actions of Palestinian Islamists responsible for a series of devastating suicide bomb attacks in Israel, and reports that Libya had donated US $1,000m. to Louis Farrakhan, the controversial leader of the Nation of Islam movement in the USA, who had visited Tripoli the previous December. In February the CIA repeated its claim that Libya was developing a secret chemical plant at Tarhuna for the manufacture of poison gas, in order to replace the Rabta facility (see above), and in March the US Secretary of Defense, William Perry, during a visit to Cairo, told the Egyptian authorities that, if necessary, the USA would use force to close down the plant. In early April President Mubarak indicated that Egypt had requested detailed data from the USA and that, if reports about the plant were confirmed, he might offer to mediate with Libya. In May the Libyan Secretary for Foreign Liaison and International Co-operation,

Omar al-Muntasser, complained to the UN Security Council that the USA was preparing an attack on Libya, on the pretext of destroying the plant at Tarhuna, and strongly denied the existence of a chemical weapons facility there. Libya instead insisted that the plant formed part of the GMR project (see Inauguration of the Great Man-made River, above). The USA repeated that it would take whatever action necessary to prevent the plant's completion, but excluded the use of chemical weapons. However, US efforts to win support for its proposal to destroy the alleged plant met with little success. Despite reports of photographic evidence confirming the plant's existence, many observers remained sceptical, although the arrest, in August, of two Germans accused of exporting computerized equipment often used in the manufacture of poison gas to Libya, reinforced the opinions of a number of US officials. Similar concerns had been expressed by the USA in June, when it was reported that Libya had signed a clandestine co-operation pact with Ukraine, which was understood to provide for the transfer of advanced weapons' technology to Libya. In December the US press published additional claims, which alleged that Ukraine had agreed to provide Libya with military equipment, including missiles, valued at $500m., in contravention of the UN arms embargo. The charges, allegedly founded on a CIA report, were denied by Ukrainian officials.

The Libyan leader's stance on the suicide bomb attacks in Israel also soured relations with the EU, which had begun to show some signs of improvement at the beginning of 1996 when Libyan and EU representatives held talks in Brussels. At the international anti-terrorism summit meeting hastily convened in Egypt in March—the so-called 'Summit of Peacemakers'—the British Prime Minister, John Major, condemned Libya and Iran for sponsoring terrorism, although the final communiqué failed to mention any state by name. Qaddafi denounced those Arab states that participated in the meeting, with the exception of Egypt. In April the South African Minister of Foreign Affairs, Alfred Nzo, on an official visit to Tripoli, called for the lifting of 'unjust sanctions' against Libya, incurring the displeasure of the United Kingdom, the USA and France. South Africa's President Nelson Mandela had earlier insisted that he would stand by countries that had supported the ANC in its struggle against apartheid and in February had issued an invitation to the Libyan leader to make an official visit to South Africa. South Africa announced that it was to appoint a non-resident ambassador to Libya. In February 1997 it was reported that President Mandela had ordered an inquiry into allegations that South Africa had illegally supplied chemical weapons to Libya since his Government had come to power.

USA IMPOSES SECONDARY SANCTIONS

In July 1996 the USA increased its pressure on Libya when the US Congress unanimously approved a controversial Iran and Libya sanctions act, which aimed to further weaken the Libyan economy as a penalty for that country's alleged support of international terrorism. The legislation had originally targeted only Iran, but had been amended to include Libya, and involved the imposition of sanctions on any non-US country investing more than US $40m. (subsequently revised to $20m.) in Libya's oil and gas industry in any one year. European Governments protested vociferously against the legislation, and promptly lodged a protest with the World Trade Organization (WTO). Trade between the EU and Libya at that time was worth some $20,000m. each year, while almost 90% of Libya's oil exports went to Western Europe where they provided around 10% of all petroleum supplies. European oil companies, particularly those of Italy and Spain were heavily involved in the Libyan petroleum industry, and were, therefore, the countries most likely to suffer as a result of the new sanctions. In response to the European challenge, the USA invoked article 21 of the General Agreement on Tariffs and Trade (GATT), which permits a signatory to break the agreement if national security interests are involved. In November a Libyan-sponsored resolution calling for the repeal of the Iran and Libya sanctions act was adopted by the UN General Assembly. Libyan diplomatic efforts, however, failed to make any progress towards the removal of UN sanctions, which were once again renewed, unchanged, in mid-November. The appointment in February 1997 of Abu Zaid Omar Dorda, a former Prime Minister, as the new Libyan

representative to the UN, was interpreted by a number of observers as an indication that Libya intended to make no further concessions, but would instead adopt an uncompromising approach to the Lockerbie affair. In January it had been reported that Libya had once more defied the UN-imposed air embargo, when an official delegation flew to Accra, Ghana. Moreover, in late March Libyan aircraft again transferred worshippers to Saudi Arabia for the annual pilgrimage, despite the fact that the UN had permitted EgyptAir to organize flights for the Libyan pilgrims. In May Qaddafi travelled by air to Niger and Nigeria. The violations were strongly condemned by the UN, but no action was taken against the Libyan regime. In April the EU and the USA came to an agreement to limit the impact of the Iran and Libya sanctions act upon European countries. Under the new arrangement the US Administration promised to protect European companies from the adverse effects of the legislation, while in return the EU agreed to withdraw its complaint to the WTO regarding an earlier US law, the Helms-Burton Act, which imposed sanctions on non-US companies involved in business with Cuba. At that time no charges had been brought against any foreign company by the USA. In July, in protest at the UN Security Council's renewal of existing sanctions and the unanimity requirement which enabled the USA to veto the lifting of sanctions, Abu Zaid Omar Dorda announced Libya's intention to no longer respect those sanctions.

EU protests at new US sanctions did not imply any change in Europe's position on Libya, and despite the visit by an EU delegation to Tripoli in June 1996, relations remained strained. Nevertheless, Qaddafi appeared to be seeking to take advantage of the divisions between the USA and the EU by working to improve European relations, particularly with France. He praised France for its pursuit of an independent foreign policy and allowed the French judge investigating the 1989 bombing of a French airliner over Niger unprecedented access to Libyan evidence during his visit to Tripoli in July, which led to the judge's decision to try *in absentia* the Libyans suspected of the attack. A declaration by German authorities in October that clear evidence was available to prove the Libyan Government's direct involvement in the 1986 bomb attack on a Berlin discotheque, which provided a pretext for the US raids against Libya 10 days later, was also a major set-back; it was announced that arrest warrants had been issued for the three Libyans believed to have been involved in the attack. Despite this development, three German deputies, who visited Libya in March 1997 as members of a parliamentary delegation responsible for relations with the UMA, recommended that regular contact between the German parliament and the GPC should continue. In the same month Libya achieved rare success in foreign policy when the Vatican resisted US pressure and established formal diplomatic relations with Libya. Pope John Paul II had often spoken out against the imposition of UN sanctions on Libya, and his officials stated that the establishment of diplomatic links with Libya took place in recognition of that country's efforts to protect freedom of religion and the Vatican's wish to see a peaceful and stable Mediterranean region. Archbishop José Sebastián Laboa became the Pope's first envoy to Tripoli, while Libya was to open a people's bureau in the Vatican City. In contrast, Libya remained excluded from co-operation initiatives between the EU and southern Mediterranean states, which were launched in Barcelona in 1995.

In October 1996 the Libyan leader provoked diplomatic outrage during the visit of Necmettin Erbakan, Turkey's first Islamist Prime Minister, when he criticized Turkey's membership of NATO and its close association with the West, urging the establishment of an independent Kurdish state. There was an angry response from Ankara and Turkey's ambassador to Tripoli was recalled. After a few months, however, the situation improved and the Turkish ambassador returned, but in June 1997 Turkey again withdrew its ambassador, after Qaddafi reportedly made remarks on Libyan television criticizing the Turkish army and Government, and denouncing military agreements between Turkey and Israel.

In February 1997 the Ministerial Council of the OAU met in Tripoli for the first major meeting of the organization to be convened outside Addis Ababa. The delegates called for an end to UN sanctions against Libya, and a committee of five ministers was established to mediate between Libya and the Western states in order to try to resolve the Lockerbie affair.

NEW DEVELOPMENTS IN THE LOCKERBIE AFFAIR

In July 1997 the Arab League, which had previously been criticized by Qaddafi for its lack of support, formally proposed that the two Libyan suspects in the Lockerbie affair be tried by Scottish judges under Scottish law in a neutral country. At an Arab League meeting in September the member states urged a relaxation of the air embargo on Libya and voted to defy UN sanctions by permitting aircraft carrying Qaddafi, and other flights for religious or humanitarian purposes, to land on their territory. In October the President of South Africa, Nelson Mandela, visited Libya, despite US disapproval, and publicly expressed support for the proposals to hold a trial of the Lockerbie suspects in a third country. Later that month the United Kingdom requested the UN to send envoys to examine the Scottish legal system, and in December, following the renewal of sanctions by the UN in November, the UN issued a report concluding that the Libyan suspects would receive a fair trial under the Scottish system. However, in February 1998 the ICJ ruled that it was competent to hear Libya's complaints that the USA and the United Kingdom were acting unlawfully by insisting on the extradition of the two Libyan suspects. The USA and the United Kingdom had attempted to prevent the case from being heard, on the grounds that intervening UN Security Council resolutions had rendered it unnecessary. Libya declared that the ICJ ruling had given its claims legitimacy and that UN sanctions should now be disregarded. Nevertheless, sanctions were renewed in March and no progress towards lifting them was achieved at a debate within the Security Council later in the same month.

In April 1998 a representative for the families of the British victims of the Lockerbie bombing and a professor of Scottish law travelled to Libya, where they met Col Qaddafi. The Libyan leader was reported to have agreed to the trial of the two Libyan suspects in The Hague. In the following month US and EU representatives concluded an agreement under which European companies would be able to invest in Iran, Libya and Cuba without incurring sanctions as set out in the so-called Iran-Libya Sanctions Act (ILSA) of 1996 and the Helms-Burton Act. In return for this concession, which had been negotiated with reference to the involvement of Total of France in Iran, EU states were reported to have agreed to monitor more carefully their exports to Libya. In June 1998 at a meeting in Ouagadougou, Burkina Faso, the OAU resolved that from September its members would cease to comply with UN sanctions against Libya unless the USA and the United Kingdom agreed to a trial being held in a neutral third country and authorized flights to Libya on humanitarian, religious or diplomatic missions with immediate effect. In the following months several African heads of state openly flouted the air embargo and flew directly to Libya for talks with Col Qaddafi. Relations with Italy, Libya's major trading partner, improved significantly. A wide-ranging accord was signed in Rome in July, in which Italy expressed regrets for its colonial past, and which provided for joint infrastructure projects, especially in the energy sector. In October the two countries signed a further agreement on technical and scientific co-operation whereby Libyans would receive training in Italy. France also appeared keen to improve relations with Libya, where French companies were actively seeking investment opportunities in the energy sector. France and Libya agreed that the six Libyans implicated in the 1989 bombing of a French airliner over Niger could be tried *in absentia*.

In late August 1998 the USA and the United Kingdom, under mounting diplomatic pressure, sought to regain the initiative in the Lockerbie affair and agreed to a trial of the two Libyan suspects in the Netherlands before a panel of Scottish judges and in accordance with Scottish law. Soon after the offer was made the UN Security Council unanimously approved a resolution (no. 1192) allowing the lifting of UN sanctions against Libya as soon as the two suspects were surrendered for trial. The USA, however, threatened to extend sanctions to include a multilateral oil embargo should Libya reject the new offer, although there seemed little likelihood that international support would be forthcoming for such a measure. Col Qaddafi gave a cautious welcome to the US and British proposal, but the

Libyan authorities later requested negotiations about the terms of a trial in the Netherlands. The USA and the United Kingdom made it clear that their offer was non-negotiable, but did agree to clarify any technical or legal points through the office of the UN Secretary-General. The Libyan Government also appointed a new, high-level legal team to represent the two suspects, headed by a former Secretary for Foreign Liaison, suggesting to some observers that the interests of the Libyan regime rather than those of the accused would now be given priority. The two suspects, Al-Amin Khalifa Fhimah and Abd al-Baset al-Megrahi, had been under virtual house arrest for some six years, with their passports confiscated by the authorities. During a British television broadcast in October, Qaddafi indicated that the two men might be guilty, but emphasized that the bombing had not been officially sanctioned and that the suspects may have been seeking their own revenge for the US air-strikes against Libya in 1986. Some analysts concluded that the Libyan leader had decided to try to resolve the conflict with the West and had withdrawn support from a number of radical political groups in an effort to refute accusations that the Libyan State sponsored terrorism. The fact that 'Abu Nidal', the leader of the pro-Palestinian Fatah Revolutionary Council, was reported to have been expelled from Libya in mid-1998 was regarded as evidence of this change. Subsequently, the Fatah Revolutionary Council accused Libya of arresting several of its members and demanded their release. By the time Kofi Annan, the UN Secretary-General, visited Libya in early December, Qaddafi had agreed to a trial in the Netherlands under Scottish law but a problem remained over US and British insistence that, if convicted, the two Libyans must serve their sentences in a Scottish prison. The Libyan leader assured Kofi Annan that he wished to resolve the Lockerbie issue, and in mid-December, just before the 10th anniversary of the bombing, the GPC expressed 'satisfaction' with the idea of a trial in the Netherlands and welcomed the UN Secretary-General's efforts to facilitate this.

In early January 1999 the head of the Libyan judiciary issued warrants for the arrest of several former US officials for their alleged involvement in air-strikes against Libya in 1986 and stated that the matter would be referred to the UN Security Council if the men were not surrendered. This was viewed as a move designed to draw attention to what Libya insists are double standards employed by the USA on issues relating to international law. Relations with the United Kingdom were further strained when a former British intelligence officer revealed details of an alleged plot by the British security services to assassinate the Libyan leader in 1996. The allegations were strongly denied by the British Government. Despite a visit to Libya by envoys of South Africa and Saudi Arabia in mid-January 1999, by late February Qaddafi had not surrendered the two suspects. The USA and the United Kingdom, increasingly frustrated by the delay, warned Libya on 25 February that unless the two suspects were surrendered within 30 days, sanctions would be strengthened. However, Libya rejected this ultimatum and the USA and the United Kingdom failed to obtain a resolution from the Security Council in support of further sanctions, to which China, France and Russia had all indicated their opposition.

In early March 1999 the six Libyans accused of bombing the French UTA airliner over Niger in 1989 were found guilty *in absentia* after a three-day trial in Paris and were sentenced to life imprisonment. The French authorities proceeded to issue international warrants for the arrest of the six men and demanded that the Libyan authorities should punish them. It appeared very unlikely that Libya would impose prison sentences on the men, who included Col Qaddafi's brother-in-law. In July 1999 Libya paid more than US $31m. in compensation to the families of the 70 people killed in the bombing of the French airliner. According to the French authorities, the payment represented 'an acknowledgement by the Libyan authorities of the responsibility of their citizens'.

In mid-March 1999, after further diplomatic efforts by South Africa, President Nelson Mandela, on a visit to Libya, announced that the Libyan authorities would release the two accused men for trial by 6 April. This was confirmed by Col Qaddafi, who announced that he had accepted South African and Saudi Arabian assurances about arrangements for the trial in the Netherlands. The Libyan Government then sent a letter to the UN

Secretary-General guaranteeing to surrender the two suspects. If the men were convicted they would serve their sentences in a Scottish prison, but the United Kingdom was reported to have agreed that the two men would be held separately from the rest of the prisoners, that UN monitors would ensure that they were not subjected to interrogation by the British or US intelligence services, and that they would have regular access to Libyan consular services. While there was much speculation about the Libyan leader's motives in finally agreeing to surrender the two men, many analysts argued that economic factors played a key role. On 5 April Al-Amin Khalifa Fhimah and Abd al-Baset al-Megrahi arrived at Valkenburg airport in the Netherlands, accompanied by the UN's chief legal counsel, Hans Corell. Neither man opposed extradition and they were placed in the custody of Scottish police-officers and transferred to Camp Zeist, near Utrecht, a former US air base, which had been designated Scottish territory for the purposes of the trial. At Camp Zeist they were formerly arrested by Scottish police and legal proceedings began when the two men appeared before a Scottish law officer to be committed for trial on charges of murder, conspiracy to murder and contravention of the 1982 Aviation Security Act. The short committal hearing was held in camera, but two UN observers were present. The trial was scheduled to begin in February 2000, after a special court agreed to the defence's request for a six-month adjournment. With the surrender of the two suspects, the UN Security Council immediately suspended the sanctions imposed on Libya in 1992, but under pressure from the USA avoided a vote on whether to approve a permanent lifting of sanctions. On 9 July the Security Council issued a statement welcoming positive developments in Libya's co-operation with the UN, and reaffirmed its intention formally to revoke sanctions 'as soon as possible'. The USA insisted that a formal lifting of UN sanctions would be premature before the trial of the Lockerbie suspects was completed, and declared that it would veto any such proposal. US sanctions against Libya—some of which dated from 1981—remained in place despite opposition from US business groups. In contrast, in September the EU removed most of its remaining sanctions against Libya, and Libya was invited to participate in the Euro-Mediterranean partnership programme initiated at Barcelona in 1995. However, the EU embargo on arms sales remained in force.

Several European countries moved quickly to strengthen political and economic links with Libya in the hope of gaining lucrative investment opportunities there. The day after the two Libyan suspects were handed over the Italian Minister of Foreign Affairs, Lamberto Dini, on a visit to Tripoli, called for Libya's full integration into the international community. In December 1999 the Italian premier, Massimo D'Alema, became the first EU premier to visit Libya for more than eight years. During the visit the two countries issued a joint statement appealing for greater international co-operation to eradicate terrorism. In July the United Kingdom had announced that it was resuming full diplomatic relations with Libya after a rupture of 15 years. The decision followed a statement by Col Qaddafi in which he accepted Libya's 'general responsibility' for the murder of a British policewoman outside the Libyan people's bureau in London in 1984 (see Qaddafi's Attempts to Quell Opposition at Home and Abroad, above). Qaddafi expressed his 'deep regret' for the incident and offered to pay compensation to the woman's family. The Libyan leader also stated that Libya would co-operate with the British police inquiry into the murder. In November the British authorities confirmed that compensation had been paid (estimated at £250,000), and a British ambassador arrived in Tripoli the following month. British trade delegations visited Libya in July and October. In January 2000, just before Libya's new envoy to the United Kingdom arrived in London, and following revelations in the press, the British Government admitted that in July 1999 its customs and excise officials had intercepted a consignment of *Scud* missile parts destined for Libya at London's Gatwick Airport. The parts were impounded, but the British authorities insisted that the incident would not affect the normalization of relations between the two countries. In February there were further allegations of involvement by the British security services in a plot by Libyan dissidents to assassinate Col Qaddafi during the mid-1990s. Libya's reaction to these revelations was restrained. Efforts by relatives of victims of the bombing of a French airliner over

Niger in 1989 to begin legal action against Qaddafi for complicity in the attack were not supported by the French Government, which considered the matter closed and was anxious to strengthen links with Tripoli. In early April 2000 Christian Pierret, Minister of State for Industry, became the first member of the French Government to visit Libya since sanctions were suspended a year earlier. In September Libya won praise from the French and German Governments for its role in securing the release of 12 Western hostages held by the Abu Sayyaf rebel Muslim group on the island of Jolo in the southern Philippines. The Qaddafi regime, which was believed to have links with Muslim separatist groups in the southern Philippines dating back to the 1970s, denied claims that it had made ransom payments of US \$12m. to secure the hostages' release, but admitted that a Libyan charitable foundation had offered to aid development projects in rebel-held areas.

In October 2000 the French Court of Appeal ruled that Qaddafi could be prosecuted in France for complicity in the 1989 bombing of the French UTA airliner over Niger. While the ruling proved embarrassing for the French Government, it was unlikely to lead to any further action and was not expected to affect the growing *rapprochement* between the two countries. On 13 March 2001 the Court of Cassation in Paris (the highest French court of appeal) overturned the ruling, on the grounds that as head of state he had immunity from such action. The families of victims of the bombing pledged to take their case to the European Court of Human Rights. In December 2000 Italy signed several agreements with Libya aimed at further improving political co-operation and increasing Italian investment.

However, Libya's relations with the EU suffered a reverse at the beginning of 2000. Although Libya had agreed to accept the terms for joining the Euro-Mediterranean partnership programme, it insisted that both Israel and the Palestinian National Authority (PNA) should be excluded. This demand was unacceptable to the EU, and in late January the President of the European Commission, Romano Prodi, withdrew an invitation to Col Qaddafi, originally made in December 1999, to visit Brussels. Some sources argued that pressure from individual EU states, notably the United Kingdom, was the real reason for Prodi's decision to cancel the visit, although officially the invitation was withdrawn on the grounds that Libya had not accepted EU conditions regarding commitment to human rights, democracy, free trade and support for the Middle East peace process. In April 2000 the Libyan leader used his main speech to the EU-OAU summit in Cairo to castigate Africa's former colonizers. However, a private meeting with Prodi was described as more positive, and Libya was courted by several European leaders eager to capitalize on the country's rehabilitation. However, there was further friction with the EU when Qaddafi claimed that EU sanctions against Austria, imposed after a new coalition Government (which included the far-right Freedom Party) came to power in that country, were the result of 'Zionist whims'. Nevertheless, in October all EU member states supported a resolution proposed by Libya in the UN General Assembly criticizing unilateral sanctions, and in November Libya was invited to participate as an observer in the Euro-Mediterranean meeting of foreign ministers in Marseille, France. France was reported to have extended a 'special invitation' to Libya in recognition of its help in securing the release of the Western hostages in the Philippines. At first Libya announced that it would not attend, but it later sent a delegation.

Meanwhile, in February 2000 the US authorities had for the first time granted a visa to Libya's ambassador to the UN, enabling him to travel from the UN headquarters in New York to Washington, DC. A month later a group of officials of the US Department of State visited Libya to determine whether security arrangements were satisfactory for US citizens to travel there; a ban on Americans visiting Libya had been in place since 1981 and was renewed in November 1999. Although the US Government strenuously denied that it had any plans to lift unilateral sanctions, the visit angered the 'Lockerbie lobby' group of relatives of US victims of the 1988 bombing. In July 2000 the US Department of Defense stated that Libya was no longer engaged in acts of terrorism and that there was no evidence that it was pursuing a chemical weapons programme. However, in early January 2001 the US Secretary of State,

Madeleine Albright, stated that US economic sanctions against Libya would be extended for another year because of continuing concerns over Libyan support for international terrorism. Earlier the Department of State had also extended for another year the ban on US passport holders travelling to Libya, even though the US consular mission to Libya had concluded that there was no reason to maintain the ban. However, Albright insisted that Libya remained unsafe because of renewed violence in the Middle East and an increase in anti-US sentiment in the region. Some observers attributed the decision to the influence of the powerful Lockerbie lobby in Washington. Although the new Administration of President George W. Bush, which took office in early 2001, was regarded as more sympathetic to the US oil companies anxious to return to Libya, and the incoming Secretary of State, Colin Powell, had been critical of the use of US sanctions, an early lifting of the US embargo or the ban on US passport holders visiting Libya appeared unlikely at this time, given the continuing influence of the Lockerbie lobby. There was speculation in the aftermath of the devastating terrorist attacks on New York and Washington, DC, on 11 September that the evolution of Libyan-US relations might be dictated by Libya's response to the suicide attacks and to US attempts to forge an international 'coalition against terrorism'. Qaddafi, who condemned the attacks, apparently indicated that Libya would not participate in such a coalition, but recognized that the USA itself had a right to take military action against targets linked to the attacks.

Meanwhile, during a visit to Russia by the Libyan Minister of Foreign Affairs in July 2000, President Vladimir Putin called for a definitive end to UN sanctions. A month earlier Russia had that it was resuming arms sales to Libya, with the first contracts reported to be worth US $100m. Other high-level political contacts followed. In December the Non-Aligned Movement called on the UN Security Council to end sanctions against Libya because it had co-operated fully in the Lockerbie trial. Although the resolution was not put to the vote, it served to demonstrate support from developing countries for Libya's position.

THE LOCKERBIE TRIAL

The trial of the two Libyans accused of the Lockerbie bombing, which had been due to start in February 2000, was adjourned until the beginning of May to allow the defence counsel more time to prepare its case. Meanwhile, in mid-February Scotland's Lord Advocate, Lord Hardie, responsible for preparing the case for the prosecution, resigned and was replaced by a former Solicitor-General, Colin Boyd, who had also been closely involved in the prosecution case. Despite some speculation, the change did not appear to be linked to the impending Lockerbie trial, although reports in the British media continued to suggest that the evidence against the two Libyans was inadequate to secure a conviction. Furthermore, doubts were raised over evidence given by key prosecution witnesses. In addition, as the US Department of State had refused to release copies of correspondence between the UN Secretary-General and the Libyan Government to families of US victims, there was concern that a deal had been agreed to ensure that senior figures in the Libyan regime would be immune from prosecution whatever the outcome of the trial.

Hearings in the trial of Al-Amin Khalifa Fhimah and Abd al-Baset al-Megrahi finally began on 3 May 2000, after a request by the prosecution in late April for a postponement of several weeks was denied by the presiding judge. There was a large media presence for the first days of the trial, but permission to televise the proceedings was refused. The two defendants were charged on three counts: murder, conspiracy to murder and contravention of the 1982 Aviation Security Act. The prosecution alleged that the two accused were members of the Libyan intelligence service and, after four years spent planning the attack, had planted a bomb in a suitcase on an Air Malta flight which was then transferred to Pan Am flight 103 at Frankfurt. The two defendants pleaded not guilty, and their defence team alleged that a small Palestinian guerrilla group, the Popular Front for the Liberation of Palestine—General Command (PFLP—GC) led by Ahmed Jibril, acting as agents of the Iranian Government, had planted the bomb in revenge for the shooting down of an Iranian civilian airliner over the Gulf by a US

warship in 1988. Given the large number of witnesses called by both prosecution and defence, the trial was expected to last for 12–18 months; however, in July it was announced that the trial was expected to be much shorter than previously anticipated. In August the CIA was ordered to hand over classified documents to the defence lawyers; the CIA's refusal fully to comply with this demand led to a three-week adjournment of the trial in late August to enable the issue to be resolved. In September the presiding judge ruled that it was permissible for a former Libyan intelligence officer who had become a CIA informant to give evidence at the trial. In late October hearings were again adjourned after the prosecution announced that it had received important new evidence from an unnamed foreign country. In August the United Kingdom and the USA had finally released the text of a controversial letter from the UN Secretary-General to Qaddafi, written in February 1999 before the transfer of the two suspects, promising that they would not be used 'to undermine the Libyan regime'. Scottish legal officers insisted that these assurances would in no way inhibit the prosecution's case. Families of US victims had for some time expressed concern that a deal had been agreed to ensure that senior figures in the Libyan regime would be immune from prosecution, whatever the outcome of the trial.

In late November, after 73 days of evidence and submissions from more than 230 witnesses, the prosecution completed its case. Much of the evidence was highly circumstantial, and a number of key witnesses proved unreliable or offered testimony that appeared to undermine the prosecution's case. Nevertheless, an attempt by the defence to have the case against one of the defendants, Fhimah, dismissed on the grounds of insufficient evidence was rejected by the judges. The defence case began in December, when lawyers sought an adjournment to give them more time to gather new evidence, which they claimed was held by the Syrian Government and which purportedly implicated the Syrian-backed PFLP—GC and the obscure Palestinian Popular Struggle Front in the bombing. The documents were thought to include information on raids on a secret PFLP—GC base in Germany, where police were reported to have found an explosive device similar to that used in the Lockerbie bombing. However, at the beginning of January 2001 the court was told that the Syrian authorities had refused to co-operate or hand over any documents. Lawyers for the defence subsequently announced that they did not intend to call the two defendants to give evidence, and concentrated instead on undermining the evidence presented by the prosecution's principal witness, Abd al-Majid Giaka, a Libyan double agent who had worked for both the Libyan intelligence services and the CIA. Some observers felt that the defence lawyers had failed to present a coherent case and expressed surprise that they had depended on weaknesses in the prosecution's case. Shortly afterwards the prosecution unexpectedly announced that it would no longer pursue the two lesser charges of conspiracy to murder and contravention of the 1982 Aviation Security Act, since it was confident of securing a conviction on the charge of murder.

On 31 January 2001 the three Scottish judges delivered their verdict. They unanimously found one of the defendants, Abd al Baset al Megrahi, guilty of the murder of 270 people and sentenced him to life imprisonment, with a recommendation that he serve a minimum of 20 years. However, Al-Amin Khalifa Fhimah was acquitted, owing to lack of proof, and immediately freed. In an 82-page judgment, the judges accepted that Megrahi was a member of the JSO, the Libyan intelligence services, 'occupying posts of fairly high rank', and while they acknowledged their awareness of what they termed 'uncertainties and qualifications' in the case, they concluded that the evidence against him combined to form 'a real and convincing pattern' which left them with no reasonable doubt as to his guilt. The judges ruled out any involvement of the PFLP—GC and the Palestinian Popular Struggle Front in the bombing, stating that they inferred from the evidence that the planning and execution of the plot was of Libyan origin. In the case of Fhimah, the judges concluded that there was no evidence that he had helped Megrahi to plant the bomb. Although the prosecution had withdrawn the allegation that Fhimah was a member of the JSO, they had relied on testimony from Giaka, who claimed that he had seen Fhimah accompany Megrahi as he carried the suitcase containing the bomb through Malta's international airport. Megrahi continued to protest his innocence, and his lawyers later lodged an appeal against the conviction. This was to be heard by five Scottish judges sitting at Camp Zeist; in the mean time, Megrahi continued to be held at Camp Zeist. In July it was reported that Megrahi's full appeal hearing would be held in the autumn.

Inevitably, the verdict raised more questions than it provided answers as regards the instigators and perpetrators of, and also the motive for, the bombing. For many, Megrahi's conviction pointed clearly to Libyan state-sponsored terrorism and to the highest level in the Libyan leadership. Others continued to maintain that Libya had been made a convenient scapegoat by the West and remained convinced that suspicions should still focus on Iran, Syria and the PFLP—GC. British relatives of the victims stated that they intended to renew their campaign for a public inquiry into the atrocity, insisting that serious questions remained unanswered. A British government spokesman stated that the United Kingdom expected the Libyan authorities to take full responsibility for the actions of their official. US relatives pledged to pursue a civil case for damages from the Libyan Government. President Bush assured them that the US Government would maintain sanctions against Libya until the Libyan authorities accepted responsibility for the bombing and agreed to compensate the families. At the end of July 2001 the US House of Representatives and the Senate voted overwhelmingly for a five year extension to ILSA (although with an option for the President to review terms of the sanctions provisions after three years). After the ruling, however, Libya's ambassador to the UN emphasized that Libya as a state had not been accused by the Scottish court, and that it was a case concerning two individuals. The day after the judgment Qaddafi announced that he would shortly reveal evidence that proved Megrahi's innocence. Four days later the Libyan leader made a long speech in Tripoli before the world's media in which he repeated that Libya was not to blame for the bombing; however, he failed to produce the new evidence, claiming only that US and British investigators had planted evidence at Lockerbie to incriminate Libya. He also maintained that Fhimah had been acquitted in order to give some credibility to the 'Western Christian justice system'. The following day Libyan protesters besieged the British embassy in Tripoli to protest at the verdict and burnt British and US flags. The demonstration was sanctioned by the Libyan authorities, but riot police later moved in and dispersed the protesters after they attempted to enter the embassy compound. These events did not, however, interrupt the normalization of relations between the United Kingdom and Libya. In March Libya's new ambassador to London, Muhammad Abu al-Qasim az-Zuai, the former justice minister, stated that Libya would accept the verdict of Megrahi's appeal and that it would not interfere with the rebuilding of good relations with the United Kingdom. In April az-Zuai acted promptly by ordering his cultural attaché and another senior Libyan diplomat back to Tripoli after the attaché allegedly attacked a leading dissident at a university lecture in London.

FOREIGN RELATIONS AFTER THE LOCKERBIE VERDICT

In June 2001 the Qaddafi Foundation, directed by Seif el-Islam Qaddafi, sponsored negotiations in Tripoli between a delegation from the Philippines headed by the Minister of Foreign Affairs, Teofisto Guingona, and representatives of the Moro Islamic Liberation Front. The negotiations were also attended by the ministers of foreign affairs of Indonesia and Malaysia. It was reported that the President's son had tried unsuccessfully to secure the release of hostages held by the Abu Sayyaf group.

Col Qaddafi immediately condemned the September 2001 suicide attacks on New York and Washington, DC, and was swift to recall that, some six years earlier, he had issued a warrant for the arrest of Osama bin Laden, whom the USA held principally responsible for the attacks, and who, at that time, had been accused of financing a radical Islamist movement in Libya intending to assassinate the Libyan leader. Shortly after the attacks the Libyan Militant Islamic Group (MIG) appeared on a list published by the US Federal Bureau of Investigation of alleged terrorist organizations linked to al-Qa'ida whose assets were to be frozen. In October and again in January 2002 the US Assistant Secretary of State for Near Eastern Affairs,

William Burns, met the head of Libyan intelligence services, Musa Kusa, in London. Kusa also held meetings with members of the CIA and the British security intelligence agency, MI5, regarding the combating of international terrorism. The Libyan team was reported to have provided US officials with information about the al-Qa'ida network, notably in the Philippines. The Libyans, for their part, requested co-operation in securing the extradition of Libyan militant Islamists living in Europe, particularly members of the MIG. Reports also suggested that an arrangement had been discussed on the Lockerbie affair. It was claimed that if Meghrahi's appeal was unsuccessful and his conviction was upheld, Libya would pay US $6,000m. (just under one-half of Libya's annual oil revenues) to families of the victims. In return Libya would be removed from the US list of states sponsoring terrorism and US sanctions would be revoked.

The 'war against terror' was one of the main topics discussed during a visit to Tripoli in late October 2001 by the French Minister for Co-operation, Charles Josselin—the first visit by a French government minister since 1992. In late November 2001 Col Abdallah Sannousi, a senior figure in the Libyan intelligence services and Qaddafi's brother-in-law (who had in 1999 been sentenced *in absentia* to life imprisonment by a Paris court for his involvement in the bombing of a French airliner over Niger 10 years earlier—see above), was placed under house arrest. His removal was regarded by some observers as confirmation that the Libyan leader wished to open a new page in relations with the West, notably the USA. In late February 2002 daily flights between Paris and Tripoli were resumed after a 14-year hiatus. The Libyan leader's eldest son, Seif al-Islam, travelled on the first flight to Paris, where he addressed a meeting at the Institut français des relations internationales.

Meanwhile, in November 2001 a German court sentenced a German woman, two Palestinians and a Libyan national to prison terms of 12–18 years' duration for carrying out a bomb attack on a West Berlin discothèque in April 1986 (see above). On the basis of new evidence from East German intelligence files, the prosecution stated that the Libyan intelligence services were implicated in the bombing, which was seen as a revenge attack for the sinking of two Libyan patrol boats in the Mediterranean by the US Navy a month earlier. The prosecution was, however, unable to prove that the Libyan leader had ordered or approved the attack. (A senior German official had claimed that, at a meeting in March 2001, Qaddafi had admitted the Libyan state's responsibility for the bombing, but the German Government refused to allow two of its senior officials to give evidence at the trial.)

Megrahi's appeal began in late January 2002 before a panel of five Scottish judges at Camp Zeist. At the centre of the appeal was new evidence from a former security guard at London's Heathrow Airport, who claimed that on the night that the Pan Am flight departed a door giving access to the loading area of Terminal 3 had been tampered with—suggesting that the bomb could have been planted in London and not in Malta, as the trial judges had concluded, thus casting doubt on the original judgment. On 16 March the five Scottish judges ruled that none of the grounds put forward by the defence was well founded, and Megrahi's appeal was unanimously rejected. He was immediately transferred to Barlinnie prison in Glasgow, Scotland, to serve his life sentence. Libya condemned the ruling as a 'political verdict' and pledged to continue efforts to free Megrahi. There were reports in May that Seif al-Islam al-Qaddafi was to assume responsibility for the Lockerbie dossier in place of Musa Kusa.

Diplomatic contacts aimed at improving relations with the USA continued. US oil companies, which have assets exceeding US $2,000m. in Libya, sought to lobby the Bush Administration, apparently concerned that unless relations improved Tripoli might terminate their concessions and allocate them to European companies. Nevertheless, relations remained strained. In late 2001 the US Department of State renewed the ban on US passport holders visiting Libya for another year, and cited Libya as one of the states it suspected of developing biological weapons. In March 2002 the US Administration named Libya as one of a number of potentially hostile states trying to establish a nuclear capability. A month earlier a Canadian intelligence report accused Libya of trying to obtain nuclear weapons. In early May John Bolton, the US Under-Secretary of State for Arms Control and International Security, condemned Libya, along with Syria and Cuba, for supporting terrorism and developing chemical and biological weapons. He maintained that since the suspension of UN sanctions in April 1999 Libya had resumed manufacturing chemical weapons at the Rabta plant and was attempting to obtain expertise in ballistic missiles. These allegations were firmly rejected by the Libyan authorities.

After much speculation that an agreement with the Libyan Government on compensation for the families of victims of the Lockerbie bombing was imminent, at the end of May 2002 a partner in the US legal firm representing the families of the Lockerbie victims claimed that Libya had made an offer amounting to US $2,700m., some $10m. per victim (substantially lower than the figure rumoured to have been put forward earlier in the year). However, it was alleged that certain conditions were attached to the offer; namely that the money would be paid into a UN escrow account and released in stages: 40% after the permanent ending of UN sanctions; 40% after the lifting of US sanctions; and the final 20% after Libya was removed from the US list of states sponsoring terrorism. Libya immediately denied that such an offer had been made. (Compensation for the families of victims of the bombing is only one of the conditions set by the international community for the permanent lifting of sanctions. It is also insisted that Libya must accept responsibility for the attack, disclose all its knowledge about the bombing, and renounce terrorism.) In early June former South African President, Nelson Mandela, visited Megrahi in prison in Glasgow to check on the conditions of his confinement. Following the conclusion of his visit, Mandela told a press conference that holding Megrahi in solitary confinement was amounted to psychological persecution and argued that he should be allowed to serve the rest of his sentence in a Muslim country, suggesting Egypt, Tunisia or Morocco as possibilities. Mandela also stated that on the basis of the views of four African judges, who had monitored the proceedings at Camp Zeist on behalf of the OAU, the trial itself was flawed and that Megrahi should be given the opportunity to make a new appeal.

In early August 2002 Mike O'Brien, a minister of the British Foreign and Commonwealth Office, visited Libya for talks with Col Qaddafi; this was the first visit by a British government minister for some 20 years. After the meeting O'Brien stated that Libya was considering making an announcement whereby it accepted 'general responsibility' for the Lockerbie bombing, while the Secretary for Foreign Affairs declared that Libya was ready 'in principle' to take steps to compensate the relatives of victims. The Libyan leader had also expressed his willingness to co-operate with the international community on issues such as weapons of mass destruction and the 'war against terror'. O'Brien welcomed these statements but emphasized that there had to be clear proof that Col Qaddafi intended to fulfil his undertakings.

RUMOURS OF AN ABORTIVE ARMY COUP AND INTERNAL DISSENT, 1993–99

During the second week of October 1993 rumours began to circulate in the Western media that a revolt by a number of army units had been crushed by the Libyan air force which had remained loyal to Qaddafi. It was claimed that the most serious clashes had occurred around Misurata and Tobruk where there had been scores of casualties. There were unconfirmed reports that Libya had closed its borders and that after three days of unrest 2,000 people had been arrested and 12 officers executed. Qaddafi's Second-in-Command, Maj. Jalloud, was reported to have been placed under house arrest. There was speculation that the coup, described in the media as the most serious challenge to the Libyan leader since 1986, had arisen as a result of differences between Qaddafi and Jalloud over the handling of the Lockerbie crisis and that the armed forces may have divided along tribal lines. Throughout the Lockerbie affair, Jalloud, who belonged to the al-Megaha tribe, was firmly opposed to surrendering the two suspects, both of whom were members of his tribe. The London-based daily *Al-Hayat* named Col Hassan al-Kabir and Col ar-Rifi Ali ash-Sharif as the leaders of the uprising and stated that while al-Kabir had been arrested, ash-Sharif had fled to Switzerland. However, doubts were expressed that a major uprising did in fact occur. Qaddafi himself condemned the rumours of an army coup in a speech on 30 October describing them as a plot by the British intelligence

services to humiliate the Libyan people. Nevertheless, it is perhaps significant that the government changes announced at the end of January 1994 placed men known for their personal loyalty to Qaddafi in key positions, suggesting that the Libyan leader felt the need to tighten his grip on power.

Libyan opposition groups in exile remained weak and divided and there was little evidence that they commanded significant support within the country. In October 1993 Muhammad Megarief, the leader of the NFSL, Maj. Abd al-Moneim al-Houni of the Co-operation Bureau for Democratic and National Forces, and Mansour Kikhia of the Libyan National Alliance (LNA) were reported to have met in either Algeria or Switzerland to discuss forming a united front against the Qaddafi regime. Abd al-Hamid al-Bakkush, the leader of the Libyan Liberation Organization, did not attend and the meeting appeared to have failed to resolve the differences between the various opposition groups. This was confirmed in February 1994 when some leading members of the NFSL announced that they had formed a breakaway movement and criticized the NFSL for failing to co-operate with other opposition groups in creating a united front against the Qaddafi regime.

Qaddafi has regularly demonstrated his intolerance of these opposition groups and has urged that his opponents abroad be hunted down and eliminated. Therefore in early December 1993, when Mansour Kikhia, a former Secretary for Foreign Liaison and, since the early 1980s, leader of the opposition LNA, disappeared while attending a meeting of the Alliance in Cairo, it was widely assumed that he had been abducted by Libyan security agents. The affair proved particularly embarrassing as Kikhia had been living in the USA, had an American wife and had only agreed to attend the meeting in Cairo after receiving personal assurances from senior Egyptian officials about his safety there. The Libyan Secretariat for Foreign Liaison and Libya's representative to the Arab League in Cairo, Ibrahim Beshari, denied Libyan involvement in the affair. Beshari stated that Kikhia presented no threat to the Libyan Government. Qaddafi told Egyptian journalists that Libya was co-operating with the Egyptian authorities to discover what had happened. Both US President Clinton and Dr Boutros Boutros-Ghali, the UN Secretary-General, appealed to President Mubarak of Egypt to investigate Kikhia's disappearance. However, although Mubarak dispatched one of his advisers to Tripoli he failed to make any progress and the Egyptian police admitted at the end of January that they had no information about Kikhia's whereabouts. Kikhia's wife continued to claim that her husband had been kidnapped by Libyan agents assisted by Egyptian security officers. In April 1995 the Arab Organization of Human Rights urged the Egyptian Government to investigate the matter and to punish those responsible for Kikhia's abduction. In late 1996 the LNA stated that it would continue to investigate Kikhia's disappearance, but many were convinced that he had been murdered. In September 1997 a report by the CIA stated that Kikhia had been kidnapped by Egyptian agents while in Cairo and extradited to Libya, where he was murdered. At the end of 1997 it was reported that an international legal committee had been formed to investigate Kikhia's disappearance and US allegations. In early 1999 the Cairo Court of Appeal criticized the Egyptian Ministry of the Interior for failing to ensure Kikhia's safety while he was visiting the country.

In early March 1994 Libyan television broadcast 'confessions' by three army officers and a student, all members of the Warfallah tribe, who had been arrested in the Bani Walid region during the army revolt in October 1993. It was the first official acknowledgement of the attempted coup. During their 'confessions' the men admitted to supplying information to the CIA, and to Muhammad Megarief, the leader of the NFSL, on military deployment, the Rabta plant, nuclear research and Col Qaddafi's own movements. The accused men stated that they had met Megarief in Zurich, Switzerland, and Madrid, Spain, in order to pass on information. The NFSL claimed that after calls for the execution of the four men, demonstrations erupted in the Bani Walid region where several protestors were arrested after setting fire to government buildings. The Libyan opposition abroad stated that 55 army officers arrested after the abortive coup had been condemned to death. At the beginning of 1996 it was reported that Col Qaddafi had overturned a court's ruling on 12 army officers of the Warfallah tribe accused of leading the abortive coup because the sentences were too lenient, and that the men had been condemned to death. According to one source, the death sentences had not been carried out in order not to antagonize the Warfallah, which had threatened retaliation if the men were killed.

Early in 1996 rumours circulated that Col Qaddafi had concentrated power within the armed forces almost exclusively in the hands of members of his own tribe and that the increasing involvement of two of his sons in government business, including financial and commercial affairs, had alienated tribal leaders, such as Cols Khalifa Ahneish, Masoud Abd al-Haft and Ahmad Qadhaf ad-Dam, who in the past had played key roles in internal security and foreign affairs. It was also claimed that the Libyan revolutionary committees were preparing to bring to trial those responsible for corruption and financial mismanagement in order to absolve Qaddafi and his immediate family of any responsibility for the country's economic problems and to provide a pretext for the elimination of opponents of the regime.

In addition to reports of continued dissent within the armed forces and the destabilizing effects of tribal rivalries, some observers argued that the Islamist opposition was the most dangerous threat to the Qaddafi regime. Despite being subjected to harsh repressive measures by the security forces for some years, Islamist opposition to the regime, strongly rooted in Cyrenaica, appears to have increased in strength, although little is known about the groups involved. In June 1995 there were a number of armed confrontations between police and Islamist militants in and around Benghazi. The regime blamed the unrest on 'extremist infiltrators' from Egypt and Sudan and independent sources confirmed that the large number of immigrants, mainly from Egypt and Sudan, seeking work in Benghazi, had created instability in the region.

There were reports of further clashes between the security services and Islamist militants in September 1995 in Benghazi, Darnah and al-Baida, in which a senior officer in the security services, Lt-Col al-Faydi, was ambushed and killed. Islamist militants calling themselves the Jama'ah al-Islamiyah al-Muqatila, or Militant Islamic Group, claimed responsibility for the September incidents and stated that it was the duty of all Muslims to overthrow the Qaddafi regime and impose *Shari'a* law. In response to these incidents, thousands of Sudanese and Egyptian workers were expelled (see below), the regime tightened its control over the country's mosques and hundreds of suspected Islamist militants were arrested. The regime also made moves to re-Islamize Libyan society, adopting laws based on the *Shari'a*. In October 1995 the London daily newspaper, *The Independent*, claimed that Col Qaddafi was fighting an underground war against the Islamist militants who threatened the stability of his regime. An attack on the Abu Saleem prison in Tripoli in November, in which some 15 dissidents escaped, was also regarded as the work of Islamist militants. In February 1996 it was reported that militants from the Militant Islamic Group (MIG) had attempted to assassinate Col Qaddafi in Sirte. After the assassination attempt, security forces carried out further arrests of suspected Islamist militants. In March, following a mass escape from the al-Kuwaifiyya prison near Benghazi during which police shot dead many of the prisoners, unrest erupted once again in and around Benghazi, Darnah and al-Baida, and there were reports of over 20 deaths in clashes between militants and the security forces. At the end of April, the MIG issued a statement claiming to have killed 15 security officers in Sirte during the previous month and to have seized weapons from police stations in Ras al-Hilal and al-Qubba. In May violent clashes were reported in Benghazi between security forces and supporters of a new opposition group, the Islamic Martyrs' Movement (IMM), which claimed responsibility for the assassinations of a number of high-ranking government officials. The movement's leader, Muhammad al-Hami was killed in July in clashes with security forces, and was later replaced by Hamzah Abu Shaltilah. In March 1997 press reports stated that Shaltilah had been dismissed and replaced by a new leader, referred to as 'Khalifah'. In June a third Islamist group, the Libya Islamic Group, claimed responsibility for the murders of eight policemen during an attack on a police training centre in Derna. A fourth group, known as the Supporters of God, was formed in September. Claims by the MIG that they had carried out an assassination attempt on Col Qaddafi in November were denied by the authorities. Throughout the second half of 1996 there were reports of clashes between Islamist groups and government forces, especially in the eastern part of the country, where several hundred people were estimated to have been killed. Few details are available about the Islamist opposition, and the degree of popular support for the various militant groups that have emerged is difficult to estimate, though the MIG, which is believed to have links with the extremist Groupe islamique armé in Algeria, appears to be the most important. There is little evidence of co-operation between the different groups or between the Islamists and the secular opposition, and it is understood that the groups' resources are limited.

The threat from the growing number of militant Islamist groups was accompanied by continued unrest within the armed forces and the alienation of tribal support for the regime. In July 1996 it was reported that an attempted coup organized by Col Khalifa Haftar, an officer who had taken part in the overthrow of the monarchy in 1969, but who had later gone into exile, had been quashed after fierce fighting in the Jabal al-Akhdar, near Darnah. In the same month bodyguards of Qaddafi's son Saadi opened fire on crowds at Tripoli's football stadium, apparently after fans began to chant anti-Government slogans following a decision by the referee that ruled in favour of a team sponsored by Saadi Qaddafi. Official Libyan reports stated that eight people were killed and 39 injured as a result of the incident. However, Western reports citing diplomatic sources put the death toll at between 20 and 50, with many others injured. At the end of August another coup attempt was uncovered, involving some 45 army officers, and said to include members of the Libyan leader's own tribe, the Qadhadhifa. Three of the coup leaders were believed to have been executed. Tight security was maintained in and around Bani Walid, the home town of officers from the powerful Warfallah tribe purportedly accused of leading the abortive coup of 1993, who were put on trial at the Supreme Military Court at the end of the year. After being convicted of spying for the CIA and trying to overthrow the regime, six senior army officers and two civilians were executed at the beginning of January 1997. The eight remaining suspects were acquitted. US officials considered the reports to be a propaganda exercise by the Libyan Government. The executions took place against the wishes of the leaders of the Warfallah tribe, and were strongly condemned by several exiled opposition groups. Some members of the Warfallah tribe, however, continued to hold senior positions in the army. In March it was reported that Maj.-Gen. Jalloud had resumed an important government role, after being removed from office in 1993 and placed under house arrest.

In late 1996 there were reports that the two exiled opposition groups, the LNA and the NFSL, had once again agreed to co-operate to bring down the Qaddafi regime, and had rejected overtures from the Libyan leader to take part in negotiations. In January 1997 Muhammad as-Sanusi, the grandson of the late King Idris who was deposed in 1969, and the heir to the Libyan throne who was living in exile in the United Kingdom, claimed to have received death threats from Qaddafi's agents. He later condemned the regime for threatening Libyan exiles and accused the security forces of having used chemical weapons in attacks against insurgents in the Jabal al-Akhdar in August 1996. A new secular opposition group, the Libyan Patriots Movement, emerged in January 1997. The group claimed to have supporters among the Libyan armed forces and announced its commitment to overthrow the Qaddafi regime by force.

At its annual meeting at Sirte in March 1997 the GPC approved legislation imposing collective punishment upon the families or tribal clans of Libyans convicted of crimes including sabotage, trafficking in arms, drugs-smuggling and assisting 'terrorists, criminals, saboteurs and heretics'. Collective punishment was to include the possibility of denial of access to water, food supplies and fuel. The so-called 'Charter of Honour' was directed principally at opponents of the regime and was strongly condemned by the leading opposition group in exile, the NFSL.

Following the GPC meeting, a number of cabinet changes were made, involving the restructuring of two secretariats. The most significant change was the division of the Secretariat of Justice and Public Security into two parts. The Secretariat of Education, Youth, Scientific Research and Vocational Training, on the other hand, was divided in three. A further reorganization of the GPC took place in December, in which the Secretariat for Planning, Economy and Trade was divided into two parts.

In June 1995 the regime passed a law forbidding foreign workers without contracts to remain in Libya, and in July began a programme of mass expulsions. Only a fraction of the Egyptian community, believed to number between 700,000 and 1m. was affected, with Sudanese and other African workers bearing the brunt of the deportations. According to the French daily newspaper *Le Monde*, by October some 40,000 Sudanese, out of a community of 400,000, had already been expelled from the country and almost half a million African workers were threatened with expulsion. The regime blamed Egyptian and Sudanese infiltrators for the outbreak of disturbances involving armed Islamist militants (see above) and justified the expulsions as a means of ridding the country of 'contagious diseases'. The expulsions were also regarded as a response to popular discontent over mounting unemployment, especially among young Libyans. However, it was the plight of Palestinian workers that caused international controversy. In a speech on 1 September Col Qaddafi repeated his threat to expel all 30,000 Palestinians resident in Libya. By the end of the month only 2,500 Palestinians had been issued with deportation orders, but their expulsion created a political crisis for the newly-formed PNA in Gaza. Lebanon, Israel and Egypt refused to receive the expelled Palestinians and many were stranded on ferries trying to cross the Mediterranean to Lebanon, and at Libya's border with Egypt, without adequate supplies of water or food. In the case of the expulsions of the Palestinians, Qaddafi stated that their ordeal demonstrated the weakness of the Oslo peace accords because the PNA lacked the power to assist them. At the end of October, after appeals from the Arab League, the Egyptian President and the PLO Chairman, Yasser Arafat, Qaddafi temporarily suspended the expulsion of Palestinians. Most of those expelled were allowed to return to Libya but, according to the UN High Commissioner for Refugees, at the end of 1996 some 200 people remained stranded on the Libyan-Egyptian border, surviving in desperate conditions. The deportation of Sudanese workers continued. In January 1996 Libya announced that it had expelled some 70,000 Sudanese and that a further 200,000 would be expelled by the end of February. However, Libya stopped the expulsion of Egyptians after President Mubarak promised to strengthen his efforts to find a solution to the Lockerbie affair and to Libya's international isolation. According to a Libyan official, some 335,000 foreign workers had been expelled by the beginning of 1996. In May 1996 Qaddafi once again threatened to expel Palestinians living in Libya, despite a new appeal from President Mubarak of Egypt. However, by October the Libyan leader appeared to have reconsidered his decision, and in November Libya invited Arab workers to apply to live in that country, due to a reported labour shortage. In January 1997 the GPC formally revoked the expulsion order, though few Palestinians appeared willing to return to Libya, and there were reports that some Palestinians still living in Libya were trying to leave the country. Subsequent reports in April 1997 suggested that the Government had, in an unexpected move, forced Palestinians remaining in refugee camps to return to Libya, and had dismantled their camps.

The Islamist opposition remained active, especially in the mountains east of Benghazi, and a number of successful arms raids against army and police posts in 1998 led to speculation that the militant Islamist groups had infiltrated the security forces. Reports of an assassination attempt on the Libyan leader by Islamist extremists near Benghazi in late May were denied by the authorities, but in the weeks that followed the security forces mounted a major offensive against Islamist strongholds in the north-eastern part of the country. A serious hip injury, which Qaddafi sustained in July, may have resulted from another assassination attempt, although official reports maintained that he had suffered an accident while exercising. In early 1998 the London-based Amnesty International published a new report on Libya listing human rights abuses, including the torture of Libyans suspected of non-violent opposition activities. The GPC convened in Sirte in mid-December, and, in addition to giving its approval to a trial in the Netherlands of the two Libyan suspects in the Lockerbie affair (see above), a number of government changes were also announced. The Secretariat for (Arab) Unity was abolished and its responsibilities assigned

to the Secretariat for Foreign Liaison and International Co-operation. The Secretariats for Justice and Public Security were merged, as were the Secretariats for Education and Vocational Training. The Secretariat for Information, Culture and Jamahiri (Mass) Mobilization was divided into two separate bodies. In some cases the restructuring of secretariats reversed decisions taken only 18 months earlier. In early 1999 Qaddafi strongly criticized the GPC for enacting a new law on polygamy which allowed Libyan men to take a second wife without the permission of the first. At the same time, unconfirmed reports appeared of high-level corruption, involving the payment of large 'commissions' by foreign companies to secure contracts in Libya and implicating relatives of the Libyan leader. During 1999 the People's Court imposed a number of harsh sentences in cases of corruption. In August, for example, it ruled that a civil servant convicted of embezzling LD 166,000 from the General Post and Telecommunications Company should have his right hand amputated, pay a large fine and serve a six-month prison sentence.

In early September 1999 extensive celebrations were held to mark the 30th anniversary of the Qaddafi regime. The Libyan authorities claimed to have contained Islamist militancy following the 1998 offensive by the security forces against Islamist strongholds in the eastern part of the country. There were some indications that the Islamist groups had been weakened militarily and were short of funds. In addition there were reports in the Arab press that Qaddafi's intelligence chief, Musa Kusa, had held talks with members of two Islamist groups—the MIG and the IMM—in order to persuade them to end their campaign of violence against the regime. Only the MIG denied that the meeting had taken place. At the same time Libyan officials also made conciliatory gestures to the opposition in exile, offering them financial inducements if they agreed to return to Libya. While there were claims that some prominent opposition figures based in the USA were prepared to continue the dialogue, the London-based NFSL completely rejected any *rapprochement* with the Qaddafi regime. Unlike the Islamists, these groups were thought to have little or no support within Libya itself. Six opposition groups—the NFSL, the Libyan National Organization, the Libyan Islamic Group, the Libyan Change and Reform Movement, the Libyan Constitutional Grouping, and the Libyan National Democratic Rally—were reported to have met in August 2000 to discuss joint action against the Qaddafi regime. However, effective co-operation between them appeared unlikely. The meeting was probably an attempt to raise their profile at a time when the Qaddafi regime had made significant progress in Libya's rehabilitation in the international community.

QADDAFI'S DECENTRALIZATION OF GOVERNMENT

In late January 2000 Qaddafi unexpectedly attended the opening session of the GPC, at the end of which he demanded that the budget for 2000 be redrafted, with a view to channelling petroleum revenues into education, health and public services. Furthermore, he urged that the current administrative system, based on General People's Committees, be abandoned in favour of an alternative form of government. Thus, at the annual meeting of the GPC held in Sirte in early March Qaddafi announced that most of the secretariats were being abolished and their functions devolved to the municipal and provincial levels. The move continued a decentralization policy introduced in the late 1980s, but was interpreted in part as a means of deflecting popular criticism away from central government by ensuring that any complaints would have to be dealt with by the relevant commune or provincial council. Significantly, however, the Libyan leader declared that the Secretariats of Foreign Liaison and International Co-operation, Finance, and Justice and Public Security would be retained and that two new secretariats would be created (African Unity and Information, Culture and Tourism), thus ensuring that key areas of government remained centralized. Policy on hydrocarbons was transferred to the National Oil Corporation (NOC) following the abolition of the energy secretariat ensuring that this vital area also remained under central control. The former Secretary for Energy, Abdallah Salem al-Badri, was appointed as head of the NOC so that continuity of policy would be maintained in this sector. A new and much smaller General People's Committee was formed, with Mubarak Abdallah ash-Shamikh (formerly Secretary for Housing and Public Utilities) as Secretary-General (effectively Prime Minister). Bashir Bu Janah and Baghdadi Mahmudi became assistant secretaries; Fawziya Bashir Shalabi was appointed Secretary of Information, Culture and Tourism; Ali Abd as-Salem at-Turayki was allocated the post of Secretary of African Unity; Abd ar-Rahman Muhammad Shalgam became Secretary for Foreign Liaison and International Co-operation; Muhammad Abu al-Qasim az-Zuai remained Secretary of Justice and Public Security and Muhammad Abdallah Bait al-Mal retained the post of Secretary for Finance. The day after these changes were announced Qaddafi indicated that the post of Co-ordinator of the General Social People's Command might develop into that of 'head of state'—a title that has not been used in Libya since 1977 and one consistently rejected by Qaddafi himself. There was some speculation that the new post might be intended for one of Qaddafi's sons—his eldest son, Seif al-Islam, was most frequently mentioned in this regard; however, there was little doubt that control would remain firmly in the hands of Qaddafi and a small group of his close confidants. By the second half of the year practical implementation of the devolution process was reported to have made little progress. In June the Secretary for Finance, Bait al-Mal, and the President of the Central Bank, Taher Jehimi, were suspended following their alleged involvement in a major corruption scandal, but in August the two men were cleared of all charges and reinstated. However Bait al-Mal was dismissed in a reorganization of the General People's Committee in October and replaced on an acting basis by Al-Ujayli Abd as-Salam Burayni. In the same reshuffle the Secretary for Justice and Public Security, Muhammad Abu al-Qasim az-Zuai, was also dismissed and replaced by Abd ar-Rahman Muhammad Shalgam; Abdallah Salem al-Badri, the influential head of the NOC, was appointed to the new post of Assistant Secretary for Services; and the Secretariat for Information, Culture and Tourism was abolished. Az-Zuai appeared to have been dismissed in reaction to the security forces' failure to act promptly during attacks by Libyan mobs on African migrant workers in the previous month (see below). In March 2001 it was announced that a new Secretariat of the Economy and Trade was to be established in the General People's Committee, under Abd es-Salem Jouir; a new governor of the Central Bank, Ahmed Abd el-Hamid was also appointed.

Ahmed Abdulkarim Ahmed became acting chairman of the NOC until October 2001, when Abd al-Hafiz Zleitni, a former Secretary for Economy and Trade, was named as the new chairman. In early November the People's Tribunal in Benghazi sentenced 47 senior officials of the Secretariat of Finance and the Central Bank, all of whom had been convicted on corruption charges, to between one and 19 years' imprisonment. Among those convicted were the current Secretary for Finance, Burayni, and his predecessor, Bait al-Mal. Ten days later, however, Burayni appeared on state television presenting the 2002 budget, suggesting that Qaddafi may have decided that the tribunal had proved too zealous in its efforts to root out corruption. In December Shukri Muhammad Ghanem, who had been director of research at OPEC, was named Secretary for the Economy Trade by the General Peoples Congress, replacing Abd es-Salem Ahmed Jouir, who had held the post for less than a year.

In November 2000 Libya hosted a symposium on HIV and AIDS, a sensitive issue in the country following the arrest in February 1999 of six Bulgarian medical personnel accused of deliberately infecting nearly 400 children at a Benghazi hospital with blood products contaminated with HIV. The Bulgarians, a doctor and five nurses, went on trial in June 2001; if convicted they could be subject to the death penalty. At an international conference on AIDS held in Nigeria in the previous month, Qaddafi had declared that the Bulgarians were acting on the orders of Western intelligence services and demanded an international 'Lockerbie–style' trial. In February 2001 Amnesty International had expressed its disquiet at the handling the case. In December 2000, meanwhile, the Libyan Association for the Control of Drugs embarked on a major programme to raise public awareness about the problem of drugs, which the authorities admitted had been present in Libyan society for some time. Meanwhile the Secretary for Justice, addressing a UN anti-crime conference in Italy, stated that Libya was particularly

vulnerable to organized crime, especially smuggling, because of its large area and long borders.

At the beginning of September 2001 Amnesty International reported that Libya's longest serving political prisoner, Ahmad az-Zubayr Ahmad as-Sanusi, had been released after 31 years' incarceration on the occasion of the Qaddafi regime's 32nd anniversary; the organization none the less expressed concern about hundreds of other political prisoners detained for more than 10 years without trial.

In February 2002 sentences were passed on some 160 people arrested in 1998 and accused of being members of the proscribed Muslim Brotherhood. Although 78 of the accused were released, two were sentenced to death and the rest received prison sentences (10 of these being life sentences). It emerged that several of those arrested had already been killed or died in custody. Despite continued intolerance of all political opposition, the Muslim Brotherhood requested dialogue with the Qaddafi regime, stating that it was committed to pursuing only peaceful activities. Also in February, Seif al-Islam al-Qaddafi, in a statement to the London-based *Ash-Sharq al-Awsat*, denied rumours that either he or another of Qaddafi's sons was being groomed to succeed their father as Libyan leader. Although he indicated that he supported reforms including the creation of an independent media, he firmly rejected political pluralism as a future option for Libya.

ICJ RULING ON AOZOU STRIP

On 3 February 1994 the ICJ ruled against Libya's claim to the Aozou strip in northern Chad. Libya and Chad had agreed in 1989 to accept the ICJ's ruling over the disputed territory. Libya's border with its southern neighbour, Chad, had been defined in 1955 in an agreement between the newly-independent State of Libya and France, then the colonial power in Chad. However, in 1973 Libya unilaterally abrogated the treaty and annexed the Aozou strip. Libya based its claim to northern Chad on the fact that the area had been part of the vast domain of the Sanusi order which had ruled much of Libya before the Italian colonial conquest in 1911. Most of the disputed strip is desert and sparsely populated. Chad regained control of the area in 1987 with the exception of a large military base built by Libya at the oasis of Aozou. After the court's ruling was announced, Libya appeared unwilling to relinquish its claim to the disputed territory and the Government of Chad reported that Libya had strengthened its military forces there. When negotiations between the two countries did begin in March, Libya demanded the release of some 500 prisoners of war captured in Chad in 1987. Then, Qaddafi suddenly announced that Libya was willing to abandon its claim to the disputed territory and a draft agreement on the withdrawal of Libyan forces was signed in Sirte on 5 April. Under the terms of the agreement the withdrawal was completed by the end of May 1994. In early June Libya signed a treaty of friendship and co-operation with Chad, but in January 1995 the President of Chad strongly denied reports in the Libyan press that plans for a union between Chad, Libya and Sudan had been agreed at a meeting of the leaders of the three countries, held in Tripoli in October 1994. A communiqué issued at the end of the meeting had merely announced that a committee had been set up to study the question of integration. It was clear that neither Chad nor Sudan had any intention of forming a union with Libya, but had agreed to discuss integration in the hope of securing Libyan financial and military assistance. In January 1997 the Chadian Government announced its intention to protest to the UN Security Council against the appearance of an official Libyan publication containing a map that showed the Aozou strip within Libyan territory.

RELATIONS WITH THE ARAB STATES AND AFRICA

Although President Mubarak has consistently resisted Qaddafi's plans for Arab unity, relations between Libya and Egypt have continued to improve in recent years. Egypt firmly opposed the UN sanctions imposed on Libya and has made strenuous diplomatic efforts to mediate between Libya and the West over the Lockerbie affair. In November 1993 President Mubarak told the newspaper *Al-Ahram* that it was in Egypt's interest for 'stability' to prevail in Libya and that relations between the two countries should remain cordial. Qaddafi's regime is seen as a bulwark against the spread of militant Islamist movements in the region and offers the prospect of much needed economic opportunities for Egypt, especially the employment of Egyptian manpower. Libya has offered to resettle 1m. Egyptian farmers on lands to be irrigated by the GMR scheme. For Libya, which has become increasingly isolated internationally through the efforts of the USA and the United Kingdom, Egypt serves as a valuable intermediary with the outside world. The close relationship between the two countries appeared to have survived the embarrassment resulting from the disappearance of Libyan opposition leader, Mansour Kikhia, in Cairo in December 1994 (see above) and Libya's strong condemnation of the Israel-PLO accord signed in September 1993. Early in 1994 the Libyan press agency, JANA, declared that Libya and Egypt were continuing to co-operate in many areas and acknowledged Egyptian efforts to persuade the West to ease sanctions against Libya. In February the Egyptian Minister of Foreign Affairs, Amr Moussa, condemned the latest round of sanctions against Libya as 'unfair' and 'coercive' and reiterated his Government's commitment to seeking a peaceful solution to the Lockerbie affair. However, Egypt's close relations with Libya provoked strong criticism from the US media at the end of 1994. Egypt was accused of abusing US aid by defending a state involved in terrorism against the USA. The Libyan Secretary of Foreign Liaison and International Co-operation, Omar al-Muntasser, condemned the attacks as an attempt to build a 'Berlin Wall' between Libya and Egypt and argued that this was yet another US media campaign to denounce Libya as a 'terrorist state' just before UN sanctions became due for review. In November 1994 Libya supported Egypt's application to join the UMA. However, political differences emerged between the states during 1995, especially as a result of Libya's outspoken opposition to the normalization of relations between a growing number of Arab states and Israel. Qaddafi was critical of Egypt's role in promoting economic co-operation between Israel and its Arab neighbours. Libya's expulsion of Egyptian workers during the second half of 1995 further soured relations, although the Egyptian Government carefully avoided any public condemnation of Libya's actions. Moreover, in October 1995 Qaddafi made a number of public statements criticizing Egypt and Mubarak for not doing enough to help Libya obtain the lifting of UN sanctions. In January 1996 the Libyan leader agreed to stop the expulsion of Egyptian workers after the Egyptian President agreed to step up his mediation efforts on behalf of Libya, although observers noted that Libya's outspoken opposition to Israel and the Middle East peace process had made Egyptian efforts at mediation over UN sanctions even more difficult. In March Col Qaddafi condemned the 'Summit of Peace-makers' held at Sharm esh-Sheikh, but carefully avoided any criticism of Egypt. In May Qaddafi held talks in Cairo with Mubarak, but caused some embarrassment to his host by issuing a new threat to expel Palestinians living in Libya. In late June, however, the Libyan leader flew to Cairo, in violation of the UN air embargo, to attend the Arab League summit convened by Mubarak in response to the election of a right-wing Government in Israel, while during Libya's debate with the USA over allegations that it was involved in the construction of a chemical weapons plant at Tarhuna (see above), Egypt refused to endorse the US claims. Recognizing Egypt as Libya's only real ally in the Arab world and as a vitally important intermediary, especially with the West, the Libyan leader continued to maintain close relations. Several meetings took place between Qaddafi and Mubarak throughout the second half of 1996 and in early December the Egyptian President made an official visit to Tripoli, at the head of a large delegation. Co-operation in security, principally directed against militant Islamist groups, was agreed during the meeting. At the end of 1996 Col Qaddafi announced that after liquidating a number of investments in Europe, Libya was to reinvest in Egypt, where Libyan government holdings were believed to total some US $440m. However, differences between the two countries, particularly regarding Egypt's relations with Israel and Col Qaddafi's outspoken opposition to the Middle East peace process, continued to put their relationship under strain.

Egypt had also been suspicious of Libya's close relations with Sudan, which supports Libyan opposition to the peace process and offers shelter to Islamist militants from Egypt. In April 1995 a Libyan delegation attended the Popular Arab and Islamic Conference in Khartoum, along with representatives of Islamist opposition groups from Algeria, Morocco and Tunisia. The meeting avoided any criticism of the Libyan Government's harsh repression of its Islamist opposition and appealed for the lifting of UN sanctions against Tripoli. However, relations between Libya and Sudan became strained during the second half of 1995, owing to Libya's expulsion of large numbers of Sudanese workers (see above). Nevertheless, the Sudanese President, Omar Hassan al-Bashir, attended the 26th anniversary of the Libyan revolution in September 1995 as an honoured guest, and in early January 1996 Abu Bakr Jaber Yunes, Co-ordinator of the General People's Committee for Defence, attended Sudan's celebrations of the 40th anniversary of its independence. Early in 1996 Libya continued to mediate in disputes between Sudan and neighbouring Uganda and Ethiopia.

Although Libya joined the UMA and Col Qaddafi assumed the presidency of the organization on 1 January 1991 for a period of six months, the Libyan leader appeared at this time to show little interest in further integration with his country's western neighbours and preferred to look east to Egypt. The union itself has made little progress and few of the agreements adopted have actually been ratified. At the sixth summit meeting, held in Tunis in April 1994, Libya, represented by Maj. Khoeldi al-Hamidi, threatened to leave the organization unless the other member states ceased to comply with the UN sanctions imposed against Libya. Of the UMA leaders, only the Algerian President, Liamine Zéroual, attended the celebrations marking the 25th anniversary of the Libyan revolution held in Tripoli in September 1994. At the beginning of 1995 Libya announced that it would not, in future, take over the presidency of the UMA nor chair any of its institutions. However, despite its threats to leave the organization, Libya continued to attend UMA meetings. It was suggested that renewed interest in the UMA may have been owing to its desire to support Egypt's application for membership and its recognition that the UMA provided Libya with a rare opportunity for contact with the EU. In June the UMA expressed its solidarity with Libya by appealing for an end to UN sanctions. Early in 1996, however, Col Qaddafi's outspoken opposition to Israel strained relations with other members of the UMA. By the end of the year Libya had made some efforts to improve relations with its Maghreb neighbours and revive the UMA, largely in order to ensure their support for Libyan efforts to obtain the lifting of UN sanctions. Relations with Tunisia on the other hand, though often strained and sometimes hostile, have become friendly since the imposition of UN sanctions. Libya has come to depend increasingly on transit facilities through Tunisia as the air embargo imposed by the UN has tightened. Tunisia has profited greatly from this transit traffic, and the remittances from the 20,000 Tunisians working in Libya represent another valuable source of foreign exchange. Despite Tunisia's strict implementation of UN sanctions and the large profits that it has made out of its role as Libya's main transit route to Europe, relations remained friendly for most of 1995. In July Tunisia requested that the UN General Assembly lift sanctions against Libya, and Tunisia was among those countries that supported Libya's unsuccessful request to attend the EU summit in Barcelona, in November. During the second half of the year, Tunisians were not included in the mass expulsion of foreign workers from Libya. However, relations deteriorated at the beginning of 1996 after Tunisia agreed to establish low-level diplomatic relations with Israel, a move that was sharply condemned by Libya. Relations were further soured in February 1996, when Tunisia placed on trial an opposition leader, Muhammad Mouada of the Mouvement des démocrates socialistes. One of the charges against him was that he had links with the Libyan intelligence services. Relations, however, improved towards the end of 1996 when Col Qaddafi made two visits to Tunis and signed a number of bilateral co-operation agreements. The Libyan leader also declared that Tunisians were welcome to work and invest in Libya. Despite misunderstandings with Algeria over Col Qaddafi's attitude towards the Front islamique du salut (FIS), the fundamentalist Islamist opposition in Algeria, Algeria has continued to support Libya in the UN and the Arab League. In April 1995 Col Qaddafi visited Algeria for talks with President Liamine Zéroual. The talks were concluded with a joint statement reviewing bilateral and economic relations and urging the UN to end sanctions against Libya. Relations between the two countries were increasingly focused on co-operation over security and the containment of Islamist militancy, and these matters were discussed when the Algerian Minister of the Interior, Mustapha Benmansour, visited Tripoli in August 1995. In April 1996 the two countries signed a security agreement to co-operate in the struggle against the threat posed by militant Islamist groups, and shortly afterwards there was speculation that the Libyan authorities had handed over some 500 Algerian members of the FIS who had taken refuge in Libya. However, relations became strained in January 1997 when it was announced that the FIS had asked Libya to mediate in their conflict with the Algerian authorities, since Libya had ostensibly broken off all links with the FIS in 1994 when Col Qaddafi had pledged to cease all support for the Islamist opposition in Algeria. Morocco supported Libya in the UN by abstaining during the vote in the Security Council in November 1993 to impose tougher sanctions on Libya. After Libya criticized Morocco for its moves towards normalizing its relations with Israel, relations improved somewhat in 1995 when King Hassan, on a visit to Washington, DC, in March, urged the US Administration to re-examine its position on sanctions against Libya in the light of their impact on the Libyan people. During 1996 both countries called for a revival of the UMA. In November 1995, after Mauritania established diplomatic relations with Israel, Libya expelled some 10,000 Mauritanian workers, withdrew its ambassador to Nouakchott, severed economic links and threatened Mauritania's status as a member of the UMA and the Arab League. In March 1997, however, diplomatic relations between the two countries were restored, despite accusations by the Mauritanian authorities earlier in the year that Libya had maintained links with a number of opposition leaders, ostensibly for the purpose of destabilizing the Mauritanian regime. Although all of Libya's neighbours remain deeply suspicious of the Qaddafi regime, they have more to fear from its collapse, an event that could have serious consequences for the stability of the whole of North Africa.

After some 30 years of promoting the virtues of Arab unity, Libya announced in October 1998 that it was downgrading its representation at the Arab League in Cairo, and in December the GPC abolished the Secretariat for (Arab) Unity. The official Libyan news agency emphasized that Libya belonged to the African continent, and from October the country's state-controlled radio station, 'Voice of the Greater Arab Homeland', changed its name to 'Voice of Africa'. Instead of his customary pan-Arab rhetoric, Qaddafi has begun to champion African self-determination, announcing that he wishes Libya to become a 'Black' country and urging Libyans to marry Black Africans. The change, which was regarded by some as merely a tactical move, reflected Qaddafi's growing frustration with Arab countries for not giving Libya stronger support on the Lockerbie issue, in marked contrast to the states of sub-Saharan Africa (see above). For some time Libya has been promoting closer relations with countries south of the Sahara, using financial assistance as an incentive, and in early 1998 initiated the Community of Sahel-Saharan States (COMESSA), comprising Burkina Faso, Chad, Mali, Niger and Sudan, in order to promote economic, social and cultural exchanges. After years of tension over the disputed Aozou strip, Libya's relations with Chad have improved dramatically. A number of bilateral agreements have been signed, and at the beginning of May the Libyan leader made a much-publicized visit to the Chadian capital, N'Djamena. In his capacity as president of COMESSA, Qaddafi attempted to mediate in a number of African disputes, although most of these initiatives had more symbolic value than substance. In addition to his efforts to mediate in the border dispute between Ethiopia and Eritrea, and between warring factions in Somalia, Sudan and Sierra Leone, Qaddafi was active in trying to end the war in the DRC between forces loyal to President Kabila and the rebel Rassemblement congolais démocratique, which is supported by Rwanda and Uganda. In late April 1999 it was announced that Qaddafi had brokered a peace agreement between Kabila and President Museveni of Uganda, which was intended to bring about a cease-fire, the deployment of an African peace-keeping force and the withdrawal of foreign troops from the DRC. Neither Rwanda nor the DRC rebels, however,

were party to the agreement. At the end of May Libyan armed forces were deployed in Uganda, and in June Qaddafi made a visit to Zambia, where he and President Chiluba arranged a meeting between the DRC President and the Rwanda-backed rebels. After visiting Zambia, the Libyan leader made a state visit to South Africa for the first time since the lifting of the UN sanctions against Libya. The Libyan leader attended the OAU summit held in Algiers in July and in September, on the occasion of the 30th anniversary of his seizure of power, he hosted an extraordinary OAU summit in Sirte. Qaddafi presented his vision of a 'United States of Africa' and demanded that Africa be given power of veto in the UN Security Council. The 'Sirte Declaration', a final document adopted by the 43 attending heads of state and government, called for the strengthening of the OAU, the establishment of a pan-African parliament, African monetary union and an African court of justice. Qaddafi's proposal for a United States of Africa was officially adopted at the OAU summit at Lomé, in July 2000, almost all the costs of which were met by Libya. (The summit also called for the permanent lifting of UN sanctions against Libya and supported Tripoli's claims for compensation against the economic cost of eight years of sanctions.) However, the proposal for a United States of Africa had to be ratified by two-thirds of OAU members before implementation, and key states such as South Africa and Nigeria expressed their reservations. Several African states were known to prefer a more cautious approach, focusing primarily on economic integration. Given the failure of Qaddafi's previous attempts to merge Libya with other states, there was widespread scepticism that his project for a united Africa would prove more successful.

Meanwhile, the Libyan leader's African ambitions suffered a set-back at the end of September, when Libyans attacked black African migrant workers, reportedly killing more than 50 (although this figure was later disputed) and forcing thousands of others to flee the country or be repatriated by their governments. African-owned businesses were destroyed, and Niger's embassy in Tripoli was looted. It was unclear exactly what triggered the violence, which began in Zuwara, west of Tripoli, but it quickly spread to other parts of the country. Qaddafi's charm offensive towards sub-Saharan Africa had proved unpopular with the majority of Libyans who had become increasingly hostile to the presence of an estimated 1m. black African migrant workers in the country. Deep-rooted racism, fear that the migrants posed a threat to Libyan culture and were responsible for a range of social problems such as crime, drugs and prostitution, and a widespread perception that migrants competed with Libyans for jobs, although in fact most of them undertook low-paid work rejected by nationals, were among the factors apparently contributing to this hostility. The security forces were evidently taken by surprise by the rapid escalation of the violence and were criticized by the GPC for failing to prevent disturbances and for delays in restoring order. Qaddafi later expressed regret at the violence and hinted that the attacks were aimed at undermining his efforts to promote African union. The GPC announced its intention formally to investigate the incidents, and in mid-October the evacuation and deportation of migrant workers from Nigeria, Chad, Niger, Sudan and Ghana commenced. In January 2001 some 331 Libyans and African immigrants were put on trial, accused of involvement in the disturbances and trying to sabotage the African unification project. On 21 May seven of the defendants were sentenced to death, 12 were given life sentences, and 152 received shorter sentences of varying duration; the remainder were acquitted.

Undeterred, in October Qaddafi embarked on a tour of the Arab world, visiting Jordan, Syria and Saudi Arabia, during which he presented a strategic proposal for Arab unity with Africa. At meetings in Jordan and Syria he declared that in the new world the Arabs were lost because they belonged to no geographical grouping and that they 'must wake up from their long sleep and be part of the African space'. Qaddafi was due to end his tour by attending the Arab League summit in Cairo called in response to renewed violence between Israel and the Palestinians. Shortly before, however, he caused embarrassment during a television interview by revealing the Egyptian draft of the final declaration of the summit, denouncing it as a sell-out and challenging Arab leaders 'to take steps that would satisfy the angry Arab masses'. Qaddafi himself then decided not to attend the summit, and his representative walked out in protest. The Libyan leader also boycotted the OIC summit in November because it did not adopt a sufficiently tough stance on Israel and the Middle East peace process. There were also rumours that the Libyan authorities were planning to introduce entry visas for nationals of other Arab countries.

In order to try to improve relations with African states undermined by the September riots, Libya offered new trade, co-operation and aid agreements with its sub-Saharan neighbours and increased its efforts to mediate in African conflicts. In November Libya was host to a pan-African summit on the civil war in the DRC. However, Qaddafi's influence with the rival parties was clearly limited, and the negotiations failed to make significant progress. At the beginning of March 2001 some 40 African heads of state were invited by the Libyan leader to a second summit meeting at Sirte. In place of Qaddafi's ambitious project for a United States of Africa more modest plans were approved to replace the OAU with a new African Union incorporating a range of pan-African institutions, including a Parliament, a Central Bank, an African Monetary Fund and a Court of Justice, but without supranational executive powers. The meeting also addressed the precarious state of the OAU's finances: Libya had already settled the arrears owed to the OAU by 10 member states, but several other states had still failed to pay their contributions. Some analysts expressed scepticism about the idea of an African parliament, pointing out that many African states were involved in armed conflicts with their neighbours and questioning the democratic credentials of some potential members. Moreover, the proposal for equal representation was opposed by states such as Nigeria and Egypt, who were apparently concerned that if such an arrangement were adopted their regional influence would be diminished. Questions were also raised about the funding of the proposed African Central Bank, given the extent of the combined external debt of the sub-Saharan region. The Arab League, at its meeting in Amman the same month, agreed to set up a committee to examine Qaddafi's proposal that the Arab states should join the new African Union. Meanwhile, South Africa, whose ambassador to Libya has been based in Tunis, announced that it was opening an embassy in Tripoli.

In May 2001, following mediation by Qaddafi, Uganda and Sudan agreed to restore diplomatic relations, which had been severed broken in 1995. At the end of May 2001 Libya sent some 100 troops to support President Ange-Félix Patassé of the Central African Republic (CAR) after an attempted *coup d'état*, and in early November dispatched another 80 soldiers to the CAR when there was another coup attempt. France was reported to have indicated its approval for Libya's role as the 'new gendarme' in the CAR. In early 2002 the Libyan troops were reinforced by military personnel from Sudan and Djibouti as part of a CEN-SAD (as COMESSA had been restyled) peace-keeping force.

In June 2001 Libya agreed to supply Ghana with 30,000 b/d of oil, half the country's requirements, on special concessionary terms with effect from August. After attending the OAU summit in Lusaka, Zambia, in July, Qaddafi visited Zimbabwe where he expressed strong support for the Government's programme of land seizures. During the visit Libya agreed to provide Zimbabwe with US \$360m to purchase petroleum products, with repayment to be made by exports of agricultural and mineral products to Libya. In January 2002 Libyan mediation helped to achieve a peace accord between the Government of Chad and the rebel Movement for Democracy and Justice operating out of the Tibesti mountains, which straddle Libya's southern border with Chad. Qaddafi's wide-ranging dealings with African states remained unpopular with many Libyans, who continued to blame social problems such as rising crime and use of drugs on the country's African migrant workers.

In early July 2002 Col Qaddafi travelled to Durban, South Africa, for the 38th and final summit of the OAU, which saw the formal creation of the new African Union, headed by South African President Thabo Mbeki. Qaddafi was accompanied by a large entourage and, according to various media reports, large quantities of cash and weaponry. While President Mbeki's speech focused on the need for democracy, good government,

the eradication of corruption, respect for human rights and peace and stability, the Libyan leader addressed his comments to the West, declaring that those who wanted to assist Africa were welcome, but not those who insisted on imposing their conditions upon African states. He heralded the birth of the African Union as his 'African dream'. During the summit Mbeki and numerous other African heads of state had tried to persuade Qaddafi to abandon his hostility towards the New Partnership for Africa's Development (NEPAD), a contract between Africa and the international community under which, in exchange for aid and investment, the African states agreed to strive towards democracy and good governance. The Libyan leader had criticized the programme for imposing a Western model of development on Africa and ignoring the continent's own traditions and religions. He also argued that African countries did not need 'numerous political parties'. His views received support especially from the poorest African states, which receive Libyan aid. After the summit Qaddafi and his entourage visited Mozambique, Zimbabwe and Malawi.

In early August 2002 the US-based human rights organization Human Rights Watch criticized the appointment of Col Qaddafi to the steering group of NEPAD, stating that while the new initiative was committed to promoting human rights and good governance, Libya had a long record of human rights abuses. Human Rights Watch also wrote to the Presidents of Nigeria, Senegal and South Africa (the other members of the NEPAD steering group), urging them to withdraw their nomination of Libya, confirmed at the previous month's Durban summit, to chair the next session of the UN Commission on Human Rights, due to begin in March 2003, or issue a clear public statement setting out the terms of African participation in the Commission consistent with NEPAD's goals.

Libyan efforts to end the civil war in Sudan involved a joint peace initiative with Egypt, and in December 1999 President Mubarak flew to Libya for talks with the Libyan leadership on the latest political crisis in Sudan. In late July 2002 Col Qaddafi attended celebrations in Cairo to mark the 50th anniversary of the Egyptian revolution and held talks with President Mubarak on the Israeli–Palestinian conflict and the peace accord between the Sudanese Government and the Sudan People's Liberation Movement. Reports in the media suggested that Libya and Egypt were displeased since they had not been consulted about the accord (which was sponsored by the Intergovernmental Authority on Development with some assistance from the USA and Norway).

At the beginning of March 2002 the Secretary-General of the Arab League, Amr Moussa, visited Tripoli after Qaddafi threatened to withdraw his country from the organization in protest at what he condemned as its ineptitude with regard to the Israeli–Palestinian conflict. The Libyan leader also rejected the peace plan put forward by Crown Prince Abdullah of Saudi Arabia in June, which proposed full normalization of relations with Israel in exchange for Israeli withdrawal from all Arab territories occupied since 1967. Colonel Qaddafi insisted on the return of all Palestinian refugees, the removal of all weapons of mass destruction from all countries in the region, and the organization of free elections under the auspices of the UN in Israel and the Palestinian territories (denied to the Libyan people throughout the period of Qaddafi's rule). Some analysts interpreted the Libyan stance as a warning to the USA that Tripoli could still disrupt Washington's Middle East policy and must therefore not be ignored. The Libyan leader did not attend the Arab League's Beirut summit, and the Libyan delegation was led by Dr Ali Abd as-Salam at-Turayki, the Secretary for African Unity, and Muhammad Qaddaf Eddam, Qaddafi's cousin and close confidant. Nevertheless, Libya pledged US \$50m. in assistance to the Palestinians.

Libya, meanwhile, continued to support attempts to revive the UMA, but little progress was made. A summit meeting of heads of state, scheduled to take place in Algiers in November 1999, was cancelled owing to renewed tensions between Algeria and Morocco. Qaddafi met several times with President Ben Ali of Tunisia, and while both countries expressed a commitment to reviving the UMA, discussions concentrated on bilateral relations: Tunisia is Libya's main trading partner in the Arab world, and in June 2000 the two countries signed an agreement to establish a free-trade zone. A summit meeting of UMA heads of state that was to have been held in Algiers in June 2002 was postponed following consultations between President Bouteflika

of Algeria and Col Qaddafi. King Muhammad of Morocco had announced that he would not attend, and it was unclear whether President Ould Sid' Ahmed Taya of Mauritania would be present.

Economy

ALAN J DAY

INTRODUCTION

Petroleum has transformed Libya from the poorest country in the world in 1951 into the country with the highest living standards in Africa (according to World Bank figures). Before the discovery of oil in commercial quantities in the 1950s, agriculture was the basis of the economy and domestic revenue covered only about one-half of the Government's ordinary and development expenditure. Between 1962 and 1968, however, national income increased from LD 131m. to LD 798m. and gross national product (GNP) increased from LD 163m. to LD 909m. Exports of petroleum during this period increased by 835%, accounting for 51% of gross domestic product (GDP) in 1968. As a result of the dramatic rise in oil prices in the 1970s, the country's GNP, according to official estimates, reached LD 3,497m. in 1975, when petroleum exports accounted for 46.3% of GDP. Oil revenues then rose steeply, reaching a peak of US $22,000m. in 1980, but fell equally sharply in the 1980s, as world oil prices declined rapidly. Estimated GNP fell from $25,984m. in 1985 to $22,300m. in 1987 and $18,400m. in 1988, before rising again, in 1989, to $23,333m., measured at average 1987–89 prices. During the greater part of the 1980s the petroleum sector accounted for 65% of GDP and 99% of export earnings, although it provided employment for less than 10% of the labour force. In 1989, according to estimates by the World Bank, Libya's GNP per head, measured at average 1987–89 prices, was $5,310. This was the highest level to be recorded among African countries, but represented an average annual decline, in real terms, of 9.2% over the period 1980–89. Libya's financial position deteriorated further in 1988–89, but then improved significantly following the Gulf crisis of 1990–91, when world oil prices rose sharply, albeit for a brief period, and generated an increase in Libyan oil revenues of nearly 25% in 1990, compared with 1989.

After the 1969 revolution, state intervention in the economy increased, in accordance with Col Qaddafi's ideas of 'Islamic socialism'. Apart, however, from the nationalization of distribution and marketing of petroleum in Libya in 1970, the Government refrained from directly taking over petroleum company assets until the dispute with British Petroleum (BP) in 1971. In September 1978 and the first two months of 1979, a large number of private companies were taken over by workers' committees. Similarly, in 1979, all direct importing business was transferred to 62 public corporations, and the issuing of licences was stopped. In March 1981, it was announced that all licences for shops selling clothes, electrical goods, shoes, household appliances and spare parts were to be cancelled, and that by the end of the year all retail shops would have to close. Retail activity became controlled by state-administered supermarkets. The whole private sector was to be completely abolished by the end of 1981, to be replaced by people's economic committees. These plans were never implemented according to schedule, and by the late 1980s Qaddafi was extolling the virtues of private enterprise.

Until the country's petroleum resources began to be exploited, not more than 25% of the population lived in the towns. This is no longer true: by 1990, according to the World Bank, the urban population comprised 70% of the total. Approximately one-half of the non-urban population is settled in rural communities, and the remainder are semi-nomads, who follow a pastoral mode of life. According to the results of the census carried out in August 1995, Libya's population was 4.8m., compared with 3.6m. at the census of July 1984; by 2000 the total was estimated by the UN to have risen to 5.3m. The country's labour force totalled an estimated 1.2m. in 1996. By the end of 1982 it was

estimated that there were 569,000 foreigners living in Libya, representing 18% of the total population. Egyptians accounted for 174,158 of these, while 73,582 were Tunisians and 44,546 were Turkish. In July 1985, however, Col Qaddafi barred Egyptians (whose numbers in Libya had fallen by 20,000 since January) from working in Libya, in retaliation against a similar measure preventing Libyans from working in Egypt. Tunisia ordered 283 Libyans (the majority of Libya's diplomats and more than 250 other Libyan nationals), accused of spying, to leave the country in August 1985, after Libya decided to expel some 30,000 Tunisian workers from Libya. It was estimated that Libya expelled or laid off more than 120,000 foreign workers during 1985 (including workers from Mali, Mauritania, Niger, and 10,000–20,000 Syrians, between August and October). Col Qaddafi maintained that the expulsions were part of a policy to achieve self-sufficiency in Libya's labour force, and not the result of economic stringency. However, remittances by foreign workers to their own countries were a substantial drain on Libya's reserves of foreign exchange, totalling some US $2,000m. in 1983, when the number of expatriate workers was at its highest level. Libya began to reduce the number of these workers in 1984, and remittances in that year were estimated to have fallen to $1,500m. In 2000 no new employment permits were issued to foreign workers, whose numbers were estimated at 46,000.

From 1980 planned mergers with Syria, Morocco and Algeria, and the military adventure into Chad, had adverse effects on the economy. The latter episode resulted in diplomatic relations being broken off with a number of West African countries. In the economic sphere, for example, Nigeria cut off uranium sales to Libya, which amounted to 500 metric tons in 1980. The purge on corruption in February 1980 increased payment delays and so deepened the reluctance of foreign companies to invest in Libya. In practical terms, little progress was made towards the 'merger' with Syria, although Libya paid off all Syria's debts to the USSR, and appeared to be moving closer to the USSR.

Relations with the USA worsened, and in March 1982 President Ronald Reagan banned imports of Libyan petroleum to the USA, and halted all exports to Libya other than food and medical supplies. Libya's perceived interference in the affairs of other nations (notably Chad) and its alleged association with international terrorism had further significant economic repercussions in January 1986, when President Reagan 'froze' Libyan assets in the USA and banned all trade between the USA and Libya. However, the effectiveness of this action was vitiated by the unwillingness of the USA's allies in Japan and Western Europe to institute a complementary economic boycott of Libya, and by the fact that assets worth some US $1,000m.–$2,000m. would have been surrendered to Libya by the US oil companies operating there if they had ceased operations immediately. These companies were given until 30 June 1986 to sell their assets to Libyan concerns, but only tenuous agreements had been reached by the time the deadline arrived. The assets were not nationalized and the companies signed agreements with Libya giving them the right to negotiate their return when circumstances allowed.

The US sanctions, rather than harming Libya, had their greatest impact on the departing oil companies, which estimated their annual losses from the oil operations that they had transferred to Libya at US $2m.–$2.5m. The withdrawal of the US petroleum companies had a greater negative effect on Libya's ability to market its petroleum than on actual levels of production, which were lower than capacity, owing to weak world demand. Petroleum lifted by US companies was formerly guaranteed an outlet through their refineries, mainly in Europe. Following the US withdrawal, Libya had to compete with other countries for sales to refineries. In June 1986 the USA banned the export to third countries of goods and technology destined for use in the Libyan petroleum industry. A three-year 'standstill agreement' between the Libyan Government and the US petroleum companies officially expired at the end of June 1989, but continued to be observed by Libya, which confirmed in March 1991 that it had no plans to dispose of the US companies' Libyan areas to third parties. In January 1991 US sanctions were renewed for a further 12-month period, and in April the US Government published a list of 48 companies, based in various countries, which it believed to be acting as agents or 'fronts' for Libyan nationals and which were therefore to be subject to the US sanctions. A supplementary list published in August 1991 added 12 companies to the total. According to the US Department of the Treasury, the mid-1993 value of Libyan assets 'frozen' in the USA since 1986 was $903m.

In addition to Libya's increasingly isolated position among both African and Arab states, during the 1980s Libya's economy was severely restricted by the effect of the low prices for petroleum consequent on the global oil glut. Revenue from sales of petroleum declined from US $22,000m. in 1980 to $5,000m. in 1988. Decreasing revenues caused serious cash-flow problems and necessitated a major revision of the 1981–85 Development Plan. Although in January 1986 the Central Bank claimed that 80% of projects under the Plan were either completed or under way, the slump in the price of oil in 1986 led to the suspension or cancellation of almost all new development projects, an outstanding exception being the 'Great Man-made River' scheme (GMR—see 'Power and Water', below). In the period 1980–89 GDP declined from $35,500m. to $23,000m. The crisis in the economy prompted Col Qaddafi to introduce a series of economic and political liberalization measures in March and April 1988. The state supermarket network, which was established in the early 1980s, was poorly organized and many basic commodities were usually unavailable, giving rise to a thriving black market. Subsequently, however, private shops were encouraged to reopen, and Col Qaddafi adopted measures to dismantle obstacles to trade and tourism with Libya's neighbours, closing customs and immigration posts along the borders with Egypt and Tunisia. Thousands of Tunisians entered Libya in 1988 to work on Libyan farms, while, along the border, a 'free zone' developed where Libyans could purchase items that were scarce in their own country. In September 1988 Qaddafi proposed an increase in 'privatization' and announced that Libyans would be able to import and export in complete freedom. In December the Government announced plans to reduce its budget deficit by removing subsidies on wheat, flour, sugar, tea and salt. However, controls on prices and on interest and exchange rates were maintained, and all important sectors of the economy remained under the effective control of the state (which in 1990 retained 70% of all Libyan salaried workers on its payroll).

At the second summit meeting of the Union of the Arab Maghreb (UMA, formed in February 1989 and comprising Algeria, Libya, Mauritania, Morocco and Tunisia), held in Algiers in July 1990, closer economic ties between the member states were proposed, including the establishment of a customs union before 1995. Moreover, a *rapprochement* with Egypt in October 1989 facilitated plans for wide-ranging economic integration and cross-border co-operation. This new relationship was one factor in Libya's decision ultimately to abide by the UN embargo that was imposed on Iraq in August 1990 because of its invasion of Kuwait (although Col Qaddafi opposed the US-led military action against Iraq). Another factor was Libya's need to take full advantage of the sudden rise in world oil prices, caused by the crisis. By increasing its output in the third and fourth quarters of the year, Libya recorded total petroleum revenues of US $9,700m. in 1990 (compared with $7,846m. in 1989) and achieved a 9.4% increase in GDP, to LD 7,816m. ($27,370m.). It also converted the 1989 current account deficit estimated at $940m. into an estimated surplus of $2,230m. in 1990. Libya thus emerged from the Gulf crisis of 1990–91 with its position enhanced both economically and diplomatically, notably in its relations with the European Community (EC, now European Union—EU), to which it was the second largest

supplier of oil. The value of petroleum revenues in 1991 amounted to about $10,000m.

Libya's economic relations with the West nevertheless continued to be complicated by allegations of official Libyan involvement in international terrorism, including the 1988 Lockerbie airliner bombing and the destruction in 1989 of a French airliner over Niger (see History). Under Resolution 748, adopted by the UN Security Council on 31 March 1992, Libya became subject to certain mandatory sanctions, in view of its failure to comply with Resolution 731 (of 12 January 1992) requiring Libyan co-operation in bringing those responsible for the terrorist actions to justice. As imposed from 15 April 1992, the sanctions included an arms embargo and the severance of air transport links with Libya, but did not, at that time, encompass a general trade embargo or any moves against Libya's exports of petroleum. Prior to their imposition, the Libyan authorities took the precaution of transferring substantial Libyan assets from West European to Middle Eastern banks.

In response to Libya's continuing non-compliance with Resolution 731, the Security Council extended the existing provisions of Resolution 748 for successive 120-day periods. The extension agreed in August 1993 was accompanied by a warning from three Council members (the United Kingdom, France and the USA) that they would seek to extend the scope of the sanctions if the situation remained deadlocked at the end of September 1993. Libyan claims that the country had suffered direct and indirect revenue losses totalling US $2,200m. during the first year of the sanctions regime were generally believed to be greatly exaggerated, the main reported trade effect of the sanctions being an increase in imports of priority items (including inputs for development projects) as a safeguard against a future UN decision to widen the scope of the sanctions.

A law promulgated by the General People's Congress (GPC) in September 1992 formally authorized the privatization of Libyan industries and permitted 'individuals or groups to exercise the liberal professions and to invest freely in the private sectors'. In July 1993 the General People's Committee issued a decree ending state control of wholesale trade, which was opened up to partnerships and limited companies. In the previous month the Committee had banned state employees from concurrently engaging in private employment. The national debate on economic reform had, in 1992, been widened by Col Qaddafi to include the proposal that 50% of the state's oil revenues should be distributed directly to citizens, and that the 'very, very big octopus' of state administration should be cut back to a minimum by privatizing most educational and health-care facilities, shutting down unprofitable state economic enterprises and devolving many defence responsibilities to local administrative units. Other leading figures, including the Governor of the Central Bank, spoke out strongly in favour of a more orthodox transition to a mixed economy. (In 1995 the GPC approved a budget provision for a direct revenue distribution scheme. The first measures towards its implementation were reported in the following year.)

In May 1993 Col Qaddafi advocated the introduction of a law to guarantee foreign capital investment in Libya. In July 1993 representatives of some 250 Libyan and Tunisian companies met in Tripoli to discuss proposals for improving economic co-operation between the two countries, including the possible establishment of new joint ventures. Delegates stressed the desirability of standardizing investment laws, pointing out that any Libyan move to introduce laws on the current Tunisian model would be consistent with the liberalization policies of the Libyan leadership.

Following the August 1993 extension of UN Security Council Resolution 748 and the subsequent circulation by the USA, France and the United Kingdom of draft proposals for stronger international action against Libya, the Libyan Government stepped up its efforts to minimize its exposure to harsher sanctions. Libya's liquid assets overseas (estimated to total US $17,000m.), if not already located in financial 'safe havens', were constantly monitored to avoid unnecessary exposure to seizure. According to the Bank for International Settlements, Libya withdrew $2,800m. of its overseas deposits in the third quarter of 1993, including an estimated $430m. from Organisation for Economic Co-operation and Development countries. The stockpiling of imported equipment for use in part-completed projects, and of spares for existing plants, was speeded up and carefully targeted on priority areas. The functions and ownership structures of Libya's fixed assets overseas (which had an estimated worth of up to $4,000m.) were analysed to assess their exposure to sanctions, and a number of deals were struck with foreign (predominantly Italian) equity partners whereby Libya relinquished control of high-profile companies.

In particular Oilinvest, the holding company through which Libya had controlled an extensive European oil refining and distribution network, was in September 1993 restructured with minority (45%) Libyan ownership, while Oilinvest's shareholding in its principal subsidiary company, Tamoil Italia, was in turn reduced to 45% and two Tamoil subsidiaries (Tamoil Transport and Chempetrol Overseas) were taken over by new owners.

The crucial Security Council vote on Libyan sanctions was delayed until 11 November 1993 because Russia (which was owed up to US $3,000m. for Soviet arms and other supplies to Libya in the 1970s and 1980s) was reluctant to endorse any measure that might prompt Libya to default on agreed payment obligations. This objection was dropped after the draft resolution was expanded to include an explicit reference to Libya's 'duty scrupulously to adhere to all its obligations concerning the servicing or repayment of foreign debt'.

Security Council Resolution 882 called on UN member states to 'freeze' all Libyan-controlled funds and financial resources abroad and to require the use of separate bank accounts for specified trade transactions; to prohibit the supply to Libya of specified items for use in the 'downstream' oil and gas sector; to shut down overseas offices of Libyan Arab Airlines and to ban the supply of civil aviation equipment and services and the renewal of aircraft insurance; and to reduce staffing levels at Libyan diplomatic missions.

The 'freeze' on Libyan funds prohibited withdrawals from, but not payments into, existing overseas bank accounts. The new 'external' bank accounts specified by the Resolution were to be set up to handle payments to foreign contractors and suppliers to the Libyan market, using revenue derived from Libyan exports of hydrocarbons and agricultural products. All transactions through such accounts had to be supported by evidence of compliance with the sanctions regulations. The petroleum and gas equipment specified in a detailed annex to Resolution 883 included pumps, loading equipment and various essential items of oil-refining equipment.

The Resolution came into force on 1 December, but the complicated administrative arrangements meant that Libyan export revenues did not begin to reach the new 'external' accounts in overseas banks until mid-January 1994, delaying payments to many foreign contractors for some weeks. Over-zealous actions by sanctions enforcers included the 'freezing' of the US assets of a Bahrain-based financial services company with a Libyan minority shareholder. This decision was rescinded in early February 1994. The UN Security Council renewed the terms of Resolution 883 for a further 120 days on 8 April.

In mid-1994 the sanctions appeared to have had no effect on the functioning of Libya's established oil and gas production facilities or the progress of development projects which had been under way when the sanctions were imposed. Many hydrocarbon facilities were not dependent on embargoed items, while others were fully supplied with stockpiled equipment. Some future projects had to be shelved for the duration of the current sanctions because they required embargoed items, but all were low-priority schemes for which no firm contracts had been awarded. There was, nevertheless, a marked decrease in the overall tempo of economic activity in Libya, and it was estimated that the country's GDP declined by 7% in both 1993 and 1994, to stand at about US $26,000m. in the latter year.

The UN sanctions remained in force in August 1995 on the same terms that applied in December 1993, the USA having failed to win UN Security Council backing for a proposal (tabled at the March and July 1995 sanctions reviews) to tighten them by imposing a total embargo on Libyan oil exports. European opposition to the US proposal had been strongest in Italy (which obtained 28% of its crude petroleum supplies from Libya). The US Government announced in April 1995 that it would examine the scope for further tightening of the USA's own unilateral sanctions against Libya.

In August 1995 the Government launched a series of mass expulsions of foreigners accused of working illegally in Libya, those affected being mainly Sudanese, Egyptians and Palestinians (the latter apparently included to make a political point about the current status of the Middle East peace process). Libya's foreign workforce was estimated to number between 1m. and 2.5m. in 1995. Unemployment was believed to have become a significant problem (with some Western estimates putting it as high as 30%) and was known to have affected increasing numbers of Libyan nationals. The expulsion of Palestinians was suspended for six months in October 1995, after which time the main targets of the government crackdown were Sudanese workers. The Palestinian expulsion order was formally rescinded in January 1997.

Having risen slightly in 1995, Libya's petroleum output showed another small increase in the first half of 1996 as the country's principal export industry continued to demonstrate that the UN sanctions regime (which remained unchanged in mid-1996) posed no significant threat to the implementation of its normal production schedules. Nor were there any reports of a slowdown in the pace of work on the GMR, which accounted for a large proportion of government spending on economic development. The level of state investment on lower-priority projects remained depressed, however, with some delays being explicitly attributed to the effects of sanctions. In certain cases (such as a major desalination scheme) the Government said it was unable to proceed to the contract stage because sanctions had made it impossible to arrange satisfactory project financing. In other cases (such as an oil refinery upgrading scheme) implementation of completed plans was deferred because the import of essential equipment was directly blocked by UN sanctions. There were also instances of international companies modifying their Libyan contract bids to allow for non-standard items to be installed instead of embargoed equipment (one example being some of the automated equipment normally installed in cement plants).

In January 1996 US President Bill Clinton extended the duration of all existing US sanctions against Libya, including 1980s measures that would otherwise have expired. Some weeks earlier the US Senate had added Libya to a bill (previously applicable only to Iran) designed to inhibit hydrocarbon investments in these countries by non-US companies. In April 1996 EU Ministers of Foreign Affairs made a formal protest to the USA about the 'extra-territoriality' of the draft legislation, which the EU regarded as a formula for a 'secondary embargo' against the mainly European companies whose commercial freedom was under threat. The Ways and Means Committee of the US House of Representatives nevertheless failed to remove the most controversial aspects of the proposed legislation when it approved a modified draft in June 1996. The Iran and Libya sanctions act completed its passage through the US Congress in the following month and was signed into law by President Clinton on 5 August 1996. It specified six forms of sanction available to the US Government: denial of access to US Export-Import Bank facilities; denial of export licences in respect of goods ordered from the USA; imposition of a ceiling of US $10m. per year on company loans from US financial institutions; withholding of permission to conduct primary dealings in US government bonds; exclusion from bidding for US government contracts; and exclusion from the US import market. A non-US company was liable to have two of these sanctions (selected by the President) imposed on it if it invested $40m. (later revised to $20m.) or more in the hydrocarbons industries of Libya or Iran in any one year, or if it violated current UN embargoes on Libya. However, the US President could decide to waive sanctions if a company's home country had 'agreed to undertake substantial measures, including economic sanctions' to prevent Libya or Iran from supporting terrorism or acquiring weapons of mass destruction, or if it had encouraged Libya to comply with UN Security Council Resolution 731 on the bringing to justice of terrorist suspects.

A resolution calling for the repeal of the US legislation was adopted by the UN General Assembly in November 1996, with EU member countries abstaining. Following the inauguration of the second Clinton Administration in January 1997, US officials indicated that there was no early intention to issue detailed guidelines on the implementation of the August 1996 legislation. A formal EU challenge to US sanctions laws, alleging violations of World Trade Organization rules, was suspended in April 1997 in order to seek a compromise settlement through informal discussions. There was minimal US reaction to reports during the first half of 1997 that the Italian company Agip, which had signed a major gas development agreement with Libya's National Oil Co some weeks before the Iran and Libya sanctions act came into force, was continuing to move towards the detailed design stage of this project.

The multilateral UN sanctions on Libya were renewed in 1996, 1997 and 1998. The Libyan Government claimed in October 1996 that UN sanctions had cost the country US $19,000m. in lost revenue by the end of 1995 (including $5,900m. from potential agricultural exports) and had contributed to the deaths of up to 21,000 Libyans (including 16,000 patients unable to obtain urgent medical treatment abroad). Preliminary estimates of Libya's economic performance in 1996 indicated a return to positive GDP growth (at a rate of 3.5% per year) for the first time since the imposition of UN sanctions in 1992. A 'purification' campaign against allegedly corrupt import-export traders led to the closure of many privately-owned small businesses in 1996.

A relaxation in May 1998 of the threat of US sanctions against countries whose companies invested in Iran was widely seen in Europe as also applying to dealings with Libya, although substantial opposition was evident in the US Congress to ending the US ban on investment in the Libyan oil industry. Following talks in Rome in July between the Italian and Libyan foreign affairs ministers, the Italian Government declared that normalization of relations between the two countries would assist Libya to return to 'co-operation with the international community', while also asserting that Libyan adherence to UN resolutions would assist the process. It was subsequently stated in Tripoli that Col Qaddafi had decreed that Italian companies should be 'given priority in all sectors' in the awarding of new government contracts.

According to unofficial estimates, Libya experienced real growth of 0.5% in 1997, the country's estimated GDP per head in that year being equivalent to about US $6,700 in terms of 'purchasing power parity'. In 1998 the economy was estimated to have declined by about 1% in real terms, reflecting the impact of a severe downturn in petroleum export prices. Libya joined other members of the Organization of the Petroleum Exporting Countries (OPEC) in a programme of production cutbacks which helped to underpin an oil price recovery during the first half of 1999. The suspension of UN sanctions against Libya in April led to an immediate intensification of contacts with non-US companies wishing to restore or strengthen their business links with Libya. Bilateral US trade sanctions were not suspended (other than to permit the export of foodstuffs and medicines to Libya), while the USA used its position in the UN Security Council to prevent the permanent lifting of the UN sanctions when they next fell due for review in July. It was, however, generally accepted that there was no likelihood of a reimposition of UN sanctions or of any positive action being taken by the USA to block other countries' economic co-operation with Libya.

In September 1999 the US Government permitted several US petroleum companies to inspect their Libyan assets. In the same month US wheat exporters resumed trade relations with the Libyan buying organization, which subsequently announced its first purchase of US wheat for 15 years. In contrast to the very slow thaw in US-Libyan economic relations, Libya's main non-US trading partners had by the end of 1999 made major efforts to achieve a full resumption of normal relations and to identify new investment opportunities in Libya. The 1999 oil price recovery was maintained in 2000, providing the Libyan Government with a strong revenue base to underpin a significant increase in infrastructural investment in its planning targets for 2001–2005. There was economic growth of around 2% in real terms in 1999, when estimated GDP per head was equivalent to US $7,900 in terms of 'purchasing-power parity' (PPP), and real growth of 5% in 2000, when GDP per head in terms of PPP was estimated at US $8,900. In that year the rate of inflation was estimated at 18.5% and some 30% of the population was unemployed. Western analysts estimated Libya's real GDP growth in 2001 at about 2% and forecast further growth of 2.5% in 2002.

The contrast between US and non-US policies towards Libya became sharper in 2001, when the renewal of US sanctions in August coincided with a further strengthening of most European countries' economic relations with Libya, assisted by the conclusion of the Lockerbie trial in January 2001 (see History) and the continuing buoyancy of petroleum prices. The Libyan Government's priority remained the lifting of US sanctions (in order that US oil companies could resume activities in Libya), to which end it appeared in May 2002 to be ready to pay compensation totalling US $2,700m. to the families of the 270 Lockerbie victims. However, amidst uncertainty about whether such an offer had been officially made, the US Government ruled out removing sanctions on Libya in the foreseeable future.

AGRICULTURE AND FISHING

Agriculture dominated the economy until the discovery of petroleum, providing around 50% of employment up until the early 1970s. By 1997 agriculture and fishing accounted for an estimated 7% of GDP and 17% of employment. The Qaddafi Government has attached high priority to agriculture, investing an estimated US $24,000m. in this sector in 1970–88. Government support for agricultural development was reaffirmed in Col Qaddafi's decision to make 1990 the 'year of agriculture', but the aim of achieving self-sufficiency in food remained a distant prospect, as in the 1990s and early 2000s Libya continued to import some 75% of its food requirements.

About 95% of Libya's land area is desert. Of the remainder, a high percentage is used for grazing, only 1.4% is arable, and 0.1% is irrigated. In mid-1970 all Italian-owned land and property in Libya, including 37,000 ha of cultivated land, was confiscated and plans were made to distribute the expropriated lands to Libyan farmers, with government credits for seed, fertilizers and machinery. Several very large contracts were awarded for reclamation and irrigation work in various scheduled areas. The best-known schemes, dating from the 1970s, are the Kufra oasis project to irrigate 10,000 ha; the Tawurgha project to reclaim 3,000 ha; the Sarir reclamation project; the Jebel al-Akhdar project; the Jefara plain project; and the Wadi Qatara reclamation project. The Wadi Jaref dam, one of the biggest in Libya, went into operation in 1976. All projects are meant to be fully integrated, providing for the establishment of farms, the building of rural roads, irrigation and drainage facilities and, in some cases, the introduction of agro-industries.

The Government invested a total of LD 700m. in agriculture over the 10-year period 1973–83. The Three-Year Plan, as revised in February 1975, provided LD 566.9m. for agricultural development and agrarian reform. The revised 1976–80 Development Plan provided LD 498m. plus LD 977m. for integral developments. Indeed, an important feature of Libya's economic planning in the 1970s was the high priority being given to agriculture. In 1975 agricultural development absorbed 21% of total budget expenditure whilst in 1976 it had risen to a corresponding 30%. In the 1978 financial year, the agricultural sector was allocated 18.9% of budgeted development expenditure and 14.6% of overall budget spending. In most other oil-rich countries, agriculture hardly received more than 10% of development funds. In 1979, however, investment in agriculture decreased, receiving only 6.4% of the general budget. In relative terms, the budget allocated to agriculture was expected to continue to decrease slightly during the 1980s, as the 1981–85 Five-Year Plan gave greater priority to industry. Nevertheless, the absolute level of expenditure on the agricultural sector was scheduled to increase. Thus, in the 1976–80 Development Plan LD 1,600m., or 21% of expenditure, were allocated to agriculture, whereas in the 1981–85 Plan the estimated expenditure on agriculture was LD 3,000m., representing about 20% of the total. This latest plan also envisaged that the proportion of the working population employed in agriculture would decline from 18.9% in 1980 to 16.8% in 1985. However, between 1983 and 1985, successive development budgets were underspent, and despite the official priority awarded to agricultural development, the agricultural sector was one of the most seriously affected, receiving 81.3% of budgeted investment in 1983, 86.9% in 1984, and only 66.7% in 1985.

In spite of the money invested in the sector, results in terms of production have been largely unsatisfactory. Climatic and soil factors will, it is hoped, cease to play such a large part in fluctuations of output, once irrigation schemes are operational and the distribution and use of fertilizers is well established. There have been signs in the production figures that this is indeed happening; according to the UN Food and Agriculture Organization (FAO), output of cereals increased from 62,000 metric tons in 1970 to 299,000 tons in 1988, while, over the same period, annual production of meat rose from 48,000 tons to 171,000 tons, root crops from 10,000 tons to 115,000 tons, soil crops from 20,000 tons to 31,000 tons and pulses from 2,000 tons to 12,000 tons. Nevertheless, in overall terms, the agricultural sector has not fulfilled expectations, and Libya continues to import around 80% of its food requirements, the value of which totalled US $1,117.3m. in 1987 (compared with $123.4m. in 1970). Problems, such as the lack of trained technicians and administrators and poor education among the farming communities, are not easily solved; Libya is obliged for the present to rely heavily on foreign expertise. The implementation of the various proposed agricultural projects has been particularly slow. In 1996 Libyan grain production amounted to some 360,000 tons, sufficient to supply about 20% of the country's cereal consumption. In 1999 Libya had an annual import requirement of between 600,000 and 700,000 tons of durum and other milling wheat and of about 700,000 tons of flour.

In 2001–02 Libya continued to invest heavily in a massive integrated water-supply project (the GMR) to serve both urban and agricultural users. This project has been under development since the 1980s and has resulted gradually in the provision of substantial additional quantities of water for coastal agricultural development (see Power and Water, below).

Animal husbandry is the basis of farming in Libya and is likely to remain so until irrigation and reclamation measures really start to take effect. During the mid-1970s the breeding of cattle for dairy produce was expanded and livestock was imported on an increasing scale from a number of sources. Breeding cattle have been supplied by the United Kingdom, and stock-raising co-operation agreements signed with Argentina, Romania and Australia. There has also been a substantial expansion in camel and poultry numbers. In 1996 livestock farming contributed about half of the value of Libya's total agricultural output of US $1,100m.

In July 1990 FAO held a special conference to raise funds to launch an emergency programme to eradicate from Libya the screw-worm fly, a parasitic insect which attacks livestock and wildlife. The fly was reported to have made its first appearance outside the western hemisphere in Libya some two years earlier, and the extent of its spread had raised fears that it would quickly infest the whole of the African continent. In January 1991 the International Fund for Agricultural Development (IFAD) launched a US $3m. pilot project as part of the programme, to which some $46m. had been pledged by February 1991. In October 1991 FAO was able to report that the screw-worm eradication programme in Libya had been successful and that the forecast continental infestation had been averted.

Of the cereal crops, barley, which is the staple diet of most of the population, is the most important, although, despite wide fluctuations from year to year in the yields of both crops, production of wheat now equals barley output. Olives and citrus fruit are grown mainly in the west of the country, and other important food crops are tomatoes, almonds, castor beans, groundnuts and potatoes, also grown mainly in the west. Dates are produced in oases in the south and on the coastal belt. As part of the Jebel al-Gharbi project, 1.5m. fig, olive and apple trees are to be planted, thus expanding the country's fruit production capacity. Esparto grass, which grows wild in the Jebel, is used for the manufacture of high-quality paper and banknotes and was formerly Libya's most important article of export.

The 1976–80 Development Plan envisaged an annual growth of 15.8% in domestic production, so that Libya would be self-sufficient in vegetables and dairy products by 1980 and would also be able to produce 92% of its fruit requirements and 75% of its meat and wheat consumption. However, these targets were too optimistic and were not achieved. In September 1984 Col Qaddafi said that, for climatic reasons, Libya had achieved only 66% self-sufficiency in wheat and barley and that 60% of meat and 40% of milk requirements were produced locally.

Although the Government has attempted some desert reclamation and afforestation projects, many have proved to be based on over-optimistic estimates of long-term environmental potential and economic return. Government-financed irrigation projects, for example, have resulted in serious groundwater depletion in north-western Libya.

The offshore waters abound in fish, especially tunny and sardines, but most of the fishing is done by Italians, Greeks or Maltese. Of special importance are the sponge-beds along the wide continental shelf. These are exploited by foreign fishermen and divers, mainly Greeks from the Dodecanese. As part of the expansion of Libya's fishing industry, the Zliten fishing port was opened in October 1983 at a cost of US $16.8m. It is designed for use by 40 trawlers and provides storage for 200 metric tons of fish, together with refrigeration facilities for up to 20 tons of fish per day. In early 1990 the Arab Fund for Economic and Social Development (AFESD) agreed to lend Libya 11m. Kuwaiti dinars for the construction of two fish canning factories. An $18m. project to construct a fishing harbour at Susa was due to be undertaken by Greek contractors in 1993–94. A $20m. project to establish a fishing port at Marsa Zuaga with a capacity for 10 trawlers and up to 70 smaller boats was at an advanced planning stage in 1996. The Marine Wealth Secretariat planned eventually to establish up to 24 new fishing ports along the Libyan coast. In 1997 the greater part of a $66.9m. loan from the Islamic Development Bank was allocated to fisheries projects. The 2001–2005 development plan encouraged foreign investment in the fisheries sector.

MINING AND ENERGY

Non-hydrocarbon mineral resources in Libya include iron ore at Wadi Shatti in the south of the country. Proposals to mine these reserves (estimated to exceed 700m. metric tons) have appeared in official development plans since the mid-1970s, but remained unimplemented at the end of the century, owing to the major cost implications of the project, which included a requirement for a 900-km rail link to transport ore to the coastal region, where steel production has been developed using imported iron ore (see Industry and Manufacturing, below). In 1997 the technical director of the Libyan Co for Iron and Steel announced that Libya was seeking foreign joint-venture partners for the development of iron-ore mining at Wadi Shatti. The 2001–2005 development plan listed non-hydrocarbon minerals as a sector in which foreign participation would be particularly welcome.

That petroleum was present in both Tripolitania and Cyrenaica had long been suspected and, for several years after Libya became independent, a large number of the bigger oil companies carried out geological surveys of the country. In 1955 a petroleum law came into force setting up a petroleum commission, which was empowered to grant concessions on a 50-50 profit-sharing basis, with parts of each concession being handed back to the Government after a given period. Under this law, concessions were granted to many US companies and to British, French and other foreign groups.

Important petroleum strikes first began to be made in 1957, and 10 years later Libya was already the fourth largest exporter in the world. The initial expansion of the Libyan petroleum industry was particularly rapid, owing to political stability, proximity to the Western European markets, and to the petroleum's lack of sulphur, which made it especially suitable for refining. The closure of the Suez Canal in 1967 was also an important factor in the growth of the industry. Production rose from 20,000 barrels per day (b/d) in 1962 to a peak of 3.3m. b/d in 1970, or 159.7m. metric tons in annual terms, equivalent to 13.6% of total output by then and future members of OPEC and to 6.8% of world oil production. Output declined steadily to 71.3m. tons in 1975 (partly because of the reopening of the Suez Canal in 1974), rose again to 100.7m. tons in 1979, but then fell in the 1980s, reaching 47.9m. tons in 1987 (its lowest level since 1964), when Libya accounted for only 5% of OPEC production and 1.7% of world output. In 1988–89 a higher level of output was recorded, however. Production accelerated in 1990, as Libya took advantage of the rise in world petroleum prices caused by the 1990–91 Gulf crisis, and in mid-1993 the production level remained well above the depressed levels of the mid-1980s.

Oil is exported from five different sea terminals, connected to the various fields by pipelines built by the five groups that have made the major finds. The pipeline system and the terminals are, however, available to other groups. The first of the five terminals to be opened was at Mersa Brega on the Gulf of Sirte (Surt), in 1961. The pipeline was built to Bir Zelten, in Cyrenaica, about 300 km south of Benghazi, where Esso Standard (Libya) had found oil in 1959. This group also operated a refinery at Mersa Brega and a gas liquefaction plant to prepare gas for shipment to Italy and Spain. The terminal for the Oasis group's Hofra field is at Ras as-Sidr, to the west of Mersa Brega. The Mobil/Gelsenberg group also found petroleum near Hofra, but built another pipeline to Ras Lanouf, just east of Ras as-Sidr. From a fourth terminal at Mersa al-Hariga, near Tobruk, a pipeline about 500 km long runs to Sarir, then the BP/Bunker Hunt concession. The terminal at Zuetina (az-Zuwaitinah) was opened in 1968 to serve the Augila and Idris fields. Here a US company, Occidental, which did not even obtain its concession until early in 1966, had found petroleum in large quantities. The Amoseas group, which produced petroleum from the Nafoora field, not far from Augila, had a pipeline connected to the Ras Lanouf terminal.

Libya has been a leader of those petroleum producers that demanded participation in petroleum activities, the company that later became the National Oil Corpn (NOC) having been founded in 1968 for that express purpose. Extensive negotiations took place between the Libyan Government and the various petroleum producers in the early 1970s, with the result that, in 1973, the Libyan Government acquired a 51% share in the Libyan operations of Agip, Conoco/Marathon/Amerada Hess, Exxon, Mobil and Occidental, while it completely nationalized the holdings of Amoseas, BP/Bunker Hunt, Shell, Texaco, California Asiatic and Atlantic Richfield. Most outstanding claims by the companies were settled in 1977, following arbitration.

At the beginning of 1980, the experienced Secretary for Petroleum, 'Izz ad-Din Mabrouk, was replaced by Abd as-Salam Muhammad Zagaar, for failing to accelerate full Libyanization of the oil industry. In a restructuring of the management of state petroleum concerns during the previous year, the NOC's operational responsibilities had been devolved to specialist subsidiary companies, leaving the NOC as a holding company responsible for strategic planning and supervision of the state oil sector. By the end of 1982 the Libyan State had an 81% interest in the Libyan operations of Elf Aquitaine, 59.2% in Oasis, 51% in Occidental and 50% in Agip. All of Exxon's Libyan interests were taken over by the state when the company withdrew in 1981, and, after a year's prevarication, Mobil, which first began operating in Libya in 1955, announced its withdrawal from exploration and production activities at the end of 1982. In mid-1985 Occidental agreed to sell 25% of its oil production and exploration facilities in Libya to the Austrian state oil company ÖMV AG. These holdings provided about one-half of Occidental's net income in 1979 and 1980, but the proportion fell to less than 20% of the total in 1984. By 1988, following the withdrawal of US companies from their Libyan operations (see below), the overall state share in oil output was 82%, with Italian, German, Austrian and French operators producing the remaining 18%.

During 1979 Libya aligned itself with Iran as a 'hawk' in terms of the international oil market, and at the beginning of 1980 raised its oil price by 28% to US $30 per barrel, only to raise it to $34.50 two weeks later. A further increase in May brought the price to $36.12 per barrel. This aggressive pricing policy continued throughout 1980, and in January 1981, the price of top-grade Zuetina was raised to $41 per barrel. In 1979 Libya's export revenue from petroleum and derivatives totalled $16,000m., and in 1980 it amounted to a record $21,919m. With the world oil glut persisting, the price of Zuetina and Brega crude was lowered to $39.9 per barrel in mid-1981, but this was still higher than most other world petroleum prices. In the summer of 1981 BP suspended liftings of Libyan petroleum, owing to its high price, and the 'spot' market price of Libyan oil then fell rapidly to $33 per barrel. Total Libyan output declined to 58.7m. metric tons in 1981 (equivalent to 1.22m. b/d), while oil revenues fell to $15,500m.

During 1982 OPEC set Libya's production ceiling at 750,000 b/d but actual production averaged 1.135m. b/d (54.7m. metric

tons in annual terms). At the end of 1982 spot prices for Libyan crude petroleum were as much as US $4 per barrel below the official price. The March 1983 OPEC agreement gave Libya a quota of 1.1m. b/d, which represented some recognition of Libya's determination to continue with relatively high levels of production. The meeting set prices for Libyan oil at $30.5 per barrel for Brega 40° crude and $29.2 for Amna 36°. During most of 1983 Libya was producing only slightly more than the set OPEC quota, and the Government's eventual petroleum revenues for the year were some $13,500m. The downward trend in oil prices on the spot market continued in 1984, during which Libyan production continued at just over 1.1m. b/d. In October OPEC decided to reduce its collective production to 16m. b/d, as a result of which Libya accepted one of the largest quota reductions, of 990,000 b/d. The country dissociated itself from the OPEC agreement on a new price structure, which was reached in January 1985, and the cost of Libya's Brega blend was held at $30.40 per barrel. However, as a large proportion of Libyan sales at the time were accounted for by barter deals involving discounts, the fact that its official price remained unchanged was of limited significance. During 1985 Libya consistently exceeded its OPEC production quota (average output during the year was 1.11m. b/d), but petroleum revenues continued to decline, falling to about $10,000m. in 1985, from $13,000m. in 1984. As market prices fell in 1986, Libya, Iran and Algeria opposed OPEC's majority policy of abandoning production restraint and seeking a 'fair' share of the world market as compensation for lower prices, advocating instead reductions in production as a means to revive prices. Accordingly, Libyan production was reduced in 1986 to an average of 1.01m. b/d (49.9m. tons), effectively anticipating the reintroduction of an OPEC production ceiling in the last four months of the year, when Libya's quota averaged some 995,000 b/d. Nevertheless, a decline in spot prices to under $10 per barrel in mid-1986 led to a severe fall in Libya's oil revenues for the year, to about $5,000m.

Another important development in 1986 was the enforced withdrawal of US petroleum companies from Libya. Having banned imports of Libyan petroleum in 1982, the US Government complemented this with a ban on imports of petroleum products in November 1985. Then, in January 1986, convinced of Libya's involvement in international terrorism, President Reagan 'froze' Libyan assets in the USA, and ordered all commercial transactions between US companies and Libya to cease by the beginning of February. The instruction was modified in February to allow about one dozen US companies in Libya (including five oil companies with equity holdings there) to continue their operations for a transitional period, while they terminated their activities. The oil companies (Occidental, Conoco, Marathon, Amerada Hess and W. R. Grace) ceased operations in Libya on 30 June, the new deadline that President Reagan had set in May. A three-year 'standstill period' officially expired at the end of June 1989, but has continued to be observed by Libya as a means of exerting pressure for the repeal of the US sanctions. Amid reports of renewed negotiations between Libya and the US companies, the Libyan Secretary for Petroleum confirmed, in March 1991, that the Government had no plans to sell the US companies' assets in Libya, adding that the companies were free to resume operations at any time.

In December 1986 OPEC imposed a ceiling of 15.8m. b/d on collective production for the first half of 1987, incorporating a reduction of 7.25% in members' quotas, which, it was hoped, would support a fixed price for OPEC petroleum of US $18 per barrel, which was applied from 1 February 1987. Libya's quota was reduced to 948,000 b/d. In June 1987 OPEC decided to retain the $18 reference price but to increase collective production by 800,000 b/d, to 16.6m. b/d, during the second half of the year, giving Libya a quota of 996,000 b/d. Although quota violations by some member states and the non-participation of Iraq made the ceiling on output a purely notional one, Libya's production in 1987 was close to its quota, at about 975,000 b/d (47.9m. metric tons in the year, its lowest output since 1964), and revenues fell below $5,000m. At meetings of OPEC held in December 1987 and May 1988, it was agreed to retain the output ceiling of 16.6m. b/d and the reference price of $18 per barrel for two further periods of six months, despite widespread quota violations, which had contributed to a renewed decline in the price of petroleum on the spot market. The price of the Brent blend, a widely traded North Sea crude (to which the Libyan blends Zuetina, Brega, Sirtica, es-Sidr, Sarir and Amna were linked in July 1988), declined to $11.20 per barrel in early September 1988. Libya's production of crude petroleum during 1988 averaged 1.055m. b/d (50.6m. tons), slightly above its OPEC quota, again yielding revenues of less than $5,000m. In November 1988 OPEC agreed to an output ceiling of 18.5m. b/d, to be imposed from January 1989. Libya's share of the total was to be 1.037m. b/d. In June 1989 oil ministers from OPEC member states met and agreed a new production ceiling of 19.5m. b/d, of which Libya was allocated a quota of 1.093m. b/d. Actual Libyan production in 1989 averaged 1.145m. b/d (54.8m. tons), yielding revenues of $7,846m., according to Libyan data. At the OPEC meeting of November 1989, quotas for the first half of 1990 were redistributed within a raised production ceiling of 22m. b/d, Libya's share being set at 1.233m. b/d. Actual Libyan output was, however, raised to 1.65m. b/d in early 1990 (allegedly to test sustainable production capacity), before being reduced to 1.35m. b/d from mid-March. At the OPEC meeting of July 1990, Libya pressed for quota parity with Kuwait but was again allocated 1.233m. b/d within an overall production ceiling of 22.5m. b/d, designed to underpin a minimum reference price of $21 per barrel.

However, the situation was then transformed by the onset of the Gulf crisis in August 1990 and by a rapid rise in world oil prices to more than US $30 per barrel. Libya refused to attend an emergency OPEC meeting held in Vienna in late August, at which it was decided to suspend quotas to allow members to take advantage of the embargoes imposed on Iraqi and Kuwaiti petroleum production. While expressing opposition to this decision, Libya proceeded to raise its production as quickly as possible, to almost 1.5m. b/d by October, with the result that its total oil revenues in 1990 increased by 23%, compared with 1989, to $9,700m. The average production level for 1990 was 1.355m. b/d (the highest annual average since 1980). Following the end of the Gulf conflict in February 1991 and the stabilization of world petroleum prices at pre-crisis levels, OPEC reimposed quotas from the second quarter of 1991, Libya's allocation being 1.425m. b/d within an overall production ceiling of 22.3m. b/d. For 1992 Libya's OPEC quota was set at 1.409m. b/d, later reduced to 1.35m. b/d from 1 April 1993 and adjusted to 1.39m. b/d from 1 October 1993. Actual Libyan output averaged 1.54m. b/d in 1991 and 1.475m. b/d in 1992 (producing revenue of at least $10,000m. per year). During 1993 Libyan oil production averaged 1.4m. b/d, a level that was steadily maintained in the first half of 1994. The monthly average spot price of Brega crude, which had fallen from over $18 per barrel to under $14 per barrel during the course of 1993, had recovered to more than $16 per barrel by the second quarter of 1994. Libyan oil output averaged 1.43m. b/d in 1994, 1.44m. b/d in 1995 and 1.45m. b/d in 1996. Libya's proven oil reserves (the largest of any African country) rose by nearly 30% in 1995 to 29,500m. barrels, remaining at this level throughout the six succeeding years, although in early 2002 the NOC confirmed that it hoped that proven reserves would increase by 35–40% by 2007. At the end of 2001 existing proven reserves were sufficient to last for 57.3 years at the current rate of production.

In March 1989 the Petroleum Secretariat was revived, after a three-year period in which control of the oil industry had been in the hands of the national companies. The revived Petroleum Secretariat then drafted plans to reorganize and develop Libya's petroleum sector, which were implemented following the appointment as Secretary for Petroleum, in October 1990, of Abdullah al-Badri, hitherto Chairman of the NOC. The changes involved a drastic reduction of the NOC's powers and the elevation to a dominant role of the Secretariat for Petroleum, to which all state oil companies were now required to report directly.

Although there was an increase in exploration activity in the early 1980s, sharp reductions in oil revenues from 1986 onwards resulted in a decline not only in exploration but also in development work on discovered fields. Moreover, the deficiencies in expertise and technology resulting from the withdrawal of US operators in 1986 (and compounded by the subsequent imposition of sanctions by the USA on Libya) were only partially compensated by European, Canadian and Asian companies. Over the decade as a whole, only some 20% of current output

was replaced by new proven reserves, while, as a result of poor state management, several established fields fell substantially below their theoretical production capacity.

Against this background, the Libyan authorities re-emphasized the need for an active exploration campaign, to which LD 200m. (US $700m.) were allocated in the NOC's 1991/92 budget. In particular, the Government was keen to evaluate the oil potential of parts of the country outside the Sirte basin in north-central Libya, where the commercial fields were grouped. There were two main areas of interest—western Libya (formerly Tripolitania) and offshore. The Bouri offshore oilfield, situated some 125 km north-west of Tripoli, was brought into production in August 1988. In April 1989 Libya's NOC and the Tunisian state petroleum enterprise, ETAP, formed a Joint Oil Co (JOC) to exploit the '7 November' oilfield straddling the two countries' continental shelf boundary, but did not finalize a development programme until May 1997, when a production-sharing contract was awarded to a Saudi-Malaysian consortium. A subsidiary of Saudi Arabia's Nimr Petroleum Co held a 55% interest and was to act as operator. Nimr's partner in this venture was a subsidiary of the Malaysian state oil company Petronas. New exploration concessions awarded to foreign oil companies in late 1990 and early 1991 included substantial offshore areas north-west of Tripoli.

Exploration also continued in other parts of the country, with some work being undertaken in the largely unexplored south. New finds continued to be made in the Sirte basin, despite the intensive exploration of previous years. In 1976, Occidental brought the new Almas field into production and the Libyan Umm al-Jawaby company also had two commercial finds, one on the eastern side of the Sirte basin and one on the west. In 1984 an oilfield with reserves estimated at 624m. barrels was discovered north-west of the Abu at-Tifl field.

In the Murzuk basin, in south-western Libya, Rompetrol of Romania was the original foreign contractor for the development of a new field (NC-115), later designated Sharara, with estimated reserves of up to 2,000m. barrels, exploitation of which required the construction of extensive oilfield storage facilities, a pipeline network and other infrastructure. By 1993 implementation of this project (originally approved in 1989) was seriously behind schedule because of financial constraints, prompting Rompetrol to sell its stake in the NC-115 field to Spain's Repsol Exploración. Also prioritized in the early 1990s were water-injection projects to increase output from certain established fields. These included the giant Sarir field in the Sirte basin, where production had seldom exceeded one-half of its capacity since nationalization, but which was scheduled to be raised from a current output of 200,000 b/d to 600,000 b/d by 1994; the field was also to supply associated gas to power-stations driving the GMR irrigation project (see Power and Water, below). In June 1992 OMV of Austria announced a promising new oil discovery in a block some 350 km south of Benghazi. It was officially claimed in 1994 that Libya was currently investing 23% of its oil revenues in petroleum exploration, production and development operations. In mid-1996 seven seismic crews were actively exploring for petroleum in Libya, compared with three or four crews in the previous year. Development of the Murzuk basin field NC-115 was meanwhile proceeding under the management of a consortium led by Repsol Exploración, which started commercial production in December 1996 and was expected to reach an output level of 200,000 b/d by the end of 2001. In June 1996 a 5,000-sq km concession in the Sirte basin was awarded to a consortium led by PanCanadian Petroleum, which undertook to spend US $17m. on exploration over a period of five years.

In February 1998 British operator Lasmo announced that a strike the previous year in the Murzuk basin, designated the Elephant field, was possibly the largest oil discovery in Libya since the mid-1980s, containing estimated reserves of over 500m. barrels. Plans were subsequently developed for the start of production from the field in late 2002 at an initial rate of 50,000 b/d, rising eventually to 150,000 b/d. Lasmo's Libyan discoveries were of major interest to the Italian energy group, ENI, which acquired Lasmo in January 2001. Further finds were announced by Petrofina of Belgium in February 1998 and by Lundin Oil of Sweden in April. Elf Aquitaine announced an offshore oil discovery in an area close to the Tunisian border in early 1999. In June 2001 Lundin announced the sale of its stake in the En Naga field, containing an estimated 100m. barrels of reserves, to the Canadian company Petro-Canada (subject to approval by the NOC).

Libya's 1997 oil output averaged 1.49m. b/d, somewhat above the country's existing OPEC quota of 1.39m. b/d. At the start of 1998 Libya's OPEC production ceiling was raised to 1.52m. b/d, this quota being subsequently reduced to 1.44m. b/d from April 1998 and to 1.32m. b/d from July 1998, as the OPEC members reacted to a sharp decline in world oil prices. Overall, Libya's 1998 oil output averaged 1.48m. b/d (0.6% less than the 1997 average), while its estimated oil revenue declined by more than 30% from around US $8,300m. in 1997 to less than $5,800m. in 1998. With effect from April 1999 Libya further reduced its official oil production ceiling to 1.23m. b/d within the framework of a new OPEC quota agreement designed to reinforce a recent strengthening in world petroleum prices (which by mid-1999 had recovered to their highest level for 18 months). Average Libyan output for the whole of 1999 was 1.43m. b/d (3.8% less than the 1998 average). In 2000 Libya's official OPEC production quota was raised to 1.32m. b/d from April and 1.36m. b/d from July, in the context of OPEC initiatives to bring oil prices back down to OPEC's target level. In practice, Libyan oil output remained above-quota throughout the first half of 2000, averaging an estimated 1.42m. b/d in the month of June. In September Libya's quota was once again raised, to 1.40m. b/d, effective from 1 October. There was a further quota increase, to 1.43m. b/d, from 1 November. Libya's average oil output for 2000 was 1.48m. b/d.

In 2001 Libya's official OPEC production quota was reduced to 1.35m. b/d from 1 February, to 1.30m. b/d from 1 April, and to 1.24m. b/d from 1 September. From 1 January 2002 it was further reduced to 1,16m. b/d. Actual average oil output in 2001 was 1,37m. b/d, and in January 2002 production was running at about 8% above the latest OPEC quota. In March 2002 Western petroleum industry sources estimated Libya's recoverable hydrocarbon reserves at 40,400m. barrels of oil equivalent (BOE) and its likely reserves yet to be proven at a further 16,500m. BOE.

In mid-2001 the NOC said that it expected Libya's sustainable oil production capacity to rise to 1.7m. b/d by the end of 2002 as development work proceeded in newer fields, while enhanced recovery projects were implemented in some older fields. A total of US $1,500m. was earmarked for investment in the upgrading of pipelines and other oil industry infrastructure in 2001–05. Libya's target for sustainable oil production capacity after 2005 was 2m. b/d. Evaluation was under way by the NOC in 2001 of the first oil company bids for exploration and production-sharing rights offered in a new licensing round, launched in 2000. Some 14 exploration blocks, divided into three packages, were included in the initial invitation for bids (which closed in January 2001), while a further 137 blocks (covering 835,000 sq km of hitherto unexplored territory) were available for subsequent licensing through a less formal bidding process with no closing date. There was strong interest in the new licensing round on the part of foreign (predominantly European) petroleum companies, stimulated in part by research suggesting that Libya was one of the world's most promising hydrocarbon exploration areas.

The appointment in November 2001 of Abd al-Hafiz Zleitni, a former Secretary of Economy and Trade, as Chairman of the NOC was received positively by the international petroleum industry, which expected that he would expedite the drafting of a new petroleum investment law easing existing restrictions on joint-venture agreements. Non-US foreign companies also hoped that the NOC would reach swift decisions on the award of new exploration licences under the round launched in 2000. However, by mid-2002 it was apparent that NOC policy was to continue to delay making new awards until US companies were permitted to resume activities in Libya. To exert pressure to that end, the NOC warned the Oasis group of US companies (Amerada Hess, Conoco, Marathon and Occidental) that their existing concessions, which were due to expire in 2005, would be reallocated to other companies if they did not resume development of them by the end of 2002. In an attempt to head off this threat, in early 2002 the US Department of State authorized the Oasis companies to renegotiate their production agreements

with the NOC, in order to facilitate their return to Libyan operations upon the lifting of sanctions.

Libya's reserves of natural gas at the end of 2001 were estimated at 1,310,000m. cu m. Marketed gas output (excluding gas flared or reinjected into the oil wells from which most Libyan gas is derived) totalled 6,780m. cu m in 1992—its highest level since 1979. Output in 2001 was 5,400m. cu m. Inaugurated in 1971, a liquefaction plant at Mersa Brega was the world's first scheme to convert flared gas into liquefied natural gas (LNG), annual exports of which, mainly to Italy and Spain, reached more than 4,000m. cu m in the mid-1970s, although they fell to under 1,500m. cu m in the 1980s, as Italy switched to cheaper Algerian supplies by gas pipeline. Further trade with Italy became impractical in 1990, when the Italian LNG import terminal was converted to accept normal-grade LNG. Spain, which still has import facilities for the high-calorie LNG currently exported by Libya, now takes the greater part of Libya's LNG exports; a new 20-year contract, for the supply of at least 1,000m. cu m per year, was signed with Enagás of Spain in March 1991. Exports to Spain totalled 1,800m. cu m in 1992, however, in 2001 they totalled just 770,000 cu m. A contract to supply Turkey with 1,500m. cu m of LNG over 25 years was signed in 1988, but implementation awaits the completion of a terminal at Marmara Ereglisi. Libya announced plans in 1993 to convert the Mersa Brega plant (which has a nominal daily capacity of 10.8m. cu m) to produce normal and low grades of LNG, rather than the high-calorie grade produced hitherto. However, when contractors who had submitted bids for this US $200m.-project studied the latest UN sanctions on Libya, it was clear that it would be impossible to carry out the work without importing equipment included on the list of embargoed items. Eager to link its own gas network with that of Algeria, in 1990 Libya initiated preparatory studies to extend its existing 670-km Mersa Brega–Homs coastal pipeline westward to the Tunisian border, with the eventual aim of linking up with the Algeria–Sicily pipeline running through Tunisia. The existing coastal pipeline had been completed by a Soviet company in 1988 and had opened in September 1989, with a capacity of 4m. cu m per year. At the same time, the concept of a direct pipeline linking Libya to Italy remained under consideration, despite previous assessments that its cost would be prohibitive. In December 1990 it was confirmed that Agip of Italy and the NOC were engaged in feasibility studies for a direct pipeline, which could form part of a massive gas development programme in Libya, costing up to $13,000m. Meanwhile, the NOC's priority plans included the development of the Kabir gasfield close to the Tunisian border, at an estimated cost of $80m., and the use of gas output from other fields to fuel the GMR irrigation project. In mid-1992 the French company Total signed a contract to take 300,000 metric tons of liquefied petroleum gas (LPG) from Libya starting in 1993 (the personal authorization of President Mitterrand was needed in view of the current UN sanctions against Libya). Agip revealed in March 1996 that it had drawn up plans to build a sub-sea pipeline to transport 8,000m. cu m of gas per year from Libya to Italy. In June 1996 (shortly before the implementation of the US 'secondary sanctions' legislation) Agip signed an addendum to a 1974 agreement with the NOC to cover gas development in onshore and offshore fields, the onshore gas to be marketed within Libya and the offshore gas to be piped to Italy. It was estimated that the so-called Western Desert gas export project would entail an investment of $4,500m. and would take four years to complete. Agip said in January 1997 that it had concluded 20-year sales agreements with Italian buyers for the full 8,000m. cu m that it planned to export each year. Because its development rights stemmed from agreements dating back to 1974, Agip said that it did not consider its Libyan gas development programme to be open to challenge as a 'new investment' under US sanctions laws.

In August 1998 Sirte Oil Co awarded a contract for the construction of a 142-km gas pipeline from Zuetina to Benghazi, while in early 1999 it awarded a contract for a 160-km pipeline between Homs and Tripoli. The latter contract included the installation of compressor stations to supply gas to a cement factory and a power-station. These projects formed part of a programme to expand the use of gas for power generation within Libya. In mid-1999 Sirte Oil Co was evaluating bids for development of a gas field at Attahaddy, 90 km north of Mersa

Brega, which was to be brought into production with a daily processing capacity of 9.8m. cu m.

In February 1999 Agip Gas (a Dutch-registered joint venture between Agip and the Libyan Government) appointed the gas division of the Italian energy group, ENI, as a project manager for the Western Desert gas export/sub-sea pipeline scheme. In December 1999 a French company (Technip Geoproduction) won the initial engineering and design contract for the project, and in February 2000 ENI concluded a sales contract with Edison International for the supply of Libyan gas to Edison's Italian power-stations. In November 2000 ENI concluded a 24-year contract to supply 2,000m. cu m of Libyan gas per year to Gaz de France. In contrast to the delay in authorizing new oil exploration (see above), the NOC and ENI in February 2002 activated the sub-sea gas export scheme by awarding the US $1,160m. contract to build the main production and gas processing facilities in Wafa to a consortium led by JGC of Japan. This was followed in June by the award of the first of three offshore packages to a consortium led by Saipem of Italy. In the same month, the China Engineering Petroleum and Construction Co was awarded a $156m. contract to build a 530-km twin gas and oil pipeline linking Wafa with a planned gas booster station at Melita.

On the marketing side, Libya concluded various agreements in the 1970s and 1980s involving the exchange of crude petroleum for specific goods or services. France, Italy, Poland, the former USSR, Yugoslavia and a number of other countries concluded barter deals with Libya, involving purchases of petroleum. Libya also has special oil arrangements with Brazil and Greece, and is committed, in principle, to reserve 4% of its output for delivery to African states. Libya's investments in the 'downstream' marketing of petroleum products in developed countries included the purchase, in 1986, of a 70% stake in the Italian Tamoil group, which subsequently provided an important overseas marketing outlet when an international oil glut developed in the late 1980s. Such overseas marketing investments are directed by the state-owned Oil Investments International Co (Oilinvest), established in 1988, while sales are effected through Chempetrol, a wholly-owned subsidiary, based in Malta.

Azzawiya refinery was opened in 1974 and enlarged in 1977 to a nominal capacity of 120,000 b/d. The other main refinery locations are at Tobruk, where a refinery with a capacity of 20,000 b/d was opened in 1986, at Ras Lanouf (near Sirte), where a 220,000-b/d refinery started production in February 1985, and at Brega, with a capacity of 10,000 b/d. Plans were announced in 1991 to build a refinery at Hymed, to be supplied from the Bouri offshore field. In the following year plans were announced for a 20,000 b/d refinery at Sebha to process crude from oilfields under development in the Murzuk basin. A $3,500m. refinery development programme was first prepared in 1993, but it was not until May 2002 that the first project was initiated with the award of a $280m. contract to LG Engineering of South Korea for the upgrading of the Azzawiya plant. Plans to upgrade the Ras Lanouf and Brega refineries were in preparation in mid-2002. Domestic consumption of refined products was estimated to be around 215,000 b/d in 2000.

INDUSTRY AND MANUFACTURING

The NOC opened its first petrochemicals plants in September 1977 at Mersa Brega, with an initial production capacity of 1,000 metric tons per day of ammonia and 1,000 tons per day of ethanol. Contracts to add 1,000 tons of ammonia capacity and 1,000 tons of urea capacity at Mersa Brega were awarded in 1978. A second urea plant with a capacity of 1,850 tons per day was opened in 1984. A chemicals complex at Abu Kammash went into production in 1980. Methanol production capacity, hitherto located mainly at the Mersa Brega complex, was supplemented in 1987 by the opening of a factory at al-Burayqah with a capacity of 2,000 tons per day. A 330,000 tons per year ethylene plant (the first of several petrochemical facilities developed around the new Ras Lanouf petroleum refinery) began production in 1987. Subsequent phases of the Ras Lanouf development included the addition of plants to produce monoethylene glycol, polyethylene (high and low density) and polypropylene.

According to the OPEC news agency, Libya invested some US $62,500m. between 1970 and 1983 to develop industry and reduce the country's dependence on the petroleum sector. The value of non-oil production activities rose from $1,610m. in 1970 to $15,280m. in 1983, and their contribution to GDP from 37% to 50%, reducing the share of the petroleum sector from 63% to 50%. An economic report covering the years 1970–86, which was released by JANA, the Libyan news agency, in September 1986, claimed that investment in the industrial sector during the period totalled LD 3,959.8m., enabling 139 projects to reach the production stage (52 food industry projects; 23 chemical and petrochemical industry factories; 17 mineral and engineering industry factories; 16 textile, clothing and leather goods factories; eight wood and paper industry factories). However, as oil revenues declined in the 1980s, the industrial sector, in common with other parts of the economy, suffered from underspending compared with budgeted figures.

In 1981 Libya started awarding contracts for construction of a steelworks at Misurata. Japan's Kobe Steel won a contract worth US $751m. for a section mill and a rod mill; a consortium of Korf Engineering of the Federal Republic of Germany and Voest Alpine of Austria won a $540m. contract for a steel production plant, while a $674m. contract for a second production plant was won by Friedrich Krupp of the Federal Republic of Germany; and two consortia, both led by Voest Alpine, won contracts for hot and cold rolling mills. In 1982 the Hyundai Engineering and Construction Co of South Korea won a contract worth $520m. to build a 480-MW power-station and a desalination plant, with a capacity of 31,500 cu m per day, to serve the steel complex. The contract for a port to handle imports of iron ore was awarded to Sezai Türkes Feyzi of Turkey. It was not until September 1990, after a series of delays caused mainly by financing difficulties when Libya's oil revenues fell significantly below target, that all the production units at the Misurata steel plant were reported to be operating, employing 3,500 Libyan nationals and 1,000 expatriate workers.

In 1991 the Misurata complex operated at about two-thirds of design capacity, producing an estimated 800,000 metric tons of steel during that year. Having failed to implement several earlier expansion plans, the Libyan Iron and Steel Co in late 1999 invited bids for a major increase in pickling capacity on a low-carbon steel line at Misurata and for reconstruction of an acid regeneration plant that had suffered fire damage in late 1997. In early 2000 bids were invited for a modernization programme at Misurata, including upgrading of existing electric arc furnaces and installation of a new ladle furnace. Liquid steel capacity was set to rise to about 2m. tons per year under this programme.

Construction work carried out under Libya's development programme gave rise to a rapidly increasing demand for cement. In 1987 cement production rose by 30%, compared with 1986, to 2.7m. metric tons, some 2m. tons less than the domestic requirement and more than 3m. less than rated capacity. In 1995 Libyan cement production exceeded local demand, with the surplus being exported to Egypt and Algeria. In November 1995 plans were announced to add 3,300 tons per day of new production capacity to a cement works at Zliten in order to meet an expected growth in demand when the GMR project entered its next phase (see Power and Water, below). The Danish company FLOTEC was awarded a contract in October 1985 to build a gypsum factory. The gypsum, which was used in cement production, would be exported to Europe. The project included the establishment of a natural gas energy plant at the factory and terminal facilities at the port of Tripoli. Other industrial diversification projects signed in 1991–92 included one with Candy Elettrodomestici of Italy for a refrigerator construction plant at Zuwara with a projected capacity of 80,000 units per year, and another with Gold Star of South Korea for a video-cassette recorder factory at Benghazi with a capacity of 70,000 recorders per year. A large pharmaceuticals plant, built by a Libyan state company in co-operation with Egyptian and Moroccan companies, opened at Rabta in September 1995. A truck assembly plant at Tripoli, owned 75% by the Libyan Government and 25% by Iveco Fiat of Italy, produced 2,961 vehicles in 1993. Investment of US $120m. was planned to increase the proportion of locally manufactured components to 40% by 1997 and to achieve a production volume of 4,000 vehicles in that year. More than 20,000 passenger cars were scheduled to be imported into Libya from South Korea and

Japan in 1995. In February 2000 Libya's first car assembly plant was opened in Tripoli by South Korea's Daewoo Corpn, acting as 'turnkey' contractor to the owner, Libyan Arab Domestic Investment Co (Ladico). Ladico subsequently invited bids for the establishment of four new car assembly plants in Libya with a combined capacity of 80,000 vehicles per year.

Many of the contracts at the peak of the construction boom in the 1970s were awarded to Turkish firms. In 1981 there were 102 Turkish companies operating in Libya, with an estimated 80,000 Turkish workers. However, falling oil revenues forced Libya to inform Turkey early in 1982 that it wanted to deduct US $70m. in oil debts from various Turkish firms. By early 1991 debts owed to Turkish contractors had reached some $600m., adversely affecting Libyan–Turkish relations, which remained strained until the following year, when a schedule of oil deliveries in lieu of debt payments was agreed in bilateral talks. By January 1995 (previously the target date for full repayment) Libya's outstanding debts to Turkish contractors were reported to have been reduced to $180m. In October 1996 Turkish government officials said that total payments arrears totalled $600m. (of which $160m. was principal and the remainder interest charges and other costs), for which the Libyan Government had issued promissory notes after a visit to Tripoli by the Turkish Prime Minister. These notes were to be honoured within three months, although it was not clear whether all payments would be made in convertible currency. The Turkish Contractors Association said in October 1996 that its members had so far carried out a total of $6,880m. worth of work in Libya and were currently contracted to work on projects worth $1,650m. South Korean companies, such as Daewoo, have also been involved in the implementation of new contracts in Libya. In May 1981 100 South Korean dockers were used to clear severe congestion at Benghazi port. The Daewoo Corpn was awarded a $337m. contract in 1985 to build sewer and water facilities, roads, pumping stations and a telephone system in Benghazi. The employment of Indian workers in Libya declined from 40,000 in the early 1980s to around 10,000 in the early 1990s, many Indian contractors having pulled out after disputes over non-payment for work carried out. In April 1995 the Libyan authorities agreed to settle $100m. of claims by Indian companies (most of them state-owned) over the next 12 months and to increase the recruitment of Indian workers in the future. At the end of 1996, when the contract to expand cement capacity at Zliten (see above) was awarded to an Iranian company, it was reported that Iranian companies were involved in negotiations for several other Libyan contracts, including reservoir and water pipeline building, railway and tramway schemes and a cattle-rearing project.

In 2000, according to Libyan officials, non-oil manufacturing contributed 12% of GDP and supplied 25%–30% of local demand for manufactures (although there was self-sufficiency in cement, iron and steel production).

POWER AND WATER

Power generation has been accorded a high priority in Libyan development planning. Since 1974 the Government has awarded several large contracts for power stations, some in association with desalination plants. During the 1976–80 period US $3,195m. were spent on power schemes. Installed generating capacity rose from 879 MW in 1975 to 1,700 MW in 1979. Under the 1980–85 plan, capacity was projected to increase from 1,950 MW to 3,878 MW. However, there were delays in power-station construction schemes, owing to lack of finance, and, according to the UN, installed capacity had declined to 1,460 MW in 1985. In 1982 an agreement was concluded with the USSR, designed to help to establish a national electricity grid by 1995, but it was not until 2000 that bids were invited to install a 1,500-km transmission line linking the east and west of the country. A 10-MW Soviet nuclear research reactor became operational at Tajura, near Tripoli, in 1982, but subsequent plans to develop a major nuclear generating plant were shelved in the mid-1980s. Work was scheduled to start in late 1993 on a three-year project to add more than 1,000 MW of new gas-turbine generating capacity at five Libyan power-stations, several of them awaiting expansion since the mid-1980s. The AFESD announced a $107m. loan package in April 1996, partly to finance improvements in Tripoli's power distribution system

and partly to finance the construction of a connection to the Egyptian electricity grid (completed in 2000). In November 1998 contracts were awarded for the construction of an AFESD-funded link between the Libyan and Tunisian electricity grids, as part of a long-term plan to integrate Libya's transmission network in a trans-national grid stretching along the North African coast. In early 1999 contracts were awarded for the installation of four 160-MW gas turbines for a power plant at Azzawiya, west of Tripoli.

Installed generating capacity in Libya in 1999 was estimated to total at least 4,500 MW. The General Electricity Corpn of Libya (Gecol) said in 2001 that it planned to invest $3,500m. to expand the country's installed generating capacity to 10,000 MW by 2010, of which 6,000 MW would be required to meet local peak demand in that year, the remaining capacity to be used to produce electricity for export. The largest plant planned in this programme was the 1,200–1,400-MW Gulf Steam power plant near Sirte, for which the contract was expected to be awarded before the end of 2002. A plan to lay a submarine cable to carry electricity from Libya to Italy was under evaluation in 2002. In January 2002 Technoprom of Russia signed a $600m. contract to undertake a 650-MW first phase expansion of the Tripoli West power station, for completion in 2005. It was envisaged that a further 650 MW would be installed in a second phase to be completed by 2010.

In 1982, prior to the unveiling of the GMR scheme (see below), plans were announced for a 462,000-cu m-per-day (cu m/d) desalination plant (Tripoli 1) to provide Tripoli with drinking water. Plans for a further 150,000 cu m/d desalination plant at Janzour, 20 km west of Tripoli, were also announced at the end of 1982. The site of Tripoli 1 was moved to Janzour in mid-1984. A water purification plant in Tobruk, with a daily capacity of 5,000 cu m for agricultural purposes (from 13,000 cu m of sewage), was inaugurated in April 1988. In 2001 three desalination plants, each with a capacity of 40,000 cu m/d, were under construction at Tobruk, Zuara and Sirte, while bidding was in progress for contracts to design three further plants at Abutoraba (40,000 cu m/d), Tripoli (250,000 cu m/d) and Benghazi (150,000 cu m/d). Five more desalination projects (four of them extensions to existing plants) with a combined capacity of 140,000 cu m/d were included in Gecol's US $900m. desalination expansion programme for 2000–10.

Libya's most ambitious project is the GMR, first announced in November 1983. Under the first stage of the irrigation and water-supply project, the Dong Ah Construction Industrial Co, from the Republic of Korea, was contracted to build a man-made river, at a cost of US $3,300m., to carry 2m. cu m of water per day along 2,000 km of pipeline from natural underground reservoirs at Tazerbo and Sarir, in the south-east Sahara desert, to Sirte and Benghazi and agricultural projects and towns on the Mediterranean coast, via Agedabia. A total of 270 wells are being drilled in the Tazerbo and Sarir areas, with the aim of irrigating approximately 280,000 ha, on which some 37,000 model farms are to be established. This is possibly the largest single contract ever awarded in the Middle East, and its cost had risen to $4,200m. by 1986. The $5,300m. second stage of the GMR will eventually pipe 2m. cu m of water per day from Sawknah to Tripoli, a distance of 600 km. Three additional stages are planned, including the extension of the first phase southward to Kufra oasis (doubling its capacity to 4m. cu m per day) and the construction of pipelines to serve the north-eastern coastal town of Tobruk (from Agedabia) and to link the eastern and western systems of the first two stages along the coast (Tripoli–Sirte), thereby creating a national water grid. If all phases are completed, there will be a total of 4,040 km of pipeline, with a water-carrying capacity of 6m. cu m/d. The eventual cost of the GMR, including agricultural infrastructure, could be as high as $25,000m., and it is thought that Libya may have difficulties in paying for it, particularly following Saudi Arabia's refusal to contribute aid. In September 1989 Dong Ah was also awarded the main contract for the second stage of the GMR, on which it began preparatory road construction in mid-1990.

With 25% of the first phase still to be completed, the entire project came under review in March 1991, owing to various unforeseen problems, including the production of heavily contaminated water from some test pumping, as a result of collapsing well screens. Nevertheless, at a grand ceremony held near Benghazi on 28 August 1991 and attended by various Arab and African leaders, the first phase of the GMR was inaugurated by Col Qaddafi, who turned on a tap starting the flow of water into one of the project's reservoirs. The increase in Libya's oil revenues in 1990–91 had eased the burden of financing this priority project, which continued to be supported by a consortium of Arab banks. The Government also remained committed to the original objective that 80% of the water supplied by the GMR would be allocated to agriculture (which already accounted for 85% of total water consumption), despite evidence that, taking into account the real unit cost of irrigation water, the cost of using it to cultivate cereals was currently some six times the prevailing world market price. Another problem was shortage of labour for the newly-created agricultural land, in the light of which the Government hoped to attract large numbers of Egyptian and Moroccan nationals to work on GMR farms. Other uncertainties surrounded the post-inauguration cost and practicalities of maintaining the GMR, it being suggested in some quarters that the weaknesses of Libya's socio-political system would result in the project's falling into disrepair. Among the special projects being assisted by the GMR Water Utilization Authority in mid-1991 were joint horticultural ventures with both private and state bodies from the Netherlands, in which particular emphasis was to be placed on the development of potato production for the lucrative north European market.

In mid-1993 the Dong Ah Construction Industrial Co, which had thus far completed 33% of the engineering and 20% of the construction work on its phase-two GMR contract, was instructed to modify certain pipeline routes and specifications in its future work schedule in ways that indicated a shift of priorities away from agricultural development in favour of accelerating the supply of water to coastal towns. The modifications effectively brought forward about half of the work originally included in phase three of the GMR plans, and would route an initial flow of 1.166m. cu m of water per day to the towns of Misurata and Khoms by 2000. Dong Ah, which at that time employed 10,000 staff on GMR projects, expected the modifications (costing an estimated US \$760m.) to add substantially to its labour requirement. At the Benghazi end of the GMR system, Dong Ah expected to link the Benghazi reservoir to the city's supply system by the end of the third quarter of 1993. The depletion rate of local groundwater sources in the Libyan coastal region was reported to be alarmingly high in 1993. By 1995 the GMR's phase-one transmission system was supplying Benghazi with 500,000 cu m of water per day, while further well-drilling was in progress to increase the volumes of water extracted at Sarir and Tazerbo. There was, however, no prospect of full utilization of the eastern trunk pipeline's transmission capacity of 2m. cu m per day until a planned network of branch pipelines was built to feed irrigation schemes. In 1995, agricultural usage of GMR water was restricted to a few small pilot schemes.

In 1995 the GMR's status as the centre-piece of Libya's economic development programme was highlighted by the inclusion in the national budget of allocations of US \$1,300m. for water transmission work and \$300m. for associated irrigation projects. Dong Ah was now employing 13,000 people on GMR works in Libya, including 2,500 at a plant manufacturing the world's largest pipes (4 m in diameter) and 4,000 involved in pipe-laying activities. Tripoli received its first supplies of GMR water via the western (phase-two) pipeline system at the beginning of September 1996. Final completion of phase two of the GMR project was scheduled for 1999. In all, the phase-two project specification, as modified in 1993, involved a total of 1,287 km of pipeline (of which 85% had been manufactured and about 70% had been laid by the start of 1996) with a daily transmission capacity of 2.5m. cu m of water drawn from 484 desert wells. The \$310m. contract to drill the last 247 of these wells was awarded to Dong Ah in April 1996 for completion within two years. In the same month Col Qaddafi informed Dong Ah that it would be awarded the contracts to build phases three and four of the GMR once designs were finalized. Phase three was intended to link Tobruk (500 km to the east) and Kufra (325 km to the south) to the phase-one supply system and to create a 180-km coastal link between the phase-one system serving Sirte and the phase-two system serving Tripoli. It would also include a 400-km pipeline from wells at Jaghboub

to the eastern coastal city of Tobruk. Intended to add almost 1.7m. cu m of water a day to the GMR network, phase three had an estimated cost of \$5,100m. and a target completion date of 2006. Phase four would involve the development of a new complex of desert wells at Waw al-Kabir in the Ghadames desert, to supply the city of Zuara and to be linked to Sirte via a 715-km pipeline system at an estimated cost of \$4,900m. The total value of Dong Ah's past and existing GMR contracts amounted to \$3,700m. for phase-one work and \$6,700m. for phase-two work.

Despite having issued a letter of intent to Dong Ah in November 1996, Libya opened phase three of the GMR to international bidding in March 1997. The position was complicated by the severe difficulties experienced by Dong Ah's parent company in South Korea as a result of the Asian economic crisis. In December 1997 the French company Dumex was reported to be the lowest bidder for the first of seven contracts for phase three of the GMR project, involving construction of a water conveyance system from Sirte to As-Sadadah linking phases one and two. However, the slump in world oil prices in 1998, and the consequential fall in Libyan oil revenues, served to delay the award of further GMR contracts. In mid-2000 (at which point the phase-two works were reported to be about 90% complete) the award of the first phase-three contract was still awaited. Contracts were awarded in June 2000 to German and Italian contractors for work (originally put out to tender in 1997) to install treatment facilities in the GMR's Tazerbo well-field, where high carbon dioxide levels were causing damage to pipework dating from phase one of the project.

In August 2000 Dong Ah applied to the GMR Authority for a 17-month extension of its contract period for phase-two works, but in November 2000 the South Korean company (which had debts of US \$2,900m.) suspended work in Libya after filing for bankruptcy. Dong Ah subsequently claimed that it was owed \$900m. for work on the GMR (including \$350m. for unfinished construction work), while Libya said in January 2001 that it would file a \$3,000m. damages claim in respect of Dong Ah's suspension of work on the GMR. Reports indicated that some \$700m. of phase-two construction work remained to be completed, as evidence emerged that the volume of water delivered via the GMR system had fallen to around 300,000 cu m daily (15% of phase-one design capacity), owing to leakage from pipelines. In March 2001 a South Korean court issued a liquidation order against Dong Ah, although the South Korean Government informed Libya that steps would be taken to ensure that the liquidation did not prevent arrangements being made to complete Dong Ah's work on the GMR (which it suggested should be taken over by Korea Express, hitherto a junior partner of Dong Ah in Libya). In the following month a Libyan delegation urged the South Korean Government to provide financial assistance to enable Dong Ah itself to complete the work. The solution eventually found was an agreement (the terms of which were not disclosed) under which Dong Ah would complete its contractual obligations with the assistance of the local Al-Nahr Co (ANC), itself a 50-50 joint venture between Dong Ah and the GMR Authority. In April 2002 SNC Lavalin of Canada took over from Dong Ah as operator and manager of the Sarir factory, which manufactured most of the pipes for the GMR.

The Government's undiminished commitment to the GMR project was shown by the selection in December 2001 of Nippon Koei of Japan to provide design and consultancy services for phase three of the project. However, reports in mid-2002 indicated that the supposed 'fast-track' first package of phase three, intended to increase the supply of water to phase one installations, had been delayed by the need to carry out further studies of the Kufra well-fields, while the contract for the Jaghboub-Tobruk pipeline was not expected to be awarded until late 2002 or early 2003.

TRANSPORT AND COMMUNICATIONS

Rapid growth in the volume of imports led to severe congestion at the main ports of Tripoli and Benghazi in the 1970s, after which these and other Libyan ports underwent large-scale expansion. It was reported in 2001 that a total of 15m. metric tons of freight was being handled each year by 10 Libyan sea ports. Libya's merchant fleet comprised 140 vessels in 2001.

A number of large road-building contracts were awarded to Egyptian companies in the 1970s and early 1980s. In 1980 an Indian company won a US $129m. contract for the construction of desert roads at a variety of locations throughout the country. The road from Tripoli to Sebha was opened at the end of 1983, providing 770 km of metalled surface. By the late 1990s Libya had around 85,000 km of roads, of which an estimated 50,000 km were paved. There have been no railways in Libya since 1964, when the Benghazi–Barce line was abandoned. In 1998 plans were announced to construct 2,178 km of track running east to west and 992 km running north to south. Talks were subsequently opened with Tunisian and Egyptian officials regarding the feasibility of cross-border links to the proposed Libyan railway. A contract to lay an initial 191 km of track and to install signalling and other facilities was awarded to China Civil Engineering Construction in March 2000. This work, scheduled for completion in 2003, formed part of the first phase of the project, linking Sirte to Ras Ajdir on the Tunisian border. Nearly two-thirds of the earthwork excavations for the 700-km Sirte-Ras Ajdir line had been completed by local contractors by mid-2001. The second phase of the project would extend the coastal line east from Sirte to Benghazi, while the third phase would further extend it from Benghazi to Musaid on the Egyptian border. Consultancy bids for second and third phase works were in preparation in 2001, while an initial feasibility study for the fourth phase of the project (a 1,500-km branch line running from Sirte via Sebha to the southern border of Libya) was being carried out by Rail India Technical and Economic Services. According to the Railway Executive Board, established to oversee the project, the Libyan railway would eventually acquire 244 diesel-electric locomotives and 8,500 other items of rolling stock and would carry 15m. tons of freight for Libyan industry and agriculture when completed.

The UN ban on international flights to Libya, which in April 1992 effectively shut down the international operations of the national carrier, Libyan Arab Airlines (LAA), led to increased use of airports in neighbouring countries. Following the suspension of UN sanctions in April 1999, regional and international airlines began to reintroduce services to Libya, while LAA opened discussions with other Middle East-based airlines with a view to leasing aircraft for international routes. The airline's fleet comprised just nine aircraft in 1999, compared with 35 (four of them leased) in the early 1990s. An agreement in principle was reached with Airbus Industrie in October 1999 to purchase 24 aircraft at such time as it became possible to proceed with such an order without contravening US trade sanctions. In May 2001 (when it seemed likely that progress on the Airbus deal would remain blocked by continuing US trade sanctions) LAA announced that it had opened negotiations with Russian and Ukrainian airframe manufacturers. In December 1999 LAA awarded an 'aircraft, crew, maintenance and insurance' contract to the Irish-based TransAer company, whereby TransAer would provide two Airbus A320 aircraft for services from Tripoli to 12 international destinations over a period of 30 months. Libyan pilots and other cockpit crew were to undergo supervision and training by TransAer staff as part of LAA's re-entry into the international aviation community. In January 2000 a French-based company, European Cargo Services, won a one-year contract to market cargo capacity on LAA in 39 countries. Flights to Libya were operated by 23 international carriers in early 2001. In 2001 the Government announced the intended improvement of the airport infrastructure and the air traffic control network. A new terminal was to be constructed at each of the four international airports.

As part of Libya's aim to create a comprehensive telecommunications network, in mid-1991 Swedish companies were awarded contracts for new installations in the south-west of the country; however, other parts of the programme, notably plans for 20 new exchanges and 182,000 extra lines in Tripoli and Benghazi, were not finalized until mid-1993. According to the International Telecommunication Union, the number of telephone mainlines increased from 59 per 1,000 people in 1995 to 109 per 1,000 in 2001. A mobile cellular telephone service was introduced in 1996, the number of subscribers reaching 9 per 1,000 people in 2001, when there were also 20,000 internet users in Libya.

TOURISM

Libyan initiatives to increase non-oil foreign currency earnings included the abandonment in the 1990s of ideological objections to the development of a mass tourism industry. However, by mid-1995 no practical steps had been taken to attract the necessary foreign investment, there being very little scope for forward planning in this area while Libya remained subject to UN sanctions. Despite the suspension of its international air links, Libya was visited by 80,000 tourists in 1994 and 85,000 tourists in 1995, when it was stated that the Government intended to invest US $1,700m. over the following five years 'to rehabilitate the tourism infrastructure'. In 1997 international consultants were appointed to draw up a plan for tourism development. Following the suspension of UN sanctions in 1999, the Government reiterated its commitment to develop Libya's still largely untapped tourism potential. In 2000 the number of visitors to Libya had increased to some 963,000; in 1999 receipts from tourism totalled US $ 28m.

In early 2001 the president of Libya's Tourism Investment and Promotion Board said that foreign investment of US $2,000m.–$3,000m. would be sought in the tourism sector during the 2001–05 development plan, with the aim of expanding the provision of hotel beds (totalling 5,000, the majority in nine hotels) to more than 60,000 and increasing tourist arrivals to 1m. per year. A master plan for tourism listed nine important sites which were to be developed as part of a strategy to offer not only conventional tourism, but also 'ecological, religious, health and sports adventure tourism projects'. In Tripoli, a 300-room hotel was due to open in 2002 as part of a $125m. shopping mall and business centre development by the Maltese Corinthia Group, whose agreement with the Libyan Government included tax and import duty concessions, while part of the project finance was loaned by the Libyan Arab Foreign Bank. Corinthia Group said in 2001 that it was planning to develop at least three more 300-room hotels to serve the tourism market in Benghazi, Sirte and Sabratha, each requiring an investment of $80m. In early 2001 a Swiss hotel chain was negotiating terms for a $40m. hotel complex in central Tripoli, while an Italian tour operator signed a contract to manage the development of a planned 145-ha coastal tourism complex near the Roman remains at Villa Silin (90 km east of Tripoli), to include up to 600 bungalows, a golf course and a desalination plant.

BUDGET, INVESTMENT AND FINANCE

Libyan planning dates back to the 1960s, with the first Development Plan running from 1963/64 to 1967/68. The second Plan ran from 1969/70 to 1973/74, and the third Plan from 1973 to 1975. Development budgets in the 1970s favoured agriculture, and the 1976–80 Development Plan, known as the Economic and Social Transformation Plan, involved a total investment of LD 9,250m. with priority given to agriculture. The overall aims of the Plan were to achieve diversity of production, thus reducing dependence on oil, to develop the economic and social infrastructure and to achieve a more equitable distribution of income and wealth. The 1981–85 Five-Year Plan was regarded as part of a major 20-year development programme, aiming at structural change in the economy to reduce its dependence on petroleum. By 1983, owing to the abrupt reversal in Libya's petroleum revenues, the targets of the Five-Year Plan for 1981–85 were not being met and major reassessments, involving substantial reductions in expenditure, had to be undertaken. The decline in government revenues curtailed budget expenditure throughout the 1980s. In the event, actual capital expenditure on development was well below the planned allocation.

Few details of the 1990 budget were made available. It was reported that expenditure on defence and subsidies was to be reduced in order to restrict the total budget deficit. As a result of the unexpected increase in income from oil exports in 1990, Libya's GDP increased by 9.4%, in comparison with 1989, to the equivalent of US $27,370m., thereby enabling the Government to allocate additional funds for the development of the oil industry and other sectors during the 1990s.

The broad outlines of the Government's 1992/93 budget were revealed in February 1993 (the penultimate month of that fiscal year). Expenditure totalled LD 2,823m. (US $9,700m.) and revenue LD 2,251m. ($7,735m.), leaving a deficit of LD 572m.

($1,965m.). Of the expected revenue, LD 1,284m. (57%) was derived from petroleum exports and the balance from taxes and duties. The total national oil revenue (including funds not earmarked for budgetary use) was expected to be about LD 3,000m. ($10,300m.). It was announced in January 1994 that Libya's budget year would henceforth coincide with the calendar year and that no budget had been in force in the nine months following the end of the last April–March budget year in 1993. No details of the 1994 budget were published, although the Government indicated that 'several billion dollars' of cutbacks had been made to take account of the impact of UN sanctions.

In July 1995 the Libyan authorities released details of the budget for that calendar year, stated partly in US dollars and partly in Libyan dinars. The foreign-currency part of the budget provided for revenue of US $8,280m. and expenditure of $9,260m., leaving a deficit of $980m. The expenditure categories included $1,600m. on water-transmission and irrigation; $700m. on the oil industry; $1,260m. on imported goods; $1,700m. on 'operating costs'; $250m. on payments to foreign companies; and $750m. on membership of international organizations. The remaining $3,000m. was earmarked for the direct distribution of grants to local families. The dinar section of the budget provided for domestic revenue of LD 1,660m. and domestic recurrent expenditure of LD 2,000m. (including LD 1,155m. on public-sector salaries), leaving a deficit of LD 340m. The 1996 budget, approved by the GPC in February of that year, provided for revenue of LD 4,518m. ($12,709m.) and expenditure of the same amount, this being Libya's first non-deficit budget for many years. The Government stated that the previous three years' budget deficits had been financed by drawings on the country's foreign reserves. The final size of the 1995 budget deficit was not revealed, although it was known that the Government had not implemented its plan to distribute lump-sum grants to Libyan families. In September 1996 the official Libyan news agency reported that 50,000 families were each to receive grants worth $5,000, under the Government's wealth redistribution programme. In March 1997 the Governor of the Central Bank told the GPC that Libya's foreign currency budget had a surplus of $680m. in 1996, when revenue on the foreign currency account had totalled $9,573m.

The sequence of balanced budgets was continued in 1997 and 1998, that for the latter year providing for a 1.3% reduction in expenditure and revenue to LD 5,311m. (US $13,760m. at the official exchange rate). It was officially stated that the 1998 budget included the allocation of LD 1,133m. ($2,935m.) to the GMR project. Figures released by the Government at the end of 1997 showed that Libya was owed some $3,273m. by various debtor nations. Debt rescheduling agreements had recently been concluded with Guinea, Guinea-Bissau and Burkina Faso, while negotiations were in progress with Pakistan and Sudan and were being sought with other debtors, including Algeria, Benin, Ethiopia, Madagascar, Mozambique, Nicaragua, Tanzania and Uganda.

Libya's 1999 budget, approved by the GPC in December 1998, provided for total expenditure of LD 4,900m. It was forecast in the budget that oil revenue would total LD 3,268m. in 1999. The Secretariat for Finance estimated the Government's actual 1998 oil revenue as LD 2,363m., nearly 35% less than the original 1998 budget forecast of LD 3,633m. (which had been based on 1997 oil export prices). After taking account of emergency spending cuts made during 1998 (notably in non-oil investment programmes), it was expected that the final 1998 accounts would show an overall deficit of some LD 650m. The 2000 budget (as redrafted in February of that year to meet Col Qaddafi's objections to certain aspects of a first draft of the budget) provided for LD 3,070m. of recurrent spending (12% less than in 1999) and LD 1,765m. of capital spending (twice as much as in 1999). The budget assumed an average oil export price of $16 per barrel in 2000, while stipulating that 80% of recurrent revenue should come from non-oil sources (including higher taxes on incomes).

Following the achievement of an estimated budget surplus equivalent to $1,400m. in 2001 (amounting to 2% of GDP), in December 2001 the GPC approved a budget for 2002 envisaging operational expenditure of LD 4,682.9m., development expenditure of LD 4,356m. and defence expenditure of LD 575m.

Western sources estimated that a budget deficit of 1.8% of GDP would be registered in 2002.

A new five-year development plan launched in 2001 called for total investment of US $35,000m., of which 60–70% would come from the public sector, and the balance from foreign investment and the Libyan private sector. The main growth targets were an average 5% per year overall and an average of 6.2% per year for the non-hydrocarbon sector. Non-hydrocarbon industries identified for foreign participation included tourism, telecommunications, mining, fisheries, and road and railway development. The main areas of investment in the development plan were the hydrocarbons, power and water sectors, all of which had major expansion programmes in place in 2001.

Before the 1969 coup most Libyan banks were subsidiaries of foreign banks. However, among the first decrees issued by the Revolution Command Council was one that required 51% of the capital of all banks operating in Libya to be owned by Libyans; the majority of directors, including the chairman, of each bank had to be Libyan citizens. Under the monarchy the Government had followed a similar policy without compulsion, and a number of foreign banks had accordingly already 'Libyanized' themselves. In December 1970 all commercial banks were nationalized, with government participation set at 51%.

In March 1993 legislation was passed authorizing Libyan citizens and companies to establish privately owned commercial banks with a minimum capitalization of LD 10m. (US $37m.). Under the same law, Libyan nationals were permitted to apply to the Central Bank of Libya for authorization to hold foreign currency in local bank accounts and to make unrestricted use of such holdings. The heavily overvalued Libyan dinar was currently being unofficially traded for convertible currencies at about one-sixth of its official exchange rate (which had been pegged to the International Monetary Fund's (IMF) special drawing right since 1986). Speaking in May 1993, Col Qaddafi said that he favoured a move towards full convertibility of the Libyan dinar at such time as 'there was adequate production' in the Libyan economy to prevent 'catastrophic' consequences.

In early November 1994 the Central Bank devalued the official exchange rate by 15.5%, from US $1 = LD 0.299 to $1 = LD 0.354, this being the fourth change in the official rate since 1992. The currency remained heavily overvalued, as its unofficial exchange rate was then about $1 = LD 3. Later the same month the Central Bank introduced a second-tier official rate of $1 = LD 1.019 'for use by local companies'. Also in November 1994 a consortium of seven local banks set up a new financial services company in Tripoli to meet the foreign currency requirements of travellers, using exchange rates 'set by supply and demand'. In early 1995 it was reported that a widening gap between official and unofficial exchange rates in Libya was pushing up the rate of price inflation, which, according to some estimates, was as high as 50%, compared with an estimated 15% in 1994. In late 1995 the unofficial exchange rate was reported to be averaging about $1 = LD 3.40. Price inflation affected mainly the growing range of 'non-essential' items whose importation was now handled by private-sector companies with little or no access to foreign exchange at the official rate. The officially recorded rates of price inflation were 4.5% in 1994 and 6% in 1995. The estimated rate of inflation in 1996 was 5.8%.

In an address to the GPC in March 1997, Col Qaddafi acknowledged that the unofficial exchange rate at that time, of about $1 = LD 3, represented a 'realistic' basis for foreign exchange transactions. However, the Central Bank's main official exchange rate was not devalued at that stage and it stood at $1 = LD 0.38 in September 1997. In early October 1998 Col Qaddafi strongly urged traders and shopkeepers to reduce their prices and announced a country-wide campaign to maintain pressure for price cuts. In November the Central Bank's main official exchange rate was devalued to $1 = LD 0.45. The unofficial exchange rate stood at around $1 = LD 3.20 in early 1999, when it was estimated that one-fifth of all currency transactions were carried out on an unofficial basis. At the beginning of 2001 Libya's official exchange rate was $1 = LD 0.55, while the second-tier commercial exchange rate was $1 = LD 1.73; there was also a special exchange rate for government transactions. A further adjustment of the official rate to $1 = LD 0.64 was followed by a major devaluation of 50.3% with effect from 1

January 2002, setting the rate at $1 = LD 1.30, in what was described as the first step towards establishing a unified market-driven parity. Analysts expected the change to increase the competitiveness of the non-oil sector, to reduce the cost of most imports and to reduce the role of the black market in currency transactions.

The growth in oil revenue in the 1970s allowed the Government to devote about one-half of its income to development expenditure, although this proportion declined in the 1980s, as petroleum revenues fell. Libya also gave generous aid abroad, in particular to the People's Democratic Republic of Yemen (PDRY), Egypt, Syria and Jordan, although the Government was somewhat capricious in implementing aid agreements. Aid was cut off from the Jordanian Government in September 1970 when it attacked the Palestinian guerrillas. Egypt was criticized over its conduct of the war with Israel, and in 1974 Libya demanded the return of a loan to Sudan. Aid to Egypt was suspended as a result of Egypt's signing the peace treaty with Israel in March 1979. There is no comparable organization in Libya to the Kuwait Fund for Arab Economic Development (KFAED), but in 1974 Libya made a contribution to the Islamic Development Bank. In 1980 Libyan aid to developing countries was US $281m., equivalent to 0.92% of GNP.

Developments in the Libyan banking sector included the establishment of joint development banks with Algeria and Turkey and an agreement to establish a joint Libyan-Mali bank. In 1977 the Libyan Arab Foreign Bank (LAFB)—effectively the 'offshore' arm of the Central Bank of Libya, and a key institution in Libyan trade finance—bought a 15.2% stake in the equity of Fiat, the Italian motor car company, for US $400m. The deal was backed by a loan to Fiat from the LAFB of $105m. repayable over 10 years (with two years' grace). Until this purchase the LAFB had pursued a cautious and selective policy of putting Libyan capital into banking, hotels and tourism in many countries, as well as joint-stock ventures in agriculture, fishing and forestry projects in some African countries. Libya appeared to regard the Fiat purchase as the vanguard of its investment in industrial countries' manufacturing bases. Libya's holdings in Italy were enlarged at the end of 1981 when the LAFB bought the bankrupt Italian sugar and steel concern, Malradi, for $450m. In September 1986, however, Libya sold its shares in Fiat for $3,000m. The Libyan ambassador to Rome denied that the sale had been prompted by the collapse of petroleum prices and the consequent shortage of foreign exchange. Other Libyan assets in Italy were frozen in mid-1986 as guarantees for Italian companies awaiting payment of millions of dollars from Libya in debt arrears. In December 1979 Kuwait and Libya signed a $1,000m. agreement to set up an Arab investment company, and in April 1980 Libya, together with Kuwait and the United Arab Emirates, decided to establish a new international insurance company. This was finally established with a capital of $3,000m. in October 1981. In September 1987 the Bankers' Trust Co of New York was ordered by a British High Court judge to release $292m. of Libyan assets placed with the bank's London branch, that had been 'frozen' by order of President Reagan in January 1986.

The LAFB increased its paid-up capital to LD 156m. in the 1991/92 fiscal year, during which it made a pre-tax profit of LD 15m. Its paid-up shares in international affiliates (including 28 international banks outside Libya) totalled LD 169.3m. In mid-1993 a proposal by the LAFB to increase its shareholding in the Athens-based Arab Hellenic Bank from 30% to 86% (thereby opening the way to the establishment of Libyan-controlled bank branches in other EC countries) was effectively halted by the Greek banking authorities. In 1992/93 the LAFB reported an increase in paid-up capital to LD 192m., an increase in net profits to LD 18.3m. and a 25% increase in total assets to LD 1,398m. The Bank's assets abroad were frozen in December 1993 under the terms of UN Security Council Resolution 883. In 1993/94 the LAFB increased its paid-up capital to LD 222m. In November 1997 the LAFB acquired a 5% stake in the newly-privatized Banco di Roma, the Governor of the Libyan Central Bank subsequently stating that the LAFB would seek a seat on the board of the Italian bank. The appointment of the Central Bank Governor as a member of the Banco di Roma board was formally announced in April 1999.

FOREIGN TRADE AND BALANCE OF PAYMENTS

Until production of petroleum began, Libya's exports consisted almost entirely of agricultural products, and its imports of manufactured goods. In 1960, for instance, imports were valued at LD 60.4m. and exports at LD 4.0m., leaving an adverse balance of LD 56.4m. (although LD 21m. of the total value of imports in 1960 was accounted for by goods imported for the account of the petroleum companies). Petroleum was first exported in the autumn of 1961, and by 1969, according to the IMF, imports totalled LD 241.3m. and exports LD 937.9m., of which LD 936.5m. was officially accounted for by crude petroleum. Although there were fluctuations within the overall trend, petroleum exports rose from LD 2,109.5m. in 1974 to LD 4,419.2m. in 1979, when they represented 99% of all Libyan exports by volume. The minute proportion of remaining exports were mainly hides and skins, groundnuts, almonds, metal scrap and re-exports.

Imports consist of a wide variety of manufactured goods, such as textiles, motor vehicles and luxury consumer goods. In the last few years imports of timber, chemicals and raw materials and, in particular, cement and building materials, have been stepped up. In addition, many foodstuffs have to be imported, for example tea, sugar, coffee and, in years of drought, wheat and flour. The value of imports increased by over 500% in 1971–79, from LD 250.4m. to LD 1,572m., whereas over the same period exports by value grew by 400%.

Since petroleum has been exported, Libya's visible trade balance has normally shown substantial surpluses. There was a general trend of increasing surpluses during the 1970s, and in 1980, when Libya's imports totalled LD 2,006.2m., and its exports LD 6,489.2m., a trade surplus of LD 4,483m., was recorded. Declining demand and lower prices for petroleum reduced the trade surplus in 1981, 1982 and 1983. Trade stabilized in 1984, but fell again in 1985 and 1986. Estimated exports in 1989 totalled US $7,320m., surpassing imports of $6,460m., a pattern which continued into the 1990s. Libya had estimated trade surpluses of $3,600m. in 1995 (exports $10,100m., imports $6,500m.) and $4,700m. in 1996 (exports $11,400m., imports $6,700m.). In 1997 there was a visible trade surplus of $2,716m. (exports $9,876m., imports $7,160m.). In 1998 the surplus fell sharply to $471m. (exports $6,328m., imports $5,857m.). In 1999 a combination of higher oil export earnings and reduced spending on imports produced a surplus of $2,974m. (exports $7,276m., imports $4,302m.), which was estimated to have increased to $3,100m. in 2000 (exports $7,700m., imports $4,600m.) and to $3,250m. in 2001 (exports $8,100m., imports $4,850m.).

In 1982 Italy (with 25.4% of total imports by value) was Libya's main supplier, followed by the Federal Republic of Germany (14.4%) and the United Kingdom (8%). In 1981 the USA (with 27.4% of Libyan exports by value), Italy (23.8%), the Federal Republic of Germany (10.3%) and Spain (6.7%) were the principal customers for Libyan exports (almost exclusively, crude petroleum). In 1977 the USA took 25% of Libya's oil exports. The USA and Western Europe together accounted for almost 90% of total oil exports from Libya. However, in 1982 all imports of Libyan oil to the USA were banned. Libyan imports from the USA fell by US $500m. from the level of $831m. in 1981. In January 1986, convinced of Libya's involvement in promoting international terrorism, President Reagan banned all trade between the USA and Libya. The USA succeeded in persuading some of its allies to reduce sharply their purchases of Libyan oil after the bombing of Tripoli and Benghazi in April 1986, but Italy, by far the largest customer for Libyan oil, actually increased its imports. The US embargo on bilateral trade with Libya reduced Libyan imports from the USA to $46.2m. in 1986, while Libyan exports to the USA amounted to a mere $1.6m.

As Libyan debts accumulated, imports from western European countries were also much reduced. Several countries, including India, Turkey and Uganda, accepted oil as payment for goods or debts owed to them by Libya. The Swedish export credit agency reached an agreement in 1991 under which it had recovered approximately US $30m. through oil purchase arrangements by mid-1994. Libya agreed in July 1995 to settle $48m. of official debt to Bulgaria and to work towards a formula for the settlement of claims of $300m. by Bulgarian companies.

Bulgarian trade with Libya had declined from $360m. in 1990 to $8m. in 1994. The Hungarian Government was reported in mid-1995 to be preparing an official approach to Libya on behalf of Hungarian companies which were owed $45m. for work carried out and goods supplied. In October 2000 the Italian export credit agency signed an interim agreement to write off $230m. of outstanding debt held by Libya.

Libya was Italy's largest regional trading partner in 1990, supplying exports (mainly petroleum) of US $4,700m. and taking Italian exports of $1,083m. Following the Gulf crisis of 1990–91, Libya's efforts to improve relations with Western Europe were encouraged by the visit of the Italian Prime Minister in June 1991 (the first by an EC Head of Government for more than 10 years), when an agreement was signed with the objective of increasing bilateral trade and Italian participation in Libyan development projects, such as the GMR irrigation scheme. Libya remained Italy's largest trading partner in 1997, with exports of $3,267.6m. and imports of $882.2m. After Italy, Libya's most important trading partners in 1997 were Germany (Libyan exports of $1,353.3m., imports of $717.8m.), Spain (Libyan exports of $825.6m., imports of $148.6m.) and Turkey (Libyan exports of $508.9m., imports of $164.4m.). In 1999 Italy took 33% of Libya's exports by value and provided 24% of imports; the corresponding figures for Germany were 24% and 12%.

In the early 1970s Libya's deficit on 'invisibles' (services and transfer payments) partly offset the visible trade surplus, leaving a fluctuating surplus on the current account, but in 1975 (when the visible trade surplus was reduced) the current account of the balance of payments went into overall deficit. Aid payments and purchases of military equipment (in 1986 Libya was estimated to owe the USSR US $4,000m.–$5,000m. for sales of arms) tended to bring about a substantial outflow on capital account—so that Libya's basic balance of payments often yielded a deficit. Government debts were estimated at $7,000m. in 1989, by which time the practice of paying debts in petroleum had become more common. International reserves totalled $4,208m. at 31 December 1978, compared with $2,131m. at the end of 1973, and by the end of 1979 the figure had risen to $6,449m. At mid-1981 foreign exchange reserves amounted to $13,444m. They declined, however, to an estimated $4,635m. in 1991. In 1980 the current account showed a surplus of $8,240m. but this was followed by a deficit of $2,978m. in 1981, and further deficits in 1982, 1983 and 1984. However, Central Bank figures showed a surplus of $2,016m. in 1985, following a decline of 33% in the value of merchandise imports and substantial reductions in capital expenditure (see Budget, Investment and Finance, above). The Central Bank reported a deficit of $252m. in 1986; a deficit of $800m. in 1987 was followed by further deficits of

$1,260m. in 1988 and $940m. in 1989. In 1990, however, the increase in oil revenues, due to the Gulf crisis of 1990–91, produced a current account surplus of $2,200m., but in 1991 the current account was roughly in balance as world oil prices reverted to their pre-crisis level. According to World Bank figures, Libya had gross international reserves of $7,225m. at the end of 1990.

By the end of 1996 Libya had an estimated external debt of US $4,200m. and estimated foreign exchange reserves of $4,900m. There was an estimated current-account surplus of $1,000m. In September 1998 Libya had debts to banks abroad of $247m. and non-bank trade credits of $279m., whereas its deposits in Western banks totalled $7,628m. Libya's balance of payments showed a current-account surplus of $1,875m. in 1997, a deficit of $391m. in 1998 and a surplus of $1,984m. in 1999. The Libyan Government announced in late 2000 that the country had no foreign debt, having registered an estimated current-account surplus of $1,400m. for the year. Foreign-exchange reserves totalled $13,619m. at the end of February 2002.

ECONOMIC PROSPECTS

Although the Government's optimistic targets for economic growth set under the 2001–05 development plan were not achieved in the plan's early stages, solid expansion was nevertheless recorded, mainly on the strength of the continuing buoyancy of world petroleum prices and the consequential healthy revenue inflow from Libya's dominant export sector. In mid-2002 most analysts expected Libya's petroleum revenues to remain healthy in the short term at least, and to provide funding for some of the Government's development plans. The full achievement of the plan targets depends on the expansion of oil and gas production, which depends in turn on whether the necessary foreign investment will be forthcoming. Such investment is likely to be available from European and Asian sources, seeking to take advantage of hydrocarbon reserves in what geologists have identified as some of the world's most promising untapped fields. However, US oil companies with an historic presence in Libya remain barred from further investment by the US Government's economic sanctions on Libya, which were renewed for a possible further five-year term in August 2001. Therefore, the Libyan Government's key goal remains the lifting of US sanctions and the resumption of investment by US oil companies, pending which it has delayed the granting of new exploration licences in promising blocks. The GMR project, to which the Government remains strongly committed despite its mediocre results to date and chronic delays in initiating its final stages, appears likely to be a continuing drain on resources.

Statistical Survey

Sources (unless otherwise stated): National Corporation for Information and Documentation; Census and Statistical Dept, Secretariat of Planning, Sharia Damascus 40, 2nd Floor, Tripoli; tel. (21) 3331731.

Area and Population

AREA, POPULATION AND DENSITY

Area (sq km)	1,775,500*
Population (census results)	
31 July 1984	
Males	1,953,757
Females	1,688,819
Total	3,642,576
August 1995 (provisional)	
Total	4,811,902†
Population (UN estimates at mid-year)‡	
1999	5,175,000
2000	5,290,000
2001	5,408,000
Density (per sq km) at mid-2001	3.0

* 685,524 sq miles.

† Comprising 4,404,986 Libyan nationals (males 2,236,943; females 2,168,043) and 406,916 non-Libyans.

‡ Source: UN, *World Population Prospects: The 2000 Revision.*

POPULATION BY REGION (1995 census, provisional figures)

Al-Batnan . . .	151,240	Misratah (Misurata)	488,573
Jebel Akhdar . .	381,165	Najghaza . . .	244,553
Banghazi (Benghazi)	665,615	Tarabulus (Tripoli) .	1,313,996
Al-Wosta . . .	240,574	Az-Zawiyah (Zawia)	517,395
Al-Wahat . . .	62,056	Jebel Gharbi . .	316,970
Al-Jufra . . .	39,335	Fazzan (Fezzan) .	314,029
Sofuljin . . .	76,401	**Total**	4,811,902

PRINCIPAL TOWNS (population at census of 31 July 1973)

Tarabulus (Tripoli,		Ajdabiyah . . .	31,047
the capital) . .	481,295	Darnah (Darna) .	30,241
Banghazi (Benghazi) .	219,317	Sabhah (Sebha) .	28,714
Misratah (Misurata) .	42,815	Tubruq (Tobruk) .	28,061
Az-Zawiyah (Zawia) .	39,382	Al-Marj . . .	25,166
Zawiyat al-Baida (Beida)	31,796	Zlitan (Zliten) . .	21,340

Mid-2000 (UN estimate, incl. suburbs): Benghazi 829,000.

Mid-2001 (UN estimate, incl. suburbs): Tripoli 1,776,000. Source: UN, *World Urbanization Prospects: The 2001 Revision.*

BIRTHS, MARRIAGES AND DEATHS

	Registered live births		Registered marriages*		Registered deaths*	
	Number	Rate (per 1,000)	Number	Rate (per 1,000)	Number	Rate (per 1,000)
1994 . .	98,423	20.1	19,190	3.9	14,036	2.9
1995 . .	88,779	17.9	21,358	4.3	13,538	4.6
1996 . .	90,428	17.8	18,743	3.7	12,281	2.4

* Registration is incomplete.

Source: UN, *Demographic Yearbook.*

Expectation of life (WHO estimates, years at birth, 2001): Males 67.5; Females 71.0) (Source: WHO, *World Health Report*).

EMPLOYMENT (official estimates, '000 persons)

	1994	1996*
Agriculture, forestry and fishing .	213.4	219.5
Mining and quarrying	29.9	31.0
Manufacturing	124.1	128.5
Electricity, gas and water	33.7	35.5
Construction	168.3	171.0
Trade, restaurants and hotels .	70.7	73.0
Transport, storage and communications . .	97.7	104.0
Financing, insurance, real estate and business		
services	18.7	22.0
Other services	434.8	439.5
Total	1,191.3	1,224.0
Libyans	1,035.2	1,092.1
Non-Libyans.	156.1	131.9

* Figures for 1995 are not available.

Health and Welfare

KEY INDICATORS

Fertility (births per woman, 2000).	3.6
Under-5 mortality rate (per 1,000 live births, 2000). . .	20
HIV/AIDS (% of persons aged 15–49, 2001).	0.24
Physicians (per 1,000 head, 1997)	1.28
Hospital beds (per 1,000 head, 1997)	4.3
Health expenditure (1998): US $ per head (PPP) . . .	290
% of GDP	3.9
public (% of total)	47.6
Access to water (% of persons, 2000)	72
Access to sanitation (% of persons, 2000)	97
Human Development Index (2000): ranking	64
value	0.773

For sources and definitions, see explanatory note on p. vi.

Agriculture

PRINCIPAL CROPS ('000 metric tons)

	1998*	1999*	2000
Wheat	140	130	125†
Barley	65	75	80†
Potatoes.	206	209	210*
Dry broad beans	12	12	13*
Almonds	30	31	31*
Groundnuts (in shell) . . .	17	17	17*
Olives	190	190	190*
Tomatoes	238	245	250*
Pumpkins, squash and gourds .	27	28	29*
Cucumbers and gherkins . .	9	10	11*
Chillies and green peppers . .	14	14	15*
Green onions and shallots .	48	50	53*
Dry onions	175	180	180*
Green peas	11	12	12*
Green broad beans . . .	14	14	15*
Carrots	23	23	24*
Other vegetables. . . .	71	74	76*
Oranges.	41	42	43*
Tangerines, mandarins, etc. . .	10	10	10*
Lemons and limes . . .	13	14	14*
Apples	45	46	47*
Apricots.	16	16	17*
Peaches and nectarines . .	9	9	10*
Plums	31	32	33*
Grapes	38	39	40*
Watermelons	210	212	215*
Cantaloupes and other melons .	25	26	27*
Figs.	28	29	30*
Dates	130	132	133*

* FAO estimate(s). † Unofficial figure.

Source: FAO.

LIVESTOCK (FAO estimates, '000 head, year ending September)

	1998	1999	2000
Horses	44	45	46
Asses	28	29	30
Cattle	180	190	210
Camels	60	70	71
Sheep	6,800	5,000	5,100
Goats	2,000	1,800	1,900
Poultry	24,000	24,500	24,800

Source: FAO.

LIVESTOCK PRODUCTS ('000 metric tons)

	1998	1999*	2000
Beef and veal	43*	15	20†
Mutton and lamb . . .	72†	50	51*
Goat meat	16†	9	9*
Poultry meat	98*	98	99
Cows' milk*	128	135	135
Sheeps' milk*	40	54	56
Goats' milk*. . . .	15	15	15
Hen eggs*	56	58	59
Wool: greasy*	8	9	9
scoured* . . .	2	2	2
Cattle hides*	7	3	3
Sheepskins*. . . .	14	6	6

* FAO estimate(s). † Unofficial figure.

Source: FAO.

Forestry

ROUNDWOOD REMOVALS
(FAO estimates, '000 cubic metres, excl. bark)

	1997	1998	1999
Sawlogs, veneer logs and logs for sleepers*	63	63	63
Other industrial wood . . .	51	52	53
Fuel wood*	536	536	536
Total	650	651	652

2000: Removals as in 1999 (FAO estimates).

* Annual output assumed to be unchanged since 1978.

Source: FAO.

SAWNWOOD PRODUCTION
(FAO estimates, '000 cubic metres, incl. railway sleepers)

	1998	1999	2000
Total (all broadleaved)* . . .	31	31	31

* Annual output assumed to be unchanged since 1978.

Source: FAO.

Fishing

(metric tons, live weight)

	1997	1998	1999
Capture*	31,877	32,511	32,450
Groupers*.	4,000	4,000	4,000
Bogue*	2,500	2,500	2,500
Porgies and seabreams* . .	4,000	4,000	4,000
Red mullet*	4,000	4,000	4,000
Jack and horse mackerels* . .	3,000	3,000	3,000
Sardinellas*	7,000	7,000	7,000
Northern bluefin tuna*. . .	1,029	1,331	1,195
'Scomber' mackerels* . . .	3,000	3,000	3,000
Aquaculture*	100	100	100
Total catch (incl. others)* . .	31,977	32,611	32,550

* FAO estimates.

Source: FAO, *Yearbook of Fishery Statistics.*

Mining

(estimates, '000 metric tons, unless otherwise indicated)

	1998	1999	2000
Crude petroleum ('000 barrels)	540,000	520,000	538,000
Natural gas (million cu m)* . .	12,600	12,400	12,000
Salt.	30	30	40
Gypsum (crude)	150	150	175

* Figures refer to gross volume. The dry equivalent (estimates, million cubic metres) was: 6,360 in 1998; 6,200 in 1999; 6,100 in 2000.

Source: US Geological Survey.

Industry

SELECTED PRODUCTS ('000 metric tons, unless otherwise indicated)

	1996	1997	1998
Olive oil (crude)	7	9	10
Paper and paperboard . . .	6	6	6
Jet fuels*	1,423	1,339	1,339
Motor spirit (petrol) . . .	1,957	1,970	1,970*
Naphthas	1,984	1,998	1,998*
Kerosene	259	274	274*
Gas-diesel (distillate fuel) oil .	4,244	4,272	4,272*
Residual fuel oils* . . .	4,799	4,834	4,834
Liquefied petroleum gas:			
from natural gas plants* .	670	682	685
from petroleum refineries .	250*	263	263*
Petroleum bitumen (asphalt) . .	103	106	106
Cement	3	3	3
Electric energy (million kWh) .	18,300	18,974	19,496

* Provisional or estimated figure(s).

1999 ('000 metric tons): Olive oil (crude) 10; Paper and paperboard 6; Cement 3.

Source: UN, *Industrial Commodity Statistics Yearbook*.

Finance

CURRENCY AND EXCHANGE RATES

Monetary Units
1,000 dirhams = 1 Libyan dinar (LD).

Sterling, Dollar and Euro Equivalents (31 May 2002)
£1 sterling = 1.875 dinars;
US $1 = 1.278 dinars;
€1 = 1.200 dinars;
100 Libyan dinars = £53.34 = $78.23 = €83.34.

Average Exchange Rate (US $ per Libyan dinar)
1995   2.8894
1996   2.7653
1997   2.6210

Note: In March 1986 the value of the Libyan dinar was linked to the IMF's special drawing right (SDR). Between November 1994 and November 1998 the official mid-point exchange rate was SDR1 = 525 dirhams (LD1 = SDR 1.90476). In February 1999 a rate of LD1 = SDR 1.577 (SDR1 = 634.1 dirhams) was introduced, but from September 1999 to September 2000 the value of the dinar fluctuated. In September 2000 a new rate of LD1 = SDR 1.4204 (SDR1 = 704.03 dirhams) was established, but in June 2001 the Libyan dinar was devalued to SDR 1.224 (SDR1 = 816.99 dirhams). The latter rate remained in effect until the end of December 2001. In January 2002 the value of the Libyan dinar was adjusted to SDR 0.608 (SDR 1 = LD 1.64474): a devaluation of 50.3%.

BUDGET (projections, LD million)

	1998*	1999
Total revenue	5,311	n.a.
Petroleum revenue	3,633	3,268
Total expenditure	5,311	4,900

* In December 1998 it was reported that petroleum revenue for the year was expected to be LD2,363 million, and that there would be an overall budget deficit of LD650 million.

INTERNATIONAL RESERVES (US $ million at 31 December)

	1999	2000	2001
Gold*	194	194	194
IMF special drawing rights . .	511	538	554
Reserve position in IMF . .	543	515	497
Foreign exchange . . .	6,226	11,408	13,749
Total	7,474	12,655	14,994

* Valued at US $42 per troy ounce.

Source: IMF, *International Financial Statistics*.

MONEY SUPPLY (LD million at 31 December)

	1999	2000	2001
Currency outside banks . . .	2,657.5	2,711.0	2,577.4
Private-sector deposits at Central Bank	133.7	200.8	297.8
Demand deposits at commercial banks	4,162.8	4,363.1	4,370.1
Total money (incl. others) . .	7,001.2	7,313.5	7,402.7

Source: IMF, *International Financial Statistics*.

COST OF LIVING
(Consumer Price Index, excluding rent, for Tripoli; base: 1979 = 100)

	1982	1983	1984
Food	134.9	152.9	169.5
Clothing	141.1	150.6	169.4
All items (incl. others) . . .	137.6	152.2	165.8

Source: ILO, *Yearbook of Labour Statistics*.

NATIONAL ACCOUNTS (LD million at current prices)
National Income and Product

	1983	1984	1985
Compensation of employees . .	2,763.1	2,865.8	2,996.2
Operating surplus	5,282.7	4,357.8	4,572.4
Domestic factor incomes . .	8,045.8	7,223.6	7,568.6
Consumption of fixed capital . .	436.1	457.5	481.6
Gross domestic product (GDP) at factor cost	8,481.9	7,681.1	8,050.2
Indirect taxes	470.0	462.2	389.0
Less Subsidies	146.7	130.0	162.2
GDP in purchasers' values . .	8,805.2	8,013.3	8,277.0
Factor income from abroad . .	200.2	142.8	122.5
Less Factor income paid abroad .	989.0	727.7	397.9
Gross national product . .	8,016.4	7,428.4	8,001.6
Less Consumption of fixed capital .	436.1	457.5	481.6
National income in market prices	7,580.3	6,970.9	7,520.0
Other current transfers from abroad	8.6	2.3	2.6
Less Other current transfers paid abroad	25.2	27.9	16.0
National disposable income .	7,563.7	6,945.3	7,506.6

Source: UN, *National Accounts Statistics*.

Expenditure on the Gross Domestic Product

	1998	1999	2000
Government final consumption expenditure	3,339	3,102	3,616
Private final consumption expenditure	8,072	8,514	7,962
Increase in stocks . . .	127	46	40
Gross fixed capital formation . .	1,397	1,536	2,281
Total domestic expenditure .	12,935	13,198	13,899
Exports of goods and services .	2,468	3,374	6,186
Less Imports of goods and services	2,661	2,433	2,690
GDP in purchasers' values . .	12,742	14,139	17,395

Source: IMF, *International Financial Statistics*.

Gross Domestic Product by Economic Activity (estimates)

	1994	1995	1996
Agriculture, forestry and fishing	601.5	680.5	782.5
Mining and quarrying	2,728.5	2,840.0	3,036.5
Petroleum and natural gas	2,559.5	2,675.0	2,822.0
Manufacturing	865.5	980.0	1,107.0
Electricity, gas and water	191.0	213.5	240.5
Construction	604.5	580.5	797.0
Trade, restaurants and hotels	1,100.0	1,190.5	1,345.5
Transport, storage and communications	846.0	925.5	1,025.5
Finance, insurance and real estate*	641.5	686.5	739.5
Public services	2,048.5	2,143.0	2,247.5
Other services	286.5	352.5	461.0
Total	9,913.5	10,592.5	11,782.5

* Including imputed rents of owner-occupied dwellings.

BALANCE OF PAYMENTS (US $ million)

	1997	1998	1999
Exports of goods f.o.b.	9,876	6,328	6,758
Imports of goods f.o.b.	−7,160	−5,857	−3,996
Trade balance	2,716	471	2,762
Exports of services	33	47	55
Imports of services	−920	−1,016	−918
Balance on goods and services	1,829	−498	1,899
Other income received	640	633	507
Other income paid	−354	−259	−218
Balance on goods, services and income	2,115	−124	2,187
Current transfers received	4	5	6
Current transfers paid	−244	−272	−210
Current balance	1,875	−391	1,984
Direct investment abroad	−282	−304	−210
Direct investment from abroad	−82	−152	−119
Portfolio investment assets	−774	−212	−3
Other investment assets	−1,040	−164	−293
Other investment liabilities	1,294	277	−346
Net errors and omissions	878	432	−372
Overall balance	1,869	−513	641

Source: IMF, *International Financial Statistics*.

External Trade

PRINCIPAL COMMODITIES
(distribution by SITC, US $ million, excl. military goods)

Imports c.i.f.	1997
Food and live animals	1,119.4
Cereals and cereal preparations	519.9
Meal and flour of wheat and meslin	185.0
Chemicals and related products	417.9
Basic manufactures	1,126.2
Textile yarn, fabrics, etc.	170.9
Iron and steel	398.2
Tubes, pipes and fittings	314.1
Machinery and transport equipment	2,012.4
Machinery specialized for particular industries	251.6
General industrial machinery, equipment and parts	554.8
Electrical machinery, apparatus, etc.	462.2
Road vehicles and parts*	562.4
Passenger motor cars (excl. buses)	314.8
Miscellaneous manufactured articles	658.5
Clothing and accessories (excl. footwear)	223.6
Total (incl. others)	5,592.9

* Data on parts exclude tyres, engines and electrical parts.

Exports f.o.b.	1997
Mineral fuels, lubricants, etc.	8,557.4
Petroleum, petroleum products, etc.	8,386.7
Crude petroleum oils, etc.	6,897.5
Refined petroleum products	1,489.2
Gasoline and other light oils	282.3
Residual fuel oils	1,206.9
Chemicals and related products	294.2
Total (incl. others)	9,028.7

Source: UN, *International Trade Statistics Yearbook*.

PRINCIPAL TRADING PARTNERS (US $ million)*

Imports c.i.f.	1997
Austria	89.0
Belgium-Luxembourg	101.1
Canada	150.5
China, People's Republic	86.9
Egypt	129.0
France (incl. Monaco)	345.5
Germany	717.8
Greece	69.8
Ireland	75.7
Italy	882.2
Japan	455.3
Korea, Republic	168.6
Malta	63.9
Morocco	117.0
Netherlands	141.7
Spain	148.6
Sweden	94.0
Switzerland-Liechtenstein	219.3
Tunisia	220.5
Turkey	164.4
United Kingdom	436.3
USA	78.7
Total (incl. others)	5,592.9

Exports f.o.b.	1997
Austria	466.0
France (incl. Monaco)	411.2
Germany	1,353.3
Greece	256.9
Italy	3,267.6
Portugal	127.2
Spain	825.6
Switzerland-Liechtenstein	393.6
Tunisia	384.7
Turkey	508.9
United Kingdom	202.0
Yugoslavia	171.6
Total (incl. others)	9,028.7

* Imports by country of origin; exports by country of destination. Figures exclude trade in gold.

Source: UN, *International Trade Statistics Yearbook*.

Transport

ROAD TRAFFIC (motor vehicles in use at 31 December)

	1995	1996
Passenger cars	794,525	809,514
Buses and coaches	1,424	1,490
Goods vehicles	342,918	356,038
Motorcycles and mopeds	1,078	1,112

Source: IRF, *World Road Statistics*.

SHIPPING

Merchant Fleet (registered at 31 December)

	1999	2000	2001
Number of vessels	142	142	140
Total displacement ('000 grt) . .	438.9	433.7	250.8

Source: Lloyd's Register-Fairplay, *World Fleet Statistics*.

International Sea-borne Freight Traffic (estimates, '000 metric tons)

	1991	1992	1993
Goods loaded	57,243	59,894	62,491
Goods unloaded	7,630	7,710	7,808

Source: UN Economic Commission for Africa, *African Statistical Yearbook*.

CIVIL AVIATION (traffic on scheduled services)

	1996	1997	1998
Kilometres flown (million) . .	4	4	4
Passengers carried ('000) . .	639	571	571
Passenger-km (million) . .	412	377	377
Total ton-km (million) . .	33	30	27

Source: UN, *Statistical Yearbook*.

Tourism

VISITOR ARRIVALS BY COUNTRY OF ORIGIN*

	1998	1999	2000
Algeria	30,776	39,193	85,181
Egypt	336,325	374,388	372,914
Morocco	20,108	24,350	23,088
Tunisia	404,716	428,871	400,843
Total (incl. others)	850,292	965,307	962,559

* Including same-day visitors (excursionists).

Source: World Tourism Organization, *Yearbook of Tourism Statistics*.

Tourism Receipts (US $ million): 18 in 1998; 28 in 1999 (Source: World Tourism Organization).

Communications Media

	1999	2000	2001
Telephones ('000 main lines in use)	550	605	610
Mobile cellular telephones ('000 subscribers)	30	40	50
Internet users ('000)	7	10	20

1994: Book production (titles) 26.
1996: Daily newspapers 4 (estimated average circulation 71,000).
1997: Radio receivers ('000 in use) 1,350; Television receivers ('000 in use) 730.

Sources: UNESCO, *Statistical Yearbook*; International Telecommunication Union.

Education

(1995/96, unless otherwise indicated)

	Institutions	Teachers	Students
Primary and preparatory:			
General	2,733*	122,020	1,333,679
Vocational . . .	168	n.a.	22,490
Secondary:			
General	n.a.	17,668	170,573
Teacher-training . .	n.a.	2,760†	23,919
Vocational . . .	312	n.a.	109,074
Universities . . .	13	n.a.	126,348

* 1993/94. † 1992/93.

Source: partly UNESCO, *Statistical Yearbook*.

Adult literacy rate (UNESCO estimates): 80.0.% (Males 90.8%; Females 68.2%) in 2000 (Source: UNDP, *Human Development Report*).

Directory

The Constitution

The Libyan Arab People, meeting in the General People's Congress in Sebha from 2–28 March 1977, proclaimed its adherence to freedom and its readiness to defend it on its own land and anywhere else in the world. It also announced its adherence to socialism and its commitment to achieving total Arab Unity; its adherence to the moral human values; and confirmed the march of the revolution led by Col Muammar al-Qaddafi, the Revolutionary Leader, towards complete People's Authority.

The Libyan Arab People announced the following:

(i) The official name of Libya is henceforth The Socialist People's Libyan Arab Jamahiriya.

(ii) The Holy Koran is the social code in The Socialist People's Libyan Arab Jamahiriya.

(iii) The Direct People's Authority is the basis for the political order in The Socialist People's Libyan Arab Jamahiriya. The People shall practise its authority through People's Congresses, Popular Committees, Trade Unions, Vocational Syndicates, and The General People's Congress, in the presence of the law.

(iv) The defence of our homeland is the responsibility of every citizen. The whole people shall be trained militarily and armed by general military training, the preparation of which shall be specified by the law.

The General People's Congress in its extraordinary session held in Sebha issued four decrees:

The first decree announced the establishment of The People's Authority in compliance with the resolutions and recommendations of the People's Congresses and Trade Unions.

The second decree stipulated the choice of Col Muammar al-Qaddafi, the Revolutionary Leader, as Secretary-General of the General People's Congress.

The third decree stipulated the formation of the General Secretariat of the General People's Congress (see The Government, below).

The fourth decree stipulated the formation of the General People's Committee to carry out the tasks of the various former ministries (see The Government, below).

In 1986 it was announced that the country's official name was to be The Great Socialist People's Libyan Arab Jamahiriya.

The Government

HEAD OF STATE*

Revolutionary Leader: Col MUAMMAR AL-QADDAFI (took office as Chairman of the Revolution Command Council 8 September 1969.

*Qaddafi himself rejects this nomenclature and all other titles.

Second-in-Command: Maj. ABD AS-SALAM JALLOUD.

GENERAL SECRETARIAT OF THE GENERAL PEOPLE'S CONGRESS
(September 2002)

Secretary: MUHAMMAD AZ-ZANATI.

Assistant Secretary for Popular Congresses: AHMAD MUHAMMAD IBRAHIM.

Assistant Secretary for Popular Committees: Dr ABD AL-KADER MUHAMMAD AL-BAGHDADI.

Secretary for Culture and Mass Mobilization: ABD AL-HAMID AS-SID ZINTANI.

Secretary for Trade Unions, Leagues and Professional Unions: ABDALLAH IDRIS IBRAHIM.

Secretary for Social Affairs: SALIMA SHAIBAN ABD AL-JABAR.

Secretary for Infrastructure, Urban Planning and Environment: Dr SALIM AHMAD FUNAYT.

Secretary for Human Resources: Dr AL-BAGHDADI ALI AL-MAHMOUDI.

Secretary for Foreign Affairs: SULEIMAN SASI ASH-SHAHUMI.

Secretary for Economy: ABD AS-SALAM AHMAD NUWEIR.

Secretary for Legal Affairs and Human Rights: MUHAMMAD ABDALLAH AL-HARARI.

Secretary for Security Affairs: MUFTAH ABD AS-SALAM BUKAR.

GENERAL PEOPLE'S COMMITTEE
(September 2002)

Secretary: MOHANDIS MUBARAK ABDALLAH ASH-SHAMIKH.

Deputy Secretary: ABDALLAH SALEM AL-BADRI.

Secretary for Justice and Public Security: MUHAMMAD ALI AL-MUSRATI.

Secretary for Finance: AL-UJAYLI ABD AS-SALAM BURAYNI.

Secretary for Foreign Liaison and International Co-operation: ABD AR-RAHMAN MUHAMMAD SHALGAM.

Secretary for African Unity: Dr ALI ABD AS-SALAM AT-TURAYKI.

Secretary for the Economy and Trade: SHUKRI MUHAMMAD GHANEM.

Secretary for Infrastructure, Urban Planning and Environment: HUTAYWISH FARAJ AL-HUTAYWISH.

Deputy Secretary for Production: AL-BAGHDADI ALI AL-MAHMOUDI.

Deputy Secretary for Services: AMMAR MABRUK AL-LUTAYYIF

Legislature

GENERAL PEOPLE'S CONGRESS

The Senate and House of Representatives were dissolved after the *coup d'état* of September 1969, and the provisional Constitution issued in December 1969 made no mention of elections or a return to parliamentary procedure. However, in January 1971 Col Qaddafi announced that a new legislature would be appointed, not elected; no date was mentioned. All political parties other than the Arab Socialist Union were banned. In November 1975 provision was made for the creation of the 1,112-member General National Congress of the Arab Socialist Union, which met officially in January 1976. This later became the General People's Congress (GPC), which met for the first time in November 1976 and in March 1977 began introducing the wide-ranging changes outlined in the Constitution (above).

Secretary-General: ABD AR-RAZIQ SAWSA.

Political Organizations

In June 1971 the Arab Socialist Union (ASU) was established as the country's sole authorized political party. The General National Congress of the ASU held its first session in January 1976 and later became the General People's Congress (see Legislature, above).

The following groups are in opposition to the Government:

Ansarollah Group: f. 1996.

Fighting Islamic Group: claimed responsibility for subversive activities in early 1996; seeks to establish an Islamic regime.

Islamic Martyrs' Movement (IMM): Spokesman ABDALLAH AHMAD.

Libyan Baathist Party.

Libyan Change and Reform Movement: breakaway group from NFSL.

Libyan Conservatives' Party: f. 1996.

Libyan Constitutional Grouping.

Libyan Democratic Movement: f. 1977; external group.

Libyan Democratic Authority: f. 1993.

Libyan Democratic Conference: f. 1992.

Libyan Movement for Change and Reform: f. 1994; based in London, United Kingdom.

Libyan National Alliance: f. 1980 in Cairo, Egypt.

Libyan National Democratic Rally.

Movement of Patriotic Libyans: f. 1997.

National Front for the Salvation of Libya (NFSL): e-mail visitor@nfsl-libya.com; internet www.nfsl-libya.com; f. 1981 in Khartoum, Sudan; aims to replace the existing regime by a democratically-elected govt; Leader MUHAMMAD MEGARIEF.

Diplomatic Representation

EMBASSIES IN LIBYA

Afghanistan: POB 4245, Sharia Mozhar al-Aftes, Tripoli; tel. (21) 75192; fax (21) 609876; Ambassador: (vacant).

Algeria: Sharia Kairauan 12, Tripoli; tel. (21) 4440025; Ambassador: MUHAMMAD SEBBAGH.

Argentina: POB 932, Sharia ibn Mufarrej al-Andalous, Tripoli; tel. (21) 4772160; fax (21) 4772258; e-mail embartrip@hotmail.com; Ambassador: MANUEL A. FERNÁNDEZ SALORIO.

Armenia: Tripoli.

Austria: POB 3207, Sharia Khalid ibn al-Walid, Garden City, Tripoli; tel. (21) 4443379; fax (21) 4440838; e-mail austroamb_tripolis@hotmail.com; Ambassador: Dr ROBERT KARAS.

Bangladesh: POB 5086, Hadaba al-Khadra, Villa Omran al-Wershafani, Tripoli; tel. (21) 900856; fax (21) 4906616; Ambassador: M. SHAFIULLAH.

Belgium: Tower 4, International Islamic Call Society Complex, Souk Ethulathah, Tripoli; tel. (21) 3350117; fax (21) 3350118; Ambassador: R. SCHRIJVERS.

Benin: POB 6676 254 rue Oumaween, Cité EC Analous, Tripoli; tel. (21) 830990; fax (21) 834569; Ambassador: LAFIA CHABI.

Bosnia and Herzegovina: POB 84373, Sharia ben Ashour, Tripoli; tel. and fax (21) 602162; Ambassador: MUHAMMAD KUPOSOVIĆ.

Brazil: POB 2270, Sharia ben Ashour, Tripoli; tel. (21) 3614894; fax (21) 3614895; e-mail brcastripoli@Ittnet.net; Ambassador: JOAQUIM PALMEIRO.

Bulgaria: POB 2945, Sharia Talha ben Abdullah 5-7, Tripoli; tel. (21) 3609988; Ambassador: LYUDMIL SPASOV.

Burkina Faso: POB 81902, Tripoli; tel. (21) 71221; fax (21) 72626; Ambassador: AMADÉ OUÉDRAOGO.

Burundi: POB 2817, Sharia Ras Hassan, Tripoli; tel. (21) 608848; Ambassador: ZACHARIE BANYIYEZAKO.

Canada: Tripoli; Chargé d'affaires a.i.: GEORGE JACOBY.

Chad: POB 1078, Sharia Muhammad Mussadeq 25, Tripoli; tel. (21) 4443955; Ambassador: IBRAHIM MAHAMAT TIDEI.

China, People's Republic: POB 5329, Andalous, Gargaresh, Tripoli; tel. (21) 830860; Ambassador: ZHAI JUN.

Cuba: POB 83738, Andalous, Gargaresh, Tripoli; tel. (21) 71346; Ambassador: RAÚL RODRÍGUEZ RAMOS.

Cyprus: POB 3284, Sharia Ad-Dhul 60, Ben Ashour, Tripoli; tel. (21) 3600499; fax (21) 3613516; Ambassador: ARGYROS ANTONIOU.

Czech Republic: POB 1097, Sharia Ahmad Lutfi Sayed, Sharia ben Ashour, Tripoli; tel. (21) 3615436; fax (21) 3615437; e-mail tripoli@embassy.mzv.cz; Ambassador: PAVEL ŘEZÁČ.

Egypt: The Grand Hotel, Tripoli; tel. (21) 605500; fax (21) 4445959; Ambassador: HANY KHALLAF.

Equatorial Guinea: Tripoli.

Eritrea: Tripoli; Ambassador: UTHMAN MUHAMMAD UMAR.

Finland: POB 2508, Tripoli; tel. and fax (21) 4831132; Chargé d'affaires: ULLA-MAIJA SUOMINEN.

France: POB 312, Sharia Beni al-Amar, Hay Andalous, Tripoli; tel. (21) 4774 891; fax (21) 4778266; internet ambafrance-ly.org; Ambassador: JEAN-JACQUES BEAUSSOU.

Germany: POB 302, Sharia Hassan al-Mashai, Tripoli; tel. (21) 3330554; fax (21) 4448968; e-mail germanembassytrip@web.de; Ambassador: DIETMAR GREINEDER.

Ghana: POB 4169, Andalous 21/A, nr Funduk-Shati, Tripoli; tel. (21) 4773379; fax (21) 4773557; e-mail ghaemb@bsisp.net; Ambassador: GEORGE KUMI.

Greece: POB 5147, Sharia Jalal Bayar 18, Tripoli; tel. (21) 3338563; fax (21) 3336689; e-mail grembtri@hotmail.com; Ambassador: Dr PANAYOTIS THEODORACOPOULOS.

Guinea: POB 10657, Andalous, Tripoli; tel. (21) 4772793; fax (21) 4773441; e-mail magatte@lttnet.net; Ambassador: EL H. ABOUB-ACAR DIONE.

Holy See: Tripoli; Apostolic Nuncio: Most Rev. LUIGI CONTI, Titular Archbishop of Gratiana (resident in Malta).

Hungary: POB 4010, Sharia Talha ben Abdullah, Tripoli; tel. (21) 605799; Chargé d'affaires: FERENC CSILLAG.

India: POB 3150, 16 Sharia Mahmud Shaltut, Tripoli; tel. (21) 4441835; fax (21) 3337560; e-mail indemtrip@mail.link.net.mt; Ambassador: APPUNNI RAMESH.

Iran: Tripoli; Ambassador: NASROLLAH MIRZAI-NASER.

Iraq: POB 974, Sharia Karji, Tripoli; tel. (21) 4778195; fax (21) 4778196; Ambassador: ANWAAR MAWOLOD THEBAN.

Italy: POB 912, Sharia Vahran 1, Tripoli; tel. (21) 3334133; fax (21) 3331673; e-mail ambasciate.tripoli@esteri.it; Ambassador: CLAUDIO PACIFICO.

Japan: Tower 4, That al-Imad Complex, Sharia Organization of African Unity, Tripoli; tel. (21) 607463; fax (21) 607462; Ambassador: AKIRA WATANABE.

Korea, Democratic People's Republic: Tripoli; Ambassador: CHOE IN SOP.

Korea, Republic: POB 4781, Gargaresh, Tripoli; tel. (21) 4831322; fax (21) 4831324; Ambassador: HUH BANG-BIN.

Kuwait: POB 2225, Beit al-Mal Beach, Tripoli; tel. (21) 4440281; fax (21) 607053; Chargé d'affaires: KHALED MOTLAQ AD-DUWAILA.

Lebanon: POB 927, Sharia Omar bin Yasser Hadaek 20, Tripoli; tel. (21) 3333733; Ambassador: MOUNIR KHOREISH.

Malaysia: POB 6309, Hai Andalus, Tripoli; tel. (21) 4830854; fax (21) 4831496; e-mail mwtripoli@lttnet.net; Ambassador: Datuk SHAPII BIN ABU SAMAH.

Mali: Sharia Jaraba Saniet Zarrouk, Tripoli; tel. (21) 4444924; Ambassador: EL BEKAYE SIDI MOCTAR KOUNTA.

Malta: POB 2534, Sharia Ubei ben Ka'ab, Tripoli; tel. (21) 3611181; fax (21) 3611180; e-mail rvellalaurenti@yahoo.com; Ambassador: Dr RICHARD VELLA LAURENTI.

Mauritania: Sharia Eysa Wokwak, Tripoli; tel. (21) 4443223; Ambassador: YAHIA MUHAMMAD EL-HADI.

Morocco: POB 908, Sharia ben Ashour, Tripoli; tel. (21) 600110; fax (21) 4445757; Ambassador: DRISS ALAOUI.

Netherlands: POB 3801, Sharia Jalal Bayar 20, Tripoli; tel. (21) 4441549; fax (21) 4440386; Chargé d'affaires: G. J. VAN EPEN.

Nicaragua: Tripoli; Ambassador: GUILLERMO ESPINOSA.

Niger: POB 2251, Fachloun Area, Tripoli; tel. (21) 4443104; Ambassador: KARIM ALIO.

Nigeria: POB 4417, Sharia Bashir al-Ibrahim, Tripoli; tel. (21) 4443038; Ambassador: Prof. DANDATTI ABD AL-KADIR.

Pakistan: POB 2169, Sharia Abdul Karim al-Khattabi 16, Maidan al-Qadasia, Tripoli; tel. (21) 4440072; fax (21) 4444698; Ambassador: KHAWAR RASHID PIRZADA.

Philippines: POB 12508, Andalous, Gargaresh, Tripoli; tel. and fax (21) 4833966; Ambassador: MUKHTAR M. MUALLAM.

Poland: POB 519, Sharia ben Ashour 61, Tripoli; tel. (21) 3615972; fax (21) 3615199; Ambassador: Dr WITOLD JURASZ.

Qatar: POB 3506, Sharia ben Ashour, Tripoli; tel. (21) 4446660; Chargé d'affaires: HASAN AHMAD ABU HINDI.

Romania: POB 5085, Sharia Ahmad Lotfi Sayed, Sharia ben Ashour, Tripoli; tel. (21) 3615295; fax (21) 3607597; e-mail amba romatrip@hotmail.com; Chargé d'affaires a.i.: MIRCEA HAS.

Russia: POB 4792, Sharia Mustapha Kamel, Tripoli; tel. (21) 3330545; fax (21) 4446673; Ambassador: ALEKSEI B. PODTSEROB.

Rwanda: POB 6677, Villa Ibrahim Musbah Missalati, Andalous, Tripoli; tel. (21) 72864; fax (21) 70317; Chargé d'affaires: CHRISTOPHE HABIMANA.

Saudi Arabia: Sharia Kairauan 2, Tripoli; tel. (21) 30485; Chargé d'affaires: MUHAMMAD HASSAN BANDAH.

Sierra Leone: Tripoli; Ambassador: el Hadj MOHAMMED SAMURA.

Slovakia: POB 5721, 3km, Hay al-Andalus, Gergarsh, Tripoli; tel. (21) 4781388; fax (21) 4781387; e-mail slovembtrp@mwc.ly; Ambassador: JÁN BÓRY.

Spain: POB 2302, Sharia el-Amir Abd al-Kader al-Jazairi 36, Tripoli; tel. (21) 3336797; fax (21) 4443743; Ambassador: PABLO BENAVIDES ORGAZ.

Sudan: POB 1076, Sharia Gargarish, Tripoli; tel. (21) 4775387; fax (21) 4774781; e-mail sudtripoli@hotmail.com; Ambassador: OSMAN M. O. DIRAR.

Switzerland: POB 439, Sharia ben Ashour, Tripoli; tel. (21) 3614118; fax (21) 3614238; Ambassador: PAUL KOLLER.

Syria: POB 4219, Sharia Muhammad Rashid Reda 4, Tripoli (Relations Office); tel. (21) 3331783; Head: MUNIR BORKHAN.

Togo: POB 3420, Sharia Khaled ibn al-Walid, Tripoli; tel. (21) 4447551; fax (21) 3332423; Ambassador: TCHAO SOTOU BERE.

Tunisia: POB 613, Sharia Bashir al-Ibrahim, Tripoli; tel. (21) 3331051; fax (21) 4447600; High Representative: MANSOUR EZZEDDINE.

Turkey: POB 947, Sharia Zaviya Dahmani, Tripoli; tel. (21) 3337717; fax (21) 3337686; Ambassador: MUFIT OZDES.

Uganda: POB 80215, Sharia ben Ashour, Tripoli; tel. (21) 604471; fax (21) 4831602; Ambassador: WILLIAM N. HAKIZA.

Ukraine: POB 4555, Sharia ben Ashour, Ares, Tripoli; tel. (21) 3608665.

United Kingdom: POB 4206, Tripoli; tel. (21) 3343630; fax (21) 3343634; e-mail belibya@hotmail.com; internet www.britain-in-libya.org; Ambassador: RICHARD DALTON (to January 2003).

Venezuela: POB 2584, Sharia ben Ashour, Jamaa al sagaa Bridge, Tripoli; tel. (21) 3600408; fax (21) 3600407; Ambassador: JULIO CÉSAR PINEDA.

Viet Nam: POB 587, Sharia Talha ben Abdullah, Tripoli; tel. (21) 833704; fax (21) 830494; Ambassador: DANG SAN.

Yemen: POB 4839, Sharia Ubei ben Ka'ab 36, Tripoli; tel. (21) 607472; Ambassador: ALI AIDAROUS YAHYA.

Yugoslavia: POB 1087, Sharia Turkia 14–16, Tripoli; tel. (21) 3334114; Ambassador: RADOMIR BOGDANOVIĆ.

Judicial System

The judicial system is composed, in order of seniority, of the Supreme Court, Courts of Appeal, and Courts of First Instance and Summary Courts.

All courts convene in open session, unless public morals or public order require a closed session; all judgments, however, are delivered in open session. Cases are heard in Arabic, with interpreters provided for aliens.

The courts apply the Libyan codes which include all the traditional branches of law, such as civil, commercial and penal codes, etc. Committees were formed in 1971 to examine Libyan law and ensure that it coincides with the rules of Islamic *Shari'a*. The proclamation of People's Authority in the Jamahiriya provides that the Holy Koran is the law of society.

Attorney-General: SALIM MUHAMMAD SALIM.

SUPREME COURT

The judgments of the Supreme Court are final. It is composed of the President and several Justices. Its judgments are issued by circuits of at least three Justices (the quorum is three). The Court hears appeals from the Courts of Appeal in civil, penal, administrative and civil status matters.

President: HUSSEIN MUKTAR AL-BUEISHI.

COURTS OF APPEAL

These courts settle appeals from Courts of First Instance; the quorum is three Justices. Each court of appeal has a court of assize.

COURTS OF FIRST INSTANCE AND SUMMARY COURTS

These courts are first-stage courts in the Jamahiriya, and the cases heard in them are heard by one judge. Appeals against summary judgments are heard by the appellate court attached to the court of first instance, whose quorum is three judges.

PEOPLE'S COURT

Established by order of the General People's Congress in March 1988.

President: ABD AR-RAZIQ ABU BAKR AS-SAWSA.

PEOPLE'S PROSECUTION BUREAU

Established by order of the General People's Congress in March 1988.

Secretary: MUHAMMAD ALI AL-MISURATI.

Religion

ISLAM

The vast majority of Libyan Arabs follow Sunni Muslim rites, although Col Qaddafi has rejected the Sunnah (i.e. the practice, course, way, manner or conduct of the Prophet Muhammad, as followed by Sunnis) as a basis for legislation.

Chief Mufti of Libya: Sheikh TAHIR AHMAD AZ-ZAWI.

CHRISTIANITY
The Roman Catholic Church

Libya comprises three Apostolic Vicariates and one Apostolic Prefecture. At 31 December 2000 there were an estimated 77,000 adherents in the country.

Apostolic Vicariate of Benghazi: POB 248, Benghazi; tel. (91) 9096563; fax (61) 9081599; Vicar Apostolic Mgr SYLVESTER CARMEL MAGRO, Titular Bishop of Saldae.

Apostolic Vicariate of Derna: c/o POB 248, Benghazi; Vicar Apostolic (vacant).

Apostolic Vicariate of Tripoli: POB 365, Dahra, Tripoli; tel. (21) 3331863; fax (21) 3334696; e-mail bishoptripolibya@hotmail.com; Vicar Apostolic Mgr GIOVANNI INNOCENZO MARTINELLI, Titular Bishop of Tabuda.

The Anglican Communion

Within the Episcopal Church in Jerusalem and the Middle East, Libya forms part of the diocese of Egypt (q.v.).

Other Christian Churches

The Coptic Orthodox Church is represented in Libya.

The Press

Newspapers and periodicals are published either by the Jamahiriya News Agency (JANA), by government secretariats, by the Press Service or by trade unions.

DAILIES

Ash-Shams: Tripoli; internet www.alshames.com.

Az-Zahf al-Akhdar (The Green March): POB 14373–6998, Tripoli; fax (21) 4772502; e-mail info@azzahfalakhder.com; internet www.azzahfalakhder.com; ideological journal of the Revolutionary Committees.

PERIODICALS

Al-Amal (Hope): POB 4845, Tripoli; internet alalmalmag.com; monthly; social, for children; published by the Press Service.

Ad-Daawa al-Islamia (Islamic Call): POB 2682, Sharia Sawani, km 5, Tripoli; tel. (21) 4800294; fax (21) 4800293; f. 1980; weekly (Wednesdays); Arabic, English, French; cultural; published by the World Islamic Call Society; Eds MUHAMMAD IMHEMED AL-BALOUSHI and ABDULAHI MUHAMMAD ABDUL-JALEEL.

Al-Fajr al-Jadid (The New Dawn): Press Building, Sharia al-Jamhariya, Tripoli; tel. (21) 3606393; fax (21) 3605728; internet www.alfajraljadeed.com; f. 1969; publ. by JANA; bi-monthly.

Economic Bulletin: POB 2303, Tripoli; tel. (21) 3337106; monthly; published by JANA.

Al-Jamahiriya: POB 4814, Tripoli; tel. (21) 4449294; internet www.aljamahiria.com; f. 1980; weekly; Arabic; political; published by the revolutionary committees.

Al-Jarida ar-Rasmiya (The Official Newspaper): Tripoli; irregular; official state gazette.

Libyan Arab Republic Gazette: Secretariat of Justice, NA, Tripoli; weekly; English; published by the Secretariat of Justice.

Risalat al-Jihad (Holy War Letter): POB 2682, Tripoli; tel. (21) 3331021; f. 1983; monthly; Arabic, English, French; published by the World Islamic Call Society.

Scientific Bulletin: POB 2303, Tripoli; tel. (21) 3337106; monthly; published by JANA.

Ath-Thaqafa al-Arabiya (Arab Culture): POB 4587, Tripoli; f. 1973; weekly; cultural; circ. 25,000.

Al-Usbu ath-Thaqafi (The Cultural Week): POB 4845, Tripoli; weekly.

Al-Watan al-Arabi al-Kabir (The Greater Arab Homeland): Tripoli; f. 1987.

NEWS AGENCIES

Jamahiriya News Agency (JANA): POB 2303, Sharia al-Fateh, Tripoli; tel. (21) 3402606; fax (21) 3402624; e-mail mail@jamahiriyanews.com; internet www.jamahiriyanews.com; branches and correspondents throughout Libya and abroad; serves Libyan and foreign subscribers.

Foreign Bureaux

Informatsionnoye Telegrafnoye Agentstvo Rossii—Telegrafnoye Agentstvo Suverennykh Stran (ITAR—TASS) (Russia): Sharia Mustapha Kamel 10, Tripoli; Correspondent GEORG SHELENKOV.

ANSA (Italy) is also represented in Tripoli.

Publishers

Ad-Dar al-Arabia Lilkitab (Maison Arabe du Livre): POB 3185, Tripoli; tel. (21) 4447287; f. 1973 by Libya and Tunisia.

Al-Fatah University, General Administration of Libraries, Printing and Publications: POB 13543, Tripoli; tel. (21) 621988; f. 1955; academic books.

General Co for Publishing, Advertising and Distribution: POB 921, Sirte (Surt); tel. (54) 63170; fax (54) 62100; general, educational and academic books in Arabic and other languages; makes and distributes advertisements throughout Libya.

Broadcasting and Communications

TELECOMMUNICATIONS

General Directorate of Posts and Telecommunications: POB 81686, Tripoli; tel. (21) 3604101; fax (21) 3604102; Dir-Gen. ABU ZAID JUMA AL-MANSURI.

General Post and Telecommunications Co: POB 886, Sharia Zawia, Tripoli; tel. (21) 3600777; fax (21) 3609515; f. 1985; Chair. FARAJ AMARI.

BROADCASTING
Radio

Great Socialist People's Libyan Arab Jamahiriya Broadcasting Corporation: POB 9333, Tripoli; POB 119, al-Baida; tel. (21) 3332451; f. 1957; broadcasts in Arabic and English from Tripoli and Benghazi; from September 1971 special daily broadcasts to Gaza and other Israeli-occupied territories were begun.

Voice of Africa: POB 4677, Sharia al-Fateh, Tripoli; tel. (21) 4449209; fax (21) 4449875; f. 1973 as Voice of the Greater Arab Homeland; adopted current name in 1998; broadcasts in Arabic, French and English; transmissions in Swahili, Hausa, Fulani and Amharic scheduled to begin in 2000; Dir-Gen. ABDALLAH AL-MEGRI.

Television

People's Revolution Broadcasting TV: POB 333, Tripoli; f. 1968; broadcasts in Arabic; additional channels broadcast for limited hours in English, Italian and French; Dir YOUSUF DEBRI.

Finance

(cap. = capital; res = reserves; dep. = deposits;
LD = Libyan dinars; m. = million; brs = branches)

BANKING
Central Bank

Central Bank of Libya: POB 1103, Sharia al-Malik Seoud, Tripoli; tel. (21) 3333591; fax (21) 4441488; internet www.cbl-ly.com; f. 1955 as National Bank of Libya, name changed to Bank of Libya 1963, to Central Bank of Libya 1977; bank of issue and central bank carrying govt accounts and operating exchange control; commercial operations transferred to National Commercial Bank 1970; Gov. and Chair. Dr TAHER E. JEHAIMI.

Other Banks

Ahli Bank: Jadu; f. 1998; private bank.

Gumhouria Bank: POB 396, Sharia Emhemed Megrief, Tripoli; tel. (21) 3333553; fax (21) 3339489; f. 1969 as successor to Barclays Bank International in Libya; known as Masraf al-Jumhuriya until March 1977; known as Jamahiriya Bank until December 2000; wholly-owned subsidiary of the Central Bank; throughout Libya; Chair. MUHAMMAD A. SHOKRI; 53 brs.

Libyan Arab Foreign Bank: POB 2542, Tower 2, Dat al-Imad Complex, Tripoli; tel. (21) 3350155; fax (21) 3350164; f. 1972; off-shore bank wholly owned by Central Bank of Libya; cap. and res LD 275.2m., dep. LD 2,560.0m. (Dec. 2000); Chair. and Gen. Man. MUHAMMAD H. LAYAS.

National Commercial Bank SAL: POB 543, HO G.S.P.L.A.J., al-Baida; tel. (21) 3612267; fax (21) 3610306; f. 1970 to take over commercial banking division of Central Bank (then Bank of Libya) and brs of Aruba Bank and Istiklal Bank; wholly owned by Central Bank of Libya; cap. LD 35m., res LD 63.4m., dep. LD 1,545.6m. (Dec. 1998); Chair. and Gen. Man. BADER A. ABU AZIZA; 49 brs.

Sahara Bank SPI: POB 270, Sharia 1 September 10, Tripoli; tel. (21) 3339804; fax (21) 3337922; f. 1964 to take over br. of Banco di Sicilia; 82% owned by Central Bank of Libya; cap. LD 525,000, res LD 52.5m., dep. LD 488.4m. (March 1988); Chair. and Gen. Man. OMAR A. SHABOU; 20 brs.

Umma Bank SAL: POB 685, 1 Giaddat Omar el-Mokhtar, Tripoli; tel. (21) 3334031; fax (21) 3332505; e-mail ummabank@umma -bank.com; internet www.umma-bank.com; f. 1969 to take over brs of Banco di Roma; wholly owned by Central Bank of Libya; cap. LD 23m., res LD 25.3m., dep. LD 1,393.8m. (Dec. 2001); Chair. and Gen. Man. AYAD DAHAIM; 50 brs.

Wahda Bank: POB 452, Fadiel Abu Omar Sq., El-Berkha, Benghazi; tel. (61) 24709; fax (61) 3337592; f. 1970 to take over Bank of North Africa, Commercial Bank SAL, Nahda Arabia Bank, Société Africaine de Banque SAL, Kafila al-Ahly Bank; 87%-owned by Central Bank of Libya; cap. LD 36m., res LD 106.1m., dep. LD 1,553.3m. (Dec. 1999); Chair. and Gen. Man. Dr MUHAMMAD M. GHADBAN; 59 brs.

INSURANCE

Libya Insurance Co: POB 64, Sharia Jamal Abdelnasser, Zawia; tel. (23) 629768; fax (23) 629490; f. 1964 (merged with Al-Mukhtar Insurance Co in 1981); all classes of insurance; Man. BELAID ABU GHALIA.

Trade and Industry

There are state trade and industrial organizations responsible for the running of industries at all levels, which supervise production, distribution and sales. There are also central bodies responsible for the power generation industry, agriculture, land reclamation and transport.

GOVERNMENT AGENCY

Great Man-made River Authority (GMRA): Tripoli; supervises construction of pipeline carrying water to the Libyan coast from beneath the Sahara desert, to provide irrigation for agricultural projects; Sec. for the Great Man-made River project ABD AL-MAJID AL-AOUD.

DEVELOPMENT ORGANIZATIONS

Arab Organization for Agricultural Development: POB 12898, Zohra, Tripoli; tel. and fax (21) 3619275; e-mail arabagri@lycos.com; responsible for agricultural development projects.

General National Organization for Industrialization: Sharia San'a, Tripoli; tel. (21) 3334995f. 1970; a public org. responsible for the devt of industry.

Kufra and Sarir Authority: Council of Agricultural Development, Benghazi; f. 1972 to develop the Kufra oasis and Sarir area in southeast Libya.

CHAMBERS OF COMMERCE

Benghazi Chamber of Commerce, Trade, Industry and Agriculture: POB 208 and 1286, Benghazi; tel. (61) 95142; fax (61) 80761; f. 1956; Pres. Dr SADIQ M. BUSNAINA; Gen. Man. YOUSUF AL-JIAMI; 45,000 mems.

Tripoli Chamber of Commerce, Industry and Agriculture: POB 2321, Sharia Najed 6–8, Tripoli; tel. (21) 3336855; fax (21) 3332655; f. 1952; Pres. ABDALLAH AL-BARONE; Dir-Gen. RAMADAN A. ZEREG; 60,000 mems.

UTILITIES
Electricity

General Electricity Company of Libya: POB 668, Tripoli; Sec of People's Cttee OMRAN IBRAHIM ABUKRAA.

STATE HYDROCARBONS COMPANIES

Until 1986 petroleum affairs in Libya were dealt with primarily by the Secretariat of the General People's Committee for Petroleum. This body was abolished in March 1986, and sole responsibility for the administration of the petroleum industry passed to the national companies which were already in existence. The Secretariat of the General People's Committee for Petroleum was re-established in March 1989 and incorporated into the new Secretariat for the General People's Committee for Energy in October 1992. This was dissolved in March 2000, and responsibility for local oil policy transferred to the National Oil Corporation, under the supervision

of the General People's Committee. Since 1973 the Libyan Government has entered into participation agreements with some of the foreign oil companies (concession holders), and nationalized others. It has concluded 85%–15% production-sharing agreements with various oil companies.

National Oil Corporation (NOC): POB 2655, Tripoli; tel. (21) 46180; fax (21) 31390; f. 1970 as successor to the Libyan General Petroleum Corpn, to undertake joint ventures with foreign cos; to build and operate refineries, storage tanks, petrochemical facilities, pipelines and tankers; to take part in arranging specifications for local and imported petroleum products; to participate in general planning of oil installations in Libya; to market crude oil and to establish and operate oil terminals; from 2000 responsible for deciding local oil policy, under supervision of General People's Committee; Chair. ABD AL-HAFIZ ZLEITNI.

  Oilinvest International: Tripoli; wholly-owned subsidiary of the NOC; Chair. and Gen. Man. AHMAD ADB AL-KARIM AHMAD.

Agip North Africa and Middle East Ltd—Libyan Branch: POB 346, Tripoli; tel. and fax (21) 3335135; Sec. of People's Cttee A. M. CREUI.

Arabian Gulf Oil Co (AGOCO): POB 263, Benghazi; tel. (61) 28931; fax (21) 49031; Chair. F. SAID.

Az-Zawiyah Oil Refining Co: POB 15715, Zawia; tel. (23) 20125; fax (23) 605948; f. 1973; Gen. Man. H. LASOUD.

Brega Oil Marketing Co: POB 402, Sharia Bashir as-Saidawi, Tripoli; tel. (21) 4440830; f. 1971; Chair. Dr DOKALI B. AL-MEGHARIEF.

International Oil Investments Co: Tripoli; f. 1988 with initial capital of \$500m. to acquire 'downstream' facilities abroad; Chair. MUHAMMAD AL-JAWAD.

National Drilling and Workover Co: POB 1454, 208 Sharia Omar Mukhtar, Tripoli; tel. (21) 3332411; f. 1986; Chair. IBRAHIM BAHI.

Ras Lanouf Oil and Gas Processing Co (RASCO): POB 1971, Ras Lanouf, Benghazi; tel. (21) 3605177; fax (21) 607924; f. 1978; Chair. MAHMUD ABDALLAH NAAS.

Sirte Oil Co: POB 385, Marsa el-Brega, Tripoli; tel. (21) 607261; fax (21) 601487; f. 1955 as Esso Standard Libya, taken over by Sirte Oil Co 1982; absorbed the National Petrochemicals Co in October 1990; exploration, production of crude oil, gas, and petrochemicals, liquefaction of natural gas; Chair. M. M. BENNIRAN.

Umm al-Jawaby Petroleum Co: POB 693, Tripoli; Chair. and Gen. Man. MUHAMMAD TENTTOUSH.

Waha Oil Co: POB 395, Tripoli; tel (21) 3331116; fax (21) 3337169; Chair. SALEH M. KAABAR.

Zueitina Oil Co: POB 2134, Tripoli; tel. (21) 3338011; fax (21) 3339109; f. 1986; Chair. of Management Cttee M. OUN.

TRADE UNIONS

General Federation of Producers' Trade Unions: POB 734, Sharia Istanbul 2, Tripoli; tel. (21) 4446011; f. 1952; affiliated to ICFTU; Sec.-Gen. BASHIR IHWIJ; 17 trade unions with 700,000 mems.

General Union for Oil and Petrochemicals: Tripoli; Chair. MUHAMMAD MITHNANI.

Pan-African Federation of Petroleum Energy and Allied Workers: Tripoli; affiliated to the Organisation of African Trade Union Unity.

Transport

Department of Road Transport and Railways: POB 14527, Sharia Az-Zawiyah, Secretariat of Communications and Transport Bldg, Tripoli; tel. (21) 609011; fax (21) 605605; Dir-Gen. Projects and Research MUHAMMAD ABU ZIAN.

RAILWAYS

There are, at present, no railways in Libya. In mid-1998, however, the Government invited bids for the construction of a 3,170 km-railway, comprising one branch, 2,178 km in length, running from north to south, and another, 992 km in length, running from east to west. The railway may eventually be linked to other North African rail networks.

ROADS

The most important road is the 1,822-km national coast road from the Tunisian to the Egyptian border, passing through Tripoli and Benghazi. It has a second link between Barce and Lamluda, 141 km long. Another national road runs from a point on the coastal road 120 km south of Misurata through Sebha to Ghat near the Algerian border (total length 1,250 km). There is a branch 247 km long running from Vaddan to Sirte (Surt). A 690-km road, connecting

Tripoli and Sebha, and another 626 km long, from Ajdabiyah in the north to Kufra in the south-east, were opened in 1983. The Tripoli–Ghat section (941 km) of the third, 1,352-km long national road was opened in September 1984. There is a road crossing the desert from Sebha to the frontiers of Chad and Niger.

In addition to the national highways, the west of Libya has about 1,200 km of paved and macadamized roads and the east about 500 km. All the towns and villages of Libya, including the desert oases, are accessible by motor vehicle. In 1996 Libya had 47,590 km of paved roads.

SHIPPING

The principal ports are Tripoli, Benghazi, Mersa Brega, Misurata and as-Sider. Zueitina, Ras Lanouf, Mersa Hariga, Mersa Brega and as-Sider are mainly oil ports. A 30-inch crude oil pipeline connects the Zelten oilfields with Mersa Brega. Another pipeline joins the Sarir oilfield with Mersa Hariga, the port of Tobruk, and a pipeline from the Sarir field to Zueitina was opened in 1968. A port is being developed at Darnah. Libya also has the use of Tunisian port facilities at Sfax and Gabès, to alleviate congestion at Tripoli. At 31 December 2001 Libya's merchant fleet consisted of 140 vessels, with a combined displacement of 250,796 grt.

General National Maritime Transport Co: POB 80173, Sharia Ahmad Sharif 2, Tripoli; tel. (21) 3333155; fax (21) 6361664; f. 1971 to handle all projects dealing with maritime trade; Chair. SAID MILUD AL-AHRASH.

CIVIL AVIATION

There are four international airports: Tripoli International Airport, situated at ben Gashir, 34 km (21 miles) from Tripoli; Benina Airport 19 km (12 miles) from Benghazi; Sebha Airport; and Misurata Airport. There are a further 10 regional airports. A US $800m. programme to improve the airport infrastructure and air traffic control network was approved in mid-2001.

Libyan Arab Airlines: POB 2555, ben Fernas Bldg, Sharia Haiti, Tripoli; tel. (21) 3614102; fax (21) 3614238; f. 1989 by merger of Jamahiriya Air Transport (which in 1983 took over operations of United African Airlines) and Libyan Arab Airlines (f. 1964 as Kingdom of Libya Airlines and renamed 1969); passenger and cargo services from Tripoli, Benghazi and Sebha to destinations in Europe, North Africa, the Middle East and Asia; domestic services throughout Libya; Chief Exec. SABRI ABDALLAH.

Tourism

The principal attractions for visitors to Libya are Tripoli, with its beaches and annual International Fair, the ancient Roman towns of Sabratha, Leptis Magna and Cyrene, and historic oases. There were 962,559 visitor arrivals in 2000; in 1999 receipts totalled some US $28m.

Department of Tourism and Fairs: POB 891, Sharia Omar Mukhtar, Tripoli; tel. (21) 3332255; fax (21) 4448385; Head of Fairs MUHAMMAD ELGADI.

General Board of Tourism: POB 91871, Tripoli; tel. and fax (21) 503041; Chair. MUHAMMAD SEALNA.

Defence

Commander-in-Chief of Armed Forces: Brig. ABU-BAKR YOUNIS JABER.

Chief of Staff of Armed Forces: Brig. MUSTAPHA KHARROUBI.

Commander of the Navy: ABD AL-LATIF AHMAD SHAKSHOUKI.

Estimated Defence Budget (2001): LD 650m.

Military Service: selective conscription; 1–2 years.

Total Armed Forces (August 2001): 76,000: army 45,000; navy 8,000; air force 23,000.

People's Militia: 40,000.

Education

Education is officially compulsory for nine years between six and 15 years of age. Primary education begins at the age of six and lasts for nine years. Secondary education, beginning at 15 years of age, lasts for a further three years. In 1997 primary enrolment included 99.9% of the relevant age-group (males 99.9%; females 99.9%). In that year secondary enrolment was equivalent to 99.9% of pupils in the relevant age-groups (males 99.9%; females 99.9%). The teaching of French was abolished in Libyan schools in 1983.

In 1958 the University of Libya opened in Benghazi with Faculties of Arts and Commerce, followed the next year by the Faculty of Science, near Tripoli. Faculties of Law, Agriculture, Engineering, Teacher Training, and Arabic Language and Islamic Studies have since been added to the University. In 1973 the University was divided into two parts, to form the Universities of Tripoli and Benghazi, later renamed Al-Fatah and Ghar Younis universities. The Faculty of Education at Al-Fatah University became Sebha University in 1983. There is a University of Technology (Bright Star) at Mersa Brega and the Al-Arab Medical University at Benghazi. Some 126,348 students were enrolled at universities in 1995/96.

Bibliography

di Agostini, Col Enrico. *La popolazione della Tripolitania.* 2 vols; Tripoli, 1917.

La popolazione della Cirenaica. Benghazi, 1922–23.

Amministrazione Fiduciaria all'Italia in Africa. Florence, 1948.

Archivio bibliografico Coloniale. Florence, Libia, 1915–21.

Allan, J. A. *Libya: the Experience of Oil.* London, Croom Helm, 1981.

Ansell, Meredith O. and al-Arif, Ibrahim M. *The Libyan Revolution.* London, The Oleander Press, 1972.

Arnold, Guy. *The Maverick State: Qaddafi and the New World Order.* London, Cassell, 1997.

Berlardinalli, Arsenio. *La Ghibla.* Tripoli, 1935.

Blunsum, T. *Libya: the Country and its People.* London, Queen Anne Press, 1968.

Burr, J. Millard and Collins, Robert O. *Africa's Thirty Years' War: Chad, Libya, and the Sudan, 1963–93.* Boulder, CO, Westview Press, 1999.

Cachia, Anthony J. *Libya under the Second Ottoman Occupation, 1835–1911.* Tripoli, 1945.

Colucci, Massimo. *Il Regime della Proprietà Fondiaria nell'Africa Italiana: Vol. I. Libia.* Bologna, 1942.

Cooley, John. *Libyan Sandstorm.* London, Sidgwick and Jackson, 1983.

Davis, John. *Libyan Politics: Tribe and Revolution.* London, I. B. Tauris, 1987.

Deeb, Mary-Jane. *Libya's Foreign Policy in North Africa.* Boulder, CO, Westview Press, 1991.

Despois, Jean. *Géographie Humaine.* Paris, 1946.

Le Djebel Nefousa. Paris, 1935.

La Colonisation italienne en Libye; Problèmes et Méthodes. Paris, Larose-Editeurs, 1935.

Dorsch, Monique and Strunz, Herbert. *Libyen: Zurück auf die Weltbühne.* Frankfurt-am-Main, Petch Lang, 2000.

Epton, Nina. *Oasis Kingdom: The Libyan Story.* New York, 1953.

Evans-Pritchard, E. E. *The Sanusi of Cyrenaica.* London, 1949.

Farley, Rawle. *Planning for Development in Libya.* London, Pall Mall, 1971.

First, Ruth. *Libya—the Elusive Revolution.* London, Penguin, 1974.

Franca, Pietro, and others. *L'Italia in Africa: Incivilimento e Sviluppo dell'Eritrea, della Somalia, e della Libia.* Rome, 1947.

Gurney, Judith. *Libya: The Political Economy of Oil.* Oxford University Press, 1996.

Hajjaji, S. A. *The New Libya.* Tripoli, 1967.

Herrmann, Gerhard. *Italiens Weg zum Imperium.* Leipzig, Goldman, 1938.

Heseltine, Nigel. *From Libyan Sands to Chad.* London, Museum Press, 1960.

Hill, R. W. *A Bibliography of Libya.* University of Durham, 1959.

Khadduri, Majid. *Modern Libya, a Study in Political Development.* Johns Hopkins Press, 1963.

Khalidi, I. R. *Constitutional Developments in Libya.* Beirut, Khayat's Book Co-operative, 1956.

El-Kikhia, Mansour O. *Libya's Qaddafi: The Politics of Contradiction.* University of California Press, 1997.

Kubbah, Abdul Amir Q. *Libya, Its Oil Industry and Economic System.* Baghdad, The Arab Petro-Economic Research Centre, 1964.

Layish, A. *Legal Documents on Libyan Tribal Society and the Process of Sedenterization: Part 1*. Wiesbaden, Harrassowirz Verlag, 1998.

Legg, H. J. *Libya: Economic and General Conditions in Libya*. London, 1952.

Lethielleux, J. *Le Fezzan, ses Jardins, ses Palmiers: Notes d'Ethnographie et d'Histoire*. Tunis, 1948.

Lindberg, J. A. *General Economic Appraisal of Libya*. New York, 1952.

Martel, André. *La Libye 1835–1990: Essai de géopolitique historique*. Paris, Presses Universitaires de France, 1991.

Martínez, L. (Ed.). 'La Libye après l'embargo', in *Monde Arabe Maghre-Machrek*, La Documentation Française, Paris. Special Number, 170 (Oct.–Dec.) 2000.

Mattes, Hans-Peter. *Die innere und aussere islamische Mission Libyens*. Munich/Mainz, Kaiser-Gruenewald, 1987.

Micacchi, Rodolfo. *La Tripolitania sotto il dominio dei Caramanli*. Intra, 1936.

Murabet, Mohammed. *Tripolitania: the Country and its People*. Tripoli, 1952.

Norman, John. *Labour and Politics in Libya and Arab Africa*. New York, Bookman, 1965.

Obeidi, Amal. *Political Culture in Libya*. Richmond, Curzon, 2001.

Owen, R. *Libya: a Brief Political and Economic Survey*. London, 1961.

Péan, Pierre. *Manipulations Africaines*. Paris, Plon, 2001.

Pelt, Adrian. *Libyan Independence and the United Nations*. Yale University Press, 1970.

Pichou, Jean. *La Question de Libye dans le règlement de la paix*. Paris, 1945.

Qaddafi, Col Muammar al-. *The Green Book*. 3 vols, Tripoli, 1976–79; Vol. I: The Solution of the Problem of Democracy, Vol. II: The Solution of the Economic Problem, Vol. III: The Social Basis of the Third Universal Theory.

Rivlin, Benjamin. *The United Nations and the Italian Colonies*. New York, 1950.

Royal Institute of International Affairs. *The Italian Colonial Empire*. London, 1940.

St. John, Ronald Bruce. *Historical Dictionary of Libya. (African Historical Dictionaries Series, No. 33)*. Lanham, MD, 1998.

Schlueter, Hans. *Index Libycus*. Boston, G. K. Hall, 1972.

Simons, Geoff and Dalyell, Tam. *Libya*. Basingstoke, Macmillan, 1996.

Steele-Greig, A. J. *History of Education in Tripolitania from the Time of the Ottoman Occupation to the Fifth Year under British Military Occupation*. Tripoli, 1948.

Vandewalle, Dirk. *Libya Since Independence—Oil and State-Building*. Ithaca, NY, Cornell University Press, 1998.

(Ed.). *North Africa: Development and Reform in a Changing Global Economy*. New York, St Martin's Press Inc, 1996.

(Ed.). *Qadhafi's Libya: 1969–1994*. London, Macmillan, 1996.

Villard, Henry S. *Libya: The New Arab Kingdom of North Africa*. Ithaca, NY, 1956.

Waddams, Frank C. *The Libyan Oil Industry*. London, Croom Helm, 1980.

Ward, Philip. *Touring Libya*. 3 vols, 1967–69.

Tripoli: Portrait of a City. 1970.

Williams, G. *Green Mountain, an Informal Guide to Cyrenaica and its Jebel Akhdar*. London, 1963.

Willimott, S. G. and Clarke, J. I. *Field Studies in Libya*. Durham, 1960.

Wright, John. *Libya: a Modern History*. London, Croom Helm, 1982.

MOROCCO

Physical and Social Geography

The Kingdom of Morocco is the westernmost of the three North African countries known to the Arabs as Jeziret al-Maghreb or 'Island of the West'. It occupies an area of 458,730 sq km (177,117 sq miles), excluding Western (formerly Spanish) Sahara (252,120 sq km), a disputed territory under Moroccan occupation. Morocco has an extensive coastline on both the Atlantic Ocean and the Mediterranean Sea. However, owing to its position and intervening mountain ranges, Morocco remained relatively isolated from the rest of the Maghreb and served as a refuge for descendants of the native Berber-speaking inhabitants of north-west Africa.

According to census results, the population at 2 September 1994 was 26,073,717. About 35% of the total were Berber-speaking peoples, living mainly in mountain villages, while the Arabic-speaking majority was concentrated in towns in the lowlands, particularly in Casablanca (which was the largest city in the Maghreb, with a population of 2,940,623 at the 1994 census), Marrakesh, the old southern capital (population 745,541), Fez (population 774,754), and Rabat (population 1,385,872, including Salé), the modern administrative capital. According to official estimates, the population in mid-2000 was 28,705,000.

PHYSICAL FEATURES

The physical geography of Morocco is dominated by the highest and most rugged ranges in the Atlas Mountain system of north-west Africa. They are the result of mountain-building in the Tertiary era, when sediments deposited beneath an ancestral Mediterranean Sea were uplifted, folded and fractured. The mountains remain geologically unstable and Morocco is liable to severe earthquakes.

In Morocco the Atlas Mountains form four distinct massifs, which are surrounded and partially separated by lowland plains and plateaux. In the north, the Rif Atlas comprise a rugged arc of mountains that rise steeply from the Mediterranean coast to heights of more than 2,200 m above sea level. There, limestone and sandstone ranges form an effective barrier to east–west communications. They are inhabited by Berber farming families who live in isolated mountain villages and have little contact with the Arabs of Tétouan (estimated population, including Larache, 878,000 at mid-1993) and Tangier (579,000) at the north-western end of the Rif chain.

The Middle Atlas lie immediately south of the Rif, separated by the Col of Taza, a narrow gap which affords the only easy route between western Algeria and Atlantic Morocco. They rise to about 3,000 m and form a broad barrier between the two countries. They also function as a major drainage divide and are flanked by the basins of Morocco's two principal rivers, the Oum er-Rbia which flows west to the Atlantic and the Moulouya which flows north-east to the Mediterranean. Much of the Middle Atlas consists of a limestone plateau dissected by river gorges and capped here and there by volcanic craters and lava flows. The semi-nomadic Berber tribes spend the winter in villages in the valleys and move to the higher slopes in summer to pasture their flocks.

To the south the Middle Atlas chain merges into the High Atlas, the most formidable of the mountain massifs, which rises to about 4,000 m and is heavily snow-clad in winter. The mountains extend from south-west to north-east, and rise precipitously from both the Atlantic lowland to the north and the desert plain of Saharan Morocco to the south. There are no easily accessible routes across the High Atlas, but numerous mountain tracks allow the exchange of goods by pack animal between Atlantic and Saharan Morocco. A considerable Berber population lives in the mountain valleys in compact, fortified villages.

The Anti-Atlas is the lowest and most southerly of the mountain massifs. Structurally it forms an elevated edge of the Saharan platform which was uplifted when the High Atlas was formed. It consists largely of crystalline rocks and is joined to the southern margin of the High Atlas by a mass of volcanic lavas which separates the valley of the river Sous, draining west to the Atlantic at Agadir, from that of the upper Draa, draining south-east towards the Sahara. On the southern side of the chain, barren slopes are trenched by gorges from which cultivated palm groves protrude.

Stretching inland from the Atlantic coast is an extensive area of lowland, enclosed on the north, east and south by the Rif, Middle and High Atlas. It consists of the Gharb plain and the wide valley of the River Sebou in the north and of the plateaux and plains of the Meseta, the Tadla, the Rehamna, the Djebilet and the Haouz farther south. Most of the Arabic-speaking people of Morocco live in this region.

CLIMATE AND VEGETATION

Northern and central Morocco experience a 'Mediterranean' climate, with warm, wet winters and hot, dry summers, but to the south this gives way to semi-arid and eventually to desert conditions. In the Rif and the northern parts of the Middle Atlas mean annual rainfall exceeds 750 mm and the summer drought lasts only three months, but in the rest of the Middle Atlas, in the High Atlas and over the northern half of the Atlantic lowland rainfall is reduced to between 400 mm and 750 mm and the summer drought lasts for four months or more. During the summer intensely hot winds from the Sahara, known as the Sirocco or Chergui, occasionally cross the mountains and desiccate the lowland. Summer heat on the Atlantic coastal plain is tempered, however, by sea breezes.

Over the southern half of the Atlantic lowland and the Anti-Atlas semi-arid conditions prevail and rainfall decreases to 200 mm–400 mm per year, becoming very variable and generally insufficient for the regular cultivation of cereal crops without irrigation. East and south of the Atlas Mountains, which act as a barrier to rain-bearing winds from the Atlantic, rainfall is reduced still further and regular cultivation becomes entirely dependent on irrigation.

The chief contrast in the vegetation of Morocco is between the mountain massifs, which support forest or open woodland, and the surrounding lowlands, which tend to be covered only by scrub growth of low, drought-resistant bushes. The natural vegetation has been depleted, and in many places actually destroyed, by excessive cutting, burning and grazing. The middle and upper slopes of the mountains are often quite well wooded, with evergreen oak dominant at the lower and cedar at the higher elevations. The lowlands to the east and south of the Atlas Mountains support distinctive species of steppe and desert vegetation, among which esparto grass and the argan tree (which is unique to south-western Morocco) are conspicuous.

NEWLY-ANNEXED TERRITORY

After independence the Moroccan Government claimed a right to administer a large area of the western Sahara, including territory in Algeria and Mauritania, and the whole of Spanish Sahara. The claim was based on the extent of Moroccan rule in medieval times. The existence of considerable deposits of phosphates in Spanish Sahara and of iron ore in the Algeria-Morocco border region further encouraged Moroccan interest in expansion. After Spanish withdrawal from the Sahara in 1976, Morocco and Mauritania divided the former Spanish Sahara (now known as Western Sahara) between them, with Morocco annexing the northern part of the territory, including the phosphate mines of Bou Craa. In August 1979 Mauritania renounced its share, which was immediately annexed by Morocco and incorporated as a new province, Oued ed-Dahab.

The current population of Western Sahara are of Moorish or mixed Arab-Berber descent with some negro admixture, who depend for their existence on herds of sheep, camels and goats which they move seasonally from one pasture to another. The main tribes are the R'gibat, Uld Delim, Izargien and Arosien. At the census of September 1982 the population of Western Sahara was estimated at 163,868; at the census of September 1994 the population had increased to 252,146. The principal towns in the area are el-Aaiún, es-Smara (formerly Smara) and Dakhla (Villa Cisneros).

The relief of most of the area is gentle. The coast is backed by a wide alluvial plain overlain in the south by extensive sand dunes aligned from south-west to north-east and extending inland over 250 km (155 miles). Behind the coastal plain the land rises gradually to a plateau surface broken by sandstone ridges that reach 300 m in height. In the north-east, close to the Mauritanian frontier, isolated mountain ranges, such as the

Massif de la Guelta, rise to over 600 m. There are no permanent streams and the only considerable valley is that of the Saguia el-Hamra which crosses the northernmost part of the area to reach the coast at el-Aaiún north of Cape Bojador. The whole region experiences an extreme desert climate. Nowhere does mean annual rainfall exceed 100 mm and over most of the territory it is less than 50 mm. Vegetation is restricted to scattered desert shrubs and occasional patches of coarse grass in most depressions. Along the coast, summer heat is tempered by air moving inland after it has been cooled over the waters of the cold Canaries current which flows offshore from north to south.

History

Revised for this edition by RICHARD I. LAWLESS

EARLY HISTORY

The Phoenicians and Carthaginians established trading posts on Morocco's coasts, and later the Romans established the province of Mauritania Tingitana in the north of the country. Muslim warriors made raids in AD 684–85 and had conquered Morocco by the eighth century. The Berber tribes of Morocco rallied to Islam, but adopted Kharijite heresies, which, together with Berber particularism, led to a great rebellion in 739–40 and the subsequent fragmentation of Morocco into small Muslim principalities.

Idris, a descendant of the Prophet Muhammad, founded the first of the great ruling Muslim dynasties in Morocco. The regime lasted from 788–89 to 985–86 but, after the death of Idris' son (828–29), fell into decline. There followed two centuries of internal conflict and tribal revolt, as well as pressures from the Umayyad Caliphate in Spain and from the Fatimid Caliphate in Ifriqiya (Tunisia and eastern Algeria) in 908–69. Subsequently, Morocco entered a glorious era, with the rise of the Almoravid religious movement among the nomadic Berbers of Sanhaja descent. The Almoravids declared Holy War (Jihad) and established control, under Yousuf ibn Tashufin (d. 1106), over all Morocco and much of Algeria, and also annexed Muslim lands in Spain. After the death of Tashufin's successor in 1142, however, Almoravid power declined rapidly.

A new religious force emerged after the death in 1130 of Muhammad ibn Tumart, a religious teacher who had gathered Berber adherents, called Almohads, around himself in the High Atlas. One of his disciples, Abd al-Mumin, led the Almohads in their conquest of the Maghreb as far east as Tripolitania and Cyrenaica in 1151–59. The Almohads prospered in the reign of al-Mansur (1184–98), who brought Muslim Spain under his control, but in 1212 they suffered a serious defeat at the hands of the Spanish Christians, and thereafter the Almohad empire began to decline. A new Berber house, the Merinids, became prominent, and by the mid-13th century they had eclipsed the Almohads. Their influence lasted for about 100 years but their attempts to reconstitute the Almohad empire were unsuccessful.

Nomadic tribes of Arab origin had penetrated the Maghreb in the 11th and 12th centuries, along with other Badawi elements during the later Almohad period. With the disintegration of the Merinid state, the Badawi tribes invaded, contributing greatly to the Arabization of the Maghreb. Until 1465 Morocco was prey to internal discords, which persisted until the emergence of the Wattasids, another Berber regime. Their pre-eminence was, however, short-lived, and they failed to halt the Portuguese and the Spaniards, who were establishing outposts along the Moroccan coasts.

A new movement of resistance to the Spaniards and Portuguese was born among the religious confraternities who now led the Jihad against the Christians. The Saadian regime arose, originating in a line of Sharifs from the Saharan side of the Atlas mountains. Ahmad al-Mansur (1578–1603) reorganized the Saadian regime under a system which exempted various Arab tribes from taxation, in return for armed services to the State. Under this system, much depended on the character of

the Sultan, as tribal rivalries erupted whenever the central government was weak or ill-directed. The period of Saadian rule, which ended in 1668, was, however, one of considerable prosperity.

Yet another wave of popular religious feeling brought to power the house of Alawi (Hasani or Filali), which originated among the Saharan Berbers and continues to reign in Morocco. Rashid II (1664–72) and Mulai Ismail (1672–1727) firmly established the regime, under which Morocco was more peaceful and united than it was ever to be again until French occupation. Mulai Ismail successfully repelled the Sanhaja Berbers, but a period of uncertainty followed his death, in the course of which one of his sons, Abdullah, was dethroned four times. His son, Sharif Muhammad ibn Abdallah (1757–90), and his immediate successors strove to maintain their power in the face of tribal dissidence and the threat of foreign intervention. However, the French conquest of Algiers in 1830 had repercussions in Morocco. Mulai Abd ar-Rahman, who was then Sultan of Morocco, gave military assistance to Abd al-Qadir, the Algerian Amir who led Muslim resistance to France, and Moroccan troops were later defeated by a French force at Wadi Isly in 1844.

A dispute over the limits of the Ceuta enclave, which had been under Spanish rule since 1580, led to a brief war between Morocco and Spain in 1860. Spanish troops defeated the Moroccans and, under the terms of the peace settlement, the Ceuta enclave was enlarged and Spain was given indemnities. Morocco also granted to Spain a territorial enclave on the Atlantic coast opposite the Canaries (Santa Cruz de Mar Pequeña, now Ifni). In 1884 Spain claimed a protectorate over the coastal zone to the south of Morocco, from Cape Bojador to Cape Blanco, the future Spanish Sahara. The borders between this territory, known as the Río de Oro, and the French possessions to the south and east were agreed between France and Spain in June 1900. A convention between France and Spain in October 1904 assigned to Spain two zones of influence, one in northern and the other in southern Morocco. The southern border of Morocco was set at 27° 40'N, beyond which were Spain's Saharan territories. The Germans now sought to intervene in Moroccan affairs and, at the conference of Algeciras in 1906, they secured the agreement of the Great Powers to the economic 'internationalization' of Morocco. A crisis in 1911, precipitated by the appearance of a German gun-boat off Agadir, ended in a Franco-German settlement whereby the Germans recognized Morocco as a French sphere of influence. In March 1912 Morocco became a protectorate of France, with a French Resident-General empowered to direct foreign affairs, control defence and introduce domestic reforms.

FRENCH RULE

Under an agreement of 1912, Spain retained its zones of influence (somewhat reduced), but these were now granted by France as the protecting power rather than by the Sultan. Gen. Lyautey, the first French Resident-General in Morocco, established effective control, before 1914, over the plains and lower plateaux of Morocco from Fez to the Atlas mountains south of Marrakesh;

then, before 1918, over the western Atlas, the Taza corridor as far as Algeria and some areas of the northern highlands. French troops helped Spain to subdue a formidable rebellion (1921–26) of the Rif tribe under Abd al-Krim. This resulted in the subjugation of the northern mountains and allowed the French to concentrate on gaining control of the Middle Atlas and the Tafilalet—a task that was accomplished by 1934, when the pacification of Morocco could be regarded as complete.

From this time, nationalist sentiment began to manifest itself in Morocco. A 'comité d'action marocaine' asked for a limitation of the protectorate. This 'comité' was dissolved in 1937, but nationalist propaganda against the French regime continued. Morocco supported France in 1939 and the Free French movement in 1942. A Party of Independence (Istiqlal), formed in 1943, demanded independence for Morocco, with a constitutional government under Sultan Muhammad ibn Yousuf, who supported the nationalist movement. Although Istiqlal had a large following in the towns, the party had little support among the conservative tribes of Morocco, who favoured Thami al-Glawi, the Pasha of Marrakesh. As a result, tension between the new and the old ideologies in Morocco increased in 1953. Sultan Muhammad ibn Yousuf had quarrelled with the French administration, and in May 1953 a number of Pashas and Cadis, led by al-Glawi, asked for his removal. The Berber tribes converged in force on the main urban centres in Morocco, and on 20 August 1953 the Sultan agreed to go into exile in Europe, but not to abdicate. Muhammad ibn Arafa, a prince of the Alawi house, was subsequently recognized as Sultan. The situation remained tense, with assassination attempts on the Sultan in 1953 and 1954, outbreaks of violence throughout Morocco in 1954–55 and intense nationalist fervour.

INDEPENDENCE—1956

Sultan Muhammad ibn Arafa renounced the throne and withdrew to Tangier in 1955. On 5 November Muhammad ibn Yousuf was recognized once more as the legitimate Sultan. A joint Franco-Moroccan declaration of 2 March 1956 stated that the protectorate agreement of 1912 was obsolete and that the French Government now recognized the independence of Morocco. A protocol of the same date covered the transitional phase before new agreements could come into effect. The Sultan would now have full legislative powers in Morocco. Henceforth a high commissioner was to represent France in the new State. France also undertook to assist Morocco in the organization of its armed forces and the reassertion of Moroccan control over the zones of Spanish influence. On 12 November 1956 Morocco became a member of the UN.

In August 1956 Istiqlal proclaimed the need to abrogate the Convention of Algeciras (1906), which had 'internationalized' the economic life of Morocco, and also to secure the withdrawal of all foreign troops from the land. Following an international conference in October, Tangier was restored to Morocco. A royal charter of August 1957 preserved the former economic and financial system in force at Tangier, which included a free money market, quota-free trade with foreign countries and a low level of taxation. In 1959 Tangier lost its special status and was integrated financially and economically with Morocco, but a royal decree of January 1962 made it once more a free port. In 1956, prior to independence, Istiqlal had envisaged the creation of a 'Great Morocco' which would include certain areas in south-west Algeria, the Spanish territories in north-west Africa and also Mauritania, together with the French Sudan (i.e. the Republic of Mali). These claims were to be reiterated by Morocco in the following years.

The problem of the Spanish territories in north-west Africa also came to the fore. Spain had recognized the independence of Morocco and had renounced the northern zone of the protectorate assigned to it in Morocco under the terms of the Franco-Spanish convention of 1912. No agreement was reached, however, on the enclaves of Ceuta and Melilla in the north, the enclave of Ifni in the south, or the Spanish territories to the south of Morocco. Since 1934 these territories had been divided in two parts—the northern Saguia el-Hamra and the southern Río de Oro—both administered jointly with Ifni, and separately from the contiguous southern zone of Spain's protectorate in Morocco. Raids on Ifni and western Sahara by Moroccan irregular forces (the 'Armée de libération du Grand Sahara') caused

serious internal unrest during 1956–58, although the Moroccan Government denied responsibility. Negotiations between Morocco and Spain, held in Portugal, led in April 1958 to an agreement whereby Spain, in accordance with the settlement reached in April 1956, relinquished the southern zone of its former protectorate. Spain retained possession of the enclaves and of Saguia el-Hamra and Río de Oro, which were renamed Spanish Sahara and separated from Ifni.

KING HASSAN II AND ROYAL DOMINANCE OF GOVERNMENT

After independence, Istiqlal remained the dominant political force and obtained a majority in the Government. At the same time Sultan Muhammad strengthened the position of the monarchy. In July 1957 Prince Moulai Hassan was proclaimed heir to the throne and in August the Sultan assumed the title of King. Istiqlal's efforts to curb the power of the monarchy were hampered by internal division. Tension between the conservative and radical wings culminated in December 1958, when a Government was formed by Abdullah Ibrahim, a leader of the radical tendency. In the following months Mehdi Ben Barka led a movement to establish a radical party organization independent of the conservative Istiqlal leadership of Allal al-Fassi. In September 1959 this new organization became an independent party, the Union nationale des forces populaires (National Union of Popular Forces—UNFP). Although the UNFP supported Ibrahim's Government, it was subjected to repressive measures by the police and the army who were under the control of the King or of 'King's men' in the Cabinet. In May 1960 a new Government was formed with the King himself as Prime Minister and Prince Hassan as his deputy. Consequently the UNFP went into opposition. On the death of King Muhammad in February 1961 the Prince ascended the throne as King Hassan II, and also became Prime Minister. In December 1962 a new Constitution, which established a constitutional monarchy and guaranteed personal and political freedoms, was approved by referendum. In January 1963 a cabinet reorganization deprived Istiqlal leaders of their government posts, and when elections for the Chamber of Representatives were held in May, both Istiqlal and the UNFP appeared as opposition parties. The King was represented by the newly formed Front pour la défense des institutions constitutionnelles (FDIC). The election, by universal direct suffrage, failed to produce the expected clear majority for the government party, the results being: FDIC 69 seats; Istiqlal 41 seats; UNFP 28 seats; independents six seats. In the following months repressive action was taken against both opposition parties. Several Istiqlal deputies were arrested for protesting against corruption and mismanagement of the election, leading the party to boycott further elections later in the year. Almost all the leaders of the UNFP were arrested in July in connection with an alleged coup attempt. Many of them were held in solitary confinement, tortured and eventually sentenced to death. In November the King relinquished the premiership and installed an FDIC Government to represent his interests.

RELATIONS IN THE MAGHREB

In July 1962 Moroccan troops entered the region south of Colomb-Béchar in Algeria—a region never officially demarcated. The Moroccan press also launched a strong campaign in support of the view that the Tindouf area in the extreme south-west of Algeria should belong to Morocco—a claim of some importance, since the area contained large deposits of high-grade iron ore and also considerable resources of petroleum and natural gas.

An arbitration commission was established by the Organization of African Unity (OAU), and Algeria and Morocco submitted evidence in support of their respective territorial claims. In February 1964 an agreement was reached to establish a demilitarized zone, and relations between the two countries subsequently improved.

Relations between Morocco and Mauritania also became more amicable. The Ministers of Information of the two States met at Cairo in July 1964 during an African Summit Conference. An understanding was reached to bring an end to the 'war' of radio propaganda and criticism hitherto conducted between Morocco and Mauritania.

INTERNAL UNREST

In August 1964 the Moroccan Government was reorganized, although it remained composed largely of FDIC members. The reshuffle was part of an attempt to attract the opposition parties back into a coalition government, since the FDIC had an inadequate majority in the Chamber of Representatives and was itself split into two factions, the Parti socialiste démocratique and the mainly Berber Mouvement populaire (MP). The weakness of the Government contributed to the tension in early 1965, as unemployment and rising prices generated discontent among the urban working class. In June King Hassan proclaimed a state of emergency, whereby he himself assumed full legislative and executive powers. Fresh elections, it was stated, would be held after the Constitution had been revised and submitted to a referendum. In October the UNFP leader, Ben Barka, disappeared in France, never to be seen again. At a subsequent French trial, Gen. Oufkir, one of the King's sturdiest supporters, was found guilty *in absentia* of complicity in Ben Barka's disappearance. Relations between Morocco and France became very strained and there were anti-government protest strikes in Morocco.

In July 1967 King Hassan relinquished the post of Prime Minister in favour of Dr Muhammad Benhima, and in 1967 and 1968 there were eight major cabinet reshuffles. Considerable student and trade union unrest continued during this period, but the King won some approval for extensive nationalization measures and a degree of land redistribution.

There was a gradual return to normal political activity in 1969, albeit under royal direction. Communal elections were held in October, although these were boycotted by opposition parties, and the successful candidates were mostly independents. Following these elections, Benhima was replaced as Prime Minister by Dr Ahmad Laraki, formerly the Minister of Foreign Affairs. A new Constitution was approved in July 1970 by over 98% of voters, despite general opposition from the main political parties, trade unions and student organizations. Elections for a new unicameral legislature were held in August. Of the 240 members, 90 were elected by direct suffrage, 90 by local councils and 60 by an electoral college. The results were that 158 elected members were independents, 60 were from the MP and 22 were from opposition parties.

In July 1971 there was an unsuccessful attempt to overthrow the King and establish a republic. A series of talks ensued between the Government and members of Istiqlal and the UNFP, who had united to form a National Front in July 1970, but the parties refused to compromise on government policies.

In March 1972 a new Constitution was promulgated, under which executive power was vested in the King. Legislative power was held by the Chamber of Representatives, with two-thirds of its members elected by universal suffrage, compared with one-half under the previous Constitution. In late April, however, King Hassan announced that the Chamber would remain dissolved, and that elections for a new Chamber would be postponed until new electoral lists had been prepared.

In August 1972 King Hassan, after surviving another attempt on his life, assumed command of the armed forces and responsibility for defence. He again appealed to opposition parties to co-operate in supervising general elections and to collaborate with the Government. However, both Istiqlal and the UNFP demanded extensive reforms, which were unacceptable to the King. The elections were postponed indefinitely, and a new Cabinet was formed in November without opposition participation.

FOREIGN RELATIONS 1967–72

Morocco continued to press its claim to Spanish-held territories in north-west Africa. In December 1967 the UN General Assembly adopted a resolution urging Spain to hold a referendum in Spanish Sahara to allow the population to determine its future. Spain accepted the principle of self-determination, but in June 1970 progress was halted, after the violent repression of riots in the Saharan town of el-Aaiún resulted in numerous deaths. Further UN resolutions in support of decolonization were adopted, and Morocco, Mauritania and Algeria each supported a rival Saharan liberation movement. In contrast, the question of Ifni was settled amicably in June 1969, when Spain ceded the small coastal enclave to Morocco.

Morocco abandoned its claim to Mauritania in 1969. Full diplomatic recognition and an exchange of ambassadors followed in 1970, and the two countries signed a treaty of solidarity and co-operation in June. Relations with France improved, and in December 1969 the diplomatic missions in Paris and Rabat were returned to full ambassadorial status for the first time since the Ben Barka affair in 1966.

In May 1970 a final agreement (ratified in May 1973) was reached in the frontier dispute with Algeria, and a joint commission agreed to maintain the boundaries of the colonial period. The disputed region of Gara-Djebilet, rich in iron ore deposits, thus became the property of Algeria, but Morocco was to be a partner in a joint company to be established to exploit the deposits.

HASSAN IN CONTROL

In March 1973 the King announced plans for the Moroccanization of sectors of the economy within two years. He also reinforced his traditional support in the rural areas by ordering the confiscation of foreign-owned lands and their redistribution among the peasantry. Since most of the landowners were French, relations between France and Morocco deteriorated again and French aid was suspended for a year, pending an agreement on compensation. In the same month relations with Spain became strained when Morocco announced the extension of its territorial waters from 12 to 70 nautical miles; in January 1974 the two countries concluded an agreement allowing a limited number of Spanish vessels to fish in Moroccan waters. Hassan's new nationalist policy also led Morocco to take a more active part in the Arab-Israeli conflict. In February 1973 troops were dispatched to the Syrian front, and during the October War further detachments were sent to Egypt; this resulted in a partial *rapprochement* between Morocco and the more radical Arab states.

Meanwhile, Morocco pursued its claim to Spanish Sahara. The development of phosphate mining in the territory presented a threat to the Moroccan economy, which was itself dependent on revenue from phosphate exports. In July 1974 the King began preparations for an international campaign for the annexation of the Sahara. Discussions with Spain in August were inconclusive, and Morocco and Mauritania rejected Spain's proposal to hold a referendum in the Sahara under UN supervision. In October the issue was debated in the UN General Assembly at the initiative of Morocco. Two months later the Assembly formally approved Morocco's suggestion that the matter be brought before the International Court of Justice (ICJ) in The Hague, the Netherlands, and the UN Special Committee on Colonialism was instructed to send a mission to the territory. The referendum that Spain had proposed was to be postponed.

In the atmosphere of national unity produced by the Sahara issue in the second half of 1974 there was a revival of political activity. New parties were formed and existing parties reorganized. Most notably the split in the UNFP (which occurred in mid-1972) was confirmed, as the Rabat section of the party became the Union socialiste des forces populaires (USFP). King Hassan again promised elections for the following year, and once more postponed them indefinitely, but even the opposition were content to give priority to the Sahara dispute. Although some political prisoners were released, harassment of opposition parties continued and they remained unrepresented in the Government.

SAHARAN TAKE-OVER

After Spain reiterated its readiness to withdraw from Spanish Sahara, it became clear that the chief conflict was between the rival North African countries and liberation movements. In October 1974 Morocco and Mauritania reached a secret agreement on the future division of the territory, which came to light in July 1975. Meanwhile, Algeria became the main target of Moroccan invective for its support of the Frente Popular para la Liberación de Saguia el-Hamra y Río de Oro (Popular Front for the Liberation of Saguia el-Hamra and Río de Oro—the Frente Polisario or Polisario Front), a Saharan liberation movement, founded in 1973, which aimed to establish an independent, non-aligned state in Spanish Sahara.

In October 1975 a UN investigative mission reported that almost all the people whom it had consulted in the territory were 'categorically for independence and against the territorial claims of Morocco and Mauritania'. Two days later the ICJ ruled in favour of self-determination for the Sahrawi people. King Hassan immediately ordered a march of 350,000 unarmed civilians to take possession of Spanish Sahara. The Green March, as it was called, began on 6 November. The Spanish authorities allowed the marchers to progress a short distance across the border before halting their advance. On 9 November Hassan abandoned the march, and on 14 November a tripartite accord was signed in Madrid, whereby Spain agreed to withdraw from Western Sahara (as the territory was redesignated) in 1976 and transfer the territory to a joint Morocco-Mauritanian administration. Algeria reacted angrily, increasing its support for the Polisario Front and making veiled threats of direct military intervention. Moroccan armed forces swiftly occupied the territory, and entered the capital, el-Aaiún, on 11 December. They encountered fierce resistance from Polisario guerrillas, and many Sahrawis fled to the Algerian border to avoid the Moroccan advance. The last Spanish troops left in January 1976, a month before they were due to depart under the terms of the tripartite agreement.

The Moroccan Prime Minister, Ahmad Osman, visited France in January 1976, and French deliveries of military equipment to Morocco were increased. In late January Algerian and Moroccan forces clashed at Amgalla, inside Western Sahara, and there was further fighting in February. On 27 February the Sahrawi Arab Democratic Republic (SADR) was proclaimed, a Saharan government-in-exile was formed in Algeria and in March Morocco severed diplomatic relations with Algeria. The prospect of outright war between the two countries receded, however, as Algeria contented itself with arming and training Polisario guerrillas for raids into Western Sahara and providing camps for civilian refugees from the area, believed to number some 60,000.

In April 1976 Morocco and Mauritania reached agreement on the division of Western Sahara. The greater part of the territory, containing most of the known mineral wealth, was allotted to Morocco, which subsequently divided it into three provinces and absorbed it into the kingdom. By placing strong army garrisons in the territory's few scattered urban settlements, the Moroccans were able to secure them against guerrilla attacks, but incursions by forces of the Polisario Front into the surrounding desert areas could not be prevented. The conveyor belt from the important Bou Craa phosphate mines to the sea was sabotaged, and clashes between the Moroccan army and Polisario forces resulted in heavy casualties on both sides. Polisario units were too strong for Mauritania's very limited armed forces in the south, and Morocco took increasing responsibility for the defence of that region. The two countries formed a joint defence committee in May 1977, following a successful Polisario raid on the Mauritanian mining town of Zouérate, in which two French nationals were killed and six captured. In November King Hassan warned Algeria that Moroccan troops would pursue Polisario forces into Algerian territory if necessary; the Algerian Government retorted that any such incursion would result in war between the two countries.

Tension was increased when France, following the release of the French captives in December 1977, launched three air attacks on the Polisario Front. Although the French Government maintained that its action was for the protection of French nationals working at the Saharan mines, and had been undertaken at the request of Mauritania, it was clear that France favoured the expansion of Moroccan interests in the area rather than those of Algeria, for both economic and strategic reasons. During 1978 intermittent fighting continued, and there was a further French air-raid in April. Proposed meetings of the OAU to discuss the issue were postponed on three occasions, revealing an apparent unwillingness on the part of many African leaders to commit themselves. The intransigence of both Morocco and Algeria was partly due to the fact that their Governments relied to a great extent on their respective Saharan policies for domestic popular support. In Morocco the various opposition parties remained united in support of the King in this respect, despite the enormous expense of the war, which accounted for at least one-quarter of the 1979 budget, and the cost of confirming Morocco's control over the Saharan provinces by installing schools, hospitals and housing for those inhabitants remaining in the area. In January 1978 the Government had announced

a Sahara Development Programme, involving proposed expenditure of US \$292m., and envisaging the settlement of Saharan nomads and the creation of a sedentary economy.

The war was having an even more severe effect on the Mauritanian economy, and this was the chief reason for the coup which took place there in July 1978. The Polisario Front immediately announced a suspension of its hostilities against Mauritania; it was soon clear that the new President, Lt-Col (later Col) Moustapha Ould Salek, would be willing to renounce the Saharan province altogether, were it not for the 10,000 Moroccan troops still stationed in Mauritania. Salek's coup was followed by renewed diplomatic activity, in which France played an important role. In September King Hassan accepted the proposal by the President of the OAU, President Gaafar Mohammed Nimeri of Sudan, that the Heads of State of six African countries (Guinea, Côte d'Ivoire, Mali, Nigeria, Tanzania and Sudan) should form a committee of 'wise men' to mediate in the dispute. Spain also became increasingly involved, although it had to safeguard its fishing rights in Moroccan waters and, more importantly, its claim to the enclaves of Ceuta and Melilla. Nevertheless, in December 1980, following harassment of Spanish fishing boats by Polisario forces, the Spanish Government gave official recognition to the Polisario Front (though not to the SADR itself) and declared its support for Saharan self-determination.

Fighting continued, and in January 1979 Polisario forces attacked the town of Tan-Tan, some distance inside Morocco's pre-1975 borders. In March the Chamber of Representatives approved the formation of a National Defence Council to formulate defence policy. This council included members of all the main political groups: independents, Istiqlal, the MP, the USFP, the Mouvement populaire constitutionnel et démocratique (MPCD), and the Parti du progrès et du socialisme (PPS). This suggested that the King was seeking to strengthen support for the war by enlarging the number and the variety of those responsible for its direction. At the same time, the Chamber of Representatives showed that its attitude was still belligerent by reaffirming Morocco's right to its Saharan territory, and recommended that the right of pursuit into foreign (i.e. Algerian) territory should be exercised.

In July 1979 Polisario forces broke their cease-fire agreement with Mauritania, and the OAU summit conference passed a resolution urging the holding of a referendum on self-determination in Western Sahara. Mauritania withdrew from the war, signing a peace treaty with the Polisario Front in August and renouncing its territorial ambitions in Western Sahara. King Hassan immediately claimed the former Mauritanian sector, and proclaimed it a Moroccan province, to be known as Oued ed-Dahab. In May 1981 elections were held for representatives from the province to the Moroccan Chamber of Representatives. Nevertheless, outside the towns, only a small area of this newly-annexed territory could strictly be said to be under Moroccan control, and, as a result, Morocco's military resources were considerably stretched. Polisario forces swiftly retaliated, and numerous battles took place during the next 18 months, often within Morocco's original borders and particularly around the garrison town of Zak. In 1980 Morocco resorted to defensive tactics, concentrating on the *triangle utile* between the towns of el-Aaiún, Bou Craa and es-Smara. This area, containing most of the population and the chief phosphate mines, was to be protected by a line of defences about 600 km long, which was completed in May 1982, and the sand wall was further extended, from Zak to the Mauritanian frontier, in 1984.

In early 1981 there were reports that Polisario, previously based only in Algeria, had established bases in Mauritania, while in March the Mauritanians blamed Morocco for an attempted coup and suspended diplomatic relations. In April Col Muammar al-Qaddafi, the Libyan leader, proposed that Mauritania and Western Sahara should unite, and the two countries issued a joint condemnation of Morocco's occupation of the territory.

DIPLOMATIC INITIATIVES

During the early years of the Western Sahara conflict, the international community gradually recognized the SADR. In November 1979 the UN General Assembly adopted a resolution confirming the legitimacy of the Polisario Front's struggle for independence, and a year later it urged Morocco to end its occupation of Western Sahara. By February 1981, the fifth anniversary of the declaration of the republic, the SADR had been recognized by about 45 governments. Earlier, at the OAU's annual summit meeting in July 1980, a majority (26 out of 50 countries) approved the admission of the SADR. Morocco, however, argued that a two-thirds majority was necessary, and threatened to leave the OAU if the SADR was admitted. The decision was referred to the committee of 'wise men', who recommended that a cease-fire be established by December, followed by a referendum, to be supervised jointly by the OAU and the UN. In June 1981, at the OAU summit conference, King Hassan agreed for the first time to a referendum, to be held according to OAU recommendations. However, Morocco still refused to negotiate directly with the Polisario Front, and insisted that the proposed referendum be based on the 1974 Spanish census of the area, which enumerated only 74,000 inhabitants. The Polisario Front stipulated that, before the poll could take place, Morocco must withdraw its troops and administration to a considerable distance inside its original borders, and allow refugees living in Algeria to return and participate in the referendum; and that an interim international administration be established. However, the conditions of the referendum were never finally agreed by all the parties concerned.

In October 1981 Moroccan aircraft were shot down by what Morocco claimed to be Soviet-built SAM-6 missiles. Mauritania was accused of allowing Polisario forces to establish bases on its soil, and of taking part in the attack itself. In response, King Hassan asked the USA for increased military assistance. In February 1982 talks were held between the Moroccan Government and Alexander Haig, then US Secretary of State, as a result of which US military aid to Morocco was tripled. In May the USA and Morocco signed a military co-operation accord providing for the establishment of US military aircraft bases on Moroccan territory in the event of crises in the Middle East or Africa. The accord, initially for six years, was to be automatically renewed unless either country gave two years' notice of cancellation.

The situation deteriorated further during that month, when the SADR delegation was admitted to a meeting of the OAU Council of Ministers in Addis Ababa, Ethiopia. The Moroccan delegation withdrew in protest, and was followed by representatives of 18 other countries. Observers considered this to be the most serious crisis within the OAU since its inception, and it was feared that the organization's very future might be at risk. Subsequent OAU meetings often had to be postponed, since no quorum could be reached. However, in June 1983 the SADR delegation agreed not to attend an OAU summit meeting in Addis Ababa, thus ending the Moroccan boycott. The issue of the continuing conflict in Western Sahara was considered again at this summit, and the meeting adopted a resolution appealing for an immediate cease-fire; for direct negotiations to be held between the Polisario Front and the Moroccan Government; and for the proposed referendum on the issue of self-determination to be held in Western Sahara before the end of the year. Morocco refused to hold talks with the Polisario Front, but once again agreed in principle to a referendum, although King Hassan stated that he would not necessarily consider Morocco to be bound by its result. Morocco and the Polisario Front failed to agree on who should be allowed to vote, and the referendum, scheduled for December 1983, did not take place.

PROGRESS TOWARDS DEMOCRACY

King Hassan won great domestic prestige and popularity from the Saharan take-over. The staging of the Green March had particularly captured the imagination of the Moroccan people. At last, Hassan felt himself secure enough to hold the long-awaited elections. With the exception of the UNFP, the opposition parties agreed to participate, despite the continuation of political trials arising from the March 1973 uprising, which resulted in heavy prison sentences for many of the accused in early 1977. Municipal elections were held in November 1976, followed by provincial elections in January 1977 and elections for professional and vocational chambers in March. At each election, independents, mostly pro-government and conservative, won more than 60% of the seats. Istiqlal and the USFP

protested against electoral irregularities and administrative interference. On 1 March four party leaders, including Muhammad Boucetta of Istiqlal and Abd ar-Rahim Bouabid of the USFP, agreed to join the Government as Ministers of State without portfolio, in the hope of ensuring that the national elections would be fairly conducted. Prior to the national elections, press censorship was abolished. In June a new Chamber of Representatives was elected, signifying a return to parliamentary democracy after 12 years of direct rule. Of the Chamber's 264 members, 176 were directly elected and 88 were chosen by an electoral college. Independents won 141 seats (including 60 by indirect election), while Istiqlal and the MP won 49 and 44 respectively, the USFP won 16 and other opposition parties 14. The new Government, announced in October, included former opposition members, notably Boucetta as Minister of Foreign Affairs, with seven other members of Istiqlal, four members of the MP and Maati Bouabid of the UNFP, whose party, however, subsequently disowned him. Thus, the King gained the co-operation of the major part of the opposition, and appeared to have succeeded in his plan to combine democracy with strong royal authority.

Among the Moroccan people support for the war appeared solid, but there were signs of discontent which could be partly attributed to the heavy cost of the fighting. During early 1979 there were numerous strikes, demanding higher wages. On 21 March Prime Minister Osman, resigned, ostensibly to devote himself to the organization of the newly-formed Rassemblement national des indépendants (RNI; in 1980 the rural branch of this party seceded to form the Parti des indépendants démocrates—PID, which included several Cabinet ministers). He was replaced by Maati Bouabid, the Minister of Justice and a former trade union leader. The new Prime Minister held talks with union leaders, after which wage rises were announced, including an increase of 40% in the minimum wage. Although this provided a temporary respite from social unrest, it could only add to the burden on the economy.

During 1980 attempts were made to cut spending on education, which accounted for nearly one-quarter of the current budget. Student strikes ensued, supported by the USFP and the PPS, and unrest continued in 1981–83. In June 1981 at least 66 people were killed in Casablanca during a general strike against reductions in food subsidies. The USFP and the trade union organization, the Confédération Démocratique du Travail (CDT), were accused of fomenting this unrest. All CDT offices were closed, and union activists were arrested. Following USFP criticism of government Saharan policy in September, its leader Abd ar-Rahim Bouabid, and other senior officials were sentenced to terms of imprisonment, and the two USFP newspapers were suspended.

Further opposition was aroused in October 1981 by the implementation of the constitutional changes approved by referendum in May 1980, particularly the clause extending the maximum period between elections to the Chamber of Representatives from four to six years: the next parliamentary elections were thus postponed until 1983. The opposition parties were angered by the prolonged life of a body which, they maintained, had been irregularly elected, and in which the majority parties were guilty of absenteeism and passivity. Consequently, all 14 USFP deputies withdrew temporarily from the Chamber of Representatives, and in November all RNI ministers lost their portfolios in a cabinet reshuffle.

Abd ar-Rahim Bouabid was pardoned in March 1982, and CDT and USFP offices were allowed to reopen in April. However, many CDT activists remained in prison and the ban on USFP newspapers was not withdrawn until 1983, when the USFP commenced publication of a new newspaper.

The result of the June 1983 municipal elections, decisively won by pro-government centre-right parties, was challenged by the opposition parties on the grounds of electoral irregularities. A general election for a new Chamber of Representatives was due to take place in September 1983 but was postponed until after the proposed referendum on Western Sahara. However, as the date of the referendum remained uncertain, legislative elections were eventually announced for September 1984. The existing Government reached the end of its six-year mandate in November 1983 and was replaced by a caretaker 'Government of national unity', formed by King Hassan. The new Government was headed by Muhammad Karim Lamrani, an administrator chosen for his lack of party affiliation (who had also been Prime Minister in 1971–72), and included representatives of the six main political parties. It was to be responsible for organizing the general election and for drafting an economic programme for 1984.

In January 1984 the Government announced imminent increases in the prices of basic foodstuffs and in education fees, prompting violent street riots in several northern towns. Troops were summoned to quell the disturbances and, in several instances, opened fire on demonstrators. Unofficial estimates of the number of civilians killed in the riots were as high as 110. The rioting eventually subsided after King Hassan announced the suspension of the planned price increases. An estimated 1,800 people were detained during the riots, many of whom subsequently received prison sentences of up to 10 years.

TEMPORARY IMPROVEMENTS IN REGIONAL RELATIONS

Relations between Morocco and Algeria improved considerably in early 1983, following a summit meeting in February between King Hassan and President Ben Djedid Chadli of Algeria. This meeting resulted in the opening in April of the Morocco-Algeria border to Moroccans resident in Algeria and Algerians resident in Morocco. The *rapprochement* continued in April with a meeting in Tangier of political parties from Morocco, Algeria and Tunisia, at which representatives appealed for the creation of a Great Arab Maghreb—a political and economic union in north-west Africa.

In August 1984 King Hassan and Col Qaddafi of Libya signed the Arab-African Federation Treaty at Oujda, Morocco, which established a 'union of states' between their countries as the first step towards the creation of a Great Arab Maghreb. The Oujda Treaty, as it became known, provided for close economic and political co-operation between Morocco and Libya, and for mutual defence in the event of attack. The treaty was to take effect only after approval by the peoples of each country. A referendum was therefore held in Morocco on 31 August, and the treaty was approved by 99.97% of voters. Libya's General People's Congress backed the agreement unanimously. Following the alliance of Algeria, Tunisia and Mauritania, through the Maghreb Fraternity and Co-operation Treaty, initiated in March 1983, and Mauritania's recognition of the SADR in February 1984, Morocco had found itself isolated in the Maghreb. By signing the treaty of union with Libya, Morocco not only gained an ally (though an unlikely one, considering the contrast between Morocco's pro-Western stance and Libya's radicalism under Qaddafi), but also persuaded Col Qaddafi to end Libyan aid to Polisario.

Polisario responded to the *rapprochement* with Libya by launching the 'Greater Maghreb Offensive', a major military initiative which resulted in widespread fighting in southern Morocco. At the same time, Muhammad Abd al-Aziz, President of the SADR, undertook an extensive African tour to gather support prior to the November 1984 summit of the OAU in Addis Ababa. As a result, the SADR delegation was seated at the summit with few objections from other states. However, Morocco resigned from the OAU in protest, thus becoming the first State to leave the organization.

Although Polisario claimed to have killed 5,673 Moroccan soldiers during 1982–85, decisive victories proved elusive, owing to Morocco's defensive strategy of building a 2,500-km wall of sand, equipped with electronic detectors, to surround Western Sahara. At the UN General Assembly in October 1985, Morocco announced a unilateral cease-fire in Western Sahara on the condition that there was no aggression against territories under its jurisdiction, and that it would be ready to hold a referendum in the territory in January 1986. However, the latter offer was withdrawn in November, after the UN Decolonization Committee supported a settlement of the conflict through direct negotiations between Morocco and the Polisario Front. The Moroccan Minister of Foreign Affairs, Abd al-Latif Filali, announced that Morocco would boycott all UN discussions on Western Sahara, as the Government considered such discussions to be futile. Proximity talks between Morocco and Polisario in April and May 1986 failed to reach a resolution, and by the end of 1985 Morocco appeared to be increasingly isolated, as 64

countries had officially recognized the SADR. Moreover, US-Moroccan relations remained uneasy, following Morocco's signature of the Oujda Treaty with Libya.

DOMESTIC AFFAIRS

About 67% of the electorate participated in elections to the Chamber of Representatives on 14 September 1984. Despite widespread gains by the USFP (which won 36 seats), the legislature was again dominated by the centre-right parties, which together controlled 206 of the 306 seats. In October King Hassan invited the leaders of the six main parties to submit their planned programmes to enable him to choose a coalition government. Meanwhile, the previous 'Government of national unity' remained in office. King Hassan finally named a new Government in April 1985. The Government, again led by Muhammad Karim Lamrani, was a coalition of four centre-right parties: the Union constitutionnelle (UC), the RNI, the MP and the Parti national démocrate (PND, as the PID had been renamed). It did not include any members of Istiqlal or the USFP, which had participated in the previous Government. The new Government's programme included increased privatization, the decentralization of health and education, and reforms of the civil service and the education system. In September 1986 Lamrani resigned, owing to ill health, and was replaced by the Deputy Prime Minister and Minister of Education, Az ad-Dine Laraki.

Meanwhile, the Government mounted a campaign of repression against organizations which it deemed to pose a threat to internal security. In August 1985 26 members of a left-wing movement, Jeunesse Islamique (Islamic Youth), were charged with plotting to overthrow the monarchy and to establish an Islamic state; in September 14 were sentenced to death. A further 28 people were charged in October with membership of a clandestine fundamentalist group, the Moudjahedine Movement, and with subversive activities. In February 1986 27 left-wing activists were imprisoned for subversion. At their trial, the prosecuting counsel had claimed that the defendants were financed by the Polisario Front. Following Arab antipathy to the Morocco-Israeli initiative in July (see below), the Government introduced anti-terrorist measures in August, including entry restrictions for visitors from Arab countries. In the same month, four foreigners were arrested on charges of possessing explosives and plotting to bomb a synagogue in Casablanca. In November three people were imprisoned for membership of an illegal Marxist-Leninist organization, al-Kaaidiyine, and for disturbing public order.

In late 1986 and early 1987 King Hassan granted a series of pardons to both political and non-political detainees. In October 1987 the authorities announced that the family of Gen. Oufkir, who had staged an abortive coup attempt in 1972, would be allowed to emigrate, after 15 years in detention. However, the family were not released until mid-1996 (see below), although Muhammad Ait Kaddour, who had been involved in one of the attempts to shoot down the King's aircraft, was pardoned after his return to Morocco.

In 1988 Morocco joined the UN Human Rights Commission and subsequently attempted to improve its reputation concerning human rights. For several years, political prisoners had held sporadic hunger strikes to focus attention on poor prison conditions, and in January 1988 the Paris-based Moroccan human rights group, the Association des Droits de l'Homme au Maroc (ADHM), organized demonstrations in France, Belgium, the Netherlands and the Federal Republic of Germany against alleged abuses of human rights in Morocco. The ADHM also drew attention to clashes between students and government forces in Fez earlier that month. The Moroccan authorities had claimed that one person died and 21 were wounded during the disturbances, but the ADHM alleged that casualties had been much more numerous, and that more than 400 subsequent arrests had been made. In May it was reported that about 12 suspected members of Ilal Amam, who had been arrested during the previous two months in a government campaign against Ilal Amam activists, had been released, along with Abdullah Zaidy, a lawyer whose arrest in December 1987 and sentence to three years' imprisonment for attacking 'sacred institutions' had attracted condemnation from the International Commission of Jurists. In the same month living conditions for political prisoners were reported to have been improved. However, the first meeting of the newly-formed human rights association, the Organisation Marocaine des Droits de l'Homme (OMDH), scheduled for late May, was postponed until the end of June, owing to government objections that some of its members were also members of 'banned extremist groups'. In August 1988 King Hassan ordered the release of 341 detainees to commemorate the 25th anniversary of the exile of Sultan Muhammad ibn Yousuf. The release of political prisoners continued, and about 2,000 were freed in the first six months of 1989. The most notable were 50 extremists, including 31 of those who had been imprisoned in February 1977 for complicity in the alleged scheme to establish a republic under the Jewish mining engineer, Abraham Serfaty.

The question of political prisoners in Morocco attracted considerable international attention during 1989 and early 1990. Between June 1989 and April 1990 a total of 2,163 political prisoners were released, despite the authorities' denial that any such prisoners existed. In June 1989 six of the Ilal Amam prisoners in Rabat jail went on hunger strike in an abortive attempt to gain the status of political prisoners. They were transferred to hospitals, where one of them died after 64 days.

The imprisonment of Islamist activists provoked condemnation from other quarters, including the Iranian Government, which had seemed unconcerned about the fate of left-wingers. As far back as 1974 Abd as-Salam Yassin had criticized the State for failing to observe Islamic precepts, and later he was imprisoned several times. It was not until 1989, however, that his followers, who had formed a group called Al Adl wa-'l Ihsan (Justice and Charity), seemed to alarm the Government, although the group had been refused official registration in 1982. In November 1989 24 of its members were charged with belonging to an unauthorized organization, holding illicit meetings and possessing documents which threatened state security. The conviction of 17 of the accused and the placing of Sheikh Yassin under house arrest led to demonstrations by the organization's followers and further arrests. In January 1990 the Government ordered the dissolution of Al Adl wa-'l Ihsan, arrested five of its members who were presumed to be its executive committee and sentenced them to terms of imprisonment ranging from nine months to two years. Four were released on appeal, while the fifth had his sentence commuted. In May thousands of Islamists demonstrated in Rabat; an estimated 2,000 were reportedly arrested, and later released.

In April 1988, prompted in part by World Bank pressure, the King announced that the State should retain sole control of strategic industries and sell the remainder, including sugar refineries, bus services and possibly water and electricity. There was considerable debate over which industries should be retained in the public sector, while the trade unions were concerned about job losses resulting from privatization of state companies. Thus, it was not until October 1989 that real progress was made, following the appointments of a new Governor of the Central Bank and of a minister in charge of privatization. In December the Chamber of Representatives approved a list of 113 enterprises to be privatized, including four leading banks, 37 hotels, the Nador steelworks and the tea and sugar monopolies. The legislation ensured that the monopolies would not fall under foreign control and that there would be opportunities for employees to buy shares in their firms; the process was expected to take six years. While foreign capital would be welcomed, the Government's priority was to create a larger national share-owning class. The moribund Bourse at Casablanca was revived. Morocco already had one of the most liberal economies in the developing world, and there were emerging plans for free-trade zones.

In late 1988 the country suffered a period of industrial unrest, as strikes took place in mines, flour mills, the petroleum refinery at Mohammadia and Air Maroc, until a series of pay settlements restored order. After the King's Throne Day speech in March 1990 (in which he appealed to the people to accept austerity because of the economic situation), demands for a general strike were ignored, following Government promises that food subsidies would be retained and that grievances would be discussed. On May Day the minimum wage was raised by 10%.

In December 1989 Hassan proposed a two-year postponement of the forthcoming general election, in order to accommodate the referendum to be held in Western Sahara. A referendum which showed that only 0.05% opposed the plan demonstrated the lack of popular interest in party politics at a time when no members of the Cabinet were party politicians. In May 1990, for the first time in the 26-year history of the Chamber of Representatives, the opposition proposed a motion expressing 'no confidence' in the Government, criticizing its record on human rights and the revised budget. Although the motion was defeated by 200 votes to 82, it remained a significant precedent.

In December 1990 more than 20 people were alleged to have been killed in Fez during a general strike, the first in Morocco since 1984. Demonstrators demanded a wage increase commensurate with rapidly rising prices; following two days of rioting, security was increased in Fez and Rabat. The Government announced that a commission was to be established to ascertain the number of persons who had been killed and the circumstances of their deaths. In late December more than 100 people were accused of rioting, and received prison sentences. In March 1991 it was estimated by a prominent human rights organization, Amnesty International, that more than 1,500 people had been detained in connection with the riots. It was widely accepted that rising frustration at the country's socio-economic problems had precipitated these events. This was confirmed when the commission published its report, which showed that the outbreak could not be attributed to organized subversion.

Industrial unrest continued throughout 1991 and into 1992. There were numerous strikes by government employees, health workers, teachers, the post office and nationalized industries. Despite the establishment of a National Council for Youth and the Future (which aimed to provide 300,000 new jobs), the problem of youth unemployment was highlighted in October, when 100,000 out-of-work graduates established a national association to present their case. Wage rises failed to keep pace with inflation, and a government announcement in early 1991 that the minimum wage would be raised by 15% was rejected by two trade unions, which demanded that it be doubled to 2,000 dirhams (about US $250) per month. In January 1992 three trade union militants received prison sentences ranging from five to 10 months.

As in other Maghreb countries, many of the unemployed saw their salvation in Islamic fundamentalism. Some of the leaders of the banned group Al Adl wa-'l Ihsan, including Sheikh Yassin, remained in detention, and in April 1991 eight other members were arrested (although subsequently released). In May Al Adl wa-'l Ihsan and other opposition groups participated in a rally in Casablanca, in which some 100,000 demonstrators demanded measures to enshrine the sovereignty of the people and reduce the powers of the King. At the same time, they denounced the proposed referendum in Western Sahara, asserting that the territory should simply be annexed to Morocco. The repression of the Front islamique du salut in Algeria was welcomed by the Government, despite apprehension that local militants might conclude that their aims were not to be achieved by the democratic process. In September the Government approached the imprisoned Al Adl wa-'l Ihsan leaders, offering recognition as a legitimate party on certain conditions, including acceptance of the monarchy and a petition for pardon. However, the leaders made their release a precondition of any negotiations, and the initiative foundered.

Despite the creation (in May 1990) of the Consultative Council on Human Rights, humanitarian organizations continued to criticize the Government. In May 1991 the OMDH, headed by Khalid Nauri, held its inaugural conference, at which speakers denounced the arbitrary treatment, and even torture, of prisoners, and the lack of contact with their families. In September 1991 Abraham Serfaty, the longest-serving political prisoner in Africa, was freed and expelled from the country. In the same month 119 prisoners were released, bringing the total for the year to more than 5,000, and the notorious Tazmamart jail, whose existence the Government never admitted, was destroyed. During the winter of 1991–92 most of the remaining prisoners who had been condemned for the attempts on the King's life in 1971 and 1972 were freed.

AN ACTIVE PERIOD IN FOREIGN AFFAIRS: 1986–92

In 1986 and 1987 Morocco made determined efforts to improve its relations with the USA and other Western nations, in order to increase military and diplomatic support for its policy in Western Sahara. In April 1986 King Hassan, as chairman of the League of Arab States (the Arab League), suspended a summit meeting, following Libya's insistence that the US raids on Libya in April should be the sole topic on the agenda. In June King Hassan proposed the foundation of a 'Maghreb Community Consultative Committee', comprising Algeria, Morocco and Tunisia, thus isolating Libya.

In July 1986 King Hassan held talks with Shimon Peres, the Israeli Prime Minister, at Ifrane, in Morocco, in an effort to salvage the peace initiative in the Middle East; he thus became the first Arab Head of State to meet an Israeli leader since the late President Anwar Sadat of Egypt. However, the meeting merely highlighted the divisions between Israel and the moderate Arab states on means of resolving the conflict in the Middle East. Arab reaction was mixed: Syria immediately suspended diplomatic relations with Morocco; Libya condemned Morocco; while Egypt, Kuwait and Jordan supported the initiative. Following criticism of the meeting, King Hassan resigned as chairman of the Arab League. In August Libya attempted to improve relations with Morocco by reaffirming support for the Oujda Treaty, but this was abrogated by Hassan at the end of the month. The Moroccan-Israeli initiative and the abrogation of the Oujda Treaty resulted in a dramatic improvement in US-Moroccan relations by September. The two countries held joint military exercises in November, and in July 1987 the US Defense Department approved the sale to Morocco of 100 tanks, suitable for use in desert terrain, along with other military equipment. Morocco re-emphasized its status as a moderate pro-Western Arab state by re-establishing diplomatic relations with Egypt in November, and in January 1988 the USA announced that Morocco was willing to allow US forces to resume 'partial activities' on Moroccan territory.

King Hassan insisted that the movement towards a unified Maghreb did not preclude Morocco's ambition to join the European Community (EC, now European Union—EU). The European Parliament had on several occasions criticized Morocco for its policy in Western Sahara and for domestic repression, but in May 1988 the West German Minister of Foreign Affairs stated that the reforms which were to be implemented in 1992 would provide Morocco with great opportunities for trade and, consequently, EC aid was substantially increased. During a visit to Morocco in March 1989 the British Prime Minister, Margaret Thatcher, said that there was no realistic possibility of Morocco's joining the EC, and in the following month, in Luxembourg at a meeting of the EC's Moroccan Co-operation Council, the Moroccan Minister of Foreign Affairs, Abd al-Latif Filali, blamed Europe for protectionism which had damaged Moroccan exports.

In January 1987 King Hassan proposed the creation of a 'reflection cell' to consider the future of the Spanish African enclaves of Ceuta and Melilla, but Spain showed no willingness to discuss their sovereignty. In July, however, the Spanish Minister of Foreign Affairs visited Rabat and agreed to further discussions on the future of the enclaves. In June 1988 a bilateral trading agreement was signed; in July discussions were held over the installation of an electric cable under the Strait of Gibraltar, and in September an agreement was signed for the construction of a pipeline across Moroccan territory, connecting the petroleum fields of Algeria with consumers in Europe. Although Spain refused to allow Polisario to reopen its office in Madrid, in October it voted against Morocco at the UN debate on Western Sahara; in protest Hassan cancelled an official visit scheduled for November. Morocco could not, however, afford to pursue the quarrel, when Spain was about to assume the presidency of the EC and a visit by Prime Minister Felipe González in May 1989 showed that amicable relations had been restored. In September King Hassan visited Spain and signed accords on defence, including joint military exercises, technology transfers and bilateral summits to be held annually.

Hassan has also played a prominent role in Arab relations. The Arab League summit meeting, held in Casablanca in May 1989, was a considerable triumph for Moroccan diplomacy since it brought Syria, with which diplomatic relations had been restored in January, together with Iraq, while Col Qaddafi of Libya consented to meet President Muhammad Hosni Mubarak of Egypt. The meeting itself was less successful, for there was acrimonious disagreement over Lebanon. However, consensus was reached on the Palestinian *intifada*, which had evoked strong emotions in Morocco. The King was appointed, together with King Fahd of Saudi Arabia and President Chadli of Algeria, to head a Tripartite Arab Committee on Lebanon in order to seek a solution to the Lebanese conflict and to advocate the Palestinian case to the world. In April 1990, following a meeting with the King, Yasser Arafat announced Hassan's intention to request the Heads of State Committee to work towards the convening of an international conference on the plight of Palestinians. He also stated that the King intended to visit the capitals of the five permanent members of the UN Security Council to draw their attention to the growing number of Soviet Jews settling in Israel. As Chairman of the Organization of the Islamic Conference (OIC), Hassan was also expected to try to persuade the US Government not to recognize Jerusalem as the capital of Israel.

THE WESTERN SAHARA CONFLICT: 1986–87

During 1986 Polisario forces attacked several foreign fishing vessels in the Atlantic, off the Western Saharan coast, which the Polisario Front terms a 'war zone'. After an outbreak of fighting between Moroccan troops and Polisario forces in February 1987, Morocco claimed to have repelled a major Polisario offensive near the Algerian border. In the same month the SADR representative in Algiers claimed that an attempted assassination of the SADR President, Muhammad Abd al-Aziz, had been foiled, and alleged that the Moroccan Minister of the Interior was implicated in the plot.

Tension in Western Sahara increased in April 1987, when Morocco completed the construction of its defensive wall on the southern border of the territory, parallel with the Mauritanian frontier. Mauritania protested that its neutrality was threatened, since Polisario troops might have to pass through Mauritanian territory to reach the Atlantic; Algeria expressed concerns and confirmed its support for Mauritania.

A *rapprochement* between Morocco and Algeria was effected in May 1987, at a summit meeting attended by King Hassan and President Chadli of Algeria, under the auspices of King Fahd of Saudi Arabia. The two leaders discussed the conflict in Western Sahara and issued a joint communiqué stating that they would remain in consultation. Before the meeting, Polisario urged Morocco to enter into direct dialogue, and attacked King Fahd's role as mediator. Later in the month, 102 Algerian prisoners in Morocco were exchanged for 150 Moroccan prisoners in Algeria, and King Hassan sent an emissary to President Chadli with proposals to establish two joint commissions to settle various bilateral disputes.

TOWARDS A SOLUTION IN WESTERN SAHARA

Meanwhile, the UN and the OAU made a concerted effort to settle the conflict in Western Sahara. In July 1987 UN missions visited Morocco, Algeria and the Congo to examine the possibility of organizing a UN-sponsored referendum on the question of self-determination in Western Sahara. In the same month there were signs of a *rapprochement* between Polisario and Morocco, following indirect talks in Geneva, under the auspices of the UN and the OAU. Afterwards, King Hassan announced that he would be willing to accept the results of the referendum, and Polisario issued a statement which welcomed some of Hassan's proposals. However, after the talks, there were clashes between Moroccan and Polisario forces near the Mauritanian border.

Polisario announced a three-week truce in November 1987 to coincide with a visit by a UN-OAU technical mission to Morocco, Western Sahara and Polisario refugee camps in Algeria, in order to assess conditions for holding a referendum. Although both Morocco and Polisario agreed on the need for a referendum, Morocco rejected Polisario's demand that the Moroccan armed forces and administration should withdraw from Western Sahara, and that the territory should be placed under an interim UN administration before the referendum. Morocco also refused to hold direct talks with Polisario representatives (a Polisario precondition of negotiations), as officially it continued to view Polisario as a front organization for Algerian mercenaries. In January 1988 Polisario renewed attacks on Moroccan positions in Western Sahara. Meanwhile, the UN announced that it was drafting detailed proposals for a cease-fire and a referendum. In April the President of the OAU, Dr Kenneth Kaunda of Zambia, visited Morocco, Western Sahara and Polisario refugee camps to discuss the conclusions of the UN technical mission. By mid-1988 a total of 71 countries had granted diplomatic recognition to the SADR.

RESTORATION OF DIPLOMATIC RELATIONS WITH ALGERIA AND MOVES TOWARDS MAGHREB UNITY

The conflict in Western Sahara was regarded by the other Maghreb nations as an obstacle to regional unity, and in late 1987 and 1988 they attempted to isolate Morocco, with the aim of forcing the kingdom to negotiate with the Polisario Front. Meanwhile, Morocco reiterated its commitment to Maghreb unity, at meetings with President Chadli of Algeria in November 1987 and with President Zine al-Abidine Ben Ali of Tunisia in February 1988, and took no part in attempts by Algeria, Libya, Mauritania and Tunisia to create a four-country Great Arab Maghreb. However, the emergence of such a power bloc was forestalled by Libya's refusal to sign the Maghreb Fraternity and Co-operation Treaty without the addition of several conditions, and in May King Hassan received the Algerian deputy leader with an invitation from President Chadli for Morocco to attend the Arab League summit in June. Hassan promptly dispatched two of his senior advisers to Algiers to hold further discussions with Chadli, and in mid-May both countries announced the re-establishment of full diplomatic relations. In May 1989 a 1972 treaty with Algeria, on the demarcation of the joint border, was ratified by Morocco. These developments were considered to be a victory for Morocco and an apparent retreat by Algeria from its previous position that diplomatic relations could be resumed only if Morocco held direct talks with Polisario. Following the *rapprochement* with Algeria, Morocco became fully involved in regional efforts to establish a Great Arab Maghreb, and in June 1988 attended the first Maghreb summit.

Diplomatic relations improved further, as it became clear that Hassan and Chadli shared similar views on Maghreb unity. They rejected the Libyan concept of a vast 'superstate' but agreed on practical steps such as the abolition of visas, harmonization in economic, cultural and technical matters and joint ventures, which had been discussed at a bilateral meeting of Algeria and Morocco in October 1988. In February 1989, at a meeting in Marrakesh, of North African Heads of State, the Union of the Arab Maghreb (UMA), grouping Morocco with Algeria, Libya, Mauritania and Tunisia, was inaugurated. The new body aimed to promote unity by allowing free movement of goods, services and labour. Hassan was appointed the first President of the UMA for the 1989/90 year. In October, at the first meeting of delegates from each national legislature, the former Prime Minister and brother-in-law of King Hassan, Ahmad Othman, was elected President of the UMA Assembly. In the same month the respective Ministers of Foreign Affairs met in Rabat and agreed to establish committees to discuss food, security, economic affairs, human resources and infrastructure. In January 1990 the national employers' organizations discussed closer co-operation, and in February a committee was created to co-ordinate petroleum policies. Plans were also drafted for the introduction of a common identity card which would serve as a travel document within the UMA. The Moroccan Chamber of Representatives endorsed two accords with Algeria, providing for the establishment of joint ventures to consider creating a second gas pipeline to transport Algerian gas through Morocco to Europe, and for closer economic and industrial relations. Morocco also increased its ties with Tunisia and Libya, which the King had visited for the first time in September 1989.

During late 1989 and early 1990 the renewal of the Polisario campaign provoked criticism of the Government within Morocco. Meanwhile, King Hassan stressed that the new alignment would not preclude Morocco's membership of the EC. Further divisions in the UMA surfaced in August 1990, following the invasion of Kuwait (see Kuwait and Iraq chapters). Whereas the other UMA members were slow to react, Morocco issued a vehement condemnation of the invasion, voted for the resolutions at the Arab summit denouncing Iraq's action and agreed to contribute to the pan-Arab force defending Saudi Arabia. In September Hassan was host in Rabat to King Hussein of Jordan and President Chadli of Algeria in an attempt to launch a new peace initiative and avoid armed conflict. Although they failed to persuade the Iraqi President, Saddam Hussain, to withdraw his troops from Kuwait, in October the Iraqi President sent his Minister of Foreign Affairs, Tareq Aziz, and a Deputy Prime Minister, to Rabat in an attempt to find a resolution. When these discussions failed, King Hassan attempted unsuccessfully to convene a summit meeting of the Arab League in November. By December some 1,500 Moroccan troops were stationed in Saudi Arabia, as part of the multinational alliance attempting to enforce Iraq's withdrawal from Kuwait.

However, in late January 1991, after pro-Iraqi demonstrations in Morocco, the Government gave implicit support to a one-day general strike (in an apparent attempt to ease domestic political pressure), organized by the principal Moroccan trade unions to express solidarity with the Iraqi people. Other members of the anti-Iraq alliance expressed concern that the Moroccan Government was not fully committed to the military campaign. In February an estimated 300,000 people demonstrated in Rabat, where they denounced the war against Iraq and demanded that the Moroccan contingent withdraw from the multinational force. The Government stressed that its troops were in the region to defend Saudi Arabia and not to force the withdrawal of Iraq from Kuwait. By late February the multinational force had liberated Kuwait from Iraqi occupation, and shortly afterwards Morocco, together with its fellow members of the UAM, demanded that the sanctions which the UN had imposed on Iraq in August 1990 be repealed immediately.

UN PEACE PLAN FOR WESTERN SAHARA

In August 1988 the UN Secretary-General, Javier Pérez de Cuéllar, who had visited Morocco in May, announced that a detailed peace plan for Western Sahara had been drafted and appealed for its prompt approval by Morocco and Polisario. The plan contained proposals for a cease-fire and a referendum to determine the status of Western Sahara, while a UN representative with wide-ranging powers and a 2,000-strong UN monitoring force were to oversee their implementation. Prior to the referendum, Morocco was to reduce its presence in Western Sahara from 100,000 to 25,000 troops, who would then be confined to barracks, while Polisario forces (totalling an estimated 8,000) were to withdraw to their bases. Eligibility to vote in the referendum was to be decided by a UN team and was expected to be limited to those enumerated in the 1974 Spanish census of the then Spanish Sahara and to those born in Western Sahara. The referendum was to offer a choice between complete independence for the territory and its integration into Morocco; it was hoped that a further option would be added, offering a large measure of autonomy for the Sahrawi people under the Moroccan crown. On 30 August Morocco and the Polisario Front formally accepted the UN peace plan, although both sides expressed reservations.

However, the UN's expectation that a cease-fire could be secured within a month, and the referendum held within six months, seemed increasingly optimistic. Moreover, the belief that the UN proposals had been unconditionally accepted by both parties was undermined when in early September 1988 the Polisario Front declared that the UN could arrange a cease-fire by the end of 1988 if Morocco was prepared to hold direct talks with its representatives. In mid-September Polisario forces attacked Moroccan troops at the Oum Dreiga section of the defensive wall, near the Mauritanian border. Polisario was reported to have deployed 2,500 men, and there were more than 200 Moroccan casualties. There was speculation that Polisario had launched the offensive to demonstrate its ability to inflict substantial damage on Morocco without Algerian support, and to emphasize the need for Morocco to hold direct negotiations before a solution could be reached. Polisario representatives maintained that all Moroccan troops, administrators and colonists must be withdrawn before the proposed referendum, but two cabinet reshuffles within a month suggested serious differences within their leadership. Meanwhile, the Moroccan Minister of Foreign Affairs, Abd al-Latif Filali, stated that, since both sides had accepted the UN proposal for a cease-fire, there was no need for direct talks. In October the UN General Assembly agreed, by 87 votes to nil with 58 abstentions (which included

Morocco and the USA), that direct talks should be held, followed by a cease-fire and a referendum.

In December 1988 there was a significant change in Morocco's stance on Western Sahara, when King Hassan agreed to meet officials of Polisario and the SADR. The meeting, held in Marrakesh in January 1989, was the first direct contact for 13 years and was reported to have been limited to exchanges of goodwill; no negotiations took place. In February Polisario announced a unilateral cease-fire. A second meeting, scheduled to take place in February, was postponed by King Hassan. Polisario put further pressure on Morocco for full negotiations by threatening to take fresh military action. By mid-March no more discussions had taken place, and Polisario resumed hostilities, bringing the six-week cease-fire to an end. In May the Polisario politburo, meeting in Tindouf, sent a message to the King complaining that the projected second round of talks had not been held and asking him to assist the peace process; at the same time it dismissed two of its members for 'infantile attitudes'. At the seventh Polisario Front Congress, held in May, Polisario reiterated its own willingness to pursue direct dialogue, and announced that, as a gesture of goodwill, 200 Moroccan soldiers would be released. Their release, however, was postponed 'for technical reasons'.

In June 1989 Pérez de Cuéllar, who had held talks with the King and the Polisario leadership in Tindouf, and visited Algeria and Mauritania, declared himself 'confident of progress in the near future'. The UN established a technical commission to expedite the peace plan which both sides had formally accepted in August 1988. The issue of entitlement to vote in any referendum on the future of Western Sahara remained unresolved, however, owing to the ambiguous status of the Moroccan settlers in the area, who now outnumbered the original inhabitants by three to two.

King Hassan's vacillation was due, in part, to the defection, in August 1989, of Omar Hadhrami (one of the six founders of the Polisario Front), two leading guerrilla commanders and the chief propagandist in Algiers. This seemed to underline splits in the movement between authentic Sahrawis and new members from Algeria and Mauritania. In addition, mass arrests had taken place in the camps, aid from Eastern Europe had ceased, and assistance from other Maghreb states was diminishing, with the result that rationing had been introduced. Hassan welcomed these 'lost sheep' back into the fold, and other defections followed. The Moroccan Government let it be known that it was ready to consider any approach from oil companies seeking concessions to prospect for petroleum deposits in Western Sahara.

In October 1989 Polisario forces launched a series of major attacks, which continued unabated for more than a month. During the offensive, 15 km of the defensive wall facing the Mauritanian border was reportedly destroyed and hundreds of Moroccan soldiers were killed. The extent of the onslaught suggested that it could not have been launched without Algerian support. During the campaign the Polisario Front demanded direct talks with the Government, but the King refused to 'negotiate with his own subjects' and announced his readiness to order his troops across international borders in pursuit of Polisario forces.

In March 1990 Pérez de Cuéllar commented that he was pleased to find 'a more propitious atmosphere' than he had encountered during his June 1989 visit, but expressed caution over any practical outcome. In April 1991 the UN Security Council approved a resolution (no. 690) which authorized the establishment of a UN Mission for the Referendum in Western Sahara (MINURSO), which was to implement the plan for a referendum on self-determination, proposed by the UN Secretary-General in 1988. A UN peace-keeping force, comprising contingents from 36 countries (including the five permanent members of the UN Security Council), was to supervise the operation. In May 1991 the Security Council approved plans for a referendum in the disputed territory, which was scheduled to take place in January 1992.

In May 1991 King Hassan visited Western Sahara (his third visit to the region since 1976), where he was met by approximately 100,000 people. In recognition of the contribution of local tribes in the conflict between Moroccan forces and the Polisario Front, the King created a new province, Assa-Zag, on the

Algerian border. The royal visit coincided with the preparations for the referendum. It was announced that a peace-keeping force of 200,000 Moroccan troops would be stationed in the area in the interim. In the same month Pérez de Cuéllar met King Hassan to discuss the UN peace plan for Western Sahara. In June Hassan granted an amnesty to all Sahrawi opponents, including members of Polisario and refugees abroad. A further unspecified number of prisoners, including left-wing leader Abraham Serfaty, were released in the following months. It was believed that the amnesty extended to refugees abroad was part of a campaign to persuade Sahrawis who were disillusioned with the Polisario Front to vote for integration into Morocco.

In July 1991 it was announced that a cease-fire in Western Sahara would come into effect on 6 September, from which date the UN special representative, Johannes Manz, would supervise the preparations for a referendum. The Moroccan presence would be reduced from about 190,000 to 65,000 troops, and MINURSO would commence operations. Morocco rejected any role for the OAU in the area, while Istiqlal and other political parties declared the referendum futile, as the return of the Saharan provinces was irreversible. The Polisario Front promised to abide by the result. Morocco, however, continued a building programme to develop the Saharan provinces.

In August 1991 a significant increase in hostilities developed, with the Polisario Front denouncing Moroccan air strikes, while the Moroccan Government stated that it was engaged in clearing 'no man's land': each side was trying to intimidate rival elements into leaving the area before the cease-fire. In addition, Polisario demanded the release of men allegedly held as prisoners of war: Morocco denied that there were any, but some 200 detainees were nevertheless released.

The main obstacle to holding the referendum was that Manz had prepared an electoral roll of about 74,000, based on the Spanish census of 1974. The Moroccans presented an alternative list of about 120,000 who, they claimed, were natives of the area or their children who had been omitted from the census because, at the time, they were refugees. The UN representatives ruled that, while applications from individuals could be considered, a block list could not. Morocco used this dispute as a pretext to prevent the deployment of MINURSO; the Polisario Front countered by repeating its former claim that the total population was 207,000, of whom 167,000 were in 'liberated areas' or in refugee camps in Algeria and Mauritania. King Hassan appealed for a postponement of the referendum, but, after meeting Polisario representatives, Pérez de Cuéllar insisted that it should go ahead.

The first 100 members of MINURSO flew into el-Aaiún, and the cease-fire took effect, as planned, on 6 September 1991. Within a fortnight, however, each side had accused the other of violating the cease-fire, while the Polisario Front alleged that the Moroccan Minister of the Interior, Driss Basri, was organizing a 'second Green March' of 170,000 people for whom temporary accommodation was being built. There were few signs that Morocco was reducing its military presence. Algerian support for the Polisario Front effectively ceased, and there were important defections from its ranks. Both sides also complained of UN bias. By the end of November MINURSO had only 240 men in the territory. Manz resigned from his post in December. The Polisario Front complained that Morocco was planting mines in 'no man's land' and arresting its supporters. Pérez de Cuéllar appeared to side with Morocco by recommending that a vote be given to anyone whose father had been born in the territory or who had had intermittent residence there for 12 years before 1974. However, this proposal was delayed in the UN Security Council and on 1 January 1992 his successor, Dr Boutros Boutros-Ghali, was asked for a report within two months; it became clear that the vote could not take place before September 1992.

In March 1992 Boutros-Ghali's report concluded that, unless there were progress by the end of May, the whole UN policy should be reconsidered. He also stated that, of the 77 violations of the cease-fire reported by MINURSO, Morocco had been responsible for 75. It was not until the end of the month that a veteran Pakistani diplomat, Yaqub Khan, was appointed as successor to Manz. He visited the area in April, and in May Boutros-Ghali announced that the two sides were to hold indirect talks under his auspices. These took place in Geneva, but proved inconclusive.

In June 1992 Driss Basri visited Western Sahara to encourage the population to enroll on the electoral register. This message was repeated by Ibrahim Hakim, who, as a former Minister of Foreign Affairs of the SADR and ambassador to Algeria, was a significant defector to Morocco in August. Hakim claimed that the Algerian Government was no longer committed to the foundation of an autonomous state in Western Sahara. He was subsequently appointed as the King's itinerant ambassador. Polisario threatened to resume hostilities if the Moroccan referendum on constitutional reform, in September, were extended to Western Sahara. In the event, however, the Ministry of the Interior announced a 100% participation of the electorate in the area, unanimously in favour of the amendments. King Hassan stated that Western Sahara would receive priority in the allocation of development funds and also that Morocco would abide by the result of the UN referendum. Polisario claimed that demonstrations in Western Sahara against the communal elections in October had been forcibly suppressed, but once more the Moroccan Ministry of the Interior announced an overwhelming rate of voter participation in the region.

Following the assassination of Muhammad Boudiaf, the Algerian Head of State, in June 1992, relations between Morocco and Algeria were strained, and the latter was reported to be increasing its aid to Polisario. In December two groups of Sahrawi notables, composed of equal numbers of representatives from within the wall and from the camps at Tindouf in Algeria, travelled to Geneva for a meeting under the chairmanship of Yaqub Khan. The Tindoufis, however, refused to negotiate, claiming that the other delegation had altered its composition.

The President of the SADR accused the UN Security Council of losing interest in the Western Sahara dispute, and in January 1993 Boutros-Ghali reported that there was little prospect of success from continuing talks on their present basis. In March he suggested three alternatives to the Council: efforts to organize talks could continue; the UN could impose the Pérez de Cuéllar list; or there could be an entirely fresh initiative. Under Resolution 809, the Council decreed that the referendum should take place before the end of 1993, with or without Polisario co-operation, that further efforts should be made to compile a satisfactory electoral list, and that Boutros-Ghali should undertake a new round of negotiations. Morocco accepted the resolution at once and, after some delay, Polisario agreed to do likewise.

In April 1993 Yaqub Khan held talks in Algiers with senior Algerian officials before meeting King Hassan in Rabat in order to prepare a report on the situation in Western Sahara. In May a senior UN diplomat, Erik Jensen, was appointed to begin work on registering voters prior to the referendum. Morocco nevertheless included its 'Saharan provinces' in the kingdom's general election, held in June. Talks in July at el-Aaiún were the first to be held in the disputed territory itself, but proved inconclusive. Morocco had enjoyed a propaganda success on the eve of the talks when a notable Sahrawi chief defected.

According to a communiqué issued by Polisario in Algiers in September 1993, the SADR President, Muhammad Abd al-Aziz, nominated a new Government for the region in that month. Bouchraya Hammoudi Bayoun was appointed to lead the Government, with the uncompromising Grahim Ghali as his Minister of Defence. In the same month it was reported that, of 1,600 UN military personnel appointed to Western Sahara, only 360 were stationed in the territory.

In November 1993 Boutros-Ghali informed the UN Security Council that, because of unresolved differences as to voter eligibility, the referendum could not take place before mid-1994. In March 1994 he announced a new approach, involving three options: to proceed with the referendum by the end of 1994, even if one or both sides in the dispute disagreed; to cancel the referendum and withdraw most of the UN peace-keeping force; or to continue with talks between Morocco and the Polisario Front in order to compile acceptable voter lists. In April Jensen stated that Polisario, after some initial misgivings, had accepted a voter registration plan proposed under Security Council Resolution 907, and that voter registration would begin in June.

In May 1994 Jensen and Driss Basri issued a joint statement that voter registration would start in el-Aaiún in early June;

however, the registration of voters did not begin until late August. Morocco had adopted familiar blocking techniques and at first refused to allow the presence of observers from the OAU at the process of identification of voters. After registration began it proved to be a slow process. In November, the date set for the completion of voter registration, the UN announced that plans to hold the referendum in February 1995 would have to be delayed because of problems of identifying potential voters. During a visit to the region at the end of November, Boutros-Ghali warned Morocco and Polisario of serious consequences if progress was not achieved in preparations for the referendum. At a meeting with Muhammad Abd al-Aziz, Boutros-Ghali tried to persuade him of the importance of encouraging voter registration. In December the UN Secretary-General stated that the referendum could be held in October 1995 but told the Security Council that a major reinforcement of UN personnel was essential if identification and registration of the large number of applications already received were to be completed in time. By February 1995 the UN had identified about 11,000 eligible voters, but differences between Morocco and Polisario over exactly who was eligible to vote remained. Polisario claimed that Morocco had settled large numbers of Moroccans in the disputed territory in order to influence the outcome of the referendum. There were violent clashes between Sahrawis and Moroccans in February during voter registration at the town of Ksabi. Although a delegation from the UN Security Council visited the territory in June to try to resolve the problems concerning voter registration, new disputes resulted in the announcement that the referendum would be delayed until January 1996. Meanwhile, during June and early July Polisario stopped co-operating with the UN commission identifying voters after a Moroccan court sentenced eight young Sahrawis to lengthy terms of imprisonment for organizing a demonstration in support of independence for Western Sahara. The sentences were subsequently commuted after the intervention of King Hassan, and Polisario resumed co-operation over voter identification. In August it was reported that Morocco had opened 40 new voter identification centres, not only in Western Sahara but also in some Moroccan towns and in its embassies abroad.

Muhammad Abd al-Aziz, who was re-elected as Polisario's Secretary-General at the organization's ninth congress held in Tindouf in August 1995, repeated that the struggle for sovereignty and independence would continue whatever the result of the referendum. Algeria reaffirmed its support for Polisario by sending three ministers to the congress but, preoccupied with its own political and economic crises, seemed unlikely to offer much practical assistance. In September it was reported that the SADR Government had been reshuffled and in the following month the first elected Saharan National Assembly, comprising 101 members elected by secret ballot, was inaugurated in Tindouf under the chairmanship of Abd al-Aziz. Polisario persisted with its campaign against Morocco by urging Spanish fishermen to ignore warnings from Morocco not to operate in Atlantic waters off Western Sahara, claiming that the fishing zone belonged to the Sahrawi people.

Progress towards a peaceful solution to the dispute was hampered by the deterioration in relations between Morocco and Algeria. Liamine Zéroual, the Algerian President, appeared to adopt a less flexible position on Western Sahara, and in August 1994 angered Morocco by referring to the territory as 'an illegally occupied country'. In December 1995, after Algeria objected to UN proposals to expedite voter registration in Western Sahara, Morocco responded angrily by obstructing the activities of the UMA of which Algeria currently held the presidency.

At intervals the UN Security Council voted to extend MINURSO's mandate on a short-term basis, although it did not set a new date for the referendum, which failed to take place in January 1996. Meanwhile, the registration process continued to be hampered by disputes between Morocco and Polisario on the identification of voters. In May 1996 the Security Council agreed to renew MINURSO's mandate until the end of November, although it voted to reduce its personnel in the territory. By November MINURSO's military component had decreased from 288 to 230, and the civilian police from 91 to nine. As the identification process remained suspended, the number of civilian posts was reduced from 410 to 170. Despite Polisario's threat to resume the armed struggle, the cease-fire remained in force, although MINURSO reported a number of violations on both sides. Although some progress was made on the exchange of prisoners of war, the identification process did not resume. MINURSO's mandate was extended in November (and again in March and September 1997), and in that month King Hassan confirmed that senior-level direct talks between his representatives and Polisario had taken place in August and September but had failed to reach any conclusive agreements.

In March 1997 the new UN Secretary-General, Kofi Annan, appointed James Baker (a former US Secretary of State) as the UN's special envoy to Western Sahara. Between June and September Baker chaired a series of direct talks between the Moroccan Government and representatives of Polisario in Lisbon, Portugal, London, United Kingdom, and Houston, Texas, USA, which he admitted had been difficult, but in mid-September a compromise agreement was reached on the highly contentious issue of who would be eligible to vote in the long-delayed referendum, which was scheduled to be held in December 1998. He appeared to have persuaded Morocco to accept a lower figure for the number of eligible voters than they had originally demanded. Agreement was also reached on the reduction of military forces of the two sides in the disputed territory, the repatriation of refugees and the release of detainees. Prime Minister Filali subsequently declared that the referendum would merely reaffirm Moroccan sovereignty over Western Sahara, which he insisted would always remain an integral part of the kingdom. In March 1998 King Hassan referred to 'an affirmative referendum', that would put an end to 'an artificial problem' that had prevented Morocco from achieving its 'territorial unity'. Morocco also continued its campaign to weaken support for Polisario in the OAU, and by September 1997 10 member states had withdrawn recognition of the SADR in return for financial assistance from Morocco. In January 1998 changes to the SADR Government appeared to strengthen the position of intransigent members of the Polisario leadership and possibly pointed to a greater control over the movement by Algerian military intelligence. Some observers, however, predicted that if Polisario failed to win the referendum, the movement would split, with much of its leadership defecting to Morocco.

Morocco's new opposition-led Government, which took office in March 1998, declared that its overriding priority was to close the dossier on 'the Moroccan Sahara' by ensuring unambiguous international recognition of the kingdom's sovereignty over this part of its territory. Responsibility for Western Sahara, however, remained firmly with the palace. In spite of the agreement brokered by James Baker in 1997, voter registration continued to be impeded by disputes, and the process had not been completed by 31 May, the date set by the UN Secretary-General for finalizing electoral lists. In June it was reported that the referendum scheduled for December 1998 had been postponed once again. Following a visit by Kofi Annan to North Africa in December, the UN set out new proposals to clarify the process of identifying which Sahrawis are eligible to vote, and set a new date for the referendum, December 1999. By October 1998 some 147,000 voters had been identified as eligible to take part in the referendum and accepted by both Morocco and Polisario. However, Morocco also insisted on the registration of a further 65,000 members of three contested tribes, on the grounds that they were Sahrawis who had migrated to southern Morocco in the late 1950s in order to escape Spanish colonial rule. Polisario accused Morocco of attempting mass registration and electoral fraud. It was reported that the new UN proposals on voter identification had been accepted by Polisario, but that Morocco had raised a number of objections. During a three-day visit to the territory in December 1998, Prime Minister el-Youssoufi pledged that Western Sahara would remain part of Morocco whatever the result of the referendum and announced a series of new infrastructure projects for the territory.

In mid-January 1999 the European Parliament adopted a resolution on Western Sahara which expressed concern that the peace process was being prolonged and urged Morocco to accept the proposals put forward by the UN Secretary-General to implement the peace plan. Later in January Morocco and Polisario reached an agreement which allowed the recording of tribal groups not already included in the identification process to resume, but the UN Security Council warned Morocco that if it did not co-operate fully MINURSO's mandate would not be renewed and the UN would withdraw from the region. Polisario declared that if the referendum did not take place, the alternative was war. In March King Hassan declared that Morocco remained committed to the UN peace plan for the territory and that the planned referendum would confirm 'the Moroccan nature of our Sahara'. Later in the year it was announced that the referendum would be delayed until July 2000. William Eagleton, a former US ambassador to Syria, replaced Charles Dunbar as the Special Representative of the UN Secretary-General for Western Sahara, and Eduardo Vetere assumed responsibility for voter identification. In late October 1999 Brig.-Gen. Claude Buze of Belgium replaced Brig. Bernd Lubenik as Chief Military Observer.

On the death of King Hassan in late July 1999, Polisario's leader, Muhammad Abd al-Aziz, sent his condolences; he praised the late king for laying the foundations for 'a democratic and modern Morocco living in peace and harmony with its neighbours', and reiterated his commitment to the referendum process. At the end of September and early October there were riots in el-Aaiún after police clashed with Sahrawis protesting at poor social and economic conditions in the territory. Local Sahrawis claimed that their peaceful protests had only become violent because Morocco's Minister of the Interior, Driss Basri, had ordered the police to use harsh methods against the demonstrators. At the beginning of November Sahrawi students staged a protest march in Rabat against police brutality. In response to the riots, Morocco's new ruler King Muhammad appeared at first to favour a policy which addressed social problems, especially unemployment, and encouraged a dialogue with the Sahrawis rather than concentrating solely on security measures. He established a Royal Commission for Sahrawi Affairs and proposed setting up an elected assembly for the territory. For its part, Polisario condemned these initiatives, claiming that Morocco was attempting unfairly to influence the population in its favour in the forthcoming referendum. Later Polisario proclaimed an *intifada* (or unarmed popular uprising) in order to put pressure on the Moroccan authorities. Before abruptly dismissing Driss Basri in November, the King had already relieved him of responsibility for Western Sahara. The senior Moroccan official in charge of liaison with MINURSO, an ally of Basri, was also subsequently replaced.

In December 1999 the UN Secretary-General, Kofi Annan, conceded that the referendum was unlikely to take place before 2002, and early in 2000, amid growing frustration within the UN at the lack of progress in voter identification, expressed doubts that the referendum would be held at all. Although more than 86,000 eligible voters had been identified, some 79,000 appeals had been lodged by those rejected under the first stage of the identification process and by March that number had risen to 130,000. By encouraging these appeals Morocco would be able to ensure further delays to the referendum timetable. In early February the leader of Polisario warned that renewed hostilities were possible if the referendum was not held before the end of 2000. Later that month the UN Secretary-General, in his report to the Security Council, drew attention to Polisario's warning and stated that if the process were delayed much longer MINURSO would become irrelevant and that there was a distinct possibility of a return to armed hostilities. Annan also stated that the UN had no provisions for enforcing the result of a referendum should one side refuse to accept it. It was against this depressing background that the Secretary-General asked James Baker to resume his role as special envoy with a mandate to explore with the parties concerned 'all ways and means to achieve an early, durable and agreed solution to the dispute'. The UN's favoured option appeared to be autonomy for Western Sahara under Moroccan sovereignty and there were reports that both the USA and France preferred to press for the widest possible autonomy for the disputed territory. However, a number of meetings in mid-2000 between Baker and representatives of the Moroccan Government and Polisario failed to make any progress and neither side was prepared to discuss Baker's suggestion of an alternative political solution to the referendum plan. Indeed, Moroccan officials threatened their country's withdrawal from the process if all Sahrawis in the 'southern provinces' and not just those found eligible under the criteria set by the UN were not allowed to vote in a referendum.

Polisario, for its part, insisted that the problems confronting the referendum were not insurmountable and that it would support any proposals put forward by the UN to allow the appeals process to begin. At a further meeting in late September chaired by Baker, Morocco indicated its willingness to begin talks on autonomy for Western Sahara. El-Youssoufi subsequently stated that his government was looking at models of regionalization adopted by other countries and was preparing plans to allow the inhabitants of the territory to administer their own affairs, but Polisario continued to reject any alternative to the referendum, which it remained confident of winning. Nevertheless, Polisario faced declining diplomatic support in Africa and Latin America, and there were reports of unrest among Sahrawi civilians under Polisario control. In December in response to Morocco's decision to allow the 2001 Paris–Dakar rally to pass through Western Sahara, Polisario threatened to end the nine-year cease-fire; however, after appeals from the UN, the OAU and Algeria it eventually decided not to resume hostilities, although the Polisario leadership warned that it remained in a state of war. A spokesman for the Moroccan Government dismissed the threat and stated that Polisario regularly made such gestures during international events for propaganda purposes.

In late February 2001 celebrations were held to mark the 25th anniversary of the declaration of the SADR at which Polisario displayed an array of military hardware. Amid growing frustration at the lack of political progress, Sahrawi refugees felt that the chance of holding the UN referendum was becoming more remote. The Polisario leadership continued to voice its threat to resume hostilities, and observers noted mounting pressure from the refugees for such action to be taken. In December 2000 Polisario had released 201 Moroccan prisoners of war, taken captive in the mid-1970s, but refused to release some 1,481 Moroccans still held in detention despite appeals from the International Committee of the Red Cross (ICRC). Polisario claimed that some 179 of its troops were being held by Morocco. In late April 2001 the UN Security Council extended MINURSO's mandate for a further three months and reaffirmed its full support for the UN settlement plan and referendum, while expressing the hope that the parties involved would continue to try and resolve problems relating to the implementation of the plan and try to agree a mutually acceptable political solution to the dispute. Annan reported with regret that thus far no progress had been made in trying to overcome the obstacles to the UN peace plan, but some sources suggested that Baker had received a pledge from Morocco that it would agree to a substantial compromise on devolution of authority for all the inhabitants of the disputed territory. Polisario remained opposed to any agreement without a referendum, but its threat to resume hostilities if the referendum were abandoned was unlikely to be supported by Algeria.

In late June 2001 the UN Security Council unanimously approved a compromise resolution encouraging Morocco and Polisario to discuss an autonomy plan for Western Sahara proposed by Annan but without abandoning the delayed referendum. The Security Council also extended MINURSO's mandate until the end of November. Under the terms of the autonomy proposal the inhabitants of Western Sahara would have the right to elect their own legislative and executive bodies and to have control over local government administration including budget and taxation, law enforcement, internal security, local economy, infrastructure, and social affairs for a period of at least five years during which Morocco would retain control over defence and foreign affairs. It also provided for the holding of a referendum on the final status of the territory within that five-year period. Questions were, however, raised to concerning why the long-delayed referendum could not immediately proceed if it was possible to hold transparent local elections in the territory. Some commentators argued that the UN, under pressure from the USA and France, had capitulated to Moroccan procrastination. Earlier in June it had been reported that Polisario had rejected a Moroccan plan for the autonomy of Western Sahara. Although the Moroccan proposals included the establishment of an elected local assembly for the territory, Sahrawis would be given control over only part of their affairs, notably in social and cultural areas, and would administer only 20% of government revenues from the territory,

with Morocco remaining responsible for foreign affairs, defence and customs. Moreover, Western Sahara would be administered by a senior official appointed by the Moroccan Government.

Polisario categorically rejected the autonomy proposals and continued to demand that the long-delayed referendum should proceed. King Muhammad however, in an interview with the French daily *Le Figaro* in September, stated tha the Western Sahara issue had been settled and that the 11 members of the UN Security Council recognised the legitimacy of Moroccan sovereignty over 'our Sahara'. At the end of October the King made his first visit to the disputed territory since coming to the throne and was reported to have received an enthusiastic welcome from crowds in el-Aaiún, the capital. Some observers described the visit as having all the appearances of a 'ceremony of allegiance' to the Moroccan crown. The Sahrawi Minister of Foreign Affairs condemned the visit as a flagrant violation of UN resolutions. King Muhammad made a second visit to the disputed territory at the end of November to complete his original programme which had been disrupted by poor weather conditions. Meanwhile, some commentators argued that Morocco's decision to withdraw its ambassador from Madrid at the end of October was taken in part because of Morocco's displeasure at Spain"s position on Western Sahara. In particular Morocco had been angered when a grouping of left-wing Spanish NGOs, well known for their support of Polisario, held a symbolic referendum on the future of the former Spanish colony in eight major towns in Andalucía in mid-October (see below). In mid-November the Moroccan authorities refused to allow Danielle Mitterrand, head of the charitable foundation France Libertés, to visit el-Aaiún for what were termed 'security reasons'. On her return to France Mitterrand, the wife of the former French President and a long-standing campaigner for the independence of Western Sahara, strongly criticized the Moroccan authorities and stated that the French embassy in Rabat had also attempted to pressure her to change her plans. She had recently visited Sahrawi refugee camps around Tindouf in Algeria, where her foundation supports various development projects, and stated that she had planned to go to Western Sahara to express solidarity with the Sahrawis. At a press conference in Paris in early December Mitterrand denounced the policy of the UN and EU on Western Sahara, which she claimed sought to make the disputed territory an integral part of the Moroccan state. She described the humanitarian situation of the Sahrawi refugees as serious: aid from the World Food Programme covered little more than a third of the food requirements of some 180,000 people living in Moroccan and Algerian camps. Disturbances broke out in es-Smara in mid–November, during which some 15 people were arrested according to the Moroccan authorities. An independent Moroccan human rights organization visited Western Sahara in January 2002 to assess the situation of the detainees, who were reported to have gone on hunger strike until the authorities agreed to an improvement in their conditions of detention. The organization reported that the disturbances in es-Smara were not political but provoked by socio-economic grievances—notably problems of employment and housing. It found that the detainees had been badly beaten and abused by uniformed and plain-clothes police, and demanded that the Ministry Justice undertake an inquiry into the arrests.

A veteran US diplomat, William Lacy Swing, took up his appointment as MINURSO head at the beginning of December 2001. However, there were reports that the mission's staff in the territory was being reduced and that the work of voter identification had effectively ceased. Within the EU, only Spain now continued to uphold the original referendum plan. On a visit to Rabat at the beginning of December President Jacques Chirac of France referred to Western Sahara as the 'southern provinces of Morocco'. Although Algerian officials denied reports in the local press that President Abdelaziz Bouteflika had accepted the Baker plan when he met US President George W. Bush in November, some commentators maintained that the price of Algeria's growing *rapprochement* with the West after the September suicide attacks on the USA would be its abandonment of the Sahrawi cause.

Meanwhile, Polisario mounted a legal challenge in the UN when Morocco granted the first oil permits in Western Sahara, one to Kerr McGee of the USA and another to TotalFinaElf of France. In early February 2002 the UN's legal counsellor stated that although the oil permits were not illegal *per se*, exploration work and production which was not in the interests of, or according to the wishes of, the Sahrawi people would represent a violation of the principles of international law. Morocco's ambassador to the UN immediately declared that everything Morocco was doing in the territory was for the benefit of the people. Polisario's UN representative urged the oil companies to suspend their activities in Western Sahara, insisting that they complicated rather than facilitated peace efforts. While the companies restrict their activities to geological evaluation they do not breach international law, but should they move to the exploration and production phase then the question of who benefits would arise. At the beginning of January 2002 Polisario released 115 Moroccan detainees who had been held for more than 20 years, angering the Moroccan authorities by high-lighting the role played by the Spanish premier, José María Aznar, in their release. According to the ICRC, some 1,362 Moroccan prisoners of war were still held by Polisario in camps around Tindouf in Algeria. The Moroccan authorities insisted that they no longer held any Polisario supporters as prisoners.

In a new report to the UN Security Council in February 2002, Kofi Annan stated that the future of the peace process in Western Sahara was rather depressing, and that in his opinion there were only four options available: that the Security Council insist on proceeding with the long-delayed referendum on self-determination; that Western Sahara become a semi-autonomous province of Morocco—an option rejected by both Polisario and Algeria; that the UN end its peace mission in the disputed territory and withdraw its military observers, risking possible confrontations between Algeria and Morocco; and the most controversial proposal, that Western Sahara be divided between Morocco and Polisario. However, the Secretary-General pointed out that while Algeria and Polisario might be willing to discuss this last option, Morocco was firmly opposed to it. Earlier Morocco's Minister of Foreign Affairs had earlier described it as a dangerous plan that would set a precedent for conflicts else-where in Africa. Meanwhile Morocco's ambassador to the UN, and most of the Moroccan press, attributed the partition plan to Algeria, claiming that the Algerian authorities wished to create a Sahrawi 'mini-state' under their protection through which Algeria would acquire an outlet to the Atlantic. Algeria's representative at the UN denied putting forward such a plan, but there was speculation that it was a personal initiative of President Bouteflika, acting without the agreement of the military *décideurs*, who regarded the Western Sahara issue as their preserve. On 26 February the UN Security Council adopted a resolution rejecting the option of a UN withdrawal from the disputed territory and setting a deadline of 30 April for the UN to decide which of the remaining three options should be pursued. On 27 February President Bouteflika made an unexpected visit to the Sahrawi refugee camps around Tindouf in western Algeria. Morocco described the visit, the first by an Algerian President, as 'provocative'. At the beginning of March King Muhammad made a two-day visit to Western Sahara, his third in four months, and convened a meeting of the Council of Ministers at the southern port of Dakhla. The visit, designed to reaffirm Moroccan sovereignty over Western Sahara, was condemned by Polisario as provocative. In late March MIN-URSO announced that Polisario had decided to allow UN mili-tary observers freedom of movement in areas controlled by their forces. According to the Moroccan authorities, restrictions on the movement of UN peace-keepers had been in force since January 2001. In late April and early May 2002 US diplomats tried unsuccessfully to persuade members of the Security Council to accept the autonomy option favoured by Morocco. Polisario had declared that if US efforts were successful it would demand the withdrawal of the UN troops from Western Sahara, a development that could lead to the renewal of hostilities between Polisario and Moroccan forces. The set-back to US efforts demonstrated that Polisario could still count on some diplomatic support internationally. On 30 April the UN Security Council renewed MINURSO's mandate for a further three months. In May Polisario signed an agreement with Fusion Oil of Australia to undertake at its own cost a 16-month integrated study of all relevant geological and geophysical data available on 'Sahrawi territorial waters'. It was assumed that the study would be based on publicly available data. When the study has

been completed Fusion (which has offshore exploration licences to the south in Mauritania, the Gambia, Senegal and Guinea-Bissau) may nominate up to three areas for future exploration licences which will only come into effect within six months of the SADR's admission to the UN.

FOREIGN POLICY SINCE THE EARLY 1990s

Morocco was determined to play a full part in world affairs in the 1990s, and in the first two years of the decade it established diplomatic relations with Namibia, South Africa (the first Arab country to do so), Viet Nam, Estonia, Ukraine and Kyrgyzstan. In August 1990 the Minister of Foreign Affairs visited all five permanent members of the UN Security Council, and in the same month, at a meeting in Turkey of OIC Ministers of Foreign Affairs, Morocco proposed to increase the group's international scope. In September Morocco and the People's Republic of China signed an agreement on co-operation in energy and mining. In the following year Crown Prince Sidi Muhammad became the most important Moroccan to visit Beijing since the establish-ment of diplomatic relations in 1958. The visit was returned by the Chinese President, Yang Shangkun. In December 1998 China and Morocco concluded several bilateral economic and cultural agreements during a visit to Beijing by Prime Minister el-Youssoufi. In October 1991 Morocco was elected to the UN Security Council for a two-year term beginning on 1 January 1992 (it had previously been a member in 1962–63).

Morocco was quick to capitalize on the goodwill that it had generated in the USA by its strong support during the Gulf War. It benefited from both bilateral aid and credits from US-dominated agencies, receiving more from the World Bank than any other country in the Middle East or North Africa. Wheat and vegetable oil were provided on credit, and Morocco acquired 20 used F-16 military aircraft for US $250m. In return, it supported the US peace initiative in the Middle East, and the King offered Morocco as a venue for the Arab-Israeli peace conference and expressed willingness to receive Prime Minister Itzhak Shamir of Israel. In August 1991 the Chairman of the Palestine Liberation Organization (PLO), Yasser Arafat, and the US Secretary of State, James Baker, visited Morocco within a few days of each other. The King made a fruitful visit to Washington, DC, in September, establishing closer relations with President George Bush, and apparently securing US sup-port for Morocco's policy on Western Sahara. He announced that a US university, specializing in science, would be established in Ifrane, with financial support from the USA and Saudi Arabia. The former US President Ronald Reagan visited the King, to the outrage of Col Qaddafi, who was further angered when Morocco, as a member of the UN Security Council, did not veto the imposition of sanctions on Libya for its refusal to surrender the suspects wanted for trial in connection with the 1988 Lock-erbie bombing. In August 1992, after Arafat had visited Rabat to discuss the forthcoming round of Middle East peace negotia-tions, Filali held talks with Baker in the USA. In April 1994 King Hassan held talks with the US Vice-President, Al Gore, during meetings culminating in the signing of the Final Act of the Uruguay Round of the General Agreement on Tariffs and Trade (GATT), which took place in Marrakesh. Morocco's rela-tions with the USA have remained close. King Hassan strongly condemned the bomb attacks on US embassies in Kenya and Tanzania in August 1998, and Morocco did not protest when the USA carried out retaliatory missile attacks against Afghanistan and Sudan. Criticism was voiced mainly by the CDT and in the left-wing press. On a visit to Morocco in February 2000 the US Secretary of Defense, William Cohen, stressed that Washing-ton's plan to expand its contracts with Algeria would not be at the expense of America's traditionally strong relations with Morocco. King Muhammad made an official visit to Washington in late June.

The Moroccan authorities strongly condemned the suicide attacks on New York and Washington, DC, of 11 September 2001, but many ordinary Moroccans held Osama bin Laden, the USA's prime suspect in the attacks, in the highest esteem for his defiance of the USA, held responsible for the suffering of the Palestinian and Iraqi peoples. In October 16 Moroccan ulema (religious scholars appointed by the Minister of Religious Endowments and Islamic Affairs) issued a *fatwa* condemning the Moroccan Government for taking part in a multi-faith ceremony held in Rabat's Roman Catholic cathedral several days after the attacks and warning against any Moroccan participation in a US-led military alliance against a Muslim state or group. The ulema expressed 'emotion' at the blow inflicted on the American people by the attacks, but urged the USA to look for the reasons why it provoked such hatred and to revise its foreign policy. Premier el-Youssoufi had taken part in the multifaith ceremony along with several ministers, and one of the King's advisers delivered a message in which he emphasized that although Morocco was a Muslim country Muslims, Christians and Jews had always lived together in 'a climate of tolerance'. On two occasions the authorities banned a protest march, planned by the main Islamist opposition Al Adl Wa-'l Ihsan, against the US-led air-offensive against bases of bin Laden's al-Qa'ida (Base) organization and its Taliban hosts in Afghanistan. In early December William Burns, the US Assistant Secretary of State for Near Eastern Affairs, visited Rabat as part of a tour of Maghreb capitals. He reaffirmed Washington's desire to promote US co-operation with the Maghreb states, and thanked the Moroccan authorities and the Moroccan people for their expressions of solidarity following the September attacks. The Moroccan security services were, meanwhile, co-operating with the US Federal Bureau of Investigation (FBI) in tracking down allgeged terrorists of Maghreb origin based in Europe.

In early April 2002, in response to the Israeli military incursions into Palestinian-controlled areas of the West Bank, US Secretary of State Colin Powell began a regional tour in Morocco. During his meeting with Powell King Muhammad suggested that, given the urgent crisis in the West Bank, it might have been advisable for him to visit Jerusalem first rather than Morocco. The daily *Le Matin*, which normally expresses the views of the palace, criticized President Bush and National Security Advisor Condoleezza Rice for their 'obsession with the Iraqi threat': such personal attacks on senior US officials are virtually unprecedented in the official Moroccan media. Over 1m. protesters took to the streets in Rabat the day before Powell's visit to express solidarity with the Palestinian people. The march was organized by the Association marocaine de soutien à la lutte du peuple palestinien and included many Islamists as well as representatives of the main political parties, trade unions and professional associations. King Muhammad made an official visit to Washington in late April, when discussions focused on the crisis in the Middle East. The Western Sahara dispute was also discussed, and there were reports that progress had been made in negotiations on a free-trade accord between Morocco and the USA. The King, accompanied by former Minister of Tourism Serge Berdugo, the leader of the Morocco's Jewish community, also met representatives of the American Jewish community. In a speech at the beginning of May, Paul Wolfowitz, the US Deputy Secretary of Defense, named Morocco as one of the Muslim states most closely involved in the 'war against terror' and religious obscurantism. He declared that such states took risks and deserved US support. Moroccan secret service agents were reported to have taken part with the US Central Intelligence Agency (CIA) in interrogating detainees held at Guantánamo Bay, Cuba, and in analysing information provided by Abu Zoubeida, a senior figure in al-Qa'ida believed to have provided details of al-Qa'ida 'cells' in Morocco, Tunisia and Libya. In early June the Moroccan authorities announced that at the beginning of May they had arrested three Saudi nationals who were alleged to be members of an Islamist cell, linked to al-Qa'ida, that was preparing terrorist attacks on US and British warships in the Strait of Gibraltar, along the lines of the attack on the USS *Cole* in Aden, Yemen, in October 2000. They were alleged to have planned to target ships based in the Spanish enclaves of Ceuta and Melilla, and the security services believed that the attacks were imminent. Two of the suspects' wives, both of Moroccan origin, had also been arrested for acting as couriers between the Saudis in Morocco and al-Qa'ida, which provided them with funds and logistical support. Morocco's Minister of the Interior attributed the success in discovering and dismantling this terrorist cell to close co-operation between Morocco's security services and their Saudi and US counterparts. The three Saudis were to be tried by a court in Casablanca.

In mid-July 2002 mediation by the US Secretary of State, Colin Powell, helped to diffuse a crisis between Morocco and Spain over the disputed island of Perejil, and resulted in an accord between the two countries on this issue (see below).

As expectations of the UMA diminished, Morocco intensified its efforts to become, if not a full member, at least a 'separate partner' of the EC. In September 1991 a proposal of the European Parliament to send observers to monitor the cease-fire and referendum in Western Sahara was officially denounced in Rabat as 'shameful blackmail'. In January 1992 the European Parliament voted against a four-year programme of aid, worth US $600m., for Morocco, in protest against alleged human rights abuses. Morocco responded by refusing to renegotiate its fishing agreement with the EC, which was due to expire in February. There were separate visits to Rabat by the EC Commissioners for European Integration and for Mediterranean Policy, to discuss a new relationship based on a free-trade zone. A new fishing agreement was signed in May, whereby Morocco would receive annual compensation of ECU 102m. In December the European Commission approved loans worth $590m. to Morocco over four years, and the European Investment Bank made a loan to improve the telecommunications system. In March 1993 the EC announced that negotiations on a form of partnership, which would include permanent political dialogue, economic co-operation, financial aid and progressive moves towards a free-trade zone, should start within a year. In December the organization's Ministers of Foreign Affairs gave their approval for the EU to negotiate with Morocco on a new Europe-Maghreb association agreement. In February 1996 Morocco signed an economic association agreement as part of the EU's plan for a 'Euro-Mediterranean partnership', leading to the gradual introduction of free trade in manufactured goods with the EU. (When the European Parliament ratified the agreement in June, it insisted on inserting a clause allowing for the accord's suspension should concerns arise regarding the violation of human rights in Morocco.) In November 1995 Morocco participated in the first Euro-Mediterranean conference held in Barcelona, Spain, at which there were appeals for greater EU investment in the Maghreb countries in order to create jobs and provide housing, thus stemming emigration and the growth of Islamist militancy. Morocco offered to host the next conference planned for 1997. Yet despite Morocco's desire for closer ties with Europe, and a series of high-level ministerial visits from EU member states during 1997, drugs-trafficking and fisheries remained sources of friction. Morocco also expressed concern that Eastern Europe rather than the countries of the southern Mediterranean had become the EU's main priority. The commitment to stronger inter-Maghreb relations, Arab-Islamic co-operation and the success of the Middle East peace process that Morocco's first opposition-led Government expressed in March 1998 was little more than formulaic. Its attention was focused primarily on Morocco's relations with the EU. Later in the year a special committee was established to address the problem of illegal immigration to Europe, and tough measures, including much longer prison sentences, were introduced for those convicted of smuggling Moroccan migrants into Europe. Despite Morocco's desire for eventual full EU membership, relations with Brussels have been strained since the end of 1999 when Morocco refused to renew the EU fisheries accord. Morocco subsequently agreed in principle to a new fisheries agreement, but the terms it proposed proved unacceptable to the EU. Romano Prodi, President of the European Commission, visited Morocco in January 2001 as part of a tour of the Maghreb states aimed at revitalizing the EU's plan for a Euro-Mediterranean partnership and urged the Moroccan Government to be more flexible in the negotiations on a new fisheries accord. However, talks on renewing the fisheries accord broke down in April.

Morocco continued to rely on France for diplomatic support in the UN Security Council and within the EC. In November 1992 Pierre Bérégovoy became the first French Prime Minister to visit Morocco since 1986. He promised to support Moroccan interests in the EC as far as he could without prejudice to French farmers. His visit was followed by that of the Minister of Foreign Trade, who announced a 50% increase in French aid. In July 1993 Edouard Balladur, the new French Prime Minister, made an official visit to Morocco, where he met King Hassan. In January 1994 the French Minister of the Interior, Charles Pasqua, visited Rabat for talks, which were believed to have covered the crisis in Algeria, Islamist terrorism, immigration, and an offer by the French Government to mediate in the dispute between Morocco and the Polisario Front. Pasqua made a private, but nevertheless controversial, visit to el-Aaiún, the first time that a senior French minister had visited the disputed territory.

After the murder of two Spanish tourists in Marrakesh in August 1994 (see below), the search for suspects spread to France, and in September French police arrested several Islamist activists, including Moroccan, Algerian and French nationals, who were alleged to have been implicated in the incident. It was claimed that they were part of Islamist terrorist cells operating on both sides of the Mediterranean. In October France expelled two Moroccan religious leaders for allegedly collecting funds for arms purchases by Islamist militant groups. In late August Morocco imposed visa requirements on Algerian nationals and others of Algerian origin, including French nationals. However, the visa requirement for French nationals of Algerian origin was quickly withdrawn, following protests from the French authorities. Filali (at that time Prime Minister and Minister of Foreign Affairs and Co-operation) visited Paris in October. An agreement on military co-operation was signed, and France promised to support Morocco in its negotiations with the EU on a partnership accord. In July 1995, moreover, the new French President, Jacques Chirac, visited Morocco. This was his first official foreign visit in his capacity as Head of State. Chirac emphasized the good relations that existed between the two countries and pledged to assist Morocco in combating Islamist extremism. The Chirac administration subsequently strengthened relations further by assisting with Morocco's external debt and by increasing project aid. In May 1996 King Hassan made a successful state visit to Paris where he was invited to address the National Assembly, an invitation criticized by France's left-wing parties because of Morocco's questionable record on human rights. After a socialist Government assumed office in France in May 1997, the new administration sought to show that Morocco remained an important partner in France's Mediterranean strategy. The Minister of Foreign Affairs, Hubert Védrine, visited Rabat in July, followed by the Prime Minister, Lionel Jospin, accompanied by the Minister of the Economy, Finance and Industry, in late December. In March 1998 the Minister of the Interior, Jean-Pierre Chevènement, held talks with his Moroccan counterpart on security issues, notably illegal immigration and drugs-smuggling. Chevènement again emphasized the great importance that France attached to its relations with Morocco which he referred to as a country 'firmly on the path of progress and modernization'. Later in the year, following a strike by several hundred Moroccan seasonal workers in Marseilles, French officials announced that visa requirements for Moroccans who work in France would be simplified. During Prime Minister el-Youssoufi's visit to Paris in October Morocco and France signed several co-operation agreements and the French Government announced an extra aid package of US $765m. and plans for a second debt-swap agreement between the two countries (see Economy). El-Youssoufi's visit was generally regarded as a success, but it was reported that some Moroccan ministers had hoped that France's socialist Government would offer more generous financial assistance to Morocco's first 'gouvernement d'alternance'. King Muhammad's first official overseas visit was to Paris in March 2000, when he asked France to support Morocco's request for a partnership with the EU and appeared to reaffirm Morocco's desire for eventual full EU membership. During the visit the French Government announced an emergency aid package worth 100m. French francs to help Morocco deal with the impact of the recent drought. In early May 2001 el-Youssoufi and Jospin presided over a meeting in Paris of the joint high committee on co-operation, the fourth annual meeting of Heads of Government of Morocco and France. The French Minister of Foreign Affairs, Hubert Védrine, and President Jacques Chirac visited Rabat in October and December respectively as part of their tours of Maghreb capitals, and decared that there was full agreement with the Moroccan Government on the 'war against terror'. The French President delighted his hosts by referring to Western Sahara as 'the southern provices of Morocco'.

Discussions continued with the Spanish Government on a proposed bridge or tunnel link across the Strait of Gibraltar, and official relations remained good. In July 1991, during a visit to Rabat by King Juan Carlos, the two countries signed a treaty of friendship. The sources of former conflict over fishing and immigration remained, but Spain seemed no longer to be concerned about its former colony of Western Sahara. Economic links between Morocco and Spain were strengthened, and Spain overtook France as the principal foreign investor in the kingdom. In July 1992 the two countries signed a 25-year agreement to build and operate the second trans-Mediterranean gas pipeline, extending from Algeria to Spain, via Morocco. In March 1993 the Ministers of Energy of Spain, Morocco and Algeria met in Rabat to discuss details, and a joint Moroccan-Spanish company, the Société pour le Pilotage de la Construction du Gazoduc Maghreb-Europe (Metragaz), was founded, with its headquarters in Casablanca. Despite improving economic links, diplomatic relations became strained in 1994, primarily because of Spanish intransigence over improved access to EU markets for Moroccan agricultural products. Morocco countered with demands for drastic reductions in EU fishing quotas, which largely affect Spanish fishermen, who hold most of the fishing licences for Moroccan waters (see Economy). Relations were not improved when, in September, Morocco criticized Spain at the UN General Assembly for its autonomy plans for the Spanish enclaves of Ceuta and Melilla. Morocco intensified its diplomatic campaign to obtain sovereignty over the territories following the final approval by the Spanish Parliament, in February 1995, of the statutes of autonomy for the two enclaves. Relations remained strained through much of 1995, partly because of the prolonged dispute over Spanish fishing rights, but improved in early 1996, following a visit by Prime Minister González of Spain in February. Spain offered financial credits and proposed a joint committee on bilateral disputes, including the sensitive issue of Ceuta and Melilla. Later in the year the new Spanish Prime Minister, José María Aznar, visited Morocco for his first overseas engagement. Crown Prince Sidi Muhammad made a state visit to Spain in May 1997 and was received by King Juan Carlos. In June a ministerial delegation, led by Prime Minister Filali, visited Madrid where talks focused on economic relations. However, the issue of Spanish fishing vessels operating in Moroccan territorial waters remained a source of friction between the two countries and in July Morocco detained a Spanish vessel, claiming that it was fishing illegally. Morocco indicated that it would not review the EU fisheries accord in 1999, an issue primarily affecting Spain. In January 1998 a joint commission was established with Spain to examine security issues, particularly illegal immigration and drugs-smuggling. The Spanish Prime Minister visited Morocco in April for talks with Prime Minister el-Youssoufi who was keen to emphasize that Morocco and Spain would never go to war over Ceuta and Melilla. Spanish concern over illegal immigration from Morocco was one of the subjects discussed at a meeting between the Moroccan and Spanish Ministers of the Interior in Tangier in August. However, after the EU fisheries accord expired in December 1999 and was not renewed, relations with Spain deteriorated sharply. Spain closed its ports to Moroccan vessels, and in early February 2000 several thousand Spaniards attacked Moroccan migrant labourers at El Ejido in southern Spain. A large number of people were injured during the violence, which lasted for three days before Spanish police were able to control the situation. The Moroccan Government demanded that those responsible for the attacks should be brought to justice. Meanwhile, in August 1999 el-Youssoufi had urged a review of the statutes of Ceuta and Melilla; however, a spokesperson for Spain's ruling Partido Popular asserted that no Moroccan sovereignty claims with regard to this issue would be considered. In January 2000 Aznar visited Ceuta and Melilla and described them as constant parts of Spain's future and stressed the 'Spanishness' of the two cities. Morocco subsequently cancelled a scheduled official visit of the Spanish Minister of Foreign Affairs (although the official reason given by the Moroccan authorities for the cancellation was that King Muhammad was on holiday). The Spanish Ministry of Foreign Affairs maintained, however, that relations in all fields remained excellent. In late July el-Youssoufi held talks in Madrid with his Spanish counterpart Aznar devoted primarily to the official visit to Spain by King Muhammad scheduled for September. During the visit it was agreed that the two countries would work together to settle their differences, notably Morocco's refusal to renew the EU fisheries accord, racist attacks on Moroccan workers in Spain and the future of the Spanish enclaves of Ceuta and Melilla. Nevertheless, relations remained strained owing to Morocco's lack of flexibility over the proposed new EU fisheries accord and attacks by Spanish fishermen on lorries carrying Moroccan exports through Spanish ports. In April 2001 Aznar described Morocco's position on the fisheries accord as 'absolutely unacceptable' and warned of the serious negative consequences Morocco's refusal to renew the accord would have on that country's relations with Spain and the EU. However, reports that Spain was planning to suspend aid to Morocco were denied by Spanish officials. Morocco also expressed concern that some 30,000 Moroccans working in Spain might be expelled after Spain introduced tough new legislation in January. Some 12,000 illegal immigrants from Morocco were expelled from Spain during 2000.

At the end of October 2001 Morocco took the unprecedented, and unexpected, step of recalling its ambassador to Madrid for consultations, provoking a diplomatic crisis with Spain. Rabat also postponed a Spanish-Moroccan summit scheduled for the end of December. Spain's Minister of Foreign Affairs declared that Spain had done nothing to warrant the recall of the ambassador. Addressing parliament, his Moroccan counterpart, Muhammad Benaissa, stated that the Spanish Government was out of step with the EU on certain 'Moroccan national issues' and with the international community's strenuous efforts to resolve this 'manufactured crisis'. While Spain's position on Western Sahara had clearly angered Morocco, Benaissa was also critical of recent border controls introduced by the Spanish authorities for Moroccans entering the Spanish enclaves of Ceuta and Melilla and imposed without prior consultations with Rabat. In addition, Benaissa stated that since the September attacks on the mainland USA Madrid had implied that there was a link between illegal immigration and terrorist networks (a number of Islamist terrorist 'cells' active in Spain had been dismantled by Spanish police in recent weeks) and had placed further restrictions on the movement of Moroccans into and out of the two Spanish enclaves. The breakdown in April of talks on renewing the EU Fisheries Accord also contributed to strained relations between the two countries. A new disagreement erupted at the end of December over maritime boundaries between the Spanish Canary Islands and Morocco's Atlantic coast after the Spanish Government granted oil exploration rights around the Canary Islands to a Spanish company, Repsol.

Relations deteriorated further in mid-July 2002 when a small detachment of Moroccan troops occupied the uninhabited rocky islet of Perejil (known as Leila to Morocco), west of the Spanish enclave of Ceuta and close to the Moroccan coastline. Morocco claimed that it was establishing a surveillance post on the island as part of its campaign against illegal emigration and drug-smuggling. Spain rejected this explanation, describing the Moroccan occupation as a 'serious incident'. Madrid insisted that since 1990 there had been an agreement that neither Morocco nor Spain would occupy the island, whereas Rabat claimed full sovereignty over the island since 1956 and the end of the Spanish Protectorate over northern Morocco and maintained that Moroccan troops had been deployed there in the past when it was deemed necessary. Spain, which proceeded to reinforce its military presence in Ceuta and the other Spanish enclave, Melilla, stated that it did not make a formal claim to sovereignty over the island, but Madrid demanded the immediate evacuation of Moroccan troops from Perejil and a return to the status quo whereby neither Spain nor Morocco occupied the island permanently, a demand supported by the EU and NATO. A week before Moroccan troops landed on Perejil, the Moroccan Ministry of Foreign Affairs had protested to the Spanish ambassador after five Spanish warships approached the Moroccan coast near al-Hoceima during a naval exercise. Some analysts suggested that the occupation of Perejil was Rabat's response to this incident, while others believed that it was designed to draw international attention to Morocco's claims to Ceuta and Melilla and perhaps to put pressure on Spain to change its position with regard to Western Sahara. A few days later Spain's ambassador to Rabat was recalled for an indefinite period, and Spanish special forces intervened and removed Moroccan troops from Perejil without casualties on either side. While Spanish officials underlined the sensitivity of the situation, they insisted

that Spanish troops would be withdrawn if King Muhammad gave assurances that his forces would not reoccupy the island. They also suggested joint use of the island in the campaign against drugs-trafficking. Morocco denounced the Spanish action as equivalent to a declaration of war, but maintained that it sought a diplomatic solution to the crisis. Morocco's stance was supported by all political parties and the Islamist organizations, and a number of popular demonstrations were held in northern Morocco in protest against the Spanish assault on Perejil. Both the Arab League and OIC expressed support for Morocco. Following mediation by the US Secretary of State, Colin Powell, Spanish forces withdrew from the island and talks in Rabat between the Spanish Minister of Foreign Affairs, Ana de Palacio, and her Moroccan counterpart towards the end of the month (the first at this level since October 2001), resulted in an accord on Perejil whereby both states agreed to return to the *status quo ante* while further discussions would be held in September to discuss some of the other issues causing friction between the two countries. This meeting was, however, cancelled by Morocco, which claimed that a Spanish aircraft had landed on the disputed islet.

Relations with Portugal were strengthened following a visit by Aníbal Cavaco Silva, the Portuguese Prime Minister, in May 1994, and the signing of a friendship and co-operation agreement. Cavaco Silva offered his support for Morocco in its negotiations with the EU. Co-operation agreements dealing with civil defence, organized crime, narcotics and visas were signed during a state visit by the Portuguese Prime Minister, António Guterres, in late 1997. Economic co-operation was the key topic under discussion when the Portuguese President, Jorge Sampaio, visited Morocco in May 1998, and el-Youssoufi's first overseas visit after becoming Prime Minister in March was to Lisbon. El-Youssoufi made a second visit to Portugal in November when six new co-operation agreements were signed. In February Morocco and Italy signed a security accord covering issues such as illegal immigration, drugs-smuggling and organized crime. In July Italy's Minister of Foreign Affairs, Lamberto Dini, visited Rabat for talks with King Hassan and el-Youssoufi on economic co-operation. During his visit a new agreement on immigration was concluded.

The UMA itself made halting progress towards its avowed goal of economic union. The Casablanca summit meeting of September 1991 was dominated by the need to agree a common policy for the forthcoming Madrid peace conference, to which it sent a joint delegation. Headquarters of the various UMA institutions were allocated, with Morocco hosting the General Secretariat, Algeria the Consultative Assembly, Mauritania the Supreme Court, Tunisia the Investment Bank, and Libya the Maghreb University and Academy of Science. In December the ministers responsible for foreign affairs, the economy and agriculture met to discuss the co-ordination of policies: there were agreements on the Maghreb Autoroute, and trade union representatives from the five countries presented a joint plea for a social charter. In February 1993, however, Prime Minister Filali announced that, at a recent meeting of the ministers of foreign affairs within the UMA, it had been decided that there should be a 'pause' in the development of a closer union; it was noted that, of the 15 conventions signed since the inauguration of the UMA, none had as yet been fully applied. The organization was further weakened during 1994 by the sharp deterioration in relations between Morocco and Algeria, including the closure of the border between the two countries, and tensions between Morocco and Tunisia over Tunisia's expulsion of several hundred alleged illegal Moroccan immigrants. The Moroccan Government protested that some of its nationals had been maltreated by the Tunisian authorities and there were mutual recriminations. In December 1995 Morocco threatened to obstruct UMA activities, accusing Algeria of interfering in the Western Sahara dispute (see above). Morocco condemned a meeting in January 1996 between the Tunisian and Mauritanian foreign ministers and the Algerian President, Liamine Zéroual, who continued to hold the UMA presidency. The meeting had been convened to resolve the dispute with Morocco. Morocco was especially critical that the UMA's Secretary-General, Mohamed Amamou, was present. As Libya did not attend, some observers believed that there was the possibility of renewed polarization in the region if the current UMA crisis was not resolved. The UMA was virtually moribund after 1994. However, following the election of Abdelaziz Bouteflika as President of Algeria in April 1999 and the suspension of UN sanctions against Libya in the same month, efforts were made to resuscitate the organization. In May Morocco sent a representative to a meeting of the UMA's 'follow-up' committee, the first to be held for three years. The meeting was attended by representatives of all five member states and the improvement in relations between Morocco and Algeria in mid-1999 (see below) aroused hopes that attempts to revive the UMA would gather pace. However, the *rapprochement* between the two neighbours proved short-lived and as relations again deteriorated the UMA heads of state summit planned for November was cancelled. In August 2000 King Muhammad met with Tunisian President Zine el-Abidine Ben-Ali in Tunis to discuss measures to be taken to attempt to reactivate the UMA. In mid-March 2001 the UMA's Council of Foreign Ministers met in Algiers to prepare for of summit of heads of state; however, Morocco was only represented by its Secretary of State for Foreign Affairs, and the meeting broke down following disagreements between Moroccan and Algerian representatives. However, Muhammad Benaissa did attend a meeting of UMA foreign ministers held in Algiers in January 2002 at which Habib Boularès of Tunisia was elected as the organization's new Secretary-General. On the sensitive issue of Western Sahara Benaissa stated that there was no question of Morocco sacrificing its 'national cause to build a Greater Maghreb'. King Muhammad announced that he would not attend the summit meeting of UMA heads of state which was due to have been held in Algiers in late June, and President Bouteflika of Algeria, after consultations with the Libyan leader, Col Qaddafi, decided to postpone the meeting.

Morocco and Algeria restored diplomatic relations in 1988, and the two countries maintained particularly strong links during early 1992, while Muhammad Boudiaf, who had lived in Morocco for more than 20 years, was Algerian Head of State. Following the assassination of Boudiaf, relations deteriorated, the frontier was closed and Algerian supplies to the Polisario Front were resumed. In January 1993, however, there was a reconciliation. Ambassadors were exchanged and the border was reopened. Relations deteriorated again in 1994, reaching their lowest ebb for many years. When the alleged leader of the Algerian Groupe islamique armé (GIA), Abd al-Hak Layada, stood trial in Algiers, he stated that, before being extradited from Morocco in September 1993, senior Moroccan army officers had asked him to eliminate certain members of the Moroccan opposition living in Algeria, together with the Polisario Secretary-General, Muhammad Abd al-Aziz. In August, after the murder of two Spanish tourists at Marrakesh, the Moroccan Ministry of the Interior issued a public statement alleging that two of the suspects sought for the killings were in the pay of the Algerian secret services, which it accused of sponsoring terrorism to destabilize the kingdom. During a massive security alert following the incident Moroccan police targeted the country's Algerian community in its search for terrorists. The Algerian Government strongly denied that it was sponsoring terrorism against its neighbour, and sealed its border with Morocco. By mid-September, however, the tension between the two countries had eased somewhat, and in a gesture of goodwill Algeria appointed a permanent ambassador to Rabat. In October the Moroccan Minister of Energy and Mines visited Algeria to attend the ceremony marking the formal start of work on the Maghreb–Europe gas pipeline. However, the frontier remained closed and visa requirements for Algerian nationals continued to be enforced. Talks between King Hassan, the Algerian Prime Minister, Mokdad Sifi, and Abd al-Latif Filali, during the OIC summit held in Casablanca in December, failed to make any significant progress. Relations remained strained throughout 1995 and at the end of the year deteriorated sharply as Morocco accused Algeria of interfering in the Western Sahara dispute. Differences between the two countries seriously threatened the future of the UMA (see above). In December 1996 the Algerian Minister of the Interior held talks in Rabat with his Moroccan counterpart. This was the first meeting of senior ministers since the border was closed in August 1994. Western Sahara remained a source of tension between the two countries and in February 1998 Gen. Khaled Nezzar, an influential former Algerian Minister of Defence, accused Morocco of demanding that Algeria

end its support for Polisario in return for the extradition of Abd al-Hak Layada. Gen. Nezzar also accused the Moroccan authorities of providing covert assistance to armed opposition groups in Algeria and allowing weapons to be smuggled across the border. Morocco strenuously denied the allegations and later in the year, as relations remained tense, the Moroccan Minister of the Interior, Driss Basri, accused Algeria of attempting to destabilize Morocco as preparations were made for the UN referendum on Western Sahara. Prime Minister el-Youssoufi attempted to achieve a reconciliation by publicly urging that the border between Algeria and Morocco should be reopened. Morocco's Minister of Territorial Administration subsequently met the leaders of Algeria's principal political parties in Tunis, and in August a meeting took place in Oran between el-Youssoufi and his Algerian counterpart. Algeria's strong support for Polisario, however, continued to obstruct any significant improvement in relations. The election of Abdelaziz Bouteflika as President of Algeria in April 1999 raised hopes of a *rapprochement*. King Hassan sent a message of congratulations to the new Algerian President and el-Youssoufi reiterated his appeal that the countries' mutual border should be reopened. President Bouteflika attended the funeral of King Hassan (see below) at the end of July and met briefly with Morocco's new ruler, King Muhammad. The improvement in relations with Algeria, however, proved short-lived. In mid-August Algeria again accused Morocco of providing a haven for its Islamist opponents after a brutal massacre of civilians by Algerian fundamentalist rebels near the Moroccan border. The long-awaited reopening of the land border between the two countries failed to take place and the press embarked on a new round of mutual accusations. The continuing Western Sahara dispute (see above) aggravated tensions between the two countries. Nevertheless, early in 2000 the Algerian Minister of Foreign Affairs, Youcef Yousfi, declared that the Western Sahara issue should not stand in the way of improved relations with Morocco. In February King Muhammad despatched a special envoy to visit President Bouteflika, who expressed his desire to improve relations with Morocco. King Muhammad and President Bouteflika held talks at the EU–OAU summit in Cairo in April, but the land frontier remained closed and the Western Sahara dispute continued to prevent any significant improvement in relations. In an interview with *Time* magazine prior to his official visit to Washington, DC, in late June, King Muhammad described the Western Sahara dispute as 'Algeria's creation'. In mid-July after it was revealed that Qatar had purchased a consignment of British arms for the Algerian armed forces worth US $7.5m., Rabat claimed that the weapons might be used to strengthen Polisario. The affair was believed to have been one of the factors which led Morocco to withdraw its ambassador from Qatar. Nevertheless, a meeting between the Moroccan and Algerian Ministers of the Interior in Rabat in mid-November—the third since the beginning of the year— was described as positive, and it was announced that a preparatory committee would meet soon to prepare for the reopening of the land border. King Muhammad and President Bouteflika met again at a conference of Francophone countries held in Yaoundé, Cameroon, in January 2001. In March Algerian and Moroccan officials attending the UN Commission for Human Rights in Geneva quarrelled publicly over the Western Sahara issue.

In the Arab world as a whole Morocco benefited both from the personal prestige of its monarch as an experienced statesman and from its support for the liberation of Kuwait. In January 1992 Arab Ministers of Foreign Affairs met in Marrakesh to agree a common strategy for the Moscow session of the Middle East peace talks. In October, just before the seventh round of the talks (held in Washington, DC), King Hassan made his most extensive tour of the Islamic world in 30 years, visiting Jordan (for the first time), Syria, Saudi Arabia, the Gulf states and Egypt. In December 1994 Morocco hosted a summit of the OIC at the request of Saudi Arabia, but King Hassan failed to engender any reconciliation between Iraq and Saudi Arabia and Kuwait, despite lengthy negotiations. King Hassan made an official visit to Egypt in May 1998 in order to strengthen bilateral relations. The King and President Mubarak signed a number of economic agreements and, in a joint statement, expressed support for the Palestinian people and urged the USA to continue its efforts to revive the Middle East peace process. In

July Morocco again hosted a meeting of the OIC's Al-Quds (Jerusalem) committee, convened in Casablanca to discuss the stalled Middle East peace process.

In September 1993, following the mutual recognition and signature of a peace accord between Israel and the PLO, the Israeli Prime Minister, Itzhak Rabin, and the Minister of Foreign Affairs, Shimon Peres, visited Rabat for talks with King Hassan. Apart from Egypt, Morocco was the only Arab state to receive the two Israeli leaders. In October a group of Moroccan industrialists, including King Hassan's economic consultant, visited Israel to attend a business conference, the first official Moroccan delegation to visit the Jewish state. Commercial links developed rapidly, and tourism was expected to expand. The Moroccan-Jewish community constitutes more than 10% of the Israeli population, and large numbers visit their country of origin every year. After talks with King Hassan in June 1994, Shimon Peres announced that the two countries had agreed to establish telecommunications links and, at a later date, to establish 'representations of some kind'. In September, as the peace process gained momentum, Morocco and Israel agreed to open 'liaison offices' in Rabat and Tel-Aviv. King Hassan had maintained discreet contacts with Israeli leaders since the 1970s. The latest move towards Israel was criticized by the opposition parties, which urged caution until a comprehensive Middle East peace settlement had been achieved. Morocco also became the first Arab state to announce that it would open a 'liaison bureau' in the Gaza autonomous area. In October 1994, during an historic appearance on Israeli television, King Hassan declared that the peace process would lead to the establishment of full diplomatic relations between Morocco and Israel, but carefully avoided stating when this would take place. He repeated Morocco's position on the restoration of Arab lands and rights, while insisting that the unconditional recognition of Israeli sovereignty within internationally agreed borders was essential. In early 1995 Morocco opened a bureau in Tel-Aviv, making it the third Arab country after Egypt and Jordan to have a representative office in Israel. However, King Hassan continued to stress that full normalization of relations between the two countries would only be achieved after the conclusion of a comprehensive Middle East peace settlement. In May King Hassan hosted talks between Peres and Yasser Arafat. In February 1996 an Israeli-Moroccan chamber of commerce was opened in Tel-Aviv. King Hassan did not attend the emergency Arab League summit in Cairo in June, convened by President Mubarak of Egypt after the new Israeli Prime Minister, Binyamin Netanyahu, and his right-wing Government rejected the 'land for peace' policies of the previous administration. It was reported that the King had taken umbrage when he was not consulted about the planning of the conference. In February 1997, as the Middle East peace process seemed close to collapse, King Hassan indicated that visits to Morocco by either Prime Minister Netanyahu or Israel's Deputy Prime Minister and Minister of Foreign Affairs, David Levy, would not be appropriate. In March the King organized a meeting in Rabat of the OIC's Jerusalem Committee, of which he was the Chairman. The committee demanded that the Israeli Government stop construction of the controversial Jewish settlement at Har Homa on the outskirts of Arab East Jerusalem, and appealed to Arab states that had begun to establish relations with Israel to reconsider these links. A threat by Morocco in April to close the Moroccan-based Bureau for Economic Development in the Middle East, established to promote economic relations between the Arab states and Israel, was withdrawn in May after US intervention. Morocco did not close its liaison office in Tel-Aviv despite King Hassan's continued refusal to have any contact with the Netanyahu administration. Although two Euro-Mediterranean summits were scheduled to be held in Marrakesh to discuss co-operation between the EU and Mediterranean countries, including Israel, the meeting planned for October was cancelled by the Moroccan Government; nevertheless, the second went ahead as scheduled in November. Along with most Arab League members, Morocco boycotted the fourth US-sponsored Middle East and North Africa Economic Conference held in Qatar in November, arguing that while the Middle East peace process remained deadlocked there was little to be gained from discussing economic co-operation with Israel. Notwithstanding, commercial and business links between Morocco and

Israel remained strong. Bilateral relations remained virtually frozen throughout 1998. In May the Moroccan legislature strongly condemned Israel, and Israel's Minister of Culture, Itzhak Levi, was refused permission to travel through Morocco when he visited the Spanish enclave of Melilla. In October Morocco refused to allow the Israeli Prime Minister to make a stopover in Rabat after attending peace negotiations in the USA. In contrast, King Hassan extended a warm welcome to Palestinian President, Yasser Arafat, who made a short visit to the Moroccan capital on his return from the USA. At the end of July, the new Israeli Prime Minister, Ehud Barak, attended the funeral of King Hassan in Rabat, where he also held informal talks with a number of Arab leaders including Yasser Arafat. In August 2000 King Muhammad chaired a meeting of the OIC's Jerusalem Committee which reaffirmed that the city should be the capital of a Palestinian state. Shortly afterwards the acting Israeli Minister of Foreign Affairs, Shlomo Ben-Ami, met with King Muhammad and his Moroccan counterpart in Agadir to discuss the Middle East peace process. Following renewed violence between Israel and the Palestinians in September–October there was growing criticism within Morocco of links with Israel, and the visit by a Moroccan delegation to the Knesset's memorial ceremony for the late King Hassan was postponed. In late October Morocco closed Israel's liaison office in Rabat and its own interest section in Tel Aviv. Earlier in the month 500,000 Moroccans had demonstrated in Rabat in support of the Palestinians—the largest protest march since the 1991 Gulf War. However, at the end of December Israel's Deputy Prime Minister and Minister of Foreign Affairs, Shimon Peres, visited Rabat to discuss US peace proposals with King Muhammad suggesting that Morocco was continuing its role as mediator between the Arab states and Israel.

There was widespread outrage in Morocco in response to the Israeli military offensive in Palestinian-controlled areas of the West Bank from the end of March 2002. A national march in solidarity with the Palestinian people took place in Rabat in early April, attracting more than 1m. people—the biggest demonstration in the Arab world. Meanwhile, there were reports in the independent Moroccan press that an apparent resurgence of anti-Semitism since the onset of the second *intifada* was causing disquiet among members of Morocco's Jewish community, who found themselves the target of verbal and even physical assaults. The Moroccan authorities remained silent on this subject, but did arrest a number of radical imams, including the leader of the Salafist Movement for Jihad, for criticizing the Moroccan and other Arab governments' alleged quiescence over the situation in the Palestinian territories. Meanwhile, in April Morocco hosted meetings between US Secretary of State Colin Powell and Crown Prince Abdullah of Saudi Arabia, and between the Crown Prince and King Abdullah of Jordan, to discuss the Israeli–Palestinian crisis.

In January 2001 a delegation of ministers and businessmen headed by Prime Minister el-Youssoufi visited Iran to prepare for closer political relations. A number of commercial agreements were signed during the visit. No senior Moroccan politician had visited Iran since the Islamic Revolution in 1979, and in 1981 Iran had severed diplomatic relations with Morocco after King Hassan allowed the Shah of Iran to take refuge in Morocco. In February 2001 King Muhammad led a large delegation to India, which resulted in the signing of a series of commercial agreements and the establishment of a joint economic council. In early February 2002 King Muhammad made an official visit to the People's Republic of China, where several co-operation agreements were signed aimed at expanding trade between the two countries. The King, who was accompanied by several senior army officers (including the head of military intelligence) also met the Chinese Minister of Defence, and there were reports that Morocco was considering purchasing arms from China. Meanwhile, in late May 2001 King Muhammad visited Senegal where he was urged by that country's President, Abdoulaye Wade, an ardent pan-Africanist, to approve Morocco's membership of the African Union, which formally replaced the OAU (from which Morocco had withdrawn in 1984, when the SADR became a member) in July 2002. King Muhammad's historic visit to Mauritania in September 2001, which was intended to inaugurate an era of improved relations between the two countries, was cut short as a result of the attacks on New York and Washington. In March 2002 it was reported that the land frontier between the two countries would be reopened after being closed for 23 years. At the end of February 2002 King Muhammad arranged a meeting in Morocco between the Presidents of Guinea, Sierra Leone and Liberia, at which the three heads of state signed a peace accord condemning the activities of non-governmental armed groups in the region, and guaranteeing total security along their common borders, the repatriation of refugees and assistance for displaced persons.

THE 1993 GENERAL ELECTION

In October 1991 various opposition parties allied to form the Mouvement national populaire (MNP), an opposition grouping under a veteran Berber politician, Mahjoubi Aherdane; in November Istiqlal and the USFP formed a united front, demanding a separation of powers, a reduction in the minimum voting age to 18 years, new electoral lists and constituency boundaries, and improvements in civil rights. The USFP was, however, weakened by the death of its veteran leader, Abd ar-Rahim Bouabid. His successor, Abd ar-Rahman el-Youssoufi, did not have the same close links with the monarchy. In April 1992 a 16th political party, the Parti de l'avant-garde démocratique socialiste (PADS, a breakaway from the USFP), was legalized. In March a trade union official and USFP politburo member, Nubir Amaoui, was sentenced to two years' imprisonment for his public criticism of the Government. In late 1992 trade union activists demonstrating to demand Amaoui's release were forcibly dispersed. Meanwhile, a prominent member of the ADHM, Ahmad Belaichi, was sentenced to three years' imprisonment for making derogatory remarks about the armed forces. In February 1993 the ADHM alleged that as many as 750 political prisoners were being detained in Morocco. However, in July, following the legislative elections, Amaoui was released, along with the leader of another, pro-Istiqlal, union, Driss Laghnimi.

In April 1992, in an address to a conference of local government bodies, the King declared that parliamentary elections would be preceded by those for regional and local councils. There was disagreement on the text of the electoral law, and the opposition parties (Istiqlal, the USFP, the PADS and the PPS) refused to enter discussions, complaining that their previous recommendations had always been ignored. Hassan, fearing that these parties would boycott the poll (rendering it meaningless), asked them to negotiate with his close associate, Reda Guedira. It was agreed that a new Constitution should be submitted to a referendum. Declaring that his status as a religious, as well as a national, leader empowered him to arbitrate, King Hassan announced the establishment of two committees: one to draft the law and the other to monitor the electoral process. In May he chaired a conference of three ministers and the leaders of five pro-government and four opposition parties, allowing them 10 days to agree on an electoral law. A law comprising 99 articles was approved, and Hassan reiterated his promise of 'transparency'. A commission, chaired by a judge and consisting of members of local authorities and party representatives, was established, with direct access to the King or to Guedira.

In June 1992 the Chamber of Representatives adopted a new electoral law, in spite of a boycott by all opposition parties. The law reduced the minimum voting age to 20 years and the minimum candidate age to 23 from 25. It also made provision for equal funding and media exposure for all parties, and was approved by 162 votes in favour, with two abstentions. The opposition parties had earlier formed the Bloc démocratique (or Koutla Dimocratya), whose expressed aims were: a minimum voting age of 18 years; a minimum age of 21 for candidates; a two-tier voting system; and an independent chairman of a new body to supervise elections.

In July 1992 King Hassan announced preparations for elections to the Chamber of Representatives, and by the end of the month registration had taken place, increasing the electorate from 7m. to 11.7m. voters. In mid-August an interim Government was appointed to ensure the fairness of the political process. The new Prime Minister, Karim Lamrani, had held the office on two previous occasions. Lamrani's Government contained just one member with party political affiliations, although the major portfolios were unchanged.

In an address to the nation in August 1992 King Hassan stated that the revised Constitution would give more responsibilities to the legislature, but emphasized that this did not mean a reduction in the sovereign's prerogatives. Under the proposed changes, ministers would be chosen by the Prime Minister but appointed by the King. A new Constitutional Council of eight members, one-half of them appointed by the King, would be created to arbitrate at the request of one-quarter of the parliamentary deputies. The revised Constitution also reaffirmed the King's commitment to human rights.

On 4 September 1992 the revised Constitution was endorsed by the Moroccan electorate. According to official results, 99.96% voted in favour (increasing to 100% in main cities, and three of the four 'Saharan provinces') and 97.25% of the 11.7m. registered voters participated. The opposition claimed that the results destroyed all credibility in the democratic process. The revised Constitution required the Government to reflect the composition of the Chamber of Representatives and to submit its programme to a vote. New legislation would be promulgated automatically one month after approval by the Chamber.

Despite protests over the result of the referendum, the Bloc démocratique contested the communal elections that took place in October 1992. The RNI became the largest party in local government, winning 18.1% of the votes cast and 21.7% of the 22,282 seats contested. The independent list, Sans appartenance politique, which, despite its name, was loyal to the Government, obtained 13.8% of the votes, and the UC 13.4%. Istiqlal emerged as the largest opposition party (with 12.5% of the votes cast), followed by the USFP. The opposition parties, however, failed to improve on their performance in the previous communal elections, despite contesting many more seats, and complained of widespread malpractice by local authorities in favour of 'loyalist' parties.

In December 1992 it was announced that the long-awaited national legislative election, the first since 1984, would not be held until 30 April 1993, to allow time for the compiling of new electoral registers. The opposition demanded that the lists should be radically revised, and the boundaries of constituencies redrawn. The authorities stated that the registers would include newly-eligible voters but rejected proposals for any other changes. In February 1993 the four leading opposition parties that formed the Bloc démocratique—Istiqlal, the USFP and two smaller parties, the PPS and the Organisation de l'action démocratique et populaire (OADP)—withdrew from the multi-party national commission responsible for overseeing the election, and threatened to boycott the poll unless the Government agreed to changes in the electoral law and register, and responded to their demands for the release of all political prisoners. In late March King Hassan announced that the election would be postponed until 25 June, to allow more time to update electoral lists and to redefine electoral boundaries. The opposition parties welcomed the King's decision and now agreed to participate in the election. Following boundary revisions (completed in late April), the Government announced that the number of seats in the Chamber of Representatives had been increased from 306 to 333. Of the total, 222 would be elected by universal adult suffrage, and the remainder by local councils and professional organizations.

At the general election, on 25 June 1993, the two main opposition parties, Istiqlal and the USFP, substantially increased the number of their seats in the Chamber (from 57 in 1984 to 91) to become the leading parties at the end of the first stage of the electoral process. The parties of the Bloc démocratique won a total of 99 seats. Although the five loyalist parties won more seats overall, the UC and the RNI secured fewer seats than in 1984. The UC had been the largest single party at the 1984 election, with 55 seats, but won only 27 seats in 1993. The MP emerged with 33 seats, two more than in 1984. According to official figures, 62.8% of the electorate voted, but observers suggested that the level of participation may have been even lower. Despite reports of abuses by local officials, polling was judged to have been fairer than in previous elections. Nevertheless, the opposition parties demanded that the election of four cabinet ministers be annulled. In the second stage of the election, held on 17 September 1993, the loyalist parties made significant gains, winning 79 of the 111 seats contested. The UC alone won 27 seats, making it the second largest party in the new Chamber (after the USFP). The USFP and Istiqlal gained only 17 seats, and el-Youssoufi, the USFP leader, resigned in protest at the attitude of the administration during the election. At the end of the second stage the five loyalist parties had 195 seats in the new Chamber, while the Bloc démocratique had 120 seats, with independents holding the remaining 18 seats.

After the election it was reported that King Hassan had agreed that the USFP and Istiqlal, as the main components of the Bloc démocratique, could form a government on condition that he appointed three principal ministers. The two parties rejected the offer and announced that they would not participate in the new Government. On 9 November 1993 the King therefore asked Karim Lamrani, who had led the interim Government appointed in August 1992 to oversee the election, to form a new Government. This was the fourth occasion on which the 74-year-old Lamrani, one of the most trusted members of the King's inner circle, had been named Prime Minister. Lamrani announced a Government largely composed of technocrats and independents. None of the ministers from the previous administration who had stood for election in June were included. Ten new ministers and five new junior ministers were appointed. Muhammad Saghou replaced Muhammad Berrada as Minister of Finance, a post that Berrada had held for eight years, and Serge Berdugo, appointed Minister of Tourism, became the first Jewish minister since 1957. Omar Azziman, a co-founder of the OMDH, was appointed to the new post of Minister-delegate responsible for Human Rights. The appointment was welcomed by Amnesty International, a persistent critic of Morocco's record in observing human rights. Amnesty appealed to the Government to release all prisoners of conscience, and presented a list of 80 Moroccans and 485 Sahrawis, whom it claimed had 'disappeared.' In late November 1993 the Chamber of Representatives adopted the Government's new programme, promising economic reforms and greater social justice.

In February 1994 there were clashes between radical Islamist and leftist students at Fez University, and courses were suspended indefinitely after the security forces intervened. At the end of the month the Government banned a 24-hour general strike (planned for 25 February), organized by the CDT to protest against declines in the standard of living. On 24 February, after 11 of its activists had been arrested in Casablanca, the CDT announced its decision to postpone the strike. A number of parliamentary by-elections were held in April, following a judicial decision to reorganize polling after complaints of irregularities during the 1993 legislative election. Of the 14 seats contested by 88 candidates in the by-elections, the USFP won two, and Istiqlal three. The RNI, which had won five of the seats in June 1993, retained only two. Nevertheless, the opposition parties again complained of irregularities during the voting.

FILALI BECOMES PRIME MINISTER AND EFFORTS TO DRAW THE OPPOSITION INTO GOVERNMENT FAIL

On 25 May 1994 Lamrani was replaced as Prime Minister by Abd al-Latif Filali, formerly the Minister of Foreign Affairs and Co-operation and another member of the King's inner circle. Filali, a former diplomat, had first held government office in 1968. The new Prime Minister was expected to promote economic liberalization more vigorously and, within a few days of his appointment, announced that he had begun consultations with all the political parties with members in the Chamber of Representatives about the political, economic and social situation of the country. After a week of consultation, however, Filali made no changes to the list of ministers presented to the King in early June. The Prime Minister retained control of the Ministry of Foreign Affairs and Co-operation. However, Ali Yata, the Secretary-General of the PPS, stated that Filali had proposed the formation of a Government of national consensus within three or four months. In July 1994 King Hassan again appealed to the opposition to join a 'government of change and renewal'. After less than a year in office, the Minister of Finance, Muhammad Saghou, was dismissed in July, for a budget policy deemed to be too lenient, and replaced by Mourad Cherif, hitherto Minister of Foreign Trade. In October Hassan continued his efforts to draw the parliamentary opposition parties into a coalition government by announcing his intention to select a Prime Minister from the ranks of the opposition. He held

separate discussions with Muhammad Boucetta, the Secretary-General of Istiqlal, and with Abd al-Wahed Radi of the USFP. The two main opposition parties agreed to the King's proposal in principle and looked to the RNI and to one of the two Berber groups as potential partners in an alternative government. However, talks between the palace and the opposition parties collapsed over the appointment of the Minister of State for the Interior and Information in the new Government. The King insisted on retaining the long-serving Driss Basri in this sensitive post, but the opposition demanded that they be allowed to make their own appointment to the ministry. The King had also insisted that the opposition should support the economic liberalization measures agreed with the IMF, implementing the privatization programme and reducing the budget deficit. In December the opposition parties rejected the Government's 1995 budget, claiming that it would adversely affect living standards and increase unemployment. They also criticized the Government for placing too great a dependence on the private sector in economic development. However, support from the loyalist parties ensured that the budget was accepted by the Chamber of Representatives.

In late January 1995 King Hassan reappointed Filali as Prime Minister and Minister of Foreign Affairs and Co-operation, and once again chose a Government drawn from loyalist parties. In February he approved a new Cabinet drawn from three of the main centre-right parties, the UC, the MP and the PND. The other two main centre-right parties, the RNI and the MNP, declined an offer to join the administration but confirmed that they would continue to support the Government in the Chamber of Representatives. Of the 35 cabinet posts, 20 portfolios were allocated to political parties, the rest to palace-appointed technocrats. Yet, despite an attempt to give the political process greater legitimacy by drawing more than one-half of the ministers from elected political parties, the King retained control of appointments to important cabinet posts. Driss Basri remained at the Ministry of the Interior and although he ceded the information portfolio—a new Ministry of Communications was created—the King could be assured that internal security would remain tightly controlled. Abd ar-Rahman Saaidi was retained as head of the Ministry of Privatization, and the politically-sensitive posts of housing and education also went to non-party palace appointees. Nine of the portfolios given to political parties went to the UC including tourism, human rights and the important post of finance and foreign investments. The MP received eight posts of which the most important were the portfolios of agriculture and foreign trade, and the PND three posts.

In June 1994 Prime Minister Filali announced that the national television service would begin broadcasting news bulletins in Tamazight, the Berber language. Since August a short news programme has been broadcast on Moroccan television with a different presenter for each of the three main Berber dialects, Tarifit (spoken in the Rif), Tamazight (centre-east) and Tachlahit (south). A few days before the broadcasts began King Hassan declared that Berber 'dialects' were an integral part of Morocco's authenticity and history and would soon be taught in state schools, at least at elementary level. He stressed, however, that Arabic remained the official language as detailed in the Moroccan Constitution. Nevertheless, these developments appeared to mark a major change in policy towards the Berber-speaking minority which constitutes more than one-third of the country's population. Berber cultural associations have flourished in recent years, attracting many young activists. Six of these associations had signed the Agadir charter in August 1991 deploring the marginalization of the Berber language and culture, appealing for the teaching of Tamazight in Moroccan schools and for Tamazight to be given national status in the Constitution alongside Arabic. By 1994 some 11 associations had signed the charter. In May 1994, after a peaceful Berberist demonstration by the Tilelli (Liberty) association at er-Rachidia demanding official recognition of Tamazight, and for the Berber language to be taught in schools, seven supporters were arrested and charged with threatening state security. The authorities claimed to have discovered documents implicating the President of Tilelli in links with 'foreign organizations'. Three of those arrested were given prison sentences, but they were released in July when King Hassan granted an amnesty to 424 prisoners following appeals by international and local human rights groups. Despite the King's declaration no action was taken in practice on teaching the Berber language in schools.

The regime remained nervous of any challenge to its authority and determined to act against organized labour, students and other dissenting groups. In June 1994 several unemployed graduates were given two-year prison sentences after holding an unauthorized demonstration to protest against corruption in local government. The penal code was also revised so that trade unionists involved in strike action over pay would be subject to prison sentences or fines. In August, after gunmen shot and killed two Spanish tourists in Marrakesh, a massive security operation was launched amid fears that the vitally important tourist industry was being targeted as part of a wider attempt to destabilize the country. Within days, two French nationals of North African origin, Algerian-born Stephane Ait-Idir and Moroccan-born Redouane Hammadi, were arrested and charged with the murders, and in the following months several hundred suspects, most of them Algerian-French or Moroccan-French, were arrested and accused of terrorist activities. In France French police arrested alleged associates of the two men charged and claimed that they belonged to Islamist terrorist cells. Seven main suspects were brought to trial in early 1995 for the Marrakesh murders. The Moroccan authorities alleged that they formed three terrorist groups: the Marrakesh group led by Ait-Idir and Hammadi, the Casablanca group led by Hamel Marzouk, and the Fez group which included a French-Algerian and three Moroccan nationals. Ait-Idir, Hammadi and Marzouk were condemned to death, the first death sentences given for political or security offences since the early 1970s, and three of the other main defendants were sentenced to life imprisonment. Twelve other suspects received prison sentences ranging from six months to 10 years. At their trial the three main defendants admitted to belonging to an Islamist terrorist group and being converted to *jihad* by a Moroccan known as Abdelilah Ziad. In August Ziad was extradited from Germany to stand trial·in France on charges of involvement in terrorist acts in both Morocco and France. Tarek Falah, also accused of taking part in the Marrakesh murders, had been extradited from Germany to France in July. The incident at Marrakesh had a damaging effect on Morocco's relations with Algeria after Morocco accused the Algerian security forces of financing terrorist groups in Morocco with the aim of destabilizing the country (see above). At his trial in Paris in December 1996 Ziad claimed that his terrorist group (the outlawed Mouvement de la jeunesse islamique marocaine), based in Paris, was responsible for organizing the Marrakesh operation and had also smuggled arms to the Armée islamique du salut in Algeria, the armed wing of the banned Front islamique du salut.

In mid-1995 the Minister of Higher Education admitted publicly for the first time that Islamist militants were gaining strength among university students. The authorities announced their intention to continue to target the ringleaders, while they would encourage other student organizations in order to counter the Islamist threat. In October 12 Moroccans and five Algerians were arrested near the Algerian border and charged with smuggling arms to the Algerian GIA. In January 1996 they received prison sentences of up to 14 years. In December 1995 Abd as-Salam Yassin, the leader of the banned Islamist movement Al Adl wa-'l Ihsan, was released after spending six years under house arrest. A week later, after addressing worshippers at a mosque and denouncing certain aspects of government policy, he was placed once again under house arrest; the authorities insisted that he was under 'police protection'. Some observers argued that this episode illustrated the Government's ambivalent attitude towards the Islamist opposition: a measure of tolerance was displayed towards the more moderate Islamist opposition (although they were refused permission to form a political party), while armed Islamist groups were severely repressed. Although small extremist Islamist groups certainly exist and are supported in particular by young militants, since the 1980s the main currents of the Islamist movement have evolved towards an 'Islamism of compromise' with the Government. Islamist groups such as Al Adl wa-'l Ihsan and Al Islah wa Attajdid (Reform and Renewal) insist that they wish to be integrated into the political system, rejecting violence and favouring the peaceful re-Islamization of society. They conduct a range of socio-cultural activities, including charitable work in the most disadvantaged areas of the major cities, and seek to gain influence in trade unions and in major political parties, such as the USFP and Istiqlal. Poor employment prospects (especially among young people), low pay, redundancies owing to the privatization of state companies, declining living standards and a severe drought not only provided fertile ground for the Islamist movement but also led to widespread strike action by many, including teachers and workers in the phosphate industry and on the railways. Although the Government attempted to promote dialogue between employers and workers, several trade unionists were imprisoned, and, amid allegations of police brutality, both unions and human rights groups condemned the Government's repressive policy in labour disputes. In mid-1995 the police presence in major cities was heightened to combat increasing levels of robbery and violence. Opposition parties accused the police of exceeding their authority by making arbitrary arrests and intimidating suspects, and in September both the police and the judiciary were strongly criticized when 26 unemployed graduates staging a peaceful demonstration at El Jadida were arrested and sentenced to six months in prison. At the end of the year the King warned that the civil service and national and local administration would have to be reformed to enable the country to confront the challenges of the next century. Conscious that retrenchment and redundancies would be strongly opposed, he appealed for dialogue with political parties and trade unions to discuss potential reforms. In December 1996 senior officials reiterated the King's message, insisting that the country could not become a modern market economy unless its bureaucracy was reformed.

In June 1995 charges against Muhammad Basri, former leader of the USFP, who had lived in exile for some 28 years after being sentenced to death (*in absentia*) for plotting against the State, were dropped, allowing him to return to Morocco. El-Youssoufi, who had resigned as Secretary-General of the USFP in 1993, agreed to resume the post in July. In the same month the PPS held its first congress for four years, at which Ali Yata was re-elected as Secretary-General.

In August 1995 King Hassan announced plans to hold a referendum to decide whether to create a second parliamentary chamber. The referendum, held on 13 September 1996, confirmed overwhelming support for the new parliamentary system, under which all members of the Chamber of Representatives would be directly elected and their term of office reduced from six to five years. A new upper house, the Chamber of Advisers, was to be established and its members chosen by electoral colleges, representing mainly local councils, with the remainder selected from professional associations and trade unions. The Chamber of Advisers would be competent to initiate legislation, issue 'warning' motions to the government and, by a two-thirds' majority vote, force its resignation. Moroccan officials denied that the role of the new upper house was to neutralize the Chamber of Representatives. The USFP and Istiqlal, together with the PPS, gave a guarded welcome to the reforms, but the OADP, their partner in the Bloc démocratique, condemned them. The USFP had either boycotted or urged its supporters to vote against the four previous revisions of the Constitution. After the referendum the OADP split when a group of officials left to form the Parti socialiste démocratique (PSD). The Ministry of Information reported that 10.17m. people had voted in favour of the King's proposal, representing 99.56% of the votes cast. Some 82.95% of the electorate participated in the referendum. In early December the Government announced that it was beginning to reform electoral procedures in preparation for the forthcoming elections; a commission, on which all officially recognized political parties were allowed representation, commenced examining electoral lists to identify irregularities. Within days the commission had identified more than 400,000 voters whose names appeared twice on the electoral lists. In mid-December a draft law was approved, providing for the establishment of elected councils in 16 new regions, including Western Sahara. Each regional council would be elected for a six-year period and would have responsibility for tax collection and the construction of schools and hospitals.

In February 1997 11 political parties, including five from the opposition, signed a political pact with the Minister of State for the Interior, Driss Basri, with the aim of 'strengthening the democratic regime based on the monarchy'. All the signatories agreed to abide by the law. The authorities conceded that they would treat all political parties equally and ban illegal practices. For their part the political parties promised to mobilize their supporters in 'a positive spirit' and not to contest, in advance, the integrity of future voting. After lengthy negotiations the authorities and the opposition parties agreed that new electoral lists would be prepared, and a national commission established to oversee the elections. The scale of irregularities in previous elections was revealed when the Moroccan press published figures indicating that 4.5m. voter registrations out of an electorate of 12m. were unreliable. The authorities appeared to have entered into the pact because they calculated that the successful integration of Morocco into the world economy required political reforms, if only to satisfy international organizations such as the World Bank and the IMF. While the official media welcomed the pact with enthusiasm, some leading members of the opposition expressed caution. There were also doubts as to whether the task of reviewing and correcting all the electoral lists could be completed in time for the general election. The Bloc démocratique announced that it would present joint candidates in some 25,000 municipal districts. The 'loyalist' parties (including the UC, the MP and the PND), which held a majority of seats in the current Chamber of Representatives, also formed a common front, the Entente nationale (or Wifaq), and adopted the same strategy. However, the small parties of the radical left felt excluded from the political process as did the Islamists. Several radical Islamist groups demanded the right to form political parties and to contest the forthcoming elections. However, although Al Islah wa Attajdid gained legal status in January 1997 after its merger with the MPCD, the authorities rejected Al Adl wa-'l Ihsan's claim for recognition as a political party.

The Moroccan authorities strongly condemned the publication of a report by the Observatoire géopolitique des drogues (based in France) presented to the EU in October 1995 on the Moroccan drugs trade, which implicated members of the royal family, former cabinet ministers, members of parliament and local government officials. Nevertheless, as part of the Government's campaign against drugs-trafficking, action was taken against several officials allegedly involved in the trade; however, some observers argued that this was merely an attempt to divert attention away from others close to the King. In April 1996 some 30 drugs-traffickers were sentenced to up to 10 years' imprisonment by a court in Salé after the country's biggest drugs trial. In the following months the Government intensified its campaign against drugs-trafficking and a record number of arrests were made. In January 1996 the Ministry of the Interior launched its largest campaign against smuggling, which targeted corrupt customs officials and resulted in the prosecution of the head of the customs and excise department and his predecessor. The campaign against the smuggling trade, believed to be extensive in Tangier and around the Spanish enclaves of Ceuta and Melilla, provoked strong criticism from opposition parties and human rights organizations for being arbitrary and unduly harsh. It also led to the resignation of the Minister-delegate to the Prime Minister, in charge of Human Rights, who described the Government's tactics against smugglers as 'collective lynching'. In June, in an attempt to placate the business community, the Government promised the employers' association that future campaigns against smuggling would be less disruptive to business. Also in June there was renewed criticism of Morocco's human rights record in the French media after three members of Gen. Oufkir's family escaped to France (see above). The family was released from detention in 1991, but had been placed under surveillance and forbidden to travel abroad. Following the much publicized escape, passports were issued to the remaining family members, including Oufkir's widow.

In early 1996 there was renewed labour unrest leading to strikes and demonstrations by public-sector employees demanding better working conditions. The unrest culminated in a general strike in June during which there were serious clashes between demonstrators and the security forces. The strike was organized by the Union Générale des Travailleurs Marocains (UGTM) and the CDT, which urged the Government to increase the minimum wage and to establish a national fund for the unemployed. Fearing more violence, the Government made concessions, and in July concluded a new accord on labour relations

with employers' associations and trade unions. The accord was signed by representatives of the UGTM, the CDT, the Confédération Générale des Entreprises du Maroc and Driss Basri. The UMT indicated that it accepted most of the points in the accord, but rising unemployment continued to provoke demonstrations against the Government, especially by unemployed graduates. After further demonstrations by unemployed graduates in May 1997, Prime Minister Filali met their representatives in June and promised to address their grievances. Nevertheless, further protests were staged in August. Although the July 1996 accord on labour relations was confirmed in July 1997, some state-sector workers expressed dissatisfaction at the new pay levels, and in September public-sector health workers went on strike for the fifth time since the beginning of the year to demand an increase in their salaries. In January 1998 the police forcibly dispersed a march by miners who were protesting about the proposed closure of a coal mine at Jerada; trade unionists accused security forces of attacking their headquarters in Jerada.

In March 1996 clashes occurred at Casablanca University between Islamist undergraduates and students affiliated to the USFP; the latter accused the Islamists of trying to 'assassinate democracy in Morocco'. There was speculation that the rift between the two student groups may have been instigated by the authorities in an attempt to weaken the Islamists' position on the campus. In January 1997 Islamist students protesting against poor facilities on campus clashed with security forces at Casablanca University and the violence quickly spread to other universities. Many students were injured in the rioting and numerous arrests were made. Some 50 undergraduates, most of them members of Al Adl wa-'l Ihsan, were later sentenced to between three months and two years in prison for their part in the disturbances. (In March the Court of Appeal substantially reduced the sentences of 25 of the students.) However, a strike in late January organized by the Union Nationale des Etudiants du Maroc, which is controlled by Al Adl wa-'l Ihsan, to protest against Government repression, did not precipitate further clashes with the security forces. In February the authorities tried to prevent Islamist students at Casablanca University from holding Friday prayers on the campus; the incident did not escalate, thanks to the intervention of the Minister of Higher Education. The Government blamed the campus unrest on poor staff–student relations, and in late January King Hassan dismissed eight university rectors and replaced them with his own appointees. In November there were further clashes between Islamist students and the security forces after the students tried to organize a strike at Casablanca and Mohammadia universities. In January 1998 supporters of Al Adl wa-'l Ihsan appealed to the Government to release the movement's leader, Abd as-Salam Yassin, who remained under house arrest.

THE 1997 LOCAL AND LEGISLATIVE ELECTIONS

The political pact signed in February 1997 (see above) was first tested in local elections held in June. A national commission, chaired by the President of the Supreme Court and including members of political parties as well as government representatives, was established to monitor the election process. Despite some complaints of irregularities, the elections for 24,253 seats on municipal councils and communes were judged to have been relatively fair with the turn-out officially estimated at 75.0%. Although the opposition Bloc démocratique achieved a much better result than in the 1992 elections, winning 31.7% of the seats, overall control of local councils was retained by the right-wing Entente nationale and the centrist grouping led by the RNI, which took 30.3% and 26.4% of the seats, respectively. During the election campaign the Bloc démocratique outlined for the first time its economic programme in an attempt to reassure the business community. In addition to the three main political groupings, five other political parties presented candidates and there were many independent contenders. The MPCD refused to take part in the elections on the grounds that it was not represented on the national election commission; however, there were claims that the authorities had put pressure on the party to withdraw because they feared that there would be strong support for radical Islamists. Notwithstanding, Al Islah wa Attajdid presented a number of independent candidates. Prior to the elections more than 100 left-wing activists were arrested, including 67 members of the PADS, for campaigning for a boycott of the electoral process. Some 26 PADS supporters were subsequently sentenced to short terms of imprisonment, having been found guilty of violating electoral and press codes.

In mid-August 1997 King Hassan appointed a new Cabinet (in which several portfolios were merged) primarily comprising technocrats, after ministers with formal party affiliation resigned at his behest in order to concentrate on their electoral campaigns for the forthcoming legislative elections. Significantly, Driss Basri retained his post as Minister of State for the Interior. Legislation promulgated later in the month detailed the composition of the future bicameral parliament: the Chamber of Representatives would comprise 325 members, directly elected for a five-year term: the Chamber of Advisers would have 270 members, selected by indirect election, of whom 162 would represent local authorities, 81 trade chambers, and 27 employees' associations. The King again appealed for legislative elections free of irregularities and repeated that his goal was to include members of opposition parties in the Government. In September the Assistant Secretary-General of Istiqlal stated that the parties of the Bloc démocratique planned to present joint candidates in the legislative elections. However, observers noted that deep rivalries still existed between its two main parties, the USFP and Istiqlal. One of the Bloc's smaller parties, the PPS, which performed poorly in the local elections, lost 40 of its members in June when they established the Front des forces démocratiques (FFD), a rival grouping. In August the PPS suffered another reverse when its leader, Ali Yata, died in a car accident.

Elections to the country's 16 new regional councils, established in December 1996 (see above), took place in October 1997. Centrist parties won control over nine of the councils. Members of the councils, elected for six years, were chosen indirectly by an electoral college comprising local provincial and prefectoral councils, salaried workers and chambers of commerce and industry, agriculture, artisans and fisheries.

Voting for the wholly-elected 325-member Chamber of Representatives in the new bicameral parliament took place on 14 November 1997. The legislative elections were considered to have been fairer than previous polls, although some complaints were registered. Of the country's legalized political parties, only the extreme left-wing PADS boycotted the elections, but the rate of voter participation was officially estimated at only 58.3% of the electorate. The Bloc démocratique, which had been widely predicted to dominate the new Chamber, won only 102 seats, 57 of which went to the USFP, while Istiqlal secured only 32 seats. The Bloc démocratique hardly improved on the number of seats it gained by direct voting in the 1993 elections and won fewer seats overall. The Entente nationale secured 100 seats, one-half of which were won by the UC, and parties of the centre-right took 97 seats (including 46 obtained by the RNI). Right-wing and centre-right parties performed much better than in direct voting in the 1993 elections. The Bloc démocratique won 34.3% of the vote, compared with 27.3% by the centre-right parties and 24.8% by the Entente nationale. The MPCD won nine seats and the leader of Al Islah wa Attajdid, Abdelilah Benkiarane, stated that the party was opposed to violence and would use its presence in the Chamber of Representatives to defend Islamic values and oppose corruption. The newly-formed FFD won nine seats, equal to the number obtained by the PPS, from which the new party had split. In an attempt to appeal to young voters, many political parties presented young candidates, with the result that 43% of deputies in the new lower chamber were under 45 years old, compared with only 14% in the previous parliament. Relatively few women stood as candidates and, as in the previous assembly, only two were elected.

Indirect elections for the new Chamber of Advisers took place on 5 December 1997. As predicted, the right and centre-right parties gained a dominant position in the upper house, winning 166 of the 270 seats. Centrist parties secured 90 seats, with the RNI emerging as the largest single party in the Chamber with 42 seats, while the Entente nationale took 76 seats. The Bloc démocratique obtained only 44 seats, of which 21 were won by Istiqlal. Smaller parties made significant gains, winning 33

seats, of which 13 went to the Parti de l'action and 12 to the FFD. Some observers anticipated that the King would use the Chamber of Advisers (which has the power to dismiss the Government) to control the Government and thereby avoid the need to intervene directly, which might damage the country's new democratic credentials. The new bicameral parliament met for the first time in January 1998 when Abd al-Wahed Radhi of the USFP was voted President of the Chamber of Representatives, and Muhammad Yalal Esaid (UC) was chosen as President of the upper chamber.

KING HASSAN APPOINTS MOROCCO'S FIRST OPPOSITION-LED GOVERNMENT

With the three main political groupings gaining roughly the same number of seats in the Chamber of Representatives, on 4 February 1998 King Hassan named Abd ar-Rahman el-Youssoufi, the veteran leader of the USFP, as Prime Minister. This was the first time that the King had chosen an opposition politician as premier. In mid-March, after weeks of difficult negotiations, el-Youssoufi formed a coalition government in which 23 of the 41 members were from the opposition Koutla Dimocratya (14 from the USFP, six from Istiqlal, and three from the PPS), three from two small opposition splinter parties, the FFD and the PSD, and nine from two centre-right parties, the RNI (six) and the MNP (three). Istiqlal, which had been the dominant political force in the early years of Moroccan independence, had not been represented in government since the early 1960s. After Istiqlal's poor performance in the legislative elections, the party's first national congress for nearly 10 years, convened in February, had chosen Abbas el-Fassi as leader in place of Muhammad Boucetta. El-Fassi had immediately reversed the party's earlier decision not to participate in the new coalition Government. Parties of the right-wing Entente nationale were not represented in the Cabinet. Although hailed as the country's first 'gouvernement d'alternance', with opposition parties taking charge of key areas of economic and social policy, the five ministers with responsibility, respectively, for the interior, foreign affairs, justice, religious endowments and Islamic affairs, together with the Secretary-General of the Government and the Minister-delegate in charge of the Administration of National Defence, were appointed directly by the King. Driss Basri retained the interior portfolio and the former Prime Minister, Abd al-Latif Filali, remained in charge of foreign affairs and co-operation. Some opposition activists were quick to point out that not only the security services but also important networks of economic influence were outside the new Prime Minister's control, restricting his room to manoeuvre.

King Hassan formally approved the new Cabinet, but warned the political parties represented in the Government that they had a duty to control their supporters in the interest of social stability. In mid-April 1998 el-Youssoufi and his senior ministers outlined an ambitious government programme, but stressed that they did not underestimate the gravity of the problems or the constraints confronting them and that there were no easy solutions. El-Youssoufi stated that his mission was to promote the democratization of the country's social and political life and pledged to raise standards of morality in public life, to promote transparency and openness in government, respect for the rule of law and for human rights, and to seek solutions through negotiation and consensus. He proposed a range of measures to tackle urgent social problems, in particular unemployment, illiteracy, acute deficiencies in basic health-care, schooling and housing, and to combat social inequalities and exclusion. Reform of public administration and the justice system was also to be undertaken. A special effort was made to reassure the private sector and to establish a 'climate of confidence' between the new Government and the business community. However, this was not to be fostered at the expense of dialogue with organized labour and employees' rights.

Perhaps inevitably, the achievements of the new Government during its first year in office fell short of expectations. On assuming the premiership, el-Youssoufi immediately ordered all civil servants, cabinet ministers and legislators to disclose their wealth and private interests. The Minister of Justice, Omar Azziman, began the enormous task of reforming the country's justice system, initiating disciplinary proceedings against some 30 magistrates, mainly on grounds of corruption.

His campaign targeted in particular the Tangier courts, which regularly hear drugs-related cases. By the end of the year nine judges had been dismissed and others suspended. In order to root out corruption and promote transparency at local government level, the King approved the creation of 16 regional courts. In the new Government's first budget, allocations to the ministries of solidarity and employment, health, housing, youth and sport, and culture were increased substantially, and for the first time there was a small reduction in that of the interior ministry. Some progress was also achieved on human rights, a personal priority of el-Youssoufi. Mary Robinson, the UN High Commissioner for Human Rights, visited Morocco in April 1998 and signed a memorandum to open a North Africa and Middle East centre in Rabat to promote and protect human rights in the region. She stated that Rabat had been chosen as the location for the new centre because of Morocco's efforts to address human rights issues. In October King Hassan declared that it was his firm determination that all outstanding human rights issues should be resolved within six months. Shortly after the King's statement, the Conseil consultatif royal des droits de l'homme (CCDH), the country's official multi-party human rights advisory council, reported that the commission investigating the fate of opponents of the regime who 'disappeared' in the 1960s, 1970s and 1980s had examined 112 cases. Some 56 of these missing persons were dead, but no details were given of how they died. Although the CCDH had examined the circumstances of 45 prisoners who had died in custody, the chairman stated that in certain cases it had been decided not to bring charges against those responsible. No names of those who had died in custody were published, with the exception of Hocine Manouzi, a militant leftist, and Abdelhak Rouissi, a trade union activist. At the same time, the CCDH reported that having examined the cases of 48 'political' prisoners, some 28, many of them members of the banned Al Adl wa-'l Ihsan, had been released, but the rest would remain in prison because they had been convicted of murder and sabotage. Independent human rights organizations, such as the Association marocaine des droits humains (AMDH), criticized the CCDH for releasing so little information about the cases they had examined and insisted that the files of those who had disappeared or died could not be closed until those responsible were brought to trial. There were calls for an independent and impartial committee to be set up to deal with these issues. Particular concern was expressed that the CCDH had not even considered two outstanding cases, that of the exiled dissident, Abraham Serfaty, and that of Abd as-Salam Yassin, the leader of Al Adl wa-'l Ihsan, who remained under house arrest. In late October, when riot police were deployed to disperse a demonstration by unemployed graduates, the Government was widely criticized in the press for its heavy-handed tactics, while the AMDH denounced the police action as a flagrant violation of free expression. Demonstrations by unemployed graduates had become commonplace outside ministries in Rabat as government efforts to improve employment prospects for graduates have met with little success. The Minister of the Interior was reported to have given the order to deploy riot police on instructions from the King and with the support of the Cabinet. Earlier in the year human rights groups had accused the authorities of 'repression' after clashes between Islamist students and security forces at Casablanca University.

In March 1999 King Hassan praised the new Government, declaring that Morocco's experience of 'alternation' was an example to others and adding pointedly that it provided a new élite with the opportunity to experience 'the hard reality of government'. In April Muhammad Benaissa, Morocco's outgoing ambassador to the USA, replaced Abd al-Latif Filali as Minister of Foreign Affairs and Co-operation. Filali had occupied the post for 14 years and no reason was given for his removal. There was speculation that dissatisfaction with Filali's handling of recent talks on Western Sahara may have precipitated the change.

Towards the end of 1998 the PPS and the PSD, which had been co-operating within the legislature, announced that from early 1999 they had decided to merge. The MPDC, which has been giving critical support to the el-Youssoufi Government, changed its name to the Parti de la justice et du développement (PJD) in order to improve its image and to distinguish itself from right and centre-right parties with similar names but very

different policies. The party gained another seat in the lower house of the legislature when its leader, Abdelilah Benkirane, won a by-election in Salé. Adb al-Latif Samlali, a former Minister of Youth and Sports, was elected secretary-general of the UC.

DEATH OF KING HASSAN

King Hassan died of a heart attack on 23 July 1999, shortly after being admitted to a hospital in Rabat. He had been in poor health for some years. His eldest son, who succeeded him as Muhammad VI, announced his father's death to the nation on state television after members of the royal family, government ministers and senior members of the armed forces had made the oath of allegiance to the new monarch. In his television address the new King appealed to the Moroccan people for 'calm and patience'. Hassan's funeral was attended by many world leaders, including US President Bill Clinton, President Jacques Chirac of France and the newly-appointed Israeli Prime Minister, Ehud Barak. Although Hassan had groomed his eldest son to succeed him, he had been reluctant to let Muhammad share power or play a role in the armed forces despite his status as a four-star general. He was never given administrative responsibilities of any importance and his public appearances were largely ceremonial.

KING MUHAMMAD TAKES CONTROL

The new King immediately demonstrated his enthusiasm for change and emerged as a strong advocate of reform and modernization. Addressing the nation for the first time, he pledged to support the multi-party system, the rule of law and respect for human rights and individual liberties. He adopted a populist style very different from that of his late father, travelled widely throughout the kingdom—including a 10-day visit to the isolated and impoverished northern Rif region, which had been virtually ignored by King Hassan—raised issues of social justice, pledged to help the poor and reduce unemployment and spoke out on sensitive social issues such as the importance of equal rights for women. Shortly after his succession the King granted an amnesty to thousands of prisoners and established an arbitration body to determine compensation for the families of political opponents who had 'disappeared' or those who had suffered arbitrary detention. In late September 1999 the King granted permission for Abraham Serfaty, the country's most prominent dissident, to return from exile in France. Two months later the family of Mehdi Ben Barka, the Moroccan opposition leader murdered in Paris in 1965, was allowed to return after spending 35 years in exile in Europe. Upon their return, the nine surviving members of Ben Barka's family immediately demanded that the Moroccan authorities publish details of past human rights abuses. In January 2000 the location was apparently revealed of Ben Barka's burial site, beneath the Courcouronnes mosque in Paris, which was constructed in the mid-1980s with finance from King Hassan II. The French Prime Minister, Lionel Jospin, announced an end to the ban on access to archives where documents relating to the abduction and murder were kept. Earlier the King had revoked a 13-year ban on public performances by a popular political satirist, Ahmed Sanoussi.

In early November 1999 the King abruptly dismissed the Minister of State for the Interior, Driss Basri, who had held the post for two decades and whose influence extended well beyond the interior portfolio. A month earlier the King had deprived Basri of responsibility for Western Sahara and for the Direction de surveillance du territoire. As the late King Hassan's closest adviser and loyal servant, Basri was closely identified with the repressive policies of the old regime. The King's decision was widely applauded, and was interpreted as a clear break with the past and a sign of his desire for a faster pace of political change. Basri was replaced by Ahmed Midaoui, a former chief of national security, and Fouad Ali el-Himma, Muhammad's chef de cabinet, became Secretary of State at the Interior Ministry. The ministry itself was expected to be reduced in size with the armed forces assuming greater responsibility for national security. The King subsequently replaced more than half of the country's provincial governors, but the task of dismantling Basri's extensive networks of allies and clients, especially at the regional level, was expected to take some time. Several new appointments were made to the security establishment, ensuring that key posts were occupied by men loyal to the new monarch.

While modernizing and changing the style of the monarchy, King Muhammad insisted on exercising the powers vested in the monarchy under the Constitution and left no doubt that, like his father, he intended to reign and rule. The King continued to dominate the political sphere, making appointments to all key posts and formulating political strategy. There was disquiet in some circles at the appearance of a number of senior army officers in prominent positions in the King's entourage. Furthermore, the King's enthusiasm and high-profile activities contrasted sharply with the opposition-led government which appeared lethargic and silent and was subject to increasing public criticism. The press accused Premier el-Youssoufi of being 'timid, passive and without imagination'. A situation whereby the Government was relegated to the role of merely carrying out the King's policies provoked unease among some Moroccans concerned that amidst much change the key features of the political system remained unchanged. El-Youssoufi's administration could point to some solid achievements but had failed to pass important legislation, notably on labour relations and women's rights, and amidst sharply deteriorating socio-economic conditions, was seen as weak on economic management.

Meanwhile, an active civil society began to occupy a more prominent part of the political sphere and was pressing for further changes and reforms, provoking tensions with the authorities. Particularly active were the associations for the defence of human rights such as 'Justice and Truth' established in October 1999 by the victims of arbitrary detention. Despite the payment of some US $14m. in compensation to past victims of repression, human rights organizations insisted that there could be no reconciliation without justice and demanded that those responsible for human rights abuses should face trial. A demonstration organized by the AMDH to mark the 52nd anniversary of the Universal Declaration of Human Rights in December was violently suppressed by the security forces, and 36 AMDH members subsequently appeared in court. Earlier the AMDH had accused three serving generals of involvement in past repression and demanded that they be put on trial. In January 2001 the authorities also banned a demonstration planned by 'Justice and Truth'. Furthermore, employers' organizations demanded greater flexibility in the rules governing employment. There was mounting discontent among trade unions and employees over pay, and a general strike was only averted in April after the Government agreed to concessions, including a 10% increase in the minimum wage and further negotiations on the proposed new labour law. These concessions, enshrined in a 'social contract to establish social peace', failed to prevent renewed industrial action by some workers. Despite government pledges to speed up the recruitment of graduates into the public sector, unemployed graduates continued to demonstrate, and in June violent clashes erupted in Rabat between protesters from the proscribed Association nationale des diplomés au chômage and the police. The security forces prevented them from marching on parliament and eventually evicted them from the headquarters of the UMT where the graduates were staging a sit-in amid scenes of violence in which 45 graduates were reported to have been injured and over 100 arrested. The Government defended its decision to use force, claiming that the protest had been unauthorized. Meanwhile, Berber cultural associations expressed dissatisfaction at plans, announced in March 2000, for the introduction of courses in Berber language in schools and universities from September, insisting that they lacked proper preparation and were intended to fail.

During 2000 the Islamist movement, whose influence extended over wide sections of society, became more visible, as both the officially recognized PJD and the banned Al Adl wa-'l Ihsan gained prominence. In early February 2000 the leader of Al Adl wa-'l Ihsan, Abd as-Salam Yassin, posted an 18-page letter addressed to King Muhammad on his internet site in which he launched a vitriolic attack on the reign of Hassan II. In it he also appealed to King Muhammad to relinquish his father's assets abroad—estimated at US $400m—in order to pay off the national debt (the royal finances have always been a highly sensitive subject) and condemned the traditional ceremony of allegiance to the monarch (*baia*) as an abomination

and sacrilegious. In mid-March Al Adl wa-'l Ihsan, together with the PJD and the League of Ulema, organized a rally in Casablanca in which an estimated 500,000 Islamists (other reports indicated 100,000–200,000 participants) protested against a controversial programme of social reforms, proposed by the Secretary of State for Social Affairs, a principal outcome of which would be to vastly improve the social status and legal rights of Moroccan women. The proposal included allocating women a third of all seats in parliament, raising the minimum age of marriage for women from 15 to 18 years, bans on polygamy and 'repudiation' as a form of divorce; and equal rights for women under a divorce settlement. The plan was regarded by Islamists as a major attack on the country's religious code of personal law. The protests forced the Government to establish a special panel to review the planned reforms, and a new law on personal statute was not expected to be promulgated before 2002. In mid-May 2001 the Yassin was released from house arrest although Al Adl wa-'l Ihsan remained prohibited. At the same time the organization's newspaper was banned along with marches planned near the border with Algeria, and Yassin was prevented from visiting members of his organization imprisoned in Kenitra. He nevertheless embarked on a country-wide tour despite claims of constant harassment by the police. In June mosques, which had been ordered to close between prayers by Basri, were allowed to open from dawn to last prayers. However, the decision was quickly reversed by the Ministry of the Interior because of fears of the politicization of the mosques. In early July security forces broke up a beach camp organized by Al Adl wa-'l Ihsan at Mahdia, some 40 km north of Rabat, arresting 49 Islamists. In early December numerous Islamists were arrested when police dispelled peaceful demonstrations in the capital and in a number of other cities organized to protest at the restrictions placed on Al Adl wa-'l Ihsan's activities and demanding its recognition as a political party. In late January 2001 22 members of Al Adl wa-'l Ihsan who had taken part in the demonstrations were sentenced to one-year terms of imprisonment by a Casablanca court, but these were later reduced on appeal to two-month suspended sentences. Courts in Fez and Rabat gave 23 other Al adl wa'l Ihsan activists short suspended sentences and fines.

Sections of the independent press acted as the driving force for change and set out to test the limits of press freedom, especially in the atmosphere of greater liberty which prevailed following Basri's removal from office. However, it quickly became apparent that comments on the monarchy, the army and Western Sahara remained subject to censure. In mid-April 2000 the authorities banned two of the most outspoken and popular weekly magazines, *Le Journal* and its Arabic companion *As-Sahifa*, after the former published an interview conducted in New York between its editor, Aboubakr Jamai, and Polisario leader, Muhammad Abd al-Aziz. Shortly afterwards three senior officials of the popular TV channel, 2M, were dismissed after the banning of *Le Journal* was reported on a news broadcast, and the Minister of Communications took charge of the channel. Meanwhile, Mustafa Alaoui, the director of the best-selling Arabic weekly, *Al-Ousbouaa al-Maghribia*, was sentenced to three months detention, suspended from practicing as a journalist for three years and ordered to pay 1m. dirhams in damages after the magazine published allegations of corruption involving the Minister of Foreign Affairs, Muhammad Benaissa. Khalid Mechbal, the editor of *Achamal*, received a six-month suspended sentence, was banned from journalism for one year and was ordered to pay damages of 100,000 dirhams for covering the same story. There was particular concern that the two men were sentenced not under the press code but under the penal code and the Syndicat national de presse marocaine protested that such a ban had not been imposed since the beginning of the French protectorate in 1912. At the end of May, however, the King granted the two men a royal amnesty, and the magazines banned a month earlier were allowed to resume publication. Nevertheless, *Reporters sans Frontières* claimed that during the first half of the year seven newspapers had been banned by the authorities. In October the Supreme Court reviewed the case of an army captain, Mustafa Adib, who had been sentenced to five years imprisonment by a military tribunal in Rabat for claiming in an interview with the French daily *Le Monde* that corruption was widespread within the Moroccan armed forces. The court ordered that Adib's sentence should be reduced to two and a half years imprisonment, but in February 2001 it rejected his renewed appeal against that sentence. Adib began a hunger strike in early March to protest against injustice and the deteriorating conditions of his detainment at Salé prison. (Captain Adib was finally freed in mid-May 2002.) Meanwhile, in November 2000 the authorities expelled the bureau chief of the Agence France-Presse bureau in Morocco for 'hostile conduct'. In early December 2000 *Le Journal, as-Sahifa* and another popular French language weekly *Demain*, were proscribed indefinitely by the Government after they published a letter written in 1974 by Muhammad Basri, a close associate of Mehdi Ben Barka, to Abderrahim Bouabid, former first secretary of the USFP and now Prime Minister el-Youssoufi claiming that leading personalities in the USFP had been implicated in the 1972 failed military coup against King Hassan. The affair provoked a widespread political crisis as according to the official history of the USFP, the party had always used non-violent methods to oppose King Hassan's authoritarian regime. Yet if the contents of the letter were to be believed its leaders had not only collaborated with those elements in the military intent on overthrowing King Hassan by force, but also with the coup's leader, Gen. Oufkir, held responsible for the death of the party's hero, Mehdi Ben Barka in 1965. El-Youssoufi insisted that the ban had been imposed not because of the letter but because the three weeklies had consistently attacked the monarchy and the army and endangered the transition to democracy. In an interview with the Spanish daily *El País*, the Prime Minister stated that he paid no attention to rumours and described the editors of the three magazines as children intoxicated with the new freedom now prevailing in Morocco and who were 'playing with fire'. In January 2001 Jamai claimed that el-Youssoufi's action exposed the growing influence of senior figures in the security apparatus opposed to greater democracy and their close alliance with the leadership of the USFP. After a wave of protests and the decision by Jamai to begin a hunger strike, the Government announced that it would allow *Le Journal* to resume publication. At the beginning of March a court in Casablanca sentenced Jamai to three months imprisonment and Ali Amar, the director-general of *Le Journal*, to two months imprisonment and ordered the payment of 2m. dirhams in damages. The two men had been charged with defamation after they approved a series of articles alleging financial irregularities during the purchase of a new residence for the Moroccan ambassador to the USA at a time when Muhammad Benaissa, the current Minister of Foreign Affairs, was Morocco's ambassador to the USA. The sentences were condemned by *Reporters sans Frontières* which quickly organized a petition to express solidarity with the two Moroccan journalists and both men announced their intention to appeal against the court's decision. In November the editor-in-chief of *Demain* was sentenced to four months' imprisonment and a fine for 'diffusion of false information', following an article which reported that one of the royal palaces might be sold to foreign interests. In December the authorities seized an issue of the magazine which carried the names of 45 people, some still holding official posts, alleged to have been responsible for human rights abuses during of King Hassan's reign. In March 2002 the lower house approved controversial new press legislation granting the courts, rather than the Prime Minister, authority to close down newspapers but retaining tough prison sentences for journalists whose writings offend the monarchy, the values of Islam or Morocco's 'territorial integrity'.

In early September 2000 King Muhammad effected a cabinet reorganization, entailing the reduction in the number of ministerial portfolios from 43 to 33. Its political composition remained largely unchanged and all but four of its members had served in the previous administration. Premier el-Youssoufi retained his post and most notable among the new appointments was the entry of two senior figures from Istiqlal into the Cabinet: the party's leader, Abbas el-Fassi, was appointed Minister of Social Development, Solidarity, Employment and Vocational Training and Muhammad Khalifa assumed the public sector and administrative reform portfolio. Doubts were, however, expressed whether the creation of three 'economic super-ministries' would actually improve the efficiency of the new administration and some analysts argued that the opportunity to create a younger and more vigorous administration capable of addressing the country's mounting social and economic problems had been lost in order to maintain the left-wing-centre-right coalition. Shortly afterwards elections were held to renew one-third of the seats in the Chamber of Advisers. The RNI won the largest number of seats, taking 14 of the 90 seats available.

The Government continued its campaign against corruption in public life. At the end of 2000 a parliamentary inquiry into the state-owned bank Crédit Immobilier et Hôtelier accused the bank's directors of widespread fraud and misappropriation of funds. Although a number of leading Moroccan politicians and economic figures were implicated in the scandal, concern was expressed that only the bank's directors would face trial. Later, a police investigation was launched into the company amid speculation of the involvement of a number of politicians, businessmen and trade union leaders in the incidents. Investigations were also proceeding into serious fraudulent activities in several other state institutions including the Caisse Nationale de Crédit Agricole, the Caisse Nationale de Securité Sociale and the Office National des Transports. The Government organized a second anti-corruption campaign in December 2001. It was reported that some 74,000 corruption cases had been referred to the courts during 2000 and 2001, including 211 major cases, compared with only 105 during the previous two decades; however, progress in these cases was slow. In a survey carried out by Transparency Maroc, an NGO campaining against corruption, one-third of respondents reported that they experienced corruption on a daily basis, with security personnel in rural areas, and local and regional government officials identified as the most corrupt. After King Muhammad met with representatives of women's groups in March 2001, he announced the establishment of a royal commission, headed by Driss Dahak, President of the Supreme Court, and including leading Islamic scholars and jurists, to revise the country's laws on personal rights and responsibilities. However, given the strength of opposition to proposals introduced in 2000 to give women greater rights (see above) doubts were raised whether this latest commission would make any progress on this sensitive and controversial issue. Members of the Association démocrate des femmes du Maroc argued that the royal commission would merely improve procedures for applying the personal status code rather than rewriting it as they demanded. Nevertheless, the King continued to show his commitment to greater rights for women by appointing women to posts of royal advisers, ambassadors and other senior public positions. In July the King appointed new *walis* (regional governors) without consulting premier el-Youssoufi, and in January 2002 granted them extensive new powers to give their actions maximum efficiency. Some observers contended that the appointment of these US-style 'city managers' in the name of decentralization and regionalization had in practice strengthened the influence of the palace at the expense of the Government.

In late March 2001 the sixth congress of the USFP—the first for 12 years—highlighted serious dissent within the party. A large group of delegates and three members of the party's political bureau, including Muhammad Nouabir Amaoui, head of the CDT, decided to boycott the meeting. Amaoui claimed that there had been irregularities in the election of delegates and an attempt to marginalize those who did not subscribe to the official party line. The CDT was opposed to the party's participation in government while the monarchy retained 'quasi-absolute powers' and was critical of the USFP-led Government's economic policies. Members of the party's youth wing (the Jeunesse socialiste) also boycotted what they described as a 'congress of apparatchiks', criticized the leadership for participating in government when all key initiatives came from the King, and demanded the establishment of a constitutional monarchy. Premier el-Youssoufi, who is also the party's first secretary, defended his record declaring that by participating in government for three years the USFP had enabled the process of democratic transition to begin and that this would not be achieved overnight. El-Youssoufi and USFP ministers attempted to persuade Amaoui to abandon his boycott as they were concerned that the CDT, which is well established among public-sector workers, could create difficulties for the Government by encouraging strike action. El-Youssoufi even proposed delaying the election to party posts until an agreement had been reached with the CDT leader. The delegates, however, insisted on proceeding, and elections were held for a new, enlarged central committee (20% of whose membership is reserved for women) and for the political bureau. El-Youssoufi was re-elected first secretary and the congress concluded with a resolution approving the party's participation in government. Furthermore it called for electoral reforms before new parliamentary elections, scheduled to be held in 2002, and for the voting age to be reduced to 18 years. In late October 2001 dissidents announced the creation of a separate political party, the Parti de congrès national unioniste, and elected Abdelmajid Bouzzoubaâ as Secretary-General. At the same time as the USFP congress was in session, the AMDH held its own conference which denounced the country's transition to democracy as a 'masquerade'. Some of the 350 delegates present were threatened with imprisonment for ignoring the Government's ban on demonstrations in December 2000 (see above), including the outgoing chairman of the association, Abderrahmane Benameur. Meanwhile following dissent within the MNP, three leading party figures, including Ahmad Moussaoui, the Minister for Youth and Sport, were expelled from its political bureau. At the end of April a co-operation agreement was signed between Moroccan officials and a delegation from Amnesty International to promote awareness of human rights issues among those who make and implement the law. Amnesty International recognized the Moroccan Government's efforts in giving independence to the official Conseil consultatif royal des droits de l'homme and in reviving the debate on the rights of women. Nevertheless, Amnesty International maintained that there were still 60 political prisoners held in Moroccan jails and that some 450 missing persons remained unaccounted for and also criticized the authorities for not bringing to justice officials responsible for human rights abuses as well as for allowing some of those suspected of such abuses to remain in their posts. While the Government continued to resist demands by human rights associations for a full independent inquiry into human rights abuses that took place during the reign of King Hassan, King Muhammad appointed a mediator to investigate future allegations of abuses by officials, including the security services.

In mid-June 2001 it was reported that the Moroccan authorities had for the first time given permission for a French judge to carry out inquiries in Morocco into the disappearance of opposition leader, Mehdi Ben Barka, in Paris in 1965. However at the end of the month a former member of the Moroccan special services, Ahmed Boukhari, purportedly confessed in an interview with the French daily *Le Monde* and the Moroccan weekly *Le Journal* that a unit of the Moroccan special services had kidnapped Ben Barka in Paris where he had died under torture. Boukhari's body had then been transported in a Moroccan military aircraft to Morocco, with the knowledge of the French intelligence services, where it was dissolved in a tank of acid at a torture and detention centre in Rabat. According to Boukhari, the bodies of dozens of opponents of King Hassan's regime had been disposed of in this way between 1961 and 1967. Boukhari, the first Moroccan secret service agent to speak out publicly about the 'dirty war' conducted against dissidents in the 1960 and 1970s, promised further revelations, and in subsequent interviews began naming those allegedly responsible. In August he was sentenced to three months' imprisonment on unrelated charges of fraud dating back to the early 1990s and after being released in November 2001 was rearrested and imprisoned for 'defamation' the following month.

At the end of July 2001, in a speech marking the second anniversary of his accession, King Muhammad sought to reaffirm his personal commitment to establishing a modern democratic state founded on fundamental public freedoms and human rights, to modernize the economy and combat poverty, and spoke of his desire to eliminate nepotism and corruption in the administration, and establish a new social contract between unions, employers and government. Amid growing public impatience and disillusionment with the new regime, some Moroccans had begun to question the new monarch's commitment to political reform and his determination to overcome resistance to change from powerful vested interests in the political and military establishment. In the same speech the King also expressed his wish to promote the country's different regional and cultural components and announced the establishment of a royal insti-

tute to 'protect, revive and promote Berber culture' and explore ways of integrating Tamazight (the principal Berber language) into the education system. At a time of violent unrest among Berbers in neighbouring Algeria, the authorities clearly wished to lay down clear boundaries for the legitimate expression of the aspirations of Morocco's large Berber-speaking population.

In September 2001 King Muhammad replaced Ahmed Midaoui as Minister of the Interior by a technocrat, Driss Jettou, one of the King's close allies. This was the first appointment to the interior portfolio from outside the security services for 40 years. No reasons were given for the hasty departure of Midaoui, who became an adviser to the King, but he had been criticized in some circles for failing to change the political culture of the the ministry under his control. Jettou, a successful industrialist, first entered government in 1993 in charge of commerce and industry, and in 1998 became Minister of Finance, Commerce and Handicrafts. In August 2001 he had been named head of the Office Chérifien des Phosphates and the royal family's representative of the board of the ONA (Morocco's the largest private company). His appointment as Minister of the Interior was interpreted as an attempt to improve the image of the monarchy in advance of parliamentary elections, which the King announced would take place as scheduled in September 2002.

In October 2001, in a break with tradition, the King announced his engagement to Salma Bennani, a well-educated member of a middle-class family from Fez. The marriage took place at the royal palace in Rabat in late March 2002. However, three days of festivities in Marrakesh scheduled for mid-April were cancelled because of the Middle East crisis arising from the Israeli reoccupation of Palestinian territories. This was the first time that the marriage of the sovereign and the identity of his wife had been made public. It was reported that Salma would accompany the King on some of his official duties.

In an interview with the French daily *Le Monde* at the end of January 2002, el-Youssoufi stated that he would stand down as Prime Minister after the elections in September but would remain Secretary-General of the USFP until the party's next congress in 2003. Accused of political 'immobility' by many Moroccans increasingly disillusioned and impatient for change, and criticized for lack of 'political courage' by the palace, el-Youssoufi defended his Government's record. For the first time, he asserted, the Government was organizing free and transparent elections that would strengthen the transition to democracy; plans were in place to provide medical cover for all citizens; and from September 2002 all children would be educated from the age of six years. He admitted that the Government's performance in economic matters could have been better, but drew attention to the burden of foreign debt and public-sector salaries, which absorbed most of the budget and severely limited the Government's room for manoeuvre, and to the devastating effects for four years of drought. The high rate of unemployment was an urgent problem that had to be addressed, but government initiatives to encourage higher levels of investment, such as the introduction of a new labour code, were being blocked by fierce opposition from the trade unions. He denied that 'cohabition' between the monarchy and the government had adversely affected the running of the country, and stated that the King was acknowledged as the cornerstone of Morocco's political system and that there was no rivalry between the palace and the Government. Shortly afterwards, however, an unsigned editorial in the USFP's daily newspaper, *Al-Ittihad al-Ichtiraki*, (of which el-Youssoufi is the editor), strongly criticized the role of one of the King's most influential advisers, André Azoulay, for encroaching on the Government's prerogatives and creating a sort of 'shadow government' in the palace. The editorial pointed out that according to political tradition royal advisers do not interfere in government or pass judgement on its actions. The previous day the USFP's Central Committee had issued a communiqué expressing the same criticisms. At the same time another party represented in the coalition Government, Istiqlal, also expressed concern about the excessive influence of King Muhammad's advisers. Some considered that since the accession of King Muhammad the Government's powers had remained limited, and that in the run-up to legislative elections it was essential for the political parties to negotiate a new division of powers between palace and government. There were those who criticized el-Youssoufi for giving priority to ensuring a smooth royal transition following the death of King Hassan at the expense of greater democracy.

THE LEGISLATIVE ELECTIONS OF SEPTEMBER 2002

In March 2002 the parties represented in el-Youssoufi's coalition Government agreed important changes to the electoral system. These included abandoning the simple majority 'first-past-the-post' system, used since 1955, in favour of proportional representation. The Government insisted that the new system would reduce fraudulent practices and increase public confidence in the political system. Some politicians, however, notably MNP leader Mahjoubi Aherdane, argued that, given high levels of illiteracy, many eligible voters would find the new voting cards difficult to understand. At least 10% of the 325 seats in the lower house were to be reserved for women. The Ministry of the Interior was to redraw electoral boundaries, prepare new electoral rolls and issue millions of new identity cards. The draft legislation proposed stringent penalties for anyone attempting to interfere with the ballot or found guilty of offering or taking bribes to influence voting. The right-wing UC condemned the Government for rushing through changes to the electoral system

only a few months before the next round of parliamentary elections. By this time there were 25 legally registered political parties, compared with 17 at the 1997 legislative elections; six of these parties had been established within the previous six months. Meanwhile, Abdelilah Benkirane, a leading figure in the 'moderate' Islamist PJD, condemned what he termed the French-speaking élite for portraying the Islamist movement as a danger to Morocco and for suggesting that the Islamists might win a landslide victory in the forthcoming elections. He stated that he expected the PJD to win some 10%–15% of the votes, compared with 4.5% in 1997. Al Adl wa-'l Ihsan stated that it would not support any other party in the elections because it did not wish to participate in a political system that it regarded as totally discredited.

At the general election held on 27 September 2002, according to official figures, el-Youssoufi's USFP again won the largest number of the 325 seats, although its representation in the Chamber of Representatives was reduced from 57 to 50 seats. Istiqlal increased its tally of seats to 48, while the PJD took 42 seats, the RNI 41, the MP 27, the MNP 18 and the UC 16; 30 seats were reserved for women. The rate of voter participation was recorded at just 51.6% of the electorate.

Economy

ALAN J. DAY

With subsequent revisions by RICHARD I. LAWLESS. Revised for this edition by RICHARD GERMAN

By the late 1970s, Morocco was seriously in debt and had a current account deficit on its balance of payments equivalent to nearly 17% of gross domestic product (GDP). In 1978 the Government introduced a three-year stabilization programme, but external factors (such as the petroleum price rise in 1979, increasing international interest rates, and a decline in revenues from phosphate exports and from migrant workers' remittances), combined with a continuing commitment to heavy expenditure on the war in Western Sahara and on subsidies for basic goods, ensured that the programme was largely ineffective. In early 1983 the Government imposed emergency import controls and reduced its expenditure. Inflation was high in the early 1980s, with increases in food prices and rising levels of unemployment particularly aggravating the living conditions of the urban poor. Reductions in public expenditure exacerbated mounting discontent, and in 1981 and 1984 provoked major strikes and violent street demonstrations.

With the support of the World Bank and the IMF, the Government introduced policies of structural adjustment in 1984 and was able to reschedule its debts towards the end of 1985. Despite good harvests in 1985 and 1986, and the fall in petroleum prices, the trade balance deteriorated. At the beginning of 1986 the World Bank expressed concern about the underlying structural weakness of the Moroccan economy and argued that stronger corrective measures were needed, including reductions in public expenditure and food subsidies. The IMF was equally concerned by the Government's fiscal and economic performance. Measures that were adopted during late 1986 and 1987 renewed confidence in Morocco's economic prospects. A firm commitment to a radical reform of the economy, involving a new emphasis on export production, trade liberalization, attraction of foreign investment and development of tourism, together with a domestic programme of privatization and encouragement of the private sector, was expressed in the 1988–92 Development Plan (see Development). Between 1988 and 1990 new IMF and World Bank support arrangements were negotiated, and debt rescheduling agreements were reached with the 'Paris Club' of creditor governments and the 'London Club' of official creditors (see Banking and Finance). In May 1989 the text of the proposed law on privatization was published, committing the Government to the transfer of the majority of state enterprises to the private sector, and in October a Ministry of Privatization was created. The law came into effect in January 1990.

In November 1991 the Minister of Finance stated that policies of structural adjustment, introduced since 1983, had produced a significant upturn in the economy. The rescheduling cycle was forecast to end by 1993, by which date the dirham would be made convertible and Morocco would return to international capital markets. In February 1992 it was announced that the IMF had approved a further credit in support of the Government's economic programme for the following year, which, according to the IMF, aimed at promoting investment, increasing productivity, strengthening the budgetary position and reorientating credit towards the private sector. The programme aimed at annual growth of 4% in GDP, a decline in inflation to 5% per year and a reduction in the current account deficit. The World Bank announced in April that it would fully support the country's adjustment programme. High priority was to be given to the development of the capital and financial markets, although concern was expressed about some social indicators, notably the high rates of infant mortality and illiteracy. In that month the Minister in charge of Planning maintained that the number of poor people in Morocco had declined from 6.6m. to 3.9m. between 1985 and 1991, and that there had been a significant reduction in the gap between rich and poor. The opposition parties disputed these claims, and argued that liberalization had widened the gap. A survey by the United Nations Development Programme and Morocco's Direction de la Statistique in 1993 estimated that 6.3m. Moroccans (almost one-quarter of the population) lived below the poverty line.

A study compiled by the IMF and released in late 1994 concluded that financial balances had been restored and the economy's structural weaknesses substantially resolved in 1993, a year which it stated 'marked a watershed for the Moroccan economy'. According to the IMF, inflation fell from 8.7% in 1986 to 5.2% in 1993, there was an overall balance of payments surplus of US $378m. in that year and the current account deficit was equivalent to 2.5% of GDP. However, growth was constrained in 1992 and 1993 as a result of drought and external pressures. The study stated that the Moroccan economy still faced significant challenges that needed to be addressed in order to move to a higher sustainable growth path, which in turn would reduce chronic unemployment and raise living standards. It identified four policy priorities: strengthening the fiscal system and accelerating financial sector reforms to free more private sector resources for investment; further liberalizing the trade and payments system and accelerating privatization to promote competition and improve resource allocation; improving the legal and regulatory environment; and elaborating a medium-term strategy to alleviate poverty and provide social protection.

In his first statement on economic policy on his appointment as Prime Minister in May 1994, Abd al-Latif Filali pledged to expedite Morocco's ambitious programme of privatization. At that time it was estimated that the debt owed by state enterprises was equivalent to about one-third of total public debt. During 1994 receipts from the sale of state assets reached 3,700m. dirhams. This was 200m. dirhams above target, and included the showpiece of the privatization programme, the holding company Société Nationale d'Investissement, which was sold for 1,669m. dirhams. In an interview that month, the Minister of Privatization, Abd ar-Rahman Saaidi, insisted that the divestment process had the support of the general public and that it had caused minimum social upheaval. Investors in privatized companies had to agree not to dismiss workers for a period of five years, and Saaidi claimed that employees, for their part, had mostly co-operated, purchasing shares and accepting management changes. He did admit, however, that problems might arise in the future as the Government proceeded to sell less profitable companies. In December 1994 Saaidi stated that out of a total of 112 companies set aside for sale to the private sector by the end of 1995, 37 had already been sold.

In March 1995 the Ministry of Privatization announced that the privatization schedule had been extended beyond 1995 and that new companies would be added to the list, including those previously considered as 'strategic' and excluded from the programme. During that month the first privatizations in the mining sector were announced (see Mining), and in April the Government and the Office Chérifien des Phosphates (OCP) stated that they were working on plans to bring private capital into Morocco's important phosphate industry (see Industry). Receipts from privatization in 1995 were estimated at 3,500m. dirhams. In January 1996 the Government launched its first issue of a new privatization bond, which was oversubscribed and raised 1,700m. dirhams (see Banking and Finance). The bonds could be converted into shares in newly-privatized companies. A second tranche of bonds was issued the following May. In November it was reported that Morocco was the market leader in Arab privatizations, although its programme had been affected by wrangles between the Ministry of Privatization and the Evaluation Organization, established to set a minimum price for privatizations. Government efforts to accelerate the privatization programme during 1997 met with some success, notably the sale of the state's remaining 62% holding in the national steel company, the Société Nationale de Sidérurgie (SONASID). Following the appointment of a new Government in March 1998, the new Minister of the Economy and Finance, Fathallah Oualalou of the left-wing Union socialiste des forces populaires (USFP), stated that privatization would continue as an important source of income and might eventually raise enough to cover some 15% of government spending. It was announced that a new programme would be launched in which the major element would be the sale of a share of the state telecommunications company, Itissalat al-Maghrib (Maroc Télécom), created following the dismantling of the Office National des Postes et Télécommunications. When the new Prime Minister Abd ar-Rahman el-Youssoufi (the USFP leader) presented his Government's policy plan to parliament in April he stated that the privatization programme would be completed 'in transparency and speed' in order to raise funds for investment in infrastructure. However, progress proved very slow and the new Government, many of whose members were drawn from the public sector, faced accusations that it was opposed to privatization. By the end of 1998, when the programme was to have been completed, only 58 of 114 firms originally listed for privatization had been sold since the programme began in 1993. While some ministers were clearly hostile to privatization on ideological grounds, the Government had little alternative but to continue the sale of state assets in order to help cover the budget deficit. Unfortunately, some of the enterprises that remain to be sold are considered unattractive to investors. After the Government's proposal for a one-year extension to the existing programme was rejected by the Chamber of Advisers,

a new privatization law was adopted in 1999 under which firms being considered for privatization were to be examined on a case-by-case basis. Financial support from the European Union (EU, formerly the European Community, EC) of some 51m. dirhams was to be used to pay for technical assistance in order to prepare public enterprises for privatization. The Government raised only half of the 2,000m. dirhams of revenues forecast from privatization during the 1998–99 fiscal year. However, the privatization programme received a welcome boost in December 2000 when the Government divested a 35% stake in Maroc Télécom for US $2,200m. A further 14% stake in the company will be floated on the stock exchange in 2002. Plans to float up to 40% of the state airline, Royal Air Maroc, on the stock exchange have been delayed until 2002. During the 1990s foreign direct investment averaged around US $450m. per year but rose sharply in 1999 to $1,700m., according to premier el-Youssoufi, largely as a result of the sale of the second global standard for mobiles (GSM) licence (see Transport and Communications). According to the Finance Ministry, foreign investment rose to $2,860m. in 2001 following the sale of the Maroc Télécom stake and the launch of administrative and tax reform programmes. The Government hopes to attract US $2,500m. in foreign investment in 2002.On a visit to Rabat in late April 1998 to open the World Bank's first resident mission in the Maghreb, the Bank's Vice-President, Kemal Dervis, stated that he expected Morocco to register significantly stronger economic growth over the following decade—averaging 6% in real terms—but emphasized the need to divide the profits of that growth more equitably. Under a five year assistance agreement beginning in 1995 Morocco received US $1,350m. from the World Bank. In November 1999 the World Bank announced a new three-year assistance programme to commence in July 2000 to help Morocco achieve stronger economic growth, reduce social disparities and carry out administrative reforms. In mid-June the IMF praised the Government's economic record but called for renewed efforts to reduce the budget deficit, emphasizing the need to abolish food subsidies and speed up privatization.

Morocco's GDP has been heavily dependent on agricultural performance. GDP grew at an average annual rate of 2.9%, in real terms, during 1978–84, although growth was depressed during several of those years, owing largely to poor harvests. Improved agricultural output in 1985 allowed GDP to rise by 6.3% in real terms, and an exceptional harvest in 1986 contributed substantially to the 8.4% growth in GDP for that year. In 1987 GDP declined by 2.6%, largely as a result of poor harvests, forcing agricultural output down by 13%, and stagnation in the phosphate sector, contributing to a 1.2% fall in output from the mining sector. A record harvest in 1988 boosted GDP growth to an estimated 10.4%. Other strong areas were manufacturing, energy production, commerce, transport and other services. In 1989, despite a good harvest, GDP grew by only 1.8%. According to official figures, GDP fell by approximately 3% in 1992, largely as a result of the drought, which reduced agriculture's share of GDP from 21% to 15%. However, according to the IMF, GDP declined by 4.1% in 1992 and grew by only 0.2% in 1993. Having grown by 10.4% in 1994 after a good harvest, Morocco's economy suffered a sharp downturn of 7.0% in 1995 primarily because of a severe drought. GDP growth of 12.0% was recorded in 1996, but the economy was again adversely affected by poor rainfall in 1997 when GDP contracted by 2.3%. According to official figures, real GDP grew by 6.5% in 1998 but fell by 0.4% in 1999 largely owing to the poor harvest that year. After a second consecutive year of severe drought real GDP growth in 2000 was estimated by official sources at 0.8% but some independent sources claimed that the economy had stagnated. With lower rainfall than expected in 2001, GDP was posted at 6.5% for that year, and is expected to grow by only around 2.5%–3% in 2002. Average inflation fell from 6.1% in 1995 to 3.0% in 1996 and 1.0% in 1997, but rose to 2.9% in 1998 before falling to 0.7% in 1999 It rose again, however, to 1.9% in 2000 before falling to 0.6% in 2001.

Unemployment remains one of the Government's most urgent problems. In 1999, according to official figures, the rate of unemployment in urban areas was 22.1% and 5.3% in rural areas, but independent sources insist that the real level of unemployment is much higher. Urban unemployment was recorded at 20.2 % in 2001.

The Government is committed to reducing the level of unemployment to 12% by 2004 and to 9% by 2009. However, with an estimated 300,000 new additions to the labour force every year the task of reducing the unemployment rate remains extremely difficult. The IMF emphasized that stronger growth in the non-agricultural sectors (which averaged only 3% per year during the 1990s) was essential to boost job creation. Shortly before his death in July 1999 King Hassan announced a three-year programme to create 60,000 new jobs annually. His successor, King Muhammad, set up the Hassan II Fund for Development and Equipment, financed by the US $1,100m. windfall from sale of the second GSM licence, one of the aims of which is to address the unemployment problem. The Government's five-year social and economic development plan (2000–04) forecasts a fall in unemployment to 12.6% in 2003. King Muhammad also insisted that priority should be given to addressing poverty and illiteracy. The 1998–99 survey by the Directon de la statistique revealed an increase in poverty levels since 1990–91 with almost one in five Moroccans, especially those in rural areas, living below the poverty line.

AGRICULTURE AND FISHERIES

About 55% of the Moroccan population live in rural areas, and by the late 1990s some 40% of the working population were employed in agriculture, livestock-raising and fishing. In 2000 the agricultural sector (including forestry and fishing) accounted for an estimated 15.8% of GDP. The cultivated area covers some 8.7m. ha of which only 1m. ha are irrigated. Large, modern farms covering much of the irrigated area, produce mainly for export and account for 80% of citrus and wine production, 33% of vegetable production and 15% of the cereals crop. The non-irrigated areas are mainly occupied by small, family farms, most of them less than 5 ha, using traditional farming methods. About 73% of the cultivated area was devoted to cereals and 22% to export crops in 2000. The principal crops are cereals (especially wheat, barley and maize), citrus fruit, as well as olives, beans, chick-peas, tomatoes and potatoes. Canary seed, cumin, coriander, linseed and almonds are also grown. Sugar beet and cane are cultivated on a large scale to substitute for imports; sugar is one of Morocco's principal food imports owing to the high level of domestic consumption. Changing climatic conditions cause substantial year-to-year variations in agricultural output. These variations, moreover, have a significant impact on the economy, affecting the level of GDP growth or decline. Severe drought in 1981—the worst for 35 years—caused cereal production to fall by 50% from 4.5m. metric tons in 1980. In 1985, when rainfall was good, cereal production increased by 41%, compared with the previous year, and in 1986 production rose again by about 47% to a record 7.7m. tons. The 1987 harvest was very disappointing, with cereal production reaching only 4.2m. tons. However, 1988 was another record year, with a bumper harvest of nearly 8m. tons. Production declined from 7.4m. tons in 1989 to 6.3m. tons in the following year. After good rains in 1991, it rose to 8.5m. tons, of which 2.2m. tons was durum wheat, 2.7m. tons soft bread wheat, 3.3m. tons barley and 335,000 tons maize. The cereal harvest decreased to 2.7m. tons in 1992, following a severe drought. It was estimated that as much as 4m. tons of wheat and barley needed to be imported as a result. In 1993 the harvest was again depleted by drought, with rainfall 60% below average. It was forecast that production of wheat, barley and maize would total approximately 2.5m. tons in that year. A record 9.4m. tons of cereals were produced in 1994 but severe drought struck again in 1995. In March 1995 it was reported that there had only been one-third of the normal rainfall and that only 60% of acreage had been planted. In May King Hassan announced that wheat production would reach only 1.6m. tons, one-quarter of the normal figure. He appealed to the public to contribute some US $200m. to a solidarity fund of $441m. to finance wheat imports. A record cereal harvest of 10m. tons was reported in 1996 when the agricultural sector grew by 78.8% in real terms, but poor rains in 1997 resulted in cereal output of only 3.4m. tons and caused a fall of 24% in agricultural value added. In addition, the Caisse Nationale de Crédit Agricole was forced to reschedule the debts of some 250,000 farmers during 1997. After heavy rains, cereal production in 1998 rose to 6.3m. tons (2.8m. tons of soft bread wheat, 1.9m. tons of barley and 1.5m. tons of

durum wheat). However, poor rains affected the 1999 cereals crop which fell to 3.76m. tons. Following a study which revealed that years of drought were becoming more frequent, the Government launched an action plan to try to increase and stabilize cereal production at around 6m. tons, including a programme aimed at increasing the amount of cereals produced on irrigated lands, and subsidies to enable farmers to plant higher quality seeds and make greater use of fertilizers. It was hoped to produce savings of US $200m. per year by reducing imports of cereals. Cereal imports averaged around 3.5m. tons per year in the late 1990s. After a second year of drought in 2000 the cereals harvest fell to an estimated 1.8m tons (940,000 tons of soft bread wheat, 410,000 tons of hard wheat and 470,000 tons of barley), only half of the 1999 crop, and cereal imports in 2000–01 were expected to rise to 5.2m. tons. Heavy rainfall in late 2000 led to an improved cereals harvest of 4.6m. tons in 2001. In 2001 Morocco produced 4.4m. tons of sugar—3.1m. tons of beet and 1.3m. tons of cane—compared with 3.3m. tons in 1997. Brazil and Thailand have been the main suppliers of sugar imports, which by 1998 accounted for about one-half of domestic consumption. In October 1997 the Ministry of Privatization offered for sale three state sugar producers for the second time. The first attempt at sale failed in 1994 because investors balked at government fixing of sugar prices. However, the sugar regime was then liberalized, with reforms culminating in the abolition of price controls in January 1997. It is envisaged that Morocco's other sugar companies, one of which owns two plants, will also be privatized in due course. The Government has signed a five-year contract to inject US $ 5.4m. into the refining company Sucrafor, where profit margins have been put under increasing pressure as costs have risen. About 2,000 farmers sell their sugar beet to the company for a total annual amount of US $9m.

Morocco is also a major food exporter. Agricultural produce accounted for 59% of total export revenue in the period 1969–73, but its importance was later eclipsed by phosphate earnings. During the late 1980s agricultural products accounted for about 25% of total exports. The main agricultural exports are citrus fruit (mainly oranges), tomatoes, and fresh and processed vegetables. Citrus production rose from 1.22m. tons in 1997 to 1.59m. tons in 1998; however, it had fallen to 979,000 tons by 2001 after a slight increase to 1.40m. tons in 2000 (although exports remained virtually unchanged). As a result of the increasing frequency of drought years, the Government set up a US $200m. fund in late 1999 to improve the irrigation network in citrus-producing areas. Efforts are also being made through financial incentives to encourage farmers to create new citrus groves. Morocco exports approximately 40% of its citrus products, of which about 70% goes to the EU. In 1990–91 France was the largest importer, accounting for almost 250,000 tons. However, it is feared that Morocco's agricultural exports may be adversely affected by growing competition from other Mediterranean countries in the EU, in particular Spain and Portugal. Under the terms of the free-trade agreement with the EU, initialled in November 1995 and signed in February 1996 (see also Balance of Payments and Trade), both parties agreed to increase trade in agricultural products. The EU agreed to raise import quotas and loosen restrictions on trading periods for tomatoes, oranges and other products, but in return EU agricultural exporters would receive favourable treatment in Morocco. In January 2000, despite strong opposition from Spain, the EU removed the 150,000 tons-per-year limit imposed on imports of tomatoes from Morocco to the EU. New talks with the EU on Morocco's agricultural exports were initiated in September 2001 but Spain and other southern European producers were expected to oppose any further concessions. Morocco also sought financial assistance from the EU to eradicate the cultivation of cannabis in the Rif mountains by creating alternative forms of employment for the rural population in an isolated and poorly-developed part of the country. In February 1998 the EU allocated US $10m. for pilot projects to encourage the cultivation of almond trees, apiculture and livestock-rearing in this region.

Livestock numbers remained relatively static until the mid-1980s, when they increased from 24.2m. in 1986 to 28.6m. in 1989. However, numbers declined during the 1990s and by 2001 they totalled an estimated 25.2m. Numbers of sheep—the most numerous species—rose from 14.6m. in 1986 to 17.5m. in 1989 before declining in the early 1990s; in 2000 the number of sheep had, however, recovered to reach 17.3m. Meat and dairy production have, nevertheless, been on the increase; meat production rose from 293,000 tons in 1987 to 589,000 tons in 2001. Morocco produces virtually all of its national meat requirements. Output of dairy products totalled 1,015,600 tons in 1987, increasing to 1,216,000 tons in 2001. In February 1992 the Ministry of Agriculture and Agrarian Reform announced a US $50m. emergency programme to save some 22m. cattle, sheep and goats that were threatened by the severe drought. Some 60,000 tons of livestock feed was distributed to those areas worst affected, and a further 100,000 tons was distributed to farmers at half the price. A further drought-related rescue plan for local farmers, launched in early 1995, involved importing 70,000 tons of barley for livestock consumption.

Financial assistance was secured for the first phase of the Upper Abda-Doukkala irrigation scheme, south-west of Casablanca, from the African Development Bank (ADB), the European Investment Bank (EIB) and the Arab Fund for Economic and Social Development (AFESD), which pledged US $181m., $74.8m. and $130m., respectively. The new scheme aimed eventually to irrigate a total of some 64,000 ha in the Doukkala region, and to increase food production for Casablanca and Rabat; all four phases were estimated to cost some 6,000m. dirhams.

In 1991 work started on the Wahada dam scheme to irrigate 100,000 ha in the Sebou and Ouerrgh valleys, with financial support from Italy, the AFESD and the Kuwait Fund for Arab Economic Development (KFAED). In January 1996 it was announced that the AFESD had agreed to lend US $56.2m. to help finance the dam's construction. The OPEC Fund for International Development agreed in February 1992 to provide a loan of $7.5m. for the Tassaouat project, which involves irrigating 44,000 ha with a new canal system and the rehabilitation of existing irrigation canals. Financial support is also being provided by the AFESD, the Saudi Fund for Development, the KFAED and the EU. In December 1992 King Hassan inaugurated the $195m. Matmata gallery project, designed to channel 600m. cu m of water per year, to irrigate 25,000 ha of the Gharb valley. In August 1993 Japan agreed to provide a loan of $127m. to the Caisse Nationale de Crédit Agricole for agriculture and fisheries projects. In February 1994 the World Bank announced that it would lend $34.7m. to provide irrigation services to some 200,000 small farmers in order to raise production in irrigated areas. In May, in one of the last major allocations from the EU's fifth financial protocol, the EIB agreed to provide $24.7m. for a five-year project to irrigate 23,000 ha in the Haouz region. The KFAED was to lend $66m. towards the project which was part of a government plan to irrigate an additional 250,000 ha by 2000. In July 1994 the World Bank provided a $121m. loan, repayable over 20 years, to support the Government's agricultural investment programme (estimated at $993m. in 1994–97) and to be used for projects in poorer regions of the country. A loan agreement was signed with the AFESD in September to provide $10m. towards the total cost of remaining works on a project for agricultural development in the Loukos basin. In November 1997 the EU approved a loan of $13.5m. to combat soil erosion in the Middle Atlas as well as credits worth $4.5m. to increase agricultural production in the Doukkala plain. In 2002 the KFAED signed an agreement for a US $36.4m. loan to finance the Arrouz dam, near the northern city of Tetuan. The project, to be completed by 2005, aims to supply drinking and irrigation water to the surrounding region. The loan will cover 54% of the project cost (estimated at US $76.1m.) and is repayable over 23 years with a 3% interest rate. The World Bank has approved a loan to fund the Irrigation Based Community Development (IBCD) programme, the first step towards the implementation of the Government's new 2020 Rural Development Strategy which calls for a more participatory, integrated approach to rural development. It aims to improve the incomes and quality of life of rural communities in 15 provinces over a 13-year period through coordinated investments in small- and medium-scale irrigation and complementary community infrastructure, including rural roads, water supply/sanitation, electrification, health and education facilities.

As a result of the increasing frequency of drought conditions, doubts have been expressed whether Morocco can succeed in increasing the irrigated area to a level that would enable it to reduce significantly the impact of years of poor rainfall. Some commentators suggested that the Government should reduce the country's dependence on agriculture through rural development programmes aimed at expanding non-agricultural activities in rural areas. It was estimated that the drought in 2000 had affected over half of the total area devoted to arable crops with agricultural production falling some 17% below the 1999 level. The Government announced that it had allocated 6,500m. dirhams for emergency measures to alleviate the effects of the drought on rural areas, and in April 2000 King Muhammad VI declared that the proceeds from the sale of the first GSM licence would be devoted to help those affected by the drought.

Fishing has become increasingly important. A separate Ministry of Fisheries, formerly the responsibility of the Ministry of Commerce, Industry and Tourism, was established in April 1981. Special financial concessions were granted to the fishing industry in 1984 to improve its export potential; in addition, state control over exports was removed. In 1988 exports of fish and fish products totalled 179,000 metric tons and accounted for 50% of all food exports and 11% of total exports. In 1990 the volume of fish available for canning decreased by an estimated 8%, largely as a result of reductions in sardine catches landed at Agadir. In 1998 landings of fish, almost all from coastal waters, totalled 698,000 tons of which 436,000 tons were sardines. In 1983 the Government signed a treaty with Spain, granting Spanish vessels certain rights in Moroccan waters in exchange for finance for infrastructural development. Bilateral agreements with Spain were renegotiated in 1987 as accords with the EC, following Spanish accession to the Community in 1986. An agreement reached in February 1988 restricted EC vessels to a catch of 95,000 tons annually in Moroccan waters, in return for licence fees and compensation worth US $48.3m. a year. Morocco also gained improved access to the European market for its canned sardine exports, the annual volume of which was to rise to 17,500 tons, compared with 14,000 tons in 1988. In February 1992, however, it was reported that the Moroccan Government had suspended talks with the EC about fishing rights for EC fleets, in retaliation for the EC's refusal to approve Morocco's fourth financial protocol in January. The 1988 agreement expired in March 1992. After lengthy negotiations, a new three-year accord came into force in May 1992, allowing 650 Spanish, 50 Portuguese and 36 other trawlers into Moroccan waters, in return for increased compensation of 102m. ECUs ($131m.). The accord also envisaged new conservation measures, the expansion of port facilities and the creation of joint marketing companies. Negotiations with the EU began at the end of March 1995 to renew the three-year fisheries agreement due to expire on 30 April. The Moroccan Government pressed for a reduction in the number of European fishing vessels allowed to operate in Moroccan waters in order to allow fish stocks to recover and for the local fishing industry to take a greater part in the industry, including European fishing boats landing catches at Moroccan ports. No agreement had been reached when the accord lapsed, but a new round of talks began in Brussels, Belgium, in May. The accord is the EU's most important external fisheries agreement and sustains an estimated 28,000 people working in the Spanish fishing and fish processing industry. Moroccan demands met with strong resistance from the Spanish fishing industry, which holds most of the fishing licences for Moroccan waters. Spanish fishermen attempted to block imports of Moroccan fish at several ports. After lengthy negotiations, a new fisheries accord was initialled with the EU in November. The four-year agreement came into effect in December, when European (mainly Spanish) fishing boats were allowed back into Moroccan waters for the first time since the end of April. Morocco won substantial concessions from the EU, which it claimed would boost the country's fishing industry and safeguard endangered fish stocks. Catches by EU fishing vessels were to be reduced by up to 40% for certain species, and European trawlers were required to unload part of their catches of squid and octopus at Moroccan ports—the proportion will rise to 30% after four years. Total compensation payments from the EU were set at $355m. over four years, and payment during the first year was increased to $162.5m., compared with $133m. under the previous agreement. In order to deal with the increase in business expected as a result of the accord, the Government announced a $233m. investment programme in April 1996 to enable fishing ports to meet additional demand. In addition, the Government embarked on a $151m. investment programme to renew the country's fishing fleet over the next four years. The programme aims to replace up to 400 fishing boats with more powerful vessels with better refrigeration equipment, enabling them to operate in the open sea and to remain at sea for longer periods. Most of the investment is expected to be provided by the private sector, although the Government agreed to contribute $23.3m. in the form of grants to finance 10%–20% of the cost of each new boat and to provide bank loan guarantees to ship-owners. In February 1996 it was reported that $7.2m. in aid from Japan would be invested in equipment to improve fishing conditions and warehouses in the provinces of Agadir and El-Hoceima. By the end of 1997 some $21m. had been spent on upgrading 320 refrigerated fishing vessels to meet EU stand-ards. In November of that year the Government announced that it planned to invest $315m. to develop fishing off its southern coasts. In April 1998 the Ministry of Public Works began evalu-ating bids for a $46m.–$51m. fishing harbour at Boujdour in the disputed Western Sahara. After the fish catch declined significantly in 1997, the Moroccan Government acted to combat the depletion of fish stocks in its territorial waters by banning all fishing for two two-month periods during the year. By 1999 the Ministry of Fisheries planned to have a new satellite sur-veillance system in place to improve monitoring of fishing activi-ties in Moroccan waters and help prevent foreign boats fishing in forbidden areas. Despite the 1996 EU fisheries accord, tensions between the Moroccan authorities and the mostly Spanish ves-sels fishing in Moroccan waters continued. Morocco indicated that it did not intend to renew the EU accord which expired at the end of 1999, and instead would seek to exploit the fish stocks in its territorial waters through joint ventures with foreign companies. In early 1998 it was reported that talks about joint ventures had begun with France and Japan. After the expiry of the EU fisheries accord in November 1999, discussions opened between Morocco and the EU on the future of co-opera-tion in this sector.

Initially the Moroccan Government was firmly opposed to any new agreement that would allow European fishing boats back into its waters and instead proposed that the EU should provide assistance for Morocco's programme to modernize its own fish-eries sector. However, after intense pressure from the EU, Morocco agreed to commence negotiations regarding a new EU fisheries agreement but set out terms that were unacceptable to the EU; they included a 50% reduction in the number of European vessels allowed to operate in Moroccan waters, a sharp reduction in the total catches permitted by European vessels, the provision that all catches by European vessels be landed at Moroccan ports, and that Moroccan citizens were to make up a quarter of those employed on European vessels. Morocco also insisted that the new agreement should be for two rather than four years and that the EU should continue compensation payments of €125m. a year despite the reduced quotas proposed. No progress was made during further talks between Morocco and the EU in 2001. Morocco's own fishing industry is strongly opposed to a new agreement with the EU, insisting that it would undermine efforts to arrest the decline in fish stocks and lead to further unemployment in the sector. Morocco has ambitious plans for its fishing industry and aims to increase production from 727,000 tons in 1999 to 1.5m tons by 2003. Fish exports in 1999 were worth 6,398m. dirhams, 9% of total exports.

In June 1992 ONA, Morocco's largest private company, signed an agreement with the Union des Coopératives de Pêcheurs de France to establish a fish-canning and marketing enterprise to market canned sardines and mackerel. In August 1995 Morocco and Russia renewed a three-year fishing accord, permitting Russian vessels to catch fish in the coastal waters off Western Sahara. The accord allows 28 Russian trawlers to fish some 200,000 tons in these waters in the first year, a substantial increase on 1994 when 17 trawlers were given permission to fish 80,000 tons. Fishing quotas for the remaining two years were to be determined by the size of fish stocks. Under the agreement all Russian catches would be marketed by a joint Russian-Moroccan company. In February 1997 Morocco signed a fisheries accord with Canada. In 2000 Morocco terminated the fishing accord with Russia.

MINING

The mining sector accounted for 2.6% of GDP in 1989 and almost one-third of Morocco's total exports, but there has been a progressive decline in the relative importance of the sector, which only accounted for an estimated 1.9% of GDP in 1996. There has also been a shift from the export of minerals to mineral derivatives. In 2000 phosphates accounted for more than 90% of the total volume of mineral output.

Morocco has about two-thirds of the world's known reserves of phosphate rock. Proven reserves are 10,600m. tons, and probable reserves 57,200m. tons. Major deposits are located at Khouribga, Youssoufia and Ben Guerir. Morocco also controls production at Bou Craa in Western Sahara, which was reopened in July 1982. With the opening of mines at Ben Guerir in 1981 and at Sidi Hajjaj in 1984, annual output capacity has gradually increased and there are long-term plans to exploit large phos-phate deposits at Meskala. A new open-cast mine opened at Sidi Chennane, south of Khouribga, in 1995 capable of producing 12m. tons of phosphate rock a year. In March 1995 the Office Chérifien des Phosphates (OCP) stated that it had the capacity to produce 30m. tons of phosphate rock a year from four open-cast mines. As a result of high phosphate prices in the early to mid-1970s, there was a decline in demand, and the volume of Moroccan exports of phosphate fell by 22% between 1979 and 1982. In the early 1980s there was a slow recovery in world demand, but international phosphate prices fell from US $49.50 per ton in 1980 to less than $40 by 1983, to $34.80 in 1986 and to $31.95 in 1987, before rising in 1988 and 1989 to $40.50. Morocco, as a result, invested heavily in the 'downstream' phos-phate derivatives industry, to increase the value of its exports (see Industry). Phosphate rock production increased from 20.9m. tons in 1996 to 23.1m. tons in 1997, while prices rose from $39.00 per ton to $40.83 per ton. Some 11m. tons of phosphates were exported in 1997 when the OCP reported that Morocco had become the world's leading exporter, overtaking the USA and accounting for almost one-third of world trade. A five-year plan was launched by the OCP in 1998 to modernize infrastructure and technology, improve productivity and reduce costs. Phosphate rock production totalled 22.8m. tons in 1999 with exports of 11.4m. tons. Sales of raw phosphates and phos-phate derivatives reached $44 per ton. During 2000 output of raw phosphates totalled 21.5m. tons, while exports totalled 10.5m. tons. As a result of an improvement in the company's performance OCP's debt fell from 220m. dirhams in 1995 to 7.50m. dirhams in 1999.

Coal production averaged between 700,000 and 800,000 metric tons per year during the 1980s but declined sharply during the 1990s with output reaching only 269,000 tons in 1998 compared with imports, mainly from South Africa, of 3.1m. tons. Most of the coal is used to generate electricity. By 2000 coal production had fallen to just 28,700 tons.

Production of crude petroleum has been negligible, reaching at most around 23,000 tons a year. Exploration for hydrocarbons intensified following the creation of the Office National de Rech-erches et d'Exploitations Pétrolières (ONAREP) in 1981. By mid-1986 agreements had been reached with numerous foreign oil companies for exploration both onshore and off shore. How-ever, the collapse in oil prices in 1986 prompted many of these companies to relinquish their interests; in any case, no major discovery had been made, apart from a gasfield owned by ONAREP in the Essaouira area. Even this, which was originally expected to satisfy 40% of Morocco's energy needs, proved, during 1985, to be more limited than anticipated. In 1991 incentives for international companies to explore for oil and gas were approved by the Chamber of Representatives, following the revision of laws which reduced the state's minimum share in agreements with international companies to 35% from 50%, reduced the minimum size of an exploration permit to 2,000 sq km from 5,000 sq km and reduced the minimum duration of an accord to eight years from 15. Two US oil companies, Ashland Exploration and Santa Fe Energy Co, were the first to sign an exploration and production-sharing agreement with ONAREP under the revised hydrocarbons code, which came into force in April 1992. The companies are exploring in a 6,000 sq km area off shore of Essaouira and Agadir, with each company holding 50% in its part of the venture and with Ashland Exploration as operator. Renewed efforts have been made to attract foreign investment in oil exploration and in early 1998 ONAREP signed agreements with Enterprise Oil Exploration of the United Kingdom, Shell Prospecting Africa, the Roc Oil Co of Australia and Lasmo Overseas Nederland covering offshore areas in southern Morocco. Between June 1997 and June 1998 ONAREP signed exploration agreements with seven prospecting companies involving total investments of US $7.5m. Later in 1998 new exploration agreements were signed with the US firm Vanco, and Saudi Arabia's Aramco. Extensive deposits of oil-bearing shale are known to exist, with a potential output of 100,000m. tons (15% of world reserves). In February 1995 the Office National de l'Electricité (ONE) signed an agreement with Pama of Israel to test oil shale from the Tarfaya deposit for power generation. Preliminary estimates suggested that the Tarfaya deposit contains some 80,000m. tons of oil shale. Gas production in the early 1980s ranged between 78,800m. cu m in 1982 and 86,600m. cu m in 1985. Four major gasfields are in production, with two others, including the Meskala field in the Essaouira area, being developed. Gas treatment facilities have been developed at Meskala. In October 1997 ONAREP announced that it had discovered reserves of some 300m. cu m of natural gas in the Gharb region near Kénitra and that after the drilling of a second well, production might reach 75,000 cu m a day. Also in October Lasmo of the United Kingdom signed an agreement to carry out surveys in the Essaouira basin in southern Morocco, which currently produces small quantities of oil and gas but where known reserves are almost exhausted. In late 1998 Cabre Maroc of Canada announced that several exploratory wells drilled in the Gharb region had produced low-sulphur gas and that additional wells would be drilled during 1999.

Amendments to the 1992 hydrocarbons law, agreed by parliament in late 1999, were aimed at encouraging further foreign investment in this sector, especially in offshore production, and included provisions to reduce the state holding in concession contracts from a minimum of 50% to a maximum of 25%. In August 2000 it was announced that Lone Star Energy, a subsidiary of Skidmore Energy of the USA, had discovered major oil and gas reserves in the Talsint block in the north-east close to the Algerian border. Estimated reserves at the first well, Sidi Belkacem 1, are modest and official predictions that total reserves at Talsint could amount to 1,500m–2000m barrels—enough to make Morocco self-sufficient in energy—were regarded by independent analysts as premature. Nevertheless, the discovery together with the attractive terms offered by the amended hydrocarbons law encouraged several international companies to convert their reconnaissance licences for offshore blocks in southern Morocco into exploration licences. In September 2000 ONAREP reported considerable interest from international oil companies when it opened bidding for eight-year exploration licences in a number of offshore blocks between Rabat and Sale. By 2002 the bidding had been extended several times to allow more oil companies to study the seismic data.

In March 2001 Energy Africa of South Africa signed three new exploration permits with ONAREP. Later that year the Government signed two further, and controversial, oil exploration agreements, both offshore in the disputed Western Sahara region which is believed to be potentially rich in oil reserves. These were with TotalFinaElf of France for the 115,000 sq km area in the Dakhla zone, and with the US-based Kerr-McGee (which already holds six reconnaissance permits with British Enterprise and Energy on the Cap Draa offshore field on the Atlantic coast) for a 110,000 sq km area in the Boujdor area, near the city of el-Aaiún. The Polisario Front, which is seeking independence for the Western Saharan region, protested the contracts to the United Nations which has determined that Morocco would be in violation of international law if it allowed foreign firms to produce oil from the disputed territory without taking into account the interests of its inhabitants. In August 1991 Gaz de France (GdF) signed two agreements with Morocco's Ministry of Energy and Mines and the Société Nationale des Produits Pétroliers (SNPP), in preparation for the second trans-Mediterranean pipeline to carry Algerian natural gas across Morocco to Europe. The SNPP, Algeria's state energy company SONATRACH, Spain's Enagas, GdF, and Germany's Ruhrgas were each to have a 19% interest, while Gás de Portugal was allocated the remaining 5%. In July 1992 Morocco and Spain

signed a 25-year agreement to build and exploit the new Maghreb–Europe gas pipeline to run from Hassi R'Mel in Algeria across Morocco and the Strait of Gibraltar to Spain. The first phase of the project was to supply 6,000m. cu m of natural gas to Spain, 1,300m. cu m to Morocco, with another 1,000m. cu m being used in Algeria. The cost of the entire pipeline was estimated at US $2,500m. Enagas was to provide an estimated $1,300m. to finance the 525-km Moroccan section. In January 1994 the pipeline's capacity had reportedly been increased by 30% to 10,000 m. cu m per year because of a new contract to supply 2,500m. cu m per year to Portugal. Following widespread reports that the work on the project was delayed and might even be cancelled because of the security situation in Algeria and rising tensions between Morocco and Algeria, the Ministers of Energy of Morocco, Spain, Portugal and Algeria met in September 1994 and reaffirmed their governments' commitment to completing the pipeline. In October 1994 the Moroccan Minister of Energy and Mines visited Algeria to attend a ceremony marking the formal start of work on the pipeline. In March 1996 it was reported that Enagas had acquired total control of Sagane, the company responsible for the construction and operation of the Moroccan section of the pipeline, by purchasing the 91% stake from the Spanish public-sector Sociedad Estatal de Participaciones Industriales for $513m. The Maghreb–Europe gas pipeline became operational in November 1996 when the first gas supplies were delivered to Spain, and the link to Portugal was completed in early 1997. The pipeline's initial capacity of 7,000 cu m a year was planned to expand to 10,000 cu m a year by 2000.

Production of iron ore, mainly from mines in the north-east of Morocco, was as high as 1.5m. metric tons in 1958, but during the next 20 years annual output declined considerably. After 1982 there was an increase in production and in 1987 total output reached 280,000 tons, although it slumped in 1988 to 156,000 tons. Production in 1990 was 149,500 tons, but by 2000 had declined to just 5,600 tons. There are plans to open new mines in the Rif mountain area. Production of iron ore is currently undertaken by the Société d'Exploitation des Mines du Rif.

Other minerals produced include barytes, lead, copper, zinc and manganese. Production of most other, non-ferrous ores had been falling, but there were signs of a recovery by the late 1980s. Apart from a sharp decline in estimated output in 1986, production of lead ore has generally increased, and the capacity of the lead smelter at Oued Heimer, operated by the Société des Mines de Zellidja, was to be expanded, following studies which indicated a high lead content in nearby deposits. Zinc production has also been increasing. In 1991 Morocco's total output of zinc ore concentrate was 47,709 tons, with exports worth US $13.3m. Production of zinc ore concentrates increased dramatically in 1993, totalling 125,700 tons, and in 2000 estimated output was 201,700 tons. Production of fluorspar at el-Hammam, near Meknès, and of barytes and cobalt concentrate also increased. Another barytes mine was opened at Zelmou, with a production capacity of 100,000 tons a year. Production of barytes rose to 322,000 tons in 1988 from 127,000 tons in 1987; output increased to 434,700 tons in 1991, but subsequently declined, totalling an estimated 320,200 tons in 2000. In the late 1980s and early 1990s output of lead averaged around 100,000 tons, and that of copper around 40,000 tons. The production of silver rose from 76 tons in 1987 to 132 tons in 1988. In an attempt to increase copper production, which had fallen in the 1980s, a major mine was developed at Bleida. Interest has been shown in the possibility of recovering uranium from the phosphate rock reserves, and exploration by the Bureau de Recherches et de Participation Minières (BRPM) has revealed traces of uranium in the upper Moulouya valley, east of Zeida, in the High Atlas. In late 1987 the BRPM signed an agreement with its French counterpart for survey work on deposits of copper, zinc and lead in the Anti-Atlas region. As a result of a project by the US Agency for International Development (USAID), US and Moroccan researchers have identified traces of nickel, cobalt and gold in the Foum Zguid region of the Anti-Atlas. There were also reports from OPEC sources that deposits of up to 20m. tons of bauxite had been discovered in Morocco. The Guemassa polymetallic mine in the High Atlas was officially opened in December 1992. In July 1993 ONA (formerly Omnium Nord

Africain), which owns and operates the mine, was seeking a $100m. loan to increase annual production to 130,000 tons of zinc, 32,000 tons of copper and 12,000 tons of lead. In May 1994 BRPM signed an agreement with Placer Outokumpu Exploration, a Canadian/Finnish company, which will invest $2m. in mineral exploration work and drilling in the Marrakesh region where the Guemassa mine is located. In May 1998 the BRPM signed a convention with Odyssey Resources of Canada, granting the firm a four-year lease for copper exploration in Alous, a town in the southern province of Taroudant. Also in May the BRPM signed a preliminary joint venture agreement with Ennex International of Ireland to develop zinc production in the Middle and High Atlas. In January 2001 the EIB agreed a loan of €30m to the mining arm of ONA for the development of the Akka gold mine in the Iourim region south of Agadir. Early in 1999 it was reported that a 10-year geological mapping project was planned to identify the country's mineral deposits for potential foreign investors. The project would be undertaken with French, British and South African assistance at a cost of some $200m. Only 20% of Morocco has currently been mapped for foreign mining operators. In early 2000 Morocco signed a memorandum of understanding with India's Ministry of Mines and Minerals to promote co-operation in the mining sector. In April: 2002 ONA dedicated a US $24m gold mine compound in Guinea and has announced plans to launch further mines in Niger in 2002 and in Burkina Faso in 2004.

In March 1995 the Ministry of Privatization announced its intention to sell the state's shareholdings in five mines: the Compagnie de Tifnout et Tighanimine, producing cobalt, in which the government holds 40% of shares; the Société Minière de Bougaffer (SOMIFER), producing 35,700 tons of copper a year, in which the state's shareholding is 34.2%; the Société Métallurgique d'Imiter (SMI), producing 236,000 tons of silver ore a year, in which the state's holding is 69.07%; the Société Anonyme Chérifienne des Etudes Minières (SACEM), producing 42,600 tons of manganese a year, in which the state's holding is 42.99%; and the Société Anonyme d'Entreprise Minière (SAMINE), producing 70,100 tons of fluorite a year, in which the state's holding is 35%. The sale, which represented the first privatization in the mining sector, had been timed to take advantage of rising international metal prices. However, the Ministry of Privatization failed to sell its shares to ONA (which holds a minority stake in the companies), after they were unable to agree on a sale price during 1995. Thus, in March 1996 the Government announced that it had put all mining companies on its privatization list on the market and was planning to sell its shares in the SMI, the Compagnie de Tifnout et Tighanimine, the SAMINE and the SOMIFER to a single bidder at a minimum price of 648.8m. dirhams ($75.3m.). The SMI, in which two-thirds of its shares were sold to ONA in 1996, recorded profits of 83.4m. dirhams in 1997, compared with 43.2m. dirhams in 1996.

INDUSTRY

In the 1980s the Government made particular efforts to promote industrial development, in order to reduce Morocco's dependence on agriculture and phosphate mining, to create employment and to reduce imports. Official policy has been to promote export-oriented industry and to encourage private-sector investment; this has been supported by the World Bank. As a result of the investment code promulgated in 1983, and amended in 1988, which provided attractive incentives for both national and foreign investors, investment rose considerably. In 1987 investment in the industrial sector increased by 32%, following growth of 25% the previous year. Investment then rose by 23% in 1988, by 39% in 1989 and by about 35% in 1990. Three-quarters of the invested funds were from private Moroccan investors; foreign investors accounted for 16% of the total in 1987 and 20% in 1988. Foreign investment (principally from France, followed by Spain and Italy) fell markedly in the early 1990s, mainly as a result of recession in Europe. Investment recovered in 1995, growing by 26%. Industrial growth slowed during 1996 to 2.6%, compared with 3.7% in 1995, but recovered in the first half of 1997 to 5.2%. Industrial growth during the first quarter of 1998 fell to 1% and expanded by only 2.4% in 1999. While chemicals benefited from strong export growth, food processing stagnated and textiles contracted due to falling

demand from overseas markets. The main industry, in terms of investment and foreign exchange earnings, is the processing of phosphates, which continues to be undertaken by the state-controlled OCP. The phosphate sector was originally excluded from the government's privatization programme, but in early 1995 plans were being considered to open this strategic sector to private capital (see below). Other industries, in order of importance, are petroleum refining, cement production, food processing, textiles and chemicals.Manufacturing remains a relatively small sector, and is primarily concerned with the processing of export commodities and the production of consumer goods. A number of state-owned industrial concerns were among the first to be offered for sale in the privatization programme. Among these were the Société des Dérivés du Sucre, in late 1992, and the Cimenterie de l'Oriental (Cior) and the Société Nationale d'Electrolyse et de Petrochimie, in early 1993. In March 1994 it was announced that three sugar companies would be offered for privatization: Şucrerie de Beni Mellal, SUTA and Sucrerie du Tadla (see also Agriculture and Fisheries). The Minister of Privatization announced that the state's remaining 22.2% share in the General Tire and Rubber Co would be sold, along with the Société Nationale de Sidérurgie (SONASID, the national steel company), the Société Marocaine de Constructions Automobiles (SOMACA) and the Société Marocaine des Fertilisants, a subsidiary of the OCP. The Government sold its remaining stake in the General Tire and Rubber Co in October, and in late September announced the privatization of the Société des Industries Mécaniques et Electriques de Fès, which makes diesel and electric motors. In January 1995 the General Tire and Rubber Co raised its capital by 20% in a stock market offering, the first newly-privatized company to do so. Although the company invested US $4.9m. in 1998–99 to increase production, it suffered from serious competition from cheaper imported products and reported losses of 49m. dirhams in 1999. In January 2001 the company suspended trading its shares on the Casablanca Stock Exchange. In February 1995 the privatization programme was expanded to incorporate some of the so-called strategic industries, including the country's two oil refineries (see below). The possibility of opening the key phosphate industry to private investment was also announced and in 1996 a 30% stake in OCP's subsidiary, Société marocaine des fertilisants (FERTIMA) was floated on the stock exchange. In late 1999 a 51% stake in FERTIMA was sold for 230m. dirhams. Early in 2000 the SOMACA car assembly plant, the textiles firm Cotef and the state tobacco company, Régie des tabacs, were listed for privatization. The privatization programme experienced its first reverse in February 1995, when the Government failed to find a buyer for SONASID; however, in 1996 a 35% share was floated on the Casablanca stock exchange, and in October 1997 the state's remaining 62% holding was sold to a consortium of local financial institutions, notably the Société Nationale d'Investissement (SNI), and Marcial Ucin, a Spanish steel company. The divestment of other less profitable industries has continued to prove troublesome. In late 1997 the Government made a new attempt to sell part of the state-owned sugar refineries, which were first offered for sale in 1994. In April 1996 the Government invited private investors to develop three new industrial zones at Tangier, Jorf Lasfar and Nouasser. International developers were asked to equip the zones and take responsibility for attracting companies to them, with the Government providing infrastructure. Total investment of some US $186m. was sought. Priority was given to the Tangier industrial zone in order to attract jobs to a deprived area. There were plans to develop a 200-ha site at an estimated cost of $87m., and to attract 1,100 enterprises, one-third of them international companies. The Nouasser zone was to cover 200 ha and Jorf Lasfar 135 ha. However, the state-owned Office de Développement Industriel failed to attract international developers and in mid-1997 the Government announced that it had asked local financial institutions to establish the Tangier and Nouasser zones on a non-commercial basis. In July three privately-owned institutions, the Banque Marocaine de Commerce Extérieur (BMCE), Banque Commerciale du Maroc (BCM) and the SNI announced that they would finance the Tangier zone which would be located near the airport and cover some 120 ha. Construction work was scheduled for completion within two years. The consortium hoped to attract foreign investment in manufacturing and warehousing. The same institutions, together with Al-Wataniya and Mutuelle Centrale Marocaine d'Assurances, two local insurance companies, were also to develop the Nouasser zone, covering 270 ha. Early in 2000 the Ministry of Industry and Commerce, in partnership with CMS Energy of the USA, appointed Fluor Daniel of the USA to carry out a feasibility study for an industrial park at Jorf Lasfar close to the OCP's industrial complex and the country's first independent power plant. The study is expected to identify industries with an interest in relocating to the proposed park and sources of investment.

Following the conclusion of an EU association agreement in February 1996 (see also Balance of Payments and Trade), the Ministry of Trade, Industry and Handicrafts published a report which claimed that some 45,000m. dirhams (US $5,287m.) would be needed over the next five years if local industries were to survive competition from EU markets after the free-trade accord became effective. Under the accord, Morocco agreed to phase out protective customs barriers on all its manufactured products over a 12-year period, with the most sensitive industries being given the longest time to adjust. The report recommended reducing energy prices, liberalizing road transport, opening public services to the private sector (so as to lower production costs for local industries), developing professional training better adapted to the needs of the private sector, reforming further the financial system, and simplifying bureaucratic procedures for manufacturers. In April 1996 the EU pledged ECU 450m. ($570m.) in grants to help Moroccan industries restructure to meet the challenge of European competition. The grant formed part of some ECU 4,685m. ($5,932m.) to be distributed by the EU to signatories of the new association agreements over a period of four to five years. It would be distributed mainly to private manufacturing companies on a project basis rather than through government agencies, with the aim of assisting them to modernize, expand and improve training. Morocco was eligible to receive additional funds from 1999, when the EU intended to offer further grants, with the largest amounts being allocated to those countries with the most successful industrial restructuring programmes. In August 1997 it was reported that the EU was to start disbursing aid promised under the free-trade accord following the initialling, in July, of a framework agreement. In addition, Moroccan industries were to receive a further ECU 450m. ($570m.) in loans from the EIB. During 1997 the Government embarked on a plan to provide financial assistance to small- and medium-sized firms, which accounted for about 90% of Moroccan industry, in order to prepare them for increased competition from the EU after 2008. Companies would be offered long-term credits at preferential rates so that they could invest in new equipment and training. In November USAID approved a loan of $10m. to support the programme, which received a further $5.5m. from the Moroccan Government. Under the terms of the EU association agreement, which came into effect in March 2000, customs duties and tariffs on goods not manufactured in Morocco are being reduced by a maximum of 25% over four years, while those on goods manufactured in Morocco remain unchanged for two years and from then on will be reduced by 10% a year. At the beginning of 2001 it had become apparent that Moroccan manufacturers had shown little interest in the *mise à niveau* programme of industrial modernization, introduced in 1998 to help private-sector firms reform their management and production processes to become competitive with European manufacturers. Only 27 firms had had their modernization plans approved involving total investment of some $150m in sharp contrast to over 1,000 companies taking part in a similar programme in Tunisia.

Morocco has invested heavily in the 'downstream' phosphates industry. Four phosphate-processing plants are in operation at Safi: Maroc Chimie I, producing phosphoric acid and fertilizers; Maroc Chimie II, producing phosphoric acid; Maroc Phosphore I—a much larger plant, opened in 1976—producing phosphoric acid and monoammonium phosphate; and Maroc Phosphore II— opened in 1982, with three sulphuric acid lines and three phosphoric acid lines. A new facility is planned at Safi with a capacity to produce 2,300 metric tons a day of sulphuric acid which will be fed into the phosphoric acid plants at the complex. The project is part of the rehabilitation and modernization

programme at Safi. The contract to prepare detailed designs for the facility was awarded in March 1997 to the French company Krebs. The phosphoric acid treatment plant at Jorf Lasfar began production in 1986. In 1987 the commissioning of two plants for phosphate calcination took place, as well as the entry into production of the fertilizer-manufacturing units of the Maroc Phosphore III and IV factories at Jorf Lasfar, producing a new type of fertilizer-diammonia. Maroc Phosphore III and IV were expected to add a further 784,000 tons of phosphoric acid per year to total production. In 1991 the OCP announced a project to develop the Maroc Phosphore V and VI fertilizer and acid production units at Jorf Lasfar, with the aim of doubling annual capacity, estimated at 4.5m. tons of sulphuric acid, 1.4m. tons of phosphoric acid and 1.2m. tons of fertilizers. In April 1995 it was announced that construction of the Maroc Phosphore units could be opened to private capital. The OCP declared in July 1997 that it planned to build a sodium tripolyphosphate plant at Jorf Lasfar, as a joint venture with Prayon-Rupel of Belgium. The US $30m. plant will have an initial capacity of 50,000 tons, rising to 100,000 tons. In 1987 the value of exports of phosphate derivatives (mainly phosphoric acid) surpassed that of phosphate rock for the first time, and in 1988 the combined value of phosphoric acid and fertilizers accounted for almost two-thirds of total exports of phosphates and phosphate derivatives. The value of exports by the OCP rose from 9,855m. dirhams in 1990 to 10,048m. dirhams in 1991. Phosphoric acid and phosphate fertilizers accounted for some 70% of sales. Exports by the OCP in 1992 declined to 8,491m. dirhams, but phosphoric acid and fertilizers continued to account for about 70% of sales revenue. After a four-year slump, OCP exports of phosphates and phosphate products rose to US $1,060m. in 1994, a 13% increase over 1993. OCP exports accounted for 28% of the country's total foreign currency earnings in 1994, compared with 25% in 1993. Exports of phosphoric acid rose from 1.6m. tons in 1996 to 1.8m. tons in 1997. The OCP has pursued a number of joint venture phosphate projects with foreign partners. In early 1996 the company signed a five-year contract with Pardeed Phosphates of India to supply 80% of its phosphate requirement, amounting to 250,000–500,000 tons a year. Having signed a partnership agreement with Troy of Mexico in August 1995, the OCP agreed a joint venture in December 1995 with Prayon-Rupel for a 130,000 tons-per-year phosphoric acid plant, but the project was not implemented until 1999. The OCP also agreed to supply Grande Paroisse of France with sufficient phosphate to feed its 180,000 tons-per-year phosphoric acid plant. Under an agreement between the OCP and Norsk Hydro of Norway signed in 1999 the OCP is to become the sole supplier of phosphates to Norsk Hydro's European plants and the two companies are to co-operate in developing speciality products using monoammonium phosphate and diammonium phosphate. A 300,000-tons-per-year phosphoric acid plant at Jorf Lasfar, a joint venture between the OCP and the Indian fertilizer group Birla, went into production in 1999. A new storage and production facility for phosphoric acid at Jorf Lafar, a joint venture between the OCP and Chambal of India, was almost complete in late 2000 and when it becomes operational will be able to process up to 1.1m. tons of rock annually. Total production of phosphoric acid rose from 2.6m. tons in 1996 to 2.7m. tons in 1997, of which 1.7m. tons were exported. Some 1.5m. tons of phosphoric acid, worth 4,800m. dirhams were exported in 1998 and 1.9m. tons were exported in 1999, worth 5,938m. dirhams.

The largest industrial project in the 1980s, outside the phosphates industry, was the Nador steel rod and bar mill, with an annual capacity of 420,000 metric tons, built by a British company, Davy Loewy, with a £75m. contract agreed in 1980. The plant began production in 1984 with an output that included wire and reinforcing rods and bars. In May 1994 it was reported that SONASID was seeking foreign investors to finance its expansion. The steel mill required considerable modernization and needed a private-sector company to provide capital and technological assistance to increase its capacity of 420,000 tons a year by building an electric arc furnace and continuous caster. Earlier, in May 1992, it was reported that SONASID planned to build a steel mini-mill near Jorf Lasfar port consisting of a 258,000 tons-per-year continuous caster and a 250,000 tons-per-year bar mill. The Government was disappointed when no buyer was found for the state's 51% holding in SONASID, which was put up for sale in early 1995. In a new attempt at a sale, SONASID was 35% privatized on the Casablanca stock exchange in July 1996, and in October 1997 the state's remaining 62% holding was sold to a consortium of local financial institutions. The consortium planned to modernize and expand the Nador plant. SONASID increased its capacity from 480,000 tons a year to 600,000 tons a year in February 1998 when it acquired Longometal Industries of Casablanca. The company recorded profits of 188m. dirhams (US $20m.) in 1997. SONA-SID's new steel plant at Jorf Lasfar is expected to come on stream in June 2002. The plant will have a capacity of 300,000 tons a year. Construction work is being carried out by Danieli and Co of Italy. The company is also carrying out feasibility studies for a 600,000 tons-per-year electric arc steel furnace to be built at either Nador or Jorf Lasfar.

In late 1994 the privately-owned Maroc Sidérurgie (Masid) announced that it was to build a steel mini-mill near Casablanca to produce 125,000 metric tons a year of steel bars and rods. The plant would include a 30-ton electric furnace, continuous billet caster and rolling mill. Masid planned to involve a European company as a partner in the project with about one-third of equity. The Banque Nationale pour le Développement Economique (BNDE) announced that it was to participate in financing the US $82m. project by providing a long-term loan of $13m. The local mining group OISMINE was to invest $27m. Liquigaz GPL of Canada and MN Dastur of India were also involved in the project, which was due to become operational in April 1997.

Petroleum refining is another major industry. The biggest refinery, located at Mohammadia and owned by the Société Anonyme Marocaine de l'Industrie du Raffinage (SAMIR), has a design capacity of 4m. tons per year but has been producing more than 5m. tons per year. CTIP of Italy won a contract to raise the refinery's capacity to 6m. tons a year. The other oil refinery, at Sidi Kacem (owned by the Société Chérifienne des Pétroles, SCP), has a capacity of 1.2m. tons a year. The two refineries, which satisfy 80% of local demand, were originally considered part of the strategic sector and not included on the list of companies listed for privatization. In March 1996, however, the Government offered for sale 25% of its holding in SAMIR worth an estimated 1,730m.–2,070m. dirhams; 70% of the shares were reserved for small investors. The offer was fully subscribed, with some 75% of buyers using the new privatization bonds (see below). The Government planned to sell a further 25% of its holding in SAMIR through the stock exchange at a later date. The demand for SAMIR shares was encouraged by reports that both the Royal Dutch/Shell Group and Total of France were interested in buying a controlling stake. In early 1996 petrol distributors expressed concern that the privatization of SAMIR might lead to an increase in the company's prices. Local distributors complained that their profit margins were already too low owing to government control of petrol prices. As a result, Mobil Oil Maroc, which had previously announced a programme to double its investment to $5m. a year, stated that it would not increase investment. In May 1997 it was announced that a Saudi-owned company (Corral Petroleum Holdings) had purchased majority stakes in SAMIR and SCP (67.7% of SAMIR's capital and 73.9% of SCP) in a privatization deal that would generate $420m. in revenues for the Government. Corral also made a commitment to invest a similar amount in the local refining industry over five years. In September 1999 the merger of the two refining companies was completed, and Corral announced plans to modernize the Mohammedia refinery. In 2001 Foster Wheeler of the USA was awarded the front-end engineering and design (FEED) contract and will also be responsible for managing the project. The $500m. expansion scheme will increase total throughput to 8m. tons per year.

One of Morocco's major import-substitution industries is cement production. The country's cement works produced a total of 3.9m. metric tons in 1987. Virtually all plants were working below capacity (average utilization of capacity was 70% in 1987), but amid indications of renewed growth in the construction industry domestic production reached 4.6m. tons in 1988 and 5.4m. tons in 1990. Cement production rose from 6.6m. tons in 1996 to 7.2m. tons in 1999. In 1990 consumption of cement increased by 16.7%, compared with the previous year, and all the country's cement production units indicated consistent

growth. Cement plants have attracted increased foreign investment in recent years, especially from France. Lafarge-Coppée of France holds a 65% interest in Cementos Marroquíes (Cemenmar), a 26.5% interest in the Cimenterie Nouvelle de Casablanca (Cinouca) and a 40% interest in Cimenterie de Meknès. Annual capacity at the Cinouca plant increased to 1.9m. tons, following the opening of a new 700,000-ton production line. Production capacity at Cemenmar's Tétouan plant, currently 250,000 tons per year, may also be increased. Lafarge-Coppée has also taken an equity share in Readymix Maroc. Another French company, Ciments Français, has a 51% share in Société des Ciments d'Agadir, which has a production capacity of 1m. tons per year, and controls 60% of Cimenterie de Safi, a 600,000 tons-per-year plant. The International Finance Corpn (IFC) has provided financial assistance for the new Safi plant (US $20.3m.) and for Cinouca's expansion programme ($17m.). In May 1994 the IFC agreed to provide $10m. to modernize Ciment du Maroc's plant at Agadir. A further $4.2m. was to be provided by a syndicate led by Banque Indosuez of France. Among the largest privatizations to have been completed by mid-1994 were holdings of the ODI, including the Ciments de l'Oriental (Cior). Holderbank Financière Glarus of Switzerland has a 51% stake in the company, which has plants at Oujda and Fez. In August 1996 the local Laraqui group sold its majority shareholding in the Asment de Temara cement plant to Portugal's Cimpor-Cimentos for $70m. The Laraqui group had earlier planned a 30% increase in production capacity at the 900,000 tons-per-year plant, but other shareholders failed to agree to the necessary capital increase. Cior is planning a $8.5m. expansion project, involving a distribution centre and a crushing plant, in the north of the kingdom. In February 1998 Lafarge Coppée announced an expansion project at its Casablanca plant, where capacity will be increased from 1.6m. tons to 2m. tons. Cement sales were reported to have fallen slightly in 1998, to 7.15m. tons, with the Lafarge group accounting for 41.6% of total sales, Cior 21.7%, Ciments du Maroc 17.2%, Asmar 10.8% and Asment 8.7%. In October 1999 Ciment du Maroc acquired Société des ciments de Marrakesh (Asmar) thus becoming the second largest firm after the Lafarge group. Total cement sales grew by only 1.1% in 1999. In March 2001 Kawasaki Heavy Industries of Japan was awarded a contract by Lafarge Maroc to build a second cement plant at Tétouan (Tétouan II). The plant will have a capacity of 960,000 tons a year and production is due to begin in 2004. In 1999 Cior announced plans for a new 1m. ton plant to be built near Settat which was scheduled to open in 2001.

In January 2002 Société Nationale d'Electrolyse & de Petrochimie (SNEP) awarded the German/Italian joint venture Uhdenora a $3.8m. contract to supply services for a chlor-alkali electrolysis plant in Mohammedia which will produce 24,000 tons per year of caustic soda and 21,300 tons of chlorine for the plastics industry. Uhdenora had previously worked for SNEP on the construction of a membrane electrolysis plant which came into operation in 1998. The Finance Ministry signed an accord with US Yasmine Enterprises Inc. in May 2002 for the construction of a canning facility in the Agadir region. The US $34m. project is intended to create over 2,000 jobs and is expected to go into production in 2003.

The food-processing industry remains of considerable importance. It produces both for export and for domestic consumption. A large quantity of grain is processed into flour locally, but imported wheat is processed at a number of mills. There are also extensive sugar processing facilities in the country (see Agriculture and Fisheries). Other food industries include fruit and vegetable processing and canning—mainly for export—and fish canning. Fruit and vegetable processing recorded low growth rates in the mid-1980s, despite the fact that manufacturers could market directly, rather than through the Office de Commercialisation et d'Exportation, which was dismantled as part of the Government's privatization programme. This sector encountered restrictions on exports by the EC from 1986, when Spain and Portugal acceded to the Community. In 1998 Morocco's food-processing industries were reported to be highly inefficient and poorly equipped to meet open competition from the large agro-industrial groups of the EU.

Textiles have been at the forefront of export-led industrial growth since the 1980s and the value of exports expanded dramatically. By the late 1990s textiles accounted for some 40% of total exports and 39% of employment in processing industries. In recent years, despite continued growth in this sector, the rate of expansion has slowed. In 1997 the textile industry grew by 5.2% and had a turnover of US $2.3m. An estimated 60% of that year's total textile production was exported. Spanish and Italian textiles firms have invested in Morocco in recent years. Tavex of Spain is majority shareholder in the Settavex textile scheme in Settat, which now employs 300 staff and produces 13.5m. metres of denim fabric a year. Settavex embarked on an expansion programme in 1998–99 to modernize its production facilities and diversify its product range. In 1999 the IFC announced plans to invest $14m. in the company. In January 1992 Carrera, an Italian textile firm, established a joint venture in Tangier with the local Nasco group to produce 2m. pairs of jeans per year. In early 1999 the American company Fruit of the Loom announced that it was transferring part of its operations from Ireland to a plant in Morocco which will employ 700 workers. Also in 1999 the Moroccan Compagnie chérifienne des textiles signed a partnership agreement with the French company Sanglar-Sicap involving co-operation in both production and marketing. Rising labour costs are presenting problems for the textile industry which remains Morocco's major exporter of manufactured goods and fears persist that some European-owned textile plants may transfer their operations to Asia if labour costs continue to rise. In January 1996 the British company Marks and Spencer denied allegations that Morocco's Société Industrielle de Confection à Mèknes—which made clothes for Marks and Spencer—was using child labour. There was concern that the gradual reduction in customs duties and tariffs provided for under the EU association agreement (see above) might be particularly damaging for the textile industry with cheap goods from outside the EU, but routed through Western Europe, flooding the local market. In late 2000 textiles accounted for 34% of exports, although manufacturers complained that their exports were being adversely affected by the overvaluation of the Moroccan dirham against the euro and by a 10% rise in the minimum wage. There were reports that several textile firms were unable to pay their workers' wages and that this had led to strike action.

In the engineering sector, there are four plants assembling cars and small utility vehicles: Renault Maroc, the Société de Promotion Industrielle et Automobile au Maroc (Peugeot-Talbot), SOMACA (Fiat), and the Société Méditerranéenne pour l'Industrie Automobile (Land Rover). Heavy trucks (16.5 metric tons and over) are manufactured by Berliet Maroc and Saida; smaller capacity vehicles are assembled by Berliet, Auto-Hall and Siab. Berliet also assembles buses, and Somami-Rahali, a Casablanca-based firm, has manufactured bus bodies for Daf chassis imported from the Netherlands. A limited range of motor vehicle components is made locally, as are tyres. Railway goods wagons, and mineral and tanker wagons are assembled by SCIF of Casablanca. In April 1994 the Ministry of Commerce, Industry and Privatization invited tenders to build and operate a plant producing an economy car for the local market and to develop the local components industry. In 1999 Yamaha of Japan and its Moroccan partner, Marocaine industrielle, financière et agricole (Mifa), announced the construction of a new factory to produce motorcycles for the local market.

In May 1996 the French/Italian electronics company, SGS-Thomson, announced that it was to spend US $300m. over the next five years expanding its two factories near Casablanca which assemble electronic components and currently employ more than 2,000 people. In October 1997 South Korea's Daewoo Corpn signed an agreement with the Government to build a car assembly plant and a semiconductor plant at the Nouasser industrial complex near Casablanca, involving an investment of $500m. The two plants were expected to create almost 6,000 jobs and generate exports of $300m. during the next five years. Daewoo launched a holding company, Daewoo-Maghreb, in June 1998 in order to implement the agreement. In 1998 the American computer firm Microsoft announced that it was establishing its regional headquarters in Casablanca, and two other US companies, Compaq and Oracle, stated that they would co-operate in opening Moroccan-based subsidiaries. In January 2001 Boeing of the USA announced a joint venture agreement with Royal Air Maroc to build an electronics component plant

at the Nouasser industrial complex to manufacture axial and general purpose wire bundles for use exclusively in Boeing aircraft. The plant, which is expected to employ around 100 people, is scheduled to open in early 2002. At the beginning of April the Franco-Italian semi-conductor manufacturer, ST Microelectronics, opened a new assembly and test plant at Bouskoura near Casablanca. Once fully equipped the $300m. plant will be able to produce 25m. integrated circuits a day and will employ 2,500 staff.

The construction industry has seen strong growth since 1997 as a result of a government programme, backed by international funding agencies, to build cheap housing to replace slums. Average real growth of 6% was recorded in 2000.

Morocco's pharmaceuticals industry comprises 24 production facilities and earned US $421m. in 1997. Almost all production is under licence, most raw materials are imported and output is almost entirely for domestic consumption. All the large plants are owned by major international companies such as Hoechst Marion Russel of Germany and Pfizer of the USA. In 1998 Britain's SmithKline Beecham opened a new $8m. pharmaceuticals plant near Rabat, and Pfizer announced that its factory at El Jadida had been chosen as one of four sites to produce the drug Viagra.

After severe droughts in 1992 and 1993 had exacerbated serious power shortages, the state power company, ONE, was forced to develop an emergency plan to increase generating capacity. Contracts for several new power stations were awarded in 1993, including the installation of 100 MW of new capacity at the CTZ-ZI power plant at Casablanca, to be built by Technip of France at a cost of US $88m. In October 1993 an agreement was signed between ONE and Tractabel of Belgium and AES of the USA to build and operate a 500-MW oil-fired power station at Mohammadia. Output from the $600m. plant was to be sold exclusively to ONE under a long-term contract. In July 1994 the EIB approved a loan of $96m. to ONE to help finance the interconnection of the Moroccan and Spanish power grids, the first power link between North Africa and Europe. The 400-kV undersea electricity link with Spain under the Strait of Gibraltar, which cost $250m., was inaugurated in June 1998. In 2000 ONE commissioned Red Eléctrica de España to carry out a feasibility study for the doubling of the capacity of the undersea link and expressions of interest were issued in 2001 from contractors to supply and install submarine cables and to expand existing terminals on either side of the channel.

In November 1994 it was reported that ONE had failed to meet payment to local distribution companies for oil shipments. State companies, including the Office National des Chemins de Fer and the Office National de l'Eau Potable, had fallen into arrears amounting to an estimated $194m. A special payment of $107m. was made to ONE in the 1995 budget to help the company overcome its payment problems.

The first of two 330-MW units at the Jorf Lasfar power station reached full load in late August 1994, having been linked to the national grid in July; the second was linked to the grid in 1995. In October 1994 ONE invited tenders to build and operate Morocco's first private power project, the Jorf Lasfar III and IV units. It was announced that the successful bidders would also receive contracts to manage the two existing units at Jorf Lasfar on a concession basis and a letter of intent to build and operate the planned Jorf Lasfar V and VI units. The US $1,600m.-contract for the privatization and expansion of the Jorf Lasfar power station was awarded to ABB Asea Brown Boveri of Switzerland and CMS Energy Corpn of the USA in 1997. By the end of 2000 the Jorf Lasfar III and IV power stations (each with a capacity of 330 MW) had become operational doubling the station's capacity to 1,362 MW. All the electricity generated at the plant is purchased by ONE which retains its monopoly over distribution. The plant is operated and maintained by CMS Energy Corpn for 30 years under the build-operate-transfer formula. Early in 1999, the Anglo-French company Alsthom won a $34m. contract to construct two high-voltage lines between the Jorf Lasfar and Mohammadia power stations.

In January 1997 ONE announced plans to build a single gas-fired power station in Tahaddart near Tangier in the north of the country because of immediate access to the Europe–Maghreb gas pipeline (so saving on fuel transport costs). This was in preference to the two facilities originally planned in Mohammadia or Kénitra in the south, which would have required the construction of a 240-km branch pipeline to feed the plants with gas. Under the terms of an agreement signed in 1998 the 400-MW combined cycle plant at Tahaddart was to be owned by ONE together with two foreign partners, Electricité de France and Endesa Sevilliana of Spain. However, in 2000 Electricité de France withdrew from the project. In 2001 ONE signed a shareholder contract for the Tahaddart Energy Company (TEC, the consortium responsible for developing the plant) with Endesa and Siemens of Germany. ONE will hold a 48% stake, Endesa 32% and Siemens a 20% stake in TEC's $62.5m. capital. The $500m. plant is scheduled to become operational in 2003. Following a visit to the Western Sahara by Prime Minister el-Youssoufi in December 1998, ONE announced a US $58m. investment programme in the disputed territory to expand the electricity grid, including a 21-MW power plant at Dakhla.

In August 1995 Lyonnaise des Eaux-Dumez of France signed an agreement with the Moroccan authorities to manage Casablanca's power and water distribution network; the agreement was approved in principle in March 1996. Opposition parties criticized the deal, arguing that it was a privatization and would lead to higher prices for consumers. Lyonnaise des Eaux-Dumez rejected these claims and stated that the agreement was neither a sale nor a privatization. Lyonnaise des Eaux plans to spend some US $3,000m. over the 30-year contract period to improve water purification, water distribution and expand the electricity network. Early in 1999 the company announced that it would spend $82m. over the next two years. In April 2000 the company won a 30-year contract to supply drinking water to Casablanca involving investment of some $29m. In May 1998 a consortium of Spanish, Portuguese and local companies signed a 30-year concession agreement to operate power, water and wastewater systems in Greater Rabat (including Salé and Temara), involving investment of 14,000m. dirhams ($1,500m.) over the concession period. Other cities were reported to be contemplating contracting private operators to manage water and sewerage services, but the Casablanca and Rabat contracts proved highly controversial and met with resistance from the employers' federation. In June 2000 it was announced that seven international consortiums had bid for the 25-year build-operate-transfer concession for the provision of water, sewerage and electricity services in the Tangier and Tétouan regions. In March 2001 Vivendi of France was awarded the contracts which involve investment of some $650m. and $750m., respectively. The project commenced in January 2002, with the first tenders for construction and equipment supply expected to be issued in 2003. The Swedish International Development Authority (SIDA) made a grant towards a feasibility study for a waste management project in Oujda (with a population of 400,000) undertaken by the Swedish Sweco consulting group in 1998. In December 2001 Sweco began the second phase, involving the design for a new waste treatment plant, providing for the pre-treatment collection of recyclable items with the remaining material deposited in a waste cell equipped with a bio-gas extraction system. The gas will be sold to ONE. There are advanced plans to build a desalination plant at el-Aaiún, which is expected to be operational by the end of 2003.

A 50 MW wind-driven power plant—the first in the Arab world—was inaugurated at Tétouan in May 2000. The plant, which cost $48m., was built and will be operated for 20 years by a consortium of Electricité de France, Compagnie Financière de Paribas and Germa. In addition three wind farms are to be built, two in the Tangier region and another in the Tarfaya region with a combined capacity of 200 MW. The projects, which are scheduled to be completed by 2005, will cost an estimated $200m. and will be carried out on a build-operate-transfer basis by an international consortium selected by ONE.

The construction of dams with hydroelectric complexes, a programme which began in the 1960s, remains an important element in the Government's strategy to increase generating capacity. In mid-1997 the AFESD agreed a loan of $100m. for the Dchar el-Oued and Aït Messaoud hydroelectric dams in the Tadla region. Construction of the dams was scheduled to begin in 1998. In March 2001 Alstom Power of France signed a US $114m. contract for the construction of a 460 MW pumped storage power plant at Afourer in the Beni Mellal region, a project for which the EIB and AFESD have agreed to provide

financial support. The project, due to be completed in 2004, involves pumping water up into two artificial storage basins. The water will then power four hydroelectric turbines, two of 165 MW capacity and two of 60 MW capacity. In October 1997 Germany's development agency, Kreditanstalt für Wiederaufbau, agreed to contribute $5.6m. to a solar energy project in the Tensift region near Marrakesh operated by ONE. A 180-MW solar-based thermal power plant is to be built at Ain Beni Mathar with financial assistance from the World Bank's Global Environment Facility; the $200m. project is scheduled for completion in 2004. Morocco is also planning the construction of a medium-capacity nuclear reactor near Rabat.

In May 1995 ONE and Sonelgaz of Algeria renewed a contract for 1995–96 under which Sonelgaz would supply 50 MW of electricity to Morocco at a cost of US $25m. Also in May ONE stated that it expected the Government to approve a $119m.-per-year investment programme to accelerate rural electrification as part of a plan to provide electricity to all rural households by 2010. Currently only 35% of rural households have electricity. The new programme is to co-ordinate two schemes for rural electrification already in progress; one financed by ONE, the other financed by local communities by creating a central fund to which both rural communities and ONE contribute. Some 1,255 villages were linked to the electricity grid in 1996. ONE announced plans to invest $445m. in 1999 to expand electricity production and continue its rural electrification programme. Japan and France agreed to provide financial assistance to link 1,127 villages to the electricity grid in 1999. Provision was made in the 1999–2000 budget for 1,500m. dirhams to be allocated annually over the next eight years to fund the rural electrification programme. By 2008 installed electricity capacity is due to rise to 6,130 MW from 4,461 MW in 2000. From 2003 the Government plans to liberalise the electricity market and allow foreign suppliers greater access. As foreign companies build and manage power stations and as the Moroccan network has greater access to foreign grids, ONE's share of electricity generation is forecast to fall to 80% by 2003 and to just 40% by 2020.

BALANCE OF PAYMENTS AND TRADE

Morocco's main sources of revenue are earnings from exports of phosphate rock and phosphate derivatives, agricultural products and manufactured goods, receipts from tourism and workers' remittances from abroad. The country's expenditure is mainly on imports of capital equipment, food and crude petroleum. After 1976 the deficit on the current account widened, as export earnings rose slowly while the cost of imports soared. In 1983 the Government took strong measures to close the export/import gap by reducing budget expenditure and by restricting imports. This reduced the trade deficit from 13,552m. dirhams in 1982 to 11,218m. dirhams in 1983. However, the continuing decline in phosphate exports (by volume and value), and the high level of food and energy imports, resulted in further increases in the trade deficit, to 15,278m. dirhams in 1984 and to 16,938m. dirhams in 1985. Only the collapse of petroleum prices during 1986 enabled the trade deficit for that year to fall by 26%, to 12,505m. dirhams. In 1987 the trade deficit fell by a further 5%, to 11,881m. dirhams. Imports in 1987 rose by only 1.9%, to 35,271m. dirhams, while exports increased in value by 5.8%, to 23,390m. dirhams. The trade deficit continued to fall in 1988, to 9,382m. dirhams, with imports of foodstuffs down by 3.9% and energy imports by 14.9%, while exports rose by 20%. The precarious nature of this improvement was revealed, however, by a sharp increase in the trade deficit in 1989, when exports declined by 5% and imports rose by 19%, compared with 1988. Even so, the improvements in the export performance of some sectors were encouraging, particularly the increase of more than 30% in export earnings from manufactured consumer goods in the first quarter of 1989. Results for the whole year, however, indicated that the trade deficit almost doubled, to 18,323.8m. dirhams. The decline in exports in 1989 was largely the result of a sharp drop in sales of phosphoric acid. In 1990 the trade deficit grew by 21% (despite an increase of 19% in exports), to 22,165m. dirhams. Imports increased by 22% in 1990, to 57,022m. dirhams. The 1990 trade deficit was equivalent to 10.5% of GDP. In 1991 the trade deficit rose to 22,437m. dirhams, despite a 7% increase in exports (to 37,283m. dirhams) and a decline in expenditure on energy imports. Imports rose to 59,720m. dirhams, of which more than one-half were semi-finished products and industrial equipment. Food exports rose by 20.6% and there was a steady growth in sales of manufactured products. Exports of phosphates and derivatives accounted for 27% of total sales. The trade deficit increased in 1992 by almost 30%, to 28,846m. dirhams. Invisible earnings (remittances from migrant workers and tourist revenues) also increased, however, so that balance-of-payment problems were not anticipated. Sales of phosphates and products decreased from 10,047m. dirhams in 1991 to 8,491.7m. dirhams in 1992. Clothing sales remained constant at 4,137m. dirhams. Oil imports increased by almost 22%, and those of wheat nearly doubled as a result of the drought, totalling 2.4m. tons in 1992. Imports of industrial machinery rose from 2,460.7m. dirhams in 1991 to 2,711m. dirhams in 1992. Figures published by the Central Bank record exports of 34,238m. dirhams in 1993 and imports of 56,368m. dirhams, giving a trade deficit of 22,130m. dirhams and a current account deficit of 4,899m. dirhams. In 1994 exports rose to 36,546m. dirhams, while imports increased by 17% to 65,963m. dirhams, resulting in a trade deficit of 29,417m. dirhams. The trade deficit continued to widen in 1995; although exports increased by 10.1% to reach 40,240m. dirhams, imports rose by 10.5% to total 72,869m. dirhams (primarily owing to a substantial increase in food imports following the severe drought), giving a deficit of 32,629m. dirhams. In 1996 the trade deficit narrowed slightly to 30,600m. dirhams as exports rose to 41,300m. dirhams and imports declined to 71,900m. dirhams. Revenue from tourism increased by almost one-quarter, to 9,000m. dirhams, and remittances from Moroccan migrants in Europe also rose, to 17,500m. dirhams. According to the Office des changes, the value of exports reached 67,057m. dirhams in 1997 with imports at 90,712m. dirhams resulting in a trade deficit of 23,655m. dirhams. The value of exports rose slightly in 1998 to 68,607m. dirhams with imports increasing more rapidly to 98,676m. dirhams resulting in a widening of the trade deficit to 30,068m. dirhams. Tourism receipts increased from 16,200m. dirhams in 1998 to 16,700m. dirhams in 1999 but transfers (of which the main component is remittances from Moroccan migrant workers) fell slightly from 18,925m. dirhams in 1998 to 18,400m. dirhams in 1999. In 1999 exports rose to 72,283m. dirhams while imports fell slightly to 97,454m. dirhams resulting in a narrowing of the trade deficit to 25,171m. dirhams. Finished goods, mainly clothing, made up almost 40% of all exports, other major exports were semi-finished goods, and food, beverages and tobacco, both of which contributed 19% of total exports. Imports comprised machinery and equipment (26%), consumer goods (23%) semi-finished goods (21%), energy (12%), food, beverages and tobacco (11%) and raw materials (7%). Tourism receipts increased from 16,754m. dirhams in 1998 to 19,211m. dirhams in 1999 but worker remittances fell slightly from 19,300m. dirhams in 1998 to 19,000m. dirhams in 1999. Tourism receipts and worker remittances have traditionally served to offset Morocco's large merchandise trade deficit, and in recent years interest payments on the foreign debt have declined. Although the deficit on the current account rose to US $1,296m. in 1995 it fell sharply to $58m. in 1996, $169m. in 1997, $146m. in 1998 and $171m. in 1999. A combination of poor export growth, large cereal imports and the high cost of oil imports led to a sharp rise in the current account deficit in 2000 to an estimated $3,560m. Exports in 2001 increased by 1.7% to $6,300m. compared to $6,190m. in 2000. This was largely attributable to the export of phosphates and their derivatives which increased by 10.7% to $1,110m. from $1,000m. in 2000, contributing to a 3.3% decrease in the trade deficit to $3,450m. Imports stabilized at $9,760m.

In 1998 the EU remained Morocco's largest trading partner accounting for more than half of all trade, although its share of the market had declined slightly in recent years. In 1998 France was the largest source of goods, providing 21.8% of imports, followed by Spain (9.7%), USA (7.3%), Italy (6.2%) and Saudi Arabia (6.2%). France was also Morocco's largest export market taking 27.2% of exports, followed by Spain (10.8%), India (6.9%), Japan (5.7%) and Italy (5.3%). In 1998 Morocco signed free-trade agreements with Hungary and Bulgaria and expanded its trade links with China. An agreement was signed with Thailand in 1999 to expand bilateral trade. Trade with the other Maghreb countries remains limited but was expected to increase, fol-

lowing the creation in 1989 of the Union of the Arab Maghreb (UMA). Numerous initiatives have been taken to encourage closer economic collaboration and integration with other members of the UMA, including the lowering of customs and tariff barriers and promotion of trade and joint ventures. Despite a great deal of rhetoric, by late 1995 the UMA had largely failed to promote greater economic co-operation between its members, and in December Morocco brought UMA activities to a standstill after it accused Algeria of interfering in the Western Sahara dispute (see History). Ambitious plans to increase bilateral trade with Egypt have not been realized. Nevertheless, Morocco and Tunisia pledged to create a free-trade zone by 2007, and in late 1999 agreed to lift duties on a large number of industrial and commercial goods with immediate effect. In June 2002 the two countries signed several co-operation accords, and are aiming to increase the value of their bilateral trade to $500m. annually.

In April 1994 Morocco hosted the signing of the GATT Uruguay round trade pact in Marrakesh. Morocco had been one of the principal supporters of the GATT agenda in the Arab world. In July 1993 the maximum customs duty on imported goods was reduced from 40% to 35%, and, in line with the government's commitment to GATT, rates on some 2,300 products (including textiles, fibres, paper and packaging, and foodstuffs) were reduced. In March 1995 the liberalization of cereal, vegetable oil and oilseed imports was postponed from April and May until July in order to give time for measures to be put in place to protect local industries. The existing quantitative restrictions are to be replaced by tariff barriers, in accordance with GATT. Measures to liberalize sugar imports were also delayed until mid-1995. In June the Government announced that it had approved the ending of the state's monopoly on petroleum imports, as part of its policy of liberalizing the energy sector. In March 1998 customs duties on imported wheat were increased significantly in an attempt to protect local farmers. As customs duties represent an important component of state revenues, Morocco has, in the past, been reluctant to accelerate the reduction of tariffs as requested by the WTO. However, under the terms of WTO accords and the 1996 free-trade accord with the EU which came into effect in March 2000 (see below) Morocco is obliged to phase out tariffs over the next decade.

Morocco's trade is likely to remain crucially dependent on Europe. In view of the importance of its trade relations with the EU, Morocco has continually sought more favourable trade agreements. A five-year agreement conferring 'partial association' on Morocco was negotiated in 1968 and came into force in 1969. A new agreement for an unlimited period was finalized in January 1976, whereby most Moroccan agricultural and industrial products were allowed free access to the EC, but with restrictions on a few crucial items, such as olive oil, citrus fruit, wine, textiles and refined petroleum products. In 1984 Morocco applied to join the EC, but, in the absence of European approval for its application, urged the Community to liberalize its trade policies; new quota agreements were signed in January 1985. The entry of Spain and Portugal into the EC in 1986 stimulated a series of discussions, in which Morocco, as one of the countries most affected, was deeply involved. It was later agreed that the voluntary quota system on manufactured goods should be abandoned, but no agreement was reached concerning agricultural exports. Proposals by the EC Commission covered the five-year transitional period up to 1990. However, Ministers of Foreign Affairs from EC member states were unable to agree on the Commission's proposals, while Morocco also expressed serious concern at what it regarded as the 'protectionism' of the EC and the inadequacy of the Community's arrangements for relations with Morocco. In July 1987 Morocco made a second application for full membership of the EC, which was rejected in October. In 1991 it was announced that the EC would provide a financial aid programme of US $5,800m. for eight Mediterranean countries, of which Morocco was to be the largest beneficiary (receiving $534m. in total funds). Concessionary loans would comprise 50%. In January 1992 the European Parliament decided to block $600m. of development aid, in protest at abuses of human rights in Morocco and in the disputed Western Sahara. Morocco then refused to conclude a new fishing accord, and agreement was not reached until May. In April the EC Commission approved a policy document envisaging a new Euro-

Maghreb partnership. In October the European Parliament eventually ratified a fourth financial protocol, according to which Morocco was to receive $580m. in new funding over four years. In July 1993 it was reported that the EU had proposed an annual increase of 3% in quotas of citrus fruit, orange juice, fruit and vegetables from Morocco in 1997–2000. In January 1995 the Government signed an agreement with the EU to bring agricultural trade regulations closer to the provisions of GATT. Under the new agreement, Morocco's preferential status in tomato exports to the EU was reduced, but exports would be allowed to maintain their traditional level of 140,000–145,000 tons per year. A minimum price was imposed for the months from November to March, Morocco's busiest export period. Moroccan farmers were prevented from selling tomatoes at less than ECU 560 ($693) per ton, compared with minimum prices stipulated under the GATT of ECU 700–750 ($866–$928) in the period from November to March and ECU 920 ($1,138.5) for the months January to March. After two years of negotiations, in February 1996 Morocco became the third Mediterranean country to sign a free-trade accord with the EU. The accord had been initialled in November 1995 after delays due to Morocco's bitter dispute with the EU over fishing rights. Under the terms of the agreement, Morocco pledged to phase out protective tariffs on EU manufactured goods entering the country over a period of 12 years, and will receive financial help from the EU to help local industries adapt to new competition. The accord forms part of the EU's wider plan to foster a new political and economic force in the Mediterranean based on free trade and political co-operation. The EU accord came into effect in March 2000. From that date customs duties and tariffs on manufactured goods not produced locally, together with raw materials and spare parts, are being reduced by a maximum of 25% over four years. Tariffs on goods which are manufactured in Morocco remain unchanged for two years and from then on will be reduced by 10% per year for 10 years. During 2000 talks took place with the EU on improved access to the European market for Moroccan agricultural exports, but any concessions in this area met strong opposition from Spain and other southern European states. Between 1996–99 under a financial package established as part of the Euro-Mediterranean partnership (the MEDA programme) the EU allocated a total of €630m. to Morocco of which €266m. was for economic modernisation and €365m. was for socio-economic projects. Some €150m. per year was expected to be allocated to Morocco under the second phase of the MEDA programme during 2000–02, with priority to be given to economic reform and structural adjustment, measures to alleviate poverty, promote the private sector, and improve environmental protection.

In March 2002 Morocco and Senegal signed six co-operation agreements covering infrastructure, communications and the avoidance of double taxation to encourage investment between the two countries. Negotiations for the creation of a future free-trade zone between Morocco and the USA were announced during King Mohammed VI's official visit to Washington in May. The Moroccan-Qatari High Joint Commission is to explore co-operation in trade and investment and the creation of a bilateral free-trade zone. The Moroccan-Guinean joint co-operation commission in Rabat has signed agreements on information, tourism, and promotion and reciprocal protection of investments. The two countries have also signed a memorandum of understanding on industrial co-operation and a protocol for the establishment in Guinea of a trade institution. Morocco imports coffee, wood and cotton from Guinea and exports clothing, footwear and canned food.

TOURISM

The tourist industry has become an increasingly important source of foreign exchange. By 1987 the total revenue earned from tourism had reached 8,000m. dirhams, representing 23% of total exports of goods and services. Only phosphates and their derivatives, and workers' remittances, brought in more foreign exchange. Tourism was undoubtedly one of the growth areas of the Moroccan economy in the 1980s, and government incentives played a significant part in its development. Special conditions drawn up in 1983 govern investment in tourism, including tax exemptions on capital goods imports, interest-free loans and, in certain circumstances, income tax exemptions for a 10-year

period. Major tourist complexes were constructed at Casablanca, Agadir, Tangier and Restinga, near Tétouan. By the end of 1988 there were more than 79,000 beds available in nearly 500 hotels, pensions and holiday villages. Most tourists stay on the southern, Atlantic coast. The total number of foreign tourist arrivals in 1987 was 1,566,254, an increase of 6.5% on the 1986 total. In 1989 the number of tourists visiting Morocco increased by 27% (to 2,515,251, compared with 1,978,420 in 1988). In 1990 some 3m. foreigners visited Morocco, increasing tourist remittances by 22%, to 10,500m. dirhams. This advance was due to a rise in the number of Algerian visitors, taking advantage of the 'open frontiers' that had been authorized by the UMA. In 1991 tourist receipts declined to 8,822.2m. dirhams, despite a 3.1% increase in arrivals, mainly accounted for by more visitors from other Maghreb countries. In 1992 the number of visitors increased to 3.3m. Tourist arrivals from Italy increased by 67.9%, and from Spain by 43.4%. There was also an increase in the number of tourists from Germany, the USA and Japan, although tourist arrivals from Algeria decreased by 19%. Tourist arrivals decreased by 9.4% in 1993 and by 22.1% in 1994 (to 2.3m.) as a result of the recession in Europe, tensions between Morocco and Algeria and the fear of terrorist attacks following the Marrakesh shooting (see History). There was a further sharp decline in 1995 when the number of tourists fell to 1.5m., resulting in a decline in revenue to 11,071m. dirhams. In late 1995 the Ministry of Tourism reported that it had closed 36 hotels and downgraded 53 as part of a programme to raise the standard of tourist facilities. Foreign tourist arrivals increased from 1.6m. in 1996 and revenue rose sharply to 14,597m. dirhams. Although tourist numbers continued to rise in 1997 to 1.8m. revenue from tourism fell to 13,780m. dirhams as a result of the decline in per caput expenditure. Tourist numbers rose to 2.0m. in 1998, and to 2.3m. in 1999 while revenue for those years totalled 16,754m. dirhams and 19,200m. dirhams, respectively. During the first 10 months of 2000 tourism revenues reached 18,000m, an increase of 11% over the same period in 1999 and provisional figures indicated that tourist arrivals totalled 2.5m. in 2000. Despite the increase in tourist numbers, the Ministry of Tourism's target of doubling numbers by the end of the 1999–2003 development plan period appeared over-ambitious. Nevertheless, the Government is planning to spend US $8,000m. on the tourist industry as part of a strategy to attract 10m. visitors by 2010. There were 2.4m.visitors in 2001, with tourism receipts of about $2,380m. However, receipts fell by nearly 30% in the first quarter of 2002, largely attributable to the adverse effects of the September 2001 attacks in the USA.

In March 1993 it was reported that five state-owned hotels in Tangier, Meknès and Casablanca (the first of 37 hotels owned by the Office National Marocain du Tourisme scheduled for privatization) had been sold. A new approach to the privatization of state holdings in hotels was announced in April, according to which the Government would sell its holdings in four- and five-star hotels to international companies as a comprehensive transaction. The 1993 budget included a reduction in the allocation to the Office National Marocain du Tourisme to 90m. dirhams, indicating the Government's commitment to disengage from the tourist industry. In May 1994 local investors purchased the Transatlantique hotel in Meknès. In January 1998 the Ministry of Privatization announced that nine state-owned hotels would be offered for sale in 1998, including seven hotels that had failed to attract buyers when they were first offered for sale in November 1997.

Recent foreign investment is providing an opportunity to revive the flagging tourist industry. In July 1996 South Korea's Daewoo Corpn announced that it would buy the Rabat Hyatt Regency hotel for US $40m. and build an extension for an additional estimated $50m. In February 1997 it was reported that the French hotel management company Accor was to open subscriptions in March for its planned $100m. fund to invest in tourism development projects in Morocco. The funds will be spent to acquire hotels, spas and other facilities. In July Accor purchased the local Moussafir hotel chain for $5m., the company's first purchase under its current investment programme in Morocco. In April it was reported that the company was in talks with the Government about financing and building a trade and leisure centre in Casablanca and a 1,200-room hotel complex in Agadir. In addition, Germany's Paradiana is to invest in two separate tourism projects (a 600-bed hotel and a holiday club) in the Agadir region, where the Société d'Aménagement de la Baie d'Agadir is trying to attract some $450m. of private investment to develop tourist facilities there. Agadir is Morocco's only significant coastal resort and the country's northern coastline lacks tourist infrastructure. To attract more foreign tourists Morocco needs to develop its coastline. In 1998 the French group Accor won a contract to manage three luxury hotels in Casablanca, and Majestic Hotels, a Saudi–British firm, announced the investment of $50m. in a tourist complex at Skhirat, south of Rabat. In early May 2001 the Office Nationale Marocaine du Tourisme confirmed that it was seeking investors to construct six beach complexes at Larache, Taghazout, Saida, Essaouira, Plage Blanche and El Jadida at a cost of some 5,200m. dirhams. It also announced that the tourism sector was to become a key element in the country's development strategy Millennium & Copthorne Hotels has been awarded a 25-year management contract to operate two 5-star hotels—the Millennium Hotel in Agadir, comprising 284 rooms and seven suites, which is scheduled for opening at the end of 2002, and the Millennium Hotel in Marrakech, with 37 guest rooms and three suites, which is scheduled to open in mid-2003.

TRANSPORT AND COMMUNICATIONS

There are 10 major ports: Casablanca, Safi, Mohammadia, Agadir, Kénitra, Jorf Lasfar, Tan Tan, Dakhla in the disputed territory of Western Sahara, along the Atlantic coast, and Nador in the north-east and Tangier in the north-west, both on the Mediterranean. Since early 1985 the major ports have been controlled by the Office d'Exploitation des Ports (ODEP). In 1985 ODEP began modernizing port equipment and facilities in a two-year development plan. In the period to 1990 ODEP planned to spend 1,350m. dirhams, more than half of which was to finance the development of ports. In 1991 several projects were announced, including a new container terminal at Casablanca, at a cost of 610m. dirhams, a 160m. dirham coal terminal at Jorf Lasfar and modernization of port equipment at ports controlled by ODEP. The World Bank was to provide loans of US $99m. to ODEP and $33m. to the central Government for the financing of these projects. The volume of traffic through all ports in 1988 reached 39.6m. tons, an increase of 12.7% over the 1987 total. In 1990 the volume was 37.9m. tons. The major goods handled include hydrocarbons and phosphates, sulphur and ammonia, triple superphosphate and phosphoric acid, citrus and other fruit, and vegetables. Of the total cargo handled in 1988, 42% went through Casablanca, 17% through Jorf Lasfar, 15% through Safi and 12% through Mohammadia. The volume of cargo traffic through Moroccan ports increased to 40.5m. tons, in 1993; the 22.1m. tons of imports included 9.5m. tons of hydrocarbons and 3.9m. tons of cereals. In March 1994 work began on a new harbour at Dakhla in Western Sahara as a centre for coastal and deep-sea fishing, including a 1,300-ha free-trade zone. In March 1996 it was reported that ODEP planned to invest 1,700m. dirhams ($200m.) in port development over the period 1996–2000. Its plans included investment of 328m. dirhams for the purchase of equipment and 144m. dirhams for infrastructure development at Casablanca, 361m. dirhams at Dakhla and 145m. dirhams at Jorf Lasfar. ODEP reported a rise in its turnover of 23% to 1,127m. dirhams in the year to the end of September 1995. In February 1996 shipping firms reported severe congestion at Casablanca owing to the Government's campaign against smuggling, which led to the arrest of a number of senior customs officials. In November 1996 the Government launched an initiative to raise interest in a $300m. investment project to build a new multi-purpose deepwater port in Tangier. The aim of the project is to divert all merchandise traffic from the existing port, which is expected to suffer from serious congestion by 2002, despite short-term expansion projects in 1996–98. Bouygues of France signed a memorandum of understanding to construct and operate the new port, known as Tangier–Atlantique, but by the end of 1999 no further progress had been made in implementing the project. In November 1997 Spain agreed credits of $4m. towards the cost of a new port at Agadir. In February 1998 ODEP announced that it was planning to spend $220m. on modernizing and expanding the country's port facilities during 1998–2002. In 1999 the EIB made a loan of $28m. to assist this programme.

In late 2000 it was reported that work had begun on an $44m. extension to the east container terminal at Casablanca port scheduled to be completed in 2002.

The railways are operated by the Office National des Chemins de Fer (ONCF). In 1989 the company planned to invest nearly 1,000m. dirhams in rail development, including projects to double the Rabat–Kénitra line and the construction of a connection between Casablanca and the city's King Muhammad V airport. Also considered were an extension of the rapid transit system which runs between Casablanca and Rabat south to El Jadida, a rail link between Taourirt and Nador in the northeast, and a controversial plan to link Marrakesh and el-Aaiún, in Western Sahara. In mid-1992 it was announced that the ADB had agreed to contribute US $84m. towards an estimated $270m. programme to improve main railway routes, in particular the Casablanca–Fez line. In January 1997, following a two-and-a-half-year period of almost no new investment, it was reported that ONCF was to start work on a $591m. (5,200m. dirhams) four-year restructuring and investment plan after securing loans to cover part of it. The plan included rehabilitating installations, modernizing the rolling stock and reorganizing the company. In April ONCF awarded a contract to double the Kénitra–Meknès railway line to a local/Spanish consortium as part of the investment programme. The World Bank agreed in May to lend ONCF $85m. to expand the domestic network and purchase seven new locomotives, while in July the EIB approved a loan for rehabilitation and upgrading work on the Marrakesh–Casablanca and the Rabat–Fez–Oujda lines. The ADB has also pledged $85m. to support ONCF's investment programme. In September 1997 Cegelec of France was awarded contracts to electrify the Kénitra–Sidi Kacem line, improve lines serving Casablanca and rehabilitate the Sidi el Aidi–Oued Zem phosphate line. In October ONCF announced that it was interested in granting concessions to private investors to build and operate new railway lines. In February 1998 three French companies began a feasibility study financed by France for a 28-km metro for Casablanca. The $588m. project (aimed to ease congestion in Casablanca) has been under consideration for some years, but the Government has been unable to raise the necessary finance for it. In 1999 it was reported that a 120-km line from Taourit to Nador was under construction at a cost of 2,000m. dirhams. In 1998 ONCF reported profits of 1m. dirhams and announced that 11.8m. passengers and 28.3m. tons of freight were carried that year. Some 1,200m. dirhams were invested by the state in the railway network during 1998. In 1999 the rail network carried 11.9m. passengers and this figure increased to 13.1m. in 2000. Freight traffic rose to 28.5m. tons in 1999 but declined to 27.1m. in 2000. Only half of the 1,907 km of track is electrified, and Moroccan railways remain in need of considerable modernization and require major new investment. In April 2002, the Government announced plans to convert ONCF into a shareholding company to prepare for further sales in the railway sector.

The road network is well developed, comprising more than 60,000 km of road, of which 50.3% is paved. Most of the roads are built to design standards appropriate for a volume of traffic substantially in advance of that which they are currently carrying. In 1998 there were 1,111,846 passenger cars and 392,602 commercial vehicles in use, as well as 19,891 motorcycles and scooters. Tonnage carried by public road freight transport under the auspices of the Office National des Transports virtually doubled between 1976 and 1986, from 6.8m. tons to 13.4m. tons, and rose to an estimated 14.7m. tons in 1988. In 1991 the Government approved a decree permitting the Société Nationale des Autoroutes du Maroc to collect tolls on Moroccan motorways. The revenue received from the tolls on the Casablanca–Rabat motorway was to be used to finance the construction of the projected Tangier–Casablanca motorway. In April 1991 four international groups were invited to rebid for the construction of the central section of the Tangier–Casablanca motorway, between Rabat and Larache, and the contract was awarded to a group of Italian companies. The US $220m. road project was to be funded by the AFESD and Italy. The AFESD agreed to a grant of $1.7m. for a study of the Maghreb Unity highway linking Nouadhibou, in Mauritania, with Benghazi, in Libya. In March 1996 contractors submitted bids for a 50-km section of the Rabat–Fez motorway between Khemisset and Sidi Allal

Bahraoui, estimated to cost some $50m.–$60m. This was the fourth of five contracts for the motorway, and in August 1996 it was awarded to Spain's OCP Construcciones. An Italian consortium was working on the section between Meknès and Khemisset, under a $75m.-contract signed in November 1995. Invitations to bid for the final section of the Rabat–Fez motorway—a 15-km section from Sidi Allal Bahraoui to Rabat—were expected to be made in 1997. The EIB and the AFESD agreed long-term loans in 1995 to cover most of the cost of the Rabat–Fez motorway. In March 1995 Japan's Overseas Economic Co-operation Fund agreed to a loan of $86.7m. towards the cost of modernizing 2,400 km of roads throughout the country and of constructing roads linking central Morocco with the northern and southern provinces. The loan is to be repaid over 10 years with a 10-year grace period. The World Bank is also contributing $140m. to the $226m. road programme, parts of which are now under construction. In June the World Bank approved a $57.6m. loan for road maintenance and management. It was reported in March and April 1997 that the Ministry of Public Works was evaluating bids for a project to build a four-lane, 112-km motorway from Casablanca to Jorf Lasfar on a build-operate-transfer-basis, and that a technical study for a 560-km road along the Mediterranean coast was to be undertaken. In February 1998 the Government announced that it was proceeding with the construction of a Mediterranean coastal highway which would link Tangier with Saidia, near the border with Algeria. Much of the construction costs would be financed by the state, but certain stretches were to be privately financed on a build-operate-transfer basis. A 30 km section of the highway linking Tangier and Laksar S'ghir opened in May 2000.

In March 1998 bids were invited for a contract to build a highway between Casablanca and Azemmour, which forms part of the Casablanca–Jorf Lasfar motorway. Four local companies which were awarded the contract to build the first tranche started work on the 16-km stretch between Casablanca and Had Soualem in July 2001. Ten local and international groups have prequalified for the two remaining sections of road—the 35-km Had Soualem-Tnine Chtouka tranche and the 28-km Tnine Chtouka-El-Jadida section. In February 1998 work began on the construction of a motorway between Casablanca and Settat, a project part-financed by the AFESD and Japan's Overseas Economic Co-operation Fund. Japan is also helping to finance a 35-km motorway between Casablanca and Mohammadia. Early in 1999 Autoroutes du Maroc, a public-private partnership, announced new investment of $100m. to develop the country's road network, including highways linking Sidi el-Yamani to Tangier and Khemisset to Fez. The state-owned road transport company, Compagnie de Transports du Maroc-Lignes Nationales (CTM-LN), Morocco's biggest bus company, was privatized in 1993. The Government's remaining 18.9% holding in the company was sold on the Casablanca stock exchange in October 1994, raising $5.5m. The offer was nearly three times oversubscribed. In May 1995 the company announced a major expansion plan over the next three years, and in November claimed that it would double its profit in 1995 to 23.9m. dirhams ($2.9m.). The company also increased its capital by 23% to 122.6m. dirhams ($14.7m.) in order to purchase new buses. In 1999 LSA Grupo of Spain won a 15-year contract to manage the bus network in the city of Marrakesh.

In February 1996 plans to construct a fixed link across the Strait of Gibraltar received new impetus when Spain and Morocco issued a joint communiqué stating their commitment to the project and announcing that they had agreed that the fixed link would be a tunnel rather than a bridge, the latter option previously favoured by Morocco. The link would involve building a 22-km single rail tunnel 900 m under the seabed; a second main tunnel would be added after the first no longer satisfied demand. The first phase, estimated to take five years and cost US $403m., would be to dig an exploratory tunnel in order to gain a better understanding of technical difficulties. It was hoped that the EU would cover just over one-third of the cost of this phase, with the private sector financing the remainder under a concession scheme. The tunnel link was expected to create jobs in Morocco and Spain and encourage the establishment of passenger and freight transport networks from other European countries to the tunnel's Spanish terminal. Prelimi-

nary investigations to determine the technical feasibility of the proposed tunnel were carried out in November 1998.

There are 10 major airports in Morocco, as well as about 50 landing strips for light aircraft. In addition, el-Aaiún in Western Sahara has an airport. In 1991 a four-year programme to expand and modernize Moroccan airports, at an estimated cost of 1,200m. dirhams, was announced. The Office National des Aéroports (ONDA) and the ADB were each to provide a 25% loan to finance the project. The remaining 50% of the cost of the programme was to be negotiated. Marrakesh-Menara airport reopened in August 1991, after the extension of the runway and work on airport buildings at a cost of US $8m. A new passenger terminal was opened in July 1992 at Casablanca's King Muhammad V airport. The airport handled 1.8m. passengers in 1991 and it was forecast that some 3.3m. passengers would pass through the airport in 1993. The ONDA plans the creation of a major industrial and commercial zone, occupying 200 ha, as the latest phase in the expansion of the airport. In 1993 a $36m. contract to build an aircraft maintenance centre at the airport was awarded to a group of US firms, led by Westinghouse Electric Corpn. In December 1992 the ADB approved a loan of $102m. to support the ONDA's plans to upgrade the infrastructure of Morocco's airports. In late 1998 the ONDA began to implement longstanding plans for a new airport at Nador, in the north-east, estimated to cost $45m. In November 1999 the AFESD granted a loan worth $32.7m. to finance a project to extend and modernize King Muhammad V airport. In 2001 the African Development Bank approved a loan to finance some of the project's foreign exchange costs, and ONDA launched the tender for the construction of a second runway. There are also plans for new terminal buildings and a new ground control system which will bring the airport in line with International Civil Aviation Organization (ICAO) standards. The total number of passengers handled by Morocco's airports is forecast to rise from 6.8m. in 2001 to 27m. in 2020. Royal Air Maroc (RAM), which was formed in 1953, is the national airline. It operates services to European and African countries, as well as to the USA. In 1988 RAM handled 1.7m. passengers, compared with 1.2m. in 1983. The number of passengers travelling by RAM increased steadily in the early 1990s, reaching 2.3m. in 1994. Tourism accounts for a significant proportion of passengers carried, although flights for business-related purposes are increasingly important. Total freight carried by air has also continued to rise. As at November 1996 RAM operated 27 aircraft, most of them Boeings. The airline's current renewal and expansion plan envisaged the purchase of two new aircraft every year until 2001. Two Boeing 737–800 aircraft ordered in 1996 were delivered in May 1998 with financing arranged by the Banque Nationale de Paris. Also in May RAM signed a co-operation agreement with Spain's national carrier, Iberia, and early in 1999 it was reported that the company wished to sign a partnership agreement with Germany's Lufthansa. RAM also signed an agreement to operate joint flights with Gulf Air, initially between Casablanca and Abu Dhabi, and in February 1999 became one of the first companies to begin regular flights to the newly opened Gaza International Airport. The company announced a sharp increase in profits during 1997/98 and aimed to carry 3.5m. passengers during 1998/99. The company has embarked on a programme to update and expand its fleet. Boeing has agreed to supply 20 medium-range and three long-range aircraft by 2012 at a cost of $1,100m. Plans for a partial privatization of RAM, involving the sale of a 40% stake in the company on the Casablanca Stock Exchange, have been postponed until 2002. An independent Moroccan company, Regional Airlines, was set up in October 1997 and operates domestic flights to six local airports and international flights to Spain and Portugal. It was announced by government officials in 2001 that RAM was expected to sign a contract with Airbus Industrie for the purchase of four A321 aircraft. With the capacity to carry up to 220 passengers, each aircraft is to be used on high-traffic-density routes including the Casablanca-Paris service.

Television and most radio services are controlled by the state, which runs a nationwide television network (Radiodiffusion-Télévision Marocaine) and nine regional radio stations broadcasting in the Arabic, French and Berber languages. There is also a commercial radio network, which broadcasts from Tangier and Nador to North Africa (Radio Méditerranée Internationale). In 1997 there were 6.6m. radios and 3.1m. television sets in Morocco. A commercial television channel for subscribers opened in 1989. In December 1994 a contract was signed between the Office National des Postes et Télécommunications (ONPT) and Siemens of Germany to install 230,000 telephone lines as part of ONPT's programme to install a total of 400,000 new lines. The company planned to increase telephone density from 3.5 lines to 10 lines per 100 inhabitants by 2000. Negotiations were taking place with Ericsson of Sweden and Alcatel of France for the remaining lines. Under an agreement signed with ONPT in March 1995 AT&T of the USA is preparing a plan for the modernization of the country's telecommunications network. ONPT stated that it wants to double the capacity of its network and introduce the latest technology. AT&T will study ways to digitalize the network and expand the use of fibre-optic links and satellites. When the study has been completed AT&T will begin negotiating to carry out part of the recommendations. In early 1996 ONPT announced that it was to invest 4,300m. dirhams (US $505.7m.) in that year on a programme to modernize and expand its network. There were plans for an additional 250,000 switching units to extend the automation system to more than 300 towns, the expansion of the GSM network to remote provinces, and increasing the number of subscribers from 1m. to 1.3m. The EIB is funding fibre optic-links between Tétouan and Agadir and a link across the Strait of Gibraltar. In February 1996 it was reported that Glenayre Electronics of the USA had been awarded a $2.6m. contract to supply and install a pager system for ONPT, initially serving 50,000 subscribers in Rabat, Casablanca, Tangier, Marrakesh, Agadir, Tétouan, Fez and Larache, to be completed in March 1997. In April 1996 it was announced that, as part of a project to restructure and modernize the country's telecommunications network funded by the World Bank, Société Eton of France had been awarded a $1m. contract to supply connection equipment, and Acome/CEAC a $2.2m. contract to supply cable.

In June 1997 the Chamber of Representatives adopted a new law heralding the liberalization of the fixed and mobile telecommunications sector. In February 1998 the state-owned ONPT was divided up and a new enterprise, Itissalat al-Maghrib (Maroc Télécom), with a monopoly of telecommunications, created as a preliminary to privatization. With the approach of privatization the company, valued at US $5,000m., has taken various measures to improve its competitiveness. In particular, the number of its mobile phone subscribers increased sharply from 400,000 in January 2000 to 2m. by the end of that year. The company also has 1.4m. fixed line subscribers and a monopoly over this sector until the end of 2001. The company's profits rose by 55% in 1999 and by 46% during the first six months of 2000. In late December 2000 the Government announced that a 35% stake in Maroc Télécom had been sold to Vivendi-Universal of France for $2,200m. A further 14% would be floated on the Casablanca Stock Exchange and foreign exchanges during 2002 with the state retaining control over the remaining 51%. Having completed a contract for the expansion of the GSM network in the main northern cities, Maroc Télécom signed a. further agreement with US telecoms equipment supplier Motorola for $47m. in 2001 in a network infrastructure expansion contract. The telecoms regulator, Agence Nationale de Réglementation des Télécommunications (ANRT), issued an international tender for the second fixed-line licence and plans to award a new international licence in 2002. Companies interested in operating the new fixed-line licence were invited apply by October 2001. A $100m. loan from the African Development Bank was approved in April 2001 to fund an information infrastructure sector development programme which is jointly financed by the World Bank. The new two-year scheme aims to introduce competition throughout the telecommunications sector and to strengthen its regulatory framework. Emphasis will be given to lowering the costs of all services and improving access to rural and deprived areas.

The sale of the second GSM licence, originally planned for 1997, took place in July 1999 generating $1,100m., more than twice the sum expected when the sale was planned. The 15-year licence was awarded to Medi Telecom, a consortium led by Telefonica of Spain together with Portugal Telecom and Moroccan investors, which pledged to invest $660m. over the following four years. The network became operational in March 2000 and had 490,000 subscribers by the end of the year. In May it was reported that three firms, Gulfsat Maghreb, Argos and Space Com had been awarded licence for the very small aperture terminal (VSAT) satellite systems by the telecoms regulator, the Agence Nationale de Réglementation des Télécommunications (ANRT), for which they paid a total of $9.3m. Several thousand users were expected within two to three years. A third private GSM licence is anticipated to be offered and in operation by 2003. Following the award in 2000 of a licence to operate satellite telecom links, Morocco Nortis, a subsidiary of the Norwegian company Telenor, launched a new high-speed internet service for businesses in October 2001.

BANKING AND FINANCE

Morocco's foreign debt rose sharply during the second half of the 1970s. In October 1980, in an attempt to control its escalating debt burden, Morocco negotiated a three-year loan from the IMF, totalling US $1,000m., the largest loan ever granted to a developing country by the Fund at that time. The terms of the loan were modified in 1982, when the progress of the economy failed to meet IMF conditions. By 1983 Morocco's debt had reached unmanageable proportions, and a new IMF agreement was negotiated as part of a debt-rescheduling arrangement with all of Morocco's creditors. Outstanding debt to the 'Paris Club' creditor countries and the Arab states was rescheduled in 1983, but negotiations with creditor banks continued until 1985. In 1985 Morocco negotiated a new arrangement with the IMF, but this encountered difficulties, as Morocco failed to achieve IMF targets in early 1986. Eventually, a new programme, with less stringent terms, was agreed in November 1986, to run until April 1988. The 'Paris Club' and the creditor banks agreed to reschedule debt repayments until the end of the IMF agreement. Meanwhile, during 1984–87 the World Bank provided finance for several sectoral adjustment programmes within a general programme to restructure and reorient the Moroccan economy. The major elements of this restructuring programme included· a shift to export-oriented production, privatization, a reduction in public expenditure, fiscal reform and tighter control over the economy as a whole. In September 1987 the World Bank declared that Morocco was 'well-poised' for economic success, as a result of its stabilization and structural adjustment programmes, and it subsequently increased its lending, to make Morocco the Bank's third largest recipient after Turkey and Pakistan, during 1987. In mid-1988 the IMF approved a new stand-by facility of SDR 220m. for the period from June 1988 to the end of 1989. The Fund generally approved of Morocco's macroeconomic performance, but was somewhat critical of fiscal policy implementation. Debt owing to the 'Paris Club' of creditor countries was rescheduled in October 1988 and again in September 1990. In December 1988 the World Bank made further finances available as part of the structural adjustment support to assist Morocco with debt management. In early 1989 negotiations began for the rescheduling of $1,400m. owing to the commercial banks of the 'London Club' and continued until April 1990, when an agreement was reached. The new accord rescheduled about $3,200m. of medium-term debt over a period of up to 20 years and reduced the interest to be paid on the debt. The existing IMF stand-by agreement expired in December 1989 but was renewed for a further eight months in July 1990. In May 1991 Spain rescheduled official debt within Morocco's 'Paris Club' accords, which included credits provided by the concessionary lending agency Fondo de Ayuda al Desarrollo, repayable over 20 years. Total debt to Spain was then estimated at 110,000m. pesetas ($1,012m.). In July the World Bank approved a $235m. loan to the financial sector, which would permit Morocco to develop domestic financial markets and to invest in private export-orientated industries. Morocco is also one of a small group of heavily-indebted countries to benefit from a World Bank Export Credit Enhanced Leverage, which provides bank guarantees and some funds for private-sector projects already receiving support from credit agencies. According to the Ministry of Finance, Morocco's external debt at the end of 1991 totalled $21,000m., of which $10,600m. was outstanding to 'Paris Club' governments, $3,600m. to the 'London Club', $3,300m. to the World Bank, $1,600m. to the USA and $600m. to the IMF.

Morocco's economic prospects improved significantly in late 1991, when Saudi Arabia and other Gulf states agreed to cancel bilateral debts estimated at around $3,600m. In February 1992 the IMF approved a stand-by credit authorizing drawings of up to SDR 91.98m. ($129m.) to support the Government's economic programme from January 1992 to March 1993. At the end of this period the Government expected to be able to return to the international capital markets and to make no further demands on IMF resources. In February the 'Paris Club' governments agreed to reschedule official debt worth $1,500m., and in March the World Bank approved a $275m. structural adjustment loan, the final loan in Morocco's economic rehabilitation, according to the country's official news agency. In August 1992, under the terms of the 'Paris Club' agreement signed in February, the USA announced that it would reschedule bilateral debt worth $101.1m. incurred up to 1983. Some $32.5m. in official development assistance was to be repaid over 20 years with a 10-year grace period and $68.6m. in consolidated debt and arrears was to be repaid over 15 years with an eight-year grace period. Figures released in May 1993 by the Ministry of Finance revealed that Morocco's external debt in 1993 was $21,305m. 'Paris Club' member states accounted for $10,549m. (about one-half of the total debt), the 'London Club' $3,525m. (17%) and international financial institutions $5,700m. (27%). Debt-service repayments in 1992 increased to $3,000m., but were projected to decrease from $2,848m. in 1993 to $2,126m. in 2000. Announcing the 1995 budget in December 1994, the Minister of Finance, Mourad Cherif, stated that the cost of servicing the external debt remained a burden with repayments in 1994 equivalent to 4.2% of gross national product. In June 1993 the Ministry of Finance introduced new rules whereby Moroccan banks or private enterprises were allowed to raise credits with foreign financial institutions to finance imports of goods and services without prior authorization.

In 1992 Morocco became the major recipient of concessionary financing from the Caisse Française de Développement, with loan commitments during the year totalling 274.5m. francs, compared with 160m. francs for Algeria and 110m. francs for Tunisia. In November it was announced that France would increase the value of its 1992 financial protocol to 1,220m. francs from 800m. francs. In mid-1993, however, the French Ministry of Finance indicated that the level of support offered under the 1993 protocol would probably be less than that for 1992. In December Spain agreed to provide a new five-year credit programme worth US $1,056m., renewing the credit line originally signed in 1988. The EU was to lend Morocco a total of ECU 438m. in 1992–96, together with funds for structural adjustment and EIB loans for the Europe-Maghreb gas pipeline. In February 1995 it was reported that Spain had renewed a credit line of $1,125m. as part of an economic and financial co-operation agreement signed in 1994. The credit line involved $375m. to be disbursed in five equal annual tranches and $750m. in export credits.

In late 1995 the Ministry of Finance estimated debt-servicing at 35% of foreign currency income and indicated that it was considering ways of reducing debt-service payments for the financial year starting 1 July 1996, including debt-equity swaps, refinancing and debt buy-backs. In January 1996 representatives of Morocco and France signed a series of bilateral agreements under which France agreed to forgive or convert 1,000m. French francs (US $203m.) of Moroccan debt, and promised further aid and technical assistance. France agreed to forgive 400m. francs of government debt on condition that this money be invested in development projects in the Rif (Morocco's main marijuana producing region); a further 600m. francs of sovereign debt was to be converted into equity of financial support for French companies investing in Morocco. In addition France would provide 340m. francs to assist with water and railway development projects, offer training and assistance to modernize and liberalize the administration, and help in the development of the country's tourist industry. Under the terms of the final accord, French and Moroccan investors were guaranteed equal treatment in both countries. France agreed to offer further financial aid in May, following a visit by King Hassan to Paris. The Caisse Française de Développement was to underwrite government bonds issued on the international market to the value of 1,500m. francs, and France would provide 1,200m.

francs in aid over the next two years to support the Government's campaign against drugs smuggling. France's aid budget to Morocco is currently 1,500m. francs a year. Although the underwriting agreement was welcomed, it was unlikely to have a significant impact on the country's overall foreign debt. During the visit of the then Spanish Prime Minister, Felipe González, in February 1996, the disbursement of a 150,000m. peseta ($1,198m.) credit package for the period to 2000 was discussed together with options for easing the terms of Morocco's $1,400m. debt to Spain. In October Spain agreed to convert $50m. of bilateral debt into investments in a similar deal to that concluded with France. In October 1997 France agreed to convert a further 1,400m. francs ($245m.) of bilateral debt into investments along the lines of the initiative concluded in January 1996 (see above). Morocco's total bilateral debt to France was estimated at $4,000m. At the same time, Spain offered to convert a further $38m. of its bilateral debt into local investment. In March Italy offered to convert $75m. of debt into local investment, and it was reported that similar debt-conversion deals were being discussed with Germany, Austria and the United Kingdom. During a visit to France by Prime Minister el-Youssoufi in October 1998, the French Government agreed to convert a further 700m. francs of debt into investments. At the same time, the United Kingdom agreed to make $42m. of 'Paris Club' debt available for conversion into equity. In early 1999 it was reported that Italy had agreed to convert some $100m. of bilateral debt into investments and to provide a further $16m. to enable small and medium-sized Moroccan firms to buy Italian exports. In March 2000 France agreed to convert a further 700m. francs of Moroccan debt into local investments. In December 1997 Morocco returned to international capital markets for the first time since 1981 when Commerzbank of Germany and Sumitomo Bank Ltd of Japan started arranging a five-year loan of $200m. The Euroloan was fully subscribed when it closed in February 1998. A Eurobond issue of around $500m., postponed from 1998 due to unfavourable market conditions, is expected to take place in 2002. Merrill Lynch and BNP Paribas were selected for the mandate to manage the issue.

In March 1998 Moody's Investors Service and Standard Poor's awarded Morocco its first international credit ratings a positive development that should enable the Government to raise additional funds on the market. According to the Ministry of Finance, Morocco's foreign debt fell from $18,000m. at the end of 1999 to $15,360m. at the end of 2000. Some independent sources, however, give somewhat higher figures estimating that debt levels fell from $19,500m. at the end of 1999 to $18,000m. at the end of 2000. The bulk of the debt is publicly guaranteed medium- and long-term debt of which 38% is owed to bilateral official creditors, 31% to multilateral agencies and the remaining 31% to private creditors, mainly commercial banks. While the proportion of the debt owed to bilateral official creditors is declining, the proportion owed to private creditors is increasing. According to World Bank figures the total cost of servicing the debt fell from $3,639m. in 1994 to $2,797m. in 1998. Principal repayments on medium- and long-term debt fell from $2,246m. in 1994 to $1,773m. in 1998 and interest payments fell from $1,393m. in 1994 to $1,024m. in 1998. The debt service ratio decreased from 31.8% in 1994 to 19.7% in 1998 and was expected to stabilize at around 19%–20% in 2000–01. Total foreign reserves rose from $3,831m. in 1995 to $5,882m. in 1999.

In December 1995 it was reported that the ADB had agreed a loan of US $225m., repayable over 12 years with a five-year grace period to support financial reforms in 1995–96. The loan agreement required the creation of a foreign exchange market, the establishment of an indirect system of currency controls, and the further development of commercial financing instruments. In January 1996 a committee comprising members of the Bank Al-Maghrib, the Ministry of Finance and commercial banks announced a number of reforms. Interest rates were freed to encourage competition between banks and to make it easier for companies to secure loans, bank reserve requirements were reduced by 5% to 15% of sight deposits and the proportion of a bank's equity that can be lent to a single client was increased from 7% to 10%. In April the Bank Al-Maghrib informed local banks that it would cease currency fixing on 2 May and allow banks to trade in foreign currencies from that date. However, local banks were reported to have requested a delay in the start of a domestic foreign exchange market as they needed time to obtain clarification on guidelines for certain types of transactions. Early in 2000 Moroccan exporters expressed growing concern about the strength of the dirham and some called for a more competitive rate. The Government, however, remained opposed to devaluation and pointed to the benefits of its policy of maintaining the relative strength of the dirham, notably low inflation. However, in April 2001 the Ministry of Finance announced a 5% devaluation in the dirham, a move regarded by some analysts as overdue and not large enough to have a significant effect on the economy

Morocco's central bank, the Bank Al-Maghrib, is the sole issuer of currency, holds and administers the State's foreign currency reserves, controls the commercial banking sector and advises the Government on its financial policies. Associated with the bank are six specialized credit institutions with specific sectoral responsibilities. There are 15 commercial banks, of which one of the most important is the Banque Marocaine du Commerce Extérieur SA (BMCE). In 1989 a new development bank, the Bank al-Amal, was established; three-quarters of its capital was to be made available in shares to Moroccans working abroad to encourage more investment from the expatriate community. The Banque Centrale Populaire (BCP, also known as Crédit Populaire du Maroc), which has specialized in handling the remittances of migrant workers for many years, was to be joined by the major Moroccan private bank, the Banque Commerciale du Maroc (BCM), which in 1989 acquired 10% of the capital of the Banque Méditerranéenne de Dépôts (BMD) in order to attract the savings of the 27,000 Moroccan workers in France who use the BMD. Several other Moroccan banks have heeded an appeal from the Minister of Finance and are extending their international activities. In February 1992 it was reported that the IFC had arranged a US $110m. credit line for four commercial banks (BCM, BMCE, Crédit du Maroc and Wafabank), the major source of term finance for the private sector. The credit lines were to be used to make five 10-year loans to small and medium-sized private-sector firms. In December the Government approved a banking law, which increased the scope for regulation in domestic banking. All local credit institutions were brought under the legislation, which also gave greater protection for savers and borrowers. In addition, the law codified rules governing business banks and other credit institutions previously excluded from legislation. In the same month it was announced that Wafabank, one of Morocco's leading privately-owned banks, was increasing its capital through the issue of shares on the Casablanca stock exchange. Other banks have been seeking foreign shareholders and increasing their capital to meet the growing demand for local banking services as the economy develops. In June 1993 the Banco Exterior de España became the first wholly-owned foreign company authorized to open a subsidiary in Morocco since the country won its independence. The BMCE took a small stake in the Banco Exterior de España and opened a branch in Madrid under a reciprocal arrangement. The long-established Citibank Maghreb offers retail banking services and has the same status as a local bank. Nevertheless, the Central Bank has proved cautious in licensing foreign institutions. In August 1993 it was reported that the Banco Central Hispano-Americano of Spain was to purchase a 15% interest in Morocco's largest bank, the BCM, subject to the approval of the Moroccan and Spanish monetary authorities, in an agreement valued at $48.8m. In October 1994 the Minister of Privatization announced the sale of most of the state's 50.4% holding in the BMCE. Some 14% of the bank's shares were offered for sale on the Casablanca stock exchange in January 1995 and another 26% were offered for sale by international tender in April, one-half restricted to local non-bank institutions and the remainder was open to all bidders. The sale of 26% of BMCE shares raised $144m., 42% more than the Government's minimum price. The new shareholders included the Royale Marocaine d'Assurances, London-based Morgan Grenfell and Co, and Morgan Stanley of the USA. The last publicly-owned shares in the BMCE were sold to the private sector in May 1997. In March 1996 the BMCE issued a global depository receipt (GDR) to boost share capital. The issue was more than four times oversubscribed and raised US $52m.; 48% of the issue was placed in Europe, 30% in the USA and 22% in

Asia. It represented the first international equity issue from Morocco and North Africa and the largest GDR transaction in the Arab world. Although small on an international scale, it was significant in Morocco where total foreign investment was estimated at $200m. Financial analysts argued that demand was high because investors were attracted by the progress made by the bank since its privatization. The funds raised by the offer will be used to expand the bank's lending activities in Morocco. In 1995 the BMCE registered assets of 33,957m. dirhams and net profits increased by 19.2% to 301m. dirhams in that year. In March 1998 BMCE established its own merchant bank, capitalized at $10.2m. Later in the year a number of foreign banks acquired shares in BMCE, while the bank reduced its holding in Crédit du Maroc to 20.25%. Early in 2000 the bank opened a representative office in London as part of its plan to establish a number of overseas offices, which was announced in 1999. In April 2002 the BMCE restructured its operations; it will be managed by an executive committee headed by the bank's president and will include a retail banking unit, major corporate accounts unit, and an international unit to manage the bank's foreign subsidiaries and representative offices. BMCE's capital stands at $139m. and its domestic network includes 201 branches and 2,850 employees.

The Government confirmed that it would privatize the BCP and the BNDE before 1999. BNDE was put on the market in May 1998 when the Government announced the sale of a minority stake in the bank. No bidder met the tender requirements, however, and it was generally agreed that the shares had been overpriced. In early 1999 the Government stated that the sale of 51% stake in the company would proceed, but by early 2000 no date had been set. In March 2001 BCP officials announced that they would soon invite bids for the role of advisor for the initial phase of the bank's privatization. The Government plans to float 20% of the bank's capital on the Casablanca Stock Exchange before the end of 2001. At the end of 2000 a parliamentary inquiry into the state-owned Crédit Immobilier et Hôtelier, which has debts totalling some 11,000m. dirhams, accused the bank's directors of poor management and widespread fraud and misappropriation of funds (see History). Banque Marocaine pour le Commerce et l'Industrie (BMCI), owned by BNP Paribas, has acquired a 99.4% stake in ABN AMRO Maroc. Under the terms of the sale, which was agreed in June 2001, BMCI will take over a network of 20 offices based in 14 Moroccan cities serving 24,000 customers.

The Government launched the first issue of its new privatization bond in January 1996. The issue originally had been planned by the Ministry of Privatization for November 1995, but was delayed when the Ministry of Finance claimed jurisdiction on the grounds that it would constitute sovereign debt. The bonds may be exchanged for shares in any of the companies to be privatized on the stock exchange in the next three years, and to make the bonds attractive to the public, holders are given priority access to shares in newly-privatized companies. Individual investors were offered the majority of the bonds, while companies, especially investment funds, were offered the remainder. The issue was handled by the BCM and Wafabank. Some 1,700m. dirhams (US $200m.) was raised through the sale of the first issue which was oversubscribed by 25%. The first test of the new bond came in March 1996, when the Government offered for sale on the stock exchange 25% of its stake in SAMIR. The offer was fully subscribed with about three-quarters of the buyers using privatization bonds. A second tranche of privatization bonds was issued in May under the same terms and conditions as the first tranche in January, although this time one-half of the bonds were reserved for institutional investment. Preliminary results indicated that demand for the second issue was lower than for the first. The Ministry of Privatization had hoped to raise 1,000m. dirhams from the second issue. However, in December 1998 the Government appeared to have decided to end the policy of issuing privatization bonds when it was announced that the Treasury would reimburse holders of existing bonds after they reach maturity.

From the beginning of 1999 the Bank al-Maghrib authorized all Moroccan banks to invest up to 10% of their equity in the Euro which became the major currency for Morocco's external transactions in January 2002. Transactions will continue to be carried out in Sterling, Swiss francs, Danish krone and Norwegian krone and separate rates for these currencies.

By 1992 the volume of transactions on the Casablanca stock exchange had risen to 1,520m. dirhams, but this increased more than threefold in 1993 (to 4,870m. dirhams) as a result of the privatization of state companies, including CTM-LN and Cior. In July 1993 it was reported that a number of decrees had been approved to convert the Casablanca exchange into a private company with stock held by brokers, to create new stock-trading bodies, to channel small savers' funds into share issues and unit trusts, and to create a stock exchange commission. A major boost to stock exchange activity in 1994 was the issue of shares worth 1,500m. dirhams in Morocco's leading private company, ONA. Local companies have turned increasingly to the stock market to raise capital through local share offers. In January 1995 the General Tire and Rubber Co raised its capital by 20% in a stock market offering, becoming the first newly-privatized company to do so. In November 1994 the bourse director forecast a turnover of 9,000m. dirhams in 1994, almost double the figure for 1993. In new moves to modernize the exchange, the Government announced in November 1994 that it had authorized the operations of the country's first stockbrokers. An agreement signed in February 1995 provided for the Société Française des Bourses and Société Interprofessionelle de Compensation des Valeurs Mobilières to conduct a US $1.2m. study on the modernization and computerization of the stock exchange and to establish a central depositary and clearing house. The stock market crises affecting several Asian countries during the second half of 1997 had little impact on the Casablanca stock exchange because only some 5% of transactions involved foreign investors. In mid-1997 the Société Marocaine de Dépôt et Crédit and the Crédit Immobilier et Hôtelier both issued bonds on the exchange. At the end of 1997 the exchange began a campaign to attract new listings, especially from small and medium-sized firms, and aimed to increase the number of companies listed from the current 49 to 100. The results, however, were disappointing, partly because of delays in the privatization programme. The number of companies listed remained at around 50; trading volumes on the exchange remained low during 1999–2000 and ended down 7.4% in 2001. Foreign participation is very limited (around 10% of total capitalization) despite the absence of any restrictions. Two new indices were launched in January 2002—the Most Active Shares Index (MADEX), which will monitor the 10 most liquid stocks on the exchange, and the Moroccan All-Share Index (MASI), which will replace the benchmark CSE index covering all stocks listed.

In August 1991 Tangier became the kingdom's first 'offshore' banking zone. It is intended to attract major international banks, and their local operations must have a minimum capital of US $500,000. Banks are offered exemption from corporation tax for 15 years, and during this period they pay a $25,000 annual licence fee. The zone is intended to compete with other Mediterranean 'offshore' zones to attract capital into the kingdom. In April 1992 Crédit Lyonnais of France became the first bank to announce its participation in the zone followed by the Banque Nationale de Paris, both with local partners. In January 1995 Attijari International, a joint venture between the local BCM and Spain's BCH capitalized at $3m., became the third bank to open in the zone. In mid-1994 it was reported that the new Euratlas Capital Development Fund, and a new investment bank, the Maghreb International Bank, would also be based in the Tangier zone.

DEVELOPMENT

The 1978 Five-Year Development Plan never came into effect, largely because of the disruption caused to the economy by the war in Western Sahara and the fall in phosphate revenues after 1975. Instead, a three-year transitional plan, which was to emphasize agriculture and industry, and attempt to reduce public expenditure, was introduced as part of the austerity measures adopted by the Government. The target for annual GDP growth was set at a modest 4.6%. Only 3% annual growth was, however, achieved in 1978 and 1979. In April 1981 a new Five-Year Development Plan came into operation, whose general aims were similar to that of its predecessor, but which envisaged a more rapid rate of GDP growth, at 6.5% a year. The level of investment was overambitious and, following the decision to

reschedule the country's external debt in 1983, many of the Plan's targets were abandoned. The Government was obliged to make severe reductions in public expenditure in order to satisfy the terms of the IMF programme. Not only were the 1983 budget commitments for capital expenditure cut by more than 20%, but even the revised targets for 1984 were reduced further. All major projects were postponed, except those already under way and likely to enhance export earnings or import savings.

The proposed 1986–88 Three-Year Plan, announced in April 1985, suggested further cuts in expenditure. Investment was to be reduced from the 1984 level of 20% of GDP to only 16.7%, while it was projected that GDP would rise by 2.9% per year. However, in late 1985 it was announced that this transitional plan was to be delayed, and a new set of proposals for a more expansionary programme was produced. These plans, however, were also deferred, largely as a result of IMF pressure, and a policy of bringing government spending more closely into balance with revenues was eventually pursued. Measures geared mainly towards tighter spending controls and the gradual reform of the fiscal system helped to reduce the treasury deficit in 1986. In October 1987 a new Five-Year Plan for 1988–92 was presented, in which 52% of funding was expected to come from the private sector. A large proportion of the investment funds was to be directed towards the newly-formed local authorities (collectivités locales), which were allocated 36,000m. dirhams. The Plan was expected to transform the current account deficit into a surplus, equivalent to 2.9% of GDP by 1992, and to enable exports to increase by 5.5% per annum. It also aimed to mobilize domestic savings for investment at a rate of 16.6% of GDP per year and to create jobs for the estimated 300,000 people entering the labour market every year. The Plan also included a reform of the public sector, envisaging the privatization of many state companies. Appropriate legislation for a privatization programme was approved by the Chamber of Representatives in April 1988 and came into force from January 1990. The six-year privatization programme was subsequently extended beyond 1995.

The 1989 budget aimed to reduce further the budget deficit, mainly by increasing tax revenue, and to limit the increase in overall state expenditure to around 7%. In the event, however, revenues failed to increase as expected, and the budget deficit was greater than had been anticipated. The treasury deficit in 1989 was equivalent to 5.7% of GDP, rather than the projected 4.4%. The 1990 budget, which had been endorsed by the Chamber of Representatives at the end of 1989, was radically revised during early 1990, while a variety of austerity measures were implemented, including a devaluation of the dirham in an attempt to improve the balance-of-payments deficit.

In accordance with the anticipated results of the 1988–92 Five-Year Plan, the main economic objectives for 1991 were to increase the rate of GDP growth to 4%–4.5%, a reduction in the annual rate of inflation to 5% (from a rate of 7%–8% in 1990) and a reduction of the budget deficit to 2% of GDP. The rise in investment in 1990 produced a more optimistic outlook for 1991. In early 1991 the Government announced that domestic savings would be encouraged, that investment would be made more efficient and that foreign trade and the public and financial sectors would be reformed, in an attempt to realize the year's economic objectives. The budget proposals for 1992 envisaged a substantial rise in social spending. Education was allocated 1,600m. dirhams (an increase of 21%), and health 552m. dirhams (an increase of more than 25%). Defence spending was to rise by 13.6%, to 10,000m. dirhams. Total spending was projected at 86,440m. dirhams, 5.5% higher than for 1991, and the deficit was to remain stable, at 1,450m. dirhams. To increase revenues, it was forecast that direct taxation would rise by 23.8%, and indirect taxes by 15.3%.

The budget proposals for 1993 envisaged a 6% increase in GDP. Overall revenue was expected to rise to 77,220m. dirhams, despite reductions in taxation. Expenditure was forecast at 80,000m. dirhams. Priority was to be given to education, public health, employment, irrigation and electric power generation. A reduction of the budget deficit was forecast, to 1% in 1993, compared with 2% in 1992 and 3% in 1991. Inflation was regarded as stable at 5.7% and foreign reserves had risen. Public investment was to increase by 11%. Debts totalling 2,700m. dirhams owed by farmers were to be rescheduled, and the

Government was to pay off public-sector arrears worth 2,603m. dirhams to ease cash-flow problems besetting local suppliers. Some 800m. dirhams was allocated to increase youth employment, and more than 15,000 jobs were to be created in public administration. Under the 1994 budget proposals, expenditure was projected to increase to 110,553m. dirhams. Of recurrent expenditure of 47,111m. dirhams, 12,900m. dirhams were allocated to education, and 9,400m. dirhams to defence. Revenues were projected at 105,352m. dirhams, including 23,719m. dirhams from indirect taxes, 17,098m. dirhams from direct taxes and 18,002m. dirhams from customs duties. The increase in recurrent expenditure was to be financed by an estimated 16% increase in tax revenues. The total projected deficit was 5,202m. dirhams. The Minister of Finance reported that debt-reservicing costs would increase by 17.3% in 1994, to 27,168m. dirhams. There was speculation that the Government's commitment to keep the budget deficit to 1.5% of GDP would be difficult to achieve because of pressure on state spending to maintain social stability. Under the 1995 budget, announced in December 1994, state spending was to be cut in most sectors in order to bring the budget deficit under control, a major priority for the Government. The Minister of Finance announced that the 1995 deficit would be around 7,000m. dirhams (US $781m.) and insisted that recourse to bank lending had to remain at reasonable levels. Official figures forecast revenues of 88,900m. dirhams in 1995 and expenditure of 91,471m. dirhams. Current spending was forecast to rise only slightly in an attempt to halt inflationary pressures in the public sector. The figure given for inflation was 4%, but other official sources put it at 5.1% in 1994. Investment spending was cut from 19,147m. dirhams in 1994 to 16,624m. dirhams in 1995. Receipts from the privatization programme, estimated at 3,500m. dirhams ($391m.) in 1995 were to be allocated to financing the investment budget and special provisions. Foreign investment was expected to reach $700m. in 1995, which, it was hoped would help cover the current account deficit. In order to reduce state spending, private sector involvement in infrastructure development would be extended to sectors such as telecommunications and communications. The budget also included incentives for stock market investment, with a reduction of the tax on share earnings from 15% to 10%. While the budget was welcomed by the business community, it was criticized by the opposition because it offered little help to the majority of the population. In late 1995 the Government approved a mini-budget for January–June 1996 to bridge the gap between December 1995 and the start of the new financial year in July 1996. Expenditure was projected at 47,900m. dirhams, of which the major item was debt-servicing and repayment, forecast at 13,700m. dirhams. Revenue was projected at 43,400m. dirhams, of which 13.2m. dirhams would be provided by indirect taxes and 5,800m. dirhams from customs duties. Value-added tax was to be raised to 20% to compensate for an anticipated fall in income and corporate taxes. Revenue from customs duties was also projected to decline as the Government began to comply with the GATT. The projected deficit was 4,500m. dirhams and was expected to be somewhat lower than the actual figure for the same period in 1995, which was higher than planned owing to the severe drought. In June 1996 the Chamber of Representatives approved the budget for July 1996–June 1997. Expenditure was forecast at 117,180.3m. dirhams, while revenue was expected to total 107,744.1m. dirhams, giving a deficit of 9,436.2m. dirhams. The draft budget for 1997/98, presented to the Chamber of Representatives in May 1997, envisaged expenditure of 126,700m. dirhams, with revenue forecast at 114,300m. dirhams, leading to a 32% increase in the fiscal deficit. In February 1998 the Government was more optimistic about the budget deficit for 1997, forecasting that if the agricultural harvest was good the overall deficit would not exceed 3.5% of GDP. Nevertheless, in a report published in March, the IMF urged the Government to cut current spending

and reduce the budget deficit. The IMF stated that the projected widening of the budget deficit in 1997–98, mainly as a result of public-sector pay increases granted in 1996, was not consistent with the need for stronger fiscal consolidation. It encouraged the Government to reduce the size of the civil service and replace food subsidies with better targeted assistance. The Minister of the Economy and Finance stated that he aimed to eliminate the budget deficit early in the next century and that the first loser would be the consumer. In April Prime Minister el-Youssoufi announced that public-sector spending would be cut in order to reduce the budget deficit. In August 1998 the Chamber of Representatives approved the draft budget for 1998–99 and it was subsequently endorsed by the upper house, the Chamber of Advisers, in late September. It envisaged a rise in total expenditure to 132,100m. dirhams, with revenues projected to increase to 118,400m. dirhams, giving a budget deficit of 13,700m. dirhams. Priority was accorded to social expenditure, with increases in allocations for health, social development, housing, youth and sports and culture; and addressing the problem of unemployment.

The 1999–2000 budget, approved by parliament in June 1999 envisaged total expenditure of 125,300m. dirhams, excluding debt service payments, with revenues projected at 109,700m. dirhams giving a budget deficit of 15,600m. dirhams (equivalent to 2.8% of GDP). Almost half of total expenditure was accorded to social sectors. In late 1999 the Minister of Economy and Finance announced that the actual budget deficit for 1998–99 was 8,100m. dirhams (2.3% of GDP), substantially lower than the projected figure as a result of spending controls, a significant increase in tax receipts and the successful management of the domestic and external debts. The Minister stated the Government was committed to achieving to further reduction in the budget deficit and set a target of 2% of GDP for 1999–2000. In December 1999 the Government adopted a five-year social and economic plan to run from 2000–04 involving a total investment of some 520,000m. dirhams (US $50,600m.) designed to improve the country's infrastructure, strengthen business and create new jobs. (The plan was approved by the Chamber of Advisers in August 2000.) Around two-thirds of the investment was expected to come from the public sector, and one third from the private sector. The plan projected an average annual growth in GDP of 5% and a reduction in the budget deficit to 1% of GDP. Meanwhile, the Government announced that from 2001 the financial year would once again run from January–December rather than from July to June. A six-month transitional budget was introduced to run from the end of the 1999–2000 fiscal year on 30 June 2000. The transitional budget envisaged GDP growth of 3% and forecast revenues at 74,880m. dirhams and expenditure at 79,650m. dirhams, resulting in a budget deficit of 4,770m dirhams, 40% lower than the deficit in July–December 1999. However, a second year of severe drought and the Government's decision to raise the minimum wage by 10% meant that these projections were unrealistic. Independent sources argued that actual revenues would certainly be lower than forecast, while expenditure would be much higher, resulting in a widening deficit. The budget for 2001 was approved by parliament in December 2000 and was based on GDP growth of 8%.

The draft budget for 2002, approved by parliament in December 2001, set revenue at 159,500m. dirhams and expenditure at 165,400m. dirhams. It was based on forecast growth of 4.5%, an inflation rate of 2.5% and an external current account deficit of 1% of GDP. The budget deficit is expected to fall to 5,900m dirhams, equivalent to 3% of GDP, from an estimated 6,600m. dirhams in 2001. The Government intended to carry out further privatizations, although revenues were expected to fall to 12,500m. dirhams from 23,300m. dirhams in 2001. The wide disparities in social services between rural and urban areas are among the main development challenges facing the country as only 45% of rural households have access to potable water and less than 20% have access to electricity.

Statistical Survey

Sources (unless otherwise stated): Direction de la Statistique, BP 178, Rabat 10001; tel. (3) 7773606; fax (3) 7773042; e-mail webmaster@statistic.gov.ma; internet www.statistic.gov.ma; Bank Al-Maghrib, 277 ave Muhammad V, BP 445, Rabat; tel. (3) 7702626; fax (3) 7706677; e-mail dai@bkam.gov.ma; internet www.bkam.ma.

Note: Unless otherwise indicated, the data exclude Western (formerly Spanish) Sahara, a disputed territory under Moroccan occupation.

Area and Population

AREA, POPULATION AND DENSITY

Area (sq km) .	710,850*
Population (census results)†	
3 September 1982	
Males .	10,205,859
Females .	10,182,358
Total	20,388,217
2 September 1994	26,073,717
Population (official estimates at mid-year)†	
1999	28,238,000
2000	28,705,000
2001	29,170,000
Density (per sq km) at mid-2001	41.0

* 274,461 sq miles. This area includes the disputed territory of Western Sahara, which covers 252,120 sq km (97,344 sq miles).
† Including Western Sahara, with a population of 163,868 (provisional) at the 1982 census and 252,146 at the 1994 census.

REGIONS (population at 1994 census)

	Area (sq km)	Population	Density (per sq km)
Sud* .	394,970	3,234,024	8.2
Tensift .	38,445	3,546,768	92.3
Centre .	41,500	6,931,418	167.0
Nord-Ouest .	29,955	5,646,716	188.5
Centre-Nord .	43,950	3,042,310	69.2
Oriental .	82,820	1,768,691	21.4
Centre-Sud .	79,210	1,903,790	24.0
Total .	710,850	26,073,717	36.7

* Including the prefectures of Boujdour, el-Aaiún, es-Smara and Oued ed-Dahab, which comprise the disputed territory of Western Sahara (area 252,120 sq km; population 252,146).

PRINCIPAL TOWNS (population at 1994 census)

Casablanca .	2,940,623	Meknès .	530,171
Rabat (capital)*	1,385,872	Tanger (Tangier) .	526,215
Fès (Fez) .	774,754	Kénitra .	448,785
Marrakech		Beni-Mellal .	386,505
(Marrakesh) .	745,541	Safi .	376,038
Oujda .	678,778	Tétouan .	367,349
Agadir .	550,200	Khouribga .	294,680

* Including Salé.

BIRTHS AND DEATHS (UN estimates, annual averages)

	1985–90	1990–95	1995–2000
Birth rate (per 1,000) .	32.8	29.1	26.8
Death rate (per 1,000) .	8.9	7.6	6.6

Source: UN, *World Population Prospects: The 2000 Revision*.

Expectation of life (WHO estimates, years at birth, 2000): Males 66.1; Females 70.4 (Source: WHO, *World Health Report*).

ECONOMICALLY ACTIVE POPULATION
(sample surveys, '000 persons aged 15 years and over)

	1999	2000	2001
Agriculture, hunting, forestry and fishing	4,048	4,010	3,900
Mining and quarrying .	58	55	
Manufacturing .	1,153	1,098	1,169
Electricity, gas and water .	40	34	
Construction. .	560	555	598
Wholesale and retail trade .	991	1,118	1,155
Transport, storage and communications .	279	297	317
Repairing .	155	158	
Restaurants and hotels .	140	155	
Financing, insurance, real estate and business services .	104	105	835
Personal and domestic services .	359	372	
General administration .	500	482	
Other community services .	440	443	976
Activities not adequately defined .	17	10	5
Total employed .	8,845	8,891	8,955
Unemployed .	1,433	1,394	1,275
Total labour force .	10,278	10,285	10,230

Health and Welfare

KEY INDICATORS

Fertility (births per woman, 2000).	3.2
Under-5 mortality rate (per 1,000 live births, 2000).	46
HIV/AIDS (% of persons aged 15–49, 2001).	0.08
Physicians (per 1,000 head, 1997) .	0.46
Hospital beds (per 1,000 head, 1997) .	0.46
Health expenditure (1998): US $ per head (PPP)	145
% of GDP .	4.4
public (% of total) .	30.0
Access to water (% of persons, 2000) .	82
Access to sanitation (% of persons, 2000) .	75
Human Development Index (2000): ranking .	123
value .	0.602

For sources and definitions, see explanatory note on p. vi.

Agriculture

PRINCIPAL CROPS ('000 metric tons)

	1998	1999	2000
Wheat .	4,378	2,154	1,381
Rice (paddy) .	20	35	25
Barley .	1,970	1,474	467
Maize .	201	136	95
Oats .	25	14	15
Sorghum .	22	18	10
Other cereals .	16	14	15
Potatoes .	1,114	1,141	1,090
Sweet potatoes .	16	7	13
Sugar cane .	1,283	1,373	1,326
Sugar beet .	2,823	3,223	2,883
Dry broad beans .	108	55	33
Dry peas .	22	11	6
Chick-peas .	58	28	15
Lentils .	25	13	13
Other pulses .	59	56	60
Almonds .	66	81	65

— continued			1998	1999	2000
Groundnuts (in shell)	.	.	45	42	45
Olives	.	.	650	386	400
Sunflower seed	.	.	62	49	19
Artichokes	.	.	26	28	41
Tomatoes	.	.	1,242	1,116	1,165
Cauliflowers	.	.	33	40	24
Pumpkins, squash and gourds	.	.	111	118	115†
Cucumbers and gherkins	.	.	36	30*	30*
Aubergines (Eggplants)	.	.	44	43*	43*
Chillies and green peppers	.	.	204	188	180
Dry onions	.	.	565	523	368
Green beans	.	.	20	31	25
Green peas	.	.	58	48	65
Carrots	.	.	229	221	210
Watermelons	.	.	259	230	219
Cantaloupes and other melons	.	.	372	340	655†
Grapes	.	.	262	274	253
Dates	.	.	85	73	74
Apples	.	.	285	303	300
Pears	.	.	31	50	30
Peaches and nectarines	.	.	39	45	48
Plums	.	.	41	51	39
Oranges	.	.	1,104	874	870
Tangerines, mandarins, clementines and satsumas	.	.	462	419	514
Lemons and limes	.	.	21	9	8
Apricots	.	.	117	106	120
Bananas	.	.	102	111	119
Tobacco (leaves)	.	.	11	4†	4*

* FAO estimate.   † Unofficial figure.

Source: FAO.

LIVESTOCK ('000 head, year ending September)

			1998	1999	2000
Cattle	.	.	2,569	2,560	2,675
Sheep	.	.	14,784	16,576	17,300
Goats	.	.	4,959	5,114	5,120
Camels*	.	.	36	36	36
Horses	.	.	147	150*	150*
Mules	.	.	524	524*	524*
Asses	.	.	980	980*	980*
Poultry	.	.	100,000	140,000	135,000

* FAO estimate(s).

Source: FAO.

LIVESTOCK PRODUCTS ('000 metric tons)

			1998	1999	2000
Beef and veal	.	.	120	130	140
Mutton and lamb	.	.	115	126	125
Goat meat	.	.	20	21	22
Poultry meat	.	.	230	260	250
Other meat	.	.	37	38	38
Cows' milk	.	.	1,051	1,130	1,150
Sheep's milk	.	.	27	27	27*
Goats' milk	.	.	35	35	35*
Butter	.	.	16	18	18
Cheese	.	.	8	8	8
Poultry eggs	.	.	180	180	175
Honey	.	.	3	3	2
Wool: greasy	.	.	38	38	40†
scoured*	.	.	17	17	17
Cattle hides (fresh)	.	.	17	18	18*
Sheepskins (fresh)	.	.	12	13	13
Goatskins (fresh)	.	.	3	3	3

* FAO estimate(s).   † Unofficial figure.

Source: FAO.

Forestry

ROUNDWOOD REMOVALS ('000 cubic metres, excl. bark)

				1998	1999	2000
Sawlogs, veneer logs and logs for sleepers	.	.	.	231	176	207
Pulpwood	.	.	.	745	394	362
Fuel wood	.	.	.	770	553	487
Total	.	.	.	1,746	1,123	1,056

Source: FAO.

SAWNWOOD PRODUCTION
('000 cubic metres, incl. railway sleepers)

			1987	1988	1989
Coniferous (softwood)	.	.	40	26	43
Broadleaved (hardwood)	.	.	40	27	40
Total	.	.	80	53	83

1990–2000: Annual production as in 1989.

Source: FAO.

Fishing

('000 metric tons, live weight)

		1997	1998	1999
Capture	.	791.6	710.4	745.4
European pilchard (sardine)	.	497.8	435.8	429.7
European anchovy	.	25.0	41.0	40.2
Chub mackerel	.	28.8	11.6	17.4
Octopuses	.	38.2	42.5	84.6
Aquaculture	.	2.3	2.1	2.8
Total catch (incl. others)	.	793.9	712.5	748.2

Note: Figures exclude aquatic plants ('000 metric tons, capture only): 8.1 in 1997; 7.0 in 1998; 5.9 in 1999.

Mining

('000 metric tons)

			1999	2000	2001
Hard coal	.	.	129.2	30.8	1.9
Crude petroleum	.	.	11.3	13.0	10.1
Iron ore†	.	.	6.6	6.5	5.0
Copper concentrates†	.	.	25.3	23.1	26.6
Lead concentrates†	.	.	114.2	117.4	110.9
Manganese ore†	.	.	29.1	25.8	13.2
Zinc concentrates†	.	.	216.2	201.7	174.8
Phosphate rock‡	.	.	22,767	19,658	20,736
Fluorspar (acid grade)	.	.	83.1	77.0	96.5
Barytes	.	.	328.9	343.6	445.8
Salt (unrefined)	.	.	156.2	162.4	231.3
Clay	.	.	22.0	30.7	40.7

* Preliminary figures.

† Figures refer to the gross weight of ores and concentrates.

‡ Including production in Western Sahara.

Industry

SELECTED PRODUCTS*
('000 metric tons, unless otherwise indicated)

	1998	1999	2000†
Cement .	7,155	7,194	7,497
Electric energy (million kWh) .	12,453	13,264	13,942
Phosphate fertilizers‡	542	481	n.a.
Carpets and rugs ('000 sq m)	618	638	n.a.
Wine§	30	49	35
Olive oil (crude) .	50	65	n.a.
Motor spirit—petrol	354	391	383
Naphthas	385	507	492
Kerosene	79	96	98
Distillate fuel oils	2,236	2,539	2,322
Residual fuel oils	1,918	2,508	2,365
Jet fuel .	272	279	282
Petroleum bitumen—asphalt .	118	116	129
Liquefied petroleum gas	252	266	239

* Major industrial establishments only.
† Preliminary figures.
‡ Estimated production in terms of phosphoric acid.
§ Source: FAO.

Source: partly UN, *Industrial Commodity Statistics Yearbook*.

Finance

CURRENCY AND EXCHANGE RATES

Monetary Units
100 centimes (santimat) = 1 Moroccan dirham.

Sterling, Dollar and Euro Equivalents (31 May 2002)
£1 sterling = 16.27 dirhams;
US $1 = 11.10 dirhams;
€1 = 10.41 dirhams;
1,000 Moroccan dirhams = £61.45 = $90.13 = €96.02.

Average Exchange Rate (dirhams per US $)
1999   9.804
2000   10.626
2001   11.303

GENERAL BUDGET (million dirhams)

Revenue	1998/99*	1999/2000*	2000†
Tax revenue .	79,681	80,813	38,807
Direct taxes	25,010	26,938	12,067
Customs receipts	12,744	12,746	6,357
Indirect taxes	34,412	36,999	18,697
Registration and stamps	3,892	4,130	1,686
Exceptional receipts	3,623	—	—
Non-tax revenue .	9,835	19,103	2,482
Monopolies, etc.	5,759	16,519	1,352
Revenue from special accounts	4,685	5,383	2,053
Total	**94,201**	**105,299**	**43,342**

Expenditure	1998/99*	1999/2000*	2000†
Ordinary expenditure	80,664	85,029	42,969
Operating expenditure .	56,789	59,405	29,936
Personnel	40,286	42,683	21,222
Interest on public debt .	17,731	18,735	9,643
Domestic	11,088	12,540	6,250
Foreign .	6,643	6,195	3,393
Price subsidies.	6,144	6,889	3,390
Investment expenditure .	17,428	17,235	11,996
Special treasury accounts (net)	4,170	5,046	2,384
Expenditure from Hassan II Fund for Economic and Social Development .	—	250	1,652
Total	**102,262**	**107,560**	**59,001**

* Figures for 1998/99 and 1999/2000 refer to the financial year ending 30 June. With effect from January 2001 the financial year was to correspond with the calendar year.
† Figures refer to the period 1 July–31 December 2000.

INTERNATIONAL RESERVES (US $ million at 31 December)

	1999	2000	2001
Gold*	193	184	169
IMF special drawing rights	85	119	123
Reserve position in IMF .	97	92	89
Foreign exchange	5,507	4,612	8,262
Total	**5,882**	**5,007**	**8,643**

* National valuation of gold reserves (704,000 troy ounces in 1999; 706,000 in 2000; 707,000 in 2001).

Source: IMF, *International Financial Statistics*.

MONEY SUPPLY (million dirhams at 31 December)

	1999	2000	2001
Currency outside banks	56,713	58,169	66,025
Demand deposits at deposit money banks .	140,895	156,545	181,092
Total money (incl. others)	**200,597**	**216,503**	**249,726**

Source: IMF, *International Financial Statistics*.

COST OF LIVING
(Consumer Price Index for urban areas; base: 1989 = 100)

	1999	2000	2001
Food	156.7	159.1	157.5
Clothing	157.6	161.3	163.5
Shelter	156.6	159.2	162.5
Household equipment	137.9	138.2	138.4
All items (incl. others)	**154.4**	**157.3**	**158.3**

NATIONAL ACCOUNTS (million dirhams at current prices)

Expenditure on the Gross Domestic Product

	1999	2000*	2001†
Government final consumption expenditure	66,146	67,689	74,619
Private final consumption expenditure	214,416	224,883	235,008
Increase in stocks	−1,984	−1,629	2,131
Gross fixed capital formation .	81,896	85,312	85,264
Total domestic expenditure	**360,474**	**376,256**	**397,022**
Exports of goods and services .	84,663	93,504	105,435
Less Imports of goods and services	99,543	115,693	119,560
GDP in purchasers' values	**345,594**	**354,068**	**382,897**
GDP at constant 1980 prices	**133,622**	**134,927**	**143,648**

* Semi-definitive figures.   † Provisional figures.

Gross Domestic Product by Economic Activity

	1999	2000*	2001†
Agriculture, hunting, forestry and fishing	52,905.2	49,570.1	60,546.4
Energy and water	27,158.9	25,263.9	26,588.9
Other mining and quarrying .	7,463.5	7,035.6	7,446.2
Other manufacturing.	59,581.8	62,267.3	64,851.4
Construction.	16,471.5	18,300.1	19,351.8
Wholesale and retail trade	66,339.3	70,682.7	72,894.8
Transport and communications	21,678.1	24,700.1	26,366.8
Public administration	49,424.0	50,489.2	58,138.0
Other services	44,695.4	45,758.9	46,712.8
GDP in purchasers' values .	**345,593.6**	**354,067.9**	**382,897.0**

* Semi-definitive figures.   † Provisional figures.

BALANCE OF PAYMENTS (US $ million)

	1998	1999	2000
Exports of goods f.o.b. . . .	7,144	7,509	7,419
Imports of goods f.o.b. . . .	−9,463	−9,957	−10,654
Trade balance	−2,319	−2,448	−3,235
Exports of services . . .	2,897	3,115	3,034
Imports of services . . .	−1,963	−2,003	−1,884
Balance on goods and services .	−1,455	−1,335	−2,085
Other income received . .	194	187	276
Other income paid . . .	−1,227	−1,172	−1,149
Balance on goods, services and income . . .	−2,489	−2,321	−2,958
Current transfers received . .	2,438	2,246	2,574
Current transfers paid . . .	−95	−96	−118
Current balance . . .	−146	−171	−501
Capital account (net) . . .	−10	−9	−6
Direct investment abroad . .	−20	−18	−59
Direct investment from abroad .	12	3	10
Portfolio investment liabilities .	24	6	18
Other investment liabilities .	−660	−4	−668
Net errors and omissions . .	160	123	148
Overall balance . . .	−640	−69	−1,078

Source: IMF, *International Financial Statistics*.

External Trade

PRINCIPAL COMMODITIES (million dirhams)

Imports c.i.f.	1999	2000	2001*
Foodstuffs, beverages and tobacco	11,540	14,210	15,348
Wheat	3,817	5,484	6,164
Energy and lubricants . .	13,000	21,657	21,874
Crude petroleum . .	8,941	14,710	14,488
Refined petroleum products .	2,507	4,802	4,744
Crude animal and vegetable products . . .	5,583	5,803	5,763
Semi-finished products . .	21,828	24,365	26,387
Chemical products . . .	3,247	3,441	3,686
Metallurgical products . .	4,679	5,403	5,533
Finished industrial capital goods	27,026	24,694	22,019
Aircraft, boats and industrial vehicles	3,454	4,000	1,958
Finished consumer products . .	24,323	28,822	29,919
Textile products . . .	10,479	10,740	12,190
Telecommunications receiving equipment . . .	995	4,501	2,398
Total (incl. others) . . .	105,931	122,527	124,081

Exports f.o.b.	1999	2000	2001*
Foodstuffs, beverages and tobacco	14,853	16,751	16,185
Citrus fruit	2,613	2,050	2,026
Crustaceans and molluscs .	4,422	6,742	4,954
Prepared and preserved fish .	1,961	2,141	2,543
Energy and lubricants . .	1,990	2,882	3,098
Crude mineral products . .	5,979	5,766	6,179
Phosphates . . .	4,462	4,129	4,687
Semi-finished products . .	13,711	17,063	17,763
Phosphoric acid . . .	5,777	5,365	5,380
Natural and chemical fertilizers	3,107	3,430	4,017
Electronic components (transistors) . . .	1,826	4,253	4,302
Finished industrial capital goods	6,776	4,798	4,449
Electric wire and cable . .	1,633	2,074	2,512
Finished consumer products . .	28,456	29,753	31,392
Manufactured garments . .	16,172	16,195	17,164
Hosiery . . .	8,070	8,935	8,861
Total (incl. others) . . .	73,617	78,827	80,440

* Provisional figures.

Source: partly Office des Changes, Rabat.

PRINCIPAL TRADING PARTNERS (million dirhams)*

Imports c.i.f.	1999	2000	2001†
Algeria	1,364.2	2,023.7	2,179.0
Argentina	704.2	1,066.8	1,651.3
Belgium-Luxembourg . .	1,866.5	1,952.2	1,762.6
Brazil	2,044.0	1,820.6	3,025.0
Canada	1,355.1	2,404.0	2,534.2
China, People's Republic . .	2,419.9	2,846.4	3,151.5
France	27,275.4	29,438.9	29,854.4
Germany	6,400.9	5,978.4	6,251.0
Iran	2,346.1	3,795.9	3,185.0
Iraq	2,481.3	5,047.6	4,640.3
Italy	5,634.1	5,809.8	6,262.0
Japan	2,359.7	2,069.4	1,889.4
Korea, Republic . . .	918.0	1,261.9	1,452.4
Netherlands	1,892.7	2,067.8	1,948.1
Russia	2,750.2	2,663.2	4,095.2
Saudi Arabia . . .	3,433.3	6,087.8	5,854.2
South Africa	837.9	938.4	1,619.0
Spain	11,771.2	12,092.6	12,806.9
Sweden	1,475.1	2,718.9	1,563.2
Switzerland . . .	1,109.2	1,209.2	1,333.6
Turkey	1,202.6	1,059.7	1,261.8
Ukraine	906.1	1,056.5	1,584.6
United Kingdom . . .	5,722.2	7,559.3	7,699.4
USA	6,929.6	6,836.1	4,557.7
Total (incl. others) . . .	105,931.0	122,526.8	124,080.7

Exports f.o.b.	1999	2000	2001†
Belgium-Luxembourg . . .	1,979.8	2,222.8	2,036.0
Brazil	473.6	730.2	915.5
France	26,309.4	26,392.1	26,391.7
Germany	4,186.8	3,916.8	3,361.0
India	3,550.4	3,297.9	2,894.3
Italy	3,728.0	5,616.3	4,599.5
Japan	2,679.8	3,009.8	2,041.3
Libya	1,130.3	668.7	660.5
Netherlands	1,420.1	1,316.4	2,184.5
Spain	7,867.3	10,220.2	12,274.2
United Kingdom . . .	6,526.6	7,560.0	6,908.8
USA	2,511.8	2,693.5	3,246.0
Total (incl. others) . . .	73,616.7	78,826.7	80,439.6

* Imports by country of production; exports by country of last consignment.
† Provisional figures.

Source: Office des Changes, Rabat.

Transport

RAILWAYS (traffic)*

	1999	2000	2001
Passenger-km (million) . .	1,875	1,956	2,019
Freight ton-km (million) . .	4,828	4,650	4,699

* Figures refer to principal railways only.

ROAD TRAFFIC (motor vehicles in use at 31 December)

	1996	1997	1998
Passenger cars	1,021,515	1,059,241	1,111,846
Goods vehicles	363,533	379,504	392,602
Motorcycles and scooters . .	19,417	19,704	19,891

Source: Ministère du Transport et de la Marine Marchande.

SHIPPING

Merchant Fleet (registered at 31 December)

	1999	2000	2001
Number of vessels . . .	496	493	485
Total displacement ('000 grt) .	448.5	466.9	461.5

Source: Lloyd's Register-Fairplay, *World Fleet Statistics*.

International Sea-borne Freight Traffic ('000 metric tons)

	1999	2000	2001
Goods loaded	24,128	23,384	24,973
Goods unloaded	28,524	29,831	32,542

CIVIL AVIATION (traffic on Royal Air Maroc scheduled services)

	1998	1999	2000
Kilometres flown (million) . .	58.8	65.0	67.9
Passengers carried ('000) . . .	3,046	3,460	3,676
Passenger-km (million) . . .	6,124	6,880	7,442
Total ton-km (million) . . .	562.9	678.4	718.5

Tourism

FOREIGN TOURIST ARRIVALS BY COUNTRY OF NATIONALITY*

	1999	2000	2001†
France	759,174	813,865	840,230
Germany	229,830	211,039	196,700
Italy	125,687	142,426	123,628
Maghreb countries . . .	60,368	63,989	71,454
Spain	241,742	232,245	200,519
United Kingdom	143,689	137,232	135,642
USA	129,707	121,068	97,072
Total (incl. others)	2,274,814	2,325,505	2,249,662

* Excluding Moroccans resident abroad (1,541,827 in 1999; 1,787,532 in 2000; 1,973,653 in 2001).
† Provisional figures.

Cruise-ship passengers: 271,274 in 1999; 180,203 in 2000; 207,260 in 2001.

Receipts from tourism (provisional, US $ million): 1,850 in 1999; 2,040 in 2000.

Communications Media

	1999	2000	2001
Television receivers ('000 in use)	4,600	4,700	n.a.
Telephones ('000 main lines in use)	1,471.0	1,425.0	1,191.3
Mobile cellular telephones ('000 subscribers)	369.2	2,342.0	4,771.7
Personal computers ('000 in use)	300	350	400
Internet users ('000)	50	100	400

1996: Book production (titles) 918, ('000 copies) 1,836; Daily newspapers 22 (average circulation 704,000 copies); Other newspapers and periodicals 699 (average circulation 3,671,000 copies).

1997: Radio receivers ('000 in use) 6,640; Telefax stations (number in use) 18,000 (estimate).

Sources: UNESCO, *Statistical Yearbook*, UN, *Statistical Yearbook*, and International Telecommunication Union.

Education

(1999/2000, unless otherwise indicated)

	Insti-tutions	Teach-ers	Pupils/Students		
			Males	Females	Total
Pre-primary . . .	33,577*	43,952	532,076	284,978	817,054
Primary					
Public . . .	5,940	121,763	1,932,806	1,565,120	3,497,926
Private . .	625	5,819	92,595	79,084	171,679
Secondary					
General					
Public . . .	1,446	84,024‡	785,550	610,346	1,393,896
Private . . .	218	4,277	26,834	18,258	45,092
Vocational . .	69	n.a.	12,810	9,981	22,791
University level*† .	68	9,667	154,314	112,193	266,507

* 1997/98 figure(s).
† Provisional; state institutions only.
‡ Including vocational teachers.

2000/01: Primary 3,842,000 (public 3,644,404; private 177,596); Secondary 1,504,367 (public 1,457,388; private 46,979); University level 265,905.
2001/02: Primary 4,029,112 (public 3,832,356; private 196,756); Secondary 1,610,753 (public 1,561,686; private 49,067); University level 260,806.

Source: mainly Ministère de l'Education Nationale.

Adult literacy rate (UNESCO estimates): 48.9% (males 61.1%; females 35.1%) in 2000 (Source: UNDP, *Human Development Report*).

Directory

The Constitution

The following is a summary of the main provisions of the Constitution, as approved in a national referendum on 4 September 1992, and as amended by referendum on 13 September 1996.

PREAMBLE

The Kingdom of Morocco, a sovereign Islamic State whose official language is Arabic, constitutes a part of the Great Arab Maghreb. As an African State, one of its aims is the realization of African unity. It adheres to the principles, rights and obligations of those international organizations of which it is a member and works for the preservation of peace and security in the world.

GENERAL PRINCIPLES

Morocco is a constitutional, democratic and social monarchy. Sovereignty pertains to the nation and is exercised directly by means of the referendum and indirectly by the constitutional institutions. All Moroccans are equal before the law, and all adults enjoy equal political rights including the franchise. Freedoms of movement, opinion and speech and the right of assembly are guaranteed. Islam is the state religion. All Moroccans have equal rights in seeking education and employment. The right to strike, and to private property, is guaranteed. All Moroccans contribute to the defence of the Kingdom and to public costs. There shall be no one-party system.

THE MONARCHY

The Crown of Morocco and its attendant constitutional rights shall be hereditary in the line of HM King Hassan II, and shall be transmitted to the oldest son, unless during his lifetime the King has appointed as his successor another of his sons. The King is the symbol of unity, guarantees the continuity of the state, and safeguards respect for Islam and the Constitution. The King appoints, and may dismiss, the Prime Minister and other Cabinet Ministers (appointed upon the Prime Minister's recommendation), and presides over the Cabinet. He shall promulgate adopted legislation within a 30-day period, and has the power to dissolve the Chamber of Representatives and or the Chamber of Advisers. The Sovereign is the Commander-in-Chief of the Armed Forces; makes appointments to civil and military posts; appoints Ambassadors; signs and ratifies treaties; presides over the Supreme Council of the Magistracy, the Supreme Council of Education and the Supreme Council for National Reconstruction and Planning; and exercises the right of pardon. In cases of threat to the national territory or to the action of constitutional institutions, the King, having consulted the President of the Chamber of Representatives, the President of the Chamber of Advisers and the Chairman of the Constitutional Council, and after addressing the nation, has the right to declare a

State of Emergency by royal decree. The State of Emergency shall not entail the dissolution of Parliament and shall be terminated by the same procedure followed in its proclamation.

LEGISLATURE

This consists of a bicameral parliament: the Chamber of Representatives and the Chamber of Advisers. Members of the Chamber of Representatives are elected by direct universal suffrage for a five-year term. Three-fifths of the members of the Chamber of Advisers are elected by electoral colleges of local councils; the remainder are elected by electoral colleges representing chambers of commerce and trade unions. Members of the Chamber of Advisers are elected for a nine-year term, with one-third renewable every three years. Deputies in both chambers enjoy parliamentary immunity. Parliament shall adopt legislation, which may be initiated by members of either chamber or by the Prime Minister. Draft legislation shall be examined consecutively by both parliamentary chambers. If the two chambers fail to agree on the draft legislation the Government may request that a bilateral commission propose a final draft for approval by the chambers. If the chambers do not then adopt the draft, the Government may submit the draft (modified, if need be) to the Chamber of Representatives. Henceforth the draft submitted can be definitively adopted only by absolute majority of the members of the Chamber of Representatives. Parliament holds its meetings during two sessions each year, commencing on the second Friday in October and the second Friday in April.

GOVERNMENT

The Government, composed of the Prime Minister and his Ministers, is responsible to the King and Parliament and ensures the execution of laws. The Prime Minister is empowered to initiate legislation and to exercise statutory powers except where these are reserved to the King. He presents to both parliamentary chambers the Government's intended programme and is responsible for co-ordinating ministerial work.

RELATIONS BETWEEN THE AUTHORITIES

The King may request a second reading, by both Chambers of Parliament, of any draft bill or proposed law. In addition, he may submit proposed legislation to a referendum by decree; and dissolve either Chamber or both if a proposal that has been rejected is approved by referendum. He may also dissolve either Chamber by decree after consulting the Chairman of the Constitutional Council, and addressing the nation, but the succeeding Chamber may not be dissolved within a year of its election. The Chamber of Representatives may force the collective resignation of the Government either by refusing a vote of confidence or by adopting a censure motion. The election of the new Parliament or Chamber shall take place within three months of its dissolution. In the interim period the King shall exercise the legislative powers of Parliament, in addition to those conferred upon him by the Constitution. A censure motion must be signed by at least one-quarter of the Chamber's members, and shall be approved by the Chamber only by an absolute majority vote of its members. The Chamber of Advisers is competent to issue 'warning' motions to the Government and, by a two-thirds' majority, force its resignation.

THE CONSTITUTIONAL COUNCIL

The Constitutional Council consists of six members appointed by the King (including the Chairman) for a period of nine years, and six members appointed for the same period—three selected by the President of the Chamber of Representatives and three by the President of the Chamber of Advisers. One-third of each category of the Council are renewed every three years. The Council is empowered to judge the validity of legislative elections and referendums, as well as that of organic laws and the rules of procedure of both parliamentary chambers, submitted to it.

JUDICIARY

The Judiciary is independent. Judges are appointed on the recommendation of the Supreme Council of the Magistracy presided over by the King.

THE ECONOMIC AND SOCIAL COUNCIL

An Economic and Social Council shall be established to give its opinion on all matters of an economic or social nature. Its constitution, organization, prerogatives and rules of procedure shall be determined by an organic law.

THE HIGH AUDIT COUNCIL

The High Audit Council exercises the general supervision of the implementation of fiscal laws. It ensures the regularity of revenues and expenditure operations of the departments legally under its jurisdiction, as it assesses the management of the affairs thereof. It is competent to penalize any breach of the rules governing such operations. Regional audit councils exercise the supervision of the accounts of local assemblies and bodies, and the management of the affairs thereof.

LOCAL GOVERNMENT

Local government in the Kingdom consists of establishing regions, governorships, provinces and communes.

REVISING THE CONSTITUTION

The King, the Chamber of Representatives and the Chamber of Advisers are competent to initiate a revision of the Constitution. The King has the right to submit the revision project he initiates to a national referendum. A proposal for a revision by either parliamentary chamber shall be adopted only if it receives a two-thirds' majority vote by the chamber's members. Revision projects and proposals shall be submitted to the nation for referendum by royal decree; a revision of the Constitution shall be definitive after approval by referendum. Neither the state, system of monarchy nor the prescriptions related to the religion of Islam may be subject to a constitutional revision.

The Government

HEAD OF STATE

HM King MUHAMMAD VI (acceded 23 July 1999).

CABINET
(September 2002)

A coalition of the Union socialiste des forces populaires (USFP); Rassemblement national des indépendants (RNI); Istiqlal; Parti du progrès et du socialisme (PPS); Mouvement national populaire (MNP); Front des forces démocratiques (FFD); Parti socialiste démocratique (PSD).

Prime Minister: ABD AR-RAHMAN EL-YOUSSOUFI (USFP).

Minister of Foreign Affairs and Co-operation: MUHAMMAD BENAISSA (RNI).

Minister of the Interior: DRISS JETTOU.

Minister of Justice: OMAR AZZIMAN.

Minister of Habous (Religious Endowments) and Islamic Affairs: ABD AL-KAEBIR M'DAGHRI ALAOUI.

Minister of Territorial Administration, the Environment, Urban Planning and Housing: MUHAMMAD EL-YAZGHI (USFP).

Minister of the Economy, Finance, Privatization and Tourism: FATHALLAH OUALALOU (USFP).

Minister of Agriculture, Rural Development, Water and Forestry: ISMAIL ALAOUI (PPS).

Secretary-General of the Government: ABDESSADEK RABII.

Minister of Industry, Commerce, Energy and Mining: MUSTAPHA MANSOURI (RNI).

Minister of Social Development, Solidarity, Employment and Professional Training: ABBAS EL-FASSI (Istiqlal).

Minister of Equipment: BOUAMAR TIGHOUANE (Istiqlal).

Minister of Transport and Merchant Navy: ABD AS-SALAM ZHINED (RNI).

Minister of National Education: ABDALLAH SAAF (PSD).

Minister of Higher Education, Professional Training and Scientific Research: NAJIB ZEROUALI OUARITI (RNI).

Minister in charge of Relations with Parliament: MUHAMMAD BOUZOUBAA (USFP).

Minister of Social Welfare, Small and Medium-sized Enterprises, Handicrafts and General Affairs of the Government: AHMAD LAHLIMI ALAMI (USFP).

Minister in charge of Human Rights: MUHAMMAD AOUJAR (RNI).

Minister of Cultural Affairs and Communications: MUHAMMAD ACHAARI (USFP).

Minister of Health: THAMI KHIARI (FFD).

Minister of Youth and Sports: AHMAD MOUSSAOUI (MNP).

Minister of Economic Planning: ABD AL-HAMID AOUAD (Istiqlal).

Minister of Public Sector and Administrative Reform: MUHAMMAD KHALIFA.

Minister of Maritime Fishing: SAÏD CHBAATOU (MNP).

Minister-delegate to the Prime Minister, in charge of the Administration of National Defence: ABD AR-RAHMAN SBAI.

Minister-delegate in charge of Rural Development: HASAN NAOUNI.

Minister-delegate in charge of Employment, Women and Family Affairs, Social Development and the Disabled: NAZHA CHAKROUNI.

There are also six Secretaries of State.

MINISTRIES

Office of the Prime Minister: Palais Royal, Le Méchouar, Rabat; tel. (3) 7762709; fax (3) 7769995; internet www.pm.gov.ma.

Ministry of Agriculture, Rural Development, Water and Forestry: Quartier Administratif, Place Abdellah Chefchaouni, BP 607, Rabat; tel. (3) 7760933; fax (3) 7763378; e-mail webmaster@mardrpm.gov.ma; internet www.madrpm.gov.ma.

Ministry of Cultural Affairs and Communications: 10 rue Beni Mellal, Rabat; tel. (3) 7762507; fax (3) 7760828; e-mail webmaster@mincom.gov.ma; internet www.mincom.gov.ma.

Ministry of Economic Planning: ave Al Haj Ahmed Cherkaoui, BP 826, 10004 Rabat; e-mail idoubba@cnd.mpep.gov.ma; internet www.mpep.gov.ma.

Ministry of the Economy, Finance, Privatization and Tourism: ave Muhammad V, Quartier des Ministères, Rabat; tel. (3) 7763171; fax (3) 7761575; internet www.mfie.gov.ma.

Ministry of Equipment: Quartier Administratif, Rabat; tel. (3) 7762811; fax (3) 7765505; internet www.mtpnet.gov.ma.

Ministry of Foreign Affairs and Co-operation: ave Franklin Roosevelt, Rabat; tel. (3) 7761583; fax (3) 7765508; e-mail mail@maec.gov.ma; internet www.maec.gov.ma.

Ministry of Habous (Religious Endowments) and Islamic Affairs: Al-Mechouar Essaid, Rabat; tel. (3) 7766801; fax (3) 7765282; e-mail webmaster@habous.gov.ma; internet www.habous.gov.ma.

Ministry of Health: 335 blvd Muhammad V, Rabat; tel. (3) 7761121; fax (3) 7768401; e-mail inas@sante.gov.ma; internet www.sante.gov.ma.

Ministry of Higher Education, Professional Training and Scientific Research: 35 ave Ibn Sina, BP 707, Rabat; tel. (3) 7774717; fax (3) 7778028; internet www.dfc.gov.ma.

Ministry in charge of Human Rights: Rabat; tel. (3) 7673131; fax (3) 7671967.

Ministry of Industry, Commerce, Energy and Mining: Rabat; tel. (3) 7761868; fax (3) 7766265; e-mail webmaster@mcinet.gov.ma; internet www.mcinet.gov.ma.

Ministry of the Interior: Quartier Administratif, Rabat; tel. (3) 7761868; fax (3) 7762056.

Ministry of Justice: Place Mamounia, Rabat; tel. (3) 7732941; fax (3) 7730772; e-mail kourout@justice.gov.ma; internet www.justice.gov.ma.

Ministry of Maritime Fishing: Rabat; e-mail webmaster@.mp3m.gov.ma; internet www.mp3m.gov.ma.

Ministry of National Education: Bab Rouah, Rabat; tel. (3) 7771822; fax (3) 7779029.

Ministry of Public Sector and Administrative Reform: Rabat; tel. (3) 7770894; fax (3) 7775690.

Ministry in charge of Relations with Parliament: Nouveau Quartier Administratif, Rabat; tel. (3) 7775124; e-mail mirepa@mcrp.gov.ma; internet www.mcrp.gov.ma.

Ministry of Social Development, Solidarity, Employment and Professional Training: Rabat; e-mail dfp@dfp.ac.ma; internet www.dfp.ac.ma.

Ministry of Territorial Administration, the Environment, Urban Planning and Housing: Rabat; e-mail info@minenv.gov.ma; internet www.minenv.gov.ma.

Ministry of Transport and Merchant Navy: rue Maa al-Ainane, Casier Officiel, BP 759, Rabat; tel. (3) 7774266; fax (3) 7779525.

Ministry of Youth and Sports: blvd lbn Sina, Rabat; tel. (3) 7680028; fax (3) 7680145; internet www.mjs.gov.ma.

Legislature

MAJLIS AN-NUAB
(Chamber of Representatives)

President: ABDELWAHED RADHI (USFP).

General Election, 27 September 2002

Party	% of votes	Seats
Union socialiste des forces populaires (USFP)	15.38	50
Istiqlal	14.77	48
Parti de la justice et du développement (PJD)	12.92	42
Rassemblement national des indépendants (RNI)	12.62	41
Mouvement populaire (MP)	8.31	27
Mouvement national populaire (MNP)	5.54	18
Union constitutionnelle (UC)	4.92	16
Front des forces démocratiques (FFD)	3.69	12
Parti national démocrate (PND)	3.69	12
Parti du progrès et du socialisme (PPS)	3.38	11
Union démocratique (UD)	3.08	10
Mouvement démocratique social (MDS)	2.15	7
Parti socialiste démocratique (PSD)	1.85	6
Parti Al Ahd	1.54	5
Alliance des libertés (ADL)	1.23	4
Parti de la gauche socialiste unifiée (PGSU)	0.92	3
Parti de la réforme et du développement (PRD)	0.92	3
Parti marocain libéral (PML)	0.92	3
Parti des forces citoyennes (PFC)	0.62	2
Parti de l'environnement et du développement (PED)	0.62	2
Parti démocratique et de l'indépendance (PDI)	0.62	2
Congrès national ittihadi (CNI)	0.31	1
Total	**100.00**	**325***

* 30 of the 325 seats were reserved for women. Of these 30 seats five were won by the USFP; Istiqlal, the PDJ and the RNI each took four seats; the MP, the MNP, the UC, the PND, the FFD and PPS all secured two seats; and the UD received one seat.

MAJLIS AL-MUSTASHARIN
(Chamber of Advisers)

President: MUSTAPHA OKACHA.

Election, 5 December 1997*

	Seats
Rassemblement national des indépendants (RNI)	42
Mouvement démocratique et social (MDS)	33
Union constitutionnelle (UC)	28
Mouvement populaire (MP)	27
Parti national démocrate (PND)	21
Istiqlal	21
Union socialiste des forces populaires (USFP)	16
Mouvement national populaire (MNP)	15
Parti de l'action (PA)	13
Front des forces démocratiques (FFD)	12
Parti du progrès et du socialisme (PPS)	7
Parti social et démocratique (PSD)	4
Parti démocratique pour l'indépendance (PDI)	4
Trade unions	
Confédération Démocratique du Travail (CDT)	11
Union Marocaine du Travail (UMT)	8
Union Générale des Travailleurs Marocains (UGMT)	3
Others	5
Total	**270**

* Of the Chamber of Advisers' 270 members, 162 were elected by local councils, 81 by chambers of commerce and 27 by trade unions.

Note: On 8 September 2000 elections were held to renew one-third of the seats in the Chamber of Advisers. 54 members were elected by local councils and 27 by chambers of commerce. The seats were allocated accordingly: RNI 14 seats; MNP 12; PND 10; MP 9; UC 8; Istiqlal 7; MDS 6; FFD 5; USFP 3; PPS 2; PA 2; PSD two; PDI one. Of the nine seats elected by trade unions the CDT won 4; the UMT 2; the UGTM 2; and the l'Union Nationale des Travailleurs du Maroc (UNMT) won one seat.

Political Organizations

Congrès national ittihadi (CNI): f. 2001; Sec.-Gen. ABDELMAJID BOUZOUBAA.

Front des forces démocratiques (FFD): 13 blvd Tariq ibn Ziad, Rabat; tel. (3) 7661625; fax (3) 7661626; f. 1997 after split from PPS; Sec.-Gen. THAMI EL-KHIARI.

Istiqlal: 4 ave Ibn Toumert, Bab el Had, Rabat; tel. (3) 7730951; fax (3) 7725354; f. 1944; aims to raise living standards and to confer equal rights on all; stresses the Moroccan claim to Western Sahara; Sec.-Gen. ABBAS EL-FASSI.

Mouvement démocratique et social (MDS): 471 ave Muhammad V, Rabat; tel. (3) 7709110; f. 1996 as Mouvement national démocratique et social after split from MNP; adopted current name in Nov. 1996; Leader MAHMOUD ARCHANE.

Mouvement national populaire (MNP): ave Imam Malik, rue el Madani Belhoussni, Souissi, Rabat; tel. (3) 7753623; fax (3) 7759761; f. 1991; centre party; Leader MAHJOUBI AHERDANE.

Mouvement populaire (MP): 66 rue Patrice Lumumba, Rabat; tel. (3) 7767320; fax (3) 7767537; f. 1958; liberal; Sec.-Gen. MOHAND LAENSER.

Mouvement populaire pour la démocratie (MPD): Leader M. EL-KHATIB.

Organisation de l'action démocratique et populaire (OADP): Résidence Maréchal Améziane, rue Bagdad, angle rue d'Agadir, BP 15797, Casablanca; tel. (2) 2262433; fax (2) 2278442; e-mail organisation.oadp@caramail.com; f. 1983; Sec.-Gen. MUHAMMAD BEN SAÏD AÏT IDDER.

Parti de l'action (PA): 113 ave Allal ben Abdallah, Rabat; tel. (3) 7206661; f. 1974; advocates democracy and progress; Sec.-Gen. MUHAMMAD EL IDRISSI.

Parti Al Ahd: f. 2002; Pres. NAJIB EL OUAZZANI.

Parti de l'avant-garde démocratique socialiste (PADS): BP 2091, 54 ave de la Résistance Océan, Rabat; tel. (3) 7200559; fax (3) 7708491; internet membres.tripod.fr/PADSMAROC/; an offshoot of the USFP; legalized in April 1992; Sec.-Gen. AHMAD BENJELLOUNE.

Parti du congrès national unioniste: Rabat; f. 2001 by dissident members of the USFP; Sec.-Gen. ABDELMAJID BOUZOUBAÂ.

Parti démocratique et de l'indépendance (PDI): Casablanca; tel. (2) 2223359; f. 1946; Sec.-Gen. ABDELWAHED MAACH.

Parti de l'environnement et du développement (PED): f. 2002; Sec.-Gen. AHMAD AL-ALAMI.

Parti des Forces citoyennes (PFC): f. 2001; Sec.-Gen. ABDERRAHIM LAHJOUJI.

Parti de la gauche socialiste unifiée (PGSU): Rabat; f. 2001; left-wing coalition comprising the OADP, the MPD, the Activistes de gauche and the Démocrates indépendants; Pres. MUHAMMAD BEN SAID AIT IDDER.

Parti de la justice et du développement (PJD): 5 rue Maati Bakhay, Rabat; tel. (3) 7208862; fax (3) 7208854; e-mail pjd@maktoub.com; f. 1967 as the Mouvement populaire constitutionnel et démocratique (MPCD); breakaway party from MP; formally absorbed members of the Islamic asscn Al Islah wa Attajdid in June 1996 and adopted current name in Oct. 1998; Sec.-Gen. ABDELKRIM KHATIB.

Parti marocain libéral (PML): f. 2002; Nat. Co-ordinator MUHAMMAD ZIANE.

Parti national démocrate (PND): 18 rue de Tunis, Rabat; tel. (3) 7732127; fax (3) 7720170; f. 1981 from split within RNI; Sec.-Gen. ABDELLAH KADIRI.

Parti de la reforme et le developpement (PRD): Rabat; f. 2001 by fmr members of the RNI; Leader ABD AR-RAHMANE KOHEN.

Parti du progrès et du socialisme (PPS): 29 ave John Kennedy, Youssoufia, Rabat; tel. (3) 7759464; fax (3) 7759476; f. 1974; successor to the Parti communiste marocain (banned in 1952), and the Parti de la libération et du socialisme (banned in 1969); left-wing; advocates modernization, social progress, nationalization and democracy; 35,000 mems; Sec.-Gen. ISMAIL ALAOUI.

Parti socialiste démocratique (PSD): 1 rue Ibn Moqla, angle les Orangers, Rabat; tel. and fax (3) 7208576; e-mail dsp1@iam.net.ma; f. 1996; breakaway party from OADP; Leader ISSA OUARDIGHI.

Rassemblement national des indépendants (RNI): 6 rue Laos, ave Hassan II, Rabat; tel. (3) 7721420; fax (3) 7733824; f. 1978 from the pro-govt independents' group that formed the majority in the Chamber of Representatives; Leader AHMAD OUSMAN.

Union constitutionnelle (UC): 158 ave des Forces Armées Royales, Casablanca; tel. (2) 2441144; fax (2) 2441141; e-mail uc@marocnet.net.ma; internet www.mincom.gov.ma/partis/uc; f. 1983; 25-member Political Bureau; Leader (vacant).

Union démocratique (UD): f. 2001; Pres. BOUAZZA IKKEN.

Union nationale des forces populaires (UNFP): 28–30 rue Magellan, BP 747, Casablanca; tel. (2) 2302023; fax (2) 2319301; f. 1959 by MEHDI BEN BARKA from a group within Istiqlal; left-wing;

in 1972 a split occurred between the Casablanca and Rabat sections of the party; Leader MOULAY ABDALLAH IBRAHIM.

Union socialiste des forces populaires (USFP): 17 rue Oued Souss, Agdal, Rabat; tel. (3) 7773905; fax (3) 7773901; e-mail usfp@mtds.com; internet www.mtds.com/~usfp; f. 1959 as UNFP, became USFP in 1974; left-wing progressive party; 100,000 mems; First Sec. ABD AR-RAHMAN EL-YOUSSOUFI.

The following group is active in the disputed territory of Western Sahara:

Frente Popular para la Liberación de Saguia el-Hamra y Río de Oro (Frente Polisario) (Polisario Front): BP 10, el-Mouradia, Algiers; tel. (2) 747907; fax (2) 747206; e-mail dgmae@mail.wissal.dz; f. 1973 to gain independence for Western Sahara, first from Spain and then from Morocco and Mauritania; signed peace treaty with Mauritanian Govt in 1979; supported by Algerian Govt; in February 1976 proclaimed the Sahrawi Arab Democratic Republic (SADR); admitted as the 51st member of the OAU in Feb. 1982 and currently recognized by more than 75 countries worldwide; its main organs are a 33-member National Secretariat, a 101-member Sahrawi National Assembly (Parliament) and a 13-member Govt; Sec.-Gen. of the Polisario Front and Pres. of the SADR MUHAMMAD ABD AL-AZIZ; Prime Minister of the SADR BOUCHRAYA HAMMOUDI BAYOUNE.

Diplomatic Representation

EMBASSIES IN MOROCCO

Algeria: 46–48 blvd Tariq Ibn Ziad, BP 448, 10001 Rabat; tel. (3) 7765591; fax (3) 7762237; e-mail algerabat@iam.net.ma; Ambassador: Dr BOUALEM BESSAIEH.

Angola: km 4.5, route des Zaêrs, BP 1318, Soussi, Rabat; tel. (3) 7659239; fax (3) 7653703; e-mail amb.angola@iam.net.ma; Ambassador: Dr LUIS JOSÉ DE ALMEIDA.

Argentina: 12 rue Mekki Bitaouri, Souissi, 10000 Rabat; tel. (3) 7755120; fax (3) 7755410; e-mail embarat@maghrebnet.net.ma; Ambassador: EDGARDO RENÉ PIUZZI.

Austria: 2 rue de Tiddas, BP 135, 10001 Rabat; tel. (3) 7764003; fax (3) 7765425; e-mail autrich@mtds.com; Ambassador: Dr MICHAEL FITZ.

Bahrain: 318 rue Beni Hassan, km 6.5, route des Zaêrs, Soussi, Rabat; tel. (3) 7656024; fax (3) 7630732; Ambassador: MUSTAFA KAMAL MUHAMMAD.

Bangladesh: 25 ave Tarek Ibn Ziad, Rabat; tel. (3) 7766731; fax (3) 7766729; e-mail bdoot@mtds.com; internet www.bangladeshembassy-morocco.org; Ambassador: Maj.-Gen. MOHAMMAD ANWAR HOSSAIN.

Belgium: 6 ave de Marrakech, BP 163, 10001 Rabat; tel. (3) 7764746; fax (3) 7767003; e-mail info@ambabel-rabat.org.ma; Ambassador: MICHEL CARLIER.

Benin: 30 ave Mehdi Ben Barka, BP 5187, Souissi, 10105 Rabat; tel. (3) 7754158; fax (3) 77754156; Ambassador: IBRAHIM ISSIRADJOU GOMINA.

Brazil: 3 rue Cadi Benjelloun, La Pinède, BP 414, 10000 Rabat; tel. (3) 7755151; fax (3) 7755291; Ambassador: LAURO BARBOSA DA SILVA MOREIRA.

Bulgaria: 4 ave Ahmed El Yazidi, BP 1301, 10000 Rabat; tel. (3) 7765477; fax (3) 7763201; Ambassador: Dr GEORGE B. KAREV.

Burkina Faso: 7 rue al Bouziri, BP 6484, Agdal, 10101 Rabat; tel. (3) 7675512; fax (3) 7675517; e-mail ambfrba@smirt.net.ma; Ambassador: ASSIMI KOUANDA.

Cameroon: 20 rue du Rif, BP 1790, Souissi, Rabat; tel. (3) 7754194; fax (3) 7750540; e-mail ambacamrabat@ifrance.com; Ambassador: MAHAMAT PABA SALÉ.

Canada: 13 bis rue Jaafar as-Sadik, BP 709, Agdal, Rabat; tel. (3) 7687400; fax (3) 7687430; Ambassador: YVES GAGNON.

Central African Republic: 42 rue Pasteur, BP 770, Agdal, 10000 Rabat; tel. (3) 7734198; Ambassador: MARTIN KOYOU KOMBELE.

Chile: 35 ave Ahmed Balafrej, Souissi, Rabat; tel. (3) 7636065; fax (3) 7636067; e-mail echilema@maghrebnet.net.ma; Ambassador: ALEJANDRO CARVAJAL.

China, People's Republic: 16 ave Ahmed Balafrej, 10000 Rabat; tel. (3) 7754056; fax (3) 7757519; Ambassador: XIONG ZHANQI.

Colombia: Residence place Otman Ibnou Affane, 3eme étage, App. no 12, angle ave 16 Novembre et rue Honaine, Agdal, 10000 Rabat; tel. (3) 7670804; fax (3) 7670802; e-mail emcora@smirt.net.ma; Ambassador: GUILLERMO SALAH ZULETTA.

Congo, Democratic Republic: 34 ave de la Victoire, BP 553, 10002 Rabat; tel. (3) 7262280; fax (3) 7631971; Ambassador: BOLENGE LUTA.

Côte d'Ivoire: 21 rue de Tiddas, BP 192, 10001 Rabat; tel. (3) 7763151; fax (3) 7762792; e-mail ambcim@dial.net.ma; Ambassador: DAOUDA DIABATÉ.

Croatia: 73 rue Marnissa, Souissi, Rabat; tel. (3) 7638824; fax (3) 7638827; e-mail croamb@acdim.net.ma.

Czech Republic: rue Ait Melloul, BP 410, Souissi, 10001 Rabat; tel. (3) 7755421; fax (3) 7755493; e-mail rabat@embassy.mzv.cz; internet www.mzv.cz/rabat; Ambassador: PAVEL JAJTNER.

Egypt: 31 rue al-Jazair, 10000 Rabat; tel. (3) 7731833; fax (3) 7706821; Ambassador: ACHRAF YUSSUF ABDELHALIM ZAÂZAÂ.

Equatorial Guinea: ave President Roosevelt, angle rue d'Agadir 9, Rabat; tel. (3) 7764793; fax (3) 7764704; Ambassador: (vacant).

Finland: 145 rue Soufiane Ben Wahb, OLM, Rabat; tel. (3) 7762312; fax (3) 7762352; e-mail admin@ambafinrab.org.ma; Ambassador: MATTI HAKKANEN.

France: 3 rue Sahnoun, 10000 Rabat; tel. (3) 7689706; fax (3) 7689720; e-mail michel.de-bonnecorse@diplomatie.fr; internet www .ambafrance-ma.org; Ambassador: MICHEL DE BONNECORSE BENAULT DE LUBIÈRES.

Gabon: ave Imam Malik, km 3.5, BP 1239, 10100 Rabat; tel. (3) 7751968; fax (3) 7757550; Ambassador: VICTOR AFOUNOUNA.

Germany: 7 rue Madnine, BP 235, 10000 Rabat; tel. (3) 7709662; fax (3) 7706851; e-mail amballma@mtds.com; internet www.amb allemagne-rabat.com; Ambassador: HANS-DIETER SCHEEL.

Greece: km 5 route des Zaiers, Villa Chems, Souissi, 10000 Rabat; tel. (3) 7638964; fax (3) 7638990; e-mail ambagrec@iam.net.ma; Ambassador: MICHEL CAMBANIS.

Guinea: 15 rue Hamzah, Agdal, 10000 Rabat; tel. (3) 7674148; fax (3) 7672513; Ambassador: MAHMADOU SALIOU SYLA.

Holy See: rue Béni M'tir, BP 1303, Souissi, Rabat (Apostolic Nunciature); tel. (3) 7772277; fax (3) 7756213; e-mail nuntius@iam.net.ma; Apostolic Nuncio: Most Rev. DOMENICO DE LUCA, Titular Archbishop of Teglata in Numidia.

Hungary: 21 blvd Jerror, Souissi, BP 5026, Rabat; tel. (3) 7750757; fax (3) 7754123; e-mail huembrba@mtds.com; Ambassador: KÁROLY GEDAI.

India: 13 ave de Michlifen, 10000 Rabat; tel. (3) 7671339; fax (3) 7671269; e-mail india@maghrebnet.net.ma; Ambassador: INDRAJIT SINGH RATHORE.

Indonesia: 63 rue Béni Boufrah, km 5.9 route des Zaêrs, BP 5076, 10105 Rabat; tel. (3) 7757860; fax (3) 7757859; e-mail rabatina@ maghrebnet.net; Ambassador: IMRON HARDJITO.

Iran: ave Imam Malik, BP 490, 10001 Rabat; tel. (3) 7752167; fax (3) 7659118; Ambassador: MUHAMMAD REDA BAKHTIARI.

Iraq: 39 blvd Mehdi Ben Barka, 10100 Rabat; tel. (3) 7754466; fax (3) 7759749; Ambassador: ABD AL-JABBAR OMAR GHANI AD-DURI.

Italy: 2 rue Idriss al-Azhar, BP 111, 10001 Rabat; tel. (3) 7720852; fax (3) 7706882; e-mail ambraba@iam.net.ma; Ambassador: GUIDO MARTINI.

Japan: 39 ave Ahmed Balafrej, Souissi, 10100 Rabat; tel. (3) 7631782; fax (3) 7750078; e-mail amb-japon@fusion.net.ma; Ambassador: HIROMI SATO.

Jordan: Villa al-Wafae, Lot 5, Souissi II, 10000 Rabat; tel. (3) 7751125; fax (3) 7758722; Ambassador: MUHAMMAD HASSAN SOLEIMANE AD-DAOUDIA.

Korea, Republic: 41 ave Mehdi Ben Barka, Souissi, 10100 Rabat; tel. (3) 7751767; fax (3) 7750189; e-mail adambco@iam.net.ma; Ambassador: JU CHUL-KU.

Kuwait: ave Imam Malik, km 4.3, BP 11, 10001 Rabat; tel. (3) 7751775; fax (3) 7753591; Ambassador: SALAH MUHAMMAD AL-BIJAN.

Lebanon: 19 ave Adb al-Karim Ben Jalloun, 10000 Rabat; tel. (3) 7760728; fax (3) 7760949; Ambassador: MOUSTAPHA HASSAN MOUSTAPHA.

Liberia: Lotissement no 7, Napabia, rue Ouled Frej, Souissi, Rabat; tel. (3) 7638426.

Libya: 1 rue Chouaïb Doukkali, BP 225, 10000 Rabat; tel. (3) 7769566; fax (3) 7705200; Ambassador: EMBAREK ABDALLAH TURKI.

Malaysia: ave Bir Kacem, Soussi, Rabat; tel. (3) 7658324; fax (3) 7658363; e-mail mwrabat@maghrebnet.net; Ambassador: SIDDIQ FIRDAUSE BIN MOHD ALI.

Mali: rue Thami Lamadour, Souissi, Rabat; tel. (3) 7759125; fax (3) 7754742; Ambassador: FOUSSEIN SY.

Mauritania: 6 rue Thami Lamdour, BP 207, Souissi, 10000 Rabat; tel. (3) 7656678; fax (3) 7656680; e-mail ambassadeur@mauritanie .org.ma; Ambassador: DAH OULD ABDI.

Mexico: 6 rue Cadi Mohamed Brebi, BP 1789, Souissi, Rabat; tel. (3) 7631969; fax (3) 7768583; e-mail embamexmar@smirt.net.ma; Ambassador: ANTONIO DE ICAZA.

Netherlands: 40 rue de Tunis, BP 329, 10001 Rabat; tel. (3) 7726780; fax (3) 7733333; e-mail nlgovrab@mtds.com; Ambassador: JOHANNES A. F. M. REVIS.

Niger: 14 Bis, rue Jabal al-Ayachi, Agdal, Rabat; tel. (3) 7674615; fax (3) 7674629; Ambassador: RAMATOU DIORI HAMANI.

Nigeria: 70 ave Omar ibn al-Khattab, BP 347, Agdal, 10001 Rabat; tel. (3) 7673856; fax (3) 7672739; nigembassy@maghrebnet.net.ma; Ambassador: LADAN ADBULLAHI SHUNI.

Norway: 9 rue Khenifra, Agdal, Rabat; tel. (3) 7764085; fax (3) 7764088; e-mail emb.rabat@mfa.no; Ambassador: OLE KRISTIAN HOLTHE.

Oman: 21 rue Hamza, Agdal, 10000 Rabat; tel. (3) 7673788; fax (3) 7674567; Ambassador: MAHMOUD BIN ALI MUHAMMAD AR-RAHMAN.

Pakistan: 11 Zankat Azrou, 10000 Rabat; tel. (3) 7762402; fax (3) 7766742; e-mail parerabat@maghrebnet.net.ma; Ambassador: Maj. Gen. (Retd) SHUJAAT ALI KHAN.

Peru: 16 rue d'Ifrane, 10000 Rabat; tel. (3) 7723236; fax (3) 7702803; e-mail lepruab@netpartners.net.ma; Ambassador: JUAN ENRIQUE AREVALO.

Poland: 23 rue Oqbah, Agdal, BP 425, 10000 Rabat; tel. (3) 7771173; fax (3) 7775320; e-mail apologne@iam.net.ma; internet www .ambpologne.ma; Ambassador: MIECZYSŁAW JACEK STEPIŃSKI.

Portugal: 5 rue Thami Lamdouar, Souissi, 10100 Rabat; tel. (3) 7756446; fax (3) 7756445; e-mail cleote@icamoes-ccrabat.pt; Ambassador: RUI GONÇALO DE BRITO E CUNHA.

Qatar: 4 ave Tarik ibn Ziad, BP 1220, 10001 Rabat; tel. (3) 7765681; fax (3) 7765774; e-mail qe-rabat@mtds.com; Ambassador: SAQR MUBARAK AL-MANSOURI.

Romania: 10 rue d'Ouezzane, 10000 Rabat; tel. (3) 7738611; fax (3) 7700196; e-mail amb.roumanie@smirt.net.ma; Ambassador: GELU VOICAN VOICULESCU.

Russia: km 4 route des Zaiers, 10100 Rabat; tel. (3) 7753509; fax (3) 7753590; e-mail consruss@mtds.com; Ambassador: YURII KOTOV.

Saudi Arabia: 43 place de l'Unité Africaine, 10000 Rabat; tel. (3) 7730171; fax (3) 7768587; e-mail ambassd@goodinfo.net.ma; Ambassador: ABD AL-AZIZ KHODJA.

Senegal: 17 rue Cadi ben Hamadi Senhaji, Souissi, 10000 Rabat; tel. (3) 7754171; fax (3) 7754149; Ambassador: DOUDOU DIOP.

South Africa: 34 rue Saadiens, Rabat; tel. (3) 7706760; fax (3) 7706756; e-mail sudaf@mtds.com; Ambassador: M. MTUTUZELI. MPEHLE.

Spain: 3 rue Madnine, BP 1354, 10000 Rabat; tel. (3) 7707600; fax (3) 7707387; e-mail infembsp@mtds.com; Ambassador: FERNANDO ARIAS-SALGADO Y MONTALVO.

Sudan: 5 ave Ghomara, Souissi, 10000 Rabat; tel. (3) 7752863; fax (3) 7752865; e-mail soudanirab@maghrebnet.net.ma; Ambassador: AHMED MEKKI AHMED YAHIA.

Sweden: 159 ave John Kennedy, BP 428, 10000 Rabat; tel. (3) 7759303; fax (3) 7758048; e-mail swedrab@mtds.com; Ambassador: NILS ANDERS PETER BRUCE.

Switzerland: Square de Berkane, BP 169, 10001 Rabat; tel. (3) 7706974; fax (3) 7705749; e-mail vertretung@rab.rep.admin.ch; Ambassador: DANIEL VON MURALT.

Syria: km 5.2, route des Zaêrs, BP 5158, Souissi, Rabat; tel. (3) 7755551; fax (3) 7757522; Ambassador: ALI HASSAN.

Thailand: 11 rue de Tiddas, BP 4436, Rabat; tel. (3) 7763328; fax (3) 7763920; e-mail thairab@wanadoo.net.ma; Ambassador: SIRIWAT SUTHIGASAME.

Tunisia: 6 ave de Fès et 1 rue d'Ifrane, 10000 Rabat; tel. (3) 7730636; fax (3) 7730637; Ambassador: SALAH BEKKARI.

Turkey: 7 ave Abdelkrim Benjelloun, 10000 Rabat; tel. (3) 7762605; fax (3) 7660476; e-mail amb-tur-rabat@iam.net.ma; Ambassador: HUSEYIN NACI AKINCI.

Ukraine: Cite OLM Soussi II, Villa 212, Rabat; tel. (3) 7657840; Ambassador: YOURI F. MALKO.

United Arab Emirates: 11 ave des Alaouines, 10000 Rabat; tel. (3) 7702085; fax (3) 7724145; e-mail uaerabat@mtds.com; Ambassador: ISSAA HAMAD BUSHAHAB.

United Kingdom: 17 blvd de la Tour Hassan, BP 45, 10001 Rabat; tel. (3) 77238600; fax (3) 7704531; e-mail britemb@mtds.com; internet www.britain.org.ma; Ambassador: HAYDON WARREN-GASH.

USA: 2 ave de Muhammad al-Fassi, Rabat; tel. (3) 7762265; fax (3) 7765661; internet www.usembassy-morocco.org.ma; Ambassador: MARGARET DEB. TUTWILER.

Venezuela: 173 ave John Kennedy, Soussi, Rabat; tel. (3) 7650315; fax (3) 7650372; Ambassador: HORACIO ARTEAGA ACOSTA.

Yemen: 11 rue Abou-Hanifa, Agdal, 10000 Rabat; tel. (3) 7674306; fax (3) 7674769; e-mail yemenembassy@iam.net.ma; Ambassador: Dr ALI MTENA HASSAN.

Yugoslavia: 23 ave Mehdi Ben Barka, Souissi, BP 5014, 10105 Rabat; tel. (3) 7752201; fax (3) 7753258; e-mail youg@iam.net.ma; Chargé d'affaires: GOLUB LAZOVIĆ.

Judicial System

SUPREME COURT

Al-Majlis al-Aala: Hay Ryad, blvd An-Nakhil, Rabat; tel. (3) 7714932; e-mail coursupreme@maghrebnet.net.ma; internet www .maghrebnet.net.ma/cour-supreme/; is responsible for the interpretation of the law and regulates the jurisprudence of the courts and tribunals of the Kingdom. The Supreme Court sits at Rabat and is divided into six Chambers.

First President: DRISS DAHAK.

Attorney-General: MUHAMMAD ABDELMOUNIM EL-MEJBOUD.

The 21 **Courts of Appeal** hear appeals from lower courts and also comprise a criminal division.

The 65 **Courts of First Instance** pass judgment on offences punishable by up to five years' imprisonment. These courts also pass judgment, without possibility of appeal, in personal and civil cases involving up to 3,000 dirhams.

The **Communal and District Courts** are composed of one judge, who is assisted by a clerk or secretary, and hear only civil and criminal cases.

The seven **Administrative Courts** pass judgement, subject to appeal before the Supreme Court pending the establishment of administrative appeal courts, on litigation with Government departments.

The nine **Commercial Courts** pass judgement, without the possibility of appeal, on all commercial litigations involving up to 9,000 dirhams. They also pass judgement on claims involving more than 9,000 dirhams, which can be appealed against in the commercial appeal courts.

The **Special Court of Justice** presides over crimes and felonies allegedly committed by Government officials or judges involving 25,000 dirhams or more.

The **Permanent Royal Armed Forces' Court** tries offences committed by the armed forces and military officers.

Religion

ISLAM

About 99% of Moroccans are Muslims (of whom about 90% are of the Sunni sect), and Islam is the state religion.

CHRISTIANITY

There are about 69,000 Christians, mostly Roman Catholics.

The Roman Catholic Church

Morocco (excluding the disputed territory of Western Sahara) comprises two archdioceses, directly responsible to the Holy See. At 31 December 2000 there were an estimated 24,000 adherents in the country, representing less than 0.1% of the population. The Moroccan archbishops participate in the Conférence Episcopale Régionale du Nord de l'Afrique (f. 1985), based in Algiers (Algeria).

Archbishop of Rabat: Most Rev. VINCENT LANDEL, Archevêché, 1 rue Hadj Muhammad Riffaï, BP 258, 10001 Rabat; tel. (3) 7709239; fax (3) 7706282; e-mail landel@wanadoo.net.ma.

Archbishop of Tangier: Most Rev. JOSÉ ANTONIO PETEIRO FREIRE, Archevêché, 55 rue Sidi Bouabid, BP 2116, 9000 Tangier; tel. (3) 9932762; fax (3) 9949117; e-mail igletanger@wanadoo.net.ma.

Western Sahara comprises a single Apostolic Prefecture, with an estimated 150 Catholics (2000).

Prefect Apostolic of Western Sahara: Fr ACACIO VALBUENA RODRÍGUEZ, Misión Católica, BP 31, 70001 el-Aaiún; tel. 893270.

The Anglican Communion

Within the Church of England, Morocco forms part of the diocese of Gibraltar in Europe. There are Anglican churches in Casablanca and Tangier.

Protestant Church

Evangelical Church: 33 rue d'Azilal, 20000 Casablanca; tel. (2) 2302151; fax (2) 2444768; e-mail eeam@lesblancs.com; f. 1920; established in six towns; Pres. Pastor JEAN-LUC BLANC; 1,000 mems.

JUDAISM

There is a Jewish community of some 8,000. In March 1999 the Moroccan authorities reopened the synagogue in Fez, established in the 17th century.

Grand Rabbi of Casablanca: CHALOM MESSAS, President of the Rabbinical Court of Casablanca, Palais de Justice, place des Nations Unies.

The Press

DAILIES

Casablanca

Assahra Al-Maghribia: 88 blvd Muhammad V, Casablanca; tel. (2) 2268860; fax (2) 2203935; f. 1989; Arabic; Dir ABD AL-HAFID ROUISSI.

Al-Bayane (The Manifesto): 62 blvd de la Gironde, BP 13152, Casablanca; tel. (2) 2307882; internet www.casanet.ma/albayane; Arabic and French; organ of the Parti du progrès et du socialisme; Dir ISMAIL ALAOUI; circ. 5,000.

Al-Ittihad al-Ichtiraki (Socialist Unity): 33 rue Emir Abdelkader, BP 2165, Casablanca; tel. (2) 2619400; fax (2) 2619405; Arabic; organ of the Union socialiste des forces populaires; Dir ABDALLAH BOUHLAL; Editor ABD AR-RAHMAN EL-YOUSSOUFI; circ. 110,000.

L'Economiste: 201 blvd Bordeaux, Casablanca; tel. (2) 2271650; fax (2) 2297285; e-mail info@leconomiste.com; internet www .leconomiste.com; f. 1991; weekly; French; Dir ABDELMOUNAÏM DILAMI: Editor NADIA SALAH; circ. 24,000.

Libération: 33 rue Emir Abdelkader, Casablanca; tel. (2) 2310062; internet www.liberation.press.ma; f.11964; French; organ of the Union socialiste des forces populaires; Dir MUHAMMAD AL-YAZGHI.

Maroc Soir: 88 blvd Muhammad V, Casablanca; tel. (2) 2268860; fax (2) 2262969; f. 1971; French; Dir DRISSI EL-ALAMI; circ. 50,000.

Le Matin du Sahara et du Maghreb: 88 blvd Muhammad V, Casablanca; tel. (2) 2268860; fax (2) 2317535; e-mail contact@ lematin.press.ma; internet www.lematin.press.ma; f. 1971; French; Dir ABD AL-HAFID ROUISSI; circ. 100,000.

Rissalat al-Oumma (The Message of the Nation): 158 ave des Forces Armées Royales, Casablanca; tel. (2) 2901925; Arabic; weekly edition in French; organ of the Union constitutionnelle; Dir MUHAMMAD ALAOUI MUHAMMADI.

Rabat

Al-Alam (The Flag): 11 ave Allal ben Abdallah, BP 141, Rabat; tel. (3) 7732419; fax (3) 7733896; f. 1946; organ of the Istiqlal party; Arabic; literary supplement on Fridays; weekly edition on Mondays; monthly edition on foreign policy; Dir ABD AL-KRIM GHALLAB; circ. 100,000.

Al-Anba'a (Information): ave Allal el-Fassi, Rabat; tel. (3) 7683967; fax (3) 7683970; internet www.alanbaa.press.ma; f. 2000; daily; Arabic; publ. by Ministry of Communication; Dir (Editorial) MUHAMMAD BELGHAZI.

Assyassa al-Jadida: 43 rue Abou Fares al-Marini, BP 1385, Rabat; tel. (3) 7208571; fax (3) 7208573; e-mail assassjdid@maghrebnet .net.ma; f. 1997; Arabic; organ of the Parti socialiste démocratique; Dir ABD AL-LATIF AOUAD: Editor TALAA ASSOUD ALATLASSI.

Al-Maghrib: 6 rue Laos, BP 469, Rabat; tel. (3) 7722708; fax (3) 7722765; f. 1977; French; organ of the Rassemblement national des indépendants (RNI); Dir MUSTAPHA IZNASNI; circ. 15,000.

Al-Mithaq al-Watani (The National Charter): 6 rue Laos, BP 469, Rabat; tel. (3) 7722708; fax (3) 7722765; f. 1977; Arabic; organ of the RNI; Dir MED AUAJJAR; circ. 25,000.

An-Nidal ad-Dimokrati (The Democratic Struggle): 18 rue de Tunis, Rabat; tel. (3) 7730754; fax (3) 7731255; Arabic; organ of the Parti national démocrate; Dir MUHAMMAD ARSALANE AL-JADIDI.

L'Opinion: 11 ave Allal ben Abdallah, Rabat; tel. (3) 7727812; fax (3) 7732181; f. 1965; French; organ of the Istiqlal party; Dir MUHAMMAD IDRISSI KAÏTOUNI; Ed. JAMAL HAJJAM; circ. 60,000.

SELECTED PERIODICALS

Casablanca

Achamal: Casablanca; weekly; Arabic; Ed. in Chief KHALID MECHBAL.

Bulletin Mensuel de la Chambre de Commerce et d'Industrie de la Wilaya du Grand Casablanca: 98 blvd Muhammad V, BP 423, Casablanca; tel. (2) 2264327; monthly; French; Pres. LAHCEN EL-WAFI.

CGEM Infos: angle ave des Forces Armées Royales et rue Muhammad Arrachid, 20100 Casablanca; tel. (2) 2986932; fax (2) 2253845; e-mail cgem@iam.net.ma; weekly; French; Admin. MOUHCINE AYOUCHE.

Construire: 25 rue d'Azilal, Immeuble Ortiba, Casablanca; tel. (2) 2305721; fax (2) 2317577; f. 1940; weekly; French; Dir TALAL BOUCHAIB.

Demain: Casablanca; f. 1997; weekly, French; Dir ALI LAMRABET.

Les Echos Africains: Immeuble SONIR, angle blvd Smiha, rue d'Anjou, BP 13140, Casablanca; tel. (2) 2307271; fax (2) 2319680; f. 1972; monthly; French; news, economics; Dir MUHAMMAD CHOUFFANI EL-FASSI; Editor Mme SOODIA FARIDI; circ. 5,000.

La Gazette du Maroc: ave des Forces Armées Royales, Tour de Habous, 13eme étage, Casablanca; tel. (2) 2313925; fax (2) 2318094; e-mail info@gazette.press.ma; internet www.gazette.press.ma; weekly; French; Dir KAMAL LAHLOU.

Al-Ittihad al-Watani Lilkouate ach-Chaabia (National Union of Popular Forces): 28–30 rue Magellan, Casablanca; tel. (2) 2302023; fax (2) 2319301; weekly; Arabic; organ of the Union nationale des forces populaires; Dir MOULAY ABDALLAH IBRAHIM.

Le Journal: Media Trust, Iman Centre, Casablanca; tel. (2) 2548700; fax (2) 2542073; e-mail media@marocnet.net.ma; internet www.lejournal.press.ma; weekly; French; news, economics; Dir ABOUBAKR JAMAI.

Lamalif: 6 bis rue Defly Dieude, Casablanca; tel. (2) 2220032; f. 1966; monthly; French; economic, social and cultural magazine; Dir MUHAMMAD LOGHLAM.

La Mañana: 88 blvd Muhammad V, Casablanca; tel. (2) 2268860; fax (2) 2203935; f. 1990; Spanish; Dir ABD AL-HAFID ROUISSI.

Maroc Fruits: 22 rue Al-Messaoudi, Casablanca; tel. (2) 2363946; fax (2) 2364041; f. 1958; fortnightly; Arabic and French; organ of the Association des Producteurs d'Agrumes du Maroc; Dir NEJJAI AHMAD MANSOUR; circ. 6,000.

Maroc Soir: 34 rue Muhammad Smiha, Casablanca; tel. (2) 2301271; fax (2) 2317535; f. 1971; French; Dir ABD AL-HAFID ROUISSI; circ. 30,000.

Matin Hebdo: 34 rue Muhammad Smiha, Casablanca; tel. (2) 2301271; weekly; Dir AHMAD AL-ALAMI.

Matin Magazine: 88 blvd Muhammad V, Casablanca; tel. (2) 2268860; fax (2) 2262969; f. 1971; weekly; French; Dir ABD AL-HAFID ROUISSI.

An-Nidal (The Struggle): 10 rue Cols Bleus, Sidi Bousmara, Médina Kédima, Casablanca; f. 1973; weekly; Arabic; organ of the Parti national démocrate; Dir IBRAHIMI AHMAD.

La Nouvelle Tribune: 1 blvd Abd al-Latif Ben Kaddour, angle blvd Zerktouni, Casablanca; tel. (2) 2940911; fax (2) 2940914; e-mail nouvelle-tribune@techno.net.ma; internet www.lanouvelle tribune.press.ma; f. 1996; weekly; French; Dir FAHD YATA; circ. 25,000.

Les Nouvelles du Maroc: 28 ave des Forces Armées Royales, Casablanca; tel. (2) 2203031; fax (2) 2277181; weekly; French; Dir KHADIJA S. IDRISSI.

Al-Ousbouaa al-Maghribia: 158 ave des Forces Armées Royales, Casablanca; f. 1984; organ of the Union constitutionnelle; Éditor MUSTAFA ALAOUI.

La Quinzaine du Maroc: 53 rue Dumont d'Urville, Casablanca; tel. (2) 2302482; fax (2) 2440426; e-mail mauro@marocnet.net.ma; f. 1951; monthly; English and French; Dir HUBERT MAURO.

Revue Marocaine de Droit: 24 rue Nolly, Casablanca; tel. (2) 2273673; quarterly; French and Arabic; Dirs J. P. RAZON, A. KETTANI.

As-Sahifa: Casablanca; weekly; Arabic; Dir ABOUBAKR JAMAI.

Les Temps du Maroc: 88 blvd Muhammad V, Casablanca; tel. (2) 2268860; fax (2) 2262969; f. 1995; e-mail contact@lematin.press.ma; internet www.tempsdumaroc.press.ma; weekly; French; Dir ABD AL-HAFID ROUISSI.

La Vie Economique: 5 blvd ben Yacine, 20300 Casablanca; tel. (2) 2443868; fax (2) 2304542; e-mail vieeco@marocnet.net.ma; internet www.marocnet.net.ma/vieeco; f. 1921; weekly; French; Pres. and Dir JEAN LOUIS SERVAN-SCHREIBER.

La Vie Industrielle et Agricole: 142 blvd Muhammad V, Casablanca; tel. (2) 2274407; 2 a month; French; Dir AHMAD ZAGHARI.

La Vie Touristique Africaine: 142 blvd Muhammad V, Casablanca; tel. (2) 2274407; fortnightly; French; tourist information; Dir AHMAD ZAGHARI.

Rabat

Al-Aklam (The Pens): Rabat; monthly; Arabic; Dir ABD AR-RAHMAN BEN AMAR.

Al-Anba'a (Information): ave Allal el-Fassi, Rabat; tel. (3) 7683967; fax (3) 7683970; internet www.alanbaa.press.ma; f. 2000; weekly; Arabic; publ. by Ministry of Communication; Dir (Editorial) MUHAMMAD BELGHAZI.

Assiassa Al-Jadida: 8 rue Sanaa, BP 1385, Rabat; tel. (3) 7208571; fax (3) 7208573; e-mail aouad@nsimail.com; f. 1996; weekly; Arabic; organ of the Partie socialiste démocratique; Dir ABDELLATIF AOUAD.

Ach-Chorta (The Police): BP 437, Rabat; tel. (3) 7723194; monthly; Arabic; Dir MUHAMMAD AD-DRIF.

Da'ouat Al-Haqq (Call of the Truth): al-Michwar as-Said, Rabat; publ. by Ministry of Habous (Religious Endowments) and Islamic Affairs; tel. (3) 7760810; f. 1957; monthly; Arabic.

Al-Haraka: 66 rue Patrice Lumumba, BP 1317, Rabat; tel. (3) 7768667; fax (3) 7768677; weekly; Arabic; organ of the Mouvement populaire; Dir ALI ALAOUI.

Al-Imane: rue Akenssous, BP 356, Rabat; f. 1963; monthly; Arabic; Dir ABOU BAKER AL-KADIRI.

Al-Irchad (Spiritual Guidance): al-Michwar as-Said, Rabat; publ. by Ministry of Religious Endowments (Awqaf) and Islamic Affairs; tel. (3) 7760810; f. 1967; monthly; Arabic.

Al-Khansa: 154 ave Souss Mohammadia, Rabat; monthly; Arabic; Dir ABOUZAL AICHA.

Al-Maghribi: Rabat; tel. (3) 7768139; weekly; Arabic; organ of the Parti de l'action; Dir ABDALLAH AL-HANANI.

At-Tadamoun: Rabat; monthly; Arabic; Dir ABD AL-MAJID SEMLALI EL-HASANI.

La Verité: Rabat; weekly; French; Chief Ed. ALLAL EL-MALEH.

La Voix du Centre: Rabat; weekly; French; Ed.-in-chief MUSTAPHA SHIMI.

Tangier

Actualités Touristiques: 80 rue de la Liberté, Tangier; monthly; French; Dir TAYEB ALAMI.

Le Journal de Tanger: 11 ave Moulay Abd al-Aziz, BP 420, Tangier; tel. (3) 7946051; fax (3) 7945709; e-mail redact@journalde tanger.com; internet www.journaldetanger.com; f. 1904; weekly; French, English, Spanish and Arabic; Dir BAKHAT ABD AL-HAQ; circ. 10,000.

NEWS AGENCIES

Maghreb Arabe Presse (MAP): 122 ave Allal ben Abdallah, BP 1049, 10000 Rabat; tel. (3) 7764083; fax (3) 7702734; e-mail direction@map.co.ma; internet www.map.co.ma; f. 1959; Arabic, French, English and Spanish; state-owned; Dir-Gen. MUHAMMAD YASSINE MANSOURI.

Foreign Bureaux

Agence France-Presse (AFP): 2 bis rue du Caire, BP 118, Rabat; tel. (3) 7768943; fax (3) 7700357; f. 1920; Dir IGNACE DALLE.

Agencia EFE (Spain): 14 ave du Kairouane, Rabat; tel. (3) 7723218; fax (3) 7732195; Bureau Chief ALBERTO MASEGOSA GARCÍA-CALAMARTE.

Informatsionnoye Telegrafnoye Agentstvo Rossii—Telegrafnoye Agentstvo Suverennykh Stran (ITAR—TASS) (Russia): 32 rue de la Somme, Rabat; tel. (3) 7750315; Dir OLEG CHIROKOV.

Inter Press Service (IPS) (Italy): Rabat; tel. (3) 7756869; fax (3) 7727183; e-mail ipseumed@hotmail.com; internet www.ips.org; Dir BOULOUIZ BOUCHRA.

Reuters (United Kingdom): 509 Immeuble es-Saada, ave Hassan II, Rabat; tel. (3) 7726518; fax (3) 7722499; Chief Correspondent (North Africa) JOHN BAGGALEY.

Xinhua (New China) News Agency (People's Republic of China): 4 rue Kadi Mekki el-Bitaouri, Souissi, Rabat; tel. (3) 7755320; fax (3) 7754319; Dir ZHUGE CANGLIN.

Publishers

Dar el-Kitab: place de la Mosquée, Quartier des Habous, BP 4018, Casablanca; tel. (2) 2305419; fax (2) 2304581; f. 1948; philosophy, history, Africana, general and social science; Arabic and French; Dir BOUTALEB ABDOU ABD AL-HAY; Gen. Man. KHADIJA EL KASSIMI.

Editions La Porte: 281 blvd Muhammad V, BP 331, Rabat; tel. (3) 7709958; fax (3) 7706476; e-mail la_porte@meganet.net.ma; law, guides, economics, educational books.

Les Editions Maghrébines: Quartier Industrial, blvd E, N 15, Sin Sebaa, Casablanca; tel. (2) 2351797; fax (2) 2355541; f. 1962; general non-fiction.

Government Publishing House

Imprimerie Officielle: ave Yacoub El Mansour, Rabat-Chellah; tel. (3) 7765024; fax (3) 7765179.

Broadcasting and Communications

TELECOMMUNICATIONS

Regulatory Authority

Agence Nationale de Réglementation des Télécommunications (ANRT): Centre d'Affaires, blvd Ar-Ryad; Hay Ryad, BP 2939,

10100 Rabat; tel. (3) 7718400; fax (3) 7716489; f. 1998; e-mail webmaster@anrt.net.ma; internet www.anrt.net.ma; Dir-Gen. OTHMANE DEMNATI.

Principal Operators

Itissalat al-Maghrib—Maroc Télécom: ave Annakhil Hay Riad, Rabat; tel. (3) 7712626; fax (3) 7714860; internet www.iam.ma; f. 1998 to take over telephone services from the ONPT; scheduled for partial transfer to private ownership in 2002; Dir ABDESSALEM AHIZOUNE.

BROADCASTING

Morocco can receive broadcasts from Spanish radio stations, and the main Spanish television channels can also be received in northern Morocco.

Radio

Radiodiffusion-Télévision Marocaine: 1 rue el-Brihi, BP 1042, 1000 Rabat; tel. (3) 7709613; fax (3) 7703208; internet www.maroc.net/rc; govt station; Network A in Arabic, Network B in French, English and Spanish, Network C in Berber and Arabic; Foreign Service in Arabic, French and English; Dir-Gen. MUHAMMAD TRICHA; Dir Radio ABD AR-RAHMAN ACHOUR.

Radio Méditerranée Internationale: 3–5 rue Emsallah, BP 2055, Tangier; tel. and fax (3) 9936363; e-mail medi1@medi1.com; internet www.medi1.com; Arabic and French; Man. Dir PIERRE CASALTA.

Voice of America Radio Station in Tangier: c/o US Consulate-General, chemin des Amoureux, Tangier.

Television

Radiodiffusion-Télévision Marocaine: 1 rue el-Brihi, BP 1042, 1000 Rabat; tel. (3) 7709613; fax (3) 7703208; internet www.maroc.net/rc; govt station; transmission commenced 1962; 45 hours weekly; French and Arabic; carries commercial advertising; Dir-Gen. MUHAMMAD TRICHA; Dir Television FAICAL LAARAICHI.

SOREAD 2M: Société d'études et de réalisations audiovisuelles, km 7.3 route de Rabat, Aïn-Sebaâ, Casablanca; tel. (2) 2667373; fax (2) 2667392; internet www.2m.tv; f. 1988, transmission commenced 1989; public television channel, owned by Moroccan Government (72%) and by private national foreign concerns; broadcasting in French and Arabic; Man. Dir NOUR EDDINE SAIL.

Finance

(cap. = capital; res = reserves; dep. = deposits; m. = million; brs = branches; amounts in dirhams unless otherwise indicated)

BANKING

Central Bank

Bank Al-Maghrib: 277 ave Muhammad V, BP 445, Rabat; tel. (3) 7702626; fax (3) 7706677; e-mail dai@bkam.gov.ma; internet www.bkam.ma; f. 1959 as Banque du Maroc; bank of issue; cap. 500m., res 4,521.0m., dep. 17,063.1m. (Dec. 1999); Gov. MUHAMMAD SEQAT.

Other Banks

ABN AMRO Bank (Maroc) SA: 47 rue Allal ben Abdallah, BP 13478, 21000 Casablanca; tel. (2) 2209191; fax (2) 2209099; f. 1948 as Société Hollandaise de Banque et de Gestion; 99.4% owned by ABN AMRO Bank NV (Netherlands); cap. 840.0m., res 551.0m., dep. 2,807.0m. (Dec. 1999); Pres. HADJ ABDERRAHAMANE BOUFTAS; 20 brs.

Arab Bank Maroc: 174 blvd Muhammad V, BP 13810, Casablanca; tel. (2) 223152; fax (2) 200233; e-mail arabbank@marocnet.net.ma; internet www.arabbank.com; f. 1975; owned by Arab Bank PLC; cap. and res 208.0m., total assets 2,358.9m. (Dec. 1998); Pres. ABDUL MAJEED SHOMAN; Gen. Man. ABDERAHIM SAHER; 9 brs.

Banque Centrale Populaire: (Crédit Populaire du Maroc): 101 blvd Muhammad Zerktouni, BP 10622, 21100 Casablanca; tel. (2) 2202533; fax (2) 2222699; e-mail bcpinternational@banquepopulairemorocco.ma; internet www.chaabinet.com; f. 1961; 51% state-owned, 49% privately-owned; scheduled for complete privatization in 2002; cap. 1,297.7m., res 4,749.5m., total assets 68,157.8m. (Dec. 1999); Pres. and Gen. Man. NOUREDDINE OMARY; 342 brs.

Banque Commerciale du Maroc SA (BCM): 2 blvd Moulay Youssef, BP 11141, 20000 Casablanca; tel. (2) 2298888; fax (2) 2268852; internet www.attijari.com; f. 1911; 20.3% owned by Banco Central Hispano; cap. 1,325.0m., res 2,901.1m., dep. 35,403.5m.

(Dec. 1999); Chair. ABD AL-AZIZ ALAMI; Gen. Mans ALI IBN MANSOUR and OMAR BENIDER; 112 brs.

Banque Marocaine du Commerce Extérieur SA (BMCE): 140 ave Hassan II, BP 13425, 20000 Casablanca; tel. (2) 2200496; fax (2) 2200512; internet www.moroccoweb.com/bmce; f. 1959; transferred to majority private ownership in 1995; cap. 1,587.5m., res 2,899.9m., total assets 46,269.1m. (Dec. 2000); Chair. and CEO OTHMAN BEN JELLOUN; 198 brs.

Banque Marocaine pour l'Afrique et l'Orient: 1 place Bandoeng, BP 11183, 20000 Casablanca; tel. (2) 2307070; fax (2) 2301673; f. 1975 to take over British Bank of the Middle East (Morocco); cap. 200.0m., res 1.4m., dep. 2,042.0m. (Dec. 1996); Chair. FARID DELLERO; Gen. Man. SAID IBRAHIMI; 29 brs.

Banque Marocaine pour le Commerce et l'Industrie SA: 26 place des Nations Unies, BP 15573, Casablanca; tel. (2) 2224101; fax (2) 2299402; e-mail bmcisg@casanet.net.ma; internet www.bmci.net.com; f. 1964; transferred to majority private ownership in 1995; cap. 763.0m., res 643.6m., dep. 22,568.4m. (Dec. 2001); Chair. MUSTAPHA FARIS; Gen. Man. JEAN-JACQUES SANTINI; 125 brs.

Banque Nationale pour le Développement Economique (BNDE): 12 place des Alaouites, BP 407, 10000 Rabat; tel. (3) 7706040; fax (3) 7703706; internet www.bnde.co.ma; f. 1959; 34.2% state-owned, 65.8% privately-owned; cap. 600.0m., res 475.8m., dep. 5,200.6m. (Dec. 1999); Chair. and Man. Dir KHALID KADIRI; 14 brs.

Citibank (Maghreb): 52 ave Hassan II, Casablanca; tel. (2) 2224168; fax (2) 2205723; f. 1967; cap. 100m., res 2.5m., dep. 612.6m. (Dec. 1996); Pres. ERIC STOCLET.

Crédit Immobilier et Hôtelier: 187 ave Hassan II, Casablanca; tel. (2) 2479000; fax (2) 2479999; e-mail cih@cih.co.ma; f. 1920; transferred to majority private ownership in 1995; cap. 1,326.7m., res 432.0m., dep. 14,406.8m. (Dec. 1999); Pres. and Gen. Man. ABDELOUAHED SOUHAÏL; 91 brs.

Crédit du Maroc SA: 48–58 blvd Muhammad V, BP 13579, 20000 Casablanca; tel. (2) 2477000; fax (2) 2477071; e-mail cdmdai@atlasnet.net.ma; internet www.creditdumaroc.co.ma; f. 1963; cap. 833.8m., res 648.1m, dep. 14,002.8m. (Dec. 2001); Chair. and CEO FRANCIS SAVOYE; 122 brs.

Société Générale Marocaine de Banques SA: 55 blvd Abd al-Moumen, BP 13090, 21100 Casablanca; tel. (2) 2200972; fax (2) 2200958; f. 1962; cap. 975.0m., res 621.6m. (Dec. 1999); Pres. ABD AL-AZIZ TAZI; 132 brs.

Société Marocaine de Dépôt et Crédit: 79 ave Hassan II, BP 296, 20000 Casablanca; tel. (2) 2224114; fax (2) 2264498; f. 1974; cap. 625.9m., res 717.8m., total assets 4,811.0m. (Dec. 1998); Chair and Gen. Man. ABD AL-LATIF IDMAHAMMA; 21 brs.

Wafabank: 163 ave Hassan II, 21000 Casablanca; tel. (2) 2200200; fax (2) 2470398; f. 1964 as Cie Marocaine de Crédit et de Banque; cap. 639.5m., res 2,250.9m., total assets 29,039.9m. (Dec. 1999); Pres. and CEO ABDELHAK BENNANI; 162 brs.

Bank Organizations

Association Professionnelle des Intermédiaires de Bourse du Maroc: 71 ave des Forces Armées Royales, Casablanca; tel. (2) 2314824; fax (2) 2314903; f. 1967; groups all banks and brokers in the stock exchange of Casablanca, for studies, inquiries of general interest and contacts with official authorities; 11 mems; Pres. ABD AL-LATIF JOUAHRI.

Groupement Professionnel des Banques du Maroc: 71 ave des Forces Armées Royales, Casablanca; tel. (2) 2314824; fax (2) 2314903; f. 1967; groups all commercial banks for studies, inquiries of general interest, and contacts with official authorities; 18 mems; Pres. ABD AL-LATIF JOUAHRI.

STOCK EXCHANGE

Bourse des Valeurs de Casablanca: ave de l'Armée Royale, Casablanca; tel. (2) 2452626; fax (2) 2452625; internet www.casablanca-bourse.com; f. 1929; Chair. DRISS BENCHEIKH.

INSURANCE

Al-Wataniya: 83 ave des FAR, 20000 Casablanca; tel. (2) 2314850; fax (2) 2313137; internet www.alwataniya.com; Dir-Gen. ABD AL-AZIZ GUESSONS.

Alliance Africaine: 63 blvd Moulay Youssef, 20000 Casablanca; tel. (2) 2200690; fax (2) 2200694; f. 1975; cap. 20m.; Pres. ABD AR-RAHIM CHERKAOUI; Dir-Gen. KHALID CHEDDADI.

Assurances Al-Amane: 122 ave Hassan II, 20000 Casablanca; tel. (2) 2267272; fax (2) 2265664; f. 1975; cap. 120m.; Pres. and Dir-Gen. MUHAMMAD BOUGHALEB.

Atlanta Assurances: BP 13685, 20001 Casablanca; tel. (2) 2491448; fax (2) 2203011; e-mail atlanta@mbox.azur.net; f. 1947; cap. 40m.; Dirs-Gen. MUHAMMAD REYAD, OMAR BENNANI.

Cie Africaine d'Assurances: 120 ave Hassan II, 20000 Casablanca; tel. (2) 2224185; fax (2) 2260150; internet www.caa.co.ma; f. 1950; Dir-Gen. JAMAL HAROUCHI.

Cie d'Assurances SANAD: 3 blvd Muhammad V, BP 13438, 20001 Casablanca; tel. (2) 2260591; fax (2) 2293813; f. 1975; Chair. MUHAMMAD AOUAD; Dir-Gen. ABD AL-LATIF TAHIRI.

CNIA Assurance: 216 blvd Muhammad Zerktouni, 20000 Casablanca; tel. (2) 2474040; fax (2) 2206081; internet www.cnia.ma; f. 1949; cap. 30m.; Pres. ABDELLATIF AL-RAYES; Dir-Gen. SAID AHMI-DOUCH.

La Marocaine Vie: 37 blvd Moulay Youssef, Casablanca; tel. (2) 2206320; fax (2) 2261971; f. 1978; cap. 12m.; Pres. HAMZA KETTANI.

Mutuelle Centrale Marocaine d'Assurances: 16 rue Abou Inane, BP 27, Rabat; tel. (3) 7766960; Pres. ABD AS-SALAM CHERIF D'OUEZZANE; Dir-Gen. YACOUBI SOUSSANE.

Mutuelle d'Assurances des Transporteurs Unis (MATU): 215 blvd Muhammad Zerktouni, Casablanca; tel. (2) 2367097; Dir-Gen. M. BENYAMNA MUHAMMAD.

La Royale Marocaine d'Assurances (RMA): 67–69 ave de l'Armée Royale, BP 13779, 20000 Casablanca; tel. (2) 2312163; fax (2) 2313884; internet www.rma.co.ma; f. 1949; cap. 1,108.0m.; Chair. OTHMAN BEN JELLOUN; Dir-Gen. SÉBASTIEN CASTRO.

Es-Saada, Cie d'Assurances et de Réassurances: 123 ave Hassan II, BP 13860, 20000 Casablanca; tel. (2) 2222525; fax (2) 2262655; e-mail es-saada@techno.net.ma; f. 1961; cap. 50m.; Pres. MEHDI OUAZZANI; Man. Dir SAÏD OUAZZANI.

Société Centrale de Réassurance: Tour Atlas, place Zallaqa, BP 13183, Casablanca; tel. (2) 2308585; fax (2) 2308672; e-mail scr@elan.net.ma; internet www.scr.co.ma; f. 1960; cap. 30m.; Chair. MUSTAPHA BAKKOURY; Man. Dir AHMAD ZINOUN.

Société Marocaine d'Assurances à l'Exportation: 24 rue Ali Abderrazak, BP 15953, Casablanca; tel. (2) 2982000; fax (2) 2252070; internet www.smaex.com; f. 1988; insurance for exporters in the public and private sectors; assistance for export promotion; Pres., Dir-Gen. MUHAMMAD TAZI; Asst Dir-Gen. ABDELKADER DRIOUACHE.

WAFA Assurance: 1–3 blvd Abd al-Moumen, BP 13420, 20001 Casablanca; tel. (2) 2224575; fax (2) 2209103; e-mail webmaster@wafaassurance.com; internet www.wafaassurance.com; Pres. SAÀD KETTANI; Dir-Gen. JAOUAD KETTANI.

Zurich Cie Marocaine d'Assurances: City Park Centre, 106 rue Abderrahmane Sahraoui, 20000 Casablanca; tel. (2) 2279015; fax (2) 2491729; Pres. and Dir-Gen. HERVÉ GIRAUDON.

INSURANCE ASSOCIATION

Fédération Marocaine des Sociétés d'Assurances et de Réassurances: 154 blvd d'Anfa, Casablanca; tel. (2) 2391850; fax (2) 2391854; f. 1958; 17 mem. cos; Pres. HAMZA KETTANI.

Trade and Industry

GOVERNMENT AGENCIES

Bureau de Recherches et de Participations Minières (BRPM): 5 ave Moulay Hassan, BP 99, 10001 Rabat; tel. (3) 7705005; fax (3) 7709411; f. 1928; state agency conducting exploration, valorization and exploitation of mineral resources; Dir-Gen. MELLE AMINA BEN-KHADRA.

Centre Marocain de Promotion des Exportations (CMPE): 23 blvd Bnou Majid el-Bahar, BP 10937, Casablanca; tel. (2) 2302210; fax (2) 2301793; e-mail cmpe@cmpe.org.ma; internet www.cmpe.org.ma; f. 1980; state org. for promotion of exports; Dir-Gen. MOUNIR M. BENSAID.

Direction de la Privatisation: 1 angle ave Ibn Sina et Oued al-Makhazine, Agdal, Rabat; tel. (3) 7689614; fax (3) 7673299; e-mail minpriv@mtds.com.; internet www.minpriv.gov.ma; privatization agency integrated with Ministry of the Economy, Finance, Privatization and Tourism; Dir NAJIB HAJOUI.

Société de Gestion des Terres Agricoles (SOGETA): 35 rue Daïet-Erroumi, BP 731, Agdal, Rabat; tel. (3) 7772834; fax (3) 7772765; e-mail sogeta@acdim.net.ma; f. 1973; oversees use of agricultural land; Man. Dir BACHIR SAOUD.

DEVELOPMENT ORGANIZATIONS

Caisse de Dépôt et de Gestion: place Moulay El-Hassan, BP 408, 10001 Rabat; tel. (3) 7765520; fax (3) 7763849; e-mail cdg@cdg.org.ma; internet www.cdg.org.ma; f. 1959; finances small-scale projects; cap. and res 2,058.1m. dirhams (Dec. 1998); Dir-Gen. MUSTAPHA BAKKOURI; Sec.-Gen. MUSTAPHA MECHAHOURI.

Caisse Marocaine des Marchés (Marketing Fund): Résidence El Manar, blvd Abd al-Moumen, Casablanca; tel. (2) 2259118; fax (2) 2259120; f. 1950; cap. 10m. dirhams; Man. HASSAN KISSI.

Caisse Nationale de Crédit Agricole (Agricultural Credit Fund): 2 ave d'Alger, BP 49, 10001 Rabat; tel. (3) 7725920; fax (3) 7732580; f. 1961; cap. 1,573.5m. dirhams, dep. 3,471.9m. dirhams; Dir-Gen. SAID IBRAHIMI.

Office pour le Développement Industriel (ODI): 10 rue Gandhi, BP 211, 10001 Rabat; tel. (3) 7708460; fax (3) 7707695; e-mail odi@odi.gov.ma; internet www.odi.gov.ma; f. 1973; a state agency to develop industry; Dir-Gen. MURAD BACHIR BOUHALI.

Société de Développement Agricole (SODEA): ave Hadj Ahmed Cherkaoui, BP 6280, Rabat; tel. (3) 7770825; fax (3) 7774798; f. 1972; state agricultural devt org.; Man. Dir M. SABBARI HASSANI LARBI.

Société Nationale d'Investissement (SNI): 60 rue d'Alger, BP 38, 20000 Casablanca; tel. (2) 2484288; fax (2) 2484303; f. 1966; transferred to majority private ownership in 1994; cap. 10,900m. dirhams; Pres. MOURAD CHERIF; Sec.-Gen. KAMAL EL-AYOUBI.

CHAMBERS OF COMMERCE

La Fédération des Chambres de Commerce et d'Industrie du Maroc: 6 rue d'Erfoud, Rabat-Agdal; tel. (3) 7767078; fax (3) 7767076; f. 1962; groups the 26 Chambers of Commerce and Industry; Pres. AHMAD M'RABET; Dir-Gen. MUHAMMAD LARBI EL HARRAS.

Chambre de Commerce, d'Industrie et de Services de la Wilaya de Rabat-Salé: 1 rue Gandhi, BP 131, Rabat; tel. (3) 7706444; fax (3) 7706768; e-mail ccisrs@ccisrs.org.ma; internet www.ccisrs.org.ma; Pres. OMAR DERRAJI; Dir ZINE EL-ABIDINE AFIA.

Chambre de Commerce et d'Industrie de la Wilaya du Grand Casablanca: 98 blvd Muhammad V, BP 423, Casablanca; tel. (2) 2264327; Pres. LAHCEN EL-WAFI.

INDUSTRIAL AND TRADE ASSOCIATIONS

Office National Interprofessionnel des Céréales et des Légumineuses: 25 ave Moulay Hassan, BP 154, Rabat; tel. (3) 7701735; fax (3) 7709626; f. 1937; Dir-Gen. ABD AL-HAI BOUZOUBAA.

Office National des Pêches: 13 rue Lieutenant Mahroud, BP 16243, 20300 Casablanca; tel. (2) 2240551; fax (2) 2242305; e-mail onp@onp.co.ma; internet www.onp.co.ma; f. 1969; state fishing org.; Man. Dir MAJID KAISSAR EL-GHAIB.

EMPLOYERS' ORGANIZATIONS

Association Marocaine des Industries Textiles et de l'Habillement (AMITH): 92 blvd Moulay Rachid, Casablanca; tel. (2) 2942085; fax (2) 2940587; e-mail amith@mail.winner.net.ma; f. 1958; mems 700 textile, knitwear and ready-made garment factories; Pres. SALAH-EDDINE MEZOUAR; Dir-Gen. ABDE LALI BERRADA.

Association des Producteurs d'Agrumes du Maroc (ASPAM): 22 rue al-Messaoudi, Casablanca; tel. (2) 2363946; fax (2) 2364041; f. 1958; links Moroccan citrus growers; has its own processing plants; Pres AHMED MANSOUR NEJJAI.

Association Professionelle des Agents Maritimes, Consignataires de Naivres, et Courtiers d'Affretement du Maroc: Iman Centre No 1, 5ème Etage, rue Arrachid Muhammad (ex rue de la Plage), Casablanca; tel. (2) 2541112; fax (2) 2541415; e-mail apram@abnet.net.ma; internet www.apram.ma; Pres. A. MAN-TRANCH.

Association Professionnelle des Cimentiers: 239 blvd Moulay Ismail, BP 3096, Casablanca; tel. (2) 2401342; fax (2) 2248208; cement manufacturers.

Confédération Générale des Entreprises du Maroc (CGEM): angle ave des Forces Armées Royales et rue Muhammad Arrachid, 20100 Casablanca; tel. (2) 2252696; fax (2) 2253839; e-mail cgem@iam.net.ma; Pres. HASSAN CHAMI.

Union Marocaine de l'Agriculture (UMA): 12 place des Alaouites, Rabat; Pres. M. NEJJAI.

UTILITIES

Electricity and Water

Office National de l'Eau Potable (ONEP): 6 bis rue Patrice Lumumba, Rabat; tel. (3) 7650695; fax (3) 7650640; e-mail onepigi@mtds.com; internet www.onep.org; f. 1972; responsible for drinking-water supply; Dir ALI FASSI-FIHRI.

Office National de l'Electricité (ONE): 65 rue Othman Ben Affan, BP 13498, 20001 Casablanca; tel. (2) 2668080; fax (2) 2220038; e-mail offelec@one.org.ma; internet www.one.org.ma; f. 1963; state electricity authority; Chair. AHMAD NAKKOUCHE.

Régie Autonome Intercommunale de Distribution d'Eau et d'Electricité de la Wilaya de Chaouia (RADEEC): industrial and commercial public body providing water and power supplies in the Chaouia region.

Régie Autonome Intercommunale de Distribution d'Eau et d'Electricité de la Wilaya de Tanger (RAID): 5 rue Oqba ibn

Naffiy, BP 286, Tangier; tel. (3) 7321414; fax (3) 7322156; water, sewerage and electricity network for Tangier; a concession to manage the services was scheduled to be awarded in 1999.

Régie d'Eau et d'Electricité (RED): Rabat; in 1998 a 30-year concession to manage Rabat's water and power grids was awarded to a consortium of Electricidade de Portugal (Portugal), Urbaser (Spain) and Alborada (Morocco).

Gas

Afriquia Gaz: rue Ibnou el-Ouennanae Ain Sebaa; Casablanca; tel. (2) 2352144; fax (2) 2352239; f. 1992; Morocco's leading gas distributor; transfer to private ownership pending; Dir-Gen. RACHID IDRISSI KAITOUNI.

MAJOR COMPANIES

Brasseries du Maroc: BP 2660, 20251 Casablanca; tel. (2) 2754646; fax (2) 2754895; f. 1919; distillery, brewery and producer of soft drinks; Dir-Gen. HAMID BOUIDAR; 2,000 employees.

Charbonnages du Maroc: Centre Minier, 60550 Jerada; tel. (5) 5821048; fax (5) 5821158; f. 1946; coal mining; Dir-Gen. BELNKADAN DRISS; 5,300 employees.

Chérifienne de Travaux Africains: blvd du Fourat; Casablanca; tel. (2) 2323317; fax 2324746; f. 1960; building and civil engineering contractors; cap. 10m. dirhams; Dir-Gen. SERGE BERDUGO; 1,500 employees.

Compagnie Marocaine des Hydrocarbures: BP 6180, angle rond Point des Sports et rue Point du Jour, blvd Abd al-Latif Benkaddour, Casablanca; tel. (2) 2296786; fax (2) 2207955; marketing of petroleum and oil products; cap. 33m. dirhams; Dir-Gen. HASSAN AGZENAI.

Compagnie Sucrière Marocaine et de Raffinage SA (COSUMAR): 8 rue el Mouatamid Ibnou Abbad, BP 3098, 20300 Casablanca; tel. (2) 2401242; fax (2) 2241071; f. 1967; sugar refining and trading; cap. 60m. dirhams; Chair. FOUAD FILALI; 3,300 employees.

Complexe Textile de Fès (COTEF): Quartier Sidi Brahim, route de Sefrou, BP 2267, 30000 Fez; tel. (5) 5641309; fax (5) 5641354; f. 1967; production of yarns and textiles; Pres. ALAMI TAZI; 1,100 employees.

Conserveries Chérifiennes: route du Djorf el-Youdi, BP 96, Safi; tel. (4) 4472513; f. 1949; fish and food processing and canning; cap. 16.2m. dirhams; Gen. Man. MUHAMMAD EL-JAMALI; 2,500 employees.

Manufacture Nationale Textile (MANATEX): 164 blvd de la Gironde, 20500 Casablanca; tel. (2) 2286655; fax (2) 2282530; f. 1957; manufacture of textiles and furnishings; Pres. OMAR KETTANI; 800 employees.

Office Chérifien des Phosphates (OCP): route d'el Jadida, BP 5196, 20101 Casablanca; tel. (2) 2230125; fax (2) 2991263; internet www.ocpgroup.ma; f. 1921; state co producing and marketing rock phosphates and derivatives; Dir-Gen. DRISS JETTOU.

ONA: 60 rue d'Alger, BP 13657, 20001 Casablanca; tel. (2) 2224102; fax (2) 2261064; f. 1919; fmrly Omnium Nord Africain; largest private co in Morocco, owns subsidiaries in food, mining, distribution, real estate and insurance industries; cap. 1,720m. dirhams (1996); Pres. FOUAD FILALI; Dir-Gen. GILLES DENISTY; 120 employees.

Phosphates de Boucraa SA (PHOSBOUCRAA): Immeuble OCP, angle route d'el Jadida et blvd de la Grande Ceinture, 20200 Casablanca; tel. (2) 2230025; fax (2) 2230565; f. 1962; production and processing of phosphate rock; cap. 328m. dirhams; Pres. MOURAD CHERIF; 3,000 employees.

Société d'Exploitation des Mines du Rif (SEFERIF): 30 Abou-Faris el-Marini, BP 436, Rabat; tel. (7) 7766350; nationalized 1967; open and underground mines produce iron ore for export and for the projected Nador iron and steel complex; Man. Dir MUHAMMAD HARRAK.

Société Marocaine de Constructions Automobiles (SOMACA): km 12, autoroute de Rabat, BP 2628, 20600 Casablanca; tel. (2) 2754848; fax (2) 2754822; f. 1959; assembly of motor vehicles; owned by Moroccan govt, Fiat, Peugeot and SNI; Pres. LARBI BELARBI; 909 employees.

Société Nationale de Sidérurgie (SONASID): BP 551, Nador; tel. (5) 6609441; fax (5) 6609442; e-mail sonasid1@iam .net.maf. 1974; iron and steel projects; cap. 390m. dirhams; transferred to private ownership in 1997; Dir-Gen. ABDALLAH SOUIBRI; 600 employees.

Société Nouvelle des Conduites d'Eau (SNCE): Résidence Kays Sahat Rabia, Al Adaouiya Agdal, 10000 Rabat; tel. (7) 7776714; fax (7) 7776674; f. 1961; manufacture of steel and cast-iron pipes and materials; cap. 67.2m. dirhams; Chair. OMAR LARAQUI; 3,000 employees.

TRADE UNIONS

Confédération Démocratique du Travail (CDT): 64 rue al-Mourtada, Quartier Palmier, BP 13576, Casablanca; tel. (2)

2994470; fax (2) 2258162; f. 1978; 400,000 mems; Sec.-Gen. MUHAMMAD NOUBIR AMAOUI.

Union Démocratique de l'Agriculture: f. 1997; Sec.-Gen. ABD AR-RAHMAN FILALI.

Union Générale des Travailleurs Marocains (UGTM): 9 rue du Rif, angle Route de Médiouna, Casablanca; tel. (2) 2282144; f. 1960; associated with Istiqlal; supported by unions not affiliated to UMT; 673,000 mems; Sec.-Gen. ABD AR-RAZZAQ AFILAL.

Union Marocaine du Travail (UMT): Bourse du Travail, 232 ave des Forces Armées Royales, Casablanca; tel. (2) 2302292; left-wing and associated with the UNFP; most unions are affiliated; 700,000 mems; Sec. MAHJOUB BEN SEDDIQ.

Union Syndicale Agricole (USA): agricultural section of UMT.

Union Marocaine du Travail Autonome: Rabat; breakaway union from UMT.

Transport

Office National des Transports (ONT): rue al-Fadila, Quartier Industriel, BP 596, Rabat-Chellah; tel. (3) 7797842; fax (3) 7797850; f. 1958; Man. Dir MUHAMMAD LAHBIB EL-GUEDDARI.

RAILWAYS

In 2001 there were 1,907 km of railways, of which 370 km were double track; 1,003 km of lines were electrified and diesel locomotives were used on the rest. In that year the network carried some 13.6m. passengers and 27.5m. metric tons of freight. All services are nationalized. A feasibility study was begun in early 1998 into the construction of a 28-km metro system in Casablanca.

Office National des Chemins de Fer (ONCF): 8 bis rue Abderrahmane El Ghafiki, Rabat-Agdal; tel. (3) 7774747; fax (3) 7774480; e-mail meziane@oncf.org.ma; internet www.oncf.org.ma; f. 1963; administers all Morocco's railways; Pres. Minister of Transport; Dir-Gen. KARIM GHELLAB.

ROADS

In 2001 there were 57,226 km of classified roads, of which 56.1% were paved.

Cie de Transports au Maroc (CTM—SA): 23 rue Léon l'Africain, Casablanca; tel. (2) 2753677; fax (2) 2765428; internet www.ctm.co.ma; agencies in Tangier, Rabat, Meknès, Oujda, Marrakesh, Agadir, El Jadida, Safi, Casablanca, es-Saouira, Fez and Ouarzazate; privatized in mid-1993 with 40% of shares reserved for Moroccan citizens; Pres. and Dir-Gen. ABDALLAH LAHLOU.

SHIPPING

According to the Ministry of Equipment, Morocco's 21 ports handled 53.2m. tons of goods in 2000. The most important ports, in terms of the volume of goods handled, are Casablanca, Mohammadia, Jorf Lasfar and Safi. Tangier is the principal port for passenger services. Construction work on new ports at Tangier (to handle merchandise traffic) and Agadir commenced in 2000.

Office d'Exploitation des Ports (ODEP): 175 blvd Muhammad Zerktouni, 20100 Casablanca; tel. (2) 2232324; fax (2) 2232325; e-mail administrateur@odep.org.ma; internet www.odep.org.ma; f. 1985; port management and handling of port equipment; Gen. Man. MUSTAPHA BERROUG.

Principal Shipping Companies

Agence Gibmar SA: 3 rue Henri Regnault, Tangier; tel. (3) 7935875; fax (3) 7933239; e-mail agemcemed@mamnet.net.ma; also at Casablanca; regular services from Tangier to Gibraltar; Chair. JAMES PETER GAGGERO; Dir YOUSSEF BENYAHIA.

Cie Chérifienne d'Armement: 5 blvd Abdallah ben Yacine, 21700 Casablanca; tel. (2) 2309455; fax (2) 2301186; f. 1929; regular services to Europe; Man. Dir MAX KADOCH.

Cie Marocaine d'Agences Maritimes (COMARINE): 45 ave de l'Armée Royale, BP 60, 20000 Casablanca; tel. (2) 2311941; fax (2) 2312570; e-mail comarine@marocnet.net.ma.

Cie Marocaine de Navigation (COMANAV): 7 blvd de la Résistance, BP 628, Casablanca 20300; tel. (2) 2303012; fax (2) 2308455; e-mail comanav@comanav.co.ma; internet www.comanav.co.ma; f. 1946; regular services to Mediterranean, North-west European, Middle Eastern and West African ports; tramping; Chair. MUHAMMAD BENHAROUGA.

Intercona SA: 31 ave de la Résistance, Tangier; tel. (3) 9322253; fax (3) 9943863; e-mail intercona@wanadoo.net.ma; f. 1943; daily services from Algeciras (Spain) to Tangier and Ceuta (Spanish North Africa); Dir-Gen. ANDRES VAZQUEZ ESPINOSA.

Limadet-ferry: 3 rue Ibn Rochd, Tangier; tel. (3) 933639; fax (3) 937173; f. 1966; operates between Algeciras (Spain) and Tangier, six daily; Dir-Gen. RACHID BEN MANSOUR.

Société Marocaine de Navigation Atlas: 81 ave Houmane el-Fatouaki, 21000 Casablanca; tel. (2) 2224190; fax (2) 2274401; f. 1976; Chair. HASSAN CHAMI; Man. Dir M. SLAOUI.

Union Maritime Maroc-Scandinave (UNIMAR): 12 rue de Foucauld, BP 746, Casablanca; tel. (2) 2279590; fax (2) 2223883; f. 1974; chemicals; Dir-Gen. ABD AL-WAHAB BEN KIRANE.

Voyages Paquet: Hôtel Royal Mansour, rue Sidi Belyout, 20000 Casablanca; tel. (2) 2311065; fax (2) 2442108; f. 1970; Pres. MUHAMMAD ELOUALI ELALAMI; Dir-Gen. NAÏMA BAKALI ELOUALI ELALAMI.

CIVIL AVIATION

The main international airports are at Casablanca (King Muhammad V), Rabat, Tangier, Marrakesh, Agadir Inezgane, Fez, Oujda, Al-Hocima, el-Aaiún, Ouarzazate and Agadir al-Massira. Construction of a new international airport at al-Aroui, located 25 km south of Nador, began in late 1998. In November 1999 the Arab Fund for Economic and Social Development granted a loan worth US $32.7m. to finance a project to extend and modernise King Muhammad V airport. The project, which includes the construction of a second runway and new terminal buildings, is expected to be completed by 2005

Office Nationale des Aéroports: Casa-Oasis, BP 8101, Casablanca; tel. (2) 2339040; fax (2) 2339051; e-mail onda@mtds.com; internet www.onda.org.ma.

Regional Airlines: Aéroport de Muhammad V, BP 12518, Casablanca; tel. (2) 2538020; fax (2) 2538411; f. 1997; privately-owned; domestic flights and services to southern Spain, Portugal and the Canary Islands; Pres. and CEO MEHDI ALAOUI.

Royal Air Maroc (RAM): Aéroport de Casablanca-Anfa; tel. (2) 2912000; fax (2) 2912087; internet www.royalairmaroc.com; f. 1953; 94.4% state-owned; scheduled for partial privatization; domestic flights and services to 35 countries in Western Europe, Scandinavia, the Americas, North and West Africa, the Canary Islands and the Middle East; CEO MUHAMMAD BERRADA.

Tourism

Tourism is Morocco's second main source of convertible currency. The country's attractions for tourists include its sunny climate, ancient sites (notably the cities of Fez, Marrakesh, Meknès and Rabat) and spectacular scenery. There are popular holiday resorts on the Atlantic and Mediterranean coasts. In 2000 foreign tourist arrivals totalled 2.46m., compared with 1.63m. in 1996. Tourist receipts in 1999 totalled US $1,850m.

Office National Marocain du Tourisme: 31 angle ave al-Abtal et rue Oued Fes, Agdal, Rabat; tel. (3) 7681531; fax (3) 7777437; e-mail visitmorocco@onmt.org.ma; internet www.morocco tourism.org.ma; f. 1918; Dir-Gen. FATHIA BENNIS.

Defence

Commander-in-Chief of the Armed Forces: HM King MUHAMMAD VI.

Estimated Defence Budget (1999): 17,300m. dirhams.

Military Service: 18 months.

Total Armed Forces (August 2001): 198,500 (army 175,000; navy 10,000; air force 13,500). Paramilitary forces: royal guard 12,000; 30,000. Reserves: 150,000.

Education

Since independence in 1956, Morocco has tried to solve a number of educational problems: a youthful and fast-growing population, an urgent need for skilled workers and executives, a great diversity of teaching methods between French, Spanish, Muslim and Moroccan government schools, and, above all, a high degree of adult illiteracy. Under the 1999/2000 budget, expenditure on education by the central Government was projected at 17,385m. dirhams (21.3% of total spending).

In 2000/01 there were 3,842,000 pupils in primary schools (including those in private schools) where syllabuses have been standardized since 1967. Great progress was made in providing new schools during 1957–64, but since then the increase in the number of places has decelerated. A decree of November 1963 made education compulsory for children between the ages of seven and 13 years, and this has now been applied in most urban areas, but throughout the country only 79% (84% of boys; 74% of girls) of the age-group attended school in 1999/2000. From September 2002 children were to be educated from six years of age. All primary teachers are Moroccan. Instruction is given in Arabic for the first two years and in Arabic and French for the next four years, with English as the first additional language.

Secondary education, beginning at the age of 13, lasts for up to six years (comprising two cycles of three years), and in 2000/01 provided for 1,504,367 pupils (excluding those in professional schools). In 1988 the secondary school graduation examination, the *baccalauréat,* was replaced by a system of continuous assessment. All secondary teachers are Moroccan, but in 1986 there were 1,461 from abroad, chiefly from France. Secondary enrolment in 1999 included 38% of the relevant age-group (boys 43%; girls 33%).

There are eight universities in Morocco, including the Islamic University of al-Quarawiyin at Fez (founded in 859), the Muhammad V University at Rabat (opened in 1957), and an English-language university, inaugurated at Ifrane in 1995. In addition, there are institutes of higher education in business studies, agriculture, mining, law, and statistics and advanced economics. In 2000/01 there was a total of 265,905 students engaged in higher education.

Adult education is supplemented by radio programmes, simplified type, and a newspaper for the newly literate. In recent years increasing attention has been given to education for girls. There are now a number of mixed and girls' schools, notably in urban areas.

Bibliography

Abu-Lughod, Janet L. *Rabat: Urban Apartheid in Morocco.* Guildford, United Kingdom, Princeton University Press, 1981.

Amin, Samir. *The Maghreb in the Modern World.* Harmondsworth, Penguin, 1971.

Ashford, D. E. *Political Change in Morocco.* Princeton U.P., 1961.

Perspectives of a Moroccan Nationalist. New York, 1964.

Ayache, A. *Le Maroc.* Paris, Editions Sociales, 1956.

Baduel, Pierre-Robert. *Enjeux Sahariens.* Paris, CNRS, 1984.

Baker, Alison. *Voices of Resistence: Oral Histories of Moroccan Women.* Albany, NY, State University of New York Press, 1998.

Barbier, Maurice. *Le Conflit du Sahara occidental.* Paris, L'Harmattan, 1982.

Barbour, Nevill. *Morocco.* London, Thames and Hudson, 1964.

Ben Barka, Mehdi. *Problèmes de l'édification du Maroc et du Maghreb.* Paris, Plon, 1959.

Option Révolutionnaire en Maroc. Paris, Maspéro, 1966.

Bennett, Norman Robert. *A study guide for Morocco.* Boston, 1970.

Bernard, Stephane. *Le Conflit Franco-Marocain 1943–1956,* 3 vols. Brussels, 1963; English translation, Yale University Press, 1968.

Berque, Jaques. *Le Maghreb entre deux guerres.* Paris, Edns du Seuil, 1962.

Brown, Kenneth. *People of Salé.* Manchester University Press, 1976.

Charrad, Mounira M. *States and Women's Rights—The Making of Postcolonial Tunisia, Algeria and Morocco.* Berkeley, CA, University of California Press, 2000.

Cohen, M. I., and Hahn, Lorna. *Morocco: Old Land. New Nation.* New York, Praeger, 1964.

Coulau, Julien. *La paysannerie marocaine.* Paris, 1968.

Daure-Serfaty, Christine. *Lettre du Maroc.* Paris, Stock, 2000.

Eickelman, Dale F. *Moroccan Islam: Tradition and Society in a Pilgrimage Center.* Princeton University Press, 1986.

Gershovich, Moshe. *French Military Rule in Morocco: Colonialism and its Consequences.* London and Portland, OR, Frank Cass, 2000.

Hall, L. J. *The United States and Morocco, 1776–1956.* Metuchen, NJ, Scarecrow Press, 1971.

Halstead, John P. *Rebirth of a Nation: the Origins and Rise of Moroccan Nationalism.* Harvard University Press, 1967.

Hassan II, King of Morocco. *Le Défi.* Paris, Albin Michel, 1976.

Hodges, Tony. *Western Sahara: the Roots of a Desert War.* London, Croom Helm, 1983.

Historical Dictionary of Western Sahara. London, Scarecrow Press, 1982.

Horton, Brendon. *Morocco: Analysis and Reform of Foreign Policy.* Economic Development Institute of the World Bank, 1990.

Julien, Charles-André. *Le Maroc face aux Impérialismes (1415–1956).* Paris, Editions Jeune Afrique, 1978.

Kaioua, Abdelkader, *Cassablanca: l'industrie et la ville, Tomes I et II.* Tours, France URBAMA, 1996.

Kay, Shirley. *Morocco.* London, Namara Publications, 1980.

Kininmonth, C. *The Travellers' Guide to Morocco.* London, Jonathan Cape, 1972.

Lacouture, J. and S. *Le Maroc à l'épreuve.* Paris, Edns du Seuil, 1958.

Landau, Rom. *The Moroccan Drama 1900–1955.* London, Hale, 1956.

Morocco Independent under Mohammed V. London, Allen and Unwin, 1961.

Hassan II, King of Morocco. London, Allen and Unwin, 1962.

The Moroccans—Yesterday and Today. London, 1963.

Morocco. London, Allen & Unwin, 1967.

Landau, Rom, and Swann, Wim. *Marokko.* Cologne, 1970.

Layachi, Azzedine. *State, Society and Democracy in Morocco: The Limits of Associative Life.* Washington DC, Georgetown University Center for Contemporary Arab Studies, 1998.

Le Tourneau, Roger. *Evolution politique de l'Afrique du Nord musulmane.* Paris, Armand Colin, 1962.

Maxwell, Gavin. *Lords of the Atlas.* London, Longmans, 1966.

Metcalf, John. *Morocco—an Economic Study.* New York, First National City Bank, 1966.

Middle East Report No. 218, Vol. 31 No. 1, Spring 2001. *Morocco in Transition.*

Mumson, Henry, Jr. *Religion and Power in Morocco.* London, Yale University Press, 1993.

Pennell, C. R. *Morocco since 1830: A History.* New York University Press, 2001.

Perrault, Gilles. *Notre Ami le Roi.* Paris, Editions Gallimard, 1991.

Perroux, F., and Barre, R. *Développement, croissance, progrès—Maroc-Tunisie.* Paris, 1961.

Robert, J. *La monarchie marocaine.* Paris, Librairie générale de droit et de jurisprudence, 1963.

Sutton, Michael. *Morocco to 1992 (Growth against the Odds).* London, Economist Intelligence Unit, 1987.

Terrasse, H. *Histoire du Maroc des origines à l'établissement du protectorat français,* 2 vols. Casablanca, 1949–50; English trans. by H. Tee, London, 1952.

Thompson, Virginia, and Adloff, Richard. *The Western Saharans.* London, Croom Helm, Totowa, NJ, Barnes and Noble, 1980.

Tiano, André. *La politique économique et financière du Maroc indépendant.* Paris, Presses universitaires de France, 1963.

Tozy, Muhammad. *Monarchie et islam politique au Maroc.* Paris, Presse de Sciences-Po, 1999.

Trout, Frank E. *Morocco's Saharan Frontiers.* Geneva, 1969.

Vermeren, Pierre. *Le Maroc en transition.* Paris, La Découverte, 2001.

Waterbury, John. *The commander of the Faithful. The Moroccan political élite.* London, 1970.

Waterson, Albert. *Planning in Morocco.* Baltimore, Johns Hopkins Press, 1963.

World Bank. *The Economic Development of Morocco.* Baltimore, Johns Hopkins Press, 1966.

Growing Faster, Finding Jobs: Choices for Morocco. 1997.

White, Gregory. *A Comparative Political Economy of Tunisia and Morocco: On the Outside of Europe Looking In.* Albany NY, State University of New York Press, 2001.

Zartman, I. W. *Morocco: Problems of New Power.* New York, Atherton Press, 1964.

OMAN

Geography

The Sultanate of Oman occupies the extreme east and south-east of the Arabian peninsula. It is bordered by the United Arab Emirates (UAE) to the north and west, by Saudi Arabia to the west and by Yemen to the south-west. A detached area of Oman, separated from the rest of the country by UAE territory, lies at the tip of the Musandam peninsula, on the southern shore of the Strait of Hormuz. Oman is separated from Iran by the Gulf of Oman, and it has a coastline of some 1,700 km (1,056 miles) on the Indian Ocean. The total area of the country is 309,500 sq km (119,500 sq miles). Disputes over the demarcation of Oman's frontiers often complicated the country's foreign relations in the past; however, in mid-1995 Oman completed the demarcation of its joint borders with both Yemen and Saudi Arabia (in May 1997 Oman and Yemen signed international border demarcation maps in Muscat), and in June 2002 it was reported that agreement had also been reached with the UAE on the demarcation of common international borders.

The first full census in Oman was held in 1993. Previous estimates of the country's population varied widely between official Omani figures and those of independent international organizations. The UN Population Division, basing its assessment on a mid-1965 figure of 571,000, estimated totals of 654,000 for mid-1970 and 984,000 for mid-1980. By 1990 the UN estimated that Oman's mid-year population had grown to 1,502,000. World Bank estimates indicated annual average population growth of 5.0% during 1990–98. According to the census of 1 December 1993, the population totalled 2,018,074, comprising 1,483,226 Omani nationals (73.5%) and 534,848 non-Omanis (26.5%). In 2001, according to official estimates the mid-year population was 2,478,000. The majority of the population are Ibadi Muslims, and about one-quarter are Hindus.

At Muscat the mean annual rainfall is 100 mm and the mean temperature varies between 20°C and 43°C (69°F and 110°F). Rainfall on the hills of the interior is somewhat heavier, and the south-western province of Dhofar is the only part of Arabia to benefit from the summer monsoon.

Oman may be divided into nine topographical areas. The largest urban area in the country is the capital region, around Muscat. Although most of the country is arid, the al-Batinah plain, which lies between the Gulf of Oman and the Hajar al-Gharbi range of mountains, comprises a fertile coastal region, and is among the most densely populated areas of the country. Another such plain is found between Raysut and Salalah, on the south-west coast in the Dhofar region, which, in total, occupies one-third of the country's area and extends northwards into the Rub al-Khali, or 'empty quarter', on Oman's western border: a rainless, unrelieved wilderness of shifting sand, almost entirely without human habitation.

Irrigation has been developed in some parts of the country, including the Dhahira area, a semi-desert plain between the south-western Hajar mountains and the Rub al-Khali, which also provides clusters of cultivable land near the wadis Dank and Ain, and the Buraini oasis. From Jebel al-Akhdar, at the southern tip of the Hajar al-Gharbi range, towards the desert in the south, lies the Interior, the country's central hill region and the most densely populated zone. The area has four main valleys, two of which (Halafein and Samail) provide the traditional route to Muscat.

The less hospitable regions are sparsely populated by groups of tribal settlers. The Hajar al-Gharbi, running parallel to the coast southwards from Oman's border with the UAE, is the home of the Rostaq, Awabi and Nakhe tribes. To the east of the Hajar range, the Sharqiya area extends south towards the Arabian Sea. It is an area of sandy plains and the home of the various Bani tribes. Musandam, separated from Oman by the UAE, is a mountainous area inhabited by the ash-Shahouh tribes. Around the eastern coast of the Arabian Sea, the Barr al-Hekkman, a group of islands and salt-plains of 650 sq km (250 sq miles), is inhabited by fishing communities.

For administrative purposes, the Sultanate is divided into eight governorates, comprising 59 *wilayat* (provinces), each under the jurisdiction of a *wali*, or provincial governor.

History

Revised for this edition by the Editorial staff

Oman was probably the land of Magan (mentioned in Sumerian tablets) with which cities such as Ur of the Chaldees traded in the third millennium BC. The province of Dhofar also produced frankincense in vast quantities, which was shipped to markets in Iraq, Syria, Egypt and the West. Roman geographers mention the city of Omana, although its precise location has not been identified, and Portus Moschus, conceivably Muscat. Oman, at various times, came under the influence of the Himyaritic kingdoms of southern Arabia and of Iran, which are believed to have been responsible for the introduction of the *falaj* irrigation systems, although legend attributes them to Sulaiman ibn Daud (Solomon).

The people of Oman come from two main ethnic stocks, the Qahtan, who migrated from southern Arabia, and the Nizar, who came in from the north. According to tradition, the first important invasion from southern Arabia was led by Malik ibn Faham, after the final collapse of the Marib dam in Yemen in the first or second century AD. Oman was one of the first countries to be converted to Islam by Amr ibn al-As, who later converted Egypt. Omanis of the tribe of al-Azd played an important part in the early days of Islam in Iraq. They subsequently embraced the Ibadi doctrine, which holds that the caliphate in Islam should not be hereditary or confined to any one family, and established their own independent Imamate in

Oman in the eighth century AD. Subsequently, although subject to invasions by the Caliphate, Iranians, Moguls and others, Oman has largely maintained its independence.

During the 10th century Sohar was probably the largest and most important city in the Arab world, while Omani mariners, together with those from Basra and other Gulf ports, went as far afield as China. When the Portuguese arrived in 1507, on their way to India, Affonso d'Albuquerque and his forces found the Omani seaport under the suzerainty of the King of Hormuz, himself of Omani stock. The towns of Qalhat, Quryat, Muscat and Sohar were already prosperous.

However, the arrival of the Portuguese in the Indian Ocean radically altered the balance of power in the area. The Portuguese established themselves in the Omani ports, concentrating principally on Sohar and Muscat, where they built two great forts, Merani (1587) and Jalali (1588). British and Dutch traders followed in the wake of the Portuguese, though they did not establish themselves by force of arms in Oman. In 1650 the Imam Nasir ibn Murshid of the Yaariba dynasty, who was also credited with a period of Omani renaissance during which learning flourished, effectively expelled the Portuguese from Muscat and the rest of Oman. The Omanis then extended their power, and by 1730 had conquered the Portuguese settlements on the east coast of Africa, including Mogadishu (now in Somalia), Mombasa (Kenya) and Zanzibar (now part of Tanzania).

The country was, however, ravaged by civil war in the first half of the 18th century, when the authority of the Imam diminished. During this period the Iranians were summoned to assist one of the contenders for the Imamate, but they were subsequently ousted by Ahmad ibn Said, who was elected Imam in 1749 and founded the al-Bu Said dynasty, one of the oldest dynasties in the Middle East, which still rules Oman. The country prospered under the new dynasty and its maritime influence revived. In about 1786 the capital of the country was transferred from Rostaq to Muscat, a move which led to a dichotomy between the coast and the interior, creating political problems between the two regions at various times.

Imam Said bin Sultan ruled Oman from 1804 until 1856. He was a strong and popular ruler, who also gained the respect and friendship of European nations, in particular the British. Treaties providing for the establishment of consular relations were negotiated with the British in 1839 (there had been earlier treaties of friendship in 1798 and 1800), the USA in 1833, France in 1844 and the Netherlands in 1877. British relations with Oman were maintained almost uninterrupted from the early 18th century until the present day, while relations with the other states concerned were less continuous.

Said bin Sultan revived Omani interest in Zanzibar and, in the latter part of his reign, spent an increasing amount of his time there. He started the clove plantations which later brought great wealth to the islands of Zanzibar and Pemba, and he founded the dynasty which ruled there until the revolution in 1964. During Said's reign, Omani dominions expanded to their greatest extent. In 1829 Dhofar became one of the constituent parts of the Sultanate and has remained so ever since.

The latter half of the 19th century was a difficult period for Oman. Not only had it lost its East African possessions, but a series of treaties with Britain to curb the slave trade also brought about a decline in the local economy, as Muscat had been an important port for this lucrative traffic.

Several insurrections took place towards the end of the 19th century, and in 1913 a new Imam was elected in the interior, in defiance of the Sultan who ruled from Muscat. This led to the expulsion of the Sultan's garrisons from Nizwa, Izki and Sumail. In the same year Sultan Faisal bin Turki, who had ruled since 1888, died, to be succeeded by his son Taimur. Efforts to come to terms with the rebels failed until 1920, when an agreement was reached between the Sultan and the principal dissidents, led by Isa bin Salih. It provided for peace, free movement of persons between the interior and the coast, limitation of customs duties and non-interference by the government of the Sultan in the internal affairs of the signatory tribes. A Treaty of Friendship with the United Kingdom, signed on 20 December 1951, recognized the full independence of the sultanate, officially called Muscat and Oman. Relations between the Imam, Muhammad bin Abdullah al-Khalili, and the Sultan remained good until the Imam's death in 1954, when rebellion again broke out under the Imam's successor, Ghalib bin Ali, who sought external assistance to establish a separate principality. In December 1955 forces under the Sultan's control entered the main inhabited centres of Oman without resistance. The former Imam was allowed by the Sultan to retire to his village, but his brother, Talib, escaped to Saudi Arabia and thence to Cairo. An 'Oman Imamate' office was established there, and the Imam's cause was supported by Egyptian propaganda. In the summer of 1957 Talib returned and established himself, with followers, in the mountain areas north-west of Nizwa. The Sultan appealed for British help, and fighting continued until early 1959, when the Sultan's authority was fully re-established. In October 1960, despite British objections, 10 Arab countries succeeded in placing the 'question of Oman' on the agenda of the UN General Assembly. In 1961 a resolution in support of separate independence for Oman failed to secure the necessary majority, and in 1963 a UN Commission of Inquiry refuted the Imamate's charges of oppressive government and public hostility to the Sultan. Nevertheless, a committee was formed to study the problem and, after its report had been submitted to the General Assembly in 1965, a resolution was adopted which, among other things, demanded the elimination of British domination in any form. The question was debated

on several further occasions until, more than a year after Sultan Qaboos's accession, Oman (as Muscat and Oman was renamed in 1970) became a member of the UN in October 1971.

TRANSFORMATION UNDER QABOOS

By 1970 Sultan Said's Government had come to be regarded as the most reactionary and isolationist in the area. Slavery was still common, and many medieval prohibitions were in force. The Sultan's insistence that petroleum revenues be used exclusively to fund defence was embarrassing for the United Kingdom, the oil companies and the neighbouring states, and provoked the rebellion that began in Dhofar province in 1964. On 23 July 1970 the Sultan was deposed (and later exiled) in a coup, led by his son, Qaboos bin Said. Qaboos, who was then 29 years of age, thus became Sultan amid general acclaim, both within the country and abroad. Sultan Qaboos intended to transform the country, using petroleum revenues for development, following the model of the Gulf sheikhdoms to the north. He asked the rebels for their co-operation, but only the Dhofar Liberation Front responded favourably. The Popular Front for the Liberation of the Occupied Arabian Gulf (reported to control much of Dhofar, and to be receiving aid, via Southern Yemen, from the People's Republic of China) and its ally, the National Democratic Front for the Liberation of the Occupied Arab Gulf, appeared to be of the opinion that the palace coup had changed little.

In August 1970 Muscat and Oman became simply the 'Sultanate of Oman'. Sultan Qaboos appointed his uncle, Tariq bin Taimur, as Prime Minister. Tariq resigned his office in December 1971, since which time the Sultan has himself presided over cabinet meetings and acted as his own Prime Minister, Minister of Defence and Minister of Foreign Affairs (and Minister of Finance in the 1990s). Priority was given to providing the basic social and economic infrastructure which the former Sultan had rigidly opposed—housing, education, communications, health services, etc. In addition, restrictions on travel were abolished, many prisoners were released, and many Omanis returned from abroad. None the less, a substantial proportion of the annual budget continued to be devoted to defence and to quelling the Dhofar insurgency.

Oman's admission to the UN in 1971 was achieved despite opposition from the People's Democratic Republic of Yemen (PDRY, formerly Southern Yemen), which supported the Popular Front for the Liberation of Oman and the Arab Gulf, formed in 1972 by the unification of the two nationalist liberation fronts. The name of this organization was changed in July 1974 to the People's Front for the Liberation of Oman (PFLO). Oman's relationship with the United Kingdom also compromised Oman's candidature for UN membership. The United Kingdom continues to supply weapons, ammunition and military advisers to the Omani Government.

The progress on social and economic reform that was achieved after 1970 did have some impact on the strength of the insurgent movement, but fighting continued until 1975. Omani forces attacked the border area of the PDRY for the first time in May 1972. In 1973 Iranian troops entered the conflict on the side of the Sultan, who also received assistance from Jordan, Saudi Arabia, the UAE, Pakistan and India. Although the Sultan's forces gradually gained the upper hand, the war was prolonged, and during October 1975 the rebels used sophisticated weapons. In December, after a new offensive, the Sultan claimed a complete victory over the insurgents. Saudi Arabia helped to negotiate a cease-fire in 1976, and an amnesty was granted to Omani nationals who had been fighting for the PFLO.

During 1975–80 only desultory conflicts took place, the majority of rebels having returned to their homes in Oman. In January 1977 Iran withdrew the bulk of its forces from Dhofar, but a token force remained until the Iranian revolution in early 1979. A renewal of the insurrection against Sultan Qaboos occurred in June 1978, when a party of British engineers was attacked in the Salalah region of Dhofar. The PFLO became largely an external force, however, and had little success in attracting adherents within Oman, despite the assassination, in 1979, of the Governor of Dhofar, and reports of renewed insurgency. In January 1981 Oman closed its border with the PDRY, and more British officers were seconded to the Omani forces as the frontier defences were put on alert. However, by

October 1982, after talks at which Kuwait and the UAE mediated, Oman and the PDRY had re-established diplomatic relations, signing an agreement on 'normalization'.

FOREIGN RELATIONS UNDER QABOOS, 1970–1989

Oman's relations with its other Arab neighbours improved considerably following the accession of Sultan Qaboos. During the reign of Sultan Said, Omani dependence on British military forces had been viewed with disfavour by its neighbours, increasing Oman's isolation in the Arab world. Since 1970, however, both Kuwait and the UAE have supplied much-needed financial support to Oman, while diplomatic relations were established with Iraq, a former supporter of the PFLO. The establishment of economic and diplomatic links with Saudi Arabia was particularly significant. Oman's support for the Israeli-Egyptian peace treaty of 1979 threatened to damage relations with some of the more uncompromising members of the League of Arab States (Arab League), but promised closer ties with the USA and with Egypt, which, at that time, undertook to respond to any request from Oman for military aid. Concern over regional security prompted Oman to join the Co-operation Council for the Arab States of the Gulf (Gulf Co-operation Council—GCC), founded in May 1981.

The strategic importance of military bases in Oman has long been recognized. After the United Kingdom withdrew its forces from Masirah island in 1977 the USA demonstrated keen interest in the territory. In February 1980 Oman began negotiations with the USA concerning a defence alliance whereby, in exchange for US military and economic aid and a commitment to Oman's security, Oman would grant the USA use of port and air base facilities in the Gulf (including Masirah island). Although direct alignment with a 'superpower' was considered to be contrary to Oman's foreign policy, the agreement was finalized in June, and was bitterly condemned by the Arab People's Congress in Libya as a concession to 'US imperialism'. The outbreak of the Iran–Iraq War in September 1980 only served to underline Oman's strategic importance, particularly with regard to the Strait of Hormuz, a narrow waterway at the mouth of the Persian (Arabian) Gulf, between Oman and Iran, through which about two-thirds of the world's sea-borne trade in crude petroleum passed at that time. The fact that Oman possesses export outlets other than the Strait brought economic advantages to the country in May 1984, as its ports handled some trade which was destined for countries within the Gulf whose commerce was threatened by an escalation of the Iran–Iraq War.

In 1981 the USA established a communications centre in Oman, and pledged more than US $200m. in 1981–83 to develop port and airport facilities in return for the right to stockpile supplies in Oman for possible use by the US Rapid Deployment Force. By 1985 the total sum spent on the improvement of facilities in Oman had risen to $300m. United States forces were permitted to make landings in Oman during the massive 'Bright Star' military exercises, held in the region in December 1981. This aroused protest from the PDRY, as it contravened a clause of the 'normalization' agreement previously made. As a result, the other Gulf states, particularly Kuwait, attempted to discourage both countries' links with the 'superpowers' by reportedly offering Oman $1,200m. to withdraw the US military facility. In a preliminary attempt to co-ordinate the Gulf's own independent defence system, the GCC focused its attention on Oman, awarding a five-year defence grant to the country in July 1983 and holding joint military exercises there in October.

In September 1985 Oman established diplomatic relations with the USSR. The move was encouraged by the peaceful relations which had been maintained between Oman and the PDRY since the resumption of diplomatic contact in 1982, and was interpreted as an indication of Oman's desire to preserve its political independence. However, an American presence was discreetly maintained, and US troops were allowed to use military bases in Oman only with the agreement of the Omani Government. The USA continued to make improvements to existing installations in the Sultanate, expanding fuel, ammunition, power and water facilities at Seeb airfield. In October 1988 Oman and the PDRY signed an agreement to increase co-operation in the sectors of trade and communications. The signing took place during the first visit to the Sultanate by a President of the PDRY since that country's independence in 1967. In January 1989 the Omani Minister of Petroleum and Minerals, Said ash-Shanfari, became the first Omani minister to visit the USSR since the establishment of diplomatic relations between the two countries in 1985. In early 1989 Oman adopted a more conciliatory policy towards Iran (in November 1987 Oman had supported the Arab League's condemnation of Iran's prolonging hostilities with Iraq), and in March the two countries established an economic co-operation committee. However, Oman's support for Iran was conditional upon the latter's efforts to achieve political stability in the Gulf region.

DOMESTIC DEVELOPMENTS SINCE 1981

A 45-member Consultative Assembly (consisting of 17 representatives of the Government, 17 representatives of the private sector and 11 regional representatives) was created in October 1981 in response to suggestions that Sultan Qaboos was not being made sufficiently aware of public opinion. In 1983 the Assembly's membership was expanded to 55, including 19 representatives of the Government. Its role, however, was confined to comment on economic and social development and recommendations on future policy. In November 1990 Sultan Qaboos announced that the Assembly was to be replaced by a new Consultative Council, comprising regional representatives, which was to be established within one year, in order to allow 'wider participation' by Omani citizens in national 'responsibilities and tasks'. In March 1991 he announced that the Council would consist of 59 elected members, who would serve three-year terms of office. The President of the Council was to be appointed by the Government. In April 21 prominent figures met to nominate three candidates (of whom one was to be appointed to the Council) for each of the country's *wilayat* (provinces). On taking office, the members of the Council were to appoint committees and executive officers. An annual meeting between the Council and members of the Government would also be held. Although the Council has no legislative power, ministers are obliged to present annual statements to it and to answer any questions addressed to them.

In December 1991 a cabinet reshuffle produced wide-ranging ministerial changes and the amalgamation of several ministries. The inaugural session of the Consultative Council was held in January 1992. Three new ministries were created in the cabinet reshuffle in January 1994, and in July it was announced that membership of the Consultative Council would be increased to 80 in 1995, allowing constituencies of 30,000 or more inhabitants to have two seats. Women were to be permitted, for the first time, to be nominated as candidates in six regions in and around the capital. In early 1995 two women were appointed to the Consultative Council.

In mid-1994 the Omani Government was reported to be employing stringent measures to curb an apparent rise in Islamic militancy in the country. In late August the security forces announced the arrest of more than 200 members of an allegedly foreign-sponsored Islamic organization, most of whom were later released. Among those arrested were two junior ministers, university lecturers, students and soldiers. In November several detainees were sentenced to death, having been found guilty of conspiracy to foment sedition; the Sultan subsequently commuted the death sentences to terms of imprisonment. In September 1995 Qais bin Abd al-Munim az-Zawawi, Deputy Prime Minister for Financial and Economic Affairs and Oman's principal financial policy-maker, was killed in a traffic accident when travelling in the same vehicle as the Sultan (who escaped unharmed). In December Ahmad bin Abd an-Nabi Macki, formerly the Minister of the Civil Service, was appointed Minister of National Economy, and also Supervisor of the restyled Ministry of Finance. In early November 1996 Fahar bin Taimour as-Said, Deputy Prime Minister for Security and Defence, died.

On 6 November 1996 Sultan Qaboos issued a decree promulgating what was termed a Basic Statute of the State, a constitutional document defining, for the first time, the organs and guiding principles of the State. Article 58 of the Statute provided for a Council of Oman, to be composed of the Consultative Council (Majlis ash-Shoura) and a new Council of State (Majlis ad-Dawlah). The latter was to be appointed from among prominent Omanis, and would function as a liaison between the

Government and the people of Oman. Later in November it was reported that 23 senior government ministers had resigned as directors of public joint-stock companies, in accordance with a stipulation in the Basic Statute that ministers should not abuse their official position for personal gain. In December a Defence Council was established by royal decree, comprising the Minister of the Royal Court, the heads of the branches of the armed and police forces and the head of internal security. The process of succession to the Sultan, as defined by the Basic Statute, required that the ruling family determine a successor within three days of the throne's falling vacant, failing which the Defence Council would confirm the appointment of a successor pre-determined by the Sultan.

In 1997 there were public signs of growing impatience with the slow pace of progress on political reform and economic development. Civil disturbances were reported in al-Hajer, 180 km west of Muscat, in May; troops were eventually deployed to end the demonstrations and disperse the crowds. University students also protested against the introduction of severe security measures on campus, which included a ban on public gatherings. Hitherto, such demonstrations had been virtually unknown in Oman and it was widely believed that budget cuts and privatization plans had created anxiety about employment prospects among the younger generation.

Voting was organized on 16 October 1997 to select candidates for appointment to the Consultative Council. Of a total of 736 candidates, 164 were chosen, from whose number the Sultan selected the 82 members of the new Council on 24 November. The two female members of the outgoing Council were returned to office. (Women from all regions had been permitted to seek nomination in the October poll.) In mid-December the Sultan issued a decree appointing the 41 members of the Council of State, which was reportedly dominated by former politicians, business leaders and academics. A further decree established the Council of Oman, which was formally inaugurated by the Sultan on 27 December.

In a cabinet reorganization in December 1997 the portfolio of Justice, Awqaf (Religious Endowments) and Islamic Affairs was separated into two ministries; Sheikh Muhammad bin Abdullah bin Zahir al-Hinai, previously Minister of Agriculture and Fisheries, was appointed Minister of Justice, and Sheikh Abdullah bin Muhammad bin Abdullah as-Salimi entered the Council of Ministers as Minister of Awqaf (Religious Endowments) and Religious Affairs. Three other ministers were replaced following their retirement. All the new ministers were Western-educated, with a strong academic background, and their appointment seemed to suggest a move towards technocratic rule in Oman. In late 1998, in what was widely regarded as a significant step towards greater democratization, the Ministers of Health and of Social Affairs, Labour and Vocational Training appeared before the Consultative Council to hear complaints and respond to questions concerning the poor performance of their ministries.

In February 2000 the Ministry of Communications was renamed and merged with the Ministry of Housing to become the Ministry of Transport and Housing, under Malek bin Sulayman al-Ma'amari, formerly Minister of Housing, and the Ministry of Posts, Telegraphs and Telephones was renamed the Ministry of Communications. A new minister, Suhail bin Mustahil bin Salem Beit Shammas, was appointed to the new communications portfolio. On 14 September voting was held to select candidates for the Consultative Council; the candidates were to be directly elected rather than selected by the Sultan, as at the previous election. A total of 541 candidates, including 21 women, stood in the election, in which 83 candidates, including two women, were elected to the Council. Although the number of people eligible to vote had tripled, to some 150,000, since the previous election, only 65% had registered their intention to vote, compared with some 90% at the previous election. Publication of final election results was postponed until 20 September, following allegations that there had been incidences of vote-buying; however, the Ministry of the Interior, responsible for investigating the claims, found no evidence of electoral malpractice. A new Majlis ad-Dawlah was appointed in October, and the Council of Oman convened for its second term on 4 November. Government changes were effected in May, June and November 2001, and in February 2002.

From late 2000 the Government undertook measures aimed at reducing the number of expatriates in Oman's labour force, a process termed 'Omanization'. In April 2001 more than 100 suspected illegal immigrants were detained by the Omani authorities, who announced that all foreign nationals employed illegally in the country who had not supplied the correct documentation within a period of two months would be liable to deportation. About 130 alleged illegal immigrants were reportedly arrested in September

FOREIGN RELATIONS SINCE THE GULF CRISIS

After the invasion of Kuwait by Iraqi troops in August 1990, the Omani Government stated that the dispute should be resolved without the use of force. When it became clear that Iraq would not withdraw from Kuwait, Oman, together with the other members of the GCC, gave its support to the deployment of a US-led defensive force in Saudi Arabia. The Omani Government expressed the view that the imposition of economic sanctions would force Iraq to withdraw from Kuwait. Oman was, however, prepared to tolerate the continuation in office of the Iraqi President, Saddam Hussain. In late November there was evidence that Oman had attempted to mediate in the crisis, when the Iraqi Minister of Foreign Affairs, Tareq Aziz, made the first official Iraqi visit to a GCC state, other than Kuwait, since August 1990.

In the aftermath of the Gulf crisis, Sultan Qaboos supported further integration among the GCC's members, and in December 1991, at the annual meeting of GCC Heads of State, he unsuccessfully proposed the creation of a GCC army. By March 1995, following Iraq's deployment in October 1994 of troops and artillery near the border with Kuwait in what was widely regarded as an attempt to effect the easing of UN economic sanctions imposed in August 1990, Oman's stance on the prolongation of economic restrictions against Iraq appeared ambivalent, urging the prompt political rehabilitation of Iraq in the region, while continuing to support the indefinite maintenance of economic sanctions. Since that time Oman has continued to support UN attempts to implement those resolutions relating to the Gulf War settlement (including a number of US and British air-strikes against strategic installations in Iraq), while attempting to draw international attention to the profound difficulties being inflicted on the Iraqi population by the maintenance of sanctions. Oman has also sought to maintain diplomatic channels with Iraq, and has urged the Iraqi authorities to seek regional rehabilitation through conciliation on issues such as alleged Kuwaiti prisoners of war (see chapter on Kuwait). In early 2002 Oman opposed attempts by the USA, as part of its 'war against terror', to garner international support for an eventual offensive against the Iraqi regime of Saddam Hussain. In July Sultan Qaboos ratified an agreement establishing a free-trade zone with Iraq.

Despite reports in February 1999 that Sultan Qaboos had communicated to US officials his opposition to aspects of US foreign policy that entailed interference in the internal affairs of other countries (a clear reference to US policy towards Iraq), in March, during a visit to Oman by the US Secretary of Defense, it was reported that the Omani Government had agreed to renew its military access agreement with the USA. In September 2001 Oman confirmed that joint Omani-British military exercises, known as Swift Sword II and scheduled to continue until mid-November, would take place despite the international tensions arising from suicide attacks in New York and Washington, DC, on 11 September. The exercises were to involve 14,000 Omani and 24,000 British soldiers, as well as over 150 aircraft and about 40 naval vessels. As elsewhere in the region, there was concern in Oman that eventual US-led military action against the al-Qa'ida (Base) network of Osama bin Laden—the USA's prime suspect in the attacks—or against the Taliban regime in Afghanistan should not be extended to target any Arab state. Street demonstrations were held in October by Omani students protesting against the war in Afghanistan. Meanwhile, during an official visit to Oman by the US Secretary of Defense, Donald Rumsfeld, in early October, it was reported that the USA was to supply Oman with 12 F-16 fighter aircraft and other advanced weaponry, at a cost of some US $1,120m.

Oman has expressed a particular desire to promote relations between the GCC states and Iran, and to support gradual political reform in the latter. In March 1991 Oman hosted a meeting at which diplomatic relations between Saudi Arabia and Iran were restored. In September 1992 the Governments of Oman and Iran signed an agreement to increase trade and economic co-operation, in particular in the sectors of transport and shipping. Further bilateral discussions were conducted in June 1998 in an attempt to formulate a strategy to combat smuggling activities across the Strait of Hormuz; a memorandum of understanding was signed to that end. However, Oman, as a GCC member, has continued to support the claims of the UAE in its territorial dispute with Iran over the sovereignty of Abu Musa and the Greater and Lesser Tunb islands.

In October 1992 Oman signed an agreement with Yemen (the Yemen Arab Republic—YAR—and the PDRY were unified in May 1990) to establish the demarcation of their border. The agreement was officially ratified in December, and in October 1993 Sultan Qaboos pledged US $21m. to finance the construction of a border road between the two countries. Relations were restored and in March 1994 Oman hosted talks with Yemen to discuss the furthering of bilateral co-operation. The efforts of Sultan Qaboos to mediate a settlement to the conflict in Yemen ended in disappointment when fighting broke out again between the two rival Yemeni factions in late April. However, the Sultanate was elected to be a non-permanent member of the UN Security Council for a two-year term from January 1994, in tribute to its mediatory role in the Middle East. In June 1995 Oman and Yemen completed the demarcation of their joint border; in the following month Oman and Saudi Arabia officially demarcated their common border. At the end of July 1996 Oman withdrew an estimated 15,000 troops from the last of the disputed territories on the Yemeni border, in accordance with the 1992 agreement. In May 1997 official representatives from both countries signed the international border demarcation maps at a ceremony in Muscat. It was also agreed to promote bilateral trade by building a new 245-km road linking the two countries. In September 1998, following a meeting of border officials from both countries, 12 economic co-operation accords were announced, as were plans for the establishment of a free-trade zone; Saudi claims that the border agreement violated sovereign Saudi territory were rejected by both countries. In June 2002 it was reported that agreement had also been reached with the UAE on the demarcation of common international borders.

In January 1994 bilateral talks were held with Egypt to promote the exchange of expertise between their respective armed forces. In April the Israeli Deputy Minister of Foreign Affairs, Yossi Beilin, participated in talks in Oman. This constituted the first official visit by an Israeli minister to an Arab Gulf state since Israel's declaration of independence in 1948. In late September 1994, moreover, Oman and the other GCC member states announced the partial ending of their economic boycott of Israel. In December the Israeli Prime Minister, Itzhak Rabin, made an official visit to the Sultanate to discuss the Middle East peace process, and in February 1995 it was announced that low-level diplomatic relations were to be established between Oman and Israel with the opening of interests sections, respectively, in Tel-Aviv and Muscat.

The agreement to establish interests sections was signed in January 1996, and in April relations between the two countries were consolidated further by a two-day official visit to Oman by Shimon Peres, the new Israeli Prime Minister. An Omani trade office was opened in Israel in August 1996, despite concerns that relations with Israel would be undermined by the uncompromising international stance adopted by the new Netanyahu Government in Israel. However, in April 1997, in accordance with an Arab League resolution adopted in March in protest at Israel's decision to construct a Jewish settlement in a disputed area of East Jerusalem, Oman suspended diplomatic links with Israel, resumed the economic boycott and withdrew from multilateral peace talks. As the Middle East peace process faltered, Oman suspended all commercial and business activities with Israel; the Government barred Israeli companies from taking part in an annual computer fair in Muscat, and two Israeli Ministry of Foreign Affairs officials were refused visas to enter Oman in order to find a permanent site for the Israeli diplomatic mission in Muscat. In late July, the Omani Ministry of Foreign Affairs announced the opening of a representative office in the Palestinian (National) Authority (PA)-administered city of Gaza, to be headed by an ambassador, and in October, in an address to the UN General Assembly, the Minister of State for Foreign Affairs, Yousuf bin al-Alawi bin Abdullah, urged UN members to encourage Israel to withdraw from the Golan Heights and southern Lebanon. Bin al-Alawi also reiterated the Government's support for the PA. In November, however, Oman attended the Middle East and North Africa economic conference in Doha, which was widely boycotted by Arab nations, owing to Israel's participation. In December Oman recalled its representative from its trade office in Tel-Aviv. In late May 1998 Sultan Qaboos formally received the first Palestinian ambassador to Oman, and in the following month Yasser Arafat, the President of the PA, visited Oman and met Sultan Qaboos during a tour of Arab states, which Arafat hoped would produce a general consensus on the organization of a pan-Arab summit to discuss the Middle East peace process. Arafat visited Oman again in mid-March 1999, hoping to secure the Sultan's support for a unilateral declaration of Palestinian statehood in May. However, in common with many Western states, the Omani Government considered that the postponement of such a declaration would be in the best interests of the Palestinian cause, particularly given the proximity of forthcoming Israeli elections; following the election of the Labour alliance's Ehud Barak as the new Israeli Prime Minister, the Omani authorities expressed renewed hopes for the future of the peace process. In October 2000, however, as the crisis in the Middle East that had erupted in late September deepened, Oman closed both its trade office in Tel-Aviv and the Israeli trade office in Muscat. Oman hosted the annual summit meeting of GCC heads of state in late December 2001, at the close of which a statement was issued blaming Israel for the collapse of the peace process and expressing support for the Palestinian leadership. Two demonstrations took place in Muscat in early April 2002 to demand an end to Israeli military incursions into Palestinian territory.

Economy

ALAN J. DAY

INTRODUCTION

Oman's economy continues to be based largely on revenue from the petroleum sector, although significant progress towards diversification has been made in recent years. Petroleum was first produced commercially in 1967, but it was not until 1970, when Sultan Qaboos bin Said assumed power, that income from petroleum was invested in the country's economic development. Subsequently, Oman's economy expanded considerably under a prudent policy of avoiding external debt while developing both public and private sectors. From the mid-1990s the Government increasingly opted to give priority to the development of the private sector through both privatization and other measures.

Oman's economic growth since the mid-1960s has been rapid but uneven. Between 1965 and 1980, according to World Bank estimates, the country's gross domestic product (GDP) increased, in real terms, by 12.5% per year, one of the highest national growth rates in the world. The comparable increase between 1973 and 1984 was 6.1% per year, a rate that was maintained at 6% during 1985. Measured in current prices, Oman's annual GDP rose from an estimated mere US $60m. in 1965 to $8,980m. in 1985. Between 1985 and 1995 it was estimated, gross national product (GNP) per head increased, in real terms, at an average rate of 0.3% per year. During 1990–95 the average annual growth rate for GDP, measured at constant prices, was 6.0%. In 1995, according to estimates by the World Bank, Oman's GNP, measured at average 1993–95 prices, was US $10,578m., equivalent to $4,820 per head; GNP per head was $4,950 in 1997. Real GDP (measured at constant 1988 prices) grew by 2.9% in 1996, by 6.2% in 1997 and by 2.7% in 1998, but fell by 0.2% in 1999, when economic policy was tightened in response to the 1998 downturn in world oil prices. In 2000 real GDP rose by an estimated 5.1%, owing mainly to growth of about 10% in the hydrocarbons sector, where a sustained recovery in petroleum prices coincided with the start of Omani liquefied natural gas (LNG) exports. In 2000 Oman's GDP per head was estimated to be about $6,700 on a conventional exchange-rate basis, or $8,000 on a 'purchasing-power parity' basis.

Revenues from petroleum have been used to underpin a series of five-year development plans, starting in 1976: the current plan covers 2001–2005. These plans have aimed to provide the country with necessary social amenities while investing further in the petroleum sector, but in recent years there has been a strong emphasis on diversification within the economy. The 1991–95 plan imposed strict limits on projected external borrowing, and again emphasized the diversification of the economy, which was to be achieved through the expansion of the private sector, and renewed stress on industry, agriculture and fisheries, mining and services. In July 1994 the Government initiated a wide-ranging privatization programme to attract private investment, particularly for infrastructure projects. In November an investment law was introduced to allow foreign nationals to own as much as 100% of 'projects contributing to the development of the national economy', particularly if they pertained to infrastructure. A new tax law was introduced in October 1996, reducing the rate of tax paid by Omani companies with 49% or less foreign ownership as part of the Government's efforts to promote foreign investment and strengthen the role of the private sector in the economy. All companies working in industry, mining, fishing, tourism and agriculture now benefit from tax exemptions which previously applied only to firms that were entirely Omani-owned. Early in 1997 the Minister of Commerce and Industry announced that all new Omani companies would be required to offer 49% of their shares to foreign ownership, a move that was not welcomed by a number of the country's major trading families who felt that this initiative would undermine their dominant position.

In the fifth Development Plan (1996–2000), emphasis was placed on the elimination of the budget deficit by 2000 through the reduction of public expenditure, the development of the non-petroleum sector and the expansion of the privatization programme. The policy of 'Omanizing' the work-force (to reduce the country's dependence on expatriate labour, thereby providing opportunities for Oman's rapidly expanding population) was given fresh impetus when, in June 1996, the Government stated that it would assume the full cost of training Omani nationals employed in the private sector and announced that a schedule of charges would be imposed on private sector companies employing foreign workers. Yet, despite the Government's 'Omanization' policy, figures for the end of 1996 revealed that expatriates made up almost two-thirds of the work-force and continued to dominate the private sector. (Indian nationals form the largest group of expatriates, comprising almost one-half of all foreign workers in 1993.) The Ministry of Social Affairs and Labour had given private sector companies until the end of 1996 to submit plans indicating how they intended to replace expatriate staff with Omanis so as to meet government quotas, but under pressure from the business community the deadline was extended to the end of 1997. Quotas for the number of Omanis employed have been set by sector: 60% of all employees in transport and storage; 45% in banks, insurance companies and estate agents; 35% in manufacturing industry; 30% in hotels and restaurants and 20% in the wholesale industry. However, finding employment for the growing number of Omanis leaving school every year is becoming an increasingly urgent problem. It was projected that annual number of school leavers would total 48,000 in 1998–2002, rising to 53,000 in 2003–07. At the end of 1996 almost 80% of

all employees in the public sector, but only 25% of private-sector workers, were Omanis. It will be difficult for the Government to increase this percentage, as the monthly salary of the majority of foreign workers in the private sector is much less than an Omani would expect to earn, and many jobs in the private sector, especially those involving manual work, are unattractive to Omani nationals. In 1998 around 22,000 foreign workers were expelled from the country by the Government. In mid-2002, according to official figures, some 538,824 foreign workers were employed in Oman's private sector, compared with just 63,179 Omanis. Occupations which were barred to non-Omanis in 2000 and 2001 included car rental businesses and the selling of audio and video cassettes. The Government's 2001–05 planning targets included the creation of 100,000 new private-sector employment opportunities for Omanis.

Annual inflation averaged just 0.3% in 1990–2000. The consumer price index fell by 0.8% in 1998, but rose by an estimated 0.4% in 1999 only to decline again, by 1.1% in 2000 and by 1.0% in 2001.

Oman is neither a member of the Organization of the Petroleum Exporting Countries (OPEC), nor of the Organization of Arab Petroleum Exporting Countries (OAPEC). However, its agreements on concessionary terms ensure that concession-holders are obliged to grant it the same privileges as those granted to members of OPEC. Oman is not, therefore, subject to controls on petroleum production and pricing, although it generally respects OPEC's policies. In the 1980s Oman benefited from its freedom to raise production levels to compensate for any loss of income resulting from the existence of large surplus stocks of petroleum during the first half of the decade. Owing to Oman's position on the southern shore of the Persian (Arabian) Gulf, the country was less vulnerable to the disruption of petroleum traffic caused by the 1980–88 war between Iran and Iraq. Although annual Omani production of crude petroleum fell from 135m. barrels in 1976 to 103m. barrels in 1980, the opening of new fields brought a recovery, with the result that production reached 137m. barrels in 1983 and rose steadily thereafter to exceed 300m. barrels for the first time in 1995. Further increases in 1996 and 1997 were followed by a slight cut-back to 327m. barrels in 1998, when Oman made a modest contribution to international efforts to arrest a decline in prices. The sharp recovery in oil prices in 1999 then stimulated a rise in Omani production to 330m. barrels, of which 309m. barrels were exported, and a 48.6% increase in oil export revenues (which were, nevertheless, 4.7% below their 1997 level). In 2000 there was a 5.8% rise in the volume of oil production and a 67% rise in oil export revenues.

Although petroleum remains the predominant feature in all aspects of the Omani economy, the development of the country's gas reserves for export and as the basis for energy-intensive industrial projects is seen as the main hope for transforming the economy in the future, especially since Oman's proven oil reserves will last for less than 16 years at present extraction rates unless new discoveries are made. An important advance towards this goal was the commencement of liquefied natural gas (LNG) exports in April 2000 (to the Republic of Korea), while the recovery in oil revenues and the revival of Asian economies enabled the Government to relaunch other major diversification projects, mostly on the basis of private sector participation. Despite the return of more moderate prices for oil on world markets in 2001 and difficulties for LNG exports associated with the collapse of the US energy corporation Enron in December 2001 (see Petroleum and Natural Gas, below), GDP growth continued to be buoyant, at an estimated 3% in 2001 and a projected 2.5% in 2002, while the Government's fiscal position remained fundamentally healthy.

AGRICULTURE AND FISHERIES

Although the relative importance of agriculture has declined sharply since the development of the petroleum industry, the sector remains a significant source of employment and income, perpetuating Oman's traditional identity as a predominantly agricultural country. The Government accepts that Oman is unlikely ever to become self-sufficient in food production, given the country's growing population and the natural shortage of water supply for agriculture. Nevertheless, substantial state investment has resulted in a notable increase in agricultural output in recent years, and the sector has continued to be an important contributor to Oman's non-oil exports.

The 1993 census indicated that 60% of arable land was under cultivation and that some 9.4% of the working population were engaged in the agricultural sector, largely in the form of subsistence farming by traditional methods. About 60% of the area under cultivation is planted with some 10m. date palms, producing between 150,000 and 175,000 metric tons of good quality dates each year. Other crops include lucerne (alfalfa), limes, mangoes, melons, bananas, papayas and coconuts. Oman is almost self-sufficient in tomatoes, cucumbers, onions and peppers. Imports of cereals increased from 52,000 tons in 1974 to 287,000 tons in 1987 and 445,800 tons in 1995. Livestock farming is practised extensively in Dhofar, which benefits from monsoon rains between June and September. Cattle are raised in the hills north of Salalah, and goats are reared in the Hajar mountains. In 2000 Oman was the leading livestock producer in the Arabian peninsula, with 980,000 goats, 330,000 sheep, 290,000 cattle and 98,000 camels, according to FAO estimates.

Agricultural GDP increased by an annual average of 8.9%, in real terms, during 1978–92, and by 5.2% and 3.2%, respectively, in 1993 and 1994. The 1986–90 Five-Year Plan emphasized the expansion of the fishing industry and the encouragement of production for export and the urban market. This was intended to reduce Oman's dependence on food imports, which cost RO 131m. (18.6% of Oman's total imports) in 1987 and RO 162.6m. in 1990. The Oman Bank for Agriculture and Fisheries was established in 1981 to provide loans to farmers, with the intention of curbing rural-to-urban migration, and in the same year a state marketing authority, the Public Authority for Marketing Agricultural Produce (PAMAP), was set up with the aim of increasing domestic consumption of local products.

By the end of 1988, which was declared to be 'Agricultural Year' by the Sultan, about 2,500 government-owned research and experimental farms had been established. In January 1989 a 10-year plan was announced for the development of the agricultural and fishing industries. In 1989 government expenditure on agriculture, forestry and fishing was only RO 27.1m. (less than 2% of the total). By 1993 government expenditure on the sector had increased to RO 40.7m., representing 3.7% of the total, but by 1998 expenditure had decreased to RO 22.1m. (1.2% of the total). During 1992–96 annual agricultural output rose from 784,200 metric tons to 1,181,800 tons, reflecting an expansion of modern techniques and intensification methods. As a result of the increase in production, the value of agricultural produce increased from RO 85.1m. in 1992 to RO 100.8m. in 1996, registering an annual increase of 4.6% (although the rate targeted in the 1991–96 Development Plan was 6.3%). Over the same period the value of agricultural exports increased from RO 31.8m. to RO 50.8m.—an average annual growth of 14.5%. In 1997 an integrated RO 12.8m. project, the Modern Poultry Farm, was initiated in Dhofar, with initial capacity to house 94,000 hens producing 55m. eggs per year, and with storage capacity for 11,000 metric tons of frozen poultry. A similar farm was subsequently established at Barqa; it was envisaged that the two farms would enable Oman to halve its annual imports of eggs and frozen chicken. In 2000 the Dhofar and Barqa farms announced plans to increase egg production to 108m. and 50m. per year respectively.

In 1999 agriculture and livestock contributed RO 107m. to Oman's GDP at current market prices, declining to RO 101m. in 2000, before increasing again to RO 103m., about 1.3% of total GDP, in 2001. Recent estimates indicate that Oman is 100% self-sufficient in dates, bananas and seasonal vegetables, 53% in milk, 46% in beef, 44% in eggs and 23% in mutton. The Government is giving particular emphasis to increasing sheep and goat production by financing the application of the latest technology to improving fertility, lowering death rates and increasing growth rates. Another government project aims to increase production of milk and other dairy products by giving dairy farmers marketing assistance and disseminating modern herd management techniques. In October 2000 the Government announced the closure of PAMAP (after an attempt to privatize it had failed), expressing confidence that with continuing state subsidies the farming industry was sufficiently mature to market itself.

Agriculture in Oman is heavily dependent on irrigation. In 1985 the Government announced that rural power and water networks were to be greatly expanded over the next five years, and in that year new dams at Khour ar-Rassagh and Wadi al-Koudh came into operation. By early 1988 a dam with a capacity of 3.6m. cu m was under construction at Wadi Jizzi in Sohar. In August 1989 three schemes to improve and expand the water distribution networks were announced: two in Nizwa and Sur, costing RO 2m. each, and one on Masirah island, at a cost of RO 500,000. In May 1990, contracts were awarded to improve water supply systems in Nizwa and Sur. The Nizwa project consisted of laying 45 km of pipeline, construction of a new section for the reservoir and the establishment of a telemetry system at a cost of RO 741,000. The Sur project involved a RO 688,000 contract to lay 10 km of transmission pipeline, 30 km of distribution pipeline and install a pumping station. In April 1991 the Ministry of Agriculture and Fisheries awarded a contract worth US $8.3m. to build two recharge dams in the Batinah coastal region. Dams already constructed at Wadi Rubkah and Wadi Taww will eventually have respective capacities of 5m. cu m and 3.7m. cu m. The Ministry of Agriculture and Fisheries also commissioned a recharge dam to be built at Wadi al-Fuleij, in Sur, at a cost of RO 1.2m., enabling a saving of 2.2m. cu m of flood water which would normally flow from the wadi into the sea.

In May 1990 the newly-created Ministry of Water Resources announced a programme for water rationalization which introduced new regulations for the registration of wells and a permit requirement for new wells. Nevertheless, irrigation still accounts for an estimated 90% of the country's water consumption and as the crops produced are of relatively low value the high rate of water usage by the agricultural sector remains a matter of concern for the Government. Oman's consumption of fresh water currently exceeds that replaced naturally by rainfall, and the depletion of groundwater supplies and sea-water intrusion into coastal aquifers have become a serious problem. A conference organized by Sultan Qaboos University in Muscat in April 1997 urged all the members of the Co-operation Council of the Arab States of the Gulf (Gulf Co-operation Council—GCC) to reduce the volume of water allocated to agriculture in order to conserve scarce supplies. However, for the Omani Government to impose additional restrictions on water use would present difficulties, given that agriculture is such a politically sensitive sector; figures for the end of 1996 indicated that agriculture employed almost half of all Omanis in the workforce and provided jobs for at least some young Omanis living in rural areas where alternative forms of employment are limited.

Fishing is a traditional and growing industry off Oman's 1,700-km coastline, where more than 150 species of fish and crustaceans having been identified, many of them commercially exploitable. Fishing and fish-processing have been developed into an important export industry over the last two decades, with emphasis on quality control and the creation of storage facilities. Although large commercial trawlers have become increasingly important, the sector remains dominated by independent fishermen using small vessels, who in 2001 were responsible for 85% of Oman's total catch. In early 2002 there were some 29,000 registered fishermen, operating about 12,000 craft, while a further 5,000 people were employed in ancillary fish industries.

In 1980 the Oman National Fisheries Co (ONFC) was formed to organize concession agreements, government trawlers and land facilities. In 1987 the ONFC was merged into the newly-formed Oman Fisheries Co (OFC), a joint-stock company in which the Government took a 24% stake. The Government's Fishermen's Incentive Fund grants substantial subsidies to the sector, while the Bank for Agriculture and Fisheries has encouraged small-scale fishing and the change from subsistence to commercial fishing. The provision, in 1990, of US aid totalling $40m. specifically for the development of the fisheries sector was an additional source of encouragement. In the fourth Five-Year Plan (1991–95) RO 200m. was allocated to the fishing industry with the objective of raising its annual growth rate, in particular by means of the creation of an industrial fishing fleet and the building of 24 new fishing ports equipped with cold-storage plants and processing facilities. By 1996 the OFC was operating nine deep-sea trawlers, an onboard fishmeal plant and a processing and freezing plant at Mutrah. The fifth Five-Year Plan (1996–2000) included annual growth rate projections of 5.6% for the fisheries sector.

During the late 1970s the annual catch was about 60,000 metric tons, and this rose steadily to reach 165,576 tons in 1988. An uneven decline in the 1990s, to 106,164 tons in 1998, was attributable to earlier overfishing and the depletion of breeding stock. Another negative factor was a decision by the European Union (EU) to suspend imports of fish from Oman in 1998 because of concerns over quality control. However, the introduction of controls to prevent overfishing and the lifting of the EU ban resulted in an increase in the total catch to 120,412 tons in 2000 (with 46,408 tons exported to more than 40 countries for a return of RO 37m.). The principal export market for fish is the United Arab Emirates, which takes nearly one-half of Omani production, followed by Saudi Arabia (20%) and the Republic of Korea (5%).

Under the sixth Five-Year Plan (2001–05) an annual growth rate of 4.3% was envisaged for the fisheries sector, while exports were projected to increase by annual averages of 16% in terms of value and 8% in terms of quantity. The longer-term aim was that the proportion of Oman's GDP contributed by fisheries should rise from about 1% in 1999 to 2% by 2020. The expansion would be driven partly by the development of aquaculture, and in particular, exploitation of the lucrative international market for shrimps, or prawns (to which end the Oman International Shrimp Co—OISC—was set up in 2000 to operate the country's first fully integrated aquaculture farm at ad-Duqm). In 2001 the Dhofar Fisheries Industries Co (DFICO) was established to run Oman's largest fish processing and canning factory at Salalah; operations were to concentrate on tuna and sardine canning and on the production of fishmeal and fish oil. By early 2002 four other modern fish processing plants, equipped to EU standards, were being operated by the OFC at Salalah, Ghala, al-Ashkarah and Masirah. In April 2002 the Government inaugurated a Japanese-financed Fish Quality Control Centre (FQCC) at al-Bustan, Muscat.

PETROLEUM AND NATURAL GAS

Since the early 1970s the economy of Oman has been dominated by the petroleum industry. In the late 1990s petroleum and gas accounted for about 75% of government revenue and around 40% of GDP. Proven oil reserves totalled 5,500m. barrels at the end of 2001, sufficient to sustain production at present rates until 2017. In 1937 Petroleum Concessions (Oman) Ltd, a subsidiary of the Iraq Petroleum Co, was granted a 75-year concession to explore for petroleum, extending over the whole area except for the district of Dhofar. A concession covering Dhofar was granted in 1953 to Dhofar Cities Service Petroleum Corpn. However, petroleum was not discovered until 1964, when deposits were found near Fahud. Commercial production began in 1967, and average output increased to around 300,000 barrels per day (b/d) in the 1970s. Production is managed by Petroleum Development Oman (PDO), in which the Government holds a 60% share, while Royal Dutch/Shell has 34%. In 1999 PDO was responsible for about 95% of Oman's crude oil output, the remainder being produced by a number of foreign concerns. In March 1997 the Minister of Petroleum and Minerals reiterated that the Government was not planning to change the ownership structure of PDO, which remains heavily dependent on managerial and technical assistance from Shell.

PDO operates two main production areas: a group of central oilfields, south-west of Muscat, and a group of southern oilfields in Dhofar. The central area was the first to be developed, and four connected oilfields together produced crude petroleum at an average rate of 341,000 b/d in 1975. When production from the three Ghaba fields started in 1976, output from the total central area reached a peak level of 368,000 b/d. From then on production declined, averaging about 250,000 b/d in early 1984. Development of the oilfields in the south has compensated for this fall. Production started at the Marmul field in 1980, and the Rima field came on stream in 1982, producing 45,000 b/d in early 1984. Further fields, at Marmul, Nimr and Sayyala, were brought into production in late 1985. A north–south pipeline connects the oilfields to the port of Mina al-Fahal, near Muscat. In June 1988 the Rajaa oilfield, situated in the Balija region of central Oman, commenced production, while the Yibal field in northern Oman came on stream in 1991. In the late 1990s two-thirds of PDO oil output was coming from the Fahud, Nimr and Yibal fields.

In mid-1995 the Government revealed plans to offer at least 10 largely untapped petroleum exploration areas (mostly in southern Oman) to international companies in order to stimulate exploration activity. In the first half of 1996 four major concessions for exploration were granted by PDO to the US companies Triton Energy and Phillips Petroleum Oman, the Japan Petroleum Exploration Co (Japex) and a joint venture between the US company, Arco, and the Portuguese-owned Partex (Oman) Corpn. Early in 1997 it was announced that the Saudi Arabian company, Nimr Petroleum, had been granted a concession to drill for oil on the south-east coast near Masirah island. In June 1998 the Government signed three exploration and production agreements with US companies—Amoco, Occidental Petroleum Corpn, and Triton—securing a minimum investment of US $80m. in exploration activities. Optimism engendered by a PDO announcement in June 1999 that a new oil find was the most significant for five years was qualified in September by a decision by Japex to abandon exploration in Oman after a decade of fruitless activity. In June 2000 PDO began production from the new Burhan and Mukhaizna oilfields in central Oman, from each of which output of 25,000 b/d was expected. The southern an-Noor field came on stream in August 2000, and further new oil and gas finds, in the south and centre of the country, were announced by PDO in the same month. Another new oil discovery was announced in February 2001.

In April 2001 Denmark's Maersk Oil Oman obtained concession agreements for two exploration blocks in western Oman. New exploration and production-sharing agreements were also signed with Novus of Australia in October 2001, Hunt Oil of the USA in November and TotalFinaElf of France in March 2002. In April 2002, moreover, Novus took over an onshore concession relinquished by Occidental, to become the biggest foreign operator in Oman in terms of acreage. These agreements left about 10 oil exploration blocks still to be awarded in the current round.

Omani oil officials estimated that the country would effectively double the size of its recoverable oil reserves if it took full advantage of the latest production technology to overcome the various difficulties posed by local geological conditions. In April 2002 PDO unveiled details of its 'Target 50' (T50) five-year plan for substantial investment in improved oil recovery (IOR) and enhanced oil recovery (EOR) programmes intended to increase the recovery rate from mature oilfields from 23% to 50% of their proven reserves. This investment was to include US $1,000m. to be spent on steam injection technology to boost production from the Mukhaizna field from 15,000 b/d to 100,000 b/d, and $200m. to be spent on a similar project in the northern Qarn Alam field, where the oil is of very high viscosity. High-pressure gas injection to increase output from the Haweel field was also planned. It was estimated that the IOR and EOR investment would more than double Oman's average oil production costs, from $3–$4 per barrel to as much as $9 per barrel.

In 1987 petroleum exports were estimated to be worth RO 1,194m., representing 82% of total revenue, and in 1988 they were worth RO 1,141.0m., according to estimates by the Central Bank. Japan is the principal recipient of Omani petroleum, taking 40.4% of the total in 1992, compared with 52.6% in 1986. Following the rise in petroleum prices precipitated by the Gulf crisis, the Government's net oil revenues rose by almost 58%, to RO 1,538m., in 1990. Oil exports rose to 252.5m. barrels in 1992 from 243.7m. in 1991. Net oil revenues fell to RO 1,241m. in 1991, rising slightly to RO 1,276m. in 1992, accounting for 79% and 77% of total revenue respectively. In January 1994 production was reduced to 720,000 b/d, in an attempt by the Government to raise prices. The plan was abandoned when it became apparent that production quotas set by OPEC would not be reduced, and PDO subsequently resumed production of an average of 800,000 b/d in 1994. In late 1994 the Government announced that it was to invest US $6,000m. in the crude petroleum production sector during 1995–98, in an attempt to increase petroleum reserves. In 1993 exports of crude petroleum provided 72.2% of total export earnings, and in 1994 the proportion increased to 74%. Petroleum exports rose from 778,000 b/d in 1995 to 811,000 b/d in 1996, when overall output averaged

885,000 b/d. However, exports to Japan fell from 272,000 b/d to 247,000 b/d. Exports to the Republic of Korea rose slightly from 147,000 b/d to 156,000 b/d, while exports to the People's Republic of China increased from 90,000 b/d to 116,000 b/d.

Exports rose to 831,000 b/d in 1997 (from total output of 900,000 b/d), but declined to 822,000 b/d in 1998 (from total output of 897,000 b/d). In 1999 exports recovered to 846,000 b/d (from total output of 910,000 b/d). In 2000 exports rose to 893,000 b/d (from total output of 961,000 b/d). As a result of increased levels of production and higher prices, the value of petroleum exports rose substantially from $4,752m. in 1995 to $5,889m. in 1996 and were only slightly lower, at $5,829m., in 1997. Oil export earnings fell sharply to $3,756m. in 1998, before recovering to $5,562m. in 1999 and rising sharply to $9,380m. in 2000. Average output in 2001 was slightly lower than the previous year, at 959,000 b/d. A return to more moderately priced oil on world markets in 2001 resulted in export revenues falling to around $7,600m. Output in the first half of 2002 averaged just 910,400 b/d, despite PDO's declared aim of achieving 1m. b/d in the medium term.

Oman's first petroleum refinery came into production at Mina al-Fahal, near Muscat, in late 1982. As a result, the value of imports of refined products was reduced from RO 49.5m. in the first half of 1982 to RO 7m. in the comparable period of 1983. It was hoped that the new refinery would satisfy domestic demand for petrol. The refinery's average throughput was 38,000 b/d in 1983, and by 1988, its capacity had risen to 80,000 b/d. Plans for construction of a second refinery at Sohar were delayed by the slump in oil prices in 1997–98, but revived following the 1999 upturn. The refinery had been originally intended for Salalah but was relocated to Sohar, where a number of integrated industries are planned. Negotiations with international oil companies commenced in October 2000 for a long-term offtake agreement for products from the proposed refinery (which would include propylene, liquefied petroleum gas, unleaded gasoline, low-sulphur gas oil, fuel oil and sulphur). After long delays over financing and other considerations, four bids were submitted in July 2002 for the $850m. contract to build the Sohar refinery. Construction of a third refinery was at that stage envisaged for Mina al-Fahal.

In June 1992 Oman signed an agreement with Kazakhstan to explore for, develop and produce petroleum and gas in that country. Later that year Oman agreed to collaborate with Kazakhstan, Azerbaijan and Russia in the 'Caspian Pipeline Consortium'. This project envisaged the construction of a pipeline to transport about 1.5m. b/d of petroleum from the former Soviet republics. Azerbaijan later withdrew from the project and after five years of disputes Russia, Kazakhstan and Oman, together with eight major oil companies, signed an agreement in April 1997 to build the pipeline. In the restructured consortium the Russian Government is the biggest shareholder, Kazakhstan holds 24% and Oman 7%. Construction work on the pipeline will cost US $2,000m.

Oman's proved reserves of natural gas totalled 70,000m. cu m at the end of 1980 and 200,000m. cu m at the end of 1990. By the end of 2001, after further discoveries, proven reserves had risen to 830,000m. cu m (sufficient to last for 62 years at the current rate of production). Oman's marketed gas output was 13,400m. cu m in 2001, compared with 8,400m. cu m in 2000, the main cause of this 60% rise being the ongoing development of liquefied natural gas (LNG) production (see below).

In September 1984 PDO embarked on a 10-year programme of exploration for unassociated gas, which, it was hoped, would enable more petroleum to be released for export. By September 1985 a total of 19 new discoveries of gas deposits had been reported. Gas production in 1985 reached 3,930m. cu m, of which 1,290m. cu m was reinjected, 900m. cu m was flared, 190m. cu m was lost and 1,550m. cu m was consumed. In 1985 PDO discovered gas reserves in Lekhwair, where it was planned, in 1989, to construct a gas injection plant in order to improve recovery levels, using surplus gas. The plant was part of a larger project to upgrade facilities at the Lekhwair field and its cost was estimated at US $100m.–$130m. In June 1990 PDO announced that it was initiating several oil pipelines and gas lift projects. In August 1990 PDO awarded a contract to develop a water flood scheme at the Lekhwair oilfield. This project was allocated $500m., enabling the scheme to have a daily capacity of 200,000 barrels of crude petroleum and 4m. cu ft of gas. In June 1986 offshore gas was discovered in the Bukha field, in the Musandam Peninsula region. Its reserves were estimated at 31.2m. barrels of condensate, 500,000m. cu ft (14,000m. cu m) of dry gas and 7.3m. barrels of associated gas. A contract to develop the gasfield was negotiated with a group led by a Canadian company, International Petroleum (IPL). At the end of 1987 natural gas was being extracted at the rate of 3.90m. cu m (140m. cu ft) per day, and by the end of the decade this was increased to 14m.–17m. cu m per day.

A pipeline links Yibal to Muscat and Sohar, and an extension of the gas pipeline network from Yibal to Izki has been completed. The scheme is intended to provide sufficient supplies from Yibal to the coast until 2010. PDO also initiated a programme to build a 26-km pipeline from Natih to Fahud. Other projects have included pipeline links from Qaharir to Marmul and Jalmu to Rima. Schemes are under way to convert domestic fuelling systems to natural gas in order to release more petroleum for export, and gas is also used to enhance the rate of petroleum recovery (by reinjection) and to power the country's copper smelter (see below). In July 1989 a proposal to expand the plant producing natural gas liquids (NGL) at Yibal was announced. In 1987 output of liquefied petroleum gas (LPG) by the National Gas Co was 35,000 metric tons, increasing to 37,000 tons in 1988.

The Government has exclusive rights to revenue from gas, and in 1988 the National Gas Co's profits reached RO 649,000, 17.5% higher than in 1987. In April 1989 Oman agreed terms for a 10-year contract to supply natural gas for the world's first floating methanol plant, beginning production by 1991. The Government agreed to sell as much as 6,343m. cu m (224,000m. cu ft) of natural gas over the period of the agreement to the consortium owning the plant, which has a capacity of 2,200 metric tons per day. In July 1989 PDO announced its largest gas discovery for 22 years, at the Saih Nihayda field in the central region. Recoverable reserves were estimated at 10,000m. cu m (350,000m. cu ft), making it Oman's fifth biggest gasfield. A further large discovery of gas, at the Saih Rawl field, was announced in March 1991. In 1992 gas revenues reached RO 63.1m. (equivalent to 3.3% of total revenue), only to decrease again to RO 57.9m. (3.3%) in 1993 and to RO 52.5m. (2.9%) in 1994. In 1991 it was announced that more than RO 44m. had been allocated for exploration and exploitation of new gas discoveries.

In February 1992 plans were announced for massive investment in a project to produce LNG, to be implemented by Oman LNG, a consortium led by the Government (51% share), Shell, Total, and various Japanese and Korean companies. The liquefaction plant was subsequently constructed at Qalhat near Sur, on the coast 150 km south of the capital, by the Chiyoda Corporation of Japan and Foster Wheeler of the USA at a cost of US $2,250m., becoming Oman's largest single construction project to date. The bulk of the finance for the plant was raised through loans from commercial firms and the balance through equity. Production began in February 2000 at a rate of 6.6m. metric tons per year, and the first LNG exports were shipped in April to the Republic of Korea under a 25-year agreement with the Korea Gas Corpn for the supply of 4.1m. tons per year. By mid-2000 long-term sales and purchase agreements had also been concluded with Japan's Osaka Gas, for 0.7m. tons per year from 2000 to 2025, and with Enron of the USA for the supply of 1.6m. tons per year of LNG to India's Dabhol Power Co over 20 years, starting in February 2002. Shorter-term customers for smaller quantities include Total of France, Coral Energy Resources of the USA and Enagas of Spain.

The sudden collapse of Enron in December 2001 caused major difficulties for Oman LNG, since it forced Dabhol—in which Enron was a major shareholder—to cancel the LNG import agreement with Oman. However, in March 2002 Oman LNG concluded a five-year agreement with Royal Dutch/Shell for the supply of 700,000 metric tons of LNG per year to that company's customers in Spain. A further agreement was negotiated in April whereby Gaz de France was to take nine spot tanker cargoes of LNG in 2002. Most crucially, in May an agreement was signed with Union Fenosa of Spain providing for the annual export to Spain, by tanker, of 1.6m. tons of LNG over a period of 20 years starting in 2006. An undertaking by Union Fenosa to invest in the long-discussed 50% 'third train' expansion of the Qalhat plant's capacity, to 9.9m. tons per year, lent new impetus to the $700m. project, for which the main construction contract was expected to be awarded by the end of 2002.

Plans are under way to drill new wells at three of the country's central gasfields, Barik, Saih Rawl and Saih Nihayda, in order to supply the amount of gas required by the Qalhat LNG plant and other planned developments, amid industry concern that existing supplies are insufficient for expected requirements. Agreements have also been signed with foreign companies for the private development of Omani gasfields, notably with Gulfstream Resources Canada in June 2000 in respect of the Hafar Block 30 concession, while joint Omani-Iranian development of the offshore Hengam/Bukha field in the Strait of Hormuz is envisaged under a 1997 agreement. Gulfstream Resources Canada declared a commercial gas discovery in 2001, while PDO announced major discoveries at Kauther in March 2001 and at Khazzan in May 2001. Revenues from gas are expected to increase rapidly now that the LNG project has become operational, and could eventually rival earnings from petroleum exports if new discoveries are made. Official projections, confirmed in October 2001, envisage cumulative new investment in the gas industry of $8,000m. by 2012, and an increase, to 15%, in the gas sector's contribution to GDP by 2020.

In 1993 the Governments of Oman and India signed a memorandum that envisaged the construction of a US $5,000m. submarine pipeline, to transport Omani natural gas to the subcontinent. The project, promoted by the state-owned Oman Oil Company (OOC), was to have been carried out in two stages involving the construction of two pipelines with a total capacity of 2,000 cu ft of gas per day and was to have been completed by 2001. In 1996, however, it was reported that the project would not proceed in the immediate future because of complex technical problems and concern that Oman would not have sufficient reserves to provide adequate supplies of gas, given its other commitments. The pipeline project was shelved in September 2002. Oman is one of the possible eventual destinations for gas from Qatar's North Field under the Dolphin project, which envisages that a pipeline to the United Arab Emirates (UAE) may be extended to Oman in about 2005 if there is sufficient demand. The Omani Government signed a memorandum of understanding with the Dolphin group in 1999, in acknowledgement that Qatari gas might be required in the longer term to meet Oman's needs.

Within Oman, engineering, procurement and construction contracts were awarded in May 2000 for two new gas pipeline projects, involving the construction of a 305-km line between Fahud and Sohar (awarded by India's Dodsal) and a 700-km line from Saih Nihayda to Salalah (awarded to an Italian-led consortium). Both due for completion by early 2003, the pipelines will transport gas to feed industries planned at Sohar (see Industry) and Salalah. The Oman Gas Company (OGC—80% government-owned and 20%-owned by the OOC), formed in March 1999, will oversee their construction, at an estimated cost of some US $570m. The addition of the new pipelines will more than double the total length of Oman's main gas transportation and transmission network (excluding the supply lines serving the LNG plant), which was estimated to be around 800 km in 2001.

INDUSTRY AND POWER

Before 1964 industry in Oman was confined to small traditional handicrafts, such as silversmithing, weaving and boat-building. The development of petroleum reserves generated activity in the construction sector, but it was not until the change of regime in 1970 that government investment in infrastructure projects and private spending on housing started a boom in construction. The 1981–85 Development Plan aimed to quadruple industrial output, giving the industrial sector an average growth rate of 36.2% per year over the Plan's term, and between 1982 and early 1984 more than 640 small and medium-sized enterprises went into operation. A large proportion of Oman's labour force in construction and industry was provided by immigrant workers from India and Pakistan.

The 1986–90 Development Plan aimed to diversify Oman's economic base as a provision against an eventual exhaustion of hydrocarbon reserves. In 1990 industry (including mining,

manufacturing, construction and power) provided 56.5% of Oman's GDP, although the proportion was reduced to 51.7% in the following year which was designated the 'Year of Industry'. In that year the Government allocated RO 24m. for industrial projects. These included a plant to manufacture 200m. glass bottles per year and another to produce 300,000 car batteries per year. The latter began production in 1992, which was also declared a 'Year of Industry' by the Sultan. In that year the Government adopted a 15-year industrial strategy, which included a liberalization of credit provision, regulations to simplify administrative procedures for business executives, and development of the infrastructure.

During 1980–94 industrial GDP increased by an annual average of 6.2%. Manufacturing industry grew by 11.6% in 1995 and 5.4% in 1996. The 1996–2000 Development Plan envisaged the expansion and diversification of Oman's industrial sector, in order to reduce the country's dependence on oil revenues, with Sohar and Sur becoming the country's principal industrial centres. Further development of the industrial sector was envisaged in the 2001–05 Development Plan, as the Government intends the sector's contribution to GDP to increase threefold, to 15%, by 2020.

Planned development projects in gas-intensive industries included a fertilizer plant, an aluminium smelter and a petrochemicals facility, although the progress of all three ventures was adversely affected by falling commodity prices, investor caution and complicated financing arrangements. In early 1997 Oman and India signed an agreement to construct a fertilizer plant at Sur, next to the Qalhat LNG complex (see Petroleum and Natural Gas, above). The plant, costing an estimated US $1,100m., is intended to produce ammonia and urea and have a capacity of 1.7m. metric tons per year. It is to be constructed and managed by the Oman-India Fertilizer Co (Omifco), in which the state-owned OOC has a 50% stake and Indian partners the other 50%. Gas feedstock for the plant is to be provided by PDO, and the Indian partners are to take most of the output. Difficulties arose in 1999 when the Indian authorities undertook a re-examination of the financial terms of the proposed venture, and one of the original Indian partners withdrew, blaming low fertilizer prices. However, in May 2000 the Indian Government approved new offtake proposals and in July 2002 financing arrangements were finalized with a view to enabling construction of the plant to start, with a scheduled completion date in 2005.

The $2,500m. aluminium smelter and the $900m. petrochemicals complex proposed in the 1996–2000 Development Plan were to be sited at Sohar, north-east of Muscat. The smelter was intended to have a capacity of 480,000 tons per year, and the petrochemicals plant was projected to produce 450,000 tons per year of ethylene and 450,000 tons per year of polyethylene. Both plants would use gas feedstock from fields in central Oman, supplied via pipeline. Despite ongoing negotiations, however, by mid-2002 financing arrangements for these projects remained unsettled, particularly in relation to the building of a gas separation plant required for the petrochemicals complex. The latter project also suffered a major set-back in October 1999 when BP Amoco of the United Kingdom withdrew from its intended 49% stake 'due to concerns over its competitive position'. A proposal put forward in 2000 to add a polypropylene unit to a planned oil refinery at Sohar (see Petroleum and Natural Gas, above) was widely regarded as a substitute for the stalled ethylene/polyethylene project.

Alongside the major industrial projects under development, the Government is encouraging small-scale industries to locate on specially-built industrial estates, hoping to attract advanced technology companies in particular. Government incentives to private industry include interest-free loans and exemption from customs duties on capital goods and raw material imports. The first such estate was established in 1985 at Rusayl, near Seeb International Airport, and by 1998 four others were in operation, at Raysut (near Salalah), Sohar, Nizwa and al-Buraimi.

In 2000 a private Omani company, Bahwan Trading, announced plans to build a fertilizer plant at Sohar with a capacity of 2,000 metric tons per day of ammonia and 3,500 tons per day of urea, using natural gas feedstock supplied via the pipeline to be built between Fahud and Sohar (see Petroleum and Natural Gas, above). By mid-2001 this project (to be managed by Sohar International Urea and Chemical Industries) was progressing towards the bidding stage. The projected start-up date for the plant was late 2005. Also announced in 2000 for projected start-up in 2005 was a planned 5,000 tons-per-day methanol plant at Sohar, likewise dependent on the supply of gas feedstock via the new pipeline. The project was initiated by an Omani private company, Omar Zawawi Establishment, in co-operation with the state-owned OOC and a German company, Ferrostaal, although in mid-2001 a formal joint-venture agreement had yet to be signed. (The function of the OOC is to invest in hydrocarbon-related joint ventures in Oman and abroad. It is funded out of a State General Reserve Fund set up by the Government in 1993 to receive the gross proceeds of 15,000 b/d of Oman's crude oil production. The assets of the Fund at end-2000 totalled $772m. The 2001 budget allocated RO 38m. of the Government's annual oil revenue to the Fund.)

Geological surveys have been undertaken to locate mineral deposits other than petroleum and natural gas. So far, sizeable reserves of copper and chromite (chromium ore) have been found. Chromite reserves, estimated at 2m. tons of medium-grade ore, exist on the coastal side of the Jebel Akhdar. The concession to develop the deposit is held by a Canadian-based company. The government-owned Oman Mining Co (OMC) began mining chromite in early 1984, and in 1986 about 5,000 metric tons were produced. In 1989 OMC was ordered to suspend the mining and export of chromite while a joint committee of the Ministries of Commerce and Industry and Petroleum and Minerals established priorities for the sector. In 1991 the new Oman Chromite Co, owned jointly by the Government (15%), private companies (45%) and public subscribers (40%), announced plans to exploit the country's chromite reserves at a rate of approximately 15,000 tons per year. By 1992 it was estimated that Oman had reserves of about 200m. tons of chromite ore at as many as 600 sites. OMC has exploited three copper mines, at Bayda, Avga and Lassail, near Sohar, north-west of Muscat, where drilling had indicated the presence of about 12m. tons of ore. In 1990 about 3,000 tons of copper ore per day was being handled from these pits. A complex for the smelting and refining of the copper ore, at Sohar, began operation in July 1983. The project cost more than US $200m., of which Saudi Arabia provided more than one-half. In 1994 bids were invited to expand the copper smelter at an estimated cost of RO 2m.–3.5m. The Yibal–Ghubra gas pipeline has been extended to the Sohar region to provide fuel, both for the smelter and for cement manufacturing. In May 2000 trials began of a 200,000-tons-per-year cement-bagging plant in Port Sultan Qaboos to be used exclusively by the Salalah-based Raysut Cement Co (which shares Omani cement production with the Oman Cement Co), amid signs of a recovery in demand for cement from less than 1.4m. tons in 1999. The value of mineral production increased by 38% during the fifth Development Plan, from RO 24.2m. in 1996 to RO 33.3m. in 2000.

The privatization of the OMC was expected to provide sufficient funds to expand the copper refinery at Sohar, increasing its capacity from 22,000–24,000 metric tons per year to 33,000 tons per year. Preliminary results from a joint study between OMC and Minproc Engineers (Australia) have indicated that the mining of copper at Hail as-Safil and Ar-Raki in Yanqul province would be economically viable, with total potential reserves of 15.25m. tons. The OMC developed a new gold mine at Yanqul in 1994, which was expected to produce 500 kg of gold annually. In July 1989 plans were announced for the construction of a plant to produce ferro-chrome near Sohar, on the Batinah coast, to begin after 1991. In August 1990, a French geological company won a RO 98,800 contract to explore for lead and zinc in the Saih Hatat and Jebel Akhdar regions. In 1991 the UN Development Programme agreed to co-operate with the Ministry of Petroleum and Minerals in a study of Oman's coal resources. The study, the cost of which was estimated at US $1m., was to examine the possibility of using coal at al-Kamil, near Sur, to generate electricity. Coal deposits exceeding 122m. tons have been discovered in the province of Bani Bu Ali, south of Sur. Estimated recoverable reserves at the two coalfields in Wadi Muswa and Wadi Fisaw are sufficient to meet the power generation needs of the Sharqiya region for the next 35–40 years. Other heavy industrial projects under consideration include plans for a hydrochloric acid plant, a silicon plant

(using locally mined quartz), a salt production plant and a new sugar refinery. In February 2000 the Oman Chloride Co opened a $26m. plant at Sohar with an annual capacity of 10m. gallons of hydrochloric acid and 4m. gallons of caustic soda.

The economic and industrial changes that have taken place in the country since 1970 have led to a need for major increases in power and water supply. Total electricity generating capacity in Oman rose from 479 MW in 1981 to 1,794 MW in 1999, when a total of 31 power plants (including many small-scale plants) were in operation. Major power stations included those at Ghubrah (dating from 1976) and Rusayl (dating from 1984), which had been expanded to capacities of 539 MW and 500 MW respectively. By 2000 nearly 90% of Oman's populated areas were connected to mains electricity supplies, and plans were progressing to complete a national grid. Muscat's Manah generating plant (dating from 1996 and expanded in 2000 to 270 MW capacity) was the Gulf region's first independent power project (IPP). Financed entirely by private capital on 'build, own, operate, transfer' terms, it is run by the United Power Company under a 20-year agreement with the Oman Government. In 2000 Oman's installed generating capacity was slightly in excess of 2,000 MW, while peak demand was slightly below 2,000 MW. With demand for electricity growing at an annual rate of 5%, projects were in place in 2001 to increase capacity to around 3,000 MW within five years. Under 'fast-track' IPP contracts awarded in 2000, the planned 285-MW al-Kamil power plant at Sharqiya Sands was scheduled to be operational by mid-2002, while a 427-MW power station (with 91,200 cu m per day of desalination capacity) was scheduled for completion at Barqa in 2003. Both projects had initial 100% foreign ownership (agreed in order to accelerate their implementation), but this was to be reduced to 65% within four years through share offerings on the Muscat Securities Market. In March 2001 a third 'fast-track' contract was concluded when Dhofar Power Company (whose 81% foreign ownership was subject to reduction to 65% in due course) won a 20-year concession to implement an integrated power project, entailing the construction and operation of a 200-MW gas-fired power station at Salalah and the acquisition of existing transmission and distribution infrastructure in the area (which the concession-holder undertook to expand to keep pace with the growth of local demand). The target date for completion of the Salalah plant was 2003.

Re-drafted legislation was expected to be introduced before the end of 2002 to pave the way for privatization of state-owned power facilities outside the Dhofar area. The Government's draft proposals called for Ministry of Electricity and Water assets and functions to be divided between a number of separate companies responsible for power generation, transmission and distribution, some of which would be opened up to 65% private ownership (although the ministry would retain ownership of smaller facilities serving rural areas). A state-owned power and water procurement company would be responsible for planning new capacity and awarding contracts, while a state-owned holding company would oversee the whole sector.

In 2000 Oman had over 20 desalination plants, whose combined capacity totalled 377,880 cu m per day. The Ghubrah power station accounted for 159,110 cu m per day of this capacity (and was scheduled to increase its output to 191,000 cu m per day in 2001).

Plans to build a wastewater system to serve Muscat, which were first proposed in 1995, made some progress in 1999, as a consortium led by the local Galfar Engineering & Contracting entered into negotiations to undertake the project on a build-own-operate-transfer basis. However, the project was being re-evaluated by the Government in mid-2001 after a change in the composition of the consortium, prompted by the withdrawal of a foreign participant. In April 1999 a consortium led by Oman Engineering Consultancy and including French and Egyptian companies was awarded an engineering design and construction supervision contract on a water-supply scheme at Sharqiya Sands, the main contract for which was awarded in June 2001 to Galfar Engineering & Contracting, in partnership with a French company. Speedier progress was made on a US $69m. water-supply scheme at al-Masarat, the main contract for which was awarded to an Egyptian company in July 2000. Construction work was scheduled to start in September, as part of a two-phase scheme to bring drinking water to towns and villages to the south of Muscat. In mid-2001 the Government commissioned a study of the possible options for commercial operation of the al-Masarat and Sharqiya Sands water supply systems on their completion. Oman's renewable water resources per caput fell from 4,000 cu m per year in 1960 to 1,133 cu m per year in 1990, and were projected to decline to 421 cu m per year by 2025. In 1999 agriculture accounted for 94% of water withdrawals, domestic consumption 3% and industry 3%.

TRANSPORT, COMMUNICATIONS AND TOURISM

Road and other communications projects have been prioritized in successive Development Plans, many having been successfully completed. Port facilities were improved by the expansion of Mina Raysut at Salalah (now known as Salalah port), and 12 new berths have been completed at Port Sultan Qaboos. In June 1990 a contract was awarded for work on the third phase of a scheme to improve facilities at Nizwa. The project involved the construction of a 140-m bridge and a 900-m bypass. In April 1992 an RO 11.7m. contract for further development of Port Sultan Qaboos was awarded to a British company, Wimpey Alawi. A new container terminal at Salalah port, a key element in the development of southern Oman, was officially opened in December 1998, and by April 1999 the port had four berths with a total handling capacity of 2m. 20-ft equivalent units (TEU). Salalah Port Services (SPS) was formed by the Omani Government, Sea-Land of the USA and Maersk of Denmark to carry out the development and holds a 30-year concession to operate, manage and procure equipment for the container port. In May 2000 SPS effectively became the port authority for Salalah, which had quickly established a major role, partly at the expense of Port Sultan Qaboos, where cargo handled fell by 10% in 1999. SPS also formed a new company to manage a free-trade zone at Salalah, extending 2 km beyond the existing port boundaries, and funded mainly by the private sector. Container traffic through Salalah in 2000 was 1,033,000 TEUs, compared with 639,003 TEUs in 1999. Handling capacity in 2001 was 2.2m. TEUs. In July 2001 the Government approved a final business plan for the Salalah free zone, drawn up by SPS and the US company Hillwood. Implementation of the first phase of the free-zone development was expected to begin before the end of 2001.

Work was under way in 2000 on the first phase of a major expansion of port facilities at Sohar, which was designated in government development plans as a future centre of hydrocarbon-based industrialization. Consultants were appointed in March 2001 to draw up a feasibility study for the operation and maintenance of the expanded port, while in May 2002 bids were invited for the second phase of the expansion. Plans to expand the port of Khasab (situated on the Strait of Hormuz) were drawn up in 2001 after it had become clear that the existing capacity was insufficient to handle the growth of trade between Oman and Iran.

Between 1970 and 1985 an estimated 6,000 km of asphalt roads and 18,500 km of dirt roads were built in Oman. In 1990 the Ministry of Communications announced proposals to build 140 km of roads and to upgrade a further 158 km, in addition to constructing 58 km of roads in al-Qabil, Ibra and Briddayah. The Dhofar Transport Co was awarded a contract in May 1990 to build a 13-km link road connecting al-Ayjah and Sur, at a cost of RO 2.5m. Another project under consideration in 1990 was the construction of a 16-km road linking the Thumrait air force base to the main Salalah—Thumrait highway, at a cost of RO 400,000. By 1994 a road linking Salalah with Sarfait, near the border with Yemen, had been completed. In May 1999 contracts were awarded for the construction of a 58-km road in Dima and at-Tayeen and the Birkat al-Manz to Sayq road. Improvement of the road network in 2000 included the award of contracts for some 700 km of new roads in the central region.

Air services to rural and outlying areas have been increased: by the end of 1984 there were rural air services to Khassab, Bayah, Buraimi, Sur and Masirah island. A major expansion programme at Seeb International Airport was completed in 1985, and in the following year more than 1.4m. passengers passed through the airport. In 1993 five international airlines began operating regular flights to Oman. In 1998 the Government appointed a financial consultant to oversee the privatization of the operation and management of Seeb International

Airport. A two-stage expansion plan for the airport envisages an increase in capacity from the current 2.8m. passengers per year to 6m. by 2004 and to 10m. by 2010, at an estimated cost of US $500m. Oman's second largest airport, at Salalah, which has been upgraded to receive cargo and passenger aircraft of all sizes, handled 180,000 passengers in 1999. In October 2001 the two airports were effectively privatized when a consortium led by BAA of the United Kingdom, and including an Omani company—the Suhail Bahwan Group, signed a 25-year agreement to manage and develop them, with the consortium taking a 75% shareholding in the privatized company.

Oman Aviation Services Company (OAS, whose activities include the provision of contract air services to Petroleum Development Oman (PDO) and the operation of a national carrier, Oman Air) made a net loss of RO 2.55m. in 2000, compared with net profits of RO 1.7m. in 1999, RO 1.8m. in 1998 and RO 3.29m. in 1997. Oman Air (established in 1993) increased its passenger numbers by about 16% to 300,000 in 2000. OAS said that its poor 2000 financial results were largely attributable to the composition of its current aircraft fleet, comprising three Fokker F27s (used for the PDO contract), two Airbus A310s, one Boeing 737-400 and two ATR-42s. In 2001 it announced plans to change its fleet over a period of three years to comprise five ATR-42s (three of them for the PDO contract), four Boeing 737-700s and one Boeing 737-800.

In 1999–2000 the expansion of the telecommunications network continued, with contracts being awarded for the expansion of the mobile telephone network in Dhofar, Muscat and al-Batinah. In July 1999 the Government announced the establishment of the Oman Telecommunications Co (Omantel), which replaced the General Telecommunications Organization, in a first step towards eventual privatization. However, a sharp downturn in the global telecommunications industry in 2001–02 forced the Government, in May 2002, to announce that the sale of a strategic stake in Omantel had been postponed owing to lack of interest from international operators. Oman has lagged behind the other Gulf states in telecommunications development, having in 1999 only 9.2 fixed telephone lines per 100 inhabitants (and a total of 220,000 in use) and only 1.6 public telephones per 1,000 inhabitants. About one-quarter of the population live in areas not linked to the fixed-line network. The number of fixed lines in use had risen to 235,300 by the end of 2001, when mobile telephone subscribers totalled 324,500 (compared with 124,000 in 1999). Work began in 2001 to install a new 7,000-line payphone system. Oman had some 120,000 internet users in 2000.

Tourism is in the early stages of development in Oman following the issue of the first tourist visas in 1990, and private-sector initiatives are being encouraged as part of the Government's strategy to turn tourism into a major revenue generator. In 1999 the number of hotels, motels and resthouses totalled 102 (compared with 32 in 1991) and the total number of beds was 7,573, the target being to have more than 10,000 rooms by 2005. Tourist arrivals rose from 279,000 in 1995 to 571,110 in 2000. Revenue from tourism in 2000 totalled RO 45.7m. Oman's 2001–05 Development Plan considered privately-developed tourism to be an important potential source of new employment opportunities, and aimed to increase the sector's share of GDP from 1% to 3% during the plan period.

In February 2002 an Omani company, Zubair Enterprises, announced plans for a US $200m. resort complex to be located at Barr al-Jissah on the Gulf of Oman, some 12 km south of Muscat. The project was scheduled for completion by mid-2005. The 500,000 sq m-development would be arranged around a group of luxury hotels with spa facilities, private apartments and cultural center, and would be entirely self-sufficient with its own power sub-station, desalination plant and fuel and water storage units. A key component of the project was the proposed construction of a road link between Barr al-Jissah and Muscat. Another major project under consideration in mid-2002 was a $800m. tourist resort to be built on the Gulf of Oman by the as-Sawadi Development Co, the first phase of which would include the construction of four hotels, two golf courses and 150 holiday villas.

BUDGET, INVESTMENT AND FINANCE

Expenditure on defence and national security in Oman has increased rapidly, with the total doubling between 1979 and 1984 and rising to 20.8% of GDP in 1985. By 1997 defence spending as a proportion of GDP had fallen to 12.2%, although the ratio rose to 13.6% in 1998. The 1996–2000 Development Plan allocated a total of RO 3,300m. for defence expenditure over the five-year period. In view of Oman's strategic importance within the GCC, defence expenditure is supported by other Council countries. The total allocation for defence in the 2001–05 Development Plan was RO 4,212m.

The targets of the 1976–80 Development Plan were relatively modest, concentrating on establishing a workable basis for light industry and agriculture. The Omani Development Bank was established in December 1977 to encourage private sector investment. The general aim of the 1981–85 Development Plan was to reduce economic dependence on petroleum, in favour of private-sector industry. The Plan included development of tourism, education, health, welfare, housing and roads. In 1984 it was announced that total spending on projects undertaken during the 1981–85 Development Plan would total RO 1,800m., 28% more than was originally envisaged.

At the end of 1985 the 1986–90 Development Plan was approved, with proposed expenditure totalling RO 9,250m. (US $26,780m.). Early in 1986, however, proposed spending was reduced to RO 8,830m. as a result of falling oil prices. The revised total was based on an estimated average petroleum price of $20 per barrel. The subsequent decline in oil prices, to less than $10 per barrel in July, necessitated further revision of proposed expenditure. Although oil prices rose above $17 per barrel by the end of 1986, the Plan was postponed for re-evaluation. In January 1991 the Government announced a fourth Development Plan, covering the period 1991–95. The plan envisaged total expenditure of RO 9,450m. The projected rate of annual GDP growth in the five years was about 6.3%. In April 1991 total development spending for the Plan period was reportedly budgeted at RO 2,107m. Of this, some RO 319m. was to be allocated to construction projects, including a hospital, housing and schools; to a $78m. extension of the airport at Seeb; to the $65m. development of Port Sultan Qaboos, gasfields and fishing ports; and to the upgrading of the Rusayl–Nizwa highway and the renovation of the Muscat water networks.

Despite the world oil surplus in the early 1980s, Oman raised its petroleum output during the 1981–85 Plan period, maintaining adequate revenues, but at a lower level than originally expected. From 1982, falling oil prices led to deficits in the annual budget. In January 1986 the rial was devalued by 10.2%, to compensate for the reduction in petroleum revenues. By 1987 the effect of the decline in oil prices was evident as expenditure decreased from RO 1,587.2m. in 1986 to RO 1,330.1m. Revenue from the petroleum sector increased from RO 521.2m. in 1986 to RO 998.0m. in 1990 (an increase of 45% over the previous year). This resulted in a reduction in the budget deficit to RO 32.8m., compared with a deficit of RO 289.5m. in 1989. In 1991 oil revenue declined to RO 777.0m., and total revenue to RO 1,261.4m. Total expenditure was RO 1,575.1m. The budget for 1995 anticipated an increase in total revenue to RO 1,847.0m., of which RO 1,352.4m. was oil revenue, and an increase in total expenditure to RO 2,159.0m., resulting in a deficit of RO 312.0m. The budget for 1996 envisaged total revenue of RO 1,934m. and expenditure of RO 2,152m., with a budget deficit forecast of RO 218m. Actual revenue and expenditure figures for the year were, however, estimated at RO 1,990.2m. and RO 2,253.7m. respectively, resulting in a deficit of RO 263.5m. The 1997 budget anticipated increases in revenue to RO 2,003m. (including RO 1,502m. from petroleum) and in expenditure to RO 2,266m., leaving a deficit of RO 263m. However, according to final figures published by the Central Bank, actual revenue for 1997, at RO 2,267.2m., was about 13% higher than the budgeted figure (largely attributable to increased earnings from petroleum). Although actual expenditure was also more than forecast (RO 2,307.3m.), the budget deficit of RO 40.1m. was equivalent to only 0.7% of GDP. The Government maintained a policy of putting any extra petroleum revenue derived from a price over US $15 a barrel, and up to $17, into the State General Reserve Fund (SGRF).

The 1996–2000 Development Plan envisaged the elimination of the budget deficit by 2000. However, after the 1998 budget had predicted a deficit of RO 295m. (based on proposed revenue of RO 2,012m. and expenditure of RO 2,307m.), declining international petroleum prices resulted in an actual budget deficit in 1998 of 375.3m., equivalent to 6.9% of GDP. Actual revenue in 1998 was RO 1,846.3m., compared with actual expenditure of RO 2,221.6m. The 1999 budget, announced by the Government in January and based on an average oil price of only US $9 per barrel, forecast a deficit of RO 631m. from revenue of RO 1,525m. ($3,961m.) and expenditure, reduced by 7%, of RO 2,156m. Non-oil income was forecast at RO 550m., the calculations including a range of new revenue-raising measures, in particular an increase in corporate taxes and taxes on luxury goods, and the introduction of higher customs duties. Increased oil revenues produced an effective fiscal surplus in 1999 equivalent to 1.8% of GDP, although the transfer of above-forecast oil revenues to the SGRF resulted in a nominal budget deficit of RO 472.9m. (equivalent to 7.8% of GDP), based on actual revenue of RO 1,796.1m. and actual expenditure of RO 2,269.0m. The 2000 budget provided for total revenue of RO 2,091m. and total expenditure of RO 2,440m., 7.7% higher than actual spending in 1999. The Government planned to issue RO 75m. of development bonds in 2000, having issued a total of RO 893m. in such bonds since 1991. Out-turn figures for 2000 showed actual revenue of RO 2,289.9m. and actual expenditure of RO 2,656.2m., leaving a nominal budget deficit of RO 366.3m. Overall, there was an effective fiscal surplus equivalent to 9.8% of GDP in 2000. An average $12 excess of the actual oil export price over the budgeted price was large enough to prompt the Government to draw down some revenues from the SGRF to finance increased capital spending in the last quarter of 2000. The estimated balance in the SGRF at the end of 2000 was equivalent to about 20% of Oman's GDP.

Oman's 2001 budget provided for revenue of RO 2,495m. (including net oil revenue of RO 1,875m.) and expenditure of RO 2,812m., leaving a nominal budget deficit of RO 317m. The assumed oil export price in this budget was $18 per barrel (compared with a 'floor' price of $22 per barrel currently used as a reference point by OPEC members). In the event, the oil export price remained about the budgeted level in 2001, with the result that the actual budget deficit was expected to be some RO 327.9m.(about 4.3% of GDP). The Government's budget for 2002 was similar to the original 2001 projections, being again based on an assumed oil export price of $18 per barrel, and providing for total revenue of RO 2,490m. and expenditure of RO 2,870m., leaving a nominal budget deficit of RO 380m. Projected expenditure in 2002 included a 12% increase in capital investment, to RO 589m., most of it earmarked for civil projects (RO 280m.) and for works to enhance the sustainability of Oman's hydrocarbons production (RO 218m.).

The 2001–05 Development Plan envisaged a fall in the nominal budget deficit to OR 138m. in 2005, when annual revenue was expected to be 5.1% higher, and expenditure 1.8% lower, than in 2001. The Plan set an overall target for economic growth of 3.5% per year, to be achieved primarily through average growth of 5.2% per year in non-oil activities (including new industries based on natural gas, whose development would require RO 1,807m. of private investment). Of the Plan's overall investment target of RO 8,118m., some RO 3,746m. represented public-sector investment (an increase of 20% compared with the corresponding target in the 1996–2000 Plan), leaving a total of RO 4,372m. to be invested by the private sector (an increase of 132% over the 1996–2000 target). The Plan envisaged stable export receipts over the period 2001–05, on the assumption that a decline in earnings from crude oil would be offset by growth in exports of LNG and other non-oil items. The target for labour market expansion in the 2001–05 plan period was 110,000 new employment opportunities for Omani nationals (compared with the previous Plan's target of 78,000 jobs), over 90% of them in the private sector. New jobs were to be created mainly through projected growth in tourism, manufacturing and construction activities. The public sector was to invest RO 35m. per year in 2001–05 in a human resources development programme, with the improvement and expansion of basic educational facilities receiving high priority.

In comparison with some other countries in the region, Oman has a small banking sector. In 2000 there were 19 banks (six national institutions, nine foreign banks and four specialized banks) operating in the Sultanate. The largest bank is the National Bank of Oman, which reportedly has 30% of the market in retail and corporate banking, and which recorded profits of RO 8.3m. in 2000. Other large institutions are Bank Muscat and Oman International Bank. Mergers have been officially encouraged to strengthen the banking sector. In April 1997, mergers were approved between the Oman Development Bank and the Oman Bank for Agriculture and Fisheries, and the Commercial Bank of Oman and the Oman Savings and Finance Bank (the latter being finalized the following August). A new bank, the Oman Alliance Bank, was launched in May 1997, while the Industrial Bank of Oman (IBO) came into being in October. It was announced in June 1998 that the Commercial Bank of Oman (Combank) had undertaken a further merger with the Bank of Oman, Bahrain and Kuwait (BOBK). A merger between Bank Muscat and the Commercial Bank of Oman at the end of 2000 left the merged entity (named BankMuscat) with the country's largest branch network (comprising 95 branches) after the sale of 16 former Commercial Bank of Oman branches to Bank Dhofar al-Omani al-Fransi. In a further consolidation at the end of 2001, BankMuscat absorbed the IBO, the new entity being formally instituted on 1 January 2002.

Between 1973 and 1986 the rial Omani was linked to the US dollar at a rate of $1 = RO 0.3454, but in January 1986 the rial was devalued by 10.2%, with the exchange rate adjusted to $1 = RO 0.3845, which has remained the official rate ever since. The Central Bank raised interest rates in April 1989, with the annual rate payable on non-government deposits increased by 1%, to 9.5%, and that on rial loans raised by 0.75%, to 11.25%. Government efforts to reduce the number of foreign staff in the banking sector succeeded in reducing their number from 60% of bank staff in 1983 to 19.4% by mid-1994. By the end of 1995 banks had to reduce their foreign staff to 10% of their workforce or face heavy penalties. The Iraqi invasion of Kuwait in August 1990 prompted panic withdrawals of deposits and increased demand for foreign currency during a 10-day period following the invasion. By late August 1990, however, the local banking system had stabilized, and by April 1991, encouraged by uncompromising government action and by encouraging reports of economic growth, deposits at local commercial banks had fully recovered from the impact of the Gulf crisis. Following the collapse of the Bank of Credit and Commerce International (BCCI) in July 1991, substantial support from the Omani Government enabled depositors and creditors in the country to be paid in full. In February 1992 the Bank Dhofar al-Omani al-Fransi acquired the 12 BCCI branches in the Sultanate.

In May 1992 the Government introduced a new law increasing the minimum requirement for a bank's paid-up capital to RO 10m., in order to encourage smaller banks to merge and thereby rationalize the banking system. Measures introduced to strengthen the banking sector included the creation of a fund in March 1995 to guarantee bank deposits. In an effort to broaden the base of local financial institutions, the Central Bank in early 1997 announced the imposition of limits on the voting shares that any individual or company can hold in a local bank. Having deregulated interest rates in 1998, the Central Bank in October 1999 reinstated a 13% ceiling on interest rates on personal loans, which had risen as high as 18% for small borrowers. The move resulted in reduced profitability for Omani commercial banks, since personal loans accounted for about 40% of total bank lending. In January 2001 legislation was introduced to raise the minimum capital requirement for Omani commercial banks from RO 10m. to RO 20m., and to set a minimum capital requirement of RO 3m. for foreign banks established in Oman. The new law also imposed ceilings on the amounts that banks were permitted to lend to their own shareholders. It made the securities trading of commercial banks subject to regulation by the Central Bank of Oman.

In 1989 Oman's first stock exchange—the Muscat Securities Market (MSM)—was opened, trading in shares in local companies with a potential total value of RO 250m. Oman's first investment fund open to non-GCC nationals was listed on the London and Muscat stock exchanges in March 1994. Subscriptions for the Oryx fund, launched to raise US $52m., closed in June. A second investment fund set up in 1994 was the UAE-Omani Joint Holding Co, with a capital of $78m. Both funds were fully subscribed. In March 1995 the stock exchanges of Muscat and Bahrain were formally linked. In November 1998 a new National Investment Fund (NIF) was established by royal decree to support the MSM by channelling RO 100m. ($260m.) from pension funds into the bourse. A new regulatory body, the Capital Market Authority (CMA), formally separated from the MSM in January 1999, in accordance with the capital market law promulgated in November 1998. The new authority was to supervise the MSM and guarantee investors' rights. After a major slump in 1998, the MSM recovered partially in 1999, boosted by the recovery in world oil prices and the entry into the market of the NIF. Further positive developments were the launch by the World Bank's International Finance Corporation (IFC) in September 1999 of a stand-alone index for the MSM and the inclusion of Oman in the IFC's composite regional indices in November. In April 2000 the CMA introduced new MSM regulations aimed at protecting shareholders by requiring quoted companies to make quarterly disclosure of financial and other information relevant to their performance. In September 2001, moreover, the CMA introduced new company listing requirements intended to promote MSM transparency.

In November 2000 the Government introduced a package of measures designed to stimulate the MSM, which had experienced a 31% decline in trading in the course of the year. In addition to offering incentives to encourage mergers between brokerage firms, the Government undertook to settle up to RO 14m. of negative equity in share trust accounts held by brokers on behalf of small investors, and to invest RO 50m. of public funds in shares traded on the MSM. In 2001 the CMA announced further regulatory initiatives intended to improve the operation of the MSM. The MSM index nevertheless remained severely depressed, falling, in mid-2001, to its lowest level since mid-1996. The index then showed a recovery, reaching a 15-month high in June 2002; but traded volumes remained low amid continuing investor doubts about the underlying financial strength of listed companies.

Oman has a free national health service, and in 1999 there were 54 hospitals and 116 health centres; more than 5,075 beds were available in 1998. There were also 96 preventive health centres, five mobile rural health centres and three maternity centres in 1990. In 1998 there were 3,061 physicians working in Oman.

FOREIGN TRADE AND BALANCE OF PAYMENTS

Oman's trade pattern continues to reflect the dominance of petroleum in the economy. In 1987 the value of non-oil exports and re-exports was RO 123.9m., equivalent to 8.3% of the value of total exports. Although by 1990, their value had risen to RO 176.2m., this still represented just 8.3% of total exports. In 1991, however, the Government's efforts at diversifying the economy began to demonstrate a degree of success, and non-oil exports and re-exports were valued at RO 244.2m., accounting for 13.0% of the total exports of RO 1,873.9m. Their value continued to increase and in 1994, they accounted for RO 503.9m. (23.6% of total exports of RO 2,132.0m.) The value of recorded imports in 1987 (when unrecorded imports were estimated at RO 55m.) was RO 700.7m. By 1990 this had risen to RO 1,030.9m. Their value continued to rise until 1994, when a 4.8% decrease (to RO 1,505.3m.) was recorded. In 1990 Oman's balance of trade showed an improvement of 56.1% compared with 1989, with recorded imports totalling RO 1,030.9m., compared with exports of RO 2,116.4m. A trade surplus was recorded each year between 1991 and 1993, and in 1994 a 29.7% increase in the trade surplus was recorded with an increase in exports, to RO 2,132.0m., and a decrease in imports, to RO 1,505.3m. The value of exports rose to RO 2,820.0m. in 1996, due to an increased volume of oil exported, as well as higher prices. Imports rose more slowly, to RO 1,760.0m., in that year, resulting in an increase in the trade surplus to RO 1,060.0m. In 1997 there was a trade surplus of RO 938.3m., from imports of RO 1,995.8m. and exports of RO 2,934.1m. In 1998, however, a trade deficit was recorded, of RO 122.5m., from imports of RO 2,117.5m. and exports of RO 2,240.0m.

Mainly as a result of a significant increase in revenue from oil and gas exports, Oman achieved a trade surplus of $2,939m.

in 1999, from exports of $7,239m. (including $5,500m. from oil) and imports of $4,300m. A further surge in the value of exports in 2000, to $11,319m. (including $9,200m. from oil), and relatively flat imports of $4,593m. more than doubled the trade surplus, to $6,726m. Provisional figures for 2001 showed a slight decline in the value of exports, to $10,918m., and a rise in imports to $5,716m., yielding a trade surplus of $5,202m. In 1999 Japan was the leading destination for Omani exports by value, taking 23%, followed by Thailand (16%), the Republic of Korea (14%), the United Arab Emirates (10%) and the People's Republic of China (9.5%), while the UAE supplied 29% of Oman's imports, ahead of Japan 18%, the UK 6% and the USA (5%) in 2000.

The principal variable factors affecting Oman's balance-of-payments performance are petroleum revenues and the level of remittances being transferred abroad by foreigners working in Oman. Statistics published by the IMF showed that the current-account deficit fell from US $2,993m. in 1998 to $369m. in 1999, and then went into a substantial surplus of $3,347m. in 2000. Remittances abroad remained almost constant, at $1,467m. in 1998, $1,438m. in 1999 and $1,456m. in 2000. Provisional figures for 2001 showed a reduced current-account surplus of $1,040m., while the forecast for 2002 was of a return to deficit, amounting to some $1,300m. Oman's foreign reserves (excluding gold) stood at $2,310m. at the end of 2000, falling to $2,277m. at the end of 2001.

In mid-June 1996 the World Trade Organization (WTO) agreed to establish a working party to negotiate terms of entry for Oman. The decision followed a commitment made by the Omani Undersecretary for Commerce and Industry to co-operate with other GCC countries in the promotion of liberal trade. In November 1999 Oman was a signatory of a GCC agreement to create a customs union in 2005, with common tariffs of 5.5% on basic goods and 7.5% on luxury items. Oman became the 139th member of the WTO in November 2000, having paved the way for its accession by introducing various measures, including bilateral trade agreements with key WTO members; new laws to protect intellectual property rights; new regulations on customs valuations and import fees; a lower maximum tax rate for branches of foreign companies (30% from 2001, compared with 50% previously); a higher ceiling for foreign participation in Omani businesses (70% from 2001, compared with 49% previously); and the authorization, from 2003, of 100% foreign ownership of companies providing specified financial services (including banking, insurance and brokerage).

In March 1997 Oman became one of the founder members of the Indian Ocean Rim Association for Regional Co-operation (IOR—ARC), which seeks to promote co-operation in trade, investment and economic development between the countries of the region. During a state visit to India in April, Sultan Qaboos signed a number of co-operation agreements to promote trade between India and Oman. India is an important source of imports to Oman, but Oman is keen to increase its small volume of exports to India.

In June 1990 the Government pledged that foreign workers would retain their tax-free status. The announcement was made after the Government had expressed its intention to impose a levy on foreign remittances, in an attempt to increase revenues. In October 1993 it was announced that income tax would be collected from all companies, whether Omani or foreign, from 1 January 1994 in order to increase government revenue. Despite its balance-of-payments surpluses, Oman has also received a substantial amount of foreign aid and loans, mainly in order to finance development projects. Oman's foreign debt declined from US $1,931m. (with a debt-service ratio of 4.6%) in 1984 to $1,875m. at the end of 1985. Until 1986, Oman enjoyed an excellent credit rating, although the sharp fall in petroleum prices altered this position, and an application for a Euroloan of $500m. in 1986 encountered difficulty in attracting a sufficient number of subscribers. At the end of 1995 Oman's total external debt was $3,107m., of which $2,563m. was long-term public debt. In that year the cost of servicing the external debt was equivalent to 7.5% of the total value of exports of goods and services. In January 1994 four international banks were awarded a mandate to raise a $300m. five-year syndicated sovereign loan to finance the fiscal deficit. In March 1997 Oman became the first GCC state to venture into the Eurobond market, with an issue that was heavily oversubscribed. In February 1999 the Government secured a $350m. five-year syndicated loan from a consortium of local and international banks, but plans for a further Eurobond issue were shelved in September in the light of the improvement in oil revenue receipts. Oman's total external debt was recorded by the IMF at $6,771m. at the end of 1999 and was estimated to have risen to $6,962m. by the end of 2000.

ECONOMIC PROSPECTS

Although not immune from the global economic downturn in the wake of the September 2001 suicide attacks on the USA, Oman is well-placed to continue its prudent deployment of relatively limited oil and gas resources to bring about economic diversification, albeit at a slower pace than previously envisaged. The Government's main short-term challenges are to bring the substantial number of development and diversification projects pending to the active stage and to implement long-discussed privatization plans, particularly with a view to creating new employment opportunities for a rapidly growing workforce. Also critical in the medium term will be the success or otherwise of the PDO programme to increase the oil recovery rate from Oman's mature oilfields to 50%.

Statistical Survey

Sources (unless otherwise stated): Ministry of National Economy, Information and Publication Centre, POB 881, Muscat 113; tel. 698900; fax 698467; e-mail mone@omantel.net.om; internet www.moneoman.gov.om; Central Bank of Oman, POB 1161, Ruwi 112; tel. 702222; fax 702253; e-mail cboresb@omantel.net.om; internet www.cbo-oman.org.

Area and Population

AREA, POPULATION AND DENSITY

Area (sq km)	309,500*
Population (census results)	
1 December 1993	
Males	1,178,005
Females	840,069
Total	2,018,074†
Population (official estimates at mid-year)	
1999	2,325,438
2000	2,401,256
2001	2,478,000‡
Density (per sq km) at mid-2001.	8.0

* 119,500 sq miles.

† Comprising 1,483,226 Omani nationals and 534,848 non-Omanis.

‡ Preliminary figure, comprising 1,826,000 Omani nationals and 652,000 non-Omanis.

GOVERNORATES (mid-2000)

	Area (sq km)	Population	Density (per sq km)
Muscat	3,900	661,145	169.5
Al-Batinah.	12,500	667,053	53.4
Musandam	1,800	34,007	18.9
Adh-Dhahira	44,000	214,997	4.9
Ad-Dakhliya	31,900	272,141	8.5
Ash-Sharqiya	36,400	306,575	8.4
Al-Wosta	79,700	20,345	0.3
Dhofar	99,300	224,993	2.3
Total	309,500	2,401,256	7.8

BIRTHS AND DEATHS (official estimates, Omani nationals only)

	1999	2000	2001
Birth rate (per 1,000). . .	30.0	32.6	28.4*
Death rate (per 1,000) . .	3.6	3.7	n.a.

* Preliminary figure.

Expectation of life (WHO estimates, years at birth, 2000): Males 69.5; Females 73.5 (Source: WHO, *World Health Report*).

ECONOMICALLY ACTIVE POPULATION
(persons aged 15 years and over, 1993 census)

	Omanis	Non-Omanis	Total
Agriculture and fishing . . .	21,993	40,789	62,782
Mining and quarrying . . .	8,076	5,991	14,067
Manufacturing	4,212	55,825	60,037
Electricity, gas and water. . .	942	3,481	4,423
Construction.	4,412	103,291	107,703
Trade, hotels and restaurants. .	12,201	91,041	103,242
Transport, storage and communications . .	11,339	12,989	24,328
Finance, insurance and real estate	5,857	11,287	17,144
Public administration and defence	134,714	25,610	160,324
Other community, social and personal services . .	34,178	76,205	110,383
Activities not adequately defined	2,056	3,786	5,842
Total employed . . .	239,980	430,295	670,275
Unemployed	32,417	2,106	34,523
Total labour force . . .	272,397	432,401	704,798
Males	248,917	387,473	636,390
Females.	23,480	44,928	68,408

Health and Welfare

KEY INDICATORS

Fertility (births per woman, 2000).	5.7
Under-5 mortality rate (per 1,000 live births, 2000). .	16
HIV/AIDS (% of persons aged 15–49, 2001). . . .	0.11
Physicians (per 1,000 head, 1998)	1.33
Hospital beds (per 1,000 head, 1990)	2.2
Health expenditure (1998): US $ per head (PPP) . .	353
% of GDP	3.6
public (% of total) . . .	81.6
Access to water (% of persons, 1999)	39
Access to sanitation (% of persons, 1999) . . .	92
Human Development Index (2000): ranking . . .	78
value	0.751

For sources and definitions, see explanatory note on p. vi.

Agriculture

PRINCIPAL CROPS ('000 metric tons)

	1998	1999	2000*
Sorghum*	2.9	2.9	3.0
Potatoes.	12.5	15.6	16.0
Tomatoes	38	42	43
Dry onions	16.0	25.0	25.5
Other vegetables*	98	98	98
Bananas	25.0*	30.1	30.5
Lemons and limes . . .	12.5	12.1	12.4
Watermelons	30.0	22.6	26.5
Mangoes	5.6	11.0	12.0
Dates	236	282	260
Papayas.	1.9	2.0	2.0

* FAO estimate(s).

Source: FAO.

LIVESTOCK ('000 head, year ending September)

	1998	1999	2000*
Asses*	28	28	29
Cattle	271	285	290
Camels*.	96	97	98
Sheep	312	327	330
Goats	940	959	980
Poultry*.	3,100	3,200	3,400

* FAO estimates.

Source: FAO.

LIVESTOCK PRODUCTS ('000 metric tons)

	1998	1999	2000
Beef and veal . . .	4.4	4.7	4.8
Camel meat	4.9	5.0	5.1
Mutton and lamb . .	12.8	12.8	12.9
Goat meat	2.8	2.9	3.0
Poultry meat . . .	4.1	4.2	4.3
Cows' milk	35.2	36.8	37.8
Sheep's milk. . . .	3.6	3.7	3.7
Goats' milk	79.8	81.2	81.4
Hen eggs*	6.5	6.8	7.0

* FAO estimates.

Source: FAO.

Fishing

('000 metric tons, live weight)

	1997	1998	1999
Capture	120.4	106.6	108.8
Demersal percomorphs . .	4.5	6.9	8.8
Groupers	3.4	5.3	4.8
Croakers and drums . .	5.5	2.2	2.1
Emperors (Scavengers) . .	5.8	6.6	7.0
Porgies and seabreams . .	4.3	4.0	6.1
Pelagic percomorphs . .	2.9	6.1	1.1
Jacks and crevalles . .	3.9	3.0	2.6
Indian oil sardine . . .	16.8	20.7	21.7
Narrow-barred Spanish mackerel . . .	5.9	3.1	3.4
Longtail tuna	5.0	4.4	4.8
Yellowfin tuna . . .	15.9	14.9	7.4
Hairtails and cutlassfishes . .	9.9	4.8	1.8
Sharks, rays, skates, etc. . .	6.7	5.0	4.3
Cuttlefish and bobtail squids	6.1	4.1	7.5
Aquaculture	—	0.0	0.0
Total catch	120.4	106.6	108.8

Source: FAO, *Yearbook of Fishery Statistics*.

Mining

('000 metric tons, unless otherwise indicated)

	1998	1999	2000
Crude petroleum ('000 barrels)	328,000	330,000	350,000
Natural gas (million cu ft) . .	367,123	408,485	547,219
Chromite	29.8	26.0	15.1
Silver (kg)	95*	236	306
Gold (kg)	575*	597	604
Marble	166.1	188.5	147.7
Limestone	1,902.0	3,808.6	3,497.1
Salt	13.8	11.2	11.7
Gypsum	165.0	180.1	131.9

* Estimate.

Source: partly US Geological Survey.

2001 (provisional figures): Crude petroleum 321,246,800 barrels; Natural gas 630,824m. cu ft.

Industry

SELECTED PRODUCTS ('000 barrels, unless otherwise indicated)

	1998	1999	2000
Kerosene	1,127.3	1,456.6	1,643.0
Motor spirit (petrol) . . .	5,225.0	4,710.9	4,856.5
Gas-diesel (distillate fuel) oils . .	6,029.1	6,297.0	6,362.7
Residual fuel oils . . .	14,948.8	14,866.2	14,796.5
Electric energy (million kWh) .	8,200	8,413	9,111

2001 (provisional figure): Electric energy 9,726m. kWh.

Finance

CURRENCY AND EXCHANGE RATES

Monetary Units

1,000 baiza = 1 rial Omani (RO).

Sterling, Dollar and Euro Equivalents (31 May 2002)

£1 sterling = 563.9 baiza;

US $1 = 384.5 baiza;

€1 = 360.9 baiza;

100 rials Omani = £177.32 = $260.08 = €277.06.

Exchange Rate

Since January 1986 the official exchange rate has been fixed at US $1 = 384.5 baiza (1 rial Omani = $2.6008).

BUDGET (RO million)

Revenue	1998	1999	2000
Petroleum revenue (net) . . .	1,240.2	1,201.6	1,721.0
Natural gas revenue . . .	63.3	57.6	73.4
Other current revenue . . .	522.7	519.8	455.3
Taxes and fees . . .	177.3	187.0	156.5
Income tax on enterprises .	40.1	36.1	41.8
Payroll tax	43.2	38.9	36.8
Customs duties . . .	61.6	80.3	46.1
Non-tax revenue . . .	345.4	332.8	298.8
Electricity	98.6	100.0	109.4
Surplus from public authorities	64.0	75.0	14.5
Income from government investments . . .	46.9	37.3	34.1
Capital revenue	9.1	13.5	7.6
Capital repayments . . .	11.0	3.6	32.6
Total	1,846.3	1,796.1	2,289.9

Expenditure	1998	1999	2000
Current expenditure . . .	1,760.4	1,808.9	2,091.9
Defence and national security	675.8	687.2	808.6
Civil ministries . . .	893.7	944.5	1,097.8
General public services . .	134.5	133.0	153.6
Education	262.4	276.8	208.8
Health	117.4	122.7	137.8
Social security and welfare .	60.7	75.3	126.5
Housing	94.2	99.2	111.7
Fuel and energy . . .	125.8	135.5	149.6
Interest payments . . .	101.6	98.8	107.1
Share of PDO expenditure* . .	89.3	78.4	78.4
Investment expenditure . . .	443.9	426.2	491.7
Civil development . . .	206.0	201.3	225.3
Fuel and energy . . .	48.7	85.4	76.0
Transport and communications	59.4	35.6	50.1
Share of PDO expenditure* . .	179.3	170.1	191.2
Participation and subsidies . .	17.3	33.9	72.6
Total	2,221.6	2,269.0	2,656.2

* Referring to the Government's share of current and capital expenditure by Petroleum Development Oman.

2001 (preliminary figures, RO million): Total revenue 2,530.0 (Oil revenue 1,875.0); Total expenditure 2,857.9.

2002 (forecasts, RO million): Total revenue 2,490.0 (Oil revenue 1,819.0); Total expenditure 2,870.0.

INTERNATIONAL RESERVES (US $ million at 31 December)

	1999	2000	2001
Gold*	68.3	68.3	80.5
IMF special drawing rights .	1.8	4.1	6.3
Reserve position in IMF . . .	68.3	64.9	81.6
Foreign exchange . . .	2,697.3	2,310.9	2,277.0
Total	2,835.8	2,448.2	2,445.4

* Valued at RO 90.8 per troy ounce until 2000, and at market-related prices from 2001.

Source: IMF, *International Financial Statistics.*

MONEY SUPPLY (RO million at 31 December)

	1999	2000	2001
Currency outside banks . . .	273.5	276.8	275.9
Demand deposits at commercial banks.	237.7	272.5	425.7
Total money	511.2	549.3	701.6

Source: IMF, *International Financial Statistics.*

COST OF LIVING (Consumer Price Index for Muscat; base: 1995 = 100)

	1998	1999	2000
Food, beverages and tobacco . .	102.9	102.7	101.4
Textiles, clothing and footwear	99.4	98.8	99.2
Rent, electricity, water and fuel	97.5	97.0	96.7
All items (incl. others) . .	99.5	100.0	98.8

2001 (base: 2000 = 100): All items 98.9 (Source: IMF, *International Financial Statistics*).

NATIONAL ACCOUNTS (RO million in current prices)

Expenditure on the Gross Domestic Product

	1999	2000*	2001†
Government final consumption expenditure . . .	1,439.7	1,580.2	1,749.6
Private final consumption expenditure	3,030.8	3,011.6	3,204.6
Increase in stocks . . . }	897.1	913.0	1,010.2
Gross fixed capital formation . . }			
Total domestic expenditure	5,367.6	5,504.8	5,964.4
Exports of goods and services .	2,888.0	4,461.0 }	1,705.0
Less Imports of goods and services	2,215.0	2,343.0 }	
GDP in purchasers' values . .	6,040.6	7,622.8	7,669.4
GDP at constant 1988 prices	5,355.6	5,628.9	n.a.

* Provisional figures.   † Preliminary figures.

Source: partly IMF, *International Financial Statistics.*

Gross Domestic Product by Economic Activity

	1999	2000*	2001†
Agriculture and livestock‡ . .	106.7	101.1	103.4
Fishing‡.	52.3	48.7	50.5
Mining and quarrying . . .	2,381.6	3,738.1	3,291.6
Crude petroleum	2,299.2	3,618.3	3,115.2
Natural gas	66.6	101.6	158.8
Manufacturing	262.3	409.3	634.8
Electricity and water. . . .	71.4	73.1	76.8
Construction.	141.2	145.4	167.3
Trade, restaurants and hotels .	825.4	857.0	932.3
Transport, storage and communications‡ . . .	436.0	448.4	494.8
Financing, insurance, real estate and business services§ . . .	678.2	690.4	700.3
Public administration and defence	688.2	715.9	766.2
Other community, social and personal services . . .	496.1	545.1	578.6
Domestic services of households	16.2	16.5	16.7
Sub-total	6,155.5	7,788.9	7,813.3
Import duties	80.3	46.1	59.6
Less Imputed bank service charge	195.2	212.2	203.5
GDP in purchasers' values . .	6,040.6	7,622.8	7,669.4

* Provisional figures.
† Preliminary figures.
‡ Excluding activities of government enterprises.
§ Including imputed rents of owner-occupied dwellings.

BALANCE OF PAYMENTS (US $ million)

	1998	1999	2000
Exports of goods f.o.b. . . .	5,521	7,239	11,319
Imports of goods f.o.b. . . .	−5,215	−4,300	−4,593
Trade balance	307	2,939	6,726
Exports of services . . .	276	273	283
Imports of services . . .	−1,633	−1,462	−1,501
Balance on goods and services .	−1,051	1,751	5,508
Other income received . . .	338	187	291
Other income paid . . .	−814	−869	−996
Balance on goods, services and income	−1,527	1,069	4,804
Current transfers paid . . .	−1,467	−1,438	−1,456
Current balance	−2,993	−369	3,347
Capital account (net) . . .	−5	−3	8
Direct investment from abroad .	101	21	23
Portfolio investment liabilities .	185	26	−36
Other investment assets . .	642	−307	−356
Other investment liabilities . .	554	325	−36
Net errors and omissions . .	751	522	−687
Overall balance . . .	−765	215	2,262

Source: IMF, *International Financial Statistics.*

External Trade

PRINCIPAL COMMODITIES (distribution by SITC)

Imports c.i.f. (RO million)	1998	1999	2000
Food and live animals . .	231.1	246.6	233.0
Dairy products and birds' eggs .	47.4	59.2	54.2
Cereals and cereal preparations	42.7	53.2	50.8
Beverages and tobacco. .	110.9	140.2	167.5
Tobacco and tobacco manufactures	89.8	122.2	149.8
Crude materials (inedible)			
except fuels	36.4	35.4	56.1
Chemicals and related products	141.6	132.5	140.4
Basic manufactures . .	396.8	263.0	267.9
Textile yarn, fabrics, etc. . .	77.5	54.8	60.0
Iron and steel	134.3	63.2	51.4
Machinery and transport			
equipment	1,010.0	744.4	838.1
Power-generating machinery and			
equipment	77.9	54.2	42.4
Machinery specialized for			
particular industries . .	143.1	97.1	113.6
General industrial machinery,			
equipment and parts . .	202.8	98.2	85.8
Telecommunications and sound			
equipment	61.8	50.2	40.4
Other electrical machinery,			
apparatus, etc. . .	87.1	61.3	61.2
Road vehicles and parts* . .	392.0	311.9	429.4
Miscellaneous manufactured			
articles	143.4	115.6	118.4
Total (incl. others) . . .	2,184.5	1,797.1	1,937.6

Exports f.o.b. (US $ million)	1997	1998	1999
Food and live animals . .	183.4	180.0	188.0
Mineral fuels, lubricants, etc.	5,829.3	3,755.7	5,562.5
Petroleum, petroleum products, ets.	5,829.2	3,755.6	5,561.8
Crude petroleum oils, etc. .	5,647.4	3,586.0	5,376.5
Refined petroleum products .	181.8	169.6	185.3
Basic manufactures . .	175.9	179.8	169.3
Machinery and transport			
equipment	917.3	906.7	838.2
Road vehicles and parts* . .	641.0	588.6	521.4
Passenger motor cars (excl.			
buses)	430.5	377.1	282.5
Parts and accessories for cars,			
buses, lorries, etc.* . .	141.2	146.2	182.8
Miscellaneous manufactured			
articles	209.8	208.2	191.4
Total (incl. others) . . .	7,630.7	5,518.8	7,230.9

* Data on parts exclude tyres, engines and electrical parts.

Source (for Exports): UN, *International Trade Statistics Yearbook*.

2001 (provisional figures, RO million): Total imports 2,229.3; Total exports 4,258.0 (Crude petroleum 2,934.8).

PRINCIPAL TRADING PARTNERS

Imports c.i.f. (RO '000)	1998	1999	2000
Australia	46,290	48,480	56,292
China, People's Republic . .	52,902	20,247	36,381
France	122,035	63,464	38,576
Germany	107,150	70,760	72,066
India	63,689	62,004	63,269
Iran	9,096	15,218	23,412
Italy	128,242	49,080	35,803
Japan	343,780	273,697	350,869
Korea, Republic . . .	41,310	37,909	66,781
Malaysia	24,849	22,737	24,837
Netherlands	47,256	57,720	45,016
Pakistan	19,985	19,980	22,872
Saudi Arabia . . .	64,652	61,167	52,942
Singapore	21,090	18,757	19,732
United Arab Emirates . .	550,766	505,314	570,891
United Kingdom . . .	159,001	122,894	112,776
USA	153,522	115,318	103,981
Total (incl. others) . . .	2,184,543	1,797,078	1,937,678

Exports f.o.b. (US $ million)	1997	1998	1999
China, People's Republic . .	1,284.6	482.7	689.2
Hong Kong	108.1	23.3	9.5
India	81.2	53.0	29.4
Iran.	175.0	160.3	120.0
Japan	1,604.2	990.2	1,674.9
Korea, Republic . . .	951.1	754.3	980.8
Philippines	270.0	208.8	166.8
Saudi Arabia . . .	72.9	101.1	116.4
Tanzania	68.0	63.2	77.2
Thailand	1,333.5	977.2	1,147.0
United Arab Emirates . .	744.9	746.1	718.1
United Kingdom . . .	64.2	53.7	79.2
USA	115.4	86.8	86.5
Yemen	59.8	136.4	91.1
Total (incl. others) . . .	7,630.7	5,518.8	7,230.9

Source (for Exports): UN, *International Trade Statistics Yearbook*.

Transport

ROAD TRAFFIC (registered vehicles at 31 December)

	1998	1999	2000
Private cars	229,029	254,214	280,977
Taxis	24,014	29,246	35,159
Commercial	110,717	117,615	124,582
Government	25,250	25,983	26,804
Motor-cycles	4,660	4,853	5,050
Diplomatic	811	945	1,113
Other	9,894	14,318	22,229
Total	404,375	447,174	495,914

SHIPPING
Merchant Fleet (registered at 31 December)

	1999	2000	2001
Number of vessels . . .	25	26	28
Total displacement ('000 grt) .	16.7	18.9	19.7

Source: Lloyd's Register-Fairplay, *World Fleet Statistics*.

International Sea-borne Freight Traffic ('000 metric tons)

	1994	1995	1996
Goods loaded	40,174	41,586	43,525
Goods unloaded	4,475	4,799	5,303

CIVIL AVIATION (traffic on scheduled services)

	1996	1997	1998
Kilometres flown (million) . .	27	26	27
Passengers carried ('000) . .	1,620	1,678	1,768
Passenger-km (million) . .	3,277	3,197	3,405
Total ton-km (million) . .	413	384	415

Note: Figures include an apportionment (one-quarter) of the traffic of Gulf Air, a multinational airline with its headquarters in Bahrain.

Source: UN, *Statistical Yearbook*.

Tourism

FOREIGN TOURIST ARRIVALS*

Country of nationality	1998	1999	2000
Bahrain	8,413	8,642	15,827
France	9,540	14,843	16,718
Germany	31,783	45,063	58,357
India	33,143	43,339	52,313
Netherlands	7,062	9,624	11,746
Philippines	3,506	4,752	12,704
Saudi Arabia . . .	9,056	12,173	17,260
Switzerland	11,535	16,397	18,810
United Arab Emirates . .	30,373	33,862	55,984
United Kingdom . . .	44,230	54,888	66,555
USA	13,918	18,456	26,789
Total (incl. others) . . .	423,953	502,788	571,110

* Figures refer to international arrivals at hotels and similar establishments.

Source: World Tourism Organization, *Yearbook of Tourism Statistics*.

Tourism receipts (RO million): 43.2 in 1998; 40.4 in 1999; 45.7 in 2000 (Source: Directorate-General of Tourism).

Communications Media

	1999	2000	2001
Television receivers ('000 in use) .	1,415	1,430	n.a.
Telephones ('000 main lines in use)	220.4	225.4	235.3
Mobile cellular telephones ('000 subscribers)	124.1	164.3	324.5
Personal computers ('000 in use)	65	80	85
Internet users ('000)	50	90	120
Daily newspapers (number) . .	5	5	n.a.
Non-daily newspapers and other periodicals (number) . .	25	25	n.a.

1996: Book production (first editions only) 7 titles.
1997 (number in use): Radio receivers 1,400,000; Facsimile machines 6,356.

Sources: mainly UNESCO, *Statistical Yearbook* and International Telecommunication Union.

Education

(2000/01)

	Insti-tutions	Teachers	Pupils/Students		
			Males	Females	Total
Pre-primary* . . .	5	347	3,792	3,197	6,989
Primary . . .	294†	9,238	130,736	122,694	253,430
Preparatory . . .	497†	8,037	77,810	69,481	147,291
Secondary . . .	177†	6,114	50,716	54,192	104,908
Higher* . . .	n.a.	1,307	8,894	7,138	16,032
University . . .	1	833	4,722	4,353	9,075

* Figures refer to 1997/98 (Source: UNESCO, *Statistical Yearbook*).
† Figure refers to 1998/99.

Adult literacy rate (UNESCO estimates): 71.7% (males 80.1%; females 61.6%) in 2000 (Source: UNDP, *Human Development Report*).

Directory

The Constitution

The Basic Statute of the State was promulgated by royal decree on 6 November 1996, as Oman's first document defining the organs and guiding principles of the State.

Chapter 1 defines the State and the system of government. Oman is defined as an Arab, Islamic and independent state with full sovereignty. Islamic law (*Shari'a*) is the basis for legislation. The official language is Arabic. The system of government is defined as Sultani (Royal), hereditary in the male descendants of Sayyid Turki bin Said bin Sultan. Article 6 determines the procedure whereby the Sultan is designated.

Chapter 2 defines the political, economic, social, cultural and security principles of the State. Article 11 (economic principles) includes the stipulation that 'All natural resources and revenues therefrom shall be the property of the State which will preserve and utilize them in the best manner taking into consideration the requirements of the State's security and the interests of the national economy'. The constructive and fruitful co-operation between public and private activity is stated to be the essence of the national economy. Public property is inviolable, and private ownership is safeguarded. Article 14 (security principles) provides for a Defence Council to preserve the safety and defence of the Sultanate.

Chapter 3 defines public rights and duties. Individual and collective freedoms are guaranteed within the limits of the law.

Chapter 4 concerns the Head of State, the Council of Ministers, Specialized Councils and financial affairs of the State. Article 41 defines the Sultan as Head of State and Supreme Commander of the Armed Forces. The article states that 'His person is inviolable. Respect for him is a duty and his command must be obeyed. He is the symbol of national unity and the guardian of its preservation and protection.' The Sultan presides over the Council of Ministers, or may appoint a person (Prime Minister) to preside on his behalf. Deputy Prime Ministers and other Ministers are appointed by the Sultan. The Council of Ministers and Specialized Councils assist the Sultan in implementing the general policy of the State.

Chapter 5 comprises a single Article (58). This states that the Council of Oman shall consist of the Majlis ash-Shoura (Consultative Council) and the Majlis ad-Dawlah (Council of State). The jurisdiction, terms, sessions, rules of procedure, membership and regulation of each shall be determined by the law.

Chapter 6 concerns the judiciary. Articles 59 and 60 state that the supremacy of the law shall be the basis of governance, and enshrine the dignity, integrity, impartiality and independence of the judiciary. Article 66 provides for a Supreme Council of the judiciary.

Chapter 7 defines the general provisions pertaining to the application of the Basic Statute.

The Government

HEAD OF STATE

Sultan: Qaboos bin Said as-Said (assumed power on 23 July 1970, after deposing his father).

COUNCIL OF MINISTERS
(September 2002)

Prime Minister and Minister of Foreign Affairs, Defence and Finance: Sultan Qaboos bin Said.
Deputy Prime Minister for the Council of Ministers: Sayyid Fahad bin Mahmoud as-Said.

Personal Representative of the Sultan: Sayyid THUWAINI BIN SHIHAB AS-SAID.

Minister of National Economy, Supervisor of the Finance Ministry and Deputy Chairman of the Financial Affairs and Energy Resources Council: AHMAD BIN ABD AN-NABI MACKI.

Minister Responsible for Defence Affairs: Sayyid BADR BIN SAUD BIN HAREB.

Minister of Legal Affairs: MUHAMMAD BIN ALI BIN NASIR AL-ALAWI.

Minister of Oil and Gas: Dr MUHAMMAD BIN HAMAD BIN SAIF AR-RUMHI.

Minister of Justice: Sheikh MUHAMMAD BIN ABDULLAH BIN ZAHIR AL-HINAI.

Minister of Awqaf (Religious Endowments) and Religious Affairs: Sheikh ABDULLAH BIN MUHAMMAD BIN ABDULLAH AS-SALIMI.

Minister Responsible for Foreign Affairs: YOUSUF BIN AL-ALAWI BIN ABDULLAH.

Minister of Information: HAMAD BIN MUHAMMAD BIN MUHSIN AR-RASHIDI.

Minister of Housing, Electricity and Water: Sheikh SUHAIL BIN MUSTAHIL BIN SALEM BEIT SHAMMAS.

Minister of Education: YAHYA BIN SAUD BIN MANSOOR AS-SULAIMI.

Minister of Higher Education: YAHYA BIN MAHFOUZ AL-MANTHARI.

Minister of Social Development: Sheikh AMIR BIN SHUWAIN AL-HOSNI.

Minister of Labour: JUMA BIN ALI BIN JUMA

Minister of Transport and Telecommunications: MALEK BIN SULAYMAN AL-MA'AMARI.

Minister of National Heritage and Culture: Sayyid HAITHAM BIN TARIQ BIN AS-SAID.

Minister of the Interior: Sayyid SAUD BIN IBRAHIM BIN SAUD AL-BUSAIDI.

Minister of Commerce and Industry: MAQBOOL BIN ALI BIN SULTAN.

Minister of Agriculture and Fisheries: Sheikh SALIM BIN HILAL AL-KHALILI.

Minister of Health: Dr ALI BIN MUHAMMAD BIN MOUSA AR-RAISI.

Minister of Regional Municipalities and the Environment: Dr KHAMIS BIN MUBARAK BIN ISA AL-ALAWI.

Minister of the Civil Service: Sheikh ABD AL-AZIZ BIN MATAR BIN SALIM AL-AZIZI.

Governor of Muscat and Minister of State: Sayyid AL-MUTASIM BIN HAMOUD AL-BUSAIDI.

Governor of Dhofar and Minister of State: Sheikh MUHAMMAD BIN ALI AL-QATABI.

Minister of the Diwan of the Royal Court: Sayyid ALI BIN HAMOUD BIN ALI AL-BUSAIDI.

Minister of the Palace Office and Head of the Office of the Supreme Commander of the Armed Forces: Maj-Gen. ALI BIN MAJID AL-MA'AMARI.

MINISTRIES

Diwan of the Royal Court: POB 632, Muscat 113; tel. 738711; fax 739427; internet www.diwan.gov.om.

Ministry of Agriculture and Fisheries: POB 467, Ruwi 113; tel. 694182; fax 695909; internet www.maf.gov.om.

Ministry of Awqaf (Religious Endowments) and Religious Affairs: POB 354, Ruwi 112; tel. 697699; e-mail admin@mara .gov.om; internet www.mara.gov.om.

Ministry of the Civil Service: POB 3994, Ruwi 112; tel. 696000; fax 601365; internet www.omanmocs.gov.om.

Ministry of Commerce and Industry: POB 550, Muscat 113; tel. 774290; fax 7717238; e-mail minister@mocioman.gov.om; internet www.mocioman.gov.om.

Ministry of Defence: POB 113, Muscat 113; tel. 704096; fax 618205.

Ministry of Education: POB 3, Muscat 113; tel. 775334; fax 704465; email info@edu.gov.om; internet www.edu.gov.om.

Ministry of Finance: POB 506, Muscat 113; tel. 738201; fax 737028; internet www.mof.gov.om.

Ministry of Foreign Affairs: POB 252, Muscat 113; tel. 699500; fax 699589.

Ministry of Health: POB 393, Muscat 113; tel. 602177; fax 601430; e-mail moh@moh.gov.om; internet www.moh.gov.om.

Ministry of Higher Education: POB 82, Ruwi 112; tel. 693148; internet www.mohe.gov.om.

Ministry of Housing, Electricity and Water: POB 1491, Ruwi 112; tel. 603906; fax 699180; internet www.mhew.gov.om.

Ministry of Information: POB 600, Muscat 113; tel. 603222; fax 601638; e-mail inform@omanet.com; internet www.omanet.com.

Ministry of the Interior: POB 127, Ruwi 112; tel. 602244; fax 696660.

Ministry of Justice: POB 354, Ruwi 112; tel. 697699; internet www.moj.gov.om.

Ministry of Legal Affairs: POB 578, Ruwi 112; tel. 605802.

Ministry of National Economy: POB 506, Muscat 113; tel. 698821; fax 698908; e-mail mone@omantel.net.om; internet www.moneoman.gov.om.

Ministry of National Heritage and Culture: POB 668, Muscat 113; tel. 602555; fax 602735; internet www.mnhc.gov.om.

Ministry of Oil and Gas: POB 551, Muscat 113; tel. 603333; fax 696972; internet www.mog.gov.om.

Ministry of the Palace Office: POB 2227, Ruwi 112; tel. 600841.

Ministry of Regional Municipalities and the Environment: POB 323, Muscat 113; tel. 696444; fax 602320.

Ministry of Social Affairs, Labour and Vocational Training: POB 560, Muscat 113; tel. 602444; fax 701515.

Ministry of Transport and Telecommunications: POB 338, Ruwi 112; tel. 697870; fax 696817; e-mail pttdiwan@omantel.net.om; internet www.comm.gov.om.

Ministry of Water Resources: POB 2575, Ruwi 112; tel. 703552; fax 701353; e-mail mwres@omantel.net.om.

COUNCIL OF OMAN

Majlis ash-Shoura
(Consultative Council)

President: Sheikh ABDULLAH BIN ALI AL-QATABI.

The Majlis ash-Shoura was established by royal decree in November 1991. Initially, members of the Majlis were appointed by the Sultan from among nominees selected at national polls, but in the September 2000 elections, members were directly elected. Two representatives are appointed from four candidates in each *wilaya* (region) of more than 30,000 inhabitants, and one from two candidates in each *wilaya* of fewer than 30,000 inhabitants. Members of the Majlis are appointed for a single three-year term of office. The Majlis elected in September 2000 comprised 83 members. The Majlis is an advisory body, the duties of which include the review of all social and economic draft laws prior to their enactment; public-service ministries are required to submit reports and answer questions regarding their performance, plans and achievements. The President of the Majlis ash-Shoura is appointed by royal decree.

Majlis ad-Dawlah
(Council of State)

President: Sheikh HAMOUD BIN ABDULLAH AL-HARITHI.

The Majlis ad-Dawlah was established in December 1997, in accordance with the terms of the Basic Statute of the State. It is also an advisory body, comprising 41 members appointed by the Sultan. Its function is to serve as a liaison between the government and the people of Oman. A new Majlis was appointed in October 2000.

Political Organizations

There are no political organizations in Oman.

Diplomatic Representation

EMBASSIES IN OMAN

Algeria: POB 216, Muscat 115; tel. 601698; fax 694419; e-mail algeria@omantel.net.om; Ambassador: CHÉRIF DERBAL.

Austria: Moosa Complex Bldg, No. 477, 2nd Floor, Way No. 3109, POB 2070, Ruwi 112; tel. 793135; fax 793669; e-mail aeiou@ omantel.net.om; Ambassador: Dr CLEMENS CORETH.

Bahrain: POB 66, Madinat Qaboos, Al-Khuwair; tel. 605912; fax 605072; Chargé d'affaires: AHMAD MUHAMMAD MAHMOUD.

Bangladesh: POB 3959, Ruwi 112; tel. 707462; fax 708495; Ambassador: AMIN AHMED CHOWDHURY.

Brunei: POB 91, Ruwi 112; tel. 603533; fax 693014; Ambassador: Pehin Dato' Haji MAHDINI.

China, People's Republic: Shati al-Qurum, Way No. 3017, House No. 1368, POB 315, Muscat 112; tel. 696698; fax 602322; Ambassador: WANG XIAOZHUANG.

Egypt: Diplomatic City, Al-Khuwair, POB 2252, Ruwi 112; tel. 600411; fax 603626; e-mail egyembmuscat@hotmail.com; Ambassador: HANI RIAD ALI.

France: Diplomatic City, Al-Khuwair, POB 208, Madinat Qaboos 115; tel. 681800; fax 681843; e-mail diplofr1@omantel.net.om; www.ambafrance-om.org; Ambassador: MICHEL TOURAINE.

Germany: POB 128, Ruwi 112; tel. 7732482; fax 7735690; e-mail diplofrg@omantel.net.om; Ambassador: WOLFGANG ERCK.

India: POB 1727, Ruwi 112; tel. 7714120; fax 7717503; e-mail indiamct@omantel.net.om; internet www.indemb-oman.org; Ambassador: SATNAM JIT SINGH.

Iran: Madinat Qaboos East, Dal, POB 3155, Ruwi 112; tel. 696944; fax 696888; Ambassador: NEMATOLLAH IAZDI.

Iraq: POB 262, Way 1737, House No. 2803, Ruwi 112; tel. 604178; fax 605112; Ambassador: KHALID ABDULLAH SALEH AS-SAMIRA'I.

Italy: Qurum Area 5, Way No. 2411, House No. 842, POB 3727, Ruwi 112; tel. 564838; fax 564846; e-mail ambmasc@omantel .net.om; Ambassador: Dr MARIO QUAGLIOTTI.

Japan: Shati al-Qurum, POB 3511, Ruwi 112; tel. 601028; fax 698720; Ambassador: ZENJI KAMINAGA.

Jordan: Diplomatic City, Al-Khuwair, POB 70, Al-Adhaiba 130; tel. 692760; fax 692762; e-mail embhkjom@omantel.net.om; Ambassador: NABIL ALI BARTO.

Korea, Republic: POB 377, 115 Madinat Qaboos; tel. 691490; fax 691495; e-mail depkomct@omantel.net.om; Ambassador: LEE YONG-HYUN.

Kuwait: Diplomatic City, Al-Khuwair, Block No. 13, POB 1798, Ruwi 112; tel. 699626; fax 600972; Ambassador: ABD AL-MOHSIN SALIM AL-HAROUN.

Malaysia: Shati al-Qurum, Villa 1611, Way 3019, POB 3939, Ruwi 112; tel. 698329; fax 605031; e-mail mwmuscat@omantel.net.om; Ambassador: Dato' MOHAMED ROZE BIN ABDUL RAHMAN.

Morocco: Al-Ensharah Street, Villa No. 197, POB 3125, Ruwi 112; tel. 696152; fax 601114; Ambassador: ALAOUI M'HAMDI MUSTAPHA.

Netherlands: Shati al-Qurum, Way 3017, Villa 1366, POB 3302, Ruwi 112; tel. 603706; fax 603778; e-mail nethmus@omantel.net.om; internet www.nlembassyoman.org; Ambassador: G. J. VAN EPEN.

Pakistan: POB 1302, Ruwi 112; tel. 603090; fax 697462; e-mail parepmct@omantel.net.om; internet www.pakemboman.ejb.net; Ambassador: KARAM ELAHI.

Philippines: POB 420, Madinat Qaboos 115; tel. 605140; fax 605176; e-mail aasakkam@omantel.net.om; Ambassador: AKMAD A. SAKKAM.

Qatar: Jameat ad-Duwal al-Arabiya Street, Diplomatic City, Al-Khuwair, POB 802, Muscat 113; tel. 691152; Ambassador: SAAD NASSER AL-HOMIDI.

Russia: Shati al-Qurum Way 3032, Surfait Compound, POB 80, Ruwi 112; tel. 602894; fax 604189; Ambassador: ALEKSANDR K. PATSEV.

Saudi Arabia: Diplomatic Area, Jamiat ad-Dowal al-Arabiya St, POB 1411, Ruwi 112; tel. 601744; fax 603540; omemb@mofa.gov.sa; Ambassador: AHMAD ALI AL-KAHTANI

Somalia: Mumtaz Street, Villa Hassan Jumaa Baker, POB 1767, Ruwi 112; tel. 564412; fax 564965; Ambassador: MUHAMMAD SUBAN NUR.

Sri Lanka: POB 95, Madinat Qaboos 115; tel. 697841; fax 697336; e-mail lankaemb@omantel.net.om; Ambassador: (vacant).

Sudan: Diplomatic City, Al-Khuwair, POB 3971, Ruwi 112; tel. 697875; fax 699065; Ambassador: ABD AL-AZIZ MARHOUM AHMAD.

Syria: Madinat Qaboos, Al-Ensharah Street, Villa No. 201, POB 85, Muscat 115; tel. 697904; fax 603895; Chargé d'affaires: ANWAR WEBBI.

Thailand: Villa No. 33–34, Madinat Qaboos East, POB 60, Ruwi 115; tel. 602684; fax 605714; Ambassador: PENSAK CHARALAK.

Tunisia: Al-Ensharah Street, Way No. 1507, POB 220, Muscat 115; tel. 603486; fax 697778; Ambassador: HATEM ESSAIEM.

Turkey: Bldg No. 3270, Street No. 3042, Shati al-Qurum, POB 47, Mutrah 115; tel. 697050; fax 697053; e-mail turemmus@ omantel.net.om; internet www.turkishembassymuscat.org; Ambassador: N. MURAT ERSAVCI.

United Arab Emirates: Diplomatic City, Al-Khuwair, POB 551, Muscat 111; tel. 600302; fax 604182; Ambassador: HAMAD HELAL THABIT AL-KUWAITI.

United Kingdom: POB 300, Muscat 113; tel. 693077; fax 693087; e-mail enquiries.muscat@fco.gov.uk; internet www.uk.gov.om; Ambassador: J. STUART LAING.

USA: Diplomatic City, POB 202, Muscat 115; tel. 698989; fax 699771; e-mail aemctric@omantel.net.om; internet www.usa .gov.om; Ambassador: RICHARD L. BALTIMORE, III (designate).

Yemen: Shati al-Qurum, Area 258, Way No. 2840, Bldg No. 2981, POB 105, Madinat Qaboos 115; tel. 600815; fax 605008; Ambassador: AHMAD DAIFALLAH AL-AZEIB.

Judicial System

Oman's Basic Statute guarantees the independence of the judiciary. The foundation for the legal system is *Shari'a* (Islamic law), which is the basis for family law, dealing with matters such as inheritance and divorce. Separate courts have been established to deal with commercial disputes and other matters to which *Shari'a* does not apply.

Courts of the First Instance are competent to try cases of criminal misdemeanour; serious crimes are tried by the Criminal Courts; the Court of Appeal is in Muscat. There are district courts throughout the country. Special courts deal with military crimes committed by members of the armed and security forces.

The Basic Statute provides for a Supreme Council to supervise the proper functioning of the courts.

An Administrative Court, to review the decisions of government bodies, was instituted in April 2001.

The office of Public Prosecutor was established in 1999 and the first such appointment was made in June 2001.

Religion

ISLAM

The majority of the population (estimated at 53.5% in 1994) are Muslims, of whom approximately three-quarters are of the Ibadi sect and about one-quarter are Sunni Muslims.

HINDUISM

According to 1994 estimates, 28.0% of the population are Hindus.

CHRISTIANITY

It was estimated that in 1994 14.7% of the population were Christians.

Protestantism

The Protestant Church in Oman: POB 1982, Ruwi 112; tel. 702372; fax 789943; e-mail pcomct@omantel.net.om; internet www.pcomct.com; joint chaplaincy of the Anglican Church and the Reformed Church of America; four inter-denominational churches in Oman, at Ruwi and Ghala in Muscat, at Sohar and at Salalah; Senior Chaplain Rev. JOHN ALDIS.

The Roman Catholic Church

A small number of adherents, mainly expatriates, form part of the Apostolic Vicariate of Arabia. The Vicar Apostolic is resident in the United Arab Emirates.

The Press

Article 31 of Oman's Basic Statute guarantees the freedom of the press, printing and publishing, according to the terms and conditions specified by the law. Published matter 'leading to discord, harming the State's security or abusing human dignity or rights' is prohibited.

NEWSPAPERS

Oman Daily Newspaper: POB 3303, Ruwi 112; tel. 701555; e-mail editor@omandaily.com; internet www.omandaily.com; daily; Arabic; Editor-in-Chief HABIB MUHAMMAD NASIB; circ. 15,560.

Ash-Shabibah: POB 3303, 112 Ruwi; tel. 795373; fax 796711; daily; Arabic; culture, leisure and sports.

Al-Watan (The Nation): POB 643, Muscat 113; tel. 591919; fax 591280; e-mail alwatan@omantel.net.om; internet www.alwatan .com; f. 1971; daily; Arabic; Editor-in-Chief MUHAMMAD BIN SULAYMAN AT-TAI; circ. 40,000.

English Language

Khaleej Times: POB 3305, Ruwi 112; tel. 700895; fax 706512; Reg. Man. SANKAR NARAYAN.

Oman Daily Observer: POB 3303, Ruwi 112; tel. 703055; fax 790524; e-mail editor@omanobserver.com; internet www.oman observer.com; f. 1981; daily; publ. by Oman Newspaper House; Chair. SULTAN BIN HAMAD BIN SAUD; Editor SAID BIN KHALFAN AL-HARTHI; circ. 22,000.

Times of Oman: POB 3770, Ruwi 112; tel. 701953; fax 799153; e-mail times@omantel.net.om; internet www.omantimes.com; f. 1975; daily; Founder, Propr and Editor-in-Chief MUHAMMAD AZ-ZEDJALI; Man. Dir ANIS BIN ESSA AZ-ZEDJALI; circ. 21,000.

PERIODICALS

Al-Adwaa' (Lights): POB 580, 113 Muscat; tel. 704353; fax 798187; weekly; Arabic; economic, political and social; Editor-in-Chief Habib Muhammad Nasib; circ. 15,600.

Al-'Akidah (The Faith): POB 1001, 112 Ruwi; tel. 701000; fax 709917; weekly illustrated magazine; Arabic; political; Editor Said as-Samhan al-Kathiri; circ. 10,000.

Business Today: Apex Press and Publishing, POB 2616, Ruwi 112; tel. 799388; fax 793316; internet www.apexstuff.com.; monthly; Editor Mohana Prabhakar.

The Commercial: POB 2002, Ruwi 112; tel. 704022; fax 795885; e-mail omanad@omantel.net.om; f. 1978; monthly; Arabic and English; business news; Man. Ayoob Chankalan; Chief Editor Hamad bin Amir al-Kasbi; circ. 7,000.

Al-Ghorfa (Oman Commerce): POB 1400, Ruwi 112; tel. 707674; fax 708497; e-mail pubrel@omanchamber.org; internet www.cham beroman.com; f. 1973; bi-monthly; English and Arabic; business; publ. by Oman Chamber of Commerce and Industry; Editor Rashid Ahmad as-Sawafi; circ. 10,500.

Jund Oman (Soldiers of Oman): POB 113, Muscat 113; tel. 613615; fax 613369; f. 1974; monthly; Arabic; illustrated magazine of the Ministry of Defence; Supervisor Chief of Staff of the Sultan's Armed Forces.

Al-Markazi (The Central): POB 1161, Ruwi 112; tel. 702222; fax 707913; f. 1975; bi-monthly economic magazine; English and Arabic; publ. by Central Bank of Oman.

Al-Mawared at-Tabeey'iyah (Natural Resources): POB 551, Muscat; publ. by Ministries of Agriculture and Fisheries and of Petroleum and Gas; monthly; English and Arabic; Editor Khalid az-Zubaidi.

Al-Mazari' (Farms): POB 467, Muscat; weekly journal of the Ministry of Agriculture and Fisheries; Editor Khalid az-Zubaidi.

An-Nahda (The Renaissance): POB 979, 113 Muscat; tel. 563104; fax 563106; weekly illustrated magazine; Arabic; political and social; Editor Taleb Said al-Meawaly; circ. 10,000.

Oman Today: Apex Press and Publishing, POB 2616, Ruwi 112; tel. 799388; fax 793316; internet www.apexstuff.com; f. 1981; bi-monthly; English; leisure and sports; Editor Emma Ventura; circ. 20,000.

Al-Omaniya (Omani Woman): POB 3303, Ruwi 112; tel. 792700; fax 707765; monthly; Arabic; circ. 10,500.

Risalat al-Masjed (The Mosque Message): POB 6066, Muscat; tel. 561178; fax 560607; issued by Diwan of Royal Court Affairs Protocol Dept (Schools and Mosques Section); Editor Jouma bin Muhammad bin Salem al-Wahaibi.

Ash-Shurta (The Police): Directorate of Public Relations, Royal Oman Police, POB 2, Muscat 113; tel. 569216; fax 562341; quarterly magazine of Royal Oman Police; Editor Director of Public Relations.

Al-Usra (The Family): POB 440, Mutrah 114; tel. 794922; fax 795348; e-mail admeds@omantel.net.om; f. 1974; fortnightly; Arabic; socio-economic illustrated magazine; Chief Editor Sadek Abdowani; circ. 15,000.

NEWS AGENCY

Oman News Agency: Ministry of Information, POB 3659, Ruwi 112; tel. 696970; e-mail info@omannews.com; internet www .omannews.com; f. 1986; Dir-Gen. Muhammad bin Salim al-Marhoon.

Publishers

Apex Press and Publishing: POB 2616, Ruwi 112; tel. 799388; fax 793316; www.apexstuff.com; f. 1980; art, history, trade directories, maps, leisure and business magazines, and guidebooks; Pres. Saleh M. Talib al-Zakwani; Editors Mohana Prabhakar, Andrea Dixon.

Arabian Distribution and Publishing Enterprise: Mutrah; tel. 707079.

Dar al-Usra: POB 440, Mutrah 114; tel. 794922; fax 795348; e-mail alusra@omantel.net.om.

Muscat Press and Publishing House SAOC: POB 3112, 112 Ruwi; tel. 795373; fax 796711.

National Publishing and Advertising LLC: POB 3112, Ruwi 112; tel. 793098; fax 708445; e-mail npanet@usa.net; f. 1987; Man. Ashok Suvarna.

Oman Establishment for Press, Printing and Publishing: POB 463, 113 Muscat; tel. 591919; fax 591280; Chair. Sultan bin Hamad bin Saud; Editor-in-Chief Said bin Khalfan el-Harthy.

Oman Newspaper House: POB 3002, 112 Ruwi; tel. 701555; fax 790523; Dir Abd al-Wahab bin Nasser al-Mantheri.

Oman Publishing House: POB 580, Muscat; tel. 704353.

Ash-Shahmi Publishers and Advertisers: POB 6112, Ruwi; tel. 703416.

Broadcasting and Communications

TELECOMMUNICATIONS

Regulatory Authority

Oman Telecommunications Regulatory Authority: Muscat; f. 2002 to oversee the privatization of OMANTEL (see below) and to set tariffs and regulate the sale of operating licences.

State-owned Company

Oman Telecommunications Company SAOC (OMANTEL): POB 789, Ruwi 112; tel. 631417; fax 697066; e-mail info@omantel .net.om; internet www.omantel.net.om; f. 1999 as successor to the General Telecommunications Organization (GTO), to facilitate transfer to private ownership; Chair. Malek bin Sulayman al-Ma'a-mari; Exec. Pres. Eng. Muhammad bin Ali al-Wahaibi.

BROADCASTING

Radio

Radio Sultanate of Oman: Ministry of Information, POB 600, Muscat 113; tel. 603222; fax 601393; e-mail omanfm@omanet.com; internet www.oman-radio.gov.om; f. 1970; transmits in Arabic 20 hours daily, English on FM 15 hours daily; Dir-Gen. Ali bin Abdullah al-Mujeni.

Radio Salalah: f. 1970; transmits daily programmes in Arabic and the Dhofari languages; Dir Muhammad bin Ahmad ar-Rowas.

The British Broadcasting Corpn (BBC) has built a powerful medium-wave relay station on Masirah island. It is used to expand and improve the reception of the BBC's Arabic, Farsi, Hindi, Pashtu and Urdu services.

Television

Sultanate of Oman Television: Ministry of Information, POB 600, Muscat 113; tel. 603222; fax 605032; internet www.oman -tv.gov.om; began broadcasting in 1974; programmes broadcast via Arabsat and Nilesat satellite networks.

Finance

(cap. = capital; res = reserves; dep. = deposits; m. = million; brs = branches; amounts in rials Omani unless otherwise stated)

BANKING

In March 2002 there were 15 commercial banks (six local and nine foreign) and three specialized banks, with a total network of 363 domestic branch offices operating throughout Oman. Legislation introduced in January 2001 increased the minimum capital requirement for Omani commercial banks from RO 10m. to RO 20m., and set a minimum capital requirement of RO 3m. for foreign banks established in Oman.

Central Bank

Central Bank of Oman: POB 1161, Ruwi 112; tel. 702222; fax 702253; e-mail cboresb@omantel.net.om; internet www.cbo -oman.org; f. 1974; cap. 250.0m., res 281.9m., dep. 107.1m. (Dec. 2000); a royal decree issued in July 2002 increased the bank's capital to RO 300.0m.; 100% state-owned; Exec. Pres. Hamoud Sangour az-Zadjali; 2 brs.

Commercial Banks

Bank Dhofar al-Omani al-Fransi SAOG: POB 1507, Ruwi 112; tel. 790466; fax 797246; e-mail info@bankdhofar.com; internet www.bankdhofar.com; f. 1990; cap. 32.0m., res 7.7m., dep. 223.6m. (Dec. 2000); Chair. Eng. Abd al-Hafidh Salim Rajab al-Aujaili; Gen. Man. Ahmad bin Ali ash-Shanfari; 21 brs.

BankMuscat SAOG: POB 134, Ruwi 112; tel. 703044; fax 707806; e-mail banking@bkmuscat.com; internet www.bankmuscat.com; f. 1993 by merger as Bank Muscat Al-Ahli Al-Omani; renamed Bank Muscat International in 1998, and as above in 1999; merged with Commercial Bank of Oman Ltd SAOG in 2000 and with Industrial Bank of Oman in 2002; 89.6% owned by Omani shareholders; cap. 45.5m., res 53.0m., dep. 1,084.7m. (Dec. 2000); Chair. Abd al-Malek bin Abdullah al-Khalili; CEO Abd ar-Razak Ali Issa; 95 brs.

Majan International Bank SAOC: POB 2717, Ruwi 112; tel. 780388; fax 780643; e-mail majanbk@omantel.net.om; internet www.majanbank.com; f. 1998—incorporated three branches of

Habib Bank AG Zurich; cap. 29.4m., res. 4.6m., dep. 89.3m. (Dec. 2000); Chair. Sheikh ADIL SAID ASH-SHANFARI; Gen. Man. SALAAM SAID ASH-SHAKSY; 6 brs.

National Bank of Oman SAOG (NBO): POB 751, Ruwi 112; tel. 708894; fax 707781; e-mail info@nbo.co.om; internet www.nbo.co.om; f. 1973; 100% Omani-owned; cap. 45.8m., res 60.1m., dep. 641.3m. (Dec. 2000); Chair. KHALFAN BIN NASSER AL-WOHAIBI; CEO STEPHEN DAVIES (acting); 54 brs.

Oman Arab Bank SAOC: POB 2010, Ruwi 112; tel. 706265; fax 797736; e-mail arabbank@gto.net.om; internet www.omanab.com; f. 1984; purchased Omani European Bank SAOG in 1994; 51% Omani-owned, 49% by Arab Bank PLC (Jordan); cap. 22.0m., res 13.4m., dep. 271.4m. (Dec. 2001); Chair. RASHAD MUHAMMAD AZ-ZUBAIR; CEO ABD AL-QADER ASKALAN; 29 brs.

Oman International Bank SAOG: POB 1727, Muscat 111; tel. 682500; fax 682800; e-mail oibintl@omantel.net.om; internet www.oiboman.com; f. 1984; 100% Omani-owned; cap. 62.9m., res 21.9m., dep. 489.5m. (Dec. 2001); Chair. NOOR BIN MUHAMMAD BIN ABD AR-RAHMAN; Gen. Man. NANI B. JAVERI; 86 brs.

Foreign Banks

Bank of Baroda (India): POB 231, Mutrah 114; tel. 714559; fax 714560; e-mail barbmust@omantel.net.om; internet www.bankofbaroda.com; f. 1976; Gen. Man. G. C. SHARMA; 3 brs.

Bank Melli Iran: POB 2643, Ruwi 112; tel. 7715160; fax 7715183; f. 1974; Gen. Man. ALI JAFFARI LOFTI.

Bank Saderat Iran: POB 1269, Ruwi 112; tel. 7733923; fax 7736478; e-mail bsimct@omantel.net.om; Gen. Man. MAHDI NALAEI.

Banque Banorabe (France): POB 1608, Ruwi 112; tel. 704274; fax 707782; f. 1981; fmrly Banque de l'Orient Arabe et d'Outre Mer; Man. (Oman) PETER S. CARVALHO.

Citibank NA (USA): POB 1994, Mutrah 114; tel. 795705; fax 795724; f. 1975; Vice-Pres. and Country Man. ZULFIQUAR ALI SULAYMAN.

Habib Bank Ltd (incorporated in Pakistan): POB 1326, Ruwi 112; tel. 7717139; fax 7715809; e-mail hbloman1@omantel.net.om; f. 1972; Exec. Vice-Pres. and Country Man. JAVED Z. KARIM; 13 brs.

HSBC Bank Middle East (United Kingdom): POB 234, Muscat 113; tel. 736041; fax 736043; f. 1948; CEO (vacant); 4 brs.

Standard Chartered Bank (UK): POB 2353, Ruwi 112; tel. 703999; fax 796864; internet www.standardchartered.com/om; f. 1968; Man. SAID SALIM AL-MUBARAK KUKOOR; 4 brs.

Development Banks

Alliance Housing Bank: POB 545, Mina al-Fahal 116; tel. 568845; fax 568001; e-mail info@alliance-housing.com; internet www.alliance-housing.com; f. 1997; state-owned; cap. 21.0m., res 3.2m., dep. 5.9m. (June 2002); Chair. AHMAD BIN SUWAIDAN AL-BALUSHI; Gen. Man. LAURIE COWELL; 7 brs.

Oman Development Bank SAOG: POB 309, Muscat 113; tel. 7712507; fax 7713100; e-mail odebe@omantel.net.om; f. 1977; absorbed Oman Bank for Agriculture and Fisheries in 1997; short-, medium- and long-term finance for development projects in industry, agriculture and fishing; state-owned; cap. 20.0m., res 0.4m., dep. 80.1m. (Dec. 2000); Chair. Sheikh YACOUB BIN HAMAD AL-HARTHY; Gen. Man. MURTADHA BIN MUHAMMAD FADHIL; 9 brs.

Oman Housing Bank SAOC: POB 2555, Ruwi 112; tel. 704444; fax 704071; f. 1977; long-term finance for housing development; 100% state-owned; cap. 30.0m., res 24m., dep. 31m. (1999); Chair. DARWISH ISMAIL ALI AL-BULUSHI; Gen. Man. ADNAN HAIDAR DARWISH AZ-ZA'ABI; 9 brs.

STOCK EXCHANGE

Muscat Securities Market: POB 3265, Muscat 112; tel. 7712607; fax 7716353; e-mail info@msm.gov.om; internet www.msm.gov.om; f. 1989; Dir-Gen. (acting) SULAYMAN BIN MUHAMMAD AR-RASHIDY.

Supervisory Body

Capital Markets Authority (CMA): POB 3359, Ruwi 112; tel. 7712722; fax 7716266; f. 2000; to regulate stock exchange; Exec. Pres. YAHYA BIN SAID ABDULLAH AL-JABRI.

INSURANCE

In 2000 there were 17 licensed insurance companies operating in Oman. Of these, seven were local firms and the remainder were branches of non-resident companies.

Al-Ahlia Insurance Co SAO: POB 1463, 112 Ruwi; tel. 709331; fax 797151; e-mail aicinsur@omantel.net.om; f. 1985; cap. 2.5m.; Chair. ADEL ABDULLAH AR-RAISI; Gen. Man. G. V. RAO.

Dhofar Insurance Co SAOG: POB 1002, 112 Ruwi; tel. 705305; fax 793641; Gen. Man. TAHER AL-HERAKI.

Al-Ittihad al-Wattani: POB 2279, 112 Ruwi; tel. 700715; fax 705595; Area Man. GEORGE A. CHIDIAC.

Muscat Insurance Co SAOG: POB 72, 112 Ruwi; tel. 695897; fax 695847; e-mail mic@omzest.com; Gen. Man. MALCOLM A. JACK.

National Life Insurance Co SAOC: POB 798, 117 Wadi Kabir; tel. 567125; fax 567124; e-mail natlife@omantel.net.om; internet www.nlicgulf.com; Gen. Man. ANDREW BENSON.

Oman National Insurance Co SAOG (ONIC): POB 2254, Ruwi; tel. 795020; fax 702569; f. 1978; cap. 2m.; Chair. SALIM BIN HASSAN MACKI; Gen. Man. MICHAEL J. ADAMS.

Oman United Insurance Co SAOG: POB 1522, Ruwi 112; tel. 703990; fax 796327; e-mail ouinsco@omantel.net.om; internet www.ouholding.com; f. 1985; cap. 2m.; Chair. SAID SALIM BIN NASSIR AL-BUSAIDI; Gen. Man. KHALID MANSOUR HAMED.

Trade and Industry

GOVERNMENT AGENCY

Omani Centre for Investment Promotion and Export Development (OCIPED): POB 25, Al-Wadi Kabir 117, Muscat; tel. 7712344; fax 7710890; e-mail info@ociped.com; internet www.ociped.com; f. 1996; promotes investment to Oman and the development of non-oil Omani exports; Dir-Gen. (Investment Promotion) MALAK AHMAD ASH-SHAIBANI; Dir-Gen. (Export Development) MEHDI BIN ALI BIN JUMA.

CHAMBER OF COMMERCE

Oman Chamber of Commerce and Industry: POB 1400, Ruwi 112; tel. 707684; fax 708497; e-mail pubrel@omanchamber.org; internet www.chamberoman.com; f. 1973; Pres. Sheikh ABDULLAH BIN SALIM AR-RAWAS; 100,000 mems (2001).

STATE HYDROCARBONS COMPANIES

National Gas Co SAOG: POB 95, CPO Seeb Airport; tel. 626073; fax 626307; f. 1979; bottling of liquefied petroleum gas; Gen. Man. P. K. BAGCHI; 83 employees.

Oman Gas Co (OGC): Muscat; f. 1999; 80% government-owned, 20% Oman Oil Co; to operate gas network and build pipelines to supply power plants in Salalah and Sohar; Chair. SARHAN SARHANI; Vice-Chair. SALIM BIN MUHAMMAD BIN SHABAAN AL-OJAILY.

Oman LNG LLC: POB 560, 116 Mina al-Fahal; tel. 707807; fax 707656; internet www.oman-lng.com; f. 1992; 51% state-owned; manages 6,600 tons-per-year liquefied natural gas plant at Qalhat; manufacturing, shipping and marketing; Chair. SALIM BIN MUHAMMAD BIN SHABAAN AL-OJAILY; CEO and Gen. Man. Dr AGNUS CASSENS.

Oman Oil Co SAOC (OOC): POB 261, al-Harthy Complex, Ruwi 118; tel. 567392; fax 567386; e-mail oman-oil@oman-oil.com; internet www.oman-oil.com; f. late 1980s; to invest in foreign commercial enterprises and oil trading operations; 100% state-owned; Chair. MAQBOOL BIN ALI BIN SULTAN; CEO DAVID C. DOUGLAS.

Oman Refinery Co LLC: POB 3568, Ruwi 112; tel. 561200; fax 561384; e-mail orc.oman1@omantel.net.om; production of light petroleum products; Man. Dir KAZUTOSHI SHIMMURO; 298 employees.

Petroleum Development Oman LLC (PDO): POB 81, Muscat 113; tel. 678111; fax 677106; internet www.pdo.co.om; incorporated in Sultanate of Oman since 1980 by royal decree as limited liability co; 60% owned by Oman Govt, 34% by Shell; production (2000) averaged 840,000 b/d from 100 fields, linked by a pipeline system to terminal at Mina al-Fahal, near Muscat; production averaged 834,000 b/d in 2001; Man. Dir STEVE OLLEREARNSHAW.

UTILITIES

As part of its privatization programme, the Omani Government is divesting the utilities on a project-by-project basis. Private investors have already been found for several municipal waste water projects, desalination plants and regional electricity providers. Listed below are the state agencies currently responsible for each utility.

Ministry of Housing, Electricity and Water: (see The Government); plans and supervises the development of the utilities in Oman.

Electricity

Oman National Electric Co SAO: POB 1393, 112 Ruwi; tel. 796353; fax 704420; f. 1978; Chair. HAMOUD BIN SONGOR BIN HASHIM; Gen. Man. M. OSMAN BAIG.

Water

Ministry of Water Resources: (see The Government); to assess, manage, develop and conserve water resources.

MAJOR COMPANIES

Construction Materials Industries SAOG: POB 1791, Ruwi 112; tel. 704603; fax 799203; e-mail cmioman@omantel.net.om; f. 1977; cap. RO 3m.; sales RO 1.0m. (1999); cap. RO 3m.; manufacture and supply of calcium silicate bricks, paving and hydrated lime and limestone products; Gen. Man. ADIL MANSOUR AL-JUMA; 120 employees.

Al-Felaij Trading and Contracting: POB 2266, Ruwi; tel. 7714481; fax 7711352; f. 1978; cap. and res RO 8m.; sales RO 6.5m. (1991); manufacture of household and industrial plastic products; Gen. Man. SHAHID BASHIR; 130 employees.

National Detergent Co SAOG: POB 3104, Ruwi; tel. 603824; fax 602145; e-mail ndcoman@omantel.net.om; internet www.ndcoman.com; f. 1980; cap. RO 1.5m., sales RO 9.2m. (2000); manufacture and marketing of detergents; Chair. ABD AL-HUSSAIN BHACKER; Gen. Man. V. SUNDARESAN; 237 employees.

Oman Cement Co SAOG: POB 560, 112 Ruwi; tel. 626626; fax 626414; e-mail omancmnt@omantel.net.om; internet www .omancement.com; f. 1977; cap. RO 33.1m., sales RO 15.5m. (2000); development and production of cement; partial privatization commenced in mid-1994; Chair. SAYYED QAHTAN YARUB AL-BUSAIDI; 362 employees.

Oman Chromite Co SAOG: POB 346, 321 Tareef Sohar; tel. 845115; fax 845155; e-mail omchromc@omantel.net.om; internet www.omchromite.com; f. 1991; cap. and res RO 1.5m., sales RO 0.2m. (1998); production of chromite; Chair. MUHAMMAD HUSSAIN KASSIM; Gen. Man. HUMAID AL-MUSLMANI.

Oman Fisheries Co SAOG: POB 2900, Ruwi 112; tel. 693032; fax 697304; e-mail samak@omantel.net.om; f. 1980 as Oman National Fisheries Co; cap. RO 12.5m., sales RO 6.0m. (2000); responsible for commercial development of fishing, processing and marketing of marine products; operates nine deep-sea trawlers, a processing and freezing plant and an onboard fishmeal plant; Chair. SALIM BIN HILAL AL-KHALILI; Gen. Man. MUHAMMAD ALAWI; 150 employees.

Oman Flour Mills Co SOAG: POB 566, Ruwi 112; tel. 711155; fax 714711; e-mail flour@omantel.net.om; internet www.oman-flourmills.com; f. 1976; cap. RO 15.8m., sales RO 28.8m. (1999); 60% state-owned; produces 800 tons per day (t/d) of various flours and 600 t/d of animal feedstuffs; Chair. RASHID BIN SALIM AL-MASOURY; 184 employees.

Oman Mining Co LLC: POB 758, 113 Muscat; tel. 669420; fax 669411; e-mail ominco@omantel.net.om; f. 1978; cap. RO 25m.; state-owned; development of copper, gold and chromite mines; Chair. MOHSIN HAIDER DARWISH; Gen. Man. M. SEXTON; 860 employees.

Oman Refreshment Co Ltd SAOG: POB 30, Muscat 113; tel. 591455; fax 591389; f. 1974; cap. RO 2.0m., sales RO 19.0m. (1999); bottling and distribution of soft drinks; Chair. ANWAR ALI SULTAN; Gen. Man. SAMI ELIAS KHASHRAM; 465 employees.

Poly Products LLC: POB 2561, Ruwi 112; tel. 626044; fax 626046; e-mail polyprod@omantel.net.om; f. 1979; sales US $20m. (1999); manufacture of flexible and rigid polyurethane foam and spring mattresses, divan and upholstered beds; Man. Dir SAID AL-HINAI; Gen. Man. SAID ANWAR AHSAN; 500 employees.

Raysut Cement Co SAOG: POB 1020, Ruwi; tel. 219122; fax 219291; e-mail raycemco@omantel.net.om; f. 1982; cap. RO 10.0m., gross profits RO 10.7m. (1999); production of cement; Chair. MUHAMMAD BIN ALAWI ALI MUQAIBEL; Man. Dir MUHAMMAD AHMAD ADH-DHEEB; 265 employees.

Shell Oman Marketing Co SAOG: POB 38, Mina al-Fahal 116; tel. 570100; fax 570121; internet www.shelloman.com; f. 1997 by merger of Shell Marketing (Oman) Ltd and Oman Lubricants Co LLC; cap. and res RO 26.0m., sales RO 146m. (2000); supply and marketing of petroleum products; Chair. and Man. Dir NICHOLAS PATTISON; 215 employees.

Yahya Costain LLC: POB 2282, 112 Ruwi; tel. 591366; fax 591981; e-mail yacostgm@omantel.net.om; internet www.yahyacostain.com; f. 1977; civil and building engineering, furniture manufacture and joinery; Chair. YAHYA MUHAMMAD NASIB; Gen. Man. T. J. HOLLOMON; 700 employees.

Transport

ROADS

A network of adequate graded roads links all the main centres of population and only a few mountain villages are inaccessible by off-road vehicles. In 1996 there were an estimated 32,800 km of roads, of which 550 km were motorways, 2,160 km national roads and 3,720 km secondary roads. There were 8,477 km of asphalt roads in 2000. In that year contracts were awarded for the construction of around 700 km of new roads in central Oman.

Directorate-General of Roads: POB 7027, Mutrah; tel. 701577; Dir-Gen. of Roads Sheikh MUHAMMAD BIN HILAL AL-KHALILI.

Oman National Transport Co SAOG: POB 620, Muscat; tel. 590046; fax 590152; operates local, regional and long-distance bus services from Muscat; Chair. TARIQ BIN MUHAMMAD AMIN AL-MANTHERI; Man. Dir SULAYMAN BIN MUHANA AL-ADAWI.

SHIPPING

Port Sultan Qaboos (Mina Sultan Qaboos), at the entrance to the Persian (Arabian) Gulf, was built in 1974 to provide nine deep-water berths varying in length from 250 ft to 750 ft (76 m to 228 m), with draughts of up to 43 ft (13 m), and three berths for shallow-draught vessels drawing 12 ft to 16 ft (3.7 m to 4.9 m) of water. A total of 12 new berths have been opened and two of the existing berths have been upgraded to a container terminal capable of handling 60 containers per hour. The port also has a 3,000-ton-capacity cold store which belongs to the Oman Fisheries Co. In the 1990s Port Sultan Qaboos underwent a further upgrade and expansion. In 1998 1,366 ships visited the port, and in 1994 2.8m. tons of cargo were handled.

The oil terminal at Mina al-Fahal can also accommodate the largest super-tankers on offshore loading buoys. Similar facilities for the import of refined petroleum products exist at Mina al-Fahal. Mina Raysut, near Salalah (now known as Salalah port), has been developed into an all-weather port, and, in addition to container facilities, has four deep-water berths and two shallow berths. In November 1998 the first phase of the Salalah port container terminal opened; phase two was completed in 1999. Salalah port is currently undergoing transformation into a free-trade zone. During 1994 203 ships called at the port. In 2001 the port handled more than 1m. 20-ft equivalent units (TEU). Loading facilities for smaller craft exist at Sohar and Khasab (both of which are being expanded), Khaboura, Sur, Marbet, Ras al-Had, Al-Biaa, Masirah and Salalah.

Directorate General of Ports and Maritime Affairs: POB 684, 113 Ruwi; tel. 700986; fax 702044; e-mail dgpma@omantel.net.om; Dir-Gen. Eng. JAMAL T. AZIZ.

Port Services Corporation SAOG: POB 133, Muscat 113; tel. 714001; fax 714007; e-mail pscco@omantel.net.om; f. 1976; cap. RO 7.2m.; jointly owned by the Govt of Oman and private shareholders; Exec. Pres. SAUD BIN AHMAD AN-NAHARI.

Salalah Port Services Co (SPS): POB 105, 118 Muscat; tel. 567188; fax 567166; e-mail mktg@salalahport.com; internet www.salalahport.com; port authority for Salalah port; CEO and Gen. Man. JACK HELTON.

CIVIL AVIATION

Domestic and international flights operate from Seeb International Airport. In 2000 some 2.7m. passengers passed through the airport; however, it is planned to increase annual passenger capacity to 12.5m. over a 25-year period. Seeb International Airport and Oman's second international airport, at Salalah (completed in 1978). are both earmarked for privatization. There are airports at Sur, Masirah, Khasab and Diba; most other sizeable towns have airstrips.

Directorate-General of Civil Aviation and Meteorology: POB 1, CPO Seeb Airport, 111 Muscat; tel. 519356; fax 519880; e-mail dgen@dgcam.com; internet www.dgcam.com.om; Dir-Gen. Eng. AHMAD BIN SAID BIN SALIM AR-RAWAHY.

Gulf Air: POB 138, Bahrain; tel. 531166; fax 530385; internet www.gulfairco.com; f. 1950 as Gulf Aviation Co; name changed 1974; jointly owned by the Govts of Bahrain, Oman and Abu Dhabi (UAE); international services to destinations in Europe, the USA, Africa, the Middle East, the Far East and Australasia; Chair. Sheikh HAMDAN BIN MUBARAK AN-NEHYAN; Pres. and CEO IBRAHIM ABDULLAH AL-HAMER.

Oman Aviation Services Co SAOG: POB 1058, Seeb International Airport; tel. 519223; fax 510805; internet www.oman-aviation .com; f. 1981; cap. RO 11m.; 35% of shares owned by Govt, 65% by Omani nationals; air-charter, maintenance, handling and catering; operators of Oman's domestic airline (Oman Air); international services to Bangladesh, India, Kuwait, Pakistan, Qatar, Saudi Arabia, Sri Lanka and the UAE; Chair. ADEL BIN ABDULLAH AR-RAIMI; Gen. Man. ROBERT BURKE.

Tourism

Tourism, introduced in 1985, is strictly controlled. Oman's attractions, apart from the capital itself, include Nizwa, ancient capital of the interior, Dhofar and the forts of Nakhl, Rustaq, and Al-Hazm. The country also possesses an attractive and clean environment, including around 1,700 km of sandy beaches. The Government promotes, in a limited capacity, high-quality adventure, cultural and marine tourism. In 2000 there were 571,110 visitor arrivals in Oman, and tourism receipts for that year totalled RO 45.7m.

Directorate-General of Tourism: Ministry of Commerce and Industry, POB 550, Muscat 113; tel. 7716527; fax 7714436; e-mail dtg@mocioman.gov.om; internet www.mocioman.gov.om; Dir-Gen. MUHAMMAD ALI SAID.

Defence

Chief of Staff of the Sultan's Armed Forces: Lt-Gen. KHAMIS BIN SALIM AL-KABANI.

Defence Expenditure (2001 budget): 926m. Omani rials.

Military service: voluntary.

Total armed forces (August 2001): 39,700: army 25,000; navy 4,200; air force 4,100. There is a 6,400-strong Royal Guard.

Paramilitary forces: 4,400: tribal Home Guard (Firqat) 4,000; police coastguard 400.

Education

Great advances have been made in education since 1970, when Sultan Qaboos came to power. Although education is still not compulsory, it is provided free to Omani citizens from primary to tertiary level, and attendance has greatly increased. Primary education begins at six years of age and lasts for six years. The next level of education, divided into two equal stages (preparatory and secondary), lasts for a further six years. In 1998/99 a new system, comprising 10 years of basic education and two years of secondary education, was introduced in 17 schools; it was to be implemented gradually throughout the country. By 2000/01 there were 1,125 schools at the primary, preparatory and secondary levels, as well as a number of private kindergartens and schools regulated by the Ministry of Education; in total, 554,845 students were in state education and 23,850 in private education in that year. As a proportion of the school-age population, the total enrolment at primary, preparatory and secondary schools increased from 25% (boys 36%; girls 14%) in 1975 to 76% (boys 78%; girls 74%) in 1997/98. Primary enrolment in 1997/98 included 76% of children in the relevant age-group (boys 78%; girls 74%), while preparatory and secondary enrolment included 67% of children in the relevant age-group (boys 68%; girls 66%). In 2000/01 there were six teacher-training colleges and four vocational institutes, together with institutes of health sciences and banking, and five technical institutes. There were seven Islamic colleges in 1995/96. Oman's first national university, named after Sultan Qaboos, was opened in late 1986, and had 9,075 students (males 4,722; females 4,353) in 2000/01. According to budget estimates, of total expenditure by the central Government in 2002, RO 331m. (11.5%) was allocated to education.

Bibliography

Aitchison, C. U. (Ed.) *Government of India Foreign Department—Collection of Treaties Relating to India and Neighbouring Countries.* Volume XII. Calcutta, 1932, reprint 1973.

Akehurst, John. *We Won a War: The Campaign in Oman 1965–75.* London, Michael Russell, 1982.

Allen, Calvin H. *Oman: the Modernization of the Sultanate.* London, Croom Helm, 1987.

Allen, Calvin H., and Rigsbee, W. Lynn. *Oman Under Qaboos: From Coup to Constitution, 1970–1996.* London, Frank Cass, 2000.

Arkless, David C. *The Secret War: Dhofar 1971/72.* London, W. Kimber, 1988.

Badger, G. P. *The History of the Imams and Sayyids of Oman, by Salilbin-Razik, from AD 661 to 1856.* Hakluyt Society, 1871, reprint 1967.

Bailey, Ronald (Ed.) *Records of Oman 1867–1960.* Slough, Archive Editions, 1988 (12 vols).

Barrault, M. *Sultanate of Oman.* Paris, M. Hetier, 1994.

Beasant, John. *Oman: The True-life Drama and Intrigue of an Arab State.* Edinburgh, Mainstream, 2002.

Bhacker, M. *Trade and Empire in Muscat and Zanzibar.* London, Routledge, 1992.

Busch, B. C. *Great Britain and the Persian Gulf 1894–1914.* University of California Press, 1967.

Clements, F. A. *Oman: A Bibliography* (2nd edn). Oxford, Clio Press, 1994.

Oman: The Reborn Land. London, Longman, 1980.

Düster, J., and Scholz, F. *Bibliographie über das Sultanat Oman.* All texts in both German and English. Hamburg, Deutsches Orient-Institut, 1980.

Eickelman, Christine. *Women and Community in Oman.* New York University Press, 1984.

Graz, Liesl. *The Omanis: Sentinels of the Gulf.* London, Longman, 1982.

Hawley, Donald. *Oman and its Renaissance* (5th edn). London, Stacey International, 1995.

Hill, Ann, and Hill, Daryl. *The Sultanate of Oman: A Heritage.* London, Longman, 1977.

Joyce, Miriam. *The Sultanate of Oman.* Westport, CT, Praeger Publishers, 1995.

Kechichian, J. *Oman and the World.* Rand, 1997.

Kelly, J. B. *Great Britain and the Persian Gulf, 1793–1880.* London, 1968.

Eastern Arabia Frontiers. London, Faber and Faber, 1964.

Landen, R. G. *Oman Since 1856.* Princeton University Press, 1967.

Lorimer, J. C. *Gazetteer of the Persian Gulf, Oman and Central Arabia.* 2 vols. Calcutta, 1908 and 1915, reprint 1970 in 5 vols, and in 1986 in 9 vols.

Maurizi, Vincenzo. *History of Seyd Said.* Cambridge, Oleander Press, 1984.

Miles, S. B. *The Countries and Tribes of the Persian Gulf.* 3rd edition, London, Frank Cass, 1966.

Morris, James (now Jan). *Sultan in Oman.* London, Faber, 1957.

Newcombe, Ozzie. *The Heritage of Oman.* Reading, Garnet, 1995.

Oman Studies Bibliographic Info. Oman Studies Centre, Pforzheim, Germany.

Owtram, Francis. *A Modern History of Oman: Formation of the State Since 1920.* London, I. B. Tauris, 2001.

Peterson, J. E. *Oman in the Twentieth Century.* London, Croom Helm, 1978.

Phillips, Wendell. *Unknown Oman.* London, Longman, 1966, reprint 1971.

Oman. A History. London, Longman, 1967, reprint 1971.

Pridham, Brian R. (Ed.). *Oman: Economic, Social and Strategic Developments.* London, Croom Helm, 1987.

Rawas, Isam ar-. *Oman in Early Islamic History.* Reading, Ithaca Press, 2000.

Riphenburg, Carol J. *Oman.* Westport, CT, Praeger Publishers, 1998.

Risso, Patricia. *Oman and Muscat: An Early Modern History.* London, Croom Helm, 1986.

Saleh, N. A. *The General Principles of Saudi Arabian and Omani Company Laws.* London, Namara Publications, 1981.

Shannon, M. O. *Oman and Southeastern Arabia: A Bibliographic Survey.* Boston, Hall, 1978.

Sirhan, Sirhan ibn Said ibn. *Annals of Oman.* Cambridge, Oleander Press, 1985.

Skeet, Ian. *Oman: Politics and Development.* London, Macmillan, 1992.

Oman before 1970: The End of an Era. London, Faber, 1985.

Solh, Raghid el- (Ed.) *Oman and the South-Eastern Shore of Arabia.* Reading, Ithaca Press, 1997.

Thesiger, Wilfred. *Arabian Sands.* London, Longman, 1959.

Townsend, John. *Oman: The Making of the Modern State.* London, Croom Helm, 1977.

Vine, Peter. *The Heritage of Oman.* London, Immel, 1995.

Ward, Philip. *Travels in Oman: on the Track of the Early Explorers.* Cambridge, Oleander Press, 1986.

Wikan, U. *Behind the Veil in Arabia: Women in Oman.* London, Johns Hopkins Press, 1982.

Wilkinson, John C. *Water and Tribal Settlement in South-East Arabia.* Oxford University Press, 1977.

The Imamate Tradition of Oman. Cambridge University Press, 1987.

Yousuf, Muhammad bin Musa al-. *Oil and the Transformation of Oman 1970–1995.* London, Stacey International, 1995.

PALESTINIAN AUTONOMOUS AREAS

Physical and Social Geography

The Palestinian Autonomous Areas are located in the West Bank and the Gaza Strip. A currently undetermined part of these areas form the territory in which an independent State of Palestine may be declared. The West Bank lies in western Asia, to the west of the Jordan river and the Dead Sea. To the north and south is the State of Israel, to the west the State of Israel and the Gaza Strip. The Israeli-Palestinian Interim Agreement on the West Bank and the Gaza Strip of September 1995 (see below and Documents on Palestine, p. 80) provides for the creation of a corridor, or safe passage, linking the Gaza Strip with the West Bank. A 'southern' safe passage between Hebron and Gaza was opened in October 1999 (although it has been closed since October 2000). Including East Jerusalem, the West Bank covers an area of 5,655 sq km (2,183 sq miles). The West Bank can be divided into three major sub-regions: the Mount Hebron massif, the peaks of which rise to between 700 m and 1,000 m above sea-level; the Jerusalem mountains, which extend to the northernmost point of the Hebron-Bethlehem massif; and the Mount Samaria hills, the central section of which—the Nablus mountains—reaches heights of up to 800 m before descending to the northern Jenin hills, of between 300 m and 400 m. The eastern border of the West Bank is bounded by the valley of the Jordan river, leading to the Dead Sea (part of the Syrian–African rift valley), into which the Jordan drains. The latter is 400 m below sea-level. Precipitation ranges between 600 mm and 800 mm on the massif and averages 200 mm in the Jordan valley; 36% of the area is classified as cultivable land, 32% grazing land, 27% desert or rocky ground and 5% natural forest. Apart from the urban centres of Bethlehem (Beit Lahm) and Hebron (Al-Khalil) to the south, the majority of the Palestinian population is concentrated in the northern localities around Ramallah (Ram Allah), Nablus (Nabulus), Jenin (Janin) and Tulkarm. In November 1988 the Palestine National Council proclaimed Jerusalem as the capital of a newly-declared independent State of Palestine. In fact, West Jerusalem has been the capital of the State of Israel since 1950. In 1967 East Jerusalem was formally annexed by the Israeli authorities, although the annexation has never been recognized by the UN (see Occupied Territories, p. 581). Under the terms of the Declaration of Principles on Palestinian Self-Rule, concluded by Israel and the Palestinians in September 1993 (see Documents on Palestine, p. 72), negotiations on the 'final status' of the city were scheduled to begin not later than the beginning of the third year of the five-year transitional period following the completion of Israel's withdrawal from the Gaza Strip and the Jericho (Ariha) area. However, despite the signing of the Wye Memorandum (see Documents on Palestine, p 86) in October 1998 (see below), 'final status' negotiations did not commence until November 1999, and are currently stalled. The future of Jerusalem is probably the most bitterly contentious of all the issues subject to 'final status' talks, and, in the opinion of some observers, may elude agreement by negotiation.

The Gaza Strip, lying beside the Mediterranean Sea and Israel's border with Egypt, covers an area of 365 sq km (141 sq miles). Crossed only by two shallow valleys, the Gaza Strip is otherwise almost entirely flat, and has no surface water. Annual average rainfall is 300 mm. Gaza City is the main population centre and the centre of administration for the Palestinian (National) Authority (PA). Ramallah is the PA's administrative centre in the West Bank.

The language of the Palestinians in the West Bank and the Gaza Strip is Arabic. The majority of the Palestinian population are Muslims, with a Christian minority representing about 2% of the Palestinian population of the territories. This minority, in turn, represents about 45% of all Palestinian Christians.

Recent History

Revised for this edition by NUR MASALHA

Until the end of the 1948 Arab–Israeli War, the West Bank formed part of the British Mandate of Palestine, before becoming part of the Hashemite Kingdom of Jordan under the Armistice Agreement of 1949. It remained under Jordanian sovereignty, despite Israeli occupation in 1967, until King Hussein of Jordan formally relinquished legal and administrative control on 31 July 1988. Under Israeli military occupation, the West Bank was administered by a military government, which divided the territory into seven sub-districts. The Civil Administration (as it later became known) did not extend its jurisdiction to the many Jewish settlements that were established under the Israeli occupation; these remained subject to the Israeli legal and administrative system. The Interim Agreement of September 1995 (see below) divided the West Bank into three zones: Areas A, B and C. By October 2000 approximately 17.2% of the West Bank (Area A) was under sole Palestinian jurisdiction and security control, but Israel retained authority over movement into and out of the zone; about 23.8% of the West Bank (Area B) was under Israeli military control, with responsibility for civil administration and public order transferred to the Palestinian authorities; the remaining 59% of the territory (Area C) was under Israeli military occupation.

An administrative province under the British Mandate of Palestine, Gaza was transferred to Egypt after the 1949 armistice and remained under Egyptian administration until June 1967, when it was invaded and occupied by Israel. Following Israeli occupation, the Gaza Strip, like the West Bank, became an 'administered territory'. Until the provisions of the Declaration of Principles on Palestinian Self-Rule (signed in 1993) began to take effect, the management of day-to-day affairs was the responsibility of the area's Israeli military commander. Neither Israeli laws nor governmental and public bodies—including the Supreme Court—could review or alter the orders of the military command to any great extent. In 2001 an estimated 42% of the Gaza Strip was under Israeli control, including Jewish settlements, military bases, bypass roads and a 'buffer zone' along the border with Israel.

TOWARDS AN INDEPENDENT PALESTINE

In accordance with the Declaration of Principles on Palestinian Self-Rule of 13 September 1993 (see Documents on Palestine, p. 72), and the Cairo Agreement on the Gaza Strip and Jericho of 4 May 1994 (ibid., p. 76), the Palestine Liberation Organization (PLO) assumed control of the Jericho area of the West Bank, and of the Gaza Strip on 17 May 1994. In November and December 1995, under the terms of the Israeli-Palestinian Interim Agreement on the West Bank and the Gaza Strip (the third 'Oslo accord'—a term referring to the role played by Norwegian diplomacy in their negotiation) signed by Israel and the PLO on 28 September 1995 (see Documents on Palestine, p. 80), Israeli armed forces withdrew from the West Bank towns of Nablus, Ramallah, Jenin, Tulkarm, Qalqilya and Bethlehem. In late December the PLO assumed responsibility in some 17 areas of civil administration in the town of Hebron. Under the terms of the Oslo accords, the PLO was eventually to assume full responsibility for civil affairs in the 400 surrounding villages, but the Israeli armed forces were to retain freedom of movement to act against potential hostilities there. In Hebron Israel effected a partial withdrawal of its troops in January 1997, but retained responsibility for the security of some 400 Jewish settlers occupying about 15% of the town. Responsibility for security in the rest of Hebron passed to the Palestinian police force, but Israel retained responsibility for security on access roads. Under the terms of the Oslo accords, Israel was to retain control over a large area of the West Bank (including Jewish settlements, rural areas, military installations and the majority of junctions between Palestinian roads and those used by Israeli troops and settlers until July 1997. Following the first phase of the redeployment and the holding, on its completion, of elections to a Palestinian Legislative Council (PLC) and for a Palestinian executive president, Israel was to effect a second redeployment from rural areas, to be completed in that month. The Israeli occupation was to be maintained in Jewish settlements, military installations, East Jerusalem and the Jewish settlements around Jerusalem until the conclusion of 'final status' negotiations between Israel and the Palestinians, scheduled for May 1999.

Subsequent postponements, and further negotiations within the context of the Oslo peace process, resulted in a new timetable for Israeli redeployment which envisaged two phases, subsequent to the Hebron withdrawal, to be completed by October 1997 and August 1998. 'Final status' discussions on borders, the Jerusalem issue, Jewish settlements and Palestinian refugees were to commence within two months of the signing of the agreement on Hebron. As guarantor of the agreements, the USA undertook to obtain the release of some Palestinian prisoners, and to ensure that Israel continued to engage in negotiations for the establishment of a Palestinian airport in the Gaza Strip and for safe passage for Palestinians between the West Bank and Gaza. The USA also undertook to ensure that the Palestinian (National) Authority (PA—appointed in May 1994) would continue to combat terrorism, complete the revision of the Palestinian National Charter (or PLO Covenant), adopted in 1964 and amended in 1968 (see Documents on Palestine, p. 69), and consider Israeli requests to extradite Palestinians suspected of involvement in attacks perpetrated on Israeli territory. By July 1998, however, conflicting interpretations of the extent of both the phased and total final redeployment (90% of the West Bank, according to the Palestinians; less than 50%, according to the Israelis) had resulted in a seemingly intractable impasse in the Oslo peace process. Those within the wider Palestinian movement who had never accepted the peace process argued that an essential weakness of the Oslo accords had made such a situation inevitable: while they, and subsequent revisions, detailed timetables for the withdrawals of Israeli armed forces, the accords did not stipulate the precise area of the territory over which the PA should thereby assume control. The implementation of the Oslo accords was further complicated by the election, in May 1996, of Binyamin Netanyahu as Israeli Prime Minister. Netanyahu formed a new coalition Government, in which his party, Likud, was the dominant force. Likud had never sought to conceal its opposition to the Oslo accords negotiated by the previous Labour Government.

By July 1998 progress on the redeployment of Israeli armed forces had been impeded for some 15 months. This paralysis emerged from the decision of the Israeli Government, announced in February 1997, to begin the construction of a new Jewish settlement on Jabal Abu Ghunaim (Har Homa in Hebrew), near Beit Sahur. Construction in this area was particularly controversial because, if completed, the new settlement would make it impossible to reach East Jerusalem from the West Bank without crossing Israeli territory, thereby prejudicing 'final status' negotiations concerning Jerusalem. In response, the Palestinians withdrew from 'final status' talks which had been scheduled to commence on 17 March. The beginning of construction work at Jabal Abu Ghunaim on the following day provoked rioting among the Palestinian population and a resumption of attacks by the military wing of the Islamic Resistance Movement (Hamas) on Israeli civilian targets. The Israeli Cabinet responded by ordering a general closure of the Palestinian areas.

Both the Jabal Abu Ghunaim (Har Homa) construction and Israel's unilateral decision to redeploy its armed forces from only 9% of West Bank territory (announced in March 1997) were regarded by many observers as a vitiation of both the Oslo and the subsequent post-Hebron agreements. These were further undermined by the publication, in the Israeli daily newspaper *Ha'aretz*, of the results of a US study which claimed that more than 25% of Jewish settlers' homes in the Gaza Strip and the West Bank were uninhabited (a claim rejected by the Israeli Central Bureau of Statistics, which argued that only 12% of the settlements were unoccupied). The same newspaper later reported that Netanyahu's original plan, evolved within the framework of the Oslo accords, eventually to relinquish 90% of the West Bank, had been revised in a new proposal—the so-called 'Allon plus' plan—to a 40% redeployment.

In June 1997 the US House of Representatives voted in favour of recognizing Jerusalem as the undivided capital of Israel and of transferring the US embassy to the city from Tel-Aviv. US President Bill Clinton was reported to have strongly disapproved of the vote, owing to its possible implications for the peace process. The decision coincided with violent clashes between Palestinian civilians and Israeli troops in Gaza and Hebron. At the beginning of July a series of meetings took place between the US Under-Secretary of State for Political Affairs, Thomas Pickering, and Israeli and Palestinian officials, with the aim of resuming negotiations between the PA and the Israeli Government. On 28 July both sides announced that peace talks were to be resumed in early August. However, on 30 July, on the eve of a scheduled visit by Dennis Ross, the US Special Co-ordinator to the Middle East, to reactivate the discussions, Hamas carried out a 'suicide bomb' attack at a Jewish market in Jerusalem, in which 14 civilians were killed and more than 150 injured. Ross cancelled his visit and the Israeli Government immediately halted payment of tax revenues to the PA and closed the Gaza Strip and the West Bank. These sanctions provoked furious protest from the Palestinians, and widespread international condemnation. In the aftermath of the suicide bombing, the PA commenced a campaign to detain members of Hamas and another militant group, Islamic Jihad. In late August, however, President Yasser Arafat convened a Palestinian national dialogue conference in Gaza, in response to the Israelis' imposition of sanctions. On this occasion, representatives of Hamas, who had boycotted a similar conference held in the previous year, agreed to participate, on the condition that the Palestinian authorities would address the issue of the Hamas members whom they were holding in detention. During the conference Arafat publicly embraced Hamas leaders and urged them, and representatives of Islamic Jihad, to unite with the Palestinian people against Israeli policies. On 26 August Hamas rejected a request from Palestinian leaders to suspend their attacks on Israeli targets.

At the beginning of September 1997, in anticipation of a visit to the Middle East by the US Secretary of State, Madeleine Albright, the Israeli authorities relaxed the closure they had imposed on the West Bank and Gaza on 30 July. On 4 September, however, a further suicide bomb attack in Jerusalem, in which eight people died (including the bombers themselves), led to the reimposition of Israeli sanctions. Hamas claimed responsibility for the attack, and the Israeli Prime Minister immediately renewed his demand that the PA should take effective action against the 'terrorist infrastructure', referring to Arafat's willingness to embrace Hamas leaders in August. The visit to the region by the US Secretary of State in mid-September failed to reactivate the peace process. During her visit, Albright reportedly stated that Israel should halt the construction of Jewish settlements on Arab lands, cease confiscations of land and the demolition of Arab dwellings, and end its policy of confiscating Palestinian identity documents. At the same time, she endorsed Netanyahu's demand that the Palestinian leadership should take more effective measures to suppress the military wing of Hamas. (In late September the Israeli authorities claimed to have traced the origin of four of the five Hamas members responsible for the recent bomb attack in Jerusalem to the West Bank village of Azira Shamaliya.) Impatience within the US Administration at the Israeli Government's apparent provocation was demonstrated by Albright's criticism of Netanyahu's decision, announced in late September 1997, to permit the construction of 300 new homes for Jewish settlers at Efrat in the West Bank.

On 28 September 1997 it was announced that, as a result of US diplomacy, Israeli and Palestinian officials had agreed to recommence negotiations in early October. The first round of talks, scheduled to begin on 6 October, would reportedly focus on the outstanding issues of the Oslo accords, in particular the opening of an airport and seaport facilities in the Gaza Strip, the establishment of a safe corridor linking Gaza with the West Bank, and the release of Palestinian prisoners from Israeli detention. A second round of talks was to commence on 13 October, at which the participants were to address the issues of security co-operation between the Palestinian and the Israeli authorities; the long-delayed redeployment of Israeli armed forces from the West Bank; Israeli expansion and construction of settlements; and questions pertaining to 'final status' negotiations.

In late September 1997 there were reports that the PA had closed some 16 institutions—mainly providers of social welfare services—with links to Hamas, and arrested 'scores' of its officials since the recent suicide bombing in Jerusalem. Hamas officials who remained at liberty, however, insisted that the organization's campaign against Israeli civilian targets would continue. In particular, the attempted assassination in the Jordanian capital, Amman, in late September of Khalid Meshaal, the head of the Hamas political bureau in Jordan, provoked warnings of retaliation both before and after official confirmation that agents of the Israeli security service, Mossad, had been responsible for the attack. In order to secure the release of its agents by the Jordanian authorities, Israel was obliged, on 1 October, to free (together with other Arab political prisoners) Sheikh Ahmad Yassin, the founder and spiritual leader of Hamas, who had been sentenced to life imprisonment in Israel in 1989 for complicity in attacks on Israeli soldiers. As had been widely predicted, Israel's release of Sheikh Yassin into Jordanian custody was swiftly followed by his return, on 6 October 1997, to Gaza, where his presence further complicated co-operation between the Israeli and Palestinian authorities on security issues. The return of Sheikh Yassin to Gaza, where he received an enthusiastic welcome from the local population, also prompted speculation concerning the possible benefits which the Palestinian leadership might derive from increased political co-operation with Hamas. However, it appeared in late October that Yassin, while prepared to promote Palestinian unity, would not approve the acceptance of even the original terms of the Oslo accords.

On 7 October 1997 talks resumed between Palestinian and Israeli negotiators on the outstanding issues of the Oslo accords, and on the following day the Palestinian President and the Israeli Prime Minister held their first meeting for eight months at the Erez check-point between Israel and the Gaza Strip. In mid-November, however, the talks remained deadlocked. In early December, following further US pressure, the Israeli Cabinet reportedly agreed in principle to withdraw troops from an unspecified area of West Bank territory. Some two weeks later, however, it remained uncertain whether Netanyahu would be able to persuade intransigent elements within his Government to endorse this decision. In early January 1998 the US Special Middle East Co-ordinator, Dennis Ross, visited Israel in a further attempt to break the deadlock regarding the redeployment of Israeli armed forces from the West Bank. However, in the second week of January the Israeli Government declared that it would not conduct such a redeployment until the PA had fulfilled a series of conditions. Among these were requirements that the Palestinian leadership should make a 'systematic and effective' effort to counter terrorism; that it should reduce the strength of its security forces from 40,000 to 24,000; and that the Palestinian National Charter should be revised to recognize explicitly Israel's right to exist. Palestinian officials maintained that these conditions had already been met when the agreement regarding the withdrawal of Israeli forces from Hebron was concluded one year earlier. There was further evidence of a hardening of the Israeli position prior to a summit meeting, scheduled to take place in Washington, DC, in the third week of January. The Israeli Cabinet issued a communiqué detailing 'vital and national interests' in the West Bank which it was not prepared to relinquish. The document asserted that Israel would, among other areas, retain control of the territory surrounding the Jerusalem region. In total, areas listed as 'vital and national interests' to Israel amounted to some 60% of all West Bank territory.

On 20 January 1998 President Clinton held discussions with the Israeli Prime Minister in Washington, DC. It was reported that the USA was seeking to persuade Israel to effect a second withdrawal of its armed forces from some 12% of the West Bank over a period of 80 days, in exchange for increased co-operation on security issues by the PA. On 25 January, however, Mahmud Abbas, the Secretary-General of the PLO Executive Committee, reported that direct contacts between the Palestinian delegation and the Israeli premier had collapsed. President Arafat was said to be seeking to convene an Arab summit meeting to discuss the deadlocked Middle East peace process.

In early March 1998 Israeli armed forces were reported to have seized a consignment of weapons that was being smuggled from Jordan across the Dead Sea, prompting speculation that the PA had begun to store arms in preparation for armed conflict with Israel in the event of an irrevocable collapse of the peace process. On 11 March widespread rioting erupted among Palestinians in the West Bank, following the shooting, by Israeli soldiers, of three Palestinian workers at a military check-point, apparently as the result of a misunderstanding.

In late March 1998 it emerged that the USA planned to present new proposals regarding the withdrawal of Israeli armed forces at separate meetings between the US Secretary of State and Arafat and Netanyahu in Europe. On 26 March Dennis Ross arrived in Jerusalem in order to present details of the latest US initiative. Although no details had been published, it appeared that the US proposals would involve an Israeli withdrawal from slightly more than 13% of West Bank territory, and a suspension of settlement construction in return for further efforts by the PA to combat Palestinian organizations engaged in campaigns of violence against Israeli targets. President Arafat sought an Israeli withdrawal from a further 30% of the West Bank, but there were indications that he might be prepared to accept an initial withdrawal from some 13% of the territory. However, it was evident that, even if a bilateral agreement could be reached, the issue of whether a subsequent withdrawal should take place prior to the commencement of 'final status' negotiations remained far more contentious. In any case, the Israeli Cabinet rejected the reported details of the new US initiative. At the end of March US Secretary of State Albright stated that the peace process was on the verge of collapse, and indicated that the USA was considering ending its involvement as a mediator.

It emerged in late April 1998 that the European Union (EU) was seeking to play a greater role in the stalled Middle East peace process. On 20 April it was reported that, during a visit to Gaza City, the British Prime Minister, Tony Blair, had obtained the agreement of President Arafat to attend a conference in London, based on the most recent US peace proposals. A summit meeting, hosted by Blair and attended by Netanyahu, Arafat and the US Secretary of State, took place in early May. At its conclusion Albright invited Netanyahu and Arafat to attend a summit meeting with US President Clinton in Washington, DC, on 12 May. The USA had reportedly proposed that the parties could proceed to 'final status' negotiations as soon as the scope of the next Israeli withdrawal from the West Bank had been agreed. However, the Israeli Government subsequently rejected the US initiative in advance of Clinton's direct participation.

In early June 1998 the details of the latest US initiative were unofficially disclosed in the Israeli press. Israel would have to agree to 'no significant expansion' of Jewish settlements and relinquish slightly more than 13% of West Bank territory over a period of 12 weeks, in exchange for increased Palestinian co-operation. The adoption by the Israeli Cabinet, in late June, of a plan to extend the boundaries of Jerusalem and construct homes there for a further 1m. people prompted incredulity at the US Department of State, and accusations by PA officials that the proposal amounted to a *de facto* annexation of territories that were officially subject to 'final status' talks. It was later reported that the Israeli Government was considering holding a popular referendum on a further withdrawal of Israeli troops from the West Bank.

On 7 July 1998 the United Nations General Assembly, in defiance of objections from the USA and Israel, approved a resolution, by a vote of 124–4, to upgrade the status of the PLO at the UN. The new provision allows the PLO to participate in debates, to co-sponsor resolutions, and to raise points of order during discussions on Middle Eastern affairs.

On 19–22 July 1998 Israeli and Palestinian delegations held direct negotiations for the first time since March 1997. They discussed the most recent US initiative to reactivate the peace process, which had been disclosed in June 1998, but the proposal was deemed unacceptable by the Israelis. In late August Netanyahu was reported to have presented a compromise plan to his Cabinet, whereby Israel would effect a full redeployment from a further 10% of the West Bank and a partial withdrawal from 3% of the Judaean desert. Arafat cautiously welcomed the plan on the following day. In late September Netanyahu and Arafat met for the first time since October 1997, at the White House in Washington, DC, and agreed to participate in a peace conference in the USA in the following month. The summit meeting, also attended by US President Bill Clinton, began at the Wye Plantation, Maryland, on 15 October 1998 (see the chapter on Israel), and culminated in the signing, on 23 October, of the Wye Memorandum (see Documents on Palestine, p. 86), which was intended to facilitate the implementation of the Interim Agreement of September 1995.

Under the terms of the Wye Memorandum, which was to be implemented within three months of its signing, Israel was to transfer a further 13.1% of West Bank territory from exclusive Israeli control (Area C) to joint Israeli-Palestinian control (Area B). An additional 14% of the West Bank was to be transferred from joint Israeli-Palestinian control to exclusive Palestinian control (Area A). The Wye Memorandum also stipulated that negotiations with regard to a third Israeli redeployment (under the terms of the Oslo accords) should proceed concurrently with 'final status' talks; that the PA should reinforce anti-terrorism measures under the supervision of the US Central Intelligence Agency (CIA); that the strength of the Palestinian police force should be reduced by 25%; that the Palestinian authorities should arrest 30 suspected terrorists (a detailed list was attached to the text); that Israel should carry out the phased release of 750 Palestinian prisoners (including political detainees); that the Palestine National Council (PNC) should annul those clauses of the PLO Covenant deemed to be anti-Israeli; that Gaza International Airport should become operational, with an Israeli security presence; and that an access corridor linking the West Bank to the Gaza Strip should be opened.

The Memorandum was endorsed by the Israeli Cabinet on 11 November 1998, and was approved by the Knesset on 17 November. Three days later Israel redeployed its armed forces from about 500 sq km of the West Bank. Of this area, some 400 sq km came under exclusive Palestinian control for both civil and security affairs. In the remaining 100 sq km the PA assumed responsibility for civil affairs, while Israel retained control over security. At the same time, Israel released some 250 Palestinian prisoners (although a majority were non-political detainees) and signed a protocol for the opening of Gaza International Airport. Israel retained the right to decide which airlines could use the airport, which was officially inaugurated by President Arafat on 24 November. However, implementation of the Wye Memorandum did not proceed smoothly, with mutual accusations of failure to observe its terms.

In the weeks prior to a visit to Israel and the Gaza Strip by the US President on 12–15 December 1998, violent clashes erupted in the West Bank between Palestinians and Israeli security forces. One cause of the unrest was a decision by the Israeli Cabinet to suspend further releases of Palestinian prisoners under the terms of the Wye Memorandum, and its insistence that Palestinians convicted of killing Israelis, together with members of Hamas and Islamic Jihad, would not be freed. On 14 December, meanwhile, in the presence of President Clinton, the PNC voted to annul articles of the Palestinian National Charter deemed to be anti-Israeli. While the Israeli Prime Minister welcomed the vote, he insisted that several further conditions had to be met before Israel would further implement its commitments under the Wye Memorandum. At a summit meeting between the US President, Netanyahu and Arafat at the Erez check-point on 15 December, Netanyahu

reiterated Israel's stance regarding the release of Palestinian prisoners. He further demanded that the Palestinians should cease incitement to violence and formally relinquish plans unilaterally to declare Palestinian statehood on 4 May 1999, the original deadline as established by the Oslo accords. At the conclusion of the meeting Netanyahu announced that Israel would not proceed with the second scheduled redeployment of its armed forces (under the Wye agreement) on 18 December 1998, claiming once again that the Palestinians had failed to honour their commitments. On 20 December the Israeli Cabinet voted to suspend implementation of the Wye Memorandum.

In early January 1999 President Arafat was still assessing his options concerning a declaration of Palestinian independence. There were indications that remonstrances from the Israeli Government and intense international pressure had prompted the Palestinian leader to consider a postponement of any unilateral declaration of statehood. In particular, the USA, EU states, Egypt and Jordan had requested that Arafat delay any declaration, at least until after the Israeli elections, scheduled for 17 May. In late January 1999 Arafat indicated that he might postpone a declaration of Palestinian statehood if he received certain assurances from Israel and the international community, notably the USA and EU, particularly with regard to the question of settlement expansion. During a tour of several European countries, Arafat was counselled by EU governments that a declaration of statehood could well result in another victory in the Israeli elections for Netanyahu and those parties which rejected the Oslo peace process outright. In mid-March Arafat embarked on an intensive international mission of diplomacy which continued into April and included the Gulf states, other parts of Asia, Europe and North America. On 23 March he met privately with President Clinton in Washington, DC. During the meeting the US President reportedly promised to press Israel for 'final status' negotiations to be commenced soon after the May elections. Meanwhile, at a summit meeting in Berlin, Germany, on 26 March, EU leaders issued their firmest commitment to date to support the creation of an independent Palestinian state. The 'Berlin Declaration' called on Israel to conclude 'final status' talks with the Palestinians within one year, and insisted that 'the creation of a democratic, viable, peaceful sovereign Palestinian state on the basis of the existing agreements and through negotiations would be the best guarantee of Israel's security and Israel's acceptance as an equal partner in the region'.

As the deadline for a final decision regarding the 4 May 1999 declaration approached, it became increasingly apparent that Arafat would be forced to capitulate under the weight of both international and domestic opinion. In late April PLO chief negotiators Mahmud Abbas and Saeb Erakat (the Minister of Local Government) visited Washington, DC, in order to secure certain assurances from the USA in return for an extension of the Oslo deadline. On 27 April the Palestinian Central Council (PCC), together with Hamas representatives, met in Gaza for final discussions. On 29 April the Council announced a postponement of any declaration on statehood until after the Israeli elections. The announcement was welcomed by Israel, the USA, and EU and Arab states; however, Palestinians in the Occupied Territories held violent protests against the decision.

Palestinians extended a cautious welcome to Ehud Barak's victory over Netanyahu in the Israeli premiership elections of 17 May 1999 (see the chapter on Israel). PA officials immediately urged Barak to break the deadlock in the Middle East peace process. However, in his victory address, the new Israeli Prime Minister insisted that he would not offer the Palestinians any fundamental concessions, prompting the Palestinian leadership to revise its expectations of immediate progress. After the elections there was a Palestinian consensus that a halt to Israel's programme of settlement expansion in the Occupied Territories (which Palestinians maintain is part of an attempt to predetermine the 'final status' borders) must be a precondition for any meaningful resumption of the peace process. On 3 June Palestinians in the West Bank declared a 'day of rage' against continuing settlement expansion there; the mass demonstrations, which were particularly violent in Hebron, followed an announcement in late May that the population of the West Bank's largest Jewish settlement, Ma'aleh Edomin, was to be expanded from 25,000 to 50,000 settlers.

The first direct meeting between Prime Minister Barak and President Arafat was held at the Erez check-point on 11 July 1999. Although both leaders repeated their commitment to restarting the peace process, Arafat was said to have been alarmed by Barak's apparent opposition to full implementation of the Wye Memorandum, his evasiveness on the issue of settlements and his seeming preoccupation with the Syrian track of the peace process (see below). During the second meeting between the Israeli and Palestinian leaders on 27 July at Erez, Barak angered Palestinians by seeking to win Arafat's approval to postpone implementation of the Wye agreement until it could be combined with 'final status' negotiations (thereby implying a 15-month delay in further redeployments of Israeli armed forces). On 1 August Barak promised to bring forward the release of 250 Palestinian prisoners if Arafat agreed to a postponement. On the same day, however, talks between the Israeli and PA delegations broke down after Arafat rejected the Israeli position. Discussions were resumed in mid-August, when Israel agreed to pursue implementation of the Wye Memorandum, and on 4 September Barak and Arafat signed the Sharm esh-Sheikh Memorandum (or Wye Two accords—see Documents on Palestine, p. 88), in the presence of US Secretary of State Albright and President Mubarak of Egypt. Under the terms of the Memorandum (which outlined a revised timetable for implementation of the outstanding provisions of the Wye agreement), on 9 September Israel released some 200 Palestinian 'security' prisoners; on the following day Israel effected the transfer of a further 7% of the West Bank to PA control.

'FINAL STATUS' NEGOTIATIONS WITH ISRAEL

A ceremonial opening of 'final status' talks between Israel and the PA took place at the Erez check-point on 13 September 1999; shortly afterwards details emerged of a secret meeting between the Israeli and Palestinian leaders to discuss an agenda for such talks. However, on 8 October the Palestinians' chief negotiator and Minister of Culture and Information, Yasser Abd ar-Rabbuh, warned that the PA would boycott 'final status' talks unless Israel ended its programme of settlement expansion. In mid-October Barak, also under pressure from left-wing groups in Israel, responded by dismantling 12 'settlement outposts' in the West Bank which he deemed to be illegal (see the chapter on Israel). Meanwhile, on 15 October Israel released a further 151 Palestinian prisoners, under the terms of Wye Two. The inauguration of the first 'safe passage' between the West Bank and Gaza Strip took place on 25 October. The opening had been delayed by almost a month owing to a dispute between Israel and the PA over security arrangements for the 44-km route, which linked the Erez check-point in Gaza to Hebron in the West Bank. Israel asserted that it would maintain almost complete control over the so-called 'southern' route and over which Palestinians would be permitted to use it. Meanwhile, the killing of a Palestinian street vendor by an Israeli soldier resulted in several days of violence between Palestinians and Israeli security forces in the West Bank town of Bethlehem.

'Final status' negotiations between Israel and the PA commenced in Ramallah on 8 November 1999, following a summit meeting held on 2 November in Oslo, Norway, between Arafat, Barak and US President Clinton. On the day before the talks opened, three bombs had exploded in northern Israel. (Israel claimed that Hamas was responsible, since the attack followed an alleged warning by the organization's military wing that it would intensify its activities in protest at Israel's settlement policies.) A further redeployment of Israeli troops from 5% of the West Bank, scheduled for 15 November, was postponed owing to disagreement over the areas to be transferred (see the chapter on Israel). Relations between the two sides worsened when on 6 December PA negotiators walked out of 'final status' talks after demanding that Israel should end immediately its policy of settlement expansion. The announcement came amid reports that settlement activity had intensified under Barak's premiership. On the following day the Israeli Prime Minister, apparently in response to US pressure, announced a halt to settlement construction while the negotiations regarding a Framework Agreement on Permanent Staus (or FAPS) were proceeding. However, the PA continued to demand the complete cessation of Jewish settlement building. On 21 December Arafat held talks in Ramallah with Barak—the first Israeli premier to

hold peace discussions in Palestinian territory. At the end of the month Israel released some 26 Palestinian 'security' prisoners as a gesture of 'goodwill'.

On 6–7 January 2000 Israeli armed forces withdrew from a further 5% of the West Bank, under the terms of Wye Two; 2% of the land was transferred from partial Palestinian control (Area B) to complete Palestinian control (Area A), while 3% shifted from Israeli control (Area C) to Area B. However, Israel announced on 16 January that a third redeployment from 6.1% of the territory (scheduled to take place on 20 January) would be postponed by three weeks until Barak had returned from peace talks with Syria in the USA. The delay was apparently due to disagreements over Arab villages on the outskirts of Jerusalem. During a meeting with Arafat in Tel-Aviv on 17 January, Barak was reported to have proposed that the deadline for reaching a FAPS be postponed for two months. Meanwhile, the explosion of a bomb in northern Israel appeared to be a further attempt by Palestinian militants to disrupt the peace process.

The approval by the Israeli Cabinet of a withdrawal of its troops from a sparsely-populated area of the West Bank led Palestinian negotiators to break off the discussions in early February 2000. On 3 February peace talks held between Arafat and Barak at Erez broke down acrimoniously, after Arafat had reportedly been angered by an Israeli map showing the proposed redeployment from a further 6.1% of the West Bank. The map included none of the Arab villages situated near East Jerusalem (as Arafat had anticipated), but instead showed various pockets of land in the north and south of the territory. On 6 February the PA announced that it was suspending peace talks with Israel. Two visits to the region by US Special Middle East Co-ordinator Dennis Ross later in that month failed to break the deadlock, and both sides acknowledged that the 13 February deadline to reach a framework agreement would elapse. On 8 February the PLO issued a document listing issues previously agreed by Israel which it claimed had not been implemented. On 2 March four members of Hamas' military wing were killed in the Israeli Arab town of Tayibbah by Israeli security forces, who claimed that the men were plotting suicide bombings inside Israel. Addressing the PLC on 7 March, Yasser Arafat's assertion that '2000 is the year of the Palestinian state…it is the year of holy Jerusalem as our capital' led to renewed fears that he intended to declare statehood even in the absence of a peace accord with Israel. On 19–20 March Israel released another 15 Palestinian 'security' prisoners. 'Final status' talks resumed between Israel and the PA on 21 March, and on the same day the redeployment of Israeli troops from a further 6.1% of the West Bank was carried out, including villages near Ramallah, Hebron, Jericho and Jenin.

Meanwhile, in early February 2000 the summary of a report on the methods of interrogation used by the Israeli security service, Shin Bet, during the Palestinian *intifada* (1987–92) was published for the first time. The report acknowledged that Palestinian detainees (and especially those in the Gaza Strip) had been 'systematically tortured' by members of Shin Bet.

On 15 February 2000 an 'historic' agreement was signed between the Vatican and the PLO, with the intention of strengthening relations between the Roman Catholic Church and a future Palestinian state. The Vatican reiterated its view that Jerusalem should be granted a special international status so that the rights of Christians, Jews and Muslims (especially the right of access to their holy sites) were protected. It also implicitly criticized Israel for its 'judaization' of Arab East Jerusalem, its settlement expansion in and around the city, and its gradual expulsion of the city's Palestinian inhabitants. Israeli officials reacted angrily to the signing of the accord. On 21 March Pope John Paul II arrived from Jordan at the beginning of an extended five-day visit to Israel and the Palestinian self-rule areas. The Pope's visit, which the Vatican insisted was purely spiritual in nature, was accorded unprecedented importance by Palestinian and Israeli leaders. The pontiff paid a symbolic visit to Dheisheh refugee camp, south of Bethlehem. Speaking at the camp, which houses some 10,000 Palestinian refugees expelled from their homes in 1948, Pope John Paul II expressed his support for justice for the refugees and indicated that they had a 'natural right to a homeland'. Riots between Palestinian youths and the police followed the speech, as Palestinians vented their frustrations with the authorities. The Pope was handed a petition prepared by Palestinian intellectuals and civic leaders, calling on him to help end the 'Israeli siege of Jerusalem'. Some Muslim leaders privately voiced concern at the visit, claiming that it was to boost the stature and influence of Christianity at the expense of Islam.

In late February 2000 the French Prime Minister, Lionel Jospin, made what became a highly controversial visit to the Palestinian territories. At a press conference in Jerusalem on 24 February Jospin had cited Hezbollah's resistance in southern Lebanon (q.v.) as an example of 'terrorist attacks'. Despite advice to the contrary, two days later the French premier gave a lecture at Birzeit University in the West Bank, during which he refused to retract his remarks concerning Hezbollah. After leaving the campus Jospin was pelted with stones and assailed with abuse from angry Palestinians. The incident developed into a major confrontation between the PA and Palestinian civil society. Arafat apologized profusely to Jospin, the PA's foreign guest and crucial European ally, and likened the stone-throwers to the 'forces of darkness'. The Palestinian President also unleashed his police and security services against the last independent university in the West Bank and Gaza. Over the next week some 120 students were rounded up and detained without charge; several were allegedly tortured, according to human rights groups. Furthermore, on 29 February the PA chief of police, Ghazi al-Jabali, decreed that henceforth marches, rallies and public meetings would require prior approval from the police, a ruling that violated the PA's own laws on public assembly.

Following further discussions between Ehud Barak and Bill Clinton in Washington, DC, on 11 April 2000, it was announced that the Israeli premier had agreed to PA demands for a greater US presence in future Israeli-Palestinian negotiations. At a meeting of the Israeli Cabinet in mid-April Barak was said to have hinted for the first time at the creation of a Palestinian entity on territory recently transferred to PA control, covering 60%–70% of the West Bank; however, Barak placed a number of conditions on the formation of such an entity, which he refused to describe as a 'state'. On 21 April Yasser Arafat held talks with President Clinton in Washington, during which Arafat reportedly asked the USA to intervene in order to prevent the continued expansion of Jewish settlements in the West Bank.

The third round of 'final status' negotiations opened at the Israeli port of Eilat on 30 April 2000. Palestinian negotiators immediately complained of the recent Israeli plan to construct 174 new housing units in the Jewish settlement of Ma'aleh Edomin. Following a tour of the Gulf states by the Palestinian President, on 7 May Barak and Arafat held a crisis meeting in Ramallah, in the presence of Dennis Ross, to discuss 'sticking and interim phase issues'. The talks were unsuccessful, however, and led to a further suspension of the peace process. Barak had reportedly proposed the transfer to full PA control of three Palestinian villages (Abu Dis, al-Azariyya and as-Sawahra) bordering Jerusalem, on condition that the third West Bank redeployment be postponed (see the chapter on Israel). The Palestinians, meanwhile, agreed that the new 13 May deadline for reaching a FAPS would not be met.

On 15 May 2000 the Palestinian chief negotiator, Yasser Abd ar-Rabbuh, resigned his post after discovering that a second round of 'secret' informal talks between the PA and Israel had been proceeding in Stockholm, Sweden, without his knowledge. The establishment of an alternative negotiating channel appeared to reflect Israel's dissatisfaction with the progress being made through the official process. The Stockholm talks, which began in early May, were led by Ahmad Quray, Speaker of the PLC for the Palestinian side, and Shlomo Ben-Ami, the Israeli Minister for Public Security, on behalf of Israel. According to Palestinian sources, the talks had been arranged by Arafat and Barak at their summit meeting in early May. Although Abd ar-Rabbuh insisted that his resignation was final, Arafat rejected it (as he had refused other resignations of discontented PA officials), reportedly stating that he had complete confidence in Abd ar-Rabbuh to lead the Palestinian delegation in the 'permanent status' talks.

On 21 May 2000 Barak ordered the suspension of the Stockholm talks, following the worst outbreak of violence to occur in the West Bank and Gaza Strip since the rioting provoked by the Israeli decision to reopen the Hasmonean tunnel in 1996. On 1 May 2000 as many as 1,000 of the 1,650 Palestinian prisoners held in Israeli gaols began a hunger strike. A few days later mass demonstrations were initiated by Palestinians throughout the self-rule areas in support of the prisoners. By 15 May, a date declared by Palestinians to be a 'day of rage' (marking *an-Nakba* or 'the catastrophe'—the anniversary of the foundation of the State of Israel in 1948), the protests had escalated into extreme violence. By the time the clashes between stone-throwing Palestinians and the Israeli security forces subsided on 18 May, seven Palestinians (including two policeman) were reported to have been killed and about 1,000 injured; some 60 Israelis were also wounded. On 21 May an Israeli child was badly hurt in a petrol bomb attack outside Jericho, which convinced Barak to suspend peace negotiations. The Palestinian prisoners ended their hunger strike at the end of May.

For some time there had been signs that the 'hard core' of the PA leadership, including Arafat and his close aides (Mahmud Abbas, Ahmad Quray, Nabil Amr and Muhammad Dahlan), would be willing to strike a deal with Israel that compromised the PA's official position. There was a deep sense of anxiety among Palestinians that their unaccountable leadership—which had agreed to go to Stockholm secretly without consulting even the PA's own Cabinet—would eventually make far-reaching concessions to Israel, compromising fundamental rights and aspirations in exchange for a nominal Palestinian state without any real substance. This concern was apparently what prompted Yasser Abd ar-Rabbuh to resign and, along with the explosion of Palestinian anger in the streets of the West Bank and Gaza in May 2000, reflected growing popular Palestinian hostility to the direction in which 'final status' negotiations were moving. Israeli draft maps of a future Palestinian state were intersected with Jewish settlements and Israeli roads, and there was no sign of a peace plan for Jerusalem or of a solution to the problem of Palestinian refugees. However, this was not the only manifestation of PA internal dissent at the 'final status' talks with Israel. Marwan Barghouthi, Fatah's leader in the West Bank, warned Arafat, without naming him, against 'deviating from our red lines'. Other Palestinian officials spoke out with unprecedented openness against Arafat's autocracy, including the way in which he was handling the 'final status' talks. The PA responded with more arrests (see Internal Affairs, below) and Yasser Arafat stepped up his campaign against critics of his administration, especially regarding the ongoing negotiations with Israel.

In late May 2000 Palestinians throughout the Occupied Territories reacted enthusiastically to Hezbollah's victory in hastening an Israeli withdrawal from southern Lebanon. At the popular level many people drew a comparison between the Lebanese victory and the Palestinians' rather different situation. In contrast, Arafat sought to play down Hezbollah's achievement, apparently to secure favour with the Israeli Government: the Palestinian President maintained in an interview with an Israeli television station that Israel's withdrawal from Lebanon had not been precipitated by Hezbollah resistance but rather by Barak's desire to implement UN Security Council Resolution 425 (see the chapter on Israel).

THE CAMP DAVID SUMMIT

US Secretary of State Madeleine Albright began a tour of Israel and the Palestinian areas in early June 2000, in an attempt to reinvigorate the peace talks. The US Government was evidently seeking to increase its diplomatic efforts in preparation for hosting a summit meeting between Barak and Arafat prior to the expiry of President Clinton's term of office in the autumn. However, even after discussions between Clinton and Arafat on 15 June in Washington, DC, and a further visit by Albright to the region in late June, little progress was reported. On 19 June Israel released three Palestinian prisoners as a 'goodwill' gesture; however, PA officials, who had expected a larger group of detainees to be freed, suspended participation in interim phase negotiations. On 21 June it was reported that the PA had agreed to a delay in the latest Israeli withdrawal from the West Bank, scheduled to take place two days later. Amid an intensification of diplomatic activity by both sides during early July, Arafat held discussions in Paris with President Jacques

Chirac of France (the current holder of the EU presidency) in an attempt to obtain EU support for his declaration of an independent Palestinian state. On 2 July the Palestinian Central Council convened and, after two days of talks, announced that the PLO would unilaterally declare statehood on or before 13 September, with Jerusalem as its capital.

On 11 July 2000 peace talks between Ehud Barak and Yasser Arafat were inaugurated by President Clinton at Camp David, Maryland, USA, in a renewed attempt to reach a FAPS. An official news black-out was imposed, and thus few details emerged about the discussions. However, on 13 July it was reported that Barak and Arafat had held their first talks in private. Arafat reportedly threatened to walk out of the negotiations in protest at US bridging proposals (which he deemed to be too close to the official Israeli position), but agreed to stay on at Camp David when Clinton withdrew the proposals. On 19 July the Israeli delegation was apparently on the verge of leaving the summit, owing to deadlock between the two sides regarding the future status of Jerusalem and the issue of Palestinian refugees. The following day, however, the summit was saved from the brink of collapse and both sets of negotiators agreed to remain at Camp David. Nevertheless, despite round-the-clock diplomatic efforts, the talks failed to break the deadlock regarding future arrangements for Jerusalem. The Camp David summit ended, without agreement, on 25 July. Progress had reportedly been reached between Israel and the PA regarding several issues (see the chapter on Israel), but the future status of Jerusalem had proved to be the main obstacle to the signing of an accord. The PA refused to accept anything less than full Palestinian sovereignty over the city's Islamic holy sites (notably the Dome of the Rock and the al-Aqsa Mosque), with East Jerusalem as the capital of a Palestinian state. Despite the failure of the summit, both sides, under the guidance of President Clinton, pledged to continue their diplomatic efforts and promised not to pursue 'unilateral actions' (apparently referring to Arafat's threat to declare Palestinian statehood). On 26 July both Israeli and Palestinian leaders returned to the Middle East. Having first visited Alexandria, Egypt, to brief President Mubarak on the outcome of the talks, Arafat returned to the West Bank and Gaza and was hailed by Palestinians as the 'hero of Jerusalem' for his refusal to grant concessions to Israel over the future of the city.

In the aftermath of the Camp David summit, during late July and August 2000 Yasser Arafat undertook a tour of several European, Arab and Asian states, in order to explain what had occurred during the talks with Israel and to discuss his anticipated declaration of Palestinian statehood. At the end of July the Palestinian leadership was angered by statements issued by President Clinton in which the US leader hinted at moving the US embassy from Tel-Aviv to Jerusalem. Amid growing international pressure, it emerged in August that the Palestinian leader had agreed, in principle, to a postponement of his statehood declaration. (The PCC announced on 10 September that it would postpone indefinitely such a declaration, although 15 November was reportedly designated as the target date.) Meanwhile, during August and September Israeli and PA negotiators continued to meet in the hope of achieving a breakthrough regarding the third redeployment of Israeli armed forces from the West Bank, as well as further prisoner releases. On 26 September Arafat and Barak held their first direct discussions since the Camp David summit. However, tensions between the two communities remained high, especially in Jerusalem, where several clashes were reported between Palestinians and the Israeli security forces. In August about 23 Palestinians had reportedly been arrested by Israeli security forces, on charges of involvement in militant Islamist 'terrorist squads'.

RELATIONS WITH OTHER ARAB STATES

After Ehud Barak's electoral victory in May 1999, one of Arafat's principal concerns was the Israeli concentration of efforts on the Lebanese and, especially, Syrian tracks of the Middle East peace process. Any shift of focus away from Israeli-Palestinian talks, with the possibility of a breakthrough in negotiations between Israel and Syria, was likely to leave the Palestinian leadership in an acutely vulnerable and isolated position. In mid-June Arafat was reported to have accused both the Jordanian and Syrian leaders of having turned their backs on the

PA. In early August a political crisis developed after the Syrian Deputy Prime Minister and Minister of Defence, Maj.-Gen. Mustafa Tlass, allegedly made highly insulting remarks about Yasser Arafat—including a claim that Arafat had 'sold Jerusalem and the Arab nation' in peace deals concluded with Israel since 1993—leading to Palestinian demands for Tlass's resignation, and the issuing, by Fatah, of a death warrant against him. Following the resumption of the Israeli-Syrian track of the peace process in December 1999, US and Israeli officials sought to reassure Arafat that negotiations on the Palestinian track would not be sidelined. When President Hafiz al-Assad of Syria died on 10 June 2000, Arafat declared three days of mourning in the Palestinian self-rule areas for the man who had once accused him of making the 'peace of cowards' with Israel. One critical reaction to the death of Assad was voiced by the PA negotiator in charge of interim talks, Saeb Erakat, who stated on 11 June that it would be difficult for President Assad's successor to be flexible in future peace talks with Israel because of Assad's uncompromising legacy. On 13 June Arafat attended the funeral of President Assad in Damascus, despite his poor relations with the Syrian regime.

Palestinians reacted to the death of King Hussein of Jordan on 7 February 1999 with great sorrow. (Of the Kingdom's more than 4m. inhabitants, around 65% are believed to be of Palestinian origin.) Three days of mourning were declared in the Palestinian territories, while Arafat travelled to Amman to pay his last respects to the man he once called a 'Zionist agent' but later praised as 'the wise man of the Arabs'. Public grief was particularly apparent in the West Bank, which King Hussein had ruled for 15 years until June 1967. For Arafat, the death of Hussein was a political disaster; the King had frequently supported Arafat in times of crisis, especially when the peace process with Israel appeared to be on the verge of collapse. Hamas leaders also paid tribute to King Hussein, recalling his efforts in Septermber 1997 to free Sheikh Ahmad Yassin from an Israeli gaol after the assassination attempt on Khalid Meshaal (see above). Only days after Hussein's death, Arafat surprised many Jordanians by proposing the establishment of a Palestinian-Jordanian confederation. The proposal (which had been put forward as part of a peace initiative in 1985, but was subsequently rejected by Hussein) was not welcomed in Jordan, where it was considered to be somewhat premature while the West Bank was still largely occupied by Israel.

INTERNAL AFFAIRS

Elections to a Palestinian Legislative Council (PLC) took place on 20 January 1996. Some 79% of the estimated 1m. eligible Palestinian voters were reported to have participated in the elections, returning 88 deputies to the 89-seat Council. (One seat was automatically reserved for the president of the PLC's executive body—the Palestinian President.) The election of a Palestinian Executive President was held at the same time as the elections to the Council. Yasser Arafat, who was opposed by one other candidate, Samiha Khalil, received 88.1% of the votes cast and took office as President on 12 February 1996. Deputies returned to the PLC automatically became members of the PNC, the existing 483 members of which were subsequently permitted to return from exile by the Israeli authorities. The PLC held its first session in Gaza City on 7 March, electing Ahmad Quray as its Speaker.

On 22–24 April 1996 the PNC held its 21st session in Gaza City. At the meeting the PNC voted to amend the Palestinian National Charter by annulling all of the Charter's clauses that sought the destruction of the State of Israel. The PNC also voted to amend all clauses contained within the Charter that were not in harmony with an agreement of mutual recognition concluded by Israel and the PLO in September 1993. On the final day of its meeting the PNC elected a new Executive Committee. In May 1996 it was reported that President Arafat had appointed the members of a Palestinian Cabinet. The appointments were approved by the PLC in July.

In late April 1997 President Arafat's audit office reported the misappropriation by PA ministers of some US $326m. of public funds. Khalid al-Qidram, the General Prosecutor of the PA, who promptly resigned in response to the findings, was reportedly placed under house arrest in early June. At the end of July a parliamentary committee, appointed by Arafat to conduct an inquiry into the affair, concluded that the Cabinet should be dissolved and that some of its members should be prosecuted. In early August the Cabinet submitted its resignation, but this was not accepted by Arafat until December. However, the Cabinet was to remain in office in a provisional capacity until new ministerial appointments were made in early 1998. There was further disruption to the Cabinet in March and April 1998, following the deaths of two ministers. Arafat's long-awaited new Cabinet was announced on 5 August and was promptly denounced by all sides. Only one prominent minister had been removed from the Cabinet, many others assuming alternative responsibilities or becoming ministers of state without portfolios. (The size of the Cabinet was increased significantly by the appointment of a number of PLC members to minister-of-state status.) Despite the immediate resignations of the newly-appointed Ministers of Higher Education (Hanan Ashrawi) and Agriculture (Abd al-Jawad Saleh), on 10 August the new Cabinet was approved by 55 votes to 28 in the PLC. Although the Cabinet was criticized by officials of the principal international organizations granting funds to the PA, in November donors agreed to grant the PA more than $3,000m., to be disbursed over the next five years.

In addition to persistent allegations of corruption within the PA, President Arafat himself has been accused of autocracy by some within the Palestinian leadership. In October 1997 Haider Abd ash-Shafi, who had played a prominent role in the peace negotiations with Israel and who was reportedly held in high popular esteem, resigned in protest at the style of Arafat's leadership and at the way in which peace talks were being conducted. There were reports in mid-November that potential successors to Arafat had initiated political manoeuvres amid enduring rumours that the President was in poor health. Among those cited as possible successors were Jibril Rajoub, the head of the Palestinian preventive security services in the West Bank, and Muhammad Dahlan, his counterpart in the Gaza Strip. It has frequently been claimed that the Palestinian security forces resort to intimidation and torture in their treatment of Palestinian detainees. Such allegations were contained in a report published by the US-based Human Rights Watch in mid-1998. In February, in its annual report, the Palestinian Independent Commission for Citizens' Rights accused security personnel of the mistreatment of prisoners in Palestinian gaols.

In March 1998 the PLC threatened to organize a vote of 'no confidence' in President Arafat's leadership, in protest at alleged corruption within the PA, the long delay in approval of the 1998 budget and the failure to hold local government elections. There was speculation that the PA had postponed these elections for fear that they would reveal widespread dissatisfaction over the lack of progress in the peace process with Israel. The PLC renewed its threat in mid-1998 in an ultimatum to the Palestinian President and the Cabinet, demanding that they respond to allegations of corruption and mismanagement and approve the budget proposals within two weeks. In September the PA chief negotiator at the peace talks and Minister of Local Government, Saeb Erakat, and the PA Minister of State for the Environment, Yousuf Abu Saffieh, were both persuaded by Arafat to withdraw their resignations, tendered in protest at inefficiency and incompetence within the PA.

President Arafat took firm action in February 1998 to suppress popular demonstrations in support of Iraq, which had exposed itself to threats of military action by the USA in the dispute over UN-conducted weapons inspections (see the chapter on Iraq). It was reported that several members of Arafat's own political movement, Fatah, had been arrested for disregarding a ban on such demonstrations, and that the publication and broadcasting of reports in support of Iraqi President Saddam Hussain had been forbidden.

In March 1998 US officials reportedly confirmed that the US CIA was assisting the Palestinian security forces in the spheres of espionage, information-gathering and interrogation, in an attempt to reassure the Israeli Government of their ability to take effective action against groups involved in attacks on Israeli targets. Later in the month the death, in mysterious circumstances, of Muhi ad-Din Sharif, the second-highest ranking member of the military wing of Hamas, the Izz ad-Din Qassim Brigades, prompted accusations by Hamas of PA collusion with Israeli security forces in his murder, and fears

that a new wave of retributive bomb attacks would be unleashed against Israeli targets. However, a succession of conflicting accusations and confessions surrounding Sharif's murder (including a number which alleged that it was the result of an internal dispute among the organization's leadership) appeared to defuse the immediate tensions in the region. In April Hamas' political leader in Jordan retracted the allegation that the PA had collaborated with Israel. In the same month it was reported that Hamas had become the dominant political force in Palestinian universities, where the organization claimed to command the allegiance of some 40% of students.

In August 1998 the Palestinian Ministry of the Interior dissolved the Palestinian Ahd Party, the Palestinian Labour Party, the Ahrar Party and the Popular Forces party, claiming that, as small individual entities which were unsuccessful in the previous legislative elections, the groups were not financially viable. According to a spokesman at the Ministry of the Interior, it was planned to merge small parties with similar ideologies, in order to increase activity.

Shortly after the signing of the Wye Memorandum, on 24 October 1998 the PA detained 11 journalists for attempting to obtain an interview with the spiritual leader of Hamas, Sheikh Ahmad Yassin (who was placed under house arrest on 29 October). On the same day the Palestinian authorities also arrested the outspoken al-Asqa cleric Sheikh Hamid Bitawi and Islamic Jihad's chief spokesman for publicly criticizing the Wye agreement. In the weeks following the agreement there was a steady erosion of press freedom in the West Bank and Gaza: several radio and television stations as well as press offices were closed down by the PA, and journalists and cameramen were imprisoned for crimes ranging from 'endangering the national interest' to reporting 'illegal' demonstrations. There was also a marked increase in self-censorship in the pro-government printed and electronic media and at the PA-controlled radio and television stations.

The PA's human rights record remained a major concern for Palestinians during 1999. In January the PLC approved a motion urging an end to political detention and the release of all those imprisoned on exclusively political charges. (The motion demanded the formation of a special committee to assess the case of every political prisoner in the Palestinian territories and submit recommendations as to which prisoners should be released; this committee was duly appointed on 15 February, and was to be headed by the Minister of Justice.) The PA responded to the PLC's immediate demands by releasing 37 political prisoners (36 Islamists and one member of the Popular Front for the Liberation of Palestine—PFLP). However, on 24 January scores of detainees linked to Hamas and Islamic Jihad began a hunger strike in Jericho and Nablus, in protest at their continued detention without trial by the Palestinian authorities. During early and mid-February thousands of Palestinians—mostly Hamas supporters—demonstrated in support of the detainees. On 6 February some 3,000 protesters marched to the PA headquarters, chanting slogans criticizing the PA's alleged 'subservience to Israel and the CIA'. (Under the terms of the Wye Memorandum, the CIA was to monitor the PA's compliance with the security provisions as part of a trilateral 'watchdog' committee involving the PA and Israel; the committee was to verify the extent to which the PA was engaged in the arrest and trial of suspected terrorists, the collection of illegal weapons and the prevention of 'incitement to violence'.)

Also in February 1999 Ghazi al-Jabali, a Gaza-based chief of police known to be an outspoken opponent of Hamas, alleged that the organization had received some US $35m. from Iran in order to carry out suicide bomb attacks against Israeli targets in order to undermine the prospects of Israeli moderates and assist Netanyahu's May 1999 election campaign (see the chapter on Israel). However, both Iran and Hamas leaders vehemently denied the allegations. Relations between the PA and Hamas were further strained following the murder of a Palestinian intelligence officer in Rafah on 1 February. On 10 March a security agent and former member of Hamas' military wing was sentenced to death for the attack, while two accomplices received lengthy prison sentences. The verdict provoked serious clashes between Palestinian police and protesters in the Gaza Strip, during which two teenagers were shot dead by police; Arafat was forced to curtail an official visit to Jordan in order to address the domestic security crisis.

Throughout May 1999 lawyers and jurists in the West Bank and Gaza organized a series of strikes and protests against the alleged 'virtual collapse of the Palestinian judicial system'. The protests followed an appeal made to Yasser Arafat by the head of the Palestinian Bar Association, Abd ar-Rahim Abu an-Nasser, to resolve the problem of continuing lawlessness in Palestinian society, to increase the number of lawyers in the territories and improve their legal training, and to appoint a new General Prosecutor of the PA (the post having been vacant for many months). On 19 June Zuheir as-Surani was appointed General Prosecutor.

Security surrounding Yasser Arafat was intensified in early June 1999, after a group of Palestinian dissidents calling themselves 'the Free Officers and the Honest People of Palestine' released a statement in which they accused leading Palestinian officials of corruption and of collaboration with Israel, and indirectly threatened to assassinate the President. Nine arrests were made by the security forces following the statement.

There was considerable criticism by Palestinian opposition groups of the Sharm esh-Sheikh Memorandum signed with Israel on 4 September 1999 (see above). Seven nationalist opposition groups denounced the PA for making more 'gratuitous concessions'. Palestinians in East Jerusalem observed a general strike in protest at the agreement, while dozens staged a sit-in at Orient House to denounce concessions by the PA on the release of political prisoners. At the same time, however, the PA continued to encourage meetings among opposition groups to agree on a unified Palestinian position on 'final status' issues. On 1 August a Palestinian national dialogue had been held in Cairo, Egypt, and included officials of Fatah and the PFLP. At the end of August representatives of nine Palestinian political factions agreed on an agenda for a comprehensive national dialogue. Three meetings were held in the West Bank town of Ramallah to discuss the convening of such a dialogue. The first, hosted by the PLO Executive Committee on 31 August, was attended by the Arab Liberation Front (ALF), the Democratic Front for the Liberation of Palestine (DFLP), Fatah, the Palestinian Democratic Union (FIDA) and the PFLP. Hamas and Islamic Jihad both declined an invitation to attend; in late August the PA had arrested several suspected activists of these two organizations. The second meeting, on 14 September, was held among FIDA, the Palestinian People's Party (PPP) and the Palestinian Popular Struggle Front (PPSF). The third, on 12 October, was attended by all seven of the political organizations, as well as Hamas and the Palestine Liberation Front (PLF). The Damascus-based opposition groups held a similar meeting in late September.

In talks in Cairo on 22–23 August 1999, Yasser Arafat and the DFLP Secretary-General, Naif Hawatmeh, agreed to set aside their differences over the Oslo peace process and to co-ordinate their positions on the 'final status' issues; it was their first meeting since 1993. The head of the PLO Political Department, Faruq Qaddumi, conducted further discussions with DFLP officials in Damascus on 2 November 1999. Meanwhile, it was reported in early September that the leader of the PFLP, George Habash, had decided to resign. (Habash resigned the party leadership on 27 April 2000 and on 8 July his deputy, Abu Ali Moustafa, was elected as his successor.) On 28 September 1999 representatives of Fatah and the PFLP met in Amman. Although the two parties failed to reach an agreement on the PFLP's participation in 'final status' talks, they issued a joint statement calling on all PLO factions to take part in an upcoming Central Council session to discuss organizational matters. Qaddumi continued discussions with PFLP leaders in Damascus on 2 November. At Arafat's request, on 16 September Israel agreed to allow the PFLP Deputy Secretary-General, Abu Ali Moustafa, to return to PA-controlled areas after more than 30 years in exile, in order to participate in reconciliation talks; Abu Ali Moustafa returned to the West Bank on 30 September. However, although the Israeli Government had also reportedly granted an entry permit to Naif Hawatmeh of the DFLP on 25 October, Hawatmeh's right of return was rescinded on 29 October, after he stated in an interview that armed struggle was legitimate as long as Jewish settlements remained in the Occupied Territories. (Earlier in the month the US Government

had removed the DFLP from its official list of terrorist organizations.) On 12 October the Israeli Supreme Court ruled that PLF head Muhammad 'Abu' Abbas was immune from trial in Israel for the 1985 *Achille Lauro* hijacking (see the chapter on Israel).

The Palestinian leadership continued to delay the PCC meeting that had been originally scheduled to take place in June 1999, after Barak's election victory in Israel. On 20 September the PA Minister of Planning and International Co-operation, Nabil Shaath, stated that the PCC's constitution committee was still working on a preliminary draft, which would contain alternative versions of articles addressing points still open to debate (for example, according to Shaath, whether the future Palestinian state would have a parliamentary or presidential system and whether the legislature, executive and judiciary would be combined or separate.) Once the draft was complete, it was to be submitted to the Palestinian leadership for review and possibly to Palestinian voters in a referendum. Revisions would then be made and a new draft submitted to legal experts for comment. On 10 October the Chief Justice of the High Court, Radwan al-Agha, abruptly ordered a number of PA judges to be transferred from their positions to posts in the West Bank, leading judges there to go on strike in protest at the decision. Meanwhile, the Chairman of the Palestinian Public Control Commission was granted ministerial status, under the terms of a presidential decree.

On 12 October 1999 the PA High Court ordered the Palestinian authorities to release immediately 34 Palestinian political detainees held in Nablus prison. By mid-November the PA had not complied. During this period the PA faced an unusual amount of popular criticism. On 17 November the Palestinian Bar Association staged a sit-in to protest against the passage of legislation requiring a lawyer to have a notarized power of attorney before representing a client. Later in the month taxi drivers held a strike in protest against tax increases, while on 22 November Palestinians staged a sit-in at the PLC in response to increased fuel prices. Others refused to pay their telephone bills after tariffs were lowered in Israel but not in the Palestinian territories. On 25–26 November there was a peaceful strike in Gaza City over price increases on basic goods, such as flour, that are controlled by PA monopolies. The strikes ended on 26 November when Arafat ordered certain price reductions and price 'caps' and opened an investigation into the telephone charges.

Such protests prompted the Chairman of the PLC, Azmi Shuaybi, on 26 November 1999 to criticize publicly the PA's lack of fiscal monitoring and accountability. Shuaybi claimed that the Administration was afraid of instituting a monitoring process because it 'would reveal the extent of public funds that are going missing'. He noted that the US $126m. that the Minister of Finance, Muhammad Zohdi an-Nashashibi, claimed to have transferred to various ministries could not be accounted for. Shuaybi added that a number of PA-run companies that received several million dollars in public funding did not report their profits to the PLC's budget committee, claiming to be private companies, yet at the same time did not pay taxes, claiming to be government enterprises. His report was followed on 27 November by a petition signed by 20 leading Palestinian academics, professionals and members of the PLC that not only accused the PA of corruption, mismanagement and abuse of power, but also implicated Arafat personally. (The petition also accused Palestinian officials of ineffectiveness in the peace talks with Israel.) The authorities responded by launching an immediate crack-down on Arafat's critics. Between 28 and 30 November PA security services arrested, interrogated or placed under house arrest 11 of the document's signatories; the other nine (all Fatah officials) were immune from prosecution because of their status as members of the PLC. At an emergency session, convened on 1 December by Arafat in Nablus, PLC members voted (by 33 votes to eight, with three abstentions and 37 absent in protest) to condemn their nine colleagues for seeking to divide the Palestinian people, but did not act on Arafat's reported wish to deprive them of their immunity. Outside the meeting thousands of Arafat supporters marched in solidarity with the PA. Returning from the session, one of the nine PLC members who had signed the anti-corruption manifesto, Mouawiyyah al-Masri, was shot and wounded by unidentified gunmen. The attack appeared to be an attempt to silence criticism of Arafat's administration, although al-Masri vowed to pursue his campaign against institutional corruption. Another PLC member was detained by the General Intelligence Service and severely beaten for participating in a sit-in supporting the signatories. Between 19 December and 6 January 2000 Arafat released the 11 detainees on bail. The PA's draconian reaction to the anti-corruption petition prompted international condemnation: statements in solidarity with the anti-corruption campaigners were signed by hundreds of Palestinians world-wide, and demonstrations were organized, including a rally of 5,000 protesters in Ramallah on 4 December. The DFLP, Hamas, Islamic Jihad and the PFLP also held a 'solidarity' meeting in Gaza on 29 November to condemn the PA response, at which they urged the Government to uphold freedom of expression.

On 10 January 2000 the PA established a Higher Council for Development, to be chaired by Arafat. The Council's role would be to ensure the transparency of the public finance system: it would handle the general revenue administration, reporting all revenue collected into a single treasury account; oversee management of all commercial and investment operations of the PA; develop a privatization strategy; oversee handing of internal and external debt policy and repayment of loans. The IMF and foreign donors praised the Council as a major step towards ending corruption and mismanagement. In mid-January Arafat ratified the Non-Governmental Organization (NGO) law, delineating the relationship beween the PA and the Palestinian NGOs; these broadly welcomed the law, despite its requirement that they register with the Ministry of the Interior rather than the Ministry of Justice. On 3 February the Legislative Council sent to Arafat for signature a draft law on the independence of the judiciary.

On 2–3 February 2000 the Central Council finally convened in Gaza with 96 of the 126 members attending. Participants represented the ALF, the DFLP, Fatah, FIDA, the PPP, the PPSF, the Islamic Salvation Party and the National Salvation Party. The PFLP presented its positions prior to the meeting but did not participate. Hamas also boycotted the session, although its Spiritual Leader, Sheikh Ahmad Yassin, attended as an observer. Invited but not attending were Islamic Jihad, the Popular Front for the Liberation of Palestine—General Command (PFLP—GC), and as-Saiqa. The Council's final communiqué urged Arafat to declare an independent Palestinian state by September at the latest, outlined consensus positions on interim and 'final status' issues and called for the reactivation of dormant PLO committees. The DFLP accepted an invitation by the PLO to join the Palestinian delegation attending the Camp David talks with Israel during July, although many opposition organizations (such as Hamas and the PFLP—GC) described the summit as 'dangerous'.

On 2 April 2000 Fares Qaddoura, a negotiator on Palestinian prisoners, declared that he would tender his resignation to the PLC, after he was attacked by security guards at Arafat's official residence in Ramallah. In a second incident, a minister responsible for environmental affairs was assaulted by six members of the Palestinian security forces, who were expected to face trial in connection with the incident. It was announced on 3 April that a new Palestinian National Council was to be established, including the PLO Executive Committee and other leading public figures; the new council's considerations were to include the issue of the Palestinian diaspora, of refugee camps in other Arab countries, and the possible participation of the Palestinians concerned in elections in those countries. At the end of June there were reports that the first draft of the constitution for a Palestinian state was complete and had been submitted to the President for approval.

At the end of May 2000 Fathi Barqawi, the chief news editor at the state-run Voice of Palestine radio station, was arrested after publicly criticizing the talks being conducted with Israel in Stockholm. During May and June a crack-down on the media by the authorities was reported, including the closure of four television and two radio stations. Dozens of people were arrested, among them members of Fatah and eight leaders of the PFLP (although most were subsequently released). In late June the police reportedly detained Arafat's adviser on refugee camp affairs, Abd al-Fattah Ghanayim, after he was said to have criticized the PA's 'secret' talks with Israel and the corruption within the PA. At the end of July a leading representative

of Hamas, Abd al-Aziz ar-Rantisi, was arrested by security forces in Gaza, on charges of defamation, incitement and sedition; he was accused of having threatened internal security by claiming that the PA negotiators who attended the Camp David summit with Israel (see above) were guilty of treason.

THE AL-AQSA UPRISING:THE RISE OF FATAH'S TANZIM AND INTRA-PALESTINIAN CO-ORDINATION

At the end of September 2000 the West Bank and Gaza became engulfed in the most serious violence seen in the territories for many years, as Palestinians demonstrated their frustration at the lack of progress in the peace process with Israel and at their failure to achieve statehood. On 28 September Ariel Sharon, leader of Israel's right-wing Likud party, visited Temple Mount/Haram ash-Sharif in Jerusalem—the site of the al-Aqsa Mosque and the Dome of the Rock—flanked by Israeli security guards. Sharon's visit to the Islamic holy sites provoked violent protests by stone-throwing Palestinians, to which Israeli security forces responded with force. The clashes spread rapidly to other Palestinian towns; by the end of October more than 140 people had died—all but eight of them Palestinians—and thousands were reportedly wounded. The perceived plight of the Palestinians received considerable international support, and there were widespread protests in other Arab capitals. Arafat and Barak visited Paris, France, on 4 October for discussions led by US Secretary of State Madeleine Albright. However, no agreement was reached on the composition of an international commission of inquiry into the causes of the clashes. Arafat and Albright continued discussions at the Egyptian resort of Sharm esh-Sheikh on the following day, but Barak returned to Israel. The Israeli authorities subsequently closed the borders of the West Bank and Gaza. On 7 October the UN Security Council issued a resolution condemning the 'provocation carried out' at Temple Mount/Haram ash-Sharif and the 'excessive use of force' employed by the Israeli security forces against Palestinians. Israeli officials, meanwhile, accused Arafat of failing to intervene to halt the violence, as members of his own organization, Fatah, joined Hamas and other militant groups in what swiftly became known as the 'al-Aqsa *intifada*'. In mid-October Israel launched rocket attacks against Arafat's headquarters in the territories, following the murder, on 12 October, of two Israeli army reservists by a Palestinian crowd in Ramallah.

In an attempt to prevent the latest Middle East crisis from developing into a major regional conflict, a US-brokered summit meeting between Barak and Arafat was convened on 16–17 October 2000 at Sharm esh-Sheikh. President Clinton announced that Israel and the PA had agreed a 'truce' to halt the spiralling violence. The two sides were also said to have agreed on the establishment of a US-appointed committee to investigate the violence. (The five-member international commission of inquiry was appointed by Clinton in early November, to be chaired by former US senator George Mitchell.) Barak, meanwhile, insisted that Arafat rearrest about 60 Islamist militants who had been released by the PA in early October. Amid renewed clashes in the Palestinian self-rule areas, the League of Arab States (the Arab League) held an emergency summit meeting in Cairo on 21–22 October and issued a strong condemnation of Israel's actions towards the Palestinians. Barak responded by announcing that Israel was calling a 'time-out' on the peace process.

The al-Aqsa *intifada* marked a new phase in the Palestinians' long struggle for independence. The leading political and military forces behind the revolt appeared to be grassroots cadres belonging to Arafat's Fatah organization, or its offshoot, the Tanzim. These consist mainly of Fatah's 'inside' leadership which emerged before and during the first *intifada* and included fighters who had been (since the Oslo accords signed since 1993) members of one or other of the PA's myriad intelligence services. It is this legacy and role that increasingly bestowed on Fatah the contradictory function of being at once the military basis of the PA's government and also its most loyal political opposition. The Fatah opposition was born not only because of the PA's increasingly incompetent performance as a 'national authority', causing a real seepage of popular support away from Fatah. It also involved the slow evolution of a political critique of the very terms of the Oslo process, where Palestinian national aspirations have been subject to a negotiating strategy based on US-led diplomacy and security co-operation with the Israeli armed forces. In its stead, Fatah 'field commanders' increasingly advocated other options aside from negotiation and diplomacy. The first was that the Palestinians should deploy popular and armed resistance against Israeli military 'outposts' and Jewish settlements situated within the PA-controlled areas, in order to increase the cost of the occupation to Israel. The new Palestinian uprising effectively created the conditions for that vision to be put into practice, with armed attacks being routinely deployed against Israeli soldiers, settlements and by-pass roads in or near Palestinian areas throughout the Occupied Territories, including East Jerusalem. It was this armed dimension that most distinguished the al-Aqsa revolt from the *intifada* that had begun at the end of 1987.

The second dimension was the shifting of the Palestinians' struggle away from what they perceived as the tutelage of US diplomacy and Israeli hegemony to the forum of the UN and the Arab world. In particular, there was a reassertion that an end to the current conflict must be conditional on Israel's full withdrawal from the territories occupied in 1967 (including East Jerusalem), the dismantlement of Jewish settlements and Israel's acknowledgement of the right of return of Palestinian refugees. The Israeli air-strikes of mid-October 2000 (see the chapter on Israel) resulted in an escalation of Palestinian outrage. Certainly, when Palestinian debate on the forthcoming Sharm esh-Sheikh summit began, there was a groundswell of Palestinian anger towards Yasser Arafat that had not been seen previously. Hundreds of Palestinians immediately rallied in Gaza on 13 October to denounce the PA; the subsequent announcement of the Sharm esh-Sheikh meeting was followed by another Gaza demonstration attended by thousands of Hamas supporters who urged Arafat not to attend the meeting. While the summit was taking place, during 16–17 October, Fatah and Hamas again organized demonstrations condemning Arafat's participation. When the 'cease-fire' arrangements between Israel and the PA were announced on 17 October, various organizations including Fatah, Hamas, Islamic Jihad, the DFLP and the PFLP denounced them and vowed to continue the *intifada*.

At the end of October 2000 there was an upsurge in violence against Israeli targets by militant Islamist groups opposed to the Oslo peace process. Israel responded by launching air-strikes against Fatah military targets in the Palestinian enclaves and announced a new policy of targeting leaders of militant Islamist organizations deemed to be involved in 'terrorist' actions. On 1 November Arafat and the Israeli Minister for Regional Co-operation, Shimon Peres, held crisis discussions in Gaza, at which they were reported to have agreed a 'cease-fire' based on the truce brokered at Sharm esh-Sheikh in October. The fragile cease-fire did not last, however, as violence between Israelis and Palestinians intensified during November (see below). Nevertheless, bilateral negotiations were resumed later in that month, partly as a result of Russian diplomatic efforts. At the end of November a partial peace plan, announced by the Israeli Government, was rejected by the PA; under the proposals Israel was said to be prepared to withdraw its troops from an additional part of the West Bank provided that the PA agree to postpone any discussion of the remaining 'final status' issues.

Although the Palestinian demonstrations during the early days of the al-Aqsa *intifada* appeared to be spontaneous and not to be orchestrated by any organization, within the first two weeks highly localized leaderships did emerge in the West Bank and Gaza, though apparently without co-ordination between them. While many of the local organizers were Fatah officials—most famously Marwan Barghouthi, who is said to attract considerable support among Palestinians in Ramallah and other parts of the West Bank—Fatah and the Tanzim, groups much vilified by Israel, seemed not to be operating on a mass scale. Claims that Fatah radiated instructions to the Palestinian masses ignored the divisions that existed within Fatah. Throughout the first two months of the al-Aqsa *intifada*, Arafat and the PA were in many ways non-present, neither organizing protests nor making a concerted effort to prevent them. Hamas and Islamic Jihad were similarly inactive as organizations. On 8 October Arafat met with the PLO Executive Committee and representatives of Hamas and Islamic Jihad to co-ordinate a joint response to Barak's threats to escalate military actions.

Arafat held similar meetings in November, but these seemed more directed towards gauging consensus and keeping Islamist groups in the fold (to present a united Palestinian front to Israel and the USA) than towards drafting battle plans.

However, an important dimension of the al-Aqsa *intifada* did emerge in the first few weeks, and was reflected in moves towards a 'national unity' among all the Palestinian factions—including the non-PLO members Hamas and Islamic Jihad. Prior to the outbreak of the *intifada*, nationalist and Islamist groups generally limited their joint discussions and co-operation efforts to achieving a broad consensus on fundamental issues: whether and how to continue the peace process, fundamental positions on 'final status' issues, and the timing of a declaration of Palestinian statehood. Since late September 2000, however, this 'national unity' was reflected in the formation of the Palestinian National and Islamic Forces (PNIF)—an umbrella movement made up of all the Palestinian factions and which laid down a calendar of mass protests and actions. The PNIF included both members of the PLO and Hamas and Islamic Jihad. Since its beginning, the driving force behind the al-Aqsa revolt has remained Arafat's Fatah movement and particularly its grassroots organization. However, the direction of the organization's policy remained determined by the decisions of local leaders rather than by orders 'from above'. The basic strategy behind Fatah's local leadership was expressed less by PA officials than by grassroots leaders such as Marwan Barghouthi in the West Bank and Saqr Habash. Modelling themselves on the final phase of Hezbollah's resistance in southern Lebanon, these two leaders described the al-Aqsa uprising as 'peaceful civilian' protests combined with 'new forms of military actions against soldiers and settlers in the Occupied Territories'. Moreover, the longer the revolt continued, the more the 'military actions' by Palestinians took precedence over peaceful ones, and stemmed in the view of many from the fractured, atomized geography which the Oslo accords had imposed on the West Bank and Gaza.

A major element of the al-Aqsa *intifada* was the importance of 'national unity' between Palestinian 'nationalist' and 'Islamist' currents, and against the Oslo accords' provision for 'security co-operation' with Israel and the US CIA. Although lending a certain religious imagery to the al-Aqsa *intifada*—due mainly to the role which Jerusalem's al-Aqsa Mosque had played in its ignition—the initial role of Hamas and Islamic Jihad in the uprising was minor but supportive. The two groups did not challenge Fatah Tanzim's leading role on either the political, diplomatic or military levels and, like Fatah, they mobilized their supporters mainly in defence of the Palestinian civilian areas. They also granted the PLO unprecedented legitimacy by attending, for the first time, sessions of its leadership and by joining the PNIF. In return for this alliance, the uprising saw the release of most Hamas and Islamic Jihad detainees from Palestinian gaols; this was the clearest evidence of the breakdown in the PA's security co-operation with Israel and the CIA. However, it was doubtful as to how long this 'national unity' would last, given the schisms that have historically divided the Palestinian nationalist and Islamist movements, both before and after the Oslo accords. One possible bone of contention could be over the range of Palestinian military actions. For the Tanzim and most of the other PLO factions, armed resistance should be confined to acts against Israeli soldiers and Jewish settlers in the Occupied Territories. Yet the Islamist groups have never explicitly accepted this distinction between Israeli civilian and military targets. On 2 November 2000 a car bomb attack in West Jerusalem left two Israelis dead; on 22 November another car bomb was exploded in the Israeli town of Hadera, killing another two civilians. Islamic Jihad claimed responsibility for the first attack, and the second bears a resemblance to Hamas' operations. The response to both attacks by Fatah and the PNIF as a whole was a resounding silence—a silence they had not felt compelled to maintain over guerrilla actions against Israeli soldiers and settlements in the Territories.

The encirclement of Palestinian towns by the Israeli army and the obstruction of roads in the West Bank and Gaza, combined with Israel's escalation of military reprisals against residential areas there, added a new dynamic to the conflict. The larger demonstrations of the first few weeks of the Palestinian uprising—which led to clashes with the Israeli army at checkpoints and major crossings, particularly near Jewish settlements—became more difficult and more costly. Given the new situation, it was no coincidence that the PNIF, comprising all nationalist and Islamist parties but separate from the PA, began issuing its leaflets on 23 October 2000. The PNIF leaflets, issued on average once a week, were generally calls for non-violent demonstrations and co-ordinated social activities, such as olive-picking. However, they urged Palestinians to organize themselves locally and suggested general strategies, such as focusing attacks on Israeli soldiers and settlers, which became standard after this period. By mid-November, the PNIF was still a nascent body that was far from having well-delineated networks on the ground, though it heralded a new chapter in intra-Palestinian co-ordination.

Prior to the outbreak of the al-Aqsa *intifada*, the PA had begun shifting more towards state-building activities and several significant events had taken place. Most importantly, on 27 August 2000 the Ministry of Local Government had begun planning elections for 350 villages and municipal councils in the West Bank and Gaza Strip. The PA had originally planned to hold local elections in June 1996, but Arafat had postponed them indefinitely and appointed Fatah loyalists as new council heads, replacing long-standing elected and popular figures. On 2 September 2000 the PA published its first new educational textbooks to replace the decades-old Egyptian and Jordanian ones. On 20 September the PA's Minister of Planning and International Co-operation, Dr Nabil Shaath, began forming a team to draft plans to transform the ministry into a foreign ministry, to appeal to foreign countries to upgrade the diplomatic status of PLO offices to that of embassies, and to otherwise standardize the Palestinian diplomatic network. PLC deputy Azmi Shu'aybi announced on 28 September the formation of a new anti-corruption coalition (consisting of PLC members, intellectuals and representatives of leading institutions), aimed at promoting and enforcing the rule of law. After the al-Aqsa clashes erupted, however, the PA shifted to crisis management. The PCC was unable to meet in full session due to economic closures, demonstrations and Israel's revocation of VIP passes. PA ministries shifted from regular project work to monitoring the damage to their sectors caused by the Israeli blockade and by Israeli air-strikes and shelling.

In November 2000 PA officials began stating repeatedly that there could be no return to the old Oslo formula in which the promise of nominal 'statehood' was traded for monumental Palestinian concessions on issues like settlements, refugees and Jerusalem. Similarly, Arafat himself increasingly opted for the 'internationalization' of the diplomatic arena. Like the majority of Palestinians, he wanted the Oslo process unshackled from what he deemed the pro-Israel bias imposed by the USA's monopoly of the negotiations and balanced by the participation of countries like Egypt, Russia and international bodies such as the UN and EU. An offshoot of the same strategy was the public Palestinian call for 2,000 UN peace-keeping troops to be sent to Gaza and the West Bank in order to ensure protection for the Palestinian people.

By November–December 2000 the al-Aqsa *intifada* was rapidly escalating into armed combat between Israel and the Palestinians. One trend was the slow decline of popular Palestinian protests in deference to armed actions, usually in reaction to Israeli military attacks. A second trend was the clear shift in power within the Palestinian national leadership brought about by the uprising, with grassroots Fatah leaders such as Marwan Barghouthi becoming major players in Palestinian politics. Moreover, institutions such as the PLC and the PA ministries— that drew their authority from the Oslo accords—effectively ceased to function or were relegated to the subsidiary role of service providers. In their stead, there was a revival in legitimacy and public loyalty towards the PLO and, above all, Fatah. Yet this meant Fatah as a national liberation movement, rather than Fatah as the 'ruling party of the PA'. On one level, it was a wholly popular development, demonstrating that Palestinian national politics had moved beyond the constraints and divisions imposed by the Oslo peace process. It also enabled a new unity among the Palestinian movements, with Hamas openly participating in Fatah-dominated bodies like the PNIF, the 'field' organization that determined the time-scale and nature of *intifada* activities. Nevertheless, this 'unity' remained largely tentative, with no real consensus between the factions about

the aims of the uprising. For example, there was a broad agreement among the PLO factions that resistance should be confined to the West Bank and Gaza Strip, since the strategic aim was to end the Israeli occupation on the basis of international legitimacy. It was less clear whether this consensus was shared by the Islamist groups, Hamas and Islamic Jihad. Arafat himself refused to consider the idea of a Palestinian 'national unity' government. As for the transformation of PA institutions into state institutions, the response was that the goal was not a formal declaration of statehood but to sustain the *intifada* to end the occupation.

In early December 2000 a court in the West Bank town on Nablus passed a death sentence on a Palestinian who had been found guilty of collaborating with Israeli secret services in the assassination of a Hamas commander. This signalled a change in policy by the PA, which in mid-January 2001 carried out the executions by firing squad of two alleged collaborators, provoking widespread criticism by human rights activists. In mid-January Hisham Mekki, the Chairman of Palestinian Satellite Television, director of the state broadcasting corporation and a close associate of Arafat, was killed by unidentified gunmen in Gaza. A militant Palestinian group, the al-Aqsa Martyrs Brigades, claimed responsibility for the attack, and accused Arafat of failing to end official corruption. Israel denied PA claims that Palestinian collaborators with Israel were behind the assassination.

In the approach both to the end of Bill Clinton's presidency in the USA in January 2001 and the Israeli premiership election in February, a further round of peace negotiations opened in mid-December 2000. The outgoing US President was reported to have proposed a peace settlement that included plans for a future Palestinian state covering the Gaza Strip and around 95% of the West Bank, as well as granting the Palestinians sovereignty over the Islamic holy sites in Jerusalem. However, the US proposals also required that the Palestinians renounce the right of return to Israel for 3.7m. refugees, which the PA deemed unacceptable. In late December the talks were ended after two Israelis were killed by Palestinian bombings in Tel-Aviv and Gaza. Moreover, at the end of the month a senior Fatah official and a prominent Jewish settler were both shot dead in the West Bank. Arafat travelled to Washington, DC, in early January 2001 to seek official clarification of the Clinton proposals, while Israel was said to have cautiously accepted the peace initiative as a basis for further discussions.

From its outbreak, there existed a rift between the 'field' leadership of the Palestinian *intifada* and the PA leadership that purported to represent the people's aspirations politically and diplomatically. Several months into the uprising—and with the arrival of an Israeli Government under Ariel Sharon in early February 2001—the rift was beginning to show signs of political confusion and internal breakdown. There were violent demonstrations by Palestinians in the Occupied Territories followed the election of Sharon, whom they held responsible for the massacre of Palestinian refugees in Lebanese camps in 1982 (at which time he was Israel's Minister of Defence). The Palestinian authorities, under strong pressure from their European and Egyptian allies, had gone to inordinate lengths, if not to get Barak re-elected, then at least not to be baled for bringing Sharon to power. This had been the main motivation for the PA to attend the Israeli-Palestinian negotiations which began on 21 January 2001 in Taba, Egypt, since they apparently knew that no agreement would be reached. Indeed, the talks ended without settlement soon afterwards, following the killing of two Israeli civilians in the West Bank for which Hamas claimed responsibility. The drift into disarray and popular resentment in the West Bank and Gaza was compounded by the absence of the PA in every public sphere except education and health and its apparent inability to alleviate the Palestinians' situation. In Gaza there were simmering clashes between Palestinian refugees and the PA's Preventive Security Force (PSF), ostensibly over the arrest of a Hamas activist. Another sign of disarray within the PA was on 1 February when the Speaker of the PNC, Salim az-Za'nun, announced that a new Palestinian body, the National Independence Commission (NIC), had been established with the support of over 100 influential Palestinians from the Occupied Territories and the diaspora. On paper, the organization called for new local and national elections and changes in the Palestinian leadership, which were precisely the internal reforms many Palestinians believed were necessary to sustain and develop the uprising. Apart from enraging Arafat (who saw az-Za'nun's move as a direct challenge to his leadership), many of the new organization's most prominent signatories, such as Hanan Ashrawi, PA representatives Saeb Erakat and Faisal Husseini (the Minister of Jerusalem Affairs), disavowed all knowledge of this initiative. The matter was quietly buried by a meeting of Fatah's Central Committee on 4 February.

On 10 March 2001 Arafat took the unusual step of addressing his people. He gave a state of the nation speech to 66 of the 88 elected members of the PLC, which was holding its first session in Gaza in over five months. On the one hand, Arafat affirmed that peace remained the 'strategic option' of the Palestinians and admitted that he was aware of the Israelis' 'need for security and stability'. On the other hand—and mindful of the Palestinian consensus brought about by the *intifada*—he repeated that Israel too must recognize the 'need and rights of the Palestinian people' and that these could not be less than those afforded them by 'international legitimacy', namely Israel's withdrawal from all Arab land occupied in 1967, including 'noble Jerusalem', and the right of return for Palestinian refugees embodied in UN General Assembly Resolution 194 of 1948. With an eye on the forthcoming Arab summit in Amman, Jordan, scheduled for late March 2001, the Palestinian leader lambasted Israel's policies of 'military escalation, siege and starvation' in the Occupied Territories and rehearsed his call for the UN to dispatch an international peace-keeping force to provide protection to Palestinian civilians.

Arafat's problem was that the *intifada* on the ground refused to be halted. Most Palestinians viewed the 'Egyptian-Jordanian' plan (see the chapter on Israel) with a combination of cynicism and indifference. A dynamic of action and reaction had developed between armed Palestinian resistance and the Israeli army that was now perilously close to being beyond control. On 17 April 2001, in response to a Palestinian mortar attack on the southern Israeli town of Sderot, the Israeli army moved tanks to the PA-controlled town of Beit Hanun in the Gaza Strip. However, as was to occur in the Palestinian territories on several occasions in subsequent months, Israeli forces were soon withdrawn from the town. On 26 April four activists belonging to Arafat's Fatah movement were killed in an explosion on Gaza's border with Egypt, including Raad Azzam, leader of the Popular Resistance Committee (PRC) that had led the armed resistance and defence of southern Gaza since the start of the uprising. The Palestinian police chief based in Gaza, Ghazi al-Jabali, insisted that the four 'policemen' had been assassinated by a remote-controlled Israeli device. Palestinians responded by renewing mortar attacks on Gaza's Jewish settlements of Gush Qatif and Kfar Darom on 28—29 April, leaving five settler children wounded. Convening a session of the PA's National Security Council (which represented all the Palestinian police and intelligence forces), on 29 April Arafat called on his followers to curb all 'security breaches', especially the mortar attacks. According to Palestinian sources he also disbanded the PRC, calling on its members to return to their original security institutions (about half of the PRC's activists are members of one or other of the PA's security forces). The Palestinian President also arrested Hamas official Abd al-Aziz ar-Rantisi over a a recent speech during which ar-Rantisi called on Palestinians to reject the Egyptian-Jordanian initiative while brandishing a Kalashnikov as the 'only way to liberate Palestine'.

The PA leadership now seemed to view engagement in any diplomatic process—no matter how futile in practical terms—as a crucial part of the struggle for sheer survival which it was reduced to waging. However, the PA needed something to show for the Palestinians' suffering and sacrifices, hence the authorities' insistence on the settlement-building moratorium as part of the 'cease-fire'. A moratorium was one of the components of the package that Israel's Government under Ariel Sharon categorically rejected. Instead the Israeli Deputy Prime Minister and Minister of Foreign Affairs, Shimon Peres, proposed limited settlement expansion to encompass 'natural growth', which the PA interpreted as meaning a licence for Israel to accelerate the pace of settlement construction.

In early June 2001 the PA agreed to implement the recommendations contained in the report of the international fact-finding committee headed by George Mitchell (the 'Mitchell Committee'), which had been published on 20 May (see Documents on Palestine, p. 90). The report's recommendations included a 'freeze' on Israeli settlement activity; a clear statement by the PA leadership demanding an end to the violent protests; an 'immediate and unconditional' end to the violence and the disengagement of forces by both sides; and the resumption of security co-operation. The report failed to support Palestinian demands for a UN peace-keeping force to be stationed in the West Bank and Gaza (a request consistently rejected by the Israeli Government and which had been blocked by a US veto at the UN Security Council vote in mid-March). On 12 June the PA also approved an extended 'cease-fire' which was negotiated by CIA Director George Tenet. The reaction of Hamas to the tentative cease-fire between Israel and the PA was rather conflicting. Hamas had claimed responsibility for a suicide bomb attack on a Tel-Aviv disco on 1 June which killed 21 Israelis. On 5 June a senior Hamas official in Gaza, Mahmud az-Zahhar, stated that Hamas would attack Israelis 'everywhere, by all means', thereby casting doubt on the viability of the recent cease-fire. Az-Zahhar declared that earlier reports that Hamas was willing to abide by the truce were due to 'miscommunications' between the group's military and political wings. Nevertheless, Hamas appeared to have reined in its suicide bombers, giving its tacit support to the fragile cease-fire and stating that it would not unleash more suicide bombers on Israel as long as Israeli troops did not kill Palestinian civilians. However, in early July both Islamic Jihad and Hamas formally declared an end to the truce. On 23–24 July clashes occurred between Palestinian militant groups and the Palestinian security forces in the Gaza Strip, following the arrest by Palestinian military intelligence of a number of militants, including members of Fatah's Tanzim.

Meanwhile, in early June 2001 Palestinians were greatly saddened by the announcement of the death (following a heart-attack) of Faisal Husseini, who, as the PA's Minister responsible for Jerusalem Affairs, had been widely respected for his moderate and conciliatory tone towards Israel. Husseini was subsequently replaced by the Minister without Portfolio with responsibility for Settlements, Ziad Abu Ziad.

During August 2001 a number of Palestinians were sentenced to death and at least 100 others were detained by the authorities, on charges of having collaborated with Israeli security services in recent attacks on senior Hamas officials. Meanwhile, the PA rejected a request by the Israeli Government that it arrest seven alleged Islamist militants, who headed a 'most wanted' list of about 100 Palestinians believed to be perpetrators of violence against Israelis. On 10 August, in response to a suicide bomb attack on a restaurant in central Jerusalem (in which at least 15 Israelis died), Israel ordered its forces to occupy a number of official PA buildings including Orient House, the *de facto* headquarters of the Palestinian administration in East Jerusalem. On 14 August Israeli armed forces entered the town of Jenin in the West Bank; this was the first time that Israel had ordered its military into land that had been transferred to full PA control under the terms of the Oslo peace process initiated in 1993. PA officials described the Israeli action as a 'declaration of war'. On 27 August 2001 the leader of the PFLP, Abu Ali Moustafa, was assassinated by Israeli troops in the West Bank. Moustafa was the highest-ranking Palestinian official to be killed by Israel under its so-called policy of 'targeted killings'. (Ahmad Saadat later assumed the PFLP leadership.) At the end of the month Israeli armed forces entered the West Bank town of Beit Jala; however, the troops agreed to a withdrawal two days later.

The unprecedented scale of the terrorist attacks launched against the World Trade Center in New York and the Pentagon in Washington, DC, on 11 September 2001 again led to an escalation of tensions in the Middle East. The suicide attacks were stated by the USA to have been perpetrated by the al-Qa'ida (Base) organization under the leadership of the Afghan-based militant Islamist Osama bin Laden. As the US Administration sought to gain support for an international 'coalition against terror', President George W. Bush placed considerable pressure on Israel and the PA to end the fighting in the West Bank and Gaza. In mid-September Yasser Arafat, who had strongly condemned the attacks, announced that he had given militant Palestinian groups 'strict orders for a total cease-fire', while the Israeli Government agreed to withdraw from PA-controlled territory in the West Bank. However, Sharon prevented a planned meeting between Arafat and Shimon Peres from taking place, stating that Israel required 48 hours without violence prior to the convening of peace talks. On 26 September Arafat and Peres finally met in the Gaza Strip, in an attempt to consolidate the 'cease-fire' arrangements outlined in the Mitchell Report. However, although there appeared initially to be a lull in the fighting, retaliatory attacks between Israelis and Palestinians resumed. According to the Palestinian Red Crescent Society, by the end of September 2001 at least 690 Palestinians had been killed and more than 16,000 injured since the start of the al-Aqsa *intifada* one year earlier. An estimated 170 Israelis had reportedly died as a result of the violence, and many more had been wounded.

IMPROVEMENT IN RELATIONS WITH SYRIA

The expected reconciliation between Arafat and Damascus, under the impact of the al-Aqsa *intifada* and after some 20 years of estrangement, was achieved during sessions of the Arab League summit held in Amman in late March 2001. Arafat met Syrian President Bashar al-Assad on the sidelines of the summit. President al-Assad called for the liberation of all Palestinian territory occupied by Israel in 1967 (including East Jerusalem), the unconditional return of all 3.7m. Palestinian refugees to their homeland, and the creation of an independent Palestinian state (with Jerusalem as its capital). The meeting indicated that the Palestinian leader had met Syria's condition that the PA commit itself to the borders of 4 June 1967. The two sides agreed on the 'unity of the tracks' in the peace process and pledged to co-ordinate and to maintain bilateral contacts. Arafat was by now spoken of as 'President of the Palestinian Authority' by the official Syrian media, and he was expected to meet President al-Assad again in Damascus on 15 April 2001. However, that meeting was subsequently postponed, as were later discussions arranged between the two leaders.

THE INTIFADA IN THE AFTERMATH OF 11 SEPTEMBER 2001

The second half of 2001 was marked by an escalation of the Palestinian uprising, with tension increasing between the PA and Israel following the latter's revived policy of assassinating leading Palestinian activists, and Palestinian suicide bombings in Jerusalem on 9 August (see above) and outside Haifa on 12 August, Israel's closure of Orient House, and its first major military incursion into a West Bank city (13–14 August). The dynamics of the situation in the West Bank were markedly changed after the 11 September attacks in the USA. Moreover, the USA's consequent launch of its 'war on terror' appeared to encourage Israel to step up the Israeli army's assaults on PA targets and ultimately to reoccupy six major Palestinian cities.

On 17 October 2001 militants from the PFLP assassinated the Israeli Minister of Tourism, Rechavam Ze'evi, in East Jerusalem. Following the killing of Ze'evi, the Israelis escalated their military campaign in PA-controlled areas of the West Bank. Although PA President Yasser Arafat denounced Ze'evi's murder, ordered Palestinian security forces to arrest the perpetrators and outlawed the armed wing of the PFLP, Ariel Sharon issued an ultimatum to the PA that they arrest and extradite Ze'evi's killers and other leading PFLP militants or face a harsh response from Israel. The Israeli Prime Minister was quick to equate the 11 September attacks on the USA with Palestinian 'violence', and by implication Arafat with Osama bin Laden.

The USA urged Sharon to show restraint. It still wanted Israel to resume talks with the PA and for the two sides to implement previous cease-fire agreements, which would facilitate US coalition-building for the 'war on terror' and the US-led military campaign in Afghanistan. In an attempt to revitalize the cease-fire arrangements, US Secretary of Defense Donald Rumsfeld toured the Middle East in early October 2001, and President Bush declared on 2 October that the creation of a Palestinian state 'has always been a part of our vision, so long as the right of Israel to exist is respected'. Bush reiterated his support for a Palestinian state through negotiations on 11 October. Apparently Sharon was angered, not only by Bush's

statement but also because Rumsfeld had not come to Israel during his regional consultations on the US 'war on terror'. Furthermore, the USA had not backed Israel's demand for the extradition of Ze'evi's assassins. Together with the EU and Russia, the USA continued to put pressure on both the PA and Israel to adhere to the cease-fire arrangement of 29 August, which had been mediated by the EU's High Representative for the Common Foreign and Security Policy, Javier Solana.

Ariel Sharon, on the other hand, rejected personal appeals by President Bush and US Secretary of State Colin Powell to resume talks with the PA, on 18 October suspending all contacts with the PA, and giving the Israeli military the green light to step up assassinations of Palestinian activists. Some right-wing Israeli politicians even called for the expulsion of Arafat from the West Bank and Gaza. In mid-October 2001 Israel deployed helicopter gunships over Palestinian cities and moved troops into the outer fringes of Jenin. On 18 October Israeli forces reoccupied Jenin, Nablus and Ramallah, while Bethlehem and Beit Jala were taken on 19 October and Qalqilya and Tulkarm on 20 October. The USA, on 22 October, condemned the Israeli invasion of PA-controlled cities in Area A by as 'unacceptable' and demanded Israel's immediate withdrawal. Israel was forced to pull back from the cities, but its army continued to occupy large sectors of territory belonging to the PA and to carry out 'targeted killings' of senior members of Hamas. The violence continued throughout late 2001 and Arafat reportedly expressed his disappointment at the lack of international pressure on the Israeli Government. Moreover, the mounting internal opposition to Arafat's policy of arresting Palestinian militants did little to strengthen his position in the Occupied Territories.

THE KARINE A AFFAIR

As the US special envoy, Anthony Zinni, returned to the region in an effort to broker an Israeli-Palestinian cease-fire, on January 3 2002 Israeli naval commandos captured a freighter ship, the *Karine A*, in the Red Sea which was alleged to be carrying 50 tons of heavy weaponry destined for the PA. The Israelis argued that the smuggling operation had been initiated by the PA leadership and approved by Yasser Arafat. They also accused Iran of involvement in the supply of weapons to the PA. Although both the Palestinian authorities and Iran denied any involvement in the shipment, the Israeli interrogation of the ship's crew (including senior members of the PA's naval forces) apparently indicated direct PA involvement. The US Administration accepted the Israeli position regarding the *Karine A* affair, declaring that it had 'convincing evidence' proving that Iran and the Lebanese Hezbollah were linked to the smuggling operation. Palestinian and Iranian spokespersons continued to deny the allegations of a strategic alliance between Iran and the PA, but US and Israeli officials insisted that the PA and Iran were working towards a military pact.

For months after the seizure of the *Karine A*, US and Israeli intelligence officials continued to claim that the affair was part of a broader relationship and accused Arafat of personally forging an alliance with Iran that included imports of Iranian heavy weapons and millions of US dollars to Palestinian guerrilla organizations in the Occupied Territories. This PA-Iranian alliance, they claimed, was worked out at a secret meeting held in Moscow in May 2001 between some of Arafat's senior aides and Iranian government officials. The meeting allegedly took place while Arafat was visiting Russian President Vladimir Putin. Palestinian spokesmen, on the other hand, dismissed the claims of an alliance between the PA and Iran and denied that Arafat had any prior knowledge of the *Karine A* shipment. They argued that the allegations were part of an attempt by Israel to justify its 'aggressive' military operations in the West Bank and Gaza Strip. Iran also denied involvement with the Palestinians or with any arms shipments. Ali Shamkhani, the Iranian Minister of Defence, stated that 'The Islamic Republic of Iran has had no military relations with Arafat, and no steps have been taken by any Iranian organization for the shipment of arms to the mentioned lands'.

THE RISE OF THE AL-AQSA MARTYRS BRIGADES

In early 2002 there was no alleviation of the violence between the Palestinians and Israel, and little prospect of a way out of the crisis for President Arafat. Moreover, the first three months of the year witnessed the rise of the al-Aqsa Martyrs Brigades, a militant offshoot of the mainstream Fatah Tanzim. The al-Aqsa Martyrs Brigades was born in the narrow alleys of the Balata refugee camp near Nablus, after many days of clashes with the Israeli army in the early months of the al-Aqsa uprising. Its founders and commanders had mostly come of age during the first Palestinian *intifada*. It is not clear how many members the al-Aqsa Martyrs Brigades has, since it has been purposely built as a loose network of regional 'cells'. In the first three months of 2002 the Brigades pursued a campaign of gun attacks against Israeli soldiers at military road-blocks in the West Bank and Gaza, and despatched suicide bombers deep into Israel. On 21 March 2002, after suicide bombers from the al-Aqsa Martyrs Brigades killed three Israelis and wounded dozens in West Jerusalem, the US State Department branded the Palestinian militia a 'terrorist organization'.

On 27 January 2002 a volunteer for the Palestinian Red Crescent Society in Ramallah became the first female suicide bomber. On 19 February the al-Aqsa Martyrs Brigades claimed joint responsibility for a raid on a West Bank check-point, in which six Israeli soldiers died. On 3 March 10 Israelis (most of them soldiers) were shot dead by a sniper from the Brigades at a West Bank check-point. The Brigades' success in orchestrating attacks led many Palestinians to believe that they could drive Israel out of the Occupied Territories, just as Hezbollah guerrillas had forced Israeli forces to withdraw from southern Lebanon. The doggedness of the Brigades also served as a counterpoint to Arafat's compromises and efforts to regain US approval by vowing to punish those responsible for the 21 March bombing and continuing discussions concerning a US-mediated cease-fire. The commanders of the al-Aqsa Martyrs Brigades answered to no higher authority and certainly not to Arafat, who made several attempts to disband the militia. That autonomy produced a curious hybrid: while the fighters remained part of the mainstream, secular Fatah movement, they adopted the strategies of radical Islamists. The Brigades' suicide bombings in early 2002 broke two Palestinian taboos: they defied Fatah's policy of confining the uprising to the West Bank and Gaza, and, for the first time, they employed women as suicide bombers. In late 2001 and early 2002, after Israel had used its air force, navy, tanks and ground forces against Palestinian refugee camps and cities in the biggest military offensive carried out by Israel in a generation, the al-Aqsa Martyrs Brigades decided to concentrate its attacks inside Israel itself. The Jerusalem bombing of 21 March, in particular, encapsulated the limits of Arafat's influence over his mainstream Fatah militia, let alone his radical Islamist opponents such as Hamas and Islamic Jihad.

THE RAMALLAH INCURSION OF MARCH 2002 AND ITS IMPACT ON PALESTINIAN INFRASTRUCTURE

Only after the Palestinians were beaten, Ariel Sharon reportedly stated in early March 2002, would negotiations be possible. The scale of Israeli attacks on Palestinian cities and refugee camps in the West Bank and Gaza was 'disproportionate and often reckless', according to an Amnesty International report. Amnesty estimated that in the six weeks from 1 March to mid-April more that 600 Palestinians had been killed and over 3,000 wounded by Israeli soldiers. By mid-March 2002 at least 1,065 Palestinians and 344 Israelis had been killed since the al-Aqsa *intifada* began in September 2000. A major escalation occurred on 11 March 2002, when the Israeli army entered Ramallah, the Palestinians' commercial and political hub in the West Bank, in what Israel said was part of a general sweep for activists and militants. The massive incursion involved some 150 tanks and was part of Israel's largest military offensive in the West Bank and Gaza Strip since the Israelis captured these territories in 1967. The incursion took place while US envoy Anthony Zinni was engaged in a renewed effort to broker a cease-fire between the two sides.

The Israelis' short-lived incursion into Ramallah resulted in huge damage to Palestinian infrastructure, affecting water and electricity supplies, the sewage system and roads—estimated by PA officials as costing tens of millions of US dollars. Twelve Palestinians were also killed during the assault on Ramallah. On 16 March 2002 Israeli tanks withdrew from the West Bank city, ending their brief reoccupation of President Arafat's power base. The Israeli army, meanwhile, announced that its forces

had left positions in two other West Bank cities but that they remained on the outskirts of Bethlehem, Nablus, Jenin and Hebron. Israeli forces also formed a cordon around Ramallah.

THE USA'S 'WAR ON TERROR' AND THE FAILURE OF US MEDIATION

Both Anthony Zinni and Israel demanded that Arafat should end the *intifada*, collect illegal weapons from militants and arrest those Palestinians wanted by Israel for 'terrorist' activities. However, the PA could not arrest the hundreds, or even thousands, of Palestinians who now participated in the regular attacks against the Israeli occupation. The reason for this was the shift in the nature of the *intifada* in recent months. If, in the initial months of the uprising, most of the attacks had been carried out by minority groups of Hamas and Islamic Jihad, now the *intifada* had apparently become the struggle of an entire nation. Deep-seated feelings of frustration, fury and desire for revenge against the Israeli state appeared to lead large numbers of Palestinian youths to be prepared to volunteer as suicide bombers. PA officials used this argument to explain their demands for the lifting of the closures, for the removal of the road-blocks, and for the Israeli army's withdrawal to the positions it held prior to September 2000. Only then, according to Arafat and Palestinian officials, would it be possible to start to bring about calm among the Palestinian population.

As Zinni pressed ahead with cease-fire talks between the PA and Israel, the Bush Administration called for a complete withdrawal of all Israeli forces from PA-controlled areas, stating that a pull back would create a better environment for the US envoy to attempt to broker a truce. Arafat urged the US to put more pressure on Israel to enable Zinni to secure a cease-fire. However, both Israel and the USA continued to repeat their demand that Arafat 'must do more' to rein in Palestinian militants and halt attacks on Israelis. Initially Zinni aimed for a declaration of a cease-fire on 20 March after he convened the joint Israeli-Palestinian security committee for discussions on how to move into the 'Tenet work plan' (the security plan prepared by CIA Director George Tenet), but he was unable to reach a co-ordinated statement by Sharon and Arafat.

The joint Israeli-Palestinian security committee met on 20 and 21 March 2002, with Zinni in attendance; however, both meetings ended without agreement. Representing the Palestinians in the meetings were Col Jibril Rajoub, the head of the PSF in the West Bank, and his Gaza counterpart Muhammad Dahlan. Besides differences of opinion between Israel and the PA as to the length of time to be allocated to the Tenet cease-fire plan before the resumption of the diplomatic process, there was also disagreement over the arrest of Palestinian militants wanted by Israel. Israel demanded the arrests of those involved in past attacks against Israelis, but the Palestinians replied that they would only detain those who intended to launch future attacks. No agreement was reached on the terms of a cease-fire.

Meanwhile, the PA continued to demand that Israel withdraw its troops to their position as at September 2000, and lift all sieges and remove all check-points around Palestinian towns and villages, as stated by the Tenet plan; the Palestinians also demanded that international observers be placed in the Occupied Territories. PA representatives insisted that, despite the difficulties posed by the Tenet plan, they would do what was required, but only if they could show the Palestinian public that there would be a immediate response from Israel, and only if the security arrangements and consequent calm would result in a renewal of the political negotiations. Israel, on the other hand, wanted the Palestinians first to take a series of steps against militant groups, including arrests, dismantling the militias and collecting weapons.

In mid-March 2002 US Vice-President Dick Cheney embarked on a visit to the Middle East, which included a trip to Israel on 18–19 March. Cheney's visit was designed to build support for the US option to widen its 'war on terror' to include Iraq. However, Arab leaders apparently informed the US Vice-President that there was little appetite in the region for an attack against Iraq while the Israeli–Palestinian violence continued. Cheney refused to meet with Arafat, although he hinted that such a meeting could take place in the near future, provided that Arafat carried out the recommendations of the Tenet plan. The US State Department had decided to designate the al-

Aqsa Martyrs Brigades as a 'terrorist organization' (see above), making it illegal to provide the group with funds and requiring banks to freeze its assets. A deep feeling of anger ran through the Palestinian leadership and print media over Cheney's refusal to hold talks with Arafat. PA officials complained bitterly about what they believed was a clearly pro-Israeli attitude expressed by Cheney, who had even refrained from commenting on the recent conditions imposed by Sharon on Arafat's freedom of movement in and out of the Palestinian territories. PA representatives also sought to turn the spotlight onto the visit of two senior officials to the Iraqi capital. The Ministers of Finance and of Economy and Trade were meeting with members of Saddam Hussein's Government in Baghdad, which pointed to a Palestinian attempt to play a part in the diplomatic manoeuvres ahead of a possible US-led strike on Iraq.

ARAFAT FAILS TO ATTEND THE BEIRUT SUMMIT

In mid-March 2002 Arafat expressed his desire to attend the Arab summit in Beirut, Lebanon, which was scheduled for 27–28 March. At the summit Saudi Arabia was to present its proposal for peace between Israel and the Arab world, in exchange for an Israeli withdrawal to the pre-1967 borders. Also in mid-March 2002 Arafat was invited to visit Spain, the then holder of the EU presidency. Israel, however, encouraged by Cheney's refusal to meet Arafat, refused to allow the PA President to attend the Arab summit. Israel had restricted Arafat's freedom of movement for months, and Sharon offered to lift the ban for Arafat to attend the summit only if there was a total cease-fire. The Israeli premier also indicated that he might not permit Arafat to return to the West Bank if there were Palestinian attacks against Israelis during the conference. Palestinians also expressed opposition to Arafat's attendance at the Beirut summit. In the opinion of some Palestinians, should Arafat deliver a moderate address in Beirut, he would come across as a 'puppet' of Sharon; but if he gave a militant speech, he would lose US support and also risk not being allowed to return to the Occupied Territories. At the close of the Beirut summit, Arab states in attendance endorsed the Saudi peace initiative that had been proposed by Crown Prince Abdullah; Israel, however, subsequently rejected the initiative. (For further details regarding the Beirut summit, see Arab–Israeli Relations 1967–2002 and also the chapters on Israel and Lebanon.)

ISRAELI REOCCUPATION OF PA-CONTROLLED AREAS

On 29 March 2002 Israel launched 'Operation Defensive Shield'—a large-scale military offensive in the West Bank in response to a series of suicide attacks by Palestinian militants and, more specifically, to a suicide bombing two days previously in Netanya (in which some 29 Israelis celebrating Passover died). This was the bloodiest attack since the start of the Palestinian uprising against Israeli occupation in September 2000. As part of its military campaign, Israeli forces broke into Arafat's presidential compound in Ramallah, where the Palestinian leader remained inside his office, effectively cut off from the rest of the city. Although Israel stated that it had no intention of harming Arafat personally, PA officials insisted that Arafat's life was in danger. On 1 April 2002 Israeli tanks entered the town of Betunya, near Ramallah, surrounding the PSF compound of West Bank security chief Jibril Rajoub and causing considerable damage to the complex. The PSF apparatus had been the strongest and most prominent of all PA forces on the West Bank.

Israeli tanks also entered Beit Jala, Bethlehem, Qalqilya, Salfit, Tulkarm, Nablus and Jenin, patrolling the streets and enforcing strict curfews that confined hundreds of thousands of Palestinians to their homes. Israeli troops had also laid siege to Jenin's refugee camp, resulting in battles with Palestinian residents of the camp who fought back with bombs and guns. Israeli soldiers also encircled hundreds of Palestinian gunmen who had barricaded themselves in Bethlehem's Church of the Nativity. Arafat, meanwhile, confined to his Ramallah headquarters, remained defiant, stating that he would prefer to die rather than be forced into exile.

It was apparent that Ariel Sharon now wanted to expel Arafat from the Territories, publicly suggesting on 2 April 2002 that

he be exiled. However, although the US Administration offered Sharon tacit support for Israel's military operation in the West Bank, US officials were not prepared to allow the Israeli Government to expel the PA President, to destroy the PA or to completely retake the areas under nominal Palestinian control. However, the Israeli offensive prevented the PA from taking effective control of the security situation in the Palestinian self-rule areas because vital Palestinian installations, including its West Bank security headquarters, had been destroyed.

During early 2002 Arab leaders accused Israel of attempting to wreck their collective call for peace which had emerged from the Beirut summit. The high levels of sympathy offered to the Palestinians from Arab nations often took the form of fund-raising events and donations being received by the PA from influential donors. Meanwhile, the UN Security Council called on Israel to withdraw from Ramallah and other PA-run towns in a resolution supported by the USA (for further details, see the chapter on Israel).

THE BATTLE FOR THE JENIN REFUGEE CAMP

The heaviest fighting between the Israeli army and Palestinian militias occurred in the refugee camp at Jenin, home to some 13,000 Palestinians. Israeli tanks had entered Jenin and surrounded the adjacent refugee camp on 3 April 2002, provoking fierce opposition from Palestinian gunmen. Many of the camp's inhabitants fled during the fighting and heavy bombardment from Israeli tanks and helicopters. The fighting in the Jenin camp lasted until 11 April. Palestinians subsequently estimated that more than 100 Palestinians had died as a result of the Israeli invasion of the camp. The UN's envoy to the Middle East, Terje Roed-Larsen, was strongly critical of Israel's actions at Jenin. However, an exact count of the number of fatalities was not possible because Israel initially barred reporters and medical personnel from the camp. After the siege of early April the Palestinians came to embrace Jenin as a symbol of wider resistance to the Israeli occupation.

THE ARREST OF MARWAN BARGHOUTHI

On 15 April 2002 Marwan Barghouthi, one of the most influential Fatah leaders in the West Bank, was detained by Israeli armed forces in Ramallah. Israel presented Barghouthi's detention as a major achievement of its reoccupation of the city, using it to counter strong international pressure against its military offensive in the West Bank. Israel accused Barghouthi of being the leader of the al-Aqsa Martyrs Brigades, although Barghouthi had never acknowledged a formal relationship with the Brigades. In recent years Barghouthi had attained the status of a 'folk hero' among most young Palestinians. His fiery speeches and almost daily media interviews—including several that he had given to Israeli television in Hebrew—had made him a defining face of the Palestinian *intifada*. Since September 2000 Barghouthi had at times appeared to disagree publicly with Arafat over the direction of the Palestinian uprising. However, Barghouthi's acumen—he never mentioned the Palestinian leader by name when criticizing his policies—and popularity had ensured his political survival. (Trial proceedings against Barghouthi began on 5 September 2002.)

On 16 April 2002 Israel reopened a detention camp in the Negev desert in order to hold some of the 6,000 Palestinians it had rounded up during the reoccupation of Palestinian towns and refugee camps. Ketziot, a tent camp in a remote part of southern Israel, had held prisoners detained throughout the first Palestinian uprising from 1987–93.

ENDING THE STAND-OFFS IN RAMALLAH AND BETHLEHEM

The stand-off at the Church of Nativity began on 2 April 2002 when Israel invaded Bethlehem and about 200 Palestinians (including militiamen, policemen, officials, clerics, and church workers) sought refuge in the shrine. By 23 April Israeli forces had pulled back from most West Bank cities, but still surrounded Arafat's compound in Ramallah and the Bethlehem church. In Ramallah, Israel demanded that Arafat hand over five men suspected of involvement in the October 2001 assassination of Rechavam Ze'evi, as well as the alleged mastermind of the *Karine A* arms shipment to the PA (see above). Although Arafat had initially refused this request, he now took pre-emptive legal action by putting the suspected assassins of Ze'evi on trial in a makeshift court, using Palestinian policemen in the Ramallah compound as judges. On 25 April the 'military field court' handed out gaol terms of between one and 18 years (with hard labour) to four men convicted of involvement in Ze'evi's assassination. The sentences were ratified by Arafat. On 28 April the Israeli Cabinet approved a US proposal aimed at ending the siege of Arafat's compound. The US plan called for US and British personnel to guard six Palestinians wanted by Israel and, in turn, Arafat was allowed to leave his headquarters and to move freely in the Palestinian areas of the West Bank and Gaza. Finally an accord based on proposals to offer militants wanted by Israel and stranded in the Church of the Nativity a choice of exile or trial in Israel, or transfer to the Gaza Strip, was devised, with US mediation. Arafat approved the dispatch of 13 Palestinians to Europe and of a further 26 to Gaza, despite strong Fatah and Hamas criticism of the agreement. On 12 May the 13 Palestinian militants were flown initially to Cyprus after leaving the Bethlehem church, on their way to permanent exile.

REOCCUPATION OF THE WEST BANK AND THE DETERIORATING HUMANITARIAN SITUATION

On 23 June 2002, after two suicide bombings in Jerusalem had killed some 26 Israelis, the Israeli military reinvaded all West Bank cities, keeping at least 600,000 Palestinians under effective house arrest with round-the-clock curfews and largely barring the media from covering its military operations. This military offensive encountered minimal Palestinian resistance and limited international criticism. Israeli tanks again surrounded Arafat's shell-damaged compound, with the President and his aides inside. As Israeli forces clamped down harder on security in the West Bank, Sharon pledged to widen the Israeli offensive against the Palestinians to the Gaza Strip.

The reoccupation of the West Bank and the prolonged curfews imposed by Israel brought about a major humanitarian crisis for the Palestinians, with UN and aid agencies having trouble getting assistance to hundreds of thousands of Palestinians there. The World Food Programme (WFP) announced that it was trying to buy thousands of metric tons of flour for an emergency distribution to 265,000 particularly vulnerable Palestinians. The Palestinian Deputy Minister of Health, Munzer Sharif, expressed particular concern about the lack of access for health workers, while a spokeswoman for the World Health Organization stated that the collapse of the PA's immunization programme and the lack of safe drinking water could lead to an outbreak of serious diseases. In Nablus, WFP estimated that some 40,000 people were in urgent need of food aid. In Qalqilya 70% of the population was said to be living below the poverty line.

GENERAL ELECTIONS AND PA REFORM ANTICIPATED

In mid-May 2002 Yasser Arafat decided to hold presidential and parliamentary elections within a year which, according to PA officials, would be part of a broader reform package of the PA. There was tremendous internal Palestinian pressure on Arafat to carry out reforms. Palestinians had long complained about widespread corruption and nepotism in the PA, but these complaints had intensified during the months of Israeli closures and invasions, which had severely disrupted everyday life. Some observers suggested that Arafat's decision to hold elections appeared to be aimed at deflecting the demands for reform expressed by many Palestinians. Previous attempts to reform Arafat's administration had led to few significant changes, with Arafat disregarding laws passed by the PLC as well as decisions by the judiciary. However, despite widespread Palestinian dissatisfaction with the PA, Arafat continued to be seen as a symbol of the Palestinian people and was not expected to face a strong challenge for leadership. Meanwhile, Israel's six-week reoccupation of the West Bank towns during April–May 2002 had strengthened a sense among many Palestinians that the PA was ineffective and unable to protect them against the Israeli military. Consequently, Arafat's waning popularity may have led him to decide to hold presidential and parliamentary elections as a way of ensuring renewed legitimacy. PA officials emphasized that the holding of elections would be on condition that

Israeli troops first withdrew to positions they had held before September 2000. The Secretary-General of the Palestinian Cabinet, Ahmad Abd-ar Rahman, declared that Arafat's decision came soon after the PLC had called for sweeping changes in the PA, including the formation of a new Cabinet within 45 days and general elections by early 2003. Minister of Planning Nabil Shaath asserted that the Palestinians also insisted that residents of Arab East Jerusalem would be permitted to vote, as they had been in the Palestinian elections held in 1996. The Palestinian Central Bureau of Statistics assessed that it would take about 60 days to compile a list of Palestinian voters, and that international monitors would be needed to ensure that the elections were conducted fairly.

Many Palestinians now cited new elections as the most important aspect of reform. The elections would be the first time that Arafat faced voters since he was overwhelmingly elected as President of the PA in 1996. The parliament's list of demands was drafted by a committee of eight legislators from Arafat's Fatah movement, who had demanded that a post of prime minister be created, with the premier to be in charge of day-to-day government operations. The planned reforms also called for a streamlining of the Palestinian security services. However, Abd-al Aziz ar-Rantisi, leader of the Hamas movement, dismissed the elections as mere cosmetic changes. Ariel Sharon, on the other hand, had proposed that a new Palestinian government be established even against the Palestinians' wishes.

On 27 May 2002 Arafat, following strong calls for reform by ordinary Palestinians and Western governments alike, named a new Cabinet that included a new minister to oversee the security forces. A few days earlier, CIA Director George Tenet had met Arafat at his Ramallah headquarters to press for the restructuring of the multiple, overlapping security agencies. Arafat streamlined down his Cabinet from 31 to 21 ministers, and brought in several new faces. In the most important change, Arafat named Abd ar-Razzak al-Yahya as the new Minister of the Interior. By appointing al-Yahya, a former PLO commander who had not held any high-profile positions in recent times, Arafat had bypassed more prominent figures. Dogged by accusations of widespread financial corruption in his administration, Arafat also named a new Minister of Finance, Dr Salam Fayyad, who had recently been employed by the IMF in Jerusalem and had called for greater financial accountability in the Palestinian Government.

PRESIDENT BUSH URGES ARAFAT TO BE REPLACED

Despite the reshuffle of the Palestinian Cabinet, Arafat remained under pressure from Europe and the USA to carry out wide-ranging 'reforms' of his government. On 24 June 2002 President Bush, in a speech concerning the Middle East, set out his Administration's plan for peace in the region. Bush called on the Palestinians to elect a 'new and different Palestinian leadership' and to adopt a new constitution with a fully empowered parliament, local-level governments and an independent judiciary. The USA and its partners would help to organize multi-party local elections by the end of the year, with national elections to follow. The President added that the PA should undertake an externally supervised overhaul of their security and police forces, dismantle 'terrorist groups' and implement financial reforms. In turn, the USA would increase humanitarian aid to the PA. Setting stiff conditions for the creation of a Palestinian state, President Bush stated that, after these steps were taken, the Palestinians would be able to count on US support for a 'provisional state of Palestine' whose final borders, capital and other aspects of sovereignty would be negotiated between Israel and the PA. The US President spoke of a political settlement being possible within three years. Bush also called on Israel to withdraw its forces to positions it had held in the West Bank on 28 September 2000 and to cease the building Jewish settlements in the West Bank and Gaza. Questions about the status of Jerusalem and the right of Palestinian refugees to return home would be dealt with during 'final status' negotiations.

Palestinian officials responded to the US President's speech by stating that the call to replace Arafat was not acceptable. In late May 2002 84 Palestinian parties, organizations and leading figures had signed a statement calling for a refusal of aid from the US Government because of its support for Israel. The signatories included leaders of the Fatah movement and Hanan Ashrawi, a prominent Palestinian legislator and internationally known commentator, Haider Abd ash-Shafi, a leading Gazan figure, the leaders of the PFLP and DFLP, heads of two Palestinian universities, and several members of the PLC.

ARAFAT'S DISMISSAL OF HIS WEST BANK
SECURITY CHIEF

In early July 2002, while the Israeli army continued its offensive in the West Bank, Yasser Arafat dismissed his most powerful security chief, Jibril Rajoub, the commander of the PSF in the West Bank, in one of the most audacious and controversial decisions taken by the Palestinian leader since the establishment of the PA in 1994. Although Arafat's motives in dismissing Rajoub were unclear, Rajoub had clearly lost credibility following the Israeli military takeover of the PSF's headquarters in Betunya four months earlier. Moreover, several Palestinian leaders, including some of Arafat's closest aides, had insinuated that Rajoub had handed over Fatah and Hamas fighters to the Israeli forces. Arafat's decision to dismiss Rajoub was first made public in the form of a statement leaked on 2 July 2002 to Western news agencies. On 5 July a terse formal statement from the PA stated that Arafat had decided to 'relieve' Rajoub of his responsibilities and to appoint in his place Zuheir Manasra, a former governor of Jenin. The decision, and particularly the way in which it was made public, angered Rajoub, who told reporters that his subordinates in the PSF would not accept Manasra as their commander and would demand that someone from 'inside the PSF' be appointed in his place. On the same day three peaceful demonstrations were staged by PSF officers

and employees in the West Bank in support of Rajoub's reinstatement. The following day several high-ranking PSF officers met Arafat in an effort to persuade him to reconsider Rajoub's position. What was clear was that Rajoub, like all PA security chiefs, had encouraged personal loyalty to himself among his subordinates. Rajoub himself met Arafat and was apparently offered several posts within the PA. Gen. Ghazi al-Jabali, the Palestinian police chief, was dismissed by Arafat in a similar fashion in early July and replaced by his deputy, Col Salim Bardini. Rajoub had been a powerful associate of Arafat, and it was difficult to see how his dismissal could strengthen Arafat's hand in the face of tremendous internal and external pressures and a multitude of problems, not least the continuing reoccupation of West Bank cities by Israeli forces and the relentless US pressure for Arafat to be replaced as the Palestinians' leader.

The entire Palestinian Cabinet resigned on 11 September 2002, in order to prevent a vote of 'no confidence' being brought against it in the PLC. (On the same day Arafat had issued a decree setting 20 January 2003 as the date of the presidential and legislative elections.) Although a new Cabinet was expected to be announced within two weeks, Arafat declared subsequently that he was unable to form a new administration while his compound in Ramallah was under Israeli occupation. Following a further Palestinian suicide bombing in Tal-Aviv, on 19 September Israel had ordered its troops into Ramallah and demolished almost all of Arafat's presidential buildings, where a number of 'wanted' militants were believed by the Israeli authorities to be sheltering. Amid strong international pressure, Israeli forces redeployed to the outskirts of the Ramallah compound on 29 September. The incumbent Palestinian ministers were to remain in office pending the formation of a new Cabinet.

Economy

Revised for this edition by the Editorial staff

INTRODUCTION

Economic conditions in the Gaza Strip, the West Bank and East Jerusalem (see Occupied Territories, p. 581) have deteriorated significantly since the signing of the Declaration of Principles on Palestinian Self-Rule in September 1993. As illustrated below, the dominant characteristic of these economies has been their dependence on Israeli markets and their consequent vulnerability to the closures imposed at various times during 1993–2002 by the Israeli authorities, mainly in response to attacks on Israeli civilians by members of militant Palestinian organizations which reject the so-called 'Oslo accords'. In November 1998 an international airport was inaugurated at Gaza; however, the implementation of further measures to reduce the dependence of the Palestinian economy, such as the opening of seaport facilities in the Gaza Strip, has been halted by the prolonged delay in implementing the Oslo accords. In October 1999 a 'southern' safe corridor between Gaza and Hebron in the West Bank was finally inaugurated. Despite this achievement, by mid-2002 the provision for a seaport at Gaza had still not been implemented (although in April 2000 a contract to construct the port was signed by the Palestinian (National) Authority (PA) and a Franco-Dutch consortium); moreover, the airport and safe passage were both closed by the Israeli authorities. In 1998 the Palestinian Central Bureau of Statistics (PCBS) estimated that 11.5% of the labour force in the West Bank and 20.9% of the labour force in the Gaza Strip were unemployed. Corresponding figures for underemployment were, respectively, 8.4% and 2.3%. By mid-2002 the PCBS estimated that 29.6% of the West Bank's and 41.7% of the Gazan labour force were unemployed. Other sources indicated that in March 1997 Israeli border closures had cost the Palestinian economy some US $5m.–$6m. per day, amounting, on an annual basis, to more than the sum of funds pledged—but not necessarily disbursed—to the PA by international donors.

Perhaps the strongest link with the Israeli economy, and the one which proved the most difficult to break, was the employ-

ment that Palestinians found within the 'Green Line', which provided many families with their livelihoods. In 1992 some 35% of the West Bank's and 45% of the Gazan labour force was employed in Israel, mainly in unskilled and semi-skilled occupations—especially in the construction industry. In 1993, following a series of attacks on Jews within Israel, the Israeli Prime Minister, Itzhak Rabin, ordered the closure of Israel's borders with the West Bank and Gaza, preventing an estimated 70,000 West Bank and some 50,000 Gazan Palestinians from travelling to work. Significantly, controls on cross-border movement were relaxed only after considerable pressure from Israeli employers; the 'reserve labour force' of some 100,000 unemployed Israelis had been reluctant to do the Palestinians' work, which was often of a low-paid, menial nature.

Since February 1996 Israel and East Jerusalem have been closed to most Palestinian residents of the West Bank and Gaza Strip. As the closures affect movement in both directions, the economy of East Jerusalem (see Occupied Territories, p. 000), deprived of West Bank markets for its goods and services, has all but collapsed. Closures have had a similarly disruptive effect within the West Bank, since they restrict communications between Palestinian towns via Israeli-controlled Jewish areas of the West Bank. Such areas comprise most of the territory of the West Bank outside Palestinian population centres.

THE ECONOMIC IMPACT OF THE AL-AQSA
UPRISING

Living standards among Palestinians in the West Bank and Gaza have deteriorated considerably as a result of the al-Aqsa *intifada*, which began at the end of September 2000, and the subsequent closure by Israel of the Palestinian territories and Gaza International Airport. The economic consequences of the military blockade have been immense, and they were expected to worsen when it was announced in September 2001 that, for security reasons, a 'buffer zone' was being established by Israel in order to seal all entry and exit points to the Territories. By that month the Palestinian Economic Council for Development and Reconstruction (PECDAR) estimated that the total monetary loss to the economy during the 12 months of the blockade was some US $5,300m., including losses incurred as a result of the replacement of long-term investment programmes by short-term projects aimed at reducing rapidly escalating levels of unemployment and poverty. According to PECDAR, the closure of Gaza's airport has had a particularly serious impact on tourism and foreign investment in the Palestinian enclaves. However, the sectors of agriculture, industry, trade and transport have also been badly affected by the political situation in the region.

The military blockade, first imposed on the Palestinian territories by Israel in immediate reaction to the al-Aqsa protests on 28 September 2000, quickly hardened into a comprehensive siege of the Palestinian economy. After 9 October the movement of people and goods across the 'Green Line' dividing the West Bank from Israel was halted. Palestinian goods were subsequently denied passage through the West Bank border crossings with Jordan, Gaza's Rafah crossings with Egypt and Israeli transit facilities. Thousands of truck-loads of goods were impounded in Israeli ports. After 14 November, the Israeli army imposed an almost complete internal closure on the territories. The economic blockade deprived the PA of the taxes on goods and salaries of those Palestinians employed in Israel. The PA also lost revenues from the commercial enterprises in which it held stakes; the highest profile of these was the Paris Casino in Jericho, which was closed in mid-October. The combination of unrest and closure brought the Palestinian economy to a near standstill. Some 125,000 workers—about a quarter of the labour force—who did regular day-labour in Israel, lost their jobs. Another 60,000 within the Occupied Territories were prevented from reaching their workplace.

In the first months of the al-Aqsa *intifada*, the Palestinian economy was losing an estimated US $9m. per day, of which $3.5m. was lost wages. The total economic loses by the end of October 2001 roughly equalled losses during the first year of the 1987–90 *intifada*. Thousands of dunums of agricultural land in the West Bank and Gaza had been demolished and numerous Palestinian buildings either destroyed or occupied by the Israeli military. Moreover, facing the prospect of starvation, many Palestinians were forced to accept UN handouts. During late 2000 and early 2001 UN workers began distributing sacks of food to around 217,000 families throughout the Territories; but despite an international appeal, the shortage of funds meant that deliveries were restricted to three-monthly intervals.

The European Union (EU) sought to play an active role in the Palestinian–Israeli conflict, both politically and economically, but largely acted as a moral voice in support of Palestinian rights. On 8 November 2000 the EU approved an emergency payment of some US $23.3m. to the PA to enable it to meet its current expenses, such as the salaries of public-sector employees. The payment was the first to be made from the EU's Special Cash Facility, a fund established in 1998 to provide refundable advances to the PA to cover current expenses at times of crisis. In December the organization pledged a further $57m. to the PA. In mid-March 2001 the EU Commissioner for External Affairs, Chris Patten, warned Israeli leaders that their economic stronghold on the Palestinian territories must be lifted. Patten stated that the EU was urging Israeli Prime Minister Sharon to transfer £36m. in tax revenue which Israel had withheld from the Palestinian administration.

In late January 2001 the Palestinian Minister of Finance, Muhammad Zohdi an-Nashashibi, requested that Arab League states transfer more of the estimated US $1,000m. of funds pledged to the PA by Arab leaders at their extraordinary summit meeting held in Cairo, Egypt, in October 2000. An-Nashashibi announced that the Palestinian economy had lost a staggering US $2,900m. since Israel ordered the closure of the West Bank on 9 October. According to PECDAR, about 64% of Palestinians were living in poverty in early 2002. The economy was in a state of paralysis, with the World Bank estimating that GDP had contracted by some 12% in 2001; productive activity had virtually ceased in much of the West Bank. Amid continued border closures, military incursions by Israel into Palestinian towns, and the destruction of much of the PA's infrastructure, the administration was effectively bankrupt.

POPULATION

According to the final results of the first census conducted by the PCBS, the Palestinian population of the West Bank and Gaza Strip totalled 2,895,683 (males 1,470,506; females 1,425,177) at 9 December 1997. Of the total population, 1,663,267 were resident in the West Bank (excluding East Jerusalem), 1,022,207 in the Gaza Strip and an estimated 210,209 in East Jerusalem. According to the census, 54% of the population (excluding the 16% resident in refugee camps) were located in urban areas, and 30% in rural areas. The population of the West Bank and Gaza increased at an average annual rate of some 3.9% in 1990–2000. The population of the Palestinian territories in mid-2000 was estimated at 3,224,504.

LABOUR FORCE

At December 1997, according to the PCBS, the strength of the Palestinian labour force (excluding East Jerusalem) aged 10 years and over was 602,092: 400,637 in the West Bank and 201,455 in the Gaza Strip. The rate of unemployment was 14.7% in the West Bank and 24.2% in the Gaza Strip. Corresponding figures for the whole of 1998 were, respectively, 11.5% and 20.9% of the labour force aged 15 years and over. In 2000, according to the results of a labour force survey conducted by the PCBS, the average level of unemployment in the Palestinian territories was 14.1%. However, by mid-2002 the PCBS estimated that 29.6% of the labour force of the West Bank and 41.7% of the Gazan labour force were unemployed, owing to the inability of Palestinians to travel to their places of employment in Israel.

NATIONAL ACCOUNTS

In 1997, according to the PCBS, the gross national product (GNP) of the West Bank and Gaza Strip, measured in current prices, totalled US $4,906m. Net factor income from abroad comprised $625m. in wage income, mainly from Palestinian workers in Israel, and $108m. in net property income from abroad. Gross domestic product (GDP) in market prices amounted to $4,173m. GDP at factor cost totalled 10,602m. new Israeli shekels in 1996. Of this total, private services (including trade, rental services and transport) contributed 38%, public services (including central and local government) 23%, industry (manufacturing, quarrying and the supply of utilities) 16%, agriculture and fishing 14%, and construction 9%. On the basis of these figures and surveys by the PCBS of the population in 1997, average GNP per head in the West Bank and Gaza Strip amounted to $1,779 in that year, while average GDP per head was $1,537. In 2000 the World Bank estimated GNP in the Palestinian territories, measured at average 1998–2000 prices, to total $4,745m., equivalent to $1,610 per head. On the basis of PCBS figures and conjectural price deflators, the World Bank has calculated that Palestinian GDP increased by 10% in real terms in 1994, but declined by 6% in 1995 and remained static in 1996. According to the PA, GDP increased, in real terms, by 4.8% in 1997 and by 7.0% in 1998. Real GDP increased by an estimated 7.4% in 1999, but decreased by some 6.2% in 2000. Real GNP rose by an estimated 8% in 1994, declining by 5% in 1995 and by 1% in 1996. On the same basis, the World Bank estimates that real GDP per head increased by 4% in 1994, but fell by 12% in 1995 and by 6% in 1996. Real GNP per head increased by 2% in 1994, but declined by 10% in 1995 and by 7% in 1996. Over the period 1994–96 real GDP per head fell by 14%, and real GNP per head by 16%. According to IMF estimates (expressed in Israeli new shekels at constant 1986 prices), in 1995–97 the GNP of the West Bank and Gaza declined at an average annual rate of 0.8%, while per-caput GNP declined at an average annual rate of 5.4%. However, during 1994–2000 Palestinian GDP expanded, in real terms, at an average annual rate of 1.9%.

CONSUMER PRICES

The annual rate of inflation in the West Bank and Gaza averaged 5.4% in 1996–2000. In the Gaza Strip an annual average inflation rate of 5.9% was recorded in 1998, while inflation averaged 4.9% in the West Bank and 6.6% in East Jerusalem. In 2001, according to the PCBS, annual consumer price inflation in the Palestinian economy averaged 1.2%, compared with 2.8% in 2000. The highest price increase in 2001 was for housing (5.3%).

AGRICULTURE

According to the PCBS, agriculture and fishing contributed 7.4% of GDP in the West Bank and Gaza Strip in 1999. According to the official labour force survey conducted in mid-2002, agriculture, hunting, forestry and fishing engaged an estimated 16.7% of the employed Palestinian labour force. Citrus fruits are the principal export crop, and horticulture also makes a significant contribution to trade. Other important crops are tomatoes, olives, cucumbers, grapes and potatoes. The livestock sector is also significant. Agro-industrial production is focused on the dairy and olive oil sectors. Although about one-half of Palestinian exports are derived from agricultural production, the sector remains orientated towards supplying local needs. Like other sectors of the economy, agricultural production and export trade are characterized by a high degree of dependence on Israel, and consequent vulnerability to Israeli border policy: some 60% of Gaza's agricultural production is exported via Israel as originating in Israel. One example is the lucrative, export-orientated production of carnations in Gaza. In 1994, of total production of 120m. flowers, only 2m. were exported directly to European markets, the remainder being distributed through Israel. Border closures and delays in the issue of transport permits have a devastating effect on the sector. Carnation production is also heavily reliant on water resources controlled by the Israeli authorities.

Expansion of agricultural production in the West Bank and Gaza is severely limited by problems with irrigation. Traditionally, wells and cisterns have accounted for some 66% of all water consumed, highland springs for some 27% and surface run-off water and water purchased from the Israeli water utilities for the remainder. Some 75% of annual rainfall is lost to evaporation. Agriculture uses about 70% of water consumed in the West Bank, but only 4% of the total land area in the West Bank is irrigated, compared with 45% within Israel. In the mid-1990s Palestinian agricultural production consumed some 152m. cu m of water annually, compared with consumption (for the same purpose) of 56m. cu m by the approximately 120,000 Jewish settlers in the West Bank. In the Gaza Strip irrigation of the important citrus crop has been affected by rising salinity in the ground-water supply. In central Gaza ground-water salinity levels are three times as high as the World Health Organization's recommended safety level. The area also suffers from a water deficit, estimated annually at approximately 50m. cu m. The Palestinian economy was seriously affected by a drought during the 1998/99 season.

The fishing industry, formerly one of the Gaza Strip's most profitable activities, has been severely constricted by Israeli military control over the area in which Palestinian boats may fish, including the prohibition of any fishing beyond a 30-km radius, established by the Israeli authorities.

INDUSTRY

Palestinian sources report that industrial activity has contributed, on average, about 10% of Palestinian GDP since the 1970s, employing some 9% of the West Bank labour force and 14% of the Gazan labour force over the same period. The IMF and PECDAR estimated the contribution of industry (excluding construction) to Palestinian GDP at 8.2% in 1994. According to the PCBS, industry (mining and quarrying, manufacturing, electricity and water supply, and construction) contributed 34.8% of the GDP of the West Bank and Gaza Strip in 1999. According to the official labour force survey conducted in mid-2002, the sector (including gas utilities) engaged about 20.6% of the labour force in the West Bank and Gaza.

Mining and quarrying accounted for 0.7% of Palestinian GDP in 1998, and engaged an estimated 0.3% of the employed labour force in 1999. Two significant gas fields were discovered off the Gazan coast in mid-1999.

A World Bank study, conducted in 1993, indicated the potential competitiveness, at free-market prices, of a sample of Palestinian enterprises. Food-processing and the production of textiles, footwear, cosmetics, cigarettes, household detergents and construction materials have all been identified as suitable for expansion through import-substitution. According to the PCBS, manufacturing enterprises in the West Bank and Gaza Strip totalled 11,559 in 1994, including 39 foreign-owned companies. Manufacturing contributed 16.5% of the GDP of the

West Bank and Gaza in 1999, according to the World Bank. In that year an estimated 15.3% of the Palestinian labour force were employed in the sector. The PCBS estimated the contribution of the construction sector to Palestinian GDP at 13.7% in 1999. In mid-2002 some 8.5% of the labour force in the West Bank and Gaza Strip were employed in construction.

The frequent closure of the West Bank and Gaza Strip by the Israeli authorities in 1993–2002 has prompted the development of free-trade industrial zones on the Palestinian side of the boundaries separating Israel from the territories. Israeli and Palestinian enterprises can continue to take advantage of low-cost Palestinian labour at times of closure, and the zones also benefit from tax exemptions and export incentives. Small and medium-sized enterprises dominate production in the three Gazan and six West Bank industrial zones. At the Erez zone, adjacent to the crossing between Israel and the Gaza Strip, textile production has emerged as a significant industry. In January 1998 the World Bank announced a loan of US $10m. to the PA for the development of the Gaza Industrial Estate project. The second phase of construction of the estate, which required total financing of $84.5m. and was expected to create as many as 50,000 jobs in the Gaza Strip, was due to commence in mid-1999. Other donors included the International Finance Corporation and the European Investment Bank.

ENERGY

According to the PCBS, the power sector—electricity and water supply—accounted for 2.0% of the GDP of the West Bank and Gaza Strip in 1998. Results of the labour force survey conducted in 1999 show that electricity, gas and water utilities employed 0.2% of the total Palestinian labour force. The Palestinian Energy Authority (PEA) was established in 1994 to develop the energy and power sectors. In addition to the Jerusalem District Electricity Co Ltd (JDECO—which supplies Jerusalem, Jericho, Bethlehem, Ramallah and Al-Birah), it was agreed to establish the Palestine Electric Co (PEC) in August 1997. The company began operations in 1999. In Gaza the distribution of electric power supply is the responsibility of 16 municipalities and village councils, which mostly purchase electricity from the Israel Electric Corporation (IEC). In the West Bank, distribution is the responsibility of 252 municipalities and village councils, of which 110 purchase electricity from the IEC, 67 receive partial supplies from village generator systems, and 75 have no formal supplies. The PEC is constructing a power plant in Gaza, while the National Electric Co (NEC)—created in 2000—plans to build a second power plant in the West Bank.

SERVICES

In 1999 the services sector contributed 57.8% of the GDP of the West Bank and Gaza Strip, according to the PCBS. Within the services sector, wholesale and retail trade contributed 12.1% of GDP, and public administration and defence 10.7%. In mid-2002, according to the labour force survey published by the same source, the services sector engaged about 62.7% of the employed labour force of the West Bank and Gaza Strip.

In 1991 the official financial services sector, comprising mainly banks and insurance companies, was estimated to employ slightly more than 1% of the Palestinian labour force. In February 1997 a stock exchange, the Palestine Securities Exchange (PSE), was inaugurated. With an initial listing of 23 companies, the aim is to develop the PSE as the foundation of a Palestinian capital market and to facilitate the investment of expatriate funds. It was estimated that 22 banks were operating in the West Bank and Gaza at the end of 1999.

EXTERNAL TRADE

Israel remains by far the largest market for goods and services from the West Bank. Trade with Israel represents some 75% of exports from, and 87% of imports to, the Territories. Prior to the *intifada*, in 1987, the West Bank recorded a trade deficit with Israel of US $420.2m.; the value of exports to Israel amounted to $160.5m., compared with imports worth $580.7m. During 1988–90 exports of goods and services from the West Bank decreased at an average annual rate of 16%, and the overall trade deficit was aggravated by the 1990–91 crisis in the Persian (Arabian) Gulf region, when the closure of borders and reduced demand affected the export of agricultural goods and manufactures to Arab markets. In 1992 the Gaza Strip recorded a trade deficit with Israel of $264.7m. (exports $63.8m., imports $328.5m.). In its trade with all countries the Gaza Strip recorded a deficit of $286.9m. (exports $79.3m., imports $366.2m.) in 1992. The value of Gazan exports to Jordan in 1992 amounted to $11.9m., while that of imports from Jordan was negligible. In its trade with all other countries, the Gaza Strip recorded a deficit of $34.1m. (exports $3.6m., imports $37.7m.) in 1992. In 1999 the value of exports (f.o.b.) to Israel was estimated at $280m., while the value of imports (c.i.f.) amounted to some $1,535m. In 1999, according to preliminary estimates, the West Bank and Gaza Strip recorded a visible trade deficit of $2,618m. and a deficit of $1,359m. on the current account of the balance of payments.

PUBLIC FINANCES

In January 1998 the PA drafted a Palestinian Development Plan for the period 1998–2000, envisaging investment expenditure of US $3,500m. The budget, expected to be completely financed by donor countries, was to allocate $1,690m. to infrastructure projects, $856m. to the public sector, $604m. to manufacturing and $304m. to private institutions. According to data released by the Israeli Ministry of Foreign Affairs in July 1997, more than 60% of the PA's revenues are derived from tax transfers by the Israeli authorities. Capital expenditure in the 1996 budget was estimated to be $173.6m. In 1997 the budget of the PA forecast revenues totalling $825.4m. and current expenditure of $863.2m. Capital expenditure in that year was some $214.4m. The aim of the Palestinian authorities is to achieve current budget surpluses from 1998, and to focus public expenditure on health, education and on investment in infrastructure. From 1998 capital expenditure under the Palestinian public investment programme was to be included in the PA's budget. In that year's budget, total revenues were estimated at $863.1m., while projected capital expenditure was $204.7m. and current expenditure was forecast at $802.6m. In 1998, according to the IMF, the PA recorded an overall budget deficit of $144.7m., equivalent to an estimated 3.4% of GDP. The 1999 budget forecast revenues totalling $1,589m. and total expenditure of $1,740m., projecting an increased deficit of $151m. In the 2000 budget, total revenues and total expenditure were both forecast at $1,386m.—the first time that the PA expected a balanced budget.

Sanctions imposed on the West Bank and Gaza Strip by the Israeli authorities in August 1997 included the partial suspension of transfers of tax revenues. One month after the closures, according to the World Bank, losses in the Palestinian territories were reported to total $4m.–$5m. per day, and tax and customs transfers suspended by the Israeli authorities amounted to $65m. The PA was reported to have been obliged to borrow heavily from local banks in order to pay the salaries of its 81,000 employees. Some funds were, in fact, released in August and September 1997, and Israel announced in October that it would release the balance of suspended transfers.

AID AND ECONOMIC DEVELOPMENT

Following the signing of the Declaration of Principles on Palestinian Self-Rule in September 1993, hopes were raised in the West Bank that future economic reconstruction would be financed from abroad. A World Bank report on the Territories estimated that a 10-year programme to construct essential infrastructure and social facilities would cost US $3,000m. The Palestine Liberation Organization (PLO), with a more ambitious Palestine Development Programme, estimated that the reconstruction of the Palestinian economy during 1994–2000 would cost $11,600m. The planners expected to generate $2,000m. from domestic savings, and the remainder from external donors; however, it was unclear how much of the total would be allocated to the West Bank if the plan were to be implemented. Following the signing of the Declaration of Principles in 1993, international donors pledged to invest some $2,900m. in the Gaza Strip and the West Bank. However, only $1,348m. of the $2,490m. pledged between 1994 and 1996 actually reached the Palestinian authorities, owing to the vicissitudes of the peace process and to donors' concerns about the accountability of the Palestinian institutions involved. In December 1997, following a meeting of

the Consultative Group of donors (to the Palestinian authorities), held under the auspices of the World Bank, a three-year economic development plan, involving projected expenditure of some $2,600m., was approved. The scheme aimed to rehabilitate the Palestinian economy and to reduce dependence on Israel. The most substantial investments that the plan envisaged were to be made in infrastructure projects, including improvements to irrigation, road construction and waste disposal. Private-sector projects, including agriculture and tourism, would also receive funds. The donor countries committed some $750m.-worth of aid for 1998, which would help to finance projects during the initial year of the development plan. For 1999 donor countries pledged to commit aid worth some $770m., although by September only $174m. had been received. In May 1999 the PA requested an additional $40m. in emergency aid, following the 1998/99 drought.

In March 2002 Arab states pledged a further US $330m. in aid to the Palestinian authorities, and in the following month international donors agreed to grant $900m. to assist the PA in rebuilding vital infrastructure destroyed during Israel's military offensive known as 'Operation Defensive Shield', and a further $300m. as emergency relief. In May UNRWA assessed that, in addition to $117m. that it had previously estimated as being necessary to fund its emergency programmes for 2002, some $70m. would be required to address the immediate humanitarian needs of Palestinians in the West Bank and Gaza arising from the recent Israeli military incursions into the Palestinian enclaves.

In January 1998 the European Commission reported that member states and institutions of the EU had pledged 1,700m. European currency units to the Palestinian authorities since the signing of the Declaration of Principles in September 1993. Total international donor commitments since that date amounted to US $2,800m.

In September 1999 the World Bank pledged US $15m. to assist with further improvements to Palestinian electricity networks. In early 2000 the PA announced the creation of a Palestinian Investment Fund and a Higher Council for Development, the latter being charged with the preparation of a comprehensive privatization strategy by May.

According to a study by the World Bank, programmes operated by the United Nations Relief and Works Agency for Palestine Refugees in the Near East (UNRWA, Part Three, International Organizations) form the basis of the social welfare system in the West Bank and Gaza Strip, since about 41% of the population there are registered refugees. At the end of June 2002, according to UNRWA, there were 626,532 registered refugees in the West Bank and 878,977 in the Gaza Strip. A number of UNRWA's programmes are directed at particularly vulnerable groups, such as the aged and the physically disabled. Palestinians working for Israeli employers are required to participate in Israel's national social security scheme. However, taxes deducted from Palestinian workers finance only very limited benefits to Palestinians because residency in Israel is a prerequisite for most Israeli schemes.

Health services in the West Bank (excluding those areas where jurisdiction has been transferred to the PA) are provided by the Israeli Civil Administration, UNRWA, private voluntary organizations and private, profit-making organizations. Institutions operated by the Israeli Civil Administration in the West Bank derive from Jordanian systems. Until 1974, when a government health insurance scheme was introduced, residents of the West Bank were entitled to free health care from these facilities. Now only members of the government health insurance scheme may receive comprehensive care at government facilities without charge. Pre-natal care and preventive services are provided by the Civil Administration free of charge to all children under the age of three years. UNRWA has traditionally provided basic health care free of charge to refugees in the West Bank and Gaza. It has also reimbursed refugees for 60% of the cost of hospital treatment obtained outside the UNRWA system. In 1991 UNRWA spent about US $8m. on health programmes in the West Bank, and $12m. on those in the Gaza Strip. UNRWA provides its services through a network of 33 health centres in the West Bank, where some 61 physicians are employed. UNRWA also operates feeding centres, dental clinics, maternity centres and a 34-bed hospital. Nine health centres in the Gaza Strip provide UNRWA services, with 82 physicians employed to care for refugees there. According to the PCBS, there were nine PA-operated hospitals in the West Bank, and

five in the Gaza Strip. In the combined territories more than 700 physicians (about one-third of all physicians practising there) work at clinics in the voluntary and private sectors.

Statistical Survey of the West Bank and the Gaza Strip

Source (unless otherwise indicated): Palestinian Central Bureau of Statistics (PCBS), POB 1647, Ramallah; tel. 2-2406340; fax 2-2406343; e-mail pcbshp@pcbs.pna.org; internet www.pcbs.org.

Note: Unless otherwise indicated, data include East Jerusalem, annexed by Israel in 1967.

Area and Population

AREA, POPULATION AND DENSITY

Area (sq km) .	6,020*
Population (census of 9 December 1997)†	
Males .	1,470,506
Females	1,425,177
Total	2,895,683
Population (official estimates at 31 December)	
1998	2,958,600‡
1999	3,084,900‡
2000	3,224,504
Density (per sq km) at 31 December 2000	535.6

* 2,324 sq miles. The total comprises: West Bank 5,655 sq km (2,183 sq miles); Gaza Strip 365 sq km (141 sq miles).

† Figures include an estimate of 210,209 for East Jerusalem and an adjustment of 83,805 for estimated underenumeration. The total comprises 1,873,476 (males 951,693; females 921,783) in the West Bank (including East Jerusalem) and 1,022,207 (males 518,813; females 503,394) in the Gaza Strip. The data exclude Jewish settlers. According to official Israeli estimates, the population of Israelis residing in Jewish localities in the West Bank (excluding East Jerusalem) and Gaza Strip was 208,300 at 31 December 2001.

‡ Figures are rounded.

GOVERNORATES (official estimates, 31 December 2000)

	Area (sq km)	Popu-lation*	Density (per sq km)
West Bank			
Janin (Jenin) .	583	220,918	378.9
Tubas .	402	40,153	99.9
Tulkarm .	246	146,027	593.6
Qalqilya.	166	79,986	481.8
Salfit .	204	53,366	261.6
Nabulus (Nablus) .	605	284,469	470.2
Ram Allah (Ramallah) and Al-Birah .	855	237,561	277.8
Al-Quds (Jerusalem)† .	345	360,710	1,045.5
Ariha (Jericho) .	593	36,209	61.1
Beit Lahm (Bethlehem) .	659	150,537	228.4
Al-Khalil (Hebron) .	997	447,209	448.6
Gaza Strip			
North Gaza .	61	216,056	3,541.9
Gaza .	74	414,741	5,604.6
Deir al-Balah .	58	169,168	2,916.7
Khan Yunus (Khan Yunis) .	108	227,679	2,108.1
Rafah .	64	139,715	2,183.0
Total .	6,020	3,224,504	535.6

* Figures exclude Jewish settlers.
† Figures refer only to the eastern sector of the city.

PRINCIPAL LOCALITIES
(estimated population at mid-2000, excluding Jewish settlers)

West Bank			
Al-Quds (Jerusalem)	228,152*	Adh-Dhahiriya .	22,989
Al-Khalil (Hebron) .	133,586	Ar-Ram and Dahiyat	
Nabulus (Nablus) .	110,966	al-Bareed .	21,027
Tulkarm .	37,589	Ram Allah (Ramallah) .	20,318
Qalqilya .	35,791	Halhul .	17,545
Yattah (Yatta) .	34,485	Dura .	17,345
Al-Birah .	31,545	Ariha (Jericho) .	16,546
Janin (Jenin) .	29,526	Qabatiya .	16,261
Beit Lahm (Bethlehem)	24,444		
Gaza Strip			
Ghazzah (Gaza) .	328,077	Beit Lahya .	44,898
Rafah .	104,192†	Deir al-Balah .	39,311
Khan Yunus (Khan		Bani Suhaylah .	26,017
Yunis) .	100,118	Beit Hanun .	24,271
Jabalyah (Jabalia) .	62,495	Tel as-Sultan Camp .	19,243
An-Nuseirat .	50,904	Al-Maghazi Camp .	19,188

* The figure refers only to the eastern sector of the city.
† Including the population of an associated refugee camp.

BIRTHS AND DEATHS (estimated)*

	1997	1998
Live births*		
West Bank .	73,586	74,891
Gaza Strip .	45,214	46,844
Deaths		
West Bank .	8,686	8,788
Gaza Strip .	4,630	4,689

* Excluding Jewish settlers.

Live births (estimates, 1999): West Bank 51,306; Gaza Strip 36,709.

Source: Ministry of Health.

MARRIAGES (number registered)

	1998	1999	2000
West Bank .	16,285	16,099	14,867
Gaza Strip .	8,115	8,775	9,023

ECONOMICALLY ACTIVE POPULATION*
('000 persons aged 10 years and over, labour force survey, 1999)

	Males	Females	Total
Agriculture, hunting, forestry and fishing	47	28	75
Mining and quarrying . . .	2	—	2
Manufacturing	79	11	90
Electricity, gas and water supply	1	—	1
Construction	132	1	133
Wholesale and retail trade . .	80	6	86
Hotels and restaurants . . .	15	—	15
Transport, storage and communications	28	1	29
Financial intermediation . . .	4	1	5
Real estate, renting and business activities	8	2	10
Public administration and defence	61	5	66
Education	27	23	50
Health and social work . . .	12	7	19
Other community, social and personal service activities . .	4	1	5
Extra-territorial organizations and bodies	2	1	3
Total employed	502	87	589
Unemployed	67	11	78
Total labour force	569	98	667
West Bank	387	75	462
Gaza Strip	182	23	205

* Figures refer to Palestinians only.

2002 (Sample survey, '000 persons aged 15 years and over, April–June): Total employed 451 (West Bank 318; Gaza Strip 133); Unemployed 229 (West Bank 134; Gaza Strip 95); Total labour force 680 (West Bank 452; Gaza Strip 228).

Health and Welfare

KEY INDICATORS

Fertility (births per woman, 1999).	5.9
Under-5 mortality rate (per 1,000 live births, 1995–99) . .	28.7
Hospital beds (per 1,000 head, 2000)	1.4
Access to water (% of persons, 2000)	96.2
Access to sanitation (% of persons, 2000)	99.6

For sources and definitions, see explanatory note on p. vi.

Agriculture

PRINCIPAL CROPS ('000 metric tons, year ending September)

	1997/98	1998/99	1999/2000
Wheat	36.5	11.1	53.4
Barley	15.7	2.8	13.9
Maize	0.8	1.7	11.9
Potatoes	58.7	52.9	47.3
Sweet potatoes	4.8	5.0	9.5
Olives	98.1	35.3	156.5
White cabbages	14.3	11.4	13.6
Tomatoes	153.7	172.0	196.1
Cauliflower	20.4	22.2	19.2
Squash	39.2	39.1	44.8
Cucumbers	108.4	109.0	135.7
Aubergines (Eggplants) . .	36.3	37.1	39.7
Chillies	14.6	9.9	11.0
Dry onions	16.7	14.0	25.6
Green kidney beans . . .	5.7	4.7	6.8
Jew's mallow	13.5	10.6	10.9
Watermelons	19.8	13.3	7.6
Musk-melons	8.9	6.0	5.7
Grapes	56.9	44.5	56.9
Plums	5.6	6.7	12.7
Oranges	103.7	97.3	76.7
Mandarins and clementines . .	18.9	18.1	12.9
Lemons	27.3	23.2	20.8
Grapefruit	10.0	5.8	4.6
Bananas	20.7	26.4	9.4
Strawberries. . . .	4.4	4.6	5.5
Figs	6.8	7.3	8.2
Guava	15.0	11.9	12.7
Almonds	5.1	3.4	4.4

LIVESTOCK ('000 head, year ending September)

	1997/98	1998/99	1999/2000
Cattle	22.1	23.9	23.7
Sheep	538.0	504.1	566.4
Goats	252.3	295.0	308.8
Chickens	40,611	50,477	45,975

Fishing

Gaza Strip (metric tons, live weight)

	1997	1998	1999*
Bogue	81	162	160
Jack and horse mackerels . .	100	115	115
Sardinellas	2,483	1,780	1,750
Chub mackerel	120	337	340
Shrimps and prawns . . .	161	161	160
Cuttlefish and bobtail squids . .	98	144	145
Total catch (incl. others) . .	3,791	3,625	3,600

* FAO estimates.

Source: FAO, *Yearbook of Fishery Statistics*.

Finance

CURRENCY AND EXCHANGE RATES

At present there is no domestic Palestinian currency in use. The Israeli shekel, the Jordanian dinar and the US dollar all circulate within the West Bank and the Gaza Strip.

BUDGET OF THE PALESTINIAN AUTHORITY
(estimates, US $ million)

Revenue	1996	1997	1998
Domestic revenue	264.6	329.4	321.1
Tax revenue	178.8	210.9	224.3
Income tax	52.4	66.0	68.4
Value-added tax	65.8	75.0	80.6
Other receipts	85.8	118.5	96.8
Revenue clearances*	419.6	496.0	542.0
Value-added tax	216.7	216.5	202.1
Petroleum excise	100.4	111.3	106.8
Total	684.2	825.4	863.1

Expenditure†	1996	1997	1998
Current expenditure	779.3	863.2	802.6
Wages and salaries . . .	402.5	470.9	466.8
Civil service	246.5	273.4	286.0
Police force	156.0	197.5	180.9
Other purposes	376.8	392.3	335.8
Capital expenditure	173.6	214.4	204.7
Total	952.9	1,077.6	1,007.3

* Figures refer to an apportionment of an agreed pool of selected tax revenues arising as a result of the *de facto* customs union between Israel and the Palestinian territories. Israel is the collecting agent for these receipts and periodically makes transfers to the Palestinian Authority.
† Excluding the cost of foreign-financed employment programmes (estimates, US $ million): 49.2 in 1996; 5.7 in 1997; 0.5 in 1998.
Source: IMF, *West Bank and Gaza Strip: Economic Developments in the Five Years Since Oslo* (1999).

1999 (estimates, US $ million): Total revenue 1,589; Total expenditure 1,740.
2000 (estimates, US $ million): Total revenue 1,386; Total expenditure 1,386 (Current 940; Capital 446).

COST OF LIVING
(Consumer Price Index; base: 1996 = 100)

	1999	2000	2001
Food	119.3	121.2	120.7
Beverages and tobacco . . .	126.9	130.2	131.9
Textiles, clothing and footwear	123.2	125.9	123.4
Housing	116.7	126.5	133.2
All items (incl. others) . .	119.9	123.3	124.8

NATIONAL ACCOUNTS (US $ million at current prices)
Expenditure on the Gross Domestic Product

	1996	1997	1998
Government final consumption expenditure	852.4	893.6	905.5
Private final consumption expenditure	4,159.5	4,196.9	4,208.8
Increase in stocks	63.1	85.8	64.4
Gross fixed capital formation . .	1,222.0	1,339.1	1,658.1
Statistical discrepancy* . . .	72.8	126.8	3.6
Total domestic expenditure	6,369.9	6,642.2	6,840.4
Exports of goods and services . .	838.9	812.6	1,017.7
Less Imports of goods and services	3,327.8	3,399.2	3,553.9
GDP in purchasers' values .	3,881.1	4,055.7	4,304.2

* Referring to the difference between the sum of the expenditure components and official estimates of GDP, compiled from the production approach.

Gross Domestic Product by Economic Activity

	1997	1998	1999
Agriculture and fishing . . .	340.6	394.7	320.0
Mining, manufacturing, electricity and water	781.7	839.6	911.1
Construction	414.4	534.9	594.4
Wholesale and retail trade . .	464.8	406.7	525.2
Transport	200.2	217.3	214.4
Financial intermediation . . .	103.6	123.6	150.5
Services	896.8	941.0	981.7
Public administration and defence	432.3	403.9	461.5
Domestic services of households	6.9	7.8	7.4
Public-owned enterprises . . .	90.0	114.5	163.5
Sub-total	3,731.3	3,984.0	4,329.7
Financial intermediation services indirectly measured . . .	−85.0	−99.0	−116.2
Taxes on imports (net) . . .	536.0	578.9	740.5
GDP in purchasers' values	4,182.2	4,463.8	4,954.0

BALANCE OF PAYMENTS
(preliminary estimates, US $ million, excluding East Jerusalem)

	1998	1999
Exports of goods f.o.b.	610.6	602.8
Imports of goods f.o.b.	−3,021.7	−3,220.7
Trade balance	−2,411.1	−2,617.8
Exports of services	394.5	471.3
Imports of services	−507.5	−522.1
Balance on goods and services . .	−2,524.1	−2,668.7
Other income received	931.5	960.6
Other income paid	−29.9	−23.2
Balance on goods, services and income	−1,622.4	−1,731.3
Current transfers received . . .	540.2	545.9
Current transfers paid	−134.7	−173.8
Current balance	−1,216.9	−1,359.2
Capital account (net)	261.1	237.3
Direct investment abroad . . .	−160.1	−169.4
Direct investment from abroad . .	218.2	188.6
Portfolio investment (net) . . .	−80.3	−106.0
Other investment (net)	656.9	918.6
Net errors and omissions	286.3	255.0
Overall balance	52.9	35.1

External Trade

PRINCIPAL COMMODITIES (US $ '000)

Imports c.i.f.	1998	1999*	2000*
Food and live animals . . .	447,195	533,787	576,490
Beverages and tobacco . . .	97,494	116,372	125,682
Crude materials (inedible) except fuels	67,185	80,194	86,610
Mineral fuels, lubricants, etc. . .	409,881	489,247	528,387
Animal and vegetable oils and fats	19,558	23,345	25,213
Chemicals and related products .	189,739	226,479	244,597
Basic manufactures	565,422	674,906	728,899
Machinery and transport equipment	386,625	461,488	498,407
Miscellaneous manufactured articles	175,642	209,652	226,424
Other commmodities and transactions	14,363	17,144	18,516
Total	2,375,102	2,835,000	3,061,800

* Estimates.

Exports f.o.b.	1998	1999*	2000*
Food and live animals . . .	61,793	64,019	66,260
Beverages and tobacco . . .	25,432	26,348	27,270
Crude materials (inedible) except fuels	17,566	18,199	18,836
Mineral fuels, lubricants, etc. . .	7,008	7,260	7,515
Animal and vegetable oils and fats	5,343	5,535	5,729
Chemicals and related products	24,631	25,518	26,412
Basic manufactures . . .	164,865	170,804	176,783
Machinery and transport equipment	20,739	21,486	22,238
Miscellaneous manufactured articles	64,397	66,717	69,052
Other commodities and transactions	1,080	1,119	1,158
Total	392,854	407,007	421,252

* Estimates.

Transport

ROAD TRAFFIC
(registered motor vehicles holding Palestinian licence, December 2000)

	West Bank	Gaza Strip	Total
Private cars	53,026	37,098	90,124
Taxis	6,090	1,173	7,263
Buses and minibuses . . .	865	177	1,042
Trucks and commercial cars . .	13,310	8,500	21,810
Motorcycles and scooters . . .	38	253	291
Tractors	1,207	1,291	2,498
Special service and other vehicles	112	169	281
Total	74,854	49,014	123,868

Tourism

ARRIVALS OF VISITORS AT HOTELS*

	1999	2000	2001
Total	316,949	335,711	60,208

* Including Palestinians (16,598 in 1999; 25,520 in 2000; 17,432 in 2001).

Communications Media

	1999	2000	2001
Telephones ('000 main lines in use)	222.2	270.0	256.9
Mobile cellular telephones ('000 subscribers)	117	285	300
Internet users ('000)	n.a.	35	60

Source: International Telecommunication Union.

Book production (1996): 114 titles; 571,000 copies (Source: UNESCO, *Statistical Yearbook*).

Education

(1999/2000)

	Institutions	Teachers	Students
Pre-primary	843	2,874	77,402
Primary	1,259*	29,186	792,990
Secondary:			
General	499†		69,788
Vocational	9		2,762
Higher:			
Universities, etc.. . . .	12	1,822	44,987
Distance-learning . . .	1	715	20,981
Other	17	467	5,157

* Schools for primary education only.
† Including schools for primary and secondary education, and including 30 schools providing both general and vocational education.

2000/01: *Pre-primary:* 811 schools; 69,247 students; *Primary:* 1,316 schools; 830,765 students; *Secondary:* 519 schools; 76,363 students.

Adult literacy rate (official estimates): 89.2% (males 94.4%; females 83.9%) in 2000.

Directory

Administration

PALESTINIAN NATIONAL AUTHORITY

Appointed in May 1994, the Palestinian National Authority (PNA), generally known internationally as the Palestinian Authority (PA), has assumed some of the civil responsibilities formerly exercised by the Israeli Civil Administration in the Gaza Strip and parts of the West Bank.

Executive President: YASSER ARAFAT (assumed office 12 February 1996).

CABINET
(September 2002)

Minister of Information and Culture: YASSER ABD AR-RABBUH (Democratic Union).

Minister of Planning and International Co-operation: Dr NABIL SHAATH (Fatah).

Minister of Finance: Dr SALAM FAYYAD.

Minister of Economy and Trade: MAHER AL-MASRI (Fatah).

Minister of the Interior: Maj.-Gen. ABD AR-RAZZAQ AL-YAHYA.

Minister of Education and Higher Education: Dr NA'IM ABU AL-HUMMUS.

Minister of Health: Dr RIYAD AZ-ZAANOUN (Fatah).

Minister of Local Government: Dr SAEB ERAKAT (Fatah).

Minister of Justice: IBRAHIM AD-DAGHMAH.

Minister of Public Works and Housing: AZZAM AL-AHMAD (Fatah).

Minister of Social Affairs: INTISAR AL-WASIR (Fatah).

Minister of Agriculture: RAFIK AN-NATSHA.

Minister of Natural Resources: Dr ABD AR-RAHMAN HAMAD (Fatah).

Minister of Labour: GHASSAN AL-KHATIB.

Minister of Tourism and Bethlehem 2002: NABIL QAIS.

Minister of Telecommunications: IMAD AL-FALOUJI (Independent).

Minister of Transport: MITRI ABU AYTAH (Independent).

Minister of Supply: ABD AL-AZIZ SHAHIN (Fatah).

Minister of Civil Affairs: JAMIL AT-TARIFI (Fatah).

Minister of Youth and Sports: ALI AL-KAWASMEH (Fatah).

Minister of Awqaf (Religious Endowments): (vacant).

MINISTRIES

Ministry of Agriculture: POB 197, Ramallah; tel. (2) 2961080; fax (2) 2961212; e-mail moa@planet.edu.

Ministry of Awqaf (Religious Endowments): POB 54825, Jerusalem; tel. (2) 6282085; fax (2) 2986401.

Ministry of Civil Affairs: Ramallah; tel. (2) 2987336; fax (2) 2987335.

Ministry of Culture: POB 147, Ramallah; tel. (2) 2986205; fax (2) 2986204; e-mail moc@gov.ps; internet www.moc.gov.ps.

Ministry of Economy and Trade: POB 1629, Ramallah; tel. (2) 2981214; fax (2) 2981207; POB 402, Gaza; tel. (8) 2826139; fax (8) 2866700; e-mail info@met.gov.ps.

Ministry of Education: POB 576, Ramallah; tel. (2) 2983254; fax (2) 2983261; e-mail moe@planet.com; internet www.moe.gov.ps.

Ministry of Finance: Sateh Marhaba, Al-Birah/Ramallah; tel. (2) 2400372; fax (2) 2405880; e-mail mofdep@hally.edu; POB 4007, Gaza; tel. (8) 2829243; fax (8) 2820696.

Ministry of Health: POB 14, al-Mukhtar St, Nablus; tel. (9) 2384772; fax (9) 2384777; e-mail moh@gov.ps; internet www.moh.gov.ps; POB 1035, Abu Khadra Center, Gaza; tel. (8) 2829173; fax (8) 2826295; e-mail mohgaza@palnet.com.

Ministry of Higher Education and Scientific Research: POB 17360, Ramallah; tel. (2) 2982600; fax (2) 2954518; e-mail minhed@planet.edu; internet www.mohe.gov.ps.

Ministry of Housing: POB 4034, Gaza; tel. (8) 2822233; fax (8) 2822235.

Ministry of Industry: POB 2073, Ramallah; tel. (2) 2987641; fax (2) 2987640; POB 4053, Gaza; tel. (8) 2826463; fax (8) 2824884; e-mail industry_wb@gov.ps; internet www.industry.gov.ps.

Ministry of Information: POB 224, Al-Birah/Ramallah; tel. (2) 2986465; fax (2) 2954043; Gaza; tel. (8) 2866888; fax (8) 2821672; e-mail minfo@gov.ps; internet www.minfo.gov.ps.

Ministry of the Interior: Gaza; tel. (8) 2829185; fax (8) 2862500.

Ministry of Jerusalem Affairs: POB 20479, Jerusalem; tel. (2) 6273330; fax (2) 6286820.

Ministry of Justice: Gaza; tel. (8) 2822231; fax (8) 2867109.

Ministry of Labour: POB 350, Ramallah Industrial Zone, Ramallah; tel. (2) 2900375; fax (2) 2900607; e-mail narman@gov.ps; internet www.mol.gov.ps; POB 4021, Gaza; tel. (8) 2829146; fax (8) 2822400.

Ministry of Local Government: Jericho; tel. (2) 2321260; fax (2) 2321240; internet www.p-ol.com/~molg.

Ministry of Planning and International Co-operation: Ramallah; tel. (2) 5747045; fax (2) 5747046; POB 4017, Gaza; tel. (8) 2829260; fax (8) 2824090; e-mail info@nmopic.pna.net; internet www.mopic.gov.ps.

Ministry of Public Works: Gaza; tel. (8) 2829232; fax (8) 2823653; e-mail mopgaza@palnet.com.

Ministry of Social Affairs: POB 3525, Ramallah; tel. (2) 2986181; fax (2) 2985239.

Ministry of Supply: Gaza; tel. (8) 2824324; fax (8) 2826430.

Ministry of Telecommunications: Ramallah; tel. (2) 9986555; fax (2) 9986556; Gaza; tel. (8) 2829171; fax (8) 2824555.

Ministry of Tourism and Antiquities: POB 534, Manger St, Bethlehem; tel. (2) 2741581; fax (2) 2743753; e-mail mota@visit-palestine.com; internet www.visit-palestine.com.

Ministry of Transport: POB 399, Ramallah; tel. (2) 2986945; fax (2) 2986943.

Ministry of Youth and Sports: POB 52, Ramallah; tel. (2) 2985981; fax (2) 2985991.

President

The first election for a Palestinian Executive President was contested on 20 January 1996 by two candidates: Yasser Arafat and Samiha Khalil. Arafat received 88.1% of the votes cast and Khalil 9.3%; the remaining 2.6% of the votes were spoilt.

Legislature

PALESTINIAN LEGISLATIVE COUNCIL

Speaker: AHMAD QURAY.

General Election, 20 January 1996

Party	Seats
Fatah	54
Independent Fatah	12
Independent Islamists	4
Popular Front for the Liberation of Palestine (PFLP)	1
Palestinian Democratic Union (FIDA)	1
Independents	16
Total	88*

* The total number of seats in the Palestinian Legislative Council—including one which is automatically reserved for the Palestinian President—is 89.

The first Palestinian legislative elections took place in 16 multi-member constituencies (including East Jerusalem) on 20 January 1996. An estimated 79% of eligible voters participated in the elections. Prior to the polls European Union observers criticized the election commission appointed by Yasser Arafat for late alterations to electoral procedure, which, it was felt, might prejudice the prospects of some candidates. Although irregularities were reported during voting, these were not regarded as sufficiently serious to compromise the final outcome. The elections were officially boycotted by all sections of the so-called Palestinian 'rejectionist' opposition, including the Islamic Resistance Movement (Hamas) and Islamic Jihad, although Hamas did endorse a list of 'approved' candidates for those voters who chose to participate. All deputies elected to the Palestinian Legislative Council (PLC) automatically became members of the Palestine National Council (PNC), the existing 483 members of which were subsequently permitted to return from exile by the Israeli authorities, in order, among other things, to consider amendments to the Palestinian National Charter (or PLO Covenant), which has largely been superseded by the agreements concluded between Israel and the PLO since September 1993. Under Palestinian legislation, the tenure of the PLC was scheduled to expire after the Israeli Government has implemented all of its outstanding obligations under the terms of the Interim Agreement of 1995 (see Recent History, above); elections were, however, scheduled to take place in January 2003.

Political Organizations

Palestine Liberation Organization (PLO): Gaza City; after the conclusion of the Cairo Agreement on the Gaza Strip and Jericho, signed by the PLO and Israel on 4 May 1994, the PLO gradually transferred its headquarters from Tunis, Tunisia, to the Gaza Strip; f. 1964; the supreme organ of the PLO is the Palestine National Council (PNC; Speaker SALIM AZ-ZA'NUN), while the PLO Executive Committee (Chair. YASSER ARAFAT; Sec.-Gen. MAHMUD ABBAS) deals with day-to-day business. Fatah (the Palestine National Liberation Movement) joined the PNC in 1968, and all the guerrilla organizations joined the Council in 1969. In 1973 the Palestinian Central Council (PCC; Chair. SALIM AZ-ZA'NUN) was established to act as an intermediary between the PNC and the Executive Committee. This 95-member Council meets when the PNC is not in session and approves major policy decisions on its behalf. Chair. YASSER ARAFAT.

The most important guerrilla organizations are:

Fatah (The Palestine National Liberation Movement): e-mail fateh@fateh.org; internet www.fateh.net; f. 1957; the largest single Palestinian movement, embraces a coalition of varying views from conservative to radical; Leader YASSER ARAFAT; Sec.-Gen. FAROUK KADDOUMI; Central Cttee (elected by Fatah's 530-member Congress, 31 May 1980): YASSER ARAFAT, SALAH KHALAF, FAROUK KADDOUMI, MAHMUD ABBAS, KHALID AL-HASSAN, HAYIL ABD AL-HAMID, MUHAMMAD GHUNAIM, SALIM AZ-ZA'NUN, RAFIQ AN-NATSHAH, HANI AL-HASAN.

Popular Front for the Liberation of Palestine (PFLP): POB 12144, Damascus, Syria; f. 1967; Marxist-Leninist; publ. *Democratic Palestine* (monthly, in English); Sec.-Gen. AHMAD SAADAT; in 1994 the PFLP announced the formation of the Democratic National Action Front (DNAF), which it described as an open political, popular forum, an extension of the PFLP.

Democratic Front for the Liberation of Palestine (DFLP): Damascus, Syria; Marxist; split from the PFLP in 1969; Sec.-Gen. NAIF HAWATMEH.

Arab Liberation Front (ALF): f. 1968; Iraqi-backed; Leader MAHMOUD ISMAIL.

Palestinian Popular Struggle Front (PPSF): f. 1967; Sec.-Gen. Dr SAMIR GHOUSHA.

Hezb ash-Sha'ab (Palestine People's Party): POB 54224, Jerusalem; tel. (2) 2960104; fax (2) 2960640; e-mail shaab@palpeople.org; internet www.palpeople.org; formerly Palestine Communist Party, admitted to the PNC at its 18th session in 1987; Sec.-Gen. SULAYMAN AN-NAJJAB.

Palestine Liberation Front (PLF): split from PFLP—GC in April 1977; the PLF split into two factions at the end of 1983, both of which retained the name PLF; one faction (Leader MUHAMMAD 'ABU' ABBAS) based in Tunis, Tunisia, and Baghdad, Iraq, and remaining nominally loyal to Yasser Arafat; the other faction belonging to the anti-Arafat National Salvation Front and having offices in Damascus, Syria, and Libya. A third group derived from the PLF was reportedly formed by its Central Cttee Secretary, Abd al-Fattah Ghanim, in June 1986. At the 18th session of the PNC, a programme for the unification of the PLF was announced, with Talaat Yaqoub (died November 1988) named as Secretary-General and 'Abu Abbas' appointed to the PLO Executive Committee, while unification talks were held. The merging of the two factions was announced in June 1987, with 'Abu Abbas' becoming Deputy Secretary-General.

Palestinian Democratic Union (FIDA): split from the DFLP in March 1990; Leader YASSER ABD AR-RABBUH; Sec.-Gen. SALEH RA'FAT.

The anti-Arafat **National Salvation Front** includes the following organizations:

Popular Front for the Liberation of Palestine—General Command (PFLP—GC): Damascus, Syria; split from the PFLP in 1968; pro-Syrian; Leader AHMAD JIBRIL.

Popular Front for the Liberation of Palestine—National General Command: Amman, Jordan; split from the PFLP—GC in 1999; aims to co-operate with the PNA; Leader ATIF YUNUS.

As-Saiqa (Vanguard of the Popular Liberation War): f. 1968; Syrian-backed; Leader ISSAM AL-QADI.

Palestine Revolutionary Communist Party: Damascus, Syria; Sec.-Gen. ARBI AWAD.

Alliance of Palestinian Forces: f. 1994; 10 members representing the PFLP, the DFLP, the PLF, the PPSF, the Palestine Revolutionary Communist Party and the PFLP—GC; opposes the Declaration of Principles on Palestinian Self-Rule signed by Israel and the PLO in September 1993, and subsequent agreements concluded within its framework (the 'Oslo accords'). The **Fatah Revolutionary Council**, headed by Sabri Khalil al-Banna, alias 'Abu Nidal', split from Fatah in 1973. Its headquarters were formerly in Baghdad, Iraq, but the office was closed down and its staff expelled from the country by the Iraqi authorities in November 1983; a new base was established in Damascus, Syria, in December. Al-Banna was readmitted to Iraq in 1984, having fled Syria. With 'Abu Musa' (whose rebel Fatah group is called **Al-Intifada**, or 'Uprising'), 'Abu Nidal' formed a joint rebel Fatah command in February 1985, and both had offices in Damascus until June 1987, when those of 'Abu Nidal' were closed by the Syrian Government. Forces loyal to 'Abu Nidal' surrendered to Fatah forces at the Rashidiyeh Palestinian refugee camp near Tyre, northern Lebanon, in 1990. 'Abu Nidal' was reported to have been found dead in Baghdad in August 2002.

The militant Islamist organizations, **Islamic Jihad** (Gen. Sec. RAMADAN ABDALLAH SHALLAH) and the **Islamic Resistance Movement** (Hamas; Spiritual Leader Sheikh AHMAD YASSIN), are also active in the West Bank and Gaza. Like the organizations represented in the Alliance of Palestinian Forces, they are strongly opposed to the Oslo accords. The formation of the **Right Movement for Championing the Palestinian People's Sons** by former members of Hamas was announced in April 1995. The movement, based in Gaza City, was reported to support the PNA.

Diplomatic Representation

Countries with which the PLO maintains diplomatic relations include:

Afghanistan, Albania, Algeria, Angola, Austria, Bahrain, Bangladesh, Benin, Bhutan, Botswana, Brunei, Bulgaria, Burkina Faso, Burundi, Cambodia, Cameroon, Cape Verde, Central African Republic, Chad, China (People's Rep.), Comoros, Congo (Dem. Rep.), Congo (Rep.), Cuba, Cyprus, Czech Republic, Djibouti, Egypt, Equatorial Guinea, Ethiopia, Gabon, Gambia, Ghana, Guinea, Guinea-Bissau, Hungary, India, Indonesia, Iran, Iraq, Jordan, Korea (Dem. People's Rep.), Kuwait, Laos, Lebanon, Libya, Madagascar, Malaysia, Maldives, Mali, Malta, Mauritania, Mauritius, Mongolia, Morocco, Mozambique, Nepal, Nicaragua, Niger, Nigeria, Norway, Oman, Pakistan, Philippines, Poland, Qatar, Romania, Russia, Rwanda, São Tomé and Príncipe, Saudi Arabia, Senegal, Seychelles, Sierra Leone, Somalia, Sri Lanka, Sudan, Swaziland, Sweden, Tanzania, Togo, Tunisia, Turkey, Uganda, United Arab Emirates, Van-

uatu, the Vatican City, Viet Nam, Yemen, Yugoslavia, Zambia and Zimbabwe.

The following states, while they do not recognize the State of Palestine, allow the PLO to maintain a regional office: Belgium, Brazil, France, Germany, Greece, Italy, Japan, the Netherlands, Portugal, Spain, Switzerland and the United Kingdom.

A Palestinian passport has been available for residents of the Gaza Strip and the Jericho area only since April 1995. In September 1995 the passport was recognized by 29 states, including: Algeria, Bahrain, Bulgaria, China (People's Rep.), Cyprus, Egypt, France, Germany, Greece, India, Israel, Jordan, Malta, Morocco, the Netherlands, Pakistan, Qatar, Romania, Saudi Arabia, South Africa, Spain, Sweden, Switzerland, Tunisia, Turkey, the United Arab Emirates, the United Kingdom and the USA.

Judicial System

In the Gaza Strip, the West Bank towns of Jericho, Nablus, Ramallah, Jenin, Tulkarm, Qalqilya, Bethlehem and Hebron, and in other, smaller population centres in the West Bank, the PNA has assumed limited jurisdiction with regard to civil affairs. However, the situation is confused owing to the various and sometimes conflicting legal systems which have operated in the territories occupied by Israel in 1967: Israeli military and civilian law; Jordanian law; and acts, orders-in-council and ordinances that remain from the period of the British Mandate in Palestine. Religious and military courts have been established under the auspices of the PNA. In February 1995 the PNA established a Higher State Security Court in Gaza to decide on security crimes both inside and outside the PNA's area of jurisdiction; and to implement all valid Palestinian laws, regulations, rules and orders in accordance with Article 69 of the Constitutional Law of the Gaza Strip of 5 March 1962. As of September 2000 the PLC had passed a total of 30 laws; others were being drafted, reviewed or awaited approval by the President.

General Prosecutor of the PNA: ZUHEIR AS-SURANI.

The Press

NEWSPAPERS

Akhbar an-Naqab: Gaza City; internet www.akhbarna.com; Arabic.

Al-Ayyam: e-mail info@al-ayyam.com; internet www.al-ayyam.com; Arabic; weekly.

Al-Ayyam al-Arabi: Ramallah; f. 1999; Arabic; daily newspaper published by PNA; Editor-in-Chief SALIM SALAMAH.

Filastin ath-Thawra (Palestine Revolution): normally published in Beirut, but resumed publication from Cyprus in November 1982; Arabic; weekly newspaper of the PLO.

Al-Hadaf: organ of the PFLP; Arabic; weekly.

Al-Haria (Liberation): organ of the DFLP; Arabic.

Al-Hayat al-Jadidah: West Bank; e-mail alhayat@p-ol.com; internet www.alhayat-j.com; f. 1994; Arabic; weekly; Editor NADIL AMR.

Al-Istiqlal: Gaza City; e-mail alesteqlal@p-i-s.com; internet www.alesteqlal.com; organ of Islamic Jihad; Arabic; weekly.

Al-Quds (Jerusalem): Jerusalem; internet www.alquds.com; Arabic; daily.

Ar-Risala (Letter): Gaza City; organ of the Islamist Construction and Democracy Party; Arabic; weekly; Editor-in-Chief GHAZI HAMAD.

Al-Watan: Gaza City; supports Hamas; Arabic; weekly.

PERIODICALS

Filastin (Palestine): Gaza City; f. 1994; Arabic; weekly.

Palestine Report: Jerusalem Media and Communications Centre, POB 25047, Nablus Rd, Jerusalem; tel. (2) 5819777; fax (2) 5829534; e-mail palreport@jmcc.org; internet www.jmcc.org/media/report online; f. 1990; English; weekly; current affairs.

Shu'un Filastiniya (Palestine Affairs): POB 5614, 92 Gr. Afxentiou St, Nicosia, Cyprus; tel. 461140; Arabic; monthly.

NEWS AGENCY

Wikalat Anbaa' Filastiniya (WAFA, Palestine News Agency): Gaza City; tel. (8) 2824056; fax (8) 2824046; e-mail wafa15@palnet.com; internet www.wafa.pna.net; formerly based in Beirut, but resumed activities in Cyprus and Tunis, November 1982; official PLO news agency; Editor ZIAD ABD AL-FATTAH.

Broadcasting and Communications

TELECOMMUNICATIONS

Palestine Telecommunications Co PLC (PalTel): POB 1570, Nablus; tel. (9) 2376225; fax (9) 2376227; e-mail paltel@palnet.net;

internet www.paltel.net; f. 1995; privately-owned monopoly; launched cellular telephone service (Palcel) in 1999; Chair. HATEM AL-HALAWANI; Dir-Gen. WALID IRSHAID.

Palestine Cellular Co (Jawal): Rafeedia St, Nablus; tel. (9) 2337370; fax (9) 2337366; internet www.myjawwal.com; f. 1999; 65% owned by PalTel, 35% state-owned; CEO Hakam Kanafani.

BROADCASTING

Palestinian Broadcasting Corpn (PBC): POB 984, Al-Birah/Ramallah; tel. (2) 2959894; fax (2) 2959893; e-mail pbc@planet.edu; Chair. RADWAN ABU AYYASH.

Sawt Filastin (Voice of Palestine): c/o Police HQ, Jericho; tel. (2) 921220; internet www.bailasan.com/pinc; f. 1994; official radio station of the PNA; broadcasts in Arabic from Jericho and Ramallah; Dir RADWAN ABU AYYASH.

Palestine Television: f. 1994; broadcasts from Ramallah and Gaza City; Dir RADWAN ABU AYYASH.

Finance

(cap. = capital; dep. = deposits; brs = branches; m. = million)

BANKING

Palestine Monetary Authority

It is intended to develop the Palestine Monetary Authority (PMA), which was established in December 1994, into the Central Bank of Palestine. In July 1995 the PMA began to license, inspect and supervise the Palestinian and foreign commercial banks operating in the Gaza Strip and the Jericho enclave in the West Bank at that time. In December 1995 the PMA assumed responsibility for 13 banks in the Palestinian Autonomous Areas over which the Central Bank of Israel had hitherto exercised control. Three currencies circulate in the Palestinian economy—the Jordanian dinar, the Israeli shekel and the US dollar. The PMA, which is seeking a reserve base of US $10m. from donors, currently has no right of issue. According to the PMA, there were 22 banks with a total of 126 branches operating in the West Bank and Gaza in December 2001. In January 2002 the banks' deposit base amounted to $3,275m. Gov. FOUAD HAMDI BESEISO; Nablus Rd, Ramallah; tel. (2) 2964786; fax (2) 2959922; e-mail info@pma-ram.pna.net; POB 4026, An-Nassera St, Gaza; tel. (8) 2825713; fax (8) 2824487; e-mail pmgaza@palnet.com; internet www.pma-palestine.org.

National Banks

Bank of Palestine Ltd: POB 50, Omar al-Mukhtar St, Gaza City; tel. (8) 2843059; fax (8) 2846025; e-mail info@bankofpalestine.com; internet www.bankofpalestine.com; f. 1960; cap. US $15.2m., res US $4.9m., dep. US $213.6m., total assets US $239.2m. (Dec. 2000); Pres., Chair. and Gen. Man. HASHEM ATA SHAWA; 19 brs in West Bank and Gaza.

Commercial Bank of Palestine PLC: POB 1799, Michael Tanous Bldg, Alawda St, Ramallah; tel. (2) 2954141; fax (2) 2953888; e-mail cbp@cbpal.palnet.com; f. 1992; total assets US $87m.; Gen. Man. KHALID MUHAMMAD GHABEISH; 4 brs.

Palestine International Bank: Al-Birah/Ramallah; tel. (2) 2983300; fax (2) 2983344; e-mail pib@pib.palnet.com; f. 1996; cap. US $20m; Chair. ABD AS-SALAM ABU ISSA.

Investment Banks

Arab Palestinian Investment Bank: POB 1260, Al-Harji Bldg, Ramallah; tel. (2) 2987126; fax (2) 2987125; e-mail apibank@palnet.com; f. 1996; Arab Bank of Jordan has a 51% share; cap. US $15m.

Palestine Investment Bank PLC: POB 3675, Al-Helal St, Al-Birah/Ramallah; tel. (2) 2407880; fax (2) 2407887; e-mail pibc@alami.net; f. 1995 by the PNA; some shareholders based in Jordan and the Gulf states; cap. US $20m.; provides full commercial and investment banking services throughout the West Bank and Gaza; Man. YOUSUF AL-QADI; 6 brs.

Al-Quds Bank for Development and Investment: POB 2384, Ramallah; tel. (2) 2961750; fax (2) 2961753; e-mail qudsbkhq@palnet.com; f. 1996; merchant bank; Dirs EID GHAYADAH, MUHAMMAD SALMAN; 3 brs.

Islamic Banks

Arab Islamic Bank: POB 631, Nablus St, Al-Birah/Ramallah; tel. (2) 2980060; fax (2) 2980065; e-mail aib@p-ol.com; internet www.p-ol.com/~alb; Regional Man. MAHER AL-KABABJI; 6 brs.

Palestine Islamic Bank: POB 1244, Omar al-Mukhtar St, Gaza City; tel. (8) 2825259; fax (8) 2825269.

Foreign Banks

Arab Bank PLC (Jordan): Regional Management: POB 1476, Ramallah; tel. (2) 2982400; fax (2) 2982444; e-mail arabbank@palnet.com; internet www.arabbank.com; f. 1930; dep. of some US $1,800m. (Jan. 2001); Senior Exec. Vice-Pres. SHUKRY BISHARA; 18 brs in the West Bank and Gaza.

Bank of Jordan PLC: POB 1328, Bahour Bldg, Al-Quds St, Ramallah; tel. (2) 2952702; fax (2) 2952705; e-mail bojreg@palnet.com; internet www.boj.com.jo; Chair. TAWFIK FAKHOURY; Gen. Man. AZIZ SHAKER; 4 brs.

Cairo Amman Bank (Jordan): POB 1870, Ramallah; tel. (2) 2983500; fax (2) 2952764; e-mail cabl@attmail.com; internet www.ca-bank.com; Regional Man. MAZEN ABU HAMDEN; 11 brs.

Jordan National Bank PLC: POB 550, Az-Zahra St, Ramallah; tel. (2) 2986310; fax (2) 2986311; e-mail jnb-ram@alqudsnet.com; internet www.ahli.com; f. 1995; Chair. ABD AL-QADER M. TASH; Regional Man. HANNA GHATTAS; 6 brs.

Other foreign banks include Egyptian Arab Land Bank, Housing Bank for Trade and Finance (Jordan), HSBC Bank Middle East (United Kingdom), Jordan Gulf Bank, Jordan Kuwait Bank, Principal Bank for Development and Agricultural Credit (Egypt), Standard Chartered Grindlays Bank Ltd (United Kingdom) and Union Bank for Savings and Investment (Jordan).

STOCK EXCHANGE

Palestine Securities Exchange (PSE): POB 128, Nablus; tel. (9) 2375946; fax (9) 2375945; e-mail psexchng@palnet.com; internet www.p-s-e.com; f. 1997; Chair. SABEIH MASRI; Gen. Man. NAIM KHUSHASHI.

INSURANCE

A very small insurance industry exists in the West Bank and Gaza.

Arab Insurance Establishment Co Ltd (AIE): POB 166, Nablus; tel. (9) 2384040; fax (9) 2384032; f. 1975; Man. Dir IBRAHIM ABD AL-HADI; Gen. Man. SHAKER HATER.

Gaza Ahliea Insurance Co Ltd: POB 1214, Al-Jalaa Tower, Remal, Gaza; tel. (8) 2824035; fax (8) 2824015; e-mail gaicnet@palnet.com; f. 1994; Chair. and Gen. Man. Dr MUHAMMAD SABAWI; 6 brs.

National Insurance Co: POB 1819, 34 Municipality St, Al-Birah/Ramallah; tel. (2) 2983800; fax (2) 2407460; e-mail nic@palnet.com; f. 1992; Chair. MUHAMMAD MAHMOUD MASROUJI; Gen. Man. AZIZ MAHMOUD ABD AL-JAWAD; 7 brs.

DEVELOPMENT FINANCE ORGANIZATIONS

Arab Palestinian Investment Co. Ltd: POB 2396, Kharaz Center, Yafa St, Industrial Zone, Ramallah; tel. (2) 2984242; fax (2) 2984243; e-mail apic@palnet.com; internet www.apic-pal.com.

Jerusalem Real Estate Investment Co: POB 1876, Ramallah; tel. (2) 2965215; fax (2) 2965217; e-mail jrei@palnet.com; f. 1996; Man. Dir WALID AL-AHMAD.

Palestine Development & Investment Co (PADICO): POB 316, Nablus; tel. (9) 2384354; fax (9) 2384355; e-mail padico@padico.com; internet www.padico.com; f. 1993; Chair. MUNIB R. AL-MASRI; Vice-Chair. NABIL GHATTAS SARRAF.

Palestinian Economic Council for Development and Reconstruction (PECDAR): POB 54910, Dahiyat Al-Barid, Jerusalem; tel. (2) 2362300; fax (2) 2347041; e-mail info@pecdar.pna.net; internet www.pecdar.org; privately-owned; Dir-Gen. Dr MUHAMMAD SHTAYYEH.

Palestine Real Estate Investment Co (Aqaria): POB 4049, Gaza; tel. (8) 2824815; fax (8) 2824845; e-mail aqaria@rannet.com; internet www.aqaria.com; f. 1994; Chair. NABIL SARRAF; Man. MUHAMMAD ISMAEL.

Trade and Industry

CHAMBERS OF COMMERCE

Bethlehem Chamber of Commerce and Industry: POB 59, Bethlehem; tel. (2) 2742742; fax (2) 2764402; e-mail bcham@palnet.com; internet www.pal-chambers.com; f. 1952; 2,500 mems.

Federation of Chambers of Commerce, Industry and Agriculture: tel. (2) 6280727; fax (2) 6280644; e-mail fpccia@palnet.com; internet www.pal-chambers.com.

Hebron Chamber of Commerce and Industry: POB 272, Hebron; tel. (2) 2228218; fax (2) 2227490; e-mail hebcham@hebronet.com; internet www.pal-chambers.com; f. 1954; 5,500 mems.

Jenin Chamber of Commerce, Industry and Agriculture: Jenin; tel. (4) 2501107; fax (4) 2503388; e-mail jencham@hally.net; internet www.pal-chambers.com; f. 1953; 3,800 mems.

Jericho Chamber of Commerce, Industry and Agriculture: POB 91, Jericho; tel. (2) 2323313; fax (2) 2322394; e-mail jercom@ hally.net; internet www.pal-chambers.com; f. 1953; 400 mems.

Jerusalem Chamber of Commerce and Industry: Jerusalem; tel. (2) 6282351; fax (2) 6272615; e-mail chamber@alqudsnet.com; internet www.pal-chambers.com; 2,050 mems.

Nablus Chamber of Commerce and Industry: POB 35, Nablus; tel. (9) 2380335; fax (9) 2377605; e-mail nablus@palnet.com; internet www.pal-chambers.com; f 1941; 4,800 mems.

Palestine Chamber of Commerce in the Gaza Strip: POB 33, Sabra Quarter, Gaza; tel. (8) 2864588; fax (8) 2821172; e-mail gazacham@palnet.com; internet www.pal-chambers.com; f. 1954; Chair. MUHAMMAD AL-QUDWAH; 14,000 mems.

Palestinian-European Chamber of Commerce: tel. (2) 894883.

Qalqilya Chamber of Commerce, Industry and Agriculture: POB 13, Qalqilya; tel. (9) 2941473; fax (9) 2940164; e-mail cham berq@hally.net; internet www.pal-chambers.com; f. 1972; 1,068 mems.

Ramallah Chamber of Commerce and Industry: POB 256, Al-Birah/Ramallah; tel. (2) 2955052; fax (2) 2984691; e-mail info@ ramallahcci.org; internet www.ramallahcci.org; f. 1950; Chair. MUHAMMAD AHMAD AMIN; Vice-Chair. YOUSUF ASH-SHARIF; 3,700 mems.

Salfit Chamber of Commerce, Industry and Agriculture: Salfit; tel. (2) 2395970; fax (2) 2574762; e-mail salfeet-chamb@ hally.net; internet www.pal-chambers.com.

Tulkarm Chamber of Commerce, Industry and Agriculture: POB 51, Tulkarm; tel. (9) 2671010; fax (9) 2675623; e-mail tul karm@zaytona.com; internet www.pal-chambers.com; f. 1945; 625 mems.

TRADE AND INDUSTRIAL ORGANIZATIONS

Union of Industrialists: POB 1296, Gaza; tel. (8) 2866222; fax (8) 2862013; Chair MUHAMMAD YAZIJI.

UTILITIES
Electricity

Palestinian Energy Authority (PEA): POB 3591, Nablus St, Al-Birah/Ramallah; tel. (2) 2986190; fax (2) 2986191; POB 3041, Gaza; tel. (8) 2808484; fax (8) 2808488; e-mail pea@palnet.com; internet www.pea.gov.ps; f. 1994; Chair. Dr ABD AR-RAHMAN T. HAMAD.

Jerusalem District Electricity Co Ltd (JDECO): internet www.jdeco.net.

National Electric Co (NEC): West Bank; f. 2000.

Palestine Electric Co (PEC): Gaza; f. 1999; Chair. SAID KHOURY; Man. Dir SAMIR SHAWWA.

Water

Palestinian Water Authority (PWA): POB 2174, Ramallah; internet www.pwa.pna.org; Dir Eng. NABIL ASH-SHARIF.

Transport

CIVIL AVIATION

Palestinian Civil Aviation Authority (PCAA): Gaza International Airport, Gaza; tel. (8) 2822800; fax (8)2823109; e-mail fzaidan@palairlines.com; internet www.gaza-airport.org; f. 1994; Gaza International Airport was formally inaugurated in November 1998 to operate services by Palestinian Airlines (its subsidiary), Egypt Air and Royal Jordanian Airline; Royal Air Maroc began to operate services to Amman, Abu Dhabi, Cairo, Doha, Dubai, Jeddah, Istanbul and Larnaca, and intend to expand their network to Europe; the airport was closed by the Israeli authorities in February 2001 and the runway seriously damaged by Israeli air-strikes in late 2001 and early 2002; Chair. and Dir-Gen. FAYEZ A. ZAIDAN.

Palestinian Airlines: POB 4043, Gaza; tel. (8) 2827834; fax (8) 2821309; e-mail commercial@palairlines.com; internet www.palair lines.com; f. 1994; state-owned; Chair. and Dir-Gen. FAYEZ A. ZAIDAN; Commercial Dir YOUSUF SHAATH.

Tourism

Although the tourist industry in the West Bank was virtually destroyed as a result of the 1967 Arab–Israeli war, by the late 1990s the sector was expanding significantly, with a number of hotels being opened or under construction. Much of the tourism in the West Bank centres around the historical and biblical sites of Jerusalem and Bethlehem. However, the renewed outbreak of Israeli–Palestinian conflict in the West Bank and Gaza Strip from late 2000 has prevented the recovery of the tourist industry.

Ministry of Tourism and Antiquities: POB 534, Bethlehem; tel. (2) 2741581; fax (2) 2743753; e-mail mota@visit-palestine.com; internet www.visit-palestine.com.

Near East Tourist Agency: POB 19015, 18 Azzahra St, Jerusalem; tel. (2) 6282515; fax (2) 6282415; e-mail operations@netours.com.

Defence

Dir-Gen. of the Palestinian National Security Forces: Maj-Gen. NASSER YOUSSEF.

Estimated Security Budget (1999): US $500m.

Paramilitary Forces (August 2001): an estimated 35,000: including Public Security Force 14,000 (Gaza 6,000; West Bank 8,000); Civil Police Force 10,000 (Gaza 4,000; West Bank 6,000); General Intelligence Force 3,000; Preventive Security Force 3,000 (Gaza 1,200; West Bank 1,800); Military Intelligence Force 500; Presidential Security Force 1,000. In addition there are small forces belonging to Coastal Police, Civil Defence, Air Force, Customs and Excise Police Force and the University Security Service.

Education

According to the World Bank, Palestinians are among the most highly educated of any Arab group. However, basic and secondary education facilities in the West Bank and Gaza Strip are described as poor. In the West Bank the Jordanian education system is in operation. Services are provided by the Israeli Civil Administration, the UN Relief and Works Agency for Palestine Refugees in the Near East (UNRWA) and private, mainly charitable, organizations. In the West Bank and Gaza schools operated by the Civil Administration enrol some 62% of all primary and secondary school students. UNRWA provides education to about 31%. In 1991 enrolment in primary schools was equivalent to about 102% of the estimated population aged 6–12 years (due to either underestimation of that population or the enrolment of over-age students). Vocational education is offered by the Civil Administration and UNWRA. All university and most community college education is provided by private, voluntary organizations. There are 20 community and teacher training colleges in the West Bank, and six universities (including an open university). The Egyptian system of education operates in the Gaza Strip, where there are two universities and one teacher training college. Palestinian education has been severely disrupted since 1987. Universities have played a major role in the political activities of the West Bank and Gaza, and were closed by the Israeli Civil Administration during 1987–1992. Education has also been disrupted during the Palestinian *intifada* which began in late 2000.

Since May 1994 the PNA has assumed responsibility for education in Gaza and parts of the West Bank. In 1999/2000, according to the Palestinian Central Bureau of Statistics (PCBS), a total of 77,402 pupils attended 843 pre-primary institutions, and 792,990 attended 1,259 primary institutions. In the same year 72,550 students attended secondary institutions. The number of teachers at pre-primary institutions in 1999/2000 was 2,874, and there were 29,186 teachers at primary and secondary schools. In that year 44,987 students attended universities or equivalent third-level institutions, while teachers numbered 1,822. In 2001/02 UNRWA operated 95 schools in the West Bank and 169 in the Gaza Strip. The number of pupils receiving education through the UNRWA programme in that year was 58,509 in the West Bank and 184,951 in the Gaza Strip. Education personnel numbered 2,432 in the West Bank and 4,951 in the Gaza Strip. In addition, UNRWA operated four vocational training centres and awarded 70 university scholarships. In 2002 UNRWA budgeted some US $84.0m. (equivalent to some $345 per student) for expenditure on Palestinian education.

Bibliography

A very large literature on the Palestinian question exists and many of these works are included in the bibliography concluding the chapter on Israel. The following are mainly volumes which have appeared since the signing of the Declaration of Principles on Palestinian Self-Rule by Israel and the PLO in September 1993.

Abu-Amr, Ziad. *Islamic Fundamentalism in the West Bank and Gaza: Muslim Brotherhood and Islamic Jihad*. Bloomington, Indiana University Press, 1995.

Ahmed, Hisham. *Hamas: from religious salvation to political transformation—the rise of Hamas in Palestinian society*. Jerusalem, The Palestinian Academic Society for the Study of International Affairs, 1994.

Artz, Donna E. *Refugees into Citizens: Palestinians and the End of the Arab–Israeli Conflict*. New York, Council on Foreign Relations, 1997.

Aruri, Naseer. *The Obstruction of Peace: the US, Israel and the Palestinians*. Monroe, Common Courage Press, 1995.

(Ed.) *Palestinian Refugees: The Right of Return*. London, Pluto Press, 2001

Ashrawi, Hanan. *This Side of Peace*. London, Simon and Schuster, 1995.

Ateek, Naim, and Prior, Michael (Eds). *Holy Land, Hollow Jubilee: God, Justice and the Palestinians*. London, Melisende, 1999.

Baron, Xavier. *Les Palestiniens: Genèse d'une nation*. Paris, Editions du Seuil, 2000.

Buchanan, Andrew S. *Peace with Justice: A History of the Israeli-Palestinian Declaration of Principles on Interim Self-Government Arrangements*. London, Macmillan, 2001.

Butt, Gerald. *Life at the Crossroads: a history of Gaza*. London, Rimal-Scorpion Cavendish, 1995.

Cattan, Henry. *The Palestine Question*. London, Saqi Books, 2000.

Cohn-Sherbok, Prof. Dan, and El-Alami, Dawoud. *The Palestine–Israeli Conflict: A Beginner's Guide*. Oxford, Oneworld Publications, 2001.

Cubert, Harold M. *The PFLP's Changing Role in the Middle East*. London, Frank Cass, 1997.

Darweish, Marwan, and Rigby, Andrew. *Palestinians in Israel: nationality and citizenship*. University of Bradford, 1995.

Finkelstein, Norman J. *The Rise and Fall of Palestine*. Minneapolis, University of Minnesota Press, 1997.

Gelber, Yoav. *Palestine, 1948: War, Escape and the Emergence of the Palestinian Refugee Problem*. Brighton, Sussex Academic Press, 2001.

Ghanem, As'ad. *The Palestinian Regime: A 'Partial Democracy'*. Sussex Academic Press, 2002.

Hamzeh, Muna. *Refugees in our own land. Chronicles from a Palestinian refugee camp in Bethlehem*. London, Pluto Press, 2001.

Karmi, Ghada, and Cotran, Eugene (Eds). *The Palestinian Exodus, 1948–98*. Reading, Ithaca, 1999.

Khalidi, Rashid. *Palestinian Identity: the construction of modern national consciousness*. New York, Columbia University Press, 1997.

Klieman, Aharon. *Compromising Palestine: A Guide to Final Status Negotiations*. New York, Columbia Universty Press, 2000.

Levenberg, Haim. *The Military Preparations of the Arab Community in Palestine 1945–48*. London, Frank Cass, 1993.

Masalha, Nur (Ed.). *The Palestinians in Israel: is Israel the state of all its citizens and 'absentees'?* Haifa, Galilee Centre for Social Research, 1993.

A Land Without a People: Israel, Transfer and the Palestinians 1949–96. London, Faber and Faber, 1997.

Mattar, Philip. *Encyclopaedia of the Palestinians*. New York, Facts on File Inc., 2000.

Mazzawi, Musa. *Palestine and the Law*. Reading, Ithaca Press, 1997.

McDowall, David. *The Palestinians—the road to nationhood*. London, Minority Rights Publications, 1995.

Milton-Edwards, Beverley. *Islamic Politics in Palestine*. London, I. B. Tauris, 1996.

Neff, Donald. *Fallen Pillars: US Policy towards Palestine and Israel, 1947–1994*. Institute for Palestine Studies, 1995.

Peleg, Ilan. *Human Rights in the West Bank and Gaza: legacy and politics*. NY, Syracuse University Press, 1995.

Robinson, Glenn E. *Building a Palestinian State: The Incomplete Revolution*. Bloomington, Indiana University Press, 1997.

Rogan, Eugene L. and Shlaim, Avi (Eds). *The War for Palestine: Rewriting the History of 1948*. Cambridge University Press, 2000.

Roy, Sara. *The Gaza Strip: The Political Economy of De-Development*. Institute for Palestine Studies, 1995.

Rubinstein, Danny. *The Mystery of Arafat*. Vermont, Steerforth Press, 1995.

Said, Edward W. *The Politics of Dispossession: the struggle for Palestinian self-determination 1969–1994*. London, Chatto and Windus, 1994.

Peace and its Discontents. London, Vintage, 1995.

The End of the Peace Process: Oslo and After. New York, Granta Books, 2000.

Schiff, Benjamin N. *Refugees unto the Third Generation—UN aid to Palestinians*. NY, Syracuse University Press, 1995.

Sherman, A. J. *Mandate Days: British Lives in Palestine, 1918–1948*. London, Thames and Hudson, 1997.

Usher, Graham. *The Oslo Agreement: Palestine and the Struggle for Peace*. London, Pluto Press, 1995.

Victor, Barbara. *Hanan Ashrawi: A Passion for Peace*. London, Fourth Estate, 1995.

Zahlan, A. B. *The Reconstruction of Palestine*. London, Kegan Paul International, 1998.

QATAR

Geography

The State of Qatar occupies a peninsula (roughly 160 km long, and between 55 km and 90 km wide), projecting northwards from the Arabian mainland, on the west coast of the Persian (Arabian) Gulf. Its western coastline joins onto the shores of Saudi Arabia, and to the east lie the United Arab Emirates (UAE) and Oman. The total area is 11,437 sq km (4,416 sq miles), and at the census of 16 March 1986 the population was 369,079, of whom fewer than one-third were native Qataris. At mid-1995, according to official estimates, the population was 640,846, but a census in March 1997 enumerated a total of only 522,023. About 60% of the total were concentrated in the town of Doha, on the east coast. A total population of 597,000 was estimated for mid-2001. Two other ports, Zakrit on the west coast and Umm Said on the east, were developed after the discovery of petroleum. Zakrit is a convenient, if shallow, harbour for the import of goods from Bahrain, while Umm Said affords anchorage to deep-sea tankers and freighters.

The climate of Qatar is hot and humid in summer, with temperatures reaching 44°C between July and September, and humidity exceeding 85%. There is some rain in winter, when temperatures range between 10°C and 20°C. Qatar is stony, sandy and barren; limited supplies of underground water are unsuitable for drinking or agriculture because of high mineral content. More than one-half of the water supply is now provided by seawater distillation processes.

History

Revised for this edition by KAMIL MAHDI

Historically, Qatar has been dominated by other Arabian, Middle Eastern or European states. Before the advent of the petroleum industry, the Qatari peninsula was sparsely populated, with its hinterland used as seasonal pasture rangeland by tribes from the Najd and Hasa regions of the Arabian mainland. Additionally, there were a few coastal settlements, mainly on the east coast, where inhabitants relied on pearling, fishing and trade. The local dominant powers in the Gulf—the Omanis and other Arabs, the Persians and the Ottomans—were gradually displaced by Europeans. The Portuguese briefly dominated that part of the Gulf during the first half of the 16th century, before being forced out by the Ottomans. During the 1760s, tribesmen of the Bani Utub settled in Zubarah (az-Zubara), on Qatar's north-west coast, where they engaged in trading and pearl-diving. Later in that century, the Khalifa section of the Utub captured Bahrain and initially ruled it from Zubarah. However, the al-Khalifa gradually moved to the more desirable Bahrain (which they continue to rule) and abandoned Zubarah and the Qatari peninsula, which was riven by tribal conflict.

By the early 19th century, the British were the dominant maritime power in the Gulf, but they paid little attention to Qatar in that they did not impose any treaty upon local tribes where there had not been any important trading ports. In 1868, the British interceded in a conflict between Bahraini forces of the al-Khalifa and Qatari tribesmen. After that, the al-Khalifa were never able to re-establish their rule over the Qatari peninsula. Muhammad ibn Thani ibn Muhammad emerged as a representative of Qatar's tribes, although sovereignty of islands and territorial waters, and Bahrain's claim to Zubarah, continued to be disputed. The peninsula came under the direct rule of the Ottoman Empire in 1872, but Turkish forces evacuated Qatar on the eve of the First World War (1914–18). The United Kingdom recognized Sheikh Abdullah ath-Thani as Ruler of Qatar, and in 1916 made a treaty with him, in accordance with its policy in Bahrain, the Trucial States (now the United Arab Emirates—UAE) and Kuwait. The Ruler of Qatar undertook not to cede, mortgage or otherwise dispose of parts of his territories to anyone except the British Government, nor to enter into any relationship with a foreign government without British consent. In return, the United Kingdom undertook to protect Qatar from all aggression by sea, and to provide support in case of an overland attack. A further treaty, concluded in 1935, extended fuller British protection to Qatar.

The discovery of petroleum in 1939 promised greater prosperity for Qatar, but development was delayed by the onset of the Second World War, and production did not begin on a commercial scale until 1949. During the 1950s, oil revenues grew rapidly, although the ruling élite benefited more from this than did the majority of the population. Qatar experienced unrest that was manifested both in conflict within the large ruling clan and in social strife. Oil and other workers came into conflict with their employers, and there were demands for popular participation and wealth redistribution. During the 1960s, there was a gradual expansion of the bureaucracy, which became the power base of the then Deputy Ruler, Khalifa bin Hamad ath-Thani, and some oil revenues were also used to finance infrastructural development; however popular disaffection continued. In January 1961 Qatar joined the Organization of the Petroleum Exporting Countries (OPEC), and in May 1970 it also became a member of the Organization of Arab Petroleum Exporting Countries (OAPEC). Qatar is a relatively minor oil-exporting country, but its development needs and its standard of living are highly dependent upon its small oil (and, more recently, gas) reserves.

In October 1960 Sheikh Ali ath-Thani, who had been Ruler of Qatar since 1949, abdicated in favour of his son, Sheikh Ahmad ath-Thani. In 1968 it was announced that British forces were to be withdrawn from the Persian (Arabian) Gulf area by 1971. As a result, Qatar attempted to associate itself with Bahrain and the Trucial States in a proposed federation. In April 1970 Sheikh Ahmad announced a provisional Constitution for Qatar, providing for a partially elected consultative assembly. Effective power remained, however, in the Ruler's hands. In May 1970 the Deputy Ruler, Sheikh Khalifa bin Hamad ath-Thani (a cousin of Sheikh Ahmad), was appointed Prime Minister. After the failure of negotiations for union with neighbouring Gulf countries, Qatar became fully independent on 1 September 1971, when the Ruler took the title of Amir. The 1916 treaty was replaced by a new treaty of friendship with the United Kingdom. In February 1972 a bloodless coup, led by Sheikh Khalifa, the Crown Prince and Prime Minister, deposed the Amir during his absence abroad. Claiming support from the ath-Thani family and the armed forces, Sheikh Khalifa proclaimed himself Amir and retained the premiership.

Qatar has generally maintained close links with Saudi Arabia, with which it signed a bilateral defence agreement in 1982, although there have been periods of tension between the two countries. In early 1981 Qatar joined the newly-established Co-operation Council for the Arab States of the Gulf (Gulf Co-operation Council—GCC). Co-operation on defence was a priority, as was underlined by the threat to the security of GCC states posed by an escalation of the war between Iran and Iraq, which had begun in 1980.

After his accession in 1972, and in accordance with the 1970 Constitution, Sheikh Khalifa decreed the first Advisory Council, to complement the Government. Its 20 members, selected by the Amir, from representatives elected by limited suffrage, were increased to 30 in 1975 and to 35 in 1988. The Advisory Council's term of office was extended by four years in 1978 and by further terms of four years in 1982, 1986, 1990, 1994 and 1998. The Advisory Council's constitutional entitlements include power to debate legislation drafted by the Council of Ministers before ratification and promulgation. It also has power to request ministerial statements on matters of general and specific policy, including the draft budget. However, the Council has no law-making powers or effective authority to investigate or challenge government decisions.

As oil revenues increased dramatically after 1973, the Government made significant social and infrastructural improvements (the oil industry had been effectively nationalized, mirroring developments in other OPEC countries at the time.) Reforms were instituted increasing expenditure on a range of public services, housing, health, welfare and non-contributory pensions. By the early 1980s a substantial programme of infrastructure construction was under way, and the provision of education, health services and public utilities to Qatar's citizens was free and generous. The rapid development required a high dependence upon expatriate labour whose numbers came to exceed those of the local population, but who lacked the rights and privileges of the latter. In May 1989 the Supreme Council for Planning (SCP) was formed to co-ordinate plans for Qatar's social and economic development. Under the direction of the heir apparent (Sheikh Hamad bin Khalifa ath-Thani), the SCP promoted industrial diversification and agricultural development with the declared aim of reducing dependence on the petroleum sector; even so, Qatar remains highly dependent on revenue from oil and, more recently, gas.

In July 1989, in the first government reshuffle since 1978, seven ministers were replaced and 11 new members were appointed to a new Council of Ministers, in which five new portfolios had been created. The Minister of Foreign Affairs, Abdullah bin Khalifa al-Attiyah, resigned in May 1990 and was replaced by Mubarak Ali al-Khatir, the former Minister of Electricity and Water. The post was later given to Hamad bin Jasim bin Jaber ath-Thani, a close ally of the present Amir. Another extensive reorganization of the Council of Ministers in September 1992 expanded its membership from 14 to 17.

COUP D'ÉTAT—SHEIKH HAMAD ASSUMES POWER

On 27 June 1995 the Deputy Amir, Heir Apparent, Minister of Defence and Commander-in-Chief of the Armed Forces, Maj.-Gen. Sheikh Hamad bin Khalifa ath-Thani, deposed the Amir, his father, in a bloodless coup. Sheikh Hamad proclaimed himself Amir, claiming the support of the ruling family and the Qatari people, but one of the reasons for his action may have been the rivalry within the historically fractious ruling family and a suspicion that power could be passed to his half-brother and rival, Abdul Aziz. Sheikh Khalifa, who was in Switzerland at the time of the coup, immediately denounced his son's actions, and vowed to return to Qatar. Although Sheikh Khalifa had effectively granted Sheikh Hamad control of the emirate's affairs (with the exception of the treasury) in 1992, a power struggle was reported to have emerged between the two in the months preceding the coup. Sheikh Khalifa was particularly opposed to his son's independent foreign policy (which had led to the strengthening of relations with both Iran and Iraq, and with Israel, thereby jeopardizing relations with Saudi Arabia and the other Gulf states), and had attempted to regain influence in policy decisions. The United Kingdom and the USA quickly recognized the new Amir, and there was evident satisfaction in some Western circles, which stemmed particularly from the new Amir's military background and his policy of rapidly developing Qatar's gas exports by relying on foreign borrowing and joint ventures. Saudi Arabia endorsed the regime shortly afterwards. In mid-July Sheikh Hamad reorganized the Council of Ministers and appointed himself Prime Minister, while retaining the posts of Minister of Defence and Commander-in-Chief of the Armed Forces. Sheikh Abdullah, Sheikh Hamad's brother, was appointed Deputy Prime Minister and Minister of the Interior. The new Amir instituted a number of reforms, including the

relaxation of press censorship and greater transparency of government procedures. There was also discussion of the separation of the financial affairs of the state from those of the ruling family, and in August 1997 the Amir announced that a draft law was being prepared to ensure this separation, although progress towards its introduction was slow. Women's issues also assumed greater prominence, and there has been an increase in the number of women appointed to positions of administrative responsibilities. In May 1998 the Amir's wife gave a newspaper interview in which she advocated reform to facilitate the participation of women in political life. The new Amir also removed travel bans and other restrictions on a number of critics of the Government, particularly those of the Arab nationalist tendency such as Dr Ali Khalifa al-Kawari, who had demanded accountability in the aftermath of the Gulf War. He also maintained relations with influential theologians, avoiding the degree of emphasis on the conservative Wahhabi trend that had dominated religious affairs under his father.

In November 1995 Sheikh Hamad announced his intention to establish an elected municipal council, although elections for this were not held until March 1999 (see below). Meanwhile, the deposed Amir took residence in the UAE, and visited Bahrain, Kuwait, Saudi Arabia, Egypt and Syria in an apparent attempt to assert his legitimacy as ruler of Qatar. In January 1996, moreover, the Minister of Foreign Affairs confirmed that Sheikh Khalifa had kept control of a substantial part of Qatar's financial reserves. In the following month security forces in Qatar were reported to have foiled an attempted coup. As many as 100 people were arrested, and a warrant was issued for the arrest of Sheikh Hamad bin Jasim bin Hamad ath-Thani, a former Minister of Economy and Trade. There were conflicting reports as to the origin of the coup plot; Sheikh Khalifa denied any involvement, although he was quick to imply that the alleged plot indicated popular support for his return. There were also unconfirmed reports that Britain's élite Special Air Service (SAS)was providing the Amir with protection against local opposition, a development which, were it to be verified, would also represent a significant shift away from his father's reliance on military support from France.

In November 1997 the trial began of 110 people (40 of whom were charged *in absentia*), accused of involvement in the attempted coup of February 1996. Hearings were immediately adjourned. In February 1998 another seven individuals, including Sheikh Hamad bin Jasim bin Hamad ath-Thani, were charged with involvement in the attempted coup. A number of those being tried *in absentia* were apprehended during 1998, among them the former deputy chief of intelligence, Abdullah Jasim al-Maliki, who was extradited from Yemen in September. In November a number of sentences were announced with five of the accused receiving 10-year prison terms. In February 2000 Sheikh Hamad bin Jasim bin Hamad ath-Thani (who had been lured from Beirut, Lebanon, to Qatar in July 1999), and 32 others (nine of whom remained outside the country), received life sentences for their role in the attempted coup; all appealed against the verdict. A further 85 defendants were acquitted. In May 2001 the Court of Appeal sentenced to death 19 of the defendants, including Sheikh Hamad bin Jasim bin Hamad ath-Thani, thereby overruling the previous sentences of life imprisonment; the court was also reported to have sentenced 20 defendants to terms of life imprisonment, and acquitted 29 others. It was suggested that the new Qatari ruler's proactive diplomacy was paying political dividends in terms of securing the co-operation of countries such as Lebanon and Yemen in addressing the Qatari regime's grievances with its domestic opponents.

Meanwhile, the Government had requested the suspension of several bank accounts held in the names of Sheikh Khalifa and a former office director, Isa al-Kawari, in five countries, pending the outcome of legal proceedings, initiated in Qatar and abroad in late July 1996, to determine the ownership of some US $3,000m.–$8,000m. in overseas assets, that were asserted by the new Amir to have been amassed by his father from state oil and investment revenues. By mid-October, however, it was reported that Sheikh Hamad and Sheikh Khalifa had been reconciled, and in February 1997 all legal proceedings were formally withdrawn. Reports of opposition activities and statements critical of the regime of Sheikh Hamad have continued to circulate abroad, and have been given prominence by some Arab newspapers. It is thought that some of these, at least, emanate from conflicts within the ath-Thani family.

On 22 October 1996 Sheikh Hamad named the third eldest of his four sons, Sheikh Jasim bin Hamad bin Khalifa ath-Thani, as heir apparent. (The rules of succession had earlier been amended, to specify that thenceforth the hereditary line would pass through the sons of the Amir.) Shortly afterwards Sheikh Hamad appointed his younger brother, Sheikh Abdullah bin Khalifa ath-Thani (the then Minister of the Interior and Deputy Prime Minister), as Prime Minister. On 30 October a new Government, which included five newly appointed ministers, was formed. A Ministry of Housing and the Civil Service was established, while the Ministry of Information and Culture was abolished. The Council of Ministers was reorganized in January 1998. Notable changes included the appointment of Sheikh Muhammad bin Khalifa ath-Thani as Deputy Prime Minister; he was succeeded as Minister of Finance, Economy and Trade by Yousuf Hussein Kamal (previously an undersecretary at the finance ministry). In March it was reported that the Ministry of Information had been reinstated, and that a National Council for Culture, Arts and Heritage had been created. In January 2001 Sheikh Abdullah bin Khalifa ath-Thani relinquished the post of Minister of the Interior (although remaining Prime Minister), which passed to Sheikh Abdullah bin Khalid ath-Thani, previously the Minister of State for the Interior. In these changes, younger members of the ruling family were promoted, together with their technocratic lay allies, giving rise to two new centres of influence. These are respectively formed around the offices of the young Crown Prince and of the Prime Minister.

In policy terms, Sheikh Hamad's Qatar has adopted a highly visible strategy of change on a broad front, and this is particularly reflected in Qatar's high-profile foreign relations. An example is the policy of maintaining a separate stance from Saudi Arabia and Qatar's other GCC partners, and its strong alliance with the USA in terms of military and economic considerations (although notably excluding the area of relations with Iraq) and also in forging relations with Israel. Domestically, the Amir's slow reforms were soon to appear conservative in comparison with the liberal atmosphere (however short-lived) that began to emerge in Bahrain after the death of its own Amir in 1999. Sheikh Hamad's moderate reform agenda included the introduction of greater accountability, particularly in the finance and oil sectors. There was considerable embarrassment, therefore, when it was revealed in January 2002 that the legal department of the British Crown Dependency of Jersey was investigating irregular payments made by a British defence company, BAE Systems, to a trust fund controlled by Qatar's Minister of Foreign Affairs, Sheikh Hamad bin Jasim bin Jaber ath-Thani. The investigation was conducted covertly and was finally abandoned in May 2002.

A particularly notable development under Sheikh Hamad was the establishment, in 1996, of a semi-independent satellite television channel, Al-Jazeera, which promoted debate, diversity of opinion and freedom of expression that are rarely tolerated in the region. Al-Jazeera swiftly acquired a wide audience, and attracted criticism from a number of governments whose own media was generally more circumspect. For example, Al-Jazeera's criticism of the Egyptian Government's failure to support the renewed Palestinian *intifada* led the Egyptian authorities to threaten to withdraw permission for the channel to broadcast via Egypt's Nilesat satellite. At the end of September 2002 the Saudi Arabian ambassador to Qatar was recalled for consultation by the Saudi Government, following a dispute with the Qatari Government over recent broadcasts made by Al-Jazeera that were deemed overtly critical of the Saudi regime. Similarly, on different occasions, the channel has been threatened with restrictive measures by the Palestinian (National) Authority (PA) and the governments of Bahrain and Kuwait. The Qatari Government's support for Al-Jazeera and its refusal to censor some relatively uncompromising reporting of sensitive security issues, has continued to provoke regional antagonism. However, some observers have noted that the channel, whose owners are closely linked with the ruling ath-Thani family, has been reluctant to highlight the growing strategic importance of the al-Udaid US military base in Qatar

itself. After the 11 September 2001 suicide attacks on the US mainland, the US Government and media complained bitterly about Al-Jazeera's critical reporting of US policy in the region and about its alleged association with supporters of the USA's prime suspect in the attacks, Osama bin Laden. Al-Jazeera was the only broadcaster to remain in Kabul throughout the US-led military intervention in Afghanistan late 2001 in pursuit of bin Laden's al-Qa'ida (Base) organization and its Taliban hosts; its offices in the Afghan capital were bombed—erroneously, according to the US authorities—by the US Air Force during the campaign. Al-Jazeera's pioneering reporting has become increasingly important for Qatar's self-image and for the Government's external projection of its high-profile diplomacy, as well as for deflecting criticism of the Government's close alliance with the US Administration and of its domestic shortcomings.

In March 1999 elections were held for the Municipal Council. They were the first elections to be held in Qatar and took place under full adult suffrage. Women were permitted to contest the elections, although no female candidate actually gained a seat on the Council, which was to have a consultative role in the operations of the Ministry of Municipal Affairs and Agriculture. The rate of participation by voters reportedly exceeded 90% in Doha, and was estimated at 60%–70% of the registered electorate in rural areas. However, the number of registered voters was low: it was estimated that only 22,000 of an eligible 40,000 actually participated in the elections. It was subsequently reported that members of the Council had objected to legislation placing the new body under the supervision of the Ministry of Municipal Affairs and Agriculture. In June Ali bin Muhammad al-Khatir, formerly Minister of State for Council of Ministers' Affairs, was appointed Minister of Municipal Affairs and Agriculture; Ali bin Saad al-Kawari replaced him as Minister of State for Council of Ministers' Affairs. In July the Amir established a 32-member commission to draft a permanent constitution which was to include an elected legislature. The commission was charged with formulating the document within three years, and a 150-clause draft Constitution was duly presented on 2 July 2002. According to the draft document, the Amir was to remain head of the executive, while a 45-member unicameral parliament, of which two-thirds were to be directly elected (the remainder being appointed by the Amir), was to have powers to legislate, review the state budget, monitor government policy and hold ministers accountable for their actions. The parliament was to have a four-year mandate. Suffrage was to be extended to all citizens, including women, aged 18 years and above. The document also guaranteed freedom of association, expression and religious affiliation and provided for the establishment of an independent judiciary. Elections to the new parliament were expected to be conducted before the end of 2005, although formal adoption of the Constitution was subject to the final approval of the Amir.

In early July 2002 the former Minister of State for Council of Ministers' Affairs, Ali bin Saad al-Kawari, was appointed Minister of Municipal Affairs and Agriculture, replacing Ali bin Muhammad al-Khatir. Muhammad bin Isa Hamad al-Mehannadi was named as the new Minister of State for Council of Ministers' Affairs.

TERRITORIAL DISPUTES WITH BAHRAIN AND SAUDI ARABIA

In April 1986 Qatar raided the island of Fasht ad-Dibal, which had been artificially constructed on a coral reef in the Persian (Arabian) Gulf, and seized 29 foreign workers who were constructing a Bahraini coastguard station on the island. Officials of the GCC met representatives of both states in an attempt to reconcile them, and to avoid a division within the Council. In May the workers were released, and the two Governments agreed to destroy the island. In July 1991 Qatar referred the demarcation of its maritime border with Bahrain and the issue of ownership of the potentially oil-rich Hawar islands (held by Bahrain) to the International Court of Justice (ICJ) in The Hague, Netherlands. In mid-1992 the Qatari Government rejected Bahrain's attempt to broaden the issue to include sovereignty over an area around Zubarah on the Qatari coast, while in April 1992 Qatar had issued a decree redefining its maritime borders to include territorial waters claimed by Bahrain. A hearing of the ICJ opened in February 1994 with the aim of determining whether the court had jurisdiction to give a ruling on the dispute. In July the ICJ invited the two countries to resubmit their dispute by 30 November, either jointly or separately. However, the two countries failed to reach agreement on presenting the dispute to the Court, and at the end of November Qatar submitted a unilateral request to continue its case through the ICJ. In February 1995, while the ICJ declared that it would have authority to adjudicate in the dispute (despite Bahrain's refusal to accept the principle of an ICJ ruling), Saudi Arabia also proposed to act as mediator between the two countries. In September, however, relations between Qatar and Bahrain soured following the Bahraini Government's decision to construct a tourism resort on the Hawar islands despite controversy over their sovereignty. In late December, furthermore, Qatar's deposed former Amir visited Bahrain and suggested that sovereignty of the Hawar islands would be returned to that country if he were restored to power. Qatar retaliated by televising interviews with exiled Bahraini Shi'ites and by publishing articles alluding to abuses of human rights in Bahrain. In mid-1996 the Qatari Government reiterated not only its rejection of Bahraini exhortations to withdraw the case from the ICJ, but also its willingness to consider Saudi involvement in negotiations, prompting renewed Bahraini claims of sovereignty over the disputed territory. During August the Bahraini authorities continued to promote a regional settlement to the dispute, proposing the convention of a bilateral summit meeting to be followed by Saudi mediation. Relations between Qatar and Bahrain deteriorated at the end of 1996 following an announcement, made by the Bahrain Government in early December, that two Qatari nationals had been arrested in Bahrain and charged with spying. (The two men were subsequently acquitted.) Qatar retaliated with public accusations of Bahraini involvement in the failed February coup attempt. Bahrain boycotted the GCC annual summit convened in Doha in December, at which it was decided to establish a quadripartite committee (comprising those GCC countries not involved in the dispute) to facilitate a solution. Attempts by the committee to foster improved relations between Bahrain and Qatar achieved a degree of success, and meetings between prominent government ministers from both countries in London, United Kingdom, and Manama, Bahrain, in February and March 1997 resulted in the announcement that diplomatic relations at ambassadorial level were to be established between the two countries by mid-1997. Qatar announced its choice of ambassador to Bahrain in early April, but Bahrain failed to reciprocate. Previously hostile media coverage of the dispute diminished as a result of these contacts, although little further progress was made. In April 1998 Bahrain alleged that the 82 documents submitted by Qatar to the ICJ in 1997 in support of its claims to sovereignty and territorial rights were forgeries. The ICJ directed Qatar to produce a report on the authenticity of the documents. Following the submission of the report, in which four experts differed in their opinion of the documents, Qatar announced that it would withdraw them. Relations with Bahrain remained tense immediately following the death of the Bahraini Amir in March 1999, but by the end of that year there had been a notable improvement, with the two countries again agreeing to exchange ambassadors and also to develop economic and financial co-operation, to facilitate travel and tourism and to form a joint committee to try to resolve their dispute. By March 2000 both countries had reportedly named their ambassadors. ICJ hearings on the territorial dispute began in May and ended in June. At that time, Bahrain suspended the joint committee pending the ruling of the ICJ. The ICJ issued its verdict in March 2001, which was binding and, even though it was considered more favourable to Bahrain, was accepted by both countries, marking a more co-operative phase in their relationship. The ruling awarded the Hawar islands to Bahrain and the shoals of Fasht ad-Dibal to Qatar, and also confirmed Qatar's jurisdiction over Zubarah and the rights of Qatar to free navigation through Bahraini waters between Hawar and Bahrain's main islands. The new maritime boundaries safeguard Qatar's ownership of the giant North Field gas reserves from any Bahraini claims, but also offers Bahrain some prospect of new hydrocarbon finds in its territorial waters. Both states proclaimed satisfaction with the ruling and announced intentions of developing their mutual co-operation, especially in the economic field. Settlement of the border issue

facilitated the development of a number of joint projects, and in September 2001 the two states signed a memorandum of understanding to build a causeway linking them; an oil and gas co-operation agreement was also signed.

In 1992 tensions arose with Saudi Arabia when Qatar accused a Saudi force of attacking the al-Khofous border post, killing two soldiers and capturing another. As a result, Qatar announced the suspension of a 1965 agreement with Saudi Arabia on border demarcation (which had never been fully ratified) and withdrew its 200-strong contingent from the GCC 'Peninsula Shield' force in Kuwait. The Saudi Government denied the involvement of its armed forces. Qatar registered its disaffection by boycotting meetings of the GCC ministers in the UAE and Kuwait in November. However, on 20 December, following mediation by President Hosni Mubarak of Egypt, Sheikh Khalifa and King Fahd of Saudi Arabia signed an agreement whereby a committee was to be established to demarcate the border between the two states. Qatar subsequently resumed attendance of GCC sessions, but in November 1994 Qatar boycotted a meeting in Saudi Arabia of GCC ministers of the interior, in protest at what it alleged to have been armed incidents on the border with Saudi Arabia in March and October. During one of the incidents, a Qatari citizen was reported to have been wounded by Saudi border guards. Finally, in June 1999 officials from Qatar and Saudi Arabia met in Riyadh, Saudi Arabia, to sign the final maps demarcating their joint border. Actual delineation of the land and sea borders between the two countries was completed in March 2001.

FOREIGN POLICY AND MILITARY DEVELOPMENTS SINCE THE GULF WAR

Qatar condemned Iraq's occupation of Kuwait in August 1990, although it had previously supported Iraq in its 1980–88 war with Iran. In late 1990 Qatar permitted the deployment of foreign forces on its territory, as part of the multinational effort to force Iraq to withdraw from Kuwait. Units of the Qatari armed forces subsequently participated in the military operation to liberate Kuwait in January–February 1991. On 23 June 1992 Qatar signed a bilateral military agreement with the USA which provided for US access to Qatari military bases and for pre-positioning of US military equipment in Qatar. Qatar resumed tentative contact with Iraq in 1993. In March 1995, during the first official visit to the country by a senior Iraqi official since the 1990–91 crisis, the then Iraqi Minister of Foreign Affairs, Muhammad Saeed as-Sahaf, attended a meeting with his Qatari counterpart, Sheikh Hamad bin Jasim bin Jaber ath-Thani, to discuss the furtherance of bilateral relations. At a press conference at the end of the visit, the Qatari minister indicated his country's determination to pursue a foreign policy independent from that of its GCC neighbours when he announced his country's support for the ending of UN sanctions against Iraq. Notwithstanding Qatar's close alliance with the USA, the Amir expressed dismay at US policy towards both Iraq and Iran during meetings with the US President in Washington, DC, in June 1997. Qatar also sent humanitarian aid to Iraq and continued to do so during the weeks of military crisis in February 1998 (see chapter on Iraq). At that time the Qatari Minister of Foreign Affairs made a visit to Baghdad to relay messages between the Iraqi President and the Amir, following which the Amir travelled to Saudi Arabia for a meeting with King Fahd to discuss the deepening crisis. After the easing of tensions in the region, the Amir met the Iraqi Minister of Foreign Affairs during the latter's presence at a meeting of foreign ministers of the Organization of the Islamic Conference (OIC) in Doha in March.

In May 1992 Qatar signed six agreements with Iran for co-operation in various sectors, including customs, air traffic and the exchange of information. In July 1993 the then Deputy Amir, Sheikh Hamad, visited Tehran, and in October an agreement was signed to establish a joint committee for co-operation in the oil and gas sector. In January 1994 Qatar hosted talks with Iran to discuss security issues and draw up plans to curb drugs-trafficking in the Gulf. Qatar chose to pursue good relations with Iran despite adverse reaction from its Arab neighbours and the USA. Iran's relations with the Arab states of the Gulf showed a marked improvement during 1997 and 1998, and as a result, both the Amir and the Minister of Foreign Affairs urged an end to the US isolation of Iran during their respective visits to the USA in June 1997 and March 1998. A further improvement in relations with Iran was evident in May 1999 when the Iranian President, Muhammad Khatami, visited Qatar.

From 1994 Qatar adopted a foreign policy that differed from that of its GCC allies on a number of key issues. Qatar declined to support a final communiqué, issued by seven other Arab states, demanding an immediate cease-fire in Yemen, arguing that it was not their place to interfere in the domestic affairs of another country. Similarly, Qatar made early contact with the Israeli Government without waiting for the peace process to be firmly established. In January discussions took place with regard to the supply of natural gas to Israel; following Arab protests, however, Qatar conceded that a sales agreement would depend on a feasibility study and on Israel's withdrawal from all Arab territories occupied in 1967. In September 1994 Qatar, along with the other GCC states, revoked aspects of the economic boycott of Israel. In early November the Israeli Deputy Minister of Foreign Affairs, Yossi Beilin, made an official visit to Qatar. An Israeli trade office was set up in Doha, and in October 1995 Qatar's Minister of Foreign Affairs was reported to have expressed his country's support for the cancellation of the direct economic boycott of Israel, even if a peace settlement in the Middle East was not achieved. In the following month Israel signed a memorandum of intent to purchase Qatari liquefied natural gas, and in April 1996 Shimon Peres made the first official visit to Qatar by an Israeli Prime Minister. However, relations deteriorated in late 1996, when Israel declared that the memorandum of intent to purchase Qatari gas had expired, although negotiations were to continue. The failure to conclude sales contracts also coincided with the election of the right-wing Likud leader, Binyamin Netanyahu, to the post of Prime Minister in Israel, and the subsequent deterioration in the prospects for a general Arab-Israeli settlement. In early November, Qatar announced that any gas sales to Israel would be dependent on the peace process and would be conducted through the huge US energy corporation Enron (which collapsed in December 2001 after revelations of massive financial irregularities). In December, Qatar condemned Israeli settlement activity in the occupied territories, and in March 1997 Qatar 'froze' relations with Israel. At the end of that month, the League of Arab States (the Arab League) passed a resolution recommending the restoration of the economic boycott against Israel and withdrawal from multilateral peace talks with that state. Qatar was heavily pressed by Arab and Islamic interests to cancel the Middle East and North Africa economic summit planned for November 1997 in Doha. (This was to be the fourth in a series of meetings gathering Israeli and Arab leaders to discuss the development of economic links in the region.) Setbacks in the peace process with Israel had cast doubt over the future of the summit, although the USA was determined that the meeting should go ahead. The Amir had also ruled out cancellation. The conference, downgraded from a 'summit', owing to the widespread Arab boycott, proceeded on 16–18 November, with the participation of a 'low-level' Israeli delegation. The Qatari Government emphasized the economic rather than the political aspects of the conference, and attempted to attract foreign investment for joint industrial projects in the country. Following the Doha conference, a dispute erupted when the Qatari Minister of State for Foreign Affairs accused Egypt (which had been vociferous in its demands for the cancellation of the conference) of conducting a campaign of vilification against Qatar. The dispute continued in the media and in the political arena for several months, and some 700 Egyptian workers, including almost all those employed by the Ministry of the Interior, had their employment in Qatar terminated. A meeting in December between the Amir and President Mubarak in Riyadh did not appear to have settled matters completely, but in early March 1998, it was announced that differences between Qatar and Egypt were to be resolved, with an exchange of ministerial visits. Later in March, the Qatari Amir visited Cairo for talks on bilateral relations. Qatar's relations with the UAE also soured at the time of the Doha meeting, but they improved following a visit by the Amir to the UAE in March 1998. Following the conference, the Qatari Government distanced itself from Israel and criticized the intransigence of the Netan-

yahu administration. A visit to Qatar by the Hamas leader of the radical Palestinian Islamist movement Hamas, Sheikh Ahmad Yassin, in June 1998 was criticized by the Israeli Government. In November 1999 Qatar agreed to receive a number of Hamas leaders who had been deported from Jordan. Prior to their expulsion, they were reported to have approached Qatar to mediate in their dispute with Jordan. In June 2001, one of the exiled Hamas leaders, Ibrahim Ghosheh, suddenly returned to Jordan aboard a scheduled Qatari Airways flight. The Jordanian Government attempted to return him, against his will, on the same aircraft; the Qatari Government refused to accept Ghosheh on the ground of his Jordanian citizenship. Jordan prevented the airliner and its crew from leaving Amman airport, and it was two weeks before the crisis was resolved and Ghosheh was allowed to remain in Jordan.

Before that, in August 1999, as Arab participation in talks with the new Israeli Government of Ehud Barak resumed, the Amir visited the PA-controlled areas, in a gesture of support for the negotiating process. Qatar was criticized by other Arab states in September 2000 following a meeting during the UN millennium summit in New York, USA, between the Amir and Barak; the meeting followed the failure of talks at Camp David, Maryland, USA, between the Israeli and Palestinian leaders. Some reports, however, suggested that relations between the Qatari Minister of Foreign Affairs and his US counterpart, Secretary of State Madeleine Albright, had deteriorated owing to US pressure that Qatar take further steps in fostering relations with Israel. In October, as the crisis in relations between Israel and the Palestinians deepened, an emergency summit meeting of the Arab League decided in Cairo to curtail relations with Israel in protest against the latter's suppression of the Palestinians. Qatar came under pressure to close the Israeli trade mission in Doha, especially after Oman, Morocco and Tunisia took similar measures. Eventually Qatar was said to have closed the mission under threat of a boycott of the OIC summit meeting which was to be held in Doha on 12–14 November. The meeting proceeded and pledged support for the Palestinians, and also provided a venue to discuss Iraq's regional political rehabilitation and the development of a dialogue between Iraq and the UN. In May 2001, however, it was reported that Israeli officials had discreetly remained in their closed Doha mission. It was also confirmed that Qatar was to host the World Trade Organization (WTO) conference in November of that year, the Qatari Government having stated that it would offer visas to critics of the WTO. However, international non-governmental organizations (NGOs) and development lobbies complained that they were finding their access to the Doha meeting severely curtailed in comparison with other international venues. Qatar's eagerness to host the conference was characteristic of recent efforts to raise its international profile (also through major sporting and other events), but the choice of Qatar as a venue also served to neutralize the growing influence of populist lobbies and pressure groups on the negotiations. The demonstrations and media attention surrounding the previous WTO meeting in Seattle, USA, was not likely to be repeated in the more restrictive social and political environment of Qatar. In the event, the emirate's pledge to permit the entry of NGO activists was rendered largely irrelevant by the expense and limited capacity of Doha hotels.

In late 1998, as relations between Iraq and weapons inspectors of the UN Special Commission (UNSCOM) deteriorated, prompting renewed US and British aerial bombardment of Iraq in December, Qatar, together with other Gulf states, attempted to distance itself from the air-strikes. In the same month, however, the USA announced plans to construct a new military base at al-Udaid in Qatar, to be completed in 2000, which was to be the largest pre-positioning site for military equipment in the world. In March 1999, in response to Qatar's criticism of the continued bombardment of Iraq, the US Secretary of Defense, William Cohen, insisted that US policy in the region was being implemented with the full support of the Qatari authorities. As Qatar's military ties with the USA grew, so military co-operation with France (Qatar's main arms supplier) was also increased, thereby underlining Qatar's pursuit of the broadest possible support. In May, during a seminar on the future of Iraqi–Kuwaiti relations, Qatar's Minister of Foreign Affairs advocated *rapprochement* with Iraq; he again raised the matter at meetings of the GCC and of the Arab League. (A free-trade agreement was concluded with Iraq in June 2002.) In April 2000 it was reported that, while visiting the Gulf region to oversee major military exercises, Cohen had entered into negotiations with Qatar to station between 30 and 40 US military aircraft in the country. The construction of a major airfield at the al-Udaid base enhanced its strategic importance within the US military network in the region.

Qatar was swift to condemn the suicide attacks in New York and Washington, DC, in September 2001, and to emphasize Qatar's opposition of terrorism in all forms and from every source. The Amir visited the USA soon after the attacks and paid his respects at the site of the New York attack.

Speculation mounted during 2002 that the US Government would extend its declared 'war against terror' to include military intervention in Iraq. However, reports emerged that the refusal at that time of the Saudi Government to allow US armed forces

to use the air command-and-control centre at the Prince Sultan airbase near Riyadh for offensive purposes against Iraq had prompted the US military to initiate the transfer of its centre of activities in the region to al-Udaid, and munitions and communications equipment were believed to have been moved to the Qatari base. The exact terms of the agreement under which the use of al-Udaid is available to the US armed forces was not known, and was thought not yet to have been formalized, despite the US removal. Some commentators discerned in the US Administration's activities in the region an assumption that the smaller Gulf states of Qatar, Bahrain and the UAE would be less able to assert their sovereignty in opposition to US military demands, but warned that this might not preclude the emergence of militant forms of opposition to such an undertaking in those states. (In November 2001 a Qatari man shot and wounded two US contractors working on construction of the US military base, before being shot dead himself.)

Economy

ALAN J. DAY

Based on an original essay by P. T. H. UNWIN

INTRODUCTION

Qatar is a largely barren peninsula, with stony and sandy soil which is generally unsuitable for arable farming. There are numerous coastal saline flats, known as *sabkha*, and the only agricultural soils are found in small depressions in the centre of the country and towards the north. Traditionally the Qatari economy was based on the nomadic farming of livestock, and on fishing and pearling. Significant reserves of petroleum in were discovered in 1939, however, providing the basis for Qatar's transformation into one of the richest countries in the region by the 1970s. In 1984, according to estimates by the World Bank, Qatar's gross national product (GNP), measured at average 1982–84 prices, was US $5,780m., equivalent to $19,010 per head. As in 1983, Qatar's GNP per head in 1984 was the second highest national level in the world, exceeded only by that of its neighbour, the United Arab Emirates (UAE). According to World Bank estimates, Qatar's GNP at constant prices fell by an average 3.3% per year between 1979 and 1989, reflecting declines in petroleum output and prices. Over the same period real GNP per head fell by an average 10% per year, owing to natural population growth and an influx of immigrant labour. The World Bank estimated Qatar's average rate of GNP growth between 1989 and 1999 as 1% per year. Qatar's 1995 GNP, measured at average 1993–95 prices, was estimated by the World Bank as $7,448m., equivalent to $11,600 per head on a conventional exchange-rate basis. In 1999 Qatar's GNP was provisionally estimated to be at least $12,000m., equivalent to $21,360 per head (using the official population estimate of 561,700).

The development of the modern Qatari economy has entailed high levels of labour immigration. In 1991 the number of indigenous Qataris was estimated at 350,000, while the World Bank estimated the total mid-year population at 506,000. A census conducted in 1997 showed a population of 522,023. In May 1997 the Government issued a directive advising private sector businesses to ensure that Qatari nationals constituted at least 20% of their work-force. In 1998 the economically active population totalled 280,122, of whom 87% were non-Qataris. Qatar's estimated total population in 2001 (as given in Central Bank statistics) was 597,000. In the mid-1980s the economy still relied heavily on petroleum revenues, but a policy of diversification meant that between 1979 and 1983 the percentage of government revenues derived from crude oil fell from 93% to 80%. The collapse in world prices for crude petroleum during 1986 nevertheless placed an increased burden on an already stressed economy. Oil revenues remained at low levels during the second half of the 1980s. Qatar has a reputation for caution in its economic policy, but in the late 1980s moves towards economic

restructuring were made, and reforms took place, in anticipation of a sharp reduction in Qatar's output of crude oil after 2010. As a result, in 1987 the Government introduced a programme of industrialization, centred on ambitious plans for the development of the North Field, the world's largest single natural gas deposit.

By 1990 the first phase of the North Field development programme was close to completion, but Iraq's invasion of Kuwait in August led to a temporary suspension of major investment projects. Production from the North Field began on 3 September 1991. By mid-1995 Qatar had secured an estimated US $4,000m. of international project finance for its industrialization programme, early implementation of which was one of the main priorities of the new Amir who took power in June 1995. By mid-1998 the total amount of project finance secured by Qatar was estimated to have exceeded $6,000m., as international bankers continued to respond positively to the emirate's development programme.

Despite a significant increase in petroleum production in 1997 and 1998, and the first liquefied natural gas (LNG) exports from Qatar, the value of the oil and gas sector of the economy (measured at current prices) declined by 25% in 1998 as a result of the sharp decline in petroleum export prices from late 1997. Overall, Qatar's nominal gross domestic product (GDP) fell by 9.2% in 1998. The divestment of a number of enterprises at the end of 1998 helped the Government to cut its budget deficit from 7.7% of GDP in 1997/98 to 4.7% of GDP in 1998/99. Following a recovery in petroleum prices in 1999, total government revenue increased significantly, producing a budget surplus for 1999/2000 equivalent to 8.6% of nominal GDP.

Foreign confidence in Qatar's industrialization strategy remained strong in 1999–2001, with successful international and domestic bond issues and the continuing availability of new bank lending for oil, gas and chemicals projects. By the end of 2001 the total amount of project finance secured by Qatar since the mid-1990s was estimated to have exceeded US $12,000m. Against this background, Qatar derived particular benefit from the continuation in 2000 of the 1999 increase in world oil prices (which coincided with continuing growth in Qatar's LNG exports as more new capacity was brought into production). The oil and gas sector of the economy grew by an estimated 53% in 1999 and 75% in 2000, producing growth in nominal GDP of 19% in 1999 and 35% in 2000, and real increases of 7% and 12% respectively. There were strong balance-of-payments surpluses on the current account in both years, and a budget surplus in 2000/01 equivalent to about 0.1% of nominal GDP. The moderation of world oil prices in 2001 resulted in a 1.8% contraction in GDP in nominal terms; but with inflation remaining minimal, real GDP growth of about 2% was achieved. Government figures indicated that GDP growth, in real terms, had averaged 11% in the four years to the end of 2001, and that per-capita GDP in 2001 was just less than US $25,000, the highest in the Middle East region by some margin. Confidence was boosted further by the announcement in May 2002 that proven gas reserves in the North Field had been revised upwards by 50%, representing an increase in the book value of Qatar's gas reserves of about $500,000m. (see Petroleum and Natural Gas, below).

AGRICULTURE AND FISHING

Qatar's agricultural activity increased steadily during the 1970s, with the number of producing farms rising from 338 in 1975 to 406 in 1979. However, during the same period the number of non-producing farms also rose, owing to increased problems of water supply and water salinity. Agriculture (including fishing) provided an estimated 0.5% of Qatar's GDP at current prices in 2001. All agricultural land in the country is owned by the Government, and most farm owners participate only indirectly in the farming process, having permanent positions in other sectors of the economy. Consequently, most farms in Qatar are administered by immigrant managers employing Omani, Palestinian, Iranian and Egyptian labour. Vegetable production has been the most successful sector of the agrarian economy, and Qatar is now thought to be self-sufficient in winter vegetables, and nearly self-sufficient in summer vegetables, with some being exported to other Gulf countries. At the end of 1991 Qatar and Iran announced plans for a US $13,000m. pipeline to carry drinking water to Qatar from Iran's Karum river. In April 1992 the Arab-Qatari Company for Vegetable Production (AQCVP) signed a $5m. contract with Dace of the Netherlands for the supply of greenhouses, sufficient to treble the company's covered growing area. In May the Government announced the provision of interest-free loans of up to QR 500,000 to farmers and fishermen, to encourage production by promoting modernization. The loans, repayable over 10 years, were to be administered by a special committee, established by the Ministry of Agriculture and Municipal Affairs. In 2000 Qatar's imports of food and live animals were valued at QR 1,212.8m., representing about 10% of total import spending. In 2000, according to FAO estimates, Qatar produced 4,100 metric tons of barley, 1,800 tons of maize, 53,400 tons of vegetables and melons and 18,000 tons of fruit and dates, as well as 35,900 tons of milk (from cows, camels, sheep and goats), 4,100 tons of poultry meat, 3,600 tons of eggs, and 7,400 tons of mutton and lamb. In 1999 a project to establish a processing and packaging plant in Doha with a planned annual capacity of 800 tons of dates and 400 tons of vegetables commenced.

Most of the country's fishing is undertaken by the Qatar National Fishing Co (QNFC), which was formed in 1966 and was nationalized in 1980. By 1985 the company had a refrigeration and processing plant near Doha, capable of handling 7 metric tons of shrimps per day. From the mid-1970s until 1980 the annual catch was estimated at about 2,000 tons. The total rose to 2,604 tons in 1981, but fell to 2,114 tons in 1983. By 1999 the total catch was 4,207.

PETROLEUM AND NATURAL GAS

The first concession to explore for petroleum in Qatar was granted to the Anglo-Persian Oil Co in 1935, and was later transferred to Petroleum Development (Qatar) Ltd. Deposits of petroleum were first discovered in Qatar in 1939, although exploration and production were delayed during the Second World War. By 1949 a pipeline had been constructed from the Dukhan oilfield, on the west coast, to Umm Said in the east, where terminal facilities had also been built, and in December of that year the first shipment of Qatari petroleum was exported. In 1952 the Shell Co of Qatar acquired a concession to develop the entire continental shelf offshore area, and by 1960 petroleum had been discovered at Idd ash-Shargi, 100 km to the east of Qatar. Soon afterwards, a second offshore oilfield was discovered, to the north-east of the first, at Maydan Mahzam, and in 1970 a third offshore field, Bul Hanine, was discovered nearby. In 1953 Petroleum Development (Qatar) Ltd was renamed the Qatar Petroleum Co, and by 1960 Qatar's onshore production had reached 60,360,000 barrels, compared with 800,000 barrels

in 1949. Qatar was admitted to membership of the Organization of the Petroleum Exporting Countries (OPEC) in 1961. In 1969 Qatar and Abu Dhabi agreed to a joint production scheme for the al-Bunduq field which straddles the border between Qatar and the UAE.

Following Qatar's attainment of full independence in 1971, the petroleum industry was reorganized, and in 1972 the Qatar National Petroleum Co was created to supervise the country's oil operations. In 1974 the Qatar General Petroleum Corpn (QGPC) was established, and new participation agreements were signed with the foreign oil companies operating in the country to give the Government a 60% share in profits. In December 1974 the Government announced its intention to purchase the remaining 40% share in the ownership of QGPC and the Shell Co of Qatar. After lengthy negotiations, the State took over the assets and rights of QGPC in September 1976, and acquired those of the Shell Co of Qatar in February 1977. QGPC was renamed Qatar Petroleum (QP) in January 2001 (see below).

Qatar's oil production varied considerably during the 1970s and the early 1980s, falling from 570,300 barrels per day (b/d) in 1973 to 437,600 b/d in 1975. By 1979 production had risen to 508,100 b/d, but it subsequently declined rapidly, and in 1982 output averaged only 332,000 b/d. However, even this reduced level of production was higher than Qatar's recommended OPEC quota of 300,000 b/d. By July 1990 Qatar's OPEC quota had been raised to 371,000 b/d. However, Iraq's invasion of Kuwait in August led to the suspension of quotas in order to allow OPEC member states to compensate for the loss of Iraqi and Kuwaiti production. Between August 1990 and February 1991 Qatari production averaged 420,000 b/d. After the liberation of Kuwait, Qatar's production quota was set by OPEC at 399,000 b/d and by the fourth quarter of 1993 Qatar's OPEC production quota was 378,000 b/d. Total oil production (including natural gas liquids) averaged 568,000 b/d in 1996, rising sharply to a record level of 694,000 b/d in 1997 and 747,000 b/d in 1998. Qatar accepted a nominal OPEC production quota of 414,000 b/d from January 1998 while continuing to lobby (based on its financial needs as OPEC's smallest producer) for a substantial quota increase to a level closer to its actual output. When OPEC made a series of supply cuts in 1998–99 to counteract the decline in world petroleum prices, Qatar agreed to reduce its actual output, adopting reference levels of 670,000 b/d from April 1998, 640,000 b/d from July and 593,000 b/d from April 1999; its formal OPEC quota remained unchanged at 414,000 b/d. Qatar's total oil production (including natural gas liquids) averaged 724,000 b/d in 1999.

Qatar's agreed reference level within the OPEC production quota system was raised in 2000 to 640,000 b/d from April, to 658,000 b/d from July, to 679,000 b/d from October and to 691,800 b/d from November as OPEC took steps to moderate excessive upward price pressures in the world oil market. Qatar's actual oil production level in 2000 (including natural gas liquids, which were not subject to OPEC quotas) averaged 796,000 b/d, an increase of 9.9% over 1999. In 2001 OPEC quotas were progressively reduced in response to a softening of market conditions, Qatar's agreed reference level being 653,000 b/d from February, 627,000 b/d from April, 601,000 b/d from September and 562,000 b/d from January 2002. Actual oil production in 2001 (including natural gas liquids) fell by 2.3% to 783,000 b/d, of which crude oil output was 681,000 b/d, significantly above the OPEC quota, although production rates in the first half of 2002 were reported to have been only about 4% above the quota. Qatar's proven oil reserves were revised upwards from 3,700m. barrels at the end of 1999, to 13,200m. barrels at the end of 2000 and to 15,200m. barrels at the end of 2001 (the latest total being equivalent to more than 55.5 years' production at the 2001 level).

Among the concessions that Qatar granted for petroleum exploitation in the 1980s was Amoco's 25-year production-sharing agreement for an 8,000-sq km area covering most of the country, except the Dukhan field and part of the north-east, which was concluded at the beginning of 1986. A six-year offshore exploration permit for 2,800 sq km was granted to Elf Aquitaine in 1988. An offshore concession agreement with the group of companies headed by Wintershall was terminated in June 1985, with the discovery of substantial quantities of gas in the area, but the consortium won a partial award against Qatar at the International Arbitration Tribunal at The Hague, Netherlands, after which a production-sharing agreement was concluded. The consortium announced plans in early 1994 for the development of facilities to produce gas and condensate for export before the end of the century. In 1995 it opened negotiations with the Dubai Government on a proposal to export gas via pipeline to Jebel Ali in Dubai. In late 1994 Wintershall had reduced its interest in the consortium from 50% to 15% and had relinquished the role of operating company. The consortium brought the ar-Rayyan field into production in November 1996 at an initial rate of 32,000 b/d. Under a July 1997 agreement with QGPC, the consortium was granted the right to develop up to 23m. cu m (800m. cu ft) per day of gas production from a defined sector of the North Field for export (via pipeline) after separation of liquids for separate marketing.

In September 1994 Occidental Petroleum secured a five-year contract, worth an estimated US $1.9m. per year, to supply technical and support services to QGPC in onshore and offshore fields. At the same time Occidental concluded a 25-year production-sharing agreement for the Idd ash-Shargi offshore field, whereby the US company would invest an estimated $700m. to raise output from around 20,000 b/d to over 90,000 b/d and would have an entitlement to 19% of the field's output. Production from this field averaged 104,000 b/d in 2000. Under QGPC's timetable for making available new exploration blocks to foreign oil companies, agreements were in force in respect of 90% of Qatar's territorial area by mid-1995. A subsidiary of the US company Pennzoil signed a four-year offshore exploration agreement on production-sharing terms in July 1994, this being Qatar's first new exploration agreement for two years. Denmark's Maersk Oil began oil production in an offshore concession area in late 1994. Output at Maersk's ash-Shaheen field increased from 30,000 b/d to 107,000 b/d in 1999, upon completion of new production facilities. An agreement on the development of another offshore oilfield (al-Khalij) was concluded in July 1995 between QGPC and the concession holders, Elf Aquitaine (55% and operator) and Agip International (45%). Production from this field, which had estimated reserves of 70m. barrels, began in 1997 at an initial rate of 30,000 b/d. In April 1996 QGPC signed an exploration and production-sharing agreement with Chevron Overseas Petroleum (the operator and majority partner in a 60:40 venture with the Hungarian Oil and Gas Co) pertaining to a 7,500-sq km offshore concession area. A programme to enhance recovery methods and to install new facilities at the onshore Dukhan field was also expected to increase output.

In early 2002 Qatar's installed crude oil production capacity totalled about 800,000 b/d, distributed among eight oilfields (Idd ash-Shargi north dome, Idd ash-Shargi south dome, ar-Rayyan, al-Khalij, Maydan Mazham, Bul Hanine, Dukhan, and ash-Shaheen). Qatar Petroleum (formerly QGPC) planned to increase Qatar's crude oil production capacity to 1.03m. b/d, and accordingly approved significant oilfield development programmes by several foreign oil companies in 2000–02. In mid-2002 preparations were being made to invite bidding for exploration licences to four more offshore blocks.

In January 2001 QGPC was renamed Qatar Petroleum (QP), notwithstanding its diversification over recent years into an ever-widening range of industries, including natural gas and petrochemicals. QP (with an authorized capital of QR 20,000m.) was a shareholder in 10 subsidiary or joint-venture companies in Qatar, and an investor in eight other companies (including five Arab joint ventures based outside Qatar) at the start of 2001. As the controller of the natural gas resources which were central to the country's industrial development strategy, QP was the dominant force in planning the development of Qatar's industrial cities, and was notably responsible for 'fast-tracking' the finalization of an independent water and power project at Ras Laffan in 2001 (see Power and Water, below). Qatar's first major refinery, at Umm Said, was commissioned in 1974 for the National Oil Distribution Co (NODCO), which had been founded in 1968 to manage the refining and distribution of oil products. (Formerly managed as a wholly-owned subsidiary of QGPC, NODCO was fully merged into QGPC during 2000.) The first Umm Said refinery had an initial capacity of 6,200 b/d, which had increased to 12,000 b/d by 1977. In 1984 it was linked to a second refinery, with a capacity of 50,000 b/d, built on an adjacent site. In 1988 two new pipelines were constructed to carry light and heavy products from Umm Said to QGPC's export terminal. In April 1990 the Umm Said refining complex was processing 62,000 b/d of crude petroleum and exporting 50,000 b/d of oil products. In 1995 QGPC announced plans to build a new refinery at Ras Laffan to process large volumes of condensate which would become available if North Field gas development proceeded according to current plans. A 'front-end' engineering and design survey was completed in 1999 for a 140,000 b/d condensate refinery at Ras Laffan, with a projected start-up date of 2004. Meanwhile, 57,000 b/d of condensate-processing capacity was to be added at the Umm Said refining complex. In June 1998 contracts were awarded to increase the total processing capacity of the Umm Said complex to 137,000 b/d. The new capacity was scheduled to be phased into production from late 2002.

Qatar's proven reserves of natural gas at the end of 2001 were estimated to total 14,400,000m. cu m (compared with 11,150,000m. cu m at the end of 2000), representing 9.3% of total world reserves at that date (when the only countries with larger reserves were Russia and Iran). In May 2002 the Government announced a major upward revision of reserves in the offshore North Field (the world's largest single deposit of non-associated gas), as a result of which the figure for total proven reserves rose to some 21,000,000m. cu m.

The North Field was discovered in the 1970s and subsequently assumed a central position in the Government's development plans. Prior to its inauguration in 1991, Qatar's gas output was drawn from a relatively small onshore deposit of non-associated gas (used mainly for power generation) and from the onshore and offshore oilfields, whose output of associated gas is processed at two plants at Umm Said. Annual gas output averaged 5,800m. cu m during the second half of the 1980s, when low output of associated gas at periods of weak oil demand prevented some gas-dependent industries from achieving optimum production levels.

The first phase of Qatar's North Field Development Project (NFDP) was designed to produce a constant 22.6m. cu m per day of gas for domestic use, together with 1.65m. metric tons per year of liquefied petroleum gas and condensate for export. Having been completed at a cost close to the budgeted US $1,300m., the first-phase facilities went into production in September 1991.

The second phase of the NFDP involved the construction of an integrated LNG complex and associated export facilities at Ras Laffan, with an annual capacity of up to 6m. metric tons of LNG, of which 4m. tons were to be shipped to Japan under a 25-year agreement with Chubu Electric Power Co. Contracts for most of the 'downstream' construction work were signed in July 1993, when the shareholders in the Qatargas company which would operate the LNG plant were QGPC (65%), Mobil (10%), Total (10%), Marubeni Corpn (7.5%) and Mitsui & Co (7.5%). Construction work on the liquefaction plant began in April 1994. A US $2,000m. 'downstream' financing package (funded by four Japanese and two European financial institutions) became available for disbursement in October 1995. A $570m. 'upstream' financing arrangement was syndicated in September 1996. Qatargas made its first condensate exports in that month and dispatched its first LNG shipment to Japan in December. Plans were proceeding in mid-2002 to increase the annual production capacity of the Ras Laffan plant (currently 7.7m. tons) to 9.2m. tons by 2004. Qatargas signed two medium-term sales and purchase agreements in May 2001 to supply a total of 9.1m. tons of LNG to the Spanish group Gas Natural between 2001 and 2009.

In a separate venture, QGPC (70%) and Mobil (30%) agreed in December 1992 to establish a new company, subsequently incorporated as the Ras Laffan Liquefied Natural Gas Co (RASGAS), with a view to developing another LNG export facility by the end of the decade, at a cost of up to US $7,500m. Output of about 10m. metric tons per year was envisaged, and the most likely export markets were seen as Japan, the Republic of Korea and Taiwan. In August 1995 RASGAS was close to signing a sales and purchase agreement with the Korea Gas Corpn (KOGAS) for the supply of 2.4m. tons of LNG per year from August 1999 (with an option for a further 1.6m. tons per year), which would effectively guarantee implementation of the project. Discussions with other potential customers had so far yielded letters of intent in respect of at least 6.6m. tons per year (from companies in Taiwan, Turkey and China) and memoranda of understanding in respect of up to 4.5m. tons per year (from Thailand and India). Having signed the KOGAS agreement, RASGAS awarded construction contracts worth an estimated $1,390m. in April 1996. In June 1997 KOGAS signed an agreement to double its LNG purchases from RASGAS to 4.8m. tons per year by 2001. RASGAS subsequently scaled up its construction programme to add the required production capacity, and shipped its first cargo of LNG in June 1999 on spot-market terms. Deliveries to KOGAS were scheduled to begin in July. In August RASGAS signed a sales and purchase agreement with an Indian company, Petronet LNG, for the supply of 7.5m. tons per year of LNG from late 2003. Plans were well advanced in mid-2002 to install additional production capacity in Qatar and receiving facilities in the west of India. In June 2001 RASGAS signed a sales and purchase agreement with the Italian company Edison to supply 3.5m. tons of LNG annually for 25 years from 2005. This agreement (the first long-term supply contract between a Gulf LNG exporter and a European importer) enabled RASGAS to proceed with plans to add a fourth production facility, which would bring its installed production capacity to 23m. tons per year by 2006.

Details of a project to export dry gas directly to Pakistan by pipeline were being finalized in 1994 by a consortium whose main sponsors were Crescent Petroleum (based in Sharjah, UAE), Brown & Root (the US company which would handle the construction work) and TransCanada PipeLines. In May 1995 Pakistan and Qatar established a joint committee to examine the technical and economic feasibility of the project. In late 1996 the French company Total joined the consortium (now named the Gulf-South Asia Gas Corpn) to take responsibility for 'upstream' development work. In March 1999 QGPC signed an outline agreement with the UAE Offsets Group (UOG) to develop and supply Qatari gas to the UAE and Oman via an undersea pipeline from Ras Laffan. Subsequent discussion of possible Qatari gas exports to Pakistan was linked to this new scheme rather than to the earlier proposals. In July 2000 a project development company, Dolphin Energy (DEL), was established by the UOG (51%), TotalFinaElf (24.5%) and Enron Corpn (24.5%) to conduct detailed negotiations with QGPC on the terms of a gas offtake agreement. In March 2001 Qatar Petroleum (the renamed QGPC) signed a commercial term sheet agreement with the UOG setting out terms and conditions for the exploitation of two North Field blocks by DEL's 'upstream' partner (TotalFinaElf) and the construction and operation by Enron Corpn of a 350-km pipeline to the UAE, through which up to 56m. cu m per day of dry gas would be exported after extraction of condensate and related products at a treatment plant at Ras Laffan. The estimated cost of the Dolphin gas project was US $3,500m. Enron Corpn withdrew from the Dolphin project in May 2001, obliging the remaining participants to reassess their development plans. In December 2001 the Dolphin group signed a development and production-sharing agreement with Qatar Petroleum (QP, the renamed QGPC), the aim being that gas sales agreements with UAE customers would be finalized in the second half of 2002 as the necessary prelude to initiating the construction of the pipeline.

In May 2000 QGPC signed a development and production sharing agreement with ExxonMobil Corpn for enhanced gas utilization in a portion of the North Field, supplies from which would be variously used for power generation within Qatar, for processing into exportable liquid products (condensates, butane and propane) and for direct export via pipeline. On the following day the Governments of Qatar and Kuwait signed a memorandum of understanding for the export of Qatari gas via pipeline to Kuwaiti power generation plants. In 2001 QP, ExxonMobil and Kuwait Petroleum Corpn finalized proposals to build a 590-km submarine pipeline to transport up to 40m. cu m of dry gas per day from Ras Laffan to az-Zour in southern Kuwait. In January 2002 the companies involved signed a project term sheet in the hope that gas sales agreements would be finalized before the end of the year. Qatari officials saw the prospective pipelines to Kuwait and the UAE as the backbone of a future Gulf gas grid which would be extended to other states in the region in due course.

Another intended use for output from Qatar's enhanced gas utilization project was as feedstock for the region's first gas-to-liquids (GTL) plants. Between June 1999 and May 2000 QGPC secured syndicated loans totalling US $1,200m. from a consortium of regional and international banks, primarily to finance its current natural gas liquids development programme at Umm Said. In July 2001 Qatar Petroleum (the majority partner) signed a 51:49 joint-venture agreement with the South African company Sasol Synfuels International to set up a GTL plant at Ras Laffan to produce 24,000 b/d of fuel, 9,000 b/d of naphtha and 1,000 b/d of liquefied petroleum gas, using Sasol's slurry phase distillation process. In the previous month Qatar Petroleum and ExxonMobil had announced a feasibility study for a 100,000 b/d GTL plant using ExxonMobil's advanced gas conversion process. By mid-2002 four other major GTL projects were under evaluation jointly with Shell International Gas, Ivanhoe Energy of Canada, Conoco and Marathon.

In March 2002 the Government announced the establishment of the Qatar Fuel Co (Wuqud) as the country's first public limited company in the local oil and gas sector, with a market capitalization of QR 150m., of which 60% was subscribed by private interests and 40% by QP. Invested with a 15-year monopoly, the new company would take over QP's responsibilities for the marketing, transportation and distribution of liquefied petroleum gas and other refined products.

Total natural gas production in Qatar in 1999 (excluding gas flared or recycled at the well-head) was 22,100m. cu m, increased from 19,600m. cu m in 1998. Total gas production rose to 29,100m. cu m. in 2000 and to 32,500m. cu m in 2001. Qatar's LNG exports by volume totalled 2,900m. cu m in 1997, 4,800m. cu m in 1998, 8,130m. cu m in 1999 and 14,040m. cu m in 2000. Japan (7,870m. cu m) and South Korea (4,410m. cu m) were the principal importers of Qatari LNG in 2000.

MANUFACTURING AND INDUSTRY

Qatar's hydrocarbons-based industrialization strategy has centred on the development of 'downstream' processing facilities for oil and gas feedstocks, coupled with some diversification into heavy industry, using local gas as a low-cost fuel source. Three core schemes were initiated at Umm Said in the late 1970s and early 1980s. These are the Qatar Fertilizer Co (QAFCO), the Qatar Petrochemical Co (QAPCO) and the Qatar Steel Co (QASCO).

The first of these projects was QAFCO, which was established in 1969 and which, since 1975, has been owned jointly by QGPC/QP (75%) and Norsk Hydro of Norway (25%). Production of fertilizers began in 1973, with gas feedstocks being supplied from the Dukhan field. Work on a second plant, QAFCO II, began in 1976 and was completed in 1979. In 1990 production totalled 708,000 metric tons of ammonia and 761,000 tons of urea. Major export markets included India and China. In 1992 QAFCO's profits reached QR 172m. Subsequent increases in QAFCO's production capacity were planned on the basis of inputs of non-associated gas supplied from the North Field. A third QAFCO plant with a capacity of 1,500 tons per day of ammonia and 2,000 tons per day of urea came into production in March 1997. In 1998 QAFCO increased production to new record levels (1.67m. tons of urea and 1.37m. tons of ammonia), although it recorded a 60% decline in profits, to QR 156m., owing to depressed world prices. In July 1999 QAFCO secured major new export orders for urea from Australia following a drive to diversify its overseas presence. Profits fell further to QR 65.5m. in 1999, but rose sharply to QR 249.6m. in 2000 following a strong recovery in world prices for ammonia and urea. In mid-2000 QAFCO announced plans to build a fourth plant with a capacity of 2,000 tons per day of ammonia and 3,500 tons per day of urea. By July 2001 QAFCO had arranged $400m. of syndicated borrowing to part-finance the fourth plant and had issued a letter of intent to its chosen contractor for the project. The estimated total cost of the project was US $535m., with a target date for completion in 2004. It would bring QAFCO's total annual capacity to 2.8m. tons of urea and 2m. tons of ammonia.

The petrochemicals facilities of QAPCO were commissioned at Umm Said during 1980 and 1981. The company was established in 1974. The plant had an initial design capacity of 280,000 metric tons of ethylene per year, but in its first year of production it produced only 132,679 tons. The plant also produces low-density polyethylene and sulphur. Sales, particularly of ethylene, were substantially below production, and in 1983 plans were cancelled for a high-density polyethylene plant at the complex. The company suffered from a shortage of ethane-rich gas, and therefore construction of an ethane recovery plant was completed in 1985. Nevertheless, QAPCO made a record loss of QR 156m. in 1985, as a result of the world-wide decline in prices of polyethylene, and a reduction in output of one-third. In early 1989 the rehabilitation of the value-control system at the ethylene plant was completed. QAPCO's performance in 1989 was much improved, with profits estimated at a record QR 420m. In September 1990 the French company Elf Atochem, and in June 1991 the Italian company Enichem, each acquired a 10% interest in QAPCO. QP holds the remaining 80%. In June 1992 QAPCO announced a programme of expansion, involving estimated expenditure of US $385m., under which ethylene capacity at Umm Said was scheduled to reach 450,000 tons in October 1995 and 525,000 tons in April 1996, while polyethylene capacity would be nearly doubled, to 365,000 tons per year, in April 1996. In 1994 QAPCO produced a record 357,000 tons of ethylene and 186,000 tons of polyethylene (representing year-on-year increases of 1.5% and 2.5% respectively) and achieved a 44% increase in profits to QR 260m. In 1998 QAPCO made a net profit of just under QR 300m. (52% less than in 1997) owing to difficult market conditions. In 1999 QAPCO's net profit rose by 30% to QR 380m. QAPCO's ethylene production totalled 480,000 tons in 1999, while output of low-density polyethylene in that year reached a record 383,000 tons. In 2000 QAPCO's net profit rose by 13% to QR 430m.

Another initiative in the field of petrochemicals was taken in 1991, when QGPC and a Canadian company, International Octane, established the Qatar Fuel Additives Co (QAFAC), which was to build a plant to produce methyl tertiary butyl ether (MTBE) and methanol. Following several restructurings, in June 1996 shareholdings in QAFAC were distributed as follows: QGPC 50%, International Octane 15%, Lee Chang Yung Chemical Industrial Corpn (of Taiwan) 15% and China Petroleum Corpn (also of Taiwan) 20%. Construction work began in 1997 on a plant with an annual capacity of 825,000 metric tons of methanol and 610,000 tons of MTBE. QAFAC commenced methanol production in June 1999 and MTBE production in the following month, and had shipped 224,000 tons of methanol and 80,000 tons of MTBE by the end of January 2000, exporting nearly half of its initial MTBE output to the USA. In 1999 legislators in California (currently the largest single market for MTBE) voted to phase out the use of MTBE in unleaded gasoline production from 2002 on health grounds. QAFAC's strong links with Taiwan (a major growth market for MTBE) meant that the company was relatively well positioned to respond to this change in demand. Feasibility studies conducted in 2000 showed that minimal plant modifications would be needed to switch part of QAFAC's capacity from MTBE to alternative products.

In May 1996 QGPC signed a preliminary agreement with a group of European companies with existing interests in Qatar (Norsk Hydro, Elf Atochem and Enichem) for a project to produce an annual 175,000 metric tons of ethylene dichloride, 230,000 tons of vinyl chloride monomer and 290,000 tons of caustic soda, using ethylene feedstock supplied by QAPCO. Participation in the new venture, called Qatar Vinyl Co (QVC), was subsequently finalized as follows: QAPCO 31.9%, Norsk Hydro 29.7%, QGPC 25.5%, Elf Atochem 12.9%. The QVC plant, built at an estimated cost of US $700m., was inaugurated in June 2001. In May 1997 QGPC signed an outline agreement with Phillips Petroleum to develop a chemicals complex which would include a 500,000 tons-per-year ethylene cracker, 467,000 tons per year of polyethylene capacity and 47,000 tons per year of hexene-1 capacity. Feedstock would be supplied from a natural gas liquids plant at Umm Said. In August 1999 Qatar Chemical Co (Q-Chem, owned 51% by QGPC and 49% by Chevron Phillips Chemical Co), secured a $750m. project-financing loan from a group of 24 regional and international banks, enabling it to award contracts for construction of the new complex at Umm Said. The scheduled completion date was 2002. In June 2001 Q-Chem's parent companies signed an agreement to develop a second petrochemicals plant, to be sited at Ras Laffan. The proposed plant would use ethane feedstock, supplied from a North Field gas processing

plant, to produce up to 1.2m. tons per year of ethylene and 750,000 tons per year of polyethylene. The proposed completion date was 2006.

The Qatar Steel Co (QASCO) began commercial production in 1978, and processes imported iron ore and local scrap for export, mainly to Saudi Arabia, Kuwait and the UAE. The Government is now the sole owner of QASCO, having acquired the holdings of the original Japanese partners (a total of 30%) in May 1997. Production levels rose continuously, from 378,544 metric tons of steel bars in 1979 to a record 565,000 tons in 1990. QASCO assumed the management of the Umm Said steel mill in early 1989. In June 1992 QASCO decided to commission a feasibility study with the aim of increasing capacity at the Umm Said plant by 140,000 tons per year, as the first stage of a plan to raise Qatari steel production to 1m. tons per year. QASCO's output in 1991 was 561,000 tons, yielding a profit of QR 127m. In 1992 production totalled 588,000 tons, yielding a profit of QR 155m., and in 1993 output reached 608,626 tons. A contract was awarded in early 1995 for the supply and installation of a 140,000-tons-per-year rolling mill to raise reinforced steel bar capacity to 470,000 tons per year. A contract was signed in May 1996 for the installation, over a period of 18 months, of an electric arc furnace with an annual output capacity of 500,000 tons of molten steel. In 1995 QASCO produced 601,000 tons of concrete-reinforcing bars and recorded a net profit of QR 210m. In February 1997 QASCO established the Qatar Hot Briquetted Iron Co (Qabico) to build a 2m. tons-per-year hot briquetted iron plant at Umm Said at an estimated cost of US $408m. Qabico was owned 31% by QASCO, 10% by QIMCO (see below) and 10% by the Qatar Shipping Co, with the remaining shares divided equally between Kuwait's Gulf Investment Corpn, Kuwait's National Industries Co and Duferco (a holding company based in the United Kingdom's Channel Islands). A further seven major development projects, involving total investment of more than $1,000m., were included in QASCO's development plans for the period to 2005. In 1998 QASCO recorded a net profit of QR 100m. The company's third electric arc furnace was commissioned in October 1999.

In addition to these major industrial schemes, many small enterprises have been established, mainly at Umm Said, now the industrial centre of the country. In 1973 the Industrial Development Technical Centre (IDTC) was founded to co-ordinate the development of non-oil related industry, and by 1983 it had reported the establishment of 72 industrial ventures. The Qatar Flour Mills Co began production at Umm Bab in 1969, and by 1985 output had reached a level of about 1,700 metric tons per day. Cement production began in Qatar at a rate of 330,000 tons per year, and was aimed solely at the domestic market. By the mid-1980s cheap imports, particularly from the UAE, had forced the Qatar National Cement Manufacturing Co (QNCMC) to reduce its prices by as much as 30%, but in 1984 production rose by 26%, to 313,000 tons, and profits for the year were QR 13.8m. In 1992 output of cement totalled 354,133 tons, output of clinker totalled 313,287 tons, and net profits were QR 25.8m. Work began in 1995 on a new 2,000-tons-per-day cement plant at Umm Bab, designed to increase Qatar's total cement capacity to 3,200 tons per day by mid-1997. The new capacity would eliminate Qatar's net import requirement for cement (of up to 700 tons per day in 1995), placing it instead in a position to become a net exporter. Other industries in the country include a ready-mix concrete factory, a plastics factory, a paint factory, a detergents company and several light industrial ventures. In July 2001 the Bahrain Aluminium Extrusion Co announced plans to set up a local subsidiary, Balexco Qatar, to build a plant with extrusion, anodizing and powder-coating facilities.

The joint-stock Qatar Industrial Manufacturing Co (QIMCO) was established in 1990 to promote industrial joint ventures. By the end of 1994 QIMCO held investments totalling QR 90.6m. in 10 projects (seven of them in the local market). There was a 29% increase in net profits (to QR 16.7m.) and a 4.6% increase in shareholders' equity (to QR 138.1m.) in 1994. In 1996 QIMCO's net profit was QR 21.5m. QIMCO, QAPCO and the Italian company Felio each held one-third of the shares in the Qatar Plastic Products Co, which went into production in November 2000.

In June 1993, in an attempt to attract foreign investment for industrial projects, the Government approved legislation to reduce the maximum rate of taxation on profits earned by foreign partners in joint ventures from 50% to 35%. In June 1997 the Government announced plans to establish a purpose-built light industrial zone to the west of Doha and to introduce a new investment law incorporating incentive schemes for companies setting up plants in designated industrial zones. The new investment law would also allow non-Qatari entities to take majority shareholdings in joint-venture projects (which were currently required to be at least 51% Qatari-owned).

POWER AND WATER

In 2000 Qatar's public electricity supply system had about 1,863 MW of installed generating capacity, of which up to 132 MW was located at the Ras Abu Aboud power station, 620 MW at the Ras Abu Fontas 'A' power station, 609 MW at the Ras Abu Fontas 'B' power station and 503 MW at supporting stations (mainly located near Doha). Peak demand (in the months of July and August) currently exceeded total capacity by 100 MW or more, necessitating some buying-in of electricity from generating plants operated by large industrial users.

Qatar has one of the world's highest levels of domestic demand for water per head of population, and one of the highest rates of dependency on desalination plants to provide drinking water. Installed desalination capacity at the main power stations in 2000 was: Ras Abu Aboud 8m. gallons per day (13.3m. cu m per year); Ras Abu Fontas 'A' 70m. gallons per day (116.1m. cu m per year); and Ras Abu Fontas 'B' 33m. gallons per day (54.7m. cu m per year).

The central planning and supervisory authority for the power and water sectors, and the managing authority for the transmission and distribution networks, is the Qatar General Electricity and Water Corpn (Kahramaa), established in April 2000 to take over these roles from the Ministry of Electricity and Water (MEW). Kahramaa also took over the MEW's responsibility for operating the Ras Abu Fontas 'A' and Ras Abu Aboud power stations and their supporting stations. The Ras Abu Fontas 'B' power station remained under the management of Qatar Electricity and Water Co (QEWC), which had taken over this station from the MEW in April 1999 under the terms of a transfer accord signed in February 1998. The QEWC (a joint-stock company established in 1990 and owned 43% by the State and 57% by private Qatari investors) sold 80% of its electricity and water output to the public distribution authority at unit prices specified in an offtake agreement forming part of the 1998 transfer accord. The drive towards private power generation accelerated in 2001 with an agreement between QEWC and Kahramaa providing for the transfer to QEWC of the power stations which Kahramaa had taken over from the MEW. The issue of introducing domestic utility charges to discourage wasteful consumption by Qatari nationals (who enjoyed free unmetered supplies of electricity and water) was first mooted in 1999, but remained unresolved in mid-2002.

In November 2000 QEWC awarded a contract to expand the generating capacity of the Ras Abu Fontas 'B' power station by 380 MW by mid-2002. A plan to add up to 30m. gallons per day of new desalination capacity at Ras Abu Fontas 'B' was being re-evaluated in mid-2002, in the light of the specifications for Qatar's first independent water and power project (IWPP). The IWPP (final bidding for which was organized by Qatar Petroleum) was to be built at Ras Laffan and brought into full production by mid-2004, with a capacity of 750 MW of electricity and 40m. gallons per day of desalinated water. A US company, AES Corpn, initialled a power and water purchase agreement in May 2001 providing for the establishment of a new utility company to implement the Ras Laffan IWPP on build-operate-transfer terms. The company would be owned 55% by AES, 25% by QEWC, 10% by Gulf Investment Corpn and 10% by Qatar Petroleum (which was to supply the plant with natural gas and also with coolant from a seawater circulation system currently under development for the benefit of new industries in Ras Laffan). Kahramaa would be the sole buyer of the IWPP's electricity output (the bulk of which would be sold to industrial end-users). Qatar's October 2000 foreign investment law permitted up to 100% foreign ownership of power plants.

TRANSPORT AND COMMUNICATIONS

The first contracts for a major port development project at Doha were awarded in mid-1993. Extensive dredging work on the 17-km port approach channel would serve the dual purpose of upgrading the maritime access facility and providing landfill material to create 360,000 sq m of new quayside space at the port and to fill some 3.55m. sq m of reclaimed land, which was designated as the site of a new international airport. Also under development at Doha was a new container terminal with two berths and a roll-on roll-off facility. Qatar's container traffic in 1999 totalled 80,000 20-foot equivalent units. At Ras Laffan, major new port facilities for LNG and condensate carriers and roll-on roll-off vessels were completed in 1995. The development plan for Ras Laffan proposed the linking of the port area to a 50 sq km industrial area surrounded by a buffer zone. In April 1996 Ras Laffan was officially designated an industrial city. Umm Said (also known as Messaieed) was officially designated as an industrial city in December 1998 and subsequently announced plans to upgrade its port facilities to handle a projected growth in trade; bids to construct a new multi-products berth were under evaluation by Qatar Petroleum in mid-2001.

In late 1997 a US firm was selected as consultant for a US $450m. roads project involving the reconstruction and upgrading of 280 km of the primary road network and the construction of 19 interchanges, including numerous bridges and underpasses. However, falling oil revenues in 1998 compelled the Government to modify its original plans and to split the construction work into several packages to be phased over a number of years. In February 2000 Qatar and Bahrain agreed to establish a committee to assess the feasibility of building a 50-km causeway between the two countries.

The Qatar Shipping Co (Q-Ship), established in 1992, was scheduled to inaugurate a passenger and car ferry service between Doha and Bahrain in late 1994, while expanding its cargo-carrying capabilities to include the transport of crude oil, liquefied petroleum gas, petrochemicals and iron ore. A QR 350m. fleet expansion programme was approved in June 1996. In 2000 Q-Ship had a fleet of seven vessels and was due to take delivery of a further two during 2002. Halul Offshore Services Co (a new 50:50 joint venture between Q-Ship and Qatar National Navigation & Transport Co) was, in mid-2001, arranging financing for the purchase of nine vessels.

The Qatar Government is a co-owner of the regional airline Gulf Air (in which Abu Dhabi, Bahrain and Oman also hold 25% interests). Each of the four shareholders in Gulf Air agreed, in May 2001, to contribute US $39.8m. of new capital to the airline, which was reported to have made heavy trading losses in the previous year. Qatar Airways, originally established by Qatari business interests in 1993, embarked on an extensive restructuring programme in 1997, one outcome of which was to bring Qatar Airways into 50% Qatari Government and 50% Qatari private ownership. In the year ending March 1999 Qatar Airways carried 910,000 passengers. In mid-2001 Qatar Airways had a fleet of 15 aircraft (of which 13 were used for scheduled passenger services to the Middle East, Europe, the Indian subcontinent and the Far East), which was to be increased to 20 aircraft by 2004 and to 22 aircraft by 2006. Despite the downturn in international air traffic after 11 September 2001, passengers carried by Qatar Airways increased by 31% in 2001 to 1.6m., and this figure was expected to increase by a further 40% in 2002, to 2.4m. However, the airline acknowledged in May 2002 that it would continue to run at a loss for at least another five years. In the same month, Qatar withdrew from the Gulf Air partnership (with Abu Dhabi, Bahrain and Oman) rather than participate in a new injection of capital into the troubled regional carrier.

Doha international airport handled an estimated 2.6m. passengers in 2000. Plans for a new passenger terminal and other expansion at the airport were elaborated in 2001, at a projected total cost of US $1,000m. In June 2002 the Government set up a special steering committee to expedite the project, owing to the need for it to be completed in time for the Asian Games to be held in Doha in December 2006 (see Services and Tourism, below).

The state-owned Qatar Public Telecommunications Corpn (Q-Tel) made a net profit of QR 307m. on a turnover of about QR 1,000m. in 1996, when it had a public network with a design capacity of 350,000 lines. The main Q-Tel network had 150,000 subscribers in 1996, while there was rapid growth in the provision of ancillary services, including mobile telephones, with 28,772 users in 1996. Q-Tel held a 10% share in the Ath-Thurraya satellite programme being developed by a consortium headed by Emirates Telecommunications Corpn. In December 1998 Q-Tel was partially privatized with 45% of its shares being sold for some US $650m. In 1999 Q-Tel recorded revenues of QR 1,281.3m. and net profits of QR 623.5m. In May 2000 it awarded a contract to the French company Alcatel to add 100,000 new lines to Q-Tel's global system for mobiles (GSM) network, which had 81,500 existing subscribers in March 2000. At the end of 2000 Q-Tel had 119,500 GSM subscribers and 160,200 fixed-line subscribers. It recorded revenues of QR 1,323.9m. and net profits of QR 724.5m. in 2000.

SERVICES AND TOURISM

In 1995 Qatar had four government hospitals, with a total of 1,122 beds, and there were 715 physicians working in official medical services. In 1988, according to the World Health Organization, there were 20 physicians, three dentists and 51 nurses for every 10,000 inhabitants in Qatar, the highest ratios for any Arab country. The Hamad General Hospital (opened in 1982) has 660 beds. In 1995 there were 25 health centres and four out-patient clinics. There is a hospital for women, with 288 beds. Social welfare developments within the country have been a high priority. Education has expanded, and by 1995/96 there were 174 primary schools in the country. The University of Qatar was established in 1977, and had 8,475 students in 1996/97.

Construction of Qatar's first privately-financed hospital (the 250-bed al-Ahli hospital in Doha) commenced in mid-2000 at a projected cost of US $54m.; it was scheduled to open in late 2002. In 1996 the Government announced proposals for the introduction of compulsory health cards costing QR 50 per five-year period for Qatari nationals, QR 100 per annum for expatriate civil servants and diplomats, and QR 200 per annum for other expatriates. Visitors to Qatar would be liable to pay 15% of the cost of local medical treatment. In early 1999 the Hamad Medical Corporation announced increased charges for the supply of medical services and medicines to expatriates and to foreign visitors. Qatar's October 2000 foreign investment law permitted hospitals and educational establishments to have up to 100% foreign ownership.

The 1997/98 budget provided funding for government housing schemes, including the completion of 900 houses already under construction and the building of 700 additional houses. In 1998 the Government was considering several initiatives to improve access to housing for Qatari nationals entering private-sector employment, including the establishment of a new bank to provide housing loans. Consideration was also being given to the introduction of pension schemes and other social security provisions to encourage Qatari nationals to take up private-sector employment. The 1998/99 budget contained provision for capital spending of QR 241m. in the health and social services sector, of which QR 190m. would finance the completion of the 700 houses provided for under the previous budget as well as the construction of 700 new housing units. The 1998/99 capital budget also allocated QR 77.4m. to education and youth welfare. The 1999/2000 budget provided for capital investment of QR 250m. in health and social services and QR 66m. in education and youth welfare. The 2000/01 capital budget allocated QR 384m. for health and social services, including QR 221m. for housing projects and QR 158m. for healthcare facilities. There was a capital provision of QR 93m. for education and youth welfare in the 2000/01 budget, including major allocations for school-building and university expansion. The 2001/02 budget provided for QR 705m. of capital investment in health and social services and QR 162m. of investment in education.

Qatar had 451,000 tourist arrivals in 1998 despite the relatively small scale of its tourism infrastructure. Tourism was being actively promoted in 2000, with four new luxury hotel developments in progress in the West Bay area, where 1,744 new hotel rooms were expected to be available by 2003. The most ambitious of the West Bay projects (with an estimated cost of up to US $130m.) involved the construction of an 18-storey, 232-room hotel, an office block and various types of residential accommodation. The state-owned Qatar National Hotels Co (QNHC, which employed 6,000 people in 2000) was scheduled to be privatized by 2004. Qatar's tourist hotels had average occupancy rates of 80% in 2000, when some 320,000 bed-nights were sold. The chairman of QNHC was appointed head of a new Qatar Tourism Authority (QTA) on its establishment in 2000. In November 2000 Qatar was awarded the right to host the 2006 Asian Games, having pledged to build a $700m. sports city to the north of Doha to accommodate 5,000 competitors. Qatar's October 2000 foreign investment law permitted up to 100% foreign ownership of hotels and tourism facilities, while hotel restaurants and selected clubs were permitted to sell alcohol to non-Muslims. In 2001 QNHC was seeking partners to develop five major tourism projects: a proposed business hotel with extensive sports and leisure attractions, to be sited at Doha Golf Club; a proposed hotel development near Ras Laffan industrial city; a proposed family theme park with a space simulator and other attractions; a proposed retail park with 'souk-style outlets and modern boutiques'; and a proposed 'eco-heritage' resort. The construction of a Museum of Islamic Arts in the area of Doha port was also planned partly with tourism in mind.

BUDGET, INVESTMENT AND FINANCE

Since 1979 the Qatari riyal has been officially pegged to the IMF special drawing right (SDR) at a rate of QR 4.7619 = SDR 1 within a permitted fluctuation margin of plus or minus 7.25%. Since 1986, however, the riyal has in reality been linked to the US dollar at a rate of QR 3.64 = $1.

Qatar's budgetary performance is very closely linked to the oil price and production levels. The increases in petroleum revenue that occurred in the 1970s resulted in large budget surpluses, which enabled Qatar to embark on its impressive programme of industrial and infrastructural projects. However, after achieving a budget surplus of QR 7,993m. in 1980, the country recorded a deficit of QR 566m. in 1983. This was largely due to the fall in petroleum exports, and, in order to alleviate the problem, government current expenditure was reduced. As a result of these cut-backs, less foreign investment was attracted to the country, and liquidity levels consequently suffered. As a result of the collapse of petroleum prices, no budget was announced for 1986/87, but it was understood that ministries were asked not to exceed the previous year's budget. Expenditure on defence, however, continued to increase, and in 1986 France agreed to supply Qatar with four *Mirage* F-1 fighter aircraft, missiles and a radar system, at a cost of US $243m. From 1989 Qatar's financial year began on 1 April.

The 1995/96 budget provided for a 10.1% rise in revenue to QR 9,204m. (assuming an average crude oil price of US $15 per barrel) and a 7.7% rise in total expenditure to QR 12,735m. (including slightly lower capital spending of QR 2,224m.). Capital spending allocations for 1995/96 were public works and infrastructure QR 931m. (including QR 198m. for roads, QR 251m. for sewerage and QR 120m. for land purchases); economic services QR 928m.; and health, social services, education and youth welfare QR 365m. The budget out-turn for that year showed a 20.0% increase in revenues (mainly owing to higher oil prices), which totalled QR 12,226m., compared with expenditure of QR 13,460m., resulting in a deficit of QR 1,234m.

The 1996/97 budget provided for total expenditure of QR 13,750m. (QR 11,530m. on current account and QR 2,220m. on capital account) and total revenue of QR 10,800m., resulting in a projected deficit of QR 2,950m. A QR 500m. package of increases in public-sector pay and allowances was announced in late June 1996. The 1996/97 out-turn figures showed higher revenues of QR 13,459m. and expenditure of QR 15,947m., producing a deficit of QR 2,488m.

The 1997/98 budget forecast provided for total expenditure of QR 16,387m. (including a 20% increase in spending on capital projects) and revenues of QR 13,397m., producing an anticipated deficit of QR 2,990m. The final out-turn figures for 1997/98 showed an actual deficit of QR 3,190m. (expenditure QR 17,932m., revenue QR 14,742m.). In 1998/99 the Government budgeted for expenditure of QR 15,659m. and revenue of QR 12,353m., leaving a deficit of QR 3,306m. However, the out-turn figures for 1998/99 showed a deficit of only QR 1,768m. (expenditure QR 16,968m., revenue QR 15,200m.), after taking account of some US $650m. (QR 2,366m.) raised from the partial privatization of Qatar Telecommunications Corporation. According to estimates published by the International Institute for Strategic Studies, Qatar's defence expenditure totalled QR 4,998m. in 1998 and QR 5,344m. in 1999. The 1999/2000 budget provided for total revenue of QR 10,530m. (including QR 5,315m. from oil and gas) and total expenditure of QR 14,136m. (including capital spending of QR 2,632m.), leaving a projected deficit of QR 3,606m. Among the revenue-raising measures implemented in the 1999/2000 fiscal year were substantial increases in the charges for entry visas and residency permits. The projected deficit in the 1999/2000 budget was based on a conservative oil price estimate of US $10 per barrel, expenditure having been budgeted at a level that would be balanced by revenue if oil prices averaged $15 per barrel. The actual out-turn figures for 1999/2000 were revenue QR 15,272m., expenditure QR 17,382m., leaving a deficit of QR 2,110m. The actual price of Qatari crude oil in 1999 averaged $17 per barrel.

The 2000/01 budget provided for revenue of QR 12,617m. and expenditure of QR 15,400m., leaving a projected deficit of QR 2,783m. The revenue projection was based on a very conservative oil price estimate in the range US $13–$15 per barrel, while expenditure was set at a level that would be balanced by revenue if oil prices averaged $18 per barrel and the rate of crude oil production averaged 594,000 b/d. Sectoral spending allocations in the 2000/01 budget included QR 1,545m. for public services and infrastructure. Overall, some QR 2,022m. was allocated for the completion of existing projects and the initiation of new schemes, it being envisaged that new schemes worth a total of QR 4,474m. would be launched before the end of the fiscal year. Preliminary out-turn figures for 2000/01 showed a budget surplus of QR 4,396m. (revenue QR 23,291m., expenditure QR 18,895m.), equivalent to 7.3% of GDP. The actual price of Qatari crude oil in 2000 averaged $27 per barrel. The 2001/02 budget provided for revenue of QR 18,057m. and expenditure of QR 17,560m., leaving a surplus of QR 497m. The revenue projection was based on an average oil price of $16.50 per barrel (whereas OPEC was currently committed to defending a 'floor' price of $22 per barrel). The expenditure projection included capital spending of QR 3,160m., including QR 2,293m. for infrastructure projects. Preliminary out-turn figures for 2001/02 showed that a sustained above-budget oil price had produced a surplus greater than the budget forecast, although no official figures had been released by mid-2002.

The 2002/03 budget provided for a 14% increase in expenditure compared with the original figure for 2001/02, to QR 20,026m., and revenue of QR 18,207m., to produce a deficit of QR 1,819m. The revenue projection was again based on a conservative assumption of an average oil price of $16.50 per barrel throughout the year. Planned expenditure included QR 4,100m. on infrastructure projects (an increase of 40%), QR 887m. on health and social services and QR 418m. on education and youth projects.

Total external debt, including project finance, grew from US $4,508m. at the end of 1995 to $9,796m. by the end of 1998, with the Government's share of Qatar's external debt (representing borrowing to finance the fiscal deficit) totalling $2,961m. (32% of GDP) in March 1999. The remainder of the country's external debt was project-related. Total external debt in July 2000 was estimated at $12,823m. (87.6% of GDP), of which $5,651m. was direct government debt, $1,654m. was government-guaranteed debt and $4,868m. was debt incurred for project development by subsidiaries of the state hydrocarbons enterprise. By the end of 2001 total external debt had risen to $13,223m., of which $7,305m. was direct government debt, $5,268m. debt incurred for project development by QP subsidiaries and $650m. other government-guaranteed debt. Having peaked at 95.5% in 1998, the external debt to GDP ratio was reduced to 76.5% by the end of 2001. Debt repayment due rose to $1,435m. in 2002 (double the 1998 figure), but was projected to fall steadily to $380m. in 2005.

The inauguration of the Qatar Industrial Development Bank (QIBD) in November 1997 brought the number of banks operating in Qatar to 15 (excluding the Central Bank), including eight foreign banks. Structured as a joint venture between the Qatar Government and local private-sector interests (mainly

banks and insurance companies), the QIBD was to provide concessionary loans to fund the fixed capital requirements of small and medium-sized industrial ventures. In October 1993 the Qatar Monetary Authority was superseded by the Qatar Central Bank, with paid-up capital of QR 50m. and overall capital and reserves totalling QR 156m. The Central Bank's end-1998 assets totalled QR 5,755.3m. (including QR 3,781.8m. of foreign assets), while the principal liabilities on its end-1998 balance sheet were currency issued to the value of QR 1,729.2m. and local banks' deposits totalling QR 828.0m. The Central Bank has supervisory powers over all banks, foreign exchange houses, investment companies and finance houses operating in Qatar. In August 1997 the Central Bank was empowered to license Qatar-based banks and finance companies to establish 'offshore' banking units, with effect from October 1997. Bahrain had previously been the only GCC member state with an 'offshore' banking sector. In February 2000 11 unlicensed investment companies were ordered by the Central Bank to cease trading and to return an estimated US $100m. to depositors. The largest Qatari commercial bank, Qatar National Bank, had total assets of QR 24,621m. in 2000, when it posted a net profit of QR 491m.

Until April 1997 trading in local companies' shares was conducted through an unofficial stock exchange which had a turnover of some US $89.3m. in 1996. In May 1997 an official Doha Securities Market (DSM), supervised by the Ministry of Finance, Economy and Trade, began trading in the shares of 17 companies and banks, the number rising to 18 by February 1998, when their market capitalization totalled QR 9,902m. (US $2,720m.) and weekly turnover was averaging QR 8.4m. ($2.3m.). In May 1998 the Qatar Arabian Investment Company (QAIC) was launched with plans for its shares to be listed on the DSM—the first listing of a dollar-denominated stock and the first open to non-Qatari investment. The market's start-up costs were funded by the Government, which planned to organize a series of share offers as part of a future privatization programme. Currently conducting business by 'floor' trading, the DSM was to be relocated in 2000 to a purpose-built exchange with a fully-computerized trading system. During the last quarter of 1998 (when the initial public offering of shares in Qatar Telecom began) the DSM had an average weekly turnover of QR 26.7m. ($7.3m.). At the end of 1999 average weekly turnover remained at about the same level. The market capitalization of the 21 companies quoted on the DSM in early 2000 was QR 18,559m. In March 2000 the right to buy and sell the shares of DSM-listed companies was extended to nationals of all GCC member-states. It was expected that the DSM's first listing of a foreign company (from Oman) would take place in 2001.

In 1997 the Government continued its practice of contracting syndicated overseas loans for general funding purposes, taking out loans of US $300m. and $200m. from consortia of international banks in the latter months of the year. A new public debt law approved in March 1998 was intended to facilitate the issue of treasury bills and bonds to finance the Government's budget deficit: the Central Bank Governor stated that the new law would also enable the bank to influence money supply and interest rates by market intervention. Under a Central Bank directive which came into force on 1 April, the maximum 6.5% interest rate on riyal deposits was abolished and banks were permitted to set their own interest rates on deposits of over 15 months' duration. Recommended by the IMF as part of financial sector reform, the changes were intended to attract more local capital into the domestic banking system and to encourage depositors to hold funds on a longer-term basis. In July 1999 the Government issued its first treasury bond, worth QR 2,000m., which was heavily over-subscribed. The three-year bonds had a face value of QR 10,000 each and carried 7.75% non-taxable interest, payable half-yearly. Trading in the bonds was to be confined to Qatari banks for one year, whereafter it was proposed to open it to companies and individuals. The Government, whose domestic borrowings totalled an estimated QR 10,800m. at the end of April 1999, saw the treasury bonds as a replacement for short- and medium-term bank credits.

In May 1998 the Commercial Bank of Qatar (CBQ) became the first local bank to secure a syndicated credit facility, signing an agreement with a group of regional and international banks under which it would borrow US $60m. for the financing of forthcoming industrial projects. At the end of June, however, the Qatari authorities postponed the Government's first Eurobond issue, owing to unfavourable conditions in emerging debt markets. The 10-year Eurobond, worth $1,000m., was subsequently successfully issued in May 1999, attracting investors from the USA (55%), Europe (25%) and the Middle East (20%). In June 2000 Qatar's second sovereign Eurobond issue raised $1,400m., nearly two-thirds of which was contributed by US investors and most of the remainder by European investors. This issue (with a 30-year term) made it possible for the Government to pay down some of its short-term debt. In December 1999 Qatar negotiated a so-called 'oil prepayment' facility with a group of international banks, effectively providing the Government with advance access to oil revenues. The facility was for $500m., repayable over five years. A further $250m., repayable over three years, was raised through a similar arrangement in early 2000. The CBQ secured a new $120m. syndicated credit facility in May 2000. A $500m. sovereign loan, repayable over seven years, was arranged for Qatar in November 2000 by Sumitomo Bank, which had been the lead arranger for previous sovereign loans in 1994, 1995 and 1996, and a co-arranger of Qatar's most recent syndicated sovereign loan in 1997.

In addition to investment in national industrial diversification, Qatar also allocated considerable sums of aid to poorer countries during the 1970s. In 1975 the level of aid was US $339m., but in 1980 the total declined to $277m., representing 4.2% of GNP. In October 1990 the Government announced that the debts owing to it by 10 Arab and African countries were to be cancelled. The World Bank estimated that Qatar extended net aid of about $1m. (0.01% of GNP) in 1991 and that its cumulative net aid over the five years 1987–91 amounted to just $4m.

In December 1995 IMF statistics for Qatar indicated total official reserves of US $694m. and total foreign assets of $787m. However, it was confirmed by the Government in the following month that a substantial tranche of Qatar's reserves had remained under the control of the former Amir, Sheikh Khalifa, following his removal from office in June 1995. The sum involved was widely reported to be in the region of $3,000m. A settlement agreement was signed in February 1997 whereby Sheikh Khalifa was understood to have formally ceded control over disputed assets.

FOREIGN TRADE AND BALANCE OF PAYMENTS

During the 1970s imports and exports grew quickly, but in the early 1980s there was a fall in Qatar's levels of trade. Imports were reduced over the period 1982–84, and in 1985 their value declined to QR 4,146.5m., the lowest annual total since 1976. The value of exports fell from QR 20,787m. in 1980 to QR 12,002m. in 1983, reflecting the reduction in petroleum exports. By 1989 the value of imports had risen to QR 4,827m. They continued to rise and were valued at QR 6,169m. in 1990 and at QR 6,261m. in 1991. Export earnings were QR 9,967m. in 1989 and QR 14,161m. in 1990, but fell to QR 11,684m. in 1991. In 1991 Japan provided 13.6% of Qatar's imports, the United Kingdom 11.8%, and the USA 11.6%. According to analysts, Japan's imports of Qatari crude petroleum in 1988 accounted for more than one-half of the estimated value of Qatar's total oil exports. In 1998 the principal source of imports (14.2%) was the USA; other important suppliers in that year were Japan, the United Kingdom, the UAE, Italy, Germany, France, and Saudi Arabia. Preliminary figures for exports in

1994 suggested that Asia (excluding Arab countries) was the principal market for exports (80.8%). The principal commodities that Qatar imports are electrical items and machinery, and there is also considerable importing of basic manufactures, food and live animals, and chemicals. Apart from its exports of petroleum, most of Qatar's export trade is with its Arab neighbours.

In 1996 Qatar had export earnings of US $3,833m. (including $2,559m. from crude oil) and imports of $2,584m., leaving a visible trade surplus of $1,249m. The 1996 balance of payments showed a current-account deficit of $1,246m. and an overall deficit of $524m. In 1997 there was a visible trade surplus of $863m. (exports $3,856m., imports $2,993m.), a current-account deficit of $1,678m. and an overall balance-of-payments deficit of $487m. Provisional trade statistics for 1998 showed export earnings of $5,030m. (including $2,995m. from crude oil and $840m. from LNG and related products), while import spending totalled $3,071m. (including $1,021m. for LNG-related construction projects), producing a visible trade surplus of $1,959m. Provisional 1998 balance-of-payments statistics showed a current-account deficit of $456m. and an overall deficit of $48m. Provisional trade statistics for 1999 showed export earnings of $7,214m. (including $4,014m. from crude oil and $1,353m. from LNG and related products) and import spending of $2,252m. (including $372m. for LNG-related construction projects), producing a visible trade surplus of $4,962m. (the highest surplus for a decade). The balance of payments showed a current-account surplus of $2,171m. and an overall surplus of $2,457m. in 1999.

Official statistics for 2000 gave Qatar's export earnings as US $11,594m. (including an estimated $6,859m. from crude oil and $3,300m. from LNG and related products) and its import spending as $2,930m., leaving a visible trade surplus of $8,664m. There was a current-account surplus of $5,417m. and an overall balance-of-payments surplus of $3,531m. Because of the normalization of world oil prices during 2001, the trade surplus contracted by 5% in that year, to $8,195m. (from exports worth $11,264m. and imports worth $3,069m.). The current-account surplus fell by 9% in 2001, to $4,940m., while the overall balance-of-payments surplus was 30% lower than in 2000, at $2,723m. Qatar's official international reserves totalled $1,318m. at the end of 2001.

ECONOMIC PROSPECTS

The very positive economic trends of recent years look set to continue in the short and medium term, as Qatar reaps the benefits of its successful use of increased oil and gas revenues since 1999 to develop its downstream activities, particularly its capacity to produce and export LNG—annual exports of which are projected to treble in the next 10 years, to some 40m. tons. The massive increase in proven gas reserves in the giant North Field announced in May 2002 will undoubtedly ensure that Qatar has ample low-cost gas output to feed its burgeoning LNG industries and also to supply the proposed gas pipelines to Kuwait and the UAE. The release of the new North Field figures prompted a decision by the US Standard and Poor's ratings agency to raise Qatar's sovereign credit rating to A–, further securing the likelihood that foreign investment will continue to flow into the country. The newly appointed Minister of Economy and Trade, Sheikh Hamad bin Faisal bin Thani ath-Thani, declared in the same month that the size of Qatar's economy would double within three to four years.

Statistical Survey

Sources (unless otherwise stated): Press and Publications Dept, Ministry of Education, POB 80, Doha; Dept of Economic Policies, Qatar Central Bank, POB 1234, Doha; tel. 4456456; fax 4413650; e-mail elzainys@qcb.gov.qa; internet www.qcb.gov.qa.

AREA AND POPULATION

Area: 11,437 sq km (4,416 sq miles).

Population: 369,079 at census of 16 March 1986; 522,023 (males 342,459; females 179,564) at census of 1 March 1997; 597,000 (provisional) at mid-2001.

Density (mid-2001): 52.2 per sq km.

Principal Towns (population of municipalities, 1997 census): Ad-Dawhah (Doha, the capital) 264,009; Ar-Rayyan 169,774; Al-Wakrah 31,702; Umm Salal 18,392; Al-Khawr (Al-Khor) 17,793.

Births and Deaths (2000): Registered live births 11,250 (birth rate 19.4 per 1,000); Registered deaths 1,173 (death rate 2.0 per 1,000). Source: mainly UN, *Population and Vital Statistics Report.*

Expectation of Life (WHO estimates, years at birth, 2000): Males 70.4; Females 75.0. Source: WHO, *World Health Report.*

Economically Active Population (persons aged 15 years and over, March 1986): Agriculture and fishing 6,283; Mining and quarrying 4,807; Manufacturing 13,914; Electricity, gas and water 5,266; Building and construction 40,523; Trade, restaurants and hotels 21,964; Transport and communications 7,357; Finance, insurance and real estate 3,157; Community, social and personal services 96,466; Activities not adequately defined 501; Total employed 200,238 (Qatari nationals 20,807; non-Qataris 179,431). Figures include 1,025 unemployed persons with previous work experience, but exclude 944 persons seeking work for the first time.

Mid-2000 (estimates in '000): Agriculture, etc. 4; Total labour force 313 (Source: FAO).

HEALTH AND WELFARE
Key Indicators

Fertility (births per woman, 2000): 3.5.

Under-5 Mortality Rate (per 1,000 live births, 2000): 14.

Physicians (per 1,000 head, 1998): 0.09.

Hospital Beds (per 1,000 head, 1995): 1.26.

Health Expenditure (1998): US $ per head (PPP): 919.
%% of GDP: 4.4.
public (% of total): 76.6.

Human Development Index (2000): ranking: 51.
value: 0.803.

For sources and definitions, see explanatory note on p. vi.

AGRICULTURE, ETC.

Principal Crops ('000 metric tons, 2000): Barley 4.1; Maize 1.8; Cabbages 2.4; Tomatoes 9.4; Cauliflowers 1.8; Pumpkins, squash and gourds 8.5*; Cucumbers and gherkins 4.8*; Aubergines (Eggplants) 5.0*; Chillies and green peppers 1.2; Dry onions 3.7; Other vegetables 11.0*; Watermelons 1.3; Cantaloupes and other melons 4.3*; Dates 16.1; Other fruits 1.9*. *FAO estimate. Source: FAO.

Livestock ('000 head, year ending September 2000): Horses 3.8*; Cattle 14.8; Camels 50.0*; Sheep 214.5; Goats 178.5; Poultry 3,835. * FAO estimate. Source: FAO.

Livestock Products ('000 metric tons, 2000): Mutton and lamb 7.4; Camel meat 1.1*; Poultry meat 4.1; Other meat 1.2*; Cows' milk 11.2; Camel's milk 13.3*; Sheep's milk 5.3; Goats' milk 6.1*; Hen eggs 3.6*. * FAO estimate. Source: FAO.

Fishing (metric tons, live weight, 1999): Groupers 913; Grunts and sweetlips 433; Emperors (Scavengers) 798; Porgies and seabreams 280; Spinefeet (Rabbitfishes) 240; Jacks and crevalles 289; Golden trevally 116; Narrow-barred Spanish mackerel 496; Total catch (incl. others) 4,207. Source: FAO, *Yearbook of Fishery Statistics.*

MINING

Production (estimates, 2000): Crude petroleum ('000 barrels) 254,000; Natural gas (million cu m) 35,000. Source: US Geological Survey.

INDUSTRY

Production (estimates, 2000, unless otherwise indicated): Wheat flour (including bran, '000 metric tons) 40 (1999); Ammonia (nitrogen content, '000 metric tons) 1,097 (reported figure); Urea (nitrogen content, '000 metric tons) 748; Motor spirit (petrol, '000 barrels) 5,500; Kerosene ('000 barrels) 4,400; Gas-diesel (Distillate-fuel) oils

('000 barrels) 5,100; Residual fuel oils ('000 barrels) 6,900; Other refinery products ('000 barrels) 2,000; Liquefied natural gas ('000 barrels) 22,000; Cement ('000 metric tons) 1,050; Crude steel ('000 metric tons) 729 (reported figure); Electric energy (million kWh) 8,170 (1998). Source: mainly US Geological Survey.

FINANCE

Currency and Exchange Rates: 100 dirhams = 1 Qatar riyal (QR). *Sterling, Dollar and Euro Equivalents* (31 May 2002): £1 sterling = 5.339 riyals; US $1 = 3.640 riyals; €1 = 2.927 riyals; 100 Qatar riyals = £18.73 = $27.47 = €29.27. *Exchange Rate:* Since June 1980 the official mid-point rate has been fixed at US $1 = QR 3.64.

Budget (QR million, year ending 31 March): 2000/01 (provisional): *Revenue:* 23,291; *Expenditure:* 18,895 (Salaries and wages 4,999, Other current expenditure 10,849, Major works and projects 1,879, Other capital expenditure 1,168).

International Reserves (US $ million at 31 December 2001): Gold 5.3; IMF special drawing rights 22.5; Reserve position in IMF 99.4; Foreign exchange 1,190.8; Total 1,318.0. Source: IMF, *International Financial Statistics.*

Money Supply (QR million at 31 December 2001): Currency outside banks 1,741; Demand deposits at commercial banks 3,479; Total money 5,219. Source: IMF, *International Financial Statistics.*

Cost of Living (Consumer Price Index for Doha; base: 1988 = 100): 137.0 in 1999; 139.3 in 2000; 141.3 in 2001.

Expenditure on the Gross Domestic Product (provisional, QR million at current prices, 1999): Government final consumption expenditure 11,810; Private final consumption expenditure 9,515; Increase in stocks 405; Gross fixed capital formation 9,107; *Total domestic expenditure* 30,837; Exports of goods and services 26,550; *Less* Imports of goods and services 12,990; *GDP in purchasers' values* 44,397. Source: UN Economic and Social Commission for Western Asia, *National Accounts Studies of the ESCWA Region* (2000).

Gross Domestic Product by Economic Activity (provisional, QR million at current prices, 2001): Agriculture and fishing 266; Petroleum and natural gas 33,180; Manufacturing 3,460; Electricity and water 675; Construction 2,030; Trade, restaurants and hotels 3,387; Transport and communications 2,180; Finance, insurance, real estate and business services 4,821; Other services 8,795; Total 58,794.

Balance of Payments (estimates, QR million, 2001): Exports f.o.b. 39,567; Imports f.o.b. −12,323; *Trade balance* 27,244; Services, private and official transfers (net) −11,294; *Current balance* 15,950; Capital (net) −5,050; *Overall balance* 10,900.

EXTERNAL TRADE

Imports c.i.f. (QR million): 12,219 in 1998; 9,098 in 1999; 11,838 in 2000.

Exports f.o.b. (QR million): 18,311 in 1998; 26,258 in 1999; 42,202 in 2000.

Principal Commodities (distribution by SITC, QR million): *Imports c.i.f.* (2000): Food and live animals 1,212.8; Crude materials (inedible) except fuels 303.3; Chemicals and related products 754.6; Basic manufactures 2,461.5; Machinery and transport equipment 5,308.6; Miscellaneous manufactured articles 1,573.8; Total (incl. others) 11,838.0. *Exports f.o.b.* (1994): Mineral fuels and lubricants 9,297.4 (Petroleum, petroleum products, etc. 8,148.9, Gas (natural and manufactured) 1,148.5); Chemicals and related products 1,187.9 (Manufactured fertilizers 420.2, Plastics in primary forms 372.3); Basic manufactures 676.0 (Iron and steel 673.6); Total (incl. others) 11,452.8 (excl. re-exports 242.3).

Principal Trading Partners (QR million): *Imports c.i.f.* (2000): Australia 224; Bahrain 145; Brazil 113; People's Republic of China 354; France 648; Germany 967; India 335; Indonesia 113; Italy 796; Japan 1,304; Republic of Korea 634; Malaysia 150; Netherlands 285; Pakistan 120; Saudi Arabia 667; Spain 152; Sweden 135; Switzerland 215; Taiwan 117; Thailand 127; United Arab Emirates 820; United Kingdom 919; USA 1,220; Total (incl. others) 11,838. *Exports f.o.b.* (incl. re-exports, 1994): States of the Co-operation Council for the Arab States of the Gulf (Gulf Co-operation Council—GCC) 1,170.0; USA 233.5; Asia (except Arab countries) 9,448.0; Australia and New Zealand 475.3; Total (incl. others) 11,695.1.

TRANSPORT

Road Traffic ('000 motor vehicles in use, 1999): Passenger cars 188.0; Commercial vehicles 88.9. Source: UN, *Statistical Yearbook.*

Shipping (international sea-borne freight traffic, '000 metric tons, 1994): *Goods loaded:* 5,853; *Goods unloaded:* 2,500. *Merchant Fleet* (registered at 31 December 2001): 68 vessels; 690,812 gross registered tons (Source: Lloyd's Register-Fairplay, *World Fleet Statistics*.)

Civil Aviation (scheduled services, 1998): Kilometres flown (million) 19; Passengers carried ('000) 1,207; Passenger-km (million) 2,653; Total ton-km (million) 357. Figures include an apportionment (one-quarter) of the traffic of Gulf Air, a multinational airline with its headquarters in Bahrain. Source: UN, *Statistical Yearbook*.

TOURISM

Tourist Arrivals ('000 foreign visitors, hotel occupants only): 327 in 1996; 435 in 1997; 451 in 1998. Source: World Tourism Organization, *Yearbook of Tourism Statistics*.

COMMUNICATIONS MEDIA

Radio Receivers ('000 in use, 1997): 256*.
Television Receivers ('000 in use, 2000): 520†.
Telephones ('000 main lines in use, 2001): 167.4†.
Facsimile Machines ('000 in use, 1996): 10.4‡.
Mobile Cellular Telephones ('000 subscribers, 2001): 178.8†.

Personal Computers ('000 in use, 2001): 100†.
Internet Users ('000, 2001): 40†.
Daily Newspapers (1996): 5 (circulation 90,000 copies)*.
Non-daily Newspapers (estimates, 1995): 1 (circulation 7,000 copies)*.
Book Production (titles, 1996): 209*.
* Source: UNESCO, *Statistical Yearbook*.
† Source: International Telecommunication Union.
‡ Source: UN, *Statistical Yearbook*.

EDUCATION

Pre-primary (1995/96): 64 schools; 321 teachers; 7,018 pupils.
Primary (1995/96): 174 schools; 5,864 teachers; 53,631 pupils.
Secondary (1994/95): 126 schools (general 123, vocational 3—1993/94); 3,858 teachers (general 3,738, vocational 120); (1995/96) 38,594 pupils (general 37,924, vocational 670).
University (1996/97): 1 institution; 643 teaching staff; 8,475 students.
Source: partly UNESCO, *Statistical Yearbook*.
Adult Literacy Rate (UNESCO estimates): 81.2% (males 80.4%; females 83.1%) in 1999. Source: UNDP, *Human Development Report*.

Directory

The Constitution

A provisional Constitution was adopted on 2 April 1970. Executive power is vested in the Amir, as Head of State, and exercised by the Council of Ministers, appointed by the Head of State. The Amir is assisted by the appointed Advisory Council of 20 members (increased to 30 in 1975 and to 35 in 1988), whose term was extended for six years in 1975, for a further four years in 1978, and for further terms of four years in 1982, 1986, 1990, 1994 and 1998. All fundamental democratic rights are guaranteed. In 1975 the Advisory Council was granted power to summon individual ministers to answer questions on legislation before promulgation. Previously the Advisory Council was restricted to debating draft bills and regulations before framing recommendations to the Council of Ministers. In March 1999 elections took place, by universal adult suffrage, for a 29-member Municipal Council, which was to have a consultative role in the operations of the Ministry of Municipal Affairs and Agriculture. In July a 32-member constitutional committee was established to draft a permanent constitution by 2002. According to the draft document, presented in July 2002, the Amir was to remain head of the executive, while a 45-member unicameral parliament, of which two-thirds were to be directly elected (the remainder being appointed by the Amir), was to have powers to legislate, review the state budget, monitor government policy and hold ministers accountable for their actions. The parliament was to have a four-year mandate. Suffrage was to be extended to all citizens, including women, aged 18 years and above. The document also guaranteed freedom of association, expression and religious affiliation and provided for the establishment of an independent judiciary. Elections to the new parliament were expected to be conducted before the end of 2005, although formal adoption of the Constitution was subject to the final approval of the Amir.

The Government

HEAD OF STATE

Amir: Maj.-Gen. Sheikh HAMAD BIN KHALIFA ATH-THANI (assumed power 27 June 1995).
Crown Prince: Sheikh JASIM BIN HAMAD BIN KHALIFA ATH-THANI.

COUNCIL OF MINISTERS
(September 2002)

Amir, Minister of Defence and Commander-in-Chief of the Armed Forces: Maj.-Gen. Sheikh HAMAD BIN KHALIFA ATH-THANI.
Prime Minister: Sheikh ABDULLAH BIN KHALIFA ATH-THANI.
Deputy Prime Minister: Sheikh MUHAMMAD BIN KHALIFA ATH-THANI.
Minister of the Interior: Sheikh ABDULLAH BIN KHALID ATH-THANI.
Minister of Foreign Affairs: Sheikh HAMAD BIN JASIM BIN JABER ATH-THANI.
Minister of Finance: YOUSUF BIN HUSSEIN KAMAL.
Minister of Economy and Trade: Sheikh HAMAD BIN FAISAL BIN THANI ATH-THANI.

Minister of Awqaf (Religious Endowments) and Islamic Affairs: AHMAD BIN ABDULLAH SALEM AL-MARRI.
Minister of Municipal Affairs and Agriculture: ALI BIN SAAD AL-KAWARI.
Minister of Justice: HASSAN BIN ABDULLAH AL-GHANIM.
Minister of Communication and Transport: Sheikh AHMAD BIN NASSER ATH-THANI.
Minister of Education: Dr AHMAD BIN KHALIFA BUSHERBAK AL-MANSOURI.
Minister of Energy, Industry, Electricity and Water: ABDULLAH BIN HAMAD AL-ATTIYA.
Minister of Public Health: Dr HAJAR BIN AHMAD HAJAR.
Minister of Civil Service Affairs and Housing: Sheikh FALAH BIN JASIM ATH-THANI.
Minister of State for Foreign Affairs: AHMAD BIN ABDULLAH AL-MAHMOUD.
Minister of State for Council of Ministers' Affairs: MUHAMMAD BIN ISA HAMAD AL-MEHANNADI.
Minister of State for the Interior: Sheikh HAMAD BIN NASSER BIN JASIM ATH-THANI.
Ministers of State without Portfolio: Sheikh AHMAD BIN SAIF ATH-THANI, Sheikh HASSAN BIN ABDULLAH BIN MUHAMMAD ATH-THANI, Sheikh HAMAD BIN SAHIM ATH-THANI, Sheikh HAMAD BIN ABDULLAH ATH-THANI, Sheikh MUHAMMAD BIN KHALID ATH-THANI, Sheikh MUHAMMAD BIN ID ATH-THANI.

MINISTRIES

Ministry of Amiri Diwan Affairs: POB 923, Doha; tel. 43882553; fax 4361212; e-mail adf@diwan.gov.qa; internet www.diwan.gov.qa.
Ministry of Awqaf (Religious Endowments) and Islamic Affairs: POB 422, Doha; tel. 4470777; fax 4327383; e-mail mela@qatar.net.qa.
Ministry of Civil Service Affairs and Housing: POB 36, Doha; tel. 4335335; fax 4446298; internet www.mcsah.gov.qa.
Ministry of Communication and Transport: POB 22228, Doha; tel. 4835522; fax 4835101.
Ministry of Defence: Qatar Armed Forces, POB 37, Doha; tel. 4404111.
Ministry of Economy and Trade: Doha.
Ministry of Education: POB 80, Doha; tel. 4333444; fax 4413886; internet www.moe.edu.qa.
Ministry of Energy, Industry, Electricity and Water: POB 2599, Doha; tel. 4832121; fax 4832024; internet www.kahramaa.com.
Ministry of Finance: POB 3322, Doha; tel. 4461444; fax 4431177.
Ministry of Foreign Affairs: POB 250, Doha; tel. 4334334; fax 4442777; e-mail webmaster@mofa.gov.qa; internet www.mofa.gov.qa.

Ministry of the Interior: POB 115, Doha; tel. 4330000; fax 4429565; internet www.moi.gov.qa.

Ministry of Justice: POB 917 (Dept of Legal Affairs), Doha; tel. 4835200; fax 4832868.

Ministry of Municipal Affairs and Agriculture: POB 820, Doha; tel. 4336336; fax 4430239; e-mail mmaa@mmaa.gov.qa; internet www.mmaa.gov.qa.

Ministry of Public Health: POB 42, Doha; tel. 4441555; fax 4446294; internet www.hmc.gov.qa.

ADVISORY COUNCIL

The Advisory Council was established in 1972, with 20 nominated members. It was expanded to 30 members in 1975, and to 35 members in 1988.

Speaker: MUHAMMAD BIN MUBARAK AL-KHOLAIFI.

Diplomatic Representation

EMBASSIES IN QATAR

Algeria: POB 2494, Doha; tel. 4662900; fax 4663658; Ambassador: MOHAMED BOUROWABA.

Bahrain: POB 24888, Doha; tel. 4839360; fax 4839360; Ambassador: ABD AR-RAHMAN MUHAMMAD AL-FATHEL.

Bangladesh: POB 2080, Doha; tel. 4671927; fax 4671190; Ambassador: ABU TAHER NAJRUL ISLAM.

Bosnia and Herzegovina: POB 876, Doha; tel. 4670194; fax 4670595; e-mail info@bosnianembassyqatar.org; internet www.bosnianembassyqatar.org; Ambassador: HUSEIN OMERSPAHIC.

China, People's Republic: POB 17200, Doha; tel. 4824200; fax 4873959; Ambassador: ZHOU XIUHUA.

Cuba: POB 12017, Doha; tel. 4672072; fax 4672074; Ambassador: JORGE LEÓN CRUZ.

Egypt: POB 2899, Doha; tel. 4832555; fax 4832196; Ambassador: MUHAMMAD ABD AL-FATTAH ABDULLAH.

France: POB 2669, Doha; tel. 4832281; fax 4832254; e-mail amba doha@qatar.net.qa; internet www.qatar.net.qa/ambadoha/ambaf; Ambassador: ALAN AZOUAOU.

Germany: POB 3064, Doha; tel. 4876959; fax 4876949; e-mail germany@qatar.net.qa; Ambassador: ROLF MEYER-OLDEN.

India: POB 2788, Doha; tel. 4672021; fax 4670448; e-mail indembdh@qatar.net.qa; internet www.indianembassy.gov.qa; Ambassador: RANJAN MATHAI.

Iran: POB 1633, Doha; tel. 4835300; fax 4831665; Ambassador: DHABEEH ALLAH NOUVERSTI.

Iraq: POB 1526, Doha; tel. 4672237; fax 4673347; Ambassador: FAKHRI HAMMUDI AD-DULAYMI.

Italy: POB 4188, Doha; tel. 4436842; fax 4446466; e-mail itembqat@qatar.net.qa; internet www.qatar.net.qa/itembqat; Ambassador: PIO LUIGI TEODORANI FABBRI POZZI.

Japan: POB 2208, Doha; tel. 4831224; fax 4832178; Ambassador: KATZUYA IKEDA.

Jordan: POB 2366, Doha; tel. 4832202; fax 4832173; Ambassador: OMAR AL-AHMAD.

Korea, Republic: POB 3727, Doha; tel. 4832238; fax 4833264; Ambassador: JAE-GOUK KIM.

Kuwait: POB 1177, Doha; tel. 4832111; fax 4832042; Ambassador: FAISAL SULAYMAN AL-MUKHAZEEM.

Lebanon: POB 2411, Doha; tel. 4477778; fax 4478817; Ambassador: AFIF AYYUB.

Libya: POB 574, Doha; tel. 4429546; fax 4429548; Chargé d'affaires: RAFAE ABD AL-QADIR AMANENA.

Mauritania: POB 3132, Doha; tel. 4836003; fax 4836015; Ambassador: MUHAMMAD AL-AMIN AS-SALEM WALD DADA.

Morocco: POB 3242, Doha; tel. 4831885; fax 4833416; e-mail moroccoe@qatar.net.qa; Ambassador: EL-HOUSSINE AZIZ.

Nepal: POB 23002, Doha; tel. 4675681; fax 4675680; e-mail rnedoha@qatar.net.qa; Ambassador: SHYAMANANDA SUMAN.

Oman: POB 1525, Doha; tel. 4670744; fax 4670747; Ambassador: NASSER BIN KHALFAN AL-KHAROOSI.

Pakistan: POB 334, Doha; tel. 4832525; fax 4832227; Ambassador: KAMAL ARIF.

Philippines: POB 24900, Doha; tel. 4831585; fax 4831595; e-mail dohape@qatar.net.qa; Ambassador: AMADO S. TOLENTINO.

Romania: POB 22511, Doha; tel. 4426740; fax 4444346; e-mail romamb@qatar.net.qa; Ambassador: MIHAI STUPARU.

Russia: POB 15404, Doha; tel. 4329117; fax 4329118; Ambassador: VIKTOR KUDRYAVTSEV.

Saudi Arabia: POB 1255, Doha; tel. 4832030; fax 4832720; Ambassador: HAMAD BIN SALEH AT-TUAIMI (recalled Sept. 2002).

Somalia: POB 1948, Doha; tel. 4832200; fax 4832182; Ambassador: SHARIF MUHAMMAD OMAR.

Sudan: POB 2999, Doha; tel. 4423007; fax 4351366; Ambassador: MUHAMMAD AHMAD MUSTAFA AD-DABY.

Syria: POB 1257, Doha; tel. 4831844; fax 4832139; Chargé d'affaires: HAJEM ABD AL-HAMED IBRAHIM.

Tunisia: POB 2707, Doha; tel. 4832645; fax 4832649; Ambassador: MOUSTAFA TLILI.

Turkey: POB 1977, Doha; tel. 4835553; fax 4835206; Ambassador: OYA INKAYA.

United Arab Emirates: POB 3099, Doha; tel. 4885111; fax 4882837; Ambassador: ABD AR-REDA ABDULLAH KHOURI.

United Kingdom: POB 3, Doha; tel. 4421991; fax 4438692; e-mail bembcomm@qatar.net.qa; Ambassador: DAVID MACLENNAN.

USA: POB 2399, Doha; tel. 4884101; fax 4884298; e-mail usis doha@qatar.net.qa; internet www.usembassy.org.qa; Ambassador: MAUREEN E. QUINN.

Yemen: POB 3318, Doha; tel. 4432555; fax 4429400; Ambassador: ABD AS-SALAM HUSSEIN AL-ANSI.

Judicial System

Independence of the judiciary is guaranteed by the provisional Constitution. All aspects pertaining to the civil judiciary are supervised by the Ministry of Justice, which organizes courts of law through its affiliated departments. The *Shari'a* judiciary hears all cases of personal status relating to Muslims, other claim cases, doctrinal provision and crimes under its jurisdiction. Legislation adopted in 1999 unified all civil and *Shari'a* courts in one judicial body, and determined the jurisdictions of each type of court. The law also provided for the establishment of a court of cassation; this was to be competent to decide on appeals relating to issues of contravention, misapplication and misinterpretation of the law, and on disputes between courts regarding areas of jurisdiction. The law also provided for the establishment of a supreme judiciary council, to be presided over by the head of the court of cassation and comprising, *inter alia*, the heads of the *Shari'a* and civil courts of appeal. The establishment of a judicial inspection system was also envisaged. An amiri decree published in June 2002 sought to establish an independent public prosecution system. Further elaboration of provisions for the creation of an independent judiciary were contained in the draft Constitution presented for amiri approval in July 2002.

Chief Justice: MUBARAK BIN KHALIFA AS-ASARI.

Public Prosecutor: Col ABDULLAH AL-MAL.

Presidency of Shari'a Courts: POB 232, Doha; tel. 4452222; Pres. Sheikh ABD AR-RAHMAN BIN ABDULLAH AL-MAHMOUD.

Religion

The indigenous population are Muslims of the Sunni sect, most being of the strict Wahhabi persuasion.

CHRISTIANITY

The Anglican Communion

Within the Episcopal Church in Jerusalem and the Middle East, Qatar forms part of the diocese of Cyprus and the Gulf. The Anglican congregation in Qatar is entirely expatriate. The Bishop in Cyprus and the Gulf is resident in Cyprus, while the Archdeacon in the Gulf is resident in Qatar.

Archdeacon in the Gulf: POB 3, Doha; Archdeacon Ven. IAN YOUNG.

The Roman Catholic Church

An estimated 60,000 adherents in Qatar, mainly expatriates, form part of the Apostolic Vicariate of Arabia. The Vicar Apostolic is resident in the United Arab Emirates.

The Press

Al-'Arab (The Arabs): POB 6334, Doha; tel. 4325874; fax 4440016; f. 1972; daily; Arabic; publ. by Dar al-Ouroba Printing and Publishing; Editor-in-Chief KHALID NAAMA; circ. 25,000.

Ad-Dawri (The Tournament): POB 310, Doha; tel. 4328782; fax 4447039; f. 1978; weekly; Arabic; sport; publ. by Abdullah Hamad al-Atiyah and Ptnrs; Editor-in-Chief Sheikh Rashid bin Owaida ath-Thani; circ. 6,000.

Gulf Times: POB 2888, Doha; tel. 4350478; fax 4350474; e-mail editor@gulf-times.com; internet www.gulf-times.com; f. 1978; daily and weekly editions; English; political; publ. by Gulf Publishing and Printing Co; Editor-in-Chief Abd ar-Rahman Saif al-Madhadi; circ. 15,000 (daily).

Al-Jawhara (The Jewel): POB 2531, Doha; tel. 4414575; fax 4671388; f. 1977; monthly; Arabic; women's magazine; publ. by al-Ahd Est. for Journalism, Printing and Publications Ltd; Editor-in-Chief Abdullah Yousuf al-Hussaini; circ. 8,000.

Nada (A Gathering): POB 4896, Doha; tel. 4445564; fax 4433778; f. 1991; weekly; social and entertainment; published by Akhbar al-Usbou'; Editor-in-Chief Adel Ali bin Ali.

Al-Ouroba (Arabism): POB 663, Doha; tel. 4325874; fax 4429424; f. 1970; weekly; Arabic; political; publ. by Dar al-Ouroba Printing and Publishing; Editor-in-Chief Yousuf Naama; circ. 12,000.

The Peninsula: POB 3488, Doha; tel. 4663945; fax 4663965; e-mail penqatar@qatar.net.qa; f. 1996; daily; English; political; publ. by Dar ash-Sharq Printing, Publishing and Distribution; Editor-in-Chief Abd al-Aziz al-Mahmoud; Man. Editor George Abraham; circ. 8,000.

Qatar Lil Inshaa (Qatar Construction): POB 2203, Doha; tel. 4424988; fax 4432961; f. 1989; publ. by Almaha Trade and Construction Co; Gen. Man. Muhammad H. al-Mijber; circ. 10,000.

Ar-Rayah (The Banner): POB 3464, Doha; tel. 4466555; fax 4350476; e-mail www.edit@raya.com; internet www.raya.com; f. 1979; daily and weekly editions; Arabic; political; publ. by Gulf Publishing and Printing Co; Editor Nasser al-Othman; circ. 25,000.

Saidat ash-Sharq: POB 3488, Doha; tel. 4662445; fax 4662450; f. 1993; monthly; Arabic; women's magazine; publ. by Dar ash-Sharq Printing, Publishing and Distribution; Editor Nasser al-Othman; circ. 15,000.

Ash-Sharq (The Orient): POB 3488, Doha; tel. 4662444; fax 4662450; e-mail webmaster@al-sharq.com; internet www.al-sharq.com; f. 1985; daily; Arabic; political; publ. by Dar ash-Sharq Printing, Publishing and Distribution House; Gen. Supervisor Nasser al-Othman; circ. 45,018.

At-Tarbiya (Education): POB 9865, Doha; tel. 4861412; fax 4880911; f. 1971; quarterly; publ. by Qatar National Commission for Education, Culture and Science; Editor-in-Chief Abd al-Aziz Faraj al-Ansari; circ. 2,000.

This is Qatar and What's On: POB 4015, Doha; tel. 4413813; fax 4413814; f. 1978; quarterly; English; tourist information; publ. by Oryx Publishing and Advertising Co; Editor-in-Chief Yousuf J. ad-Darwish; circ. 10,000.

Al-Ummah: POB 893, Doha; tel. 4447300; fax 4447022; e-mail m_dirasat@islam.gov.qa; internet www.islam.gov.qa; f. 1982; bi-monthly; Islamic thought and affairs, current cultural issues, book serializations.

Al-Watan: POB 22345, Doha; tel. 4652244; fax 4660440; e-mail feedback@al-watan.com; internet www.al-watan.com; f. 1995; daily; Arabic; political; publ. by Dar al-Watan Printing, Publishing and Distribution; Editor-in-Chief Ahmad Ali al-Abdullah; circ. 25,000.

NEWS AGENCIES

Qatar News Agency (QNA): POB 3299, Doha; tel. 4450319; fax 4438316; e-mail qna@qatar.net.qa; internet www.qatarnewsagency.com; f. 1975; affiliated to Ministry of Foreign Affairs; Dir and Editor-in-Chief Ahmad Jassim al-Humar.

Publishers

Qatar National Printing Press: POB 355, Doha; tel. 4448453; fax 4449550; Man. Abd al-Karim Deeb.

Ali bin Ali Media and Publishing: POB 75, Doha; tel. 4313245; fax 4411251; e-mail publishing@alibinali.com; internet www.alibinali.com; publishers of *Qatar Telephone Directory and Yellow Pages.*

Dar al-Ouroba Printing and Publishing: POB 52, Doha; tel. 4423179.

Dar ash-Sharq Printing, Publishing and Distribution: POB 3488, Doha; tel. 4662444; fax 4662450; e-mail webmaster@al-sharq.com; Editor-in-Chief Abd al-Aziz al-Mahmoud; circ. 22,000.

Gulf Publishing and Printing Co: POB 533, Doha; tel. 4466555; fax 4424171; e-mail gm@gulftimes.com; internet www.gulf-times.com; Gen. Man. Muhammad Allam Ali.

Oryx Publishing and Advertising Co: POB 3272, Doha; tel. 413813; fax 4413814.

Broadcasting and Communications

TELECOMMUNICATIONS

Qatar Telecommunications Corpn (Q-Tel): POB 217, Doha; tel. 4400400; fax 4413904; e-mail webmaster@qtel.com.qa; internet www.qtel.com.qa; f. 1987; majority state-owned; provides telecommunications services within Qatar; Chair. Sheikh Abdullah bin Muhammad ath-Thani; Gen. Man. Hamad al-Attiya.

BROADCASTING
Regulatory Authority

Qatar Radio and Television Corpn (QRTC): Doha; f. 1997; autonomous authority reporting directly to the Council of Ministers.

Radio

Qatar Broadcasting Service (QBS): POB 3939, Doha; tel. 4894444; fax 4882888; f. 1968; govt service transmitting in Arabic, English, French and Urdu; programmes include Holy Quran Radio and Doha Music Radio; Dir Muhammad A. al-Kuwari.

Television

Al-Jazeera Satellite Channel: POB 23123, Doha; tel. 4890890; fax 4885333; internet www.aljazeera.net; f. 1996; 24-hr broadcasting; Pres. Hamad bin Thamer ath-Thani; Editor-in-Chief Ibrahim Helal.

Qatar Television Service: POB 1944, Doha; tel. 4894444; fax 4874170; f. 1970; operates two channels; Dir Muhammad Jasim al-Ali (acting); Asst Dir Abd al-Wahab Muhammad al-Mutawa'a.

Finance

(cap. = capital; res = reserves; dep. = deposits; m. = million; brs = branches; amounts in Qatar riyals unless otherwise stated)

BANKING
Central Bank

Qatar Central Bank: POB 1234, Doha; tel. 4456456; fax 4413650; e-mail webmaster@qcb.gov.qa; internet www.qcb.gov.qa; f. 1966 as Qatar and Dubai Currency Board; became Qatar Monetary Agency in 1973; renamed Qatar Central Bank in 1993; cap. 1,140.9m., dep. 836.1m., currency in circulation 1,729.2m. (Dec. 1999); Gov. Abdullah bin Khalid al-Attiya; Dep. Gov. Sheikh Abdullah bin Said Abd al-Aziz ath-Thani.

Commercial Banks

Al-Ahli Bank of Qatar QSC: POB 2309, Doha; tel. 4326611; fax 4444652; e-mail ahlibk@qatar.net.qa; f. 1984; cap. 182.8m., res 23.4m., dep. 1,784m. (Dec. 2001); Chair. Saleh bin Mubarak al-Khulaifi; Gen. Man. Qasim M. Qasim; 8 brs.

Commercial Bank of Qatar QSC: Grand Hamad Ave, POB 3232, Doha; tel. 4900000; fax 4438182; e-mail info@cbq.com.qa; internet www.cbq.com.qa; f. 1975; owned 30% by board of directors and 70% by Qatari citizens and organizations; cap. 197.8m., res 224.3m., dep. 3,558.6m. (Dec. 2000); Chair. Abdullah bin Khalifa al-Attiya; Gen. Man. Andrew Stevens; 12 brs.

Doha Bank: Grand Hamad Ave, POB 3818, Doha; tel. 4456600; fax 4416631; e-mail dohabank@qatar.net.qa; internet www.dohabank.com.qa; f. 1979; cap. 184.6m., res 442.8m., dep. 5,490.0m. (Dec. 2001); Chair. Sheikh Fahad bin Muhammad bin Jaber ath-Thani; Gen. Man. Salah Muhammad Jaidah; 13 brs in Qatar and 1 overseas.

Grindlays Qatar Bank QSC: POB 2001, Suhaim bin Hamad St, Doha; tel. 4473700; fax 4473710; e-mail qatarenq@qa.standardchartered.com; f. 2000 (previously a branch of ANZ Grindlays Bank, f. 1956);cap 75.0m.; total assets 1,043.4m. (Dec. 2001); Gen. Man. J. F. Murray.

Qatar Industrial Development Bank: POB 22789, Doha; tel. 4421600; fax 4350433; e-mail qidb@qatar.net.qa; internet www.qidb.com.qa; f. 1996; inaugurated Oct. 1997; state-owned; provides long-term low-interest industrial loans; cap. 200m.; Chair. Sheikh Abdullah bin Saud ath-Thani.

Qatar International Islamic Bank QSC: POB 664, Doha; tel. 4332600; fax 4444101; e-mail qiibit@qatar.net.qa; f. 1990; cap. 90m., res 84.2m., dep. 1,714.9m. (Dec. 2000); Gen. Man. Abd al-Basit ash-Shaibei; 3 brs.

Qatar Islamic Bank SAQ: POB 559, Doha; tel. 4409409; fax 4412700; e-mail qibt@qatar.net.qa; f. 1983; cap. 250.0m., res 54.0m., dep. 3,326.3m. (Dec. 2000); Chair. and Man. Dir KHALID BIN AHMAD AS-SUWAIDI; Gen. Man. MARWAN AWAD; 8 brs.

Qatar National Bank SAQ: POB 1000, Doha; tel. 4407407; fax 4413753; e-mail webmaster@qatarbank.com; internet www .qatarbank.com; f. 1965; owned 50% by Govt of Qatar and 50% by Qatari nationals; cap. 1,038.2m., res 3,439.3m., dep. 23,358.6m. (Dec. 2001); Chair. Minister of Finance; Chief Exec. SAID BIN ABDULLAH AL-MISNAD; 30 brs in Qatar and 3 abroad.

Foreign Banks

Arab Bank PLC (Jordan): POB 172, Doha; tel. 4437979; fax 4410774; e-mail arabbank@qatar.net.qa; f. 1957; total assets 1,100m. (Dec. 1996); Regional Man. GHASSAN BUNDAKJI; Dep. Man. SAAD AD-DIN ELAYAN; 2 brs.

Bank Saderat Iran: POB 2256, Doha; tel. 4414646; fax 4430121; e-mail bsiiran@qatar.net.qa; f. 1970; Man. MUHAMMAD ZAMANI.

BNP Paribas (France): POB 2636, Doha; tel. 4433844; fax 4410861; e-mail qatar.paribas@paribas.com; internet qatar.bnpparibas.com; f. 1973; Gen. Man. CHRISTIAN DE LA TOUCHE.

HSBC Bank Middle East (United Kingdom): POB 57, Doha; tel. 4382222; fax 4416353; e-mail hsbcqa@qatar.net.qa; internet www .britishbank.com; f. 1954; total assets US $550m. (1999); CEO CHRIS MEARES; Gen. Man. J. P. PASCOE; 2 brs.

Mashreq Bank PSC (UAE): POB 173, Doha; tel. 4413213; fax 4413880; f. 1971; Gen. Man. KHALED GAMAL ELDIN.

Standard Chartered PLC (UK): POB 29, Doha; tel. 4414252; fax 4413739; f. 1950; total assets 725m.; Gen. Man. ARIF MANSOOR.

United Bank Ltd (Pakistan): POB 242, Doha; tel. 4424400; fax 4424600; e-mail ubldoha@qatar.net.qa; f. 1970; Gen. Man. and Vice-Pres. RAI MANSOOR AHMAD KHAN.

STOCK EXCHANGE

Doha Securities Market (DSM): Al-Khaleej Insurance Co Bldg, Doha; f. 1997; 23 cos listed; Dir GHANIM AL-HAMMADI.

INSURANCE

Doha Insurance Co: POB 7171, Doha; tel. 4335000; fax 4657777; e-mail dohainsco@qatar.net.qa; f. 1999 as public shareholding co; cap. 127m. (1999); Chair. Sheikh NAWAF BIN NASSER BIN KHALID ATH-THANI; Gen. Man. BASSAM HUSSAIN.

Al-Khaleej Insurance Co (SAQ): POB 4555, Doha; tel. 4414151; fax 4430530; e-mail alkhalej@qatarnet.qa; internet www.alkh alej.com; f. 1978; cap. 24m.; all classes except life; Chair. ABDULLAH BIN MUHAMMAD JABER ATH-THANI; Gen. Man. MUHAMMAD AMER TAHA.

Qatar General Insurance and Reinsurance Co SAQ: POB 4500, Doha; tel. 4417800; fax 4437302; e-mail management@qgirc.com; internet www.qgirc.com; f. 1979; cap. 30m. (1997); all classes; Chair. and Man. Dir Sheikh ALI BIN SAUD ATH-THANI; Gen. Man. GHAZI ABU NAHL.

Qatar Insurance Co SAQ: POB 666, Doha; tel. 4490490; fax 4831569; e-mail qatarins@qatar.net.qa; f. 1964; cap. 36m. (1995); all classes; the Govt has a majority share; Chair. Sheikh KHALID BIN MUHAMMAD ALI ATH-THANI; Gen. Man. KHALIFA A. AS-SUBAYI; br. in Dubai.

Qatar Islamic Insurance Co: POB 12402, Doha; tel. 4413413; fax 4447277; f. 1993; cap. 20m. (1995).

Trade and Industry

DEVELOPMENT ORGANIZATION

Department of Industrial Development: POB 2599, Doha; tel. 4832121; fax 4832024; govt-owned; conducts research, development and supervision of new industrial projects; Dir-Gen. MAJID ABDULLAH AL-MALKI.

CHAMBER OF COMMERCE

Qatar Chamber of Commerce and Industry: POB 402, Doha; tel. 4621131; fax 4622538; e-mail qcci@qatar.net.qa; internet www.qatar.net.qa/qcci; f. 1963; 17 elected mems; Pres. Sheikh HAMAD BIN JASIM BIN MUHAMMAD ATH-THANI; Dir-Gen. Dr MAJID ABDULLAH AL-MALKI.

STATE HYDROCARBONS COMPANIES

Qatar Petroleum (QP): POB 3212, Doha; tel. 4491491; fax 4831125; e-mail webmaster@qp.com.qa; internet www.qp.com.qa; f. 1974 as the Qatar General Petroleum Corpn (QGPC), name changed 2001; cap. QR 20,000m.; the State of Qatar's interest in companies active in petroleum and related industries has passed to the Corpn; has responsibility for all phases of oil and gas industry

both onshore and offshore, including exploration, drilling, production, refining, transport and storage, distribution, sale and export of oil, natural gas and other hydrocarbons; Chair. Minister of Energy, Industry, Electricity and Water; Vice-Chair. HUSSAIN KAMAL.

Qatar Petroleum wholly or partly owns: Qatar Fertilizer Co (QAFCO), Ras Laffan LNG Co Ltd (Rasgas), Gulf Helicopters Co (GHC), Qatar Vinyl Co (QVC), Qatar Chemical Co (Q-Chem), Qatar Fuel Additives Co Ltd (QAFAC), Qatar Clean Energy Co (QACENCO), Qatar Electricity and Water Co (QEWC), Qatar Shipping Co (Q-Ship), Arab Maritime Petroleum Transport Co (AMPTC), Arab Petroleum Pipelines Co (SUMED), Arab Shipbuilding and Repair Yard Co (ASRY), Arab Petroleum Services Co (APSC) and Arab Petroleum Investments Corpn (APICORP); and also the following:

Qatar Liquefied Gas Co (QATARGAS): POB 22666, Doha; tel. 4736000; fax 4736666; internet www.qatargas.com; f. 1984 to develop the North Field of unassociated gas; cap. QR 500m.; QP has a 65% share; ExxonMobil and TotalFinaElf hold 10% each; the Marubeni Corpn and Mitsui and Co of Japan hold 7.5% each; Chair. Minister of Energy, Industry, Electricity and Water; Vice-Chair. and Man. Dir FAISAL MUHAMMAD AS-SUWAIDI.

Qatar Petrochemical Co (QAPCO) SAQ: POB 756, Doha; tel. 4777111; fax 4771346; e-mail information@qapco.com.qa; internet www.qapco.com; f. 1974; QP has an 80% share; 10% is held by ATOFINA (France), and 10% by ENICHEM (Italy); total assets QR 2,439m. (2000); operation of petrochemical plant at Umm Said; produced 535,215 metric tons of ethylene, 382,029 tons of low-density polyethylene, and 40,873 tons of solid sulphur in 2001; Gen. Man. HAMAD RASHID AL-MOHANNADI.

UTILITIES

Qatar General Electricity and Water Corpn (Kahramaa): POB 41, Doha; tel. 4845484; fax 4845496; internet www.kahramaa.com; f. 2000; state authority for planning, implementation, operation and maintenance of electricity and water sectors; Chair. Minister of Energy, Industry, Electricity and Water.

Qatar Electricity and Water Co (QEWC): POB 22046, Doha; tel. 4858585; fax 4831116; e-mail qewc@qatar.net.qa; f. 1990; 57% privately-owned; has responsibility for adding new generating capacity in Qatar; Gen. Man. FAHAD HAMAD AL-MOHANNADI.

MAJOR COMPANIES

AKC Contracting: POB 2760, Doha; tel. 4665576; fax 4665579; e-mail akcqatar@qatar.net.qa; f. 1975; building, plumbing, joinery, landscaping, etc.; sales QR 48m. (2000); Man. Dir ISSA A. R. AL-MANNAI; Gen. Man. JOHN W. FOX; 700 employees.

Arab-Qatari Co for Dairy Production: POB 8324, Doha; tel. 4601107; fax 4600516; e-mail ghadeerr@qatar.net.qa; f. 1985; cap. p.u. QR 45m.; production of dairy products, ice creams and fruit juices; Man. Dir SHAMSEDDIN HUSSAINI.

Arab-Qatari Co for Poultry Production: POB 3606, Doha; tel. 4729042; fax 4729028; produces between 1m. and 2.5m. broiler chickens, and between 10m. and 25m. eggs, per year; Dir ISMAIL FAITI AL-ISMAIL.

Kassem Darwish Fakhroo & Sons (KDS): POB 92, Doha; tel. 4422781; fax 4426378; e-mail kdsgroup@qatar.net.qa; f. 1911 (corporate group 1971); electrical, mechanical and civil contractors, general trading, manufacturers; Chair. KASSEM DARWISH FAKHROO; Man. Dir HASSAN DARWISH; 1,000 employees.

Mideast Constructors Ltd (MECON): POB 3325, Doha; tel. 4415025; fax 4415174; e-mail mecon@qatar.net.qa; f. 1975; sales QR 300m. (2001); mechanical and electrical instrumentation, heating, ventilating and air-conditioning, and civil engineering and contracting; Chair. AHMAD AL-MANNAI; Gen. Man. ROBERT M. WALKER; 550 employees.

National Industrial Gas Plants (NIGP): POB 1391, Doha; tel. 4422116; fax 4435030; e-mail nigp@qatar.net.qa; f. 1954; production of industrial gases (oxygen, carbon dioxide, nitrogen, argon and acetylene), liquid gases (oxygen, nitrogen and argon), and dry ice, hydrostatic pressure testing of high-pressure cylinders; Pres. M. H. ALMANA; 125 employees.

Qatar Fertilizer Co (QAFCO) SAQ: POB 50001, Umm Said; tel. 4779779; fax 4770347; e-mail info@qafco.com; internet www .qafco.com; f. 1969; sales QR 700m. (1999); produced 1,371,380 metric tons of ammonia and 1,668,157 tons of urea in 1998; owned by QP (75%) and Norsk Hydro (25%); Chair. ABDULLAH H. SALATT; Man. Dir KHALIFA AS-SUWAIDI; 852 employees.

Qatar Flour Mills Co SAQ: POB 1444, Doha; tel. 4671816; fax 4671611; e-mail qfmco@qatar.net.qa; f. 1968; cap. QR 56.8m., sales QR 52.2m. (1998); produced 33,000 metric tons of flour and 11,500 tons of bran in 1993; Chair. Sheikh AHMAD BIN ABDULLAH ATH-THANI; Gen. Man. SAID ABBAS; 250 employees.

Qatar Industrial Manufacturing Co (QIMCO): POB 16875, Doha; tel. 4673555; fax 4670344; e-mail qimco@qatar.net.qa; internet www.qimco.com; f. 1989 to establish domestic and international industrial ventures; cap. QR 100m.; sales QR 90.9m. (1998); operates seven subsidiaries; Qatar Saudi Gypsum Co, Qatar Jet Fuel Co, Qatar Metal-Coating Co, Modern Detergent Co, Gulf Ferro Co, National Paper Co, Qatar Sand-Treatment Plant; Chair. Sheikh ABD AR-RAHMAN BIN MUHAMMAD JABER ATH-THANI; Gen. Man. ABDULLAH AL-ABDULLAH.

Qatar National Cement Co SAQ: POB 1333, Doha; tel. 4664800; fax 4667846; f. 1965; cap. QR 81.3m., sales QR 171.9m. (2000); produced 1,029,000 metric tons of ordinary Portland and sulphate-resisting cement in 2000; Chair. SALEM BIN BUTTI AN-NAIMI; Gen. Man. MUHAMMAD ALI AS-SULAITI; 430 employees.

Qatar National Plastic Factory: POB 5615, Doha; tel. 4689977; fax 4689922; f. 1977; production of polyethylene bags, film and UPVC pipes; Chair. MUHAMMAD BIN ABDULLAH AL-ATTIYA; Gen. Man. KHALID MUHAMMAD AL-ATTIYA; 130 employees.

Qatar Steel Co (QASCO): POB 50090, Steel Mill, Umm Said; tel. 4778778; fax 4771424; the plant was completed in 1978, and produced 601,000 tons of concrete-reinforcing steel bars in 1995; 100% govt-owned; Chair. YOUSUF KEMAL; Man. Dir NASSER MUHAMMAD AL-MANSOURI.

Qatar Hot Briquetted Iron Co (Qabico): POB 50090, Umm Said; f. 1997 by QASCO (31%), Duferco (16.3%), Gulf Investment Corpn (16.3%), National Industries Co (16.3%), Qatar Industrial Manufacturing Co (10%), Qatar Shipping Co (10%); capacity 2m. tons.

Readymix (Qatar) WLL: POB 5007, Doha; tel. 4653070; fax 4651534; e-mail rmq@qatar.net.qa; f. 1978; production of ready-mixed concrete; Gen. Man. W. D. FORDE.

Qatar Quarry WLL: POB 5007, Doha; tel. 4653070; fax 4651534; e-mail rmq@Qatar.net.qa; f. 1983; production of aggregates, road materials and armour rock; Gen. Man. W. D. FORDE.

Transport

ROADS

In 1991 there were some 1,191 km of surfaced road linking Doha and the petroleum centres of Dukhan and Umm Said with the northern end of the peninsula. The total road network in 1999 was estimated to be 1,230 km. A 105-km road from Doha to Salwa was completed in 1970, and joins one leading from Al-Hufuf in Saudi Arabia, giving Qatar land access to the Mediterranean. A 418-km highway, built in conjunction with Abu Dhabi, links both states with the Gulf network. A major upgrading of the national road network was planned for the first years of the 21st century. In September 2001 a Danish consortium was appointed to carry out a feasibility study for the construction of a planned causeway (the Friendship Bridge) linking Qatar with Bahrain, with an anticipated completion date of 2006.

SHIPPING

Doha Port has nine general cargo berths of 7.5 m–9.0 m depth. Total length of berths is 1,699 m. In addition, there is a flour mill berth, and a container terminal (with a depth of 12.0 m and a length of 600 m) with a roll-on roll-off berth at the north end, is currently under construction. Cold storage facilities exist for cargo of up to 500 tons. At Umm Said Harbour the Northern Deep Water Wharves consist of a deep-water quay 730 m long with a dredged depth alongside of 15.5 m, and a quay 570 m long with a dredged depth alongside of 13.0 m. The General Cargo Wharves consist of a quay 400 m long with a dredged depth alongside of 10.0 m. The Southern Deep Water Wharves consist of a deep water quay 508 m long with a dredged depth alongside of 13.0 m. The North Field gas project has increased the demand for shipping facilities. A major new industrial port was completed at Ras Laffan in 1995, providing facilities for LNG and condensate carriers and roll-on-roll-off vessels.

Customs and Ports General Authority: POB 81, Doha; tel. 4457457; fax 4413563; Dir of Ports G. A. GENKEER.

Qatar National Navigation and Transport Co Ltd (QNNTC): West Bay, Al-Tameen St, POB 153, Doha; tel. 4468666; fax 4468777; e-mail navigation@qnntc.com; internet www.qatar.net.qa/qnntc; f. 1957; 100%-owned by Qatari nationals; shipping agents, stevedoring, chandlers, forwarding, shipowning, repair, construction, etc.; Chair. SALEH MUBARAK AL-KHOLEILI; Vice-Chair. and Chair. of Exec Cttee Sheikh ABDULLAH MUHAMMAD JABER ATH-THANI.

Qatar Shipping Co QSC (Q-Ship): POB 22180, Doha; tel. 4315500; fax 4315565; e-mail qshipops@qship.com; internet www.qship.com; f. 1992; oil and bulk cargo shipping; Chair. SALEM B. AN-NAIMI; Gen. Man. NASSER AR-ROMAIHI.

CIVIL AVIATION

Doha International Airport is equipped to receive all types of aircraft. In 1998 some 2.4m. passengers used the airport. Upgrading of the airport, at an estimated cost of US $600m., was expected to increase passenger-handling capacity to 8m. by 2006. Qatar withdrew from Gulf Air, which it had owned jointly with Bahrain, Oman and Abu Dhabi, in May 2002.

Civil Aviation Authority: POB 3000, Doha; tel. 4428177; fax 4429070; Chair. and Man. Dir ABD AL-AZIZ MUHAMMAD AN-NOAIMI.

Doha International Airport: POB 73, Doha; tel. 4622222; fax 4622044; Dir ABDULLAH BIN AHMAD ATH-THANI.

Gulf Helicopters: POB 811, Doha; tel. 4333888; fax 4352287; e-mail mohd@gulfhelicopters.com; internet www.gulfhelicopters.com; f. 1974; owned by QP; Chair. ABDULLAH BIN HAMAD AL-ATTIYA.

Qatar Airways: POB 22550, Doha; tel. 4621717; fax 4621533; e-mail infodesk@qatarairways.com; internet www.qatarairways.com; f. 1993; services to more than 20 international destinations; CEO AKBAR AL-BAKER.

Tourism

Qatar's tourist industry is small, owing to its limited infrastructure. Some 451,000 tourists visited the country in 1998. By 2000, however, tourism was being actively promoted and Qatar's reputation as a venue for international conferences and sporting events was growing.

General Tourism Authority (GTA): Doha; f. 2002; affiliated with Council of Ministers; Chair. Sheikh ABDULLAH BIN AHMAD ATH-THANI; Gen. Man. DAVID TEWELDE.

Defence

Estimated Defence Budget (2001): QR 5,300m.

Total armed forces (August 2001): 12,330: army 8,500; navy 1,730 (incl. marine police); air force 2,100.

Education

All education within Qatar is provided free of charge, although it is not compulsory, and numerous scholarships are awarded for study overseas. In the academic year 1999/2000 there was a combined total of some 75,000 students at all levels of regular education in Qatar; there were about 44,000 students in private schools. In 1995/96 there were 7,018 children receiving pre-primary education. Primary schooling begins at six years of age and lasts for six years. In 1995/96 the 174 primary schools were attended by 53,631 pupils. The next level of education, beginning at 12 years of age, is divided between a three-year preparatory stage and a further three-year secondary stage, with a total of 38,594 pupils in 1995/96. There are specialized religious, industrial, commercial and technical secondary schools for boys; the technical school admitted its first students in 1999/2000, as did two scientific secondary schools (one for girls). In 1995 the equivalent of 86% of all children in the relevant age-group (boys 87%; girls 86%) were enrolled at primary schools, while the comparable ratio for secondary enrolment was equivalent to 80% (boys 80%; girls 79%). In 1994/95 some 1,193 Qataris were sent on scholarships to higher education institutions abroad, in other Arab countries, the United Kingdom, France or the USA. The University of Qatar was established in 1977, and comprises faculties of education, science, humanities and social sciences, administration and economics, engineering, and Islamic studies. In the academic year 1996/97 there were 8,475 students and a teaching staff of 643. The 2002/03 budget allocated QR 418m. for education and youth welfare.

Bibliography

Abdulla, Yousof Ibrahim Al-. *A Study of Qatari-British Relations 1914–1945*. Orient Publishing and Translation, 1981.

Graham, Helga. *Arabian Time Machine: Self-Portrait of an Oil State*. Heinemann, 1978.

Mallakh, Ragaei El-. *Qatar, Energy and Development*. Croom Helm, 1985.

Nab, Ibrahim Abu. *Qatar: A Story of State Building*. Ministry of Information, Qatar, 1977.

Nafi, Zuhair Ahmed. *Economic and Social Development in Qatar*. Frances Pinter, 1983.

Othman, Nasser Al-. *With Their Bare Hands: the Story of the Oil Industry in Qatar*. Longman, 1984.

For further titles, see the Bibliography sections for Bahrain and the United Arab Emirates.

SAUDI ARABIA

Physical and Social Geography of the Arabian Peninsula

The Arabian peninsula is a distinct geographical unit, delimited on three sides by sea—on the east by the Persian (Arabian) Gulf and the Gulf of Oman, on the south by the Indian Ocean, and on the west by the Red Sea—while its remaining (northern) side is occupied by the deserts of Jordan and Iraq. This isolated territory, extending over some 2.5m. sq km (about 1m. sq miles), is divided politically into several states. The largest of these is Saudi Arabia, which occupies 2,240,000 sq km; to the east and south lie much smaller territories where suzerainty and even actual frontiers are disputed in some instances. Along the shores of the Persian Gulf and the Gulf of Oman there are, beginning in the north, the State of Kuwait, with two adjacent zones of 'neutral' territory; then, after a stretch of Saudi Arabian coast, the islands of Bahrain and the Qatar peninsula, followed by the United Arab Emirates and the much larger Sultanate of Oman. Yemen occupies most of the southern coastline of the peninsula, and its south-western corner.

PHYSICAL FEATURES

Structurally, the whole of Arabia is a vast platform of ancient rocks, once continuous with north-east Africa. Subsequently a series of great fissures opened, as the result of which a large trough, or rift valley, was formed and later occupied by the sea, to produce the Red Sea and Gulf of Aden. The Arabian platform is tilted, with its highest part in the extreme west, along the Red Sea, and it slopes gradually down from west to east. Thus the Red Sea coast is often bold and mountainous, whereas the Persian Gulf coast is flat, low-lying and fringed with extensive coral reefs which make it difficult to approach the shore in many places.

Dislocation of the rock strata in the west of Arabia has led to the upwelling of much lava, which has solidified into vast barren expanses, known as *harras*. Volcanic cones and flows are also prominent along the whole length of the western coast as far as Aden, where peaks rise to more than 3,000 m above sea-level. The mountains reach their highest in the south, in Yemen, with summits at 4,000 m, and the lowest part of this mountain wall occurs roughly half-way along its course, in the region of Jeddah, Mecca, and Medina. A principal reason for the location of these three Saudi Arabian towns is that they offer the easiest route inland from the coast, and one of the shortest routes across Arabia.

Further to the east the ancient platform is covered by relatively thin layers of younger rocks. Some of the strata have been eroded to form shallow depressions; others have proved more resistant, and now stand out as ridges. This central area, relieved by shallow vales and upstanding ridges and covered in many places by desert sand, is called the Najd, and is considered to be the homeland of the Wahhabi sect, which now rules the whole of Saudi Arabia. Further east, practically all the land lies well below 300 m in altitude, and both to the north and to the south are desert areas. The Nefud in the north has some wells, and even a slight rainfall, and therefore supports a few oasis cultivators and pastoral nomads. South of the Najd, however, lies the Rub' al-Khali, or Empty Quarter, a rainless, unrelieved wilderness of shifting sand, too harsh for occupation even by nomads.

Most of the east coast of Arabia (al-Hasa) is low-lying, but an exception is the imposing ridge of the Jebel al-Akhdar ('Green Mountain') of Oman, which also produces a fjord-like coastline along the Gulf of Oman. Another feature is the large river valleys, or *wadis*, cut by river action during an earlier geological period, but in modern times almost, or entirely, dry and partially filled with sand. The largest is the Wadi Hadramawt, which runs parallel to the southern coast for several hundred km; another is the Wadi Sirhan, which stretches north-westwards from the Nefud into Jordan.

CLIMATE

Because of its land-locked nature, the winds reaching Arabia are generally dry, and almost all the area is arid. In the north there is a rainfall of 100 mm–200 mm annually; further south, except near the coast, even this fails. The higher parts of the west and south do, however, experience appreciable falls—rather sporadic in some parts, but copious and reliable in areas adjacent to the Red Sea.

Because of aridity, and hence relatively cloudless skies, there are great extremes of temperature. The summer is overwhelmingly hot, with maximum temperatures of more than 50°C, which are intensified by the dark rocks, while in winter there can be general severe frost and even weeks of snow in the mountains. Another result of the wide variations in temperature is the prevalence of violent local winds. Also, near the coast, atmospheric humidity is particularly high, and the coasts of both the Red Sea and the Persian Gulf are notorious for their humidity. Average summer temperatures in Saudi Arabia's coastal regions range from 38°C to 49°C (100°F–120°F), sometimes reaching 54°C (129°F) in the interior, or falling to a minimum of 24°C (75.2°F) in Jeddah. The winters are mild, except in the mountains. Winter temperatures range from 8°C (46.4°F) to 30°C (86°F) in Riyadh, and reach a maximum of 33°C (91.4°F) in Jeddah.

Owing to the tilt of the strata eastwards, and their great elevation in the west, rain falling in the hills near the Red Sea apparently percolates gradually eastwards, to emerge as springs along the Persian Gulf coast. This phenomenon, borne out by the fact that the flow of water in the springs greatly exceeds the total rainfall in the same district, suggests that water may be present underground over much of the interior. Irrigation schemes to exploit these supplies have been developed, notably in the Najd at al-Kharj, but results have been fairly limited.

ECONOMIC LIFE

Over much of Arabia, life is based around oases. Many wells are used solely by nomads for watering their animals, but in some parts, more especially the south, there is regular cultivation. Yemen, in particular, has a well-developed agriculture, showing a gradation of crops according to altitude, with cereals, fruit, coffee and qat (a narcotic) as the chief products. Other agricultural districts are in Oman and in the large oases of the Hedjaz (including Medina and Mecca). However, conditions in Arabia are harsh, and the population depends partly on resources brought in from outside, such as revenues from pilgrims. A major change in the economy of Saudi Arabia and the Gulf States resulted from the exploitation of petroleum, the revenues from which transformed those States.

RACE, LANGUAGE AND RELIGION

The inhabitants of the centre, north and west are of almost unmixed Mediterranean stock—lightly built, long-headed and dark. In coastal districts of the east, south and south-west, intermixture of broader-headed and slightly heavier peoples of Armenoid descent is a prominent feature; and there has been some exchange of racial type with the populations on the Iranian shores of the Persian Gulf and Gulf of Oman. Owing to the long-continued slave trade, negroid influences from Africa are also widespread. On this basis it is possible to delimit two ethnic zones within Arabia: a northern, central and western area, geographically arid and in isolation, with a relatively unmixed racial composition; and the coastlands of the south, south-west and east, showing a mixed population. A recent result of the rapid economic growth in the petroleum-producing countries has been the influx of large numbers of expatriates from the developed countries of the Western world, and labourers from developing countries further east. The official language of Arabia is Arabic, which is spoken by almost all of the population.

As its borders enclose the holy cities of Mecca and Medina, Saudi Arabia is the centre of the Islamic faith. About 85% of Saudi Muslims belong to the Sunni sect of Islam, the remainder being Shi'ites. Except in the Eastern Province, Sunni rites prevail.

History

Revised for this edition by JON LUNN

ANCIENT AND MEDIEVAL HISTORY

For the most part, Arabian history has been the account of small pockets of settled civilization, subsisting mainly on trade, in the midst of nomadic tribes. The earliest urban settlements developed in the south-west, where the flourishing Minaean kingdom is believed to have been established in the 12th century BC. This was followed by the Sabaean and Himyarite kingdoms, which lasted until the sixth century AD. The term 'kingdom' in this connection implies a loose federation of city states rather than a centralized monarchy. As an important trading station between east and west, southern Arabia was brought into early contact with the Persian and Roman empires, and thereby with Judaism, Zoroastrianism, and later Christianity. Politically, however, the south Arabian principalities remained independent.

By the end of the sixth century the centre of power had shifted to the west coast, to the Hedjaz cities of at-Ta'if, Mecca and Medina. While the southern regions fell under the control of the Sasanid rulers of Persia, the independent Hedjaz grew in importance as a trade route between the Byzantine Empire, Egypt, and the East. From the fifth century, Mecca was dominated by the tribe of Quraish. Meanwhile, the central deserts remained nomadic, and the inhospitable east coast remained, for the most part, under Persian influence.

The flowering and development of Arabism from the 7th century AD, inspired by the Prophet Muhammad (the founder of Islam) proceeded, for the most part, outside the Arabian peninsula itself. The Islamic unification of the Near and Middle East reduced the importance of the Hedjaz as a trade route. Mecca retained a unique status as a centre of pilgrimage for the whole Islamic world, but Arabia as a whole, temporarily united under Muhammad and his successors, soon drifted back into disunity. Yemen was the first to break away from the weakening Abbasid Caliphate in Baghdad, and from the ninth century onwards a variety of small dynasties established themselves in San'a, Zabid, and other towns. Mecca also had its semi-independent governors, though their proximity to Egypt made them more cautious in their attitude towards the Caliphs and the later rulers of that country, particularly the Fatimids of the 10th to 12th centuries. In Oman, in the south-east, a line of spiritual Imams arose who before long were exercising temporal power. To the north the Arabian shores of the Persian Gulf provided a home for the fanatical Carmathian sect, whose influence at times extended as far as Iraq, Syria, Mecca, and Yemen.

THE OTTOMAN PERIOD

Arabia remained unsettled until the beginning of the 16th century, when the whole peninsula came under the nominal suzerainty of the Ottoman Sultans in Istanbul. Their hold was never very strong, even in the Hedjaz, and in Oman and Yemen native lines of Imams were once again exercising unfettered authority before the end of the century. More important for the future of the peninsula was the appearance of European merchant adventurers in the Indian Ocean and the Persian (Arabian) Gulf. The Portuguese were the first to arrive, in the 16th century, and they were followed in the 17th and 18th centuries by the British, Dutch and French. By the beginning of the 19th century the United Kingdom had supplanted its European rivals and had established its influence firmly in the Gulf and, to a lesser extent, along the southern coast.

The political structure of Arabia was now beginning to develop along its modern lines. Yemen was already a virtually independent Imamate; Lahej broke away in the middle of the 18th century, only to lose Aden to the United Kingdom in 1839 and to become the nucleus of the Aden Protectorate. To the north of Yemen was the principality of the Asir, generally independent, though both countries were occupied by the Turks from 1850 until the outbreak of the First World War. The Hedjaz continued to be a province of the Ottoman Empire. In 1793 the Sultanate of Oman was established with its capital at Muscat, and during the 19th century all the rulers and chieftains along the Persian Gulf coast, including Oman, the sheikhdoms of the Trucial Coast, Bahrain and Kuwait, entered into 'exclusive' treaty relations with the British Government. The United Kingdom was principally concerned with preventing French, Russian and German penetration towards India, and suppressing the trade in slaves and weapons.

Meanwhile, the Najd, in the centre of Arabia, was the scene of another upheaval with religious inspirations. The puritanical and reforming Wahhabi movement, launched in the middle of the 18th century, had by 1800 grown so powerful that its followers were able to capture Karbala and Najaf in Iraq, Damascus in Syria, and Mecca and Medina in the Hedjaz. They were defeated by Muhammad Ali of Egypt, acting in the name of the Ottoman Sultan, in 1811–18 and again in 1838, but the Wahhabi ruling house of Sa'ud continued to rule in the interior until 1890, when the rival Rashidi family, which had Turkish support, seized control of Riyadh.

In 1901 a member of the deposed Sa'udi family, Abd al-Aziz ibn Abd ar-Rahman, set out from Kuwait, where he had been living in exile, to regain the family's former domains. In 1902, with only about 200 followers, Abd al-Aziz captured Riyadh, expelled the Rashidi dynasty and proclaimed himself ruler of the Najd. Later he recovered and consolidated the outlying provinces of the kingdom, resisting Turkish attempts to subjugate him. Having restored the House of Sa'ud as a ruling dynasty, Abd al-Aziz became known as Ibn Sa'ud. To strengthen his position, Ibn Sa'ud instituted the formation of Wahhabi colonies, known as Ikhwan ('Brethren'), throughout the territory under his control. The first Ikhwan settlement was founded in 1912, and about 100 more were established, spreading Wahhabi doctrines to communities in remote desert areas, over the next 15 years. These colonies formed the basis of a centralized organization which was to prove a powerful instrument in later years. By the outbreak of the First World War (1914–18), Ibn Sa'ud was effectively the master of central Arabia, including the Hasa coast of the Persian Gulf.

EVENTS, 1914–26

When Turkey entered the war on the side of Germany in October 1914, Arabia inevitably became a centre of intrigue, if not necessarily of military action. British influence was paramount along the eastern and southern coasts, where the various sheikhs and tribal chiefs from Kuwait to the Hadramawt lost no time in severing their remaining connections with the Ottoman Empire. On the other hand, the Turks had faithful allies in Ibn Rashid of the Shammar, to the north of the Najd, and in Imam Yahya of Yemen. The Turks also maintained garrisons along the west coast. In the centre, Ibn Sa'ud, who, in 1913, had accepted Turkish recognition of his occupation of the Hasa coast, enjoyed friendly relations with the British-controlled Government of India.

British military strategy developed, as the war dragged on, into a two-pronged offensive against the Turks from both Egypt and the Persian Gulf. In the implementation of this plan opinions were divided on the extent to which use could be made of the Arab population. The Indian Government on the eastern wing, while favouring the pretensions of Ibn Sa'ud, preferred to see the problem in purely military terms, and opposed any suggestion of an Arab revolt. This, however, was the scheme favoured by the Arab Bureau in Cairo, whose views eventually prevailed in London. They were alarmed at the Ottoman declaration of a *jihad* (holy war) and possible repercussions in Egypt and North Africa. Negotiations were started at a very early stage with Arab nationalist movements in Syria and Egypt, but these met with comparatively little success. More progress was made when the British negotiators turned their attentions to the Sharif of Mecca, Hussein, a member of the Hashimi family which had ruled in Mecca since the 11th century AD. The support of such a religious dignitary would be an effective counter to Turkish claims. Hussein was inclined to favour the Allied cause, but it was only after he had elicited from the British (in the MacMahon correspondence—see Documents on Palestine, p. 50) promises that he believed would meet Arab nationalist aspirations that he decided to move. On 5 June 1916 he proclaimed Arab independence and declared war on the Turks. By November he felt sufficiently confident to claim the title of King of the Hedjaz. Military operations continued throughout the winter, and in July 1917 the port of Aqaba was captured and the Hedjaz cleared of Turkish troops except for a beleaguered garrison in Medina.

Arabia thereafter remained comparatively peaceful, and was not even greatly disturbed by the complicated post-war political manoeuvres in the Middle East. Hussein was a rather ineffectual spokesman for the Arab point of view at the peace conferences and over the allocation of mandates, and as a result forfeited the favour of the British Government. When, therefore, he was unwise enough to challenge the growing power of his former rival Ibn Sa'ud, he found himself entirely without support. Ibn Sa'ud's stature had been steadily growing since the end of the war. In November 1921 he had succeeded in supplanting the house of Ibn Rashid and annexing the Shammar, and a year later he was recognized by the Government of India as overlord of Hayil, Shammar and Jawf. On 5 March 1924 Hussein laid claim to the title of Caliph, made vacant by the deposition of the Ottoman Sultan. His claims were nowhere recognized, and Ibn Sa'ud overran the Hedjaz in a campaign of a few months, captured Mecca and forced Hussein's abdication. Hussein's eldest son, Ali, continued to hold Jeddah for another year, but was then ousted, and on 8 January 1926 Ibn Sa'ud proclaimed himself King of the Hedjaz. At first the Najd and the Hedjaz formed a dual kingdom, but on 23 September 1932 they were merged to form the Kingdom of Saudi Arabia.

THE KINGDOM OF SAUDI ARABIA*

Ibn Sa'ud's new status was recognized by the United Kingdom in the Treaty of Jeddah of 1927, while Ibn Sa'ud, in his turn, acknowledged his rival Hussein's sons, Abdullah and Faisal, as rulers of Transjordan and Iraq, and also the special status of the British-protected sheikhdoms along the Gulf coast. The northern frontier of his domains had previously been established by the Hadda and Bahra agreements of November 1925, which set the Mandate boundaries as the limit of his expansion. The border with Yemen was settled in 1934 after protracted negotiations and a brief war.

In the years that followed, the new King's priority remained the unification and development of his country. The colonization policy which he had begun in 1912 was pursued vigorously; land settlements were established and unruliness among the bedouin was suppressed. The modernization of communications was initiated, and the need for economic development emphasized. The main damage that Saudi Arabia suffered during the Second World War was economic. The pilgrimage traffic declined to almost nothing, and in April 1943 it was necessary to include Saudi Arabia as a beneficiary of Lend-Lease, the arrangement whereby the USA supplied equipment to allied countries.

Saudi Arabia's production of crude petroleum increased steadily as new oilfields were developed. In October 1945 a petroleum refinery opened at Ras Tanura, and two years later

work started on the Trans-Arabian Pipeline (Tapline), to connect the Arabian oilfields with ports on the Mediterranean Sea in Lebanon. Petroleum first reached the Lebanese port of Sidon on 2 December 1950. In the same month the Saudi Arabian Government and the Arabian-American Oil Co (Aramco) signed a new agreement providing for equal shares of the proceeds of petroleum sales. In 1956 a government-owned National Oil Co was formed to exploit areas not covered by the Aramco concession.

Saudi Arabia was a founder member of the League of Arab States (the Arab League), formed in 1945, and initially played a loyal and comparatively inconspicuous part. Ibn Sa'ud sent a small force to join the fighting against Israel in the summer of 1948. When the solidarity of the League began to weaken, it was natural that he should side with Egypt and Syria rather than with his old dynastic enemies, the rulers of Iraq and Jordan. In the course of time, however, he began to turn once more to internal development, and in 1950 and 1951 he concluded an agreement for a US $15m. loan, as well as a four-point agreement and a mutual assistance pact. However, the real basis of development was the revenue from the developing petroleum industry. This was sufficient to justify the announcement, in July 1949, of a $270m. Four-Year Plan, whose main feature was an ambitious programme of railway development. Apart from this, the King's policy was one of cautious modernization at home, and the enhancement of Saudi Arabian prestige and influence in the Middle East and in world affairs generally.

AFTER IBN SA'UD

On 9 November 1953 King Ibn Sa'ud died, at the age of 71, and was succeeded by Crown Prince Sa'ud ibn Abd al-Aziz, who had been appointed Prime Minister in the previous month. Another of the late King's sons, Faisal ibn Abd al-Aziz, replaced Sa'ud as Crown Prince and Prime Minister. The policy of strengthening the governmental machine, and of relying less on one-man rule, was continued by the formation of new ministries and a regular Council of Ministers. In March 1958, bowing to pressure from the royal family, King Sa'ud conferred on Crown Prince Faisal full powers over foreign, internal and economic affairs, with the professed aim of strengthening the machinery of government and of centralizing responsibilities. In December 1960, however, the Crown Prince resigned as Prime Minister, and the King assumed the premiership himself. In the following month, a high planning council, with a team of international experts, was formed to survey the country's resources, and there followed steady progress in the modernization of the country.

Throughout his reign, King Sa'ud regarded his role as that of a mediator between the conflicting national and foreign interests in the Arab Middle East. He refused to join either the United Arab Republic (UAR) or the rival Arab Federation. Relations with Egypt ranged from the mutual defence pacts between Egypt, Syria and Saudi Arabia in October 1955 (which Yemen and Jordan also signed a year later) to the open quarrel in March 1958 over an alleged plot to assassinate President Nasser. Subsequently, relations improved. The Saudi Government also played a leading role in bringing the Arab governments together after Egypt's nationalization of the Suez Canal in July 1956 and the Israeli, British and French military action in the Sinai peninsula in November. In 1961 Saudi Arabia supported the Syrians in their break with the UAR, and in general, relations with that country deteriorated. By 1964, however, in spite of the tensions over the revolution in Yemen, King Sa'ud attended the Cairo conference on the Jordan waters dispute in January, and in March, after a meeting in Riyadh, diplomatic relations with the UAR were resumed.

FAISAL IN POWER

In March 1964 King Sa'ud relinquished all real power over the affairs of the country to his brother, Crown Prince Faisal, who had again acted as Prime Minister intermittently during 1962, and continuously since mid-1963. The rule of Prince Faisal was expected to result in many concessions to 'Westernization', such as more cinemas and television, with more profound social and economic reforms to follow. The change of power, by which King Sa'ud retired as active monarch, was supported in a statement by the *'ulama* council of religious leaders (Council of Ulema) 'in the light of developments, the King's condition of health, and

---

* For subsequent developments in the rest of the Arabian peninsula, see separate chapters on Bahrain, Kuwait, Oman, Qatar, the United Arab Emirates (UAE) and Yemen.

his inability to attend to state affairs'. In November 1964 Sa'ud was forced to abdicate in favour of Faisal. The new King retained the post of Prime Minister, and in March 1965 appointed his half-brother, Khalid ibn Abd al-Aziz, to be Crown Prince. On 24 August 1965 King Faisal confirmed his stature as an important Arab leader when he concluded an agreement at Jeddah with President Nasser of the UAR on a peace plan for Yemen.

Although the Yemen issue remained unresolved, there was evidence of Saudi Arabia's genuine anxiety that a solution should be found, even though in April 1966 the construction of a military airfield near the frontier brought protests from the Republican Government of Yemen and the UAR. Representatives of Saudi Arabia and the UAR met in Kuwait in August 1966 in an attempt to implement the Jeddah agreement, but relations with both the UAR and the Arab League continued to be tense.

THE SIX-DAY WAR, AND AFTER

In the June 1967 Arab–Israeli war, Saudi forces collaborated with Jordanian and Iraqi forces in action against Israel. At a summit conference of Arab leaders held in Khartoum at the end of August 1967 Saudi Arabia agreed to provide £50m. of a total £135m. fund to assist Jordan and the UAR in restoring their economic strength after the hostilities with Israel. An agreement was also concluded with President Nasser on the withdrawal of UAR and Saudi military support for the warring parties in Yemen. By way of recompense for these concessions, Saudi Arabia persuaded other Arab states that it was in their best interests to resume shipments of petroleum to Western countries—supplies had been suspended for political reasons after the war with Israel.

The internal political situation was disturbed by abortive coups in June and September 1969. Plans for both seem to have been discovered in advance, the only visible evidence being the arrests of numbers of army and air force officers. In Yemen the royalist cause, which the Saudi Government had strongly supported, appeared to be within sight of victory early in 1968. By mid-1969, however, its remaining adherents had largely been driven into exile and the civil war seemed to have come to an end, although further hostilities were reported during late 1969 and early 1970. Discussions between San'a representatives and Saudi officials took place in 1970, and the Yemen Arab Republic (YAR) was officially recognized in July. Relations with Southern Yemen (subsequently the People's Democratic Republic of Yemen—PDRY) deteriorated, however, and in December 1969 the two countries fought an extensive battle on the disputed frontier: Saudi Arabia won easily, mainly because of its superior air power.

REPERCUSSIONS OF THE OCTOBER WAR

When the Arab–Israeli war of October 1973 broke out and US aid to Israel continued, Saudi Arabia, despite its traditionally good relationship with the West, led a movement by all the Arab petroleum-producing countries to exert political pressure by cuts in petroleum production. Since there was no immediate response from the USA, members of the Organization of the Petroleum Exporting Countries (OPEC—of which Saudi Arabia is a member) placed an embargo on petroleum supplies to that country and to several other developed Western countries. Supplies to the West were not cut off entirely, but it was announced that production would be progressively reduced until attitudes towards support for Israel changed. Western nations attempted to repair their links with the petroleum-producing countries, who were debating among themselves how far they should wield the 'oil weapon' to achieve their ends.

As the possessor of 40% of the Middle East's petroleum reserves, and one-quarter of world reserves, Saudi Arabia, together with Egypt, was in the very forefront of negotiations. It soon became apparent, however, that the Saudis held different views from those of other producer nations (notably Libya, Algeria and Iran) on the extent to which their control of petroleum supplies could safely be used to put pressure on the West. It was feared in Riyadh that too much of this pressure would have unwanted economic repercussions. The more radical OPEC members wanted to retain the petroleum embargo until a satisfactory outcome to the October hostilities was reached. At a meeting in March 1974, however, Saudi Arabia pressed for a

resumption of supplies to the USA and, when this was agreed, resisted any moves to increase prices for petroleum, which had risen to nearly four times the pre-hostilities level. It was reported that, in order to achieve their aim, the Saudis had threatened to leave OPEC and to lower prices unilaterally. Reluctantly, therefore, the more radical OPEC members agreed to a price freeze.

Meanwhile, in negotiations with consumer countries, the Saudis made it clear that the continued supply of petroleum was dependent not only on a change in attitudes towards Israel but on assistance to Saudi Arabia itself in industrializing and diversifying its economy, in preparation for such time as reserves of petroleum would be depleted. The USA, in particular, showed itself eager to satisfy these conditions, and an important economic and military co-operation agreement was signed in May 1974.

ASSASSINATION OF FAISAL, ACCESSION OF KHALID

On 25 March 1975 King Faisal was assassinated by one of his nephews, Prince Faisal ibn Masaed ibn Abd al-Aziz. There were fears of a conspiracy, but it soon became clear that the assassin had acted on his own initiative. King Faisal was succeeded by Crown Prince Khalid, who also became Prime Minister, and who appointed one of his brothers, Fahd ibn Abd al-Aziz (Minister of the Interior since 1962), to be Crown Prince and First Deputy Prime Minister.

No major change of policy followed Khalid's succession. He quickly announced that Saudi Arabia would follow the late King Faisal's policies of pursuing Islamic solidarity and the strengthening of Arab unity, and that Saudi Arabia's objectives remained 'the recovery of occupied Arab territories' and the 'liberation of the City of Jerusalem from the claws of Zionism'.

In March 1976 Saudi Arabia established diplomatic relations with the PDRY. Although the two countries had been ideological enemies since the PDRY achieved independence (as Southern Yemen) in 1967, they were both concerned about the presence of Iranian forces in Oman. A Saudi Arabian loan was made to the PDRY, and it was expected that, in return, the Yemenis would abandon their support for the People's Front for the Liberation of Oman.

An indication of the growth in stature of Saudi Arabia in Arab affairs in the late 1970s was its key role in October 1976 in bringing about the Riyadh summit—a meeting that was instrumental in ending the civil war in Lebanon and also brought about reconciliation between Egypt and Syria. Saudi Arabia also asserted its influence at the OPEC summit in Doha in December 1976, when the country, along with the UAE, showed itself firmly committed to a petroleum price rise of only 5%, while the other OPEC countries insisted on a 10% rise.

Saudi Arabia supported President Anwar Sadat of Egypt, fearing that his fall from power would result in the ascendancy of Egypt's political left. When Sadat visited Israel in November 1977, Saudi Arabia gave him discreet support in his peace initiative. This position, however, was abandoned following the signing of the Egyptian-Israeli treaty in the following spring. At the Arab summit meeting held in April 1979, Saudi Arabia aligned itself with the 'moderate' states in supporting the sanctions against Egypt which had been outlined at the Arab League meeting in the previous November. In July 1979 the Saudi Government withdrew from its arms manufacturing consortium with Egypt. Nevertheless, flights between Egypt and Saudi Arabia continued, and there was no ban on the employment of Egyptian workers in Saudi Arabia.

In domestic affairs, the Saudi Government was content to allow social change to unfold gradually, although the country's vast petroleum wealth and the development plans of 1975–80 and 1980–85 brought about a great improvement in communications, welfare services and the standard of living in general.

The stability of the kingdom and the hegemony of the royal family were abruptly undermined when some 250 armed 'traditionalist' dissidents seized and occupied the Grand Mosque at Mecca on 20 November 1979, the eve of the Islamic year AH 1400. The insurgents, led by Juhaiman ibn Seif al-Otaibi, attempted to force the estimated 50,000-strong congregation (the majority of whom were subsequently released) to recognize one of their number, Muhammad ibn Abdullah al-Qatami, as the Mahdi (or 'Guided One' of Islamic theological tradition—a prophet sent to replace corruption and evil with justice and law at the end of time). Reports of the siege became increasingly confused, the authorities apparently convinced, at least initially, that the insurgents were drawn from the disaffected quarters of the country's Shi'a minority, although al-Otaibi was known to be from one of the most pre-eminent Sunni families of the Najd. Al-Otaibi declared that the corruption, ostentation and 'Westernization' of the as-Sa'ud dynasty had necessitated such a response. The Council of Ulema issued special dispensation to the security forces to use arms to end the siege, which continued for two weeks, before the rebel 'purists' were defeated; al-Qatami was one of 102 insurgents killed during the liberation of the Mosque, while al-Otaibi was one of 63 rebels executed following the siege. More than 100 Saudi troops and 27 civilians were killed during the operation to relieve the Mosque.

SAUDI ARABIA IN THE 1980s

The siege of the Grand Mosque revealed a degree of popular unease in Saudi Arabia. Although the royal family retained a firm grip on power, the existing system entitled as many as 5,000 Saudi princes to royal privileges, and there was widely-rumoured disenchantment with the royal family's conspicuous consumption and privilege. An eight-man committee under the chairmanship of Prince Nayef, Minister of the Interior, was appointed in March 1980 to draft a 200-article 'system of rule' based on Islamic principles. It was announced that a consultative assembly would be formed to act as an advisory body, although the assembly was not inaugurated until 1993 (see below). Saudi Arabia's geo-political position, however, added to the unease. With the PDRY already in the Soviet sphere of influence, with the YAR concluding an agreement to purchase armaments from the USSR in November 1979, and with the Soviet invasion of Afghanistan in December, Saudi Arabia regarded itself as increasingly vulnerable. This feeling was intensified by the outbreak of war between Iran and Iraq in September 1980, which caused further instability in the region. Saudi Arabia initially supported Iraq, but later came to fear that Iranian retaliation might take the form of agitating Saudi Arabia's Shi'a minority (which had rioted violently in the Eastern Province in late 1979). Saudi Arabia therefore concentrated on consolidating its position in the early 1980s. Defence spending became a major feature of Saudi Arabia's current expenditure, largely involving the purchase or loan of armaments and military equipment from the USA. In March 1981 the USA agreed to sell to Saudi Arabia five AWACS (airborne warning and control systems) aircraft in addition to the four that were supplied under US control after the outbreak of the Iran–Iraq War.

In May 1981 Saudi Arabia joined five other Gulf states in founding the Co-operation Council for the Arab States of the Gulf (Gulf Co-operation Council—GCC), a pact for economic co-operation but also with some emphasis on the formation of a military alliance and a collective security agreement. The GCC made preliminary moves towards the co-ordination of its members' defences in November 1982, when it was agreed that its own Rapid Defence Force (RDF) would be formed. This decision was ratified in October 1983, when member countries participated in the 'Peninsula Shield' joint military exercises in Oman. Saudi Arabia's defence forces form a large part of the RDF's military strength.

Saudi Arabia was one of the leading mediators in the negotiations that ended the 1981 missiles crisis in Lebanon, and became increasingly involved in trying to find a solution to the Arab–Israeli question and the issue of Palestinian autonomy. The basis of Saudi Arabia's policy with regard to these questions was the eight-point 'Fahd Plan', first publicized by Crown Prince Fahd in August 1981. The plan (see Documents on Palestine, p. 68) caused concern in the remainder of the Arab world because it recognized the legitimacy of Israel, by implication, although Saudi Arabia was reluctant to admit this. The plan was due to be discussed at an Arab summit meeting in Morocco in November, but there was disagreement over its implications and the summit quickly broke up in disarray.

ACCESSION OF FAHD

King Khalid died suddenly on 13 June 1982 and was succeeded by his younger brother, Crown Prince Fahd. Owing to Khalid's ill health, Fahd had already exercised considerable power. Fahd also became Prime Minister, and he appointed a half-brother, Abdullah ibn Abd al-Aziz (Commander of the National Guard since 1962), to be Crown Prince and First Deputy Prime Minister. The previous Saudi policy of positively seeking a solution to the Palestine question, inflamed still further by the Israeli move into Lebanon in June, was continued. The Saudi Government was unwilling to exercise the political influence over Syria (particularly concerning Syrian involvement in Lebanon) that Western countries assumed it to have, demonstrating clearly its priority of Arab unity. In February 1984 Crown Prince Abdullah expressed support for the Syrian position in Lebanon, demanding a withdrawal of US marines from the area.

After 1982 there was a considerable slump in government revenues from petroleum. Supportive loans to other Arab countries, including Syria and Iraq, proved to be a significant burden on the kingdom's finances. Donations to Iraq were widely thought to have totalled US $25,000m. by April 1984, and there seemed little likelihood that Saudi Arabia would abrogate the responsibility that it had assumed for supporting Iraq in its war with Iran. Under an agreement reached in the first year of the Iran–Iraq War, Saudi Arabia and Kuwait sold up to 310,000 barrels per day (b/d) of oil (250,000 b/d from the Neutral/Partitioned Zone and the remainder from Saudi Arabia) through the Arabian Oil Co, the proceeds of which went to Iraq, to compensate it for lost export capacity. In mid-1987, however, Saudi Arabia assured Iran that it was selling only a negligible amount of oil on Iraq's behalf.

As the war between Iran and Iraq showed signs of escalating towards the end of 1983 and in early 1984, Saudi Arabia appeared to be in danger of becoming involved militarily in the conflict. In April 1984 a Saudi Arabian merchant ship, a tanker loading at Iran's Kharg island oil terminal, was struck by missiles from Iraqi fighter aircraft. In retaliatory incidents in May, Iranian aircraft attacked two more tankers, one of which was travelling in Saudi Arabian waters. In response, Saudi Arabia approached the USA to request help in improving its defence systems, by extending its air defence zone (with the new 'Fahd Line'), and by mobilizing its defences to patrol the region. At a meeting of the UN Security Council in May, the GCC countries tried unsuccessfully to secure a general condemnation of Iran's behaviour in the war. However, they were supported by Egypt, a move which heralded an improvement in relations between Egypt and the more moderate Arab countries. The willingness of the USA to become involved in safeguarding the Strait presented problems for the Gulf countries, since GCC policy countenanced the intervention of either superpower only in a case of urgent need, and the Gulf States retained certain reservations in their otherwise good relations with the USA concerning, for example, US policy in Lebanon. Therefore, Saudi Arabia refused to give the USA access to military facilities on its territory in the event of a major escalation of the war between Iran and Iraq.

Saudi Arabia's concern for the development of its own defences was apparent in 1985, and was reflected particularly in the announcement of the 'Peace Shield' defence programme in February. The project, which was not expected to be complete before the mid-1990s, aimed to provide Saudi Arabia with a computerized command, control and communications system for all of its air defences, and also involved the establishment of factories producing avionics and telecommunications equipment. Other defence projects under way in 1985 included plans for the formation of a joint strike force involving Saudi Arabia and its allies in the Gulf region, and the construction of the King Khalid military city, which was eventually to accommodate 70,000 people. In June 1986 a controversial sale of military equipment was agreed between Saudi Arabia and the USA. The deal, which was initially valued at US $3,000m., was reduced to $265m. when plans to supply 800 *Stinger* anti-aircraft missiles and 60 advanced fighter aircraft were cancelled, owing to strong Congressional opposition. Also in June another controversial agreement was signed between the two countries for the sale of five US-built AWACS aircraft, worth $8,600m. Saudi Arabia's co-operation became essential to the US naval convoys, which began to escort reflagged Kuwaiti tankers through the Persian Gulf in June, following an increase in attacks on shipping in the Gulf by Iran and Iraq during the year. The escalation of tension in the Gulf, exacerbated by the presence of US and Soviet naval forces, resulted in the adoption of Resolution 598 by the UN Security Council on 20 July 1987, which urged an immediate cease-fire. Iraq agreed to observe a cease-fire if Iran would also, but Iran prevaricated, attaching conditions to its acceptance of the Resolution. In November, at an extraordinary meeting of the Arab League in Amman, Jordan, representatives of the member nations, including Saudi Arabia, unanimously condemned Iran for prolonging the war against Iraq, deplored its occupation of Arab (i.e. Iraqi) territory, and urged it to accept Resolution 598 without preconditions.

In early 1985, following a visit by the Saudi Minister of Foreign Affairs, Prince Sa'ud al-Faisal, to Tehran, Ali Akbar Velayati, his Iranian counterpart, visited Riyadh in an attempt to improve relations between the two countries. However, in May two bombs exploded in the Sulmaniya district of Riyadh, killing one person and injuring three others. The Iranian-based Islamic Jihad group claimed responsibility and threatened that this was the beginning of a major bombing campaign within the country. Relations between Saudi Arabia and Iran deteriorated further in 1987, following clashes on 31 July between Iranian pilgrims and Saudi security forces during the *Hajj* (the annual pilgrimage of Muslims to the Islamic holy city of Mecca). Saudi Arabia reported that 402 people, of whom 275 were Iranians, were killed in the disturbances. Confusion surrounded exactly what took place in Mecca. Iran alleged that Saudi security forces opened fire on Iranian pilgrims, and accused Saudi Arabia and the USA of planning the incident. Mass demonstrations followed in Tehran, the Saudi embassy was sacked and Iranian leaders vowed to avenge the pilgrims' deaths by overthrowing the Saudi ruling family. Saudi Arabia, on the other hand, denied that any shooting took place, and insisted that the deaths occurred during a stampede caused by Iranian pilgrims, following unlawful political demonstrations in support of Ayatollah Khomeini. The Mecca incident renewed fears in Saudi Arabia, which had first been aroused after the Islamic revolution in Shi'ite Iran in 1979, that the minority Saudi Shi'ite community would rebel against the Sunni majority, to which the Saudi royal family belongs. In March 1988 the Saudi Arabian Government announced its intention of temporarily limiting the number of pilgrims to Mecca from abroad during the *Hajj* season, which was to begin in mid-July. National quotas would be allocated on the basis of 1,000 pilgrims for every 1m. citizens. This formula gave Iran a quota of 45,000. Iran's supreme religious leader, Ayatollah Khomeini, insisted that 150,000 Iranians, the same number as in 1987, would perform the *Hajj*, and that he would not prevent them from staging political protests at Mecca. In the event, Iran decided not to send pilgrims on the *Hajj*. Saudi Arabia severed its diplomatic relations with Iran in April 1988.

In October 1986 Sheikh Ahmad Zaki Yamani was dismissed from office by King Fahd, after serving for 24 years as Minister of Petroleum and Mineral Resources. His dismissal was interpreted as a sign of King Fahd's dissatisfaction with the OPEC 'fair share' policy, adopted at the end of 1985, whereby OPEC abandoned its system of official quotas for petroleum production in an attempt to regain its share of the world market. Sheikh Hisham Nazer, the Minister of Planning, was subsequently confirmed as the new Minister of Petroleum and Mineral Resources, and in April 1988 he was appointed as the first Saudi Arabian chairman of Aramco, the largest oil company operating in Saudi Arabia.

In November 1987 Saudi Arabia resumed full diplomatic relations with Egypt, following a decision taken by the Arab League that permitted member states to restore relations with Egypt at their own discretion. Relations had been severed in 1979, following the signing of a peace treaty between Egypt and Israel.

In March 1988 the disclosure that Saudi Arabia had taken delivery of an unspecified number of Chinese medium-range missiles provoked threats by Israel of a pre-emptive strike on the missiles' base at al-Kharj. The USA subsequently warned Israel against taking such action. In April, however, it was reported that King Fahd, in an unprecedented move, had requested the replacement of the US ambassador, following his delivery of an official complaint from the USA concerning Saudi Arabia's purchase of the missiles. In May the US Senate voted to ban sales of military equipment to Saudi Arabia (or to any

other nation that had taken delivery of such missiles), unless the President could certify that the country purchasing the missiles had no chemical, biological or nuclear warheads with which to equip them.

Following the refusal of the US Congress to supply military equipment to Saudi Arabia, the kingdom signed an agreement with the United Kingdom, valued at a record US \$20,000m., for the supply of fighter-bomber aircraft, trainer aircraft, helicopters and minesweepers and the construction of two huge airbases in collaboration with Ballast Nedam of the Netherlands.

In October 1988 four Saudi Arabian Shi'a Muslims, convicted of sabotaging a petrochemicals plant and collaborating with Iran, were executed. In an attempt to demonstrate Saudi Arabia's intention of improving relations with Iran, it was decreed that the Saudi official media would halt their campaign of attacks on that country. However, in late 1988 and early 1989 two senior Saudi Arabian intelligence officers, posing as diplomats in an attempt to trace members of the pro-Iranian Shi'a group believed to be responsible for the aforementioned sabotage, were assassinated in Turkey and in Thailand.

In December 1988 the Soviet Deputy Minister of Foreign Affairs visited Saudi Arabia to discuss the conflict in Afghanistan. Saudi Arabia, along with Sudan, recognized the Afghan *mujahidin* Government-in-exile, formed following the Soviet withdrawal, and, at a meeting of the Organization of the Islamic Conference (OIC) in March, it urged other countries to do likewise. However, the exclusion by the Government-in-exile of the eight *mujahidin* opposition groups based in Iran angered the Iranian authorities. Moreover, the issue of compensation for the families of the Iranian pilgrims who died in the July 1987 riots remained unresolved. Iran boycotted the pilgrimage for the second time in July 1989, owing to Saudi Arabia's refusal to abandon the quota system agreed in March 1988 by the OIC. Two explosions, which killed one pilgrim and wounded 16 in Mecca during the *Hajj*, widened the rift between the two countries. Iran blamed the USA and Saudi Arabia for the bombings, while the Saudis accused Iran of promoting terrorism. Saudi Arabia failed to send condolences upon the death of Ayatollah Khomeini, illustrating the deterioration in relations with Iran. Iranian pilgrims boycotted the *Hajj* for the third successive year in 1990, and Iran claimed that the Saudi Arabian Government opposed their participation. However, Saudi Arabian officials said that Iranian pilgrims were welcome on condition that Iran observed the allocated quota.

Relations between Saudi Arabia and other Gulf states improved in 1989. In March King Fahd signed a non-aggression pact with Iraq, a development apparently designed to ease concerns among conservative Arab Gulf states about Iraq's political ambitions following the war between Iran and Iraq. In April Saudi Arabia announced that it would help Iraq to rebuild the nuclear reactor that had been destroyed by Israel, on condition that the installation be used for peaceful purposes. In August documents ratifying the November 1988 agreement concluded by Kuwait and Saudi Arabia, concerning the property of citizens of the two countries in the Neutral Zone, were signed and exchanged at the Kuwaiti Ministry of Foreign Affairs. King Fahd's visit to Egypt in March 1989 was viewed as signifying the end of Egypt's isolation from the Arab world. Both countries declared their support for efforts to create a Palestinian state and denounced Israeli repression of the Palestinians in the occupied West Bank and Gaza Strip.

Defence remained a major concern in Saudi Arabia. In March British Aerospace revealed that the value of the defence agreements signed by Saudi Arabia and the United Kingdom in 1985 and 1988 (see above) could ultimately reach £150,000m., representing one of the biggest arms contracts in history. In the same month, allegations that bribery was used to secure the contract led to an official investigation in the United Kingdom. Saudi Arabia denied the allegations, stating that the sale was agreed by the two Governments without the use of intermediaries.

OPERATION DESERT SHIELD AND ITS IMPLICATIONS

Saudi Arabia's concern about its capacity to defend itself and its fears of Iraqi expansionism were substantiated in August 1990, when Iraq invaded and annexed Kuwait and proceeded to deploy armed forces along the Kuwaiti–Saudi Arabian border. King Fahd decided that he had no option but to request—in accordance with Article 51 of the UN Charter—multinational armed forces to deploy in Saudi Arabia in order to deter an attack on the country by Iraq. Thus 'Operation Desert Shield' was launched (see the chapters on Kuwait and Iraq).

King Fahd condemned the Iraqi invasion of Kuwait and offered refuge to the Amir of Kuwait, and Kuwait established a Government-in-exile at Ta'if. Meanwhile, Saudi Arabia stressed the role of Egyptian, Moroccan, Pakistani, Bangladeshi, Kuwaiti and Syrian contingents in the multinational force. By so doing, it sought to counter allegations—made by President Saddam Hussain of Iraq principally, but also by the Palestine Liberation Organization (PLO) and all those opposed to the USA's policies in the Middle East—that, by allowing the deployment of US forces in its defence, it had allowed itself to become an instrument of US strategic interests in the Gulf. The perception, in the Arab world, of Saudi Arabia as such an instrument threatened the whole of its diplomacy, by which it set great store, and which was based not only on the country's wealth, its leading role in OPEC and its custodianship of the holy cities, but also on the standing of King Fahd. Saudi Arabia stressed that the presence of the multinational defensive force was temporary.

There was a shift in the pattern of Saudi Arabia's foreign relations after the onset of the Gulf crisis in August 1990. The co-operation of the USSR, within the structures of the UN, was regarded as vital to the defence of Saudi Arabia, and in September Saudi Arabia and the USSR re-established diplomatic relations after a rupture lasting 50 years. Syria, aware of the diplomatic benefits that it could gain, committed forces to the defence of Saudi Arabia.

Meanwhile, Saudi Arabia implemented retaliatory measures against Jordan and Yemen for the equivocal stance that they had adopted towards Iraq's invasion of Kuwait. In late September 1990 Saudi Arabia expelled some diplomats from Iraq, Jordan and Yemen, while emergency supplies of oil to Jordan were terminated. Privileges enjoyed by the estimated 1.5m. Yemeni expatriate workers in Saudi Arabia were withdrawn; more than 300,000 of the expatriates returned to Yemen. In early November discussions on the restoration of diplomatic relations were held between Saudi Arabia and Iran.

By early January 1991 some 30 countries had contributed ground troops, aircraft and warships to the multinational force based in Saudi Arabia and the Gulf region, although the USA played the principal logistical role in the operation. The entire Saudi Arabian armed forces (some 67,500 men) were mobilized in defence of the country. Financial contributions to the cost of the multinational force were received from all over the world.

In mid-January 1991, following the failure of international diplomatic efforts to effect Iraq's withdrawal from Kuwait, the US-led multinational force launched a military campaign ('Operation Desert Storm') to liberate Kuwait, as authorized by the UN Security Council's Resolution 678, which had been adopted in late November 1990. As part of its response to the aerial bombardment which began the campaign, Iraq launched 35 *Scud* missiles against mainly urban targets in Saudi Arabia, and made similar attacks against Israel. Most of the missiles were intercepted by advanced air defence systems that had been installed by the USA, although one of those that struck Saudi Arabia demolished a US barracks near Dhahran, killing 28 soldiers, in February. Many Saudi installations, including desalination plants, were threatened by the release into the Gulf by Iraq of an estimated 4m. barrels of Kuwaiti petroleum; however, the long-term effects of the spillage were eventually considered to be less devastating than had been feared. In late January Iraqi forces entered Saudi Arabia, briefly occupying the town of Ras al-Khafji, close to Saudi Arabia's border with Kuwait, before being repelled by US, Saudi Arabian and Qatari units. Other Iraqi incursions in the same region were likewise repelled, and there was no further fighting on Saudi Arabian territory. In early February Iraq formally severed diplomatic relations with Saudi Arabia, and by the end of that month, when hostilities were suspended, Saudi Arabian casualties included at least 26 killed and 10 missing.

Following the liberation of Kuwait and the declaration of a cease-fire in late February 1991, the Kuwaiti Prime Minister and other members of his Government returned to Kuwait from Saudi Arabia in early March, followed subsequently by the Amir. Also in early March, Saudi Arabia, the remaining members of the GCC, Egypt and Syria agreed to form an Arab peace-keeping force in the Gulf region, as part of a draft plan on security and economic co-operation. Later in the month the withdrawal of coalition forces from bases in Saudi Arabia began. The return to Iraq of an estimated 62,000 Iraqi prisoners of war, held in camps in Saudi Arabia, also began in March. In April Saudi Arabia announced its decision to give refuge to an estimated 50,000 Iraqis, many of whom had participated in an unsuccessful revolt against Saddam Hussain's regime in the previous month. In early May the GCC member states endorsed US proposals for an increased Western military presence in the Gulf region, as a deterrent to any future military aggression. Meanwhile, diplomatic relations between Saudi Arabia and Iran were re-established in late March 1991, and Iranian pilgrims resumed attendance of the *Hajj*, their numbers regulated in accordance with Saudi Arabia's quota system.

DOMESTIC AND FOREIGN CHALLENGES, 1991–95

In February and May 1991 two petitions were presented to King Fahd appealing for more extensive Islamization in areas as diverse as the armed forces, the press and all administrative and educational systems. The first petition bore the signatures of as many as 100 senior Saudi religious dignitaries, including that of Sheikh Abd al-Aziz ibn Baz, the most influential Saudi theologian. Following the second petition, the Government immediately sent security force personnel to visit leading signatories, some of whom were forbidden to travel abroad. In June the Government's Higher Judicial Council issued a statement warning the signatories of the consequences of issuing any further criticism against the King. The creation of the Higher Judicial Council, within the Ministry of Justice, was considered to be an institutional challenge to the judicial powers of the 'ulama (religious scholars) in Saudi Arabia. Reform of the judicial system was one of the principal aims of the petition, as it stipulated the establishment of a supreme judiciary council with the authority to implement Islamic laws, which would conflict with the powers of the existing Higher Judicial Council. The petitions illustrated the growing assertiveness and restlessness of Islamic conservatives in the domestic debate on the political future of the country, which intensified after the Gulf crisis of 1990–91. On the other hand, the growth of liberal opposition was illustrated in April, when 43 intellectuals and businessmen published an open letter requesting the King to establish national and municipal councils and to curb the excesses of the Islamic religious police, the *mutaween*. At the end of January 1992, however, there were widespread reports of repression of fundamentalist Islamist dissent. On 29 January it was reported that the Minister of Justice had ordered the deposition of Sheikh Abd al-Ubaykan, the president of Riyadh's main court, who had criticized government policies in his Friday sermons and opposed the deployment of US troops on Saudi Arabian soil and the Middle East peace conference, which had begun (in Madrid, Spain) in October 1991. At the end of the month it was reported that 20 Muslim clerics had been arrested in recent weeks, and a preacher dismissed and condemned to 80 lashes for criticizing the Saudi women's association. Meanwhile, in September 1991 it was disclosed that 37,000 of the 541,000 US troops who had been deployed in Saudi Arabia during the Gulf War remained, in a non-military capacity, in the country. However, resistance to closer military co-operation came from both Islamic fundamentalists within the kingdom, and from pro-Israeli elements in the US Congress. Nevertheless, in September President Bush announced that he was authorizing the sale of 72 F-15 aircraft to Saudi Arabia.

In February 1992 15 Iraqi opposition leaders met in Riyadh in an attempt to form a united front to depose Saddam Hussain. The conference, held amid strict security, was interpreted as an indication that Saudi Arabia was prepared to be more forthright in its opposition to the Iraqi President.

A royal decree issued in March 1992 announced the creation of a Consultative Council within six months. Its members were to be selected by the King every four years, but were not to have any legislative powers. Two further decrees provided the framework for the creation of regional authorities and for a 'basic law of government', equivalent to a written constitution.

However, in an interview in a Kuwaiti newspaper, King Fahd stated that Islam favoured 'the consultative system and openness between a ruler and his subjects', rather than free elections. In September Sheikh Muhammad al-Jubair, hitherto Minister of Justice, was appointed Chairman of the Consultative Council.

In November 1992 a major reorganization of the 18-member Council of Ulema was instigated by royal decree. Among 10 new members appointed by the King was the new Minister of Justice, Abdullah ibn Muhammad ash-Sheikh. In a speech in December King Fahd warned the religious community not to use public platforms to discuss secular matters. He also denounced the spread of Islamist fundamentalism, and referred to attempts by 'foreign currents' to destabilize the kingdom. In May 1993 Saudi authorities disbanded the Committee for the Defence of Legitimate Rights (CDLR), established by a group of six prominent Islamic scholars and lawyers, less than two weeks after its formation. The six founders of the committee were also dismissed from their positions, and their spokesman, Muhammad al-Masari, was arrested. In the following month it was reported that an accommodation had been reached between the Saudi authorities and an opposition Shi'a organization, the Reform Movement, whereby members of that organization undertook to cease 'dissident' activities, in return for permission to return to Saudi Arabia and for the release of a number of Shi'a Muslims held in detention there. In April 1994 members of the CDLR, including al-Masari (who had recently been released from custody), relocated their organization to London, United Kingdom.

In August 1993 four royal decrees had defined the membership and administration of the new Consultative Council (Majlis ash-Shoura), and outlined new rules governing the composition and procedure of the Council of Ministers. The Consultative Council was to consist of 60 men selected by King Fahd from the educated and professional classes. It was to meet regularly in full session, and eight committees were to be established to review the activities of Government. The composition of the Council did not lead observers to expect many challenges from it to government policies. In relation to the Council of Ministers, King Fahd set fixed limits for the cabinet's term of office and that of each cabinet member. Many incumbent ministers had occupied the same portfolio since the mid-1970s.

In September 1993 a further decree concerned a provincial system of government, the last of the constitutional reforms promised in March 1992. The decree defined the nature of government for the 13 regions, as well as the rights and responsibilities of their governors, and created councils of officials and citizens for each province to monitor development and to advise the government. Each council was to meet four times a year under the chairmanship of its governor. By the end of 1993 both the Consultative Council and the provincial councils had been opened.

During 1994 the Saudi Government was the subject of a series of accusations of corruption and malpractice, made by foreign journalists and Saudi citizens residing abroad. In June Muhammad al-Khiweli, a high-ranking diplomat at the Saudi mission to the UN headquarters in New York, sought political asylum in the USA, accusing the Saudi Government of human rights violations, terrorism and corruption. In the same month another Saudi diplomat residing in the USA, Ahmad az-Zahrani, levelled similar accusations against the Government and sought asylum in the United Kingdom. The defections caused embarrassment to the US and British Governments, which appeared averse to jeopardizing commercial and political ties with Saudi Arabia. In August, none the less, al-Khiweli was granted asylum in the USA. Meanwhile, az-Zahrani was denied political asylum in the United Kingdom, and in November the British authorities announced their intention to deport him. During 1995 the British Government sought, unsuccessfully, to deport Muhammad al-Masari, although in January 1996 the British authorities ordered his deportation to the Caribbean island of Dominica. The Saudi Government was reported to have demanded his expulsion, and prominent British defence and aerospace companies were believed to have exerted pressure on the Government to concede to Saudi Arabia's demands in order to secure the continuation of lucrative trade agreements with that country. In March the Chief Immigration Adjudicator in the United Kingdom recommended that the Government should

reconsider al-Masari's application for political asylum. In April 1996 al-Masari was granted exceptional leave to remain in the United Kingdom for a period of at least four years, although he was not granted asylum. Meanwhile, reports emerged of a split within the CDLR; in April it was announced that al-Masari would continue to lead the reorganized CDLR, while Dr Saad al-Faqih, the former Secretary-General of the CDLR, would lead the rival Islamic Reform Movement.

In September 1994 more than 1,000 people, including clerics and academics, most of whom had attended a demonstration in Buraidah, 300 km to the north-west of Riyadh, to protest at the arrest of two religious leaders who had allegedly been agitating for the stricter enforcement of *Shari'a* law, were themselves reportedly arrested. The Government subsequently confirmed that 110 arrests had been made, but in mid-October announced that 130 of the 157 people arrested in September had since been released. In early October the King approved the creation of a Higher Council for Islamic Affairs, under the chairmanship of Prince Sultan ibn Abd al-Aziz, the Second Deputy Prime Minister and Minister of Defence and Civil Aviation, in what was widely interpreted as a measure to limit the influence of militant clerics and to diminish the authority of the powerful Council of Ulema.

The Government's plan eventually to replace the expatriate work-force with Saudi nationals was given fresh impetus in late 1994 with the strict enforcement of the kingdom's residency law, which resulted in the expulsion or voluntary repatriation of more than 100,000 illegal immigrants between December 1994 and February 1995. In June 1995 an opposition activist, Abdullah Abd ar-Rahman al-Hudhaif, was sentenced to 20 years' imprisonment for his part in an attack on a security officer and for maintaining links with the CDLR in London. In mid-August, however, al-Hudhaif was reported to have been executed. No explanation was given for the increase to his sentence. A further nine opposition activists were reported to have received prison sentences ranging from three to 18 years, and, according to Amnesty International, as many as 200 'political suspects' remained in detention in the kingdom. The increase in the number of executions in Saudi Arabia during 1995—primarily for those convicted of drugs-smuggling or murder—provoked international criticism. Between January and October 1995 a total of 191 people (including six women) received the death penalty, compared with 53 during the whole of 1994, and 85 in 1993.

In mid-1992 there were signs of a *rapprochement* between Saudi Arabia and Jordan, as well as the PLO; King Fahd sent best wishes to King Hussein for a speedy recovery from an operation in the USA, and the Saudi Arabian Minister of Foreign Affairs received the Palestinian envoy to Riyadh, the first indication of a reconciliation since the outbreak of the Gulf crisis. In January 1994 King Fahd met PLO leader Yasser Arafat for the first time since the Gulf crisis and pledged US $100m. towards the reconstruction of the Gaza Strip and Jericho, the two sites for Palestinian interim self-rule agreed by Israel and the PLO in their 1993 Declaration of Principles. In September 1994 Saudi Arabia, in common with the other GCC members, agreed to a partial removal of the economic boycott of Israel. In April 1995 Saudi Arabia became the first Arab country to recognize passports issued by the Palestinian (National) Authority (PA) for Palestinians in Gaza and Jericho. In June the Council of Ministers approved the import of goods made within the area controlled by the PA. In July 1995 Jordan's Minister of Foreign Affairs met his Saudi counterpart in Riyadh, the first high-level visit made by a Jordanian official since the Gulf crisis.

In September 1992 the Government sent a memorandum to the Government of Yemen in an attempt to expedite demarcation of the Saudi–Yemeni border. Sporadic negotiations, through the medium of a joint border commission, continued into 1993 but stalled in 1994 as a result of renewed civil war in Yemen. It became apparent that the Saudi Government's allegiance lay with the secessionists, and, following their defeat in July 1994, tensions between the two countries increased. Relations deteriorated further in January 1995, when the two countries failed to renew the 1934 Ta'if agreement (renewable every 20 years), which delineated their *de facto* frontier. Following military clashes between the two sides, and intense mediation by Syria, a joint statement was issued in January 1995, in which Saudi Arabia and Yemen undertook to halt all military activity in the border area; it was subsequently agreed to pursue the demarcation of the disputed border area by a joint committee. In late February the Saudi and Yemeni Governments signed a memorandum of understanding that reaffirmed their commitment to the legitimacy of the Ta'if agreement and provided for the establishment of six joint committees to delineate the land and sea borders and to develop economic and commercial ties. In March the joint Saudi-Yemeni military committee, also established by the memorandum, held its first meeting in Riyadh. In June President Saleh of Yemen visited the kingdom, accompanied by a high-ranking delegation. This was the first official Yemeni visit since February 1990. At the end of September 1992 Qatar accused a Saudi military force of attacking a border post at al-Khofous, killing two soldiers and capturing a third. In October Qatar suspended the 1965 border agreement with Saudi Arabia, and in the same month it was reported that Qatar was to withdraw its contingent of 200 troops from the GCC 'Peninsula Shield' force, stationed in Kuwait. However, in late December 1992, following mediation by President Hosni Mubarak of Egypt, the Qatari Amir, Sheikh Khalifa, signed an agreement with King Fahd to establish a committee which was to demarcate the border between the two states. In late November 1994 Qatar boycotted a GCC ministerial session in Riyadh, in protest at alleged armed incidents on the Saudi–Qatari border earlier in that year; the Saudi Government, however, denied the allegations. In August 1995, following the coup in Qatar, the new Amir, Sheikh Hamad, visited Saudi Arabia to hold talks with King Fahd. Some observers argued that the visit, the Amir's first trip abroad since assuming power, demonstrated Sheikh Hamad's willingness to resume good relations with the kingdom.

In July 1995 officials from Saudi Arabia and Oman signed documents to demarcate their joint borders. In the same month it was reported that Saudi Arabia and Kuwait had made progress on the demarcation of their mutual sea border.

POLITICAL DEVELOPMENTS SINCE 1995

In August 1995 King Fahd announced the most far-reaching reshuffle of the Council of Ministers for two decades, although no changes were made to the portfolios held by members of the royal family. The key portfolios of finance and national economy and of petroleum and mineral resources were allocated to younger, though highly experienced, officials. Dr Sulaiman Abd al-Aziz as-Sulaim, hitherto Minister of Commerce, replaced Sheikh Muhammad Ali Aba al-Khail (who had managed the kingdom's finances for 20 years) as Minister of Finance and National Economy. Sheikh Hisham Mohi ad-Din Nazer was replaced as Minister of Petroleum and Mineral Resources by Ali ibn Ibrahim an-Nuaimi, hitherto President of the government-controlled oil company, Saudi Aramco. Nevertheless, the portfolio changes were not expected to result in any major alterations to the kingdom's strategic policies. Some observers regarded the appointment of a new, Western-educated, Minister of Information, Dr Fouad ibn Abd as-Salam ibn Muhammad Farsi, as more significant, possibly signalling the imminent liberalization of Saudi Arabia's press regulations. In October the new Minister of Finance and National Economy resigned, citing ill health; he was replaced by an experienced government official, Dr Abd al-Aziz al-Abdullah al-Khuwaiter, hitherto Minister of State and Minister of Education, Agriculture and Water, who was, in turn, replaced by Dr Ibrahim Abd al-Aziz al-Assaf (hitherto Minister of State) in January 1996.

In early July 1997 King Fahd issued a decree increasing the membership of the Consultative Council from 60 to 90 when it began its second term later that month. Following the expiry of an amnesty for illegal immigrants in mid-October, the Government announced that more than 500,000 immigrant workers without valid documentation had left the country, while a further 300,000 had obtained the necessary work permits.

In November 1995 a car bomb exploded outside the offices of the Saudi Arabia National Guard in Riyadh, which was being used temporarily by US civilian contractors to train Saudi personnel. Seven foreign nationals (including five US citizens) were killed as a result of the explosion, and a further 60 were injured. Responsibility for the bomb was claimed by several organizations, including the Islamic Movement for Change,

which earlier in the year had warned that it would initiate attacks if non-Muslim Western forces did not withdraw from the Gulf region. In April 1996 four Saudi nationals were arrested in connection with the attack; in their confessions they claimed to have been influenced by Islamist groups outside the kingdom. The accused were executed at the end of the following month, despite anonymous threats of retaliation if the sentences were carried out. According to Amnesty International, their trial had been conducted in secret and they had been denied access to lawyers. The reliability of their confessions was also questioned. Amnesty International issued a report in 1997 in which the organization condemned the Saudi justice system as 'blatantly unfair', denouncing a lack of judicial supervision which permitted the widespread use of torture, amputation and execution.

In late June 1996 19 US personnel were killed, and as many as 400 others (including 147 Saudi, 118 Bangladeshi and 109 US citizens) were injured, when an explosive device attached to a petroleum tanker was detonated outside a military housing complex in al-Khobar, near Dhahran. Saudi officials pledged increased security measures in the kingdom, and offered a substantial reward for information leading to the arrest and prosecution of those responsible for the explosion (believed to be Islamist militants). Earlier in the year US officials had reportedly been critical of the Saudi authorities' investigation of the November 1995 bomb explosion, and of the swift execution of the alleged perpetrators. It was reported in early November 1996 that some 40 Saudis were being held on suspicion of involvement in the bombing. Scant information regarding the Saudi authorities' investigation into the attack emerged in late 1996, prompting speculation that Saudi Shi'a groups with possible links to Iran were being held responsible for the atrocity, rather than the same Sunni extremist factions that were widely believed to have been responsible for the November 1995 car bomb (see above).

Saudi-US relations had been placed under increasing strain as a result of the bomb attack and subsequent investigation. However, in June 1997 a Saudi citizen, Hani Abd ar-Rahim as-Sayegh, was deported from Canada to the USA to face charges in connection with the June 1996 bombing. Suspicions of Iranian involvement in the explosion were repeatedly denied by Iran. In September, however, the USA announced that there was insufficient evidence to secure a conviction, and as-Sayegh would thus not be tried in the USA. Saudi Arabia subsequently applied for as-Sayegh's extradition; in October 1999, following the announcement by the Saudi Arabian Minister of the Interior that the country's security forces possessed information regarding as-Sayegh's involvement in the bombing, as-Sayegh was extradited to Saudi Arabia. In May 1998 Saudi Arabia had declared that the bombing had been perpetrated by Saudi Arabians acting independently, although the USA continued to investigate alleged Iranian involvement. Several Saudi nationals were arrested in January 2001 in connection with the bombing. In June US investigators indicted 14 individuals on charges relating to the explosion, although three of them remained at large in June 2002 when the Saudi authorities announced that sentences had been passed on a number of the detainees. Meanwhile, as-Sayegh remained in custody in Saudi Arabia.

Sheikh Abd al-Aziz ibn Baz, who had been appointed Grand Mufti in 1993, died in May 1999; he was succeeded as Grand Mufti by Sheikh Abd al-Aziz ibn Abdullah ash-Sheikh. In June 1999 a minor cabinet reorganization was effected in which four new members were appointed to the Council of Ministers; Muhammad ibn Ali al-Fayez was also appointed to the newly-created post of Minister of the Civil Service. In July four new appointments were made to the Majlis to replace those who had joined the Council of Ministers.

In November 1999 the Government announced that it planned to introduce independent personal identification cards for women for the first time. However, Saudi Arabia continued to be the subject of heavy criticism from international human rights groups. Amnesty International accused the Saudi authorities of arresting scores of people as suspected political or religious opponents during 1999, including so-called Arab Afghan veterans and Shi'a and Sunni Muslim critics. In November, a female relative of the exiled Muhammad al-Masari, on a visit from the United Kingdom, was arrested and detained for a month before being released without charge. Allegations of torture and ill-treatment of detainees continued, and at least 29 people were reported to have been executed during 1999 after trials which, according to Amnesty International, fell far short of international standards. The Government repudiated the allegations, and issued an invitation to the Special Rapporteur of the UN Commission on Human Rights on the independence of judges and lawyers to visit the country in order to study the Saudi justice system, although no date was set for such a visit.

In January 2000 a Supreme Petroleum and Minerals Council was established by royal decree, and in April the Cabinet approved broad guide-lines for the issuing of tourist visas; a supreme commission to promote tourism within the kingdom was subsequently established. Also in April the Government had approved a new and more liberal foreign investment law and the creation of a General Investment Authority as part of its efforts to open up the economy and attain membership of the World Trade Organization. In May it announced that government ministers would no longer be permitted to hold company positions while in office, with the exception of those in the state-owned Saudi Aramco.

In June 2000 the Government announced the establishment of a new Council of the Royal Family, to be headed by Crown Prince Abdullah. Although no reasons for the establishment of this new body were given, observers suggested that it reflected a view that more formal structures for consultation were required within a royal family that now included more than 4,000 princes. The new Council met for the first time in August. In the same month the Government continued its efforts to improve its reputation on human rights issues by announcing that it would sign the UN Convention on the Elimination of All Forms of Discrimination against Women. However, the impact of this announcement was muted by its insistence that it would enter reservations regarding any section of the Convention that it deemed to violate *Shari'a* (Islamic) law. Observers claimed that there was a link between this announcement and the appointment of a Saudi woman, Thuraya Ahmad Obeid, to the post of Director of the UN Fund for Population Activities in October. In the same month two Saudi nationals hijacked a Saudi Arabian Airlines passenger flight, *en route* from Jeddah to the United Kingdom, reportedly to protest against human rights abuses in Saudi Arabia and the presence of US and British troops on Saudi territory. The aircraft eventually landed in the Iraqi capital, Baghdad, and the hijackers were taken into custody by the Iraqi authorities. The Iraqi authorities refused extradition requests from Saudi Arabia and the Saudi authorities subsequently decided not to pursue the matter.

In December 2000 Saudi Arabia agreed to allow former Pakistani Prime Minister Nawaz Sharif to reside in the country following his expulsion by Pakistan's military regime. In the same month a British citizen was seriously injured by a bomb blast in Riyadh and a US national was arrested in connection with other recent explosions that had killed one Briton and injured three others. The authorities attributed this wave of bomb explosions to criminal or personal rivalries rather than to the activities of militant Islamic groups. In February 2001 three expatriates (a Briton, a Canadian and a Belgian) were detained by the Saudi authorities in connection with the attacks. In August three more expatriates (all Britons) were detained and their alleged confessions were broadcast on Saudi television. (In February 2002 it was alleged by the families of four of the detainees that the suspects had been tortured in the course of their interrogation by the security services; however, in April it emerged that three Britons had been sentenced, by a secret court in a preliminary judgment in October 2001 and February 2002, to 18 years' imprisonment, and there was an unconfirmed report that another Briton and a Canadian had been sentenced to death—a final verdict was still pending and the suspects, who had since retracted their 'confessions' had lodged numerous appeals against the verdicts.)

In early March 2001 35 pilgrims died and 160 others were injured in a stampede at Jumarat Bridge, near Mecca. The authorities announced that 1.4m. pilgrims had attended that year's *Hajj*.

In June 2001 King Fahd inaugurated the third term of the Consultative Council (Majlis ash-Shoura). A government decree

further increased its size from 90 to 120 members. In September King Fahd appointed Prince Nawaf bin Abd al-Aziz to replace Prince Turki al-Faisal bin Abd al-Aziz as the head of the intelligence services. Prince Nawaf was known to be a close associate of Crown Prince Abdullah and there was speculation that his appointment was the result of a power-struggle within the Saudi royal family.

DIPLOMATIC DEVELOPMENTS SINCE 1995

The normalization of relations which had been agreed between Saudi Arabia and Jordan got under way in November 1995 with the appointment of a Saudi ambassador to Jordan. Relations were further consolidated in February and August 1996 when King Hussein of Jordan met Crown Prince Abdullah in Saudi Arabia.

Tensions persisted between Saudi Arabia and Yemen over the demarcation of the border between the two countries. In December 1995 both countries denied that there had been further military clashes on the land border. Meetings of the joint committees continued into 1996, and in July the two countries signed a border security agreement. Despite further reported tensions, negotiations on border demarcation continued in 1997. In November, however, armed clashes on the border resulted in the deaths of three Saudis and one Yemeni border guard. In that month it was reported that Saudi Arabia had sent a memorandum to the UN stating that it did not recognize the 1992 border agreement between Yemen and Oman and claiming that parts of the area concerned were Saudi Arabian territory. The Saudi objection to the agreement was widely believed to be related to its attempts to gain land access to the Arabian Sea, via a corridor between Yemen and Oman, which it had thus far been denied in its negotiations with Yemen. In July Yemen submitted a memorandum to the Arab League refuting the Saudi claim to the land and stating that the Saudi protests contravened the Ta'if agreement signed by that country. During June and July 1998 there were further land and sea clashes around a group of Red Sea islands in the disputed maritime border region. In July it was reported that three armed Yemenis had been killed on the island of Duwaima (area 6 sq km), as a result of an exchange of gunfire with a Saudi border patrol. According to the Saudi authorities, the patrol had acted in self-defence against the men, who were part of a small military presence that Yemen had established on the island during June and early July. The Saudi Government maintained, moreover, that some three-quarters of the island was marked as Saudi territory under the terms of the Ta'if agreement. In late July the Saudi Minister of Foreign Affairs visited his Yemeni counterpart to discuss the escalation of hostilities. A joint military committee meeting was convened in early August 1998, but limited significant progress was made. Relations between Saudi Arabia and Qatar over the demarcation of their mutual border were again strained in December 1995 when Qatar boycotted the closing session of the annual GCC summit, in protest at the selection of a Saudi national as the new GCC Secretary-General (in preference to a Qatari candidate). In January 1996, in apparent retaliation, Crown Prince Abdullah received Qatar's deposed Amir in Riyadh. None the less, in March Qatar formally announced its acceptance of the new GCC Secretary-General, and in the following month Qatar and Saudi Arabia agreed to accelerate the completion of their border demarcation (initially scheduled for the end of 1994).

Relations with Iran, which were strained at the beginning of 1997 owing to allegations of Iranian involvement in the al-Khobar bombing, subsequently improved, and by mid-1997 it was announced that a Saudi-Iranian summit was planned for later in the year. In September Iran Air resumed flights to Saudi Arabia for the first time since the 1979 revolution. The installation of the new Government of President Sayed Muhammad Khatami in Iran, in August 1997, facilitated further *rapprochement*; the new Minister of Foreign Affairs, Kamal Kharrazi, toured Saudi Arabia and other GCC states in November, and Crown Prince Abdullah attended the Conference of Heads of State of the OIC in Tehran in December. An Iranian delegation, led by former President Ali Akbar Hashemi Rafsanjani, began a 10-day visit to Saudi Arabia in late February 1998. The formation of a joint ministerial committee for bilateral relations was announced at the end of the visit. Some tensions remained, however, notably with regard to Saudi Arabia's insistence that there should be no political rallies as part of the *Hajj*: Iran had urged its pilgrims to protest against the USA and Israel. In May, in what was widely seen as an attempt to maintain good relations with Iran, the Minister of the Interior stated that the Saudi Government was satisfied that the al-Khobar bombing had been carried out by Saudi nationals with no foreign assistance.

In late 1997, as tensions mounted between the Iraqi authorities and weapons inspectors of the UN Special Commission (UNSCOM), Saudi Arabia firmly advocated a diplomatic solution. In February 1998 Saudi Arabia stated that it would not allow the USA to use Saudi territory as a base for air-strikes against Iraq, and reiterated its desire for a diplomatic solution. As relations deteriorated once again between Iraq and UNSCOM in late 1998 Saudi Arabia again asserted that it would not allow its territory to be used as a base for US-led air-strikes against Iraq, although it was later claimed that discreet support had been given which included the use of its bases. Iraqi allegations, in February 1999, that Saudi pilots had taken part in bombing raids over Iraq were vehemently denied by the Saudi authorities.

Relations with Afghanistan deteriorated during 1998, and in September Saudi Arabia withdrew its chargé d'affaires from that country and asked the Afghan chargé d'affaires to leave Saudi Arabia. No official reason was given, but it was widely attributed to the presence in Afghanistan of the exiled Saudi-born dissident, Osama bin Laden, who was held responsible for the bombing of two US embassies in Africa in August. Saudi Arabia had previously enjoyed good relations with Afghanistan, and was one of only three states to have recognized the Taliban Government in that country. In October Saudi Arabia was reported to have requested bin Laden's extradition from Afghanistan, although the request was denied.

Crown Prince Abdullah travelled widely abroad in 1998–99, in what was generally perceived as an effort to raise his international profile as King Fahd's health deteriorated.

In March 1999 Saudi Arabia held talks with Iran in an effort to mediate in its dispute with the UAE over the Tunb islands. Despite tensions between the GCC and Iran in that month, following a statement by the GCC which condemned both Iran's recent military exercises near the islands and its claim to them, and emphasized UAE sovereignty over the islands, bilateral relations continued to improve, and in May the Iranian President made an official visit to Saudi Arabia; Khatami was the first Iranian Head of State to visit Saudi Arabia since the Revolution. In July 2000 the two Governments announced that they were close to signing a security agreement, which aimed to combat crime, terrorism and drugs-trafficking. Saudi Arabia emphasized that this was not a defence pact. The agreement was finally signed in April 2001 during a visit to Tehran by the Saudi Minister of the Interior, Prince Nayef bin Abd al-Aziz. The agreement pointedly excluded arrangements for extradition, despite US claims that Iran might have been involved in the 1996 al-Khobar bombing.

Relations between Saudi Arabia and the UAE deteriorated as a result of the *rapprochement* with Iran (although Saudi Arabia insisted that improved relations with Iran would not be achieved at the expense of its relations with any other country) and in March 1999 the UAE boycotted a meeting of GCC ministers responsible for petroleum production in protest at Saudi exploration of an oilfield in disputed territory prior to an agreement being reached.

From mid-1999 some success appeared to have been achieved in the diplomatic efforts to resolve border disputes between Saudi Arabia and its neighbours. In June officials from Saudi Arabia and Qatar met in Riyadh to sign the final maps demarcating their joint border. In March 2001 the two countries signed what was described as a final agreement on the demarcation of their joint border. The Saudi and Yemeni Ministers of Foreign Affairs signed a final agreement on the demarcation of their mutual land and maritime borders in June 2000. The agreement incorporated the 1995 Memorandum of Understanding and the 1934 Treaty of Ta'if (with minor amendments), and included a mutual pledge to end support for opposition groups. However, sections of the eastern border reportedly remained undefined,

and in August three Saudi border guards and one Yemeni soldier died in clashes reported in the border area. In the following month the Saudi Council of Ministers approved an agreement ending the long-running maritime border dispute with Kuwait. Final maps delineating that border were signed by officials from both sides in January 2001. In June 2001 the Saudi-Yemen Co-ordination Council was reconvened for the first time since the Gulf War.

During 2000 and into 2001 Saudi Arabia, allied with Kuwait, continued to oppose wider Arab initiatives to improve relations with Iraq. Saudi Arabia also supported the maintenance of full UN sanctions against Iraq. The Government did not condemn major US and British-led air-strikes on Iraq in August 2000 and February 2001, and dismissed Iraqi calls for an emergency summit meeting of Gulf states following the first wave of attacks. Iraq repeated its accusation that Saudi Arabia's policy on Iraq was being dictated by the USA. In June 2001 Saudi Arabia accused Iraq of launching 11 raids on Saudi border posts during the preceding months. Iraq denied the allegations.

Saudi Arabia played a prominent role in the decision taken at the 21st GCC summit in December 2000 to increase the strength of the GCC's RDF to 22,000 personnel. A US $70m. telecommunications project to link the military headquarters of all six members of the GCC was also agreed at the summit.

In a sign of an improvement in relations with Libya, in October 2000 Muammar al-Qaddafi made his first visit to Riyadh for 20 years. No details were given of the agenda for what both sides called 'consultations'.

The collapse of the Middle East peace process and the eruption of the al-Aqsa *intifada* by the Palestinians from late September 2000 led to a more active Saudi role in wider Arab diplomatic initiatives. Saudi Arabia's priority was to support a unified Arab effort to revive the peace process while displaying solidarity with the Palestinians. Saudi Arabia opposed calls for all Arab states to terminate diplomatic relations with Israel. In October 2000 Crown Prince Abdullah visited wounded Palestinians being treated in Saudi hospitals and announced that King Fahd had personally donated US $8m. to 'the heroes of the al-Aqsa *intifada*'. By the end of that month a public fund-raising campaign had amassed more than $40m. In November 2000 Saudi Arabia threatened to pull out of a scheduled OIC summit in Qatar because Qatar had refused to close the Israeli trade office in the capital, Doha. The threat was withdrawn following the formal closure of the office. At the summit meeting of the Arab League held in Amman in March 2001 Saudi Arabia joined with other states in agreeing to send emergency aid to the Palestinians and in condemning the USA's failure to support the dispatch of a UN-sponsored international observer force to Israel and the Palestinian territories. It also endorsed calls for senior Israeli public figures to face an international war crimes tribunal and for a feasibility study to be initiated regarding a revival of the Arab boycott of Israel.

In April 2001 Saudi Arabia gave its support to Egyptian-Jordanian proposals to end the violence and revive 'final status' talks. At the same time the Government urged the new US Administration of President George W. Bush to become more engaged in the peace process. In June Saudi Arabia indicated its support for the recommendations of the Mitchell Report on the causes of the violence between Israel and the Palestinians. Saudi displeasure at US disengagement was demonstrated by the refusal of Crown Prince Abdullah to accept invitations to visit Washington, DC, for a meeting with President Bush. Tensions between Saudi Arabia and the USA were exacerbated in June 2001 when the US authorities issued indictments against 13 Saudi nationals and one Lebanese national for complicity in the 1996 al-Khobar bombing. The Saudi authorities complained of lack of consultation and insisted that any trials should take place in Saudi Arabia.

During 2001 a number of the younger members of the Saudi royal family, most notably Prince Talal ibn Abd al-Aziz, openly expressed support for the creation of an elected assembly in Saudi Arabia. Certainly, there was considerable Saudi interest in the democratic experiment underway in Bahrain during 2001 (see chapter on Bahrain), but there were few signs that similar moves were being considered seriously within the kingdom itself.

DOMESTIC DEVELOPMENTS AFTER 11 SEPTEMBER 2001

Following the terrorist attacks on New York and Washington, DC, on 11 September 2001, in which up to 15 Saudi nationals were believed to have been involved, the authorities declared their determination to identify and apprehend sympathizers of Osama bin Laden (whose al-Qa'ida terrorist network was held by the USA to be principally responsible for the attacks) within Saudi Arabia and subsequently took action to 'freeze' their financial assets. An undisclosed number of people were detained, and there were reports that the assets of 66 people and organizations named by the US authorities as suspected sponsors of terrorism had been 'frozen' by the end of October. More than 40 Saudi nationals were detained in the USA following the attacks, including two members of the royal family, although they were subsequently released. There was considerable media speculation in the West that tensions between the two countries might jeopardize the continued existence of US military bases on Saudi soil. (In January 2002 the Saudi Government issued an official denial that it was to request that all US military forces leave the country.) No missions were flown from US bases in Saudi Arabia during the US-led military campaign against the Taliban regime in Afghanistan, which began in October, although command-and-control facilities at Prince Sultan airbase were utilized. A variety of dissident clerics within Saudi Arabia issued fatwas threatening the excommunication of the royal family should it support the US-led offensive. In December the authorities requested that Saudi nationals detained by US military personnel following the overthrow of the Taliban regime (some of whom were subsequently transferred with other foreign nationals to the US military base at Guantánamo Bay, Cuba) be repatriated for trial. These requests were denied by the US authorities, but in June 2002 a Saudi delegation of interior and foreign ministry officials was reported to have been allowed access to the Saudi prisoners (thought to number more than 100). In January 2002 it was announced that the Saudi Arabian Monetary Agency had been tasked with drafting legislation to combat the 'laundering' of illicit funds through the banking system. In March the Minister of the Interior, Prince Nayef ibn Abd al-Aziz, confirmed that the Government had co-operated with US efforts to 'freeze' the assets overseas of the Somali and Bosnian branches of a major Riyadh-based Islamic charity, the al-Haramain Charitable Foundation, because of its alleged links to al-Qa'ida. In mid-June the Saudi security services announced that seven Saudis and one Sudanese national (all believed to be members of al-Qa'ida) had been arrested several months earlier, following an unsuccessful missile attack on the Prince Sultan airbase; the men remained in detention. The announcement was made only days before a British banker was killed by a car bomb near his home in Riyadh. At the end of June an attempt on the lives of an American couple working in Riyadh, using an almost identical explosive device, was narrowly prevented. In late September a German citizen was killed in a car bomb attack in the Saudi capital. These incidents heightened international concerns about the hidden extent of militant Islamist activity within the kingdom.

In March 2002, at least 14 schoolgirls died in a fire in Mecca after the religious police reportedly stopped them from fleeing a blazing school building because they were improperly dressed. The case provoked unprecedented criticism of the religious police in the Saudi media, and the department responsible for female education (whose director was dismissed) was subsequently merged with the Ministry of Education.

It was announced in mid-September 2002 that the Ministry of Agriculture and Water had been divided into two ministries; the former Saudi ambassador to the United Kingdom, Ghazi al-Gosaibi, was named as the new Minister of Water.

FOREIGN POLICY AFTER 11 SEPTEMBER 2001

Under evident pressure from the USA, Saudi Arabia severed diplomatic relations with the Taliban regime in Afghanistan in late September 2001, in response to the suicide attacks on New York and Washington, DC, on 11 September. Although the USA's prime suspect in the attacks, the Afghan-based Osama bin Laden, was born to a wealthy Saudi Arabian family, the Saudi authorities emphasized that bin Laden had long been deprived of any connections with his country of birth. Crown

Prince Abdullah visited Washington shortly after the attacks, and conveyed to the US Secretary of State, Colin Powell, the support of the Saudi people for efforts to eliminate terrorism. However, Saudi Arabia warned against any 'vengeful' response to the atrocities, and in common with the other Arab states attempted to influence the USA to avoid any action through its 'war against terror' that might lead to an escalation of the conflict between Israel and the Palestinians. The Saudi Government made it clear that it would not participate in the proposed military action against Afghanistan. When the US-led coalition embarked on a military intervention to overthrow the Taliban regime in Afghanistan in October, the Saudi authorities accepted the legitimacy of military action but opposed the bombing of civilians, calling on Osama bin Laden and Taliban leader Mullah Omar to surrender and stand trial. In January 2002 Saudi Arabia was one of four chairing countries at an international donors' conference on Afghanistan held in Tokyo, Japan. The Saudi Government announced that it would provide up to US $220m. in aid to Afghanistan during 2002–05.

During October and November 2001, Saudi Arabia was the subject of considerable criticism in the US media for its alleged complicity in the emergence of global Islamist terror networks, but the ruling family vigorously defended the country's reputation and urged the US authorities to play a more active role in the conflict between Israel and the Palestinians. Media representations of Saudi Arabia were gradually modified as the US Administration sought to ensure that its 'war against terror' was not interpreted as a 'war of civilizations'. However, relations between the two countries were placed under renewed strain in August 2002 after a group representing 900 relatives of victims of the September 2001 attacks filed a civil suit in Washington, DC, against senior Saudi ministers and institutions (and the Government of Sudan) seeking compensation amounting to US $1,000,000m. for their alleged funding of al-Qa'ida activities. Saudi investors reacted angrily to the suit, threatening in response to withdraw from the USA some $750,000m. in Saudi investments.

The Saudi Government welcomed President Bush's announcement in November 2001 that the USA supported the creation of a Palestinian state and would be launching a new diplomatic initiative to end the violence between Israelis and Palestinians. However, following the successful overthrow of the Taliban regime in late 2001, Saudi Arabia made clear its opposition to any moves to extend the 'war against terror' to Iraq. Indeed, Saudi Arabia, encouraged by the mediation of the Arab League, was indicating by the beginning of 2002 that it was ready for cautious *rapprochement* with Iraq.

The introduction of the idea of *rapprochement* with Iraq was carefully synchronized with the launch of a new peace proposal for Israel and the Palestinians, formulated by Crown Prince Abdullah. While concerned to maintain its pro-Palestinian credentials—by playing an active role in support of a revived Arab economic boycott of Israel, for example—the Saudi Government also apparently saw the advantage of a diplomatic initiative that might help to improve its troubled relations with the USA. In an interview with a US newspaper in mid-February 2002 Crown Prince Abdullah described a proposal in which Arab relations with Israel were fully 'normalized' in exchange for the creation of a Palestinian state based on pre-1967 borders. Although the plan was significantly lacking in detail, the USA and European countries seized on the possibilities that it presented for a return to political negotiations. The proposal was welcomed by the Palestinian leadership, and Israel's response was cautiously positive. In the weeks preceding the Arab League summit meeting held in Beirut, Lebanon, on 27–28 March there were intense diplomatic efforts to consolidate Arab support for the proposals. (In order to secure the agreement of Lebanon and Syria, Crown Prince Abdullah agreed to a reformulation whereby 'normal relations' would follow a 'comprehensive peace', explicitly involving Israeli withdrawal from the Golan Heights and Shebaa Farms; reference to a 'just solution' to the Palestinian right of return in accordance with UN General Assembly Resolution 194 was also added.) The plan received UN support on 12 March in Security Council Resolution 1397 (see Documents on Palestine, p. 98), in which the Security Council explicitly endorsed the creation of a Palestinian state for the first time.

Saudi insistence that Yasser Arafat should be present at the Arab League summit or the peace proposals would not be formally endorsed was ultimately abandoned following US and European pressure, and the plan was unanimously approved in Beirut. The summit also declared firm opposition to any idea of further allied military action against Iraq. (Crown Prince Abdullah and the Vice-President of Iraq's Revolutionary Command Council, Izzat Ibrahim, publicly embraced at the summit.) Crown Prince Abdullah also stated that Saudi Arabia was opposed to the maintenance of UN sanctions against Iraq and reiterated its refusal to allow the use of US military bases for allied air-strikes against Iraq. In June 2002 it was reported that the Arar border crossing from Saudi Arabia to Iraq was to be reopened within four weeks, providing a fifth land route for Iraqi trade under the UN oil-for-food arrangement. In the same month it was reported that the Saudi authorities were considering the negotiation of a free-trade agreement with Iraq.

However, this moment of Saudi political pre-eminence in the Arab world was short-lived. The uncompromising Israeli military intervention in the West Bank from late March 2002, following an escalation in the number and frequency of Palestinian suicide attacks on Israeli civilians underlined the absence of short-term proposals for ending the violence in the Saudi peace plan. Both Syria and Egypt displayed a lack of enthusiasm for the plan, despite having endorsed it formally. From the beginning of April the Saudi peace plan became incorporated into tentative US proposals for an international peace conference on the Middle East. Late in the month Crown Prince Abdullah met President Bush in Washington, DC, and urged the USA to do more to end the Israeli reoccupation of the West Bank. However, the Saudi Government was also increasingly critical of the Palestinian 'suicide' attacks, and during a meeting between Crown Prince Abdullah and Presidents Hosni Mubarak

and Bashar al-Assad in Egypt, in mid-May, the participants rejected 'all forms of violence'. In June President Mubarak, who had been displeased by the way in which the Saudi plan had displaced Egypt from its traditional role as leading Arab interlocutor between Israel and the Palestinians (he did not attend the Beirut summit in person), put forward fresh peace proposals of his own. The importance and relevance of the Saudi plan continued to diminish, and there was little sign of concerted activity by the follow-up committee established at the Beirut summit. Saudi Arabia responded warily to President Bush's 'landmark speech' on the Middle East peace process in late-June, welcoming Bush's acceptance of the principle of Palestinian statehood but criticizing his insistence on prior reform of Palestinian institutions and his effective repudiation of Yasser Arafat as a negotiating partner. Moreover, in September 2002, following intense pressure from the US and British Governments, the Saudi Minister of Foreign Affairs conceded that the Saudi authorities might be prepared to approve the use of military bases in Saudi Arabia for a future US-led attack on Iraq, if the Iraqi authorities were to continue to reject UN resolutions demanding the unconditional return of weapons inspectors to Iraq, and if such a military undertaking were to be conducted under UN auspices.

At the GCC summit convened in Muscat, Oman, in late December 2001, Saudi Arabia was instrumental in concluding agreements to establish a Supreme Joint Defence Council and to work to achieve monetary union and a single GCC Council by 2010. Crown Prince Abdullah also acknowledged that the GCC had failed to fulfil expectations since its creation in 1981.

Relations between Saudi Arabia and Iran, which have improved considerably since 1997, were further strengthened following the 11 September 2001 terrorist attacks on New York and Washington, DC, as the two countries co-operated in seeking to oppose the emergence of anti-Islamic sentiment in the West.

Economy

Revised for this edition by the Editorial staff

The economy of Saudi Arabia is dominated by petroleum, of which the country is by far the largest producer within the Organization of the Petroleum Exporting Countries (OPEC). Saudi Arabia has received massive revenues from petroleum exports (particularly since the dramatic increase in international petroleum prices in 1973–74), which it has used, in part, to finance an ambitious programme of infrastructural development and modernization, as well as far-reaching programmes for health, social and educational purposes. Substantial budgetary allocations have also been made to the country's armed forces and to the purchase of sophisticated weaponry from abroad. Public sector employment and pay expanded rapidly and heavy consumer and producer subsidies were introduced. The rapid increase in the levels of government and private expenditure absorbed the budget and foreign-exchange surpluses, and led to substantial deficits and increased borrowing since the late 1980s. Nevertheless, major sectors of the economy and the population's standard of living remain heavily dependent upon government subsidies, and there continues to be a need for reform, which is most strongly advocated during periods of depressed international petroleum prices. Conservative and strictly Islamic in orientation, the Saudi ruling family has consistently favoured a pro-Western, market-orientated economic strategy and has placed great reliance on Western and Japanese expertise for the development of the country's petroleum and other sectors. There remains a substantial expatriate contribution to the management of various economic sectors, although Saudi nationals have come increasingly to the fore, especially in the petroleum and gas industries. Throughout the economy, expatriates form the majority of the work-force. Emphasis has been placed, under recent development plans, on the promotion of 'downstream' oil industries, such as refining and petroleum derivatives, and progress has also been made in developing the country's non-oil industries.

Whereas in the 1970s and early 1980s Saudi Arabia's exports consisted almost entirely of petroleum, by the late 1980s non-oil exports represented more than 10% of total value. A similar pattern was apparent in the structure of gross domestic product (GDP), enhanced by a sharp fall in petroleum production in the mid-1980s. Having achieved an average annual growth rate of 10.6% in the period 1968–80, Saudi Arabia's GDP declined, in real terms, at an average rate of 1.2% per year over the decade 1980–90, largely because petroleum output was reduced from a peak of almost 10m. barrels per day (b/d) in 1980 to 3.6m. b/d in 1985 (see Petroleum, below). Although production rose to more than 5m. b/d in 1988 and 1989, depressed international prices resulted in substantially reduced revenues, with adverse consequences for the current account and national budget, both of which moved into deficit. The situation was transformed by the Gulf crisis of 1990–91, as a result of which Saudi Arabia entered a new period of economic growth. The cost of the conflict to the Saudi Government was substantial, being estimated at between US $50,000m. and $65,000m., with the result that the current-account and budget deficits rose sharply in 1990–91. However, partly to compensate for the loss of Iraqi supplies, Saudi Arabia was able to increase its petroleum production to more than 8m. b/d, as international petroleum prices rose sharply because of the crisis. Overall GDP exceeded $100,000m. in 1990, for the first time since 1983, and stood at $108,640m. in 1991. The growth rate of GDP, in real terms, was estimated to be around 1% in 1992. GDP declined by 0.6% in 1993, but increased again by 0.5% in 1994, compared with 10.8% in 1990 and 9.8% in 1991. GDP increased, in real terms, by an annual average of 2.0% in 1990–2000. The Government reactivated a range of major projects under the 1990–95 Five-Year Plan, aiming, in particular, at industrial diversification and import substitution. According to World Bank figures, Saudi Arabia's gross national product (GNP) per head declined at an average annual rate of 3.4%, in real terms, over the period 1980–91 (when the population increased by an estimated 4.6% per year). During 1990–99, it was estimated, GNP per head declined, in real terms, at an average rate of 1.4% per year. During 1990–2000 the population increased by an annual average of 2.7%. In 1999 GNP was estimated at $139,365m., equivalent to $6,900 per head. However, in 1998 Saudi Arabia's continued dependence on petroleum was again highlighted. Declining oil prices led to a sharp decrease in revenues and GDP at current prices declined by 11.5%. The recovery of petroleum prices from the second half of 1999 again transformed short-term Saudi economic prospects. Although real GDP declined by 0.8% in 1999, there were increases of 4.9% in 2000 and 1.2% in 2001. The impact of these increases on economic activity, employment and living standards will only be reflected through the Government's responses to the new economic opportunities, and it is likely that the previous accumulation of public debt will dictate initial caution in increasing government expenditure.

In 1993 and 1994 the Saudi Government came under increasing pressure to improve the public finances; many years of deficit budgeting having helped to raise the Government's net outstanding domestic debt to an estimated 318,000m. riyals (equivalent to about 76% of annual GDP) in the latter year. An attempt to achieve a balanced budget in 1994 was unsuccessful, despite reductions in planned spending and lengthy delays in payments to contractors. The 1995 budget, introduced at the start of the year, combined further spending cuts with an unprecedented initiative to increase domestic revenues through the imposition of higher charges for a range of state-subsidized goods and services. This tightening of fiscal discipline coincided with favourable external factors in 1995 (notably a year-on-year rise of about 20% in the average oil export price at a time of strong growth in non-oil exports). In the 1996 budget total expenditure was 'frozen' at the 1995 level, while total revenue was expected to fall by nearly 3% if oil export prices declined as forecast. However, oil prices increased in 1996 to their highest average levels since 1990, with the result that total government revenue exceeded the budget forecast by some US $12,100m. (34.6%). Most of the additional revenue was used to fund increased spending, and some $5,900m. of payments arrears to domestic creditors were settled by the Government. Saudi Arabia's estimated GDP in 1996 was $136,000m., and the Ministry of Finance and National Economy estimated the rate of real GDP growth to be 5% in that year, although IMF estimates were lower, at 1.4%. By 1995 domestic debt had reached 405,000m. riyals (86% of GDP), and by 1998 the Government's domestic debt was equivalent to 115.7% of GDP. However, by 2000 national debt was estimated to account for 85%–90% of GDP.

In sharp contrast to the two preceding budgets, Saudi Arabia's 1998 budget seriously overestimated the level of oil export prices, which in the first half of the year suffered their steepest decline since 1986. It was clear in mid-1998 that efforts were being made throughout the public sector to hold capital and recurrent expenditure below the levels originally budgeted. Some large projects were scaled down or postponed, public-sector wages and recruitment were 'frozen', and payments to contractors were withheld for the maximum allowable settlement periods (often 180 days). In 1998 the decline in petroleum revenues resulted in an increase in the budget deficit, to 48,400m. riyals, which was financed primarily by domestic borrowing; domestic debt in that year was estimated to have exceeded 100% of GDP. Another large deficit, of 36,300m riyals, was recorded in 1999, but a surplus of 22,700m. riyals was achieved in 2000 owing to an improvement in petroleum revenues. A deficit of 25,000m. riyals was recorded in 2001 (equivalent to 3.6% of GDP). Budget forecasts for 2002 envisaged a deficit of 45,000m. riyals.

AREA AND POPULATION

The area of Saudi Arabia has been estimated at 2,240,000 sq km (864,869 sq miles), but, since not all of the borders have been defined, it is not possible to arrive at a precise figure. The results of a census held in September 1992 recorded the total population as 16,948,388, of whom 12,310,100 (males 50.5%, females 49.5%) were Saudi Arabian citizens and 4,638,300 (males 70.4%, females 29.6%) were foreign nationals. The census

results reflected the country's dependence on foreign contract labour in most areas of employment outside administration, banking and certain state enterprises. By mid-2000 the population was estimated to have increased to 22,010,000. Total civilian employment in Saudi Arabia was estimated at 5,771,800 in 1991 and by 1999 had increased to 7,176,300. It was estimated that more than three-quarters of Saudi Arabia's population resided in urban areas in 1990 (compared with less than one-half at the end of the 1960s).

A comprehensive socio-economic survey of the royal capital, Riyadh, published by the Riyadh Development Authority in 1992, provided detailed examples of recent trends in the composition of the urban population and labour force in Saudi Arabia. Between 1986 and 1991, the survey showed, the area of land under development in Riyadh had almost doubled, while the population had likewise risen to 2,073,800, comprising 1,334,800 Saudi nationals and 739,000 non-nationals. Net migration into the city accounted for more than one-third of the total population increase over this period. Some 153,000 Egyptians constituted the largest group of foreign nationals in Riyadh in 1991, a large number of Yemenis having been forced to leave the country after Iraq's invasion of Kuwait in 1990. The next largest group of non-nationals in 1991 comprised Syrians, Jordanians and Iraqis. The survey showed that 60% of Riyadh's 1991 population was aged less than 20 years, and just 2% aged more than 60, and that the average age of the Saudi nationals was 17.1 years. Total employment in the city was 584,779 in 1991, nearly 40% higher than in 1986, with Saudi nationals filling 254,182 jobs in 1991. The employment of women (severely restricted by Islamic custom) nearly doubled to 83,000 (of whom 72,000 were non-nationals) between 1986 and 1991, virtually all of the employed Saudi females in Riyadh being engaged in professional and technical positions. Riyadh's unskilled work-force (accounting for 28% of all jobs in the city) was almost entirely composed of foreign nationals in 1991, whereas Saudi citizens held nearly 50% of professional and technical jobs and about 73% of clerical jobs. According to UN estimates, the population of Riyadh (including suburbs) had risen to 4,761,000 by 2001.

In February 1995 the Saudi Government stated that more than 100,000 illegal immigrants had left the country in the preceding four months, which had seen strict enforcement of the residency laws. Saudi employers were reminded that they could be fined as much as US $13,000 and imprisoned for up to three months for employing illegal workers. In July the Government announced that its 'strategic goal' was the eventual elimination of expatriate labour, which would entail acceptance by Saudi citizens of employment 'in all kinds of work and at all levels'. In December 1995 the Ministry of the Interior estimated the expatriate population at 6.2m., drawn from 190 different countries. Of these, some 4m. were employees and the remainder were dependants of employees. Expatriate remittances abroad totalled 38,100m. riyals ($10,160m.) in the first nine months of 1995. The Government urged the private sector to create 660,000 new jobs for Saudi citizens by the end of the decade. From the beginning of 1996 the Government began to enforce quotas for the employment of Saudi citizens in various sectors of the economy, including some types of manual and clerical employment. The minimum Saudi element which the affected industries were required to employ varied from 5% to 40% of the company work-force. Local private-sector employers held consultations in 1996 with a view to adopting standard contracts of employment and standard salary ranges for different occupations, the suggested minimum salaries for Saudi citizens being significantly higher than the suggested maximum salaries for expatriates doing similar work. In December 1996 government figures estimated the expatriate population at 6.5m. Employment sectors targeted for 'Saudiization' in 1997 included transport (employing 5% of the total labour force), as well as commerce and financial services, where a number of occupations have been reserved for Saudis. The number of expatriates employed by the Government in that year was 104,000 (including 51,000 in the health sector and 44,000 in education), compared with 119,500 in 1992. A three-month amnesty for illegal foreign residents in mid-1997 led to 500,000 people leaving the kingdom; a further 300,000 obtained the necessary work permits. The issuing of entry visas to Yemeni citizens, suspended since the 1990–91 Gulf crisis, was resumed in 1998, although Yemenis were now required to comply with standard Saudi work permit regulations which had previously been waived. More than 400,000 Yemenis were believed to be working in Saudi Arabia in early 1998. In July 1998 the Saudi Government restricted the duration of public-sector employment contracts for expatriates to a maximum of 10 years in most categories of employment. In 2000 government figures estimated the expatriate population to be 5.8m. In July 2002 the Ministry of Labour and Social Affairs instructed recruitment agencies to stop issuing new visas to non-Saudis seeking employment in 22 professions, believed to include administrative and procurement managers, car salesmen, public relations officers and secretaries. This latest example of the Government's policy of 'Saudiization' of the work-force brought to 36 the total number of occupations to which expatriate access was now restricted or denied.

DEVELOPMENT PLANS

Since 1970 the development of the Saudi economy has been guided by a series of five-year plans. The first Plan (1970–75) was a relatively modest programme costing 56,223m. riyals, of which 32,762m. riyals was allotted to economic and social development. However, after the rise in petroleum revenues in 1973–74 (see Petroleum, below), the Government found itself in possession of vast financial resources and determined to embark on a massive programme of industrialization and modernization. Hence the second Five-Year Plan (1975–80) provided for expenditure of 498,230m. riyals (about US $142,000m.).

A major feature of the second Plan was a project to increase industrial output, creating two new industrial cities, one at Jubail on the Gulf coast and the other at Yanbu on the Red Sea. Development of the two sites was to take 10 years and cost around US $70,000m. Jubail was to have three petroleum refineries, six petrochemical plants, an aluminium smelter and a steel mill, as well as support industries, an industrial port and large-scale urban development. Yanbu was planned on a slightly smaller scale: two petroleum refineries, a natural gas processing plant, a petrochemical complex, other lighter industries, an industrial port and a new urban area. The Yanbu industries were to be supplied by an oil pipeline and a gas pipeline across the Arabian peninsula from the Eastern Province. There were also plans to expand existing industrial and commercial sites, at Dammam in particular. The Government pursued the goals of the second Plan with great determination, and the results were, on the whole, successful. Although the main industrial projects fell behind schedule, infrastructure grew apace, endowing the country with the basic transport and communications facilities required by a modern industrial state.

Consequently, the third Five-Year Plan (1980–85) was intended to shift the emphasis from infrastructure projects to the productive sectors, with particular importance accorded to agriculture and the aim of achieving 'food security' by being less dependent on imported foodstuffs. The Plan stressed the need for manpower training, to reduce reliance on foreign labour, and for Saudi private investors to be encouraged to play a more prominent role in the economy. Planned investment for the five-year period was set at 782,000m. riyals (about US $235,000m.), but this total did not include defence spending, the largest item of expenditure under the previous Plan.

The fourth Five-Year Plan (1985–90) envisaged a total expenditure of 1,000,000m. riyals at current prices, of which 500,000m. riyals were allocated to development projects in the civilian sector. Four essential policy themes underlay the Plan: greater operational efficiency; an emphasis on non-oil revenue-generating activities, particularly industry, agriculture and financial services; a campaign to develop private-sector involvement and initiatives; and the need for further economic and social integration among the countries of the Co-operation Council of the Arab States of the Gulf (Gulf Co-operation Council—GCC). Within the details of the Plan, considerable emphasis was also given to raising desalination capacity, the expansion of irrigation and power facilities, a review of subsidies, the reduction of expatriate labour, the development of new industrial estates, and the expansion of health services.

By mid-1988, the fourth Development Plan was widely considered to have fallen short of its targets, mainly as a result of the steep decline in oil revenues following the collapse in oil prices

in 1986. The implementation of many projects, in particular those involving public utilities, had been delayed.

Direct military spending was to receive 312,500m. riyals of the fourth Plan's allocation, sustaining the emphasis already given to defence by the Government. As a consequence of the Iran–Iraq War, large sums of money had already been spent on defence, in particular on the Peace Shield defence system announced in 1985. The programme would provide a computerized command, control and communications system for Saudi Arabia's air defences. In early 1986 another major defence contract, worth about £7,500m., was signed with the British Government for the supply of 48 *Tornado* fighter-bomber aircraft from the European Panavia consortium, 30 *Hawk* trainer aircraft from British Aerospace and 30 *Pilatus* trainers. In July 1988 a new agreement, which more than doubled the value of the original contract, was signed. It included a revised £1,000m. offset programme which involved bilateral investments by Saudi and British companies. In addition to aircraft, the agreement envisaged the supply of ships and the construction of two huge airbases.

The fifth Five-Year Development Plan (1990–95) envisaged a total expenditure of 753,000m. riyals. Owing to the crisis in the Gulf following the invasion of Kuwait by Iraq, Saudi Arabia increased military spending, and about 34% (255,000m. riyals) of total expenditure in the fifth Plan was to be allocated to defence. The six major themes of the Plan were: the expansion of government revenue, in particular from non-oil sources; increased reliance on the private sector; further job opportunities and training for the Saudi Arabian labour force; import substitution and the promotion of exports; the diversification of economic activities into non-oil areas; and a balanced development of the regions. Under the Plan, the encouragement of Saudi Arabian industry, notably in the construction sector, was to be reinforced by a ruling that at least 30% of the value of government contracts must be awarded to Saudi Arabian companies.

The sixth Development Plan, for the period 1995–2000, was designed to achieve average annual growth of 3.8%. Priority was to be given to measures to balance the national budget by the end of the planning period (including reductions in direct and indirect price subsidies); to the development of a privatization programme; to increasing the proportion of Saudi nationals in the private-sector work-force; and to bringing about greater private-sector participation in infrastructural and other development projects. However, the Plan was based on overly optimistic petroleum prices and state revenues and assumed the ability to sustain a high rate of growth in government investment. In the event, fluctuating petroleum prices resulted in lower than predicted revenues and consequently disrupted expenditure. Overall real GDP growth for the first three years of the Plan was recorded at 1.2% annually, with oil and non-oil sector growth of 1.6% and 1.0%, respectively. (The plan had predicted annual oil sector growth of 3.8% and annual non-oil sector growth of 3.9%.) Petroleum prices declined sharply in 1998, causing overall GDP to decrease by some 11.5% measured at current prices, although GDP at constant prices showed an increase of 2.8% over the previous year owing to increased oil production.

A new Five-Year Plan, the seventh, for the period 2000–2005, aimed to create 817,000 additional jobs for Saudi workers, mainly in the private sector. The Plan envisaged increased private investment, and increased growth for the private and non-oil sectors, with overall growth in real GDP averaging 3.16% per year. The Plan is reliant upon the success of economic reforms, which encourage the participation of both the domestic private sector and international corporations through programmes of liberalization and administrative and economic reforms; the expected participation of international oil companies in the Saudi gas, power, refining and petrochemical industries was particularly encouraging for the Plan's targets for private sector growth.

In mid-1999 the Government announced the creation of a Supreme Economic Council (SEC), which is intended to increase investment, create jobs for Saudi citizens and increase private sector participation in the economy. The SEC, chaired by Crown Prince Abdullah, is designed to accelerate decision-making and to enable the co-ordinated and effective implementation of policies. Its membership comprises relevant government ministers, and it has a consultative committee of private sector representatives as well as academics and professional experts.

AGRICULTURE AND FISHING

Agriculture (including forestry and fishing), contributed only 5.1% of GDP in 2001, although the sector employed an estimated 9.8% of the working population in 1999. Its contribution to GDP increased from 3.3% in 1984, mainly as the result of the decline in revenue from petroleum that Saudi Arabia began to experience in the mid-1980s. During the third Five-Year Plan (1980–85), the output of the agricultural sector expanded, in real terms, at an average rate of 8.7% per year, compared with its projected growth rate of 5.4%. Agricultural production increased by an annual average of 7.4% in 1985–93; however, in 1994 output declined by 11.7%. Cultivation is confined to oases and to irrigated regions, which comprise only 2% of the total land area. About 39% of land is used for low-grade grazing. Although the Ministry of Agriculture and Water reported that the area of cultivated land in Saudi Arabia had increased to approximately 2.5m. ha by 1988, a considerable area of this land lay fallow and only about 600,000 ha were under regular cultivation. The Grain Silos and Flour Mills Organization (GSFMO) had announced in August 1993 that it would buy no wheat in 1994 from the six main commercial producers, while imposing quota restrictions on purchases from smaller commercial farmers, who would be entitled to an 'incentive' price of US $400 per ton. The aggregate government subsidy to wheat farmers was estimated to have reached $1,300m. per year before the production cut-backs started. At the end of 1994 the Government announced that its planned levels of wheat purchases from farmers were 2.3m. metric tons in 1995/96 and 2m. tons in 1996/97, with wheat exports being discontinued in 1996/97. Thereafter, annual wheat production would be maintained in balance with the prevailing level of domestic consumption (expected to be around 1.8m. tons annually in coming years), with a limited margin of surplus production for the country's strategic stockpile of grain. However, wheat harvests were 1.2m. tons in 1996 and 1.8m tons in 1997. The decline in output was due to the sharp reduction in subsidies and the reduced plantings by farmers experiencing delays in payment. FAO figures for 1997 showed wheat consumption of 2.2m. tons. The consequent shortfall was covered by drawing down local stocks. Output of barley also declined sharply in 1996, to 400,000 tons; 5m. tons of barley were imported in 1997.

Watermelons, tomatoes, dates and grapes are produced in significant numbers. In 1996 the Government embarked on the third phase of a programme to combat red beetle infestation in date palms (which had caused the European Union—EU—to ban imports of Saudi dates). Some 850,000 trees were to be cut down over a period of four months, bringing the total number felled since the launch of the programme to more than 1m. In 1998 the Government allocated 74.3m. riyals for the purchase of 21,000 metric tons of locally-grown dates (most of which were to be distributed to the poor).

The importance of developing the agricultural sector as a means of reducing imports has been emphasized by the Government. In 1987 an increase in local output reduced food imports to 65% of total food requirements, compared with 83% in 1980. The cost of imported food declined from US $4,669m. in 1984 to $2,799m. in 1987 and increased to $5,500m. in 1991. By 1994 the cost of food imports had fallen to $3,035m. At the start of 1998 the Government banned imports of specified fruits and vegetables from five countries—Egypt, Jordan, Lebanon, Syria and Turkey—which did not themselves permit the import of Saudi Arabian fruit and vegetables. Syria had been an important supplier of Saudi Arabia's tomato imports (worth $53m. in 1996), while Turkey and Egypt had provided most of Saudi Arabia's onion imports (worth $38m. in 1996). In February 1998 the Government announced new import tariffs on food products to protect local farmers. It subsequently banned the import of 10 types of vegetable during Saudi Arabia's own harvesting seasons for the crops concerned.

Saudi Arabia is subject to important natural limitations on the development of agriculture, principally the scarcity of water. Agriculture accounts for 85%–90% of water demand in the kingdom, which is met mostly by non-renewable groundwater reserves. The Government has initiated an ambitious pro-

gramme to increase the country's water supply, including surveys for underground water resources (20 main aquifers had been identified by 1983, nine of which were being exploited), construction of dams, irrigation and drainage networks, combined with distribution of fallow land, settlement of bedouin and the introduction of mechanization. The eventual aim of the programme was to raise agricultural production to the level of near self-sufficiency in all foods. Consequently, budgetary allocations for the agricultural sector increased considerably. The third Five-Year Plan (1980–85) projected spending on agriculture at 7,975m. riyals, and on water (mainly desalination plants) at no less than 52,979m. riyals, although much of this was to be used for developing urban water supplies. Surveys that were conducted in the 1960s indicated a potential for greatly increasing agricultural output by means of irrigation. Under the 1985–90 Plan, 50,000 ha of land were to be drained or irrigated, and 8,000 ha were to be converted into pasture land.

In 1981, according to FAO estimates, 395,000 ha of land were irrigated. A number of important projects have been undertaken by the Government. The Al-Hasa irrigation and drainage scheme, inaugurated in December 1971, was completed over five years at a cost of 260m. riyals. It is the country's largest agricultural scheme, benefiting about 50,000. The Faisal Model Settlement scheme, which cost 100m. riyals, has involved extensive land reclamation and irrigation, and provided permanent farmland and housing for 1,000 bedouin families. The Wadi Gizan dam, inaugurated in March 1971, has a reservoir with a capacity of 71m. cu m of water and was built at a cost of 42m. riyals. A second dam at Wadi Najran, completed in 1980, has added a further 68m. cu m to water storage capacity in the Gizan Najran area. The Abha dam, in the Asir region, was opened in April 1974, with a reservoir capacity of 2.4m. cu m. In all, the kingdom operated a total of 104 dams in 1983.

Apart from lack of water, the major constraint on Saudi agriculture is shortage of labour, as the population is drawn away from rural areas by the attractions of urban development, and most farm workers are expatriates. The Government is countering the drift to the towns by improving rural facilities, but the future of Saudi agriculture must lie in capital-intensive, water-efficient farming. A major success has been achieved with dairy farming, using the most modern technical expertise from Sweden, Denmark and Ireland. In 1988 Masstock Saudia, a joint venture established by Ireland and Saudi Arabia in 1976, had 12 farms throughout the kingdom and a herd of 11,000 cows, yielding an average 7,900 litres of milk per year. The Saudi Arabian Agriculture and Dairy Co (SAADCO) was formed in 1980, and by the end of 1984 had 15,000 cows and a 60 sq km farm at al-Kharj. By 1986 Saudi Arabia was self-sufficient in eggs and broiler chickens. Subsidized milk powder from the EU constitutes the main competition to local production, and by 1997 milk production had increased to 700m. litres, sufficient for some 40% of total domestic requirements. Meat, dairy and other livestock production remains dependent upon various imported inputs.

Government incentives to farmers are substantial. Interest-free loans are available through the Agricultural Bank, set up in 1963, and a total of 9,209 loans, valued at 1,551m. riyals, were disbursed by the bank in 1985/86. Chemical fertilizers, domestic or imported, are distributed at half-price. There are also large subsidies available to local farmers for the purchase of farm machinery (amounting to 45% of the total cost of the item), irrigation pumps and imported rearing stock. In response to these incentives, the agricultural sector expanded by more than 6% per year in the early 1980s. As a result of declining revenue from petroleum in the early 1980s, expenditure on agriculture was reduced. Total planned lending under the fifth Development Plan was set at 14,411m. riyals, compared with 61,000m. riyals disbursed during the third Plan. In 2000 the Agricultural Bank disbursed 6,147 loans amounting to 1,112.2m. riyals.

Criticism of Saudi Arabia's agricultural policy has concentrated on the high depletion rate of the non-renewable fossil aquifers from which farmers draw most of their water supply. It was estimated in 1992 that the water-table in Qassim (the principal wheat-growing area) had fallen by 100 m in the previous decade. The export of subsidized wheat has also been criticized, and it has been calculated that dairy farming in Saudi

Arabia uses 1,500 litres of water per litre of milk production. In March 1997 the Government outlined its progress in implementing more responsible policies. Cut-backs in the production of cereal crops (see above) had reduced the over-extraction of groundwater for irrigation from 6,990m. cu m in 1992 to 1,850m. cu m in 1996, while 500 cattlefeed projects had been phased out because of their high water requirement.

Agricultural GDP increased by an average of 0.9% per year in 1990–2000; the sector's GDP increased by 1.4% in 2000, according to provisional estimates. During 1999 the total productive cultivated area was increased by 6.5% to 1.2m. ha and total agricultural production increased by 3.7%, to 325,000 metric tons. These results were achieved partly as a result of increasing the area under grain and fruit by 10.3% and 29.8% respectively.

The fishing industry has grown in recent years, and by 2000 the total catch had reached 49,650 metric tons. New projects launched by the Saudi Fisheries Co (SFC) in the early 1990s included a facility to convert fish to fodder, a processing factory and the purchase of shrimping vessels. The SFC reported in June 1992 that stocks of shrimps in the Gulf had been almost destroyed by pollution, caused by the Gulf hostilities.

PETROLEUM

The most important industry in Saudi Arabia is the production of crude petroleum and petroleum products. Saudi Arabia is the major petroleum producer in OPEC, accounting for 29.0% of the organization's output in 2001, and is one of the three principal producers in the world, with 11.8% of global oil output in 2001, ahead of the USA (9.8%) and Russia (9.7%). Saudi Arabia's proven reserves of petroleum at the end of 2001 totalled 261,800m. barrels (24.9% of the world total and 32.0% of the OPEC total), sufficient to maintain production at 2000 levels for 85.0 years. Production is from 14 major oilfields, in particular Ghawar, Abqaiq, Safaniya and Berri. Ghawar is generally accepted as the world's largest oilfield, while Safaniya is the world's largest offshore field. The kingdom also enjoys equal rights with Kuwait to the petroleum reserves of the Saudi Arabia-Kuwait Neutral/Partitioned Zone, which totalled 5,000m. barrels at the start of 1993.

In 1933 a concession was granted to Standard Oil Co of California to explore for petroleum in Saudi Arabia. The operating company, the Arabian-American Oil Co (Aramco), began exploration in that year, and discovered petroleum in commercial quantities in 1938. By 1945, four oilfields had been discovered, and the necessary facilities had been established to satisfy demands for crude petroleum and refined products. Other US companies gradually acquired shares in Aramco and by 1948 Standard Oil, Texaco and Exxon each owned a 30% share, with Mobil accounting for the remaining 10%.

In November 1962 the Government created the General Petroleum and Mineral Organization (PETROMIN) as the instrument for increasing state participation in the petroleum and gas industries. In accordance with the action of other Arab petroleum-producing states, the Saudi Government acquired a 25% share in Aramco in January 1973. A 100% take-over of the company was agreed in 1980 (for the subsequent creation of Saudi Aramco, see below).

The expansion of Saudi Arabia's petroleum output in the 1960s and 1970s was spectacular. Production increased from about 62m. metric tons (equivalent to 1.3m. b/d) in 1960 to 178m. tons (3.8m. b/d) in 1970, and to 412m. tons (8.5m. b/d) in 1974. This growth in output was accompanied by rising prices for petroleum, culminating in the huge increases of October and December 1973, which almost quadrupled the cost per barrel. The Government's petroleum revenues increased dramatically, from US $1,214m. in 1970 to $22,573m. in 1974. The price rises reflected OPEC's collective will to exploit a favourable market situation.

After the events of 1973–74, however, Saudi Arabia emerged as a powerful conservative and pro-Western influence in OPEC, using its high potential output to hold down the price of petroleum. In the depressed market of 1975 the country's production of crude petroleum declined to 344m. metric tons (7.1m. b/d), but in 1977 it rose to a new peak of 455m. tons (9.2m. b/d), with government revenues at US $36,540m. This increase in output

resulted from a disagreement within OPEC over pricing; a compromise on pricing policy was reached in July.

For most of 1978 the supply of petroleum was plentiful, prices remained steady, and Saudi Arabia kept its production below 8.5m. b/d. With the outbreak of the Iranian revolution in late 1978, however, the situation was transformed. To compensate for the Iranian shortfall, Saudi Arabia increased production to more than 10m. b/d. The country's total output for 1978 was 410m. tons (8.3m. b/d), with government revenue from petroleum reaching US $32,234m. Output was maintained at around 9.5m. b/d for most of 1979, but prices increased sharply, as intense anxiety over petroleum supplies seized the industrialized West. Despite Saudi efforts, the price of the country's petroleum rose rapidly. The price of one grade, Saudi light crude, increased from $13.3 per barrel at the start of 1979 to $28 per barrel in May 1980, the most rapid rise since 1973–74. Since Saudi Arabia's total output for 1979 was 470m. tons (9.5m. b/d) and prices doubled in the course of the year, government revenues from petroleum reached a new peak of $48,435m.

The Saudi Government raised production in the last quarter of 1980 to 10.3m. b/d to compensate for output lost as a consequence of the Iran–Iraq War, giving a record total production for the year of 493m. metric tons (9.99m. b/d), which remains the peak output level for any one year. Prices continued to drift upwards, Saudi light crude reaching US $32 per barrel by the end of 1980, and total government revenues from petroleum in that year were $84,466m., which represented an increase of 74% over the previous year's figure. During the first nine months of 1981, however, Saudi efforts to hold down prices finally began to have a real effect. Reduced demand, combined with the continued high level of Saudi output (maintained at more than 10m. b/d), made it difficult to sell petroleum at the official level and impossible for prices to rise any further. In October 1981, in an attempt to restore a unified price structure, Saudi Arabia induced OPEC to accept a package involving a $2 rise in the market price to $34 per barrel, accompanied by a cut in Saudi output to a ceiling of 8.5m. b/d. Total Saudi output for 1981 fell marginally, to 491m. tons (9.98m. b/d), but government revenues from petroleum reached a record level of about $102,000m.

During 1982 world demand for petroleum continued to fall and, after a further OPEC meeting in March, the Saudi Government declared a new upper limit of 7.5m. b/d for the country's production. In reality, output had already dropped below that figure. Total production for 1982 was 328m. metric tons, an average of only 6.6m. b/d, and the petroleum sector's output, as a proportion of real GDP, declined by 36.1% during the year 1982/83. Finally, in March 1983, OPEC bowed to market pressure. The member states agreed to reduce the market price by 15%, to US $29 per barrel, and to limit total OPEC output to 17.5m. b/d. Total Saudi output for 1983 was 256m. tons (5.2m. b/d), and in 1984 production levels fell once again, to 233m. tons (4.8m. b/d), yielding revenues of $46,000m. Since 1984 Saudi Arabia has been involved in barter agreements, whereby petroleum is exchanged for other goods, particularly aircraft and military equipment.

Saudi Arabia's petroleum is mostly exported by tanker from terminals on the Gulf coast. In 1981 PETROMIN completed construction of a Trans-Arabian pipeline to Yanbu on the Red Sea coast. The pipeline, designed to carry some 1.9m. b/d (mainly for export from a Red Sea tanker terminal), shortens the export route to Western Europe and North America by about 3,500 km. A new pipeline, linking the Iraqi oilfields to the Trans-Arabian pipeline, was completed in 1985, allowing Iraq and Saudi Arabia to share the pipeline until 1989, when a direct pipeline, with a capacity of 1.6m. b/d, was planned to link Iraqi oilfields to Yanbu.

In the 1980s Saudi Arabia acted as a 'swing producer' within OPEC, adjusting its own production levels in order to keep overall production by OPEC member states within the organization's recommended limits. However, the lack of agreement among OPEC members on pricing and production, and the loss of revenue resulting from Saudi Arabia's much lower production levels, culminated in a major change of policy in late 1985. Saudi Arabia abandoned its former role and increased sales, with petroleum exports in the last quarter of 1985 at their highest since the end of 1983. Nevertheless, total production in

1985 was only 173m. metric tons (3.6m. b/d), yielding revenues of US $27,000m. At the end of 1985 OPEC decided to end its official quota policy and to seek a greater share of the world market, to offset falling prices. As a result of a surge in production, international prices for crude petroleum fell precipitously in 1986, dipping below $10 per barrel in July. Accordingly, although Saudi Arabian output in 1986 rose to 251m. tons (5.2m. b/d), oil revenues fell to $20,000m.

In 1986 a policy aimed at limiting production and increasing prices was implemented. The policy was proposed by the newly-appointed Minister of Petroleum and Mineral Resources, Sheikh Hisham Nazer, at an OPEC meeting held in December, whereby a target price for crude petroleum of US $18 per barrel was to be supported by an arrangement ensuring strict output quotas, with a production ceiling for the first half of 1987 of 15.8m.b/d, a reduction of 7.25% in each country's quota compared with December. Saudi Arabia, which was allotted a nominal quota of 4,133,000 b/d, was again effectively the 'swing producer'. The new production agreement came into effect on 1 January 1987. In practice, however, production in the first half of 1987 was consistently below the ceiling and prices stabilized at slightly above the reference level of $18 per barrel.

In June 1987 OPEC members agreed to maintain the reference price of US $18 per barrel in the second half of that year, but to increase their collective production by 800,000 b/d, to 16.6m. b/d. Under the revised arrangements, Saudi Arabia was allocated a quota of 4,343,000 b/d, its actual average output in 1987 being close to the quota, at 4.36m. b/d (annual production 212m. metric tons), yielding revenues of $25,000m. However, consistent over-production by OPEC members caused a renewed decline in the price of crude petroleum, which fell below $12 per barrel in September 1988. Total Saudi Arabian production in 1988 rose to 257m. tons (5.26m. b/d), but revenues fell to around $20,000m. In November OPEC agreed to form a committee, comprising representatives of eight member states, to monitor the production quotas of all members and to supervise adherence to the agreed production levels. At the same meeting OPEC agreed a collective production quota of 18.5m. b/d, of which Saudi Arabia's share was to be 4,524,000 b/d, to take effect from January 1989 and to operate for the first six months of the year. At the mid-1989 OPEC conference the production ceiling was raised to 19.5m. b/d, and in November quotas were redistributed within a new ceiling of 22m. b/d. Total Saudi Arabian output for the year was slightly reduced, at 256m. tons (5.2m. b/d), with revenues at $24,000m.

The OPEC meeting in Geneva in July 1990 was held in an atmosphere of increasing tension, caused by Iraq's threats of military action against those countries—principally the United Arab Emirates (UAE) and Kuwait—which it had accused of exceeding their production quotas. At the meeting Iraq sought to raise OPEC's minimum reference price for crude petroleum to US $25 per barrel, but, in the event, OPEC's ministerial council adopted a price of $21 per barrel and fixed a new production ceiling of 22.5m. b/d for the remainder of 1990. Quotas for individual countries remained unchanged (Saudi Arabia's at 5.38m. b/d), except that of the UAE, which was raised to 1.5m. b/d.

By mid-August 1990 'panic buying' of crude petroleum, following Iraq's invasion of Kuwait at the beginning of the month, had caused 'spot' market prices almost to double. Saudi Arabia announced that it would increase its production of crude petroleum by 2m. b/d unless OPEC agreed to hold an emergency meeting and claimed that the Geneva agreement was now obsolete. Petroleum prices had risen to about US $28 per barrel, and OPEC production—since Iraqi and Kuwaiti supplies could no longer be marketed—was some 4m. b/d below the ceiling agreed at the July meeting.

An emergency meeting of OPEC was duly held in August 1990, at which it was agreed to allow members to increase production rates above the quotas fixed in July. Iraq and Libya were absent from the meeting, and Iran refused to endorse the agreement. By early September petroleum prices had risen above US $30 per barrel in London and New York. Saudi Arabia was reported to have increased production to 7.4m. b/d, and to be exporting more than 7m. b/d. Despite OPEC's decision to increase production, the fear of hostilities in the Gulf caused prices to rise above $40 per barrel for the first time in almost a

decade. During 1990 as a whole, Saudi Arabian production averaged 6.4m. b/d (annual production 312m. metric tons), producing revenues of $31,500m.

OPEC quotas remained in effective suspension throughout 1991, and Saudi Arabia took advantage of the absence of Iraqi and Kuwaiti petroleum to increase its output to an average of 8.2m. b/d (annual production was almost 400m. metric tons, the highest level since 1981), of which only 1m. b/d was for domestic use. Although international petroleum prices eventually fell, they remained higher than the pre-crisis level, so that Saudi oil revenues rose to US $43,450m. in 1991. Despite being allocated a ceiling of 7,887,000 b/d by OPEC in mid-February 1992, Saudi Arabia demanded a minimum quota of 8m. b/d and Saudi crude oil production remained significantly above 8m. b/d throughout 1992, its final average for the year being 8,377,800 b/d. Saudi Arabia accepted an OPEC ceiling of 8,395,000 b/d for the first quarter of 1993, and 8m. b/d thereafter. Average oil export earnings were estimated at $3,568m. per month for the first half of 1993 and around $3,040m. per month for the remainder of the year, when prices weakened significantly. Saudi Arabia's 1993 crude oil production averaged 8,131,700 b/d, having been cut back to fractionally more than 8m. b/d by the last quarter of the year. Output averaged 8,006,700 b/d in 1994 and 8,018,000 b/d in 1995. In 1996 Saudi Arabia's output of crude oil averaged 8,150,000 b/d, while the kingdom's total oil production (including natural gas liquids) averaged 8,920,000 b/d.

Prior to the stimulus to its petroleum industry that the Gulf crisis provided, Saudi Arabia had undertaken a major reorganization of state structures responsible for the sector. This included the conversion of PETROMIN into a holding company and the creation of several affiliated operating companies with responsibilities for exploration, refining, marketing and shipping. The first of these, Petrolube, was established in February 1988, to operate the lubricating oil blending plants in Jeddah, Riyadh and Jubail. The most important of the successor companies was the Saudi Arabian Marketing and Refining Co (SAMAREC), formed in 1989 to manage petroleum refining and distribution for the Saudi domestic market and to handle state exports of refined products.

In April 1989 the Saudi Arabian Oil Co (Saudi Aramco) was formed to take control of the nationalized Aramco assets. It is an independent enterprise with the right to establish companies and initiate projects. In addition, a new Supreme Oil Council was formed to take responsibility for the country's petroleum industry. Chaired by King Fahd, the council's members included private businessmen as well as government ministers: an indication of the Government's desire to involve the private sector in the management of the economy. In June 1993 the Government effectively abolished SAMAREC, and placed its operations, together with other PETROMIN oil interests, under the management of Saudi Aramco. A new 12-member Supreme Council for Petroleum and Mineral Affairs was formed in January 2000 under the Chairmanship of King Fahd. It was responsible for all policy relating to oil and gas affairs, including any agreements with international oil companies and for general policy guide-lines for Saudi Aramco.

In June 1989 Saudi Aramco announced that three major development projects would be proceeding as planned: the expansion of the east-west pipeline to carry crude petroleum (Petroline); the upgrading of facilities at the Safaniya and Uthmaniya oilfields; and the development of two wet crude handling and gas-gathering facilities at the onshore Uthmaniya field. The expansion of Petroline's overall capacity from 3.6m. to 4.8m. b/d (completed in 1993) was the largest scheme to have been undertaken in the petroleum sector for several years. In the same month it was stated that new oilfields in the al-Hawtah region, south of Riyadh, were commercially viable, and that further exploration would be undertaken; subsequent evaluation indicated a production capacity of up to 170,000 b/d of high-quality crude. In June 1991 a US company, McDermott International, was awarded a contract for work on offshore pipelines at the Zuluf oilfield, as part of the kingdom's plan to raise petroleum production capacity to 10m. b/d by the mid-1990s. By mid-1994 sustainable production capacity had reached the target level, representing a very substantial margin of excess capacity in current market conditions.

Saudi Aramco nevertheless decided in May 1995 to initiate a major development programme in the Shayba oilfield, situated on the border with Abu Dhabi, some 600 km from the closest gathering facility in the established Saudi oilfields. Discovered in 1968, the Shayba field contained estimated reserves of up to 7,000m. barrels of very light (40°–42° API gravity) crude containing only 0.7% sulphur. Development of the field had first been considered in 1989, since when the pattern of world oil demand had undergone a significant shift towards premium-priced light crudes. Saudi Aramco expected this trend to continue, assuring the company of a relatively rapid recovery of its development costs (estimated at US $2,500m.) when the field was brought into production. Meanwhile, Saudi Aramco's policy of reducing production of heavy crude in favour of lighter grades was facilitated by the inauguration of the al-Hawtah field in late 1994, with a production capacity of 150,000 b/d of 44°–50° API 'super-light' crude. An adjacent 'super-light' field was discovered in early 1995. The Haradh oilfield, containing 34° API crude, was due to begin producing in 1996, with an initial capacity of 300,000 b/d (to be doubled by late 1998).

In 1997 Saudi Arabia's output of crude oil (excluding Neutral Zone output) averaged 8,358,000 b/d, while total Saudi Arabian oil production (including natural gas liquids and the Saudi share of Neutral Zone crude oil output) averaged 9,375,000 b/d. Saudi Arabia's OPEC crude oil production quota, which had stood at 8m. b/d since April 1993, was raised to 8,761,000 b/d at the start of January 1998 in line with an OPEC agreement on 9.5% quota increases for most member states. World oil prices subsequently fell sharply (touching their lowest levels for 12 years in 'spot' trading in March) against a background of depressed demand in key Asian import markets, prompting OPEC members to undertake a fresh review of quotas. Under revised OPEC quota agreements (supported by several non-OPEC exporting countries) Saudi Arabia introduced a reduced crude oil output ceiling of 8,461,000 b/d with effect from April, with a further reduction of 225,000 b/d from July. Estimates of Saudi Arabia's average crude oil production in the second quarter of 1998 gave Saudi Aramco's own-account output as 8,250,000 b/d (including 150,000 b/d of natural gas liquids produced at the well-head); Saudi Aramco's Abu Saafa output (produced for the benefit of Bahrain) as 150,000 b/d; and the Saudi share of Neutral Zone output as 290,000 b/d. In June production began at the Shayba oilfield and reached its target capacity of 500,000 b/d in August. With Saudi Arabia continuing to make full use of its agreed OPEC production ceiling, the proportion of extra-light crude in Saudi Aramco's output increased as output of other grades was cut back initially to accommodate the Shayba output, and subsequently as a result of OPEC production restraints in late 1998. Saudi Aramco decided in June (while prospective contractors were drawing up tenders for the work) to postpone implementation of a project to double the production capacity of the Haradh oilfield. There were no other 'upstream' oil development projects on Saudi Aramco's planning agenda, with the government concentrating on development of gas production. Nevertheless, during Crown Prince Abdullah's international tour in September 1998 he held meetings with senior executives of foreign oil companies, generating optimism about the possibility of foreign participation in upstream Saudi oil activities. A number of companies subsequently submitted proposals for investment in the Saudi upstream sector, although Saudi Arabia stated that participation would only be allowed in projects involving non-associated gas, petrochemicals and refining. In July 2000 the Minister of Foreign Affairs, Prince Sa'ud al-Faisal as-Sa'ud, was appointed to lead negotiations with international oil companies over proposed investments in designated gas, refining and petrochemical projects, in partnership with Saudi Aramco.

In February 2000 negotiations for the renewal of a concession in the Saudi portion of the Neutral Zone, which had been operated by the Japanese-owned Arabian Oil Company for 40 years, ended without agreement, following Saudi Arabian demands for major Japanese investment, including a commitment to a major railway project from the Eastern province to the north of the country. Saudi Aramco subsequently established the Aramco Gulf Operations Co to operate the concession.

Petroleum prices declined further in late 1998, and in March 1999 Saudi Arabia negotiated further production cuts with

OPEC and non-OPEC producers (effective from 1 April). Saudi Arabia reduced production by 585,000 b/d, to 7,438,000 b/d, as part of a total pledged reduction of some 2m. b/d. As a result of this round of production cuts, petroleum prices increased substantially; by March 2000 the Brent Crude marker price had reached almost US $30 per barrel. In that month OPEC agreed to reverse its March 1999 production cuts with the aim of maintaining prices in the range $22–$28 per barrel. Prices declined only briefly before again increasing, and in June, under pressure from the USA, OPEC again agreed to raise its output, this time by 500,000 b/d, giving Saudi Arabia a production quota of 253,000 b/d. By July 2000 almost all OPEC members except Saudi Arabia were producing very close to their sustainable production capacity, giving Saudi Arabia a particularly strong role in the market. Continued high prices resulted in a unilateral declaration by Saudi Arabia that it would increase production by a further 500,000 b/d. Another OPEC meeting was held in September at which further quota increases were agreed, bringing the total OPEC production ceiling, effective from 1 October, to 26,200,000 b/d, with Saudi Arabia allocated 8,512,000 b/d. Two downward adjustments were made in early 2001, effective from 1 February and 1 April, in an attempt to reverse the negative impact on world prices of a decline in demand in the latter part of 2000. In July 2001, in an effort to stabilize the price of petroleum in the face of a slowdown in the world economy, OPEC agreed to reduce total production by 1m. b/d, effective from September. Saudi Arabia's overall quota decreased to 7,541,000 b/d as a result. In September OPEC ministers gave an undertaking to maintain oil-price stability in the uncertain economic climate following the terrorist attacks on the USA, while Saudi Arabia signalled its preparedness unilaterally to increase production to cover any shortages in world oil markets. In late October Saudi Arabia, together with Venezuela, Iran, the UAE and non-OPEC Oman all declared themselves in favour of a further cut in production. However, diplomacy undertaken by Saudi Arabia's Minister of Petroleum and Mineral Resources, Ali ibn Ibrahim an-Nuaimi and President Chávez of Venezuela, had apparently made no progress in achieving its objective of persuading Mexico, Norway and Russia, all key non-OPEC producers, to support the Organization's management strategy. An extraordinary meeting of the OPEC conference convened in Vienna on 14 November observed that 'as a result of the global economic slowdown and the aftermath of the tragic events of 11 September 2001, in order to achieve a balance in the oil market, it will be necessary to reduce the supply from all oil producers by a further 2m. b/d, bringing the total reduction in oil supply to 5.5m. b/d from the levels of January 2001, including the 3.5m. b/d reduction already effected by OPEC this year'. On 28 December, at a consultative meeting of the OPEC conference, convened in Cairo, OPEC confirmed its decision to implement a reduction of 1.5m. b/d in its overall production from 1 January 2002. Saudi Arabia agreed to reduce production from 7.5m. b/d to 7.1m b/d. Adherence to these revised quotas would reduce OPEC's total production from 23.2m. b/d to 21.7m. b/d. During 2001 OPEC's production of crude had declined by 720,000 b/d, or 2.7%, compared with 2000, with a fall in Saudi Arabian production of some 350,000 b/d accounting for almost 50% of the total reduction within OPEC. At an extraordinary ministerial conference held in Vienna on 26 June, OPEC agreed to maintain production at the prevailing level until the end of September 2002.

INDUSTRY, GAS AND MINING

Saudi Arabia has expended substantial oil revenues in financing major industrial projects under successive development plans (see Development Plans, above). The cornerstone of the industrialization programme is the construction of refineries and processing industries to exploit the country's huge reserves of petroleum and natural gas (Saudi Arabia had published proven gas reserves of 6,220,000m. cu m at the end of 2001). The major projects are being undertaken as joint ventures between the State and foreign companies.

Following its absorption of SAMAREC in mid-1993, Saudi Aramco took charge of the management of the entire range of state petroleum-refining and product-marketing interests. As well as handling the marketing of products from Saudi Aramco's Ras Tanura plant, SAMAREC had operated refineries at

Jeddah, Riyadh and Yanbu and had been responsible for marketing the state share of output from export-oriented refineries at Jubail, Yanbu and Rabigh. Saudi Arabia's installed refinery capacity totalled 1,865,000 b/d in 1992, an increase of 1m. b/d since 1984. At the refineries' aggregate throughput level of about 1.5m. b/d of crude oil in 1992, the volume of refined products available for marketing through state channels was slightly more than 1m. b/d., of which about two-thirds was sold on the home market and the remainder exported. In 1999 Saudi Arabia had an installed refining capacity of 1,710,000 b/d and a domestic demand for refined products of 1,335,000 b/d. Total refining capacity at the end of 2001 was 1,816,000 b/d.

One effect of the reorganization was the deferment of a proposed US $4,000m. programme to upgrade the oil-refining facilities which had fallen within SAMAREC's sphere of influence for planning purposes. A separate $1,000m. upgrading programme for the Ras Tanura refinery was under way by mid-1994. In 1995 Saudi Aramco acquired full ownership of the Rabigh export refinery (built in 1985 as a joint venture with a Greek company) and announced plans for a $2,000m. upgrading programme at this plant. A heavily modified programme (costed at $800m.) was put out to tender in June 1998. As a result of declining petroleum prices and decreasing revenues the Rabigh upgrade was cancelled in October, although it was suggested as a possible project for foreign participation less than two years later. In mid-1998 the current phase of upgrading work at the Ras Tanura refinery, providing sufficient gasoline capacity to supply the kingdom's expected domestic demand until 2002, was completed. Recent shortfalls in Saudi gasoline production had been covered by imports from one of Saudi Aramco's overseas refining affiliates.

An important element of Saudi Arabia's overall product-marketing strategy for the 1990s is the acquisition by Saudi Aramco of refining interests in petroleum-importing countries. In November 1988 Saudi Aramco entered into a joint venture with Texaco, whereby it gained access to a refining and marketing network spanning 26 states in the southern and eastern USA. In 1991 Saudi Aramco acquired a 35% equity interest in South Korea's largest refining company, Ssangyong Oil, which had 265,000 b/d of installed capacity.

In 1993 Saudi Aramco was actively studying proposals for further joint ventures with established refiners in Asia, Europe and the USA, with a view to raising its effective overseas refining capacity to around 3m. b/d. There was also a complementary programme to acquire oil storage capacity in major overseas importing centres, in furtherance of which Saudi Aramco announced in mid-1993 that it was to buy a 34.4% interest in a 17m.-barrel import terminal at the Dutch port of Rotterdam. In February 1994 Saudi Aramco acquired a 40% shareholding in the Philippine company Petron, which, through its 155,000 b/d Bataan refinery and its associated transportation and retailing network, currently supplied 41% of the Philippine market for refined products. In the following month a Saudi businessman acquired Sweden's largest oil firm, OK Petroleum, which had a refining capacity of 265,000 b/d and which obtained part of its current crude supply from Saudi Aramco. In March 1996 Saudi Aramco acquired a 50% shareholding in a Greek company, Motor Oil Hellas Corinth Refineries, and its marketing affiliate, Avin Oil. The refining company's 100,000 b/d Corinth plant supplied a chain of 700 Avin petrol stations.

A plan to build a refinery and associated facilities in northern India, conceived as a joint venture by Hindustan Petroleum Corpn and Saudi Aramco (which would supply 115,000 b/d of Saudi crude), was approved in principle by the Indian Government in mid-1996. Saudi Aramco was a minority partner in two Chinese joint-venture refineries in 1995. In early 1996 its efforts to acquire a majority share in one of these ventures was blocked by China's state petrochemical company SINOPEC (the existing majority partner), which also rejected Saudi Aramco's proposals for creating a third joint venture. The stumbling-block in the latter case was the Chinese Government's requirement for joint-venture refineries to export at least 70% of their output in order to generate foreign currency earnings. In July 1997 an agreement was reached between Texaco, Shell Oil Co and Saudi Aramco to merge their refining and marketing operations in the eastern and Gulf coast regions of the USA. A new jointly-owned company, Motiva Enterprises, was established in mid-

1998 to take control of the 820,000 b/d of US refining capacity and the various service-station networks covered by the merger, which also entailed the dissolution of Star Enterprise (Saudi Aramco's 50-50 joint venture with Texaco). Saudi Arabia's Minister of Petroleum and Mineral Resources said in June 1997 that the volume of Saudi crude oil supplied to overseas refining affiliates was projected to rise from 3.2m. b/d to 4m. b/d as Saudi Aramco continued to expand its world-wide interests.

The Saudi Basic Industries Corpn (SABIC), founded in 1976, is Saudi Arabia's main non-oil industrial enterprise, including among its holdings many major gas-utilization projects. Chief among them is the petrochemical development at Jubail, Jeddah and Yanbu. In 1983 the Saudi Methanol Co (ar-Razi) plant at Jubail, which cost 900m. riyals and has a capacity of 500,000 metric tons per year, became the first venture to begin production. It was followed by a further four new projects in 1984: the National Methanol Co (Ibn Sina) plant at Jubail, the Saudi Petrochemical Co (Sadaf) plant at Jubail, producing ethylene, ethylene dichloride, styrene, ethanol and caustic soda; the Al-Jubail Petrochemical Co (Kemya) plant, producing linear low-density polyethylene (LLDPE); and the Saudi Yanbu Petrochemical Co (Yanpet) plant, producing ethylene, ethylene glycol, LLDPE and high-density polyethylene. In 1985 two new plants also came into operation at Jubail: the Arabian Petrochemical Co (Petrokemya) plant, producing ethylene; and the Eastern Petrochemical Co (Sharq) plant, producing LLDPE and ethylene glycol. In March 1989 production of methyl-tertiary-butyl ether (MTBE), a lead substitute for petrol, was initiated by one of SABIC's joint ventures, the Saudi-European Petrochemical Co (Ibn Zahr), at Jubail. In the same month Petrokemya began the production of plastic resin polystyrene, with the aim of producing 100,000 tons per year, while the annual output of ethylene was scheduled to reach 500,000 tons in 1993, increasing total ethylene capacity to 2.9m. tons per year. In July PVC production capacity at Ibn Hayyan was 100,000 tons per year. SABIC experienced severe problems in selling its products, as major market areas began to impose tariff restrictions in 1985. The company has, however, been able to sell a large volume of products in the Far East and in Europe, despite the tariffs.

In March 1991 SABIC expanded its marketing network when it opened a new ethylene glycol terminal in Italy to improve service to Italian and other southern European clients. In 1991 SABIC owned two European terminals for liquid products (in Italy and in the Netherlands), as well as three storage terminals for plastic resins, situated in Belgium, France and the United Kingdom. In June Ibn Zahr signed contracts for the construction of a polypropylene plant with a capacity of 200,000 metric tons per year and a new MTBE plant with a capacity of 700,000 tons per year. Altogether, Saudi Arabia holds 13% of the world MTBE market, and private Saudi firms had been planning further expansion when it became apparent that the demand for MTBE could fall dramatically as a result of fears about its adverse effects on health. Features of SABIC operations in 1991 included the completion of expansion at the National Plastics Co (Ibn Hayyan), to a capacity of 300,000 tons per year, and of the Saudi Methanol Co (ar-Razi), to a capacity of 1.2m. tons per year. Following the start of polypropylene production at Jubail, SABIC was in 1994 manufacturing all five thermoplastics and was inviting joint-venture proposals to produce more than 30 categories of finished product, ranging from clingfilm to footwear. Saudi Arabia's consumption of plastic resins per caput was forecast to approach European levels by 2000.

In 1995 the Arabian Industrial Fiber Co began production of polyester fibre; future plans included the installation of an aromatics and purified terephthalic acid complex at Yanbu. This and other expansion and diversification projects within the SABIC group were expected to increase SABIC's annual production capacity to 30m. metric tons by 2000. SABIC's combined production stood at 25m. tons in 1995, and was expected to rise to 48m. tons by 2010. In 1996 SABIC marketed 17m. tons of products, having increased its total production volume to 23m. tons (including 12.3m. tons of chemicals, more than 2m. tons of plastics, 2.8m. tons of steel and more than 4m. tons of fertilizer). A fall in international prices for many petrochemical products caused SABIC's profits to decrease by almost 30% to 4,412m. riyals in 1996.

In 1997 SABIC's total production rose by 3% to 23.7m. metric tons, while its marketed production rose by 4.5% to 18.39m. tons, comprising 9.2m. tons of petrochemicals, 2.85m. tons of steel, 2.8m. tons of fertilizers, 2.3m. tons of plastics, 1.1m. tons of industrial gases and 140,000 tons of polyester products. Turnover rose by 15.3% to 24,023m. riyals in 1997, while net profits rose by 4.3% to 4,600m. riyals. In 1998, however, net profits declined by some 50%, to 2,020m. riyals. A company spokesman said that SABIC's competitive position had been eroded in 1998 because the decline in world oil prices (which benefited overseas petrochemicals manufacturers using oil-derived feedstocks) had occurred at a time when Saudi Arabia's gas-based factories were absorbing a 50% rise in their own feedstock costs. SABIC's poor performance in 1998 affected the company's ability to proceed with its planned investment. A programme of restructuring, in which a number of separate affiliates were established, was initiated; the affiliates were expected to enter into joint ventures with private national and international companies and were also expected to prove more attractive to project finance. SABIC's declining profits forced the company's affiliates to approach creditor banks in order to reschedule debts from earlier expansion projects. In September 1999 three SABIC affiliates (the Saudi Iron and Steel Co (Hadeed), the Arabian Industrial Fiber Co (Ibn Rushd) and Ibn Zahr) were reported to be engaged in talks to restructure finance totalling some US $2,500m.

A joint venture with Taiwan Fertilizer Co, Saudi Fertilizer Co (Samad), has an annual capacity of 500,000 metric tons of urea. In August 1983 its production was 167,760 tons, but by the beginning of 1985 it had reached its full capacity. In early 1985 the Saudi Arabian Fertilizer Co (SAFCO) and SABIC formed a company to build a 1,500 tons-per-day ammonia plant at Jubail. In 1988 SAFCO produced 176,591 tons of ammonia, 284,994 tons of urea, approximately 91,728 tons of sulphuric acid and 17,839 tons of melamine. In 1991 SAFCO had a net income of 167m. riyals and announced plans for the construction of a new fertilizer complex at Jubail, at an estimated cost of 1,400m. riyals. Saudi Arabia's third fertilizer manufacturer, the National Chemical Fertilizer Co, opened a factory at Jubail in 1987. The aggregate annual capacity of Saudi Arabian fertilizer plants exceeded 3m. tons in 1993 and was targeted to reach 4m. tons before the end of the decade. The producing companies (all affiliates of SABIC) signed a 'services agreement' in January 1994 to consolidate many of their operational and management functions. In 1997 SAFCO's net profit fell by 29% to 438m. riyals, reflecting (notably) the impact of China's termination of fertilizer imports in the latter part of the year. Its net profit for the first half of 1998 was 110m. riyals, some 62% lower than the first-half profit in 1997. SAFCO's figures for the first half of 1999 showed a loss, but during the equivalent period in 2000 there was a profit of 86m. riyals. The main factor in these fluctuations is the unstable market.

The Saudi Iron and Steel Co (Hadeed), based in Jubail, is a joint venture with Germany's Korf-Stahl. In 1991 Hadeed began exporting iron products to Far East and South-East Asian countries. In July a shipment of about 10,000 metric tons of reinforcing bars and wire rod coils was exported to Japan, and further sales to Singapore, Taiwan and South Korea, in July and August, raised exports to more than 40,000 tons. In 1985 production of steel was 1.18m. tons, and in 1986 output increased to 1.9m. tons. An expansion programme, for which a seven-year loan of 500m. riyals was signed in August 1991, was intended to increase steel capacity at Hadeed's Jubail plant to 2m. tons per year. In 1991 self-sufficiency was achieved within the Saudi Arabian steel industry, which expanded to satisfy construction requirements within the kingdom and other GCC countries. Steel output from the expanded Hadeed plant reached a record 2.54m. tons in 1996. A contract to build a rolling mill at Jubail with an annual capacity of 850,000 tons of flat steel products was awarded in 1996. The rolling mill had come on stream by June 2000, and at that time, an existing plant, the Jeddah Steel Rolling Mill (Sulb) with a capacity of 140,000 tons of steel rods and bars per year, was closed down as it was not suitable for expansion. Existing Hadeed facilities undergoing expansion and upgrading in 1997 included a rod mill, a section and bar mill and an electric arc furnace. In September 1999, as a result of cash-flow difficulties, Hadeed sought to restructure

loans of 4,725m. riyals. It also postponed further capacity expansion in Jubail and was forced to negotiate with its creditors without the provision of a guarantee from SABIC, its holding company.

In the private sector, in mid-1988 the National Industrialization Co (NIC) announced plans to construct a steel foundry at Dammam with a capacity of 10,000 metric tons per year, at an estimated cost of 117m. riyals. Construction work was expected to reach completion in 1991. NIC is also planning the construction of a steel wire plant at Jubail, with a provisional capacity of about 50,000 tons per year, to produce specialized steel wires and related wire products. In 1990 profits fell from 17m. riyals in 1989 to 14m. riyals. This decline was attributed to the failure of certain companies, in which NIC has shareholdings, to announce dividends. The reduction in profits continued to reflect NIC's poor performance in its delayed implementation of the many industrial projects that it had initiated. In 1994 NIC reported a net profit of 9.4m. riyals (55% less than in 1993). In the late 1990s the NIC was reported to be working on a US $570m. propane dehydrogeneration and polypropylene scheme.

One of SABIC's most notable joint venture proposals was agreed in 1983 between SABIC and private Saudi Arabian investors. Called the National Gas Co (Gas), it was expected to produce 146,000 metric tons of nitrogen and 438,000 tons of oxygen per year by 1985. Further joint ventures, agreed in 1984, included a partnership with Italy and Finland to produce fractionated gases.

The success of these ventures depends, to a large extent, on effective marketing, and all partners are bound to market at least 40% of production in their own countries. The basis for such ambitious heavy industrial schemes is a gas-gathering project, Master Gas System (MGS), which is being implemented by Saudi Aramco. Natural gas will provide the raw material for the petrochemicals industry and an energy source for the steel plant. The scheme was initiated in 1975, when it was expected to cost US $5,000m. and to produce 156m. cu m per day. By the time of its completion in 1982, however, the first phase of the scheme had cost an estimated $12,000m., with a capacity of 98m. cu m per day. In January 1998 Saudi Aramco increased its charge to industrial users of ethane and methane. The new tariff covered about two-thirds of the estimated replacement cost to Saudi Aramco as operator of the MGS. Three processing plants have been built (at Berri, Shedgum and Uthmaniyah) to separate out natural gas liquids (NGLs) from methane, and two fractionation plants, at Juaymeh on the Gulf coast and at Yanbu on the Red Sea, process the NGLs into ethane, liquefied petroleum gas (LPG) and condensate. Gas is carried to Yanbu through the 1,200-km Trans-Arabian pipeline. The Berri, Shedgum and Juaymeh plants had all started production by mid-1980, the Uthmaniyah plant began operating in 1981, and the Yanbu plant started in 1982. Apart from fuelling industrial development, the scheme was to have made Saudi Arabia one of the world's largest exporters of LPG, with shipments of about 650,000 b/d. In 1991, however, SAMAREC amended its LPG price-indexing mechanism, owing to the exceptional volatility of the LPG market. As a result, SAMAREC introduced an upper limit on the permitted volume of exported LPG, in order to compensate for any rapid change in prices. In June 1992 SAMAREC signed 15 five-year contracts for the supply of a total of 42m. metric tons of LPG to Japanese, South Korean, British and Saudi Arabian companies. There are also facilities for the recovery of sulphur: three plants, with a combined annual capacity of about 1.3m. barrels, came into operation in 1981, and total sales in 1982 reached 800,000 tons.

Most of the gas which is produced in Saudi Arabia is associated gas (i.e. it is found in conjunction with petroleum), so the decline in petroleum output in the mid-1980s led to shortfalls in the production of gas and its 'downstream' products. Work on the second phase of the MGS scheme is under way, aiming to exploit associated gas from offshore fields and to reduce the problem of gas shortages created by declines in production of petroleum. The installed processing capacity of the MGS in 1993 was estimated at 121.8m. cu m per day, based on crude oil output of about 8.2m. b/d. Saudi Aramco's refinery at Ras Tanura has been producing NGLs since 1962, and production totalled 155m. barrels in 1982. Recovery of NGLs from associated gases rose by

27%, from 420,946 b/d in 1989, to 533,229 b/d in 1990. Similarly, production of refined products at Ras Tanura increased from 174m. barrels in 1989 to 192m. barrels in 1990, with significant increases in the output of jet fuel and fuel oil. There were plans to exploit unassociated gas, independent of petroleum extraction, by 1986. The Khuff reservoir of unassociated gas in the Ghawar oilfield, estimated to contain more than one-half of Saudi Arabia's natural gas reserves, was scheduled to yield 20m. cu m per day. Saudi Arabia's marketed output of natural gas in 2001 (excluding gas flared or reinjected into oil wells) totalled 53,700m. cu m. Expansion schemes under way in 1997 (including the development of a major new gathering facility at Hawiya for unassociated gas) were designed to increase the installed processing capacity of the MGS to 195m. cu m per day by 2001. However, the programme began to fall behind schedule in early 1998 when the bids submitted for the main phases of the installation work were unacceptably high. Saudi Aramco subsequently re-examined the project specifications and invited contractors to submit new tenders for the work; contracts were awarded in late 1998 and early 1999, with part financing from a Saudi bank. In June 2001 three major gas concessions, in South Ghawar, Shaybah and the Red Sea, were awarded to eight foreign oil companies, including Exxon Mobil, Shell Oil Co and BP. The concessions marked the return of foreign companies into Saudi Arabia's fuel industry since it was nationalized in 1975. Total investment arising from the concessions was estimated at US $25,000m.

The Government is encouraging Saudi private enterprise to develop smaller-scale industries. A total of eight industrial estates offer basic infrastructure and services at minimal charge, credit is available on favourable terms, and selected products are protected by duties on imports. The Saudi Industrial Development Fund (SIDF) was established in 1974 to provide concessionary loans to private investors, and the NIC was established in 1984, by private investors, to develop and control investment by private individuals. By 1991 the SIDF had an authorized capital of 8,000m. riyals and had granted 1,404 loans, amounting to 18,738m. riyals. During 1996 the SIDF approved 109 loans totalling 2,429m. riyals. The building materials sector, and in particular the cement industry, is flourishing, as are electrical equipment manufacturing, the production of chemical rubber and plastics, and food processing and soft drinks. National cement output of 14.1m. metric tons in 1992 covered 98% of the rapidly rising domestic demand, prompting five of the kingdom's seven publicly-traded cement companies to announce expansion plans, which would increase total cement production capacity by almost one-third, to 18.5m. tons per year. Cement imports increased to 2m. tons in 1994. Saudi Arabia's annual demand for all types of cement in 1996 was 17.3m. tons (including 16m. tons of Portland cement). In 1997 Saudi cement production fell by 6% to 15.4m. tons; 14m. tons were consumed locally, 1.3m. tons were exported and the remainder stockpiled. Saudi Arabia's installed cement production capacity rose to 22.7m. tons per year in 1998, following the establishment of an eighth producing company. Cement production increased to 16.4m. tons in 1999 and 18.2m. tons in 2000.

In 1991 the Ministry of Industry and Electricity approved a licence for the newly-established Saudi Industrial Development Co (SIDC) to build a ceramics plant in the Western Province. The scheme would involve a total investment of 311m. riyals. The output of the new plant and that of the Saudi Ceramics Co, based in Riyadh, was expected to satisfy 80% of the domestic market. As part of its policy to stimulate the Saudi private sector, the Government sold 30% of SABIC's capital in 1984. In 1990 there were 2,255 factories in operation, of which the metals industry accounted for 28.1%, building materials 24.8%, and food and beverages 16%. A public flotation of shares in the SIDC in mid-1992, intended to raise 250m. riyals, was vastly oversubscribed. The SIDC planned to invest in various industrial projects, including a US $64m. pharmaceuticals factory. The number of industrial licences issued in 1996 was more than treble the level of 1989, and at that time authorized capital nearly doubled, to 7,300m. riyals.

At the end of 1994 the Minister for Industry and Electricity stated that the Saudi manufacturing sector currently had an invested capital of more than US $40,000m., annual production

of more than $15,000m. and annual exports of more than $3,000m., although its share of GDP was less than half of the Government's 22% planning target. Nearly $26,000m. was currently invested in chemicals and plastics enterprises; nearly $5,300m. in the manufacture of building materials, ceramics and glass; $3,500m. in production of machine tools and finished metal goods; $2,400m. in food and beverage production; $1,100m. in basic metal industries; $1,100m. in paper and printing; and $533m. in the manufacture of textiles, clothing and leather. In 1997 Saudi Arabia's first sugar refinery, with the capacity to produce 500,000 metric tons per year from imported raw sugar, began production at Jeddah, and there were plans to increase its capacity by 47%, to 765,000 tons per year, by the end of 2002.

Non-oil mineral production includes limestone (for cement manufacture), gypsum, marble, clay and salt. Substantial deposits of bauxite, iron ore and magnesite, as well as copper, gold, lead, zinc, silver and some uranium, are known to exist. A mine at Mahd adh-Dhahab, with 1.2m. metric tons of ore (including gold), was inaugurated in 1983. Construction of a gold-mining town began at the end of 1994, and annual output of gold from the mine reached 3.5 tons in 1991, with estimated reserves of 1,123,000 tons. In 1997 the mine's reserves were estimated to be more than 2m. tons and in 1996 157,000 oz of gold, 479,000 oz of silver and 900 tons of copper were produced. Production of zinc concentrate, at an annual rate of up to 10,000 tons, was due to begin in 1997. In 1991 there were 495 known sites of gold deposits in Saudi Arabia, of which 31 were estimated to contain more than 1,000 kg each and a further 99 were estimated to contain at least 100 kg each. In 1986 large quantities of gold were discovered in the Sukhaybarat area, and in 1991 the Saudi Company for Precious Metals (a joint venture between PETROMIN and a Swedish company, Boliden) began gold production, which reached 978 kg by the end of the year. By the end of 1996 cumulative production had reached 13,000 kg of fine gold. Reserves at Sukhaybarat were estimated at 8.4m. tons. The private-sector Arabian Shield Development Co was awarded a 30-year mining lease in 1993 for the al-Masane area of south-western Saudi Arabia, where substantial deposits of copper, zinc, gold and silver were known to exist. Feasibility studies were in progress in 1994 for a proposed US $50m. mining project and associated plans to create zinc-processing facilities at Yanbu. At the end of 1996 the project was granted an industrial licence after preparing plans envisaging annual yields of 31,270 tons of zinc, 8,750 tons of copper, 13,100 oz of gold, 550,000 oz of silver and 12 tons of bullion (98% silver and 2% gold). At the end of 1997 the US-owned Arabian Shield Development Co set up the Arabian Shield Company for Mining Industries as a joint venture with the Saudi-owned Al-Mashreq Company for Mining Investments. Financial backers of the Arabian Shield project included the SIDF, which agreed to provide a $38m. interest-free loan. In 1994 the Government invited applications to develop a recently evaluated iron ore deposit at Wadi Sawawin in north-western Saudi Arabia. It was estimated that an investment of $550m. would be needed to develop an open-pit mine and ore beneficiation facility for the production of pellets at an annual rate of 2.2m. tons for 25 years. There are 213m. tons of proven phosphate-bearing ore (averaging 21% phosphoric anhydride content) at al-Jalamid in the far north of Saudi Arabia. In May 1994 the Government invited proposals for the extraction from these reserves of 4.5m. tons of phosphate concentrate per year, to be transported by slurry pipeline to Jubail as feedstock for a proposed 2.9m. tons-per-year diammonium phosphate plant. A feasibility study was initiated in 1993 on proposals to establish a 150,000 tons-per-year copper smelter and refinery at Yanbu.

Strategic control of the minerals sector is exercised by the Directorate-General of Mineral Resources (DGMR). In 1997 the state-owned Saudi Arabian Mining Company (Ma'aden) was established to take over existing state interests in the non-oil mining sector and to serve as a vehicle for future state mining ventures. Ma'aden had an initial capital of 4,000m. riyals. In addition to taking sole ownership of the Mahd adh-Dhahab mine, where 1997 gold production was around 170,000 oz, Ma'aden inherited PETROMIN's 50% interest in the Sukhaybarat gold mine, whose 1997 production was around 90,000 oz. Ma'aden was granted a 30-year gold mining lease at al-Amar

(220 km south-west of Riyadh) in September 1997 and a 30-year gold and silver mining lease at al-Hajar (350 km south-east of Jeddah) in May 1998. The al-Hajar mine is expected to produce about 55,000 oz per year of gold and 235,000 oz per year of silver. The company said that it aimed to double Saudi Arabia's gold production by 2001. Demand for gold in Saudi Arabia (one of the top five consuming countries) increased by 8% to 199 tons in 1997. Ma'aden is also to exploit magnetite deposits near Hail.

ELECTRICITY AND WATER

Saudi Arabia's electricity system has to satisfy rapidly growing urban and industrial demand, and also to supply power for small, widely-scattered rural settlements. Until the 1970s, generation was controlled by a large number of small companies: 26 of them were operating in the Eastern Province alone. The main aim was to create regional grids, each operated by a single company. In 1977 the companies operating in the Eastern Province merged into a single Saudi Consolidated Electric Co (SCECO-East), managed by Aramco. A unified company for the southern region (SCECO-South) was formed in 1979. The other unified regional companies are SCECO-West and SCECO-Central. Northern areas continued to be supplied by separately-controlled local plants in 1994. SCECO-Central imports about 40% of its supply from SCECO-East via the only connection between two regional grids. Total sales of electric power increased from 1,690m. kWh in 1970 to 55,201m. kWh in 1988/89, of which 15,524m. kWh were used by industry. An increasing amount of electricity is now produced in association with sea-water desalination. Demand increased during the 1990s, and a major programme for the expansion of capacity was planned, coupled with a campaign to reduce wasteful consumption (accounting for an estimated 30% of current electricity usage). By 1999 installed generating capacity totalled 23,438 MW. In 1997 the number of electricity subscribers rose by 115,000 to 3.15m., and by 1997, according to government estimates, demand was growing at an annual rate of 16% (the Government's long-term forecast for 1995–2020 envisaged annual growth of 4.5%). A wide range of development options, including national and international private sector participation, were under review in 1997 as the Government considered the practicalities of sustaining an expansion of generating capacity at an average rate of 1,500 MW–2,000 MW per year. In April 1997 contractors were invited to bid for a new power station development on a 'build-own-operate' basis, although in mid-1998 it was reported that a conventional 'turnkey' bidder seemed likely to win the contract. During the Islamic year 1420 (April 1999–April 2000) electricity consumption increased by 4.7%, to 4,999.8m. kWh, while the total installed generating capacity (excluding energy generated by desalination plants) increased to 21,679 MW and the number of subscribers increased to 3,518,433.

The state body with overall responsibility for the Saudi electricity system is the General Electricity Corpn, founded in 1976. The Corporation has been especially active in establishing power networks in rural areas. By 1982 SCECO-South was implementing its own rural schemes, including the largest single rural project, Tihama rural electricity supply programme, costing an estimated 4,000m. riyals. By August 1984 the overall target of the 1980–85 Development Plan, which was to provide 80% of the population with electricity and water, had already been reached. Substantial additional progress has since been made in this field with the aid of heavy government subsidies, which necessitated a considerable financial burden. As a result the Government has been preparing the electricity sector for eventual privatization. In November 1998 it was announced that the 10 existing power companies (four Saudi Consolidated Electric Companies and six smaller regional power-generating companies) were to be merged into the Saudi Electricity Company (SEC), which would also take over rural electric power provision from the General Electricity Corpn. A new higher structure of tariffs was to be introduced prior to SEC's incorporation and the new company was to be mandated to collect tariffs more effectively. A regulatory body was to be established within one year of SEC's incorporation. Greater efficiency was to be achieved through the further development of a national electricity network.

Urban water supply has been a major challenge. At one time the exploitation of underground resources appeared to be the best solution, but this has encountered technical difficulties. However, aquifers at depths as great as 1,700 m are to be tapped. The largest projects are at Riyadh: the Minjur aquifer began supplying the city in 1979, and the huge Wasia aquifer produced 200,000 cu m of water per day in 1983, while an additional 110,000 cu m per day were supplied by Salbakh and Buwaib. The construction of dams throughout the kingdom, as a means of preserving rainwater, has also expanded in recent years. By 2000 the total number of dams in Saudi Arabia was 197 (with aggregate storage capacity of 809m. cu m). A further 11 dams were under construction in 2001. Water (renewable underground and surface water, rain water and recycled sewage water) consumed by the agricultural sector totalled some 18,000m. cu m in 2000; renewable underground water accounted for 40% of this total.

Desalination projects are the responsibility of the Saline Water Conversion Corpn (SWCC), which is the world's largest producer of desalinated water. Jeddah already receives 350,000 cu m per day, or 91% of its water, from the SWCC, and massive new plants at Jubail and al-Khobar are due to supply the Eastern Province. In 1991 the Western Province Water and Sanitary Disposal Department approved contracts worth 327m. riyals to undertake three maintenance programmes in Mecca and Jeddah. A pipeline carries water from the Jubail plant inland to Riyadh. In the mid-1990s the Shuaiba desalination plant was pumping 35m. gallons to Mecca and 15m. gallons to Ta'if daily. The 1985–90 Plan foresaw investment of 31,789m. riyals in water projects. The aim was to increase desalination capacity to 1.8m. cu m per day by 1990. Emphasis was to be placed on developing water reuse and surface water resources for direct use and for recharging aquifers. In 1991 a contract worth 31m. riyals was awarded to As-Saiqh Trading to implement an expansion project in Yanbu, and a contract worth 15m. riyals was awarded to Al-Fahd Corporation for Trading, Contracting and Industry to work on one of a series of projects to dispose of rising ground water in Riyadh. The SWCC had a 1996 project budget of 1,900m. riyals (unchanged from 1995), of which an estimated 800m.–1,000m. riyals was required for maintenance work on existing installations. Water output in 1996 was around 2.36m. cu m (520m. gallons) per day, while the SWCC's electricity generating capacity was around 3,000 MW (due to rise to 4,500 MW on completion of the current expansion programme). In 2000 the SWCC had 27 plants, with a combined capacity of about 2m. cu m (450m. gallons) per day. Total production of desalinated water increased by 6.7% in 2000, to 827.1m. cu m (equivalent to some 30% of total world production).

TRANSPORT, COMMUNICATIONS AND TOURISM

Until 1964 the only surfaced roads, besides those in the petroleum network, were in the Jeddah-Mecca-Medina area. Since then, roads have been given priority, and at the end of 2000 there were about 155,237 km of roads, of which about 31% were paved. In 2001 plans were unveiled to build 3,950 km of major roads (at a cost of US $5,400m.) in order to link the main cities with remote provinces. A causeway linking Bahrain with the Saudi mainland was opened in late 1986. It is open for 24 hours per day, although trucks and lorries may only use it at off-peak times. Saudi Arabia's national bus operator, the Saudi Public Transport Co (SAPTCO), whose 1,700 vehicles serve mainly inter-city routes), made a net profit of 82.6m. riyals in the first half of 1994.

The main seaports are at Jeddah, Yanbu and Gizan on the Red Sea and at Dammam and Jubail on the Gulf. A programme of rapid expansion and modernization was undertaken by the Saudi Ports Authority (SEAPA) in the late 1970s which improved facilities, particularly at Jubail, Yanbu and Gizan. In 1988 the expansion of exports from the agricultural and industrial sectors led to a revival in cargo-handling, despite the continuing decline in the volume of imports. The emergence of the industrial ports of Jubail and Dammam as important export centres was prompted by the decision, in 1987, to reduce port tariffs for industrial and some agricultural goods produced locally by 50% and to extend the period of free storage from two to 10 days. Jeddah port, however, has continued to suffer from the decline in imported cargo, and therefore SEAPA agreed in late 1988 to revise the regulations to allow transhipment. An estimated 12,000 vessels use Saudi Arabian portsannually, which, in 2002 had a total of 183 organized and mechanized berths (137 at six commercial ports and 46 at two industrial ports). The volume of cargo (excluding crude petroleum) handled by Saudi ports in 2001 totalled 100.6m. metric tons (68.9m. tons of exports and 31.7m. tons of imports). A programme was introduced in 1997 to 'commercialize' the operation of the main ports by offering 10-year operations, maintenance and management leases to private-sector contractors, who would derive their income from stevedoring fees charged to port users and would pay a proportion of their income to SEAPA as royalties. In 1983 Saudi Arabia became the 40th member of the London-based International Maritime (now Mobile) Satellite Organization (INMARSAT). Vela, the shipping arm of Saudi Aramco, owns one of the world's largest fleets of oil-tankers, which in 1994 included 23 vessels classified as very large or ultra-large crude carriers. In 1997 the National Shipping Company of Saudi Arabia (NSCSA) made a net profit of 5m. riyals, compared with a net loss of 77.5m. riyals in 1996. Primarily an operator of container and general cargo services, the NSCSA also owned five very large crude carriers, currently on long-term charter to Vela.

In the late 1980s Saudi Arabia established satellite transmission and reception stations, facilitating direct telephone dialling to most of the rest of the world. About 50,000 new telephone lines became available in mid-1996, on completion of the first phase of a US $3,950m. scheme to add 1.5m. digital lines to the system over a seven-year period. In 2001 there were an estimated 3.2m. telephone lines installed, the current planning aim being to reach a 'teledensity' of at least 30 lines per 100 inhabitants within five years. The number of mobile cellular telephone users in the kingdom increased from 174,700 in 1996 to 316,100 in 1997 and had reached an estimated 2.5m. by 2001. In April 1998 a royal decree authorized the transfer of state-run telecommunications interests to a new Saudi Telecommunications Company (STC) with an initial capital of 12,000m. riyals. It was intended that STC, once established as a profitable commercial enterprise, should become the subject of Saudi Arabia's first major privatization exercise. In July 2002 the Saudi Communications Commission issued new legislation which provided a comprehensive framework for deregulation of the telecommunications sector. Private involvement was, meanwhile, introduced into the provision of postal services in June 1998, when the first three-year licences were issued to applicants wishing to set up privately-run post offices in six areas of the kingdom.

There are 25 commercial airports in the kingdom. The principal international airports are at Jeddah (King Abd al-Aziz), Dhahran (the Eastern Province International Airport) and Riyadh (King Khalid). In the late 1970s plans were announced for new airports in the three main regions. King Fahd International Airport in Dhahran came into operation in 1990. The new Riyadh airport, inaugurated in November 1983, cost some US $5,000m. to build and is one of the world's largest. More than 25m. passengers, including 16m. on domestic flights, passed through Saudi Arabian airports on normal flights in 1996. There were also 864,000 passengers on special flights for Muslim pilgrims. In July 1998 the Government drew up plans to introduce departure taxes for all non-pilgrim travellers on international routes, the proposed rates being 50 riyals at airports and 20 riyals at seaports. Total passenger numbers in 2000 increased to 27.5m., while 467,000 metric tons of cargo were carried in the same year.

The Government operates the national carrier, Saudi Arabian Airlines, which links important Saudi cities and operates regular flights to many foreign countries. In October 1995 it signed an agreement to purchase 61 new aircraft from the US companies Boeing and McDonnell Douglas at an estimated total cost of US $7,500m. New hangars and maintenance facilities were expected to cost a further $600m. Delivery of the new fleet was to begin in September 1996 and be completed within three to five years, while payment for the aircraft would be made over a period of up to 10 years. It was intended that the introduction of the new fleet would be accompanied by a campaign to improve the airline's competitiveness (the Government's declared aim being to open the airline to private investment as soon as its

operations had been suitably restructured). Use of the name Saudia (introduced in 1972) was phased out at the end of 1996 and replaced by the full name Saudi Arabian Airlines. In 1996 the airline carried 11.7m. passengers, including 3.87m. on international services, and handled 225,473 metric tons of freight, 65% of it on international routes. By mid-2001 the airline was taking delivery of new aircraft at the rate of three to four per month, and expected to have 58 of its new fleet in operation by the end of 2000.

Saudi Arabia has the only rail system in the Arabian peninsula; in 2000 it carried 853,780 passengers and 1.6m. metric tons of freight. The principal lines are a 571-km single-track railway which connects the port of Dammam, on the Gulf, with Riyadh, and a 322-km line, linking Riyadh with Hufuf, which was inaugurated in May 1985. In early 1995 plans to create a 120-km rail link between Dammam and Jubail, at an estimated cost of 920m. riyals, were presented to potential industrial users and development authorities by the Saudi Railway Organization, which forecast an annual revenue yield of between 140m. and 170m. riyals if the scheme was implemented. In 1991 it was announced that an automated light railway service was to be built, to take pilgrims from parking areas to the Grand Mosque, as part of the project to develop the holy places in Mecca and Medina. The project was estimated to cost US $100m.

In 1996 several tourism development projects, representing a total investment of some 15,000m. riyals, were under way in Saudi Arabia, many of them designed to appeal primarily to Saudi citizens wishing to holiday in their own country. (Saudi citizens spent an estimated 6,700m. riyals on foreign tourism in 1995.) The largest single tourism development was the new town of al-Buhairat, being built at a cost of 4,800m. riyals to provide a wide range of accommodation and leisure facilities on the Red Sea coast at 45 km north of central Jeddah (and about 15 km from Jeddah's international airport). Designed to house a population of about 18,000 when fully developed, al-Buhairat was due to receive its first residents before the end of 1996. Another town-sized development, Durrat al-Arus, was under construction on an island at the mouth of the Gulf of Salman, north of al-Buhairat. Costing 1,300m. riyals and including a racecourse, golf-course, marina, theme park and aqua park, Durrat al-Arus was scheduled to open in mid-1996 and to complete all its planned attractions by 1998. Most tourism facilities under development on Saudi Arabia's Gulf coast in 1996 were smaller in scale. Developments in the Half Moon Bay area, south of al-Khobar, included the an-Nakheel tourist village, a complex of 120 villas under construction at a cost of 124m. riyals. During 2000 Saudis spent some 54,000m. riyals on foreign tourism, while tourism receipts totalled 6,750m. riyals; at the end of 2000 there were 518 hotels with some 50,000 rooms.

FOREIGN TRADE

The total value of the country's exports, of which more than 90% was provided by petroleum before 1988, rose from 138,242m. riyals in 1978 to 362,885m. riyals in 1980, but by 1985 had decreased to 99,536m. riyals, before increasing again, to 166,339m. riyals in 1990. Total exports, including re-exports, increased to 227,443m. riyals in 1997, declined to 145,388m. riyals in 1998, and then reached an estimated 190,084m. riyals in 1999. Sales of petroleum and petroleum products accounted for 88.5% of total export revenue in 1999. The estimated value of total exports in 2000 was 290,553m. riyals (of which amount some 267,750m. riyals—92.2%—was for petroleum and petroleum products). The principal customers for Saudi Arabia's exports in 1999 were the USA (taking 19.6% of the total), Japan (15.0%), the Republic of Korea (10.7%) and Singapore (5.8%). Other important sources of foreign exchange are the local expenditure of foreign companies and the pilgrimage traffic.

The value of Saudi Arabia's imports increased from 69,180m. riyals in 1978 to 139,335m. riyals in 1982, but fell to 85,564m. riyals in 1985, and by 1990 had increased to 90,282m. riyals. By 2001 imports were an estimated 116,931m. riyals. The main categories of imports are machinery and mechanical appliances, transport equipment, base metals, chemicals and textiles. In 2000 the kingdom's major suppliers were the USA (accounting for 19.2% of total imports), Japan (10.4%), Germany (8.0%), the United Kingdom (6.5%) and Italy (4.2%). The main items to be imported from Japan are cars, pick-up trucks and spare parts. Cars and machinery are the main imports from the USA, and from the United Kingdom military equipment is pre-eminent.

In 1990 the visible trade surplus increased by 150%, to US $22,889m., as a result of exports worth $44,414m. (an increase of 56.5% over 1989) and imports worth $21,525m. (an increase of 11.9%). Although the visible trade surplus decreased to $16,522m. (exports $42,395m., imports $25,873m.) in 1993, by 1996 the visible trade surplus was $35,370m. (exports $60,729m., imports $25,358m.). The decline in petroleum prices in 1998 severely affected trade in Saudi Arabia, reducing the visible trade surplus to $11,287m. (exports $38,822m., imports $27,535m.). In 1999, following the recovery of international petroleum prices, Saudi Arabia recorded a visible trade surplus of 25,039m. riyals (exports 50,757m., imports 25,717m.). The visible trade surplus increased to 49,843m. riyals in 2000 (exports 77,584m., imports 27,741m.), but decreased to 44,387m. riyals (exports 73,032m., imports 28,645m. riyals) in 2001.

Saudi Arabia's current-account surplus increased dramatically from US $2,520m. in 1973 to $23,025m. in 1974, under the influence of the increases in the price of petroleum, and in 1980 it reached $41,503m. The impact of the fall in petroleum output in 1982 was dramatic: the decline in export revenues was far greater than the drop in imports, and by 1983 a deficit of $16,852m. had been recorded. The deficit had decreased to $4,152m. by 1990, but in 1991 extraordinary items arising out of the Gulf conflict were largely responsible for a sharp increase in the overall current-account deficit to $27,546m. (that year's deficit on services being $35,896m., while net transfers abroad totalled $20,235m. and net unearned income totalled $6,767m.). The deficit decreased in the early 1990s and in 1996 the current account showed its first surplus (of $681m.) for 14 years. A further surplus, of $305m., was recorded in 1997. In 1998, however, owing to the decline in petroleum prices, a deficit of $13,150m. was recorded. In 1999, as oil prices recovered, a current account surplus of 412m. riyals was recorded and this increased to 14,336m. riyals in 2000 and 14,502m. riyals in 2001.

In June 1993 Saudi Arabia, which had held observer status to the General Agreement on Tariffs and Trade (GATT) since 1985, submitted an application for full membership. Negotiations with GATT's successor body, the World Trade Organization (WTO), have been prolonged and are unlikely to be completed before 2003. WTO membership appears to have become a major government objective, and a number of liberalization measures have been introduced in an apparent attempt to counter objections to WTO accession. In April 2000 new investment regulations were approved; these would permit wholly foreign-owned companies to benefit from all the tax concessions and infrastructure and financial support available to Saudi firms. Saudi Arabia had earlier raised the price of its gas feedstock to its domestic petrochemical industry, and began slowly liberalizing its financial markets and permitting foreigners to own property in the country. This represents a politically contentious restructuring of the economy and its regulatory system, and it is part of a wider reform programme; however, other measures, such as further regulation of intellectual property rights and removal of subsidies, may also be needed.

FINANCE

Since mid-1977, and particularly since July 1978, the Saudi Arabian Monetary Agency (SAMA) has made a series of frequent small adjustments in the exchange rate of the Saudi riyal against the US dollar. The riyal was devalued seven times in 1984, and following three further adjustments in the first six months of 1985, the exchange rate stood at $1 = 3.645 riyals in June. This rate remained unchanged until June 1986, when a rate of $1 = 3.745 riyals was established. Despite heavy pressure after mid-1993 from speculators, who maintained that the riyal was overvalued at a time of weak oil prices, the Government ruled out any devaluation, accepting a rise in Saudi interest rates at the end of 1993 in order to defend the existing exchange rate. SAMA, established in 1952, acts as a central bank.

At the end of 1977 Saudi Arabia's international reserves totalled US $30,034m. and were surpassed only by those of the Federal Republic of Germany. From April 1978 Saudi Arabia's reserves were redefined to exclude foreign exchange cover against the note issue, then about $5,300m. Under the new

definition, reserves declined to $16,756m. in October 1979, but then made a sharp recovery, rising to $32,422m. at the end of 1981. Reserves declined to $25,181m. in December 1985, and by December 1990 had declined further, to $11,897m. (including gold valued at $229m.). By the end of 1993 total reserves stood at only $7,649m., following heavy expenditure to finance the international action against Iraq in 1990–91 and to purchase new military equipment in the aftermath of the crisis. From 1996 figures for reserves reflected a change in the methodology for classifying foreign assets. Figures for reserves minus gold at the end of the year totalled $14,876m. at the end of 1997, decreasing to $14,220m. at the end of 1998 and recovering to $16,997m. at the end of 1999. By the end of 2000 reserves minus gold stood at $19,585m.

Until September 1997 there were 12 commercial banks in Saudi Arabia, of which three were wholly Saudi and nine joint ventures. The largest Saudi commercial bank is the National Commercial Bank (NCB). In that month the United Saudi Commercial Bank merged with the Saudi Cairo Bank to form the United Saudi Bank, making the total number of banks 11. In terms of its capital, the new bank is the third largest in the kingdom. In mid-1999 the United Saudi Bank completed a further merger, with the Saudi American Bank, reducing the total number of banks to 10.

Specialized credit institutions provide project finance: the SIDF, set up by the Government in 1974, is a major source. It grants low-interest loans for up to 50% of the total cost of a project (up to 80% in the case of electricity projects). The SIDF is managed by Chase Manhattan Bank. The Public Investment Fund (PIF), established in 1972, finances large-scale commercial and industrial projects in the public sector. In 1984 the National Industrialization Co was established by private investors: its object is to encourage and plan development in the private sector.

Another major state financial institution which assists in the country's development is the Real Estate Development Fund (REDF), whose capital has been raised successively from 240m. riyals to 23,800m. riyals. The REDF provides a home-loan scheme under which purchasers are required to pay 80% of loan principal. The Saudi Agricultural Bank, set up in 1963, offers medium- and short-term loans for farmers. The Saudi Credit Bank was set up in 1973 to advance interest-free loans to low-income Saudis for purposes such as getting married or carrying out home repairs.

Saudi banks have become more outward-looking, and the most obvious example of this trend is the 55% Saudi-owned Saudi International Bank, which opened as a fully-fledged merchant bank in London, United Kingdom, in March 1976. SAMA holds 50% of the capital, while the NCB and Riyad Bank have 2.5% each. The principal non-Saudi partner in the enterprise is the Morgan Guaranty Trust Co, a US bank, which also provides management. The first wholly private Saudi bank abroad—As-Saudi Banque—opened in Paris, France, in the autumn of 1976. Riyad Bank has a share in the Paris-based Union de Banques Arabes et Françaises, and in the Gulf Riyad Bank in Bahrain. The NCB has small stakes in European-Arab Holding and the Compagnie Arabe et Internationale d'Investissement, both based in Luxembourg, and in the Amman-based Arab-Jordanian Investment Bank, which opened in the spring of 1978.

In 1988 the performance of the banking sector improved, although the recovery was not uniform among all the 12 commercial banks. The United Saudi Commercial Bank, Riyad Bank and the Arab National Bank increased their profits, but NCB recorded no profit and the Saudi Cairo Bank trebled its losses. The main reason for the poor performance of the banking sector in the mid-1980s was the domestic recession, but they also needed to make substantial provision against loan losses. In 1985 SAMA began requiring banks to report their non-performing loans. In March 1987 King Fahd ordered the central bank to establish a committee to arbitrate in bank loan disputes. By mid-1988 the outstanding loans and advances disbursed by the Saudi Agricultural Bank, the Saudi Credit Bank, the PIF, the SIDF and the REDF totalled 166,600m. riyals. In 1992 the Saudi commercial banking sector experienced very strong growth. The audited accounts released by the 11 publicly-quoted banks showed aggregate assets of 234,233m. riyals, an increase of 13.4% on the 1991 total, and aggregate profits of 3,712m.

riyals, a rise of nearly 29% on the previous year's level. A 30% increase in Saudi banking profits in 1993 was followed by a 4% fall in 1994, when commercial banks' aggregate net income totalled 4,808m. riyals. In 1998 Saudi Arabia's 11 commercial banks had aggregate assets of 386,032m. riyals, compared with 357,947m. riyals in 1997, when aggregate net profits were 6,588m. riyals. In the first half of 1999 the commercial banks' total assets increased to 412,565m. riyals, and profits also increased by 6.7%.

During the course of 1994 banks came under increasing pressure to provide short-term credit facilities to companies affected by delays in government payments to contractors undertaking public-sector projects. By the last quarter of the year, when some payments were more than 12 months overdue, a total of 18,750m. riyals was believed to be involved, causing senior bankers to appeal for urgent government action to resolve the situation. The Government subsequently undertook to release cash payments to contractors that were owed less than 10m. riyals, and had by late April 1995 reduced its debt to such contractors by an estimated 3,000m.–5,000m. riyals. Contractors owed more than 10m. riyals were, in March 1995, issued with government bonds maturing at different dates between March 1996 and September 1997 and carrying fixed coupons of between 6.5% and 7.25%. The bonds were negotiable through the banking system and could be used as security against commercial borrowing. The March 1995 bond issue covered a total of 5,200m. riyals owed to 120 local and foreign companies. Between January and March 1996 the Government issued negotiable non-interest-bearing certificates to the value of an estimated 9,500m. riyals to Saudi farmers who were awaiting official payments (mainly for grain production). Contractors' bonds worth an estimated 4,000m. riyals, and maturing between April 1998 and April 2002, were issued to corporate creditors in April 1996. In January 1998 the Saudi Government secured a seven-year sovereign loan of US $4,330m. from a consortium of international banks to finance the purchase of a new fleet of US aircraft for the national carrier Saudi Arabian Airlines. In mid-1998 Saudi Aramco renewed an existing $2,000m. five-year revolving credit facility and opened negotiations with international banks for a new $2,000m. syndicated loan repayable over four years.

In May 1987 Saudi Arabia opened its first stock-exchange trading floor in Riyadh, under the jurisdiction of SAMA. However, the Central Trading Hall was closed indefinitely less than a month after it had opened, owing to technical problems and to disagreement about procedures between the Ministry of Finance, which is responsible for SAMA, and the Ministry of Commerce. Shares are traded by banks and independent brokers, and in 1990 SAMA introduced an electronic trading system. Although the market is limited, the value of traded shares rose by 80% in 1991, compared with 1990, to some 8,000m. riyals, and share prices increased overall by about 70%. In 1995 shares were being traded in 69 companies with a market capitalization of 153,400m. riyals. In 1997 market capitalization was about 218,750m. riyals and the value of shares traded was 62,060m. riyals. It was estimated that the Government owned about 25% of all quoted shares in 1997 and that a single large corporation (SABIC) accounted for 21% of total market capitalization in that year. A Saudi Arabia Investment Fund was launched in June 1997 by Saudi American Bank as a vehicle for indirect market participation by non-GCC investors. Saudi Arabia's insurance market, in which about 80 companies and agencies were active in 1992, was worth some 1,870.5m. riyals in gross written premiums in that year.

In July 1989 Saudi Arabia signed a syndicated loan for US $660m., apparently the first international borrowing by the Saudi Government for a quarter of a century. There was a reluctance during the 1980s and 1990s to raise funds publicly, owing to the memory of the 1950s when an excess of borrowing led to economic crisis.

Owing to the Saudi Government's own budget deficit, in 1991 it was forced to sign a term-loan worth US $4,500m. with international banks, in addition to borrowing $2,500m. in foreign currency from domestic banks. It was agreed that the larger Saudi banks would lend a maximum of $400m. each to the Government, while the smaller banks would lend $50m.–$100m. each. The major part of the foreign borrowing was believed to be

needed to defray costs incurred as a result of the multinational military assistance provided to Saudi Arabia during the Gulf crisis in 1990–91. In November 1991 SAMA announced the kingdom's first issue of Treasury bills, starting with issues of up to 2,000m. riyals per week, to finance the budget deficit. The Government's other main public financing instrument is medium-term development bonds, first introduced in 1988. The first repayment of $900m. to international banks under the terms of the 1991 loan was made on schedule in May 1994. In April 1994 the Government had signed a new loan agreement under which a syndicate of local banks would lend the Ministry of Finance and National Economy $1,300m. over seven years, with two years' grace. Repayment of the international banks' 1991 loan was completed in May 1995. In 1996 SAMA accepted an invitation to join the Bank for International Settlements. In June 1998 the Government made its third issue of contractors' bonds, worth an estimated total of 5,000m.–6,000m. riyals; maturity periods ranged from one to five years and rates of interest payable ranged from 5.67% to 5.95%. In July the Government indicated that wheat farmers would receive a total of 2,200 riyals for their 1996 harvest but did not specify whether payment would be made in cash or certificates.

AID

Between 1973 and 1989 grants and concessionary loans that Saudi Arabia made available to developing countries totalled US $59,470m., representing 5.5% of GNP and placing the kingdom fourth in the world list of donors of aid. Among OPEC members, Saudi Arabia is by far the largest donor of aid, having contributed more than 80% of OPEC allocations in the period 1980–89. Between 1972 and 1983 aid totalling $25,568m. was provided to other Islamic states, where most aid is sent. The country has generally been the principal contributor to the various Arab funds that have been established to help poor Arab and poor African states, as well as to the IMF oil facilities. In April 1981 Saudi Arabia made a $10,000m. loan to the IMF for two years. Following further loans, the country was estimated to have advanced $15,000m. by 1984. It has also lent large sums to the World Bank at commercial rates. The Saudi Fund for Development (SFD), established in 1974, makes concessionary loans to Africa, Asia and Latin America, as well as to the Arab world. Financial support was given to Iraq during its war with Iran from 1980 to 1988, and in 1983 a substantial loan was granted to France. In March 1989 Saudi Arabia donated $85.5m. to the Palestine Liberation Organization (PLO), the last tranche of a 10-year programme of payments to the organization. A further $6m. per month during 1989 was pledged for Palestinians in the Israeli-occupied territories. In the period 1975–91 the SFD granted 277 loans to 61 countries, totalling 18,727m. riyals.

In May 1991 Saudi Arabia gave US $3,650m. in cash payments towards the US military effort in the Gulf War. The USA had so far received $8,186m. in cash for its military contribution. In July the Saudi Government approved a loan worth 64m. riyals to Egypt by the SFD, to build an expressway from Asyut to Cairo. In the same month the USA received a further $850m. for costs incurred during the Gulf crisis. Saudi Arabia pledged $16,839m. in total, and as of August the outstanding balance was $4,110m. In that month the Government announced its intention to give Turkey $1,000m. worth of free crude petroleum, in addition to supplies that Turkey had already received, worth $1,600m., to compensate for the adverse effects of the Gulf crisis on the Turkish economy, and also paid $175m. of its $1,000m. pledge to the United Kingdom towards that country's military costs during the Gulf War. Bangladesh was to receive aid worth $100m. to help in the rebuilding of infrastructure that was destroyed during the flood disaster in May 1991. In June 1997 $2.4m. of exceptional aid was given to the UN Relief and Works Agency for Palestine Refugees in the Near East.

BUDGETS

Government revenues from petroleum traditionally provide more than 90% of the State's budget revenue. The 1994 budget provided for the first balanced budget since 1982, at 160,000m. riyals. However, this revenue projection proved to be wholly unrealistic, and in the 1995 budget statement the Government's 1994 revenue was stated as 120,000m. riyals, leaving a deficit of 40,000m. riyals. In the 1995 budget provision was made for total expenditure of 150,056m. riyals and total revenue of 135,000m. riyals, leaving a 1995 budget deficit of 15,056m. The expenditure total in the budget did not include spending of 1,088m. riyals by the municipal and water sector or 2,175m. riyals by the state telephone company, funded out of the service providers' charges to users. On the revenue side of the 1995 budget, the Government used a very conservative oil price forecast of US $14 per barrel while imposing new or higher charges for a range of subsidized items, including fuel, power, water, telecommunications and transport. Other measures included substantial rises in visa fees for foreign workers. The total yield from domestic revenue-raising measures in 1995 was expected to exceed 9,000m. riyals.

The 1996 budget provided for total expenditure of 150,000m. riyals and total revenue of 131,500m. riyals, leaving a deficit of 18,500m. riyals. Less than half of the 1996 expenditure total was attributed to specific sectors in the budget announcement, the specified allocations being those for education (18.4%), health and social development (8.9%), transport and communications (6.1%), domestic subsidies (4.6%), infrastructure, industry and electricity (4.1%), and municipalities and water (3.6%). As in 1995, the revenue estimates assumed an average oil export price of US $14 per barrel, whereas the actual price of Saudi Arabia's main export grade averaged $17.73 per barrel in the first half of 1996 (compared with $16.26 per barrel in the first half of 1995). This price increased further in the second half of 1996 to $18.56 per barrel, boosting actual revenue for 1996 to 179,100m. riyals. Expenditure was revised upwards to 198,100m. riyals, leaving a deficit of 19,000m. riyals. Of the 48,100m. riyals of additional expenditure in 1996, some 22,000m. riyals were used to reduce the Government's indebtedness to domestic creditors. The 1997 budget provided for revenue of 164,000m. riyals and expenditure of 181,000m. riyals, leaving a deficit of 17,000m. riyals. Levels of taxation and subsidy remained unchanged in the 1997 budget, which included no new revenue-raising measures.

Oil export prices remained above budgeted levels in 1997, with the result that actual revenue for that year totalled 205,500m. riyals. Expenditure was revised upwards to 221,272m. riyals, leaving a deficit of 15,772m. riyals. The 1998 budget provided for total revenue of 178,000m. riyals and total expenditure of 196,000m. riyals, resulting in a deficit of 18,000m. riyals. Sectoral spending allocations itemized in the budget announcement were 45,595m. riyals (23.3% of total expenditure) for education, 19,700m. riyals (10%) for health and social development, 11,750m. riyals (6%) for transport and communications, 10,655m. riyals (5.4%) for infrastructure, industry and electricity, 7,640m. riyals (3.9%) for municipal services and water, 7,271m. riyals (3.7%) for domestic subsidies and social insurance, and 5,000m. riyals (2.5%) for state development organizations and funds. Independent analysts estimated that some 31.5% of the total 1998 budget was earmarked for spending on defence and national security. The Government's 1998 revenue projections assumed an average oil export price of about US $14.50 per barrel. However, the actual price of the kingdom's main export grade averaged only $11.46 per barrel

during the first half of 1998, compared with an average of $17.05 per barrel for the whole of 1997, resulting in actual revenue of 141,608m. riyals in 1998. Expenditure was reduced slightly, to 190,060m. riyals, increasing the deficit to 48,452m. riyals. The budget for 1999 envisaged a deficit of 44,000m. from revenue of 121,000m. riyals and expenditure of 165,000m. riyals. Sectoral spending allocations detailed in the 1999 budget were 42,900m. riyals (26% of total expenditure) for education, 18,700m. riyals (11.3%) for health and social development, 5,200m. riyals (3.2%) for transport and communications, 8,500m. riyals (5.2%) for infrastructure, industry and electricity, and 6,600m. riyals (4.0%) for municipal services and water. The increase in petroleum prices from the second half of 1999 resulted in increased revenue, of 147,000m. riyals, in that year. Expenditure was also increased, to 181,000m. riyals, although the deficit was reduced slightly, to 34,000m. riyals. The budget for 2000 predicted revenue of 157,000m. riyals and expenditure of 185,000m., with a resultant deficit of 28,000m. riyals, although revised figures for 2000 indicate a surplus of 45,000m riyals as a result of sustained high prices for petroleum for much of the year.

EDUCATION, HEALTH AND SOCIAL SECURITY

Within the Government's development policy, considerable emphasis has been placed on the improvement of education, health services and other aspects of social security. The number of schools and institutes of higher education increased from some 3,000 in 1970 to more than 20,000 in 1997, with the number of students increasing from 547,000 to 4.2m. over the same period. There are plans to expand the universities at Umm al-Qura, Jeddah and Medina. The number of hospitals under the control of the Ministry of Health increased from 47 in 1970 to 290 in 1998, with medical and paramedical personnel increasing from 4,494 to almost 100,000, and the number of beds to 43,000. In early 1991 there were four hospital beds for every 1,000 inhabitants, a ratio similar to that in the USA. In 1994 there were 1,668 health centres. In August the Ministry of Health announced that work would soon commence on the construction of 2,000 additional primary health care centres and that the possibility of establishing a comprehensive health insurance programme was being studied. In December 1995 the Government introduced a compulsory health insurance scheme for expatriate workers, 80% of the cost of contributions being borne by employers and 20% by employees. Total disbursements of social security payments increased from 41.7m. riyals (to 198,000 beneficiaries) in 1970 to 1,537m. riyals (to 314,117 beneficiaries) in 1985/86. The budget allocation for expenditure on health and social services in 2000 was 16,381m. riyals (8.9% of total expenditure), compared with the 1999 allocation of 15,152m. riyals (9.2%). Housing has also been an important part of government policy, and it is estimated that since 1974 more than 500,000 housing units have been constructed throughout the kingdom: about half by the Government and half by the private sector. By late 1991 a total of 477,000 housing units had been wholly or partly funded by the REDF. All adult Saudi Arabians, if not independently wealthy, are entitled to a plot of land and a loan of US $80,000 with which to build a home. In 1988 a total of 347,260 people received the loan.

Statistical Survey

Sources (unless otherwise indicated): Kingdom of Saudi Arabia, *Statistical Yearbook*; Saudi Arabian Monetary Agency, *Annual Report* and *Statistical Summary*.

Area and Population

AREA, POPULATION AND DENSITY

Area (sq km)	2,240,000*
Population (census results)	
9–14 September 1974	7,012,642
27 September 1992†	
Males	9,479,973
Females	7,468,415
Total	16,948,388
Population (official estimates at mid-year)	
1998	20,665,000
1999	21,334,000
2000	22,010,000
Density (per sq km) at mid-2000	9.8

* 864,869 sq miles.

† Of the total population at the 1992 census, 12,310,100 (males 50.5%; females 49.5%) were nationals of Saudi Arabia, while 4,638,300 (males 70.4%; females 29.6%) were foreign nationals. (Figures are rounded to the nearest '00.)

SAUDI ARABIA-IRAQ NEUTRAL ZONE

The Najdi (Saudi Arabian) frontier with Iraq was defined in the Treaty of Mohammara in May 1922. Later a Neutral Zone of 7,044 sq km was established adjacent to the western tip of the Kuwait frontier. No military or permanent buildings were to be erected in the zone and the nomads of both countries were to have unimpeded access to its pastures and wells. A further agreement concerning the administration of this zone was signed between Iraq and Saudi Arabia in May 1938. In July 1975 Iraq and Saudi Arabia signed an agreement providing for an equal division of the diamond-shaped zone between the two countries, with the border following a straight line through the zone.

SAUDI ARABIA-KUWAIT NEUTRAL ZONE

A Convention signed at Uqair in December 1922 fixed the Najdi (Saudi Arabian) boundary with Kuwait. The Convention also established a Neutral Zone of 5,770 sq km immediately to the south of Kuwait in which Saudi Arabia and Kuwait held equal rights. The final agreement on this matter was signed in 1963. Since 1966 the Neutral Zone, or Partitioned Zone as it is sometimes known, has been divided between the two countries and each administers its own half, in practice as an integral part of the State. However, the petroleum deposits in the Zone remain undivided and production from the onshore oil concessions in the Zone is shared equally between the two states' concessionaires.

PRINCIPAL TOWNS (population at 1992 census)

Riyadh (royal capital)	2,776,096	At-Ta'if . .		416,121
Jeddah (administra-		Tabouk . .		292,555
tive capital) . .	2,046,251	Buraidah . .		248,636
Makkah (Mecca) .	965,697	Hufuf . .		225,847
Al-Madinah (Medina)	608,295	Al-Mobarraz .		219,123
Dammam . . .	482,321	Khamis-Mushait .		217,870
		Ha'il (Hayil) .		176,757

2000 (UN estimates, incl. suburbs) Jeddah 3,192,000; Mecca 1,335,000; Medina 891,000; Dammam 764,000 (Source: UN, *World Urbanization Prospects: The 2001 Revision*).

2001 (UN estimates, incl. suburbs) Riyadh 4,761,000 (Source: UN, *World Urbanization Prospects: The 2001 Revision*).

BIRTHS AND DEATHS (UN estimates, annual averages)

	1985–90	1990–95	1995–2000
Birth rate (per 1,000) . . .	40.2	37.5	34.9
Death rate (per 1,000) . . .	6.0	5.0	4.4

Source: UN, *World Population Prospects: The 2000 Revision*.

Expectation of life (WHO estimates, years at birth, 2000): Males 68.1; Females 73.5 (Source: WHO, *World Health Report*).

EMPLOYMENT ('000 persons)

	1999
Agriculture, hunting, forestry and fishing	557.9
Mining and quarrying	112.1
Manufacturing	589.0
Electricity, gas and water.	93.5
Construction.	1,019.7
Trade, restaurants and hotels.	1,036.6
Transport and communications	299.2
Finance and real estate services	2,217.2
Government services	916.2
Other community and personal services . . .	334.9
Total	**7,176.3**
Saudi nationals	3,172.9
Non-Saudi nationals	4,003.4

Mid-2000 (estimates in '000): Agriculture, etc. 600; Total labour force 6,095 (Source: FAO).

Health and Welfare

KEY INDICATORS

Fertility (births per woman, 2000).	5.8
Under-5 mortality rate (per 1,000 live births, 2000). .	29
Physicians (per 1,000 head, 1997)	1.66
Hospital beds (per 1,000 head, 1997)	2.3
Health expenditure (1998): US $ per head (PPP) . .	459
% of GDP	4.1
public (% of total) . .	77.5
Access to water (% of persons, 2000)	95
Access to sanitation (% of persons, 2000) . . .	100
Human Development Index (2000): ranking . . .	71
value	0.759

For sources and definitions, see explanatory note on p. vi.

Agriculture

PRINCIPAL CROPS ('000 metric tons)

	1998	1999	2000
Wheat	1,734	2,046	1,800*
Barley	250	192	200*
Millet	12	7	7†
Sorghum	199	204	204†
Potatoes.	347	394	394†
Tomatoes	498	277	277†
Pumpkins, squash and gourds† .	79	80	80
Cucumbers and gherkins† .	122	125	125
Aubergines (Eggplants)† . .	79	80	80
Dry onions	171	95	95†
Carrots	51	65	65†
Okra†	58	59	59
Other vegetables† . . .	610	615	615
Citrus fruit†	88	89	89
Grapes	141	116	116†
Watermelons	372	285	285†
Cantaloupes and other melons†	141	141	141
Dates	648	712	712†
Other fruits†	274	275	275

* Unofficial figure.   † FAO estimate(s).

Source: FAO.

LIVESTOCK ('000 head, year ending September)

	1998	1999	2000*
Asses*	100	100	100
Camels	415	400*	400
Cattle	294	297	297
Sheep	7,421†	7,576†	7,576
Goats	4,350	4,305	4,305
Poultry*	130,000	130,000	130,000

* FAO estimate(s).   † Unofficial figure.

Source: FAO.

LIVESTOCK PRODUCTS ('000 metric tons)

	1998	1999	2000
Beef and veal . . .	19	19	19*
Mutton and lamb . . .	65†	70†	70*
Goat meat	20	21	21*
Poultry meat . . .	395†	418†	418*
Camel meat* . . .	53	50	50
Cows' milk* . . .	581	601	601
Sheep's milk* . . .	74	75	75
Goats' milk* . . .	72	71	71
Camels' milk* . . .	88	84	84
Poultry eggs	136	136	136*
Wool: greasy* . . .	10	10	10
Cattle hides (fresh) . . .	3	3	3*
Sheepskins (fresh) . . .	11	12	12
Goatskins (fresh). . .	4	4	4

* FAO estimate(s).   † Unofficial figure.

Source: FAO.

Fishing

(metric tons, live weight)

	1997	1998	1999
Capture	49,314	51,329	46,897
Groupers and seabasses . .	4,403	4,978	5,007
Snappers and jobfishes . .	2,148	2,391	1,997
Emperors (Scavengers) . .	6,904	4,773	6,844
Porgies and seabreams . .	2,481	2,796	2,803
Spinefeet (Rabbitfishes) . .	2,173	1,823	1,788
Carangids	5,925	5,469	6,065
Narrow-barred Spanish			
mackerel	5,511	7,032	6,294
Indian mackerel . . .	1,990	2,072	2,066
Penaeus shrimps . . .	7,011	7,812	3,892
Aquaculture	4,690	5,101	5,052
Nile tilapia	3,775	3,212	3,631
Total catch	54,004	56,430	51,949

Source: FAO, *Yearbook of Fishery Statistics.*

Mining

('000 metric tons, unless otherwise indicated)

	1998	1999	2000
Crude petroleum (million metric			
tons)* . . .	444.5	411.9	441.4
Natural gas (million cu metres)*†	46,800	46,200	49,800
Silver (kilograms)‡ . . .	13,840	10,470	9,300§
Gold (kilograms)‡ . . .	5,100	4,570	3,800§
Salt (unrefined) . . .	140§	200	200§
Gypsum (crude) . . .	330§	380	400§
Pozzolan§	145	140	150

* Including 50% of the total output of the Neutral or Partitioned Zone, shared with Kuwait.
† On a dry basis.
‡ Figures refer to the metal content of concentrate and bullion.
§ Estimated production.

2001: Crude petroleum 422.9m. metric tons; Natural gas 53,700m. cu metres.

Sources: partly US Geological Survey and *BP Statistical Review of World Energy*.

Industry

SELECTED PRODUCTS

(including 50% of the total output of the Neutral Zone; '000 metric tons, unless otherwise indicated)

	1996	1997	1998
Nitrogenous fertilizers (a)*† . .	1,064	981	1,080
Phosphatic fertilizers (b)*. . .	130	120	137
Jet fuel†	2,900	2,770	2,440
Motor spirit (petrol) . . .	11,844	11,309	12,242†
Naphtha†	5,182	4,948	5,356
Kerosene†	5,200	5,066	4,420
Gas-diesel (distillate fuel) oils .	25,735	24,514	23,352†
Residual fuel oils . .	27,114	24,834	26,500†
Lubricating oils† . . .	750	752	755
Petroleum bitumen (asphalt)† .	1,460	1,480	1,500
Liquefied petroleum gas:			
from natural gas plants† .	17,200	17,200	17,203
from petroleum refineries† .	920	920	922
Cement	16,391	15,448	15,776
Crude steel‡ . . .	2,683	2,539	2,356
Electric energy (million kWh) .	103,353	107,289	112,691†

1999 ('000 metric tons): Nitrogenous fertilizers (a)* 1,004†, Phosphatic fertilizers (b)* 150; Cement 16,381; Crude steel‡ 2,610†.

* Production in terms of (a) nitrogen or (b) phosphoric acid.
† Provisional or estimated figure(s).
‡ Data from the US Geological Survey.

Source: UN, *Industrial Commodity Statistics Yearbook.*

2000 ('000 metric tons): Cement 18,107; Crude steel 2,973 (Source: US Geological Survey).

Finance

CURRENCY AND EXCHANGE RATES

Monetary Units
100 halalah = 20 qurush = 1 Saudi riyal (SR).

Sterling, Dollar and Euro Equivalents (31 May 2002)
£1 sterling = 5.493 riyals;
US $1 = 3.745 riyals;
€1 = 3.515 riyals;
100 Saudi riyals = £18.21 = $26.70 = €28.45.

Exchange Rate
Since June 1986 the official mid-point rate has been fixed at US $1 = 3.745 riyals.

BUDGET ESTIMATES (million riyals)

Revenue	1999	2000	2001
Petroleum revenues	75,881	117,895	169,000
Other revenues	45,119	39,105	46,000
Total	121,000	157,000	215,000

Expenditure	1999	2000	2001
Human resource development. .	42,792	49,284	53,010
Transport and communications .	5,197	5,534	5,732
Economic resource development .	4,418	5,955	5,629
Health and social development .	15,152	16,381	18,089
Infrastructure development .	1,707	2,067	2,532
Municipal services	5,400	5,710	7,224
Defence and security	68,700	74,866	78,850
Public administration and other government spending .	16,458	19,277	37,372
Government lending institutions* .	420	436	411
Local subsidies	4,756	5,490	6,151
Total	165,000	185,000	215,000

* Including transfers to the Saudi Fund for Development (SFD).

1999 (revised figures, million riyals): Total revenue 147,454; Total expenditure 183,841.
2000 (revised figures, million riyals): Total revenue 258,065; Total expenditure 235,322.
2001 (revised figures, million riyals): Total revenue 230,000; Total expenditure 255,000.
2002 (estimates, million riyals): Total revenue 157,000; Total expenditure 202,000.

INTERNATIONAL RESERVES (US $ million in December)

	1999	2000	2001
Gold*	221	210	202
IMF special drawing rights . .	152	191	242
Reserve position in IMF . . .	1,355	1,359	2,558
Foreign exchange	15,490	18,036	14,796
Total	17,218	19,796	17,798

* Valued at SDR 35 per troy ounce.

Source: IMF, *International Financial Statistics*.

MONEY SUPPLY (million riyals in December)

	1999	2000	2001
Currency outside banks . .	55,060	51,019	49,249
Demand deposits at commercial banks	101,756	114,691	130,450
Total money	156,816	165,710	179,699

Source: IMF, *International Financial Statistics*.

COST OF LIVING (Consumer Price Index for all cities; base: 1988 = 100)

	1999	2000	2001
Food, drink and tobacco . . .	118.6	117.5	118.2
Housing	122.6	122.8	122.8
Textiles and clothing . . .	88.1	83.4	81.2
House furnishing	99.2	99.1	97.7
Medical care	102.8	103.6	103.5
Transport and communications .	130.6	131.0	126.8
Entertainment and education . .	103.8	101.5	100.7
All items (incl. others) . .	113.3	112.6	111.7

NATIONAL ACCOUNTS
Expenditure on the Gross Domestic Product
(million riyals at current prices)

	1999	2000	2001*
Government final consumption expenditure	154,094	183,804	188,695
Private final consumption expenditure	252,217	258,126	255,784
Increase in stocks	9,421	8,903	5,135
Gross fixed capital formation . .	118,196	123,324	126,609
Total domestic expenditure .	533,928	574,157	576,223
Exports of goods and services .	210,231	308,473	292,913
Less Imports of goods and services .	140,570	175,973	170,733
GDP in purchasers' values .	603,589	706,657	698,403
GDP at constant 1999 prices .	603,589	632,906	640,413

* Preliminary figures.

Gross Domestic Product by Economic Activity
(million riyals at current prices)

	1999	2000	2001*
Agriculture, forestry and fishing .	34,443	34,973	35,708
Mining and quarrying:			
Crude petroleum and natural gas	173,102	259,847	238,492
Other	2,464	2,552	2,650
Manufacturing:			
Petroleum refining . . .	18,021	21,084	20,671
Other	44,779	47,206	49,425
Electricity, gas and water . .	2,899	3,015	3,152
Construction	39,437	41,724	43,018
Trade, restaurants and hotels .	45,992	47,832	49,506
Transport, storage and communications	27,893	29,103	30,500
Finance, insurance, real estate and business services:			
Ownership of dwellings . .	42,221	43,056	43,835
Other	31,603	33,073	34,462
Government services . . .	116,789	119,123	123,753
Other community, social and personal services	21,377	22,176	23,130
Sub-total	601,020	704,764	698,302
Import duties	9,634	9,650	8,077
Less Imputed bank service charge .	7,065	7,758	7,976
GDP in purchasers' values . .	603,589	706,656	698,403

* Preliminary figures.

BALANCE OF PAYMENTS (US $ million)

	1999	2000	2001
Exports of goods f.o.b. . . .	50,757	77,584	73,032
Imports of goods f.o.b. . . .	−25,717	−27,741	−28,645
Trade balance	25,039	49,843	44,387
Exports of services . . .	5,380	4,785	5,182
Imports of services . . .	−18,855	−25,262	−19,307
Balance on goods and services .	11,564	29,367	30,262
Other income received . . .	5,811	3,349	4,130
Other income paid . . .	−2,887	−2,869	−4,650
Balance on goods, services and income	14,489	29,847	29,742
Current transfers paid . . .	−14,077	−15,511	−15,240
Current balance	412	14,336	14,502
Direct investment from abroad .	−780	−1,884	20
Portfolio investment assets . .	11,712	−9,394	−2,798
Other investment assets . . .	−10,678	−3,943	−12,343
Other investment liabilities . .	2,149	3,549	−1,289
Overall balance	2,815	2,665	−1,909

Source: IMF, *International Financial Statistics*.

External Trade

PRINCIPAL COMMODITIES (million riyals)

Imports c.i.f.	1998	1999	2000*
Live animals and animal products	5,107	5,313	5,693
Vegetable products	6,868	7,637	8,302
Prepared foodstuffs, beverages, spirits, vinegar and tobacco .	4,761	4,192	5,531
Products of chemical or allied industries .	9,249	9,494	9,565
Plastics, rubber and articles thereof	3,753	3,488	4,141
Textiles and textile articles . .	7,464	6,494	6,674
Pearls, precious or semi-precious stones, precious metals, etc. .	6,263	5,113	4,575
Base metals and articles of base metal	10,743	8,808	8,934
Machinery and mechanical appliances; electrical equipment; sound and television apparatus	22,486	25,187	24,984
Vehicles, aircraft, vessels and associated transport equipment .	20,706	15,201	20,062
Total (incl. others) . . .	112,397	104,980	113,470

Exports†	1998	1999	2000*
Mineral products . . .	121,973	168,298	270,950
Crude petroleum . .	98,840	136,321	219,470
Refined petroleum products .	23,133	31,977	51,480
Petrochemicals . . .	9,961	9,189	12,125
Construction materials . .	2,737	2,808	2,712
Agricultural, animal and food products	1,663	1,768	1,700
Total (incl. others) . . .	145,389	190,084	295,755

* Provisional, preliminary or estimated figures.
† Including re-exports (million riyals): 1,796 in 1998; 1,869 in 1999; 1,886 (provisional) in 2000.

2000 (revised totals, million riyals): Imports 113,240; Exports 290,553 (Mineral products 265,750).
2001 (preliminary figure, million riyals): Imports 116,931.

PRINCIPAL TRADING PARTNERS (million riyals)

Imports c.i.f.	1998	1999	2000*
Australia	1,978	2,273	2,905
Belgium	1,386	1,558	1,707
Brazil	1,658	1,650	2,314
Canada	1,176	1,321	1,083
France	5,862	4,421	4,686
Germany	7,052	7,648	9,111
India	3,058	2,770	3,132
Indonesia	1,696	1,508	1,700
Italy	4,667	4,424	4,769
Japan	9,666	9,650	11,850
Korea, Republic . . .	3,884	3,801	3,795
Malaysia	814	890	1,152
Netherlands	1,829	1,971	2,387
Spain	1,813	1,962	1,609
Sweden	1,373	1,441	1,813
Switzerland	4,828	3,523	3,694
Taiwan	1,545	1,258	1,161
Turkey	1,316	985	853
United Arab Emirates . .	1,842	2,213	2,208
United Kingdom . . .	9,535	8,456	7,330
USA	23,984	19,882	21,840
Total (incl. others) . . .	112,397	104,980	113,470

Exports (incl. re-exports)	1997	1998	1999
Australia	2,060	1,271	1,591
Bahrain	6,272	4,387	5,560
Brazil	3,908	2,210	2,216
France	8,950	5,456	7,469
Germany	2,612	1,514	1,886
Greece	2,638	2,128	2,321
India	9,251	6,083	8,175
Indonesia	1,653	2,280	3,318
Italy	8,004	4,908	4,428
Japan	39,361	21,668	28,496
Korea, Republic . . .	23,149	13,886	20,429
Netherlands	10,612	6,043	7,845
Pakistan	1,948	1,520	2,562
Philippines	3,606	2,021	2,828
Singapore	15,645	8,697	11,107
Spain	4,230	3,048	3,388
Taiwan	5,696	3,476	4,185
Thailand	2,980	1,607	2,100
Turkey	3,496	2,320	1,944
United Arab Emirates . .	7,375	4,912	4,710
USA	34,603	23,695	37,185
Total (incl. others) . . .	227,443	145,388	190,084

Transport

RAILWAYS (traffic)

	1998	1999	2000
Passenger journeys ('000) . .	646.2	770.4	853.8
Freight carried ('000 metric tons) .	2,100.0	1,800.0	1,600.0

ROAD TRAFFIC (motor vehicles in use at 31 December)

	1989	1990	1991
Passenger cars	2,550,465	2,664,028	2,762,132
Buses and coaches . . .	50,856	52,136	54,089
Goods vehicles	2,153,297	2,220,658	2,286,541
Total	4,754,618	4,936,822	5,103,205

1996 (estimates): Passenger cars 1,744,000; Buses and coaches 23,040; Goods vehicles 1,169,000; Total 2,935,000.

Source: IRF, *World Road Statistics*.

SHIPPING

Merchant Fleet (vessels registered at 31 December)

	1999	2000	2001
Oil tankers			
Vessels	25	24	26
Displacement ('000 grt) . .	218	219	224
Others			
Vessels	247	252	248
Displacement ('000 grt) . .	989	1,041	909
Total vessels	272	276	274
Total displacement ('000 grt) .	1,208	1,260	1,133

Source: Lloyd's Register-Fairplay, *World Fleet Statistics*.

International Sea-borne Freight Traffic ('000 metric tons*)

	1988	1989	1990
Goods loaded	161,666	165,989	214,070
Goods unloaded	42,546	42,470	46,437

* Including Saudi Arabia's share of traffic in the Neutral or Partitioned Zone.

Source: UN, *Monthly Bulletin of Statistics*.

2001 ('000 metric tons, excluding crude oil): Goods loaded 68,894; Goods unloaded 31,668.

CIVIL AVIATION (traffic on scheduled services)

		1996	1997	1998
Kilometres flown (million)	. .	118	117	120
Passengers carried ('000) .	.	11,706	11,738	11,816
Passenger-kilometres (million)	.	18,980	18,949	18,820
Total ton-km (million)	. .	2,592	2,650	2,645

Source: UN, *Statistical Yearbook*.

2000: 27.5m. passengers carried; 467,000 metric tons of cargo carried.

Tourism

		1996	1997	1998
Tourist arrivals ('000)	. . .	3,458	3,594	3,700
Tourist receipts (US $ million)	.	1,308	1,420	1,462

Source: World Tourism Organization, *Yearbook of Tourism Statistics*.
1999: 4.8m. tourist arrivals.
2000: 6,750m. riyals in tourism receipts.

PILGRIMS TO MECCA FROM ABROAD*

		1990/91	1991/92	1992/93
Total	. . . . . .	720,102	1,015,664	992,813

* Figures relate to Islamic lunar years. The equivalent dates in the Gregorian calendar are: 23 July 1990 to 11 July 1991; 12 July 1991 to 30 June 1992; 1 July 1992 to 19 June 1993.

2000/01: (5 April 2000 to 24 March 2001): 1,363,992 pilgrims.

Communications Media

	1999	2000	2001
Television receivers ('000 in use) .	5,500	5,700	n.a.
Telephones ('000 main lines in use)	2,706.2	2,964.7	3,232.9
Mobile cellular telephones ('000 subscribers)	836.6	1,375.9	2,528.6
Personal computers ('000 in use)	1,200	1,300	1,400
Internet users ('000 in use) . .	100	200	300

1995 (estimate): 150,000 facsimile machines in use.
1996: 13 daily newspapers; 185 non-daily newspapers.
1997: 6,250,000 radio receivers in use.

Sources: UNESCO, *Statistical Yearbook*; International Telecommunication Union.

Education

(1999/2000)

		Institutions	Teachers	Students
Pre-primary*	. . . . .	893	7,703	85,484
Primary .	. . . . .	12,415	190,570	2,285,328
Intermediate	. . . .	6,104	86,686	1,073,175
Secondary (general) .	. .	3,290	55,277	755,419
Teacher-training .	. . .	18	1,807	24,655
Technical and vocational .	. .	77	5,214	50,004
University colleges	. . .	75	10,554	190,478

* Figures refer to 1996/97. Source: UNESCO, *Statistical Yearbook*.

Adult literacy rate (UNESCO estimates): 76.3% (males 83.1%; females 66.9%) in 2000 (Source: UNDP, *Human Development Report*).

Directory

The Constitution

The Basic Law of Government was introduced by royal decree in 1992.

Chapter 1 defines Saudi Arabia as a sovereign Arab, Islamic state. Article 1 defines God's Book and the Sunnah of his prophet as the constitution of Saudi Arabia. The official language is Arabic. The official holidays are Id al-Fitr and Id al-Adha. The calendar is the Hegira calendar.

Chapter 2 concerns the system of government, which is defined as a monarchy, hereditary in the male descendants of Abd al-Aziz ibn Abd ar-Rahman al-Faisal as-Sa'ud. It outlines the duties of the Heir Apparent. The principles of government are justice, consultation and equality in accordance with Islamic law (*Shari'a*).

Chapter 3 concerns the family. The State is to aspire to strengthen family ties and to maintain its Arab and Islamic values. Article 11 states that 'Saudi society will be based on the principle of adherence to God's command, on mutual co-operation in good deeds and piety and mutual support and inseparability'. Education aims to instil the Islamic faith.

Chapter 4 defines the economic principles of the State. All natural resources are the property of the State. The State protects public money and freedom of property. Taxation is only to be imposed on a just basis.

Chapter 5 concerns rights and duties. The State is to protect Islam and to implement the *Shari'a* law. The State protects human rights in accordance with the *Shari'a*. The State is to provide public services and security for all citizens. Punishment is to be in accordance with the *Shari'a*. The Royal Courts are open to all citizens.

Chapter 6 defines the authorities of the State as the judiciary, the executive and the regulatory authority. The judiciary is independent, and acts in accordance with *Shari'a* law. The King is head of the Council of Ministers and Commander-in-Chief of the Armed Forces. The Prime Minister and other ministers are appointed by the King. It provides for the establishment of a Consultative Council (Majlis ash-Shoura).

Chapter 7 concerns financial affairs. It provides for the annual presentation of a state budget. Corporate budgets are subject to the same provisions.

Chapter 8 concerns control bodies. Control bodies will be established to ensure good financial and administrative management of state assets.

Chapter 9 defines the general provisions pertaining to the application of the Basic Law of Government.

The Government

HEAD OF STATE

King FAHD IBN ABD AL-AZIZ AS-SA'UD (acceded to the throne 13 June 1982).

Crown Prince: ABDULLAH IBN ABD AL-AZIZ AS-SA'UD.

COUNCIL OF MINISTERS
(September 2002)

Prime Minister: King FAHD IBN ABD AL-AZIZ AS-SA'UD.

First Deputy Prime Minister and Commander of the National Guard: Crown Prince ABDULLAH IBN ABD AL-AZIZ AS-SA'UD.

Second Deputy Prime Minister, Minister of Defence and Civil Aviation and Inspector General: Prince SULTAN IBN ABD AL-AZIZ AS-SA'UD.

Minister of Public Works and Housing: Prince MUTAIB IBN ABD AL-AZIZ AS-SA'UD.

Minister of the Interior: Prince NAYEF IBN ABD AL-AZIZ AS-SA'UD.

Minister of Foreign Affairs: Prince SA'UD AL-FAISAL AS-SA'UD.

Minister of Petroleum and Mineral Resources: Eng. ALI IBN IBRAHIM AN-NUAIMI.

Minister of Labour and Social Affairs: ALI IBN IBRAHIM AN-NAMLA.

Minister of Agriculture: Dr ABDULLAH IBN ABD AL-AZIZ IBN MUAMMAR.

Minister of Water: GHAZI AL-GOSAIBI.

Minister of Education: Dr MUHAMMAD IBN AHMAD AR-RASHID.

Minister of Higher Education: Dr KHALID IBN MUHAMMAD AL-ANGARI.

Minister of Communications: Dr NASIR IBN MUHAMMAD AS-SALOUM.

Minister of Finance and National Economy: Dr IBRAHIM IBN ABD AL-AZIZ AL-ASSAF.

Minister of Planning and acting Minister of Posts, Telegraphs and Telephones: KHALED IBN MUHAMMAD AL-QUSAIBI.

Minister of Information: Dr FOUAD IBN ABD AS-SALAM IBN MUHAMMAD FARSI.

Minister of Industry and Electricity: Dr HASHIM IBN ABDULLAH IBN HASHIM YAMANI.

Minister of Commerce: USAMA IBN JAFAAR IBN IBRAHIM FAQIH.

Minister of Justice: Dr ABDULLAH IBN MUHAMMAD IBN IBRAHIM ASH-SHEIKH.

Minister of Pilgrimage (Hajj) Affairs: IYAD IBN AMIN MADANI.

Minister of Municipal and Rural Affairs: Dr MUHAMMAD IBN IBRAHIM AL-JARALLAH.

Minister of Awqaf (Religious Endowments), Dawa, Mosques and Guidance Affairs: SALEH IBN ABD AL-AZIZ MUHAMMAD IBN IBRAHIM ASH-SHEIKH.

Minister of Health: Dr USAMA IBN ABD AL-MAJID SHUBUKSHI.

Minister of the Civil Service: MUHAMMAD IBN ALI AL-FAYEZ.

President of the General Presidency of Youth Welfare: Prince SULTAN IBN FAHD IBN ABD AL-AZIZ AS-SA'UD.

Minister of State and Secretary-General of the Supreme Commission for Tourism: Prince SULTAN IBN SALMAN IBN ABD AL-AZIZ.

Ministers of State: Dr MUHAMMAD IBN ABD AL-AZIZ IBN ABDULLAH IBN HASSAN ASH-SHEIKH, Dr MUTLIB IBN ABDULLAH AN-NAFISA, Dr ABD AL-AZIZ IBN IBRAHIM AL-MANIE, Dr MUSAID IBN MUHAMMAD AL-AYBAN, Dr MADANI IBN ABD AL-QADIR ALAQI, Dr ABD AL-AZIZ AL-ABDULLAH AL-KHUWAITER, Prince ABD AL-AZIZ IBN FAHD AS-SA'UD.

MINISTRIES

Most ministries have regional offices in Jeddah.

Council of Ministers: Murabba, Riyadh 11121; tel. (1) 488-2444.

Ministry of Agriculture: Airport Rd, Riyadh 11195; tel. (1) 401-6666; fax (1) 404-4592; e-mail info@agrwat.gov.sa; internet www.agrwat.gov.sa.

Ministry of Awqaf (Religious Endowments), Dawa, Mosques and Guidance Affairs: Riyadh 11232; tel. (1) 473-0401; internet www.islam.org.sa.

Ministry of the Civil Service: POB 18367, Riyadh 11114; tel. (1)402-6900; fax (1) 403-4998; internet www.mcs.gov.sa.

Ministry of Commerce: POB 1774, Airport Rd, Riyadh 11162; tel. (1) 401-2222; fax (1) 403-8421.

Ministry of Communications: Airport Rd, Riyadh 11178; tel. (1) 404-3000; fax (1) 403-1401.

Ministry of Defence and Civil Aviation: POB 26731, Airport Rd, Riyadh 11165; tel. (1) 476-9000; fax (1) 405-5500; internet www.pca.gov.sa.

Ministry of Education: POB 3734, Airport Rd, Riyadh 11481; tel. (1) 402-9500; fax (1) 404-1391; e-mail webmaster@moe.gov.sa; internet www.moe.gov.sa.

Ministry of Finance and National Economy: Airport Rd, Riyadh 11177; tel. (1) 405-0000; fax (1) 401-0583; internet www.mof.gov.sa.

Ministry of Foreign Affairs: Nasseriya St, Riyadh 11124; tel. (1) 401-5000; fax (1) 403-0159; internet www.mofa.gov.sa.

Ministry of Health: Airport Rd, Riyadh 11176; tel. (1) 401-5555; fax (1) 402-9876; internet www.moh.gov.sa.

Ministry of Higher Education: King Faisal Hospital St, Riyadh 11153; tel. (1) 441-9849; fax (1) 441-9004; internet www.mohe.gov.sa.

Ministry of Industry and Electricity: POB 5729, Omar bin al-Khatab St, Riyadh 11432; tel. (1) 477-6666; fax (1) 477-5441.

Ministry of Information: POB 570, Nasseriya St, Riyadh 11161; tel. (1) 406-8888; fax (1) 404-4192; internet www.saudinf.com.

Ministry of the Interior: POB 2933, Airport Rd, Riyadh 11134; tel. (1) 401-1111; fax (1) 403-1185.

Ministry of Justice: University St, Riyadh 11137; tel. (1) 405-7777.

Ministry of Labour and Social Affairs: Omar bin al-Khatab St, Riyadh 11157; tel. (1) 477-8888; fax (1) 478-9175; internet www.mol.gov.sa.

Ministry of Municipal and Rural Affairs: Nasseriya St, Riyadh 11136; tel. (1) 441-8888; fax (1) 441-7368; internet www.momra.gov.sa.

Ministry of Petroleum and Mineral Resources: POB 247, King Abd al-Aziz Rd, Riyadh 11191; tel. (1) 478-1661; fax (1) 478-1980; internet www.mopm.gov.sa.

Ministry of Pilgrimage (Hajj) Affairs: Omar bin al-Khatab St, Riyadh 11183; tel. (1) 404-3003; fax (1) 402-2555.

Ministry of Planning: POB 358, University St, Riyadh 11182; tel. (1) 401-3333; fax (1) 404-9300; e-mail info@planning.gov.sa; internet www.planning.gov.sa.

Ministry of Posts, Telegraphs and Telephones: Sharia al-Ma'azer, Intercontinental Rd, Riyadh 11112; tel. (1) 463-4444; fax (1) 405-2310.

Ministry of Public Works and Housing: POB 56095, Ma'ather St, Riyadh 11554; tel. (1) 407-3618; internet www.mpwh.gov.sa.

Ministry of Water: Riyadh.

MAJLIS ASH-SHOURA
(Consultative Council)

In March 1992 King Fahd issued a decree to establish a Consultative Council of 60 members, whose powers include the right to summon and question ministers. The composition of the Council was announced by King Fahd in August 1993, and it was officially inaugurated in December of that year. Each member is to serve for four years. The Council's membership was increased to 90 when its second term began in July 1997; it was increased further, to 120, in May 2001.

Chairman: SALIH IBN HUMAYD.

Vice-Chairman: ABDULLAH IBN UMAR IBN MUHAMMAD IBN NASIF.

Secretary-General: HAMOUD IBN ABD AL-AZIZ AL-BADR.

Diplomatic Representation

EMBASSIES IN SAUDI ARABIA

Algeria: POB 94388, Riyadh 11693; tel. (1) 488-7171; fax (1) 482-1703; Ambassador: ABD AL-KARIM GHARIB.

Argentina: POB 94369, Riyadh 11693; tel. (1) 465-2600; fax (1) 465-3057; e-mail earab@nesma.net.sa; Ambassador: LUIS DOMINGO MENDIOLA.

Australia: POB 94400, Riyadh 11693; tel. (1) 488-7788; fax (1) 488-7973; Ambassador: ROBERT J. TYSON.

Austria: POB 94373, Riyadh 11693; tel. (1) 480-1217; fax (1) 480-1526; e-mail aeriyadh@shabakah.net.sa; Ambassador: Dr HARALD WIESNER.

Bahrain: POB 94371, Riyadh 11693; tel. (1) 488-0044; fax (1) 488-0208; Ambassador: ISSA MUHAMMAD AL-KHALIFA.

Bangladesh: POB 94395, Riyadh 11693; tel. (1) 419-6665; fax (1) 419-3555; e-mail bdootriyadh@zajil.net; Ambassador: MAHBOOB ALAM.

Belgium: POB 94396, Riyadh 11693; tel. (1) 488-2888; fax (1) 488-2033; e-mail ambelgium@saudionline.com.sa; Ambassador: FRANZ MICHILS.

Bosnia and Herzegovina: POB 94301, Riyadh 11693; tel. (1) 456-7914; fax (1) 454-4360; Ambassador: SENAHID BISTRIĆ.

Brazil: POB 94348, Riyadh 11693; tel. (1) 488-0018; fax (1) 488-1073; e-mail arabras@nesma.net.sa; Ambassador: LUÍS SÉRGIO GAMA FIGUEIRA.

Burkina Faso: POB 94330, Riyadh 11693; tel. (1) 465-2244; fax (1) 465-3397; e-mail burkinafaso.ksa@arab.net.sa; Ambassador: OUMAR DIAWARA.

Cameroon: POB 94336, Riyadh 11693; tel. (1) 488-0022; fax (1) 488-1463; e-mail ambacamriyad@ifrance.com; Ambassador: MOHAMADOU LABARANG.

Canada: POB 94321, Riyadh 11693; tel. (1) 488-2288; fax (1) 488-1997; Ambassador: MELVYN L. MACDONALD.

Chad: POB 94374, Riyadh 11693; tel. and fax (1) 465-7702; Ambassador: al-Hajji DJIME TOUGOU.

China, People's Republic: POB 75231, Riyadh 11578; tel. (1) 482-4246; fax (1) 482-1123; Ambassador: YU XINGZHI.

Côte d'Ivoire: POB 94303, Riyadh 11693; tel. (1) 482-5582; fax (1) 482-9629; e-mail ambciryd@digi.net.sa; Ambassador: LANCINA DOSSO.

Denmark: POB 94398, Riyadh 11693; tel. (1) 488-0101; fax (1) 488-1366; e-mail dkembassyriyadh.dk; internet www.dkembassyriyadh.dk; Ambassador: SVEN ERIK NORDBERG.

Djibouti: POB 94340, Riyadh 11693; tel. (1) 454-3182; fax (1) 456-9168; Ambassador: IDRISS AHMAD CHIRWA.

Egypt: POB 94333, Riyadh 11693; tel. (1) 465-8425; fax (1) 465-2800; Ambassador: FATHY ASH-SHAZLY.

Ethiopia: POB 94341, Riyadh 11693; tel. (1) 477-5285; fax (1) 476-8020; e-mail ethembsa@shabakah.net.sa; Ambassador: Ato MUHAMMAD ALI.

Finland: POB 94363, Riyadh 11693; tel. (1) 488-1515; fax (1) 488-2520; Ambassador: HEIKKI PUURUNEN.

France: POB 94009, Riyadh 11693; tel. (1) 488-1255; fax (1) 488-2882; e-mail diplomatie@ambafrance.org.sa; internet www.ambafrance.org.sa; Ambassador: BERNARD POLETTI.

Gabon: POB 94325, Riyadh 11693; tel. (1) 456-7173; fax (1) 470-0669; Ambassador: NABIL KOUSSOU INAMA.

Gambia: POB 94322, Riyadh 11693; tel. (1) 465-1320; fax (1) 462-1481; e-mail gamemruh@digi.net.sa; Ambassador: ALIEU NGUM.

Germany: POB 94001, Riyadh 11693; tel. (1) 488-0700; fax (1) 488-0660; Ambassador: Dr HARALD KINDERMANN.

Ghana: POB 94339, Riyadh 11693; tel. (1) 454-5122; fax 450-9819; e-mail ghanaemb@naseej.com; Ambassador: ABD AR-RAZAQ MUYHIDEEN HASSAN TAHIR.

Greece: POB 94375, Riyadh 11693; tel. (1) 480-1975; fax (1) 480-1969; Ambassador: PAUL APOSTOLIDES.

Guinea: POB 94326, Riyadh 11693; tel. (1) 488-1101; fax (1) 482-6757; Ambassador: el-Hadj ABOUL KARIM DIOUBATÈ.

Hungary: POB 94014, al-Waha District, Ahmad Tonsy St 23, Riyadh 11693; tel. (1) 454-6707; fax (1) 456-0834; e-mail huemb.ryd@nournet.com.sa; Ambassador: TAMÁS VARGA.

India: POB 94387, Riyadh 11693; tel. (1) 488-4144; fax (1) 488-4750; e-mail ieriyadh@shabakah.net.sa; Ambassador: TALMIZ AHMAD.

Indonesia: POB 94343, Riyadh 11693; tel. (1) 488-2800; fax (1) 488-2966; Ambassador: Dr ISMAIL SUNY.

Iran: POB 94394, Riyadh 11693; tel. (1) 488-1916; fax (1) 488-1890; Ambassador: MUHAMMAD REZA NURI-SHARUDI.

Ireland: POB 94349, Riyadh 11693; tel. (1) 488-2300; fax (1) 488-0927; Ambassador: MICHAEL COLLINS.

Italy: POB 94389, Riyadh 11693; tel. (1) 488-1212; fax (1) 488-1951; e-mail info@italia-as.org; internet www.italia-as.org; Ambassador: TORQUATO CARDILLI.

Japan: POB 4095, Riyadh 11491; tel. (1) 488-1100; fax (1) 488-0189; Ambassador: MINORO TAMBA.

Jordan: POB 94316, Riyadh 11693; tel. (1) 488-0051; fax (1) 488-0072; Ambassador: HANI KHALIFAH.

Kazakhstan: POB 94012, Riyadh 11693; tel. (1) 470-1839; fax (1) 454-7781; e-mail kazruh@ae.net.sa; Ambassador: BAGHDAD AMREYEV.

Kenya: POB 94358, Riyadh 11693; tel. (1) 488-1238; fax (1) 488-2629; Ambassador: ALI MUHAMMAD ABDI.

Korea, Republic: POB 94399, Riyadh 11693; tel. (1) 488-2211; fax (1) 488-1317; Ambassador: KIM CHUNG-KI.

Kuwait: POB 94304, Riyadh 11693; tel. (1) 488-3401; fax (1) 488-3682; Ambassador: ABD AR-RAHMAN AHMAD AL-BAKR.

Lebanon: POB 94350, Riyadh 11693; tel. (1) 419-7000; fax (1) 419-2767; Ambassador: ZOUHEIR HAMDAN.

Libya: POB 94365, Riyadh 11693; tel. (1) 454-4511; fax (1) 456-7513; Ambassador: MUHAMMAD SA'ID AL-QASHSHAT.

Malaysia: POB 94335, Riyadh 11693; tel. (1) 488-7100; fax (1) 482-4177; Ambassador: Datuk Haji MOKHTAR BIN Haji AHMAD.

Mali: POB 94331, Riyadh 11693; tel. (1) 464-5640; fax (1) 419-5016.

Malta: POB 94361, Riyadh 11693; tel. (1) 463-2345; fax (1) 463-3993; e-mail maltaemb@shabakah.net.sa; Ambassador: SAVIOUR P. GAUCI.

Mauritania: POB 94354, Riyadh 11693; tel. (1) 464-6749; fax (1) 465-8355; Ambassador: BABA OULD MUHAMMAD ABDULLAH.

Mexico: POB 94391, Riyadh 11693; tel. (1) 482-8218; fax (1) 482-8379; e-mail embamex@embamex.org.sa; Ambassador: EDGARDO FLORES RIVAS.

Morocco: POB 94392, Riyadh 11693; tel. (1) 481-1858; fax (1) 482-7016; Ambassador: ABD AL-KRIM SEMMAR.

Nepal: POB 94384, Riyadh 11693; tel. (1) 402-4758; fax (1) 403-6488; Ambassador: NARAYAN S. THAPA.

Netherlands: POB 94307, Riyadh 11693; tel. (1) 488-0011; fax (1) 488-0544; internet www.holland.org.sa; Ambassador: P. LAGENDIJK.

New Zealand: POB 94397, Riyadh 11693; tel. (1) 488-7988; fax (1) 488-7912; Ambassador: LAURIE MARKES.

Niger: POB 94334, Riyadh 11693; tel. and fax (1) 464-2931.

Nigeria: POB 94386, Riyadh 11693; tel. (1) 482-3024; fax (1) 480-1828; e-mail nigeriaryd@zajil.net; Ambassador: Alhaji AHMAD AL-GAZALI.

Norway: POB 94380, Riyadh 11693; tel. (1) 488-1904; fax (1) 488-0854; e-mail emb.riyadh@mfa.no; Ambassador: SVEIN ANDREASSEN.

Oman: POB 94381, Riyadh 11693; tel. (1) 482-3120; fax (1) 482-3738; Ambassador: HAMAD H. AL-MO'AMARY.

Pakistan: POB 94007, Riyadh 11693; tel. (1) 488-7272; fax (1) 488-7953; Ambassador: Lt-Gen. (retd) ASAD DURRANI.

Philippines: POB 94366, Riyadh 11693; tel. (1) 488-0835; fax (1) 488-3945; Ambassador: ROMULO M. ESPALDON.

Portugal: POB 94328, Riyadh 11693; tel. (1) 462-2115; fax (1) 462-3365; Ambassador: JOSÉ MANUEL WADDINGTON MATOS PARREIRA.

Qatar: POB 94353, Riyadh 11461; tel. (1) 482-5544; fax (1) 482-5394; Ambassador: M. ALI AL-ANSARI.

Russia: POB 94308, Riyadh 11693; tel. (1) 481-1875; fax (1) 481-1890; Ambassador: IGOR A. MELIKHOV.

Rwanda: POB 94383, Riyadh 11693; tel. (1) 454-0808; fax (1) 456-1769; Ambassador: SIMON INSONERE.

Senegal: POB 94352, Riyadh 11693; tel. (1) 454-2144; fax (1) 264-7675; Ambassador: MODOU DIA.

Sierra Leone: POB 94329, Riyadh 11693; tel. (1) 464-3982; fax (1) 464-3662; e-mail slembrdh@zajil.net; Ambassador: Alhaji AMADU DEEN TEJAN-SIE.

Singapore: POB 94378, Riyadh 11693; tel. (1) 465-7007; fax (1) 465-2224; Chargé d'affaires a.i.: ANTHONY CHNG.

Somalia: POB 94372, Riyadh 11693; tel. (1) 464-3456; fax (1) 464-9705; Ambassador: ABD AR-RAHMAN A. HUSSEIN.

South Africa: POB 94006, Riyadh 11693; tel. (1) 456-2982; fax (1) 454-3727; e-mail embriyad@ogertel.com; Ambassador: (vacant).

Spain: POB 94347, Riyadh 11693; tel. (1) 488-0606; fax 488-0420; e-mail embespsa@mail.mae.es; Ambassador: RAMÓN ANSOÁIN GARRAZA.

Sri Lanka: POB 94360, Riyadh 11693; tel. (1) 454-2368; fax (1) 454-9748; e-mail lankaemb@shabakah.net.sa; Ambassador: NOWFEL SALY JABIR.

Sudan: POB 94337, Riyadh 11693; tel. (1) 488-7979; fax (1) 488-7729; Ambassador: Dr ATTALLA H. BASHIR.

Sweden: POB 94382, Riyadh 11693; tel. (1) 488-3100; fax (1) 488-0604; e-mail ambassaden.riyadh@foreign.ministry.se; internet www.swedemb.org.sa; Ambassador: AKE KARLSSON.

Switzerland: POB 94311, Riyadh 11693; tel. (1) 488-1291; fax (1) 488-0632; Ambassador: DOMINIK M. ALDER.

Syria: POB 94323, Riyadh 11693; tel. (1) 482-6191; fax (1) 482-6196; Ambassador: MUHAMMAD KHALID AT-TALL.

Tanzania: POB 94320, Riyadh 11693; tel. (1) 454-2839; fax (1) 454-9660; Ambassador: Prof. A. A. SHAREEF.

Thailand: POB 94359, Riyadh 11693; tel. (1) 488-1174; fax 488-1179; e-mail thaiemry@awalnet.net.sa; Chargé d'affaires: SOMSAKDI SURIYAWONGSE.

Tunisia: POB 94368, Riyadh 11693; tel. (1) 488-7900; fax (1) 488-7641; Ambassador: KACEM BOUSNINA.

Turkey: POB 94390, Riyadh 11693; tel. (1) 482-0101; fax (1) 488-7823; email turkemb@concept.net.sa; Ambassador: TÜRKEKUL KURT-TEKIN.

Uganda: POB 94344, Riyadh 11693; tel. (1) 454-4910; fax (1) 454-9264; e-mail ugariyadh@arab.net.sa; Ambassador: Dr MOHAMMED AHMED KISUULE.

United Arab Emirates: POB 94385, Riyadh 11693; tel. (1) 482-9652; fax (1) 482-7504; Ambassador: ISSA K. AL-HURAIMIL.

United Kingdom: POB 94351, Riyadh 11693; tel. (1) 488-0077; fax (1) 488-2373; e-mail Information.Riyadh@fco.gov.uk; internet www.ukm.org.sa; Ambassador: Sir DEREK PLUMBLY.

USA: POB 94309, Riyadh 11693; tel. (1) 488-3800; fax (1) 488-7360; e-mail usisriyadh@yahoo.com; internet www.usembassy.state.gov/riyadh/; Ambassador: ROBERT W. JORDAN.

Uruguay: POB 94346, Riyadh 11693; tel. (1) 462-0739; fax (1) 462-0648; e-mail ururia@mcimail.com; Ambassador: CARLOS A. CLULOW.

Uzbekistan: Riyadh; Ambassador: ULUGBEK ISROILOV.

Venezuela: POB 94364, Riyadh 11693; tel. (1) 476-7867; fax (1) 476-8200; Ambassador: NORMAN PINO.

Yemen: POB 94356, Riyadh 11693; tel. (1) 488-1769; fax (1) 488-1562; Ambassador: KHALED ISMAIL AL-AKWA'A.

Judicial System

Judges are independent and governed by the rules of Islamic *Shari'a*. The following courts operate:

Supreme Council of Justice: consists of 11 members and supervises work of the courts; reviews legal questions referred to it by the Minister of Justice and expresses opinions on judicial questions; reviews sentences of death, cutting and stoning; Chair. Sheikh SALIH AL-LIHAYDAN.

Court of Cassation: consists of Chief Justice and an adequate number of judges; includes department for penal suits, department for personal status and department for other suits.

General (Public) Courts: consist of one or more judges; sentences are issued by a single judge, with the exception of death, stoning and cutting, which require the decision of three judges.

Summary Courts: consist of one or more judges; sentences are issued by a single judge.

Specialized Courts: Article 26 of the judicial system stipulates that the setting up of specialized courts is permissible by Royal Decree on a proposal from the Supreme Council of Justice.

Religion

ISLAM

Arabia is the centre of the Islamic faith, and Saudi Arabia includes the holy cities of Mecca and Medina. Except in the Eastern Province, where a large number of people follow Shi'a rites, the majority of the population are Sunni Muslims, and most of the indigenous inhabitants belong to the strictly orthodox Wahhabi sect. The Wahhabis originated in the 18th century but first became unified and influential under Abd al-Aziz (Ibn Sa'ud), who became the first King of Saudi Arabia. They are now the keepers of the holy places and control the pilgrimage to Mecca. In 1986 King Fahd adopted the title of Custodian of the Two Holy Mosques. The country's most senior Islamic authority is the Council of Ulema.

Mecca: Birthplace of the Prophet Muhammad, seat of the Great Mosque and Shrine of Ka'ba, visited by 1,363,992 Muslims in the Islamic year 1421 (2000/2001).

Medina: Burial place of Muhammad, second sacred city of Islam.

Grand Mufti and Chairman of Council of Ulema: Sheikh ABD AL-AZIZ IBN ABDULLAH ASH-SHEIKH.

CHRISTIANITY

The Roman Catholic Church

A small number of adherents, mainly expatriates, form part of the Apostolic Vicariate of Arabia. The Vicar Apostolic is resident in the United Arab Emirates.

The Anglican Communion

Within the Episcopal Church in Jerusalem and the Middle East, Saudi Arabia forms part of the diocese of Cyprus and the Gulf. The Anglican congregations in the country are entirely expatriate. The Bishop in Cyprus and the Gulf is resident in Cyprus, while the Archdeacon in the Gulf is resident in Qatar.

Other Denominations

The Greek Orthodox Church is also represented.

The Press

Since 1964 most newspapers and periodicals have been published by press organizations, administered by boards of directors with full autonomous powers, in accordance with the provisions of the Press Law. These organizations, which took over from small private firms, are privately owned by groups of individuals experienced in newspaper publishing and administration (see Publishers).

There are also a number of popular periodicals published by the Government and by the Saudi Arabian Oil Co, and distributed free of charge. The press is subject to no legal restriction affecting freedom of expression or the coverage of news.

DAILIES

Arab News: POB 10452, Jeddah 21433; tel. (2) 639-1888; fax (2) 639-3223; e-mail editorial1@arabnews.com; f. 1975; English; publ. by Saudi Research and Marketing Co; Editor-in-Chief KHALED AL-MAEENA; circ. 110,000.

Al-Bilad (The Country): POB 6340, Jeddah 21442; tel. (2) 672-3000; fax (2) 671-2545; f. 1934; Arabic; publ. by Al-Bilad Publishing Org.; Editor-in-Chief QUINAN AL-GHOMDI; circ. 66,210.

Al-Jazirah (The Peninsula): POB 354, Riyadh 11411; tel. (1) 487-0000; fax (1) 487-1201; e-mail chief@al-jazirah.com; internet www.al-jazirah.com; Arabic; Gen. Man. ABD AR-RAHMAN BIN FAHD AR-RASHAD; Editor-in-Chief KHALID IBN HAMAD AL-MALIK; circ. 94,000.

Al-Madina al-Munawara (Medina—The Enlightened City): POB 807, Makkah Rd, Jeddah 21421; tel. (2) 671-2100; fax (2) 671-1877;

internet www.almadinah.com; f. 1937; Arabic; publ. by Al-Madina Press Est; Chief Editor USAMA AS-SIBA'IE; circ. 46,370.

An-Nadwah (The Council): Jarwal Sheikh Sayed Halabi Bldg, POB 5803, Mecca; tel. (2) 520-0111; fax (2) 520-3055; f. 1958; Arabic; publ. by Mecca Printing and Information Establishment; Editor Dr ABD AR-RAHMAN AL-HARTHI; circ. 35,000.

Okaz: POB 1508, Seaport Rd, Jeddah 21441; tel. (2) 672-2630; fax (2) 672-4297; e-mail 104127.266@compuserve.com; f. 1960; Arabic; Editor-in-Chief HASHIM ABDU HASHIM; circ. 107,614.

Ar-Riyadh: POB 2943, Riyadh 11476; tel. (1) 442-0000; fax (1) 441-7417; internet www.alriyadh.com.sa; f. 1965; Arabic; publ. by Al-Yamama Publishing Establishment; Editor TURKI A. AS-SUDARI; circ. 150,000 (Sat.–Thurs.), 90,000 (Friday).

Riyadh Daily NP: POB 2943, Riyadh 11476; tel. (1) 441-7544; fax (1) 441-7116; English; publ. by Yamama Publishing Establishment; Editor-in-Chief TALA'T WARFA.

Saudi Gazette: POB 5576, Jeddah 21432; tel. (2) 672-2775; fax (2) 672-7621; e-mail news@saudigazette.com.sa; internet www.saudigazette.com.sa; f. 1976; English; publ. by Okaz Org.; Editor-in-Chief Dr AHMAD AL-YOUSSUF; circ. 60,000.

Al-Watan: POB 15156, Airport Road, Abha; tel. (7) 227-3333; fax (7) 227-3590; internet www.alwatan.com.sa; f. 1998; publ. by Assir Establishment for Press and Publishing; Asst Man. Dir Dr MAMDOUH A. BA-OWAIDAN.

Al-Yaum (Today): POB 565, Dammam 31421; tel. (3) 858-0800; fax (3) 858-8777; e-mail admin@alyaum.com; internet www.alyaum.com; f. 1965; Editor-in-Chief MUHAMMAD AL-WAEEL; circ. 80,000.

WEEKLIES

Al-Muslimoon (The Muslims): POB 13195, Jeddah 21493; tel. (2) 669-1888; fax (2) 669-5549; f. 1985; Arabic; cultural and religious affairs; publ. by Saudi Research and Marketing Co; Editor-in-Chief Dr ABDULLAH AR-RIFA'E; circ. 68,665.

Saudi Arabia Business Week: POB 2894, Riyadh; English; trade and commerce.

Saudi Economic Survey: POB 1989, Jeddah 21441; tel. (2) 651-4952; fax (2) 652-2680; e-mail walid@saudieconomicsurvey.com; internet www.saudieconomicsurvey.com; f. 1967; English; a weekly review of Saudi Arabian economic and business activity; Publr S. A. ASHOOR; Gen. Man. WALID S. ASHOOR; circ. 2,500.

Sayidati (My Lady): POB 4556, Madina Rd, Jeddah 21412; tel. (2) 639-1888; fax (2) 669-5549; Arabic; women's magazine; publ. by Saudi Research and Marketing Co; Editor-in-Chief MATAR AL-AHMADI.

Al-Yamama: POB 851, Riyadh 11421; tel. (1) 442-0000; fax (1) 441-7114; f. 1952; Editor-in-Chief ABDULLAH AL-JAHLAN; circ. 35,000.

OTHER PERIODICALS

Ahlan Wasahlan (Welcome): POB 8013, Jeddah 21482; tel. (2) 686-2349; fax (2) 686-2006; monthly; flight journal of Saudi Arabian Airlines; Gen. Man. and Editor-in-Chief YARUB A. BALKHAIR; circ. 150,000.

Al-Faysal: POB 3, Riyadh 11411; tel. (1) 465-3027; fax (1) 464-7851; monthly; f. 1976; Arabic; culture, education, health, interviews; Editor-in-Chief Dr YAHYA MAHMOUD IBN JUNAID.

Al-Manhal (The Spring): POB 2925, Jeddah; tel. (2) 643-2124; fax (2) 642-8853; f. 1937; monthly; Arabic; cultural, literary, political and scientific; Editor NABIH ABD AL-QUDOUS ANSARI.

Majallat al-Iqtisad wal-Idara (Journal of Economics and Administration): King Abd al-Aziz University, POB 9031, Jeddah 21413; twice a year; Chief Editor Prof. ABD AL-AZIZ A. DIYAB.

The MWL Journal: Press and Publications Department, Rabitat al-Alam al-Islami, POB 537, Mecca; fax 544-1622; monthly; English; Dir MURAD SULAIMAN IRQISOUS.

Ar-Rabita: POB 537, Mecca; tel. 543-3583; fax 543-1488; Arabic; Man. Editor MUHAMMAD AL-ASAD.

Saudi Review: POB 4288, Jeddah 21491; tel. (2) 651-7442; fax (2) 653-0693; f. 1966; English; monthly; newsletter from Saudi newspapers and broadcasting service; publ. by International Communications Co; Chief Editor SAAD AL-MABROUK; circ. 5,000.

Ash-Sharkiah-Elle (Oriental Elle): POB 6, Riyadh; monthly; Arabic; women's magazine; Editor SAMIRA M. KHASHAGGI.

As-Soqoor (Falcons): POB 2973, Riyadh 11461; tel. (1) 476-6566; f. 1978; 2 a year; air-force journal; cultural activities; Editor HAMAD A. AS-SALEH.

At-Tadhamon al-Islami (Islamic Solidarity): Ministry of Pilgrimage (*Hajj*) Affairs, Omar bin al-Khatab St, Riyadh 11183; monthly; Editor Dr MUSTAFA ABD AL-WAHID.

At-Tijarah (Commerce): POB 1264, Jeddah 21431; tel. (2) 651-5111; fax (2) 651-7373; e-mail jcci@mail.gcc.com.bh; f. 1960; monthly;

publ. by Jeddah Chamber of Commerce and Industry; Chair. Sheikh ISMAIL ABU DAUD; circ. 8,000.

NEWS AGENCIES

International Islamic News Agency (IINA): POB 5054, Jeddah 21422; tel. (2) 665-2056; fax (2) 665-9358; e-mail iina@ sps.net.sa; internet www.islamicnews.org; f. 1972; operates under OIC auspices; Dir Gen. ABD AL-WAHAB KASHIF.

Islamic Republic News Agency (IRNA) (Iran): Riyadh; f. 2001; Dir-Gen. ABDOLLAH NASIRI.

Saudi Press Agency: c/o Ministry of Information, POB 7186, Riyadh 11171; tel. (1) 462-3333; fax (1) 462-6747; e-mail wass@spa .gov.sa; internet www.spa.gov.sa; f. 1970; Dir-Gen. BADI KUIAYYEM.

Publishers

Assir Establishment for Press and Publishing: POB 15156, Abha; tel. (7) 227-3333; fax (7) 227-3590; f. 1998; publishes *Al-Watan*; cap. 200m.; Chair. and Acting Dir-Gen. FAHD AL-HARITHI.

Al-Bilad Publishing Organization: POB 6340, As-Sahafa St, Jeddah 21442; tel. (2) 672-3000; fax (2) 671-2545; publishes *Al-Bilad* and *Iqra'a*; Dir-Gen. AMIN ABDULLAH AL-QARQOURI.

Dar ash-Shareff for Publishing and Distribution: POB 58287, Riyadh 11594; tel. (1) 403-4931; fax (1) 405-2234; f. 1992; fiction, religion, science and social sciences; Pres. IBRAHIM AL-HAZEMI.

Dar al-Yaum Press, Printing and Publishing Ltd: POB 565, Dammam 31421; tel. (3) 843-5058; fax (3) 843-0064; e-mail humaidan@zajil.net; f. 1964; publishes *Al-Yaum*.

International Publications Agency (IPA): POB 70, Dhahran 31942; tel. (3) 895-4925; fax (3) 895-4925; publishes material of local interest; Man. SAID SALAH.

Al-Jazirah Corpn for Press, Printing and Publishing: POB 354, Riyadh 11411; tel. (1) 441-9999; fax (1) 441-2536; e-mail marketing@al-jazirah.com; f. 1964; 42 mems; publishes *Al-Jazirah* and *Al-Masaeyah* (both dailies); Dir-Gen. SALAH AL-AJROUSH; Editor-in-Chief KHALID EL-MALEK.

Al-Madina Press Establishment: POB 807, Jeddah 21421; tel. (2) 671-2100; fax (2) 671-1877; f. 1937; publishes *Al-Madina al-Munawara*; Gen. Man. AHMED SALAH JAMJOUM.

Makkah Printing and Information Establishment: POB 5803, Jarwal Sheikh Sayed Halabi Bldg, Mecca; tel. (2) 542-7868; publishes *An-Nadwah* daily newspaper.

Okaz Organization for Press and Publication: POB 1508, Jeddah 21441; tel. (2) 672-2630; fax (2) 672-8150; publishes *Okaz, Saudi Gazette* and *Child*.

Saudi Publishing and Distributing House: Al-Jouhara Bldg, South Block, Bughdadia, Medina Road, POB 2043, Jeddah 21451; tel. (2) 642-4043; fax (2) 643-2821; f. 1966; publishers, importers and distributors of English and Arabic books; Chair. MUHAMMAD SALAHUDDIN.

Saudi Research and Publishing Co: POB 4556, Jeddah 21412; tel. (2) 669-1888; fax (2) 669-5549; e-mail arabnews@arabnews.com; internet www.arabnews.com; publishes 17 titles incl. *Arab News, Asharq al-Awsat, Al-Majalla, Al-Muslimoon* and *Sayidati*; Chair. Prince AHMAD IBN SALMAN.

Yamama Publishing Establishment: POB 2943, Riyadh 11476; tel. (1) 442-0000; fax (1) 441-7116; publishes *Ar-Riyadh* and *Al-Yamama*; Dir-Gen. SAKHAL MAIDAN.

Broadcasting and Communications

TELECOMMUNICATIONS

Saudi Communications Commission (SCC): Riyadh; f. 2001; ind. regulatory authority; Gov. MUHAMMAD JAMIL MULLA.

Saudi Telecommunications Co: Riyadh; internet www.stct.com.sa; f. 1998; provides telecommunications services in Saudi Arabia; scheduled for privatization; cap. 12,000m. riyals; Pres. KHALED AL-MOLHEM.

BROADCASTING

Radio

Saudi Arabian Broadcasting Service: c/o Ministry of Information, POB 60059, Riyadh 11545; tel. (1) 401-4440; fax (1) 403-8177; 24 medium- and short-wave stations, including Jeddah, Riyadh, Dammam and Abha, broadcast programmes in Arabic and English; 23 FM stations; overseas service in Bengali, English, Farsi, French, Hausa, Indonesian, Somali, Swahili, Turkestani, Turkish and Urdu; Dir-Gen. MUHAMMAD AL-MANSOOR.

Saudi Aramco FM Radio: Bldg 3030 LIP, Dhahran 31311; tel. (3) 876-1845; fax (3) 876-1608; f. 1948; English; private; for employees of Saudi Aramco; Man. ESSAM Z. TAWFIQ.

Television

Saudi Arabian Government Television Service: POB 7971, Riyadh 11472; tel. (1) 401-4440; fax (1) 404-4192; began transmission 1965; 112 stations, incl. six main stations at Riyadh, Jeddah, Medina, Dammam, Qassim, Abha, transmit programmes in Arabic and English; Dir-Gen. ABD AL-AZIZ AL-HASSAN (Channel 1).

Saudi Arabian Government Television Service Channel 2: POB 7959, Riyadh 11472; tel. (1) 442-8400; fax (1) 403-3826; began transmission 1983; Dir-Gen. ABD AL-AZIZ S. ABU ANNAJA.

Finance

(cap. = capital; res = reserves; dep. = deposits; m. = million; brs = branches; amounts in Saudi riyals unless otherwise stated)

BANKING

At the end of 2000 the Saudi Arabian banking system consisted of: the Saudi Arabian Monetary Agency, as central note-issuing and regulatory body; 11 commercial banks (three national and eight foreign banks); and five specialist banks. There is a policy of 'Saudi-ization' of the foreign banks.

Central Bank

Saudi Arabian Monetary Agency (SAMA): POB 2992, Riyadh 11169; tel. (1) 463-3000; fax (1) 466-2963; e-mail info@sama.ksa.org; internet www.sama.gov.sa; f. 1952; functions include stabilization of currency, administration of monetary reserves, regulation of banking and issue of notes and coins; res 2,103.7m., dep. 61,843.7m., total assets 154,301.8m. (June 2001); Gov. Sheikh HAMAD SA'UD AS-SAYARI; 10 brs.

National Banks

National Commercial Bank (NCB): POB 3555, King Abd al-Aziz St, Jeddah 21481; tel. (2) 649-3333; fax (2) 644-6468; e-mail contact@alahli.com; internet www.alahli.com; f. 1950; cap. 6,000m., res 2,051m., dep. 88,757m. (Dec. 2001); Chair. and Man. Dir Sheikh ABDULLAH SALIM BAHAMDAN; 270 brs.

Ar-Rajhi Banking and Investment Corpn (ARABIC): POB 28, Riyadh 11411; tel. (1) 460-1000; fax (1) 460-0922; e-mail contactus@ alrajhibank.com.sa; internet www.alrajhibank.com.sa; f. 1988; operates according to Islamic financial principles; cap. 2,250m., res 3,189m., dep. 37,536m. (Dec. 2000); Chair. and Man. Dir Sheikh SULAYMAN BIN ABD AL-AZIZ AR-RAJHI; 362 brs.

Riyad Bank Ltd: POB 22601, King Abd al-Aziz St, Riyadh 11416; tel. (1) 401-3030; fax (1) 404-2707; internet www.riyadbank.com.sa; f. 1957; cap. 4,000m., res 4,195m., dep. 55,161m. (Dec. 2001); Chair. RASHED A. AR-RASHED; Pres. and CEO TALAL I. AL-QUDAIBI; 180 brs.

Specialist Bank

Arab Investment Co SAA (TAIC): POB 4009, King Abd al-Aziz St, Riyadh 11491; tel. (1) 476-0601; fax (1) 476-0514; e-mail taic@ taic.com; internet www.taic.com; f. 1974 by 17 Arab countries for investment and banking; cap. US $400m., res $57m., dep. $1,372m. (Dec. 2000); Chair. Dr MUHAMMAD SULAYMAN AL-JASSER; Dir-Gen. Dr SALIH AL-HUMAIDAN; 1 br, 3 offices throughout Middle East.

Banks with Foreign Interests

Al-Bank as-Saudi al-Fransi (Saudi French Bank): POB 56006, Riyadh 11554; tel. (1) 404-2222; fax (1) 404-2311; e-mail communica tions@alfransi.com; internet www.alfransi.com; f. 1977; Saudi shareholders 68.9%, Crédit Agricole Indosuez 31.1%; cap. 1,800m., res 1,732m., dep. 32,836m. (Dec. 2000); Chair. IBRAHIM A. AT-TOUQ; Man. Dir BERTRAND P. VIRIOT; 57 brs.

Arab National Bank (ANB): POB 56921, Riyadh 11564; tel. (1) 402-9000; fax (1) 402-7747; e-mail marketing@anb.com.sa; internet www.anb.com.sa; f. 1980; Arab Bank plc, Jordan, 40%, Saudi shareholders 60%; cap. 1,500m., res 1,800m., dep. 26,273m. (Dec. 2001); Chair. ABD H. AL-JABR; Man. Dir and CEO NEMEH SABBAGH; 117 brs.

Bank al-Jazira: POB 6277, Jeddah 21442; tel. (2) 651-8070; fax (2) 653-2478; e-mail info@baj.com.sa; internet www.baj.com.sa; 94.17% Saudi-owned; cap. 600m., res 55m.; dep. 4,412m. (Dec. 2000); Chair. ADEL MUHAMMAD FAKEIH; Gen. Man. and CEO MISHARI I. AL-MISHARI; 13 brs.

Gulf International Bank (Bahrain): POB 93413, Riyadh 11673; tel. (1) 218-0888; fax (1) 218-0088; f. 2000; Man. ZAFER AL-KALALI.

Saudi American Bank (SAMBA): POB 833, Riyadh 11421; tel. and fax (1) 477-4770; internet www.samba.com.sa; 74% owned by Saudi nationals, 23% by Citibank NA, USA, 2% by Banque du Caire, Egypt, 1% by Bank Melli Iran; merged with United Saudi Bank in 1999; cap. 4,000m., res 4,232m., dep. 67,609m. (Dec. 2000); Chair. ABD AL-AZIZ IBN HAMAD AL-GOSAIBI; Man. Dir ARTHUR M. DE GRAFFANRIED; 43 brs.

Saudi British Bank: POB 9084, Riyadh 11413; tel. (1) 405-0677; fax (1) 405-0660; e-mail pr@sabb.com.sa; internet www.sabb.com.sa; 60% owned by Saudi nationals, 40% by HSBC Holdings BV; f. 1978; cap. 1,600m., res 1,666m., dep. 38,028m. (Dec. 2000); Chair. Sheikh ABDULLAH MUHAMMAD AL-HUGAIL; Man. Dir DAVID HODGKINSON; 80 brs.

Saudi Hollandi Bank (Saudi Dutch Bank): POB 1467, Riyadh 11431; tel. (1) 401-0288; fax (1) 403-1104; e-mail csc@ shb.com.sa; internet www.saudihollandibank.com; a joint-stock co; f. 1977 to assume activities of Algemene Bank Nederland NV in Saudi Arabia; ABN AMRO Bank (Netherlands) 40%, Saudi citizens 60%; cap. 630m., res 1,193m., dep. 18,744m. (Dec. 2000); Chair. Sheikh SULEYMAN A. R. AS-SUHAIMI; Man. Dir HENRIK G. MULDER; 40 brs.

Saudi Investment Bank (SAIB): POB 3533, Riyadh 11481; tel. (1) 477-8433; fax (1) 477-6781; internet www.saib.com.sa; f. 1976; provides a comprehensive range of traditional and specialized banking services; cap. 1,000m., res 885m., dep. 12,512m. (Dec 2001); Chair. Dr ABD AL-AZIZ O'HALI; Pres. and Gen. Man. SA'UD AS-SALEH; 13 brs.

Government Specialized Credit Institutions

Real Estate Development Fund (REDF): POB 5591, Riyadh 11139; tel. (1) 479-2222; fax (1) 479-0148; f. 1974; provides interest-free loans to Saudi individuals and cos for private or commercial housing projects; cap. 70,841 (1993); loans granted amounted to 1,900m. in 2000; Gen. Dir AHMAD AL-AKEIL; 25 brs.

Saudi Arabian Agricultural Bank (SAAB): POB 1811, Riyadh 11126; tel. (1) 402-3911; fax (1) 402-2359; f. 1963; cap. 10,000m. (1982); loans disbursed amounted to 803.9m. in 2000; Controller-Gen. ABDULLAH SAAD AL-MENGASH; Gen. Man. ABD AL-AZIZ MUHAMMAD AL-MANQUR; 70 brs.

Saudi Credit Bank: POB 3401, Riyadh 11471; tel. (1) 402-9128; f. 1973; provides interest-free loans for specific purposes to Saudi citizens of moderate means; loans disbursed amounted to 321.3m. in 2000; Chair. SAID IBN SAIED; Dir-Gen. MUHAMMAD AD-DRIES; 24 brs.

STOCK EXCHANGE

The Saudi Arabian Monetary Agency (see Central Bank, above) operates the Electronic Securities Information System. At mid-2000 shares in 75 companies were being traded. In 2001 691m. shares amounting to 83,602m. riyals were traded.

INSURANCE COMPANIES

In 2000 there were 99 insurance companies, agencies and brokerage offices operating in Saudi Arabia.

Amana Gulf Insurance Co (E.C.): POB 6559, Jeddah 21452; tel. and fax (2) 665-5692.

Arabia Ace Insurance Co Ltd (E.C.): POB 276, Dammam 31411; tel. (3) 832-4441; fax (3) 834-9389; internet www .khereiji.com; cap. US $1m.; Chair. Sheikh ABD AL-KARIM AL-KHEREIJI; Man. Dir TAJUDDIN HASSAN.

Independent Insurance Co of Saudi Arabia Ltd: POB 1178, Jeddah 21431; tel. (2) 651-7732; fax (2) 651-1968; f. 1977; all classes of insurance; cap. US $1m.; Pres. KHALID TAHER; Man. JULIAN D. SHARPE.

Insaudi Insurance Co (E.C.): POB 3984, Riyadh 11481; tel. (1) 476-7711; fax (1) 476-1213.

Islamic Arab Insurance Co: POB 430, Jeddah; tel. (2) 671-0000; fax (2) 617-1027; e-mail iaic@dallah.com.

Al-Jazira Insurance Co Ltd: POB 153, al-Khobar 31952; tel. and fax (3) 895-3445.

National Company for Co-operative Insurance (NCCI): POB 86959, Riyadh 11632; tel. (1) 218-0100; fax (1) 218-0102; e-mail ncci@ncci.com.sa; internet www.ncci.com.sa; f. 1985 by royal decree; owned by three govt agencies; auth. cap. 500m.; Chair. SULAYMAN AL-HUMMAYYD; Man. Dir and Gen. Man. MOUSA AR-RUBAIAN; 13 brs and sales offices.

Ar-Rajhi Insurance Co: POB 22073, Jeddah 21495; tel. (2) 651-1017; fax (2) 651-1797.

Ar-Rajhi Islamic Co for Co-operative Insurance: POB 42220, Jeddah 21541; tel. (2) 651-4514; fax (2) 651-3185.

Red Sea Insurance Group of Cos: POB 5627, Jeddah 21432; tel. (2) 660-3538; fax (2) 665-5418; e-mail redsea@anet.net.sa; internet www.redsains.com; f. 1974; insurance, development, and reinsurance; cap. US $9m. (1998); Chair. KHALDOUN B. BARAKAT.

Royal & Sun Alliance Insurance (Middle East) Ltd (E.C.): POB 2374, Jeddah 21451; tel. (2) 671-8851; fax (2) 671-1377; e-mail alalamiya@dmp.net.sa; managed by Royal & Sun Alliance Insurance Group, London; total assets US $51m. (2000). Chair. WAHIB S. BINZAGR; Man. Dir P. W. HEAD.

Saudi Continental Insurance Co: POB 2940, Riyadh; tel. (1) 479-2141; fax (1) 476-9310; f. 1983; all classes of insurance; cap. US $3m.; Chair. OMAR A. AGGAD; Gen. Man. J.A. McROBBIE.

Saudi National Insurance Co EC: POB 5832, Jeddah 21432; tel. (2) 660-6200; fax (2) 667-4530; Gen. Man. OMAR S. BILANI.

Saudi Union National Insurance Corpn: POB 2357, Jeddah 21451; tel. (2) 667-0648; fax (2) 667-2084.

Saudi United Insurance Co Ltd: POB 933, al-Khobar 31952; tel. (3) 894-9090; fax (3) 894-9428; f. 1976; all classes of insurance and reinsurance except life; cap. US $5m.; majority shareholding held by Ahmad Hamad al-Gosaibi & Bros; Chair. and Man. Dir Sheikh ABD AL-AZIZ HAMAD AL-GOSAIBI; Dir and Gen. Man. ABD AL-MOHSIN AL-GOSAIBI; 6 brs.

U.C.A. Insurance Co (E.C.): POB 5019, Jeddah 21422; tel. (2) 653-0068; fax (2) 651-1936; e-mail ucajed@hotmail.com; f. 1974 as United Commercial Agencies Ltd; all classes of insurance; cap. US $8m.; Chair. Dr GHAITH R. PHARAON; Senior Vice-Pres. MACHAAL A. KARAM.

Al-Yamamah Insurance Co Ltd: POB 41522, Riyadh 11531; tel. (1) 477-4498; fax (1) 477-4497.

Trade and Industry

DEVELOPMENT ORGANIZATIONS

Arab Petroleum Investments Corpn: POB 1547, al-Khobar 31932; tel. (3) 887-0555; fax (3) 887-0404; f. 1975; affiliated to the Organization of Arab Petroleum Exporting Countries; specializes in financing petroleum and petrochemical projects and related industries in the Arab world and in other developing countries; shareholders: Kuwait, Saudi Arabia and the United Arab Emirates (17% each), Libya (15%), Iraq and Qatar (10% each), Algeria (5%), Bahrain, Egypt and Syria (3% each); authorized cap. US $1,200m.; subscribed cap. $460m. (Dec. 1996), Chair. ABDULLAH A. AZ-ZAID; Gen. Man. RASHEED AL-MARAJ.

General Investment Fund: c/o Ministry of Finance and National Economy, Airport Rd, Riyadh 11177; tel. (1) 405-0000; f. 1970; provides government's share of capital to mixed capital cos; 100% state-owned; cap. 1,000m. riyals; Chair. Minister of Finance and National Economy; Sec.-Gen. SULAYMAN MANDIL.

National Agricultural Development Co (NADEC): POB 2557, Riyadh 11461; tel. (1) 404-0000; fax (1) 405-5522; e-mail info@ nadec-sa.com; internet www.nadec-sa.com; f. 1981; interests include 4 dairy farms, 40,000 ha for cultivation of wheat, barley, forage and vegetables and processing of dates; the govt has a 20% share; chief agency for agricultural development; cap. 400m. riyals; Chair. Minister of Agriculture and Water; Dir MUHAMMAD AL-BUBTAIN.

National Industrialization Co (NIC): POB 26707, Riyadh 11496; tel. (1) 476-7166; fax (1) 477-0898; e-mail general@nic.com.sa; internet www.nic.com.sa; f. 1985 to promote and establish industrial projects in Saudi Arabia; cap. 600m. riyals; 100% owned by Saudi nationals; CEO MOAYYED AL-QURTAS.

Saudi Arabian General Investment Authority (SAGIA): POB 1267, Riyadh 11431; tel. 448-4533; fax 448-1234; e-mail alshareef@ sagia.org; internet www.sagia.org; f. 2000 to promote foreign investment; Gov. Prince TURKI IBN ABD AL-AZIZ AS-SA'UD.

Saudi Fund for Development (SFD): POB 50483, Riyadh 11523; tel. (1) 464-0292; fax (1) 464-7450; e-mail info@sfd.gov.sa; internet www.sfd.gov.sa; f. 1974 to help finance projects in developing countries; cap. 31,000m. riyals (1991); had financed 317 projects by 1999; total commitments amounted to 26,447m. riyals; Chair. Minister of Finance and National Economy; Vice-Chair. and Man. Dir MUHAMMAD A. AS-SUGAIR.

Saudi Industrial Development Fund (SIDF): POB 4143, Riyadh 11149; tel. (1) 477-4002; fax (1) 479-0165; f. 1974; supports and promotes local industrial development, providing medium-term interest-free loans; also offers marketing, technical, financial and administrative advice; cap. 7,000m. riyals (1996); loans disbursed amounted to 1,100m riyals in 2000; Chair. HAMAD BIN SAUD AS-SAYYARI; Dir-Gen. SALEH ABDULLAH AN-NAIM.

CHAMBERS OF COMMERCE

Council of Saudi Chambers of Commerce and Industry: POB 16683, Riyadh 11474; tel. (1) 405-3200; fax (1) 402-4747; e-mail council@saudichambers.org.sa; internet www.saudichambers.org

.sa; comprises one delegate from each of the chambers of commerce in the kingdom; Chair. ISMAIL ABU DAWOOD; Sec.-Gen. USAMAH M. AL-KURDI.

Abha Chamber of Commerce and Industry: POB 722, Abha; tel. (7) 227-1818; fax (7) 227-1919; e-mail Abhachamber@arab .net.sa; Pres. ABDULLAH SAEED AL-MOBTY; Sec.-Gen. HAMDI ALI M. AL-MALIKI.

Al-Ahsa Chamber of Commerce and Industry: POB 1519, al-Ahsa 31982; tel. (3) 852-0458; fax (3) 857-5274; Pres. ABD AL-AZIZ SULAYMAN AL-AFALIQ.

Ar'ar Chamber of Commerce and Industry: POB 440, Ar'ar; tel. (4) 662-6544; fax (4) 662-4581; Sec.-Gen. MATAB MOZIL AS-SARRAH.

Al-Baha Chamber of Commerce and Industry: POB 311, al-Baha; tel. (7) 727-0291; fax (7) 828-0146; Pres. SAID ALI AL-ANGARI; Sec.-Gen. YAHYA AZ-ZAHRANI.

Eastern Province Chamber of Commerce and Industry: POB 719, Dammam 31421; tel. (3) 857-1111; fax (3) 857-0607; e-mail info@chamber.org.sa; internet www.chamber.org.sa; f. 1952; Chair. ABD AR-RAHMAN RASHID AR-RASHID; Sec.-Gen. IBRAHIM ABDULLAH AL-OLAYAN.

Federation of Gulf Co-operation Council Chambers (FGCCC): POB 2198, Dammam 31451; tel. (3) 826-5943; fax (3) 826-6794; e-mail fgccc@zajil.net; Pres. SALIM H. ALKHALILI; Sec.-Gen. MUHAMMAD A. AL-MULLA.

Ha'il Chamber of Commerce and Industry: POB 1291, Ha'il; tel. (6) 532-1060; fax (6) 533-1366; e-mail aza100@concept.net.sa; Pres. MUBARAK F. AS-SALAMAH; Sec.-Gen. KHADDAM AS-SALIH AL-FAYEZ.

Jeddah Chamber of Commerce and Industry: POB 1264, Jeddah 21431; tel. (2) 651-5111; fax (2) 651-7373; e-mail customer service@jcci.org.sa; internet www.jcci.org.sa; f. 1946; 26,000 mems; Chair. ABD AHMAD ZEINAL ALIREZA; Sec.-Gen. Dr MAJED A. AL-KASSABI.

Jizan Chamber of Commerce and Industry: POB 201, Jizan; tel. (7) 322-5155; fax (7) 322-3635; Pres. Dr SALEH AZ-ZAIDAN.

Al-Jouf Chamber of Commerce and Industry: POB 585, al-Jouf; tel. (4) 624-9060; fax (4) 624-0108; Pres. MA'ASHI DUKAN AL-ATTIYEH; Sec.-Gen. AHMAD KHALIFA AL-MUSALLAM.

Al-Majma' Chamber of Commerce and Industry: POB 165, al-Majma' 11952; tel. (6) 432-0268; fax (6) 432-2655; Pres. FAHD MUHAMMAD AR-RABIAH; Sec.-Gen. ABDULLAH IBRAHIM AL-JAAWAN.

Mecca Chamber of Commerce and Industry: POB 1086, Mecca; tel. (2) 534-3838; fax (2) 534-2904; f. 1947; Pres. ADEL ABDULLAH KA'AKI; Sec.-Gen. ABDULLAH ABD AL-GAFOOR TOUJAR-ALSHAHI.

Medina Chamber of Commerce and Industry: POB 443, King Abd al-Aziz Rd, Medina; tel. (4) 838-8909; fax (4) 838-8905; Sec.-Gen. Dr SALEH D. AL-HARTI.

Najran Chamber of Commerce and Industry: POB 1138, Najran; tel. (7) 522-2216; fax (7) 522-3926; Sec.-Gen. MAKHFOOR ABDULLAH AL-BISHER.

Al-Qassim Chamber of Commerce and Industry: POB 444, Buraydah, Qassim; tel. (6) 381-4000; fax (6) 381-2231.

Al-Qurayat Chamber of Commerce and Industry: POB 416, al-Qurayat; tel. (4) 642-6200; fax (4) 642-3172; Pres. OTHMAN ABDULLAH AL-YOUSEF; Sec.-Gen. JAMAL ALI AL-GHAMDI.

Riyadh Chamber of Commerce and Industry: POB 596, Riyadh 11421; tel. (1) 404-0044; fax (1) 402-1103; e-mail rdcham ber@rdcci.org.sa; f. 1961; acts as arbitrator in business disputes, information centre; Chair. Sheikh ABD AR-RAHMAN AL-JERAISY; Sec.-Gen. HUSSEIN ABD AR-RAHMAN AL-AZAL; 23,000 mems.

Tabouk Chamber of Commerce and Industry: POB 567, Tabouk; tel. (4) 422-2736; fax (4) 422-7387; Pres. ABD AL-AZIZ M. OWADEH; Sec.-Gen. AWADH AL-BALAWI.

Ta'if Chamber of Commerce and Industry: POB 1005, Ta'if; tel. (2) 736-6800; fax (2) 738-0040; Pres. IBRAHIM ABDULLAH KAMAL; Sec.-Gen. Eng. YOUSUF MUHAMMAD ASH-SHAFI.

Yanbu Chamber of Commerce and Industry: POB 58, Yanbu; tel. (4) 322-7878; fax (4) 322-6800; f. 1979; produces quarterly magazine; 5,000 members; Pres. Dr TALAL ALI ASH-SHAIR; Sec.-Gen. OSMAN NAIM AL-MUFTI.

STATE HYDROCARBONS COMPANIES

General Petroleum and Mineral Organization (PETROMIN JET): POB 7550, 21472 Jeddah; tel. (2) 685-7666; fax (2) 685-7545; works in conjunction with the Ministry of Petroleum and Mineral Resources to oversee petroleum industry; Chair. and Exec. Asst ABDULLAH O. ATTAS (acting).

Arabian Drilling Co: POB 708, Dammam 31421; tel. (3) 887-2020; fax (3) 882-6588; e-mail adcgen@al-khobar.oilfield.slb.com; f. 1964; PETROMIN shareholding 51%, remainder French private cap.; undertakes contract drilling for oil (on shore and off shore),

minerals and water both inside and outside Saudi Arabia; Chair. SULAYMAN J. AL-HERBISH; Man. Dir SAAD ABDULLAH SAAB.

Arabian Geophysical and Surveying Co (ARGAS): POB 535, al-Khobar 31952; tel. (3) 882-9122; fax (3) 882-9060; f. 1966, with the General Petroleum and Mineral Organization (PETROMIN) having a shareholding of 51%; remainder provided by Cie Générale de Géophysique; geophysical exploration for petroleum, other minerals and groundwater, as well as all types of land, airborne and marine surveys; Chair. AHMAD MUHAMMAD GHAZZAWI; Man. Dir HABIB M. MERGHELANI.

Petromin Marketing (PETMARK): POB 50, Dhahran Airport 31932; tel. (3) 890-3883; f. 1967; operates the installations and facilities for the distribution of petroleum products in the Eastern, Central, Southern and Northern provinces of Saudi Arabia; Pres. and CEO HUSSEIN A. LINJAWI.

Saudi Arabian Oil Co (Saudi Aramco): POB 5000, Dhahran 31311; tel. (3) 875-4915; fax (3) 873-8490; e-mail webmaster@ aramco.com.sa; internet www.saudiaramco.com; f. 1933; previously known as Arabian-American Oil Co (Aramco); in 1993 incorporated the Saudi Arabian Marketing and Refining Co (SAMAREC, f. 1988) by merger of operations; holds the principal working concessions in Saudi Arabia; operates five wholly-owned refineries (at Jeddah, Rabigh, Ras Tanura, Riyadh and Yanbu) with total capacity of more than 1m. barrels per day; Pres. and CEO ABDULLAH S. JAMA'AH; Exec. Vice-Pres. (Exploration and Production) SADAD AL-HUSSEINI.

Saudi Arabian Lubricating Oil Co (PETROLUBE): POB 1432, Jeddah 21431; tel. (2) 661-3333; fax (2) 661-3322; f. 1968; 71% owned by Saudi Aramco, 29% by Mobil; for the manufacture and marketing of lubricating oils and other related products; production 199m. litres (1988); cap. 110m.; Pres. KHALID M. ALAGIL.

Saudi Aramco Lubricating Oil Refining Co (LUBEREF): POB 5518, Jeddah 21432; tel. (3) 638-5040; fax (2) 636-6932; f. 1975; owned 70% by Saudi Aramco and 30% by Mobil; production 3,800,000 barrels; Chair. SALIM S. AL-AYDH; Pres. and CEO MUHAMMAD ALI AL-HARAZY.

Saudi Aramco Mobil Refinery Co Ltd (SAMREF): POB 30078, Yanbu; tel. (4) 396-4000; fax (4) 396-0942; f. 1981; operated by Saudi Aramco and Mobil, capacity 360,000 b/d; Pres. and CEO MUHAMMAD A. MISFER.

Saudi Aramco Shell Refinery Co (SASREF): POB 10088, Jubail 31961; tel. (3) 357-2000; fax (3) 358-9667; e-mail k.al-buainain@pr.sasrefalj.simis.com; internet www.shell.com; operated by Saudi Aramco and Shell; capacity 300,000 b/d; exports began in 1985; Chair. ABD AL-AZIZ M. AL-HOKAIL.

Saudi Basic Industries Corpn (SABIC): POB 5101, Riyadh 11422; tel. (1) 401-2033; fax (1) 401-2045; internet www.sabic.com; f. 1976 to foster the petrochemical industry and other hydrocarbon-based industries through jt ventures with foreign partners, and to market their products; 70% state-owned; production 35m. tons (2001); Chair. Minister of Industry and Electricity; Vice-Chair. and CEO MUHAMMAD AL-MADY.

Projects include:

Al-Jubail Petrochemical Co (Kemya): POB 10084, Jubail 31961; tel. (3) 357-6000; fax (3) 358-7858; f. 1980; began production of linear low-density polyethylene in 1984, of high-density polyethylene in 1985, and of high alfa olefins in 1986, capacity of 330,000 tons per year of polyethylene; jt venture with Exxon Corpn (USA) and SABIC; Pres. ABD AL-AZIZ I. AL-AUDAH; Exec. Vice-Pres. CLAY LEWIS.

Arabian Petrochemical Co (Petrokemya): POB 10002, Jubail 31961; tel. (3) 358 7000; fax (3) 358-4480; e-mail otaibifr@petro kemya.sabic.com; produced 2.4m. tons of ethylene, 135,000 tons of polystyrene, 100,000 tons of butene-1; 570,000 tons of propylene, 100,000 tons of butadiene and 150,000 tons of benzene in 2001; wholly-owned subsidiary of SABIC; owns 50% interest in ethylene glycol plant producing 610,000 tons per year of monoethylene glycol, 65,000 tons per year of diethylene glycol and 3,900 tons per year of triethylene glycol; Chair. HOMOOD AT-TUWAIJRI; Pres. KHALID S. AR-RAWAF.

Eastern Petrochemical Co (Sharq): POB 10035, Jubail 31961; tel. (3) 357-5000; fax (3) 358-0383; f. 1981 to produce linear low-density polyethylene, ethylene glycol; total capacity 660,000 tons of ethylene glycol and 280,000 tons of polyethylene per year; a SABIC jt venture; Pres. IBRAHIM S. ASH-SHEWEIR.

National Industrial Gases Co (Gas): POB 10110, Jubail 31961; tel. (3) 357-5700; fax (3) 358-5542; total capacity of 876,000 tons of oxygen and 492,750 tons of nitrogen per year; jt venture with Saudi private sector; Pres. ABDULLAH MUJBEL AL-JALAWI.

National Plastic Co (Ibn Hayyan): POB 10002, Jubail 31961; tel. (3) 358-7000; fax (3) 358-4736; f. 1984; produces 390,000 tons per year of vinylchloride monomer and 324,000 tons per year of polyvinylchloride; jt venture with Lucky Group (Republic of Korea), SABIC and three other cos; Pres. KHALED AR-RAWAF.

Saudi-European Petrochemical Co (Ibn Zahr): POB 10330, Jubail 31961; tel. (3) 341-5060; fax (3) 341-2966; f. 1985; annual capacity 1.4m. tons of methyl-tertiary-butyl ether (MTBE), 0.3m. tons of propylene; SABIC has a 70% share, Ecofuel, Nesté Corpn and APICORP each have 10%; Pres. SAMI AS-SUWAIGH.

Saudi Methanol Co (ar-Razi): POB 10065, Jubail Industrial City 31961; tel. (3) 357-7820; fax (3) 358-0838; e-mail emt@arrazi.com; f. 1979; capacity of 3,158,000 tons per year of chemical-grade methanol; total methanol exports in 2001 were 3,248,000 tons; jt venture with a consortium of Japanese cos; Pres. NABIL A. MANSOURI; Exec. Vice-Pres. H. MIZUNO.

Saudi Petrochemical Co (Sadaf): POB 10025, Jubail 31961; tel. (3) 357-3000; fax (3) 357-3142; f. 1980; to produce ethylene, ethylene dichloride, styrene, crude industrial ethanol, caustic soda and methyl-tertiary-butyl-ether (MTBE); total capacity of 4,710,000 tons per year; Shell (Pecten) has a 50% share; Pres. MOSAED S. AL-OHALI.

Saudi Yanbu Petrochemical Co (Yanpet): POB 30139, Yanbu; tel. (4) 396-5000; fax (4) 396-5006; f. 1980; to produce 820,000 tons per year of ethylene, 600,000 tons per year of high-density polyethylene and 340,000 tons per year of ethylene glycol; total capacity 1,692,200 tons per year by 1990; Mobil and SABIC each have a 50% share; Pres. ALI AL-KHURAIMI; Exec. CEO P. J. FOLEY.

Foreign Concessionaires

Arabian Oil Co Ltd (AOC): POB 256, Ras al-Khafji 31971; tel. (3) 766-0555; fax (3) 766-2001; f. 1958; holds concession (2,200 sq km at Dec. 1987) for offshore exploitation of Saudi Arabia's half-interest in the Kuwait-Saudi Arabia Neutral Zone; Pres. KEIICHI KONAGA; Chief Exec. General Affairs. AHMAD IBRAHIM AL-ASFOUR.

Saudi Arabian Texaco Inc: POB 363, Riyadh; tel. (1) 462-7274; fax (1) 464-1992; also office in Kuwait; f. 1928; fmrly Getty Oil Co; holds concession (5,200 sq km at Dec. 1987) for exploitation of Saudi Arabia's half-interest in the Saudi Arabia-Kuwait Neutral Zone.

UTILITIES

Utilities Co (Uco): Jubail; f. 1999; owned equally by Royal Commission for Jubail and Yanbu, Public Investment Fund, Saudi Aramco and SABIC; cap. 2,000m. riyals; to provide utilities in industrial cities of Jubail and Yanbu.

Electricity

Electricity Services Regulatory Authority (ESRA): Riyadh; f. 2001 to regulate the power industry and to recommend tariffs for the sector; Gov. FAREED ZEDAN.

Saudi Electricity Co (SEC): POB 57, Riyadh 11411; tel. (1) 403-2222; fax (1) 405-1191; f. 2000 following merger of 10 regional companies; joint-stock co; cap. 33,758m.; to organize the generation, transmission and distribution of electricity into separate operating companies; Chair. Minister of Industry and Electricity; CEO SULAYMAN A. AL-QADI.

Water

Saline Water Conversion Corpn (SWCC): POB 4931, 21412 Jeddah; tel. (2) 682-1240; fax (2) 682-0415; provides desalinated water; 24 plants; capacity 2m. cu m per day (1994); Dir-Gen. ABD AL-AZIZ OMAR NASSIEF.

MAJOR COMPANIES
Figures for sales and capital, etc. are in Saudi riyals.

Saleh & Abd al-Aziz Abahsain Co Ltd: POB 209, al-Khobar 31952; tel. (3) 898-4045; fax (3) 899-0114; e-mail abahsain@zajil.net; internet www.abahsain.net; f. 1946; trade in general heavy machinery and machinery for construction and engineering; Pres. And CEO ABD AL-AZIZ IBRAHIM ABAHSAIN; Gen. Man. SHAUKAT RIAZ SHEIKH; 2,080 employees.

Alhamrani Group: POB 1229, Jeddah 21431; tel. (2) 682-7777; fax (2) 683-6085; f. 1953; retail and distribution services for automotive industry; automatic banking and security equipment; construction materials and airport and aviation services; sales 2,631m., cap. 90m. (1998); Chair. MUHAMMAD A. AL-HAMRANI; CEO SIRAJ A. AL-HAMRANI; 2,800 employees.

Haji Hussein Alireza & Co Ltd: POB 8, Jeddah 21411; tel. (2) 647-2233; fax (2) 648-3010; e-mail info@alireza.com; internet www.alireza.com; f. 1845; engineering, supply, installation, maintenance and training for computer and telecommunications networks; security systems; precision engineering; sales 1,527m., cap. 100m. (2000); Pres. AHMAD Y. Z. ALIREZA; Gen. Man. YAHIA TEWFIQ HASSAN; 1,400 employees.

Alpha Trading and Shipping Ltd: POB 205, Jeddah 21411; tel. (2) 644-3216; fax (2) 642-1188; e-mail alphajeddah@zajil.net; f. 1946; trade in foodstuffs, raw materials and commodities; sales 630m.

(1999); Chair. ABD AL-QADIR MUHAMMAD AL-FADL; Man. Dir ANDREAS ELLINAS.

Arab Supply and Trading Corporation (ASTRA Group): POB 254, Tabouk; tel. (4) 422-0400; fax (4) 428-1584; e-mail astra@nour net.com.sa; f. 1976; farming; manufacturing; wholesale and retail trade; medical and pharmaceutical products and services; sales 883m., cap. 250m. (1999); Chair. SABIH AT-TAHER AL-MASRI; Man. Dir KAMIL A. SADEDIN; 4,500 employees.

Arabian Cement Co Ltd: POB 275, Jeddah 21411; tel. (2) 682-8270; fax (2) 682-9989; f. 1954; produces ordinary Portland cement and sulphate-resistant cement; subsidiary company Cement Product Industry Co Ltd; cap. 600m. (1999); Chair. Prince TURKI IBN ABD AL-AZIZ AS-SA'UD; Dir-Gen. Eng. MUHAMMAD NAJIB KHEDER; 870 employees.

Consolidated Contractors Co WLL: POB 234, Riyadh 11411; tel. (1) 465-0311; fax (1) 464-5963; f. 1965; general construction and engineering projects including infrastructure and heavy industry; major shareholders are members of Saudi royal family; parent company Consolidated Contractors Group, Athens (Greece); sales 896.2m., cap. 1m. (1999); Gen. Man. HAMID AMIN; 421 employees.

Dallah al-Baraka Group: POB 430, Jeddah 21411; tel. (2) 671-0000; fax (2) 671-3603; e-mail webmaster@albaraka.com; internet www.albaraka.com; f. 1969; divided into business, finance and media divisions; industrial investment; agriculture; trading; real estate; transport; tourism; construction; financial services; communications; satellite broadcasting; sales 15,006m., cap. 3,750m. (1998); Pres. SALEH ABDULLAH KAMEL; 37,000 employees.

Eastern Province Cement Co: POB 4536, Dammam 31412; tel. (3) 827-3330; fax (3) 827-1923; f. 1994; cap. 645m., sales 196m. (1998); Chair. AHMAD ABDULLAH AZ-ZAMEL; Gen. Man. ABD AL-AZIZ AL-JAMAL; 725 employees.

Al-Faisalia Group: POB 16460, Riyadh 11464; tel. (1) 462-4266; fax (1) 464-0498; f. 1970; sale, installation and management of electrical, electronic and telecommunications equipment; computers; petrochemicals; dairy and agricultural products; sales 2,000m., cap. 375m. (1999); Chair. MUHAMMAD ABDULLAH AL-FAISAL; Man. MUHAMMAD ABD AR-RAHMAN AL-ARIEFY; 3,000 employees.

Grain Silos and Flour Mills Organization: POB 3402, Riyadh 11471; tel. (1) 464-9864; fax (1) 463-1943; f. 1972; autonomous body formally responsible to the Ministry of Agriculture; production of flour and animal feeds for domestic consumption; grain capacity 585,999 tons (1988); Chair. Minister of Agriculture and Water; Dir-Gen. SALEH AS-SULAYMAN; 1,830 employees.

Hoshan Company Ltd—Hoshanco: POB 509, Riyadh 11421; tel. (1) 416-2323; fax (1) 465-6248; e-mail hoshanco@hoshanco.com.sa; internet www.hoshanco.com.sa; f. 1964; office furniture and equipment, telecommunications, engineering, information technology and microfilm products; sales 220m. (2000); Chair. AHMAD AL-HOSHAN; Gen. Man. ANAS YAFI; 600 employees.

Jadawel International Group: POB 250, Dhahran Airport 31932; tel. (3) 894-7733; fax (3) 894-5306; f. 1982; electrical and mechanical contractors; sales 1,764m., cap. 600m. (1999); CEO MUHAMMAD IBN ISA AL-JABER; Finance Man. KHALIL OKASHA; 1,230 employees.

Jamjoon Corporation for Commerce and Industry: POB 59, Jeddah 21411; tel. (2) 671-5995; fax (2) 671-5210; e-mail jamjoom-co@ogertel.com; f. 1971; general construction, operation and maintenance services; import and distribution of air-conditioning, heating, refrigeration, power-generating, water treatment and desalination equipment; shipping and navigation; environmental pollution control; sales 1,141m., cap. 64.1m. (1999); Chair. and CEO Sheikh ABD AL-QAFAR MUHAMMAD JAMJOON; 1,700 employees.

Al-Jubail Fertilizer Co (Samad): POB 10046, Jubail 31961; tel. (3) 341-6488; fax (3) 341-7122; f. 1979; capacity of 620,000 tons per year of urea, 40,000 tons per year of ammonia, 150,000 tons per year of 2-ethyl hexanol, 50,000 tons per year of di-octyl phtalate and 180,000 tons per year of ISO-butaraldehyde; jt venture between SABIC and Taiwan Fertilizer Co; Pres. ABDULLAH AL-BARAK; Gen. Man. Operations JIMMY CHEN; 517 employees.

Isam Khairy Kabbani Group: POB 5338, Jeddah 21422; tel. (2) 667-2000; fax (2) 665-8079; f. 1968; contracting including roof works, concrete works; oil and gas pipelines; hydrocarbons plants; wholesale and retail trade in construction materials, electrical goods, tools, hardware and food products; sales 698m. (1999); Chair. Sheikh ISAM KABBANI; Dir HASSAN ISAM KABBANI; 1,650 employees.

Kingdom Holding Company: POB 2, Riyadh 11321; tel. (1) 488-1111; fax (1) 481-1542; f. 1980; project financing, contracting and trading; sales 16,980m., cap. 37,064m. (1998); Chair. and CEO Prince WALID IBN AT-TALAL.

Manufacturing and Building Co Ltd (MABCO): POB 52743, Riyadh 11573; tel. (1) 498-1222; fax (1) 498-4807; f. 1977; manufacture of pre-cast components for construction of buildings; sales 150m. (1977); cap. p.u. 100m.; Pres. OMAR ABD AL-FATTAH AGGAD; Gen. Man. WAJIH AL-BAZ; 500 employees.

Al-Marai Company Ltd: POB 8524, Riyadh 11492; tel. (1) 470-0005; fax (1) 470-1555; f. 1976; agricultural management and dairy farming; jt venture with Masstock International (UK/N. Ireland); sales 1,250m., cap. 200m. (1999); CEO ABD AR-RAHMAN A. AL-MOHANA; Gen. Man. CHRIS LEDWIDGE; 2,900 employees.

Marei bin Mahfouz Group & Co Ltd: POB 734, Mecca; tel. (2) 550-0088; fax (2) 550-0099; e-mail bmahfouz@sps.net.sa; internet www.binmahfouz.net; f. 1970; manufacturer; investor in real estate; import and export; wholesale and retail; medical services; sales 1,250m., cap. 25m. (1999); Chair. MAREI MUBARAK BIN MAHFOUZ; Gen. Man. ABDULLAH MAREI BIN MAHFOUZ; 1,150 employees.

Napco Group: POB 538, Dammam 51411; tel. (3) 847-3040; fax (3) 847-1504; e-mail rbitar@napcogroup.com; f. 1956; manufacture and wholesale trade in plastics; sales 810m. (2000); Man. Dir JAMAL ABD AR-RAHMAN AL-MOAIBED; 2,146 employees.

National Gas and Industrialisation Co (GASCO): POB 564, Riyadh 11421; tel. (1) 401-4806; fax (1) 401-4088; e-mail puch@gasco sa.com; f. 1963; supply and transportation of liquefied petroleum gas (LPG); sales 1,050m., cap. 500m. (1999); Chair. ABDULLAH AN-NUAIM; Gen. Man. ABD AL-AZIZ AL-HEDAITHY; 1,520 employees.

National Glass Industries Co (Zoujaj): POB 88646, Riyadh 11672; tel. (1) 477-0045; fax (1) 477-0087; f. 1990; sales 53.8m., cap. 200m. (1998); manufacture of glass products; Chair. Eng. MUBARAK AL-KHAFRA; Gen. Man. ABD AR-RAHMAN BIN ZARAH; 275 employees.

National Gypsum Co: POB 187, Riyadh 11411; tel. (1) 495-3730; fax (1) 463-0612; f. 1958; sales 123m., cap. 144m. (1999); Chair. ABDULLAH F. AT-THUNAYAN; Man. Dir AMR M. KHASHOGGI; 450 employees.

National Methanol Co (Ibn Sina): POB 10003, Jubail 31961; tel. (3) 340-5500; fax (3) 340-5506; e-mail ibnsina@ibnsina.com; began commercial production of chemical-grade methanol in November 1984; capacity 1m. tons per year; began commercial production of methyl-tertiary-butyl ether (MTBE) in May 1994; capacity 900,000 tons per year; jt venture of SABIC, Hoechst-Celanese Corpn (USA) and PanEnergy Corpn (USA); Pres. ABD AR-RAHMAN AL-GARAWI; 348 employees.

National Pipe Co Ltd: POB 1099, al-Khobar 31952; tel. (3) 857-0535; fax (3) 857-0962; f. 1978; manufacture and marketing of spiral-welded steel pipes for oil and gas transmission; sales 208m. (1996); cap. 50m.; Chair. TEYMOUR ALIREZA; Gen. Man. EIJI MIKAMI; 345 employees.

Olayan Financing Company: POB 8772, Riyadh 11492; tel. (1) 477-8740; fax (1) 478-0988; internet www.olayangroup.com; f. 1948; investment in industrial development and technology projects; sales 3,988m., cap. 10,000m. (1999); Chair. KHALED S. OLAYAN; Gen. Man. IMTIAZ H. HYDARI; 8,600 employees.

Qassim Cement Co: POB 345, Buraidah, Qassim; tel. (6) 381-0795; fax (6) 381-6187; internet www.qcc.com.sa; f. 1976; production of 2,000 tons per day; Hon. Chair. Prince ABDULLAH AL-FAISAL AS-SA'UD; Chair. Prince SULTAN AL-ABDULLAH AL-FAISAL AS-SA'UD; 580 employees.

Ar-Rajhi Co for Industry and Trade: POB 4130, Riyadh 11491; tel. (1) 447-0088; fax (1) 448-9256; f. 1972; production of foodstuffs, fruit beverages and packaging; Chair. SULAYMAN ABD AL-AZIZ AR-RAJHI; Man. Dir ABDULLAH M. AN-NAIM; 800 employees.

Riyadh Cables: POB 26862, Riyadh 11496; tel. (1) 265-0850; fax (1) 265-1423; f. 1984; manufacture of electrical cables; sales 1,396.1m., cap. 240m. (1999); Chair. HAMDI SA'ADUDDIN AZ-ZAIM; 1,561 employees.

Saad Trading and Contracting Co: POB 3250, al-Khobar 31952; tel. (3) 882-2220; fax (3) 882-8699; f. 1986; design; building and construction contracting; engineering; building maintenance; sales 1,494m., cap. 10m. (1999); CEO MA'AN ABD AL-WAHID AS-SANEE; Gen. Man. STUART F. SMITH; 5,350 employees.

Mahmood Saeed Collective Co: POB 17013, Jeddah 21484; tel. (2) 636-0020; fax (2) 637-9093; f. 1957; manufacture of soft drinks and packaging, bedding, perfume and cosmetic products; import of textiles; Chair. MAHMOOD MUHAMMAD SAEED QASSIM; Man. Dir RASHID MAHMOOD SAEED; 2,250 employees.

As-Safi Dairy Establishment: POB 10525, Riyadh 11443; tel. (1) 461-0077; fax (1) 462-9647; f. 1979; dairy products; Pres. MUHAMMAD AL-AREEFY; Gen. Man. MUHAMMAD ASH-SHONAIFY; 1,670 eployees.

Saudi Arabian Amiantit Co (Amiantit): POB 589, Dammam 31421; tel. (3) 857-2160; fax (3) 857-9771; f. 1968; production and marketing of pipes, fibreglass and rubber products; sales 646m., cap. 350m. (1999); Pres. ABD AL-AZIZ S. AL-JARBOU; Gen. Man. TOUFIC ABAHUSSAIN; 1,140 employees.

Saudi Arabian Fertilizer Co (SAFCO): POB 11044, Jubail 31961; tel. (3) 341-1100; fax (3) 341-1257; f. 1965; produced 353,744 tons of urea, 225,735 tons of ammonia, 98,535 tons of sulphuric acid and 20,240 tons of melamine in 1993; owned 41% by SABIC, 10% by its staff and 49% by private Saudi investors; sales 793.3m., cap. 2,000m. (2000); Chair. MUHAMMAD H. AL-MADY; 700 employees.

Saudi Arabian Mining Co (Ma'aden): POB 68861, Riyadh 11537; tel. (1) 472-1222; fax (1) 472-1333; internet www.maaden.com.sa; f. 1997; produced 7 tons of gold in 1997; Pres. ABDULLAH AD-DABBAGH.

Saudi Cable Group: POB 4403, Jeddah 21491; tel. (2) 638-1405; fax (2) 637-5447; e-mail wsg@xenel.com; f. 1975; manufacture of building wires, power and telecommunication cables including fibre optic cables, copper and aluminium rod, PVC compounds, information technology products, power transmission and distribution products, turnkey services; sales 769.6m.; cap. 500m. (1999); Chair. KHALID ALIREZA; Pres. WAHIB A. LINJAWI; 2,600 employees.

Saudi Cement Co: POB 306, Dammam 31411; tel. (3) 834-4500; fax (3) 834-5460; e-mail scc@saudicement.com.sa; internet www.sau dicement.com.sa; f. 1955; cap. 1,020m.; Chair. Sheikh WALID AHMAD JUFFALI; Gen. Man. ABD AL-AZIZ M. SHOWAIL; 1,830 employees.

Saudi Ceramic Co: POB 3893, Riyadh 11481; tel. (1) 464-4244; fax (1) 465-2124; e-mail info@saudiceramics.com; internet www.sau diceramics.com; f. 1977; manufacture and marketing of ceramics; sales 194.5m., cap. 250m. (1999); Chair. SAAD AL-MOJEL; Gen. Man. SULAYMAN ALKHELAIFI; 1,300 employees.

Saudi Fisheries Co (SFC): POB 6535; Dammam 31452; tel. (3) 857-3979; fax (3) 857-2493; e-mail fishsales@saudi-fisheries.com; internet www.saudi-fisheries.com; f. 1981; sales 176.5m., cap. 100m. (1999); Chair. Minister of Agriculture and Water; Gen. Man. ABD AL-LATIF IBRAHIM AL-AJAJI; 1,500 employees.

Saudi Iron and Steel Co (Hadeed): POB 10053, Jubail 31961; tel (3) 357-1100; fax (3) 358-5000; f. 1979; produced more than 2.5m. tons of steel reinforcing bars, coils of wire rod and light sections in 1999; Pres. MUTLAQ AL-MORISHED; 3,383 employees.

Saudi Pharmaceutical Industries and Medical Appliances Corpn (Spimaco): POB 20001, Riyadh 11455; tel. (1) 477-4481; fax (1) 477-3961; e-mail general@spimaco.com.sa; internet www.spi maco.com.sa; f. 1986; sales 511m., cap. 600m. (1999); manufacture of pharmaceutical products; Chair. Dr SALEH ABD AL-AZIZ AL-OMAIR; Gen Man. Dr ABDULLAH A. ABD AL-KADER; 505 employees.

Saudi Plastic Products Co Ltd (SAPPCO): POB 2828, Riyadh 11461; tel. (1) 448-0448; fax (1) 446-1392; f. 1969; manufacture and supply of UPVC pipes and fittings; cap. 75m.; total assets 194m.; Man. Dir FAISAL AL-FALEH; 150 employees.

Saudi United Fertilizers Co (Al-Asmida): POB 4811, Riyadh 11412; tel. (1) 478-1304; fax (1) 478-9581; f. 1975; import and export of agricultural fertilizers, pesticides, forage seeds, field sprayers and agricultural machinery; Man. Dir SAMIR ALI KABBANI.

Saudia Dairy and Foodstuff Co Ltd (SADAFCO): POB 5043, Jeddah 21422; tel. (2) 651-9340; fax (2) 653-1595; internet www.sad afco.com; f. 1977; manufacture and distribution of food products and beverages; sales 965.3m. (2000); Man. Dir AHMAD M. AL-MARZOUKI; Gen. Man. KEVIN BAXTER; 2,100 employees.

Savola Group: POB 14455, Jeddah 21424; tel. (2) 657-3333; fax (2) 648-4119; e-mail habib@savola.usa.com; production of food and beverages; sales 2,162.6m, cap. 550m. (1998); Chair. and Man. Dir ADEL MUHAMMAD FAKEIH; 4,000 employees.

Southern Province Cement Co: (Head Office) POB 548, Abha; tel. (7) 227-1500; fax (7) 227-1003; internet www.awanet/commerce/spcco/sapco2.asp; f. 1974; sales 566.9m., cap. 1,050m. (2000); Chair. Prince KHALID IBN TURKI AT-TURKI; Gen. Man. Eng. AMER SAEED BARGAN; 1,313 employees.

As-Subeaei United Company: POB 749, Jeddah 21421; tel. (2) 672-2288; fax (2) 672-5924; e-mail Jeddah@alsubeaei.com; f. 1934; import and distribution of foodstuffs, textiles, furniture, hardware and gold; money exchange; sales 720m., cap. 10m. (1999); Chair. MUHAMMAD IBRAHIM AS-SUBEAEI; Sec. C. H. ABD AL-JALEEL; 150 employees.

As-Suwaiket Trading and Contracting Co: POB 691, Dhahran Airport 31932; tel. (3) 857-9780; fax (3) 857-2904; f. 1947; general contracting; electro-mechanical engineering; telecoms and electronics; drilling, wells and pipeline services; sales 2,130m., cap. 50m. (1999); Pres. MUBARAK ABDULLAH AS-SUWAIKET; 1,200 employees.

Tamimi Co: POB 172, Dammam 31411; tel. (3) 847-4050; fax (3) 847-1592; e-mail tamimi-ho@al-tamimi.com; internet www.al -tamimi.com; f. 1964; pipeline construction, mechanical and civil construction, industrial catering, real estate; cap. 20m.; Chair. TALAL A. TAMIMI.

At-Tayyar Travel Group Co Ltd: POB 52660, Riyadh 11573; tel. (1) 463-3133; fax (1) 465-6049; e-mail altayyar@altayyargroup.com; internet www.altayyargroup.com; f. 1983; travel and tourism; customs clearance services; shipping; car hire; advertising; sales 944m., cap. 4.3m. (1999); Chair. and CEO NASSER AT-TAYYAR; 620 employees.

Yamama Saudi Cement Co: POB 293, Riyadh 11411; tel. (1) 405-8288; fax (1) 403-3292; e-mail yamama-company@hotmail.com; f. 1961; cap. sales 277m., cap. 450m. (1998); production and marketing of cement; Gen. Man. SAUD AD-DABLAN; 1,180 employees.

Yanbu Cement Co: (Head Office) POB 5330, Jeddah 21422; tel. (2) 653-1555; fax (2) 653-1420; e-mail sales@yanbucement.com; internet www.yanbucement.com; f. 1977; sales 385m., cap. 1,050m. (1998); Chair. Prince MESHAL IBN ABD AL-AZIZ; Dir-Gen. Dr SAUD SALEH ISLAM.

Az-Zamil Group: POB 9, al-Khobar 31952; tel. (3) 894-4888; fax (3) 895-1248; e-mail webmaster@zamil.com; internet www.zamil.com; f. 1930; involved in real estate and land development as well as the marketing of products from numerous subsidiary companies, including Az-Zamil Aluminium Factory Ltd, Zamil Soule Steel Building Co Ltd, Yamama Factories, Arabian Gulf Construction Co Ltd, Bahrain Marble Factory, Az-Zamil Nails and Screws Factory, Saudi Plastics Factory; Pres. MUHAMMAD A. AZ-ZAMIL; Gen. Man. MUHAMMAD SAID BATARFI; 7,500 employees.

TRADE UNIONS

Trade unions are illegal in Saudi Arabia.

Transport

RAILWAYS

Saudi Arabia has the only rail system in the Arabian peninsula. The Saudi Government Railroad comprises 719 km of single and 157 km of double track. In addition, the total length of spur lines and sidings is 348 km. The main line, which was opened in 1951, is 578 km in length; it connects Dammam port, on the Gulf coast, with Riyadh, and passes Dhahran, Abqaiq, Hufuf, Harad and al-Kharj. A 310-km line, linking Hufuf and Riyadh, was inaugurated in May 1985. A new 2,000-km network, linking Riyadh to the north of the kingdom and connecting Jubail to Dammam, was under consideration in early 2002. A total of 854,000 passengers travelled by rail in the kingdom in 2000, and 1.6m. metric tons of freight was carried by the railways in the same year.

Saudi Railways Organization: POB 36, Dammam 31241; tel. (3) 871-5151; fax (3) 833-6337; Pres. K. H. AL-YAHYA.

ROADS

Asphalted roads link Jeddah to Mecca, Jeddah to Medina, Medina to Yanbu, Ta'if to Mecca, Riyadh to al-Kharj, and Dammam to Hufuf as well as the principal communities and certain outlying points in Aramco's area of operations. During the 1980s the construction of other roads was undertaken, including one extending from Riyadh to Medina. The trans-Arabian highway, linking Dammam, Riyadh, Ta'if, Mecca and Jeddah, was completed in 1967. A causeway linking Saudi Arabia with Bahrain was opened in November 1986. A 317-km highway linking Riyadh to Qassim was completed in the late 1980s. At the end of 2000 there were 155,237 km of roads, of which 15,113 km were main roads (including motorways), 9,021 km were secondary roads and 23,221 km were asphalted agricultural roads. Metalled roads link all the main population centres.

Saudi Public Transport Co (SAPTCO): POB 10667, Riyadh 11443; tel. (1) 454-5000; fax (1) 454-2100, f. 1979, operates a public bus service throughout the country and to neighbouring countries; the Govt holds a 30% share; Chair. Dr NASIR AS-SALOOM; CEO Dr ABD AL-AZIZ AL-OHALY.

National Transport Co of Saudi Arabia: Queen's Bldg, POB 7280, Jeddah 21462; tel. (2) 643-4561; specializes in inward clearance, freight forwarding, general and heavy road haulage, re-export, charter air freight and exhibitions; Man. Dir A. D. BLACKSTOCK; Operations Man. I. CROXSON.

SHIPPING

Responsibility for the management, operation and maintenance of the commercial ports of Jeddah, Dammam, Yanbu, Dhiba and Jizan, the King Fahd Industrial Ports of Jubail and Yanbu, and the oil port of Ras Tanura, as well as a number of minor ports, began to be transferred to the private sector after 1997, but all ports remain subject to regulation and scrutiny by the Ports Authority. Some 95% of Saudi Arabia's imports and exports pass through the country's sea ports. An estimated 12,000 vessels visit annually. In 2002 there were 183 mechanized and organized berths. In 2001 the total cargo handled by Saudi Arabian ports, excluding crude petroleum, was 100.6m. metric tons, compared with 68.2m. tons in 1990/91. Some 1.8m. passengers were also embarked and disembarked in 2001.

Jeddah is the principal commercial port and the main point of entry for pilgrims bound for Mecca. It has berths for general cargo, container traffic, 'roll on, roll off' (ro-ro) traffic, livestock and bulk grain shipments, with draughts ranging from 8 m to 16 m. The port also has a 200-ton floating crane, cold storage facilities and a fully-equipped ship-repair yard. In 1997 a total of 4,515 vessels called at Jeddah Islamic Port. Some19.7m. tons of cargo, excluding crude petroleum, were handled and 1.1m. passengers were processed in 2001.

Dammam is the second largest commercial port and has general cargo, container, ro-ro, dangerous cargo and bulk grain berths. Draughts at this port range from 8 m to 13.5 m. It has a 200-ton floating crane and a fully-equipped ship-repair yard. In 1997 a total of 2,430 vessels called at King Abd al-Aziz Port in Dammam. 12.1m. tons of cargo, excluding crude petroleum, were handled in 2001.

Jubail has one commercial and one industrial port. The commercial port has general cargo, bulk grain and container berths with ro-ro facilities, and a floating crane. Draughts at this port range from 12 m to 14 m. In 1997 a total of 183 vessels called at Jubail Commercial Port, and 1.9m. tons of goods, excluding crude petroleum, were handled in 2001. The industrial port has bulk cargo, refined and petrochemical and ro-ro berths, and an open sea tanker terminal suitable for vessels up to 300,000 dwt. Draughts range from 6 m to 30 m. In 1997 a total of 1,032 vessels called at King Fahd Industrial Port in Jubail; 35.6m. tons of cargo, excluding crude petroleum, were handled in 2001.

Yanbu, which comprises one commercial and one industrial port, is Saudi Arabia's nearest major port to Europe and North America, and is the focal point of the most rapidly growing area, in the west of Saudi Arabia. The commercial port has general cargo, ro-ro and bulk grain berths, with draughts ranging from 10 m to 12 m. It also has a floating crane, and is equipped to handle minor ship repairs. In 1997 a total of 77 vessels called at Yanbu Commercial Port, and less than 1.7m. tons of cargo, excluding crude petroleum, were handled in 2001. The industrial port has berths for general cargo, containers, ro-ro traffic, bulk cargo, crude petroleum, refined and petrochemical products and natural gas liquids, and a tanker terminal on the open sea. In 1997 a total of 1,388 vessels called at King Fahd Industrial Port in Yanbu; the port handled 27.8m. tons of cargo, excluding crude petroleum, in 2001.

Jizan is the main port for the southern part of the country. It has general cargo, ro-ro, bulk grain and container berths, with draughts ranging from 8 m to 11 m. It also has a 200-ton floating crane. In 1997 a total of 752 vessels called at Gizan Port, and 1.5m. tons of cargo, excluding crude petroleum, were handled in 2001.

Dhiba port, on the northern Red Sea coast, serves the Tabouk region. It has three general cargo berths with a ro-ro ramp, and passenger-handling facilities. Maximum draught is 10.5m. In 1997 a total of 490 vessels called at Dhiba, and 0.3m. tons of cargo, excluding crude petroleum, were handled in 2001.

In addition to these major ports, there are a number of minor ports suitable only for small craft, including Khuraiba, Haql, al-Wajh, Umlujj, Rabigh, al-Lith, Qunfoudah, Farasan and al-Qahma on the Red Sea coast and al-Khobar, Qatif, Uqair, Darin and Ras al-Khafji on the Gulf coast. Ras Mishab, on the Gulf coast, is operated by the Ministry of Defence and Civil Aviation.

Saudi Ports Authority: POB 5162, Riyadh 11422; tel. (1) 405-0005; fax (1) 405-3508; internet www.ports.gov.sa; f. 1976; regulatory authority; Chair. Dr FAYEZ I. BADR; Vice-Chair. and Dir-Gen. MUHAMMAD IBN ABD AL-KARIM BAKR.

Dammam: POB 28062, Dammam 31188; tel.(3) 833-2500; fax (3) 857-1727; Dir-Gen. NAEEM IBRAHIM AN-NAEEM.

Dhiba: POB 190, Dhiba; tel. (4) 432-1060; fax (4) 432-2679; Dir-Gen MUHAMMAD ASH-SHAREEF.

Jeddah: POB 9285, Jeddah 21188; tel. (2) 647-1200; fax (2) 647-7411; Dir-Gen. MUHAMMAD AL-GHAITHI.

Jizan: POB 16, Jizan; tel. (7) 317-1000; fax (7) 317-0777; Dir-Gen. ALI HAMOUD BAKRI.

Jubail: POB 547, Jubail 31951; tel. (3) 357-8000; fax (3) 357-8011; Dir-Gen. MUTHANNA ISA AL-QURTAS.

Yanbu: POB 30325, Yanbu; tel. (4) 396-7000; fax (4) 396-7037; Dir-Gen. Dr HUMOOD SAADI.

Arabian Petroleum Supply Co Ltd: POB 1408, Al-Qurayat St, Jeddah 21431; tel. (2) 637-1120; fax (2) 636-2366; Chair. Sheikh MUHAMMAD YOUSSUF ALI REZA; Gen. Man. E. D. CONNOLLY.

Baaboud Trading and Shipping Agencies: POB 7262, Jeddah 21462; tel. (2) 642-1468; fax (2) 644-0912; Chair. AHMAD M. BAABOUD; Man. Dir ABOUD M. BAABOUD.

Bakry Navigation Co Ltd: POB 3757, Jeddah 21481; tel. (2) 651-9995; fax (2) 651-2908; Chair. Sheikh A. K. AL-BAKRY; Man. Dir G. A. K. AL-BAKRY.

National Shipping Co of Saudi Arabia (NSCSA): POB 8931, Riyadh 11492; tel. (1) 478-5454; fax (1) 477-8036; e-mail prmail@nscsa.com.sa; internet www.nscsa.com; f. 1979; transportation of crude petroleum and petrochemical products; routes through Red Sea and Mediterranean to USA and Canada; Chair. SULEIMAN J. AL-HERBISH; CEO ZIYAD FAHAD AD-DUGAITHER.

Saudi Lines: POB 66, Jeddah 21411; tel. (2) 642-3051; regular cargo and passenger services between Red Sea and Indian Ocean ports; Pres. M. A. BAKHASHAB PASHA; Man. Dir A. M. BAKHASHAB.

Saudi Shipping and Maritime Services Co Ltd (TRANSHIP): POB 7522, Jeddah 21472; tel. (2) 642-4255; fax (2) 643-2821; e-mail tranship@dmp.net.sa;

Chair. Prince Sa'ud ibn Nayef ibn Abd al-Aziz; Man. Dir Capt. Mustafa T. Awara.

Shipping Corpn of Saudi Arabia Ltd: POB 1691, Arab Maritime Center, Malik Khalid St, Jeddah 21441; tel. (2) 647-1137; fax (2) 647-8222; Pres. and Man. Dir Abd al-Aziz Ahmad Arab.

CIVIL AVIATION

King Abd al-Aziz International Airport, which was opened in 1981, has three terminals, one of which is specifically designed to cope with the needs of the many thousands of pilgrims who visit Mecca and Medina each year. The airport handled 12.1m. passengers in 2001. King Khalid International Airport, at Riyadh, opened in 1983 with four terminals. It handled 8.7m. passengers in 2001. A third major airport, King Fahd International Airport (with an initial handling capacity of 5.2m. passengers per year), opened in the Eastern Province in 1994. Some 2.7m. passengers used the airport in 2001. Overall, the country's airports were used by 29.8m. passengers in 2001. There are 25 commercial airports in the kingdom.

Presidency of Civil Aviation (PCA): POB 887, Jeddah 21165; tel. (2) 640-5000; fax (2) 640-2444; internet www.pca.gov.sa; Pres. Dr Ali Abd ar-Rahman al-Khalaf.

National Air Services Co: Riyadh; f. 1998; privately-owned; cap. SR60m.; Chair. Yousuf al-Maimani.

Saudi Arabian Airlines: POB 620, Jeddah 21231; tel. (2) 686-0000; fax (2) 686-4552; internet www.saudiairlines.com; f. 1945, began operations in 1947; in 1999 carried 13.3m. passengers, its fleet numbering 126 aircraft; regular services to 25 domestic and 52 international destinations; scheduled for privatization; Chair. Prince Sultan ibn Abd al-Aziz; Dir-Gen. Khaled A. ibn al-Bakr; Exec. Vice-Pres. (operations) Adnan ad-Dabbagh.

Tourism

All devout Muslims try to make at least one visit to the holy cities of Medina, the burial place of Muhammad, and Mecca, his birthplace. In 2000 there were 518 hotels in the kingdom, with a total of more than 50,000 rooms. Tourist numbers increased to 4.8m. in 1999, and receipts from tourism amounted to 6,750m. riyals in 2000. A total of 1,363,992 foreign pilgrims visited Mecca in the Islamic year ending in March 2001.

In 2000 the Government decided to issue tourist visas for the first time. A Supreme Commission for Tourism, to develop the tourist industry in Saudi Arabia, was subsequently established.

Saudi Hotels and Resort Areas Co (SHARACO): POB 5500, Riyadh 11422; tel. (1) 481-6666; fax (1) 480-1666; f. 1975; Saudi Govt has 40% interest; cap. SR500m.; Chair. Musaad as-Senany; Dir-Gen. Abd al-Aziz al-Ambar.

Defence

Chief of the General Staff: Gen. Saleh ibn Ali al-Muhaya.

Director-General of Public Security Forces: Brig.-Gen. Abdullah ibn ash-Sheikh.

Commander of Land Forces: Lt-Gen. Hussein al-Qabeel.

Commander of Air Force: Maj. Abd al-Aziz ibn Muhammad Hunaiydi.

Commander of the Navy: Vice-Adm. Fahd ibn Abdullah ibn Muhammad ibn Abd ar-Rahman as-Sa'ud.

Defence Budget (estimate, 2001): 78,850m. riyals.

Military Service: male conscription (18–35 years of age).

Total Armed Forces (August 2001): 126,500 (army 75,000; navy 15,500; air force 20,000); air defence forces 16,000; national guard 75,000 active personnel.

Paramilitary Forces (August 2001): 10,500 frontier force and 4,500 coastguard.

Education

The educational system in Saudi Arabia resembles that of other Arab countries. Educational institutions are administered mainly by the Government. The private sector plays a significant role at the first and second levels, but its total contribution is relatively small compared with that of the public sector.

Pre-elementary education is provided on a small scale (with 85,484 children enrolled in 1996/97), mainly in urban areas. Elementary or primary education is of six years' duration and the normal entrance age is six. The total number of pupils at this stage in 1999/2000 was 2,285,328, with 190,527 teachers. Intermediate education begins at 12 and lasts for three years. The total number of pupils at this stage in 1999/2000 was 1,013,175, with teachers numbering 86,686. Secondary education begins at 15 and extends for three years. After the first year, successful pupils branch into science or arts groups. The total number of pupils at this stage in 1999/2000 was 755,419, with 55,277 teachers. Enrolment of children in the primary age-group increased from 32% in 1970 to 61% (boys 63%; girls 60%) in 1996. Over the same period enrolment at intermediate and secondary schools rose from 9% to 61% (boys 65%; girls 57%). The proportion of females enrolled in Saudi Arabian schools increased from 25% of the total number of pupils in 1970 to 47.5% in 2000.

Industrial and commercial schools can be entered after the completion of the intermediate stage. In 1990/91 there were eight industrial schools, 22 commercial schools and one agricultural school. In addition, there were seven higher technical and four higher commercial colleges offering two-year courses. Vocational craft-training institutes are maintained in numerous centres, providing courses in electrical, mechanical and allied trades. In 1999/2000 a total of 50,004 students attended 77 technical and vocational institutes.

In the 1999/2000 academic year 399,338 students were enrolled in higher education. Tertiary institutions in that year included 75 university colleges and 72 colleges exclusively for women. Construction of the first private university, in partnership with a US technology institute, was scheduled to begin in late 2002. Government expenditure on education in 2001 was provisionally estimated at SR 53,010m., equivalent to 25% of total expenditure.

Bibliography

Abir, Mordechai. *Saudi Arabia: Society, Government and the Gulf Crisis*. London, Routledge, 1993.

Anderson, Irvine H. *Aramco, the United States, and Saudi Arabia: a study in the dynamics of Foreign Oil Policy, 1935–50*. Princeton University Press, 1982.

Anderson, Prof. Sir Norman. *The Kingdom of Saudi Arabia*. London, Stacey International, 1977.

Atlas of Saudi Arabia. London, Edward Stanford, 1978.

Benoit-Méchin, S. *Ibn Séoud ou la naissance d'un royaume*. Paris, Albin Michel, 1955.

Brown, E. Hoagland. *The Saudi-Arabia-Kuwait Neutral Zone*. Beirut, 1964.

De Gaury, Gerald. *Faisal*. London, Arthur Barker, 1969.

Dequin, Horst. *Saudi Arabia's Agriculture and its Development Possibilities*. Frankfurt, 1963.

Fandy, Mamoun. *Saudi Arabia and the Politics of Dissent*. Basingstoke, Palgrave, 1999.

Farsy, Fouad Al-. *Saudi Arabia. A Case Study in Development*. London, Kegan Paul International Ltd, 1981.

Modernity and Tradition: Saudi Equation. London, Kegan Paul International, 1990.

Field, Michael. *The Merchants: The Big Business Families of Arabia*. London, John Murray, 1984.

Furtig, Henner. *Iran's Rivalry with Saudi Arabia Between the Gulf Wars*. Reading, Ithaca Press, 2000.

Helms, Christine Moss. *The Cohesion of Saudi Arabia*. London, Croom Helm, 1981.

Hobday, Peter. *Saudi Arabia Today: An Introduction to the Richest Oil Power*. London, Macmillan, 1978.

Holden, David, Johns, Richard, and Buchan, James. *The House of Saud*. London, Sidgwick & Jackson, 1981.

Howarth, David. *The Desert King: Ibn Sa'ud*. New York, NY, McGraw Hill, 1964.

Jerichow, Anders. *The Saudi File: People, Power and Politics*. Richmond, Curzon Press Ltd, 1998.

Lees, Brian. *Handbook of the Sa'ud family of Saudi Arabia*. London, Royal Genealogies, 1980.

Long, David E. *The Kingdom of Saudi Arabia*. Gainesville, FL, University Press of Florida, 1998.

Mackey, Sandra. *The Saudis*. London, Harrap, 1987.

McLoughlin, Leslie. *Ibn Saud, Founder of a Kingdom*. London, Macmillan, 1993.

Montague, Carolyn. *Industrial Development in Saudi Arabia*. London, Committee for Middle East Trade, 1987.

Niblock, Tim. *State, Society and Economy in Saudi Arabia*. London, Croom Helm, 1981.

Philby, H. St. J. B. *Arabia and the Wahhabis*. London, 1928.

    Arabia. London, Benn, 1930.

    Arabian Jubilee. London, 1951.

    The Empty Quarter. London, 1933.

    The Land of Midian. London, 1957.

    A Pilgrim in Arabia. London, 1946.

    Saudi Arabia. London, 1955.

Quandt, Willam B. *Saudi Arabia in the 1980s: Foreign Policy, Security and Oil*. Oxford, Basil Blackwell, 1982.

Robinson, Jeffrey. *Yamani: The Inside Story*. London, Simon and Schuster, 1988.

Sarhan, Samir (Ed.). *Who's Who in Saudi Arabia*. Jeddah, Tihama, and London, Europa, 3rd edn, 1984.

Troeller, Gary. *The Birth of Saudi Arabia: Britain and the Rise of the House of Sa'ud*. London, Frank Cass, 1976.

Van der Meulen, D. *The Wells of Ibn Sa'ud*. John Murray, 1957.

Vassiliev, Alexei. *The History of Saudi Arabia*. London, Saqi Books, 1998.

Wilkinson, John. *Arabia's Frontiers*. London, I. B. Tauris, 1991.

Williams, K. *Ibn Sa'ud: the Puritan King of Arabia*. London, Cape, 1933.

Winder, R. Bayly. *Saudi Arabia in the Nineteenth Century*. London, Macmillan, 1965.

Yamani, Hani A. Z. *To be a Saudi*. London, Janus, 1998.

Yamani, Mai. *Changed Identities: The Challenge of the New Generation in Saudi Arabia*. London, Royal Institute of International Affairs, 1999.

SPANISH NORTH AFRICA

Geography

Spanish North Africa comprises Ceuta and Melilla, two enclaves within Moroccan territory, and several rocky islets off the Moroccan coast. The average temperature is 17°C.

CEUTA

The ancient port and walled city of Ceuta is situated on a rocky promontory on the North African coast overlooking the Strait of Gibraltar, the Strait here being about 25 km wide. Ceuta was retained by Spain as a plaza de soberanía (a presidio, or fortified enclave, over which Spain has full sovereign rights) when Morocco became independent from France in 1956, and is administered as part of Cádiz Province. Ceuta now functions as a bunkering and fishing port. Ceuta occupies an area of 19.7 sq km. In November 2001 its population was 71,505.

MELILLA

Melilla is situated north of the Moroccan town of Nador, on the eastern side of a small peninsula jutting out into the Mediterranean Sea. It was retained by Spain as a plaza de soberanía when Morocco became independent in 1956, and is administered as part of Málaga Province. Melilla is an active port. The territory's area totals 12.5 sq km. In November 2001 its population was estimated to be 66,411 (including the islets separately mentioned below).

THE PEÑÓN DE VÉLEZ DE LA GOMERA, PEÑÓN DE ALHUCEMAS AND CHAFARINAS ISLANDS

These rocky islets are administered with Melilla. The Peñón de Vélez de la Gomera is situated 117 km south-east of Ceuta, lying less than 85 m from the Moroccan coast, to which it is connected by a narrow strip of sand. This rocky promontory, of 1 ha in area, rises to an altitude of 77 m above sea-level, an ancient fortress being situated at its summit. The Peñón de Alhucemas lies 155 km south-east of Ceuta and 100 km west of Melilla, being 300 m from the Moroccan coast and the town of al-Hocima. It occupies an area of 1.5 ha. The uninhabited rocks of Mar and Tierra lie immediately to the east of the Peñón de Alhucemas. The three Chafarinas Islands (from west to east: Isla del Congreso, Isla de Isabel II and Isla del Rey) are situated 48 km east of Melilla and about 3.5 km from the Moroccan fishing port of Ras el-Ma (Cabo de Agua). The islands are of volcanic origin, their combined area being 61 ha. Spain maintains small military bases on some of the islets.

History

CEUTA

Ceuta was conquered by Juan I of Portugal in 1415. Following the union of the crowns of Spain and Portugal in 1580, Ceuta passed under Spanish rule and in 1694, when Portugal was formally separated from Spain, the territory requested to remain under Spanish control. During the 16th, 17th and 18th centuries Ceuta endured a number of sieges by the Muslims. Ahmad Gailan, a chieftain in northern Morocco, blockaded the town in 1648–55. The Sultan of Morocco, Mulai Ismail (1672–1727), attacked Ceuta in 1674, 1680 and 1694, after which he maintained a blockade against the town until 1720. Ahmad Ali ar-Rifi, a chieftain from northern Morocco, made yet another unsuccessful assault in 1732. A pact of friendship and commerce was negotiated between Spain and Morocco at Aranjuez in 1780, a peaceful agreement following in the next year over the boundaries of the Ceuta enclave. In 1844–45 there was a sharp dispute once more about the precise limits of Ceuta. Further disagreement led to the war of 1859–60. Spanish forces, after an engagement at Los Castillejos, seized Tetuán from Morocco. Following another battle at Wadi Ras in March 1860 the conflict came to an end. A settlement was then made, which enlarged the enclave of Ceuta and obliged Morocco to forfeit to Spain 100m. pesetas as war indemnities. In 1974 the town became the seat of the Capitanía General de Africa.

MELILLA

Spain secured control of Melilla in 1556, the town having been conquered in 1497 by the ducal house of Medina Sidonia, which had been empowered to appoint the governor and seneschal with the approval of the Spanish Crown. The Rif tribesmen attacked Melilla in 1562–64. Later still, the Sultan of Morocco, Mulai Ismail (1672–1727) assaulted the town in 1687, 1696 and 1697. Sultan Muhammad b. Abdallah (1757–90) besieged Melilla in 1771 and 1774. An agreement concluded between Spain and Morocco in 1780 at Aranjuez led, however, in the following year, to a peaceful delimitation of the Melilla enclave. There was a brief period of tension in 1844 and, subsequently, in 1861, under the terms of an agreement signed after Spain's Moroccan campaign of 1860, Melilla's boundaries were extended. Conflict with the Rif tribesmen gave rise in 1893–94 to the so-called 'War of Melilla', which ended with a settlement negotiated at Marrakesh. It was not until 1909 that Spanish forces, after a hard campaign, occupied the mountainous hinterland of Melilla between the Wadi Kert and the Wadi Muluya— a region in which, some 15 km behind Melilla, were situated the rich iron mines of Beni Bu Ifrur. In July 1921 the Rif tribes, under the command of Abd al-Krim, defeated a Spanish force near Annual and threatened Melilla itself. Only in 1926, with the final defeat of the Rif rebellion, was Spanish control restored over the Melilla region. Melilla was the first Spanish town to rise against the government of the Popular Front on 17 July 1936, at the beginning of the Spanish Civil War.

OTHER POSSESSIONS

The Chafarinas Islands came under Spanish control in 1847. The Peñón de Alhucemas was occupied in 1673. The Peñón de Vélez de la Gomera, about 80 km further west, came under Spanish rule in 1508, was then lost not long afterwards and reoccupied in 1564. All three possessions are, like Melilla, incorporated into the province of Málaga. Spanish sovereignty over the uninhabited island of Perejil, which lies north-west of Ceuta, is uncertain.

RECENT EVENTS

Since 1939 both Ceuta and Melilla have been ruled as integral parts of Spain, though this arrangement is disputed in the territories. All those born in Ceuta, Melilla and the island dependencies are Spanish citizens and subjects. Both Ceuta and Melilla have municipal councils (ayuntamientos), and are administered as an integral part of Spain by an official (Delegado del Gobierno) directly responsible to the Ministry of the Interior in Madrid. This official is usually assisted by a government sub-delegate. There is also one delegate from each of the ministries in Madrid.

In October 1978 King Hassan of Morocco attempted to link the question of the sovereignty of Melilla to that of the return of the British territory of Gibraltar to Spain, and in November King Hassan stated his country's claim to Ceuta and Melilla. In October 1981 Spain declared before the UN that Ceuta and Melilla were integral parts of Spanish territory. In April 1982, however, the Istiqlal, a Moroccan political party, demanded action to recover the territories from Spain, and in March 1983 the Moroccan Government blocked the passage of goods across the frontiers of Ceuta and Melilla. In August the movement of Moroccan workers to Ceuta, Melilla and also Gibraltar was restricted.

From 1984 there was increasing unease over Spanish North Africa's future. Following the opening of the Spanish frontier with Gibraltar, in early 1985 Morocco reiterated its claim to Ceuta and Melilla. King Hassan indicated, however, that he desired a political solution to the problem. Spain continued to reject any comparison between the two enclaves and Gibraltar; however, in July 1985 the leaders of the nationalist parties of both Ceuta and Melilla visited Gibraltar for talks with the Chief Minister, in an effort to secure support for their cause.

Details of the enclaves' new draft statutes, envisaging the establishment of two local assemblies, with jurisdiction over such matters as public works, agriculture, tourism, culture and internal trade, were announced in August and approved by the central Government in December 1985. Unlike Spain's other regional assemblies, however, those of Ceuta and Melilla were not to be vested with legislative powers, and this denial of full autonomy was much criticized in the two enclaves. In March 1986 up to 20,000 people took to the streets of Ceuta in a demonstration to demand autonomy.

Meanwhile, the introduction by the central Government of a new aliens law in July 1985 required all foreigners resident in Spain to register with the authorities or risk expulsion. In Ceuta most Muslims possessed the necessary documentation. However, in Melilla (where the Muslim community was estimated to number 27,000, of whom only 7,000 held Spanish nationality) thousands of Muslims staged a protest against the new legislation in November 1985, as a result of which the central Government gave an assurance that it would assist the full integration into Spanish society of Muslims in Ceuta and Melilla, and promised to improve conditions in the territories. In December an inter-ministerial commission, headed by the Minister of the Interior, was created to formulate plans for investment in the enclaves' social services and other public facilities.

Tension in Melilla was renewed in December 1985, when 40,000 members of the Spanish community attended a demonstration in support of the new aliens law. In January 1986 the brutality with which the police dispersed a peaceful rally by Muslim women provoked widespread outrage. In addition to the hunger strike already being undertaken by a number of Muslims, a two-day general strike was called. In February 1986, however, the Ministry of the Interior in Madrid and the leaders of the Muslim communities of Ceuta and Melilla reached agreement on the application of the aliens law. A joint commission to study the Muslims' problems was to be established, and a census to determine those eligible for Spanish citizenship was to be carried out. The agreement was denounced as unconstitutional by the Spanish populations of the enclaves. The Minister of the Interior visited the territories in April and reiterated that the implementation of the aliens law (the deadline for registration having been extended to 31 March 1986, following three postponements) would not entail mass expulsions of Muslim immigrants.

After negotiations with representatives of the Muslim community, in May 1986 the Government agreed to grant Spanish nationality to more than 2,400 Muslims resident in the enclaves. By mid-1986, however, the number of Muslims applying for Spanish nationality in Melilla alone had reached several thousand. As a result of the delays in the processing of the applications by the authorities, Aomar Muhammadi Dudú, the leader of the newly-founded Muslim party, Partido de los Demócratas de Melilla (PDM), accused the Government of failing to fulfil its pledge to the Muslim residents.

At the general elections of June 1986 the ruling Partido Socialista Obrero Español (PSOE) was successful in Ceuta, but was defeated by the centre-right Coalición Popular (CP) in Melilla, the latter result indicating the strong opposition of local Spaniards to the Government's plan to integrate the Muslim population. Tight security surrounded the elections in Melilla, where 'parallel elections', resulting in a vote of confidence in the PDM leader, were held by the Muslim community. The

elections were accompanied by several days of unrest, involving right-wing Christians and local Muslims, and there were further violent clashes between the police and Christian demonstrators demanding the resignation of the Government Delegate in Melilla, Andrés Moreno.

In August 1986 work began on the census of Muslim residents in Ceuta and Melilla. In the same month Juan Díez de la Cortina, Secretary-General of the extreme right-wing Partido Nacionalista (Español) de Melilla, was arrested on suspicion of planning a terrorist attack against the Government Delegate in Melilla. Following talks in Madrid between representatives of the main political parties in Melilla and the Ministry of the Interior, concessions to the enclave included the replacement of Andrés Moreno as Government Delegate by Manuel Céspedes. The Madrid negotiations were denounced by Aomar Muhammadi Dudú, the Muslim leader of Melilla, who nevertheless in September agreed to accept a senior post in the Ministry of the Interior in Madrid, with responsibility for relations with the Muslim communities of Spain.

In October 1986 it was reported that Dudú had travelled to Rabat for secret discussions with the Moroccan Minister of the Interior. In November Muslim leaders in Melilla announced that they wished to establish their own administration in the enclave, in view of the Madrid Government's failure to fulfil its promise of Spanish citizenship for Muslim residents. The Spanish Minister of the Interior, however, reiterated an assurance of the Government's intention to carry out the process of integration of the Muslim community. Later in the month, Muslim traders staged a four-day closure of their businesses to draw attention to their plight, and thousands of Muslims took part in a peaceful demonstration, reaffirming support for Dudú, who had resigned from his Madrid post after only two months in office. (Dudú subsequently went into exile in Morocco and lost the support of Melilla's Muslim community.) A similar protest, to have taken place in Ceuta in December, was banned by the Spanish authorities.

In January 1987 the Spanish Minister of the Interior paid an official visit to Morocco. King Hassan proposed the establishment of a joint commission to seek a solution to the problem of the Spanish enclaves, but the proposal was rejected by Spain. There was a serious escalation of tension in Melilla in early February, when a member of the Muslim community died from gunshot wounds, following renewed racial clashes. Police reinforcements were flown in from Spain to deal with the crisis, numerous demonstrators were detained. Several prominent Muslims were charged with sedition and transferred to a prison in Almería on the Spanish mainland, but were released shortly afterwards. In March King Hassan of Morocco reaffirmed his support for the Muslims of the Spanish enclaves, and later warned that a serious crisis in relations between Rabat and Madrid would arise if Spain were to grant autonomy to the territories.

In April 1987 Spanish and Moroccan troops participated in joint manoeuvres on Moroccan territory adjacent to Melilla, as part of a programme of military co-operation. In early May thousands of Melilla residents attended a demonstration in favour of autonomy for the enclave. In July, following a visit to Rabat by the Spanish Minister of Foreign Affairs, King Hassan declared that agreement had been reached on the holding of talks on the question of Ceuta and Melilla. The Spanish Government, however, denied the existence of such an agreement, maintaining that the issue was not negotiable.

In August 1987 there was renewed unrest in Ceuta, following the death of a Muslim at the hands of the security forces. In February 1988 it was announced that, in accordance with European Community (EC, now European Union—EU) regulations, Moroccan citizens would in due course require visas to enter Spain. Entry to Spanish North Africa, however, was to be exempt from the new ruling. In March, however, a group of Muslims occupied the office in Melilla responsible for the processing of applications for Spanish nationality in protest at its alleged inefficiency. Of the 8,000 applications presented, it was claimed, fewer than one-half had been granted.

In March 1988 it was announced that the central Government and the main opposition parties in Madrid had reached a broad consensus on the draft autonomy statutes for the Spanish External Territories; however, in July a senior member of the ruling PSOE acknowledged that the party's Programme 2000 contained contradictory proposals regarding Ceuta and Melilla. Although it was envisaged that Spain would retain the territories, the possibility of a negotiated settlement with Morocco was not discounted. In late July, seven years after the enclaves' first official request for autonomy, the central Government announced that the implementation of the territories' autonomy statutes was to be accelerated. Revised draft statutes were submitted by the PSOE to the main opposition parties for consideration. The statutes declared Ceuta and Melilla to be integral parts of Spain and, for the first time, the Spanish Government undertook to guarantee financial support for the territories. A further innovation contained in the revised draft provided for the establishment of mixed commissions to oversee the movement of goods and services through the territories. As previously indicated by the Spanish Government, the two Spanish North African assemblies were to be granted 'normative' rather than legislative powers. Each new assembly would elect from among its members a city president. It was later also revealed that the revised statutes encompassed only the enclaves of Ceuta and Melilla, thus excluding the associated Spanish North African islands, and that they had been erroneously incorporated in the preliminary statutes, approved in December 1985. Although remaining the responsibility of the Spanish Ministry of Defence, these islands were not, therefore, to become part of any Spanish autonomous region.

In October 1988 the Moroccan Minister of Foreign Affairs formally presented his country's claim to Ceuta and Melilla to the UN General Assembly. An official visit by King Hassan to Spain, scheduled for November, was indefinitely postponed without explanation, and in Melilla a Muslim group acknowledged that it had been in receipt of financial assistance from the Moroccan Government. None the less, during a visit to Ceuta in December a Spanish government official stated that the enclaves would be granted autonomy during the present Government's term of office. In January 1989, however, King Hassan reiterated Morocco's claim to Ceuta and Melilla. A planned visit to Rabat by the Spanish Minister of Foreign Affairs was postponed, but in March Narcís Serra, the Spanish Minister of Defence, travelled to Morocco for consultations with King Hassan on security matters. In April the Spanish Government and the Partido Popular (PP), the main opposition party, reached agreement on the revised statutes for Ceuta and Melilla. In May the Spanish Prime Minister and King Hassan met in Casablanca for discussions on the situation in the Middle East. King Hassan paid an official visit to Spain in September 1989. The question of Spanish North Africa was not discussed, although King Hassan reiterated his country's claim to the territories, while discounting the use of force as a means of settling the dispute. Spain and Morocco agreed to hold annual summit meetings, in order to improve relations.

At the general election held in October 1989 the ruling PSOE retained its Ceuta seats, despite allegations by the opposition PP that many names on the electoral register were duplicated. In Melilla, however, the election results were declared invalid, following the discovery of serious irregularities. At the repeated ballot held in March 1990, at which some 52% of the electorate voted, both Senate seats and the one Congress seat were won by the PP, the latter result stripping the PSOE of its overall majority in the Madrid lower chamber. The Government Delegate in Melilla claimed that voting irregularities had again occurred.

Relations between Spain and Morocco were again strained in March 1990, when Spanish fishermen blockaded Algeciras and other ports (thereby disrupting communications with Ceuta) in protest at the Moroccan authorities' imposition of greatly-increased penalties on Spanish fishing vessels found to be operating without a licence in Moroccan waters. Following negotiations between the EC and Morocco, Spain agreed to grant financial compensation to Morocco. In the same month a Moroccan government minister repeated his country's claim to Spanish North Africa, maintaining that, with the accession of Namibia to independence, Ceuta and Melilla were the last vestiges of colonialism in Africa. In April the Spanish Government decided to open negotiations with the political groupings of Ceuta and Melilla, the autonomy statutes having been presented for discussion in the territories. It was confirmed that the enclaves were to remain an integral part of Spain, and that they were to be granted self-government at municipal, rather than regional, level. The Spanish Government's decision provoked a strong reaction from Moroccan political parties, which were united in their denunciation of the perceived attempt to legalize Spanish possession of the territories. In June a two-hour strike in Ceuta, in support of demands for full autonomy for the enclave, was widely observed.

In July 1990 a Moroccan opposition party, Istiqlal, announced that it was initiating a new campaign to press for the 'liberation' of Ceuta and Melilla. In the following month Istiqlal organized a protest march through the streets of Martil, a Moroccan town 40 km from Ceuta. The Muslim community of Ceuta, however, expressed its concern at these developments.

In mid-August 1990 Spain granted its Government Delegate in Melilla direct powers to expel illegal residents from the territory. In December a Spanish delegation, led by Prime Minister Felipe González, travelled to Morocco, where the first of the planned regular summit meetings between the Spanish and Moroccan premiers took place. Among the topics discussed was the forthcoming implementation (in May 1991) of new visa requirements for North Africans entering Spain, which had caused dismay in the Muslim community. Special arrangements were to apply to Moroccan citizens who worked in, or travelled regularly to, Ceuta and Melilla.

Elections for the 25-member municipal councils of Ceuta and Melilla were held in May 1991, and in each territory the PSOE Mayor was replaced. In Ceuta Francisco Fraiz Armada of the Progreso y Futuro de Ceuta (PFC) became Mayor. In Melilla, where the PP had secured 12 of the 25 seats, Ignacio Velázquez Rivera of the right-wing Partido Nacionalista de Melilla (PNM) was elected Mayor of the enclave.

In July 1991, in Rabat, the Spanish and Moroccan heads of government signed a treaty of friendship. In addition to the promotion of co-operation in the fields of economy, finance, fisheries, culture and the judiciary, agreement was also reached on Spanish military aid to Morocco. Shortly afterwards the Moroccan Minister of the Interior, Driss Basri, and a cabinet colleague unexpectedly accepted an invitation from the Spanish Minister of the Interior to visit Ceuta, their brief trip being the first ever visit by members of the Government of King Hassan.

The draft autonomy statutes of Ceuta and Melilla were submitted to the Congress of Deputies in Madrid for discussion in October 1991. During the debate the PP accused the PSOE of supporting Moroccan interests. In November thousands of demonstrators, many of whom had travelled from the enclaves, attended a protest march in Madrid (organized by the Governments of Ceuta and Melilla), in support of demands for autonomy for the territories. In early 1992, however, the central Government confirmed that the assemblies of Ceuta and Melilla were not to be granted full legislative powers. In May a general strike in Ceuta, to protest against this denial of full autonomy, was widely supported.

In mid-1992 relations between Spain and Morocco were dominated by the issue of illegal immigration. In addition to the problem of the large numbers of Moroccans trying to enter mainland Spain, there had been a sharp increase in the numbers of those from other (mainly West African) countries attempting to gain entry to Europe via Morocco and the two Spanish enclaves. In July the Spanish Minister of Foreign Affairs flew to Rabat for discussions on the problem.

In March 1993 it was revealed that Spain would require the permission of NATO before employing its most modern military equipment in the defence of the enclaves, which were excluded from NATO's security 'umbrella'. In the same month, in an attempt to bring about the transfer of powers to the territories, the PP submitted its own draft statute for Melilla to the central Government, which immediately condemned the document as unconstitutional. All political parties in Melilla, except the PSOE, demanded that a local referendum be held on the issue of autonomy. At the subsequent general election held in June, the PSOE of Ceuta lost its one seat in Congress and its two seats in the Senate to the PP. In Melilla, however, the PSOE candidate defeated the incumbent PP Congress member; the PP also lost one of its two seats in the Senate.

In February 1994 the Mayor of Ceuta, Francisco Fraiz Armada, was obliged to resign, following the Supreme Court's ratification of a lower court ruling that barred him from holding public office for six years. His disqualification resulted from his involvement in irregularities in the housing sector in 1984, when unauthorized evictions had been carried out. He was replaced by Basilio Fernández López, also of the PFC.

In March 1994 King Hassan declared his opposition to the forthcoming adoption of the autonomy statutes, repeating Morocco's claim to the territories. Representatives of Ceuta were particularly critical of delays in the presentation of the final statutes to the Cortes in Madrid, and urged the central Government and the opposition PP to bring the matter to a speedy conclusion. In the same month King Juan Carlos of Spain received a delegation from Melilla, led by the Mayor, Ignacio Velázquez Rivera, who emphasized the necessity for a swift adoption of the enclave's autonomy statute and conveyed his citizens' concern at the Moroccan monarch's recent statement. In September the final statutes of autonomy were finally approved by the Spanish Government, in preparation for their presentation to the Cortes. The statutes provided for 25-member local assemblies with powers similar to those of the municipal councils of mainland Spain. Morocco, however, announced that it was initiating a new diplomatic campaign to reassert its claim over the territories.

The proposals for limited self-government were generally acceptable in Melilla but not in Ceuta, where, in October 1994, a general strike received widespread support. An estimated 20,000 residents of Ceuta participated in a demonstration to demand equality with other Spanish regions and full autonomy for the enclave. Earlier in the month, following expressions of concern regarding the territories' protection in the event of Moroccan aggression, the Minister of Defence confirmed that Spain would continue to maintain an appropriate military presence in Ceuta and Melilla. In December more than 2,000 citizens of Ceuta attended a demonstration in Madrid to demand full autonomy.

Following their approval by the Congress of Deputies in December 1994, the autonomy statutes were ratified by the Senate in February 1995. This approval of the statutes by the Spanish Cortes was denounced by the Moroccan Government, which, upon taking office in March, declared that the recovery of Ceuta and Melilla was to be one of its major objectives. In April responsibility for two explosions in Ceuta was claimed by the Organización 21 de Agosto para la Liberación de los Territorios Marroquíes Usurpados, a Muslim group that demanded the return of the territories to Morocco, and which the Spanish Government suspected was now receiving covert assistance from the Moroccan authorities.

In September 1994 Morocco had demanded that its fisheries agreement with the EU be renegotiated and that quotas be drastically reduced. In late April 1995 hundreds of Spanish fishing vessels, including some from Ceuta, were obliged once again to withdraw from Moroccan waters, following the EU's failure to renegotiate the agreement with Morocco. In May, as anti-Moroccan sentiment grew, there were violent scenes when Spanish fishermen and farmers attempted to obstruct the entry of Moroccan produce into the ports of southern Spain. The protests were renewed in late August. Negotiations between the EU and Morocco continued intermittently in mid-1995, and in October Morocco agreed to accept a four-year accord (rather than the three-year arrangement it had originally demanded) on the basis of decreases in fish catches. Morocco also agreed to reduce its claim for financial compensation. Vessels from EU nations, mainly Spain, were therefore able to return to Moroccan waters in late November. The accord entered into force in January 1996.

Elections for the new local assemblies were held in May 1995. In Ceuta the PP won nine of the 25 seats, the PFC six, the nationalist Ceuta Unida four and the PSOE three. Basilio Fernández López of the PFC was re-elected Mayor/President, heading a coalition with Ceuta Unida and the PSOE. Mustafa Mizziam Ammar, leader of the Partido Democrático y Social de Ceuta (PDSC), became the first Muslim candidate ever to be elected in the territory. Fewer than 57% of those eligible voted in Ceuta. In Melilla, where the level of participation was less than 62%, the PP won 14 of the 25 seats, the PSOE five seats, Coalición por Melilla (CpM), a new Muslim grouping, four seats and the right-wing Unión del Pueblo Melillense (UPM) two

seats. Ignacio Velázquez (PP/PNM) returned to the position of Mayor/President.

In Ceuta concern about the level of illegal immigration from sub-Saharan Africa increased during 1995. By mid-1995 these immigrants, many of whom were without documentation and claimed to have fled from war-ravaged countries such as Rwanda, were estimated to total more than 300. In October a violent confrontation occurred between about 150 Africans and the security forces, the latter being joined by citizens' vigilante groups, during which a policeman was shot and seriously injured. An investigation into the shooting discounted the possibility that an African demonstrator had been responsible. Nevertheless, more than 100 illegal immigrants were transferred to a detention centre on the Spanish mainland, while 15 Africans who were alleged to have led the riot were imprisoned in Ceuta. In an attempt to curtail illegal immigration, Ceuta's frontier with Morocco was strengthened.

A general election was held in March 1996. In Ceuta the three PP delegates to the Cortes in Madrid were re-elected. In Melilla the PSOE lost its seat in the lower house to the PP, which also took both seats in the Senate. Following the installation of the PP administration in Madrid, both Government Delegates in the territories were replaced. At the end of March thousands of Muslims took part in a demonstration, organized by the CpM, to protest against their marginal position in society.

In July 1996 the Mayor/President of Ceuta, Basilio Fernández López of the PFC, resigned after seven months at the head of a minority administration, and was replaced by Jesús Fortes Ramos of the PP, who urged that the enclave be considered a full autonomous region. In September the Secretary-General of NATO confirmed that Ceuta and Melilla would remain outside the alliance's sphere of protection if Spain were to be fully integrated into NATO's military structure.

In mid-1996 attention focused once again on the issue of illegal immigration from Africa. Both Ceuta and Melilla appealed to the EU for financial assistance to counter the problems arising from the enclaves' attractive location as an entry point to Europe and from the recent implementation of the EU's Schengen Convention permitting the free movement of persons among the accord's signatory countries. In June, following disturbances involving refugees from Central Africa during which several people were injured, a total of 103 immigrants were flown from Melilla to detention centres on the Spanish mainland and thence, only hours later in a clandestine, and subsequently highly controversial, operation, were expelled via the Canary Islands to various sub-Saharan countries. As the exodus of migrants from Africa continued, the Spanish authorities intercepted numerous small boats in the Strait of Gibraltar, while in September 1996 representatives of the International Committee of the Red Cross (ICRC) declared that its supplies were insufficient to feed the 406 (mainly Moroccan and Algerian) immigrants located at an encampment in Ceuta. In October the Spanish Minister of the Interior met his Moroccan counterpart in Madrid for discussions, which resulted in an agreement on the establishment of two joint commissions to address the specific problems of illegal immigration and drugs-trafficking.

In the following month the Spanish Minister of the Interior travelled to Rabat for further discussions on the issues of illegal immigration and drugs-trafficking. For the first time since the signing of a joint accord in 1992, Morocco agreed to the readmission of illegal immigrants held in the Spanish enclaves. In December 1996, the Spanish Ministry of the Interior announced that in 1996 a total of 1,552 illegal Moroccan immigrants had been detained in Ceuta, while 2,321 had been detained in Melilla. The central Government subsequently allocated emergency funding to meet the immediate needs of the immigrants. In early 1997 concern grew that much of the illegal immigration from Morocco was being controlled by networks involved in the smuggling of drugs and tobacco, and the first joint police operation with Morocco was undertaken against these networks.

In March 1997, in Melilla, a motion of censure against Ignacio Velázquez resulted in the Mayor/President's defeat, owing to the defection to the opposition of two PP councillors, Enrique Palacios and Abdelmalik Tahar. The latter subsequently absconded to the Canary Islands. The opposition then declared Enrique Palacios to be Mayor/President, although the central Government continued to recognize Ignacio Velázquez as the rightful incumbent. In May Enrique Palacios alleged that at the election of May 1995 that party had employed irregular tactics in its campaign for the support of Muslim voters. Also in May 1997, for the first time, the Mayor/Presidents of Ceuta and Melilla attended a conference of the autonomous regions' presidents, held in Madrid. Despite the attempted 'coup' in Melilla, the territory was represented by Ignacio Velázquez. In November 1997, from Tenerife, Abdelmalik Tahar accused Ignacio Velázquez and five associates of having subjected him to blackmail and threats, as a result of which he had relinquished his seat on the Council, thereby permitting the PP to replace him and to regain its majority. In December 1997 Tahar, who was now under police protection, declared to the investigating judge that he had been offered a substantial bribe. Following an appeal by Enrique Palacios and a judicial ruling that permitted the successful revival of the motion of censure against Ignacio Velázquez in February 1998, Palacios took office as Mayor/President of Melilla, accusing his predecessor, furthermore, of serious financial mismanagement. A new motion of censure, presented by the PP urging that (despite the bribery charges against him) Ignacio Velázquez be restored to office, was deemed to be illegal and therefore rejected in a decree issued by Enrique Palacios. In July Enrique Palacios accused the PP of having employed public funds to secure the votes of some 2,500 Muslims at the 1995 local elections, the bribes reportedly having taken the form of building materials for the purposes of residential repairs. The allegations were denied by the PP.

In June 1997 police reinforcements were drafted into Melilla, following renewed disturbances in which one immigrant died. More than 100 illegal immigrants were immediately returned to Morocco as part of a special security operation, and on the same day of action a total of 873 Moroccans were denied entry to Melilla. (More than 10,000 Moroccans daily continued to cross the border legally, in order to work in the enclave.) In July a young Moroccan was shot and wounded, and two civil guards were injured, during a confrontation on the Melilla border. In August various non-governmental organizations (NGOs) condemned the rudimentary conditions in which some 800 illegal immigrants were being held in Melilla. It was further announced that a Melilla reception centre housing about 100 Algerians was to close, owing to unsatisfactory conditions. In the same month hundreds of Moroccan children, who had been begging on the streets of Melilla, were returned to their homeland. The increasing involvement of organized criminal gangs in such activities continued to cause disquiet. Following an incident involving Moroccan immigrants, in which 15 cars were destroyed by fire, the Melilla Government accused the Moroccan authorities of facilitating the entry of the illegal immigrants. In August the Spanish General Prosecutor demanded emergency measures to address the immigrant crisis, having already urged the Ministry of the Interior in June to find an immediate solution.

In September 1997, as Melilla commemorated the 500th anniversary of its foundation by the Spanish, various Moroccan political parties renewed their denunciation of Spain's 'colonial' occupation of the territory. In the same month, at the UN General Assembly in New York (USA), the Moroccan Prime Minister denounced the situation in Ceuta and Melilla.

In December 1997 the Spanish Government announced that 1,206 sub-Saharan Africans were to be transferred from Ceuta and Melilla to the mainland. In late December the authorities effected the first transfers to Spain, where the illegal immigrants were received by various NGOs. The Minister of the Interior announced that two new reception centres were to be built in Ceuta and Melilla.

In January 1998 three police-officers were injured and six immigrants were detained, as a result of a confrontation in offices of the ICRC in Melilla, where about 50 immigrants from central Africa staged a demonstration against the criteria for transfer to mainland Spain. About 200 Algerians, protesting against delays in their transfer, also demonstrated outside government offices. As the territories' borders were strengthened and both maritime and street patrols increased, in February 1998 it was announced that during the course of the previous year 4,358 illegal immigrants had been expelled from Ceuta. In March 1998, in Melilla, a demonstration by Algerian immigrants left three people injured. On the occasion of the Spanish Prime Minister's visit to Morocco in April 1998, his newly-appointed Moroccan counterpart requested that Spain review its policy on Ceuta and Melilla.

In September 1998 the Government of Melilla rejected Morocco's offer of dual nationality for the citizens of the two enclaves, and later urged the Spanish Government to lodge a protest with the Moroccan authorities. In January 1999 the Ceuta authorities expelled more than 100 Moroccans, including 60 children, all of whom lacked documentation. In March, however, the Spanish General Prosecutor ordered the police force of Ceuta to suspend expulsions of destitute minors.

In January 1999 the PP Senator for Melilla, Aurel-Gheorghe Sava, announced his resignation owing to an internal party dispute. He was replaced by Beatriz Caro. In the same month, after 12 years' exile in Morocco, Aomar Muhammadi Dudú, the former Muslim leader, returned to Melilla, in preparation for the local elections to be held in June. In February, as the internal crisis within the local party grew, the PP lost a motion of censure against Enrique Palacios.

In February 1999 it emerged that the two enclaves were being used extensively by drugs-traffickers for the purpose of 'money-laundering' operations. The Ministry of Economy and Finance began an inquiry into these irregular movements of substantial amounts of foreign exchange. In March the Ministry of the Interior initiated an investigation into allegations of corruption in the prison and security services of Ceuta, the accusations again related to the trade in illicit drugs. By mid-1999 there was serious concern in Ceuta over the increasing number of drugs-related shootings. In July 1999 48 arrests were made in Melilla following a police operation to dismantle a network believed to be responsible for the illegal 'laundering' of funds derived from drugs-trafficking.

In early 1999 it was conceded that the security barrier on Ceuta's border with Morocco was proving inadequate. The project, which had been funded by the EU, remained unfinished, despite having been initiated some five years earlier. Further improvements were therefore announced, which were to incorporate 17 surveillance towers, two additional fences of more than 3 m in height (bringing the total to four, running parallel to a patrol road), thermal cameras and fibre optic sensors. Security on the beaches was also strengthened. The improvements were finally completed in February 2000. Between January and July 1999 alone a total of 21,411 illegal immigrants were apprehended on Ceuta's frontier and returned to Morocco. Meanwhile, work progressed on a new reception centre in Ceuta to replace the inadequate facilities of the Calamocarro camp, where in mid-1999 more than 1,000 illegal immigrants, mainly from sub-Saharan Africa, were being held. The centre was completed in May 2000 at a cost of 2,800m. pesetas; it had accommodation for 130 immigrants. In September 1999, in one of the most serious disturbances to date, damage estimated at 20m. pesetas was caused during rioting at a reception centre in Melilla, where 300 illegal immigrants were accommodated. The inmates alleged that they were being mistreated by the security guards. Following the disturbances, eight Algerian immigrants were accused of public disorder and arson, and were transferred to prison. There were increasing numbers of disturbances at Ceuta reception centres in 2000 and 2001.

In Morocco, meanwhile, King Hassan died in July 1999. In August the Moroccan Prime Minister urged Spain to open negotiations on the future of Ceuta and Melilla. In the same month the Spanish Prime Minister paid a brief visit to Rabat. During his discussions with the newly-enthroned King Muhammad, the issue of Ceuta and Melilla was not raised.

At the elections of June 1999, the most successful party in both Ceuta and Melilla was the Grupo Independiente Liberal (GIL), recently founded by Jesús Gil, the controversial Mayor of Marbella. The GIL secured 12 of the 25 seats in the local assembly of Ceuta and seven of the 25 in Melilla. Antonio Sampietro Casarramona of the GIL replaced Jesús Fortes Ramos of the PP as Mayor/President of Ceuta. In Melilla the two newly-elected PSOE councillors defied a central directive to vote with the five PP delegates (in order to obstruct the accession of the GIL to the city presidency), and instead gave their support to Mustafa Aberchán Hamed of the CpM, which had won five seats. Aberchán was thus elected to replace

Enrique Palacios as Mayor/President of Melilla. In mid-July Aberchán and the GIL agreed to form a minority Government. The two rebel PSOE councillors subsequently relinquished their seats. In August a replacement PSOE delegate claimed that a representative of Aberchán had offered him a bribe in exchange for the renunciation of his seat. The fact that his predecessor had relinquished her seat, and then attempted to withdraw her resignation, led to intense speculation that she had also been offered a bribe. Similar allegations of malpractice were made in Ceuta.

In September 1999, following a rift between the CpM and the GIL, the Mayor/President of Melilla was attempting to form a minority Government with representatives of the Partido Independiente de Melilla (PIM), recently established by Enrique Palacios. In October, however, Mustafa Aberchán reached a broad accommodation with members of the PP and UPM that enabled him to remain in office. In November the Melilla branch of the GIL announced that it was to operate independently of the mainland party. In the same month, following a new agreement between Aberchán and the GIL, the GIL announced its intention to renew its participation in the Government of Melilla. As a result, the socialist councillors withdrew from the administration. In early December Aberchán announced the composition of a new coalition Government. Crispin Lozano, the local leader of the GIL, was appointed First Vice-President, while Enrique Palacios of the PIM became Second Vice-President. In the same month Ignacio Velázquez, the former PP Mayor/President of Melilla, was barred from public office for six years, having been found guilty of neglecting his duty during his period in office. He was, however, cleared of charges relating to the misappropriation of public funds. In January 2002, Velazquez resigned as Councillor of the Presidency, after the Supreme Court upheld his conviction.

In January 2000 José María Aznar visited Spanish North Africa, the first visit by a Spanish Prime Minister for 19 years. His decision to visit in his capacity as leader of the PP, however, rather than as head of government, was severely criticized in Ceuta and Melilla, while, in protest, the Moroccan Government cancelled the planned visit to Rabat of the Spanish Minister of Foreign Affairs (although the official reason given by the Moroccan authorities for the cancellation was that King Muhammad was on holiday). At the general election held on 12 March 2000, Ceuta's three PP representatives in Madrid, one deputy and two senators, all secured re-election. The PP also retained Melilla's three seats in the Spanish legislature.

In February 2000 the Spanish Government liberalized Spain's immigration laws, thereby provoking a dramatic rise in clandestine immigration. In February an operation to prevent the entry into Ceuta of some 500 migrants from sub-Saharan Africa led to violent confrontation between the migrants and the authorities, while in May the Government of Ceuta estimated that more than 25,000 potential immigrants, mainly Moroccans, were awaiting an opportunity to travel to southern Spain. It was also revealed in May that some 700,000 persons had been refused admission to Spanish North Africa during 1999. In the same month, during a visit to Morocco, the Spanish Prime Minister admitted that the new immigration legislation would need to be revised, as, since its entry into force, more than 82,000 immigrants had applied for Spanish residency permits. Large numbers of immigrants continued to enter the two enclaves throughout mid-2000 and clashes between migrants and the security forces continued to be reported. The immigration law reforms entered into force on 23 January 2001, intended to assist those seeking asylum but offering severe penalties to illegal immigrants and to traffickers in and employers of illegal immigrants. Under the law, those entering the country illegally could be deported within 48 hours of apprehension; illegal workers would be deprived of the right to strike and to join a union, and their use of public services would be limited; illegal immigrants would gain the right to remain in the country only after five years of employment, rather than the two years previously specified. Protests against the reforms were staged in Spanish North Africa, as in Spain. In 2000–01, with reception centres full on a number of occasions, Ceuta experienced increasing difficulties in supplying temporary residence for illegal immigrants.

In June 2000, in Melilla, four policemen were arrested for their involvement in one of the principal immigrant trafficking networks. Three organizers of a similar network were detained in Ceuta in November, and two further networks were uncovered there in April 2001. A further immigrant trafficking ring was uncovered in June 2001, and later in that month the section chief of the Capitanía Marítima de Ceuta and the crew of two fishing vessels were arrested for their alleged involvement in immigrant trafficking. In November 2000 the border guard of the Tarajal frontier between Ceuta and Morocco announced an indefinite strike, protesting against the lack of resources and personnel. In the resulting delays and closures of the border, three policemen were injured when 800 Moroccans attempted to force entrance to Ceuta. In late August police intercepted some 800 Moroccan immigrants who were attempting to take advantage of a high level of traffic at the Tarajal border crossing in Ceuta during an annual trade fair. The following month, the Government announced that the identification papers of Moroccans attempting to enter Ceuta and Melilla would henceforth be more closely examined. Furthermore, in October, two members of the Civil Guard were imprisoned for trafficking in illegal immigrants from Pakistan.

In Melilla, in early May 2000 two GIL deputies and one UPM representative defected to the opposition. Aberchán declared that, despite his Government's loss of its majority, he would not resign. The opposition subsequently announced that they would request a vote of 'no confidence' in Aberchán's government at the earliest opportunity. Later in the month the national leadership of the PP and the PSOE met in Madrid in order to negotiate a solution to the political crisis in Melilla. The two parties agreed that, if Aberchán's Government were removed from office, they would form a coalition government in partnership with the UPM, whose leader, Juan José Imbroda Ortiz, would be nominated Mayor/President. In early July the remaining five GIL members left the Government and joined the opposition. The opposition subsequently introduced a motion of censure against Aberchán, whom they accused of nepotism, a lack of transparency and of harassment of the opposition. Aberchán, who described the accusations as being racially motivated, announced that the CpM was to withdraw from the legislature. In mid-July some 2,000 Muslim citizens of Melilla demonstrated in support of Aberchán. At the same time the Vice-President of Melilla, Enrique Palacios, suspended the motion of censure by decree, reportedly without having consulted Aberchán. (Palacios was subsequently barred from public office for seven years, having been found guilty of perverting the course of justice.) The opposition, who had criticized the decree as 'illegal and possibly criminal', later successfully overturned the decree in the courts, and the vote on the motion of censure against Aberchán was therefore able to proceed. The motion was adopted on 17 September, with the support of 16 of the 25 deputies, and Imbroda was elected as Mayor/President. In late 2000 four members of the GIL announced their departure from the party. In early January 2001 five Ceuta councillors resigned their posts and announced their departure from the GIL, thus depriving the party of its majority in the Assembly. On 24 January a motion of censure was brought against Sampietro by the PP, PSOE, PDSC and one of the former GIL councillors, Aida Pietra. The motion was carried on 10 February, with the support of 17 of the 25 deputies, and Juan Jesús Vivas Lara of the PP was appointed Mayor/President of Ceuta. A new Council was subsequently announced, including the five 'rebel' councillors (now members of the Grupo Mixto). During July two councillors and one vice-councillor resigned, necessitating a Council reshuffle.

In early September 2000, following a ruling in the Spanish courts that Ceuta and Melilla could not be considered to be autonomous communities, the ruling GIL proposed in the Ceuta Assembly that the Spanish Government grant Ceuta greater autonomy. Discussions on the proposal, which proved highly emotive, led to disturbances within the Assembly. The motion was subsequently carried by a majority vote, despite the opposition of the PP and PSOE and the abstention of the PDSC.

Morocco's withdrawal of its ambassador from Madrid in October 2001 further worsened the strained relations between that country and Spain. In December, a confrontation developed when the Spanish authorities attempted to seize a vessel, allegedly laden with narcotics, which the Moroccans had already been pursuing through their own waters. In February 2002 the Spanish Ministry of Foreign Affairs again rejected the Moroccan Government's comparison of the status of Ceuta and Melilla with that of Gibraltar, as talks between the Spanish and British governments regarding the British territory progressed.

The situation deteriorated in mid-July 2002, when a small detachment of Moroccan troops occupied the uninhabited rocky islet of Perejil (Leila), west of Ceuta. Morocco claimed that it was establishing a surveillance post on the island as part of its campaign against illegal emigration and drugs-trafficking. Spain, however, objected to the presence of the troops on the island, citing an accord made by the two countries in 1990 whereby both countries agreed not to occupy the territory. The Moroccan Government claimed that it had had full sovereignty over the island since 1956 and maintained that Moroccan troops had been deployed there in the past. Madrid responded by demanding the immediate evacuation of Moroccan troops from Perejil, receiving the support of the EU and NATO. Although not making a formal claim of sovereignty over the island, Spain proceeded to increase its military forces in Ceuta and Melilla

On 17 July the Spanish ambassador to Rabat was recalled for an unlimited period, and Spanish special forces removed Moroccan troops from Perejil without casualties on either side. The Government offered to withdraw its troops if King Muhammad gave assurances that Moroccan forces would not reoccupy the island. They also suggested joint use of the island in the campaign against drugs-trafficking. Morocco denounced the Spanish action as equivalent to a declaration of war, but insisted on a diplomatic solution to the crisis. Following mediation by the US Secretary of State, Colin Powell, Spanish forces withdrew from the island on 18th July. The Spanish Minister of Foreign Affairs, Ana de Palacio, and her Moroccan counterpart, Muhammad Benaissa, subsequently concluded an accord on Perejil under which both states agreed to return to the status quo ante. On 30 July, however, King Muhammad demanded that Ceuta and Melilla be ceded to Morocco. In subsequent months the Moroccan authorities frequently closed border crossings to Ceuta and Melilla, while Spanish border patrols tightened security. A further meeting between the Moroccan and Spanish Ministers of Foreign Affairs, scheduled for late September, was cancelled by Morocco.

Economy

CEUTA AND MELILLA

Ceuta and Melilla, both free ports, are in fact of little economic importance, while the other possessions, with a population in 1982 of 312, mostly military personnel and fishermen, are of negligible significance. The chief reason for Spanish retention of these areas was their predominantly Spanish population. The registered population of Ceuta has grown fivefold in the last century, and continues to grow at an average annual rate of 0.6% (compared with the Spanish average of 0.2%). Melilla, however, has suffered a decline in population, owing to a lack of economic opportunities. Between 1970 and 1996 the population declined by 2.2% overall in both cities, although the proportion of Arab residents has greatly increased, particularly in Melilla. There are large numbers of immigrants from Morocco.

In 1991 Ceuta's gross domestic product (GDP) was 33.6% below the average for the whole of Spain, while that of Melilla was 30.5% below. In the same year the average disposable family income of Ceuta was only 76.85% that of Spain, the figure in Melilla being 84.76%. Social security benefits accounted for 22.75% of the average family income in Ceuta and 24.25% in Melilla. In 1992 the GDP of the two territories totalled 133,767m. pesetas, equivalent to 1,072,607 pesetas per head. In 1995 the territories' combined GDP per head was 11.61% below the average for the whole of Spain. In that year, compared with 1994, the GDP of Ceuta and Melilla increased by 1.98%. In 1996 GDP per head was estimated to have increased by 1.58% in Ceuta and by 1.68% in Melilla. By 1996, although the two territories' income per head was below the average for Spain, family income per caput being 0.83% below the Spanish average in Ceuta and 6.04% above in Melilla, purchasing power was 3.03% higher in Ceuta and 6.55% higher in Melilla. An unofficial report issued in October 1996 classified Melilla as by far the poorest city in Spain. In 1997, compared with the previous year, the GDP of Ceuta increased by 2.82%, while that of Melilla expanded by 2.76%, among the lowest growth rates in Spain. In 1998 GDP in Ceuta was 119,673m. pesetas and GDP in Melilla was 92,703m. pesetas, while GDP per head was equivalent to 76.6% of the average for Spain in Ceuta and 71.3% of the Spanish average in Melilla. The following year GDP in Ceuta grew by 3.24%, and accounted for 74.53% of the national average. In 2001 the combined GDP for both territories was €1,840m.

The hinterland of the two cities is small. Development is restricted by the lack of suitable building land. Ceuta, in particular, suffers from intermittent water shortages. In September 1995 tenders were invited for the construction of a desalination plant in the territory, which would be capable of processing 12,000 cu m of sea water per day (rising to 16,000 cu m). The apparent shortcomings of the territories' infrastructure were

demonstrated in Melilla in November 1997 by the rupture of a large water-storage tank. The resultant flood killed 11 people, injured 41 and caused damage estimated at more than 1,350m. pesetas.

Agriculture, Industry and Tourism

Most of the population's food has to be imported, with the exception of fish, which is obtained locally. Sardines and anchovies are the most important items. In 1998 344.4 metric tons of fish were landed in Ceuta. A large proportion of the tinned fish is sold outside Spain. More important to the economies of the cities is the port activity; most of their exports take the form of fuel supplied—at very competitive rates—to ships. Most of the fuel comes from the Spanish refinery in Tenerife. Ceuta's port is the busier, receiving a total of 11,804 ships in 1998. Apart from the ferries from Málaga and Almería in mainland Spain, Melilla's port is not so frequented and its exports are correspondingly low. Imports in Ceuta in 2000 totalled 38,547mm. pesetas. Textile materials accounted for 6,114m. pesetas, articles of clothing 3,699m. pesetas, and fuel and lubricants 9,664m. pesetas. The leading sources of imports in that year were China (22.1%), Italy (14.0%) and South Korea (13.4%). Ceuta's main exports are frozen and preserved fish, foodstuffs and beer, as well as supplies of fuel and water to ships entering the port. Commercial agricultural activity in the territories is negligible, and industry is limited to meeting some of the everyday needs of the cities. There is a local brewery in Ceuta.

Tourism previously made a significant contribution to the territories' economies. Almost 1m. tourists visited Ceuta in 1986, attracted by duty-free goods. High ferry-boat fares and the opening of the Spanish border with Gibraltar in 1985, however, had an adverse effect on the enclaves' duty-free trade, and tourist numbers declined to 64,684 in 2000. Successive defence cuts led not only to fears for Spanish North Africa's security but also to losses in income from military personnel stationed in the territories.

In 2000 the economically active population of the two enclaves totalled 65,600, of whom 8,400 were unemployed, 4,200 were employed in the construction sector, 2,100 in industry and 300 in agriculture, hunting, forestry and fishing; 42,200 were employed in the services sector. In 1996 the civil service employed 2,904 workers in Ceuta and 2,877 in Melilla. By March 2002, the number of unemployed in the two enclaves declined to an estimated 4,200.

Finance and Inward Investment

In 1986 the Spanish Government announced that it was to grant 6,500m. pesetas to Ceuta and 8,500m. to Melilla for the purposes of infrastructural development. In 1989 a campaign to attract more investment to Ceuta began. Tax concessions and other incentives were offered. In the three years to 1990 the Spanish Government's investment in Melilla totalled 32,000m. pesetas. Ceuta received 9,000m. pesetas for the purposes of public works, and its health service was allocated 347m. pesetas. In early 1993 investment of a further 18,000m. pesetas for housing and transport projects in Melilla was announced. In Ceuta the apparent lack of banking controls and alleged corruption at senior levels drew criticism in April 1993, when evidence of the territory's use as a 'money-laundering' centre for the proceeds of drugs-trafficking was revealed. A sum of more than 25,000m. pesetas was believed to be involved. Furthermore, in December fraudulent operations, allegedly involving almost 100m. pesetas and in which two civil servants were implicated, were uncovered at the city hall of Ceuta. Following Spain's intensification of security at its frontier with Gibraltar in 1995–96, many drug and tobacco smugglers were believed to have relocated their bases to Ceuta.

Upon the accession of Spain to the European Community (EC, now European Union—EU) in January 1986, Ceuta and Melilla were considered as Spanish cities and European territory, and joined the Community as part of Spain. They retained their status as free ports. The statutes of autonomy, adopted in early 1995, envisaged the continuation of the territories' fiscal benefits. On 28 February 2002, euro notes and coins entered circulation as sole legal tender in the enclaves. In June 1994 the EU announced substantial regional aid: between 1995 and 1999 Ceuta and Melilla were to receive totals of ECU 28m. and ECU 45m., of which ECU 20m. and ECU 18m., respectively, were to be in the form of direct aid. With assistance from the European Social Fund, a programme of employment and vocational training for Melilla was announced in 1996. In 1997 projected state investment in Ceuta and Melilla was 7,786m. pesetas, compared with 6,363m. pesetas in 1996. Ceuta's budget for 1999 was estimated at 22,000m. pesetas. As a proportion of GDP per head in relation to the EU average, the estimate for Ceuta rose from 37.0% in 1960 to 66.2% in 1996, while that for Melilla increased from 30.8% in 1960 to 70.9% in 1996. The comparable figures for Spain as a whole were 57.2% in 1960 and 76.2% in 1996.

The average annual rate of inflation in 1996 was 2.2% in Ceuta and 3.6% in Melilla, compared with 4.5% in the two enclaves in 1995. In the 12 months to December 1997 and again in the year to December 1998 the inflation rate was 1.9% in Ceuta and Melilla combined. In the 12 months to December 1999 the rate of inflation rose to 2.2%; the rate was 3.5% in the year to December 2000.

Statistical Survey

Ceuta

Sources (unless otherwise stated): Administración General del Estado, Beatriz de Silva 4, 51001 Ceuta; tel. (956) 512616; fax (956) 511893; Instituto Nacional de Estadística, Paseo de la Castellana 183, 28046 Madrid; tel. (91) 5839301; fax (91) 5839086; e-mail info@ine.es; internet www.ine.es.

AREA, POPULATION AND DENSITY

Area: 19.7 sq km (7.6 sq miles).

Population (census results): 67,615 at 1 March 1991; 71,505 at 1 November 2001.

Density (1 November 2001): 3,630 per sq km.

Births, Marriages and Deaths (2000): Live births 1,013 (birth rate 13.6 per 1,000); Marriages 295 (marriage rate 4.0 per 1,000); Deaths 440 (death rate 5.9 per 1,000).

Expectation of Life (Ceuta and Melilla, years at birth, 1998–99): Males 73.7; Females 80.0.

Immigration and Emigration (1998): Immigrants 2,114; Emigrants 1,695.

Economically Active Population (incl. Melilla, '000 persons, 2000): Agriculture, hunting, forestry and fishing 2.1; Industry 2.1; Construction 4.2; Services 42.2; Total employed 57.2; Unemployed 8.4; Total labour force 65.6.

AGRICULTURE, ETC.

Agriculture: Agricultural activity in the territory is negligible, and the majority of the population's food, with the exception of fish, is imported.

Fishing (metric tons, live weight): Total catch 408.4 in 1996; 357.0 in 1997; 344.4 in 1998. Source: *Ceuta—Memoria de la situación socioeconomica y laboral de la ciudad.*

FINANCE

Currency and Exchange Rates: 100 cent = 1 euro (€). *Sterling and Dollar Equivalents* (31 May 2002): £1 Sterling = 1.5625 euros; US $1 = 1.0653 euros; 100 euros = £64.00 = $93.87. *Average Exchange Rate* (euros per US $): 0.9386 in 1999; 1.0854 in 2000; 1.1175 in 2001. Note: The local currency was formerly the Spanish peseta. From the introduction of the euro, with Spanish participation, on 1 January 1999, a fixed exchange rate of €1 = 166.386 pesetas was in effect. Euro notes and coins were introduced on 1 January 2002. The euro and local currency circulated alongside each other until 28 February, after which the euro became the sole legal tender. Some of the figures in this Survey are still in terms of pesetas.

Cost of Living (incl. Melilla, Consumer Price Index at December; base: 1992 average = 100): 127.5 in 1999; 132.3 in 2000; 134 in 2001 (excluding Melilla).

Gross Domestic Product (estimates, million euros, incl. Melilla): 1,682.5 in 1999; 1,767.8 in 2000; 1,840.2 in 2001.

Gross Domestic Product by Economic Activity (estimates, million euros, incl. Melilla, 2001): Agriculture, hunting, forestry and fishing 2.9; Industry 147.8 (incl. Energy 25.9, Construction 95.6); Services 1,586.0; *Sub-total* 1,736.7; *Less* Imputed bank service charges 68.4; *GDP at basic prices* 1,668.3; Taxes (less subsidies) on products 171.8; *GDP in purchasers' values* 1,840.2.

EXTERNAL TRADE

Principal Commodities: *Imports* (million pesetas, 2000): Fuel and lubricants 9,664; Electronics and computers 1,020; Milk and dairy products 2,531; Textile materials 6,114; Articles of clothing 3,699; Artisan-made textiles 1,824; Total (incl. others) 38,547. *Exports:* Ceuta supplies fuel and water to ships entering the port. Other exports include frozen and preserved fish, beer and foodstuffs.

Principal Trading Partners (percentages, 2000): *Imports:* China 22.1; Germany 5.5; Indonesia 4.5; Italy 14.0; Netherlands 10.1; Russia 4.4; South Korea 13.4; United Kingdom 3.65.

Volume of Trade (million pesetas, 2000): Imports 38,547; Exports 15,309. Source: *Ceuta—Memoria de la situación socioeconomica y laboral de la ciudad.*

2001 (million euros): Total imports 244.4; Total exports 110.2.

TRANSPORT

Road Traffic: Vehicles entered (2000): 212,747; Vehicles departed (2000): 219,603.

Shipping (2000): Goods loaded 287,070 metric tons, Goods unloaded 1,228,950 metric tons; Passenger arrivals 1,229,000; Passenger departures 1,269,000.

TOURISM

Visitor Arrivals: 84,719 in 1998; 71,448 in 1999; 64,684 in 2000.

Tourist Nights: 129,841 in 1998; 203,843 in 1999; 158,777 in 2000.

EDUCATION

Pre-primary (1999/2000): 2 schools; 2,699 students.

Primary (1999/2000): 23 schools; 8,419 students; 353 teachers (incl. pre-primary).

Secondary (1999/2000): 5 schools; 4,174 students; 421 teachers.

Vocational (1998/99): 2 centres; 1,035 students; 27 teachers.

Melilla

Sources (unless otherwise stated): Instituto Nacional de Estadística, Paseo de la Castellana 183, 28046 Madrid; tel. (91) 5839301; fax (91) 5839086; e-mail info@ine.es; internet www.ine.es.

AREA, POPULATION AND DENSITY

Area: 12.5 sq km. (4.8 sq miles).

Population (census results): 56,600 at 1 March 1991; 66,411 at 1 November 2001.

Density (1 November 2001): 5,312 per sq km.

Births, Marriages and Deaths (2000): Live births 1,223 (birth rate 18.6 per 1,000); Marriages 503 (marriage rate 7.7 per 1,000); Deaths 438 (marriage rate 6.8 per 1,000).

Expectation of Life: see Ceuta.

Immigration and Emigration (1998): Immigrants 2,409; Emigrants 1,948.

Economically Active Population: see Ceuta.

FINANCE

Currency and Exchange Rates: see Ceuta.
Cost of Living: (Consumer Price Index at December; base: 1992 average = 100): 134 in 2001; (Previous years, see Ceuta).
Gross Domestic Product: see Ceuta.

EXTERNAL TRADE

Melilla is a duty-free port. Most imports are from Spain but over 90% of exports go to non-Spanish territories. The chief export is fish.

TRANSPORT

Road Traffic: Vehicles registered (2000): 3,184. Source: Dirección General de Tráfico, Madrid.
Shipping (1999): Goods loaded 145,000 metric tons; Goods unloaded 622,000 metric tons.
Civil Aviation (1999): Passengers transported 260,000; Goods transported 644 metric tons.

EDUCATION

Pre-primary (1999/2000): 1 school; 2,598 students.
Primary (1999/2000): 14 schools; 8,097 students; 464 teachers (incl. pre-primary).
Secondary (1999/2000): 8 schools; 3,952 students; 450 teachers.
Vocational (1998/99): 1 centre; 696 students; 22 teachers.

Directory

Ceuta

GOVERNMENT
(September 2002)

Delegación del Gobierno: Beatriz de Silva 4, 51001 Ceuta; tel. (956) 512523; fax (956) 513671; e-mail roberto@ceuta.map.es; Government Delegate in Ceuta LUIS VICENTE MORO DÍAZ.

Deputy elected to the Congress in Madrid: FRANCISCO ANTONIO GONZÁLEZ PÉREZ (PP). Representatives to the Senate in Madrid: JOSÉ LUIS MORALES MONTERO (PP), NICOLÁS FERNÁNDEZ CUCURULL (PP). Commandant-General: FERNANDO LÓPEZ DE OLMEDO

COUNCIL OF GOVERNMENT

Mayor/President of Ceuta: JUAN JESÚS VIVAS LARA (PP).
Vice-President and Councillor of Co-ordination and Communication: CRISTINA BERNAL DÚRAN.
Councillor of Development: NICOLÁS FERNÁNDEZ CUCURULL.
Councillor of the Environment: JUAN ANTONIO RODRÍGUEZ FERRÓN.
Councillor of the Economy and Employment: JUAN JOSÉ ROSALES FERNÁNDEZ.
Councillor of Education and Culture: ADELAIDA ALVAREZ RODRÍGUEZ.
Councillor of Finance: ALFONSO CONEJO RABANEDA.
Councillor of the Presidency and the Interior: EMILIO CARREIRA RUIZ.
Councillor of Public Health, Consumer Affairs and Sport: JUSTO OSTALÉ BLANCO.
Councillor of Public Works: MUSTAFA MIZZIAN AMAR.
Councillor of Social Services: MOHAMMED MOHAMMED CHAIB.
Councillor of Tourism: AIDA PIEDRA RUBIO.
Councillor of Youth and Festivals: FRANCISCO TORRES CANTERO.
Presidency of Ceuta: Plaza de Africa s/n, 51001 Ceuta; tel. (956) 528200; fax (956) 514470; internet www.ciceuta.es.
Council of Co-ordination and Communication: Plaza de Africa s/n, 51001 Ceuta; tel. (956) 528200.
Council of Development and the Environment: Plaza de Africa s/n, 51001 Ceuta; tel. (956) 528200; e-mail fomento@ciceuta.es, medioambiente@ciceuta.es.
Council of the Economy and Employment: Plaza de Africa s/n, 51001 Ceuta; tel. (956) 528200; e-mail economia@ciceuta.es; presupuestos@ciceuta.es.
Council of Education and Culture: Plaza de Africa s/n, 51001 Ceuta; tel. (956) 528200; e-mail cultura@ciceuta.es.
Council of Finance: Padilla, Edif. Ceuta Center, 51001 Ceuta; tel. (956) 528200; e-mail hacienda@ciceuta.es.
Council of the Presidency and the Interior: Plaza de Africa s/n, 51001 Ceuta; tel. (956) 528200; e-mail presidencia@ciceuta.es.

Council of Human Resources: Plaza de Africa s/n, 51001 Ceuta; tel. (956) 528200.
Council of Public Health, Consumer Affairs and Sport: Avda Barcelona s/n, 51001 Ceuta; tel. (956) 528200; e-mail sanidad@ciceuta.es.
Council of Public Works: Plaza de Africa s/n, 51001 Ceuta; tel. (956) 528200.
Council of Social Services: Padilla, Edif. Ceuta Center, 51001 Ceuta; tel. (956) 528200; e-mail bsocial@ciceuta.es.
Council of Tourism: Padilla, Edif. Ceuta Center, 51001 Ceuta; tel. (956) 528200; fax (956) 528247; e-mail turismo@ciceuta.es; internet www.turiceuta.com.
Council of Youth and Festivals: Plaza de los Reyes s/n, 51001 Ceuta; tel. (956) 510654; e-mail participacion@ciceuta.es.

COUNCIL

Election, 13 June 1999

	Seats
Grupo Independiente Liberal (GIL)	12
Partido Popular (PP)	8
Partido Socialista Obrero Español (PSOE)	2
Partido Democrático y Social de Ceuta (PDSC)	3
Total	**25**

POLITICAL ORGANIZATIONS

Ceuta Unida (CEU): Ceuta; nationalist party; Sec.-Gen. JOSÉ ANTONIO QUEROL.

Grupo Independiente Liberal (GIL): Ceuta; f. 1999; Leader ANTONIO SAMPIETRO CASARRAMONA.

Izquierda Unida: Gral. Yaque, 4-1°, 11701 Ceuta; tel (956) 513558; fax (956) 513558; left-wing electoral alliance; Leader MUSTAFA HASSEN.

Partido Democrático y Social de Ceuta (PDSC): Bolivia 35, Ceuta; Muslim party; Leader MUSTAFA MIZZIAM AMMAR.

Partido Independiente de Ceuta: B. Príncipe Alfonso, Fuerte 6, 51003 Ceuta; Leader HAMED MOHAMED LIAZID.

Partido Popular (PP): Real 90 Bajo Izquierda, 51001 Ceuta; tel. (956) 518139; fax (956) 511636; e-mail opceuta@pp.es; internet www.pp.es; fmrly Alianza Popular; centre-right; Pres. PEDRO GORDILLO DURÁN.

Partido Socialista Obrero Español (PSOE): Ceuta; socialist workers' party; Leader FRUCTUOSO MIAJA.

Partido Socialista del Pueblo de Ceuta (PSPC): Carretera del Embalse 10, 11704 Ceuta; dissident group of PSOE; Leader JUAN LUIS ARÓSTEGUI.

Progreso y Futuro de Ceuta (PFC): Poligono Virgen de Africa s/n, Ceuta; Leader FRANCISCO FRAIZ ARMADA.

There are branches of the major Spanish parties in Ceuta, and also various civic associations. The **Asociación Ceuta y Melilla (Acyme)** is based in Granada (Pres. FRANCISCO GODINO), and is opposed to the limited autonomy of the enclaves. The **Organización 21 de Agosto para la Liberación de los Territorios Marroquíes Usurpados** resumed its activities in 1995.

JUDICIAL SYSTEM

Tribunal Superior de Justicia de Andalucía, Ceuta y Melilla: Plaza Nueva, 10, Palacio de la Real Chancillería, 18071 Granada, Spain; tel. (958) 002600; fax (958) 242156; Pres. AUGUSTO MÉNDEZ DE LUGO Y LÓPEZ DE AYALA.

RELIGION

The majority of the European inhabitants are Christians, almost all being adherents of the Roman Catholic Church. Most Africans are Muslims, totalling about 13,000 in 1991. There were about 500 Hindus in 1995. The Jewish community numbers several hundred.

Christianity
The Roman Catholic Church

Bishop of Cádiz and Ceuta: ANTONIO CEBALLOS ATIENZA (resident in Cádiz); Vicars-General: MANUEL DE LA PUENTE SENDÓN, FRANCISCO CORRERO TOCÓN; Plaza de Nuestra Señora de Africa, 11701 Ceuta; tel. (956) 517732; fax (956) 513208; e-mail obispadoceuta@planalfa.es.

THE PRESS

El Faro de Ceuta: Sargento Mena 8, 51001 Ceuta; tel. (956) 524148; fax (956) 524147; e-mail elfaro@retemail.es; f. 1934; morning; Dir CARMEN ETXARRI PUIDO; Editor-in-Chief ROCÍO ABAD DE LOS SANTOS; circ. 5,000.

El Periódico de Ceuta: Ampliación Muelle de Poniente P-104-10, 11701 Ceuta; tel. (956) 513348; fax (956) 513669.

El Pueblo de Ceuta: Independencia 11, 1°, 51001, Ceuta; tel. (956) 514367; fax (956) 517650; e-mail elpueblo_redaccion@teleline.es; daily; Dir and Editor-in-Chief SALVADOR VIVANCOS CANALES.

Press Association

Asociación de la Prensa: Sargento Mena 8, 51001 Ceuta; tel. (956) 524148.

BROADCASTING
Radio

Onda Cero Radio Ceuta: Delgado Serrano, 1, 1°drcha. 51001 Ceuta; tel. (956) 200068; fax (956) 200179; Dir RAFAEL ROMAGUERA MENA.

Radio Ceuta: Real 90, Portón 4, 1° Dcha, 51001 Ceuta; tel. (956) 511820; fax (956) 516820; f. 1934; commercial; owned by Sociedad Española de Radiodifusión (SER); Dir ANTONIO ROSA GUERRERO.

Radio Nacional de España: Real 90, 51001 Ceuta; tel. (956) 524688; fax (956) 519067; Dir EDUARDO SÁNCHEZ DORADO.

Radio Popular de Ceuta/COPE: Sargento Mena 8, 1°, 11701 Ceuta; tel. (956) 524200; fax (956) 524202; Dir DANIEL OLIVA.

Television

Televisión Ceuta: Ceuta; tel. (956) 514417; Dir MANUEL GONZÁLEZ BOLORINO.

FINANCE
Banking

Banco Bilbao Vizcaya Argentaria (BBVA): Plaza de los Reyes s/n, 51001 Ceuta; tel. (956) 511611; 3 brs.

Banco de España: Plaza de España 2, 51001 Ceuta; tel. (956) 511805; fax (956) 513108.

Banco Español de Crédito (Banesto): Camoens 6, 51001 Ceuta; tel. (956) 513009.

Banco Popular Español: Paseo del Revellín 1, 51001 Ceuta; tel. (956) 510740.

Banco Santander Central Hispanoamericano (BSCH): Paseo del Revellín 17, 51001 Ceuta; tel. (956) 511371; 2 brs.

Caja de Ahorros y Pensiones de Barcelona 'la Caixa': Ceuta.

Caja Duero: Sargento Coriat, 5, 51001,Ceuta; tel (956) 518040; fax (956) 517019; 1 br.

Caja Madrid: Plaza de los Reyes s/n, 51001 Ceuta; tel. (956) 510942; 6 brs.

Insurance

MAPFRE: Cervantes 14, 51001 Ceuta; tel. (956) 519638; fax (956) 513916.

Utilities

Empresa de Alumbrado Eléctrico de Ceuta SA: Beatriz de Silva 2, Ceuta; generates and transmits electricity; Rep. ALBERTO RAMÓN GAITÁN RODRÍGUEZ.

TRADE AND INDUSTRY

Cámara Oficial de Comercio, Industria y Navegación: Muelle Cañonero Dato s/n, 51001 Ceuta; tel. (956) 509590; fax (956) 509589; e-mail sgeneralceuta@camaras.org; internet www.ceuta.com; Pres. LUIS MORENO NARANJO; Sec.-Gen. MARIÁ DEL ROSARIO ESPINOSA SUÁREZ.

Confederación de Empresarios de Ceuta: Teniente Arrabal 2, 51001 Ceuta; tel. (956) 516912; employers' confederation; Pres. MIGUEL ANGEL AZCOITIA LEÓN; Sec.-Gen. EVARISTO RIVERA GÓMEZ.

Trade Union

Confederación Sindical de Comisiones Obreras (CCOO): Alcalde Fructuoso Miaja 1, 11701 Ceuta; tel. (95) 6516243; fax (95) 6516991; e-mail ccooce@ctv.es; internet www.ccoo.es; 1,721 mems (1999); Sec.-Gen. JOSÉ MARIA FIDALGO.

TRANSPORT

Much of the traffic between Spain and Morocco passes through Ceuta; there are ferry services to Algeciras, Melilla, Málaga and Almería. The ferry service contract was due to be renegotiated in July 2001. Plans for an airport are under consideration. Helicopter services to Málaga are provided by Helisureste.

Compañía Trasmediterránea: Muelle Canoero Dato 6, 51001 Ceuta; tel. (956) 509532; fax (956) 522239; internet www.trasmediterranea.es.

TOURISM

Visitors are attracted by the historical monuments, the Parque Marítimo and by the museums, as well as by the Shrine of Our Lady of Africa. There were 64,684 visitors to Ceuta in 2000. In that year Ceuta had four hotels and 19 hostels.

Oficina Municipal de Turismo: Alcalde Sánchez Prados, 51001 Ceuta; tel. (956) 528146; e-mail turismo@ciceuta.es; internet www.turiceuta.com.

Patronato Municipal de Turismo: Estacion Maritima s/n, 51001 Ceuta; tel. (956) 506275.

DEFENCE

Military authority is vested in a commandant-general (see Government). The enclaves are attached to the military region of Sevilla. In August 2001 Spain had 8,100 troops deployed in Spanish North Africa, compared with 21,000 in mid-1987. Two-thirds of Ceuta's land area are used exclusively for military purposes.

EDUCATION

The conventional Spanish facilities are available. In higher education, links with the University of Granada are maintained.

Melilla

GOVERNMENT
(September 2002)

Delegación del Gobierno: Avda de la Marina Española 3, 52001 Melilla; tel. (95) 2675840; fax (95) 2672657; e-mail puri@melilla.map.es; Government Delegate in Melilla: ARTURO ESTEBAN ALBERT.

Deputy elected to the Congress in Madrid: ANTONIO GUTIÉRREZ MOLINA (PP-UPM). Representatives to the Senate in Madrid: CARLOS A. BENET CAÑETE (PP-UPM), JUAN JOSÉ IMBRODA ORTIZ. Commandant-General: FRANCISCO DÍEZ MORENO.

COUNCIL OF GOVERNMENT

Mayor/President of Melilla: JUAN JOSÉ IMBRODA ORTIZ (UPM).

First Vice-President and Councillor of the Environment: RAFAEL HERNÁNDEZ SOLER.

Second Vice-President and Councillor of Culture: FRANCISCO JAVIER MARTÍNEZ MONREAL.

Councillor of the Economy, Finance and Heritage: FRANCISCO SUÁREZ REYES.

Councillor of Education, Tourism and Sports: JOAQUÍN GONZÁLEZ MOLERO.

Councillor of Labour and Human Resources: INÉS URDIALES MORENO.

Councillor of the Presidency: ANTONIO MIRANDA MENTILLA.

Councillor of Public Works and Territorial Affairs: ERNESTO RODRÍGUEZ MUÑOZ.

Councillor of Social Development and Health: MARÍA ISABEL QUESADA VÁZQUEZ.

Presidency of Melilla: Plaza de España 1, 52001 Melilla; tel. (95) 2699100; fax (95) 2674800; internet www.camelilla.es.

Council of Culture: Plaza de España 1, 52001 Melilla; tel. (95) 2699193; fax (95) 2674394.

Council of the Economy, Finance and Heritage: Plaza de España 1, 52801 Melilla; tel. (95) 2699219; fax (95) 2699103.

Council of Education, Tourism and Sports: General Prim 1, 52001 Melilla; tel. (95) 2681950; fax (95) 2264328; e-mail cej01@melilla500.com.

Council of the Environment: Plaza de España 1, 52001 Melilla; tel. (95) 2699134.

Council of Labour and Human Resources: Plaza de España 1, 52001 Melilla; tel. (95) 2699102; fax (95) 2699103.

Council of the Presidency: Plaza de España 1, 52001 Melilla; tel. (95) 2699140.

Council of Public Works and Territorial Affairs: Jiménez Iglesias 30, 52071 Melilla; tel. (95) 2699100; fax (95) 2680255.

Council of Social Development and Health: Avda de la Marina Española 12, 52004 Melilla; tel. (95) 2676790; fax (95) 2678080; e-mail cbs01@melilla500.com.

COUNCIL

Election, 13 June 1999

	Seats
Grupo Independiente Liberal (GIL)	7
Coalición por Melilla (CpM)	5
Partido Popular (PP)	5
Partido Independiente de Melilla (PIM)	3
Unión del Pueblo Melillense (UPM)	3
Partido Socialista Obrero Español (PSOE)	2
Total	25

POLITICAL ORGANIZATIONS

Coalición por Melilla (CpM): c/ Querol, 46, Melilla; Leader MUSTAFA ABERCHÁN HAMED.

Grupo Independente Hispano Bereber: c/ Garcia Cabrelles, 23, Melilla.

Grupo Independiente Liberal (GIL): Melilla; f. 1999; Leader CRISPIN LOZANO.

Partido de los Demócratas de Melilla (PDM): Avda del General Aizpuru 29, Melilla; f. 1985; Muslim party; Leader ABDELKÁDER MOHAMED ALÍ.

Partido Independiente de Melilla (PIM): Avda Juan Carlos I Rey 23, 1° Izqda, Melilla; f. 1999; Leader ENRIQUE PALACIOS.

Partido Popular (PP): Roberto Cano 2, 1° Izqda, POB 384, 52001 Melilla; tel. (95) 2681095; fax (95) 2684477; centre-right; Pres. ANTONIO GUTIÉRREZ MOLINA.

Partido Social Demócrata de Melilla (PSDM): c/ General O'Donnell, n°8-1° izda, Melilla; f. 1998.

Partido Socialista de Melilla-Partido Socialista Obrero Español (PSME-PSOE): Cándido Lobera 7-1°, Melilla; tel. (95) 2681820; socialist workers' party; favours self-government but not full autonomy; Leader JAVIER DE PRO.

Unión del Pueblo Melillense (UPM): Ejército Español 7, 1°, Apdo 775, 52001 Melilla; tel. (95) 2681987; fax (95) 2684677; e-mail www.lanzadera.com/melilla; f. 1985; right-wing; Pres. DANIEL CONESA MÍNGUEZ; Sec.-Gen. GUILLERMO MERINO BARRERA.

There are branches of the major Spanish parties in Melilla, and also various civic associations.

RELIGION

As in Ceuta, most Europeans are Roman Catholics. The registered Muslim community numbered 20,800 in 1990. The Jewish community numbered 1,300. There is also a Hindu community.

Islam

Comisión Islámica de Melilla (CIM): c/ Garcia Cabrelles 13, Melilla; Pres. ABDERRAMAN BENYAHYA.

THE PRESS

Diario Sur: Avda Juan Carlos I Rey 19, 1°, Izqda, Melilla; tel. (95) 2681854; fax (95) 2683908; Perm. Rep. AVELINO GUTIÉRREZ PÉREZ.

El Faro de Melilla: General Marina 11, 1°, 52001 Melilla; tel. (95) 2690050; fax (95) 2680010; e-mail faromeli@arrakis.es; Dir JUAN ANTONIO CALLEJA FLÓREZ.

Melilla Hoy: Polígono Industrial SEPES, La Espiga, Naves A-1/A-2, 52006 Melilla; tel. (95) 2690000; fax (95) 2675725; e-mail redaccionmelillahoy@arrakis.es; f. 1985; Dir IRENE FLORES SÁEZ; Editor-in-Chief MARÍA ANGELES JIMÉNEZ PADILLA; circ. 2,000.

El Telegrama de Melilla: Polígono El Sepes, Calle La Espiga, Nave A-8, 52006 Melilla; tel. (95) 2691443; fax (95) 2691469; e-mail eltelegrama@eltelegrama.com; internet www.eltelegrama.com; Dir RAFAEL MARTOS VILCHEZ.

News Agency

Agencia EFE: Candido Lobera 4, 1° Izqda, 52001 Melilla; tel. (95) 2685235; fax (95) 2680043; Correspondent PILAR SALAS DURÁN.

Press Association

Asociación de la Prensa: Crtra Alfonso XII, Edif. Miguel de Cervantes, Bloque 5 Bajo, 52006 Melilla; tel. (95) 2679121; Pres. ANGEL MORÁN JIMÉNEZ.

BROADCASTING

Radio

40 Melilla: Muelle Ribera 1°, 29805 Melilla; tel. (95) 2681708; fax (95) 2681573; Dir ANTONIA RAMOS PELÁEZ.

Antena 3: Edif. Melilla, Urbanización Rusadir, 29805 Melilla; tel. (95) 2688840; Dir TOÑI RAMOS PELÁEZ.

Cadena Rato: Melilla; Dir ANGEL VALENCIA.

Dial Melilla: Urbanización Rusadir, Edif. Melilla, 52005 Melilla; tel. (95) 2673333; fax (95) 2678342; Representative NURIA FERNÁNDEZ.

Ingar Radio: Abdelkader 3 bajo, 52000 Melilla; tel. (952) 682100.

Onda Cero Radio Melilla: Músico Granados 2, 52004 Melilla; tel. (95) 2691283; fax (95) 2824209; Dir JOSÉ JESÚS NAVAJAS TROBAT.

Radio Melilla: Muelle Ribera 1, 52005 Melilla; tel. (95) 2681708; fax (95) 2681573; commercial; owned by Sociedad Española de Radiodifusión (SER); Dir ANTONIA RAMOS PELÁEZ.

Radio Nacional de España (RNE): Duque de Ahumada 5, 52001, Melilla; tel. (95) 2681907; fax (95) 2683108; state-controlled; Rep. MONTSERRAT COBOS RUANO.

Television

A fibre optic cable linking Melilla with Almería was laid in 1990. From March 1991 Melilla residents were able to receive three private TV channels from mainland Spain: Antena 3, Canal+ and Tele 5.

FINANCE

Banking

The following banks have branches in Melilla: Banco Bilbao Vizcaya Argentaria (2 brs), Banco de España, Banco Español de Crédito (Banesto), Banco Popular Español, Banco Santander Central Hispanoamericano and Caja de Ahorros y Pensiones de Barcelona 'la Caixa'.

Insurance

MAPFRE: Avda Democracia 9, 52004 Melilla; tel. (95) 2673189; fax (95) 2674977.

TRADE AND INDUSTRY

Cámara Oficial de Comercio, Industria y Navegación: Cervantes 7, 52001 Melilla; tel. (95) 2684840; fax (95) 2683119; f. 1906; Pres. MARGARITA LÓPEZ ALMENDÁRIZ; Sec.-Gen. MARÍA JESÚS FERNÁNDEZ DE CASTRO Y PEDRAJAS.

Confederación de Empresarios de Melilla: Paseo Marítimo Mir Berlanga 26 Entreplanta, Apdo de Correos 445, 29806 Melilla; tel. (95) 2678295; fax (95) 2676175; f. 1979; employers' confederation; Pres. MARGARITA LÓPEZ ALMENDÁRIZ; Sec.-Gen. JERÓNIMO PÉREZ HERNÁNDEZ.

Trade Union

Confederación Sindical de Comisiones Obreras (CCOO): Plaza 1° de Mayo s/n, 3°, 29803 Melilla; tel. (95) 2676535; fax (95) 2672571; e-mail orga.melilla@melilla.ccoo.es; internet www.ccoo.es; 1,314 mems (1999); Sec.-Gen. MÁXIMO GARCÍA AGÜERA.

TRANSPORT

There is a daily ferry service to Málaga and a service to Almería. Melilla airport, situated 4 km from the town, is served by daily flights to various destinations on the Spanish mainland, operated by Iberia and by Melilla Jet/Pauknair. There are also services to Madrid and Granada.

Compañía Trasmediterránea: Avda General Marina 1, 52001 Melilla; tel. (95) 2681635; fax (95) 2682685; e-mail correom@ trasmediterranea.es; internet www.trasmediterranea.es; operates ferry service between Melilla and mainland Spain.

Empresa C.O.A.: Estación de Autobuses, Melilla; tel. (95) 2672616; operates bus services throughout the city.

TOURISM

There is much of historic interest to the visitor, while Melilla is also celebrated for its modernist architecture. Melilla had 19 hotels in the late 1980s. Further hotels, including a luxury development, were under construction in the 1990s.

Dirección Provincial Comercio y Turismo: Calle Cervantes, 29801 Melilla; tel. (95) 2681906.

Oficina Provincial de Turismo: Pintor Fortuny 21, 52004 Melilla; tel. (95) 2675444; fax (95) 2691232; e-mail cevtt@melilla500.com.

Viceconsejería de Turismo: Calle Pintor Fortuny 20, Palacio de Congresos y Exposiciones, 52004 Melilla; tel. (95) 2675444; fax (95) 2691232; e-mail cevtt@melilla500.com; internet www.camelilla.es; part of Council of Culture; Dir JAVIER MATEO FIGUEROA.

DEFENCE

See Ceuta. More than one-half of Melilla's land area is used solely for military purposes.

EDUCATION

In addition to the conventional Spanish facilities, the Moroccan Government finances a school for Muslim children in Melilla, the languages of instruction being Arabic and Spanish. In 1982 only 12% of Muslim children were attending school, but by 1990 the authorities had succeeded in achieving an attendance level of virtually 100%. The Spanish open university (UNED) maintains a branch in Melilla. In August 2001 it was announced that children in primary education could choose to attend classes in the Islamic religion.

The Peñón de Vélez de la Gomera, Peñón de Alhucemas and Chafarinas Islands

These rocky islets, situated respectively just west and east of al-Hocima (Alhucemas) and east of Melilla off the north coast of Morocco, are administered with Melilla. The three Chafarinas Islands lie about 3.5 km off Ras el-Ma (Cabo de Agua). The Peñón de Alhucemas is situated about 300 m from the coast. The Peñón de Vélez de la Gomera is situated about 80 km further west, lying 85 m from the Moroccan shore, to which it is joined by a narrow strip of sand. A small military base is maintained on the Peñón de Vélez, while a military garrison of fewer than 100 men is stationed on the Peñón de Alhucemas, and a garrison of about 100 Spanish soldiers is maintained on the Isla del Congreso, the most westerly of the Chafarinas Islands. A supply ship calls at the various islands every two weeks. Prospective visitors must obtain the necessary military permit in Ceuta or Melilla.

Bibliography

Areilza, J. M. de, and Castiella y Maíz, F. M. *Reivindicaciones de España*. Madrid, 1941.

Baeza Herrazti, A. (Ed.). *Ceuta hispano-portuguesa*. Ceuta, Instituto de Estudios Ceutíes, 1993.

Boucher, M. *Spain in Africa* (3 articles, *Africa Institute Bulletin*, May–July 1966).

Ceuta y Melilla en las relaciones de España y Marruecos. Madrid, Instituto Español de Estudios Estratégicos, Centro Superior de Estudios de la Defensa, 1997.

Las comunidades europeas y el norte de Africa. Actas del primer simposium-debate sobre Melilla, Asociación de Estudios Hispano-Africanos, 1987.

Domínguez Sánchez, C. *Melilla*. Madrid, Editorial Everest, 1978.

Europa Ethnica (Vol. 1-2). *Ceuta and Melilla—Spain's presence on African soil*. Vienna, Braumüller, 1999.

Habsbourg, O. D. E. *Européens et Africains: L'Entente Nécessaire*. Paris, Hachette, 1963.

Lafond, P. *Melilla*. Barcelona, Lunwerg Editores, 1997.

Mir Berlanga, F. *Melilla en los Siglos Pasados y Otras Historias*. Madrid, Editora Nacional, 1977.

Resumen de la Historia de Melilla. Melilla, 1978.

Patronato Municipal de Turismo. *Ceuta—La España Inédita*. Madrid, 1988.

Pélissier, R. *Los Territorios Españoles de Africa*. Madrid, 1964.

Tello Amondareyn, M. *Ceuta: Llave principal del estrecho*. Ceuta, Instituto de Estudios Ceutíes, 1994.

SYRIA

Physical and Social Geography

W. B. FISHER

Before 1918 the term 'Syria' was rather loosely applied to the whole of the territory now forming the modern states of Syria, Lebanon, Israel and Jordan. To the Ottomans, as to the Romans, Syria stretched from the Euphrates to the Mediterranean, and from the Sinai to the hills of southern Turkey, with Palestine as a smaller province of this wider unit. Although the present Syrian Arab Republic has a much more limited extension, covering 185,180 sq km (71,498 sq miles), some present-day Syrians refer from time to time to a 'Greater Syria' as a desirable but possibly remote aspiration. None the less, there is evidence of the attachment to the idea of a 'Greater Syria' in current Syrian policy towards Israel and, especially, Lebanon.

The frontiers of the present-day state are largely artificial, and reflect to a considerable extent the interests and prestige of outside powers—Britain, France and the USA—as these existed in 1918–20. The northern frontier with Turkey is defined by a single-track railway line running along the southern edge of the foothills—probably the only case of its kind in the world; while eastwards and southwards boundaries are highly arbitrary, being straight lines drawn for convenience between salient points. Westwards, the frontiers are again artificial, although less crudely drawn, leaving the headwaters of the Jordan river outside Syria and following the crest of the Anti-Lebanon hills, to reach the sea north of Tripoli.

PHYSICAL FEATURES

Geographically, Syria consists of two main zones: a fairly narrow western part, made up of a complex of mountain ranges and intervening valleys; and a much larger eastern zone that is essentially a broad and open platform dropping gently towards the east and crossed diagonally by the wide valley of the Euphrates river.

The western zone, which contains over 80% of the population of Syria, can be further subdivided as follows. In the extreme west, fronting the Mediterranean Sea, there lies an imposing ridge rising to 1,500 m above sea-level, and known as the Jebel Ansariyeh. Its western flank drops fairly gradually to the sea, giving a narrow coastal plain; but on the east it falls very sharply, almost as a wall, to a flat-bottomed valley occupied by the Orontes river, which meanders sluggishly over the flat floor, often flooding in winter, and leaving a formerly malarial marsh in summer. Further east lie more hill ranges, opening out like a fan from the south-west, where the Anti-Lebanon range, with Mount Hermon (2,814 m), is the highest in Syria. Along the eastern flanks of the various ridges lie a number of shallow basins occupied by small streams that eventually dry up or form closed salt lakes. In one basin lies the city of Aleppo, once the second town of the Ottoman Empire and now the largest city of Syria. In another is situated Damascus, irrigated from five streams and famous for its clear fountains and gardens—now the capital of the country. One remaining sub-region of western Syria is the Jebel Druse, which lies in the extreme south-west, and consists of a vast outpouring of lava, in the form of sheets and cones. Towards the west this region is fertile, and produces good cereal crops, but eastwards the soil cover disappears, leaving a barren countryside of twisted lava and caverns. Owing to its difficulty and isolation, the Jebel Druse has tended socially and politically to act independently, remaining aloof from the rest of the country.

The entire eastern zone is mainly steppe or open desert, except close to the banks of the Euphrates, the Tigris and their larger tributaries, where recent irrigation projects have allowed considerable cultivation on an increasing scale. The triangularly-shaped region between the Euphrates and Tigris rivers is spoken of as the Jezireh (jazira, island), but is in no way different from the remaining parts of the east.

The presence of ranks of relatively high hills aligned parallel to the coast has important climatic effects. Tempering and humid effects from the Mediterranean are restricted to a narrow western belt, and central and eastern Syria show marked continental tendencies: that is, a very hot summer with temperatures often above 38°C (100°F) or even 43°C, and a moderately cold winter, with frost on many nights. Very close to the Mediterranean, frost is unknown at any season, but on the hills altitude greatly reduces the average temperature, so that snow may lie on the heights from late December to April, or even May. Rainfall is fairly abundant in the west, where the height of the land tends to determine the amount received; but east of the Anti-Lebanon mountains the amount decreases considerably, producing a steppe region that quickly passes into true desert. On the extreme east, as the Zagros ranges of Persia are approached, there is once again a slight increase, but most of Syria has an annual rainfall of less than 250 mm.

ECONOMIC LIFE

There is a close relationship between climate and economic activities. In the west, where up to 750 mm or even 1,000 mm of rainfall occur, settled farming is possible, and the main limitation is difficult terrain. From the Orontes valley eastwards, however, natural rainfall is increasingly inadequate, and irrigation becomes necessary. The narrow band of territory where annual rainfall lies between 200 mm and 380 mm is sometimes spoken of as the 'Fertile Crescent', since it runs in an arc along the inner side of the hills from Jordan through western and northern Syria as far east as Iraq. In its normal state a steppeland covered with seasonal grass, the Fertile Crescent can often be converted by irrigation and efficient organization into a rich and productive territory. Such it was in the golden days of the Arab caliphate; now, after centuries of decline, it has been revived. From the 1950s onwards, a marked change was seen and, initially because of small-scale irrigation schemes and the installation of motor pumps to raise water from underground artesian sources, large areas of the former steppe began to produce cotton, cereals and fruit. Syria used to have a surplus of agricultural production, especially cereals, to export to Jordan and Lebanon, neither of which are self-sufficient in foodstuffs. It was expected that production would increase with the eventual doubling of Syria's irrigated area (by 640,000 ha) as the Euphrates Dam at Tabqa developed fully. However, only about 60,000 ha had been irrigated by 1988; difficulties have been experienced in irrigating part of the designated area and some experts believe that perhaps 300,000 ha may be impossible to develop according to the original plans. Over the last few years, production of cereals and cotton has declined, partly owing to lack of technical and management skills, and partly to drought. High military expenditure has also reduced available development funds.

As a result of its relative openness and accessibility and its geographical situation as a 'waist' between the Mediterranean and the Persian (Arabian) Gulf, Syria has been a land of passage, and for centuries its role was that of an intermediary, both commercial and cultural, between the Mediterranean world and the Far East. From early times until the end of the Middle Ages there was a flow of traffic east and west that raised a number of Syrian cities and ports to the rank of international markets. Since the 1930s, following a long period of decline and eclipse resulting from the diversion of this trade to the sea, there has been a revival of activity, owing to the new elements of air transport and the construction of oil pipelines from Iraq.

In addition, Syria was able to develop its own deposits of petroleum and phosphate; and its greatly improved political standing (as, temporarily at least, the successor of Egypt as the leading politically activist Arab state) brought economic benefits. The Syrian economy became stronger, and the country was able to 'balance' between the Soviet and Western political groups, although the cost of wars and internal political uncertainties eroded some development gains. After 1981, however, Syria became more isolated from its Arab neighbours, and the policy of balance, both in external and internal affairs, was less successful. In response to the collapse of communism in Eastern Europe and the diminution of Soviet influence, Syria's foreign policy has remained, above all, pragmatic. This was clearly illustrated by the country's allying itself with the Western powers and the 'moderate' Arab states against Iraq in 1990/91, in return for diplomatic and economic gains.

RACE AND LANGUAGE

Racially, many elements can be distinguished in the Syrian people. The nomads of the interior deserts are unusually pure specimens of the Mediterranean type, isolation having preserved them from intermixture. To the west and north there is a widely varying mosaic of other groups: the Kurds and Turkish-speaking communities of the north, and the Armenians, who form communities in the cities; groups such as the Druzes, who show some affinity to the tribes of the Persian Zagros, and many others.

As a result, there is a surprising variety of language and religion. Arabic is spoken over most of the country, but Kurdish is widely used along the northern frontier and Armenian in the cities. Aramaic, the language of Christ, survives in three villages.

History

Revised for this edition by JON LUNN

ANCIENT HISTORY

From the earliest times, Syria has experienced successive waves of Semitic immigration—the Canaanites and Phoenicians in the third millennium BC, the Hebrews and Aramaeans in the second, and, unceasingly, the nomad tribes infiltrating from the Arabian peninsula. This process has enabled Syria to assimilate or reject, without losing its essentially Semitic character, the alien invaders who, time and again, in the course of a long history, have established their domination over the land. Before Rome assumed control of Syria in the first century BC, the Egyptians, the Assyrians and the Hittites, and, later, the Persians and the Macedonian Greeks had all left their mark to a greater or lesser degree. Damascus is claimed to be the oldest capital city in the world, having been continuously inhabited since about 2000 BC, and Aleppo may be even older. Under Roman rule the infiltration and settlement of nomad elements continued, almost unnoticed by historians, save when along the desert trade routes a Semitic vassal state attained a brief importance as, for example, the kingdom of Palmyra in the Syrian desert, which the Emperor Aurelian destroyed in AD 272 or, later still, when the Byzantines ruled in Syria, the Arab state of Ghassan, prominent throughout the sixth century AD as a bulwark of the Byzantine Empire against the desert tribes in the service of Sasanid Persia.

ARAB AND TURKISH RULE

When, after the death of the Prophet Muhammad in AD 632, the newly-created power of Islam began a career of conquest, the populations of Syria, Semitic in their language and culture and, as adherents of the Monophysite faith, ill-disposed towards the Greek-speaking Orthodox Byzantines, did little to oppose the Muslims, from whom they hoped to obtain a greater measure of freedom. The Muslims defeated the Byzantine forces at Ajnadain in 634, seized Damascus in 635, and, by their decisive victory on the Yarmouk river (636), virtually secured possession of all Syria. From 661 to 750 the Umayyad dynasty ruled in Syria, which, after the conquest, had been divided into four military districts or junds (Damascus, Homs, Urdun, i.e. Jordan, and Palestine). To these the Caliph Yazid I (680–83) added a fifth, Kinnasrin, for the defence of northern Syria, where in the late seventh century, the Mardaites, Christians from the Taurus, were making serious inroads under Byzantine leadership. Under Abd al-Malik (685–705), Arabic became the official language of the state, in whose administration, hitherto largely carried out by the old Byzantine bureaucracy, Syrians, Muslim as well as Christian, now had an increasing share. For Syria was now the heart of a great Empire, and the Arab army of Syria, well trained in the ceaseless frontier warfare with Byzantium, bore the main burden of imperial rule, taking a major part in the two great Arab assaults on Byzantium in 674–78 and in 717–18.

The new regime in Syria was pre-eminently military and fiscal in character, representing the domination of a military caste of Muslim Arab warriors, who governed on the basic assumption that a large subject population, non-Muslim and non-Arab in character, would continue indefinitely to pay tribute. But this assumption was falsified by the gradual spread of Islam, a process which meant the progressive diminution of the amount of tribute paid to the state, and the consequent undermining of the fiscal system as a whole. In theory, conversion meant for the non-Arab convert (*mawla*; in the plural, *mawali*) full social and economic equality with the ruling caste, but in practice it was not enough to be a Muslim, one had to be an Arab as well. The discontent of the *mawali* with their enforced inferiority expressed itself in an appeal to the universal character of Islam, an appeal which often took the form of religious heresies, and which, as it became more widespread, undermined the strength of the Arab regime.

To the ever-present fiscal problems of the Arab state and the growing discontent of the *mawali* was added a third and fatal weakness: the hostility between those Arab tribes that had arrived in Syria with or since the conquest, and those which had infiltrated there at an earlier date. The Umayyad house strove to maintain a neutral position over and above the tribal feuds; but from the moment when, under the pressure of events, the Umayyads were compelled to side with one faction to oppose the other (Battle of Marj Rahit, 684), their position was irretrievably compromised.

When in AD 750, with the accession of the Abbasid dynasty, the centre of the Empire was transferred to Iraq, Syria, jealously watched because of its association with the former ruling house, became a mere province, where in the course of the next hundred years, several abortive revolts, inspired in part by the traditional loyalty to the Umayyads, failed to shake off Abbasid control. During the ninth century Syria was the object of dispute between Egypt and Baghdad. In 878 Ahmad ibn Tulun, Governor of Egypt, occupied it and, subsequently, every independent ruler of Egypt sought to maintain a hold, partial or complete, over Syria. Local dynasties, however, achieved from time to time a transitory importance, as did the Hamdanids (a Bedouin family from northern Iraq) who, under Saif ad-Daula, ruler of Aleppo from 946–967, attained a brief ascendancy, marked internally by financial and administrative ineptitude, and externally by military campaigns against the Byzantines which did much to provoke the great Byzantine reconquest of the late 10th century. By the treaty of 997, northern Syria became Byzantine, while the rest of the country remained in the hands of the Fatimid dynasty which ruled in Egypt from 969. Fatimid control remained insecure and from about 1027 a new Arab house ruled at Aleppo—the Mirdasids, who were soon to disappear before the formidable power of the Seljuq Turks. The Seljuqs, having conquered Persia, rapidly overran Syria (Damascus fell to them in 1075) but failed to establish there a united state. As a result of dynastic quarrels, the Seljuq domination disintegrated into a number of amirates: Seljuq princes ruled at Aleppo and

Damascus, a local dynasty held Tripoli and, in the south, Egypt controlled most of the littoral.

This political fragmentation greatly favoured the success of the First Crusade which, taking Antioch in 1098 and Jerusalem in 1099, proceeded to organize four feudal states at Edessa, Antioch, Tripoli and Jerusalem, but did not succeed in conquering Aleppo, Homs, Hama, and Damascus. From the death of Baldwin II of Jerusalem in 1131, the essential weakness of the crusading states began to appear. Byzantium, the Christian state of Lesser Armenia, and the Latin principalities in Syria never united in a successful resistance to the Muslim counteroffensive which, initiated by the Turkish general Zangi Atabeg of Mosul, developed rapidly in the third and fourth decades of the century. Zangi, who seized Aleppo in 1128, and the Latin state of Edessa in 1144, was succeeded in 1146 by his able son Nur ad-Din, who by his capture of Damascus in 1154 recreated in Syria a united Muslim power. On Nur ad-Din's death in 1174, the Kurd Saladin, already master of Egypt, assumed control of Damascus and, in 1183, seized Aleppo. His victory over the Crusaders at Hattin (July 1187) destroyed the kingdom of Jerusalem. Only the partial success of the Third Crusade (1189–92) and, after his death in 1193, the disintegration of Saladin's empire into a number of separate principalities, made it possible for the Crusaders to maintain an ever more precarious hold on the coastal area of Syria. The emergence in Egypt of the powerful Mamluk sultanate (1250) meant that the end was near. A series of military campaigns, led by the Sultan Baibars (1260–77) and his immediate successors, brought about the fall of Antioch (1268) and Tripoli (1289), and, with the fall of Acre in 1291, the disappearance of the crusading states in Syria.

Before the last crusading states had been reduced, the Mamluks had to encounter a determined assault by the Mongols until, in 1260, the Mongol army of invasion was crushed at the Battle of Ain-Jalut, near Nazareth. The Mongol Il-Khans of Persia made further efforts to conquer Syria in the late 13th century, negotiating for this purpose with the papacy, the remaining crusader states, and Lesser Armenia. In 1280 the Mamluks defeated a Mongol army at Homs; but in 1299 were themselves beaten near the same town, a defeat which enabled the Mongols to ravage northern Syria and to take Damascus in 1300. Only in 1303, at the Battle of Marj as-Suffar, south of Damascus, was this last Mongol offensive finally repelled.

The period of Mamluk rule in Syria, which endured until 1517, was on the whole one of slow decline. Warfare, periodic famine, and not least, plague (there were four great outbreaks in the 14th century, and in the 15th century 14 more recorded attacks of some severity) produced a state of affairs which the financial rapacity and misrule of the Mamluk governors and the devastation of Aleppo and Damascus by Timur (1400–01) served only to aggravate.

The ill-defined protectorate which the Mamluks asserted over Cilicia and considerable areas of southern Anatolia occasioned, in the late 15th century, a growing tension with the power of the Ottoman Turks, which broke out into inconclusive warfare in the years 1485–91. When to this tension was added the possibility of an alliance between the Mamluks and the rising power of the Safavids in Persia, the Ottoman Sultan Selim I (1512–20) was compelled to seek a decisive solution to the problem. In August 1516 the battle of Marj Dabik, north of Aleppo, gave Syria to the Ottomans, who proceeded to ensure their continued hold on the land by conquering Egypt (1517). Turkish rule, during the next three centuries, although unjustly accused of complete responsibility for a decay and stagnation which appear to have been well advanced before 1517, brought only a temporary improvement in the unhappy condition of Syria, now divided into the three provinces of Damascus, Tripoli, and Aleppo. In parts of Syria the Turkish pashas in reality administered directly only the important towns and their immediate neighbourhood; elsewhere, the older elements such as Bedouin emirs and Turcoman chiefs were left to act much as they pleased, provided the due tribute was paid. The pashas normally bought their appointment to high office and sought in their brief tenure of power to recover the money and bribes they had expended in securing it, knowing that they might at any moment be replaced by someone who could pay more for the post. Damascus alone had 133 pashas in 180 years. As the control of the Sultan at Constantinople became weaker, the pashas obtained greater freedom of action, until Ahmad Jazzar, Pasha of Acre, virtually ruled Syria as an independent prince (1785–1804).

The 19th century saw important changes. The Ottoman Sultan Mahmoud II (1808–39) had promised Syria to the Pasha of Egypt, Muhammad Ali, in return for the latter's services during the Greek War of Independence. When the Sultan declined to fulfil his promise, Egyptian troops overran Syria (1831–33). Ibrahim Pasha, son of Muhammad Ali, now gave to Syria, for the first time in centuries, a centralized government strong enough to hold separatist tendencies in check and to impose a system of taxation which, if burdensome, was at least regular in its functioning. But Ibrahim's rule was not popular, for the land-owners resented his efforts to limit their social and political dominance, while the peasantry disliked the conscription, the forced labour, and the heavy taxation which he found indispensable for the maintenance of his regime. In 1840 a revolt broke out in Syria, and when the Great Powers intervened on behalf of the Sultan (at war with Egypt since 1839), Muhammad Ali was compelled to renounce his claim to rule there.

Western influence, working through trade, through the protection of religious minorities, and through the cultural and educational efforts of missions and schools, had received encouragement from Ibrahim Pasha. The French Jesuits, returning to Syria in 1831, opened schools, and in 1875 founded their University at Beirut. The American Presbyterian Mission (established at Beirut in 1820) introduced a printing press in 1834, and in 1866 founded the Syrian Protestant College, later renamed the American University of Beirut. Syria also received some benefit from the reform movement within the Ottoman Empire, which, begun by Mahmoud II, and continued under his successors, took the form of a determined attempt to modernize the structure of the Empire. The semi-independent pashas of old disappeared, the administration being now entrusted to salaried officials of the central Government; some effort was made to create schools and colleges on Western lines, and much was done to deprive the landowning classes of their feudal privileges, although their social and economic predominance was left unchallenged. As a result of these improvements, there was, in the late 19th century, a revival of Arabic literature which did much to prepare the way for the growth of Arab nationalism in the 20th century.

MODERN HISTORY

By 1914 Arab nationalist sentiment had made some headway among the educated and professional classes, and especially among army officers. Nationalist societies like al-Fatat soon made contact with Arab nationalists outside Syria—with the army officers of Iraq, with influential Syrian colonies in Egypt and America, and with the Sharif Husain of Mecca. The McMahon Correspondence (July 1915–March 1916—see Documents on Palestine, p. 50) encouraged the Arab nationalists to hope that the end of the First World War (1914–18) would mean the creation of a greater Arab kingdom. This expectation was disappointed, for as a result of the Sykes-Picot Agreement, negotiated in secret between England, France, and Russia in 1916 (see Documents on Palestine, p. 50), Syria was to become a French sphere of influence. At the end of the war, and in accordance with this agreement, a provisional French administration was established in the coastal districts of Syria, while in the interior an Arab government came into being under Amir Faisal, son of the Sharif Husain of Mecca. In March 1920 the Syrian nationalists proclaimed an independent kingdom of Greater Syria (including Lebanon and Palestine); but in April of the same year the San Remo Conference gave France a mandate for the whole of Syria, and in July, French troops occupied Damascus.

By 1925 the French, aware that the majority of the Muslim population resented their rule, and that only among the Christian Maronites of the Lebanon could they hope to find support, had carried into effect a policy based upon the religious divisions so strong in Syria. The area under mandate had been divided into four distinct units; a much enlarged Lebanon (including Beirut and Tripoli), a Syrian Republic, and the two districts of Latakia and Jebel Druse. Despite the fact that the French rule gave Syria a degree of law and order which might have rendered possible the transition from a medieval to a more modern form of society, nationalist sentiment opposed the mandate on principle, and deplored the failure to introduce full representative institutions and the tendency to encourage separatism amongst the religious minorities. This discontent, especially strong in the Syrian Republic, became open revolt in 1925–26, during the course of which the French twice bombarded Damascus.

The next 10 years were marked by a hesitant and often interrupted progress towards self-government in Syria, and by French efforts to conclude a Franco-Syrian treaty. In April 1928 elections were held for a Constituent Assembly, and in August a draft Constitution was completed; but the French High Commissioner refused to accept certain articles, especially Article 2, which, declaring the Syrian territories detached from the old Ottoman Empire to be an indivisible unity, constituted a denial of the separate existence of the Jebel Druse, Latakia, and the Lebanese Republic. After repeated attempts to reach a compromise, the High Commissioner dissolved the Assembly in May 1930 and, on his own authority, issued a new Constitution for the State of Syria, much the same as that formerly proposed by the Assembly, but with those modifications which were considered indispensable to the maintenance of French control. After new elections to a Chamber of Deputies (January 1932), negotiations were begun for a Franco-Syrian treaty, to be modelled on that concluded between the United Kingdom and Iraq in 1930, but no compromise could be found between the French demands and those of the nationalists who, although in a minority, wielded a dominant influence in the Chamber and whose aim was to limit both in time and in place the French military occupation, and to include in Syria the separate areas of Jebel Druse and Latakia. In 1934 the High Commissioner suspended the Chamber indefinitely. Disorders occurred early in 1936 which induced the French to send a Syrian delegation to Paris, where the new Popular Front Government showed itself more sympathetic towards Syrian aspirations than former French governments had been. In September 1936 a Franco-Syrian treaty was signed which recognized the principle of Syrian independence and stipulated that, after ratification, there should be a period of three years during which the apparatus of a fully independent state should be created. The districts of Jebel Druse and Latakia would be annexed to Syria, but would retain special administrations. Other subsidiary agreements reserved to France important military and economic rights in Syria. It seemed that Syria might now enter a period of rapid political development; but the unrest caused by the situation in Palestine, the crisis with Turkey, and the failure of France to ratify the 1936 treaty were responsible, within two years, for the breakdown of these hopes.

In 1921 Turkey had consented to the inclusion of the Sanjak of Alexandretta in the French mandated territories, on condition that it should be governed under a special regime. The Turks, alarmed by the treaty of 1936, which envisaged the emergence of a unitary Syrian state including, to all appearance, Alexandretta, now pressed for a separate agreement concerning the status of the Sanjak. After long discussion the League of Nations decided in 1937 that the Sanjak should be fully autonomous, save for its foreign and financial policies which were to be under the control of the Syrian Government. A treaty between France and Turkey guaranteed the integrity of the Sanjak, and also the Turco-Syrian frontier. Throughout 1937 there were conflicts between Turks and Arabs in the Sanjak, and in Syria a widespread and growing resentment, for it was clear that sooner or later Turkey would ask for the cession of Alexandretta. The problem came to be regarded in Syria as a test of Franco-Syrian co-operation, and when, in June 1939, under the pressure of international tension, Alexandretta was finally ceded to Turkey, the cession assumed in the eyes of Syrian nationalists the character of a betrayal by France. Meanwhile, in France itself, opposition to the treaty of 1936 had grown steadily; and in December 1938 the French Government, anxious not to weaken its military position in the Near East, declared that no ratification of the treaty was to be expected.

Unrest in Syria led to open riots in 1941, as a result of which the Vichy High Commissioner, Gen. Dentz, promised the restoration of partial self-government; while in June of the same year, when in order to counter Axis strategy the Allies invaded Syria, Gen. Catroux, on behalf of the Free French Government, promised independence for Syria and the end of mandatory rule. Syrian independence was formally recognized in September 1941, but the reality of power was still withheld, with the effect that nationalist agitation, inflamed by French reluctance to restore constitutional rule and by economic difficulties owing to the war, became even more pronounced. When at last elections were held once more, a nationalist Government was formed, with Shukri al-Kuwatli as President of the Syrian Republic (August 1943).

Gradually all important powers and public services were transferred from French to Syrian hands; but conflict again developed over the Troupes Spéciales, the local Syrian and Lebanese levies which had existed throughout the mandatory period as an integral part of the French military forces in the Levant, and which, transferred to the Syrian and Lebanese Governments, would enable them to form their own armies. Strongly supported by the newly-created League of Arab States (the Arab League), Syria refused the French demand for a Franco-Syrian Treaty as the condition for the final transfer of administrative and military services which had always been the main instruments of French policy. In May 1945 disturbances broke out which ended only with British armed intervention and the evacuation of French troops and administrative personnel. The Troupes Spéciales were now handed over to the Syrian Government, and with the departure of British forces in April 1946 the full independence of Syria was achieved.

UNSTABLE INDEPENDENCE

After the attainment of independence Syria experienced a long period of instability. Syria found itself aligned at this time with Egypt and Saudi Arabia against the ambitions of the Hashemite rulers of Iraq and Jordan. These rivalries, together with the profound disappointment felt in Damascus over the Arab failures in the war of 1948–49 against Israel, were the prelude to three *coups d'état* in 1949. Dislike of continued financial dependence on France, aspirations towards a greater Syria, the resentments arising out of the unsuccessful war against the Israelis—all help to explain the unrest inside Syria.

The intervention of the army in politics was itself a cause of further tension. Growing opposition in the Syrian Chamber of Deputies to the army's dominance resulted in yet another *coup d'état* in December 1951. Syria now came under the control of a military autocracy with Col Shishakli as head of state. The Chamber of Deputies was dissolved in December 1951; a decree of April 1952 abolished all political parties in Syria. After the approval of a new Constitution in July 1953 Shishakli became President of Syria in August of that year. The formation of political parties was now allowed once more. Members of the parties dissolved under the decree of April 1952 proceeded, however, to boycott the elections held in October 1953, at which President Shishakli's Movement of Arab Liberation obtained a large majority in the Chamber of Deputies. Politicians hostile to the regime of President Shishakli established in November a Front of National Opposition, refusing to accept as legal the results of the October elections and declaring as their avowed aim the end of military autocracy and the restoration of democratic rule. Demonstrations in Damascus and Aleppo in December led soon to the flight of Shishakli to France. The collapse of his regime early in 1954 meant for Syria a return to the Constitution of 1950. New elections held in September 1954 brought into being a Chamber of Deputies notable for the large number of its members (81 out of 142) who might be regarded as independents grouped around leading political figures.

INFLUENCE FROM ABROAD

There was still, however, much friction in Syria between those who favoured union or at least close co-operation with Iraq and those inclined towards an effective *entente* with Egypt. In August 1955 Shukri al-Kuwatli became President of the Republic. His appointment was interpreted as an indication that pro-Egyptian influence had won the ascendancy in Syria. On 20 October 1955 Syria made with Egypt an agreement for the creation of a joint military command with its headquarters at Damascus.

The USSR, meanwhile, in answer to the developments in the Middle East associated with the Baghdad Pact, had begun an intensive diplomatic, propaganda and economic campaign of penetration into the region. In the years 1954–56 Syria, the only Arab state where the Communist Party was legal, made a number of barter agreements with the USSR and its associates in Eastern Europe. A report from Cairo intimated, in February 1956, that Syria had joined Egypt in acquiring arms from the USSR.

At the end of October 1956 there occurred the Israeli campaign in the Sinai peninsula, an event followed, in the first days of November, by the armed intervention of the United Kingdom and France in the Suez Canal region. On 30 October the Syrian President left Damascus on a visit to the USSR. A state of emergency was declared in Syria. Reports from Lebanon revealed on 3 November that Syrian forces had disabled the pipelines carrying Iraqi oil to the Mediterranean. The damage that Syrian elements had done to the pipelines earned the sharp disapproval of such Arab states as Iraq and Saudi Arabia, both of whom were now faced with a severe loss of oil revenues. The Syrian Government declared that it would not allow the repair of the pipelines until Israel had withdrawn its troops from Gaza and the Gulf of Aqaba. Not until March 1957 was it possible to restore the pipelines, Israel having in the mean time agreed to evacuate its forces from the areas in dispute.

UNION WITH EGYPT

The Syrian National Assembly, in November 1957, passed a resolution in favour of union with Egypt. The formal union of Egypt and Syria to constitute one state under the title of the United Arab Republic (UAR) received the final approval of the Syrian National Assembly on 5 February 1958. President Gamal Abd an-Nasser of Egypt, on 21 February, became the first head of the combined state. A central Cabinet for the UAR was established in October 1958, also two regional executive councils, one for Syria and one for Egypt. A further move towards integration came in March 1960, when a single National Assembly for the whole of the UAR, consisting of 400 deputies from Egypt and 200 from Syria, was instituted.

Syrian dissatisfaction with the union grew over the next three years, as administrators and officials of Egyptian origin came to hold influential positions in the Syrian Region, and on 28 September 1961 there occurred in Syria a military *coup d'état* which aimed—successfully—at the separation of Syria from Egypt and at the dissolution of the UAR. President Nasser recognized the *fait accompli*. Most foreign states swiftly granted formal recognition to the Government in Damascus. On 13 October Syria again became a member of the UN. A provisional Constitution was promulgated in November and elections for a Constituent Assembly took place on 1 December 1961.

The regime thus established in Syria rested on no sure foundation. At the end of March 1962 the Syrian army intervened once more, bringing about the resignation of Dr Nazim Kudsi, the President of the Republic, and also of the ministers who had taken office in December 1961. After demonstrations at Aleppo, Homs and Hama in April 1962, Dr Kudsi was reinstated as President, but further ministerial resignations in May pointed to the existence of continuing tensions within the Government.

THE REVOLUTION OF 1963

A military junta, styled the National Council of the Revolutionary Command, seized control in Damascus on 8 March 1963. In May the Baathists (members of the Arab nationalist socialist party) took measures to purge the armed forces and the administration of personnel known to favour a close alignment with Egypt. A new Government, formed on 13 May and strongly Baathist in character, carried out a further purge in June and at the same time created a National Guard recruited from members of the Baath movement. These measures led the pro-Egyptian elements to attempt a *coup d'état* at Damascus on 18 July 1963. The attempt failed, however, with considerable loss of life. On 27 July Maj-Gen. Amin al-Hafiz, Deputy Prime Minister and Minister of the Interior, became President of the National Council of the Revolutionary Command, a position equivalent to head of state.

BAATH SOCIALISM

The nationalization of all Arab-owned banks in 1963, and of various industrial enterprises, also the transfer of land to the peasants—all had contributed to bring about much dissatisfaction in the business world and among the influential landed elements. The Baath regime depended for its main support on the armed forces which had, however, been recruited in no small degree from the religious minorities in Syria, including adherents of the Alawi faith (a schism of the Shi'ite branch of Islam)—most Syrians being, in fact, of Sunni or orthodox Muslim allegiance. In general, conservative Muslims tended to oppose the Baath Government under guidance of the *'ulama* (scholars/lawyers) and of the Muslim Brotherhood. The mass of the peasant population was thought to have some pro-Nasser sympathies; the small working class was divided between pro-Nasser and Baathist adherents; the middle and upper classes opposed the domination of al-Baath. The unease arising out of these frictions and antipathies took the form of disturbances and finally of open revolt—soon suppressed—at Hama (April 1964).

On 25 April 1964 a provisional Constitution had been promulgated, describing Syria as a democratic socialist republic forming an integral part of the Arab nation. A Presidential Council was established on 14 May 1964, with Gen. Hafiz as Head of the State.

The as yet undeveloped petroleum and other mineral resources of Syria were nationalized in 1964, together with other industrial concerns. On 7 January 1965 a special military court was created with wide powers to deal with all offences, of word or deed, against the nationalization decrees and the socialist revolution.

A National Council, almost 100 strong, was established in August 1965 with the task of preparing a new constitution which would be submitted to a public referendum. Meeting for the first time on 1 September 1965, it created a Presidential Council, of five members, which was to exercise the powers of a head of state.

RADICAL REACTION

The tensions hitherto visible in al-Baath were, however, still active. Two groups stood ranged one against the other—on the one hand the older, more experienced politicians in al-Baath, less inclined than in former years to insist on the unrestrained pursuit of the main Baathist objectives, socialism and Pan-Arab union, and, on the other hand, the extreme left-wing elements, doctrinaire in their attitude and enjoying considerable support amongst the younger radical officers in the armed forces.

The tensions thus engendered found expression in a new *coup d'état* on 23 February 1966. A military junta representing the extreme radical elements in al-Baath seized power in Damascus and placed under arrest a number of personalities long identified with al-Baath and belonging to the international leadership controlling the organization throughout the Arab world—among them Michel Aflaq, the founder of al-Baath; Gen. Hafiz, the Chairman of the recently established Presidential Council; and Salah ad-Din Bitar, the Prime Minister of the displaced administration.

ARAB–ISRAELI WAR OF 1967

The friction ever present along the frontier between Syria and Israel had provoked violent conflict from time to time during recent years, particularly in the region of Lake Tiberias. Now, in the winter of 1966–67, the tension along the border began to assume more serious proportions. Israel, in October 1966, protested to the UN Security Council about guerrilla activities from Syria across the frontier into Israeli territory. In April 1967 mortars, cannon and air force units from Syria and Israel were involved in fighting south-east of Lake Tiberias.

The continuing tension on the Syrian-Israeli frontier was now to become a major influence leading to the war that broke out on 5 June 1967 between Israel and its Arab neighbours Egypt, Syria and Jordan. During the course of hostilities, which lasted six days, Israel defeated Egypt and Jordan and then, after some stubborn fighting, outflanked and overran the Syrian positions on the hills above Lake Tiberias. With the breakthrough accomplished, Israeli forces made a rapid advance and occupied the town of Quneitra about 65 km from Damascus. On 10 June Israel and Syria announced their formal acceptance of the UN proposal for a cease-fire; however, Syria effectively boycotted the Arab summit conference held at Khartoum in August 1967, and in September the Baath Party of Syria rejected all idea of a compromise with Israel. A resolution adopted by the UN Security Council in November, urging the withdrawal of the Israelis from the lands occupied by them during the June war and the ending of the belligerency which the Arab Governments had until then maintained against Israel, was rejected by Syria, which alone maintained its commitment to a reunified Palestine.

STRUGGLE FOR POWER 1968–71

The ruling Baath Party had for some years been divided into two main factions. Until October 1968 the dominant faction had been the 'progressive' group led by Dr Atassi and Dr Makhous, the premier and foreign minister respectively. This group was distinguished by its doctrinaire and Marxist-orientated public pronouncements and by the strong support it received from the USSR. It held that the creation of a strong one-party state and economy along neo-Marxist lines was of paramount importance, overriding even the need for a militant stand towards Israel and for Arab unity.

By October 1968 the Government felt particularly insecure, partly owing to a feud with the new Baath regime in Iraq, and at the end of the month a new Cabinet was formed including several members of the opposing 'nationalist' faction. This group took less interest in ideological questions and favoured a pragmatic approach to the economy, improved relations with Syria's Arab neighbours and full participation in the campaign against Israel, including support for the *fedayin* movement. Its leader was Lt-Gen. Hafiz al-Assad, who assumed control of the all-important Ministry of Defence. His critical attitude to the powerful Soviet influence on the Government led to a prolonged struggle with the 'progressive' leadership. Cabinet reshuffles took place in March and May, but both Dr Atassi and Gen. Assad retained their positions. During the spring of 1969 a number of communists were arrested or sent into exile, and the leader of the Syrian Communist Party, still technically an illegal organization, flew to Moscow.

General Assad attempted to take over the Government in February 1969 but was forestalled by Soviet threats that if he did so all military supplies, economic and technical aid, and trade agreements would end. This would have caused a major disruption to the national economy and the armed forces, and the 'nationalists' were obliged to yield. In May Gen. Mustafa Tlass, the Chief of Staff of the army and Gen. Assad's principal assistant, led a military delegation to the People's Republic of China to negotiate the purchase of military equipment. The incident indicated a new independence from Moscow. Some observers also saw this independence in the creation of a joint military command with Iraq (with whom relations improved during the spring) and Jordan. Relations with Lebanon worsened, owing to Syria's support of the Lebanese *fedayin* movement, containing many Syrian members. During 1968–70 this appeared to direct much of its activity towards bringing down the precarious Lebanese Government, presumably in the hope that a more militantly anti-Israel ministry would take power.

In November 1970, following a reported coup attempt backed by Iraq in August, the struggle between the two factions of the Baath Party culminated in Gen. Assad's seizure of power. Dr Atassi, who was in hospital at the time, was placed under guard and a retired general, Salah Jadid, Assistant Secretary-General of the Baath Party and leader of the civilian faction, was arrested. Other members of the civilian wing were arrested or fled to Lebanon. The coup was precipitated by attempts by Jadid and his supporters to oust Assad and Tlass from their posts. This power struggle had become acute as a result of differences over support for the Palestine guerrillas during the fighting with the Jordanian army in September. Jadid and Yousuf Zeayen, a former Prime Minister, controlled the movement of tanks from Syria into Jordan to support the Palestinian guerrillas' efforts against the Jordanian army; this was opposed by Assad and the military faction. Their approach to the Palestinian problem was more akin to Nasser's and they wanted to avoid giving any provocation to Israel, because they considered the Syrian armed forces to be unready to offer adequate resistance.

ASSAD IN POWER

There was no obvious opposition to the military *coup d'état*. Ahmad Khatib became acting President and Gen. Assad Prime Minister and Secretary-General of the Baath Party. A new

Regional Command of the party was formed. Following amendments to the 1969 provisional Constitution in February 1971, Gen. Assad was elected President for a seven-year term in March. In the following month Maj.-Gen. Abd ar-Rahman Khlefawi became Premier and Mahmoud al-Ayoubi was appointed Vice-President. In February the first legislative body in Syria since 1966, the People's Assembly, was formed. Of its 173 members, 87 represented the Baath Party.

The Nasserite leanings of the new regime in foreign policy soon became apparent. Although Syria continued to reject the November 1967 UN Security Council Resolution (No. 242), relations with the UAR and Jordan improved, and Syria's isolation in the Arab world was soon reduced. Syria's willingness to join a union with the UAR, Sudan and Libya almost immediately became apparent and agreement on federation with Libya and the UAR was reached in April 1971, but the Federation had little effect.

After coming to power, the Assad regime increased the Syrian army's control over the Palestinian guerrilla group as-Saiqa (Vanguard of the Popular Liberation War). In April 1971 guerrilla operations against Israeli positions from the Syrian front were banned by the Government. Then, at the beginning of July, some guerrilla units were forced out of Syria into southern Lebanon, and arms destined for them and arriving from Algeria were seized by the Syrian authorities. Yet, after the Jordanian Government's final onslaught on the Palestinian guerrillas in northern Jordan in July, Syria closed its border and in August severed diplomatic relations. Egyptian mediation reduced the chances of a more serious conflict developing, but diplomatic links remained severed with Jordan until October 1973. Relations with the USSR improved during the last half of 1971 and in 1972, and in May Marshal Andrei Grechko, the Soviet Minister of Defence, visited Damascus. However, Syria was not at that time prepared to sign a friendship treaty with the USSR, as had Egypt and Iraq. On the other hand, the Syrian Government, which had been broadened in March 1972 to include representatives of parties other than the Baath, like the communists, did not follow Egypt's example in July and expel its Soviet advisers.

In December 1972 Maj.-Gen. Khlefawi resigned from the post of Prime Minister for health reasons, and a new Government was formed by Mahmoud al-Ayoubi, the Vice-President, who allotted 16 out of 31 government portfolios to members of the Baath Party. A new Syrian Constitution, proclaiming socialist principles, was approved by the People's Assembly in January 1973 and confirmed by a referendum in March. The Sunni Muslims were dissatisfied that the Constitution did not recognize Islam as the state religion, and, as a result of their pressure, an amendment was made declaring that the President must be a Muslim. Under the Constitution, freedom of belief was guaranteed, with the state respecting all religions, although the Constitution recognized that Islamic jurisprudence was 'a principal source of legislation'. In 1972 a National Charter created a National Progressive Front (NPF), a grouping of the Baath Party and its allies. Elections were held in March 1973 for the new People's Assembly, under the aegis of the Front, and 140 of the 186 seats were won by the Progressive Front, while 42 seats were won by independents and four by the opposition.

THE FOURTH ARAB–ISRAELI WAR AND ITS AFTERMATH

On 6 October 1973 Egyptian and Syrian forces launched a war against Israel, in an effort to regain territories lost in 1967. On both the Egyptian and Syrian fronts, complete surprise was achieved, giving the Arabs a strong initial advantage, much of which they subsequently lost. (See Arab–Israeli Relations 1967–2001, p. 00.) Although Egypt signed a disengagement agreement with Israel on 18 January 1974, fighting continued on the Syrian front, in the Golan Heights area, until a disengagement agreement was signed on 31 May, after much diplomacy by the US Secretary of State, Dr Henry Kissinger (see Documents on Palestine, p. 61).

Syria continued to maintain an uncompromising policy in the Middle East, especially regarding the Palestinian question, and after the 1973 war it received vast amounts of Soviet military aid in order fully to re-equip its forces. Syria's strong support for the Palestine Liberation Organization (PLO) was vindicated in October 1974 at the Arab summit meeting in Rabat, Morocco, where the PLO's claim to the West Bank was formally recognized. By June 1976, however, Syria was in the position of invading Lebanon to crush the Palestinians, and finding most of the remainder of the Arab world agreeing to send a peace-keeping force to Lebanon to quell the conflict.

FOREIGN AFFAIRS 1975–78

This reversal for Syria arose out of a lengthy chain of events. An improvement in relations with Jordan took place in 1975, with King Hussein visiting Damascus in April and President Assad visiting Amman in June. A joint military and political command was set up between the two countries, and by the spring of 1977 their customs, electricity networks and education systems were unified. Plans were made for the eventual union of the two countries. Relations between Syria and Jordan deteriorated, however, after Jordan appeared to give guarded support to Egyptian President Anwar Sadat's peace initiative in November 1977.

The second Egyptian-Israeli disengagement agreement in Sinai, signed in September 1975, met with Syria's strong condemnation. Syria accused Egypt of acting without the agreement of other Arab states and, by agreeing to three years of peace with Israel, of weakening the general Arab position and betraying the Palestinians.

Syria had shown considerable interest in the Lebanese civil war since its outbreak in April 1975. Initially, Syria wanted to protect the position of the Palestinians in Lebanon and perhaps also to further plans for a 'Greater Syria', sending in about 2,000 as-Saiqa troops in January 1976. After having secured a cease-fire, Assad pledged that he would control the Palestinians in Lebanon, and the core of the PLO, under Yasser Arafat, began to be apprehensive that they would be dominated by Syria. By early June 1976 the fighting in Lebanon was so fierce that Syria felt obliged to intervene militarily and overtly. This time Syria's intervention was welcomed by the Christian right-wing parties and condemned by the Palestinians and the Muslim left (and also Egypt).

A meeting of the Arab League ministers of foreign affairs on 8–9 June 1976 agreed that an Arab peace-keeping force should be sent to Lebanon to effect a cease-fire. After some delay, a peace-keeping force, consisting of Syrian and Libyan troops in equal proportions, did arrive in Lebanon, but the fighting continued unabated until October, when Arab summit meetings, in Riyadh, Saudi Arabia, and Cairo, secured a more lasting cease-fire. A 30,000-strong Arab Deterrent Force, consisting largely of Syrian troops, was given authority at the Arab summit meetings to maintain the peace. President Assad's prestige, in Syria and the Arab world, was considerably strengthened by this success. Relations with Egypt improved after a tacit understanding that Syria would end its criticism of the September 1975 Egyptian-Israeli agreement on Sinai in return for Egypt's acceptance of Syrian intervention in Lebanon.

In August 1976 Syria's Prime Minister, Mahmoud al-Ayoubi, was replaced by his predecessor, Gen. Khlefawi. He held office until March 1978, when he was succeeded by Muhammad Ali al-Halabi, previously Speaker of the People's Assembly.

Relations with the USSR, which had been extremely poor during most of 1976, improved after the October summit meetings and were consolidated when Assad visited Moscow in April 1977. With Iraq, however, relations remained poor. Iraq shut off the flow of petroleum from its Kirkuk oilfield to the Syrian port of Banias in protest at Syria's intervention in Lebanon. Another Iraqi grievance was Syria's use of water from the Euphrates river for irrigation projects. When an attempt to assassinate the Syrian Vice-Premier and Minister of Foreign Affairs, Abd al-Halim Khaddam, was made in December 1976, sources in Syria were swift to blame terrorists trained in Iraq. Relations between Syria and Egypt deteriorated again as a result of President Sadat's peace initiative in November 1977. President Assad strongly criticized the move and diplomatic relations between the two countries were severed in December.

Syria's rift with Egypt widened further after Sadat and Prime Minister Menachem Begin of Israel signed the Camp David agreements (see Documents on Palestine, p. 63) in the USA in September 1978. The third summit meeting of the 'Steadfast-ness and Confrontation Front', comprising Arab countries strongly opposed to Egypt's attempt to make a separate peace with Israel, met in Damascus in late September 1978. When the Egyptian-Israeli peace treaty was finally signed in March 1979 (see Documents on Palestine, p. 65), Syria joined most of the other Arab League states at a meeting in Baghdad that endorsed political and economic sanctions against Egypt.

Egypt's *rapprochement* with Israel led to a brief improvement in Syria's relations with Iraq. In October 1978 Syria and Iraq signed a 'national charter for joint action' in which the eventual intention was complete political and economic union between the two countries. Although the oil pipeline from Iraq to Banias was reopened, the scheme for union collapsed when an internal conspiracy in Iraq in July 1979 was attributed to Syrian intrigue.

DIFFICULTIES OF THE EARLY 1980s

Although President Assad was easily returned for a second seven-year term of office in February 1978, there was growing evidence of internal dissatisfaction in Syria. Important government posts were largely in the hands of Alawites, a minority Muslim sect to which Assad belonged, and, after 1977, assassinations of Alawites became an increasing problem. In June 1979 more than 60 army cadets, most of them thought to be Alawites, were massacred. The slaughter was officially attributed to the Muslim Brotherhood, who were also held responsible for subsequent killings.

President Assad's attempts to end this violence met with little lasting success. In January 1980 he appointed a new Council of Ministers with Dr Abd ar-Rauf Kassem as Prime Minister. Militias of workers, peasants and students were set up, but were ineffective in helping the regular authorities to curb violence.

During the spring of 1980 the number of Soviet advisers in the country increased to more than 4,000, and in October 1980 Syria signed a 20-year treaty of friendship and co-operation with the USSR. By 1986 Syria had received an estimated US $12,000m.–$13,000m. in military loans from the USSR since 1973. A proposed merger between Syria and Libya, announced in September 1980, came to nothing.

At the outbreak of war between Iraq and Iran in September 1980, Syria supported Iran, on account of its own long-standing distrust of the rival Baath Party in Iraq. A crisis with Jordan soon developed, partly because of Syrian allegations that Muslim Brotherhood treachery was being planned from within Jordan and partly because of Jordan's support for Iraq in the Iran–Iraq War. Towards the end of 1980 Syrian and Jordanian troops faced each other across the frontier; conflict was only averted by Saudi mediation.

Syria's biggest distraction, however, was its involvement in Lebanon. The 30,000 Syrian troops of the Arab Deterrent Force had been in Lebanon since 1976, and had been a severe drain on Syrian resources. In the summer of 1980 the Phalangist militia consolidated its position in Lebanon and came to occupy the town of Zahle in the Beka'a valley, east of Beirut. Clashes developed in the Zahle area between Syrian troops and the Phalangist militia, and the Christian forces found themselves under siege in Zahle in April 1981. Syria maintained that Zahle and the Beka'a valley were vital to its security against Israel. Israeli aircraft made repeated sorties into Lebanon, and at the end of April Syria moved surface-to-air (SAM) missiles into the Beka'a valley after two Syrian helicopters had been shot down by Israeli planes. A prolonged international crisis developed, with a serious threat of war between Israel and Syria. After Saudi and Kuwaiti mediation, however, the siege of Zahle was lifted at the end of June, and the Phalangist militia withdrew. The SAM missiles remained in the Beka'a valley, as the Syrians maintained that this was a separate issue.

In the following year, however, there were a number of reversals for President Assad. In December Israel formally annexed the Golan Heights, a development which prompted Syria to try to obtain more arms from the USSR. A huge car bomb explosion in Damascus in November was attributed to the Muslim Brotherhood, and this was followed by further indications of incipient unrest, culminating in February 1982 in an uprising in Hama which lasted for nearly three weeks. This was eventually suppressed by Assad's forces with brutal ferocity, and, although it was again attributed to the Muslim

Brotherhood, other opposition elements were also involved. On 20 February the National Alliance of the Syrian People was formed, as an opposition grouping of 19 factions drawn from, among others, Baathists, Nasserites, Christians, Alawites and the Muslim Brotherhood.

These problems were completely overshadowed, however, by the Israeli invasion of Lebanon in June 1982. Israeli forces quickly reached Beirut, trapping the PLO guerrillas there; the Syrian missiles in the Beka'a valley were destroyed and the Syrian presence in northern Lebanon, in the form of the Arab Deterrent Force, was rendered impotent. In August agreement was reached on the evacuation of PLO and Syrian forces from Beirut, and their withdrawal, supervised by an international peace-keeping force, took place between 21 August and 1 September. The number of evacuees was estimated to be more than 14,500. No change occurred in the relative positions of Syrian and Israeli forces in Lebanon as a whole, however.

In January 1983, shortly after the start of negotiations between Lebanon and Israel for an agreement covering the withdrawal of foreign forces from Lebanon, Syria took delivery of a number of Soviet SAM-5 anti-aircraft missiles. Soviet *Scud* ground-to-ground rockets were already deployed with Syrian forces, but the SAM missiles, with a range of 240 km, posed a potential threat to aircraft over Lebanon, parts of Jordan and over Israel almost as far as Jerusalem. Two bases were built to accommodate the missiles: one at Dumeir, north of Damascus, and the other at Shinshar, near Homs. These missiles had never before been deployed outside the USSR and Eastern Europe, and the arrival of the technicians who were employed to operate the system was thought to have increased the number of Soviet military personnel in Syria to 6,000.

Syria opposed all US-sponsored diplomatic initiatives to achieve peace between Lebanon and Israel, and categorically rejected President Ronald Reagan's proposed settlement of the Palestinian question, based on an eventual Palestine-Jordan confederation, which he announced on 1 September 1982. (Arab proposals for a settlement were defined later that month at Fez, Morocco—see Documents on Palestine, p. 68.) Finally, on 17 May 1983, after almost six months of talks, an agreement was reached between Lebanon and Israel announcing the end of hostilities and imposing a time limit of three months for the withdrawal of foreign troops from Lebanon. The agreement, formulated by the US Secretary of State, George Shultz, was rejected outright by President Assad, who refused to withdraw Syrian forces from northern Lebanon—thus creating a stalemate with Israel, which refused to leave Lebanon unless the Syrians and the PLO did so first. President Assad insisted on Israel's unconditional withdrawal, declaring that the status of Syrian troops, invited into Lebanon by the Lebanese Government in 1976, could not be compared with that of the invading Israeli forces. He stated that the agreement between Israel and Lebanon placed unacceptable limitations on Lebanon's sovereignty and threatened Syrian security.

THE STRUGGLE FOR CONTROL OF THE PLO

By July 1983 the position was little changed. About 40,000 Syrian troops, camped in the Beka'a valley, and around 8,000–10,000 PLO guerrillas, entrenched in the eastern Beka'a and northern Lebanon, faced some 25,000 Israelis in the south of the country. Neither side seemed eager for war, but, equally, neither was prepared to withdraw. Syria, which continued to supply, and, effectively, to control the militias of the Lebanese Druze and Shi'ite factions in their struggle with the Lebanese Government and the Christian Phalangists in and around Beirut, began to address itself to destabilizing the regime of President Amin Gemayel of Lebanon by trying to unite Lebanese opposition groups in a pro-Syrian 'national front'. Syria was also supporting Palestinian rebels involved in the struggle for power within the PLO which erupted in the Beka'a valley in May, fundamentally over dissatisfaction with what radical Fatah members viewed as the compromise diplomacy of the PLO Chairman, Yasser Arafat, which, they believed, had been responsible for the Palestinians' humiliation in Beirut in 1982. Arafat accused Syria and Libya of inspiring the revolt in order to win control of the PLO, and at the end of June he travelled to Damascus to receive a personal letter of support from President Yurii Andropov of the USSR, only to be ordered out of the

country by the Syrian authorities. Syrian forces now faced armed opposition in Lebanon, not only from the Israeli army, but also from Sunni Muslims in Tripoli, Maronite Christians in the centre of the country, and guerrillas loyal to Arafat in the Beka'a valley.

Syrian and rebel PLO forces, led by 'Abu Musa' and 'Abu Saleh', finally trapped Arafat in the Lebanese port of Tripoli in November 1983. After fierce fighting a truce, arrived at through the mediation of Saudi Arabia, allowed Arafat and some 4,000 of his followers to leave Lebanon in December, in five Greek ships, under UN protection. Syria had failed to gain control of the Palestine Liberation Movement, though it had been instrumental in effecting a dilution of Arafat's authority within the PLO. This became apparent in a series of reconciliation talks held between several of the rival Palestinian factions (though not those that had sent troops against Arafat in Tripoli) in the first half of 1984. The agreements reached at these talks saw the PLO seeking to move towards a more collective style of leadership.

Syria's progress towards a position of pre-eminence in the Arab world was eroded during 1984, as the rehabilitation of Egypt continued. Syria dissented from the decision to readmit Egypt to membership of the Organization of the Islamic Conference (OIC) in March, and opposed Jordan's restoration of diplomatic relations with Egypt in September and King Hussein's alliance with Yasser Arafat. Syria's attempt to wrest control of the PLO from Yasser Arafat succeeded in splitting the movement. Arafat retained his leadership of the bulk of the organization and manoeuvred it towards an emergent moderate Arab alliance including Egypt, Jordan, Iraq and Saudi Arabia.

SYRIAN INFLUENCE IN LEBANON

Although Israel withdrew its forces from Beirut, redeploying them along the Awali river, south of the capital, in September 1983, Syria's army remained entrenched in northern Lebanon. There were occasional exchanges of fire between Syrian forces around Beirut and aircraft and naval guns of the US fleet standing off shore in support of the US contingent in the multinational peace-keeping force in Beirut. The state of civil war existing in and around Beirut eventually compelled the evacuation of the multinational force in the first three months of 1984.

In March 1984 President Gemayel of Lebanon was forced to succumb to the controlling influence of Syria in Lebanese affairs. He abrogated the 17 May 1983 agreement with Israel, as President Assad had always insisted that he should, and reconvened the National Reconciliation Conference of the rival Lebanese factions (which had first met in Geneva in November 1983) in Lausanne, Switzerland, under pressure from Syria to agree constitutional reforms which would give the majority Muslim community of Lebanon greater representation in government. In return, Gemayel received guarantees of internal security from Syria. These involved Syrian agreement to restrain the Druze and Shi'ite Amal militias (led by Walid Joumblatt and Nabih Berri, respectively) which relied on Syria to continue their armed struggle. The National Reconciliation Conference failed to produce the results hoped for by Syria, and marked the beginning of the rapid disintegration of the Lebanese National Salvation Front, comprising leading Lebanese opponents of President Amin Gemayel, which had been created, with Syrian backing, in July 1983. At the Conference a member of the Front, former Lebanese President Sulayman Franjiya, vetoed Syrian plans for constitutional changes in Lebanon involving the diminution of the powers of the President, traditionally a Maronite Christian. Despite careful Syrian orchestration, the Conference broke up without having agreed any reforms of the Lebanese system of government.

In April 1984, however, President Gemayel returned to Damascus to gain approval from President Assad for plans for a government of national unity in Lebanon, giving equal representation in the cabinet to Muslims and Christians. Assad accepted the terms of composition of the Government under the premiership of Rashid Karami (who had been Prime Minister of Lebanon on 10 previous occasions); Gemayel was to retain the presidency. Walid Joumblatt and Nabih Berri greeted their appointment to posts in the new Lebanese Cabinet on 30 April, and the very idea of a government of national unity under a

Christian President, with scepticism. Nevertheless, both agreed to participate in the Government. Inter-factional fighting, which continued and intensified in Beirut, threatened the existence of the new Lebanese Government.

INTERNAL TENSION

In November 1983 President Assad suffered what was thought to be a heart attack, though this was denied by the Syrian authorities. He recovered, but his evidently weakened condition aroused speculation regarding his eventual successor. During and after Assad's illness, potential rivals for the succession made displays of military force in and around Damascus, involving various units of the armed forces, to establish the strength of their claims to power. Prominent among these was Rifaat Assad, the President's brother and commander of the 20,000–30,000-strong defence brigades which effectively controlled Damascus and defended the regime's authority. On 4 March 1984 the Council of Ministers, under Prime Minister Abd ar-Rauf Kassem, resigned. Kassem was then invited to form a new Council of Ministers to fill four vacancies arising as a result of the deaths of ministers; this was the first ministerial reshuffle for four years. At the same time President Assad appointed an unprecedented three Vice-Presidents. Rifaat Assad was made Vice-President for Military and National Security Affairs; Abd al-Halim Khaddam, the former Minister of Foreign Affairs, was made Vice-President for Political Affairs; and Zuheir Masharkah was promoted from his post as a regional secretary of the Baath Party to become Vice-President for Internal and Party Affairs. Ostensibly, President Assad's intention was to ease his workload after his illness, but another possible motive for the appointment of three Vice-Presidents was to distribute power evenly between his potential successors, giving none an overall advantage. Rifaat Assad thus gained some recognition of his claim to the succession and retained control of the defence brigades; but the regular army (Assad's power-base in what was, essentially, a military dictatorship) was still commanded by officers loyal to President Assad, including the Chief of Staff, Gen. Hikmat Shehabi, who was responsible for the appointment and dismissal of senior army officers, and a rival of Rifaat Assad.

In what was seen as a disciplinary measure against those principally responsible for the confrontations between military units which took place in and around Damascus after President Assad's illness in November 1983, Rifaat Assad, Gen. Ali Haydar (commander of the Special Forces élite army unit), and Gen. Shafiq Fayyadh (commander of the Third Armoured Division) were sent as part of a delegation to Moscow in June 1984. While the rest of the delegation returned to Syria within one week, these three were apparently not permitted to do so. Rifaat Assad was sent to Geneva, Switzerland, and Gens Haydar and Fayyadh to Sofia, Bulgaria, into what appeared to be temporary exile. While Rifaat Assad was abroad, the defence brigades were absorbed into the army, with the exception of a few units which were put under the command of Rifaat Assad's son-in-law. Rifaat Assad was finally permitted to return to Syria in November and was given responsibility for national security affairs. President Assad was re-elected for a third seven-year term of office in February 1985 and appeared to have regained much of his former authority. A ministerial reshuffle took place in April.

THE IRAN–IRAQ WAR AND OIL SUPPLIES

Syria's reliance on Iran for supplies of crude oil for processing at its oil refineries (see Economy), which occurred as a direct result of its support for Iran in the Iran–Iraq War, was exposed as a serious weakness in 1984, as hostilities in the conflict began to affect the passage of oil tankers in the Gulf. Attacks on shipping were made by both sides in the first half of the year, threatening Syria's oil link with Iran. President Assad attempted to restrain Iran from widening the conflict and endangering vital oil supplies. An agreement on the continued delivery of Iranian oil to Syria was reached in May, but attacks on Gulf shipping by both Iran and Iraq continued. A Soviet attempt to bring about a reconciliation between the rival Baathist regimes in Syria and Iraq, involving the reopening of the oil pipeline between Kirkuk, in Iraq, and Banias, in Syria, made no progress.

ISRAEL'S WITHDRAWAL FROM LEBANON

By means of Syrian mediation, a security plan for Beirut was agreed and put into operation at the beginning of July 1984. The plan met with only limited success, and the extent of Syria's influence with its Lebanese allies came into question when, in September, even the threat of force failed to win Walid Joumblatt's unequivocal approval of an extension of the security plan to allow the Lebanese army into the Druze stronghold of the Chouf mountains. In September Syria arranged a truce to end fighting in Tripoli between the pro-Syrian Arab Democratic Party and the Sunni Muslim Tawheed Islami (Islamic Unification Movement). This prepared the way for the Lebanese army to enter the city in November, under the terms of an extended security plan, backed by Syria, to assert the authority of the Lebanese Government in Beirut, Tripoli and south of the capital. On this occasion, Walid Joumblatt's opposition to the plan's provisions for the army to take control of the coastal road south of Beirut appeared to have tacit Syrian approval. However, the plan finally went ahead in January 1985.

Syria approved Lebanese participation in talks with the Israelis to co-ordinate the departure of the Israeli Defence Force (IDF) from southern Lebanon with other security forces, in order to prevent an outbreak of civil violence. A series of talks had begun in an-Naqoura (Lebanon) in November 1984 but had repeatedly foundered on the question of which forces should take the place of the IDF. Under Syrian influence, the Lebanese wanted the UN Interim Force in Lebanon (UNIFIL) to police the Israel–Lebanon border (as it had been mandated to do in 1978), and the Lebanese army to deploy north of the Litani river, between UNIFIL and the Syrians in the Beka'a valley. Israel was not convinced of the competence of the Lebanese army, and wanted UNIFIL to be deployed north of the Litani, while the Israeli-backed, so-called 'South Lebanon Army' (SLA) patrolled the southern Lebanese border. In the absence of an agreement, Israel withdrew from the talks, and on 14 January 1985 the Israeli Cabinet voted to take steps towards a three-phased unilateral withdrawal to the international border.

On 10 June 1985 Israel announced the accomplishment of the third and final phase of the withdrawal, taking its forces behind the southern Lebanese border and leaving a protective buffer zone inside Lebanon, policed by the SLA with IDF support. Although Syria was evidently determined to retain control of events in Lebanon, the Israeli withdrawal offered the opportunity of reducing its costly military presence in the north and east of the country. At the end of June and the beginning of July Syria withdrew an estimated 10,000 troops from the Beka'a valley, leaving some 25,000 in position.

SYRIA LOSES ITS GRIP ON LEBANON

In March 1985 Dr Samir Geagea, a regional commander of the Christian Lebanese Forces (LF) militia, rebelled against the Phalange Party leadership and the extent to which it was prepared to accept the Syrian influence in Lebanese affairs, particularly as manifested in President Gemayel's apparent willingness to accommodate Syrian-backed plans for constitutional reform favouring the Muslim majority in Lebanon. Geagea immediately secured the support of the greater part of the LF and threatened to set up an independent Christian administration. Syria, though unwilling to be drawn into the civil-military entanglement in Lebanon, feared the necessity of having to send troops into Christian east Beirut to quell the revolt, which threatened to precipitate the partition of Lebanon along sectarian lines, creating a number of unstable mini-states close to the Syrian border which would be vulnerable to exploitation by Syria's enemies. Syria accused Israel of inciting the revolt. It ended, however, in May, when the LF elected a new leader, Elie Hobeika, who announced his readiness to negotiate with Syria and its Druze allies.

The extent of Syria's diminishing influence over the actions of its allies in Lebanon was repeatedly demonstrated by its inability to prevent renewed inter-factional fighting in Beirut. On 17 April 1985 Prime Minister Rashid Karami, a Sunni Muslim, tendered his resignation, partly over the failure of the Council of Ministers to agree to reinforce the army, which was engaged in heavy fighting against elements of Samir Geagea's rebel LF around Sidon, and partly over attacks on Sunni Muslims by the Shi'ite Amal militia. The Shi'ites had combined with the Druze in trying to eliminate the Sunni Murabitoun militia, which had joined forces with members of the PLO, whose numbers in Beirut were growing again. Amal hoped to prevent the re-emergence anywhere in Lebanon of a PLO power-base that might attract Israeli military retaliation. Karami withdrew his resignation later on 17 April and, on a subsequent visit to Damascus, was persuaded to remain as Prime Minister and ensure the survival of the Government of national unity.

In May and June 1985, however, Syria itself backed Amal in attempting to suppress a resurgence of the PLO (in particular the pro-Arafat wing of the movement) in the Palestinian refugee camps of Sabra, Chatila and Bourj el-Barajneh in Beirut. Many of the estimated 5,000 mostly pro-Arafat Palestinians who had infiltrated Lebanon since the Israeli withdrawal became inevitable, had made their way to Beirut. Walid Joumblatt's Druze militia refused to assist its former allies in imposing a siege on the camps, but Amal had the support of the predominantly Shi'ite sixth brigade of the Lebanese army. In the bloody battle for the camps, which spanned May and June, more than 600 people were killed, but Amal failed to take control. An unforeseen development was the extent to which pro- and anti-Arafat PLO factions united to resist the attack on the Palestinian community. On 17 June a fragile, Syrian-sponsored cease-fire agreement was reached in Damascus between Amal and the Palestinian National Salvation Front (PNSF), representing the pro-Syrian, anti-Arafat element in the camps.

Weeks of fighting between Christians and Muslims along the 'Green Line' dividing east and west Beirut, and between Muslims and Druze in the west of the capital, preceded an attempt to enforce another Syrian-sponsored security plan for the city. The plan was introduced in July 1985, after 13 Muslim and Druze leaders had met to discuss it in Damascus. Under the terms of the plan, Muslim west Beirut was to comprise five security zones; the militias were to leave the streets and close their offices, with the police taking their place, supported by a unit of the Sixth Army Brigade. These measures were meant to lay the foundations for the extension of the plan to Christian east Beirut and the renewal of inter-sectarian dialogue on political and constitutional reform. However, more heavy fighting soon rendered the plan ineffective.

President Assad was able to demonstrate that he retained some command over events in Lebanon when his intercession was instrumental in securing the release of 39 American hostages from a hijacked TWA airliner, who had been detained at secret locations in Beirut since 17 June 1985 by members of the extremist Shi'ite group Hezbollah. Assad threatened to sever relations with Hezbollah and to provide no further aid if the hostages were not released. The hostages were freed and driven to Damascus on 30 June.

Four weeks of intensive fighting between rival militias in the Lebanese port town of Tripoli in September and October 1985 were interpreted as part of Syria's campaign to prevent the re-emergence of the pro-Arafat wing of the PLO in Lebanon. The pro-Arafat, Sunni Muslim Tawheed Islami and the pro-Syrian, Alawite Arab Democratic Party fought for control of the town and its port, which was allegedly being used to distribute weapons and supplies to Arafat loyalists in other parts of the country. A cease-fire was agreed in Damascus in November, and troops of the Syrian army moved into the town.

THE ABORTIVE NATIONAL AGREEMENT IN LEBANON

A month of negotiations, under Syrian auspices, between the three main Lebanese militias, the Druze forces, Amal and the LF, which began in October 1985, led to the preparation of a draft accord for a politico-military settlement of the civil war. The agreement was finally signed by the three militia leaders (Walid Joumblatt, Nabih Berri and Elie Hobeika) on 28 December, in Damascus. It provided for an immediate cease-fire and for an end to the state of civil war within one year; the militias would be disbanded, and the responsibility for security would pass to a reconstituted and religiously-integrated army, supported by Syrian forces. The accord sought the immediate establishment of a national coalition government which would preside over the abolition of the 'confessional' system of power-sharing government and the creation of a secular administration. It also recognized Lebanon's community of interest with

Syria and envisaged a 'strategic integration' of the two countries in the fields of military relations, foreign policy and security.

It was always doubtful that the Damascus accord could be implemented. President Gemayel, who had not been consulted during the drafting of the agreement, refused to endorse it, and at the end of December 1985 clashes erupted in east Beirut between elements of the LF who supported the agreement and those loyal to President Gemayel who resented the concessions that had been made on their behalf by Elie Hobeika. In January 1986 Hobeika was forced into exile, and Samir Geagea resumed command of the LF, urging the renegotiation of the Damascus agreement. The long round of inter-sectarian clashes in Beirut resumed in earnest on 22 January.

Fighting between Palestinian guerrillas and Shi'ite Amal militiamen for control of the refugee camps in the south of Beirut, which had continued sporadically ever since a cease-fire nominally took effect in June 1985, escalated into major exchanges on 19 May 1986. The Palestinian refugee camps of Sabra, Chatila and Bourj el-Barajneh were increasingly under the control of guerrillas loyal to Yasser Arafat, who were continuing to return to Lebanon. Syria appeared to be powerless to prevent the resurgence of the PLO in Lebanon, despite the efforts of the Syrian-backed Amal militia to keep Palestinian and radical pro-Iranian Hezbollah guerrillas, who were growing in strength, away from the Israeli security zone inside the southern Lebanese border. The PLO claimed that the number of guerrillas in Lebanon in 1986 exceeded the 14,300 who, according to its own figures, had been evacuated from Beirut in 1982. Independent estimates assessed the number in Beirut at several thousands.

THE SYRIAN ARMY RETURNS TO BEIRUT

Leaders of the Muslim communities in Lebanon met Syrian Government officials in Damascus, and agreed to impose a cease-fire around the Palestinian refugee camps in Beirut on 14 June. The cease-fire, which effectively reduced the fighting to exchanges of sniper fire, proved to be the first element in a Syrian-sponsored peace plan for Muslim west Beirut. About 1,000 Lebanese troops were deployed in west Beirut at the end of June. The Amal, Druze and Murabitoun militias were ordered to close their offices and to leave the streets. Crucial to their co-operation in the plan was the appearance in Beirut, for the first time since 1982, of uniformed Syrian soldiers (several hundred in number), supported by members of the Syrian security service, *Mukhabarat* ('information'), under the command of Brig.-Gen. Ghazi Kena'an. The security plan was successful in its limited objective of curbing the activities of militias in west Beirut, but the plan (and Syria's visible involvement in it) was strongly opposed in Christian east Beirut, and the Syrians hesitated over extending the plan into the southern suburbs, which contained the majority of the city's Palestinian refugees and was controlled by the radical Shi'ite Hezbollah, backed by Iran, which Syria was concerned not to offend.

RAPPROCHEMENT WITH JORDAN

Syria opposed the joint Jordanian-Palestinian agreement, which was signed by King Hussein and Yasser Arafat in Amman in February 1985, and its proposals for a Middle East peace settlement. In August, with Algeria, Lebanon, Libya and the PDRY, Syria boycotted the extraordinary meeting of the Arab League in Casablanca, Morocco, which was convened partly to consider the Amman accord. The PLO's persistent refusal to acknowledge the UN Security Council Resolutions (Nos 242 and 338) on the Palestinian issue, and a series of terrorist incidents in the second half of 1985 in which the PLO was implicated, reducing its credibility as a potential partner in peace negotiations and also reducing the prospects that the joint peace initiative would make progress, led King Hussein to seek a reconciliation with Syria. Relations between Jordan and Syria had been poor since 1979, when Syria had accused Jordan of harbouring anti-Syrian groups. The Prime Ministers of the two countries met in Damascus in November 1985, and agreed on the need for 'joint Arab action' to achieve peace in the Middle East. At subsequent talks in Riyadh in October, Jordan and Syria rejected 'partial and unilateral' solutions (ruling out separate negotiations with Israel) and affirmed their adherence to the 1982 Fez plan, omitting all reference to the Jordanian-

Palestinian peace initiative. In February 1986 King Hussein withdrew from his political alliance with Yasser Arafat, and in April Jordan appointed its first ambassador to Syria since 1980.

Syria severed diplomatic relations with Morocco in July 1986, after King Hassan held talks with Prime Minister Shimon Peres of Israel.

BOMB ATTACKS IN SYRIA

On 13 March 1986 a bomb exploded in Damascus, causing an estimated 60 deaths and wounding about 110. Syria blamed Iraqi agents for the attack. Then, on 15 April, bombs exploded, almost simultaneously, in five Syrian towns. Further bomb attacks were carried out on public transport targets in several towns, including Damascus, before the end of the month. In May the Government admitted that 144 people had been killed, and 149 injured, during the bombing campaign in April. According to the Voice of Lebanon radio station, a hitherto unknown Syrian group (the 17 October Movement for the Liberation of the Syrian People) claimed responsibility for the campaign, and its message suggested that it was a pro-Iraqi, militant Islamist organization.

SYRIA AND INTERNATIONAL TERRORISM

Although it failed to provide conclusive proof of Syrian involvement, the USA claimed that there was evidence of a link between Syria and the Palestinian terrorists who carried out attacks on Rome and Vienna airports in December 1985, and on a discothèque in West Berlin in April 1986. The USA attacked the Libyan cities of Tripoli and Benghazi in that month, as punishment for alleged Libyan involvement in international terrorism, and reserved the right to use force against other countries that had proven links with terrorist operations. President Assad denied that Syria was sponsoring terrorism, and refused to restrict the activities of Palestinian groups (including the Abu Nidal faction, the Fatah Revolutionary Council) on Syrian territory, which, he claimed, were 'cultural and political'.

In October 1986 a Jordanian national, Nezar Hindawi, was convicted in the United Kingdom of attempting to plant a bomb on an Israeli airliner at London's Heathrow airport in the previous April. The British Government claimed to have proof of the complicity of Syrian diplomats in the affair, and, on 24 October, severed diplomatic relations with Syria. One month later, three Syrian diplomats were expelled from West Germany, after a court in West Berlin ruled that the Syrian embassy in East Berlin was implicated in the bombing of a discothèque in the West of the city in April. In November the member states of the European Community (EC, now European Union—EU), with the exception of Greece, imposed limited diplomatic and economic sanctions against Syria, as did the USA and Canada (both of which recalled their ambassadors to Syria). Syria persistently denied any involvement in international terrorism, and by April 1987 several EC countries had made tentative advances to Syria, seeking to upgrade diplomatic relations, and only the United Kingdom continued to insist on a ban on high-level (ministerial) contacts. Within the EC, France in particular had been an unenthusiastic supporter of the sanctions demanded by the British Government, mindful of the crucial role that Syria had to play in the Middle East peace process, and of the need for its co-operation in securing the release of Western hostages being held by militant Islamist groups in Beirut. For its part, Syria appeared to be anxious to be seen to dissociate itself from terrorist groups and to use its influence in Lebanon to free Western hostages. In June 1987 it was reported that the offices of Abu Nidal's Fatah Revolutionary Council, near Damascus, had been closed, and many of its members expelled, by the Syrian authorities, and that Abu Nidal himself had moved to Libya. The EC, with the exception of the United Kingdom, ended its ban on ministerial contacts with Syria in July, and financial aid was resumed in September, although a ban on the sale of arms to Syria remained in force. The United Kingdom, although it had withdrawn its opposition to its EC partners' restoration of contacts with Syria, remained sceptical as to the true extent of Syria's rejection of terrorism, and alleged that Abu Nidal's group was still active in Lebanon, in the Syrian-controlled Beka'a valley.

PAX SYRIANA IN LEBANON

In October 1986 the Syrian-backed resistance to the re-emergence of the pro-Arafat PLO in Lebanon spread from Beirut to the Palestinian refugee camps around Tyre and Sidon, which were besieged by the forces of Amal. In February 1987 Syria reportedly asked Amal to abandon the blockade of the camps, but the respite for the inhabitants of the camps of Bourj el-Barajneh, in Beirut, and Rashidiyah, near Tyre, where supplies were allowed in, proved to be brief, and the siege of the other camps remained in force.

In February 1987 fierce fighting occurred in west Beirut between Amal forces and an alliance of Druze, Murabitoun and Communist Party militias. Muslim leaders appealed for Syria to intervene to restore order, and about 4,000 Syrian troops were deployed in west Beirut on 22 February. The Syrian force (which was soon increased to some 7,500 troops) succeeded in enforcing a cease-fire in the central and northern districts of west Beirut, and moved into areas occupied by Hezbollah, killing 23 Hezbollah members and forcing others to return to their stronghold in the southern suburbs, into which the Syrians still declined to venture.

A Syrian-supervised cease-fire at the embattled Palestinian refugee camps in Beirut took effect on 6 April 1987. The cease-fire agreement was negotiated by representatives of Syria, Amal and the pro-Syrian Palestine National Salvation Front (PNSF), and brought an end to the worst fighting. Members of the PNSF and Arafat loyalists had made common cause in defence of the camps, and their alliance was a contributory factor in the reunification of the PLO under Arafat's leadership, which took place at the 18th session of the Palestine National Council (PNC) in the Algerian capital in April, turning the Syrian-backed PNSF into a rump, depriving it of the support of the largest and most influential groups that had rebelled against Arafat in 1983. The PNC adopted a resolution committing itself to improving PLO relations with Syria.

In January 1988, avowedly as a gesture of support for protests by Palestinians living in Israeli-occupied territories, Nabih Berri, the leader of Amal, announced the lifting of the siege of the Palestinian refugee camps in Beirut and southern Lebanon. On 21 January Syrian troops replaced Amal militiamen and soldiers of the Sixth Brigade of the Lebanese army in positions around the Beirut camps, and the 14-month siege of Rashidiyah camp, near Tyre, was ended. However, PLO guerrillas loyal to Yasser Arafat refused to withdraw from their positions overlooking Ain al-Hilweh, interrupting the withdrawal of Amal from around Rashidiyah.

A new political crisis overtook Lebanon in mid-1987, which emphasized the division between the Muslim and Christian communities and the extent of the problem that Syria faced in its attempts to oversee a political settlement. The Lebanese Prime Minister, Rashid Karami, who had tendered his resignation on 4 May, as a result of the Cabinet's failure to agree on measures to alleviate the country's acute economic problems, was assassinated on 1 June. Although it was not clear who was responsible for Karami's death, the Muslim community strongly suspected the Christian section of the divided Lebanese army and the Christian LF militia. Karami, a Sunni Muslim, had been a firm ally of Syria and had been one of the leaders who invited Syrian troops into Beirut in February, in the face of Christian opposition. Syria had yet to confront the problem of Christian-controlled east Beirut, to where no attempt had been made to extend the security plan.

RELATIONS WITH IRAN AND IRAQ

A realignment of Syrian policy towards Iran, which became more apparent during 1987, led to an increasingly uneasy relationship between the two countries. As international opinion turned against Iran in the Iran–Iraq War and moves were made to engineer a diplomatic settlement of the conflict, Syria's support for Iran became more of a liability. The USSR was critical of Syria's stance (reportedly withholding sales of arms to Syria in July), and, as the only Arab country apart from Libya to support Iran, Syria incurred the displeasure of other Arab states. Libya, meanwhile, switched its allegiance to Iraq in September. Syria's concern to regain the favour of Western nations and to play a full role in proposed Middle East peace initiatives by distancing itself from Islamist fundamentalist and anti-Arafat terrorist groups, and by seeking the release of Western hostages in Lebanon, brought it into dispute with Iran. Syrian troops in Beirut did not venture into the southern suburbs where Hezbollah was based, but, after their deployment in February and to Iran's obvious annoyance, they harassed Hezbollah members and limited their freedom of movement in the parts of Lebanon under the group's effective jurisdiction. Syria also controlled the entry of Iranians into the country, and in June sent tanks and members of the Special Forces to surround the camps of Hezbollah militiamen and several hundred Iranian Revolutionary Guards, who were stationed at Ba'albek in the Beka'a valley. Syria was evidently concerned about the destabilizing influence of Hezbollah's brand of Islamist militancy, which aimed to create in Lebanon an Islamic republic on the Iranian model.

Syria's relations with Iran were further strained by the kidnapping in June 1987 of Charles Glass, an American journalist, allegedly by Hezbollah. This was the first abduction of a Westerner in west Beirut since the Syrian army assumed responsibility for security there in February, and was the cause of annoyance and embarrassment to Syria, which was eager to improve its relations with the USA. When, four weeks later, Glass escaped from his captors, his freedom was attributed to Syrian mediation with Hezbollah. Syrian influence was also instrumental in securing the release in September of a West German hostage, one of 23 Western captives being held in south Beirut. At the beginning of September the US ambassador to Damascus, who had been recalled to Washington, DC, in November 1986, returned to Syria, and the US Government withdrew its opposition to operations by US oil companies in Syria.

Assad and President Saddam Hussain of Iraq were reported to have met secretly in Jordan in April 1987, at the instigation of King Hussein of Jordan and Crown Prince Abdullah of Saudi Arabia. In November the two leaders held talks with King Hussein and other leaders at an extraordinary summit meeting of the Arab League in Amman, Jordan. The summit, which had been convened by King Hussein to discuss the Iran–Iraq War, produced a unanimous statement expressing solidarity with Iraq, condemning Iran for prolonging the war and for its occupation of Arab (i.e. Iraqi) territory, and urging it to observe the cease-fire proposals contained in UN Security Council Resolution 598. It was widely reported that Syria had been offered financial inducements by Saudi Arabia (Syria's principal source of aid), Kuwait and other Gulf states to realign its policy on the Iran–Iraq War with majority Arab opinion, as well as compensatory supplies of oil, should such a realignment result in Iran's withholding oil shipments. However, after the summit meeting, Syria announced that it had succeeded in obstructing an Iraqi proposal that Arab states should sever diplomatic relations with Iran, that a reconciliation with Iraq had not taken place, and that Syrian relations with Iran remained fundamentally unchanged. Syria had used its veto to prevent the adoption of an Iraqi proposal to readmit Egypt to membership of the Arab League, but it could not prevent the inclusion in the final communiqué of a clause permitting individual member nations to re-establish diplomatic relations with Egypt. By mid-February 1988 11 Arab countries, including Iraq, had resumed diplomatic links with Egypt.

In July 1987 Syria and Turkey signed a security protocol in which both agreed to curb the activities on their soil of terrorist and separatist groups carrying out operations against the other. Turkey believed that guerrilla attacks in its south-eastern provinces had been organized by Kurdish exiles in Damascus. Turkey also assured Syria that the series of dams that it was building on the Euphrates river would not be deliberately used in such a way as to deprive Syria of vital water supplies further downstream.

GOVERNMENT CHANGES

A major government reshuffle was implemented in November 1987, following the resignation of the Prime Minister, Abd ar-Rauf al-Kassem. His Government had been accused of corruption and inefficiency, and of failure to solve the country's severe economic problems. Earlier, four ministers (in June those of Agriculture and of Construction; and, in October, those of Industry and of Supply and Internal Trade) had been forced to

resign, following accusations of mismanagement leading to votes of 'no confidence' in the People's Assembly. Mahmoud az-Zoubi, the Speaker of the People's Assembly, was appointed Prime Minister on 1 November. His Council of Ministers contained 15 new members.

SYRIAN AND IRANIAN SURROGATES CLASH IN LEBANON

The Syrian-brokered lifting of the siege of the Palestinian refugee camps in January 1988, was a carefully calculated move. In cynical terms it was politically inexpedient for Syria to continue to employ its proxy, Amal, in its attempt to suppress the PLO in Lebanon, at a time when the Palestinian *intifada* (uprising) in the Israeli-occupied territories (see below) was attracting widespread sympathy (particularly among Arab states) to the plight of the Palestinians and increasing support for Arafat's 'mainstream' PLO. By suspending Amal's campaign against the (pro-Arafat) PLO, Nabih Berri's Amal forces could be deployed against the Iranian-backed Hezbollah, whose strength was viewed by Syria as a threat to its own ambitions to control Lebanon.

Amal's attacks were initially directed against Hezbollah bases in southern Lebanon, and clashes (the first military confrontation between the two groups) occurred at the end of March 1988 in the Nabatiyah area. On 9 April Amal claimed to have captured Hezbollah's last stronghold in the south, at Siddiqin, while Iranian Revolutionary Guards stationed at Sharqiyah and Jibshit had been ordered to leave the area.

On 5 May 1988 fighting broke out between the Amal and Hezbollah militias (the latter supported by Iranian Revolutionary Guards) in the southern suburbs of Beirut. Attempts to impose a cease-fire through Iranian and Syrian mediation failed, and Syrian troops became involved in the fighting on 13 May when Hezbollah guerrillas, who had wrested control of about 90% of the 36-sq km southern suburbs from Amal, briefly advanced into a Syrian-controlled area of west Beirut. On 15 May 7,500 Syrian troops encircled the southern suburbs, ready to advance into the enclave to restore order, while intensive negotiations took place between Syria and Iran, neither of which, despite their divergent ambitions in Lebanon, was eager to alienate the other. On 27 May several hundred Syrian troops moved into the southern suburbs of Beirut to enforce a cease-fire agreement reached by Syria, Iran and their militia proxies on the previous day. When the Syrian deployment was complete, Amal and Hezbollah were to close down their military operations in all parts of the southern suburbs, except in areas adjoining the 'Green Line' which separated west Beirut from the Christian-controlled east of the city, where they would continue to be allowed to post their men. On 3 June, in accordance with the agreement, Nabih Berri announced the disbandment of the Amal militia in Beirut and the Beka'a valley (areas under Syrian control) and all other areas of the country except the south (which was not controlled by Syrian troops).

ARAFAT LOYALISTS DRIVEN OUT OF BEIRUT

In April 1988 a reconciliation was reported to have taken place between President Assad and Yasser Arafat, though Assad continued to insist on the severance of all relations between Arafat's Fatah and Egypt. The two leaders held discussions (their first since Arafat's expulsion from Syria in 1983) when Arafat attended the funeral in Damascus of Khalil al-Wazir ('Abu Jihad'), the military commander of the Palestine Liberation Army. At the end of April Arafat loyalists in the Palestinian refugee camps of Chatila and Bourj el-Barajneh in Beirut, possibly interpreting Syria's support for the Palestinian *intifada* and subsequent indications of a *rapprochement* between their leader and Assad as evidence of the Syrian President's waning commitment to the revolt within the PLO, attempted to drive out the fighters belonging to the Syrian-backed group, al-Fatah Intifada (Fatah Uprising), led by PLO dissident 'Abu Musa'. The Syrian troops who had surrounded the camps in April 1987, did not attempt to intervene in the fighting but, with Syria's other surrogate in Lebanon's factional conflict, the Amal militia, otherwise occupied, they allowed reinforcements to reach the rebel Fatah group. On 27 June 1988 the Arafat loyalists in the camp of Chatila were overrun and surrendered to the forces of 'Abu Musa'. On the following day, Syria granted 100 PLO guerrillas safe passage from Chatila to the Palestinian camp at Ain al-Hilweh, near Sidon. On 7 July Bourj el-Barajneh, Yasser Arafat's last stronghold in Beirut, fell to 'Abu Musa' and 120 Arafat loyalists were evacuated to Ain al-Hilweh.

LEBANON FAILS TO ELECT A NEW PRESIDENT

Amin Gemayel's term of office as President of Lebanon was due to expire on 22 September 1988 and the National Assembly was required to elect a new President prior to that date. Three main contenders for the presidency (traditionally a post occupied by a Maronite Christian) emerged: Gen. Michel Awn, the Commander-in-Chief of the armed forces; Raymond Eddé, the exiled leader of the Maronite Bloc National; and Sulayman Franjiya, President of Lebanon between 1970 and 1976. The latter did not announce his candidacy until 16 August 1988, two days before the election was scheduled to take place, and the news immediately united President Gemayel and Samir Geagea, the commander of the Christian LF militia, in opposition to Franjiya's candidature, on the grounds that he represented Syrian interests. It was Franjiya who, as President, had invited Syria to intervene militarily in Lebanon to end the civil war in 1976.

On 18 August 1988 only 38 of the 76 surviving members of the National Assembly attended the session at which the new President was to be elected. The President of the National Assembly declared the session inquorate and the election was postponed. It was strongly alleged that a number of Christian deputies had been intimidated, threatened or forcibly prevented from attending the election by the LF and soldiers under the command of Gen. Awn. Consultations between Syria and the USA (initiated in mid-1988) resumed during September to find a compromise candidate for the presidency. It was reported that they had agreed to support the candidacy of Mikhail ad-Daher, a deputy in the National Assembly, but Christian leaders in Lebanon repeated their rejection of any candidate imposed upon them by foreign powers.

A second attempt to stage the presidential election was made on 22 September 1988, but, again, the session of the National Assembly failed to achieve a quorum. Only minutes before his term of office was due to expire, President Gemayel appointed a six-member interim military Government, composed of three Christian and three Muslim officers, led by Gen. Awn, to rule until a new President was elected. Muslim politicians had refused to participate in an interim civilian government headed, contrary to the Constitution, by a Maronite Prime Minister, Pierre Hélou, instead of a Sunni Muslim. The three Muslim officers named in the interim military Government refused to take up their posts, while the two Christian members of the existing civilian Government surrendered their posts in recognition of the authority of the interim military administration. Lebanon was plunged into a constitutional crisis, with two Governments, one Christian, in east Beirut, and one predominantly Muslim, in west Beirut, claiming legitimacy. Syria refused to recognize the interim military Government and there were fears that, unless a new President could be elected, the fact of dual authority would formalize what was already an effective partition of the country into Christian and Muslim cantons.

The new interim military Government was regarded with suspicion by the LF militia, which feared that it would seek an accommodation with Syria in order to further the presidential ambitions of Gen. Awn. In February 1989 there was a major confrontation between the LF and Lebanese army brigades (both Christian and Muslim) loyal to Gen. Awn. While neither side achieved a decisive victory, the authority of the Lebanese army (which had been steadily eroded) was restored as a result of the clashes. On 17 February, after having suffered heavy losses, the LF was ordered by its commander, Samir Geagea, to withdraw from many parts of east Beirut. In response to allegations by Gen. Awn that it was levying illegal taxes, the LF agreed to close its 'customs point' in east Beirut, and Geagea subsequently claimed that both the LF and the Lebanese army were united in the aim of expelling Syrian forces from Lebanon.

GENERAL AWN'S 'WAR OF LIBERATION'

In March 1989 the most violent clashes for two years erupted in Beirut between Christian and Muslim brigades of the Lebanese army, loyal to Gen. Awn, and Syrian-backed Muslim militia,

positioned on either side of the 'Green Line'. While the immediate cause of the fighting was the blockade of illegal ports in west and south Beirut by Christian forces, Gen. Awn declared at a press conference on 14 March that his Government had decided to take all measures for the immediate withdrawal of Syrian forces from Lebanon.

During the ensuing six months Gen. Awn's self-declared 'war of liberation' developed into one of the most violent confrontations of the Lebanese conflict, causing heavy casualties in both the Christian and Muslim communities. Syria's claim that its forces were not directly involved in the hostilities was regarded as highly disingenuous, but most observers doubted whether Gen. Awn realistically expected to achieve the withdrawal of Syrian forces from Lebanon by military means. Rather, his aim was perceived to be the 'internationalization' of the Lebanese conflict in order to increase diplomatic pressure on Syria to effect such a withdrawal.

The ferocity of the fighting and the scale of the casualties prompted several diplomatic initiatives to secure a peace settlement (for a full account, see the chapter on Lebanon). However, successive plans for peace foundered on the question of the withdrawal of Syria's estimated 35,000–40,000 troops in Lebanon, on which Gen. Awn insisted as an essential condition of any cease-fire agreement. At an emergency summit meeting of Arab leaders in Casablanca during 23 May–28 May 1989, the proposal (supported by Egypt, Iraq, Jordan and the PLO) that Syria should immediately withdraw its troops from Lebanon was abandoned in response to Syrian opposition.

By August 1989 it had become clear that Syria was prepared to disregard international censure of its role in Lebanon and to wage a war of attrition against the Lebanese army. Its refusal to consider any compromise with regard to the withdrawal of its forces stemmed from the long-standing strategic consideration of its need to control Lebanon in order to guard against any Israeli strike in the Beka'a valley. However, Syria was restrained from using its overwhelming military superiority to impose its authority on 'Christian Lebanon' by several factors. Initially, Syria feared that Israel might come to the defence of Lebanese Christians in the event of a full-scale military assault on the Christian enclave. Also, for economic reasons, it was anxious to avoid any further deterioration of its relations both with Western countries and the USSR, which such an assault might have provoked.

In September 1989 the Tripartite Arab Committee on Lebanon announced details of a seven-point plan for peace in Lebanon which, unlike its previous diplomatic initiatives, did not demand the withdrawal of Syrian forces from Lebanon. Rather, in recognition of the futility of attempting to persuade Syria to withdraw its forces, diplomatic efforts in support of the new peace plan now concentrated on persuading Gen. Awn to accept its terms. The proposals envisaged a cease-fire (to be supervised by a Lebanese security committee under the auspices of the Assistant Secretary-General of the Arab League, Lakhdar al-Ibrahimi); the ending of the Syrian naval blockade of the Christian enclave; and the convening of the Lebanese National Assembly to discuss a 'charter of national conciliation' drafted by the Tripartite Committee. The new plan presented Gen. Awn with a dilemma, since he had already, on previous occasions, rejected its principal proposals. At the same time, it had become clear that the 'war of liberation' was being fought in vain. The evacuation in early September of US diplomatic personnel and the closure of the US embassy in Beirut, in response to alleged threats of 'Christian terrorism', were widely regarded as signalling the end of Awn's hopes of achieving his aim though international intervention. Moreover, by September more than 800 people were reported to have been killed, and more than 2,000 injured, in the six months since the escalation of the hostilities. The Christian population (those who had not already fled Beirut), which had at first enthusiastically supported the 'war of liberation', was badly demoralized. On 22 September, following reports that the French Minister of Foreign Affairs had warned him that he could expect no international assistance if he refused to accept the Tripartite Arab Committee's latest proposals, Gen. Awn announced that he had abandoned the 'war of liberation' against Syria and agreed to the seven points of the Committee's peace plan for Lebanon. However, he subsequently vowed to continue the war by political means until the liberation was complete.

For Syria, therefore, the problem remained of how to impose its authority on Christian Lebanese by means other than military force, since, ultimately, it had been international pressure that had forced Gen. Awn to abandon his campaign. On 25 September it was announced that the Lebanese National Assembly would convene in Saudi Arabia on 30 September to discuss political reforms aimed at ending the Lebanese conflict. The proposed reforms included the transfer of executive powers from the Christian Maronite President to the Sunni Muslim Prime Minister; the ending of sectarianism in the army and the civil service; and an increase in the number of seats in the National Assembly, from 99 to 108.

In October 1989 the Lebanese National Assembly endorsed a charter of national reconciliation (the Ta'if agreement—for full details, see the chapter on Lebanon), which envisaged a continuing role for the Syrian armed forces in Lebanon by stipulating that they should assist in the implementation of a security plan incorporated in the agreement. The endorsement of the charter by the National Assembly was denounced by Gen. Awn as a betrayal of Lebanese sovereignty, since Christian deputies to the Assembly had reportedly assured Gen. Awn that they would permit concessions on the question of political reform in Lebanon only in exchange for a full withdrawal of Syrian forces.

Following a meeting of the newly-formed Lebanese Cabinet on 28 November 1989, it was announced that Gen. Awn had again been dismissed as Commander-in-Chief of the Lebanese army, and that Gen. Emile Lahoud had been appointed in his place. It was feared that Syrian forces would now launch an assault on Awn's stronghold in Baabda, east Beirut. Samir Geagea, the commander of the LF, announced that, in the event of such an assault, the LF would fight beside Gen. Awn, even though the Ta'if agreement had, to a large extent, been facilitated by the co-operation of Lebanon's Maronite leaders. Geagea's refusal to reject the Ta'if agreement led Gen. Awn to declare the LF to be an ally of Syria, and precipitated intense fighting between Awn's forces and the LF in early 1990 for control of the Christian enclave in Beirut.

Fighting continued in Beirut until Syria intervened decisively in October 1990, when thousands of its troops were deployed to evict Gen. Awn from the presidential palace at Baabda, after President Elias Hrawi of Lebanon had requested the troops' assistance. Christian resistance to the legitimization of Syrian influence in Lebanon had finally been broken, paving the way for the full implementation of the Ta'if agreement.

THE INTIFADA AND THE SHULTZ PLAN

In December 1987 a violent Palestinian uprising against Israeli occupation of the West Bank and Gaza Strip erupted in the Occupied Territories. At the end of February 1988, with the *intifada* showing no sign of moderating in intensity, the US Secretary of State, George Shultz, embarked on a tour of Middle Eastern capitals, including Damascus, in an attempt to solicit support for a new peace initiative. The Shultz Plan proposed an international peace conference and direct talks between Israel and each of its adversaries (excluding the PLO), and an interim period of limited autonomy for Palestinians in the Territories, pending a permanent negotiated settlement (for full details, see Documents on Palestine, p. 69). President Assad stopped short of rejecting the plan outright, but, in certain fundamental respects, it was impossible for any Arab leader to accept: it failed to recognize the right of the PLO to participate in peace negotiations or the right of the Palestinians to self-determination. Further talks between Shultz and Assad in April failed to reconcile the two sides.

At the beginning of June 1988 an extraordinary summit meeting of the Arab League was held in Algiers to discuss the *intifada* and the Arab–Israeli conflict in general. The final communiqué of the summit, endorsed by all 21 League members, including Syria, rendered the Shultz Plan effectively moribund by demanding the participation of the PLO in any future peace conference, endorsing the Palestinians' right to self-determination and urging the establishment of an independent Palestinian state in the West Bank. Syria, alone of all the Arab states, refused to recognize the independent Palestinian State, proclaimed at the 19th session of the PNC in Algiers in November.

FOREIGN RELATIONS 1988–90

The cease-fire in the Iran–Iraq War, which came into force on 20 August 1988, created a number of problems for Syria. As the sole Arab supporter of Iran, Syria was already isolated, and the cessation of hostilities presented Iraq with an opportunity to settle old scores with its Baath rival, initially by attempting to thwart Syrian plans for domination over Lebanon. In September Iraq was reportedly supplying arms and money to the Christian LF in Lebanon and, following the failure of the Lebanese National Assembly to elect a new President, Iraq proclaimed its support for the interim military administration appointed by President Gemayel, which was opposed by Syria. After March 1989, when the 'war of liberation' waged by the Lebanese army against Syrian forces in Lebanon began, Iraq became the principal supplier of arms to the Lebanese army. The expression of Syrian–Iraqi rivalry by proxy in Lebanon also complicated attempts by the Arab League to achieve a cease-fire there following the escalation of hostilities in March 1989, since it was feared that the withdrawal of Syrian forces from Lebanon might provoke a direct confrontation between Iraq and Syria.

Syria found itself on the same side as Iraq in a dispute with Turkey over the diversion of water from the Euphrates river in order to fill the reservoir supplying Turkey's newly-constructed Atatürk dam. In January 1990 Syria lodged a formal complaint with Turkey over the effects of the diversion on Syria's water and electricity supplies. However, the Turkish Government rejected the complaint, claiming that it had increased the supply of water to Iraq and Syria by 50% between November 1989 and January 1990 in order to make good the loss of water caused by the diversion in early 1990. The Syrian and Turkish Ministers of Foreign Affairs met in Turkey in June to discuss relations, in particular the sharing of the Euphrates waters.

SYRIA AND THE 1990–91 GULF CRISIS

Syria was eager to exploit the diplomatic opportunities arising from Iraq's invasion of Kuwait in August 1990, and, in particular, to improve its relations with the USA and Egypt. In December 1989 Egypt and Syria had agreed to re-establish diplomatic relations after a rupture lasting almost 12 years, and in May 1990 President Hosni Mubarak of Egypt visited Syria, the first such visit by an Egyptian leader since 1977.

Syria supported Egypt's efforts to co-ordinate Arab responses to Iraq's invasion of Kuwait, and agreed, at an emergency summit meeting of the Arab League, held in Cairo on 10 August 1990, to send troops to Saudi Arabia as part of a pan-Arab deterrent force supporting the US effort to deter an Iraqi invasion of Saudi Arabia. Despite widespread popular support among Syria's Palestinian population for the Iraqi President, Saddam Hussain, Syria committed itself to the demand for an unconditional Iraqi withdrawal from Kuwait, and later in August the first contingent of Syrian troops was deployed in Saudi Arabia, joining a US-led multinational force. Syria claimed that its troops were in Saudi Arabia purely for defensive purposes.In late October 1990 the objections of the United Kingdom prevented the EC from removing the economic sanctions which it had applied against Syria since 1986. By late November 1990, however, it became apparent that Syria's participation in the US-led multinational force was transforming its relations with the West, when diplomatic ties were restored between Syria and the United Kingdom. By the beginning of December an estimated 20,000 Syrian troops had been deployed in Saudi Arabia.

In mid-January 1991 President Saddam Hussain of Iraq rejected a message from President Assad, who sought to persuade him that Iraq's occupation of Kuwait benefited Israel alone. Following attacks by Iraqi *Scud* missiles on Israel, Syria warned Israel not to become militarily involved in the Gulf crisis, and implied that it might be obliged to withdraw from the multinational force in the event of an Israeli attack on an Arab state. Subsequent statements, however, indicated that Syria would tolerate limited Israeli retaliation against Iraq for the missile attacks.

In early 1991 the overwhelming military defeat of Iraq by the US-led multinational force placed Syria in a stronger position with regard to virtually all of its major regional concerns. Syria consolidated the improvement in relations with Egypt, which had begun in December 1989, and laid the foundation for increased co-operation in matters of regional security. In early March 1991 the foreign ministers of the members of the GCC—Saudi Arabia, Kuwait, Qatar, Bahrain, the United Arab Emirates (UAE) and Oman—met their Egyptian and Syrian counterparts in Damascus to discuss regional security. The formation of an Arab peace-keeping force, comprising mainly Egyptian and Syrian troops, was subsequently announced. In early May, however, Egypt announced its decision to withdraw all of its forces from the Gulf region within three months, thus casting doubt on the future of joint Syrian-Egyptian security arrangements.

Syria's decision to ally itself, in opposition to Iraq, with the Western powers and the so-called 'moderate' Arab states led the USA to realize that it could no longer seek to exclude it from any role in the resolution of the Arab–Israeli conflict. After the conclusion of hostilities with Iraq, US diplomacy focused on seeking to initiate negotiations between Israel, the Arab states, including Syria, and Palestinian representatives. The loss of credibility that the PLO had suffered as a result of its support for Iraq in the Gulf War left all the Arab states in a stronger position to dictate the final terms of a peace settlement with Israel, and was especially gratifying to Syria, which had long opposed Yasser Arafat's leadership.

Despite attempts in early May 1991 by both the USA and the USSR to create sufficient common ground between Israel and Syria for peace negotiations to begin, Baker stated that there were still 'significant' differences between Israel and Syria regarding the holding of a Middle East peace conference. Syria remained adamant that talks with Israel should take place within the framework of an international conference, with the full participation of the UN, and that afterwards such a conference should reconvene at regular intervals. Israel remained opposed both to UN participation and to the reconvening of the conference after an initial session had been held. The USA, for its part, excluded the possibility of holding a peace conference without Syrian participation.

In mid-July 1991 President Assad agreed for the first time (following a meeting with the US Secretary of State) to participate in direct negotiations with Israel at a regional peace conference, for which the terms of reference would be a comprehensive peace settlement based on UN Security Council Resolutions 242 and 338. By agreeing to participate on the terms proposed by the USA, Syria decisively increased the diplomatic pressure on Israel to do likewise. On 4 August the Israeli Cabinet formally agreed to attend a peace conference on the terms proposed by the USA and the USSR.

NEGOTIATIONS WITH ISRAEL 1993–2000

By late October 1993—following an initial, 'symbolic' session of the conference held in Madrid, Spain, in October 1991, and attended by Israeli, Syrian, Egyptian, Lebanese and Palestinian-Jordanian delegations—11 sessions of bilateral negotiations had been held between Israeli and Syrian delegations. In April 1992 they had proceeded to debate the precise meaning of UN Security Council Resolution 242, but the Israeli Government continued firmly to reject any exchange of occupied land—including the Golan Heights—in return for a peace settlement. In May, owing to the failure of bilateral negotiations to achieve any progress towards a peace settlement, Syria and Lebanon refused to attend multilateral discussions, convened in Belgium, Austria, Canada and Japan, to discuss, among other issues, water resources and the question of Palestinian refugees. Following the final dissolution of the USSR in December 1991, and the consequent erosion of its position as a potential counterfoil to the USA's Middle Eastern policies, Syria remained obliged actively to support and participate in the US peace initiative. With regard to other regional issues, however, the Syrian Government appeared determined not to acquiesce in the interests of the USA, announcing, in mid-April 1992, that it would continue to maintain air links with Libya, in defiance of the sanctions that the UN had imposed on that country (see the chapter on Libya). In late April, in an attempt to allay suspicions of its Middle Eastern policies, the US Administration formally assured the Syrian Government that it had no hostile intentions towards it.

The sixth round of bilateral negotiations between Israeli and Syrian delegations, which commenced on 24 September 1992 in

Washington, DC, and lasted for a month, seemed at times to be close to achieving real progress on the issue of the Golan Heights. The new Labour-dominated coalition Government in Israel (elected in mid-July) reportedly indicated its willingness to consider some form of compromise, although there was no sign that it was prepared to meet Syria's minimum demand: Israel's full and unconditional compliance with UN Security Council Resolution 242, which requires, *inter alia*, the withdrawal of Israeli armed forces from territories occupied in 1967.

Initially, the Declaration of Principles on Palestinian Self-Rule (see Documents on Palestine, p. 72), signed by Israel and the PLO on 13 September 1993, drew a guarded response from Syria. Subsequently, however, President Assad indicated that he had serious reservations about the agreement, and that he regarded the secret negotiations between Israel and the PLO which had led to it as having weakened the united Arab position in the ongoing peace process with Israel. It appeared that Syria would not actively oppose the agreement, but there was no sign that it would cease to support those Palestinian factions, such as the Damascus-based Popular Front for the Liberation of Palestine—General Command (PFLP—GC), which had vowed to do so. Syria reportedly feared that Israel might now view the terms of the Declaration of Principles as a model for an agreement with Syria on the Golan Heights (i.e. the exchange of only a partial withdrawal of Israeli armed forces from the Golan Heights for a comprehensive peace settlement).

In January 1994 Syria agreed to resume bilateral negotiations with Israel. On 16 January President Assad met with US President Bill Clinton for talks in Geneva aimed at giving fresh momentum to the talks. The Israeli Prime Minister, Itzhak Rabin, responded by announcing that a referendum would have to be held in Israel on the issue of withdrawal from the Golan Heights; Syria's Minister of Foreign Affairs, Farouk ash-Shara', claimed that this would contravene international law. Bilateral discussions continued in Washington, DC, on 24 January, but were temporarily suspended on 27 February following the murder of some 30 Muslim worshippers at a mosque in Hebron on the West Bank by a right-wing Jewish extremist. Assad continued to reject proposals to hold 'secret' talks with Israel, and ignored Israeli demands to prevent attacks by Lebanese militia groups on the Israeli forces in southern Lebanon. In late April Warren Christopher, the US Secretary of State, visited the Middle East in an apparent attempt to break the deadlock over the Golan Heights. Under the Israeli plan, to be phased over a period of eight years, Syria would initially be granted control over the four Druze settlements in the Golan Heights, the next stage would involve the closure of Israeli settlements in the Golan, and the final phase would be a full-scale withdrawal. In May, when an agreement was signed between Israel and the PLO providing for Palestinian self-rule in the Gaza Strip and Jericho, Syrian officials remained sceptical, arguing in favour of a united Arab approach to the peace settlement. Syria similarly expressed dissatisfaction at the agreement reached between Israel and Jordan in early June, accusing the two sides of placing obstacles in the way of reaching a comprehensive regional peace settlement.

The US Special Co-ordinator to the Middle East, Dennis Ross, met with Israeli and Syrian leaders in September 1994 as speculation grew about possible secret talks between the two countries. In Israel Itzhak Rabin faced growing public discontent over the prospect of withdrawal from the Golan Heights, and in late September a group of Labour party members submitted a proposal to the Knesset to table a law requiring the Government to secure an absolute majority in order to withdraw from the Golan. The Middle East peace process was again curtailed in mid-October following the events in the Gulf (see the chapter on Kuwait). On 18 October a group of 300 Syrian Jews were allowed to emigrate to Israel in what was seen as a gesture of goodwill on the part of the Syrian Government towards its Israeli neighbour. President Clinton attended the signing of the peace treaty between Israel and Jordan on 26 October, and on the following day he visited Syria—the first visit to the country by a US President for 20 years. Pressure on President Assad to reach an agreement with Israel over the Golan Heights increased following the Israeli-Jordanian treaty, and it was reported that Assad might be considering Israel's proposal for a phased withdrawal but over a shorter period of time. In mid-March 1995—more than a year after their suspension—discussions between Syria and Israel finally resumed, although initially involving only the ambassador of each country to the USA.In late May 1995 Israel and Syria concluded a 'framework understanding on security arrangements', in order to facilitate the participation in the negotiations of the two countries' chiefs of staff. Israel stated publicly for the first time that it had proposed a four-year timetable for the withdrawal of its armed forces from the Golan Heights, but that Syria had insisted on one of 18 months. In June the Israeli Minister of Foreign Affairs, Shimon Peres, referred to the Golan as 'Syrian territory', while the Israeli President, Ezer Weizman, clearly stated that Israel was negotiating on the basis of a full withdrawal to the international border. None the less, opinion polls in Israel suggested that the majority of the population was against full withdrawal, in particular Jewish settlers in the Golan itself. President Assad spoke publicly about the peace process for the first time in June and took the unprecedented step of actually referring to Israel by name. In late June the Israeli and Syrian chiefs of staff held talks in Washington, DC. Syria was reported to have proposed a means of demilitarization in the Golan Heights whereby Syria would demilitarize 10 km on its side of the border for every 6 km demilitarized by Israel. However, neither Government was prepared to release further details of the negotiations. Syria's willingness to compromise on demilitarization failed to give a new impetus to the peace talks, which had reportedly stalled over Israel's insistence on retaining its early-warning system on Mount Hermon. There were also differences over the delineation of the final border between the two countries, with Syria insisting on a return to the border that existed before the 1967 war, and Israel demanding a return to the pre-1948 border. Syria blamed Israel for the lack of progress, and many observers concluded that Israeli Prime Minister Rabin had decided not to try to reach a full settlement with Syria until after the Israeli elections due to take place in 1996. In October President Assad stated that Syria was willing to accept Israeli air surveillance over the Golan Heights but not radar monitoring. US diplomatic efforts failed to achieve a resumption of peace talks. In November, on becoming Israeli Prime Minister after the assassination of Itzhak Rabin, Shimon Peres declared that seeking peace with Syria would be his top priority. He immediately strengthened the Israeli negotiating team and called for the talks to be expanded to cover a range of political issues in addition to military questions. Syria welcomed Peres' initiative, and the two countries concluded a 10-point agreement to act as a framework for new negotiations. A new round of US-sponsored talks began at the end of December in Maryland, USA, and continued in January and February 1996. According to US officials, some progress was made, and there were rumours that agreement had been reached in principle on border issues. US Secretary of State Christopher visited Damascus in February to assure President Assad that despite Peres' decision to call an early election in May, the Israeli premier remained determined to negotiate a settlement with Syria. The USA clearly hoped that a Labour victory in the elections would put Peres in a strong position to make concessions to Syria and that a preliminary agreement might be reached before the US presidential election in November 1996.

A series of suicide bomb attacks in Israel in late February and early March 1996, in which more than 50 Israelis died, shattered support for the peace process in Israel. As part of the tough stance Prime Minister Peres adopted following the attacks, and against US advice, he broke off negotiations with Syria. Despite pressure from the USA and Egypt, President Assad refused to attend the 'summit of peacemakers' at Sharm esh-Sheikh, Egypt, which was convened in March in response to these attacks. Syria claimed that the summit meeting was simply an attempt to support the embattled Israeli Prime Minister and argued that the only effective means of saving the peace process was to reconvene the Madrid conference. After the summit Israel demanded that Syria should explicitly condemn terrorism before it would resume peace talks. Syria stated that it did condemn terrorism, but claimed that violent resistance to Israeli occupation was a legitimate right of the Palestinians. Syria also rejected demands by Israel and the USA that it

should close down the offices in Damascus of radical Palestinian groups opposed to the peace process.

Negotiations suffered a further reverse in April 1996, when Israel launched 'Operation Grapes of Wrath', a massive bombardment of Lebanon in response to Hezbollah rocket attacks on Kiryat Shmona and other northern settlements (see below). Some analysts argued that this offensive confirmed Syrian interpretations of the objectives of Prime Minister Peres—that neutralizing Hezbollah would not only bring advantages in terms of security, but would also allow Israel to take a tougher stance in its negotiations with Syria on the Golan Heights and southern Lebanon. Having failed to achieve these objectives, when both Syria and Lebanon refused to yield to Israeli and US demands, Peres gave priority once again to negotiations with the Palestinians and it appeared that talks with Syria might be suspended for a long time.

During the approach to the Israeli elections at the end of May 1996, Shimon Peres told voters that he doubted whether a peace agreement could be reached with Syria without returning all of the Golan Heights, and added that he had always been prepared to make territorial compromises over the Golan. His right-wing challenger, Likud leader Binyamin Netanyahu, in contrast, repeated his pledge that he would only negotiate with Syria on the understanding that Israel retained control over the Golan Heights. Netanyahu's unexpected victory in the elections and the subsequent formation of a right-wing Government in Israel was greeted with alarm in Syria, which condemned the new administration as 'a cabinet of rabbis, racists and generals'. Addressing the Knesset in June, Prime Minister Netanyahu appealed for the reopening of unconditional peace talks with Arab states but rejected the 'land-for-peace' policies of his Labour predecessor and told deputies that his emphasis would be on security. He insisted that retaining sovereignty over the Golan Heights must be the basis of any peace settlement with Syria. When the new Israeli Minister of Foreign Affairs, David Levy, suggested that Israel might meet Syria 'half-way' on the Golan problem, his statement was immediately disavowed by Netanyahu's spokesman, who insisted that only statements made by the Prime Minister reflected Israeli policy on these issues. The final communiqué of the emergency Arab League summit meeting held in Cairo at the end of June urged the new Israeli Government not to abandon the 'land-for-peace' principle. It appealed for the removal of all Israeli settlements on the Golan Heights and its return to Syria. In response, however, the Israeli premier stated that Israel should wait at least two generations before even discussing the possibility of giving up the Golan Heights, even if Syria agreed to normalize relations with Israel.In early August 1996, during a visit to Israel's 'security zone' in southern Lebanon, Netanyahu warned that further attacks by Hezbollah guerrillas might provoke Israeli reprisals against Syria. Tensions mounted as the Syrian Chief of Staff claimed that the military option was still open to Syria in its dispute with Israel, and intelligence sources reported the redeployment of large numbers of Syrian troops from Lebanon to new positions in Syria, possibly to reinforce the western defences of the capital. An offer by Netanyahu to withdraw Israeli troops from southern Lebanon, on condition that Hezbollah forces be disarmed and that both Lebanon and Syria agree to prevent them launching any new attacks on northern Israel, was rejected by President Assad. Such a move would have denied Syria the option of using Hezbollah to exert pressure on Israel while leaving Israel firmly in control of Golan. The Syrian President insisted that peace negotiations could only resume if Netanyahu's Government honoured earlier agreements and understandings reached with Itzhak Rabin and Shimon Peres. President Assad stated that, before his assassination, Prime Minister Rabin had given a commitment to the USA that Israel would withdraw from the whole of the Golan Heights. However, Netanyahu declared that he was under no obligation to abide by what he referred to as 'theoretical statements' made by his predecessor during the course of negotiations, and insisted that peace talks must be without prior conditions.

At the end of December 1996 Syria blamed Israel for a bomb attack on a bus in Damascus, although most observers believed that responsibility for the attack lay elsewhere (see below). During the early part of 1997 the Israeli Government's determination to proceed with the controversial Jewish settlement at Har Homa in Arab East Jerusalem, and the collapse in negotiations between Israel and the Palestinian (National) Authority (PA), further obstructed the Israeli-Syrian peace initiative. In February Israel announced that new Jewish settlements were to be constructed on the Golan, and in July withdrawal from the Golan was made conditional on approval by two-thirds of the Knesset. In April the Israeli press accused Syria of developing weapons of mass destruction, including missiles armed with lethal nerve gas capable of hitting targets inside Israel. Damascus denied the allegations. In August President Assad invited a delegation of Israeli Arabs, including members of the Knesset, to Damascus, on what was only the second visit of its kind. Assad informed them that he thought a withdrawal from the Golan was unlikely while Netanyahu remained Prime Minister. Meanwhile, Western military analysts reported that Syria had deployed new 200T-55MV main battle tanks, supplied by Ukraine, in forward positions near the Golan Heights.

Syria was sceptical that the US-brokered Wye River Memorandum (see Documents on Palestine, p. 86), signed in October 1998 by Israel and the PA, would increase the likelihood of a lasting peace in the Middle East; President Assad reiterated demands for a resumption of 'land-for-peace' negotiations. In early November the Syrian-based militant Islamic Jihad claimed responsibility for a bomb attack in Jerusalem, and threatened further attacks in opposition to the Wye agreement. In mid-February 1999 Syria apparently rejected an Israeli proposal to resume discussions, stating its intention to postpone talks until after the Israeli general election, scheduled for May. In early 1999 Israel urged the Syrian Government to exert its influence to end Hezbollah attacks on Israeli forces in southern Lebanon, and to curb the group's activities during the Israeli election campaign. Following the defeat of Binyamin Netanyahu and his Likud party on 17 May, Israel's new Prime Minister, Ehud Barak (of the Labour-led One Israel coalition), reportedly proposed a five-phase plan to conclude a peace with Syria and to effect an Israeli withdrawal from southern Lebanon. Syria responded by demanding that Barak should uphold his pre-election pledge to withdraw from Lebanon within one year of his election and to resume peace negotiations from their point of deadlock in 1996. None the less, Syria welcomed Barak's election victory, and in late June 1999 President Assad was reported to have described Barak as a 'strong and sincere' man with a 'real desire' to achieve peace with Syria. However, Syria strongly condemned air-strikes carried out by Israel on central and southern Lebanon at the end of June, which were alleged to have been wholly attributable to the outgoing Netanyahu administration. At the inauguration of the new Israeli Cabinet on 6 July, Barak promised to negotiate a bilateral peace with Syria, based on UN Security Council Resolutions 242 and 338, apparently signalling to Damascus his intention to return most of the occupied Golan Heights to Syria in exchange for peace and normalized relations. In mid-July, prior to a meeting in Washington, DC, between Barak and US President Clinton, Syria reportedly warned dissidents of Palestinian organizations based in Damascus to cease their military operations against Israel and was believed to have temporarily disrupted the supply of weapons from Iran to Hezbollah guerrillas in southern Lebanon. Moreover, on 20 July Syria reported a 'cease-fire' with Israel, although disagreements remained, most notably over the point at which previous peace negotiations had been suspended. On 4 September, when Israel and the Palestinian National Authority (PA) signed the Sharm esh-Sheikh Memorandum ('Wye Two'—see Documents on Palestine, p. 88, and the chapter on Israel), the US Secretary of State, Madeleine Albright, held talks with President Assad in Damascus. However, nothing tangible was agreed regarding the resumption of peace talks with Israel. On 22 September Albright held discussions with Syria's Minister of Foreign Affairs, Farouk ash-Shara', in New York, USA. Meanwhile, at the end of the month Albright angered Israelis when, for the first time, she openly declared US support for Syrian demands for a complete Israeli withdrawal from the Golan Heights.

Increased hopes of a resumption of Israeli-Syrian talks were tempered by continuing public disagreement over whether, as Syria claimed, the then Israeli Premier, Itzhak Rabin, had agreed, during the previous round of negotiations in 1994–96,

to a full Israeli withdrawal to its pre-1967 border. Israel asserted that it had only agreed to withdraw to the pre-1948 border between Palestine and Syria. Nevertheless, on 8 December 1999, reportedly as a result of diplomatic efforts by US President Bill Clinton and secret meetings between Israeli and Syrian officials, Israel and Syria agreed to resume direct negotiations at ministerial level. Announcing the resumption of talks, Clinton stated that they would resume 'from the point where they left off'. He did not, however, specify where that point was.

The first round of discussions between the Syrian Minister of Foreign Affairs, Farouk ash-Shara', and the Israeli premier, Ehud Barak, was opened by the US President on 15 December 1999 in Washington, DC. The talks commenced despite an increase in tension in southern Lebanon, and made little progress. Both sides, however, emphasized their determination to end the state of war between their two countries, and Barak reiterated Israel's willingness in principle to return the Golan Heights to Syria (although, as ever, the question remained as to what each side deemed that to mean). Israeli and Syrian officials agreed to resume discussions in January 2000. In late December 1999 there were reports that Syria and Israel had agreed an informal 'cease-fire' in order to limit the conflict in Lebanon.

A second round of senior-level talks was held on 3–10 January 2000 in Shepherdstown, West Virginia, USA, with the participation of President Clinton, after Syria and Israel had agreed on the establishment of four committees to discuss simultaneously the issues of borders, security, normalization of relations, and water sharing. However, during the eight days of talks, differences emerged as to what should be the priorities for negotiations. Israel argued for security arrangements and the normalization of relations, while Syria insisted that the question of the Golan Heights be resolved first. As the talks proved to be inconclusive, on 7 January the US Government presented a 'draft working document' to both Syrian and Israeli negotiating teams, intended to act as the basis for a framework agreement. The document, which set out the key issues requiring resolution, was duly endorsed and both Syria and Israel pledged to reconvene for further discussions on 19 January. In mid-January, however, bilateral relations again deteriorated. Syria accused Israel of having leaked the framework document, and repeated its claim that Israel was reneging on promises made during the 1994–96 round of talks. Syrian officials now demanded a 'written' commitment from Israel to withdraw from the Golan Heights prior to a resumption of talks, while Israel demanded the personal involvement of President Assad in the peace process and that Syria take action to restrain Hezbollah in southern Lebanon. Within days of the announcement, on 17 January 2000, that the talks scheduled to begin two days later had been postponed indefinitely, violence intensified further in southern Lebanon. The informal 'cease-fire' ended in late January, following the killing by Hezbollah of a senior SLA commander.

In late February 2000 Barak was reported to have admitted that Israel had indeed agreed to withdraw from all of the Golan Heights ahead of the 1994–96 talks. However, he also indicated the intention of a unilateral Israeli withdrawal from southern Lebanon. This was confirmed in early March when the Israeli Cabinet voted unanimously to withdraw its forces from Lebanon by 7 July 2000, even in the absence of an Israeli-Syrian peace settlement. Israel also sought to increase the pressure on Syria by increasing the proportion of voters on the Golan Heights that would be required to approve, in a referendum, any deal on a handover to Syria.

On 26 March 2000 President Assad held discussions with US President Clinton in Geneva, amid expectations of a renewed breakthrough in Syrian-Israeli relations. Clinton reportedly conveyed a proposal from Israel that would involve continued Israeli sovereignty over a narrow strip of land along the north-eastern shore of Lake Tiberias which under the pre-1967 border had been part of Israel. This strip of land had become a crucial means of access to the water of Lake Tiberias for Israel. Syria was willing to grant access but not sovereignty. It was clear that water security was a vital issue for both sides. Israeli demands that it be permitted to operate a military early-warning station on Mount Hermon remained a sticking-point. Syria reiterated its willingness to allow a third party to run such a station, but not Israel itself.

The Clinton-Assad meeting thus failed to reach an agreement that would allow a resumption of the peace negotiations. As violence escalated in southern Lebanon, hardening Israeli attitudes were further demonstrated by the decision of the Government, on 13 April 2000, to end its suspension of the building of Jewish settlements on the Golan Heights. Attention switched back towards the Israeli-Palestinian track of the Middle East peace process, assuaging Palestinian anxieties that Syria might unilaterally pursue a peace settlement with Israel. In early May the foreign ministers of Syria, Egypt and Saudi Arabia held talks regarding the peace process in the Syrian city of Palmyra. The meeting was viewed as an attempt to present a united Arab front to the USA and Israel, especially in the approach to the Israeli withdrawal from southern Lebanon. It was later reported that Egypt and Saudi Arabia had pledged military support to Syria in the event of an Israeli attack. The death on 10 June 2000 of President Hafiz Assad (see below), and domestic preoccupations with the issue of his succession, inevitably stalled the Israeli-Syrian track even further.

SYRIAN DOMINANCE IN LEBANON DURING THE 1990s

By aligning itself with the Western powers and the moderate Arab states against Iraq in August 1990, Syria had obtained a free rein to consolidate its interests in Lebanon. In October it had acted to suppress the revolt led by Gen. Michel Awn (see above) as the first step towards the implementation of the Ta'if agreement. The Ta'if agreement stipulated a formal role for Syrian forces in Lebanon, assigning to them the responsibility for maintaining security there until the various Lebanese militias had been disbanded and the Lebanese army could itself assume that role. The implementation of the Ta'if agreement accelerated in the aftermath of Iraq's military defeat by the US-led multinational force in February 1991, and it culminated in the signing, in May, of a treaty of 'fraternity, co-operation and co-ordination' between Syria and Lebanon.

In late May 1992 there was international concern at the escalating tension between Israel and Syria, as expressed in southern Lebanon. Syria feared that the USA might permit Israel to undermine, militarily, the implementation of the Ta'if agreement. The possibility of direct conflict between Syrian and Israeli armed forces arose from Syria's decision to allow Hezbollah fighters to continue to mount attacks on northern Israeli settlements, in the belief that only by continued coercion would Israel withdraw from occupied Arab territories. By the same token, the Israeli Government cited attacks by Hezbollah fighters in justification of its refusal to comply with UN Security Council Resolution 425 and withdraw its armed forces from the southern Lebanese 'buffer zone'. In July 1993 Israeli armed forces launched their most intense offensive ('Operation Accountability') against the positions of Hezbollah and other guerrilla factions in southern Lebanon since 'Operation Peace for Galilee' in 1982. Israeli aircraft were also reported to have attacked Syrian army positions in the Beka'a valley. Many civilians were killed and more than 250,000 Lebanese were forced to flee from their homes. Mediation by the USA and Syria produced an informal 'understanding' between Israel and Hezbollah whereby fighting was to be confined to the southern 'security zone'. However, Hezbollah continued to strike at Israeli targets, provoking Israeli reprisals. In April 1996, little more than a month before the Israeli general elections, there was a new escalation in the conflict in southern Lebanon. After Hezbollah fighters fired rockets into northern Israel, wounding 36 people, and killed an Israeli soldier in the security zone, Prime Minister Peres launched 'Operation Grapes of Wrath' during which, for almost two weeks, Israel attacked targets in the southern part of the 'security zone', the Beka'a valley and (for the first time in 14 years) the southern suburbs of Beirut. In the face of international pressure to bring about a cease-fire, the US Secretary of State, Warren Christopher, turned to Syria to resolve the crisis. After a week of shuttle diplomacy by the Secretary of State, a cease-fire 'understanding' was reached, under which, as in 1993, it was agreed effectively to confine the conflict to the security zone. The 'understanding' also provided for the establishment of an Israel-Lebanon Monitoring Group (ILMG), comprising representatives of Syria, Lebanon, Israel, France and the USA, to oversee the cease-fire.

In late March 1992 some Syrian troops began to withdraw from Beirut, in preparation for the withdrawal of all Syrian armed forces to eastern Lebanon by September (in accordance with the Ta'if agreement). However, Syrian influence on Lebanese internal affairs remained pervasive, and was regarded by some observers as having contributed to the resignation of the Lebanese Government in May. The former Lebanese Prime Minister, Omar Karami, alleged that, had it not been for Lebanon's close relations with Syria, Western economic aid to Lebanon would have been more substantial, and the economic crisis that had led to his Government's resignation less severe.

The decision of the new Lebanese Government to hold elections to the National Assembly in August and September 1992, before the redeployment of Syrian armed forces to eastern Lebanon had taken place, attracted strong criticism both in Lebanon and abroad. Lebanese Maronites and other Christian groups, and Western governments argued that the continued presence of the Syrian forces would prejudice the outcome of the elections. However, the Lebanese Government argued that its own army was still unable to guarantee the country's security in the absence of the Syrian armed forces, and that the timetable for elections, as stipulated by the Ta'if agreement, should be observed. Syria claimed that the continued presence of its forces did not contravene the Ta'if agreement, which allowed for them to remain to assist the Lebanese Government until constitutional reforms had been fully implemented. There was no doubt, however, that the electoral process had been severely compromised in the eyes of Christian, especially Maronite, Lebanese. In many Maronite constituencies the participation of the electorate was very low, although there was not—as some Maronite leaders urged—a total boycott. Other Maronite leaders adopted a more pragmatic approach, acknowledging Syria's domination of Lebanon as a *fait accompli*. In October 1995 President Assad gave his support to the Lebanese Prime Minister's proposal to extend Lebanese President Elias Hrawi's term of office by another three years, a measure subsequently approved by 110 of the 128 Lebanese deputies in the National Assembly. Parliamentary elections held in mid-1996 produced an Assembly dominated by pro-Syrian supporters of Prime Minister Hariri. The largely Christian opposition parties had little success, and there were allegations of vote-rigging. During the elections Syria redeployed an estimated 10,000–12,000 of its troops from Lebanon to more secure positions in Syria, amid speculation that Damascus feared Israeli attacks. In September the Commander of the Israeli-backed SLA, Gen. Antoine Lahad, suggested that Israel might carry out a unilateral withdrawal from southern Lebanon but would hold Syria responsible for any new attacks on northern Israel. Shortly beforehand, the Israeli Prime Minister had put forward a similar proposal which had been immediately rejected by Syria (see above). In mid-December a bus carrying Syrian workers was attacked in a predominantly Christian area, prompting swift action by the Lebanese authorities who arrested some 50 government opponents, (most of whom were subsequently released). In response to the attack the Syrian Vice-President, Abd al-Halim Khaddam, accused Lebanese opposition leaders of conspiring with Israel against Syria.

Lebanon's Constitutional Court overturned the results of the 1996 elections in four parliamentary seats, accusing Syria of intimidating voters. In 1997 the US-based Human Rights Watch accused Syrian forces of seizing over 100 Lebanese and Palestinians in Lebanon and detaining them in Syria. It called on the Lebanese President and Prime Minister publicly to condemn such abuses of human rights and for Syrian forces to be held accountable for crimes they committed in Lebanon. In August fighting again escalated in southern Lebanon between Syrian-backed Hezbollah guerrillas and Israeli troops supporting the SLA. The rising death toll among Israeli soldiers in Israel's self-declared 'security zone' led to renewed demands within Israel for a unilateral withdrawal of its forces from Lebanon. In August the head of the Maronite Church, Cardinal Nasrallah Pierre Sfeir, an outspoken critic of the Syrian presence in Lebanon, stated that Damascus was interfering in every aspect of life and undermining the country's right to self-determination. However, the Lebanese Prime Minister, Rafik Hariri, repeated that the Syrian presence was necessary to guarantee domestic security and was in accordance with the 1989 Ta'if agreement. In September the US Secretary of State, Madeleine Albright, visited

Beirut and pledged to support a 'free and democratic sovereign Lebanon', a comment which was interpreted as a reference to Syria's control over the country's internal and external affairs.

At the beginning of April 1998 the Lebanese and Syrian Governments rejected an offer by Israel to withdraw from its 'security zone' in southern Lebanon, providing that there were adequate security guarantees for its northern border. Damascus dismissed the proposal as propaganda designed by the Netanyahu Government to improve Israel's image in the West. At the same time, Israel's request for direct negotiations with Lebanon concerning security issues in southern Lebanon led Damascus to suspect that the Israeli authorities were seeking to undermine Syrian dominance in Lebanon. In mid-October 1998 Syrian influence in Lebanon was evident in the selection of Gen. Emile Lahoud as the new Lebanese President, and the subsequent appointment of a Lebanese government of national unity (see the chapter on Lebanon). In late December Lebanon and Syria signed a bilateral trade agreement, in preparation for the customs union between the two countries which entered into effect on 1 January 1999. Syrian efforts to forge ever closer relations with Lebanon continued during 1999. Ten years after the Ta'if agreement some 30,000 Syrian troops remained deployed in Lebanon. In October both Governments reaffirmed their commitment to support one another, and further agreements were signed in the spheres of foreign relations, business and the environment.

Following the breakdown in direct talks between the Syrian and Israeli Governments at Shepherdstown in January 2000 (see above), there was a marked increase in attacks against Israeli forces in southern Lebanon by Hezbollah fighters. This, in turn, sparked retaliatory raids by Israel against Lebanese targets. However, on 5 March Israel announced that it would unilaterally withdraw from southern Lebanon by 7 July, regardless of whether peace agreements had been secured with Lebanon or Syria. The Syrian Minister of Foreign Affairs, Farouk ash-Shara', warned that this would be a 'suicidal' course of action in the absence of such peace settlements. Israel's phased withdrawal ultimately disintegrated to become a rapid retreat as the Israeli-backed SLA fled and Hezbollah intensified its military actions. Israel's occupation of southern Lebanon finally came to an end on 24 May 2000, several weeks ahead of schedule. Hezbollah declared the withdrawal to be a vindication of its strategy of armed resistance. However, Syria's response was somewhat muted, and it was careful to ensure that its soldiers were not seen to be trying to fill the vacuum created by the Israeli withdrawal. Hezbollah forces effectively took over southern Lebanon following Israel's withdrawal. At the end of July a small contingent of UNIFIL started to redeploy close to Lebanon's border with Israel, and in early August the Lebanese army and security forces entered the territory to take charge of general security. However, Hezbollah remained in control of the actual border, the so-called 'Blue Line'. (For further details regarding the Israeli withdrawal, see the chapters on Israel and Lebanon.)

OTHER DIPLOMATIC DEVELOPMENTS 1995–2000

Throughout 1995–96 Syria's relations with the USA were largely dominated by the US-sponsored peace negotiations with Israel (see above). However, in August 1995, after reports that the Damascus office of Hamas had threatened to attack US interests, the USA urged Syria to strive to prevent Syrian-based Palestinian groups opposed to the peace process from carrying out any such attack. Syria denied that any of these groups was planning to carry out 'military acts' against US targets. The expulsion of the Palestinian 'rejectionist' groups from its territory was believed to be the key prerequisite for Syria's removal from the US list of countries that sponsor terrorism. In early 1996 bilateral relations deteriorated. The USA blamed the collapse of Israeli-Syrian peace negotiations on President Assad's intransigence, and the US Department of State became increasingly exasperated with the Syrian regime as it attempted to broker a cease-fire in southern Lebanon. Prospects for Middle East peace declined dramatically after the right-wing victory in the Israeli elections in May 1996, and Syria appealed to the USA to abandon its perceived pro-Israeli bias in favour of a more balanced approach towards the peace process. In November 1997 efforts by Damascus to combat drugs production and trafficking

in Lebanon's Beka'a valley (largely controlled by the Syrian army) were rewarded when President Clinton removed both Lebanon and Syria from the list of states allegedly producing or trafficking in illegal drugs. However, as long as Syria continued to support Hezbollah in southern Lebanon, it was likely to remain on the US list of countries sponsoring terrorism. Efforts by the Syrian Government to involve the EU in the peace negotiations with Israel, in order to counterbalance the USA's role, met with little success, although Syria was invited to participate in the first Euro-Mediterranean conference held in Barcelona, Spain, in November 1995. During the conference Syria's Minister of Foreign Affairs, Farouk ash-Shara', clashed with his Israeli counterpart over the Nuclear Non-proliferation Treaty. Syria continued to press for greater EU involvement in the Middle East peace process, and in particular welcomed France's efforts to bring about a cease-fire in Lebanon after renewed fighting between Hezbollah and Israeli forces in April 1996, although it recognized that French influence was likely to be modest compared with that of the USA. In October 1996 President Jacques Chirac visited Damascus and announced the rescheduling of some 1,900m. French francs of debt arrears owed to France. Following a visit to Damascus in October 1997 by Manuel Marín, a Vice-President of the European Commission, Syria indicated that it was prepared to enter negotiations towards a free-trade agreement with the EU. In late 1997 Israeli officials visited Paris for talks with the French Government regarding the resumption of peace negotiations with Syria, and in November 1997 and January 1998 the French Minister of Foreign Affairs, Hubert Védrine, held talks in Damascus. In November 1997 Jacques Poos, Luxembourg's Minister of Foreign Affairs and leader of an EU mission to the Middle East, met President Assad in Damascus and indicated that the EU supported Syria's demand that Israel withdraw completely from the Golan Heights. In mid-July 1998 President Assad held discussions with President Chirac in France—the Syrian leader's first state visit outside the Middle East (with the exception of US-Syrian meetings in Switzerland) since 1976. The French President expressed support for the rejection by Syria of Israel's recent proposal for withdrawal from southern Lebanon. In mid-July 1999 Spain became the first EU country to sign a loan agreement with Syria, covering credit facilities worth some US $55m. In the second half of 1999 EU governments stepped up their involvement in efforts to bring about a resumption of direct talks between Syria and Israel. During a visit to Israel in October, Finnish President Martti Ahtisaari proposed that Helsinki could be a venue for future discussions. However, US predominance as peace-broker in the Middle East meant that the proposal was not borne out.

At the end of 1997 Russia also joined diplomatic efforts to revive peace negotiations between Syria and Israel. The Russian Deputy Minister of Foreign Affairs, Viktor Posvalyuk, held talks in Damascus and Jerusalem in December 1997, but angered Israelis by supporting Syria's position that negotiations should begin at the point at which they had stalled in February 1996 (see above). There were visits to Damascus by a number of senior Russian officials in early 1998, and a Syrian-Russian committee, which had been set up in 1993 to co-ordinate bilateral relations, held its first meeting. Amid speculation that the strong links that had existed between Damascus and Moscow during the Soviet era were being re-established, in mid-November 1998 Syria and Russia signed a military agreement whereby Russia would assist in the modernization of Syria's defence systems and provide training to military personnel. However, in late January 1999 Syria denied Western reports that it was receiving military assistance from Russia in the development of chemical weapons. On 5–6 July President Assad visited Moscow at the head of a high-level Syrian delegation—his first visit to the Russian capital since the disintegration of the USSR. (The Syrian leader had postponed a scheduled visit to Moscow in April, apparently owing to the presence in the city of the then Israeli Minister of Foreign Affairs, Ariel Sharon.) Assad held talks with the then President Boris Yeltsin and his premier, Sergei Stepashin, which were reported to be successful: topics discussed included the Middle East peace process, military and technical co-operation between the two countries and the issue of Syria's debt to Russia (estimated to be more than US $10,000m.). Russia reiterated its support for Syria's demand for a complete Israeli withdrawal from the Golan Heights and southern Lebanon, and that Israeli-Syrian peace negotiations be resumed from the point at which they stalled in 1996. In May 2000 it was reported that a major arms deal had been concluded whereby Russia had agreed to supply Syria with defence equipment, worth $2,000m., to upgrade its air force and air-defence system.

Following a meeting of the Syrian, Iranian and Turkish Ministers of Foreign Affairs in Tehran in September 1995, a statement was issued reaffirming their commitment to the territorial integrity of Iraq and warning against foreign interference in Iraq's internal affairs. Although Syria had become a centre for elements of the Iraqi opposition, the Syrian regime was concerned that the disintegration of Iraq could set a dangerous precedent for its own minorities, and also feared that Saddam Hussein might be replaced by a pro-Western regime. In November the Syrian Minister of Foreign Affairs accused Israel of trying to destroy Iraq by plotting its division into Kurdish, Sunni and Shi'a regions. It was alleged that President Assad had conducted a clandestine meeting with the Iraqi President, Saddam Hussein, on the Syrian-Iraqi border in May 1996 to discuss common issues including Turkey's military agreement with Israel, although some sources maintained that the meeting was only attended by their representatives. In May 1997 an economic delegation from Syria, including the Chairman of the Federation of Syrian Chambers of Commerce, visited Baghdad for talks with the Iraqi trade minister, Muhammad Mahdi Salih, about securing contracts for Syrian exports to Iraq following implementation of the UN 'oil-for-food' agreement. A high-level Iraqi trade delegation visited Damascus in the following month. Commenting on the visit, the Syrian Vice-President, Abd al-Halim Khaddam, stated that his Government's decision to reopen trade links with Baghdad, after an interlude of 18 years, was largely due to concern that Turkey was seeking to monopolize trade with Iraq in order to impose its economic domination over the country. However, it seemed more likely that the decision was influenced by Syria's concern about Turkey's military co-operation with Israel and Ankara's military operations against the Kurdistan Workers' Party (Partiya Karkeren Kurdistan—PKK) in northern Iraq. On 2 June border crossings between the two countries were reopened, and each country closed down radio stations that had been broadcasting propaganda against the other since the late 1970s. By September 1997 several large contracts for Syrian exports of food and medical supplies to Iraq had been signed, and it was agreed that the Syrian ports of Tartous and Latakia would receive goods in transit for Iraq. Baghdad also reportedly requested that Syria reopen the oil pipeline linking Iraq's Kirkuk oilfields to the Mediterranean terminal of Banias in Syria, which had been closed since 1982. At the end of 1997 the Iraqi Deputy Prime Minister, Tareq Aziz, was received in Damascus by the Syrian Minister of Foreign Affairs, Farouk ash-Shara', the first public meeting between senior ministers of the two countries for 17 years. There were reports that ash-Shara' had subsequently gone to Riyadh with a letter from President Assad to King Fahd of Saudi Arabia, setting out proposals for reintegrating Iraq into the Arab 'fold'. In early February 1998, when the US sought regional support for renewed air-strikes against Iraq, Syria strongly opposed such action. To emphasize this point, President Assad received the Iraqi Minister of Foreign Affairs in Damascus on 10 February, the first time that he had met publicly with a senior Iraqi official since the early 1980s. At the end of March 1998 the Syrian Minister of Health, Iyad ash-Shatti, became the first Syrian minister to visit Baghdad for almost 20 years. The Syrian Government expressed strong criticism regarding air-strikes carried out by the USA and United Kingdom against Iraq in late 1998, and attacks against Iraqi air-defence targets in 1999–2002.

Relations with Iran deteriorated in late 1995 after the Syrian regime voiced support for the UAE in its dispute with Tehran over Abu Musa and the Greater and Lesser Tunb islands. In protest, Hassan Habibi, an Iranian Vice-President, and Kamal Kharrazi, the Iranian Minister of Foreign Affairs, cancelled a visit to Damascus, and there were attacks on Syria in the Iranian press. Following Iraq's invasion of Kuwait in 1990 Syria continued to strengthen its links with Saudi Arabia and the Gulf states, while assuring Tehran that it remained committed

to maintaining the 'strategic' relationship with Iran. There were signs of an improvement in Syrian-Iranian relations in February 1996 when a joint committee to co-ordinate bilateral co-operation was set up. Shortly afterwards, when Syria expressed support for the Bahrain Government, it was careful to avoid any reference to alleged Iranian involvement in the unrest on Abu Musa. In August a Syrian delegation, led by the Prime Minister, met senior Iranian government officials in Tehran. During this visit, President Rafsanjani called for closer bilateral links to confront the threat posed by the USA and Israel. In July 1997 President Assad visited Tehran. However, there were reports that Syrian interest in a triple alliance with Iran and Iraq, to counter growing military co-operation between Israel, Turkey and the USA, had not met with a positive response from Iranian officials, owing to continuing tensions between Iran and Iraq. Nevertheless, in September 1998 Iran, Iraq and Syria agreed to the formation of a joint forum to co-ordinate their foreign policy (see above). Iran was swift to explore the possibilities for further improving its relations with Syria following the death of President Hafiz Assad in June 2000 and the accession of his son, Bashar, to the presidency. Within a week of the latter's assumption of the presidency, Ali Akbar Velayati, Iran's former foreign affairs minister, visited Damascus. In August, meanwhile, rail links were resumed between Iraq and the Syrian city of Aleppo, an event which was widely viewed as confirming the *rapprochement* between the two countries.

Syria's relations with Turkey remained strained, owing to continuing disagreements over cross-border water supplies, and over the Kurds. Although the two countries have a provisional accord for sharing water from the Euphrates river, whereby Turkey allows a flow of 500 cu m per second of water into Syria, they have failed to conclude a permanent accord, and both Syria and Iraq are concerned that new dam projects in Turkey, especially the Birecik dam, will reduce the volume of Euphrates water downstream. Both Syria and Iraq have also blamed Turkey for increased pollution levels in the water they receive. At the end of 1995 Syria retaliated by announcing that it would reduce the water supply to Turkey from the Orontes river. Syria also used its support for the rebel PKK to put pressure on its powerful neighbour. The PKK was known to have bases in the Syrian-controlled Beka'a valley in Lebanon, and at the end of 1995 Kurdish fighters crossed the Turkish border from Syria and launched attacks on Turkish military targets. In February 1996 Turkey accused the Syrian Government of giving refuge to the PKK leader, Abdullah Öcalan, and demanded his extradition to Turkey. Bilateral relations deteriorated sharply in April after it was revealed that Turkey and Israel had signed a military accord earlier in the year allowing the Israeli air force to use Turkish military airfields for training purposes. The Syrian press denounced the treaty, declaring that Israel had extended its 'security zone' to the borders of Iran and warning that Turkey should respect its historical links with the Arab world. The crisis between Syria and Turkey was aggravated at the end of April 1996 when Turkey temporarily closed the flood gates of the Euphrates dams for 'technical reasons', resulting in water rationing in Damascus on the eve of the festival of Id al-Adha and provoking widespread concern in the Arab world. When a series of small bombs exploded in Syrian cities in May there was speculation that the Turkish Government might be responsible and that they were in response to Syria's support for the PKK separatists, particularly as the apartment of the PKK leader in Damascus had reportedly been a target. Although the Syrian Government denied that the bombings had taken place, it was reported to have arrested several hundred ethnic Turks in retaliation. The Turkish media blamed Syria's banned Muslim Brotherhood for the explosions.

Some commentators argued that the military accord between Turkey and Israel was part of an emerging strategic partnership in the Middle East (to replace the Middle East peace process) involving an alliance of Turkey, the USA, Israel and Jordan in order to form a military front against those states in the region perceived as enemies of the West. The new partnership threatened to leave Syria dangerously isolated. After Turkey's first Islamist-led Government took office in July 1996, the Syrian ambassador to Ankara was one of the first envoys to visit the new Turkish Prime Minister, Necmettin Erbakan. While in opposition, Erbakan's Refah party had strongly criticized Turkey's military accord with Israel and had urged closer relations with neighbouring Arab and Muslim countries. Once in government, Erbakan did indicate his desire for a political solution to the dispute with the PKK but pressure from the military caused him to revert to the official line, condemning PKK terrorism. In addition, military co-operation with Israel was expanded, again at the insistence of the military, which regarded the accord as a means of exerting pressure on Syria for its support of the PKK. Relations with Turkey deteriorated once again in May 1997, when it launched another military operation against PKK bases in northern Iraq. Syria reportedly mobilized troops on its border with Turkey and called on Ankara to withdraw its forces from Iraq. Also in May the Turkish authorities accused Syria of helping Kurdish dissidents to set up television transmitters along the border with Turkey so that Kurds living in south-eastern Anatolia could receive programmes broadcast by the pro-PKK Kurdish-language channel, MED-TV. During the eighth Conference of the OIC in Tehran in early December, at which Turkey faced implicit criticism for its military co-operation with Israel, the Syrian Minister of Foreign Affairs, Farouk ash-Shara', stated that Ankara had agreed not to renew its agreement with Israel. This was later denied by Turkish officials.

Tension between Syria and Turkey increased considerably in October 1998, when Turkey threatened to invade Syria if its demands for an end to alleged Syrian support for the separatist PKK were not met. The Turkish authorities also demanded the extradition of Abdullah Öcalan (who, they claimed, was directing PKK operations from Damascus) and insisted that Syria renounce its historic claim to the Turkish province of Hatay. In early October the Turkish armed forces Chief of General Staff announced that a state of 'undeclared war' existed between Syria and Turkey. The latter's aggressive stance was viewed by Syria as evidence of a Turkish-Israeli military and political alliance, and as a result both Syria and Turkey ordered troops to be deployed along their joint border. By mid-October mediation efforts, particularly by Egyptian President Hosni Mubarak, and Syrian assurances that Öcalan was not residing in Syria, allowed a degree of normalization in relations. In late October, following two days of negotiations near the southern Turkish city of Adana, Turkey and Syria signed an agreement whereby the PKK was to be banned from entering Syrian territory, while the organization's active bases in Syria and Lebanon's Beka'a valley were to be closed. Turkey and Syria also agreed mutual security guarantees, and resolved to invite Lebanon to participate in further negotiations on the issue of PKK activity. During 1999 Syrian concerns regarding the close nature of Turkish-Israeli relations persisted. However, it was reported in March 2000 that Syrian and Turkish officials were holding discussions in Damascus on a memorandum of principles, intended to establish a new framework for future bilateral relations.

The election of the right-wing Likud Government in Israel at the end of May 1996 resulted in closer contacts between Syria, Egypt, Jordan and the PA. After informal talks between Syria, Egypt and Saudi Arabia, an Arab League summit was convened in Cairo at the end of June. Although Syria's more militant proposals, including a 'freeze' on existing relations with Israel and the reintroduction of the Arab economic boycott of Israel, were opposed by the moderate Arab states, the summit was widely seen as a success for Syria. Also at the summit, Turkey was urged to reconsider its military agreement with Israel (see above). The Egyptian President, Hosni Mubarak, had condemned this agreement fearing that it would further undermine Egypt's regional role, and had pledged his support for President Assad. In the following months, as hopes for the peace process collapsed, there were regular consultations between Syrian and Egyptian officials. At the Cairo summit King Hussein had accused the Syrian authorities of sponsoring terrorist operations in Jordan in an attempt to destabilize the kingdom. Syria's relations with Jordan had become increasingly acrimonious since Jordan signed a separate peace agreement with Israel in 1994, and Syrian officials claimed that Jordan was working with Israel and Turkey to undermine President Assad's regime. However, after direct talks between King Hussein and President Assad at the summit, bilateral relations were said to have improved, and in August the King met Assad again in Da-

mascus—his first visit to Syria since 1994. Following this visit, the Syrian authorities arrested a number of Palestinians and other Arabs deemed to have been implicated in organizing attacks in Jordan or in Israel through Jordan, and the two countries agreed to reopen talks to resolve their differences over the use of water from the Yarmouk river.

In mid-October 1998 the Jordanian Foreign Minister presented the Syrian chargé d'affaires in Amman with a list of 239 Jordanians allegedly missing in Syria, and a further 190 whom it claimed were imprisoned there; the Jordanian Government demanded 'immediate answers' from Syria as to their whereabouts. The Syrian authorities reportedly denied the claims, stating that most of those listed were in fact members of Palestinian organizations linked with Jordan, and who had violated Syrian laws; they agreed, however, to investigate the matter. In early February 1999 President Assad unexpectedly attended the funeral of King Hussein of Jordan, and reportedly held a private meeting with the new King, Abdullah; this was Assad's first visit to Jordan for five years. King Abdullah made his first official visit to Syria in late April. During talks with President Assad, the two leaders urged a resumption of the peace process and agreed to increase bilateral co-operation. In late May four Jordanian prisoners were released by the Syrian authorities. In that month Syria began to supply Jordan with water for a period of four months, in order to ease Jordan's drought. In late June Syria welcomed Jordan's decision not to participate in joint Turkish-Israeli naval exercises, scheduled for the following month; similar exercises in 1998 had led to a diplomatic crisis with Syria. In late July 1999 King Abdullah visited Syria, amid Jordanian concerns that any peace agreement concluded by Israel and Syria might isolate and undermine the Palestinian cause in future negotiations. In early August the joint Jordanian-Syrian higher committee met in Amman, under the chairmanship of both countries' premiers—the first time in almost a decade that a senior Syrian delegation had visited Jordan's capital; a bilateral trade accord was signed. Regarding the issue of Jordanian prisoners held in Syria, Prime Minister Mahmoud az-Zoubi stated that many of the prisoners had been released under a general amnesty in July (see below) and that the 'very few' who remained in detention in Syria were non-political prisoners. Later in August Syria agreed to allow the free circulation of Jordanian newspapers and publications after a 10-year ban. A further 17 Jordanian prisoners were reportedly released from Syrian gaols in March 2000. Following the death of President Hafiz Assad in June, King Abdullah was among the most prominent mourners and one of the first to initiate substantive contacts with the new President. He visited Bashar al-Assad in Damascus on 19 July for talks regarding bilateral issues; Syria again agreed to supply Jordan with drinking water over the summer months of 2000.

During the Cairo summit held in June 1996, President Mubarak of Egypt also persuaded Hafiz Assad to meet the PA President, Yasser Arafat. The two men had been bitter rivals for many years and had not met since 1993 (when Assad condemned Arafat for signing the Oslo accords); however, the meeting improved relations between the two men. One month later Arafat visited Damascus and his foreign affairs adviser, Farouk Kaddumi, held talks with leaders of Palestinian groups which were opposed to the Oslo accords and which were based in the Syrian capital. Early in 1997 there were reports that the Syrian authorities had warned the PFLP and other Palestinian groups based in Damascus that if they continued to organize military operations against Israel from Syria their offices would be closed down. There were similar reports in July 1999. In early August a diplomatic crisis developed between Syria and the PA, after the Syrian Deputy Prime Minister and Minister of Defence, Maj.-Gen. Mustafa Tlass, publicly accused Arafat of having 'sold Jerusalem and the Arab nation' in peace agreements concluded with Israel since 1993, and made other personal insults against the Palestinian leader. The PA demanded that Tlass resign, while President Assad was reportedly angered by the Minister's remarks. In late 1999 there were reports of a heavy Syrian-instigated crack-down on members of Fatah, the Palestinian political movement headed by Arafat, in Palestinian refugee camps in southern Lebanon.

INTERNAL AFFAIRS 1990–2000

In May 1990 elections were held to the People's Assembly, in which the number of seats was increased from 195 to 250. Candidates representing the Baath Party were elected to 134 seats, 54% of the total, compared with 66% of the total in elections held in 1986. Other parties that had joined the Baath Party-dominated National Progressive Front (NPF) were elected to 33 seats, while independent candidates were elected to 84 seats. Some 60% of the electorate were reported to have participated in the elections, which were contested by 9,765 candidates.

There was speculation during 1991 that President Assad was preparing to introduce a degree of liberalization into Syria's political system, widely regarded as one of the most autocratic in the world. In December it was announced that 2,864 political prisoners were to be released. In March 1992 Assad indicated that new political parties might in future be established in Syria. However, he rejected the adoption by Syria of foreign democratic frameworks as unsuited to the country's level of economic development. In late June a limited reshuffle of the Council of Ministers took place.

In January 1994 the future stability of the regime became uncertain when Assad's eldest son, Basel, who had been expected to succeed his father as President, died in a motor accident. The President's second son, Bashar, was instructed to assume the role previously carried out by his brother, in order to avoid a power struggle. In June the Minister of Electricity, Kamal al-Baba, was dismissed following two years of electricity shortages and power cuts. In August 16 senior officials, including the Special Forces commander, Ali Haidar, were removed from office in an apparent attempt by Assad to consolidate his position, weaken the influence of the old guard and improve the country's international stance. At the People's Assembly elections held on 24 August more than 7,000 candidates were presented, but turn-out at the polls was recorded at just over 50% of the electorate. The coalition parties in the NPF maintained their dominant position, winning 167 seats; the remaining seats were won by independent candidates. Leading business people were reported to be among the 158 newly-elected members. At the inaugural session of the new Assembly, on 14 November, the Prime Minister, Mahmoud az-Zoubi, announced a programme of major economic reforms. A report by a prominent human rights organization, Amnesty International, published in April 1995, concluded that although some attempts had been made to improve human rights in Syria, further reforms were still urgently needed.

In November 1995 rallies were held across the country to mark President Assad's 25 years in power, and some 1,200 political prisoners, including members of the banned Muslim Brotherhood, were released. It appeared that the Muslim Brotherhood was no longer seen as a threat to the regime, and a number of the organization's leading figures, among them the former Secretary-General, Abd al-Fattah Abu Ghuddah, were allowed to return from exile. Also in November the Minister of Tourism, Amin Abu ash-Shamat, was replaced by Danhu Daoud, a Minister of State. In May 1996 Syrian officials denied reports of a series of bomb explosions in Damascus, Aleppo and Latakia, amid speculation that the attacks had been carried out with Turkish involvement (see above). However, a Jordanian source subsequently claimed that they were intended to trigger an army coup involving Sunni Muslim officers supported by the US and Israeli intelligence services. Later that month, Abd al-Majid at-Tarabulsi, the Minister of Awqaf (Islamic Endowments), died; he was succeeded by Muhammad Abd ar-Ra'uf Ziyadah. Musallam Muhammad Hawwa was appointed Minister of State for Cabinet Affairs, but rumours of a major cabinet reshuffle, including the replacement of Mahmoud az-Zoubi as premier, proved unfounded.

Towards the end of 1996 there were several reports that President Assad was in poor health, provoking more speculation about the succession. Syrian officials quickly condemned such reports as 'malicious lies' aimed at destabilizing the country, and stated that the President had undergone minor surgery although he was expected to require a long period of convalescence. President Assad continued to prepare his surviving son, Bashar, for high office but Bashar himself was reported to be reluctant to assume a leading role. In the early months of 1997 a poster campaign in support of Bashar appeared in towns and cities throughout the country, and, in a sermon during the festival of Id al-Fitr, the Mufti of Damascus referred to Bashar as his father's successor. The Mufti also acknowledged Bashar's role in heading the Government's campaign against corruption. In June 1996 Nadir an-Nabulsi, then Minister of Petroleum and Mineral Wealth, was dismissed after corruption charges were made against him relating to the period when he headed the Al-Furat Petroleum Company. When a bomb exploded on a bus in Damascus at the end of December, killing 11 people, there was speculation that it may have been related to the Government's anti-corruption drive and the investigations into the business affairs of the President's family. Few details were released about the incident, but an official statement accused Israel of responsibility for the attack. In early 1997 President Assad's brothers, Jamil and Rifaat, both came under investigation for their business dealings, and, as a result, Jamil was sent into exile in Paris. Towards the end of 1997 there were reports that Bashar al-Assad had been given new responsibilities in economic policy-making, notably in the promotion of privatization and foreign investment, in addition to heading the campaign against corruption and overseeing Syrian interests in Lebanon (especially contacts with the Maronite Christian community), although he still had no specific political post. In February 1998 President Assad dismissed his brother Rifaat from his position as one of Syria's three Vice-Presidents, a post which he had held since 1984. For much of this period, however, Rifaat had been out of favour and living in exile, but he had been allowed to return to Syria in 1992 for the funeral of his mother and had remained in the country. There were reports that Rifaat and his son Sawmar had recently become more active in politics and business and that Rifaat still enjoyed a measure of popularity with some sections of the armed forces. In early July 1998 Maj.-Gen. Hikmat ash-Shehabi retired as Chief of Staff of the Armed Forces, a post that he had held since 1973. He was replaced by his deputy, Maj.-Gen. Ali Aslan. There was speculation that ash-Shehabi, for many years a close associate of President Assad, might be appointed Vice-President. At the same time the head of the General Intelligence Directorate, Bashar an-Najjar, was dismissed from his post for unspecified irregularities and replaced by Gen. Mahmoud ash-Shaqqa, a former chief of military intelligence in the Quneitra region and commander of the Syrian troops sent to Saudi Arabia during the 1991 Gulf War. These changes prompted speculation regarding the possible appointment of Bashar al-Assad to a senior political post and a cabinet reshuffle that would bring economic reformers into the Government. Meanwhile, it was reported in mid-June 1998 that some 225 political prisoners had been released since the beginning of the month, including leading members of the Muslim Brotherhood, communists and associates of Salah Jadid, the leader of the civilian branch of the Baath party ousted from power by Assad in 1970.

Elections to the People's Assembly were held on 30 November and 1 December 1998, and, as in the 1994 election, the NPF, led by the ruling Baath Party, won 167 of the 250 seats. In late January 1999 a report by Amnesty International demanded the release of more than 300 Lebanese, Palestinian and Jordanian political prisoners (many of whom, the organization alleged, were prisoners of conscience) from Syrian gaols. In the same month the incoming People's Assembly voted unanimously to nominate President Assad for a fifth term in office. Assad's re-election was confirmed in a national referendum held on 11 February. There was widespread speculation that the President would begin his new term of office by forming a new Government, and that possible changes might include the promotion of his son Bashar to the vice-presidency. (The President's son had already been promoted to the rank of army colonel in January, and it was reported that he had also been granted new powers over the management of state finances and other important domestic matters.) By appointing his son as Vice-President, Assad would confirm the growing speculation both in Syria and elsewhere that he was accelerating the process of preparing Bashar for succession.

In June 1999 the Syrian authorities were reported to be carrying out an 'unprecedented' campaign, led by the President's son, to counter corruption in public office. (Several leading officials and businessmen were subsequently imprisoned, while in early October, following a nine-month trial, a former director of Syria's intelligence service received a lengthy prison sentence for alleged corruption and embezzlement of public funds.) In mid-July President Assad issued a general amnesty for prisoners convicted of certain 'economic' crimes, and for those who had deserted the army or evaded military service. The amnesty was to affect hundreds (some reports claimed thousands) of prisoners, including a number of Muslim Brotherhood activists. In late September a huge wave of arrests was carried out by security forces in Damascus and Latakia against supporters of President Assad's brother Rifaat; according to some reports, about 1,000 people were detained by the authorities. The arrests were believed to be linked to the succession issue, since Rifaat, also viewed as a possible successor to Assad, had in recent months sought to increase his public profile in Syria. Moreover, in late October the Syrian authorities closed down a port in Latakia which they claimed had been built illegally by Rifaat. The action provoked several days of violent clashes between Rifaat's supporters and the security forces, in which, according to certain sources, hundreds of people were killed or injured. However, the Government dismissed such reports, and denied claims that the security forces had acted for political reasons. In November the Government warned Rifaat, who was once again in exile, that he would be prosecuted should he return to Syria. Bashar's elevation to the status of heir apparent was further confirmed when, in early November, he held discussions with French President Jacques Chirac in Paris. However, that Bashar's status was not accepted by all sections of the Assad clan was demonstrated by reports that a son-in-law of the President, and ally of Bashar, had been shot by Maher, the President's youngest son, and was receiving medical treatment in France for his wounds.

In early February 2000 a report by Amnesty International alleged that in recent months several hundred Syrians (including a number of Islamists) opposed to a future peace accord with Israel had been arrested. It was also reported early in that month that Syria's military intelligence chief, Gen. Ali Duba, had been removed from his post, owing to alleged 'administrative offences'; he was replaced by his deputy, Maj.-Gen. Hassan Khalil.

The long-awaited government reorganization was finally announced on 7 March 2000, when President Assad selected the former governor of Aleppo, Muhammad Mustafa Mero, as the new Prime Minister, having accepted the resignation of Mahmoud az-Zoubi, who had occupied the post since 1987, and his administration. The new Cabinet, announced on 13 March 2000, included 22 new ministers (among whom were a number of younger technocrats and supporters of Bashar al-Assad), although President Assad's trusted stalwarts retained the crucial defence, interior and foreign affairs portfolios. However, a new Minister of Information, Adnan Omran, was appointed, raising hopes that Syria's media might be allowed greater freedom in the future. There was speculation that President Assad intended that the new administration would accelerate social and economic reforms in the country, continue the fight against corruption, and resume peace negotiations with Israel.

Mahmoud az-Zoubi's fall from political prominence proved to be rapid. On 10 May 2000 the former Prime Minister was expelled from the Baath Party for alleged 'irregularities and abuses' during his period in office; his assets were subsequently seized and he was expected to stand trial on charges of corruption. However, on 21 May it was reported by the Syrian authorities that az-Zoubi had committed suicide as the Chief of Police was arriving at his home to escort him to court.

DEATH OF PRESIDENT HAFIZ ASSAD

As preparations were under way for the first general congress of the Baath Party to be held since 1985, on 10 June 2000 President Hafiz Assad died following a heart attack. Although his health had long been poor, the reaction both in Syria and abroad was initially one of shock. Assessments of Assad's legacy tended to focus more on his international impact—his commitment to pan-Arabism, his implacable opposition to Israel and his role in later years as a stabilizing influence in the Middle East—and much less on his domestic record, where, according to many observers, he had displayed an indifference to human rights and democratic values, had until his later years proved

tolerant of official corruption, and had presided over a long period of economic stagnation.

SUCCESSION OF BASHAR AL-ASSAD

While the First Vice-President, Abd al-Halim Khaddam, assumed the role of acting President, the death of Hafiz Assad necessitated an acceleration of the succession process. The general congress of the Baath Party had been expected to see the promotion of his son Bashar to high office. Now, however, the accession to power was far more dramatic. By the time of his father's burial in the family's home town of Qardaha on 13 June 2000—attended by many world leaders and foreign dignitaries—the People's Assembly had unanimously voted to amend the Constitution to lower the minimum age required to be attained by the President from 40 to 34 years, Bashar's exact age. The Regional Command of the Baath Party then hastened to nominate Bashar as head of state. On 11 June a decree was passed promoting him from his then rank of Staff Colonel to Lieutenant-General, and making him Commander-in-Chief of the Armed Forces. The speed of Bashar's accession was partly prompted by worries that the late President's exiled brother Rifaat would challenge Bashar's legitimacy. This he did on 13 June, claiming that the assumed succession by his nephew was unconstitutional. Bashar's supporters were also worried that members of the Baath Party's 'old guard' might challenge his appointment. Hikmat ash-Shehabi, who had retired in 1998 as Commander-in-Chief of the Armed Forces, had left the country for the USA shortly before Hafiz Assad's death, amid rumours that he was about to be indicted on corruption charges. However, he returned to the country in July 2000, and the Syrian authorities stated that they had no plans to prosecute him.

The general congress of the Baath Party, which began, as scheduled, on 17 June 2000, became principally a forum to legitimize Bashar's accession to power. On the final day of the congress, on 20 June, Bashar was elected Secretary-General of the party. On 27 June the People's Assembly met to set a date for a referendum on Bashar's presidential candidacy, thereby approving his nomination. The referendum, held on 10 July, produced a 97.29% vote in favour of the succession of the sole candidate, Bashar. The new President took the oath of office on 17 July, three days ahead of the expiry of the 40 days of official mourning proclaimed following the death of his father. In his speech, Bashar al-Assad emphasized his commitment to reviving the Syrian economy and promised greater freedom of expression in the country, provided that any criticism of his administration was constructive. The new President also undertook to uphold his father's legacy in foreign policy—above all, his firm stance regarding the Golan Heights.

BASHAR'S EARLY YEARS IN POWER

Within days of his accession to power and the ending of the period of official mourning, Bashar was the object of appeals from within Syrian society. A group of 44 Islamic and professional figures sent him an 'open letter' on 21 July 2000 urging him to liberalize the political system while honouring the foreign policy objectives of his father. Bashar responded by calling on Syrians to avoid making him the beneficiary of a 'cult of personality' and, from late July, by releasing a significant number of political prisoners, mainly members of the Muslim Brotherhood and the Communist Action Party. Representatives of the Muslim Brotherhood in exile welcomed the action but demanded that all political prisoners be released and that repressive laws be repealed. (The presidential amnesty was said to have excluded Jordanian and Palestinian prisoners.)

Bashar al-Assad's accession to the Syrian presidency thus appeared to have proceeded remarkably smoothly. However, it remained too early to view his accession to power as complete. Bashar's early actions suggested a leader who sought to modernize Syria in both the economic and political spheres. However, his strategy appeared to be a gradualist one. The pursuit of rapid and large-scale change was thought likely to lead the new President into direct conflict with the 'old guard' in the party and state bureaucracy, which remained largely intact and very powerful. Although Bashar promised to review the existing restrictive laws on forming political parties, there were were no indications that he was willing to allow the dominance of the Baath Party to be seriously challenged. In addition, the spectre of Rifaat and his supporters within the Assad family had not yet been entirely vanquished. Furthermore, the need to assuage traditionalists at home appeared to limit Bashar's scope to innovate in the field of foreign policy, where his father's legacy retained overwhelming popular support, although some scope did appear to exist to lower Syria's profile in Lebanon (see below).

In September 2000 a group of prominent business figures announced that they were interested in forming a new political party: the Syrian Social National Party, banned since the early 1970s, appeared to be being revived. In the following month a group of 99 writers and intellectuals issued a declaration calling for an end to martial law, in force since 1963. When the National Assembly deputy, Mamun Homsi, attacked the excessive powers of the various security agencies and called for their merger into one organization, it was reported that Bashar had rejected calls for her to face official sanctions. In November 2000 a further 600 political prisoners were released. Amnesty International welcomed this development, although it claimed that over 900 political prisoners still remained in Syrian detention. In December Mezzeh prison in Damascus, which has long been a notorious location for the imprisonment of political opponents, was closed. A government decree in the same month liberalized the laws regarding the importing of foreign films.

In November 2000 Syria experienced some of its bloodiest rural conflict for many years in the Suweida region. Tensions between the majority Druze population and local Bedouin nomads over land-use rights led to violence in which over 20 people died. The Syrian army was forced to intervene to end the fighting.

Meanwhile, hopes rose that Bashar's commitment to greater openness and freedom in Syria was genuine. The President's personal popularity at home increased further in January 2001, when he married Asmaa al-Akhras, who had worked in the United Kingdom as a financial analyst and appeared to be a woman of modern tastes and views. Civil society organizations, including a number that focused on human rights issues, became increasingly confident about operating openly and publicly. Emboldened by the positive signals coming from the Syrian authorities, in January Riad Seif, an outspoken parliamentarian who, along with former political prisoner Michel Kilo, had formed a civil society group called the Committee of Friends of Civil Society, declared that he intended to form a new political party, to be called the Movement for Social Peace, and that he had applied for official permission to do so. Seif declared that the party's political philosophy would be 'liberal' and 'nationalist'. In the same month a 'manifesto' containing over 1,000 signatures was handed to the authorities, calling for martial law to be lifted. The Government responded by stating that the country's emergency laws had been 'frozen'. In February a prominent cartoonist and associate of the new President, Ali Farzat, announced that he had been given permission to publish a weekly private newspaper, to be called *Ad-Dumari* (Lamplighter). This was the first private newspaper to be published in Syria for 38 years.

However, there were already indications that some members of the Government were worried that changes were occurring too fast and too radically. In December 2000 a woman was detained on charges of defamation for the dissemination of a cartoon featuring the new President that was deemed offensive. In February 2001 a well-known writer, Nabil Suleiman, was attacked and beaten by unknown persons. In March Vice-President Abd al-Halim Khaddam warned civil society groups not to threaten 'national unity'; he announced that henceforth such groups should apply to the authorities 15 days in advance for permission to hold meetings. The freedom to travel abroad which political critics had enjoyed over the previous few months began to be restricted again. Government officials criticized calls for martial law to be lifted. These developments appeared to confirm fears that any increased political freedom in Syria would be at the discretion of the ruling Baath Party, rather than by right.

A report published in April 2001 by the UN Human Rights Committee concerning Syria's record in implementing the International Covenant on Civil and Political Rights showed just how far Syria still had to travel if the process of political liberalization was to erase the authoritarian legacies of the past. The Committee raised concerns regarding the number of criminal offences punishable by death, the continuing use of administrative detention, a long legacy of extra-judicial executions and 'disappearances' of persons, systematic torture in prisons, violations of the right to fair trial and the fact that martial law did remain in force. The Committee also called for the establishment by the Syrian Government of an independent commission of inquiry to investigate past extra-judicial executions and 'disappearances'.

President Bashar al-Assad sought to capitalize on the visit of Pope John Paul II to Syria in early May 2001 to increase further his prestige at home. He emphasized Syria's religious tolerance and strongly reaffirmed the country's unconditional insistence on the return in full of the Golan Heights (see below). However, the visit of the Pontiff precipitated a number of other prisoner releases, including the journalist Nizar Nayyuf, who had been in gaol for nine years for publishing 'false information'. Nayyuf had gone on hunger strike ahead of the visit. However, in late June Nayyuf was again briefly detained by military intelligence, only to be released on the orders of the President.

The contradictory signals concerning human rights issues that had characterized Bashar's rule thus far continued in late 2001. During August and September of that year, following attempts by certain organizations to hold meetings without official permission, there was a major crack-down on civil society activists and political critics. Among those arrested were Riad Seif, Nizar Nayyuf, Mamun Homsi and veteran communist leader and long-term political detainee Riad at-Turk. Increasing co-operation between sections of the Muslim Brotherhood and the Communist Action Party was reportedly one reason behind the authorities' growing reluctance to tolerate dissent. The activists faced a range of charges, including attempting to change the Constitution by illegal means, forming a secret society and, in the case of at-Turk, fomenting sectarian strife and calling for armed insurrection. In October it was announced that another notorious detention centre, Tadmur prison, was to be closed. In November there was another wave of prisoner releases, this time focused upon members of banned Communist groups and the Muslim Brotherhood. For the first time, none of those released was required to sign an oath pledging to forego political activity in the future. In February 2002 the Government agreed to allow private broadcasters to operate for the first time in 50 years. However, they would only be permitted to broadcast music and advertisements. In March 2002 Seif and Homsi were each sentenced to five years in prison. Other political trials continued. However, the activity of civil society was far from wholly extinguished by the official restrictions. In April there were street protests in Damascus against Israel's *de facto* re-occupation of the West Bank, at which domestic issues were also raised.

In December 2001 President Bashar al-Assad carried out a long-anticipated reorganization of the Syrian Cabinet. While it left the crucial defence and foreign affairs' portfolios unchanged, the reshuffle did increase the number of independent-minded technocrats in the Government. Amongst them were Ghassan ar-Rifai, who took over at the Ministry of Economy and Foreign Trade from one of the architects of Syria's centralized economy, Muhammad Imadi, and Dr Issam az-Zaim, the new Minister of Industry. The reshuffle came one month after Syria had lodged a formal application to join the World Trade Organization. However, the new technocrats in the economic ministries were to report to the new Deputy Prime Minister for Economic Affairs, Muhammad al-Hussain, a known conservative. Maj.-Gen. Ali Hammoud, head of the Department of General Security, was appointed as Minister of the Interior. There were indications that al-Assad was seeking to rationalize the number of intelligence services within Syria, bringing in a new generation of senior officers. Overall, the Baath Party's presence in government was reduced from 26 to 19 posts, while the number of independents was increased from five to seven. The reshuffle was accompanied by a reorganization of the army's leadership that affected some 800 middle-ranking officers.

Bashar's continuing commitment to combating corruption was further illustrated in December 2001 when two cabinet ministers in the discredited former Government of Mahmoud az-Zoubi were gaoled for 10 years, on charges of the misuse of funds of the state-owned Syrian Arab Airlines. In May 2002 one of them was also found guilty of bribery and the abuse of power, incurring a further 10-year sentence. In March 2002 al-Assad dismissed 23 officials at the Ministry of the Interior for 'misconduct'. Fifteen officials at the Ministry of Transport were arrested on corruption charges in the same month and the Director-General of the Commercial Bank of Syria was also detained.

In early June 2002 the Zaysun dam, north of the Orontes river, collapsed, leaving at least 20 dead and thousands homeless. Over 1,200 ha of cultivated land in northern Syria and southern Turkey were inundated. The Syrian Government initiated an investigation into the disaster and called for international assistance to help the victims.

In late June 2002 the Supreme State Security Court sentenced Riad at-Turk to two-and-a-half years in gaol, on charges of seeking to change the Constitution by illegal means. He was, however, acquitted on other counts.

DIPLOMATIC DEVELOPMENTS UNDER BASHAR AL-ASSAD

In late July 2000 Bashar al-Assad indicated a desire to resume talks with Israel in the near future, although he was eager to emphasize the continuity of Syrian policy concerning the Middle East peace process. However, the rapidly deepening crisis on the Israeli-Palestinian track meant that no practical steps towards the resumption of discussions took place. Syria had been swift to blame Israel for the failure of Israeli-Palestinian efforts to agree a framework agreement for a permanent settlement at talks held in mid-July at Camp David, Maryland, USA, and warned that there was a danger of a fresh Palestinian *intifada* against Israel. Syria also condemned suggestions by President Clinton that the USA was considering moving its embassy in Israel from Tel-Aviv to Jerusalem.

Relations between Israel and Syria became further strained from late September 2000, when intense fighting broke out between Palestinians and Israeli forces in the West Bank and Gaza Strip. Syria declared its solidarity with what quickly became known as the al-Aqsa *intifada*. As tensions increased throughout the Middle East, Israel accused Syria of involvement in the abduction of Israeli military personnel by Hezbollah in southern Lebanon. During an emergency summit meeting of the Arab League held in Cairo on 21–22 October 2000 Syrian Minister of Foreign Affairs ash-Shara' urged all Arab countries to sever diplomatic ties with Israel and supported calls for the establishment of a war crimes tribunal to try Israeli 'war criminals'. In November Syria boycotted a Euro-Mediterranean summit because it felt that the EU had failed to condemn Israel's alleged excessive use of force against Palestinian protesters in the Occupied Territories. In the same month Syria welcomed the decision of Egypt and Jordan to withdraw their ambassadors from Israel.

The death of President Assad in June 2000 and the outbreak of the al-Aqsa *intifada* at the end of September at last created the conditions for decades of mistrust between Fatah and Syria to be overcome. PA officials appealed to the Syrian authorities to release the remaining Palestinian detainees held in Syrian prisons. In December seven Palestinians were released into Lebanese custody. At an Arab League summit in Amman, Jordan, on 27–28 March 2001, Bashar al-Assad and Yasser Arafat held a bilateral meeting at which they declared that their reconciliation was complete. At the same summit Syria supported a decision to investigate the feasibility of reviving the Arab boycott of Israel.

As the Palestinian uprising continued, Syria was forthright in its condemnation of Israel's actions in the West Bank and Gaza, and displayed considerable caution towards all efforts to end the violence and restart the Oslo peace process that appeared to fall short of a comprehensive solution (particularly following the electoral victory in February 2001 of the right-wing Ariel Sharon). The Syrian regime was heavily critical of what it perceived as US bias towards Israel, and it continued to host radical Palestinian factions that reject peace negotiations with Israel. During the visit of Pope John Paul II to Syria in May, Bashar al-Assad took the Roman Catholic leader to parts of the Golan Heights occupied by Israel between 1967–74, provoking Israeli criticism that the Pope had allowed himself to be used for propaganda purposes. However, the country had no appetite for a resumption of military conflict with Israel. This was reflected in its policy in Lebanon, which remained the most likely immediate cause of renewed conflict between Israel and Syria. Israel's withdrawal from southern Lebanon in May 2000 had not extended to the long-disputed Shebaa Farms area, which Israel claimed was part of Syria and was therefore subject to settlement only as part of a peace deal with Syria itself. Syria, for its part, asserted that Shebaa Farms was Lebanese territory and criticized the UN's support for the Israeli position. In November 2000 Hezbollah attacked an Israeli patrol in the area, provoking retaliatory Israeli air-strikes. Hezbollah attacks continued over the coming months. In January 2001 Israel began constructing a concrete security fence some 500 m north of the UN-delineated border (the 'Blue Line') between Israel and Lebanon. Syria protested to the UN, which intervened to force Israel to cease construction of the border fence. In March it was the turn of the UN to face Syrian criticism, following its announcement that UNIFIL's size was to be scaled down. Syria viewed this as a means of compelling Lebanese forces to move into the border area and maintain security. It did not wish to see Hezbollah's freedom of action curtailed, and joined with the Lebanese Government in affirming that security for Israel would only come with the signing of a comprehensive Middle East peace settlement. In April, accusing Syria of supporting the attacks by Hezbollah, Israel responded by bombing a Syrian radar station 35 km east of Beirut. Syria condemned the bombing and stated that it would respond at the appropriate time, but showed no signs of replying in kind. In June 2001 Syria welcomed reports that the UN Secretary-General, Kofi Annan, had stated that the UN now acknowledged that Shebaa Farms should be considered part of Lebanon. The Shebaa Farms stand-off provided Syria with a further pretext for continuing its presence in Lebanon. However, this did not mean that the situation remained completely unchanged following the Israeli withdrawal from southern Lebanon. Responding to growing calls from within Lebanese political circles, President Bashar al-Assad began a careful and cautious process of reducing the scale of the Syrian presence during his early years in office.

Following the death of President Hafiz Assad on 10 June 2000, public mourning in Lebanon had been at a level comparable to that in Syria itself. The Lebanese authorities took steps to censor any local or international media comment that was critical of Assad's legacy. The Lebanese President, Emile Lahoud, the Prime Minister, Selim al-Hoss, and the National Assembly President, Nabih Berri, all attended Assad's funeral on 13 June. On 15 June Hezbollah platoons marched through the late President's home village to salute their patron for a final time. However, following the end of the period of official mourning in late July, Maronite Christian deputies called on the new Syrian President to release all Lebanese political prisoners being held in Syria. A coalition of Christian political parties in Lebanon urged the Lebanese people to boycott parliamentary elections scheduled for 27 August and 3 September 2000, on the grounds that Syria would dictate the outcome of the poll. The results of voting, at which the Syrian-sponsored Government of Selim al-Hoss was resoundingly defeated by former premier Rafik Hariri, and subsequent demands from elements in Lebanon for a reorganization or withdrawal of Syrian forces (for further details, see the chapter on Lebanon), served to intensify speculation as to Syria's future role in Lebanese affairs. None the less, Syrian officials had played a significant role in consultations leading to the formation of a new Lebanese Government, under Rafik Hariri, in October. In addition, Syria's allies in the south, Nabih Berri's Amal and Hezbollah, had won a comprehensive electoral victory in the elections. In November the Syrian foreign minister Farouk ash-Shara' stated that the issue of Syrian 'redeployment' would be addressed in accordance with the 1989 Ta'if agreement. In December 2000, in an important move to address a long-standing Maronite Christian grievance, Syria released 46 Lebanese prisoners and allowed them to return to Lebanon.

During the first half of 2001 the pressure on Syria to make a significant gesture in terms of military redeployment grew progressively more intense. Traditional allies such as Druze leader Walid Joumblatt joined with Maronite Christian groups in calling for Syrian troop withdrawals. Finally, on 14 June 2001 the Syrian army began a complete pull-out of its estimated 6,000 troops stationed in Beirut and Mount Lebanon governorates. The redeployment was completed on 19 June. Syrian officials claimed that the decision to withdraw from Beirut and Mount Lebanon had been taken some time ago, but that tension in southern Lebanon had postponed implementation of the manouevre. Most of the troops were reported to have returned to Syria (although some were said to have redeployed in the Beka'a valley). However, hundreds of intelligence officers were left in place in the capital.

Relations between Syria and Iraq improved steadily during Bashar al-Assad's early years in the presidency. Syria strongly opposed the continuation of UN sanctions against Iraq, including US- and British-led efforts to modify them to create a regime of 'smart' sanctions. Despite international criticism, in particular from the USA, increasing quantities of Iraqi oil were exported to Syria outside the framework of UN sanctions (a disused oil pipeline was reopened for this purpose in November 2000). Rail links were resumed in August of that year, after an interruption of some 20 years, and in November the Iraqi Minister of Foreign Affairs, Tareq Aziz, flew to Damascus on the first direct flight abroad by a senior Iraqi official since 1991. In January 2001, the two countries announced that they had worked out a detailed plan to share water resources. Syria condemned US–British air-strikes on Baghdad in February.

Relations between Syria and Turkey remained uncertain. In January 2001 a high-level military delegation visited Turkey to discuss the normalization of diplomatic ties, but little progress was made. A key impediment remained the issue of water resources. The headwaters of the Tigris and Euphrates rivers lie in Turkey. A positive sign for the longer term lay in increased co-operation over border security between the two countries. In June 2002, in a breakthrough in relations, the two countries signed a military training agreement.

The Syrian Government condemned the suicide attacks carried out on New York and Washington, DC, on 11 September 2001. However, the extent to which the Syrian Administration would be prepared actively to support the US Administration of George W. Bush in its demands for a 'world-wide coalition' to fight the terrorist threat remained unclear in the immediate aftermath of the attacks. In early October 2001 Syria was elected as a non-permanent member of the UN Security Council for the years 2002–03. There were no US objections. While Syrian support for Hezbollah in Lebanon and the Palestinian militant Islamist organization Hamas kept Syria on the US list of 'state sponsors of terrrorism' when the US State Department released its report in May 2002, details emerged in June of its co-operation with US efforts to combat the radical Islamist al-Qa'ida network. Syria confirmed that there had been extensive intelligence sharing, most notably with regard to an alleged participant in the events leading up to the 11 September 2001 attacks on the USA, Muhammad Haydar Zammar, who had been extradited from Morocco to Syria in connection with alleged terrorist activities. Zammar, a Syrian-born German citizen, was alleged to have recruited some of the hijackers involved in the attacks.

While relations between Syria and the USA did thaw somewhat following the 11 September 2001 attacks, their divergent positions on the Middle East peace process prevented genuine *rapprochement*. As violence continued between Israel and the Palestinians, Hezbollah renewed attacks on Israeli outposts in the Shebaa Farms area in October and November 2001. The USA warned Damascus that it would not be able to restrain Israel should such attacks continue. It was unclear whether Syria had even been consulted by Hezbollah prior to its military action. Syria was not welcoming of the Middle East peace plan first proposed by the Crown Prince Abdullah in February–March 2002, which initially contained no reference to the Golan Heights or Shebaa Farms. The plan was subsequently amended to incorporate clear reference to their return to Syria as part of a 'comprehensive peace' settlement. Syria endorsed the plan at the Beirut summit of the Arab League on 27–28 March but showed little regret as it was rapidly overtaken by events.

Syria condemned the *de facto* Israeli reoccupation of the West Bank at the end of March 2002 but, in response to US and European pressure, Bashar al-Assad joined with President Mubarak and Crown Prince Abdullah at a meeting in Sharm esh-Sheikh in mid-May in rejecting 'all forms of violence'. This appeared to bring Syria into line with other Arab states in condemning Palestinian suicide attacks on Israeli civilians. As Hezbollah attacks on the Shebaa farms intensified in early April, Syria announced that it was withdrawing its forces from central and southern Lebanon in accordance with the 1989 Ta'if agreement. The redeployment left most of the estimated 25,000 Syrian troops in Lebanon deployed along the Lebanon–Syria border. Two units remained near Beirut to support the Lebanese army. This was widely interpreted as a move to ensure that Syria could not so plausibly be held responsible for Hezbollah's military actions against Israel. Few saw it as presaging the end of Syrian influence over Lebanon. US Secretary of State Colin Powell met President al-Assad in Damascus in mid-April to underscore US concerns and warn Syria once again that Israel held it responsible for the Hezbollah attacks. Israeli military aircraft flew over Syrian positions in the Beka'a valley in early May, prompting anti-aircraft fire from the Syrian troops. At the same time, in response to US pressure, Hezbollah forces unexpectedly withdrew from the border area with Israel.

On his visit to Damascus in mid–April 2002 Colin Powell also sought Syrian support for a US-sponsored Middle East peace conference. Bashar al-Assad displayed little enthusiasm for the proposal, given its backing by Israeli Prime Minister Ariel Sharon. He also rejected the US and Israeli emphasis on the prior reform of Palestinian institutions before peace negotiations could resume in earnest. Syria was also critical in late June of President Bush's 'landmark' speech on the Middle East peace process, accusing the USA of ignoring existing Arab proposals and following an agenda considered by the Arab world as entirely set by Israel.

Another impediment to improved relations with the USA was Syria's position on Iraq. In December 2001 Syria denied US allegations that it had been receiving 150,000 barrels of oil per day from Iraq in defiance of UN sanctions. In April 2002 it was reported that an arms shipment destined for Iraq had reached its destination in February via the Syrian port of Latakia. Syria accused the USA of being behind these reports and reiterated its opposition to Iraq becoming the next military target in the 'war against terror'. In mid-May Syria endorsed UN Security Council Resolution 1409, which revised the sanctions regime in force against Iraq by removing restrictions on 'civilian goods'. Its support for the resolution was widely viewed as reluctant.

Economy

ALAN J. DAY

INTRODUCTION

Syria covers an area of 185,180 sq km (71,498 sq miles), of which about 45% is considered to be arable land. The remainder consists of bare mountain, desert and pastures capable of sustaining only nomadic populations. Of the total cultivable area of 8.7m. ha, little more than 1980–1990 was estimated to be 3.6%. Census totals in September 1970, September about 70% is under cultivation. The average annual increase in Syria's population during 1981 and September 1994 were 6,304,685,

9,052,628 and 13,782,315 respectively. Between 1993 and 1999 the average annual rate of population growth was estimated to be 2.7%. Official Syrian estimates gave the population as 16,320,000 in 2000 and 16,720,000 in 2001.

There has been a continuing movement from village to town. In 1965 about 40% of the population were classified as urban. By 1999 the proportion had risen to 54%. The urban population increased at an annual rate of 4.4% in 1980–90, almost identical to the 4.5% of 1965–80. The process of urbanization has put a strain on services in the cities. One of the achievements of President Hafiz al-Assad's regime was to extend development projects to rural areas, notably through the ambitious rural electrification programme. The population of Damascus and its surrounding province approximately doubled between 1959 and 1973, from more than half a million to an estimated 1.46m. According to UN estimates, the city had an estimated population of 2,195,000 at mid-2001. The population of Aleppo, estimated at 466,026 in 1959, had risen to some 2,229,000 by mid-2000, while Homs had a population of about 811,000. The distribution of employment changed markedly between the mid-1960s and the early 1990s, reflecting industrial growth and the expansion of the service sector. In 1993 (when Syria had a total economically active population of 3.86m.) agriculture, forestry and fishing employed 32.6% of the labour force, compared with 52% in 1965. It was estimated in 1993 that the public sector (excluding the armed forces) employed about 31% of the Syrian labour force, and that the total number of Syrians supported by public-sector employment (including employees' dependants) was approaching 6m.

The Syrian economy must be viewed against a background of regional geopolitics and the internal political developments that have taken place since the Baath Party came to power in 1963. As a 'confrontation state', a portion of whose land has been under Israeli occupation since 1967, Syria has incurred significant levels of defence expenditure, amounting to more than one-half of the country's recurrent budget in some financial years. (In the late 1990s Syria's planned defence expenditures were estimated to be equivalent to 30%–40% of the total national budget, although in 1998 and 1999 actual outlays on defence were estimated to be equivalent to less than 20% of the national budgets. In 1999 estimated defence spending by Syria was equivalent to 5.6% of gross domestic product (GDP) or US $60 per head of population, compared with estimated Israeli defence spending equivalent to 8.9% of GDP or $8,846 per head of population.) At the same time, its position as a regional power has encouraged Syria to intervene elsewhere in the area, notably in Lebanon, where it has had a costly military presence since 1976. The continuing involvement in Lebanon, combined with the threat of outright war with Israel and the history of bad relations with neighbouring Iraq (which have, in turn, influenced relations with the moderate Arab states of the Persian (Arabian) Gulf), have all affected the Syrian economy. In 1976–77, for example, Iraq decided to stop pumping petroleum through Syria to the Mediterranean coast, thus depriving the Government in Damascus of valuable transit revenues and the benefits of easily accessible petroleum supplies at a favourable price. The pipeline was closed again in 1982, but Syria was subsequently able to buy oil from Iran at concessionary rates. (For the controversial reopening of the pipeline in 2000, see Mining and Energy, below.)

During Syria's three-year union with Egypt (the United Arab Republic—UAR) from 1958 to 1961, agrarian reform and nationalization were introduced. The country's first Five-Year Plan was inaugurated during the union, and covered the period 1961–65. The nationalization programme was reversed after the dissolution of the union, and the land reform law was amended in favour of the landowners. However, in June 1963, following the Baath-dominated coup, all amendments to the agrarian reform law were abrogated, and the law itself was made even stricter. The banks were nationalized in that year, and a rigorous nationalization of industry and trade was begun in 1965. By the time that Hafiz al-Assad seized power in November 1970, there had been a radical transformation of the country's economic structure, with the economic power of the landowners, merchants and industrialists greatly weakened, and the public sector dominant.

President Assad relaxed the state's control of the economy somewhat after coming to power, partly in an attempt to widen his power base: he introduced some liberalization of foreign trade early in his presidency; a foreign investment law was promulgated in 1971; and this was followed by several related articles of legislation.

The Arab–Israeli war of October 1973 caused damage to Syria estimated at US $1,800m. Latakia port, the Banias and Tartous oil terminals and the huge Homs complex in central Syria, which then housed the country's only petroleum refinery and generated more than 40% of its power needs, were virtually destroyed. The reconstruction effort necessary to restore the Syrian economy was immense, but the Government acted swiftly, introducing measures of economic liberalization to encourage investment, in early 1974. Business confidence gradually began to return, to the extent that the third Development Plan (1971–75) ended with a flourish of unprecedented growth. This, in turn, prompted the Government to reinforce investment incentives in certain sectors and to initiate an ambitious fourth Development Plan for the period 1976–80, only to find itself confronted, once again, with the economic repercussions of regional political problems.

The fifth Development Plan (1981–85) and its successor (1986–90) concentrated on trying to finish projects already under way rather than launching ambitious new schemes. The growth targets set by the fifth Plan were noticeably more modest than those in the fourth, but even these were not achieved.

In the late 1980s, the economy was in a state of crisis, with the population suffering increasing hardship. According to the IMF, Syria's total reserves minus gold in mid-1986 stood at only US $10m., although by the end of 1987 reserves had risen to $223m., the highest end-of-year total since 1984. At the end of 1988 reserves of foreign exchange amounted to $191m. The scarcity of foreign exchange caused a shortage of spare parts and raw materials for industry, and production was substantially below capacity, with some factories ceasing production altogether. Corruption and mismanagement in the state industrial and agricultural sectors also affected output. The economic crisis led to the imposition of strict curbs on the 'black market' and on the issuing of import licences, which created difficulties for the private sector. Budget expenditure was reduced in real terms during the late 1980s, and zero or negative economic growth rates were recorded from 1986 to 1988.

The 1980 friendship treaty with the USSR and Syria's alleged links with international terrorism affected US aid to the country. In 1983 such aid was halted altogether. Syria's alleged involvement in international terrorism also affected the flow of aid from the European Community (EC, now European Union—EU) and from individual European countries. Lending by multinational institutions was, meanwhile, hampered by the slow rate of project implementation and, for a period, by Syria's debt arrears. Syria has, however, traditionally enjoyed considerable support from the various Arab aid organizations.

Participation in the US-led multinational force against Iraq in 1990–91 was calculated to increase Syria's access to aid from the USA, the EC and the 'moderate' Arab states, among other diplomatic benefits. In the event, Syria was widely regarded as the main regional beneficiary of the war, particularly in the economic sphere. Bolstered by higher world oil prices, GDP grew by more than 5% in real terms in 1991 and the trade balance went into healthy surplus. At the same time there was a major influx of aid from various sources, while economic deregulation and new tax incentives helped to stimulate private investment by local and foreign businesses. On the negative side, the collapse of the USSR in 1991 presaged economic problems for Syria, to the extent that large sectors of its economy had been orientated towards exporting low-quality goods to the USSR.

Syria's leading exports remain petroleum, cotton and phosphates, which depend on the volatile world commodity markets and, in the case of cotton, on agricultural policies and the unreliable rainfall in much of the country. The services sector, dependent on tourism and transit trade, remains extremely vulnerable to the political situation in the region.

In the first half of the 1990s the main constraints on Syria's economic development were the poor condition of much of the physical infrastructure and the inefficient administration within highly centralized public-sector organizations. The disbursal of available funding for important public-sector projects was frequently delayed for long periods by procedural obstacles, while the financing of some private-sector projects was greatly complicated by Syria's complex foreign-exchange rules and limited banking services. Despite these and other impediments, the rate of real economic growth was estimated to have averaged 6% annually over the five year period 1991–95. Over the same period Syria received about US $2,500m. of project aid from abroad (including $855m. of loans from the Kuwait Fund for

Arab Economic Development—KFAED) and obtained provisional offers of up to $1,000m. of additional aid for proposed future projects

Japan's Overseas Economic Co-operation Fund lent more than US $800m. between 1991 and 1995 for power-generation projects. However, US aid to Syria (halted for political reasons in 1983) remained suspended, while Syria's access to up to $472m of EU aid funds was largely blocked because of disputes over Syria's debt arrears to certain EU member states. (At the end of 1995 only ECU 7.9m. in grants—for banking reforms and electricity sector management—had been extended to Syria under current EU aid protocols covering a total of ECU 354m., the bulk of this total being European Investment Bank (EIB) funding blocked by the moratorium on new EU lending to Syria.) The Arab donors that provided the bulk of project aid to Syria in 1991–95 included the national development funds of Kuwait, Saudi Arabia and Abu Dhabi and various Gulf-based multilateral agencies, notably the Arab Petroleum Investments Corpn and the Arab Fund for Economic and Social Development (AFESD). As well as extending development aid, Saudi Arabia reportedly provided substantial financial backing for Syrian purchases of Russian weapons after the Gulf crisis.

In September 1997 Syria made its largest ever single repayment of foreign debt, having reached an agreement with the World Bank to settle arrears accumulated since the 1980s (see Foreign Trade and Balance of Payments, below). An important agreement for the settlement of bilateral debt had earlier been negotiated with France, bringing Syria closer to an unblocking of multilateral EU funds (eventually achieved in late 2000 when Syria reached a debt settlement agreement with Germany). None the less, the pace of economic reform and government decision-making within Syria remained chronically slow, prompting public criticism from several quarters. In April 1997 the AFESD made it clear that Syria could not expect long-standing offers of project aid to be held open indefinitely. In the same month prominent members of the Syrian business community estimated that projects worth up to US $1,300m. had been lost in recent years because prospective Arab investors had encountered severe difficulty conducting business in Syria. According to the World Bank, gross national product (GNP) in 1997 was $16,643m. ($1,120 per head) on a conventional exchange-rate basis, equivalent to $45,000m. ($3,000 per head) on a 'purchasing-power parity' (PPP) basis. During 1990–97, it was estimated, GNP per head increased, in real terms, at an average annual rate of 3.3%. The World Bank estimated Syria's GNP at constant prices (and conventional exchange rates) as $15,800m. ($1,030 per head) in 1998 and $15,200m. ($970 per head) in 1999. According to provisional government statistics, Syria's GDP increased at an average annual rate of 5.7%, in real terms, in 1990–99. According to unofficial estimates, GDP in 1999 was equivalent to $42,200m. ($2,650 per head) on a PPP basis. The average annual rate of inflation was 8.7% in 1990–99. Consumer prices increased by an average of only 2.3% in 1997, subsequently falling by 1.2% in 1998 and by 0.5% in 1999.

During the course of 1998—a year of sharply falling oil export prices—there was a steady decline in Syria's real GDP growth rate as the economy moved closer to recession. In 1999, when the agricultural sector was affected by the onset of severe drought, there was an estimated decline of 1.5%–2% in real GDP. Syria's low or negative GDP growth rates over the period 1998–2000 exacerbated the country's underlying unemployment problem (the rate of job creation having rarely kept pace with the growth of the working-age population in recent years). Between 1984 and 1999 the total recorded labour force (including only those seeking employment) nearly doubled in size, from 2.37m. to an estimated 4.70m., while the official rate of unemployment rose from 4.6% to 8.6% over the same period. Most unofficial estimates indicated an overall unemployment rate in the range 15%–20% in 1999, although some opponents of the Government cited higher estimates that took account of such factors as the widespread under-employment of well qualified university graduates.

Western analysts of Syria's recent economic performance have highlighted the many institutional obstacles to the development process, including the banking, tax and legal systems, and were particularly critical of the way in which 'Law 10' of 1991 had so far provided a major stimulus to private-sector imports but had failed to attract large-scale private investment in new industrial projects. Advocates of economic reform welcomed the appointment in March 2000 of a new Government, under the leadership of Dr Muhammad Mustafa Mero, committed to addressing such issues and to introducing wide-ranging anti-corruption measures. The subsequent accession to the presidency of Bashar al-Assad, already identified as a supporter of the new Government's economic programme, reinforced Syrian expectations that significant measures to liberalize the economy were in prospect. An important indicator was the adoption by the ruling Baath Party's general congress in June 2000 of resolutions advocating legislation to assist the private sector and reduce bureaucratic obstacles to private-sector initiative. The party congress also expressed support for reform of the tax system in order to stimulate production and exports. However, the congress was at pains to stress that its support for 'activation of the national private sector' should not be taken to imply support for 'liquidation of the public sector through accelerating privatization'. By August 2000 some changes had already been announced to investment, banking and foreign-exchange rules, and external support for reformist policies had included a pledge of EU aid 'to increase the competitiveness of the private business sector in view of Syria's progressive transition towards a market economy'. In July of that year the Syrian Government announced a £S50,000m. programme to address the problem of unemployment, with the aim of creating 440,000 jobs over a five-year period. In 2000 real GDP grew by an estimated 3% under the stimulus of a sustained upturn in oil export prices, producing a rise in GDP per head to an estimated US $3,300 on a PPP basis.

Continuing strong oil export earnings in 2001 and a recovery in the agricultural sector underpinned further modest GDP growth of about 2% in 2001, with consumer-price inflation remaining low at 1.5%, although the current account went into a deficit of around $300m. after recording a surplus of $1,061m. in 2000. By mid-2002 the available economic data indicated further GDP growth of about 2% over the year, although the current account was expected to go further into deficit.

AGRICULTURE

Agriculture retains its position as a mainstay of the Syrian economy, despite the existence of a traditionally strong trading sector and partially successful attempts at industrialization. The agricultural sector employed about one-third of the economically active population throughout the 1990s; the sector engaged some 28.4% of the total labour force in 1999. In 2000 agriculture contributed 24.1% of Syria's GDP at current market prices (equivalent to 29.6% of GDP at constant 1995 prices). The main areas of cultivation form a narrow strip of land along the coast, from the Lebanese to the Turkish frontiers, which enjoys a Mediterranean climate, is exceedingly fertile and produces fruit, olives, tobacco and cotton. East of this strip lies the northward continuation of the Lebanon range of mountains, which falls sharply on the east to the Orontes river valley, whose marshes have been reclaimed to form one of Syria's most fertile areas. In central Syria this valley joins the steppe-plain, about 150 km wide, which runs from the Jordanian borders north-eastward towards the Euphrates valley. The plain is traditionally Syria's major agricultural area, with cereals as the principal crops. Also in this region are the country's main cities, Damascus, Homs, Hama and Aleppo. The importance of this plain is now being rivalled by a fourth area, the Jezira, which lies between the Euphrates in Syria and the Tigris in Iraq. Although fertile lands along the banks of the Euphrates and its tributaries had previously been cultivated, the Jezira's value was recognized only in the early 1950s, when large-scale cotton cultivation was introduced in former pasture lands. It has since greatly increased its output with the development of the Euphrates Dam, and the Government has made efforts to promote the social and economic development of this previously neglected area.

One of the chief characteristics of Syria's agricultural performance, in the absence of any established large-scale irrigation system, has been an extreme fluctuation in annual output, owing to wide variations in rainfall. Dependence on rainfall for good harvests is illustrated by the Central Bureau of Statistics' general indices for agricultural production, which show fluctuations from 78 in 1979 to 109 in 1983, to 99 in 1984, to 104 in 1985 and to 110 in 1986 (1980 = 100). In 1989 agricultural output by value fell by nearly 20%. By the early 1990s, however, the implementation of irrigation schemes and investment in modern techniques had begun to yield results in the shape of higher and more consistent output, especially of cereal crops.

As a consequence of agrarian reform legislation introduced in 1958, the area of unused cultivable land (excluding fallow) increased from 1,892,000 ha in 1963 to 2,825,000 ha by 1970. Suspicion of government intentions was gradually tempered, however, by the relaxation of the reform law and, under the post-1970 Assad administration, by a number of significant amendments. Out of agricultural investments accounting for a sizeable 35% of total investment under the third Five-Year Plan (1971–75), the Government devoted the largest share to the Euphrates dam project (see Power and Water, below). The main task for the fourth Development Plan (1976–80) was to put the dam's stored waters to work and to irrigate an additional 240,000 ha of land in the Euphrates basin by the end of the decade. However, statistics for 1984 showed that only some 60,000 ha had actually been irrigated, which means that it will be a very long time before the final Euphrates irrigation target of 640,000 ha (which, it was originally intended, would be achieved by the end of the century) is reached. In the mean time, emphasis has been placed not only on the Euphrates, but also on other irrigation schemes, including those on the Yarmouk river (on which three pumping stations and 400 km of canals are being constructed to irrigate about 300 ha of farmland) and in the Ghab, in order to increase the area available for the cultivation of cereals, sugar beet and cotton. In September 1987 Jordan and Syria signed an agreement on the use of the waters of the Yarmouk, whereby the countries undertook to share irrigation systems and the power from a hydroelectricity plant associated with the al-Wahdeh dam, which was to be built on the Yarmouk in Jordan. In 1999 Syria made 8m. cu m of Yarmouk water available to Jordan, but the supply was reduced to 3.5m. cu m in 2000 and 2m. cu m in 2001 (when the river's flow was less than 20% of normal) owing to drought. Jordan and Syria agreed in April 2001 to refrain from using Yarmouk water for the irrigation of summer crops in the current circumstances.

With the Euphrates scheme having produced somewhat disappointing results, the Government gave increasing attention to the rain-fed areas, which account for 84% of the total cultivated area. In the southern provinces of Dera'a and Suweidiya a US $76.3m. project began in the mid-1980s to increase food production and improve living standards on 25,400 ha of rainfed land. The project was funded by the World Bank ($22m.), the International Fund for Agricultural Development (IFAD, $18m.), and the UN Development Programme ($2.2m.). Syria has benefited from the presence near Aleppo of the International Centre for Agricultural Research in the Dry Areas (ICARDA), one of the 13 centres throughout the world of the Consultative Group on International Agricultural Research (CGIAR). ICARDA is attempting to improve yields and farming systems in areas of low and medium rainfall throughout the Middle East.

In January 1993 the EIB agreed to finance the construction of the 65m. cu m ath-Thawra earthfill dam on the Snobar river, designed to irrigate 10,500 ha of land in the Latakia area. Scheduled for completion in 1994, the project would stimulate cultivation of market-garden crops, mainly for local consumption, and would facilitate tree planting to combat soil erosion. Later in 1993, bids were invited from Western consultants for the redesign of unimplemented irrigation schemes originally drawn up by East European firms in the mid-1980s. The main redesign contract (to be funded by the KFAED) related to a proposed 5-km dam on the Khabour river, which formed part of a scheme to irrigate 40,000 ha of farmland in north-eastern Syria. The unimplemented designs for this scheme had been prepared by a Bulgarian firm in 1985.

Although medium-staple cotton had been grown in Syria for many years, it was the high prices prevalent after the Second World War and during the Korean War that provided the greatest impetus to cotton production. In the early 1950s the previously neglected Jezira area was opened up for large-scale agriculture on a new capital-intensive basis, relatively free from traditional agricultural relations, still semi-feudal in the rest of the country. Syria's output of unginned cotton increased from 38,000 metric tons in 1949 to 220,800 tons in 1954. The area under cotton increased from 25,300 ha in 1949, to 78,000 ha in 1950 and to 250,000 ha in 1971/72. By 1987/88 this area had declined to 128,000 ha, but in the following year it increased to 165,000 ha, and the area designated for cotton in 1989/90 was 170,000 ha.

Petroleum overtook cotton as Syria's most valuable source of export earnings in 1974, as cotton exports (raw, yarn and textiles) declined, both in value and volume. Output of cotton lint was 200,000–250,000 metric tons per year in 1968–73, but by the 1980/81 season it had declined to 117,800 tons. Production subsequently recovered, and in 1983/84 a record cotton crop of 523,418 tons yielded 194,000 tons of cotton lint, although there was a decline in cotton output, to 125,931 tons of lint in 1986/87. Cotton export earnings rose from £S453m. in 1982 to £S1,076m. in 1984, but dropped to £S391m. in 1986. The 1987/88 crop was affected by bad winter weather, and this, combined with the decrease in area, yielded only 95,000 tons of lint. The 1988/89 crop yielded 116,000 tons of lint, and total cotton production rose to 441,000 tons in 1989/90 and to 555,000 tons in 1990/91. The official prices payable to Syrian farmers for their cotton have been progressively increased in recent years, but the sector has suffered to some extent from competition from other major crops. The local textile industry (historically one of the Syrian economy's leading sectors) uses an appreciable proportion of the cotton crop, its average lint requirement being about 50,000 tons a year in the early 1990s and 100,000 tons a year at the end of the decade. Syria's cotton crop totalled 600,000 tons in 1995, 760,000 tons in 1996 and a record 1m. tons in 1997 (when it accounted for some 6.3% of export earnings). The volume of ginned cotton reached 345,100 tons in 1997. In 1998 Syria produced 340,100 tons of ginned cotton. The cotton crop accounted for some 9.4% of export earnings in 1998. A 21% tax on cotton and cotton textile production was abolished in June 1999, in order to stimulate production and exports. In the 1999/2000 season (beginning in August 1999) Syria produced 315,000 tons of cotton lint. In the 2000/01 season estimated lint production was 370,000 tons, from 1.1m. tons of seed cotton grown on 270,000 ha of land. The estimated domestic demand for cotton lint in that season was 110,000 tons, leaving an exportable balance of 260,000 tons.

One of the crops that has competed with cotton is sugar beet. The Government has been keen to foster a domestic sugar industry, and the area planted with beet rose from 22,000 ha in 1980 to 35,700 ha in 1984. However, the failure of the domestic refining industry to perform as planned has led to a drastic reduction in the beet area, to 13,200 ha in 1986. The harvest of sugar beet declined from 1.3m. metric tons in 1984 to 412,000 tons in 1985, rising to 440,000 tons the following year. Production rose again, to 457,000 tons, in 1987, but declined to 222,000 tons in 1988. It rose again to 412,000 tons in 1989, to 422,000 tons in 1990 and to 637,000 tons in 1991. In 1992 production reached 1.4m. tons, declining slightly, to 1.2m. tons, in 1993 and rising again, to 1.4m. tons, in 1994. Production remained at 1.4m. tons in 1995, then fell sharply to 974,000 tons in 1996. However, production of sugar beet recovered to 1.1m. tons in 1997, 1.2m. tons in 1998, and 1.3m. tons per year in 1999 and 2000. Production of refined sugar by local factories reached a peak of 206,000 tons in 1983 but dropped to 54,000 tons in 1985, rising only marginally to 57,000 tons in the following year. The decline in the sugar industry was partly the result of the fall in the world price of sugar. In the mid-1970s, when Syria started to develop the industry, prices were high, while those of cotton were low. Imports of sugar fluctuated during the 1980s. Those of raw sugar rose from 96,600 tons in 1985 to 261,200 tons in 1986, while those of refined sugar declined from 321,700 tons to 268,200 tons. In 1994 the state sugar refining company was obliged to import 128,000 tons of raw sugar, in order to fulfil its 1994 production target of 260,000 tons of refined sugar (about 48% of current consumption). Construction of a new 129,000-tons-per-year sugar refinery was scheduled to begin in 1995. In that year the Government gave its approval to proposals to build Syria's first privately-owned sugar refinery, with an output capacity of 100,000 tons per year. The refinery would be sited at Tartous and would process imported raw sugar.

Syria's cereals crop is also of prime importance, accounting in 1993 for nearly 80% of the £S45,000m. spent on crop purchases by the agricultural marketing authorities. Wheat and barley together occupied 2.65m. ha in 1985, two-thirds of the total cropped area. Output of both crops has varied considerably from year to year, depending on the rainfall. (About 40% of Syria's wheat is produced on irrigated land, while virtually all barley is grown in wholly rain-fed areas.) In 1987/88 the cereals harvest more than doubled, to almost 5m. metric tons, including more than 2m. tons of wheat. However, low rainfall in early 1989 adversely affected the harvest, leading to substantial decreases. Wheat production was 2m. tons in 1990, 2.1m. tons in 1991 and 3m. tons in 1992. Barley production was 1m. tons in 1990, after which efforts were made to stabilize yields in marginal growing areas. (During the 1980s the average annual barley yield had ranged from as little as 235 kg per ha to as much as 1,044 kg per ha.) The Government's 1994 barley production target of 1.5m. tons was underfulfilled by 50% because of weather-related crop damage. About 300,000 tons of maize (sufficient to supply 60% of the state fodder company's requirement) were produced in 1993.

In 1993 the wheat harvest reached 3.6m. metric tons, placing a severe strain on available storage space despite the construction of 15 additional grain silos over the previous year. The state grain marketing authorities launched an emergency programme to build 13 more silos during 1994 and to expand local flour-milling capacity, which fell far short of current requirements. The main reasons for the strong upturn in wheat production in 1993 were favourable rainfall, improved cultivation techniques, and increases in areas planted (attributable partly to price liberalization to improve the financial returns to farmers). Syria's annual wheat consumption was around 2.2m. tons in the early 1990s, while national flour-milling capacity was around 1.35m. tons, necessitating a heavy reliance on Lebanese mills to process part of the Syrian wheat harvest. Despite some weather damage, the 1994 wheat harvest totalled 3.7m. tons. Wheat production in 1995 was just under 4.2m. tons. Contracts were awarded in late 1994 for the construction of five new flour mills to increase Syria's annual milling capacity by 750,000 tons by 1998. In 1996 the wheat harvest totalled almost 4.1m. tons and the barley harvest was 1.5m. tons. Up to 5.3m. tons of wheat were held in storage in 1996, when Syria exported cereals to the value of US $150m. It was reported in May 1997 that Syria was to export $14m. worth of wheat to Bulgaria in settlement of debts owed to Bulgarian state enterprises. Cereals production declined in 1997, owing to low rainfall in the traditional wheat-growing areas. Wheat output was some 3m. tons, while that of barley fell to just under 1m. tons. It was reported in December that the OPEC Fund for International Development had agreed to provide a loan of $6m. to help finance the construction of four new grain silos, each with a capacity of 100,000 tons. In 1998 an area of over 1.7m. ha was planted to wheat, yielding a harvest of 4.1m. tons and permitting exports of 600,000 tons. Barley production in 1998 was 869,000 tons. In 1999 Syria's worst drought for decades reduced that year's wheat production to 2.7m. tons (some 32% below the previous five-year average), while barley production fell to 426,000 tons, about 73% below the previous five-year average. In 2000 wheat production was estimated at 3.1m. tons and barley production at 213,000 tons. Having been a net exporter of about 500,000 tons of wheat per year during 1996–1998, Syria was a minor importer in the drought-affected years of 1999 and 2000. Private-sector imports of wheat and wheat flour were permitted from 1999 as inputs for the production of food items that would ultimately be exported from Syria. Formerly a net exporter of about 350,000 tons of barley per year, Syria imported an estimated 584,700 tons in 1999 and 740,000 tons in 2000. Annual maize production fell from 285,000 tons in 1998 to 155,000 tons in 1999, and then rose to an estimated 180,000 in 2000. Imports of maize (primarily to meet the demand for poultry feed) increased from 632,800 tons in 1999 to an estimated 750,000 tons in 2000. A return to more normal rainfall in 2001 yielded a strong recovery in cereal and other agricultural production, although no official figures were available as at mid-2002.

There are several other actual and potential agricultural exports. Tobacco production averaged around 15,000 metric tons per year, and exported about 3,000 tons per year, during the early 1990s; production has risen in recent years, now averaging some 24,000 tons. There is also considerable scope for expansion in the production of fruit and vegetables. Syria has embarked on a project to double production of citrus fruit. In 1990 it produced 171,000 tons of oranges. By 1998 production had risen to 439,000 tons (although it fell to 357,000 tons in 1999, before rising again, to some 400,000 tons, in 2000). Output of tomatoes, potatoes and onions in 2000 totalled an estimated 610,000 tons, 450,000 and 95,000 tons, respectively. Demand for fruit and vegetables is necessitating imports from other sources, including Lebanon. In recent years there have, at times, been shortages of fruit and vegetables, partly as a result of the official curbing of imports in general. Syria does export a certain amount of fruit and vegetables, and in 1986 such exports included 33,512 tons of potatoes, 415 tons of onions, 5,935 tons of lentils, 1,788 tons of dried figs and 4,183 tons of watermelons. Fruit growers who had expanded production for export to guaranteed markets in the former Soviet Union suffered some losses when trade was cut back after the late 1980s. Production of grape and apple juice was due to start in 1995 at a new processing plant near Damascus which aims to provide growers with an assured outlet for a proportion of these crops. In 1998 Syria produced around 2.21m. tons of vegetables (compared with 2.15m. tons in 1997). The fruit harvest in 2000 included an estimated 315,000 tons of melons (including watermelons), 400,000 tons of grapes, 320,000 tons of apples, 65,000 tons of apricots and 27,000 tons of plums. Syria's production of olives increased from 401,000 tons in 1999 to 866,500 tons in 2000, when there were 64.3m. trees planted on 477,900 ha of land. The country consumes around 85,000 tons of olives and 75,000 tons of olive oil per year. The bulk of the additional production in 2000 was exported.

Stockraising is another important branch of agriculture. In 2000 there were an estimated 920,000 cattle, 1.1m. goats and 14.5m. sheep. Almost 1.7m. tons of milk was produced in that year. The Government announced in March 1999 that livestock farming would be relatively unaffected by the drought at that time because plentiful fodder stock had been set aside for use in such circumstances. However, it subsequently became clear that there was a substantial import requirement for barley in 1999/2000 (see above) to compensate for losses of animal feed and forage. The Government, which planned to import only 200,000 tons through public-sector agencies, authorized private-sector imports of barley, while FAO and the World Food Programme jointly approved a US $5.46m. emergency programme to assist drought-hit herders over the period October 1999 to March 2000.

MINING AND ENERGY

Production of phosphates started from mines in the Palmyra area in 1972. A sudden rise in world phosphate prices in 1974 took the price of Syrian rock up to US $53 per metric ton, despite its high chlorine content and low quality. Prices and production subsequently fluctuated. Under the provisions of the 1981–85 Plan, phosphate production was expected to reach 5m. tons per year by 1985, but actual output was considerably less than this figure. Production declined from 1.46m. tons in 1982 to 1.23m. tons in 1983. It rose to 1.51m. tons in 1984 but fell to 1.2m. tons in 1985. In 1986 production rose to 1.6m. tons, and exports increased from 694,000 tons, worth £S75.6m., in 1985, to 1.3m. tons, worth £S150m. Production in 1987 amounted to almost 2m. tons. In 1998 phosphate output totalled 2.49m. tons, of which 1.84m. tons were exported. Production was 2.12m. tons in 1999. Government planning targets advocate the modernization of equipment and the adoption of more efficient processing methods in order to increase annual output to 4m. tons.

Syria was formerly thought to have no petroleum reserves. The Iraq Petroleum Co group had rights throughout Syria but abandoned them in 1951 after failing to find petroleum in commercial quantities. Concessions were granted to an independent US operator in 1955 and to a West German-led consortium in 1956. These led to the discovery of petroleum—first of the Karatchouk field, in the north-eastern corner of the country, then of the Suweidiya field, and finally of the field at nearby Rumelan. However, in addition to the cost of extraction being high, the petroleum from all three oilfields was of low quality. The petroleum found at Karatchouk had a density of 19° API and a sulphur content of 4.5%, while that found at Suweidiya had a density of 25° API and a 3.5% sulphur content. In 1964, several years before any of the three fields had begun production on a commercial basis, Syria became one of the first Arab states to discard the notion of petroleum concessions and to nationalize its petroleum operations. Even at that early stage, Syria's industrial planners were anxious to use the country's petroleum not only for export in its crude state, but also as a raw material for domestic industry. For the next 10 years all exploration and exploitation was conducted solely by the state-owned General Petroleum Authority and its offshoot, the Syrian Petroleum Co (SPC), with Soviet assistance.

Output from Suweidiya started in July 1968 and totalled 1m. metric tons in the first year, of which 833,000 tons were exported. Output in 1969, when the Karatchouk field began to produce, failed to reach expectations, totalling only 3.2m. tons, of which 2.3m. tons were exported. The October War in 1973 reduced production from a level of 6.3m. tons in the previous year to just 5.4m. tons, recovering in 1974 to 6.2m. tons. Production remained at about that level in the late 1970s; by the early 1980s, with oil prices falling and its known petroleum reserves being exhausted, Syria was actually a net importer of petroleum. From the mid-1980s, however, the petroleum industry was transformed by the discovery of large reserves of high-quality crude oil near Deir ez-Zor by a consortium of foreign oil companies.

The new discoveries were the result of the reversal of the Government's 'no-concessions' policy in the mid-1970s. In May 1975 the first Syrian concession to be won by any Western company for over 15 years was awarded to a US group, on production-sharing terms heavily tilted in the Government's favour and stipulating that US $20m. be invested in exploration off shore. In June 1975 the Government took its new policy one stage further by offering a dozen onshore oil concessions for international bidding. Altogether, 50,000 sq km were to be made available. The oil companies' response to the invitation was initially slow, and when the first US group, Tripco, relinquished its concession in March 1976 no other company had come forward to join the search. In July 1977, however, a US-Syrian consortium called Samoco took up a concession in the Deir ez-Zor area, and in December another concession, in Raqqa province, was taken by Shell subsidiaries, Syria Shell Petroleum Development and Pecten Syria Co. Both Shell and Samoco insisted on a larger share of eventual petroleum production than was agreed between the Government and Tripco. This softening of terms reawakened the interest of other firms, including Chevron of the USA.

By 1983, however, Samoco, Chevron and Rompetrol of Romania (which was exploring west of Hassakeh) had all followed Tripco in relinquishing their concessions, leaving Pecten and Marathon of the USA as the only foreign operators in the country. In early 1983 Pecten, together with Royal Dutch Shell and Deminex of the Federal Republic of Germany, assumed control of Samoco's concession area. At the end of 1984 it was revealed that the consortium had discovered reserves of high-quality crude oil at ath-Thayyem, near Deir ez-Zor. In 1985 the three foreign partners and the SPC formed the Al-Furat Petroleum Co (AFPC) to develop the concession. Full commercial production began in September 1986, adding an initial 60,000 barrels per day (b/d), or 3m. metric tons per year, to Syria's total production capacity. Because the oil from the field is light crude (36° API), with a very low sulphur content, it has considerably reduced the need to import light crudes for blending with heavy Syrian ones at Syrian refineries. Previously Syria had imported between 5m. and 6.6m. tons of oil every year. Related to the main ath-Thayyem field are the later discoveries of the al-Ward, al-Asharah, ash-Shula and al-Kharata fields. In May 1989 it was reported that ath-Thayyem was producing 65,000 b/d, with output from the related fields bringing the total output of this system to 100,000 b/d out of total Syrian production in 1989 of 15.2m. tons (310,000 b/d).

Marathon had discovered gas reserves capable of producing 450m. cu m per day at a well named Cherrife 2 in 1982, and had made a further gas and condensate discovery in mid-1985, at ash-Shair. In December 1988, after a long period of resisting government pressure to develop gas reserves, Marathon agreed to a production-sharing scheme, with investment of up to US $20m. in converting the oil-fired Muhardeh and Banias power stations to gas. The agreement was the first in Syria to include a gas sales clause. Turkey has expressed an interest in developing Syrian gas reserves (estimated at 225,000m. cu m in 1992) with a view to possible export to Turkey.

Syria's crude oil production reached 21.1m. metric tons (405,000 b/d) in 1990, 24.5m. tons (470,000 b/d) in 1991 and 26.9m. tons (520,000 b/d) in 1992, about two-thirds of the latter total being light crude and the balance heavy crude. Syrian oil output averaged 570,000 b/d in both 1993 and 1994, rising to 600,000 b/d in 1995. Average oil output subsequently fell to 590,000 b/d in 1996 and 580,000 b/d in 1997 and 1998. Average output then rose slightly to 584,000 b/d in 1999 before falling by 7.1%, to 555,000 b/d in 2000 and to 551,000 b/d in 2001. Syria's proven oil reserves totalled 2,500m. barrels at the end of 2001 (unchanged since the previous year), sufficient to maintain the average 2001 rate of production for a further 12.5 years.

While AFPC continued to widen the scope of its own development programme (which included increasing use of water-injection techniques to maintain production from 'mature' oilfields), Elf Aquitaine of France was preparing to increase or commence production from new wells in the Atallah North and Jafra areas of the Deir ez-Zor field in 1993, while the Shell, Tullow Oil, Unocal and Occidental companies were engaged in active oil exploration programmes in other parts of the country. During the third quarter of 1994 Syrian oil output reached 615,000 b/d following the completion of current oilfield development programmes. Oil exploration activity was very limited and was currently yielding disappointing results. In late 1994 Shell (whose investment in Syria over the previous decade totalled about US $3,000m., 90% of which had so far been recouped) signed a new exploration agreement covering areas previously relinquished by BP and Total. Unocal had ceased exploration in Syria by the end of 1994. Tullow Oil was in mid-1996 preparing to develop a small Euphrates Basin oilfield (the Kishma field) discovered in 1995. In mid-1996 about 66% of Syria's oil output was produced by AFPC, 24% by SPC and 10% by Elf Aquitaine.

From the late 1980s the Government's desire to maximize oil output was apparent in the easing of state bureaucratic constraints on the sector. Nevertheless, foreign companies continued to be deterred by the difficulties they experienced in Syria, added to which the prospects of major new discoveries were seen as limited. An estimated 65% of Syria's geological structures remained unexplored in 1993, when the Government's policy on oil development terms was broadly based on prevailing Egyptian practices. According to a comparative survey of 101 oil-producing countries, published in February 1995 by a Swiss company, Petroconsultants, Syria had the least attractive fiscal climate for oil exploration companies. The foreign oil companies operating in Syria in 1995 were understood to have urged the Government to allow 40% recovery of development costs (compared with the existing 25% cost-recovery allowance) and to introduce accelerated cost-recovery procedures for existing operators (by allowing production from established wells to be offset against the development costs of new wells).

In February 1997 MOL was awarded a 5,000 sq km oil exploration block east of Palmyra. An exploration and production agreement covering a five-block exploration area totalling 4,201 sq km was concluded in the following month with a consortium made up of subsidiaries of Elf Aquitaine (40%), Japan's Sumitomo Development Co (30%) and Malaysia's Petronas (30%). In May Syria Shell Petroleum Development was granted a new exploration block in the Euphrates basin. At the end of 1997 the Government concluded two new agreements with international companies, Croatia's INA—Naftaplin and Sweden's Svenska Petroleum Exploration, to explore in the Palmyra and Deir ez-Zor areas, and was reported to be negotiating as many as three further such agreements. Government plans were subsequently revealed in June 1998 to invite companies to explore for oil and gas for the first time off shore in the Mediterranean. In November Tullow Oil, which had experienced a major fall in output from its Syrian oilfield during the course of the year, announced that it was abandoning its Syrian operations because they were no longer commercially viable.

In February 2000 Syria Shell announced its first new oil discoveries since 1993, in its Zenobia exploration contract area in the north-east, although no significant proven reserves in the field had been confirmed by mid-2002. In May 2000 Tanganyika Oil Co (a Canadian affiliate of Sweden's Lundin Oil) was granted exclusive rights to the Oude development block, comprising 403 sq km close to Syria's north-eastern border with Turkey. Output of heavy crude from the block's one producing field (operated by SPC since the late 1970s) had declined steadily for some time, and the new arrangement signalled the Syrian Government's acceptance of a need for foreign capital and technology to maximize the potential of SPC's older fields. Tanganyika Oil undertook to invest a minimum of US $5m. in modern gravity displacement pumping techniques in the first two years of the new agreement. In July 2001 the Government invited bids for oil and gas exploration rights in five blocks with a total area of 26,000 sq km, whose development would be subject to production-sharing agreements. A further 11 blocks totalling 63,000 sq km were opened for bidding in June 2002, the SPC's aim being that licences to all 16 blocks would be granted by the end of 2002. Motivating the SPC in promoting new exploration was the gradual fall in production from existing fields and fears that Syria could become a net importer of oil unless new discoveries were made. For the same reasons, the SPC was in mid-2002 actively pursuing plans for the application of advanced oil recovery technology to increase output from its main producing fields in north-eastern Syria.

The generally poor quality of Syrian petroleum until the late 1980s, together with opposition on the part of some of the major oil companies to Syria's nationalization experiment, combined, at the outset of the country's petroleum development, to cause considerable marketing difficulties. However, with increasing sales (particularly to Greece, France, Italy and the USSR), crude petroleum became Syria's most important export. The value of exports of petroleum and petroleum products soared from £S291.2m. in 1972 to £S1,607.5m. in 1974 and to £S6,253m. in 1980, but it fell subsequently as a result of the slump in world oil prices. In 1981 Syria became a net importer of petroleum by value for the first time since petroleum exports began in the mid-1970s, recording a deficit on its trade in petroleum of £S262m. There was a surplus of £S189m. in the petroleum account in 1982, although deficits of £S123m. and £S767m. were recorded in 1983 and 1984. In 1986 oil imports were halved, from 5.4m. metric tons in 1985, to 2.7m. tons, while exports fell from 7.4m. tons to 6.3m. tons—an oil trade surplus of 3.7m. tons, worth £S346m. (compared with a surplus of £S315m. in 1985). In 1986 sales of oil and oil products accounted for 42% of total exports by value, compared with 74% in 1985, the decline being caused by lower oil prices. By 1990 oil and other minerals accounted for 45% of Syria's merchandise exports by value, and in 1991 exports of oil were valued at £S17,218m. The volume of oil exports fluctuated within the range of 300,000 b/d to 360,000 b/d in early 1994, at which point the state marketing company had 21 term customers abroad and was seeking to conduct an increasing proportion of its business through term contracts rather than sales on the spot market. In mid-1995 the estimated volume of Syria's oil exports was 320,000 b/d. The country's oil export earnings totalled £S21,007m. (nearly 60% of total merchandise exports by value) in 1993 and £S20,190m. in 1994. Oil exports were worth US $2,499m. in 1995, $2,748m. in 1996 and $2,509m. in 1997, equivalent, respectively, to 64.7%, 65.7% and 61.8% of total merchandise exports. In 1998, a year of severely depressed world oil prices, Syria earned an estimated $1,700m. from oil exports (54.2% of estimated merchandise exports). Syrian oil exports were estimated to be worth around $2,200m. in 1999 and $3,500m. in 2000.

The capacity of petroleum refineries in Syria totalled 11.4m. metric tons per year (228,000 b/d) at 1 January 1988, comprising 5.4m. tons per year (102,000 b/d) at the Homs refinery and 6m. tons per year (126,000 b/d) at the Romanian-built refinery at Banias, which came on stream in 1980. For a long time, however, the Banias plant operated at considerably below capacity, owing to repeated shortfalls in deliveries of crude petroleum. It was this problem that delayed construction of the refinery, as its specifications had to be altered to enable it to process different grades of crude and thus reduce its dependence on uncertain Iraqi supplies, which were subsequently discontinued by Syria's closure of the Kirkuk–Banias pipeline, which had a capacity of 500,000 b/d. The sixth expansion of the Homs refinery was

carried out by Technoexport of Czechoslovakia. The seventh expansion was to have entailed construction of a base lube oil complex with a capacity of 100,000 tons per year but, owing to Syria's budgetary constraints, this project was replaced by one for a plant to process used lubricating oils, with a capacity of 30,000 tons per year, to be increased to 40,000 tons per year. In 1994 the Government accepted the recommendations of a 1992 study by a US consultancy which advocated a major restructuring of both existing refineries in order to boost their output of light products. About half of the current refining capacity was devoted to the production of heavy fuel oil, Syrian demand for which was due to fall substantially in coming years as new gas-fired power stations were constructed. Also in 1994, a private-sector business backed by Saudi Arabian and other Gulf region investors announced plans (approved in principle by the Syrian Government) to build a new oil refinery in Syria with a capacity of about 100,000 b/d, while the Government put forward unrelated proposals for a new 60,000 b/d refinery near the Deir ez-Zor oilfields. Syria's crude oil refining capacity stood at 242,140 b/d at the end of 2001. Royalties for the transit of foreign crude petroleum through Syrian territory were for many years more valuable than indigenous production. Two pipelines carry petroleum from the Kirkuk oilfield, in Iraq, through Syria. One, built in 1934, leads on to a terminal at Tripoli in Lebanon. The second IPC pipeline, completed in 1952, branches off at Homs to the Syrian terminal at Banias. A third pipeline, belonging to the Trans-Arabian Pipeline Co (Tapline) which used to carry 24m. metric tons of Saudi crude petroleum per year to a terminal near Sidon in Lebanon, crosses about 150 km of Syrian territory, much of which was occupied by Israel in 1967. After nationalizing the Iraq Petroleum Company in June 1972, the Iraqi Government took over payment of royalties to Syria and in January 1973, after lengthy negotiations, Syria and Iraq signed a transit agreement which provided both for transit dues and the supply of petroleum for Syria's own domestic use. However, the flow of petroleum through the Kirkuk–Banias pipeline has been interrupted more than once since then. Throughput was suspended in 1976, when negotiations between Iraq and Syria on renewing the financial clauses of the transit agreement broke down, with Iraq demanding higher prices for its petroleum (to match the 1973–74 increases) and Syria seeking a proportionate increase in transit fees. For more than two years Iraq refused to use the pipeline, instead directing its petroleum southward to the Gulf and also via Turkey, through a pipeline that came on stream in 1977. The short-lived improvement in Iraqi–Syrian political relations in late 1978, combined with the world shortage of petroleum arising from the Iranian revolution, brought a resumption of pumping from Kirkuk to Banias in 1979, but this was halted yet again in September 1980 at the start of the Iran–Iraq War. When, despite the continuation of the war, Iraq recommenced exports of petroleum on a limited scale, the situation in the Gulf put Syria in a relatively stronger position and the Iraq–Syria pipeline came into use again in February 1981. However, Syria remained dissatisfied with the transit royalties, stating that in 1981 the pipeline cost US $31m. to operate but brought revenues of only $25.7m. In April 1982, having signed an agreement to buy 8.7m. tons of petroleum per year from Iran, Syria closed the Kirkuk–Banias pipeline to Iraqi petroleum. With the closure of the pipeline, concessional supplies from Iran played an important part in fulfilling Syria's oil import needs. From 1982 onwards yearly agreements were negotiated with Iran for the supply of oil: typically, 1m. tons supplied free to the Syrian army and the rest at a discount. The oil agreements were, however, plagued by political disagreements between the two countries, and by Syria's mounting oil debt to Iran, which was reported in mid-1986 to be at least $1,500m. For some periods Iranian oil supplies were halted altogether. In April 1987, 12-month agreements were signed for the supply of 1m. tons of oil free of charge to the Syrian army, and 2m. tons at OPEC prices on a cash-payment basis. A new one-year agreement, allowing for the supply of 1m. tons of free oil, was reached in April 1988. The smaller quantity of oil involved in the recent agreements reflected the impact that the Deir ez-Zor production has had on Syria's oil import needs. In June 1989, the Syrian Minister of Petroleum stated that Iran had made no deliveries of 'free' oil since the end of 1988.

In July 1998 Iraq and Syria agreed to reopen the Kirkuk–Banias IPC pipeline, which was subsequently restored to good working order on both sides of the border (and was reportedly available for use from March 2000). From late 2000 it was widely reported that Iraq was pumping oil to Syria without seeking formal clearance from UN sanctions administrators. The reported rate of supply of Iraqi crude to Syrian refineries was 140,000 b/d–150,000 b/d, this being the amount by which Syria was able to increase exports of its own crude oil in December 2000. In February 2001 the US Secretary of State, Colin Powell, stated that he had received assurances from President Assad that Syria accepted that Iraqi oil imported through the Kirkuk–Banias pipeline should be 'under the same kind of [UN] control as other elements of the sanctions regime'. In February 2002, however, the British Government informed the UN Security Council that Syria was continuing to violate UN sanctions by importing up to 200,000 b/d of Iraqi oil. Meanwhile, in November 2001 Syria had signed an agreement with Iraq for the construction of a new US \$200m. pipeline from Kirkuk to Banias to replace the ageing IPC link.

Syria's limited proven reserves of natural gas were estimated at 240,000m. cu m in 2001, about three-quarters of them owned by the SPC and located mainly in the Palmyra and other northeastern regions. Major gas development projects were initiated in the 1990s to bring the gas to population centres in the west and south, and to fuel electricty generation at power stations supplying Damascus, Homs and other cities, while further exploration resulted in a limited number of new discoveries being announced in the late 1990s. Production of gas rose five-fold in the 1990s, reaching an average of about 16m. cu m per day in 2000 and being targeted to reach 30m. cu m per day by 2005. The Government's stated aims are to substitute natural gas for oil in power generation in order to free up as much oil as possible for export and to make Syria a net exporter of liquefied gas, as well as to use gas feedstock to increase the country's production of fertilizers.

In November 1998 Conoco and what became TotalFinaElf, bidding in partnership, were awarded a contract (which was ratified by the Syrian legislature in April 1999) to develop gas resources in the Deir ez-Zor area. Costing an estimated US \$430m., this 'Desgas' project entailed the gathering and processing of associated gas currently being flared off in existing oilfields, and the bringing into production of the hitherto undeveloped Tabiyeh gas condensate field. Conoco (the lead partner) and Elf Aquitaine were to act as service contractors to SPC during the project's development phase and its first four years of production (at a target rate of 4.2m. cu m per day), after which SPC would take over as operator of the production facilities. The engineering, procurement and construction contract for this project, awarded to Kvaerner ENC in March 2000, called for the construction of two processing trains, six compressor stations, a 180-km gathering system and a 270-km pipeline link to the national gas grid serving the main population centres in western Syria. Completion of the system was achieved in September 2001, several months ahead of schedule.

Syria is involved in various regional gas pipeline projects, both as a potential supplier and as an importer and transshipment centre of gas from nearby countries. In January 2001 Syria signed an agreement with Egypt and Lebanon envisaging the construction of a US \$1,000m. underwater gas pipeline from the Egyptian fields on the Mediterranean coast to the Lebanese port of Tripoli and then onwards to Turkey via Syria. This was followed by the signature in December 2001 of an agreement providing for the supply of Syrian gas to Lebanese power stations from late 2002 and entailing the construction of a 45-km pipeline, situated mainly within Lebanon, with a capacity of 6m. cu m per day (although an initial supply rate of 1.5m. cu m per day was envisaged). Syria is also a partner in the plan finalized in June 2001 for an overland pipeline which would supply Egyptian gas to Jordan from 2003 and would later be extended to the Syrian port of Banias and potentially to Lebanon, Turkey and Cyprus.

MANUFACTURING AND INDUSTRY

A remarkable industrial boom, mainly based on textiles, occurred in Syria shortly after independence and was the principal cause of the dissolution of the customs union with Lebanon

in 1959, since the protectionist policies adopted by the Syrian Government to safeguard this growth came into direct conflict with Lebanon's free-trade tradition. Since then the industrial (manufacturing and mining) sector has grown steadily. In 1971, for the first time, it replaced agriculture as the main generator of wealth, accounting for 19.5% of Syria's GDP, compared with 19.1% for agriculture. Manufacturing output expanded strongly in the early 1980s, with the index of production rising from 108 in 1982 to 167 in 1983 (1980 = 100). Until the early 1990s, however, production stagnated, with the industrial index standing at 163 in 1986. In some sectors there was a marked decline in 1986: the wood and furniture index fell from 80 to 14; that for paper, printing and binding from 252 to 165; and that for the main mineral industries from 175 to 132. The target for average annual industrial growth under the 1976–80 Development Plan was an ambitious 15.4%, while the investment allocation for the industrial sector was £S11,289m., representing 20.8% of the total. There was something of a change of policy, thereafter, partly because of disappointing growth rates in this sector, and industry's allocation under the 1981–85 Plan fell to 16.6% of the total, or £S16,899m. In Syria's national accounts, the industrial sector comprises manufacturing, with mining, electricity, gas and water. In terms of GDP at constant 1980 prices, the value of mining, manufacturing and utilities fell by 17% in 1984, to £S7,622m. In 1985 it rose by 5%, to £S7,997m. Figures showed a further increase of 33% in 1986, to £S10,767m. However, this is likely to have been caused by increases in the output of oil and phosphates, rather than the result of an improvement in the performance of the manufacturing sector in general. In 1999, according to preliminary government data, the industrial sector contributed 27.0% of GDP at current market prices (equivalent to 33.4% of GDP at constant 1995 prices). The real GDP of the industrial sector increased by an average of 5.7% per year during 1990–96, by 2.8% in 1997 and by 2.5% in 1998.

Syria's phosphate reserves (see Mining and Energy, above) have enabled the establishment of a phosphatic fertilizer industry. Production at a Romanian-built triple superphosphate (TSP) plant at Homs, costing US \$180m., began in 1981 with an annual capacity of 450,000 metric tons of TSP. Production of phosphatic fertilizers rose from 68,333 tons in 1981 to 192,720 tons in 1986. An ammonia urea plant was completed at Homs in 1979, with a daily capacity of 1,000 tons of ammonia, of which 600 tons was to be used to manufacture 1,050 tons of urea per day. Production of nitrogenous fertilizers increased from 59,607 tons in 1981 to 116,543 tons in 1982. In 1984 and 1985 production was 110,206 tons and 104,000 tons, respectively, rising to 109,919 tons in 1986. In December 1986 Syria and the USSR signed a protocol on co-operation in the phosphate industry, providing for the annual volume of Syrian phosphate exports to the USSR to rise to 6m. tons by 2000. (After the collapse of the USSR in 1991, Syria sought to renegotiate such contracts with Russia and other successor republics.) Plans for the construction of a new TSP plant near Palmyra, which have been under study since the 1980s, were reportedly revived in 1997. Estimated to cost between \$350m. and \$450m., the plant would have a capacity of 500,000 tons per year. In March 1998 international bids were invited for another long-delayed project for the construction of an ammonia and urea plant (with a daily production capacity of 1,000 tons and 1,750 tons respectively).

The iron and steel industry, centred on Hama, comprises a smelter (capacity 120,000 metric tons per year), a rolling mill and a steel pipe plant, built by firms from West Germany and Switzerland. The potential for developing Syria's own deposits of iron ore, estimated at about 530m. tons, has been studied by Indian consultants. After the 1990–91 Gulf crisis, Saudi Arabia pledged funding for a new US \$1,000m. iron and steel complex at az-Zara (near Hama), which would have an annual capacity of 700,000 tons and specialize in coils, bars and industrial sections. The original proposal was shelved in 1994, but in October 1998 the Syrian Government made it known that the project was once again under active consideration. Syria's cement output (once targeted to reach 6m. tons by 1980) amounted to 2.85m. tons in 1982. However, completion of a big cement works at Tartous in 1983, together with other factories at Adra, Hama, Musulmiya and Aleppo, brought output to 4.3m. tons in 1985. In 1993 Syrian cement demand was expected to total 5m. tons, which was roughly in balance with the country's current production capacity. An import requirement emerged again in 1994, when Jordan was among the sources of supplies to meet the shortfall. In 1995 Syria's estimated cement demand was between 6m. and 6.5m. tons, while local cement production was around 3.2m. tons. Annual demand was forecast to reach 10m. tons by the end of the century. Having allocated a total of £S1,810m. to modernize, expand and refurbish existing state-owned cement plants, the Government was in mid-1996 evaluating bids for a project to add 1m. tons per year of new capacity at Hama. A letter of intent for this project was awarded to an Iranian company in 1999. The KFAED was to provide $71m. towards the project, the total cost of which was estimated at $198m. The Syrian press reported in July 2001 that construction work would soon begin at Hama. Production of cement in 1998 was just over 5m. tons. In June 2000 the Higher Council for Investment gave its approval to a proposal by a consortium of Syrian, Egyptian and Saudi Arabian investors to build a 3m.-tons-per-year cement plant at Abu Shammat, 80 km north of Damascus. The estimated cost of this project was $540m. Syria's seven sugar refineries supplied nearly one-half of local demand of 550,000 tons in 1994, when plans were announced to build an eighth plant which would raise the country's total sugar refining capacity to 389,000 tons per year. Export sales by the state-owned General Establishment of Food Industries (including, notably, olive oil) averaged around $1.5m. per month in 1998, more than double the average for 1997. In early 1999 a Saudi Arabian company was granted approval to establish a new olive-pressing plant in Syria, with a capacity of 15,000 tons of olive oil per year.

Other established industries include the manufacture of textiles, rubber, glass and paper, and the assembly of tractors, refrigerators and television receivers. Plans for a motor car assembly plant were postponed following the financial difficulties of 1976, and cars have since been imported in large numbers from Japan. However, a new private-sector scheme to assemble pick-up trucks, jeeps and small passenger vehicles was approved in principle by the Government in August 1994. To be based on the import of kits supplied by the US manufacturer General Motors, the proposed plant would begin production within two years of final approval for the project and would reach its full capacity of 30,000 vehicles per year within seven years. Food processing industries have also been developed. Contracts to build four new cotton spinning mills were awarded between 1992 and 1997. In 1999 a 15,000-tons-per-year mill at Latakia was already in production, while a 12,000-tons-per-year extension was being commissioned. A 15,000-tons-per-year plant at Idleb was due to start production by the end of 1999, while a 24,000-tons-per-year plant at Jebla was scheduled for completion in 2001. In November 1999 the General Organization for Textile Industries secured a US $70m. loan from the Abu Dhabi Fund for Development to finance a proposed new 15,000-tons-per-year cotton mill at Tartous.

Despite the dominance of large-scale state industries, the private sector has continued to play an important role in industrial manufacture. In 1986 the private sector accounted for 56% of the production of refrigerators, 62% of paints, 23% of biscuits, 100% of olive oil and 34% of detergents. Since 1991 Syria's economic policy has been officially described as 'pluralist', a term indicating 'equal co-existence' of the public, private and mixed sectors of the economy. The Government's annual budgets for the years 1991 to 1994 provided for a total of £S42,000m. of public capital investment in public-sector production industries (equal to 27% of the projected private-sector investment in so-called 'Law 10' production industries approved over the same period). Under Law 10 of May 1991, encouragement was given to Syrian and foreign investment in industrial ventures, particularly in the light industry sector. To qualify for 'Law 10' status, a project had to involve investment of more than £S10m. and had to secure the approval of the Higher Council for Investment, whose project evaluation criteria took particular account of the amount of foreign capital to be invested; compatibility with national development plans; utilization of advanced or innovatory technology; the amount of new employment to be created; and the utilization of locally available resources. Approved projects were entitled to five or more years' exemption from profit, dividend and real-estate taxes, and were subject to a

liberalized regime of import regulations and exchange controls (including unrestricted repatriation of profits for foreign investors). At the start of 1995 the total number of approved 'Law 10' projects was 1,251, involving projected investment of £S232,800m. and the creation of up to 87,346 new jobs. Inward transfers of funds were expected to cover nearly 77% of the average amount invested, with expatriate Syrians providing much of this 'foreign' investment. (It was generally believed that a significant proportion of private capital investment from abroad was in reality a repatriation through legitimate channels of undeclared wealth that had originally left Syria through clandestine channels.) The transport sector accounted for nearly 53% of all projects approved (although only 25% of projected total investment), with car import schemes predominating. The agricultural sector accounted for just 26 projects costing an estimated £S17,800m. Some 565 projects, involving projected investment of £S155,300m., were approved in production industries, including food processing (217 projects worth £S45,900m.), metal goods and construction materials (146 projects worth £S69,400m.), chemical goods (104 projects worth £S14,300m.) and textiles and clothing (75 projects worth £S21,600m.). By early 1995 a total of 65 'Law 10' manufacturing enterprises had started production and a further 135 manufacturing projects were under active development. The generally slow implementation of approved manufacturing projects stemmed in part from the need to raise equity finance (often on a large scale) as a substitute for commercial loan finance, which was virtually unobtainable within Syria and very difficult to obtain from abroad. The first 'Law 10' project financed in part by a commercial loan was a chemicals plant (25% owned by the Syrian Ministry of Industry) that was due to start production in early 1997. A $4.4m. seven-year loan for this project was granted in August 1996 by the German investment agency DEG. One of the first 'Law 10' projects under majority foreign ownership (a food and beverages plant, 60%-owned by Nestlé of Switzerland) went into production in May 1997. In September 1994 the management of public-sector enterprises was placed on a new footing under the terms of a legislative decree empowering the directors of such enterprises to operate 'on a commercial basis' without the need to seek government approval for their business plans.

In 1998 a number of amendments were made to 'Law 10' in order to improve the incentives to investment. These included the removal of a 75% limit on the proportion of output that could be exported; an increase in the permissible level of foreign representation on company boards; additional tax incentives for projects outside Damascus and Aleppo; and the extension of 'Law 10' benefits to holding companies. In May 2000 legislation was enacted to permit foreign investors to own or lease land needed for 'Law 10' projects; to extend by two years the tax-exemption period for 'Law 10' projects sited in remote areas; and to reduce to 25% the rate of corporate taxation levied after the expiry of 'Law 10' tax-exemption periods. In July a group of leading Saudi Arabian businessmen, headed by Syrian-born Wafic Said, established the Arab Investment Holding Co, capitalized at US $100m., to invest in new 'Law 10' ventures in Syria. In September the Syrian Tyre Co, a 'Law 10' company that is 82.5% owned by a US investor of Syrian origin, began work on a factory in Deraa, scheduled for completion in early 2002 at an estimated cost of $90m. The plant would have a production capacity of 2.1m. tyres per year and would seek to compete in regional and world markets for its products. At the end of 2000 the cumulative total of 'Law 10' approvals (excluding cancelled projects) was 1,640 projects, involving projected investment of £S334,000m. and the creation of up to 96,000 jobs. There was a net fall of £S19,000m. in the projected investment total during 2000 as a result of cancellations by investors.

POWER AND WATER

The centre-piece of Syria's 1971–75 five-year plan was the Euphrates dam project, on which construction work began in 1968. Nearly one-quarter of public investment over this planning period was earmarked for its implementation, with £S950m. allocated for the dam itself and £S643m. for land reclamation and development in the Euphrates basin. The project involved the construction of a dam 4.6 km long and 60 m high, with a width of 500 m at the bottom. The reservoir thus created, Lake Assad, was designed to hold 12,000m. cu m of water, operating eight turbines and enabling the long-term irrigation of 640,000 ha of land, including 550,000 ha by 1990. The scheme was undertaken with the help of 1,200 Soviet technicians and about £S600m. in Soviet financial assistance, under an agreement reached with the USSR in April 1966. By 1977, however, only 100 Soviet experts remained on the site. The entire project was formally opened in early 1978, although the dam's first turbines had started to operate, ahead of schedule, in early 1974. Despite its advantages, the dam has exacerbated friction between Syria and Iraq, which also relies on water from the Euphrates river. Disputes over water rights reached a crisis point in 1974–75, when Turkey started to fill the reservoir behind its Keban dam, also on the Euphrates, at the same time as Syria started to fill Lake Assad, leaving Iraq with much less water than usual. Tension over this issue subsided in 1977–78, but resurfaced in 1984 between Syria and Turkey after the latter had started work on its new Atatürk dam. It is thought that the Atatürk dam and the associated South East Anatolian project (GAP) could remove 5,000m. cu m of water per year, or more, from the Euphrates, once they are completed, in or around 2015.

In 2001—following several years of serious drought in Syria—the authorities considered a range of possible long-term solutions to the water supply problems of major urban areas, including the construction of desalination plants and long-distance pipelines. In the immediate term, stringent water rationing was in force in Damascus, where the drying of important springs and wells caused the authorities to shut off the capital's piped water supply for 20 hours each day (compared with 16 hours previously) from July of that year. Plans to carry out detailed feasibility studies for a proposed US $1,000m. bulk water supply system for Damascus remained to be implemented in mid-2002 because of delays in evaluating bids from engineering consultants. In the Latakia region, work was proceeding in 2002 on the As-Sinn reservoir and dam project, with completion expected in 2003. The project (involving a total storage capacity of 200m. cu m) was intended to provide year-round supplies for urban and agricultural use in the Latakia area. In a blow to Syria's water supply infrastructure, the Zeyzoun dam north of Hama collapsed in early June 2002 when almost full to its 70m. cu m capacity; over 20 people were killed in the resultant flood.

Since its inauguration in 1978, the Euphrates dam, with its eight 100-MW turbines, has made an important contribution to power generation in Syria. However, from an early stage extensive Turkish exploitation of the Euphrates waters often reduced the level of water in Lake Assad to such an extent that only three turbines could operate. In July 1987 Turkey undertook to use 500m. cu m of water from the Euphrates per year for irrigation until agreement was reached with Syria and Iraq on the use of the river's waters. Syria has considered various ways of overcoming its power shortage. There has long been talk of a nuclear power plant, possibly using uranium obtained from local phosphate deposits. Four Western companies were short-listed to carry out the pilot study for a 1,200-MW station in 1979/80, but none was ever given the go-ahead. In mid-1983 Syria and the USSR signed a protocol whereby both sides were to study the construction of Syria's first nuclear power station, but little progress appeared to have been made in this direction before the disintegration of the USSR in 1991. In 1998, however, Russia reached agreement with Syria on a resumption of the nuclear co-operation programme initiated under the Soviet regime, this being followed by the signature of an agreement in May 1999 for the construction of two nuclear reactors in Syria.

In recent years Syria has suffered frequent interruptions in the supply of electric power. Electricity demand soared owing to rapid industrialization in the 1970s, and the Euphrates Dam did not, as was hoped, meet Syria's growing needs, as shortfalls in its water supply due to erratic rainfall and Turkish offtake upstream were compounded by an almost total lack of maintenance of the dam and its generating plant. By early 1993 the generating capacity of the dam was thought to be barely 150 MW, while its actual output fell below 100 MW at some points, contributing to chronic power shortages which led to electricity supplies being cut off for seven or more hours per day. Many Syrian businesses relied on diesel generators to keep factories running. An ambitious programme of power station construction

launched in the 1980s was increasingly geared to the exploitation of local natural gas resources as a fuel source, but failed to keep pace with the growth of demand because of chronic delays between the planning and construction stages. (Only three contracts were finalized between 1983 and 1992.) In 1993 Syria was estimated to have a total of 1,900 MW of operational generating capacity (10.5% hydro, 63% thermal and 26.5% gas-turbine) out of a theoretical installed capacity of 3,002 MW (30% hydro, 51% thermal and 19% gas-turbine), while the minimum operational capacity needed to meet current demand was estimated to be 2,500 MW. Demand was officially projected to rise to 3,284 MW in 1995 and 4,882 MW in 2000. In a bid to rectify the situation, the authorities approved heavy, aid-financed investment in electricity generation in the early 1990s. Work has since been completed on the 600-MW Jandar plant, financed by Japan, and is continuing on the Saudi-financed 1,000-MW plant in Aleppo. Another important generating project carried out in recent years has been the installation of eight 128-MW turbines in various locations by an Italian company, with finance from Kuwait. In early 1997 Mitsubishi Heavy Industries of Japan was awarded the contract to construct a 600-MW plant at Az-Zara. This plant was completed in late 2000. A major refit of the 680-MW Banias power station was completed by Japanese contractors in April 2001. Nearly US $1,000m.-worth of Japanese funds were provided for Syrian power projects between 1989 and 2001. In August 1995 the AFESD extended a $100m. loan for a project to link the Syrian and Jordanian electricity networks, and in June 1996 it made a further $86.7m. available to finance a link between the Syrian and Turkish electricity networks. It was reported in March 1998 that Siemens of Germany had secured the contract to construct two sub-stations serving the grid interconnection with Jordan. Earlier, at the end of 1997, the Government issued a decree allowing Syria's first independent power project to proceed as a 100% private venture. The developers, a Belgian/Syrian partnership, plan to build a 600-MW plant at al-Bardeh, 150 km north of Damascus.

In 2001 Syria initiated the construction of several new electricity sub-stations, funding for which had been obtained from the European Investment Bank. Other sources of finance for a major programme to modernize and upgrade the electricity distribution system by the end of 2005 were the AFESD, the Abu Dhabi Fund for Development and the Islamic Development Bank. The two last-named organizations were also responsible for funding a project to upgrade the Tishrin power station (put out to tender in 2001), while the Kuwait Fund for Arab Economic Development (KFAED) was to fund a project to convert the Italian-equipped Nasiriyeh power station to combined-cycle operation.

TRANSPORT AND COMMUNICATIONS

The regional political situation has not helped Syria in developing its ports. Operations at the ports of Latakia and Tartous (both equipped to handle transit traffic bound for the Gulf) were adversely affected by the closure of the border with Iraq in 1982. The volume of goods handled at the two ports declined markedly after 1981, when it totalled 7.63m. metric tons. In 1985 the total was 5.5m. tons, and in 1986 4.37m. tons. In mid-1996 the Government announced plans for a major expansion of port capacity, as recommended in studies submitted by the Japan International Co-operation Agency. Total port capacity in Syria was targeted to reach 19.3m. tons per year by 2003 (6.2m. tons at Latakia, 5.4m. tons at Tartous and 7.7m. tons at a new port to be developed near Tartous), rising to 29.1m. tons per year by 2010 (11.4m. tons at Latakia, 7.7m. tons at Tartous and 10m. tons at the proposed new port). Existing port capacity in 1996 was 9.5m. tons per year (4.4m. tons at Latakia and 5.1m. tons per year at Tartous) and in that year Latakia handled just under 3m. tons of cargo, and Tartous 4.14m. tons. In mid-1997 Tartous had two Finnish straddle carriers and four British dockside cranes on order, while Latakia (currently lacking specialized container-handling equipment) was negotiating to buy four ship-to-shore gantry cranes. The reopening of Syria's land border with Iraq at the start of June 1997 was followed by a Syrian request to the UN that Syrian seaports be added to the list of approved transit points for Iraq's humanitarian imports under the UN-administered 'oil-for-food' scheme. Shipments bound for Iraq subsequently contributed to a rise in Syrian transit trade. The Government announced in May 2000 that it was seeking a US $100m. loan from Japan to finance the modernization of port facilities at Latakia and Tartous. In March Al-Sham Shipping, a 'Law 10' company (see Manufacturing and Industry, above) with Syrian and Saudi Arabian shareholders, announced an $18.5m. order for two multi-purpose container vessels.

At the start of 1997 the national airline, Syrian Arab Airlines, had a 16-strong fleet comprising two Boeing 747s, six Boeing 727s, three Tupolev 154s, two Tupolev 134s and three Caravelles. No new aircraft had been purchased since the early 1980s, although some Boeings had been acquired as gifts from Kuwait and Abu Dhabi. Six Airbus A320 aircraft were ordered from Airbus Industrie at the end of 1996, the first of these aircraft being delivered in October 1998 and the second in April 1999. In 1999 Syrian Arab airlines carried 580,591 passengers on international routes and 87,763 passengers on domestic routes, representing a load factor of 48.2%. In 2000 the airline had 380 employees for every aircraft in its fleet, compared with the current industry average of 60 employees per aircraft.

In June 1997 the General Establishment for Syrian Railways signed a contract to purchase 30 new diesel locomotives from the Anglo-French company GEC Alsthom. Separate negotiations were in progress with other Western companies bidding for a contract to refit 32 of Syria's existing fleet of 140 (mainly Soviet-built) diesel locomotives. In 1997 Iranian consultants began an outline study of proposals to build a metro system in Damascus. Similar proposals had been studied by Soviet consultants in the early 1980s.

Syria had an estimated 26,300 km of paved highways in 1999, of which 880 km were classed as expressways. A US $206.5m. contract was awarded in 2001 for the construction of a 100-km four-lane highway from Latakia to Ariha, financed by loans from the AFESD and KFAED.

A contract to install 600,000 new telephone lines (double the existing number) was awarded to Siemens of Germany in mid-1991. International telecommunications services were upgraded in December 1994 with the inauguration of a new submarine cable linking Syria and Lebanon with Cyprus. In 1996 Syria had an efficient modern telephone system with a total of more than 2m. lines installed and was planning to establish a GSM (global standard for mobiles) system in the near future. In mid-1998, as part of a new programme to expand the telephone system by 1.65m. lines, Ericsson of Sweden signed a contract valued at US $120m. for the supply and installation of digital switching systems for 1m. new lines. Samsung Electronics of South Korea was reported to have secured the contract for rural fibre optic links. The expansion programme was being financed by loans from the AFESD, KFAED and the Abu Dhabi Development Fund. Two separate GSM pilot schemes were launched in February 2000 with a combined capacity to serve 60,000 subscribers. In April 2001 they were superseded by two permanent GSM networks, one operated by Investcom (a Lebanese company equipped by Ericsson) and the other by Syriatel (a subsidiary of the Egyptian company Orascom Telecom, equipped by Siemens). Both networks were operated under 15-year build-own-operate contracts which had been awarded by the state-run Syrian Telecommunications Establishment (STE) in that January. STE was to receive royalties of 30% of the operators' revenue for the first three years, 40% for the next three years and 50% thereafter. The operators were required to expand the capacity of their networks in stages, with an ultimate target of 850,000 subscribers each.

TOURISM

Tourist traffic declined from 774,500 tourists in 1979 to 346,800 in 1982, but rose to 565,000 in 1984, largely because of an arrangement whereby Iranians visited Syria in part-payment for Iranian oil supplies. The number of Iranian visitors dropped from 157,200 in 1984 to 132,600 in 1985, and there was a decline in the overall number of tourists to 486,700. In 1986, however, the number of Iranian tourists rose to a record 174,000 and the total number of tourists reached 567,700. The number of tourists from Western Europe remained modest—by far the largest number in 1986 came from West Germany (17,100) and France (14,800), followed by the United Kingdom and Italy, each with

5,600. Western tourists have for many years been deterred by instability in the region and by fear of terrorist attacks. Since 1978, a number of joint public-private sector companies, in which the Government has a minority interest, have been set up.

In 1993 Syria was visited by 2.9m. tourists, generating US $700m. of tourism revenue. A joint private and public sector consortium was in 1994 preparing to invite construction bids for a $70m. resort development near Tartous, to include hotel and bungalow accommodation, sports facilities, restaurants and shops. Work on this project had still to start in mid-1996 because of difficulties in arranging financing. Construction of a $10m. tourism complex in the Shabaa area (south of Damascus) began in early 1996. The main shareholder in the Shabaa complex was a Saudi Arabian company. The construction, with Saudi investment, of a 350-room five-star hotel and associated facilities in Damascus was scheduled to start in 2001. The first stage of the $25m. Happy Land amusement park opened near Damascus in April 1998. More than 3.0m. tourists (again mainly from Arab states) visited Syria in 2000, when tourist receipts were some $474m. In April 2000 a $19m. contract was awarded for the construction over a period of 22 months of a Sheraton hotel at Aleppo with 179 standard rooms and 17 suites.

In 2000 tourism contributed about 4% of Syria's GDP, generating over US $1,500m. of hard-currency earnings. A new 20-year sectoral development programme aimed to double the tourism industry's share of GDP by 2020. The main planning targets for that year were a total provision of around 175,000 hotel beds (compared with 35,000 in 2000 and 21,600 in 1981) and annual visitor numbers of more than 7m. Incentives to foreign investors in tourism projects included concessionary arrangements in respect of land purchase, taxation, import duty and repatriation of profits. In December 2000 Kuwaiti investors received planning permission for a proposed tourism development at Lake Assad, to include two villages, a golf course, water amusement parks and related facilities. In July 2001 Syria's Minister of Tourism announced that over 80 tourism-related projects were currently 'under development' and that 64 proposed projects were open to private-sector investment. Despite a downturn in tourism in the wake of the 11 September 2001 terrorist attacks on the USA, projects in progress in mid-2002 included the construction of a $120m. marina and accommodation complex at Tartous and of new luxury hotels in Damascus and Aleppo. The Government's revised five-year economic reform programme, published in July 2002, envisaged that revenue from tourism would show a 13% annual growth rate by 2004 and would help to offset a potential decline in oil revenue in the longer term.

BUDGET, INVESTMENT AND FINANCE

In 1972 Syria's method of valuing exports, other than cotton and crude petroleum, was transferred from the official exchange rate (then US $1 = £S3.80) to the 'parallel' (free) market rate ($1 = £S4.30), which meant a *de facto* devaluation of Syrian currency in relation to most transactions. The 'parallel' market was discontinued in July 1973 and remained suspended for nearly eight years. In April 1981, in an attempt to mobilize remittances to finance imports by the private sector and thereby reduce pressure on the Syrian pound, the Government announced that remittances from abroad and other private sector 'invisible' earnings would be convertible into Syrian currency at a freely floating 'parallel' rate. At the same time, it imposed very tight restrictions on private businesses wishing to open letters of credit for imports. These were not eased until late 1984, and even then importers were advised that suppliers might have to wait nearly a year to receive payment. In late 1984 there was also an official reduction in the Syrian currency's value in terms of the tourist exchange rate, which was adjusted from $1 = £S7 to $1 = £S8. From September 1985, resident Syrians were permitted to open accounts in foreign currency at the Commercial Bank of Syria, to be used for imports. In the previous year this concession had been granted to foreigners and non-resident Syrians. In early 1986 there was a major currency crisis, with the value of the Syrian pound on the 'black' market dropping to $1 = £S17, or more. There were widespread arrests of currency dealers, and large quantities of gold and foreign currency were seized. The effect of these measures was to bring about a short-term appreciation in the value of the currency, but it soon began to depreciate once more, weakened by Syria's shortage of reserves of foreign exchange. Between October 1985 and October 1986 the Syrian pound lost 50% of its value against the US dollar. In August 1986 one of Syria's five exchange rates was devalued from $1 = £S11.75 to $1 = £S22, a level more comparable with the 'black' market rate, which fell to $1 = £S24–£S25 at the end of 1986, when the tourist exchange rate stood at $1 = £S9.75. The fixed official rate for government accounts and strategic imports remained at $1 = £S3.925, as it had been since April 1976. 'Decree 24' of September 1986 rendered currency smugglers liable to prison terms of 15–25 years, and smugglers of precious metals to terms of three to 10 years. Possession of hard currency was classed as a criminal offence punishable by imprisonment. Although it was rarely enforced, the latter provision was seen by Syrian businesses as a disincentive to legitimate trading activity and demands for its repeal were repeatedly made in the first half of the 1990s by advocates of economic liberalization. 'Decree 24' was finally repealed in April 2000, when new foreign-exchange regulations were introduced with a maximum penalty of five years' imprisonment for serious currency infringements. In September 1987 the Syrian pound, according to the official exchange rate, was devalued from $1 = £S3.925 (a level maintained since 1976) to $1 = £S11.20–£S11.25—a move that many observers considered to be long overdue.

Subsidies have been paid to Syria by other Arab countries since the Khartoum summit meeting of 1967. They were reinforced at the Rabat summit of 1974, which resulted in the promise of an annual US $1,000m. to Syria in its capacity as a 'confrontation state'. The Baghdad summit of 1978 pledged to increase these subsidies to $1,800m. per year for a period of 10 years. The amount of Arab aid which Syria actually received reached $690m. in 1975 but dropped to only $355m. in 1976. The amounts received in 1979 and 1980 were estimated at $1,600m. and $1,400m., respectively, but donations were adversely affected by the Iran–Iraq War (in which Syria's former backers provided financial support to Iraq, while Syria sided with Iran) and by the erosion of the financial surpluses that OPEC countries accumulated before the decline in oil prices. Aid to Syria from the Gulf states was estimated to have dropped to $600m.–$700m. in 1986, although it has been difficult to gauge with any true accuracy the amount of aid from Gulf states under the Baghdad summit agreement. Saudi Arabia has been the most consistent of the Arab states in honouring its aid commitments to Syria. Political actions by the Syrian leadership that have met with the approval of 'moderate' Arab states are often accompanied by reports of large sums being channelled from Saudi Arabia. Thus it was widely believed that Syria received a substantial 'reward' for attending the Arab summit held in Amman in November 1987, which was critical of Iran's actions in the Iran–Iraq War. Moreover, Syria's participation in the US-led multinational force against Iraq in the Gulf War of 1991 led to further 'rewards' in the form of special aid totalling more than $1,000m.

In 1979, as a result of the pledges made at the Baghdad summit, a marked increase in defence spending raised Syria's total budget expenditure to £S22,600m. By 1985 the total had increased to £S42,984m. (US $10,950m.), with defence, at £S13,000m., continuing to take a major share of current spending. The 4% nominal increase in total expenditure compared with an annual rate of inflation estimated at 10%. Investment expenditure under the 1985 budget was estimated at only £S19,436m., compared with £S17,886m. in 1984 and £S17,981m. in 1983. In the 1986 budget total spending amounted to £S37,091m., a substantial drop in real terms, taking inflation into account. In the 1987 budget expenditure was cut by 4.4% to £S35,443m. Current expenditure was reduced by 14.1% to £S23,029m. Defence received the largest single allocation (£S14,327m., accounting for 62.2% of current expenditure), while agriculture was allocated about 20% (£S3,500m.) of total investment spending, compared with almost 25% in 1986. The 1988 draft budget was the first for a number of years to feature a substantial increase in spending. Total expenditure was raised by more than one-fifth, to £S51,545m., compared with actual spending of £S35,443m. in 1987. Current expenditure rose from £S23,029m. to £S29,665m., and investment spending from £S12,414m. to £S21,880m. Of revenues of £S51,545m., taxes,

aid and services were budgeted to provide £S34,848m. and the state sector surplus £S16,697m. The 1989 and 1990 budgets provided for expenditure of £S57,413m. and £S61,875m. respectively. The 1991 budget set expenditure at £S84,690m. and envisaged an effective deficit of £S13,676m., although this was treated as exceptional financing in order to achieve a technical balance. The 1992 budget was also technically balanced, providing for expenditure and revenue of £S93,043m.; this represented a nominal spending increase of almost 10% over 1991, although after allowing for inflation of 20% budgeted spending was lower in real terms. The 1992 expenditure total consisted of £S56,793m. in current spending and £S36,250m. in investment, with defence accounting for 26% of current spending (considerably less than in previous years), education 20% and health 5%. The largest allocation in the investment budget, some 26%, was for agriculture and irrigation. The effective deficit in the 1992 budget was equivalent to 20.9% of total revenue, to be funded by concessional loans totalling £S13,904m. and other foreign loans totalling £S5,607m.

The 1993 budget provided for total expenditure of £S123,018m., including £S27,869m. for defence (up 2.5% on 1992) and £S12,671m. for electricity, water and gas (up 157% on 1992). Overall, investment spending was nearly twice as high as in 1992, and represented about half of total budgeted spending for 1993. The effective deficit was equal to 34.9% of the total budget in Syrian pounds, the borrowing elements on the revenue side being concessional loans of £S9,000m., other foreign loans totalling £S22,868m. and domestic loans of £S11,026m. (compared with a zero requirement for domestic loans in the 1992 budget). The real increase in foreign borrowing between 1992 and 1993 was estimated to be around 6.5% in dollar terms after allowance was made for the Government's use of an exchange rate of US $1 = £S43 (rather than the official accounting rate of $1 = £S11.2) to calculate this component of the 1993 budget. The overall size of the deficit was nevertheless criticized by several deputies during the budget debate in the Syrian legislature (which formally adopted the Government's proposals on 9 May 1993). The 1994 budget provided for total expenditure of £S144,162m. (17.2% higher than in 1993) and total revenue of £S106,890m., leaving a deficit of £S37,272m. Current spending accounted for 53% of the 1994 expenditure total. Public-sector wages were raised by 30% in May 1994, while price increases were announced for electricity, petrol and many other items. In the same month the currency exchange rate used to levy customs duties on items other than basic commodities and most industrial raw materials was changed from $1 = £S11.2 to $1 = £S23. (The former rate continued to apply to the 'basic' import category.) There was a further selective modification of exchange-rate policy at the start of 1995, when the rate applicable to most sales or purchases of foreign currency through the Syrian banking system was changed from £S23 to £S42 per dollar. The free-market exchange rate for the Syrian pound (as determined by informal currency trading in Lebanon) averaged $1 = £S49 in the first half of 1995, having remained fairly stable for more than two years. From October 1995 the exchange rate of $1 = £S42 was applied to the prices charged to foreign visitors for hotel accommodation. It was estimated that four-fifths of all officially sanctioned foreign-exchange transactions in Syria were based on this rate of exchange at the end of 1995. The oil industry (hitherto required to use a rate of $1 = £S11.20) was permitted to switch to a rate of $1 = £S22.95 from January 1996 and to the main rate of $1 = £S42 from August 1996.

Syria's 1995 budget provided for expenditure of £S162,040m. (12.4% higher than in 1994) and revenue of £S125,718m. (17.6% higher than in 1994), leaving a deficit of £S36,322m. (2.5% less than the 1994 deficit). Recurrent items made up 54.3% of expenditure in the 1995 budget. The 1996 budget provided for total expenditure of £S188,049.9m. A budgetary deficit of £S1,577m. was recorded in that year. Recurrent spending totalled £S95,977m. (51.2% of total expenditure), including £S36,463m. (19.5% of total expenditure) for defence. Syria's 1997 budget provided for total expenditure of £S211,125m. and a supplementary allocation of £S10,200m. was announced in August 1997 to cover payments connected with Syria's debt settlement agreement with the World Bank. The 1998 budget provided for total expenditure of £S237,300m. (£S117,700m. for current expenditure and £S119,600m. for investment expenditure). This was 12.4% higher than in 1997, although 5.7% of that increase was the result of an adjustment to the exchange rate of the Syrian pound against the dollar. The 1999 budget provided for total expenditure of £S255,300m. (representing a nominal increase of 7.5% over the 1998 budget) and total revenue of £S244,300m. The 1999 budget was not formally submitted to the legislature until the end of that year, government departments having meanwhile operated on the basis of their 1998 spending allocations, restricting any capital investment to projects approved in 1998.

The budget for 2000 (enacted in June of that year) provided for total expenditure of £S275,400m. (including investment expenditure of £S132,000m.), representing a nominal increase of 7.9% over the 1999 budget. The budget provided for total revenues of £S263,141m., reportedly incorporating an oil price forecast of US $20 per barrel (whereas the actual oil export price averaged more than $25 per barrel in 2000). It was subsequently reported that the 2000 budget out-turn was in surplus as a result of above-forecast revenue and below-forecast expenditure. In November 2000 the Government abolished price subsidies for white sugar, of which 1.5 kg per month had been available to each Syrian for £S9 (about 56% of the current cost price), and for rice (the subsidized entitlement to which had been 750 g per month for £S7). The 2001 budget was submitted to the legislature in late October 2000 and approved in early December, prior to the start of the new financial year. Reportedly incorporating an oil price forecast of $24 per barrel, it provided for total revenue of £S312,798m. and total expenditure of £S322,000m., of which £S161,000m. was investment expenditure (a 22% increase over the investment budget for 2000), £S123,680m. was current expenditure, and £S37,320m. was an allocation for debt repayments and price subsidies.

In July 2001 Syria's Minister of State for Planning Affairs declared that he expected the public sector to provide 69% of all new capital investment over the five years to 2005, with a primary focus on infrastructure projects. It was the Government's aim to raise annual development investment (including private investment) to a level equivalent to 27% of GDP by 2005. The Minister also reiterated the Government's preference for reform, rather than privatization, of public-sector bodies, which the authorities would seek to make 'independent, accountable and market-oriented'. Although the 2001 budget included a significantly increased provision for capital expenditure, project implementation remained generally slow, highlighting the persistence of established attitudes in the public sector.

As given parliamentary approval in November 2001, the Government's 2002 budget provided for expenditure of £S356,400m., a 10% increase on the 2001 budgeted figure. No details of anticipated revenues were published, although officials stated that they would be approximately equal to expenditure and would include an unspecified amount of foreign borrowing. Budget allocations in 2002 included £S184,000m. for infrastructural investment, notably on transport, communications and water and electricity distribution, £S131,900 for public-sector spending and £S40,500m. for debt servicing (mostly on debts still owed to the former Soviet-bloc countries). Approval of the 2002 budget was accompanied by the launching of a five-year economic reform programme focusing on job creation and administrative reform and anticipating real GDP growth of 3% a year in 2002–04. In July 2002 the Government published a revised two-phase programme of structural and legal reforms covering 2002–03 and 2004–06, envisaging that annual GDP growth of 4% would be achieved by 2006. Under the revised programme a significant share of planned investment of about £S33,000m. would be allocated to the private industrial sector and to the development of tourism (see Tourism, above).

In October 1996 the exchange rate applicable to most foreign-exchange transactions was devalued from US $1 = £S42 to $1 = £S43.50, and the rate decreased further, to $1 = £S45, in July 1997; the Government stated that it intended to use the latter rate to calculate the 1998 budget (previous budgets were based on multiple exchange rates). The free-market value of the currency in the latter part of 1997 averaged around $1 = £S50, having shown little variation over a long period of stable trading. From October 1996 Syrians were permitted to open hard-cur-

rency deposit accounts in Syria without declaring the origin of their funds, but there was no formal repeal of the 1986 law forbidding possession of hard currency and no measures were introduced to make it possible to buy hard currency through the Syrian banking system. In these circumstances, Syrians continued to rely on the Lebanese banking system for most foreign-exchange transactions: the total amount of hard currency held in private foreign-exchange accounts in Syria in early 1999 was only $6.5m. In August 1998 the principal exchange rate used by Syrian banks was slightly devalued to $1 = £S46. The free-market value of the currency at this time was around $1 = £S52, which continued to be the rate in mid-2002.

In 1998 deposits in local currency in the state post office's savings accounts increased substantially after being declared exempt from inheritance tax. It was reported in late 1998 that the Government had authorized the post office to invest as much as one-half of its deposits in investment projects, a move that would potentially channel more than £S12,000m. into productive investment. In March 1999 it was announced that the Government was finalizing plans to establish an export bank with a capitalization of £S1,000m. In April 2000 a decree was passed to allow foreign banks to set up branches within Syria's free-zone areas (currently sited at Deraa, Damascus, Latakia, Aleppo and Tartous and planned for three further locations). Early interest in the new scheme (which did not provide access to the mainstream Syrian economy) was confined to Lebanese bankers. By March 2001 six Lebanese banks had obtained licences to set up branches in Syrian free zones, and two of them had opened their first such branches. The capital requirement for such ventures was US $10m. In January 2001 the Commercial Bank of Syria was authorized to carry out a limited range of foreign currency transactions on the basis of a variable market-related exchange rate (initially set at $1 = £S50.20, compared with the actual free-market rate of $1 = £S52.50 at that time). Generally regarded as a pilot scheme to prepare the way for further reforms, the new facility was available to Syrian residents travelling abroad as pilgrims or for the purpose of undergoing medical treatment. The actual free-market rate for the Syrian currency in early August 2001 was $1 = £S53.48.

In April 2001 the Syrian legislature approved bills to safeguard banking secrecy and to allow the establishment of mainstream private banks throughout the country. Practical implementation of the law on private commercial banking (which ended a public-sector monopoly dating from the bank nationalizations of 1963) was expected to be a relatively lengthy process, dependent on the introduction of detailed regulations. The key provisions of the legislation were that each private bank should have a minimum capital of US $30m., should have majority (51% or more) Syrian ownership and should not be more than 5% owned by any single individual. The Central Bank of Syria was to supervise the new private banks while continuing to supervise the existing state-owned banks (which the Government intended to leave in place to face competition from the private sector). Provision was made for the state to set up new banking ventures as a minority (25% or less) partner of private interests.

Further legislation (Law 23) adopted in December 2001 and enacted in March 2002 consolidated the legal framework for the establishment and operation of private banks in Syria 'as private or joint venture companies with shareholdings'. It also created a regulator for the sector, the Monetary and Credit Council, which would be chaired by the Governor of the Central Bank. The new Council would have as an eventual objective the introduction of a floating exchange rate for the Syrian pound to replace the existing complex system of 'official', 'customs' and 'commercial' rates and the consequential widespread use of the black market for currency transactions. The passage of Law 23 quickly resulted in several applications being received by the Central Bank from investor groups in other Arab countries wishing to set up private banks in Syria. In June 2002 Syria became the 156th member of the Multilateral Investment Guarantee Agency (MIGA), through which foreign investors in Syria and Syrian companies investing abroad became eligible for risk coverage.

FOREIGN TRADE AND BALANCE OF PAYMENTS

Commerce has traditionally been a major occupation of Syria's towns, especially of Damascus and Aleppo which lie on the main east–west trade route. There have been, however, some radical changes in both the direction and the composition of Syria's trade over the years. During the mid-1960s Syria's principal suppliers were among the Eastern European bloc. In 1968 the USSR and Czechoslovakia together provided more than 20% of all imported goods. In 1974, although the value of their supplies had increased, those two countries accounted for just under 7.2% of the total. Meanwhile, the value of Syria's imports over the six-year period had risen nearly four-fold, reaching £S4,571m. in 1974, and the bulk of the increase had resulted from flourishing trade ties with Western Europe. In the 1980s, the pendulum swung back in favour of the Eastern bloc again. The trend towards the East was reinforced during this period by trade agreements with Eastern bloc countries and by the willingness of some of these to accept barter deals and thereby accommodate Syria's shortage of foreign exchange. Yugoslavia, for example, agreed in 1985 to take almost one-third of Syrian phosphate exports in return for construction machinery, iron and steel, timber, pharmaceuticals and medical equipment. Czechoslovakia also agreed to exchange engineering equipment for phosphates and farm produce, while Romania was a close trading partner for some years. The USSR, after signing a friendship treaty with Syria in 1980, followed this up with an agreement to boost bilateral trade to the equivalent of some US $2,600m. in the five years up to 1985. This was renewed for a further five years in 1985. The fields in which Soviet companies were active in Syria included transport, the oil industry, the phosphate industry, agriculture, power generation, and the search for reserves of water. Another friendship and co-operation treaty, this time with Bulgaria, was signed in May 1985. In 1980 socialist countries took 16.1% of Syria's exports, and in 1986 the proportion rose to 46.4%. The proportion of Syria's imports supplied by socialist countries rose from 14.6% in 1985 to 20.2% in 1986. However, the EC's share also increased, from 29.9% to 34.8%, while that of Iran declined from 17.8% to 6.8%, as a result of the fall in Iranian oil imports. After the post-1989 changes in Eastern Europe and the disintegration of the USSR in 1991, the pendulum swung again towards trade with the West. Exports to the USA increased to $206.6m. in 1991 (from $150.4m. in 1990), while imports fell from $52.1m. to $27.1m.

Syria's exports increased dramatically during the 1970s, mainly owing to large increases in the value of petroleum sales. Largely as a result of the decline in oil prices and the volume of exports, Syria's export earnings declined every year between 1980 and 1986. From £S8,273m. in 1980, the value of exports fell to £S6,427m. in 1985 and £S5,199m. in 1986. Exports in 1987 nearly trebled, in terms of local currency, to £S15,200m., although these figures used an exchange rate of US $1 = £S11.20, which did not replace the former rate of US $1 = £S4.05 until early 1988. In terms of US dollars, the value of exports in 1987 increased by only 6%, to $1,356m.

In view of the country's alarming shortage of foreign exchange, there have been strict curbs on imports (although large amounts of goods are smuggled into the country). In 1981 the value of imports totalled £S19,781m. In 1985 the figure was £S15,570m., and in 1986 there was a drop of 31.9%, to £S10,611m. The adjustment in the exchange rate affected import figures, in local currency, with an almost three-fold increase in 1987 to £S27,900m. In terms of US dollars, however, there was a 6% drop, to US $2,492m. The trade deficit declined from $1,360m. in 1986 to $1,136m. in 1987. The USSR was Syria's leading trade partner in 1986, taking 29.7% of Syria's exports, and providing 10.1% of its imports. Syria's second biggest customer was Italy (12.1%), followed by Romania (9.4%) and the Federal Republic of Germany (4.1%). Its second biggest supplier was the Federal Republic of Germany (9.1%), followed by France (8.7%) and Italy (7.5%). Iran, previously Syria's largest supplier, fell to fifth place, with a 6.8% share.

In March 1990 the Government announced a trade surplus of £S10,430m. for 1989. The value of exports was reported to have totalled £S33,740m., while that of imports amounted to £S23,310m. However, local analysts cast doubt upon the accuracy of these figures, observing that few of the goods smuggled into Syria from Lebanon were recorded in trade statistics.

Furthermore, it was noted that at least three exchange rates applied to imports: the official fixed rate of US $1 = £S11.225; an 'incentive' rate of $1 = £S20.22; and a free-market rate of $1 = £S45. Since it was unclear on which rate the calculation of the trade balance had been based, it was impossible to ascertain the accuracy of the Government's figures in hard currency terms. The IMF estimated Syria's 1990 trade surplus as $2,094m. (exports $4,156m., imports $2,062m.). According to official statistics, a 1991 trade surplus of £S7,438m. (exports £S38,504m., imports £S31,066m.) was followed by a deficit of £S4,459m. in 1992 (exports £S34,719m., imports £S39,178m.) and a further deficit of £S11,151m. in 1993 (exports £S35,318m., imports £S46,469m.). Within the overall trade balance for 1991 there was a public-sector trade surplus of £S10,364m. and a private-sector deficit of £S2,926m. In 1992 public-sector trade was in surplus by £S12,713m. while private-sector trade was in deficit by £S17,172m. In 1993 the public-sector surplus fell to £S8,761m. while the private-sector deficit increased to £S19,912m. 'Law 10' of May 1991 (see Manufacturing and Industry, above) was an important factor in a sharp rise in private-sector imports from £S16,575m. in 1991 to £S28,752m. in 1993. In June 1992 the Minister of Economy and Foreign Trade stated that there was a need to set up a special Syrian export bank. Five years later the Government was still 'studying the possibility' of such a step.

In May 1993 the Government launched an unprecedentedly thorough campaign against smuggling across the Lebanese border, causing the black-market price of illegally imported US-manufactured cigarettes (the main indicator of the level of smuggling activity) to triple within a month. The Government subsequently announced that a state trading organization would in future import foreign cigarettes for sale at the prices which smugglers had been charging before the clamp-down (when the trade in illegal cigarette imports had been worth an estimated US $1m. per day).

IMF statistics gave Syria's 1993 visible trade deficit as $273m. (exports $3,203m., imports $3,476m.), the 1994 deficit as $1,275m. (exports $3,329m., imports $4,604m.), the 1995 deficit as $146m. (exports $3,858m., imports $4,004m.) and the 1996 deficit as $338m. (exports $4,178m., imports $4,516m.). In 1997 Syria recorded a trade surplus of $454m. (exports $4,057m., imports $3,603m.). IMF figures for 1998 showed that the value of Syrian exports had fallen by nearly 23%, to $3,142m. (the main factor being a 32% decline, to $1,700m., in oil export earnings during a year of depressed world prices). Spending on imports (which in 1997 had been sharply reduced in response to restrictive government policies) decreased further, to $3,320m., resulting in a visible trade deficit of $178m. Syria's principal source of imports in 1999 was Germany (7.0%), followed by France (5.7%), Italy (5.6%) and Turkey (5.0%). The main market for exports was Italy (26.6%), followed by France (20.6%), Turkey (9.3%) and Saudi Arabia (8.4%). The principal exports in 1999 were crude petroleum, vegetables and fruit, and textiles, while the principal imports were base metals and manufactures, foodstuffs, and machinery. Public-sector visible trade was in surplus by $1,940m. in 1997 and $1,228m. in 1998, while private-sector visible trade was in deficit by $1,486m. in 1997 and $1,406m. in 1998. Syria's trade statistics for 1999 showed total export earnings of $3,806m. (reflecting an upturn in oil export prices) and import spending of $3,590m., producing a visible trade surplus of $216m. and a current-account surplus of $201m. In 2000 a decline in the volume of Syria's oil production was more than offset by further strong growth in oil prices, which resulted in exports increasing by 35% in value to $5,146m. With imports increasing marginally to $3,723m., the trade surplus therefore rose sharply to $1,423m., while the current account showed a surplus of $1,061m.

Syria's entire system of foreign trade, based on laws dating back to 1952, came under review in 1993 as the Government studied the extent to which current import and export controls were hampering the growth of private-sector enterprises. In September 1997 the Government removed a £S300,000 ceiling on the total value of approved locally produced goods that Syrian travellers were permitted to carry abroad. This was interpreted as a move to encourage the growth of 'informal' trade across the recently reopened border with Iraq. It was reported in June 1998 that an agreement had been reached with Saudi Arabia to establish a free-trade regime under the Arab League free-trade protocol (which called on Arab states to reduce tariffs on mutual trade by 10% per year from 1998). Earlier in 1998 the Syrian Government had agreed to establish a free-trade regime with Lebanon. By early 2001 Iraq, Qatar and the UAE had also agreed to establish free-trade regimes, while Syria was seeking agreements with Egypt, Tunisia, Libya, Jordan, Oman, Morocco and Yemen. Negotiations for an association agreement between Syria and the EU entered their seventh round in July 2001. In July 2000 the Syrian Government lifted a ban (in force for the past 35 years) on the importation of petrol-fuelled cars by private citizens. Such imports were now permitted for cars up to two years old purchased with hard currency earned from exports (within a ceiling of 10% of export proceeds deposited in the Commercial Bank of Syria). Import permits were required and cars continued to attract high rates of customs duty.

Syria's annual receipts of official development aid (ODA) were in the US $600m.–$700m. range in 1984–87, falling to $191m. in 1988 and to $127m. in 1989, rising to $650m. in 1990 (when ODA represented 4.4% of GNP) and falling to $373m. in 1991. Syria's debt arrears to funding institutions, particularly the World Bank, have, however, created problems. The arrears to the World Bank led to disbursements of new loans being 'frozen' in late 1986; in mid-1991 Syria's debt to the Bank was estimated at more than $300m. Political events have at times cast a shadow over Western official aid. In November 1983 the US Congress voted for US economic aid to Syria to be terminated; already in 1981 Congress had decided to 'freeze' $138.2m. in aid instalments totalling $227.8m. West Germany cut off aid in late 1986, after two Jordanians were sentenced for a bomb attack in Berlin in which Syria was implicated—a line of credit suspended since 1980 had only been restored in 1985. In 1987 aid was restored. The EC imposed a *de facto* 'freeze' on its aid to Syria in late 1986, but aid was resumed after the visit of the EC's North-South commissioner, Claude Cheysson, to Damascus in September 1987. In the third EC protocol, which came into effect at the start of 1993, Syria was allocated ECU 146m. A fourth EC protocol, providing for an allocation of ECU 158m., failed to secure the necessary support when it was submitted to the European Parliament for approval in March of that year. Syria's total external debt (including military debt to the former Soviet bloc countries of about $10,000m.) was estimated by the World Bank to have been $16,815m. at the end of 1991, compared with $3,549m. in the early 1980s. However, the debt-service ratio as a percentage of exports was reduced from 15.6% in 1986 to 3.9% in 1990. The World Bank's estimate of Syria's end-1993 external debt was $19,975m. (over 70% of which was classified as 'bilateral concessional'), while total debt service paid during 1993 was estimated as $289m. Nearly $4,000m. of the end-1993 debt consisted of arrears to official creditors, about 10% of these arrears being owed to the World Bank, about 30% to creditors of the Organisation for Economic Co-operation and Development (OECD) and the balance to the former Soviet Union and other East European countries.

In May 1994 the Minister of Economy and Foreign Trade stated that Syria was currently making interest payments of US $6m. per month on its World Bank debt of about $500m., and was seeking to negotiate arrangements whereby the Government would pay off one-third of the debt while a 'friends of Syria' donor group would pay off the remainder. He ruled out the option of a formal IMF/'Paris Club' arrangement as 'unacceptable in our political climate'. He said Syria was currently settling its outstanding debts to the export credit agencies of several Western European states; that it had reduced its indebtedness to commercial banks to about $500m. through repayments and restructuring agreements; and that it regarded its military debt to the former Soviet Union as a matter for discussion 'in its proper context as a mutual obligation'. It had been reported in April 1994 that Syria had sought an 80% write-off of military debt during exploratory talks with Russian officials. Sweden and Belgium were among the OECD countries whose export credit agencies reached agreements with Syria in 1994 in respect of relatively minor debts. However, Syria's main OECD bilateral creditors (among which France, Japan and Germany were each owed arrears of more than $100m.) were still seeking settlements in mid-1995. Negotiations with Germany were complicated by the inclusion of an estimated $500m.

of Syrian debt to former East Germany within Syria's total debt of around $640m. to the unified state. The World Bank estimated Syria's end-1994 external debt as $20,557m., including arrears of principal totalling $4,563m. and arrears of interest totalling $1,400m. The Bank estimated that Syria paid $398m. in debt service in 1994 (out of a total of $1,530m. due for payment in that year).

In October 1996 France announced a debt settlement agreement involving the 'forgiving' of a reported 900m. French francs (US $175m.) of arrears of interest and the rolling-over of a further 1,000 French francs ($195m.) of debt. In July 1997 the Syrian Government signed an agreement to settle its debt to the World Bank. Arrears of principal totalling $269.5m. were repaid in full on 1 September 1997, while arrears of interest totalling $256.9m. were to be repaid in instalments over five years from 1 October 1997. It was reported in September 1997 that Syria was negotiating with the Islamic Development Bank to settle around $300m. of payments' arrears. By mid-1998 Syria's only remaining unresolved debt problems of significance were with Germany and Russia. In November 1998 Italy (currently Syria's largest export market and second largest import supplier) agreed an aid programme for 1999–2001, under which loans and grants totalling as much as $65m. were to be made available for agricultural, energy, health, agro-industrial, environmental and scientific projects.

In August 1999 Syria agreed a formula for settling US $502m. of debt owed to Iran. The International Finance Corporation approved its first project in Syria (an equity investment in an irrigation technology company) in December 1999, this being the first World Bank Group project in Syria for 13 years. The World Bank subsequently confirmed that Syria continued to meet all of its obligations under its 1997 debt settlement agreement with the Bank. Syria's repayments of commercial debt to Japan (under a 1995 rescheduling agreement) became 'erratic' in 1999, but were brought back on schedule after Syria's change of government in March 2000. Discussions on Syria's continuing debt dispute with Germany resumed in February 2000, leading to the signature in November of an agreement to reschedule the repayment of $572m. of debt over 20 years from 2001. In April 2000 the Romanian Government announced a debt recovery scheme covering the greater part of Syria's outstanding communist-era debt to Romania. In May it was reported in Western aviation journals that Russia had agreed to upgrade the Syrian air force and air defence systems (implying that there were now no unresolved military debt disputes between Russia and Syria). In December the European Investment Bank, which had made no new development loans to Syria for the past decade, announced a $75m. loan for improvements to the electricity supply network. The World Bank estimated that Syria's total external debt at end-2000 was $21,655m. (127.5% of nominal GDP), compared with an end-1999 figure of $22,340m. (140.5% of GDP).

Total official reserves (excluding gold) fluctuated considerably in the 1980s. At mid-1986 they declined to only US $10m., but by the end of 1988 they had increased to $191m. Net foreign assets rose from $2,000m. at the end of 1989 to $3,700m. at the end of 1990. At the end of 1996 Syria's net foreign assets totalled $8,901m., having risen by more than 50% since 1994, as world oil prices improved.

ECONOMIC PROSPECTS

With its population increasing annually by around 2.5%, Syria's current real GDP growth rate of about 2% a year is well below the estimated 5% rate needed to produce significant economic progress for the country as a whole. A key question is whether the recent increase in oil and gas exploration activity will yield new discoveries that will significantly boost Syria's proven oil and gas reserves, the exploitation of which has underpinned recent economic development. The Government points out that only about 40% of some 800 potentially hydrocarbon-bearing structures in Syria have been drilled so far. However, industry analysts note that no major discoveries have been made since the early 1990s and warn that unless new reserves are found Syria will become a net oil and gas importer within little more than a decade. Against this background, future economic progress is likely to depend in large part on the success of efforts to promote downstream oil and gas activities and non-oil industrial enterprises, which will depend on whether Syria can begin to attract substantial foreign investment. This, in turn, will depend on whether the Government delivers real liberalization of what is still a largely state-controlled economy and implements the range of structural and legal reforms promised since 1990.

Statistical Survey

Source (unless otherwise stated): Central Bureau of Statistics, rue Abd al-Malek bin Marwah, Malki Quarter, Damascus; tel. (11) 3335830; fax (11) 3322292.

Area and Population

AREA, POPULATION AND DENSITY

Area (sq km)	
Land	184,050
Inland water	1,130
Total	185,180*
Population (census results)†	
8 September 1981	9,052,628
3 September 1994	
Males	7,048,906
Females	6,733,409
Total	13,782,315
Population (official estimates at mid-year)†	
1999	16,110,000
2000	16,320,000
2001	16,720,000
Density (per sq km) at mid-2001	90.8

* 71,498 sq miles.

† Including Palestinian refugees, numbering 193,000 at mid-1977.

PRINCIPAL TOWNS (population at census of 3 September 1994)

Damascus (capital) .	1,394,322	Hama	264,348
Aleppo	1,582,930	Rakka	165,195
Homs	540,133	Al-Qamishli . .	144,286
Latakia . . .	311,784	Deir ez-Zor . .	140,459

Mid-2000 (UN estimate, incl. suburbs): Aleppo 2,229,000; Homs 811,000.
Mid-2001 (UN estimate, incl. suburbs): Damascus 2,195,000.

Source: UN, *World Urbanization Prospects: The 2001 Revision.*

REGISTERED BIRTHS, MARRIAGES AND DEATHS

	Births	Marriages	Deaths
1991	396,309	96,656	43,910
1992	404,948	106,545	46,308
1993	399,330	114,979	46,032
1994	407,395	115,994	43,981
1995	429,414	120,146	44,904
1996	446,958	126,561	46,540
1997	437,286	126,407	46,223
1998	442,012	130,835	50,511

Expectation of life (WHO estimates, years at birth, 2000): Males 69.3; Females 72.4 (Source: WHO, *World Health Report*).

ECONOMICALLY ACTIVE POPULATION
(sample survey, persons aged 10 years and over, 1999)*

	Males	Females	Total
Agriculture, hunting, forestry and fishing	799,181	364,491	1,163,672
Mining and quarrying . . .	10,159	709	10,868
Manufacturing	477,477	43,257	520,734
Electricity, gas and water . .	3,386	—	3,386
Construction	568,909	13,473	582,382
Trade, restaurants and hotels . .	623,085	24,110	647,195
Transport, storage and communications	216,727	7,800	224,527
Financing, insurance, real estate and business services . . .	27,092	6,382	33,474
Community, social and personal services	660,339	248,903	909,242
Total employed	3,386,355	709,125	4,095,480
Unemployed	268,703	163,075	431,778
Total labour force	3,655,058	872,200	4,527,258

* Figures refer to Syrians only, excluding armed forces.

Health and Welfare

KEY INDICATORS

Fertility (births per woman, 2000)	3.8
Under-5 mortality rate (per 1,000 live births, 2000) . .	29
HIV/AIDS (% of persons aged 15–49, 1994)	0.01
Physicians (per 1,000 head, 1997)	109
Hospital beds (per 1,000 head, 1997)	4.0
Health expenditure (1998): US $ per head (PPP) . . .	109
% of GDP	4.0
public (% of total)	51.5
Access to water (% of persons, 2000)	80
Access to sanitation (% of persons, 2000)	90
Human Development Index (2000): ranking	108
value	0.691

For sources and definitions, see explanatory note on p. vi.

Agriculture

PRINCIPAL CROPS ('000 metric tons)

	1998	1999	2000
Wheat	4,111.6	2,691.5	3,105.5
Barley	868.8	425.5	211.9
Maize	285.0	181.0	190.3
Potatoes	492.3	496.5	484.8
Sugar beet	1,202.2	1,330.4	1,175.3
Chick-peas	84.6	28.9	64.5
Lentils	154.1	43.5	73.0
Almonds	67.2	57.7	62.3
Olives	785.0	400.5	866.1
Cottonseed	635.2	602.0	703.2
Cabbages	71.5	57.1	42.9
Lettuce	59.1	49.7	46.3
Tomatoes	555.2	610.2	753.2
Cauliflowers	57.3	50.4	29.8
Pumpkins, squash and gourds	121.7	100.0	100.5*
Cucumbers and gherkins	126.7	125.0*	125.0*
Aubergines (Eggplants)	155.8	128.0*	128.0*
Chillies and green peppers	38.4	33.4	43.0
Green onions and shallots	44.1	42.0	42.0*
Dry onions	104.8	91.0	71.9
Oranges	439.0	356.6	407.1
Lemons and limes	68.0	82.9	83.5
Apples	362.0	283.7	286.8
Apricots	67.2	62.9	78.9
Cherries	56.0	54.1	56.3
Peaches and nectarines	43.1	41.6	42.0
Grapes	590.0	387.0	409.5
Watermelons	402.5	258.5	201.5
Cantaloupes and other melons	67.4	45.0*	45.0*
Figs	47.0	41.8	44.1
Cotton (lint)	326.0	306.2	360.0

* FAO estimate.

Source: FAO.

LIVESTOCK ('000 head, year ending September)

	1998	1999	2000
Horses*	28	29	30
Mules*	19	19	20
Asses*	195	196	198
Cattle	932	978	984
Camels*	8	8	8
Sheep	15,425	13,998	13,505
Goats	1,101	1,046	1,050
Chickens	20,422	21,009	21,476

* FAO estimate.

Source: FAO.

LIVESTOCK PRODUCTS ('000 metric tons)

	1998	1999	2000
Beef and veal	43.4	46.7	47.1
Mutton and lamb	154.2	176.7	184.1
Chicken meat	97.2	104.4	106.6
Cows' milk	1,118.8	1,143.4	1,156.4
Sheep's milk	581.9	445.9	445.6
Goats' milk	78.7	65.9	70.3
Cheese	96.6	87.9	92.9
Butter and ghee	17.5	14.6	14.4
Hen eggs	116.4*	124.0	116.5
Wool: greasy†	29.9	26.6	25.7
scoured	15.0	12.8	13.0†
Cattle hides	6.7	7.2	7.3
Sheepskins	25.7	29.5	30.7

* Unofficial figure.   † FAO estimate.

Source: FAO.

Forestry

ROUNDWOOD REMOVALS ('000 cubic metres, excl. bark)*

	1998	1999	2000
Sawlogs, veneer logs and logs for sleepers	16	16	16
Other industrial wood	19	19	19
Fuel wood	16	16	16
Total	50	50	50

* Assumed unchanged since 1993 (FAO estimates).

Sawnwood production ('000 cubic metres): 9 per year in 1991–2000.

Source: FAO.

Fishing

(metric tons, live weight)

	1997	1998	1999
Capture	6,131	7,097	7,945
Freshwater fishes	3,557	4,347	5,345
Demersal percomorphs	450	626	530
Aquaculture	5,596	7,233	6,079
Common carp	4,451	5,786	4,930
Tilapias	1,100	1,372	1,065
Total catch	11,727	14,330	14,024

Source: FAO, *Yearbook of Fishery Statistics.*

Mining

('000 metric tons, unless otherwise indicated)

	1997	1998	1999
Crude petroleum ('000 cubic metres)	33,177	33,140	33,320
Phosphate rock	2,471	2,494	2,127
Salt (unrefined)	119	178	104
Natural asphalt	115	154	114

Source: Central Bank of Syria, *Quarterly Bulletin.*

Industry

SELECTED PRODUCTS ('000 metric tons, unless otherwise indicated)

	1996	1997	1998
Cotton yarn (pure)	43	53	60
Silk and cotton textiles	15	25	25
Woollen fabrics (metric tons)	0.2	2.7	4.9
Plywood ('000 cu metres)	87.6	78.3	79.8
Cement	4,817	4,838	5,016
Glass and pottery products	58	69	57
Soap	18	18	21
Refined sugar	181	176	89
Olive oil	127	78	145
Other vegetable oils and fats	36	53	65
Cottonseed cake	117	194	226
Manufactured tobacco	9	10	10
Electricity (million kWh)	17,278	18,259	19,841
Refrigerators ('000)	155.2	138.2	136.9
Washing machines ('000)	80	71.5	68.5
Television receivers ('000)	123.8	128.2	150.5

1999 ('000 metric tons, unless otherwise indicated): Cotton yarn (pure) 62; Cement 5,134; Refined sugar 158; Olive oil 80; Other vegetable oils and fats 50; Cottonseed cake (estimate) 103; Electricity (million kWh) 21,568.
2000 ('000 metric tons, unless otherwise indicated): Cement 4,632; Olive oil 165; Other vegetable oils and fats 70; Cottonseed cake (estimate) 161; Electricity (million kWh) 23,952.

Sources: mainly Central Bank of Syria, *Quarterly Bulletin*; FAO; UN, *Monthly Bulletin of Statistics.*

Finance

CURRENCY AND EXCHANGE RATES

Monetary Units

100 piastres = 1 Syrian pound (£S).

Sterling, Dollar and Euro Equivalents (31 May 2002)

£1 sterling = £S16.464;
US $1 = £S11.225;
€1 = £S10.537;
£S1,000 = £60.74 sterling = $89.09 = €94.90.

Exchange Rate

Between April 1976 and December 1987 the official mid-point rate was fixed at US $1 = £S3.925. On 1 January 1988 a new rate of $1 = £S11.225 was introduced. In addition to the official exchange rate, there is a promotion rate (applicable to most travel and tourism transactions) and a flexible rate. For calculating the value of transactions in the balance of payments, the Central Bank of Syria used the following average exchange rates: $1 = £S44.88 in 1997; $1 = £S49.27 in 1998; $1 = £S48.83 in 1999.

BUDGET (estimates, £S million)

Revenue	1997	1998	1999
Taxes and duties. . . .	69,296.0	75,516.0	82,686.0
Services, commutations and revenues from state properties and their public investments .	18,574.0	20,054.0	19,409.0
Various revenues . .	48,108.0	60,385.0	65,500.0
Supply surplus . . .	44,516.0	47,081.0	50,314.0
Exceptional revenues. . .	30,631.0	34,264.0	37,391.0
Total	211,125.0	237,300.0	255,300.0

Expenditure	1997	1998	1999
Community, social and personal services	116,167.5	127,432.7	144,087.7
Agriculture, forestry and fishing .	24,220.4	25,059.0	24,580.5
Mining and quarrying . .	8,471.1	8,964.9	8,635.2
Manufacturing	14,033.4	17,049.1	16,734.8
Electricity, gas and water. .	27,004.4	25,168.2	23,538.7
Building and construction .	1,216.2	1,225.3	1,117.6
Trade	3,435.6	3,732.3	3,369.7
Transport, communications and storage	11,012.4	17,679.9	20,288.8
Finance, insurance and companies	1,164.0	1,388.6	1,147.0
Total (incl. others)	211,125.0	237,300.0	255,300.0

2000 (projections, £S million): Revenue 263,000; Expenditure 275,400.
2001 (projections, £S million): Revenue 312,798; Expenditure 322,000.
2002 (projections, £S million): Revenue 356,400; Expenditure 356,400.

CENTRAL BANK RESERVES (US $ million at 31 December)

	1986	1987	1988
Gold*	29	29	29
Foreign exchange	144	223	193
Total	173	252	222

* Valued at $35 per troy ounce.

Source: IMF, *International Financial Statistics.*

MONEY SUPPLY (£S million at 31 December)

	1999	2000	2001
Currency outside banks . . .	182,184	203,863	229,266
Demand deposits at commercial banks	121,471	151,753	176,845
Total money (incl. others) . .	313,318	368,670	419,916

Source: IMF, *International Financial Statistics.*

COST OF LIVING
(Consumer Price Index for Damascus; base: 1990 = 100)

	1998*	1999	2000
Food and beverages	169	162.3	159.0
Electricity, gas and other fuels	267	268.3	269.2
Clothing and footwear . .	248	252.6	252.3
Rent	197	198.2	199.0
All items (incl. others) . . .	188	184.3	182.9

* Figures are rounded.

Source: ILO, *Yearbook of Labour Statistics.*

NATIONAL ACCOUNTS (£S million at current prices)

Expenditure on the Gross Domestic Product

	1998	1999	2000
Government final consumption expenditure	88,521	86,857	98,403
Private final consumption expenditure	542,374	575,866	579,627
Gross capital formation . . .	162,446	153,706	155,757
Total domestic expenditure .	793,341	816,429	833,787
Exports of goods and services . .	241,316	264,704	326,715
Less Imports of goods and services	244,213	262,041	263,868
GDP in purchasers' values .	790,444	819,092	896,634
GDP at constant 1995 prices .	675,888	662,396	666,567

Source: IMF, *International Financial Statistics.*

Gross Domestic Product by Economic Activity

	1997	1998	1999*
Agriculture, hunting, forestry and fishing	192,162	232,283	196,743
Mining and quarrying . . .			
Manufacturing	184,938	179,687	221,416
Electricity, gas and water. . .			
Construction	28,102	29,470	27,433
Trade, restaurants and hotels. .	149,054	152,130	152,866
Transport, storage and communications	86,409	88,876	104,053
Finance, insurance, real estate and business services . . .	29,459	29,971	35,095
Government services	60,056	61,789	64,859
Other community, social and personal services . . .	15,136	15,935	18,498
Non-profit private services . .	253	303	364
GDP in purchasers' values .	745,569	790,444	821,327

* Preliminary figures.

Source: Central Bank of Syria, *Quarterly Bulletin.*

BALANCE OF PAYMENTS (US $ million)

	1998	1999	2000
Exports of goods f.o.b. . . .	3,142	3,806	5,146
Imports of goods f.o.b. . . .	−3,320	−3,590	−3,723
Trade balance	−178	216	1,423
Exports of services . . .	1,666	1,651	1,700
Imports of services . . .	−1,491	−1,612	−1,667
Balance on goods and services.	−3	255	1,456
Other income received . .	369	356	345
Other income paid . . .	−839	−899	−1,224
Balance on goods, services and income	−473	−288	577
Current transfers received . .	533	491	495
Current transfers paid . . .	−2	−2	−10
Current balance . . .	58	201	1,062
Capital account (net)	27	80	63
Direct investment from abroad .	82	263	270
Other investment assets . .	1,422	1,332	1,049
Other investment liabilities .	−1,308	−1,422	−1,711
Net errors and omissions . .	153	−195	−192
Overall balance . . .	434	259	541

Source: IMF, *International Financial Statistics.*

External Trade

PRINCIPAL COMMODITIES (£S million)

Imports c.i.f.	1997	1998	1999*
Cotton textiles, other textile goods and silk	4,287.4	4,376.4	4,279
Mineral fuels and oils . . .	1,914.6	1,747.6	1,212
Sugar	1,700.1	1,622.7	1,796
Other foodstuffs	5,268.1	4,880.7	5,945
Machinery and apparatus . .	6,863.8	6,422.8	5,600
Base metals and manufactures .	6,703.5	7,203.7	7,273
Chemicals and pharmaceutical products	4,320.8	3,756.1	3,738
Transport equipment . . .	3,452.4	3,797.5	3,807
Paper and paper products . .	1,336.7	1,259.1	1,400
Resins, artificial rubber, etc. . .	3,071.5	2,929.5	2,503
Total (incl. others) . . .	45,210.7	43,725.5	43,010

Exports f.o.b.	1997	1998	1999*
Raw cotton	2,772.6	3,065.3	1,745
Wheat	2,142.0	1,062.8	272
Textiles	3,200.1	2,430.1	2,805
Vegetables and fruit (fresh and prepared)	3,332.2	3,887.3	4,026
Crude petroleum	24,396.4	15,472.7	24,470
Total (incl. others) . . .	43,953.0	32,443.4	38,880

* Figures are rounded.

Source: Central Bank of Syria, *Quarterly Bulletin.*

PRINCIPAL TRADING PARTNERS (£S million)

Imports c.i.f.	1997	1998	1999*
Belgium	1,546.7	1,547.6	1,227
Bulgaria	454.8	295.0	376
China, People's Republic .	1,626.2	1,570.9	1,425
Czechoslovakia (former) . .	400.8	455.1	300
Egypt	558.2	640.7	492
France	1,797.1	2,393.6	2,465
Germany	3,680.6	3,099.7	3,031
India	667.0	625.8	634
Italy	3,275.7	2,854.7	2,424
Japan	1,666.6	1,744.2	1,756
Netherlands	912.3	1,067.6	938
Romania	1,615.1	903.2	863
Russia	1,127.3	932.1	887
Saudi Arabia	1,286.7	1,021.7	1,124
Spain	756.6	688.4	642
Turkey	2,414.8	2,098.4	2,137
United Kingdom	1,095.4	1,050.2	995
USA	2,926.7	2,085.8	1,963
Total (incl. others) . . .	45,210.7	43,725.0	43,010

Exports f.o.b.	1997	1998	1999*
Egypt	342.2	329*	391
France	8,650.6	5,707.9	8,013
Germany	666.8	581.1	330
Italy	10,783.3	7,031.3	10,337
Jordan	750.7	473.7	439
Kuwait	467.7	591.5	581
Lebanon	3,702.4	2,778.6	1,537
Russia	1,135.4	519.5	498
Saudi Arabia	2,389.0	2,632.7	3,260
Spain	2,450.5	1,605.9	2,670
Turkey	4,409.7	3,348.2	3,599
United Kingdom	646.7	319.6	927
USA	151.6	181*	503
Total (incl. others) . . .	43,953.1	32,442.5	38,880

* Figures are rounded.

Source: Central Bank of Syria, *Quarterly Bulletin.*

Transport

RAILWAYS (traffic)

	1996	1997	1998
Passenger-km ('000) . . .	453,886	294,126	181,575
Freight ('000 metric tons) . .	4,655	4,939	4,983

ROAD TRAFFIC (motor vehicles in use)

	1996	1997	1998
Passenger cars	139,592	138,460	138,900
Buses and coaches . . .	33,970	47,453	40,143
Lorries, trucks, etc. . . .	251,451	262,060	282,664
Motor cycles	88,490	87,361	88,121

SHIPPING

Merchant Fleet (registered at 31 December)

	1999	2000	2001
Number of vessels	223	219	215
Total displacement ('000 grt) .	440.1	465.4	498.2

Source: Lloyd's Register-Fairplay, *World Fleet Statistics.*

International Sea-borne Traffic

	1996	1997	1998
Vessels entered ('000 net reg. tons)	2,901*	2,640	2,622
Cargo unloaded ('000 metric tons) .	4,560	4,788	5,112
Cargo loaded ('000 metric tons) .	1,788	2,412	2,136

* Excluding Banias.

Source: mainly UN, *Monthly Bulletin of Statistics* and *Statistical Yearbook.*

CIVIL AVIATION (traffic on scheduled services)

		1996	1997	1998
Kilometres flown (million)	. .	11	12	13
Passengers carried ('000) .	. .	599	694	665
Passenger-km (million)	. .	1,068	1,235	1,410
Total ton-km (million)	. .	113	127	140

Source: UN, *Statistical Yearbook*.

Tourism

FOREIGN VISITOR ARRIVALS (incl. excursionists)*

Country of nationality	1998	1999	2000
Iran	152,866	199,307	221,380
Iraq	36,375	58,136	85,439
Jordan	477,747	513,783	538,493
Kuwait	66,931	65,868	69,075
Lebanon	827,039	868,051	995,235
Saudi Arabia	245,785	273,161	283,653
Turkey	169,912	186,770	182,801
Total	2,463,724	2,681,534	3,014,758

* Figures exclude Syrian nationals resident abroad.

Source: World Tourism Organization, *Yearbook of Tourism Statistics*.

Tourism receipts (US $ million): 1,190 in 1998, 1,360 in 1999; 474 in 2000 (Source: World Bank, *World Bank Atlas*).

Communications Media

	1999	2000	2001
Television receivers ('000 in use) .	1,070	1,080	n.a.
Telephones ('000 main lines in use)	1,600.4	1,675.2	1,807.6
Mobile cellular telephones ('000 in use)	4.0	30.0	200.0
Personal computers ('000 in use) .	230	250	270
Internet users ('000)	20	30	60

1992: Book production 598 titles.
1996: Daily newspapers 8 (average circulation 287,000 copies).
1997 ('000 in use): Radio receivers 4,150.
1998 ('000 in use): Facsimile machines 22.

Sources: UNESCO, *Statistical Yearbook*; UN, *Statistical Yearbook*; International Telecommunication Union.

Education

(1996/97)

	Insti-tutions	Teachers	Pupils/Students		
			Males	Females	Total
Pre-primary . .	1,096	4,427	52,627	45,524	98,151
Primary . .	10,783	114,689	1,433,385	1,256,820	2,690,205
Secondary:					
General . .	n.a.	52,182	469,032	396,010	865,042
Vocational .	n.a.	12,479	44,895	47,727	92,622
Higher:*					
Universities, etc.	n.a.	4,733	101,819	65,367	167,186
Others . . .	n.a.	n.a.	25,167	23,381	48,548

* Figures refer to 1994/95.

Source: UNESCO, *Statistical Yearbook*.

Pupils/Students (1999/2000): Pre-primary 115,613 (males 61,458; females 54,155); Primary 2,774,922 (males 1,470,800; females 1,304,122); General secondary 955,272 (males 511,702; females 443,570). Source: Ministry of Education.

Adult literacy rate (UNESCO estimates): 74.4% (males 88.3%; females 60.5%) in 2000 (Source: UNDP, *Human Development Report*).

Directory

The Constitution

A new and permanent Constitution was endorsed by 97.6% of the voters in a national referendum on 12 March 1973. The 157-article Constitution defines Syria as a 'Socialist popular democracy' with a 'pre-planned Socialist economy'. Under the new Constitution, Lt-Gen. Hafiz al-Assad remained President, with the power to appoint and dismiss his Vice-President, Premier and government ministers, and also became Commander-in-Chief of the Armed Forces, Secretary-General of the Baath Socialist Party and President of the National Progressive Front. Legislative power is vested in the People's Assembly, with 250 members elected by universal adult suffrage (84 seats are reserved for independent candidates).

Following the death of President Hafiz al-Assad on 10 June 2000, the Constitution was amended to allow his son, Lt-Gen. Bashar al-Assad, to accede to the presidency. Bashar al-Assad also became Commander-in-Chief of the armed forces, Secretary-General of the Baath Socialist Party and President of the National Progressive Front.

The Government

HEAD OF STATE

President: Lt-Gen. Bashar al-Assad (assumed office 17 July 2000).

Vice-Presidents: (First) Abd al-Halim Khaddam (responsible for Political and Foreign Affairs); (Second) Muhammad Zuheir Masharkah (responsible for Internal and Party Affairs).

COUNCIL OF MINISTERS
(September 2002)

Prime Minister: Dr Muhammad Mustafa Mero.

Deputy Prime Minister and Minister of Defence: Maj.-Gen. Mustafa Tlass.

Deputy Prime Minister in charge of Public Services: Eng. Muhammad Naji Otri.

Deputy Prime Minister in charge of Economic Affairs: Muhammad al-Hussain.

Deputy Prime Minister and Minister of Foreign Affairs: Farouk ash-Shara'.

Minister of Information: Adnan Omran.

Minister of the Interior: Maj.-Gen. Ali Hammoud.

Minister of Supply and Internal Trade: Bassam Muhammad Rostom.

Minister of Local Government: Hilal al-Atrash.

Minister of Education: Dr Mahmoud as-Sayed.

Minister of Higher Education: Dr Hasan Risha.

Minister of Electricity: Munib Assad Saim ad-Daher.

Minister of Culture: Najwa Qassab Hassan.

Minister of Transport: Eng. Makram Obeid.

Minister of Economy and Foreign Trade: Ghassan ar-Rifai.

Minister of Petroleum and Mineral Resources: Ibrahim Haddad.

Minister of Industry: Dr Issam az-Zaim.

Minister of Finance: Muhammad al-Atrash.

Minister of Housing and Utilities: Ayman Wanli.

Minister of Justice: NABIL AL-KHATIB.

Minister of Agriculture and Agrarian Reform: NOUR ED-DIN MOUNA.

Minister of Irrigation: Eng. RADWAN MARTINI.

Minister of Communications: BASHIR AL-MUNJID.

Minister of Health: Dr MUHAMMAD IYAD ASH-SHATTI.

Minister of Construction: HASSAN AL-ASWAD.

Minister of Awqaf (Islamic Endowments): MUHAMMAD ABD AR-RA'UF ZIYADAH.

Minister of Labour and Social Affairs: GHADA AL-JABI.

Minister of Tourism: SAADALLAH AGHA AL-QALLA.

Minister of Presidential Affairs: HAYTHAM DUWAIHI.

Minister of State for Emigration Affairs: NASIR QADDOUR.

Minister of State for the Environment: ADNAN KHAZAM.

Ministers of State: FAISAL JAWISH, ABD AL-KARIM SAYED YOUSUF, ABD AN-NASSER ABD AL-MU'TI DAOUD.

MINISTRIES

Office of the President: Damascus; internet www.assad.org.

Office of the Prime Minister: rue Chahbandar, Damascus; tel. (11) 2226000.

Ministry of Agriculture and Agrarian Reform: rue Jabri, place Hedjaz, Damascus; tel. (11) 2213613; fax (11) 2216627; e-mail agre-min@syriatel.net; internet www.syrianagriculture.org.

Ministry of Awqaf (Islamic Endowments): Rukeneddin, Damascus; tel. (11) 4419079; fax (11) 419969.

Ministry of Communications: nr Majlis ash-Sha'ab, Damascus; tel. (11) 2227033; fax (11) 2246403.

Ministry of Construction: rue Sa'dallah al-Jaberi, Damascus; tel. (11) 2223595.

Ministry of Culture: rue George Haddad, ar-Rawda, Damascus; tel. (11) 3331556; fax (11) 3320804.

Ministry of Defence: place Omayad, Damascus; tel. (11) 7770700.

Ministry of Economy and Foreign Trade: rue Maysaloun, Damascus; tel. (11) 2213514; fax (11) 2225695; e-mail econ-min@net.sy; internet www.syrecon.org.

Ministry of Education: rue Shahbander, al-Masraa, Damascus; tel. (11) 4444703; fax (11) 4420435; internet www.syrianeducation.org.

Ministry of Electricity: BP 4900, rue al-Kouatly, Damascus; tel. (11) 2223086; fax (11) 2223686.

Ministry of Finance: BP 13136, rue Jule Jammal, Damascus; tel. (11) 2239624; fax (11) 2224701; e-mail mof@net.sy.

Ministry of Foreign Affairs: ave Shora, Muhajireen, Damascus; tel. (11) 3331200; fax (11) 3320686.

Ministry of Health: rue Majlis ash-Sha'ab, Damascus; tel. (11) 3311020; fax (11) 3311114; e-mail health-min@net.sy.

Ministry of Higher Education: ave Kasem Amin, ar-Rawda, Damascus; tel. (11) 3330700; fax (11) 3337719.

Ministry of Housing and Utilities: place Yousuf al-Azmeh, as-Salheyeh, Damascus; tel. (11) 2217571; fax (11) 2217570; e-mail mhu@net.sy.

Ministry of Industry: BP 12835, rue Maysaloun, Damascus; tel. (11) 2231834; fax (11) 2231096; e-mail min-industry@syriatel.net; internet www.syr-industry.org.

Ministry of Information: Imm. Dar al-Baath, Autostrade Mezzeh, Damascus; tel. (11) 6622141; fax (11) 6617665; e-mail moi@net.sy; internet www.moi-syria.com.

Ministry of the Interior: rue al-Bahsah, al-Marjeh, Damascus; tel. (11) 2238682; fax (11) 2246921.

Ministry of Irrigation: rue Fardoss; tel. (11) 2212741; fax (11) 3320691.

Ministry of Justice: rue an-Nasr, Damascus; tel. (11) 2214105; fax (11) 2246250.

Ministry of Labour and Social Affairs: place Yousuf al-Azmeh, as-Salheyeh, Damascus; tel. (11) 2210355; fax (11) 2247499.

Ministry of Petroleum and Mineral Resources: BP 40, al-Adawi, Insha'at, Damascus; tel. (11) 4451624; fax (11) 4463942; e-mail mopmr@net.sy; internet www.mopmr-sy.org.

Ministry of Supply and Internal Trade: opposite Majlis ash-Sha'ab, as-Salheyeh, Damascus; tel. (11) 2219044; fax (11) 2219803.

Ministry of Tourism: Barada St, Damascus; tel. (11) 2233183; e-mail min-tourism@mail.sy; internet www.syriatourism.org.

Ministry of Transport: BP 134, rue al-Jalaa, Damascus; tel. (11) 3336801; fax (11) 3323317.

Legislature

MAJLIS ASH-SHA'AB
(People's Assembly)

Speaker: ABD AL-QADIR QADDURAH.

Election, 30 November and 1 December 1998

Party	Seats
Baath Party	135
Communist Party	8
Arab Socialist Unionist Party	7
Syrian Arab Socialist Union Party	7
Arab Socialist Party	6
Socialist Unionist Democratic Party	4
Independents	83
Total	**250**

Political Organizations

The **National Progressive Front (NPF)**, headed by President Assad, was formed in March 1972 by the grouping of the following five parties:

Arab Socialist Party: Damascus; a breakaway socialist party; contested the 1994 election to the People's Assembly as two factions; Leader ABD AL-GHANI KANNOUT.

Arab Socialist Unionist Party: Damascus; Leader SAMI SOUFAN; Sec.-Gen. SAFWAN QUDSI.

Baath Arab Socialist Party: National Command, BP 9389, Autostrade Mezzeh, Damascus; tel. (11) 6622142; fax (11) 6622099; e-mail baath-n@net.sy; internet www.albaath.com; Arab nationalist socialist party; f. 1947; result of merger of the Arab Revival (Baath) Movement (f. 1940) and the Arab Socialist Party (f. 1940); brs in most Arab countries; in power since 1963; supports creation of a unified Arab socialist society; Sec.-Gen. Lt-Gen. BASHAR AL-ASSAD; Asst Sec.-Gen. ABDULLAH AL-AHMAR; Regional Asst Sec.-Gen. Dr SULEIMAN QADDAH; more than 800,000 mems in Syria.

Communist Party of Syria: Damascus; tel. (11) 448243; f. 1924; until 1943 part of joint Communist Party of Syria and Lebanon; Sixth Party Congress January 1987; contested the 1994 election to the People's Assembly as two factions; Sec.-Gen. YOUSUF FAISAL; Sec. Gen. of Political Bureau RIAD AT-TURK.

Syrian Arab Socialist Union Party: Damascus; tel. (11) 239305; Nasserite; Sec.-Gen. SAFWAN KOUDSI.

A sixth party, the **Socialist Unionist Democratic Party**, contested the elections held to the People's Assembly in May 1990 and August 1994 as a member of the National Progressive Front. There is also a **Marxist-Leninist Communist Action Party**, which regards itself as independent of all Arab regimes.

An illegal Syrian-based organization, the **Islamic Movement for Change (IMC)**, claimed responsibility for a bomb attack in Damascus in December 1996.

Two new political organizations were formed in early 2001: the **Grouping for Democracy and Unity** (nationalist; Sec.-Gen. MUHAMMAD SAWWAN) and the **Movement for Social Peace** (prodemocratic; Leader RIAD SEIF); however, the latter was reportedly disbanded later that year.

Diplomatic Representation

EMBASSIES IN SYRIA

Afghanistan: BP 12217, ave Secretariat, West Villas, Mezzeh, Damascus; tel. (11) 6112910; fax (11) 6133595; Chargé d'affaires: Sheikh ABDULLAH MOHSENI.

Algeria: Immeuble Noss, Raouda, Damascus; Ambassador: SALEM BOUJOUMAA.

Argentina: BP 116, rue Ziad ben Abi Soufian, Raouda, Damascus; tel. (11) 3334167; fax (11) 3327326; Ambassador: HERNÁN ROBERTO PLORUTTI.

Australia: Immeuble Dakkak, 128A rue Farabi, East Villas, Mezzeh, Damascus; tel. (11) 6664317; fax (11) 6621195; Ambassador: JIM DALLIMORE.

Austria: BP 5634, Immeuble Mohamed Naim ad-Deker, 152A rue Farabi, East Villas, Mezzeh, Damascus; tel. (11) 6116730; fax (11) 6116734; e-mail autdam@scs-net.org; Ambassador: Dr MICHAEL LINHART.

Belgium: BP 31, Immeuble du Syndicat des Médecins, rue al-Jalaa, Abou Roumaneh, Damascus; tel. (11) 3332821; fax (11) 3330426; Ambassador: PHILIPPE HENRI ARCQ.

Brazil: BP 2219, 7 rue Kassem Amin, Damascus; tel. (11) 3335770; fax (11) 3330054; e-mail braemsyr@net.sy; Ambassador: GUILHERME FAUSTO DA CUNHA BASTOS.

Bulgaria: 4 rue Chahbandar, Damascus; Ambassador: GEORGI YANKOV.

Canada: BP 3394, Damascus; tel. (11) 6116692; fax (11) 6114000; Ambassador: F. D. PILLARELLA.

Chile: BP 3561, 45 rue ar-Rachid, Damascus; tel. (11) 3338443; fax (11) 3331563; e-mail echilesy@scs-net.org; Ambassador: LUIS LILLO.

China, People's Republic: 83 rue Ata Ayoubi, Damascus; Ambassador: SHI YANCHUN.

Cuba: Immeuble Istouani and Charbati, 40 rue ar-Rachid, Damascus; tel. (11) 3339624; fax (11) 3333802; e-mail embacubasy@net.sy; Ambassador: ORLANDO LANCÍS SUÁREZ.

Cyprus: BP 9269, 106 Akram al-Ojjeh, Eastern Mezzeh-Fursan, Damascus; tel. (11) 6130812; fax (11) 6130814; Ambassador: PLATONAS KYRIAKIDES.

Czech Republic: BP 2249, place Abou al-Ala'a al-Maari, Damascus; tel. (11) 3331383; fax (11) 3338268; e-mail damascus@embassy.mzv.cz; Chargé d'affaires: OTTO HOLUBAR.

Denmark: BP 2244, rue Chekib Arslan, Abou Roumaneh, Damascus; tel. (11) 3331008; fax (11) 3337928; e-mail dk-emb@cyberia.net.lb; Ambassador: OLE WØHLERS OLSEN.

Egypt: Damascus; tel. (11) 3330756; Ambassador: Dr MUHAMMAD AHMAD ISMAIL.

Finland: BP 3893, Immeuble Yacoubian, Hawakir, West Malki, Damascus; tel. (11) 3338809; fax (11) 3734740; Ambassador: ANTTI KOISTINEN.

France: BP 769, rue Ata Ayoubi, Damascus; tel. (11) 3327992; fax (11) 3338632; e-mail ambafr@net.sy; internet www.amb-damas.fr; Ambassador: JEAN-FRANÇOIS GIRAULT.

Germany: BP 2237, 16 rue Abd al-Mun'im Riyad, al-Malki, Damascus; tel. (11) 3323800; fax (11) 3323812; e-mail german emb@net.sy; Ambassador: Dr GUNTER MULACK.

Greece: BP 30319, Immeuble Pharaon, 11 rue Farabi, Mezzeh, Damascus; tel. (11) 6113035; fax (11) 6114920; e-mail grembdam@mail.sy; Ambassador: VASSILIS PAPAIOANNOU.

Holy See: BP 2271, place Ma'raket Ajnadin, Malki, Damascus (Apostolic Nunciature); tel. (11) 3332601; fax (11) 3327550; e-mail noncesy@mailosy; Apostolic Nuncio: Most Rev. DIEGO CAUSERO; Titular Archbishop of Grado.

Hungary: BP 2607, 102 rue al-Fursan, East Villas, Mezzeh, al-Akram, Damascus; tel. (11) 6110787; fax (11) 6117917; e-mail hung emb@net.sy; Ambassador: BALÁZS BOKOR.

India: BP 685, Immeuble Yassin Noueilati, 40/46 ave Adnan al-Malki, Damascus; tel. (11) 3739082; fax (11) 3326231; e-mail ind embsy@net.sy; Ambassador: K. M. MEENA.

Indonesia: BP 3530, 10 rue as-Salam 17, Mezzeh Eastern Villa, Damascus; tel. (11) 6119630; fax (11) 6119632; e-mail kbridams @cyberia.net.lb; internet www.welcome.to/kbri-damascus; Ambassador: ZARKOWI SOEJOETI.

Iran: Autostrade Mezzeh, nr ar-Razi Hospital, Damascus; Ambassador: Hojatoleslam MUHAMMAD HASSAN AKHTARI.

Italy: 82 ave al-Mansour, Damascus; tel. (11) 3338338; fax (11) 3320325; e-mail italemb@net.sy; internet www.ambitsir.org; Ambassador: LAURA MIRACHIAN.

Japan: 15 ave al-Jala'a, Damascus; tel. (11) 339421; Ambassador: RYUJI ONODERA.

Jordan: rue Abou Roumaneh, Damascus; tel. (11) 3334642; fax (11) 3336741; Ambassador: AHMAD JALAL AL-MUFLEH.

Korea, Democratic People's Republic: rue Fares al-Khouri-Jisr Tora, Damascus; Ambassador: JONG CHUN GUN.

Kuwait: rue Ibrahim Hanano, Damascus; Ambassador: AHMAD ABD AL-AZIZ AL-JASSEM.

Libya: Abou Roumaneh, Damascus; Head of People's Bureau: AHMAD ABD AS-SALAM BIN KHAYAL.

Mauritania: ave al-Jala'a, rue Karameh, Damascus; Ambassador: MUHAMMAD MAHMOUD OULD WEDDADY.

Morocco: rue Farabi Villas Est, Mezzeh, Damascus; tel. (11) 6110451; Ambassador: IDRIFF DHAHAQ.

Netherlands: BP 702, Immeuble Tello, rue al-Jalaa, Abou Roumaneh, Damascus; tel. (11) 3335119; fax (11) 3339369; Ambassador: R. VAN SCHREVEN.

Norway: BP 7703, rue Ahmad Shawki; tel. (11) 3322072; fax (11) 3337114; e-mail emb.damas@mfa.no; Ambassador: SVEIN SEVJE.

Oman: BP 9635, rue Ghazzawi, West Villas, Mezzeh, Damascus; tel. (11) 6110408; fax (11) 6110944; Ambassador: Sheikh HILLAL BIN SALIM AS-SIYABI.

Pakistan: BP 9284, rue al-Farabi, East Villas, Mezzeh, Damascus; tel. (11) 6132694; fax (11) 6132662; Ambassador: AFZAL AKBAR KHAN.

Panama: BP 2548, Apt 7, Immeuble az-Zein, rue al-Bizm, Malki, Damascus; tel. (11) 224743; Chargé d'affaires: CARLOS A. DE GRACIA.

Poland: BP 501, rue George Haddad, Abou Roumaneh, Damascus; tel. (11) 3333010; fax (11) 3315318; e-mail dampol@cyberia.net.lb; Ambassador: JACEK CHODOROWICZ.

Qatar: BP 4188, 20 Immeuble Allawi, place Madfa, Abou Roumaneh, Damascus; tel. (11) 336717; Ambassador: FAHD FAHD AL-KHATER.

Romania: BP 4454, 8 rue Ibrahim Hanano, Damascus; tel. (11) 3327570; fax (11) 3327572; e-mail ro.dam@net.sy; Ambassador: ION DOBRECI.

Russia: rue d'Alep, Boustan al-Kouzbari, Damascus; Ambassador: ALEKSANDR I. ZOTOV.

Saudi Arabia: ave al-Jala'a, Damascus; Ambassador: ABDULLAH BIN SALEH AL-FADL.

Slovakia: BP 33115, place Mezzeh, rue ash-Shafei, East Villas, Damascus; tel. (11) 6132114; fax (11) 6132598; e-mail slov embdk@net.sy; Ambassador: IVAN ZACHAR.

Somalia: ave Ata Ayoubi, Damascus; Ambassador: (vacant).

Spain: BP 392, rue ash-Shafi, Mezzeh East, Damascus; fax (11) 6132941; Ambassador: JAVIER NAVARRO.

Sudan: Damascus; tel. (11) 6111405; fax (11) 6112904; Ambassador ABD AL-HAFIZ IBRAHIM.

Sweden: BP 4266, rue Chakib Arslan, Abou Roumaneh, Damascus; tel. (11) 3327261; fax (11) 3327749; e-mail ambassaden.damaskus@foreign.ministry.se; Ambassador: VIOLA FURUBJELKE.

Switzerland: BP 234, 2 rue ash-Shafi, East Villas, Mezzeh, Damascus; tel. (11) 6111972; fax (11) 6111976; e-mail swissemb@net.sy; Ambassador: ROBERT MAYOR.

Tunisia: BP 4114, 6 rue ash-Shafi, blvd Fahim, Mezzeh, Damascus; tel. (11) 6132700; fax (11) 6132704; e-mail at.damas@net.sy; Ambassador: MUHAMMAD HASSAIRI.

Turkey: BP 3738, 56–58 ave Ziad bin Abou Soufian, Damascus; tel. (11) 3331370; fax (11) 3339243; e-mail sambe@mfa.gov.tr; Ambassador: OGUZ CELIKKOL.

Ukraine: Mezzeh, East Villas, 14 rue as-Salam, Damascus; tel. (11) 6113016; fax (11) 6121355; e-mail ukrembassy@mail.sy.

United Arab Emirates: Immeuble Housami, 62 rue Raouda, Damascus; Ambassador: SALIM RASHID AL-AQROUBI.

United Kingdom: BP 37, Immeuble Kotob, 11 rue Muhammad Kurd Ali, Malki, Damascus; tel. (11) 3739241; fax (11) 3731600; e-mail british.embassy.damascus@fco.gov.uk; Ambassador: HENRY G. HOGGER.

USA: BP 29, 2 rue al-Mansour, Damascus; tel. (11) 33331324; fax (11) 2247938; e-mail acsdamascus@state.gov; internet www.usembassy.state.gov/damascus; Ambassador: THEODORE KATTOUF.

Venezuela: BP 2403, Immeuble at-Tabbah, rue Lisaneddin bin al-Khateb, place Rauda, Damascus; tel. (11) 3336863; fax (11) 3333203; e-mail embavenez@net.sy; Ambassador: IVAN URBINA ORTIZ.

Viet Nam: Damascus; tel. (11) 333008; Ambassador: LE THANH TAM.

Yemen: Abou Roumaneh, Charkassieh, Damascus; Ambassador: ABDULLAH HUSSAIN BARAKAT.

Yugoslavia: BP 739, ave al-Jala'a, Damascus; tel. (11) 3336222; fax (11) 3333690; Chargé d'affaires: JOVAN VUJASINOVIĆ.

Note: Syria and Lebanon have very close relations but do not exchange formal ambassadors.

Judicial System

The Courts of Law in Syria are principally divided into two juridical court systems: Courts of General Jurisdiction and Administrative Courts. Since 1973 the Supreme Constitutional Court has been established as the paramount body of the Syrian judicial structure.

THE SUPREME CONSTITUTIONAL COURT

This is the highest court in Syria. It has specific jurisdiction over: (i) judicial review of the constitutionality of laws and legislative decrees; (ii) investigation of charges relating to the legality of the election of members of the Majlis ash-Sha'ab (People's Assembly); (iii) trial of infractions committed by the President of the Republic in the exercise of his functions; (iv) resolution of positive and negative jurisdictional conflicts and determination of the competent court between the different juridical court systems, as well as other bodies exercising judicial competence. The Supreme Constitutional Court is composed of a Chief Justice and four Justices. They are appointed by decree of the President of the Republic for a renewable period of four years.

Chief Justice of the Supreme Court: NASRAT MOUNLA-HAYDAR, Damascus; tel. (11) 3331902.

COURTS OF GENERAL JURISDICTION

The Courts of General Jurisdiction in Syria are divided into six categories: (i) The Court of Cassation; (ii) The Courts of Appeal; (iii) The Tribunals of First Instance; (iv) The Tribunals of Peace; (v) The Personal Status Courts; (vi) The Courts for Minors. Each of the above categories (except the Personal Status Courts) is divided into Civil, Penal and Criminal Chambers.

(i) **The Court of Cassation:** This is the highest court of general jurisdiction. Final judgments rendered by Courts of Appeal in penal and civil litigations may be petitioned to the Court of Cassation by the Defendant or the Public Prosecutor in penal and criminal litigations, and by any of the parties in interest in civil litigations, on grounds of defective application or interpretation of the law as stated in the challenged judgment, on grounds of irregularity of form or procedure, or violation of due process, and on grounds of defective reasoning of judgment rendered. The Court of Cassation is composed of a President, seven Vice-Presidents and 31 other Justices (Councillors).

(ii) **The Courts of Appeal:** Each court has geographical jurisdiction over one governorate (Mouhafazat). Each court is divided into Penal and Civil Chambers. There are Criminal Chambers which try felonies only. The Civil Chambers hear appeals filed against judgments rendered by the Tribunals of First Instance and the Tribunals of Peace. Each Court of Appeal is composed of a President and sufficient numbers of Vice-Presidents (Presidents of Chambers) and Superior Judges (Councillors). There are 54 Courts of Appeal.

(iii) **The Tribunals of First Instance:** In each governorate there are one or more Tribunals of First Instance, each of which is divided into several Chambers for penal and civil litigations. Each Chamber is composed of one judge. There are 72 Tribunals of First Instance.

(iv) **The Tribunals of Peace:** In the administrative centre of each governorate, and in each district, there are one or more Tribunals of Peace, which have jurisdiction over minor civil and penal litigations. There are 227 Tribunals of Peace.

(v) **Personal Status Courts:** These courts deal with marriage, divorce, etc. For Muslims each court consists of one judge, the 'Qadi Shari'i'. For Druzes there is one court consisting of one judge, the 'Qadi Mazhabi'. For non-Muslim communities there are courts for Roman Catholics, Orthodox believers, Protestants and Jews.

(vi) **Courts for Minors:** The constitution, officers, sessions, jurisdiction and competence of these courts are determined by a special law.

PUBLIC PROSECUTION

Public prosecution is headed by the Attorney-General, assisted by a number of Senior Deputy and Deputy Attorneys-General, and a sufficient number of chief prosecutors, prosecutors and assistant prosecutors. Public prosecution is represented at all levels of the Courts of General Jurisdiction in all criminal and penal litigations and also in certain civil litigations as required by the law. Public prosecution controls and supervises enforcement of penal judgments.

ADMINISTRATIVE COURTS SYSTEM

The Administrative Courts have jurisdiction over litigations involving the state or any of its governmental agencies. The Administrative Courts system is divided into two courts: the Administrative Courts and the Judicial Administrative Courts, of which the paramount body is the High Administrative Court.

MILITARY COURTS

The Military Courts deal with criminal litigations against military personnel of all ranks and penal litigations against officers only. There are two military courts: one in Damascus, the other in Aleppo. Each court is composed of three military judges. There are other military courts, consisting of one judge, in every governorate, which deal with penal litigations against military personnel below the rank of officer. The different military judgments can be petitioned to the Court of Cassation.

Religion

In religion the majority of Syrians follow a form of Islamic Sunni orthodoxy. There are also a considerable number of religious minorities: Shi'a Muslims; Ismaili Muslims; the Ismaili of the Salamiya district, whose spiritual head is the Aga Khan; a large number of Druzes, the Nusairis or Alawites of the Jebel Ansariyeh (a schism of the Shi'ite branch of Islam, to which President Assad belongs, who comprise about 11% of the population) and the Yezidis of the Jebel Sinjar, and a minority of Christians.

The Constitution states only that 'Islam shall be the religion of the head of the state'. The original draft of the 1973 Constitution made no reference to Islam at all, and this clause was inserted only as a compromise after public protest. The Syrian Constitution is thus unique among the constitutions of Arab states (excluding Lebanon) with a clear Muslim majority in not enshrining Islam as the religion of the state itself.

ISLAM
Grand Mufti: AHMAD KUFTARO.

CHRISTIANITY
Orthodox Churches
Greek Orthodox Patriarchate: His Beatitude IGNATIUS HAZIM, Patriarch of Antioch and all the Orient, BP 9, Damascus; has jurisdiction over Syria, Lebanon, Iran and Iraq.

Syrian Orthodox Patriarchate: BP 914, Bab Touma, Damascus; tel. (11) 447036; Syrian Orthodox Patriarch: His Holiness IGNATIUS ZAKKA I IWAS, Patriarch of Antioch and All the East; the Syrian Orthodox Church includes one Catholicose (of the East), 30 Metropolitans and one Bishop, and has an estimated 3m. adherents throughout the world.

The Armenian Apostolic Church is also represented in Syria.

The Roman Catholic Church

Armenian Rite

Patriarchal Exarchate of Syria: Exarchat Patriarcal Arménien Catholique, BP 22281, Bab Touma, Damascus; tel. (11) 5433438; fax (11) 5431988; f. 1985; represents the Patriarch of Cilicia (resident in Beirut, Lebanon); 4,000 adherents (31 December 2001); Exarch Patriarchal Bishop JOSEPH ARNAOUTIAN.

Archdiocese of Aleppo: Archevêché Arménien Catholique, BP 97, rue 33 at-Tilal, Aleppo; tel. (21) 2213946; fax (21) 2235303; e-mail armen.cath@mail.sy; 17,000 adherents (31 December 2000); Archbishop BOUTROS MARAYATI.

Diocese of Kamichlié: Evêché Arménien Catholique, BP 17, Al-Qamishli; tel. (53) 424211; fax (53) 426211; 4,000 adherents (31 December 2000); Bishop (vacant).

Chaldean Rite

Diocese of Aleppo: Evêché Chaldéen Catholique, BP 4643, 1 rue Patriarche Elias IV Mouawwad, Soulémaniyé, Aleppo; tel. (21) 4441660; fax (21) 4600800; 15,000 adherents (31 December 2000); Bishop ANTOINE AUDO.

Latin Rite

Apostolic Vicariate of Aleppo: BP 327, 19 rue Antaki, Aleppo; tel. (21) 2210204; fax (21) 2219031; e-mail vicariatlatin@mail.sy; f. 1644; 10,000 adherents (31 December 2000); Vicar Apostolic ARMANDO BORTOLASO, Titular Bishop of Raphanea.

Maronite Rite

Archdiocese of Aleppo: Archevêché Maronite, BP 203, 57 rue Fares-El-Khoury, Aleppo; tel. (21) 2248048; fax (21) 2248048; 4,105 adherents (31 December 2000); Archbishop YOUSSEF ANIS ABI-AAD.

Archdiocese of Damascus: Archevêché Maronite, BP 2179, 6 rue ad-Deir, Bab Touma, Damascus; tel. (11) 5430129; fax (11) 5435105; 8,000 adherents (31 December 2000); Archbishop RAYMOND EID.

Diocese of Latakia: Evêché Maronite, BP 161, rue Hamrat, Tartous; tel. (43) 223433; fax (43) 322939; 28,000 adherents (31 December 2000); Bishop MASSOUD MASSOUD.

Melkite Rite

Melkite-Greek-Catholic Patriarchate: Patriarcat Grec-Melkite Catholique, BP 22249, 12 ave az-Zeitoon, Bab Charki, Damascus; or BP 70071, Antélias, Lebanon; tel. (11) 5433129; fax (11) 5431266 (Damascus); or (4) 413111; fax (4) 525655; e-mail (Lebanon) gcp@pgc-lb.org (Antélias); jurisdiction over 1.5m. Melkites throughout the world (including 215,000 in Syria); Patriarch of Antioch, Alexandria and Jerusalem S. B. GREGOIRE III LAHAM. The Melkite Church includes the patriarchal sees of Damascus, Cairo and Jerusalem and four other archdioceses in Syria; seven archdioceses in Lebanon; one in Jordan; one in Israel; and six Eparchies (in the USA, Brazil, Canada, Australia, Venezuela and Mexico).

Archdiocese of Aleppo: Archevêché Grec-Catholique, BP 146, place Farhat, Aleppo; tel. (21) 2213218; fax (21) 2223106; e-mail gr.melkcath@mail.sy; 20,000 adherents (31 December 2000); Archbishop JEAN-CLÉMENT JEANBART.

Archdiocese of Busra and Hauran: Archevêché Grec-Catholique, Khabab, Hauran; tel. (15) 855012; 27,000 adherents (31 December 2000); Archbishop BOULOS NASSIF BORKHOCHE.

Archdiocese of Homs: Archevêché Grec-Catholique, BP 1525, rue El-Bahri, Boustan ad-Diwan, Homs; tel. (31) 482587; fax (31) 464582; e-mail melkiteh@scs-net.org; 48,000 adherents (31 December 2000); Archbishop ABRAHAM NEHMÉ.

Archdiocese of Latakia: Archevêché Grec-Catholique, BP 151, rue al-Moutannabi, Latakia; tel. (41) 460777; fax (41) 467002; 10,000 adherents (31 December 2000); Archbishop NICOLAS SAWAF.

Syrian Rite

Archdiocese of Aleppo: Archevêché Syrien Catholique, 1 rue Ibn ar-Rumi, Azizié, Aleppo; tel. (21) 2241200; fax (21) 2246651; 8,000 adherents (31 December 2000); Archbishop ANTOINE CHAHDA.

Archdiocese of Damascus: Archevêché Syrien Catholique, BP 2129, 157 rue Al-Mustaqeem, Bab Charki, Damascus; 6,400 adherents (31 December 2000); tel. and fax (11) 5432312; e-mail ftouma@mail.sy; Archbishop GREGORIOS ELIAS TABÉ.

Archdiocese of Hassaké-Nisibi: Archevêché Syrien Catholique, BP 6, Hassaké; tel. (52) 320812; fax (52) 316340; 6,320 adherents (31 December 2000); Archbishop JACQUES BEHNAN HINDO.

Archdiocese of Homs: Archevêché Syrien Catholique, BP 368, rue Hamidieh, Homs; tel. (31) 221575; 10,000 adherents (31 December 2000); Archbishop THÉOPHILE GEORGES KASSAB.

The Anglican Communion

Within the Episcopal Church in Jerusalem and the Middle East, Syria forms part of the diocese of Jerusalem (see the chapter on Israel).

Protestant

National Evangelical Synod of Syria and Lebanon: BP 70890, Antélias, Lebanon; tel. (04) 525030; fax (04) 411184; e-mail nessl@minero.net; f. 1920; 80,000 adherents (2002); Gen. Sec. Rev. ADEEB AWAD.

Union of the Armenian Evangelical Churches in the Near East: BP 110-377, Beirut, Lebanon; tel. 565628; fax 565629; e-mail uaecne@cyberia.net.lb; f. 1846 in Turkey; comprises about 30 Armenian Evangelical Churches in Syria, Lebanon, Egypt, Cyprus, Greece, Iran, Turkey and Australia; 7,500 mems (1995); Pres. Rev. MEGRDICH KARAGOEZIAN; Office Dir Pastor SEBOUH TERZIAN.

The Press

Since the Baath Arab Socialist Party came to power, the structure of the press has been modified according to socialist patterns. Most publications are issued by political, religious or professional associations (such as trade unions), and several are published by government ministries. Anyone wishing to establish a new paper or periodical must apply for a licence.

The major dailies are *Al-Baath* (the organ of the party), *Tishrin* and *Ath-Thawra* in Damascus, *Al-Jamahir al-Arabia* in Aleppo, and *Al-Fida'* in Hama.

PRINCIPAL DAILIES

Al-Baath (Renaissance): BP 9389, Autostrade Mezzeh, Damascus; tel. (11) 6622142; fax (11) 6622099; e-mail baath-n@net.sy; f. 1946; morning; Arabic; organ of the Baath Arab Socialist Party; Gen. Dir and Chief Editor TURKI SAQR; circ. 45,000.

Barq ash-Shimal (The Syrian Telegraph): rue Aziziyah, Aleppo; morning; Arabic; Editor MAURICE DJANDJI; circ. 6,400.

Al-Fida' (Redemption): Al-Wihdat Press, Printing and Publishing Organization, BP 2448, Dawar Kafr Soussat, Damascus; tel. (11) 225219; morning; Arabic; political; publishing concession holder Osman Alouini; Editor A. Aulwani; circ. 4,000.

Al-Jamahir al-Arabia (The Arab People): United Association of Journalists, BP 2448, Damascus; tel. (21) 214309; fax (21) 214308; Arabic; political; Chief Editor MORTADA BAKACH; circ. 10,000.

Al-Oroubat: Al-Wihdat Press, Printing and Publishing Organization, BP 2448, Dawar Kafr Soussat, Damascus; tel. (11) 225219; morning; Arabic; circ. 5,000.

Ash-Shabab (Youth): rue at-Tawil, Aleppo; morning; Arabic; Editor MUHAMMAD TALAS; circ. 9,000.

Syria Times: Tishrin Foundation for Press and Publication, BP 5452, Corniche Meedan, Damascus; tel. (11) 2247359; fax (11) 2247049; e-mail syriatimes@teshreen.com; internet www.teshreen.com/syriatimes; English; Editor FOUAD MARDOUD; circ. 15,000.

Ath-Thawra (Revolution): United Association of Journalists, BP 2448, Damascus; tel. (11) 2210850; fax (11) 2216851; e-mail thawra@net.sy; internet www.thawra.com; morning; Arabic; political; Editor-in-Chief (vacant); circ. 40,000.

Tishrin (October): Tishrin Foundation for Press and Publication, BP 5452, Corniche Meedan, Damascus; tel. (11) 2131100; fax (11) 2231374; e-mail daily@teshreen.com; Arabic; Chief Editor KHALAF AL-JARAAD; circ. 50,000.

Al-Wihdat (Unity): Al-Wihdat Press, Printing and Publishing Organization, Latakia; Arabic.

WEEKLIES AND FORTNIGHTLIES

Al-Ajoua' (The Air): Compagnie de l'Aviation Arabe Syrienne, BP 417, Damascus; fortnightly; Arabic; aviation; Editor AHMAD ALLOUCHE.

Ad-Doumari (Lamplighter): Damascus; f. 2001; weekly; Arabic; political satire; privately-owned; Publr ALI FARZAT.

Al-Esbou ar-Riadi (The Sports Week): Immeuble Tibi, ave Fardoss, Damascus; weekly; Arabic; sports; Asst Dir and Editor HASRAN AL-BOUNNI; circ. 14,000.

Al-Fursan (The Cavalry): Damascus; Arabic; political magazine; Editor RIFAAT AL-ASSAD.

Homs: Homs; weekly; Arabic; literary; Publisher and Dir ADIB KABA; Editor PHILIPPE KABA.

Al-Iqtisadiya: f. 2001; weekly; Arabic; economic; privately-owned; Editor WADDAH ABD AR-RABBO.

Jaysh ash-Sha'ab (The People's Army): Ministry of Defence, BP 3320, blvd Palestine, Damascus; f. 1946; fortnightly; Arabic; army magazine; published by the Political Department of the Syrian Army.

Kifah al-Oummal al-Ishtiraki (The Socialist Workers' Struggle): Fédération Générale des Syndicats des Ouvriers, rue Qanawat, Damascus; weekly; Arabic; labour; published by General Federation of Labour Unions; Editor SAID AL-HAMAMI.

Al-Masirah (Progress): Damascus; weekly; Arabic; political; published by Federation of Youth Organizations.

Al-Maukef ar-Riadi (Sport Stance): Al-Wihdat Press, Printing and Publishing Organization, BP 2448, Dawar Kafr Soussat, Damascus; tel. (11) 225219; weekly; Arabic; sports; published by Al-Wihdat Press, Printing and Publishing Organization; circ. 50,000.

An-Nas (The People): BP 926, Aleppo; f. 1953; weekly; Arabic; Publisher VICTOR KALOUS.

Nidal al-Fellahin (Peasants' Struggle): Fédération Générale des Laboureurs, BP 9389, Autostrade Mezzeh, Damascus; weekly; Arabic; peasant workers; Editor MANSOUR ABU AL-HOSN; circ. 8,100.

Ar-Riada (Sport): BP 292, near Electricity Institute, Damascus; weekly; Arabic; sports; Dir NOUREDDINE RIAL; Publisher and Editor OURFANE UBARI.

As-Sakafat al-Usbouiya (Weekly Culture): BP 2570, Soukak as-Sakr, Damascus; weekly; Arabic; cultural; Publisher, Dir and Editor MADHAT AKKACHE.

Sawt ash-Shaab (Voice of the People): Damascus; f. 1937, but publication suspended in 1939, 1941, 1947 and 1958; relaunched in 2001; fortnightly; Arabic; organ of the Communist Party of Syria.

Tishrin al–Usbouiya (October Weekly): Damascus; e-mail weekly@teshreen.com; weekly.

Al-Wehdawi (Unionist): Damascus; f. 2001; weekly; Arabic; organ of the Arab Socialist Unionist Party.

Al-Yanbu al-Jadid (New Spring): Immeuble Al-Awkaf, Homs; weekly; Arabic; literary; Publisher, Dir and Editor MAMDOU AL-KOUSSEIR.

OTHER PERIODICALS

Al-Arabieh (The Arab Lady): Syrian Women's Association, BP 3207, Damascus; tel. (11) 3316560; monthly; Editor S. BAKOUR.

Ad-Dad: rue Tital, Wakf al-Moiriné Bldg, Aleppo; monthly; Arabic; literary; Dir RIAD HALLAK; Publisher and Editor ABDULLAH YARKI HALLAK.

Ecos: BP 3320, Damascus; monthly; Spanish; general.

Al-Fikr al-Askari (The Military Idea): BP 4259, blvd Palestine, Damascus; f. 1950; 6 a year; Arabic; official military review published by the Political Dept of the Syrian Army; Editor NAKHLE KALLAS.

Flash: BP 3320, Damascus; monthly; English and French; general.

Al-Ghad (Tomorrow): Association of Red Cross and Crescent, BP 6095, rue Maysat, Damascus; tel. (11) 2242552; fax (11) 7777040; monthly; environmental health; Editor K. ABED-RABOU.

Al-Irshad az-Zirai (Agricultural Information): Ministry of Agriculture and Agrarian Reform, rue Jabri, Damascus; tel. (11) 2213613; fax (11) 2216627; 6 a year; Arabic; agriculture.

Al-Jundi al-Arabi (The Arab Soldier): BP 3320, blvd Palestine, Damascus; monthly; published by the Political Department of the Syrian Army.

Al-Kalima (The Word): Al-Kalima Association, Aleppo; monthly; Arabic; religious; Publisher and Editor FATHALLA SAKAL.

Al-Kanoun (The Law): Ministry of Justice, rue an-Nasreh, Damascus; tel. (11) 2214105; fax (11) 2246250; monthly; Arabic; juridical.

Al-Maaloumatieh (Information): National Information Centre, BP 11323, Damascus; tel. (11) 2127551; fax (11) 2127648; e-mail nice@net.sy; f. 1994; quarterly; computer magazine; Editor ABD AL-MAJID AR-RIFAI; circ. 10,000.

Al-Ma'arifa (Knowledge): Ministry of Culture, rue ar-Rouda, Damascus; tel. (11) 3336963; f. 1962; monthly; Arabic; literary; Editor ABD AL-KARIM NASIF; circ. 7,500.

Al-Majalla al-Batriarquia (The Magazine of the Patriarchate): Syrian Orthodox Patriarchate, BP 914, Damascus; tel. (11) 4447036; f. 1962; monthly; Arabic; religious; Editor SAMIR ABDOH; circ. 15,000.

Al-Majalla at-Tibbiya al-Arabiyya (Arab Medical Magazine): rue al-Jala'a, Damascus; monthly; Arabic; published by Arab Medical Commission; Dir Dr Y. SAKA; Editor Prof. ADNAN TAKRITI.

Majallat Majma' al-Lughat al-Arabiyya bi-Dimashq (Magazine of the Arab Language Academy of Damascus): Arab Academy of Damascus, BP 327, Damascus; tel. (11) 3713145; fax (11) 3733363; e-mail mla@net.sy; f. 1921; quarterly; Arabic; Islamic culture and Arabic literature, Arabic scientific and cultural terminology; Chief Editor Dr SHAKER FAHAM; circ. 1,600.

Al-Mawkif al-Arabi (The Arab Situation): Ittihab al-Kuttab al-Arab, rue Murshid Khatir, Damascus; monthly; Arabic; literary.

Monthly Survey of Arab Economics: BP 2306, Damascus; BP 6068, Beirut; f. 1958; monthly; English and French editions; published by Centre d'Etudes et de Documentation Economiques, Financières et Sociales; Dir Dr CHAFIC AKHRAS.

Al-Mouallem al-Arabi (The Arab Teacher): National Union of Teachers, BP 2842-3034, Damascus; tel. (11) 225219; f. 1948; monthly; Arabic; educational and cultural.

Al-Mouhandis al-Arabi (The Arab Engineer): Order of Syrian Engineers and Architects, BP 2336, Immeuble Dar al-Mouhandisen, place Azme, Damascus; tel. (11) 2214916; fax (11) 2216948; e-mail @lbosea@net.sy; f. 1961; 4 a year; Arabic; scientific and cultural; Dir Eng. M. FAYEZ MAHFOUZ; Chief Editor Dr Eng. AHMAD AL-GHAFARI; circ. 50,000.

Al-Munadel (The Militant): c/o BP 11512, Damascus; fax (11) 2126935; f. 1965; monthly; Arabic; magazine of Baath Arab Socialist Party; Dir Dr FAWWAZ SAYYAGH; circ. 100,000.

An-Nashra al-Iktissad (Economic Bulletin): Damascus Chamber of Commerce; tel. (11) 2218339; fax (11) 2225874; e-mail dcc@net.sy; f. 1922; quarterly; finance and investment; Editor GHASSAN KALLA; circ. 3,000.

Risalat al-Kimia (Chemistry Report): BP 669, Immeuble al-Abid, Damascus; monthly; Arabic; scientific; Publisher, Dir and Editor HASSAN AS-SAKA.

Saut al-Forat: Deir ez-Zor; monthly; Arabic; literary; Publisher, Dir and Editor ABD AL-KADER AYACHE.

Ash-Shourta (The Police): Directorate of Public Affairs and Moral Guidance, Damascus; monthly; Arabic; juridical.

As-Sinaa (Industry): Damascus Chamber of Commerce, BP 1305, rue Mou'awiah, Harika, Damacus; tel. (11) 2222205; fax (11) 2245981; monthly; commerce, industry and management; Editor Y. HINDI.

Souriya al-Arabiyya (Arab Syria): Ministry of Information, Immeuble Dar al-Baath, Autostrade Mezzeh, Damascus; tel. (11) 6622141; fax (11) 6617665; monthly; publicity; in four languages.

At-Tamaddon al-Islami (Islamic Civilization Society): Darwichiyah, Damascus; tel. (11) 2215120; fax (11) 2233815, e-mail raweyah@cyberia.net.lb; f. 1932; monthly; Arabic; religious; published by At-Tamaddon al-Islami Association; Pres. of Asscn AHMAD MOUAZ AL-KHATIB.

At-Taqa Wattanmiya (Energy and Expansion): BP 7748, rue al-Moutanabbi, Damascus; tel. (11) 233529; monthly; Arabic; published by the Syrian Petroleum Co.

Al-Yakza (The Awakening): Al-Yakza Association, BP 6677, rue Sisi, Aleppo; f. 1935; monthly; Arabic; literary social review of charitable institution; Dir HUSNI ABD AL-MASSIH; circ. 12,000.

Az-Zira'a (Agriculture): Ministry of Agriculture and Agrarian Reform, rue Jabri, Damascus; tel. (11) 2213613; fax (11) 2244023; f. 1985; monthly; Arabic; agriculture; circ. 12,000.

PRESS AGENCIES

Syrian Arab News Agency (SANA): BP 2661, Baramka, Damascus; tel (11) 2228239; fax (11) 2220365; e-mail sana@net.sy; internet www.sana-syria.com; f. 1966; supplies bulletins on Syrian news to foreign news agencies; 14 offices abroad; 14 foreign correspondents; Dir-Gen. GHAZI AD-DIB.

Foreign Bureaux

Agencia EFE (Spain): Damascus; Correspondent ZACHARIAS SARME.

Agence France-Presse (AFP): BP 2400, Immeuble Adel Charaj, place du 17 avril, Damascus; tel. (11) 428253; Correspondent JOSEPH GHASI.

Agenzia Nazionale Stampa Associata (ANSA) (Italy): Hotel Méridien, BP 2712, Damascus; tel. (11) 233116; f. 1962; Correspondent ABDULLAH SAADEL.

Allgemeiner Deutscher Nachrichtendienst (ADN) (Germany): Damascus; tel. (11) 332093; Correspondent FRANK HERRMANN.

Associated Press (AP) (USA): c/o Hotel Méridien, BP 2712, Damascus; tel. (11) 233116; internet www.ap.org.

Deutsche Presse-Agentur (dpa) (Germany): c/o Hotel Méridien, BP 2712, Damascus; tel. (11) 332924.

Kuwait News Agency (KUNA) and Reuters (UK) are also represented in Syria.

Publishers

Arab Advertising Organization: BP 2842-3034, 28 rue Moutanabbi, Damascus; tel. (11) 2225219; fax (11) 2220754; e-mail sy-adv@net.sy; internet www.elan-sy.com; f. 1963; exclusive government establishment responsible for advertising; publishes *Directory of Commerce and Industry, Damascus International Fair Guide, Daily Bulletin of Official Tenders*; Dir-Gen. TALEB QADI AMIN.

Damascus University Press: Damascus; tel. (11) 2215100; fax (11) 2236010; f. 1946; arts, geography, education, history, engineering, medicine, law, sociology, social sciences; Dir HUSSEIN OMRAN.

Institut Français d'Etudes arabes de Damas: BP 344, Damascus; tel. (11) 3330214; fax (11) 3327887; e-mail ifead@net.sy; internet www.univ-aix.fr/ifead; f. 1922; sociology, anthropology, Islamic archaeology, history, language, arts, philosophy, poetry, geography, religion; Dir FLORÉAL SANAGUSTIN.

OFA-Business Consulting Center—Documents Service: BP 3550, 67 place Chahbandar, Damascus; tel. (11) 3318237; fax (11) 4426021; e-mail ofa@net.sy; internet www.ofa-holding.com; f. 1964; numerous periodicals, monographs and surveys on political and economic affairs; Dir-Gen. SAMIR A. DARWICH. Has two affiliated branches, OFA-Business Consulting Centre (foreign company representation and services) and OFA-Renseignements Commerciaux (Commercial enquiries on firms and persons in Syria).

The Political Administration Press: BP 3320, blvd Palestine, Damascus; publishes *Al-Fikr al-Askari* (6 a year) and *Jaysh ash-Sha'ab* (fortnightly) and *Al-Jundi al-Arabi* (monthly).

Syrian Documentation Papers: BP 2712, Damascus; f. 1968; publishers of *Bibliography of the Middle East* (annual), *General Directory of the Press and Periodicals in the Arab World* (annual), and numerous publications on political, economic, literary and social affairs, as well as legislative texts concerning Syria and the Arab world; Dir-Gen. LOUIS FARÈS.

United Association of Journalists: BP 2448, Damascus; tel. (11) 2210850; fax (11) 2216851; publishes *Al-Jamahir al-Arabia* and *Ath-Thawra* (dailies).

Al-Wihdat Press, Printing and Publishing Organization (Institut al-Ouedha pour l'impression, édition et distribution): BP 2448, Dawar Kafr Soussat, Damascus; tel. (11) 225219; publishes *Al-Ouroubat, Al-Fida'* and *Al-Wihdat* (dailies), *al-Maukef ar-Riadi* (weekly) and other commercial publications; Dir-Gen. FAHD DIYAB.

Broadcasting and Communications

TELECOMMUNICATIONS

Syrian Telecommunications Establishment (STE): rue Mezzeh, Damascus; tel. (11) 6122400; fax (11) 6121240; e-mail ste-gm@syriatel.net; internet www.syriatel.net; f. 1975; Chair. (vacant).

BROADCASTING
Radio

Directorate-General of Radio and Television: place Omayyad, Damascus; tel. (11) 720700; f. 1945; broadcasts in Arabic, French, English, Russian, German, Spanish, Portuguese, Hebrew, Polish, Turkish, Bulgarian; Dir-Gen. KHUDR OMRAN; Dir SAFWAN GHANIM.

Television

Directorate-General of Radio and Television: (see Radio); services started in 1960; Dir-Gen. Dr FAYEZ AS-SAYEGH; Dir of Television: M. ABD AS-SALAM HIJAB.

Finance

(cap. = capital; res = reserves; dep. = deposits;
m. = million; brs = branches; amounts in £S)

BANKING
Central Bank

Central Bank of Syria: BP 2254, place At-Tajrida al-Mughrabia, Damascus; tel. (11) 2212642; fax (11) 2213076; e-mail mrksybabn @mail.sy; internet www.syrecon.org; f. 1956; cap. 10m., dep. 391,275m., total assets 773356m. (Dec. 2001); Gov. Dr MUHAMMAD BASHAR KABBARA; 11 brs.

Other Banks

Agricultural Co-operative Bank: BP 4325, rue at-Tajehiz, Damascus; tel. (11) 2213461; fax (11) 2241261; f. 1888; Chair. and Dir-Gen. Dr ALI ARAFAT; 106 brs.

Commercial Bank of Syria: BP 933, place Yousuf al-Azmeh, Damascus; tel. (11) 2218890; fax (11) 2216975; e-mail cbos@mail.sy; f. 1967; govt-owned bank; cap. and res 8,197m., dep. 309,545m., total assets 743,000m. (Dec. 2001); Chair. MAHMOUD NADIM MISKAL; Dep. Chair. and Gen. Man. TARREK SARRAJ; 53 brs.

Industrial Bank: BP 7578, Immeuble Dar al-Mohandessin, rue Maysaloon, Damascus; tel. (11) 2228200; fax (11) 2228412; f. 1959; nationalized bank providing finance for industry; cap. 100m.; Chair. ABD AL-QADIR OBEIDO; 13 brs.

Popular Credit Bank: BP 2841, 6e étage, Immeuble Dar al-Mohandessin, rue Maysaloon, Damascus; tel. (11) 2227604; fax (11) 2211291; f. 1967; government bank; provides loans to the services sector and is sole authorized issuer of savings certificates; cap. 25m., dep. 2,313m., res 42,765m. (Dec. 1984); Pres. and Gen. Man. MUHAMMAD HASSAN AL-HOUJJEIRI; 50 brs.

Real Estate Bank: BP 2337, place Yousuf al-Azmeh, Damascus; tel. (11) 2218602; fax (11) 2237938; f. 1966; govt-owned bank; provides loans and grants for housing, schools, hospitals and hotel construction; cap. 1,000m. (Dec. 1999); Chair. and Gen. Man. MUHAMMAD AHMAD MAKHLOUF; 13 brs.

Syrian Lebanese Commercial Bank SAL: BP 118701-1135127, Damascus; fax (11) 2243224; Chair. and Gen. Man. MAHMOUD NADIM MISKAI.

INSURANCE

Syrian General Organization for Insurance (Syrian Insurance Co): BP 2279, 29 rue Ayyar, Damascus; tel. (11) 2218430; fax (11) 2220494; f. 1953; auth. cap. 1,000m.; a nationalized company; operates throughout Syria; Chair. and Gen. Man. GHASSAN BAROUDIT; Assistant Gen. Man.and Admin. Dir SULAYMAN AL-HASSAN.

Trade and Industry

STATE ENTERPRISES

Syrian industry is almost entirely controlled and run by the State. There are national organizations responsible to the appropriate ministry for the operation of all sectors of industry, of which the following are examples:

Cotton Marketing Organization: BP 729, rue Bab al-Faraj, Aleppo; tel. (21) 2238486; fax (21) 2218617; f. 1965; governmental authority for purchase of seed cotton, ginning and sales of cotton lint; Pres. and Dir-Gen. Dr AHMAD SOUHAD GEBBARA.

General Company for Phosphate and Mines (GECOPHAM): BP 288, Homs; tel. (31) 420405; fax (31) 412961; e-mail gecopham@ net.sy; f. 1970; production and export of phosphate rock; Gen. Dir Eng. FARHAN AL-HUHSSIN.

General Organization for the Exploitation and Development of the Euphrates Basin (GOEDEB): Raqqa; Dir-Gen. Dr Eng. Dr AHMAD SOUHAD GEBBARA.

General Organization for Food Industries (GOFI): BP 105, rue al-Fardous, Damascus; tel. (11) 2225290; fax (11) 2245374; e-mail foodindustry@mail.sy; f. 1975; food-processing and marketing; Chair. and Gen. Dir KHALIL JAWAD.

General Organization for the Textile Industries: BP 620, rue Fardoss, Damascus; tel. (11) 2216200; fax (11) 2216201; f. 1975; control and planning of the textile industry and supervision of textile manufacture; 13 subsidiary cos.; Dir-Gen. MOUSTAFA JAWEESH.

Syrian Petroleum Company (SPC): BP 2849, rue al-Moutanabbi, Damascus; tel. (11) 2228298; fax (11) 2225648; f. 1958; state agency; holds the oil and gas concession for all Syria; exploits the Suweidiya, Karatchouk, Rumelan and Jbeisseh oilfields; also organizes exploring, production and marketing of oil and gas nationally; Dir-Gen. Dr Eng. MUHAMMAD KHADDOUR.

Al-Furat Petroleum Company: BP 7660, Damascus; tel. (11) 6183333; fax (11) 6184444; e-mail afpc@afpc.net.sy; internet www.afpc-sy.com; f. 1985; owned 50% by SPC and 50% by a foreign consortium of Syria Shell Petroleum Development B.V. and Deminex Syria GmbH; exploits oilfields in the Euphrates river area; Chair. HAITHAM GHANEM; Gen. Man. JOHN MALCOLM.

DEVELOPMENT ORGANIZATIONS

State Planning Commission: Parliament Square, Damascus.

Syrian Consulting Bureau for Development and Investment: Damascus; independent; Chair. NABIL SUKKAR.

CHAMBERS OF COMMERCE

Federation of Syrian Chambers of Commerce: BP 5909, rue Mousa Ben Nousair, Damascus; tel. (11) 3337344; fax (11) 3331127; e-mail syr-trade@mail.sy; internet www.fedcommsyr.org; f. 1975; Pres. Dr RATEB ASH-SHALLAH; Gen. Sec. Dr ABD AR-RAHMAN AL-ATTAR.

Aleppo Chamber of Commerce: BP 1261, Aleppo; tel. (21) 2238236; fax (21) 2213493; e-mail alepchmb@mail.sy; internet www.aleppochamber.com; f. 1885; Pres. M. SALEH AL-MALLAH; Sec. MUHAMMAD MANSOUR.

Alkalamoun Chamber of Commerce: BP 2507, rue Bucher A. Mawla, Damascus; fax (11) 778394; Pres. M. SOUFAN.

Damascus Chamber of Commerce: BP 1040, rue Mou'awiah, Damascus; tel. (11) 2211339; fax (11) 2225874; e-mail dcc@net.sy; internet www.dcc-sy.com; f. 1890; Pres. Dr RATEB ASH-SHALLAH; Gen. Dir HISHAM AL-HAMWY; 11,500 mems.

Hama Chamber of Commerce and Industry: BP 147, rue al-Kouatly, Hama; tel. (33) 233304; fax (33) 517701; e-mail ham -coci@net.sy; f. 1934; Pres. IZZAT AL-HABBAL; Dir ABD AR-RAZZAK AL-HAIT.

Homs Chamber of Commerce and Industry: BP 440, rue Abou al-Of, Homs; tel. (31) 471000; fax (31) 464247; e-mail hcc-i@net.sy; internet www.homschamber.org; f. 1938; Pres. Dr Eng. TARIF AKHRAS; Dir M. FARES AL-HUSSAMY.

Latakia Chamber of Commerce: rue al-Hurriyah, Latakia; Pres. JULE NASRI.

CHAMBERS OF INDUSTRY

Aleppo Chamber of Industry: BP 1859, rue al-Moutanabbi, Aleppo; tel. (21) 339812; f. 1935; Pres. MUHAMMAD M. OUBARI; 7,000 mems.

Damascus Chamber of Industry: BP 1305, rue Harika Mou'awiah, Damascus; tel. (11) 2215042; fax (11) 2245981; Pres. Dr YEHYA AL-HINDI; Dir-Gen. Dr ABD AL-HAMID MALAKANI.

EMPLOYERS' ORGANIZATIONS

Fédération Générale à Damas: Damascus; f. 1951; Dir TALAT TAGLUBI.

Fédération de Damas: Damascus; f. 1949.

Fédération des Patrons et Industriels à Lattaquié: Latakia; f. 1953.

Order of Syrian Engineers and Architects: BP 2336, Immeuble Al Mohandessin, place Azmeh, Damascus; tel. (11) 2214916; fax (11) 2216948; e-mail @lbosea@net.sy; Pres. M. FAYEZ MAHFOUZ.

UTILITIES
Electricity

Public Establishment for Electricity Generation and Transmission (PEEGT): BP 3386, rue Nessan 17, Damascus; tel. (11) 2223086; fax (11) 2229062; e-mail peegt@net.sy; internet www.peegt-syria.org; f. 1965; renamed 1994; state-owned; operates eleven power stations through subsidiary companies; Dir-Gen. Dr A. AL-ALI.

TRADE UNIONS

Ittihad Naqabat al-'Ummal al-'Am fi Suriya (General Federation of Labour Unions): BP 2351, rue Qanawat, Damascus; f. 1948; Chair. 'IZZ AD-DIN NASIR; Sec. MAHMOUD FAHURI.

Transport

RAILWAYS

In 1998 the railway system totalled 2,450 km of track.

Syrian Railways: BP 182, Aleppo; tel. (21) 2213900; fax (21) 2228480; e-mail cfs.syria@net.sy; f. 1897; Pres. and Dir-Gen. Eng. MUHAMMAD IYAD GHAZAL.

General Organization of the Hedjaz-Syrian Railway: BP 134, place Hedjaz, Damascus; tel. (11) 2215815; fax (11) 2227106; f. 1908; the Hedjaz Railway has 347 km of track (gauge 1,050 mm) in Syria; services operate between Damascus and Amman, on a branch line of about 24 km from Damascus to Katana, and there is a further line of 64 km from Damascus to Serghaya; Dir-Gen. S. AHMED.

ROADS

Arterial roads run across the country linking the north to the south and the Mediterranean to the eastern frontier. At 31 December 1999 Syria's total road network was 43,381 km, including 31,189 km of highways, main or national roads and 9,191 km of secondary or regional roads. In 1996 work was scheduled to commence on the first stage of a project costing £S1,800m. to improve the road linking Rakka with Deir ez-Zor. In 2001 the Syrian Government awarded a contract for the construction of a 100-km, four-lane highway, connecting the eastern port town of Latakia with Ariba in the northern governorate of Aleppo, at an estimated cost of US $207m. The project was to be financed by loans from the Kuwaiti-based Arab Fund for Economic and Social Development (AFESD) and the Kuwait Fund for Arab Economic Development (KFAED).

General Co for Roads: BP 3143, Aleppo; tel. (21) 555406; f. 1975; Gen. Man. Eng. M. WALID EL-AJLANI.

PIPELINES

The oil pipelines that cross Syrian territory are of great importance to the national economy, representing a considerable source of foreign exchange. In the late 1990s a number of gas pipelines, linking gas fields in the Palmyra area to Aleppo and Lebanon, were under construction.

Syrian Co for Oil Transport (SCOT): BP 13, Banias; tel. (43) 711300; fax (43) 710418; f. 1972; Dir-Gen. MUHAMMAD DOUBA.

SHIPPING

Latakia is the principal port; the other major ports are at Banias and Tartous. A project to expand the capacities of Latakia and Tartous, and to construct new port facilities near Tartous, commenced in 1997.

General Directorate of Syrian Ports: BP 505, Latakia; tel. (41) 473333; fax (41) 475805; Dir-Gen. ALI RAZZOUK.

Syrian General Organization for Maritime Transport: BP 730, 2 rue Argentina, Damascus; tel. (11) 2226350.

Abdulkader, Abu Bakr: Arwad, Latakia; operates a fleet of 5 general cargo vessels.

Delta Marine Transport: rue de Baghdad, Latakia; tel. (41) 222426; fax (41) 222760.

Ismail, A. M., Shipping Agency Ltd: BP 74, rue Marilyas, Tartous; tel. (43) 220543; operates 8 general cargo vessels; Man. Dir MAHMOUD ISMAIL.

Muhieddine Shipping Co: BP 779, rue du Port, Tartous; tel. (43) 220510; fax (43) 317139; operates 7 general cargo ships.

Riamar Shipping Co Ltd: Al Kornish ash-Sharki, BP 284, Immeuble Tarwin, rue du Port, Tartous; tel. (43) 314999; fax (43) 212616; e-mail tarekg@scs-net.org; operates 6 general cargo vessels; Chair. and Man. Dir ABD AL-KADER SABRA.

Samin Shipping Co Ltd: BP 315, rue al-Mina, Tartous; tel. (43) 318835; fax (43) 318834; operates 10 general cargo ships.

Syro-Jordanian Shipping Co: BP 148, rue Port Said, Latakia; tel. (41) 471635; fax (41) 470250; e-mail syjomar@net.sy; f. 1976; operates 2 general cargo ships; transported 70,551 metric tons of goods in 1992; Chair. OSMAN LEBBADY; Tech. Man. M. CHOUMAN.

CIVIL AVIATION

There is an international airport at Damascus, and the upgrading of Aleppo airport, to enable it to handle international traffic, is planned.

Directorate-General of Civil Aviation: BP 6257, place Nejmeh, Damascus; tel. (11) 3331306; fax (11) 2232201.

Syrian Arab Airlines (Syrianair): BP 417, 5th Floor, Social Insurance Bldg, Youssef al-Azmeh Sq., Damascus; tel. (11) 2220700; fax (11) 224923; e-mail syr-air@syriatel.net; f. 1946, refounded 1961 to succeed Syrian Airways, after revocation of merger with Misrair; domestic passenger and cargo services (from Damascus, Aleppo, Latakia and Deir ez-Zor) and routes to Europe, the Middle East, North Africa and the Far East; Chair. and Man. Dir Capt. ADNAN ANWAR SHUJAA.

Tourism

Syria's tourist attractions include a pleasant Mediterranean coastline, the mountains, town bazaars and antiquities of Damascus and Palmyra, as well as hundreds of deserted ancient villages in the north-west of the country. In 2000 some 3m. tourists visited Syria, generating estimated revenues of US $474m.

Ministry of Tourism: Barada St, Damascus; tel. (11) 2233183; e-mail min-tourism@mail.sy; internet www.syriatourism.org; f. 1972; Counsellor to the Minister Mrs SAWSAN JOUZY.

Middle East Tourism: BP 201, rue Fardoss, Damascus; tel. (11) 2211876; fax (11) 2246545; f. 1954; Pres. MUHAMMAD DADOUCHE; 7 brs.

Syrian Arab Co for Hotels and Tourism (SACHA): BP 5549, Mezzeh, Damascus; tel. (11) 2223286; fax (11) 2219415; f. 1977; Chair. DIRAR JUMA'A; Gen. Man. ELIAS ABOUTARA.

Defence

Commander-in-Chief of the Armed Forces: Lt-Gen. BASHAR AL-ASSAD.

Minister of Defence and Deputy Commander-in-Chief of the Armed Forces: Maj.-Gen. MUSTAFA TLASS.

Chief of Staff of the Armed Forces: Maj.-Gen. HASSAN AT-TURKMANI.

Air Force Commander: Gen. MUHAMMAD AL-KHOULI.

Special Forces Commander: Gen. ALI HABIB.

Defence Budget (2001): £S44,000m.

Military Service: 30 months (Jewish population exempted).

Total Armed Forces (August 2001): (estimated) 321,000 (army (estimated) 215,000, air defence command (an army command; estimated) 60,000, navy (estimated) 6,000, air force 40,000); reserves 354,000 (army 280,000; air force 70,000; navy 4,000).

Paramilitary Forces: (estimated) 108,000 (Gendarmerie—under control of Ministry of Interior—8,000, Baath Party Workers' Militia (estimated) 100,000).

Education

Primary education, which begins at six years of age and lasts for six years, is officially compulsory. In 1996/97 there were 2,690,205 pupils in primary education, equivalent to 91% of children in the relevant age-group (males 95%; females 87%). Secondary education, beginning at 12 years of age, lasts for a further six years, comprising two cycles of three years each. In 1996/97 there were 957,664 pupils in secondary education, equivalent to 38% of children in the relevant age-group (males 40%; females 36%). By 1999/2000 the number of pupils at the primary level had risen to 2,774,922 (males 1,470,800; females 1,304,122), while the number of pupils in general secondary education (excluding vocational courses) was 955,272 (males 511,702; females 443,570).

There are agicultural and technical schools for vocational training, and higher education is provided by the universities of Damascus, Aleppo, Tishrin (the October University, in Latakia) and Homs (the Baath University, formerly the Homs Institute of Petroleum). There were 167,186 students enrolled at the universities in 1994/95. The main language of instruction in schools is Arabic, but English and French are widely taught as second languages. Expenditure on education by all levels of government in 1996 amounted to £S25,555m.

Bibliography

Abd-Allah, Dr Umar. *The Islamic Struggle in Syria*. Berkeley, Mizan Press, 1984.

Abu Jaber, Kamal S. *The Arab Baath Socialist Party*. New York, Syracuse University Press, 1966.

Asfour, Edmund Y. *Syrian Development and Monetary Policy*. Harvard, 1959.

Batatu, Hanna. *Syria's Peasantry, the Descendants of its Lesser Rural Notables, and Their Politics*. NJ, Princeton University Press, 1999.

Davis, Scott C. *The Road from Damascus: A Journey through Syria*. Seattle, Cune Press, 2002.

Degeorge, Gérard. *Syrie*. Paris, Editions Hermann.

Devlin, John F. *Syria: A Profile*. London, Croom Helm, 1982.

Drysdale, Alastair, and Hinnebusch, Raymond A. *Syria and the Middle East Peace Process*. New York, Council on Foreign Relations, 1992.

Ehteshami, A., and Hinnebusch, R. *Syria and Iran: Middle Powers in a Penetrated Regional System*. London, Routledge, 1997.

Fedden, Robin. *Syria: an Historical Appreciation*. London, 1946.

Syria and Lebanon. London, John Murray, 1966.

Glubb, J. B. *Syria, Lebanon, Jordan*. London, Thames and Hudson, 1967.

Haddad, J. *Fifty Years of Modern Syria and Lebanon*. Beirut, 1950.

Helbaoui, Youssef. *La Syrie*. Paris, 1956.

Heydemann, Steven. *Authoritarianism in Syria: Institutions and Social Conflict, 1946–1970*. Ithaca, NY, Cornell University Press, 1998.

Hinnebusch, Raymond E. *Authoritarian Power and State Formation in Ba'thist Syria: army, party and peasant*. Oxford, Westview Press, 1990.

Hitti, Philip K. *History of Syria; including Lebanon and Palestine*. New York, 1951.

Homet, M. *L'Histoire secrète du traité franco-syrien*. New edn, Paris, 1951.

Hopwood, Derek. *The Russian presence in Syria and Palestine 1843–1914*. Oxford, 1969.

Hourani, Albert H. *Syria and Lebanon: A Political Essay*. New York, 1946.

Hureau, Jean. *La Syrie aujourd'hui*. Paris, Editions Afrique.

Kienle, Eberhard (Ed.). *Contemporary Syria: Liberalization between Cold War and Cold Peace*. London, I. B. Tauris, 1994.

Lawson, Fred H. *Why Syria Goes to War: Thirty Years of Confrontation*. Cornell University Press, 1996.

Lloyd-George, D. *The Truth about the Peace Treaties, Vol. II.* (London, 1938).

Longrigg, S. H. *Syria and Lebanon Under French Mandate*. Oxford University Press, 1958.

Ma'oz, Moshe. *Syria and Israel: from war to peace-making*. Oxford University Press, 1995.

Mirza, Nasseh Ahmad. *Syrian Isma'ilism: The Ever Living Line of Imamate AD 1100–1260*. Richmond, Curzon Press, 1996.

Perthes, Volker. *The Political Economy of Syria Under Asad*. London, I. B. Tauris, 1995.

Petran, Tabitha. *Syria*. London, Benn, 1972.

Pipes, Daniel. *Greater Syria: the History of an Ambition*. New York, Oxford Unversity Press, 1990.

Rabinovich, Itamar. *The Brink of Peace. The Israeli-Syrian Negotiations*. Princeton University Press, 1999.

Rabbath, E. *Unité Syrienne et Devenir Arabe*. Paris, 1937.

Rathmell, Andrew. *Secret War in the Middle East: The Covert Struggle for Syria, 1949-1961*. London, I. B. Tauris, 1995.

Runciman, Steven. *A History of the Crusades*. London, Vol. I 1951, Vol. II 1952.

Seale, Patrick and Hourani, Albert. *The Struggle for Syria*. London, I. B. Tauris, 1986.

Springett, B. H. *Secret Sects of Syria and the Lebanon*. London 1922.

Stark, Freya. *Letters from Syria*. London, 1942.

Thubron, C. A. *Mirror to Damascus*. London, Heinemann, 1967.

Tibawi, A. L. *Syria*. London, 1962.

American Interests in Syria 1800–1901. New York, Oxford University Press, 1966.

A Modern History of Syria. London, Macmillan, 1969.

Torrey, Gordon H. *Syrian Politics and the Military*. Ohio, State University, 1964.

Tritton, A. S. *The Caliphs and their Non-Muslim Subjects*. London, 1930.

Van Dam, Nikolaos. *The Struggle for Power in Syria*. London, Croom Helm, 1979.

Weulersse, J. *Paysans de Syrie et du Proche Orient*. Paris, 1946.

Yamak, L. Z. *The Syrian Social Nationalist Party*. Cambridge, MA, Harvard University Press, 1966.

Ziadeh, N. *Syria and Lebanon*. New York, Praeger, 1957.

Zisser, Eyal. *Asad's Legacy: Syria in Transition*. London, C. Hurst & Co, 2000.

TUNISIA

Physical and Social Geography

D. R. HARRIS

Tunisia is the smallest of the countries that comprise the 'Maghreb' of North Africa, but it is more cosmopolitan than Algeria or Morocco. It forms a wedge of territory, 163,610 sq km (63,170 sq miles) in extent, between Algeria and Libya. It includes the easternmost ridges of the Atlas Mountains but most of the country is low-lying and bordered by a long and sinuous Mediterranean coastline that faces both north and east. Ease of access by sea and by land from the east has favoured the penetration of foreign influences and Tunisia owes its distinct national identity and its varied cultural traditions to a succession of invading peoples: Phoenicians, Romans, Arabs, Turks and French. It was more effectively arabized than either Algeria or Morocco and remnants of the original Berber-speaking population of the Maghreb are confined, in Tunisia, to a few isolated localities in the south.

At the April 1994 census the population was 8,785,364 and the overall density was 57.9 per sq km. Most of the people live in the more humid, northern part of the country, and at the 1994 census about 7.7% (674,100) lived in Tunis. Situated where the Sicilian Channel links the western with the central Mediterranean and close to the site of ancient Carthage, Tunis combines the functions of capital and chief port. No other town approaches Tunis in importance, but on the east coast both Sousse (population 125,000 in 1994) and Sfax (population 230,900) provide modern port facilities, as does Bizerta (population 98,900) on the north coast, while some distance inland the old Arab capital and holy city of Qairawan, now known as Kairouan (population 102,600), serves as a regional centre. Other sizeable towns include Ariana (152,700), Ettadhamen (149,200) and Gabès (98,900). The population had reached an estimated 9,673,000 by mid-2001.

The principal contrasts in the physical geography of Tunisia are between a humid and relatively mountainous northern region, a semi-arid central expanse of low plateaux and plains, and a dry Saharan region in the south. The northern region is dominated by the easternmost folds of the Atlas mountain system which form two separate chains, the Northern and High Tell, separated by the valley of the River Medjerda, the only perennially flowing river in the country. The Northern Tell, which is a continuation of the Algerian Tell Atlas, extends along the north coast at heights of between 300 m and 600 m. South of the Medjerda valley lies the broader Tell Atlas, which is a continuation of the Saharan Atlas of Algeria, and comprises a succession of rugged sandstone and limestone ridges. Near the

Algerian frontier these reach a maximum height of 1,544 m at Djebel Chambi, the highest point in Tunisia, but die away eastward towards the Cap Bon peninsula, which extends northeast to within 145 km of Sicily.

South of the High Tell or Dorsale ('backbone') central Tunisia consists of an extensive platform sloping gently towards the east coast. Its western half, known as the High Steppe, comprises alluvial basins rimmed by low, barren mountains, but eastward the mountains give way first to the Low Steppe, a gravel-covered plateau, and ultimately to the flat coastal plain of the Sahel. Occasional watercourses cross the Steppes, but they flow only after heavy rain and usually fan out and evaporate in salt flats, or sebkhas, before reaching the sea.

The central Steppes give way southward to a broad depression occupied by two great seasonal salt lakes or shotts. The larger of these, the Shott Djerid, lies at 16 m below sea-level and is normally covered by a salt crust. It extends from close to the Mediterranean coast near Gabès almost to the Algerian frontier and is adjoined on the north-west by the Shott ar-Rharsa, which lies at 21 m below sea-level. South of the shotts Tunisia extends for over 320 km into the Sahara. Rocky, flat-topped mountains, the Monts des Ksour, separate a flat plain known as the Djeffara, which borders the coast south of Gabès, from a sandy lowland partly covered by the dunes of the Great Eastern Erg.

The climate of northern Tunisia is Mediterranean in type, with hot, dry summers followed by warm, wet winters. Average rainfall reaches 1,500 mm in the Kroumirie Mountains, the wettest area in north Africa, but over most of the northern region it varies from 400 mm to 1,000 mm. The wetter and least accessible mountains are covered with forests in which cork oak and evergreen oak predominate, but elsewhere lower rainfall and overgrazing combine to replace forest with meagre scrub growth. South of the High Tell rainfall is reduced to between 200 mm and 400 mm annually, which is insufficient for the regular cultivation of cereal crops without irrigation, and there is no continuous cover of vegetation. Large areas of the Steppes support only clumps of wiry esparto grass, which is collected and exported for paper manufacture. Southern Tunisia experiences full desert conditions. Rainfall is reduced to below 20 cm annually and occurs only at rare intervals. Extremes of temperature and wind are characteristic and vegetation is completely absent over extensive tracts. The country supports only a sparse nomadic population except where supplies of underground water make cultivation possible.

History

Revised for this edition by RICHARD I. LAWLESS

EARLY HISTORY

By 550 BC Carthage had achieved a position of commercial and naval supremacy in the Mediterranean. The empire reached its height in the course of the fourth century BC but was later challenged by the Roman Republic. The Punic Wars (264–241 BC, 218–201 BC and 149–146 BC) ended in the total destruction of the Carthaginian Empire and its incorporation within the empire of Rome. Carthage was rebuilt by the Emperor Augustus and intensive colonization brought a new prosperity. During the first two centuries AD Carthage was accounted the empire's second city but, with the decline of Rome's power, the city was lost to the Vandals (AD 439), to be recovered for the Byzantine Empire in 533–34. Byzantine rule was by no means secure:

the tendency of the local governors to reject the control of Constantinople was compounded by religious dissent among the native Berber population, who adopted Christian heresies in opposition to imperial rule. It was, however, the rise of Islam in Arabia and its rapid expansion after the death of the Prophet (632) that led to the destruction of Byzantine power and to the Arab invasion of North Africa. Arab control was finally established there with the conquest of Carthage in 698 and the foundation of Tunis. Islam spread rapidly among the Berbers, but they adopted Kharijite heresies; the eighth century was dominated by Berber-supported risings, manifestations of militant Islam against the central Government, and constant revolts among the occupying Arab forces. In the last years of the

Umayyad dynasty (overthrown 748–50) Tunisia escaped completely from imperial control: the new dynasty of the Abbasids, ruling from Iraq, retook Qairawan, the centre of Arab rule in the Maghreb, but lost it in 767, and a period of complete anarchy ensued. Tunisia was restored to Abbasid control in 800 and Ibrahim ibn Aghlab was appointed tributary ruler of Ifriqiya—corresponding roughly to present-day Tunisia.

For most of the ninth century the country was relatively prosperous, but the Aghlabid dynasty began to decline from 874 and was finally overthrown between 905 and 909 by the Fatimids, fanatical adherents of the heretical doctrines of Shi'ism, who pursued a vigorous policy of expansion and conquest; by 933 Fatimid rule was established throughout the Maghreb. Between 943 and 947 a Berber revolt took place, but it was effectively suppressed, allowing Tunisia to enjoy a certain amount of prosperity for the subsequent 25 years. In 969–70 the Fatimids gained control of Egypt and Syria: three years later Mahdiya was abandoned for the new capital of Cairo, and the Government of Tunisia was handed over to the Berber Zirid family. The golden age of Zirid rule was brought to an end in 1050 when the dynasty transferred its allegiance to the orthodox caliph at Baghdad. The economy crumbled and the country lapsed into political fragmentation. In 1087 Italian forces from Pisa and Genoa took Mahdiya, allowing the Zirids to continue as its rulers. Early in the 12th century the Zirids renewed their loyalty to Cairo, but were expelled by the Normans in 1148. Norman rule in Tunisia was over by 1160, and for the next 50 years Tunisia formed part of the empire of the caliphs of Marrakesh (the Almohads). In the 13th century the authority of Baghdad was briefly restored over Tunisia: a strong provincial government was established in 1207 under the Berber family of the Hafsids, who had held the governorship of Tunis since 1184. For most of the 13th century they ruled over North Africa from Tripoli to central Algeria but, in the face of tribal and Arab unrest, the town of Jerba fell into Christian hands (1284–1337). In the reign of Abu'l-Abbas (1370–94) the fortunes of the dynasty revived, but by the end of the 15th century the Hafsid Empire was disintegrating and Tunisia had become involved in the struggle between the Spanish and Ottoman forces for control of the Mediterranean.

By 1520 Bougie, Tripoli and Jerba had fallen to Spain; then in 1534 Khair ed-Din (Barbarossa), high admiral of the Ottoman fleet, drove the Emir al-Hasan from Tunis. In 1535 a great Spanish naval expedition recaptured the town, and al-Hasan was returned as the Emperor's vassal. In 1542 he was deposed by his son Ahmad, who made a final attempt to reunite Tunisia against Spain. The defeat of Ahmad at the siege of Malta (1565) which, together with the Spanish naval victory of Lepanto six years later, ended the struggle for maritime supremacy. The Pasha of Algiers stationed a garrison in Tunis in 1564, only to be expelled briefly (1572) in the aftermath of Lepanto; but in 1574 an Ottoman expedition put an end to Spanish power in Tunis and to the Hafsid dynasty itself.

Direct Ottoman rule was brief, a military revolt in Tunisia in 1591 reducing the power of the Pasha, the representative of the sultan, to a cipher. State affairs were assumed by one of the 40 deys, or high officers of the Ottoman army of occupation. By about 1600 the diwan, or governing council, shared a pre-eminent place with the taifa, or guild of corsair chiefs. By about 1606 the *de facto* independence of Tunisia had been recognized, although it was to remain nominally part of the Ottoman Empire for more than 250 years.

In the first half of the 17th century trade and commerce flourished, but from about 1650 the deys' power declined, authority passing to the beys, originally subordinate in rank. Hammuda, bey from 1659–63, became master of the entire country, and his family—the Muradids—retained power until 1702. This was a period of decline, with tribal unrest and incursions from Algiers. With the accession of Hussain Ali Turki in 1705, a new line of beys brought some semblance of order. The remainder of the 18th century passed fairly uneventfully, with some prosperity, despite uncertain relations with Algeria and the growth of European naval power in the Mediterranean.

After the Napoleonic Wars the European powers forced the bey, Mahmud (1814–24), to suppress the activities of the corsairs, which had provided a considerable part of state revenues. The French occupied Algiers in 1830, and reduced Algeria to colonial status; for the next 50 years Tunisia desperately tried to avoid the same fate. Increasingly the influence of France and Britain, and later Italy, became apparent through the activities of their consuls. The beys Ahmad (1837–55) and Muhammad (1855–59) attempted reforms, but merely intensified dependence on France. The next bey, Muhammad as-Sadiq (1859–82), promulgated a constitution (suspended 1864). Increased taxes, however, provoked tribal rebellion, and in 1869 the bey was obliged to accept financial control by France, Britain and Italy. Imminent financial collapse prompted France to intervene, and French forces invaded Tunisia in April 1881. They encountered little resistance and the Treaty of Kassar Said was signed, under which the bey remained the nominal ruler, while French officials administered military, financial and foreign affairs.

FRENCH PROTECTORATE

The Treaty of Mersa (1883) formally established a French protectorate over Tunisia and brought the actual Government of the country under French control, effective power passing to the French Resident-General. The international control commission was abolished in 1884, the currency was reformed along French lines in 1891, and the extra-territorial privileges of other Europeans were abrogated. Encouraged by large-scale grants of land, there was a considerable influx of settlers from France, and also from Italy, especially after 1900. Besides being confronted with the task of sustaining the economy, which they tackled by investment in the development of the country's resources, the French encountered rivalry from Italy and a rise of Tunisian nationalism.

Tunisian cultural and political life absorbed many French ideas, but was also influenced by movements in other parts of the Islamic world. An attempt to emulate the Young Turk reformers in the Ottoman Empire was the foundation, in 1908, of the Young Tunisian Movement, which demanded the restoration of the authority of the bey together with democratic reforms. The achievement of independence in eastern Arab countries after the First World War, and the example of the nationalist movement in Egypt, inspired Tunisians with a greater national consciousness, and in 1920 the Destour (Constitution) movement was formed under the leadership of Sheikh ath-Tha'libi, one of the founders of the Young Tunisians.

The Destour appealed for a self-governing constitutional regime with a Legislative Assembly. French attempts to conciliate opinion by administrative reforms, dating from 1920 with the formation of economic councils on which Tunisians were represented, failed to satisfy the more radical elements, and, confronted with further nationalist activity, the French administration resorted to repressive measures. Sheikh ath-Tha'libi was exiled in 1923, and in 1925 the Destour movement was dissolved. It was revived in the early 1930s but soon split, the former leaders of the Destour being accused of collaboration with France by younger members eager for political action on a broad front. In 1934 the Néo-Destour (New Constitution) Party was formed, led by Habib Bourguiba, a Tunisian lawyer. The party employed methods of widespread political agitation as a result of which Bourguiba was exiled. After the victory of the Popular Front in France in 1936 he returned to Tunisia, but little was achieved in direct negotiations with the new French Government. The Néo-Destour became a powerful organization, its influence extending to all parts of the country, and its strength was proved in a successful general strike in 1938. Widespread clashes with the police followed, martial law was proclaimed, some 200 nationalists were arrested, and both the Destour and Néo-Destour parties were dissolved.

At the outbreak of the Second World War Tunisian opinion rallied in favour of France, and when Italy entered the war some 23,000 Italians in Tunisia were interned. With the fall of France Tunisia came under Vichy rule, and Bizerta, Tunis and other ports were used by Germany and Italy to supply their armies in Libya until the defeat of the Axis forces by the Allies in 1943 restored French authority. The bey, Muhammad al-Monsif, was accused of collaboration with the Axis powers and deposed; he was replaced by his cousin, Muhammad al-Amin.

GROWING AUTONOMY

The virtual restoration of peace in 1944 brought a relaxation of political restrictions and during the following years there was renewed agitation for political change. As a result of subsequent French repression, Habib Bourguiba went into exile in Cairo in 1945 but his chief lieutenant, Salah Ben Yousuf, remained in Tunisia. The French authorities turned their attention to political reforms, and by beylical decrees in 1945 the Council of Ministers and the Grand Council (an elected body with equal French and Tunisian representation) were reorganized, the authority of the latter being extended. These measures did not satisfy the nationalists, who demanded complete independence. Later in 1946 a government was formed under Muhammad Kaak, which included an increased number of Tunisians (moderate leaders being appointed after the Destour and Néo-Destour had refused to participate); the French, however, retained ultimate control.

Bourguiba returned to Tunisia in 1949. In April 1950 the Néo-Destour proposed the transfer of sovereignty and executive control to Tunisian hands, under a responsible government with a Prime Minister appointed by the bey and an elected National Assembly which would draft a democratic constitution. Local French interests would be protected by representation on municipal councils, and Tunisia would co-operate with France on equal terms. These proposals received a reasonable response in France, and a new Tunisian Government was formed in August 1950, composed of an equal number of Tunisian and French ministers, with Muhammad Chenik as Prime Minister and Salah Ben Yousuf as Minister of Justice. The object of the new Government was stated to be the gradual restoration of Tunisian sovereignty, in co-operation with France. Despite strong opposition to these developments from the European settlers (some 10% of the population), further reforms were effected in September 1950 and February 1951, when French advisers to the Tunisian ministers were removed and the Resident-General's control over the Council of Ministers was diminished.

Peaceful progress towards autonomy came to a halt, however, owing to growing settler opposition, procrastination on the part of the French Government and consequent alienation of the nationalists. Tunisian resentment erupted in strikes and demonstrations in early 1952. The Néo-Destour had formed an intimate alliance with the influential trade union movement, and many leaders held office in both organizations. In February Bourguiba and other Néo-Destour leaders were arrested on the order of the new Resident-General, Jean de Hauteclocque, and a wave of violence spread throughout the country, culminating in the arrest and removal from office of the Prime Minister, and the imposition of French military control.

A new Government was formed under Salaheddine Baccouche, and a French-inspired scheme designed to lead to eventual internal autonomy was announced in April 1952. Meanwhile, the now-proscribed Néo-Destour took its case to Cairo and the UN General Assembly. Against a background of increasing terrorism, countered by French repressive action, and in the face of opposition from both the Néo-Destour and the settlers, little in the way of reform could be achieved. The bey at first refused to sign French reform decrees, and when he yielded in December under the threat of deposition, the proposals were promptly repudiated by the Néo-Destour.

Terrorist activities continued and a settler counter-terrorist organization, the 'Red Hand', came to prominence. The situation approached civil war in 1953, with bands of *fellagha* active in the western highlands and around Bizerta and terrorism and counter-terrorism in the towns. In July 1954 the newly-formed French Government, led by Pierre Mendès France, offered internal autonomy for Tunisia, with France retaining responsibility only for defence and foreign affairs. The French proposals were accepted, and in August a new Tunisian Government was formed, headed by Tahar Ben Ammar and containing three members of the Néo-Destour as well as moderate nationalists. Negotiations with the French Government opened in Carthage in September. The talks had reached deadlock when the Mendès France Government fell in February 1955, but they resumed in March and a final agreement was signed in Paris on 2 June.

The accord granted internal autonomy to Tunisia while protecting French interests and preserving Tunisia's close links with France. France retained responsibility for foreign affairs, defence (including the control of frontiers) and internal security. Although the agreement was supported by a majority of the Néo-Destour, the extremist wing, headed by the exiled Salah

Ben Yousuf, and the old Destour and Communist elements, opposed it, as did the settlers' organizations. An all-Tunisian Council of Ministers was formed in September 1955 by Tahar Ben Ammar, with members of the Néo-Destour holding six of the 12 posts.

Habib Bourguiba had returned from three years' exile in June 1955, to be followed by Salah Ben Yousuf in September. In October Ben Yousuf was expelled from the Néo-Destour for opposition to the recent agreement and for 'splitting activities'. A Néo-Destour party congress at Sfax in November endorsed the agreement, but reaffirmed that the party would be satisfied only with independence and demanded the election of a constituent assembly. Clashes between 'Bourguibist' and 'Yousufist' factions followed, and in December a conspiracy to create a terrorist organization to prevent the implementation of the agreement was discovered. Ben Yousuf fled to Tripoli in January 1956, and many suspected 'Yousufists' were placed in detention. At the same time *fellagha* activity revived, rebel bands became active in the remoter parts of the country and acts of terrorism were committed against both French settlers and members of the Néo-Destour.

INDEPENDENCE

On 27 February 1956 a Tunisian delegation led by Bourguiba began independence negotiations with the French Government in Paris. In a protocol signed on 20 March, France formally recognized the independence of Tunisia and its right to exercise responsibility over foreign affairs, security and defence, and to raise a national army. A transitional period was envisaged during which French forces would gradually be withdrawn from Tunisia, including Bizerta.

Elections for the Constituent Assembly, held on 25 March 1956, resulted in all 98 seats being won by candidates of the National Front, all of whom acknowledged allegiance to the Néo-Destour. The elections were boycotted by the 'Yousufist' opposition. Habib Bourguiba became Prime Minister on 11 April, leading a Government in which 16 of the 17 ministers belonged to the Néo-Destour.

In the early years of independence Tunisia's relations with France were dominated by the question of the evacuation of French forces. A Tunisian demand for their withdrawal was rejected in July 1956 by the French Government, which was preoccupied with the deteriorating situation in Algeria. Bourguiba visited Paris in September in an attempt to promote a mediated settlement in Algeria based on French recognition of Algeria's right to independence, but hopes of progress in this direction were shattered by the French kidnapping in October of five leading Algerian nationalists. Tunisia immediately severed diplomatic relations with France, anti-French riots erupted, and there were clashes between French troops and Tunisian demonstrators resulting in deaths on both sides.

Measures were taken in early 1957 to strengthen Tunisia's relations with its neighbours. In January a treaty of good-neighbourliness was signed with Libya, as a step towards establishing a 'Great Arab Maghreb', and in March a 20-year treaty of friendship was concluded with Morocco.

The bey, Muhammad al-Amin, had been the object of constant criticism from Tunisian nationalist leaders, who accused him of reluctance to participate actively in the struggle for independence. After independence his remaining powers were eroded and on 25 July 1957 the Constituent Assembly voted to abolish the monarchy, proclaim Tunisia a republic and invest Bourguiba with the powers of Head of State.

RELATIONS WITH FRANCE

Although diplomatic relations with France had been resumed in January 1957, differences between the two Governments concerning the Algerian revolt persisted. The most serious Franco-Tunisian incident during the Algerian war occurred in February 1958, when French aircraft from Algeria attacked the Tunisian border village of Sakhiet Sidi Yousuf, the scene of several clashes the previous month. The Tunisian Government's reaction was to sever diplomatic relations with France, to forbid all French troop movements in Tunisia, to demand the immediate evacuation of all French bases, including Bizerta, and to take the matter before the UN Security Council. French troops were blockaded in their barracks, and the extra-territorial status of Bizerta, from which French warships were banned, was abolished. In addition some 600 French civilians were expelled from the frontier area and five of the seven French consulates were closed.

British and US mediation was accepted, and on 15 April 1958 it was agreed that all French troops would be evacuated and Tunisian sovereignty over Bizerta recognized; at the same time the French consulates would be reopened and the cases of the expelled French civilians examined. When further clashes between Tunisian and French forces occurred in May, a state of emergency covering the whole country was proclaimed and Tunisia again took the matter to the UN Security Council.

A new phase in Franco–Tunisian relations began with the accession to power of Gen. de Gaulle in June 1958. An agreement was concluded on 17 June under which French troops stationed outside Bizerta were to be withdrawn during the next four months, while negotiations for a provisional agreement on Bizerta were to follow. Restrictions on French troops were removed and diplomatic relations resumed. By October the only French troops remaining in Tunisia were in Bizerta.

The eradication of French interests had meanwhile commenced. In June 1958 the French-owned transport services and in August the electricity services of Tunis were nationalized. In November President Bourguiba announced proposals for the purchase of all agricultural land in Tunisia owned by French citizens by 1960, and for its redistribution to landless Tunisians.

POLITICAL CONSOLIDATION

With the improvement of relations with France, the Tunisian Government was able to consolidate its internal position, by restructuring the Néo-Destour Party and by instituting court proceedings against members of the former regime and 'Yousufist' opponents. Prince Chadli, the eldest son of the bey, and former Prime Ministers Tahar Ben Ammar and Salaheddine Baccouche were among those tried in late 1958 on charges that included the misuse of public funds and collaboration with the French authorities; sentences imposed ranged from heavy fines to imprisonment and loss of civic rights. Salah Ben Yousuf (*in absentia*) and 54 of his supporters were charged with plotting to assassinate President Bourguiba, smuggling arms from Libya, and aiming to overthrow the Government. Ben Yousuf and eight others were sentenced to death, with most of the remainder receiving long prison sentences.

This trial widened the breach between Tunisia and the United Arab Republic (UAR—Egypt), from where Ben Yousuf had been conducting his activities. In October 1958 Tunisia had joined the Arab League, only to withdraw from a meeting of its council 10 days later, after accusing the UAR of attempting to dominate the organization. Diplomatic relations with the UAR were severed later in the month on the grounds of its alleged complicity in the 'Yousufist' attempt to assassinate President Bourguiba. On the eve of Ben Yousuf's trial, Bourguiba announced the capture of Egyptian officers who had secretly entered Tunisia to assist subversive elements to overthrow his Government.

On 1 June 1959 a new Constitution was promulgated, providing for the election of a President with a five-year mandate (renewable three times consecutively). The President was empowered to formulate the general policy of the state, choose the members of the Government, hold supreme command of the armed forces and make all appointments to civil and military posts. The Constitution also provided for the election of a national assembly for five years and required the approval of the assembly for the declaration of war, the conclusion of peace and the ratification of treaties. In elections which followed on 8 November President Bourguiba was elected unopposed, and all 90 seats in the new National Assembly were won by the Néo-Destour, their only opponents being the Communists.

THE BIZERTA CRISIS

The forging of cordial relations with France continued during 1959–60. A trade and tariff agreement was signed in September 1959, and further agreements on technical co-operation and the transfer of property of the French State in Tunisia to the Tunisian Government were concluded. In October President Bourguiba announced his support for President de Gaulle's offer of self-determination for Algeria, and Tunisia subsequently

acted as intermediary between France and the Algerian rebels in moves towards a negotiated settlement.

None the less, Tunisia continued to press for the return of the Bizerta base, and in July 1961 President Bourguiba made a formal demand for its return and repeated the claim (first made in 1959) to Saharan territory in Algeria adjacent to the south-western part of Tunisia. Demonstrations ensued against the continued French occupation of Bizerta, and fighting between Tunisian and French troops began around the Bizerta base and in the disputed area of the Sahara. In mid-July diplomatic relations were again severed, and Tunisia requested a meeting of the UN Security Council. The fighting ended on 22 July with the French in firm control of the base and town of Bizerta, more than 800 Tunisians having been killed. In the south a Tunisian attempt to seize the fort of Garat el-Hamel also failed. A subsequent visit to Bizerta by the UN Secretary-General, Dag Hammarskjöld, in an attempt to promote a settlement, was unsuccessful. According to a French statement released in late July, France wished to continue to use the base while a state of international tension persisted but was prepared to negotiate with Tunisia over its use during this period.

The immediate results of the Bizerta crisis were a *rapprochement* between Tunisia and other Arab states, a deterioration in relations with the West and an improvement of relations with the communist bloc. The final settlement of the dispute occupied the remainder of 1961 and much of 1962. The Algerian ceasefire in March 1962 benefited Franco-Tunisian relations, and the French installations at Menzel Bourguiba, near Bizerta, were handed over to Tunisia on 30 June. In March 1963 agreement was reached on the transfer of some 370,000 acres of French-owned agricultural land to the Tunisian Government. Other agreements, on trade and finance, were reached, in order to reduce Tunisia's balance-of-payments deficit with France.

Although Algerian independence had been warmly welcomed by Tunisia, the extremist doctrines of the new state conflicted with Tunisian moderation and relations quickly deteriorated. In January 1963 the Tunisian ambassador was recalled from Algiers on the grounds of alleged Algerian complicity in a recent unsuccessful attempt on the life of President Bourguiba, in which 'Yousufists' in Algeria, as well as supporters of the old Destour and army elements, were implicated. Moroccan mediation facilitated a conference of the Maghreb states in Rabat in February, at which the Tunisians demanded the cessation of 'Yousufist' activities in Algeria. After further negotiations a frontier agreement between Tunisia and Algeria was signed in July.

EXPROPRIATION

In May 1964 the Tunisian National Assembly enacted legislation authorizing the expropriation of all foreign-owned lands (some 300,000 ha). The French immediately suspended, then cancelled, all financial aid. This nationalization of foreign-owned land was a step towards the development of socialism in the agrarian sector of the economy. The Néo-Destour's commitment to 'Tunisian socialism' was emphasized in the change of the party's name to the Parti socialiste destourien (PSD—Destour Socialist Party) prior to the presidential and general elections in November 1964, in which President Bourguiba was again elected unopposed and the PSD, the only party to present candidates, won all 90 seats in the National Assembly.

From 1964 onwards, domestic politics became more settled and the Government concentrated its attention on economic development. The hold of the PSD on the country was strengthened and President Bourguiba's position was unchallenged.

FOREIGN POLICY

After 1964 Tunisia's relations with the world beyond the Arab states and Africa were influenced by the need for foreign aid, most of which was received from Western countries where the moderation of Tunisian policies inspired confidence. Tunisia also made cautious overtures towards the communist bloc. Some economic assistance was obtained from the USSR while Tunisia maintained its non-aligned position. Diplomatic relations with the People's Republic of China were established, following a visit to Tunisia by the Chinese Premier, Zhou Enlai, in January 1964. Nevertheless, President Bourguiba publicly criticized Chinese policies, in particular the policy of encouraging revolution in Africa.

Relations with the rest of the Arab world continued to be the focus of President Bourguiba's attention and the source of bitter controversy. In April 1965 he openly attacked Arab League policy on Palestine and advocated a more flexible approach, including direct negotiations with Israel over the UN partition plan of 1948. This provoked severe criticism from the Arab states (excepting Morocco, Libya and Saudi Arabia). After violent demonstrations in Cairo and Tunis, the UAR and Tunisia withdrew their respective ambassadors. Tunisia's refusal at the end of April to follow the example of other Arab League states in severing relations with the Federal Republic of Germany, which had exchanged ambassadors with Israel, widened the rift. A conference of Arab Heads of State at Casablanca, Morocco, in May, at which Tunisia was not represented, categorically rejected Bourguiba's proposal that Israel should be asked to cede territory to the Palestinian refugees in return for recognition by the Arab states, and reaffirmed their determination to effect the complete overthrow of Israel. In an open letter to those attending, Bourguiba accused the Egyptian President, Gamel Abd an-Nasser, of attempting to use the Arab League as an instrument of UAR national policy and of interfering in the affairs of every Arab state; Tunisia was not prepared to take part in the debates of the Arab League under such circumstances. In October 1966 Tunisia announced the complete severance of diplomatic relations with the UAR.

The Six-Day War between Israel and the Arab states in June 1967 led to immediate reconciliation in the Arab world. Tunisian troops were dispatched to the front, but the Israeli success was so swift and the cease-fire came so soon that they were recalled before they had reached the scene of the fighting. Diplomatic relations between Tunisia and the UAR were restored, and Tunisia was represented at the Arab summit meeting in Khartoum in September, when Arab nations agreed to neither recognize nor negotiate with Israel.

In May 1968, however, following criticism of President Bourguiba by the Syrian Prime Minister, who charged him with having betrayed the Arab struggle in Palestine, the Syrian chargé d'affaires and his staff in Tunis were accused of inciting subversive activities and expelled. At a meeting in Cairo in September, the Arab League refused to hear a statement from the Tunisian delegate criticizing the Arab attitude, particularly that of the UAR, towards Israel. Tunisia subsequently announced its intention to boycott future meetings of the League. Nevertheless, Tunisia reaffirmed its support for the Palestine Liberation Organization (PLO).

An exchange of visits by the Ministers of Foreign Affairs of Tunisia and Algeria in early 1969 resulted in an improved climate for negotiation on the demarcation of their common frontier and on economic matters, especially those arising from the nationalization by each country of property owned by nationals of the other. In January 1970 the two countries signed a treaty of co-operation and friendship.

THE FALL OF AHMAD BEN SALAH

During 1964–69 the chief issue in internal affairs was the campaign to collectivize agriculture, implemented under the leadership of Ahmad Ben Salah, Minister of Finance and Planning. The programme encountered widespread opposition in affected areas and disagreement within the ruling party itself. In September 1969 the policy was abandoned; Ben Salah was stripped of all office, arrested, tried and sentenced to 10 years' hard labour. However, he escaped from prison in February 1973 and took refuge in Europe, from where he issued statements condemning President Bourguiba for acting against the people in the interests of a privileged class, and became the leader of the radical Mouvement de l'unité populaire (MUP—Popular Unity Movement), which was declared illegal in Tunisia.

Ben Salah was the first of several ministers to experience a sharp reversal of fortune. In November 1969 President Bourguiba appointed Bahi Ladgham as Prime Minister, but in October 1970 replaced him by Hédi Nouira. A year later the President declared that Nouira would be his successor. In March 1973 Ladgham resigned from all his political posts. Mahmoud Mestiri was the next minister to fall into disgrace. As Minister of the Interior in 1970 and 1971, he demanded the liberalization

of the Government. Consequently he was dismissed from the Council of Ministers in September 1971, expelled from the party in 1972 and from the National Assembly in May 1973. When a revision of the Constitution was finally proposed in March 1973, it included almost none of the measures suggested by Mestiri to modify the presidential nature of the Government. Indeed, during the next two years Bourguiba and Prime Minister Nouira consolidated their power. In September 1974 the ninth party congress of the PSD elected Bourguiba as President-for-life of the party and confirmed Nouira in the post of Secretary-General. Bourguiba appointed a new political bureau of 20 members, including 14 ministers, confirming a tendency to draw the PSD and the Government closer together. In November Bourguiba was re-elected unopposed as President of Tunisia, and in the National Assembly elections all 112 PSD candidates were returned, also without opposition. The Assembly voted amendments to the Constitution, designating the Prime Minister as the President's successor and allowing for the appointment of a President-for-life, a post to which the Assembly elected Bourguiba in March 1975. Constitutional reforms in December 1975 increased presidential powers still further.

UNION WITH LIBYA

In June 1970 the President's son, Habib Bourguiba, Jr, was replaced as Minister of Foreign Affairs by Muhammad Masmoudi. From that date relations with the more radical Arab states and with extremist powers outside the area improved. Normal relations were resumed with the UAR and Syria, and Tunisia rejoined the Arab League.

In January 1974, after a meeting between President Bourguiba and Col Muammar al-Qaddafi, the Libyan leader, on the island of Djerba, it was announced that Tunisia and Libya had agreed to form a union. The Djerba Agreement was greeted with general surprise for, despite an improvement in relations between the two countries in previous years, Bourguiba had always shown himself to be hostile to such a union. Bourguiba was to be president of the new state, with Qaddafi as his deputy. It would seem that the Djerba Agreement was managed by Muhammad Masmoudi, without the consent of Prime Minister Nouira, who was out of the country at the time. Nouira returned swiftly to Tunisia, and Masmoudi was dismissed from his post in the Government and the PSD.

In the aftermath of this confused affair, relations with Libya were tense. The Libyans continued to urge fulfilment of the Djerba Agreement, and in 1975 Bourguiba expressed concern at the increase in strength of the Libyan army. Another source of contention between the two countries was the delimitation of their respective sectors of the continental shelf, in which important deposits of petroleum were to be found. In June 1977 both sides agreed to submit to arbitration by the International Court of Justice (ICJ) and agreement was finally reached in February 1982. In October 1977 a joint statement was issued, saying that Tunisia and Libya had agreed to 'reactivate mutual co-operation' and establish a scheme to link the electricity networks of the two countries, while experts were to discuss the possibility of other joint ventures. Relations with Algeria also improved in 1977, after Tunisia had abandoned its attempts at conciliation in the Western Sahara dispute (in which it sided with Morocco): a co-operation agreement was signed in July by the respective Ministers of the Interior.

DOMESTIC UNREST

By 1977, with President Bourguiba in his seventies and in poor health, there was growing uncertainty over the future of the system of government that he had dominated for so long. Hédi Nouira, his designated successor, appeared to lack the powerful personality that had kept Bourguiba in command of the country, and there were signs of a succession struggle in the increasing demands for the free development of a pluralist democracy from, among others, former ministers Ahmad Ben Salah, in exile, and Ahmad Mestiri, leader of the unofficial Mouvement des démocrates socialistes (MDS—Social Democrats). The arrest and trial (in mid-1977) of 33 members of the MUP, on charges of threatening state security and defaming the President, indicated the continuing hostility of the Government to any form of organized opposition.

Meanwhile, however, a more effective political force was beginning to make itself felt. After a number of strikes by workers in 1976, a 'social contract' was formulated in early 1977 between the Government and the Union Générale des Travailleurs Tunisiens (UGTT—General Union of Tunisian Workers) under the leadership of Habib Achour, involving inflation-linked pay rises for the duration of the 1977–81 Development Plan. In spite of this agreement there were further strikes in various sectors of industry in late 1977, in demand of better pay and conditions, and backed by the UGTT, which was becoming (particularly through its weekly newspaper *Ach-Cha'ab*) an increasingly vocal critic of government policy and an outlet for political dissenters. In December Muhammad Masmoudi, the former Minister of Foreign Affairs, returned from exile in Libya and declared his support for the UGTT, thereby underlining its potential as a political force. Tahar Belkhodja, the Minister of the Interior, was dismissed in late December, after having suggested that the unrest should be attributed to social and economic problems, such as a rapidly increasing population and severe unemployment. Six other moderate members of the Council of Ministers resigned in sympathy, but President Bourguiba reaffirmed his support for Nouira by forming a new Government in which the dissidents were replaced mainly by civil servants and technocrats, all of whom could be expected to accept Nouira's tough policy; in addition, Bourguiba appointed his son, Habib Bourguiba, Jr, as special adviser.

In January 1978 Achour resigned from the political bureau and central committee of the PSD after pressure from members of the UGTT who felt that his dual role had become unacceptable. The UGTT national council appealed for urgent changes in the method of government and an end to the use of 'intimidation' in suppressing strikes and demonstrations. In late January the union organized a general strike as a warning to the Government and in retaliation for attacks on union offices. Rioting ensued in Tunis and several other cities, the army intervened and at least 51 people were killed, while hundreds more were injured; a state of emergency was declared and a curfew imposed. Hundreds of demonstrators were arrested, tried and imprisoned, and Achour and other members of the UGTT executive were also taken into custody and charged with subversion. The Government accused the UGTT of a long-standing conspiracy against the State and hinted at foreign backing, presumably from Libya.

There was considerable international criticism of the irregular conduct of the trial of Achour and 30 other union leaders, which began in August 1978. Nevertheless, Achour was sentenced to 10 years' hard labour, and prison sentences were also passed on all but six of the other defendants. Under a new Secretary-General, Tijani Abid, the UGTT expressed regret at the recent events and declared its willingness to co-operate with the Government. Although Achour was pardoned by President Bourguiba in August 1979, he remained under house arrest; 263 others serving prison terms for their involvement in the riots had been pardoned in May, but it was nevertheless clear that the power of the UGTT as a source of opposition had, for the moment, been crushed.

In July 1979 the National Assembly approved an amendment to the electoral code, allowing, for the first time, the number of candidates in legislative elections to be twice the number of seats although it remained unclear whether members of parties other than the PSD would be permitted to stand. At the PSD congress in September, the need to 'open up' the party to new adherents and original ideas was emphasized, but the Prime Minister rejected the idea of a multi-party system and a 'national pact' proposed two years previously by the MDS. The main opposition groups—the MUP, the MDS and the Parti communiste tunisien (PCT—the Communist Party)—declared that they would boycott the legislative elections in November, since participation would indicate support of the present system (and would presumably not have been permitted in any case, since none of the groups had official party status). The rate of participation in the elections was substantially lower than on previous occasions, reaching only 81%, compared with an average of 95%.

In January 1980 there was an attack on the town of Gafsa in western Tunisia by guerrillas, originally estimated to number 300, although only 60 were later brought to trial. The Tunisian

armed forces quickly regained control of the town, but 41 deaths were reported. Responsibility for the attack was claimed by a hitherto unknown group, the Tunisian Armed Resistance, which declared that it aimed to free Tunisia from the 'dictatorship' of the PSD. The Tunisian Government claimed that the attackers were Tunisian migrant workers who had been trained in Libya and encouraged to make the attack in order to destabilize the Bourguiba administration: diplomatic relations with Libya were suspended. Libya expressed its incredulity at these allegations, and referred to the incident as a 'popular uprising'. Nevertheless, the attack caused international concern, particularly in France, which sent military transport aircraft to Gafsa and naval vessels to the Tunisian coast, while the USA also offered to expedite military supplies. The Gafsa attack was condemned by the more established opposition groups within Tunisia, engendering a temporary national solidarity, although the same groups condemned the execution of 13 of the guerrillas which took place in April.

MOVES TOWARDS POLITICAL LIBERALIZATION

The sudden illness of Hédi Nouira in February 1980 renewed political uncertainty. The Minister of Education, Muhammad Mzali, was appointed as temporary government co-ordinator and in April as Prime Minister, thereby becoming Bourguiba's successor under the terms of the Constitution. The new Government headed by Mzali included a member of the MDS and three of the ministers who had resigned in 1977 in protest at the harsh measures taken against strikers. In December Tahar Belkhodja, the former Minister of the Interior who had been dismissed in 1977, was readmitted to the Government. Most political prisoners were released during 1980, and in January 1981 a pardon was granted to nearly 1,000 members of the UGTT who had been convicted of involvement in the 1978 riots. Greater tolerance was also shown towards opposition parties: in mid-1980 permission was granted to the MDS to publish two weekly periodicals, and in the following February an amnesty was granted to all members of the proscribed MUP, except its leader-in-exile, Ahmad Ben Salah. In April 1981 President Bourguiba declared that he saw no objection to the emergence of political parties provided that they rejected violence and religious fanaticism and were not dependent 'ideologically or materially' on any foreign group (which suggested that Islamic fundamentalists would not be welcome candidates). The congress elected a new PSD central committee of 80 representatives, some 75% of whom had not previously been members of the committee.

An extraordinary congress of the UGTT was also held in April 1981, the first since the riots of January 1978. Of the 13 members of the executive committee elected by the congress, 11 were former committee members who had been imprisoned in 1978. The new Secretary General—Taieb Baccouche—was the first non-PSD member to be elected to this post. Habib Achour was released in December 1981 and allowed to reassume his position as leader of the UGTT.

The process of installing a multi-party system continued with the announcement of legislative elections for November 1981; Bourguiba promised that any participating group that gained a minimum of 5% of the votes cast would be officially recognized as a political party. Several parties refused to take part in the elections under these conditions. In July the one-party system ended with the official recognition of the PCT. As a former officially recognized political party (banned since 1963), the PCT was not required to fulfil the 5% condition laid upon the other groups. In contrast to this apparent political liberalization, as many as 50 leading members of the Mouvement de la tendance islamique (MTI—Islamic Tendency Movement) were arrested and given prison sentences in September. The Government continued to regard the MTI, a relatively moderate Islamic group, as a dangerous influence.

Although the PCT, the MUP and the MDS presented candidates in the November 1981 legislative elections, the result was an emphatic victory for the Front national, a joint electoral pact formed by the PSD and the UGTT, which gained 94.6% of votes cast and won all 136 seats in the new Assembly. The other parties all failed to win 5% of the vote, and consequently none was given official recognition. Formal protests of electoral irregularities were made by the three opposition groups. The

MDS and the MUP were finally accorded official status in November 1983.

FURTHER UNREST

In January 1984 widespread rioting and looting broke out. The immediate cause was a substantial increase in the price of bread and the abolition of government subsidies on flour and other staple foods, but the disturbances were also linked to long-standing grievances, including the high level of unemployment (particularly among the young), and to unrest amongst Islamist groups. Rioting started in the south of the country, but spread to the northern cities of Sfax, Gabès and Tunis. On 3 January the Government declared a state of emergency, and troops were brought in to control street demonstrations. The resulting clashes between troops and demonstrators left 89 people dead and 938 injured, according to official figures, and more than 1,000 people were arrested. After a week of disturbances President Bourguiba personally intervened to reverse the price rises, and order was re-established.

An official inquiry into the cause of the riots accused the Minister of the Interior, Driss Guiga, of exploiting the violence for his own political ends and of failing to inform the President of the magnitude of the disturbances. Guiga had been dismissed by President Bourguiba in January 1984 and subsequently left the country. The vacant portfolio was granted to Prime Minister Mzali, whose position was considerably strengthened by the downfall of his former rival for the presidential succession. In June Guiga was tried *in absentia* for high treason and sentenced to 15 years' imprisonment.

Throughout 1984 and in early 1985 Tunisia was troubled by a series of strikes in the public sector. The strikers demanded increases in public-sector salaries, which had been frozen for two years. In April 1985 riot police surrounded the UGTT headquarters, after the union urged a general strike in support of the demands of public-sector strikers. The UGTT subsequently postponed the strike, pending talks with government negotiators. However, in early May, the UGTT announced that negotiations had collapsed and that it would refuse to participate in the municipal elections later that month. The MDS, the PCT and the MUP also boycotted the elections. Nevertheless, there was a turn-out of 92.8% (compared with only 66.8% for the equivalent elections in 1980), which the PSD interpreted as a vote of support for its policies. In July the UGTT declared the start of a campaign of renewed strike action. In the same month the union's newspaper, *Ach-Cha'ab*, was suspended by the Government for six months. In October the police occupied the UGTT headquarters and arrested union leaders. Local UGTT committees were dissolved and replaced by pro-government committees. By early November about 100 UGTT leaders had been arrested, including the union's Secretary-General, Habib Achour, but many were released later in the month. In December the UGTT executive committee agreed to replace Achour with a provisional Secretary-General, on condition that the Government released the union members who were still in detention and reinstated workers who had been dismissed for taking industrial action. In January 1986 the UGTT's administrative commission, considering that these conditions had not been met, voted to reinstate Achour as Secretary-General. In the same month, however, Achour was imprisoned on a charge of theft, dating from 1982. (In April he was sentenced to a further two years' imprisonment for alleged mismanagement of union funds, and in December his sentence was extended by another four years.) In May the UGTT elected a 'moderate', Ismaïl Lajeri, as Secretary-General.

The Tunisian Government's refusal to condemn the US raid on Libya in April 1986 prompted considerable popular disquiet, and anti-US sentiment was suppressed by the authorities. Ahmad Mestiri, leader of the MDS, was jailed for organizing a demonstration, and several magazines (including the MDS weekly and two PCT periodicals) were seized by the Government. The authorities suspended publication of three magazines for six months. The appointment of Gen. Zine al-Abidine Ben Ali, who was regarded as immoderate, as Minister of the Interior, in late April, was considered a significant change in domestic policy.

BOURGUIBA ATTEMPTS TO TIGHTEN HIS GRIP ON POWER

In early 1986 Habib Bourguiba, Jr, was suspended from his post of special adviser, owing to his opposition to the series of arrests in late 1985. In the following months President Bourguiba announced several ministerial reshuffles, which gradually weakened the position of Muhammad Mzali, the Prime Minister, who had been regarded as Bourguiba's potential successor. During the 12th congress of the PSD in June, Bourguiba apparently confirmed Mzali's position as Secretary-General of the PSD, yet he dispensed with the ballot to elect the members of the PSD central committee, and personally appointed 90 members, none of whom was an associate of Mzali. In July Mzali was replaced as Prime Minister by Rachid Sfar (previously Minister of Finance), and was dismissed as Secretary-General of the PSD. Mzali subsequently fled to Algeria, and was later sentenced *in absentia* to one year's imprisonment for crossing the border illegally, to a further three years' imprisonment for defamatory comments against Tunisian leaders, and to 15 years' hard labour for mismanagement of public funds.

A general election for a new National Assembly was held in November 1986, but was boycotted by the opposition parties. The PSD won all 125 seats, opposed by only 15 independent candidates. There was a high level of participation (82.9% of the electorate), according to official figures, although these were disputed by the opposition.

By 1987 the Government had consolidated its control over the UGTT, and left-wing militancy was no longer perceived as a threat. In December 1986 the UGTT elected a new 18-member executive bureau, and an apparently moderate Secretary-General, Abd al-Aziz Bouraoui. In January 1987 Bourguiba presided over the opening of an extraordinary congress of the UGTT, during which the union confirmed its support of the PSD and approved a new union charter. Habib Achour was released on humanitarian grounds in May. In the same month, Bourguiba pardoned 13 members of the Rassemblement socialiste progressiste (RSP), who had been sentenced to six months' imprisonment for illegal assembly.

SUPPRESSION OF ISLAMIST ACTIVISTS

Meanwhile, President Bourguiba had become increasingly concerned that 'Islamic fundamentalism' was a threat to his regime, and attempts were made to suppress Islamist activity. In July 1986 four Islamist activists were sentenced to death, and some 22 others were imprisoned, for a series of offences. Numerous arrests were reported by human rights organizations, following clashes between Islamists and left-wing students at the University of Tunis in early 1987. In March 1987 the Secretary-General of the MTI, Rached Ghanouchi, was arrested on charges of violence and collusion with foreign powers to overthrow the Government. Later in the month, Tunisia severed diplomatic relations with Iran, after Tunisians, suspected of terrorist offences, were arrested in France and Djibouti. The Tunisian Government accused Iranian diplomats in Tunis of subversive acts, including the recruitment of Tunisian Islamists to perpetrate terrorist acts abroad, and thus undermine Tunisia's relations with friendly states. The Government also claimed to have evidence of an Iranian plot to overthrow Bourguiba, and to establish a pro-Iranian fundamentalist administration in Tunisia. On this pretext, a series of arrests of Islamists ensued. According to the authorities, 1,500 people were detained, although opposition parties estimated that the total reached more than 3,000. The arrests were condemned by the Ligue tunisienne des droits de l'homme (LTDH—Tunisian League of Human Rights), and in April the opposition parties issued a communiqué, warning against a return to repressive practices and demanding guarantees for the freedom of the trade unions and the universities. There were further arrests after clashes between police units and Islamists during an anti-government demonstration in April. Later in the month, the Secretary-General of the LTDH, Khemais Chamari, was arrested and accused of disseminating false information and defaming the State. (Chamari was later released on parole, and was acquitted in January 1988.) In May the Government approved the creation of the Association for the Defence of Human Rights and Public Liberty, as a rival to the LTDH, which the Government accused of being pro-MTI. In June 37 Islamists, mostly students, were sentenced to terms of imprisonment of between two and six years for taking part in illegal demonstrations in April and for defaming Bourguiba. In August 13 foreign tourists were injured by bomb explosions, and the Government promptly insisted that the MTI was responsible, despite the publication of a statement from a radical group, Islamic Jihad, claiming responsibility. Six young Tunisians later confessed to planting the bombs, and stated that they were members of the MTI. They alleged that the bombings were part of an operation to damage the tourist trade on which Tunisia depended. In September the trial opened of 90 Islamists, accused of threatening state security and of plotting against the Government. The conduct of the trial was criticized by opposition parties and human rights groups. Despite the prosecution's demand that all 90 defendants should receive the death penalty, only seven were sentenced to death, five of them *in absentia*. Fourteen defendants were acquitted, and 69 (including Rached Ghanouchi) received prison sentences.

FOREIGN RELATIONS IN THE 1980s

In the 1980s President Bourguiba continued to pursue a moderate, pro-Western foreign policy. After the attack on Gafsa in January 1980, Tunisia strengthened its links with the USA and the two countries established a US-Tunisian military commission in November 1981.

Tunisian relations with other Maghreb countries improved considerably in the early 1980s. In March 1983 a meeting was held in Tunisia between President Bourguiba and President Ben Djedid Chadli of Algeria. Discussions on the normalization of relations between the two countries, the demarcation of the frontier and common industrial projects resulted in the drafting of the Maghreb Fraternity and Co-operation Treaty. At the subsequent ratification of the treaty by the Tunisian National Assembly, appeals were made for closer relations between the Maghreb states of Algeria, Libya, Mauritania, Morocco and Tunisia, and the introduction of a common political structure. Mauritania signed the treaty in December 1983.

However, relations with Libya reached a dangerously low ebb in August 1985 after Tunisia expelled 283 Libyan nationals, including most of the Libyan diplomats in Tunis, on charges of spying, in retaliation against Col Qaddafi's decision to expel some 30,000 Tunisians working in Libya. Qaddafi threatened to use military force to resolve the dispute, and Tunisia's armed forces were placed on alert before Morocco offered to mediate between the two countries. In September Tunisia severed diplomatic relations with Libya, following the expulsion of four Libyan diplomats who had been accused of sending letter-bombs to Tunisian journalists.

In response to the Libyan military threat, Tunisia's links with the USA were strengthened. However, in October 1985 relations between the two countries were soured, following the bombing by Israeli aircraft of the headquarters of the PLO, near Tunis. At the UN Security Council, the USA abstained on a Tunisian resolution condemning the raid, but resisted Israeli pressure to veto the motion. By March 1986 relations between the USA and Tunisia had improved, following a visit by US Vice-President George Bush. However, the US raid on Libya in the following month proved to be a further source of embarrassment for the Tunisian Government, which refused to condemn or to approve the US action and thus angered members of opposition parties and Islamists. Demonstrations ensued and many opposition figures were arrested (see above).

Meanwhile, there was growing Tunisian ambivalence over the PLO presence in Tunis. Following the Israeli raid on the PLO headquarters, a group of Palestinians 'hijacked' an Italian cruise liner, the *Achille Lauro*, off the Egyptian coast. The USA made it clear that it would not allow the hijackers to return to the PLO headquarters in Tunis, and the Tunisian authorities refused to let the Egyptian aircraft carrying the hijackers and a PLO official land in Tunisia (see chapter on Egypt). Although there was speculation in late 1986 that the PLO would move its headquarters out of Tunisia, as a result of increasing restrictions imposed on its activities by the Tunisian Government, in October the organization decided to remain in Tunisia but with a considerably reduced number of staff.

Relations with Libya began to improve in March 1987, when President Bourguiba met a representative of the Libyan Government to discuss the issue of compensation for Tunisian workers,

and the restoration of capital to companies expelled from Libya in 1985. In early 1987 Libya produced a written undertaking not to interfere in Tunisia's internal affairs. In July flights were resumed by Tunisia's national airline, TunisAir, to Tripoli. Following Col Qaddafi's proposals to unify Libya and Algeria, Bourguiba and President Chadli of Algeria issued a joint communiqué in July, announcing that discussions had taken place on how to develop the unity of the Maghreb region, although it seemed that Bourguiba had agreed to increased co-operation between the Maghreb states, rather than merger. In September Tunisia announced that the dispute with Libya over the expulsion of the Tunisian workers had been resolved, and consular ties were resumed in the following month, when the border between the two countries was reopened.

BOURGUIBA'S DECLINE

In the second half of 1987 President Bourguiba's behaviour became increasingly erratic. In September the appointments were announced of a new Minister of Cultural Affairs, Director of the PSD Political Bureau, Director-General of the Tunisian broadcasting company, and editor of the state-owned newspaper, *al-Amal*. A few days later, in early October, Bourguiba revoked the appointments and dismissed Rachid Sfar from the premiership. Ben Ali was appointed Prime Minister, with responsibility for internal affairs, and Secretary-General of the PSD. A few weeks later, a new director of the PSD was appointed. In late October Bourguiba carried out a minor cabinet reshuffle in which the Ministry of Finance was divided into two portfolios and a Ministry of the National Economy was created.

Meanwhile, ministers, concerned about Bourguiba's behaviour, began to examine provisions in the Constitution that would allow for the retirement of the President. Reports emerged that Bourguiba was demanding a retrial of the Islamists who had been sentenced in September 1987 (see above), with the aim of having the death sentence imposed on all 90 defendants. A disagreement about the fate of the Islamists allegedly ensued between Bourguiba and Ben Ali, and it was rumoured in early November that Bourguiba intended to dismiss Ben Ali. Meanwhile, a plot to overthrow Bourguiba was disclosed, allegedly involving about 150 people, both military and civilian.

BEN ALI TAKES OVER

On 7 November 1987 seven doctors declared that President Bourguiba was unfit to govern, owing to senility and ill health, and, in accordance with the Constitution, the Prime Minister, Zine al-Abidine Ben Ali, was sworn in as President. There was no apparent opposition to Ben Ali's takeover, which had been approved in advance by the majority of ministers and senior military officers. President Ben Ali declared that he would continue to implement existing foreign and economic policies, but announced plans to revise the Constitution and to permit greater political freedom. He appointed Hedi Baccouche as Prime Minister, and a new Council of Ministers was announced, which omitted four ministers closely associated with Bourguiba. Later in November, Ben Ali formed a National Security Council (comprising himself, the Prime Minister, the Minister of State for Defence, the Minister of Foreign Affairs and the Minister of the Interior) to safeguard internal security. The Council subsequently announced that 76 people, including members of the army and national guard, police, customs officers and members of the MTI, had been arrested on suspicion of plotting against the State.

On assuming power, President Ben Ali immediately began to effect a policy of national reconciliation. The publication was permitted of opposition newspapers that had been suspended by the Bourguiba administration, although radio and television networks continued to be controlled. In late November 1987 the National Assembly approved legislation that limited to four days the length of time during which a person could be held in police custody without the authority of the public prosecutor: the length of time during which a person could be held on remand was limited to six months for most offences. In December the State Security Court was abolished, along with the post of Prosecutor-General. In the same month, 2,487 political and non-political detainees were released, including 608 MTI members and Ahmad Mestiri, the leader of the MDS. In January 1988 405 political prisoners were released, and in

March Ben Ali granted amnesty to a further 2,044 political and common-law detainees.

Ben Ali also initiated attempts to normalize relations between the Government and the UGTT, as a result of which the two rivals for the leadership of the UGTT, Habib Achour and Abd al-Aziz Bouraoui, agreed to renounce their union responsibilities as a first step towards the reconciliation of the 'radical' and 'moderate' factions of the union. In May 1988 Ben Ali ordered the release of Rached Ghanouchi, the leader of the MTI. Ahmad Ben Salah, the exiled leader of the MUP, was also pardoned, and he returned to Tunisia in June.

Meanwhile, the new Government continued to consolidate its power. The size of the PSD political bureau was reduced from 20 to 13 members in December 1987. Nine new members were appointed, including seven members of the Council of Ministers formed in November, all of whom were close associates of President Ben Ali. In January 1988 the PSD won all the seats at five by-elections to the National Assembly with a comfortable majority, although the PCT alleged electoral malpractice. In a government reorganization in the following month, Ben Ali assumed the defence portfolio and appointed a Secretary of State for Security Affairs.

POLITICAL LIBERALIZATION

In accordance with his promises after assuming power, President Ben Ali introduced proposals to increase political freedom and to introduce a more democratic system of government. In February 1988 the central committee of the PSD announced that the party's name had been changed to the Rassemblement constitutionnel démocratique (RCD—Democratic Constitutional Assembly). In July the National Assembly approved a series of proposals to reform the Constitution. Under the amendments, the post of President-for-life was abolished, and the President was to be elected by universal suffrage every five years, and limited to two consecutive terms in office. A maximum age of 70 years was to be introduced for presidential candidates. If the presidency fell vacant before the end of the term of office, the President of the National Assembly, rather than the Prime Minister, was to assume presidential powers until elections were held, but was himself prohibited from becoming a candidate. The reforms also redefined the role of the Prime Minister as a co-ordinator of government activities rather than as leader of the government.

In April 1988 legislation was passed by the National Assembly instituting a multi-party system, although, in order to gain legal recognition, political parties had to uphold the aims of, and work within, the Constitution, and were not to be permitted to pursue purely religious, racial, regional or linguistic objectives. Gifts and donations to political parties were to be supervised by the Minister of the Interior, in order to prevent foreign interference. In July the National Assembly modified the Press Code, relaxing its repressive tendencies. In the same month, Tunisia became the first Arab nation to ratify the UN convention against torture and other inhumane or degrading treatment. In late July, as part of an amnesty extended to 932 detainees, Tunisia's remaining 180 classified political prisoners were released, and a further 1,075 people charged with political crimes or under police surveillance had their civil liberties restored. The beneficiaries of this amnesty included 50 Islamists arrested in 1987; members of the UGTT; Tunisians involved in the attack on Gafsa in 1980; and supporters of Salah Ben Yousuf, who had been arrested in 1963. (However, about 170 prisoners accused of terrorist acts remained in detention.)

In a major ministerial reshuffle in July 1988, seven ministers who had served under Bourguiba were dismissed, leaving Hedi Baccouche, the Prime Minister, as the only prominent member of the Council of Ministers to have served under the two Presidents. In an apparent move to separate the RCD from the state apparatus, as a prelude to a multi-party system, the Director of the RCD Political Bureau lost his right to sit in the Council of Ministers and the public health portfolio was allocated to Saadadine Zmerli, the President of the LTDH, who was not a member of the RCD. Ben Ali also divided the Ministry of Economy into a Ministry of Trade and Industry and a Ministry of Energy and Mines.

At the first congress of the RCD in late July 1988, President Ben Ali pledged that he would establish a multi-party system

with fair elections and freedom of expression. In accordance with Ben Ali's appeal for pluralism, Ahmad Mestiri, the leader of the MDS, and Muhammad Belhadj Amor, the leader of the Parti de l'unité populaire (PUP), were invited to address the congress, and both endorsed the policies of the Ben Ali Government. Ben Ali was re-elected as president of the RCD, despite speculation, following the recent cabinet reshuffle, that he would relinquish his party post. The perpetuation of ties between the RCD and the Government was also reflected in the appointments of Hedi Baccouche, the Prime Minister, as Vice-President of the party, and of the Minister of Foreign Affairs, the Minister of the Interior and the Governor of the Central Bank (who held cabinet rank) as members of the new streamlined seven-member political bureau. There was also concern over the disclosure that Ben Ali had personally appointed 122 members of the RCD's enlarged 200-strong central committee.

Ben Ali restated his desire to 'open a new page of pluralism and democracy' at the beginning of consultations held in September 1988 on a Tunisian 'National Pact' to present the aims and values of the administration. Participants in the consultations included representatives from national organizations (the UGTT, employers' organizations, youth and women's groups, etc), the Secretary-Generals of the RCD, the MDS, the PCT and the PUP, and the leaders of the unofficial political parties (the leftist RSP, the liberal Parti social pour le progrès—PSP, the MUP and the MTI). Later that month, the RSP and the PSP were granted legal recognition. Earlier in August, Rached Ghanouchi had announced that the MTI accepted the law on political parties and respected the Constitution, especially the personal status code enshrining women's rights.

Ben Ali was faced with the problem of integrating the Islamists into the political system without totally abandoning the secularism of the Bourguiba regime, and he succeeded in establishing good relations with their leader. Following the release of leading fundamentalists in September and November 1988, Ghanouchi stated that the era of injustice was over. Stress was laid upon the Arab and Islamic identity of Tunisia, the *Azzan* and prayers were broadcast on television, *Hijri* dates appeared on official documents, and the seventh-century religious college, the Zeitouna, was given the status of a university. The MTI, transformed into a political party (Hizb an-Nahdah or Parti de la renaissance), was, none the less, denied official status.

On the first anniversary of his rise to power Ben Ali announced a National Pact, which was designed to show Tunisia as a country ready for democracy. Basic freedoms were guaranteed, although political parties could be formed only with the approval of the Minister of the Interior. Elections, not due until 1991, were brought forward to April 1989. In November 1988 a new political party, the Union démocratique unioniste (UDU), was legalized, and began to develop Arab nationalist and unionist policies.

During this period old associates of Bourguiba were indicted for corruption and embezzlement of considerable sums: Mahmoud Skhiri was sentenced to five years' imprisonment, Tahar Belhodja (*in absentia*) to five years, Mahmoud Belhassine to 10 years and a heavy fine, while Mzali's request, from abroad, for rehabilitation was refused. Moreover, Ben Ali dismissed Habib Ammar, one of his oldest and closest associates (whose son had been involved in a smuggling case), from the Ministry of the Interior.

THE APRIL 1989 ELECTIONS

In February 1989, in an attempt to establish national consensus and also to guarantee the election of some non-RCD candidates, Ben Ali invited the leaders of the six opposition parties to present themselves to the electorate as a coalition. The offer was rejected, although the parties had previously agreed to support Ben Ali as sole candidate for the presidency. In a drastic purge conducted at local level, the RCD readopted only 20 of its 125 retiring members. The Communists, fearing humiliation at the polls, declined to participate. Hizb an-Nahdah, forbidden from campaigning as a party, presented 'independent' candidates in 19 of the 25 constituencies, in which a total of 480 candidates contested 141 seats. The National Assembly elections were the first multi-party elections in Tunisia since 1981; the level of participation was 76% of the 2,700,000 eligible voters. The RCD won all 141 seats, with 80% of the votes cast, while the

Islamist independents replaced the MDS as the main opposition force, taking 13% of the total votes and 25% of votes in many constituencies. Opposition allegations of widespread electoral fraud were denied by the RCD. Ben Ali was confirmed as President by 99% of voters.

On 11 April 1989 a new Council of Ministers of 32 members was announced. Although the leading members, headed by Baccouche, were retained, the cabinet represented a new political generation. With an average age of 48 years, most ministers were too young to have taken part in the struggle for independence, and 28 of them had not held any office under Bourguiba. In addition, they were drawn from the whole country (one-third from the deprived south) rather than predominantly from Bourguiba's own Sahel area. Technocrats were given portfolios to address what Ben Ali defined as the main problems: foreign debts, expensive subsidies, a cumbersome and expensive public sector, unemployment and regional policies. As a conciliatory gesture to the opposition, the liberal Mohammed Charfi, a leading member of the LTDH, was placed in charge of education and scientific research, while Daly Jazi, a founding member of the MDS, was appointed as Minister of Public Health.

POLITICAL DEVELOPMENTS

However, the National Pact failed to curb political dissent in the country, and tensions were exacerbated by the imposition of essential economic reforms. In April 1989 Ben Ali announced a general amnesty, which restored civil and political rights to 5,416 people condemned by the former regime, many of whom were Islamist activists. The remaining 48 Islamist prisoners, sentenced in 1987 for plotting against Bourguiba, were released in May 1989. In September Ben Ali dismissed his Prime Minister, Hedi Baccouche, following a disagreement over economic policy; Baccouche was replaced by Hamed Karoui, hitherto Minister of Justice. In November a further 1,354 people, including Bourguiba's close associates Mahmoud Skhiri and Tahar Belkhodja, were granted amnesty. In one of the few political trials, the leader of a breakaway faction of the MUP was sentenced in August to one year's imprisonment for defamation of the President (but was released in November); six communists were later imprisoned for similar offences. In May 1990 an Islamist leader, Professor Moncef Ben Salem, was sentenced to three years' imprisonment for criticizing the Government in an Algerian fundamentalist newspaper.

In late 1989 taxes were lowered in an attempt to reduce evasion, and Ben Ali announced a 10% increase in wages. However, the President failed to gain popular support and appeared increasingly autocratic, declaring that he alone would decide the pace and course of reform. The conflict between the country's need for reform and modernization and the traditional Islamic values held by certain factions was seemingly insoluble. The Government was also concerned that Islamists were receiving financial aid from foreign sources. After the April 1989 elections, Rached Ghanouchi went into voluntary exile in Paris, and a lawyer, Abd al-Fatha Mourou, assumed the leadership of an-Nahdah within Tunisia. In June official recognition of an-Nahdah was refused, on the grounds that 15 of its leaders had not yet regained their civil rights. Ben Ali also demanded that an-Nahdah clarify its position on the rights of women, and reiterated his opposition to the concept of a religious political party. In December a second application for registration was refused, although an-Nahdah was permitted to publish a weekly journal, al-Fajr. (The an-Nahdah weekly, al-Moustaqbal, had been closed down in the previous year.)

Following their failure to secure legal recognition, the Islamists increased their political agitation and gained support among students. In December 1989 96 students began a hunger strike after the Government tried to divide its opponents by dissolving the Theological Faculty of the Zeitouna University. A campus police station in Kairouan was ransacked, and casualties were reported on the campus at Sfax. In February 1990 the protests culminated in clashes between police and students belonging to the Union Générale des Etudiants Tunisiens (UGET), an organization allied to an-Nahdah. About 600 student activists were detained, and some were briefly drafted into the army. The Government accused an-Nahdah of exploiting the students and of inciting unrest among the work-force, including a strike by 10,000 municipal workers. Political tension increased following severe floods in late January 1990, which killed 30 people and caused damage to property totalling more than US $400m. Some 800 demonstrators, incited by Islamist leaders who condemned the Government's dilatory relief efforts, attacked government offices in Sidi Bou Zid, and 26 were arrested. Ben Ali subsequently pledged $445m. towards relief work. (In April five men were sentenced to three months' imprisonment for leading the riots.)

The Government was keen that municipal elections, due to be held in June 1990, should be viewed as a serious stratagem towards multi-party democracy. In January Prime Minister Karoui invited opposition leaders for discussions on the amendment of the electoral code and access to the media. However, the discussions were boycotted by three of the recognized opposition parties and by an-Nahdah, and little progress was made. In May the electoral law was amended to introduce a form of proportional representation in the forthcoming municipal elections. The winning party was to gain only 50% of the seats, while the remaining seats were to be divided between all the parties, according to the number of votes received. However, the six legal opposition groups and an-Nahdah boycotted the elections, held on 10 June, on the grounds that they were neither free nor fair. The RCD won control of all but one of the 245 municipal councils, taking 3,750 council seats. The remaining 34 seats were won by independent candidates, many of whom were former members of the RCD. According to official sources, an estimated 79.3% of the electorate voted. In the same month publication of al-Fajr was suspended, following an article by exiled leader Rached Ghanouchi that strongly criticized the Tunisian Government.

Disagreement over government policy regarding the Gulf crisis, and in particular the stance adopted concerning Iraq, was the apparent cause of the replacement, in late August 1990, of the Minister of Foreign Affairs, Ismaïl Khelil, by Habib Boularès (a prominent journalist and a former Minister of Culture and Information under Bourguiba).

In October 1990 it was reported by the human rights organization, Amnesty International, that although more than 10,000 common-law and political prisoners had benefited from amnesty measures since Ben Ali's accession to the presidency, human rights abuses, of which members of unregistered political groups were often the victims, continued. In the following month Ben Ali pardoned 113 prisoners, and announced the formation of a national commission on human rights (to be known as the Comité supérieur des droits de l'homme et des libertés fondamentales—CSDHLF). In March 1991 an amnesty was announced for a further 836 prisoners. The human rights commission was inaugurated in April.

In November 1990 several members of an-Nahdah were arrested, following the discovery of explosives that were allegedly to have been used for terrorist activities. An-Nahdah's senior officials denied that the movement was involved in terrorism. In the same month it was announced that the authorities had dismantled an 'Islamic network' that had allegedly been planning an Islamist revolution. In late December senior officials of an-Nahdah were arrested, together with more than 100 other people, and accused of attempting to establish an Islamic state. The arrests provoked demonstrations by Islamist militants in January 1991, and in the same month thousands of Tunisians took part in pro-Iraqi demonstrations, following the outbreak of war between Iraq and the US-led multinational force. In February further demonstrations by Islamists were violently suppressed. In the same month the co-ordinator of the MUP, Brahim Hayder, was sentenced to three months' imprisonment on a charge of attempting to disturb public order (after having condemned the Government's banning of a pro-Iraqi demonstration in January).

In February 1991 the Minister of the Interior, Abd-al Hamid Escheikh, whose attitude towards recent Islamist manifestations of support for Iraq had apparently been regarded by his government colleagues as insufficiently uncompromising, was replaced by Abdallah Kallel, hitherto Minister of Defence. Habib Boularès assumed the defence portfolio. Escheikh's dismissal was announced within hours of an armed attack, allegedly by an-Nahdah supporters, on RCD offices in Tunis, as a result of which one person was said to have been burned to death. In March Abd al-Fatha Mourou and the two other members of the an-Nahdah executive committee who were still at liberty in Tunis (four members were reported to be in detention at this time, two had fled the capital to evade arrest, while Rached Ghanouchi remained in exile) responded to government pressure, denouncing violent acts committed in the name of an-Nahdah and 'freezing' their activities within the movement. However, tensions persisted, and in May two students were killed in a clash with the police. The students' union, UGET, was disbanded by the authorities after the police claimed to have found weapons and subversive material linked to an-Nahdah, and riot police were posted outside centres where the annual baccalaureate examinations were being held. Also in May some 300 people, including about 100 members of the security forces, were arrested in connection with an alleged Islamist plot: the Government claimed that it had been planned to assassinate Ben Ali and other government members in October. In June five Islamists were sentenced to death (two *in absentia*) for their part in the attack on the RCD headquarters. The executions of the three who were in detention took place in October, this reportedly being only the second occasion on which death sentences had been implemented since Ben Ali's accession to power.

In July 1991 Amnesty International reported that it had received accounts of the systematic torture of more than 100 prisoners, most of whom were suspected members of an-Nahdah. The Government requested the newly-created CSDHLF to investigate, and its findings, published in October, showed that there had indeed been abuses, but concluded that these had not been officially sanctioned. About 140 prisoners, many of them political, were released in November (on the anniversary of the President's accession to power), and the sentences of more than 900 other detainees were reduced. In March 1992 a further report by Amnesty International, which detailed the arrests of some 8,000 people—mostly suspected members of an-Nahdah—over an 18-month period, and cited 200 cases of the torture and ill-treatment of detainees, as well as the deaths in custody of at least seven Islamists, was immediately condemned by the Tunisian authorities as 'baseless'. However, the Government, while denying that any detainee in Tunisia could be classified as a prisoner of conscience, later conceded that some violations of human rights had been committed, and announced that it would investigate allegations of the abuse of detainees. Meanwhile, new restrictions were imposed on organizations such as the LTDH, which in July 1991 had criticized restrictions on press freedom. In June 1992 the LTDH was dissolved by its leadership, following the introduction of legislation which, in establishing new distinctions between the competences of political parties and hitherto quasi-political associations such as the LTDH, effectively banned members of the latter from participation in political life.

In addition to an apparently unsuccessful attempt to persuade Abd al-Fatha Mourou and his supporters to form a 'moderate' Islamic party, Ben Ali began to court the legalized opposition. In March 1991 he received opposition leaders and ordered that they should receive funds for party expenses and propaganda and that the police should not harass their activities. Ben Ali also appeared anxious to end the RCD's monopoly of power in the National Assembly, and offered not to present RCD candidates for nine by-elections pending to the legislature. However, the opposition, demanding a wider reform of the electoral system, boycotted the elections, and the vacant seats were taken by RCD candidates. The relatively high level of participation by voters, ranging from 69.5% to 92.4%, was interpreted as an indication of popular support for the Government's uncompromising attitude towards an-Nahdah. In December Ben Ali announced that changes to the electoral code, to be formulated in co-operation with opposition parties, would be implemented during 1992, with the aim of ensuring greater representation at the national level for parties other than the RCD. The opposition resumed a dialogue with the Government in January 1992, although its cohesion was undermined by a number of incidents: Ahmed Ben Salah and Muhammad Mzali, both still in exile, were reported to have declared support for an-Nahdah, and Ahmad Mestiri resigned from the MDS in early 1992, apparently in response to internal party differences which resulted in the 'suspension' of the activities within the MDS of three members of the party's political bureau.

Government changes in October 1991 resulted in the promotion of Abdallah Kallel to the rank of Minister of State. At the same time Ben Ali appointed a close associate, Abd al-Aziz Ben Dhia, to replace Habib Boularès at the Ministry of Defence. (Boularès was subsequently appointed President of the National Assembly.) In March 1992, at the beginning of the Islamic month of Ramadan, a new Ministry of Religious Affairs was created. Further government changes in June included the creation of a Ministry of International Co-operation and Foreign Investment, as well as the appointment of Ben Ali's adviser on human rights, Sadok Chaabane, as Minister of Justice. In the following month the composition of the Council of Ministers was again modified.

Suppression of an-Nahdah continued, with widespread arrests and a large security presence on the streets. In July 1992 more than 100 people, said to belong to the Islamist terrorist group 'Commandos du sacrifice', were put on trial at the Tunis military tribunal. The accused, who included army, police and customs officials, were charged with conspiring to take power by force and plotting to assassinate the President. During the trial, an-Nahdah's official spokesman insisted that the Commandos du sacrifice were not part of the an-Nahdah movement and denied the existence of any plot to overthrow the State. Habib Laasoued, alleged to be the leader of the Commandos, also denied any link with an-Nahdah, which he described as a rival movement. At the same time, almost 200 alleged an-Nahdah members were put on trial for plotting to take power by force. Throughout both trials there were allegations of irregularities in the conduct of the hearings and of human rights abuses. Many of the accused claimed that torture had been used to extract a confession. In August the courts announced long prison sentences for the defendants. Among those receiving life sentences were three exiled an-Nahdah leaders, Rached Ghanouchi, Salah Karkar and Habib Moknil. It was claimed that Ghanouchi had received funds from the Governments of Iran, Sudan and Saudi Arabia to overthrow the Tunisian regime and was organizing violent Islamist revolution. These mass trials were seen as the culmination of the Tunisian Government's long campaign against an-Nahdah, whose organizational structures within the country were largely destroyed and its leaders imprisoned or forced into exile. Abdallah Kallel claimed that 'a Tunisian terrorist network' had been completely dismantled. Some members of opposition parties accused President Ben Ali of using the threat of 'Islamic fundamentalism' as an excuse to delay long-promised democratic reforms. In August 1993 it was reported that Ghanouchi (sentenced to life imprisonment *in absentia* in 1992) had been granted political asylum in the United Kingdom, despite the Tunisian Government's efforts to obtain his extradition. The British Foreign and Commonwealth Office emphasized that the decision to grant Ghanouchi asylum had been taken by the Home Office (responsible for internal affairs) and was not a matter of foreign policy.

FOREIGN POLICY UNDER BEN ALI

President Ben Ali continued to pursue a moderate, pro-Western foreign policy. Relations with the USA remained cordial, and, during discussions on political and economic issues in March 1988 with the Tunisian Government, the US Secretary of State, George Shultz, announced US support for Ben Ali's political reforms. In April the US Secretary of Defense, Frank Carlucci, visited Tunis to discuss Tunisia's military debt to the USA, which totalled US $400m. In June the Tunisian administration authorized two US banks to refinance the debt. The Tunisian Government attempted to improve relations between the USA and Libya after the shooting down of two Libyan aircraft in January 1989. It was hampered by the strength of popular sentiment, with anti-US demonstrations occurring across the country. During an official visit to the USA in May 1990, Ben Ali met the US President, George Bush, to discuss the issue of peace in the Middle East. He also urged continued economic support from Western nations and an increase in US investment.

However, the new Tunisian Government was also interested in extending its co-operation with other Western nations. A military co-operation accord was reached with Spain in December 1987 and adopted by the Tunisian National Assembly in May 1988. Under the terms of the accord, the two countries were to establish joint ventures for the research, development and production of military equipment, to exchange military personnel and to conduct joint military exercises on each other's territory. Earlier, in January, the United Kingdom announced that it was willing to assist in the training and equipping of Tunisian security forces. In April the Tunisian Government received a military delegation from the Federal Republic of Germany, with the intention of gaining German military co-operation. In September Ben Ali discussed economic co-operation with President François Mitterrand, during a state visit to France. Co-operation between France and Tunisia was strengthened following visits by Laurent Fabius, the President of the French National Assembly, in December, and by Roland Dumas, the Minister of Foreign Affairs, in May 1989. During a state visit to Tunisia in June President Mitterrand promised greater investment in Tunisia; in August four agreements concerning financial aid were reached. The Turkish Prime Minister, Turgut Özal, also visited Tunisia. Although the two countries reached some trade agreements, Tunisia refused a request to recognize the 'Turkish Republic of Northern Cyprus'. In March 1990 a military co-operation agreement was signed with Turkey.

Following Iraq's invasion of Kuwait in August 1990 (see the chapter on Iraq), President Ben Ali condemned the deployment of a US-led multinational force in the Gulf region, arguing that it was neither in the interests of Arabs nor of world peace. He refused to attend an emergency summit meeting of the Arab League, held in Cairo, and, in an apparent attempt to undertake a central mediatory role, asked that the meeting be postponed while he visited Baghdad to persuade the Iraqi President, Saddam Hussain, of the need for a settlement. His official pronouncements against intervention by Western nations were apparently influenced by the growing Arab nationalist support for Iraq within Tunisia. This solidarity was reflected in the formation of a new political organization, the National Committee for Support to Iraq, which comprised most opposition parties and professional associations. The Committee demanded a suspension of diplomatic relations with countries, such as Egypt and Saudi Arabia, which supported intervention in the Gulf region, and the enlistment of Tunisian volunteers to be sent to Iraq. In late August Ben Ali sent a number of emissaries to Arab and Western nations, as part of a diplomatic initiative to prevent war in the Gulf. In September Tunisia restored diplomatic relations with Iran, which had been suspended in 1987 after Tunisia had accused Iran of supporting fundamentalist opponents of then President Bourguiba.

RELATIONS WITHIN THE MAGHREB

Under the Ben Ali administration, relations with Libya improved dramatically, with the result that Tunisia was able to play a more active role in the development of Maghrebin unity. In December 1987 full diplomatic relations were resumed with Libya, after Libya had agreed to pay US $10m. in indemnities to the Tunisian workers expelled in 1985 and to reimburse Tunisian assets, which had been frozen in Libya. Subsequently the Tunisian, Algerian and Mauritanian ministers responsible for foreign affairs met to discuss the possibility of Libya becoming a signatory to the Maghreb Fraternity and Co-operation Treaty of 1983, as a prelude to the creation of a Great Arab Maghreb. In January 1988 President Chadli of Algeria visited Tunisia and held further discussions with Ben Ali on the issues of the Great Arab Maghreb, bilateral co-operation and a lasting settlement for the Moroccan-occupied Western Sahara. Ben Ali discussed these matters again with the Moroccan Prime Minister, Az ad-Dine Laraki, at the beginning of February.

In January 1988 Col Qaddafi postponed a scheduled visit to Tunisia to demonstrate his displeasure at the Tunisian Government receiving the commanders of the US and French navies. In February, however, the visit took place, and, following talks, Ben Ali and Col Qaddafi stated that they had agreed to abolish entry visas for Tunisians and Libyans crossing the Tunisian–Libyan border, and to abide by the judgment of the ICJ concerning the delineation of their respective sectors of the continental shelf in the Gulf of Gabès. Several days later, Ben Ali, Col Qaddafi and President Chadli of Algeria met and expressed their determination to encourage co-operation between the Maghreb countries. In June Ben Ali attended the

first summit meeting of the five heads of the Maghrebin countries in Algiers (for further details, see Algeria, History). In May Ben Ali and Col Qaddafi had held an unscheduled summit on the island of Djerba. The two leaders signed an agreement providing for a social and economic union of the two countries, the free movement of people and goods across their common frontier, the establishment of a common identity card system and the freedom to live, work and own property in the respective countries. A number of joint industrial, economic and cultural projects were initiated immediately after the summit. In August Ben Ali visited Col Qaddafi in Libya and signed a series of co-operation agreements and an agreement concerning the settlement of the dispute over the continental shelf in the Gulf of Gabès. During the visit, a technical commission was established to examine means of accelerating co-operation and merger between Tunisia and Libya. In September an agreement was signed establishing a joint Tunisian-Libyan company, which would exploit the '7 November' oilfield on the continental shelf in the Gulf of Gabès. An agreement to link the two countries' electricity grids was signed.

Taking advantage of the open frontier, an estimated 1m. Libyan tourists visited Tunisia, spending so much money that shortages of goods in the shops were reported. A new motorway from the frontier to Sfax was constructed to facilitate their entry. At least 30,000 Tunisians found employment in Libya. During a visit to Tunisia in December 1988, Col Qaddafi addressed the National Assembly, stating that he favoured 'constitutional unity' between the two countries but would not try to impose it. He returned with President Chadli of Algeria in February 1989.

Ben Ali was influential in the movement towards Maghreb unity, by convincing President Chadli that unity would be impossible without the participation of Morocco; he had no wish to continue in a subordinate role in the Maghreb Fraternity and Co-operation Treaty. Tunisia was put in charge of the working party dealing with human and social affairs and security, and played a significant role in all the meetings of ministers and heads of state, arguing for gradual progress towards unity.

Tunisia initially seemed the most committed member of the newly-created Union of the Arab Maghreb (UMA), while Col Qaddafi appeared reluctant to implement agreements, such as the joint exploration of the Gulf of Gabès and the financing of infrastructure programmes in Tunisia. The Tunisian Prime Minister, Hedi Baccouche, visited Tripoli in July 1989, in an attempt to promote economic co-operation, although little practical progress was achieved. During a preliminary meeting of ministers responsible for foreign affairs in January 1990 the Tunisian minister proposed a series of measures, all of which were approved, including the creation of a permanent secretariat (preferably based in Tunis), the expansion of the Consultative Council to 100 members, the establishment of commissions to examine joint projects in food production, economy and finance, infrastructure and human resources, and negotiations with other groups, particularly the European Community (EC).

In February 1990 the Minister of the Economy proposed a single energy market for North Africa, with free trade in electricity, petroleum and natural gas, the linkage of grids and extension of pipelines. In the same month the first meeting of the Human Resource Committee, attended by ministers of education, was held, and special passport controls were provided for North African visitors at Tunis airports. In March a television service, broadcast throughout North Africa, was established in Tunis. Also in March the newly-appointed Tunisian Minister of Foreign Affairs, Ismaïl Khelil, proposed that the EC should reschedule debts to provide for training and the creation of jobs in North Africa, with the aim of reducing emigration to Europe. Official sources estimated that 1.8m. Maghrebis worked in Europe (with a further 600,000 working illegally), while the number of unemployed within the UMA totalled at least 2m. The UMA also raised the issue of racial attacks upon their citizens in the EC. In June 1990 President Ben Ali proposed an agreement between the EC and UMA, which would guarantee the rights of North Africans working in Europe.

RELATIONS WITH OTHER ARAB NATIONS

Tunisia's status as a moderate Arab state was maintained under Ben Ali. Following discussions with PLO representatives and members of the Egyptian Government, the Tunisian Government announced in January 1988 that it would be resuming diplomatic relations with Egypt. (Relations had been severed by Tunisia in 1979 after Egypt signed the Camp David Agreement with Israel.) Meanwhile, Hedi Baccouche, the Tunisian Prime Minister, toured the Arab Gulf states, which ranked among Tunisia's major sources of economic aid, to explain to Arab leaders the new administration's domestic and foreign policies. Baccouche reaffirmed Tunisia's support for the Gulf states, which feared an extension of the Iran–Iraq War, thus seeming to rule out the possibility that the Ben Ali Government would restore diplomatic relations with Iran in the near future. In April Baccouche visited Egypt and concluded several bilateral agreements. In January 1989 Dr Boutros Boutros-Ghali, then Minister of State for Foreign Affairs, became the first Egyptian minister to visit Tunisia for 10 years.

Meanwhile, Tunisia was the scene of another Israeli operation against the PLO. In April 1988 'Abu Jihad', the military commander of the PLO, was assassinated at his home near Tunis in a combined operation by the Israeli secret service, Mossad, and Israeli army and naval commando forces. The Israeli operation was a source of embarrassment for the Tunisian authorities, as it was revealed that Mossad operatives had been based in Tunisia for some time before the assassination was carried out. After discovering evidence that an Israeli military aircraft (apparently carrying sophisticated equipment with which to 'jam' telecommunications) had passed close to Tunisian airspace when 'Abu Jihad' was killed, the Tunisian Government lodged a complaint with the UN Security Council. Later in April, the Council adopted a resolution condemning 'the Israeli aggression against Tunisian territory'.

In March 1990 Ben Ali made the first visit to Cairo by a Tunisian President since 1965, and signed several agreements on bilateral co-operation with Egypt. Relations with Saudi Arabia also remained cordial; in March the Saudi-Tunisian Joint Commission met to discuss eight projects, financed by Saudi Arabia, and in July the Saudi Arabian Minister of Defence visited Tunis. Despite the high level of co-operation between the two countries, the Tunisian Government was concerned about the extent of Saudi support for Tunisian Islamists. In April the Iraqi Deputy Prime Minister visited Tunis, where he signed a bilateral trade agreement. In September a majority of members of the Arab League decided to move the League's headquarters from Tunis (where it had been 'temporarily' established in 1979) back to its original site in Cairo. The Tunisian Government protested at the decision and the League's Tunisian Secretary-General, Chedli Klibi, resigned.

RELATIONS WITH THE ARAB WORLD AFTER THE GULF WAR

After the cease-fire in the Gulf War in February 1991, Tunisia sought to restore links that had been strained by its support for Iraq (a policy which probably prompted the replacement of the pro-Baathist Habib Boularès as Minister of Foreign Affairs by the less abrasive Habib Ben Yahia). Although Kuwait had withdrawn its ambassador from Tunis, Ben Ali sent a cordial message to the Amir, congratulating him upon regaining his sovereignty. Ben Ali undertook a tour of the Gulf region in November. Soon after his appointment Ben Yahia went to Cairo in an attempt to re-establish cordial relations. The Egyptian and Tunisian ministers responsible for the interior met twice to discuss the problems posed by Islamist activists, and made arrangements for the exchange of intelligence. A trade pact was signed with Syria in August 1991, following an earlier visit to Damascus by Ben Yahia. In February 1992 further bilateral agreements covered co-operation in education and other fields.

Conversely, when in April 1991 the Iraqi Deputy Minister, Tareq Aziz, visited the Maghreb, Ben Ali, alone among the regional heads of state, refused to receive him, claiming fatigue and the need to prepare for a visit to the People's Republic of China. The Iraqi aircraft that had taken refuge in Tunis during the crisis were not returned, but Tunisia did join the other UMA countries in appealing for the ending of sanctions against Iraq. Sudan had co-operated closely with Tunisia in the attempt to prevent the outbreak of war in the Gulf region, and Lt-Gen. Omar Hassan Ahmad al-Bashir, the Sudanese Head of State, visited Tunis in March 1991. However, in October Tunisia withdrew its ambassador from Khartoum, alleging that Sudan had been supporting Islamist terrorists. In July 1992 Sudan announced the closure of its embassy in Tunis, in protest against the Tunisian authorities' alleged suppression of the Islamist movement. In December a series of agreements was signed with Oman and relations between the two countries were described as exemplary. In mid-1993 there were signs that relations with Kuwait, badly strained during the Gulf crisis, might improve. In June Habib Ben Yahia made his first visit to Kuwait since the crisis, and President Ben Ali, in a letter to the Amir of Kuwait, sought improved relations. After a hostile reception from Kuwaiti politicians and from the press, Ben Yahia was forced to cut short his visit. However, after a visit to Tunis in April 1994 by the Kuwaiti Minister of Foreign Affairs and First Deputy Prime Minister, Sheikh Sabah al-Ahmad al-Jaber as-Sabah, it was reported that normal diplomatic relations would be restored. Later in 1994 the first co-operation agreement with Kuwait since the Gulf crisis was signed during a visit to Tunis by the Kuwaiti Minister of Education. In early 1996, during a visit to Kuwait by Sadok Rabah, the Tunisian Minister of Social Affairs, to encourage more investment in Tunisia, Kuwait's Minister of Foreign Affairs spoke of his pleasure at the continuing improvement in relations between the two countries. Efforts to improve relations with Kuwait were finally rewarded in April 1996 when bilateral co-operation was restored during a visit to Tunis by a high-level Kuwaiti delegation led by Sheikh Saad al-Abdullah as-Salim as-Sabah, the Crown Prince and Prime Minister. During the visit agreements were signed with the Kuwait-based Arab Fund for Economic and Social Development (AFESD) for loans worth US $45m., the first to Tunisia since the Gulf crisis. At the same time, Tunisia continued to maintain good relations with Iraq. In September 1995 Ben Ali had visited Jordan, Syria and Qatar as part of the Government's efforts to improve relations with other Arab states. In early 1997 the Egyptian Prime Minister, Kamal Ahmad al-Ganzouri, visited Tunis where he signed several economic and cultural co-operation agreements. Both countries pledged to work together to increase bilateral trade, and agreement was reached in principle on the creation of a free-trade zone. In early 1998 the two countries signed an agreement in Cairo at a meeting of the Tunisian-Egyptian Joint Higher Committee to dismantle customs duties over the next 10 years. A state visit to Tunis by the Amir of Qatar, Sheikh Hamad bin Khalifa ath-Thani, in June 1997, provided further evidence of the gradual improvement in Tunisia's relations with the Gulf states since the 1991 Gulf War. In January 1998 two small opposition parties, the RSP and the UDU, with the support of the UGTT, organized a meeting to express support for Iraq in its dispute with the UN. The Tunisian Government has regularly urged the UN to lift sanctions against Iraq. Also in January the Council of Arab Interior Ministers, meeting in Tunis, approved the draft of an Arab anti-terrorism agreement. In mid-1998 Tunisia and Jordan agreed to establish a free-trade zone and to work to increase commercial relations which, however, remained very limited. The new King of Jordan, Abdullah II, visited Tunis in June 1999 and shortly afterwards Prime Minister Karoui held talks in Amman with his Jordanian counterpart. American and British air strikes against Iraq in December were strongly criticized by the Government, and condemned by the Chamber of Deputies and by several opposition parties. However, there were no street demonstrations in support of Iraq, although security around the US embassy in Tunis was increased. In January 1999 President Ben Ali repeated his appeal for the lifting of sanctions against Iraq, in order 'to end the suffering of the Iraqi people'. The Iraqi Minister of Foreign Affairs, Muhammad Saeed as-Sahaf, visited Tunis in February and contacts at ministerial level continued during the year. In May Tunisia signed a trade agreement with Iraq, and Tunisia's trade minister, Mondher Zenaidi, made a number of visits to Baghdad to discuss bilateral trade under the UN's 'oil-for-food' programme for Iraq. By the end of 1999 Tunisia was reported to have won contracts worth $200m. to supply goods to Iraq since the 'oil-for-food' programme began. In November President Ben Ali held talks in Egypt with President Mubarak, and in a joint statement the two leaders called for a revival of the Arab League and for progress in creating an Arab free-trade zone. Early in 2000 it was reported that Tunisia was well disposed to Egypt's plan for a North

African common market consisting of Egypt, Tunisia, Algeria and Morocco, an initiative encouraged by the USA. Later the two countries signed several co-operation agreements dealing with commercial, social and cultural relations. Sheikh Salim Sabah as-Salim as-Sabah, Kuwait's defence minister, visited Tunis in November 1999 for talks on further military co-operation between the two countries.

Responding to pressure from public opinion, in October 2000 Tunisia defied the air embargo against Iraq and sent two aircraft to Baghdad carrying humanitarian and medical aid. A trade delegation led by the Minister of Trade, Mondher Zenaidi, travelled on one of the flights. Tunisia expressed deep regret at the US and British air-strikes against targets near Baghdad in mid-February 2001. During a visit to Tunis by Iraqi Vice-President, Taha Yassin Ramadan, in late February the two countries signed a free-trade agreement. In the same month President Mubarak of Egypt made an official visit to Tunis to discuss the escalation in violence between Israel and the Palestinians and efforts to revive the UMA. Also in February 2001 after Al-Jazeera, a Qatari private satellite channel, broadcast live interviews with leading human rights activist, Moncef Marzouki, exiled an-Nahda leader Rachid Ghanouchi and other leading Tunisian dissidents, Tunisia responded by recalling its ambassador from Qatar.

Tunisia claimed to have played a leading role, together with Norway, in the secret talks between the PLO and Israel which led to the signing of the Declaration of Principles on Palestinian Self-Rule in September 1993. At that time the PLO headquarters had been based near Tunis for more than 10 years. Tunisia welcomed the breakthrough in PLO-Israeli relations, and shortly afterwards an Israeli delegation arrived in Tunis for talks with Tunisian and PLO officials. Salah Masawi, the director-general of foreign relations, declared that there was no obstacle to Tunisia's establishing diplomatic relations with Israel, but that the Tunisian Government was waiting for another North African state to make the first move; it was assumed that he was referring to Morocco, which had maintained contacts with Israel through the Moroccan Jewish community for some years (see chapter on Morocco). After meeting Ben Yahia in Tunis in December, Warren Christopher, the US Secretary of State, announced that progress was being made in the normalization of relations between Tunisia and Israel. The Tunisian Ministry of Foreign Affairs welcomed the PLO-Israeli Cairo Agreement of May 1994 on implementing Palestinian self-rule in Gaza and Jericho. The PLO offices in Tunis were closed in June, as Yasser Arafat and the Palestinian leadership prepared to move to Gaza, where the newly-appointed Palestinian National Authority (PNA) was to be established. At a meeting with President Ben Ali at the end of June Chairman Arafat thanked Tunisia for the 'warm hospitality' the PLO had received since its offices were transferred from Beirut to Tunis in 1982. The official farewell ceremonies for Arafat in July were attended by Ben Ali.

As the Palestinians departed, Tunisia made new moves towards the normalization of relations with Israel. The first party of Israeli tourists to visit Tunisia since independence arrived in June 1994 (following an agreement made in October 1993 with Yossi Beilin, the Israeli Deputy Minister for Foreign Affairs—the first senior Israeli to visit Tunisia), and direct telephone links were established with Israel in July. In October the Tunisian and Israeli ministers responsible for foreign affairs met at the UN General Assembly in New York and agreed in principle to open interests sections (which Tunisia referred to as 'economic channels') in the Belgian embassies in Tunis and Tel-Aviv. At a meeting at the US State Department in Washington, DC, with Warren Christopher and the Israeli Minister of Foreign Affairs, Shimon Peres, Habib Ben Yahia stated that this was the first step towards full diplomatic relations. In October an agreement on co-operation in environmental affairs was signed between the two countries during a visit to Tunis by the Israeli Minister of the Environment. In December Haim Madar, the Grand Rabbi of Tunisia's small Jewish community, made his first visit to Israel. In February 1995 Tunisia, together with Israel, Morocco, Mauritania and Egypt, took part in talks with NATO in Brussels, Belgium, on security co-operation. Before the talks the Secretary-General of NATO, Willy Claes, had made the controversial statement that he saw Islamist

extremism as the biggest single threat to the West since the collapse of communism. In March Tunisia participated in naval exercises off the Tunisian coast with Israel, Canada, Morocco, Algeria, Egypt and four of the Arab Gulf states. These attempts to co-operate with Israel provoked criticism from some Arab quarters. In April a Tunisian liaison office was opened in the Gaza Strip; a second office was expected to be installed in Jericho. In October Yasser Arafat met President Ben Ali in Tunis to review progress made on the implementation of Palestinian self-rule. After the Palestinian elections in January 1996, Tunisia indicated that it was satisfied that progress had been made in the peace process and an agreement was reached with Israel to proceed with low-level diplomatic relations from April. Tunisia thus became the fourth Arab state to establish diplomatic relations with Israel, after Egypt, Jordan and Morocco. The move, agreed in principle in October 1994, was opposed by only one of the six legal opposition parties, but strongly condemned by Rached Ghanouchi, the exiled leader of an-Nahdah. At the same time Tunisia agreed to recognize passports issued by the PNA. In April 1996 Israel opened an interests office in the Belgian embassy in Tunis; however, Tunisia delayed sending its own representative to Tel-Aviv in response to Israeli attacks on southern Lebanon. Nevertheless, some contacts between the two countries were made. However, after the victory of Binyamin Netanyahu in the Israeli elections in May and the formation of a right-wing Government, the process of normalization was expected to decelerate. President Ben Ali attended the emergency Arab summit meeting in Cairo in June and, as current Chairman of the Arab League, made one of the two keynote speeches. After the conference he defended the actions of those countries that had taken steps to normalize relations with Israel, stating that they were intended 'to push the peace process forward'. However, in November the Tunisian leadership condemned Israeli intransigence towards the peace process and criticized the building of Jewish settlements in the occupied territories. The normalization of relations was suspended, the head of the Tunisian interests office in Tel-Aviv departed in August 1997 and the only remaining Tunisian diplomat returned to Tunis early in 1998. The Israeli interests office in Tunis was closed in July 1998. However, after the appointment of a new government in Israel headed by Labour leader, Ehud Barak, and a revival of the Middle East peace process, relations improved, and the Israeli interests office in Tunis reopened in October 1999. Early in 2000 Tahar Sioud, Secretary of State for Foreign Affairs, became the first senior Tunisian official to visit Israel where he held talks with the Israeli Minister of Foreign Affairs, David Levy. They discussed the Middle East peace process and agreed to establish a joint committee for trade and tourism. Sioud also met Yasser Arafat, who travelled to Tunisia in April to attend the funeral of ex-president Habib Bourguiba. In late October, in response to violent clashes between Israel and the Palestinians, Tunisia again closed its interests section in Tel-Aviv and imposed a freeze on normalization of relations with the Jewish state. Many Tunisians remained deeply hostile towards Israel, and several large pro-Palestinian demonstrations were held, including one led by Ben Ali and the Palestinian leader, Yasser Arafat. However, the protests were carefully controlled by the authorities, and university students were forbidden to hold their own demonstrations in support of the Palestinians.

In early April 2002 a tanker lorry exploded outside a synagogue on the island of Djerba, in southern Tunisia. As many as 19 people were killed, most of them foreign tourists, and 20 others wounded. A spokesman for the Israeli Ministry of Foreign Affairs immediately insisted that it was an anti-Semitic 'terrorist' attack linked to Israel's military offensive in Palestinian-controlled areas of the West Bank. The Tunisian authorities initially claimed that the explosion had been an accident, but some days later announced that it had been a 'premeditated criminal act'. A number of Arabic newspapers immediately carried claims that the al-Qa'ida (Base) organization of Osama bin Laden—the principal suspect in the September 2001 attacks on New York and Washington, DC, was responsible, and in late June the Qatar-based satellite television station Al-Jazeera broadcast a statement by a spokesman for al-Qa'ida, asserting that the attack had been perpetrated in the name of al-Qa'ida in protest against Israel's actions against the Palestinians.

Within the UMA, Tunisia was chosen as the site of the new Maghreb Investment and Foreign Trade Bank. A Tunisian diplomat, Muhammad Amamou, was appointed UMA Secretary-General and represented the UMA at the opening session of the Middle East peace conference in Madrid, Spain, in October 1991. Tunisia was the only UMA member to contribute personnel to the UN monitoring body, MINURSO, in Western Sahara (see the chapter on Morocco). In January 1993 Tunisia assumed the annual presidency of the UMA. The Government emphasized its determination to reactivate the process of Maghreb union, as well as dialogue with the EC. However, according to a statement made by the Moroccan Minister of Foreign Affairs, Abd al-Latif Filali, in February 1993, following a meeting of the five UMA member states in Tunis, it had been decided to allow a 'pause' for reflection in the process of developing Maghreb union. Tunisian officials stressed that Ben Ali's presidency had been a success and that 11 co-operation agreements had been signed during his one-year term of office, including plans for a Maghreb free-trade zone. Yet, in reality, he failed to give new impetus to the organization, largely because two of its members, Algeria and Libya, remained preoccupied with their own problems: Algeria plunged into civil war by escalating Islamist violence, and Libya subjected to even tighter UN sanctions. The summit meeting that should have marked the end of Tunisia's presidency was delayed three times and did not take place until April 1994. At the meeting, Ben Ali handed over the presidency to Liamine Zéroual, the new Algerian Head of State. Neither King Hassan of Morocco nor Col Qaddafi of Libya were present. Although at least 40 accords had been adopted by the UMA, only five had been ratified by all five member states, indicating that little progress had been made in translating rhetoric into reality in developing a unified Maghreb. During 1994 tensions between Tunisia and Morocco (see below) and between Morocco and Algeria merely added to the problems affecting the UMA. There were reports that Tunisia was hostile to Egypt's request in November to join the UMA, and would oppose Egyptian membership. In February 1995 Ben Ali sent a letter to the leaders of the other four member states urging them to try to overcome the obstacles facing the UMA by joint action. However, little progress was made, and in late 1995 Morocco blocked UMA activities because of alleged Algerian interference in the Western Sahara dispute. Tunisia regretted Morocco's action and continued its diplomatic efforts to revive the Union. During 1996 Tunisia concentrated on attempting to engender a reconciliation between Algeria and Morocco. Its efforts appeared to have met with some success when in October Algeria proposed a new UMA summit and Morocco was reported to have agreed in principle to the meeting. At the end of 1996 both Algeria and Morocco appealed for a revival of the UMA. On a visit to Tunis in October Col Qaddafi also expressed renewed interest in the UMA. Nevertheless, the UMA remained virtually moribund, although Tunisia continued to insist that the organization could be revived. During a state visit to Morocco in March 1999, President Ben Ali and King Hassan agreed to work to resuscitate the UMA, which Ben Ali referred to as 'an irreversible fateful choice' for Tunisia. Following the suspension of UN sanctions against Libya in April, some tentative moves were made to revive the organization. In May Tunisia was represented at the first session of the UMA Follow-up Committee to be held for more than three years. All five member states attended, but, despite continuing Tunisian diplomatic efforts, plans for a heads of state summit meeting in Algiers in November—the first for five years—were cancelled owing to renewed tensions between Algeria and Morocco. During a visit to Egypt in November, President Ben Ali stated that Tunisia was favourably disposed to Egypt's request to join the UMA. Tunisia continued its efforts to revivify the UMA during 2000, hosting visits by King Muhammad VI of Morocco in May, President Bouteflika of Algeria in June and Col Qaddafi of Libya in August. A summit meeting of ministers responsible for foreign affairs of the five UMA member states was arranged, and proceeded in the Algerian capital in mid-March 2001. However, the meeting, which was to have made preparations for the first summit meeting of UMA heads of state since 1995, quickly broke down following disagreements between Moroccan and Algerian representatives, although it was agreed to hold further talks in October. At a meeting of foreign ministers in Algiers in January

2002 former Tunisian Minister of Foreign Affairs Habib Boularès, was appointed UMA Secretary-General to replace another Tunisian, Muhammad Amamou, who had stepped down because of ill health. The Moroccan Minister of Foreign Affairs, Muhammed Benaissa, attended the meeting, but informed journalists that with regard to Western Sahara there was no question of Morocco's sacrificing its 'national cause' to build a Greater Maghreb. The UMA heads of state summit that was to have been held in Algiers in June was cancelled after King Muhammad of Morocco and President Maawiya Ould Sid'Ahmed Taya of Mauritania announced that they would not be attending. President Ben Ali had recently made a brief visit to Libya in an attempt to salvage the summit but failed to persuade Col Qaddafi, who was angered by the quarrel between Algeria and Morocco over Western Sahara, to attend the meeting. The two Tunisian and Libyan leaders also discussed further developments in bilateral relations.

The decision by the UN Security Council in April 1992 to impose sanctions against Libya over the Lockerbie affair (see the chapter on Libya) was reluctantly accepted by Tunisia. Although flights to and from Libya were suspended, Tunisia acknowledged popular feeling and the close economic ties between the two countries by insisting that land and sea links would remain open. The Libyan sanctions created a mini-boom in southern Tunisia, amid a sharp increase in cross-border trade and in transit traffic, but relations deteriorated sharply in September, when the Libyan leader remarked that Tunisia had no future and was doomed to unite with either Libya or Algeria. This outburst provoked an indignant response from President Ben Ali, who drew attention to Tunisia's achievements and commented that the Libyan people were suffering from the consequences of a crisis for which they were not responsible. Despite these differences, the Tunisian Government made efforts to negotiate a solution to the Lockerbie affair. In April 1993 Ben Ali visited Libya and consulted with President Mubarak of Egypt in a further attempt to resolve the deadlock between Libya and the West in the approach to the UN Security Council's sanctions review. Failure to resolve the Lockerbie affair also frustrated Ben Ali's efforts to forge closer relations between the UMA and the European Union (EU, as the EC had become). On a visit to Tunis in December 1993, the French Minister of Defence left the President in no doubt that Libya's membership of the UMA was a serious impediment to closer relations between the UMA and the EU. There were reports of a flourishing black market as Tunisian traders took advantage of the overvalued Libyan dinar and heavily subsidized prices to import cheap food into southern Tunisia. In July 1993 representatives of some 250 Libyan and Tunisian companies met in Tripoli to examine ways of strengthening business relations in the formal sector of the economy. As a result of UN sanctions, Tunisia became the main point of entry for international companies working in Libya—international flights to Tunis link with Djerba, from where there are ferry services to Libya. However, a new dispute occurred in October 1994 when Libya claimed that cholera had broken out in Tunisia and stated that all travellers from Tunisia would be vaccinated at the border if they did not possess a vaccination certificate. Tunisia retaliated by stating that bubonic plague had broken out in Libya and that anyone entering the country from Libya had to present a hospital certificate confirming that they did not have the disease. Some hundreds of travellers were stranded at the border with both countries blaming the other for the disruption. It was not until late November that the travel restrictions were lifted. There was speculation that Libya's actions in this affair may have been a response to Tunisian moves towards the normalization of relations with Israel announced in October. Discussions on economic co-operation resumed in July 1995 and relations improved in the second half of 1995. In September Tunisia appealed for the lifting of UN sanctions against Libya and also supported Libya's request to take part in the Euro-Mediterranean summit held in Barcelona (Spain) in November. A series of economic agreements were signed in October when the Tunisian Prime Minister met the Secretary-General of the Libyan General People's Committee. President Ben Ali held talks with Col Qaddafi in January 1996. However, relations between the two countries became strained after Libya criticized Tunisia's decision to establish low-level diplomatic relations with Israel.

Nevertheless, a Tunisian delegation led by the Prime Minister attended a meeting in Tripoli in July, and relations between the two countries improved after a visit to Tunis by Col Qaddafi in October where he addressed the National Assembly. Several agreements on investment, trade and co-operation were signed subsequently and progress was made on a number of joint economic projects during 1997. Trade and economic co-operation increased during 1998, although a number of joint projects remained at the planning state. Towards the end of the year President Ben Ali visited Tripoli and invited Col Qaddafi to visit Tunisia. The Libyan Secretary for Foreign Liaison and International Co-operation, Omar al-Muntasir, visited Tunis in February 1999 at the same time as the US Secretary of Defense, William Cohen, who asked President Ben Ali to show more support for UN sanctions against Libya and to use his influence with Qaddafi to persuade Libya to surrender the two suspects in the Lockerbie affair. In January, however, Ben Ali had repeated an appeal for the lifting of sanctions against Libya 'to end the suffering of the Libyan people', arguing that sanctions had also aggravated regional tensions and undermined Tunisia's own economic development plans. Nevertheless, Tunisia did not follow some sub-Saharan African states in openly flouting the air embargo. President Ben Ali held talks with Col Qaddafi at the OAU summit meeting in Algiers in July, and the Libyan leader visited Tunis on his return from the meeting. Ben Ali attended the special OAU summit meeting in Libya in early September which coincided with extensive celebrations to mark the 30th anniversary of Qaddafi's regime. After Ben Ali visited Libya in June the two countries signed an agreement to establish a free-trade zone. Tunisia was Libya's principal trading partner in the Arab world.

Tunisia's relations with Algeria continued to be dominated by the Islamist issue. In December 1991 Rached Ghanouchi and other senior an-Nahdah members were reportedly expelled from Algeria to Sudan. Relations with Algeria improved appreciably after the second round of Algerian elections were suspended in January 1992, and Tunisia welcomed the appointment of Muhammad Boudiaf as Chairman of the High Council of State, as well as the suppression of Algeria's Islamist movement. In February 1993 Boudiaf's successor, Ali Kafi, visited Tunis. During his stay he exchanged letters with President Ben Ali to ratify the official demarcation of the 1,000-km border between Tunisia and Algeria. Ben Ali and Kafi also expressed their determination to work together to counter the threat of terrorism in the region. In December the Algerian and Tunisian ministers responsible for foreign affairs met at Tabarka, Tunisia, to celebrate the final demarcation of the frontier between the two countries, the precise line of which had been disputed for some years after independence. The new Algerian Head of State, Liamine Zéroual, visited Tunis for the UMA summit meeting in April 1994 and held further talks with Ben Ali after the meeting ended. The two leaders issued a statement expressing their commitment to democracy, pluralism and the promotion of human rights; and condemning fanaticism and extremism. Zéroual's appeals for dialogue with Algeria's banned Front islamique du salut (FIS) seem certain to have alarmed Ben Ali, who had rejected any negotiations with the Tunisian Islamist opposition. During 1994 there were reports that several thousand Algerians, mainly professionals, had taken refuge in Tunisia since the conflict began in Algeria, many of whom had experienced difficulty in finding jobs. After the attack by Algerian Islamist militants against a Tunisian frontier post in February 1995, security along the border was strengthened. The Tunisian Government welcomed Zéroual's victory in the Algerian presidential elections in November and the press hailed it as a triumph against terrorism and extremism. President Ben Ali continued to urge the Algerian Government to take decisive action against Islamist extremists. Some difficulties that had arisen over the employment of Algerians in Tunisia and over trade relations between the two countries appeared to have been resolved when Prime Minister Karoui visited Algiers in June 1996. The Algerian Prime Minister, Ahmed Ouyahia, made a reciprocal visit to Tunis in December and indicated his support for Tunisia's efforts to revive the UMA. President Ben Ali held talks with Algeria's new president, Abdelaziz Bouteflika, at the OAU summit meeting in Algiers in July 1999 and again during the special OAU summit meeting in Libya in

September, during which they discussed improving bilateral co-operation and the revival of the UMA. In April 2000 Bouteflika was one of the few heads of state to attend the funeral of Habib Bourguiba, the leader of Tunisia's struggle for independence and the country's first president. In mid-May the Tunisian authorities announced that their security forces had repulsed a cross-border attack by a group of Algerian Islamist guerrillas linked to Hassan Hattab's Da'wa wal Djihad, during which three militants were killed and two Tunisian soldiers injured. The incident, the most serious since 1995, occurred shortly after Tunisia signed a customs agreement with Algeria aimed at combating smuggling which, Algeria insists, helps to finance its radical Islamist opponents. However, sections of the Algerian press claimed that the Ben Ali regime was deliberately using the threat of violence spilling over the border from its western neighbour to justify continued political repression at home. Nevertheless, in June President Bouteflika visited Tunis, where he addressed the Tunisian parliament. President Ben Ali made an official visit to Algiers in February 2002 to discuss bilateral relations and reviving the UMA. Earlier, in April and November 2001, the Algerian army Chief of Staff, Gen. Muhammad Lamari, had visited Tunis for talks with Ben Ali and his military and security officials about intensifying the battle against Islamist militants, better surveillance of their borders to prevent Tunisian and Algerian members of al-Qa'ida from returning to their country of origin, and dismantling North African Islamist networks in Europe. It was reported that numerous Islamist activists from Tunisia, who had taken refuge in Algeria and joined local GIA groups, had been arrested and handed over to the Tunisian authorities.

Tunisia's normally good relations with Morocco were strained in May 1994 after Tunisia expelled some 600 Moroccans who the authorities claimed were living there without permission or had broken Tunisian laws. Towards the end of the year the Tunisian authorities expelled several hundred Moroccans, claiming that they were trying to enter Italy as illegal immigrants. The Moroccan Government protested that some of its nationals had been maltreated by the Tunisian police. Relations remained strained during 1995 as a result of further expulsions of Moroccan workers and students. In early 1996 Tunisia condemned Morocco for trying to block UMA activities in retaliation for alleged Algerian interference in the Western Sahara dispute. Relations were further strained by criticism from Moroccan non-governmental organizations of the prison sentences imposed on opposition politicians Muhammad Mouada and Khemais Chamari (see below). However, after a visit to Rabat by Karoui in September, a commitment was made to improve economic and political co-operation. In November both countries appealed for the revival of the UMA. This message was repeated in March 1999 when President Ben Ali made a state visit to Rabat. During the visit a free-trade agreement was signed between the two countries as part of a plan to increase bilateral trade. Morocco's new ruler, King Muhammad VI, visited Tunis in May. President Ben Ali made an official visit to Morocco in July 2001 at the invitation of King Muhammad, when discussions were held about increasing bilateral trade.

RELATIONS WITH THE NON-ARAB WORLD SINCE THE GULF WAR

For a brief period in the aftermath of the Gulf War, Tunisia's stance during the crisis was seen to have damaged relations with those countries that had participated in the effort to liberate Kuwait, while reports, most notably by Amnesty International, of abuses of human rights in Tunisia continued to cause international disquiet. In February 1991 the USA reduced the level of economic aid to Tunisia (see Economy), and military aid was entirely discontinued, although subsequent investment agreements with the USA indicated a rapid improvement in relations. A visit by François Mitterrand in July 1991 (the French President's first visit to an Arab country since the end of the Gulf War) was interpreted as a sign of French support for the Ben Ali administration's campaign against Islamist extremists. In December 1992 considerable anger was provoked in Tunisia by the trial, in Paris, of a group of mainly Tunisian suspects. Among these was the brother of President Ben Ali, who was sentenced *in absentia* to 10 years' imprisonment for drugs-trafficking offences. In February 1993 the Tunisian Minister of the Interior, Abdallah Kallel, during a visit to Paris, criticized the French authorities for granting asylum to Tunisian Islamist militants. The election of a new French Government in March 1993 was, however, well received in Tunisia. The French Minister of Foreign Affairs, Alain Juppé, visited Tunisia in June 1994 and after talks with Ben Ali, he stated that relations between the two countries were good, but that he was anxious that Tunisia should resolve the remaining cases of compensation to former French residents for property left behind in Tunisia after independence. When the French Minister of the Interior, Charles Pasqua, visited Tunis in October for a meeting on security co-operation, he pledged that the French Government would not allow France to become a base for Islamist activists. In January 1995 the French and Tunisian ministers responsible for the interior met in Tunis with their counterparts from Italy, Spain, Portugal, Algeria and Morocco to discuss security matters arising from Islamist militancy. They condemned 'terrorism, fundamentalism and every form of extremism and fanaticism' and agreed to exchange information on a regular basis. In their declaration at the end of the meeting the ministers sought to link illegal immigration into Europe and the growing traffic in drugs and arms to the rise in 'Islamist extremism'. Jacques Chirac's election to the French presidency was welcomed by the Tunisian authorities and it was hoped that the new French administration would support Tunisia in its negotiations with the EU and maintain an unyielding policy towards Islamist militants in France. In June the French police arrested a number of Tunisians and Algerians living in France who, it was alleged, were part of a network providing arms to Islamist groups in Algeria and to the Front islamiste tunisien, described as a splinter group of an-Nahdah. The new French Minister of the Interior, Jean-Louis Debré, visiting Tunis in September, urged all Mediterranean states to form a common front against 'these terrorists'. In October President Chirac made a state visit to Tunisia during which he praised Ben Ali for his achievements in promoting modernization, democracy and social harmony in the country. He promised that French aid to Tunisia during 1995 would be increased to 1,100m. French francs. In April 1996 the second Franco–Tunisian parliamentarians' conference met in Paris at which delegates discussed bilateral relations and EU co-operation with the Mediterranean states. However, Ben Ali's state visit to France, which should have taken place in September, was cancelled amid speculation that the President feared public criticism of Tunisia's human rights record. There had been widespread criticism in France of the arrest and imprisonment of Mouada and Chamari (see below). Mouada had been arrested only three days after Chirac's visit to Tunis. The release of the two politicians in December, together with promises of political reforms, helped to improve relations, and during a visit to Tunis in February 1997 by the French Minister of Defence, Charles Millon, agreement was reached on further military co-operation to include joint military manoeuvres, arms supply and the training in France of Tunisian army officers. In May Karoui held talks with Chirac in Paris, and in August the new French Minister of Foreign Affairs, Hubert Védrine, on his first visit to Tunis, stated that relations between the two countries remained close and that the French administration would continue to assist the Tunisian Government's political and economic reform programme. Ben Ali's state visit to Paris finally took place at the end of October. French leaders acknowledged Tunisia's difficult regional position and pledged continued support for economic reforms, but appealed for further progress in democracy and human rights. Although the French press was highly critical of the Ben Ali regime, there were no hostile street demonstrations and during the visit two economic agreements were signed, providing additional French financial support for the Tunisian economy. The long-standing dispute over French-owned property in Tunisia was also resolved. Towards the end of 1998 the Chamber of Deputies passed a law enabling French owners to sell properties acquired in Tunisia during the colonial period and to repatriate the proceeds without restrictions. At a meeting of the Franco-Tunisian inter-governmental commission in Tunis in January 1999 the two countries agreed to promote French investment in small and medium-sized Tunisian companies. While economic co-operation continued to develop, relations at the political level were soured by highly critical reports about the Ben Ali regime

in the French media during the Tunisian presidential and parliamentary elections in October 1999. On a visit to Tunis in early 2000 the French Minister of Foreign Affairs described relations between the two countries as 'solid and constructive' and confirmed that a visit by France's premier, Lionel Jospin, would take place before the end of the year. He also hoped that progress towards greater democracy and public liberties would 'continue and consolidate'. In early April President Chirac, together with interior minister Jean-Pierre Chevènement and Philippe Séguin, a former president of the National Assembly, attended the funeral in Monastir of ex-president Habib Bourguiba. France was the only Western country to be represented by senior political figures. Later that month, however, the case of Taoufiq Ben Brik, a Tunisian journalist who staged a hunger strike in protest at official harassment (see below), led to new strains in relations with France. The case attracted much attention in the French press, which renewed its attack on Tunisia's human rights record. Indeed, it provoked the strongest criticism of Tunisia by France since Ben Ali came to power. The French Government evidently made representations on several occasions and President Chirac himself telephoned Ben Ali to express concern over the affair. The Tunisian authorities reacted angrily and accused France of leading a malicious campaign against Tunisia. Ben Ali made a public protest, and the state-controlled press gave prominent coverage to denunciations of France. Later in the year relations appeared to have improved, and the suspension imposed by the Tunisian authorities on the leading French daily newspapers was lifted. Relations with the former colonial power were always uneasy, but France remained Tunisia's principal ally within the EU. However, there was renewed tension in early 2001 when the French Government criticized the growing use of violence against human rights activists and called on the Tunisian authorities to allow the LTDH and the press to operate freely. In March 2001 the Tunisian authorities launched a virulent campaign in the local press against foreign interference in the country's internal affairs, directed mainly at France, which it condemned for criticizing Tunisia's human rights record. In April 2001 the national bureau of the French Socialist Party announced that it could not consider maintaining normal relations with the RCD while the country's human rights organizations were reduced to silence. The RCD described the decision as 'unusual and unacceptable'. Plans by the French Secretary of State for Co-operation and Francophonie, Charles Josselin, to meet with a group of prominent human rights activists and representatives of civil societies during a visit to Tunisia in early May angered the Tunisian authorities, who cancelled part of Josselin's official programme. As a result Josselin decided to postpone his visit, which had been designed to renew dialogue between France and the Ben Ali regime. Josselin's visit eventually took place at the beginning of June and included separate meetings with LTDH president Mokhtar Trifi, Mohamed Charfi, and Bechra Belhaj Hmida, president of the Association des femmes démocrates. However, later in the month relations between the two countries again became strained, following the arrest and imprisonment of the CNLT spokesperson, Sihem Ben Sedrine, after she toured Europe to speak about the human rights situation in Tunisia. Josselin informed Slaheddine Maâoui, Tunisian Minister-delegate to the Prime Minister in charge of Human Rights, Communications and Relations with the National Assembly, that the affair had aroused strong emotions in France, while members of the Paris-based Reporters sans frontières briefly occupied the Office tunisien du tourisme in Paris. This last action was denounced by Maâoui as 'irresponsible and unacceptable', while the Tunisian official news agency condemned the occupation as 'a criminal act'. Visiting Tunis in late July Danielle Mitterrand, in her capacity as President of the Fondation France-Libertés, visited Tunis, expressed support for several opposition figures and defenders of human rights and held meetings with Moncef Marzouki, Judge Mokhtar Yahyaoui (see below) and representatives of the LTDH. Although she was unable to secure meetings with Sihem Ben Sedrine or Muhammad Mouada, Mitterrand stated that her mission had been successful. The French Minister of Youth and Sport attended the 14th meeting of the Mediterranean Games held in Tunis in early September despite requests by Reporters sans frontières for the minister to boycott the proceedings because of Tunisia's violations of human rights. There was, furthermore, strong criticism of the appointment of former Minister of the Interior Habib Ammar as head of the organizing committee of the games. Gen. Ammar, had established the Brigade d'investigation et de recherches in the 1980s, and had later been commander of the national guard, was accused by Reporters sans frontières of crimes of torture.

Following the suicide September 2001 attacks on New York and Washington, DC, there appeared to be a swift reassessment on the part of the French authorities of their attitude to the Ben Ali regime. The French Minister of Foreign Affairs, Hubert Védrine, visited Tunis in October, and in December Jacques Chirac held talks with Ben Ali during a tour of Maghreb capitals. The Chirac declared that the French and Tunisian governments were in complete agreement on the need to eradicate international terrorism, and angered the Tunisian opposition by praising Ben Ali for his 'exemplary policy of combating terrorism'. Just before Chirac's visit, the Tunisian authorities had allowed Moncef Marzouki to leave the country to take up a university post in France. At a meeting of the Commission mixte franco-tunisienne in Paris at the end of January, chaired by Hubert Védrine, his Tunisian counterpart, Habib Ben Yahia, emphasized that democracy must be developed in security and stability and accused the Islamists of exploiting human rights issues as part of their campaign to take power.

Robert Pelletreau, the US Assistant Secretary of State, visited Tunis in December 1995 for talks with President Ben Ali and leading ministers. He praised the country's economic reforms, stated that military co-operation between the two countries would continue and announced that any threat to Tunisia would be viewed 'with concern' by the US administration. In May 1997 a senior-level delegation, led by Tunisia's Minister of National Defence, visited Washington, DC, to attend a meeting of the joint committee for military co-operation. Reports, in early 1998, that Tunisia's close relations with Libya and Iraq (see above), and its refusal to host the next economic conference on the Middle East and North Africa, had caused a rift in relations with the USA, appeared to have been exaggerated. In June, during a visit to Tunis, the US Under-Secretary of State, Stuart Eizenstat, praised Tunisia as a 'model for the developing world' and proposed a new economic partnership with the USA to encourage structural change and to promote greater US investment. Although a Tunisian request for US military aid was not granted, the meeting of the Tunisian-American military committee, postponed in May, took place in September, attended by the US Under-Secretary of State for the Middle East and North Africa, Ronald Neumann, and the US Under-Secretary of State for Defense, Walter Slocombe. At the same time, Tunisia's Minister of International Co-operation and Foreign Investment, Muhammad Ghannouchi, led a high-level delegation to Washington where two new trade agreements with the USA were drawn up. In early April 1999 the US First Lady, Hillary Rodham Clinton, visited Tunisia as part of a North African tour promoting women's rights. Later in the year Martin Indyk, the Assistant Secretary of State for Near Eastern Affairs, met President Ben Ali for talks on the Middle East peace process and on efforts to revive the UMA. Several US delegations visited Tunisia in early 2000, probably linked in part to the fact that Tunisia had just begun a two-year term on the UN Security Council. In January the Minister of Defence visited Washington, DC, for one of the regular meetings of the Tunisian-American military committee. In early April Stuart Eizenstat, Deputy Secretary in the US Department of the Treasury, represented the USA at the funeral in Monastir of ex-president Habib Bourguiba. Eizenstat had been actively promoting greater economic co-operation between the USA, Tunisia and its Maghreb neighbours, Morocco and Algeria, but excluding Libya and thus presenting a problem for Tunisia, which was anxious to maintain good relations with Tripoli. In a report to the US Senate Committee on Foreign Relations in February 2001 the US Department of State strongly criticized Tunisia's human rights record, alleging that prisoners were regularly tortured by the security forces and deploring the Government's influence over the judiciary in some political cases. However, the new US Administration of George W. Bush continued to regard Tunisia as an important strategic ally, and, as had previous presidencies, appeared to disregard these criticisms.

Following the September 2001 suicide attacks on New York and Washington, DC, President Ben Ali vehemently denounced those who had carried out the attacks and reiterated Tunisia's 'principled and deeply-anchored stand against terrorism in all its forms and manifestations'. In contrast to the 1991 Gulf War, there were no popular demonstrations against the US bombing of Afghanistan, although some observers believed that Tunisian popular opinion was sympathetic to bin Laden. In December William Burns, US Assistant Secretary of State for Near Eastern Affairs, visited Tunis as part of a tour of Maghreb capitals. During talks with Ben Ali he reaffirmed Washington's interest in promoting US co-operation with the Maghreb states and thanked the Tunisian leadership and the Tunisian people for their expressions of solidarity following the September attacks. Tunisian security services were co-operating with the IS Federal Bureau of Investigation to track terrorists of Tunisian origin based in Europe. In April 2001 Italian police had arrested a number of Tunisians suspected of belonging to the Milan 'cell' of the Algerian-based Groupe salafiste pour la prédication et le combat, or Da'wa wal Djihad, which was alleged to be providing logistical support for, and planning terrorist attacks in Europe on behalf of, al-Qa'ida. The Italian police believed that more Tunisians were members of the Da'wa wal Djihad network which had cells in several European countries. Following the attacks on the USA sections of the Tunisian press accused the banned Islamist party an-Nahda, the leadership of which is based in Europe, of having links with al-Qa'ida: these allegations were strongly denied by an-Nahda representatives.

President Oscar Luigi Scalfaro of Italy visited Tunis in November 1993 for a two-day visit to increase bilateral trade and to discuss Mediterranean security issues. Italy is Tunisia's second largest trading partner (after France) and the third biggest source of foreign investment. Italy was anxious to ensure the continued co-operation of the Tunisian authorities in trying to curb illegal immigration from Tunisia. During 1994 the Tunisian authorities made several well-publicized arrests of groups of illegal emigrants—including Tunisians, Moroccans and Libyans—who were trying to enter Italy from Tunisia. However, the arrival in Tunisia of former Italian Prime Minister, Bettino Craxi, sentenced *in absentia* by the Italian courts to serve 18 years in prison for corruption, proved embarrassing for the Tunisian authorities. Craxi, who maintained close links with the Tunisian leadership, was reported to be too ill to leave his villa near Hammamet. The Italian authorities also began investigations into the Italian export credit agency's relations with the Maghreb states, which caused delays in Italian trade credits for Tunisia. In June 1995 Italy requested that Tunisia extradite Craxi; however, the matter proved complicated because the extradition agreement between the two countries excluded political offences. When the new Tunisian Minister of Foreign Affairs, Abd ar-Rahim Zouari, visited Rome in March 1997, Italian officials appealed for an agreement between the two countries on the repatriation of illegal immigrants from Tunisia. In May Tunisia and Italy signed a co-operation agreement following a meeting held in Rome between the two Heads of State. Later in the year relations became strained when Tunisia seized several Italian boats which it claimed were fishing illegally in Tunisian waters. Problems over fishing zones and illegal immigration continued to cause friction with Italy in 1998. After meeting President Ben Ali in Tunis in June, the Italian Prime Minister, Romano Prodi, insisted that these were minor problems and could easily be resolved. In July, however, a sharp increase in illegal immigrants from Tunisia provoked an angry rebuke from the Italian Minister of Foreign Affairs, who accused the Tunisian authorities of not doing enough to stem the flow. The row quickly subsided, and in August the two countries signed an accord under which Tunisia agreed to do more to prevent Tunisians from entering Italy illegally and to take back those illegal immigrants apprehended by the Italian authorities in exchange for a substantial aid package. Later in the year the two countries agreed to promote greater maritime co-operation, in order to improve detection of illegal immigrants into Italy from Tunisia, and to reduce illegal fishing by Italian vessels in Tunisian waters. Nevertheless, disputes over fishing rights continued to cause some friction between the two countries, but co-operation on Tunisian immigration to Italy made some progress. During the second half of 2000 new agreements

were signed with Italy on defence co-operation and the employment of Tunisian workers. In November Enrico Letta, Italy's
Minister of Industry, Commerce and Handicrafts and Foreign
Trade, visited Tunis to discuss ways of increasing Italian investment. Italy had established a TD 40m. credit line to assist joint
ventures between Tunisian businesses and Italian investors. In
April 2001, and after the September attacks on the USA, Italian
police arrested a number of Tunisians who were accused of
belonging to the Milan cell of Da'wa wal Djihad (see above). The
issue of terrorism was discussed during visits to Tunis by the
Italian President, Carlo Azeglio Ciampi, and Minister of Foreign
Affairs, Renato Ruggiero, in October, and by the Italian Prime
Minister, Silvio Berlusconi, in November. Progress in handling
questions of illegal immigration and fishing rights resulted in
an improvement in bilateral relations.

Relations with Spain were strengthened in October 1995
when a treaty of friendship and co-operation was signed during
a visit to Tunis by the Spanish Prime Minister, Felipe González.
King Juan Carlos of Spain had visited Tunisia in November
1994 and President Ben Ali had made an official visit to Spain
in May 1991. The first annual meeting between leaders of the
two countries, as agreed under the 1995 treaty of friendship
and co-operation, was held in Madrid in January 1997 and
attended by the Tunisian Prime Minister, Hamed Karoui.
Although the meeting dealt with economic co-operation, the
Spanish Prime Minister, José María Aznar, appealed for a
further improvement in Tunisia's record on human rights.
Karoui insisted that there were no political prisoners in Tunisia,
only Islamist militants convicted of terrorist acts. The issue of
human rights and political freedoms had also been raised when
the Tunisian Minister of Foreign Affairs held talks with his
Spanish counterpart in Madrid in July 1996. Prime Minister
Aznar again visited Tunis in May 1998 for the annual meeting
between senior officials and urged Spanish firms to take greater
advantage of investment opportunities in Tunisia. He held talks
with President Ben Ali on a number of foreign policy issues. A
visit to Tunis by the Spanish, Prime Minister in late September
2001 was devoted mainly to discussions about the international
coalition against terrorism.

In December 1993 the EU's Council of Ministers mandated
the European Commission to begin talks with Tunisia on a new
partnership agreement to replace the co-operation agreement
signed in 1976. The Tunisian Ministry of Foreign Affairs welcomed the talks, which it described as 'a political signal' marking
European approval of Tunisia's progress towards political pluralism and its respect for human rights. During talks with the EU
which began in Brussels in March 1994, Tunisian negotiators
expressed their support for free entry of European goods into
Tunisia, but wanted tariffs to be lowered gradually, additional
financial assistance to make its industries more competitive
with their European counterparts and higher guaranteed quotas
for its olive oil exports to Europe. The European Commission
was reported to have impressed on EU governments that a new
partnership agreement with the Maghreb states was essential,
since strengthening their economies would lessen Islamist violence and stem the flow of emigrants to Europe. Negotiations
were not completed until July 1995 when Tunisia became the
first southern Mediterranean country to sign a new economic
association agreement as part of the EU's plan for a 'Euro-
Mediterranean partnership'. The agreement involves the gradual removal of tariffs on industrial imports from the EU, a
high-risk strategy for the country's vulnerable manufacturing
sector (see Economy). In May 1996 the European Parliament
had for the first time passed a resolution condemning Tunisia's
treatment of opposition politicians and strongly criticizing its
human rights record. The resolution reiterated that the 1995
association agreement required Tunisia to respect democratic
principles and human rights and urged the European Commission to persuade the Tunisian Government to meet these obligations. The resolution was greeted with an indignant response
from the Tunisian Government and from several opposition
parties. The association agreement was formally implemented
in March 1998 after it had been ratified by all EU member
states. At the first meeting of the EU–Tunisia Association
Council in July, the Austrian Minister of Foreign Affairs, Wolfgang Schüssel, raised EU concerns over civil liberties in Tunisia
and stated that the EU would wish to discuss such issues

without restrictions. However, despite receiving numerous
highly critical reports from international human rights organizations about the situation in Tunisia, the EU did not condemn
the Ben Ali regime's human rights record and preferred to focus
on the country's stability while insisting that some progress
was being made towards greater democracy. Early in 2000
Tunisia, which is keen to increase its agricultural exports to
Europe, opened preliminary talks with the EU about the liberalization of trade in agricultural goods. The Ben Brik affair (see
below) provoked renewed criticism of Tunisia's human rights
record in the European Parliament, and in June some of its
deputies demanded that the association agreement should be
suspended. In November 1996 the establishment of Eurofor, the
rapid action force for the southern Mediterranean region, by
France, Italy, Spain and Portugal, was criticized by the Tunisian
authorities. Despite assurances that the force was for defence,
peace-keeping and humanitarian missions, Tunisia's Minister
of Foreign Affairs declared that it was incompatible with the
tradition of dialogue his country had sought to create between
the northern and southern shores of the Mediterranean. Nevertheless, Tunisia continued military co-operation with its
Western allies, and in November 1999 a NATO delegation held
talks in Tunis about the Tunisian armed forces taking part in
that organization's humanitarian operations. The President of
the European Commission, Romano Prodi, visited Tunis in
January 2001 as part of a tour of the Maghreb aimed at reviving
the Euro-Mediterranean partnership. During his visit he met
with a delegation from the LTDH. It was reported that Tunisia
had become increasingly disillusioned with the EU accord,
arguing that European financial support had not been sufficient
to offset the losses resulting from the progressive reduction of
tariffs on European imports and the costs of preparing the
economy for free trade. Tension also resulted from what the
Tunisian Government perceived as EU interference in the country's internal affairs, notably criticism of its human rights
record.

In November 1993 Tunisia hosted a meeting of the ministers
responsible for foreign affairs of the members of the OAU.
Shortly before the meeting, Tunisia invited the South African
Minister of Foreign Affairs, Pik Botha, to make an official visit,
at the end of which both countries agreed to establish diplomatic
relations. In May 1994 Tunisia announced that diplomatic relations with South Africa would soon be established and ambassadors exchanged. In April President Ben Ali assumed the
presidency of the OAU for 12 months and in June Tunis hosted
the 30th annual summit meeting of the OAU. South Africa
attended for the first time. As Chairman of the OAU, Ben Ali
appealed for a new partnership between Europe and Africa
and urged industrialized nations to assist African countries by
improving their terms of trade and through debt rescheduling.
Ben Ali made a state visit to South Africa in April 1995 where
he had talks with President Nelson Mandela and addressed the
South African Parliament. With Tunisia holding the chairmanship of the OAU, Tunis became the venue for a series of meetings
sponsored by that organization in the first half of 1995, including
a summit meeting held in April to discuss the prevention,
management and solution of conflicts in Africa. In 1998 Tunisia
supported the OAU's demand for two permanent seats for Africa
on the UN Security Council. Tunisia has repeatedly called
for an enlargement of the Security Council to make it more
representative. Tunisia joined the Community of Sahel-Saharan
States (CEN-SAD, formerly COMESSA) at the organization's
third summit held in Khartoum, Sudan, in February 2001.

In early 2001 Prime Minister Ghannouchi became the first
Tunisian prime minister to visit Iran since the 1979 Revolution.
Tunisia had severed diplomatic relations with Iran after the
Revolution, and during the 1980s had accused Tehran of sup-
porting Islamist militancy in Tunisia.

THE ELECTIONS OF 1994

In December 1992 President Ben Ali announced that presidential and parliamentary elections would be held in March 1994.
Promising a revised electoral law and an up-to-date voting
register, the President predicted that political pluralism in
Tunisia would be consolidated. The ruling RCD held its second
congress at the end of July 1993 (the first was in 1988, following
Ben Ali's takeover and the renaming of the party) and nominated

Ben Ali as its candidate for the forthcoming presidential election. The party was reported to have 1.6m. members, including 60,000 elected cadres, linked through 321 federations and 27 co-ordinating committees in Tunisia and one in Paris. Leaders of the legal opposition parties, of which the largest was the MDS, were present at the congress, and Ben Ali used the opportunity to reiterate his commitment to bring the opposition into the new parliament. On 7 November 1993, the sixth anniversary of his takeover, Ben Ali formally announced that he would stand for a second term as President. Once again he was the only candidate and was supported by all the legal opposition parties. The UGTT endorsed the President's candidature at its December congress. Under the terms of the new electoral system, the number of seats to be contested in the National Assembly was increased to 163. Of these, 144 were to be contested according to the existing majority list or 'first past the post' system, which gave all 141 seats in the old chamber to the RCD, but the remaining 19 seats would be distributed at a national level among the parties according to their proportion of the total vote. Ben Ali commended the system as one that would 'achieve pluralism in the National Assembly through the representation of political parties according to their weight and influence in society'. Other reforms to the voting system brought to an end the controversial practice of sponsorship for candidates. The State also agreed to contribute to the election expenses of candidates. Some of the opposition parties felt that the long-awaited electoral reform did not go far enough and that the number of seats allocated on a proportional basis should have been larger. Nevertheless, all six legal parties, the MDS, the Mouvement de la rénovation (MR—which incorporated some of the members of the disbanded PCT), the RSP, the PUP, the UDU and the PSP, which had boycotted all elections since 1989 because they maintained that the results were manipulated by the RCD, accepted the new formula and indicated that they would take part. There were appeals from the opposition for equal access to the state-controlled media during the election campaign and complete freedom to hold public meetings without interference by the authorities. Their acceptance of the extremely modest and largely cosmetic electoral reform measures were regarded by many as a clear indication of the weakness of the legal and secular opposition parties, reduced to an obedient official opposition to the ruling party.

Despite government claims that an-Nahdah's organization had been destroyed in Tunisia, a high level of security was maintained. In early 1994 Noufal Ziadi, the Secretary-General of the UGET, condemned the permanent presence of police on university campuses and complained about restrictions placed on union activity. The LTDH (dissolved in June 1992) began rebuilding its regional networks in January 1994. In April, in an unusually outspoken declaration, some 200 intellectuals denounced the regime's paranoia about security and alleged a sharp decline in human rights and freedom of speech. In a report published in January Amnesty International had claimed that the Government's prominent role in international human rights organizations served to mask its own serious and systematic violations of human rights. Amnesty reported that, over the previous three years, thousands of suspected political opponents had been subjected to arbitrary arrest, held illegally, incommunicado, in prolonged detention, tortured or ill-treated and imprisoned after unfair trials.

The presidential and legislative elections held on 20 March 1994 brought few surprises. President Ben Ali was re-elected for a second term, winning 99.9% of the vote, according to official sources, which also reported that 94.9% of eligible voters had participated in the election. Abderrahmane el-Hani, a lawyer and leader of a political party not recognized by the Government, and Moncef Marzouki, the former president of the LTDH and a persistent critic of the regime's human rights record, had both been arrested after announcing their intention to stand for the presidency. In July Moncef Marzouki was freed provisionally and there was speculation that his trial might be postponed indefinitely if he withdrew from politics. However, in December he was prevented from travelling to New York to receive an award from the US-based Human Rights Watch.

In the parliamentary elections the RCD swept to victory, winning 97.7% of the vote and taking all 144 seats allocated under the majority list system. The six legal opposition parties

secured only 2.3% of the vote, but, under the new electoral formula, the MDS was allocated 10 of the 19 'guaranteed' seats reserved for parties which did not secure a majority in the constituencies, the MR four seats, the UDU three seats, and the PUP two seats. In his address to the new National Assembly in April, Ben Ali proclaimed that Tunisia had achieved political pluralism and declared its commitment to strengthen democracy and human rights.

In contrast to the 1989 election, there were few complaints from opposition parties about the conduct of the 1994 poll. However, the LTDH claimed that secrecy of voting had not always been assured and accused the authorities of interfering with a number of opposition campaign meetings. When Boujamaa Rmili, an official of the MR, condemned the election as 'a scandal', he was quickly arrested and detained for a week. There were few foreign observers because, in the approach to the elections, the regime had moved to control the foreign press and television. Several French and British newspapers were banned, the British Broadcasting Corporation's correspondent in Tunis was expelled and a French television team deported for their alleged hostile attitude and 'intolerable attacks on Tunisia's dignity'. Local journalists who expressed criticism of the regime suffered harassment, dismissal and even imprisonment.

The opposition parties drawn into the National Assembly by the offer of a handful of seats had little power and did not threaten the dominant position of the ruling party and the President. Supporters of the regime claimed that democracy had to be introduced gradually or Tunisia would suffer the instability and violence that had engulfed neighbouring Algeria. There were appeals for further electoral reform from the leader of the largest opposition party, the MDS, and from the LTDH.

TUNISIA AFTER THE 1994 ELECTIONS

In August 1994, in interviews with the foreign press, President Ben Ali stated that democracy had to be introduced gradually in Tunisia and that freedom of expression on its own would not bring development or create employment. He renewed his attack on 'Islamic fundamentalists' and argued that religious extremists only found support where there was poverty. His Government sought to achieve political stability by pursuing policies that addressed social and economic problems and that helped the country's poorest regions and sections of society.

Following the transfer of the two leaders of the Algerian FIS from prison to house arrest in September 1994, the leader of an-Nahdah, Rached Ghanouchi, in exile in the United Kingdom, urged the Tunisian Government to follow Algeria's example and open dialogue with the Islamist opposition. In August Ghanouchi himself had been criticized by two senior members of an-Nahdah for favouring a policy of confrontation with the Tunisian authorities which they claimed had led to the imprisonment of large numbers of party members. From exile in Paris, El Azhar Abaab issued a statement urging an-Nahdah to disband and the Government to release imprisoned party activists and allow those living in exile to return to Tunisia. Some days later, another member of the an-Nahdah leadership, Fouad Mansour Kassem, resigned from the party which he claimed was on the verge of collapse. There were reports that another group of activists had established a radical Islamist party, committed to armed struggle against the Tunisian authorities. In early 1995 a Paris court ordered the deportation of Salah Karkar, the co-founder of an-Nahdah 'for active support for a terrorist movement'. Karkar had lived in exile in France since 1988 after being condemned to death *in absentia* by a Tunisian court in 1987.

In February 1995 there were reports of an attack on a Tunisian frontier post at Tamerza, near Tozeur in the southwest of the country, by an Islamist group based across the border in Algeria, in which six Tunisian soldiers were killed. Algeria's radical Groupe islamique armé (GIA) claimed responsibility for the attack. The Tunisian authorities initially denied that the incident had taken place; however, they later conceded that the guards had been killed, most probably by Islamist militants. They also denied a report in the London-based *Al-Hayat* newspaper in March that Tunisian forces were assisting the Algerian Islamist guerrillas. Some observers considered the Tamerza attack as a GIA warning to the Tunisian Government against assisting Algeria in its struggle to destroy the Islamist opposition; others regarded it as an attempt to obtain weapons. Tunisia is known to have co-operated with Algeria on security matters for some years and the co-operation may have extended beyond sharing intelligence.

In February 1995 a number of trade union officials were arrested and detained for several days after a strike by school teachers, and in March Moncef Marzouki was prevented from travelling to Belgium where he was to have delivered a series of lectures. In June it was reported that a court order imposed on Marzouki, refusing him permission to leave the country, had been lifted.

At local elections held in May 1995 the RCD won control of all municipal councils and received 99.9% of the votes cast. Independent candidates and members of five legal opposition parties, represented in 47 of the 257 constituencies, won only six of the 4,090 seats; however, this was the first time since 1956 that the opposition had been represented on municipal councils. The RCD rejected allegations made by the MDS of irregularities in the electoral procedure, including inadequate access for observers. The result highlighted the impotence of the secular opposition parties which failed to offer an attractive alternative to the ruling party. Given the lack of interest in the elections, the official figure of a 92.5% turn-out appeared unrealistically high.

In July 1995 the Government introduced a law imposing strict controls on the use of satellite dishes and in September stopped broadcasts to Tunisia by the Italian television channel Rai Uno. Opposition deputies condemned the law on satellite dishes and accused the Government of imposing even tighter controls on the media.

In September 1995 Muhammad Mouada, the Secretary-General of the MDS, sent a letter to President Ben Ali expressing disquiet at what he referred to as a return to 'a regime of a hegemonic and dominating single party', and complaining that the repressive measures introduced to control society were more extensive and systematic than under the Bourguiba regime. Mouada argued that the current climate encouraged public indifference to politics and provided favourable ground for violence and extremism. He proposed a political plan which, he argued, would lead gradually to political pluralism and democracy. Under Mouada's leadership the MDS had agreed to participate in the 1994 legislative elections, and had supported both the regime's intransigent approach to the Islamist opposition and its economic liberalization programme. Mouada's letter was regarded as an expression of the party's frustration at not receiving any reward for supporting the regime. In early October, the day after the MDS made the letter public, Mouada was arrested and charged with maintaining secret contacts with foreign agents, endangering the country's security and accepting money from a foreign country. The security forces claimed to have found documents at his home that indicated that he had received substantial sums of money from Libya. A Libyan informer alleged that the payments were for secret political and military information about Tunisia. In November Khemais Chamari, the deputy leader of the MDS, was stripped of his parliamentary immunity, in order to allow judicial charges (relating to Mouada's trial) to be brought against him. At his trial, Mouada, who was known for his pan-Arab beliefs and sympathy for Libya, insisted that his contacts with Libya had been strictly within bounds acceptable for politicians. His lawyers argued that the incriminating documents found at his home had been falsified.

In November 1995 President Ben Ali promised electoral reform to enable the opposition parties to win more seats at the next municipal elections, and financial subsidies for the four opposition parties represented in the National Assembly. He also pardoned Hamma Hammani and Muhammad Kilani of the Parti des ouvriers communistes tunisiens (POCT), both serving long prison sentences, and in December held talks with the leaders of the two centrist opposition parties represented in the National Assembly, the UDU and the PUP. While these moves were considered to be an attempt to improve relations with the opposition, most observers were convinced that the treatment of Mouada was more indicative of the authoritarian nature of the regime, and its refusal to tolerate criticism or permit genuine political pluralism. In February 1996 Mouada was sentenced to

11 years in prison. Chamari was detained in May, and in July was sentenced to five years' imprisonment for breaching security proceedings relating to Mouada's trial. Both men denied the charges made against them and their harsh sentences were strongly condemned by international human rights organizations and the European Parliament. Mouada's arrest and detention provoked a bitter struggle for leadership of the MDS between supporters of Ismail Boulahya, a critic of Mouada's policies, and a faction led by Muhammad Ali Khalfallah. Boulahya, recognized as the new MDS Secretary-General by the Tunisian authorities, convened an extraordinary party congress in April 1997 at which it was decided to increase the MDS political bureau from nine to 11 members and to require the national council (rather than the congress) to elect future leaders.

In December 1996 President Ben Ali announced plans to amend the electoral law in an attempt to increase the number of opposition deputies in the National Assembly. Political parties would need to win only 3% of the vote to become eligible for parliamentary seats distributed by proportional representation (compared with 5% in the 1994 election). Opposition parties would also be represented in municipal councils owing to a proposed amendment preventing any one party from holding more than 80% of the seats. Ben Ali promised legislation to provide more state funds for recognized political parties. Observers interpreted these moves as an attempt by the Tunisian leadership to improve its image abroad without undermining the ruling party's dominant position in the political system. Ben Ali's announced reforms were followed by the conditional release of Mouada and Chamari at the end of December, together with Muhammad Hedi Sassi, imprisoned for being a member of the POCT. There were rumours that the French Government had made discreet approaches to the Tunisian authorities to grant the two MDS leaders a presidential pardon. Despite their release, Mouada and Chamari remained under police surveillance. Their prison sentences had only been suspended and their civil rights were not restored. In by-elections held at the end of 1996 the seat at Ben Arous (formerly held by Chamari) was won by a candidate presented by the PUP and the UDU, which had formed an alliance earlier in the year, while the seat at Medenine was won by the RCD. Voter turn-out at Ben Arous, which was not contested by the RCD, was less than 5%, demonstrating once again that the opposition parties lacked popular support among an increasingly cynical electorate.

In late 1997 it was announced that the law was to be strengthened to restrict the activities of Tunisian critics who spread false information to 'foreign parties', a move clearly directed at Tunisian activists with links to international human rights organizations (see below). In April, when several trade unionists appealed for greater democracy and criticized the UGTT leadership for collaborating with the Government, a number were promptly arrested. In May the Council of Ministers approved draft legislation on constitutional amendments which included proposals to widen the scope of referendums, lowering the minimum eligible age for candidates for the National Assembly (from 25 to 23 years) and obliging political parties to denounce all forms of violence, extremism, racism and segregation. In August, just before the French Minister of Foreign Affairs visited Tunis, the authorities ended the house arrest of Mouada, and lifted police surveillance of him. However, in December, after returning from a visit to France and the United Kingdom, during which he met exiled members of the Tunisian opposition, including some from an-Nahdah, Mouada was arrested again and questioned by the police. He was subsequently charged with attempting to destabilize the regime in alliance with a 'terrorist network'. Meanwhile, the split in the MDS between the faction led by Ismail Boulahya and that led by Muhammad Ali Khalfallah, which was opposed to collaboration with the Ben Ali regime, deepened and virtually paralysed the party. The continuing detention of former Head of State Habib Bourguiba, who remained under effective house arrest and was rarely permitted visitors, led to some public protest in late 1997. Towards the end of 1997 a number of political reforms that had first been announced by Ben Ali in 1996 were approved by the National Assembly and incorporated into the Constitution. The reforms that, according to the Government would 'strengthen democracy', included a guarantee that opposition parties should win at least 20% of the seats in the National Assembly; no party was to be allowed to hold more than 80% of seats on municipal councils; the minimum age of parliamentary candidates was to be reduced from 25 to 23 years; citizens with Tunisian mothers (in addition to those with Tunisian fathers) were to be allowed to stand for parliament; all political parties would have to respect republican values, human rights and the rights of women and not be based on religion, language, race or region, or have links with foreign countries; and the President was to be allowed to hold a referendum on issues of national importance. In a speech in November, on the 10th anniversary of his takeover, Ben Ali announced further political reforms including a formula to increase the number of candidates at the presidential election scheduled to be held in October 1999; an extension to the powers of the Constitutional Council; and reform of the law on the issue of passports to improve freedom of movement. In the same speech, the President announced that the post of Secretary of State for Information (whose role had been to disseminate government propaganda and censor those who criticized the regime) had been abolished and told journalists that they should abandon self-censorship and help stimulate public debate on political issues. He also urged members of the National Assembly to engage in more vigorous debate in the Assembly on policy issues. Given the strict controls over the press and the regime's intolerance of criticism from opposition politicians, genuine debate either in the press or in the Assembly seemed unlikely. Some commentators dismissed the proposals as a façade created by the authoritarian regime merely to impress Tunisia's European allies, notably France.

In early 1998 reports of high-level government corruption became more widespread and included claims that members of the country's political élite had profited unfairly from the recent privatization of public companies. As some of the reports came from within the Government, there was speculation that they were being spread by people who resented the wealth and privileges acquired by families close to President Ben Ali.

At its congress in July 1998 the RCD endorsed Ben Ali's candidature for a third term of office in the presidential elections due to take place in late October 1999. In his speech to delegates President Ben Ali emphasized his commitment to gradual change and to balancing economic liberalization with social justice and integrating Tunisia into the world economy without destroying its identity. The party congress approved the Government's decision to increase the proportion of seats in parliament allocated to the opposition parties to 20% at the next legislative elections; urged the RCD to develop stronger relations with non-governmental organizations and associations throughout the country; and agreed that it was necessary to press ahead with industrial modernization, reform of the country's financial system and efforts to increase both domestic and foreign investment. The Congress also recommended reform of the welfare system, which would require more affluent families to pay for their own healthcare and for higher education. Support was expressed for the Government's plan to reduce the cost of food subsidies and to ensure that subsidies benefited those in greatest need. The RCD's central committee was enlarged from 200 to 236 members.

In December 1998 university students went on strike in protest at the introduction of new aptitude tests for teacher training. Three university teachers were arrested for being members of the banned POCT. One of them was also accused of being an organizer of the strikes. Demonstrations by high school students occurred in several towns in February 1999, provoked by concerns over the baccalaureate examination, which determines access to higher education. Police arrested many of the demonstrators, several students were injured and there were unconfirmed reports that a number had been killed. An underlying cause of the unrest was reported to be the relatively limited number of places currently available in higher education. The Government announced ambitious plans to increase the number of students in higher education to 205,000 by 2001, and to 300,000 by 2010. However, graduate unemployment was already high and unrest among young Tunisians was likely to remain a serious political problem for the Ben Ali regime.

Early in 1999 parliament approved an amendment to the Constitution, whereby the number of candidates eligible to stand for president was increased. Under the terms of the amendment, leaders of opposition parties could stand for the presidency provided that they had led their party for five consecutive years, and that their party had at least one seat in the Chamber of Deputies. Previously candidates for the presidency had to obtain the support of 30 members of parliament or mayors, which effectively disqualified all those who were not nominees of the ruling RCD. Muhammad Belhadj Amor, the leader of the PUP, later announced his intention to stand for the presidency and Abderrahmane Tlili, the Secretary-General of the UDU, was also expected to stand. The two men are regarded as close allies of Ben Ali, whose victory in the forthcoming election was not in doubt. Muhammad Harmel, the leader of the MR, was too old to stand (candidates must not be over 70 years of age), and Ismail Boulahya had led the MDS for less than five years. The amendment, however, was valid only for the 1999 presidential elections, suggesting that further changes to the Constitution may be introduced at a later date in order to allow President Ben Ali to stand for a fourth consecutive term of office in 2004. In the approach to the presidential and parliamentary elections the opposition parties remained weak and divided, with little popular support. The largest of them, the MDS, remained split into rival factions and was reported to have been unable to agree on an election manifesto. There were also reports of divisions within the PSL. Efforts by the Secretary-General of the RSP, Nejib Chebbi, to persuade all six legal opposition parties to form an electoral alliance with the trade unions and independent groups failed to win support.

During the first part of 1999 the trial of some 139 Tunisians on charges of drugs-smuggling concluded with many of those convicted being sentenced to between one and 35 years' imprisonment. The defendants included members of the interior ministry's anti-drugs squad, police officers, customs officials, TunisAir stewards and members of prominent families. Lawyers for the defence claimed that some confessions had been obtained under torture and insisted that the leaders of the drugs-trafficking business had escaped prosecution because they had high-level connections. It was Tunisia's biggest drugs trial and was held *in camera*, with no reports appearing in the local media, increasing popular suspicions that the traffickers had connections with senior figures within the regime.

In late April 1999 the President made a number of changes to the Council of Ministers. Muhammad Jeri, who has been one of Ben Ali's close associates for many years, was replaced as Minister of Finance by Tawfik Baccar, the Minister of Economic Development. There were reports that Jeri's efforts to increase tax revenues in order to compensate for a reduction in import duties caused by the implementation of Tunisia's association agreement with the EU had alienated the country's business community. Abd al-Latif Saddam replaced Baccar at the economic development ministry. The Minister of the Environment and Land Planning, Muhammad Medhi Melika, one of Ben Ali's nephews, was replaced by Feiza Kefi, and Mustapha Bouaziz, Minister of State Domains was replaced by Ridha Grira, who had been Government Secretary-General. Despite continued speculation that the President would appoint a new Prime Minister committed to a faster pace of economic reform, the conservative Hamed Karoui retained his post.

At the 19th congress of the UGTT Ismail Sahbani was re-elected Secretary-General for a third five-year term. Under his leadership relations with the Government have been relatively harmonious after the confrontations of the 1980s, but Sahbani has faced criticism from within the union for not opposing privatization and reform of the labour law. In April 2000 a number of activists in the UGTT were arrested after criticizing Sahbani's policies. In July prison sentences were imposed on several members of the banned POCT, which, despite years of repression, retained a core of support mainly in the universities. At the end of the year the UGTT accused the police of using violent methods to stop a peaceful march of its members to the memorial of Ferhat Hached, a former leader of the union murdered in 1952.

The Tunisian authorities continued to maintain that the country was immune to Islamist extremism because of progressive social policies and the strict application of the law. However, they were concerned that networks of Islamist militants still existed abroad, especially in certain European countries, and that these groups were determined to undermine Tunisia's stability. At a meeting in July 1995 with ministers of foreign affairs from several Mediterranean countries, President Ben Ali stated that Islamist militants granted political asylum in Western countries had abused their status, and he appealed for co-operation in containing 'fanaticism, extremism and terrorism'. In January 1996 the Arab League, meeting in Tunis, adopted a proposal sponsored by Tunisia for a 'code of conduct' to combat 'terrorism', referring primarily to Islamist extremism. The Tunisian Minister of Foreign Affairs, Habib Ben Yahia, appealed for an international code of conduct against terrorism at the 'Summit of Peace-makers', hastily convened in Egypt in March after the spate of suicide bomb attacks in Israel, and again criticized countries that gave asylum to Islamist extremists. From his exile in the United Kingdom, Rached Ghanouchi warned that unless all parties were allowed to participate in the political system, Tunisia could experience violent conflict in the future, like its neighbour Algeria. In November 1995 Ghanouchi was one of a group of Tunisian opposition leaders in exile who published a statement in the London-based newspaper *Al-Hayat* petitioning for a return to democracy. In early 1996 Ghanouchi stated that he was working with other opposition leaders, including former Prime Minister Muhammad Mzali, to form an alliance committed to a democratic Tunisia. He declared that all Tunisians, whether or not they held Islamist sympathies, had become the victims of the authoritarian regime, and claimed that an-Nahdah differed from Tunisia's other Islamist groups in that it had rejected armed struggle and favoured peaceful political change. In December Ben Ali once again refused to legalize an-Nahdah and proposed constitutional amendments in order to proscribe political parties based on race, region or religion (see above).

During 1995–96 concern continued to be expressed over human rights violations in Tunisia. The US Department of State's report on human rights in Tunisia during 1995 noted that serious problems still remained and that the Government continued to 'stifle freedoms of speech, press and association'. The LTDH's annual report included accounts of violations of the freedom of the press, the illegal detention of suspects, the banning of political parties, and poor conditions inside prisons—despite claims by an internal commission of inquiry into the country's prisons (established by the President) that conditions had greatly improved. In September 1995 the LTDH issued a statement which denounced the deaths in suspicious circumstances of two prisoners. Amnesty International's annual report on Tunisia, published in November, described widespread and systematic human rights abuses and argued that internal commissions of inquiry by the authorities were ineffectual. In January 1996 Najib Hosni, a lawyer who had defended an-Nahdah activists, was sentenced to eight years' imprisonment. It was alleged that he had falsified documents, but Amnesty International insisted that he had been prosecuted for his human rights activities and claimed that he had been tortured during the 18 months that he was detained without trial. In May two other leading human rights activists, Moncef Marzouki, a former President of the LTDH, and Frej Fennich, the Director of the Arab Institute of Human Rights, were arrested. Later that month a court found that, as a private association, the LTDH could continue to select its members. The Ministry of the Interior had insisted that the organization should be open to anyone, leading to fears that it would be infiltrated by political opponents. Meanwhile, the European Parliament passed a resolution in May which strongly criticized Tunisia's human rights record and made special reference to Marzouki's treatment. Several of Tunisia's European allies also openly criticized the country's record on human rights (see above). In December Hosni was granted a presidential pardon at the same time as Mouada and Chamari were released from prison. Their release may have been a response to criticism from abroad, but it did not signal greater tolerance of political opponents. In early 1997 the head of Amnesty International's local branch was arrested and detained for several days, prompting renewed complaints of human rights abuses in Tunisia. In May an-Nahdah announced the death in prison of one of its founder members, Sheikh Mabrouk Zren, and cited other cases of political activists who had died or contracted illnesses while in detention. Ironically, Tunisia was unanimously elected to the UN Human Rights

Commission in May, and soon afterwards the Government tried to improve relations with the LTDH, describing the organization as a 'national asset' but urging it to prove its 'patriotism and sense of responsibility'. In a report on Tunisia published in June, Amnesty International stated that while the Government expressed its commitment to human rights, it was guilty of 'a widening circle of repression', affecting families (particularly wives) and associates of political opponents, and that large-scale human rights abuses continued to take place. Amnesty later joined several other international organizations in appealing to the regime to stop its 'campaign of intimidation' against human rights activists. After several Tunisian human rights activists were refused permission to attend a conference at the European Parliament, a group of parliamentary members announced that they planned to introduce another resolution in the Parliament condemning Tunisia for human rights abuses. In July, during a speech to mark the 40th anniversary of the declaration of the Republic, President Ben Ali vigorously denounced critics of his regime, insisting that in every possible way Tunisia was a state of law and a country of human rights. He accused prominent Tunisian human rights activists of spreading lies about their country and stated that they were guilty of 'a form of high treason'. In September Khemais Ksila, the Vice-President of the LTDH, was arrested after publishing a statement attacking the Government and sending it to a French news agency. He was sentenced to three years' imprisonment in February 1998 for divulging false information likely to upset public order. The sentence was later upheld by the appeal court. At the end of March Radhia Nasraoui, a lawyer well-known for defending political and human rights activists, and married to Hamma Hammani of the POCT, was charged with several offences including links with a terrorist organization and incitement to rebellion. Reporting on human rights practices in 1997, the US State Department recorded an improvement in the Tunisian Government's performance, but claimed that it continued to commit serious offences, including the physical abuse of prisoners, harassment of government critics, and significant restrictions on the freedom of speech and press, while demonstrating a pattern of intolerance to public criticism. In a report published in early 1998 the Arab Commission of Human Rights stated that there had been an increase in human rights abuses in Tunisia and claimed to have evidence relating to the torture of political opponents. Human rights activists in France demanded the release of Khemais Ksila, and a Paris-based group set up a defence committee to campaign for his release in the UN, the EU, the Arab League and the OAU. A report by Article 19, a London-based anti-censorship organization, condemned press restrictions imposed by the Ben Ali regime and urged the EU to put pressure on the Tunisian authorities to respect press freedoms. At the first meeting of the EU-Tunisia Association Council in July, Wolfgang Schüssel, the Austrian Minister of Foreign Affairs, indicated that as part of the political dimension of Tunisia's association agreement, the EU would wish to discuss its concerns over civil liberties in Tunisia. In September the Brussels-based Human Rights Watch urged the EU to play a more active role in reducing human rights abuses in Tunisia and sent an open letter to the European Parliament stating that there had been little change in the human rights situation in Tunisia, with hundreds of political prisoners held in custody and many cases of torture during interrogation. At the same time, Tunisia was elected to the Human Rights Committee of the UN for a four-year period. In November three international human rights organizations published reports expressing strong criticism of Tunisia. Amnesty International stated that despite the regime's attempts to improve its human rights image, human rights abuses had in fact escalated. The Fédération internationale des ligues des droits de l'homme (FIDH) accused the Tunisian authorities of practising torture systematically, and listed 500 specific cases including at least 30 in which prisoners had died. The UN Committee against Torture denounced the security forces and police for their cruel practices, including torture, which had sometimes resulted in death. The Tunisian authorities vigorously denied the allegations made by the three organizations, claiming that their reports did not represent reality and that Tunisia was a country of 'openness, democracy and tolerance'.

The 50th anniversary of the Universal Declaration of Human Rights was celebrated with meetings, seminars and exhibitions portraying what the authorities claimed to be Tunisia's own achievements in the field of human rights, and emphasizing that the most fundamental rights were to food, health, education and work. At the end of 1998 the Chamber of Deputies resolved that the power to withdraw a citizen's passport should be transferred from the Ministry of the Interior to the courts, while the Government announced that community service would replace short prison sentences, where appropriate, in accordance with the international Charter for Civil and Political Rights. Reporting on human rights in Tunisia during 1998, the US State Department pointed to the continuance of serious abuses, referring again to the torture and physical abuse of prisoners by the security forces, harassment of government critics, and significant restrictions on freedom of assembly and association, adding that the judiciary remained under Government control and that due process of law was not always observed. Meanwhile, the President announced changes to the penal code in order to improve procedures relating to the arrest and detention of citizens.

BEN ALI'S THIRD PRESIDENTIAL TERM

In Tunisia's first contested presidential election since independence, held on 24 October 1999, two candidates opposed Zine al-Abidine Ben Ali, the current President—Abderrahmane Tlili, Secretary-General of the UDU and Muhammad Belhadj Amor, Secretary-General of the PUP. They obtained less than 1% of the total vote between them. Ben Ali's victory was never in doubt—he won 99.44% of the vote—and the presence of the other two candidates was a risk-free strategy to give the illusion of greater political pluralism. In parliamentary elections held at the same time, the ruling RCD swept to victory, securing 91.6% of votes cast and winning all 148 of the contested seats in the National Assembly. Of the 34 seats reserved for the opposition parties and distributed according to the number of votes gained, the MDS received 13, the UDU seven, the PUP seven, the MR five and the PSL, represented for the first time, two. Once again the RSP failed to win enough votes to secure representation in the assembly. Together the opposition parties did increase their proportion of the vote compared with the 1994 elections—from 2.3% to 6.4%—and were allocated 19% of seats in the assembly compared with only 12% in 1994. However, despite the President's declaration that the elections heralded a new order of multiparty politics, the ruling RCD retained a massive majority in the new assembly. On this occasion, unlike in the past, the legal opposition parties voiced few criticisms of the elections, which Tunisian and international observers declared to have been free and fair. Two Tunisian human rights activists—Marzouki and Ben Jaafar—who did make critical comments, were detained for questioning, and during the election period the authorities prevented the distribution of several foreign newspapers which had published reports critical of the regime. Despite the high turn-out, most Tunisians showed little interest in the election campaign. After the elections, Muhammad Belhadj Amor resigned as Secretary-General of the PUP and was replaced by Muhammad Bouchiha, while Naceur Ben Ameur was appointed to the new post of president of the party's central council.

Ben Ali was sworn in as President on 15 November 1999, and, in an address to the nation, set out the priorities for his third term of office. He declared that the task of reducing unemployment would be his 'priority of priorities', promised new legislation to ensure greater transparency in the electoral process and to guarantee freedom of the press, and pledged to strengthen the judicial system to improve the protection of human rights, and reform the education system and the administration.

Shortly after the elections Ben Ali appointed Muhammad Ghannouchi as Prime Minister in place of Hamed Karoui who had held the premiership for a decade. The decision followed months of speculation that the President would appoint a new Prime Minister committed to a faster pace of economic reform. Ghannouchi, international co-operation and finance minister since 1992, is an economist with wide experience in economic planning, finance and investment and in negotiations with the major international financial agencies. Other cabinet changes included the transfer of Habib Ben Yahia from defence to foreign affairs, a portfolio he held for much of the 1990s; Muhammad Jegham, who had headed the presidential office, became the new defence minister; Ali Chaouch was replaced as interior minister by Abdallah Kallel, who had held the justice portfolio; Fethi Merdassi replaced Ghannouchi as international co-operation and foreign investment minister, having served as Ghannouchi's deputy; Dali Jazi moved from higher education to head a new ministry of communications, human rights and relations with parliament; Sadok Chaabane, a former justice minister, took over the higher education portfolio; Abd al-Aziz Ben Dhia, Secretary-General of the RCD and a former defence minister, was appointed to the new post of Minister of State and Special Adviser to the President. While most of the changes involved a redistribution of cabinet posts among long-serving political figures close to the President, there were a number of newcomers including Bechir Tekkari, a lawyer, appointed as justice minister, and Jalloul Jaribi, the head of Zitouna University, who became religious affairs minister. At the same time, a number of changes were made to the membership of the RCD's political bureau. Abderrahim Zouari, a former education minister, replaced Abd al-Aziz Ben Dhia as Secretary-General, although Ben Dhia remained a member of the political bureau; Chedli Neffati, the social affairs minister, returned to the political bureau after an absence of three years, and Said Ben Mustapha and Ali Chaouch were removed.

In early November 1999 Ben Ali ordered the release of some 600 political prisoners as part of an amnesty under which some 1,800 prisoners were freed and another 1,200 had their sentences reduced. Most of the political prisoners freed were members of the banned Islamist party, Hizb an-Nahdah, but also included some POCT members. Meanwhile, Abderraouf Chamari, formerly deputy leader of the MDS and a leading human rights activist, who had been sentenced to one year in prison for allegedly slandering the authorities, had been released after only two months of his sentence, and shortly afterwards Khemais Ksila, vice-president of the LTDH, sentenced to three years' imprisonment in early 1998, was also released. Early in 2000 the former MDS leader, Muhammad Mouada, was released from house arrest.

In February 2000 unrest broke out in the south-east of the country as anti-Government demonstrations by high school students and young unemployed Tunisians turned violent. The unrest appeared to have begun in the small towns of Jebeniana, Zarzis and El Hamma, where high school students were reported to have attacked public buildings and clashed with the police. While the authorities insisted that the unrest only lasted for a few hours and was limited to a small area, other sources claimed that the rioting lasted for several days and spread beyond the south-east to Sfax, Tunisia's second-largest city, and even to the outskirts of the capital. Some reports indicated that hundreds of students had been arrested, but the authorities stated that only 33 students would face trial. Although on a much smaller scale than the 1984 riots which also began in the south, commentators noted that as a result of the authorities' intolerance of even peaceful protest, some Tunisians were increasingly prepared to resort to violent actions.

On 6 April 2000 Habib Bourguiba, Tunisia's first President, died at the age of 96. The funeral two days later at Bourguiba's home town of Monastir was a deliberately low-key affair, and the authorities ordered state television not to broadcast live coverage of the ceremony. Nevertheless, tens of thousands of Tunisians lined the route of the funeral procession, and in Sfax hundreds of students demonstrated against the Ben Ali regime. At the beginning of the month, Taoufiq Ben Brik, Tunis correspondent for the Swiss daily *La Croix* and several other European newspapers, had begun a hunger strike in protest at police harassment directed not only against himself but also his family and supporters. In March Ben Brik had been charged with diffusion of false information and defamation of the country's institutions after he wrote several articles for the European press critical of the Ben Ali regime. The affair attracted unprecedented attention in the international press, with French newspapers in particular devoting considerable coverage to human rights abuses in Tunisia, and several senior European politicians raised the issue with the Tunisian authorities. Within Tunisia dissidents became more outspoken in their criticism of the regime and argued that civil society was finally reawakening to resist the regime's 'strategy of fear'. In early May, apparently under strong European pressure, the authorities backed down, returned Taoufiq Ben Brik's passport, lifted the ban on him travelling abroad and released his brother, Jelal, who had been arrested when he tried to visit Taoufiq's house. In response, Ben Brik ended his hunger strike, which had lasted for 42 days, and left for France. (He subsequently returned to Tunisia in early September.) The affair led to a number of other hunger strikes by human rights activists and political prisoners and by several Tunisian political exiles in Europe including an-Nahdah leader Rached Ghanouchi. The repercussions of the Ben Brik affair were also felt in Government circles. Ben Ali quickly replaced Dali Jazi, the minister with responsibility for human rights, with Afif Hendaoui and also made changes among senior staff at the ministry of information, in the state-controlled media and at the official press agency. At the same time, the President replaced a number of senior military officers including Gen. Salah Laouani, head of the *Brigades d'ordre publique* and Gen. Gmati, commander of the National Guard, who had both been closely involved in Ben Ali's takeover in 1987.

At the end of May 2000 a prominent Tunisian journalist, Riad Ben Fadhel, was shot and seriously wounded outside his home in Tunis. Three days before the attack, Ben Fadhel, a former editor of the Arabic edition of *Le Monde Diplomatique*, had published an article in the French daily *Le Monde* in which he warned against amending the Constitution to allow Ben Ali a fourth presidential term.

In municipal elections held at the end of May the ruling RCD retained control of all municipal councils, winning 93% of the 4,128 seats contested. Official figures estimated turn-out at 84%, compared with 92.5% in 1995. The ruling party stood unopposed in 175 of the 257 constituencies, with the opposition parties presenting candidates in only 60 constituencies and independent candidates standing in only 22. The RCD, in contrast, presented candidates in every constituency. Although independent and opposition candidates won 243 seats compared with only six (out of 4,090) in 1995, they had been expected to win more than 800 seats following the introduction of new electoral rules in 1997, under which no party was supposed to hold more than 80% of seats on municipal councils. The new rules, however, were only applied in those constituencies where opposition parties presented candidates. Of the 176 seats won by opposition parties, the MDS took 78, the PUP 42, the UDU 35, the PSL 12 and the MR nine. The RSP boycotted the elections claiming that political conditions did not lend themselves to fair competition. Later in the year divisions were evident within the PSL when its leader and treasurer were accused of misappropriating party funds and one of its two deputies was expelled. The MDS failed to overcome the internal disputes. At the party's conference in early 2001 Ismail Boulahya was re-elected leader; however, his opponents, including seven deputies, refused to accept the result and called for a new conference to be held. Meanwhile, the authorities banned the RSP's newspaper, *Al-Mawkef*, for publishing articles on the trials of human rights activists.

During a visit to London (United Kingdom) in June 2000 Moncef Marzouki, a leading human rights activist, announced that a national democratic conference was planned for early December to lay the foundations for a democratic state in Tunisia within a decade. This was Marzouki's first overseas visit in four years, and during his stay in London he met exiled an-Nahdah leader Rached Ghanouchi. Marzouki, the spokesman for the Conseil national des libertés en Tunisie, a grouping of some 35 Tunisian dissidents, founded in late 1998 but officially banned, expressed the hope that members of an-Nahdah would participate in the proposed conference, thus bringing together the hitherto divided secular and Islamist opponents of the Ben Ali regime. In June two members of the banned POCT were released from prison after staging a hunger strike, and in August Taoufiq Chaib, a member of the outlawed an-Nahdah party, was given a presidential pardon after his health deteriorated sharply following a hunger strike lasting more than six weeks. In July officials from Amnesty International and the FIDH were refused permission to visit Tunisia, and Moncef Marzouki, spokesman for the CNLT, was dismissed from his university post after publicly criticizing the Tunisian

authorities during a visit to Europe. Marzouki received a one-year prison sentence in December, having been convicted of belonging to an illegal organization and disseminating false information. Marzouki had also criticized the management of Tunisia's Fonds de solidarité nationale. Representatives of several international human rights groups attended Marzouki's trial, as did diplomats from France, the United Kingdom and the USA. Marzouki appealed against the judgment, and in early March 2001 was refused permission to travel to Paris, where he had been invited to attend a medical conference.

In September 2000 Ismail Sahbani, Secretary-General of the UGTT, was forced to resign and was later arrested on charges that included forgery. His deputy, Abdessalem Jerad, replaced him as Secretary-General. As leader of Tunisia's largest trade union Sahbani had fostered good relations with the Government and with employers and had generally supported Ben Ali's economic policies, but this had provoked much criticism from the union's members. In October the LTDH held its first congress since 1995 at which a radical lawyer, Mokhtar Trifi, was elected president together with a new executive committee, which included supporters of illegal left-wing and Islamist groups. A faction of the ruling RCD was defeated, and several of its candidates declared that there had been irregularities in the conduct of the election and took legal action to overturn the results. The authorities proceeded to suspend the organization's newly elected leadership until the court announced its ruling on the case. Delegates condemned the suspension as 'a political move disguised as legal action', and the Government's action was also criticized abroad, notably by the UN Secretary-General's special representative for human rights and the European Parliament. In February 2001 a court declared the election result null and void, and in early March legal action was taken against Mokhtar Trifi for diffusion of false information and refusal to submit to a court ruling. New elections were to be held under the supervision of the previous leadership but no date was set. Meanwhile, the organization's headquarters remained closed. Following the 'freeze' imposed on activities of the LTDH, the European Parliament demanded an immediate end to the repression of human rights groups in Tunisia. In November 2000 14 alleged members of an illegal Islamist organization, Ansar, were sentenced to between two and 17 years' imprisonment for undermining state security through illicit contacts with Iranian agents.

In November 2000 President Ben Ali emphasized his strong commitment to human rights and announced a series of initiatives aimed at furthering the democratization process and promoting human rights in Tunisia. The measures included: state compensation to anyone taken into custody or imprisoned unlawfully and later found to be innocent; improved access to legal aid; legislation to improve conditions in the country's prisons and to guarantee prisoners' rights; the transfer of responsibility for the prison system to the justice ministry rather than the interior ministry; a revised press code reducing censorship and prosecution of journalists without good reason, removing imprisonment for infringements of the code, and removing the charge of 'defamation of public order'. In return for these changes the President called on journalists and publishers to prepare a code of ethics in order to protect journalism from excesses. However, despite the promise of greater press freedom, the authorities prevented the distribution of the magazine *Jeune Afrique*, published in Paris, when it carried a profile of Muhammad Talbi, a Tunisian human rights activist.

In a reshuffle of the Council of Ministers in January 2001 President Ben Ali replaced the Minister of the Interior, Abdallah Kallel, by the Government Secretary-General, Abdallah Kaabi, who was himself replaced by Muhammad Rachid Kechiche; the Minister of National Defence, Muhammad Jegham, was replaced by Dali Jazi, a former minister with responsibilities for human rights; Faïza Kéfi was moved from Minister of the Environment and Land Planning to Minister of Professional Training and Employment, to be replaced by Muhammad Nabli; Moncer Rouissi was moved from Minister of Professional Training and Employment to Minister of Education, where he replaced Ahmed Iyadh Ouederni who was appointed to the new post of Minister, Secretary-General of the Presidential Office. Muhammad Raouf Najar was moved from Minister of Children, Youth and Sport to head the Government audit office, and was replaced by Abderrahim Zouari, the Secretary-General of the RCD; Mondher Zenaidi was moved from Minister of Trade to Minister of Tourism, Leisure and Handicrafts and was replaced by Tahar Sioud, a Secretary of State for Foreign Affairs. In February Slaheddine Maâoui, the former Minister of Tourism, Leisure and Handicrafts, was appointed to the sensitive post of Minister delegate to the Prime Minister in charge of Human Rights, Communications and Relations with the National Assembly, where he replaced Afif Hindaoui, who had only held the post from mid-2000. Although there were few changes to senior ministerial posts, the number of under-secretaries was increased from 12 to 24. Most of those appointed to these posts were less than 40 years old and were university graduates brought in to improve the Government's management of the economy and to accelerate the pace of economic reform. At the same time a number of changes were made to the RCD's political bureau: the Prime Minister, Muhammad Ghannouchi, became a member, Ali Chaouch returned to the post of Secretary-General and Muhammad Jeghem was replaced by Dali Jazi.

In mid-January 2001 a Tunisian living in exile in Switzerland began legal proceedings against Abdallah Kallel, the former interior minister who was receiving medical treatment in Geneva at that time, on the grounds that he had been tortured in the Ministry of the Interior in 1992. However, by the time the Swiss police began to investigate the allegations, Kallel had left the country. Shortly afterwards Ben Ali appointed Kallel to the post of presidential councillor. Also in February, following the refusal by the Government to authorize a new opposition newspaper, *Kaws el-Karama*, a Tunisian dissident and editor of the newspaper, Jalel Zoghlani, brother of journalist Taoufiq Ben Brik (see above), was attacked and wounded by six armed men, while some 100 armed police surrounded his apartment for more than 24 hours; he subsequently went on hunger strike in protest. Omar Mestiri of the CNLT and Abdelmoumen Belanes, a former political prisoner and member of the POCT, were both beaten by the security forces when they tried to visit Zoghlani. In the same month Taoufiq Ben Brik had his documents confiscated at Tunis airport on his return from an extended visit to France. In March Khedija Cherif, leader of the Tunisian Association des femmes démocrates and a member of the CNLT, was beaten and insulted by the security forces outside the CNLT headquarters; she had suffered a similar attack outside a Tunis court earlier in the month, when her documents were seized. Also in March police were accused of assaulting several members of the CNLT, when they broke up a meeting. In April the LTDH condemned the assault and confiscation of documents of its vice-president, Souhair Belhassen, at Tunis airport on her return from a visit to France. To many observers it appeared that the state was now ordering physical attacks against dissidents rather than prosecuting them through the courts. Also in April human rights organizations held demonstrations in Tunis and Paris calling for the release of the human rights lawyer and CNLT member Najib Hosni. In the early 1990s Hosni had been sentenced to eight years in prison and banned from practising as a lawyer. Although he had been released from jail after serving two and a half years of his sentence the ban had remained in place. In late 2000 he was arrested for violating the ban and forced to serve the remaining five and a half years of his sentence. Hosni was given a presidential pardon and freed in mid-May 2001.

In late March 2001 almost 100 moderate figures in civil society signed a petition denouncing President Ben Ali's plans to amend the Constitution to allow him a fourth term in office, accusing him of corruption and nepotism. Among the signatories was Mohammed Charfi, a former minister of education who, in a long interview with *Le Monde*, stated that Ben Ali's ultimate goal was to make himself President for life. Charfi pledged to campaign to prevent this and to restore democracy and respect for human rights. He asserted that he remained opposed to the Islamists but deplored the fact that a large number of supporters of the Islamist movement remained in prison. Charfi also alleged that corruption had reached such a level that it was beginning to undermine the country's economic development. Meanwhile, an-Nahdah released a joint communiqué with a dissident faction of the MDS, led by Muhammad Mouada, in which they proposed a National Democratic Front of opposition groups, uniting Islamists and liberals against the Ben Ali regime. Its aim was to

work for 'a genuinely pluralistic alternative with a real popular and political credibility' and to oppose the perpetuation of one-party rule and a 'royal presidency'. However, profound differences between the Islamists and the secular opponents of the Ben Ali regime make such an alliance unlikely. Moreover, serious doubts remained as to whether an-Nahdah was prepared to accept a pluralistic alternative. On 19 June Mouada was arrested and imprisoned for allegedly breaking the terms of his conditional release, imposed in December 1996 (see above). Mouada's arrest was believed to be in response to recent statements by several Tunisian opposition figures, broadcast by Arab television stations popular with many Tunisians. Earlier in the month there were reports that a growing number of prisoners, including members of an-Nahdah, were engaged in hunger strikes with the aim of securing a general amnesty, and that four human rights activists had also announced a hunger strike in order to obtain the return of their passports which had been arbitrarily confiscated by the Ministry of the Interior.

Some observers argued that Ben Ali's entourage was split into two factions. One group was opposed to any political change that was not purely cosmetic; they believed that ordinary Tunisians were more interested in their economic and material well-being than in civil liberties. This group was reported to have powerful networks in the interior ministry and support from within the President's family. The other group, drawn from a younger generation, was deeply concerned about Tunisia's image abroad and favoured greater openness, although it was unclear whether the group favoured major concessions such as allowing effective opposition parties and transparent government. In early April the Minister in charge of Human Rights, Communications and Relations with the National Assembly, Slaheddine Maâoui, gave an interview to *Le Monde* in which he stated that the Government must recognize and speak out about problems of human rights in Tunisia. He vigorously condemned an assault by police in March against Khedija Cherif (see above) and confirmed that the police-officer responsible had been disciplined. He recognized that official censorship of the internet, notably where it concerned human rights, was 'absurd and counter-productive' and was only justified in the case of certain subversive sites. Finally, he promised greater press freedom and gave a personal pledge that journalists who spoke out would not be penalized if they remained within the law. Some commentators argued that Maâoui's remarks should be interpreted in the context of the presidential election due in 2004, and that Ben Ali might be willing to accept a limited measure of democratization in order to secure a fourth term of office. Rumours circulated that the President might agree to appoint a Prime Minister from the moderate opposition and give him greater powers. However, the issue of *Le Monde* that carried the interview with Maâoui was censored on the orders of the presidency.

In late April 2001 President Ben Ali instructed the Ministry of the Interior to investigate all alleged abuses by the security forces against Tunisian citizens and to ensure that those found guilty were punished. In May the President gave his first interview to a Tunisian newspaper since assuming power, in which he expressed his commitment to accelerating the pace of democratic change and reaffirmed that those responsible for human rights abuses would be brought to justice. To reinforce his message the President made various conciliatory gestures, ordering the release of a number of political prisoners. At the same time a court ruled that the LTDH could resume its activities. Under revisions to the press code announced in May the offence of 'defamation of public order' was abolished, together with prison sentences for some violations of the code. On the whole, however, the changes did little to encourage freedom of expression, with the regime maintaining tight surveillance over the local press and foreign publications. The revisions were condemned by the Association des journalistes tunisiens as completely inadequate.

In June 2001 Sihem Ben Sedrine, spokesperson for the CNLT, was arrested and imprisoned by the authorities on her return from London, where she had given an interview to the Arab television station, Al-Mustaquilla, an important forum through which members of the Tunisian opposition have expressed their views. During the interview Ben Sedrine had exposed details of a corruption scandal allegedly involving a close relative of

President Ben Ali. Also in June Mokhtar Trifi, president of the LTDH, launched a campaign calling for a general amnesty law, an initiative that was supported by Moncef Marzouki and Mohammed Charfi, and later by the Secretary-General of the UGTT, Abdessalem Jerad. In early July Judge Mokhtar Yahyaoui addressed an open letter to President Ben Ali condemning the pressure exerted by the regime on judges, forcing them to give judgments 'dictated in advance, to which there was no appeal and which were not in accordance with the law'. This was the first time that a senior member of the judiciary had spoken out publicly in this way and his remarks commanded particular attention as Yahyaoui was unaffiliated to any political party or group and had a reputation for integrity and professionalism. Yahyaoui was suspended from duty and deprived of his salary, and in December was dismissed from his post. The Association des magistrats tunisiens, which in late May had passed a resolution calling for the independence of the judiciary, issued a communiqué expressing support for judge Yahyaoui. In early June 80 judges had circulated an unsigned manifesto on the internet stating that they were prepared to fight to restore the 'honour and dignity' of the Tunisian legal system. In Paris several associations expressed their support for judge Yahyaoui, and the FIDH took up the case with the UN Special Rapporteur of the Commission on Human Rights on the independence of judges and lawyers. At the end of July, in a speech marking the 44th anniversary of the Republic, Ben Ali stressed the importance of applying the law and of punishing those who disregarded it in the name of democracy and civil liberties, and rejected demands for the release of opponents of the regime and an end to the prosecution of others. Ben Ali did not refer to the controversial question of a fourth presidential term of office, but the RCD, the pro-Government press and various associations appealed to him to stand. At the end of September the RCD's central committee nominated Ben Ali as the party's official candidate for the 2004 presidential election.

Amnesty International declared that holding the 14th meeting of the Mediterranean Games in Tunis in early September 2001 should not obscure the fact that some 1,000 political prisoners were still held in Tunisian gaols, where they were subjected to what the organization termed cruel and degrading treatment. The meeting was well-organized but failed to attract the level of international attention that the Tunisian authorities had hoped for.

In early October 2001 Ben Ali effected a minor reorganization of the Council of Ministers following the appointment of Faiza Kefi, Minister of Professional Training and Employment, as Tunisia's ambassador to Paris. Her ministerial responsibilities were taken over by Néziha Zarrouk, hitherto Minister for Family and Women's Affairs. In by-elections in seven constituencies in late October the ruling RCD won all the seats; only four opposition parties—the MDS, PUP, UDU and PSL—presented candidates but, in contrast to the RCD, did little campaigning. As a result the RCD increased its seats in the Chamber of Deputies to 149, leaving the opposition parties with 33 seats.

In late October 2001, in an interview with *Le Monde*, Kamel el-Taief, a former political adviser to Ben Ali and until the early 1990s a close ally of the President, spoke out for the first time against the Ben Ali regime, stating that the country was ruled by a 'mafia' linked to the President's family and that Tunisians were scandalized by the widespread corruption and angered by the lack of civil liberties. He claimed that opposition existed within the regime, and that even some ministers were opposed to the Ben Ali 'clique' and the ruling party. He spoke of being subjected to numerous forms of intimidation since his estrangement from the ruling circle in 1995, and accused the officials of ordering a campaign of harassment against him. El-Taief was arrested in November and sentenced to one year's imprisonment in early February 2002. Shortly before President Chirac of France visited Tunis in December 2001 the Tunisian authorities decided to lift the travel restrictions imposed on Moncef Marzouki to enable him to leave Tunisia to take up a university post in France. At the end of November Marzouki had appealed to international human rights organizations, stating that his home was under continuous police surveillance, that he was forbidden to work, travel, write, or telephone, and that he had been had been deprived of his civil and political rights. Meanwhile the Geneva-based Organisation mondiale contre la

torture claimed that the murder of a human rights activist and high-ranking official of the Ministry of Foreign Affairs, Ali Saidi, in Gafsa in December 2001, was political. At the end of January 2002 Muhammad Mouada was again given a conditional release from prison after a nine-day hunger strike. Although forbidden to engage in any political activity, he reaffirmed his commitment to continue the struggle for a democratic regime in Tunisia. At the beginning of February, after spending some four years in hiding from the police, Hamma Hammani, leader of the POCT, and two other party members were brought before a Tunis court. The three men had come out of hiding to protest against the nine-year prison sentences imposed on them *in absentia* in 1999 for belonging to a banned political party. The court, however, confirmed the original sentences and sentenced one of the men, Samir Taamallah, to an additional two years' imprisonment for contempt of court. The men were sentenced without being given an opportunity to speak and in the absence of their lawyers. Despite the presence of numerous international observers, diplomats and journalists, there were violent scenes involving plain-clothes police both inside and outside the court. A representative of the FIDH declared that the men had committed no violent acts and had been condemned simply for their political views. The Tunisian lawyers' association staged a strike to protest at the conduct of the trial. In late March the Court of Appeal reduced the sentences to 38 months for Hammani and 21 months for his two associates. At the end of June Radia Nasraoui, Hammami's wife, announced that she was beginning an indefinite hunger strike in an attempt to secure the immediate and unconditional release of her husband. Hammani was not included in the group of prisoners granted a presidential pardon on the 25 July, the anniversary of independence. At the end of July Radia Nasraoui gave a press conference at the headquarters of the FIDH in Paris, in which she condemned the Ben Ali regime and was criticized those countries, including France, that praised the Tunisian authorities. She declared that her hunger strike was not just to demand the release of her husband, but to draw attention to the lack of freedom in Tunisia and the harsh conditions under which political prisoners, whether communists, Islamists or nationalists, were held. An official of the French Ministry of Foreign Affairs stated that it was following Nasraoui's case with interest and had taken up the matter with the Tunisian authorities on humanitarian grounds. Meanwhile, the Tunisian authorities had issued a communiqué criticizing the foreign media's treatment of the Nasraoui affair. In early August, shortly after returning to Tunisia, Nasraoui announced that she was ending her hunger strike but would continue the struggle and planned to create an association against torture.

At the beginning of February 2002 three alleged Islamists were brought before a military tribunal in Tunis accused of having links with al-Qa'ida. Some 31 other suspects were being tried *in absentia*, including a Tunisian arrested by Italian police in April 2001 (see above). At the end of March 2002 a prisoner serving a 16-year sentence for membership of an-Nahda died following a hunger strike.

In late April 2002, two weeks after the tanker bomb attack on the Djerba synagogue (see above) President Ben Ali replaced the Minister of the Interior and the Director of National Security, the two most senior officials responsible for internal security. Hedi M'henni, hitherto Minister of Social Affairs, replaced Abdallah Kaâbi at the Ministry of the Interior, and Mahammad Hedi Ben Hassine, a retired general and former director of military security, replaced Ali Ganzaoui as head of national security. In early March the CNLT, presenting its annual report in Paris, strongly condemned what it termed the manipulation of the justice system by the Ben Ali regime and called for the restoration of an independent judiciary. At its congress held in Djerba in early February 2002 the UGTT pledged to re-establish its independence from the Ben Ali regime, to encourage links with other groups within civil society, and to promote greater democracy within the organization itself. Delegates expressed solidarity with the strike by the lawyers' association (see above), called for respect for civil liberties, expressed support for the embattled LTDH, and demanded an end to legal proceedings against POCT leader Hamma Hammani. Later, however, the Secretary-General, Abdessalem Djerad, declared that Ben Ali could count on the support of workers and trade unionists in his efforts 'to consolidate the foundations of the Republican regime'. At the end of April some 13 senior officers in the Tunisian armed forces—among them Brig.-Gen. Abdelaziz Skik, who had been appointed army chief of staff in mid-2001, were killed when the helicopter in which they were travelling crashed as the officers were returning from a visit to a military base in the Kef region near the frontier with Algeria. Col Rachid Ammar was named as Skik's successor.

CONSTITUTIONAL CHANGES 2002

In November 2001, in a speech marking the 14th anniversary of his accession to power, Ben Ali announced what he termed a 'fundamental reform' of the constitution, although he gave few details of the proposed changes. He declared that he wished to bring about an improvement in the country's political system in order to prepare Tunisia for the future. While he expressed his grateful thanks to all those Tunisians who had pledged their loyalty and appealed to him to continue as President, he made no reference to changing the Constitution in order to allow him to seek a fourth term. Nevertheless, most commentators concluded that Ben Ali was determined to secure a fourth mandate and that the proposed changes to the Constitution would probably include increasing the number of presidential candidates, so as to lend greater credibility to the 2004 elections, and the addition of a clause devoted to upholding human rights and liberties. The PDP, the dissident faction of the MDS not represented in parliament, together with the unrecognized Forum démocratique pour le travail et les libertés, led by Mustapha Ben Jaafar, and the Congrès pour la république, founded by Moncef Marzouki, set up a 'democratic co-ordination committee' to campaign against a fourth mandate for Ben Ali and to press for an amnesty for political prisoners, freedom of expression and the independence of the judiciary. Opposition to a fourth term for Ben Ali was also voiced by the PSL (which nominated its leader, Mounir Beji, as a candidate in the 2004 presidential elections), the CNLT and various human rights groups. In December the PUP became the first legal opposition party to express support for Ben Ali's candidature. At the end of February 2002 the Chamber of Deputies met in special session to examine proposals for revisions to the Constitution prepared by a team of experts headed by Abdelaziz Ben Dhia, special adviser to the President. The proposed revisions included the creation of a second chamber, the Chamber of Councillors, to ensure better representation of the regions and professional bodies; and the removal of restrictions on the number of times

the presidential mandate could be renewed. Presidential elections would be required to involve more than one candidate. After discussions in the Chamber of Deputies the revisions would be put to a referendum, which Ben Ali announced would be held in conditions of transparency with observers and journalists from neighbouring and friendly countries allowed to monitor the proceedings. Legal political parties taking part in the referendum campaign would benefit from financial assistance and access to radio and television. The opposition Ettajdid's political bureau deplored the fact that the proposals had been presented to parliament without prior consultation with opposition parties or civil society, and later was the only party represented in parliament to condemn the referendum. The CNLT described the proposals as a manoeuvre to reinforce the absolute powers of the President. There was particular concern that under the proposed changes the Head of State would enjoy legal immunity during his term of office, and also after the end of his mandate for actions carried out during his term of office. Disquiet was also expressed by democrats at the inclusion of a clause demanding that all citizens have a duty to show loyalty towards Tunisia, because of concern that such a vague statement would be open to many interpretations. At the beginning of April the Chamber of Deputies adopted the proposals which were put to a referendum held on 26 May. In the final draft the maximum age for presidential candidates had notably been increased from 70 to 75 years, giving Ben Ali (who would be 68 years of age at the 2004 election) the opportunity to seek two additional mandates and fuelling speculation that he intended to make himself 'President for life'. While the PDP demanded a boycott of the referendum, the first official results indicated that 99.52% of voters had approved the changes, with voter participation put at 95%. An editorial in the French daily *Le Monde* declared that Ben Ali had used the 26 May referendum to mount his own '*coup d'état*' without criticism from the West. At the beginning of June the authorities closed down a popular website TUNeZINE and arrested its founder, Zouhair Yahyaoui (nephew of the dissident judge Mokhtar Yahyaoui) for 'disseminating false information'. Zouhair Yahyaoui's website had become extremely popular in Tunisia and abroad, especially among young people, providing a daily newsletter and discussion forums. Some commentators considered that TUNeZINE, which had been particularly critical of the conduct of the recent referendum, had become the first victim of official action against a new form of resistance which had more influence on the young than the mainstream opposition leaders.

Economy

Revised for this edition by RICHARD GERMAN

Tunisia covers an area of 163,610 sq km (63,170 sq miles). More than one-third of the urban population live in the Greater Tunis area. Most of the towns, and also the greater part of the rural population, are concentrated in the coastal areas. In the centre and the south, the land is infertile semi-desert, the population scattered, the standard of living very low, and the rate of growth of the population higher than in the north. The results of the 1999 census indicated that the population totalled 9,442,000, compared with 8,795,000 at the previous census in 1994. Some 62.4% of Tunisians were urban dwellers. The annual population growth rate had continued to fall, to 1.3% compared with 1.7% in 1994 and 2.5% in 1984. In 1998 the UN Population Fund (UNFPA) reported that Tunisia had the lowest annual rate of population increase in the Arab world and noted that 50% of Tunisian women used modern methods of contraception, the highest proportion in Africa and the Middle East. By 1999 the average size of household had fallen to 4.9 persons, compared with 5.2 persons in 1994, and life expectancy had increased to 71.2 years for women and 68.8 years for men. Some 31% of the population were under the age of 15 years in 1999 compared with 37% in 1990. The concentration of the population along the eastern coast had become more pronounced, and by 1999 43% of all Tunisians lived in Tunis and the surrounding region.

According to the Institut National de la Statistique, the population totalled 9,673,000 at mid-2001.

The capital and main commercial centre is Tunis (population 674,100, according to the 1994 census), which, together with the adjacent La Goulette, is also the chief port. There are about 50,000 Europeans in Tunis, mainly French and Italians, their numbers having decreased rapidly since independence. Other towns of importance include Sfax (population 230,900 in 1994), which is the principal town in the south, the second port and the centre for exports of phosphates and olive oil; Ariana (152,700); Ettadhamen (149,200); Sousse (125,000); and Kairouan (102,600). Some 600,000 Tunisians are estimated to reside abroad, relieving the domestic employment situation and providing a source of foreign exchange earnings through workers' remittances from overseas. The Government is trying to encourage Tunisians to work in Saudi Arabia and in other countries bordering the Persian (Arabian) Gulf, in order to offset the reduction in demand for Tunisian workers in traditional markets, especially France. Even greater efforts were needed to accommodate the 30,000 Tunisian workers who were expelled from Libya in 1985.

Tunisia's development record in the 1970s was fairly impressive, with gross domestic product (GDP), measured in current prices, increasing from US \$4,339m. (\$773 per head) in 1975 to \$8,667m. (\$1,356 per head) in 1980. In the early 1980s, however, the economy entered a period of turbulence. Output of petroleum reached a peak level in 1980, and the countryside was devastated by a series of droughts. Measured at constant 1980 prices, GDP (in purchasers' values) declined from TD 3,736m. in 1981 to TD 3,718m. in 1982, but growth averaged 5.3% per year in 1983–85. Meanwhile, the deficit on the current account of the balance of payments remained at an unacceptably high level, resulting in a worrying increase in external debt (totalling \$4,880m. at the end of 1985). These problems culminated in 1986, when the sudden fall in the international price of petroleum resulted in a balance-of-payments crisis, which forced the Government to seek assistance from the International Monetary Fund (IMF). As agricultural output declined, GDP fell by 1.4%, in real terms, in 1986. With the IMF's assistance, the Government adopted a radical economic programme for the 1987–91 period, designed to provide a secure basis for the economy until the next decade, by which time it was anticipated that Tunisia would have become a net energy importer. The strategy depended on an increase in exports of agricultural and manufactured goods, a rise in revenues from tourism, and severe reductions in the Government's investment budget. Meanwhile, trade was to be liberalized, and the Tunisian dinar was to be devalued, in an attempt to maintain export competitiveness. The economy recovered in 1987, as a result of an increase in the international price of petroleum, an abundant harvest and the success of government measures to control public spending and to encourage higher output, exports and foreign investment. Accordingly, GDP expanded by 5.5%, in real terms, and the current account deficit fell to the equivalent of 0.6% of GDP. However, in 1988 the combined effects of severe drought and locust damage on the harvest, and a fall in the oil price, reduced GDP growth to 1.5%, although the current account of the balance of payments showed an annual surplus (of \$216m.) for the first time since 1974. In 1989 GDP increased by 3.5%, with the help of a substantial expansion in the tourism sector and higher remittances from workers abroad, although the current account was in deficit by \$160m. (1.6% of GDP). In 1990 an ample harvest of cereals and a rise in the petroleum price contributed to real GDP growth of 6%, but the current account deficit increased to \$523m. (4.1% of GDP).

In 1988 the IMF and the World Bank provided financial support for a medium-term adjustment programme for 1988–91. The policies of the 1987–91 programme were continued under the new programme, with emphasis being placed on the acceleration of the process of trade liberalization, the strengthening of the financial sector, the restructuring of state enterprises and the introduction of tax reforms. By 1989 substantial progress had been made and the programme was viewed as highly successful. In March 1991, however, it was announced that austerity measures would have to be adopted in order to counter the effects of the Gulf War on exports, tourism revenues and external funding sources. In protest at Tunisia's ambivalence at the time of the crisis, Kuwait and Saudi Arabia withdrew planned investment and aid totalling US \$412m. and \$200m. respectively, while the USA reduced aid from \$59m. in 1990 to a projected \$19m. in 1991. Against this background the Government obtained a one-year extension to its agreement with the IMF and also secured balance-of-payments support from the World Bank and other sources. By the end of 1991 mid-year forecasts of zero GDP growth that year had been revised to projected growth of 3.5%, reflecting a record harvest, a recovery in tourism and an upturn in the industrial sector. As a result, both the trade deficit (\$874m.) and the current account deficit (\$191m., or 1.5% of GDP) showed improvements in 1991, and GDP growth of 6.5% was forecast for 1992. In July 1992 a new Five-Year Plan (1992–96) was inaugurated, amid optimism that Tunisia was set to become North Africa's leading centre of venture capital and technology. At the same time, it was announced that the Government would not be seeking an IMF facility to replace the Extended Fund Facility (EFF) which had expired in mid-1992. GDP growth of 7.8% was recorded in 1992, followed by growth of only 2% in 1993, when there were falls in agricultural, mining and oil production. The economy grew by 3.3% in 1994, when the effects of an accelerated decline in agricultural output (owing mainly to drought conditions)

were offset by strong growth in tourism, transport and industry, including export-orientated manufacturing, and by 2.4% in 1995. GDP grew by 6.9% in 1996, a significant rise which in large part was the result of a good agricultural performance and, according to official estimates, by 5.6% in 1997, although some independent sources put the figure at just over 5%. Unemployment, particularly acute in the poorer south, centre and north-west, remained a problem, affecting an estimated 15% of the economically active population by 1997 according to official figures, but around 20% according to some independent sources. GDP grew by 5% in 1998, according to Government figures, and by 6.2% in 1999. By the late 1990s GDP per head had risen to \$2,100, the highest in the Maghreb. Despite a sharp contraction in agriculture as a result of poor rainfall, the central bank estimated that real GDP grew by 5% in 2000, with both the industrial and service sectors recording strong growth. This suggested that as a result of diversification, the economy was able to withstand the impact of periodic droughts. Average inflation fell from 3.1% in 1998 to 2.7% in 1999, and remained subdued at 2.9% in 2000. The IMF estimates that economic growth averaged 5.5% during the period 1996–2001, evidence that gradual liberalization of the economy has produced results in terms of productivity, growth, and economic diversification. Real GDP grew by 5% in 2001 despite a contraction in agricultural output caused by a third consecutive year of drought. Inflation dropped to 1.9%, its lowest rate for over a quarter of a century.

In July 1995 Tunisia signed a new trade agreement with the European Union (EU) under which Tunisian manufacturers would be exposed to increasingly strong competitive pressures from 1996 onwards (see also Industry; External Trade). It was expected that there would be significant inflows of EU official assistance and European private investment during the 12-year trade liberalization period. According to government officials, Tunisia's closer association with Europe would help to ensure that a critical phase of the industrialization process was realistically planned and adequately funded. The agreement formally came into force in March 1998, although Tunisia began dismantling trade barriers to EU industrial goods in January 1996. In April 1998 it was announced that the EU had agreed to grant Tunisia US \$10.7m. to support the Government's privatization programme and assist the Tunisian economy's adjustment to growing competition from the EU under the free-trade agreement. The grant was to be disbursed over five years and was made on condition that the Government accelerated the divestment of state-owned companies. Despite pressure from the World Bank, the IMF and Tunisia's own central bank over the preceding decade, the Government had moved relatively slowly to privatize public companies, fearing that this would lead to reductions in the workforce and aggravate unemployment. According to the Minister of Economic Development an annual average of six firms were privatized in 1987–94, and 15 per year in 1994–97. The Government raised around TD 350m. (\$308m.) from the programme during 1987–97. In 1998 the Ministry of Economic Development publicly stated the objectives of the privatization programme: public companies would not simply be sold to the highest bidder and financial offers would be balanced by other considerations, such as investment plans, the number of jobs to be retained, transfer of technology and export plans. The programme would also be carried out with greater 'transparency'. By this time there was some evidence that political resistance to privatization had become weaker and that the Government accepted that an acceleration in the sale of public companies was essential to strengthen the economy. During 1998 the sale of two state-owned cement companies for TD 409m. (\$366m.)—slightly more than total receipts from privatization during the previous 10 years—appeared to mark a new phase in the programme. As a result of these sales, Tunisia did not have to seek external commercial funding in 1998. The privatization programme continued to make progress in 1999 but the amount of revenue raised was well below government projections. During the first half of 2000 two more state-owned cement companies were sold for a total of TD 361.5m. and as a result a substantial rise in privatization revenues was expected by the end of the year. According to official sources 138 companies were privatized between 1987 and March 2000 raising around TD 1,268m. The largest receipts were from the sale of companies in the construction materials, tourism and trade sectors. The results for 2001 fell short of Government objectives, which was largely attributed to the offered prices being lower than targeted. Of 41 enterprises (with combined assets of TD 1,840m.) scheduled to be privatized, only 15 small companies were sold, raising TD 44m. In January 2002 the Government announced a new programme to sell 26 companies, five of which would be sold by an Initial Public Offering (IPO).

At the beginning of his third term of office in November 1999, President Ben Ali declared that reducing unemployment was his 'priority of priorities'. A Fonds national pour l'emploi was set up with initial capital of TD 60m. to help people secure employment by financing training and work programmes, and by providing financial assistance to those wishing to establish their own businesses. The President also highlighted the importance of increasing both domestic and foreign investment, improving the competitiveness of the economy and strengthening exports. The new Prime Minister, Muhammad Ghannouchi, formerly Minister of International Co-operation and Foreign Investment, was expected to set a faster pace of economic reform than his predecessor. Although the 1999 census revealed a marked improvement in the standard of living—most Tunisian households now have electricity and three-quarters have piped water—poverty remains widespread, despite the work of the Fonds de solidarité nationale established in 1993 to improve infrastructure in less developed areas and to provide financial assistance to poor families. In 2000 Tunisia won praise from the IMF for a strong economic performance and outstanding social achievements by regional standards (poverty incidence having been reduced from 13% in 1980 to 4%), but concern was expressed that despite the creation of new jobs the unemployment rate remained virtually unchanged. Its recommendations included accelerating the privatization programme, allowing local and foreign investment in the services sector and liberalizing foreign trade. The World Bank also identified unemployment as Tunisia's greatest problem and stated that annual growth rates of 6%–7% would have to be achieved in order to reduce it. Higher levels of domestic and foreign investment, faster export growth and further structural reforms were essential in order to achieve higher growth rates. However, some analysts were pessimistic about Tunisia's ability to attract a significantly higher level of foreign investment, arguing that many foreign investors were deterred by the repressive policies of the Ben Ali regime and evidence of widespread corruption and nepotism. In 2002 the IMF issued a generally positive report on Tunisia's economy, although unemployment remained high at 15%. It stressed the importance of continued privatization, cuts in subsidies, restructuring of the banking and financial sector, and multilateral trade liberalization. It also stated that the past years of robust economic growth could be curtailed by the impact on tourism of the September 11 2001 terrorist attacks in the USA, and by a further drop in agricultural production as a result of continued drought.

AGRICULTURE

About two-thirds of the total area of Tunisia is suitable for farming. For agricultural purposes the country is composed of five different areas: the mountainous north, with its large fertile valleys; the north-east, including the Cap Bon, where the soil is especially suitable for the cultivation of oranges and other citrus fruit; the Sahel, where olives grow; the centre, with its high tablelands and pastures; and the south, with oases and gardens, where dates are prolific. Harvests vary considerably in size, determined by the uncertain rainfall, since cultivation is largely by dry farming and irrigation is, as yet, limited. The main cereal crops are wheat, barley, maize, oats and sorghum. Fruit is also important, with grapes, olives, dates, oranges and figs grown for export as well as for the local market.

In recent years Tunisia has been importing increasing amounts of cereals, as local production has failed to keep pace with population growth. During the 1960s the agricultural sector grew at only about 1.5% per year, but exceptional weather conditions and improved irrigation in 1971 and 1972 resulted in excellent agricultural yields, and during the fourth Plan period (1973–76) good weather, except in 1974, led to an average annual growth rate of 3%. The 1977–81 Plan envisaged annual

growth of 3.5% and the 1982–86 Plan projected average annual growth at 5%, as a higher proportion of investment was allocated to the agricultural sector. However, these targets were not reached, owing to poor crop conditions in 1977, 1982 and 1986. The collapse in agricultural output was particularly severe in 1986. The 1987–91 Plan projected annual growth of 6% per year, and directed even more investment to agriculture. In 1988, however, agricultural output declined drastically as a result of drought and a plague of locusts. Agriculture's contribution to GDP declined from 22% in 1965 to 12% in 1990. However, a record cereal harvest reversed the trend in 1991, when agriculture's share of GDP increased to 19.6%. Owing to population increase, the average index of food production per caput fell to 87 in the period 1988–90 (1979–81 = 100). By 1997 the proportion of the labour force engaged in agriculture had fallen to 25.7%, from 49% in 1965. In 1993 agriculture's share of GDP was 16.9%, and the total value of exports from this sector (TD 392.6m.) was some TD 7.4m. more than spending on agricultural and food imports. In 1994 the surplus in agricultural trade amounted to TD 48.4m. (exports TD 526.7m., imports TD 478.3m.). By 1995 agriculture's contribution to GDP had declined to 13.4%, increasing to 15.9% in 1996. During 1980–90 agricultural GDP rose by an annual average of 2.8%; however, agricultural GDP declined by an annual average of 0.1% in 1990–96. According to official figures, the agricultural sector grew by 12.4% in 1999, higher than the overall rate of growth in GDP. The budget for 2000 forecast growth at 3.5%, but in practice agricultural GDP contracted by 1% according to official figures and by 5% according to some independent sources. Although the 2001 budget forecast growth at 6.5%, there was a 1.5% contraction in agricultural output due to the drought. The deficit in agricultural trade increased to TD 364.6m. from TD 189.2m. in 2000 (with imports valued at TD 1143.1m. and exports at TD 778.5m.) The means by which self-sufficiency should be achieved has been the subject of political debate since the early 1970s. During 1960–69 the basis of the Government's agrarian reform programme lay in the formation of collective 'agricultural units'. These units, consisting of at least 500 ha, were to be operated as collectives in order to consolidate small peasant holdings and, later, to exploit land expropriated from French farmers or acquired from owners of large or medium-sized farms. The system was controlled through credits provided by the Agricultural Bank. By 1968 some 220 state co-operatives were in existence and several hundred more were being created. However, opposition to the scheme was widespread, and there were revelations of unsatisfactory performance, heavy debts and misappropriation of state funds. These discoveries were instrumental in the downfall and disgrace of Ben Salah, whose position was already weakened by the displeasure of foreign aid donors with his agricultural policies.

Following Ben Salah's downfall, farmers were given a chance to opt out of the state co-operatives, which were later dismantled. Meanwhile, the National Assembly approved legislation allowing for the eventual division of large private estates among individual farmers or private co-operatives. The Government also introduced a number of measures to stimulate output, including the provision of funds for mechanization, a reduction in taxes, and the introduction of subsidies for purchases of fertilizers and seed. By 1975 about 50% of the total cultivated area of 9m. ha was privately owned, a further 2.1m. ha were worked by private co-operatives and the remainder was farmed by state or religious institutions. In April 1974 a 'supervised credits scheme' was announced, whereby small and medium-sized farms could apply for short-term supervised credits to improve farming methods. It was hoped that this would encourage crop diversification.

The Government's agricultural policy subsequently came to reflect several concerns: one was to achieve self-sufficiency, thus saving on expensive food imports which the country could ill afford, and a second was to reduce regional imbalance by developing rural areas. By making funds available for agriculture, the authorities hoped to stem rural depopulation. The 1982–86 Plan allocated about 16% of total investment to agriculture, compared with only 13% in the previous Plan. In the 1987–91 Plan, investment in agriculture increased further, to about 20% of total proposed investment, a particular aim being to increase the role of the private sector in the financing of agriculture.

In June 1989 the World Bank agreed to provide Tunisia with credit of US $84m. to finance the second phase of a seven-year agricultural reform programme launched in 1986. During the second phase of the programme it was intended to increase the share of the private sector in agricultural production, fortify agricultural support services and reform pricing and marketing structures. The need to boost domestic production was regarded as increasingly urgent since, by the mid-1980s, the value of Tunisia's agricultural exports was less than one-half that of its agricultural imports. In June 1990 the Government introduced the first stage of a further reform programme, financed by the World Bank, to improve agricultural extension and research. Under the 1992–96 Plan emphasis was to be given to encouraging private investment in agro-industrial ventures, with a view to maximizing export and food-processing potential.

By 1999 official sources indicated that Tunisia had achieved self-sufficiency in dairy products, vegetables and fruit and was almost self-sufficient in red meat. In 1999 Tunisia recorded a surplus in food trade, with exports increasing by 29% and imports falling by 18%. Investment in the agricultural sector reached TD 854m. in 1999 and rose to TD 920m. in 2000, just over one-half of which was from private sources.

The fragmentation of land-holdings and the need to consolidate them into larger, more efficient units, remains a major obstacle to increasing the profitability of the agricultural sector. However, after the experiences of the 1960s, attempts to consolidate small land-holdings became a highly sensitive subject for the Government. Nevertheless, speaking in November 1997, President Ben Ali announced that there would be national debate on land reform to find ways of amalgamating small agricultural land-holdings into more efficient units. The scale of the problem was highlighted by the Ministry of Agriculture in early 1998 when it reported that while the area devoted to agriculture—some 5.3m. ha—was beginning to decline as farmland was taken over for urban and industrial uses, the number of land-holders had increased from 326,000 in 1962 to 471,000 in 1995, with the average size of land-holdings declining from 16 ha to 11 ha. According to government estimates, farms on non-irrigated land must be at least 50 ha to be efficient, but the vast majority of land-holdings were well below this threshold and just over one-half were under 5 ha. Consequently many farms were too small to be profitable, and this discouraged investment and the use of modern farming methods. One-third of landowners were part-time farmers and there were many absentee landlords. In January 1998 the Minister of Agriculture announced that state-owned farms would be leased to foreign investors with expertise in livestock and vineyard management. Investment in agriculture was reported to have increased substantially during the first half of 1998. Investment by private companies leasing state land totalled TD 33m., compared with TD 18m. during the corresponding period of 1997.

A major programme of water development, including the construction of a number of dams for irrigation and flood prevention, was being implemented under the supervision of the World Bank. The Sidi Salem dam, with a capacity of 500m. cu m per year, opened in May 1982, and the Sidi Saad dam, near Kairouan, irrigating more than 4,000 ha, formally opened in the following month. Germany was financing the construction of the Bou Heurtna dam in Jendouba, which would irrigate 20,000 ha. In the late 1980s construction began on a pipeline linking the Sidi Salem dam and the partly-built Sejnane dam with the water plant at Mateur. The saline water from Sidi Salem was to be mixed with the water from Sejnane at the plant, and was to be used to supply Tunis and to irrigate the northern cereal- and citrus fruit-growing areas. In the mid-1980s Tunisia's national water storage capacity was 1,500m. cu m and some 80,000 ha of land were irrigated. In mid-1992 two major dam projects, at El-Houareb and Sejnane, were near completion. Between 1990 and 1999 the total irrigated area was expanded by more than one-third, from 256,000 ha to 345,000 ha, as part of a 10-year programme under which six large dams, 110 hillside dams, 547 reservoirs, 1,580 deep wells and 57 waste-water treatment plants were constructed, increasing available water resources from 2,070m. cu m to 3,043m. cu m (the country's total accessible water resources were estimated at 3,900m. cu m). In addition, water-efficient irrigation methods were utilized on over one-half of the irrigated land. By

2006 the Government planned to increase the irrigated area to 400,000 ha and to extend the use of water-efficient irrigation methods to virtually the entire irrigated area. A further 11 dams were planned, with a total capacity of 350m. cu m, and a network of pipelines was to be built linking all the country's main dams so that water could be transferred as required from one reservoir to another. In addition another 50 new hillside dams were to be constructed. By 2001 work on the 1.3m. cu m Zerga dam in the Tabarka region in northern Tunisia near the Algerian border was in progress and would be completed in September 2003. Two other dams were to be built in the Tabarka region; the Kebir dam and the Moula dam, and a fourth new dam was planned near Bizerta In the long term there were plans to transport some of the water to central and southern parts of the country. Part of the cost of these projects was being provided by the Arab Fund for Economic and Social Development (AFESD). In 2002 Agence Française de Développement (AFD) extended a €25m. loan to finance a drinking water project and the Abu Dhabi Development Fund granted a $25m. loan to construct 20 small dams for rainwater collection in the mountainous areas. It was also reported that the Islamic Development Bank (IDB) had provided a $5m. loan to the Tunisian National Bank for agricultural development. A World Bank report in 2000 warned that unless more efficient use were made of water resources and realistic prices were charged for water, especially to farmers, Tunisia would face a serious water shortage by 2015. It stated that 80% of Tunisia's exploitable water resources (3,100m. cu m a year) were already being utilized and that the remainder would be brought into use over the next decade. 80% of current water use was for irrigation, 12% for drinking, 6% for industry and 2% by the tourism sector, but demand for water outside the agricultural sector was rising as a result of population growth, an increase in per head consumption and growing demands from industrial users. Consequently, the World Bank predicted that it was only a matter of time before there was a major water shortage. The report stated that growing cereals on irrigated land was not cost effective and pointed out that in the southern oases one-half of the water used for irrigation was wasted. It suggested that farmers should be charged for the real cost of water in order to shift water use away from agriculture, and that within the agricultural sector farmers should concentrate on high value-added crops, rather than subsistence crops such as cereals. Competition in agricultural products from the EU from 2008 was another reason for a shift to high value products. However, so far the Government has been reluctant to make farmers pay the real cost of the water they use for irrigation.

Grown in a belt across the northern part of the country, wheat is the most important cereal crop. The Government guarantees the price to the grower and, among other incentives, pays the transport costs of merchants. The Government has encouraged the spread of the Mexican dwarf wheat, and this variety now accounts for more than one-tenth of Tunisia's output. Production of wheat and barley totalled 606,000 metric tons during the disastrous 1985/86 season, but output increased to 1.9m. tons in 1986/87. In 1987/88, however, production fell sharply, to 292,000 tons, as a result of severe drought and the worst plague of locusts to affect the country for 30 years. Total cereal production reached 636,000 tons in 1989, but increased to 1.6m. tons in 1990, despite floods in January 1990, which necessitated the import of large amounts of grain. In 1991 there was a record cereal harvest of 2.6m. tons, falling in 1992 to 2.2m. tons. The 1993 cereal harvest totalled 1.9m. tons, but in 1994 drought conditions reduced the harvest to 650,000 tons. There was another poor harvest in 1995, resulting in a substantial increase in food imports. Spending on imports of cereals was TD 124.1m. in 1990, TD 65m. in 1991, TD 80.1m. in 1992 and TD 95.2m. in 1993. Improved rainfall in the 1995/96 growing season boosted the size of the 1996 cereal harvest to around 2.8m. tons. However, poor rains in 1996/97 reduced the 1997 cereal harvest to just over 1m. tons. As a result of the poor harvest, and increased domestic consumption, some 2m. tons of cereals were imported in 1997 at a cost of TD 347m. The 1998 cereal harvest was estimated at 1.67m. tons. Cereal imports during the first half of 1998 rose to 1.2m. tons, at a cost of TD 233.2m. The cereal harvest grew to 1.81m. tons in 1999, but after poor rainfall in the early months of the year fell to 1.1m. tons in 2000. A series of relief measures were introduced by the Government to help farmers affected by the drought. The cereal harvest for 2001 was estimated at 1.82m. tons after heavy rainfall at the end of 2000. However, in 2001–02 Tunisia experienced one of the worst droughts in more than 50 years. Government estimates put output at only 0.6m. tons for 2002, with demand projected at 2.5m. tons. It was reported that cereal imports had increased by 5% during the first quarter of 2002.

Grapes are grown around Tunis and Bizerta. Wine production reached a peak of 1,986,000 hl in 1963. However, annual output had declined to one-third of this amount by the end of the 1970s. Production increased from 513,000 hl in 1982 to 680,000 hl in 1984, but fell to only 210,000 hl in 1988. By the early 1990s average annual output was around 340,000 hl, and there was new investment in vineyards. Some 90,000 hl of wine, worth TD 12.5m., was exported in 1993.

The size of Tunisia's annual harvest of olives fluctuates considerably, owing partly to the two-year flowering cycle of the tree. Tunisia is usually the world's fourth largest producer of olive oil. Production reached 180,000 metric tons in 1975/76, but declined in subsequent years. The value of Tunisia's exports of olive oil has fluctuated dramatically since the late 1960s, reaching a peak of TD 70m. in 1974, but falling steeply in the late 1970s. Exports recovered in the mid-1980s, totalling TD 54m. in 1986, TD 66m. in 1987 and TD 71m. in 1988. Output of olive oil in 1991/92 reached a record 280,000 tons, falling to less than half this tonnage in the following year. Exports of olive oil rose from 96,473 tons (worth TD 158.4m.) in 1992 to 122,630 tons (worth TD 179.1m.) in 1993. Radical reforms of the export marketing system for olive oil included the ending in 1994 of a requirement to negotiate all export contracts through the industry's national marketing board. In the 1993/94 season olive oil production totalled 210,000 tons. It then fell sharply to 75,000 tons in 1994/95 and declined further to between 60,000 and 70,000 tons in 1995/96 because of continuing drought conditions. Olive oil output in 1996/97 reached a record 310,000 tons, and a sharp increase in olive oil exports, to 126,000 tons, worth TD 288m., helped to boost agricultural and food exports during 1997. As a result of the poor harvest of 1995/96, exports for 1996 amounted to only 29,000 tons. Poor rains in early 1997 reduced olive oil production in 1997/98 to 90,000 tons. Exports in 1998 totalled 124,000 tons, worth TD 226m. Production during the 1998/99 season doubled compared with the previous year and exports of olive oil increased substantially. Olive oil exports make up about 50% of all food exports and around 5% of total exports. In 1998 the Government abolished export taxes on olive oil and introduced a number of other measures to increase exports and improve the quality of the oil produced. Tunisia's annual export quota to the EU was increased from 46,000 to 50,000 tons in 2001 (see External Trade). Efforts were being made to find new markets in the USA and Canada, and to increase domestic consumption, which averaged around 50,000–60,000 tons annually.

Citrus fruits are grown mainly in the Cap Bon peninsula. Production declined from 220,000 metric tons in 1980/81 to 165,000 tons in 1981/82. The annual crop rose to around 250,000 tons in 1985/86 and 1986/87. In 1992/93 citrus production totalled 281,000 tons, and in 1993 exports totalled 23,640 tons, worth TD 9.6m. Production then declined to 210,000 tons in 1993/94 and 194,000 tons in 1994/95. Although output recovered to 221,000 tons in 1995/96, there was a decline in production to 211,000 tons in the 1996/97 harvest, with exports totalling only 16,100 tons. Output rose to 230,000 tons in 1997/98, but was forecast to decline to 210,000 tons in 1998/99 (including 104,000 tons of oranges, 28,000 tons of clementines, 26,000 tons of mandarins and 17,000 tons of lemons). Output rose to 225,000 tons in 1999–2000 and to 271,000 tons in 2000–01. Tunisia's production of dates totalled 81,200 tons in 1990, 74,700 tons in 1991 and 74,800 tons in 1992, with average annual exports of 18,200 tons over the same period. Date exports of 18,510 tons in 1993 (in which year production totalled 90,000 tons) were worth TD 47.5m. Date production declined to 86,000 tons in 1994 (worth TD 55.5m.). There was a fall of about 12% in the 1996 date harvest (compared with a 13.5% increase in the previous year), output totalling 74,000 tons. Production in 1997/98 was estimated at 95,000 tons, rising to a record 103,000 tons in 1998/99. The increase in production was achieved as a result

of investment in new date plantations and efforts to improve the quality of the crop. Production fell slightly, to 102,000 tons, in 1999–2000 and the quality of the crop was adversely affected by high temperatures. Consequently, exports declined by some 26% to 20,300 tons, compared with 1998–99, and their value fell from TD 70m. to TD 54m. The 2000–01 date harvest was estimated at 107,000 tons. Dates were mainly exported to the EU, principally France, but new markets were being developed, especially in Asia and North America. Production of sugar beet was 291,000 tons in 1992 and totalled 300,000 tons in 1996. A sugar refinery at Béja is able to process 1,850 tons per day. A second refinery, at Ben Bechir in Jendouba governorate, was commissioned in 1983, with an annual capacity of 40,000 tons of sugar. Spending on sugar imports totalled US $91.5m. in 1994 and $72.7m. in 1995. Government efforts to increase sugar beet production by persuading farmers to grow the crop in rotation with cereals have not achieved the targets that were hoped for, and less than 3,000 ha of sugar beet was planted in 1998. Production fell by 77% to 20,700 tons in 2000. Imports have been increasing and cost TD 92m. in 1997. Other crops include tomatoes, chillies and peppers, melons, watermelons and almonds.

During the drought in 1987–88 the Government introduced measures to protect livestock, including the distribution of state-subsidized fodder to farmers, a reduction of the price of animal feedstuffs, a programme to import lucerne and bran, and a vaccination campaign. In 2001, according to FAO estimates, Tunisia's livestock included 1.45m. goats, 6.6m. sheep, 795,000 cattle and 43m. poultry.

Sfax is the main centre of the industry, which has received substantial state investment in recent years, including finance for the modernization of the fleet, the upgrading of some 30 fishing ports, and for research and training. The Government has also sought to reduce overfishing in the gulf of Gabès by developing fishing grounds in the north. The total catch rose steadily from 31,686 metric tons in 1975 to 102,570 tons in 1988, but declined steadily thereafter to 83,600 tons in 1995. Production rose to 89,000 tons in 1997, of which 17,000 tons were exported. Among its traded food commodities, the value of Tunisia's fish exports was second only to that of olive oil in 1995–99. More than two-thirds of fishing vessels are concentrated in the south, along the Gulf of Gabès, but as a result of pollution and overfishing this region produces slightly less than 50% of the country's total catch. Some 42% of the catch is produced from the ports of Sousse, Mahdia and Monastir in the central region, while the northern coastline is underexploited. In a modernization of the fishing industry's infrastructure, fish-processing factories were brought up to European standards, in order to increase production and improve the quality of fish products. Incentives were given to develop fishing along the northern coastline and limits were placed on fishing in the Gulf of Gabès. Government investment in a port and fleet modernization programme resulted in a slow increase in the total catch, which reached 93,300 tons in 1999. Tunisia signed a two-year agreement with Morocco in 2000 to promote co-operation in the fisheries sector, including joint ventures in fishing and fish processing industries. In 2000 the catch reached 95,600 tons, of which 13,700 tons (valued at TD 120m.) were exported.

A US $69m. forestry development loan was approved by the World Bank in 1993 to finance the planting of trees on 25,000 ha of land, together with related schemes to promote the growth of forestry in Tunisia.

Two institutions have been established to address the problem of Tunisia's insufficient agricultural output. The Agence de Promotion des Investissements Agricoles was created in 1982 to channel funds into productive projects, notably the development of new cash crops. In early 1983 the Banque Nationale du Développement Agricole (BNDA) was founded to ease investment in the agricultural sector. Although fully Tunisian-owned, the BNDA's funds—initially TD 140m.—were subscribed equally by Kuwait and the EC (European Commission, now the EU). In 1990 the BNDA and the Banque nationale de Tunisie (BNT) merged to form a new commercial bank based in the agricultural sector, designated the Banque Nationale Agricole (BNA).

MINERALS

Petroleum, formerly Tunisia's principal source of export earnings, was overtaken as a source of revenue by textiles and agricultural exports in the late 1980s. The collapse of petroleum prices in the mid-1980s resulted in a fall in export earnings from a peak of TD 665m. in 1980 to TD 341m. in 1986, although in 1987 earnings recovered to TD 418m. By 1990 exports of hydrocarbons were worth TD 533.4m. In 1991, despite a 15% increase in oil output, export revenues fell to TD 489.8m., while spending on energy imports amounted to TD 365.8m. (TD 429.4m. in 1990). In 1992 there was a surplus of TD 141.3m. in energy-sector trade (exports TD 538.4m., imports TD 397.1m.), but in 1993 export earnings fell by 19.4% to TD 434.2m., some TD 22.9m. below spending on imports (up 15.1% to TD 457.1m.). Energy exports totalled TD 442m. in 1994, TD 437m. in 1995 and TD 563m. in 1996, when they accounted for 10% of the value of total exports. The Government expected energy exports to remain at around this level until 1999, but to decline to TD 367m. in 2000 and to TD 320m. in 2001, when they were forecast to account for only 4% of the value of total exports. In 1996 imports of petroleum and petroleum products totalled US $482.4m.; imports of gas totalled $148.7m. Intensive exploration for petroleum has been carried out in Tunisia since the discovery of hydrocarbons in neighbouring Algeria. In May 1964 a subsidiary of Ente Nazionale Idrocarburi (ENI), the Italian state energy enterprise, discovered petroleum at al-Borma, in southern Tunisia, near the Algerian border. When the discovery was announced, the Tunisian Government took a 50% share in the al-Borma operating company. The crude petroleum extracted from the al-Borma oilfield is transported to the terminal at La Skhirra on the Gulf of Gabès via a 'spur' pipeline which links with the pipeline from the oilfields at Zarzaitine and Edjeleh, in Algeria. The crude petroleum is then transported from La Skhirra to the refinery at Bizerta.

In 1968 Tunisia's second oilfield came into operation at Douleb, 200 km north of al-Borma. A pipeline was subsequently built, connecting the Douleb oilfield to the terminal at La Skhirra. Other oilfields include Tamesmida, on the Algerian border south-west of Douleb, which was joined to the Douleb-La Skhirra pipeline in 1969; and Bihrat and Sidi al-Itayem, both of which began producing in 1972. Important discoveries of petroleum were made off shore at Ashtart, east of Sfax in the Gulf of Gabès, and these deposits accounted for more than one-quarter of Tunisia's total output in the mid-1980s. The Ashtart oilfield was originally operated by Elf Hydrocarbures Tunisie (EHT—a wholly-owned subsidiary of Elf Aquitaine of France) and the Tunisian state oil company, Entreprise tunisienne d'activités pétrolières (ETAP), which also operated the Douleb oilfield. In 1997 EHT was bought by Arco of the USA, which currently has a 50% holding in the Ashtart field. A US $200m. investment programme to halt the decline in production at Ashtart was completed at the end of 1997. Early in 2000 Arco announced that it had sold its 50% stake in the Ashtart field to Preussag Energie of Germany. The field currently produces some 15,000 barrels per day (b/d) and contains reserves estimated at 35m. barrels.

Other new Tunisian oilfields include, in the south, Makhrouga, Larich and Debbech, which are being developed by the Société d'Exploitation des Permis du Sud, FINA of Belgium, and ETAP; the Tazerka field in the Gulf of Hammamet, operated by Shell with AGIP Africa, a subsidiary of ENI, and ETAP; the Isis field in the Gulf of Gabès, for which the concession is held by Shell, Tunirex, Total-CFP and AGIP; the Ezzaouia offshore field, operated by Marathon Oil of the USA; the Rhemoura onshore field, in the Karkemna concession of British Gas (BG) Tunisie; and the Belli field, also operated by Marathon Oil.

A dispute with Libya over demarcation of territorial waters in the Gulf of Gabès, where promising discoveries of petroleum had been made, was settled in February 1982. A ruling by the International Court of Justice (ICJ) delimited the two countries' offshore territories around a boundary approximately 26° east from the land border to latitude 34°10′30″ north, where it deviates 52° east. (In December 1985 Tunisia's application to the ICJ for a revision of its judgment was rejected.) In August 1989 a joint Tunisian-Libyan company was established to exploit the '7 November' oilfield in the Gulf of Gabès. However, this company, known as Joint Oil, failed to attract any foreign partners for some years. After 1980, US petroleum companies began to obtain permits for drilling rights in Tunisia. Promising discoveries included the offshore Cosmos well, near Hammamet, located by EHT, gas and condensate discoveries in the Douz area, found by the US company Amoco, the el-Bibane well in the extreme south, discovered by Marathon Oil, and the two offshore Maamoura wells, near Hammamet, discovered by the Italian company, AGIP. In mid-1991 Marathon Oil was given permission to explore for oil and gas in a new area of 1,760 sq km at Grombalia, which is situated close to the Abiod gas-production structure, south-east of Tunis; Marathon Petroleum Grombalia, a new subsidiary of Marathon Oil, would finance all exploration costs. In 1985 the Government improved the terms of its petroleum exploration law to encourage prospecting companies to develop new discoveries. In 1986, however, the collapse of energy prices prompted many oil companies to reduce the scale of their operations, and the Government was forced to introduce an even more favourable law in April 1987. In 1990 23 foreign companies held permits for drilling rights in Tunisia, attracted by the range of financial incentives offered by the Government to encourage exploration and development. In the late 1990s, despite the absence of a major petroleum strike for many years, foreign oil companies remained interested in Tunisia and at the end of 1997 Pluspetrol of Argentina, Anadarko Petroleum Corpn of the USA, AGIP of Italy and Mobil of the USA, were among the companies engaged in exploration work. In early 1998 Germany's Preussag Energie announced the discovery of petroleum in a second well in the Guebiba field in which it had a 49% holding (the remainder being held by ETAP). In 1997 Preussag bought the oil interests of BG Tunisie in Guebiba along with four other small onshore fields, namely Al Ain, Gremda, Rhemoura and El Hajeb, as well as the Cercina offshore field. Production at the offshore al-Biban field began in March 1998, operated by Centurion Energy International of Canada. The field, with estimated recoverable reserves of 6m. barrels of petroleum, produced 4,000 b/d and crude oil exports began in May. In April Petro-Canada signed a two-year exploration agreement for Tunisia's Berkane basin, working jointly with ETAP. The area is relatively unexplored, but substantial oil discoveries have been made in adjacent areas in Algeria. Early in 2000 it was reported that initial exploration work at the '7 November' oilfield by a consortium of the Saudi-owned Nimr Petroleum and Petronas, Malaysia's state oil company, had proved disappointing, and additional seismic tests were to be conducted before any further drilling was undertaken. It had been hoped that the field would contain major reserves. At the same time, Centurion Energy continued preliminary work at its Al-Manzah field where reserves were estimated at 15m. barrels. A new and more flexible hydrocarbons law came into effect in February 2000, providing incentives to encourage further oil and gas exploration by international companies. In 2002 Tunisia and Algeria agreed to create a joint venture company specializing in oil and natural gas research and exploration as part of a new programme to boost bilateral relations.

At the end of 1998 production was reported to have begun at the Didon offshore field in the Gulf of Gabès, operated by a partnership of Medex Petroleum of France and Soco International of the USA. The field was producing 5,000–7,000 b/d, and recoverable reserves were estimated at 6m. barrels. At the same time, Ecumed Petroleum Grombalia, a subsidiary of Centurion Energy International of Canada, announced a small oil strike in its Grombalia concession area in northern Tunisia and CMS Energy of the USA announced a modest oil and gas find in its Baguel concession in southern Tunisia. Early in 1999 MOL of Hungary began petroleum production from the Sabria West-1 well in the Kebili area in southern Tunisia. According to the Minister of Industry the incentives provided by the new hydrocarbons law had attracted small independent oil companies as well as a number of international companies to Tunisia. By the end of 2000 45 reconnaissance and exploration licences were in operation and 12 wells had been drilled compared with only five in 1999. In February 2000 ETAP had launched bids for 20 new exploration blocks but by the end of the year no significant discoveries had been reported. Nevertheless, Centurion Energy continued to develop its Al Manzah field, where production from the first two wells reached 4,850 b/d, and Coparex Netherlands began drilling three wells in the offshore Isis field, east of Sfax, which had estimated reserves of 12m. barrels and where production, forecast at 15,000 b/d, was due to begin in mid-2001. In early 2001 a pipeline with a capacity of 22,000 b/d was completed, extending 126 km to link the Sidi al-Kilani oilfield to the petroleum storage facilities at La Skhirra. Sidi al-Kilani was Tunisia's third largest oilfield, producing about 13,000 b/d. It was operated by the Kuwait Foreign Petroleum Exploration Co.

At 1 January 1998 Tunisia's reserves of petroleum were estimated at 300m. barrels, sufficient to maintain output (at 1997 levels) for 9.4 years. Production has exceeded 4m. metric tons per year since 1970, and reached a peak level of 5.6m. tons in 1980. In 1991 production from the Ezzaouia field reversed the downward trend of petroleum production, which by mid-1992 was running at 120,000 b/d, while domestic consumption amounted to 90,000 b/d. It was hoped that further exploration, and the development of known deposits, might result in an increase in output from the mid-1990s. Total output in 1992 was 5.2m. tons. Tunisia's oil output totalled 4.7m. tons in 1993, 4.4m. tons in 1994, 4.3m. tons in 1995 and 4.2m. tons in 1996. Production fell to below 3.8m. tons in 1997 and was estimated at 3.7m. tons in 1998. Output rose slightly, to 3.9m. tons, in 1999 and exports rose by 4.5%. Output in 2000 was estimated to have declined to 3.7m. tons as production from the development of small new fields failed to compensate for falling production at El Borma. Output was forecast to increase slightly in 200102 as a result of new production from the Isis field. Some two-thirds of all petroleum production comes from the El Borma, Ashtart and Sidi Kilani fields.

Tunisia's main petroleum refinery, at Bizerta, has a capacity of 2.0m. metric tons per year. Plans to increase the capacity of the Bizerta refinery to 3m. tons a year were abandoned and an alternative project was subsequently conceived: in March 1997 the Government selected the local Offshore-Mediterranean Refining Co (ORC) to establish and operate a new refinery at La Skhirra. The refinery's ultimate capacity was to be 6m. tons a year; however, in 2001 the project had not begun.

Tunisia became a member of the Organization of Arab Petroleum Exporting Countries (OAPEC) in March 1982. In 1986, however, Tunisia withdrew from the organization, owing to the decline in the country's oil output.

In February 1998 an attempt by the Government to sell shares in Tunisia Oil Fields Contractors, in which the state had a majority holding, failed to meet an acceptable price and tenders were reissued in July. The Société d'assistance et de ravitaillement offshore Tunisie and the Société nationale de distribution du pétrole were among other state-owned companies to be offered for sale in 1998 as part of the Government's accelerated privatization programme (see above).

Tunisia's reserves of natural gas are estimated at about 100,000m. cu m. Almost all of the country's gas production came from the al-Borma field until 1995, when the offshore Miskar field was brought on stream by British Gas International Tunisia (BGIT), which invested US $600m. to develop the field, the biggest foreign investment ever made in the country. The Miskar project, completed in early 1997, is now the country's major gasfield, supplying more than 90% of total national production. BGIT is under contract to deliver 4.5m. cu m per day (cu m/d) of gas to the Société tunisienne d'électricité et du gaz (STEG) for the first five years, rising to 5.7m. cu m/d thereafter. The 4.5m. cu m/d delivery rate was achieved on a sustained basis from June 1996, and by early 1998 production had reached 5.2 m. cu m/d. In March 1998 it was reported that BGIT was seeking a review of the price formula in its agreement with STEG to supply gas from the Miskar field. The gas price was indexed to that of high-sulphur fuel petroleum, which fell sharply along with other petroleum prices and reduced BGIT's returns from the Miskar project. BGIT also announced that it is ready to invest $400m. in the development of a new offshore gasfield, Hasdrubal, located just south of the Miskar field. Initial discoveries suggested that future production from the Hasdrubal field could average 5m. cu m/d. Both the Miskar and Hasdrubal fields are part of BGIT's Amilcar permit, held jointly with ETAP. In early 1999 BGIT awarded a contract to increase the capacity of the Hannibal gas treatment plant near Sfax, which treats gas from the Miskar field, to 5.5m. cu m/d. Fol-

lowing ratification of a new hydrocarbons law in early 2000, a new gas pricing agreement between BGIT and STEG paved the way for BGIT to invest $450m. to increase output from the Miskar field and develop the new Hasdrubal field. In 1997 CMS Nomeco International of the USA announced a $30m. investment programme to develop the El Franig and Baguel gasfields in the south-west of the country, where gas and condensates estimated at 1.7m. metric tons of oil equivalent have been discovered. The development programme included the construction of a 115-km pipeline opened in 1998 to link the fields to the national pipeline system. The fields are owned jointly by Nomeco and ETAP. In early 1998 Preussag Energie of Germany announced that it was to develop the offshore Chergui gasfield in the Gulf of Gabès where recoverable reserves were estimated at 2,000m. cu m of natural gas. Tunisia's total gas production rose from 127m. cu m in 1995 to 1,985m. cu m in 2000 (production from El Borma fell from 121m. cu m to 83m. cu m between 1995 and 1999, while that from Miskar increased from 2m. cu m to 1,622m. cu m).

The Miskar field was scheduled to produce about 168m. cu ft/d until 2001, increasing to 230m. cu ft/d from that date under the terms of an agreement between BGIT and STEG made in mid-2000. The Transmed gas pipeline constructed to supply Algerian natural gas to Italy crosses Tunisia and became operational in 1983. Tunisia's royalty was equivalent to 5.25% of all gas transported in the pipeline. Liftings from the pipeline became a new source of natural gas for STEG. Work to expand the annual capacity of the Transmed pipeline from 16,000m. cu m to 24,000m. cu m was completed during 1997. In 2000 Tunisia's royalties in kind from the Transmed pipeline amounted to 1,274m. cu m of gas. As part of an agreement signed in 1997, Tunisia and Libya are to build a gas pipeline to supply southern Tunisia with Libyan gas. Tunisia's gas consumption reached 2.9m. tons of oil equivalent in 2000, 78% of which was used to generate electricity. Demand is expected to rise to at least 5m. tons of oil equivalent by 2020, and possibly as high as 9.5m. The construction of a gas pipeline from Libya, to be completed in 2003, will provide a new source of supply in addition to the gas that Tunisia receives from the Transmed pipeline in the form of dues.

Tunisia is the world's fourth-largest producer of calcium phosphates, which are chiefly mined from six large deposits in central Tunisia. Output of calcium phosphates totalled 5.6m. metric tons in 1994. Phosphates and phosphatic fertilizers have long been an important source of export revenue. After remaining fairly static at 3.0m.–3.8m. tons per year in 1970–78, production of natural phosphates increased steadily after 1979, when it exceeded 4.1m. tons. Annual phosphate output was slightly more than 6m. tons annually in 1987–89. The phosphate sector was affected by low world prices in 1986, and a recovery plan was implemented, aiming to reduce production costs and to increase output to 6m. tons annually in 1986–88. Government policy was to develop new resources and to concentrate efforts on the local manufacture of highly profitable fertilizer and phosphoric acid. Only about 25% of phosphate output was exported as raw phosphate rock, and production of triple superphosphate (TSP) and phosphoric acid increased dramatically in the early 1980s. Output of TSP reached 956,800 tons in 1986, an increase of more than 400,000 tons in 10 years, and 985,800 tons in 1987, while production of phosphoric acid rose from 93,000 tons in 1973—the first year of production—to 593,300 tons in 1987, and to 856,100 tons in 1988. Because the phosphate rock is of low quality, the processing plants use special methods to produce phosphoric acid and phosphatic fertilizers. The Compagnie des Phosphates de Gafsa (CPG), which mines phosphate rock in the Gafsa area, plans to maintain annual production at less than 6m. tons, developing new mines as existing ones become exhausted. Most of the fertilizer plants are at Gabès, but in 1985 a new plant was opened at M'Dilla, near the Gafsa mines, while a plant to produce superphosphoric acid opened at La Skhirra. However, a project to exploit the phosphate reserves at Sra Ouertane, in the north-west, was postponed, owing to the Government's budgetary problems. In July 1989 Tunisia was granted a loan of US $34m. by the Kuwait Fund for Arab Economic Development in order to finance the renovation of its phosphate fertilizer plants.

In 1991 production of raw phosphates fell by 30% compared with 1990, although export revenues fell by only 19%, to TD 14m. Exports of phosphatic fertilizers fell by 4% in 1991, to TD 241m., mainly owing to a 35% decline in sales of ammonium nitrate to the Iraqi market. The value of exports of phosphoric acid, however, increased by 27% to TD 156m. The 1991 results reflected continuing problems in the Tunisian phosphates industry, especially within the CPG, as well as the disappearance of traditional markets in Eastern Europe. In 1992 the CPG doubled the volume of its export sales from 425,888 metric tons to 956,109 tons, while its domestic sales (to the state processing company Groupe Chimique) totalled 5.1m. tons. In 1991 the two companies had recorded combined losses of TD 522m. A government restructuring programme, announced in 1993, envisaged plant closures among other rationalization measures, including an eventual merger of the two companies. The CPG's phosphate production totalled 6.1m. tons in 1992 and 6.4m. tons in 1993 (85% from underground mines and the balance from surface mines). Tunisia's exports of phosphorus pentoxide and phosphoric acid were worth TD 166.2m. in 1994, while exports of phosphatic fertilizers totalled TD 112.1m. Initiatives to gain new export outlets in 1994 included co-operation with Brazil, with a view to increasing that country's imports of Tunisian phosphates from 90,000 tons to 170,000 tons per year. Production of raw phosphate by the CPG reached 7.2m. tons in 1997, of which some 1.3m. tons were exported and the remainder was sold to Groupe Chimique for conversion into phosphoric acid and fertilizers. Some 7.8m. tons of raw phosphate were produced in 1999, increasing to 8.3m. in 2000.

Production of iron ore has steadily declined since independence, when it was more than 1m. metric tons per year. Output was 310,000 tons (gross weight) per year during 1984–86, compared with 275,000 tons in 1982 and 400,000 tons in 1981. In 1995 output was 225,000 tons and remained at much the same level during the late 1990s before falling to 183,300 tons in 2000. The ore's iron content is approximately 53%.

Lead is mined in the northern coastal region, and zinc in the north-west. In 1980 the Société tunisienne d'expansion minière announced a US $50m. investment programme to expand production. Output of zinc concentrates totalled 17,400 metric tons in 1989, but fell to 9,400 tons in 1991. Production declined to 4,100 tons in 1992 and 1,300 tons in 1993 before rising to 12,900 tons in 1994, and to 44,200 in 1995. Output of lead concentrates, which totalled 14,000 tons in 1980, has been falling steadily, and reached only 3,400 tons in 1987 before declining to 1,300 tons in 1991. Production totalled 1,400 tons in 1992 and 500 tons in 1993, increasing to 2,000 tons in 1994, and to 7,000 tons in 1995. The Bougrine lead and zinc mine, operated by the Société Minière de Bougrine (SMB), the country's first private mine, opened in 1994 after an investment of $80m., but was closed in October 1996 as a result of financial problems. In 1997 Inmet Mining Corpn of Canada sold its 49% holding in SMB to Breakwater Resources of Canada, which reopened the mine in May 1998. By the end of 1998 it was operating at full capacity (97,000 tons of zinc and 12,000 tons of lead). Reserves were estimated as sufficient for 10 years' production, and Breakwater Resources announced plans to invest TD 10m. in the mine in 1999. In February 2000 Billiton UK Resources BV signed an agreement with Aurora Gold Corpn of Canada to invest in initial exploration work in the Hammala area for high grade zinc minerals. Also in 2000 Consolidated Global Minerals of Canada took over five exploration permits for zinc and lead in northern Tunisia, together with a small zinc mine in Fej Lahdoun, from the Office National des Mines.

INDUSTRY

Tunisia's industrial sector ranges from the traditional activities, such as textiles and leather, to 'downstream' industries based on the country's phosphate reserves. During the period of the 1973–76 Plan, the industrial sector grew by 7.4% instead of the 10.2% planned. In 1977 the sector grew by only 4.2%, mainly because of a sharp fall in agri-business and the food processing industries. With the exception of the textile industries, the sector's performance improved in 1978, with a 10.6% growth rate, mainly because of higher output in three sectors: construction materials, mechanical and electrical industries. The growth rate of manufacturing industries fell to 3% in 1982, but rose to

around 9% per year in 1983, 1984 and 1985, in accordance with the 1982–86 Development Plan. In the late 1980s private sector small and medium-sized businesses became increasingly prominent, and the Government made considerable progress in attracting foreign venture capital to the industrial sector, as well as in promoting Tunisia as a regional centre for high technology. Figures issued by the Société de participation et de promotion des investissements (SPPI) in early 1992 showed that in 1990–91 the SPPI had supported 22 joint venture projects involving total investment of TD 34m. According to the Agence de promotion des investissements (API), declarations of investment intent by local and international companies were 2% higher in 1991 than in 1990, although the impact of the Gulf crisis had contributed to a 20% decline in foreign investment applications in 1991. In June 1992 the new post of Minister of International Co-operation and Foreign Investment was created to signal the Government's commitment to industrial expansion. In 1992 new foreign investment in Tunisian manufacturing industry was estimated at TD 52m., out of total foreign investment of TD 160m. Although the bulk of foreign investment (see also Planning) remained in the energy sector, in 1997 investment in manufacturing industry reached TD 85.7m. Much of the new investment was reported to be in the high technology sector, particularly electronics. Foreign direct investment rose sharply in 1998, with some TD 409m. accounted for by the sale of two state-owned cement plants to Spanish and Portuguese firms (see below). Also in 1998 a number of new measures were introduced to encourage private investment in small and medium-sized enterprises, notably by raising the level of contributions made by the Fonds de promotion et de décentralisation industrielle to investment projects, especially in regional development areas. Foreign investment in manufacturing industry fell to TD 198m. in 1999 before recovering sharply to TD 688m. in 2000 (although this figure included the sale of state-owned cement and chemical assets). In 2001 it declined again to TD 221m.

During the 1982–86 Development Plan period, the Government concentrated on large investment projects, until it was forced by budgetary constraints to alter its strategy in 1986. The 1987–91 Plan reflected this change, with more investment in small projects and a greater emphasis on attracting private investment into industry. Exports of industrial goods (excluding energy) rose steadily in the period of the 1987–91 Plan, reaching TD 1,812.6m. in 1990. Textiles and leather contributed TD 1,325m. to this total, mechanical and electrical items TD 416.4m., and other industries TD 254.7m. Under the 1992–96 Plan, the 6% annual GDP growth target was to be achieved mainly by means of expansion in the manufacturing and services sector. Exports from the manufacturing sector rose from TD 2,240m. in 1992 (out of total exports of TD 3,550m.) to TD 3,794m. in 1996 (out of total exports of TD 5,372m.). In 1992 textiles and leather contributed TD 1,546m., mechanical and electrical goods TD 433m. and other industries TD 261m. In 1996 textiles and leather contributed TD 2,743m., mechanical and electrical goods TD 675m. and other industries TD 376m. During the 1992–96 Plan period industrial production grew by 5.8% a year, according to the Government, although independent sources reported a much lower figure. According to official figures, investment in industry totalled TD 3,100m. during the Plan period. Under the 1997–2001 Development Plan industrial production was projected to grow by 6.9% a year, with investments in industry forecast to reach TD 1,200m. over the five-year period. In 1998 industry was reported to generate some 25% of GDP and to employ some 590,000 people, around one-fifth of the workforce. Official sources indicated that the manufacturing sector grew by 6% in 1999, with exports from this sector totalling TD 6,200m. (a 6.5% increase). Total investment in manufacturing industry in 1999 grew by 10.6% to TD 1,300m., with high levels of investment reported in export-orientated companies. Despite growing competition from the EU as tariffs were lifted on European manufactured goods, this sector grew at the same pace in 2000 and 2001, with higher growth recorded in textiles (12%) and mechanical and electrical industries (14%).

More than one-half of Tunisia's industry is located in Tunis. Other industrial centres are Sousse, Sfax, Gabès, Bizerta, Gafsa, Béja and Kasserine. Major new industrial estates were under development near Tunis and Sfax in 1994. In the past, manufacturing tended to concentrate on processing raw materials, especially foodstuffs, and was aimed at meeting local demand. In an attempt to attract foreign investment and to promote exports, the Government ratified a new industrial investment code during 1987. This law simplified and extended the provisions in the legislation of 1973 and 1981. A new code, adopted in November 1989, laid down guidelines for the activities of service companies, the aim being to increase private-sector investment; by mid-1992 some 600 new companies had been established in the services sector. Other government initiatives included the approval of special legislation early in 1992 for the creation of 'offshore' free-trade zones for new industries. Site preparation for the 46-ha Bizerta zone began in late 1993. The aim of the zone's shareholders (42% banks, 32% public-sector companies, 26% private-sector companies) was to attract TD 60m. of new investment from Europe, North America and South-East Asia and to generate TD 120m. of exports per year. The Bizerta zone opened in the late 1990s, initially with 20 businesses (10 industrial companies, four trading companies and six banks) on site. A free-trade zone at Zarzis (near Tunisia's border with Libya) was undergoing expansion from 12 ha to 20 ha in the second half of 1996, in response to strong demand for accommodation from manufacturing, trading and services companies. It was announced in February 1997 that the Government intended to invite private investors to equip and operate three industrial zones at sites in Bizerta, Menzel Bourguiba and M'Saken. The plan was part of a larger programme to establish 26 industrial zones throughout the country under the ninth five-year Plan covering 1997–2001 (see Planning, below). This would include 16 zones in coastal regions, five in central Tunisia and one in the interior. A shortage of prepared sites for manufacturing industry was reported to have been a factor in discouraging industrial expansion and thwarting efforts to increase foreign investment in this sector.

The textiles sector is the most important in manufacturing and exports. By early 1999 there were an estimated 250,000 workers employed by 1,800 firms, 700 of which had foreign owners or partners. Earnings from textile exports in 2001 totalled TD 4,020m., representing 42% of all export earnings. Virtually all textile exports go to the EU, especially to France, Germany, Italy and Belgium. In the shoe and leather goods sector about a third of firms produce exclusively for export, principally shoes. The sector employs some 36,000 workers and in 2000 had exports valued at TD 463m.In order of importance, the other leading sectors are: construction materials, mechanical and electro-mechanical products, chemicals, and paper and wood. Tunisia also manufactures glass, furniture, batteries, paint and varnish, and rubber goods. Ceramics are made at Nabeul, while sugar is refined at Béja and carpets are handwoven at Kairouan. A cellulose factory and paper pulp plant at Kasserine uses locally grown esparto grass. The metallurgical, mechanical and electrical industries are expanding steadily. The al-Fouladh steel complex at Menzel Bourguiba, near Bizerta, is supplied with iron ore from Tamera and Djerissa. In 2000 it had an annual capacity of 237,000 metric tons of iron bars, wire and small sections, and plans are in hand to increase the complex's capacity to 400,000 tons per year. Another steel mill, with a capacity of 100,000 tons per year, is sited at Bizerta.

In 1983 a farm machinery complex, managed by the Complexe mécanique de Tunisie, began production. A scheme to manufacture tyres for the local market and for export was commissioned in 1986, with the assistance of an Italian company, Pirelli, the Government having nationalized the largest US investment in Tunisia—the Firestone Tyre and Rubber Co's tyre factory at Menzel Bourguiba in 1980. In early 1988 production of diesel engines commenced at a plant at Sakiet Sidi Youssef, on the Algerian-Tunisian border. The plant, managed by the Société maghrébine de fabrication de moteurs thermiques, had an initial annual capacity of 25,000 diesel engines. Later in 1988 it was announced that joint ventures with Mercedes and Volkswagen would be established to produce car components. In November 1991 General Motors of the USA announced the reopening of its joint venture vehicle assembly plant at Kairouan, which was to produce up to 4,000 light commercial vehicles per year for the North African market. Known as Industries Mécaniques Maghrébines, the joint venture had been launched in 1982, but

was suspended in 1988. Also active in vehicle assembly in Tunisia is Saab-Scania of Sweden. Local assembly of Mercedes-Benz buses, imported from Germany in kit form, began in 1994 at the rate of 60 vehicles per year. In 1995 Tunisia had 50 export-orientated automobile components manufacturers whose combined output was worth an estimated TD 22m. in that year. Although the total value of their output in 1996 rose to TD 28m., this still fell well short of the Government's ambitions for a key sector in its industrial strategy. In early 1998 METS, a subsidiary of Germany's Draxlmaier, and Leonische Drahtwerke of Germany, both announced plans to expand their production of electrical car components in Tunisia by building new plants at Sousse. In April United Technologies Corpn opened a factory producing wire harnesses for Peugeot's car assembly plant in Spain and announced plans to double output by the end of the year.

In the high technology sector, several computer companies located operations in Tunisia. Plans for a special 'offshore' high technology zone, to be located in Tunis, were under consideration in mid-1992. By 1993 a 40-ha site near Tunis-Carthage airport had been chosen for development, and financing of up to US $100m. was being sought. Citing successful Malaysian 'technology parks' as its model, the Government regarded the venture as a means of encouraging the transfer of technology, creating jobs for graduates and attracting foreign investment.

Cement production during the late 1990s averaged around 4.7m. metric tons and totalled 5.4m. tons in 2000. Several new cement plants were planned or under construction, while existing ones were being expanded. A cement works at Oum al-Khelil, built by Fives-Cail Babcock of France, started production in 1980. A works at Enifida, constructed by Japan's Kawasaki Heavy Industries, Marubeni Corpn and C. Itoh, was commissioned in 1983. In January 1988 a white cement works at Feriana entered production. The plant, established as a joint project with Algeria, had an annual capacity of 210,000 tons, enough to meet both domestic and Algerian needs. In 1998 two state-owned cement plants were sold as part of the Government's privatization programme: the Société des ciments de Jebel Oust (producing 1.2m. tons a year) to Cimpor of Portugal for TD 241m., and the Société des ciments d'Enfida (producing 1.2m. tons a year) to Uniland of Spain for TD 168m. Cimpor announced plans to expand production at the Société des ciments de Jebel Oust to 1.9m. tons and to export some of the plant's output. The sale of the two plants provided the bulk of revenue obtained from privatization during 1998. The Société des ciments de Gabès (1m. tons per year capacity), was sold in early 2000 to another Portuguese firm for TD 311m. and in May an Italian firm purchased the Société des ciments artificiels de Tunis (CAT) for TD 50.5m. The Government failed to sell the Société des ciments d'Oum El-Khelil during 2000, and it was decided that the country's sixth plant, the Société des ciments de Bizerte, would remain under state ownership. In 2001 a $56m. contract was awarded to double the capacity of the Enfida plant. The EIB extended a EUR20m. loan to CAT for plant modernization and expansion at Ben Arous, which is expected to be completed in 2004.

The chemical industry has received special attention from the Government, its share of industrial output having fallen from 13% in 1970 to 9% by 1989. The principal activity within this sector has been the processing of phosphate rock into phosphatic fertilizers and phosphoric acid by the state-owned Industries chimiques maghrébines at Gabès and by 'mixed' (partly state-owned) companies at Sfax. In 1988 reforms for the chemical sector were announced, including consolidation of companies' capital and long-term restructuring of their debts. In 2000 the state-owned Chemical Products and Detergents Company (SPCD) and the Cosmetics, Detergents and Perfumes Company (CODEPAR) were sold to a Dutch multinational company. Under the terms of the association agreement with the EU (see External Trade), Tunisia will dismantle trade barriers to EU industrial goods in stages over a 12-year period; barriers to those products that would be most competitive with Tunisian manufactured goods were to be phased out over the full period. The Ministry of Industry estimated that as many as 2,000 companies could collapse as a result of increased competition from the EU unless efforts were made to improve productivity and the quality of their goods. Almost two-thirds of the 384 firms that applied for help from SOS Entreprise, a government body established in 1995 to assist ailing companies, were in the manufacturing sector. The vast majority were family-run businesses, suffering from poor management, a shortage of capital, low levels of training and outdated technology. The EU pledged to provide financial support to Tunisia for adjustment programmes designed to prepare the manufacturing industry for competition from EU member states. These included a 'mise à niveau' programme of industrial modernization to help private-sector firms reform their management and production processes to become competitive with European manufacturers. In addition to receiving financial support from the EU, the programme was also funded by the World Bank and by two Tunisian state funds, the Fonds de promotion et de maîtrise de technologie and the Fonds pour le développement de la compétitivité industrielle. In April 1998 the EU agreed a grant of TD 12.5m. (US $10.7m.) for the mise à niveau project and a further grant of TD 12.5m. to support the privatization of state-owned companies on condition that the Government's divestment programme was improved and accelerated. By the end of 2000 over 1,600 companies had registered to take part in the mise à niveau programme. Some 848 of these companies had received approval of their modernization plans, involving a total investment of TD 1,600m. A survey found that companies taking part in the programme had achieved an increase in turnover of 15%, growth in exports of 13% and a 6.6% increase in employment levels. From the beginning of 2000 the programme was extended to sections of the services sector linked to industry and by the end of the year 69 services companies had joined the programme. From January 2000, under the terms of the EU association agreement, tariffs were lifted on the first group of European manufactured goods that are also produced in Tunisia, increasing competition for the Tunisian manufacturing sector. Later in the year the Union tunisienne de l'industrie, du commerce et de l'artisanat, representing Tunisian employers, stated that Tunisian manufacturers should be given more time to complete their modernization programmes, but it seemed unlikely that the schedule for lifting tariff barriers would be slowed down. It was also argued that the first phase of the modernization programme was too limited because it aimed to modernize only 2,000 of Tunisia's 45,000 companies; the Government was urged to simplify and widen the programme to encourage more firms to join. By 2001 the programme covered 1,834 companies, of which 1,027 received approval for their restructuring plans involving a total investment of TD 1,914m. (which includes TD 265m. in Government subsidies). The programme has increased profitability by about 40% in the companies concerned. In early 1998 it was reported that the Government planned to strengthen craft industries, which employed some 220,000 workers, accounted for 3% of GDP and earned TD 177m. in export revenue. A training commission was to be established, and improvements made to the quality and diversity of products, to marketing, and to the provision of loans.

Production of electricity for public use was 4,536m. kWh in 1989, compared with 2,429m. kWh in 1980. Most of this was generated by thermal means; hydroelectric power was of lesser importance. The Government prepared ambitious plans for new generating units in the early 1980s. However, implementation of these plans was postponed, owing to budgetary constraints and a fall in demand, and funding was reallocated to development of the power distribution network. In the light of the economic upturn, which followed the Gulf crisis, the Government confirmed, in June 1992, that the British/French GEC Alsthom group had been contracted to build a 350-MW combined-cycle power-station at Sousse, at an estimated cost of US $250m. Completion of this plant would raise Tunisia's total installed capacity to 1,680 MW. At the end of 1997 the General Electric Co of the USA completed the installation of two 120-MW gas turbines at the new Bir M'Cherga power-station and won the contract to supply and install a 120-MW gas turbine at the Bouchemma power-station near Gabès. At the same time ETAP announced that it was building a 16-MW power-station on the Ezzaouia oilfield using gas that is currently flared. The electricity generated would be sold to STEG. The national electricity grid served over 75% of the country in 1994, and was due to provide 90% coverage by 1996 if planning targets for rural electrification were met. In March 1996 legislation was

introduced to end STEG's monopoly on power generation, government policy being to open up power-station construction, operation and ownership to private investors. In early 1998 Carthage Power Co, a consortium of Community Energy Alternatives of the USA, Marubeni Corpn of Japan and Sithes Energies, a Franco-Japanese group, was awarded the contract for the country's first private power-station at Radès (also known as Radès II). The 470-MW combined-cycle plant would run on natural gas and fuel petroleum. Carthage Power would build, own and operate the new plant and sell electricity to STEG, which retained its monopoly on prices and distribution. After complicated negotiations over financing the project, Alsthom Construction was awarded the $180m. engineering and construction contract. Work on the plant began in July 1999 and it was expected to become operational in 2002. In 2000 Sithes Energies sold its 32.5% holding in the project to the other two partners so that Community Energy Alternatives had a 60% stake and Marubeni Corpn a 40% stake. A 500 MW gas-fuelled electricity plant is to be built by BG at Sfax, in association with either STEG or ENAP; this is scheduled to come into operation in 2005. The plant will cost $200m. and will use gas from Miskar and later from the new Hasdrubal field. Tunisia is already linked to Algeria and Morocco through a 220-kV grid and in early 1999 contracts were awarded for the construction of a 220-kV link between the electricity grids of Tunisia and Libya. Red Eléctrica of Spain and Transenergie of Canada were awarded the contract to advise the two Governments on implementing the connection in 2001.

In late 1997 the Agence de maîtrise de l'énergie announced plans to install 1m. sq m of solar panels to generate power equivalent to 120,000 metric tons of petroleum by 2010. A pilot project involving the installation of 50,000 sq m of solar panels was being funded by the International Fund for the Environment. In 1998 STEG signed a contract with Endesa of Spain to build a wind power station on Cap Bon at an estimated cost of US $10m. By 2010 Tunisia hoped that about one-quarter of its energy requirements would come from renewable sources. Also in 1998 the European Investment Bank (EIB) announced a loan of $54m. to Tunisia, to help meet the cost of expanding the country's power transmission and supply network during 1998–2001. In 2002 the EIB extended a €150m. loan under the 2002–06 Development Plan to modernize Tunisia's electricity transmission network.

In 2000 total electricity production increased to 10,097m. kWh and consumption to 8,975m. kWh. Consumption was forecast to rise to 17,800 gWh by 2010, requiring a doubling of installed capacity, from 1,900 MW in 1998 to 4,000 MW in 2010, in order to raise production to 20,000 gWh.

TRANSPORT AND COMMUNICATIONS

Tunisia inherited a relatively modern system of road and rail communications from the period of colonial rule. Substantial work was being carried out to modernize and extend the existing highway and railway networks. Tunisia has some 20,000 km of primary and secondary roads, most of which are surfaced and relatively well-maintained. In 1995 the Government announced a US $88.7m. programme (including $51.5m. loaned by the World Bank) to improve over 1,000 km of rural roads. After 1995 the Government's policy on motorway building was to seek private-sector financing for the construction of toll roads. It was intended that public-sector investment should be channelled into the maintenance and improvement of existing roads, some 500 km of roads being scheduled for upgrading in 1996. In November 1998 the Government announced that construction would begin on two new sections of motorway, one from Tunis to Bizerta and another from Bizerta to Menzel Bourguiba; and that feasibility studies would be carried out on motorways from Tunis west to Mejez el-Bab and from M'Saken to Sfax. The Japan Bank for International Cooperation (JBIC) provided a $94m. loan to construct a 50-km. tranche from El-Jem to Sfax in 2002.

Part of the revenue generated from the privatization programme would be devoted to motorway construction. At the same time, it was announced that the Tunisian section of the proposed trans-Maghreb highway would be completed by 2001 rather than 2011, the date announced by the Government two years earlier. It was hoped that much of the construction work would be undertaken by the private sector; however, private investors have shown little interest in this or any other road project. Nevertheless, by mid-2000 construction had begun on the Tunis-Bizerta motorway, a $120m. project funded in part by a loan from the AFESD. By late 1998 there were 776,000 licensed vehicles in the country, including 446,000 private cars and 190,000 transport vehicles. About one-half of the total number of vehicles were owned by people living in the Greater Tunis area. In 2000 the National Transport Company and the 12 regional transport companies carried 311m. and 288m. passengers respectively (an increase of 3%). Privately-owned mass transit urban lines in the Greater Tunis area carried 6.4m. passengers.

Tunisia's 2,190-km rail network is operated by the state-owned Société nationale des chemins de fer tunisiens (SNCFT) and consists of a north-south coastal line and four east-west branch lines to Jendouba, Le Kef, Kasserine, and Tozeur. Passenger numbers increased from 27.7m. in 1995 to 35.6m. in 2000, but freight traffic remained relatively unchanged at around 2,283m. km a year. The surface metro system serving the capital, Tunis, is being expanded with financial assistance from the EIB and Kreditanstalt für Wideraufbau of Germany. A new 6 km–7 km-line is being built linking the central station to the southern suburb of El Mourouj and over 3 km of existing track is being upgraded. Ten new stations are being constructed, together with bus and metro interchanges, and new rolling stock was to be purchased.

There are international airports at Tunis-Carthage, Djerba-Zarzis, Monastir-Skanès, Sfax-Thyna, Tabarka-7 Novembre, Tozeur-Nefta and Gafsa-Ksar (opened in late 1998). The second phase of the Tunis-Carthage airport expansion project, to increase passenger capacity from 3.5m. to 4.5m. per year, was completed in April 1998. The country's airports handled 8.3m. passengers in 1997, an increase of 12.5% over 1996, as a result of a rise in the number of foreign tourists. In early 2000 work was in progress to enlarge the capacity of Monastir-Skanès airport from 3.5m. to 5m. passengers and Djerba-Zarzis airport from 2m. to 4m. passengers. At the same time, a French company won a US $10m. contract for technical studies for a new international airport to be built at Enfida, some 60 km south of Tunis. On completion of the first phase of this project in 2004, the airport will be capable of handling 5m. passengers and, after further expansion schemes, it is scheduled to become Tunisia's largest airport, with a capacity of 30m. passengers. Another new airport is to be built near the port of Gabès. Tunisia's airports handled a total of 91,100 aircraft and 9.6m. passengers in 2000. The national airline, TunisAir, carried 3.5m. passengers in 2000. In 1995 the state's 85% shareholding in the company was reduced to 45.2% as part of the Government's privatization programme, and in mid-1995 the company announced that it would offer 20% of its capital to public subscription. A further 20% stake in TunisAir was listed for privatization in 1999. The company brought forward its plans to update its fleet and placed orders for 15 new aircraft with Airbus and Boeing for delivery during 1998–2005. Three new Boeings and two new Airbuses were delivered in 1999. As well as modernizing its fleet, the company has made efforts to improve passenger services and to reduce operating costs. Nevertheless, net profits fell sharply in 1997 resulting in a fall in the value of the company's shares. In 1999 TunisAir signed an agreement with Air France under which the two airlines would co-ordinate their flights between Tunisia and France (which represent two-fifths of TunisAir's services) and co-operate in aircraft maintenance and staff training. Co-operation agreements were signed with Royal Air Maroc and Delta Airlines of the USA in 2000. The company reported losses of TD 29m. on a turnover of TD 613m. in 2000 (compared with a net profit of TD 13m. in 1999 on a turnover of TD 588m.) which it attributed in part to the rise in fuel prices. Staff cuts and price increases were announced, in an attempt to remedy the situation. Carthage Airlines, a new private charter airline set up by local businessmen, began flights in 2001. Nouvel Air, another charter airline, carried 985,000 passengers in 2000. Overall passenger numbers on charter flights increased by 22%.

The state-owned shipping company, the Compagnie tunisienne de navigation (CTN), began operating in 1971 and carried around 25% of total trade in 1985. Although the Government

announced in mid-1995 that it wanted to privatize the company, no action was taken. The CTN has not been profitable and in recent years has begun a restructuring programme, abandoning non-profitable routes and offering incentives to reduce the workforce by one-third. It has also started renewing its fleet. In 2000 it handled 1.38m. tons of goods, representing 5.7% of port traffic.

In early 1984 a contract was awarded to a Turkish firm for the expansion of the port at Gabès. A new commercial port at Zarzis, near Djerba, was constructed shortly afterwards. In May 1990 the World Bank agreed to provide a loan of US $17m. towards rural road improvement, and $80m. towards the development of railways and ports. In March 1992 the Office des ports nationaux tunisiens announced a project to upgrade facilities in the Tunis-Goulette-Radès area. La Goulette and Radès are being provided with new quays and computerized facilities funded in part by the EIB, and there are plans to upgrade container handling capacity. Following criticism from the business community about the inefficiency of Tunisian ports and the consequent long delays in handling cargo, in late 1997 the Government stated that it planned to involve the private sector in port management and cargo handling, thereby ending the monopolies of the state-owned Office des ports nationaux tunisiens and the Société tunisienne d'acconage et de manutention. Early in 2001 it was reported that all commercial port activities were to be privatized. The number of ships entering Tunisia's main ports increased from 5,938 in 1995 to 6,184 in 2000; almost one-half of this traffic was handled by Tunis-La Goulette-Radès. Under the 1997–2000 Development Plan, investment of TD 4,600m. ($4,000m.) was projected for the transport sector, including finance for the construction of 1,500 km of new roads, the extension of Tunis, Monastir and Djerba airports and the creation of a second railway track between Tunis and Sousse.

Investment of some TD 1,500m. (US $1,300m.) was allocated to the telecommunications sector under the 1997–2001 Development Plan, with the aim of increasing the number of telephone lines to 1m. In early 1998 the country's first global standard for mobiles (GSM) cellular phone system, installed by Alcatel of France for the state telecommunications company, Tunisie Télécom (at a cost of $20m.), started operating for 30,000 subscribers in the Tunis-Nabeul-Hammamet region. By 2000 the network had 50,000 subscribers and its capacity was being expanded by Alcatel of France and Ericsson of Sweden to 300,000 subscribers by mid-2001. In early 2000 Tunisie Télécom announced that by the end of the year there would be 1m. fixed telephone lines, 200,000 GSM lines and 11,000 lines serving a rural network. The Government had given priority to strengthening the telecommunications sector, which is regarded as a weak point in the country's otherwise well-developed infrastructure. In March 2001 the Ministry of Communications invited international tenders for the country's first private GSM licence. However, owing to unexpectedly low offers, the Government postponed the sale. Some of the bid requirements were relaxed and the tender was reissued in October. Against strong competition from Spanish Telefónica and Kuwaiti Telecom, Orascom Telecom of Egypt was awarded the licence for $454m. in 2002.

The sale of 40.6% of shares in the state-owned Société tunisienne d'entreprise de télécommunications (SOTETEL) began in June 1998 and Siemens of Germany was reported to have bought a 12% stake in the company for some US $1.2m.

FINANCE AND BUDGET

The Banque centrale de Tunisie (BCT) is the sole bank of issue of Tunisia's national currency, the dinar, and it performs all the normal central banking functions. On 1 March 1994 a new foreign exchange market opened in Tunis, bringing to an end the BCT monopoly on quoting prices for the dinar against hard currencies. At the beginning of 2000 the Governor of the BCT stated that the Tunisian economy was not yet ready for full convertibility of the dinar, which he ruled out 'for the foreseeable future'. In addition to 13 commercial banks, the Government has established eight development institutions to channel aid into the economy. Other development institutions, such as the World Bank, have established credit programmes with the development banks. A major development since 1981 has been the creation of joint-venture banks with other Arab countries. These include the Banque Tuniso-Koweïtienne de développement, Société Tuniso-Saoudienne d'investissement et de développement,

Banque de coopération du Maghreb Arabe, and the Banque de Tunisie et des Emirats d'investissement. In October 1991 it was announced that Tunis was to be the headquarters of the Banque Maghrébine d'investissement et de commerce extérieur, a development bank established by the five members of the Union of the Arab Maghreb (UAM). The Government introduced legislation in 1994 to tighten the regulation of several areas of banking activity, and (in a separate initiative included in the 1994 budget) ordered Tunisian banks to set aside 50% of their profits to cover an estimated US $3,000m. of bad debts, to meet a capital adequacy requirement of 5%, to cease making unsecured loans and to reduce their exposure to any single sector to no more than 25%. Thereafter, additional efforts were made to increase competition, improve efficiency and to bring the banking system up to international standards. As a result the banking system has become stronger, but competition is still limited in a sector dominated by the state, and the burden of substantial bad debts has made it difficult for the banks to raise money overseas. The Government has also begun to tackle the problem of bad debts. Some TD 1,000m. is owed by state-owned firms and an estimated one in five Tunisians with a bank loan is more than a year in arrears. The five main commercial banks, in which the state has either a controlling interest or a major stake, bear most of the burden of bad debts. By the late 1900s a restructuring of the whole banking system was under way, aimed at reducing the number of banks and making them more efficient. The programme has been promised financial assistance worth some $400m. from the World Bank, the African Development Bank and the EU. As part of the reforms the Government has taken over TD 720m. of non-performing loans made to state companies, and plans to tighten operating standards and begin privatizing state banks. The merger of the Société tunisienne de banque, the Banque de développement économique de Tunisie (BDET) and the Banque nationale de développement touristique was completed in December 2000. The new bank retained the name Société tunisienne de banque. As Tunisia's largest bank, capitalized at TD 124.3m., it became the country's first bank to offer a full range of services and was expected to be able to compete internationally. The state retains 50% of its equity, but the bank may be privatized at a later date. The Union internationale des banques (following a failed merger with the Banque de Tunisie et des Emirats d'investissement in 1998) and Banque du Sud are included in the Government's privatization programme for 2002. In 2001 the Arab Banking Corpn, which already operated an 'offshore' subsidiary, ABC Tunis, opened an onshore commercial bank, ABC Tunisia. The offshore banking sector was regulated by legislation, enacted in 1976, which placed strict limits on the banks' activities. Offshore banks include Tunis International Bank, Alubaf International Bank and North Africa International Bank. Complaints from the offshore banks about lack of business led to reductions in staffing levels and to the withdrawal of National Bank of Abu Dhabi in 1984. These complaints were heeded by the Central Bank and the Ministry of Finance, and in March 1985 they approved the text of a law that was to give offshore banks greater freedom to do business in the local currency and to participate in dinar treasury operations. The law was approved by the National Assembly towards the end of 1985. In June 1995 Tunisia's first merchant bank, International Maghreb Merchant Bank, began operating with a paid-up capital of TD 3m. Shareholders included the International Finance Corpn, French and Austrian banks, the local Maghreb Finance Group and private Saudi Arabian investors, together with the British-based initiator of the project, London Court Securities. The new bank's aim was to specialize in project and corporate finance and in privatization and stock market activities, initially within Tunisia, but with a view to subsequent expansion into the wider Maghreb region. A second merchant bank, the Banque d'affaires de Tunisie, opened in 1997, with the Société tunisienne de banque as the major shareholder, together with the BDET and banks from Morocco, the United Kingdom, Spain, Italy and France. The new merchant bank specialized in privatization and in the restructuring of company finances. In February 1998 the Banque internationale arabe de Tunisie raised US $40m. through the issue of global depository receipts. This was Tunisia's first international equity offering. According to official figures, offshore bank resources increased to $1,508.7m. in 2000

from $1,455.7m. in 1999. Client deposits reached $350.5m. and banking activity generated proceeds of $102.7m., representing an increase of 14% over 1999.

The availability of local savings for investment has meant, firstly, that the need for foreign borrowings to finance development projects has been greatly reduced; and, secondly, that the local financial markets have expanded and become more sophisticated to meet the demand for loans. To encourage domestic savings, interest rates on deposits and loans were raised in September 1977, and the official discount rate increased from 5% to 5.75%. Overall, national savings accounted for about 80% of total investment in the fifth Development Plan (1977–81), compared with a projected 65%. Since the early 1980s, the Government has been studying various proposals for tax reform, and in July 1988 64 taxes on turnover, production and consumer goods were replaced by a new value-added tax (VAT), which by 1991 was yielding 30% of tax receipts. However, with total tax receipts still only equivalent to 2.4% of GDP, in late 1991 the Government introduced measures to increase the tax base, including a strengthened inspectorate. Other sources of government income include petroleum and gas revenues, profits from state monopolies and, increasingly, the proceeds from the privatization of state assets. In June 1994 the Government issued five- and 10-year treasury bonds which were open to the public for the first time. In 1996 the scope of VAT was extended to cover all retail activities (including those of small shops), and steps were taken to strengthen the tax inspection and enforcement systems. VAT and other indirect taxes were expected to play an increasingly important revenue-raising role as customs tariffs were progressively reduced under the terms of Tunisia's trade agreement with the EU (see External Trade, below).

In November 1994 a law was introduced to convert the state-run Tunis stock exchange, the Bourse des Valeurs Mobilières, (then dealing actively in only 20 companies' shares) into a private company, regulated by an independent monitoring body. The creation of an independently administered exchange with streamlined trading procedures was expected to facilitate the Government's privatization programme. Shares in various transport, hotel and industrial companies were initially scheduled for sale in the second half of 1995 at the rate of one flotation per month, but this timetable was modified when the market showed signs of over-rapid expansion. Regulations were introduced in mid-1995 to make it easier for foreign investors to do business on the Tunis stock exchange, with the proviso that no quoted company's share capital could be more than 10% foreign-owned without the permission of the Tunisian authorities. (The investment regulations allowed foreign ownership of non-quoted companies' shares to reach 30% before permission was required.) In 1997 the limit on foreign ownership of companies was raised to 49.9%. Yet, despite government efforts to stimulate the stock market, by the end of 1998 fewer then 40 firms were listed, many of them banks, and few foreign investors had shown interest. Activity increased sharply during 1999 when share-trading activity more than doubled. In particular, there was renewed interest from foreign investors in blue-chip stocks such as TunisAir and the Société tunisienne d'entreprises de télécommunications (SOTETEL). By the end of the year capitalization had grown from TD 2,500m. to TD 3,300m. The Government hoped to increase the number of companies listed to 200 by the end of 2003, principally by encouraging private and privatized companies to consider listing. However, although the stock market remained buoyant during 2000, with growing interest from foreign investors, by 2001 the number of firms listed had only increased to 45. In 2002 the Government introduced additional investment incentives, including further tax concessions, for foreign investors.

Tunisia made use of the Eurocurrency market for the first time in 1977 and obtained a US $125m. loan to finance industrial development. In early 1979 a $100m. loan was arranged, through a consortium of international banks, to finance the Tunisian section of the Algeria-Italy gas pipeline. In early 1981 the Compagnie financière immobilière et touristique was able to raise $25m. for seven years at 0.5% above the London interbank offered rate—a very low spread for a developing country. During the period of the 1982–86 Development Plan, borrowing remained at a relatively high level, although the Government managed to attract concessionary loans for development projects, especially from France and the Federal Republic of Germany. In May 1986 the Government raised $120m. on the international markets, but this proved to be the last international loan before the balance-of-payments crisis in mid-1986.

Under a medium-term IMF-sponsored programme for 1988–91, the Government committed itself to the reduction of the central government deficit, which was to be achieved by liberalizing external trade and pricing mechanisms, and by restructuring and, in some cases, 'privatizing' state enterprises. In addition, as stated above, the Government attempted to enhance its revenue base by implementing various tax reforms. In 1989 the principal objectives of the IMF's three-year extended programme, including the reduction of the central government deficit, had been, in part, achieved. As a reflection of this success, Tunisia requested that the amount of credit available in the three-year EFF be reduced from US $275m. to $183m. However, the effects of the 1991 Gulf crisis undermined adjustment efforts, and in June 1991 Tunisia became only the second country ever to request an extension of, and restoration of full access to, the IMF's EFF. This was granted, effectively extending the reform programme for a further year. In mid-1992 it was reported that the Government would not be seeking an IMF facility to replace the EFF, which had recently expired.

Following this extension, in December 1991 the World Bank approved a three-year loan of US $250m. in support of Tunisia's restructuring programme, the total cost of which was estimated at almost $400m. In March 1992 a structural adjustment loan of ECU 40m. was granted by the EC, while the balance of funds required was made available by Japan and the Arab Monetary Fund. In addition, in December 1991 the Tunisian Government took the unprecedented step of issuing treasury bills to finance its budget deficit, while in June 1992 Tunisia raised a syndicated loan of $110m. on the international market. In March 1994 a further loan of ECU 20m. was granted by the EU. The World Bank approved a loan of $280m. in 1998, bringing the total value of its loans to Tunisia during 1996–98 to $750m. World Bank funds support projects in agriculture, health, education, transport, tourism and export promotion. Under the terms of the MEDA aid programme, which became available following the signing of the Tunisia-EU association agreement in 1995, loans to Tunisia totalled ECU 380m. ($426m.) by the end of 1998. In addition, Tunisia had received a further ECU 200m. in loans from the EIB.

The Government's 1991 budget provided for a 10% rise in expenditure, to TD 4,080m., and a deficit of TD 410m., which, in the event, widened to over TD 500m. The 1992 budget envisaged an 11.4% increase in expenditure and a reduction in the deficit to TD 320m. The Five-Year Plan for 1992–96 set as a target the reduction of the budget deficit to 1.2% of GDP. The 1993 budget projected expenditure totalling TD 4,950m. Sources of revenue included TD 330m. US ($352m.) in foreign credits, to be extended by the World Bank ($149m.), Japan ($59m.), the African Development Bank ($42.6m.), France ($42.6m.), the USA ($32m.) and Italy ($27m.). The average annual inflation rate in 1987–91 was about 7%, the aim being to reduce the rate to 5% over the period 1992–96. From 8.3% in 1991, the annual rise in the consumer price index fell to 5.8% in 1992 and to 4% in 1993. The 1994 budget provided for expenditure of TD 5,515m., of which 52% was current spending and 19% was capital investment, the remaining 29% being the debt-servicing requirement. Revenue was budgeted at TD 4,312m., leaving a deficit of TD 1,203m. to be financed by government borrowing, 28% of which would come from foreign loans. Over 47% of expenditure was linked to social policy, and spending to alleviate the impact of structural economic reform on the poorer sections of society included TD 230m. in price subsidies for basic commodities. Sectoral spending allocations included TD 304m. for agricultural projects. The 1995 budget provided for total expenditure of TD 6,595m. and total revenue of TD 4,951m., leaving an overall deficit of TD 1,644m. to be financed by government borrowing. Further liberalization measures in 1995 would reduce to 15% the proportion of domestic consumer items subject to retail price control, while there would be a reduction to 9.5% in the proportion of imported goods for which import permits were required. The Government's inflation target for 1995 was 4.5%, compared with recorded inflation of 4.7% in 1994. In May

1995 statutory minimum wages were increased by 4.6%, to TD 132.9 per 40-hour week in industry and to TD 4.5 per day in agriculture. The 1996 budget provided for total expenditure of TD 7,230m. and total revenue of TD 5,235m., leaving a deficit of TD 1,995m. Inflation dropped to 3.7% from 6.3% in 1995. In the budget for 1997, the Government planned a spending increase of 10.8% to TD 8,010m. and a deficit of TD 2,546m. Actual expenditure in 1997 was higher than budgeted (totalling TD 8,200m.) and there was a significant shortfall in revenue. In the budget for 1998 projected spending was increased to TD 9,000m., with revenues forecast to rise to TD 5,700m., leading to an increase in the overall deficit to TD 3,300m. Taxation was expected to account for some 83% of total revenue. Notably, VAT was to be increased by 1%, to 18%, in order to offset the loss of customs revenue following the implementation of Tunisia's trade agreement with the EU. The budget was based on inflation at 3.8% and real GDP growth of 5.4%. The 1999 budget was based on inflation at 3.6% and real GDP growth of 6.3%. Exports of goods and services were projected to rise by 9.7%, with imports rising by only 1.4%. Total investment in the economy was to rise by 14.8% to TD 6,490m.—some 25.8% of GDP. Government spending was forecast to rise to TD 9,590m., with almost two-thirds devoted to social sectors, including training and job creation, and infrastructure. The 2000 budget was based on real GDP growth of 6%, with the budget deficit projected at 2.7% of GDP. Almost two-thirds of revenue (projected at TD 10,510m.) was to come from tax and non-fiscal revenue, with the rest from borrowing. A sharp rise in tax revenues was forecast (with tax increases on tobacco, alcohol and cars) in order to compensate in part for a fall in customs revenue as tariffs are removed under the terms of the EU accord. Operating expenditure was to rise from TD 4,104m. in 1999 to TD 4,347m., with almost two-thirds devoted to health, education, training and research. Development expenditure was set to rise from TD 1,939m. in 1999 to TD 2,113m., with the implementation of many new projects in water management and infrastructure. Just over one-half of total investment during the year was to come from the private sector. The IMF estimated that, excluding grants and privatization receipts, the actual budget deficit for 2000 was TD 786m. (2.9% of GDP) compared with a projected TD 947m. The 2001 budget was set at TD 10,800m. based on real GDP growth of 6.2% and inflation at 3% with the budget deficit projected to fall to 2.4% of GDP. Current spending was forecast to increase by 7.2%, taking into account wage increases and the recruitment of additional public sector workers in the health and education sectors. Tax receipts were expected to increase by 8.6%, following the introduction of more efficient collection procedures. Total investment was forecast to increase by 10% to TD 7,800m. (equivalent to 26.4% of GDP), 55% of which was derived from the private sector. The budget also set out the Government's economic priorities for 2001, which included creating new jobs, increasing investment, improving the competitiveness of the economy, promoting agriculture and fishing, and continuing to reform the financial sector. The IMF estimated that, excluding grant and privatization receipts, the actual budget deficit was 3.5% of GDP in 2001. The 2002 budget was set at TD 11,533m. with the budget deficit projected to fall to 2.2% of GDP. Expenditure is estimated to rise by 6.6% and inflation to 3%.

Tunisia's deficit on its balance of trade (see External Trade) was traditionally offset by earnings from tourism and remittances from Tunisians working abroad, so that the overall position on current payments was roughly in balance until 1975. In that year the fall in petroleum prices and the slump in demand for phosphates widened the visible trade gap so seriously, despite continuing good harvests, that the current balance showed a deficit of TD 227.2m., compared with TD 90.9m. in 1974. Over the next decade, the deficit rose steadily, reaching TD 1,076m. in 1984. A severe cutback on imports reduced the deficit to TD 844m. in 1985, TD 50m. in 1986 and TD 78m. in 1987. In 1988 the trade deficit increased substantially as a result of a poor harvest and low petroleum prices; but, partly owing to a large increase in receipts from tourism, the current account of the balance of payments recorded a surplus of TD 52m. However, in 1989 the current account registered a deficit of TD 312.5m., equivalent to 3.6% of GDP, as a result of an increase in food imports after severe drought, and in capital goods imports, owing to the recovery of foreign investment. In 1990 the current-account deficit widened to TD 580m. because of the negative impact of the Gulf crisis, which also contributed to a further large deficit, of TD 527.3m., in 1991. A deterioration in the country's terms of trade contributed to an increase in the current-account deficit to TD 662.3m. in 1992. A current-account deficit of TD 860m. in 1993 was followed by an estimated deficit of TD 839m. in 1994 and TD 735m. in 1995, representing 4.3% of GDP. However, as a result of a decline in the trade deficit, together with higher receipts from tourism and worker remittances, the current-account deficit was reduced to TD 466m. in 1996, equivalent to 2.4% of GDP. The current account deficit rose to TD 655m. in 1997 (3.1% of GDP), and TD 769m. in 1998 (3.4% of GDP), but fell to TD 525m. in 1999 (2.1% of GDP). As a result of the widening of the trade deficit, the current account deficit increased to TD 1,126m. in 2000, equivalent to 4.2% of GDP. The IMF estimated a similar deficit in 2001. The Government launched a 30,000m.-yen ($295m.) placement on the Japanese bond market in early 1994 to help cover Tunisia's balance-of-payments deficit, having chosen to borrow in yen to obtain a favourable interest rate. Part of this yen borrowing was subsequently swapped into French francs. The Government returned to the Japanese bond market in February, April and September 1995 (to bring its cumulative borrowing from this source to 85,000m. yen—about $870m.) and again in October 1996 and August 1997. In September Tunisia launched its first 'Yankee bond' for $400m. In December 1995 Tunisia sought a $100m. syndicated sovereign loan on the international market, where the response was such that the amount borrowed was doubled to $200m. when the loan was finalized in the following month. A further syndicated loan of $150m. (an amount 50% higher than the Government originally asked for) was signed in September 1996. In 1999 Tunisia entered the Eurobond market for the first time, raising $242m. in 10-year bonds. In July 2000 the Government launched a 50,000m.-yen global Samurai bond. In March 2001 Tunisia successfully launched a sovereign bond for 55,000m. yen ($450m.),almost double the amount originally planned. This was followed by a further issue—a 30-year global bond for an additional 20,000m. yen ($167m.). In April 2002 the Government launched a 10-year global dollar bond for $650m.

Almost 600,000 Tunisians were resident abroad in 1993, when remittances from migrant workers amounted to TD 600m. ($588m.), some 18% higher than in 1992. Workers' remittances increased from TD 696m. in 1994 to TD 712m. in 1995, TD 798m. in 1996 and TD 846m. in 1997. Some 90% of remittances come from Tunisians working in Western Europe, and 60% from France alone. Remittances increased to TD 902m. in 1998 (of which TD 676m. was in currency and TD 226m. was in kind—mostly motor vehicles) and to TD 1,020m. in 1999 (TD 732m. in currency and TD 288m. in kind). In 2000 they increased to TD 1,091m. (TD 810m. in currency, an increase of 10.7%, and TD 281m. in kind)

PLANNING

It was not until 1961, when the 10-year perspective plan was formulated, that the Government laid down comprehensive plans for development. The broad lines of policy that had been put forward in the perspective plan were embodied in the first Three-Year Plan (1962–64) and then successive Four-Year Plans (1965–68, 1969–72 and 1973–76). These were followed by successive Five-Year Plans covering 1977–81, 1982–86, 1987–91,1992–96 and 1997–2001. The tenth Development Plan, covering 2002–06, was introduced in June 2002.

Although Tunisia has relied to a considerable extent on petroleum to underpin economic growth, it has to plan for a future in which it is likely to be a net importer of fuel. Because of petroleum, the country's exports during the 1977–81 Development Plan period grew faster, in constant prices, than imports did—by 14.6% per year, compared with import growth of 8.9%. The 1982–86 Plan was designed to introduce the economic adjustments necessary to prepare Tunisia for an era of reduced income from petroleum. Stringent controls were to be maintained on the external debt and the balance of payments, while non-petroleum exports were to be encouraged, and various incentives given to increase employment. However, most of the Plan's targets were not achieved. Growth in real GDP averaged

about 3% per year, instead of the projected figure of 6% per year, and job creation totalled about 200,000, compared with the Plan's target of 270,000. Investment spending rose above the targeted level, contributing to a worrying rise in the current-account deficit and the external debt. The need for revised measures became apparent in 1986, when the collapse of international petroleum prices coincided with a poor harvest and a bad tourist season. In this situation, the Government brought forward its 1987–91 Plan, which constituted a radical attempt to restructure the economy and to reduce dependence on petroleum exports. The objectives of the 1987–91 Plan were more modest than those of its predecessors, with annual GDP growth targeted at 4% and job creation at 240,000, compared with total expected demand for about 345,000 jobs during the Plan period. The various structural reforms, to be implemented with the assistance of the World Bank, were intended to promote non-petroleum exports, which were expected to increase by 8% per year, compared with the 2% growth rate achieved during 1982–86. One of the major instruments of economic reform has been the devaluation of the dinar, which has been maintained at a rate that competes with the currencies of other Mediterranean exporters, such as Greece, Spain and Portugal. As well as stimulating exports, the depreciation of the currency assists the tourism industry, which has become a major source of foreign exchange.

Investment was estimated to total about TD 10,400m. during the 1987–91 Development Plan, representing a substantial reduction, in real terms, compared with the 1982–86 period. A higher proportion of investment was directed into agriculture (20%, compared with 16% in the 1982–86 Plan). To compensate for reduced state investment, the Government envisaged that 52% of total investment would come from the Tunisian private sector, and also sought to attract TD 6,000m. in external investment support. The 1992–96 Plan was introduced in July 1992 and envisaged total investment of TD 17,400m., of which 52.3% would be generated by the private sector, and the creation of 320,000 jobs. Public expenditure would be focused on health, education, housing and services, with priority for investment in transport and communications; and emphasis would also be placed on regional development, particularly in western Tunisia. Also planned were further reductions in subsidies on consumer and other products; the disposal of all state assets except in strategic sectors, such as electricity generation; the elimination of price controls on manufactured goods; and the introduction of selective charges for health, education and other services. Assuming the implementation of fundamental reforms (the introduction of free-trade zones and a relaxation of exchange controls, leading to full convertibility of the Tunisian dinar), it was projected that an average GDP growth rate of 6% per year could be attained in the period 1992–96. In reality, GDP grew at about 4.5% per year over the period, and the Government sought to improve economic performance on all fronts in the 1997–2001 Development Plan (see below).

Since the early 1970s there has been a notable change in Tunisian policy regarding foreign private investment. The law of April 1972 provided a package of incentives to attract foreign and also domestic capital to establish manufacturing industries producing solely for export. By 1980 a total of about 250 export-orientated projects had been established under the 1972 decree, employing some 25,000 people. Companies from Germany, France, Belgium and the Netherlands predominated, with about 65% in the textile sector. In 1973 a special organization, the API, was established to centralize investment activities. Legislation was introduced in 1974 to promote investment in domestic-orientated manufacturing. In 1985 the API approved schemes with a total value of TD 504m., compared with a total of TD 583m. in 1984. Of the 1985 total, the largest single allocation (TD 142m.) was for the manufacture of construction materials, ceramics and glass. Mechanical and electrical industries received TD 123m. during that year, and food industries TD 100m. Investments receiving the API's approval created a total of 27,000 jobs in 1985, compared with nearly 30,000 in 1984. The private sector provided nearly two-thirds of the 1985 investment total, and created nearly 90% of the jobs. In August 1987 the API was merged with the Centre national d'études and the Agence foncière industrielle. The revamped API was to conduct feasibility studies, organize industrial training schemes and establish industrial zones. In September 1990 Tunisia created an Employment and Training Bank, financed by the World Bank, to help the country's labour force to adapt to changing patterns in employment.

A revised foreign investment law, which took effect in January 1994, was designed to unify existing sectoral codes, to update legislation relating to investment and to stimulate investment in priority areas, including high-technology and export-orientated industries. Emphasis was placed on the fulfilment of broad policy objectives, such as job creation, decentralization and technology transfer. Drafting of the law began in February 1992 as a condition of Tunisia's structural adjustment loan from the World Bank. In June 1995 the Government announced that major infrastructural projects would in future be open to private-sector investment. The first areas to be opened up would be power-station and motorway construction and management. Other areas listed by the Government included water and sewerage systems; desalination plants; solid waste treatment plants and controlled dumping facilities; land reclamation and pollution control schemes; and large-scale tourism developments. In early 1996 the Government was in negotiation with the World Bank over the conditions for obtaining loans of about US $250m. per year over a period of three years. The Bank advocated in particular the early implementation of 'a serious programme of privatization'; a radical reform of the banking sector to improve its competitiveness and flexibility; and the removal of many remaining bureaucratic obstacles to foreign investment in Tunisia. In July the Government drafted a list of 112 companies to be offered for privatization and adopted a target of $500m. for sales of state-owned assets over the next three years. The World Bank subsequently announced its approval of three loans: $60m. to establish employment and training services for workers affected by economic restructuring; $38.7m. to strengthen institutions supporting private-sector industries; and $75m. to improve the competitiveness of Tunisian companies during the transition to freer trade with the EU.

In December 1996 the Government announced new measures to encourage foreign investment. The measures, to be implemented during the period 1997–2001, included allowing foreign investors to buy up to 49% of any local company without prior authorization (the limit had been 10% for companies listed on the Tunis stock exchange and 30% for other companies); simplifying procedures for foreign investment in agricultural joint ventures; opening up engineering and technical consulting to foreign investment; and lowering interest rates on business loans and social welfare contributions by employers. The limit on foreign ownership of companies listed on the stock exchange was raised to 49.9% in 1997. However, despite efforts to attract foreign investors, the level of investment outside the hydrocarbons sector has fluctuated according to the level of privatization receipts (see also Industry). According to Central Bank figures, total foreign direct investment reached TD 543m. in 1994 but fell back to TD 305m. in 1995 and TD 272.5m. in 1996. Having recovered to TD 403m. in 1997, foreign investment then rose sharply to TD 760m. in 1998 before falling back to TD 437m. in 1999. Following a substantial rise in 2000 (including privatization receipts) to TD 1,068m., foreign investment declined to TD 665m. in 2001.The 1997–2001 Development Plan set the following economic targets. GDP was to grow by an average of 6% in real terms each year, a target which implied average annual growth of 7% in manufacturing and services and 4.3% in agriculture. The unemployment rate, at 15.5% in 1996, was to fall to 13% by 2001, while average inflation over the five-year period was targeted at 3.7%, down from 4.8% in 1992–96. The budget deficit was to be reduced to an average of 2.6% of GDP from 3.5% in 1992–96, and the current-account deficit was to narrow to 2.2% of GDP in 2001. External debt (see Foreign Aid, below) was to increase in absolute terms, but fall as a percentage of GDP (to 40.9%, compared with 51.1% in 1996). The investment plan envisaged total spending of TD 42,000m. over the five-year period, of which the government budget would provide TD 33,775m.; the remainder was to be funded by external financing. In early 2000 the Government indicated that almost three-quarters of the objectives of the plan would have been achieved by the end of the year. According to the Ministry of Economic Development, capital investment in the economy

during the first three years of the plan totalled TD 17,200m. compared with the target of TD 17,800m. Some 52% of investment came from the private sector compared with the projected 56%.

The 2001–06 Development Plan envisages a 60% increase in private-sector contribution to the economy, raising foreign investment to TD 850m. The Government has set a per capita growth rate target of 4.8% and a 5.4% annual economic growth rate by 2006. The third tranche of the Economic Adjustment Loan (ECAL), negotiated with the World Bank, the African Development Bank and the EU in support of the five-year plan, was approved in 2001.

EXTERNAL TRADE

Tunisia's trade deficit grew steadily during the 1960s and 1970s. The deficit in 1987 totalled TD 738m., compared with TD 892m. in 1986 and TD 844m. in 1985. In 1988, as a result of severe drought and a plague of locusts, the cost of imports rose by 26.2% (with food imports up by 53% compared with 1987) and the trade deficit increased to TD 1,112m. (imports TD 3,167m., exports TD 2,055m.), despite a 16% rise in export revenues. The trade deficit for 1990 was TD 1,800m., which represented a 29% increase over the 1989 level. In 1991 the trade deficit narrowed to TD 1,372m., but it rose again in 1992, to TD 2,121.8m., primarily because of a rise in imports. According to World Bank estimates, the average annual growth rate of exports by value fell from 10.8% in 1965–80 to 4.8% in 1980–90, while the growth of imports showed a sharper decline, from 10.4% in 1965–80 to 1.1% in 1980–90. Exports in 1990 covered only 64% of imports, compared with 67% in 1989. The ratio of exports to imports has remained close to 60% for most of the period since 1960.

Petroleum and its derivatives were the main source of export earnings from the mid-1970s to the mid-1980s. However, the slump in petroleum prices in 1986 caused export earnings from petroleum to fall from TD 604m. in 1985 to TD 340m. in 1986. Petroleum was overtaken as the largest export, in terms of value, by textiles, worth TD 389m. in 1986, compared with TD 283m. in 1985. In 1987 petroleum prices recovered and Tunisian export earnings from petroleum accordingly increased to TD 418m., although they declined to TD 331m. in 1988. Exports of crude petroleum were worth a total of TD 506m. in 1989, TD 451m. in 1990, and TD 411m. in 1991. Meanwhile, exports of textiles continued to grow, earning TD 511m. in 1987, rising to TD 1,325m. in 1991. Other major exports include agricultural products (such as seafood, olive oil, dates, citrus fruits and vegetables), leather goods and phosphates.

Tunisia's main imports are machinery, raw cotton and cotton yarn, chemicals and related products, food and live animals, crude petroleum (grades not produced locally) and petroleum products, clothing and accessories, iron and steel, and cereals and cereal preparations. In 1986 imports of capital goods were worth TD 505m., while food imports cost TD 288m. Semi-finished products cost TD 557m. in 1986, and energy imports TD 199m., a substantial reduction from TD 308m. in 1985. In 1987 total imports rose slightly, to TD 2,509m., compared with TD 2,308m. in 1986. The value of total imports increased to TD 3,167m. in 1988, to TD 4,151m. in 1989, to TD 4,852m. in 1990 and to TD 4,789m. in 1991.

Under an agreement reached with the EC in January 1976, the import levy on Tunisian olive oil was abolished and tariffs on all other Tunisian agricultural products imported into EC countries were lowered. Nevertheless, Tunisia was disappointed with the way in which the agreement was implemented, in particular with delays in lifting restrictions on imports of olive oil. In June 1977 the EC quota of textiles and clothing imports was reduced. This measure severely affected the Tunisian textile and clothing industries, although Tunisia did not, in fact, fulfil its EC quotas in 1978, as a result of a two-month strike in the industry early in the year. Nevertheless, negotiations on this issue continued into 1979, and in March Tunisia signed an agreement, under pressure from the EC, to limit its textile exports to EC countries in 1979 and 1980. In return, Tunisia sought a five-year freeze on its obligations to eliminate tariff barriers relating to goods imported from the EC. Tunisia registered its anxiety about the possible consequences of the entry of Spain and Portugal into the EC in January 1986, as the two countries are Tunisia's main agricultural competitors. In mid-

1985 the European Commission announced a plan to guarantee Tunisian exports to the EC at levels prevailing in the early 1980s. In December 1990 Tunisia was one of the states to benefit from a new 'horizontal' trade and co-operation agreement between the EC and Mediterranean non-Community countries. In September 1990 Tunisia had become a contracting party to the General Agreement on Tariffs and Trade (GATT), in a move designed to increase exports to foreign markets.

In 1995 Tunisia exported goods to the value of US $5,474.6m. (19.4% up on the 1994 total) and imported goods to the value of $7,903.1m. (21.9% more than in 1994), leaving a visible trade deficit of $2,428.5m. (27.9% higher than in 1994). The 1995 import total was boosted by increased imports of foodstuffs (primarily as a result of Tunisia's continuing drought), chemicals and related products, and basic manufactures. The export total was improved by substantial increases in earnings from machinery and transport equipment, clothing and accessories, and chemicals and related products, which rose by 31.2%, 26.2% and 23.4%, respectively, compared to 1994. Exports of agricultural products declined markedly. The sectoral shares of 1995 export earnings were textiles and leather 47.5%; chemicals and related products 11.9%; machinery and transport equipment 9.4%; agriculture and food products 8.7%; and minerals, fuels and lubricants 8.5%. Of Tunisia's three largest trading partners, France had a surplus of $488.2m. in 1995 (exports to Tunisia $2,024.6m., imports from Tunisia $1,536.4m.); Italy had a surplus of $187.6m. (exports $1,209.0m., imports $1,021.4m.); and Germany had a surplus of $132.7m. (exports $993.7m., imports $861.0m.). Overall, the EU supplied 71.5% of Tunisian imports and bought 79.0% of Tunisian exports in 1995. Trade grew strongly in 1997, with total imports rising from TD 7,543m. in 1996 to TD 8,756m. (an increase of 16.1%), while exports increased from TD 5,372m. to TD 6,148m., (a rise of 14.4%). In July 1997 the Government abolished its 5% export duty and doubled the term of export licences to two years in order to stimulate exports. The Conseil supérieur de l'exportation was created, chaired by President Ben Ali, who stated that it was essential to reduce bureaucratic constraints on exporters. Exports were forecast to rise by an average of 13% a year to total TD 8,803m. ($7,707m.) by 2001, with textiles and leather, together with chemical and phosphate exports, increasing their share of the total and energy exports continuing to decline. Exports rose to TD 6,532m. in 1998, with imports rising to TD 9,476m. Consequently, the trade deficit widened to TD 2,944m., a rise of nearly 13% over 1997. Imports of capital goods and raw materials for the textiles industry increased significantly. Export growth was largely the result of increased sales of manufactured goods, notably textiles, but also of electrical and mechanical goods, together with shoes and leather. Exports rose to TD 6,967m. in 1999 and imports to TD 10,061m., resulting in a further widening of the trade deficit, to TD 3,094m. Exports from the food processing and mechanical goods industries expanded significantly, while in contrast textile exports grew very slowly. There was a sharp increase in energy and equipment imports, but imports of foodstuffs fell as a result of the good harvest. Exports in 2000 increased to TD 8,005m. and imports to TD 11,728m. resulting in a trade deficit of TD 3,723m., nearly 20% higher than 1999. According to the IMF, total exports as a share of GDP rose from 28.5% in 1990 to 33% in 2001, in which year the value of exports increased by 18.7% to TD 9,503.7m. and the value of imports by 16.4% to TD 13,658.3m., resulting in a trade deficit of TD 4,154.6m. (equivalent to 11.8% of GDP). Exports from the textile sector and the mechanical engineering and electrical industries recorded significant growth. The import value increase was the result of a 25% rise in consumer goods, a 19.5% rise in raw materials and semi-finished products, and a 7.2% increase in capital goods. In July 1995 Tunisia signed a free-trade agreement with the EU, scheduled to take effect from the start of 1996. Its main provisions were as follows. EU capital goods and semi-finished goods not manufactured in Tunisia (accounting for 12% of Tunisia's imports from the EU at that time) would be exempt from import duty from the date the agreement entered into force. EU exports of specified goods that were also manufactured in Tunisia (accounting for 28% of Tunisian imports from the EU) would be subject to the progressive elimination of import duties over a period of five years after entry into force. Duties on EU

exports of goods that were deemed to be 'more sensitive' in the Tunisian economic context (accounting for 30% of Tunisian imports from the EU) would be phased out over a period of 12 years. Duties on EU exports of goods that were deemed to be 'most sensitive' (29.5% of Tunisian imports from the EU at that time) would be maintained for the first five years of the agreement before being phased out over a seven-year period. Duties on traditional handicraft and textile products (constituting 0.5% of Tunisian imports from the EU) would not be phased out under the agreement. During the 12-year transition period following the agreement's entry into force, Tunisia would have the option of reimposing import duties of up to 25% on EU exports that were considered to threaten emerging industries in Tunisia, provided that such duties did not affect more than 15% of all imports from the EU and were not maintained for more than five years. Tunisia (which already had duty-free access to the EU market for industrial goods) would benefit from a limited relaxation of EU quota and tariff restrictions on some agricultural exports, although olive oil exports to the EU remained subject to existing restrictions. In January 2000 negotiations began with the EU on the extension of free trade to agricultural products; an agreement on agricultural trade came into effect on 1 January 2001. The agreement raised the annual quota of olive oil exports that enter the EU duty free from 46,000 metric tons to 50,000 tons, with further annual increases to a maximum of 56,000 tons by 2005. Olive oil exports account for about one-half of all Tunisia's agricultural exports. It also fixed the quantities of other agricultural exports permitted to enter the EU duty free. The EU's quota for soft wheat exports to Tunisia was raised to 460,000 tons, and a quota for 100,000 tons of vegetable oil exports was also introduced. Earlier it was reported that the Government called for EU financial support for an agricultural modernization programme similar to the 'mise à niveau' programme in place for the industrial and services sectors.

The Tunisian Government expected that investment of around TD 2,200m. (60% for the restructuring and modernization of businesses and 40% for infrastructural development and other initiatives to improve the business environment) would be required during the first five years of exposure to increased competition. Detailed preparatory studies had indicated that about one-third of Tunisian industrial companies were likely to be put out of business by the new trade measures, while a further third would find the transition difficult. Under the agreement, the EU pledged to provide financial assistance to help the Tunisian economy adjust to growing competition from EU member states, including support for the Government's industrial restructuring programme (see Industry), training and the promotion of the private sector. The EU was to provide ECU 330m. (US $300m.) in loans over the period 1996–99, and by early 1998 it was reported that some ECU 250m. had already been allocated. It took more than two and a half years for all 15 EU member states to ratify the free-trade agreement, which did not come into force formally until March 1998. However, Tunisia began implementing the agreement from 1 January 1996, when import duties on EU capital goods were abolished. In January 2000 tariffs were removed on the first group of European manufactured goods also produced in Tunisia, exposing Tunisian manufacturing industries to increased competition. Some 40% of imports of EU industrial goods entered Tunisia without duties. It was estimated that Tunisia would incur a revenue shortfall of some $1,500m. between 1997 and 2001 as a result of the removal of tariff barriers. By the end of 1998 EU loans to Tunisia under the terms of the free-trade agreement totalled ECU 380m. with a further ECU 200m. in loans from the EIB having been disbursed. Tariff reduction moved ahead broadly as scheduled in 2001, decreasing to 28.3% from 35.9% in 2000.

Free-trade agreements were signed with Jordan and Egypt in 1998 and with Morocco in 1999, in the hope of increasing bilateral trade. Trade with Libya has increased in recent years, but represents only a tiny fraction of Tunisia's local external trade.

In 2002 Tunisia signed trade co-operation agreements with Iran, Egypt, Portugal and Morocco. The agreement with Morocco aims to increase the value of bilateral trade to $500m. annually.

Exchanges stood at $151.8m. in 2001, as against $122m. in 2000).

TOURISM

During 1961–72 total tourist arrivals grew at a rate of 30% annually. Tourism was the nation's principal source of foreign currency from 1968 to 1976 (when it was overtaken by petroleum). In the 1980s the number of annual tourist arrivals fluctuated wildly, owing to the effects of recession in Western European countries on the whole Mediterranean tourist industry. Tunisia has experienced difficulties in competing with other holiday destinations, such as Greece, Spain and Morocco, and foreign tourists have been deterred from visiting Tunisia by terrorist incidents and the bombing of Libya by the USA in 1986. The number of foreign visitors totalled 3.3m. in 1989 and 3.2m. in 1990. Tourist arrivals increased steadily thereafter, to 3.9m. in 1994, and 4.1m. in 1995. Although the number of tourist arrivals fell slightly, to 3.9m., in 1996, numbers increased to 4.3m. in 1997, mainly as a result of a rise in arrivals from Europe, and reached 4.72m. in 1998. Almost two-thirds of tourists came from Europe, and the remainder from other Maghreb countries. Germany is the main country of origin of tourists, followed by France, Italy and the United Kingdom. There are four main centres for tourists: Hammamet, Sousse, Djerba and Tunis. A major tourist development was built along the coast north of Sousse, and in 1998 work began on the Marina Hammamet-Sud, a new development including a 740-berth marina, hotels and commercial buildings. The BNDT promotes and finances three types of ventures: construction of new hotels; modernization of existing hotels; and other activities related to tourism, such as transport, housing and real estate. The substantial devaluation of the dinar in mid-1986 enabled the Tunisian tourist industry to compete with Mediterranean rivals. In November 1987 the Government announced a series of incentives to encourage the development of tourism in the Sahara, with the aim of attracting tourists, who generally arrive in the summer to stay at the seaside resorts, to Tunisia throughout the year. However, Saharan tourism did not grow as rapidly as expected, with tourists continuing to choose coastal resorts and making only short excursions into the Sahara. As a result, by 1997 hotels in the Saharan region had accumulated debts of TD 35m. (US $30m.). In January 1998 President Ben Ali announced a number of measures to expand tourism in the area, including the rescheduling of hotel debts and an increase in direct air connections from European cities to the regional capital, Tozeur. The 1987–91 Development Plan envisaged that tourism would overtake petroleum as the principal source of foreign exchange, providing Tunisia with an average of TD 600m. per year. In 1988 receipts from tourism amounted to about $1,300m. In 1989 receipts from tourism totalled $951m.; arrivals in 1990 declined slightly and tourist receipts in that year were $900m. Receipts from tourism were estimated at TD 950m. ($1,037m.) in 1992, up from $770m. in the previous year, and reached TD 1,114m. ($1,092m.) in 1993. In 1994 the tourism sector grew by 5.1% and accounted for one-half of all new jobs created in that year. Tourism receipts in 1994 amounted to TD 1,317m. ($1,404m.). In 1995 tourist arrivals rose by 7%, while estimated earnings from tourism increased to TD 1,323m. Tourist revenues grew from TD 1,413m. in 1996 to TD 1,540m. in 1997, an increase of 9%, and to TD 1,710m. in 1998, a rise of 10.3%. The Ministry of Tourism began implementing its own five-year plan in 1998 to improve the training of employees in the tourism sector. During 1999 the Office national du tourisme tunisien began promoting Tunisian tourism using the slogan 'quality and variety', in an attempt to attract wealthier tourists to the Saharan resorts. Tourism revenues continued to grow, reaching TD 1,710m. in 1998 and TD 1,950m. in 1999. The number of foreign tourist arrivals grew to 4.8m. in 1999 (of which almost three-quarters were from Europe) and there was a sharp increase in the number of tourist nights, to 35.3m. However, revenue per tourist was low at $340, compared with $468 for Morocco and $850 for Egypt. In 1999 tourism contributed 6.2% of GDP and provided 16% of the country's foreign exchange earnings. The tourism sector was reported to employ 70,000 people and provide indirect employment to some 200,000. Tourism revenues rose to TD 2,100m. in 2000 when some 5.2m. tourists visited the country, a rise of some 7% on the previous year. Despite a sharp decline in the fourth quarter, receipts increased to TD 2.400m. in 2001 with 5.4m. tourist arrivals.

FOREIGN AID

The principal sources of economic aid for Tunisia continue to be Western countries and international institutions. The World Bank Group has been the most important multilateral donor, providing loans and credits for investment in a variety of projects. The African Development Bank is another large multilateral donor. Tunisia's largest bilateral donor is France, which provides annual packages of mixed credits. In August 1989 an agreement was signed, under the terms of which France agreed to extend to Tunisia three new credit lines and a grant totalling 1,060m. French francs. In August 1990 Tunisia and France renewed the financial agreement, which comprised a loan of 1,000m. French francs. Protocols signed with France in late 1993 granted Tunisia a total of more than 900m. French francs. One of the agreements, signed in November, granted 277m. French francs for exceptional balance of payments aid. Other important bilateral donors are the USA and the Gulf Arab states, although these countries have reduced lending, owing to recent budgetary constraints. In February 1991 the US Government announced its decision to reduce sharply its aid to Tunisia, owing to the country's muted support for Iraq during the Gulf crisis (1990–91). In recent years Japan has extended substantial credit to Tunisia for the purchase of Japanese goods and services. Tunisia's receipts of official development aid rose from US $178m. in 1984 to $316m. in 1988, $283m. in 1989, $393m. in 1990 and $322m. (2.5% of GNP) in 1991. Germany agreed to provide Tunisia with $33.4m. of development aid in 1994. During the second half of the 1990s Tunisia continued to obtain substantial external funds, principally from the World Bank, the EU and OECD countries. The Ministry of International Co-operation and Foreign Investment reported that 38 financial agreements had been signed in 1998, resulting in TD 1,100m. ($965m.) in foreign aid and loans. The major source of assistance was the World Bank, which is providing some $250m. each year. In 2001 agreements were reached for TD 1,150m. in bilateral and multilateral foreign loans and grants, compared with TD 1,350m. in 2000 and TD 811m. in 1999.

Tunisia's total foreign debt increased from US $3,526m. in 1980 to $8,475m. in 1992. As a proportion of total exports of goods and services, the cost of debt-servicing rose correspondingly, from 14.8% to 20.6%. During the period of the 1982–86 Development Plan, Tunisia's total debt increased rapidly, owing partly to the appreciation of the US dollar in the early 1980s. As a proportion of Tunisia's GNP, the country's total external debt increased from 41.6% in 1980 to 73.9% in 1987. In 1991 the ratio stood at 66.2%. At the end of 1995 Tunisia's external debt was $10,820m., while the cost of debt-servicing was equivalent to 16.9% of the value of exports of goods and services. Total foreign debt increased to $11,379m. in 1996. Most of it was public or publicly guaranteed medium- to long-term debt. Debt-service payments totalled $1,466m. in 1996 when the debt-service ratio stood at 16.4%.

After a decline in 1998, to $10,850m., in 1999 total foreign debt had risen to $11,872m., of which $9,487m. was long-term public debt. The debt-servicing ratio was 15.9% in 1999, up from 15.4% in 1998. Under the terms of the 2000 budget, external borrowing was set at TD 1,500m., compared with TD 1,117m. in 1999 and TD 977m. in 1998. In 2000 total foreign debt was $11,500m. and the debt servicing ratio was 22.6%. According to the IMF, total external debt rose to 60.2 % of GDP from 59.6% of GDP in 1999. Foreign exchange reserves rose to TD 2,810m. at the end of 2001.

Statistical Survey

Source (unless otherwise stated): Institut National de la Statistique, Ministère du Développement Economique, 70 rue ach-Cham, 1002 Tunis; tel. (1) 891-002; fax (1) 792-559; e-mail INS@e-mail.ati.tn; internet www.ins.nat.tn.

Area and Population

AREA, POPULATION AND DENSITY

Area (sq km)	
Land	154,530
Inland waters	9,080
Total	163,610*
Population (census results)	
30 March 1984	6,966,173
20 April 1994	
Males	4,447,341
Females	4,338,023
Total	8,785,364
Population (official estimates at mid-year)	
1999	9,455,900
2000	9,563,500
2001	9,673,300
Density (per sq km) at mid-2001	59.1

* 63,170 sq miles.

GOVERNORATES (population at 1 July 2001)

	Area (sq. km)	Population	Density (per sq km)
Tunis	346	932,500	2,695.1
Ariana	498	373,400	749.8
Ben Arous	761	456,700	600.1
Manouba	1,060	321,100	302.9
Nabeul	2,788	641,200	230.0
Zaghouan	2,768	155,600	56.2
Bizerte	3,685	523,200	142.0
Béja	3,558	318,800	89.6
Jendouba	3,102	427,700	137.9
Le Kef	4,965	281,200	56.6
Siliana	4,631	256,700	55.4
Kairouan	6,712	567,500	84.6
Kasserine	8,066	420,700	52.2
Sidi Bouzid . . .	6,994	401,400	57.4
Sousse	2,621	501,100	191.2
Monastir	1,019	421,100	413.2
Mahdia	2,966	371,400	125.2
Sfax	7,545	820,100	108.7
Gafsa	8,990	330,500	36.8
Tozeur	4,719	97,400	20.6
Kébili	22,084	142,800	6.5
Gabés	7,175	335,000	46.7
Médenine	8,588	427,100	49.7
Tataouine	38,889	149,000	3.8
Total	163,610	9,673,300	59.1

PRINCIPAL COMMUNES (population at 1994 census)

Tunis (capital) . . .	674,100	Kairouan (Qairawan) .	102,600
Sfax (Safaqis) . . .	230,900	Gabés	98,900
Ariana	152,700	Bizerta (Bizerte) . .	98,900
Ettadhamen . . .	149,200	Bardo	72,700
Sousse	125,000	Gafsa	71,100

Mid-2001 (UN estimate, incl. suburbs): Tunis 1,927,000 (Source: UN, *World Urbanization Prospects: The 2001 Revision*).

BIRTHS, MARRIAGES AND DEATHS*

	Registered live births		Registered marriages		Registered deaths	
	Number	Rate (per 1,000)	Number	Rate (per 1,000)	Number	Rate (per 1,000)
1990 . .	205,345	25.4	55,612	6.8	45,700	5.6
1991 . .	207,455	25.2	59,010	7.1	46,500	5.6
1992 . .	211,649	25.2	64,700	7.6	46,300	5.5
1993 . .	207,786	24.1	54,120	6.3	49,400	5.7
1994 . .	200,223	22.7	52,431	5.9	50,300	5.7
1995 . .	186,416	20.8	53,726	6.0	52,000	5.8
1996 . .	178,801	19.7	56,349	6.2	40,817	5.5
1997 . .	173,757	18.9	57,861	6.3	42,426	5.6

Birth rate (per 1,000): 17.9 in 1998; 16.9 in 1999; 17.1 in 2000.
Death rate (per 1,000): 5.6 in 1998; 5.7 in 1999; 5.6 in 2000.

* Birth registration is reported to be 100% complete. Death registration is estimated to be about 73% complete. UN estimates for average annual death rates are: 8.5 per 1,000 in 1980–85, 7.3 per 1,000 in 1985–90, 6.4 per 1,000 in 1990–95. UN estimates for average annual birth rates are: 33.7 per 1,000 in 1980–85, 30.9 per 1,000 in 1985–90, 24.1 per 1,000 in 1990–95.

Expectation of life (WHO, estimates, years at birth, 2000): Males 69.2; Females 73.4 (Source: WHO, *World Health Report*).

EMPLOYMENT ('000 persons aged 15 years and over at 20 April 1994)

	Males	Females	Total
Agriculture, forestry and fishing .	393.7	107.3	501.0
Manufacturing	244.7	211.0	455.7
Electricity, gas and water* . .	34.4	2.4	36.8
Construction	302.6	3.2	305.8
Trade, restaurants and hotels† .	277.8	37.8	315.6
Community, social and personal services‡	503.9	163.2	667.1
Activities not adequately defined .	28.6	10.0	38.6
Total employed	1,785.7	534.9	2,320.6

* Including mining and quarrying.
† Including financing, insurance, real estate and business services.
‡ Including transport, storage and communications.

Mid-2000 (estimates in '000): Agriculture, etc. 942; Total labour force 3,826 (Source: FAO).

Health and Welfare

KEY INDICATORS

Fertility (births per woman, 2000)	2.2
Under-5 mortality rate (per 1,000 live births, 2000). . .	28
HIV/AIDS (% of persons aged 15–49, 1994). . . .	0.04
Physicians (per 1,000 head, 1997)	0.70
Hospital beds (per 1,000 head, 1997)	1.7
Health expenditure (1998): US $ per head (PPP) . . .	326
% of GDP . . .	5.3
public (% of total) . . .	41.3
Human Development Index (2000): ranking	97
value	0.722

For sources and definitions, see explanatory note on p. vi.

Agriculture

PRINCIPAL CROPS ('000 metric tons)

	1998	1999	2000
Wheat	1,354	1,390	850
Barley	303	420	240
Other cereals	11	9	5
Potatoes	295	320	295
Sugar beet	122	77	18
Broad beans (dry)	34	45	47*
Peas (dry)	3†	14*	14†
Chick-peas	12	9	8*
Almonds	59	58	60
Olives	950	1,125	1,000*
Sunflower seed	10*	10†	10†
Tomatoes	663	930	950
Artichokes	23	19	17
Spinach*	38	38	38
Chillies and green peppers	189	185	190
Dry onions	143	127	133*
Pumpkins, etc.†	50	50	50
Cucumbers and gherkins†	33	33	33
Green peas†	23	24	24
Green broad beans†	25	25	25
Carrots†	40	40	40
Watermelons	300*	350	360*
Grapes	114*	138	141*
Dates	103	103	104
Apples	83	97	108*
Pears	54	50	54*
Peaches and nectarines	65	70	73*
Oranges	122	105	115*
Tangerines, mandarins, clementines and satsumas	40	38	38†
Lemons and limes	15	17	17†
Grapefruit and pomelos†	50	50	50
Apricots	27	30	30*

* Unofficial figure(s).   † FAO estimate(s).

Source: FAO.

LIVESTOCK (FAO estimates, '000 head, year ending September)

	1998	1999	2000
Horses	56	56	56
Mules	81	81	81
Asses	230	230	230
Cattle	770	780	790
Camels	231	231	231
Sheep	6,600	6,600	6,600
Goats	1,300	1,350	1,400
Chickens	36,000	38,000	43,000
Turkeys	2,400	2,800	2,900

Source: FAO.

LIVESTOCK PRODUCTS ('000 metric tons)

	1998	1999	2000
Beef and veal	53	58	60
Mutton and lamb	50	53	54
Poultry meat	90	104	115
Cows' milk	740	817	908
Sheep's milk	17	17*	17*
Goats' milk	12	12*	12*
Hen eggs*	75	80	80
Wool: greasy*	9	9	9
scoured*	6	6	6
Cattle hides	5	5	5
Sheepskins	8	8	8

* FAO estimate(s).

Source: FAO.

Forestry

ROUNDWOOD REMOVALS (FAO estimates, '000 cu m, excl. bark)

	1998	1999	2000
Sawlogs, veneer logs and logs for sleepers	21	21	21
Pulpwood	75	75	75
Other industrial wood	117	118	118
Fuel wood	2,066	2,080	2,094
Total	2,279	2,294	2,308

Source: FAO, *Yearbook of Forest Products*.

SAWNWOOD PRODUCTION (FAO estimates, '000 cu m, incl. sleepers)

	1998	1999	2000
Coniferous (softwood)	7	7	7
Broadleaved (hardwood)	14	14	14
Total	20	20	20

Source: FAO, *Yearbook of Forest Products*.

Fishing

('000 metric tons, live weight)

	1997	1998	1999
Common pandora	2.5	3.0	3.1
Sargo breams	3.2	2.1	3.0
Bogue	2.2	2.5	3.9
Jack and horse mackerels	6.3	3.9	5.6
Sardinellas	8.1	6.3	7.5
European pilchard	10.8	8.9	13.4
Chub mackerel	4.1	3.2	3.5
Caramote prawn	4.4	3.8	4.7
Common cuttlefish	6.5	4.9	6.6
Common octopus	5.7	3.1	2.3
Total catch (incl. others)	87.0	88.1	92.1

Source: FAO, *Yearbook of Fishery Statistics*.

Mining

('000 metric tons, unless otherwise indicated)

	1998	1999	2000
Crude petroleum ('000 barrels)	30,570	30,960	28,207
Natural gas (million cu m)	1,899	1,819	2,220
Iron ore: gross weight	220	219	182
metal content	119	119	98
Lead concentrates (metric tons)†	4,272	6,589	6,602
Zinc concentrates (metric tons)†	31,368	49,066	41,247
Phosphate rock‡	7,901	8,006	8,339
Barite (Barytes) (metric tons)	8,011	530	3,702
Salt (marine)	473	447	481
Gypsum (crude)*	100	100	100

* Estimated production.

† Figures refer to metal content of concentrates.

‡ Figures refer to gross weight. The estimated phosphoric acid content (in '000 metric tons) was: 2,370 in 1998; 2,400 in 1999; 2,500 in 2000.

Source: US Geological Survey.

Industry

SELECTED PRODUCTS ('000 metric tons, unless otherwise indicated)

	1997	1998	1999
Superphosphates.	349	362	384
Phosphoric acid	604	629	905
Cement .	4,378	4,588	4,864
Electric power (million kWh)	8,389	8,958	n.a.
Beer ('000 hl)	780	813	911.9
Cigarettes (million units) .	7,735	9,813	11,066
Wine ('000 hl)	372	352	469
Olive oil .	96	200	180
Flour	697	708	721.3
Refined sugar	75	101	123.5
Crude steel .	195	171	231
Quicklime	471	483	475
Motor gasoline	362	294*	n.a.
Kerosene	119	127*	n.a.
Diesel oil	571	560*	n.a.
Residual fuel oil .	646	635*	n.a.

Source: partly UN, *Industrial Commodity Statistics, Yearbook.*

2000 ('000 metric tons, unless otherwise indicated): Cement 5,647.3; Beer ('000 hl) 1,065.7; Wine ('000 hl) 413.3; Olive oil 225; Flour 745.5; Refined sugar 103.2.
2001 ('000 metric tons, unless otherwise indicated): Cement 5,720.4; Beer ('000 hl) 1,087.2; Wine ('000 hl) 336.0; Olive oil 115; Flour 755.6; Refined sugar 102.2.
* Estimate.

Finance

CURRENCY AND EXCHANGE RATES

Monetary Units
1,000 millimes = 1 Tunisian dinar (TD).

Sterling, Dollar and Euro Equivalents (31 May 2002)
£1 sterling = 2.101;
US $1 = 1.432 dinars;
€1 = 1.345 dinars;
100 Tunisian dinars = £47.60 = $69.81 = €74.37.

Average Exchange Rate (dinars per US $)
1999   1.1862
2000   1.3707
2001   1.4387

BUDGET (million dinars)*

Revenue†	1997	1998	1999
Taxation	5,224	5,884	6,427
Taxes on income, profits, etc.	1,113	1,294	1,387
Social security contributions	993	1,114	1,220
Taxes on payroll or work-force	78	69	79
Taxes on property	78	83	98
Domestic taxes on goods and services	2,112	2,438	2,733
Value-added tax .	1,170	1,443	1,625
Excises .	722	775	858
Taxes on international trade	736	751	731
Import duties	717	742	723
Export duties	11	9	9
Other current revenue	702	691	750
Capital revenue	7	5	6
Total	5,933	6,579	7,183

Expenditure‡	1997	1998	1999
General public services	474	549	659
Defence	379	411	424
Public order and safety	548	584	624
Education	1,192	1,263	1,395
Health	437	465	491
Social security and welfare	1,030	1,170	1,327
Housing and infrastructure	237	264	287
Recreational, cultural and religious affairs and services	166	182	207
Economic affairs and services .	1,029	1,092	1,151
Agriculture, forestry and fishing	394	418	474
Transport and telecommunications	110	111	184
Other purposes	1,126	1,135	1,302
Total	6,618	7,115	7,866
Current .	5,283	5,644	6,153
Capital .	1,335	1,471	1,713

* Figures refer to the consolidated accounts of the central Government, including administrative agencies and social security funds. The data exclude the operations of economic and social agencies with their own budgets.
† Excluding grants from abroad (million dinars): 66 in 1997; 89 in 1998; 83 in 1999. Also excluded are receipts from privatization (million dinars): 3 in 1997; 418 in 1998; 1 in 1999.
‡ Excluding net lending (million dinars): 186 in 1997; 108 in 1998.
Source: IMF, *Tunisia: Statistical Appendix* (February 2001).

State Budget (million dinars): *Revenue:* 6,872.5 in 2000; 7,105.4 (estimate) in 2001; 7,561.0 (projection) in 2002. *Expenditure:* 7,524.2 in 2000; 8,025.5 (estimate) in 2001; 8,261.0 (projection) in 2002.

CENTRAL BANK RESERVES (US $ million at 31 December)

	1999	2000	2001
Gold*	3.5	3.2	3.0
IMF special drawing rights	26.5	3.9	1.7
Reserve position in IMF .	27.7	26.3	25.3
Foreign exchange	2,207.3	1,780.9	1,962.2
Total	2,265.0	1,814.2	1,992.2

* National valuation.
Source: IMF, *International Financial Statistics.*

MONEY SUPPLY (million dinars at 31 December)

	1999	2000	2001
Currency outside banks	1,994	2,229	2,376
Demand deposits at commercial banks .	3,435	3,779	4,169
Total money (incl. others)	5,794	6,369	6,926

Source: IMF, *International Financial Statistics.*

COST OF LIVING (Consumer Price Index; base: 1990 = 100)

	1999	2000	2001
Food	150.0	156.7	159.4
Housing	140.7	144.5	148.5
Clothing	163.4	164.7	167.5
Transport	147.3	150.0	153.4
All items (incl. others)	150.8	155.2	158.2

NATIONAL ACCOUNTS (million dinars at current prices)

Expenditure on the Gross Domestic Product

	1999	2000	2001
Government final consumption expenditure	3,836	4,165	4,527
Private final consumption expenditure	14,900	16,181	17,476
Increase in stocks	210	260	403
Gross fixed capital formation . .	6,278	7,020	7,510
Total domestic expenditure .	25,224	27,626	29,915
Exports of goods and services . .	10,501	11,784	13,686
Less Imports of goods and services	11,052	12,725	14,843
GDP in purchasers' values . .	24,672	26,685	28,759
GDP at constant 1990 prices .	16,415	17,181	18,029

Source: IMF, *International Financial Statistics.*

Gross Domestic Product by Economic Activity

	1999	2000*	2001*
Agriculture and fishing . . .	3,210.4	3,297.5	3,347.0
Mining (excluding hydrocarbons) .	209.7	234.4	220.1
Manufacturing (excluding hydrocarbons) . . .	4,469.6	4,847.5	5,325.6
Hydrocarbons, electricity and water	1,161.9	1,287.5	1,351.9
Construction and public works .	1,121.0	1,252.4	1,391.2
Transport and telecommunications	1,906.0	2,138.3	2,390.7
Trade, finance, etc.	5,139.9	5,610.0	6,071.4
Hotels and restaurants . . .	1,540.1	1,632.4	1,713.0
Non-market services . . .	3,335.0	3,593.4	3,913.5
Sub-total	22,094.4†	23,893.7†	25,724.4
Less Imputed bank service charges	722.2	793.9	862.6
GDP at factor cost . . .	21,372.2	23,099.8	24,861.8
Indirect taxes, *less* subsidies . .	3,299.3	3,585.5	3,931.3
GDP in purchasers' values . .	24,671.6	26,685.3	28,793.1

* Provisional figures.   † Including adjustment.

BALANCE OF PAYMENTS (US $ million)

	1998	1999	2000
Exports of goods f.o.b. . . .	5,724	5,873	5,840
Imports of goods f.o.b. . . .	−7,875	−8,014	−8,092
Trade balance	−2,152	−2,141	−2,252
Exports of services . . .	2,757	2,920	2,767
Imports of services . . .	−1,257	−1,234	−1,219
Balance on goods and services .	−651	−455	−704
Other income received . .	90	89	94
Other income paid . . .	−947	−978	−1,036
Balance on goods, services and income	−1,507	−1,344	−1,646
Current transfers received . .	852	920	854
Current transfers paid . . .	−20	−18	−29
Current balance . . .	−675	−442	−821
Capital account (net) . . .	61	59	3
Direct investment abroad. . .	1	−3	−1
Direct investment from abroad .	650	350	752
Portfolio investment liabilities .	33	10	−20
Other investment assets . . .	−508	−228	−624
Other investment liabilities . .	313	954	541
Net errors and omissions . . .	−12	38	−34
Overall balance . . .	−138	738	−205

Source: IMF, *International Financial Statistics.*

External Trade

PRINCIPAL COMMODITIES (distribution by SITC, US $ million)

Imports c.i.f.	1997	1998	1999
Food and live animals . . .	672.8	646.4	506.1
Cereals and cereal preparations .	324.1	303.4	240.2
Crude materials (inedible) except fuels	400.7	374.8	351.1
Mineral fuels, lubricants, etc. .	634.9	436.7	559.2
Petroleum, petroleum products, etc.	512.3	359.6	443.4
Refined petroleum products . .	361.6	261.4	286.2
Chemicals and related products	663.8	710.8	673.6
Basic manufactures . . .	2,152.9	2,474.0	2,296.5
Textile yarn, fabrics, etc. . .	1,245.3	1,440.9	1,330.8
Woven cotton fabrics* . .	575.5	666.5	605.8
Bleached and mercerized fabrics*	539.3	634.6	574.1
Woven fabrics of man-made fibres*	339.2	410.4	379.0
Iron and steel	258.2	318.3	270.5
Machinery and transport equipment	2,349.2	2,554.9	2,848.5
Machinery specialized for particular industries . .	368.3	458.3	456.5
General industrial machinery, equipment and parts . .	388.4	443.6	406.6
Electrical machinery, apparatus, etc.	598.5	693.3	633.3
Road vehicles and parts† . .	526.4	527.2	612.3
Passenger motor cars (excl. buses)	284.2	254.2	323.2
Other transport equipment† . .	165.2	122.5	445.5
Aircraft and associated equipment	3.5	90.4	252.6
Miscellaneous manufactured articles	879.5	932.2	908.3
Clothing and accessories (excl. footwear)	492.5	517.4	476.2
Total (incl. others)	7,947.0	8,347.3	8,336.9

* Excluding narrow or special fabrics.
† Excluding tyres, engines and electrical parts.

Exports f.o.b.	1997	1998	1999
Food and live animals . . .	253.0	277.5	250.4
Mineral fuels, lubricants, etc. .	504.6	369.3	414.6
Petroleum, petroleum products, etc.	503.8	369.1	414.6
Crude petroleum oils, etc. . .	376.2	282.1	380.9
Animal and vegetable oils, fats and waxes	268.1	199.6	341.5
Fixed vegetable oils and fats .	267.9	199.4	341.3
Olive oil	263.7	188.8	321.0
Chemicals and related products	694.5	723.1	673.1
Inorganic chemicals . . .	334.0	331.7	312.7
Inorganic chemical elements, oxides and halogen salts . .	256.1	246.6	230.7
Manufactured fertilizers . .	279.7	303.7	288.6
Basic manufactures . . .	517.5	568.1	582.6
Machinery and transport equipment	602.3	738.2	723.7
Electrical machinery, apparatus, etc.	475.8	601.4	585.7
Equipment for distributing electricity	215.3	257.8	252.0
Miscellaneous manufactured articles	2,527.9	2,708.2	2,639.7
Clothing and accessories (excl. footwear)	2,298.6	2,474.2	2,375.0
Total (incl. others)	5,559.4	5,737.9	5,788.0

Source: UN, *International Trade Statistics Yearbook.*

PRINCIPAL TRADING PARTNERS (million dinars)*

Imports c.i.f.	1999	2000	2001
Algeria	63.1	119.9	119.1
Belgium	382.6	402.5	478.6
China, People's Republic . .	103.4	138.2	187.8
France	2,694.1	3,088.1	3,544.7
Germany	1,122.0	1,126.3	1,322.6
Italy	1,856.4	2,243.4	2,620.3
Japan	251.1	239.3	254.6
Libya	281.4	437.7	466.0
Netherlands	218.4	244.7	251.2
Spain	417.2	468.4	624.1
Sweden	98.6	161.9	223.9
Switzerland	92.0	109.2	150.0
United Kingdom	210.2	283.6	343.1
USA	433.7	540.8	562.1
Total (incl. others)	10,070.5	11,738.0	13,658.3

Exports f.o.b.	1999	2000	2001
Algeria	50.0	84.3	109.0
Belgium	401.6	406.1	464.2
France	1,835.0	2,145.7	2,751.3
Germany	974.5	1,001.8	1,114.0
India	179.0	149.1	118.3
Italy	1,575.1	1,842.2	2,207.0
Libya	286.5	288.9	357.5
Netherlands	211.1	280.7	233.9
Spain	389.3	434.4	460.4
United Kingdom	121.4	175.7	226.3
Total (incl. others)	6,966.9	8,004.8	9,503.7

* Imports by country of production; exports by country of last destination.

Transport

RAILWAYS (traffic)

	1997	1998	1999
Passengers carried ('000) . .	31,303	32,194	34,406
Passenger-kilometres (million) .	1,094	1,130	1,200
Freight carried ('000 metric tons) .	12,388	12,619	12,548
Freight net ton-kilometres (million)	2,338	2,351	2,365

ROAD TRAFFIC (estimates, motor vehicles in use at 31 December)

	1997	1998	1999
Passenger cars	415,200	445,600	482,700
Commercial vehicles . . .	217,100	233,000	250,300

Source: UN, *Statistical Yearbook*.

SHIPPING

Merchant Fleet (vessels registered at 31 December)

	1999	2000	2001
Number of vessels . . .	79	78	77
Total displacement ('000 grt) .	199.5	208.3	202.7

Source: Lloyd's Register-Fairplay, *World Fleet Statistics*.

International Sea-borne Freight Traffic ('000 metric tons)

	1999	2000	2001
Goods loaded*	6,783	6,367	6,777
Goods unloaded	13,154	14,424	14,971

* Excluding Algerian crude petroleum loaded at La Skhirra.

CIVIL AVIATION (traffic on scheduled services)

	1996	1997	1998
Kilometres flown (million) . .	18	24	27
Passengers carried ('000) . .	1,371	1,779	1,888
Passenger-km (million) . .	2,118	2,479	2,683
Total ton-km (million) . .	212	249	266

Source: UN, *Statistical Yearbook*.

Tourism

FOREIGN TOURIST ARRIVALS BY NATIONALITY ('000)

	1999	2000	2001
Algeria	616.4	611.6	623.1
Austria	138.3	110.2	114.8
Belgium	132.4	139.8	150.7
France	893.7	997.9	1,047.4
Germany	1,036.3	1,011.3	934.7
Italy	354.6	393.9	398.3
Libya	603.1	685.2	1,016.6
Switzerland	110.2	118.4	114.2
United Kingdom	261.9	299.4	314.7
Total (incl. others)	4,813.7	5,057.2	5,387.3

Receipts from tourism (million dinars): 1,950 in 1999; 2,095.1 in 2000; 2,343.0 in 2001.

Communications Media

	1999	2000	2001
Television receivers ('000 in use) .	1,800	1,900	n.a.
Telephones ('000 main lines in use)	850.4	n.a.	15,056.2
Mobile cellular telephones ('000 subscribers)	55.3	n.a.	389.2
Personal computers ('000 in use) .	145	219	230
Internet users ('000)	30	100	400

Radio receivers ('000 in use): 2,060 in 1997.
Facsimile machines (number in use): 31,000 in 1997.
Daily newspapers: 8 (average circulation 280,000) in 1996.
Non-daily newspapers: 25 (estimated average circulation 900,000) in 1996.

Sources: UNESCO, *Statistical Yearbook*, UN, *Statistical Yearbook*, and International Telecommunication Union.

Education

	1999/2000	2000/01	2001/02
Institutions			
Primary	4,497	5,406	4,518
Secondary	1,301	1,323	1,356
Higher	101	114	128
Teachers			
Primary	60,912	60,706	60,556
Secondary	52,432	55,155	57,821
Pupils			
Primary	1,413,795	1,373,904	1,325,707
Secondary	965,607	1,015,996	1,074,391
Higher	180,044	207,388	225,102

Adult literacy rate (UNESCO estimates): 71.0% (males 81.4%; females 60.6%) in 2000 (Source: UNDP, *Human Development Report*).

Directory

The Constitution

A new Constitution for the Republic of Tunisia was promulgated on 1 June 1959 and amended on 12 July 1988; further amendments were approved by referendum on 26 May 2002. Its main provisions are summarized below:

NATIONAL ASSEMBLY

Legislative power is exercised by the National Assembly, which is elected (at the same time as the President) every five years by direct universal suffrage. Every citizen who has had Tunisian nationality for at least five years and who has attained 20 years of age has the right to vote. The National Assembly shall hold two sessions every year, each session lasting not more than three months. Additional meetings may be held at the demand of the President or of a majority of the deputies.

Note: The constitutional amendments approved in May 2002 envisaged the establishment of a second legislative chamber, the Chamber of Councillors.

HEAD OF STATE

The President of the Republic is both Head of State and Head of the Executive. He must be not less than 40 years of age and not more than 75 (not more than 70, prior to the May 2002 amendments). The President is elected by universal suffrage for a five-year term. The amendments approved in May 2002 removed restrictions on the renewal of the presidential mandate (previously, this was renewable twice consecutively). The President is also the Commander-in-Chief of the army and makes both civil and military appointments. The Government may be censured by the National Assembly, in which case the President may dismiss the Assembly and hold fresh elections. If censured by the new Assembly thus elected, the Government must resign. Should the presidency fall vacant for any reason before the end of a President's term of office, the President of the National Assembly shall take charge of affairs of the state for a period of 45 to 60 days. At the end of this period, a presidential election shall be organized. The President of the National Assembly shall not be eligible as a presidential candidate.

COUNCIL OF STATE

Comprises two judicial bodies: an administrative body dealing with legal disputes between individuals and state or public bodies, and an audit office to verify the accounts of the state and submit reports.

ECONOMIC AND SOCIAL COUNCIL

Deals with economic and social planning and studies projects submitted by the National Assembly. Members are grouped in seven categories representing various sections of the community.

The Government

HEAD OF STATE

President: ZINE AL-ABIDINE BEN ALI (took office on 7 November 1987; re-elected 2 April 1989, 20 March 1994 and 24 October 1999).

COUNCIL OF MINISTERS
(September 2002)

Prime Minister: MUHAMMAD GHANNOUCHI.

Minister of State, Special Adviser to the President: ABD AL-AZIZ BEN DHIA.

Minister of National Defence: DALI JAZI.

Minister of the Interior: HEDI M'HENNI.

Minister, Secretary-General of the Presidential Office: AHMAD IYADH OUEDERNI.

Minister of Justice: BÉCHIR TEKKARI.

Minister of Foreign Affairs: HABIB BEN YAHIA.

Minister of Religious Affairs: JALLOUL JERIBI.

Minister of International Co-operation and Foreign Investment: FETHI MERDASSI.

Minister of Finance: TAOUFIK BACCAR.

Minister of Economic Development: ABD AL-LATIF SADDAM.

Minister of Industry: MONCEF BEN ABDALLAH.

Minister of Trade: TAHAR SIOUD.

Minister of Agriculture: SADOK RABAH.

Minister of State Domains and Property Affairs: RIDHA GRIRA.

Minister of Equipment and Housing: SLAHEDDINE BELAÏD.

Minister of the Environment and Land Planning: MUHAMMAD NABLI.

Minister of Transport: HOUCINE CHOUK.

Minister of Tourism, Leisure and Handicrafts: MONDHER ZENAIDI.

Minister of Communications: AHMAD FRIAÂ.

Minister of Education: MONCER ROUISSI.

Minister of Higher Education: SADOK CHAÂBANE.

Minister of Culture: ABDELBAKI HERMASSI.

Minister of Public Health: HABIB M'BAREK.

Minister of Social Affairs: CHEDLI NEFFATI.

Minister of Professional Training and Employment: NÉZIHA ZARROUK.

Minister of Children, Youth and Sport: ABDERRAHIM ZOUARI.

Minister of Family and Women's Affairs: NÉZIHA BEN YEDDER.

Minister-delegate to the Prime Minister in charge of Human Rights, Communications and Relations with the National Assembly: FETHI HOUDI.

Minister delegate to the Prime Minister in charge of Scientific Research and Technology: ABD AL-KARIM ZBIDI.

Government Secretary-General: MUHAMMAD RACHID KECHICHE.

There are, in addition, 24 Secretaries of State.

MINISTRIES

Ministry of Agriculture: 30 rue Alain Savary, 1002 Tunis; tel. (71) 786-833; fax (71) 799-457; e-mail mag@ministeres.tn.

Ministry of Children and Youth: ave Muhammad Ali Akid, Cité Nationale Sportive, al-Menzah, 1004 Tunis; tel. (71) 841-433; fax (71) 789-047; e-mail mje@ministeres.tn.

Ministry of Communications: 3 bis rue d'Angleterre, 1000 Tunis; tel. (71) 359-000; fax (71) 352-353; e-mail mcom@ministeres.tn.

Ministry of Culture: 8 rue du 2 Mars 1934, la Kasbah, 1006 Tunis; tel. (71) 562-661; fax (71) 574-580; e-mail mcu@ministeres.tn.

Ministry of Economic Development: Place de la monnaie, 1000 Tunis; tel. (71) 351-515; fax (71) 787-234; e-mail mde@ministeres.tn.

Ministry of Education: ave Bab Benat, 1030 Tunis; tel. (71) 263-336; fax (71) 569-230; e-mail med@ministeres.tn.

Ministry of the Environment and Land Planning: Centre Urbain Nord, 2080 Ariana, Tunis; tel. (71) 704-000; fax (71) 702-431; e-mail meat@ministeres.tn.

Ministry of Equipment and Housing: 10 blvd Habib Chita, Cité Jardin, 1002 Tunis; tel. (71) 842-244; fax (71) 780-397; e-mail meh@ministeres.tn.

Ministry of Family and Women's Affairs: 2 rue d'Alger, 1000 Tunis; tel. (71) 332-781; fax (71) 349-900; e-mail maff@email.ati.tn.

Ministry of Finance: place du Gouvernement, 1008 Tunis; tel. (71) 571-888; fax (71) 963-959; e-mail mfi@ministeres.tn.

Ministry of Foreign Affairs: place du Gouvernement, la Kasbah, 1006 Tunis; tel. (71) 660-088; e-mail mae@ministeres.tn.

Ministry of Higher Education: ave Ouled Haffouz, 1030 Tunis; tel. (71) 786-300; fax (71) 786-711; e-mail mes@ministeres.tn.

Ministry of Industry: 37 ave Kheireddine Pacha, 1002 Tunis; tel. (71) 289-368; fax (71) 892-350; e-mail mind@ministeres.tn.

Ministry of the Interior: ave Habib Bourguiba, 1000 Tunis; tel. (71) 333-000; fax (71) 340-888; e-mail mint@ministeres.tn.

Ministry of International Co-operation and Foreign Investment: 98 ave Muhammad V, 1002 Tunis; tel. (71) 798-522; fax (71) 799-069; e-mail mciie@ministeres.tn.

Ministry of Justice: 31 ave Bab Benat, 1006 Tunis; tel. (71) 560-502; fax (71) 586-106; e-mail mju@ministeres.tn.

Ministry of National Defence: blvd Bab Menara, 1030 Tunis; tel. (71) 560-240; fax (71) 561-804; e-mail mdn@ministeres.tn.

Ministry of Professional Training and Employment: 10 ave Ouled Haffouz, 1005 Tunis; tel. (71) 790-838; fax (71) 794-615; e-mail mfpe@ministeres.tn.

Ministry of Public Health: Bab Saâdoun, 1006 Tunis; tel. (71) 560-545; fax (71) 567-100; e-mail msp@ministeres.tn.

Ministry of Religious Affairs: 176 ave Bab Benat, 1009 Tunis; tel. (71) 570-147; fax (71) 570-283; e-mail mar@ministeres.tn.

Ministry of Social Affairs: 25 ave Bab Benat, 1006 Tunis; tel. (71) 567-502; fax (71) 568-722; e-mail mas@ministeres.tn.

Ministry of State Domains: 19 ave de Paris, 1000 Tunis; tel. (71) 341-644; fax (71) 342-410; e-mail mdeaf@ministeres.tn.

Ministry of Tourism, Leisure and Handicrafts: 1 ave Muhammad V, 1001 Tunis; tel. (71) 341-077; fax (71) 332-070; e-mail info@tourismtunisia.com; internet www.tourismtunisia.com.

Ministry of Trade: 37 ave Kheireddine Pacha, 1002 Tunis; tel. (71) 892-313; fax (71) 792-420; e-mail mcmr@ministeres.tn.

Ministry of Transport: rue 8006 Montplaislir par l'ave Muhammad V, Tunis; tel. (71) 781-824; fax (71) 790-149; e-mail mtr@ministeres.tn.

President and Legislature

PRESIDENT

Presidential Election, 24 October 1999

Candidate	Votes	% of votes
Zine al-Abidine Ben Ali	3,269,067	99.45
Muhammad Belhadj Amor	10,492	0.32
Abderrahmane Tlili	7,662	0.23
Total*	3,287,221	100.00

* Excluding 8,779 invalid votes.

ASSEMBLÉE NATIONALE

President: Fouad Mebazaa.

Election, 24 October 1999

Party	Votes	%	Seats
Rassemblement constitutionnel démocratique	2,831,030	91.59	148
Mouvement des démocrates socialistes	98,550	3.19	13
Union démocratique unioniste . .	52,612	1.70	7
Parti de l'unité populaire . . .	52,054	1.68	7
Mouvement de la rénovation . . .	32,220	1.04	5
Parti social libéral	15,024	0.49	2
Rassemblement socialiste progressiste	5,835	0.19	0
Independents	3,737	0.12	0
Total*	3,091,062	100.00	182†

* Excluding 9,036 spoilt ballot papers.

† Under the terms of an amendment to the electoral code adopted by the National Assembly in 1998, 34 of the 182 seats in the National Assembly were reserved for candidates of opposition parties. These were allotted according to the proportion of votes received nationally by each party.

Political Organizations

Ettajdid (Renewal): Tunis; f. 1993; legal.

Congrès pour la République: Tunis; f. 2001; Leader MONCEF MAR-ZOUKI.

Mouvement des démocrates socialistes (MDS): Tunis; in favour of a pluralist political system; participated in 1981 election and was officially recognized in Nov. 1983; Political Bureau of 11 mems, National Council of 60 mems, normally elected by the party Congress; Sec.-Gen. ISMAIL BOULAHYA.

Mouvement de la rénovation (MR): 6 rue Metouia, 1000 Tunis; tel. (71) 256-400; fax (71) 240-981; f. 1993; Sec.-Gen. MUHAMMAD HARMEL.

Mouvement de l'unité populaire (MUP): Tunis; supports radical reform; split into two factions, one led by AHMAD BEN SALAH, living in exile until 1988; the other became the Parti de l'unité populaire (see below); Co-ordinator BRAHIM HAYDER.

Parti Démocratique Progressiste (PDP): Tunis; f. 1983 as Rassemblement socialiste progressiste, officially recognized in Sept. 1988; changed name as above in 2001; leftist; Sec.-Gen. NEJIB CHEBBI.

Parti de la renaissance—Hizb an-Nahdah: Tunis; formerly Mouvement de la tendance islamique (banned in 1981); Leader RACHED GHANOUCHI; Sec.-Gen. Sheikh ABD AL-FATHA MOUROU.

Parti des ouvriers communistes tunisiens (POCT): Tunis; illegal; Leader HAMMA HAMMANI.

Parti social libéral (PSL): 38 rue Gandhi, 1001 Tunis; tel. and fax (71) 341-093; f. 1988; officially recognized in Sept. 1988 as the Parti social pour le progrès; adopted present name in 1993; liberal; Pres. MOUNIR BEJI; Vice-Pres. HOSNI LAHMAR.

Parti de l'unité populaire (PUP): 7 rue d'Autriche, 1002 Tunis; tel. (71) 289-678; fax (71) 796-031; split from MUP (see above); officially recognized in Nov. 1983; Leader MUHAMMAD BOUCHIHA.

Rassemblement constitutionnel démocratique (RCD): blvd 9 avril 1938, Tunis; e-mail info@rcd.tn; internet www.rcd.tn; f. 1934 as the Néo-Destour Party, following a split in the Destour (Constitution) Party; renamed Parti socialiste destourien in 1964; adopted present name in Feb. 1988; moderate left-wing republican party, which achieved Tunisian independence; Political Bureau of nine mems, and a Cen. Cttee of 200, elected by the party Congress; Chair. ZINE AL-ABIDINE BEN ALI; Vice-Chair. HAMED KAROUI; Sec.-Gen. ALI CHAOUCH.

Rassemblement national arabe: Tunis; banned in 1981; Leader BASHIR ASSAD.

Union démocratique unioniste (UDU): Tunis; officially recognized in Nov. 1988; supports Arab unity; Sec.-Gen. ABDERRAHMANE TLILI.

Diplomatic Representation

EMBASSIES IN TUNISIA

Algeria: 18 rue de Niger, 1002 Tunis; tel. (71) 783-166; fax (71) 788-804; Ambassador: SMAÏL ALLAOUA.

Argentina: 10 rue al-Hassan et Houssaine, al-Menzah IV, 1002 Tunis; tel. (71) 231-222; fax (71) 750-058; e-mail fetune@mrecic.gov.ar; Ambassador: HÉCTOR TEJERINA.

Austria: 16 rue ibn Hamdiss, BP 23, al-Menzah, 1004 Tunis; tel. (71) 751-091; fax (71) 767-824; e-mail autriche@ambassade_autriche.intl.tn; Ambassador: Dr MAXIMILIAN PAMMER.

Bahrain: 72 rue Mouaouia ibn Soufiane, al-Menzah VI, Tunis; tel. (71) 750-865; Ambassador: JASSIM BUALLAY.

Belgium: 47 rue du 1er juin, BP 24, 1002 Tunis; tel. (71) 781-655; fax (71) 792-797; Ambassador: DANIEL LEROY.

Brazil: 37 ave d'Afrique, BP 64, al-Menzah V, 1004 Tunis; tel. (71) 232-538; fax (71) 750-367; Ambassador: LUIZ JORGE RANGEL DE CASTRO.

Bulgaria: 5 rue Ryhane, Cité Mahragène, 1082 Tunis; tel. (71) 798-962; fax (71) 791-667; Ambassador: TCHAVDAR TCHERVENKOV.

Canada: 3 rue du Sénégal, place d'Afrique, BP 31, Belvédère, 1002 Tunis; tel. (71) 796-577; fax (71) 792-371; Ambassador: JACQUES SIMARD.

China, People's Republic: 41 ave Jugurtha, Mutuelleville, Tunis; tel. (71) 282-090; Ambassador: ZHU BANGZAO.

Congo, Democratic Republic: 11 rue Tertullien, Notre Dame, Tunis; tel. (71) 281-833; Ambassador: MBOLADINGA KATAKO.

Côte d'Ivoire: 7 rue Fatma al-Fahria, BP 21, Belvédère, 1002 Tunis; tel. (71) 796-601; fax (71) 798-852; Ambassador: KOUASSI GUSTAVE OUFFOUÉ.

Cuba: 20 ave du Golfe Arabe, al-Menzah VIII, 1004 Tunis; tel. (71) 712-844; fax (71) 714-198; Ambassador: JORGE MANFUGAS-LAVIGNE.

Czech Republic: 98 rue de Palestine, BP 53, Belvédère, 1002 Tunis; tel. (71) 780-456; fax (71) 793-228.

Denmark: 5 rue de Mauritanie, BP 254, Belvédère, 1002 Tunis; tel. (71) 792-600; fax (71) 790-797; e-mail dannebrog@planet.tn; Ambassador: HERLUF HANSEN.

Djibouti: Tunis; Ambassador: ALI ABDOU MUHAMMAD.

Egypt: ave Muhammad V, Quartier Montplaisir, rue 8007, Tunis; tel. (71) 792-233; fax (71) 794-389; Ambassador: MAHDI FATHALLA.

France: 1 place de l'Indépendance, 1000 Tunis; tel. (71) 358-111; fax (71) 358-198; e-mail courrier@ambafrance-tn.org; Ambassador: YVES AUBIN DE LA MESSUZIÈRE.

Germany: 1 rue al-Hamra, Mutuelleville, BP 35, 1002 Tunis-Mutuelleville; tel. (71) 786-455; fax (71) 788-242; Ambassador: Dr CHRISTOPH DERIX.

Greece: 6 rue Saint Fulgence, Notre Dame, 1082 Tunis; tel. (71) 288-411; fax (71) 789-518; e-mail amb.grec@planet.tn; Ambassador: PETROS AVIERINOS.

Hungary: 12 rue Achtart, Nord Hilton, Tunis; tel. (71) 780-544; fax (71) 781-264; e-mail huembtun@planet.tn; Ambassador: Dr GYÖRGY SZATHMÀRY.

India: 4 place Didon, Notre Dame, Tunis; tel. (71) 787-819; fax (71) 783-394; e-mail india_emb@emb_india.intl.tn; Ambassador: RAM MOHAN.

Indonesia: BP 63, al-Menzah, 1004 Tunis; tel. (71) 860-377; fax (71) 861-758; e-mail ss.alink@kbritun.intl.tn; Ambassador: IS ISNAEDI.

Iran: 10 rue de Docteur Burnet, Belvédère, 1002 Tunis; tel. (71) 792-578; Ambassador: JAHAN BAKHSH MOZAFARI.

Iraq: ave Tahar B. Achour, route X2 m 10, Mutuelleville, Tunis; tel. (71) 890-633; Ambassador: Dr ISAM SHARIF.

Italy: 37 rue Gamal Abd an-Nasser, 1000 Tunis; tel. (71) 321-811; fax (71) 324-155; e-mail seg.ambit@email.ati.tn; Ambassador: ARMANDO SANGUINI.

Japan: 10 rue Mahmoud al-Matri, BP 95, Belvédère, 1002 Tunis; tel. (71) 285-937; fax (71) 786-625; Ambassador: YOSHIKAZU SUGITANI.

Jordan: 87 ave Jugurtha, Mutuelleville, Tunis; tel. (71) 288-401; Ambassador: NABIH AN-NIMR.

Korea, Republic: 16 rue Caracalla, Notre Dame, BP 297, 1082 Tunis; tel. (71) 799-905; fax (71) 791-923; Ambassador: CHOE IN-SOP.

Kuwait: 40 route Ariane, al-Menzah, Tunis; tel. (71) 236-811; Ambassador: MEJREN AHMAD AL-HAMAD.

Libya: 48 bis rue du 1er juin, Tunis; tel. (71) 236-666; Ambassador: ABD AL-ATTI OBEIDI.

Mauritania: 17 rue Fatma Ennechi, BP 62, al-Menzah, Tunis; tel. (71) 234-935; Ambassador: MOHAMED LAMINE OULD YAHYA.

Morocco: 39 ave du 1er juin, Tunis; tel. (71) 782-775; fax (71) 787-103; Ambassador: ABD AL-KADER BENSLIMANE.

Netherlands: 6–8 rue Meycen, Belvédère, BP 47, 1082 Tunis; tel. (71) 797-724; fax (71) 785-557; Ambassador: Baron BENTINCK VAN SCHOONHETEN.

Norway: 20 rue de la Kahéna, BP 9, 1082 Tunis; tel. (71) 802-158; fax (71) 801-944; e-mail noramb@planet.tn; Ambassador: WILLUM STEEN.

Pakistan: 7 rue Ali ibn Abi Talib, BP 42, al-Menzah VI, 1004 Tunis; tel. (71) 234-366; fax (71) 752-477; Ambassador: Vice-Adm. (rtd) SHAMOON ALAM KHAN.

Poland: 5 Impasse No. 1, rue de Cordoue, El Manar I, Tunis; tel. (71) 873-837; fax (71) 872-987; e-mail polamba.tunis@email.ati.tn; Ambassador: RAFAL KARPINSKI.

Portugal: 2 rue Sufétula, Belvédère, 1002 Tunis; tel. (71) 893-981; fax (71) 791-189; Ambassador: MANUEL MOREIRA DE ANDRADE.

Qatar: 2 Nahj al-Hakim Bourni, Belvédère, Tunis; tel. (71) 285-600; Chargé d'affaires: MAJID AL-ALI.

Romania: 18 ave d'Afrique, al-Menzah V, 1004 Tunis; tel. (71) 766-926; fax (71) 767-695; e-mail amb.roumanie@planet.tn; Chargé d'affaires a.i.: NICOLAE IORDACHE.

Russia: 4 rue Bergamotes, BP 48, 2092 el Manar I, Tunis; tel. (71) 882-446; fax (71) 882-478; e-mail russie@emb_rus.intl.tn; Ambassador: VENIAMIN V. POPOV.

Saudi Arabia: 16 rue d'Autriche, Belvédère, Tunis; tel. (71) 281-295; Ambassador: Sheikh ABBAS FAIK GHAZZAOUI.

Senegal: 122 ave de la Liberté, Tunis; tel. (71) 282-544; Ambassador: IBRA DEGUENE KA.

Somalia: 6 rue Hadramout, Mutuelleville, Tunis; tel. (71) 289-505; Ambassador: AHMAD ABDALLAH MUHAMMAD.

South Africa: 7 rue Achtart, Nord Hilton, 1082 Tunis; tel. (71) 800-311; fax (71) 796-742; e-mail sa@emb-safrica.intl.tn; internet www.southafrica.itnl.tn; Ambassador: AUBREY MASIZE J. MFABE.

Spain: 22-24 ave Dr Ernest Conseil, Cité Jardin, 1002 Tunis; tel. (71) 782-217; fax (71) 786-267; Ambassador: SENEN FLORENSA PALAU.

Sudan: 30 ave d'Afrique, Tunis; tel. (71) 238-544; fax (71) 750-884.

Sweden: Les Berges du Lac, Lot 12-01-03, Tunis; tel. (71) 860-580; fax (71) 860-810; e-mail ambsuedetunis@planet.tn; Ambassador: STAFFAN ÅBERG.

Switzerland: Immeuble Stramica, BP 501, Les Berges du Lac, 1025 Tunis; tel. (71) 962-997; fax (71) 965-796; e-mail swissembtun@email.ati.tn; Ambassador: PETER VON GRAFFENRIED.

Syria: 119 Azzouz Ribai-Almanar 3, Tunis; tel. (71) 888-188; Ambassador: Dr SAMI GLAIEL.

Turkey: 30 ave d'Afrique, BP 134, al-Menzah V, Tunis; tel. (71) 750-668; fax (71) 767-045; Ambassador: HÜSEYIN PAZARCI.

Ukraine: 30 rue du docteur Burnet, Mutuelleville, 1002 Tunis; tel. (71) 849-861; fax (71) 840-866.

United Arab Emirates: 15 rue du 1er juin, Mutuelleville, Tunis; tel. (71) 783-522; Ambassador: HAMAD SALEM AL-MAQAMI.

United Kingdom: 5 place de la Victoire, 1000 Tunis; tel. (71) 341-444; fax (71) 354-877; e-mail british.emb@planet.tn; internet www.british-emb.intl.tn; Ambassador: ROBIN KEALY.

USA: 144 ave de la Liberté, 1002 Tunis; tel. (71) 782-566; fax (71) 789-719; internet usembassy.state.gov/tunis; Ambassador: RUST DEMING.

Venezuela: 30 rue de Niger, 1002 Tunis; tel. (71) 285-075; Ambassador: JOSÉ ANTONIO QUIJADA SÁNCHEZ.

Yemen: rue Mouaouia ibn Soufiane, al-Menzah VI, Tunis; tel. (71) 237-933; Ambassador: RASHID MUHAMMAD THABIT.

Yugoslavia: 4 rue de Libéria, 1002 Tunis; tel. (71) 783-057; fax (71) 796-482; e-mail yuamb.1@gnet.tn; Ambassador: MOMCILO BOJOVIC.

Judicial System

The **Cour de Cassation** in Tunis has three civil and one criminal sections. There are three **Cours d'Appel** at Tunis, Sousse and Sfax, and 13 **Cours de Première Instance**, each having three chambers, except the **Cour de Première Instance** at Tunis which has eight chambers. **Justices Cantonales** exist in 51 areas.

Religion

The Constitution of 1956 recognizes Islam as the state religion, with the introduction of certain reforms, such as the abolition of polygamy. An estimated 99% of the population are Muslims. Minority religions include Judaism (an estimated 2,000 adherents in 1993) and Christianity. The Christian population comprises Roman Catholics, Greek Orthodox and French and English Protestants.

ISLAM

Grand Mufti of Tunisia: Sheikh MUHAMMAD HABIR BELKHODJA.

CHRISTIANITY

Reformed Church of Tunisia: 36 rue Charles de Gaulle, 1000 Tunis; tel. (71) 327-886; e-mail williambrown@bigfoot.com; internet members.truepath.com/ertunis; f. 1880; c. 100 mems; Pastor WILLIAM BROWN.

Roman Catholic Church: 4 rue d'Alger, 1000 Tunis; tel. (71) 335-831; fax (71) 335-832; e-mail eveche.tunisie@gnet.tn; f. 1964; Bishop of Tunis Most Rev. FOUAD TWAL; 22,000 adherents (2000).

The Press

DAILIES

Ach-Chourouk (Sunrise): 10 rue ach-Cham, Tunis; tel. (71) 834-000; fax (71) 830-337; Dir SLAHEDDINE AL-AMRI; circ. 70,000.

El-Horria: 8 rue de Rome, Tunis; tel. (71) 352-255; Arabic; organ of the RCD; Dir MUHAMMAD HEDI TRIKI; circ. 50,000.

La Presse de Tunisie: 6 rue Ali Bach-Hamba, Tunis; tel. (71) 341-066; fax (71) 349-720; e-mail contact@lapresse.tn; internet www .lapresse.tn; f. 1936; French; Dir MONCEF GOUJA; circ. 40,000.

Le Quotidien: 25 rue Jean Jaures, 1000 Tunis; f. 2001; French; Dir SLAHEDDINE AL-AMRI; circ. 30,000.

Le Renouveau: 8 rue de Rome, 1000 Tunis; tel. (71) 352-255; fax (71) 351-927; internet www.tunisieinfo.com/LeRenouveau/; f. 1988; organ of the RCD; French; Dir ZOHRA BEN ROMDHANE; Editor ZINE AMARA.

As-Sabah (The Morning): blvd du 7 novembre, BP 441, al-Menzah, 1004 Tunis; tel. (71) 717-222; fax (71) 718-420; e-mail info@assabah .com.tn; internet www.tunisie.com/Assabah; f. 1951; Arabic; Dir HABIB CHEIKHROUHOU; circ. 50,000.

As-Sahafa: 6 rue Ali Bach-Hamba, Tunis; tel. (71) 341-066; fax (71) 349-720; www.sahafa.com; f. 1936; Arabic; Dir MONCEF GUUJA.

Le Temps: 4 rue Ali Bach-Hamba, Tunis; tel. (71) 340-222; f. 1975; French; Dir HABIB CHEIKHROUHOU; circ. 42,000.

PERIODICALS

Afrique Economie: 16 rue de Rome, BP 61, 1015 Tunis; tel. (71) 347-441; fax (71) 353-172; e-mail iea@planet.tn; f. 1970; monthly; Dir MUHAMMAD ZERZERI.

Al-Akhbar (The News): 1 passage d'al-Houdaybiyah, Tunis; tel. (71) 344-100; f. 1984; weekly; general; Dir MUHAMMAD BEN YOUSUF; circ. 75,000.

Les Annonces: 6 rue de Sparte, BP 1343, Tunis; tel. (71) 350-177; fax (71) 347-184; f. 1978; 2 a week; French/Arabic; Dir MUHAMMAD NEJIB AZOUZ; circ. 170,000.

Al-Anouar at-Tounissia (Tunisian Lights): 10 rue ach-Cham, 1002 Tunis; tel. (71) 331-000; fax (71) 340-600; SLAHEDDINE AL-AMRI; circ. 165,000.

L'Avenir: 26 rue Gamal Abd an-Nasser, BP 1200, Tunis; tel. (71) 258-941; f. 1980; weekly; organ of Mouvement des démocrates socialistes (MDS).

Al-Bayan (The Manifesto): 87 ave Jughurta, Belvédère, 1002 Tunis; tel. (71) 791-098; fax (71) 796-400; f. 1977; weekly; general; Dir HÉDI DJILANI; circ. 120,000.

Al-Biladi (My Country): 15 rue 2 mars 1934, Tunis; f. 1974; Arabic; political and general weekly for Tunisian workers abroad; Dir HÉDI AL-GHALI; circ. 90,000.

Bulletin Mensuel de Statistiques: Institut National de la Statistique, 70 rue Ech-cham, BP 265, 1080 Tunis; tel. (71) 891-002; fax (71) 792-559; e-mail ins@email.ati.tn; internet www.ins.nat.tn; monthly.

Conjoncture: 37 ave Kheireddine Pacha, 1002 Tunis; tel. (71) 784-223; fax (71) 782-742; f. 1974; monthly; economic and financial surveys; Dir HOSNI TOUMI; circ. 5,000.

Démocratie: Tunis; f. 1978; monthly; French; organ of the MDS; Dir HASSIB BEN AMMAR; circ. 5,000.

Dialogue: 15 rue 2 mars 1934, Tunis; tel. (71) 264899; f. 1974; weekly; French; cultural and political organ of the RCD; Dir NACEUR BECHEKH; circ. 30,000.

Etudiant Tunisien: Tunis; f. 1953; French and Arabic; Chief Editor FAOUZI AOUAM.

Al-Fajr (Dawn): Tunis; f. 1990; weekly; Arabic; publ. of the Hizb an-Nahdah movement; Dir HAMADI JEBALI (imprisoned Jan. 1991).

Al-Falah: rue Alain Savary, al-Khadra, 1003 Tunis; tel. (71) 800-800; fax (71) 797-292; weekly; agricultural; Dir ABD AL-BAKI BACHA; Editor GHARBI HAMOUDA; circ. 7,000.

Al-Fikr (Thought): Tunis; f. 1955; monthly; Arabic; cultural review.

L'Hebdo Touristique: rue 8601, 40, Zone Industrielle, La Charguia 2, 2035 Tunis; tel. (71) 786-866; fax (71) 794-891; f. 1971; weekly; French; tourism; Dir TIJANI HADDAD; circ. 5,000.

IBLA: Institut des Belles Lettres Arabes, 12 rue Jemaâ el-Haoua, 1008 Tunis; tel. (71) 560-133; fax (71) 572-683; e-mail ibla@gnet.tn; 2 a year; French; social and cultural review on Maghreb and Muslim-Arab affairs; Dirs J. FONTAINE and D. BOND; circ. 800.

Al-Idhaa wa Talvaza (Radio and Television): 71 ave de la Liberté, Tunis; tel. (71) 287-300; fax (71) 781-058; f. 1956; fortnightly; Arabic language broadcasting magazine; Dir Gen. ABD AL-HAFIDH HERGUEM; Editor WAHID BRAHAM; circ. 10,000.

Irfane (Children): 6 rue Muhammad Ali, 1000 Tunis; tel. (71) 256-877; fax (71) 351-521; f. 1965; monthly; Arabic; Dir-Gen. RIDHA EL OUADI; circ. 100,000.

Jeunesse Magazine: 6 rue Muhammad Ali, 1000 Tunis; tel. (71) 256-877; fax (71) 351-521; f. 1980; monthly; Arabic; Dir-Gen. RIDHA EL OUADI; circ. 30,000.

Journal Officiel de la République Tunisienne: ave Farhat Hached, 2040 Radès; tel. (71) 299-914; fax (71) 297-234; f. 1860; the official gazette; French and Arabic editions published twice weekly by the Imprimerie Officielle (The State Press); Pres. and Dir-Gen. ROMDHANE BEN MIMOUN; circ. 20,000.

Al-Maoukif: Tunis; weekly; organ of the Rassemblement socialiste progressiste; Dir AHMAD NEJIB CHABI.

Al-Maraa (The Woman): 56 blvd Bab Benat, 1006 Tunis; tel. (71) 567-845; fax (71) 567-131; e-mail unft@email.a.t.i.tnf. 1961; monthly; Arabic/French; political, economic and social affairs; issued by the Union Nationale de la Femme Tunisienne; Pres. CHEDLIA BOUKHCHINA; circ. 10,000.

Le Mensuel: Tunis; f. 1984; monthly; economic, social and cultural affairs.

Al-Moussawar: 10 rue ach-Cham, Tunis; tel. (71) 289-000; fax (71) 289-357; weekly; circ. 75,000.

Outrouhat: Tunis; monthly; scientific; Dir LOTFI BEN AISSA.

Ar-Rai (Opinion): Tunis; f. 1977 by MDS; weekly; opposition newspaper; Dir HASSIB BEN AMAR; circ. 20,000.

Réalités: 85 rue de Palestine, Belvédère, BP 227, 1002 Tunis; tel. (71) 788-313; fax (71) 893-489; f. 1979; weekly; French/Arabic; Dir TAÏEB ZAHAR; circ. 25,000.

At-Tariq al-Jadid (New Road): 6 rue Metouia, Tunis; tel. (71) 246-400; fax (71) 350-748; e-mail sof@realites.com.tn; internet www.tunisieinfo.com/realites; f. 1981; organ of the Mouvement de la rénovation; Editor MUHAMMAD HARMEL.

Tounes al-Khadra: rue Alain Savary, 1003 Tunis; tel. (71) 800-800; fax (71) 798-598; f. 1976; monthly; agricultural, scientific and technical; Dir ABD AL-BAKI BACHA; Editor GHARBI HAMOUDA; circ. 5,000.

Tunis Hebdo: 1 passage d'al-Houdaybiyah, Tunis; tel. (71) 344-100; fax (71) 355-079; internet www.tunishebdo.com.tn; f. 1973;

weekly; French; general and sport; Dir M'HAMEÓ BEN YOUSUF; circ. 35,000.

Tunisia News: rue 8601, 40, Zone Industrielle, La Charguia 1, 2035 Tunis; tel. (71) 786-866; fax (71) 794-891; e-mail haddad.tijani@planet.tn; f. 1993; weekly; English; Dir TIJANI HADDAD; circ. 5,000.

NEWS AGENCIES

Tunis Afrique Presse (TAP): 7 ave Slimane Ben Slimane, 2092 al-Manar, Tunis; tel. (71) 889-000; fax (71) 883-500; f. 1961; Arab, French and English; offices in Algiers, Rabat, Paris and New York; daily news services; Chair. and Gen. Man. BRAHIM FRIDHI.

Foreign Bureaux

Agence France-Presse (AFP): 45 ave Habib Bourguiba, Tunis; tel. (71) 337-896; fax (71) 352-414; e-mail pvro.afp@gnet.tn; Chief PATRICK VAN ROEKEGHEM.

Agencia EFE (Spain): 126 rue de Yougoslavie, 1000 Tunis; tel. (71) 321-497; fax (71) 325-976; e-mail manostos@gnet.tn; Chief MANUEL OSTOS LÓPEZ.

Agenzia Nazionale Stampa Associata (ANSA) (Italy): Tunis; Chief MANUELA FONTANA.

Informatsionnoye Telegrafnoye Agentstvo Rossii— Telegrafnoye Agentstvo Suverennykh Stran (ITAR—TASS) (Russia): Tunis; Chief VIKTOR LEBEDEV.

Inter Press Service (IPS) (Italy): 80 ave Tahar Ben Ammar, al-Menzah IX, 1013 Tunis; tel. (71) 880-182; fax (71) 880-848; f. 1976; Chief ABD AL-MAJID BEJAR.

Kuwait News Agency (KUNA): Tunis; tel. (71) 717-624; fax (71) 718-062.

Reuters (United Kingdom): 3 rue Ibn Rachiq, BP 369, Belvédère, 1002 Tunis; tel. (71) 787-711; fax (71) 787-454; Senior Correspondent ABD AL-AZIZ BARROUHI.

Rossiiskoye Informatsionnoye Agentstvo—Novosti (RIA— Novosti) (Russia): 102 ave de la Liberté, Tunis; tel. (71) 283-781; Chief NICOLAS SOLOGUBOVSKII.

Saudi Press Agency (SPA): Tunis.

Xinhua (New China) News Agency (People's Republic of China): 6 rue Smyrne, Notre Dame, Tunis; tel. (71) 281-308; Dir XIE BINYU.

Publishers

Addar al-Arabia Lil Kitab: 4 ave Mohieddine El Klibi, al-Manar, BP 32, al-Manar 2, 2092 Tunis; tel. (71) 888-255; fax (71) 888-365; f. 1975; general literature, children's books, non-fiction; Dir-Gen. REBAH DEKHILI.

Agence de Promotion de l'Industrie (API): 63 rue de Syrie, Belvédère, 1002 Tunis; tel. (71) 792-144; fax (71) 782-482; e-mail api@api.com.tn; internet www.tunisieindustrie.nat.tn; f. 1987 by merger; responsible for the implementation of the Government's policies relative to the promotion of the industrial sector; provides a support structure for companies and promoters; 23 regional offices; Gen. Man. KHELIL LAGIMI.

Bouslama Editions: 15 ave de France, 1000 Tunis; tel. (71) 243-745; fax (71) 381-100; f. 1960; history, children's books; Man. Dir ALI BOUSLAMA.

Ceres Productions: rue Lac Victoria, Immeuble Lac des Cygnes, 2035 Les Berges du Lac; tel. (71) 960-980; fax (71) 960-977; e-mail nbic.ceres@planet.tn; f. 1964; art books, literature, novels; Pres. MUHAMMAD BEN SMAIL.

Dar al-Amal: 8 rue de Rome, Tunis; tel. (71) 352-255; f. 1976; economics, sociology, politics; Dir-Gen. MAHMOUD MEFTAH.

Dar al-Kitab: 5 ave Bourguiba, 4000 Sousse; tel. (73) 25097; f. 1950; literature, children's books, legal studies, foreign books; Pres. TAIEB KACEM; Dir FAYÇAL KACEM.

Dar as-Sabah: Centre Interurbain, BP 441, al-Menzah, 1004 Tunis; tel. (71) 717-222; fax (71) 718-366; f. 1951; 200 mems; publishes daily and weekly papers which circulate throughout Tunisia, North Africa, France, Belgium, Luxembourg and Germany; Dir-Gen. MONCEF CHEIKHROUHOU.

Institut National de la Statistique: 70 rue Ech-Cham, BP 265, 1080 Tunis; tel. (71) 891-002; fax (71) 792-559; e-mail ins@email .ati.tn; internet www.ins.nat.tn; publishes a variety of annuals, periodicals and papers concerned with the economic policy and devt of Tunisia.

Librairie al-Manar: 60 ave Bab Djedid, Case Postale 179, 1008 Tunis; tel. (71) 253-224; fax (71) 336-565; e-mail librairie.almanar@planet.tn; f. 1938; general, educational, Islam; Man. Dir HABIB M'HAMDI.

Maison Tunisienne d'Edition: Tunis; f. 1966; all kinds of books, magazines, etc.; Dir ABDELAZIZ ACHOURI.

En-Najah—Editions Hedi Ben Abdelgheni: 11 ave de France, 1000 Tunis; tel. (71) 334-246; fax (71) 336-471; Arab and French books, Koranic texts.

Société d'Arts Graphiques, d'Edition et de Presse: 15 rue 2 mars 1934, La Kasbah, Tunis; tel. (71) 264-988; fax (71) 569-736; f. 1974; prints and publishes daily papers, magazines, books, etc.; Chair. and Man. Dir HASSEN FERJANI.

Sud Editions: 79 rue de Palestine, 1002 Tunis; tel. (71) 785-179; fax (71) 792-905; f. 1976; Arab literature, art and art history; Man. Dir M. MASMOUDI.

Government Publishing House

Imprimerie Officielle de la République Tunisienne: ave Farhat Hached, 2040 Radès; tel. (71) 434-211; fax (71) 434-234; f. 1860; Man. Dir ROMDHANE BEN MIMOUN.

Broadcasting and Communications

TELECOMMUNICATIONS

Société Tunisienne d'Entreprises des Télécommunications (SOTETEL): rue des Entrepreneurs, Zone Industrielle, la Charguia 2, 1080 Tunis; tel. (71) 703-345; internet www.sototel.com.tn; transferred to private ownership in 1998.

Tunisie Télécom: 41 rue Asdrubal, 1002 Tunis; tel. (71) 801-717; fax (71) 800-777; internet www.tunisietelecom.tn; CEO KHÉDIJA GHARIANI; Gen. Man. AHMED MAHJOUB.

BROADCASTING

Radio

Etablissement de la Radiodiffusion-Télévision Tunisienne (ERTT): 71 ave de la Liberté, 1002 Tunis; tel. (71) 847-300; fax (71) 781-058; e-mail presidence@ertt.net.tn; internet www.radiotunis.com; govt service; broadcasts in Arabic, French, Italian, Spanish and English; stations at Gafsa, El-Kef, Monastir, Sfax, Tataouine and Tunis (three); Pres. RAOUF BASTI.

Television

Etablissement de la Radiodiffusion-Télévision Tunisienne: (see Radio).

Office National de la Télédiffusion (ONT): 13 rue de Bizerte, 1006 Tunis; tel. (71) 794-609.

Television was introduced in northern and central Tunisia in January 1966, and by 1972 transmission covered the country. A relay station to link up with European transmissions was built at al-Haouaria in 1967, and a second channel was introduced in 1983.

Finance

(cap. = capital; dep. = deposits; res = reserves; m. = million; brs = branches; amounts in dinars unless otherwise stated)

BANKING

Central Bank

Banque Centrale de Tunisie (BCT): 25 rue Hédi Nouira, BP 369, 1080 Tunis; tel. (71) 340-588; fax (71) 354-214; e-mail bct@bct.gov.tn; internet www.bct.gov.tn; f. 1958; cap. 6.0m., dep. 2,099.8m., res 20.2m., total assets 4,666.8m., (Dec. 1999); Gov. MUHAMMAD DAOUAS; 10 brs.

Commercial Banks

AMEN Bank: ave Muhammad V, 1002 Tunis; tel. (71) 835-500; fax (71) 834-770; e-mail amen.bank@amenbank.com.tn; internet www.amenbank.com.tn; f. 1967 as Crédit Foncier et Commercial de Tunisie; changed name as above in 1995; cap. and res 85.3m., total assets 1,348.5m. (Dec. 1998); Chair. and Pres. RACHID BEN YEDDER; Gen. Man. AHMED EL KARM; 73 brs.

Arab Banking Corpn Tunisie: ABC Building, rue du Lac d'Annecy, Les Berges du Lac, 1053 Tunis; tel. (71) 861-861; fax (71) 860-921; e-mail abc.tunis@arabbanking.com; internet www.arabbanking.com; f. 2000; cap. 18m.; CEO EZZEDINE SAIDANE; 3 brs.

Arab Tunisian Bank: 9 rue Hédi Nouira, POB 520, 1001 Tunis; tel. (71) 351-155; fax (71) 349-278; e-mail atbbank@atb.com.tn; internet www.atb.com.tn; f. 1982; cap. 46.2m., dep. 810.5m. (Dec. 2000); Dir-Gen. HAMMOUDA BELKHODJA; 30 brs.

Banque de l'Habitat: 21 ave Kheireddine Pacha, BP 242, 1002 Tunis; tel. (71) 785-277; fax (71) 784-417; e-mail banquehabitat@bh.fin.tn; f. 1984; 57.4% govt-owned; cap. and res 79.3m., total assets 1,590.7m. (Dec. 1998); Chair. TAHAR BOURKHIS; 49 brs.

Banque Internationale Arabe de Tunisie (BIAT): 70–72 ave Habib Bourguiba, BP 520, 1080 Tunis; tel. (71) 340-733; fax (71) 340-680; e-mail abderrazak.lahiani@biat.com.tn; internet www.biat.com.tn; f. 1976; cap. 100.0m., res 99.6m., dep. 1,994.8m. (Dec. 2000); Pres. MOKHTAR FAKHFAKH; 92 brs.

Banque Nationale Agricole: rue Hédi Nouira, 1001 Tunis; tel. (71) 831-000; fax (71) 835-551; f. 1989 by merger of the Banque Nationale du Développement Agricole and the Banque Nationale de Tunisie; cap. 100.0m., res 226.5m., dep. 2,453.3m. (Dec. 2000); Chair. MUHAMMAD FERID BEN TANFOUS; Gen. Man. FADHEL BEN OTHMAN; 140 brs.

Banque du Sud: 95 ave de la Liberté, 1002 Tunis; tel. (71) 849-400; fax (71) 782-663; e-mail courier@banksud.com.tn; internet www.banksud.com.tn; f. 1968; cap. 100.0m., res 42.6m., dep. 969.1m. (1999); Pres. LAROUSSI BAYOUDH; 86 brs.

Banque de Tunisie SA: 2 rue de Turquie, BP 289, 1001 Tunis; tel. (71) 332-188; fax (71) 347-756; e-mail finance@bt.com.tn; f. 1884; cap. 40.0m., res 60.6m., dep. 944.7m. (Dec. 2001); Chair. and Man. Dir FAOUZI BEL KAHIA; 5 brs and 77 agencies.

Citibank N.A.: 55 ave Jugurtha, BP 72, Belvédère, 1001 Tunis; tel. (71) 790-066; fax (71) 785-556; f. 1989; cap. 10m., total assets 387m. (Dec. 1998); Gen. Man. NAYERA N. AMIN; 2 brs.

Société Tunisienne de Banque (STB): rue Hédi Nouira, BP 638, 1001 Tunis; tel. (71) 340-477; fax (71) 348-400; internet www.stb.com.tn; f. 1957; 50% govt-owned; merged with Banque Nationale de Développement Touristique and Banque de Développement Economique de Tunisie in 2000; cap. 124.3m., res 228.6m., dep. 2,281.0m. (Dec. 2000); Chair. and Gen. Man. ALI DEBAYA; 113 brs.

Union Bancaire pour le Commerce et l'Industrie: 139 ave de la Liberté, Belvédère, 1002 Tunis; tel. (71) 340-635; fax (71) 328-823; e-mail dg@ubci.com.tn; internet www.ubci.com.tn; f. 1961; cap. 35.0m., res 82.9m., dep. 875.4. (Dec. 2000); affiliated to Banque Nationale de Paris Intercontinentale; Pres. and Gen. Man. SLAH EDDINE BOUGERRA; 39 brs.

Union Internationale de Banques SA: 65 ave Habib Bourguiba, BP 109, 1000 Tunis; tel. (71) 347-000; fax (71) 353-090; e-mail nessafiuib@planet.tn; f. 1963 as a merging of Tunisian interests by the Société Tunisienne de Banque with Crédit Lyonnais (France) and other foreign banks, including Banca Commerciale Italiana; cap. and res 97.5m., total assets 1,323.1m. (Dec. 1998); scheduled for privatization in 2002; Pres. and Gen. Man. BRAHIM SAÂDA; 94 brs.

Merchant Banks

Banque d'Affaires de Tunisie (BAT): Les Berges du Lac, 1001 Tunis; tel. (71) 860-080; fax (71) 861-081; f. 1997; cap. 3m.; Gen. Man. ARNAUD DINASHIN.

International Maghreb Merchant Bank (IM Bank): Immeuble Maghrebia, Bloc B, 2035 Tunis; tel. (71) 860-816; fax (71) 860-057; f. 1995; auth. cap. 3m., total assets 3.1m. (Dec. 1995); Pres. MONCEF CHEIKH-ROUHOU; CEO KACEM BOUSNINA.

Development Banks

Banque Arabe Tuniso-Libyenne pour le Développement et le Commerce Extérieur: 25 ave Kheireddine Pacha, BP 102, Belvédère, 1002 Tunis; tel. (71) 781-500; fax (71) 782-818; f. 1983; promotes trade and devt projects between Tunisia and Libya, and provides funds for investment in poorer areas; cap. 100.0m., res 17.6m., dep. 38.7m. (Dec. 1999); Chair. SAID M'RABET.

Banque de Coopération du Maghreb Arabe: ave Muhammad V, BP 46, Belvédère, 1002 Tunis; tel. (71) 780-311; fax (71) 781-056; f. 1981, began operations 1982; finances jt devt projects between Tunisia and Algeria; cap. and res US $53.7m., total assets $77.8m. (Dec. 1998); Chair. ABDELKARIM LAKEHAL; Gen. Man. CHAFIK BEN HAMZA.

Banque de Tunisie et des Emirats d'Investissement: 5 bis Blvd Muhammad Badra, 1002 Tunis; tel. (71) 783-600; fax (71) 783-756; scheduled to merge with Union Internationale de Banques.

Banque Tunisienne de Solidarité: 56 ave Muhammad V, 1002 Tunis; tel. (71) 849-400; fax (71) 847-352; e-mail BTS@e-mail.ati.tn; f. 1997; provides long-term finance for small-scale projects; cap. 30m.; Pres. ANOUAR BELARBI.

Banque Tuniso-Koweïtienne de Développement: 10 bis ave Muhammad V, BP 49, 1001 Tunis; tel. (71) 340-000; fax (71) 343-106; e-mail ask@btkd-bank.com; internet www.btkd-bank.com; f. 1981; provides long-term finance for devt projects; cap. 100m., res 74.9m. (Dec. 2000); Dir-Gen. ANOUAR BELARBI.

Société Tuniso-Séoudienne d'Investissement et de Développement (STUSID): 32 rue Hédi Karray, BP 20, 1002 Tunis; tel.

(71) 718-233; fax (71) 719-515; e-mail stusid@gnet.tn; f. 1981; provides long-term finance for devt projects; cap. and res 173.8m., total assets 237.3m. (Dec. 1998); Chair. Dr MAHSOUN BAHJET JALAL; Pres. ABDELGHAFFAR EZZEDDINE.

'Offshore' Banks

Alubaf International Bank: BP 51, rue Montplaisir, Belvédère, 1002 Tunis; tel. (71) 783-500; fax (71) 793-905; e-mail alub.tn@gnet.tn; f. 1985; cap. US $25.0m., res 5,618m., dep. 49,210m. (Dec. 2000); Pres. MUHAMMAD ABDULJAWAD; Gen. Man. FARAG ALI GAMRA.

Arab Banking Corpn Tunis: ABC Bulding, rue du Lac d'Annecy, Les Berges du Lac, 1053 Tunis; tel. (71) 861-861; fax (71) 860-921; e-mail abc.tunis@arabbanking.com; internet www.arabbanking.com; f. 1993; cap. US $6m., res 5,645m.; Gen. Man. EZZEDINE SAIDANE.

Beit Ettamwil Saudi Tounsi (BEST): 88 ave Hédi Chaker, 1002 Tunis; tel. (71) 790-000; fax (71) 780-235; f. 1983; cap. US $50m., total assets $156.0m. (Dec. 1996); Pres. Dr SALAH JEMIL MALAIKA.

North Africa International Bank: BP 485, 1080 Tunis; tel. (71) 950-800; fax (71) 950-840; f. 1984; cap. US $30.0m., res $12.0m. (2001); Pres., Chair. and Gen. Man. SADDIQ M. HIJJAJI.

Tunis International Bank: 18 ave des Etats-Unis d'Amérique, BP 81, 1002 Tunis; tel. (71) 782-411; fax (71) 782-479; e-mail tib1-tib@planet.tn; f. 1982; cap. US $25.0m., res 9.6m., dep. 185.3m. (Dec. 2000); Chair. ZOUHAIR KHOURI; 3 brs.

STOCK EXCHANGE

Bourse de Tunis: Centre Babel, Bloc E, Zone Montplaisir, 1002 Tunis; tel. (71) 799-414; fax (71) 789-189; e-mail hamdi.bannour@bvmt.com.tn; internet www.bvmt.com.tn; Chair. AHMED HADDOUEJ.

INSURANCE

Caisse Tunisienne d'Assurances Mutuelles Agricoles: 6 ave Habib Thameur, 1069 Tunis; tel. (71) 340-933; fax (71) 332-276; f. 1912; Pres. MOKTAR BELLAGHA; Dir-Gen. MEZRI JELIZI.

Cie d'Assurances Tous Risques et de Réassurance (ASTREE): 45 ave Kheireddine Pacha, BP 780, 1002 Tunis; tel. (71) 792-211; fax (71) 794-723; f. 1950; cap. 4m. dinars; Pres. and Dir-Gen. MUHAMMAD HACHICHA.

Cie Tunisienne pour l'Assurance du Commerce Extérieur (COTUNACE): ave Muhammad V/Montplaisir I, rue 8006, 1002 Tunis; tel. (71) 783-000; fax (71) 782-539; e-mail cotunace2@email.ati.tn; internet www.cotunace.com.tn; f. 1984; cap. 5m. dinars; 65 mem. cos; Pres. and Dir-Gen. MONCEF ZOUARI.

Lloyd Tunisien: 7 ave de Carthage, 1000 Tunis; tel. (71) 340-911; fax (71) 340-909; f. 1945; fire, accident, liability, marine, life; cap. 1m. dinars; Chair. and Man. Dir ABD AL-KARIM MERDASSI.

Société Tunisienne d'Assurance et de Réassurance (STAR): ave de Paris, Tunis; tel. (71) 340-866; fax (71) 340-835; f. 1958.

Tunis-Ré (Société Tunisienne de Réassurance): ave Muhammad V, Montplaisir 1, POB 133, 1082 Tunis; tel. (71) 844-011; fax (71) 787-573; e-mail tunis.re@email.ati.tn; f. 1981; various kinds of reinsurance; cap. 24.4m. dinars; Chair. and Gen. Man. MUHAMMAD EL-FATEH MAHERZI.

Trade and Industry

GOVERNMENT AGENCIES

Centre de Promotion des Exportations (CEPEX): 28 rue Ghandi, 1001 Tunis; tel. (71) 350-344; fax (71) 353-683; e-mail cepexedpuc@attmail.com; f. 1973; state export promotion org.; Pres. and Dir-Gen. HAMDANE BEN OTHMAN.

Foreign Investment Promotion Agency (FIPA): 63 rue de Syrie, 1002 Tunis; tel. (71) 792-144; fax (71) 782-971; e-mail fipa.tunisia@mci.gov.tn; internet www.investintunisia.tn; f. 1995; Dir-Gen. ABDESSALEM MANSOUR.

Office du Commerce de Tunisie (OCT): 1 rue de Syrie, 1060 Tunis; tel. (71) 682-901; Dir-Gen. MUHAMMAD AMOR.

CHAMBERS OF COMMERCE AND INDUSTRY

Chambre de Commerce et d'Industrie de Tunis: 1 rue des Entrepreneurs, 1000 Tunis; tel. (71) 350-300; fax (71) 354-744; e-mail ccitunis@planet.tn; f. 1885; 25 mems; Pres. JILANI BENM'BAREK.

Chambre de Commerce et d'Industrie du Centre: rue Chadli Khaznadar, 4000 Sousse; tel. (73) 225-044; fax (73) 224-227; f. 1895; 25 mems; Pres. KABOUDI MONCEF; Dir FATEN BASLY.

Chambre de Commerce et d'Industrie du Nord-Est: Tom Bereaux Bizerte Center, Angle rues 1er Mai, Med Ali, 7000 Bizerte;

tel. (72) 431-044; fax (72) 431-922; f. 1903; 5 mems; Pres. KAMEL BELKAHIA; Dir MOUFIDA CHAKROUN.

Chambre de Commerce et d'Industrie de Sfax: 10 rue Tahar Sfar, BP 794, 3018 Sfax; tel. (74) 296-120; fax (74) 296-121; e-mail ccis@ccis.org.tn; internet www.ccis.org.tn; f. 1895; 35,000 mems; Dir IKRAM MAKNI.

INDUSTRIAL AND TRADE ASSOCIATIONS

Agence de Promotion de l'Industrie (API): 63 rue de Syrie, 1002 Tunis; tel. (71) 792-144; fax (71) 782-482; e-mail api@api.com.tn; www.tunisieindustrie.nat.tn; f. 1987 by merger; co-ordinates industrial policy, undertakes feasibility studies, organizes industrial training and establishes industrial zones; overseas offices in Belgium, France, Germany, Italy, the United Kingdom, Sweden and the USA; Pres. and Dir-Gen. KHELIL LAGIMI.

Centre Technique du Textile (CETTEX): ave des Industries, Zone Industrielle, Bir El Kassaa, 2013 Ben Arous, BP 279, Tunis; tel. (71) 381-133; fax (71) 382-558; e-mail cettex@textiletunisia.com.tn; responsible for the textile industry; Dir MONJI JLAIEL.

Cie des Phosphates de Gafsa (CPG): Cité Bayech, Gafsa; tel. (76) 22022; f. 1897; production and marketing of phosphates; Pres. MUHAMMAD AL-FADHEL KHELIL.

Entreprise Tunisienne d'Activités Pétrolières (ETAP): 27 ave Kheireddine Pacha, BP 367, 1002 Tunis; tel. (71) 782-288; fax (71) 784-092; responsible for exploration and investment in hydrocarbons.

Office des Céréales: Ministry of Agriculture, 30 rue Alain Savary, 1002 Tunis; tel. (71) 790-351; fax (71) 789-573; f. 1962; responsible for the cereals industry; Chair. and Dir-Gen. A. SADDEM.

Office National des Mines: 24 rue 8601, BP 215, 1080 Tunis; tel. (71) 787-366; fax (71) 794-016; f. 1963; mining of iron ores; research and study of mineral wealth; Chair. and CEO MOHAMMED FADHEL ZER-ELLI.

Office National des Pêches (ONP): Le Port, La Goulette, Tunis; tel. (71) 275-093; marine and fishing authority; Dir-Gen. L. HALAB.

Office des Terres Domaniales (OTD): 30 rue Alain Savary, 1002 Tunis; tel. (71) 800-322; fax (71) 795-026; e-mail otd@email.ati.tn; f. 1961; responsible for agricultural production and the management of state-owned lands; Dir BECHIR BEN SMAIL.

UTILITIES
Electricity and Gas

Société Tunisienne de l'Electricité et du Gaz (STEG): 38 rue Kemal Atatürk, BP 190, 1080 Tunis; tel.(71) 341-311; fax (71) 349-981; e-mail dpsc@steg.com.tn; f. 1962; responsible for generation and distribution of electricity and for production of natural gas; Pres. and Gen. Man. MUHAMMAD MONCEF BOUSSEN; 35 brs.

Water

Société Nationale d'Exploitation et de Distribution des Eaux (SONEDE): Ave Slimane ben Sliman el-Manar 2,Tunis; tel. (71) 887-000; fax (71) 881-000; e-mail commuson@gnet.tn; f. 1968; Pres. and Dir. Gen. MABROUK ABDELLAZIZ

MAJOR COMPANIES

Bata Tunisienne SA: route de Mornag, Km 7, Ben Arous, Tunis; tel. (71) 384-155; (71) 382-798; e-mail bata@tunis.bata.com; f. 1935; manufacture of shoes and sandals; Dir-Gen. LASSAD MZAH; 350 employees.

Compagnie Générale des Salines de Tunisie (COTUSAL): 19 rue de Turquie, 1001 Tunis; tel. (71) 347-666; fax (71) 336-163; f. 1949; production of edible and industrial sea salt; Man. Dir NOR-BERT DE GUILLEBON; 450 employees.

Entreprise Ali Mheni (EAM): 12 bis rue de Russie, BP 609, 1000 Tunis; tel. (71) 332-433; fax (71) 323-001; f. 1934; construction and civil engineering, public works, building; Pres. and Dir-Gen. RAOUF MHENI; 4,500 employees.

Grands Ateliers du Nord SA: GP 1 Km 12, az-Zahra Hammam-Lif, Tunis; tel. (71) 438-077; fax (71) 439-748; e-mail info.gam@poulina.com.tn; f. 1975; manufacture of agricultural equipment, electrical home appliances and office furniture; sales TD 30m., cap. p.u. TD 16m. (2001); Pres. ABDELAZIZ GUIDARA; 1,000 employees.

Groupe Chimique Tunisien: 7 rue du Royaume d'Arabie Saoudite, 1002 Tunis; tel. (71) 784-488; fax (71) 783-495; f. 1947; production of Phosphoric acid and fertilizers; Chair. RAFAA DKHIL.

Industries Maghrébines de l'Aluminium (IMAL): 14 rue 8612 Z.I. Charguia I, 2035 Tunis; tel. (71) 795-979; fax (71) 782-074; f. 1964; manufacture and distribution of aluminium products; cap. p.u. TD 450,000; Chair. MONCEF EL-HORRY; 50 employees.

Industries Mécaniques Maghrébines (IMM): Kairouan; tel. (77) 722-028; fax (77) 722-685; e-mail latrous.tahas@gnet.tn; f. 1982; ownership 20% General Motors, 10% Isuzu Motors, 70% local investors; production of light commercial vehicles; Man. Dir TAHAR LATROUS.

Skanes Meubles: route de Sousse, 5000 Monastir; tel. (73) 501-333; fax (73) 501-339; f. 1962; manufacture of furniture and hotel equipment, toys; Pres. RIDHA BCHIR.

Société Industrielle de Pêches et de Conserves Alimentaires SA: ave Habib Bourguiba, 2014 Megrine-Riadh; tel. (71) 295-500; fax (71) 295-722; fish, fruit and vegetable processing and canning; Dir-Gen. ALI MABROUK; 150 employees.

Société Tunisienne Automobile, Financière, Immobilière et Maritime (STAFIM): 85 ave Louis Braille, 1003 Tunis; tel. (71) 785-055; fax (71) 782-467; f. 1932; sales of cars, spare parts, engines and mechanical machinery; Dir-Gen. DOMINIQUE DOUROUZE.

Tunisienne de Conserves Alimentaires (TUCAL): Route de Mateur, Km 8.5, 2010 La Manouba; tel. (71) 601-833; fax (71) 601-251; manufacture and distribution of canned food products; Pres. and Gen. Man. AMOR BEN SÉDRINE.

TRADE AND OTHER UNIONS

Union Générale des Etudiants de Tunisie (UGET): 11 rue d'Espagne, Tunis; f. 1953; 600 mems; Pres. MEKKI FITOURI.

Union Générale Tunisienne du Travail (UGTT): 9 rue de Grèce, Tunis; e-mail ugtt.relaintl@planet.tn; f. 1946 by FARHAT HACHED; affiliated to ICFTU; mems 360,000 in 23 affiliated unions; 18-member exec. bureau; Sec.-Gen. ABDESSALEM DJERAD.

Union Nationale des Agriculteurs (UNA): 6 ave Habib Thameur, 1000 Tunis; tel; (71) 246-920; fax (71) 349-843; f. 1955; Pres. BACHA ABD AL-BAKI.

Union Nationale de la Femme Tunisienne (UNFT): 56 blvd Bab Benat, Tunis; tel. (71) 561-845; fax (71) 567-131; e-mail unft@email.ati.tn; f. 1956; 100,000 mems; promotes the rights of women; 27 regional delegations; Pres. CHEDLIA BOUKHCHINA; Vice-Pres. FAIZA AZOUZ.

Union Tunisienne de l'Industrie, du Commerce et de l'Artisanat (UTICAL): 103 ave de la Liberté, Belvédère, 1002 Tunis; tel. (71) 780-366; fax (71) 782-143; f. 1946; mems: 15 national federations and 170 syndical chambers at national levels; Pres. HEDI JILANI.

Transport

RAILWAYS

In 1999 the total length of railways was 2,168 km. A total of 34.4m. passengers travelled by rail in Tunisia in that year.

Société du Métro Léger de Tunis (SMLT): 60–62 ave Jean-Jaurès, BP 4, 1002 Tunis; tel. (71) 348-555; fax (71) 338-100; f. 1981; operates light railway system in and around Tunis (total length 53 km); Pres. and Dir-Gen. CHEDLY HAJRI.

Société Nationale des Chemins de Fer Tunisiens (SNCFT): Bâtiment La Gare Tunis Ville, Place Barcelona, 1001 Tunis; tel. (71) 333-343; fax (71) 344-045; f. 1956; state org. controlling all Tunisian railways; Pres. and Dir-Gen. ABD AL-AZIZ CHAÂBEN.

ROADS

In 1996 there were an estimated 23,100 km of roads. Of these, 6,240 km were main roads and 7,900 km secondary roads.

Société Nationale des Transports (SNT): 1 ave Habib Bourguiba, BP 660, 1025 Tunis; tel. (71) 259-422; fax (71) 342-727; f. 1963; operates 190 local bus routes with 1,034 buses; Chair. and Man. Dir CHEDLY HAJRI; Gen. Man. MONCEF CHENITI.

Société Nationale de Transport Interurbain (SNTRI): ave Muhammad V, BP 40, Belvédère, 1002 Tunis; tel. (71) 784-433; fax (71) 786-605; e-mail drn@sntri.com.tn; f. 1981; Dir-Gen. SASSI YAHIA.

There are 12 **Sociétés Régionales des Transports**, responsible for road transport, operating in different regions in Tunisia.

SHIPPING

Tunisia has seven major ports: Tunis-La Goulette, Radès, Bizerta, Sousse, Sfax, Gabès and Zarzis. There is a special petroleum port at La Skhirra.

Office de la Marine Marchande et des Ports: Bâtiment Administratif, Port de la Goulette, 2060 La Goulette; tel. (71) 735-300; fax (71) 735-812; maritime port administration; Pres. and Dir-Gen. ALI LABIEDH.

ie Générale Maritime: Résidence Alain Savary, Bloc D7, Apt 74, 1003 Tunis; tel. and fax (71) 860-430; e-mail logwan.girgen@gnet.tn; Chair. ELIAS MAHERZI.

Cie Méditerranéenne de Navigation: Tunis; tel. (71) 331-544; fax (71) 332-124.

Cie Tunisienne de Navigation SA (CTN): 5 ave Dag Hammarskjoeld, BP 40, 1001 Tunis; tel. (71) 341-777; fax (71) 350-976; f. 1959; state-owned; brs at Bizerta, Gabès, La Skhirra, La Goulette, Radès, Sfax and Sousse; Chair. M. YONSAA.

Gabès Marine Tankers: Immeuble SETCAR, route de Sousse, km 13, 2034 Tunis; tel. (71) 445-644; fax (71) 454-650; Chair. FÉRID ABBES.

Gas Marine: Immeuble SETCAR, route de Sousse, km 13, 2034 Ez-Zahra; tel. (71) 454-644; fax (71) 454-650; Chair. HAMMADI ABBES.

Hannibal Marine Tankers: 10 rue 8161, Cité Olympique, 1003 Tunis; tel. (71) 807-032; fax (71) 773-805; Gen. Man. AMEUR MAHJOUB.

Société Tunisienne de Navigation Maritime (PETRONAV): Immeuble Saâdi, BP 85, 2080 Ariana; tel. (71) 861-125; fax (71) 861-780; Chair. HICHEM KHATTECH.

SONOTRAK: 179 ave Muhammad Hédi Khefacha, Gare Maritime de Kerkenna, 3000 Sfax; tel. (74) 498-216; fax (74) 497-496; e-mail jabeur.m@planet.tn; Chair. TAOUFI JRAD.

Tunisian Shipping Agency: Zone Industrielle, Radès 2040, BP 166, Tunis; tel. (71) 448-379; fax (71) 448-410; e-mail tsa.rades@planet.tn; Chair. MUHAMMAD BEN SEDRINE.

CIVIL AVIATION

There are international airports at Tunis-Carthage, Sfax, Djerba, Monastir, Tabarka, Gafsa and Tozeur. In January 2000 it was announced that a new airport was to be built at Enfidha, 100 km south of Tunis. The new airport was to be operational by mid-2004.

Office de l'Aviation Civile et des Aéroports: BP 137, Aéroport International de Tunis-Carthage, 1080 Tunis; tel. (71) 754-000; fax (71) 755-133; f. 1972; air traffic control and airport administration; Pres. and Dir-Gen. ABDERRAHMEN TLILI.

Nouvelair Tunisie: Zone Touristique Dkhila, 5065 Monastir; tel. (73) 520-600; fax (73) 520-666; e-mail info@nouvelair.com.tn; internet www.nouvelair.com; f. 1989 as Air Liberté Tunisie; name changed as above in 1996; Tunisian charter co; flights from Tunis, Djerba and Monastir airports to Scandinavia and other European countries; Chair. AZIZ MILAD; Gen. Man. SAMI ZITOUNI.

Tuninter: BP 1080, Immeuble Securas ZI Charguia 11, 1080 Tunis; tel. (71) 701-717; fax (71) 712-193; e-mail tuninter@mail.gnet.tn; f. 1992; Tunisian charter co; Man. Dir ABD AL-KARIM OUERTANI.

TunisAir (Société Tunisienne de l'Air): blvd du 7 novembre 1987, 2035 Tunis; tel. (71) 700-100; fax (71) 700-897; internet www.tunisair.com.tn; f. 1948; 45.2% govt-owned; 20% of assets privatized in 1995; flights to Africa, Europe and the Middle East; Pres. and Dir-Gen. RAFAA DEKHIL.

Tunisavia (Société de Transports, Services et Travaux Aériens): Immeuble Saadi Spric, Tour CD, 1082 al-Menzah, Tunis; tel. (71) 717-600; fax (71) 718-100; e-mail tunisaviasiege@planet.tn; internet www.tunisavia.com.tn; f. 1974; helicopter and charter operator; Pres. AZIZ MILAD; Dir-Gen. JILANI BENM'BAREK.

Tourism

The main tourist attractions are the magnificent sandy beaches, Moorish architecture and remains of the Roman Empire. Tunisia contains the site of the ancient Phoenician city of Carthage. Tourism, a principal source of foreign exchange, has expanded rapidly, following extensive government investment in hotels, improved roads and other facilities. The number of hotel beds increased from 71,529 in 1980 to 188,600 in 1999. In that year foreign tourist arrivals totalled 4.8m. (compared with 4.7m. in 1998). Receipts from tourism in 1999 totalled 1,950m. dinars.

Office National du Tourisme Tunisien: 1 ave Muhammad V, 1001 Tunis; tel. (71) 341-077; fax (71) 350-997; e-mail info@tourismtunisia.com; internet www.tourismtunisia.com; f. 1958; Dir-Gen. FAKHREDDINE MESSAI.

Defence

Chief of Staff of the Army: Col RACHID AMMAR.

Chief of Staff of the Navy: Adm. HABIB FEDHILA.

Chief of Staff of the Air Force: Gen. RIDHA ATTAR.

Defence Budget (2000): 461m. dinars.

Military Service: 1 year (selective).

Total Armed Forces (estimates, August 2001): 35,000 (army 27,000; navy 4,500; air force 3,500).

Paramilitary Forces (August 2001): 12,000 National Guard.

Education

Education is compulsory in Tunisia for a period of nine years between the ages of six and 16. Primary education begins at six years of age and normally lasts for six years. Secondary education begins at 12 years of age and lasts for seven years, comprising a first cycle of three years and a second cycle of four years. In 1997 the total enrolment at primary schools was equivalent to 99.9% of the school-age population (99.9% of boys; 99.9% of girls). In that year the total enrolment at secondary schools included 74.3% of children in the relevant age-group (76.2% of boys; 72.4% of girls).

Proposed administrative budget expenditure on education was 1,395m. dinars in 1999, representing 17.7% of total government spending.

Arabic is the first language of instruction in primary and secondary schools, but French is also used. French is used almost exclusively in higher education. The University of Tunis was opened in 1959/60. In 1988 the university was divided into separate institutions: one for science, the other for arts. It has 54 faculties and institutes. In 1986 two new universities were opened, at Monastir and Sfax. In 1999/2000 a total of 180,044 students were enrolled at universities in Tunisia.

Bibliography

Anthony, John. *About Tunisia.* London, 1961.

Ardant, Gavriel. *La Tunisie d'Aujourd'hui et Demain.* Paris, 1961.

Ashford, Douglas E. *Morocco-Tunisia: Politics and Planning.* Syracuse University Press, 1965.

Azaiez, Tahar Letaief. *Tunisie, changements politiques et emploi (1956–1996).* Paris, L'Harmattan, 2000.

Basset, André. *Initiation à la Tunisie.* Paris, 1950.

Belkhodja, Tahar. *Les trois décennies de Bourguiba.* Paris, Arcanteres-Publisud, 1998.

Ben Brik, Taoufik. *Une si douce dictature: chroniques tunisiennes 1990–2000.* Paris, La Découverte: Reporters sans Frontières, 2000.

Ben Salem, Mohamed. *L'Antichambre de l'Indépendance.* Tunis, CERES Productions, 1988.

Bessis, Sophie, and Belhassen, Souhayr. *Bourguiba Tome 1: A la conquête d'un destin (1901–1957).* Paris, Jeune Afrique Livres, 1988.

Bourguiba, Habib. *La Tunisie et la France.* Paris, 1954.

   Hadith al-Jamaa. (Collected Broadcasts) Tunis, 1957.

Brunschvig, Robert. *La Tunisie au haut Moyen Age.* Cairo, 1948.

Camau, Michel. *Tunisie au présent. Une modernité au-dessus de tout soupçon?* Paris, Centre National de la Recherche, 1987.

Cambon, Henri. *Histoire de la régence de Tunisie.* Paris, 1948.

Charrad, Mounira M. *States and Women's Rights—The Making of Postcolonial Tunisia, Algeria and Morocco.* Berkeley, CA, University of California Press, 2000.

Depois, Jean. *La Tunisie, ses Régions.* Paris, 1959.

Duvignaud, Jean. *Tunisie.* Lausanne, Editions Rencontre, 1965.

Duwaji, Ghazi. *Economic Development in Tunisia.* New York, Praeger, 1967.

Garas, Félix. *Bourguiba et la Naissance d'une Nation.* Paris, 1956.

Guen, Moncef. *La Tunisie indépendante face à son économie.* Paris, 1961.

Joffe, E. G. H. Editor. *North Africa: Nation, State and Region.* London, Routledge, 1993.

Knapp, W. *Tunisia.* London, Thames and Hudson, 1972.

Laitman, Leon. *Tunisia Today: Crisis in North Africa.* New York, 1954.

Ling, Dwight D. *Tunisia, from Protectorate to Republic.* Indiana University Press, 1967.

Memmi, Albert. *Le Pharaon.* Paris, Julliard, 1988.

Micaud, C. A. *Tunisia, the Politics of Moderation.* New York, 1964.

Moore, C. H. *Tunisia since Independence.* Berkeley, University of California Press, 1965.

Murphy, Emma C. *Economic and Political Change in Tunisia: from Bourguiba to Ben Ali.* London, St Martin's Press, 2000.

Nerfin, M. *Entretiens avec Ahmed Ben Salah.* Paris, F. Maspero, 1974.

Perkins, Kenneth J. *Historical Dictionary of Tunisia* (African Historical Dictionaries, No. 45). Metuchen, NJ, and London, The Scarecrow Press, 1989.

Raymond, André. *La Tunisie.* Series *Que sais-je,* No. 318, Paris, 1961.

Rudebeck, Lars. *Party and People: A Study of Political Change in Tunisia.* London, C. Hurst, 1969.

Salem, Norma. *Habib Bourguiba, Islam and the Creation of Tunisia.* London, Croom Helm, 1984.

Sylvester, Anthony. *Tunisia.* London, Bodley Head, 1969.

Tlatli, Salah-Eddine. *Tunisie nouvelle.* Tunis, 1957.

White, Gregory. *A Comparative Political Economy of Tunisia and Morocco: On the Outside of Europe Looking In.* Albany NY, State University of New York Press, 2001.

World Bank. *Tunisia's Global Integration and Sustainable Development: Strategic Choices for the 21st Century.* World Bank, 1997.

Ziadeh, Nicola, A. *The Origins of Tunisian Nationalism.* Beirut, 1962.

TURKEY

Physical and Social Geography

W. B. FISHER

Turkey is, in a remarkable sense, passage land between Europe and Asia, having land frontiers with Greece, Bulgaria, Armenia, Georgia, the Nakhichevan autonomous enclave of Azerbaijan, Iran, Iraq and Syria. The west, the richest and most densely populated part of Turkey, looks towards the Aegean and Mediterranean seas and is very conscious of its links with Europe. However, in culture, racial origins and ways of life, there are frequent reminders of Turkey's geographical situation primarily as a part of Asia.

Turkey consists essentially of the large peninsula of Asia Minor, which has strongly defined natural limits; sea on three sides (the Black Sea to the north, the Aegean to the west, and the Mediterranean to the south), and high mountain ranges on the fourth (eastern) side. The small region of European Turkey, containing the cities of İstanbul (Constantinople) and Edirne (Adrianople), is, on the other hand, defined by a purely artificial frontier, the exact position of which has varied considerably since the 19th century, according to the fluctuating fortunes and prestige of Turkey itself. Another small territory, the Hatay, in southern Turkey and centred on İskenderun (Alexandretta) is bordered to the west by the Mediterranean sea and to the east by Syria, from which it was acquired as part of a diplomatic bargain in 1939.

PHYSICAL FEATURES

The geological structure of Turkey is extremely complicated, and rocks of almost all ages occur, from the most ancient to most recent. Broadly speaking, Turkey consists of a number of old plateau blocks, against which masses of younger rock series have been squeezed to form fold mountain ranges of varying size. As there were several of these plateau blocks, rather than just one, the fold mountains run in many different directions, with considerable irregularity, and hence no simple pattern can be discerned—instead, one mountain range gives place to another abruptly, and we can pass suddenly from highland to plain or plateau.

In general outline Turkey consists of a ring of mountains enclosing a series of inland plateaux, with the highest mountains to the east, close to Armenia and Iran. Mount Ararat is the highest peak in Turkey, reaching 5,165 m, and there are neighbouring peaks almost as high. In the west the average altitude of the hills is distinctly lower, though the highest peak (Mount Erciyas or Argaeus) is over 3,900 m. The irregular topography of Turkey has given rise to many lakes, some salt and some fresh, and generally more numerous than elsewhere in the Middle East. The largest, Lake Van, covers nearly 4,000 sq km.

Two other features may be mentioned. Large areas of the east and some parts of the centre of Asia Minor have been covered in sheets of lava which are often of such recent occurrence that soil has not yet been formed—consequently wide expanses are sterile and uninhabited. Secondly, in the north and west, cracking and disturbance of the rocks has taken place on an enormous scale. The long, indented coast of the Aegean Sea, with its numerous oddly shaped islands and estuaries, is due to cracking in two directions, which has split the land into detached blocks of roughly rectangular shape. Often the lower parts have sunk and been drowned by the sea. The Bosphorus and Dardanelles owe their origin to this faulting action, and the whole of the Black Sea coast is due to subsidence along a great series of fissures. Movement and adjustment along these cracks has by no means ceased, so that at the present day earthquakes are frequent in the north and west of Turkey.

Because of the presence of mountain ranges close to the coast, and the great height of the interior plateaux (varying from 800 m to 2,000 m), Turkey has special climatic conditions, characterized by great extremes of temperature and rainfall, with wide variation from one district to another. In winter, conditions are severe in most areas, except for those lying close to sea-level. Temperatures of –30°C to –40°C can occur in the east, and snow lies there for as many as 120 days each year. The west has frost on most nights of December and January, and (again apart from the coastal zone) has an average winter temperature below 1°C. In summer, however, temperatures over most of Turkey exceed 30°C, with 43°C in the south-east. There can hence be enormous seasonal variations of temperature—sometimes over 50°C, among the widest in the world.

Rainfall, too, is remarkably variable. Along the eastern Black Sea coast, towards the Georgian frontier, over 2,500 mm fall annually; but elsewhere, amounts are very much smaller. Parts of the central plateau, being shut off by mountains from the influence of sea winds, are arid, with annual totals of under 250 mm, and expanses of salt steppe and desert are frequent. Like Iran, Turkey also has a 'dead heart', and the main towns of Anatolia, including Ankara, the capital, are placed away from the centre and close to the hills, where rainfall tends to be greater and water supplies better.

It is necessary to emphasize the contrast that exists between the Aegean coastlands, which, climatically, are by far the most favoured regions of Turkey, and the rest of the country. Round the Aegean, winters are mild and fairly rainy, and the summers hot, but tempered by a persistent northerly wind, the Meltemi, or Etesian wind, which is of great value in ripening fruit, especially figs and sultana grapes.

ECONOMIC LIFE

The variety of geographical conditions within Turkey has led to uneven development, intensified by poor communications, due to the broken nature of the topography. Roads are relatively few, railways slow and often circuitous, and whole districts—sometimes even considerable towns—are accessible only by unsurfaced track. Many rivers flow in deep gorges near their sources and either meander or are broken by cascades in their lower reaches, so that none are navigable.

Thus, we find that the west of Turkey, situated close to the Aegean Sea, is by far the most densely peopled and the most intensively developed. Since 1923, however, attempts have been made to develop the Anatolian plateau and the districts in the extreme east, which, following the expulsion and massacre of the Armenians in 1914–18, for a time supported only a very scanty population. Development in the central plateau has been aided by the exploitation of several small, but on the whole valuable, mineral deposits, and by irrigation schemes to improve agriculture. A certain degree of industrialization (mainly undertaken by state-sponsored and -owned organizations) has also grown up, based on Turkish-produced raw materials—cotton, wool, mohair, beet-sugar, olive oil and tobacco. The eastern districts present a more intractable problem, and development so far has been slower.

The considerable increase of population in recent years (an annual average of 2.2% in 1985–90, 1.5% in 1990–98 and 2.5% in 1999–2001) has led to intensification of settlement and to an increase in the use of available land for cultivation. Because of the strategic importance of the country, there has been a considerable pro-gramme of road-building, largely financed by the USA. The absorption of Turkish labour in Western Europe (chiefly Germany) provides useful extra revenue from remittances.

RACE AND LANGUAGE

Racially, the bulk of the Turkish people show an inter-mixture of Mediterranean and Armenoid strains. In the western half of the country the two are more or less equally represented; but further east the proportion of Armenoids steadily increases until, towards the former Soviet and Iranian borders, they become almost universal. Much of south-eastern Turkey is inhabited by Kurds, a people of Indo-European descent; estimates of their number range from 3m. to more than 8m. Turkey also has less important racial elements; there would seem to be small numbers of proto-Nordics in the north and west, and some authorities suggest a racial relationship between Galatia (the modern district of Ankara) and ancient Gaul. The Ottoman Turks were, in the main, of Turki (western Mongoloid) ancestry but, in the view of some authorities, their contribution to the ethnic stocks of Turkey was small, since they were really an invading tribal group that became an aristocracy and soon intermarried with other peoples. There are also numbers of Caucasians—particularly Circassians and Georgians—who have contributed to the racial structure of Turkey; and during

1951 a further element was added by the arrival of many thousands of Bulgarian Muslims who had been deported from their own country.

The Turkish language, which is of central Asiatic origin, is spoken over most, but by no means all, of the country. This was introduced into Turkey in Seljuq times, and was written in Arabic characters, but, as these are not really well adapted to the sound of Turkish, Roman (i.e. European) script has been compulsory since 1928. In addition, there are a number of non-Turkish languages. Kurdish is widely spoken in the south-east, along the Syrian and Iraqi frontiers; and Caucasian dialects, quite different from either Turkish or Kurdish, occur in the north-east. Greek and Armenian were once widespread but, following the deportations which began in the 1920s, both forms of speech are now current only in the city of İstanbul, where considerable numbers of Greeks and Armenians still live.

History

Revised for this edition by ALAN J. DAY

ANCIENT HISTORY

The most ancient written records so far found in Asia Minor date from the beginning of the second millennium BC. They are in Assyrian, and reveal the existence of Assyrian trading colonies in Cappadocia. These documents, together with a growing amount of archaeological evidence, show an important Copper Age culture in Central Anatolia in the third and early second millennia. Later in the second millennium the greater part of Asia Minor fell under the rule of the Hittites, whose empire flourished from about 1600 BC to about 1200 BC, and reached its apogee in the 14th and 13th centuries, when it became one of the dominant states of the eastern Mediterranean. After the break-up of the Hittite Empire, Asia Minor was split up among a number of dynasties and peoples—Phrygians, Cimmerians, Lydians and others—about whom not very much is known. Towards the end of the Hittite period the Greeks began to invade the Aegean coast, and entered on a long struggle with the native states that is reflected in the story of the Trojan War. Greek culture spread in western Anatolia, which was gradually incorporated into the Hellenic world. A series of political changes, of which the most important are the Persian conquest in 546 BC, the conquest of Alexander in 334 BC, and the constitution of the Roman province of Asia in 133 BC, did not impede the steady spread of Greek language and culture in the cities.

In AD 330, the Emperor Constantine inaugurated the new city of Constantinople, on the site of the old Greek trading settlement of Byzantium. This city at once became the capital of the East Roman and then of the Christian Byzantine Empire. Asia Minor was now the metropolitan province of a great empire, and grew in wealth, prosperity and importance. Under Byzantine rule Greek Christianity, already firmly established in Roman times, spread over most of the peninsula.

SELJUQS AND OTTOMANS

At the beginning of the 11th century a new conquest of Anatolia began—that of the Turks. The early history of the Turkish peoples is still obscure. Some references in the ancient biography of Alexander show them to have been established in Central Asia at the time of his conquests, and Turkish tribal confederacies played an important part in the invasions of Europe from late Roman times onwards. The name 'Turk' first appears in historical records in the sixth century AD, when Chinese annals speak of a powerful empire in Central Asia, founded by a steppe people called Tu-Kiu. It is from this state that the oldest surviving Turkish inscriptions have come. From the seventh century onwards the Central Asian Turks came into ever closer contact with the Islamic peoples of the Near East, from whom they adopted the Islamic faith and the Arabic script, and with them much of the complex civilization of Islam. From the ninth century Turks entered the service of the Caliphate in increasing

numbers, and soon came to provide the bulk of its armies, its generals and, eventually, its rulers.

From the 10th century whole tribes of Turks began to migrate into Persia and Iraq, and in the 11th century, under the leadership of the family of Seljuq, the Turks were able to set up a great empire comprising most of the eastern lands of the Caliphate. The Muslim armies on the Byzantine frontier had long been predominantly Turkish, and in the course of the 11th century they began a great movement into Anatolia which resulted in the termination of Byzantine rule in most of the country and its incorporation in the Muslim Seljuq Sultanate. A Seljuq prince, Süleyman ibn Kutlumush, was sent to organize the new province, and by the end of the 12th century his successors had built up a strong Turkish monarchy in Anatolia, with its capital in Konya (the ancient Iconium). Under the rule of the Anatolian Seljuqs, which in various forms lasted until the 14th century, Anatolia gradually became a Turkish land. Masses of Turkish immigrants from further east entered the country and a Turkish, Muslim civilization replaced Greek Christianity.

In the late 13th century the Sultanate of Konya fell into decay, and gradually gave way to a number of smaller principalities. One of these, in north-western Anatolia, was ruled by a certain Osman, or Othman, from whom the name Ottoman is derived. The Ottoman state soon embarked on a great movement of expansion, on the one hand in Anatolia, at the expense of its Turkish neighbours, on the other in the Balkans. Ottoman armies first crossed to Europe in the mid-14th century, and by 1400 they were masters of much of the Balkan peninsula as well as almost all of Anatolia. The capital was moved first from Bursa to Edirne and then, in 1453, to Constantinople, the final conquest of which from the last Byzantine emperor completed the process that had transformed a principality of frontier-warriors into a new great empire. Constantinople, called İstanbul by the Turks, remained the capital of the Ottoman Empire until 1922. The wave of conquest was by no means spent. For more than a century Ottoman arms continued to advance into Central Europe, while in 1516–17 Sultan Selim I destroyed the Mamluk sultanate and incorporated Syria and Egypt into the Empire. During the reign of Sultan Süleyman I (1520–66), known as the Magnificent in Europe, the Ottoman Empire was at the height of its power.

The decay of the Empire is usually dated from the death of Süleyman. In the West great changes were taking place. The Renaissance and the Reformation, the rapid development of science and technology, the emergence of strong, centralized nation states with constantly improving military techniques, the deflection of the main routes of international trade from the Mediterranean to the open seas, all combined to strengthen Turkey's Western adversaries while leaving her own resources unchanged or even diminished, and contributing to her cultural and economic stagnation. By the end of the 17th century the weakness of the Ottoman state was manifest. During the 18th century Austria and Russia made the main territorial advances in the Balkans and in the Black Sea area, while Britain and France were content with commercial and diplomatic privileges. In a succession of wars one province after another was lost, while internal conditions worsened. During the 19th century Britain and France began to play a more active role. British policy was generally to support the Turks against their impatient heirs. In 1854 Britain and France went to war at the side of Turkey in order to check Russian ambitions, and in 1877–78 British diplomatic intervention was effective to the same end. Meanwhile, nationalist ideas had spread from the West to the subject peoples of the Empire, and one by one the Serbs, Greeks, Romanians and Bulgarians succeeded in throwing off Ottoman rule and attaining independent statehood.

The first serious attempts at reform by the Turks themselves occurred during the reign of Selim III (1789–1807). During the 19th century a series of reforming sultans and ministers worked on a programme of development and modernization which, though it fell short of its avowed objectives, nevertheless transformed the face of the Ottoman Empire and began a process of change, the effects of which are still visible. In 1878 the reforming movement came to an abrupt end and until 1908 the Empire was ruled by Abd al-Hamid II, who ruthlessly repressed every attempt at liberal thought and reform. In 1908 the secret opposition group known as the Young Turks seized power and, in a wave of revolutionary enthusiasm, inaugurated a Constitution, parliamentary government and a whole series of liberal reforms. However, internal dissension, then foreign wars, combined to turn the Young Turk regime into a military dictatorship. In 1911 the Italians suddenly started a war against Turkey which ended with their gaining Libya and the Dodecanese Islands; in 1912–13 a Balkan alliance succeeded in wresting from the Empire most of its remaining possessions on the continent of Europe. Finally, in October 1914, Turkey entered the war on the side of the Central powers. During the reign of Abd al-Hamid, German influence had been steadily increasing in Turkey and the process continued under the Young Turks. It was also helped by the growing friendship between the Western powers and Russia, as Germany was the only power that seemed ready to support the Turks against Russian designs. German officers reorganized the Turkish army; German businessmen and technicians extended their hold on the economic resources of the country and German engineers and financiers began the construction of the famous Baghdad railway which was to provide direct rail communication between Germany and the Middle East.

The Turkish alliance was of immense military value to the Central powers. The Turkish armies, still established in Syria and Palestine, were able to offer an immediate and serious threat to the Suez Canal and to the British position in Egypt. By their dogged and successful defence of the Dardanelles they prevented effective co-operation between Russia and the Western powers. Their position as the greatest independent Muslim state, and their prestige among Muslims elsewhere, created a series of problems in the British and French Empires.

Despite their weakness and exhaustion after two previous wars, the Turks were able to wage a bitter defensive war against the Allies. After two unsuccessful attempts, a new British attack from Egypt and from India succeeded in expelling the Turks from Palestine, Syria, and most of Iraq. Defeated on all sides and cut off from their allies, the Turks abandoned the struggle and signed an armistice at Mudros on 30 October 1918. French, Italian and British occupation forces moved into Turkey.

For some time the victorious powers were too busy elsewhere to attend to the affairs of Turkey and it was not until the San Remo Conference of April 1920 that the first serious attempt was made to settle the Turkish question. Meanwhile, the victors were busy quarrelling among themselves. Partly, no doubt, with the idea of forestalling Italian ambitions, the British, French, and US Governments agreed to a Greek proposal for a Greek occupation of İzmir (Smyrna) and the surrounding country, and on 15 May 1919 a Greek army, under cover of Allied warships, landed there. The integrity of this move later became a cause for concern within the Allied camp, and in October the Inter-Allied Commission in İstanbul condemned it as 'unjustifiable' and as 'a violation of the terms of the Armistice'. The conse-

quences of the invasion for Turkey were momentous. Now, it was no longer the non-Turkish subject provinces and the Ottoman superstructure of the Turkish nation that were threatened, but the Turkish homeland itself. Moreover, the Greeks, unlike the Western Allies, showed that they intended to stay, and that their aim was the incorporation of the territories they occupied into the Greek kingdom. The Turkish reaction to this danger was vigorous and immediate. The Nationalist movement, hitherto limited to a small class of intellectuals, became the mass instrument of Turkish determination to preserve the integrity and independence of the homeland. A new leader appeared to organize their victory.

THE RISE OF ATATÜRK

Mustafa Kemal, surnamed Atatürk in 1934, was born in Salonika, then an Ottoman city, in 1880. After a promising career as a regular army officer, he achieved his first active command in Libya in 1911, and thereafter fought with distinction in the successive wars in which his country was involved. After his brilliant conduct of the defence of Gallipoli he fought on various fronts against the Allies, and at the time of the Armistice held a command on the Syrian front. A month later he returned to İstanbul, and at once began to seek ways and means of getting to Anatolia to organize national resistance. At length he was successful, and on 19 May 1919—four days after the Greek landing in İzmir—he arrived at Samsun, on the Black Sea coast, ostensibly in order to supervise the disbanding of the remaining Turkish forces. Instead he set to work at once on the double task of organizing a national movement and raising a national army.

Meanwhile the Allied powers were at last completing their arrangements for the obsequies of the Turkish Empire. After a series of conferences, a treaty was drawn up and signed by the Allied representatives and those of the Sultan's Government at Sèvres, on 10 August 1920. The Treaty of Sèvres was very harsh—far more so than that imposed on Germany. This treaty was, however, never implemented. While the Allies were imposing their terms on the Sultan and his Government in İstanbul, a new Turkish state was rising in the interior of Anatolia, based on the rejection of the treaty and the principles on which it was founded. On 23 July 1919 Mustafa Kemal and his associates convened the first Nationalist congress in Erzurum, and drew up a national programme. Delegates from all over the country attended a second congress, held in September. An Executive Committee, presided over by Kemal, was formed, and chose Ankara, then a minor provincial town, as its headquarters. Ankara soon became the effective capital of the Nationalist movement and forces. It was there that they issued the famous National Pact, the declaration that laid down the basic programme of the Kemalist movement, renouncing the Empire and the domination of the non-Turkish provinces, but demanding the total and unconditional independence of all areas inhabited by Turks. This declaration won immediate support, and on 28 January 1920 was approved even by the legal Ottoman Parliament sitting in İstanbul. The growth of the Nationalist movement in İstanbul alarmed the Allies, and on 16 March British forces entered the Turkish part of the city and arrested and deported many Nationalist leaders. Despite this reverse, followed by a new anti-Nationalist campaign on the part of the Sultan and his political and religious advisers, the Kemalists continued to advance. On 19 March Kemal ordered general elections, and at the end of April a National Assembly of 350 deputies met in Ankara and voted the National Pact. The Sultan and his Government were declared deposed, a provisional constitution promulgated and a government set up with Mustafa Kemal as President.

There remained the military task of expelling the invaders. The Greco–Turkish war falls into three stages, covering roughly the campaigns of 1920, 1921 and 1922. In the first campaign the Nationalists, hopelessly outmatched in numbers and material, were badly defeated and the Greeks advanced far into Anatolia. Turkish resistance was, however, strong enough to impress the Allies, who, for the first time, accorded a certain limited recognition to the Nationalist Government and proclaimed their neutrality in the Greco–Turkish war. The second campaign began with Greek successes, but the Turks rallied and defeated the invaders first at İnönü—from which İsmet Pasha, who commanded the Turkish forces there, later took his surname—and then, on 24 August 1921, in a major battle on the Sakarya river, where the Turkish forces were under the personal command of Mustafa Kemal. This victory considerably strengthened the Nationalists, who were now generally realized to be the effective Government of Turkey. The French and Italians withdrew from the areas of Anatolia assigned to them under the Treaty of Sèvres and made terms with the new Government. The Soviets, now established on Turkey's eastern frontier, had already done so at the beginning of the year.

A period of waiting and reorganization followed, during which the morale of the Greek armies was adversely affected by political changes in Greece. In August 1922 the third and final phase of the war of independence began. The Turkish Army drove the Greeks back to the Aegean and on 9 September reoccupied İzmir. Mustafa Kemal now prepared to cross to Thrace. To do so he had to cross the Straits, still under Allied occupation. The French and Italian contingents withdrew, and, after a menacing pause, the British followed. On 11 October an armistice was signed at Mudanya, whereby the Allied Governments agreed to the restoration of Turkish sovereignty in Eastern Thrace. In November the Sultan's Cabinet resigned and the Sultan himself went into exile. Turkey once more had only one Government and İstanbul, the ancient seat of empire, became a provincial city, ruled by a governor appointed from Ankara.

The peace conference opened in November 1922 and the treaty was finally signed on 24 July 1923. It recognized complete and undivided Turkish sovereignty and the abolition of the last vestiges of foreign privilege. The only reservation related to the demilitarization of the Straits, which were not to be fortified without the consent of the powers. This consent was given at the Montreux Conference in 1936.

THE TURKISH REPUBLIC

The military task was completed, and the demands formulated in the National Pact had been embodied in an international treaty. There remained the greater task of rebuilding the ruins of long years of war and revolution—and of remedying those elements of weakness in the Turkish state and society that had brought Turkey to the verge of extinction. Mustafa Kemal saw the solution of Turkey's problems in a process of Westernization—in the integration of Turkey, on a basis of equality, in the modern Western world. Between 1922 and 1938, the year of his death, Kemal carried through a series of far-reaching reforms.

The first changes were political. After the deposition of Sultan Vahdeddin in November 1922, a brief experiment was made with a purely religious sovereignty and Abd al-Mejid was proclaimed as Caliph but not Sultan. The experiment was not successful. Abd al-Mejid followed his predecessor into exile and on 29 October 1923 Turkey was declared a Republic, with Kemal as President. The Kemal regime was effectively a dictatorship—though without the violence and oppression normally associated with that word in Europe. A single party, the Cumhuriyet Halk Partisi (CHP—Republican People's Party), formed the main instrument for the enforcement of government policy. The Constitution of 20 April 1924 provided for an elected parliament, which was the repository of sovereign power. Executive power was to be exercised by the President and a cabinet chosen by him.

The next object of attack was the religious hierarchy already weakened by the removal of the Sultan-Caliph. In a series of edicts the Ministry of Religious Affairs was abolished, the religious orders disbanded, religious property sequestrated and religious instruction forbidden. With the religious leaders in retreat, the attack on the old social order began. Certainly the most striking reforms were the abolition of the fez and the Arabic script, and the adoption of the Latin script. But these were probably less important in the long run than the abrogation of the old legal system and the introduction of new civil and criminal codes of law adapted from Europe. In 1928 Islam itself was disestablished and the Constitution amended to make Turkey a secular state.

Not the least of the problems that faced Mustafa Kemal was the economic one. Turkey needed capital. Rather than risk the independence of Turkey by inviting in foreign capital at a time of weakness, Kemal adopted the principle of *étatisme*, and made it one of the cardinal doctrines of his regime. From 1923 to 1933 the State's main achievement was in railway construction, nearly doubling the length of line in that period. At the same time efforts were made towards establishing other industries. While often wasteful and inefficient, state-sponsored industry was probably the only form of development possible at the time without recourse to foreign aid.

The foreign policy of the Republic was, for a long time, one of strict non-involvement in foreign disputes, and the maintenance of friendly relations with as many powers as possible. In 1935–36, however, Turkey co-operated loyally in sanctions against Italy, and thereafter the growing threat of German, and more especially Italian, aggression led to closer links with the West and in 1938 steps were taken to strengthen economic links between Turkey and the United Kingdom.

The establishment of the Republic also put an end to the prospect of Kurdish independence offered by the Treaty of Sèvres. The Kurds were opposed to Kemal's secularist and nationalist policies and in 1925 rose up in revolt after the abolition of the Caliphate. They were ruthlessly crushed. A more nationalist uprising in 1930 and a further revolt against the repressive actions taken by the Government were also suppressed. The Kurdish provinces remained rigorously policed, garrisons were established in larger towns and Kurdish leaders were exiled. The Kurdish language was made illegal and the Government refused to recognize any aspect of the Kurds' separate ethnic identity, calling them 'mountain Turks'.

The death of Kemal Atatürk in November 1938 was a great shock to Turkey. He was succeeded as President by İsmet İnönü (formerly known as İsmet Pasha), who announced his intention of maintaining and carrying on the work of his predecessor. The new President was soon called upon to guide his country through a very difficult time. As early as 12 May 1939 a joint Anglo-Turkish declaration was issued, stating that 'the British and Turkish Governments, in the event of an act of aggression leading to war in the Mediterranean area, would co-operate effectively and lend each other all the aid and assistance in their power'. This prepared the way for the formal Anglo-French-Turkish Treaty of Alliance, signed on 19 October. It had been hoped that this Treaty would be complemented by a parallel treaty with the USSR, but the equivocal attitude of the Soviet Government, followed by the Stalin-Hitler Agreement of August 1939, made this impossible, and the Turks proceeded with the Western alliance in the face of clearly expressed Soviet disapproval. They protected themselves, however, by Protocol II of the treaty, stipulating that nothing in the treaty should bind them to any action likely to involve them in war with the USSR.

TURKEY DURING THE SECOND WORLD WAR

The fall of France, the hostile attitude of the Soviet Government and the extension of German power over most of Europe led the Turkish Government to the conclusion that nothing would be gained by provoking an almost certain German conquest. While continuing to recognize the Alliance, therefore, they invoked Protocol II as a reason for remaining neutral. In June 1941, when German expansion in the Balkans had brought the German armies within 100 miles of İstanbul, the Turkish Government further protected itself by signing a friendship and trade agreement with Germany. However, the agreement stipulated that Turkey would still maintain her treaty obligations to Britain.

The German attack on the USSR, and the consequent entry of that country into the Grand Alliance, brought an important change to the situation, and the Western powers increased their pressure on Turkey to enter the war. The main consideration holding Turkey back from active participation in the war was mistrust of the USSR, and the widespread feeling that Nazi conquest and Soviet 'liberation' were equally to be feared. While stopping short of actual belligerency, however, the Turks, especially after 1942, entered into closer economic and military relations with the West and aided the Allied cause in a number of ways. In August 1944 they broke off diplomatic relations with Germany and on 23 February 1945 declared war on Germany in order to comply with the formalities of entry to the United Nations (UN) Conference.

The war years subjected Turkey to severe economic strains. These, and the dangers of armed neutrality in a world at war, resulted in the imposition of martial law, of closer police surveillance and of a generally more authoritarian form of government. Between 1945 and 1950, came a further series of changes, no less remarkable than the great reforms of Atatürk. When the Charter of the UN was introduced for ratification in the Turkish Parliament in 1945, a group of members, led by Celâl Bayar, Adnan Menderes, Fuad Köprülü and Refik Koraltan, tabled a motion suggesting a series of reforms in the law and the Constitution that would effectively ensure inside Turkey those liberties to which the Turkish Government was giving its theoretical approval in the Charter. The Government rejected the motion and the motion's sponsors were forced to leave the party. In November, however, under pressure of a by now active and informed public opinion, President İnönü announced the end of the single-party system and in January 1946 the opposition leaders registered the new Demokratik Parti (DP—Democratic Party).

TURKEY UNDER THE DEMOCRATIC PARTY

In July 1946 new elections gave the DP opposition 70 out of 416 parliamentary seats and there can be little doubt that completely free elections would have given them many more. During the years that followed the breach in the dictatorship grew ever wider and a series of changes in both law and practice ensured the growth of democratic liberties. Freedom of the press and of association were extended, martial law was ended and on 15 February 1950 a new electoral law was approved, guaranteeing free and fair elections. In May 1950 a new general election was held, in which the DP won an overwhelming victory. Celâl Bayar became President and a new Cabinet was formed, with Adnan Menderes as Prime Minister. The new regime adopted a more liberal economic policy, involving the partial abandonment of *étatisme* and the encouragement of private enterprise, both Turkish and foreign. For a time the stability and progress of the Republic seemed to be threatened by the growing activities of groups of religious fanatics, whose programme appeared to require little less than the abrogation of all the reforms achieved by the Turkish revolution. After an attempt on the life of the liberal journalist Ahmet Emin Yalman in November 1952, the Government took more vigorous action against what were called the 'forces of clericalism and reaction'. Many arrests were made and in mid-1953 the National Party, accused of complicity in reactionary plots, was briefly outlawed and legislation was passed prohibiting the exploitation of religion for political purposes. The relations between the two main parties, after a temporary improvement in the face of the common danger of reaction, deteriorated again in the course of 1953–54, though not to such an extent as to imperil national unity. On 2 May 1954, in Turkey's third general election since the war, the DP won a resounding victory.

In view of the smallness and weakness of the opposition parties and the immense parliamentary majority of the DP, it was inevitable that sooner or later divisions would appear within it. In October 1955 a serious crisis culminated in the dismissal or resignation from the party of 19 deputies. These were later joined by others and formed a new party, the Freedom Party.

Conflict between the Government and opposition was sharpened by the decision taken to advance the date of the general elections by more than eight months, to 27 October 1957. The three opposition parties—Republicans, Freedom and National Parties—first intended to present a united front, but the electoral law was changed to make this impossible. They were therefore obliged to present separate lists in each constituency, and so, although the combined votes won by opposition candidates were slightly more than 50% of the total, the DP again emerged triumphant, though with a diminished majority.

FOREIGN AFFAIRS 1945–60

In foreign affairs, both the CHP and the DP Governments followed a firm policy of unreserved identification with the West in the Cold War. From May 1947 the USA extended economic and military aid to Turkey on an increasing scale, and in 1950 a first indication of both the seriousness and the effectiveness of Turkish policy was given with the dispatch of Turkish troops to Korea, where they fought with distinction. In August 1949 Turkey became a member of the Council of Europe, and early

in 1952 acceded to full membership of the North Atlantic Treaty Organization (NATO), in which it began to play an increasingly important part. Thereafter other arrangements were made by which Turkey accepted a role in both Balkan and Middle Eastern defence. This culminated in November 1955 in Turkey's joining the Baghdad Pact, in which the country subsequently played a major role.

In January 1957 the USA announced a new programme of economic and military assistance for those countries of the area which were willing to accept it. At a further meeting held in Ankara the Muslim states belonging to the Baghdad Pact expressed their approval of this 'Eisenhower Doctrine'. The USA in March made known its decision to join the military committee of the Baghdad Pact and later in March Turkey promised to co-operate with the USA against all subversive activities in the Middle East. It was announced that financial aid would be forthcoming from the USA for the economic projects previously discussed between the members of the Baghdad Pact.

From 1958 Turkey was actively involved in settling terms for the constitution of an independent Cyprus. These were eventually agreed between Turkey, Greece, the United Kingdom and the Greek and Turkish Cypriots. Cyprus achieved independence in August 1960.

Adherence to NATO and the Central Treaty Organization (CENTO) remained the basis of Turkey's foreign policy during the late 1950s. By the beginning of 1960, however, Turkey's relations with the USSR were becoming less antipathetic.

THE 1960 REVOLUTION

Economic difficulties continued to be one of the main preoccupations of the Turkish Government. The development plans envisaged since 1950 had been pursued with financial aid from the USA and from such bodies as the World Bank. These policies had been accompanied by inflationary pressures, an unfavourable trade balance, decreased imports, a shortage of foreign exchange and, since the agricultural population was in receipt of subsidies from the Government, a higher demand for consumer goods which aggravated the prevalent inflation. Social and economic unease tended to reveal itself in a drift of people from the villages to the towns, the population of centres like Ankara, İstanbul, İzmir, Bursa and Adana being considerably increased during recent decades.

The influences leading to the revolution had long been at work. Hostility between the DP and the opposition CHP grew steadily more marked, and was sharpened towards the end of 1959 by suspicions that the DP was planning to hold elections in the near future, ahead of schedule. It was feared that these would, if necessary, be rigged to keep the DP in power indefinitely.

In May 1959 political tension between the two main parties had already broken into violence during a political tour of Anatolia conducted by the opposition leader İsmet İnönü. The Government banned all political meetings. Blows were struck in the National Assembly and the opposition walked out.

Much the same pattern of events ushered in the final breakdown a year later. At the beginning of April 1960 İsmet İnönü undertook another political tour of Anatolia. At one point troops were called on to block his progress. The opposition tried, but failed, to force a debate in the Assembly, while the DP set up a commission of inquiry, composed entirely of its own supporters, to investigate 'the destructive and illegal activities of the CHP'. Again the National Assembly was the scene of violence, and all political activity was suspended for three months.

At the end of April, student unrest led to the imposition of martial law. As administrator of martial law, the Turkish army found itself, contrary to its traditions, involved in politics. A group of officers decided that their intervention must be complete if Turkey was to return to Kemalist principles. In the early hours of 27 May President Bayar, Prime Minister Menderes, most Democratic deputies and a number of officials and senior officers were arrested. The Government was replaced by a Committee of National Unity headed by Gen. Cemal Gürsel, a much respected senior officer who had fought with Atatürk at Gallipoli.

The coup was immediately successful and almost bloodless. The Menderes regime was accused of breaking the Constitution and moving towards dictatorship. The officers insisted that they were temporary custodians of authority and would hand over to the duly constituted civilian authorities. A temporary Constitution was quickly agreed, pending the drafting of a final new one. During this interval legislative power was vested in the Committee of National Unity, and executive power in a Council of Ministers, composed of civilians as well as soldiers. On 25 August, however, 10 of the 18 ministers were dismissed, leaving only three civilians in the Government. Gen. Gürsel was President of the Republic, Prime Minister and Minister of Defence. The courts were declared independent. Commissions were set up to inquire into the alleged misdeeds of the Menderes regime.

Although the new regime encountered political opposition, particularly among the peasants and around İzmir, a stronghold of Menderes, the main problems facing it were economic. The former regime had been heavily in debt. Austerity measures, including restrictions on credit, had to be put into operation and an economic planning board was set up to work out a long-term investment plan with the aid of foreign experts.

THE RETURN TO CIVILIAN GOVERNMENT

The Committee of National Unity, which originally consisted of 37 members, was reduced to 23 on 13 November 1960. This purge completed, preparations for a return to political democracy continued. A new Assembly, to act as a temporary parliament, was convened at the beginning of January 1961. It consisted of the 23 members of the Committee of National Unity, acting jointly with a House of Representatives of 271 members, both elected and nominated. In this the CHP predominated. At the same time party politics were again legalized and a number of new parties emerged. Some of them proved short-lived, but one, the Adalet Partisi (AP—Justice Party), founded by Gen. Ragip Gümüşpala, who had been Commander of the Third Army at the time of the *coup d'état*, attracted the support of many former adherents of the DP, which had been declared illegal.

A special committee of the Assembly framed a new Constitution which had some significant changes from the 1924 version. It provided for a court to determine the constitutionality of laws, for a bicameral legislature (comprising a National Assembly and a Senate), and it included a reference to 'social justice' as one of the aims of the State. These constitutional developments took place against the background of the trial of the accused members of the Menderes regime. The trial was held on the small island of Yassiada in the Bosphorus, where the accused had been confined after arrest, and lasted from October 1960 to August 1961. The sentence of the court was pronounced on 15 September. There were 15 death sentences, 12 of which, including that on Bayar, were commuted to life imprisonment. Adnan Menderes, Fatin Zorlu, the former Minister of Foreign Affairs, and Hasan Polatkan, the former Minister of Finance, were duly hanged. In September 1990, following a prolonged campaign by right-wing factions (including the ruling Anavatan Partisi—ANAP—Motherland Party), the bodies were exhumed and buried in İstanbul with state honours.

The trial, in 1960, inevitably absorbed the attention of the country, and there were many reminders that sympathy for the former regime and its leaders was far from dead. The most serious set-back for the authorities, however, appeared in the results of the referendum on the new Constitution. This was approved by 6,348,191 votes against 3,934,370, and the large minority was taken as an indication of continuing loyalty to the DP.

The campaign preceding elections in October 1961, perhaps because the Yassiada trials were ruled out as a subject for discussion, proved unexpectedly quiet. On 15 October the elections gave the CHP 173 seats and the AP 158 seats in the National Assembly, and 36 and 70 respectively in the Senate. The CHP had failed to achieve an overall working majority and a coalition became necessary. The election results were also further evidence of latent support for the DP. Parliament opened on 25 October 1961, whereupon the transfer of power from the military to civilians was made. The next day Gen. Gürsel, the only candidate, was elected President. However, forming a government proved a much harder process. On 10 November İsmet İnönü, leader of the CHP, was asked to form a government and, after much hesitation and strong pressure from the army, the AP agreed to join forces with its rival. A new Cabinet was formed with İnönü as Prime Minister, Akıf İyidoğan of the AP

as Deputy Prime Minister, and 10 more ministers from each of the two coalition parties.

The Government received criticism, both from those who thought the army did too much (i.e. that civil liberties were still circumscribed) and those who thought it did too little (i.e. that it did not crush all signs of counter-revolution). The resignation of İnönü at the end of May 1962 weakened the extremists in the AP, who had wanted to grant an amnesty to former supporters of Menderes. They were now face to face with the army, the original architects of the 1960 revolution, and many of them felt it wise to moderate their demands. By the end of June 1962 İnönü had formed a coalition Government composed of 12 ministers from the CHP, six from the New Turkey Party, four from the Republican Peasants' Nation Party, and one independent minister.

RAPPROCHEMENT WITH THE USSR

The first months of 1964 were overshadowed by an attempt on the life of İnönü in February, and by the situation in Cyprus, where the fate of the Turkish minority created strong feeling on the mainland. İnönü's critics claimed that he had displayed a considerable lack of foresight by failing to intervene on the island with force when the trouble started. Diplomatic efforts towards a solution failed and public disaffection grew, not only with Greece, but also with Turkey's western allies, in particular the USA and the United Kingdom, which were accused of being lukewarm in their support of Turkey's case. İnönü, though moving with characteristic caution, gave a warning that the alliance with the West, the basis of Turkey's foreign policy since the war, was in danger. To reinforce his warning, several steps were taken to improve relations with the USSR. Initially, the Soviet Government had appeared to side with Greece on the question of Cyprus; however, diplomatic approaches were made in both Moscow and Ankara. At the end of October Feridum Cemal Erkin was the first Turkish Minister of Foreign Affairs to visit the USSR for 25 years. On the issue of Cyprus, the USSR appeared to have moved closer to the Turkish point of view, the communiqué which ended Erkin's talks speaking favourably of a solution 'by peaceful means on the basis of respect for the territorial integrity of Cyprus, and for the legal rights of the two national communities'. Erkin's journey was followed up in January 1965 by the visit to Ankara of a Soviet parliamentary delegation. A trade pact between the two countries followed in March.

DEMIREL GOVERNMENT

For all this, the question of Cyprus continued to give the opposition ammunition with which to harass the İnönü Government. At the Senate elections in June 1964 the AP won 31 out of the 51 seats contested, thus increasing its already large majority in this house. Its success was clouded by the death of the party's leader, Gen. Gümüşpala. In November Süleyman Demirel was elected leader in his place, although he was without a seat in Parliament. İnönü survived more than one narrow vote of confidence, but was finally defeated on 13 February 1965 during voting in the National Assembly on the budget—the first time that the term of a Turkish Government had been ended in this way. After a short delay a coalition Government was formed from the four opposition parties—the AP, the New Turkish Party, the Republican Peasants' Party and the Millet Partisi (National Party). An independent senator, Suat Ürgüplü, became Prime Minister.

At the general election of 11 October 1965, the AP under Demirel won an overall majority. In spite of its working majority, the Demirel Government proved only marginally more successful than its predecessors in achieving its objectives. However, elections in June 1966 for one-third of the seats in the Senate showed that the AP was not losing popularity. Meanwhile, in March President Gürsel was succeeded by Senator Cevdet Sunay.

To some extent this success was attributed to the innate conservatism of the rural population, who may have been alarmed by İnönü's statement that the CHP was left of centre. This position was not approved by all the party—some thought that it went too far, others not far enough. A convention of the party in October 1966 showed a victory for the left-wingers. Bülent Ecevit, Minister of Labour in 1961–65, was elected

Secretary-General of the party, with the declared intention of turning it into a party of democratic socialism. Six months later 48 senators and members of the National Assembly, led by Turhan Feyzioğlu, a former minister, resigned from the party on the grounds that it was falling into a 'dangerous leftist adventure'. This was denied by Ecevit and İnönü, who supported him. They claimed that, on the contrary, their progressive policies would pre-empt the policies of, and undermine support for, other left-wing parties and therefore represented the best barrier against communism.

In May 1967 a majority of dissidents came together to form the Reliance Party, which proclaimed its opposition to socialism and its belief in the 'spiritual values of the Turkish nation'. In June Ecevit forced a fresh election of the CHP executive, and by securing the elimination of two left-wing representatives he was able to emphasize that his party remained left of centre rather than left wing.

In March 1968 a new electoral law was approved, in spite of the protests of a united opposition, which threatened the electoral chances of all the smaller parties but was thought to be particularly aimed at the Türkiye İşçi Partisi (TIP—Turkish Workers' Party), which was accused by the Government of using communist tactics.

Turkey's relations with its allies deteriorated in 1966. The Turkish press's campaign against US bases in Turkey led to a riot in Adana in March. Together with these manifestations against Turkey's formerly most stalwart ally, an effort by the Demirel Government to make its whole foreign policy more flexible was undertaken.

The touchstone of Turkey's foreign relations continued to be Cyprus. In 1967 this perennial problem oscillated between near settlement and near war. On 15 November the situation suddenly deteriorated as a result of attacks by Greek Cypriots on the island's Turkish enclaves. Two days later the National Assembly voted by 432 votes to one to authorize the Government to send troops to foreign countries—i.e., to fight in Cyprus. There were daily Turkish flights over the island, and the likelihood of war increased. As a result of strong intervention by US and UN intermediaries, however, a more serious conflict was avoided. On 3 December the Greeks undertook to withdraw their troops from the island and the Turks to take the necessary measures to ease tension. By February 1968 the situation had been so far restored that direct efforts to agree on a negotiated settlement for Cyprus were once again under way.

MILITARY INTERVENTION

Demirel's AP Government was faced with the growing problem of political violence from early 1968 onward. Disorder in the universities, emanating from non-political educational grievances and from clashes between political extremists of the right and the left, took an increasingly violent form. Students staged anti-US riots, and in June 1969 troops were summoned to prevent extremists from disrupting examinations. The fighting between right- and left-wing factions became more serious in 1970, with firearms and petrol bombs being used and a number of political murders taking place.

Parliamentary politics also became rather confused. Elections in October 1969 produced an enlarged majority for the AP, but the party soon split, a number of Demirel's right-wing opponents forming a new Demokratik Parti (DP—Democratic Party). Party strengths became almost impossible to calculate, as factions and alliances formed and dissolved, and on crucial votes the support of Government and the combined opposition parties was almost equally balanced. A new party, the Milli Nizam Partisi (MNP—National Order Party), with right-wing policies and theocratic tendencies, was formed in January 1970 by Prof. Necmettin Erbakan.

Throughout 1970 and the early part of 1971, political and social unrest continued, with outbreaks of violence among students, in the trade unions and by Kurdish separatist groups. Factional disputes prevented the Government from taking effective action, and on 12 March 1971 the Chief of the General Staff and the army, navy and air force commanders delivered a memorandum to the President. They accused the Government of allowing the country to slip into anarchy and of deviating from Atatürk's principles. They threatened that, unless 'a strong and credible government' were formed at once, the armed forces

would take over the administration of the State. Later that day the Demirel Government resigned.

MILITARY DOMINATION OF POLITICS

A new Government was formed by Dr Nihat Erim, with the support of both the AP and the CHP. Bülent Ecevit, the CHP Secretary-General, resigned from office and refused to collaborate. Erim's programme promised sweeping reforms in taxation, land ownership, education, power and industry, but the Government's attention was first directed to the suppression of political violence. The military ultimatum was followed by further bombings, kidnappings and clashes between right- and left-wing students and between students and police. On 28 April 1971, martial law was proclaimed, initially for one month, in 11 provinces, including Ankara and İstanbul.

Newspapers were suppressed, strikes were banned and large numbers of left-wing supporters were arrested. The MNP was dissolved in May 1971 and the Turkish Labour Party in July. The murder of the Israeli Consul-General in İstanbul by the Turkish People's Liberation Army provided the military authorities with an opportunity to round up nearly 1,000 suspects in İstanbul alone, including many journalists, writers and intellectuals. In September Erim introduced a number of amendments to the Constitution, limiting individual civil rights and the autonomy of universities and radio and television stations, in addition to placing restrictions on the press and trade unions and giving the Government powers to legislate by decree. Erim's proposal to use the new powers to introduce sweeping social and economic reforms, supported by the armed forces, was opposed by the AP. Cabinet crises in October and December led to the formation of a new coalition Government, again headed by Erim, but his proposals for taking further executive powers were opposed by the four major parliamentary parties, and in April 1972 he resigned. President Sunay rejected a Government formed by Suat Ürgüplü, but in May a Government drawn from the AP, National Reliance Party and CHP, headed by Ferit Melen, was approved. There was a shift to the left within the CHP in May; the veteran party leader İsmet İnönü resigned after 34 years as Chairman, and was replaced by Bülent Ecevit. Meanwhile, the terrorist activities of the Turkish People's Liberation Army continued, and martial law was prolonged at two-month intervals.

In July 1972, dissident CHP members, opposing the dominance of the left wing led by Ecevit, formed the Republican Party. In November the CHP withdrew its support from the Melen coalition Government, but its five ministers preferred to leave the party and stay in the Council of Ministers. This caused further resignations from the CHP, including that of İsmet İnönü and 25 other deputies and senators. A number of these dissidents, together with the National Reliance Party and the Republican Party, joined to form the Cumhuriyetci Güven Partisi (CGP—Republican Reliance Party) in February 1973. The CHP, without its right wing, began actively to oppose the Melen Government, which it considered to be dominated by the armed forces, and martial law, under which, it was alleged with increasing frequency, arbitrary arrests and torture were perpetrated. In March, for the first time, the CHP voted against the extension of martial law.

President Sunay's term of office expired in March 1973. Gen. Gürler resigned his post as Chief of Staff in order to stand for the presidency, his candidature receiving the strong support of the armed forces. He was opposed by members of the Justice and Democratic parties, while the CHP decided to abstain from voting as a protest against military interference in the election and the censorship of electoral news in Ankara. Despite obvious military support for Gen. Gürler, 14 ballots failed to produce a result, and eventually the AP, CHP and CGP agreed on a compromise candidate, Senator Fahri Korutürk, former Commander-in-Chief of the Navy, who had no party political affiliation. He was elected President on 6 April 1973. The following day Melen resigned, and was succeeded as Prime Minister by Naim Talû, an independent senator, who formed a Government with AP and CGP participation.

The Talû Government, although considered to be merely a caretaker administration to last until the general election, scheduled for October 1973, brought about a number of reforms, and during its term of office the armed forces gradually withdrew from political affairs. A Land Reform Law, distributing some 8m. acres to 500,000 peasants, was enacted in June 1973, and measures were taken to prevent foreign domination of the mining and petroleum industries. A strong element within the armed forces felt that the time had come to return to a strictly military role, and that martial law had achieved its objective by duly eradicating extremism. Gen. Sancar, who became Chief of Staff when Gen. Gürler resigned to make his unsuccessful attempt to become President, was opposed to military intervention in politics, and retired 196 senior officers. Martial law was gradually lifted, and came to an end in September.

FOREIGN POLICY DEVELOPMENTS

The traditional hostility between Turkey and Greece revived following the Greek announcement in February 1974 that petroleum had been found in Greek territorial waters in the Aegean. This led to a dispute over the extent of national jurisdiction over the continental shelf and territorial waters, with both sides making aggressive moves in Thrace and the Aegean. Turkey began a hydrographical survey of the continental shelf in this area, claiming oil exploration rights in the eastern Aegean. The Aegean issue contributed to making the possibility of a confrontation with Greece, rather than the USSR, the dominating issue of Turkish foreign policy during the late 1970s. The potentially tense situation in the Aegean was overshadowed by a coup in Cyprus in July 1974.

This coup was carried out by the Cypriot National Guard, led by officers from Greece, apparently with the support of the Greek military regime. Declaring its intention of protecting the Turkish community in Cyprus and preventing the union of Cyprus with mainland Greece, Turkey proclaimed a right to intervene as a guarantor state under the Zürich agreement of 1959. On 20 July 1974 Turkish troops landed in Cyprus, and rapidly won control of the area around Kyrenia on the northern coast. The Turkish intervention in Cyprus was followed by negotiations between Turkey, Greece and the United Kingdom. Turkey pressed for the creation of an independent federal Cypriot state, with population movements to give the Turkish community their own sector in the north. The intransigence of both Greeks and Turks, and Greece's rejection of a possible cantonal solution put forward by Turkey, led to a further successful advance by the Turkish forces in Cyprus. When a second cease-fire was called on 16 August, Turkey controlled about one-third of the total area of Cyprus.

The sector under Turkish control, all of Cyprus north of a line running from Morphou through Nicosia to Famagusta, contained more than half the livestock, citrus plantations and mineral reserves of Cyprus, with access to two major seaports. The flight of Greek Cypriot refugees from the north effectively left the Turks free to take over the administration and economy, and establish a *de facto* partition of the island. The Turkish Cypriots unilaterally declared a 'Turkish Federated State' in northern Cyprus on 13 February 1975, and continued pressing for the establishment of a bi-regional federal state system in Cyprus. Greek and Turkish foreign ministers held talks in Rome, Italy, in May on outstanding disputes between the two countries, with the future of Cyprus among the main topics. The Greek–Turkish Aegean dispute was also discussed, including the issue of ownership of the rights to petroleum exploration in the area, the equitable division of the Aegean continental shelf and the question of airspace control in the area. The dispute was submitted to the International Court of Justice (ICJ) in the Hague, The Netherlands. In April 1978 Turkey refused to recognize the jurisdiction of the Court on this question, preferring to try to negotiate a political settlement, and in October the ICJ ruled that it was not competent to try the issue.

The USA imposed an embargo on military aid and the supply of arms to Turkey in February 1975 on the grounds that US military equipment had been used in the Turkish invasion of Cyprus in July 1974 and that Turkey had failed to make substantial progress towards resolving the Cyprus crisis. In July 1975 Turkey implemented counter-measures, including the take-over of US bases in Turkey. After lengthy negotiations a new bilateral defence agreement was reached between the two countries in March 1976, but the agreement was not ratified, owing to the strength of the Greek lobby in the US Congress.

In January 1978, at the beginning of his term of office, Ecevit stated that his foreign policy would be aimed at the exploration at the highest level of possible compromises between Greece and Turkey. A summit meeting took place at Montreux, Switzerland, on 9 March, at which the progress made in personal relations between Ecevit and the Greek Prime Minister, Konstantinos Karamanlis, contributed to a general lessening of tension in the Aegean.

In response to a US statement about the linkage of the arms embargo relaxation and US arms aid, Ecevit turned to the USSR to demonstrate that Turkey had alternatives for its national defence. In April 1978 a trade pact was agreed between the two countries, and in June a friendship document was signed which Ecevit claimed not to be in conflict with Turkey's NATO responsibilities. In response to this *rapprochement* with the USSR, the US Congress ended the arms embargo in October and four key US bases in Turkey were reopened. Finally, after lengthy negotiations, a five-year defence and economic co-operation agreement was signed on 29 March 1980. In return for economic aid to help Turkey modernize its army and fulfil its NATO obligations, the USA was to obtain access to more than 25 military establishments, allowing expanded surveillance of the USSR. The USA's readiness to come to an agreement increased after the Soviet invasion of Afghanistan in December 1979, which heightened Turkey's strategic importance.

Some progress was achieved in the Greek-Turkish Aegean dispute in February 1980. On 22 February Turkey revoked 'Notam 714' which claimed Turkish control of all air traffic over the eastern half of the Aegean. In response, Greece revoked its civil aviation notice of 1974 which declared the Aegean unsafe and banned all flights except its own. However, the dispute flared up again in June when Turkey held its annual NATO Sea Wolf air and naval manoeuvres in the Aegean, with Greece demanding flight plans for areas that Turkey did not regard as being within Greek airspace. In July Turkish Airlines resumed flights to Athens from İstanbul and Ankara. Intercommunal talks on Cyprus, sponsored by the UN, were resumed in June 1979 but were adjourned after a week with no agreement reached.

ECEVIT GOVERNMENT

General elections for the National Assembly and for 52 Senate seats were held on 14 October 1973. In the National Assembly the CHP, with 185 seats, replaced the AP as the largest party, but failed to win an overall majority. The CHP was believed to have won many votes from former supporters of the banned TIP, while the AP lost support to the DP and a new organization, the Milli Selamet Partisi (MSP—National Salvation Party). This last, led by Prof. Necmettin Erbakan, had been founded in 1972 to replace his banned MNP, sharing its traditionalist, Islamic policies, and became the third largest party in the new National Assembly. Prime Minister Talû resigned, but then remained in office for a further three months while negotiations on the formation of a coalition government continued. Despite this parliamentary crisis, the armed forces remained aloof from politics. Eventually, on 25 January 1974, a Government was formed by the CHP and the MSP, with Bülent Ecevit as Prime Minister and Erbakan as his deputy. The Council of Ministers was composed of 18 CHP members and seven from the MSP.

The new Government, an apparently unlikely coalition of the left-of-centre CHP and the reactionary MSP, proclaimed its reforming intentions, but made concessions to the demands of its Muslim supporters, who tended to deviate from Atatürk's strictly secular principles. In February 1974 Turkey was for the first time represented at a summit meeting of the Organization of the Islamic Conference (OIC). Despite the appointment of an MSP deputy as Minister of the Interior, the main lines of the Ecevit Government's policy seemed to be of a reforming, liberal nature, intended to remove the more excessive aspects of the police state created during the period of military intervention.

The land reform passed by the Talû administration came into operation in a pilot project in Urfa province, and in July 1974 the ban on opium production, introduced under US pressure in 1972, was rescinded—a move which, together with the successful handling of the Cyprus question, increased Ecevit's popularity. The differences between the MSP and the CHP had been submerged during the Cyprus crisis, but once more became apparent in September. On 16 September 1974 Ecevit announced that he had decided to resign, as the coalition was no longer viable, to seek a stronger mandate in new elections. The Council of Ministers resigned two days later. However, new elections were not held immediately, and President Korutürk sought to find a coalition government. Turkey remained without a parliamentarily approved government for more than six months. In November Prof. Sadi Irmak attempted unsuccessfully to form an interim coalition to prepare for new elections in 1975, but remained in office in an interim capacity while efforts were made to form a new government. Internal unrest increased during the lengthy government crisis, with serious clashes between opposing political factions and between students.

DEMIREL RETURNS TO POWER

In March 1975 Süleyman Demirel returned to power, leading a right-wing coalition, the Nationalist Front, consisting of four parties: Demirel's AP, the MSP, the CGP and the neo-fascist Milliyetçi Hareket Partisi (MHP—Nationalist Action Party) founded by Col Alparslan Türkeş, who became Deputy Prime Minister. In the Council of Ministers, the AP occupied 16 of the seats, the MSP eight, the CGP four, and the MHP two. However, the precarious nature of this coalition meant that the Government had to avoid taking radical measures that would upset the co-operation between the four parties. This prevented Demirel's Government from tackling the pressing problems of a deteriorating economy and increasing political violence, for Erbakan refused to countenance the austerity measures demanded by the IMF while Türkeş stood in the way of a crackdown on political violence, most of which the 'Grey Wolves' of the MHP were thought to have instigated. The weakness of the coalition also hampered progress towards a settlement of the Cyprus question, with Demirel having to make concessions to the militant views of the extreme right wing represented by Erbakan's MSP. Between 1974 and 1977 the fortunes of the MSP changed drastically and their representation in the National Assembly was reduced from 48 to 24. Erbakan became increasingly discredited, while support for the MHP improved substantially. It combined anti-communism, Islamic values and a desire for centrally-directed free enterprise with a nationalism that would dispense with democracy. Meanwhile, the MHP was able to build up a system of militant cadres by placing its supporters in the police and civil service.

In spite of its difficulties, the Demirel Government continued in power by suspending all action over controversial issues, such as the economy, Cyprus and Greece and relations with the European Community (EC, now European Union—EU) and NATO, pending the general election scheduled for October 1977. Increasing political violence throughout Turkey and especially in the universities, between left- and right-wing groups, persuaded the authorities to bring forward the general election to June. The political inactivity was matched by economic paralysis as it became clear that the economy was overloaded with short-term debt and banks struggled to meet foreign-currency bills of payment.

However, the election of June 1977 failed to produce the hoped-for decisive majority. While the CHP increased its share of seats in the National Assembly to 213 out of 450, the AP also increased its share from 149 to 189 seats. Ecevit, the leader of the CHP, formed a Council of Ministers but failed to agree a coalition with the smaller parties, and a week later was defeated in a vote of confidence in the legislature. Demirel, the leader of the AP, was subsequently invited to form a new Government and on 1 August a coalition came to power which gave key ministerial posts to members of the MSP and the MHP. As a result there was penetration of the university and college administrations by extreme right-wing factions and a consequent flare-up of violence on campuses. By mid-December one-third of the universities were shut and 250 people had died in political violence.

Frustration at the coalition's powerlessness led to the progressive diminution of the AP's support in the National Assembly between October and December 1977 as members resigned. By 27 December the coalition could muster only 214 votes and Ecevit was preparing a new coalition. Following a vote of 'no confidence' in the legislature, the Demirel Government resigned on 31 December and formed a caretaker administration. On 2 January 1978 Ecevit formed a new Government.

ECEVIT RETURNS TO POWER

After the chaos of Demirel's administration, the appointment of Ecevit as Prime Minister was greeted with great popular enthusiasm; his popular support, however, was not reflected in the National Assembly. His majority was dependent upon the support of defectors from the AP, to 10 of whom he gave places in the Council of Ministers, while the number of deputies who had changed allegiances had resulted in a 'pool' of about 20 independents. Radical reforms were urged on Ecevit, but the insecure parliamentary majority, the country's economic weakness, and the unwanted reputation of the CHP in the conservative rural areas as a radical party, enjoined on him the necessity for caution. He began a painstaking, relentless purge of right-wing elements in the public administration. He adopted an economic stabilization programme, signed a stand-by arrangement with the IMF (providing for a total of US $450m. over two years) and began work on restructuring the severe short-term debt burden. He was, however, unable to secure the huge amounts of international financial assistance necessary to make the stabilization programme work and few of the targets were reached. Inflation continued at about 60%–70%, unemployment reached 20% and, for lack of raw materials, industry was working half-time. Nevertheless, Ecevit was unwilling to take further austerity measures demanded by the IMF as a condition for further aid. Moreover, political violence continued to escalate. Although calm returned to the universities, elsewhere more and more people were killed in acts of terrorism. Both the police force and the internal security forces (MIT) were riven by factions of left and right which rendered them unable to intervene. Here, too, the process of purging extremists was begun, and in September 1978 Ecevit replaced the Chief of Security. However, while the civilian tools of authority remained weak and unreformed, the maintenance of law and order depended on the armed forces and Ecevit was forced to ask the gendarmerie to undertake policing duties in urban areas. By December more than 800 people had been killed, particularly in the eastern provinces. These new areas of violence reflected a change of tactics by the MHP, which during 1978 campaigned in central and eastern Anatolia where the traditional elements of society had been least affected by modernization and were most threatened by its arrival. Türkeş's appeal to nationalism gained him supporters, particularly in areas where Turks lived with other ethnic groups, notably the Kurds. The violence culminated in December at the south-eastern town of Karamanmaraş in the most serious outbreak of ethnic fighting since the 1920s. There the historic enmity between the orthodox Sunni majority and the Alevi (Shi'a) minority had been exacerbated by the activities of right- and left-wing agitators. On 21 December the Alevis turned the funeral of two members of the left-wing teachers' association, murdered the day before, into a large-scale demonstration. The mourners were fired on by Sunni supporters of Türkeş and indiscriminate rioting erupted. After three days, more than 100 people had been killed, at least 1,000 had been injured and large parts of the Alevi quarters had been reduced to ruins. The MIT had failed to alert the Government to the incidents leading up to the massacre, and order was not restored until the army intervened on 24 December.

MARTIAL LAW

The violence led to the imposition of martial law on 26 December 1978. Although he had long been urged to take this step by Demirel, Ecevit had refused in view of Turkey's previous experiences of martial law. Martial law was imposed for two months (renewed subsequently at two-monthly intervals) in 13 provinces, all—except İstanbul and Ankara—in the east, although the mainly Kurdish areas of the south-east were excluded to prevent friction. Ecevit announced that it was to be 'martial law with a human face', and instituted a co-ordination committee for its implementation comprising himself, Gen. Kenan Evren, the Chief of the General Staff, and Lt-Gen. Sahap Yardimoğlu, the Chief Martial Law Administrator. Special military courts were established to hear cases of those arrested for martial law violations. However, even these new measures proved insufficient to curb the violence, which was now endemic.

In April 1979 a crisis developed on the political front when six ministers, members of the group of defectors from the AP, issued a public memorandum criticizing Ecevit for taking insufficient account of their views and demanding tougher measures to combat political violence, particularly by left-wing groups, and Kurdish separatism. They also demanded a redirection of economic policies to allow more Western investment and greater freedom for private enterprise. The gulf between these views and those of Ecevit's left-wing supporters in the CHP became more and more pronounced, and the impossibility of reconciling the left- and right-wing elements in the coalition became clear. In response to the growth of Kurdish separatism, and alarmed by Kurdish violence in Iran, Ecevit agreed to extend martial law into six more provinces, all in the Kurdish south-east. Three CHP deputies promptly resigned, reducing the party's minority representation in the National Assembly to 211 out of 450.

As violence continued, the authorities imposed an all-day curfew in İstanbul and Ankara on May Day in 1979, to prevent riots at the traditional parades. A march planned by the more radical of the union confederations, Devrimci İşçi Sendikaları Konfederasyonu (DİSK), was banned and the army ordered the arrest of its entire leadership, a severe blow to Ecevit's reputation as a champion of workers' rights and an indication of the army's increasing involvement in politics. During the next few months Ecevit's parliamentary majority gradually dwindled after a series of resignations by CHP deputies, and in October by-elections the AP achieved substantial gains. Ecevit's Government resigned on 16 October. Eight days later Demirel formed a new Government with the backing of the rightist MHP and the MSP, affording the Government a majority of four. His Council of Ministers was entirely composed of moderate and uncontroversial AP deputies, in an effort to avoid antagonizing the left-wing faction in the National Assembly and jeopardizing his slender majority.

With no reduction in the level of violence by the beginning of 1980, the armed forces again intervened. On 2 January the Turkish generals issued a public warning to all political parties, criticizing them for arguing and urging them to reach a consensus of opinion on anti-terrorist measures. Under threat of greater military intervention, the National Assembly immediately began to debate a package of anti-terrorist legislation proposed by the Government. In spite of this threat, the bill was defeated on 15 January, when the MSP voted against it, and sectarian and political killings continued at an average rate of 10 per day. By February 20 provinces were under martial law. At this time a number of left-wing papers were shut down, and in May the Türkiye Emekçi Partisi (Workers' Party of Turkey) was dissolved by the Constitutional Court. Once again May Day processions were banned and violence broke out.

The instability of the Government was illustrated by parliamentary inability to choose a new President after Korutürk's term expired in April 1980. This again provoked criticism from Gen. Kenan Evren, Chief of the General Staff. Neither the right nor the left was prepared to compromise on the choice of candidate, and after much indecision Ihsan Sabri Çağlayangil took office as acting President. In June the CHP tabled a censure motion intended to force the resignation of the Government before the summer recess. However, the 22 MSP deputies voted against the motion, in spite of their opposition to Demirel's pro-Western, pro-NATO stance, and the Government survived the motion by one vote. By August political violence had almost reached the proportions of civil war. Although martial law continued to be extended every two months in 20 out of the 67 provinces, clashes between right and left had caused some 2,000 deaths since the beginning of the year. Meanwhile, inflation and foreign debts continued to escalate, food and power shortages and unemployment were widespread and the political infighting continued. At the beginning of September Demirel attempted to bring forward the elections (scheduled for June 1981), which he hoped would give his party a majority and the power to deal with the country's crisis. However, this move was defeated by the opposition and the Government remained paralysed, unable to make important decisions or implement vital measures.

THE 1980 COUP AND ITS AFTERMATH

On 11 September 1980 the armed forces, led by Gen. Evren, seized power in a bloodless coup, the third in 20 years. There appeared to be three main reasons for their intervention: the failure of the Government to deal with the country's political and economic chaos, the ineffectiveness of the police force, and, more immediately, the sudden resurgence of Islamist fundamentalism. This development was particularly evident at a rally in August, during which Erbakan and the MSP appealed for the restoration of Islamic (*Shari'a*) law. The leaders of the coup formed a five-man National Security Council (NSC), sworn in on 18 September. The Chairman of the NSC, Gen. Evren, became head of state. Martial law was extended to the whole country and the legislature was dissolved. On 21 September the NSC appointed a mainly civilian Council of Ministers, with a retired naval commander, Bülent Ulusu, as Prime Minister and Turgut Özal as Deputy Prime Minister and Minister for Economic Affairs. The new Government's main aims were to eradicate all possible sources of terrorism and political violence and to reduce the power of political extremists, to uphold Kemalist principles, to honour all foreign debts and existing agreements, and to return the country to democratic rule after the establishment of law and order. Former political leaders, suspected terrorists and political extremists were detained, while all political activity was banned and trade union activities were restricted. A stringent programme of austerity was introduced by Özal. In October the NSC drafted a seven-point provisional Constitution which provided the generals with unlimited powers for an indefinite period.

By February 1981 the new Government claimed to have eliminated the main left-wing terrorist groups, including the powerful guerrilla organization Dev Yol. By May 1982, according to varying reports, between 43,000 and 100,000 suspected left- and right-wing activists had been detained. The authorities also imposed harsh measures on Kurdish nationalist organizations, believing them to be supported by forces in the Eastern bloc. By May 1982 there had been a number of mass trials of Kurdish activists, especially members of the left-wing separatist Partiya Karkeren Kurdistan (PKK—Kurdistan Workers' Party). Censorship of the press was not officially imposed, but extremist publications were banned and the press and other media placed under strict self-censorship. By October more than 66,000 suspects were said to have been arrested, including the leaders of the MHP and the MSP, together with a large number of trade unionists and the editors of some leading newspapers. The new Government succeeded in reducing the level of political violence in Turkey and in establishing law and order. However, the likelihood that this had been achieved only at the expense of human rights caused concern among the Western Governments: Turkey was banned from the Council of Europe, EC aid was suspended, and fellow-members of NATO urged Turkey to return to democratic rule as soon as possible.

In October 1981 a Consultative Assembly was formed to draft a new Constitution and to prepare the way for a return to parliamentary rule. It comprised five members of the NSC and 160 others, of whom 40 were appointed directly by the NSC and the remaining 120 chosen by the same body from candidates put forward by the governors of the 67 provinces. All former politicians (who had been banned from political activity in April) were excluded, and on 16 October all political parties were disbanded and their assets confiscated. A new Constitution was approved by referendum on 7 November 1982, with a 91% majority—despite widely-expressed objections that excessive powers were to be granted to the President, while judicial powers and the rights of trade unions and the press were to be curtailed. An appended 'temporary article' automatically installed Gen. Evren as President for a seven-year term. The opposition was not allowed to canvass openly against the new Constitution. Under the Constitution, power was vested in the President, enabling him to dissolve the legislature, delay laws, call elections and make all key public appointments.

Following the referendum, the military regime dismissed left-wing university professors, closed newspapers, tightened press censorship and held mass trials of labour leaders and others. In May 1983 the President revoked the 30-month ban on political activity and allowed political parties to be formed under strict rules. All the former political parties, which had been dissolved in October 1981, were to remain proscribed, along with 723 former members of the legislature and leading party officials who were banned from active politics for 10 years. By the end of May it was clear that proscribed political parties were resurfacing under new names and with new titular leaders. The first new political party to be banned, on 31 May, was the Great Turkey Party, whose leader was Husamettin Cindoruk. This party was the reconstructed AP, with discreet backing from Süleyman Demirel. In response, Demirel loyalists formed the Dogru Yol Partisi (DYP—True Path Party). The President gave support to the Milliyetçi Demokrasi Partisi (MDP—Nationalist Democracy Party), led by Gen. Turgut Sunalp, in the hope that it would become the main centre-right party in the new Parliament. On the centre-left the Sosyal Demokrasi Partisi (SDP—Social Democratic Party) was formed, under the leadership of Prof. Erdal İnönü, and won support from the former CHP (although Bülent Ecevit recommended boycotting the new political system); however, the SDP was banned on 24 June. The Halkçi Parti (HP—Populist Party), led by Necdet Calp, had military approval as a centre-left party.

CIVILIAN RULE RETURNS UNDER ÖZAL

A general election was held on 6 November 1983, and parliamentary rule was restored, with a 400-seat unicameral Grand National Assembly (Büyük Millet Meclisi). Election was on the basis of proportional representation (with a minimum requirement of 10% of the total votes, to discourage small parties), voting was compulsory and every candidate had to be approved by the military council.

The President banned a total of 11 parties from participating in the general election. Unexpectedly, the conservative ANAP, led by Turgut Özal, won 211 of the 400 seats in the Grand National Assembly. The party had been allowed to participate only because the President felt that it would be no threat to the two parties that the military leadership favoured. However, the armed forces' preferred party, the centre-right MDP, was beaten into third place, with the centre-left HP coming second. The result reflected the great popularity of Özal, stemming from his performance while head of the State Trading Organization and later as Deputy Prime Minister and Minister for Economic Affairs. He was appointed Prime Minister and named his Council of Ministers in December.

The result of the election suggested a decisive rejection of military rule, and this view was strengthened when local elections were held on 25 March 1984. Three parties that had been banned from the general election—the SDP, the DYP and the Refah Partisi (RP—Welfare Party)—were allowed to contest the local elections. ANAP received about 40% of the total votes (almost identical to the November general election result), with the moderate left-wing SDP obtaining 23.3% of the votes. Thus, the main opposition in the country to ANAP was a party not represented in the Grand National Assembly, a fact which gave rise to further speculation about the undemocratic nature of the general election. The HP and the MDP fared badly, winning less than 10% of the votes each. In November 1985 the HP and the SDP, the main opposition parties within and outside the Grand National Assembly respectively, merged to form a single party, the Sosyal Demokrat Halkçi Parti (SHP—Social Democratic Populist Party). However, the left-wing opposition was split as a result of the formation, a few days later, of the Demokratik Sol Parti (DSP—Democratic Left Party), led by Rahsan Ecevit (wife of ex-Prime Minister Bülent Ecevit) and drawing support from the former CHP.

The civilian Government's main priorities were economic, although corruption continued to be a problem; in October 1984 the Minister of Finance and Customs, Vural Arikan, was dismissed by President Evren after accusing the Minister of the Interior (who had resigned shortly before) of allowing the police to torture customs officials who had been accused of corruption. The press and labour unions were put under strict control, despite a few civilian appointments to important posts formerly held by the military. The police were given further widespread powers to maintain law and order and to ensure that there was no return to the political violence prevalent in Turkey during the late 1970s.

The MDP voted to disband itself in May 1986. Many of its members joined the new right-wing Hür Demokrat Partisi

(HDP—Free Democratic Party), which was formed by Mehmet Yazar, the former President of the Union of Chambers of Commerce and Industry. In December the HDP merged with ANAP, and the right-wing Vatandas Partisi (VP—Citizen Party, formed earlier in the year) merged with the DYP (although the VP's leader, Vural Arikan, became an independent); the DSP became a legitimate parliamentary group (i.e. it had more than 20 deputies in the Grand National Assembly) when several deputies from the SHP defected and joined its ranks. By the end of 1986, therefore, there were four recognized parliamentary groups in the Grand National Assembly—ANAP, the SHP, the DSP and the DYP.

In May 1987 it became apparent that there were rifts within ANAP when its Secretary-General, Mustafa Tasar, resigned after criticizing the party's increasingly powerful Islamic fundamentalist wing. ANAP fared well, however, in the mayoral elections in June, winning 55 of the 84 seats contested. The DYP also proved its continuing popularity by winning 17 seats, whilst the SHP won only six seats and the DSP just three.

Concern continued throughout the 1980s and the early 1990s regarding the persistent and widespread use of torture of political prisoners. In December 1985 a case brought before the Human Rights Commission of the Council of Europe by five European countries, alleging that Turkey had violated the European Convention for the Protection of Human Rights and Fundamental Freedoms, was settled out of court. Turkey agreed to rescind all martial law decrees within 18 months, to introduce an amnesty for political prisoners and to allow independent observers from the Council of Europe to monitor progress. In July 1987 all martial law decrees in Turkey were repealed; by that time an official state of emergency had been declared in a total of nine provinces. The Government's signing, in January 1988, of UN and Council of Europe agreements denouncing torture, however, received a cynical response from both the local and the international media. In November the eight-year state of emergency in İstanbul was revoked.

In November 1987 Dr Nihat Sargin and Haydar Kutlu, the respective leaders of the banned Workers' Party of Turkey and the Turkish Communist Party, returned to Turkey after seven years of self-imposed exile, with the intention of merging their two parties to form a new Turkish United Communist Party. They were both arrested at Ankara airport and were charged with offences under the Turkish penal code, which specifically outlawed communist organizations and the dissemination of Marxist-Leninist ideas. At their trial, which began in June 1988, both men alleged that they had been tortured. In May 1990 they were released from detention for the remainder of the trial, in anticipation of significant changes to the articles of legislation that had declared communist parties illegal. In June it was reported that an application for legal status for the Turkish United Communist Party, put forward by the two men, had been rejected. In July 1989, at the end of a seven-year trial of members of the banned Dev Yol, a military court sentenced seven left-wing extremists to death, 39 to life imprisonment and more than 300 to gaol terms of up to 21 years for activities dating back to the time of the 1980 military coup. In April 1990 it was estimated that 25,000 people had been detained for political reasons since 1980.

A sharp increase in outbreaks of urban terrorism in early 1990, coupled with a perceived increase in the influence of fundamentalist thought, led to widespread fears of a return to the extremist violence of the late 1970s. The increase in terrorist attacks by Islamist and left-wing groups was exacerbated by the Government's stance in the conflict in the Persian (Arabian) Gulf (see below). A series of attacks were unleashed against Western targets in Turkey, including US civilians, diplomatic missions and offices of several national airlines and banks in İstanbul and Ankara.

In early April 1991 the Grand National Assembly approved draft anti-terrorism legislation. Presented as a move towards greater liberalization and democratization, the bill contained provisions for the abolition of controversial articles of the penal code which had proscribed the formation of religious or communist political parties, for the early release of as many as 35,000 prisoners, for the commuting of the death sentence for more than 250 prisoners and for a relaxation of the ban on the use of minority languages. By mid-April it was reported that some 5,000 political prisoners had already been released as a result of the new bill. In July Turkey's Constitutional Court again refused to afford legal status to the Turkish Communist Party.

FURTHER STEPS TOWARDS DEMOCRACY

In a national referendum held in September 1987 a narrow majority approved the repeal of the restrictions imposed on over 200 politicians in 1981, which prohibited them from taking an active part in public life for a period of 10 years. This result enabled Bülent Ecevit to assume the leadership of the DSP, while Süleyman Demirel was elected as leader of the DYP. As the polls for the referendum closed, the Prime Minister, who had campaigned against the repeal of the ban, immediately announced that a general election would be held on 1 November (a year earlier than required). A few days later, the Grand National Assembly approved legislation enabling a general election to be held at such short notice, by eliminating the procedure of primary elections within each party. After protests and threats of an electoral boycott by the opposition parties, however, the Government postponed the general election until 29 November, thus enabling primary elections to be held. Seven parties contested the general election, which was the first free election in Turkey since the 1980 military coup. ANAP obtained 36.3% of the votes cast (which, because of the 'weighted' electoral system, meant that it was allotted 292 of the seats in the Grand National Assembly, now enlarged from 400 to 450 seats), while the SHP (24.7% of the votes) won 99 seats and the DYP (19.1% of the votes) won 59 seats. Since the country's proportional representation system required a party to obtain at least 10% of the national vote in order to be represented in the Grand National Assembly, none of the four other parties contesting the election (including the DSP, with 8.5% of the votes, and the RP, with 7.2%) won seats. Özal formed a new, expanded Council of Ministers in December. In February 1988 the Sosyalist Parti (Socialist Party), the first overtly socialist political party in Turkey since the 1980 coup, was formally established.

In August 1988 Özal made an unsuccessful attempt to pass a new piece of legislation through the Constitutional Court, which would have enabled local elections (normally held every five years) to take place up to one year in advance. A national referendum, held in the following month, to decide whether to adopt this amendment and to bring forward the holding of local elections (scheduled for March 1989) by five months, to November, illustrated the widespread public dissatisfaction with the Government and its policies, with only 35% of the total votes cast in favour of Özal's proposed amendment, which was, consequently, not adopted.

At the local elections, which proceeded throughout Turkey in late March 1989, ANAP obtained only 22% of the total votes, while the SHP and the DYP won 28% and 26%, respectively. The ruling party's defeat included the loss of control of the local councils in the country's three largest cities (Ankara, İstanbul and İzmir) to the SHP. A few days after these elections, Özal implemented an extensive ministerial reshuffle, aimed at restoring public confidence in the Government. In the following month the Prime Minister requested and won from the Grand National Assembly a vote expressing confidence.

ÖZAL BECOMES PRESIDENT

In mid-October 1989 Özal declared his candidacy for the presidential election to be conducted in the Grand National Assembly on 31 October. Despite a boycott of the election by SHP and DYP deputies, who claimed that Özal no longer had a popular mandate, and attempts by a second ANAP candidate to divide support, Özal received the simple majority required in the third round of voting (having failed to secure the two-thirds' majority of the 450 deputies necessary for victory in the first two rounds), polling 263 of the votes. On 9 November Özal succeeded Gen. Kenan Evren as President, and unexpectedly appointed Yıldırım Akbulut, the Speaker of the Grand National Assembly and a former Minister of the Interior, to succeed him as Prime Minister. Akbulut was subsequently elected as party leader. Towards the end of 1989 the parliamentary position of the SHP was seriously undermined when a number of SHP deputies resigned in protest at the expulsion of six Kurdish deputies who had attended a Kurdish conference in Paris, France, earlier in the year. Rumours of division within ANAP were confirmed in early 1990 when two ministers resigned, both expressing disenchantment with party policy and leadership. In March Bedrettin Dalan, a former Mayor of İstanbul and an ANAP party member, announced his intention of forming a new Demokratik Merkez Partisi (DMP—Democratic Centre Party), which was expected to attract many disaffected ANAP supporters.

At an ANAP party congress convened on 15 June 1991 former Minister of Foreign Affairs Mesut Yılmaz defeated Prime Minister Yıldırım Akbulut in a contest for the party leadership. The following day Akbulut resigned as Prime Minister, and on 17 June, in accordance with the Constitution, President Özal invited Yılmaz to head a new administration. On 23 June Yılmaz announced the composition of a new, radically-altered Council of Ministers and the next day he assumed the premiership. The appointment of Yılmaz (the leader of the liberal faction within ANAP) and the composition of the Council of Ministers was widely interpreted as an attempt to balance the influence of the liberal and fundamentalist movements within the Government. In August the Government announced that general elections (not legally required until November 1992) would be conducted in October 1991 in response to demands by the opposition SHP and DYP, which claimed that ANAP no longer commanded sufficient popular support to govern effectively.

THE 1991 GENERAL ELECTION

At the general election held on 20 October 1991 the DYP, under the leadership of Süleyman Demirel, received an estimated 27.3% of the votes cast, narrowly defeating ANAP (with 23.9%) and the SHP (with 20.6%). Although the DYP failed to attract the level of support necessary for the formation of a single-party government, Demirel assumed the premiership at the head of a coalition comprising members of the DYP and the SHP. The Grand National Assembly approved the Council of Ministers, including 12 SHP members (with the deputy premiership assigned to SHP party leader Erdal İnönü) and 20 DYP members, later in the month. On 25 November the coalition partners announced a programme for political and economic reform that included the drafting of a new constitution, improvements in anti-terrorist legislation and matters of human rights, and increased levels of cultural recognition and of autonomy in local government for Kurds in Turkey. While international observers were impressed by Demirel's apparent commitment to human rights (the establishment of a separate Ministry of Human Rights, to be headed by an ethnic Kurd, was promptly announced), the formal adoption of amendments to the criminal procedure code, designed to discourage torture (including a proposed reduction in the length of periods of legitimate police detention), were impeded by a lack of consensus within the coalition Government. Although the DYP and the SHP had performed well at municipal elections conducted in early June 1992 (increasing their combined share of national support to 58%, compared with 48% in the October 1991 general election), the reactivation of the CHP in September 1992 (as a result of the adoption of more lenient guide-lines for the formation of political parties) threatened to undermine left-wing support for the Government.

FOREIGN AFFAIRS, 1980–93

Turkey is recognized as a key member of NATO, both on account of its strategic position in Europe and because it is the only NATO member of the OIC. However, in the early 1980s the NATO countries were divided over support for the Turkish Government: while the USA promised to accelerate the flow of aid to Turkey, EC countries were considering the suspension of aid. In January 1982 the European Parliament voted to suspend relations with Turkey, and in March the EC decided to 'freeze' aid to Turkey.

In September 1986 Turkey was readmitted to associate membership of the EC, when the Turkish-EC Association Council (which was established in 1963, but had been suspended since the army coup in 1980) met for talks in Brussels, Belgium. Turkey, however, failed to gain access to the suspended EC aid. In April 1987 Turkey made a formal application to become a full member of the EC. Overruling Greek objections, the EC Council of Ministers agreed to submit the application to the Commission of the European Communities to formulate its opinion on the merits of the case. In April 1988 a meeting of the Turkish-EC Association Council in Luxembourg was postponed indefinitely after objections by the Turkish delegation to a reference to Cyprus, inserted at the request of the Greek delegates, in the EC's opening statement. In December 1989 the Commission of the European Communities effectively rejected Turkey's application, at least until 1993. The Commission emphasized that the completion of a single European market was necessary before any enlargement could take place, and cited factors including Turkey's unsatisfactory human rights record, high rate of inflation, dependence upon the rural population and inadequate social security provisions as falling short of EC expectations.

The Turkish Government responded positively to requests from the USA for logistical aid following the forcible annexation of Kuwait by Iraq in August 1990, and in September the defence and economic co-operation agreement (which provides for the US military presence in Turkey) was extended. In mid-January 1991 a resolution to extend the war powers of the Government and effectively endorse the unrestricted use of Turkish air bases by coalition forces was agreed by the Grand National Assembly. On the following day US aircraft began bombing missions into north-east Iraq from NATO bases inside south-east Turkey. In February and March the US Government announced substantial increases in military and economic aid to Turkey for 1991 and 1992.

Although Greece and Turkey had agreed to ease tensions in April 1982, relations were further strained when the Turkish-backed 'Turkish Federated State of Cyprus' made a unilateral declaration of independence in November 1983. Turkey is the only country to have recognized this state, the 'Turkish Republic of Northern Cyprus' ('TRNC'), and to have exchanged ambassadors with it (in May 1984). In July 1986 Turgut Özal became the first Turkish Prime Minister to make an official visit to the 'TRNC'. Tension between Greece and Turkey came to a head in March 1987 when a disagreement between the two countries over petroleum-prospecting rights in disputed areas of the Aegean Sea almost resulted in the outbreak of military conflict. Relations between Turkey and Greece improved considerably, however, in 1988: in February the Turkish Government officially annulled a decree, issued in 1964, that curbed the property rights of Greek nationals living in Turkey. In return, the Greek Prime Minister, Andreas Papandreou, officially accepted Turkey's status as an associate member of the EC by signing the Protocol of Adaptation (consequent on Greece's accession to the EC) to the EC-Turkey Association Agreement in April, which the Greek Government had hitherto refused to do. The situation deteriorated somewhat, however, later in the same month, when Greece insisted on linking the possibility of Turkey's entry into the EC with the ending of the Turkish presence in Cyprus. In May the Greek Minister of Culture became the first Greek minister to visit Turkey since 1974, and in the following month Özal became the first Turkish premier to visit the Greek Prime Minister in Athens for 36 years. In February 1990 relations again deteriorated, following violent clashes in Greece between Christians and the Muslim minority in western Thrace.

In late 1984 tension arose between the USA and Turkey over a congressional resolution condemning alleged massacres of Armenians by Turks during the First World War. The resolution eventually lapsed, and the USA granted military aid, but the tension remained. The Turkish Government was angered once again in February 1987 when the European Parliament adopted a report 'deploring' the alleged massacres.

Turkey protested vehemently against the campaign of forced assimilation launched by the Bulgarian authorities in late 1984, whereby ethnic Turks living in Bulgaria (estimated to number about 1.5m.) were forced to adopt Slavonic names and were banned from practising Muslim religious rites. Despite some improvement in relations, in 1989 the Bulgarian authorities began to deport hundreds of Turks to Turkey, and continued to deny the existence of an ethnic-Turkish minority in their country. The official explanation was that the ethnic Turks were, in fact, Slavs whose ancestors had been forcibly converted to Islam. In late May the Bulgarian authorities altered their policy and issued passports and exit visas to at least 150,000 Turks who wished to enter Turkey. In response, the Turkish Government opened the border and publicly stated its commit-

ment to accepting all the ethnic Turks as refugees from Bulgaria. By mid-August an estimated 310,000 had crossed into Turkey, but more than one-third of that number had returned to Bulgaria by February 1990, as a result of disillusionment with conditions in Turkey and the proposed abolition of the assimilation campaign by a new Bulgarian administration.

Following the formal dissolution of the USSR in December 1991, the Turkish Government sought to further its political, economic and cultural influence in the Central Asian region, and in particular to forge strong links with the six Muslim states of the former Soviet Union. In June 1992 leaders of 11 countries, including both Turkey and Greece and six former Soviet republics, established a Black Sea economic alliance (now the Organization of the Black Sea Economic Co-operation—BSEC—based in İstanbul), and expressed their commitment to promoting greater co-operation with regard to transport, energy, information, communications and ecology.

TURKEY AND THE IRAQI KURDS

In August 1988 the Iraqi armed forces launched a major offensive against Kurdish separatists in northern Iraq. Thousands of Kurdish refugees (an estimated 100,000–150,000 by early September) fled to the Turkish border, where, after initial hesitation, the Turkish Government admitted them on 'humanitarian grounds' and provided asylum in makeshift camps. In addition, the Turkish Government refused a request by Iraq to allow Iraqi forces to pursue Kurdish guerrillas in Turkish territory. However, the Government made it clear that the refuge being given to the Iraqi Kurds was only temporary. Iraq offered an amnesty to the Iraqi Kurds in Turkey in September, but very few returned. By August 1989 there were still about 36,000 Iraqi Kurds living in three camps in eastern Turkey, yet the Turkish authorities continued to refuse to recognize them officially as political refugees.

Following the Iraqi invasion of Kuwait in August 1990, the Turkish Government swiftly complied with UN proposals for economic sanctions against Iraq. Despite the increase in the number of Turkish troops in the border region and the deployment of additional US and NATO aircraft in south-east Turkey in early 1991, President Özal continued to stress that Turkey had no intention of opening a second military front against Iraq and that Turkish forces would continue to guarantee Iraq's 'territorial integrity'.

During high-level talks, conducted in Turkey between senior Turkish foreign ministry officials and the leaders of Kurdish groups within Iraq in early 1991, Turkey had endorsed the notion of some form of autonomy for Iraqi Kurds within Iraqi territory and had also agreed to open its border for humanitarian aid to areas of northern Iraq which had been reportedly liberated by Kurdish rebels in the aftermath of the Gulf conflict. By the beginning of April, however, having suffered serious reversals at the hands of the Iraqi armed forces, more than 500,000 Iraqi refugees (mainly Kurds) were reported to be fleeing to the Turkish border. Although the Turkish Government formally announced the closure of the border, claiming that it was unable to accommodate such a large-scale exodus (some 10,000 refugees, many of them ethnic Turks, had already been recently received by Turkish authorities), and appealed to the UN Security Council to consider the plight of the refugees and to take immediate action to ensure their safety, by mid-April it was estimated that some 600,000 refugees (including 400,000 within Turkish borders) were encamped in the mountainous border region. While reports of the appalling conditions confronting the refugees gave rise to grave international concern and the initiation of an ambitious humanitarian aid programme (with US Air Force transport planes from the İncirlik air base distributing supplies to the refugees), the Turkish minister of state in charge of the relief effort criticized Western governments for their slow response to the crisis. Following intense international pressure, the Turkish authorities (who had contained the refugees in the border region in the hope that a protected buffer zone would be created to accommodate the Kurds on flatlands just inside the Iraqi border rather than on equivalent land at a much greater distance inside Turkey) began to make provision for the removal of up to 20,000 of those refugees in greatest need of medical attention to better conditions at an existing camp at Silopi, inside Turkey. In mid-April, in accordance with a UN-approved proposal to establish temporary 'safe havens' for the refugees in northern Iraq, Turkey agreed to allow coalition forces to use Turkish facilities to help the refugees, under UN auspices. By mid-May it was estimated that some 200,000 refugees had returned to Iraq, while 89,000 remained in Turkey (65,000 at Hakkâri and 24,000 at Sirnak) and a further 162,000 were still encamped on the Iraqi side of the border with Turkey.

Following the completion of the first phase of the international relief effort for the Kurdish refugees and the subsequent withdrawal of coalition forces, the Turkish Government agreed to the deployment in south-east Turkey of a 3,000-strong multinational 'rapid reaction force' which would respond to any further act of aggression by Iraq against the Kurds in the newly-created 'safe havens'. The force, to be jointly commanded by the USA and Turkey (the latter would reserve the right to veto attacks against Iraq launched from Turkish territory or airspace) was to include a 1,000-strong Turkish battalion. In September 1991 the Government approved a 90-day extension for the presence, in south-east Turkey, of a small allied air-strike force, and subsequently its mandate was granted six-month extensions. All allied ground forces, however, were withdrawn in October.

POLICY TOWARDS THE TURKISH KURDS, 1980–93

During the 1980s the potential threat of separatism among the Kurds in the south-east of the country was a continuing problem. Despite the fact that there are an estimated 3m.–8m. Kurds in Turkey, they are not officially recognized as a separate ethnic group and it is illegal to speak Kurdish. In 1984 the outlawed PKK, which advocates the creation of a Kurdish national homeland in Turkey and is led by Abdullah Öcalan, launched a violent guerrilla campaign against the Turkish authorities in the south-eastern provinces. The Government responded by arresting suspected Kurdish leaders, dispatching more security forces to the region, establishing local militia groups, and imposing martial law in nine troubled provinces. By July 1987, however, martial law had been replaced by a state of emergency under a district governor in all of these provinces. In spite of this concession, the violence continued and the PKK began to concentrate its attacks on the local militia and civilians. In April 1990 the Government introduced severe measures to combat ethnic unrest, including harsh restrictions on the media and an increase in the powers of local officials to outlaw strikes and impose internal banishment. Violence continued to escalate, however, and in April and May clashes between rebel Kurds, security forces and civilians left 140 dead, marking the bloodiest period of the conflict since August 1984.

In early 1991, in the context of the Kurdish uprising in Iraq, President Özal sought to alleviate mounting tension among Turkish Kurds by announcing the Government's decision to review existing legislation proscribing the use of languages other than Turkish and by allowing Kurds to celebrate openly the Kurdish new year for the first time. By mid-1991, however, a new wave of violence between PKK guerrillas and security forces had erupted in the south-eastern provinces. In July three people were killed and more than 100 wounded when security forces clashed with some 20,000 mourners attending the funeral of a murdered Kurdish rights activist in Diyarbakir. The conflict entered a new phase when, in late 1991 and early 1992 (in retaliation for continuing cross-border attacks on Turkish troops), government fighter aircraft conducted numerous sorties into northern Iraq in order to attack suspected PKK bases there. In the course of these raids many civilians and refugees (mainly Iraqi Kurds) were reportedly killed, prompting international observers and relief workers publicly to call into question the integrity of the exercises. In October 1991 the Iraqi Government lodged formal complaints with the UN, denouncing Turkish violations of Iraq's territorial integrity. In April 1992 negotiations with Syria resulted in the reactivation of a 1987 security agreement designed to curb the activities of the PKK in the border region.

In late 1992 Turkish air and ground forces (in excess of 20,000 troops), conducted further attacks upon PKK bases inside northern Iraq, hoping to take advantage of losses inflicted upon the Kurdish rebels by a simultaneous offensive, initiated by Iraqi Kurdish *peshmerga* forces in October, with the aim of forcing the PKK from Iraq. By mid-December most Turkish ground forces had been withdrawn from Iraqi territory, and in January 1993 the Turkish military offensive was redirected against PKK strongholds in south-eastern Turkey.

ÇILLER BECOMES PRIME MINISTER

On 16 May 1993 Süleyman Demirel succeeded Turgut Özal as President, after being elected in the third round of voting by the Grand National Assembly. (Özal had died in April as a result of heart failure.) In early June Minister of State Tansu Çiller was elected to the DYP party leadership, and subsequently assumed the premiership as Turkey's first female Prime Minister. Çiller announced the composition of her Council of Ministers in late June. While all 12 SHP ministers retained their portfolios, the replacement of several prominent DYP ministers was interpreted as an attempt by the Prime Minister to consolidate support for her premiership.

On taking office as Prime Minister, Çiller was immediately confronted with a dramatic increase in separatist violence. The PKK ended its unilateral cease-fire, which had been announced in March 1993, by declaring 'war' on all Turkish targets. There followed a wave of bomb explosions in Turkish tourist resorts and abductions of foreign nationals by the PKK, as well as a series of attacks upon Turkish diplomatic missions and business interests in Europe. The Government responded by postponing measures to allow the use of the Kurdish language in schools and the media, and by withdrawing plans to give a degree of local autonomy to the south-eastern provinces. At the same time the armed forces, which numbered 150,000–200,000 in the south-east of the country, were given a virtual free hand against the PKK.

The pro-Kurdish Halkın Emek Partisi (HEP—People's Labour Party) was outlawed in July 1993. The Government cancelled all public investment in the south-east of the country, while it was estimated that there had been 2,000 deaths in the region as a result of the conflict between June and December 1993. In March 1994 'mainstream' parliamentarians voted to strip seven members of the Demokrasi Partisi (DEP—Democratic Party, the successor to HEP) and one independent Kurdish deputy of their parliamentary immunity from prosecution, and six deputies were subsequently detained. On 16 June Turkey's Constitutional Court banned the DEP and ruled that its 13 deputies should be expelled from the Grand National Assembly, owing to associations with the PKK. In August the six deputies detained since March, along with two DEP deputies arrested in July, went on trial on charges of supporting separatist movements. In December they were found guilty and received prison sentences of between three-and-a-half and 15 years, despite international protests (although the length of time already served in prison was sufficient to enable the immediate release of two of the deputies). At the end of October 1995 the Supreme Court released two of the deputies. However, it upheld the sentences of the four deputies remaining in prison.

In March 1995 about 35,000 Turkish troops were sent into northern Iraq in a military operation aimed at forcing the PKK out of its bases near the border. The PKK was reported, however, to have obtained advance knowledge of the incursion and to have withdrawn to areas inaccessible to the Turkish forces. Under increasing international pressure, including the temporary suspension of relations by the Council of Europe parliamentary assembly and the suspension of military trade with Turkey by certain countries, Turkish troops withdrew by early May. Nevertheless, there was a further incursion into northern Iraq by some 3,000 Turkish troops in July 1995, by which time the official death toll arising from the PKK conflict was estimated at more than 19,000.

Even as Çiller struggled to contain and defeat the PKK, she was confronted by tensions within the governing coalition, with the minority coalition partner, the SHP, suspicious of plans for privatization. It was widely expected that the Government would suffer heavy electoral defeats in the local elections of March 1994; however, the beneficiary was not the main opposition party, ANAP, but the Islamic conservative RP. The RP, which had campaigned against inflation and high interest rates and against Turkey's ties to NATO and the EU (as the EC had become), won 19% of the votes and took control of both Ankara and İstanbul.

In May 1994 Çiller sought to consolidate relations with the SHP, and simultaneously to deflect international criticism of Turkey's human rights record in the south-eastern provinces, by announcing plans to open up the political arena to groups that had been outlawed since the 1980 military coup. All restrictions on political activity were to be abolished, the voting age was to be reduced to 18 from 21 and deputies were to be allowed to transfer allegiance between parties.

Despite continuing dissension within the Government, and the resignation of several cabinet ministers, Çiller's coalition held together throughout the remainder of 1994, sustained, not least, by mutual fear of the RP. In November the Grand National Assembly approved legislation enabling the sale of some 100 state enterprises. Çiller's position appeared to be strengthened by the merger of the SHP and the CHP in February 1995, the merged party taking on the latter's name under the leadership of Hikmet Cetin. The merger led to a new coalition agreement and a consolidation of the Government's parliamentary majority. However, Çiller encountered considerable resistance from the Grand National Assembly in relation to her proposals for 'democratization', as first disclosed in May 1994. In June 1995 deputies from the RP and from within Çiller's own DYP successfully blocked the majority of these proposals. This placed in jeopardy the customs union between the EU and Turkey, the terms of which had been agreed in March and which was scheduled to come into effect at the end of the year, subject to ratification by the European Parliament (which had threatened to veto the agreement unless there was significant progress on raising standards of human rights in Turkey). At the end of July Çiller secured approval from the Grand National Assembly for several democratization measures, including the lowering of the minimum voting age and the removal of certain restrictions on trade unions and political participation. In addition, the number of parliamentary seats was to be increased by 100, to 550.

Relations with Greece deteriorated in 1994 following Greece's signing of the UN Convention on the Law of the Sea, which would permit the extension of its territorial waters in the Aegean Sea from six to 12 nautical miles. The Turkish Government, fearing the loss of shipping access to international seas, insisted that any expansion of territorial waters would be considered an act of aggression on the part of Greece, to which Turkey would respond. As the Convention entered into force in mid-November 1994, both sides conducted military exercises in the Aegean. Tensions between the two countries were manifest in early 1995 during negotiations to conclude a customs union between the EU and Turkey. Greece finally withdrew its opposition to the agreement in March, following the adoption of a formal timetable for accession negotiations to commence with Cyprus. In June the Grand National Assembly granted the Government military powers to defend the country's interests in the Aegean, following ratification of the Law of the Sea Convention by the Greek parliament.

In early September 1995, following the election of Deniz Baykal as the new leader of the CHP, the party's government ministers submitted their resignation, to enable Baykal to re-negotiate the coalition arrangement with the DYP. Talks between Baykal and Çiller revealed substantial differences between the two leaders. By 20 September the leaders had failed to secure the future of the coalition, forcing President Demirel to accept the Prime Minister's resignation. On the following day Demirel asked Çiller to form a new government. She announced its composition in early October, having secured the backing of the MHP and the DSP parliamentary groups, although the latter was dependent on Çiller's resolution of the trade dispute at that time involving an estimated 350,000 striking public-sector workers. A week later the new administration lost a vote of confidence conducted in the Grand National Assembly by 230 to 191 votes, hindered by several defections from its own DYP party. (The 'rebel' deputies were subsequently expelled from the DYP.) On 16 October Baykal revealed that a tentative agreement had been reached with the DYP leadership for the re-establishment of the DYP-CHP coalition. On 17 October Demirel assigned Çiller the task of forming the next government. Çiller conceded that an early general election would have to be conducted, at the end of the year, in order to secure future political stability. At the end of October Demirel approved a new coalition administration, formed by Çiller with the CHP. The Council of Ministers, which included several independent deputies, secured a vote of confidence in the Grand National Assembly on 5 November, obtaining 243 votes to 171.

THE ISLAMISTS ENTER GOVERNMENT

The overriding objective of Tansu Çiller's caretaker administration prior to the general election, scheduled for 24 December 1995, was to secure endorsement by the EU of the long-proposed customs union. In October 1995 the Supreme Court cancelled the charges against four Kurdish former deputies, while the Grand National Assembly voted to amend the 'anti-terror' laws, one of the outstanding concerns of the European Parliament, in order to permit greater freedom of expression. The customs union was finally approved by the European Parliament on 13 December, and entered into force on 1 January 1996.

During the election campaign domestic issues, such as the high rate of inflation, were the dominant concerns. The outcome of the election failed to resolve the country's political uncertainties: the RP won 158 of the 550 seats in the enlarged Grand National Assembly, having obtained 21.4% of the votes cast, while the DYP secured 135 seats (19.2%), ANAP 132 seats (19.7%), the DSP 76 seats (14.6%) and the CHP 49 seats (10.7%). The remaining votes were shared among smaller parties, which gained no representation.

President Demirel gave the RP, as the largest party in the new Grand National Assembly, the first opportunity to form a government. Protracted negotiations between the parties ensued over the next two months. Despite RP leader Necmettin Erbakan's apparently conciliatory approach, the party failed to secure the secular coalition partner that it needed to form the first predominantly Islamic government in the history of modern Turkey. The question increasingly became whether the two secular right-wing parties, the DYP and ANAP, could agree terms for a coalition that would prevent the formation of an RP administration. Finally, on 28 February 1996 ANAP and the DYP concluded an agreement. A rotating premiership arrangement was to be undertaken, according to which the ANAP leader, Mesut Yılmaz, was to occupy the office in the first year. The DYP was given most of the economic ministries, while ANAP took control of the defence and security portfolios. The new coalition still needed the support of the DSP if it was to control an absolute majority in the Grand National Assembly, but a formal arrangement proved impossible to secure.

Within weeks it was evident that the DYP-ANAP coalition would not last long, not least because of the intense personal animosity between Yılmaz and Çiller. During April and May 1996 the RP won two parliamentary votes to initiate corruption investigations against Çiller, on both occasions with significant support from ANAP deputies. Meanwhile, the opposition parties questioned the credibility of the Government following a ruling of the Constitutional Court to annul the vote of confidence that the coalition received in March. By the end of May Çiller was publicly urging Yılmaz to resign. The political uncertainty was seriously damaging the economy. The atmosphere of crisis within the country was deepened by an unsuccessful attempt to assassinate President Demirel on 19 May. In early June the Grand National Assembly, with the support of DYP deputies, voted to debate a censure motion on the Government; however, on 6 June Yılmaz resigned.

On 7 June Necmettin Erbakan was invited to form a government, and negotiations to establish a new coalition began. The DYP entered into discussions with the RP for the first time. On 28 June the two parties reached agreement, and the new coalition won a confidence vote in the Grand National Assembly on 8 July. Erbakan, as leader of the RP, became Prime Minister, while Çiller assumed the deputy premiership and foreign affairs portfolio. In addition, the DYP was awarded the defence, interior and education ministries and responsibility for the Treasury. The new Government announced that its objective was to secure political and economic stability; it promised to pursue further European integration and undertook to honour existing international and strategic agreements, providing they did not threaten national interest.

Nevertheless, Turkey had entered a new, potentially contradictory, era. It had moved closer to Europe even as it had sworn in its first Islamist-led government. Almost immediately

Erbakan embarked on a tour of Middle East and Asian Islamic countries, while there was continuing uncertainty over the future of the agreement reached in February 1996 between Turkey and Israel, providing for co-operation in military training, which had led Syria, Egypt and Iran to express anxiety that Turkey was abandoning the Islamic camp. Similar uncertainty prevailed over the long-term prospects for continued use of Turkish bases by allied forces engaged in 'Operation Provide Comfort' in northern Iraq, although at the end of July a five-month extension of the mandate was approved. Relations with the USA, however, became strained in the first months of the new administration. In August Turkey and Iran signed an agreement authorizing the construction of a pipeline between the two countries and enabling the sale of natural gas from 1999. The accord was concluded days after the entry into force of US legislation threatening punitive measures against countries undertaking substantial investment commitments in Iran. In early September Turkey was reportedly not consulted before US air-strikes were launched against Iraqi government troops in northern Iraq, and the Turkish authorities refused permission for the use of Turkish bases to pursue the operation.

However, there were policy areas where continuity seemed more assured under a government led by the RP. The RP leadership pledged itself to firm action against the PKK. In late June 1996 more than 30 members of the principal pro-Kurdish nationalist grouping, the Halkın Demokrasi Partisi (HADEP—People's Democracy Party), including its leader Murat Bozlak, were detained following disturbances at a party congress and were subsequently arraigned on charges of encouraging separatism. Civilian clashes with police occurred in Ankara and İstanbul during June and July at demonstrations of support for some 300 PKK prisoners who were on hunger strike as a protest against their treatment and conditions of confinement. Some 12 detainees died while refusing sustenance, prompting widespread international criticism at the Government's intransigence. Meanwhile, at the end of July the Grand National Assembly approved an extension of the state of emergency in the south-eastern provinces, despite the RP's electoral campaign commitment to reverse the situation, and the Turkish army intensifed its efforts to combat the PKK in the south-east and in northern Iraq. In August the Government approved legislation granting extensive powers of martial law to the governors of all 76 provinces, in a move which suggested the imminent repeal of the controversial 'state of emergency' law, which in November was extended for a further four months in nine of the 10 south-eastern provinces in which it had previously been applied. In August legislation was also endorsed that relaxed curbs on the Kurdish language and culture and facilitated increased investment in the south-east. In October, however, the European Parliament blocked aid to Turkey worth US \$470m., because of continuing concerns regarding the country's human rights record. Following the US raids on northern Iraq in early September, the Turkish Government proposed the establishment of an exclusion zone along its entire border with Iraq in order to prevent an influx of refugees and to eradicate separatist violence from the region. Turkey argued for the ending of UN sanctions against Iraq, which would allow it to begin purchasing Iraqi petroleum, and the renegotiation of 'Operation Provide Comfort', which, it was claimed, had produced a political vacuum in northern Iraq, which was being exploited by the PKK. The 'Operation Provide Comfort' mandate expired on 31st December 1996, and a more limited aerial surveillance operation, 'Northern Watch', which was to monitor Iraq's compliance with UN resolutions, was established. In December, in accordance with the 'oil-for-food' agreement (Security Council Resolution 986) agreed between the UN and Iraq in May, a fixed quantity of Iraqi oil began to be exported through Turkey, in order to enable Iraq to purchase supplies of medicine and food.

The Government suffered a serious legal defeat in December 1996 when the European Court of Human Rights (ECHR) ruled that Turkey, as the effective power in the 'TRNC', had breached the European Convention on Human Rights by denying a Greek Cypriot woman access to her property in Kyrenia since the 1974 invasion. The ruling was expected to open the way for compensation claims against Turkey (a signatory to the Convention) by other displaced Greek Cypriots. (In January 1999, however, Turkey refused to pay the compensation; failure to comply with the ECHR ruling could result in expulsion from the Council of Europe.)

YILMAZ REPLACES ERBAKAN

In the context of persistent rumours of an imminent military coup and a new censure motion against the Government, tabled in protest at proposals to introduce Islamic reforms, a meeting of the military-dominated National Security Council (NSC) on 28 February 1997 led to the publication of an 18-point memorandum setting out recommendations to ensure the protection of secularism in Turkey. On 5 March, under intense pressure, Erbakan reluctantly signed the memorandum, whereby the Government was committed to increasing the length of compulsory state education from five to eight years, to closing unauthorized Islamist schools and acting against Muslim brotherhoods (*Ikhwan*); to halting the employment of soldiers expelled from the army for fundamentalist activities; and to reducing co-operation with Iran.

Although the immediate political crisis had apparently been resolved, DYP dissidents began to call for the dissolution of the Government and the organization of early elections. In June 1997, following increasing opposition, including the demand by the NSC that the implementation of the 18-point programme be accelerated, the narrow defeat of a censure motion and the loss of his parliamentary majority, Erbakan resigned. However, President Demirel selected not Çiller (despite agreements concluded at the formation of the 1996 coalition) but ANAP leader Mesut Yılmaz to form a new coalition. On 30 June Yılmaz was appointed Prime Minister, having successfully gained the support of the DSP and the recently-founded Demokrat Türkiye Partisi (DTP—Democratic Turkey Party), along with that of several DYP defectors, to form a coalition with a nominal 12-seat majority. The new Government's programme, announced on 7 July, stressed its commitment to secularism and echoed many of the recommendations of the 18-point memorandum drawn up by the NSC (including the controversial education reforms). The Government received a vote of confidence from the Grand National Assembly on 12 July. Legislation promulgating the education reforms secured parliamentary approval in mid-August, as did a press amnesty law which suspended the sentences of imprisoned editors (believed to number at least six) who had been convicted of publishing articles posing a threat to national security. Later that month the trial began of a total of 48 members of the security forces, including 11 officers, for the murder of a journalist in 1996. Doubts were raised about the effectiveness of the trial when the defendants failed to attend the court; delays to the case resulted in demonstrations in İstanbul in January 1998. In March, however, five of the officers were sentenced to more than seven years' imprisonment, while the remaining six were acquitted.

On 16 October 1997 Turkey agreed an out-of-court settlement in a case of alleged torture that had been taken to the ECHR. Later that month a human rights activist, Esber Yagmurdereli, was sentenced to 23 years' imprisonment for supporting terrorist activity and disseminating separatist propaganda. Following both foreign and domestic condemnation of his detention, he was released in November ostensibly on the grounds of ill health. On 27 November the ECHR ordered Turkey to pay compensation to six former DEP deputies who had been detained for two weeks without trial and to three Kurdish women whose homes had been destroyed by the army. On 11 March 1998 10 members of the security forces were acquitted of torturing 14 students who were subsequently convicted of belonging to a proscribed organization and sentenced to between five and 12 years' imprisonment. At the end of the month five of the students were released, pending their retrial on lesser charges. During late 1997 and early 1998 detainees at Erzurum gaol protested against prison conditions, staging an extended hunger strike and taking hostages to reinforce their claims.

Meanwhile, in May 1997 the armed forces launched their most ambitious military incursion into northern Iraq to date in pursuit of PKK activists, in an operation entailing the mobilization of some 50,000 troops. The army claimed that the Iraqi-Kurdish Kurdistan Democratic Party (KDP), which was reported to have clashed ferociously with the PKK during 1996, invited its intervention. The incursion prompted a muted international response, when compared with the military intervention of 1995; the USA had been 'disengaging' from northern Iraq for some months and appeared content for Turkey to assume some of its former responsibilities. The most severe critics of the exercise were Iran and Syria, who accused Turkey of seeking to establish a permanent military presence in northern Iraq. A further offensive against PKK positions in northern Iraq in October was accompanied by the lifting of the 10-year-old state of emergency in three of the nine south-eastern provinces (Bitlis, Batman and Bingöl). The continuing emergency rule in the other six provinces and the Turkish military presence in northern Iraq were seen as indicative of a Turkish intention to create an informal cross-border security zone to prevent further incursions by Kurdish rebels.

FOREIGN RELATIONS 1997–99

At the end of April 1997 the Greek and Turkish ministers responsible for foreign affairs held bilateral talks in Malta under EU auspices, during which it was agreed that each country would establish a committee of experts to help resolve bilateral disputes. The two committees were to be separate and independent and were to communicate through the EU. In July, at a NATO summit in Madrid, Spain, direct talks took place between Demirel and the Greek Prime Minister, Konstantinos Simitis (the first such meeting for three years). An agreement was signed on 8 July whereby both sides pledged to respect the other's sovereign rights and to renounce violence, and the threat of violence, in their dealings with each other. Later in July, following earlier statements from Turkey expressing the hope that Greece would revoke its veto on EU aid, Greece stated that the veto would not be removed unless Turkey agreed to international arbitration over the disputed islet of Imia/Kardak.

In July 1997 Turkey announced the formation of a joint committee to implement partial integration between Turkey and the 'TRNC', in response to the EU's agreement to commence accession talks with Cyprus. Turkey also declared in September that should the EU continue to conduct membership talks with the Greek Cypriot Government, then it would seek further integration with the 'TRNC'. However, Yılmaz and Simitis held a cordial meeting later in November and agreed to explore confidence-building measures. Throughout 1997 and early 1998 relations were strained by mutual accusations of violations of airspace and territorial waters. The most serious incident occurred in October 1997, when Greece accused Turkey of harassing an aircraft carrying the Greek Minister of Defence. In January 1998 Turkey declared that a Greek plan to extend its territorial waters from six to 12 miles was unacceptable, as were plans to open several Aegean islets for settlement. In June new tensions arose over Cyprus when six Turkish military aircraft landed at a 'TRNC' airfield in response to the landing a week earlier of Greek military aircraft at Paphos. In the following month President Demirel paid an official visit to the 'TRNC' (in response to an unprecedented visit to Greek Cyprus by President Stefanopoulos of Greece the previous month), amid a show of Turkish military force to mark the 24th anniversary of the 1974 intervention. At the same time Yılmaz reiterated Turkey's threat to take retaliatory military action if the Greek Cypriot Government implemented its plan to deploy Russian-supplied missiles before the end of 1998.

Relations with the EU were further strained by announcements in December 1997 that Turkey would not be included in negotiations for the enlargement of the EU, but that it would be invited to a newly-created European Conference, which was to include both EU and non-EU states. Turkey stated that it would not attend such a conference and that it would also cease negotiations on Cyprus, human rights and the Aegean disputes. The deadlock persisted in 1998–99, aggravated by the opening of substantive accession negotiations between the EU and the Greek Cypriot Government in November 1998.

In January 1999 Turkey accused Greece of escalating tension in the Aegean and urged reconciliation through talks and negotiations. Relations with Greece deteriorated in early 1999 following repeated Turkish accusations of Greek support for the PKK; Greece denied the accusations, and Öcalan was later captured at the Greek embassy in Kenya (see below). In March Turkey alleged that Greece had unilaterally suspended 'confidence-building' talks on the dispute in the Aegean, and denied a claim that Turkish aircraft had violated Greek airspace. However, relations between the two countries improved considerably in August 1999, following the positive political and humanitarian response of the Greek Government to the earthquake that devastated Turkey in that month (see below).

Meanwhile, following negotiations, it was announced at the end of September 1997 that full diplomatic relations were to be resumed with Iran. In September President Demirel called for talks with Syria and Iran on the use of the Euphrates' waters.

DOMESTIC DIFFICULTIES PERSIST

On 16 January 1998 the Constitutional Court issued a judgment banning the RP on the grounds that it had a 'hidden' fundamentalist agenda and had conspired against the secular order. In addition, former Prime Minister Erbakan and six other RP officials were banned from holding political office for five years. A month later some 100 former RP deputies joined the new Fazilet Partisi (FP—Virtue Party), which had been founded in December 1997 under the leadership of Ismail Alptekin, and by early March the FP had become the largest party in the Grand National Assembly.

Public demonstrations followed the military's insistence on the strict enforcement of the ban on wearing Islamic dress in public buildings, notably educational establishments. 10,000 people attended the largest of these demonstrations in İstanbul at the end of February 1998. The Government subsequently stated that the ban would not be strictly enforced, and in mid-March survived its third censure motion, which was presented against the Minister for Education for his handling of the issue of Islamic dress. At the end of the month, however, the NSC criticized the Government for advocating a relaxation of the enforcement of anti-Islamic legislation; the Government subsequently proposed further measures to curb Islamist radicalism, and the universities announced their decision to enforce the dress code.

Also in March 1998, the Court of Appeals ruled that former Prime Minister Çiller could not be prosecuted over allegations that she had misused government funds during her premiership. While admitting that she had withdrawn substantial sums from a secret government 'slush fund', Çiller had claimed that she could not disclose the destination of the money for reasons of national security. In May the Grand National Assembly confirmed that an inquiry would be conducted into corruption allegations against Prime Minister Yılmaz connected with tendering for government contracts. In early June Yılmaz announced that he would resign at the end of the year to make way for a broadly-based caretaker government which would oversee the holding of early legislative elections in April 1999. In August 1998 12 former RP politicians, including Erbakan and FP leader Recai Kutan, were charged with illegally diverting funds from the party prior to its dissolution. (In October 1999 their assets were frozen while the trial continued.) An investigation into Çiller's financial affairs was begun in September 1998.

In November 1998 the Grand National Assembly approved an investigation into the Minister of Public Works and Housing, Yaşar Topçu, on charges that he misused his office in the tender for the İzmit Bay Project. In the same month a parliamentary commission, owing to insufficient evidence, dismissed corruption charges against Çiller. Also in November Erbakan was acquitted on charges of slandering the judiciary, and Minister of State Güneş Taner was removed from office following a parliamentary censure motion arising from corruption allegations. In December Çiller's husband was acquitted on charges of falsifying documents.

Following corruption allegations against Prime Minister Yılmaz connected with the privatization of the Türk Ticaret Bankası, on 25 November 1998 the Grand National Assembly approved a motion of 'no confidence' in the Government, which subsequently resigned. Protracted political manoeuvring resulted in the formation, in January 1999, of an interim administration headed by Ecevit, comprising members of the DSP and independents. Also in January, a motion was filed for the dissolution of the pro-Kurdish nationalist Halkın Demokrasi Partisi (HADEP—People's Democracy Party), owing to its alleged links with the PKK; in March, however, the Constitutional Court ruled that HADEP was to be allowed to contest the elections.

ÖCALAN CAPTURED

Relations with Syria, which had already deteriorated in July 1998 (owing to Syria's repeated claim to the Hatay region of Turkey), worsened in early October after Turkey threatened the use of force if Syria did not expel PKK leader Abdullah Öcalan (known to be residing in that country) and close down terrorist training camps both in Syria and the Beka'a valley in Lebanon. It was reported that 10,000 Turkish troops had been deployed near the border; the Turkish ambassador to Syria was also recalled. Egypt and, later, Iran both attempted to mediate in the dispute, and following a meeting of Turkish and Syrian officials in late October an agreement was signed under which Syria would not allow the PKK to operate on its territory. Öcalan was also forced to leave the country.

Turkey had recalled temporarily its ambassador to Italy in October 1998 after that country hosted a meeting of the Kurdish parliament-in-exile. Relations deteriorated further following the arrest of Öcalan upon his arrival in Italy in November, as a result of Italy's refusal to extradite him to Turkey and of his application for asylum. Anti-Italian demonstrations were held in Turkey, and Italian goods were boycotted; Turkey also threatened to end diplomatic relations if Öcalan's asylum requests were granted. PKK attacks in the south-east were reported during November, and government operations against the PKK continued. Öcalan's request for asylum was denied, and in January 1999 Öcalan was reported to have left Italy. His subsequent whereabouts were unclear, but on 15 February Öcalan was captured at the Greek embassy in Kenya and returned to Turkey. Widespread Kurdish protests were held throughout Europe.

Öcalan was charged with treason on 23 February 1999, and held personally responsible for the deaths of some 30,000 people during the 15-year Kurdish struggle for autonomy. PKK violence in protest at the trial continued in that month. In April a further operation was launched against the PKK, involving the deployment of some 15,000 Turkish troops in northern Iraq. Some foreign journalists were permitted to observe Öcalan's trial, conducted on the prison island of Imrali, but Öcalan's lawyers claimed that they had been prevented from providing a proper defence. During the proceedings Öcalan depicted himself as a moderate, called for a PKK cease-fire and declared his willingness to negotiate a peace agreement for the Kurdish region if his life was spared. On 29 June, however, he was found guilty and sentenced to death, whereupon his lawyers lodged an appeal in Turkey and also applied to the ECHR for a ruling that the sentence breached the European Convention on Human Rights.

1999 GENERAL ELECTION

On 18 April 1999 early elections took place to the 550-seat Grand National Assembly. Some 87% of the electorate voted, and the DSP became the largest party in the Grand National Assembly with 136 seats, closely followed by the MHP (129 seats) and the FP (111). ANAP and the DYP obtained 86 seats and 85 seats respectively; three seats were won by independents. HADEP performed strongly in the south-east, but failed to secure the 10% of the national vote necessary for a seat in the Grand National Assembly. The CHP leader, Deniz Baykal, resigned following the poor performance of his party. President Demirel on 3 May invited Bülent Ecevit to form a new administration, and on 28 May a three-party coalition Government, composed of the DSP, the MHP and ANAP, was announced. The new Government commanded 351 seats in the Grand National Assembly, and was thus the first since 1995 to command an overall parliamentary majority. In the same month the Chief Prosecutor instituted a court case against the FP, with the aim of dissolving the party. At that time the FP was involved in controversy after one of its female deputies had arrived at the Grand National Assembly for her investiture wearing an Islamic headscarf.

NATURAL DISASTERS—EXTERNAL AND DOMESTIC DEVELOPMENTS

A major earthquake, measuring 7.4 on the Richter scale, devastated the industrial region of north-west Turkey on 17 August 1999, killing more than 17,000 people, injuring 40,000, leaving an estimated 600,000 homeless and inflicting huge damage on the economy. On 12 November a second earthquake in the same area, measuring 7.2 on the Richter scale, killed a further 700 people. Widespread public anger focused on the slow response of state institutions, particularly the armed forces, to the disaster, and on the endemic corruption which had allowed many sub-standard apartment blocks to be constructed in a region known to be vulnerable to earthquakes.

International assistance in the wake of the earthquakes included considerable help from Greece, which Turkey reciprocated when Athens was struck by an earthquake in September 1999. Encouraged by US President Bill Clinton during his visit to Turkey in November, there was a marked improvement in Turkish-Greek relations, which in turn contributed to Greek acceptance of the decision of the EU summit meeting in Helsinki, Finland, in December to grant Turkey the status of a candidate for EU membership. Although no date was set for actual negotiations, pending improvement in Turkey's observance of human and democratic rights, Ankara responded by encouraging the Turkish Cypriots to participate in long-sought UN-sponsored negotiations on the Cyprus problem, although there seemed little prospect of a solution in the near future. An exchange of visits by the Greek and Turkish Ministers of Foreign Affairs in January and February 2000, the first for nearly 40 years, confirmed the *rapprochement*; during these visits several bilateral agreements were signed and a joint working group on the reduction of military tensions in the Aegean region was established.

In September 1999 unrest broke out in prisons across the country as a result of the poor conditions and overcrowding; 10 prisoners were killed and a number of guards were held hostage. The Minister of Justice asserted that he would not resign over the unrest; he later announced that a special force was to be established to ensure prison security. Some 100 people were arrested in İstanbul while trying to issue a press release on the prison incidents. Unrest continued in prisons in late 1999 and early 2000. In February 2000 a protocol was signed providing for the education of prison inmates.

Although the Court of Appeals and the Chief Prosecutor rejected Abdullah Öcalan's appeal against his death sentence, the Government on 12 January 2000 granted a stay of execution until such time as the ECHR had considered the PKK leader's case. In February the PKK leadership declared a cease-fire and reportedly removed the proscribed word 'Kurdistan' from the organization's title. However, the Turkish authorities were not convinced by this initiative, and not only continued to harass pro-Kurdish HADEP politicians but also, in April, launched a new offensive against alleged Kurdish guerrillas in northern Iraq, claiming that the PKK was re-establishing positions near the Turkish border despite its cease-fire declaration.

SEZER ELECTED PRESIDENT—EU AND ARMENIAN CONTROVERSIES

On 29 March 2000 the Grand National Assembly rejected constitutional amendments proposed by the Government, including measures that sought to reduce the presidential term of office from seven to five years, introduce direct presidential elections, and allow an incumbent Head of State to seek re-election—the specific aim of this last provision being to enable President Demirel to serve a second term. Following a second rejection of the amendments on 5 April, on 5 May the Assembly elected Ahmet Necdet Sezer, hitherto President of the Constitutional Court and the Government's nominee, as Turkey's 10th President, with 330 votes out of 533 in a third round of voting. In July Mesut Yılmaz was appointed Deputy Prime Minister and State Minister and was given special responsibility for EU affairs.

Although the Prime Minister had nominated Sezer for the presidency, the two came into conflict in August 2000 when the President refused to sign a decree giving the Government authority, subject to appeal, to dismiss civil servants suspected of supporting Islamist groups or of being sympathetic to Kurdish separatism. Inspired by the strongly secular military establishment and reportedly aimed at some 3,000 civil servants believed to have such tendencies, Sezer rejected the decree as unconstitutional on the grounds that it had not been enacted by parliamentary legislation. He did, however, emphasize that he shared the

Government's concern about threats to the secular system. The decree had been partly motivated by the discovery, in early 2000, of evidence that the Hezbollah Islamist group had conducted a long-running campaign of torture and murder against Kurdish and other opponents of the Government with the backing of elements in the civil service and military.

Deterioration of relations with Greece in October 2000 over controversial NATO military exercises was followed in November by a clash with the EU over the terms of the accession partnership agreement, which would govern Turkish entry negotiations. In particular, Turkey objected to the inclusion in the EU draft text of a specification that the political criteria by which Turkish suitability would be judged included observance of human rights, a resolution of the longstanding dispute with EU member Greece on the delimitation of the Aegean Sea and its willingness to promote a Cyprus settlement based on UN resolutions. Turkey's anger at the inclusion of these conditions was speedily demonstrated by its joint decision with the Turkish Cypriot leader, Rauf Denktaş, that he should withdraw from the current UN-sponsored talks on Cyprus. The dispute was partially resolved in December by the inclusion of a new subheading referring to 'political dialogue' before the political criteria section of the EU text, so that Turkey could claim that the criteria were not a condition for progress on its membership application. However, no date was set for the opening of negotiations, and the EU was subsequently critical of Turkey's programme for meeting the requirements of accession, published in March 2001, for not adequately addressing the problems identified by the EU in the accession partnership agreement.

The European Parliament's adoption in November 2000 of a resolution condemning the 'genocide' of Armenians in Ottoman Turkey during World War I further strained EU-Turkish relations. Moreover, a similar motion was passed by the French Parliament and signed into law by President Chirac in January 2001. Turkey responded to the latter initiative by recalling its ambassador from Paris and by applying immediate economic sanctions on French companies active in Turkey. In the Grand National Assembly, several draft laws were tabled providing for recognition of France's 'genocide' of Muslim Algerians during the 1954–62 war of independence.

SERIOUS PRISON UNREST—FEBRUARY 2001 FINANCIAL CRISIS AND AFTERMATH

At least 30 prisoners and two security personnel were killed in mid-December 2000 when paramilitary forces launched assaults on hundreds of political prisoners in 20 prisons. The inmates were staging hunger strikes in protest against the Government's plan to move them to new 'F-type' prisons with small cells, because their existing large dormitories were often controlled by political groups or criminal gangs. Ignoring prisoners' protests that they would be isolated and vulnerable to abuse in the new prisons, the authorities began the transfers after regaining control, sparking further hunger strikes. These resulted in the deaths of 57 prisoners by mid-September 2002, even though the Government announced that no more 'F-type' prisons would be built after the present programme had been completed.

Meanwhile, Turkey had experienced its worst financial crisis for many years in late February 2001, when the Government was forced to float the lira. The crisis was triggered by a public clash between President Sezer and Prime Minister Ecevit at a meeting of the National Security Council on 19 February. Ecevit walked out when the President accused him of protecting Ministers suspected of corruption. The immediate reaction of the markets was a massive flight of capital and a collapse in share prices. After three days of abortive resistance, the Government released the lira from its 'peg' with the US dollar on 22 February, thereby effectively devaluing the currency by about a third. Consequential price increases provoked large protest demonstrations and rumours of an imminent military coup. Ecevit resisted opposition calls for his resignation, instead appointing Kemal Derviş, hitherto a senior World Bank official, as Minister of State responsible for economic policy with extensive new powers.

Derviş quickly drew up a recovery plan, envisaging the implementation of long-delayed privatization and liberalization measures, and applied to the IMF for emergency support. Protracted negotiations ensued, during which the IMF insisted on key steps

being taken before it would agree to new loans, including the closure of loss-making, state-owned banks and privatization of the telecommunications industry. After the Government had secured parliamentary approval for these and other measures in early May 2001, the IMF on 15 May approved additional stand-by credit of US \$8,000m., bringing total IMF resources available to Turkey to \$19,000m. Continued opposition within the ruling coalition to the privatization of telecommunications in particular impelled the IMF to suspend disbursements to Turkey in late June, but they were resumed on 12 July after the Government had reassured the IMF about its commitment to economic reform and privatization. Five days later Enis Öksüz of the MHP, a leading opponent of the restructuring programme, resigned as Minister of Transport and Communications after further turmoil on the exchange markets had reduced the value of the lira to little more than half its pre-February level. He was replaced by his party colleague Oktay Vural.

BANNING OF VIRTUE PARTY—OTHER PARTY DEVELOPMENTS, 2001–02

In common with its three Islamist predecessors, the FP was banned by the Constitutional Court on 22 June 2001 with immediate effect and ordered to surrender its assets to the state, on the grounds that the party had become the focus of anti-secular activities in breach of the Constitution. The Court also ordered the expulsion from the Grand National Assembly of two FP deputies for particular anti-secular offences, the remaining FP deputies being required to become independents. Kutan described the ruling as 'a blow to Turkey's search for democracy and law', while Ecevit regretted the decision because of its potential to destabilize the political situation at a sensitive time for the economy. On 25 June the former SP deputies walked out of the Assembly, declaring that they would not return until constitutional amendments had been enacted to restrict the grounds for outlawing political parties.

In July 2001, with the support of about half the former FP deputies, Kutan announced the formation of a new Islamist party, to be called Saadet ('Prosperity'), stating that it would seek to protect religious rights, but would not challenge the secular basis of the Turkish state. Most of the remaining FP deputies declared their support for a more reformist Islamist party, the AK Party (Justice and Development Party, or 'White' Party), founded in August by the former mayor of İstanbul, Recep Tayyıp Erdogan. At the end of July the ECHR ruled by four votes to three that the Turkish Constitutional Court had not violated the European Convention on Human Rights in January 1998 in proscribing the RP (the predecessor of the FP). The AK quickly emerged not only as the stronger of the two successor Islamist parties, but also the best-supported party in the country in opinion polls. In what appeared to be a concerted establishment campaign against Erdogan, the Constitutional Court ruled in January 2002 that the AK leader's conviction on a sedition charge in 1999 had disqualified him from politics, and banned him from standing in the next general election. The electoral commission confirmed the decision in June 2002. Also banned for similar reasons were Necmettin Erbakan, Murat Bozlak, the HADEP leader, and Akin Birdal, a prominent human rights activist.

Following further crack-downs on alleged Kurdish dissidents by the security forces, the PKK announced in mid-April 2002 that it had re-formed itself as the Congress for Freedom and Democracy in Kurdistan (KADEK), with the imprisoned Öcalan as its leader. It was stated that the successor party did not seek an independent Kurdistan, but rather full rights for Kurds to be taught, to publish and to broadcast in Kurdish as equal citizens of a 'united and democratic Turkey'. Turkish officials dismissed the move as a tactical ploy, adopted because the PKK had been declared an 'international terrorist organization' by the USA, the United Kingdom and other governments, and also claimed that the PKK's armed wing had not been disbanded. Meanwhile, in the same month the ECHR ruled that the banning of the pro-Kurdish HEP in 1993 had breached the European convention and fined Turkey €40,000, while in June the Court awarded damages of €50,000 each to the 13 former HEP members who had been expelled from the Grand National Assembly in 1994. In between these reverses, the Turkish Government welcomed an EU decision in May to designate both the PKK and the far-left Revolutionary People's Liberation Party—Front (DHKP—C) as 'terrorist organizations'. (In September 2001 the DHKP—C had been linked with Turkey's first suicide bombing, in which two İstanbul policemen and the bomber had been killed.)

TROOP DEPLOYMENT IN AFGHANISTAN— EXTERNAL RELATIONS, 2001–02

The Grand National Assembly in October 2001 gave the Government authority to send Turkish troops abroad to participate in the US-led military operation against al-Qa'ida and Taliban forces in Afghanistan (mounted in the wake of the September suicide attacks on the USA) and also to allow more foreign troops to be stationed in Turkey. In December the US Secretary of State, Colin Powell, visited Ankara in the course of a 10-nation tour to rally support for military action in Afghanistan. The following month, as Ecevit had talks with President George W. Bush in Washington, DC, Turkey supplied a contingent of 50 soldiers to the multinational International Security Assistance Force (ISAF) being deployed in Afghanistan. After some hesitation, until the Government had secured US assurances of financial compensation, Turkey took over from the United Kingdom as commander of ISAF in June 2002 for six months. None the less, in the same month Ecevit stated publicly that he did not support the apparent US intention to remove the Saddam Hussein regime in Iraq by military force. In particular the Government feared a break-up of the Iraqi state and the creation of a Kurdish state in northern Iraq that could be used to foster Kurdish nationalism in its own territory, and the possible mass exodus of Iraqi Kurds into Turkey. There were also concerns about the disruption to Turkish-Iraqi trade and economic co-operation that any US attack would bring. It was estimated that the Gulf War of 1991 and subsequent sanctions had cost the Turkish economy some US $30,000m.–$40,000m.

An Ankara-backed decision by the Turkish Cypriots to return to the UN negotiating table in Cyprus in January 2002 helped to reactivate the process of *rapprochement* between Turkey and Greece, as required by the EU as a precondition for the opening of formal accession negotiations with Turkey. Senior Turkish and Greek officials met in Ankara in March to discuss the Aegean Sea delimitation and related issues, and were reported to have agreed to submit intractable differences to the ICJ. The two sides also signed an agreement for the construction of pipeline through which Turkey would supply gas to Greece. However, the failure of the Cyprus talks to make a breakthrough by the June target-date set by the UN raised the prospect that Cyprus would be admitted to the EU without a prior political settlement on the island—a course to which Turkey remained vehemently opposed. By September there had still been no substantive progress in the talks.

2002 GOVERNMENT CRISIS—CALLING OF EARLY ELECTION

Early in October 2001 the Government secured the Grand National Assembly's approval of several amendments to the Constitution intended to facilitate Turkey's accession to the EU, including an easing of the ban on the Kurdish language. The following month the Grand National Assembly approved revisions to the Civil Code under which women obtained equal status with men in the sphere of the family. However, there remained strong parliamentary opposition, particularly from the MHP, to abolishing the death penalty—a key EU requirement—and to giving legislative force to other human rights reforms. On the economic front, moreover, the international downturn caused by the September suicide attacks on the USA frustrated Turkish hopes of a speedy recovery and necessitated the conclusion in February 2002 of a new three-year agreement

with the IMF, providing for stand-by credit of US $16,000m. (including $4,000m. rolled over from the previous credit).

The political deadlock deepened in early May 2002 when Ecevit became seriously incapacitated by illness and injury but rejected demands that he should stand down. He also resisted calls for an early general election not only from the opposition, but also from within the ruling coalition. The crisis appeared to be defused in early June, when the MHP agreed to remain in the Government while allowing the human rights legislation and the abolition of capital punishment to be approved in the Grand National Assembly by an alliance of the other two coalition parties and opposition members. The Government was also able to revoke the state of emergency in two of the four mainly-Kurdish provinces in the south-east. In the following month, however, Ecevit's continuing infirmity and refusal to resign resulted in a major challenge to his leadership from within the DSP. After Ecevit had dismissed Hüsamettin Özkan as Deputy Prime Minister, İsmail Cem resigned as Minister of Foreign Affairs, while more than 60 DSP members of the Grand National Assembly defected from the party, thus depriving the Government of its parliamentary majority. Şükrü Sina Gürel, who was regarded as a hard-liner on Cyprus and other regional issues, replaced both Cem and Özkan.

Derviş also announced his resignation from the Government in July 2002, but was persuaded by the President to remain in office to reassure the financial markets and the IMF. He was nevertheless present when Cem and Özkan launched a new pro-EU formation, called the Yeni Turkiye Partisi (YTP—New Turkey Party), as opinion polls indicated that none of the three existing coalition parties would surmount the 10% barrier in an election. The new party joined the widespread calls for an early poll, to which the increasingly isolated Ecevit was forced to bow after the MHP officially voiced its support for an election. As confirmed by the Grand National Assembly at the end of July, a general election was set for 3 November 2002, nearly 18 months ahead of schedule. This decision cleared the way for the Grand National Assembly's formal approval in early August of the delayed human rights and other reforms, including the abolition of the death penalty except in time of war, the ending of the ban on broadcasting in languages other than Turkish, authorization of Kurdish teaching in regulated private schools, the lifting of penalties for criticism of the armed forces and other state institutions, the easing of restrictions on public demonstrations and association, greater freedom for non-Muslim religions, the redefinition of police duties and powers, and the revision of press laws and regulations.

Despite the calling of an early election, Ecevit lost another member of the Government on 7 August 2002, when Yaşar Okuyan (of ANAP) resigned as Minister of Labour and Social Security, reportedly because of opposition from employers to a draft law to expand the rights of workers. Three days later the disarray of the Government was confirmed by the delayed resignation of Derviş, after he had concluded a further round of negotiations with the IMF to secure the release of the latest tranche of stand-by credit. Replaced by Masum Türker of the DSP, Derviş stated that he would work with Cem and the YTP to build a new secular coalition which reflected modern social liberal principles. After weeks of uncertainty, Derviş opted at the end of August to join the CHP, the historic party of Atatürk but unrepresented since the 1999 election, with the declared aim of restoring it to parliamentary dominance on the secular left.

On 20 September 2002 Turkey's highest electoral board confirmed the Constitutional Court's decision to prohibit Erdogan, Erbakan, Bozlak and Birdal from taking part in the November election. However, despite its leader's ban, the AK remained the most popular party in early October. The military and more mainstream politicians remained sceptical of Erdogan's newly professed pro-European views, and continued to regard his party as Islamist.

Economy

ALAN J. DAY

Based on an earlier article by DAVID SEDDON

INTRODUCTION

Turkey is about 1,450 km (900 miles) long and some 500 km (300 miles) wide, covering an area of 779,452 sq km (300,948 sq miles). The October 1985 census recorded a population of 50,664,458, and that of October 1990 showed the population to be 56,473,035. These totals excluded Turks working abroad, the largest number of whom are in Germany. The census results indicated an average annual population increase between 1985 and 1990 of 2.2%, compared with 2.6% between 1980 and 1985. Turkey's population density was 65.0 per sq km in October 1985, and had increased to 87.0 per sq km by mid-2001. The results of the national census conducted in November 1997 showed the population to have increased to 62.9m., indicating an average annual rate of growth of 1.5% since 1990. İstanbul, the country's largest city, had a population of 9.2m. (7.2m. in 1990), followed by Ankara (the capital) with 3.7m. and İzmir with 3.1m. By mid-2001 Turkey's population was officially estimated to have risen to 67.8m.

The country possesses great natural advantages: the land yields good grain and a wide variety of fruit and other products; it is rich in minerals; and it has a number of natural ports. The climate is varied and, on the whole, favourable, although communications are hindered by the mountain ranges that ring the Anatolian plateau to the north, east and south. Despite these advantages, Turkey has economic output, infrastructural development and gross national product (GNP) per caput well below that of other members of the Organisation for Economic Co-operation and Development (OECD). In consequence, millions of Turks have gone abroad to seek economic betterment, notably to become 'guest workers' in Germany.

GNP expanded, in real terms, by an average of 7% annually between 1970 and 1978. However, in the severe economic and social crisis of the late 1970s, growth slowed to the extent that an actual decline of 1.1% was recorded in 1980. In 1980–90 GNP at constant 1987 prices increased by an annual average of 5.5%, with a growth rate of 9.2%, the highest for more than a decade, in 1990. In 1991 the adverse effects of the Gulf War contributed to growth of just 0.9%, with GNP amounting to US $109,078m. GNP growth improved in both 1992 and 1993, but, after a severe financial crisis early in 1994 and an austerity programme in April, GNP contracted by 6.1% in that year. The decline in the economy was successfully reversed during 1995, when GNP growth of 8% was achieved, a level that was sustained (7.9%) in 1996. The strongest sectoral growth in both 1995 and 1996 was recorded in trade and industry. Figures published by the OECD revealed that although income per head rose by 6.1% in 1995, to $2,928, the wealthiest 20% of the population had an income of $8,037 per head, while the poorest had only $717, giving Turkey the worst income distribution of all OECD countries except Mexico. In 1997, according to World Bank estimates, GNP rose by 8.6% to $199,300m. ($3,130 per head) on a conventional exchange-rate basis. On a 'purchasing-power parity' (PPP) basis, GNP was equivalent to $412,000m. ($6,470 per head). In 1998 adverse external factors such as the major financial crisis in Russia (Turkey's second most important trading partner) contributed to a reduction in GNP growth to 3.9%, yielding GNP of $200,530m. ($3,160 per head) on a conventional exchange-rate basis, or $419,000m. ($6,594) on a PPP basis. Gross domestic product (GDP) in that year was recorded by the OECD at $200,800m. In 1990–1998, according to the World Bank, GNP had increased at an average annual rate of 2.9%.

A further sharp decline in the economic growth rate was already predicted for 1999 when two major earthquakes in north-western Turkey in August and November, measuring 7.4 and 7.2 on the Richter scale respectively, inflicted huge damage on industry and infrastructure, resulting in an actual decline in GNP of 6.4%, to US $185,136m. ($2,878 per head), together with a 5% contraction in GDP, to $190,800m. In addition to killing some 18,000 people, injuring over 40,000 and making an estimated 600,000 homeless, the earthquakes destroyed thousands of factories and facilities in Turkey's industrial heartland, and the cost of repairing the damage was estimated at between $5,000m. and $20,000m. As well as being pledged substantial foreign assistance and being admitted to the official list of European Union (EU) candidate countries (see Foreign Trade and Balance of Payments, below), the Government introduced special taxation measures intended to raise some $1,400m. for reconstruction. Furthermore, in December 1999 it concluded a stand-by arrangement with the IMF under which it was to receive some $4,000m. over three years in support of a wide-ranging economic restructuring and anti-inflation programme.

By mid-2000 recovery appeared to be under way, GDP having increased by 5.6% in the first quarter. In November, however, the underlying weakness of the economy was again exposed by a major banking and stock market crisis, in which the Central Bank expended some US $7,000m. supporting the lira, before the Government secured an additional stand-by facility of $7,000m. from the IMF in December. Earlier expectations of GDP growth of around 5% in 2000 were accordingly disappointed, although expansion of 3.5% was recorded, with GDP totalling $198,800m. according to the OECD ($455,500m. at PPP), producing GDP per head of $3,000 ($6,800 at PPP), while GNP was estimated at $201,972m. A Central Bank plan to restore credibility to the currency after a decade of high inflation, by introducing a new lira on 1 January 2001 equivalent to TL1m., was shelved.

The respite proved to be only temporary. Following a public clash between the President and the Prime Minister in February 2001 over the latter's alleged failure to combat corruption, the financial system went into near-meltdown in Turkey's worst economic crisis in recent years. A massive flight of capital forced the Government to float the lira and to accept an immediate devaluation of over a third (see Budget, Investment and Finance, below). Consequential consumer price increases of a third or more sparked widespread protest demonstrations, amidst rumours that another military takeover was imminent. Difficult negotiations with the IMF resulted in approval in May of further stand-by credit equivalent to US $8,000m. (bringing the total granted to Turkey since December 1999 to a record $19,000m.), but only on even stricter conditions that long-promised economic restructuring and counter-inflationary measures would at last be implemented, including reductions in consumer subsidies, reform of the banking sector and privatization of state-owned enterprises. In the wake of the crisis, which was aggravated by the economic effects of the September 2001 suicide attacks on the USA, anticipated GDP growth of 4.5% in 2001 became in reality a contraction of 7.4%, while GNP fell by 9.4% and inflation rose to 68.5%. Total GDP in 2001 declined to $148,166m. by exchange-rate calculation and to $427,000m. at PPP, giving respective GDP per-caput figures of $2,226 and $6,419.

The continuing economic crisis necessitated the conclusion in February 2002 of a new agreement with the IMF for stand-by credit of about US $16,000m., on the basis of renewed pledges of structural reform (see Budget, Investment and Finance, below). However, the political crisis which developed in mid-2002 and the calling of an early general election for early November created new uncertainties for the economy both domestically and internationally. During the second quarter of 2002 the official rate of unemployment rose to 9.6% of the total registered labour force and to 13.9% in the non-agricultural sector (from 6.9% and 10.7% respectively a year earlier).

AGRICULTURE AND FISHING

Turkey relies substantially on agriculture (and is the largest producer and exporter of agricultural products in the Middle East and North African region), although the sector's overall role has shrunk considerably over recent decades and Turkey has not been self-sufficient in food production in recent years, even though some 45% of the active labour force is engaged in agriculture. The agricultural sector has been constrained by high rates of interest and inflation, structural deficiencies such as fragmented and small land holdings, a lack of grassroots farmers' organizations, poor marketing facilities, inefficient open-market price formation and dependence on government subsidies (amounting directly or indirectly to some $11,500m. in 2000, or 4% of GNP). Efforts to remedy such deficiencies formed part of the Government's structural reform programme in the wake of the financial crises of November 2000 and February 2001, in the context of Turkey's aspiration to be admitted to EU membership and its undertakings to the IMF.

Nearly 25m. ha, or about one-third of total land area, are in some sort of agricultural use, although the area devoted to permanent crops fell from 4.1% in 1980 to 3.2% in 1996, while irrigated land rose from 9.6% to 15.4% of cropland over the same period. Of Turkey's 4m. agricultural units, about 60% are small, the average size of a family farm being only 6 ha. The principal agricultural exports by value are hazel-nuts, cotton, tobacco, grapes and citrus fruits. Other important crops are barley, sunflower and other oilseeds, maize, sugar beet, potatoes, tea and olives.

During the period 1963–70 Turkey's agricultural output rose by only 2.5% annually, mainly because insufficient emphasis had been placed on agriculture in both the first and second economic development plans. However, with the introduction of land reforms and the improved utilization of land, machinery and farmer education resources, agricultural production in 1971 increased by some 30%. In 1975 real expansion in agriculture was 10.9%, but such good results were infrequent and the expansion targets set in successive five-year plans were not met. In 1978 the rise in output was only 2.7%, while in 1981 it was just 0.3%. The rate of increase has fluctuated considerably in recent years and although inadequate rainfall in 1989 caused agricultural output to contract by 10.8%, during 1980–90 agricultural output increased by an annual average of 1.3%. In 1990–96 an average annual increase of 1.2% was recorded. In 1995 an increase in output of only 2% was attained, but growth was stronger in 1996, averaging 5.2%, largely due to exceptionally strong growth during the last three months of the year. Agricultural production then declined by about 2% in 1997, but favourable weather conditions led to an increase of 9.3% in 1998. The 1999 earthquakes resulted in a 5.2% decline in that year. Agriculture provided 59.4% of total export revenue in 1979, but the proportion declined to around 20% in the late 1980s and to 13.6% in 1994, increasing to 15.8% in 1999 and then falling to 13.9% in 2000, in which agricultural exports were valued at US $3,828m. compared with $4,440m. the previous year. The agricultural sector, including forestry and fishing, contributed 14.3% of GDP in 1998, 14.9 % in 1999 and 14.2% in 2000. In 2001 the sector contributed 12.5%.

Government policy is to increase agricultural productivity and to improve animal husbandry, but budget constraints restrict project financing. The funds that are available come mainly from international sources, notably the World Bank. However, there is increasing foreign commercial interest in developing Turkish agro-industry, particularly for Middle East export markets. In an attempt to alleviate the poverty of the south-eastern provinces of Turkey, the Government drew up the South-East Anatolia Programme (GAP) in the early 1980s, covering a total area of 74,000 sq km. Some 495 projects were integrated into GAP, which envisaged the construction of 22 dams on the Tigris and Euphrates rivers and their tributaries, 19 power plants and an irrigation network with the potential to cover 8.5m. ha. GAP has been affected by delays resulting from attacks by Kurdish separatists and disputes over financing. In 1994 two water pipelines were opened. At the end of that year GAP had cost

US $11,000m. and required an estimated $21,000m. for its scheduled completion by 2005.

About one-half of the cultivated area is devoted to cereals, of which the most important is wheat. The principal wheat-growing area is the central Anatolian plateau, but the uncertain climate causes wide fluctuations in production. Barley, rye and oats are other important crops grown on the central plateau. Maize is grown along the Black Sea coastal regions, and leguminous crops in the İzmir hinterland. Rice, normally sufficient for domestic needs, is grown in various parts of the country. In the 1990s the annual wheat harvest has usually stayed above the high level of 18m. metric tons, owing to good weather, improved cultivation methods and increased levels of irrigation. In 1993 there was a particularly good harvest of 21m. tons, although export earnings remained at a relatively low level of about US $70m. In 1994 output was 17.5m. tons, with no improvement in export earnings. Output rose to 18.0m. tons in 1995, 18.5m. tons in 1996, 18.6m. tons in 1997 and 21m. tons in 1998, but decreased to 18m. tons in 1999 from 9.4m. ha devoted to wheat. Wheat production was estimated to have increased to 21m. tons in 2000. Output of barley and oats also declined in 1999 (and increased slightly in 2000); 7.7m. tons of barley were produced (compared with 9.0m. tons in 1998) and 290,000 tons of oats (310,000 tons in 1998). However, rice and rye production increased slightly in 1999 (and remained at a similar level in 2000); 350,000 tons of rice were produced in 2000(compared with 315,000 tons in 1998) and 260,000 tons of rye, also in 2000 (232,000 tons in 1998). Maize output has steadily decreased in recent years; 2.3m. tons in 1998, 2.3m. tons in 1999 and an estimated 2.1m. tons in 2000.

Cotton has traditionally been Turkey's main export earner, grown mainly in the İzmir region and in the district round Adana, in southern Turkey. In recent years it has lost some of its traditional importance, although the irrigation of agricultural land in the eastern Haran region has enhanced production. Production of cotton lint decreased from 851,487 metric tons in 1995 to an estimated 791,000 tons in 2000, while cottonseed output increased from 1,287,527 tons in 1995 to 1,314,660 tons in 1999. The value of cotton exports rose to US $782m. in 1998, from $674m. in 1997. Sugar beet production increased during the same period, from 11.2m. tons in 1995 to an estimated 18m. tons in 2000, as the result of a 25% increase in the land area devoted to the crop to 440,000 ha.

Turkey produces what is regarded as a particularly fine type of tobacco for consumers. The three principal producing regions are the Aegean district, the Black Sea coast and the Marmara-Thrace region. The bulk of the crop is produced in the Aegean region, where the tobacco is notable for its light golden colour and mild taste. The finest tobacco is grown on the Black Sea coast, around Samsun. Although a traditional Turkish export, its relative position as an export has been declining in recent years. Most of Turkey's tobacco exports go to buyers in the USA and East European countries. The size of the crop fluctuates considerably: in 1993 it reached a record level of 324,000 metric tons (matched only in 1976) but fell to 204,000 tons by 1995. Production increased to 286,000 tons in 1997, but declined to 262,000 tons in 1998, further declining to 260,000 tons in both 1999 and 2000. In 1999 260,000 ha were devoted to the crop, compared with 210,000 ha in 1995. The value of tobacco exports fell to US $587m. in 1998, from $683m. in 1997. In 1984 the Government permitted the first legal imports of foreign cigarettes in more than 40 years, breaking the monopoly over sales and distribution held by the state-owned tobacco and beverages agency, Tekel. Several international tobacco companies have started negotiations to manufacture cigarettes locally and one joint-venture operation has been established at Bitlis in the south-east of the country to produce cigarettes for export. A new cigarette factory in İzmir, as part of a joint venture between the US tobacco company Philip Morris and the local Sabanci group, produces popular US brands for the domestic market. Tekel, however, has responded by raising capacity and output and improving the quality of its brands, notably by producing cigarettes with Virginia tobacco. As required by the IMF, the Government in January 2002 secured parliamentary approval for large cuts in state subsidies to tobacco farmers, as a preparatory step to privatizing Tekel.

The coastal area of the Aegean, with mild winters and hot, dry summers, produces grapes, citrus and other fruits, figs and olives. Exports of dried figs were valued at US $53m. in 1993, France being the main customer. Production of figs declined from 300,000 metric tons in 1995 to 255,500 tons in 1998, but recovered to 275,000 tons in 1999 before falling back to 260,000 tons in 2000. The outstanding product, however, is the sultana type of raisin. Turkey normally ranks second in the world as a sultana producer, but in good years becomes the largest producer in the world. Sultana harvests varied from 85,000 tons in 1976 to 138,000 tons in 1989, when exports were worth $72m., while in 1994 total exports of dried fruits were valued at $747m. In 1997 the sultana harvest was 233,000 tons, increasing to 250,000 tons in 1998 and declining to an estimated 214,000 tons in 1999. Production of grapes rose to 3.7m. tons in both 1996 and 1997, but declined to 3.6m. tons in 1998 and to 3.4m. tons in 1999. Production was estimated to have increased to 3.6m. tons in 2000. In contrast, the citrus fruit sector expanded steadily from 1995 to 2000; annual production of oranges increased from 842,000 to 1,035,000 tons, mandarins from 453,000 to and estimated 560,000 tons and grapefruit from 65,000 to 140,000 tons. Other significant fruit production in 2000 included 2.3m. tons of apples, 430,000 tons of peaches, 360,000 tons of pears, 500,000 tons of apricots, 300,000 tons of cherries, 190,000 tons of plums, 129,000 tons of strawberries, 58,000 tons of pomegranates and 34,000 tons of bananas. In other categories, production of tuber crops (mainly potatoes and onions) rose from 7.8m tons in 1995 to 8.8m. tons in 2000 and vegetables from 18.3m. tons to 20.3m. tons, whereas output of pulses declined from 1.8m. tons to 1.3m. tons over the same period.

The Black Sea area, notably around Giresun and Trabzon, produces the greatest quantity of hazel-nuts (filberts) of any region in the world, having been grown there since 300 BC. A harvest of 580,000 metric tons was recorded in 1996, when exports of hazel-nuts were valued at US $578.6m., the crop remaining at the same level in 1998 before declining to 470,000 tons in 2000. Substantial amounts of walnuts, almonds and pistachios are also grown, the 2000 crops totalling 138,000 tons, 46,500 tons and 65,000 tons respectively.

Tea is grown at the eastern end of the Black Sea, around Rize, and in other areas. Production has increased from the early 1980s to total 178,000 metric tons in each of 1998, 1999 and 2000.

Turkey is also an important producer of oilseeds, principally sunflower, groundnuts, soybeans and sesame, total oilseed production rising to 1.2m. metric tons in 2000. It also produces olive oil, some of which is exported. Production fluctuates, partly because of the two-year flowering cycle of olive trees. Olive oil production increased from 40,000 tons in 1997, to 180,000 tons in 1998, but decreased to 54,000 tons in 1999 when 600,000 tons of olives were harvested, compared with 1,650,000 tons in 1998 and 510,000 tons in 1997. In 2000 olive oil production increased to 180,000 tons when the olive harvest remained constant at 600,000 tons.

Steady, if uneven, progress has been made in the acquisition by Turkish farmers of modern agricultural equipment and machinery. While numbers of wooden and animal-drawn ploughs in use fell, respectively, from 317,000 and 433,000 in 1995 to 178,000 and 309,000 in 1999, Turkey's farms were equipped with 924,446 tractors and 83,674 milking machines in 1999, compared with 776,863 and 35,593 respectively in 1995. According to World Bank figures, the number of tractors per 1,000 agricultural workers in Turkey increased from 38 in 1980 to 57 in 1996.

Turkey was, until 1972, one of the seven countries with the right to export opium under the UN Commission on Narcotic Drugs. Much opium was, however, exported illegally, particularly to the USA and Iran; partly as a result of pressure from the US Government, the Turkish Government made the cultivation of opium poppies illegal in 1972, but the ban was ended in July 1974 and the flowers are grown in certain provinces under strict controls. Opium gum is no longer tapped from the living plant. The poppy pods (opium straw) are sold to the Government, which processes them into concentrate for export as the basis for morphine and other drugs.

Sheep and cattle are raised on the grazing lands of the Anatolian plateau. Stock-raising forms an important branch of the economy. The sheep population (29.4m. in 2000) is mainly of the Karaman type and is used primarily as a source of meat and milk. The bulk of the clip comprises coarse wool suitable only for carpets, blankets and poorer grades of clothing fabric. However, efforts have been made in recent years to encourage breeding for wool, and there are some 200,000 Merino sheep in the Bursa region. The Angora goat produces the fine, soft wool known as mohair. Turkey is one of the world's largest producers of mohair, with an average output of about 9,000 metric tons per annum. Poultry-meat has displaced traditional meats such as lamb, mutton and goat in domestic consumption patterns and government projects aiming to increase the low milk yields and meat productivity of Turkish herds have been implemented.

In January 1998 Turkey agreed to grant the EU major trade concessions on exports of EU food and farm products to the country. The Government agreed to unlimited imports of EU breeding cattle and up to 70% reductions on import duties for some 19,000 metric tons of frozen beef per year from the EU. Turkey also accepted annual imports from the EU, without duty, of 200,000 tons of wheat, 100,000 tons of barley, 52,000 tons of corn, 46,000 tons of malting barley, 28,000 tons of rice and 60,000 tons of soy oil. The EU also became entitled to export 80,000 tons of sugar to Turkey at half the normal duty rates. These concessions were agreed despite the EU's exclusion of Turkey from the list of countries eligible to join the organization. Following the EU decision taken in December 1999 to admit Turkey to the list of candidates for membership (see Foreign Trade and Balance of Payments, below), Turkey's agricultural sector faced particular difficulties in adapting to the requirements of future EU membership and to the reduction in state subsidies for wheat and other agricultural produce as stipulated under the series of reform programmes agreed with the IMF in 1999–2001 (see Budget, Investment and Finance, below). Also controversial were the requirements to privatize state-owned enterprises in the agri-food sector and to grant full autonomy to agricultural sales unions and co-operatives. Pending the opening of negotiations on Turkish membership of the EU, the European Commission has been providing financial assistance for a national programme for the control and eradication of foot-and-mouth disease in Turkey, as well as co-operating on raising veterinary and phytosanitary arrangements to EU standards.

Turkey has 8,333 km of coastline and some 1,200 inland water resources, but fishing potential has been curtailed by overfishing, pollution and ecological changes. Although the fisheries sector grew by 8% in 1997 and by 6% in 1998, it accounted for only 2% of overall agricultural production in the latter year and only 0.3% of GNP in 1999. The development of aquaculture in inland waters has been one of the aims of the GAP (see above), while the Black Sea Fishery Improvement Project aims to increase catches within a sustainable framework. In 1998 a five-year project for increasing turbot production was launched at the Black Sea port of Trabzon, with Japanese technical and financial assistance. In 1999 there were 17,475 Turkish fishing vessels and 55,000 fishermen were licensed, while 200,000 people were directly employed in the fishing industry and 2m. indirectly employed. In 2001 the fisheries sector contributed TL 110,946m. to GNP (0.5%).

MINERALS AND MINING

Turkey has a diversity of rich mineral resources, including large quantities of bauxite, borax, chromium, copper, iron ore, manganese and sulphur. The mining and quarrying sector employed some 134,000 workers in 1999. Mineral exports earned US $2,316.6m. in 1994 and $2,243.0m. in 1995, representing about 10% of the value of total exports. In 1998 the mining industry recorded growth of 6.8%–8.4% by state-owned enterprises and 0.4% in the private sector. About 60% of all mineral output, and all coal production, derives from state-owned enterprises. The most important state-owned enterprise in the mining sector is Etibank, which works through its subsidiaries, Eregli Coal Mines, East Chromium Mines, Turkish Copper, Keban Lead Mines and Keçiborlu Sulphur Mines. During the early 1960s state-owned enterprises increased their predominance over the private sector, with an investment programme that was supported by the Mining Investment Bank, established in 1962. The policy of encouraging the private sector to play a greater part in the mining industry, through the establishment of the Turkish Mining Bank Corpn in 1968, has failed to overcome the general reluctance of private investors to view mining as a worthwhile area for long-term investment, with the result that the private sector is under-capitalized. An additional factor militating against the development of mining has been the long-held suspicion of foreign investment in mining. A law enacted in 1973 restricted foreign participation in mining development projects. However, this restriction was relaxed in January 1980, allowing up to 49% foreign participation in mining ventures. Since then, negotiations have proceeded slowly between Etibank and potential foreign partners for copper, lead and other mineral mining. In 1983 Etibank entered into a joint venture agreement with a US company, Phelps Dodge, for copper mining. Etibank's banking and mining operations were separated in 1993, in the initial phase of privatization, which was completed in 1998.

Bituminous and anthracite coal is found at and around Zonguldak, on the Black Sea coast. The seams are steeply inclined, much folded and strongly faulted. The coal is generally mined by the longwall system or a variation of it. These mines constitute Etibank's largest operation, and the coalfield is the largest in this part of the world, including the Balkans. Most of the seams are of good coking quality, the coke being used in the steel mills at nearby Karabük. In 1998 total coke production amounted to 2.2m. metric tons, compared with 2.5m. tons in 1997 and 3.2m. tons in 1996. Lignite is found in many parts of central and western Anatolia, and possible total reserves are estimated at up to 8,000m. tons. In 1999 production of lignite by public-sector enterprises amounted to 64.9m. tons, being used to produce almost 50% of Turkey's electricity output. Seams located in western Turkey are operated by the West Lignite Mines. The other main mines are at Soma, Degirmisaz and Tunçbilek. Lignite deposits at Afsin Elbistan are being developed, with extensive German and international financial assistance, as part of an ambitious integrated energy project designed to increase capacity generating by 1,360 MW. In 1999 some 40,000 people were employed in the sector (compared with 64,000 in 1990). In 2000 Turkey's output of coal and lignite was 63.0m. tons, falling slightly to 60.2m. tons in 2001. Proven coal reserves stood at 3,700m. tons at end-2001, sufficient to sustain the current production rate for 54 years.

Practically all of Turkish iron ore comes from the Divrigi mine, situated between Sivas and Erzurum, in the north-east of the country, and operated by the Turkish Iron and Steel Corpn (Erdemir). The average grade of ore is from 60% to 66%; reserves have been estimated at 28m. metric tons. Output of iron ore increased from 1.7m. tons in 1979 to 5.5m. tons in 1992. Production totalled 3.4m. tons in 1996.

Turkey is one of the world's largest producers of chromite (chromium ore). The richest deposits are in Güleman, south-eastern Turkey, in the vicinity of İskenderun; in the area around Eskişehir, north-west Anatolia; and between Fethiye and Antalya on the Mediterranean coast. The Güleman mines, producing 25% of the country's total, are operated by East Chromium Mines under Etibank. Other mines are owned and worked by private enterprise. Little chromium is used domestically and the mineral is the principal earner of foreign exchange among Turkey's mining exports. Output of chromite fell from a peak of 0.8m. metric tons of ore, mined in 1977, to less than 0.5m. tons per year in the early 1980s, but recovered to reach 1.5m. tons in 1989. However, production decreased again to around 0.6m. tons in 1992 with exports valued at US $32m. In 1993 output decreased further, and export earnings fell to $18m. Production recovered to 2.1m. tons in 1995, the bulk in the private sector.

Copper has been mined in Turkey since ancient times. Current production, conducted entirely by Etibank, comes from the Ergani Mines, at Maden in Elâziğ, and the Morgul Copper Mine, at Borçka in Çoruh province. Production of blister copper has tended to fluctuate, decreasing from 36,000 metric tons in 1986 to 28,578 tons in 1994. In 2001 25,000 tons of blister copper were produced. Most of the output is exported to Germany, the United Kingdom and the USA. Known reserves of copper ore are estimated at 90m. tons.

Eskişehir, in north-west Anatolia, is the world's leading centre for meerschaum mining. Meerschaum, a soft white mineral which hardens on exposure to the sun and looks like ivory, has long been used by Turkish craftsmen for pipes and cigarette holders.

Manganese, magnesite, lead, sulphur, salt, asbestos, antimony, zinc and mercury are important mineral resources. Of these, manganese ranks first in importance. Deposits, worked by private enterprise, are found in many parts of the country, but principally near Eskişehir and in the Eregli district. Lead is mined at Keban, west of Elâziğ. Production of sulphur (public sector only), mainly from the Keciborlu mine, in Isparta province, totalled 39,000 metric tons in 1987. Antimony is mined in small quantities near Balikesir and Nigde. An important find of mercury deposits, which may amount to 440,000 tons, has been made at Sizma, in Konya province. Large uranium deposits have been discovered in the Black Sea, between 1 km and 2 km below sea-level. Turkey's first commercially viable silver mine was opened in January 1988. In April 1996 a project to develop Turkey's first gold mine (reserves were discovered in 1990) near Bergama, in İzmir province, was finally approved.

The Uludağ (Bursa) tungsten deposits, carrying an average grade of 0.43% WO_3, are among the richest in the world. Etibank and the German firm of Krupp are jointly working these deposits. Output of tungsten ore reached 3,400 metric tons in 1979. Other minerals are barytes, perlite, phosphate rock, boron minerals, cinnabar and emery (Turkey supplies more than 80% of the world market for emery).

Turkey's bauxite deposits are now supplying the aluminium complex which was built, with Soviet aid, at Seydişehir. The plant's initial annual capacity was 60,000 metric tons of aluminium but this is to be expanded to 120,000 tons. The plant will also produce alumina for export, and semi-finished products. The reserves at Seydişehir are estimated at more than 30m. tons.

Petroleum was first discovered in Turkey in 1950, and all subsequent discoveries have been in the same area, in the south-east of the country. It is mostly heavy-grade petroleum with a fairly high sulphur content. Production of crude petroleum has fluctuated since it reached 3.5m. metric tons in 1973. Because of the small size of Turkey's main oilfields in the fractured terrain of the south-eastern Hakkari Basin, it declined steadily between 1980 and 1985. Production increased in the early 1990s and reached 3.9m. tons in 1993. In 1996 production totalled 3.5m. tons and declined slightly to 3.4m. tons in 1997, to 3.2m. tons in 1998, to 2.9m. tons in 1999, to 2.7m. tons in 2000 and to 2.6m, in 2001. Turkey also currently produces about 900m. cu m of natural gas per year, its largest non-associated field being the offshore Marmara Küzey field in the Thrace-Gallipoli basin of the Sea of Marmara. In July 2001 it was announced that gas had been discovered in Mersin and İskenderun bays in south-western Turkey, while in March 2002 the new Gocerler gas field in the Thrace basin began production 16 months after its discovery. Domestic consumption of petroleum in 2001 was estimated at 662,000 b/d and gas consumption at 15,500m. cu m, so that about 90% of oil requirements and 95% of gas consumption had to be imported. Imports of mineral fuels and oils rose from US $5,375.3m. in 1999 to $9,529.3m. in 2000, when they accounted for 17.5% of the value of total imports. In 2001 such imports declined to $8,288.6m., although representing an increased share (20.5%) of total imports. Saudi Arabia is Turkey's main supplier of oil, with substantial volumes also imported from Iran, Libya and Iraq (see below). Russia supplies 70% of Turkey's gas imports, most of the balance coming from Algeria and Nigeria.

Three main companies produce petroleum: the Turkish Petroleum Corpn (TPAO), a 99% state-owned Turkish company, and subsidiaries of the Royal Dutch/Shell Group and the US Mobil group. Proven petroleum reserves as at 1 January 2002 were 296m. barrels, sufficient to maintain the existing production level for only 11 years, while proven gas reserves were some 8,775m. cu m. Possible reserves have consistently been put at much higher figures by TPAO, although sporadic exploration in the south-east and in the Aegean has failed to make new finds. In 1983 the Government introduced a new law intended to liberalize conditions for foreign companies, enabling them to export as much as 35% of any onshore petroleum that they discovered, and up to 45% of any offshore output. At first, major foreign oil companies were dubious about Turkey as a viable political and economic base, but in 1984 quickening interest resulted in the signing of several joint-venture exploration agreements by new foreign major oil companies with TPAO.

Refining and other downstream operations are dominated by the state-owned Turkish Petroleum Refining Co (TÜPRAS), which has four refining complexes: Batman in the southeast, Aliaga near İzmir, İsmit near İstanbul, and the Central Anatolian Refinery at Kirikkale near Ankara. TÜPRAS is planning to build a fifth refinery near Yarimca in western Turkey, to be completed by 2007 at a cost of US $750m. Of the country's total refining capacity of 720,000 b/d, TÜPRAS has a market share of about 80% and has recently instituted a modernization programme to switch to lighter refined products. The country's largest refinery, at İsmit, with a capacity of 226,000 barrels per day (b/d), suffered extensive fire damage following an earthquake in August 1999. Turkey's sole private refinery is ATAS, near Mersin on the Mediterranean coast, a joint venture of Mobil, Shell British Petroleum and a local company.

Having privatized a 31.5% stake in TÜPRAS (for $2,300m.) in 2000, the Government confirmed in July 2001 that its holding would be reduced to under 50% by a further offering. In 2000 the Government had also privatized a majority stake in Petrol Ofisi (POAS), the dominant petroleum distributor, while plans were also drawn up for partially privatizing the state oil and gas pipeline authority, BOTAŞ. In May 2001 a law was passed liberalizing the country's gas market, ending BOTAŞ's monopoly in gas importation and separating the company into units for gas importation, transport, storage and distribution by 2009 preparatory to their privatization (except for the transport unit). In July 2002 the Government announced that it intended to sell its remaining 25.8% stake in POAS to the majority private shareholder. Responding to IMF pressure, the Government confirmed in the same month that it intended to privatize most of the rest of the country's energy sector during 2003.

TPAO operates a 500-km pipeline running from the oilfields around Batman to Dörtyol on the Gulf of İskenderun. A 986-km pipeline from Kirkuk, in northern Iraq, to Turkey has a capacity of 1.5m. b/d. Completion and full commissioning of a second pipeline, alongside the first, took place in July 1987. Until August 1990, when economic sanctions were imposed on Iraq by the UN, the twin pipeline from Kirkuk to Turkey's Mediterranean terminal at Ceyhan carried about one-third of Iraq's oil exports. The closure of the pipeline for more than six years is estimated to have cost BOTAŞ more than US $400m. per year in lost revenues. In March 1996 Turkey and Iraq signed a memorandum of understanding determining conditions for the future reopening of the pipeline. Following Iraqi acceptance, in May of that year, of a UN proposal to permit limited oil sales (up to a value of $2,000m. over a six-month period, amounting to an estimated 800,000 b/d) in order to purchase humanitarian supplies, the pipeline was scheduled to open in mid-September. However, the agreement was postponed by the UN in early September, owing to Iraqi military activities against its Kurdish population, and oil did not start to flow through the pipeline until December. The reopening of the pipeline did little to curb the large-scale smuggling of Iraqi oil into Turkey, costing the Turkish treasury large sums in lost tax revenue. Turkey's National Security Council (NSC) launched a new operation in March 2000 to suppress oil smuggling, not only from Iraq but also from Iran, Georgia, Azerbaijan, Syria and Bulgaria, and by July claimed to have reduced such activity by 50%.

Turkey is looking to the Caspian Sea and Central Asia to provide the bulk of its future oil and gas needs, and is involved in several projects to develop supplies there. In 1994 TPAO became part of the Azerbaijan International Operating Company (AIOC), a consortium of foreign petroleum companies in a production-sharing agreement with Azeri state oil company SOCAR, to develop offshore oilfields in the Caspian Sea. TPAO also became a partner in the Azeri Shah Deniz field in 1996 and has established a petroleum exploration company with the Government of Kazakhstan.

Oil and gas transportation is a controversial issue in the Caspian Sea and Central Asia regions. Turkey, Russia and Iran are competing to route the rich energy resources of Azerbaijan, Kazakhstan, Turkmenistan and Uzbekistan through their territories en route to Western markets. Turkey is advocating a 1,730-km oil pipeline that would transport 1m. b/d of Azeri and Kazakh Caspian Sea oil from Baku in Azerbaijan through Georgia and then across Turkey to the Mediterranean port of Ceyhan, at an estimated cost of up to US $4,000m. The Governments of Turkey, the USA and Azerbaijan have all declared their support for the Baku–Ceyhan route, which would reduce dependence of Caspian Sea energy exports on Russia and bypass Iran. In November 1999 Turkey, Azerbaijan, Georgia and Kazakhstan signed a legal framework agreement to enable what was renamed the Baku–Tbilisi–Ceyhan pipeline to proceed. The proposed pipeline was boosted by the signature in Baku in December 2000 of an agreement under which seven international petroleum companies agreed to finance a $25m. engineering feasibility study, these companies becoming members of the Main Export Pipeline Company (MEPCO). In February 2001, moreover, ChevronTexaco of the US, which had previously opposed the pipeline, announced its willingness to join MEPCO, while the following month a memorandum of understanding on the pipeline was signed in Astana, the Kazakh capital, by the Governments of Turkey, Azerbaijan, Georgia and Kazakhstan. Construction of the Turkish section of the pipeline began in September 2002 with a target-date for completion in late 2004. However, doubts remained about the project's economic viability, centring on whether sufficient quantities of oil would be available from Azerbaijan and Kazakhstan under the required timetable, and about whether the Kazakh Government would make a definitive commitment to the pipeline. In March 2002 SOCAR reduced its stake in MEPCO from 45% to 25%, distributing 20% among other participating companies. In June it sold an additional 5% stake to TotalFinaElf of France, but rejected the admission of ChevronTexaco to MEPCO.

Turkey's enthusiasm for the oil pipeline to Ceyhan is based in part on its concern to restrict the use of the Bosphorus to export petroleum. In 1994 Turkey imposed stricter controls for ships transporting hazardous goods through the Bosphorus, effective from 1 July, following a collision in March. Russia, which exports some 70% of its oil exports by means of the Bosphorus, protested at the measure. An agreement signed in April 1997 to build a pipeline with an initial capacity of 560,000 b/d, rising to 1.5m. b/d, from the Kazakhstan oilfields to the Russian Black Sea port of Novorossiisk was likely to increase tensions between Turkey and Russia regarding the export of petroleum via the Bosphorus.

Demand for natural gas is projected to rise dramatically in Turkey over the next two decades, to 54,000m. cu m in 2010 and 83,000m. cu m in 2020, with the main consumers expected to be industry and power plants in view of the Government's identification of gas as the preferred fuel for future power generation for economic, environmental and regional political reasons. In this context, Turkey has set itself the goal of diversifying its sources of gas, given the inability of domestic production to meet its future requirements. In December 1997 Turkey and Russia signed a 25-year contract (the so-called 'Blue Stream' agreement) for a large increase in Russian natural gas supplies. The gas will mostly be delivered via a 1,210-km dual pipeline which, when built (at an estimated cost of US $13,500m.), will run from Isobilnoye in southern Russia under the Black Sea to the Turkish port of Samsun and on to Ankara. What will be the world's deepest underwater gas pipeline may eventually be extended overland to Lebanon, Syria and Israel. The agreement envisages the import of an additional 3,000m. cu m of gas per year through the pipeline, with its throughput rising to 16,000m. cu m by 2010. Russian supplies received through the Black Sea pipeline would supplement those received by Turkey through the existing pipeline route (crossing Ukraine, Moldova, Romania and Bulgaria), so that Russia would continue to provide at least half of Turkey's total annual demand for imported gas well into the 21st century. In March 2000 Russia's Gazprom and ENI of Italy, the two main companies involved in the 'Blue Stream' project, announced that $1,600m. of initial Japanese financing had been arranged, following which work on above-ground sections of the pipeline began in both Turkey and Russia. In early August 2001, moreover, a huge construction ship carrying cranes for laying the under-water pipeline passed through the Bosphorus en route for the Black Sea, where the laying of the first 'Blue Stream' line was completed in March 2002 and work on the second began in June. By mid-2002 the Turkish onshore section of the pipeline was in place and the Russian section was scheduled for completion in September, so that the first supplies could be pumped in late 2002.

New natural gas supplies are now coming to Turkey via a pipeline from Iran, for which a US $20,000m. agreement was concluded in August 1996, for the construction of a 1,400-km pipeline from Tabriz, in Iran, to Ankara. Despite US disapproval, Turkey proceeded with the project and awarded the contract for the construction of the first section of the pipeline, from the Iranian border to Erzerum, in early 1997; the second section, from Erzerum to Ankara, was to be built at a later date. Each country is responsible for financing the section of the pipeline in its own territory. According to a further agreement, signed in December 1996 with Turkmenistan, Turkey was to import 3,000m. cu m of natural gas each year from Turkmenistan, via the Tabriz–Ankara pipeline, in the place of Iranian gas, until such gas was available. In late July 1997 the USA announced that it would not oppose the construction of the US $1,600m. gas pipeline from Turkmenistan into Iran, because it would not technically violate US-imposed sanctions against Iran and because Turkey's agreement to purchase Turkmen gas would make it less reliant on supplies from Iran. Under the original schedule, the Tabriz–Erzerum section of the pipeline was to have been completed by 1999, with initial deliveries of gas rising from 3,000m. cu m per day to 10,000m. cu m per day in 2005. Following delays in completion, for which each side blamed the other, an agreement was reached in January 2000 that deliveries would commence in mid-2001. However, in late July 2001 inauguration of the pipeline was postponed because of what Turkey described as technical difficulties on the Iranian side, although Iran denied that it was to blame for the further delay. The pipeline was eventually inaugurated in January 2002, it being expected that Iranian supplies of gas to Turkey would rise from 3,000m. cu m in 2002 to 10,000m. cu m by 2007. In March 2002 Turkey signed an agreement with Greece providing for the extension of the Tabriz-Erzerum pipeline to Alexandroupolis in northern Greece, for onward transmission to Western European markets.

A separate scheme for the shipment of gas from Turkmenistan to Turkey is the Trans-Caspian Pipeline (TCP), on which BOTAŞ signed an agreement with Turkmenistan in May 1999 envisaging the construction of a 1,690-km pipeline running under the Caspian and via Azerbaijan and Georgia to Turkey. To be constructed by a consortium headed by the US Bechtel Corpn at an estimated cost of US $2,000m., the pipeline would carry up to 30,000m. cu m of gas per year to Turkey, with additional gas possibly being sent onwards to Europe. However, although Turkish officials endorsed the TCP plan and argued that Turkey's anticipated future gas needs would support more than one new pipeline, sceptics saw the TCP proposal as a direct competitor to the 'Blue Stream' and other pipeline projects and pointed out that major gas reserves recently discovered in Azerbaijan's Shah Deniz field are much closer to Turkey than Turkmen gas. Pending further progress on the TCP project, in March 2001 Turkey signed a bilateral agreement with Azerbaijan providing for the supply of gas, mainly from the Shah Deniz, field over 15 years, starting in 2005 with 2,000m. cu m and rising to 6,500m. cu m from 2008. It is envisaged that the gas will be supplied through a 1,000-km pipeline running from Baku to Erzerun via Georgia. In late 2001 the Azeri and Georgian parliaments ratified the necessary transit agreements for the pipeline, the construction of which was scheduled to start in late 2002 for completion by the end of 2004 at a projected cost of $1,000m. The pipeline would have an initial capacity of 22,000m. cu m a year, rising to 30,000m. cu m, and so would be able to pipe gas from Turkmenistan when, and if, the TCP was constructed to Baku.

Two other gas pipelines under active consideration by Turkey are an underwater pipeline linking Egypt's offshore Mediterranean gas fields with Turkey via the Gaza Strip, Israel, Lebanon and Syria; and a 1,300-km overland pipeline from Kirkuk in Iraq to Turkey's Mediterranean coast. In November 1999 the Turkish Government stated that the Kirkuk pipeline proposal, on which a provisional agreement had been signed in 1997, had been revived as a serious possibility. In January 2000 the Government announced the creation of a special department to expedite pipeline development, with particular responsibility for insurance and international arbitration issues, which was to co-ordinate and clarify the various projects for new oil and gas pipelines to Turkey.

Pending the completion of more of the gas pipeline projects, Turkey has signed a number of agreements to import supplies of liquefied natural gas (LNG). Imports of LNG from Algeria, equivalent to 3,000m. cu m per year of natural gas, began in 1994 and were to continue for a 20-year period. LNG is also imported from Nigeria, and plans exist for annual imports of LNG from Qatar equivalent to 2,000m. cu m of natural gas. The state pipeline agency, BOTAŞ, has tendered a project to build a terminal at Alinga with the capacity to store 4,000 cu m of LNG, and other LNG terminals are planned at Ereglisi and İzmit Bay.

MANUFACTURING AND INDUSTRY

The leading role in the process of inaugurating industrialization in the 1930s was played by the State economic enterprises (SEEs). However, by the beginning of the 1970s the private sector accounted for nearly one-half of industrial output and its rate of capital investment had become almost equal to public sector investment. The Government announced its long-awaited plans for privatization of the SEEs in May 1987. Initially, the Government's stake in 22 private companies would be sold, followed by the denationalization of the more efficient and profitable SEEs. As a first step, one-half of the Government's shareholding of 40% in Teletas, a telecommunications company, was sold to the private sector in early 1988. A sharp fall in share prices on the İstanbul Stock Exchange (ISE) then slowed the privatization programme. Five state-owned cement works were sold directly to a French company (although the completion of this sale was suspended in 1991), and USAS, an aircraft services firm, was sold directly to a Scandinavian airline in early 1989. The fact that these were sold directly to foreign companies, rather than to the public on the ISE, attracted widespread criticism. As the ISE recovered at the end of 1989, the Government proceeded with the sale of its minority shareholdings in private-sector companies. Such holdings in six companies were sold in early 1990. Subsequent privatizations enjoyed varying degrees of success. Small portions of state-owned shareholdings were sold in a number of major companies such as Petkim, the petrochemicals giant, and Erdemir, the iron and steel complex. In the first half of 1992 the Demirel Government undertook five such sales, with estimated total revenue of TL 552,000m. In July 1992 the Government announced the sale of 11 state cement companies, which together accounted for 18% of total cement production in Turkey. In late 1992 and 1993 the privatization programme continued at a steady rate, but under the Çiller Government few sales were completed. In July 1994 legislation to accelerate privatization was declared to be unconstitutional by the Constitutional Court, although new legislation was approved in November. None the less, the programme generated only US $354m. in 1994 and $576m. in 1995 (of target revenue for that year of $5,000m.).

Although every Government from the mid-1980s claimed that privatization was a key part of economic policy, only US $3,500m. had been raised from the sale of state enterprises by 1997. However, proceeds from privatization in 1998 were projected to increase dramatically as the coalition Government under Mesut Yılmaz reactivated the process. In May 1998 the Privatization Administration (OIB) sold a 12.23% stake in Türkiye İş Bankası (one of the country's leading commercial banks) for $651m., while in July it accepted a bid of $1,160m. for a 51% holding in the petrol distributor Petrol Ofisi (POAS). However this bid effectively lapsed some weeks later when the prospective buyer (a consortium of four local firms) failed to secure the necessary finance. In April the OIB called off the privatization of POAS, having previously been obliged to defer the sale of several other organizations in the second half of 1998 in the light of adverse market trends and pre-election political uncertainties. In July 1999, however, following a change of government, the OIB relaunched the privatization programme—a key element of the economic restructuring programme agreed with the IMF in December (see Budget, Investment and Finance, below). The sale of a 51% stake in POAS was finally completed in March 2000 (for $1,260m.), while a 31.5% stake in TÜPRAS was sold in April (for $2,300m.). Other enterprises earmarked for early complete or partial privatization included Türk Telekom, the Erdemir Iron and Steel

Corpn, the İskenderun Iron and Steel Works (İsdemir) and Petkim, as well as national carrier Turkish Airlines (THY) and parts of the power generation industry. Privatizing a strategic stake in Türk Telekom proved to be especially controversial. A first offer of a 33.5% stake was abandoned after no bids had been received by the 15 September 2000 deadline, whereupon the proposal was restructured so that the purchaser would obtain majority management rights. In the wake of the massive financial crisis of February 2001, privatization of a 51% stake in Türk Telekom (currently valued at $10,000m.) was a condition of further IMF assistance. The disposal received reluctant parliamentary approval in May, under the basis that the Government would retain a 'golden share' giving it the power to block any onward disposal thought to be undesirable.

The privatization programme was further delayed by the impact of the crisis in 2001, in which industrial output declined by 9% and the contribution of the industrial sector to GNP fell by 7%. In a letter of intent to the IMF in July 2002, the Government stated that the Privatization Agency had adopted a new strategy for reducing the state's holding in TÜPRAŞ to under 50% by end-2002, through a tender for a strategic partner and/or the placement of exchangeable bonds, since a public offering was not feasible in current market conditions. The Government continued that it had just reduced its stake in Erdemir to below 50% by means of a sale to an investment fund, that its remaining 25.8% stake in POAS would shortly be sold to the existing strategic investor and that at least 51% of the shares in Petkim would be offered by October. The letter expressed confidence that these and other sales would meet the indicative target of US $700m. in privatization proceeds in 2002. As regards other plans, the letter recorded that 'road maps' had been drawn up for the privatization of Türk Telekomünikayson, the Tekel tobacco and alcohol monopoly and the Seker sugar company, that all state-owned thermal generation and electricity distribution assets would be offered in February 2003 (with the exception of projects eligible for Treasury guarantee) and that two distribution subsidiaries of the BOTAŞ pipeline company would be privatized by the end of 2003.

Turkey's recent high growth rates have been industry-led. The share of industry in the economy increased from 12% of GDP in 1952 to 35.4% in 1998. However the sector's share decreased slightly in 1999 (34.8%) and 2000 (34.6%). Growth in the manufacturing sector has been the most noticeable, under the stimulus of the Government's export incentive scheme, although, latterly, domestic demand has equalled the demand made on manufacturing for exports. In 1986 the manufacturing sector expanded by a record 10.5%, followed by growth of 10.1% in 1987. The 1994 financial collapse caused the manufacturing sector to contract by 8.4% although an expansion in the manufacturing sector of 13.5% was reported in 1995. Further expansion of 7.5% in 1996 and 11.2% in 1997 was followed by growth of only 1.8% in 1998. Between 1980 and 1998 the share of industrial products in total exports increased from 36% to 77.4%. A 5% fall in industrial output in 1999 was followed by recovery to 5.6% expansion in 2000, during which lower interest rates helped to boost consumer demand, especially for motor-cars and household appliances. The industrial production index (1995 = 100) stood at 123 at the end of 2000.

Production of such goods as paper, cotton and woollen yarn, cotton and woollen fabrics, refined fuels and petroleum products, steel products and glassware began a significant recovery in the early 1980s. Overall, the average annual growth rate of industrial GDP was 7.8% in 1980–90, and 5.0% in 1990–98.

Textiles and clothing manufacture accounts for some 39% of Turkey's export sales. Exports of textiles rose by 5.9% in 1998 to US $3,551.6m., while overseas sales of clothing increased by 5.4% to $7,058.2m. The industry employs around one-fifth of Turkey's industrial workers, accounting for more than 8% of industrial production.

Inaugurated in the late 1930s, the iron and steel industry in Turkey has been one of the fastest-growing in the world and prospects continue to be relatively good, following difficulties in the early 1980s. Both private and public manufacturers complain of dumping by European and Asian companies. Public sector capacity is 4.6m. metric tons per year and private sector capacity 2.7m. tons per year. Total output of crude steel reached 14.3m. tons in 2000. In July 1996 an agreement was signed with the European Coal and Steel Community (part of the EU) for the elimination of duties by both sides, with effect from 1 August 1996. The value of exports of iron and steel declined to US $1,598m. in 1998, from $2,004m. in 1997. Slight increases, to $1,737m. and $1,865m., were recorded in 1999 and 2000 and exports increased dramatically, to $2,448m., in 2001.

Cement production, on the strength of the expansion in the construction industry (owing largely to the Government's mass housing programme), rose to a record 20m. metric tons in 1986. Production has continued to increase, in spite of occasional declines in years when the economy as a whole has done badly, and output stood at 30.1m. tons in 2001. The industry is now almost entirely privately owned as a result of the privatization programme.

Among food industries, the state-controlled sugar industry is the most important. In 1994 total production of raw sugar was 1.7m. metric tons, with the private sector accounting for only slightly over 25% of this total. Total production declined slightly to 1.3m. tons in 1995, but rose to 1.8m. tons in 1996, to 2.0m. tons in 1997, to 2.5m. tons in 1998 and to 2.9m. tons in 1999. In 2000, however, there was a decrease to 2.2m. tons, before an increase to 2.8m. tons in 2001.

The paper and board industry is dominated by the state-owned SEKA corporation, which has one old-established mill at İzmir, with an annual capacity of 126,000 metric tons of paper and board, plus six mills which have been opened since 1971. Total output of paper and board was relatively stable at around 400,000 tons annually (including 136,000 tons of newsprint and 78,000 tons of Kraft paper in 1994). However, 1998 saw an increase in production to 644,000 tons, followed by a decline to 528,000 in 1999. In July 2000 the OIB privatization authority sold two major SEKA factories, in Dalaman and Çaycuma, for a total of US $59m.

The motor vehicle industry was established after 1956, and by 1971 had become the largest industrial employer after the textile sector, accounting for about 5% of total industrial output. After several years of suppressed demand and low capacity utilization in the early 1980s, the outlook began to improve in 1983. In 1988 output of cars (local versions of Fiat, Ford and Renault models) increased by 12.7%, to 120,800, and by 1993 output had nearly trebled to just fewer than 345,000. Despite a sharp decline in the output of cars in 1994, to 201,000, as a result of the currency crisis that hit the economy, a number of foreign manufacturers have expressed interest in local production ventures in view of Turkey's expanding domestic market and, since the start of 1996, its advantageous trading relationship with the EU, under the customs union agreement. In 1994 a Toyota assembly plant began operations, and in 1996 Honda was proceeding with the construction of a car plant, in association with Anadolu Endustri Holding AŞ, at a cost of US $50m., while Oyak-Renault, the Turkish subsidiary of Renault of France, announced plans to build a $362m. plant, which would employ more than 1,000 workers. In early 1997 it was reported that Volvo of Sweden planned to invest DM 300m. in a factory at Bursa, to produce buses for export to the Middle East and Russia. The new plant, a joint venture with Ulosoy Holding, was to begin production by 2000. Although car production decreased in 1996 (the first year of customs union with the EU), to 207,575, total vehicle output for 1996 rose by 2% to 348,467, however, as a result of a sharp increase in the production of buses, tractors and trucks. The domestic car industry faced the prospect of further problems in 1997, following a government decision to allow all Turkish citizens to import one used car from abroad, on condition that they deposit DM 50,000 in a state bank. Production of vehicles made by the Republic of Korea's Hyundai Motor Co was inaugurated in September 1997 at a plant near İzmit. The plant's initial output of 60,000 cars per year will eventually double when it reaches full capacity. It was announced in March 1998 that the US Ford Motor Co and the local Otosan had agreed in principle to build a $500m. car plant in Turkey, with a planned capacity of 120,000 vehicles per year. In 1997 car sales rose to 344,800, but while sales of imported cars rose by 118%, sales of those produced in Turkey increased by only 21%. Sales of light commercial vehicles increased to 118,800 units. Total motor-vehicle sales in 2000 reached a record 465,000 units, of which 55% were imported (compared with 30% in 1999).

In 1970 Turkey's first petrochemicals complex, situated at İzmit, began production of ethylene, polythene, polyvinyl chloride (PVC), chlorine and caustic soda. There is another petrochemicals plant at Aliaga, while a third is planned at Yumurtalık. They are operated by the state-owned firm Petkim. In 1994 the output of artificial fertilizers (excluding potassic fertilizers) totalled 4.0m. metric tons, although this increased to 5.3m. tons by 1998. The state-owned Turkish Nitrates Corpn has a nitrate plant at Kutahya, a triple superphosphate plant at Samsun and a superphosphate plant at Elâziğ. There are several privately-owned fertilizer plants, including triple superphosphate plants at İskenderun and Yarimca. Turkey produces 75% of its requirements of fertilizers and, when new plants are completed, it will be self-sufficient.

Other manufacturing industries include tobacco, chemicals, pharmaceuticals, metal working, engineering, leather goods, glassware and ferrochrome.

The power sector, along with the transport, communications and tourism sector, has continued to hold priority in the Government's development programmes for every year since 1989. Official sources indicated that domestic power production rose by 10.5% in 1996, but still failed to keep pace with increase in demand, which grew by 12%. In spite of the progress made in power plant construction in recent years, many more units will have to be built to meet an expected increase in demand of 8%–10% annually in the two decades to 2020. Gas-fired plants will generate most new capacity. The growth in energy consumption is estimated to require an additional 2,000 MW of new capacity annually, and the Ministry of Energy and Natural Resources has estimated that capacity must rise threefold, to 65,000 MW, between 1998 and 2010 and to about 100,000 MW by 2020. Even with increasing private sector input, most new capacity will have to be provided by the state.

Output from stations operated by the Turkish Electricity Board currently accounts for about 60% of all electricity generated, while chartered companies and private generators provided the remainder. Total output stood at 94,862m. kWh in 1996, rising to 103,150m. kWh in 1997, 110,900m. kWh in 1998, 116,441m. kWh in 1999, 124,922m. kWh in 2000 and 123,001m. kWh in 2001. Thermal sources accounted for about 62% of the 1998 total power generation and hydroelectricity the remainder. In mid-1995 construction of a gas-fuelled generating station in Marmara was initiated by a consortium of one Turkish and three foreign companies. The power plant, which was estimated to cost US $540m., had a potential capacity of 3,600m. kWh. In November 1995 an agreement was signed with foreign creditors and contractors for the construction of the 672-MW Birecik hydroelectric plant on the Euphrates river. The agreement was the first of many planned build-operate-transfer (BOT) schemes, under which the ownership of the plant was to be transferred to the Turkish Government once it became fully operational and profitable, or after a period of 15 years.

More controversial among new hydroelectric power projects is the proposed 1,200-MW Ilisu dam on the Tigris river in south-eastern Turkey, which has been strongly opposed on environmental and social grounds as its reservoir will displace up to 30,000 people and submerge the ancient Kurdish town of Hasankeyf and its numerous historical monuments. The dam is also opposed by Syria and Iraq on the grounds that the Tigris water flow would be reduced, although Turkey denies that this would be the case. The British Government in 2000–01 delayed a decision on whether to grant export credit guarantees to engineering company Balfour Beattie to underwrite its involvement in construction of the dam, amidst vociferous opposition to the project from environmentalists and also in Parliament. In the event, Balfour Beattie announced its withdrawal from the project in November 2001, as did Impregilo of Italy, while in February 2002 the Swiss UBS bank withdrew as financial adviser. Another similarly controversial dam is proposed for the Coruh river at Yusefeli in north-eastern Turkey. Up to 15,000 people, mostly from Turkey's Georgian minority, are expected to lose their homes if the project proceeds as planned. In March 2002 the UK-based AMEC construction company announced its withdrawal from the Yusefeli dam project, citing purely commercial reasons. Turkish officials responded by insisting that construction of the Ilisu and Yusefeli dams would go ahead as planned.

In November 2000 contracts were awarded for the construction of a 160-km system of pipelines and collection points for the pumping of fresh water from the mouth of the River Melen on the Black Sea to İstanbul, where rapidly increasing population and urbanization placed a serious strain of existing water supplies. Work on the US $1,180m. project, which included a 5.5-km sub-sea pipeline across the Bosphorus and was intended to supply 1,180m. cu m of water a year when fully operational, was expected to start in late-2001, for completion in 2004.

From mid-1996 preparations were undertaken for the construction of the country's first nuclear generator, at Akkuyu on the southern Mediterranean coast. The US $4,000m. plant was put out to tender in December 1996 and construction was to have been completed in 2005. The 1,300-MW plant would have supplied some 2% of Turkey's energy needs. In July 2000, however, the Government announced that the project, which had attracted much environmentalist and regional opposition, had been shelved indefinitely on cost grounds, although it might be reconsidered in the future, should nuclear technology improve.

Turkey has imported electricity from Bulgaria for some time, and in March 1997 Ankara signed a new five-year energy agreement with that country. Turkey also imports power from Georgia and Iran, and has signed a memorandum of understanding with other Black Sea Economic Co-operation (BSEC) members to examine the creation of a regional power grid. Other recent initiatives to diversify supply sources include the signature in May 1999 of an agreement for Turkmen electricity to be supplied to Turkey.

Joint-venture defence manufacturing with foreign partners is a major element of foreign investment in Turkish industry (a development that began with the US $4,000m. agreement concluded in 1983 with the US Government and a US company, General Dynamics, to assemble and later manufacture F-16 fighter aircraft at Murted outside Ankara). The Defence Industry and Support Administration (DIDA), established in 1985, was to co-ordinate Turkey's 10-year programme, costing $15,000m., to modernize the armed forces. The modernization was to involve, to a large extent, locally manufactured equipment and weapons. In July 1988 a joint-venture manufacturing agreement for multi-launch rocket systems was signed by a US company and a state-owned munitions company. According to the agreement, 180 rocket launchers were to be produced at a plant near Burda. Some of the launchers were to be bought by DIDA and the remainder were to be exported. In late 1988 a consortium (including a US company and the Turkish company Nurol) was awarded a contract to manufacture armoured personnel carriers in Turkey. Turkey currently exports a range of weapons including F-16 fighter aircraft and armoured personnel carriers. In August 1998 it was reported that Turkish Aerospace Industries (TAI) had awarded a $200m. contract to install radar systems on 80 F-16s to a joint venture between a local company and the US Lockheed Martin Corpn. The Turkish firm was already working on a contract to install radar systems on another 160 Turkish F-16s. Earlier, in June, the Government suspended talks with France's Aerospatiale over a $441m. short-range anti-tank missile production contract after the French National Assembly voted in May to adopt a resolution recognizing the genocide of Armenians in Turkey in 1915. In July 1998 it was announced that the Turkish Ministry of Defence had signed a $558m. contract with a German company for the construction of four 1,400-ton submarines. After the adoption in late 2000 of a further French parliamentary resolution recognizing the Armenian genocide, Turkey in February 2001 cancelled a $205m. contract with a French company for the modernization of 80 F-16 Turkish warplanes and also excluded French companies from the bidding for a projected road link across the Bay of İzmit.

TOURISM

Tourism is one of Turkey's fastest growing industries and is an important source of foreign currency. In 1996 some 8.6m. tourists visited Turkey, generating US $5,650m. in revenue. While these figures represent a substantial improvement on the previous decade, a huge potential still remains unrealized. One problem over the past few years has been the escalation of Kurdish nationalist activity which has frequently spilt over into the tourist resorts of the West, severely damaging the prospects of the tourism industry. Tourist arrivals increased to 9.7m. in 1997 and decreased slightly to 9.4m. in 1998, generating revenue of $7,002m. and $7,177m. respectively. However, revenue decreased to $5,203m. in 1999, as the result of a decline in arrivals of 20.6% owing to political unrest and earthquake-related disruption. The number of tourist arrivals recovered in 2000 to 10.4m., producing revenue of $7,636m. The tourism sector performed well in 2001 despite the country's economic and financial crisis, the number of arrivals increasing to 11.6m., although lower individual spending by tourists resulted in revenue generated being below target, at about $8,090m. (about 4% of GNP). In the first half of 2002, moreover, arrivals were about 5% higher than in the first half of 2001. Germany (with 24.8%) was the main source of tourists in 2001, followed by the United Kingdom (7.3%), Russia (6.5%), Bulgaria (4.7%), France (4.5%) and the USA (3.7%).

In October 1999 the Privatization Administration invited bids for various state-owned tourist assets, including hotels and land, as part of the Government's strategy of promoting private sector development of the tourism sector. Plans were also drawn up in 2000–01 for the diversification of tourism away from coastal resorts, to inland attractions such as hot springs and to winter sports, with the aim bringing tourists to Turkey throughout the year rather than mainly in the summer season. The Government's longer-term objective was the arrival of 60m. tourists a year by 2020, generating annual revenue of US $50,000m.

BUDGET, INVESTMENT AND FINANCE

Successive Five-Year Economic Development Plans have aimed at the long-term target of self-sustained economic growth (independent of foreign loans), devoting a large proportion of investment to mining and manufacturing industry. In May 1989 the Government published the sixth Five-Year Plan (1990–94), which envisaged an average annual growth rate of 7%, reaching 8.3% in 1994. Private sector investments were targeted to grow at an average annual rate of 11%, with growth reaching 15% by the end of the Plan period. The surplus on the current account of the balance of payments was expected to increase throughout the period, to reach US $2,500m. in 1994, while exports were projected to grow at an average rate of 15% per year, and to exceed $22,000m. by 1994. In September 1994 the preparation for the seventh Plan was postponed by one year; an intermediary target plan was implemented in 1995. In May 1995 the Government published the seventh Plan, for the period 1996–2000, which envisaged economic growth increasing to an annual 7.1%. The eighth Five-Year Plan, for the period 2001–05, was approved by the Grand National Assembly in June 2000 and set the following main economic goals: the allocation of resources to rebuild social and economic infrastructures in eastern and south-eastern Turkey which had been damaged in the Kurdish separatist struggle; a progressive tightening of public expenditure; and improvement of the financial position of small businesses and artisans.

The Central Bank (Merkez Bankası), the sole bank of issue, started its operations on 3 October 1931. It controls exchange operations and ensures the monetary requirements of certain state-owned enterprises by the discounting of bonds issued by these institutions and guaranteed by the treasury. However, legislation adopted in 1987 awarded the Government wide-ranging powers over the Central Bank, that could, if applied, theoretically reduce the bank to the level of an ordinary state bank. In June 1999 a law was approved providing for the reform of the financial sector. The legislation, which came into effect in early 2000, incorporated core principles of the Basle Committee on Banking Supervision relating to risk-based capital requirements, loan administration procedures, auditing practices and credit risk issues, and envisaged the establishment of an independent Regulatory and Supervisory Board for Banking, whose members (appointed for six-year terms) were to be nominated by the treasury, the Ministry of Finance, the Central Bank, the state planning organization, the Capital Markets Board and the Banks' Association of Turkey. This new body would monitor the observance of financial regulations (which had hitherto been regularly breached by some smaller institutions) and would have powers to order the merger or acquisition of institutions

experiencing financial difficulty. In early 1999 Turkey had 74 banks, of which 38 were small family-controlled concerns. At least 14 of these concerns were in difficulties in 1999 because of over-lending to affiliated companies, eight being taken over by the Central Bank via the Savings Deposit Insurance Fund with bad debts of some US $5,000m. In June 2000 the Central Bank initiated preparations for the restructuring and sale of the eight banks, possibly as a merged group or groups, as part of a longer term programme of privatization of the state-owned banking sector.

The principal sources of budgetary revenue are income tax, import taxes and duties, taxes and fees on services, and revenues from state monopolies. In late 1984 the Government introduced value-added tax to replace the previous unwieldy system of production taxes.

From 1989 onwards political instability affected the Government's ability to implement its economic plans. The appointment of Tansu Çiller as Prime Minister in 1993 was a popular choice with the business community, but while she quickly identified economic priorities internal problems hampered attempts to implement reform. In 1993 the budget deficit tripled that of the previous year to reach TL 122,000,000m., or 9.2% of GNP. In early 1994 two US credit rating agencies downgraded Turkey's credit rating, which resulted in a 'run' on foreign currencies. The value of the lira was officially devalued by 12% against the US dollar; however the currency continued to plummet. Interest rates rose to 150%–200% as the Government and the Central Bank desperately tried to bring the financial markets under control. In early April the Government announced a programme of austerity measures to reduce the budget deficit, lower inflation and restore domestic and international confidence in the economy. The programme included a 'freezing' of wages, price increases of up to 100% on state monopoly goods, as well as longer-term restructuring measures such as the closure of loss-making state enterprises and an accelerated privatization process. By May the lira stabilized at around TL 30,000 to the dollar, having stood at some TL 16,000 at the beginning of the year. In August the value of the lira fell once more but was steadied at a rate of TL 34,000 per dollar, following an increase in interest rates from 70% to 240%. The austerity measures then began to have a measure of success, the markets stabilized and the lira stayed below 40,000 to the dollar until the end of the year. The measures also helped to restore a degree of international confidence in the Turkish economy and to secure an IMF stand-by loan, approved in July, of SDR 610m. (approximately US $873m.). The budget deficit for 1994 was substantially reduced in real terms and totalled TL 146,000,000m., or 3.7% of GNP. None the less, the budget deficit continued to exert serious inflationary pressure on the economy and to attract much domestic and international criticism. The Government continued to borrow heavily on the domestic market, although foreign borrowing became prohibitively expensive because of the crisis and was thus reduced. Domestic debt stood at TL 799,100,000m. at the end of 1994 (compared with TL 356,555,000m. at the end of 1993). Meanwhile, Turkey's foreign debt came down to US $65,601m., from more than $67,000m. in 1993. The pressure of servicing both the domestic and external debt boosted the rate of inflation, which rose dramatically to 106.3% in 1994, from 66.1% in 1993.

The inflationary pressure on the economy remained strong in 1995, when the annual rate of inflation declined only slightly, to 93.6%, and the actual budget deficit increased to TL 320,000,000m. Çiller abandoned the 14-month IMF stand-by agreement in September, after the collapse of her Government. The resultant political uncertainty and negotiations were accompanied by the largest series of strikes since the 1970s, which caused the closure of ports and a halt in production at state-owned industrial and transport companies. By October the strike action was costing the country an estimated US $500m. in lost export revenue and production, and threatened to undermine attempts to control inflation and restore economic stability. Prior to the general election in December, Çiller was able to settle the public-sector wage dispute, and, more importantly, to secure ratification of the EU customs union, which entered into force on 1 January 1996 (see Foreign Trade and Balance of Payments, below).

The general election of December 1995 failed to produce a clear victory for any one party, and the period of uncertainty that followed precluded the adoption of any stabilizing measures to improve the economic situation. In June a new Government was established, led by the Islamic fundamentalist Welfare Party (RP), with the True Path Party (DYP) as a coalition partner. In early July the new administration approved an increase in the minimum wage and salary increases of 50% for state workers and pensioners. During his first five months in office, RP Prime Minister Necmettin Erbakan announced three economic packages which, he claimed, would raise a total of US $30,000m. in revenue, to meet the pay awards and limit the budget deficit. They included the sale of state-owned land, housing and real estate, a 6% levy on short-term foreign financing of imports (mainly consumer goods), measures to attract hard currency held abroad by Turkish banks, and the leasing of uncompleted power plants. The new Government stated that the main aspects of its economic programme were: a commitment to a free-market economy; lower inflation and a steady growth rate; lower taxation for producers; greater efforts to attract foreign investment; an acceleration in the privatiza-tion programme; an emphasis on investment in infrastructure projects; and economic planning to achieve long-term solutions. It transpired that the budget deficit for the whole of 1996 was TL 1,215,000,000m., representing 8.2% of GNP, while the annual rate of inflation fell only slightly to 82.4%.

At the end of November 1996 the Grand National Assembly approved the Erkaban Government's ambitious and controver-sial budget for 1997, in which he vowed to increase expenditure, end domestic borrowing and yet produce a 'zero-deficit' through a massive increase in government income from privatization. Dubbed the 'dream' budget, it totalled TL 6,254,920,000m., but encountered strong criticism from political opponents and from the country's business community. The Government's privatiza-tion plans received a welcome boost in January 1997, when the Constitutional Court gave its approval to the sale of a major stake in the state company, Türk Telekom, although there were objections to a number of Erbakan's revenue-raising packages, notably his attempt to sell large public real estate holdings and lease state-owned power projects. Early in 1997 Erbakan made new promises of additional pay increases to state workers and pensioners, over and above those included in the 1997 budget, which did little to inspire confidence in the Government's econ-omic competence.

The coalition Government of Prime Minister Yılmaz, which took office in mid-1997, made a determined effort in its first year to stem the rise in inflation and improve economic management, notably by accelerating privatization. Revised economic targets for 1997 were announced, including: growth in GNP of 5.5%–6%, compared with the previous target of 4%, based on a 5.7% increase in GNP during the first quarter of 1997; a reduction in the trade deficit, from US $20,500m. to $20,000m.; and a budget deficit at the end of the year of TL 2,400,000m., including a supplementary budget of TL 2,000,000m. In fact, GNP expanded by an impressive 8.6% in 1997, whereas inflation worsened to 99%. By July 1998 year-on-year inflation had fallen to 72% from 101% in January. The reduction was achieved largely through a 'freeze' in public sector prices. In June the Government signed an accord with the IMF under which the Fund would monitor the Turkish economy for 18 months. The agreement, which committed the Government to keeping a tight rein on public expenditure and boosting privatization and tax receipts, set targets for wholesale inflation of 50% by the end of 1998 and 20% by the end of 1999. Tax reform legislation, passed in July, reduced the tax burden for most people and aimed to encourage full declaration of earnings. However, in the same month the Government was forced to compromise on its pledge to keep down public sector pay rises when it agreed to an immediate 20% rise, with a further 10% for the three months from October. In 1998 the Government recorded an actual budget deficit of TL 3,697,824,000m. (equivalent to 6.7% of GNP) from expenditure of TL 15,585,376,000m. and revenue of TL 11,887,552,000m., although the primary budget, excluding expenditure on debt servicing, showed a surplus of TL 2,479,000,000m. The inflation reduction target was not met, with the consumer price index rising by 70% in 1998.

Following the elections held in April 1999, the new Govern-ment declared its intention to implement a programme of struc-tural reforms. It was announced in early July that the IMF monitoring programme introduced in 1998 would remain in place in preparation for an application for an IMF stand-by arrangement. The increasing need for social security reform, and the importance attached to it by the IMF, led the Government to publish a draft bill proposing an increase in the pensionable retirement age, from 38 to 58 for women and from 43 to 60 for men, over a 10-year period. Legislation to reform the financial sector was enacted in June, and in the same month the Govern-ment imposed a 20% ceiling on public-sector pay increases, despite trade union demands that increases be linked to the prevailing inflation rate of more than 60%. On 13 August constitutional amendments were approved permitting interna-tional arbitration in disputes between state bodies and foreign investors and allowing the privatization of state-owned utilities. The lack of international arbitration clauses in contracts for BOT projects had previously deterred many potential foreign partners from investing in infrastructure development, including high-priority work in the energy sector.

The 1999 budget, adopted in June, envisaged a deficit of TL 9,236,000,000m. (including debt-servicing requirements), equivalent to 11.6% of GNP. Budgeted expenditure for 1999 was TL 27,266,000,000m., including TL 10,300,000,000m. for debt servicing, while revenue totalled TL 18,030,000,000m. The anticipated surplus on the 1999 primary budget (excluding interest payments) was TL 1,064,000,000m. The increase in the 1999 debt-servicing requirement (which was 67% higher than in 1998) was the result of a larger than expected rise in the interest payable on the Government's domestic borrowing. In fact, the disruption of state finances caused by the earthquakes of August and November contributed to a primary budget deficit equivalent to 2.7% of GNP, while consumer price inflation during the year was recorded at 68.8%.

The 2000 budget, approved in December 1999, provided for a deficit after debt-servicing of TL 14,383,000,000m., equivalent to 11.5% of GNP, although a projected 70% increase in tax receipts, to TL 24,000,000,000m., was expected to contribute to a primary budget surplus of 2.2% of GNP (3.7% excluding earthquake-related expenditure). In the previous month the Grand National Assembly had approved a new 'national solid-arity' tax law, intended to raise in excess of TL 700,000,000m. (about US $1,360m.) to finance post-earthquake reconstruction. The specific measures included an additional 5% tax on 1998 corporate earnings and on personal earnings exceeding TL 12,000m.; a tax of between 4% and 19% (depending on maturity date) on proceeds from government bonds issued before 1 December 1999; a doubling of motor vehicle and real estate tax in 2000; a 25% surcharge on mobile telephone fees; a charge of TL 600,000 on every bank cheque written; special transaction taxes on lotteries, domestic airline fares and gun licences; and authorization to increase petroleum products consumption tax from 300% to 500%. The new tax on government bonds resulted in a 6% fall in share values on the ISE, with particularly heavy losses being sustained by banks as major holders of such bonds.

The 2000 budget was a key component of the Government's economic restructuring programme for the period 2000–02; the first tranche of an SDR 2,892m. (about US $3,800m.) IMF stand-by credit was released following the Fund's approval of the programme in December 1999. With the ambitious goal of increasing the rate of GNP growth to 5.8% in 2002, its key elements were 'up-front' fiscal adjustment to achieve a stable primary budget surplus of around 4% of GNP; a more diversified debt management policy and increased privatization to contain the burden of interest payments; reduction of consumer and wholesale price inflation to 25% and 20%, respectively, in 2000 and to 7% and 5%, respectively, in 2002; a firm exchange-rate commitment supported by consistent incomes policies; and structural reform to strengthen public finances, reduce inequali-ties in the tax burden and curb waste in public expenditure. As part of the anti-inflation programme, a new 'exchange rate substitution' policy took effect on 1 January 2000, under which the managed peg used since 1994 was abandoned in favour of a peg set according to a pre-determined devaluation rate (20% in 2000), itself set against a 'basket' of the US dollar and the euro. The IMF arrangement was supplemented in May 2000 by a World Bank 'economic reform loan' of $750m. with a maturity of 15 years including a five-year grace period.

The Government's sale of a 51% stake in Petrol Ofisi in March 2000 (for US $1,260m.) and of a 31.5% stake in Tupras in April (for $2,300m.) were the main components of first-half proceeds from privatization of some $5,000m., so that the full-year target of $7,600m. was likely to be exceeded in the second half, during which the sale of a 20% stake in Türk Telekom was scheduled. The Government also raised $2,500m. from the sale to a Turkish-Italian consortium of a third global system for mobiles (GSM) licence. First-half GDP growth of over 5% compared with the same period in 1999 suggested that the economy was recovering from the 1999 set-back, although consumer price inflation remained well above the Government's 25% target for 2000. However, the Government's intentions were again frustrated by a major banking liquidity crisis and flight of capital in November 2000, during which the Central Bank expended $7,000m. of its reserves in supporting the lira before the IMF eased the situation in December by granting a supplemental reserve facility of SDR 5,800m. (about $7,000m.). Another package of reforms agreed with the IMF included the familiar objectives of curbing inflation, reducing the budget deficit and expediting privatization. The resultant 2001 budget provided for expenditure of TL 48,400,000,000m. and revenue of TL 43,100,000,000m, the projected deficit of TL 5,300,000,000m. representing 3.5% of anticipated GNP. It also envisaged economic growth of 4.5% in 2001 (compared with 3.5% in 2000) and a reduction in consumer price inflation from 39% in 2000 to 12% in 2001.

No sooner had the new programme been introduced than Turkey's gravest economic crisis in three decades struck in February 2001, as a result of a public clash between President Sezer and Prime Minister Ecevit over the latter's alleged inaction against ministers and officials suspected of corruption. The immediate reaction of the markets was a fall in the share price index to over 60% below its 2000 high, capital flight involving the movement of some US $5,000m. out of Turkey on 19 February alone and a rise in overnight interest rates to the equivalent of 4,000% annually, as the Central Bank mounted an abortive effort to defend the lira. Bowing to market forces, the Government on 22 February ended the 'crawling peg' with the US dollar and allowed the lira to float freely, with the result that its value fell by 36% over two days. Ecevit responded by appointing a new Central Bank governor and installing Kemal Derviş, hitherto a senior World Bank official, as Minister of State responsible for economic policy, charged in particular with securing yet another IMF bail-out. To that end, Derviş quickly drew up a 'recovery' plan featuring the familiar ingredient of a radical restructuring of the banking sector, including the placing of the three main state-owned banks under a joint administration headed by technocrats, liquidation of other insolvent banks and full independence for the Central Bank. Also envisaged was speedy action to privatize debt-laden, state-owned enterprises long earmarked for disposal, beginning with a 51% stake in Türk Telekom and including major stakes in Turkish Airlines and the state sugar, alcohol and tobacco monopolies.

Protracted negotiations with the IMF resulted in approval being given on 15 May 2001 to an additional stand-by facility of SDR 6,000m. (about US $8,000m.), bringing the total made available to Turkey since December 1999 to SDR 15,100m. (the largest package in the IMF's history), of which Turkey had by mid-May drawn SDR 8,100m. (about $10,000m.). In addition, the World Bank undertook to provide further loans of up to $2,500m. The IMF approved the latest facility only after the Turkish Government had secured parliamentary approval of its 'recovery' plan in the face of strong opposition from corporatist forces who claimed that Turkey was surrendering its national economic sovereignty. However, the strength of such opposition, not least within the ruling coalition, raised immediate doubts about the Government's commitment to reform, with the result that the IMF suspended disbursements in late June, thus provoking further sharp depreciation of the lira (to just over 50% of its pre-February value) and a further slump in share prices. The disbursements were resumed on 12 July after the Government had given new assurances, in particular on its commitment to reform of the banking sector and to privatization of Türk Telekom, and in early August the IMF Executive Board 'com-mended the Turkish authorities on the strong implementation of their ambitious economic reform programme'. However, the Government's hopes that GDP contraction could be contained to 3% in 2001 were shattered by the negative effects on the already beleaguered Turkish economy of the global economic slowdown, aggravated by the effects of the September 2001 suicide attacks on the USA. The outcome was that Turkey's GDP shrank by 7.4% in 2001 (and GNP by 9.4%), while inflation almost doubled to 68.5% year-on-year and the budget deficit came in at 17.2% of GNP.

As approved in December 2001, the 2002 budget once again aspired to correct persistent fiscal imbalances, providing for expenditure of TL 97,831,000,000m. (17% less in real terms than in 2001) and revenue of TL 70,918,000,000m., with the projected deficit of just under TL 27,000,000,000m. corresponding to about 10% of anticipated GNP. At the same time, the budget provided for a public sector primary surplus of 6.5% of GNP. A resumption of economic growth at 3%–4% was forecast for 2002, while the Government aimed to reduce the annual inflation rate to 35%. An accompanying restatement of economic reform objectives included the completion of the restructuring of the banking sector by the end of 2002, improved transparency in the use of public funds, enhancement of the private sector through a revitalized privatization programme, and the removal of obstacles to foreign and domestic investment. In January 2002 parliamentary approval was given to legislation aimed at eliminating corruption from the public procurement process and also to a sharp reduction in subsidies for tobacco farmers preparatory to the intended part-privatization of Tekel, the state-owned tobacco and alcohol monopoly.

The 2002 budget package and associated measures secured the endorsement of the IMF, which, on 4 February 2002, approved a new three-year stand-by credit of SDR 12,800m. (about US $16,000m.) for Turkey, which was able to draw SDR 7,300m. immediately. The new arrangement replaced the December 1999 stand-by credit as expanded in May 2001, the remaining undisbursed element of which (SDR 3,300m.) was folded into the new credit. By August 2002 Turkey had drawn SDR 9,000m., although in approving the release of a third tranche on 7 August the IMF warned that the latest political crisis in Ankara had unsettled domestic financial markets and revealed 'vulnerabilities' showing that strict adherence to the reform programme was essential.

A heavy burden of foreign debt, contracted in the late 1970s and extended through subsequent reschedulings, has severely hampered the Government's structural adjustment efforts, which have also been complicated by rising domestic debt. At the end of 1998 foreign debt stock totalled US $101,000m., while domestic debt totalled $44,500m. During 1998 the Government borrowed a total of $2,400m. on international capital markets (later raised to $2,600m. through the issue of additional bonds). In 1999 its international borrowing target (as formulated prior to the August earthquake) was about $3,000m., plus an estimated $1,000m. for project financing. At the end of 1999 the outstanding external debt stock totalled $111,215m., while domestic debt totalled TL 26,679,144,000m. in March 2000, the corresponding figures rising to $119,600m. at end-2000 and TL 90,332,000,000m. by June 2001 respectively. By the end of 2001 domestic debt had risen to TL 122,199,000,000m., while external debt had fallen to $115,100m.

FOREIGN TRADE AND BALANCE OF PAYMENTS

Turkey has had a persistent foreign trade deficit since 1947. But, following the economic reforms of 1980 and the introduction of free-market, export-led policies, the deficit decreased in the early 1980s. In 1990 the deficit more than doubled, to US $9,555m., owing to the overvalued lira, the continuing liberalization of the import regime and the phasing out of direct subsidies to exporters. Foreign trade performance was much improved by 1994, with exports of $18,390m. and imports of $22,606m., bringing the trade deficit down to $4,216m. In 1995, however, while exports increased to $21,975m., imports rose sharply to $35,187m., resulting in a trade deficit of $13,212m. Figures for 1996 showed that exports increased to $32,446m. but imports rose to $43,028m., producing a trade deficit of $10,582m. In 1997 a deficit of $15,398m. was recorded from exports of $32,631m. and imports of $48,029m. The deficit in

1998 was reduced to $14,220m. from exports of $31,220m. and imports of $45,440m., and was further reduced in 1999 to $10,447m., from exports of $29,326m. and imports of $39,773m. In 2000, however, the deficit more than doubled to $22,341m., from exports of $31,214m. and imports of $53,555m. The post-February 2001 domestic economic crisis and the effects of the September 2001 terrorist attacks on the USA resulted in a sharp fall in imports in 2001 to $38,916m., although exports improved to $34,379m., producing a visible trade deficit of $4,537m.

Turkey's trade deficit has been partly offset, for some time, by a net surplus on invisible earnings (services and transfers), particularly helped by expatriate workers' remittances. A major contributor to the invisibles balance since the early 1980s has been the contribution from Turkish contractors, who, although arriving late for the growth in the Middle East construction industry, quickly made their mark. Like other foreign firms, however, their fortunes have been linked to fluctuations in the price of petroleum and the availability of development revenues. Since the disintegration of the USSR, Turkish contractors have been turning their attention to Russia, Azerbaijan and the Turkic republics of Central Asia, with considerable success. In March 1997 a Russian official stated that 150 Turkish contractors were working on 200 construction projects in Russia, worth some US $5,000m., making Turks the leading foreign contractors in that country.

Workers' remittances have long been an important source of foreign exchange. These totalled US $4,197m. in 1997 and $5,397m. in 1998, but fell to $4,576m. in 1999 before rising slightly to $4,603m. in 2000. In 2001 they fell sharply to $2,837m. Receipts from tourism, also an important source of foreign exchange, totalled $7,002m. in 1997 and $7,177m. in 1998, but fell to $5,203m. in 1999 because of political unrest and earthquake-related disruption to the tourist trade. They recovered to $7,636m. in 2000 and increased further to a provisional $8,090m. in 2001. A current-account deficit of $2,437m. was recorded in 1996, increasing to $2,679m. in 1997, and, although a surplus of $1,984m. was recorded in 1998, a deficit, of $1,360m., was again recorded in 1999. In 2000 the current-account deficit increased to an unprecedented $9,819m., due to an over-valued lira, rising oil prices and strong domestic demand. Partly because of a slump in imports, the current account showed a surplus of $3,396m. in 2001, but was expected to revert to a deficit position in 2002. The overall balance of payments recorded a small deficit of $441m. in 1998, which increased sharply to $5,204m. in 1999 owing to a decline in inward capital investment. In 2000 Treasury borrowing on the international capital markets and a doubling of net capital inflow to $9,400m, financed the record current-account deficit without difficulty, contributing to a overall balance-of-payments surplus of $2,934m. In the crisis year of 2001, however, a deficit of $12,888m. was recorded. Turkey receives large inflows of foreign currency from unrecorded trade with Eastern Europe and Russia (known as the 'suitcase trade'), which do not appear in official current-account statistics. Estimates have suggested that these unrecorded revenues may be as high as $5,000m.–$10,000m.

Turkey's principal imports in 2001 by value were machinery and transport equipment (with 31.7%), mineral fuels and lubricants (20.5%), basic manufactures (16.4%) and chemicals (15.4%). The principal exports were basic manufactures (24.0%), machinery and transport equipment (22.9%) and clothing and accessories (excluding footwear) (21.3%). The EU is Turkey's principal trading partner, with Germany alone taking 17.2% of all Turkish exports in 2001 and supplying 13.2% of all imports. A customs union with the EU came into effect in January 1996 (see below) and a supplementary agreement on trade in iron and steel products, concluded in July of that year, means that, in theory, there is free trade between Turkey and EU countries in all goods except agricultural products. As analysts had predicted, there was a rapid increase in imports from the EU in 1996, with imports rising by 19%, as Turkey removed remaining trade tariffs, with the result that the trade gap between Turkey and the EU widened. Turkey's trade with Russia and with the Central Asian republics of Azerbaijan, Uzbekistan, Kazakhstan and Kyrgyzstan, grew rapidly in the 1990s. While official Turkish exports to Russia totalled US $1,200m. in 1995, some

analysts believed that the figure would rise to $6,000m. if the so-called 'suitcase trade' were taken into account. In 2001 Russia (8.6%) was the third largest supplier of Turkish imports.

In 1963 the Government signed an association agreement with the EC, under which Turkey was granted financial aid and preferential tariff quotas. A package of minor improvements was introduced at the end of 1976 and the association agreement was revised in July 1980, offering Turkey a five-year financial aid package. Since the military coup of September 1980, aid from EC countries has become increasingly dependent upon the restoration of democracy and human rights in Turkey. NATO countries have been divided on support for the Ankara regime: in December 1981 the USA promised to accelerate aid to Turkey, but in March 1982 EC aid worth US $586m. was 'frozen'. This aid remained blocked, despite the reconvening of the Turkey-EC Association Council in September 1986. In 1987 Turkey submitted an application for full EC membership, followed by a concerted diplomatic effort to win support for its application in Europe. The 'frozen' aid was partly released in early 1988. At the end of 1989 the European Commission published its report in response to Turkey's application for full membership. The report drew attention to both economic and political problems in Turkey, as well as the country's unsatisfactory human rights record, and proposed that negotiations should not start until after 1992. Although an agreement to construct a customs union as of 1 January 1995 was secured in 1993, its establishment was postponed in late 1994, owing to persisting concerns regarding the Turkish Government's record on human rights, democracy and the rule of law. Negotiations in early 1995 finally concluded an agreement, which was signed at a meeting of the EU-Turkey Association Council in March. The accord was formally ratified by the European Parliament in December, and came into effect on 1 January 1996. The impact of the removal of commercial barriers (except those on agricultural goods) was expected to stimulate trade between the two sides and to promote greater competitiveness among Turkish industries. The EU was to provide ECU 1,800m. over a five-year period, in order to assist the implementation of the new trade regime and to alleviate any initial hardships resulting from the agreement. However, some $470m. in EU adjustment funds to support the customs union was blocked in September 1996 by Greece, and by the European Parliament as a result of concern over Turkey's human rights record.

Turkey's relations with the EU remained strained throughout 1996, and they suffered a further set-back in December 1997 when the EU decided to exclude Turkey from the list of countries eligible to join the organization in the near future. Although the European Commission subsequently published a strategy in March 1998 for enhancing co-operation by building on the customs union which came into force in 1996, EU financial assistance to Turkey remained blocked at the insistence of Greece. However, the improvement in Greek-Turkish relations in the wake of the August 1999 earthquake resulted in Greece ending its veto on EU aid to Turkey and also backing the decision of the EU summit in Helsinki, Finland, in December to grant Turkey the status of a candidate for EU membership, although actual negotiations remained dependent on an improvement in Turkey's observance of human and democratic rights. In December 2000 an EU-Turkey accession partnership agreement was concluded, providing a introduction to future negotiations. Pending their start, however, Turkey was not included in the allocation of European Parliament seats and qualified majority voting rights to the prospective new members, as agreed under the Treaty of Nice. In March 2001 the Government published a detailed programme for meeting the requirements of EU membership, setting out plans for the harmonization of economic, social and administrative structures with the EU's *acquis communautaire*. However, the Government acknowledged that implementation of the programme would not be possible unless Turkey found solutions to its deep-seated economic weaknesses. The post-February 2001 economic crisis created further difficulties for Turkey's EU application, although the Government remained firmly committed to the goal of membership. By September 2002 Turkey had enacted many of the constitutional, legal and human rights reforms required by the EU; but no date had been set for the opening of formal accession negotiations.

In recent years the US Government's intended military and economic aid to Turkey has been affected by the determination of Congress to institute severe cuts in retaliation for the Turkish Government's refusal to modify its support for the 'Turkish Republic of Northern Cyprus'. The Congress has also attempted to withhold certain portions of aid in order to encourage greater respect for human rights in the Turkish Government's treatment of Kurdish separatists. In August 1994 Prime Minister Çiller refused US military and economic aid amounting to US \$453m., owing to its conditional element. In June 1996 the US House of Representatives vetoed a \$25m. foreign aid allocation to Turkey, in part because of Turkey's land blockade of Armenia. However, the US Senate later authorized the release of some \$12m., without conditions. Turkey incurred further US displeasure when Ankara signed a trade agreement with Cuba in August 1996, and when Prime Minister Erbakan made controversial visits to Iran and Libya.

At the end of August 1997, following a recommendation of the NSC, the Government indicated that the illegal barter trade with northern Iraq would be brought under control, to raise urgently required tax revenues. For some years Turkish traders had exchanged a variety of goods for cheap Iraqi diesel oil, to be resold in Turkey at prices far lower than those recommended officially. Although this thriving border trade was in violation of UN sanctions against Iraq, it was tolerated since it provided an important source of foreign currency for the Kurdish population of northern Iraq. Petrol Ofisi, the state-owned petroleum distributor, was henceforth to buy, sell and tax the diesel, to raise an estimated US \$900m. per year in revenue for the Government.

Under a Free Zones Law of 1985, Turkey has set up a number of special sites within the country deemed to be outside the customs border. Consequently, they are exempt from foreign trade and other regulations, providing Turkish and foreign companies operating within them with special incentives. The free zones established by 2001 were Mersin (1987), Antalya (1987), Aegean (1990), İstanbul Atatürk Airport (1990), Trabzon (1992), İstanbul-Leather (1995), Eastern Anatolia (1995), Mardin (1995), İstanbul International Stock Exchange (1997), İzmir Menemen-Leather (1998), Rize (1998), Samsun (1998),

İstanbul Thrace (1998), Kayseri (1998), Europa (1999), Gaziantep (1999) and Adana Yumurtalık (1999).

ECONOMIC PROSPECTS

The major financial crises of November 2000 and, in particular, of February 2001 again exposed Turkey's chronic underlying weaknesses and the failure of successive governments to correct them. The new IMF programme agreed after the November 2000 crisis was quickly followed by another in May 2001 and a third in February 2002 after Turkey had been badly affected by the post-11 September international economic downturn and had suffered its second-biggest annual GDP contraction since 1945. Like its predecessors, the latest programme focuses on curbing inflation and the budget deficit, revitalizing productive sectors by means of the privatization of inefficient state enterprises, eliminating subsidies and strengthening the legal framework for foreign investment. Under the new arrangements the IMF has demonstrated increased rigour in monitoring the Government's implementation of the programme and a greater willingness to halt disbursements from IMF facilities as soon as any shortcomings become apparent, while the Government's resolve has been strengthened by its awareness that reform is essential if Turkey is to make progress towards the goal of admission to the EU. Under this discipline, a modest recovery began in the first half of 2002 (including a reported 8.2% increase in GDP during the second quarter of the year compared with the same period in 2001), putting the Government on course to achieving GDP growth of around 3% over the full year and to regaining 2000 output levels by 2004.

It was clear, however, that the disparate three-party coalition Government of Bülent Ecevit had remained in power through the crises only because of the absence of a credible alternative government. When the coalition imploded in July 2002 and an early general election was called for November, new uncertainties were created for future economic prospects, particularly over whether a new administration would accept the IMF and EU stipulations followed hitherto. Also clouding Turkey's economic horizon as the election approached was the looming prospect of US-led military action against the Saddam Hussein regime in neighbouring Iraq, into which Turkey would inevitably be drawn, at least indirectly, as the USA's principal military ally in the region.

Statistical Survey

Source (unless otherwise stated): Türkiye İş Bankası AŞ, Economic Research and Planning Dept, İstiklal Cad. 300, Beyoğlu, İstanbul; tel. (212) 2927764; fax (212) 2498298; internet www.isbank.com.tr.

Area and Population

AREA, POPULATION AND DENSITY

Area (sq km)	779,452*
Population (census results)	
21 October 1990	
Males	28,607,047
Females	27,865,988
Total	56,473,035†
30 November 1997	62,865,574
Population (official estimates at mid-year)‡	
1999	65,819,000
2000	66,835,000
2001	67,829,000
Density (per sq km) at mid-2001	87.0

* 300,948 sq miles. The total comprises Anatolia (Turkey in Asia or Asia Minor), with an area of 755,688 sq km (291,773 sq miles), and Thrace (Turkey in Europe), with an area of 23,764 sq km (9,175 sq miles).

† Comprising 50,497,586 in Anatolia and 5,975,449 in Thrace.

‡ Source: State Institute of Statistics.

PRINCIPAL TOWNS

(estimated population at mid-1997, within municipal boundaries)

İstanbul . . .	8,274,921		Malatya . . .	330,312
Ankara (capital) .	2,937,524		Gebze . . .	264,170
İzmir (Smyrna) .	2,130,359		Denizli . . .	253,848
Adana . . .	1,131,198		Siirt . . .	246,642
Bursa . . .	1,095,842		Erzurum . . .	246,535
Gaziantep . . .	789,056		Tarsus . . .	246,206
Konya . . .	628,364		Kahramanmaraş .	245,772
Mersin (İçel) . .	587,212		Elâzığ . . .	228,815
Antalya . . .	564,914		Van . . .	219,319
Diyarbakır . . .	479,884		Sultanbeyli . .	211,068
Kayseri . . .	475,657		İzmit (Kocaeli) . .	210,068
Eskişehir . . .	470,981		Manisa . . .	207,148
Urfa . . .	405,905		Batman . . .	203,793
Samsun . . .	339,871			

Source: UN, *Demographic Yearbook*.

Mid-2000 (UN estimates, '000 incl. suburbs): İstanbul 8,953; Ankara (capital) 3,155; İzmir (Smyrna) 2,214; Bursa 1,166; Adana 1,091; Gaziantep 757.

Mid-2001 (UN estimate, '000 incl. suburbs): Ankara 3,208.

Source: UN, *World Urbanization Prospects: The 2001 Revision*.

BIRTHS, MARRIAGES AND DEATHS

	Registered live births		Registered marriages		Registered deaths	
	Number	Rate (per 1,000)	Number	Rate (per 1,000)	Number	Rate (per 1,000)
1994	1,383,000	22.8	462,415	7.7	401,000	6.6
1995	1,381,000	22.4	463,105	7.6	405,000	6.6
1996	1,379,000	22.0	486,734	7.9	408,000	6.5
1997	1,340,000	21.5	518,856	8.3	395,000	6.3
1998	1,339,000	21.1	485,112	7.6	402,000	6.3
1999	1,405,000	21.8	n.a.	n.a.	438,000	6.8
2000	1,504,000	22.3	n.a.	n.a.	439,000	6.5
2001	1,507,000	22.0	n.a.	n.a.	463,000	6.7

Sources: UN, *Demographic Yearbook* and *Population and Vital Statistics Report*; State Institute of Statistics.

Expectation of life (WHO estimates, years at birth, 2000): Males 66.8; Females 72.5 (Source: WHO, *World Health Report*).

ECONOMICALLY ACTIVE POPULATION*
(sample surveys, '000 persons aged 12 years and over, October)

	1997	1998	1999
Agriculture, hunting, forestry and fishing	8,219	9,534	10,096
Mining and quarrying	176	171	134
Manufacturing	3,602	3,300	3,117
Electricity, gas and water	111	106	78
Construction	1,323	1,335	1,192
Trade, restaurants and hotels	2,916	2,901	2,944
Transport, storage and communications	926	953	863
Financing, insurance, real estate and business services	516	516	520
Community, social and personal services	3,024	3,142	3,107
Total employed	20,815	21,958	22,049
Males	15,364	15,587	15,167
Females	5,450	6,371	6,882
Unemployed	1,545	1,547	1,730
Total labour force	22,360	23,505	23,779

* Excluding armed forces.

Source: ILO.

WORKERS ABROAD ('000)

	1997	1998*	1999
Australia	21	17	13
Austria	51	48	55
Belgium	38	27	27
CIS	40	25	25
France	73	96	79
Germany	740	731	741
Libya	6	6	3
Netherlands	65	56	48
Saudi Arabia	120	115	115
Switzerland	34	34	33
Total (incl. others)	1,264	1,219	1,206

* Figures at October.

WORKERS' REMITTANCES FROM ABROAD (US $ million)

	1999	2000	2001
Total	4,576	4,603	2,835

Source: Secretariat of the State Planning Organization.

Health and Welfare

KEY INDICATORS

Fertility (births per woman, 2000)	2.5
Under-5 mortality rate (per 1,000 live births, 2000)	45
HIV/AIDS (% of persons aged 15–49, 1999)	<0.1
Physicians (per 1,000 head, 1998)	1.21
Hospital beds (per 1,000 head, 1996)	2.5
Health expenditure (1998): US $ per head (PPP)	172
% of GDP	4.9
public (% of total)	71.9
Access to water (% of persons, 2000)	83
Access to sanitation (% of persons, 2000)	91
Human Development Index (2000): ranking	85
value	0.742

For sources and definitions, see explanatory note on p. vi.

Agriculture

PRINCIPAL CROPS ('000 metric tons)

	1998	1999	2000
Wheat	21,000	18,000	21,000
Rice (paddy)	315	340	350
Rye	232	233	260
Barley	9,000	7,700	8,000
Maize	2,300	2,297	2,100*
Oats	310	290	312
Dry beans	242	247†	247†
Chick peas	600	560*	540*
Lentils	540	380*	380*
Vetch	145	170†	170†
Broad beans (dry)	43	42†	42†
Potatoes	5,250	6,000	5,350
Onions (dry)	2,270	2,500	2,200
Garlic (dry)	106	110†	110†
Tomatoes	6,600	7,800*	6,800*
Cabbages (incl. black)	712	732†	732†
Carrots	232	240†	240†
Melons and watermelons	5,725	5,800*	5,800*
Aubergines (Eggplants)	915	850†	850†
Apples	2,450	2,500	2,300
Grapes	3,600	3,400	3,550
Pears	360	360*	360*
Hazel-nuts (Filberts)	580	530	470
Figs (dried)	255	275	260
Walnuts	120	140*	138*
Pistachios (in shell)	35	40	65
Almonds	36	42*	46.5*
Chestnuts	55	60†	60†
Oranges	970	1,100	1,035
Lemons and limes	390	520*	460*
Tangerines, mandarins, etc.	480	500*	560*
Peaches and nectarines	410	400	430
Plums	200	190†	190†
Apricots (incl. wild)	540	500†	500†
Cherries (incl. sour)	290	300†	300†
Cotton (lint)	871	791†	791
Tobacco (leaves)	262	260	260
Sugar beet	21,941	16,854	18,000
Sesame seed	26	27†	27
Sunflower seed	860	950	825
Olives	1,650	600	1,700
Olive oil	180	54	180
Tea (made)	177.9	178†	178†

* FAO estimate(s).   † Unofficial figure.

Source: FAO.

LIVESTOCK ('000 head, year ending September)

	1998	1999	2000
Horses	345	330	330*
Mules	142	133	133*
Asses	640	603	603*
Cattle	11,185	11,031	10,900†
Buffaloes	194	176	175†
Camels	1	1	1*
Pigs.	5	5	5*
Sheep	30,238	29,435	29,435*
Goats	8,376	8,057	8,057*
Chickens	166,273	180,000*	200,000*
Ducks	1,829	1,339	1,339*
Geese	1,795	1,771	1,771*
Turkeys	5,328	3,805	3,805*

* FAO estimate(s).   † Unofficial figure.

Source: FAO.

LIVESTOCK PRODUCTS ('000 metric tons)

	1998	1999	2000
Beef and veal	359	365*	371*
Buffalo meat.	4.8	4.9	5
Mutton and lamb . . .	317*	313*	313†
Goat meat	57*	55*	55†
Horse meat	2.3	2.1	2.1
Poultry meat	509.1	532.9	594.9
Cows' milk	8,832	8,800†	8,700†
Buffalo milk	80	66.2†	66.2†
Sheep milk	813	785†	785†
Goats' milk	246	225†	225†
Butter and ghee	118.1	117	116
Cheese	129.6	128.4	127.7
Hen eggs*	694.4	660	715
Honey	67.5	71†	71†
Wool (greasy)	44.4	44.3†	44.3†
Cattle and buffalo hides . .	37.9	36.2	36.2
Sheepskins	56.6	55.4	55.4
Goatskins	7.4	7	7

* FAO estimate(s).   † Unofficial figure.

Source: FAO.

Forestry

ROUNDWOOD REMOVALS ('000 cubic metres, excl. bark)

	1998	1999	2000
Sawlogs, veneer logs and logs for sleepers	4,846	4,933	5,178
Pulpwood	1,588	1,610	1,534
Other industrial wood . .	3,545	3,522	3,719
Fuel wood	7,689	7,550	7,336
Total	17,668	17,615	17,767

Source: FAO.

SAWNWOOD PRODUCTION ('000 cubic metres, incl. railway sleepers)

	1998	1999	2000
Coniferous (softwood) . . .	2,101	2,280	2,542
Broadleaved (hardwood) . . .	1,889	2,020	2,141
Total	3,990	4,300	4,683

Source: FAO.

Fishing

('000 metric tons, live weight)

	1997	1998	1999
Capture	459.2	487.2	575.1
Common carp . . .	16.0	20.0	17.8
Blue whiting . . .	15.0	27.2	17.0
Whiting . . .	15.5	13.2	14.1
Mullets	42.5	45.4	46.8
European pilchard . . .	20.5	23.6	22.0
European anchovy . . .	241.0	228.0	350.0
Atlantic bonito	7.8	24.0	17.9
Aquaculture	45.5	56.7	63.0
Trout	28.5	34.6	38.6
Total catch	504.6	543.9	638.1

Note: Figures exclude aquatic plants and aquatic mammals.

Source: FAO, *Yearbook of Fishery Statistics.*

Mining

('000 metric tons)

	1999	2000	2001
Crude petroleum	2,939	2,748	2,551
Lignite	64,897	59,686	56,542
Coal	2,738	3,330	3,639
Copper (blister)	43	30	25

Source: Secretariat of the State Planning Organization.

Industry

SELECTED PRODUCTS
('000 metric tons, unless otherwise indicated)

	1999	2000	2001
Paper*	1,349	1,566	n.a.
Cotton yarn	126	n.a.	n.a.
Woollen yarn	8	n.a.	n.a.
Cotton fabrics (million metres) .	177	n.a.	n.a.
Woollen fabrics (million metres) .	28	n.a.	n.a.
Raki (million litres) . . .	79 }	759	764
Beer (million litres) . . .	669		
Cigarettes	119	123	126
Crude steel	14,309	14,325	n.a.
Pig-iron	315	n.a.	n.a.
Cement	34,216	36,237	30,125
Sugar (raw)*	2,921	2,162	2,755
Commercial fertilizers† . .	3,216	n.a.	n.a.
Electrolytic copper‡ . . .	43	n.a.	n.a.
Polyethylene	217	225	207
Polyvinyl chloride compositions§	191	177	147
Coke‖¶	2,144	2,811	2,090
Motor spirit (petrol) . . .	3,412	2,758	3,027
Kerosene ('000 barrels)¶ . .	730	638*	n.a.
Fuel oils	6,584	6,532	7,250
Tractors (number) . . .	24,864	35,908	15,054
Domestic refrigerators ('000) .	2,102	2,355	2,237
Domestic washing machines ('000)	1,227	1,391	1,022
Vacuum cleaners ('000) . .	1,067	1,173	591
Television receivers ('000) .	6,940	8,789	8,025
Passenger motor cars ('000) .	222	306	227
Buses and minibuses ('000) .	32	47	12
Electricity (million kWh) .	116,441	124,922	123,001

* Data from FAO.   † Excluding potassic fertilizers.

‡ Private sector only.

§ Including precipitated calcium carbonate.

‖ Including semi-coke.

¶ Data from US Geological Survey.

Source (unless otherwise indicated): mainly Secretariat of the State Planning Organization.

Finance

CURRENCY AND EXCHANGE RATES

Monetary Units

100 kuruş = 1 Turkish lira (TL) or pound.

Sterling, Dollar and Euro Equivalents (31 May 2002)

£1 sterling = 2,114,216 liras;
US $1 = 1,441,478 liras;
€1 = 1,353,115 liras;
10,000,000 Turkish liras = £4.730 = $6.937 = €7.390.

Average Exchange Rate (liras per US $)

1999	418,783
2000	625,219
2001	1,225,588

CONSOLIDATED BUDGET (TL '000 million)*

Revenue	2000	2001	2002*
General budget	33,040,903	51,143,596	70,918,000
Taxation	26,503,698	39,767,892	57,911,000
Taxes on income	10,503,316	15,647,113	19,027,000
Income tax	6,212,977	11,578,894	15,401,000
Corporate tax	2,356,787	3,675,662	3,595,000
Interest tax	1,640,655	382,208	31,000
Taxes on goods and services	11,363,785	18,135,668	28,625,000
Domestic value-added tax	4,487,808	7,289,376	10,608,000
Petroleum consumption tax	3,268,774	5,658,565	10,509,000
Banking and Institutions Transactions tax	858,154	1,511,194	1,588,000
Stamp tax	704,478	834,256	1,345,000
Taxes on foreign trade	4,289,401	5,551,053	9,560,000
Value-added on imports	3,891,746	5,149,317	8,892,000
Non-tax revenue	3,486,493	7,398,155	7,007,000
Property	1,548,821	4,490,549	2,845,000
Special revenue and funds	3,050,712	3,977,549	6,000,000
Funds	2,206,054	2,933,055	5,000,000
Annexed budget revenues	399,240	668,946	300,000
Total	33,440,143	51,812,542	71,218,000

Expenditure	2000	2001	2002*
Personnel	9,978,784	15,203,977	21,891,000
Wages	1,708,554	2,538,942	3,200,000
Other current expenditure	3,635,153	5,164,362	7,783,230
Ministry of National Defence	2,326,906	3,220,858	5,350,000
Investment expenditure	2,475,116	4,139,803	5,735,940
Transfers	30,615,975	55,870,862	62,720,830
Interest payments	20,439,862	41,064,609	42,795,000
Domestic debt interest	18,791,862	37,949,301	36,900,000
Foreign debt interest	1,648,000	3,570,308	5,895,000
Tax rebates	1,632,049	2,918,178	3,400,000
VAT rebates on exports	770,983	1,691,353	2,000,000
Social security payments	3,321,098	5,112,000	7,930,000
Payments to retirement fund	1,775,000	2,625,000	400,000
Payments to institution for the self-employed	1,050,685	1,437,000	1,740,000
Agricultural subsidies	358,501	1,032,578	2,125,000
Fund appropriation	1,995,073	1,480,501	300,000
Total	46,705,028	80,379,004	98,131,000

* Projections.

Source: General Directorate of Public Accounts, Ministry of Finance.

INTERNATIONAL RESERVES

(US $ million at 31 December)

	1999	2000	2001
Gold*	1,011	1,009	1,008
IMF special drawing rights	—	22	4
Reserve position in IMF	155	147	142
Foreign exchange	23,191	22,313	18,733
Total	24,357	23,491	19,887

* National valuation.

Source: IMF, *International Financial Statistics.*

MONEY SUPPLY

(TL '000 million at 31 December*)

	1999	2000	2001
Currency outside banks	1,887,150	3,196,940	4,462,300
Demand deposits at deposit money banks	2,399,720	3,392,530	5,544,100
Total money (incl. others)	4,307,100	6,612,070	10,044,400

* Figures are rounded.

Source: IMF, *International Financial Statistics.*

COST OF LIVING

(Consumer Price Index for urban areas at December; base: 1994 = 100)

	1998	1999	2000
Food	1,410.3	2,186.3	2,907.3
Clothing	1,517.1	2,195.9	2,981.5
Household expenditures	1,154.4	1,813.8	n.a.
Medical and personal care	1,575.9	2,696.8	4,071.5
Transport	1,477.8	2,865.1	3,658.1
Cultural and recreational expenditures	1,392.2	2,206.5	3,014.5
Dwelling expenditures*	1,570.9	2,973.2	4,350.4
All items	1,455.4	2,456.6	3,415.5

* Rent is assumed to be fixed.

December 2001 (base: December 2000 = 100): All items 168.5.

NATIONAL ACCOUNTS

Expenditure on the Gross Domestic Product

(TL '000,000 million at current prices)

	1998	1999	2000
Government final consumption expenditure	6,633	11,748	17,496
Private final consumption expenditure	36,123	55,928	88,978
Increase in stocks	−212	1,149	2,428
Gross fixed capital formation	12,839	16,931	27,688
Total domestic expenditure	55,383	85,756	136,590
Exports of goods and services	12,713	17,972	29,755
Less Imports of goods and services	14,573	20,801	38,940
Sub-total	53,523	82,926	127,424
Statistical discrepancy	−1,090	−5,510	−2,442
GDP in purchasers' values	52,433	77,416	124,982
GDP at constant 1987 prices	117	111	119

Source: IMF, *International Financial Statistics.*

Gross Domestic Product by Economic Activity

(TL '000 million, at current prices)

	1999	2000	2001
Agriculture, forestry and fishing	11,851,055	17,540,631	23,427,659
Mining and quarrying	883,737	1,422,903	2,128,387
Manufacturing	14,839,451	23,888,136	36,730,882
Electricity, gas and water	2,250,677	3,716,743	7,015,153
Construction	4,362,039	6,483,106	9,202,185
Wholesale and retail trade	14,750,945	24,906,513	37,867,860
Transport, storage and communications	10,868,376	17,645,564	28,462,322
Financial institutions	4,228,349	4,698,024	6,639,387
Ownership of dwellings	3,465,420	5,772,955	8,491,506
Other private services	2,830,826	4,430,360	6,704,663
Government services	8,781,478	12,633,650	18,781,015
Private non-profit institutions	272,486	477,141	918,063
Sub-total	79,384,839	123,615,726	186,369,082
Import duties	2,314,575	5,065,425	6,573,910
Less Imputed bank service charges	4,284,141	4,097,693	11,534,431
GDP in purchasers' values*	77,415,272	124,583,458	181,408,563

* Based on unrounded data.

BALANCE OF PAYMENTS (US $ million)

	1999	2000	2001
Exports of goods f.o.b. . . .	29,325	31,664	34,379
Imports of goods f.o.b. . . .	–39,768	–54,041	–38,916
Trade balance	**–10,443**	**22,377**	**–4,537**
Exports of services	16,398	19,484	16,028
Imports of services	–8,953	–8,149	–6,898
Balance on goods and services.	**–2,998**	**–11,042**	**4,593**
Other income received . . .	2,350	2,836	2,753
Other income paid	–5,887	–6,838	–7,753
Balance on goods, services and income	**–6,235**	**–15,044**	**–407**
Current transfers received . .	5,294	5,317	3,861
Current transfers paid . . .	–119	–92	–58
Current balance	**–1,360**	**–9,819**	**3,396**
Direct investment abroad. . .	–645	–870	–497
Direct investment from abroad .	783	982	3,267
Portfolio investment assets . .	–759	–593	–788
Portfolio investment liabilities .	4,188	1,615	–3,727
Other investment assets . . .	–2,571	–2,138	–156
Other investment liabilities . .	3,674	10,449	–12,296
Net errors and omissions . . .	1,894	–2,560	–2,087
Overall balance	**5,204**	**–2,934**	**–12,888**

Source: IMF, *International Financial Statistics*.

External Trade

PRINCIPAL COMMODITIES
(distribution by SITC, US $ million, excl. military goods)

Imports c.i.f.	1999	2000	2001
Crude materials (inedible) except fuels	2,521.8	3,304.1	2,434.7
Mineral fuels, lubricants, etc. .	5,375.3	9,529.3	8,288.6
Petroleum, petroleum products, etc.	3,482.2	5,642.7	4,665.0
Gas (natural and manufactured) .	1,466.8	3,078.7	3,119.3
Chemicals and related products	6,303.8	7,414.7	6,242.4
Organic chemicals . . .	1,361.3	1,760.1	1,397.6
Medicinal and pharmaceutical products	1,159.3	1,344.8	1,345.3
Plastics in primary forms. . .	1,259.4	1,561.9	1,200.4
Basic manufactures . . .	6,539.4	8,465.1	6,634.8
Textile yarn, fabrics, etc. . .	1,906.9	2,135.8	1,920.7
Iron and steel	1,564.8	2,422.2	1,795.6
Machinery and transport equipment	15,378.5	20,508.6	12,826.7
Power-generating machinery and equipment	1,200.2	1,428.5	1,956.9
Machinery specialized for particular industries . .	1,819.0	2,340.1	1,638.3
General industrial machinery, equipment and parts . .	1,990.0	2,182.6	1,809.1
Office machines and automatic data processing machines .	1,206.9	1,594.7	781.1
Telecommunications and sound equipment	2,348.6	3,009.8	1,206.1
Road vehicles and parts* . .	3,003.4	5,432.2	1,814.1
Miscellaneous manufactured articles	2,749.4	3,381.2	2,695.7
Total (incl. others) . . .	**40,687.3**	**54,502.9**	**40,474.8**

Exports f.o.b.	1999	2000	2001
Food and live animals . . .	3,190.3	2,890.7	3,277.4
Vegetables and fruit . . .	2,132.7	1,816.9	2,127.8
Chemicals and related products	1,120.6	1,242.9	1,343.1
Basic manufactures . . .	6,071.9	6,585.4	7,475.2
Textile yarn, fabrics, etc. . .	3,477.8	3,705.7	3,936.2
Non-metallic mineral manufactures	856.8	1,015.3	1,091.5
Iron and steel	1,737.3	1,864.5	2,447.5
Machinery and transport equipment	5,036.8	5,740.5	7,132.2
Telecommunications and sound equipment	753.0	944.5	987.2
Electrical machinery, apparatus, etc. (excl. telecommunications and sound equipment) . .	1,017.7	1,163.0	1,422.7
Road vehicles and parts* . . .	1,438.3	1,520.5	2,295.8
Miscellaneous manufactured articles	7,640.4	7,928.4	8,128.2
Clothing and accessories (excl. footwear)	6,516.0	6,586.0	6,655.5
Total (incl. others)	**26,587.2**	**27,774.9**	**31,128.9**

* Including air-cushion vehicles.
Source: Secretariat of the State Planning Organization.

PRINCIPAL TRADING PARTNERS (US $ million, excl. military goods)

Imports c.i.f. (excl. grants)	1999	2000	2001
Austria	508	n.a.	n.a.
Belgium-Luxembourg . . .	1,133	1,661	890.3
China, People's Republic . . .	895	n.a.	n.a.
France	3,127	3,532	2,284
Germany	5,880	7,198	5,334
Iran	636	n.a.	n.a.
Italy	3,192	4,333	3,480
Japan	1,393	1,621	1,307
Korea, Republic	871	n.a.	n.a.
Libya	502	n.a.	n.a.
Netherlands	1,315	1,585	1,042
Russia	2,374	3,887	3,476
Saudi Arabia	579	961	771
Spain	1,262	1,678	1,062
Sweden	1,444	1,440	544
Switzerland	749	891	683
Ukraine	774	982	758
United Kingdom	2,190	2,748	1,800
USA	3,080	3,911	3,253
Total (incl. others)	**40,687**	**54,503**	**40,507**

Exports f.o.b.	1999	2000	2001
Algeria	408	384	421
Austria	312	n.a.	n.a.
Belgium-Luxembourg . . .	624	647	681
Egypt	467	376	421
France	1,570	1,657	1,893
Germany	5,475	5,180	5,362
Italy	1,683	1,789	2,333
Netherlands	932	874	890
Russia	763	644	923
Saudi Arabia	367	387	492
Spain	763	714	945
Switzerland	268	n.a.	n.a.
United Arab Emirates . . .	391	n.a.	n.a.
United Kingdom	1,830	2,037	2,173
USA	2,437	3,135	3,121
Total (incl. others) . . .	**26,587**	**27,775**	**31,186**

Source: Secretariat of the State Planning Organization.

Transport

RAILWAYS (traffic)

	1997	1998	1999
Passenger-km (million) . .	5,840	6,160	6,147
Freight ton-km (million) . .	9,717	8,377	8,265

Source: UN, *Statistical Yearbook.*

ROAD TRAFFIC (motor vehicles at end of February)

	2000	2001	2002
Passenger cars	4,422,180	4,534,803	4,539,944
Minibuses	235,885	239,381	239,525
Buses and coaches . . .	118,454	119,306	119,357
Small trucks.	794,459	833,175	836,438
Trucks	394,283	396,493	396,668
Motorcycles and mopeds . .	1,011,284	1,031,221	1,032,079
Special purpose vehicles . .	55,677	57,490	57,766

Source: State Institute of Statistics.

SHIPPING

Merchant Fleet (registered at 31 December)

	1999	2000	2001
Number of vessels . . .	1,152	1,153	1,146
Total displacement ('000 grt) . .	6,324.6	5,832.7	5,896.7

Source: Lloyd's Register-Fairplay, *World Fleet Statistics.*

International Sea-borne Freight Traffic ('000 metric tons)

	1998	1999	2000*
Goods loaded†	24,756	37,332	25,476
Goods unloaded	78,168	58,080	77,916

* Estimate.
† Excluding livestock and timber.
Source: UN, *Monthly Bulletin of Statistics.*

CIVIL AVIATION (Turkish Airlines)

	1995	1996	1997*
Number of passengers ('000) . .	8,599	9,281	10,405
Freight handled (metric tons)† .	90,846	91,688	109,242

* Figures are provisional.   † Cargo and mail.

Tourism

TOURISTS BY COUNTRY OF ORIGIN*

Country	1999	2000	2001
Bulgaria.	259,075	381,545	540,437
France	270,280	449,727	523,777
Germany	1,388,787	2,277,505	2,881,550
Greece	146,871	218,092	189,028
Iran.	351,937	380,819	327,067
Italy	79,029	218,768	315,134
Romania	483,184	265,128	180,941
Russian Federation . . .	n.a.	677,152	757,121
Syria	102,444	122,417	109,723
United Kingdom	814,889	915,286	845,932
USA	395,006	515,284	428,989
Yugoslavia (former) . . .	213,776	128,383	125,818
Total (incl. others) . . .	7,487,285	10,428,153	11,619,909

* Including same-day tourists.
Sources: State Institute of Statistics; World Tourism Organization, *Yearbook of Tourism Statistics.*

Tourism receipts (million US $): 5,203 in 1999; 7,636 in 2000; 8,090* in 2001 (Source: Secretariat of the State Planning Organization).
* Provisional.

Communications Media

	1999	2000	2001
Television receivers ('000 in use) .	n.a.	29,500	n.a.
Telephones ('000 main lines in use)	18,054.0	18,395.2	18,900.9
Mobile cellular telephones ('000 subscribers)	8,121.5	16,133.4	20,000
Personal computers ('000 in use) .	2,200	2,500	2,700
Internet users ('000)	1,500	2,000	2,500

Source: International Telecommunication Union.

Radio receivers ('000 in use): 11,300 in 1997.
Facsimile machines (number in use): 108,014 in 1997.
Book production (titles): 6,546 in 1996.
Daily newspapers (number): 57 in 1996; (Circulation, '000) 5,600 in 1996.
Non-daily newspapers (number): 1,468 in 1996.
Sources: UNESCO, *Statistical Yearbook,* and UN, *Statistical Yearbook.*

Education

(1998)

	Institutions	Teachers	Total pupils/ students
Pre-primary	6,868	10,979	204,000
Primary	45,112	317,795	9,625,400
Secondary:			
General	2,598	71,344	1,282,600
Vocational and teacher training	3,367	74,559	998,000
Higher	1,222	60,129	1,465,000

Source: UN, *Statistical Yearbook for Asia and the Pacific.*

Adult literacy rate (UNESCO estimates): 85.1% (males 93.5%; females 76.5%) in 2000 (Source: UN Development Programme, *Human Development Report*).

Directory

The Constitution

In October 1981 the National Security Council (NSC), which took power in September 1980, announced the formation of a Consultative Assembly to draft a new constitution, replacing that of 1961. The Assembly consisted of 40 members appointed directly by the NSC and 120 members chosen by the NSC from candidates put forward by the governors of the 67 provinces; all former politicians were excluded. The draft Constitution was approved by the Assembly in September 1982 and by a national referendum in November. Its main provisions are summarized below:

Legislative power is vested in the unicameral Grand National Assembly, with 400 deputies, who are elected by universal adult suffrage for a five-year term. Executive power is vested in the President, who is elected by the Grand National Assembly for a seven-year term and is empowered to appoint a Prime Minister and senior members of the judiciary, the Central Bank and broadcasting organizations; to dissolve the Grand National Assembly; and to declare a state of emergency entailing rule by decree. Strict controls on the powers of trades unions, the press and political parties were also included. An appended 'temporary article' automatically installed the incumbent President of the NSC as Head of State for a seven-year term, assisted by a Presidential Council comprising members of the NSC.

An amendment adopted in June 1987 increased the number of deputies in the Grand National Assembly from 400 to 450. The number was increased to 550 in a further amendment adopted in July 1995.

The Government

HEAD OF STATE

President: AHMET NECDET SEZER (took office 16 May 2000).

COUNCIL OF MINISTERS
(September 2002)

A coalition of the Demokratik Sol Partisi (DSP), the Milliyetçi Hareket Partisi (MHP) and the Anavatan Partisi (ANAP).

Prime Minister: BÜLENT ECEVIT (DSP).

Deputy Prime Minister and Minister of State: DEVLET BAHÇELI (MHP).

Deputy Prime Minister and Minister of State: MESUT YILMAZ (ANAP).

Deputy Prime Minister and Minister of State, and Minister of Foreign Affairs: ŞÜKRÜ SINA GÜREL (DSP).

Ministers of State: MASUM TÜRKER, TUNCA TOSKAY (MHP), MEHMET KEÇECILER (ANAP), M. ZEKI SEZER, FARUK BAL (MHP), ALI DOĞAN, MEHMET KOCABATMAZ, RAMAZAN MIRZAOĞLU (MHP), YILMAZ KARAKOYUNLU (ANAP), MELDA BAYER, ŞUAYIP ÜŞENMEZ (MHP), EDIP SAFTER GAYDALI (ANAP), ERDOĞAN TOPRAK, REŞAT DOĞRU (MHP), HÜSEYIN TAYFUN İÇLI, TAYYIBE GÜLEK.

Minister of Justice: AYSEL CELIKEL.

Minister of National Defence: SABAHATTIN ÇAKMAKOĞLU (MHP).

Minister of the Interior: MUZAFFER ECEMIŞ.

Minister of Finance: SÜMER ORAL (ANAP).

Minister of National Education: NECDET TAKIN.

Minister of Public Works and Housing: ABDÜLKADIR AKCAN (MHP).

Minister of Health: OSMAN DURMUŞ (MHP).

Minister of Transport and Communications: NACI KINACIOGLU (MHP).

Minister of Agriculture and Rural Affairs: HÜSNÜ YUSUF GÖKALP (MHP).

Minister of Labour and Social Security: NEJAT ARSEVEN.

Minister of Trade and Industry: AHMET KENAN TANRIKULU (MHP).

Minister of Energy and Natural Resources: ZEKI ÇAKAN (ANAP).

Minister of Culture: BURHAN SUAT ÇAGLAYAN.

Minister of Tourism: MUSTAFA TAŞAR (ANAP).

Minister of Forestry: NAMI ÇAĞAN (DSP).

Minister of the Environment: FEVZI AYTEKIN (DSP).

MINISTRIES

President's Office: Cumhurbaşkanlığı Köşkü, Çankaya, Ankara; tel. (312) 4685030; fax (312) 4271330; e-mail cankaya@tccb.gov.tr; internet www.cankaya.gov.tr.

Prime Minister's Office: Başbakanlık, Bakanlıklar, Ankara; tel. (312) 4189056; fax (312) 4180476; e-mail info@basbakanlik.gov.tr; internet www.basbakanlik.gov.tr.

Deputy Prime Minister's Office: Başbakan yard. ve Devlet Bakanı, Bakanlıklar, Ankara; tel. (312) 4191621; fax (312) 4191547.

Ministry of Agriculture and Rural Affairs: Tarım ve Köyişleri Bakanlığı, Şehit Adem Yavuz Sok. 10, 06140 Kızılay, Ankara; tel. (312) 4191677; fax (312) 4177168; e-mail admin@tarim.gov.tr; internet www.tarim.gov.tr.

Ministry of Culture: Kültür Bakanlığı, Atatürk Bul. 29, 06050 Opera, Ankara; tel. (312) 3090850; fax (312) 3126473; e-mail kultur@kultur.gov.tr; internet www.kultur.gov.tr.

Ministry of Energy and Natural Resources: Enerji ve Tabii Kaynaklar Bakanlığı, İnönü Bul. 27, Ankara; tel. (312) 2126915; fax (312) 2864769; e-mail webmaster@enerji.gov.tr; internet www.enerji.gov.tr.

Ministry of the Environment: Gevre Bakanlığı, Eskişehir Yolu 8, 06530 Ankara; tel. (312) 2879965; fax (312) 2852742.

Ministry of Finance: Maliye Bakanlığı, Dikmen Cad., Ankara; tel. (312) 4250018; fax (312) 4250058; e-mail bshalk@maliye.gov.tr; internet www.maliye.gov.tr.

Ministry of Foreign Affairs: Dişişleri Bakanlığı, Yeni Hizmet Binası, 06520 Balgat, Ankara; tel. (312) 2873556; fax (312) 2873869; internet www.mfa.gov.tr.

Ministry of Forestry: Orman Bakanlığı, Atatürk Bul., Bakanlıklar, Ankara; tel. (312) 4176000.

Ministry of Health: Sağlık Bakanlığı, Yenişehir, Ankara; tel. (312) 4312486; fax (312) 4339885; e-mail adres@saglik.gov.tr; internet www.saglik.gov.tr.

Ministry of the Interior: İçişleri Bakanlığı, Bakanlıklar, Ankara; tel. (312) 4181368; fax (312) 4181795.

Ministry of Justice: Adalet Bakanlığı, 06440 Bakanlıklar, Ankara; tel. (312) 4196050; fax (312) 4173954.

Ministry of Labour and Social Security: Çalışma ve Sosyal Güvenlik Bakanlığı, İnönü Bul. 42, 06100 Emek, Ankara; tel. (312) 4170727; fax (312) 4179765; internet www.calisma.gov.tr.

Ministry of National Defence: Milli Savunma Bakanlığı, 06100 Ankara; tel. (312) 4254596; fax (312) 4184737; e-mail meb@meb.gov.tr; internet www.msb.gov.tr.

Ministry of National Education: Milli Eğitim Bakanlığı, Attatürk Bul., Bakanlıklar, Ankara; tel. (312) 4191410; fax (312) 4177027; internet www.meb.gov.tr.

Ministry of Public Works and Housing: Bayındırlık ve İskan Bakanlığı, Vekaletler Cad. 1, 06100 Ankara; tel. (312) 4255711; fax (312) 4180406.

Ministry of Tourism: Turizm Bakanlığı, İsmet İnönü Bul. 5, 06100 Bahçelievler, Ankara; tel. (312) 2128300; fax (312) 2128391; internet www.turizm.gov.tr.

Ministry of Trade and Industry: Sanayi ve Ticaret Bakanlığı, Eskişehir yolu üzeri 7 km Ankara; tel. (312) 2860365; internet www.sanayi.gov.tr.

Ministry of Transport and Communications: Ulaştırma Bakanlığı, Sok. 5, Emek, Ankara; tel. (312) 2124416; fax (312) 2124930; internet www.ubak.gov.tr.

Legislature

BÜYÜK MİLLET MECLİSİ
(Grand National Assembly)

Speaker: OMER IZGI.

General Election, 18 April 1999

Party	% of votes	Seats
Demokratik Sol Parti (DSP) . . .	22.19	136
Milliyetçi Hareket Partisi (MHP) . . .	17.98	129
Fazilet Partisi (FP)	15.41	111
Anavatan Partisi (ANAP)	13.22	86
Doğru Yol Partisi (DYP)	12.01	85
Independents	0.87	3
Others*	18.32	—
Total	100.00	550

* Including Cumhuriyet Halk Partisi (8.71%) and Halkın Demokrasi Partisi (4.75%).

Political Organizations

Political parties were banned from 1980–83. Legislation enacted in March 1986 stipulated that a party must have organizations in at least 45 provinces, and in two-thirds of the districts in each of these provinces, in order to take part in an election. A political party is recognized by the Government as a legitimate parliamentary group only if it has at least 20 deputies in the Grand National Assembly.

In mid-1992, following the adoption of more lenient guidelines for the formation of political parties (proposed by the Demirel Administration), several new parties were established, and the left-wing CHP, dissolved in 1981, was reactivated.

AK Partisi (Justice and Development Party): f. 2001; Islamist-orientated; Leader RECEP TAYYIP ERDOĞAN.

Anavatan Partisi (ANAP) (Motherland Party): 13 Cad. 3, Balgat, Ankara; tel. (312) 2865000; fax (312) 2865019; e-mail anavatan@anap.org.tr; internet www.anap.org.tr; f. 1983; supports free-market economic system, moderate nationalist and conservative policies, rational social justice system, integration with the EU, and closer ties with the Islamic world; Chair. MESUT YILMAZ; Sec.-Gen. YAŞAR OKUYAN.

Büyük Birlik Partisi (BBP) (Great Unity Party): Tuna Cad. 28, Yenişehir, Ankara; tel. (312) 4340923; fax (312) 4355818; e-mail bbp@bbp.org.tr; internet www.bbp.org.tr; f. 1993; Chair. MUHSIN YAZICIOĞLU.

Cumhuriyet Halk Partisi (CHP) (Republican People's Party): Çevre Sok. 38, Ankara; tel. and fax (312) 4685969; e-mail chpbim@chp.org.tr; internet www.chp.org.tr; f. 1923 by Kemal Atatürk, dissolved in 1981 and reactivated in 1992; merged with Sosyal Demokrat Halkçı Parti (Social Democratic Populist Party) in February 1995; left-wing; Leader DENIZ BAYKAL; Sec.-Gen. TARHAN ERDEM.

Değişen Türkiye Partisi (DEPAR) (Changing Turkey Party): Aşağlı Öveçler 6, Cad. 78, Sok. 15/2, Dikmen, Ankara; tel. (312) 4794875; fax (312) 4795964; e-mail webmaster@depar.org; internet www.depar.org; f. 1998; Chair. GÖKHAN ÇAPOĞLU.

Demokrasi ve Barış Partisi (DBP) (Democracy and Peace Party): Menekşe 1, Sok. 10-A/7, Kızılay, Ankara; tel. (312) 4173587; f. 1996; pro-Kurdish; Leader REFIK KARAKOÇ.

Demokrat Türkiye Partisi (DTP) (Democratic Turkey Party): Mesnevi Sok 27, Ankara; tel. (312) 4420151; fax (312) 4421263; e-mail sevginazlioglu@dtp.org.tr; internet www.dtp.org.tr; Leader İSMET SEZGIN.

Demokratik Sol Partisi (DSP) (Democratic Left Party): Fevzi Çakmak Cad. 17, Ankara; tel. (312) 2124950; fax (312) 2213474; e-mail akguvercinist@dsp.org.tr; internet www.dsp.org.tr; f. 1985; centre-left; drawing support from members of the fmr Republican People's Party; Chair. BÜLENT ECEVIT; Sec.-Gen. ZEKI SEZER.

Doğru Yol Partisi (DYP) (True Path Party): Selanik Cad. 40, Kızılay, Ankara; tel. (312) 4191818; fax (312) 4176090; internet www.dyp.org.tr; f. 1983; centre-right; replaced the Justice Party (f. 1961 and banned in 1981); Chair. TANSU ÇILLER; Sec.-Gen. NURHAN TEKINEL.

Emeğin Partisi (EMEP) (Labour Party): Ulufeci Sok Fındıkoba Ishani 2/2, Kocamustafapasa, İstanbul; tel. (212) 5884332; fax (212) 5884341; e-mail info@emep.org; internet www.emep.org; Pres. Levent Tüzel.

Halkın Demokrasi Partisi (HADEP) (People's Democracy Party): 2 Cadde, 32 Sok 37, Ankara; tel. (312) 2852200; fax (312) 2852297; e-mail hadepgm@yahoo.com; internet www.hadep.org.tr; f. 1994; pro-Kurdish nationalist party; Chair. MURAT BOZLAK.

İşçi Partisi (IP) (Workers' Party): Mithatpaşa Cad. 10/8, Sıhhıye, Ankara; tel. (312) 4352999; fax (312) 4343386; e-mail ip@ip.org.tr; internet www.ip.org.tr; f. 1992; Chair. DOĞU PERINÇEK.

Liberal Demokratik Parti (LDP) (Liberal Democratic Party): Gazi Mustafa Kemal Bul., 108/18 Maltepe, 06570 Ankara; tel. (312) 2323374; fax (312) 4687597; e-mail info@ldp.org.tr; internet www.ldp.org.tr; f. 1994; Chair. BESIM TIBUK.

Millet Partisi (MP) (Nation Party): İstanbul Cad., Rüzgarlı Gayret Sok. 2, Ankara; tel. (312) 3127626; fax (312) 3127651; internet www.mp.org.tr; f. 1992; Chair. AYKUT EDIBALI.

Milliyetçi Hareket Partisi (MHP) (Nationalist Action Party): Karanfil Sokak 69, 06640 Bakanlıklar, Ankara; tel. (312) 4195956; fax (312) 2311424; e-mail mhp@mhp.org.tr; internet www.mhp.org.tr; f. 1983; formerly the Conservative Party; Leader DEVLET BAHÇELI; Sec.-Gen. KORAY AYDIN.

Özgürlük ve Dayanisma Partisi (ODP) (Freedom and Solidarity Party): Necatibey Cad. 23/11, Ankara; e-mail ozgurluk@odp.org.tr; internet www.odp.org.tr; f. 1996; Leader UFUK URAZ.

Saadet Partisi (SP) (Felicity Party): f. 2001; replaced conservative wing of Islamic fundamentalist and free-market advocating Fazilet Partisi (Virtue Party), which was banned in June 2001; Leader RECAI KUTAN.

Türkiye Komünist Partisi (TKP) (Communist Party of Turkey): Osmanağa Mahallesi Nüzhet Efendi Sok 38, Kadıköy, İstanbul; tel. (216) 4185351; fax (216) 3461137; e-mail tkp@tkp.org.tr; internet www.tkp.org.tr; f. 1981 as the Party of Socialist Power, name changed as above in 2001; Gen. Sec. KEMAL OKUYAN.

Yeniden Doğuş Partisi (YDP) (Rebirth Party): Sağlık Sok 3, Sıhhıye, Ankara; tel. (312) 4356565; fax (312) 4356564; f. 1992; Chair. HASAN CELAL GÜZEL.

Yeni Parti (YP) (New Party): Rabat Sok 27, Gaziosmanpaşa, Ankara; tel. (312) 4469254; fax (312) 4469579; f. 1993; Leader YUSUF BOZKURT ÖZAL.

Yeni Turkiye Partisi (YTP) (New Turkey Party): f. 2002; comprised of former DSP politicians; Leader İsmail Cem.

The following proscribed organizations were engaged in an armed struggle against the Government:

KADEK (Congress for Freedom and Democracy in Kurdistan): internet www.pkk.org; f. 1978, as the Partiya Karkeren Kurdistan (PKK) (Kurdistan Workers' Party); 57-member directorate; launched struggle for an independent Kurdistan in 1984; ceased activities in 2000; assumed present name in April 2002; Chair. ABDULLAH ÖCALAN.

Devrimici Halk Kurtuluş Cephesi (DHKP—C) (Revolutionary People's Liberation Party—Front): e-mail dhkc@ozgurluk.org; internet www.ozgurluk.org/dhkc; left wing faction of Dev-Sol; subsumed parent organization in 1996.

Diplomatic Representation

EMBASSIES IN TURKEY

Afghanistan: Cinnah Cad. 88, 06551 Çankaya, Ankara; tel. (312) 4381121; fax (312) 4387745; Ambassador: Dr ABD AS-SALAM AUSEM.

Albania: Ebuziya Tevfik Sok 17, Çankaya, Ankara; tel. (312) 4416103; fax (312) 4416104; Ambassador: SAIMAR BALA.

Algeria: Şehit Ersan Cad. 42, 06680 Çankaya, Ankara; tel. (312) 4687719; fax (312) 4687619; Ambassador: RABAH HADID.

Argentina: Uğar Mumcu Cad. 60/3, 06700 Gaziosmanpaşa, Ankara; tel. (312) 4462062; fax (312) 4462063; Ambassador: JOSÉ PEDRO PICO.

Australia: Nenehatun Cad. 83, 06680 Gaziosmanpaşa, Ankara; tel. (312) 4461180; fax (312) 4461188; e-mail ausemank@ibm.net; internet www.embaustralia.org.tr; Ambassador: JONATHAN PHILP.

Austria: Atatürk Bul. 189, Kavaklıdere, Ankara; tel. (312) 4190431; fax (312) 4189454; e-mail austroambtr@superonline.com; Ambassador: Dr MARIUS CALLIGARIS.

Azerbaijan: Cemal Nadir Sok 20, Çelikler Apt, Çankaya, Ankara; tel. (312) 4412620; fax (312) 4412600; Ambassador: MEHMET NEHROZODLU ALIEV.

Bangladesh: Cinnah Cad. 78/7–10, Çankaya, Ankara; tel. (312) 4392750; fax (312) 4392408; Ambassador: MAHBOOB ALAM.

Belarus: Han Sok 13/1–2, Gaziosmanpaşa, Ankara; tel. (312) 4463042; fax (312) 4460150; Ambassador: MIKALAY LEPESHKO.

Belgium: Mahatma Gandhi Cad. 55, Gaziosmanpaşa, Ankara; tel. (312) 4468247; fax (312) 4468251; e-mail ankara@diplobel.org; Ambassador: ALEXIS BROUHNS.

Bosnia and Herzegovina: Turan Emeksiz Sok. 3/9, Park Evleri, B Blok, Gaziosmanpaşa, Ankara; tel. (312) 4273602; fax (312) 4273604; Ambassador: NERKEZ ARIFHODŽIĆ.

Brazil: Reşit Galip Cad., İlkadım Sok 1, Ankara; tel. (312) 4481840; fax (312) 4481838; Ambassador: LUIZ ANTÔNIO JARDIM GAGLIARDI.

Bulgaria: Atatürk Bul. 124, 06680 Kavaklıdere, Ankara; tel. (312) 4671948; fax (312) 4672574; Ambassador: VIKTOR VALKOV.

Canada: Nenehatun Cad. 75, 06700 Gaziosmanpaşa, Ankara; tel. (312) 4599200; fax (312) 4599361; e-mail ankra@dfait-maeci.gc.ca; Ambassador: MICHAEL LEIR.

Chile: Reşit Galip Cad., İrfanli Sok 14/1-3, Gaziosmanpaşa, Ankara; tel. (312) 4473418; fax (312) 4474725; e-mail echile@mbox .marketweb.net.tr; Ambassador: PEDRO BARROS.

China, People's Republic: Gölgeli Sok 34, 06700 Gaziosmanpaşa, Ankara; tel. (312) 4360628; fax (312) 4464248; Ambassador: YAO KUANGYI.

Croatia: Kelebek Sok 15/A, Gaziosmanpaşa, Ankara; tel. (312) 4469460; fax (312) 4366212; Ambassador: Dr I. TOMIĆ.

Cuba: Komşu Sok 7/2, 06690 Çankaya, Ankara; tel. (312) 4394110; fax (312) 4414007; Ambassador: JORGE CASTRO BENÍTEZ.

Czech Republic: Uğur Mumcu Cad. 100/3, 06700 Gaziosmanpaşa, Ankara; tel. (312) 4461244; fax (312) 4461245; e-mail ankara@ embassy.mzv.cz; Ambassador: JOZEF BRAUN.

Denmark: Kırlangıç Sok 42, 06700 Gaziosmanpaşa, Ankara; tel. (312) 4667760; fax (312) 4684559; e-mail danemb@ada.net.tr; internet www.danimarka.org.tr; Ambassador: CHRISTIAN HOPPE.

Egypt: Atatürk Bul. 126, 06680 Kavaklıdere, Ankara; tel. (312) 4261026; fax (312) 4270099; Ambassador: MAHDI FATHALLAH.

Finland: Kader Sok 44, 06700 Gaziosmanpaşa, Ankara; tel. (312) 4261930; fax (312) 4680072; Ambassador: BJÖRN EKBLOM.

France: Paris Cad. 70, 06540 Kavaklıdere, Ankara; tel. (312) 4681154; fax (312) 4679434; e-mail ambafr@ada.net.tr; Ambassador: BERNARD GARCIA.

Georgia: Abdullah Cevdat Sok 15, Çankaya; Ankara; tel. (312) 4426508; fax (312) 4421507; Ambassador TARIEL LEBANIDZE.

Germany: Atatürk Bul. 114, 06680 Kavaklıdere, Ankara; tel. (312) 4555100; fax (312) 4266959; Ambassador: Dr RUDOLPH SCHMIDT.

Greece: Ziya ül-Rahman Cad. 9–11, 06610 Gaziosmanpaşa, Ankara; tel. (312) 4368860; fax (312) 4463191; Ambassador: YANNIS KORANDIS.

Holy See: Birlik Mah. 3, Cad. 37, PK 33, 06552 Çankaya, Ankara (Apostolic Nunciature); tel. (312) 4953514; fax (312) 4953540; e-mail vatican@tr.net; Apostolic Nuncio: Most Rev. EDMOND FARHAT, Titular Archbishop of Byblus.

Hungary: Sancak Mah. 1. Cad. 30, Yıldı, Çankaya, Ankara; tel. (312) 4422273; fax (312) 4415049; Ambassador: Dr GYÖRGY KÉRY.

India: Cinnah Cad. 77/A, 06680 Çankaya, Ankara; tel. (312) 4382195; fax (312) 4403429; Ambassador: K. GAJENDRA SINGH.

Indonesia: Abdullah Cevdet Sok 10, 06552 Çankaya, Ankara; tel. (312) 4382190; fax (312) 4382193; Ambassador: SOEMARSO H. SUEB-ROTO.

Iran: Tahran Cad. 10, Kavaklıdere, Ankara; tel. (312) 4682820; fax (312) 4682823; Ambassador: SAYED MUHAMMAD HUSEIN LAVASANI.

Iraq: Turan Emeksiz Sok 11, 06700 Gaziosmanpaşa, Ankara; tel. (312) 4687421; fax (312) 4684832; Ambassador: FAROK A. YAHYA.

Ireland: Uğur Mumcu Cad 88, MNG Binası B Blok Kat 3, Gazios-manpaşa 06700 Ankara; tel. (312) 4466172; fax (312) 4468061; e-mail ireland@superonline.com; Ambassador: SÉAN WHELAN.

Israel: Mahatma Gandhi Cad. 85, Gaziosmanpaşa, Ankara; tel. (312) 4463605; fax (312) 4261533; e-mail israel@marketweb.net.tr; Ambassador: URI BAR-NER.

Italy: Atatürk Bul. 118, Kavaklıdere, Ankara; tel. (312) 4265460; fax (312) 4265800; e-mail itaamb@superonline.com; internet www.itaamb.org.tr; Ambassador: Dr VITTORIO CLAUDIO SURDO.

Japan: Reşit Galip Cad 81, Gaziosmanpaşa, Ankara; tel. (312) 4460500; fax (312) 4372504; Ambassador: ATSUKO TOYAMA.

Jordan: Dede Korkut Sok 18, 06690 Çankaya, Ankara; tel. (312) 4402054; fax (312) 4404327; Ambassador: Dr MOUSA SULAYMAN BRAIZAT.

Kazakhstan: Ebuziya Tevfik Sok 6, Çankaya, Ankara; tel. (312) 4412301; fax (312) 4412303; e-mail kazank@ada.net.tr; Ambassador: KANAT B. SAUDABAYEV.

Korea, Republic: Cinnah Cad., Alaçam Sok 5, 06690 Çankaya, Ankara; tel. (312) 4684822; fax (312) 4682279; Ambassador: BYUNG WOO YU.

Kuwait: Reşit Galip Cad. Kelebek Sok 110, Gaziosmanpaşa, Ankara; tel. (312) 4450576; fax (312) 4466839; Ambassador: ABDULLAH AL-MURAD.

Kyrgyzstan: Boyabat Sok 24, GOP, Ankara 11; tel. (312) 4468408; fax (312) 4468413; e-mail kirgiz-o@tr-net.net.tr; Ambassador: AMANBEK KARIPKULOV.

Lebanon: Kızkulesi Sok 44, Gaziosmanpaşa, Ankara; tel. (312) 4467486; fax (312) 4461023; Ambassador: JAFFER MUAVI.

Libya: Cinnah Cad. 60, 06690 Çankaya, Ankara; tel. (312) 4381110; fax (312) 4403862; e-mail ashaabiankara@hotmail.com; Ambassador: MOHAMED A. MANGUSH.

Lithuania: Mahatma Gandhi Cad 17/8–9, Gaziosmanpaşa, Ankara; tel. (312) 4470766; fax (312) 4470663; e-mail lrambasd@ada.net.tr.

Macedonia, former Yugoslav republic: Filistin Sok 30/2, Gazios-manpaşa, Ankara; tel. (312) 4469204; fax (312) 4469206; Ambassador: TRAJAN PETROVSKI.

Malaysia: Mahatma Gandhi 58, 06700 Gaziosmanpaşa, Ankara; tel. (312) 4463547; fax (312) 4464130; Ambassador: ABDUL JALIL HARON.

Mexico: Reşit Galip Cad. Rabat Sok 16, Ankara; tel. (312) 4460335; fax (312) 4462521; e-mail enriqueb@dominet.in.com.tr; Ambassador: ENRIQUE BUJ FLORES.

Moldova: Kaptanpasa Sok 49, Ankara; tel. (312) 4465527; fax (312) 4465816; Ambassador: ION BOTNARU.

Mongolia: Koza Sok 109, Gaziosmanpaşa, Ankara; tel. (312) 4467977; fax (312) 4467791.

Morocco: Reşit Galip Cad., Rabat Sok 11, Gaziosmanpaşa, Ankara; tel. (312) 4376020; fax (312) 4471405; Ambassador: BABANA EL-ALAOUI.

Netherlands: Uğur Mumcu Cad. 16, 06700 Gaziosmanpaşa, Ankara; tel. (312) 4460470; fax (312) 4463358; e-mail nlgovank@ domi.net.tr; internet www.dutchembassy.org.tr; Ambassador: I. H. GOSSES.

New Zealand: PK 162, İran Cad. 13/4, 06700 Kavaklıdere, Ankara; tel. (312) 4679054; fax (312) 4679013; e-mail newzealand@ superonline.com; Ambassador: ALAN COOK.

Norway: Kelebek Sok 18, 06700 Gaziosmanpaşa, Ankara; tel. (312) 4478690; fax (312) 4478694; e-mail emb.ankara@mfa.no; Ambassador: FINN K. FOSTERVOLL.

Oman: Mahatma Gandhi Cad. 63, 06700 Gaziosmanpaşa, Ankara; tel. (312) 4470630; fax (312) 4470632; Ambassador: MUHAMMAD AL-VAHIBI.

Pakistan: İran Cad. 37, 06700 Gaziosmanpaşa, Ankara; tel. (312) 4271410; fax (312) 4671023; e-mail parepank@marketweb.net.tr; Ambassador: QAZI HUMAYUN.

Philippines: Mahatma Gandi Cad. 56, Gaziosmanpaşa, Ankara; tel. (312) 4465831; fax (312) 4465733; e-mail jochar@surf.net.tr; Ambassador: JOSE LINO B. GUERRERO.

Poland: Atatürk Bul. 241, 06650 Kavaklıdere, Ankara; tel. (312) 4675619; fax (312) 4678963; e-mail polamb@ada.net.tr; internet www.polonya.org.tr; Chargé d'affaires a.i.: GRZEGORZ MICHALSKI.

Portugal: Kuleli Sok 26, 06700 Gaziosmanpaşa, Ankara; tel. (312) 4461890; fax (312) 4461892; e-mail embport@domi.com.tr; Ambassador: ANTÓNIO MONTEIRO PORTUGAL.

Qatar: Karaca Sok 19, 06610 Gaziosmanpaşa, Ankara; tel. (312) 4411364; fax (312) 4411544; Ambassador: Dr HASSAN ALI HUSSEIN EN-NIMAH.

Romania: Bükreş Sok 4, 06680 Çankaya, Ankara; tel. (312) 4271243; fax (312) 4271530; e-mail romania@attglobal.net; Ambassador: GEORGE CIAMBA.

Russia: Karyağdı Sok 5, 06692 Çankaya, Ankara; tel. (312) 4392122; fax (312) 4383952; Ambassador: ALEKSANDR LEBEDEV.

Saudi Arabia: Turan Emeksiz Sok 6, Gaziosmanpaşa, Ankara; tel. (312) 4685540; fax (312) 4274886; Ambassador: NAJI MUFTI.

Slovakia: Atatürk Bul. 245, 06692 Kavaklıdere, Ankara; tel. (312) 4675075; fax (312) 4682689; e-mail slovakya@optima.net.tr; Ambassador: JAN LISUCH.

Slovenia: Küpe Sok 1/3, Gaziosmanpaşa, Ankara; tel. (312) 4056007; fax (312) 4466887.

South Africa: Filistin Cad. 27, Gaziosmanpaşa, Ankara; tel. (312) 4464056; fax (312) 4466434; e-mail saemb@ada.net.tr; internet www.southafrica.org.tr; Ambassador: THOMAS WHEELER.

Spain: Abdullah Cevdat Sok 8, 06680 Çankaya, Ankara; tel. (312) 4380392; fax (312) 4395170; Ambassador: JESÚS ATIENZA.

Sudan: Koza Sok 51, Gaziasmanpaşa, Ankara; tel. (312) 4413885; fax (312) 4413886; e-mail sudani@superonline.com.tr; Ambassador: Dr BAHA'ALDIN HANAFI.

Sweden: Katip Çelebi Sok 7, 06692 Kavaklıdere, Ankara; tel. (312) 4664558; fax (312) 4685020; Ambassador: HENRIK LILJEGREN.

Switzerland: Atatürk Bul. 247, 06692 Kavaklıdere, Ankara; tel. (312) 4675555; fax (312) 4671199; e-mail 100634.3643@ compuserve.com; Ambassador: ANDRÉ FAIVET.

Syria: Sedat Simavi Sok 40, 06680 Çankaya, Ankara; tel. (312) 4409657; fax (312) 4385609; Chargé d'affaires a.i.: MAMDOUH HAIDAR.

Tajikistan: Mahatma Gandhi Cad. 36, Gaziosmanpaşa, Ankara; tel. (312) 4461602; fax (312) 4463621; Chargé d'affaires a.i.: ROU-STAM DODCNOV.

Thailand: Çankaya Cad. Kader Sok 45/3, 06700 Gaziosmanpaşa, Ankara; tel. (312) 4673059; fax (312) 4277284; e-mail thai ank@mbex.marketweb.net.tr; Ambassador: KAROON RUECHUYOTHIN.

Tunisia: Kuleli Sok 12, 06700 Gaziosmanpaşa, Ankara; tel. (312) 4377812; fax (312) 4377100; e-mail atunisia@superonline.com; Ambassador: MOHAMED LESSIR.

'Turkish Republic of Northern Cyprus': Rabat Sok 20, 06700 Gaziosmanpaşa, Ankara; tel. (312) 4462920; fax (312) 4465238; Ambassador: NAZIF BORMAN.

Turkmenistan: Koza Sok 28, Çankaya, Ankara; tel. (312) 4417122; fax (312) 4417125; Ambassador: NUR MUHAMMAD HANAMOV.

Ukraine: Sancak Mahallesi, Sok. 206, 8470, 17 Yildyz, Çankaya, Ankara; tel. (312) 4415499; fax (312) 4406815; e-mail emb_tr@mfa.gov.ua; Ambassador: Dr IHOR DOLHOV.

United Arab Emirates: Reşit Galip Cad. Şairler Sok. 28, Gaziosmanpaşa, Ankara; tel. (312) 4476861; fax (312) 4475545; Ambassador: SALEM RASHED SALEM AL-AGROOBI.

United Kingdom: Şehit Ersan Cad. 46/A, Çankaya, Ankara; tel. (312) 4553344; fax (312) 4553351; e-mail britembank@ celik.net.tr; internet www.britishembassy.org.tr; Ambassador: Sir DAVID LOGAN.

USA: Atatürk Bul. 110, 06540 Kavaklıdere, Ankara; tel. (312) 4686110; fax (312) 4670019; internet www.usis-ankara.org.tr; Ambassador: W. ROBERT PEARSON.

Uzbekistan: Willy Brand Sok. 13, Çankaya, Ankara; tel. (312) 4413871; fax (312) 4427058; e-mail uzbekembassy@superonline .com; Ambassador: ABDULAKHAT JALILOV.

Venezuela: Cinnah Cad. 78/2, Çankaya, Ankara; tel. (312) 4387135; fax (312) 4406619; e-mail venezemb@dominet.in.com.tr; Ambassador: RAMÓN DELGADO.

Yemen: Fethiye Sok 2, 06700 Gaziosmanpaşa, Ankara; tel. (312) 4462637; fax (312) 4461778; Ambassador: MUHAMMAD ABDULLAH AL-GAIFI.

Yugoslavia: Paris Cad. 47, 06450 Kavaklıdere, Ankara; tel (312) 4260236; fax (312) 4278345; e-mail yugoslav@tr.net; Ambassador: ZORAN S. POPOVIC.

Judicial System

Until the foundation of the Turkish Republic, a large part of the Turkish civil law—the laws affecting the family, inheritance, property, obligations, etc.—was based on the Koran, and this holy law was administered by special religious (*Shari'a*) courts. The legal reform of 1926 was not only a process of secularization, but also a radical change of the legal system. The Swiss Civil Code and the Code of Obligation, the Italian Penal Code and the Neuchâtel (Cantonal) Code of Civil Procedure were adopted and modified to fit Turkish customs and traditions.

According to current Turkish law, the power of the judiciary is exercised by judicial (criminal), military and administrative courts. These courts render their verdicts in the first instance, while superior courts examine the verdict for subsequent rulings.

SUPERIOR COURTS

Constitutional Court: Consists of 11 regular and four substitute members, appointed by the President. Reviews the constitutionality of laws, at the request of the President of the Republic, parliamentary groups of the governing party or of the main opposition party, or of one-fifth of the members of the National Assembly, and sits as a high council empowered to try senior members of state. The rulings of the Constitutional Court are final. Decisions of the Court are published immediately in the Official Gazette, and shall be binding on the legislative, executive, and judicial organs of the state. **Chair:** MUSTAFA BUMIN.

Court of Appeals: The court of the last instance for reviewing the decisions and verdicts rendered by judicial courts. It has original and final jurisdiction in specific cases defined by law. Members are elected by the Supreme Council of Judges and Prosecutors. **Chair:** SAMI SELCUK.

Council of State: An administrative court of the first and last instance in matters not referred by law to other administrative courts, and an administrative court of the last instance in general. Hears and settles administrative disputes and expresses opinions on draft laws submitted by the Council of Ministers. Three-quarters of the members are appointed by the Supreme Council of Judges and Public Prosecutors, the remaining quarter is selected by the President of the Republic.

Military Court of Appeals: A court of the last instance to review decisions and verdicts rendered by military courts, and a court of first and last instance with jurisdiction over certain military persons, stipulated by law, with responsibility for the specific trials of these

persons. Members are selected by the President of the Republic from nominations made by the Military Court of Appeals.

Supreme Military Administrative Court: A military court for the judicial control of administrative acts concerning military personnel. Members are selected by the President of the Republic from nominations made by the Court.

Court of Jurisdictional Disputes: Settles disputes among judicial, administrative and military courts arising from disagreements on jurisdictional matters and verdicts.

The Court of Accounts: A court charged with the auditing of all accounts of revenue, expenditure and government property, which renders rulings related to transactions and accounts of authorized bodies on behalf of the National Assembly.

Supreme Council of Judges and Public Prosecutors: The President of the Council shall be the Minister of Justice, and the Under-Secretary to the Minister of Justice shall serve as an *ex-officio* member of the Council. Three regular and three substitute members from the Court of Appeals, together with two regular and two substitute members of the Council of State, shall be appointed to the Supreme Council by the President of the Republic for a four-year term. Decides all personnel matters relating to judges and public prosecutors.

Public Prosecutor: The law shall make provision for the tenure of public prosecutors and attorneys of the Council of State and their functions. The Chief Prosecutor of the Republic, the Chief Attorney of the Council of State and the Chief Prosecutor of the Military Court of Appeals are subject to the provisions applicable to judges of higher courts.

Military Trial: Military trials are conducted by military and disciplinary courts. These courts are entitled to try the military offences of military personnel and those offences committed against military personnel or in military areas, or offences connected with military service and duties. Military courts may try non-military persons only for military offences prescribed by special laws.

Religion

ISLAM

More than 99% of the Turkish people are Muslims. However, Turkey is a secular state. Although Islam was stated to be the official religion in the Constitution of 1924, an amendment in 1928 removed this privilege. After 1950 subsequent governments have tried to re-establish links between religion and state affairs, but secularity was protected by the revolution of 1960, the 1980 military takeover and the 1982 Constitution.

Diyanet İşleri Reisi (Head of Religious Affairs in Turkey): Prof. MUSTAFA SAIT YAZICIOĞLU.

CHRISTIANITY

The town of Antioch (now Antakya) was one of the earliest strongholds of Christianity, and by the the 4th century had become a patriarchal see. Formerly in Syria, the town was incorporated in Turkey in 1939. Constantinople (now İstanbul) was also a patriarchal see, and by the 6th century the Patriarch of Constantinople was recognized as the Ecumenical Patriarch in the East. Gradual estrangement from Rome developed, leading to the final breach between the Catholic West and the Orthodox East, usually assigned to the year 1054.

In 1986 it was estimated that there were about 100,000 Christians in Turkey.

The Orthodox Churches

Armenian Patriarchate: Ermeni Patrikliği, 34480 Kumkapı, İstanbul; tel. (212) 5170970; fax (212) 5164833; e-mail arm.pat .ist@amicus.com; f. 1461; 65,000 adherents (1999); Patriarch MESROB II.

Bulgarian Orthodox Church: Bulgar Ortodoks Kilisesi, Halâskâr Gazi Cad. 319, Şişli, İstanbul; Rev. Archimandrite GANCO ÇOBANOF.

Greek Orthodox Church: The Ecumenical Patriarchate (Rum Ortodoks Patrikhanesi), Sadrazam Ali Paşa Cad. No. 35, TR-34220 Fener-İstanbul; tel. (212) 5319671; fax (212) 5349037; e-mail www.elpidof@attglobal.net; internet www.patriarchate.org; Archbishop of Constantinople (New Rome) and Ecumenical Patriarch BARTHOLOMEOS I.

The Roman Catholic Church

At 31 December 2000 there were an estimated 31,945 adherents in the country.

Bishops' Conference: Conferenza Episcopale di Turchia, Ölçek Sok 83, Harbiye, 80230 İstanbul; tel. (212) 2480775; fax (212)

2411543; f. 1987; Pres. Mgr Franceschini Ruggero (Titular Bishop of Sicilibba).

Armenian Rite

Patriarchate of Cilicia: f. 1742; Patriarch Nerses Bedros XIX Tarmouni (resident in Beirut, Lebanon).

Archbishopric of İstanbul: Sakızağacı Cad. 31, PK 183, 80072 Beyoğlu, İstanbul; tel. (212) 2441258; fax (212) 2432364; f. 1830; Archbishop Hovhannes Tcholakian.

Byzantine Rite

Apostolic Exarchate of İstanbul: Hamalbaşı Cad. 44, PK 259, 80070 Beyoğlu, İstanbul; tel. (212) 2497104; fax (212) 2411543; f. 1861; Vicar Delegate Louis Pelâtre, Titular Bishop of Sasima.

Bulgarian Catholic Church: Bulgar Katolik Kilisesi, Eski Parmakkapı Sok. 15, Galata, İstanbul.

Chaldean Rite

Archbishopric of Diyarbakır: Hamalbaşı Cad. 48, 80070 Beyoğlu, İstanbul; tel. (212) 2440351; fax (212) 2932064; Archbishop Paul Karatas.

Latin Rite

Metropolitan See of İzmir: Church of St Polycarp, Necatibey Bul. 2, PK 267, 35212 İzmir; tel. (232) 4840531; fax (232) 4845358; e-mail padrestefano@hotmail.com; Archbishop of İzmir Giuseppe Germano Bernardini.

Apostolic Vicariate of Anatolia: Uray Cad. 85, PK 35, 33001 Mersin; tel. (324) 2320578; fax (324) 2320595; e-mail curiaves@future.net.tr; e-mail vic.ap@softhome.com; f. 1990; Vicar Apostolic Ruggero Franceschini, Titular Bishop of Sicilibba.

Apostolic Vicariate of İstanbul: Ölçek Sok 83, 80230 Harbiye, İstanbul; tel. (212) 2480775; fax (212) 2411543; f. 1742; Vicar Apostolic Louis Pelâtre, Titular Bishop of Sasima.

Maronite Rite

The Maronite Patriarch of Antioch, Cardinal Nasrallah Pierre Sfeir, is resident in Lebanon.

Melkite Rite

The Greek Melkite Patriarch of Antioch, Gregoire III Laham, is resident in Damascus, Syria.

Syrian Rite

The Syrian Catholic Patriarch of Antioch, Ignace Pierre VIII Abdel Ahad, is resident in Beirut, Lebanon.

Patriarchal Vicariate of Turkey: Sarayarkası Sok 15, PK 84, 80090 Ayazpaşa, İstanbul; tel. (212) 2432521; fax (212) 2490261; Vicar Patriarchal Rev. Yusuf Sağ.

The Anglican Communion

Within the Church of England, Turkey forms part of the diocese of Gibraltar in Europe. The Bishop is resident in England.

Archdeacon of the Aegean: Canon Jeremy Peake (resident in Vienna, Austria).

JUDAISM

In 1996 it was estimated that there were about 25,000 Jews in Turkey.

Jewish Community of Turkey: Türkiye Hahambaşılığı, Yemenıcı Sok 23, Beyoğlu, 80050 Tünel, İstanbul; tel. (212) 2938794; fax (212) 2441980; e-mail jcommnty@atlas.net.tr; Chief Rabbi David Asseo.

The Press

Almost all İstanbul papers are also printed in Ankara and İzmir on the same day, and some in Adana. Among the most serious and influential papers are the dailies *Milliyet* and *Cumhuriyet*. The weekly *Gırgır* is noted for its political satire. The most popular dailies are the İstanbul papers *Sabah, Hürriyet, Milliyet* and *Zaman; Yeni Asır*, published in İzmir, is the best-selling quality daily of the Aegean region. There are numerous provincial newspapers with limited circulation.

PRINCIPAL DAILIES

Adana

Yeni Adana: Abidinpaşa Cad. 56, Adana; tel. (322) 3599006; fax (322) 3593655; e-mail yeniadana@ttnet.net.tr; f. 1918; political; Propr Çetin Remzi Yüreğir; Chief Editor Yalçın Remzi Yüreğir; circ. 2,000.

Ankara

Ankara Ticaret: Rüzgârlı Sok O. V. Han 2/6, Ankara; tel. (312) 4182832; f. 1954; commercial; Man. Editor Nuray Tüzmen; Chief Editor Muammer Solmaz; circ. 1,351.

Belde: Rüzgarlı Gayret Sok 7/1, Ulus, Ankara; tel. (312) 3106820; f. 1968; Propr İlhan İşbilen; circ. 3,399.

Tasvir: Ulus Meydanı, Ulus İş Hanı, Kat 4, Ankara; tel. (312) 4111241; f. 1960; conservative; Editor Ender Yokdar; circ. 3,055.

Turkish Daily News: Hülya Sok 45, 06700 GOP, Ankara; tel. (312) 4475647; fax (312) 4468374; e-mail tdn-f@tr.net; internet www.turkishdailynews.com; f. 1961; English language; Publisher İlhan Çevik; Editor-in-Chief İlnur Çevik; circ. 54,500.

Türkiye Ticaret Sicili: Karanfil Sok 56, Bakanlıklar, Ankara; f. 1957; commercial; Editor Yalçın Kaya Aydos.

Vakit: Konya Yolu 8km, 68 Balgat, Ankara; tel. (312) 2877906; f. 1978; Man. Editor Nali Alan; circ. 3,384.

Yeni Tanin: Ankara; f. 1964; political; Propr Burhanettin Göğen; Man. Editor Ahmet Tekeş; circ. 3,123.

Yirmidört Saat: Gazeteciler Cemiyeti Çevre Sok 35, Çankaya, Ankara; tel. (312) 1682384; f. 1978; Propr Beyhan Cenkçi.

Eskişehir

Istikbal: Köprübaşı Değirmen Cad. 19/4, Eskişehir; tel. (222) 2318975; fax (222) 2345888; f. 1950; morning; Editor Vedat Alp.

Gaziantep

Olay (Event): Gaziantep; Man. Erol Maras.

İstanbul

Akşam: Davutpaşa Cad. 34, Zeytinburnu, İstanbul; tel. (212) 4493000; fax (212) 4819561; internet www.aksam.com.tr.

Apoyevmatini: İstiklâl Cad., Suriye Pasajı 348, Beyoğlu, İstanbul; tel. (212) 2437635; f. 1925; Greek language; Publr Dr Y. A. Adaşoğlu; Editor İstefan Papadopoulos; circ. 1,200.

Bugün: Medya Plaza Basın Ekspres Yolu, 34540 Güneşli, İstanbul; tel. (212) 5504850; fax (212) 5023340; f. 1989; Propr Önay Bilgin; circ. 184,884.

Cumhuriyet (Republic): Türkocağı Cad. 39, 34334 Cağaloğlu, İstanbul; tel. (212) 5120505; fax (212) 5138595; internet www.cumhuriyet.com.tr; f. 1924; morning; liberal; Man. Editor Hikmet Çetinkaya; circ. 75,000.

Dünya (World): Yil Mahallesi 100, 34440 Bağcilar, İstanbul; tel. (212) 6290808; fax (212) 6200313; internet www.dunya.com; f. 1952; morning; economic; Editor-in-Chief Nezih Demirkent; circ. 50,000.

Fotomaç: Medya Plaza Basın Ekspres Yolu, 34540 Güneşli, İstanbul; tel. (212) 5504900; fax (212) 5028217; f. 1991; Chief Officer İbrahim Seten; circ. 250,000.

Günaydın-Tan: Alayköşkü, Cad. Eryilmaz Sok 13, Cağaloğlu, İstanbul; tel. (212) 5120050; fax (212) 5260823; f. 1968; Editor-in-Chief Seckin Turesay.

Hürriyet: Babiali Cad. 15–17, Guneslikoy, 34540 Bakırköy, İstanbul; tel. (212) 5550050; fax (212) 5156705; internet www.hurriyet.com.tr; f. 1948; morning; independent political; Propr Aydın Doğan; Chief Editor Ertuğrul Özkök; circ. 542,797.

Meydan (Nationalism): Yüzyıl Mahallesi, Mahmutbey Viyadüğü Altı, İkitelli, 34410 Cağaloğlu, İstanbul; tel. (212) 5056111; fax (212) 5056436; f. 1990; Propr Refik Aras; Ed. Ufuk Guldemir.

Milli Gazete: Çayhane Sok 1, 34040 Topkapı, İstanbul; tel. (212) 5674775; fax (212) 5674024; f. 1973; pro-Islamic; right-wing; Editor-in-Chief Ekrem Kızıltaş; circ. 51,000.

Milliyet: Doğan Medya Center, Bağcilar, 34554 İstanbul; tel. (212) 5056111; fax (212) 5056233; internet www.milliyet.com.tr; f. 1950; morning; political; Publr Aydın Doğan; Editor-in-Chief Derya Sazak; circ. 630,000.

Nor Marmara: İstiklâl Cad., Solakzade Sok 5, PK 507, İstanbul; tel. (212) 2444736; f. 1940; Armenian language; Propr and Editor-in-Chief Rober Haddeler; Gen. Man. Ari Haddeler; circ. 2,200.

Sabah (Morning): Medya Plaza, Basın Ekspres Yolu, Günesli, İstanbul; tel. (212) 5504810; fax (212) 5028143; internet www.sabah.com.tr; Propr Dinç Bilgin; Editor Zafer Mutlu; circ. 550,000.

Tercüman: Sercekale Sok 4, 34370 Topkapı, İstanbul; tel. (212) 5017505; fax (212) 5446562; f. 1961; right-wing; Propr Sedat Colak; Chief Editor Nazif Okumus; circ. 32,869.

Türkiye (Turkey): Çatalçeşme Sok 17, 34410 Cağaloğlu, İstanbul; tel. (212) 5120050; fax (212) 5209362; e-mail bulend@ihlas.net.tr; internet www.turkiyegazetesi.com; f. 1970; Editor-in-Chief Kenan Akın; circ. 450,000.

Yeni Nesil (New Generation): Sanayi Cad., Selvi Sok 5, Yenibosna, Bakırköy, İstanbul; tel. (212) 5846261; fax (212) 5567289; f. 1970 as *Yeni Asya*; political; Editor-in-Chief UMIT SIMSEK.

Yeni Şafak: Yenidoğan Mah., Şenay Sokak 2, Kat 1, Bayrampaşa, İstanbul; tel. (212) 6122390; fax (212) 6121944; internet www .yenisafak.com.tr.

Yeniyüzyıl: Medya Plaza Basın Ekspres Yolu, 34540 Güneşli, İstanbul; tel. (212) 5028877; fax (212) 5028295; Editor KEREM ÇALI-SKAN.

Zaman (Time): Çobançeşme, Kalendar Sok 21, 34530 Yenibosna, İstanbul; tel. (212) 6393450; fax (212) 6522423; e-mail okurhatti @zaman.com.tr; internet www.zaman.com.tr; f. 1962; morning; political, independent; Man. Editor ADEM KALAC; circ. 210,000.

İzmir

Rapor: Gazi Osman Paşa Bul. 5, İzmir; tel. (232) 4254400; f. 1949; Owner DINÇ BILGIN; Man. Editor TANJU ATEŞER; circ. 9,000.

Ticaret Gazetesi: 1571 Sok 16, 35110 Çınarlı, 35110 İzmir; tel. (232) 4619642; fax (232) 4619646; e-mail ticinfo@unimedya.net.tr; internet www.ticaretgazetesi.com; f. 1942; commercial news; Editor-in-Chief AHMET SUKÜTI TÜKEL; Man. Editor CEMAL M. TÜKEL; circ. 5,009.

Yeni Asır (New Century): Yeni Asır Plaza, Ankara Cad. 3, İzmir; tel. (232) 4615000; fax (232) 4610757; e-mail yeniasır@yeniasır.com.tr; internet www.yeniasir.com.tr; f. 1895; political; Man. Editor AYDIN BILGIN; Editorial Dir HAMDI TÜRKMEN; circ. 60,000.

Konya

Yeni Konya: Mevlâna Cad. 4, Konya; tel. (332) 2112594; f. 1945; political; Man. Editor M. NACI GÜCÜYENER; Chief Editor ADIL GÜCÜYENER; monthly circ. 1,657.

Yeni Meram: Babu Aksaray Mah. Piroğlu Sok 4, Konya; tel. (332) 3512699; fax (332) 3507565; e-mail yenimeram@yenimeram.com; internet www.yenimeram.com; f. 1949; political; Propr M. YALÇIN BAHÇIVAN; Chief Editor TUFAN BAHÇIVAN; monthly circ. 44,000.

WEEKLIES
Ankara

EBA Briefing: Bestekar Sok 59/3, Kavaklıdere, Ankara; tel. (312) 4685376; fax (312) 4684114; f. 1975; publ. by Ekonomik Basın Ajansı (Economic Press Agency); political and economic survey; Publrs YAVUZ TOLUN, MELEK TOLUN.

Ekonomi ve Politika: Kavaklıdere, Ankara; f. 1966; economic and political; Publisher ZIYA TANSU.

Türkiye İktisat Gazetesi: Karanfil Sok 56, 06582 Bakanlıklar, Ankara; tel. (312) 4184321; fax (312) 4183268; f. 1953; commercial; Chief Editor MEHMET SAĞLAM; circ. 11,500.

Turkish Economic Gazette: Atatürk Bul. 149, Bakanlıklar, Ankara; tel. (312) 4177700; publ. by UCCET.

Turkish Probe: Hülya Sok. 45, 06700 GOP, Ankara; tel. (312) 4475647; fax (312) 4468374; English language; Publr A. ILHAN ÇEVIK; Editor-in-Chief ILNUR ÇEVIK; circ. 2,500.

Antalya

Pulse: PK 7, Kemer, Antalya; tel. and fax (242) 8180105; e-mail uras@ada.net.tr; internet www.turkpulse.com; politics and business; English; published online; Publr VEDAT URAS.

İstanbul

Aktüel: Medya Plaza Basın Ekspres Yolu, 34540 Güneşli, İstanbul; tel. (212) 5504870; e-mail aktuel@birnumara.com.tr; internet aktuel.birnumara.com.tr; f. 1991; Gen. Man. GÜLAY GÖKTÜRK; Man. Editor ALEV ER.

Bayrak: Çatalçeşme Sok 50/5, 34410 Cağaloğlu, İstanbul; tel. (212) 5275575; fax (212) 5268363; f. 1970; political; Editor MEHMET GÜNGÖR; circ. 10,000.

Doğan Kardes: Türbedar Sok 22, Cağaloğlu, İstanbul; f. 1945; illustrated children's magazine; Editor ŞEVKET RADO; circ. 40,000.

Elegans: Valikonağı Cad. Y.K.V. Binası K:5 D:3 Nişantaşı 80220 İstanbul; tel. (212) 2336506; fax (212) 2412738; e-mail editor@yu mak.com.tr; internet www.elegans.com.tr; f. 1985; social, economic, and global issues; Editor-in-Chief MURAT BEKDIK.

Ekonomik Panaroma: Büyükdere Cad. Ali Kaya Sok 8, 80720 Levent, İstanbul; tel. (212) 2696680; f. 1988; Gen. Man. AYDIN DEMIRER.

Ekonomist: Hürgüç Gazetecilik AŞ Hurriyet Tesisleri, Kireçocaği Mevkii, Evren Mah., Güneşli Köy, İstanbul; tel. (212) 5500050; f. 1991; Gen. Man. ADIL ÖZKOL.

Gırgır: Alayköşkü Cad., Çağaloğlu, İstanbul; tel. (212) 2285000; satirical; Propr and Editor OĞUZ ARAL; circ. 500,000.

İstanbul Ticaret: İstanbul Chamber of Commerce, Ragip Gümüş-pala Cad. 84, 34378, Eminönü, İstanbul; tel. (212) 5114150; fax (212) 5131565; f. 1958; commercial news; Publr MEHMET YILDIRIM.

Nokta: Gelisim Yayinlari, Buyukdere Cad., Ali Kaya Sok 8, 80720 Levent, İstanbul; tel. (212) 2782930; fax (212) 2794378; Editor ARDA USKAN; circ. 60,000.

Tempo: Hürgüç Gazetecilik AŞ Hürriyet Tesisleri, Güneşli, İstanbul; tel. (212) 5500081; f. 1987; Dir SEDAT SIMAVI; Gen. Man. MEHMET Y. YILMAZ.

Türk Dünyası Araştırmalar Dergisi: Hürgüç Gazetecilik AŞ Hürriyet Tesisleri, Güneşli, İstanbul; tel. (212) 5500081; Dir SEDAT SIMAVI; Gen. Man. MEHMET Y. YILMAZ.

PERIODICALS
Ankara

Azerbaycan Türk Kültür Dergisi: Vakıf İş Hanı 324, Anafartalar, Ankara; f. 1949; literary and cultural periodical of Azerbaijani Turks; Editor Dr AHMET YAŞAT.

Bayrak Dergisi: Bestckar Sok 44/5, Kavaklıdere, Ankara; f. 1964; Publr and Editor HAMI KARTAY.

Bilim ve Teknik: Bilim ve Teknik Dergisi Tübitak, Atatürk Bul. 221, Kavaklıdere, 06100 Ankara; tel. (312) 4270625; fax (312) 4276677; e-mail bteknik@tubitak.gov.tr; internet www.biltek .tubitak.gov.tr; f. 1967; monthly; science; Propr NAMIK KEMAL PAK; Man. Editor RAŞIT GÜRDILEK.

Devlet Opera ve Balesi Genel Müdürlügü: Ankara; tel. (312) 3241476; fax (312) 3107248; f. 1949; state opera and ballet; Gen. Dir. RENGIM GOKMEN.

Devlet Tiyatrosu: Devlet Tiyatrosu Um. Md., Ankara; f. 1952; art, theatre.

Eğitim ve Bilim: Kızılırmak Sok 8, Kocatepe, Ankara; tel. (312) 4174202; fax (312) 4175365; e-mail tedgmrk@superonline.com; 4313488; f. 1928; quarterly; education and science; publ. by the Turkish Educational Asscn (TED); Editors GÜLTEKIN ÖZDEMIR, Dr MARGARET SÖNMEZ; circ. 500.

Elektrik Mühendisliği Mecmuası: Gülden Sok. 2/A Güvenevler, Kavaklıdere, Ankara; f. 1954; publ. by the Chamber of Turkish Electrical Engineers; Pres. SEFA GÖMDENIZ.

Karınca: Türk Kooperatifçilik Kurumu, Mithatpaşa Cad. 38/A, 06420 Kızılay, Ankara; tel. (312) 4316125; fax (312) 4340646; f. 1934; monthly review publ. by the Turkish Co-operative Asscn; Editor Prof. Dr CELÂL ER; circ. 5,000.

Maden Tetkik Arama Genel Müdürlüğü: İnönü Bul., Ankara; f. 1935; 2 a year; publ. by Mineral Research and Exploration Institute of Turkey; English Edition *Bulletin of Mineral Research and Exploration* (2 a year).

Mimarlık (Architecture): Konur Sok 4, Kızılay, Ankara; tel. (312) 4173727; fax (312) 4180361; e-mail mimarlarodasi@superonline .com; internet www.mimarlarodasi.org.tr; f. 1963; every 2 months; publ. by the Chamber of Architects of Turkey; Editor KADRI ATABAŞ; circ. 12,500.

Mühendis ve Makina: Sümer 2 Sok 36/1-A, 06640 Demirtepe, Ankara; tel. (312) 2313159; fax (312) 2313165; f. 1957; engineering; monthly; Publr Chamber of Mechanical Engineers; Propr MEHMET SOĞANCI; Editor YÜKSEL KÖKEN; circ. 30,000.

Teknik ve Uygulama: Konur Sok 4/4, 06442 Kızılay, Ankara; tel. (312) 4182374; f. 1986; engineering; every 2 months; publ. by the Chamber of Mechanical Engineers; Propr İSMET RIZA ÇEBI; Editor UĞUR DOĞAN; circ. 3,000.

Türk Arkeoloji ve Etnoğrafya Dergisi (General Directorate of Monuments and Museums): Kültür Bakanlığı, Anıtlar ve Müzeler Genel Müdürlüğü-II. Meclis Binası Ulus, Ankara; tel. (312) 3105363; fax (312) 3111417; archaeological.

Türk Dili: Türk Dil Kurumu, Atatürk Bul. 217, 06680 Kavaklıdere, Ankara; tel. (312) 4286100; fax (312) 4285288; e-mail tdili@ tdk.gov.tr; internet www.tdk.gov.tr; f. 1951; monthly; Turkish literature and language; Editor Prof. Dr ŞÜKRÜ HALUK AKALIN.

Turkey—Economic News Digest: Karanfil Sok 56, Ankara; f. 1960; Editor-in-Chief BEHZAT TANIR; Man. Editor SADIK BALKAN.

Turkish Review: Atatürk Bul. 203, 06688 Kavaklıdere, Ankara; tel. (312) 4671180; fax (312) 4682100; f. 1985; 4 a year; cultural, social and economic; English; publ. by the Directorate General of Press and Information; Chief Officers MURAT ERSAVCI, OSMAN ÜNTÜRK, NAZAN ER, MINE CANPOLAT.

Türkiye Bankacılık: PK 121, Ankara; f. 1955; commercial; Publisher MUSTAFA ATALAY.

Türkiye Bibliyografyası: Milli Kütüphane Başkanlığı, 06490 Bahçelievler, Ankara; tel. (312) 2126200; fax (312) 2230451; e-mail katalog@mkutup.gov.tr; internet www.mkutup.gov.tr; f. 1928; monthly; Turkish national bibliography; publ. by the Turkish National Library, Cataloguing and Classification Dept; Dir AHMET ÇELENKOĞLU.

Türkiye Makaleler Bibliyografyası (Bibliography of Articles in Turkish Periodicals): Milli Kütüphane Başkanlığı, 06490 Bahçelievler, Ankara; tel. (312) 2126200; fax (312) 2230451; e-mail bibliografya@mkutup.gov.tr; internet www.mkutup.gov.tr; f. 1952; monthly; Turkish articles, bibliography; publ. by the Turkish National Library, Bibliography Preparation Dept; Dir SEMA AKINCI.

İstanbul

Arkeoloji ve Sanat Dergesi (Archaeology and Art Magazine): Hayriye Cad. 3/5 Çorlu Apt., Beyoğlu 80060, İstanbul; tel. (212) 2456838; fax (212) 2456877; e-mail info@arkeolojisanat.com; internet arkeolojisanat.com; f. 1978; bimonthly; publ. by Archaeology and Art Publications; Publr and Editor NEZIH BAŞGELEN; English-Language Submissions Editor BRIAN JOHNSON.

Bankacılar: Nıspetıye Cad. Akmerkez, B3 Blok. Kat 13–14, 80630 Etiler, İstanbul; tel. (212) 2820973; fax (212) 2820946; publ. by Banks' Asscn of Turkey; quarterly.

İstanbul Ticaret Odası Mecmuası: Gümüşpala Cad. 84, 34378 Eminönü, İstanbul; tel. (212) 5114150; fax (212) 5131565; f. 1884; quarterly; journal of the İstanbul Chamber of Commerce (ICOC); English; Editor-in-Chief CENGIZ ERSUN.

Musiki Mecmuası (Music Magazine): Sem'i Bey Sok 19/3, Yıldızbakkai, Kadiköy 81130, İstanbul; tel. (216) 3306299; e-mail etemungor@hotmail.com; f. 1948; monthly; music and musicology; Editor ETEM RUHI ÜNGÖR.

Nûr (the Light): Nuruosmaniye Cad., Sorkun Han 28/2, 34410, Cağaloğlu, İstanbul; tel. (212) 5277607; fax (212) 5208231; e-mail sozler@ihlas.net.tr; internet www.sozler.com.tr; f. 1986; religion; Publr MEHMET NURI GÜLEÇ; Editor CEMAL UŞAK; circ. 10,000.

Pirelli Mecmuası: Büyükdere Cad. 117, Gayrettepe, İstanbul; tel. (212) 2663200; fax (212) 2520718; e-mail bilyay@ibm.net; f. 1964; monthly; Publr Türk-Pirelli Lâstikleri AS; Editor UĞUR CANAL; circ. 24,500.

Présence (Aylık Dergi): Ölçek Sok 82, 80230 Harbiye, İstanbul; tel. and fax (212) 2408801; f. 1986; 10 a year; publ. by the Apostolic Vicariate of İstanbul; Gen. Man. FUAT ÇÖLLÜ.

Ruh ve Madde Dergisi (Spirit and Matter): Ruh ve Madde Publications and Health Services Co., PK 9, 80072 Beyoğlu, İstanbul; tel. (212) 2431814; fax (212) 2520718; e-mail bilyay@bilyay.org.tr; internet www.ruhvemadde.com; f. 1959; organ of the Foundation for Spreading the Knowledge to Unify Humanity; Editor HALUK HACALOGLU.

Sevgi Dünyası (World of Respect): Aydede Cad. 4/5, 80090 Taksim, İstanbul; tel. (212) 2504242; f. 1963; monthly; social, psychological and spiritual; Publr and Editor Dr REFET KAYSERILIOĞLU.

Turkey: Ihlas Holding Merkez Binasi, Ekim Cad. 29, 34520 Yenibosna, İstanbul; tel. (212) 4542530; fax (212) 4542555; e-mail img@img.com.tr; internet www.img.com.tr; f. 1982; monthly; English language, economics; Editor MEHMET SOZTUTAN; circ. 43,000.

Türkiye Turing ve Otomobil Kurumu Belleteni: Oto Sanayi Sitesi Yanı 4, Levent, İstanbul; tel. (212) 2828140; f. 1930; quarterly; publ. by the Touring and Automobile Club of Turkey; Publr Prof. NEJAT ÖLCAY; Editor ÇELIK GÜLERSOY.

Varlık: Ayberk Ap. Piyerloti Cad. 7–9, Çemberlitaş, 34400 İstanbul; tel. (212) 5226924; fax (212) 5162004; e-mail varlik@varlik.com.tr; internet www.varlik.com.tr; f. 1933; monthly; literary; Editors FILIZ NAYIR DENIZTEKIN, ENVER ERCAN; circ. 4,000.

İzmir

İzmir Ticaret Odası Dergisi: Atatürk Cad. 126, 35210 İzmir; tel. (232) 4417777; fax (232) 4837853; f. 1927; every 2 months; publ. by Chamber of Commerce of İzmir; Sec.-Gen. Prof. Dr İLTER AKAT; Man. ÜMIT ALEMDAROĞLU.

NEWS AGENCIES

Anadolu Ajansı: Mustafa Kemal Bul. 128/C, Tandogan, Ankara; tel. (312) 2317000; fax (312) 2312174; e-mail disyayin@anadolu ajansi.com.tr; internet www.anadoluajansi.com.tr; f. 1920; Chair. ALI AYDIN DUNDAR; Gen. Dir BEHIÇ EKŞI.

ANKA Ajansı: Büklüm Sok 20–22, Kavaklıdere, Ankara; tel. (312) 4172500; fax (312) 4180254; e-mail anka@ankaajansi.com.tr; Dir-Gen. MÜŞERREF HEKIMOĞLU.

Bagımsız Basın Ajansı (BBA): Saglam Fikir Sok 11, Esentepe, İstanbul; tel. (212) 2122936; fax (212) 2122940; e-mail bba@bba.tv; internet www.bba.tv; f. 1971; provides camera crewing, editing and satellite services in Turkey, the Balkans, the Middle East and the former Soviet republics to broadcasters worldwide.

EBA Ekonomik Basın Ajansı (Economic Press Agency): Bestekar Sok 59/3, Kavaklıdere, 06680 Ankara; tel. (312) 4685376; fax (312) 4684114; e-mail ebainfo@superonline.com; internet www.ebanews .com; f. 1969; private economic news service; Propr MELEK TOLUN; Editor YAVUZ TOLUN.

Hürriyet Haber Ajansı: Hürriyet Medya Towers, Güneşli, 34544 İstanbul; tel. (212) 6770365; fax (212) 6770372; e-mail ucebeci@ hurriyet.com.tr; f. 1963; Dir-Gen. UĞUR ÇEBECI.

İKA Haber Ajansı (Economic and Commercial News Agency): Atatürk Bul. 199/A-45, Kavaklıdere, Ankara; tel. (312) 1267327; f. 1954; Dir ZIYA TANSU.

Milha News Agency: Doğan Medya Center, Bağcılar, 34554 İstanbul; tel. (212) 5056111; fax (212) 5056233.

Ulusal Basın Ajansı (UBA): Meşrutiyet Cad. 5/10, Ankara; Man. Editor OĞUZ SEREN.

Foreign Bureaux

Agence France-Presse (AFP): And Sok 8/13, Çankaya, Ankara; tel. (312) 4689680; fax (312) 4689683; e-mail afpank@ada.net.tr; Correspondent FLORENCE BIEDERMANN.

Agenzia Nazionale Stampa Associata (ANSA) (Italy): Sedat Simavı Sok 30/5, Ankara; tel. (312) 4406084; fax (312) 4405029; Correspondent ROMANO DAMIANI.

Associated Press (AP) (USA): Tunus Cad. 87/3, Kavaklıdere, Ankara; tel. (312) 4282709; Correspondent EMEL ANIL.

Bulgarska Telegrafna Agentsia (BTA) (Bulgaria): Hatır Sok. 25/6, Gaziosmanpaşa, Ankara; tel. (312) 4273899; Correspondent LUBOMIR GABROVSKI.

Deutsche Presse-Agentur (dpa) (Germany): Yesil Yalı Sok, Liman Apt 6/6 Yesilköy, İstanbul; tel. (212) 5738607; Correspondent BAHADETTIN GÜNGÖR.

Informatsionnoye Telegrafnoye Agentstvo Rossii— Telegrafnoye Agentstvo Suverennykh Stran (ITAR—TASS) (Russia): Romşu Sok 7/7, Ankara; tel. (312) 4405781; fax (312) 4391955; e-mail tassankara@superonline.com; Correspondent ANDREI PALARIA.

Reuters: Emirhan Cad. 145/A, Dikilitaş Beşiktaş, 80700 İstanbul; tel. (212) 2750875; fax (212) 2116794; e-mail turkey.marketing@ reuters.com; internet www.reuters.com/turkey; Gen. Man. SAMEEH EL-DIN.

United Press International (UPI) (USA): Cağaloğlu, İstanbul; tel. (212) 2285238; Correspondent ISMET IMSET.

Xinhua (New China) News Agency (People's Republic of China): Horasan Sok 16/4, Gaziosmanpaşa, Ankara; tel. (312) 4361456; fax (312) 4465229; Correspondent WANG QIANG.

Zhongguo Xinwen She (China News Agency) (People's Republic of China): Nenehatun Cad. 88-2, Ata Apartmanı, Gaziosmanpaşa, Ankara; tel. (312) 4362261; Correspondent CHANG CHILIANG.

AFP also has representatives in İstanbul and İzmir; AP is also represented in İstanbul.

JOURNALISTS' ASSOCIATION

Gazeteciler Cemiyeti: Cağaloğlu, İstanbul; tel. (212) 5138300; fax (212) 5268046; f. 1946; Pres. NECMI TANYOLAÇ; Sec. RIDVAN YELE.

Publishers

Altın Kitaplar Yayınevi Anonim ŞTİ: Celal Ferdi Gökçay Sok, Nebioğlu Han, Kat. 1, Cağaloğlu, İstanbul; tel. (212) 5268012; fax (212) 5268011; e-mail info@altinkitaplar.com.tr; internet www .altinkitaplar.com; f. 1959; fiction, non-fiction, biography, children's books, encyclopaedias, dictionaries; Publrs FETHI UL, TURHAN BOZKURT; Chief Editor MÜRSIT UL.

Arkadas Co Ltd: Mithatpaşa Cad. 28C, 06441 Yenisehir, Ankara; tel. (312) 4344624; fax (312) 4356057; e-mail arkadas@arkadas .com.tr; internet www.arkadas.com.tr; f. 1979; fiction, educational and reference books; Dir of Publs MELTEM ÖZDEMIR.

Arkeoloji ve Sanat Yayınları (Archaeology and Art Publications): Hayriye Cad. 3/4 Çorlu Apt., Beyoğlu 80060 İstanbul; tel. (212) 2456838; fax (212) 2456877; e-mail info @arkeolojisanat.com; internet www.arkeolojisanat.com; f. 1978; classical, Byzantine and Turkish studies, art and archaeology, numismatics and ethnography books; Publr NEZIH BAŞGELEN; Senior Editor BRIAN JOHNSON.

Bilgi Yayınevi: Meşrutiyet Cad. 46/A, Yenisehir, 06420 Ankara; tel. (312) 4318122; fax (312) 4317758; e-mail info@bilgiyayinevi.com.tr; internet www.bilgiyayinevi.com.tr.

IKI NOKTA (Research Press & Publications Industry & Trade Ltd): Moda Cad. 180/10, Kadıköy, 81300 İstanbul; tel. (216) 3490141; fax (216) 3376756; e-mail info@ikinokta.com; internet www.ikinokta.com; humanities; Pres. YÜCEL YAMAN.

İletişim Yayınları: Klodfarer Cd Iletisim Han 7/2, Cağaloğlu, 34400 İstanbul; tel. (212) 5162263; fax (212) 5161258; e-mail iletisim@iletisim.com.tr; internet www.iletisim.com.tr; f. 1984; fiction, non-fiction, encyclopaedias, reference; Gen. Man. NIHAT TUNA.

Inkilap Kitabevi: Ankara Cad. 99, Sirkeci, İstanbul; tel. (212) 5140610; fax (212) 5140612; e-mail posta@inkilap.com; internet www.inkilap.com; f. 1935; general reference and fiction; Man. Dirs N. FIKRI, J. FIKRI, E. FIKRI.

Kabalci Yayınevi: Himaye-i Etfal Sok 8-B, 34410 Cağaloğlu, İstanbul; tel. (212) 5268685; fax (212) 5136305; e-mail info@ kabalci.com.tr; internet www.kabalci.com.tr; art, history, literature, social sciences; Pres. SABRI KABALCI.

Kök Yayıncılık: Konur Sok. 8/6, 06550 Kızılay, Ankara; tel. (312) 4172868; fax (312) 4315013; f. 1987; childcare, education, health; Editor OSMAN CAN.

Metis Yayınları: Ipek Sok. 9, 80060 Beyoğlu, İstanbul; tel. (212) 2454509; fax (212) 2454519; e-mail metis@turk.net; internet www.metisbooks.com; f. 1982; fiction, literature, non-fiction, social sciences; Dir SEMIH SÖKMEN.

Nurdan Yayınları Sanayi ve Ticaret Ltd Sti: Prof. Kâzim Ismail Gürkan Cad. 13, Kati 1, 34410 Cağaloğlu, İstanbul; tel. (212) 5225504; fax (212) 5125186; e-mail info@nurdan.com.tr; internet www.nurdan.com.tr; f. 1980; children's and educational; Dir NURDAN TÜZÜNER.

Parantez Yayınları AŞ: Istikal Cad. 212 Alt Kat 8, Beyoğlu, İstanbul; tel. and fax (212) 2528567; e-mail parantez@yahoo.com; internet www.planet.com.tr/bilisim/parantez; f. 1991; Publr METIN ZEYNIOĞLU.

Payel Yayınevi: Cağaloğlu Yokusu Evren han Kat 3/51, 34400 Cağaloğlu, İstanbul; tel. (212) 5284409; fax (212) 5118233; f. 1966; science, history, literature; Editor AHMET ÖZTÜRK.

Remzi Kitabevi AŞ: Selvili Mescit Sok 3, 34440 Cağaloğlu, İstanbul; tel. (212) 5139424; fax (212) 5229055; e-mail post@remzi .com.tr; internet www.remzi.com.tr; f. 1927; general and educational; Dirs EROL ERDURAN, ÖMER ERDURAN, AHMET ERDURAN.

Saray Medikal Yayın Tıc Ltd Sti: 168 Sok. 5/1, Bornova, İzmir; tel. (232) 3394969; fax (232) 3733700; e-mail eozkarahan@ novell.cs.eng.dev.edu.tr; f. 1993; medicine, social sciences.

Seckin Yayınevi: Saglik Sok. 19B, 06410 Sihhiye, Ankara; tel. (312) 4353030; fax (312) 4352472; e-mail yayin@seckin.com.tr; internet www.seckin.com.tr; f. 1959; accounting, computer science, economics, law.

Türk Dil Kurumu (Turkish Language Institute): Atatürk Bul. 217, 06680 Kavaklıdere, Ankara; tel. (312) 4268124; fax (312) 4285288; e-mail bilgi@tdk.gov.tr; internet tdk.gov.tr; f. 1932; non-fiction, research, language; Pres. Prof. Dr ŞÜKRÜ HALUK AKALIN.

Varlık Yayınları: Ayberk Ap. Piyerloti Cad. 7–9, Çemberlitaş, 34400 İstanbul; tel. (212) 5129528; fax (212) 5162004; e-mail varlik@varlik.com.tr; internet www.varlik.com.tr; f. 1946; fiction and non-fiction books; Dirs FILIZ NAYIR DENIZTEKIN, OSMAN DENIZTEKIN.

Government Publishing House

Ministry of Culture: Directorate of Publications, Necatibey Cad. 55, 06440 Kızılay, Ankara; tel. (312) 2315450; fax (312) 2315036; e-mail ydyimlar@kutuphanelergmgov.tr; internet www.kultur .gov.tr; f. 1973; Dir ALI OSMAN GÜZEL.

PUBLISHERS' ASSOCIATION

Türkiye Yayıncılar Birliği Derneği (The Publishers' Association of Turkey): Kazım Ismail Gürkan Cad. 12, Ortaklar Han Kat 3/17, Cağaloğlu, İstanbul; tel. (212) 5125602; fax (212) 5117794; e-mail info@turkyaybir.com.tr; internet www.turkyaybir.org.tr; f. 1985; Pres. ÇETIN TÜZÜNER; Sec. METIN CELAL ZEYNIOĞLU; 230 mems.

Broadcasting and Communications

TELECOMMUNICATIONS

General Directorate of Communications: 90 Str. no. 5, 06338 Ankara; tel. (312) 2128088; fax (312) 2121775; regulatory authority; Dir-Gen. HAYRETTIN SOYTAS.

Türk Telekomünikayson AŞ: Ankara; internet www.telekom .gov.tr; 51% privatized in 2001, further sale pending in late 2002; provides telecoms services throughout Turkey; Dir-Gen. İBRAHIM HAKKI ALPTÜRK.

Turkcell: Ankara; internet www.turkcell.com.tr; subsidiary of Turk Telekomunikayson AŞ; provides mobile cellular services.

BROADCASTING
Regulatory Authority

Türkiye Radyo ve Televizyon Üst Kurulu (Turkish Radio and Television Supreme Council): Bilkent Plaza B2 Blok, Bilkent, 06530 Ankara; tel. (312) 2662013; fax (312) 2661964; e-mail rtuk2@ttnet .net.tr; responsible for assignment of channels, frequencies and bands, controls transmitting facilities of radio stations and TV networks, draws up regulations on related matters, monitors broadcasting and issues warnings in case of violation of the Broadcasting law; Chair SEDAT NURI KAYIS.

Radio

Türkiye Radyo ve Televizyon Kurumu (TRT) (Turkish Radio and Television Corpn): Oran Sitesi, B Blok Kat 9, 06450 Oran, Ankara; tel. (312) 4901797; fax (312) 4905936; internet www.trt.net.tr; f. 1964; controls Turkish radio and television services incl. four national radio channels; Dir-Gen. YÜCEL YENER; Head of Radio ÇETIN TEZCAN.

Voice of Turkey; PK 333, 06443 Yenişehir, Ankara; tel. (312) 4909800; fax (312) 4909845; e-mail englishservice@tsr.gov.tr; internet www.tsr.gov.tr; foreign service of the TRT; Man. Dir DANYAL GÜRDAL.

There are also more than 50 local radio stations, an educational radio service for schools and a station run by the Turkish State Meteorological Service. The US forces have their own radio and television service.

Television

Türkiye Radyo ve Televizyon Kurumu (TRT): (Turkish Radio and Television Corpn): Oran Sitesi Turan Günes Bul. A Block Kat 6, 06450 Oran, Ankara; e-mail nilgun.artun@trt.net.tr; internet www.trt.net.tr; five national channels in 2000 and two satellite channels broadcasting to Europe; Head of Television NILGÜN ARTUN; Dir Ankara TV GÜRKAN ELÇI.

In addition there are also 11 other TV stations, including cable networks. These are; ATV (www.atv.com.tr), Cine 5 (www.cine5 .com.tr), Kanal D (www.kanald.com.tr), Kanal 6 (www.kanal6.com .tr), Kral TV (www.kraltv.com.tr), No1 TV (www.levi.com.tr/no1tv), NTV Online (www.ntv.co.tr), Show TV (www.showtv.net), Star (www.star.com.tr), TGRT (www.tgrt.com.tr), and NTVMSNBC (www.ntvmsnbc.com).

Finance

(cap. = capital; res = reserves; dep. = deposits; m. = million; brs = branches; amounts in Turkish liras unless otherwise stated)

The Central Bank of the Republic of Turkey was originally founded in 1930, and constituted in its present form in 1970. The Central Bank is the bank of issue and is also responsible for the execution of monetary and credit policies, the regulation of the foreign and domestic value of the Turkish lira jointly with the government, and the supervision of the credit system. In 1987 a decree was issued to bring the governorship of the Central Bank under direct government control.

Several banks were created by special laws to fulfil specialized services for particular industries. Etibank operates primarily in the extractive industries and electric power industries; the Ziraat Bankası makes loans for agriculture; the Emlâk Bankası participates in construction and in industrial undertakings.

The largest of the private sector Turkish banks is the Türkiye İş Bankası, which operates 854 branches.

There are several credit institutions in Turkey, including the Sınai Kalınma Bankası (Industrial Development Bank), which was founded in 1950, with the assistance of the World Bank, to encourage private investment in industry by acting as underwriter in the issue of share capital.

There are numerous co-operative organizations, including agricultural co-operatives in rural areas. There are also a number of savings institutions.

In 1990 the Turkish Government announced plans to establish a structure for offshore banking. A decree issued in October 1990 exempted foreign banks, operating in six designated free zones, from local banking obligations.

In June 1999 an independent supervisory body, the Regulatory and Supervisory Board for Banking, was established by law to monitor the financial sector. The treasury, the Ministry of Finance, the Central Bank, the state planning organization, the Capital Markets Board and the Banks' Association of Turkey were each to nominate one member to the Board for a six-year term. The Board was operational from mid-2000. Other legislation passed in June

1999 incorporated core principles of the Basle Committee on Banking Supervision relating to risk-based capital requirements, loan administration procedures, auditing practices and credit risk issues.

BANKING

Regulatory Authority

Bancacılık Düzenleme ve Denetleme Kurumu (BDDK) (Banking Regulation and Supervisory Agency): Atatürk Bulvaı 191, 06680 Kavaklidere, Ankara; tel. (312) 4556500; fax (312) 4240877; e-mail bilgi@bddk.org.tr; internet www.bddk.org.tr; Chair. ENGIN AKCAKOCA.

Central Bank

Türkiye Cumhuriyet Merkez Bankası AŞ (Central Bank of the Republic of Turkey): Head Office, İstiklal Cad. 10, 06100 Ulus, Ankara; tel. (312) 3103646; fax (312) 3107434; e-mail info@tcmb.gov.tr; internet www.tcmb.gov.tr; f. 1931; bank of issue; cap. 25,000.0m., res 2,390,298,019m., dep. 22,572,549,565m. (Dec. 2000); Gov., Pres. and Chair. SUREYYA SERDEGEÇTI; 21 brs.

State Banks

Türkiye Cumhuriyeti Ziraat Bankası (Agricultural Bank of the Republic of the Turkish Republic): Bankalar Cad. 42, 06107 Ulus, Ankara; tel. (312) 3122957; fax (312) 3101135; e-mail zbmail@ziraat bank.com.tr; internet www.ziraatbank.com.tr; f. 1863; absorbed Türkiye Emlâk Bankası AŞ (Real Estate Bank of Turkey) in July 2001; cap. 261,305,000m., res 179,789,000m., dep. 14,587,301,000m. (Dec. 2000); Chair. and Pres. SAFA OCAK; Gen. Man. Dr NIYAZI ERDOĞAN; 1,177 brs.

Türkiye Halk Bankası AŞ: Esikişehir Yolu, 2 Cad. 63, Söğütözü, 06520 Ankara; tel. (312) 2892000; fax (312) 2892378; e-mail dciner@halkbank.com.tr; internet www.halkbank.com.tr; f. 1938; absorbed Turkiye Öğretmenler Bankası TAŞ in May 1992; cap. 315,901,000m., dep. 8,894,332,000m. (Dec. 2000); Chair. A. VURAL AKIŞIK; Gen. Man. EMEL ÇABUKOĞLU; 804 brs.

Türkiye İhracat Kredi Bankası AŞ (Türk Eximbank) (Export Credit Bank of Turkey): Milli Müdafa Cad. 20, 06100 Bakanlıklar, Ankara; tel. (312) 4171300; fax (312) 4257896; e-mail ankara@eximbank.gov.tr; internet www.eximbank.gov.tr; f. 1987; fmrly Devlet Yatırım Bankası AŞ (f. 1964); cap. 529,513,000m., res 71,658,000m., total assets 4,445,213,000m. (Dec. 2001); extends credit to exporters, insures and guarantees export transactions; Chair., CEO and Gen. Man. H. AHMET KILIÇOĞLU; 2 brs.

Türkiye Vakıflar Bankası TAO (Foundation Bank of Turkey): Atatürk Bul. 207, 06683 Kavaklıdere, Ankara; tel. (312) 4557575; fax (312) 4684541; e-mail international@vakifbank.com.tr; internet www.vakifbank.com.tr; f. 1954; cap. 319,666,000m., res 959,290,000m., dep. 7,140,585,900m. (Dec. 2001); Chair. and Gen. Man. İRFAN ERCIYAS; 301 brs.

Principal Commercial Banks

Akbank TAŞ: Sabancı Center, 4 Levent, 80745 İstanbul; tel. (212) 2699822; fax (212) 2818188; internet www.akbank.com.tr; f. 1948; cap. 500,000,000m., res 57,486,000m., dep. 4,375,895m. (Dec. 2000); Chair. EROL SABANCI; CEO and Gen. Man. ZAFER KURTUL; 606 brs.

Alternatifbank AŞ: Cumhuriyet Cad. 22–24, Elmadağ, 80200 İstanbul; tel. (212) 3156500; fax (212) 2331500; e-mail sakir.somek@abank.com.tr; internet www.abank.com.tr; cap. 93,416,000m., dep. 315,879,000m. (Dec. 2000); Chair. TUNCAY ÖZILHAN; CEO ALEV GÖÇMEZ; 27 brs.

Bank Ekspres AŞ: Istınye Yokuşu, 80860 Istınye, İstanbul; tel. (212) 2852525; fax (212) 2854646; e-mail bilgi@bankekspres.com.tr; internet www.bankekspres.com.tr; f. 1992; taken into govt control in Oct. 1998; cap 30,000,000m. (Dec. 1998), dep. 164,287,000m., total assets 221,932,000m. (Sept. 1998); Chair MUHSIN YENER GÜRMEN; Pres. and CEO DOGAN TUNALI; 26 brs.

Denizbank AŞ: Büyükdere Cad 110, Esentepe, 80496 İstanbul; tel. (212) 3550800; fax (212) 2747993; e-mail info@denizbank.com; internet www.denizbank.com; f. 1997; cap. 42,960,000m., res 7,137,078m., dep. 347,310,992m. (Dec. 2000); Pres. and CEO HAKAN ATEŞ; Chair. Dr VEYSI SEVIG.

Eskişehir Bankası TAŞ (Esbank): Meşrutiyet Cad. 141, 80050 Tepebaşı, İstanbul; tel. (212) 2517270; fax (212) 2432396; e-mail webmaster@esbank.com.tr; internet www.esbank.com.tr; f. 1927; taken into govt control in Dec. 1999; cap. 45,000,000m., res 8,878,806m., dep. 443,897,966m. (Dec. 1998); Chair. MESUT EREZ; Gen. Man. CANKUT LAC; 84 brs.

Etibank AŞ: Emirhan Cad. 145, Atakule B Blok, 80700 Dikilitaş, Beşiktaş, İstanbul; tel. (212) 2368585; fax (212) 2584360; e-mail mail@etibank.com.tr; internet www.etibank.com.tr; f. 1935; privat-

ized 1998; absorbed Esbank and Interbank AS in July 2001; cap. US $70m., dep. $830m. (March 1999); Chair. DINC BILGIN; Gen. Man. ZEKI ÜNAL; 151 brs.

Finansbank AŞ: Büyükdere Cad. 129, 80300 Mecidiyeköy, İstanbul; tel. (212) 2167070; fax (212) 2161217; internet www.finansbank.com; f. 1987; sold to Banque National de Paris in mid-2001; cap. 304,759,480m., res −105,275,721m., dep. 914,927,701m. (Dec. 2000); Man. Dir Dr ÖMER ARAS; 73 brs.

İktisat Bankası TAŞ: Büyükdere Cad. 165, 80504 Esentepe, İstanbul; tel. (212) 2747111; fax (212) 2747028; internet www.iktisatbank.com.tr; f. 1927; cap. 30,000,000m.; res 419,355,000m., dep. 264,679,000m. (Dec. 1999); Chair. TEVFIK ALTINOK; Pres. DOĞAN TUNALI; 28 brs.

Kentbank AŞ: Süzer Plaza Askerocagi Cad 15, Elmadag, Şişli, 80200 İstanbul; tel. (212) 3343434; e-mail ugurg@kentbank.com.tr; internet www.kentbank.com.tr; f. 1992; cap. 68,901,000m., res −26,302m., dep 412,420,000m. (Dec. 1999); Gen. Man. and CEO VEYSEL BILEN; 74 brs.

Koçbank AŞ: Barbaros Bulvari, Morbasan Sokak, Koza Iş Merkezi-C Blok Balmumcu, İstanbul; tel. (212) 2747777; fax (212) 2672987; e-mail fim@kocbank.com.tr; internet www.kocbank.com.tr; f. 1986; cap. 283,135,000m., res −42,704,000m., dep. 2,151,501,000m. (Dec. 2000); Chair. BURHAN KARAÇAM; Gen. Man. HALIL EGÜR; brs 112.

Körfezbank: Maçka Cad. Bronz Sok, Maçka Palas, 80210 Teşuikiye, İstanbul; tel. (212) 2191111; fax (212) 2194112; e-mail cemb@korfezbank.com.tr; internet www.korfezbank.com.tr; f. 1988; cap. 324,866,000m., res −172,451,000m., dep. 689,110,000m. (Dec. 2000); Pres. and CEO HÜSNÜ AKHAN; 9 brs.

Oyak Bank AŞ: Büyükdere Cad., Ali Kaya Sok. 4, Polat Plaza A Blok, 80620 Levent, İstanbul; tel. (212) 3252929; fax (212) 2808716; e-mail gm@oyakbank.com.tr; internet www.oyakbank.com.tr; f. 1990; cap. 62,749,000m., res −5,461,586m., dep. 213,717,968m. (Dec. 2000); Chair. ALI CANER ONER; Gen. Man. A. MEHMET ÖZDENIZ; 177 brs.

Pamukbank TAŞ: Büyükdere Cad. 82, 80450 Gayrettepe, İstanbul; tel. (212) 2752424; fax (212) 2758606; internet www.pamukbank.com.tr; f. 1955; cap. 170,000,000m., res 649,967,000m., dep. 3,137,439,000m. (Dec. 2000); taken into govt control in June 2002; Chair. MEHMET EMIN KARAMEHMET; Pres. and CEO AHMET TUREL AYAYDIN; 196 brs.

Şekerbank TAŞ: Atatürk Bul. 171, 06680 Kavaklıdere, 06680 Ankara; tel. (312) 4179120; fax (312) 4178233; e-mail seker1@sekerbank.com.tr; internet www.sekerbank.com.tr; f. 1953; cap. 30,000,000m., res 654,893,000m., dep. 70,237,000m. (Dec. 2000); Chair. KAMIL ÖZDEMIR; Gen. Man. HASAN BASRI GÖKTAN; 182 brs.

Sümerbank AŞ: Buyukdere Cad. 106, Esentepe, 80280 Istanbul; tel. (212) 3364000; fax (212) 3364989; e-mail corrbanking@sumer bank.com.tr; internet www.sumerbank.com.tr; f. 1933; taken into govt control in Dec. 1999; absorbed Türkiye Tütüncüler Bankasi Yaşarbank AŞ in Jan. 2001 and Ulusal Bank TAS in Apr. 2001; sale pending in mid-2001; cap. 17,500,000., res 7,577,173m., dep. 244,406,954m. (Dec. 1998); Chair. and Gen. Man. ATILLA TAŞDEMIR; 87 brs.

Tekstilbank AŞ: Abide-i Hürriyet Cad. Geçit Sok 10, 80270 Şişli, İstanbul; tel. (212) 2241313; fax (212) 2241334; internet www.tekstilbank.com.tr; f. 1986; cap. 40,000,000m., res 22,714,000m., dep. 404,945,000m. (Dec. 2000); Chair. MUSTAFA ŞENDAĞ; CEO PULAT AKÇIN; Gen. Man. GIM GÜZELAYDINLI; 23 brs.

Toprakbank AŞ: Büyükdere Cad. 23, 80220 Şişli, İstanbul; tel. (212) 2332211; fax (212) 2255800; e-mail toprakbank@toprakbank.com.tr; internet www.toprakbank.com.tr; f. 1992; cap. 131,080,000m., res −22,754,000; dep. 736,270,000m. (Dec. 2000); Chair. and Gen. Man. CEMALETTIN HASDEMIR; 165 brs.

Türk Dış Ticaret Bankası AŞ (Turkish Foreign Trade Bank): Yıldız Posta Cad. 54, 80280 Gayrettepe, İstanbul; tel. (212) 2744280; fax (212) 2725278; internet www.disbank.com.tr; f. 1964; cap. 100,000,000m., res 186,490,395m., dep. 976,159,686m. (Dec. 2000); Chair. M. Ç. HACALOĞLU; Gen. Man. FAIK AÇIKALIN; 105 brs.

Türk Ekonomi Bankası AŞ: Meclisi Mebusan Cad. 35, 80040 Fındıklı, İstanbul; tel. (212) 2512121; fax (212) 2496568; internet www.teb.com.tr; f. 1927; fmrly Kocaeli Bankası TAŞ; cap. 69,602,000m., res 32,983,000m., dep. 662,304,000m. (Dec. 2000); Chair. YAVUZ CANEVI; Man. Dir. Dr AKIN AKBAYGIL; 10 brs.

Türk Ticaret Bankası AŞ (Turkbank): Yildiz Posta Cad. 2, 80280 Gayrettepe, İstanbul; tel. (212) 2885900; fax (212) 2886113; internet www.turkbank.com.tr; f. 1913; cap. 109,249,236m., res −104,228,585m., dep. 520,482,945m. (Dec. 1999); Chair. ERDAL ARSLAN (acting); Gen. Man. ISMET TUĞUL (acting); 258 brs.

Türkiye Garanti Bankası AŞ (Garantibank): Büyükdere Cad. 63, 80670 Maslak, İstanbul; tel. (212) 3353240; fax (212) 3353535; e-mail mutlus@garanti.com.tr; internet www.garantibank.com; f. 1946; merged with Osmanli Bankasi AŞ (f. 1863) in Dec. 2001; cap.

807,313,000m., dep. 7,394,925,000m., total assets 9,791,928,000m. (Dec. 1999); Chair. FERIT FAIK ŞAHENK; Pres., CEO, and Gen. Man. ERGUN ÖZEN; 283 brs.

Türkiye İmar Bankası TAŞ: Büyükdere Cad. Doğuş Han. 42-46, 80290 Mecidiyeköy, İstanbul; tel. (212) 2670607; fax (212) 2665514; internet www.imarbankasi.com.tr; f. 1928; cap. 140,000,000m., res 5,603,107m., dep. 1,306,751,463m. (Dec. 2001); Chair. KEMAL UZAN; Gen. Man. HILMI BAŞARAN; 171 brs.

Türkiye İş Bankası AŞ (İşbank): İş Kuleleri, Büyükdere Cad., 80620 Levent, İstanbul; tel. (212) 3160000; fax (212) 3160900; e-mail halkla.iliskiler@isbank.com.tr; internet www.isbank.com.tr; f. 1924; cap. US $44m., res US $226m., dep. US $7,029m. (Dec. 2000); Chair. Dr AHMET KIRMAN; CEO and Gen. Man. ERSIN OZINCE; 854 brs.

Yapı ve Kredi Bankası AŞ: Yapı Kredi Plaza, Blok D, Büyükdere Cad., 80620 Levent, İstanbul; tel. (212) 3397000; fax (212) 2781289; e-mail yi@ykb.com; internet www.ykb.com.tr; f. 1944; cap. 1,000,507,000m., res 611,629,000m., dep. 5,823,567,000m. (Dec. 2000); Chair. RONA YIRCALI; CEO NACI SIĞIN; 414 brs.

Development and Investment Banks

Park Yatırım Bankası AŞ: Büyükdere Cad., Meşeli Sok 9, Kat 4, 80620 Levent, İstanbul; tel. (212) 2814820; fax (212) 2780445; e-mail webmaster@parkmaster.com.tr; internet www.parkbank .com.tr; f. 1992; cap. 2,000,000m., res 374,264m., dep. 3,885,680m. (Dec. 1998); Chair. HASAN KARAMEHMET; Gen. Man. RIZA SUAT GÖKDEL.

Sınai Yatırım Bankası AŞ (Industrial Investment Bank): Büyükdere Cad. 129, Esentepe, 80300 İstanbul; tel. (212) 2131600; fax (212) 2131303; e-mail form@syb.com.tr; internet www.syb .com.tr; f. 1963; cap. 22,500,000m., res 30,166,236m., dep. 15,123,746m. (Dec. 2000); Chair. CAHIT KOCAÖMER; Pres. and Gen. Man.HALIL EROĞLU.

Türkiye Kalkınma Bankası AS (Development Bank of Turkey): İzmir Cad. 35, Kızılay, 06440 Ankara; tel. (312) 4171220; fax (312) 4183967; e-mail tkb@tkb.com.tr; internet www.tkb.com.tr; f. 1975; cap. 75,000,000m., res 37,275,314m. (Dec. 2000); Pres. and Gen. Man. TACI BAYHAN; 6 brs.

Türkiye Sınai Kalkınma Bankası AŞ (Industrial Development Bank of Turkey): Meclisi Mebusan Cad. 161, Findikli, 80040 İstanbul; tel. (212) 3345050; fax (212) 2432975; e-mail ergund@tskb.com.tr; internet www.tskb.com.tr; f. 1950; cap. 28,000,000m., res 9,215,000m. (Dec. 2000), total assets 525,824,000m. (Dec. 2001); Chair. ISMET CAHIT KOCAÖMER; Pres. and Gen. Man. HALIL EROĞLU; 2 brs.

Foreign Banks

ABN AMRO NV (Netherlands): İnönü Cad. 13/17, Taksim, Gümüş-suyu, 80090 İstanbul; tel. (212) 2938802; fax (212) 2492008; f. 1921; Gen. Man. ALBERT MEIJER; 1 br.

Arap Türk Bankası AŞ (Arab Turkish Bank): Vali Konağı Cad. 10, PK 380, 80223 Nişantaşı, İstanbul; tel. (212) 2250500; fax (212) 2250526; e-mail webmaster@arabturkbank.com; internet www .arabturkbank.com.tr; f. 1977; cap. 62,846,515m., res 3,991,596m., dep. 66,497,837m. (Dec 2000); 54% owned Arabbanks; Chair. HALUK L. SOMERSAN; Gen. Man. MUHAMMAD NAJIB H. EL-JAMAL; 6 brs.

Banca di Roma (Italy): Büyükdere Cad. Üç Yol Mevlik, Noramin Is Merkezi Kat 5, Maslak, 80670 İstanbul; tel. (212) 2859310; fax (212) 2769425; f. 1911; cap. 26,777m., res 5,868m. (Dec. 1992); Gen. Man. VALERIO BERT; 2 brs.

Bank Mellat (Iran): Büyükdere Cad. Binbirçiçek Sok 1, PK 67, 80620 Levent, İstanbul; tel. (212) 2798015; fax (212) 2846214; e-mail mellat@mellatbank.com; f. 1982; cap. and res US $2.1m., dep. US $18.4m. (Dec. 2001); Chair. MOSTAFA BEHESHTI ROUY; 3 brs.

BNP-Ak-Dresdner Bank AŞ: 1 Levent Plaza, Büyükdere Cad. 173, A Blok Kat. 8, Levent, İstanbul; tel. (212) 3395700; fax (212) 3395705; e-mail fininst@bnp-ak-dresdner.com.tr; internet www.bnp -ak-dresdner.com.tr; f. 1985; cap. 24,000,000m., res 35,493,472m., dep. 388,258,656m. (Dec. 2000); Pres. and Chair. AKIN KOZANOĞLU; Gen. Man. Dr ROLF SUTTER.

Chase Manhattan Bank (USA): Kat 11, Atakule A Blok, Emirhan Cad. 145, Beşiktaş, 80700 İstanbul; tel. (212) 2279700; fax (212) 2279729; f. 1984; Gen. Man. I ANTIKA; 1 br.

Citibank NA (USA): Büyükdere Cad. 100, Maya Akar Centre, 24th Floor, 80280 Esentepe, İstanbul; tel. (212) 2887700; fax (212) 2887760; e-mail dardo.sabarots@citicorp.com; internet www .citicorp.com; f. 1981; Gen. Man. SEBASTIAN PARADES; 3 brs.

Credit Agricole Indosuez Türk Bank AŞ (France): Büyükdere Cad. Plaza C Blok K Yapi Kredi Plaza, Levent, 80620 İstanbul; f. 1990; tel. (212) 2797070; fax (212) 2826301; e-mail indosuez@ turk.net; cap. 11,265,000m., res 2,900,000m. (Dec. 2001); Pres. HENRI GUILLEMIN; Gen. Man. GILLES SERRA.

Cyprus Turkish Co-operative Central Bank Ltd ('TRNC'): PO Box Mersin 10; tel. (392) 2273398; fax (392) 2276787; internet

www.koopbank.com; f. 1959; cap. and res 4,344,363m., dep. 117,722,019m. (Dec. 2000); Chair. AHMET ALPER; Gen. Man. Dr TUNCER ARIFOĞLU; 12 brs.

Habib Bank Ltd (Pakistan): Abide-i Hürriyet Cad. 12, PK 8, 80222 Şişli, İstanbul; tel. (212) 2460235; fax (212) 2340807; e-mail habibbank@fornet.net.tr; f. 1983; cap. 50,000m., res 2,125m., dep. 158,207m. (Dec. 1998); Gen. Man. A. B. TÜRKAY; 1 br.

HSBC Bank AŞ: Büyükdere Cad. 2, Levent, 80620 İstanbul; tel. (212) 2751900; fax (212) 2826020; internet www.hsbc.com.tr; f. 1990 as Midland Bank AŞ, name changed as above in 1999; acquired Demirbank TAŞ (f. 1953) in 2001; Chair. KEITH R. WHITSON; CEO PIRAYE Y. ANTIKA.

Kuwait Turkish Evkaf Finance House: Büyükdere Cad. 97, Mecidiyeköy, 80300 İstanbul; tel. (212) 2752435; fax (212) 2752419; e-mail kuveytturk@kuveytturk.com.tr; internet www.kuveytturk .com.tr; f. 1988; cap. 21,630,000m., res −6,315,931m., dep. 280,948,931m. (Dec. 2000); CHAIR. MUHAMMED S. AL OMAR; Gen. Man. UFUK UYAN; brs 24.

Société Générale SA (France): Akmerkez E-3, Nispetiye Cad., Blok Kat. 9, Eitler, 80600 İstanbul; tel. (212) 2821942; fax (212) 2821848; f. 1990; Gen. Man. ERIC FAIVRE; 1 br.

Turkish Bank AŞ ('TRNC'): Valikonağı Cad. 7, 80200 Nişantaşı, İstanbul; tel. (212) 2250330; fax (212) 2250353; e-mail dmm@ turkishbank.com; internet www.turkishbank.com; f. 1982; cap. 3,327,000m., res 812,448m., dep. 79,884,401m. (Dec. 2000); Chair. HAMIT B. BELLI; 13 brs.

Westdeutsche Landesbank Girozentrale (Germany): Ebulula Mardin Cad., Maya Park Towers, 80630 İstanbul; tel. (212) 3392500; fax (212) 3522258; f. 1990; Gen. Man. JOHN CHRISTOPHER DUTHIE; 2 brs.

Banking Organization

Banks' Association of Turkey: Nıspetıye Cad. Akmerkez B3 Blok. Kat 13–14, 80630 Etiler, İstanbul; tel. (212) 2820973; fax (212) 2820946; e-mail gensek@tbb.org.tr; internet www.tbb.org.tr; f. 1958; Chair. OSMAN TUNABOYLU (acting); Sec.-Gen. Dr EKREM KESKIN.

STOCK EXCHANGE

İstanbul Menkul Kıymetler Borsası (İMKB): 80860 İstinye, İstanbul; tel. (212) 2982371; fax (212) 2982500; e-mail dis@ imkb.gov.tr; internet www.ise.org; f. 1866; revived in 1986 after being dormant for about 60 years; 125 mems of stock market, 150 mems of bond and bills market; Pres. and CEO OSMAN BIRSEN; Senior Vice-Chair ARIL SEREN.

INSURANCE

Anadolu Sigorta TAŞ (Anadolu Insurance Co): Rıhtım Cad. 57, 80030 Karaköy, İstanbul; tel. (212) 2516540; fax (212) 2432690; internet www.anadolusigorta.com.tr; f. 1925; Chair. BURHAN KAR-AGÖZ; Gen. Man. AHMET YAVUZ.

Ankara Sigorta TAŞ (Ankara Insurance Co): Bankalar Cad. 80, 80020 Karaköy, İstanbul; tel. (212) 2521010; fax (212) 2524744; f. 1936; Chair. and Gen. Man. Dr SEBAHATTIN BEYAZ.

Destek Reasürans TAŞ: Abdi İpekçi Cad. 75, 80200 Maçka, İstanbul; tel. (212) 2312832; fax (212) 2415704; f. 1945; reinsurance; Pres. ONUR ÖKTEN; Gen. Man. İBRAHIM YAYCIOĞLU.

Doğan Sigorta AŞ: Serdarı Ekrem Sok 48, 80020 Kuledibi, İstanbul; tel. (212) 2516374; fax (212) 2516379; f. 1942; fire, marine, accident; Chair. T. GÜNGÖR URAS.

Güven Sigorta TAŞ: Bankalar Cad. 812, 80000 Karaköy, İstanbul; tel. (212) 2547900; fax (212) 2551360; e-mail bilgeoy@ govensigorta.com; internet www.guvensigorta.com.tr; f. 1924; all branches of insurance; Chair. and Gen. Man. HAYATI CETIN.

Hür Sigorta AŞ: Büyükdere Cad., Hür Han 15/A, 80260 Şişli, İstanbul; tel. (212) 2322010; fax (212) 2463673; Chair. BÜLENT SEM-ILER; Gen. Man. GÜNER YALÇINER.

İMTAŞ İttihadı Milli Sigorta TAŞ: Büyükdere Cad. 116, 80300 Zincirlikuyu, İstanbul; tel. (212) 2747000; fax (212) 2720837; f. 1918; Chair. Prof. Dr ASAF SAVAŞ AKAT; Gen. Man. MUSTAFA AKAN.

İstanbul Reasürans AŞ: Güneş Plaza, Büyükdere Caddesi No. 110 Kat 9, 80280 Esentepe-Şişli/İstanbul; tel. (212) 3556891; fax (212) 2173723; f. 1979; Chair. HASAN ALTANER; Gen. Man. GÜLGÜN ÜNLÜOĞLU.

Koç Allianz Sigorta AŞ: Bağlarbaşı, Kısıklı Cad. 11, 81180 Altuni-zade, İstanbul; tel. (212) 3101250; fax (212) 3101349; e-mail kocallianz@kocallianz.com.tr; f. 1923; Chair. M. RAHMI KOÇ; Gen. Man. GÜNEL BAŞER.

Milli Reasürans TAŞ: Teşvikiye Cad. 43–57, 80200 Teşvikiye, İstanbul; tel. (212) 2314730; fax (212) 2308608; e-mail info@ millire.com; internet www.millire.com; f. 1929; premium income

257,433,972m., total assets 250,959,762m. (Dec. 2001); Chair. Prof. Dr AHMET KIRMAN; Dir and Gen. Man. CAHIT NOMER.

Şeker Sigorta AŞ: Meclisi Mebusan Cad. 87, Şeker Sigorta Hanı, PK 519, 80040 Fındıklı, İstanbul; tel. (212) 2514035; fax (212) 2491046; e-mail info@sekersigorta.com.tr; internet www.sekersigorta.com.tr; f. 1954; Chair. HASAN BASRI GÖKTAN; Gen. Man. KÂMIL YIĞIT.

Tam Sigorta AŞ: Meclisi Mebusan Cad. 27/1, Setüstü, Kabataş, İstanbul; tel. (212) 2934064; fax (212) 2517181; f. 1964; all types of insurance except life; Chair. REHA BAVBEK; Gen. Man. MEHMET NEZIR UCA.

Türkiye Genel Sigorta AŞ: Meclisi Mebusan Cad. 91, 80040 Salıpazarı, İstanbul; tel. (212) 2520010; fax (212) 2499651; f. 1948; Chair. MEHMET E. KARAMEHMET; Gen. Man. HULUSI TAŞKIRAN.

Yapi Kredi Sigorta AŞ: Büyükdere Cad. 161, 80506 Zincirlikuyu, İstanbul; tel. (212) 3360606; fax (212) 2751668; e-mail kcirak@yksigorta.com.tr; internet www.yksigorta.com.tr; f. 1944; Chair. HALUK CILLOV; Gen. Man. ERHAN DUMANLI.

Trade and Industry

GOVERNMENT AGENCY

Özelleştirme İdaresi Başkanlığı (Privatization Administration): Hüseyin Rahmi Gürpınar Sok. 2, Çankaya, 06680 Ankara; tel. (312) 4411500; fax (312) 4403271; e-mail info@oib.gov.tr; internet www.oib.gov.tr; co-ordinates privatization programme; Pres. UGUR BAYAR.

DEVELOPMENT ORGANIZATIONS

Turkish Atomic Energy Authority: Prime Minister's Office, 06530 Ankara; tel. (312) 2876536; fax (312) 2871224; e-mail erdener.birol@taek.gov.tr; internet www.taek.gov.tr; f. 1956; controls the development of peaceful uses of atomic energy; 11 mems; Pres. Prof. Dr ERDENER BIROL; Sec.-Gen. EROL BARUTÇUGIL.

Turkish Electricity Authority (TEAS) (Nuclear Power Plants Department): İnönü Bul. 27, 06440 Ankara; tel. (312) 2229855; fax (312) 2127853; state enterprise to supervise the construction and operation of nuclear power plants; attached to the Ministry of Energy and Natural Resources; Head of Dept NEVZAT ŞAHIN.

CHAMBERS OF COMMERCE AND INDUSTRY

Union of Chambers of Commerce, Industry, Maritime Commerce and Commodity Exchanges of Turkey (UCCET): 149 Atatürk Bul. 149, Bakanlıklar, Ankara; tel. (312) 4184325; fax (312) 4254854; e-mail info@info.tobb.org.tr; f. 1952; represents 335 chambers and commodity exchanges; Pres. FUAT MIRE; Sec.-Gen. ŞEFIK TOKAT.

Ankara Chamber of Commerce: Ato Sarayi Eskişehir Yolu Söğütözü Mahallesi Cad. 5, Ankara; tel. (312) 2857950; fax (312) 2863446; internet www.atonet.org.

Ankara Chamber of Industry: Atatürk Bul. 193/4-5, Kavaklıdere, Ankara; tel. (312) 4171200; fax (312) 4175205; e-mail aso@aso.org.tr; internet www.aso.org.

İstanbul Chamber of Commerce (ICOC): Reşadiye Cad. 84,34378 Eminönü, İstanbul; tel (212) 5114150; fax (212) 5131565; internet www.ito.org.tr; f 1882; more than 230,000 mems; Chair. MEHMET YILDIRIM.

İstanbul Chamber of Industry: Meşrutiyet Cad. 118, Tcpcbaşi, İstanbul; tel. (212) 2522900; fax (212) 2934398; e-mail mkabasahal@iso.org.tr.

İzmir Chamber of Commerce: Atatürk Cad. 126, 35210 İzmir; tel. (232) 4417777; fax (232) 4837853; e-mail info@izto.org.tr; internet www.izto.org.tr; f. 1885; Pres. EKREM DEMIRTAŞ; Sec.-Gen. Prof. Dr İLTER AKAT.

EMPLOYERS' ASSOCIATIONS

Türk Sanayicileri ve İşadamları Derneği (TÜSİAD) (Turkish Industrialists' and Businessmen's Association): Meşrutiyet Cad. 74, 80050 Tepebaşı, İstanbul; tel. (212) 2495448; fax (212) 2491350; e-mail webmaster@tusiad.org; internet www.tusiad.org; f. 1971; 451 mems; Pres. TUNCAY ÖZILHAN; Chair. ERKUT YÜCAOĞLU; Sec.-Gen. Dr HALUK R.TÜKEL.

Türkiye İşveren Sendikaları Konfederasyonu (TİSK) (Turkish Confederation of Employers' Associations): Meşrutiyet Cad. 1/4-5, 06650 Kızılay, Ankara; tel. (312) 4183217; fax (312) 4184473; e-mail gensec@tisk.org.tr; internet www.tisk.org.tr; f. 1962; represents (on national level) 20 employers' associations with 1,200 affiliated member employers or companies; official representative in labour relations; Pres. REFIK BAYDUR; Sec.-Gen. BÜLENT PIRLER.

UTILITIES

Electricity

Türkiye Elektrik Üretim-İletim AŞ (TEAŞ-Turkish Electricity Authority): İnönü Bul. 27, 06440 Ankara; tel. (312) 2229855; fax (312) 2127853; attached to Ministry of Energy and Natural Resources.

MAJOR COMPANIES

Aksa (Akrilik Kimya San. AŞ): Miralay Şekipbey Sok. Ak Han 15–17, Kat. 5/6, Gumuşsuyu, İstanbul; tel. (212) 2514500; fax (212) 2514507; internet www.aksaakrilik.com.tr; cap. and res TL 36,372,449m., sales TL 70,882,043m. (1998); produces acrylic fibres and general chemical products; Pres. ALI DINÇKÖK; 850 employees.

Akçansa Çimento Sanayi ve Ticaret AS: Kat 7–10 Akatlar, 80630 İstanbul; tel. (212) 2841520; fax (212) 8836841; f. 1967; cap. and res TL 58,127,030m., sales TL 67,299,884m. (1998); production of cement, Chair A. ÇELENK; Gen. Man. OKAN ERDEM; 996 employees.

Aktas Elektrik: Ankara Asfalti, Kozyatagi Yan Yolu, 81090 Erenkoy, İstanbul; tel. (216) 3842960; fax (216) 3720744; f. 1975; cap. and res TL 6,594,445m., sales TL 36,306,112m. (1997); electricity generation and distribution; 450 employees.

Arçelik AŞ: 41460 Çayırova, İstanbul; tel. (212) 3954515; fax (212) 3952727; e-mail cemolp@arcelik.com.tr; turnover US $1,400m. (1998); produces domestic appliances; Pres. SUNA KIRAÇ; 3,434 employees.

Aygaz AŞ: Büyükdere Cad. Aygaz Han 145/1, 80300 Zincirikuyu, İstanbul; tel. (212) 2743000; fax (212) 2883151; cap. and res TL 14,591,692m., sales TL 59,404,791m. (1997); wholesale of liquefied petroleum gas; Chair. R. M. KOÇ; Gen. Man. ÜNAL CINGIR; 645 employees.

Beko Elektronic AŞ: Beylik Düzü Mevkii, 34901 Büyükçekmece, İstanbul; tel. (212) 8722000; fax (212) 8722013; e-mail celalk@beko.com.tr; f. 1966; produces electronic consumer goods; Pres. A. I. ÇUBUKÇU; 2,000 employees.

Boru Hatları ile Petrol Taşıma AŞ (BOTAŞ): 4 Cad. Bilkent Plaza A-2 Blok, 06530 Bilkent, Ankara; tel. (312) 2972000; fax (312) 2660734; e-mail mailbox@botas.gov.tr; internet www.botas.gov.tr; state-owned, but partial privatization pending in 2001; operator of petroleum and gas pipelines; Dir-Gen. GÖKHAN BILDACI; 1,900 employees.

Brisa—Bridgestone Sabanci Tire Manufacturing and Trading Co Inc: Sabanci Centre Kule 2, Kat. 7-9, 80745 4 Levent, İstanbul; tel. (212) 2780021; fax (212) 2811681; cap. and res TL 29,567,151m., sales TL 52,933,997m. (1997); manufactures tyres; Pres. SAKIP SABANCI; 1,628 employees.

Çolakoğlu Metalurji AŞ: Kemeraltı Cad. Karaköy Ticaret Merkezi 24, Kat. 6, Karaköy, İstanbul; tel. (212) 2520000; fax (212) 2495588; e-mail colmet@superonline.com; manufactures steel wire rod in coils, reinforcing bars, billets; Pres. MEHMET ÇOLAKOĞLU; 1,110 employees.

Çukurova Çelik Endüstrisi AŞ: Meclisi Mebusan Cad. Salıpazarı Yokuşu 1, 80040 Salıpazarı, İstanbul; tel. (212) 2513737; fax (212) 2511286; f. 1978; manufactures steel billets, reinforcing bars and wire rods; Gen. Man. MEHMET KUZEYLI; 796 employees.

Çukurova Elektrik AŞ: Seyhan Baraji, PK 239, 01322 Adana; tel. (322) 2350681; fax (322) 2350256; f. 1952; cap. and res TL 18,119,352m., sales TL 53,427,087m. (1997); manufactures electrical appliances; Chair. CEM CENGIZ UZAN; Gen. Man. ERKAN MANAVOĞLU; 715 employees.

Ege Biracilik ve Malt Sanayii AŞ: Kemelpasa Cad. 51, 35070 Işıkkent, İzmir; tel. (232) 4362200; fax (232) 4361940; e-mail efes01@egenet.com.tr; cap. and res TL 4,256,582m., sales TL 42,322,590m. (1998); production of food and beverages; Pres. KAMIL YAZICI; Gen. Man. SEMIH MAVIŞ.

Enka Holding Investment Co Inc: Balmumcu Mahallesi, Bestekar Şevki Bey Cad., ENKA II Binası, Beşiktaş, İstanbul; tel. (212) 2740970; fax (212) 2728869; internet www.enka.com; f. 1957; contracting, industry, trading, tourism, banking and engineering with 44 specialized subsidiaries; Co-founder and Chair. ŞARIK TARA; Man. Dir VAHITTIN GÜLERYÜZ; 18,000 employees.

Erciyas Biracilik ve Malt Sanayii AŞ: Eski Londra Asalti, 22 Haznedar Mevkli, PK 1, 34592 Bahcelievler, İstanbul; tel. (212) 6429100; fax (212) 5566204; f 1966; cap. and res TL 9,127,804m., sales TL 20,032,519m. (1997); food and beverages; Chair. KAMIL YAZICI; Gen. Man. ERDAL TUNCA; 413 employees.

Ereğli Demir ve Çelik Fabrikalari TAŞ (Erdemir): Uzunkum 7, Karadeniz, 67330 Ereğli; tel. (372) 3232500; fax (372) 3163969; internet www.erdemir.com.tr; f. 1960; partially privatized in mid-2002; cap. and res TL 239,410,049m. (1998); manufactures steel and iron products; Pres. YALÇIN AMANVERMEZ; 7,002 employees.

Ford Otomotiv San AŞ: Ankara Asfaltı 4 KM, Uzunçayır Mevkii, 81302 Kadıköy, İstanbul; tel. (216) 3267060; fax (216) 3390861; f. 1959; cap. and res TL 73,106,250m., sales TL 461,164,836m. (2001); manufactures passenger cars, trucks and engines; Chair. RAMI KOÇ; 4,300 employees.

Goodyear Lastikleri TAŞ: Büyükdere Cad. Maslak Meydanı 41, Maslak İş Merkezi, Levent, İstanbul; tel. (212) 2852168; fax (212) 2766225; e-mail nedret_turkkusu@goodyear.com; manufactures tyres; Pres. W. HOWE; 2,000 employees.

Hyder Mühendislik Müşavirlik Ltd Şirketi: Eston Gamli Evler, Mavi Gam Apt. Kat. 17, Daire 71 İstanbul; tel. (216) 4691261; fax (216) 4191263; e-mail ceting@ultratv.net; internet www.hydertur.com; transport and environmental infrastructure, industrial facilities.

ISDEMIR (İskenderun Iron and Steel Works Co): İsdemir General Directorate, 31319 İskenderun; tel. (326) 7583000; fax (326) 7551184; e-mailisdemir@bi.net.tr; internet www.isdemir.com.tr; f. 1975; state-owned, but earmarked for privatization; manufactures steel and iron; Chair. and Dir-Gen. A. NECIP EBEGIL; 11,000 employees.

İzmir Pamuk Mensucatı TAŞ: 1201 Sok. 11, PK 106, Halkapınar, İzmir; tel. (232) 4339810; fax (232) 4339782; f. 1914; manufacturers and exporters of cotton goods; Chief Exec. CAN TANCI.

Koç Holding AŞ: Nakkaştepe Aziz Bey Sok. 1, 80207 Kuzguncuk, İstanbul; tel. (216) 3414650; fax (216) 3431944; internet www.koc.com.tr; f. 1926; cap. and res TL 47,739,745m.; construction and engineering with 116 specialized subsidiaries; manufacturers of consumer durables; Chair. RAHMI KOÇ; Vice-Pres. NECATI ARIKAN; 35,530 employees.

Kordsa Sabancı Dupont Endüstriyel İplik ve Kord Bezi Sanayi ve Ticaret AŞ: Sabancı Centre Kule 2, Kat. 5, 80745 4 Levent, İstanbul; tel. (212) 2810012; fax (212) 2810027; e-mail kordsainfo@kordsa.com.tr; internet www.kordsa.com.tr; manufactures cord fabric; part of Haci Omer Sabanci Holding; Pres. GÜLER SABANCI; 971 employees.

Mercedes-Benz Türk AŞ: Burmalı Çeşme Sok. Askeri Fırın Yolu 2, 34022 Davutpaşa, İstanbul; tel. (212) 5670409; fax (212) 5770402; manufactures civil and military vehicles; Pres. EIKE LIPPOLD; 2,300 employees.

Metaş (İzmir Metalurji Fabrikası TAŞ): Kemalpaşa Cad. Işıkkent Girişi, 35070 İzmir; f. 1958; tel. (232) 4334010; fax (232) 4334041; construction group; steel producers and exporters; Chair. ATTILA ŞNOL; Gen. Man. NIYAZI ALTAN.

Migros Türk TAŞ: Caferaga Mah., Damga Sok. 23/25, 81300 Kadıköy, İstanbul; tel. (216) 4181910; fax (216) 3491293; f. 1954; cap. and res TL 5,740,606m., sales TL 71,518,266m. (1997); retail, marketing and distribution; Chair. INAN KIRAÇ; Gen. Man. BÜLEND ÖZAYDINKLI; 5,355 employees.

Oyak—Renault Otomobil Fab. AŞ: Emirhan Cad. Barbaros Plaza Blok C 145, Kat. 6, 80700 Dikilitaş, İstanbul; tel. (212) 2270000; fax (212) 2594545; manufactures automobiles; Pres. ALI BOZER; 4,500 employees.

Paşabahçe Cam San. ve Tic. AŞ: Ankara Asfalti İçmeler Mevkii 81700 Tuzla, İstanbul; tel. (212) 3503286; fax (212) 3504256; e-mail ctokel@sisecam.com.tr; f. 1934; glass tableware and gift exporters; Gen. Man. GULSIM ANKI; 15,000 employees.

Petkim Petrokimya Holding AŞ: PK 12, 35801 Aliaga, İzmit; tel. (262) 6163240; fax (262) 6161248; state-owned, but earmarked for privatization in late 2002; produces petrochemicals; Pres. MEHMET YILMAZ; 6,000 employees.

Petrol Ofisi (POAS): Ayazağa Büyükdere Cad. 37, 80670 Maslak, İstanbul; tel. (212) 3291500; fax (212) 3291898; internet www.petrol-ofisi.com.tr; f. 1941; 74.2% privatized, sale of remaining govt-owned share of 25.8% pending in 2002; cap. and res TL 37,022,425m., sales TL 571,168,495m. (1997); distribution of petroleum and petroleum products, Gen. Man. M. KOREL AYTAC; 6,369 employees.

Sasa Sun'i ve Sentetik Elyaf San. AŞ: Sabancı Centre Kule 2, 80745 4 Levent, İstanbul; tel. (212) 2785088; fax (212) 2786201; e-mail sasa@sasa.com.tr; internet www.sasa.com.tr; f. 1966; cap. and res TL 29,191,760m., sales TL 58,222,515m. (1997); manufactures synthetic yarns and fibres; Pres. ÖMER SABANCI; 4,000 employees.

Söktaş: Cumhuriyet Mah. Karasuluk Mevkii, PK 32, 09201 Söke; tel. (256) 5182255; fax (256) 5184539, e-mail soktas@soktas.com.tr; f. 1971; cap. and res TL 5,744,834m., sales 13,861,647m. (1998); manufacturers and exporters of raw and finished cotton fabric and thread; Gen. Man. MUHARREM KAYHAN; 1,400 employees.

Tat Konserve Sanayii A Ş: İstiklal Cad. 347/4, 80050 Beyoğlu, İstanbul; tel. (212) 2523600; fax (212) 2455133; f. 1967; cap. and res TL 5,979,036m., sales 10,828,555m. (1997); tomato products; Chair. S. KIRAC; Gen. Man. NAMIK BAYRAKTAROĞLU; 2,335 employees.

TDÇ Isl. Genel Müd Karabük D.C. Mües. Müd: Karabük; tel. (372) 4182001; fax (372) 4182110; manufactures iron, steel, coke and napthalene; Vice-Pres. COŞKUN AKTEM; 9,000 employees.

Tekfen Insaat ve Tesisat AŞ: Tekfen Sitesi, 80600 Etiler, İstanbul; tel. (212) 2576100; fax (212) 2659869; e-mail tekfen@tekfen.com.tr; internet www.tekfen.com.tr; construction; Pres. ERHAN ONER; 2,650 employees.

Tofaş (Türk Otomobil Fab. AŞ): Büyükdere Cad. 145/5, 80300 Zincirlikuyu, İstanbul; tel. (212) 2753390; fax (212) 2753988; internet www.tofas.com.tr; f. 1968; cap. and res TL 39,309,124m.; sales TL 167,625,459m. (1968); manufactures automobiles and automobile parts; Pres. SUNA KIRAÇ; 3,911 employees.

Trakya Cam Sanayii AŞ: Barbaros Bul. 125, Bsiktas, İstanbul; tel. (288) 4362240; fax (288) 4173126; cap. and res TL 23,923,530m., sales TL 30,768,200m. (1997); production of glass; Chief Exec. ALPASLAN AKINCI; 1,552 employees.

Türk Pirellı Lastikleri AŞ: Büyükdere Cad. 117, Gayrettepe, İstanbul; tel. (212) 2752280; fax (212) 2726077; internet www.pirelli.com; manufactures and distributes tyres; Pres. BÜLENT ECZAC-IBASI; 1,250 employees.

Turkish Petroleum Corpn (TPAO): Mustafa Kemal Mah. II Cad. 86, 06520 Bakanlıklar, Ankara; tel. (312) 2869100; fax (312) 2869000; e-mail tpaocc@petrol.tpao.gov.tr; internet www.tpao.gov.tr; f. 1954; Turkey's largest State Economic Enterprise; explores for, drills and produces crude petroleum and natural gas; Chair. and Gen. Man. OSMAN DEMIRAĞ; 3,912 employees.

Türkiye Petrol Rafinerileri AŞ (TÜPRAŞ): PK 211–212, 41002 Körfez, İzmit; tel. (262) 5270600; fax (262) 5270658; f. 1983; 31.5% privatized in 2000, plan for Government share to be reduced to under 50% confirmed in July 2002; cap. and res TL 17,344,002m., sales TL 87,583,604m. (1998); refining of crude oil; Gen. Man. M. ERGUN KURAN; 4,480 employees.

Türkiye Şeker Fabrikaları AŞ: Mithatpaşa Cad. 14, 06100 Yenişehir, Ankara; tel. (312) 4359815; fax (312) 4317225; produces sugar and manufactures machinery used in sugar production; Gen. Dir Dr SELIM YÜCEL; 14,677 employees.

Tütün, Tütün Mamülleri, Tuz ve Alkol İşletmeleri Genel Müdürlüğü (TEKEL): Atatürk Bul. 27, Unkapanı, İstanbul; tel. (212) 5321078; fax (212) 5320527; e-mail makbay@tekel.gov.tr; internet www.tekel.gov.tr; f. 1862; sales TL 2,116,395,993m. (2000); production and distribution of tobacco products, alcohol and salt; Pres. MEHMET AKBAY; 36,578 employees.

Uzel Makine Sanayi AŞ: Topçular, Kışla Cad. 5, 34147 Rami, İstanbul; tel. (212) 5670841; fax (212) 5764595; f. 1953; cap. and res TL 17,344,002m., sales TL 87,583,604m. (1998); manufactures tractors, wheels, brakes and automobile springs; Pres. AHMET UZEL; 1,767 employees.

Vestel: Ambarli, Petrol Ofisi Dolum Tesisleri Yolu, 34840 Avcilar, İstanbul; tel. (212) 6907600; fax (212) 6907664; internet www.vestel.com.tr; manufacturing; Chair AHMET NAZIF ZORLU; CEO Dr METIN CAĞLAR.

Zihni Group: Rıhtım Cad. Zihni Han 28/30, 80030 Tophane, İstanbul; tel. (212) 2511515; fax (212) 2435325; e-mail info@zihni.com.tr; internet www.zihni.com.tr; f. 1930; integrated sea and land transport company specializing in imports and exports.

TRADE UNIONS

Confederations

DİSK (Türkiye Devrimci İşçi Sendikaları Konfederasyonu) (Confederation of Progressive Trade Unions of Turkey): Cad. Abide-I Hürriyet 117, Kat. 5-6-7, Şişli, İstanbul; tel. (212) 2910005; fax (212) 2342075; e-mail disk-f@tr.net.tr; internet www.disk.org.tr; f. 1967; member of ICFTU, ETUC and TUAC; 26 affiliated unions; Pres. SÜLEYMAN ÇELEBI; Sec.-Gen. MURAT TOKMAK.

Türk-İş (Türkiye İşçi Sendikaları Konfederasyonu Genel Başkanlığı) (Confederation of Turkish Trade Unions): Bayındır Sok 10, Yenişehir, Ankara; tel. (312) 4333125; fax (312) 4336809; e-mail turkis@turkis.org.tr; f. 1952; member of ICFTU, ETUC, ICFTU-APRO and OECD/TUAC; 32 national unions and federations with 1.7m. mems; Pres. BAYRAM MERAL; Gen. Sec. HÜSEYIN KARAKOÇ.

Principal DİSK Trade Unions

Bank-Sen (Türkiye Devrimci Banka ve Sigorta İşçileri Sendikası): Nakiye Elgun Sok 117, Şişli, İstanbul; tel. (212) 2321000; fax (212) 2311911; Pres. VEYSEL KALAY; 15,000 mems.

Basın-İş (Türkiye Basın İşçileri Sendikası) (Press Workers' Union): İstanbul; f. 1964; Pres. YILMAZ ÖZDEMIR; Gen. Sec. DERVIŞ BOYOĞLU; 5,000 mems.

Birlesik Metal-İs (Birlesik Metal İşçileri Sendikası): Tünel Yolu Cad. 2, 81110 Bostancı, Kadıköy, İstanbul; tel. (216) 3622091;

fax (216) 3736502; e-mail info@birlesikmetal.com; Gen. Sec. MUZAFFER ŞAHIN; 58,800 mems.

Demiryol-İş (Türkiye Demiryolu İşçileri Sendikası) (Railway Workers): Necatibey Cad., Sezenler Sok 5, 06430 Yenişehir, Ankara; tel. (312) 2318029; fax (312) 2318032; internet www.sendikaonline.com; f. 1952; Pres. ERGÜN ATALAY; Gen. Sec. HÜSEYIN DEMIR; 25,000 mems.

Deri-İş (Türkiye Deri İşçileri Sendikası) (Leather Industry): Ahmet Kutsi Tecer Cad. 12/6, Merter, İstanbul; tel. (212) 5048083; fax (212) 5061079; f. 1948; Pres. NUSRETTIN YILMAZ; Gen. Sec. ALI SEL; 11,000 mems.

Dev. Sağlık-İş (Türkiye Devrimci Sağlık İşçileri Sendikası) (Health Employees): İstanbul; f. 1961; Pres. DOĞAN HALIS; Gen. Sec. SABRI TANYERI; 15,000 mems.

Genel-İş (Türkiye Genel Hizmet İşçileri Sendikası) (Municipal Workers): Çankırı Cad. 28, Kat 5-9, Ulus, Ankara; tel. (312) 3091547; fax (312) 3091046; f. 1983; Pres. ISMAIL HAKKI ÖNAL; Gen. Sec. ATILA ÖNGEL; 50,000 mems.

Gıda-İş (Türkiye Gıda Sanayii İşçileri Sendikası): Ahmet Kutsi Tecer Cad. 12/3, 34010 Merter, İstanbul; tel. (212) 5751540; fax (212) 5753099; Pres. MEHMET MUHLACI; Gen. Sec. YURDAKUL GÖZDE; 31,000 mems.

Koop-İş (Türkiye Kooperatif ve Büro İşçileri Sendikası) (Cooperative and Office Workers): İzmir Cad. Fevzi Çakmak Sok 15/11-12, Yenişehir, Ankara; tel. (312) 4300855; f. 1964; Pres. AHMET BALAMAN; Gen. Sec. AHMET GÜVEN; 29,000 mems.

Limter-İş (Liman, Tersane Gemi Yapım Onarım İşçileri Sendikası) (Harbour, Shipyard, Ship Building and Repairs): İcmeler Tren İstasyonu Yanı 12/1, Tuzla, İstanbul; tel. (216) 3955271; f. 1947; Pres. EMIR BABAKUŞ; Gen. Sec. ASKER ŞIT; 7,000 mems.

Nakliyat-İş (Nakliye İşçileri Sendikası) (Transportation Workers): Guraba Hüseyin Ağa Mah. Kakmacı Sok 10, Daire 11 Vatan Cad. Tranvay, Durağı Karşısı, Aksaray, İstanbul; tel. (212) 5332069; Pres. ŞEMSI ERCAN; Gen. Sec. NEDIM FIRAT.

OLEYİS (Otel, Lokanta, Eğlence Yerleri İşçileri Sendikası) (Hotel, Restaurant and Places of Entertainment Workers' Union): Necatibey Cad. 96/1-3, Kızılay, Ankara; tel. (312) 2311845; fax (312) 2311846; e-mail oleysis@oleyis.org.tr; internet www.oleyis.org.tr; f. 1947; Pres. ENVER ÖKTEM; Gen. Sec. ETHEM KAYNAR OLGUNER; 4,000 mems.

Petkim-İş (Türkiye Petrol, Kimya ve Lastik Sanayii İşçileri Sendikası): İzmir Cad., Fevzi Çakmak Sok. 7/13, Ankara; tel. (312) 2300861; fax (312) 2299429; Pres. MUSTAFA KARADAYI; 18,000 mems.

Sosyal-İş (Türkiye Sosyal Sigortalar, Eğitim, Büro, Ticaret Kooperatif Banka ve Güzel Sanatlar İşçileri Sendikası) (Banking, Insurance and Trading): Necatibey Cad. Sezenler Sok. Lozan Apt. 2/14, Yenişehir, Ankara; tel. (312) 2318178; fax (312) 2294638; Pres. ÖZCAN KESGEÇ; Gen. Sec. H. BEDRI DOĞANAY; 31,000 mems.

Tekstil İşçileri Sendikası: Ahmet Kutsi Tecer Cad. 12/1, Merter, İstanbul; tel. (212) 6429742; fax (212) 5044887; Pres. RIDVAN BUDAK; 45,000 mems.

Tümka-İş (Türkiye Tüm Kağıt Selüloz Sanayii İşçileri Sendikası): Gündoğdu Sok 19/3, Merter, İstanbul; tel. (212) 5750843; Pres. SABRI KAPLAN; 3,000 mems.

Other Principal Trade Unions

Denizciler (Türkiye Denizciler Sendikası) (Seamen): Rıhtım Cad., Denizciler Sok. 7, Tophane, İstanbul; tel. (212) 2929081; fax (212) 2933938; e-mail selimataergin@hotmail.com; f. 1959; Pres. TURHAN UZUN; Gen. Sec. ÇEMIL YENIAY; 4,272 mems.

Fındık-İş (Fiskobirlik İşçileri Sendikası) (Hazel-nut producers): Giresun; Pres. AKÇIN KOÇ; Gen. Sec. ERSAIT ŞEN.

Hava-İş (Türkiye Sivil Havacılık Sendikası) (Civil Aviation): İncirli Cad., Volkan Apt., 68/1 Bakırköy, İstanbul; tel. (212) 6601495; fax (212) 5719051; e-mail havais@mail.turk.net; Pres. ATILAY AYÇIN; Gen. Sec. MUSTAFA YAĞCI; 7,000 mems.

Liman-İş (Türkiye Liman ve Kara Tahmil İşçileri Sendikası) (Longshoremen): Necatibey Cad., Sezenler Sok 4, Kat. 5, Sıhhıye, Ankara; tel. (312) 2317418; fax (312) 2302484; e-mail liman-is@tr-net.net.tr; f. 1963; Pres. RAIF KILIÇ; Gen. Sec. ERDING ÇAKIR; 5,000 mems.

Şeker-İş (Türkiye Şeker Sanayii İşçileri Sendikası) (Sugar Industry): Karanfil Sok 59, Bakanlıklar, Ankara; tel. (312) 4184273; fax (312) 4259258; f. 1952; Pres. ÖMER ÇELIK; Gen. Sec. FETHI TEKIN; 35,000 mems.

Tarım-İş (Türkiye Orman, Topraksu, Tarım ve Tarım Sanayii İşçileri Sendikası) (Forestry, Agriculture and Agricultural Industry Workers): Bankacı Sok 10, 06700 Kocatepe, Ankara; tel. (312) 4190456; fax (312) 4193113; e-mail tarim-is@tr.net; f. 1961; Pres. BEDRETTIN KAYKAÇ; Gen. Sec. İ. SABRI KESKIN; 40,500 mems.

Tekgıda-İş (Türkiye Tütün, Müskirat Gıda ve Yardımcı İşçileri Sendikası) (Tobacco, Drink, Food and Allied Workers' Union of Turkey): 4 Levent Konaklar Sok, İstanbul; tel. (212) 2644996; fax (212) 2789534; e-mail bilgi@tekgida.org.tr; internet www.tekgida.org.tr; f. 1952; Pres. HÜSEYIN KARAKOÇ; Gen. Sec. MUSTAFA TÜRKEL; 176,000 mems.

Teksif (Türkiye Tekstil, Örme ve Giyim Sanayii İşçileri Sendikası) (Textile, Knitting and Clothing): Ziya Gökalp Cad. Aydoğmuş Sok 1, Kurtuluş, Ankara; tel. (312) 4312170; fax (312) 4357826; f. 1951; Pres. ZEKI POLAT; 80,000 mems.

Tez-Koop-İş (Türkiye, Ticaret, Kooperatif, Eğitim, Büro ve Güzel Sanatlar İşçileri Sendikası) (Commercial and Clerical Employees): Üç Yıldız Cad. 29, Subayevleri, Ayınlıkevler, 06130 Ankara; tel. (312) 3183979; fax (312) 3183988; f. 1962; Pres. SADIK ÖZBEN; Gen. Sec. H. FARAK ÜSTÜN; 30,000 mems.

Türk Harb-İş (Türkiye Harb Sanayii ve Yardımcı İşkolları İşçileri Sendikası) (Defence Industry and Allied Workers): İnkılap Sok 20, Kızılay, Ankara; tel. (312) 4175097; fax (312) 4171364; f. 1956; Pres. İZZET CETIN; Gen. Sec. NURI AYCICER; 35,000 mems.

Türk-Metal (Türkiye Metal, Çelik, Mühimmat, Makina ve Metalden Mamul, Eşya ve Oto, Montaj ve Yardımcı İşçileri Sendikası) (Auto, Metal and Allied Workers): Kızılırmak Mah., Adalararası Sok. 3, Eskişehir Yolu 1 km, 06560 Söğütözü, Ankara; tel. (312) 2844010; fax (312) 2844018; e-mail metal@superonline.com; f. 1963; Pres. MUSTAFA ÖZBEK; Vice-Pres. ÖZBEK KARAKUS; 247,000 mems.

Yol-İş (Türkiye Yol, Yapı ve İnşaat İşçileri Sendikası) (Road, Construction and Building Workers' Unions): Sümer 1 Sok 18, Kızıloy, Ankara; tel. (312) 2324687; fax (312) 2324810; f. 1963; Pres. BAYRAM MERAL; Gen. Sec. TEVFIK ÖZÇELIK; 170,000 mems.

Transport

RAILWAYS

The total length of the railways operated within the national frontiers is 10,922 km (2000), of which 8,671 km are main lines, 2,122 km are electrified, and 2,505 km are signalled. A new direct rail link between Ankara and İstanbul, cutting the distance from 577 km to 416 km, is expected to be completed by 2000. There are direct rail links with Bulgaria to Iran and Syria. A new line connecting Turkey with Georgia is expected to be completed by 2000. İstanbul operates an 18-km light railway system, and opened its first metro line in September 2000. Both systems are being expanded. Ankara and İzmir both operate metro railways.

Türkiye Cumhuriyeti Devlet Demiryolları İşletmesi Genel Müdürlüğü (TCDD) (Turkish Republic State Railways): Talatpaşa Bul., 06330 Gar, Ankara; tel. (312) 3090515; fax (312) 3123215; e-mail tcddapk@superonline.com; internet tcdd.gov.tr; f. 1924; operates all railways and connecting ports (see below) of the State Railway Administration, which acquired the status of a state economic enterprise in 1953, and a state economic establishment in 1984; 479 main-line diesel locomotives, 78 main-line electric locomotives, 1,031 passenger coaches and 16,624 freight wagons; Chair. of Board and Gen. Dir VEDAT BILGIN.

ROADS

At 1 January 2000, 1,746 km of motorways were open to traffic and nearly 511 km of motorways were under construction; the total length of the highway network was 62,672 km and the total length of village roads was 319,218 km. In 1999 there were 59,894 km of roads in the maintenance programme.

Bayındırlık ve İskan Bakanlığı, Karayolları Genel Müdürlüğü—KGM (General Directorate of Highways): Yücetepe, 06100 Ankara; tel. (312) 4252343; fax (312) 4186996; e-mail info@kgm.gov.tr; internet www.kgm.gov.tr; f. 1950; Dir-Gen. DINÇER YIĞIT.

SHIPPING

At the end of 2001 Turkey's merchant fleet comprised 1,146 vessels and had an aggregate displacement of 5,896,708m. grt.

General-purpose public ports are operated by two state economic enterprises. The ports of Bandırma, Derince, Haydarpaşa (İstanbul), İskenderun, İzmir, Mersin and Samsun, all of which are connected to the railway network, are operated by Turkish State Railways (TCDD) (see above), while the smaller ports of Antalya, Giresun, Hopa, Tekirdağ and Trabzon are operated by the Turkish Maritime Organization (TDI).

Turkish Maritime Organization (TDI): Genel Müdürlüğü, Karaköy, İstanbul; tel. (212) 2515000; fax (212) 2495391.

Port of Bandırma: TCDD Liman İşletme Müdürlüğü, Bandırma; tel. (266) 2234966; fax (266) 2236011; Port Man. OKKES DEMIREL; Harbour Master RUSEN OKAN.

Port of Derince: TCDD Liman İşletme Müdürlüğü, Derince; Port Man. ALI ARIF AYTAÇ; Harbour Master HAYDAR DOĞAN.

Port of Haydarpaşa (İstanbul): TCDD Liman İşletme Müdürlüğü Haydarpaşa, İstanbul; tel. (212) 3379988; fax (212) 3451705; Port Man. NEDIM OZCAN; Harbour Master İSMAIL SAFAER.

Port of İskenderun: TCDD Liman İşletme Müdürlüğü, İskenderun; tel. (326) 6140047; fax (326) 6132424; Port Man. HILMI SÖNMEZ; Harbour Master İSHAK ÖZDEMIR.

Port of İzmir: TCDD Liman İşletme Müdürlüğü, İzmir; tel. (232) 4632252; fax (232) 4632248; Port Man. GÜNGÖR ERKAYA; Harbour Master MEHMET ONGEL.

Port of Mersin: TCDD Liman İşletme Müdürlüğü, Mersin; tel. (324) 2330687; fax (324) 2311350; Port Man. FAHRI SAYILI; Harbour Master RACI TARHUSOĞLU.

Port of Samsun: TCDD Liman İşletme Müdürlüğü, Samsun; tel. (362) 4357616; fax (362) 4317849; Port Man. SAFFET YAMAK; Harbour Master Capt. ARIF H. UZUNOĞLU.

Private Companies

Deniz Nakliyatı TAŞ (Turkish Cargo Lines): Meclisi Mebusan Cad. 151, 80040 Fındıklı, İstanbul; tel. (212) 2522600; fax (212) 2512696; f. 1955; privatization pending 1997; regular liner services between Turkey and Mediterranean, Adriatic, Red Sea, US Atlantic, and Indian and Far East ports; Gen. Man. NEVZAT BILICAN; 17 general cargo ships, 4 roll-on, roll-off, 8 bulk/ore carriers.

İstanbul Deniz Otobusleri Sanayi ve Ticaret AŞ: POB 81110, Bostanci, İstanbul; tel. (216) 3628013; fax (216) 3620443; ferry company; Chair. MUSTAFA ACIKALIN; Man. Dir BINALI YILDIRIM; 23 vessels.

Kiran Shipping Group of Companies: Fahrettin Kerim Gorkay Cad. 22, Denizcilar İş Merkezi B Blok Kat 2, 81190 Altunizade, İstanbul; tel. (216) 3916150; fax (216) 3916168; Chair. TURGUT KIRAN; Man. Dir TAMER KIRAN; 16 vessels.

Ozsay Seatransportation Co Inc: Iskele Sok Ozsay Bldg 44 Kat 3, 81320 Kadikoy, İstanbul; tel. (216) 3451827; fax (216) 3469532; Pres. IHSAN KALKAVAN; Man. Dir OZNUR CALIS; 10 vessels.

Pinat Gida Sanayi ve Ticaret AŞ: Pak Ismerkezi Prof. Dr Bulent Tarcan Sok 5/3, 80290 Gayrettepe, İstanbul; tel. (212) 2747533; fax (212) 2750317; e-mail pinat@pinat.com.tr; Pres. ENGIN PAK; Man. Dir ALPAY CITAK; 7 vessels.

T.D.I Sehir Hatlan İşletmesi: Mayis Han, Bahcekapi 27, 34420 Sirkeci, İstanbul; tel. (212) 5264020; fax (212) 2495391; 14 vessels.

Türkiye Denizcilik İşletmeleri Denizyolları İşletmesi Mudurlugu (TDI): Meclisi Mebusan Cad. 18, 80040 Salıpazarı, İstanbul; tel. (212) 2521700; fax (212) 2515767; internet www.tdi.com.tr; ferry company; Chair. ERKAN ARIKAN; Man. Dir Kadir Kurtoğlu; 5 vessels.

Vakif Deniz Finansal Kiralama AŞ: Rihtim Cad. 201 Tahir Han kat 6, PK 853, 80040 Karaköy, İstanbul; 15 vessels.

Yardimci Shipping Group of Companies: Aydintepe Mah. Tersaneler Cad. 50 Sok 7, 81700 Tuzla, İstanbul; tel. (216) 4938000; fax (216) 4928080; e-mail moliva@turk.net; Chair. KEMAL YARDIMCI; Man. Dir HUSEYIN YARDIMCI; 11 vessels.

Shipping Associations

SS Gemi Armatörleri Motorlu Taşıyıcılar Kooperatifi (Turkish Shipowners' Asscn): Meclisi Mebusan Cad., Dursun Han, Kat. 7, No 89, Salıpazarı İstanbul; tel. (212) 2510945; fax (212) 2492786; f. 1960; Pres. GÜNDÜZ KAPTANOĞLU; Man. Dir A. GÖKSU; 699 vessels; 5,509,112 dwt (1993).

Türk Armatörler Birliği (Turkish Shipowners' Union): Meclisi Mebusan Cad. Dursun Han, Kat. 7 No. 89, Salıpazarı, İstanbul; tel. (212) 2453022; fax (212) 2492786; f. 1972; 460 mems; Pres. ŞADAN KALKAVAN; Co-ordinator HAKAN ÜNSALER; 8,780,436 dwt (1997).

Vapur Donatanları ve Acenteleri Derneği (Turkish Shipowners' and Shipping Agents' Asscn): Mumhane Cad. Emek İş Hanı Kat. 3 No. 31, Karaköy, İstanbul; tel. (212) 2443294; fax (212) 2432865; e-mail vapurd@vda.org.tr; internet www.vda.org.tr; f. 1902; worldwide agency service; Pres. Capt. M. LEBLEBICIOĞLU; Man. Dir C. KAPLAN.

CIVIL AVIATION

There are airports for scheduled international and internal flights at Atatürk (İstanbul), Esenboğa (Ankara), Adnan Menderes (İzmir and Trabzon), while international charter flights are handled by Adana, Dalaman and Antalya. Fifteen other airports handle internal flights only.

Alfa Hava Yolları AŞ (Alfa Airlines Inc.): Fatih Cad. 21, Günesli, 34540 İstanbul; tel. (212) 6303348; fax (212) 6575869; e-mail hkeser@airalfa.com.tr; internet www.airalfa.com.tr; f. 1992; charter services to Europe; Man. Dir. NECMETTIN METINER.

Eurosun Airlines (ESN): Fener Mah, Bul. Ozgurluk, Melda 2/7, Antalya 07134; tel. (242) 3235060; fax (242) 3241252; f. 1999, as Air Rose, assumed present name in June 2000; charter flights to European destinations; Man. Dir. MESUT SENER.

İstanbul Hava Yolları AŞ (Istanbul Airlines): Firuzköy Yolu, Bağlar İçi Mevzii 26, 34850 Avcılar, İstanbul; tel. (212) 5092100; fax (212) 5938742; internet www.istanbulairlines.com.tr; f. 1985; charter services from major Turkish cities to European destinations; Gen. Man. SAFI ERGIN.

Onur Air Taşımacılık AŞ: Senlik Mahallesi, Gatal Sok. 3, 34810 Florya, İstanbul; tel. (212) 6632300; fax (212) 6632319; internet www.onurair.de; f. 1992; regional and domestic passenger and cargo charter services; Chair. CANKUT BAGANA.

Pegasus Hava Taşımacılığı AŞ: İstasyon Cad. 24, Kat. 1, 34800 Yeşilyurt, İstanbul; tel. (212) 6632934; fax (212) 5739627; internet www.pgtair.com; f. 1989; charter services; Chair. S. ALTUN; Gen. Man. L. J. LOWTH.

Sky Airlines: Jalan Cad., Suite 41, Baranaklar-Anatalya 07100; tel. (242) 3237576; fax (242) 3237567; f. 2000; regional passenger charter flights; CEO TALHA GORGULU.

Sonmez Hava Yolları: 9 km Yakova Yolu, PK 189, Bursa; tel. (224) 2610440; fax (224) 2465445; f. 1984; scheduled flights and dedicated freight; Chair. ALI OSMAN SÖNMEZ.

SunExpress: Fener Mahallesi Sinanoghu Cad., Oktay Airport, PK 28, 07100 Antalya; tel. (242) 3234047; fax (242) 3234057; e-mail sunexpress@condor.de; internet www.sunexpress.de; f. 1990; charter and scheduled passenger and freight; serves European destinations; Man. Dir PAUL SCHWAIGER.

Top Air: Atatürk Havalimani, E-Kapısı, Polis Okulu Arkası, 34640 Sefaköy, İstanbul; tel. (212) 5416040; fax (212) 5985060; e-mail info@topair.com.tr; internet www.topair.com.tr; f. 1990; charter and scheduled flights for tour operators.

Türk Hava Yolları AO (THY) (Turkish Airlines Inc.): Genel Müdürlük Binas, Atatürk Hava Limanı, 34830 Yeşilköy, İstanbul; tel. (212) 6636300; fax (212) 6634744; e-mail turkishairlines@thy.com; internet www.turkishairlines.com; f. 1933; majority state-owned, but earmarked 51% privatization in 2001; extensive internal network and scheduled and charter flights to destinations in the Middle East, Africa, the Far East, Central Asia, the USA and Europe; Pres. and CEO YUSUF BOLAYIRLI.

Tourism

Visitors to Turkey are attracted by the climate, fine beaches and ancient monuments. Tourism is being stimulated by the Government, and the industry is expanding rapidly. In 2001 provisional receipts from tourism were a record US $8,090m., compared with $7,636m. in 2000, while the number of tourists increased from 7.5m. in 1999 to 10.4m. in 2000 and 11.6m. in 2001.

Ministry of Tourism: İsmet İnönü Bul. 5, Bahçelievler, Ankara; tel. (312) 2128300; fax (312) 2128391; e-mail tbtgmos@tr-net.net.tr; internet www.tourism.gov.tr; f 1963; Dir-Gen. of Establishments YENAL ÜNSEL; Dir-Gen. of Information MUSTAFA SYAHHAN; Dir-Gen. of Investments HALUK AKAR.

Defence

Chief of General Staff: Gen. HILMI OZKOK.

Ground Forces Commander: Gen. TAHIR AYTAC YALMAN.

Navy Commander: Vice-Adm. BULENT ALPKAYA.

Air Force Commander: Gen. CUMHUR ASPARAK.

Gendarmerie Commander: Gen. SENER ERUYGUR.

Defence Budget (2001): estimated at TL 5,875,000,000m.

Military Service: 18 months.

Total Armed Forces (August 2001): 515,100 (including an estimated 391,000 conscripts): army 402,000 men, navy 53,000 men, air force 60,100 men.

Paramilitary Forces: 152,200: 150,000 gendarmerie, 2,200 coastguard.

Education

When the Turkish Republic was formed, the Ministry of Education became the sole authority in educational matters, replacing the dual system of religious schools and other schools. One of the main obstacles to literacy was the Arabic script, which required years of study before proficiency could be attained. In 1928, therefore, a Turkish alphabet was introduced, using Latin characters. At the same time the literary language was simplified, and purged of some of its foreign elements. In 2001 estimated Government expenditure on education amounted to TL 7,497,000,000m., or 9.4% of total budget expenditure.

PEOPLE'S SCHOOLS

This change of script created a need for schools in which reading and writing in the new alphabet could be taught to adults. Temporary institutions, known as 'people's schools' or 'national schools', were established throughout Turkey. During the winter months these schools gave instruction in reading and writing and other basic subjects to men and women beyond the normal school age. Between 1928 and 1935 about 2m. people received certificates of proficiency. Since then, education in Turkey has made significant advances.

PRIMARY EDUCATION

Primary education may be preceded by an optional pre-school establishment which serves 3–6 year old children. In 1998 there were 6,868 such schools, with 10,979 teachers. In the same year 200,000 children were enrolled at pre-schools.

According to the 'Basic Law of National Education', the education of children between the ages of six and 14 is compulsory. Basic Education Institutes are organized to provide eight years of education and are essentially a combination of primary school and middle school. Primary education, therefore, comprises two cycles, the first consisting of five years at primary school and the second of three years at middle school. The transition from a system of primary and middle schools to that of a single eight-year basic education school was introduced throughout the country from September 1997.

Primary education is now entirely free, and co-education is the accepted basis for universal education. The number of schools has risen from 12,511 in 1950 to 45,112 in 1998, and the number of teachers from 27,144 to some 317,795. In 1998 some 9.6m. children were enrolled at primary schools. In 1996 enrolment at primary schools included 99% of children in the relevant age-group (males 102%; females 96%).

SECONDARY EDUCATION

The reorganization of the system of secondary education began in the early 1920s. This period of education lasts for a minimum of three years after primary education and provides for students who intend to proceed to higher educational institutions. Secondary education encompasses general high schools, or lycées, and vocational and technical high schools. In addition, since 1992/93, 'open' high schools have provided secondary education opportunities to young working people through the media and other new technologies.

The lycée takes the student up to the age of 17 or 18 years, and those who wish to proceed to an institute of higher education must pass the state matriculation examination. The study of a modern language (English, French or German) is compulsory. In 1998 there were 5,965 such schools, with 145,903 teachers. In the same year 200,000. children were enrolled in secondary education. In 1996 enrolment at secondary schools included 51% of children in the relevant age-group (males 59%; females 43%).

INFORMAL EDUCATION

Informal education comprises teaching and guidance outside of the formal education system, which aims to ensure all citizens obtain reading, writing and other essential skills. Since 1932, reading-rooms have been established in every town and many villages. They are centres of social and cultural life and provide evening classes. Their libraries, meeting-halls and recreational facilities are open to all. In the towns there are also evening trade schools which provide technical training for adults, and travelling courses are sent out to the villages. Other informal education is provided for children of secondary school age through apprenticeship training.

HIGHER EDUCATION

Higher educational institutions in Turkey were founded, and are administered, by the State. These institutions include the universities and the higher professional schools. In 1998 there were 1,222 institutes of higher education (including universities, teacher training colleges and other technical and vocational institutions). The number of students enrolled at universities and equivalent institutes of higher education was 1.5m. in that academic year.

TECHNICAL EDUCATION

The problem of technical education began to be seriously considered first in 1926; specialists were invited from Europe and America, and a plan was drawn up for perfecting the existing vocational schools and for founding new ones to meet the economic needs of each region. In 1995/96 there were 3,678 technical and vocational lycées, giving training to some 1.3m. students. Plans were made for evening schools to train craftsmen and for the founding of teachers' technical training high schools. In addition, there are colleges for commerce, tourism, communication, local administration and secretarial skills.

TEACHERS' TRAINING

In Turkey teachers' training colleges are divided into three basic categories: two-year teacher-training institutes which train teachers for primary schools, three-year teacher-training institutes which train teachers for middle schools and higher teacher-training schools offering a four-year course qualifying teachers for the lycées. Students of the higher teacher-training schools take specialist subject courses in the relevant university faculty and their pedagogy courses in the higher teacher-training schools.

Bibliography

GENERAL

Abramowitz, Morton (Ed.). *Turkey's Transformation and the American Policy*. Washington, DC, Century Foundation Press, 2001.

Allen, H. E. *The Turkish Transformation*. Chicago, 1935.

Armstrong, H. C. *Grey Wolf: Mustafa Kemal: an Intimate Study of a Dictator*. London, 1937.

Auboyneau & Fevret. *Essai de bibliographie pour l'Empire Ottomane*. Paris, 1911.

Bahrampour, Firouz. *Turkey, Political and Social Transformation*. New York, Gaus, 1967.

Barkley, Henri J. (Ed.) *Reluctant Neighbour: Turkey's Role in the Middle East*. US Institute of Peace Press, 1997.

Bean, G. E. *Aegean Turkey*. London, Benn, 1966.

Turkey's Southern Shore. London, Benn, 1968.

Berkes, Niyazi. *The Development of Secularism in Turkey*. London, C. Hurst and Co, 1999 (2nd edition; first published 1964).

Bisbee, Eleanor. *The New Turks*. London, Greenwood Press.

The People of Turkey. New York, 1946.

Cohn, Edwin J. *Turkish Economic, Social and Political Change*. New York, Praeger, 1970.

Cooke, Hedley V. *Challenge and Response in the Middle East: The Quest for Prosperity, 1919–1951*. New York, 1952.

Cornell Erik. *Turkey in the 21st Century: Opportunities, Challenges, Threats*. Richmond, Curzon Press, 1999.

Dodd, Clement H. *Politics and Government in Turkey*. Manchester University Press, 1969.

Edgecumbe, Sir C. N. E. *Turkey in Europe*. New York, Barnes and Noble, 1965.

Eren, Nuri. *Turkey Today and Tomorrow*. New York, 1964.

Frey, F. W. *The Turkish Political Elite*. Cambridge, MA, MIT Press, 1965.

Gökalp, Ziya. *Turkish Nationalism and Western Civilisation*. London, 1960.

Hale, William. *Aspects of Modern Turkey*. Epping, Bowker Publishing, 1977.

Harris, George S. *The Origins of Communism in Turkey*. Stanford, CA, Hoover Institution, 1967.

Heyd, Uriel. *Foundations of Turkish Nationalism: the Life and Teachings of Ziya Gökalp*. London, Luzac and Harvill Press, 1950.

Language Reform in Modern Turkey. Jerusalem, 1954.

Hotham, David. *The Turks*. London, John Murray, 1972.

Houston, Christopher. *Islam, Kurds and the Turkish Nation State*. Oxford, Berg, 2001.

Howe, Marvine. *Turkey Today: A Nation Divided over Islam's Revival*. Boulder, CO, Westview Press, 2000.

Ibrahim, Ferhad, and Gurbey, Gulistan (Eds). *The Kurdish Conflict in Turkey: Obstacles and Chances for Peace and Democracy*. Palgrave, 2001.

Jenkins, Gareth. *Context and Circumstance: The Turkish Military and Politics*. Oxford, Oxford University Press, 2001.

Kamer, Heinz. *A Changing Turkey: Challenges to Europe and the US*. Washington, DC, Brookings Institution Press, 2000.

Karpat, Kemal. *Turkey's Politics, The Transition to a Multi-Party System*. Princeton, 1959.

Kazamias, A. M. *Education and the Quest for Modernity in Turkey*. London, Allen and Unwin, 1967.

Keyder, Caglar. *State and Class in Turkey*. London, Verso, 1987.

Kinnane, Dirk. *The Kurds and Kurdistan*. Oxford, 1965.

Kinross, Lord. *Within the Taurus*. London, 1954.

    Europa Minor: Journeys in Coastal Turkey. London, 1956.

    Turkey. London, 1960.

    Atatürk. London, Weidenfeld & Nicolson, 1964.

Kişlali, Ahmet Taner. *Forces politiques dans la Turquie moderne*. Ankara, 1967.

Koray, Enver. *Türkiye Tarih Yayınları Bibliografyası 1729–1950; A Bibliography of Historical Works on Turkey*. Ankara, 1952.

Kürger, K. *Die Türkei*. Berlin, 1951.

Lamb, Harold. *Suleiman the Magnificent: Sultan of the East*. New York, 1951.

Lewis, Bernard. *The Emergence of Modern Turkey*. London and New York, Oxford University Press, revised edn 1970.

Lewis, G. L. *Turkey* ('Nations of the Modern World' series). London, 1955; 3rd edn, New York, Praeger, 1965.

Liel, Alon. *Turkey in the Middle East: Oil, Islam and Politics*. Boulder, CO, Lynne Reiner, 2001.

Linke, L. *Allah Dethroned*. London, 1937.

Lukach (Luke), Sir Harry Charles. *The Old Turkey and the New*. London, Geoffrey Bles, 1955.

Mellaart, James. *Earliest Civilizations of the Near East*. London, Thames and Hudson, 1965.

    Çatal Hüyük. London, Thames and Hudson, 1967.

Newman, Bernard. *Turkish Crossroads*. London, 1951.

    Turkey and the Turks. London, Herbert Jenkins, 1968.

Orga, Irfan and Margarete. *Atatürk*. London, 1962.

Ozeygin, Gul. *Untidy Gender: Domestic Service in Turkey (Women in the Political Economy)*. Philadelphia, PA, Temple University Press, 2000.

Pettifer, James. *The Turkish Labyrinth: Atatürk and the New Islam*. London, Viking, 1997.

Plate, Herbert. *Das Land der Türken*. Graz, Wien, Köln, Verlag Styria, 1957.

Pope, Nicole and Hugh. *Turkey Unveiled: Atatürk and After*. London, John Murray, 1997.

Poulton, Hugh. *Top Hat, Grey Wolf and Crescent: Turkish nationalism and the Turkish Republic*. London, Hurst and Co, 1997.Ringman, Jonathan, Hutchings, Roger, and Simpson, John. *Atatürk's Children: Turkey and the Kurds*. Herndon, VA, Cassell Academic, 2001.

Robins, Philip. *Turkish Foreign Policy since the Cold War*. London, C. Hurst, 2002.

Salter, Cedric. *Introducing Turkey*. London, Methuen, 1961.

Shankland, David. *Islam and Society in Turkey*. Huntingdon, Eothen Press, 1999.

    (Ed.) *The Turkish Republic at Seventy-Five Years*. Huntingdon, Eothen Press, 1999.

Stark, Freya. *Ionia*. London, 1954.

    Lycian Shore. London, 1951.

    Riding to the Tigris. London, 1956.

Steinhaus, Kurt. *Soziologie der turkischen Revolution*. Frankfurt, 1969.

Szyliowicz, Joseph S. *Political Change in Rural Turkey: Erdemli*. The Hague, Mouton, 1966.

Toynbee, A. J. *The Western Question in Greece and Turkey*. London, Constable, 1923.

Toynbee, A. J., and Kirkwood, D. P. *Turkey*. London, 1926.

    Lycian Shore. London, 1956.

Tunaya, T. Z. *Atatürk, the Revolutionary Movement and Atatürkism*. Istanbul, Baha, 1964.

Vali, Ferenc A. *Bridge across the Bosphorus: the Foreign Policy of Turkey*. Johns Hopkins Press, 1970.

Ward, Barbara. *Turkey*. Oxford, 1942.

Ward, Robert E., and Rustow, Oankwart A. (Eds). *Political Modernizations in Japan and Turkey*. Princeton University Press, 1964.

Webster, D. E. *The Turkey of Atatürk: Social Progress in the Turkish Reformation*. Philadelphia, 1939.

Winrow, Gareth. *Turkey and the Caucasus: Domestic Interests and Security Concerns*. London, Royal Institute of International Affairs, 2001.

Yalman, A. E. *Turkey in my Time*. University of Oklahoma Press, 1956.

HISTORY

Ahmad, Feroz. *The Young Turks*. Oxford University Press, 1969.

    The Turkish Experiment in Democracy 1950–1975. London, Hurst, for Royal Institute of International Affairs, 1977.

Alderson, A. D. *The Structure of the Ottoman Dynasty*. Oxford, 1956.

Allen, W. E. D., and Muratoff, P. *Caucasian Battlefields: A History of the Wars on the Turco-Caucasian Border, 1828–1921*. Cambridge, 1953.

Barchard, David. *Turkey and the West*. London, Routledge and Kegan Paul, 1985.

Birand, Mehmet Ali. *The Generals' Coup in Turkey: An Inside Story of September 12, 1980*. Oxford, Brassey's, 1987.

Boghossian, Roupen. *Le Conflit Turco-Arménien*. Beirut, Altapress, 1987.

Cahen, Claude. *Pre-Ottoman Turkey*. London, Sidgwick & Jackson, 1968.

Cassels, Lavender. *The Struggle for the Ottoman Empire, 1717–1740*. London, John Murray, 1967.

Coles, Paul. *The Ottoman Impact on Europe*. London, Thames and Hudson, 1968; New York, Brace and World, 1968.

Davison, Roderic H. (updated by Dodd, Clement H.). *Turkey. A short History*. Huntingdon, Eothen Press, 3rd edn, 1998.

Geyikdagi, Mehmet Yaşar. *Political Parties in Turkey: The Role of Islam*. New York, Praeger, 1986.

Goodwin, Jason. *Lords of the Horizons: A History of the Ottoman Empire*. New York, Henry Holt, 1999.

Gurney, O. R. *The Hittites*. London, 1952.

Hale, William. *The Political and Economic Development of Modern Turkey*. London, Croom Helm, 1981.

Kasaba, Resat. *The Ottoman Empire and the World Economy: The Nineteenth Century*. Albany, NY, State University of New York Press, 1989.

Kazancigil, Ali, and Ozbudun, Ergun (Eds). *Atatürk: Founder of a Modern State*. London, Hurst, 1981.

Kedourie, Elie. *England and the Middle East: The Destruction of the Ottoman Empire, 1914–1921*. Cambridge, 1956.

Kinzer, Stephen. *Crescent and Star: Turkey between Two Worlds*. New York, Farar, Straus and Giroux, 2001.

Kushner, David. *The Rise of Turkish Nationalism*. London, Frank Cass, 1980.

Landau, Jacob M. *Pan-Turkism: A Study in Irredentism*. London, Hurst, 1981.

Lewis, Bernard. *Istanbul and the Civilization of the Ottoman Empire*. University of Oklahoma Press, 1963.

Lewis, Geoffrey. *La Turquie, le déclin de l'Empire, les réformes d'Ataturk, la République moderne*. Belgium, Verviers, 1968.

Liddell, Robert. *Byzantium and Istanbul*. London, 1956.

Lloyd, Seton. *Early Anatolia*. London, 1956.

Mango, Andrew. *Atatürk*. London, John Murray, 1999.

Mantran, Robert. *Histoire de la Turquie*. Paris, 1952.

McDowall, David. *A Modern History of the Kurds*. London, I. B. Tauris & Co Ltd, 1996.

Miller, William. *The Ottoman Empire and its Successors, 1801–1927*. Cambridge, 1934.

Moorehead, A. *Gallipoli*. London, Wordsworth Editions, 1997.

Olsson, Tord, Ozdalga, Elisabeth, and Raudvere, Catharina (Eds). *Alevi Identity*. Richmond, Curzon Press, 1999.

Ostrogorsky, G. *History of the Byzantine State*. Oxford, 1956.

Pfeffermann, Hans. *Die Zusammenarbeit der Renaissance Päpste mit den Türken*. Winterthur, 1946.

Price, M. Philips. *A History of Turkey: From Empire to Republic*. London, 1956.

Quataert, Donald. *The Ottoman Empire, 1700–1922*. Cambridge University Press, 2000.

Ramsaur, E. E. *The Young Turks and the Revolution of 1908*. Princeton University Press, 1957.

Rice, David Talbot. *Art of the Byzantine Era*. New York, Praeger, 1963.

    Byzantine Art. London, Penguin, 1962.

Rice, Tamara Talbot. *The Seljuks*. London, 1962.

Robinson, Richard D. *The First Turkish Republic*. Harvard University Press, 1963.

Rugman, Jonathan, and Hutchings, Roger. *Atatürk's Children: Turkey and the Kurds*. London, Cassell, 1996.

Runciman, Sir Steven. *The Fall of Constantinople, 1453*. Cambridge University Press, 1965.

Shaw, Stanford. *History of the Ottoman Empire*. Cambridge University Press, 1976.

Sumner, B. H. *Peter the Great and the Ottoman Empire*. Oxford, 1949.

Vaughan, Dorothy. *Europe and the Turk: A Pattern of Alliances, 1350–1700*. Liverpool, 1954.

Vere-Hodge, Edward Reginald. *Turkish Foreign Policy, 1918–1948*. London, 2nd revised edition, 1950.

Volkan, Vamik D. and Itzkowitz, Norman. *Turks and Greeks, Neighbours in Conflict*. Huntingdon, Eothen Press, 1994.

Walder, David. *The Chanak Affair*. London, Hutchinson, 1968.

ECONOMY

Insel, Ahmet. *La Turquie entre l'Ordre et le Développement*. Paris, l'Harmattan, 1984.

Issawi, Charles. *The Economic History of Turkey*. University of Chicago Press, 1980.

Rittenberg, Libby (Ed.) *The Political Economy of Turkey in the Post-Soviet Era*. Westport, CT, Praeger Publishing, 1998.

Shorter, Frederic C. (Ed.). *Four Studies on the Economic Development of Turkey*. London, Cass, 1967; New York, Kelley, 1968.

THE UNITED ARAB EMIRATES

ABU DHABI   DUBAI   SHARJAH   RAS AL-KHAIMAH
UMM AL-QAIWAIN   AJMAN   FUJAIRAH

Geography

The coastline of the seven United Arab Emirates (UAE) extends for nearly 650 km (400 miles) from the frontier of the Sultanate of Oman to Khor al-Odaid, on the Qatari peninsula, in the Persian (Arabian) Gulf, interrupted only by an isolated outcrop of the Sultanate of Oman which lies on the coast of the Persian Gulf to the west and the Gulf of Oman to the east at the Strait of Hormuz. Six of the emirates lie on the coast of the Persian Gulf, while the seventh, Fujairah, is situated on the eastern coast of the peninsula, and has direct access to the Gulf of Oman. The area is one of extremely shallow seas, with offshore islands and coral reefs, and often an intricate pattern of sandbanks and small gulfs as a coastline. There is a considerable tide. The waters of the Gulf contain abundant quantities of fish, hence the important role of fishing in local life.

The climate is arid, with very high summer temperatures; and, except for a few weeks in winter, air humidity is also very high. The total area of the UAE has been estimated at 77,700 sq km (30,000 sq miles), relatively small compared with neighbouring Oman and Saudi Arabia, and it has a rapidly growing population, totalling 2,377,453 at the census of December 1995. In 1999 the population was estimated to be 2,938,000. The population is concentrated in the emirates of Abu Dhabi and Dubai, the principal commercial regions of the country. Abu Dhabi is the largest emirate, with an area of about 67,350 sq km and a population of 928,360 at the December 1995 census. The town of Abu Dhabi, with a population of 471,000 in 2001 (including suburbs) according to UN estimates, is also the capital of the UAE. The most important port is Dubai, the capital of the UAE's second largest state; according to UN estimates, the population of the town of Dubai (including suburbs) was 886,000 in 2000. Its significance derives from its position on one of the rare deep creeks of the area, and it now has a very large transit trade.

Many inhabitants are still nomadic Arabs, and the official language is Arabic, which is spoken by most of the native inhabitants. Arabs are outnumbered, however, by non-Arab immigrant workers. In the coastal towns there are many Iranians, Indians, Pakistanis and Africans. Most of the native inhabitants are Muslims, mainly of the Sunni sect.

History

Revised for this edition by Jon Lunn

In the early 16th century the Portuguese commercial monopoly of the Gulf area was challenged by other European traders. The Portuguese ascendancy in the East gradually declined, and in 1650 they evacuated Oman, losing their entire hold on the Arabian shore. There followed a period of commercial and political rivalry between the Dutch and the British. The initial Dutch predominance weakened and in 1766 came practically to an end, while the British were consolidating their position in India.

Both European and Arab pirates were very active in the Gulf during the 17th, 18th and early 19th centuries. Attacks on British-flag vessels led to British expeditions against the pirates and eventually, in 1818, against the pirate headquarters at Ras al-Khaimah and other harbours along the 240 km of 'Pirate Coast'. In 1820 a general treaty of peace, for suppressing piracy and slave traffic, was concluded between Great Britain and the Arab tribes of the Gulf. It was signed by the principal sheikhs of the Pirate Coast and Bahrain. A strong British squadron was stationed at Ras al-Khaimah to enforce the treaty.

Piracy persisted and accordingly, in 1835, the sheikhs agreed, in a 'maritime truce', not to engage, under any circumstances, in hostilities by sea during the pearl-diving season. The advantages of this were so noticeable that the sheikhs willingly renewed the truce for increasing periods until, in May 1853, a 'treaty of maritime peace in perpetuity' was concluded, establishing a 'perpetual maritime truce' on the newly-named 'Trucial Coast' (also called Trucial Oman). It was supervised by the British Government, to whom the signatories would refer any breach. The British did not interfere in wars between the sheikhs on land.

Towards the end of the 19th century, France, Germany and Russia showed increasing interest in the Gulf area, and in 1892 Britain entered into separate but identical 'exclusive' treaties with the Trucial rulers, whereby the sheikhs undertook not to cede, mortgage or otherwise dispose of parts of their territories to anyone except the British Government, nor to enter into any relationship with a foreign government, other than the British, without British consent. Britain had already undertaken to protect the states from outside attack in the perpetual maritime treaty of 1853.

In 1820, when the general treaty was signed, there were only five Trucial states. In 1866, on the death of the Chief Sheikh of Sharjah, his domains were divided among his four sons, the separate branches of the family being established at Sharjah, Ras al-Khaimah, Dibba and Kalba. Kalba was incorporated into Sharjah in 1952, when its ruler agreed to accept all existing treaties between the United Kingdom and the Trucial States, as did the ruler of Fujairah. This involved recognizing the British Government's right to define state boundaries, to settle disputes between the Trucial sheikhdoms and to render assistance to the Trucial Oman Scouts, a force of some 1,600 men, officered and paid for by the United Kingdom, which was founded in 1952.

In 1952, on British advice, a trucial council was established, at which all seven rulers met at least twice a year, under the chairmanship of the political agent in Dubai. Its object was to encourage the pursuit of a common policy in administrative matters, possibly leading to a federation of the states.

The advent of the commercial production of petroleum in mid-1962 gave Abu Dhabi a great opportunity for development. A major obstacle to this development was removed in August 1966, when Sheikh Shakhbut bin Sultan an-Nahyan, the ruler of Abu Dhabi since 1928, was deposed. The ruling family replaced Shakhbut by his younger brother, Sheikh Zayed bin Sultan. The subsequent history of Abu Dhabi has been indicative of a society suddenly transformed by the acquisition of immense wealth. In 1966 petroleum was discovered in neighbouring Dubai, which also benefited greatly from the petroleum boom.

In June 1965 Sheikh Saqr bin Sultan of Sharjah was deposed. In spite of an appeal to the UN, supported by Iraq and the

United Arab Republic (now Egypt), the accession of his cousin, Sheikh Khalid bin Muhammad, proceeded without incident.

Intending to relocate its major military base in the Middle East, the United Kingdom started work in 1966 on a base in Sharjah, which by 1968 had become the principal base in the Gulf. However, British forces had been withdrawn from the area by the end of 1971. The Trucial Oman Scouts, based in Sharjah, were proposed as the nucleus of a federal security force after the British withdrawal, but some states, notably Abu Dhabi, were already creating their own defence forces.

In order to avoid disputes over the ill-defined state borders, those between Qatar, Abu Dhabi and Dubai were settled early in 1970—although not without objection from Saudi Arabia, whose territorial claims overlapped those of Abu Dhabi to a considerable extent. In late 1974 a border agreement was signed with Saudi Arabia on the Liwa oases, whereupon Saudi Arabia recognized the United Arab Emirates (UAE) and ambassadors were exchanged.

The original proposals for the formation of a federation (after the British had withdrawn) included Bahrain and Qatar, as well as the seven Trucial States, but these larger and more developed states eventually opted for separate independence. On 1 December 1971 the United Kingdom terminated all existing treaties with the Trucial States. On the following day Abu Dhabi, Dubai, Sharjah, Umm al-Qaiwain, Ajman and Fujairah formed the UAE, and a treaty of friendship was made with the United Kingdom. The federation approved a provisional constitution, which was to expire after five years, when a formal constitution would be drafted. However, the provisional constitution was repeatedly renewed until 1996, and this lent a flexibility to the developing emirates, allowing the process of centralization to follow a gradual course and averting any serious dispute which could arise from an emirate's contravention of formal constitutional decrees. At independence, Sheikh Zayed, the ruler of Abu Dhabi, took office as the first President of the UAE. Sheikh Rashid bin Said al-Maktoum, the ruler of Dubai since 1958, became Vice-President, while his eldest son, Sheikh Maktoum bin Rashid (Crown Prince of Dubai), became Prime Minister. In December 1991 the UAE became a member of both the League of Arab States (the Arab League) and the UN. In February 1972 Ras al-Khaimah became the seventh member of the federation.

In January 1972 the Ruler of Sharjah, Sheikh Khalid, was killed by rebels under the leadership of his cousin, Sheikh Saqr, who had been deposed in 1965. The rebels were captured, and Sheikh Sultan bin Muhammad succeeded his brother as ruler, confirming a continuation of the late Khalid's relatively liberal principles of government, and Sharjah's membership of the UAE.

Although the UAE remained one of the most conservative Arab states, it gave considerable support to the Arab cause in the October War of 1973 and participated in the associated petroleum cut-backs and boycotts. It was the first state to impose a total ban on exports of petroleum to the USA, and subsequently supported the Arab ostracism of Egypt which followed the negotiation of the Camp David agreements between Egypt and Israel in 1978 and the subsequent 1979 peace treaty between the two countries.

TOWARDS GREATER CENTRALIZATION

Alongside the presidency, judiciary and Supreme Council (ministerial cabinet), the UAE also instituted a consultative and 'supervisory' legislature called the Federal National Council. This body consists of 40 members, distributed as follows: eight seats each for Abu Dhabi and Dubai; six each for Sharjah and Ras al-Khaimah; and four each for Ajman, Umm al-Qaiwain and Fujairah. It first met in February 1972. However, real power still resides with members of the ruling families. In December 1973 the separate Abu Dhabi Government was disbanded and, in a ministerial reshuffle, some of its members became federal ministers. Most notably, the Abu Dhabi minister responsible for petroleum, Dr Mana bin Said al-Oteiba, became the first federal Minister of Petroleum and Mineral Resources. The government reorganization involved a considerable extension of central authority and was a further step towards the integration of the seven sheikhdoms. In May 1975, at a session of the Supreme Council, the seven emirs gave their consent, in

principle, to further steps towards centralization. In November Sharjah merged the Sharjah National Guard with the Union Defence Force, and also granted control of its broadcasting station to the Federal Ministry of Communications, its police to the Ministry of the Interior and its courts to the Ministry of Justice. The Sharjah flag was abolished in favour of the federal tricolour. Fujairah and Abu Dhabi both discontinued the use of their flags.

The merger of the main defence forces (the Union Defence Force, the Abu Dhabi Defence Force and the Dubai Defence Force) was finally agreed in early May 1976, when Gen. Sheikh Khalifa bin Zayed an-Nahyan, the Crown Prince of Abu Dhabi, was made deputy supreme commander (Sheikh Zayed became supreme commander). In November the provisional constitution was amended so that the right to levy armed forces and acquire weapons was placed exclusively in the hands of federal government.

During 1976 Sheikh Zayed, impatient with the slow rate at which the emirates were achieving centralization, threatened not to stand for a second term as President of the UAE in November. In the event, he was re-elected unanimously after the Supreme Council had granted the federal Government greater control over defence, intelligence services, immigration, public security and border control. A reshuffle of the Council of Ministers followed in January 1977, with ministers chosen on the principle of individual merit rather than equitable representation of the seven emirates. The new 40-member Federal National Council, which was inaugurated on 1 March, included only seven members of the first five-year session (1971–76).

Mounting pressure from within the emirates for a more united federation led, in 1978, to the setting up of a joint Cabinet-Federal National Council committee to discuss methods of achieving this. Events in Iran in 1979 and the resultant security threat prompted a full meeting of the Council of Ministers and the Federal National Council in February. The outcome of this was a 10-point memorandum advocating the abolition of all internal borders, the unification of defence forces and the merging of revenues in a federal budget. This plan was subsequently submitted to the Supreme Council.

Despite their widespread support in the emirates, these proposals aggravated the long-standing rivalry between Abu Dhabi, the financial mainstay of the federation, and Dubai, which had become increasingly critical of the centralized federal Government. Dubai rejected the memorandum completely and, together with Ras al-Khaimah, boycotted a Supreme Council meeting in March 1979.

It was thought that the deadlock had been broken, at least temporarily, when Sheikh Rashid, ruler of Dubai, replaced his son as Prime Minister of the federal Government (while retaining the vice-presidency) in July 1979. A new Council of Ministers was formed, preserving a similar balance of power between the emirates as before. Ras al-Khaimah integrated its defence force with the federal force, and both Abu Dhabi and Dubai pledged to contribute 50% of their revenues from petroleum to the federal budget. Dubai's forces, however, remained, in practice, a separate entity. Further attempts at integration included the construction of national roads, the installation of telecommunications, and the central planning and financing of health, education and agriculture. In November 1981 Sheikh Rashid was re-elected Prime Minister by the Supreme Council, and Sheikh Zayed was re-elected President.

FOREIGN POLICY AND THE IRAN–IRAQ WAR

With the outbreak of war between Iran and Iraq in 1980, the UAE became vulnerable to external forces over which it had no control. Iran's repeated threats to close the Strait of Hormuz to traffic carrying exports of petroleum from Gulf countries represented a grave potential danger to states such as the UAE, which depend on revenues from petroleum. Partly in response to Iranian threats, the UAE joined with five other Gulf states to form the Co-operation Council of the Arab States of the Gulf (Gulf Co-operation Council—GCC) in March 1981, to work towards economic, political and social integration in the Gulf. The GCC's primary concern initially was to develop greater economic co-operation, but this gave way to concern over the region's ability to defend itself. A bilateral defence agreement was signed with Saudi Arabia in 1982, and, in accordance with

GCC policy, the UAE has substantially increased its defence expenditure.

In August 1987 a Panamanian-registered supertanker, the *Texaco Caribbean*, struck a mine (presumed to be of Iranian origin) 13 km off the coast of the UAE, near the port of Fujairah. The Government of the UAE declared Fujairah port a danger zone and banned all commercial shipping from a surrounding area of 100 sq km, while minesweeping operations were carried out. At the end of August the UAE gave provisional permission for the use of its ports as a base for British minesweeping operations. In April 1988 the Mubarak oilfield, which belongs to the emirate of Sharjah and is located 30 km off the coast of the UAE, was closed for two months, following an attack on its installations by forces involved in the Iran–Iraq War.

The decline in revenues from petroleum in the mid-1980s had little effect on the comfortable lifestyle of the UAE, although certain development plans were postponed or rescheduled. One effect of decreased revenue was a greater commitment to local co-operation both within the UAE and among Gulf countries in general. Thus, bilateral agreements with Oman, Qatar, the People's Democratic Republic of Yemen and Iraq were made for the purpose of mutual aid in educational, scientific and cultural development. The establishment, in November 1985, of diplomatic relations with the USSR was expected to lead to increased bilateral trade.

In November 1987 the UAE restored diplomatic relations with Egypt, following the adoption of a resolution at a summit meeting of the Arab League, which permitted member states to resume relations with Egypt at their own discretion.

The escalation of tension in the Gulf, exacerbated by the presence of US and Soviet naval forces, had resulted in the adoption of Resolution 598 by the UN Security Council on 20 July 1987, which urged an immediate cease-fire. In November, at an extraordinary meeting of the Arab League in Amman, Jordan, representatives of the member states, including the UAE, unanimously condemned Iran for prolonging the war against Iraq, deplored its occupation of Arab (i.e. Iraqi) territory, and urged it to accept Resolution 598 without pre-conditions.

DEVELOPMENTS IN DOMESTIC POLITICS

In October 1986 the provisional federal Constitution was renewed for a further five years, and Sheikh Zayed and Sheikh Rashid were unanimously re-elected to the posts of President, and Vice-President and Prime Minister, respectively.

An attempted coup took place in Sharjah in June 1987, when Sheikh Abd al-Aziz, a brother of the ruler (Sheikh Sultan bin Muhammad al-Qasimi), issued a statement, in his brother's absence, which announced the abdication of Sheikh Sultan, on the grounds that he had mismanaged the economy. (Sharjah had incurred debts estimated at US \$920m. in mid-1987, as the result of an extravagant programme of construction ordered by the ruler.) However, Dubai intervened and convened a meeting of the Supreme Council of Rulers, which endorsed Sheikh Sultan's claim to be the legitimate ruler of Sharjah, and restored him to power. As a result of the attempted coup, Sheikh Abd al-Aziz was given the title of Crown Prince and granted a seat on the Supreme Council. In July Sheikh Sultan formed an executive council in Sharjah, comprising the heads of local government departments and other individuals selected by him, to assist in the administration of the public affairs of the emirate. Sheikh Sultan also signed an agreement with bank creditors, whereby Sharjah's loan repayments would be rescheduled until 1993. In February 1990, however, Sheikh Sultan removed his brother from the post of Crown Prince and revoked his right to succeed him. In July Sheikh Sultan appointed Sheikh Ahmad bin Muhammad al-Qasimi, the head of Sharjah's petroleum and mineral affairs office, as Deputy Ruler of Sharjah. He was not given the title of Crown Prince. On 7 October the Ruler of Dubai, Prime Minister and Vice-President of the UAE, Sheikh Rashid bin Said al-Maktoum, died. He was succeeded in all of his offices by his eldest son, Sheikh Maktoum bin Rashid al-Maktoum. In November a reorganization of ministerial portfolios took place. In October 1991 the Supreme Council confirmed Sheikh Zayed and Sheikh Maktoum as, respectively, President and Vice-President, each for a further five-year term. The provisional federal Constitution was also renewed for a further period of five years.

In 1991 the UAE became involved in a major international financial scandal, when, in July, the regulatory authorities in seven countries abruptly closed down the operations of the Bank of Credit and Commerce International (BCCI), in which the Abu Dhabi ruling family and agencies had held a controlling interest (77%) since April 1990. The termination of the bank's activities followed the disclosure by an auditor's report, commissioned by the Bank of England, of systematic, large-scale fraud by BCCI authorities (perpetrated before April 1990). By the end of July 1991 BCCI's activities had been suspended in all 69 countries in which it had operated. A compensation plan, drawn up by the bank's majority shareholders, was delayed in December 1992, when three prominent creditors, who had objected to a clause that would require recipients of compensation to waive any further claims against Abu Dhabi in respect of the BCCI scandal, initiated appeal proceedings and it was not until February 1995 that a compensation agreement, worth a total of US \$1,800m., received judicial authorization in Luxembourg. In February 1996 the UAE Central Bank formally revoked the licence of the BCCI, and in May the Abu Dhabi authorities made a payment of \$1,550m. to BCCI's liquidators, Touche Ross (a further \$250m. was to be held in an escrow account for release at a later date). In October 1998 it was announced that the auditors of the BCCI were to pay \$195m. in settlement of a \$11,000m. claim for negligence. By 1999 two payments, totalling some \$4,500m., had been made to BCCI creditors, and a third payment, of more than \$1,000m., was made in May 2000. A dispute between the liquidators and the emirate of Sharjah was resolved in May when Sharjah's ruler, Sheikh Sultan, agreed to pay \$76m. in settlement of a \$460m. claim which had arisen from a \$41m. loan made to Sharjah by the BCCI in 1975. Further difficulties were experienced in the banking sector in 1999, when an expatriate businessman defaulted on loans and bank credits estimated to total some \$866m.; subsequent investigations into his business revealed fraudulent activity. The Central Bank called an emergency meeting to discuss the recovery of the monies owed, and UAE banks were later criticized by the police for their lack of vigilance in potential fraud cases.

Meanwhile, in February 1994 Sheikh Zayed issued a decree whereby a wide range of crimes, including murder, theft, adultery and drugs-related offences, would be tried in *Shari'a* (Islamic religious law) courts rather than in civil courts, and in April 1995 the Council of Ministers approved the introduction of the death penalty for drugs dealers and smugglers.

In January 1995 a decree was issued by the Ruler of Dubai, Sheikh Maktoum bin Rashid al-Maktoum, naming Sheikh Muhammad bin Rashid al-Maktoum as Crown Prince. The decree also named Sheikh Hamdan bin Rashid al-Maktoum as Deputy Ruler of Dubai. In June 1996 legislation designed to make the provisional constitution permanent was endorsed by the Federal National Council, following its approval by the Supreme Council of Rulers. At the same time Abu Dhabi was formally designated capital of the UAE. Sheikh Zayed was subsequently re-elected to the presidency.

In late March 1997 there was a cabinet reorganization—the first for seven years. Although the key finance, defence and foreign affairs portfolios did not change hands, new appointees included Sheikh Fahim bin Sultan al-Qasimi as Minister of Economy and Commerce and Sheikh Abdullah bin Zayed an-Nahyan, son of the UAE President, as Minister of Information and Culture. Muhammad Khalfan bin Kharbash, appointed Minister of State for Finance and Industry, was regarded as the head of a new 'clique' of Western-educated technocrats whose influence in domestic politics was expected to grow.

In January 2001, in an address to the Federal National Council, the Minister of Information and Culture was reported to have urged a review of certain articles of criminal law, in force since 1980, which prohibit journalists from reporting on contentious matters relating to legislation and from criticizing public institutions. In April 2001 Dubai's Director-General of Ports and Customs, Dr Obeid Saqer bin Busit, was sentenced to 27 years' imprisonment, having been convicted on two charges of corruption arising from abuse of his position; bin Busit was the highest ranking civil servant ever to have been tried for corruption in the UAE. Six other defendants (three UAE nationals and three Pakistani expatriates) were also convicted—

among them the head of Dubai's Hamriya port, who was found guilty of four charges and sentenced to 31 years' custody. The arrests had been ordered personally by Dubai's Crown Prince in early February, following a two-year investigation, and it was subsequently reported that the federal Minister of Justice and Islamic Affairs and Awqaf (Religious Endowments) had proposed the establishment of an anti-corruption commission and the institution of more stringent legislation to counter corruption. There were, however, subsequent reports that those convicted in the customs fraud had been pardoned.

Following the suicide attacks on New York and Washington, DC, on 11 September 2001, the UAE's banking sector was subject to considerable international scrutiny, after US investigators claimed to have discovered evidence of financial transactions between banks in the UAE and certain banks in the USA used by those involved in the September attacks (one of whom was a UAE national). Mustafa Ahmad, a Dubai-based associate of Osama bin Laden (whose al-Qa'ida terrorist network was held responsible for the attacks by the US authorities) was reported to have acted as the conduit for funds. At the end of September 2001 the Central Bank ordered the 'freezing' of assets in the UAE belonging to 27 individuals and organizations accused by the USA of being actively involved in the promotion of terrorism. In October 2001 a decree was passed which sought to prohibit the 'laundering' of funds through the UAE's banking sector; henceforth all banks would be required to inform the Central Bank of the receipt or transfer of amounts in excess of US $10,900. Those convicted on charges connected to 'money-laundering' activities, furthermore, would receive increased fines and prison sentences of up to seven years. The decree also formally established a national commission to seek to combat such practices. However, the Hawala finance system—a traditional alternative remittance system operating outside the control of the conventional banking sector—was unaffected by the changes; much of the funding destined for terrorist activities is believed to be channelled in this way. In June 2002 it was reported that the police in Dubai had made their first ever arrests on charges of 'money-laundering'; the detainees were believed to include both Arabs and Europeans.

The UAE celebrated the 30th anniversary of its creation in December 2001, when the rulers of the constituent states of the UAE re-elected Sheikh Zayed bin Sultan an-Nayhan as President for another five-year term. While noting its fundamental stability, independent commentators had suggested that the federal structure of the UAE had weakened during the previous decade, owing, in part, to the economic preponderance of Abu Dhabi and the weakness of some of the northern emirates, but also because of the inability of the federal Government to develop its own sources of income. Reports of tensions over the issue of succession within the ruling house in Abu Dhabi were also believed to be undermining stability, although Sheikh Zayed's eldest son, Khalifa, who is Chairman of the Supreme Petroleum Council, is widely expected to succeed his father. Industrial safety concerns emerged during 2002 after 27 workers were killed when the Dubai dry docks flooded in March and an unknown number of construction workers were killed and injured when the roof of a new power plant under construction at the Jebel Ali industrial centre near Dubai city collapsed in August.

FOREIGN RELATIONS

Iraq's occupation of Kuwait, in August 1990, caused political and economic crisis throughout the Gulf region. The UAE responded by supporting resistance to Iraqi aggression, and on 20 August the UAE ordered all nationals to join the armed forces for six weeks' military training. At the same time it was announced that armed forces opposing Iraq's aggression would be granted military facilities in the UAE. Units from the British and French air forces were among those which were subsequently stationed there. In February 1991, after the outbreak of hostilities between Iraq and a US-led multinational force, UAE air force conducted four raids against Iraqi targets.

Tension between the UAE and Iran was not confined to matters relating to the GCC; there was also a territorial dimension. Rival claims to the island of Abu Musa had been made by Sharjah and Iran in 1970, when petroleum exploration began. In 1971 agreement was reached to divide any oil revenues. In

August 1992, however, it was reported that Iran had annexed Abu Musa after 20 years of joint control. It was claimed that Iranian authorities had denied landing permission to more than 100 residents of the island who were returning from Sharjah, and that Iran was refusing a compromise agreement. Iran subsequently claimed sovereignty over Abu Musa, together with the Greater Tunb and Lesser Tunb islands. Discussions between representatives of the countries' Ministers of Foreign Affairs were convened in Abu Dhabi at the end of September, but collapsed almost immediately, with Iran refusing to discuss ownership of two of the three islands. At a GCC summit meeting in Abu Dhabi in December it was demanded that Iran reverse the 'virtual annexation' of the islands. In April 1993 a GCC statement expressed satisfaction at recent developments and support for bilateral negotiations. In the same month it was reported that all persons who had been expelled from (or refused entry to) Abu Musa in 1992 had been permitted to return. Both the UAE and Iran periodically proclaimed their commitment to direct talks; however, by late 1994 no significant progress had been made towards resolving the conflict, and in December the UAE announced its intention to refer the dispute to the International Court of Justice. In February 1995 it was alleged that Iran had deployed air defence systems on the islands. In November officials from the UAE and Iran, meeting in Qatar, failed to reach agreement on establishing an agenda for ministerial-level negotiations. In March 1996 relations between the two countries deteriorated further when Iran opened an airport on Abu Musa; in the following month Iran established a power station on the island of Greater Tunb. Although talks were held in March 1997, no solution was reached, and in June the UAE protested to the UN about a pier which, it alleged, Iran had constructed on Greater Tunb. The GCC has supported UAE claims to the islands but has also welcomed an Iranian offer to open dialogue. In March 1999 the GCC issued a statement criticizing Iranian naval exercises near the disputed islands. At that time, the UAE was also highly critical of a developing *rapprochement* between Iran and Saudi Arabia, the latter having offered to mediate in the dispute over the islands. Relations with Saudi Arabia deteriorated further following a visit to that country by President Muhammad Khatami of Iran, although the Saudi authorities insisted that any *rapprochement* with Iran would not be achieved at the expense of its relations with any other country. In November a tripartite committee, established by the GCC and comprising representatives of Oman, Qatar and Saudi Arabia, announced that it would continue in its efforts to facilitate a settlement. At the end of the month Sheikh Zayed decided not to attend a meeting of GCC leaders in Saudi Arabia, in protest at the lack of attention given to the dispute with Iran by the other members of the GCC, at a time when they were increasingly moving towards improved relations with Iran. In December the UAE renewed its request for Iran to enter into direct negotiations or to agree to international arbitration over the islands and in March 2000, following a statement by Iran that it would be prepared to negotiate over the islands, the UAE said that it welcomed Iran's statement, but would refer it to the tripartite GCC committee. By mid-2002 no significant progress had been made towards a resolution of the territorial dispute, but hopes for direct negotiations on the issue were encouraged later in the year by news that President Khatami was to undertake an official visit to Abu Dhabi in December.

The UAE boycotted a meeting of GCC oil ministers in March 1999, in protest at the decision by Saudi Arabia to begin petroleum production on disputed territory prior to an agreement being reached on the ownership of the land. In May the UAE and Oman signed an agreement demarcating their joint border, and documents to formalize the settlement were signed by both sides in June 2002.

In July 1994 the UAE signed a defence agreement with the USA which extended the agreement signed in 1991 in the aftermath of the Gulf conflict. This coincided with the announcement of plans to reduce the size of the UAE armed forces by 10,000, to 50,000. In January 1995 the UAE concluded a defence agreement with France which provided for 'consultations' in the event of aggression against or threats to UAE territory. A similar agreement was reportedly under negotiation with the United Kingdom. However, negotiations stalled for a period, owing to the reluctance of the British Government to accept the extension of UAE jurisdiction over British troops deployed there. A defence agreement was finally signed in November 1996 whereby the United Kingdom undertook to defend the UAE in the event of an external attack. The UAE is expanding its air force as part of a 10-year weapons procurement programme, worth an estimated US $15,000m. In December 1997 the Government signed a contract for the modernization of its 33 *Mirage* 2000 jets, and for the purchase of 30 new *Mirage* 2000-9 fighter aircraft, and in May 1998 it was announced that 80 US F-16 fighter aircraft had been ordered (at a cost of at least $6,000m.), representing the largest defence purchase in the country's history. Abu Dhabi provides 80% of the UAE's total military manpower and defence budget. Some analysts have criticized the overly politicized and decentralized nature of arms procurements: ordnance is far from standardized, with each emirate operating its own internal paramilitary forces.

In mid-October 1995, while addressing a meeting of the new ambassadors in the UAE, Sheikh Zayed announced that it was 'time for reconciliation' with Iraq and appealed for the easing of UN sanctions against that country to relieve the suffering of the Iraqi people. In January 1997 the UAE sent a shipment of aid containing food and medicine to Iraq to help alleviate the desperate situation of Iraqi children. In late 1997, as the crisis developed between Iraq and weapons inspectors of the UN Special Commission (UNSCOM, see the chapter on Iraq), the UAE persisted in its reconciliatory stance towards Iraq, refusing US requests to allow the deployment of US fighter aircraft in the UAE, and strongly advocating a diplomatic solution. A further shipment of medicine and food aid from the UAE arrived in Iraq in February 1998. In June the UAE reiterated its support for an end to the economic blockade against Iraq, and in August it was announced that the UAE was to restore diplomatic ties with Iraq, although there was no indication of how soon this would take place.

The UAE reopened its embassy in the Iraqi capital in April 2000. However, the Ruler of Fujairah was criticized in Iraq following a speech, at the UN Millennium Summit in New York in September, in which he called on Iraq to apply all pertinent UN resolutions, particularly those related to the issue of prisoners of war. Although Iraq's Minister of Trade visited Abu Dhabi in early December, where he was received by Sheikh Zayed, the UAE lent its support to a declaration of the GCC annual summit meeting that urged Iraq to conform with UN Security Council Resolutions: it was generally considered that

the Emirates had been compelled to endorse the declaration in return for emphasis of GCC support for the UAE in its territorial dispute with Iran. Addressing the Arab Inter-Parliamentary Union in late February 2001, Sheikh Zayed none the less urged Arab states to work together towards an end to the sanctions regime in force against Iraq; the UAE President also appealed for concerted Arab support for the UAE in its territorial dispute with Iran.

The UAE severed diplomatic relations with the Taliban regime in Afghanistan in late September 2001, in response to the devastating terrorist attacks against New York and Washington, DC, on 11 September. Hitherto, the UAE had been one of only three states to maintain ties with the Taliban, although relations had been downgraded to chargé d'affaires level and an air link between Dubai and Kabul had been suspended in compliance with UN sanctions imposed against Afghanistan in late 2000. Bin Laden was now the US Administration's principal suspect in orchestrating the September 2001 suicide attacks in the USA. After diplomatic relations were severed, the UAE's Minister of Foreign Affairs stated that the Emirates had made 'intense efforts' to persuade the Taliban authorities to hand over bin Laden so that he might stand trial in an international court. In common with the other GCC members, the UAE pledged support for the USA in its efforts to bring to justice the perpetrators of acts of terrorism, and in apparent demonstration of this a suspected militant Islamist wanted for questioning in France was extradited to that country at the beginning of October. Nonetheless, the UAE emphasized that the success of the USA's 'global coalition' against terrorism must be linked to a resumption of the Arab-Israeli peace process and expressed concerns that military action should not target any Arab state. At the Arab League summit meeting convened in Beirut, Lebanon, on 26–28 March 2002, the Minister of State for Foreign Affairs, Sheikh Hamdan bin Zaid an-Nahyan, declared the UAE to be opposed to any future US-led attack on Iraq as a potential second phase in the US Government's declared 'war against terror'.

At the GCC summit meeting convened in Muscat, Oman, in late December 2001, the UAE joined with other member states in agreeing to establish a Supreme Joint Defence Council and to formulate a joint strategy on terrorism. A new GCC combined defence force was to be established by 2004 under joint GCC command. Meanwhile, GCC ministers also reiterated their condemnation of Iran's continuing occupation of three islands claimed by the UAE (see above).

Economy

Dr P. T. H. UNWIN

Revised for this edition by JON LUNN

INTRODUCTION

Prior to the discovery of petroleum, the economy of the seven sheikhdoms, or emirates, that comprised the Trucial States was based on pearling, fishing, trade and a limited amount of agriculture. In the 19th century, piracy, as defined by the Western powers that became dominant in the area, also formed an important source of income for the coastal tribes. Since 1958, when petroleum was first discovered off Abu Dhabi, and in particular since June 1962, when it was first exported, the economy of the area has undergone dramatic change. The pace of this change increased appreciably following independence in 1971, leading to the creation of the federal state of the United Arab Emirates (UAE), and the increases in the price of oil dictated by the Organization of the Petroleum Exporting Countries (OPEC), of which the UAE is a member. In 1998, according to estimates by the World Bank, the UAE's gross national product (GNP), measured at average 1996–98 prices, was US $48,673m. equivalent to $17,870 per head. According to later World Bank estimates gross domestic product (GDP) increased at an average annual rate of 2.9% in 1990–2000, although GDP

per head declined by an average of 1.6% over the same period. GDP totalled AED 163,750m. in 1996, AED 181,179m. in 1997, and AED 170,666m. in 1998.

Abu Dhabi and Dubai, the principal petroleum producers, dominate the economy of the UAE, while the northern emirates remain relatively undeveloped, and there is little co-ordination in the economic affairs of the emirates. The UAE is less dependent than other petroleum-producing countries on the hydrocarbons sector (crude oil accounted for only 25% of GDP in 1999), and Dubai is of particular importance as an entrepôt for regional trade. The sharp decline in international petroleum prices in 1998 caused GDP to decline by 5.8% in that year and led to predictions of slow economic growth in 1999. However, by September 1999 prices had increased dramatically, and by the end of the year a recovery was well under way. Despite the anticipated decline in Government revenue in 1999, no spending cuts were enforced, with the emirates focusing on ways to maximize revenues; Abu Dhabi continued with its privatization programme, divesting the electricity and water sector along with telecommunications; Dubai encouraged self-reliance and greater profitability among its state enterprises; and the northern emirates continued to expand non-oil-sector activities. Social welfare reforms were also instituted in 1999. With effect from September, UAE nationals working for private companies were to be entitled to the same social security and pension benefits as UAE nationals in the public sector. A General Authority for Pensions and Social Security was established to invest employer and employee contributions and to operate the new social security and pension arrangements (which took effect for public sector employees in May of that year). In May 2001 Dubai revoked the entitlement of expatriates to free health care.

The sustained recovery in international petroleum prices was the principal factor contributing to a 23.4% increase in the value of the UAE's exports and re-exports in 2000, compared with a 4.1% increase in spending on imports; the value of non-hydrocarbons exports increased by 3.4%. Declining international petroleum prices and a general downturn in the global economy in the aftermath of the terrorist attacks on the USA in September 2001 led to a deceleration in the rate of growth; according to figures published by the UAE Central Bank in July 2002, economic growth of 1.3% was recorded in 2001, with GDP totalling AED 217,000m. Non-oil GDP was reported to have increased by 3.7%, to AED 169,000m. (accounting for 77.9% of total GDP). Forecasts for 2002 anticipated a further deceleration in the rate of growth, but a significant recovery was envisaged in 2003 based on rising international petroleum prices. The draft federal budget for 2002 projected a primary deficit of AED 2,169m., with increased spending allocations, notably in the areas of education, health, social security, power and water and infrastructure development. Dubai's banking regulations were reviewed following the emergence of evidence that the terrorist attacks in the USA had been funded, in part, through a Dubai-based bank account (see below). In December 2001, unofficial reports claimed that Dubai was receiving more than 100,000 b/d of crude petroleum from Abu Dhabi to help it through the economic slump brought about by the attacks in September 2001. Economic projections for 2002 began to be revised upwards from March 2002 onwards, as petroleum prices recovered more quickly than expected, returning to September 2001 levels.

The UAE covers approximately 77,700 sq km, most of which is either sand desert or *sibakh* (salt flats). At the March 1968 census its population was 179,126. The pace of the UAE's rapid economic change can be seen in the dramatic increase in population during succeeding years: it reached 1,042,099 by the December 1980 census, and results from the December 1985 census indicated that the population had grown by 55.7% in the intervening five years, to 1,622,464, of whom about 670,000 were inhabitants of Abu Dhabi. The December 1995 census recorded a population of 2.38m., of whom 928,360 lived in Abu Dhabi, 674,100 in Dubai, 400,400 in Sharjah and the remainder in the other emirates. During 1994–2000 the population increased by an annual average of be 4.0%. In 2000 the population was officially estimated to be 3,108,000. The largest relative increases in population have been in the smallest emirates, reflecting their policy of economic expansion. The unequal distribution of the sexes (with males accounting for about two-thirds of the total population) indicates the large amount of immigration that has been necessary to sustain the country's economic growth. Foreign workers comprise some 80% of the population; in Dubai, the figure is estimated to be nearer 90%. There have been strong demands for the redeployment of labour from non-Arab Asians to Arabs. In a government drive against illegal immigrants, up to 200,000 Asian workers were estimated to have left the country by November 1996. Despite a consequent increase in labour costs, the Government justified its actions on the grounds of the need to avoid cultural dilution and political unrest. However, more than 40% of UAE nationals are under 15 years of age and many currently lack the required skills. In 2000 it was estimated that the total number of people in employment was 1,779,000, of whom 7.9% were engaged in agriculture and fishing (compared with 21% in 1965), 33.4% in industry (32% in 1965) and 58.7% in services (47% in 1965). Overall, the labour force was estimated by the World Bank to have increased by an average of 3.7% in 1994–2000.

Despite progress in the UAE towards political integration, co-ordination in economic policies has proved to be difficult to accomplish. Abu Dhabi's wealth tends to overshadow the other emirates but, at the same time, it is the main factor which holds the seven emirates together. Dubai's strategy of diversification away from reliance on the oil industry over the last decade, reflecting progressively depleted petroleum reserves, thus far has produced mixed results. Apart from the difference between Abu Dhabi and Dubai over participation in the petroleum industry, the two main emirates have tended to pursue independent strategies in developing their various industries. An important instrument of development policy is the federal budget, which is essentially concerned with the implementation of federal infrastructure policy. Individual emirates also draw up separate budgets for municipal expenditure and local projects. The Constitution provides for social services, such as health and education, to come under federal control. In the 1970s Abu Dhabi contributed more than 90% of the federal budget revenue, but by 1990 its share had fallen to about 80%, with Dubai contributing about 16%. Abu Dhabi continues to dominate the UAE economy. As a result of depressed petroleum prices from 1983, overall GDP declined in some subsequent years, but in 1989 the economic recovery which followed the cease-fire in the Iran–Iraq War enabled a number of industrial projects, postponed in the mid-1980s, to be revived. GDP in that year increased by 15.9%, to AED 100,976m. (US $27,506m.), and in 1990 the combination of increased oil production and higher prices produced a massive increase in GDP, to AED 125,266m. ($34,110m.).

Iraq's invasion of Kuwait in August 1990 initially had a destabilizing effect upon the UAE economy. Work on development projects was suspended and banks lost between 15% and 30% of their deposits in August and September. More than 8,000 Kuwaitis fled to the UAE. Higher shipping insurance premiums acted as a restraint on trade. By the end of 1990, however, work on development projects had resumed, and confidence in the economy had revived as a result of the 54% increase in the revenue which the UAE had earned from its sales of petroleum in the course of the year. At $21,100m., the value of these sales was more than sufficient to meet the additional expenses which the UAE incurred as a result of the crisis in the Gulf. A large part of these expenses arose from the financial support it gave to the military operations of the anti-Iraq coalition; and from aid granted to those countries for which the economic effects of the crisis were most severe. (The UAE donated £275m. towards the cost of British and US $4,067m. towards the cost of US military operations. It also made a contribution of $1,469m. to the Gulf Financial Crisis Co-ordination Group.) After the liberation of Kuwait in February 1991 the UAE announced ambitious expenditure plans in both the petroleum and non-petroleum sectors. The UAE also benefited from participation in Kuwait's reconstruction programme, in the aftermath of its liberation, and from a revival of regional trade after the war. The UAE placed orders worth an estimated $12,050m. for defence equipment in 1993. Cumulative UAE defence spending during the 1990s was forecast to total about $20,000m. Under the country's 'offset' rules, foreign defence contractors winning orders worth more than $10m. were required to reinvest, over a seven-year period, 60% of the value of such orders in approved projects beneficial to the UAE economy.

Relatively steady revenues from petroleum exports and rapidly growing non-oil trade provided a strong financial base to support the Government's ambitious plans for industrial expansion and diversification through the 1990s. By 1997 the non-oil sector was estimated to contribute some 70% of GDP. In 1999 the mining sector contributed 25.4% of GDP and services 48.5%.

PETROLEUM AND GAS

The economy of the UAE is dominated by petroleum. At the end of 2001 the UAE's proven oil reserves totalled 97,800m. barrels (9.3% of world reserves and 11.9% of OPEC reserves). At the end of 2001 the UAE's proven reserves of natural gas totalled 6,010,000m. cu m (3.9% of world reserves). In 1996 91.4% of total reserves (5,300,000m. cu m) were in Abu Dhabi. Between 1971 and 1980 the UAE's revenue from petroleum increased about 25-fold, and, particularly between 1973 and 1976, the economy expanded very rapidly. In this period, public-sector spending increased at an annual rate of 72%. The second half of the 1970s, however, was a period of retrenchment, and there was a major recession in the mid-1980s. Owing to the surplus of petroleum supplies in the 1980s, government revenue from exports of petroleum was greatly reduced. Japan, which is the largest customer for crude petroleum from the UAE, imported 26.8% of its total crude oil requirements from the UAE in 1995. The petroleum sector's contribution to GDP declined from 63% in 1980 to 32% in 1996. In 1997, as a result of declining petroleum prices, the sector's contribution to GDP decreased further, to 29%. Meanwhile, non-oil GDP grew by 7.2% from 1996 to 1997; while manufacturing constituted an impressive 15.9% of total GDP in 1997. Nonetheless, crude oil exports still constituted about 40% of total commodity exports in 1997. Thus, lower international oil prices in 1998 led to a 5% decline in the UAE's real GDP, although the economy recovered strongly with the revival in oil prices from the second half of 1999. The oil sector's contribution to GDP declined to just 20.3% as a result of the depressed world price for oil in 1998, but the sector recovered sufficiently to contribute 25.0% of GDP in 1999.

In 1983 Abu Dhabi produced 69.9% of the UAE's petroleum output, Dubai 29.5% and Sharjah 0.5%. Output rose rapidly, from an average of 14,200 barrels per day (b/d) in 1962 (the first year of production) to 1,059,000 b/d in 1971. Output nearly doubled to 1,998,700 b/d in 1977 before falling gradually to 1,133,743 b/d in 1981—lower than in any year since 1971. Under the terms of an OPEC agreement in March 1983, the UAE was accorded a production quota of 1.1m. b/d.

During 1985–1988 the UAE regularly exceeded its OPEC production quota. The UAE was widely acknowledged to be the most flagrant over-producer in the Organization and repeatedly rejected the quotas that it had been allocated, claiming that they were inconsistent with the country's large reserves and disproportionate to the quotas allotted to other OPEC member states. After the abandonment of oil-pricing agreements at an OPEC meeting held in Vienna in October 1985, the UAE's production rose appreciably. In December OPEC decided to abandon production restraint and to seek a larger share of the market. By March 1986 it was apparent that Abu Dhabi had raised production levels by almost 30%, while at the same time halving prices in an attempt to maintain its revenue. The UAE's total production rose from 805,000 b/d at the end of 1985 to 1.7m. b/d in July 1986.

In June 1988 the Supreme Petroleum Council was formed, following the issuing of a presidential decree which proposed the abolition of the Department of Petroleum and the dissolution of the board of directors of the Abu Dhabi National Oil Co (ADNOC), in an attempt to unify the Government's petroleum policy and planning activities. The 11-member Council, headed by Sheikh Khalifa bin Zayed an-Nahyan, assumed the former responsibilities of ADNOC's directors and of the Department of Petroleum, namely the administration and supervision of all the country's petroleum affairs. At its November 1988 meeting, OPEC members agreed to form a committee, consisting of representatives of eight member states, to monitor the production quotas of all members and to supervise adherence to the levels allocated.

Iraq's invasion of Kuwait in August 1990 led to the suspension of OPEC quotas as member states agreed to compensate for the loss of Iraqi and Kuwaiti production of petroleum due to the UN's mandatory trade embargo. The UAE's average output during the 1990–91 Gulf crisis was 2.4m. b/d, 63% more than its quota figure of July 1990. Increased production was accompanied until January 1991 by higher 'spot' prices. With the outbreak of hostilities between the US-led multinational force and Iraq, prices began to decline to pre-conflict levels. Having reached a maximum price of $32 per barrel in October 1990, by February 1991 the 'spot' price of Dubai crude petroleum had fallen to less than $15 per barrel. In March OPEC agreed to lower production levels by 5% in the second quarter of the year. The UAE agreed to reduce its level of production to 2.320m. b/d. From March 1992 the UAE's OPEC quota was set at 2.244m. b/d, which the UAE appeared to be observing, notwithstanding Abu Dhabi's decision to proceed with a $5,000m. development programme designed to add an extra 600,000 b/d of oil production capacity by 1996. In 1992 crude oil production averaged 2,283,200 b/d. UAE petroleum production fluctuated little during 1993–96, hovering around its OPEC quota (set in April 1993) of 2.161m. b/d.

In November 1997, at a meeting of OPEC members convened in Jakarta, Indonesia, production quotas were increased to reflect actual production (many OPEC members, including the UAE, exceeded their quotas in 1997) and the expected increase in demand in 1998; the UAE's new quota was 2.366m. b/d. However, declining petroleum prices in 1998 led to production cuts. In March both OPEC and non-OPEC members agreed to reduce production, and in June, following a further decrease in prices, the UAE pledged to reduce production to 2.157m. b/d compared with average output of 2.270m. b/d in May. In addition to the declining petroleum prices, the UAE was also more directly affected by the economic crisis in Asia, as more than 50% of its exports in 1996 went to Japan, South Korea and Singapore. Petroleum prices continued to decline, and in March 1999 the UAE agreed to reduce production further, to 2.000m. b/d (effective from 1 April), in conjunction with both OPEC and non-OPEC countries in an effort to stabilize the market. By mid-1999 a notable recovery in world petroleum prices had been achieved as a result. Following a continued rise in petroleum prices in 2000, the UAE agreed to raise its level of production to 2.219m. b/d, effective from 1 July. The recovery continued for much of 2000, with prices at times in August–October exceeding their highest levels since the Gulf crisis. It was agreed to raise output from 1 October, to 2.289m. b/d, and further from 31 October, as a result of which the UAE's quota increased by 44,000 b/d. Production quotas were reduced by OPEC in early 2001, in an effort to counter a downward trend in world prices as demand fell. Thus, from 1 February the UAE agreed a reduction in output of 132,000 b/d, to 2.201m. b/d; and a further decrease, to 2.113m. b/d, was effected from 1 April. However, these decreases failed sufficiently to offset the impact on prices of the slowing of international demand, necessitating a further round of production cuts from 1 September whereby the UAE's production quota was reduced to 2.025m. b/d (of an OPEC total of 23.201m. b/d. Following the terrrorist attacks on New York and Washington, DC, later in the same month, international demand slumped even further. The UAE's production quota was reduced by 131,000 b/d to 1.894m b/d. from 1 January 2002.

Whereas in the past much gas was simply burnt off, increasingly the UAE has exploited this resource both for internal energy usage, and as a lucrative source of export earnings. A US $1,000m. onshore gas development programme (OGD-2) at the Habshan natural gas complex near the Bab oil and gas field, was inaugurated in 1998, and was completed in early 2001. The associated $700m. Asab gas project was completed in 1999, and will support industries in Ruwais. Tendering is due in late 2002 for the third phase of the onshore gas development programme (OGD-3) and the second phase of the Asab gas development project. Both are to be completed by 2005 at an estimated total cost of US $2,500m.

During 1999 memoranda of understanding were signed between Qatar, Oman and the UAE, providing for the construction of a gas pipeline to link Qatar to Abu Dhabi, Dubai, Oman and Pakistan, at an estimated total cost of US $10,000m., over a seven-year period. Gas from this project, called Dolphin, will be distributed between UOG (UAE Offsets Group) and ADNOC, according to agreements signed in October 1999. The UAE hopes that the anticipated extension of Dolphin from Oman to Pakistan will materialize as planned in 2005, as UAE investors are keen on developing gas-consuming power plants in the latter country. Qatar, which has huge reserves of unassociated gas in the North Field, is expected to supply 30,000m. cu m of gas per year as part of the scheme. The project has been promoted heavily by Abu Dhabi in response to increasing shortages of gas for power generation in that emirate. In late 2001, two production-sharing agreements were signed by Qatar Petroleum and Dolphin Energy Ltd. By mid-2002 UOG had selected its two private partners for the project—TotalFinaElf and Occidental Petroleum Corporation.

Abu Dhabi

The first company to obtain a concession to explore for petroleum in Abu Dhabi was the Trucial Coast Development Oil Co, which was granted a concession over the entire territory in 1939. In 1962 the consortium was renamed the Abu Dhabi Petroleum Co (ADPC), and during the 1960s it gradually relinquished much of its concession. Agreements made in the early 1970s gave ADNOC, founded in 1971, an eventual 60% share, backdated to 1 January 1974. ADNOC has a monopoly over distribution and is responsible for all petroleum installations and oil-based industries in the emirate. The second largest oil company in Abu Dhabi was founded in 1954 as Abu Dhabi Marine Areas Ltd (ADMA), which in 1971 was a consortium of British Petroleum (BP) and Compagnie Française des Pétroles (CFP). In 1972 BP sold 45% of its shares to the Japan Oil Development Co (JODCO) and by 1974 the Abu Dhabi Government, in the form of ADNOC, had acquired a 60% share. In 1977 ADNOC and ADMA agreed to establish a new company, ADMA-OPCO (with the same shareholders as ADMA), for offshore work, and in 1978 the Abu Dhabi Company for Onshore Oil Operations (ADCO) was formed from ADPC for onshore work. These two companies produced 93% of Abu Dhabi's petroleum in 1979, and the remaining four companies in the emirate, the Abu Dhabi Oil Company Ltd, the Total Abu al-Bukhoosh Co, the Al-Bunduq Company Ltd and Amerada Hess, produced about 7%. The main onshore oilfields are the Murban, Bu Hasa and Asab fields, while the main offshore ones are Umm Shaif (which produced an average 133,599 b/d in 1983) and Lower Zakum (average 71,912 b/d in 1983). This level was broadly maintained into the 1990s. With the onset of the Gulf crisis in August 1990 and the suspension of OPEC quotas, Abu Dhabi provided 75% of the UAE's expanded production, at levels of up to 1.8m. b/d.

Two new discoveries of petroleum were reported in 1982, and during 1983 ADNOC drilled a total of 16 exploration wells. In 1985 two further offshore oilfields came into operation, with the Sateh field producing at 10,000 b/d and the Umm ad-Dalkh field producing at 25,000 b/d. However, the oil glut and reductions in OPEC production quotas for the UAE led to a fall in output prior to the last quarter of 1985. During the last quarter of 1985, however, Abu Dhabi raised production considerably in order to offset declines in prices, and the unfavourable prospects for the oil industry in the short term also led to the postponement of two schemes to increase the rate of recovery from the Sahil and Bab fields. In August 1986 Abu Dhabi was producing approximately 1.3m. b/d, but during 1987 some rationalization of ADNOC's activities took place. ZADCO and UDECO were merged, and by 1988 ADCO was operating only four rigs, compared with 15 in mid-1986, but exploration drilling increased in 1989. In March 1991 Abu Dhabi announced that, as part of a US $7,000m. development plan (1991–95), $2,800m. was to be spent on doubling exports of liquefied natural gas (LNG), increasing long-term production capacity from 2m. b/d to 2.6m. b/d and doubling refining capacity to more than 250,000 b/d. Formal approval had been obtained for the release of the estimated $500m. that was needed to expand capacity at the onshore Bab field and the offshore Upper Zakum field. At the Bab field ADCO aimed to increase capacity from 60,000 b/d to 350,000 b/d. The capacity at the Upper Zakum field was to be increased by 200,000 b/d. Small discoveries that had been ignored over the past decade were also to be reappraised. In late 1994 the broad division of crude oil production within Abu Dhabi was 425,000 b/d from ADMA-OPCO offshore fields, 470,000 b/d from the Upper Zakum offshore field and 920,000 b/d from ADCO's onshore fields. At 1 January 1995 proven oil reserves in Abu Dhabi were 92,200m. barrels (92.6% of the UAE total).

The Government has consistently sought to develop its 'downstream' production, and its first refinery, at Umm an-Nar, came 'on stream' in 1976 with a capacity of 15,000 b/d. A second refinery, at Ruwais, went into operation in June 1981. The Ruwais refinery, which after expansion was originally planned to achieve an output of 300,000 b/d, was producing to a capacity of only 71,000 b/d in 1985 and 1986, after declines in demand had led to cut-backs in the scale of expansion. By 1991 its capacity had fallen to 50,000 b/d. Work on a 60,000 b/d extension of the Umm an-Nar refinery was completed in 1984. In 1993 the capacity of the Umm an-Nar refinery was raised to 85,000 b/d, bringing total refining capacity in Abu Dhabi to 215,500 b/d. The Ruwais refinery produced 132,050 b/d in 1999. In 1994 aggregate refinery throughputs in the UAE averaged 226,000 b/d. The long-standing proposal to expand the Ruwais refinery finally received government approval in January 1995, allowing planners to draw up detailed specifications for a major upgrading package which was expected to cost between US $1,300m. and $1,900m. As well as the construction of two condensate processing plant units, the expansion is expected to include a 420-MW–450-MW power plant, a 30,000 cu m-per-day desalination facility and a major seawater system. In early 1988 the Abu Dhabi-based International Petroleum Investment Co (IPIC) began to develop its refinery interests elsewhere, by purchasing a 10% interest in a Madrid-based refinery, Compañia Española de Petróleos, for $123m. This ensured a secure outlet for 60,000 b/d of Abu Dhabi's crude petroleum. The interest was doubled in early 1989. IPIC (which is jointly owned by ADNOC and the Abu Dhabi Investment Authority) announced plans in May 1994 to acquire a 20% interest in the Austrian energy and chemicals group OMV. During the 1970s there were several plans for the development of petrochemical industries in the emirate, but one of the few to come to fruition was the fertilizer complex at Ruwais, Ruwais Fertilizer Industries (FERTIL), of which two-thirds is owned by ADNOC and one-third by Total-CFP. FERTIL produced 600,000 tons of ammonia and urea in 1994. In 1995 ADNOC announced outline proposals for a major new petrochemical development at Ruwais, to be undertaken after the forthcoming expansion of the Ruwais oil refinery. In November 1998 a contract was awarded for the construction of a 600,000 tons-per-year ethane cracker on the Abu Dhabi Polymers Company complex at Ruwais. Further contracts, for the construction of two 225,000 tons-per-year polyethylene units were awarded in mid-1999. The complex began production in December 2001.

Abu Dhabi's exports of petroleum are transported through two main terminals. The Jebel Dhanna terminal was completed in 1963. Additional installations, finished in 1974, increased the export capacity of ADPC's Murban petroleum to 1,280,000 b/d. ADMA-OPCO's Umm Shaif and Zakum petroleum is exported through the Das terminal. Two smaller terminals exist at Abu al-Bukhoosh and Mubarraz. At the beginning of 1980 ADNOC and JODCO began work on a new terminal, costing $750m., on Delma island. As a result of the onshore petroleum expansion plans announced in March 1991, Jebel Dhanna was also to be expanded. Three new tanks were ready for commissioning in late 1992.

During the early 1970s much of the gas produced in association with petroleum was flared off, but in 1977 an LNG plant at Das island started recovering offshore associated gas, and in 1981 the GASCO plant began onshore gas collection. In 1981 a new gasfield was found underlying the offshore Zakum oilfield, and in 1984 exploration began in Abu Dhabi's share of the Khuff formation, thought to be one of the largest offshore gasfields in the world.

In 1983 the Abu Dhabi Gas Liquefaction Co (ADGAS) borrowed US $500m. to upgrade its Das island complex by building three new LNG storage tanks and four for liquefied petroleum gas (LPG), together with vapour recovery units. The Thamama C Gas project came on stream in 1984, processing gas from the Thamama C foundation of the Bab field. In 1988 Das island produced 2.48m. tons of LNG, 7.8% above design capacity, for export to ADGAS's sole long-term contract customer for LNG, Japan's Tokyo Electric Power Co. A third LNG production train and 34m. cu m per day of additional gas-gathering facilities were completed in 1994, raising the plant's capacity to 5m. tons per year. In early 1995 ADGAS made several LNG shipments to Belgian, Spanish and French importers under single-cargo sales agreements. It subsequently secured short-term contracts to supply a total of nearly 1m. tons of LNG to the same customers between July 1995 and April 1996.

ADNOC's ambitious plans for the further expansion of its 'upstream' gas industry include the Asab field gas development scheme (AGD) and the onshore gas development programme (OGD) (see above).

Dubai

Dubai is the second largest producer of petroleum in the UAE. In 1994 crude oil contributed an estimated 20.1% of Dubai's GDP. By early 1994 output was down to an estimated 275,000 b/d, and steps were being taken to slow the rate of decline through increased use of enhanced recovery techniques. Output had risen to an estimated 320,000 b/d by mid-1994 following the drilling of new wells. Two years later, when Dubai's estimated oil output was around 300,000 b/d, independent analysts were forecasting a decline to around 250,000 b/d in 1997 and to less than 200,000 b/d in 1998, as offshore reservoirs approached exhaustion.

In 1963 Conoco acquired the earlier petroleum concession, held from 1937 to 1961 by Iraq Petroleum Co, and formed the Dubai Petroleum Co (DPC), concentrating on offshore production. In 1954 CFP and Hispanoil had obtained an onshore concession, and formed Dubai Marine Areas Ltd (DUMA). In 1963 DPC acquired a 50% share in DUMA's concession and then released some of its shares to other companies, so that by the late 1960s CFP, Hispanoil, Continental Oil, Texaco, Sun Oil and Wintershall all had shares in DUMA–DPC's concession. By 1974 the Government of Dubai had acquired a 60% share in participation in DUMA–DPC. Nevertheless, the former concessionaire companies continued to operate under the same conditions until, in 1979, the Government decided to buy back 50% of the production to market it directly.

Although petroleum was first discovered in Dubai in 1966, production did not begin until 1969. Output averaged 34,236 b d in 1970, rising to 362,346 b/d in 1978. Output is mainly from the two offshore oilfields of Fateh and South West Fateh, but some petroleum is also lifted from the Rashid and Falah offshore fields. In May 1982 a major new onshore discovery was made in the Margham field, and by 1988 production reached 40,000 b/d of condensate from 15 wells. In April 1989 a 59-km pipeline, linking the Margham field with the gas-processing plant at Jebel Ali, was brought into operation. During the 1970s Dubai's natural gas was flared off, but in 1980 a gas treatment plant, owned by the Dubai Natural Gas Co (DUGAS), began operations. Dubai's gas reserves are estimated at 125,000m. cu m, and the DUGAS plant, at Jebel Ali, began operations with a treatment capacity of 3m. cu m. In 1985 the plant had a production capacity of between 825 and 850 metric tons per day (t/d) of propane, 600 t/d of butane and 850 t/d–900 t/d of condensate. Most of the production from the plant has been shipped to Japan in the past. In 1988 DUGAS and two foreign companies, ASCO (of the USA) and BP, signed an agreement to process associated gas from the Margham field at Jebel Ali. Previously this gas had been flared. Construction of a new DUGAS plant to produce methyl-tertiary-butyl ether, a lead substitute in petrol, was completed in February 1995. In July 1997 the Dubai-based Emirates National Oil Corpn awarded a contract for the construction of a condensate processing plant to an Italian company, Technipetrol. The plant was due to be operational by late 1998, and was expected to produce 60,000 b/ d of naphtha, jet fuel and diesel for sale in the local market. The installation of an unleaded petrol plant was also planned at Jebel Ali.

Because of its vibrant industrial sector, and its decision to begin to use gas rather than oil to supply its power stations, Dubai was expected to increase its gas consumption by 7% per year until at least 2005. The largest consumer is the Dubai Electricity and Water Authority (DEWA). In February 1998 Abu Dhabi agreed to supply Dubai with gas (which was previously supplied mainly by Sharjah). To meet rising demand, the gas and condensate-bearing capacity at the Margham field at Jebel Ali is to be expanded. From 2005, Dubai will draw on supplies from the regional Dolphin project (see above).

Sharjah

Production of petroleum began in Sharjah in 1974, with the Mubarak field producing at the rate of 60,000 b/d. The field lies in a 'protocol area', which is occupied by Iran, and in the north it lies in Iranian territorial concessions for hydrocarbons exploration. Sharjah has production and drilling rights, but shares production and revenue with Iran. This situation caused considerable difficulties following the onset of hostilities between Iran and Iraq, and in 1984 oil exploration was interrupted when Iranian patrol boats arrived near Abu Musa island. The security problems facing Sharjah became more apparent when Iranian naval forces attacked the Mubarak oilfield in April 1988, thereby causing its closure for a period of two months. The field has brought Sharjah revenues of around AED 20m. per year. At the end of 1980 Amoco announced a major new onshore discovery of petroleum and natural gas. Exports of crude petroleum from this Sajaa field started in mid-1982 at a rate of 25,000 b/d. The emirate's total production in

1983 exceeded 50,000 b/d. It is estimated that Sharjah maintained production levels at an average of 65,000 b/d during 1987–90, although in 1991 output was about 25% lower, owing to problems at the Mubarak field. By 1992 output from the Mubarak field had fallen to 8,000 b/d.

Export revenues from Sharjah's two gasfields, Sajaa 1 and Sajaa 2, were expected substantially to reduce Sharjah's international debt, which was estimated at between US $600m. and $700m. in 1986, and average production from the Sajaa fields in 1986 reached 16.98m. cu m per day. However, the collapse of the price of petroleum weakened Sharjah's ability to repay its international debt. A pipeline costing $190m. was completed in 1984, to carry gas from the Sajaa fields to power stations in Ras al-Khaimah, Fujairah, Ajman and Umm al-Qaiwain, and in 1985 this pipeline had a capacity of 60,000 b/d of condensate and 1.1m. cu m per day of gas. Following the settlement of the border dispute between Sharjah and Dubai in 1985, a 24-in (60-cm) gas pipeline was built to supply gas from the Sajaa field to Dubai's power and desalination plant at Jebel Ali. An agreement was also reached in 1983 for Amoco to drill six wells over the ensuing 15 months, to bring the capacity of the Sajaa field to 14.2m. cu m per day. An LPG plant began production in July 1986, with a capacity of 13,000 b/d of mixed LPGs, 7,500 b/d of propane, 6,000 b/d of butane and 6,000 b/d of condensate. Many projects were postponed during the recession of the mid-1980s, but the economic revival following the 1990–91 Gulf crisis enabled the Government to revive development plans. In July 1992 the Amoco Sharjah Oil Co (owned 60% by the Sharjah Government and 40% by Amoco Corpn) announced significant new gas discoveries, and in 1993 plans were announced to expand Sharjah's gas-processing capacity by 60% in 1994. A new contract to supply gas to power stations in the northern emirates was awarded by the UAE federal authorities in June 1994. It was estimated that 50%–60% of Sharjah's dry gas production was piped to Dubai in 1995, with the remainder going to Sharjah and the northern emirates' power stations. Production of condensates and natural gas liquids was 40,000 b/ d–45,000 b/d in 1995. In December 1995 Amoco Corpn signed a memorandum of understanding with the Government of Oman whereby the US company was granted exclusive representation to market Omani gas in the UAE. Amoco's proposal was to build a pipeline from Oman's gas fields to Amoco Sharjah's gas-treatment plant, which would be expanded to handle a greatly increased throughput. (Gas demand in Dubai and the northern emirates was forecast to rise by as much as 34m. cu m per day within six years.)

FAL Petroleum Co (owned by a Sharjah businessman) announced in late 1995 that it had purchased an existing Canadian oil refinery for shipment to Sharjah and reassembly on a free-zone site at Hamriyya, where it was scheduled to begin producing 20,000 b/d of petroleum products in late 1997.

Ajman, Fujairah, Ras al-Khaimah and Umm al-Qaiwain

Of the remaining emirates, Ras al-Khaimah appears to have the largest reserves of petroleum and natural gas. Offshore discoveries, made in 1976 and 1977, proved not to be commercially exploitable, but Gulf Oil made new discoveries off the west coast in 1981. In the same year, an onshore concession was granted to a consortium of Amoco and Gulf Oil, and, following seismic tests, Gulf Oil announced significant discoveries of petroleum and gas in the second offshore test well, Saleh One X, in February 1983. The well started production in February 1984, at 5,000 b/d, followed in April by Saleh Two X at 3,500 b/d, and production there has since increased. At the beginning of 1985, however, Ras al-Khaimah was producing oil at a rate of only between 8,000 b/d and 10,000 b/d. A new well, Saleh Four X, began operating in February 1985, with a production rate of between 7,000 b/d and 8,000 b/d of oil, and a further well, Saleh Five X, was 'spudded' in April. In 1987 production was only 11,000 b/d, most of the revenue from which was used to finance exploration and development. By the end of 1987 a seventh well had been 'spudded' in the Saleh field, and production was reported to be about 12,000 b/d. By mid-1986 the four-stage programme to establish a 'downstream' oil industry in Ras al-Khaimah, at a cost of US $45m.–$50m., had been completed. This consists of pipelines from the Saleh field to the mainland, separation and stabilization facilities, onshore storage facilities for 500,000 barrels, and an LPG plant. In 1991 the Omani Government agreed to allow gas from its Bukha offshore field to be processed at Ras al-Khaimah. Output was expected to be limited to around 5,000 b/d of condensate, 800 b/d of LPG and 40 cu ft of 'dry' gas per day. The emirate has been processing gas at Khor Khuwair since 1985, but utilization has been minimal. In January 1996 a new company, Ras al-Khaimah Oil and Gas, whose principal shareholder was a US investor, signed an agreement to undertake onshore and offshore exploration work in the emirate.

Umm al-Qaiwain's first well was 'spudded' in 1981, and a Canadian concession in the emirate was due to start production in 1985. Exploration continues in Umm al-Qaiwain, as it does in Ajman, where drilling for petroleum finally began in 1982. In July 1983 Ajman formed the Ajman National Oil Co (AJNOC), with a capital of US $37m. In February 1984 it was announced that two Canadian oil companies had been granted offshore concessions in Fujairah, and in 1988 Broken Hill Petroleum of Australia conducted a seismic survey off shore from the emirate. Further exploration of the northern emirates featured prominently in the UAE's 1991–95 development plan. In late 1995 a 30,000 b/d refinery, purchased second-hand from a major multinational by the Greek company Metro Oil, went into production in Fujairah upon completion of more than 12 months' reassembly work. The refinery's product mix was configured to supply the needs of shipping using Fujairah's bunkering facilities. In 1995 Fujairah's deep-water port was one of the world's largest bunkering stations. It had about 500,000 cu m of product storage capacity and was well placed to act as a bulk oil trade centre for the Gulf and the Indian sub-continent. A major new tank-terminal venture, with a projected initial capacity of 465,000 cu m and a projected final capacity of 700,000 cu m, was under development in Fujairah in 1996 by a consortium led by Royal Van Ommeren (a Dutch company with world-wide oil storage interests).

INDUSTRY

Since the UAE was formed in 1971, the diversification of the economy away from petroleum has been a clearly stated government policy. The development of an integrated infrastructure and extensive construction work took place in the 1970s, and this early industrial development was manned largely by immigrant labour. It was estimated that by 1982 the labour force of the UAE was 559,960, of whom a large majority—in some sectors over 90%—were non-nationals. In the early 1980s, anxiety over the large number of Asian workers and unemployment led to the enforcement of a restrictive labour-law and stricter visa regulations, making it increasingly difficult for overseas casual labourers to settle in the UAE. However, by 1986, when the expatriate work-force in Dubai totalled only 75,070, the decline of the economy had led to a reversal of this policy, and the Government had begun to encourage immigrant labourers earning incomes above a certain level to bring their families with them. A survey conducted by the UAE Ministry of Economy and Industry in 1988 indicated the poor productivity of capital invested in manufacturing industry in the UAE, a lack of new technology and the low level of wages paid to the mainly Asian work-force.

In 1987 non-oil manufacturing industry contributed 11% of GDP (compared with 4% in 1980), but in 1990 the proportion declined to 7.3%, its value being AED 9,300m. In 1994 this sector contributed 8.3% of GDP, with a value of AED 11,160m.

The federal Ministry of Electricity and Water is responsible for 11 power stations: at Umm al-Qaiwain, Falaj al-Mualla, Dhaid, Masfut, Manama, Uzun, Masafi, Fujairah, Qidfa and Dibba. On the east coast a 33-kV overhead transmission system were installed, and a number of small contracts were issued in 1980 to link the remainder of the power supply system in this area. In 1982 the power stations at Qidfa and Ghalilah began operations, resulting in a 97% rise in power output in the northern emirates during the first nine months of the year. Dubai, Ras al-Khaimah, Sharjah and Abu Dhabi are responsible for their own power. In addition to the old diesel, gas and steam stations, Abu Dhabi's power is provided by the Umm an-Nar East and West stations, Units 9 and 10, a new 600-MW station at Bani Yas, and stations at Sadiyat and al-Ain. Until recent years, the Government of Abu Dhabi operated power and elec-

tricity services directly through the Abu Dhabi Water and Electricity Department (ADWED). However, in early 1998 a government committee recommended that ADWED be transformed into a semi-autonomous regulatory body called the Abu Dhabi Water and Electricity Authority (ADWEA), and that Abu Dhabi's power stations should be partially or totally privatized. In April 1989 it was announced that the Taweela A power station, under construction since 1984, would begin operation in August, supplying Abu Dhabi with 250 MW of power and 20m. gallons of water per day (g/d). The second phase, originally approved in January 1987 and recently completed, entailed the construction of a power station (Taweela B) with a capacity of 732 MW, and a desalination unit with a capacity of 76m. g/d. Work on the Taweela project was interrupted by the Gulf crisis of 1990–91. Further delays were caused by the decision, in March 1991, to invite retenders for construction of Taweela B, with a view to securing a bid closer to the sum allocated for the project. In the event, the 'turnkey' contract was awarded for the Taweela B project in July 1992, to a Zürich-based consortium. The al-Taweelah Power Company was to manage the Taweelah B facility; with the addition of two new gas-turbine units its capacity would rise to 1,220 MW.

Expenditure on power has often been subject to budgetary constraints, but, with demand rising by about 10% per year, the Government has decided to press rapidly ahead with expansion projects. By 1994 the total installed capacity of the UAE's power stations was 5,000 MW, while the anticipated demand in 2000 was 7,500 MW. In April 1997 the Abu Dhabi Government approved the US $700m. expansion of the Taweela A power and desalination plant to be implemented as an independent power project. Under its new owners, the Emirates CMS Power joint venture, it assumed full-scale production of electricity and desalinated water in 2001. Plans have also been announced for the expansion of the Jebel Ali E station by 232 MW to 472 MW, and for the construction of a new power station, Jebel Ali G, with a capacity of 440 MW. A major generation station built at Mirfa, near Ruwais, already supplies many villages and islands in Abu Dhabi with 246 MW and 16.2m. gallons of water per day. It will soon expand its capacity via an $80m. investment by the new al-Mirfa Power Company. Similar upgrading is planned for the Umm al-Nar plant, run by a private company of the same name. In April 2002 ADWEA invited bids from foreign companies for a 40% stake in the new project company that is to be established for the upgrading of Umm an-Nar. In December 1999 bids were received for a 1,500 MW plant at Shuweihat, west of Abu Dhabi, to be operational by 2004. In August 2001 the US/UK joint venture CMS Energy and International Power signed a 20-year power and water purchase agreement for the first phase of the project; CMS has taken a 40% stake in a new utility company, the Shuweihat CMS International Power Company, while ADWEA has secured a 60% stake. In December loan financing agreements were signed for the first phase and Siemens were awarded the 'turnkey' contract to build the plant. Fisia Italimpianti was awarded the contract to build the associated desalination plant.

At a more strategic level, the UAE federal Government plans to enter the second stage of a US $1,000m. plan to create a regional power grid in the GCC region. Before the UAE can join, however, it must ensure that it unifies its own power grid by connecting stations along its western coast with those in the centre. By mid-2002 the Federal Ministry of Electricity and Water were reported to be close to approving a draft study for the Emirates' National Grid Project (ENG). The cost of the project was expected to be AED 630m.–680m.

The lack of water resources has led to much investment in the provision of fresh water. This has been achieved by building new underground wells, and desalination plants—22 in 1985 and 82 by 1999. The latter supply about 200m. g/d to the federation, and meet 82% of its total water needs. However, both expedients carry problems: wells have dangerously lowered the water table, while desalination plants have proven costly for the poorer northern emirates, and are strategically vulnerable to attack. By 1985 there were 22 desalination plants in the UAE. In 1982 annual water demand was estimated at 565m. cu m, of which agriculture used 410m. cu m. Examples of projects which have been completed are: a 3.3m. g/d desalination plant associated with the power station at Qidfa, in Fujairah, and a reverse osmosis desalination plant, with a capacity of 3.6m. g/d, at Ajman. Four 50 MW steam turbines, and two 18,000-cu m-per-day multi-stage flash desalination units were built at Raafah, in Umm al-Qaiwain. A project to divert water from two Turkish rivers, the Ceyhan and the Seyhan, to the Gulf along two pipelines, totalling 5,000 km in length, has been discussed, but has never come close to implementation. By January 1995 Abu Dhabi had an installed desalination capacity of 110m. g/d and was proceeding with six new projects which would add an additional 84m. g/d of capacity. Of the 81m. g/d of desalinated water supplied to Abu Dhabi city in 1994, 44m. g/d was for domestic use and the remainder for horticultural use. Dubai had 30m. g/d of excess desalination capacity in 1995, the completion of new water plants at power stations having eliminated the water authority's need to purchase up to half of Dubai's fresh water supply from a desalination facility attached to the Dubai Aluminium Co (DUBAL) complex. Plans were announced in 1995 to install a total of about 8m. g/d of new desalination capacity in the northern emirates of Fujairah, Ajman and Ras al-Khaimah. In July 1997 the federal Ministry of Electricity and Water awarded an AED 235m. contract to the local Emirates Trading Agency for the supply and installation of five new desalination units in the northern emirates.

Abu Dhabi

Abu Dhabi City is a thriving metropolis of more than 600,000 people. Oil contributes about one-quarter of this emirate's GDP, but Abu Dhabi also derives income from massive investment in overseas assets, estimated at about US $150,000m. Most of Abu Dhabi's heavy industry is centred on the Jebel Dhanna-Ruwais industrial zone, 250 km west of Abu Dhabi city, which was officially opened by Sheikh Zayed in March 1982. In 1979 the General Industries Corpn (GIC) was set up to co-ordinate non-petroleum development, and by early 1981 it was involved in a paper bag factory, a brick works, a concrete block factory, a steel-rolling mill, and an animal feed plant, all of which had begun production in the preceding two years. An industrial bank, the Emirates Industrial Bank, was founded in 1983 to fund new industrial projects. Light industry is concentrated in the al-Musalah area, just over the bridges joining Abu Dhabi island to the mainland. In 1985 there was a total of 221 industrial units in Abu Dhabi. A bottling plant for Coca-Cola opened in 1989, and the construction of a plant to manufacture 6,000 tons of polyurethane blocks per year has been announced. The government-owned Abu Dhabi Investment Co (ADIC) launched an industrial investment programme in 1993. In 1995 the GIC was finalizing plans to sell five industrial plants with an estimated combined valuation of AED 700m., this being the UAE's first privatization initiative since 1985 and the first in which the intended means of privatization was a series of share offers through the UAE's informal stock market. In February 1996 the GIC announced that shares worth AED 300m. in several of its food processing companies would be distributed to social security recipients, low-income employees and small shareholders. New projects under active evaluation by the GIC in mid-1996 included the construction of a rolling mill at Taweela to manufacture steel bars for the local building industry. In June 1997 it was reported that the GIC had launched an AED 100m. industrial loan fund to support private sector participation in small and medium-sized industrial ventures in the emirate. The joint venture, The Abu Dhabi Polymers Company, began production of polyethylene in December 2001.

A joint-stock company called Abu Dhabi Ship Building (ADSB) was established in 1995 with the US company Newport News (40%) and the Abu Dhabi Government (18.5%) as founding shareholders. The remaining 41.5% of the share capital was raised through a heavily over-subscribed public offering. ADSB's repair and construction facilities for naval and merchant vessels were to be located initially at an established dry dock at Mussafah pending construction of a purpose-built yard with a projected completion date of 1999.

A decree was issued in July 1996 to establish Abu Dhabi's first free zone on Saadiyat island, east of Abu Dhabi city. It is currently investing US $3,300m. to develop storage, transportation and trading facilities for various commodities, from ores, grain and foodstuffs to precious metals and gems. The island is currently being linked to Abu Dhabi city by a 6-km bridge. In August 1997 it was announced that both local and international investors would be offered a $1,700m. equity stake in the initial public offering in the Saadiyat Free Zone Authority (SFZA) which will regulate the free zone. A project development company will build and operate the facilities on the island under a 25-year renewable concession agreement.

Dubai

Dubai has taken the lead in developing non-petroleum industry (which could explain how in 1983, when the UAE witnessed a narrowing of its trade surplus, Dubai's increased by 30%, despite a 14% decline in petroleum revenues). Dubai accounts for 70% of the Emirates' non-oil trade, attracting foreign investors as an offshore financial, business and tourism centre. Based on a plan first drafted in 1993, Dubai projects non-oil GDP growth of up to 7% annually until 2015. This has been centred on the Jebel Ali port and industrial area, 30 km west of Dubai city. The decision to build a new deep-sea port was taken in August 1976, and there were 15 km of quays by mid-1981. The port possessed 67 berths by 1988, and is the largest man-made harbour in the world. In 1989 Jebel Ali Port handled 9.97m. tons of cargo. The older Port Rashid had 35 berths by mid-1984. By 1985 there was a total of 305 industrial units in Dubai. Despite a reduction in trade through Dubai's ports in the immediate aftermath of Iraq's invasion of Kuwait in August 1990, owing to raised war risk insurance premiums, shipping container tonnage in 1990 rose by 79% and general cargo tonnage by 61% compared with 1989. In May 1991 a new company, the Dubai Ports Authority (DPA), was established to take over the running of Port Rashid and Jebel Ali. Dubai's ports played an important role as transhipment points for Kuwait's reconstruction programme.

The first major plant to begin production was an aluminium smelter, owned by DUBAL, which commenced operations at the end of 1979. It was built at a cost of US $800m., and initially had an installed capacity of 135,000 metric tons of aluminium ingots per year. By 1988 production had increased to 163,445 tons, of which Japan purchased 64%. Asian countries are major customers of the plant. In May 1989 work began on the expansion of the plant by more than 40%, to a capacity of 240,000 tons per year. In January 1995 DUBAL announced plans to expand its production capacity to 372,600 tons per year by early 1997 at a cost of $503m., of which $253m. would be financed out of company resources and the balance through a five-year syndicated bank loan. A further expansion of production capacity, to 525,000 tons per year (at a cost of $725m.), was completed in early 2000. Dubai Investment PJSC envisages that its $160m. aluminium rolled products plant will be operational in 2004.

In 1979 another industrial plant, cable manufacturer DUCAB, came into production. Its sales of cables were worth a record AED 212m. ($57.7m.) in 1993, when it won major new export orders in Asian markets. In 1994 DUCAB produced nearly 20,000 tons of copper and aluminium cable. In 1995 it expanded its product range to include specialist lead-sheathed cables for the oil, gas and petrochemical industries. Initially, DUCAB was jointly owned by BICC of the United Kingdom and the Dubai Government, but in June 1997 the Abu Dhabi Government bought a 35% share in the company.

In May 1980, in an effort to promote Dubai's industrial development, Sheikh Rashid decreed that Jebel Ali should be a free-trade zone. The Jebel Ali Free Zone Authority, which offers the advantages of duty-free trade, was finally inaugurated, under full foreign ownership, in early 1985 (see Trade, Transport and Tourism). By mid-1994 around 630 companies had set up businesses in the Jebel Ali Free Zone, and new companies were arriving there at an average rate of 15 per month. Major foreign companies locating there included Xerox, Union Carbide, 3M, Black and Decker, Mitsubishi, York International, BP Amoco Arabian Agencies and Shell Markets. Local firms at Jebel Ali include Dubai's National Cement Co and the National Flour Mills, which began production in 1987. A new sugar refinery with a daily capacity of 2,400 tons was due to go into production in late 1994. In 1990 a warehouse and distribution facility for the Sony Corpn and a US $3m. manufacturing plant for the Kavoos Co of Iran, to make raw materials for paint production, were opened. Jebel Ali Free Zone has become an important distribution point for Kuwait's reconstruction programme. In 1990 investments in the zone reached AED 1,500m., a 50% increase on 1989 levels. A second area for light industry has also been developed around the extended port area of Mina Rashid in Dubai itself. The garment-manufacturing sector has expanded dramatically, with the value of exports rising from an insignificant level in 1985 to $227.1m. in 1993. The industry is concentrated in Jebel Ali, where 25 factories were established by mid-1988, mostly by Indian businessmen. However, punitive quotas, introduced by the USA, have caused some units to close. The economic importance of this sector to the UAE is diminished by the fact that all raw materials and labour are imported, mainly from India.

In April 1993 the authorities introduced a new law that explicitly excluded licensed national firms from the offshore provisions of the original free-trade zone legislation (see Trade, Transport and Tourism, below), confirmed their liability to the provisions of Dubai's standard company laws, and made the granting of a licence subject to proof of at least 51% UAE or GCC ownership of the company concerned and at least 40% locally added value in its products. It was hoped that the removal of former ambiguities would encourage more local companies to take advantage of the infrastructure benefits of manufacturing within the zone.

In 1994 (which saw a marked decline in textile and garment exports) the Jebel Ali Free Zone Authority adopted a policy of not granting new licences to garment manufacturers, on the grounds that it did not wish to encourage labour-intensive industries. By early 1995 the total number of companies using the zone was about 735, drawn from 70 countries in all parts of the world. Distribution and sales operations (often serving markets far beyond the Gulf region) outnumbered manufacturing and assembly operations by about two to one, although manufacturing and assembly accounted for four-fifths of total investment in the zone. An Indian company announced in early 1995 that it was to invest US $27m. at Jebel Ali to establish a nylon tyre cord factory with an annual capacity of 18,000 metric tons. In mid-1996 India's Southern Petroleum Industries Corpn (SPIC) announced plans to locate a fertilizer plant at Jebel Ali to serve the Indian market. At that time more than 1,000 companies were operating in the Jebel Ali free zone.

Investment in 'high-technology' ventures such as computer assembly fell well short of targets set by the Free Zone Authority, which was currently making special efforts to attract this type of venture. Dubai inaugurated its US $200m. Internet City (DIC), a 25 sq km collection of offices to attract international names in 'e-commerce' in October 2000. By September 2000 180 companies had apparently rented all available space in DIC, which includes an internet university. The terrorist attacks on New York and Washington, DC, in September 2001 led to the short-term closure by some foreign companies of their offices in Dubai and the cancellation of a number of conferences, but Dubai's significant spending on infrastructure projects, which rose by 24.2% in 1999–2001, looked set to continue.

The Northern Emirates

Industrial development in the remaining emirates has been based largely on the construction industry and port expansion. Two container ports have been developed in Sharjah, where there is also a lubricating oil plant, a rope factory, the Sharjah Oxygen Co, a factory making plastic pipes and a cement plant producing 700 tons per day. The Gulf Industries Complex in Sharjah's industrial zone was opened in 1981, producing furniture and household utensils. In April 1982 a fodder factory at Mina Khaled, operated by the Gulf Company for Agricultural Development, was opened. An LPG plant came into operation on the site in July 1986. According to a study by the Emirates Industrial Bank, Sharjah was the focus of 35% of the UAE's industrial installations in 1987. Total capital investment in Sharjah increased from AED 461m. in 1977 to AED 997m. in 1987, while the number of employees doubled, from 3,173 to 6,840, over the same period. Sharjah's industrial sector registered 48% growth in 1988. After 1996 Sharjah, already well established as a centre for light industry, set up its fifteenth industrial park on the border with Dubai. Here, units produce perfumes, clothing, furniture, paint, plastic pipes, ready-mix concrete and building materials.

Ras al-Khaimah has developed a valuable export business in aggregate (stones used in making concrete) from the Hajar Mountains. The first explosives factory in the Gulf was opened there in 1980, and a pharmaceutical factory was opened in 1981. The emirate has a cement factory, an asphalt company and a lime kiln, and in 1981 the Ras al-Khaimah Company for White Cement was established to build the Gulf's first white cement factory at Khor Khuwair. This joint Kuwaiti-UAE venture commenced operations in March 1986, producing 300,000 tons of white cement per year.

At the end of 1980 the Government of Fujairah established a department of industry and economy to organize industrial development. Fujairah has factories producing marble, tiles, rockwool (asbestos) insulation, concrete blocks, tyres and shoes, and many of these industries use materials from the Hajar mountains, where surveys have indicated significant quantities of copper, chromite, talc and magnesium. Commercial production of 1,600 tons per day began at a new cement plant in Dibba in 1982, when Fujairah's US $4.9m. rockwool factory also started operations, with an annual capacity of 5,000 tons. Cement production capacity was due to rise to 2,500 tons per day during 1996. A new port with 11 berths was opened in Fujairah in 1982. Traffic at the port increased after Iraq's invasion of Kuwait in August 1990 as shippers attempted to avoid the war risk insurance premiums levied on the Gulf ports of Abu Dhabi and Dubai. In 1990 traffic at the port of Fujairah increased by 50% compared with 1989. A crushing plant, designed to produce 3m. tons per year of aggregate for cement production, went into production in May 1985. A five-year Development Plan, announced in 1988, included proposals for a $100m. industrial suburb and a $140m. break-shipment warehouse project. Fujairah outlined ambitious development plans in 1991, based on significant investment by the GCC member states. These include a Gulf railway, with the spur of the line connecting with the port of Fujairah, and a petrochemical complex. A free-zone facility in Fujairah was the base for 55 enterprises in mid-1995. Its total trade volume in the first half of 1995 was 6,152m. tons (principally foodstuffs, textiles, electronic goods, medical equipment, packaging and steel commodities) with a value of AED 260m.

Umm al-Qaiwain has concentrated on construction, and the newly-formed Umm al-Qaiwain Cement Industries Co plans to build a cement works producing 1m. tons per year to add to the one already in existence. Currently, however, the UAE's annual cement capacity is 8.4m. tons, which is four times the level of local demand of 2m. tons, and consequently the UAE's eight cement works are seeking to implement a production quota system. Cement production and related activities are likely to remain the dominant sector of the economy of Umm al-Qaiwain. Plans, announced in 1986, for the construction of an aluminium smelter, at a cost of US $1,200m., were abandoned in 1988, and the smelter will now be built in Qatar. Umm al-Qaiwain has also followed Dubai's example by establishing a free zone by royal decree in 1987.

Ajman, the smallest emirate, has a cement factory, a dry dock and a ship repair yard. There is a pressing need for improved infrastructure in Ajman. In December 2001 an international consortium was awarded a wastewater concession by the Ajman Government. In 1991 the federal Government announced plans for a 240-MW increase in the electricity production capacity of the northern emirates. Contracts to install an extra 210 MW of capacity were awarded in late 1994. Plans were being drawn up in 1995 for new west-coast electricity distribution links between Ras al-Khaimah, Ajman and Umm al-Qaiwain, while a proposal to link the northern emirates to the Abu Dhabi grid was under consideration as a future development option. In January 1997 the federal Ministry of Electricity and Water signed contracts for the interconnection of the west-coast power distribution network in the northern emirates.

AGRICULTURE

Since the establishment by FAO of an agricultural experimental station at Digdagga (Ras al-Khaimah) in 1955, agriculture in the UAE has undergone a major transformation. Traditionally, agriculture was based on nomadic pastoralism, in association with some oasis cultivation on the east coast and at Liwa, Dhaid, al-Ain and Falaj al-Mualla. This cultivation was totally dominated by dates. Although dates are still the major crop in terms of area cultivated, the production of vegetables has increased dramatically, particularly in Abu Dhabi, and now accounts for the largest revenues.

In April 1984 a ban was announced on imports of those foods in which the UAE is self-sufficient, during growing seasons. This expansion has been implemented through the creation of a widespread government extension service. In general, agricultural inputs are provided to farmers at about one-half of their real cost, with the Government subsidizing fertilizers, seeds and pesticides at 50% of cost. A central laboratory for the Ministry of Agriculture and Fisheries was officially opened near al-Ain in April 1982. In 1982 official figures stated that total production of fruit and vegetables reached 343,500 metric tons. In that year the value of vegetable production was AED 773m., of a total GNP of AED 119,700m. Some of this had, in the past, gone to waste, and in 1983 the Government established the Public Corporation for Agricultural Produce to ensure that surplus vegetables were shared between the emirates, and to package and store produce. Agricultural production increased from 39,000 tons in 1972 to more than 600,000 tons per year in the late 1980s, while the area of cultivable land increased from about 48,000 ha to more than 250,000 ha in 1994. Date production rose from 62,000 tons in 1986 to an estimated 318,000 tons in 2000, while tomato production increased from 42,000 tons in 1990 to an estimated 780,000 tons in 2000. Government figures indicate that in al-Ain the number of farms increased from 980 in 1979 to 1,939 in 1983, with an increase in farm area over the same period from 43,000 dunums to 82,668 dunums. The area of forest in the al-Ain region also increased, from 10,617 ha in 1978 to 13,433 ha in 1983.

There are a number of large-scale agricultural enterprises in the UAE. By 1981 there were three private dairy farms, four poultry farms, a French-sponsored fresh vegetable concern at al-Ain, and a government wheat project on 600 ha at al-Oha, near al-Ain. During 1984 the Arab Company for Animal Production's farm in Ras al-Khaimah was reported to be producing 16,000 cartons of milk and yoghurt daily from its 600 cows. A US $26m. poultry farm has been built at Fujairah. This produces 3.5m. birds and 11m. eggs per year. In 1989 the UAE produced about 13,000 tons of poultry, making the country 45% self-sufficient. Output of eggs reached 170m. in 1989, satisfying 70% of domestic requirement. A vegetable-canning factory was opened at al-Ain in 1986. In 2000 the UAE produced an estimated 30,000 tons of poultry meat, and output of eggs totalled 13m. tons.

The increased cultivation of vegetables and, in particular, the extensive forestry programme have led to severe problems with the water tables. Between 1976 and 1980 1,545 new wells were dug by government teams, and it seems that at least this number were also dug privately. The consequent fall in the water table has been dramatic, especially near the coast. In 1980 the water table in Ras al-Khaimah fell by 3.37m. In places this has led to increased salinity of soil and water. Encroachment of seawater was also reported in 1982, when it apparently penetrated as far as 20 km inland in the northern emirates. As a result, several farms went out of production. The Government has attempted to alleviate the problem through the construction of desalination plants (see Industry) and catchment dams, such as those opened in 1982 at Wadi Ham and Wadi Bih. At the end of 1982 the Government barred the drilling of new wells in parts of the northern emirates. In November 1982 the Tebodin Co of the Netherlands began a comprehensive study of the fresh water needs of the four smallest emirates until 2011, to enable the Ministry of Electricity and Water to formulate policies for those emirates. In 1983 a new dam was opened in Fujairah, with a capacity of 10m. cu m of rain-water, and plans were laid for the construction of a 17,000 cu m-per-day desalination plant at Ajman. Despite the problems facing the UAE concerning its water supply, plans were shelved in 1984 for the construction of eight recharge dams. During 1987 Abu Dhabi's Executive Council announced plans to drill a further 200 artesian wells in three parts of the emirate to supply farmers with yet more water for irrigation purposes. Further plans for the western region in 1988 included the construction of small desalination plants to treat brackish water pumped by free pumps, and the cultivation of 600 ha, using sprinklers and drip irrigation. In

1990 Abu Dhabi announced its intention to cultivate 1,300 ha in Abu Dhabi, the western region and al-Khaten. In order to irrigate this land 100 wells were to be sunk and two reservoirs were to be built. A large fossil-water reservoir was discovered at a depth of 70 m in the Liwa area of Abu Dhabi's western region in 1996, prompting the announcement of a 630-well drilling programme. In 2002, the federal Ministry of Agriculture and Fisheries acknowledged that pressure on groundwater resources was still increasing, and stated that it intended to create more stations for treatment of sewerage water to be used for the irrigation of public parks and forests. Shortage of groundwater had reached 2,100m. cu m by 1999.

By 2000, the UAE was expected to reach 100% self-sufficiency in wheat, and 95% self-sufficiency in fish, although in 1985 it was reported that over-fishing in breeding areas was beginning to have adverse effects on the fishing industry. The total catch was 95,129 tons in 1990, when there were 10,611 full-time fishermen, compared with about 4,000 in 1980. It was estimated in 1993 that the current annual catch of 97,200 tons exceeded local demand for fish by about 27,200 tons. Part of this surplus was exported and part was returned to the sea (there being no fish-processing industry in the UAE to provide a market for it). In 1998 the total catch was 114,739 tons.

By 2000 the contribution of the agricultural sector to non-oil GDP had risen to 6.3% from 4.5% in 1995. The number of workers in the sector increased from 91,112 to 120,242 during the same period. The total area cultivated had reached 475,000 ha, representing 6% of the land area of the UAE.

TRADE, TRANSPORT AND TOURISM

During the 1970s the UAE's earnings from exports of petroleum enabled the country to retain a healthy overall balance of trade. In the early 1980s decreases in the levels of the UAE's petroleum production resulted in a relative decline in the country's trade surplus. The Iran–Iraq War brought considerable problems for the economies of other countries in the region, but Dubai continued to benefit from its trade links with Iran. In 1990, as a result of increased oil export volume and firmer oil prices, occasioned by the Gulf crisis, the trade surplus increased to AED 37,000m., from AED 20,387m. in 1989. Trade surpluses were markedly lower between 1992–94, but from 1995 they began steadily to rise. Both exports and imports rose, but the rate of growth of the former outstripped the latter. In 1995 the trade surplus was AED 22,600m. (exports and re-exports AED 114,000m., total imports AED 91,400m.), increasing to AED 29,500m. in 1996 (exports and re-exports AED 130,700m., total imports AED 101,200m.) and to AED 30,300m. in 1997 (exports and re-exports AED 139,500m., total imports AED 109,100m.). The trend towards a rapidly rising trade surplus since 1995 was, however, brought to an end by the economic slowdown and decline in petroleum prices brought about by the terrorist attacks on New York and Washington, DC, in September 2001. The trade surplus for 2001 decreased to AED 16,500m. (exports and re-exports AED 139,460m., total imports AED 123,000m.), and forecasts for 2002 anticipated a surplus of only AED 4,700m.

The principal commodity groups in the UAE's imports are basic manufactures, machinery and transport equipment, and food and live animals. The leading purchasers of crude petroleum from Abu Dhabi are Japan, Western Europe and the Far East. All of Sharjah's petroleum exports go to the USA. In 1993 the leading suppliers of imports into the UAE were Japan, China, the USA, the United Kingdom and India. The UAE was admitted to GATT membership in March 1994, and to its successor, the World Trade Organization, in February 1996.

One way in which trade has been allocated is through the designation of free-trade zones, such as Jebel Ali and Port Zayed. From April 1982 customs duty in Dubai and Sharjah was lowered from 3% to 1%, to bring it in line with Abu Dhabi. In 1983 all the emirates introduced a 4% unified import tariff, following a GCC unified economic agreement in 1981, although this tariff was not uniformly applied throughout the federation until August 1994 (when individual emirates formally abandoned inconsistent customs practices). Imports from within the GCC area were exempt from the 4% tariff, as were many industrial raw materials, agricultural inputs, medicines and certain food items. The GCC unified tariff has not been properly observed by other member states within the region since it was agreed in 1981. The UAE supported a relaunch of this regional initiative at the December 2001 GCC summit in Muscat, Oman, at which it was agreed that a 5% unified tariff would come into effect in January 2003. Since the cease-fire in the Gulf War, several lines which had operated to the east coast during the conflict have returned to the Gulf, and investment in the free-trade zones has risen. The Jebel Ali Free Zone offers various incentives to investors, including: the right to 100% foreign ownership; the absence of taxes, import or export duties; and the right to full repatriation of profits and capital, as well as an ample supply of cheap labour.

The modern internal transport system of the UAE was largely developed in the late 1960s and the 1970s, when main roads were constructed to link all the major cities. The petroleum retailer Emarat (formerly known as Emirates General Petroleum Corpn) operated a network of 168 service stations in 1996. One of the characteristics of the country's economy over recent years has been the expansion in the number of major airports. Over 11.6m. passengers and 637,000 tons of cargo passed through the UAE's airports in 1995. There are six international airports in the UAE, 16 other paved airports, 18 airports with unpaved runways and two heliports. The busiest international airport is Dubai, which was expected to double its capacity to 12m. passengers by the end of 2000. In 1993 Dubai airport handled 5.67m. passengers and 218,264 tons of cargo, and was considering plans to increase its annual cargo-handling capacity from 250,000 to 350,000 tons. In late 1995 plans were announced to expand the airport, which will increase handling capacity to 12m. passengers a year by 2000, and in 1996 some 8.5m. passengers used the airport.

In 1985 Dubai founded its own airline, Emirates Airlines, which by late 1995 was flying to 38 destinations. In 1992 Emirates Airlines announced a US $1,000m. investment plan to purchase new aircraft over a 10-year period. Contracts have since been signed with Boeing (for seven B777 aircraft) and Airbus Industrie (for 16 A330-200 airliners). In July 2000 Emirates Airlines became the first world airline to place an order for a new Airbus A3XX 'super jumbo', with delivery scheduled for 2006. In 1997/98 Emirates Airlines carried 3.68m. passengers and 200,138 tons of cargo, achieving net profits of AED 262.4m. There is strong competition from Gulf Air, which enjoys considerable regional superiority. However, Emirates Airlines appears likely to challenge that superiority in the years ahead. In November 2001 the airline announced that it would buy new aircraft to the value of $15,000m., and would increase its fleet from 36 to 100 aircraft by 2010. The target for through-passengers at Dubai International Airport by the same date was 30m. In May 2001 a further $1,400m. expansion plan for Dubai airport had been announced.

Abu Dhabi has two international airports—the main one handled over 3m. passengers in 1995—which are being upgraded and expanded in a five-year, $500m. investment programme, financed by the Abu Dhabi Government. The new Sharjah international airport handles the bulk of the UAE's air-cargo as well as providing up-to-date facilities for passengers. The other UAE airports are in Fujairah and Ras al-Khaimah.

Port facilities have also been greatly expanded over recent years. The UAE has a total of 15 commercial ports, which between them handle over 33m. tons of cargo a year. Fujairah port's container throughput rose to 480,000 20-foot-equivalent units (TEUs) from 188,129 TEUs in 1987. Container traffic at Mina Rashid was 557,521 TEUs in 1988, while at Mina Jebel Ali the total freight handled was 4,475,175 metric tons. In 1992 the Dubai Ports Authority's area of operations (taking in Mina Rashid and Mina Jebel Ali) was ranked as the world's sixteenth busiest container port, with combined traffic of 1.48m. TEUs, shared almost equally between the two locations. In 1998 these two ports handled more than 36m. metric tons of cargo. The number of vessels calling at the Dubai ports in 1992 was 8,253, and the amount of general cargo handled, excluding petroleum, totalled 2.8m. tons. In 1998 the Dubai Ports Authority's area of operations handled 2.8m. TEUs. In that year the Abu Dhabi port of Mina Zayed handled 4,368,007 tons of general cargo. Total container traffic at the UAE's six major ports was some 3.5m. TEUs for 1995 (of which 2.15m. TEUs passed through the Dubai ports). There are plans for a new port at Taweela in

Abu Dhabi to serve the proposed industrial zone. Substantial development is planned for the site with a new shipbuilding facility, and a gas processing facility to treat offshore Khuff gas before it is delivered to Jebel Ali in Dubai. In June 2002 the shipbuilding facility was opened, with a 2,000-ton shiplift capable of raising vessels with a length of 85 m, and two assembly halls where as many as six ships can be built simultaneously. The facility will allow for the construction of military corvettes for the UAE navy.

The UAE tourism industry, which in 1993 catered for more than 1m. visitors for the first time, underwent rapid expansion from 1995 as several major development schemes neared completion while others were at earlier stages of construction. In Dubai, the principal centre for UAE tourism (with 1,768,000 visitors in 1996), the main emphasis was on diversification into luxury beach and resort developments catering predominantly for holidaymakers rather than the business travellers who constituted the core clientele of many of Dubai's older-established hotels. Promotion of the UAE as a year-round destination for 'sunshine tourism' was aimed in the mid-1990s mainly at the upper end of the European, Japanese and American markets. The completion of the world's tallest hotel—the Bourj al-Arab, or 'Tower of the Arabs'—in December 1999, was expected to attract large numbers of tourists to Dubai. In May 2001 an ambitious project to develop 120 km of coastline in Dubai was announced. Known as the Palm Islands Project, the development was expected to reach completion by early 2004, despite the downturn in tourism arising from the terrorist attacks on New York and Washington, DC, in September 2001. The project involves the construction of 2,000 residential villas, up to 40 hotels and a host of other tourist facilities.

COMMUNICATIONS

According to recent estimates, there are more mobile telephones (about 1m.) in the UAE than land-lines. Analysts further predict that the demands of business will require 9.3m. telephone lines by 2013. Nearly 70% of households have satellite dishes, and the UAE is ranked seventh world-wide in the use of paging services. The UAE has 22 radio stations and 15 television stations. The Government has been particularly enthusiastic about the possibilities of multi-media, internet and 'e-commerce' (see above). Indeed, the GCC region (including the UAE) has 15 times higher 'internet penetration' than the Arab world as a whole. In February 2000 the UAE created an Electronic Commerce and Media Zone to encourage international and regional Arab media firms to relocate. In April 2000 the UAE and India signed a protocol on co-operation in the field of information technology. However, a law of 1988 still applies, which encourages self-censorship in the UAE's established newspapers, and may dissuade media concerns to move to the UAE. Furthermore, a 'hacker' spread alarm on UAE internet servers in early 2000, making many government figures think more cautiously about the pitfalls of this 'new economy'. In October 2001 an 'e-government' initiative was launched, reinforcing the UAE's reputation as a regional pioneer in this area. The publicly-owned telecoms monopoly, Etisalat, announced in January 2002 that it expected the number of internet subscribers to reach 310,000 in 2002, with the number of actual users exceeding 1m.

BANKING AND FINANCE

The unit of currency in the UAE is the dirham, which was created in 1973 to replace the Bahraini dinar and the Qatar/Dubai riyal, formerly used in the emirates. With effect from March 1996, 'AED' superseded 'Dh' as the Central Bank's official abbreviation for the currency unit. The dirham is linked officially to the IMF's Special Drawing Right but in practice to the US dollar. In December 2001, the GCC summit in Muscat agreed to establish a single currency for the region, to be called the dinar, by January 2010. A central monetary institution, the UAE Currency Board, was established in 1973, but inter-emirate rivalry prevented it from being given full central banking powers. This has led to a rapid multiplication of banks in the country. The Currency Board, managed mainly by expatriates, was able to bring only a little order to the banking free-for-all. A moratorium on the opening of new banks was imposed in 1975, lifted temporarily and then re-imposed with a let-out for international banks of restricted licences (which allow all operations except domestic retail banking), only five of which have opened. In December 1980 the UAE Central Bank replaced the Currency Board, and the rulers of Abu Dhabi and Dubai agreed to place one-half of their national revenues with the new institution. In April 1981 the moratorium on new banks was lifted again but in May the governor of the Central Bank announced that no foreign banks would be granted new branch licences. In July 1981 the Central Bank became more aggressive and told all foreign banks that they had until 1984 to reduce their operations to eight branches each. One way in which some banks tried to minimize the impact of this legislation was by becoming locally incorporated, with a 60% UAE shareholding. By the end of 1983, however, all foreign banks had complied with the legislation and reduced their number of branches to eight. Early in 1982 the Central Bank again intervened to keep a high level of liquidity in the country by imposing a 30% interest-free reserve requirement on dirham loans placed outside the UAE for less than one year, replacing the former 15% charge, imposed in May 1981, for loans up to three months.

Other disruptions to the banking sector were announced in early 1983. The ruler of Abu Dhabi decided that foreign banks should pay a tax of 20% on profits; and the Central Bank, implementing certain clauses of the 1980 bank law, established an upper limit on borrowing by individual bank directors and boards of directors. Despite this, many banks continued to do well in the early 1980s. In 1982 Umm al-Qaiwain opened its first locally incorporated bank, the National Bank of Umm al-Qaiwain. However, the general 'ceiling' of 5% on loans to individual directors led to the collapse, in 1983, of the Union Bank of the Middle East, which had loaned its Chairman, Abd al-Wahab Galadari, monies representing 25%–30% of the bank's total lending. The Central Bank forced his resignation in November, and established a committee of bankers and businessmen to take over the management of the bank. By mid-1986, Abd al-Wahab Galadari's creditors had received a payment of 75% from the official receivers, which amounted to US $321m. Other banks seem to have adopted policies in accordance with the Central Bank's requirements.

A further development in the banking sector was the establishment, in 1983, of the Emirates Industrial Bank, with an authorized capital of AED 500m., to provide loans to new industries. Towards the end of 1984, in an attempt to discourage capital outflow, the Central Bank announced increases in the percentage of demand deposits accepted by local banks which would have to be placed with the Central Bank. The Central Bank's concern over the liquidity of many of the country's smaller banks has continued, and in 1985 a Central Bank circular obliged each of the UAE's banks to provide a detailed account of its financial operations, thus proving the existence of its inner reserves. This move was followed by a series of mergers involving the country's smaller banks.

The collapse of the price of petroleum in 1986, and the deepening recession of the mid-1980s, caused an increasing number of problems for the majority of the banks in the UAE. In mid-1986 the Central Bank announced several measures that were aimed at imposing restraint in financial matters. The new measures, in particular, prohibited banks operating in the UAE from making unsecured loans. In 1987 provision for loan losses was reduced, and in 1988 the Central Bank announced that UAE banks were in a position to withstand bad debts (i.e. debts unlikely to be repaid). During 1987 a presidential decree specified that, in future, all debt cases would be considered by the civil court rather than the *Shari'a* court, and a further decree spread considerable confusion by announcing that in all cases interest should not exceed the amount of the principal debt. Initially Iraq's invasion of Kuwait in August 1990 severely affected confidence in the banking sector. According to UAE spokesmen, however, the banking sector overcame the negative effects of the Gulf crisis by virtue of speedy action by the Central Bank to ensure liquidity and confidence in the 47 existing commercial banks, whose consolidated balance sheet total increased by 9.5%, to US $35,300m., in the second half of 1990. However, the effective failure of the National Investments and Security Corpn (NISCORP) in September 1991, after recording losses of $35m., impelled the federal authorities to seek to restore confidence by appointing a new Governor of the Central Bank. Total bank assets rose by 10% in 1991, to AED 142,000m.

In 1995, when 19 local and 28 foreign banks were active in the UAE, aggregate bank assets totalled AED 180,892m. (the highest such figure in any Arab state except Saudi Arabia). By June 1998 the total assets of commercial banks had reached AED 207,077m.

Inflation and the growth of bank credit have both been reduced since 1980. In mid-1994 the inflation rate was estimated to be around 6.5% per annum. By 2000 annual inflation averaged just 2.0%. The average rate of inflation for 1990–99 was 3.9% per year.

The UAE had been considering the establishment of a stock exchange since 1985, and the Dubai Financial Market (DFM) finally opened in March 2000. By May 2001 the DFM had 10 listed companies, and had a market capitalization of AED 26,562m. An Abu Dhabi stock exchange is also planned. In May 1997 it was reported that public subscription in the UAE's first mutual fund was to be invited at the beginning of June. Launched and managed by the Emirates Bank Group, the fund would provide the first opportunity for non-UAE nationals to invest in the UAE's equities market. The fund's launch came at a time of increased activity in the UAE stock market. On the informal market, trading volumes had risen by 100% during the previous two years, boosted by the establishment of several new joint stock companies. Several new public offerings are reportedly planned, in advance of the establishment of the long-awaited stock exchange. Several banks have diversified their operations in recent years, notably the Abu Dhabi Commercial Bank, which has introduced Islamic banking, and the British Bank of the Middle East (now HSBC Bank Middle East), which has established a regional treasury centre. In June 1999 the Council of Ministers approved a draft law on the structure of the formal stock exchange; the law has yet to be approved by the Federal National Council. The stock exchange is to be established on Saadiyat island where the Government hopes to establish a regional financial centre. While the DFM was initially affected by the adverse economic impact of the the terrorist attacks in New York and Washington, DC, in September 2001, by the beginning of 2002 the market had recovered. However, levels of investor interest remain relatively low. In February 2002 the creation of the Dubai International Finance Centre (DIFC) was announced, with an initial emphasis upon asset management, Islamic finance and back-office operations. There has been some speculation that this move constitutes nothing more than a repackaging exercise and concerns have been expressed that there might not be demand in the Gulf region for two such centres, given Bahrain's established track-record in this area. However, the DIFC received a boost in May 2002 when the World Bank announced its intention to be the first international financial institution to issue a bond, valued at US $100m., through the Centre. In the previous month the Dubai Government had announced that it would establish a metals and commodities centre for trading in diamonds and gold and other important metals; the Dubai Metals and Commodities Centre is to be created as a free-trade zone offering a 50-year tax moratorium and 100% foreign ownership possibilities to resident companies.

In many economic matters, the individual emirates tend to pursue their own separate policies, although they rarely publish detailed budgets. Abu Dhabi and, to a lesser extent, Dubai, are by far the biggest contributors to the federal budget. Abu Dhabi has not published its budgets since 1984, although in 1988 total expenditure of AED 3,600m. was announced. In 1994 the Abu Dhabi Government announced a 20% spending cut-back for the current year, to be followed by a further 20% cut-back in its 1995 budget. It did not, however, specify the amounts involved, and was generally assumed to be indicating broad objectives rather than imposing binding targets. In 1996 Abu Dhabi was reported to have received revenue of AED 36,332m. and incurred expenditure of AED 62,353m., resulting in a deficit of AED 26,021m., while Dubai recorded a deficit of AED 512m. (from revenue of AED 7,922m. and expenditure of AED 8,434m.). In the same year, Sharjah recorded a surplus of AED 162m. (from revenue of AED 1,456m. and expenditure of AED 1,345m.) and Ras al-Khaimah recorded revenues of AED 217m. and expenditure of AED 254m., resulting in a deficit of AED 37m.

The 1995 federal budget provided for total spending of AED 17,949m. and total revenue of AED 16,903m., leaving a deficit of AED 1,046m. The deficit rose gradually, if unspectacularly, during 1996–2001. By 1999 there was a deficit of AED 2,665m. from revenue of AED 20,245m. and expenditure of AED 22,910m. The draft budget for 2002, announced in March, projected a deficit of AED 2,169m. from revenue of AED 20,987m. and expenditure of AED 23,156m. The decrease in the deficit, despite a continuing rise in expenditure, was attributed to the strong performance of most of the non-oil sectors of the economy.

Sheikh Zayed bin Sultan an-Nahyan, the ruler of Abu Dhabi and President of the UAE, was a founding shareholder of the Bank of Credit and Commerce International (BCCI). In 1988 BCCI became involved in a scandal when two of its US subsidiaries were accused of 'laundering' profits from trade in illegal drugs. With the bank's problems mounting, Sheikh Zayed and Abu Dhabi agencies purchased a 77% stake in BCCI in mid-1990 and sought to formulate a plan for reconstructing BCCI. In September 1990 the headquarters of BCCI were moved from London to Abu Dhabi. The reconstruction plan was thought to involve dividing BCCI into three separately capitalized entities registered in London, Hong Kong and Abu Dhabi, respectively, and with the holding company based in Abu Dhabi. Abu Dhabi invested as much as US $1,000m. in BCCI. These plans, however, were pre-empted when BCCI was closed on 5 July 1991 in seven countries after a report by its auditors, Price Waterhouse, commissioned by the Bank of England, alleged major and systematic fraud by the bank. Within days BCCI operations had been suspended in most of the 69 countries in which it had operated. The UAE protested at the lack of prior consultation before BCCI's closure.

The closure of BCCI caused hardship amongst traders, businessmen and shippers in the UAE. The UAE Government stated that it would compensate private depositors. Abu Dhabi's intention appeared to be to reconstruct the bank as a Middle East and Asian bank. On 3 August 1991 the Bank of Credit and Commerce (Emirates) changed its name to the Union National Bank. It was intended that BCCI's 40% shareholding should be purchased in order to sever all ties with the parent bank. In mid-1992 the Abu Dhabi-based majority shareholders in the former BCCI warned creditors that their offer of 30% compensation payment was final. Creditors, however, appeared unwilling to accept this and ready to risk litigation. In July Abu Dhabi was criticized, in a draft of the official British report of the BCCI collapse, for withholding information as to the scale of the fraud from the Bank of England. In October it was reported that 90% of BCCI's creditors had voted to accept the joint liquidators' plan, but in mid-1993 the objections of a minority of creditors (who were pursuing their case in the Luxembourg courts) continued to delay acceptance of the plan. The Ministry of Justice in Abu Dhabi stated in July 1993 that 13 senior managers of BCCI would go on trial in October on charges including forgery of documents, concealment of banking losses, and making false loans. All but one of the 13 defendants were convicted at the conclusion of the trials in May 1994 (although two convictions were later overturned on appeal).

In January 1995 a Luxembourg court approved a revised settlement plan (already approved by courts in London and the Cayman Islands) under which the Abu Dhabi Government and ruling family would contribute US $1,800m. in compensation payments to BCCI creditors world-wide over a period of three years. In May 1996 the Abu Dhabi Government signed an agreement implementing the settlement plan, whereby $1,550m. was to be paid directly to the liquidators and $250m. was to be paid into an escrow account for later release. The liquidators' stated intention was to pay a first dividend of about 20% of creditors' claims in mid-1996. Subsequent dividends were expected to increase the total compensation paid to 30%–40% of the amount claimed. The UAE Central Bank formally removed BCCI from its banking register in April 1996 (the closing date for compensation claims from UAE depositors). In November 1996 it was announced that the first payments would be made in December of that year. In September 1999 BCCI's liquidators announced that a third payment to creditors was to be made within six months, taking the level of returns to 55%. Earlier that year the liquidators initiated legal action in an attempt to recover some AED 1,691m. from the ruler of Sharjah, Sheikh Sultan bin Muhammad al-Qasimi.

With effect from July 1993, the UAE Central Bank introduced new banking regulations whereby the minimum ratio for capital adequacy was raised to 10% (2% higher than the internationally recommended minimum). Moreover, the legal definition of a bank's 'core' capital and its 'supplementary' capital was respecified in accordance with current international standards. All on- and off-balance-sheet items were required to be ranked according to a schedule of risk. Banks were required to maintain a minimum level of 10% of total risk-weighted assets relative to their capital base, in which 'core capital' must reach a minimum of 6% of total risk-weighted assets, while 'supplementary capital' would be considered only up to a maximum of 67% of core capital. Banks would henceforth be required to report to the Central Bank every three months.

In October 1993 the Central Bank issued a circular tightening the banking regulations still further from the beginning of 1994 (with provision for deferral on a case-by-case basis until the end of 1995). This circular limited any bank's exposure to the following proportion of its capital base: 25% if the exposure was to a government-owned commercial entity; 5% to a director or board member, and no more than 25% in aggregate to the bank's whole board; 6% in aggregate to bank employees; 7% to one of its shareholders, or a single borrower, or a group of related borrowers; 20% to a subsidiary or affiliate. There were also ceilings on funded inter-bank exposures, letters of credit and guarantee, and other contingent liabilities. Banks were required to report large exposures (including those of subsidiaries) to the Central Bank on a quarterly basis, a large exposure being defined in the circular as all exposures to a single borrower or a group of related borrowers that total 7% or more of a bank's capital base. The Central Bank later agreed to exclude contingent liabilities from its definition of a large exposure, which was to be calculated after deductions for provisions, cash collateral and deposits under lien. The Central Bank also agreed to draw up a list of acceptable securities against which banks would be permitted to lend without reference to the 'large exposure' limits. During 1994 UAE banks increased their capital by more than US $200m. to comply with international adequacy standards and UAE banking regulations.

In February 1995 a total of 53 leading corporate and individual members of the Dubai business community and ruling family (including nine financial institutions) announced the establishment of a new joint-stock company, Dubai Investments, in which they would hold 45% of the shares. The remaining 55% of the shares were sold to the public two months later through a heavily over-subscribed flotation (open to all UAE nationals) managed by Emirates Bank International. Dubai Investments had an authorized capital of AED 1,300m. Its stated aims included the establishment and acquisition of interests in a wide range of economic activities, including agricultural, mining, services, insurance and tourism ventures within the UAE and, in the longer term, suitable ventures in other countries. The new company announced its first equity investment (in a fibre-optic manufacturing venture in the Jebel Ali Free Zone) in February 1996. In November 1996 Dubai Investments announced that it had acquired majority stakes in three local companies and that it planned to build a new industrial park close to the Jebel Ali Free Zone and port.

In late 1997 reports of instability were denied by Mashreq Bank. The Central Bank issued a statement affirming the strong position of the bank, which later announced net profits of AED 486m. for 1997, the largest in local banking history. In March 1998 the Central Bank was obliged to intervene and provide short-term liquidity in support of Dubai Islamic Bank. There was some speculation that the discovery of fraudulent practices had prompted the crisis. At that time, legislation was being prepared to strengthen the role of the Central Bank and to enforce stricter regulation of the financial sector. In May 1999 the Central Bank called an emergency meeting with four local and nine foreign banks to discuss proposals for the recovery of debts of AED 479m. accrued by an expatriate businessman whose clients had defaulted on payments.

The reputation of the UAE's banking system was the subject of renewed scrutiny following the terrorist attacks on New York and Washington, DC, in September 2001, when it emerged that financial transactions between branches of Citibank in the UAE and the USA had provided the means to finance the attacks. In late-September 2001 the UAE Central Bank 'froze' the assets of some 27 individuals and organizations accused of sponsoring terrorist activities; at least 62 private bank accounts were suspended. In October a decree was passed which sought to prohibit the 'laundering' of funds through the UAE's banking sector; henceforth all banks would be required to inform the Central Bank of the receipt or transfer of amounts in excess of US $10,900. Those convicted on charges connected to 'money-laundering' activities, furthermore, would receive increased fines and prison sentences of up to seven years. The decree also formally established a national commission to seek to combat such practices. However, the Hawala finance system—a traditional alternative remittance system operating outside the control of the conventional banking sector—was unaffected by the changes; much of the funding destined for terrorist activities is believed to be channelled in this way

DEVELOPMENT PLANNING

Until 1981, development expenditure in the UAE came from the annual federal budget, and there was no attempt at detailed long-term integrated economic planning, although Abu Dhabi did have a loose development plan for 1977–79. The end of the 1970s saw a great increase in health facilities in the country, with the number of hospital beds available rising from 1,750 in 1979 to 3,500 in April 1981. This increase was partly brought about through the completion of two major new hospitals at al-Ain. In 1986 the UAE had 28 hospitals and 119 clinics. In 1989 a total of 10 new primary health care centres were planned, at a cost of AED 10m.–12m. each. In 1990 the UAE had one doctor for every 1,040 inhabitants and one nurse for every 500 inhabitants, and in 1994 there was one doctor for every 598 inhabitants. The infant mortality rate in 1995 was 16 per 1,000 live births, compared with 87 per 1,000 in 1970. In 1993 99% of the population had access to public health services. In January 1995 the Government increased the annual fee for a compulsory health card to AED 300 for each adult non-citizen and AED 100 for each adult citizen. In 1999 the UAE had 51 hospitals with 6,835 beds, and at the end of 1997 there were 5,000 doctors and 10,000 nurses in the country. Social welfare reforms were instituted in that year (see above). By 2000 the cost of social services—some US $13,200m.—had exceeded 20% of the UAE's GDP, the largest percentage in the Arab world.

The first Five-Year Plan was intended to have been implemented in 1981, to run until 1985, but the fall in revenues from petroleum severely restricted initial proposals. Overall expenditure was estimated to be AED 16,000m. for the five years, with Abu Dhabi receiving 21%, Fujairah 12.5%, Sharjah 10.8%, Ras al-Khaimah 9.4%, Umm al-Qaiwain 7.7%, Dubai 5.3%, and Ajman 4.4%. The Plan initially predicted an overall increase of 20% in the country's GDP up to 1985. However, in 1983 alone GDP fell by 13.5%, and in 1981–85 GDP, at constant 1990 prices, declined by an annual average of 2.3%. The Plan

also allocated AED 3,800m. to the agricultural sector, which was expected to expand at an annual rate of 10.3%. It was hoped, in particular, to improve productivity and marketing services, and to aim for the best possible use of water resources. Of the AED 16,000m. which was to be spent in the Plan, AED 3,500m. was for investment projects and AED 8,400m. for schemes already under construction. The experience of the first five-year plan for the UAE meant that there was little enthusiasm for a second and the emirates of the UAE returned to a more flexible approach to defining and planning development priorities. In early 1989 Abu Dhabi announced that the emirate planned to spend about AED 14,800m. in the next decade on infrastructure and development. A total of AED 875m. was allocated to the construction of 85 schools (as part of the fifth education plan), of which 41 were scheduled to be completed by the beginning of the 1990/91 academic year.

In November 1996 the Abu Dhabi Government established a consultative committee for the development of the emirate. The committee was to develop and facilitate procedures for businesses seeking to invest in the emirate. Its establishment was in keeping with Abu Dhabi's overall policy of encouraging greater private sector investment, of which the planned privatization of electricity and water installations was a key aspect. In the same month Dubai unveiled its first strategic development plan, setting out an ambitious programme aimed at achieving economic diversification, high non-oil sector growth and increased productivity by 2010. The plan envisaged annual GDP growth of 5% over the next 15 years, fuelled by a 6%–7% annual increase in the non-oil sector contribution to GDP. The plan envisaged capital investments of AED 44,500m. over the next five years, with funding for projects proceeding from both the Government and the private sector.

The UAE, however, has not only been concerned with its own development. Abu Dhabi, through its Fund for Arab Economic Development (ADFAED), has been a major source of international aid. ADFAED was set up in 1971 with a capital of US $120m.; its commitments up to the end of 1980 totalled $800m. However, in 1982, as a result of declining revenues from petroleum, the UAE reduced its foreign aid budget to AED 6,500m. from AED 9,400m. in 1981. Aid continued to decline during the 1980s, but in 1988 ADFAED signed loans totalling AED 151m. ($41.1m.), compared with AED 15.6m. ($4.2m.) in 1987. The ADFAED was renamed the Abu Dhabi Fund for Development at the end of 1993 (reflecting its involvement in projects in some non-Arab countries).

On 22 April 1991 the UAE agreed, as part of the GCC, to establish a Gulf Development Fund, with a capital of US $10,000m. for an initial 10-year period. The fund was to provide new finance for those Middle East countries whose economies are relatively weak. Finance will be aimed at the private sector and will be incorporated into World Bank and IMF programmes.

Statistical Survey

Area and Population

AREA, POPULATION AND DENSITY

Area (sq km)	77,700*
Population (census results)	
December 1985	1,622,464
17 December 1995 (provisional)	
Males	1,579,743
Females	797,710
Total	2,377,453
Population (official estimates at mid-year)	
1998	2,780,000
1999	2,938,000
2000	3,108,000
Density (per sq km) at mid-2000	40.0

* 30,000 sq miles.

POPULATION BY EMIRATE (preliminary figures, mid-1997)

	Area (sq km)	Population*	Density (per sq km)*
Abu Dhabi	67,350	1,000,000	14.8
Dubai	3,900	737,000	189.0
Sharjah	2,600	435,000	167.3
Ras al-Khaimah . . .	1,700	153,000	90.0
Ajman	250	133,000	532.0
Fujairah	1,150	83,000	72.2
Umm al-Qaiwain . . .	750	39,000	52.0
Total	77,700	2,580,000	33.2

* Source: IMF, *UAE—Recent Economic Developments* (December 1998).

PRINCIPAL TOWNS (population at December 1980 census)

Abu Dhabi (capital)	. 242,975	Sharjah . . .	. 125,149
Dubai . .	. 265,702	Al-Ain . . .	. 101,663

Source: UN, *Demographic Yearbook*.

Mid-2000 (UN estimate, incl. suburbs): Dubai 886,000 (Source: UN, *World Urbanization Prospects: The 2001 Revision*).

Mid-2001 (UN estimate, incl. suburbs): Abu Dhabi 471,000 (Source: UN, *World Urbanization Prospects: The 2001 Revision*).

BIRTHS AND DEATHS (UN estimates, annual averages)

	1985–90	1990–95	1995–2000
Birth rate (per 1,000) . . .	27.0	19.6	16.0
Death rate (per 1,000) . . .	3.9	3.7	3.6

Source: UN, *World Population Prospects: The 2000 Revision*.

1995: 4,779 registered deaths (death rate 2.1 per 1,000).

1996: 47,050 registered live births (birth rate 19.3 per 1,000.

Source: UN, *Population and Vital Statistics Report*.

Expectation of life (WHO estimates, years at birth, 2000): Males 72.3; Females 76.4 (Source: WHO, *World Health Report*).

ECONOMICALLY ACTIVE POPULATION ('000 persons)

	1995*	2000
Agriculture, hunting and forestry	96.8	129.6
Fishing	8.1	10.8
Mining and quarrying	30.3	40.8
Manufacturing	143.6	195.0
Electricity, gas and water supply	13.1	17.5
Construction	253.8	340.1
Wholesale and retail trade; repair of motor vehicles, motorcycles and personal and household goods	183.1	246.6
Hotels and restaurants	45.8	61.9
Transport, storage and communications . .	93.8	126.2
Financial intermediation	16.7	22.8
Real estate, renting and business activities	33.5	45.3
Public administration and defence; compulsory social security	175.1	235.4
Education	49.2	69.5
Health and social work	23.6	33.3
Other community, social and personal service activities	40.0	53.8
Private households with employed persons . .	103.2	147.4
Extra-territorial organizations and bodies . .	1.2	1.7
Not classifiable by economic activity . . .	0.9	1.2
Total employed	1,311.8	1,779.0
Unemployed	24.1	41.0
Total labour force	1,335.9	1,820.0
Males	1,180.1	1,587.7
Females	155.8	232.3

* Census figures.

Source: ILO, *Yearbook of Labour Statistics*.

Health and Welfare

KEY INDICATORS

Fertility (births per woman, 2000)	3.1
Under-5 mortality rate (per 1,000 live births, 2000). . .	9
HIV/AIDS (% of persons aged 15–49, 1994). . . .	0.18
Physicians (per 1,000 head, 1997)	1.81
Hospital beds (per 1,000 head, 1996)	2.64
Health expenditure (1998): US $ per head (PPP) . . .	739
% of GDP	4.1
public (% of total)	79.7
Access to water (% of persons, 2000)	—
Access to sanitation (% of persons, 2000)	—
Human Development Index (2000): ranking	46
value	0.812

For sources and definitions, see explanatory note on p. vi.

Agriculture

PRINCIPAL CROPS ('000 metric tons)

	1998	1999	2000
Cabbages	30.8	53.7	58.1
Spinach .	16.0	16.5	16.7
Tomatoes	743.0	750.0*	780.0*
Cauliflower . . .	18.8	19.6	17.1
Pumpkins, squash and gourds	30.5	31.0	31.3
Cucumbers and gherkins .	15.0	16.9	14.8
Aubergines (Eggplants) . .	24.2	25.9	28.1
Green onions and shallots .	16.2	20.2	16.5
Lemons and limes . .	19.6	18.5	18.1
Watermelons . . .	9.0	12.2	14.0*
Cantaloupes and other melons .	62.2	63.0*	64.0*
Mangoes	10.0	9.7	10.3*
Dates	290.4	305.0*	318.0*

* FAO estimate.

Source: FAO.

LIVESTOCK ('000 head, year ending September)

	1998	1999	2000*
Cattle	98	106	110
Camels*	190	195	200
Sheep	437	467	467
Goats	1,128	1,207	1,200
Chickens*	12,300	13,680	14,650

* FAO estimates.

Source: FAO.

LIVESTOCK PRODUCTS ('000 metric tons)

	1998	1999	2000
Beef and veal	14.3	15.0	15.3
Camel meat	11.5	12.3	12.0
Mutton and lamb . . .	23.0	23.4	23.4
Goat meat	7.4	7.9	7.9
Chicken meat	26.4	29.3	29.9
Cows' milk	8.6*	8.7†	8.7†
Camels' milk	29.4	31.5	30.6
Sheep's milk	8.7	9.3	9.0
Goats' milk	26.1	27.9	27.2
Hen eggs	13.9	13.0	13.3

* Unofficial figure.   † FAO estimate.

Source: FAO.

Fishing

('000 metric tons, live weight)

	1997	1998	1999
Capture	114.4	114.7	117.6
Groupers	7.2	7.3	7.4
Snappers and jobfishes . .	3.7	3.7	3.8
Emperors (Scavengers) . .	12.2	12.3	12.6
Jacks and crevalles . .	7.4	7.4	7.6
Carangids	6.2	6.8	7.0
Indian oil sardine . . .	4.1	4.1	4.1
Sardinellas	9.2	9.2	9.5
Stolephorus anchovies . .	10.3	10.3	10.6
Narrow-barred Spanish mackerel	7.1	7.1	7.3
Longtail tuna	3.7	3.7	3.7
Indian mackerel . . .	4.7	4.7	4.8
Aquaculture	0.0	0.0	0.0
Total catch	**114.4**	**114.7**	**117.6**

Source: FAO, *Yearbook of Fishery Statistics*.

Mining

	1998	1999	2000
Crude petroleum (million barrels)*	880	756	900
Natural gas (million cu metres)†	37,070	38,500	39,000

* Estimate.

† On a dry basis.

Source: US Geological Survey.

Industry

SELECTED PRODUCTS ('000 metric tons, unless otherwise indicated)

	1995	1996	1997
Jet fuels*	2,585	2,474	2,972
Motor spirit (petrol) . . .	1,498	1,464	1,507
Naphthas*	700	983	1,072
Kerosene*	150	144	173
Gas-diesel (distillate fuel) oil .	3,367	3,332	3,807
Residual fuel oils . . .	1,962	1,860	1,982
Liquefied petroleum gas:			
from natural gas plants .	4,137*	4,464	5,052
from petroleum refineries . .	396*	404	462
Electric energy (million kWh)*	19,070	19,737	20,571

* Provisional or estimated figure(s).

Source: UN, *Industrial Commodity Statistics Yearbook*.

Finance

CURRENCY AND EXCHANGE RATES

Monetary Units

100 fils = 1 UAE dirham (AED).

Sterling, Dollar and Euro Equivalents (31 May 2002)

£1 sterling = 5.3865 dirhams;
US $1 = 3.6725 dirhams;
€1 = 3.4474 dirhams;
100 UAE dirhams = £18.57 = $27.23 = €29.01.

Exchange Rate

The Central Bank's official rate was set at US $1 = 3.671 dirhams in November 1980. This remained in force until December 1997, when the rate was adjusted to $1 = 3.6725 dirhams.

FEDERAL BUDGET (million UAE dirhams)*

Revenue	1996	1997†	1998‡
Emirate contributions . . .	12,555	13,520	13,949
Abu Dhabi	11,355	12,320	12,749
Dubai	1,200	1,200	1,200
Other receipts	5,517	6,108	5,946
Enterprise profits . . .	1,989	2,302	2,319
Electricity and water . .	322	323	324
Other fees and charges . .	3,206	3,483	3,303
Total	**18,072**	**19,628**	**19,895**

Expenditure	1996	1997†	1998‡
Current expenditure . . .	16,456	17,591	19,410
Interior and defence . .	8,110	8,466	8,741
Education and health . .	4,237	4,535	4,804
Other ministries . . .	2,055	2,217	3,116
Subsidies and transfers . .	2,016	2,153	2,449
Foreign grants . . .	38	220	300
Development expenditure . .	497	529	1,343
Loans and equity . . .	0	67	640
Total	**16,953**	**18,187**	**21,393**

* Excluding the operations of the seven emirate governments.

† Provisional.

‡ Projections.

Source: IMF, *UAE—Recent Economic Developments* (December 1998).

INTERNATIONAL RESERVES (US $ million at 31 December)

	1999	2000	2001
Gold*	90.7	90.7	90.7
IMF special drawing rights . .	6.2	4.0	2.2
Reserve position in IMF . . .	291.7	214.7	225.9
Foreign exchange†	10,377.1	13,303.9	13,918.2
Total	10,765.7	13,613.3	14,237.0

* Valued at US $228 per troy ounce.
† Figures exclude the Central Bank's foreign assets and accrued interest attributable to the governments of individual emirates.

Source: IMF, *International Financial Statistics*.

MONEY SUPPLY (million UAE dirhams at 31 December)

	1999	2000	2001
Currency outside banks . . .	10,272	10,017	10,537
Demand deposits at commercial banks	19,980	24,050	28,927
Total money	30,252	34,067	39,464

Source: IMF, *International Financial Statistics*.

COST OF LIVING (Consumer Price Index; base: 1990 = 100)

	1995	1996	1997*
Food, beverages and tobacco . .	122.2	126.3	134.8
Clothing and footwear . . .	128.4	134.8	143.5
Housing (incl. rent)	135.8	137.1	132.0
Furniture, etc.	125.8	130.1	134.3
Transport and communications .	120.2	126.7	143.9
Recreation and education . .	133.7	138.7	147.4
All items (incl. others) . .	129.3	133.5	137.9

* Preliminary.

Source: IMF, *UAE—Recent Economic Developments* (December 1998).

NATIONAL ACCOUNTS (million UAE dirhams at current prices)
National Income and Product

	1988	1989	1990
Compensation of employees . .	25,226	26,769	27,996
Operating surplus	49,193	60,848	81,633
Domestic factor incomes .	74,419	87,617	109,629
Consumption of fixed capital . .	14,382	15,127	16,078
Gross domestic product (GDP) at factor cost	88,801	102,744	125,707
Indirect taxes, *less* subsidies . .	−1,695	−1,768	−1,699
GDP in purchasers' values .	87,106	100,976	124,008
Factor income from abroad . .	9,940	10,600	10,900
Less Factor income paid abroad .	9,690	10,178	12,200
Gross national product . .	87,356	101,398	122,708
Less Consumption of fixed capital .	14,382	15,127	16,078
National income in market prices	72,974	86,271	106,630
Other current transfers from abroad (net)	−1,040	−744	−11,000
National disposable income .	71,934	85,527	95,630

Source: UN, *National Accounts Statistics*.

Expenditure on the Gross Domestic Product

	1996	1997	1998
Government final consumption expenditure	26,150	28,100	28,640
Private final consumption expenditure	74,410	86,232	90,662
Increase in stocks	2,300	2,150	2,180
Gross fixed capital formation . .	40,940	48,757	49,154
Total domestic expenditure .	143,800	165,239	170,636
Exports of goods and services .	125,800	128,613	115,030
Less Imports of goods and services	105,850	112,673	115,000
GDP in purchasers' values .	163,750	181,179	170,666

Source: IMF, *International Financial Statistics*.

Gross Domestic Product by Economic Activity

	1997	1998*	1999*
Agriculture and fishing . . .	6,052	6,325	6,541
Mining and quarrying . . .	54,815	36,676	49,365
Crude oil	54,221	36,057	48,726
Manufacturing	22,009	22,458	24,009
Electricity and water	3,729	3,841	4,014
Construction	15,612	16,392	16,319
Wholesale and retail trade; repair of motor vehicles, motorcycles and personal and household goods	19,994	20,931	21,690
Restaurants and hotels . . .	3,139	3,395	3,560
Transport, storage and communications	11,972	13,347	13,818
Financial institutions and insurance	11,042	11,677	12,174
Real estate and business services .	17,102	17,496	17,421
Government services	18,465	20,010	20,873
Other community, social and personal services	4,514	4,758	4,942
Sub-total	188,445	177,306	194,726
Less Imputed bank service charge	3,985	4,159	4,271
Total	184,460	173,147	190,455

* Estimates.

Source: *Middle East Economic Digest*.

BALANCE OF PAYMENTS (estimates, million UAE dirhams)*

	1995	1996	1997†
Exports of goods f.o.b. . . .	114,000	130,700	139,500
Imports of goods c.i.f. . . .	−91,400	−101,200	−109,100
Trade balance	22,600	29,500	30,300
Services and other income (net) .	6,200	8,800	8,100
Balance on goods, services and income	28,800	38,300	38,400
Current transfers (net) . . .	−12,800	−13,900	−13,900
Current balance . . .	15,900	24,300	24,600
Short-term private capital . .	1,300	−6,300	−6,100
Other capital	9,500	6,000	4,800
Net errors and omissions . . .	−24,100	−21,800	−22,200
Overall balance	2,600	2,200	1,100

* Figures are rounded to the nearest 100 million dirhams.
† Preliminary.

Source: IMF, *UAE—Recent Economic Developments* (December 1998).

External Trade

PRINCIPAL COMMODITIES

Imports c.i.f. (million UAE dirhams)	1994	1995	1996
Vegetable products	2,397	4,249	4,610
Products of chemical or allied industries	2,957	4,390	4,893
Plastics, rubber and articles thereof	1,980	3,220	3,709
Textiles and textile articles	9,247	10,423	11,781
Pearls, precious or semi-precious stones, precious metals, etc.	2,516	2,507	2,178
Base metals and articles of base metal	3,797	7,635	7,598
Machinery and mechanical appliances; electrical equipment; sound and television apparatus	12,589	20,523	20,760
Vehicles, aircraft, vessels and associated transport equipment	4,906	6,990	9,480
Miscellaneous manufactured articles	1,946	2,580	3,040
Total (incl. others)	78,246	78,466	85,625

Source: IMF, *UAE—Recent Economic Developments* (December 1998).

Exports f.o.b. (US $ million)	1994	1995	1996
Crude petroleum, etc.	10,518.1	11,312.3	13,176.8
Refined petroleum products	1,541.1	2,809.1	2,838.4
Gas (natural and man.)	678.9	1,262.5	1,549.1
Total (incl. others)	20,906.0	24,332.0	21,237.0

Source: UN, *International Trade Statistics Yearbook*.

PRINCIPAL TRADING PARTNERS (US $ million)

Imports	1995	1996
Australia	282	341
Belgium-Luxembourg	251	233
China, People's Republic	1,844	2,039
France (incl. Monaco)	874	948
Germany	1,620	1,411
India	1,290	1,414
Indonesia	498	579
Iran	269	308
Italy (incl. San Marino and Vatican)	1,377	1,275
Japan	2,079	2,278
Korea, Republic	1,256	1,235
Malaysia	373	392
Netherlands	372	385
Pakistan	217	247
Saudi Arabia	751	743
Singapore	211	229
Spain	199	239
Switzerland-Liechtenstein	291	262
Thailand	441	487
United Kingdom	1,646	1,738
USA	1,763	2,494
Total (incl. others)	20,984	22,638

Exports*	1991†	1992†	1993
Bahrain	34.7	43.3	147.4
Congo, Republic	17.7	0.0	0.7
France (incl. Monaco)	22.9	20.3	26.2
Germany	45.6	54.2	112.6
India	12.4	22.1	143.8
Japan	244.3	148.7	141.0
Korea, Republic	35.3	42.4	56.7
Kuwait	20.0	36.5	267.0
Netherlands	9.2	35.5	108.6
Oman	70.5	72.9	73.5
Pakistan	15.2	14.9	140.2
Saudi Arabia	19.1	35.0	215.0
Thailand	22.0	19.2	38.9
United Kingdom	28.0	89.9	87.6
USA	26.1	45.7	101.1
Yemen	20.2	35.5	129.7
Total (incl. others)	754.4	899.3	3,764.2

* Excluding crude petroleum.   † Excluding re-exports.

Source: UN, *International Trade Statistics Yearbook*.

Transport

ROAD TRAFFIC ('000 motor vehicles in use)

	1994	1995	1996
Passenger cars	332.5	321.6	346.3
Commercial vehicles	87.2	84.2	89.3

Source: UN, *Statistical Yearbook*.

SHIPPING

Merchant Fleet (registered at 31 December)

	1999	2000	2001
Number of vessels	322	350	341
Total displacement ('000 grt)	786.5	978.8	746.4

Source: Lloyd's Register of Shipping, *World Fleet Statistics*.

International Sea-borne Shipping
(estimated freight traffic, '000 metric tons)

	1988	1989	1990
Goods loaded	63,380	72,896	88,153
Crude petroleum	54,159	63,387	78,927
Other cargo	9,221	9,509	9,226
Goods unloaded	8,973	8,960	9,595

Source: UN, *Monthly Bulletin of Statistics*.

CIVIL AVIATION (traffic on scheduled services)*

	1996	1997	1998
Kilometres flown (million)	82	85	94
Passengers carried ('000)	4,063	4,720	5,264
Passenger-km (million)	11,352	13,519	15,633
Total ton-km (million)	1,743	2,107	2,403

* Figures include an apportionment (one-quarter) of the traffic of Gulf Air, a multinational airline with its headquarters in Bahrain.

Source: UN, *Statistical Yearbook*.

Tourism

ARRIVALS BY NATIONALITY

Country	1998	1999	2000
Egypt	77,876	85,259	94,058
France	52,136	65,755	60,955
Germany	100,958	147,736	171,519
India	175,237	216,219	235,493
Iran	127,571	137,678	154,861
Pakistan	97,827	115,441	136,061
Russia	331,026	232,081	228,785
United Kingdom	229,631	293,025	337,865
USA	75,805	94,502	100,547
Total (incl. others)*	2,990,539	3,392,614	3,906,545

* Total includes domestic tourists.

Dubai tourism receipts (US $ million): 562 in 1998; 607 in 1999.

Source: partly World Tourism Organization, *Yearbook of Tourism Statistics.*

Education

(1996/97, unless otherwise indicated)

| | Teachers | Pupils/Students | | |
		Males	Females	Total
Pre-primary	3,110	28,920	26,704	55,624
Primary	16,148	134,817	124,692	259,509
Secondary				
General	9,832*	88,644	90,195	178,839
Vocational . . .	249	n.a.	n.a.	1,925
University	728†	4,519	11,694	16,213
Other higher† . . .	354	627	1,110	1,737

* Figure refers to 1995/96.

† Figure(s) refer to 1991/92.

Source: UNESCO, *Statistical Yearbook.*

Adult literacy rate (UNESCO estimates): 76.3% (males 75.0%; females 79.3%) in 2000 (Source: UNDP, *Human Development Report*).

Communications Media

	1999	2000	2001
Television receivers ('000 in use) .	740	760	n.a.
Telephones ('000 main lines in use)	975.2	1,020.1	1,052.9
Mobile cellular telephones ('000			
subscribers)	832.3	1,428.1	1,909.3
Personal computers ('000 in use)	300	400	n.a
Internet users ('000) . . .	400	735	900

1996: Daily newspapers 7 (combined circulation 384,000 copies).
1997 ('000 in use): Radio receivers 820; Facsimile machines 50.

Sources: UNESCO, *Statistical Yearbook*; UN, *Statistical Yearbook*; International Telecommunication Union.

Directory

The Constitution

A provisional Constitution for the UAE took effect in December 1971. This laid the foundation for the federal structure of the Union of the seven emirates, previously known as the Trucial States.

The highest federal authority is the Supreme Council of Rulers, which comprises the rulers of the seven emirates. It elects the President and Vice-President from among its members. The President appoints a Prime Minister and a Council of Ministers. Proposals submitted to the Council require the approval of at least five of the Rulers, including those of Abu Dhabi and Dubai. The legislature is the Federal National Council, a consultative assembly comprising 40 members appointed by the emirates for a two-year term.

In July 1975 a committee was appointed to draft a permanent federal constitution, but the National Council decided in 1976 to extend the provisional document for five years. The provisional Constitution was extended for another five years in December 1981, and for further periods of five years in 1986 and 1991. In November 1976, however, the Supreme Council amended Article 142 of the provisional Constitution so that the authority to levy armed forces was placed exclusively under the control of the federal Government. Legislation designed to make the provisional Constitution permanent was endorsed by the Federal National Council in June 1996, after it had been approved by the Supreme Council of Rulers.

The Government

HEAD OF STATE

President: Sheikh ZAYED BIN SULTAN AN-NAHYAN, Ruler of Abu Dhabi (took office as President of the UAE on 2 December 1971; re-elected 1976, 1981, 1991, 1996 and 2 December 2001).

Vice-President: Sheikh MAKTOUM BIN RASHID AL-MAKTOUM, Ruler of Dubai.

SUPREME COUNCIL OF RULERS
(with each Ruler's date of accession)

Ruler of Abu Dhabi: Sheikh ZAYED BIN SULTAN AN-NAHYAN (1966).

Ruler of Dubai: Sheikh MAKTOUM BIN RASHID AL-MAKTOUM (1990).

Ruler of Sharjah: Sheikh SULTAN BIN MUHAMMAD AL-QASIMI (1972).

Ruler of Ras al-Khaimah: Sheikh SAQR BIN MUHAMMAD AL-QASIMI (1948).

Ruler of Umm al-Qaiwain: Sheikh RASHID BIN AHMAD AL-MU'ALLA (1981).

Ruler of Ajman: Sheikh HUMAID BIN RASHID AN-NUAIMI (1981).

Ruler of Fujairah: Sheikh HAMAD BIN MUHAMMAD ASH-SHARQI (1974).

COUNCIL OF MINISTERS
(September 2002)

Prime Minister: Sheikh MAKTOUM BIN RASHID AL-MAKTOUM.

Deputy Prime Minister: Sheikh SULTAN BIN ZAYED AN-NAHYAN.

Minister of the Interior: Lt-Gen. Dr MUHAMMAD SAID AL-BADI.

Minister of Foreign Affairs: RASHID ABDULLAH AN-NUAIMI.

Minister of Finance and Industry: Sheikh HAMDAN BIN RASHID AL-MAKTOUM.

Minister of Defence: Sheikh MUHAMMAD BIN RASHID AL-MAKTOUM.

Minister of Economy and Commerce: Sheikh FAHIM BIN SULTAN AL-QASIMI.

Minister of Information and Culture: Sheikh ABDULLAH BIN ZAYED AN-NAHYAN.

Minister of Communications: AHMAD BIN HUMAID AT-TAYER.

Minister of Public Works and Housing: RAKKAD BIN SALEM AR-RAKKAD.

Minister of Higher Education and Scientific Research: Sheikh NAHYAN BIN MUBARAK AN-NAHYAN.

Minister of Health: HAMAD ABD AR-RAHMAN AL-MADFA.

Minister of Electricity and Water: HUMAID BIN NASSER AL-OWAIS.

Minister of Labour and Social Affairs: MATEER HUMAID AT-TAYER.

Minister of Planning: Sheikh HUMAID BIN AHMAD AL-MU'ALLA.

Minister of Petroleum and Mineral Resources: OBEID BIN SAIF AN-NASIRI.

Minister of Agriculture and Fisheries: SAID MUHAMMAD AR-RAGABANI.

Minister of Education and Youth: ALI ABD AL-AZIZ ASH-SHARHAN.

Minister of Justice, Islamic Affairs and Awqaf (Religious Endowments): MUHAMMAD NAKHIRA ADH-DHAHERI.

Minister of State for Cabinet Affairs: SAID KHALFAN AL-GHAITH.

Minister of State for Finance and Industry: MUHAMMAD KHALFAN BIN KHARBASH.

Minister of State for Foreign Affairs: Sheikh HAMDAN BIN ZAYED AN-NAHYAN.

Minister of State for Affairs of the Supreme Council: Sheikh MAJEED BIN SAID AN-NUAIMI.

Director-General of the President's Office: Sheikh MANSOUR BIN ZAYED AN-NAHYAN.

FEDERAL MINISTRIES

Office of the Prime Minister: POB 12848, Dubai; tel. (4) 3534550; fax (4) 3530111.

Office of the Deputy Prime Minister: POB 831, Abu Dhabi; tel. (2) 4451000; fax (2) 4450066.

Ministry of Agriculture and Fisheries: POB 213, Abu Dhabi; tel. (2) 6662781; fax (2) 6654787; e-mail maf@uae.gov.ae; internet www.uae.gov.ae/maf.

Ministry of Communications: POB 900, Abu Dhabi; tel. (2) 6651900; fax (2) 6651691.

Ministry of Defence: POB 46616, Abu Dhabi; tel. (4) 4461300; fax (4) 4463286.

Ministry of Economy and Commerce: POB 901, Abu Dhabi; tel. (2) 6265000; fax (2) 6215339; e-mail moec@uae.gov.ae; internet www.uae.gov.ae/moec.

Ministry of Education and Youth: POB 295, Abu Dhabi; tel. (2) 6213800; fax (2) 6313778; internet www.education.gov.ae.

Ministry of Electricity and Water: POB 629, Abu Dhabi; tel. (2) 6274222; fax (2) 6269738; e-mail moew@uae.gov.ae; internet www.uae.gov.ae/moew.

Ministry of Finance and Industry: POB 433, Abu Dhabi; tel. (2) 6726000; fax (2) 6768414; e-mail mofi@uae.gov.ae; internet www.uae.gov.ae/mofi.

Ministry of Foreign Affairs: POB 1, Abu Dhabi; tel. (2) 6652200; fax (2) 6668015; e-mail mofa@uae.gov.ae.

Ministry of Health: POB 848, Abu Dhabi; tel. (2) 6330000; fax (2) 6726000; e-mail moh@uae.gov.ae; internet www.uae.gov.ae/moh.

Ministry of Higher Education and Scientific Research: POB 45253, Abu Dhabi; tel. (2) 6428000; fax (2) 6427262; e-mail mohe@uae.gov.ae; internet www.uae.gov.ae/mohe.

Ministry of Information and Culture: POB 17, Abu Dhabi; tel. (2) 4453000; fax (2) 4452504; e-mail mic@uae.gov.ae.

Ministry of the Interior: POB 398, Abu Dhabi; tel. (2) 4414666; fax (2) 4414938.

Ministry of Justice and Islamic Affairs and Awqaf (Religious Endowments): POB 260, Abu Dhabi; tel. (2) 6814000; fax (2) 6810680; e-mail moia@uae.gov.ae; internet www.uae.gov.ae/moia.

Ministry of Labour and Social Affairs: POB 809, Abu Dhabi; tel. (2) 6671700; fax (2) 6665889; e-mail molsa@uae.gov.ae.

Ministry of Petroleum and Mineral Resources: POB 59, Abu Dhabi; tel. (2) 6651810; fax (2) 6664573; e-mail mopmr@uae.gov.ae.

Ministry of Planning: POB 904, Abu Dhabi; tel. (2) 6271100; fax (2) 6269942; e-mail mop@uae.gov.ae; internet www.uae.gov.ae/mop.

Ministry of Public Works and Housing: POB 878, Abu Dhabi; tel. (2) 6651778; fax (2) 6665598; e-mail mpwh@uae.gov.ae.

Ministry of State for Affairs of the Supreme Council: POB 545, Abu Dhabi; tel. (2) 6323900; fax (2) 6344225.

Ministry of State for Cabinet Affairs: POB 899, Abu Dhabi; tel. (2) 6811106; fax (2) 6812968; e-mail moca@uae.gov.ae; internet www.uae.gov.ae/moca.

Ministry of State for Finance and Industrial Affairs: POB 433, Abu Dhabi; tel. (2) 771133; fax (2) 793255.

Ministry of State for Foreign Affairs: POB 1, Abu Dhabi; tel. (2) 6660888; fax (2) 6652883.

Legislature

FEDERAL NATIONAL COUNCIL

Formed under the provisional Constitution, the Council is composed of 40 members from the various emirates (eight each from Abu Dhabi and Dubai, six each from Sharjah and Ras al-Khaimah, and four each from Ajman, Fujairah and Umm al-Qaiwain). Each emirate appoints its own representatives separately. The Council studies laws proposed by the Council of Ministers and can reject them or suggest amendments.

Speaker: MUHAMMAD BIN KHALIFA AL-HABTOUR.

Diplomatic Representation

EMBASSIES IN THE UNITED ARAB EMIRATES

Afghanistan: Abu Dhabi; POB 5687, Abu Dhabi; tel. (2) 661244; fax (2) 655310 (reopened February 2002).

Algeria: POB 3070, Abu Dhabi; tel. (2) 448943; fax (2) 447068; Ambassador: MUHAMMAD MELLOUH.

Argentina: POB 3325, Abu Dhabi; tel. (2) 4436838; fax (2) 4431392; e-mail embar@emirates.net.ae; Ambassador: MARIO QUADRI CASTILLO.

Bahrain: POB 3367, Abu Dhabi; tel. (2) 6657500; fax (2) 6674141; Ambassador: Sheikh AHMAD BIN KHALIFA AL-KHALIFA.

Bangladesh: POB 2504, Abu Dhabi; tel. (2) 4465100; fax (2) 4464733; e-mail banglaad@emirates.net.ae; Ambassador: HASAN MASHHUD CHOUDHURY.

Belgium: POB 3686, Abu Dhabi; tel. (2) 319449; fax (2) 319353; Ambassador: HENRY O. LOBERT.

Belize: POB 43432, Abu Dhabi; tel. (2) 333554; fax (2) 330429; Ambassador: ELHAM S. FREIHA.

Bosnia and Herzegovina: POB 43362, Abu Dhabi; tel. (2) 6444164; fax (2) 6443619; Chargé d'affaires a.i.: SALKO ČANIĆ.

Brazil: POB 3027, Abu Dhabi; tel. (2) 665352; fax (2) 654559; Ambassador: JOSÉ FERREIRA LOPES.

Brunei: POB 5836, Abu Dhabi; tel. (2) 4491100; fax (2) 4491567; e-mail kbdauh98@emirates.net.ae; Ambassador: Dato MALAI Haji AHMAD BIN SYED Haji MASHOR.

Canada: POB 6970, Abu Dhabi; tel. (2) 4456969; fax (2) 4458787; internet www.dfait-maeci.gc.ca/world/embassies/abudhabi; e-mail abdbi@dfait-maeci.gc.ca; Ambassador: DAVID HUTTON.

China, People's Republic: POB 2741, Abu Dhabi; tel. (2) 434276; fax (2) 435440; Ambassador: ZHANG ZHIJUN.

Czech Republic: POB 27009, Abu Dhabi; tel. (2) 782800; fax (2) 795716; Chargé d'affaires: JOSEF KOUTSKY.

Egypt: POB 4026, Abu Dhabi; tel. (2) 445566; fax (2) 449878; Ambassador: BAHAA ELDIN MOSTAFA REDA.

Eritrea: POB 2597, Abu Dhabi; tel. (2) 331838; fax (2) 346451; Ambassador: MUHAMMAD OMAR MAHMOUD.

Finland: POB 3634, Abu Dhabi; tel. (2) 6328927; fax (2) 6325063; e-mail finemb@emirates.net.ae; internet www.finabu.com; Ambassador: RISTO REKOLA.

France: POB 4014, Abu Dhabi; tel. (2) 4435100; fax (2) 4434158; e-mail ambafr@emirates.net.ae; internet www.ambafrance.org.ae; Ambassador: FRANÇOIS GOUYETTE.

Germany: POB 2591, Abu Dhabi; tel. (2) 4435630; fax (2) 4455712; e-mail germemb@emirates.net.ae; internet www.germemb.org.ae; Ambassador: Dr ALEXANDER MÜHLEN.

Greece: POB 5483, Abu Dhabi; tel. (2) 6654847; fax (2) 6656008; e-mail grembauh@emirates.net.ae; Ambassador: GEORGE ZOIS.

Hungary: POB 44450, Abu Dhabi; tel. (2) 6660107; fax (2) 6667877; e-mail hungexad@emirates.net.ae; Chargé d'affaires a.i.: IVAN P. NOVAK.

India: POB 4090, Abu Dhabi; tel. (2) 6664800; fax (2) 6651518; e-mail indiauae@emirates.net.ae; internet www.indiaembassyuae.org; Ambassador: K. C. SINGH.

Indonesia: POB 7256, Abu Dhabi; tel. (2) 454448; fax (2) 455453; Ambassador: ABDULLAH FUAD RACHMAN.

Iran: POB 4080, Abu Dhabi; tel. (2) 447618; fax (2) 448714; e-mail iranemb@emirates.net.ae; internet www.iranembassy.org.ae; Ambassador: KAMAL SADEQI.

Italy: POB 46752, Abu Dhabi; tel. (2) 4435622; fax (2) 4434337; e-mail ambital@emirates.net.ae; internet www.italian-embassy .org.ae; Ambassador: DOMENICO PEDATA.

Japan: POB 2430, Abu Dhabi; tel. (2) 4435969; fax (2) 4434219; Ambassador: TOSHIO MOCHIZUKI.

Jordan: POB 4024, Abu Dhabi; tel. (2) 4447100; fax (2) 4449157; Ambassador: EID KAMEL AR-RODAN.

Kenya: POB 3854, Abu Dhabi; tel. (2) 666300; fax (2) 652827; Ambassador: MUDE DAE MUDE.

Korea, Republic: POB 3270, Abu Dhabi; tel. (2) 4435337; fax (2) 4435348; e-mail keauhlee@emirates.net.ae; Ambassador: SUN-YONG KANG.

Kuwait: POB 926, Abu Dhabi; tel. (2) 446888; fax (2) 444990; Ambassador: IBRAHIM AL-MANSOUR.

Kyrgyzstan: Abu Dhabi.

Lebanon: POB 4023, Abu Dhabi; tel. (2) 4492100; fax (2) 4493500; e-mail libanamb@emirates.net.ae; Ambassador: HASSAN BERRO.

Libya: POB 5739, Abu Dhabi; tel. (2) 450030; fax (2) 450033; Chargé d'affaires: ABDUL HAMID ALI SHAIKHY.

Malaysia: POB 3887, Abu Dhabi; tel. (2) 4482775; fax (2) 4482779; e-mail mwadhabi@emirates.net.ae; Ambassador: Dato' Syed HUSSEIN AL-HABSHEE.

Mauritania: POB 2714, Abu Dhabi; tel. (2) 462724; fax (2) 465772; Ambassador: TELMIDI OULD MUHAMMAD AMMAR.

Morocco: POB 4066, Abu Dhabi; tel. (2) 433963; fax (2) 433917; Ambassador: ABDELLAH AZMANI.

Netherlands: POB 46560, Abu Dhabi; tel. (2) 6321920; fax (2) 6313158; e-mail nlgovabu@emirates.net.ae; Ambassador: JOSEPH P. M. WOLFSWINKEL.

Norway: POB 47270, Abu Dhabi; tel. (2) 6211221; fax (2) 6213313; e-mail emb.abudhabi@mfa.no; Ambassador: ULF CHRISTIANSEN.

Oman: POB 2517, Abu Dhabi; tel. (2) 463333; fax (2) 464633; Ambassador: SULTAN AL-BUSAIDI.

Pakistan: POB 846, Abu Dhabi; tel. (2) 447800; fax (2) 447172; Chargé d'affaires: ABDUL RAZZAK SOOMRO.

Philippines: Abu Dhabi; tel. (2) 345665; fax (2) 313559; Ambassador: JOSEPH GERARD B. ANGELES.

Poland: POB 2334, Abu Dhabi; tel. (2) 4465200; fax (2) 4462967; e-mail polcon99@emirates.net.ae; internet www.plembassy.gov.ae; Chargé d'affaires: MIROSLAW ADAMCZYK.

Qatar: 26th St, Al-Minaseer, POB 3503, Abu Dhabi; tel. (2) 435900; fax (2) 434800; Ambassador: ABDULLAH M. AL-UTHMAN.

Romania: 9 Sudan St, Sector 2/35, POB 70416, Abu Dhabi; tel. (2) 6666346; fax (2) 6651598; e-mail romaniae@emirates.net.ae; Ambassador: IOAN EMIL VASILIU.

Russia: POB 8211, Abu Dhabi; tel. (2) 721797; fax (2) 788731; Ambassador: OLEG DERKOVSKII.

Saudi Arabia: POB 4057, Abu Dhabi; tel. (2) 445700; fax (2) 448491; Ambassador: SALEH MUHAMMAD AL-GHUFAILI.

Slovakia: POB 3382, Abu Dhabi; tel. (2) 6321674; fax (2) 6315839; e-mail slovemb@emirates.net.ae; Ambassador: PETER ZSOLDOS.

Somalia: POB 4155, Abu Dhabi; tel. (2) 669700; fax (2) 651580; Ambassador: HUSSEIN MUHAMMAD BULLALEH.

South Africa: Madinat Zayed, an-Najdah St, 8th St, Villa 12A, POB 29446, Abu Dhabi; tel. (2) 6337565; fax (2) 6333909; e-mail saemb@emirates.net.ae; internet www.southafrica.co.ae; Ambassador: YUSUF SALOOJEE.

Spain: POB 46474, Abu Dhabi; tel. (2) 213544; fax (2) 342978; Ambassador: MANUEL POMBO.

Sri Lanka: POB 46534, Abu Dhabi; tel. (2) 6426666; fax (2) 6428289; e-mail lankemba@emirates.net.ae; Ambassador: J. B. NAKKAWITA.

Sudan: POB 4027, Abu Dhabi; tel. (2) 666788; fax (2) 654231; Chargé d'affaires: MOHIEDDIN SLAIM AHMED.

Switzerland: POB 46116, Abu Dhabi; tel. (2) 6274636; fax (2) 6269627; e-mail swiemadh@emirates.net.ae; Ambassador: FRANÇOIS BARRAS.

Syria: POB 4011, Abu Dhabi; tel. (2) 4448768; fax (2) 4449387; Ambassador: H. E. AHMAD HALLAK.

Thailand: POB 47466, Abu Dhabi; tel. (2) 6421772; fax (2) 6421773; e-mail thaiauh@emirates.net.ae; Ambassador: SNANCHART DEVA-HASTIN.

Tunisia: POB 4166, Abu Dhabi; tel. (2) 6811331; fax (2) 6812707; e-mail ambtunad@emirates.net.ae; Ambassador: MUSTAPHA TLILI.

Turkey: POB 3204, Abu Dhabi; tel. (2) 6655466; fax (2) 6662691; e-mail tcabudbe@emirates.net.ae; Ambassador: ERCAN ÖZER.

Ukraine: POB 45714, Abu Dhabi; tel. (2) 327586; fax (2) 327506; e-mail emb_ae@mfa.gov.ua; Ambassador: Dr OLEH SEMENETS.

United Kingdom: POB 248, Abu Dhabi; tel. (2) 6326600; fax (2) 6345968; e-mail britembc@emirates.net.ae; internet www.britain -uae.org; Ambassador: PATRICK M. NIXON.

USA: POB 4009, Abu Dhabi; tel. (2) 4436691; fax (2) 4435441; e-mail paoabud@exchange.usia.gov; internet www.usembabu.gov.ae; Ambassador: MARCELLE M. WAHBA.

Yemen: POB 2095, Abu Dhabi; tel. (2) 448454; fax (2) 447978; Ambassador: Dr ABDULLAH HUSSAIN BARAKAT.

Judicial System

The 95th article of the Constitution of 1971 provided for the establishment of the Union Supreme Court and Union Primary Tribunals as the judicial organs of State.

The Union has exclusive legislative and executive jurisdiction over all matters that are concerned with the strengthening of the federation, such as foreign affairs, defence and Union armed forces, security, finance, communications, traffic control, education, currency, measures, standards and weights, matters relating to nationality and emigration, Union information, etc.

President Sheikh Zayed signed the law establishing the new federal courts on 9 June 1978. The new law effectively transferred local judicial authorities into the jurisdiction of the federal system.

Primary tribunals in Abu Dhabi, Sharjah, Ajman and Fujairah are now primary federal tribunals, and primary tribunals in other towns in those emirates have become circuits of the primary federal tribunals.

The primary federal tribunal may sit in any of the capitals of the four emirates and have jurisdiction on all administrative disputes between the Union and individuals, whether the Union is plaintiff or defendant. Civil disputes between Union and individuals will be heard by primary federal tribunals in the defendant's place of normal residence.

The law requires that all judges take a constitutional oath before the Minister of Justice and that the courts apply the rules of *Shari'a* (Islamic religious law) and that no judgment contradicts the *Shari'a*. All employees of the old judiciaries will be transferred to the federal authority without loss of salary or seniority.

In February 1994 President Sheikh Zayed ordered that an extensive range of crimes, including murder, theft and adultery, be tried in *Shari'a* courts rather than in civil courts.

Chief Shari'a Justice: AHMAD ABD AL-AZIZ AL-MUBARAK.

Religion

ISLAM

Most of the inhabitants are Muslims of the Sunni sect. About 16% of the Muslims are Shi'ites.

CHRISTIANITY

Roman Catholic Church

Apostolic Vicariate of Arabia: POB 54, Abu Dhabi; tel. (2) 4461895; fax (2) 4465177; e-mail apvicar@emirates.net.ae; responsible for a territory covering most of the Arabian peninsula (including Saudi Arabia, the UAE, Oman, Qatar, Bahrain and Yemen), containing an estimated 1,400,000 Catholics (31 December 2000); Vicar Apostolic Fr GIOVANNI BERNARDO GREMOLI, Titular Bishop of Masuccaba.

The Anglican Communion

Within the Episcopal Church in Jerusalem and the Middle East, the UAE forms part of the diocese of Cyprus and the Gulf. The Anglican congregations in the UAE are entirely expatriate. The Bishop in Cyprus and the Gulf resides in Cyprus, while the Archdeacon in the Gulf is resident in Qatar.

Chaplain, St Andrew's Church: Rev. STEVE COLLIS, St Andrew's Church, POB 262, Abu Dhabi; tel. (2) 4461631; fax (2) 4465869; e-mail standrew@emirates.net.ae.

The Press

The Ministry of Information and Culture has placed a moratorium on new titles.

Abu Dhabi

Abu Dhabi Magazine: POB 662, Abu Dhabi; tel. (2) 214000; fax (2) 348954; f. 1969; Arabic, some articles in English; monthly; Editor ZUHAIR AL-QADI; circ. 18,000.

Directory

Adh-Dhafra: POB 4288, Abu Dhabi; tel. (2) 328103; Arabic; weekly; independent; publ. by Dar al-Wahdah.

Emirates News: POB 791, Abu Dhabi; tel. (2) 451446; fax (2) 453662; e-mail emrtnews@emirates.net.ae; f. 1975; English; daily; publ. by Al-Ittihad Press, Publishing and Distribution Corpn; Chair. Sheikh ABDULLAH BIN ZAYED AN-NAHYAN; Man. Editor PETER HELLYER; circ. 21,150.

Al-Fajr (The Dawn): POB 505, Abu Dhabi; tel. (2) 478300; fax (2) 474326; Arabic; daily; Man. Editor OBEID AL-MAZROUI; circ. 28,000.

Hiya (She): POB 2488, Abu Dhabi; tel. (2) 474121; Arabic; weekly for women; publ. by Dar al-Wahdah.

Al-Ittihad (Unity): POB 791, Abu Dhabi; tel. (2) 452206; fax (2) 455126; f. 1972; Arabic; daily and weekly; publ. by Al-Ittihad Press, Publishing and Distribution Corpn; Man. Editor OBEID SULTAN; circ. 58,000 daily, 60,000 weekly.

Majed: POB 791, Abu Dhabi; tel. (2) 4451804; fax (2) 4451455; Arabic; e-mail majid-magazine@emi.co.ae; internet www. emi.co.ae; f. 1979; weekly; children's magazine; Man. Editor AHMAD OMAR; circ. 145,300.

Ar-Riyada wa-Shabab (Sport and Youth): POB 2710, Dubai; tel. (4) 444400; fax (4) 445973; Arabic; weekly; general interest.

UAE and Abu Dhabi Official Gazette: POB 899, Abu Dhabi; tel. (2) 660604; Arabic; daily; official reports and papers.

UAE Press Service Daily News: POB 2035, Abu Dhabi; tel. (2) 44292; f. 1973; English; daily; Editor RASHID AL-MAZROUI.

Al-Wahdah (Unity): POB 2488, Abu Dhabi; tel. (2) 478400; fax (2) 478937; f. 1973; daily; independent; Man. Editor RASHID AWEIDHA; Gen. Man. KHALIFA AL-MASHWI; circ. 20,000.

Zahrat al-Khaleej (Splendour of the Gulf): POB 791, Abu Dhabi; tel. (2) 461600; fax (2) 451653; f. 1979; Arabic; weekly; publ. by Al-Ittihad Press, Publishing and Distribution Corpn; women's magazine; circ. 10,000.

Dubai

Akhbar Dubai (Dubai News): Department of Information, Dubai Municipality, POB 1420, Dubai; f. 1965; Arabic; weekly.

Al-Bayan (The Official Report): POB 2710, Dubai; tel. (4) 688222; fax (4) 688222; f. 1980; owned by Dubai authorities; Arabic; daily; Editor-in-Chief Sheikh HASHER MAKTOUM; circ. 82,575.

Emirates Woman: POB 2331, Dubai; tel. (4) 2824060; fax (4) 2827593; e-mail annabel@motivate.co.ae; f. 1979; Motivate Publishing; English; monthly; fashion, health and beauty; Editor ANNABEL KANTARIA; circ. 18,690.

Gulf News: POB 6519, Dubai; tel. (4) 447100; fax (4) 441627; e-mail editorial@gulf-news.co.ae; internet www.gulf-news.co.ae; f. 1978; An-Nisr Publishing; English; daily; two weekly supplements, *Junior News* (Wednesday), *Gulf Weekly* (Thursday); Editor-in-Chief OBAID HUMAID AT-TAYER; Editor FRANCIS MATTHEW; circ. 86,900.

Al-Jundi (The Soldier): POB 2838, Dubai; tel. (4) 3433033; fax (4) 3433343; e-mail mod5@emirates.net.ae; f. 1973; Arabic; monthly; military and cultural; Editor Brig. KHAMIS BIN HASHER; circ. 4,000–7,000.

Khaleej Times: POB 11243, Dubai; tel. (4) 4382400; fax (4) 4390519; e-mail ktimes@emirates.net.ae; internet www .khaleejtimes.com; f. 1978; a Galadari enterprise; English; daily; free weekly supplement, *Weekend* (Friday); Man. Dir QASSIM MUHAMMAD YOUSUF; Editor S. NIHAL SINGH; circ. 70,000.

Trade and Industry: POB 1457, Dubai; tel. (4) 280000; fax (4) 2028597; e-mail dcciinfo@dcci.org; internet www.dcci.org; f. 1975; Arabic and English; monthly; publ. by Dubai Chamber of Commerce and Industry; circ. 26,000.

What's On: POB 2331, Dubai; tel. (4) 2824060; fax (4) 2824436; e-mail editor-wo@motivate.co.ae; f. 1979; Motivate Publishing; English; monthly; Exec. Editor IAN FAIRSERVICE; circ. 17,905.

Ras al-Khaimah

Akhbar Ras al-Khaimah (Ras al-Khaimah News): POB 87, Ras al-Khaimah; Arabic; monthly; local news.

Al-Ghorfa: POB 87, Ras al-Khaimah; tel. (7) 333511; fax (7) 330233; f. 1970; Arabic and English; free monthly; publ. by Ras al-Khaimah Chamber of Commerce; Editor ZAKI H. SAQR.

Ras al-Khaimah Magazine: POB 200, Ras al-Khaimah; Arabic; monthly; commerce and trade; Chief Editor AHMAD AT-TADMORI.

Sharjah

Al-Azman al-Arabia (Times of Arabia): POB 5823, Sharjah; tel. (6) 356034.

The Gulf Today: POB 30, Sharjah; tel. (6) 5591919; fax (6) 5532737; e-mail tgtmkt@alkhaleej.co.ae; f. 1995; English; daily; circ. 38,000.

Al-Khaleej (The Gulf): POB 30, Sharjah; tel. (6) 625304; fax (6) 598547; f. 1970; Arabic; daily; political, independent; Editor GHASSAN TAHBOUB; circ. 82,750.

Sawt al-Khaleej (Voice of the Gulf): Sharjah; tel. (6) 358003.

Ash-Sharooq (Sunrise): POB 30, Sharjah; tel. (6) 598777; fax (6) 599336; f. 1970; Arabic; weekly; general interest; Editor YOUSUF AL-HASSAN.

At-Tijarah (Commerce): Sharjah Chamber of Commerce and Industry, POB 580, Sharjah; tel. (6) 5116600; fax (6) 5681119; e-mail scci@emirates.net.ae; internet www.sharjah.gov.ae; f. 1970; Arabic/English; monthly magazine; circ. 50,000; annual trade directory; circ. 100,000.

UAE Digest: Sharjah; tel. (6) 354633; fax (6) 354627; English; monthly; publ. by Universal Publishing; commerce and finance; Man. Dir FARAJ YASSINE; circ. 10,000.

NEWS AGENCIES

Emirates News Agency (WAM): POB 3790, Abu Dhabi; tel. (2) 454545; fax (2) 454694; f. 1977; operated by the Ministry of Information and Culture; Dir IBRAHIM AL-ABED.

UAE Press Service: POB 2035, Abu Dhabi; tel. (2) 820424.

Foreign Bureaux

Agenzia Nazionale Stampa Associata (ANSA) (Italy): POB 44106, Abu Dhabi; tel. (2) 454545.

Kuwait News Agency (KUNA): Apartment 907, 9th Floor, Building No. 728, Zayed I St, Khalidiya, Abu Dhabi; tel. (2) 666994; fax (2) 666935.

Reuters (UK): POB 7872, Abu Dhabi; tel. (2) 328000; fax (2) 333380; Man. JEREMY HARRIS.

Publishers

Al-Ittihad Press, Publishing and Distribution Corpn: POB 791, New Airport Rd, Abu Dhabi; tel. (2) 455555; fax (2) 451653; Chair. KHALFAN BIN MUHAMMAD AR-ROUMI.

All Prints: POB 857, Abu Dhabi; tel. (2) 338235; publishing and distribution; Partners BUSHRA KHAYAT, TAHSEEN S. KHAYAT.

Motivate Publishing: POB 2331, Dubai; tel. (4) 824060; fax (4) 824436; e-mail motivate@emirates.net.ae; f. 1979; books and magazines; Dirs OBAID HUMAID AT-TAYER, IAN FAIRSERVICE.

Broadcasting and Communications

TELECOMMUNICATIONS

Ministry of Communications: (see Ministries, above); regulatory authority.

Emirates Telecommunications Corpn (Etisalat): POB 3838, Abu Dhabi; tel. (2) 283333; fax (2) 725456; internet www.etisalat .co.ae; provides telecommunications services throughout the UAE; privatization pending in 1998.

Radio

Abu Dhabi Radio: Abu Dhabi; tel. (2) 451111; fax (2) 451155; f. 1968; broadcasts in Arabic over a wide area; also broadcasts in French, Bengali, Filipino and Urdu; Dir-Gen. ABD AL-WAHAB AR-RADWAN.

Capital Radio: POB 63, Abu Dhabi; tel. (2) 451000; fax (2) 451155; English-language FM music and news station, operated by the Ministry of Information and Culture; Station Manager AIDA HAMZA.

Dubai Radio and Colour Television: POB 1695, Dubai; tel. (4) 370255; fax (4) 374111; broadcasts domestic Arabic and European programmes; Chair. Sheikh HASHER MAKTOUM; Dir-Gen. ABD AL-GHAFOOR SAID IBRAHIM.

Ras al-Khaimah Broadcasting Station: POB 141, Ras al-Khaimah; tel. (7) 851151; fax (7) 353441; two transmitters broadcast in Arabic and Urdu; Dir Sheikh ABD AL-AZIZ BIN HUMAID.

Sharjah Broadcasting Station: POB 155, Sharjah; broadcasts in Arabic and French.

Umm al-Qaiwain Broadcasting Station: POB 444, Umm al-Qaiwain; tel. (6) 7666044; fax (6) 7666055; e-mail uaqfm@emirates .net.ae; f. 1978; broadcasts music and news in Arabic, Malayalam, Sinhala and Urdu; Gen. Man. ALI JASSEM.

UAE Radio and Television—Dubai: POB 1695, Dubai; tel. (4) 3369999; fax (4) 3374111; e-mail dubairtv@emirates.net.ae; internet www.ecssr.ac.ae/05uae.6television.html; broadcasts in Arabic and English to the USA, India and Pakistan, the Far East, Australia and New Zealand, Europe and North and East Africa; Chair. Sheikh

HASHEM MAKTOUM; Dir-Gen. AHMED SAEED AL-GAOUD; Controller of Radio HASSAN AHMAD.

Television

Dubai Radio and Colour Television: (see Radio).

UAE Radio and Television-Dubai: (see Radio); Controller of Programmes NASIB BITAR.

UAE TV—Abu Dhabi: POB 637, Abu Dhabi; tel. (2) 452000; fax (2) 451470; internet www.ecssr.ac.ae/05uae.6television.html; f. 1968; broadcasts programmes incorporating information, entertainment, religion, culture, news and politics; Dir-Gen. ALI OBAID.

UAE Television—Sharjah: POB 111, Sharjah; tel. (6) 361111; fax (6) 541755; f. 1989; broadcasts in Arabic and Urdu in the northern emirates; Executive Dir MUHAMMAD DIAB AL-MUSA.

Finance

(cap. = capital; dep. = deposits; res = reserves; m. = million; brs = branches; amounts in dirhams, unless otherwise indicated)

BANKING

Central Bank

Central Bank of the United Arab Emirates: POB 854, Abu Dhabi; tel. (2) 6652220; fax (2) 66652504; e-mail uaccbadm@emirates .net.ae; internet www.uaecb.gov.ae, f. 1973; acts as issuing authority for local currency; superseded UAE Currency Board December 1980; auth. cap. 300m.; total assets 50,136m. (Dec. 2000); Chair. MUHAMMAD EID AL-MURAIKHI; Gov. SULTAN NASSER AS-SUWAIDI; 6 brs.

Principal Banks

Abu Dhabi Commercial Bank (ADCB): POB 939, Abu Dhabi; tel. (2) 6962222; fax (2) 6776499; internet www.adcbuae.com; f. 1985 by merger; 65% govt-owned, 35% owned by private investors; cap. 1,250.0m., res 1,911.9m., dep. 15,604.8m. (Dec. 1999); Chair. FADHEL SAEED AD-DARMAKI; CEO and Man. Dir KHALIFA MUHAMMAD HASSAN; 37 brs.

Abu Dhabi Islamic Bank: POB 313, Najda St, Abu Dhabi; tel. (2) 6343000; fax (2) 6342222; e-mail adib@adib.co.ae; internet www .e-adib.com; f. 1997; cap. 1,000m., res 36.4m., dep. 3,034.9m. (Dec. 2000); Chair. OBAID SAIF AN-NASSERI; CEO ABD AR-RAHMAN ABD AL-MALIK.

Arab Bank for Investment and Foreign Trade (ARBIFT): POB 46733, ARBIFT Bldg, Hamdan St, Tourist Club Area, Abu Dhabi; tel. (2) 6721900; fax (2) 6777550; e-mail arbiftho@emirates.net.ae; internet www.arbift.com; f. 1976; jointly owned by the UAE Govt, the Libyan Arab Foreign Bank and the Banque Extérieure d'Algérie; cap. 570.0m., res 659.3m., dep. 4,463.1m. (Dec. 2001); Chair. Dr ABD AL-HAFID ZLITNI; Gen. Man. IBRAHIM M. LOOTAH; 2 brs in Abu Dhabi, 1 in Dubai, 1 in al-Ain.

Arab Emirates Investment Bank PJSC: POB 5503, Dubai; tel. (4) 2222191; fax (4) 274351; e-mail aeibank@emirates.net.ae; cap. 40.9m., res 8.9m., dep. 143.5m. (Dec. 1999); Chair. KHALID MUHAMMAD SAEED AL-MULLA; Gen.-Man. SAJJAD AHMAD.

Bank of Sharjah Ltd: POB 1394, Sharjah; tel. (6) 5694411; fax (6) 5694422; e-mail bankshj@emirates.net.ae; internet www .bank-of-sharjah.com; f. 1973; cap. 220m., res 112.5m., dep. 1,484.6m. (Dec. 2000); Chair. AHMAD AN-NOMAN; Gen. Man. VAROUJ NERGUIZIAN; brs in Abu Dhabi and Dubai.

Commercial Bank of Dubai PSC: POB 2668, Deira, Dubai; tel. (4) 3523355; fax (4) 3520444; e-mail cbd-ho@cbd.co.ae; internet www.cbd.co.ae; f. 1969; cap. 409.9m., res 643.6m., dep. 4,974.7m. (Dec. 1999); Chair. AHMAD HUMAID AT-TAYER; Gen. Man. OMAR ABD AR-RAHIM LEYAS; 15 brs.

Commercial Bank International PLC: POB 4449, Dubai; tel. (4) 2275265; fax (4) 2279038; e-mail cbiho@emirates.net.ae; internet www.cbiuae.com; f. 1991; cap. 230.2m., res 96.6m., dep. 2,015.2m. (Dec. 2001); Chair. and Man. Dir SALEH AHMAD ASH-SHALL.

Dubai Bank: Dubai; f. 2002; cap. 300.0m.

Dubai Islamic Bank PLC: POB 1080, Dubai; tel. (4) 2953000; fax (4) 2954000; internet www.alislami.com; f. 1975; cap. 1,000.0m., res 159.8m., dep. 9,864.8 (Dec. 2000); Chair. Dr MUHAMMAD KHALIFAN BIN KHARBASH; 9 brs.

Emirates Bank International PJSC: POB 2923, Dubai; tel. (4) 2256256; fax (4) 2268005; e-mail pnd@emiratesbank.com; internet www.emiratesbank.com; f. 1977 by merger; 77% owned by Govt of Dubai; cap. 734.7m., res 2,685.1m., dep. 13,482.5m. (Dec. 2000); Chair. AHMAD HUMAID AT-TAYER; Gen. Man. CHARLES NEIL; 25 brs in UAE.

First Gulf Bank: POB 3662, Sheikh Zayed St, Abu Dhabi; tel. (2) 6394000; fax (2) 6217721; e-mail fgbabd@emirates.net.ae; f. 1979;

cap. 360m., res 135.9m., dep. 1,798.3m. (Dec. 2000); Chair. Sheikh TAHNOON BIN ZAYED AN-NAHYAN; Man. Dir AHMED SAIF AN-NASRI; 5 brs.

Investbank PLC: Al-Borj Ave, POB 1885, Sharjah; tel. (6) 5695550; fax (6) 5694442; e-mail sharjah@invest-bank.com; internet www .invest-bank.com; f. 1975; cap. 300m., res 158.7m., dep. 2,018.3m. (Dec. 2001); Chair. Dr ABDULLAH OMRAN TARYAM; 5 brs.

MashreqBank PSC: POB 1250, Deira, Dubai; tel. (4) 2229131; fax (4) 2226061; internet www.mashreqbank.com; f. 1967 as Bank of Oman; adopted present name 1993; cap. 715.9m., res 837.6m., dep. 18,777.8m. (Dec. 2001); Chair. ABDULLAH AHMAD AL-GHURAIR; Man. Dir and CEO ABD AL-AZIZ AL-GHURAIR; 30 brs.

Middle East Bank PJSC: POB 5547, Deira, Dubai; tel. (4) 2256256; fax (4) 2255322; e-mail pnd@emiratesbank.com; internet www .emiratesbank.com/meb; f. 1976; subsid. (99.8%-owned) of EBI; cap. 500.0m., res 137.0m., dep. 1,554.1m. (Dec. 2000); Vice-Chair. FARDAN BIN ALI AL-FARDAN; 14 brs.

National Bank of Abu Dhabi (NBAD): POB 4, Abu Dhabi; tel. (2) 6666800; fax (2) 6655329; internet www.nbad.co.ae; f. 1968; owned jointly by Abu Dhabi Investment Authority and UAE citizens; cap. 941.6m., res 2,545.6m., dep. 27,729.6m. (Dec. 2001); Chair. Sheikh MUHAMMAD BIN HABROUSH AS-SUWAIDI; CEO MICHAEL H. TOM-ALIN; 51 brs in UAE.

National Bank of Dubai PJSC: POB 777, Dubai; tel. (4) 2222111; fax (4) 2283000; e-mail contactus@nbd.co.ae; internet www.nbd .co.ae; f. 1963; cap. 864.5m., res 3,609.3m., dep. 27,595.0m. (Dec. 2001); Chair. Dr KHALIFA MUHAMMAD AHMAD SULAYMAN; Gen. Man. R. DOUGLAS DOWIE; 31 brs.

National Bank of Fujairah: POB 887, Fujairah; tel. (9) 2224513; fax (9) 2224516; e-mail fujairah@emirates.net.ae; internet www .nbf.co.ae; f. 1982; owned jointly by Govt of Fujairah (36.78%), Govt of Dubai (9.78%), and UAE citizens and cos (51.25%); cap. 330.0m., res 145.0m., dep. 2,034.6m. (Dec. 2001); Chair. Sheikh SALEH BIN MUHAMMAD ASH-SHARQI; Gen. Man. MICHAEL H. WILLIAMS; 5 brs.

National Bank of Ras al-Khaimah PSC: POB 5300, Ras al-Khaimah; tel. (7) 2281127; fax (7) 2283238; e-mail nbrakho@ emirates.net.ae; f. 1976; cap. 250.0m., res 228.6m., dep. 1,853.7m. (Dec. 2001); Chair. Sheikh KHALID BIN SAQR AL-QASIMI; Gen. Man. J. G. HONEYBILL; 11 brs.

National Bank of Sharjah: POB 4, Al-Borj Ave, Sharjah; tel. (6) 5681000; fax (6) 5680101; e-mail nbsmail@emirates.net.ae; f. 1976; commercial bank; cap. 314.8m., res 158.1m., dep. 1,273m. (Dec. 2000); Chair. Sheikh SULTAN BIN MUHAMMAD AL-QASSIMI; Gen. Man. SAID MUHAMMAD; 9 brs.

National Bank of Umm al-Qaiwain PSC: POB 800, Umm al-Qaiwain; tel. (6) 7655225; fax (6) 7655440; e-mail edpnbuaq@ emirates.net.ae; f. 1982; cap. 250.0m., res 100.4m., dep. 1,204.8m. (Dec. 2000); Chair. Sheikh SA'UD BIN RASHID AL-MU'ALLA; Man. Dir and CEO Sheikh NASSER BIN RASHID AL-MU'ALLA; 10 brs.

Union National Bank: POB 3865, Abu Dhabi; tel. (2) 6741600; fax (2) 6786080; e-mail feedback@unb.co.ae; internet www.unb.co.ae; f. 1983; fmrly Bank of Credit and Commerce (Emirates); cap. 679.4m., res 501.1m., dep. 10,573.0m. (Dec. 2000); Chair. Sheikh NAHYAN BIN MUBARAK AN-NAHYAN; CEO MUHAMMAD NASR ABDEEN; 10 brs in Abu Dhabi, 5 brs in Dubai, and one each in al-Ain, Sharjah, Ras al-Khaimah and Fujairah.

United Arab Bank: POB 25022, Sharjah; tel. (6) 5733900; fax (6) 5733907; e-mail uarbae@emirates.net.ae; f. 1975; affiliated to Société Générale, France; cap. 227.3m., res 130.6m., dep. 1,286.0m. (Dec. 2000); Chair. Sheikh FAISAL BIN SULTAN AL-QASSIMI; Gen. Man. BERTRAND GIRAUD; 9 brs.

Development Banks

Emirates Industrial Bank: POB 2722, Abu Dhabi; tel. (2) 339700; fax (2) 319191; f. 1982; offers low-cost loans to enterprises with at least 51% local ownership; 51% state-owned; cap. 200m.; Chair. MUHAMMAD KHALFAN KHIRBASH; Gen. Man. MUHAMMAD ABD AL-BAKI MUHAMMAD.

United Arab Emirates Development Bank: Abu Dhabi; tel. (2) 344986; f. 1974; participates in development of real estate, agriculture, fishery, livestock and light industries; cap. 500m.; Gen. Man. MUHAMMAD SALEM AL-MELEHY.

Foreign Banks

ABN AMRO Bank NV (Netherlands): Istiqlal St, POB 22401, Abu Dhabi; tel. (2) 6335400; fax (2) 6330182; f. 1974; POB 2567, Deira, Dubai; tel. (4) 3512200; fax (4) 3511555; POB 1971, Sharjah; tel. (6) 5093101; fax (6) 5360099; internet www.abnamro-uae.com; cap. 223m., total assets 3,677m. (1999); Man. (Abu Dhabi) BRICE ROPION.

Al-Ahli Bank of Kuwait KSC: POB 1719, Deira, Dubai; tel. (4) 2681118; fax (4) 2684445; e-mail abkdub@emirates.net.ae; Chair. MURAD YOUSUF BEHBEHANI.

Arab-African International Bank (Egypt): POB 1049, Dubai; tel. (4) 2223131; fax (4) 2222257; e-mail aaibdxb@emirates.net.ae; internet www.aaibank.com; f. 1970; POB 928, Abu Dhabi; tel. (2) 6323400; fax (2) 6216009; e-mail aaib@emirates.net.ae; f. 1976; Chair. Dr FAHD AR-RASHID; Gen. Man. (Dubai) MUHAMMAD FARAMAOUI.

Arab Bank PLC (Jordan): POB 875, Abu Dhabi; tel. (2) 334111; fax (2) 336433; f. 1970; POB 11364, Dubai; tel. (4) 228845; fax (4) 285974; POB 130, Sharjah; tel. (6) 353994; fax (6) 357182; POB 4972, Ras al-Khaimah; tel. (7) 228473; fax (7) 222837; POB 300, Fujairah; tel. (9) 222050; fax (9) 568249; POB 17, Ajman; tel. (6) 422431; fax (6) 426871; Man. NAIM KHUSHASHI; 8 local brs.

Bank of Baroda (India): POB 3162, Dubai; tel. (2) 538093; fax (2) 536962; e-mail barbaead@emirates.net.ae; f. 1974; Chair. K. KANNAN; CEO PAR KASH SINGH; also brs in Abu Dhabi, al-Ain, Deira (Dubai), Sharjah and Ras al-Khaimah.

Bank Melli Iran: Regional Office and Main Branch, POB 1894, Dubai; tel. (4) 221462; fax (4) 269157; e-mail bmirodxb@ emirates.net.ae; f. 1969; Regional Dir AZIZ AZIMI NOBAR; brs in Dubai, Abu Dhabi, al-Ain, Sharjah, Fujairah and Ras al-Khaimah.

Bank Saderat Iran: POB 700, Abu Dhabi; tel. (2) 225155; fax (2) 225062; POB 4182, Dubai; tel. (4) 221161; fax (4) 215961; also Sharjah, Ajman, Fujairah and al-Ain; Man. ALI VERDI.

Banque Banorabe (France): POB 4370, Dubai; tel. (4) 2284655; fax (4) 2236260; POB 5803, Sharjah; tel. (6) 5736100; fax (6) 5736080; e-mail banorabe@emirates.net.ae; f. 1974; fmrly Banque de l'Orient Arabe et d'Outre Mer; Chair. and Gen. Man. Dr NAAMAN AZHARI; UAE Regional Man. BASSEM M. AL-ARISS.

Banque du Caire (Egypt): POB 533, Abu Dhabi; tel. (2) 224900; fax (2) 225881; POB 1502, Dubai; tel. (4) 715175; fax (4) 713013; POB 254, Sharjah; tel. (6) 5739222; fax (6) 5739292; POB 618, Ras al-Khaimah; tel. (7) 332245; fax (7) 334202; Gulf Regional Man. FOUAD ABD AL-KHALEK TAHOON.

Banque Libanaise pour le Commerce SA (France): POB 4207, Dubai; tel. (4) 222291; fax (4) 279861; e-mail blcad@emirates.net.ae; POB 854, Sharjah; tel. (6) 724561; fax (6) 727843; e-mail blcdxbrm@emirates.net.ae; POB 3771, Abu Dhabi; tel. (2) 270909; fax (2) 268851; POB 771, Ras al-Khaimah; UAE Regional Man. ELIE N. SALIBA.

Barclays Bank PLC (UK): POB 2734, Abu Dhabi; tel. (2) 275313; fax (2) 268060; POB 1891, Zabeel, Dubai; tel. (4) 351555; fax (4) 366700; Corporate Dir of Gulf JONATHAN PINE.

BNP Paribas (France): POB 2742, Abu Dhabi; tel. (2) 6267800; fax (2) 6268638; POB 7233, Dubai; tel. (4) 2225200; fax (4) 2225849; Gen. Man. (Abu Dhabi) LUC FICHTER; Gen. Man. (Dubai) MICHEL DUBOIS.

Citibank NA (USA): POB 749, Dubai; tel. (4) 522100; fax (4) 524942; f. 1963; POB 346, Sharjah; tel. (6) 354511; POB 999, Abu Dhabi; tel. (2) 742484; fax (2) 334524; POB 294, Ras al-Khaimah; POB 1430, al-Ain; Gen. Man. AHM BIN BREK.

Credit Agricole Indosuez Gulf (France): POB 9256, Dubai; tel. (4) 3314211; fax (4) 3313201; f. 1975; POB 46786, Abu Dhabi; tel. (2) 6267500; fax (2) 6275581; f. 1981; Regional Man. FRANÇOIS RIVIER.

El Nilein Industrial Development Bank (Sudan): POB 6013, Abu Dhabi; tel. (2) 326453; Man. ABDULLAH MAHMOUD AWAD.

Habib Bank AG Zurich (Switzerland): POB 2681, Abu Dhabi; tel. (2) 322838; fax (2) 351822; f. 1974; POB 1166, Sharjah; POB 3306, Dubai; Joint Pres. H. M. HABIB; Vice-Pres. HATIM HUSAIN; 8 brs throughout UAE.

Habib Bank Ltd (Pakistan): POB 888, Dubai; tel. (4) 268171; fax (4) 260198; f. 1967; POB 897, Abu Dhabi; tel. (2) 325665; fax (2) 333620; f. 1975; Sr Vice-Pres. JAVED AKHTAR CHATTHA; 6 other brs in UAE.

HSBC Bank Middle East (United Kingdom): POB 66, Dubai; tel. (4) 3535000; fax (4) 35315641; e-mail hsbcuae@emirates.net.ae; internet www.banking.middleeast.hsbc.com; f. 1946; total assets US $7,832m. (1999); Dep. Chair. ANDREW DIXON; CEO MUKHTAR HUS-SAIN; 8 brs throughout UAE.

IntesaBCI SpA: POB 3839, Abu Dhabi; tel. (2) 274224; fax (2) 273709; Dep. Chief Man. DANIÈLE PANIN.

Janata Bank (Bangladesh): POB 2630, Abu Dhabi; tel. (2) 344542; fax (2) 348749; POB 3342, Dubai; tel. (4) 281442; fax (4) 246023; Chair. MUHAMMAD ALI; Man. Dir M. A. HASHEM; brs in al-Ain, Dubai and Sharjah.

Lloyds TSB Bank PLC (UK): POB 3766, Dubai; tel. (4) 3422000; fax (4) 3422660; e-mail ltsbbank@emirates.net.ae; f. 1977; Area Man. RICHARD STOCKDALE.

National Bank of Bahrain BSC: POB 46080, Abu Dhabi; tel. (2) 335288; fax (2) 333783; Sr Man. FAROUK KHALAF.

National Bank of Oman SAOG: POB 3822, Abu Dhabi; tel. (2) 348111; fax (2) 321043; Man. O. R. QUADRI.

Rafidain Bank (Iraq): POB 2727, Abu Dhabi; tel. (2) 335882; fax (2) 326996; Gen. Man. ZANAIB TALEB.

Standard Chartered Bank (UK): POB 240, Abu Dhabi; tel. (2) 330077; fax (2) 341511; POB 999, Dubai; tel. (4) 520455; fax (4) 526679; POB 5, Sharjah; tel. (6) 357788; fax (6) 543604; POB 1240, al-Ain; tel. (3) 641253; fax (3) 654824; Gen. Man. COLIN AVERY.

United Bank Ltd (Pakistan): POB 1367, Dubai; tel. (4) 3552020; fax (4) 3514525; ubldra@emirates.net.ae; POB 237, Abu Dhabi; tel. (2) 6391507; fax (2) 6315052; e-mail ublman@emirates.net.ae; f. 1959; Gen. Man. SHAUKAT MIR; 8 brs in UAE.

Bankers' Association

United Arab Emirates Bankers' Association: POB 44307, Abu Dhabi; tel. (2) 6272541; fax (2) 6274155; e-mail ebauae@emirates.net.ae; internet www.eba_ae.com; f. 1983.

STOCK EXCHANGE

Dubai Financial Market (DFM): World Trade Centre, POB 9700, Dubai; tel. (4) 3055555; fax (4) 3314924; e-mail ekazim@dfm.co.ae; internet www.dfm.co.ae; f. 2000; 11 listed cos; market capitalization AED 34,392m. (August 2002); Dir-Gen. ESSA ABD AL-FATTAH KAZIM.

A second trading floor, the Abu Dhabi Stock Exchange (ADSE), is also planned.

INSURANCE

Abu Dhabi National Insurance Co (Adnic): POB 839, Abu Dhabi; tel. (2) 6264000; fax (2) 6268600; e-mail adnic@ emirates.net.ae; internet www.adnic-uae.com; f. 1972; subscribed 25% by the Govt of Abu Dhabi and 75% by UAE nationals; all classes of insurance; Chair. and Gen. Man. KHALAF A. AL-OTAIBA.

Al-Ahlia Insurance Co: POB 128, Ras al-Khaimah; tel. (7) 221479; f. 1977; Chair. Sheikh OMAR BIN ABDULLAH AL-QASSIMI; 3 brs.

Al-Ain Ahlia Insurance Co: POB 3077, Abu Dhabi; tel. (2) 4459900; fax (2) 4456685; e-mail alainins@emirates.net.ae; internet www.alaininsurance.com; f. 1975; Chair. MUHAMMAD BIN J. R. AL-BADIE ADH-DHAHIRI; Gen. Man. M. MAZHAR HAMADEH; brs in Dubai, Sharjah, Tarif, Ghouifat and al-Ain.

Dubai Insurance Co PSC: POB 3027, Dubai; tel. (4) 2693030; fax (4) 2693727; e-mail dubins@emirates.net.ae; f. 1970; Chair. MAJID AL-FUTTAIM.

Sharjah Insurance Co: POB 792, Sharjah; tel. (6) 5686690; fax (6) 5686545; e-mail sirco@emirates.net.ae; internet www.sharjahinsurance.co.ae; f. 1970; Gen. Man. MUHAMMAD FAWZI NAJI.

Union Insurance Co: Head Office: POB 460, Umm al-Qaiwain; tel. (6) 666223; POB 4623, Dubai; POB 3196, Abu Dhabi; Gen. Man. L. F. DOKOV.

Trade and Industry

DEVELOPMENT ORGANIZATIONS

Abu Dhabi Development Finance Corpn: POB 814, Abu Dhabi; tel. (2) 6441000; fax (2) 6440800; e-mail opadfdmn@emirates.net.ae; purpose is to provide finance to the private sector; Chair. Sheikh KHALIFA BIN ZAYED AN-NAHYAN; Dir-Gen. SAEED KHALFAN MATAR AR-ROMAITHI.

Abu Dhabi Fund for Development (ADFD): POB 814, as-Salam St, Abu Dhabi; tel. (2) 6441000; fax (2) 6440800; e-mail opadfdmn@ emirates.net.ae; f. 1971; purpose is to offer economic aid to other Arab states and other developing countries in support of their development; cap. AED 4,000m.; Dir-Gen. SAEED KHALFAN MATTAR AR-ROMAITHI.

Abu Dhabi Investment Authority (ADIA): POB 3600, Abu Dhabi; tel. (2) 213100; f. 1976; responsible for co-ordinating Abu Dhabi's investment policy; Chair. Sheikh KHALIFA BIN ZAYED AN-NAHYAN; Pres. Sheikh MUHAMMAD HABROUSH AS-SUWAIDI; 1 br. overseas.

Abu Dhabi Investment Company (ADIC): POB 46309, Abu Dhabi; tel. (2) 658100; fax (2) 650575; e-mail adic@emirates.net.ae; internet www.adic.co.ae; f. 1977; investment and merchant banking activities in the UAE and abroad; 98% owned by ADIA and 2% by National Bank of Abu Dhabi; total assets AED 5,947m. (1997); Chair. HAREB MASOOD AD-DARMAKI; Gen. Man. HUMAID DARWISH AL-KATBI.

Abu Dhabi Planning Department: POB 12, Abu Dhabi; tel. (2) 727200; fax (2) 727749; f. 1974; supervises Abu Dhabi's Development Programme; Chair. MUSALLAM SAEED ABDULLAH AL-QUBAISI; Under-Sec. AHMED M. HILAL AL-MAZRUI.

General Industry Corpn (GIC): POB 4499, Abu Dhabi; tel. (2) 6214900; fax (2) 6325034; e-mail info@gic.co; www. gic.co.ae; f. 1979; responsible for the promotion of non-petroleum-related industry; Chair. Sheikh HAMAD BIN TAHNOON AN-NAHYAN; Deputy Dir-Gen. SUHAIL MUHAMMAD AL-AMERI.

International Petroleum Investment Co (IPIC): POB 7528, Abu Dhabi; tel. (2) 336200; fax (2) 216045; f. 1984; cap. US $200m.; state-owned venture to develop overseas investments in energy and energy-related projects. Chair. JOUAN SALEM ADH-DHAHIRI; Man. Dir KHALIFA MUHAMMAD ASH-SHAMSI.

Sharjah Economic Development Corpn (SHEDCO): Sharjah; tel. (6) 371212; industrial investment co; jt venture between Sharjah authorities and private sector; auth. cap. AED 1,000m.; Gen. Man. J. T. PICKLES.

CHAMBERS OF COMMERCE

Federation of UAE Chambers of Commerce and Industry: POB 3014, Abu Dhabi; tel. (2) 6214144; fax (2) 6339210; e-mail fcciauh@emirates.net.ae; POB 8886, Dubai; tel. (4) 2212977; fax (4) 2235498; e-mail fccidxb@emirates.net.ae; internet www.fcci .uae.com; f. 1976; 7 mbr chambers; Pres. SAEED SAIF BIN JABER AS-SUWAIDI; Sec.-Gen. ABDULLAH SULTAN ABDULLAH.

Abu Dhabi Chamber of Commerce and Industry: POB 662, Abu Dhabi; tel. (2) 6214000; fax (2) 6215867; e-mail services@adcci .gov.ae; internet www.adcci-uae.com; f. 1969; 45,000 mems; Pres. SAID SEIF BIN JABER AS-SUWAIDI; Dir-Gen. MUHAMMAD OMAR ABDULLAH.

Ajman Chamber of Commerce and Industry: POB 662, Ajman; tel. (6) 422177; fax (6) 427591; e-mail ajmchmbr@emirates.net.ae; internet www.ajcci.co.ae; f. 1977; Pres. HAMAD MUHAMMAD ABU SHIHAB; Dir-Gen. MUHAMMAD BIN ABDULLAH AL-HUMRANI.

Dubai Chamber of Commerce and Industry: POB 1457, Dubai; tel. (4) 280000; fax (4) 211646; e-mail dcci@dcci.gov.ae; internet www.dcci.org; f. 1965; 40,000 mems; Pres. HASSAN BIN ASH-SHEIKH; Dir-Gen. ABD AR-RAHMAN GHANEM AL-MUTAIWEE.

Fujairah Chamber of Commerce, Industry and Agriculture: POB 738, Fujairah; tel. (9) 222400; fax (9) 221464; e-mail fujccia@ emirates.net.ae; Pres. SAID ALI KHAMAS; Dir-Gen. SHAHEEN ALI SHAHEEN.

Ras al-Khaimah Chamber of Commerce, Industry and Agriculture: POB 87, Ras al-Khaimah; tel. (7) 333511; fax (7) 330233; e-mail rakchmbr@emirates.net.ae; f. 1967; 800 mems; Pres. ALI ABDULLAH MUSSABEH; Dir-Gen. ALI MUHAMMAD ALI AL-HARANKI.

Sharjah Chamber of Commerce and Industry: POB 580, Sharjah; tel. (6) 5116600; fax (6) 5681119; e-mail scci@ sharjah.gov.ae; internet www.sharjah.gov.ae; f. 1970; 25,000 mems; Chair. AHMAD MUHAMMAD AL-MIDFA'A; Dir-Gen. SAID OBEID AL-JARWAN.

Umm al-Qaiwain Chamber of Commerce and Industry: POB 436, Umm al-Qaiwain; tel. (6) 656915; fax (6) 657056; Pres. ABDULLAH RASHID AL-KHARJI; Man. Dir SHAKIR AZ-ZAYANI.

STATE HYDROCARBONS COMPANIES
Abu Dhabi

Supreme Petroleum Council: POB 898, Abu Dhabi; tel. (2) 602000; fax (2) 6023389; f. 1988; assumed authority and responsibility for the administration and supervision of all petroleum affairs in Abu Dhabi; Chair. Sheikh KHALIFA BIN ZAYED AN-NAHYAN; Sec.-Gen. YOUSUF BIN OMEIR BIN YOUSUF.

Abu Dhabi National Oil Co (ADNOC): POB 898, Abu Dhabi; tel. (2) 6020000; fax (2) 6023389; e-mail adnoc@adnoc.com; internet www.adnoc.com; f. 1971; cap. AED 7,500m.; state company; deals in all phases of oil industry; owns two refineries: one on Umm an-Nar island and one at Ruwais; Habshan Gas Treatment Plant (scheduled for partial privatization); gas pipeline distribution network; a salt and chlorine plant; holds 60% participation in operations of ADMA-OPCO and ADCO, and 88% of ZADCO; has 100% control of Abu Dhabi National Oil Company for Oil Distribution (ADNOC-FOD), Abu Dhabi National Tanker Co (ADNATCO), National Drilling Co (NDC) and interests in numerous other companies, both in the UAE and overseas; ADNOC is operated by Supreme Petroleum Council, Chair. Sheikh KHALIFA BIN ZAYED AN-NAHYAN; Gen. Man. YOUSUF BIN OMEIR BIN YOUSUF.

Subsidiaries include:

Abu Dhabi Co for Onshore Oil Operations (ADCO): POB 270, Abu Dhabi; tel. (2) 6040000; fax (2) 669785; shareholders are ADNOC (60%), British Petroleum, Shell and Total (9.5% each), Exxon and Mobil (4.75% each) and Partex (2%); oil exploration, production and export operations from onshore oilfields; average production (1990): 1.2m. b/d; Chair. YOUSUF BIN OMEIR BIN YOUSUF; Gen. Man. KEVIN DUNNE.

Abu Dhabi Drilling Chemicals and Products Ltd (ADDCAP): POB 46121, Abu Dhabi; tel. (2) 6029000; fax (2) 6029010; e-mail addcap@emirates.net.ae; f. 1975; production of drilling chemicals and provision of marine services; wholly-owned subsidiary of ADNOC; Chair. YOUSUF BIN OMEIR BIN YOUSUF; Gen. Man. MAHFOUD A. DARBOUL ASH-SHEHHI.

Abu Dhabi Gas Co (ATHEER): POB 345, Abu Dhabi; tel. (2) 6020000; fax (2) 6027150; processing and distribution of natural gas.

Abu Dhabi Gas Industries Co (GASCO): POB 665, Abu Dhabi; tel. (2) 6041111; fax (2) 6047414; started production in 1981; recovers condensate and LPG from Asab, Bab and Bu Hasa fields for delivery to Ruwais natural gas liquids fractionation plant; capacity of 22,000 tons per day; ADNOC has a 68% share; Total, Shell Gas and Partex have a minority interest; Chair. SAHAIL AL-MAZROUI; Gen. Man. PHILIPPE HILAIREAUD.

Abu Dhabi Gas Liquefaction Co (ADGAS): POB 3500, Abu Dhabi; tel. (2) 6061111; fax (2) 6065456; f. 1973; owned by ADNOC, 51%; British Petroleum (BP), 16%; Total, 8%; Mitsui and Co, 22%; Mitsui Liquefied Gas Co, 3%; operates LGSC and the LNG plant on Das Island which uses natural gas produced in association with oil from offshore fields and has a design capacity of approx. 2.3m. tons of LNG per year and 1.29m. tons of LPG per year; the liquefied gas is sold to the Tokyo Electric Power Co, Japan; Chair. A. N. AS-SUWEIDI; Gen. Man. P. J. CARR.

Abu Dhabi Marine Operating Co (ADMA-OPCO): POB 303, Abu Dhabi; tel. (2) 6060000; fax (2) 6065062; operates a concession 60% owned by ADNOC, 40% by Abu Dhabi Marine Areas Ltd; f. 1977 as an operator for the concession; production (1984): 67,884,769 barrels (8,955,721 metric tons); Chair. YOUSUF BIN OMEIR BIN YOUSUF; Gen. Man. HENRY BACCONNIER.

Abu Dhabi Oil Refining Co (TAKREER): POB 3593, Abu Dhabi; tel. (2) 6027000; fax (2) 6065062; refining of crude oil; production of chlorine and related chemicals.

ADNOC Distribution: POB 4188, Abu Dhabi; tel. (2) 771300; fax (2) 722322; e-mail adnoc-fod@adnoc-fod.co.ae; internet www.adnoc-fod.co.ae; 100% owned by ADNOC; distributes petroleum products in UAE and worldwide; Chair. YOUSUF BIN OMEIR BIN YOUSUF; Gen. Man. JAMAL JABER ADH-DHAREEF.

National Drilling Co (NDC): POB 4017, Abu Dhabi; tel. (2) 316600; fax (2) 317045; e-mail ndcisc@emirates.net.ae; drilling operations; Chair. ABDULLAH NASSER AS-SUWAIDI; Gen. Man. NAJEEB HASSAN AZ-ZAABI.

National Petroleum Construction Co Ltd (NPCC): POB 2058, Abu Dhabi; tel. (2) 5549000; fax (2) 5549111; e-mail npccnet@emirates.net.ae; f. 1973; 'turnkey' construction and maintenance of offshore facilities for the petroleum and gas industries; cap. AED 100m.; Chair. YOUSEF OMAR BIN YOUSEF; Gen. Man. AQEEL A. MADHI.

Ajman

Ajman National Oil Co (AJNOC): POB 410, Ajman; tel. (6) 421218; f. 1983; 50% govt-owned, 50% held by Canadian and private Arab interests.

Dubai

DUGAS (Dubai Natural Gas Co Ltd): POB 4311, Dubai (Location: Jebel Ali); tel. (4) 846000; fax (4) 846118; wholly owned by Dubai authorities; Dep. Chair. and Dir SULTAN AHMED BIN SULAYEM.

Dubai Petroleum Co (DPC): POB 2222, Dubai; tel. (4) 846000; fax (4) 846118; holds offshore concession which began production in 1969; wholly owned by Dubai authorities; Pres. S. L. CORNELIUS.

Emirates General Petroleum Corpn (Emarat): POB 9400, Dubai; tel. (4) 444444; fax (4) 444292; f. 1981; wholly owned by Ministry of Finance and Industry; distribution of petroleum; Gen. Man. AHMAD MUHAMMAD AL-KAMDA.

Emirates National Oil Co (ENOC): POB 6442, Enoc House, 4th Floor, al-Qutaeyat Road, Dubai; tel. (4) 3374400; fax (4) 3031221; e-mail webmaster@enoc.co.ae; f. 1993; responsible for management of Dubai-owned cos in petroleum-marketing sector; Chief Exec. HUSSAIN M. SULTAN.

Emirates Petroleum Products Co (Pvt.) Ltd: POB 5589, Dubai; tel. (4) 372131; fax (4) 3031605; f. 1980; jt venture between Govt of Dubai and Caltex Alkhaleej Marketing; sales of petroleum products, bunkering fuel and bitumen; Chair. Sheikh HAMDAN BIN RASHID AL-MAKTOUM.

Sedco-Houston Oil Group: POB 702, Dubai; tel. (4) 224141; holds onshore concession of over 400,000 ha as well as the offshore concession formerly held by Texas Pacific Oil; Pres. CARL F. THORNE.

Sharjah

In 1999 a Supreme Petroleum Council was established in Sharjah. Chaired by Ahmad bin Sultan al-Qasimi, it was to assume the responsibilities of the Petroleum and Mineral Affairs Department.

Petroleum and Mineral Affairs Department: POB 188, Sharjah; tel. (6) 541888; Dir ISMAIL A. WAHID.

Sharjah Liquefied Petroleum Gas Co (SHALCO): POB 787, Sharjah; tel. (6) 5543666; fax (6) 5548799; e-mail shalco@emirates .net.ae; f. 1984; gas processing; 60% owned by Sharjah authorities, 25% Sharjah Amoco-Oil Co, 7.5% each Itochu Corpn and Tokyo Boeki of Japan; Gen. Man. SALEH ALI.

Umm al-Qaiwain

Petroleum and Mineral Affairs Department: POB 9, Umm al-Qaiwain; tel. (6) 666034; Chair. Sheikh SULTAN BIN AHMAD AL-MU'ALLA.

UTILITIES
Abu Dhabi

A decree issued in late February 1998 restructured the Abu Dhabi utilities sector in preparation for its privatization.

Abu Dhabi Water and Electricity Authority (ADWEA): POB 6120, Abu Dhabi; tel. (2) 6943333; fax (2) 6943491; internet www.adwea.gov.ae; f. 1999 to oversee the privatization of the water and electricity sectors; Chair. Sheikh DIAB BIN ZAYED AN-NAHYAN.

Abu Dhabi Distribution Co: POB 219, Abu Dhabi; tel. (2) 642300; fax (2) 6426033; e-mail customerservice@addc.co.ae; internet www.adwea.gov.ae/addc; f. 1999; distribution of water and electricity.

Abu Dhabi Transmission and Dispatch Co: POB 173, Abu Dhabi; tel. (2) 6414000; fax 92) 6426333; internet www.adwea .gov.ae/transco; f. 1999.

Abu Dhabi Water and Electricity Co (ADWEC): POB 51111, Abu Dhabi; tel. (2) 6943333; fax (2) 6425773; internet www.adwea .gov.ae/adwec; f. 1999.

Al-Ain Distribution Co: POB 1065, al-Ain; tel. (3) 7636000; fax (3) 7632025; e-mail aadc@aadc.cc; internet www.adwea.gov.ae/ aadc; f. 1999; distribution of water and electricity.

Bayounah Power Co.: POB 3477, Abu Dhabi; tel. (2) 731100; fax (2) 730403; internet www.adwea.gov.ae/bpc; f. 1999.

Al-Mirfa Power Co: POB 32277, Abu Dhabi; tel. (2) 8833044; fax (2) 8833011; e-mail mirfa@emirates.net.ae; internet www.adwea.gov.ae/ampc; f. 1999; to control Mirfa and Madinat Zayed plants; capacity 300 MW electricity per day, 16m. gallons water per day; Chair. ABDULLAH AL-AHBABI; Gen. Man. PHILIP GRAHAM TILSON.

Al-Taweelah Power Co: POB 32255, Abu Dhabi; tel. (2) 5627000; fax (2) 5627055; internet www.adwea.gov.ae/atpc; f. 1999.

Emirates CMS Power Co: POB 47688, Abu Dhabi; tel. (2) 5067100; fax (2) 5067157; e-mail jnash@cmsenergy.com; internet www.adwea.gov.ae/ecpc; f. 1999; owns and operated the Al-Taweelah plant; Man. Dir ALBERT G. BRANTLEY.

Umm an-Nar Power Co: POB 33488, Abu Dhabi; tel. (2) 5582700; fax (2) 5582405; internet www.adwea.gov.ae/uanpc; f. 1999.

Dubai

Dubai Electricity and Water Authority (DEWA): POB 564, Dubai; tel. (4) 3244444; fax (4) 3248111; e-mail dewa@ dewa.gov.ae; internet www.dewa.gov.ae.

Northern Emirates (Ajman, Fujairah, Ras al-Khaimah and Umm al-Qaiwain)

Ministry of Electricity and Water: (see Ministries, above).

Sharjah

Sharjah Electricity and Water Authority (SEWA): Sharjah; tel. (2) 5288888; fax (2) 5288000; internet www.sewa.gov.ae.

MAJOR COMPANIES
Abu Dhabi

Admak General Contracting Co: POB 650, Abu Dhabi; tel. (2) 5542200; fax (2) 5543134; e-mail admak@emirates.net.ae; f. 1968 as M. A. Kharafi, in 1981 adopted present name; general civil engineering and road contractors; part of the M. A. Kharafi Group of Kuwait; Man. Dir MOHSEN KAMEL MOSTAFA; Exec. Dir SAID A. FOTOUH; 2,600 employees.

Arabconstruct International Ltd: POB 238, Abu Dhabi; tel. (2) 322668; f. 1967; general civil works, construction, engineering and contracting; cap. AED 12m.; Chair. and Propr ADNAN M. DERBAS; 1,500 employees.

International Aluminium: POB 2329, Abu Dhabi; tel. (2) 325326; specialist contractors, design, manufacture and erection of high-rise applications; Propr HUSSAIN GHULAM HAJIPOUR.

Mechanical and Civil Engineering Contractors (MACE) Ltd: POB 2307, Abu Dhabi; tel. (2) 666462; fax (2) 662616; Chair. and Man. Dir WILLIAM A. T. HADDAD; 1,200 employees.

Nitco Concrete Products: POB 654, Abu Dhabi; tel. (2) 344255; f. 1980; production and supply of ready-mix concrete, concrete fences and paving stones; sales AED 15m. (1981/82); cap. AED 8m.; Chair. FARAH ABD AR-RAHMAN HAMED; Man. Dir ABDULLAHI FARAH.

Pilco (Pipeline Construction Co): POB 2021, Abu Dhabi; tel. (2) 554500; fax (2) 559053; e-mail pilco@emirates.net.ae; f. 1968; fabrication of steel, piping, tanks, pressure vessels and machine components; general services to the oil industry; Gen. Man. E. N. HAWA; 200 employees.

Ash-Shaheen Gypsum Products Est: POB 2618, Abu Dhabi; tel. (2) 554673; fax (2) 662116; f. 1978; fabrication of gypsum blocks for use in dry wall partitioning; Dirs OBAID AL-MANSOURI, FRANÇOIS LAMA.

Ajman

Ajman Mosaic Co: POB 406, Ajman; tel. (6) 422104; production of marble and terrazzo; Chair. Sheikh HUMAID.

Dubai

Al-Ahmadiah Contracting and Trading: POB 2596, Dubai; tel. (4) 3450900; fax (4) 3450327; e-mail ahmadiah@emirates.net.ae; f. 1970; building and civil engineering contractors; Pres. and Propr Sheikh HASHER MAKTOUM JUMA AL-MAKTOUM; Vice-Pres. Col MUHAMMAD MUBARAK IESA; Dir S. K. JOSHI; 1,500 employees.

Dubai Aluminium Co (DUBAL): POB 3627, Dubai; tel. (4) 8846292; fax (4) 8846919; e-mail sales@dubal.co.ae; internet www.dubal.co.ae; f. 1979; production of primary aluminium; capacity of 30m. gallons of potable water per day; produces about 550,000 tons of cast metal per annum; Chair. Sheikh HAMDAN BIN RASHID AL-MAKTOUM; CEO IAN RUGERONI.

Fibroplast Industries Co (PVT) Ltd: POB 10192, Dubai; tel. (4) 257575; f. 1977; manufacture of glass fibre-reinforced polyester pipes, tanks, fittings; sales AED 49.8m. (1982); cap. AED 8m.; Chair. ABD AL-GHAFFAR HUSSAIN; Man. Dir W. NAJARIAN; 187 employees.

Al-Futtaim Tower Scaffolding (PVT) Ltd: POB 5502, Dubai; tel. (4) 2858861; fax (4) 2858592; f. 1975; manufacture of scaffolding and steel products; general fabrication; Chair. MAJID MUHAMMAD AL-FUTTAIM; Gen. Man. V. M. G. RAMAN; 150 employees.

Al-Ghurair Group: POB 1, Dubai; tel. (4) 2693311; fax (4) 2691852; f. 1960/61; general contracting, banking, import and export, aluminium extrusion and manufacture of aluminium doors, windows, etc., PVC pipes, tiles and marbles, cement and mineral waters; gold and exchange dealers, owners of grain silos and flour mills, printing press, packaging factory, real estate dealers; cap. AED 1,000m.; Chair. SAIF AHMAD MAJED AL-GHURAIR; Vice-Chair. ABDULLAH AHMAD MAJED AL-GHURAIR; 5,000 employees.

Gulf Eternit Industries Co Ltd: POB 1371, Dubai; tel. (4) 2857256; fax (4) 2852498; e-mail info@gulf-eternit.com; internet www.gulf-eternit.com; f. 1971; design, manufacture and installation of piping systems for industrial, petrochemical, municipal, civil and irrigation applications; sales AED 245.5m., cap. AED 50m. (1998); Pres. FOUAD MAKHZOUMI; Exec. Vice-Pres. Dr OMAR ASHER.

Al-Habtoor Group LLC: POB 25444, Dubai; tel. (4) 3431111; fax (4) 3431140; e-mail habtoor@emirates.net.ae; internet www .habtoor.com; f. 1970; civil and building contracting; engineering; hotels and catering; insurance; leasing; transport services; Chair. KHALAF A. AL-HABTOOR; about 6,000 employees.

Bin Hussain Aluminium Factories: POB 1535, Dubai; tel. (4) 2660643; fax (4) 2661567; f. 1973; process and fabrication of aluminium doors, windows, shop fronts, balustrades, rolling shutters, etc.; Chair. YOUSUF ASH-SHALI.

Bin Ladin Contracting group UAE: POB 1555, Dubai; tel. (4) 691500; tel. 45991; fax (4) 691350; e-mail binladin@emirates.net.ae; internet www.saudi-binladin-group.com; f. 1967 in UAE; civil engineering, roadworks, piling, ground services and building, electrical contracting; Man. Dir ABU BAKR SALIM AL-HAMID; 4,000 employees.

National Cement Co PSC: POB 4041, Dubai; tel. (4) 3388885; fax (4) 3388886; e-mail cement@emirates.net.ae; production and sale of cement; Chair. MUHAMMAD A. AL-GHURAIR.

Ash-Shirawi Contracting Co LLC: POB 33539, Dubai; tel. (4) 2852306; fax (4) 2859255; e-mail valrani@ascontg.com; f. 1971; building and civil engineering contractors, supply of building materials; Chair. ABDULLAH ASH-SHIRAWI; 150 employees.

United Foods Co PSC: POB 5836, Dubai; tel. (4) 3382688; fax (4) 3381987; e-mail aseel@emirates.net.ae; internet www.aseelandsafi .com; f. 1976; manufacture and trading of hydrogenated vegetable oil and edible oils; Chair. SAEED MUHAMMAD AL-MULLA; Gen. Man. M. TAWFIQ BAIG; 100 employees.

Unity Construction Co (UNCO) Ltd: POB 16638, Dubai; tel. (4) 2667870; fax (4) 2615309; f. 1972; building and civil works contracting; Chair. SEIF RASHID HAMARAIN; Gen. Man. HRAYR SOGHOMONIAN; 600 employees.

Fujairah

Fujairah Cement Industries: POB 600, Fujairah; tel. (9) 2223111; fax (9) 2227718; f. 1979; cement manufacture and supply; Chair. Sheikh HAMAD BIN SAIF ASH-SHARQI; Gen. Man. NASSER ALI KHAMAS; 225 employees.

Ras al-Khaimah

Alltek Emirates Ltd: POB 1569, Ras al-Khaimah; tel. (7) 668865; fax (7) 668977; manufacture and marketing of spray plasters, decorative paints and limestone powder.

Raknor (PVT) Ltd: POB 883, Ras al-Khaimah; tel. (7) 2668351; fax (7) 2668910; f. 1976; manufacture of concrete blocks; Chair. Sheikh SA'UD BIN SAQR AL-QASSIMI; Gen. Man. SAMI RIDA SAMI.

Sharjah

CME Contracting Marine Engineering: POB 1859, Sharjah; tel. (6) 354511; f. 1975; turnkey industrial projects, water and electricity plants, construction, building, marine works; joint venture between Chair. and German cos Klaus Stuff, Helma Greuel-Mainz; Chair. Dr F. AL-GAWLY; 323 employees.

Conforce Gulf Ltd Co: POB 289, Sharjah; tel. (6) 591433; f. 1979; building contractor, exporter of building and electrical materials; Man. ABDULLAH MUHAMMAD BUKHATIR.

Dafco Trading and Industrial Co WLL: POB 515, Sharjah; tel. (6) 593333; fax (6) 596531; f. 1980; general contracting trading company; operates factories producing bricks and concrete; Man. M. AL-FARHAN.

General Enterprises Co: POB 1150, Sharjah; tel. (6) 331727; fax (6) 336470; general trading and contracting; Gen. Man. Sheikh AHMAD BIN MUHAMMAD SULTAN AL-QASIMI.

Gulf Building Materials Co Ltd (GBM): POB 1612, Sharjah; tel. (6) 354683; production and supply of building materials: cement, marble and aluminium.

Hempel Paints (Emirates) LLC: POB 2000, Sharjah; tel. (6) 5283307; fax (6) 5281491; f. 1976; manufacture and sale of paints for offshore marine, domestic and industrial use; Chair. SA'UD ABD AL-AZIZ AR-RASHID; CEO and Gen. Man. JOHN R. SPENDLOVE.

Sharjah Electrodes: POB 2019, Sharjah; tel. (6) 5331000; fax (6) 5337244; f. 1976; manufacture and distribution of arc welding electrodes and wire nails; Man. Dir. MUHAMMAD ABDULLAH AL-KHAYYAL.

Umm al-Qaiwain

Umm al-Qaiwain Aluminium Co (UMALCO): Umm al-Qaiwain.

Umm al-Qaiwain Asbestos and Cement Industries Co: POB 547, Umm al-Qaiwain; tel. (6) 671772; fax (6) 671011; Chair. Sheikh SA'UD BIN RASHID AL-MU'ALLA.

Transport

ROADS

Roads are rapidly being developed in the United Arab Emirates, and Abu Dhabi and Dubai are linked by a good road which is dual carriageway for most of its length. This road forms part of a west coast route from Shaam, at the UAE border with the northern enclave of Oman, through Dubai and Abu Dhabi to Tarif. An east coast route links Dibba with Muscat. Other roads include the Abu Dhabi–al-Ain highway and roads linking Sharjah and Ras al-Khaimah, and Sharjah and Dhaid. An underwater tunnel links Dubai Town and Deira by dual carriageway and pedestrian subway. In 1998 there was a total road network of roads of 1,088 km, of which 253 km were motorways and 139 km were main roads.

SHIPPING

Dubai has been the main commercial centre in the Gulf for many years. Abu Dhabi has also become an important port since the opening of the first section of its artificial harbour, Port Zayed. There are smaller ports in Sharjah, Fujairah, Ras al-Khaimah and Umm al-Qaiwain. Work on a dry-dock scheme for Dubai was completed in 1979. It possesses two docks capable of handling 500,000-ton tankers, seven repair berths and a third dock able to accommodate 1,000,000-ton tankers. The Dubai port of Mina Jebel Ali has the largest man-made harbour in the world.

Abu Dhabi

Abu Dhabi Seaport Authority: POB 422, Port Zayed, Abu Dhabi; tel. (2) 6730600; fax (2) 6731023; e-mail Mrktdept@emirates.net.ae;

internet www.portzayed.gov.ae; f. 1972; administers Port Zayed; facilities at the port include 21 deep-water berths and five container gantry cranes of 40 metric tons capacity; cold storage 20,500 metric tons; in 2000 Port Zayed handled 315,810 20-ft equivalent units (TEUs); Chair. Sheikh SAID BIN ZAYED AN-NAHYAN; Dir MUBARAK MUHAMMAD AL-BUAINAIN.

Abu Dhabi National Tanker Co (ADNATCO): POB 2977, Abu Dhabi; tel. (2) 277733; fax (2) 272940; subsidiary company of ADNOC, operating owned and chartered tankships, and transporting crude petroleum, refined products and sulphur; Chair. NASSER AHMAD AS-SUWAIDI; Gen. Man. BADER M. AS-SUWAIDI.

Abu Dhabi Petroleum Ports Operating Co (ADPPOC): POB 61, Abu Dhabi; tel. (2) 333500; fax (2) 333567; e-mail adppoc@emirates.net.ae; f. 1979; manages Jebel Dhanna, Ruwais, Das Island, Umm an-Nar and Zirku Island SPM terminal, Mubarraz; cap. AED 50m.; 60% owned by ADNOC, 40% by LAMNALCO Kuwait; Chair. YOUSUF BIN OMEIR BIN YOUSUF; Gen. Man. KHALIFA M. AL-GOBAISI.

National Marine Services Co (NMS): POB 7202, Abu Dhabi; tel. (2) 339800; fax (2) 211239; operate, charter and lease specialized offshore support vessels; cap. AED 25m.; owned 60% by ADNOC and 40% by Jackson Marine Corpn USA; Chair. SOHAIL FARES AL-MAZRUI; Gen. Man. Capt. HASSAN A. SHAREEF.

Dubai

Dubai Ports Authority (DPA): POB 17000, Dubai; tel. (4) 8815000; fax (4) 8816093; e-mail mktg@dpa.co.ae; internet www.dpa.co.ae; storage areas and facilities for loading and discharge of vessels; supervises ports of Jebel Ali and Mina Rashid; handled 3m. TEUs in 2000; Chair. SULTAN AHMAD BIN SULAYEM; Man. Dir JAMAL MAJID BIN THANIAH.

Dubai Drydocks: POB 8988, Dubai; tel. (4) 3450626; fax (4) 3450116; e-mail drydocks@drydocks.gov.ae; internet www.drydocks.gov.ae; f. 1983; state-owned; dry-docking and repairs, floating dock, tank cleaning, construction of vessels and floating docks, conversions, galvanizing plant, dredging, etc.; Chief Exec. KEITH BURGESS.

Sea Bridge Shipping: POB 8458, Dubai; tel. (4) 379858; fax (4) 372600; cargo ships; Chair. S. RAMAKRISHNAN; Man. Dir L. B. CULAS.

Vela International Marine: POB 26373, City Towers 2, Sheikh Zayed Road, Dubai; tel. (4) 312800; fax (4) 315675; operates tankships; Chair. DHAIFALLAH F. ALUTAIBI; Man. Dir ADEL M. AD-DULAIJIN.

Fujairah

Fujairah Port: POB 787, Fujairah; tel. (9) 2228800; fax (9) 2228811; f. 1982; offers facilities for handling full container, general cargo and roll-on roll-off traffic; handled 565,723 TEUs in 1999; Chair. Sheikh SALEH BIN MUHAMMAD ASH-SHARQI; Harbour Master TAMER MASOUD.

Ras al-Khaimah

Mina Saqr Port Authority: POB 5130, Ras al-Khaimah; tel. (7) 668444; fax (7) 668533; Port operators handling bulk cargoes, containers, general cargo and 'roll on, roll off' traffic; govt-owned; Chair. Sheikh MUHAMMAD BIN SAQR AL-QASIMI; Man. DAVID ALLAN.

Sharjah

Sharjah Ports and Customs Department: POB 510, Sharjah; tel. (6) 281666; fax (6) 281425; the authority administers Port Khalid and Port Khor Fakkan and offers specialized facilities for container and roll-on roll-off traffic, reefer cargo and project and general cargo; in 1999 Port Khalid handled 90,972 TEUs of containerized shipping, and Port Khor Fakkan 989,028 TEUs; Chair. (Ports and Customs) Sheikh SAUD BIN KHALID AL-QASIMI; Dir-Gen. ABD AL-AZIZ SULAIMAN AS-SARKAL.

Fal Shipping Co Ltd: POB 6600, Sharjah; tel. (6) 286666; fax (6) 280861; operates tankships; Chair. ABDULLA JUMA AS-SARI; Gen. Man. MUHAMMAD OSMAN FADUL.

Umm al-Qaiwain

Ahmed bin Rashid Port and Free Zone Authority: POB 279, Umm al-Qaiwain; tel. (6) 7655882; fax 7651552; e-mail abrpaftz@emirates.net.ae.

CIVIL AVIATION

There are six international airports at Abu Dhabi, al-Ain (Abu Dhabi), Dubai, Fujairah and Ras al-Khaimah, and a smaller one at Sharjah, which forms part of Sharjah port, linking air, sea and overland transportation services. In 1995 a total of 11.6m. passengers used the six UAE airports, 3.3m. of them passing through

Abu Dhabi airports; and in 1996 a record 8.5m. passengers used Dubai airport.

Civil Aviation Department: POB 20, Abu Dhabi; tel. (2) 757500; responsible for all aspects of civil aviation; Chair. HAMDAN BIN MUBARAK AN-NAHYAN.

Abu Dhabi Aviation: POB 2723, Abu Dhabi; tel. (2) 449100; fax (2) 449081; f. 1976; domestic charter flights; Chair. HAMDAN BIN MUBARAK AN-NAHYAN; Gen. Man. MUHAMMAD IBRAHIM AL-MAZROUI.

  Emirates Air Service: POB 2723, Abu Dhabi; tel. (2) 757021; fax (2) 449100; f. 1976 as Abu Dhabi Air Services; overhaul, engine and avionics servicing, component repairs and complete refurbishment.

Emirates Airline: POB 686, Dubai; tel. (4) 2951111; fax (4) 2955817; e-mail corpcom@emiratesairline.com; internet www .emiratesairline.com; f. 1985; services to 52 destinations worldwide; owned by the Dubai Govt; in 2000/01 the airline carried 5.7m. passengers and 335,194 tons of freight; Chair. Sheikh AHMAD BIN SAID AL-MAKTOUM; Group Man. Dir. MAURICE FLANAGAN.

Falcon Express Cargo Airlines: Dubai International Airport, POB 93722, Dubai; tel. (4) 2826886; fax (4) 2823125; e-mail feca@ emirates.net.ae; f. 1995; dedicated courier freight.

Gulf Air Co: POB 5015, Sharjah; tel. (6) 356356; fax (6) 354354; internet www.gulfairco.com; f. 1950; jointly owned by Govts of Bahrain, Oman, Qatar and Abu Dhabi since 1974; flights worldwide; Pres. and Chief Exec. SALIM BIN ALI BIN NASSER.

Tourism

Tourism is an established industry in Sharjah, and plans are being implemented to foster tourism in other emirates, notably in Abu Dhabi and Dubai. In 1994 foreign visitors to the UAE totalled more than 1.9m., compared with 616,000 in 1990. In 1999 some 2.5m. tourists visited Dubai.

Department of Tourism and Commerce Marketing: POB 594, Dubai; tel. (4) 2230000; fax (4) 2230022; e-mail info@ dubaitourism.co.ae; internet www.dubaitourism.com.ae.

Dubai Information Department: POB 1420, Dubai; Dir OMAR DEESI.

Fujairah Tourism Bureau: POB 829, Fujairah; tel. (9) 231554; fax (9) 231006; e-mail fujtourb@emirates.net.ae; internet www .fujairah-tourism.com; f. 1995; Chair. Sheikh SAEED ASH-SHARQI; Dir WAHID BIN YOUSSEF.

National Corporation for Tourism and Hotels (NCTH): Abu Dhabi; 20% owned by Government of Abu Dhabi.

Ras al-Khaimah Information and Tourism Department: POB 141, Ras al-Khaimah; tel. (7) 751151; Chair. Sheikh ABD AL-AZIZ BIN HUMAID AL-QASIMI.

Sharjah Commerce and Tourism Development Authority: POB 26661, 11th Floor, Crescent Tower, Buheirah Corniche, Sharjah; tel. (6) 5562777; fax (6) 5563000; e-mail sctda@

sharjahcommerce-tourism.gov.ae; internet www.sharjah-welcome .com; f. 1980; Dir. MUHAMMAD SAIF AL-HAJRI.

Defence

The Union Defence Force and the armed forces of the various emirates were formally merged in May 1976, although difficulties have since been experienced (see History). Abu Dhabi and Dubai retain a degree of independence. Military service is voluntary.

Chief of Staff of Federal Armed Forces: Lt-Gen. MUHAMMAD BIN ZAYED AN-NAHYAN.

Total armed forces (August 2001): 65,000 (army 59,000; navy est. 2,000; air force 4,000).

Defence Budget (2000): AED 14,500m.; federal expenditure on defence has been substantially reduced since the early 1980s, but procurement and project costs are not affected, as individual emirates finance these separately. In 1992 a scheme was announced to draft thousands of local men and women into the army, and to replace the estimated 30% expatriate section of the army with nationals.

Education

Primary education is compulsory, beginning at six years of age and lasting for six years. Secondary education, starting at the age of 12, also lasts for six years, comprising two equal cycles of three years. As a proportion of all school-age children, the total enrolment at primary and secondary schools was equivalent to 85% in 1996 (males 85%; females 85%), compared with only 61% in 1970. Secondary enrolment included 71% of children in the relevant age-group in 1996 (males 68%; females 74%). The UAE is engaged in expanding education, which is regarded as a unifying force for the future of the federation. As a result, major accomplishments in the provision of education have been achieved within the emirates. By 1985/86 there were an estimated 255,000 students at all stages of education in the country as a whole, compared with 141,424 in 1980/81 and about 109,000 in 1978/79. In 1996/97 a total of 55,624 children attended government kindergartens, and 259,509 attended primary schools in the UAE. At the same time, secondary enrolment totalled 180,764. There are primary and secondary schools in all the emirates, and further education in technical fields is available in the more advanced areas. Teachers from other Arab countries, most notably Kuwait, Egypt and Jordan, supplement the UAE's native teaching staff; of a total of 8,859 teachers in 1983, only 646 were UAE nationals. Many students receive higher education abroad. The UAE has one university, at al-Ain in Abu Dhabi, where 16,213 students were enrolled in 1996/97. The four higher colleges of technology (two for male and two for female students) in Abu Dhabi admitted a total of 1,150 students in 1992/93, all of whom were citizens of the UAE. Federal government expenditure in 1995 included AED 2,699m. for education (15.1% of total expenditure by the central Government). A literacy and adult education programme is in operation.

Bibliography

Abdullah, M. Morsy. *The Modern History of the United Arab Emirates*. London, Croom Helm, 1978.

Abed, Ibrahim al-, and Hellyer, Peter (Eds). *The United Arab Emirates*. London, Trident Press, 2001.

Albaharna, H. M. *The Legal Status of the Arabian Gulf States*. Manchester University Press, 1969.

Amni, Sayed Hassan. *International and Legal Problems of the Gulf*. Menas Press, 1981.

Bulloch, John. *The Gulf*. London, Century Publishing.

Busch, B. C. *Britain and the Persian Gulf 1894–1914*. University of California Press, 1967.

Cordesman, Anthony H. *The Gulf and the Search for Strategic Stability*. Mansell, 1984.

Daniels, John. *Abu Dhabi: A Portrait*. London, Longman, 1974.

Fenelon, K. G. *The United Arab Emirates: an Economic and Social Survey*. London, Longman, 1973.

Gabriel, Erhard F. (Ed.). *The Dubai Handbook*. Ahrensburg, Germany, Institute for Applied Economic Geography, 1989.

Ghareeb, Edmund, and Abed, Ibrahim al- (Eds) *Perspectives on the United Arab Emirates*. London, Trident Press, 1997.

Hawley, Donald Frederick. *Courtesies in the Trucial States*. 1965.

The Trucial States. London, George Allen and Unwin, 1971.

Hay, Sir Rupert. *The Persian Gulf States*. Washington, DC, Middle East Institute, 1959.

Heard-Bey, Dr Frauke. *From Trucial States to United Arab Emirates*. London, Longman, 1982.

  The Arabian Gulf States and the Islamic Revolution. Bonn, German Institute for Foreign Policy Research.

Khalifa, Ali Mohammad. *The United Arab Emirates: Unity in Fragmentation*. London, Croom Helm, 1980.

Lienhardt, Peter, and Shahi, Ahmed al- (Ed.). *Shaikhdoms of Eastern Arabia*. New York, St Martin's Press, 2001.

McLachlan, Keith, and Joffé, George. *The Gulf War—A Survey of Political Issues and Economic Consequences*. London, Economist Intelligence Unit, 1984.

Mann, Clarence. *Abu Dhabi: Birth of an Oil Sheikhdom*. Beirut, Khayats, 1964.

Marlowe, John. *The Persian Gulf in the 20th Century*. London, Cresset Press, 1962.

Miles, S. B. *The Countries and Tribes of the Persian Gulf*. 3rd edn, London, Cass, 1966.

Ministry of Information and Culture. *United Arab Emirates: A Record of Achievement, 1979–81*. Abu Dhabi, 1981.

Oteiba, Mani Said al-. *Petroleum and the Economy of the United Arab Emirates*. London, Croom Helm, 1977.

   Essays on Petroleum. London, Croom Helm, 1982.

Peck, M. C. *The UAE—A Venture in Unity*. London, Croom Helm.

Qasimi, Sultan bin. *Myth of Arab Policy in the Gulf*. London. Croom Helm, 1986.

Sadiq, Muhammad T., and Snavely, William P. *Bahrain, Qatar and the United Arab Emirates: Colonial Past, Present Problems, and Future Prospects*. Lexington, MA, Heath, 1972.

Sakr, Nadwi. *The UAE to 1990–One market or Seven?* (Special Report No. 238). London, Economist Intelligence Unit, 1986.

Taryam, A. O. *The Establishment of the UAE*. London, Croom Helm.

Wilson, Graeme. *Father of Dubai: Sheikh Rashid bin Saeed Al-Maktoum*. Dubai, Media Prima, 1999.

Yorke, V., and Turner, L. *European Interests and Gulf Oil*. Royal Institute of International Affairs/Gower, 1986.

Zahlan, Rosemarie Said. *The Origins of the United Arab Emirates*. London, Macmillan, 1978.

YEMEN

Geography

On 22 May 1990 the Yemen Arab Republic (YAR) and the People's Democratic Republic of Yemen (PDRY) merged to form the Republic of Yemen. Yemen consists of the south-west corner of the Arabian peninsula—the highlands inland, and the coastal strip along the Red Sea; and the former British colony of Aden (195 sq km or 75.3 sq miles) and the Protectorate of South Arabia (about 333,000 sq km), together with the islands of Perim (13 sq km) and Kamaran (57 sq km). The Republic of Yemen lies at the southern end of the Arabian peninsula, approximately between longitude 43°E and 56°E, with Perim Island a few kilometres due west, in the strait marking the southern extremity of the Red Sea; and Socotra in the extreme east. Yemen has frontiers with Saudi Arabia and Oman, although atlases have shown considerable variation in the precise boundaries of the three countries, or sometimes have not indicated them at all. (A final agreement on delineation of the border with Saudi Arabia, with the exception of some eastern sections, was signed in mid-2000, while the border with Oman was officially demarcated in 1995.) The capital of the Republic of Yemen is San'a, which lies on the al-Jehal plateau (2,175 m above sea-level).

Physically, Yemen comprises the dislocated southern edge of the great plateau of Arabia. This is an immense mass of ancient granites, once forming part of Africa, and covered in many places by shallow, mainly horizontal layers of younger sedimentary rocks. The whole plateau has undergone down-warping in the east and elevation in the west, so that the highest land (over 3,000 m) occurs in the extreme west, near the Red Sea, with a gradual decline to the lowest parts (under 300 m) in the extreme east. The whole of the southern and western coasts of Yemen were formed by a series of enormous fractures, which produced a flat but very narrow coastal plain, rising steeply to the hill country a short distance inland. Percolation of molten magma along the fracture-lines gave rise to a number of volcanic craters, now extinct, and one of these, partly eroded and occupied by the sea, forms the site of Aden port.

An important topographic feature is the Wadi Hadramawt, an imposing valley running parallel to the coast at 160 km–240 km distance inland. In its upper and middle parts, this valley is broad, and occupied by a seasonal torrent; in its lower (eastern) part it narrows considerably, making a sudden turn south-eastwards and reaching the sea. This lower part is largely uninhabited, but the upper parts, where alluvial soil and intermittent flood water are available, support a farming population.

Rainfall is generally scarce, but relatively more abundant on the highlands and in the west. The climate of the highlands is considered to be the best in all Arabia since it experiences a regime rather like that of East Africa: a warm, temperate and rainy summer, and a cool, moderately dry winter with occasional frost and some snow. Aden receives 125 mm of rain annually, all of it during winter (December–March), whilst in the lowlands

of the extreme east, it may rain only once in five or 10 years. In the highlands a few miles north of Aden, falls of up to 760 mm occur, for the most part during summer, and this rainfall also gradually declines eastwards, giving 380 mm–500 mm in the highlands of Dhofar. As much as 890 mm of rain may fall annually on the higher parts of the interior, off the Red Sea coast, with 400 mm–500 mm over much of the plateau; but the coast receives less than 130 mm generally, often in the form of irregular downpours. There is, therefore, the phenomenon of streams and even rivers flowing perennially in the western highlands but failing to reach the coast.

Ultimately, to the north and east, rainfall becomes almost negligible, as the edges of the Arabian Desert are reached. This unusual situation of a reversal in climatic conditions over a few miles is thought to be the result of two streams of air; an upper one, damp and unstable in summer, and originating in the equatorial regions of East Africa; and a lower current, generally drier and related to conditions prevailing over the rest of the Middle East. In this way the low-lying coastal areas have a maximum of rainfall in winter, and the hills of Yemen a maximum in summer. Temperatures are everywhere high, particularly on the coastal plain, which has a southern aspect: mean figures of 25°C (January) to 32°C (June) occur at Aden town, but maxima of more than 38°C are common. Owing to this climate gradation from desert temperate conditions, Yemen has a similar gradation of crops and vegetation. In the interior, off the Red Sea coast, the highest parts appear as 'African', with scattered trees and grassland. Crops of coffee, qat, cereals and vegetables are grown, while, lower down, 'Mediterranean' fruits appear, with millet and, where irrigation water is available, bananas. The date palm is the only tree to grow successfully in the coastal region.

To the east, except on the higher parts, which have a light covering of thorn scrub (including dwarf trees which exude a sap from which incense and myrrh are derived), and the restricted patches of cultivated land, the territory is devoid of vegetation. Cultivation is limited to small level patches of good soil on flat terraces alongside the river beds, on the floor and sides of the Wadi Hadramawt, or where irrigation from wells and occasionally from cisterns can be practised. The most productive areas are: Lahej, close to Aden town; two districts near Mukalla (about 480 km east of Aden), and parts of the middle Hadramawt. Irrigation from cisterns hollowed out of the rock has long been practised, and Aden town has a famous system of this kind, dating back many centuries. Today, however, the main system of irrigation is provided by floodwater.

The area of Yemen is approximately 536,869 sq km (207,286 sq miles) and its population was 14,587,807 at the census of 16 December 1994. The official estimate of total population at mid-2001 was 18,863,000, giving a population density of 35.1 persons per sq km.

History

RICHARD I. LAWLESS

Based on an earlier article by ROBIN BIDWELL

PRE-ISLAMIC YEMEN

In the millennium before Christ there were three centres of civilization in the Arabian peninsula; one in the north-west around Madain Salih, the second based in Bahrain and in what is now the United Arab Emirates (UAE); and the third, the most advanced, in the Yemen. Traditional Arab genealogists

assign to the Yemenis a different ancestor (*Qahtan*) from that of the northern tribes (*Adnan*). Yemen was unique amongst ancient civilizations in that it was not dependent on a great river, but relied upon rainfall to irrigate terraced fields, controlling the waters by a sophisticated system of dams, of which the one at Marib was famous throughout Arabia. In addition to flourishing agriculture, the incense trade and the use of its ports as a link between India, China, Africa and the Mediterranean made it one of the richest regions of the ancient world. References in the Bible and Classical authors and archaeology indicate that it had a social structure that endured into the 20th century: towns with an hereditary literate class, trades divided into noble and ignoble, settled agriculturalists and, separate from these, tribesmen who were sometimes soldiers and sometimes predators. The chronology is uncertain, but it is clear that about 110 BC the whole area including what are now parts of Saudi Arabia and Oman came under the domination of the Himyarites whose rule continued almost until the rise of Islam at which time, after half a century of Abyssinian rule, Yemen had recently been conquered by the Persians.

EARLY ISLAMIC YEMEN

The Persian *satrap* appears to have accepted an invitation from the Prophet to adopt Islam and, according to tradition, the whole of the great tribe of Hamdan, the ancestors of the Hashid and Bakil tribes, were converted in a single day by Muhammad's son-in-law Ali; this forged a link between them and the Hashemites which lasted until the Revolution of 1962. Although huge numbers of Yemenis served in the Islamic armies (which conquered territories from the Atlantic to the borders of China), for a while it seemed that Yemeni particularism might prove too strong to accept a religion of foreign origin, and a series of revolts occurred. The Caliphs of Baghdad took little interest in such a remote area and in 822 their local governor, Ibn Ziyad, revolted and reunited most of the old Himyarite state under his own rule from the city of Zabid. Although short-lived, this had the effect of splitting the Yemen away from the main Arab Empire and reasserted its individuality.

The second half of the ninth century was a period of religious strife as the Ismailis attempted to seize control of the Yemen. In 1037, while the Ismailis were ruling in Cairo, a local chieftain conquered most of the old Himyaritic area and ruled it from San'a in their name. The Sulayhid dynasty survived in great prosperity for almost a century, but as it declined local governors asserted their independence. In 1174, the great Saladin (Salah ad-Din al-Ayyubi), who had overthrown the Ismailis in Egypt, sent his brother to destroy their adherents in Yemen and once again most of south-west Arabia was governed by a single ruler. The Ayyubids remained for half a century and left affairs in the hands of an official, ar-Rasul, who later assumed an independent sovereignty.

The Rasulids, from their capital at Taiz, had diplomatic relations with Persia, India and China and were so effective that they were able to organize a trilateral campaign by land and sea against a rebellious vassal in Dhofar. Their state, in turn, disintegrated and the area was totally fragmented when the Portuguese attacked Aden in 1513.

FROM THE SIXTEENTH TO THE EARLY NINETEENTH CENTURY

The fear that the Portuguese might establish a presence in southern Arabia which could serve as a base to attack the Holy Places led to the intervention of the Ottoman Sultan. An army, using firearms for the first time in the area, succeeded in installing a Pasha in San'a who ruled almost all of the historic Yemen. The Zaidis in the mountains remained detached and in the east the Kathiri family established a semi-independent state in Hadramawt, although they acknowledged Ottoman sovereignty. The discovery of the route to India round the Cape practically destroyed the importance of Aden as an entrepôt, but, from *c.* 1600, British and Dutch traders travelled to Mocha to buy coffee and sell textiles.

At about the same time a new Zaidi Imam launched a guerrilla war against the Turks who, after nine years' fighting, agreed to leave him in control of the area north of San'a. His son launched a religious and national war which, in 1636, led to their departure. He and succeeding Imams brought the whole of South Arabia, including Dhofar and Asir under their rule.

Once more central authority declined and in 1728 the Governor of Lahej and Aden proclaimed himself an independent Sultan and his example was followed in Asir and most of the South. By the time the explorer Niebuhr visited San'a in 1763

the writ of the Imam was only valid in San'a, Taiz and the Tihamah.

In 1804 the Wahhabis occupied Mecca and Medina and also penetrated into the Tihamah. Some years later the Ottoman Sultan, as Protector of the Holy Places, requested his vassal Muhammad Ali, Pasha of Egypt, to expel them. This he did and went on to take over the Tihamah and monopolize the coffee trade; in 1837 he bought control of Taiz.

In 1834, taking advantage of the plundering of an Indian vessel flying the British flag, the Bombay Government sent Captain Haines of the Indian navy to exact restitution and at the same time to negotiate for the purchase of Aden (a valuable fuelling station between Britain and India). The Sultan of Lahej, fearing that it might be seized by the Egyptians, agreed to sell but then reneged on the deal. His son then tried to kidnap Haines in order to repossess the document and this provided a pretext for an attack in which Aden was stormed on 19 January 1839.

In 1841 as part of a general peace settlement Muhammad Ali Pasha evacuated his troops from Yemen. A period of lawlessness ensued, during which the Imam requested a treaty of protection with the British. Haines, who was at that time Political Agent in Aden, was ordered to refuse. The Turks decided to reassert control and in 1849 they occupied Hodeida.

THE BRITISH IN ADEN 1839–1918

At the time of the conquest, Aden was in a state of dilapidation with about 600 inhabitants, but Haines had the vision to realize that it could be built into a great port to serve the hinterland and resume its historic role as an entrepôt. In seven years the population rose to 25,000. After repelling two attempts by the Sultan of Lahej to recapture the town, Haines sought the friendship of the local tribes by giving small subsidies to their leaders, often through the Sultan of Lahej, and by abstaining from interference in their internal affairs. Aden became a free port in 1850 and from 1869 benefited from the substantial increase in shipping that resulted from the opening of the Suez Canal, although until 1881 it was not master of its own water supply. Aden was a military base, secured by the acquisition of Perim Island and Little Aden, which had been sought by the French, and occupation of part of the Somali coast which ensured that no hostile power could dominate the entrance to the Red Sea. The Kuria Muria Islands were a gift to Queen Victoria from Saiyid Said of Oman.

In the early 1870s the Turks in San'a established contact with some of the tribes, including those of Hadramawt, that had been at least nominally subject to the Ottoman Sultan during the first occupation. This alarmed the British who presented Constantinople with a list of nine tribes that they regarded as under their sphere of influence and in which they would oppose Turkish interference. The Turks occupied part of the Sultanate of Lahej, but withdrew in December 1873 after strong diplomatic action in Constantinople. The British then consolidated their position with a series of treaties, similar to the Exclusive Treaties with the Gulf Sheikhdoms, signed with the tribes, who, in return for protection against outside attack and regular subsidies, undertook to refrain from correspondence with foreign powers to whom they were not to cede any territory without approval. These events were significant in Yemeni history because for the first time southern Arabia was formally divided into two distinct territories separated by a boundary which was apparent to the tribes and recognized by international agreement.

Despite proposals by the British Foreign Office that Aden should be taken over by the Colonial Office, it continued to be administered as part of the Bombay presidency. Consequently, Aden began to adopt a distinctly Indian style of government and trade. Despite the emergence of small numbers of educated local Arabs, the increasing use of English and Urdu words and expressions made its colloquial language difficult for outsiders to understand and it took on a cultural identity of its own which was quite different from the traditional Arab background of San'a.

THE TURKS IN YEMEN AND THE FIRST WORLD WAR

The Turks had occupied Hodeida in 1849 and, after concluding a treaty with the Imam, proceeded to settle in San'a but were expelled with heavy casualties by its inhabitants. There followed twenty years of near-anarchy until the opening of the Suez Canal enabled Constantinople to send large reinforcements by sea as part of its general policy of reasserting its position in Arabia. San'a was occupied again in 1871 and while the Zaidis were left alone, the rest of the country was virtually controlled by occupying forces despite frequent skirmishes with the tribes. Yemen was regarded as a place of exile for Ottoman officials whose financial dishonesty and lax morals caused great resentment.

In 1891 Muhammad Hamid ad-Din was elected Imam and, taking the regnal name assumed by the leader of the seventeenth century revolt, he issued a proclamation denouncing the religious unworthiness of the Turks to rule the country, once again showing the symbiosis of Zaidi doctrine and Yemeni nationalism. Soon all the highlands rallied to him but Constantinople retaliated by sending a notoriously ruthless Pasha who crushed the rebellion. The Turks then attempted to modernize their administration, but the secular nature of many of their reforms alienated the Shafai inhabitants of the Tihamah and Hujariyah.

In 1904 Muhammad's son, Yahya, succeeded him as Imam and called for a new uprising. In addition to their immorality and secularization, he was particularly incensed by the Turkish agreement with the British to delimit a frontier which he regarded as recognizing the separation of territory he considered as part of historic Yemen. Despite the deployment of almost 100,000 troops, the Turks were unable to destroy Yahya's tribal levies and in 1911, anxious to redeploy their troops to confront the Italian invasion of Tripoli and imminent war in the Balkans, they concluded with him the treaty of Da'an. Yahya conceded that the Ottoman Sultan was responsible for the defence and foreign affairs of the Islamic community as a whole, including Yemen, in return for non-interference in the religious and legal affairs of the Zaidis: in effect he was left in control of the Highlands while the Turks ruled the Tihamah where unrest continued.

Despite several British efforts to buy his support after the outbreak of war in 1914, Yahya remained loyal to the treaty. The Turks, by exploiting British military incompetence, occupied Lahej and besieged Aden for over three years. Having failed to win over Yahya, the British sought to undermine his position by providing the intensely ambitious *de facto* independent ruler of Asir, Said Muhammad Ali al-Idrisi, with the financial means to subvert the Hashid and Bakil tribes and encouraged plots to overthrow the Imam. Yahya also resented apparent British support for the pretensions of Sharif Hussain of Mecca to be King of the Arabs and the seizure of Kamaran, just off the Yemeni coast. The Turks occupied the north-western part of the Protectorate, tried unsuccessfully to incite the tribes east of Aden and only withdrew after their Government, defeated elsewhere, sought an armistice.

BRITISH RELATIONS WITH THE IMAM YAHYA

After the war, relations between Yahya and the British Government were extremely uncordial. They deteriorated further when, upon the withdrawal of the Turks from territories within the recognized area of the Aden Protectorate, Yahya sent his troops to replace the Turkish contingent while the British seized Hodeida and encouraged al-Idrisi to extend his influence in the Tihamah where, as a Shafai, he was preferred to the Zaidi Imam. When Hodeida was evacuated, al-Idrisi was allowed to occupy it. The British then attempted to conciliate Yahya in the same way as had been the strategy with other Peninsular rulers, most of whom received subsidies from Britain in return for accepting direction in their foreign affairs. A mission sent for the purpose was detained in Tihamah by Shafai tribesmen opposed to the Imam. Negotiations lingered on because the British wished to discuss details of a frontier which Yahya, claiming by right of inheritance all that had once been ruled by his Himyaritic ancestors, declared had no legal existence. He also denied the right of the authorities in Aden to have relations with the Protectorate chiefs whom he regarded as Yemeni subjects. After a serious incident in 1928 the British bombed Taiz and other cities and Yahya agreed to withdraw his troops.

In 1933 Yahya, aware of the probability of war with Ibn Sa'ud on his northern frontier, settled his dispute with the British. In the Treaty of San'a, signed in February 1934, he tacitly accepted the boundaries agreed between Britain and the Turks, although he considered this as merely permitting Aden to administer part of his territory. In deference to his claims, no further boundary pillars were erected and no further survey carried out. It was agreed that no changes would be made in the boundaries for 40 years after which the matter would be discussed again. The British elevated Yahya's status by recognizing him as King. The treaty ushered in a period of generally peaceful coexistence which lasted for the rest of the reign of Imam Yahya. He resented the toleration of his political opponents in Aden while the British were concerned about his apparent friendship with Fascist Italy, although during the Second World War he remained strictly neutral.

POST-WAR ADEN AND THE HINTERLAND

In 1937, in addition to the hinterland, the Colonial Office had taken control of Aden itself. In 1947 a nominated Legislative Council for Aden was established and in 1949 the first elections, for a township authority, were held. Meanwhile, the town was transformed by the construction of a refinery, and the efficient bunkering service that followed ensured that Aden, still a free port, was by 1957 fourth after London, Liverpool and New York in the amount of shipping that it handled. Local industries were created to satisfy the needs of a population which trebled within a few years and increased still further after the British Government's Defence White Paper of 1957 made the Colony the largest British military base outside Europe. The increase in prosperity enabled the Government in Aden to establish what were, at the time, the best social services in the Arab world. Most who came to work in Aden were from the North, and locally-born Arabs were outnumbered by Yemeni immigrants.

There was no evidence of discontent with colonial rule before December 1947, when there was a general strike, followed by riots in which more than 100 people were killed, as a protest against British policy in Palestine. Subsequently three nationalist groups emerged—the Aden Association, which aimed at eventual independence within the Commonwealth, to be achieved by co-operation; the South Arabian League, seeking independence for a united Colony and Protectorate under the Sultan of Lahej; and a radical United National Front, demanding union with Yemen and Muscat as a republic.

These movements were supported by the freest press in the Arab world, but it was the rise of a trade union movement that strengthened their position. At a time when the voice of Nasser could be heard through the newly-invented transistor radios, the Imam's union with Egypt led to the first talk of 'the occupied South', and, when a reform gave the elected members a majority on the Legislative Council, the question arose of votes for immigrants from North Yemen, who constituted the majority of trade unionists. When, in January 1959, voting was held for 12 seats, there was a boycott by many Arabs: nine Arabs, two Somalis and an Indian were elected.

After the Treaty of San'a, the administration in Aden believed that more should be done for the Protectorate, and the first measure was to appoint a political officer and to enlist local tribesmen to police their own areas. There was a considerable increase in security, and progress was made in educational, health and agricultural matters. In 1937 the Qu'aiti Sultan of Mukalla had become the first ruler to bind himself to accept a resident adviser and 'for the welfare of his state to accept his advice in all matters except those concerning Muhammadan religion and custom'. Within five years the area had an effective, locally-run administration, directed by a State Council.

The hinterland was divided into the Eastern and Western Aden Protectorates (the EAP and the WAP, respectively). The EAP comprised the Hadramawt, the coastal strip of Mahra and the associated island of Socotra, and two minor Wahidi sultanates to the west of Mukalla with a total population estimated at 326,000. The WAP consisted of 17 states and various territories where there was no administration of any sort and which were never even visited by government officials, Arab or English.

Advisory treaties were later signed with the other states of the EAP and with many of those of the WAP. Their effect depended upon the working relationship that the adviser could establish with his local ruler for he had no executive powers. A

Sultan who rejected 'advice' tendered through the Governor could be deposed, but this needed the approval of the Secretary of State for the Colonies, who often had little time for the misconduct of a minor sheikh. An Arab chief who was knowledgeable about the area and who was liked or feared by the people, could normally impose his views upon a transitory British official. In practice the sultanates were not colonies because they enjoyed a large degree of independence, albeit hampered by financial dependence on the British.

During the Second World War British intervention increased because of the need to maximize local production of food. By 1954 the number of chiefs in relation with Aden had grown to more than 50 and this incensed the Imam who imposed his own interpretation of the Treaty of San'a, which he declared to have been violated. He therefore initiated a determined effort to incite the tribes to revolt against Christian encroachments. This caused the Governor, Sir Tom Hickinbotham, to reverse the old policy of relying on tribal particularism in order to prevent union against the British and to attempt to form a federal union which would create a distinct South Arabian nation. He attempted, but failed, to impose a ready-made formula, which made no mention of eventual independence and was unsuited to local conditions.

The idea of federation, despite its failure, provoked the Imam into intensifying his efforts to arouse subversion. He was assisted by Egyptian and Russian advisers and technicians. Violent incidents culminated in the spring of 1958, when an estimated 1,000 dissidents besieged a British political officer in a fort near the frontier while, at the same time, bombs were being thrown in Aden Colony. The idea of federation also encouraged the Sultan of Lahej to attempt to unite South Arabia under his own rule and consequently began to recruit adherents in other states while at the same time he talked of joining the Arab League and of employing Egyptian advisers. He was deposed.

The double threat from Lahej and Yemen, which would become more dangerous when Badr, known to be pro-Nasser, succeeded his father; the fact that the increase in economic activity made the existence of customs posts every few miles an absurd inconvenience; and the possibility that oil would be discovered in Hadramawt which would be unlikely to share its benefits unless there was some form of unity, revived the idea of federation. The British authorities primed the most trusted amirs with financial rewards and promises and feigned surprise when the rulers of six WAP states, Beihan, Audhali, Fadhli, Dhala, Lower Yafa and the Upper Aulaqi Sheikhdom travelled to Britain to request assistance in forming a federation.

THE MUTAWAKILITE KINGS (1919–1962)

During the war in 1914 Yahya had only exerted authority in the Zaidi areas and after the departure of the Turks, al-Idrisi made a determined effort to assume control of the Shafai areas. In 1920, however, the British discontinued his subsidy and his supporters decreased. He died in 1923, leaving feuding successors and a situation in which both Yahya and Ibn Sa'ud could intervene. Although a certain amount of fighting was involved, Yahya managed to bring both Zaidi and Shafai areas under either his own control or that of friendly chiefs. British officials travelling to San'a to negotiate the treaty of 1934 were astonished at the tranquillity of the country, which contrasted strongly with the insecurity prevailing in the Aden Protectorate.

Yahya managed to retain some Turkish soldiers and officials to form a backbone for his administration but otherwise he relied upon the traditional allies of the Imamate—the Saiyids and the traditional literate class of Qadis and upon the Hashid and the Bakil to comprise an armed force.

Yemen, before the discovery of petroleum in the Peninsula, was practically the only state that was self-supporting and Yahya saw no need for foreigners who might interfere with his independence and corrupt his people. Not even Arab states were permitted to establish embassies in San'a, foreign newspapers were forbidden, prospecting for petroleum or minerals was prohibited and though some weapons were obtained from Italy, Yahya ensured that it exercised no political influence. His determination to reconstruct the Himyarite 'empire' led to maladroit encroachments in Asir and Najran which culminated in a war with Saudi Arabia. An army under the future King Faisal advanced through the Tihamah, capturing Hodeida, but

Ibn Sa'ud, unwilling to commit his troops to fighting in the mountains and to risk European intervention, made peace on generous terms, although Yahya had to withdraw his claims to Asir and Najran. Towards the end of his reign, Yahya joined the Arab League and the UN, uniting with other Arabs in opposition to Zionism.

Yahya had allowed young men to study abroad and had even sent some to Baghdad for military training. They returned convinced of the backwardness of Yemen and formed an opposition group, the *Ahrar*, the Free Yemenis, based in Aden where they received support in the local press. They were financed by merchants who wished to end royal monopolies. Yahya had provoked some of the religious leaders by breaking Zaidi tradition in requiring oaths of allegiance to his son Ahmad as Crown Prince. This particularly affronted the influential Saiyid Abd Allah al-Wazir who considered his right to the throne at least equal to that of Ahmad. These dissidents coalesced in a 'Sacred National Pact' which would establish a constitutional Imamate under al-Wazir, and enlisted tribal outlaws who in February 1948 assassinated Yahya in the first post-war coup in the Arab world.

Ahmad, though personally unpopular, managed to rally the tribes because of the shock of the murder, the failure of the new regime to attract support at home or abroad, and a promise that his tribal followers might sack San'a. He moved the capital to Taiz and ruled as autocratically as his father had done, showing the same immense knowledge of the country and intuitive understanding of the causes of local events. He survived a failed military coup and several assassination attempts.

He ended the country's isolation, admitting resident ambassadors, giving concessions to oil prospectors, accepting Soviet aid to develop Hodeida harbour and a Chinese-built road up to San'a. He maintained the claim to rule the whole of South Arabia and his dislike of the British, intensified by suspicions that they had connived at the murder of his father and by their adoption of a forward policy in the Aden Protectorate at a time when imperialism was in retreat elsewhere. In 1953, with the support of other Arab states, he raised the issue with the UN. He feared that the British might formally annex Shabwa, where there was believed to be oil. His officials fomented trouble across the frontier, attracting malcontents with arms and money. In order to acquire arms he signed a treaty in 1955 with Saudi Arabia and Egypt and later made agreements with several Eastern Bloc countries. Criticism grew of his reactionary and arbitrary policies, but he disconcerted his opponents by joining with Egypt and Syria in the United Arab States, which implied the backing of Nasser, the champion of radical Arab nationalism. In April 1959 Ahmad was the first Imam ever to leave the country, travelling to Rome, Italy, for treatment for morphine addiction. The unnatural union did not survive Egyptian intervention during his absence and he denounced it. Consequently, hostility to Nasser led to a *rapprochement* with the British. He reverted to morphine addicton after another assassination attempt and gradually allowed Badr to assume power before his death in September 1962.

THE FEDERATION OF SOUTH ARABIA

After a treaty in which the British extended to the new entity, as a whole, the Protectorate Treaties previously concluded with its individual members, the federation came into existence in February 1959. The British would continue to meet the cost of its defence. Its ultimate aim, for which the Colonial Secretary pledged help to prepare, was independence. A new capital, al-Ittihad, was built and Sultans, sitting as the Supreme Council, constituted its only political and legislative organ. The ruler of each state, eventually numbering 17, had to be given a cabinet portfolio. The federation, dependent on British officials and British finances, initially appeared to be an instrument for British foreign policy and was never recognized by Arab Governments, many of which worked to destroy it. Nevertheless, considerable economic and some social progress was made, and in 1961 the federation acquired its own armed forces, consisting of five infantry battalions, an armoured car regiment with signals and administrative units.

In 1961 the British Government, believing that the security of the base in Aden was threatened by the turbulence engendered by trade union activists, now calling themselves the

People's Socialist Party, decided to overwhelm the nationalists there by merging the Colony into the new federation. Britain would retain sovereignty over the Colony. Many Aden politicians were strongly opposed, but enough were coerced or bribed and some genuinely supported it. A motion to unite was forced through the Legislative Council in September 1962 and took effect from January 1963, but many, particularly the intellectuals, never ceased to resent the way in which merger was brought about. All those with grievances found a ready hearing amongst those in the British Labour Party who were ideologically opposed to a government of Sultans.

Mutual jealousies amongst the rulers meant that the federation had neither a president nor a prime minister and its titular head was the Chairman of the Supreme Council—an office which rotated monthly. The important states of the EAP refused to join and the British declined to coerce them although federal leaders saw their membership as vital. A constitutional conference arranged for December 1963 had to be postponed when a grenade was thrown amongst the rulers assembled at Aden airport, and it did not take place until June 1964. The leaders assembled in London, England, were relentlessly intimidated by the Colonial Secretary, Duncan Sandys, to the extent that one of the founding Sultans defected, joining the nationalist opposition in Cairo, Egypt. It was announced, however, that independence would come in 1968 and that in the interim there would be a president and a prime minister, an elected assembly and complete arabization of the civil service. These reforms were not implemented, for there was no agreement as to who should occupy the principal offices and outside Aden there was still no real administrative structure and no political organization to mobilize the people in support of the federation. The rulers, in offices in the capital, started to lose touch with what was occurring in their home states. Aden remained under a state of emergency imposed after the grenade attack and there was an increasing tendency amongst British officials to see its population as 'disloyal' in comparison with the 'trustworthy' Sultans.

The Yemeni Revolution had brought bribed Egyptian officers to the frontier to incite subversion. With their encouragement, young men from the Protectorates, inspired by the ideals of Arab nationalism, formed the National Liberation Front (NLF, which was allegedly entirely financed by Egypt) announcing in a declaration of 14 October 1963 that they intended not merely to expel the British from South Arabia, but to make a socialist revolution. Their first triumph was to provoke a tribal revolt in Radfan which was suppressed by the use of British troops, helicopters and even heavy bombers. The campaign attracted wide publicity and led to criticism by left-wingers in Britain and the Arab world which seriously damaged the image of the federation, in whose name it was undertaken. Further denunciation followed the destruction of a Yemeni fort after Egyptian aircraft had dropped bombs on the territory of the federal Government which then invoked the Defence Treaty with Britain. The anti-colonial group at the UN became increasingly interested in the area, passing, in 1963, Resolution 1949 which called for self-determination for South Arabia, elections under UN supervision and the removal of the British base. Doubts about the future of the federation increased after the election of Harold Wilson as the Prime Minister of the British Government in October 1964.

In April 1964, visiting San'a, Nasser had sworn 'by Allah, to expel the British from all parts of the Arabian peninsula' and a campaign of urban terror was launched to make Aden ungovernable. It was estimated that between December 1963 and May 1966, 60 people were killed and 350 injured in Aden alone, one-third of the casualties being British. On joining the federation Aden had been permitted a chief minister and Abd al-Qawi Makkawi, appointed to that post in March 1965, appeared more anxious to appease the terrorists than to collaborate with the British. He denounced the state of emergency and the banning of the NLF. After Makkawi had publicly refused to condemn the murder of a respected official, he was dismissed by the Governor, Sir Richard Turnbull, who suspended the Constitution and imposed direct colonial rule in September 1965. He went into exile, joined soon afterwards by Asnaj and they and the NLF amalgamated, as a result of Egyptian

pressure, to form the Front for the Liberation of Occupied South Yemen (FLOSY).

Financial difficulties and the need to conciliate internal party opposition led the Wilson Government, in February 1966, to announce that there was no further need for the Aden base— the defence of which had been the paramount reason for creating the federation. Moreover, there would be no further British military presence in South Arabia after independence in 1968. The federal leaders, realizing that they had isolated themselves from much of the Arab world by supporting the British, felt betrayed and defenceless. Around the same time militants of the NLF became more radical, finding the ideas of Mao and Guevara more to their liking than those of the bourgeois Nasser and of the FLOSY leaders and, by bank robberies and extortion, they freed themselves from financial dependence on Egypt. Assisted by fellow tribesmen in the police force and the federal armed forces, they fought the British and at the same time wrested control of the Aden streets from FLOSY. Aden was still formally a Colony and the British refused to allow the federal Government to use its own forces to improve security there and its members started to lose confidence in their own future and attempted to negotiate on a basis of Resolution 1949. In December 1966 the NLF declared itself the sole representative of the people of South Arabia.

The British Government was now preoccupied with withdrawing from South Arabia with the minimum cost in British lives and with the lesser objective of leaving a stable government behind. Various expedients were tried, including inviting help from Nasser and from the UN, promising a short-term security cover and working for an alliance between the federal Government and the NLF, with which secret contacts were established. It was even hoped that Saudi Arabia might take over responsibility for the area. There was also a desperate attempt to organize a new administration under an Adeni premier, after a brief but bloody military mutiny in June 1967 but this failed owing to the jealousies of the tribal ministers.

The NLF started to take control of state after state in the hinterland and on 4 September 1967 the High Commissioner stated that the federal Government had ceased to exist. Although the NLF was known to have extreme left-wing views, the British preferred it to the pro-Nasser FLOSY and assisted its assumption of power. FLOSY, deprived of external support as a result of the Egyptian withdrawal from Yemen, was defeated with heavy losses after the federal army declared support for the NLF. The handover to the NLF was formalized by a meeting at Geneva, Switzerland, after which force and threats were used by the British to prevent any of the federal rulers from returning home.

REVOLUTION AND EGYPTIAN INTERVENTION IN THE NORTH

The Imam Ahmad died on 19 September 1962 and Badr assumed the throne. Nasser welcomed this development as it seems likely that he had sanctioned a coup against Ahmad but ordered its postponement on his death as he regarded Badr as an ally who would support his version of Arab nationalism. His instructions were, however, disregarded by the Commander-in-Chief, Field Marshal Abd al-Hakim Amer, who was anxious to find an independent and profitable source of revenue for the Egyptian army. With the help of Egyptian officers, Yemeni officers on the night of 26/27 September bombarded the palace of Badr and announced that he had been assassinated. A senior officer, Col Abd Allah Sallal, who does not seem to have been involved in the coup, was proclaimed President in the expectation that he would later be replaced. Within days, in order to 'oppose any foreign intervention', Egyptian troops arrived with such speed that they had clearly been deployed beforehand, in anticipation of the coup.

The Royalists rallied under Badr's uncle, Hassan, who was proclaimed Imam and called for the tribes to rally to him. Although many supported the new Imam, the traditional allies of the Imamate, the Hashid and Bakil, whose chiefs had suffered at the hands of Ahmad, did not. Hassan set up a government in Saudi Arabia and also received help from the federal rulers of the south, with the connivance of the British. In October the Royalists captured Marib in the east but were repelled at Sada in the north. The Egyptians, knowing that this could not have been achieved without Saudi help, bombed Saudi towns and the two countries appeared on the brink of open war. Sallal called for all-out war, proclaimed a republic of the Arabian peninsula and demanded the return of Najran and Asir.

In November 1962 Badr reappeared, gave a press conference, and resumed the Imamate. The Americans, believing that the republic controlled the whole country and anxious to conciliate Nasser, recognized the new regime but the British who were better informed, did not and their legation was closed. The Yemen Arab Republic (YAR) was admitted to the UN.

Sallal promoted himself Field Marshal and was determined to rule. However, despite several attempts to secure constitutional legitimacy, he was never able to do so. Practically without local adherents, he had to rely on the Egyptians, who, though they often treated him with contempt, were unable to find a more convincing representative. The Egyptian forces were increased, in 1963 numbering about 28,000, and in April the UN attempted to bring about the disengagement of Egyptian and Saudi forces by providing an Observer Mission (UNYOM) but as it was not forbidden to contact the royalists, it proved totally futile and was withdrawn in September 1964.

Many Yemenis came to realize that their country was merely providing a battlefield on which Nasser and King Faisal were contesting the leadership of the Arab world. Moderate republicans and moderate royalists therefore attempted to make a peace between Yemenis at a conference at Erkowit in Sudan in October 1964. They agreed that both Badr and Sallal should relinquish power and that Egyptian forces should be asked to leave, but the initiative failed owing to the intransigence of the Egyptians and of Sallal. A cease-fire was proclaimed, but it lasted only a few days and was followed by a series of royalist successes, which left them in control of one-third of the country. The republicans split and the moderates, led by the Prime Minister, Ahmad Nu'man, tried to make peace but were again frustrated by Sallal's belligerence.

Nasser, realizing that he could not win a war which was becoming extremely unpopular at home, tried to end it by negotiating with King Faisal on the basis that he would withdraw his forces, now estimated at 50,000 provided the Saudis stopped supplying the royalists. Negotiations continued until the publication of a British 'white paper' on defence in February 1966, with the statement of the intended departure from Aden by 1968.

For the next year there was a stalemate—which the armed forces, subsidized by at least one side and with unusual opportunities to loot—were in no hurry to end. Egyptian military activity was confined to bombing and poison gas attacks, while the royalists were divided by internal feuds in the absence of Badr through ill-health.

The situation was transformed by the Egyptian defeat, by Israel, in the June War of 1967. At the Khartoum Summit, Nasser, now dependent upon Saudi Arabian financial assistance, agreed to withdraw his troops from Yemen. This was opposed by Sallal who feared for his own position but the withdrawal of Egyptian troops was nevertheless completed by the end of November, by which time he was out of the country on his way to seek alternative support from the Eastern Bloc. No one rallied to his support, there was no bloodshed and he was succeeded by a three-man Council headed by Qadi Abd ar-Rahman al-Iryani who had been one of the old *Ahrar* but had also been an adviser to the Imam Ahmad.

The royalists launched a major offensive and in December they began a three-month siege of San'a. The republicans, led by Gen. Hassan al-Amri, conducted a vigorous defence in which they were supported firstly by Soviet aircraft and secondly by the NLF which had by then taken power in Aden and which sent volunteers who succeeded in opening the road from Hodeida. Al-Amri, without the Egyptian forces previously thought indispensable, succeeded in reconquering much of the country, helped by intensified royalist feuding which led to the brief deposition of Badr by his cousin Muhammad bin Hussain. Many tribal chiefs defected.

By February 1970 King Faisal had decided that he could tolerate the moderate republic of al-Iryani, a pious Muslim, and indeed use it as an ally against the communist South. He therefore terminated all aid to the royalists and 'ordered' them to cease fighting. Nearly all except members of the ruling family

returned and were integrated in the new regime which was then recognized by Saudi Arabia and the United Kingdom. It was estimated that during the war 200,000 Yemenis, 4% of the population, had been killed. Although the Egyptians had done some good work in improving education and other social services, they had also installed a ponderous bureaucracy, modelled on the one in Cairo, which was quite unsuitable for Yemeni needs.

THE SOUTH GOES LEFT (1967–1978)

Qahtan ash-Shaabi, the only one amongst the chiefs of the NLF with sufficient seniority to be credible as a statesman, had emerged as their leader at their first Congress at Taiz in 1965. He led the delegation to the Geneva talks and upon the formal take-over of sovereignty on 30 November 1967 he proclaimed himself President, Prime Minister and Commander-in-Chief. He at once declared South Yemen a unitary state, abolished the old sheikhdoms and demanded the abandonment of all tribal bloodfeuds. Other parties were banned, the press was controlled, a State Security Supreme Court was created and quickly established firm control throughout the country by means of a police force trained by East Germans. An uprising amongst the Aulaqis, who had been the greatest beneficiaries of the federation but who also had preferred FLOSY to the NLF, was crushed with such savagery that henceforth they played little part in affairs and an attempt by the Sharif of Beihan, with Saudi backing, to regain his state was defeated.

Relations with the United Kingdom deteriorated rapidly as advisers who had remained to assist in the build-up of new armed forces were expelled and replaced by Soviet advisers who also provided arms. The handing over to Muscat by the British of the Kuria Muria islands caused bitterness in Aden. Although it was believed that the USA had given covert help to the NLF when it was a clandestine anti-British movement, their military attaché was given 24 hours' notice to leave, and the controlled press made much of their connections with Israel and with Saudi Arabia which had emerged as the principal enemy of the new state.

On the day he assumed office ash-Shaabi declared that 'the aim of our Revolution has been since the beginning to unite both parts of Yemen. We are all one people'. He appointed one of the most influential NLF leaders, Abd al-Fattah Ismail, as Minister of Yemeni Unity Affairs; a similar ministry was set up in San'a. No ambassadors were appointed between the two Governments, whose relations were handled by these ministries. North and South helped each other against local opponents and there was talk of a Greater Yemen embracing Asir, Najran and even Muscat.

The country was in a desperate financial plight as a result of the ending of British subsidies and the departure of the large, free-spending expatriate community which coincided with the closure of the Suez Canal which had been Aden's only other source of income. Faced with the problem of actually running the country, ash-Shaabi showed a definite pragmatism by refusing to dismantle working institutions. Although he had been imprisoned by Nasser, ash-Shaabi believed, like the Egyptian leader, in egalitarianism, imposed by firm authority, and was in no way a communist. Opposing him was an extreme left group, under the leadership of Ismail and Ali Salim al-Baid which called for a complete new beginning with 'scientific socialism' based on rural soviets, collectivization of land, a people's militia, nationalization of banks and foreign trade and the export of revolution throughout the Peninsula. These policies divided the party at the Zinjibar Congress of March 1968 and the leftist view prevailed. Ash-Shaabi, however, persuaded the army that its status would be threatened by the proposed militia and, on his behalf, it arrested his leading opponents.

Ash-Shaabi had, however, been alarmed by the strength of the extremists and he moved to the left. He spoke of the socialist path and the redistribution of land. He took control of imports although he was still anxious to encourage the investment of foreign capital. He called on the Saudi people to overthrow their monarch and provided bases for the Dhofari rebels. His numerous visits abroad included Moscow and Pyongyang (North Korea) among the destinations. These moves, at a time when the YAR was moving into the Saudi orbit, led to verbal hostilities between San'a and Aden.

Ash-Shaabi had released his left-wing opponents and even included some of them in his Government. In June 1969 he quarrelled over the posting of an officer with the Minister of the Interior, Muhammad Ali Haitham, a man with very similar political views, and dismissed him. Haitham, who had considerable influence with the army and with the tribes, thereupon joined forces with the left, and later that month, in a bloodless coup, ash-Shaabi and his cousin, Prime Minister Faisal Abd al-Latif, were deposed. He was replaced by a five-man Presidential Council, chaired by Salim Rubai Ali and including Ismail and Haitham, who was appointed Prime Minister. The shift to the left was signalled immediately by the recognition of East Germany by the new Minister of Foreign Affairs, Ali Salim al-Baid. In October, having called on all Arab countries to follow his lead, he severed diplomatic relations with the USA.

There followed a period of harsh repression with constant speeches about conspiracies, mass arrests with special courts untrammelled by ordinary law 'to review anti-state activity'. Large numbers of citizens, some estimated up to a quarter of the population, fled abroad. The army, whose commander escaped to Taiz, and the police, were subjugated through purges and indoctrination. Military training started in schools. Ismail encouraged the spread of party branches throughout the country.

The Government called for revolution in 'the Occupied Gulf' and refused to recognize the independence of Bahrain, Qatar and the UAE. There was a frontier clash with Saudi Arabia at al-Wadiah in November 1969. Such strong support was given to the rebels in Dhofar that they also succeeded in capturing Salala. Haitham, however, worked to improve relations with the YAR and in November 1970 was the first South Yemeni Prime Minister to visit Taiz where he urged unification. A new Constitution, with its adoption of the name People's Democratic Republic of Yemen (PDRY) was announced. Drawn up by an East German and an Egyptian, its commitment to socialism, tolerance of Islam, stress on the rights of women, and vesting of all power in the party differed greatly from the Constitution adopted shortly afterwards in the YAR. This, drawn up after intensive local consultations, was, more than any other recent Arab Constitution, based on Islamic principles, with a constitutional court of *'ulama* (ulema), empowered to ensure that laws were based on Islamic principles.

Abd al-Fattah Ismail, as Secretary-General, was immersed in party and doctrinal affairs, building a following amongst the urban proletariat. Ali, the Chairman, visited the People's Republic of China, returning inspired by Maoist ideas of spreading the revolution in the countryside by encouraging the seizure of land by the peasants and in 1970 he signed a series of decrees nationalizing businesses and concentrating most economic activities in the hands of the state. In the same year Aden ceased to be a free port. Aid from the USSR alone kept the country afloat. Facing the problem of actually administering a country in a perpetual economic crisis, Haitham tried to moderate foreign and domestic policies to encourage foreign and local investment. His colleagues, Ali and Ismail, both adopted a more dogmatic approach and conspired against him. He was replaced in August 1971 by Ali Nasser Muhammad, the Minister of Defence. There followed a new wave of purges and arrests.

The Constitutions of 1970 had shown that there was no common ideological grounds between North and South Yemen and the financial dependence of one on Saudi Arabia and the other on the USSR prevented any move towards unity: indeed neither the Cabinet of the PDRY nor that of the YAR contained a Minister of Unity Affairs. The situation was intensified by the presence on Northern territory of thousands of exiles from the South, armed and funded by Saudi Arabia. Border incidents followed their incursions and a leading northern tribal sheikh was lured across the frontier and murdered with 60 of his followers. In San'a, army officers, who were partly funded by Saudi Arabia, called for war to end communism in the South. Each side accused the other of increasingly grave acts of aggression and in September there was widespread fighting which continued for several days, in the course of which the North captured Kamaran. An Arab League mission mediated a cease-fire and then, on 28 October 1972, to general amazement, an agreement was reached in Cairo, Egypt, which provided for a single unified state, with one flag, one capital, one leadership,

with single legislative, executive and judicial organs. A formal Treaty of Union was signed between the two Presidents in Tripoli, Libya in November.

Eight committees were set up to discuss the details of unification with instructions to finalize proceedings within a year, after which a new Constitution would be put to a referendum. Saudi Arabia and the USSR both publicly welcomed the union but each feared that its own protégé would be the weaker partner and become submerged beneath the predominance of the opposing party. Conservatives in San'a, who had contacts with Saudi Arabia, put obstacles in the way of progress and when in May 1973 a leading opponent of unification was murdered, it was generally believed that Aden had been responsible. President al-Iryani personally favoured unification but admitted that little progress had been made by the committees. After his removal from office, prospects for unity seemed to increase, for his successor, Lt-Col Ibrahim al-Hamadi, established cordial personal relations with Ali; each felt the support of the other would be beneficial in internal politics in which each was under threat, and in foreign affairs in weakening dependence on their respective patrons. They agreed on a gradual approach to unity through economic co-operation and in February 1977 they constituted a council of themselves and senior ministers to meet every six months. A joint diplomatic mission toured the oil states. There was speculation that there would be an important announcement concerning unification when al-Hamadi visited Aden in October 1974 but, two days before he was due to arrive, he was murdered. After his death Lt-Col Ahmad ibn Hussein al-Ghashmi, his successor, established closer contacts with the Saudis and relations with Aden deteriorated.

The death of King Faisal enabled the establishment of diplomatic relations with Saudi Arabia and in August 1977 Ali visited Riyadh. A cease-fire was announced with Oman. Kuwait and Abu Dhabi provided aid. Relations with Britain improved and the Aden refinery was taken over by agreement. In October 1977 at the UN Ali made preliminary overtures to the USA. He tried to maintain equal loyalty to the USSR and the People's Republic of China. All these moves angered Ismail who wanted friendship exclusively with the USSR and with Cuba which provided instructors. The foreign policy of the PDRY followed an erratic course as the two leaders struggled for control. Ismail managed to send troops to assist the new revolution in Ethiopia, the success of which was vitally important to the USSR. Ali, meanwhile, had arranged to receive an envoy from the USA.

It seems that at this juncture Ali attempted to establish with al-Ghashmi the same close ties that he had had with al-Hamadi. He sent a special messenger in whose briefcase a bomb, possibly placed by an agent of Ismail, exploded, killing both the YAR President and the envoy. Fighting immediately broke out in Aden, either because Ali attempted to arrest his opponents or Ismail ordered an attack, in which it is said Soviet and Cuban elements took part, on the presidential palace. Ali was captured, found guilty of numerous crimes and executed.

THE NORTH GOES RIGHT (1970–1978)

Abd ar-Rahman al-Iryani, who had succeeded Sallal, played an indispensable role in national reconciliation after eight years of war. An obviously pious Muslim with a liberal background, he had to take account of a central government weakened by the war, conservative tribal sheikhs and the *'ulama*, and young modernisers and townsfolk anxious for reform against a background of financial crisis with an army demanding expensive new equipment. He played a major part in drafting a Constitution which was a real attempt to find a political system suitable to the country. Consequently, the first (indirect) elections in Yemeni history took place in April 1971.

In foreign affairs he succeeded in creating good relations with all the Arab states and with the West without alienating the USSR. The YAR could reasonably be described as a neutral country, despite its government's dependence on Saudi Arabia for financial aid. This largesse was also extended to influential individuals, especially the tribal chiefs whose domination of the Consultative Council hampered moves towards the unity with the South agreed in 1972.

Within a month of its signature, its principal architect, the Prime Minister Mohsin al-Aini, a man of leftist tendencies but influential tribal background, resigned. Al-Iryani appointed a deeply religious conservative, Qadi Abdullah al-Hajari to succeed al-Aini. Al-Hajari immediately went to Riyadh to re-assure the Saudis and received financial aid in return for re-nouncing the Yemeni claim to Asir and Najran. Al-Hajari made no attempt at administrative reform in a period of inefficiency and corruption and executed several supporters of unification. In August 1973, al-Iryani went into exile to show his discontent but returned to build up support against his Prime Minister whom, in February 1974, he felt strong enough to replace by the more competent and progressive Dr Hassan Makki. In June a plot backed by Iraq to overthrow the regime was discovered and al-Iryani opposed any strong action. When the army and tribal leaders threatened a coup, he resigned and went to live in Syria.

His successor was Lt-Col Ibrahim al-Hamadi, not a tribesman but a member of the Qadi class, who appointed al-Aini as his Prime Minister. He suspended the Constitution and the Consultative Council. Al-Hamadi gradually became immensely popular, with inspiring oratory, evident honesty and sincerity and his youth (he was about 30). He seemed to represent a new generation and engendered new hope after decades of harsh rule and civil war. He and al-Aini made a determined effort to eradicate corruption but in January 1975, feeling the need of a technocrat with financial expertise, al-Hamadi appointed Abd al-Aziz Abd al-Ghani as Prime Minister.

During 1975 al-Hamadi travelled widely, visiting nearly every Arab country, Iran and Europe. He returned with financial aid which would enable him to launch new projects and reduce dependence on Saudi Arabia, thus realizing one of his main objectives. He was concerned to develop rural areas on which he concentrated the ambitious development plan of 1977. He paid special attention to the Shafais and enlisted their help in making the army less a monopoly of Zaidi tribal notables. He aimed at a strong centralized state with wide political participation and he encouraged the emergence of the leftist National Democratic Front (NDF). These moves offended the practically independent northern chiefs, some of whom rebelled and were consequently bombed by the airforce. On the night of 11/12 October 1977 al-Hamadi and his brother were murdered. The assassins were never caught nor were the motives for the crime established. He was succeeded by the Chief of Staff, Ahmad al-Ghashmi, a tribesman of the Hashid confederation. A Shafai officer attempted to incite an uprising in Taiz but al-Ghashmi, with the help of the Zaidi tribes, crushed it and the rebels with other members of the NDF sought refuge in Aden where Ismail hoped to use them to bring about unity by overthrowing the Government in San'a. Al-Ghashmi therefore loosened ties with Aden and strengthened relations with Saudi Arabia. He spoke of democracy and nominated a 99-man Consti-tutional Assembly which was to prepare the way for eventual elections. Preoccupied with day-to-day affairs, he had neither the ability nor the time to make a mark on Yemeni history before his murder on 24 June 1978.

ABD AL-FATTAH ISMAIL AND ALI NASSER MUHAMMAD (1979–1986)

After the execution of Ali in July 1978 several days of heavy fighting ensued with a new flood of refugees to the North. Ali Nasser Muhammad became Chairman of the Presidential Council to which were added the communist, Ali Badeeb and the former guerrilla, Ali Antar. Ismail succeeded in his ambition of changing the NLF into a 'Vanguard Party'—the Yemen Socialist Party (YSP)—with stringent rules for admission and discipline and which contained all his close collaborators, including al-Baid. In December Ismail became Head of State.

The YAR, now led by Col Ali Abdullah Saleh, blamed Aden for the murder of al-Ghashmi and prevailed upon the other Arab states to suspend relations with the PDRY. In February 1979 the PDRY launched an attack against the North in an effort to bring about unity by force. In well-planned attacks the main frontier towns were captured and the YAR army appeared to be on the verge of disintegration. Other Arab states inter-vened and on 30 March in Kuwait the two Presidents signed an agreement to unite, almost identical with that signed nearly seven years before.

In January 1980 it was stated that 134 articles of a constitu-tion had been agreed. Previously, Ismail had visited the USSR where he signed a Treaty of Friendship which appeared more intimate than those with other Arab states. There was general surprise when on 20 April 1980 he resigned on grounds of ill health, was given an honorary title and went into exile in the USSR.

Ali Nasser Muhammad resumed the Presidency and although he still maintained the Soviet alliance he showed that it was not exclusive by visiting Saudi Arabia, where he established his Muslim credentials by performing *umrah*. He also attended the Islamic Summit in Ta'if. Saudi Arabia gave generous help after floods in March 1982 in which it was estimated that 500 people had perished and 64,000 were made homeless. The hostility to Oman which had existed since independence and continued despite the defeat of the Dhofari rebels nearly a decade before finally ended with an agreement to exchange ambassadors, although this did not happen for several years.

The departure of Ismail did not end Aden's support for the NDF which was extremely active in 1980 and 1981. The two Yemens also adopted different stances in the Iran–Iraq War. San'a was, however, angered by not being allowed to join the Co-operation Council of the Arab States of the Gulf (Gulf Co-operation Council—GCC) and drew nearer to Aden. After a visit by Saleh, in December 1981, Muhammad agreed to reduce help to the NDF and the two Presidents laid down common foreign policy goals in which Saleh appeared to make concessions. They constituted themselves the Supreme Yemeni Council, which would hold regular meetings to discuss the practical details of unification. They also set up joint ministerial committees. Sessions in San'a in August 1983 and in Aden in March 1984 showed some co-ordination of foreign policy. In January 1985 the PDRY and the YAR agreed to co-operate in joint exploitation of natural resources.

Local elections were held in 1981 in which the YSP announced that it had received 94.6% support. Despite nearly 20 years of official condemnation of tribalism, it was noticeable that the President entrusted more and more posts to people from his native Dathina and Abyan. However, when in March 1985 Muhammad decided to divest himself of the premiership, a Saiyid from Hadramawt, Haidar Abu Bakr al-Attas, succeeded him.

In February 1985 Ismail returned from exile and was later given a place on the politburo. He was clearly concerned that Muhammad regarded the purity of Marxist-Leninist dogma as secondary to the practical needs of the country. In January 1986 Muhammad's attempt to arrest or kill his opponents at a meeting of the politburo was only partially successful and trig-gered a brief but intensive civil war in which at least 2,000, including 55 senior party figures, were killed. The tribes of Dathina rallied to his side while those of the north-west fought to avenge Ali Antar, who had been killed in the Politburo fighting. Ismail disappeared and his body was never found: al-Baid, of whom Muhammad had hoped to rid himself, escaped. Some 6,000 foreigners were evacuated to Djibouti. Muhammad fled to Ethiopia where he was joined by the navy which had remained loyal to him. During the battle Saleh closed the frontier to prevent YAR tribesmen from joining either side.

ALI ABDULLAH SALEH AS PRESIDENT OF THE YAR (1978–1990)

Evidence that the assassination of al-Ghashmi in October 1974 was plotted from outside the YAR is provided by the fact that no group in San'a was prepared to take advantage of the incident. There was no obvious successor so a temporary Presi-dential Council was formed in 1978, under the chairmanship of the politically neutral Speaker of the Constitutional Assembly, Qadi Abd al-Karim al-Arshi. Nearly a month later the Assembly, by a large majority, elected as President, Lt-Col Ali Abdullah Saleh, commander of the Taiz military area, who was, like his predecessor, a tribesman of the Hashid. He appointed al-Arshi Vice-President and Abd al-Ghani retained his portfolio as Prime Minister. At first his position was extremely precarious and he was fortunate to escape assassination in September and to survive what appeared to be an attempted military coup, with backing from Aden, in October. The Shafai South, restless since the murder of al-Hamadi, was stirred up by the NDF, based on Aden. There were also reports of fighting in the regions of Sada, Marib and Jawf and the YAR appeared on the point of collapse as Saleh was forced to revert back to the old Imamate policy of relying on the Hashid and Bakil to deal with internal threats. Only the intervention of other Arab states saved the country from complete disaster during the war with the South in September 1979.

Over the next few years Saleh acquired the skills, shown by the old Imams, required to rule an unusually difficult country. He also made a persistent effort to win support by increasing public participation in government. One of his first speeches promised 'real democracy', starting with municipal elections which took place in 1979. Later that year he appointed a 15-man Consultative Council and expanded the membership of the Constituent Assembly. In February 1980 he announced that there would be a general election and in May he set up a 'committee for national dialogue' to prepare for it. He also launched a new party, the Unified Yemeni Organization, with a charter that comprised both the principles of the Revolution and the 'sublime principles of Islam'. In October he called into being a National Assembly of 1,000 representatives, 700 of whom were elected through elections in co-operatives which met in August 1982.

Progress towards elections was disrupted by increased activity by the NDF, whose leader, Sultan Ahmad Omar, stated that he would only participate if the Government committed itself to a series of measures which included land reform, nationalization of industry and less dependence on Saudi Arabia. The NDF overran considerable areas during 1981 but then Aden decreased its support and the Zaidi tribes, worried about the advance of the 'godless', rallied to the support of Saleh. Early in 1982 Saleh ordered a full-scale offensive, defeated the NDF and allowed the survivors to be reintegrated in the North.

In October 1980 there had been a change of Prime Minister when Abd al-Ghani, the Shafai economist, was replaced by another technocrat, an agricultural economist, Dr Abd al-Karim al-Iryani, a member of the Qadi class. In general Saleh's policy was to choose competent officials and not to interfere in administrative matters.

In foreign policy Saleh avoided total commitment either to the East or the West. The Saudis provided enough aid to keep his Government solvent but not enough to permit total economic independence. At the UN, the YAR abstained from voting on the Afghanistan question. Saleh's ministers sought aid and investment from the West but Saleh also needed to obtain Soviet arms and exert pressure on Aden to reduce its backing for the NDF. As a result relations between the YAR and Saudi Arabia were downgraded. Saleh refused to endorse the US Rapid Deployment Force but did not join the Tripartite Pact of Libya, Ethiopia and the PDRY formed to denounce it. The Republic did not join the GCC but sent volunteers to fight for Iraq against Iran. In December 1982 the YAR provided a base for 2,000 Palestine Liberation Organization (PLO) guerrillas after their expulsion from Beirut.

In 1984 Saleh revisited Moscow and signed a treaty of friendship similar to those concluded by the USSR with Syria and the PDRY, but refused to Libya. About the same time it was announced that although the USSR had failed to find oil in the YAR, the USA had succeeded in doing so. Western help was essential for its exploitation and also in the development of agriculture to which the Government attached almost equal importance. Also, in the same year, the YAR signed a five-year trade and aid agreement with the EC.

In November 1982 an earthquake devastated central Yemen, resulting in the deaths of more than 3,000 people and causing damage worth an estimated US $3,000m. In December al-Iryani was put in charge of reconstruction and Abd al-Ghani replaced him as Prime Minister. In 1985 al-Iryani was given the newly-created post of Chairman of the Supreme Council for Petroleum and Mineral Resources and another well-known economist, Dr Muhammad Said al-Attar was appointed Deputy Prime Minister and Minister of Development. Much of the attention of the Government had to be devoted to economic matters as the country exported less than 1% of the value of its imports. Until its petroleum could be fully exploited, the YAR was dependent upon aid and remittances from citizens working abroad and had to observe the utmost austerity in restricting imports. There was, however, a great improvement in the infrastructure with the spread of roads and electricity. A particularly striking fea-

ture of the 1980s was the emergence of educated women, holding responsible posts in business and administration. Central Government control was loose in the tribal areas with the mountain tribes benefiting both from Saudi subsidies and from smuggling goods across its border.

In May 1983 Saleh unexpectedly resigned, announcing that he would not stand for re-election. The Assembly, however, unanimously re-elected him for a further five years. In July 1985 the YAR held its first free elections when 17,500 representatives were elected to local councils working for co-operative development. About one-half of the electorate voted and the polls were seen as a significant development which would eventually bring into political life educated young Yemenis and weaken the powers of the tribal sheikhs. On 5 July 1988 the long-postponed general election took place for 128 seats in the new 159-member Consultative Council which replaced the old Constituent Assembly. The remaining 31 members were appointed by the President. More than a million registered to vote, including 60,000 women, and more than 1,200 candidates stood for election. None of the 15 women candidates was successful. Approximately one-sixth of the elective seats, including all six constituencies in San'a were won by candidates sympathetic to the Muslim Brotherhood and many others to tribesmen of conservative background. The Consultative Council was to have a life of five years and was empowered to legislate, to ratify treaties and supervise the work of government, in which it could request a vote expressing 'no confidence'. Its first action was to re-elect Saleh for another five years by 152 votes to none with two abstentions and five absentees. The post was strengthened by no longer having to share power with the Military Command Council. Saleh announced his aim to achieve democracy without repression, claimed that there were no political prisoners and stated that he would give priority to agriculture and industry making use of local materials. Abd al-Ghani was reappointed as Prime Minister. Subsequent events showed that the Consultative Council operated more freely than almost any other in the Arab world, criticizing government policies despite the intensification of a personality cult of the President.

In foreign policy Saleh aimed at being on good terms with as many states as possible by avoiding involvement in other people's quarrels. The exploitation of petroleum, which was first exported in December 1987, required investment and technology from most major states. In Arab matters the YAR tried to work through bilateral agreements through which joint committees arranged co-operation over a wide range of activities. In November 1987, following an Arab League decision that members might resume diplomatic relations with Egypt, the YAR did so and in mid-1988 President Mubarak visited San'a. The Government tried to maintain good relations with both Iraq and Syria and the Prime Minister negotiated aid agreements with both countries for the development of the petroleum industry. In October 1988 the Organization of the Islamic Council met in San'a, the first time that the city had hosted an international gathering on such a large scale. Saleh visited Pakistan and China, where he obtained aid worth US $42m. In January 1989 President Saddam Hussain of Iraq visited San'a in order to thank Yemeni troops for their participation in the war with Iran. In the same year the YAR became a founder-member of the Arab Co-operation Council (ACC), with Jordan, Iraq and Egypt. The ACC was formed with the object of creating an Arab Common Market of those states that were ineligible to join the GCC, allowing free movement of labour and capital within the bloc and hoping to double trade between its members in the next few years.

Despite occasional frontier incidents, the outcome of local rivalries rather than government policies, relations with Saudi Arabia were generally good. The Saudi-Yemeni Co-ordinating Committee, formed in 1975, continued to meet to distribute aid. In May 1989 Saudi Arabia lifted almost all restrictions imposed on Yemeni emigrant workers, giving them almost equal rights with Saudi citizens. At various stages of the process towards unity with the South, Saleh travelled to Saudi Arabia to reassure King Fahd.

The USSR continued to provide training and technical personnel and in January 1990 Saleh visited the USA for the first time and was saluted by President Bush as 'a pillar of stability'.

Saleh took every opportunity to put forward the case for the Palestinians and returned with increased aid.

Following a bomb explosion in the Grand Mosque in San'a in March 1989, three alleged members of the Muslim Brotherhood were summarily executed. In August 12 people were killed in the Marib area when tribesmen opposed the introduction of vehicle registration (which made smuggling more difficult). Following reports of unrest amongst Zaidi tribesmen who realized that the Shafais would be a majority in a united Yemen, their leader, the Paramount Sheikh of the Hashid who had been one of the most influential figures in the country for nearly 30 years, claimed that tribesmen should retain their right to bear arms. Religious leaders, too, continued to regard the Southerners as atheistic communists and to oppose unification.

THE PDRY 1986–1990

When Ali Nasser Muhammad attempted his coup in January 1986, the Prime Minister, Haidar Abu Bakr al-Attas, was on a mission to India, which he interrupted by visiting Moscow, USSR, hoping for some intervention to achieve a peace settlement. Upon his return, he assumed Muhammad's posts as President and Secretary-General of the YSP and appointed as Prime Minister the Deputy Prime Minister and Minister of Fisheries, Dr Yasin Said Numan. As a result of casualties and mass arrests of Muhammad's supporters, the Council of Ministers, the Politburo and the Central Committee underwent drastic changes. The first problem of the new regime was to restore a situation of normality. There were reports of three assassination attempts aimed at al-Attas. Muhammad had taken refuge in the North, where he was allegedly joined by numerous armed supporters. It was uncertain whether Saleh would be willing or able to prevent Muhammad and his supporters launching an invasion but, with assistance from the USSR, he managed to counteract any such action. Most of Muhammad's supporters who had been detained were gradually released and al-Attas succeeded, by a series of amnesties, in persuading most of those who had fled to return, including the entire navy which had sailed to Ethiopia. By October it was felt safe to hold the delayed general election in which 176 candidates contested the 111 seats in the Supreme People's Council. Al-Attas was elected President for five years but it became apparent that al-Baid, Secretary-General of the YSP, held an equally important post.

In December 1986 the Supreme Court began the public trial of Muhammad and 93 others (48 of whom, including the ex-President, were tried *in absentia*) on charges of treason and terrorist activities. After a year, death sentences were passed on 35 of the defendants (19, including Muhammad, still *in absentia*). There were international appeals for clemency and al-Attas commuted 24 of the death sentences to life imprisonment. Only five were actually executed and in May 1988 Muhammad was offered a retrial if he returned voluntarily. Later that year 35 of the remaining 59 prisoners, including three former ministers, were released. In January 1990, prior to unification, there was a general amnesty for all political offenders.

At a time when it was imperative to neutralize Muhammad and his followers, much power appeared to rest with the military, particularly in the hands of his tribal opponents from the north-west, to the extent that the fourth Congress of the YSP in June 1987 expressed concern about 'opportunist rightists' in the armed forces. Despite the glorification of Ismail, Ali Antar and other 'martyrs' of January 1986, there appeared to be little change in either the internal affairs or foreign policy of the new regime. In the same year al-Attas stated that the relationship with the USSR was the 'corner-stone' of government policy and there was close co-operation in trade, petroleum and economic matters. The USSR replaced the weapons destroyed in January 1986 and agreed to continue aid until 2005.

Nevertheless one of the first visits that al-Attas made as President of the PDRY was to assure King Fahd of Saudi Arabia that there would be no further encouragement to incite revolutionary activities against the Saudi Government. It was noticeable that King Fahd did not, unlike his brother Faisal, finance or arm exiled opponents of the Aden regime. A joint ministerial commission was established, several projects were financed, and the Saudis were the first to give aid after disas-

trous floods in March 1989. The reconciliation with Oman continued and in October 1988 al-Attas became the first PDRY Head of State to visit Muscat. Amidst references to 'brotherhood', several agreements were signed including one to delimit the frontier. Other Gulf states provided aid. Relations with Ethiopia, a supporter of Muhammad during the fighting of January 1986, were restored as were those with Somalia which had been strained since Ismail had sent troops to oppose the advance into the Ogaden in the war of 1977. As part of the PDRY's attempt to present a more moderate image abroad, diplomatic relations were restored with Morocco, and with Egypt as soon the Arab League lifted its veto. Al-Attas visited Baghdad, Iraq, in July 1988, and later there was an agreement to increase the processing of Iraqi petroleum at Aden refinery with Iraqi crude piped across Saudi Arabia to Yanbu. Dr Abd al-Aziz adh-Dhali in 1989 became the first PDRY Minister of Foreign Affairs to visit an EC capital, and also in 1989 William Waldegrave of the British Foreign Office was the first British Minister to visit Aden since independence. Al-Attas stated that the USA had been approached for the resumption of relations, which were, in fact, restored just before unification. The PDRY therefore ended its separate existence with no outstanding feuds and indeed had achieved international recognition by election to the UN Security Council. In January 1990 al-Attas opened a regional peace conference called by the Organization for Afro-Asian Solidarity, attended by 45 states with a call for withdrawal of all fleets from the Red Sea, the Gulf and the Indian Ocean: Western nations, Iran and Israel were not invited.

Meanwhile, the domestic economy had collapsed after two decades of ideologically-led mismanagement and people were on the verge of starvation. Despite some pressure from military leaders, the USSR under the leadership of Gorbachev stated that there was no need for the Aden base after the end of the cold war and Soviet aid declined from US $400m. in 1988 to $50m. in 1989. In 1989 the communist regimes of Eastern Europe started to collapse. There changes were set in motion by a popular revolt but in the PDRY they were introduced by the Government. In early July the YSP set up six working parties to study a comprehensive list of changes, including that of its own role and relationship with the state, and concerning economic, administrative and cultural affairs. There had long been a chronic shortage of housing and it was announced that private individuals might build for sale or rent; then private ownership of hotels and factories was permitted. Adenis were encouraged to invest their capital locally with exemptions from taxes and tariffs. Foreign investors might transfer profits abroad. In particular investment was sought in petroleum, tourism and the port of Aden. In December the Government promised to compensate owners of shares in the banks nationalized in 1969. Just before unification the Government announced that the properties of exiles would be restored. The ponderous communist bureaucracy was dismantled and government monopolies, such as that of supplying ships, were ended. In February 1990 plans were published to re-establish Aden as a free zone.

Al-Baid put forward a programme for political *perestroika*, including a rotating presidency, civil rights and correction of 'wrong stands on Arab and Islamic culture and religion'. In October Numan stated that a multi-party system was 'very necessary for democracy' and that the private sector should 'play its true role in economic developments'. Al-Baid said that things had gone wrong because of the 'leftist adventurist tendency rather than right-wing deviationism'. Pluralism and democracy were more important than ideology. The Institute of Scientific Socialism was renamed the Institute of Social Sciences while the two ash-Shaabis and Salim Rubai Ali were rehabilitated as they had been condemned in the 'absence of democratic thought'. Citizens were given the right to travel abroad. There were local elections, the fifth since independence but the first with any real choice of candidates.

In December 1989 the YSP ended its monopoly and the formerly outlawed Nasserite party applied for recognition and was quickly followed by the Yemeni Unity Party (YUP), the first to have members both South and North of the frontier. Even the partisans of former President Muhammad were able to form the Unionist Democratic Party. In January 1990 the ban on foreign publications was lifted and later permits were issued for a range of independent newspapers and journals.

The relaxation of controls triggered inflation which, in turn, provoked an unprecedented series of strikes for higher pay. The first, on 13 January 1990, was at the petroleum refinery and was followed by strikes in the electricity, banking, textile and fishing industries. Workers claimed that the cost of living had risen by 30% and wages had not kept pace. The Government made concessions and the strikes were usually of short duration.

THE ROAD TO UNIFICATION

Presidents Saleh and Ali Nasser Muhammad had established a good working relationship but during the fighting in Aden in January 1986, San'a remained neutral and abstained from commenting upon events in Aden. The new regime of President al-Attas quickly declared its commitment to unity but the situation was complicated by the presence of Muhammad and his followers in camps just north of the frontier. Gradually the conciliatory policy of the Aden Government led many of them to go home and those that remained refrained from provoking any confrontational incidents between the two states.

In July 1986 both Heads of State met for the first time as participants in a summit in Tripoli, Libya. Although an agreement was not reached they consulted again in September and Saleh stated that he would give priority to unity. Although the exiles were inactive, their presence still caused difficulties and after a death sentence had been passed on Muhammad, Aden demanded his extradition which San'a refused. Kuwait tried to mediate a settlement of the refugee problem but it was still a high priority when al-Baid went to San'a in July 1987 in the hope of co-ordinating economic and social policies. Meanwhile, there had been disputes concerning the exact location of the frontier which had never been delimited and was particularly vague in the area of Shabwa where it was anticipated that petroleum would be found. In December 1987 al-Iryani denied that there had been armed clashes but in the following April there were reports that both sides were reinforcing their border troops. Saleh declared that the long-standing dispute could only be resolved through unification and in May al-Baid travelled to San'a and negotiated a series of agreements. The Higher Yemeni Council, the Joint Ministerial Committee and other joint committees were reconstituted. There was a declaration that there should be no recognition of frontiers drawn up during foreign occupation or during the reign of the Imamate, existing border posts would be replaced by new ones, jointly manned, movement between the two states should be unrestricted, troops should be withdrawn from frontier areas and there should be joint exploitation of a zone of 2,200 sq km in the Marib/Shabwa area which would be demilitarized. Saleh travelled to Riyadh, Saudi Arabia, to reassure King Fahd that this *rapprochement* was not directed against Saudi Arabia, while Muhammad declared that he welcomed the agreement. The first practical results were the abolition of the need for passports for travel between North and South and a meeting of the Ministers of Petroleum who agreed on the establishment of the Yemeni Company for Investment in Oil and Mineral Resources for joint exploitation of Marib/Shabwa. The head office was in San'a, its capital was US $10m. and it was soon able to announce that it had received 45 bids from international oil companies. The Southern Minister of Petroleum said that neither North nor South could develop properly unless they were united while al-Baid spoke of 'creating unified economic interests that would be a material basis for the political success of unity'. A major objective was to revive the port of Aden as a free zone and to provide it with a larger and more prosperous hinterland. It was clear that neither state could finance its own development unilaterally or attract enough outside help but through unification this would be possible. The Arab Fund for Economic and Social Development (AFESD) agreed to provide $18m. and subsequently $63m. to link the two electricity systems. It appeared that the two Yemens were now set upon at least economic integration.

However, a financial crisis, leading to *perestroika*, started in Aden shortly afterwards, and in the general ferment the stability of the YAR became more attractive. In November 1989 al-Iryani and the Assistant Secretary-General of the YSP, Salim Salih Muhammad spent three days in San'a discussing a 136-article Constitution, based on agreements reached by the constitutional committee established following the war in 1979. It was published while Saleh was in Aden and he proposed that it should be referred to both Legislatures and then be put to a referendum; this set a target date for unification of November 1990. Al-Baid emphasized that unity in Yemen should be seen as a step towards full Arab unity. Delegations were sent to all the Arab countries to inform them of Yemen's intention to form a single state. The PDRY removed obstacles to a joint foreign policy by ending its last diplomatic dispute, including the restoration of relations with the USA and an invitation to Sultan Qaboos of Oman to visit Aden. The ACC had no objection to the adherence of the PDRY. It was agreed that the YSP and the General People's Congress (GPC), which was regarded as its northern equivalent, should preserve their independence and that there should be room for political parties; the YUP, set up in January 1990, was the first to recruit from both North and South. In the same month al-Iryani travelled to Aden to discuss preparations for elections and for merging the Ministries of the Interior. Plans were announced for a merger of the state airlines. A new press law was introduced in both states. A few days later the two Cabinets held a joint meeting in San'a. All political prisoners were released and a joint committee set up to negotiate with other political parties. This led to an agreement concluded in April that there should be no foreign funding nor campaigning in mosques or barracks and Saleh welcomed 'a multi-party system provided that it is of Yemeni origin'. In February there was a second joint Cabinet meeting, in Aden, at which 46 laws were approved on such matters as customs procedures, taxation, trade unions and education. Plans were drawn up for a single currency from a unified central bank and later Aden promised pay rises to ensure parity with wages in the North. After a brief summit in Mukayras, south of the frontier, Saleh visited Riyadh, Saudi Arabia, and announced that King Fahd supported unity 'totally and without limit', although many doubted that he would really welcome a united democratic Yemen on his southern flank. The USSR, USA and the People's Republic of China welcomed the prospect of unity.

In early March 1990 there was a prolonged summit in Taiz, Aden and again in Taiz, which ended without a communiqué, suggesting that problems had arisen. There still appeared to be opposition amongst hard-line communists in Aden while in the North dissatisfaction amongst religious and tribal leaders was more public. There were reports of fighting in the Saada and of tribesmen receiving Saudi arms and money. A leading Muslim Brother attacked 40 articles of the proposed Constitution as unislamic and demanded that the *Shari'a* should be the only source of law. There was concern over Aden's tolerance of alcohol and freedom given to women. In a four-day meeting in San'a in April Saleh and al-Baid decided to pre-empt the opposition by bringing forward the date of unification to 22 May. On 4 May both currencies were declared legal tender. On 21 May the agreement to unite was passed unanimously in Aden but in San'a three Islamic fundamentalist members walked out and five abstained amid demonstrations by their supporters. The following day a joint session of the two Assemblies elected a five-man Presidential Council, headed by Saleh (promoted to the rank of General), al-Baid (Vice-President), Salim Salih Muhammad, Abd al-Ghani and the former Speaker, al-Arshi.

The priorities of the Government of the Republic of Yemen, which were announced in late May 1990, were to develop the country's economic infrastructure and to improve relations with other Arab states. In particular, the Government was committed to resolving long-standing border disputes with neighbouring Saudi Arabia and Oman. In July 1990 both President Mubarak of Egypt and the Chairman of the PLO, Yasser Arafat, visited Yemen and were reported to have discussed regional issues with President Saleh.

In September 1990 it was reported that more than 30 new political parties had been formed in Yemen since unification. The Yemeni Islah Party (YIP), an Islamic party with widespread support in the new House of Representatives, was regarded as the most important of the new parties.

In November 1990 the Government established a Supreme Council for National Defence, which would be responsible for military mobilization and wartime civil defence. The council would be authorized to declare war and states of emergency. It was to be chaired by the President and would comprise the Vice-President and various members of the Council of Ministers.

In mid-May 1991 the people of Yemen voted in a referendum on the Constitution for the unified state. A few days earlier religious fundamentalists and sympathizers, among whom were members of the YIP, demonstrated about the role of Islam under the proposed Constitution, and urged a boycott of the referendum: a clause in the Constitution stated that *Shari'a* law would be the main source of legislation, but the Islamists stipulated that *Shari'a* law should be the only source of legislation. Those who participated in the referendum approved the new Constitution by a large majority, although fewer than 50% of the electorate registered to vote. Members of the YIP and other opposition groups claimed that irregularities in the voting procedure had rendered the result null and void.

YEMEN'S RESPONSE TO THE GULF CRISIS

In August 1990 Iraq's invasion and annexation of Kuwait placed the Government of Yemen in an especially difficult position. The economy of Yemen was heavily dependent on trade with, and aid from, Iraq, and also on aid from Saudi Arabia, which normally hosts very large numbers of Yemeni expatriate workers. Moreover, there was evidence of widespread popular support in Yemen for President Saddam Hussain of Iraq. These factors explained the Government's equivocal response to the Iraqi invasion of Kuwait and to subsequent developments in the Gulf region. In the immediate aftermath of the invasion the Government condemned Iraq, but also criticized the arrival of US and other Western military forces to defend Saudi Arabia. At the summit meeting of leaders of Arab League member states, held in Cairo on 10 August 1990, Yemen voted against the proposal to send Arab forces to Saudi Arabia as part of a multinational force to deter aggression by Iraq. Yemen also abstained in the UN Security Council vote to impose economic sanctions on Iraq. By late August, however, the Government appeared to be committed to implementing the UN sanctions against Iraq, albeit reluctantly. In October the Yemeni Minister of Foreign Affairs, Abd al-Karim al-Iryani, announced that Yemen would support any measures taken to achieve a peaceful withdrawal of Iraqi troops from Kuwait, but that this should result in the withdrawal of all foreign forces from the area.

Yemen's relations with Saudi Arabia deteriorated as a result of Yemen's initial strong opposition to the presence of foreign armed forces in the Gulf and to the ambiguous stance it subsequently adopted in this respect. On 15 September 1990, in what was regarded as a retaliatory action, Saudi Arabia announced that it had withdrawn the privileges which Yemeni workers in Saudi Arabia had previously enjoyed. This resulted in an exodus from Saudi Arabia of an estimated 500,000–800,000 Yemeni workers during October and November, which caused widespread economic and social disruption. The expulsion and return of the Yemeni workers not only caused a reduction in the country's income from remittances sent home by the expatriates, but also led to a serious increase in unemployment.

In November 1990 the Yemeni Government voted against the UN Security Council resolution to authorize the multinational contingent stationed in the Gulf to use 'all necessary means' against Iraq in order to remove its forces from Kuwait if they had not withdrawn by 15 January 1991. This prompted a visit to Yemen by the US Secretary of State, James Baker, in an attempt to persuade Yemen to modify its position concerning the UN resolution. In late November the Minister of Foreign Affairs, Abd al-Karim al-Iryani, visited France, Germany and Algeria in the hope of gathering support to prevent the UN Security Council resolution from being passed. In December Yemen assumed the chair of the UN Security Council (which rotates on a monthly basis) and the Government increased its efforts to mediate in the Gulf crisis: the Vice-President of Yemen, Ali Salim al-Baid, met King Hussein of Jordan, in Amman, and the Iraqi President, Saddam Hussain, in Baghdad, for talks concerning the crisis. In January 1991 Yemen presented a peace plan in an attempt to prevent war in the Gulf; the plan included an Iraqi withdrawal from Kuwait, the withdrawal of the multinational military force, and the holding of an international conference on the Arab–Israeli conflict. Despite numerous diplomatic initiatives undertaken by the Yemeni Government, prior to the UN deadline of 15 January, the peace plan failed to prevent the outbreak of war in the Gulf on 16–17 January. Following the US-led military offensive against Iraq, Yemen

issued a statement in which it condemned the action, and hundreds of thousands of Yemenis demonstrated in support of Iraq. Later in January it was confirmed that US aid to Yemen was to be severely reduced, apparently as a result of Yemen's policy towards Iraq.

POLITICAL AFFAIRS AFTER REUNIFICATION

The two government parties, the Northern GPC and the Southern YSP, had agreed to share power equally until elections were held in November 1992 but within months of the referendum there were reports that extreme members of each were increasing their stocks of weapons for use against the other. Due to the disparity in the population—10m. in the North and two million in the South—posts had to be found in the North for southerners, who were regarded as secularists, indeed as former communists, and whose presence was resented. Northerners were shocked by the unislamic lifestyle of many in Aden and by the enhanced role of women. The deaths and injuries in both cities that attended an Aden–San'a football match were indicative of the mutual animosity.

In September 1991 a YSP official was murdered; in December two more were killed at a party meeting in Ibb, where a fourth was killed in February. Two were later wounded in Sa'ada and another killed in Taiz. In April 1992, the Minister of Justice, Abd al-Wasi Salam, a YSP leader, survived after gunmen opened fire on his car; there was suspicion that the attempt was connected with his imminent departure for Muscat for frontier negotiations. In May the house of Salim Salih Muhammad, a YSP representative on the Presidential Council, was attacked. Only three days later there was a bomb at the house of the Prime Minister who denied that it had any connection with the Oman dispute. In June the YSP claimed, but the Government denied, that there had been an attack on the home of the editor of their newspaper and the brother of the Prime Minister was murdered in the southern port of Shihr: this was seen as an attempt to disrupt the unification process as he had played no part in politics. In July, in circumstances that are disputed, a colonel, a member of the YSP central committee, 'killed himself' after a shootout in which two policemen were also killed: his car which had failed to stop at a road-block was found to be full of weapons. A former Deputy Prime Minister of the PDRY, Anis Hassan Yahya, escaped assassination in Aden and at the beginning of August security forces defused a mine outside the house in San'a of the former Prime Minister Muhammad Ali Haitham. The YSP also claimed that several of their local officials had been shot dead in provincial towns, mainly in the North of the country. However, in September there were reports of bomb attacks on the homes of leading GPC members.

One of the ways in which the YSP could assert its strength was through its control of the trade unions, particularly in Aden. President Saleh declared industrial unrest unpatriotic but in March 1992 100,000 workers in Aden brought everything from the airport to government services and the university to a halt. They threatened a three-day stoppage unless wages were raised by 40%, a job creation scheme for people expelled from Saudi Arabia and a price 'freeze' were implemented. They later settled for a wage increase of 25%, backdated to January, and a barely credible promise to keep prices at 1991 levels. Different labour grievances then emerged as the staff of the government newspaper in Aden went on strike for parity of wages with their colleagues in the San'a press.

A human rights organization, Amnesty International, asserted that all political prisoners in the South had been released before reunification, although there were possibly 25 in the North. No executions had taken place although there had been five amputations of hands. Much forcibly-nationalized property in the South was restored to its former owners and journalists sacked under Ismail were reinstated. In May 1992 an amnesty was extended to former President Ali Nasser Muhammad and five of his associates.

The Government estimated that the Gulf crisis had cost the Yemeni economy US $3,000m., and although some of this was recouped by the sale of petroleum concessions, the economic situation remained serious. Only 20% of debt repayments were met. In March 1992 the budget envisaged a deficit of $1,000m. The general economic conditions and social unrest proved fertile soil for Islamic fundamentalists, who provided education and other services which the state could not. The question of the place of the *Shari'a* in the legal system continued to provoke controversy. The YIP became, after the two government parties, the next strongest and probably displaced the YSP in the North. It seemed, however, likely to split between its religious and its tribal leadership and even within its tribal element. It was also attacked by some religious leaders, such as Sheikh Ahmad ash-Shami (Secretary-General of the al-Haq party), as an instrument of Saudi Arabia and in thrall to old-fashioned tribal sheikhs. President Saleh was said to have guaranteed Vice-President al-Baid that his position would not be affected whatever the result of the elections, but that other parties would join the government. Meanwhile, the estimated 30–40 political parties were encouraged to merge in order to reduce electoral confusion.

FOREIGN AFFAIRS AFTER THE GULF WAR

Yemen's stance during the Gulf War was not quickly forgotten in the Arabian peninsula and, one year later, relations with some of its states were still frosty. On the first anniversary of reunification the only Arab head of state to attend was Yasser Arafat, although Yemen had tried to establish its Arab credentials by raising the question of Israeli settlements at the UN Security Council, and by denying that it had approved an Israeli plan to resettle the remaining 1,500 Yemeni Jews. In mid-1992 French, British and US Jewish groups mounted a diplomatic campaign in order to organize the discreet departure from Yemen of the small remaining Jewish community. The Yemeni response was that, whereas emigration was open to all its citizens, emigration to Israel was forbidden by the Constitution. Israel claimed in July 1993 to have secretly airlifted about 250 Yemeni Jews into the country, although the Yemeni Government denied all knowledge of the affair.

In addition to its resentment at Yemen's attitude to the Gulf crisis, Saudi Arabia, which had ceased its financial support of some US $600m. per year and had expelled immigrant workers constituting about 8% of the total population of Yemen, disliked Yemen's new political pluralism and free press, and, in any case, can scarcely have been enthusiastic about reunification. Saudi Arabia delayed the sale of its 49% share-holding in the San'a-based airline Yemenia, thus preventing the company's merger with the Adeni airline Alyemda. Contrary to previous practice, Saudi visas were required from Yemeni *Hajj* pilgrims. More seriously, in April 1992, Saudi Arabia warned the four oil companies, including British Petroleum (BP), that were prospecting in the eastern desert in an area where the frontier had not been precisely delimited that they were trespassing on Saudi territory, and, to the great indignation of the Yemenis, the companies ceased work. A similar threat to the US Hunt Oil Co was said to have been withdrawn after an intercession by President Bush. The frontier dispute continued, with the Saudis claiming that the Yemenis were not serious about wanting a settlement while the Yemenis felt that the dispute was being prolonged to sabotage their development. In September 1992, however, a committee of experts assembled in Riyadh to discuss the border dispute. No apparent progress was made, either on this occasion, or at further meetings in October and November. The process was subsequently suspended during Ramadan and the Yemeni elections, but in August 1993, against a background of improved relations between Yemen and Saudi Arabia, the committee assembled for a fifth round of talks aimed at solving the dispute. Little progress had been made by January 1994 when the talks entered their seventh round. Nevertheless, the Minister of Foreign Affairs, Muhammad Salim Basindwa, appointed because of his good relations with the Gulf states, declared that improving relations with Saudi Arabia was his top priority and the eighth round of talks concerning demarcation took place in April.

The Saudis also disapproved of Yemen's increasing friendship with Iran. Both the Iranian Minister of Foreign Affairs, Velayati, and the Speaker of the Majlis, Mahdi Karrubi, visited San'a, and agreements were signed for co-operation in a range of fields. There were proposals for a joint fishing company and for processing Iranian petroleum at Aden refinery. The GCC stopped funding the expansion of Aden port, and Kuwait instructed its airline not to sell tickets to Yemenis. In mid-1993 it was reported that the Ministers of Foreign Affairs of Kuwait

and Yemen were to meet in Vienna, Austria, reflecting a gradual improvement in relations between the two states. The meeting was subsequently cancelled, however, following opposition from the Speaker of the Kuwaiti National Assembly. Yemen's one ally in the Arabian peninsula was Oman, with frequent high-level visitors exchanging messages between Sultan and President. In December 1991 President Saleh said that the agreement on frontier delimitation, envisaged in the Oman–PDRY reconciliation of 1988, would be concluded within two weeks. However, opposition arose, as it was believed that Yemen would relinquish nearly 6,000 sq miles of territory, and the YUP and the local Mahra authorities challenged the Government's right to do so. In October 1992 Yemen and Oman signed an agreement to establish the demarcation of their border. The agreement was officially ratified in December and co-operation between Yemen and Oman in the areas of construction, transport and commerce was subsequently envisaged. In April 1993 the two countries agreed on measures to open border points and increase bilateral trade.

Relations with the three remaining GCC member states also showed signs of gradual improvement. In February 1993 Sheikh Muhammad al-Maktoum, the UAE Minister of Defence, visited Yemen, and in the following month his visit was returned by the Yemeni Minister of Planning and Development. In June 1993 the Yemeni Minister of Foreign Affairs, Muhammad Basindwa, declared that improving relations with the Gulf states was his highest priority, and in the following month he visited Bahrain.

In August 1991 al-Iryani flew to Egypt and relations were repaired, although Cairo later rejected Yemen's proposal for a revival of the ACC, initially without Iraqi participation. Yemen's relations with the other ACC member, Jordan, were cordial, and in September 1991, during a visit to Amman, Prime Minister al-Attas signed a series of agreements for co-operation in trade, agriculture, educational exchanges and tourism. In the same month, Yemen and Iraq signed a cultural agreement, and in May 1992 Iraq undertook to provide teachers to support Yemen's campaign to develop education. Yemen continued to oppose sanctions against Iraq, but in March 1993 Saddam Hussain sent his half-brother to San'a to protest at Yemeni attempts to improve its relations with the Gulf states.

Reconciliation with the Western powers was smoother. The USA, unwilling to offend its more important GCC allies, let it be known that its attitude would depend upon Yemen's actions in the Security Council and over human rights, but in August 1991 it agreed to sell Yemen 300,000 tons of subsidized wheat, more than ever before. Yemen fully supported the US Middle-East peace initiative. US firms were chosen to draw up the master plan for Aden free port and a feasibility study for a gas-fired power station in Marib. In January 1992 the Deputy Secretary of State for Energy, Hanson Moore, visited the country.

The British had been less upset than their allies over Yemen's attitude to the Gulf War, and relations were fully restored in time for a successful visit by al-Iryani to London in February 1992. Al-Baid had already visited Britain in August 1991, followed by a financial team to seek investment in the free port. British firms won various contracts including one to prospect for gold in the Hadramawt and another to print new currency. The cordiality of relations between Britain and Yemen was confirmed by a successful visit of the Yemeni Minister of Planning and Development to London.

In the West there was a growing belief that Yemen had developed into the most genuine democracy in the Arab world—a sentiment articulated by the French Minister of Foreign Affairs on a visit in October 1991. The EC sent a parliamentary delegation to San'a in June 1992 and in the same month the German President, Dr Richard von Weizsäcker, made a state visit during which he promised aid. The Yemeni Chief of Staff, Brig.-Gen. al-Busheiry, also visited Paris. The problems of investment were discussed in July at a conference in Geneva at which the presence of Qatar gratified the Yemenis. The need for aid and also the broad range of the participants in the development of its oil industry—including Japan, Indonesia, Norway and Canada—kept Yemen active diplomatically, although financial difficulties forced the closure of 16 Yemeni embassies at the end of 1992.

Yemen had increasingly been drawn into the affairs of its neighbours across the Red Sea. In July 1991 Yemeni officials collaborated with French diplomats to settle disputes in Djibouti. After the fall of Lt-Col Mengistu, ships of the Ethiopian navy took refuge in Aden: Zimbabwe's Minister of Foreign Affairs helped to mediate and the fleet returned home. More serious was the crisis that arose from the civil war in Somalia, which obliged Yemen to give refuge to more than 60,000 Somali refugees during 1992 and 1993. The Yemeni Government had great problems in accommodating and feeding them. Finally an agreement was reached whereby Yemen would accept further refugees on the understanding that the UN should take responsibility for their welfare.

THE 1993 ELECTIONS AND THE ENSUING POLITICAL CRISIS

In spite of the climate of unrest, voter registration for the legislative elections, scheduled for 27 April 1993, took place between 15 January and 16 February. An outbreak of attacks on expatriate workers prompted a warning, in February, that the Government could not guarantee the safety of expatriate residents owing to the threat of certain hostile Yemeni tribes. There were 3,400 candidates for the 301 seats in the House of Representatives, many standing as independents. Of the major political parties presenting candidates, the GPC, led by the President, Ali Abdullah Saleh, and the YSP, led by the Vice-President, Ali Salim al-Baid, were the largest. The two other major parties were the YIP, widely reported to have received substantial financial assistance from Saudi Arabia, led by Sheikh Abdullah bin Hussain al-Ahmar, and the Baath (Renaissance) party, led by Mujahid Abu Shuarib. There were also more than 40 smaller parties, but most of them were in alliance with one of the four major parties.

After lively campaigning in the months preceding the elections, the turn-out on election day was very high. International observers expressed broad satisfaction with the conduct of the elections, the first nation-wide, multi-party elections based on universal suffrage in the Arabian peninsula. Inevitably there were reports of disturbances in several towns and accusations of fraudulent practices by both of the leading parties. When the results were announced the GPC had, not surprisingly, won the majority of the vote and gained 123 of the 301 seats, most of them in the former YAR. The YIP took second place with 62 seats, again mainly in the former YAR, with the YSP relegated to third place with 56 seats, most of them in the former PDRY. The Baath party took seven seats, minor parties five seats and independents 47 seats. Of the 50 women candidates who stood for election, two won seats.

After the election the YIP is reported to have threatened to boycott the new House of Representatives unless it was admitted to government. The three main parties eventually agreed to form a coalition, with the GPC and YSP each taking two seats on the Presidential Council and the YIP the one remaining seat. The YIP was also allocated six posts in the Council of Ministers, but these did not include the portfolios of education and finance which the party had demanded. However, the leader of the YIP, Sheikh Abdullah bin Hussain al-Ahmar, became Speaker of the House of Representatives. The YSP leadership was disappointed by the election results and became increasingly apprehensive and resentful about the emerging alliance between the GPC and the YIP. The GPC found it easier to co-operate with the YIP on a number of important political issues, especially proposed constitutional changes, than with the YSP; this co-operation was assisted by the fact that the GPC leader's tribe, the Sanhan, belonged to the Hashid tribal federation, of which the YIP leader was the paramount Sheikh. In August 1993 the Vice-President refused to take part in the Government and decided to return to Aden. His departure from San'a marked the official beginning of a political crisis that was to lead to civil war. This crisis intensified following a series of assassinations of YSP officials, including the Vice-President's nephew, who was shot in Aden on 29 October. It was widely rumoured in San'a that these assassinations were ordered by the President's 'entourage', notably his brother and three half-brothers who commanded key military units and the security services.

In an attempt to put pressure on President Saleh to make concessions that would restore southern influence, the Vice-President had issued an 18-point list of demands in September. They included security and military reforms and decentralization to allow each governorate more freedom in administrative and financial affairs. In November al-Baid declared that the North was attempting to annex the South rather than unifying with it. Efforts to mediate between the two factions by Oman, Jordan, PLO Chairman Arafat, the USA and the *'ulama* (religious scholars) failed to resolve the crisis, while the departure of the Vice-President and other southern officials including the Prime Minister, Haidar al-Attas, brought the business of government to a standstill, aggravating already chronic economic problems. Riots in San'a and Taiz in early January 1994 reflected popular discontent at rising prices and the falling value of the Yemeni riyal. Meanwhile the security situation in the country continued to deteriorate. There were more political killings—al-Baid claimed that more than 150 YSP members had been killed since May 1990—and further kidnappings of foreign nationals.

Amidst the deepening political crisis a National Dialogue Committee was formed with representatives from across the political spectrum, to try to work out a formula acceptable to both factions. After months of discussions and deliberations, the committee drew up a 'Document of Pledge and Agreement' on 18 January 1994 which incorporated many of the demands made by al-Baid in his 18-point list. The document proposed major constitutional reform that would clearly define the powers of the Presidential Council, the President and the Vice-President, devolution of power from central government to local and regional assemblies, the restructuring of the armed forces and the arrest and trial of those responsible for the wave of assassinations largely directed at YSP officials. On 20 February the President and Vice-President signed the document at a public ceremony in Amman, Jordan, attended by representatives from Oman, the USA, France, the PLO and the Arab League. There was no reconciliation between the two Yemeni leaders however; they refused to shake hands after signing the document and al-Baid demanded that Saleh order the immediate arrest of his brothers. Al-Baid and his principal lieutenants walked out on follow-up talks and further strained relations with the President by visiting Saudi Arabia and the Gulf states to seek support for their cause. Some analysts argued that President Saleh had no intention of honouring the concessions made in Amman, but only wanted to gain time, having already chosen the military option. The real intentions of the southern leadership were also unclear. Several observers maintained that while some of the YSP leaders wanted secession, the majority had sought to escalate the political crisis in order to topple the President and take over a united Yemen.

The day after the ceremony there were clashes between rival military units in the southern province of Abyan and in other parts of the country. After unification the armed forces of the former YAR and PDRY had not been integrated; the GPC continued to control the northern forces and the YSP those of the south. The fighting that continued sporadically for some months involved not only forces under the command of the GPC and the YSP, but also YSP forces loyal to the former South Yemen President, Ali Nasser Muhammad, as well as tribal militias which used the opportunity to promote their own interests. The GPC was reported to have mobilized the powerful Hashid tribal federation, while the YSP called on the support of their traditional rivals, the Bakil tribes. At the beginning of March a joint military committee of northern and southern officers, Jordanian and Omani officers and the US and French military attachés, attempted to disengage the widely dispersed and intermixed rival military units. Jordan, Oman, Egypt and the UAE all made diplomatic efforts to mediate between the two main rival factions but made no progress. In April both Oman and Jordan withdrew from the joint military committee.

THE CIVIL WAR

On 27 April 1994, the anniversary of the general election, a major tank battle took place between rival army units at Amran, some 60 km to the north of San'a. It was the biggest clash between the opposing forces since the crisis began. Some 200 tanks were involved in the fighting; 85 tanks were reported to have been destroyed and more than 400 soldiers killed or wounded. Both sides claimed that the other attacked first. The

YSP claimed that the attack was tantamount to a declaration of war, while the President accused al-Baid of secessionism and pledged to fight to defend the unity of the country. During the night of 4 May fighter aircraft under the command of the YSP attacked northern airports at San'a, Taiz and Hodeida, the presidential palace in San'a, the country's two main power stations, Hodeida port, and petroleum storage and pipeline facilities at Marib. Northern aircraft retaliated on 5 May, badly damaging the airport at Aden. The northern military command reported pitched battles in several areas along the old frontier between the YAR and PDRY and claimed that southern forces had suffered heavy losses in seven of the country's 17 provinces. The civil war had begun in earnest. The President declared a 30-day state of emergency and dismissed the Vice-President. France announced that it was evacuating its nationals and the USA advised its citizens to leave. On 10 May Prime Minister al-Attas, a southerner, was dismissed after he appealed for outside forces to help end the civil war. The Minister of Petroleum and Minerals, Hussainoun, was among other YSP members dismissed from their posts in the Council of Ministers. On 21 May al-Baid proclaimed the breakaway 'Democratic Republic of Yemen' (DRY) and began diplomatic efforts to secure recognition of the old frontier. Al-Attas, the former Prime Minister of Yemen, who had joined the secessionist government in Aden, travelled to Egypt to seek the backing of Arab moderates and appealed to the West for support and recognition for the southern government. Al-Baid was named President of the new state, with a five-man Presidential Council drawn from a range of political and tribal affiliations, including the opposition League of the Sons of Yemen, the Nasserite Federation for the Liberation of South Yemen, and the wing of the YSP associated with the ex-President of the PDRY, Ali Nasser Muhammad. The breakaway state adopted the same Constitution as the North, and the same legal system, based on Islamic law. President Saleh denounced the secession, offering an amnesty to all those in the former PDRY who rejected it, with the exception of al-Baid and 15 other YSP leaders.

As northern forces advanced on Aden, Saudi Arabia together with Bahrain, Oman, the UAE and Egypt requested a meeting of the UN Security Council to discuss the Yemeni conflict. San'a's UN representative strongly objected to what it considered interference in its internal affairs. Nevertheless, on 1 June 1994 the Security Council unanimously adopted Resolution 924, appealing for an immediate cease-fire and requesting the dispatch of a UN commission of inquiry to assess prospects for a renewed dialogue between the belligerents. It also urged an immediate cessation of the supply of arms and other materials that might contribute to the conflict. The Resolution, which Prince Bandar bin Sultan, the Saudi Arabian ambassador to Washington, was reported to have played an important role in drafting, deliberately omitted any direct endorsement of Yemeni unity. Two days later the UN Secretary-General, Dr Boutros Boutros-Ghali, appointed the much respected former Algerian Minister of Foreign Affairs, Lakhdar al-Ibrahimi, as his special envoy and head of the fact-finding mission. Spokesmen for the North and South welcomed al-Ibrahimi's appointment and promised their full co-operation. However, before the commission of inquiry began its work, the Ministers of Foreign Affairs of the GCC, meeting on 4–5 June, issued a statement effectively blaming the North for the conflict and implicitly recognizing the DRY. The Ministers warned that continued hostilities would have repercussions for the GCC states, forcing them to adopt appropriate measures against 'the party that does not abide by the cease-fire'. Only Qatar dissented. While Saudi Arabia maintained that its only concern was to prevent the destabilization of the region, many observers argued that the YSP leadership, given the smaller military forces under its command, would not have declared independence unless it had the support of its powerful neighbour. The Government in San'a condemned the GCC statement and Dr Abd al-Karim al-Iryani, the Minister of Planning and Development and principal political counsellor to President Saleh, maintained that they had clear evidence that arms purchased with Saudi funds were being supplied to the South. The North accused Saudi Arabia of encouraging the secessionists in order to create a new petroleum emirate in the Hadramawt under Saudi influence and providing it with an outlet to the Indian Ocean. One of the principal oil concessions

in Hadramawt is held by the Nimr company, owned by the Saudi Arabian Ibn Mahfouz family, who were originally from the Hadramawt. Saudi Arabia had not forgiven Yemen for its support for Iraq during the Gulf crisis and feared that a united and democratic Yemen would threaten its supremacy in the Arabian peninsula. Despite official statements of strict neutrality in the conflict, it was widely believed that Egypt was hostile to the North because the GPC leadership had allowed Egyptian Islamist militants to train in camps set up in Yemen under the protection of Sheikh Abd al-Majid az-Zindani, the leading ideologue of the YIP and a member of Yemen's Presidential Council. Sheikh Zindani was reported to have raised 63m. riyals for the northern war effort through collections from mosques and religious associations. Support for the North came from Iraq, Iran and Sudan. The South accused both Iraq and Sudan of providing military assistance to the North, accusations which Iraq and Sudan denied.

By the first week in June 1994 northern forces were besieging the southern capital of Aden and there were reports of air attacks on strategic installations and heavy shelling and artillery fire from northern forces. On 6 June, shortly after the arrival of the UN commission of inquiry, San'a agreed to observe a cease-fire, as did the South. Al-Ibrahimi managed to secure the agreement of both factions to the formation of a monitoring body to police the truce, but when San'a suggested that the joint military committee should be revived, Aden objected and demanded a full UN multinational peace-keeping force and the withdrawal of northern forces to behind the old frontier between the YAR and the PDRY. The cease-fire lasted only six hours. Talks arranged in Cairo by al-Ibrahimi also collapsed because San'a insisted that it would only negotiate with the YSP in the context of a united Yemen, whereas the South demanded that negotiations should be between two independent states. The southern negotiating team, led by Muhsin bin Farid, the 'Deputy Prime Minister' of the self-proclaimed DRY, walked out of the talks and appealed for UN intervention to enforce a truce and punish the North for continuing its assault on Aden. Southern officials admitted publicly in mid-June that they were being supplied with arms by 'friendly Arab countries'. On 17 June it was reported that military equipment, including 30–40 tanks and more than 100 missiles, had been unloaded at the port of Mukalla in the south over the past two weeks. Later in June there were reports that the South had acquired new MiG-29 fighter planes from Eastern Europe, with Gulf funding, and was using its air power to bomb the Marib oilfields.

At the end of June 1994 the UN Secretary-General reported that UN efforts to mediate between the two rival factions had made no progress. He expressed concern that the fighting had not stopped and drew attention to the deteriorating humanitarian situation. The Security Council, meeting on 29 June, adopted Resolution 931 which requested that the Secretary-General continue to mediate between the two factions in order to secure a durable cease-fire and called for a monitoring force to supervise the truce. The Resolution was seen as a setback for supporters of the self-proclaimed DRY who had urged the UN to condemn the North for the continued fighting and to initiate moves that might extend to the official recognition of the DRY. Several observers pointed to the critical role of the USA which finally decided to support a unified Yemen and warned Saudi Arabia against interfering. Despite talks in Moscow on 30 June and again in New York on 2 July on implementing and supervising a cease-fire, northern forces continued their advance and by 4 July had entered northern districts of Aden which was without water or electricity. On 7 July Aden surrendered to northern forces and the self-proclaimed DRY collapsed. Al-Baid fled to Oman, and his 'Vice-President', Abd ar-Rahman al-Jifri, to Saudi Arabia, from where he pledged to continue the struggle against the North. President Saleh reported that 931 civilians and soldiers had been killed in the civil war and 5,000 had been wounded, although others claimed that the death toll was much higher. It was estimated that the war against the southern secessionists had cost the central government US $8,000m. Saleh estimated that it would cost US $7,500m. in post-war reconstruction. Following the announcement of a general amnesty and the termination of the state of emergency, southern Yemeni soldiers began returning to the country. There were reports that during the dismantling of the southern army, irregular tribal forces carried off much of the army's military equipment.

THE AFTERMATH OF THE CIVIL WAR

After the fall of Aden to northern forces, the victorious North pledged to work for national reconciliation. On 7 July 1994 a document was submitted to the UN Secretary-General stating that military operations would cease immediately, a general amnesty would be declared, democracy and political pluralism, together with human rights, freedom of speech and of the press would be respected, and national dialogue within the framework of constitutional legitimacy would be resumed. These statements were reaffirmed during a meeting of the Council of Ministers in Aden on 12 July, in which it was declared that all northern military units would return to barracks. (In August, moreover, President Saleh announced that party membership would no longer be permitted within the armed forces.) A committee was formed to implement the reconstruction of Aden, which was named as the country's economic capital. However, UN attempts to bring the two opposing sides together for talks in Geneva at the end of July failed. Al-Iryani of the GPC, who had been scheduled to meet al-Attas of the YSP for talks in the presence of UN mediator Lakhdar al-Ibrahimi, denied that any negotiations were under way and stated that the UN had no further role to play as any discussions between the different parties would take place within Yemen itself. After a meeting of the YSP politburo in Damascus, Syria, under Secretary-General Salim Salih Muhammad, a statement was issued condemning the secession and appealing for unity and reconciliation, and a return to the principles incorporated in the Document of Pledge and Agreement signed in Amman earlier in the year. In September the YSP in Yemen elected a new politburo, none of whose members had been involved in the declaration of the DRY. The politburo elected Ali Saleh Obad as the new Secretary-General of the YSP. In the following month remnants of the secessionist administration, now grouped around Abd ar-Rahman al-Jifri in the newly-formed National Opposition Front, also appealed for a settlement on the basis of the Amman agreement, but while declaring that they hoped to achieve their aims through dialogue, they did not preclude resorting to armed struggle. From exile in Oman, al-Baid had declared that he was retiring from politics.

On 28 September 1994 the House of Representatives in San'a adopted a series of constitutional reforms which greatly strengthened the position of the President, including the abolition of the Presidential Council. Following the defeat of the secular YSP and the dispersal of its military and political power base, the Islamist YIP began asserting its authority. As part of the constitutional reforms *Shari'a* (Islamic law) became the only, rather than the principal, source of legislation, and the last references to the specific rights of women were removed from the Constitution. On 1 October Saleh was re-elected President of the Republic and despite much rhetoric about reconciliation, the YSP was excluded from the new Government. During an interview in early 1995 President Saleh stated that he did not preclude the eventual reintegration of the YSP into the power structure, but only after it had reformed and was prepared to 'respect constitutional rules'. In the new Council of Ministers appointed by the President on 6 October, the GPC retained the majority of posts but the YIP increased its membership from six to nine, including the influential portfolios of education and justice. The South was represented in the new Council of Ministers by four ministers, together with Vice-President Maj.-Gen. Abd ar-Rabbuh Mansur Hadi, all of whom were now standing as members of the GPC but were former allies of the Ali Nasser Muhammad faction.

Despite its minority representation in government, the YIP was the most influential party in the country with the best and most dynamic organization. Its officials were active in the towns and even in remote parts of the countryside, and its broad-based constituency included the tribes, the commercial bourgeoisie and the influential Muslim Brotherhood. In September the YIP congress elected members of the Muslim Brotherhood to most of its key posts. Yet despite the ascendancy of its ideologues, the YIP moved cautiously and was careful in its public statements to stress its commitment to political pluralism and to a market economy, while condemning violence and terrorism in all its

forms. The YIP Assistant Secretary-General, Abd al-Wahab al-Ansi, interviewed in early 1995, stated that if the party obtained an absolute majority in the next election, it would not monopolize power since it believed it was necessary to have the co-operation of all Yemeni political groupings in order to solve the problems of underdevelopment. However, statements by the party's leader, Sheikh Abdullah bin Hussain al-Ahmar, and the Chairman of its *majlis*, Sheikh Abd al-Majid az-Zindani, contradicted the YIP's stated commitment to a pluralist democratic system. For their part, YIP ministers acted with discretion but determination. The Minister of Education, Abd Ali al-Qubati, for example, did not overturn existing teaching programmes; however, he did increase the hours devoted to Koranic studies at the expense of science teaching, suspend teachers suspected of socialist and secular sympathies and replace them with Islamist teachers recruited from Sudan or Egypt. He also gradually phased out co-educational classes in schools and in the university in the southern provinces, and 'recommended' that female teachers and students observe the proper dress code. The Minister of Justice, Dr Abd al-Wahab Lufti ad-Daylami, dismissed women judges whose appointment had survived from the former PDRY, stating that they were totally incompetent in Islamic law. The YIP and the GPC, meanwhile, co-operated to destroy the YSP and appeared determined to 'Islamize' the southern provinces. The Government seized all properties belonging to the YSP, and thousands of civil servants suspected of socialist sympathies were dismissed. Both parties blamed southern officials and the YSP for widespread corruption despite the complexity of the problem which could not be ascribed to a single party or faction. Nevertheless in early 1995 there were reports of tensions between the GPC and the YIP, which appeared to have become increasingly dissatisfied with its role in government. Differences emerged over economic policy, for example, with the GPC apparently accepting as inevitable at least some of the economic reforms recommended by the World Bank and the IMF, whereas the YIP expressed its opposition to the introduction of austerity measures. Some observers argued that the eclipse of the YSP, the only obstacle to the growing influence of the Islamists, could lead to the weakening of political pluralism, the erosion of basic liberties and the eventual emergence of a new single-party dictatorship under the YIP, with or without President Saleh.

In early February 1995 13 opposition parties from across the political spectrum formed a common front to oppose the ruling GPC/YIP coalition. The new Democratic Coalition of Opposition adopted as its platform the Document of Pledge and Agreement signed before the civil war and urged the Government to abide by its terms. The new bloc demanded that the Government act without delay to implement the economic measures endorsed by the House of Representatives at the end of November 1994 and to eradicate corruption in the country's administration. Because of increasing government interference in what had been a free press, with opposition papers being targeted for harassment by the authorities, and widespread illiteracy, the new coalition stated that it would take its campaign to the people by the use of audio-cassettes.

The economic repercussions of the civil war presented additional problems for the Government in the form of a number of popular protests and civil disturbances, particularly in the south. In September 1994 hundreds demonstrated in Abyan province in protest at water and electricity shortages and the price of basic foodstuffs, which in some instances had increased fivefold. In February 1995 more than 150 wholesalers were arrested in San'a for their alleged role in inflating prices. In late March and early April, moreover, following the devaluation of the riyal and the doubling of the price of fuel, demonstrators clashed with police in Aden, San'a and Dhamar, resulting in more than 50 arrests and three deaths. The activities of Islamist militants, meanwhile, posed a potential threat to internal stability. In early September 1994 some 20 people were reported to have been killed in clashes with the security forces in Abyan province, following the destruction of three Muslim saints' shrines by Islamist militants who deemed them idolatrous. In April 1995 Islamist militants were involved in skirmishes in Hadramawt province, resulting in the deaths of two members of the Hussainain tribe, after they levelled similar accusations at the tribe for unislamic burial practices.

In a reorganization of the Council of Ministers in mid-June 1995 the GPC increased its share of portfolios at the expense of independents, with the result that the Council consisted entirely of members of the GPC and the YIP. Later in the month President Saleh was re-elected head of the GPC at the party's first general assembly to be held since 1988, and was given the new title of party Chairman. The Deputy Prime Minister and Minister of Foreign Affairs, Abd al-Karim al-Iryani, assumed Saleh's previous position of Secretary-General, and the post of party Vice-Chairman was taken by the country's Vice-President, Abd ar-Rabbuh Mansur Hadi. In accordance with a decision to rationalize and restructure the party, the permanent committee, elected to represent the constituencies, was reduced to 300 members, and the size of the politburo, elected by the permanent committee, was reduced from 23 to seven members. Meanwhile, the government continued to pursue a policy of decentralization and was reported to have granted the governorates a degree of control over their own budgets and greater freedom in appointing local officials. New provincial governors were appointed, and in April the President announced the demobilization of some 50,000 troops as part of a plan to rationalize the armed forces.

The tensions which had emerged between the GPC and the YIP in early 1995 continued as the year progressed, with differences over many aspects of policy becoming more pronounced. While some elements in the YIP were keen to further Islamist influence over the country's banking system, the GPC was in favour of its privatization. The YIP, which had established its own system of educational establishments, quite separate from the state-run education system, was also opposed to the GPC's aim of educational integration and unification. During 1994–95 these religious schools enrolled 326,484 pupils, 13% of total school enrolment in that year. The YIP also declared its opposition to the development of the free-trade zone at Aden, arguing that it would attract large numbers of non-Yemenis and thereby undermine the country's Islamic identity. In November YIP ministers boycotted the weekly meeting of the Council of Ministers in protest at a newspaper report that claimed the party was colluding with Islamist radicals. Relations between the YIP and the GPC continued to deteriorate. The YIP expressed its opposition to economic reforms recommended by the World Bank, and criticized the GPC for attending an economic summit meeting in Jordan, in October, at which representatives of Israel were present. Moreover, in December the YIP Minister of Trade and Supply, Muhammad Ahmad Afandi, resigned from his post, citing political and economic differences with the GPC. (In January 1996 responsibility for the portfolio was given to a GPC member, Abd ar-Rahman Muhammad Ali Othman.) A new Minister of Education was appointed in October 1996.

The situation in the southern governorates remained tense. There was widespread frustration and resentment in the south that commitments to reconciliation and reconstruction were not honoured by the Government in San'a after the end of the civil war. With the collapse of the YSP, the southern governorates felt increasingly marginalized and neglected, and reconstruction work in the south has been mainly financed by foreign governments and organizations. Violent outbreaks continued in 1996 with explosions in Aden and other southern towns. In June 19 people died in riots in Mukalla and a bomb attack on the Egyptian embassy in July was blamed on 'separatist elements'. Although the exiled National Opposition Front denied responsibility, the group's leader, former Vice-President al-Baid, issued a statement reaffirming his commitment to a separate southern state and for a referendum to secure better terms for the southern governorates. He warned of further violence if these issues were not addressed. At the end of September new anti-government demonstrations occurred in Hadramawt but were quickly suppressed. Attempts by Islamists to enforce stricter public morality in the southern governorates were believed to have contributed to the continuing unrest. In November Ali Nasser Muhammad (a former President of the PDRY, in exile since 1986) returned to Yemen at the invitation of President Saleh. He insisted that he did not seek a political role, but there was speculation that the GPC might urge him to mediate with the south.

THE 1997 ELECTIONS

Tensions between the GPC and its coalition partner, the YIP, increased in the weeks preceding Yemen's second multi-party elections. In October 1996 the YIP took part in a press conference organized by six opposition parties which criticized the registration process, demanded a revision of new voter lists and called for changes to the independent committee responsible for organizing the elections. Some parties indicated that they might boycott the elections unless action was taken. The YIP held talks with several opposition parties including the ideologically-opposed YSP. In an earlier interview, the Prime Minister had played down the recent conflicts between the GPC and the YIP, arguing that each party merely wished to emphasize its distinct political identity as the elections approached. He also expressed support for the emergence of an effective opposition and for the return of the YSP to an active role, but stipulated that the party should first dissociate itself from the secessionists. In December the GPC announced plans to bring the YIP-controlled religious institutes into the state education system. This was seen as a direct challenge to the YIP, as the institutes are used for Islamic indoctrination and recruitment. Discussion of the subject within the Council of Ministers prompted YIP ministers to walk out, but the plan was later approved during a further meeting which the YIP ministers did not attend. Despite their differences the leaders of both parties met in January 1997 and renewed their coalition agreement. Earlier, opposition parties had accused both the GPC and the YIP of monopolizing access to the state-controlled media and using public funds for their election campaigns.

In the elections, held on 27 April 1997, the GPC swept to victory winning 187 of the 301 seats, 64 more than in 1993. With almost two-thirds of all seats, the GPC secured a clear majority in the new parliament. Its only serious rival, the YIP, secured only 53 seats, compared with 62 in 1993. Many candidates from the party's radical Islamist wing were defeated in the elections, while the more traditional tribal elements retained their seats. The party leader, Sheikh Abdullah bin Hussain al-Ahmar, the head of the Hasid tribal federation, was re-elected parliamentary speaker. The YSP, which won 56 seats in 1993, boycotted the elections along with several other opposition groupings. They claimed that the elections would not be fair because of irregularities in voter registration. Nevertheless, some YSP members did stand as independents. In total, independent candidates increased their representation from 48 to 54 seats. Of these, 39 declared their support for the GPC and six for the YIP. The GPC increased its representation throughout the country, particularly in the south, which, in 1993, had been dominated by the YSP. Only four parties were represented in the new parliament compared with eight in 1993.

The Government, which for months had mounted a campaign to encourage people to register to vote, estimated that voter turn-out on election day was around 80%; foreign observers put the figure at 60%. Some procedural improvements were made, such as the introduction of party symbols on ballot slips to aid illiterate voters. However, as in 1993, the election process was characterized by demonstrations and outbreaks of violence in which at least 20 people were reported to have been killed, and all parties except the GPC made accusations of fraudulent practices. International observers, including the US National Democratic Institute and the mainly European Joint International Observer Group in Yemen, were invited by the Government to monitor the elections, and although they were critical of some aspects of the elections, on balance, they pronounced them reasonably free and fair. In May a new Council of Ministers was named; 25 of the 29 members were GPC members, three were independents and there was one members of al-Haq, a conservative Islamic party which won no seats in the 1997 election. The GPC emphasized that they were 'participants' and not partners in government. An independent, Faraj Said bin Ghanim, was appointed Prime Minister. A number of GPC members retained their portfolios, and among the new appointments was a former Governor of the Central Bank, Alawi Salih as-Salami, who became Minister of Finance. As a result of their move to opposition, the YIP forfeited all its ministerial portfolios and consequently its control over the Ministry of Education, and immediately after the election the President confirmed that the YIP's religious institutes would be incorporated in the state education system and their finances and curriculum brought into line with state schools. In a move seen by many as the first step towards the creation of an upper house of parliament, President Saleh appointed 59 members to a new Consultative Council, designed to broaden the base of participation. Although lacking executive or legislative authority, the Council has a committee structure which parallels that of the Council of Ministers and was given a mandate to draft laws on local administration including the reorganization of provincial boundaries, a politically sensitive issue. In December the House of Representatives approved the promotion of President Saleh from lieutenant-general to the rank of field marshal.

After two bombs exploded in Aden at the end of July 1997 120 people were arrested throughout the southern governorates, mainly members of those opposition parties which had boycotted the 1997 elections. The authorities claimed that the opposition parties were responsible for the bombings, but Abd ar-Rahman al-Jifri, the leader of the League of the Sons of Yemen, insisted that the bombs had been planted by the Yemeni Government in an attempt to discredit the opposition. Later in the year the authorities stated that most of those detained had been released, but the opposition claimed that the majority of the men were still in prison and that two of the detainees had died after being tortured. The arrests provoked demonstrations during August and September in Mukalla, the capital of the Hadramawt, where support for the exiled separatist leader Ali Salim al-Baid remains strong. The demonstrators were also reacting to a decision by the newly formed Consultative Council to divide the province of Hadramawt into two parts, a move which was interpreted as an attempt to isolate the coastal areas, including the towns of Mukalla and Shihr (where the YSP retains a strong presence) from the interior of the province. At the end of October several car bombs exploded in Aden. No casualties were reported and some 27 men were arrested and charged, including Nabil Kenani, a Syrian who was alleged to have confessed to working for Saudi Arabia's intelligence services. The Saudi Arabian authorities, however, denied any involvement in the bombing campaign, and the decision by the Yemeni Government to report the confession was interpreted by some as an attempt to divert attention away from mounting popular discontent in the country. Kenani was subsequently sentenced to death after being convicted of involvement in the bombing, and the sentence was upheld by the Aden Court of Appeal in November 1999. In December 1997 several members of the YSP and the League of the Sons of Yemen imprisoned in Mukalla staged a hunger strike; after their health deteriorated President Saleh ordered their release.

Elsewhere in the country the Government's economic reforms were provoking widespread and often violent protests. In October 1997, after fuel prices were increased, local people in Dhammar, Marib and al-Jawf protested by blocking roads to the capital. Tribal leaders supported the protesters' actions and the authorities responded by dispatching troops to reopen the roads. At Dhammar three people died and many were injured in clashes between armed tribesmen and the security forces. Foreigners were no longer considered immune from violent attacks, and there was a sharp increase in the number of kidnappings of foreign residents and tourists, mainly by tribes seeking to extract material benefits from the state or to demonstrate their dissatisfaction with certain government actions. In November 1997 Brig. Hussain Muhammad Arab, the Minister of the Interior, linked the increase in the number of kidnappings with the Aden bombings, describing them as part of a campaign to 'tarnish Yemen's image and shake its stability'. In the same month 31 people alleged to be 'foreign agents' were put on trial in San'a charged with attacking and robbing military posts.

In a report published in March 1997 Amnesty International described Yemen as a 'major violator of human rights' despite having ratified or acceded to most human rights treaties and incorporated many of their safeguards into its domestic legislation. The report criticized the activities of the political branch of the security forces and the dramatic increase in the use of the death penalty since 1990, and alleged the systematic use of torture in prisons and the arbitrary arrest and detention of political opponents. It also listed abuses against women. The Deputy Prime Minister expressed surprise at the criticism, but

the Government promised to investigate the alleged abuses and gave assurances that the political security branch would be brought under judicial control. At the beginning of April the European Parliament urged the European Commission to put pressure on the Yemeni authorities to improve the country's human rights record, and a new co-operation agreement signed with the EU at the end of the month (replacing the 1984 agreement) was made conditional on progress both in human rights and democracy in Yemen. Later in the year Amnesty International deplored the increase in extra-judicial punishments and instances where international standards to ensure fair trials were disregarded. In a number of cases, following lenient sentencing, crowds of armed civilians took the law into their own hands and the authorities made little effort to curb the increase in vigilante activity. In October a formal Yemeni application for membership of the Commonwealth (former British) was rejected on the grounds that Yemen did not meet the required standards in terms of democracy, the rule of law and respect for human rights. In February 1998 Mansur Rajih, who had been adopted as a prisoner of conscience by several human rights organizations, was released after 15 years in prison under threat of execution.

At the end of March 1998 the year-long trial of 15 members of the separatist southern Yemeni leadership during the 1994 civil war finally came to an end. Five of the men, including the former Yemeni Vice-President, Ali Salim al-Baid, and former Prime Minister Haidar al-Attas, were condemned to death, three, including Abd ar-Rahman al-Jifri, were sentenced to 10 years in prison, five received suspended sentences and two were acquitted. All the accused, who fled abroad after the southern secessionists were defeated by northern forces, were tried *in absentia* and it was thought unlikely that they would be extradited. In April it was reported that more than 2,000 people had demonstrated in the southern town of Mukalla in protest at the death sentences and that three people had been killed and several injured. There were further bomb explosions in Aden at the end of May and violent clashes between demonstrators and police in the southern province of Abyan. Kidnapping of foreigners by tribesmen continued; there were 21 actual kidnappings in 1997 and six attempts and 16 kidnappings in the early part of 1998, and little prospect of those involved being arrested. In April 1998 President Saleh instructed the Consultative Council to find a way of ending the practice, and later instructed the Council to form a permanent committee to study the issue of vengeance-related violence in Yemeni society. In June three British journalists were arrested for filming illegally in Yemen and were only released following diplomatic exchanges. The Government claimed that the murder of a group of nuns in July was the work of 'deranged extremists'. In August a decree was issued whereby the maximum legal penalty imposable on conviction of kidnapping was increased to death.

In late March 1998 the Prime Minister, Faraj Said bin Ghanim, left for Switzerland, ostensibly for medical treatment, but on his return to Yemen in late April he resigned from the premiership, after only eleven months in office. He stated that corruption and incompetence among his ministers had prompted his resignation. Bin Ghanim subsequently became head of the Consultative Council. The President appointed the Minister of Foreign Affairs, Abd al-Karim al-Iryani, to head a provisional administration, and in mid-May al-Iryani was confirmed in the post when a new Government was announced. There were three new appointees to the enlarged Council of Ministers, but apart from bin Ghanim only one minister, an independent, departed. The most significant change was the promotion of Abd al-Qadir Bajammal, the former Minister of Planning and Development, to the post of Deputy Prime Minister and Minister of Foreign Affairs. Presenting the new Government's programme to parliament on 1 June, al-Iryani pledged to continue wider-ranging reforms to tackle the country's economic problems and to begin implementing comprehensive administrative, employment and legal reforms. The Government also indicated that it would proceed with efforts to settle the long-standing border dispute with Saudi Arabia (see below). On 7 June the new Government won a vote of confidence from parliament on its policy programme, with 226 members voting in favour, 17 against and 26 abstentions.

The Government's decision, in mid-June 1998, to increase prices of fuel and some basic foodstuffs by up to 40% with immediate effect led to a week of riots and demonstrations in the capital and several other towns, including Taiz, Dhammar, Ibb and Marib. Official sources stated that some 34 people had been killed and 102 injured in the violence, but opposition sources abroad claimed that up to 100 people had died in the unrest. Some 21 soldiers were reported to have been killed on 26 June when the security forces tried to reopen the road from Marib to San'a which had been blocked by tribesmen; an estimated 20-30 tribesmen were reported to have died in the clashes around Marib. On 29 June Hunt Oil stated that its oil pipeline from Marib to the Red Sea had been punctured by bullets fired by protesters, but was still operational. The southern provinces were reported to have been relatively quiet, but there was a large peaceful demonstration at Mukalla on 30 June urging the President to reverse the price rises. A group of five opposition parties issued a statement blaming the Government for the rioting and urging it to reverse its 'wrong policies' because they were impoverishing the people. Al-Iryani, however, told parliament that the price rises would not be cancelled, but that fuel prices would not be increased again for another four years. Officials accused members of the YIP of direct involvement in the disturbances. (The YIP had announced its intention to bring down the al-Iryani Government.) By the end of June the security forces appeared to have brought the disturbances in the towns under control, but in early July there were reports that tribesmen had seriously damaged the oil pipeline from Marib to the Red Sea. According to the *Yemen Times*, the cost of repairs would exceed US $1m., although both the Government and Hunt Oil played down the seriousness of the incident. At the same time at least two explosions were reported in Aden. By the end of the year there had been 17 separate attacks on the Marib oil pipeline since June, and the Government responded by forming a committee charged with protecting oil installations. A Yemeni source reported that in mid-November an attempt was made to assassinate President Saleh in ad-Dali. Four local men disguised as soldiers are alleged to have attempted to attack the President's motorcade, but their equipment failed. A later report accused an exiled opposition group based in London, United Kingdom, of planning the attack. At the end of November the YSP held its first congress for over a decade, at which the secretary-general, Ali Said Obad, accused the Government of a campaign of harassment and intimidation. He reaffirmed that his party was committed to reconciliation and national unity. Earlier in the month President Saleh had denounced the YSP for having a policy of 'conspiracy and liquidation', and had criticized the opposition parties in general for failing to respond to the Government's efforts to foster multi-party democracy.

At the end of December 1998 the spate of kidnappings took a more serious and tragic turn when 16 Western tourists were taken hostage in the southern province of Abyan and four of the hostages (three Britons and an Australian) were killed during a rescue operation by the security forces. In this incident, the tourists had not been kidnapped by tribesmen but by the so-called 'Islamic Army of Aden-Abyan', a small faction of the Yemeni Islamist group, Islamic Jihad, whose commander, Zain al-Abdin al-Mihdar (alias Abu Hassan), was captured during the rescue attempt along with two of his accomplices. Islamic Jihad has a number of international connections dating back to the war in Afghanistan, including Osama bin Laden (see the chapter on Saudi Arabia), and operates a military training camp in the mountains of southern Yemen, which the Yemeni authorities have been trying to close for some time. Much uncertainty surrounded precisely who killed the four tourists. The kidnappers had used them as 'human shields', but it was unclear whether the security forces had only opened fire after the kidnappers had begun killing the hostages or whether they had been hit in crossfire between the kidnappers and the security forces during the rescue attempt. The actions of the security forces were heavily criticized in the British media. Abu Hassan later admitted in court that he had given instructions to kill male hostages if the security forces opened fire, but two of the hostages who died were women. The incident sparked a diplomatic row between Britain and Yemen, with British officials accusing the Yemeni authorities of ignoring their advice to seek a negotiated end to the kidnapping (see below). The motive

for the kidnapping was also unclear. It was suggested that it may have been a reprisal for the US-British air strikes against Iraq earlier in December. It was reported that the kidnappers sought the release of Sheikh Salih Haidara al-Atawi, the leader of Islamic Jihad, who had been arrested in mid-December following clashes between Jihad militants and the security forces. It was also claimed that the kidnapping was linked to an extremist Islamist group based in London known as 'Supporters of the *Shari'a*' and led by an Egyptian, Abu Hamza al-Masri (see below). After the incident, the Islamic Army of Aden called for the overthrow of the Government and its replacement by a broad-based administration including ulema, tribal chiefs and notables. In May 1999 a court in Zinjibar sentenced the three kidnappers to death, but the men immediately appealed against their sentences. Having adopted a tough stance against hostage-taking, some observers felt that the Government's authority would be undermined if the executions were not carried out. This was the first kidnapping for many years in which hostages had died. However, there were also fears of reprisals from the men's tribal and religious supporters if they were executed. The Islamic Army had already threatened to assassinate the Minister of the Interior. Furthermore, the group's leader, Abu Hassan, was reported to have a number of high-level contacts, including the President's half-brother, Ali Muhsin al-Ahmar. It should also be remembered that the Government of San'a has its own links with Islamists living in the south, and persuaded many of them to assist its forces in suppressing the southern secessionists during the 1994 civil war. They may have been made promises which the Government then failed to honour.

A few days before the kidnapping in Abyan, the Yemeni authorities had arrested five young British Muslims and an Algerian (who had been living in Britain) in connection with an alleged plot to bomb the British consulate and a British-built church in Aden. The authorities claimed that the men were members of a London-based extremist Islamist group, 'Supporters of the *Shari'a*', and had been sent to Yemen by the group's leader, Abu Hamza al-Masri, a veteran of the Afghan war, to take part in a terrorist campaign there. The families of the men, however, insisted that they were in Yemen simply to learn Arabic. Abu Hamza's group was reported to have had links with the Islamic Army of Aden-Abyan for some time, and in October 1998 the group had issued a communiqué in Arabic on behalf of the Islamic Army, warning 'unbelievers' to leave the Arabian Peninsula. It later emerged that one of the British Muslims arrested was the stepson of Abu Hamza. The Yemeni authorities claimed that the London-based group was implicated in both the alleged bomb plot in Aden and the kidnappings in Abyan. Abu Hamza admitted that he had had a telephone conversation with the leader of the Islamic Army during the Abyan kidnapping, and some maintained that the Western tourists had been taken hostage in order to secure the release of those arrested for the alleged Aden bomb plot. At a press conference in London on 20 January 1999 Abu Hamza called for the overthrow of the Yemen Government and warned non-Muslims against visiting Yemen on pain of death.

The six suspects went on trial in Aden at the end of January 1999, accused of membership of an armed group and of planning to commit acts of sabotage against Yemeni and foreign interests in Aden. The men all denied the charges and retracted their confessions, declaring that they had been obtained under torture. Meanwhile Abu Hamza's teenage son, Mustafa Kamil, was arrested in Abyan along with two Britons, an Algerian and two members of the Islamic Army implicated in the kidnapping of the Western tourists. Kamil was reported to have 'confessed' that he had been encouraged by his father to undertake *jihad* (holy war) and had arrived in Yemen to join the Islamic Army. Kamil, the two Britons and the Algerian were put on trial in Aden together with the original six suspects. At the end of February one of the British lawyers involved in their defence was arrested and then expelled from Yemen. He claimed that he had been beaten and threatened by the security forces. In mid-March British police arrested Abu Hamza in London for questioning, but released him three days later. Abu Hamza had earlier issued a new threat on behalf of the Islamic Army, warning the British and US ambassadors to leave Yemen. In April the judge in the Aden trial agreed to an independent medical examination of the defendants, after the defence insisted that their confessions had been obtained under torture. The medical team concluded that the defendants had not been tortured, but their findings were contested by the defence. In August the court in Aden found the 10 defendants guilty as charged; seven were sentenced to terms of imprisonment of three to seven years, while the other three were given shorter sentences which they were regarded as having already served while awaiting trial. The men appealed against their convictions and in response the prosecution also lodged an appeal arguing that the sentences imposed by the judge had been too lenient. The appeal court rejected both appeals in September, and the judge ordered that two of the three men who had already served their sentences but were still in prison at that time should be released and allowed to leave the country, along with the third man who had been released earlier on medical grounds. All three were subsequently allowed to return to the United Kingdom. In April 2000 Yemen's Supreme Court upheld the prison sentences imposed on the remaining five Britons in 1999. Their families insisted that they would continue the campaign to secure the men's release, and there was some speculation that all five Britons would not serve the full sentences and would be repatriated. The Yemeni authorities continued to accuse Abu Hamza of being the main instigator of recent terrorist operations in Yemen, and to condemn the United Kingdom for refusing to extradite him to Yemen. The United Kingdom, however, insisted that after investigating Abu Hamza's activities it had no grounds for deporting him. In October 1999, after two unsuccessful appeals, Abu Hassan was executed. His two accomplices later had their sentences commuted to life imprisonment. There were reports that the Government had come under strong pressure, notably from the YIP leader, Sheikh Abdullah bin Hussein al-Ahmar, to take decisive action against the kidnappers. After the arrest at the end of October of two men alleged to be the new leaders of the Islamic Army of Aden-Abyan, the authorities claimed that the group now consisted of only small, low-level units which were under close surveillance by the security forces. In response to Abu Hassan's execution the group had threatened to strike against Western interests in Yemen. Meanwhile the Government announced the creation of a separate court to try kidnappers and those involved in acts of sabotage against oil pipelines.

Nevertheless, the kidnapping of foreigners by tribesmen continued. After the Abyan incident, the Yemen authorities had given assurances to their Governments that force would not be used to secure hostages' release. In July 1999 two French nationals, four Belgian and a Canadian oil worker were kidnapped by tribesmen in separate incidents, but later released unharmed after mediation by government officials.

In April 1999, after a number of YSP members were attacked in Dali in the south, the party accused the Government's security forces of responsibility and also blamed the Government for the car crash the same month in which a member of the YSP's political bureau, Abdallah Majid Ali, was killed. In June two people were killed and another four injured when a bomb exploded in central Aden, and in August a car bomb killed another two people in the city. The same month a grenade thrown in a busy market place in San'a killed seven people. The authorities denied that these violent incidents were politically motivated—the Islamic Army of Aden-Abyan had claimed responsibility for at least one of the attacks. Nevertheless in June the security forces had arrested 16 people alleged to be members of the Islamic Army, and it was claimed that they were found in possession of firearms and explosives. Later the authorities stated that the men had links with the London-based 'Supporters of the Shari'a' and were planning a campaign of assassinations and acts of sabotage in Yemen.

THE 1999 PRESIDENTIAL ELECTION

In July 1999 parliament approved only two candidates to contest Yemen's first direct presidential election, scheduled for September. Under the Constitution, candidates were required to gain the support of 10% of the 301-member parliament. Out of 253 votes cast, the incumbent President Saleh, who had the backing of the ruling GPC and the YIP, which together control most of the seats in parliament, secured 182 votes. Najib Qahtan ash-Shaabi, the son of the first President of South Yemen, who although a member of the GPC was standing as an independent,

also qualified with 39 votes. Another independent, Khalid az-Zarraka, who took 25 votes, and Ali Saleh Obad, the YSP leader, with only seven votes, failed to qualify. The YSP has no parliamentary presence, having boycotted the 1997 parliamentary elections, but Obad's nomination had been supported by all the main opposition parties. In response to the exclusion of Obad, the YSP and the other opposition parties questioned whether an election in which both candidates were members of the same party could be considered constitutional—the Constitution specifies that presidential elections must be 'competitive'—adding 'we have one candidate competing with this shadow'. Shaabi, who has been a member of parliament since 1992, told a press conference that, if he won the election, he would combat all the evils of Yemeni society, including the chewing of qat and blood feuds, and also promised to promote full political and social rights for women.

As expected, Ali Abdullah Saleh won 96.3% of the votes cast in the election, held on 23 September, in which some two-thirds of the eligible voters participated according to official figures. Abd al-Qadir Bajammal, the deputy premier and Minister of Foreign Affairs, described the opposition's decision to boycott the election as 'undemocratic' and claimed that some YSP members in the Hadramawt had defied the party's leadership and taken part in the election. He went on to warn the YSP that it faced extinction if the party boycotted parliamentary elections scheduled for 2001. After being sworn in for the five-year term as President, Saleh gave an address to parliament in which he spoke out against nepotism and corruption in public life. Shortly afterwards he appointed his eldest son, Ahmed, as commander of a newly-formed élite special forces unit charged with combating terrorism and with responsibility for dealing with kidnappings. Later Ahmed, a GPC member of parliament, was appointed head of the Republican Guard, encouraging speculation that the President was preparing to make him heir apparent. Although President Saleh denied this, he stated that his son might wish to become a presidential candidate. In late November, President Saleh again condemned corruption and mismanagement within the country's bureaucracy, and according to some reports was particularly critical of the Ministry of Foreign Affairs. At a special cabinet meeting in December the President reproached ministers for failing to press ahead with economic reforms, especially the establishment of more efficient measures to raise revenues.

At the end of January 2000, parliament finally approved a bill setting out the structure and powers of local and regional government. The new law established district and governorate councils, with governors and district managers appointed by the President while their deputies will be elected. No date was set for local elections, although the Minister for Parliamentary and Legal Affairs indicated that they would be held at the same time as the new parliamentary elections, and it was unclear whether or not the new local councils would be given any financial authority. The opposition had called for all local officials to be elected and for local councils to be given extensive tax-raising powers. It seemed unlikely, however, that the Government would agree to devolve substantive powers to the new local councils, especially those in the south. Meanwhile, it was reported that the Government was considering enlarging the Consultative Council from 59 to 101 members, including some women, and extending the current four-year legislative term to six years.

The central Government remained incapable of imposing its authority and the rule of law over many parts of the country. The kidnapping of Westerners by tribesmen seeking to extract concessions from the Government continued, despite the imposition of the death penalty for the offence. Official sources first blamed 'foreign hands' for the kidnappings, usually a reference to Saudi Arabia, but later accused the YIP of being behind the abduction of an American oil worker. In March 2000 Qiyari tribesmen abducted the Polish ambassador in San'a, apparently in retaliation for the arrest the previous day of Sheikh Khaled al-Qiyari on security grounds. The authorities again claimed that 'foreign hands' were behind recent kidnappings in order to destabilize Yemen. The following day a Dutch development worker and his Yemeni colleague were killed in their office in the capital. In June a Norwegian diplomat and his son were kidnapped by northern tribesmen, and during a police operation to rescue them the diplomat was killed in the cross-fire. Later that month an Italian archaeologist was taken hostage by northern tribesmen demanding the release from prison of one of their kinsmen. The archaeologist was later released unharmed. There were reports that the Government was taking a tough stance on kidnapping, imposing long prison sentences and in some cases the death sentence on those convicted of the offence; in early September, for example, Yemeni television announced that 10 people had been sentenced to death for kidnapping and murder. Nevertheless, incidents involving the kidnapping of foreigners continued. At the end of November a Swedish national was taken hostage near Marib by northern tribesmen. The man was released after more than two weeks amid speculation that the authorities had given in to their demands for a ransom and immunity from prosecution in order to avoid an armed rescue operation. In January 2001 a German engineer working with the oil company Preussag was abducted but released unharmed several days later after negotiations between the tribesmen and the authorities. Later that month there were reports that two Italian women had been kidnapped near Marib but released unharmed after a few hours.

In February 2000 there were reports of rioting in Dali governorate near Aden, where support for the YSP is traditionally strong, and several explosions in Dali city. The security forces made numerous arrests. In the same month several Jihad militants were arrested in Shabwah governorate after violent clashes with the security forces. Later there were further clashes between security forces and the opposition in Dali province, where government buildings were attacked and several soldiers killed. In March the opposition claimed that 5,000 people had taken part in a 'silent march' in Dali organized to secure the release of two YSP activists detained by the security forces. It was one of a number of demonstrations held there to protest against the repressive measures of the central Government in San'a. In April the authorities closed down the YSP's provincial headquarters in Dali, and reports in *Ash-Sharq al-Awsat* suggested that 50–100 YSP activists were arrested. In late May celebrations in Aden to mark the 10th anniversary of unification were deliberately low-key, and the two-day festivities in the southern capital were only attended by the Vice-President, Abd ar-Rabbuh Mansur Hadi. In January 2001 there were five small explosions in Aden. A church in the At-Tawahi area and the offices of the official news agency SABA were among the targets. The authorities claimed that the Islamic Army of Aden-Abyan was responsible for these attacks and were reported to have made several arrests. The violence was not restricted to the southern provinces. In August the deputy assistant governor of San'a was assassinated by armed men; some claimed that Islamists were responsible, others attributed the murder to feuding tribesmen. In January, meanwhile, there were reports that a bomb had been found at the home of the Minister of the Interior, Hussain Muhammad Arab.

At the end of August 2000 the YSP held its party congress in San'a. Ali Saleh Obad was re-elected party leader, and the congress elected a new central committee which included several YSP members living in exile, notably Ali Salim al-Baid who led the southern secessionists during the 1994 civil war and was later sentenced to death *in absentia* (see above). Delegates supported the border agreement with Saudi Arabia, but denounced the constitutional changes proposed by President Saleh (see below). In response to the election of al-Baid and other exiled members to the central committee, in September the Government threatened to ban the YSP. During the following months the authorities continued to threaten the party with dissolution, but no action was taken: banning the YSP would have alienated international donors and provoked further unrest in the southern provinces. Nevertheless intimidation of the YSP by the security services continued. In January 2001 an explosion that badly damaged the YSP's headquarters in Shaab, in Dali governorate, was believed by many to be the work of the Political Security Organization.

NEW CONSTITUTIONAL CHANGES

At the end of November 2000, afer two months of debate, the House of Representatives ratified several important amendments to the Constitution. The amendments, proposed by President Saleh, included extending the parliamentary term from four to six years and the presidential term from five to seven years, increasing the size of the Consultative Council from 59 members to 111, and strengthening the powers of the executive. Under the new measures the President would be empowered to dissolve the legislature and call new elections within 60 days (hitherto, a national referendum had been required to approve the reasons for the dissolution); the role of the House of Representatives was reduced to one of 'monitoring' the executive, rather than 'directing and monitoring' it; and large parts of the Constitution could henceforth be changed without prior approval by national referendum. In addition, the amended constitution required presidential candidates to obtain the endorsement of 5% of a combined vote of the appointed Consultative Council and the elected House of Representatives (in place of 10% of the latter chamber alone). Legislative elections due in April 2001 were postponed until 2003, although in a speech in late May 2000 to commemorate the 10th anniversary of unification Saleh had promised that they would proceed as scheduled. The President justified extending the term of parliament on the grounds that this would save money; he also suggested that the expanded Consultative Council would be more democratic as a result of the addition of economists and other technocrats. The Supreme Opposition Council—a coalition of opposition parties including the YSP, al-Haq, the Nasserite Unionist Popular Organization and the Arab Socialist Baath Party—condemned the changes as anti-democratic because they increased the powers of the President and executive. In their view, extending the life of parliament would prevent them from participating in the legislature for another two years, during which time the GPC would retain its dominant position. Critics of the Government argued that an extended Consultative Council could hardly be more democratic since the President would continue to appoint all its members, and expressed concern that the powers of the Council had been increased at the expense of the elected legislature. They pointed out that the new rules governing presidential elections would in practice make it more difficult for opposition candidates to stand, as they would now have to obtain approval from the Consultative Council appointed by the President as well as the House of Representatives. Some analysts interpreted the extension of the president's term of office as yet another indication that President Saleh intended to establish a 'royal' presidency. Most YIP members of parliament were also unhappy with the amendments but they nevertheless voted in favour of the proposed changes, suggesting that the party's leadership had come to an arrangement with the Government and its members had been persuaded to vote accordingly. In late December President Saleh announced that the constitutional amendments would be put to a referendum on 20 February 2001 (as required under the existing Constitution), at the same time as local elections (see below).

The official results of the referendum revealed that 77.5% of valid votes were in favour of the constitutional revisions: The amendments were required to secure more than 50% of the vote in order to become law: thus despite substantial opposition this was a favourable result for the Government. Both the YIP and the YSP had urged their supporters to vote against the changes. Before the poll rumours circulated that the Government had put pressure on civil servants to vote in favour of the amendments. Turn-out by voters was, however, very low with only 2.6m. Yemenis casting valid votes.

LOCAL ELECTIONS

At the end of December 2000 President Saleh announced that the long-delayed local elections would take place on February 20, 2001 (at the same time as the referendum on the constitutional amendments). Local elections had been promised since unification in 1990 as the final stage in the construction of a democratic framework, and under existing legislation should have been held at the same time as parliamentary elections. Some commentators suggested that the Government decided to proceed with local elections rather than wait until April 2003 (the new date scheduled for parliamentary elections) to provide an additional incentive for its supporters to turn out in large numbers and vote in the referendum on constitutional changes, and thus persuade Western critics of its commitment to democratic principles. In practice, these same critics considered that the local elections would do little to advance the democratic process as only councillors at district and governorate levels were to be elected, with senior local government officials continuing to be appointed by the Government. Furthermore, successful candidates would only serve for two years as new local elections were scheduled for April 2003 (in tandem with the delayed legislative elections). The opposition parties of the Supreme Opposition Council, which had all been weakened by their decision to boycott the 1997 parliamentary elections, declared that they would participate in the local elections. The YSP nevertheless described them as 'basically ornamental'. Initially the YIP declared that it would only take part if voter lists were amended; however, in January the party announced that it would participate after the personal intervention of President Saleh, who attended one of its meetings and urged the party not to boycott the poll.

Polling was (as many had predicted) marred by more than 100 violent incidents, and some reports suggested that at least 45 people died on the day of the poll and during the subsequent counting of votes. An independent and a Nasserite Unionist candidate in al-Bayda and a YIP candidate in Ibb were among those killed. Reports suggested that many of the incidents involved rival supporters of the ruling GPC and the YIP, and arose from complaints of irregularities and malpractice. The YIP accused the GPC of gaining unfair advantage by using the official media, the army and public funds to boost its campaign, while for its part the GPC accused the YIP—which had campaigned extensively through the mosques—of 'terrorism'. Earlier the independent National Democratic Institute (NDI), a non-governmental organization based in the USA, had criticized the Government for restricting access by opposition parties to the media, especially television and radio. The *Yemen Times* reported that during the count at Marib the army had been confronted by heavily-armed tribesmen and YIP supporters after soldiers attempted to remove a number of ballot boxes when it became clear that the YIP was in the lead. Voting was unable to proceed or had to be suspended at some 200 polling stations because of violent incidents or because of organizational problems such as failure to deliver ballot boxes or incorrect ballot papers. Some of the problems experienced may have resulted from the fact that the Supreme Elections Committee (SEC) had been given only three months to prepare for a poll that involved 26,000 candidates competing for 7,000 seats, requiring a far greater organizational effort than the last parliamentary election. In a report published in August 2000 the NDI had advised the Government to postpone local elections (then scheduled for April 2001) because it did not believe that the SEC would have sufficient time to make the necessary arrangments for polling to be 'credible'. The NDI considered that SEC officials did not have adequate demographic data to draw boundaries for local councils and that the voter registration system was seriously flawed and in need of major revisions. The NDI criticized the Government for failing to advance the democratic process and of not doing enough to encourage women to participate in the electoral process. Other sources accused the SEC of managing the poll to give unfair advantage to the GPC. It was expected that the final results of the local elections would not be known for some time. Soon after voting had come to an end, however, the SEC announced preliminary results, indicating that the GPC had won 62% of seats, followed by the YIP, which had taken 22%, with the remainder of the seats going to the YSP and independents. The GPC's share of the vote was about the same as in the 1997 legislative elections, with the YIP's share increasing slightly from 18%. In contrast, the YSP did not appear to have performed well—with poor results even in its traditional stronghold of Aden. It was suggested that many southerners had become disillusioned with a party whose policies no longer seemed relevant to their needs and whose leadership was seen as divided and incompetent. The army newspaper, *26 September*, described the elections as 'an expression of a better future' and 'a luminous spot on the road of national gains'. For its part, the *Yemen Times* commented that despite more than a decade of experience with democracy and political pluralism 'we have not got any closer to really allowing the Yemeni people to decide freely and objectively what is right for the future of the country'. At the end of March some 10,000 protesters, most of them YIP supporters, surrounded the

SEC's offices in San'a. The YIP claimed that its candidates had won seats in Arhab, Khawlan, al-Jubahin and as-Salafiya, but that these seats had been fraudulently awarded to the GPC. Many results remained in dispute. All the opposition parties declared that they would reject the final official results of the local elections, and demanded that a new round of voting should be held. The SEC, however, refused to consider holding new elections.

In April 2001 President Saleh replaced Abd al-Karim al-Iryani as Prime Minister by Abd al-Qadir Bajammal, hitherto Deputy Prime Minister and Minister of Foreign Affairs. There had been rumours that relations between al-Iryani and President Saleh had become increasingly strained, particularly over the constitutional amendments. Al-Iryani was also known to be in poor health, and disillusioned after his efforts to introduce economic reforms had met with strong opposition both within the Government and in the legislature. Bajammal, a southerner from Hadramawt and a former government minister in the PDRY, had joined the GPC after unification. Shortly after his appointment the new premier dismissed some 17 ministers in a major cabinet reorganization. The enlarged Council of Ministers included 22 newcomers—among them Yemen's first female minister, Prof. Wahiba Fare'e, rector of Queen Arwa University, who was appointed to the new post of Minister of State for Human Rights. Southerners were appointed to the key ministries of Defence, Oil and Transport. The new Minister of Finance, Alawi Salih as-Salami (a respected figure in international financial circles), was also appointed Deputy Prime Minister. Ahmad Muhammad Sufan, who retained the planning and development portfolio, and Ahmad Abd ar-Rahman as-Samawi, who remained Governor of the Central Bank, were also regarded as experienced and capable reformers. President Saleh called on the new Government to act to curb corruption and fulfil the people's aspirations in education, development and industry. The official media praised the new appointments as a sign of 'change and modernization', but some critics insisted that the new ministers were too inexperienced while others described the changes as merely cosmetic. At the end of April President Saleh appointed the new Consultative Council. Among the new appointees were 11 ministers from the outgoing al-Iryani administration and several members of opposition parties. For the first time the new council included three female members. In the past the council had mainly been composed of technocrats, and the appointment of a significant number of political figures appeared to confirm its politicization.

The new Government's programme included a controversial measure to incorporate religious institutes (estimated to number some 400, with 250,000 students) into the state education system. These institutes, basically Koranic schools, developed in North Yemen in the 1970s primarily to counteract the spread of Marxist ideas from the PDRY, but by the 1990s had come to be widely regarded as a vehicle for YIP propaganda and recruitment. Following unification in 1992 legislation was adopted to integrate the institutes into the state education system, but the law was never implemented because at that time the GPC regarded the YIP as a useful ally against the YSP. Some commentators suggested that the decision of the Bajammal Government to implement the law was related to the fact that during the February 2001 local elections the YIP had presented a serious challenge to the GPC and had accused the ruling party of malpractice (see above). After a fierce gun battle in early July resulted in the deaths of 11 soldiers investigating the bombing of the main Marib—Red Sea oil pipeline, the GPC issued a statement claiming that 'YIP mercenaries' had perpetrated the attack on the pipeline and ambushed the soldiers in an effort to persuade the Government not to bring the religious institutes under its control. The YIP rejected these allegations, insisting that GPC members had carried out the attack in order to 'spread sedition'. In early August the YIP and six other opposition parties announced that they were suspending all dialogue with the Government on amendments to the new electoral law, in protest against the Government's decision to raise fuel prices by 70%. In mid-July President Saleh was flown to a clinic in Germany and remained there for several days before returning to Yemen. Although officials stated that the President had merely been undergoing a routine health assessment, there was some speculation as to his level of fitness and about who would succeed him in the event of his incapacity or death (there being no obvious candidate as his son, Ahmed, was considered to be too young and inexperienced).

A new series of abductions of foreign nationals by tribesmen began in May 2001 when a Bulgarian doctor was kidnapped from a hospital in al-Bayda governorate. At the end of the month a German student was abducted in San'a but was later released when police mounted an assault on the premises where he was being detained. In the past Western governments have been highly critical of such actions being undertaken by the security forces because of the danger they present to the lives of the hostages. At the end of September a German diplomat who had been kidnapped in San'a in late July was finally released. Although it was at first believed that Islamic Jihad had been responsible for the abduction, this was subsequently denied by the group's leader, and it later emerged that members of the Jahm tribe from the Marib area had carried out the kidnapping. Also in September a member of the Nihm tribe (also from the Marib area) kidnapped a Chinese national from San'a; the hostage was released some weeks later after negotiations with the security forces. At the same time inter-tribal conflicts intensified; in August some 25 tribesmen were killed in a feud between the Wadiah and al-Oseimat tribes near San'a, and in October a land dispute between two tribes in Marib and Hajjah governorates claimed 16 lives.

GOVERNMENT GROWS MORE INTOLERANT OF OPPOSITION

The final results of the February 2001 local elections were never published, a strong indication that opposition parties, notably the YIP, had performed well. In the months following the election the YIP had become increasingly outspoken in its criticsm of the Government, and in July tensions were exacerbated when *As-Sahwa*, the YIP's weekly newspaper, claimed that the GPC was making efforts to forge closer ties with Israel. At the end of July the Prime Minister announced that the Government was going to abolish some three-quarters of the 400 local councils only five months after the local elections, claiming that most of the newly elected councillors lacked the education and management skills to run the councils efficiently. Outside observers had warned that high levels of illiteracy in Yemen represented a serious constraint on the introduction of local councils. Nevertheless, the move suggested government disquiet at the level of control exercised by opposition parties over many of the councils. Prime Minister Bajammal also rejected demands from the opposition that the heads of local and provincial councils should be elected rather than appointed by the Government. Changes to the composition of the seven-member Supreme Elections Committee (SEC), established in 1993 to oversee elections and referendums, were also announced. Under the terms of a new electoral law approved by parliament later in the year, all seven members of the SEC, who had previously been appointed by the President from a list of candidates approved by at least two-thirds of deputies, henceforth were to be appointed directly by the President. Shortly afterwards, President Saleh appointed a new committee in which four members were from the ruling GPC, with one member from each of the YIP, YSP and the Nasserite Unionist Popular Organization. At first the YIP threatened to boycott the new committee but withdrew the threat when the President indicated that he would simply replace the YIP candidate with a member of his own party. In November the Government finally began implementing the 1992 legislation bringing 'independent' religious institutes under the control of the Ministry of Education (see above). In the following months some religious institutes were closed down and their foreign students deported. In January 2002 the private al-Iman University run by Sheikh Abd al-Majid az-Zindani, the Chairman of the YIP's Shura Council, was also briefly closed down. Sheikh az-Zindani, notorious for his fierce anti-Western and anti-Jewish rhetoric, was reported to have assumed a low public profile in late 2001, as his University was regarded by many as an academic centre of Islamist extremism where a culture of intolerance was promoted. In the aftermath of the 11 September 2001 terrorist attacks on the US mainland, the Government maintained that the closures were part of the ongoing 'war against terror' (see below). By February 2002 it was reported

that some 600 foreign students enrolled in religious institutes had been deported.

Traditional animosities between natives of the north and south were again highlighted in December 2001 when a number of former ministers and intellectuals, including former Minister of the Interior, Hussain Muhammad Arab, announced the establishment of a forum to defend the rights of citizens of the former PDRY. They denounced alleged discrimination practised by the central Government against southerners after the civil war in 1994, and were particularly incensed at the Government's dismissal of thousands of southern civil servants and military personnel under its reforms of the civil service. These tensions were reported to have strained relations between President Saleh and his southern Vice-President, Abd ar-Rabbuh Mansur Hadi. In an attempt to assuage feelings of resentment in the south, the Government encouraged exiled southerners to return to Yemen, and indicated that it might consider an amnesty for the five southern secessionist leaders condemned to death in *absentia* in 1998 (see above). President Saleh personally supervised the return from exile of a prominent southerner, Salem Saleh Muhammad. On his return Salem Saleh made a statement recognizing the current leadership of the YSP, and at a meeting of the party's central committee in April 2002 he was appointed to the YSP's political bureau. Some commentators suggested that Salem Saleh might be considered a good candidate to become YSP leader since he appeared to be acceptable to the authorities. However, in an interview in mid-May with the London-based *Ash-Sharq al-Awsat*, the YSP's Secretary-General, Ali Saleh Obad, stated that this view was being promoted by the authorities and not by the party. Obad also declared that at the recent meeting of the central committee the party had reiterated its demand for the return of those secessionists condemned *in absentia* after the 1994 civil war, including former Vice-President, Ali Salim al-Baid, who remained a member of the YSP's central committee. The YSP maintained that it did not recognize the verdicts against the secessionists and encouraged them to return to Yemen, even if they were to be imprisoned as a result. Obad rejected any suggestion of an alliance with the GPC at the next elections and declared that his party would remain in opposition. Obad also expressed the opinion that if and when parliamentary elections were held, they were unlikely to be conducted in a free and fair fashion. Following the central committee meeting the YSP renewed its call for national reconciliation, and criticized US-Yemeni ties, accusing the Government of disseminating false information about security co-operation 'to avoid speaking frankly to the Yemeni masses'. In mid-June the YSP called for the sentences against those secessionists condemned *in absentia* in 1998 to be revoked, for a general amnesty to be granted to all persons punished for political reasons related to past conflicts, and for the return of all those forced into exile for political reasons.

In February 2002 it was reported that the Ministry of the Interior had closed down *Ash-Shoma'a*, an independent weekly, following a dispute with the editor-in-chief, who had written articles accusing senior government officials of corruption. Some time before six journalists working on the weekly had been arrested, but they were later released on instructions from President Saleh. In May three Yemeni journalists working for *Ath-Thawri*, the YSP's weekly publication, were arrested after writing a series of articles criticizing government policies and calling for equality for all citizens. They were accused of 'encouraging confessional, regional and secessionist sentiments, criticizing the President and inciting the public against the ruling regime'; they were sentenced to five months' imprisonment in early June, but in July a court of appeal ordered their release subject to guarantees that they would appear at future hearings.

In early March 2002 four people were killed in clashes between rival tribal clans in Ibb governorate provoked by disputes over water rights. Soon after, further clan fighting left 11 people dead and 32 injured. In an interview with *The Yemen Times* in mid-June Sheikh Yahya al-Ukaymi, a pre-eminent native of the al-Jawf region, rejected allegations that the tribal areas were a 'breeding ground' for terrorism, although he acknowledged that elements of terrorist groups such as al-Qa'ida might take advantage of the poverty and chaos that characterized these areas. Al-Ukaymi denied that his tribe was sheltering al-Qa'ida suspects, claiming it was attempting to locate al-Qa'ida supporters and bring them to justice. In early July London-based Arabic press sources reported that a military helicopter had been fired on by tribesmen in the al-Jawf region, slightly injuring a senior military officer, Brig. Ali Muhammad Saleh, Deputy Chief-of-Staff and head of the Security Committee of the SEC. The officers on board had been visiting military units stationed in the al-Jawf governorate and border areas. According to local sources, tribesmen had opened fire because they feared that the helicopter was about to fire on their villages. Some weeks before President Saleh had named al-Jawf as one of three governorates where the authorities had declared a state of high alert to prevent possible terrorist attacks, and the security forces had targeted a number of local tribes believed to be sheltering suspected al-Qa'ida members (see below). The attack on the helicopter occurred shortly after the most prominent tribal leader in al-Jawf governorate, Sheikh Amin al-Ukaymi, a member of the YIP and commander of al-Jawf's border guard, had been detained briefly by military police in San'a when he and his companions refused to surrender their weapons. (In early February the Council of Ministers had banned the carrying of weapons in public in San'a and other major cities for all but official security purposes.) The Minister of Defence was charged with investigating the helicopter incident, and a military team demanded the immediate surrender of those responsible. Meanwhile, several tribal leaders from al-Jawf were attempting to act as mediators to reduce tensions between local tribes and the armed forces.

Ongoing disputes between the Government and opposition were characterized by claims and counter-claims of corruption. In late March 2002, opposition parties launched a media campaign accusing Prime Minister Bajammal of presiding over a network of corruption within government agencies. In his defence the Prime Minister declared that he was aware of corruption in government institutions and was determined to eradicate it by all possible means since it was discouraging foreign investment in Yemen. In mid-June, during the inauguration of the First Forum on Restructuring Civil Service Units, Prime Minister Bajammal, in turn, accused the opposition parties of corrupt practices, accusing some of their senior officials of offering and accepting financial inducements to and from foreign diplomats in Yemen. In mid-March, meanwhile, some 20 university students had been injured in clashes with the police in Hodeida following a dispute between the university authorities and the YIP-controlled students' union. Police were reported to have fired into the air in an effort to disperse the students and subsequently to have arrested some 15 of them.

In April 2002 an organization describing itself as the Sympathizers of al-Qa'ida claimed responsibility for a series of explosions targeting the offices of the secret police, the Political Security Organization (PSO), and the homes of some of its senior officials, although no one was injured. The organization later issued an ultimatum through the Yemeni media threatening further bomb attacks unless the authorities released 173 of their comrades whom they claimed were being detained by the PSO. In early May the organization claimed responsibility for an explosion close to the homes of the Prime Minister and of the deputy director of the PSO. President Saleh largely dismissed the threat posed by the organization and insisted that the small number of al-Qa'ida activists in Yemen were being carefully monitored by the security services. However, some local commentators argued that in their zeal to co-operate with the US authorities in the hunt for suspected supporters of al-Qa'ida, the authorities had ignored domestic political considerations and should reconsider their policies, especially the detention of suspects for long periods without trial. At the beginning of July a car bomb exploded outside the home in San'a of Brig. Fadhi al-Kawsee, the senior security official for Amran governorate.

At the end of May 2002 Prime Minister Bajammal confirmed that parliamentary elections would be held in 2003 and promised that they would not be complicated by the problems that had beset previous elections as the country had struggled to reach political and democratic maturity. In mid-June a spokesman for the SEC stated that the committee had completed work on the electoral division of the country and that new registration lists would be drawn up to replace the existing ones which, it had been claimed, contained many mistakes,

irregularities and forgeries. In addition the SEC warned that any party found to have provoked violence or to have endangered the election process in any constituency would incur the financial costs of conducting a fresh election in that constituency and would be banned from taking part. Every party was to be entitled to have a representative in every polling station, and all national and international organizations were to be allowed to supervise the electoral process. The opposition, however, declared that the new electoral districts had not been agreed by all of the country's political parties and had been drawn up to favour the GPC. In response, the SEC stated that it had taken into account the opinions of political parties as well as social figures and neutral persons and was confident that the new electoral map would satisfy the majority of people. In early August the opposition parties issued a communiqué stating that they were refusing to participate in the registration committees (created to monitor the enrolment process for forthcoming elections) because the SEC had decreed that representation on the committees would be determined by the proportion of votes obtained by parties at the 2001 local elections. This arrangement was, again, considered overly favourable to the ruling GPC.

In late June 2002 political security police in al-Dali arrested Sheikh Abdullah Sa'tar, a member of the YIP's higher committee. According to official sources, Sa'tar had not obtained permission to deliver political speeches in mosques and had been detained to prevent mosques from becoming 'arenas for political strife and centres for propagating the messages of the political parties'. Sa'tar was believed to have angered President Saleh by speaking out about state corruption and accusing the Government of responsibility for widespread poverty and unemployment in the country. Sa'tar insisted that he was a 'moderate' Islamist and that if people such as himself were prevented from criticizing the Government it would open the way for extremism and fanaticism. Sa'tar insisted that his detention undermined political pluralism and multi-party politics and democracy in Yemen. Sa'tar was promptly released after YIP leader Sheikh Abdullah al-Ahmar intervened on his behalf with President Saleh. Sheikh al-Ahmar declared that although he did not agree with the content of Sa'tar's rhetoric, his detention was unconstitutional and illegal. Meanwhile, the YIP leader called an extraordinary session of the party's higher committee to discuss what it regarded as exceptional illegal measures taken by the Government against its members and supporters in the months preceding the forthcoming parliamentary elections scheduled for 2003. In early August President Saleh issued a decree establishing a National Security Agency with responsibility for collecting and analyzing intelligence information on all 'hostile activities directed from abroad which constitute a threat to national security', and for proposing measures to confront them. The new agency was expected to co-operate with similar organizations in other countries.

FOREIGN RELATIONS AFTER THE CIVIL WAR

In the aftermath of the civil war President Saleh quickly embarked on a diplomatic offensive to isolate the secessionists and ensure that they could not regroup in neighbouring countries, most of which had supported the South during the two-month conflict. Oman and Djibouti promised the prompt return of military equipment brought there by the fleeing southern forces, and most states, including Egypt, expressed their support for a unified Yemen. Relations with Oman were strengthened further in June 1995 when the demarcation of the Yemeni–Omani border (initiated in 1992) was officially completed. Relations with Sudan also improved and Iran showed growing interest in Yemen and began providing some medical assistance. However, the arrival of militants from Algeria's banned Front islamique du salut (FIS), and later from the extremist Groupe islamique armé (GIA), provoked a strong protest from the Algerian Government and in January 1995 Algeria recalled its ambassador from San'a. The YIP was known to have provided military training and political indoctrination for Islamist militants from Algeria and also from Egypt, while declaring publicly that the party supported an end to violence in Algeria and dialogue leading to free, multi-party elections. The Yemeni Government strongly denied the existence of training camps for militant Islamists until 1995 when President Saleh, on a visit to Cairo, declared that his security forces had discovered a cell of the militant Egyptian group, Islamic Jihad, and offered to exchange members of the group for Yemeni separatists based in Cairo. Towards the end of 1997 the Yemeni authorities were reported to have arrested a number of Yemeni and foreign Islamist militants, including the so-called 'Arab Afghans', possibly in a move to curb the activities of the more extremist elements within the YIP.

Long-standing difficulties with Yemen's powerful neighbour, Saudi Arabia, continued to dominate foreign relations. After the civil war ended, Saudi Arabia provided assistance for the reconstruction of Aden hospital, and promises of further assistance for health projects were made during a visit by Saudi Arabia's Deputy Minister of Health in December 1994, the first sign since the end of the Gulf war that Saudi Arabia might begin to resume financial aid to Yemen. Yemen promised to begin a new chapter in its relations with Saudi Arabia based on 'co-operation, security and stability'. However, in late December tensions between the two countries increased over the disputed border, and there were reports of armed clashes between Saudi and Yemeni forces in disputed territory. The Saudi Minister of Defence, Prince Sultan ibn Abd al-Aziz Abd as-Sa'ud, was reported to have told Prime Minister Abd al-Aziz Abd al-Ghani that the Saudi air force would bomb Yemen unless it withdrew military units stationed in certain frontier areas. A large Saudi force of 20,000 men, together with 400 tanks, armoured vehicles and pieces of heavy artillery, penetrated some 70 km inside Yemeni territory. The intervention of the Syrian Vice-President, Abd al-Halim Khaddam, defused the situation and produced a compromise in January 1995. After a month of difficult negotiations the two countries signed a memorandum of understanding in Mecca on 26 February, establishing the basis for future discussions. Under the memorandum, Yemen accepted the terms of the 1934 Ta'if agreement, which had lapsed in 1994, thereby effectively conceding sovereignty over the provinces of Najran, Gizan and Asir, which were annexed by Saudi Arabia in 1934. Although the Ta'if agreement dealt principally with the border area in the north-west of the country, Yemen's Minister of Foreign Affairs succeeded in ensuring that future talks would deal with the entire length of the border between the two countries. The memorandum signed in Mecca provided for the establishment of six joint committees to delineate the land and sea borders and develop economic and commercial ties; both sides also agreed that they would not permit their country to become 'a base and centre for aggression' against the other. If the negotiations did not lead to agreement, the memorandum provided for international arbitration, a point initially rejected by Prince Sultan. On 8 March 1995 the memorandum was approved by the Yemeni Council of Ministers and later in the month the joint Yemeni-Saudi military committee, established by the memorandum, held its first meeting in Riyadh. In early June President Saleh and a high-ranking delegation visited Saudi Arabia, constituting the first official visit to that country since February 1990. In a joint statement, issued at the end of the visit, the two Governments expressed their satisfaction with the memorandum of understanding and, in addition, pledged their commitment to strengthening economic, commercial and cultural co-operation. Yemen clearly hoped that the memorandum would lead to the normalization of relations with Saudi Arabia, and that negotiations could lead to the return of at least some of the 800,000 Yemeni workers expelled from Saudi Arabia during the Gulf crisis, as well as the resumption of significant Saudi aid. By the end of 1995 some progress had been made in implementing the February memorandum of understanding as the various joint committees began their work. The military committee produced plans to reduce troop levels in border areas, and border controls between the two countries were relaxed, allowing an increase in trade. Notably, the Saudi Government agreed to allow Yemenis to seek work in the kingdom, declaring that the Saudi Ministry of Labour would begin issuing work permits to Yemenis provided they had a Saudi sponsor. It was assumed that many Yemenis expelled in 1990 would return to their former employers and businesses in the kingdom, although it was thought unlikely that the level of emigration would be as great as before the expulsion. In December 1995 reports of armed clashes along the disputed border were denied by Saudi Arabia and early in 1996 the two countries reached a preliminary agreement on their land

frontier. Talks also began on the delimitation of the maritime boundary between the two countries. In July, the two countries signed a bilateral security agreement aimed mainly at combating cross-border drugs-trafficking, but also at preventing Yemen from becoming a refuge for radical Saudi dissidents. In the past Yemen had been accused of providing refuge for foreign dissidents, particularly members of Islamist groups, but since mid-1995 the Government has moved to arrest and extradite many such dissidents, including the Arab *mujahidin* who fought in Afghanistan against the Soviet occupation. The two countries concluded a new trade agreement in September 1996. During August and September 1996 a number of high-level meetings were held between Saudi and Yemeni officials, including a visit to San'a by the Saudi Minister of Defence, responsible for negotiations with Yemen, and the Minister of the Interior. After the elections in Yemen, in May 1997, President Saleh stated that he would visit Saudi Arabia in order to seek a settlement of the border issue, as little progress had been made since the signing of the preliminary agreement. However, tensions between the two countries quickly re-emerged. After a visit to Jeddah, the new Minister of Foreign Affairs, Abd al-Karim al-Iryani, a noted critic of Saudi Arabia, complained that he had not been treated with the correct diplomatic protocol. The Yemeni press immediately launched a campaign accusing the Saudis of trying to destabilize Yemen in order to strengthen their hand in the border negotiations. After border clashes were reported in late June and early July, the interior ministers of the two countries held urgent talks which both Governments declared would lead to an early and permanent settlement of the border dispute. However, the joint committees set up under the 1995 memorandum of understanding (see above) had failed to reach any common positions and tensions arose again after the Saudi-owned television station in London, the Middle East Broadcasting Corporation, transmitted an interview with the southern Yemeni leader, al-Baid, who was on trial *in absentia* in Yemen. Later in 1997, after further high-level meetings between the two sides, including a meeting between President Saleh and Prince Sultan, the Yemeni press suggested that a settlement of the border dispute was imminent. However, in October al-Iryani accused Saudi Arabia of supporting the tribal unrest in Yemen, and the Yemeni authorities also claimed to have evidence that Saudi Arabia was involved in a series of bombings in Aden (see above). Further border clashes occurred in November in which several soldiers were reported to have been killed. At the end of November al-Iryani held talks with King Fahd and Crown Price Abdullah in Riyadh but no progress was made towards a settlement. In early December al-Iryani stated that Yemen might take the dispute to international arbitration if negotiations remained deadlocked. Despite the renewal of immigration visas for Yemenis in May 1998, for the first time since the end of the 1991 Gulf crisis, the border dispute flared up again at the end of the month, when it was reported that Saudi forces had occupied several islands in the Red Sea, which are also claimed by Yemen, and expelled the resident population. While this was regarded as an attempt by Saudi Arabia to establish its own claim to the area, some also interpreted it as signalling Saudi disapproval of the new Yemeni Government headed by al-Iryani. The occupation may also have been motivated, in part, by Saudi Arabia's desire to prevent Yemen supporting Ethiopia in its dispute with Eritrea. In July Saudi Arabian forces shelled the disputed islands, killing three Yemenis, only one week after they had crossed the land border to take part in pacification operations against local tribes supported by Saudi Arabia in their struggle against the Yemeni Government. There were protests from President Saleh, but the two countries later agreed to work towards a peaceful solution to their differences. A joint military committee meeting attended by the respective Chiefs of Staff was held in August, but only agreements governing 'guarantees and rules' between the two countries were concluded.

By the early part of 1999 it was reported that only a few minor technicalities prevented the two countries reaching an agreement on the disputed border. Talks continued, but after the Joint Committee for Demarcation met for the seventeenth time in November, the two sides appeared to be no closer to reaching a settlement. According to some observers, Saudi Arabia's reluctance to finalize an agreement was due to rivalries within the royal family over the succession. Whereas Crown Prince Abdullah was believed to favour an early settlement, his brother and main rival, Prince Sultan, took a hard-line stance towards Yemen and was opposed to it. Amidst growing frustration in Yemen, President Saleh was reported to have urged Saudi Arabia to honour the accord which he signed in Italy in 1997 with Prince Sultan (see above), at which most of the disputed border from Jebel Thaniyah to the border with Oman had evidently been settled, at least in basic outline. The President also stated that Saudi Arabia was now insisting on a revision of the 1934 Ta'if agreement, dealing principally with the north-western portion of the border, on which a new agreement had been reached in 1995 (see above). At the same time, President Saleh again suggested that international arbitration might be the only way of achieving a settlement to the long-running dispute, a proposal to which Saudi Arabia remained strongly opposed. To demonstrate its displeasure Saudi Arabia expelled 3,000 Yemeni workers from the kingdom in December, amidst renewed tensions between the two countries. In January 2000 serious border clashes broke out between Yemeni and Saudi forces in which some ten Yemeni soldiers were reported to have been killed. In February the USA offered to mediate between the two parties, but the offer was politely rejected by Saudi Arabia. Some commentators were predicting that it might take years before a settlement was finally reached. However, in late May Crown Prince Abdullah attended celebrations in San'a to mark the tenth anniversary of Yemeni unification, and in June the two countries signed an agreement described as 'a final and permanent' treaty for maritime and land borders. The new treaty incorporated both the 1934 Ta'if agreement and the 1995 memorandum of understanding (see above), but did not define the entire frontier. The maritime border was clearly defined, along with the north-western section of the land frontier which, with some minor amendments, confirmed the line set out in the Ta'if agreement. But the long eastern section of the border, running from Jabel Thar to the intersection of the Saudi, Oman and Yemen borders, remained undefined, and the treaty merely stated that the two sides had agreed to demarcate this sector 'in an amicable way' without making specific arrangement for settling disputes. The two Governments agreed to appoint an international company to demarcate the border and produce maps which, following approval by both sides, would form part of the agreement. The new treaty also incorporated a number of clauses from the 1995 memorandum of understanding not directly related to the border. The two sides agreed to promote economic, commercial and cultural relations and not to allow their territories to be used as bases for aggression or for political, military or propaganda purposes against the other. It was reported that in political circles in San'a the new agreement was being hailed as an event as memorable as the unification of North and South Yemen a decade before. There were high hopes that improved relations with their powerful neighbour would bring economic rewards, improving prospects for Yemeni workers in the kingdom and encouraging Saudi investment in Yemen. Both countries denied rumours that Saudi Arabia had agreed to support Yemen's application for membership of the GCC, and that the privileges enjoyed by Yemeni workers in the kingdom before the 1990–91 Gulf crisis would be restored, were denied by both countries, although Saudi Arabia was expected to allow more Yemeni workers to enter the country. The border agreement was ratified by Yemen's House of Representatives and appeared to have popular support, even though some opposition groups insisted that efforts should have been made to recover territories lost under the 1934 Ta'if accord. In July the interior ministers of the two countries agreed a timetable for implementing the new accord, and after further discussions by a joint Saudi-Yemeni technical committee in October a German firm, Hansa Luftbild, was awarded the contract to delineate the border. The company had been involved in demarcating the border between Oman and Saudi Arabia and between Oman and Yemen. After a visit to Yemen by Saudi Arabia's Minister of the Interior, Prince Nayef ibn Abd al-Aziz as-Sa'ud, in January 2001 a joint statement was issued indicating that progress was being made on implementing the border agreement and that the next step would be to consider ways of organizing border authorities and crossings.

The first significant sign of improved relations with Saudi Arabia came in December 2000, when the two countries held the first meeting of their joint co-operation council for more than 10 years. Saudi Arabia pledged US $300m. in loans for development projects and agreed to reschedule $330m. of Yemeni debt. Pledges were also made on co-operation in education, health, trade, investment, transport and civil aviation. The issue of Yemeni workers in the kingdom would be addressed at a later meeting. With the border accord in place President Saleh declared that Yemen would reduce the size of its armed forces in order to cut military expenditure. In April 2001 there were reports that Yemen and Saudi Arabia had signed a contract worth US $1000m. with Hansa Luftbild authorizing the company to demarcate the border, and had reached an agreement on the location of four border crossing-points which would be open throughout the year. At the same time reports indicated that the withdrawal of Saudi and Yemeni troops from their respective sides of the border, as set out under the accord, was almost complete. Another meeting of the joint co-operation council was held in June, attended by Saudi Arabia's defence minister, Prince Sultan ibn Abd al-Aziz, together with 16 other Saudi ministers. The main priority was strengthening trade relations between the two countries, but Prince Sultan stated that all political, economic and military issues should be considered together.

In 1995 the participation of the USA in the negotiations between Yemen and Saudi Arabia was believed to have played an important role in securing at least a provisional agreement between the two countries and was seen as marking another stage in the gradual normalization of relations between Yemen and Western countries. On a visit to San'a in October 1997, the US Assistant Secretary of State for Middle East and Near East Affairs, Martin Indyk, expressed continued US support for all measures to strengthen security and stability in the region and stated that Washington was keen to promote and expand co-operation with Yemen. He praised the Yemeni Government for their 'rational approach' to the border dispute with Saudi Arabia. In late May and December 1998 the Commander-in-Chief of the US Central Command, Anthony Zinni, visited Yemen for talks with President Saleh on military co-operation and in November US and Yemeni forces carried out one of a series of joint military exercises. Zinni made a third visit to Yemen in April 1999 when he inspected the work of American military staff assisting Yemen's mine-clearance programme. The visit fuelled rumours that the Government was planning to offer the USA military facilities in the island of Socotra, at the entrance of the Gulf of Aden, despite strenuous denials by President Saleh. In March the editor of an opposition newspaper, *Al-Haqq*, was arrested after the paper published a report accusing the Government of allowing the USA to use Socotra as a military base. The US military has a commercial agreement under which its ships may refuel at Aden, but it seems unlikely that the US wishes or indeed requested to station military personnel in Yemen in a permanent basis. In May Yemen's foreign minister indicated that the US would be permitted to use the country's military bases on a temporary basis but only if this was part of an operation that was in Yemen's interests. Despite increased military co-operation and a general improvement in bilateral relations the two countries remained divided on policy towards Iraq and Iran. Yemen for example had condemned as 'flagrant aggression' US and British air-strikes against Iraq in December 1998 known as 'Operation Desert Fox' (see below). Meanwhile the USA expressed concern when part of a consignment of T-55 tanks purchased by Yemen from Poland found their way to Sudan. There were similar anxieties in Washington after the Czech Republic agreed in September 1999 to sell Yemen 100 T-54 and T-55 tanks because of fears that some of this weaponry might also be destined for Sudan or even Iraq. In July 2000 the Czech Republic confirmed that it had dispatched 30 T-55 tanks to Yemen and planned to deliver another 76 tanks by the end of the year. In May Russia had also sent a consignment of tanks to Yemen. As President Saleh had stated that Yemen was committed to reducing military expenditure following the border accord with Saudi Arabia, these shipments inevitably aroused suspicions that, despite the criticisms voiced by the USA, Yemen was continuing to purchase arms destined for sale to 'pariah' states such as Sudan.

In February 2000 the State Department again offered to mediate in the border dispute between Yemen and Saudi Arabia but the offer was rejected by Riyadh. Shortly before, it was reported that representatives of the exiled southern opposition group led by Abd ar-Rahman al-Jifri (see above) had held talks with State Department officials in Washington. In late March, President Saleh made an official visit to Washington, DC, where he held talks with President Bill Clinton and senior members of his Administration which were reported to have covered aid, plans for increased military co-operation and regional issues, notably the Middle East peace process. In April the US Department of State reported that Yemen remained a 'safe haven' for terrorist groups, in part because the Government had only limited control over much of the interior of the country and its borders. It noted that the Palestinian Hamas (Islamic Resistance Movement) was allowed to maintain an official representative in Yemen, and that members of the Algerian GIA and Egyptian Islamic Jihad, or those sympathetic to these groups, were living openly in Yemen. Concern was also expressed by the State Department about human rights and the significant limitations placed on democratic institutions such as elections.

In mid-October 2000 17 US naval personnel were killed and 38 wounded in a suicide bomb attack against the destroyer *USS Cole* while it was refuelling at Aden. At first President Saleh stated that there had been an explosion on board the US vessel, but he later conceded that there had been a terrorist attack and offered full co-operation in investigating the incident. US sources immediately pointed to a link between the suicide bombers and the militant Islamist Osama bin Laden, and suggested that even if bin Laden was not directly involved in the attack on the *USS Cole* he may well have inspired those responsible, whose aim was to deter the USA from its political engagement and military involvement in the Middle East. According to the Yemeni Government, some of those detained after the attack were members of the Egyptian-based Islamic Jihad with links to Osama bin Laden. However, three Yemeni Islamist groups claimed responsibility for the attack, the Islamic Army of Aden-Abyan and two previously unknown groups— Muhammad's Army and the Islamic Deterrence Force. The US Administration defended its policy of refuelling ships at Aden, stating that 25 ships had been safely refuelled there in the last 18 months. Addressing the US Senate's Armed Services Committee, Gen. Anthony Zinni, recently retired as commander of US forces in the Middle East, insisted that the decision to allow US ships to refuel at Aden had not been made for political reasons and argued that the Yemeni port had appeared a safer location to refuel than many others in a volatile region. He rejected any suggestion that the navy might have compromised security to support the political goal of improving US-Yemeni relations. In December Yemeni officials announced that six people accused of being involved in the attack on the *USS Cole* would go on trial in January 2001. The accused included some civil servants who were alleged to have provided forged papers. Early in 2001, however, the Yemeni authorities announced that the trial would be delayed, and it was reported that US officials had requested more time to gather additional evidence. Co-operation between the Yemeni and US teams investigating the attack had proved difficult, but in late November 2000 the two sides had come to an agreement which defined their respective roles in the investigation. Nevertheless, in an interview with *The Washington Post* in December, President Saleh stated that US officials would not be allowed to question Yemeni suspects unless Yemeni investigators were present, and insisted that Yemen would not consider any requests for the extradition of Yemeni suspects. As a result, it was uncertain exactly when the trial would take place. In April 2001 it was reported that another three suspects had been arrested. In early July William Burns, the new US Assistant Secretary of State for Near Eastern Affairs, visited San'a for discussions about security issues. Meanwhile, the US embassy had closed its consular division for a month following fears of a 'terrorist threat'. The Yemeni authorities continued to complain of the intrusive behaviour of US officials of the Federal Bureau of Investigation (FBI) investigating the *USS Cole* incident, but towards the end of 2001 Yemen was reported to have provided Washington with important information regarding the case. In November the official newspaper *26 September* published claims that the individual suspected of planning the attack had subsequrntly sought refuge in Afghanistan. He man was named as Muhammad Omar al-Harazi, and was also believed to have been one of the principal organizers of the 1998 attacks on the US embassies in Kenya and Tanzania. In February 2002 it was reported that the trial of eight of the suspects in the bombing of the *USS Cole* had been postponed at the request of the US authorities because of the possibility that new information about the case would be obtained during interrogation of al-Qa'ida and Taliban prisoners captured by US military forces in Afghanistan in late 2001 and held in detention at the US military base at Guantánamo Bay, Cuba.

The Russian news agency TASS reported that a military delegation from Yemen had visited Moscow in March 2000 for talks with armaments companies about the purchase of military equipment. President Saleh subsequently denied that any arms deals were being negotiated, but it was thought that some military purchases could take place following successful negotiations with Moscow over outstanding debt to the former USSR.

In February 1995 President Saleh visited the Netherlands, Germany and France, concluding a number of new aid agreements and other joint projects. In April the United Kingdom announced that its aid programme for Yemen would be resumed at a modest level, and in June Japan stated that it was prepared to reactivate fully its economic aid programme for Yemen. After the parliamentary elections in May 1997 Saleh again visited a number of European capitals securing promises of increased aid, help with outstanding debts and new co-operation agreements. In mid-November he made an official visit to the United Kingdom, the first visit by a Yemeni head of state since Britain's evacuation of Aden in 1967. However, relations between the two countries became strained at the end of 1998 when a diplomatic row broke out over a kidnapping incident in southern Yemen in which three British tourists were killed during a rescue operation mounted by the security forces (see above). Britain complained that Yemen had ignored advice to seek a negotiated settlement to the kidnapping, and accused the Yemeni authorities of failing to provide a full account of the rescue attempt. The row deepened when eight British nationals were arrested in connection with an alleged plot to carry out a series of bomb attacks in Aden. Yemen insisted that both the kidnapping incident and the alleged bomb plot were linked to a London-based Islamist group, 'Supporters of the *Shari'a*', and accused Britain of harbouring terrorists. The matter continued to sour relations with Britain during 1999, especially after the eight British nationals were convicted in August and five of them sentenced to three to seven years' imprisonment (see above). In September President Saleh again accused Britain of harbouring the leader of 'Supporters of the *Shari'a*', Abu Hamza al-Masri. In October 2000, shortly after the suicide bomb attack against the *USS Cole* at Aden, there was a large explosion at the British embassy in San'a. British officials stated that an explosive device thrown over the perimeter wall had struck the embassy's generator. There were no injuries to embassy staff, and a man was later arrested by the Yemeni authorities and charged with the attack. The Yemeni Government had initially claimed that the explosion was caused by a malfunctioning generator. It was unclear whether there was any link between the two attacks, but some analysts suggested that they were probably triggered, as violence escalated in the West Bank and Gaza Strip, by mounting Arab anger at the USA and its Western allies for their support for Israel. In July 2001 four Yemenis were found guilty of planning and carrying out the attack on the embassy and were sentenced to between four and 15 years' imprisonment. Two of those convicted had pleaded guilty, stating that the attack was in retaliation for Israeli violence against the Palestinians. The other two pleaded not guilty, claiming that they had been coerced into making confessions. During the early stages of the trial one defendant had claimed to work for Yemeni intelligence, while another stated that a Libyan diplomat had commissioned the attack. Both later retracted these statements.

Early in 1998 the President visited Malaysia (a country with which Yemen has long-established links), China and Indonesia. Relations with Oman improved after June 1995, when a border demarcation agreement, initiated in 1992, was completed. By mid-1996 the last remaining troops had been withdrawn from the border area, and agreements on economic co-operation and investment had been signed. Later in the year the two countries agreed to set up a free-trade zone near the border. In early 1997 agreements were signed to improve air and road links between the two countries, and at the end of May final demarcation maps for their joint border were signed. Although Saudi Arabia had not formally opposed the 1992 agreement, it was reported in April 1998 that Saudi Arabia claimed some of the territory covered in the border demarcation agreement between Yemen and Oman. There was speculation that these claims might be linked to Saudi Arabia's ambitions to secure a corridor to the Arabian Sea between Yemen and Oman. In early July 1995, following a statement made in the previous month by Kuwait's Deputy Prime Minister and Minister of Foreign Affairs, Sheikh Sabah al-Ahmad al-Jaber as-Sabah, which stipulated that Yemen would have to officially demand Iraq's implementation of the UN Security Council's resolutions before Yemeni-Kuwaiti relations could be normalized, the GPC issued a policy statement requiring Iraq's implementation of the aforementioned resolutions. In September a delegation of Kuwaiti trade unionists visited Yemen and at the end of the year the Kuwait-based AFESD agreed to support a development project in Yemen. However, relations with Kuwait remained strained. In October Yemen's Minister of Foreign Affairs, Abd al-Karim al-Iryani, had accused Kuwait of supporting the southern separatists in the civil war. In December 1996 Kuwait opposed the Yemeni application for GCC membership, which was rejected two months later. This decision provoked acrimonious exchanges in the Kuwaiti and Yemeni press, although in early 1997 Yemen did succeed in joining the Indian Ocean Rim Association for Regional Co-operation which promotes co-operation in trade, investment and economic development. In June 1998 the Minister of Foreign Affairs, Dr Abd al-Qadir Bajammal, stated that Yemen would not repeat its request to join the GCC. Yemen's Minister of Foreign Affairs visited Kuwait in May 1999, at the invitation of the Kuwaiti Government, in order to formalize the normalization of relations between the two countries. During the visit the Yemen embassy in Kuwait, closed since the Gulf crisis, was reopened, and later Yemen offered to try and secure information about Kuwait prisoners of war held in Iraq. In May 2000 Kuwait's Minister of Foreign Affairs attended celebrations to mark the 10th anniversary of Yemeni unification.

After the Gulf War the Yemen Government continued to express solidarity with Iraq and urged an end to the UN oil embargo on Iraq. Popular feeling in Yemen remained fiercely pro-Iraqi. A parliamentary delegation and a senior official of the GPC visited Baghdad in October 1995. During the crisis in relations between Iraq and the USA in February 1998 President Saleh cut short a visit to Indonesia to attend discussions on the crisis in Abu Dhabi, and security forces in San'a were reported to have dispersed unlicensed demonstrations against the US and British military build-up in the Gulf. In December Yemen strongly condemned 'Operation Desert Fox', and thousands of Yemenis took part in peaceful demonstrations in San'a against the US and British air-strikes against Iraq. However, President Saleh failed to secure sufficient support from other Arab leaders for an Arab League summit on Iraq. In a speech on foreign policy at the end of May 2000 President Saleh expressed concern about the suffering of the Iraqi people and called for an end to economic sanctions against Baghdad. In October Yemen dispatched a humanitarian flight to Iraq carrying food and medicines together with a ministerial delegation including the Ministers of Foreign Affairs and of Information, having in advance secured clearance for the flight from the UN Sanctions Committee. While the Yemeni Government remained sensitive to pro-Iraqi popular feeling, it appeared anxious to alienate neither the USA nor Saudi Arabia and Kuwait by its policy towards Iraq.

Yemen has built good relations with Iran. On a visit to Tehran in early 1999, Yemen's foreign ministers held talks with President Khatami and praised Iran for its contribution to peace and stability in the Gulf region. Earlier Yemen had urged Arab Gulf states to recognize the role that Iran could play in the region's security. In April 1999 a delegation from the self-proclaimed 'Republic of Somaliland' visited Yemen, which currently shelters some 40,000 refugees from the long-running civil war in Somalia.

In late 1996 a Libyan-sponsored conference of opponents of the Middle East peace process was held in San'a and several GPC members attended. However, in an interview in January 1997, the Minister of Foreign Affairs stated that the Yemeni Government was not opposed to the peace process and supported the principle of 'land-for-peace'. Although Yemen traditionally maintains a hard-line stance towards Israel, it agreed to attend the fourth Middle East and North Africa economic conference held in Doha, Qatar, in November 1997 at which an Israeli delegation was present. Leading Arab states, including Egypt and Saudi Arabia. had refused to take part in the summit. Later in September 1999 Yemen attended a meeting in New York of Arab foreign ministers and the Israeli foreign minister hosted by the US Secretary of State. The following month a leading Israeli daily, *Yedioth Aharonoth*, carried a report that Yemen was involved in secret talks with Israel. Officials in San'a denied the report, but some observers suggested that Yemen may well have been involved in unofficial approaches about normalization of relations with Israel. The official line from San'a remained support for an independent Palestinian state, and an insistence on Israel's withdrawal from the Golan Heights and southern Lebanon. It appeared unlikely that there would be any moves to establish diplomatic relations with Israel until a comprehensive Middle East peace settlement had been concluded. Nevertheless, early in 2000 Yemen agreed to allow Israeli Jews of Yemeni origin to visit the country using special permits issued by the UN. President Saleh stated that any further easing of travel restrictions for Israelis would be dependent on progress in the Middle East peace process. At least five groups of Israeli tourists visited Yemen in the following months, despite a warning issued by the Israeli Ministry of Foreign Affairs that it did not advise its citizens to visit Yemen until there had been improvements in security. Popular opinion in Yemen remained strongly opposed to any improvement in relations with the Israel, and Sheikh Abdullah bin Hussain al-Ahmar, the Speaker of the House of Representatives and leader of the YIP, strongly condemned the visits. Rumours of secret contacts between the two countries continued, and *Az-Zaman* reported that a senior official from the Israeli Ministry of Foreign Affairs had visited Yemen at the end of March for talks with senior officials including the Prime Minister. In late May President Saleh stated that Israelis of Yemeni origin would no longer be permitted to travel to Yemen because Israel had tried to exploit the concession by portraying it as a move towards normalization of relations between the two countries. The Israeli Government subsequently stated that continuing concerns about security in Yemen meant that any Israeli citizens travelling to Yemen would have to obtain permission from the Israeli Ministry of the Interior.

In October 2000, as violence between Israel and the Palestinians escalated, President Saleh urged all Arabs to support the Palestinian cause. Tens of thousands of Yemenis marched through San'a to protest against the killing of Palestinian civilians by Israeli troops. In November Sheikh Abdullah bin Hussain al-Ahmar urged Yemenis to boycott US goods because of the USA's support for Israel. Yasser Arafat, President of the Palestinian (National) Authority, visited San'a in December for talks with President Saleh, who was reported to have reiterated Yemen's support for an independent Palestinian state with Jerusalem as its capital, and for Palestinian resistance to Israeli occupation.

In November 1995 there were reports that Eritrean troops had attempted to land on the Red Sea island of Greater Hanish, one of three islands (the others being Lesser Hanish and Zuqar) claimed by both Yemen and Eritrea. The attempted invasion had apparently been prompted by Yemen's announced intention to develop Greater Hanish as a tourist resort, and its subsequent refusal to comply with an Eritrean demand that the island be evacuated. Negotiations in Yemen and Eritrea in late November and early December failed to defuse the crisis, and on 15 December fighting broke out between the two sides, resulting in the deaths of six Eritrean and three Yemeni soliders. On 17 December Yemen and Eritrea agreed to a cease-fire, to be monitored by a commission comprising a senior official from each country and two US diplomats. None the less, fighting was renewed the following day and Eritrean forces succeeded in occupying Greater Hanish. The cease-fire was subsequently adhered to, and some 180 Yemeni soliders (captured during the fighting) were released at the end of the month. Attempts by the Ethiopian and Egyptian Governments to broker an agreement between the two sides proved unsuccessful. In late January 1996 France assumed the role of mediator. On 21 May representatives of Eritrea and Yemen signed an arbitration accord in Paris, France, whereby the two sides agreed that they were prepared to submit the dispute to an international tribunal. France and the USA subsequently undertook to observe and supervise military movements in the area around the disputed islands. In August, however, Eritrean troops occupied Lesser Hanish and Yemen threatened to send troops to force them to withdraw. After intervention by the UN and France, Eritrea withdrew its forces and in October the two countries reaffirmed their agreement to allow an international arbitration panel to settle the dispute. The five-member panel began work in January 1997 and in October 1998 awarded the main Hanish islands to Yemen while Eritrea was given two groups of tiny islets and fishing rights in Yemen waters. Eritrea accepted the ruling and withdrew its forces from the islands soon after the arbitration panel's decision was announced. Yemen assumed control of the majority of the Hanish islands on 1 November. In December 1999 the panel concluded its work, declaring that the maritime boundary between Yemen and Eritrea should be the median line between the coastlines of the two countries and rejected Eritrean claims to mineral rights on certain Yemeni islands. However, the panel was careful to define the maritime boundary between the two countries only as far as 15° 42′10″ N (a point just north of Jebel ath-Thayr islands) so as to avoid areas that might be claimed by Saudi Arabia. Yemen had requested that the boundary be defined as far north as latitude 16° N, a move strongly opposed by Saudi Arabia. Despite some misgivings, both Yemen and Eritrea indicated that they would accept the decision, but relations between the two countries remained strained. In October Yemen had signed a joint security agreement with Eritrea's neighbour, Ethiopia, at a time when the two states were engaged in a long and bitter war.

YEMEN AND THE 'WAR AGAINST TERROR'

After the terrorist attacks on New York and Washington on 11 September 2001 US commentators frequently identified Yemen as one of those states believed to be harbouring militant Islamists and described it as a possible target for future US-led military intervention as part of the US Government's declared 'war against terror'. President Saleh, who was no doubt determined to avoid the diplomatic isolation and economic sanctions that followed Yemen's support for Iraq during the 1990–91 Gulf crisis, immediately pledged full support for the USA's global campaign against terrorism. On his arrival in San'a at the end of September the new US ambassador, Edmund Hull, a former co-ordinator for counter-terrorism at the US State Department, declared Yemen to be a partner rather than a target in the 'war against terror'. For their part, the Yemeni authorities were anxious to demonstrate their willingness to co-operate with the US authorities on security issues. Yemeni security forces were instructed to detain all Yemeni nationals suspected of having links with Osama bin Laden (the fugitive Saudi-born leader of the al-Qa'ida terrorist network) while many 'Arab Afghans' were arrested and deported. The Central Bank later 'froze' a number of bank accounts belonging to organizations and individuals, on the basis of information supplied by the US intelligence sources.

Security co-operation with the US Administration brought diplomatic and financial benefits to Yemen, but also served to intensify popular animosity towards the USA for its uncompromising support for Israel and its continuing bombing campaign against Iraq. According to a survey conducted by *The Yemen Times*, a majority of Yemenis were opposed to the US bombing of Afghanistan; several anti-US demonstrations were reported—one such protest, held in Amran in late October, attracted some 30,000 marchers. At the same time, a group of the country's leading Islamic scholars condemned any form of co-operation with the USA or its allies, as did opposition parties—notably the YIP. Responding to expressions of popular resentment towards the USA, President Saleh emphasized that any US-led military action should be undertaken only in accordance with guide-lines established by the UN and should seek to

minimize casualties among Muslim civilians. On several occasions the President also described Yemen as a victim of the rise of global terrorism, pointing to kidnappings and violent anti-government activities.

Some hardliners within the US political establishment continued to demand that Yemen be targeted in the 'war against terror', arguing that the country was likely to provide refuge to many al-Qa'ida militants fleeing Afghanistan. During a visit to Washington, DC, in late November 2001, President Saleh held talks with President Bush, Secretary of State Colin Powell and Central Intelligence Agency (CIA) Director George Tenet, and reaffirmed his Government's commitment to close co-operation with the international anti-terrorism coalition. President Saleh promised to crush Islamist extremism in Yemen, and to arrest suspects sought by the US authorities and allow US investigators to interrogate them. There were reports that, in return, the US Administration had promised US $150m. in bilateral aid, and had pledged support for Yemen in its requests for assistance from the World Bank and the IMF. Intelligence co-operation was to be increased, and the USA offered assistance in training Yemen's security forces. In mid-December a unit of Yemen's élite Republican Guard, commanded by President Saleh's son, Ahmed, launched a series of attacks on the village of al-Hossoun, in Marib province, where two suspected members of al-Qa'ida were believed to have taken refuge among the Abeidah tribe. The operation was a spectacular failure and the heavily armed unit was forced to withdraw after some 19 soldiers were killed. The al-Qa'ida suspects evaded capture and six months later both men were believed to be still hiding in tribal areas in the north-east of the country. The incident highlighted the ability of the tribes, many of which are better armed and organized than the security forces, successfully to defy the central Government. The US Assistant Secretary of Defense, Paul Wolfowitz, acknowledged that the US Government had called on Yemen to make greater efforts in the battle against terrorism and stated that the US Administration had been concerned for some time that the Government in San'a did not appear to control the area close to the border with Saudi Arabia, where they believed several al-Qa'ida members had gone to ground.

The US embassy in San'a was closed in mid-January 2002 after an alleged senior al-Qa'ida commander held by US forces in Afghanistan told interrogators of a planned attack against the embassy. In early February a team of Yemeni investigators visited the Guantánamo base in Cuba where the USA was holding Taliban and al-Qa'ida prisoners in order to assist in questioning some 20–30 Yemeni nationals held there; Yemenis formed the second-largest national group in detention (after suspects from Saudi Arabia). On 12 February, on the basis of information obtained during these interrogations, US officials issued a warning that a Yemeni national, named as Fawaz Yahya Ar-Rabeei, was planning an attack on the US mainland or against US interests in the Gulf region on that day. The Yemeni authorities stated that they had increased security measures to protect US interests in the country and had arrested five Yemeni nationals suspected of belonging to a 15-member al-Qa'ida terrorist cell led by ar-Rabeei. According to the armed forces' newspaper, *26 September*, one of the Yemenis, who blew himself up while fleeing from police, was a relation of one of the 11 September hijackers and of one of the suspects in the *USS Cole* bombing. At the end of the month CIA Director George Tenet visited Yemen to discuss co-operation in tracking down further al-Qa'ida suspects. President Saleh stated during an interview that 84 terrorist suspects had been arrested during the current anti-terrorism campaign, and although he denied the existence of al-Qa'ida bases in Yemen, he admitted that some suspected terrorists had been employed in government departments or agencies but not in the military and security forces. In early March a US official stated that the US Government was preparing to send about 100 troops to Yemen to assist Yemeni forces in apprehending al-Qa'ida suspects. *The Wall Street Journal*, however, claimed that the USA was preparing to send several hundred troops to Yemen. US Vice-President Dick Cheney made a brief visit to Yemen in mid-March—the first visit by a senior US official since 1986—as part of a diplomatic tour of the Middle East region. For security reasons Cheney did not leave the airport. His talks with President Saleh were reported to have focused on the Israeli–Palestinian crisis,

Yemen's role in the 'war against terror', and Iraq. Official sources reported that three teams of US military advisers and trainers, each with 20–30 members, were being sent to Yemen. Eight political parties in Yemen issued a statement condemning Cheney's visit and accusing the USA of seeking military domination of the region. The day after the visit two grenades were thrown at the US embassy in San'a but no one was injured in the explosions. In May a young university student was sentenced to 10 years' imprisonment for the attack. It was believed that he had acted alone; at his trial he declared that he had carried out the attack in support of the Palestinian cause. Earlier, in mid-March, a British man had been shot and seriously injured in the port city of Hodeida. The Israeli military intervention in Palestinian-controlled areas of the West Bank at the end of March provoked popular demands for Yemen to end security co-operation with the USA, and on several occasions large crowds tried to protest outside the heavily-protected US embassy in the capital. The embassy was closed again in late April for several days after receiving another warning of a possible terrorist attack. Shortly after the embassy reopened, a large explosion and gunfire was heard nearby. Also in April there were several bomb attacks against offices of Yemen's secret police, the PSO and the homes of its officials. A new radical Islamist group calling itself Sympathizers of al-Qa'ida claimed responsibility for the attacks, and also issued threats of 'suicide' attacks against the intelligence services and senior political figures unless al-Qa'ida suspects held at PSO headquarters were released (see above). In mid-April opposition parties called for action against US economic and oil interests in the Arab region because of the US Government's apparent unconditional support for what they termed 'Israeli terrorist attacks in Palestine', and demanded an end to all forms of co-operation between Yemen and the USA. At the same time the Yemeni House of Representatives, where the GPC enjoys a strong majority, called on Arab and Muslim countries to suspend all forms of co-operation with both the USA and the United Kingdom until they renounced their 'one-sided policies towards Israel'. Nevertheless, security co-operation with the US Government continued. President Saleh announced that a team of 40 US military experts had arrived in Yemen to provide counter-terrorism training for the security forces. The USA was also helping to install computers and surveillance equipment at airports and border crossings to monitor those entering and leaving the country more closely. It was also reported that new terms had been agreed for refuelling US ships at the port of Aden, including a provision that would allow US marines to assist with security at the port. US officials, however, stated that there were no immediate plans to resume refuelling at Aden, use of the port having been suspended after the attack on the USS Cole in October 2000. However, in early May 2002 a spokesman for President Saleh declared that Yemen would not grant military facilities to the USA or any other country at any of its ports. In late May Prime Minister Bajammal defended the continuing co-operation with the USA in the 'war against terror' and insisted that Yemen could only benefit from US military training expertise. In late June the Commander of allied forces in Afghanistan, Gen. Tommy Franks, visited San'a for talks with President Saleh which focused on further co-operation between the two countries in anti-terrorism activities, and particularly the scope for US military and economic assistance to Yemen. Meanwhile, at a seminar organized by the Yemen Centre for Future Studies, attended by journalists, lawyers, and some parliamentary deputies, speakers appeared to confirm that some al-Qai'da terrorist cells were indeed operating in Yemen and would become stronger in the future unless the authorities took decisive action to dismantle them. However, in early July Sheikh Abdullah al-Ahmar, the YIP leader, rejected official claims that the 84 people being held in custody in Yemen were linked to al-Qa'ida and insisted that the accusations against them had been made merely to appease the US Administration. Moreover, al-Ahmar claimed that hundreds of Yemenis had been detained by the authorities since 11 September 2001 and Yemen's decision to co-operate with the USA in the 'war against terror'.

Close co-operation with the USA brought some diplomatic rewards at the regional level. In December 2001 the GCC granted Yemen membership of four of its non-political commit-tees and there was unanimous support for Yemen eventually being admitted to full membership of the organization, although the Omani Foreign Minister stated some time later that this process would take at least 10 years. In January 2002 Qatar's Council of Ministers ratified an agreement on security co-operation with Yemen. In mid-March Egypt's Minister of the Interior visited San'a for talks on co-operation against terrorism. Relations with Egypt had been strained during the 1990s owing to Yemen's refusal to extradite Egyptian nationals accused of belonging to the banned Islamic Jihad. In February, however, the Yemeni authorities had arrested a number of Egyptian nationals during their campaign to shut down certain religious institutes. This campaign, however, created tension with Indonesia and Malaysia. In February, after 44 Indonesian students studying in Yemen were arrested, the Indonesian ambassador protested to the Yemeni authorities and demanded their immediate release, warning that their continued detention could undermine the good relations between the two countries. The Yemeni authorities resolved that those students who had been studying at the Dar al-Hadith schools in Marib and Saada would be deported and in future all Indonesian students wishing to study in Yemen would be obliged to obtain permission from the Indonesian Government and pursue their studies at an establishment recognized and approved by the Yemeni authorities. During February and March a number of Malaysian students were detained on suspicion of being involved in political and terrorist activities, while others fled and sought refuge in the Malaysian embassy. Reports suggested that some 300 Malaysians were studying in Yemen, many of them at al-Iman University.

In mid-February 2002, in an interview with *Al-Hayat*, President Saleh was reported to have warned the US Government that a US-led attack on Iraq, as part of its 'war against terror', would jeopardize the continued support of its traditional allies in the Arab region. However, Saleh was careful to emphasize his own ongoing efforts to persuade the Iraqi authorities to accept the return of UN weapons inspectors. In March Iraqi Vice-President Taha Yassin Ramadan visited San'a and conveyed a communication from Saddam Hussain to the President concerning developments in the region, in preparation for the Arab League summit meeting to be held in Beirut, Lebanon at the end of the month. In early August, in an interview with *The Yemen Times*, the Iraqi ambassador to Yemen praised Yemen's official stance on the Iraqi issue, noting that the Yemeni Government was continuing to urge the international community to end sanctions against Iraq and to denounce the frequent threats made against the Iraqi administration. At the end of March, as Israel undertook an uncompromising military intervention in Palestinian-controlled areas of the West Bank, thousands of Yemenis demonstrated across the country in support of the Palestinian cause. They also called for an end to UN sanctions against Iraq and expressed their opposition to any US military action in that country. In a message to the Secretary-General of the Arab League at the beginning of April, President Saleh urged Arab states to break contacts with Israel and to end all moves towards normalization of relations with the Jewish state. Shortly afterwards, the House of Representatives called on Arab and Muslim states to donate money to the Palestinian *intifada*, urging those states that had established relations with Israel to end all co-operation and invoking the use of oil embargoes to force concessions from the West on this issue. There were demands that Israel withdraw immediately from Palestinian lands and comply with all UN resolutions pertinent to the Arab–Israeli conflict. In mid-April more than 100,000 demonstrators took part in a protest march through San'a organized by the YIP to protest against the action of the Israeli armed forces in the Palestinian-controlled areas. In a televised address President Saleh urged Yemenis to support the Palestinians by donating blood and money. Meanwhile, a delegation led by the Head of the PLO's political department, Farouk Kaddoumi, visited San'a to inform Yemeni officials about the latest developments in the West Bank. The delegation also met the YIP leader, Sheikh al-Ahmar. In mid-June the Assistant Secretary-General of Syria's ruling Baath Party attended the third regional conference of the Baath Arab Socialist Party held in San'a. Concurrent discussions with President Saleh covered Yemeni-Syrian co-operation and the Israeli–Palestinian crisis.

At the end of June President Saleh led a Yemeni delegation to Sudan to attend celebrations marking the anniversary of the National Salvation Revolution, and he later held talks with President (Lt-Gen.) Omar Hassan Ahmad al-Bashir.

Economy

ALAN J. DAY

INTRODUCTION

Despite possessing substantial oil and gas resources and a significant proportion of agriculturally productive land, Yemen has been consistently ranked in the lower ranges of the world's low-income countries. According to official Yemeni estimates, Yemen's gross national product (GNP) was US $7,386m. ($404 per head) in 2000 on a conventional exchange-rate basis, compared with $4,949m. ($321 per head) in 1995. Measured by the World Bank on the basis of purchasing-power parity (PPP), GNP amounted to an estimated $14,000m. ($770 per head) in 2000. In 1989, the last year before Yemeni unification, the World Bank had estimated Yemen's GNP per head as $650 (conventionally measured), based on aggregated data for the then Yemen Arab Republic (YAR, or North Yemen) and the People's Democratic Republic of Yemen (PDRY, or South Yemen). These estimated statistics, suggesting a significant decline in GNP per head in the years following unification in May 1990, appear to be broadly consistent with the turbulent course of events in the new Republic of Yemen. Early plans for economic development and integration were quickly disrupted by the Gulf crisis of 1990–91, particularly by the UN trade embargo on Iraq, which Yemen applied with some reluctance in view of its close economic links with that country. Also damaging was the enforced return of up to 1m. Yemeni workers from Saudi Arabia and other Gulf states and the consequential loss of crucial remittance income. Financial difficulties associated with the crisis obliged the Government to adjust economic policy, notably by reducing expenditure and food subsidies, with the result that social unrest increased in 1992. During the following year the Government appeared to be moving towards the introduction of fundamental structural reforms, but in 1994 normal economic planning was again disrupted by a political crisis, associated on this occasion with the onset of civil war.

Unification created a country of 536,869 sq km with a population estimated at 11,282,000 in mid-1990, excluding up to 2.5m. Yemenis working abroad, mainly in Saudi Arabia. Of the two components, the YAR had a population of 9,274,173 (including nationals abroad) in 1986, while the PDRY had a population of 2,345,266 in 1988. The YAR had fared better economically, achieving a GNP per head of US $640 by 1988 (according to the World Bank), whereas the PDRY's equivalent statistic was $430. The results of Yemen's first post-unification census, carried out on 16 December 1994, indicated a total population of approximately 14.6m. (23% of whom lived in urban areas). The resident population at mid-2001 was estimated as 18,863,000. The World Bank estimated a rate of population increase averaging 2.8% in 1994–2000. A household budget survey conducted in 1998 indicated that the proportion of Yemen's population living in poverty (as defined by current UN measures of living standards) rose from 19% in 1992 to 33% in 1998, with the main concentrations of poverty in rural areas.

In the mid-1980s the economic prospects of both the YAR and PDRY were significantly improved by the discovery of hydrocarbons in commercial quantities, and the perceived need for rapid joint development of their oil and gas sectors was a major factor in the two countries' decision to unite. Prior to unification, both countries had sought to promote development by means of three- or five-year plans which called for large inflows of foreign aid, but both had usually failed to achieve their targets. The YAR's second five-year plan had been disrupted in December 1982 by a major earthquake in Dhamar province which killed about 3,000 people and caused an estimated US $650m. of damage. In 1983, moreover, there was a slump in earnings from the remittances of North Yemenis working abroad, caused by cut-backs in petroleum production, reduced revenues and, hence, less profitable employment in the petro-leum industries of Saudi Arabia and the Gulf States. These factors caused a crisis in the economy of the YAR, leading to the introduction of austerity measures. However, in 1984 the country's prospects improved, following increases in aid for the relief of the earthquake region. In July 1984 petroleum was discovered in the YAR, and was being produced at a rate of 180,000 barrels per day (b/d) by the time of unification in May 1990.

The onset of the crisis in the Persian (Arabian) Gulf region in August 1990 seriously disrupted the unified Yemen's economy, especially when the Government, after some hesitation, decided to adhere to UN sanctions against Iraq and Iraqi-occupied Kuwait. Prior to the crisis Yemen had been greatly dependent on trade with, and aid from, both Iraq and, to a lesser extent, Kuwait. It had also relied heavily, for balance-of-payments purposes, on hard currency remittances from Yemeni workers in Saudi Arabia and the Gulf States, who returned home in large numbers, especially from Saudi Arabia, which in late September 1990 terminated Yemeni workers' privileges in retaliation for Yemen's opposition to the US-led military build-up in the Gulf. In October 1990 the Government, in support of a request for special aid from the international community, calculated its actual and prospective losses in 1990–91 at US $1,686m. Later Yemeni estimates of the overall cost of the crisis included one by President Saleh in May 1991 putting Yemen's total prospective losses, including 1992, at over $3,000m. Moreover, in April 1991 the Government valued property and assets lost by Yemeni nationals forced to leave Saudi Arabia at $7,900m. By then the total number of returnees from Saudi Arabia was estimated by Yemeni officials at up to 1m., representing a 10% increase in the country's population and giving rise to serious social problems and pressure on scarce resources. Against this background, the World Bank co-ordinated international moves to provide emergency aid and credits for Yemen totalling $245m. Aggravating Yemen's problem was a foreign debt said to be in excess of $7,000m.

In November 1991 President Saleh conceded that Yemen was experiencing an economic crisis, with unemployment between 25% and 30%, and lost aid and other negative effects producing a 50% shortfall in government receipts compared with the original 1991 budget. In response, the Government implemented austerity measures, including cuts in food subsidies and defence expenditure, and co-operated informally with the IMF and other international agencies in adjusting short-term economic policy. On the positive side, activity in the oil and gas sectors accelerated sharply in 1991–92, on the strength of discoveries of significant new reserves, although output from existing oilfields declined in 1992, when government oil revenues remained modest in relation to the country's current financial needs. By mid-1993 there were signs that relations with Saudi Arabia and other states of the Gulf Co-operation Council (GCC) were beginning to improve, and in August 1993 oil production started to rise when the first shipments were made from a newly-developed field.

In 1994 political events led once more to deep economic crisis as the armed conflict of May–July further destabilized the deficit-ridden public finances and burdened the country with a costly agenda of post-war repair work to be undertaken before the normal development programme could resume. An initial assessment of civil war damage by UNDP put the cost of essential repairs to basic infrastructure and services in the Aden area at between US $100m. and $200m., and in mid-August the UN launched an appeal for $22m. of emergency aid to cover the immediate needs of the population of the southern war zone for the next six months. The Yemen Government estimated the overall cost of the war at $4,000m., and anticipated a $3,500m. spending requirement for reconstruction work. Widespread shortages of food, water and electricity continued to be reported in many parts of the country in September 1994, when a particular cause of popular discontent was the five-fold rise in prices of some basic foodstuffs since early July. In mid-September the World Bank authorized the expenditure of $35m. on emergency reconstruction work in five sectors of the economy, while UNDP announced a $4m. distribution of food aid in the war-affected areas over a period of two months. Countries which extended various types of emergency aid through national agencies included Italy, Germany, the Netherlands and the USA. The World Bank package utilized funds that formed part of Yemen's accumulated entitlement to $345m. of International Development Association (IDA) concessionary finance for projects whose implementation had been delayed by bureaucratic inefficiencies in Yemen. The package included $21m. for the power sector but only $700,000 for the water sector, which had already secured some bilateral aid. Allocations for health, education, agriculture and fisheries were to be spent mainly on the replacement of looted equipment and supplies. It was subsequently estimated by the IMF that Yemen's real gross domestic product (GDP), measured at constant 1990 prices, had declined at an average annual rate of 0.2% in the period 1991–94, while consumption per head had declined by an average 26.5% per year and the inflation rate had averaged 57.3% per year.

Prior to the outbreak of civil war, the Yemen Government had discussed the prospects for structural economic reform in some detail with experts from the World Bank, whose primary recommendation was that the Government should curb the fiscal deficit, adjust the currency exchange rate and adopt a disciplined monetary policy as first steps in any reform programme. A delegation of World Bank and IMF officials visited San'a in January 1995 to reassess the situation and draw up proposals for immediate remedial action. It was estimated at this point that prices were rising at an annual rate of 60% despite direct and indirect government subsidies totalling more than US $400m. per year, while the unemployment rate was around 30%, despite widespread overmanning throughout the public sector. By late March the inflation rate was reported to have risen to 100%, and the unemployment rate to 50%, as the country awaited a major economic policy initiative by the Government. The main components of this initiative were price increases and other measures to curb the budget deficit; adoption of a more liberal exchange-rate policy; and a commitment to implement wide-ranging structural reforms (to be finalized in consultation with the IMF and World Bank) from 1996 onwards. Implementation of an IMF-approved reform programme began on schedule in January 1996, and in July the Government published a detailed development plan for the remainder of the decade. At the end of 1996 the World Bank congratulated the Yemeni Government on its 'remarkable success' in stabilizing the currency and reducing the rate of price inflation (which by November 1996 was less than 10% on an annualized basis). In June 1997 a consultative group of 26 international aid donors met in Brussels, Belgium, to review the implementation of Yemen's structural adjustment programme. The World Bank, the IMF and other major donors agreed that progress to date had exceeded all expectations and expressed strong confidence in the future of the programme. The meeting pledged a total of $1,800m. in aid to Yemen over the next three years. In July 1999 the IMF, which had approved a new support package for Yemen in late 1997, commended the Government for 'pushing ahead effectively with its reform programme' in the 'difficult circumstances' arising from the 1998 downturn in oil export prices. In April 1999 the World Bank indicated its willingness to consider up to $700m. of new lending to Yemen over the next three years, subject to satisfactory implementation of existing Bank-funded projects. The strong recovery in international oil prices in 1999 and 2000 was accompanied by a significant upturn in Yemen's oil production capacity, so that the Government began to enjoy a more favourable environment for the implementation of economic reforms.

Yemen's nominal GDP at current prices rose from 1,132,619m. riyals in 1999 to 1,379,812m. riyals in 2000, in which year the main sectoral components were oil and gas (33.7%); agriculture, forestry and fisheries (15.3%); transportation, storage and com-

munications (10.3%); wholesale and retail trade (8.7%); financial institutions and real estate (7.8%); manufacturing, including oil refining (7.5%); and construction (4.3%). The oil and gas sector has a particular prominence in Yemen's nominal GDP statistics, which directly reflect large swings in world oil prices and changes in currency exchange rates against the US dollar (in which world oil prices are denominated). The rise in oil prices from late 1999 (which coincided with an upturn in Yemen's oil production capacity) boosted the sector's share of GDP from one-quarter in 1999 to more than one-third in 2000, a level largely maintained in 2001, a year in which oil prices were moderated but remained buoyant. According to the IMF, Yemen's real GDP at constant prices increased at an average annual rate of 5.6% in the period 1995–99 (9.8% for the oil and gas sector and 4.7% for the non-oil economy), while real consumption per head grew at an average rate of 2.9% per year and inflation averaged 25.3% per year. The IMF estimated the year-on-year growth rates in real GDP as 7.9% in 1995, 2.9% in 1996, 8.1% in 1997, 4.9% in 1998 and 3.7% in 1999.

In 2000 the rate of real GDP growth was 5.1%, but in 2001 it declined to an estimated 3.3% owing to a stabilization of oil production and a decline in non-oil GDP growth. In 2001 the Yemeni Government finalized its five-year development plan for the period 2001–2005, having previously adopted a far-reaching structural reform programme (including privatization and public-sector rationalization) drawn up in consultation with advisers from the IMF and World Bank. The plan incorporated a detailed poverty reduction strategy designed to reduce the estimated 40% of the population living below internationally recognized levels of poverty and to address associated social problems. The Government's broad economic policy objectives were to continue the process of structural reform in order to provide conditions 'conducive to an acceleration of growth led by private-sector activity and investment and characterized by a free and open economy, domestic financial stability and external viability', while at the same time ensuring 'a significant improvement in social indicators'. Yemen's border treaty with Saudi Arabia, concluded in June 2000, was widely portrayed in Yemen as an event of major economic significance, opening the way to substantial increases in trade, investment and economic cooperation. There was significant oil industry interest in Yemen's subsequent development of oil exploration blocks in areas adjacent to the Saudi border, the first such block being allocated to the company responsible for one-half of Yemen's current oil output. In December 2000 Saudi Arabia agreed to resume economic aid to Yemen, confirming the full normalization of relations after a decade of estrangement.

The international economic downturn in the aftermath of the 11 September 2001 terrorist attacks on the US mainland posed some difficulties for Yemen, notably in terms of increased transport costs and dwindling tourism receipts; but oil revenues remained healthy, underpinning a forecast 4% GDP growth rate in 2002 and further efforts to diversify the economy. The consumer price index rose by an annual average of 11% in 2000, 12% in 2001 and a projected 16% in 2002, whilst the official rate of unemployment fell from 35% in 2000 to 18% in 2001.

AGRICULTURE AND FISHING

The contribution of the agriculture, forestry and fisheries sector to GDP declined unevenly from 24.2% in 1990 to 15.3% in 2000; but the sector remains a disproportionately large source of employment in Yemen. Agriculture provided 58% of male employment and 95% of female employment among the 77% of Yemen's population who lived in rural areas at the time of the December 1994 census. The 1999 labour market survey showed that the sector employed 1.9m. persons (1.1m. men and 0.8m. women), representing about 54% of those in employment. The real annual growth rate of agricultural production averaged 4.5% in the decade to 2000. Only 6% of Yemen's land area is categorized by the World Bank as arable (and only one-half of this as 'crop land'), while 7% is classed as forest and woodland and 30% as permanent pasture. The remaining 57% is largely desert and scrub. Of a total cultivable area of 1.7m. ha, 1.1m. ha were in cultivation in 2000, with 65% being devoted to cereals, 11% to fodder, 9% to cash crops such as cotton, 9% to fruit and 6% to vegetables.

The greater part of the arable land is in the western part of the country, which is the most fertile area of the Arabian peninsula, with a long tradition of intensive cultivation by smallholders. The wide range of climatic conditions across the hillsides, mountains, valleys, coastal plains and highland plateaux of western Yemen make it possible to cultivate a diversity of crop types, including dates, tobacco and cotton on the drought-prone Tihama plain and in coastal areas further to the south; coffee (at altitudes above 1,300 m); the qat bush (mainly at altitudes between 1,500 m and 2,500 m); sorghum or durra (at altitudes up to 3,000 m); and other cereals including wheat, barley and maize. Traditional fruit and vegetable crops in the highland areas include citrus fruits, apricots, peaches, grapes, tomatoes and potatoes, while newer crops encouraged since the 1970s under agricultural development programmes (often backed by bans on fruit and vegetable imports) include water-melons, cucumbers, peas, cauliflowers and lettuces. Mangoes, bananas and papayas are grown at lower altitudes where subtropical conditions prevail. The less favourable climate and terrain of Yemen's desert interior restrict agricultural production mainly to the wadi areas with sufficient water resources to support farming. The fertile Wadi Hadramawt, extending across 160 km of eastern Yemen, is the largest wadi system in the Arabian peninsula. Livestock farming and animal herding are important activities in most parts of Yemen, supplying much of the local demand for meat and dairy products and providing a small exportable surplus of hides and skins.

Agricultural development projects, mainly financed by foreign aid, featured prominently in the development plans of the former YAR and PDRY and have remained a priority since unification. Established in 1993, the Fish and Agriculture Promotion Fund (FAPF) had by 2001 financed some 3,340 programmes and projects, including more than 700 in the field of irrigation and water construction. Other bodies include the Tihama Development Authority (TDA), which was set up with aid from the International Fund for Agricultural Development (IFAD), the IDA and other sources to oversee the development of irrigation systems, water storage schemes and ground-water exploitation in the Tihama region. The TDA's Wadi Sihan project is designed to irrigate an initial 5,700 ha of land. The building of a major new Marib dam at Wadi Abida was completed in 1986 with financing from the Abu Dhabi Fund for Development. The dam has a storage capacity of 390m. cu m and is designed to provide perennial irrigation for 6,000 ha of cereal crops, with 5,000 ha of intermittent irrigation. Plans for a second development phase of the Marib dam scheme were finalized in 2000. Small-scale dam-building projects have been undertaken in many other wadi areas throughout Yemen. A major scheme was inaugurated in eastern Yemen in the 1980s to increase production on 3,225 ha of agricultural land in Hadramawt. Third-phase work on this scheme—originally scheduled for completion by 1996 as an irrigation project—was to be extended to include flood control systems designed to provide better protection against exceptionally heavy rainfall (the area having suffered extensive flood damage in early 1989). A $21.3m. IDA credit was approved in 2000 for the first phase of a project to improve state irrigation systems over a total area of 90,000 ha of agricultural land.

Fish catches were around 50,000 tons in the former PDRY and 21,000 tons in the former YAR in the mid-1980s. It has long been recognized that the Arabian Sea fishing grounds off southern Yemen and, to a lesser extent, the Red Sea grounds off western Yemen, have considerable untapped development potential. Ongoing fisheries expansion schemes at the time of unification in May 1990 included a long-term programme in the south which was then mid-way through its third phase. Fourth-phase funding was subsequently secured in 1991–92 from IDA, IFAD and the European Community (EC, now European Union—EU). Yemen's fish-canning factories at Mukalla and Shukra were in mid-1998 seeking new investment (possibly involving privatization) to double their production capacity. In 1999 the Yemeni fish catch totalled 123,607 tons, about 90% of which was marketed within Yemen. Whereas the Government's planning target was to achieve an annual catch of 168,000 tons by 2000, the actual catch in that year was 134,733 tons (valued at 19,209m. riyals), the 9% increase on 1999 being attributed to improved fishing methods and techniques.

Yemen's trade in agricultural produce is heavily in deficit, annual production of such exportable cash crops as coffee and cotton having remained at fairly modest levels (around 28,000 tons and 11,000 tons respectively in 2000) while local production of staple food crops has supplied a diminishing proportion of local demand. Efforts to increase cereals output have been hampered by uncertain rainfall, so that Yemen has continued to rely on imports of wheat in particular, at an annual level of 2m.–3m. tons in recent years. Aggregate production of cereals rose to 911,304 tons in 1999 (including 167,402 tons of wheat and 547,920 tons of sorghum and millet), but fell to 757,932 tons in 1999 (including 139,563 tons of wheat and 464,240 of sorghum and millet) and to 735,317 tons in 2000 (including 141,884 tons of wheat and 440,300 tons of sorghum and millet). Nevertheless, the added value of the agricultural sector as a whole rose by 3.7%, to 192,199m. riyals at current prices, in 2000, a year in which the production of vegetables increased to 774,908 tons (from 759,820 tons in 1999), production of fodder increased to 14.1m. tons (from 14m. tons in 1999), production of cash crops (cotton, sesame, tobacco and coffee) increased to 68,963 tons (from 65,010 tons in 1999) and production of fruit increased to 590,796 tons (from 578,573 tons in 1999). According to official figures, Yemen had 1.34m. cattle in 2000, 4.8m. sheep, 4.3m. goats and 190,000 camels.

The true balance between food crops and cash crops in the agriculture of Yemen is difficult to assess accurately, because a key crop, the mildly narcotic qat, is not reliably recorded in official statistics. There is no doubt that the qat bush is by far the most profitable cash crop, although its growers are not eligible for such benefits as concessionary agricultural loans and do not have access to export markets (qat use being banned in neighbouring Arab countries). Inside Yemen, however, the chewing of qat leaves is a regular social ritual for the majority of the adult population. Chewing sessions take place every day from 2 p.m. to sunset, the former PDRY's 'weekend only' restriction having been abolished after Yemeni unification. Qat growing occupies a significant proportion of Yemen's best agricultural land—between 50,000 ha and 70,000 ha in the mid-1980s, and an estimated 120,000 ha in the late 1990s—and entails weekly irrigation, accounting for an estimated 16% of national water usage. Moreover, qat grows year-round, permanently occupying land that might have been used for crop rotation. Qat has no nutritional value. The World Bank has estimated that Yemen's internal trade in qat generates at least 25% of gross domestic product (GDP) and 16% of employment. A 1998 estimate by Yemeni analysts suggested that qat-chewing sessions occupied up to 20m. man-hours each day and that current spending on qat exceeded the value of the national budget. Many regular users are said to spend 25% to 50% of their total incomes on qat; some users as much as 66% of income. A conservative estimate published in the late 1990s suggested that purchases of qat accounted for an average 5%–10% of total household expenditure in all except the desert regions of Yemen. A 20% tax on retail sales of qat yielded 1,600m. riyals in 1999 despite serious enforcement problems. Critics of qat cultivation in Yemen include experts on water resource depletion. A World Bank study of regional water resources, published in 1997, described Yemen as the most 'water stressed' country in the Middle East and North Africa, with only 176 cu m of water available per head of population per year from renewable underground reserves, compared with a regional average of 1,250 cu m and a world average of 7,500 cu m. ('Availability' in this context is the maximum rate of extraction from aquifers without causing irreversible depletion of reserves.) In 1994, the report said, Yemen pumped an estimated 2,800m. cu m of water from aquifers whose sustainable withdrawal rate was 2,100m. cu m per year. With all available surface water resources in full use, more than 60% of Yemen's total 1994 water supply was from aquifers, and 93% of the withdrawals from aquifers were for agricultural use. Sustainable patterns of water use on farms with traditional terraced irrigation systems had been critically disrupted by the introduction of modern tube-well technology in response to the pressure of rapid population growth over the past 20 years. The San'a basin, containing 10% of Yemen's population, faced complete exhaustion of its aquifers within 10 years if extraction from them continued at its 1994 rate of 224m. cu m per year. There were at least 45,000 groundwater wells in

Yemen in 1994, when the depths of some newly drilled wells in the San'a basin exceeded 2,000 m. Underground water levels near Amran (a major centre of the qat trade) fell by 30 m in the first half of the 1990s. The 1997 World Bank study said that the Government had, in effect, contributed to Yemen's water crisis by banning the importation of qat (which is also cultivated in Ethiopia, Somalia and Kenya), banning the importation of fruit and vegetables, and failing to abolish all subsidies on the price of diesel (the main fuel for water pumps). Yemen's new Prime Minister acknowledged in mid-1998 that the water crisis was his country's 'greatest problem'. There was, he said, a case for differential pricing in the agricultural sector to curb wasteful usage by qat growers. In May 1999 it was announced that President Saleh had ceased to use qat and had launched a campaign to encourage other prominent Yemenis to follow his example. Qat-chewing in public buildings and during working hours was banned in late 1999. Nevertheless, qat production was officially recorded as having risen to 108,043 tons in 2000, from cultivated land totalling 102,934 ha, yielding revenues of 64,178m. riyals.

MINING AND ENERGY

Although it does not qualify for membership of the Organization of the Petroleum Exporting Countries (OPEC), Yemen is a significant producer of crude petroleum and natural gas, revenue from which provides crucial support for the state budget and investment programme. The sector's contribution to GDP rose from 6% in 1994 to 33.7% in 2000, in which year petroleum accounted for 75.8% of the Government's revenue compared with 64.1% in 1999. At the end of 2001 Yemen's proven reserves of petroleum (virtually all situated in fields discovered between 1984 and 1993) totalled 4,000m. barrels, sufficient to maintain the current level of production for 24.2 years.

The discovery in July 1984 of significant oil deposits in the Marib/al-Jawf region, in the north-east of the YAR, was followed by discoveries across the border in the neighbouring Shabwa region of the PDRY. Small-scale production of crude oil began in the YAR at the end of 1985, and in the PDRY in mid-1987. Talks between the YAR and PDRY Governments on closer economic co-operation led to the establishment in January 1989 of a joint company to administer oil exploration and development rights in a cross-border area totalling 2,200 sq km. At the time of Yemeni unification in May 1990 aggregate oil output averaged 180,000 b/d, of which less than 10,000 b/d was produced in the former PDRY's Shabwa region. The first-phase development work in Shabwa was carried out by Soviet contractors, who suspended their oilfield production operations in mid-1990 pending completion of a pipeline link to the port of Bir Ali on the Gulf of Aden. The 200-km Bir Ali pipeline was inaugurated in May 1991 with a rated capacity of 100,000 b/d, greatly exceeding the installed output capacity of the Shabwa wells.

Concession rights in the former YAR's Marib/al-Jawf oilfields were held by a US-South Korean consortium whose operating company was Yemen Hunt Oil Co (a subsidiary of Hunt Oil of the USA). Yemen Hunt Oil's annual average production reached nearly 170,000 b/d in 1988 following the completion in 1987 of a 440-km pipeline running west from Marib to a Red Sea export terminal at Ras Isa, offshore from the port of Salif. The rated capacity of the Ras Isa pipeline was 225,000 b/d, expandable to 400,000 b/d if required in the future. Installations on the Alif oilfield (the first of the Marib/al-Jawf fields to go into production) include a 10,000 b/d 'topping' (primary distillation) plant which came on stream in April 1986 to supply gasoline, diesel and fuel oil for local consumption. Proposals were put forward in 1999 to expand the capacity of this plant to between 15,000 b/d and 20,000 b/d, the state-owned Yemen Oil Refining Co having made it known in October 1998 that it was seeking to take over ownership of the plant with a view to securing new foreign investment in an expansion scheme. In an exploration block immediately to the east of the Marib/al-Jawf concession area, the Jannah oilfield was brought into production by a separate Hunt Oil subsidiary (Jannah Hunt Oil Co) as operator for a consortium of US, French, Kuwaiti and Russian oil companies. The Jannah field's output, which is transported to the coast via the Ras Isa pipeline, averaged 15,000 b/d on start-up in October 1996 and reached an estimated 67,000 b/d in 2000.

After Yemeni unification more than 10 significant oilfields were discovered in the 1,260 sq km Masila exploration block in the eastern Hadramawt region. Canadian Occidental Petroleum (CanOxy), the operating company in this block, made its first oil shipment in August 1993 via a 140-km pipeline built to link the Masila fields to an export terminal west of the port of ash-Shihr on the Gulf of Aden. Yemen's average annual oil output rose from 210,000 b/d in 1993 to 345,000 b/d in 1994 (about 45% of the 1994 total coming from Masila). In the East Shabwa concession area, immediately west of the Masila fields, Total-CFP (the operator for a consortium of French, Kuwaiti, US and Australian oil companies) brought the Kharir oilfield into production at the end of 1997 at an initial rate of 20,000 b/d. Output from East Shabwa, which is transported via CanOxy's Masila export pipeline, was targeted to reach 30,000 b/d by 1999. Expectations of production growth in the main Shabwa exploration areas (situated 200 km west of the East Shabwa block) were not fulfilled in the 1990s despite extensive exploration work. In 1991 Nimir Petroleum (a Cayman-registered company owned by private Saudi Arabian oil interests) paid an exceptionally high premium to obtain the operating licence for the only Shabwa block with established production facilities (in the Ayadh field linked to the Bir Ali pipeline). However, Nimir's output from the Ayadh field did not exceed 5,000 b/d and was around 3,500 b/d when the company suspended production during Yemen's civil war in 1994. Nimir subsequently sought improved financial terms, bringing the Ayadh field back into production in 1997 at an initial rate of 1,500 b/d after the legislature had approved an amended production-sharing agreement. At the end of 2000, however, Nimir abandoned the Ayadh field and relinquished its other concession interests in Yemen.

In mid-1997 a total of 167,602 sq km of Yemeni territory—including some of the least intensively explored parts of the Arabian peninsula—was divided into 56 oil exploration blocks, of which 31 then remained open to bids from prospective concession holders. Competition between foreign oil companies for new oil concessions had been strongest in Yemen's 1991–92 licensing round, which included notably Shabwa blocks regarded at that time as prime development sites. Disappointing exploration results in the Shabwa region caused several companies to opt for non-renewal of their agreements in 1994–95, while Nimir Petroleum, as the operator of a producing Shabwa field, suspended production until it secured improved terms (although it later abandoned the field—see above). Prior to the start of small-scale production in the East Shabwa block, Total-CFP successfully negotiated for a 70% cost-recovery allowance (compared with a previous government offer of a 40% allowance). There was a general improvement in 1995–96 in the terms offered to new concession-holders, including an increase of 5% in average cost-recovery allowances, and the Government made particular efforts during 1997 to attract new investment in smaller blocks and blocks that had been assessed as marginal on the basis of previous exploration work. Foreign companies signing new oil exploration agreements or renewing existing agreements in 1997–98 included Transglobe Energy, First Calgary Petroleum and Calvalley Petroleum (all of Canada), Kerr McGee Corpn (of the USA), MOL (of Hungary), Preussag Energie (of Germany) and three British companies, Mayfair Petroleum, Dove Energy and Oil and Gas Mine Co (OGMC, owned by Yemeni interests). In 1997 the state-owned Yemen Oil and Gas Corpn was authorized to acquire minority equity stakes (of 15% to 25%) in newly awarded exploration blocks. In late 1999 the Government announced that Yemen's next oil licensing round would incorporate improved incentives for investment, including reductions in concession-holders' initial 'signature' payments, reductions in minimum royalty rates, and increases in cost-recovery allowances. Five onshore and two offshore blocks were opened to bidding on the improved terms in early 2000. Later in the year the Government indicated its intention to offer four new blocks in areas covered by Yemen's June 2000 border treaty with Saudi Arabia.

Yemen's total oil output averaged 350,000 b/d in 1995, 355,000 b/d in 1996 and 370,000 b/d in 1997. In April 1998, when production was running at 386,500 b/d, the contributions of the respective producing companies were 200,000 b/d from CanOxy's Masila block, 140,000 b/d from Yemen Hunt's Marib/al-Jawf block, 25,000 b/d from Jannah Hunt's Jannah block,

20,000 b/d from Total-CFP's East Shabwa block and 1,500 b/d from Nimir Petroleum's Shabwa block. The estimated government share of April 1998 oil output was just over 200,000 b/d, of which about 115,000 b/d was exported and the remainder consumed locally. Yemeni crude oil was normally priced with reference to standard international benchmarks—thus in 1997–98 Marib light crude was priced at parity with North Sea Brent crude, while Masila crude was priced at a specified discount relative to Brent. The Government's reported oil export revenue rose from US $958m. in 1996 to a record $1,012m. in 1997, reflecting an increase in production during a period of relatively strong export prices. In the first half of 1998, however, a slump in the world oil market cut the average price of Yemen's main export grade by 32% (from $17.27 per barrel in January–June 1997 to $11.80 per barrel in January–June 1998). Over the same period the state share of Yemeni oil output declined by an estimated 20%, resulting in a fall of 45% in the Government's reported oil export revenue.

Yemen was one of several non-members of OPEC to make a public pledge of support for OPEC production cuts designed to counteract the 1998 price slump. A March 1998 statement from Yemen's Ministry of Oil and Mineral Resources said that a Yemeni oil production cut-back of 2%–3% was to be introduced (although the state oil corporation continued to forecast an 11% production increase by the end of 1998). In the event, average 1998 oil output was 380,000 b/d (2.7% higher than the 1997 average); the Government's average share of output in 1998 was 189,000 b/d, of which 107,120 b/d was exported; and the Government's 1998 oil export revenue totalled $453.8m. (a fall of more than 55% compared with 1997). In 1999 production increases were reported from several areas (including Masila, where output averaged 210,000 b/d in the second quarter of the year, and Jannah, where output reached 65,000 b/d in the third quarter of the year), while export prices recovered from the depressed levels of 1998. Overall, Yemen's average oil output rose by 4.6% to 395,000 b/d in 1999. In 2000 Yemen's oil output was 160.6m. barrels, from an average of 440,000 b/d, representing revenues of 605,712m. riyals, compared with 417,284m. riyals in 1999 and 201,159m. riyals in 1998. Production in 2001 rose to an average of 458,000 b/d, well below initial government plans for output levels approaching 500,000 b/d. In November 2001, amidst considerable oil industry scepticism, the Government declared its aim of increasing production to an average of 550,000 b/d in 2002.

In early 2002 the reported distribution of oil output in Yemen was 230,000 b/d from the Masila block operated by Nexen (the new name adopted by CanOxy in November 2000); 122,000 b/d from Yemen Hunt's Marib/al-Jawf block; 67,000 b/d from Jannah Hunt's Jannah block; between 28,000 and 30,000 b/d from the East Shabwa block operated by TotalFinaElf (formerly Total-CFP); and 12,500 b/d from the Howarin block, which was brought into production in November 2000 by the Norwegian company DNO (operator for a consortium including Canada's Transglobe Energy). Companies which announced new oil finds in Yemen in 2000 included Vintage Petroleum (operator of the Damis block, where its partner was Transglobe Energy) and Dove Energy (which declared the Shayroos field commercial in December 2000). Adair Yemen (the local affiliate of Adair International Oil and Gas) was the operator in an exploration block relinquished by Hunt Oil and TotalFinaElf on expiry of a joint licence. Four new blocks in territory bordering Saudi Arabia (and unavailable for exploration until the conclusion of the June 2000 border treaty) were opened to bidding in late 2000. Nexen (in partnership with Occidental Petroleum) was awarded the first of these blocks in early 2001, while a second was secured in mid-2001 by a consortium of PanCanadian Petroleum, the Spanish company Cepsa (as operator) and the Austrian company OMV. Occidental Petroleum secured a new block elsewhere in Yemen in early 2001. The two remaining border blocks were reported to be the subject of intense competition between foreign oil companies. Seven blocks in other areas of Yemen were included in a licensing round in 2001, and it was announced that up to 40 more blocks were to be made available in 2002.

At the end of 2001 Yemen had proven reserves of natural gas totalling 480,000m. cu m, discovered both separately and in association with oil by companies drilling in oil concession areas

(the main discoveries of non-associated gas having been made in the Marib/al-Jawf and Jannah blocks). Throughout the first half of the 1990s various proposals were put forward for a major gas development project centred on the export of liquefied natural gas (LNG). In March 1997 the Yemeni legislature approved the establishment of a consortium to organize the planned project. As constituted in October 1997, the consortium comprised Total-CFP (the project leader, with a 36% interest), the state-owned General Gas Corpn (21%), Hunt Oil (15.1%), Exxon (14.5%) and the South Korean companies Yukong (8.4%) and Hyundai (5%). It was envisaged that gas would be piped from Marib to a liquefaction plant on the Gulf of Aden with an export capacity of 5.3m. metric tons per year. However, the consortium's sole memorandum of understanding, with the Turkish company Botas, was not renewed on its expiry at the end of 1997, by which time many target markets in Asia were experiencing severe economic downturns. In May 1998 discussions were opened with BG UK Holdings regarding the possible supply of Yemeni LNG to an import terminal under construction on the west coast of India by British Gas International. The Yemen Government was meanwhile awaiting the completion of a feasibility study on the economics of creating a local gas supply grid and of establishing gas-fired power plants in Yemen. Gas production in 2000 was officially recorded at 463m. tons of oil equivalent (compared with 413m. tons in 1999), yielding revenue of 4,020m. riyals.

In May 2000 the consortium responsible for Yemen's planned LNG export project (now operating under the name Yemen Liquefied Natural Gas Co) announced its decision to invite bids for the project's engineering, procurement and construction contracts. The consortium had yet to conclude any firm sales and purchase agreements for Yemeni LNG. The published project specifications included a liquefaction plant with two LNG trains (each capable of producing 3.1m. tons per year), a 300-km gas supply pipeline and two smaller pipelines. By the end of 2000 the consortium had received several bids for each of the project's construction contracts. It had not, however, secured any customers for the LNG it proposed to produce. Its marketing efforts were similarly unproductive in 2001 and in the first half of 2002, so that the project remained dormant, although it retained the support of the Government.

Yemen's principal non-hydrocarbon mine and quarry products include rock salt, limestone, marble, gypsum, granite, basalt and clay. This sector contributed only 0.1% of GDP in 2000, when Yemen produced 2.5m. tons of quarried stone, 819,000 tons of sand and gravel aggregate, 154,000 tons of salt and 43,000 tons of gypsum. Deposits of copper, nickel, zinc, lead, coal, iron, sulphur, silver, gold and uranium are known to exist. Improved mapping and evaluation of hard mineral resources have been prioritized by the post-unification Government, which has obtained financial assistance from the World Bank, UNDP and IDA for surveying work. The Government is particularly interested in the possibility of Yemen becoming a significant producer of gold, which Soviet surveyors first discovered at Medden (50 km west of Mukalla) in the early 1980s. Gold-prospecting licences were held by Irish, Dutch and British companies in 1992, and in 1993 prospecting rights in a further 30,000 sq km were granted to a Yemeni company. In 1997 a Canadian company, Menora Resources, was carrying out a pre-feasibility drilling programme at Medden, where the measured resource of gold was recorded at 280,000 oz. In early 1998 the Yemen Government announced that five companies were currently engaged in mineral prospecting, including exploration for zinc and lead, and that new gold discoveries had been made by Canadian, US and Indonesian prospecting companies. In July 2000 a Canadian company signed an agreement to develop nickel, copper and cobalt deposits in the Haja region.

MANUFACTURING AND INDUSTRY

The industrial sector, broadly defined to include manufacturing, construction and the supply of electricity, gas and water, contributed 12.4% of GDP in 2000, compared with 18% in 1994. Within this total, manufacturing (including oil refining) accounted for an estimated 7.5% of GDP in 1999, compared with 14% in 1994. Excluding oil refining, manufacturing accounted for 4.9% of GDP in 2000, compared with 13.4% in 1994. The largest industrial plant in Yemen at the time of unification in 1990 was the former BP oil refinery at Aden, opened in 1954 when Aden was among the world's busiest seaports. The Government designated Aden as the 'economic capital' of the unified state, its aim being to re-establish the port as a major regional trading centre incorporating an industrial free-trade zone. By 2000 Yemen had 33,972 industrial establishments with a total of 114,869 employees, including 383 employing 10 or more people.

The state-owned Aden Refinery Co, set up by the former PDRY Government when the predominantly export-orientated Aden refinery was nationalized in 1977, obtained crude oil processing contracts from various countries during the 1980s, including India, Saudi Arabia, Libya, Kuwait, Iran, Algeria, Iraq and the USSR. At the time of the Iraqi invasion of Kuwait in August 1990, Iraq (30,000 b/d) and Kuwait (20,000 b/d) were the Aden refinery's principal suppliers of preferentially priced crude oil. Part of unified Yemen's own recently developed crude oil production (which in mid-1990 came wholly from oilfields in the former YAR) was subsequently diverted from its intended export markets in order to cover the refinery's loss of imports resulting from the UN embargo on trade with Iraq and Iraqi-occupied Kuwait. Only about one-third of the refinery's nominal processing capacity of 170,000 b/d was in use in the early 1990s, when the Government of unified Yemen was seeking financing for a two-phase modernization programme to raise that capacity by 80,000 b/d (the first 30,000 b/d at an estimated cost of US $150m., and the final 50,000 b/d at an estimated cost of $200m.). The Aden refinery was shut down for some weeks during and immediately following the 1994 civil war after several of its storage tanks were destroyed in the fighting. There was no major damage to the distillation facilities, and the plant was operating at its normal pre-war production volume by early August 1994. In early 1995 the refinery was processing crude oil from Yemen, Malaysia, Iran and Oman and producing an average 95,000 b/d of refined products.

At the end of 1995 the Aden refinery was processing an average 60,000 b/d of domestic crude and 40,000 b/d of imported crude. In 1996 detailed specifications were drawn up for upgrading works that would entail the construction of a new smaller processing facility at Aden to provide some continuity of supply during a shutdown of the existing plant. Having put the upgrading project out to three successive rounds of tendering, the Government decided in late 1997 to seek private investment in the Aden Refinery Co with the aim of financing the upgrading work out of the proceeds of share sales to local and foreign investors. The principle of returning the company to majority private ownership was approved by the Council of Ministers in May 1998. In December 2000 the Prime Minister said that preparations were being made to seek a private buyer for an initial 51% stake in the project, and the Government reaffirmed its commitment to the project in November 2001. In an unrelated development, a private Yemeni company secured a US $300,000 grant from the US Trade and Development Agency in June 1997 towards a feasibility study for a proposed new oil refinery on northern Yemen's Red Sea coast, near the Ras Isa oil export terminal. A further feasibility study for this project was initiated in May 2002 by the US-based VECO Consultants, which was also studying the feasibility of upgrading the small Marib oil refinery to double its capacity to 20,000 b/d.

A plant for blending lubricating oils was opened at Taiz in May 1996. The US $20m. plant, with an annual production capacity of 60,000 metric tons, was 30% owned by Mobil and Royal Dutch/Shell and 70% owned by a Yemeni firm which had previously distributed imported lubricants. In 1993 unified Yemen achieved self-sufficiency in bottled liquefied petroleum gas (LPG—for which there had previously been a $40m. annual import requirement), following the opening of a bottling plant at San'a.

Non-hydrocarbon manufactures in the former PDRY included textiles, agricultural implements, cigarettes, ginned cotton, liquid batteries, animal feedstuffs, construction materials (including cement blocks, tiles and bricks), crystallized sea salt, food and drink products, plastic products and aluminium goods. It was the policy of the post-unification Government that Yemeni businesses affected by the former PDRY's nationalization policies should in due course be returned to their former private owners. The Arabian peninsula's only brewery, in the Aden

suburb of Mansura, was forced to close down in 1994 in the aftermath of the civil war. Industrial development in the former YAR was aimed primarily at achieving self-sufficiency in food processing, clothing and construction materials and at developing traditional occupations using local raw materials, including textiles, leather goods, basketry, jewellery and glass making. In the mid-1980s one-third of the loans to YAR businesses by the Industrial Bank of Yemen were for food and drink production. Other sectors of particular interest to the bank were construction materials; light and household chemicals and plastics; light engineering; woodworking; and electrical and mechanical services. The relatively modest scale of unified Yemen's manufacturing base was illustrated by 1997 estimates showing that local flour production was around 210,000 metric tons per year, while imports of flour were currently around 800,000 tons per year. Contracts were awarded in late 1997 for a 1,500-tons-per-day flour mill and associated silos at Aden (inaugurated in October 1999) and for a 600-tons-per-day flour mill and associated silos at the Red Sea port of Salif (scheduled for completion in 2000).

The state-owned Yemen Corpn for Cement Production and Marketing (also known as Yemen Cement Co) had an installed production capacity of 1.25m. metric tons per year in 2000 at its plants at Bajil (established in 1973 and expanded in 1983 to 250,000 tons capacity), Amran (established in 1982 with a capacity of 500,000 tons) and Mafraq (established in 1993 with a capacity of 500,000 tons). Production from these plants (which were reported to be operating at close to maximum capacity in 2000) was sufficient to supply an estimated 40%–50% of Yemen's annual demand for cement, the balance being supplied by imports from neighbouring countries (reported to include some unrecorded illegal imports). Bids were submitted in January 2002 for a contract to add up to 1.2m. tons of new capacity to the Amran plant, the contract being subsequently awarded to Ishikawajima-Harima Heavy Industries of Japan. Planning permission was granted in 1998 for the construction of a private-sector cement factory. In 1997 a US $120m. iron smelter was under construction in Abyan. Its developer, the United Company for Mineral Industries (owned by Bugshan Steel of Saudi Arabia), anticipated that three-fifths of the smelter's raw materials would consist of scrap iron available within Yemen and that the remainder would be imported.

The centre-piece of unified Yemen's industrial development strategy is a commercial and industrial free-zone development at Aden, modelled on similar initiatives in other developing countries. Inaugurated in May 1991 (at which time 50 industrial projects had already received outline approval), the zone was to be developed in stages over a period of years. A proposal submitted by US consultants in 1993 recommended total investment of US $5,600m. in four phases over a period of 25 years, centred on the development of port infrastructure to take full advantage of Aden's potential as a transhipment centre for the container traffic of regional ports situated further away from the main international shipping lanes. The plan included proposals for new harbour facilities, an airport extension, a new 300-MW gas-turbine power station and new manufacturing infrastructure, and recommended that development be on a fully-privatized basis. The Yemen Free Zones Public Authority (YFZPA) subsequently announced its intention to seek full privatization of all administrative operations at the port and airport, to countenance full private ownership of the proposed extensions, and to open up Aden's existing port and airport facilities to some form of joint-venture participation by private interests.

In March 1996 the YFZPA finalized an agreement whereby a company called Yemen Investment and Development International (Yeminvest) became the concession holder and project co-ordinator for the Aden development programme. Ownership of Yeminvest from October 1997 was 51% by Yemen Holdings (owned by Saudi Arabian private interests) and 49% by PSA Corpn (formerly known as the Port of Singapore Authority). PSA was to manage and operate a new Aden container terminal for 20 years following completion of the first phase of construction, scheduled for March 1999. Costing up to US $280m., the first-phase works included dredging harbour channels, building six quays and a new transhipment terminal, installing a small power plant, equipping the terminal with cranes and other facilities and providing access roads and other ancillary features. The handling capacity of the terminal would be 500,000 20-foot-equivalent units (TEUs) per year. It was intended that completion of the port facilities should be followed by the development of a 1,350-ha site for export-orientated industries; modernization and improvement of infrastructure and facilities and expansion of cargo-handling capacity at Khormaksar international airport; construction of a new power station; and (as the final phase of the development programme) construction of a World Trade Centre complex including 100,000 sq m of office space and 9,300 sq m of exhibition space. According to Yeminvest's initial revenue projections, the free-zone development would be self-financing by its seventh year, with the container port playing an important income-generating role. The Yemen Government's entitlement to revenue from free-zone operations was to rise gradually from 25% to 100% over the 25-year life of the concession.

The Aden container terminal opened on schedule in March 1999, on completion of the bulk of the first-phase development work. Its first regular user, American President Lines, stepped up its transhipment volumes from April 1999 (having made a corresponding reduction in its use of the Sri Lankan port of Colombo). A British shipping consortium, Beacon, began to call at the Aden terminal on a trial basis in August 1999. The container terminal's average monthly throughput exceeded 15,000 TEUs in the last quarter of 1999. Annual throughput rose from 247,913 TEUs in 2000 to 377,367 TEUs in 2001, despite a 15% fall in traffic following the events of 11 September 2001. Construction work on the initial phase of the Aden free zone's industrial and commercial estate (known as Aden Distripark) began in January 2001. Basic infrastructure for an area of 30 ha was scheduled for completion by September 2001. At the start of 2001 about 30% of the available first-phase space had been reserved, mainly by Yemeni companies. In March 2001 Yeminvest signed a memorandum of understanding for the largest project so far planned for the estate, namely a sugar refinery with a capacity of 200,000 metric tons per year of refined sugar and 13,000 tons of molasses. Yemen Sugar Co, owned 50% by the US company Adair International Oil and Gas, 40% by a private Yemeni company and 10% by a US sugar company, aimed to supply both the Yemeni domestic market and regional (primarily East African) export markets. The proposed sugar refinery would include a 21-MW power station which would supply some of its electricity output to other users of the free zone.

Yemen's General Investment Authority (GIA), established in 1991 to encourage and supervise new investment in Yemen (including investment by Yemenis resident abroad) was in 1998 operating within the framework of recently amended investment laws offering an extensive range of tax and other incentives. GIA promotional campaigns placed particular emphasis on investment in labour-intensive export industries, including the manufacture of textiles, for which Yemen offered the advantage of quota-free access to the EU, the USA and other main markets.

POWER AND WATER

The electricity, gas and water sector contributed an estimated 0.7% of Yemen's GDP in 2000 (compared with 0.8% in 1994). A main planning priority in the power sector after unification in 1990 was to link the electricity grids of the former YAR and PDRY. This was finally achieved in July 1997 at a total cost of US $64m. (of which $54m. was funded by the Arab Fund for Economic and Social Development—AFESD). It was estimated that Yemen's nominal electricity generating capacity from all sources (including small public supplies not connected to the national grid, as well as private diesel generators in remote areas) did not exceed 700 MW in 1997. The World Bank estimated that the Public Electricity Corpn's total 1997 installed capacity was a nominal 596 MW, of which only 408 MW was effectively available because of the technical limitations of Yemen's power plants and distribution lines. High growth of energy demand—stimulated partly by subsidized tariffs—had placed Yemen's electricity supply system under severe pressure for some years. San'a had experienced particularly bad power shortages since 1993, and some generating and transmission facilities had suffered damage in the 1994 civil war. In 1997 the Government drew up a $51m. emergency power project to

cover Yemen's electricity needs until the year 2001. As submitted to IDA (from which funding was sought) the project called for the rapid installation of 30 MW of additional generating capacity at the Dhahban power plant serving San'a; the rehabilitation of 20 MW of existing diesel generating capacity at the same plant; and the improvement of transmission lines to ensure that the plant's increased output was fully available to the grid. Work on the installation of 30 MW of new oil-fired generating capacity began in December 1998 and was scheduled for completion by the end of 1999.

At mid-2002 Yemen had a total installed generating capacity of 700 MW and was expected to have need of an additional 500 MW by 2010; the cost of installing the additional capacity was expected to exceed US $600m. Pending the creation of new capacity, industry sources maintained that power shortages could be partly remedied by recovering the 30% of current electricity output lost as a result of the inefficiency of the national grid. In May 2002 the Yemen Government initialled an agreement for the operation of a proposed independent power project put forward by Marib Power Co Yemen, a joint venture between Delma Power Co (based in the USA) and Consolidated Contractors International Co (based in Greece). Under these proposals a gas-fired plant with an initial generating capacity of 400 MW would be constructed near Marib on build-own-operate terms and would supply electricity at significantly lower cost than existing oil-fired plants.

Major water-supply initiatives in post-unification Yemen included a project to bring drinking water to 45,000 people in over 100 villages to the north of Aden. The first phase of this project, involving the drilling of wells in the coastal Wadi Bani and the construction of the means of raising the water 1,500 m to the Laboos plateau, was under way in late 1991. The Radaa water supply and sanitation project, involving the supply of drinking water to some 30,000 people, was also under way. Aden's water supply system and sewerage facilities were severely disrupted during the civil war in 1994, and serious water shortages continued to be reported three months after the end of the fighting in the city. UN agencies identified an emergency requirement for essential repairs costing up to US $5m. to water and sewerage infrastructure. New water and sewerage schemes under consideration in 1996 included a pilot project to improve the water supply in Taiz (for which $10m. was to be provided by the World Bank) and the construction of a waste-water treatment plant in San'a (to be financed by the World Bank, the AFESD and the OPEC Fund for International Development). Two loan agreements relating to water and waste-water projects in San'a were approved by the Yemeni legislature in May 1999 (the sums involved being $25m. from the World Bank and KD 18m. from the AFESD). The first phase of the waste-water project was put out to tender in 2001.

According to a World Bank study, about 88% of Yemen's urban households had access to piped water supplies in 1997, although such supplies were often erratic and interruptions of up to eight weeks could be experienced in some areas. (See Agriculture and Fishing, above, for details of Yemen's underlying water shortage.) In some large cities, including Taiz and San'a, more than one-fifth of the population depended on private-sector water suppliers. It was estimated that two-thirds of all water consumed in San'a in 1997 was provided by these largely unregulated private suppliers. About 90% of Yemen's urban households were estimated to have access to adequate waste-water facilities, although in the majority of cases these took the form of closed pit systems rather than public sewer networks. The disposal of solid waste was a particular problem in urban Yemen in the mid-1990s, as municipal collections tended to be limited to market areas and main streets, leading to accumulations of rubbish in side streets and to uncontrolled dumping of waste outside towns. Laws on environmental protection and waste management were introduced in 1995 to provide a basis for improving this situation.

TRANSPORT AND COMMUNICATIONS

Transportation, storage and communications contributed 10.3% of GDP in 2000, compared with 14.6% in 1994.

In 1999 Yemen had 69,263 km of roads, 12% of which were asphalted and a further 24% of which were classed as paved roads. In 2000 883,429 road vehicles (64% of them commercial vehicles) were in use. Road-building and maintenance are important development priorities, and have been funded to a large extent by foreign aid donors in recent years. After Yemeni unification in 1990 there was an increased emphasis on the improvement of road links across the former YAR–PDRY border. In 1993 the Government of Oman agreed to finance a highway across Oman's newly opened border with Yemen. Road-building schemes scheduled to go to tender in 1998 included 180 km in the south (between Aden and Mukalla) and 65 km in the west (between Salif and Hodeida), both of which were to be financed by the World Bank. More than 800 km of existing roads were included in upgrading plans under consideration in 1998.

The port of Aden, developed around a natural deep harbour, was ideally placed to benefit from the growth of international Suez Canal traffic during the period of British colonial rule. Its trade was especially hard hit by the closure of the Canal from 1967 to 1975 and the subsequent failure of the PDRY Government to respond adequately to changing shipping patterns (including the rapid growth of containerization). The first phase of a major modernization and expansion of Aden's port facilities was completed in 1999 (see Industry and Manufacturing, section). The state transport sector in Aden, including existing port operations, made a net profit of 424m. riyals on a turnover of 1,200m. riyals in 1997. The port's existing freight and distribution services were transferred to seven private contractors in mid-1998 as part of the Government's privatization programme. The volume of imports passing through Aden's established port facilities (i.e. excluding traffic through the newly opened container terminal) exceeded 1.7m. metric tons in 1999, having doubled since 1997. The main port serving the easternmost region of Yemen is Mukalla, an important fishing centre with deep-water harbour facilities developed during the 1980s. The region's main oil export terminal is situated about 35 km east of Mukalla. The main port on Yemen's Red Sea coast is Hodeida, which was greatly expanded in the 1970s and 1980s in line with the growth in the import trade of the former YAR. The selection of Aden as unified Yemen's commercial capital in 1990 implied some slow-down in the future expansion of port facilities at Hodeida. The port of Mocha, situated south of Hodeida (and therefore closer to Aden) cancelled many of its own expansion plans after unification. In contrast, the port of Salif, north of Hodeida, benefited in the 1990s from its proximity to Yemen's Red Sea oil export terminal at Ras Isa.

Aden's international airport at Khormaksar was extensively upgraded in the late 1980s with Soviet financial assistance. However, its terminal building, capable of handling 250,000 passengers annually, was damaged in the 1994 civil war. Repairs to the terminal, as well as the construction of a new control tower and related technical facilities, were included in a World Bank-supported airport rehabilitation project which was put out to tender at the beginning of 1998. In June 1999 a US $24m. contract was awarded for the project, which was scheduled for completion over a period of 30 months. Yemen's other international airports are at San'a (scheduled for future upgrading under plans approved in mid-2002), Hodeida, Taiz and Mukalla. There are 12 main local airports for domestic flights. In total, Yemen had 50 airports and airfields in 1999, and most towns were linked by internal air services. Yemen's national carrier, Yemen Airways or Yemenia, was established in May 1996 through the merger of the former YAR airline (also called Yemenia) and the former PDRY airline (Al-Yemen, previously known as Alyemda). Saudi Arabian Airlines held a 49% shareholding in the merged airline, which took delivery of two Airbus A310-300 aircraft in March 1997. There were substantial increases in domestic and international air fares from April 1995 onwards as part of the Government's subsidy reduction programme. Yemenia carried 479,700 international passengers and 251,300 domestic passengers in 1999. A major fleet renewal programme—involving the replacement of four Boeing 737s, three Boeing 727s and four Dash 7s—was under consideration in 1998. An agreement was signed in 2001 to lease three Boeing 737-800s for eight years from 2002.

Yemen has modern international telecommunications links via satellite stations and microwave relays, as well as relatively good links between major centres within the country. However, many smaller towns and rural areas still had fairly limited telephone networks in the mid-1990s, while there was a gener-

ally inadequate provision of lines within urban centres. Overall, Yemen had only 1.29 fixed telephone lines per 100 inhabitants in 1996. There were 8,800 cellular telephone subscribers in the same year (although mobile telecommunications services, suspended during the 1994 civil war, were not restored until September 1996). Contracts worth US $3m. were awarded in November 1996 for an expansion of the telephone network within San'a and the upgrading of links between San'a and other population centres. In March 1997 Japan announced a $29m. loan to help finance the installation of more than 50,000 additional telephone lines in Aden. In late 1997 the French company Alcatel (currently working at 45 locations in Yemen) was awarded a $14m. contract to install 82,000 new lines throughout the country. Alcatel subsequently won a contract to install a modern telecommunications system on Socotra island. In 1999 Yemen's analogue mobile telephone network (set up in 1992) had 18,000 subscribers, more than 60% of them based in San'a. A new mobile satellite communications service, serving the hydrocarbons, agricultural and tourism sectors, was licensed in June 1999. In the same month the Government announced its intention to seek two service providers to set up competing GSM (global standard for mobiles) networks in Yemen. The two GSM contracts were awarded in July 2000, when it was expected that GSM services would be available nation-wide within two years. The provision of fixed telephone lines by the state-owned Yemen Telecom Corpn totalled 417,100 (2.38 per 100 inhabitants) in 2000. International telephone services are provided by TeleYemen, owned 51% by Cable & Wireless and 49% by Yemen Telecom Corpn.

TOURISM

In 1982 the PDRY and YAR Governments established the Yemen Tourism Co to promote 'package' tours to both countries. In 1987 about 28,000 tourists visited the PDRY. In 1989 the YAR was visited by 55,088 tourists, who spent an estimated US $22m. In 1995 there were 61,400 tourist arrivals in unified Yemen, more than half of them from European countries, generating an estimated revenue of $50m. Yemen's largest tourism company, Universal Travel and Tourism, had links with some 300 overseas tour operators in Europe, the USA and Japan in 1995, when several major hotel developments were in progress to cater for a projected rise in visitor numbers. The main developer was the Tourism Investment Co (50% owned by Universal Travel and Tourism). Yemen earned around $55m. from tourism in 1996, when there were 229 registered hotels in the country. An Egyptian-led consortium submitted proposals in mid-1998 for a tourism resort development on the thinly populated Yemeni island of Socotra (where conservation of the natural environment was an issue of major concern to international environmental experts). All aspects of Socotra's future development, including tourism projects, came under review in 2001 as part of an EU-funded study of the island's medium-term planning options.

A total of 87,600 tourists visited Yemen in 1998, generating an estimated revenue of US $84m. This 3.8% rise in tourist arrivals (from 80,500 in 1997) occurred despite an increase during 1998 in kidnappings of tourists by tribal communities with grievances against the central Government. In an incident of a more serious nature at the end of the year, four foreign hostages were killed during an armed clash between government forces and a militant extremist group. Tourist numbers then fell by one-third, to 58,370, in 1999 as a result of adverse publicity about Yemen's internal security situation, remaining depressed in 2000 as kidnappings and terrorist attacks continued to be reported. Estimated revenue from tourism in 1999 was $48.4m. Financial aid was secured from the EU in August 2000 for the development of a detailed action plan to revive Yemen's tourism industry. The decline in tourist numbers coincided with a growth in the provision of hotel accommodation. The number of hotels in Yemen doubled between 1996 and 2000, with the result that occupancy rates of 30% or less were reported in 2000. Nevertheless, according to official statistics, the number of tourist arrivals recovered to 72,836 in 2000, with one-third coming from Europe and one-third from other countries in the Middle East region. However, the 11 September 2001 terrorist attacks on the US mainland had a notable adverse effect on tourism, receipts from which fell to $63m. for the year as a whole.

BUDGET, INVESTMENT AND FINANCE

After unification, the respective currencies of the two former Yemeni states were legal tender in the Republic of Yemen and could be used at a rate of 1 (South) Yemeni dinar = 26 (North) Yemeni riyals until 20 June 1996, when the old dinar was formally abolished and the riyal became the sole currency unit for the unified Yemen. In mid-1993, when the standard official exchange rate was US $1 = 12.01 riyals (as it had been since February 1990), the black-market value of the Yemeni currency was approximately $1 = 46 riyals (reflecting, in part, the country's annual inflation rate of about 200% at that time). In 1992 the Government had introduced a 'customs rate' of $1 = 18 riyals for all non-essential imports, and in May 1993 it had introduced an 'incentive rate' of 25 riyals to the dollar for oil companies and tourists.

In the unified state's first budget, for 1991, expenditure was projected at 50,980m. riyals (compared with an aggregate figure of 46,256m. riyals in 1990) and revenue at 35,218m. riyals (24,704m. in 1990). The resultant forecast deficit of 15,762m. riyals represented a 27% reduction against the 1990 combined deficit of 21,552m. riyals. The biggest allocation in the 1991 budget was for defence (12,700m. riyals), followed by investment and development (11,000m. riyals) and education (8,300m. riyals). The investment and development allocation did not include loans and grants from external sources, which were seen as crucial for offsetting losses attributable to the Gulf crisis.

The 1992 budget provided for estimated revenue of 45,778m. riyals and expenditure of 58,114m. riyals, and thus for a deficit of 12,336m. riyals. The Government's financial projections for the year envisaged: that its foreign-exchange resources would total US $2,185m. to meet anticipated commitments of $2,349m. (as against resources of $1,836m. and outgoings of $2,212m. in 1991); that imports of wheat, flour, rice and essential drugs would cost $368m.; that all foreign debt obligations would be met in 1992; and that defence spending would be reduced by 12% compared with 1991. The Government did not publish budget proposals for 1993, and was assumed to be organizing its finances on a month-to-month basis, using its 1992 spending as a guide-line for the current year. According to press reports (said to be based on internal Finance Ministry records), actual spending in 1992 had totalled 58,060m. riyals (of which 53,637m. riyals was current spending), while actual revenue had amounted to only 32,008m. riyals (about one-third of estimated GNP). The largest single component of expenditure in 1992 was the public-sector salary bill, reported to total 32,735m. riyals. In 1994 the Government again failed to reach any agreement on a national budget, and was assumed to be maintaining a form of month-to-month accounting system until May, when established procedures were disrupted by the onset of civil war.

According to estimates published by independent Yemeni economists in January 1994, the Government spent 74,000m. riyals in 1993 and collected revenue of 32,000m. riyals, leaving a deficit of 42,000m. riyals, equivalent to more than one-third of the current GDP (which was estimated to be between 110,000m. and 120,000m. riyals). It was not known how the budget deficit had been financed. Following the end of the civil war in July 1994, the Government stated that it planned to issue bonds to raise funds for post-war reconstruction work. The Yemeni currency's unofficial exchange rate against the US dollar, which had declined to 80 riyals before the outbreak of hostilities, fell below 100 riyals for the first time during June 1994. Retrospective budget statistics for 1994, published long after the end of that year, showed total revenue of 41,384m. riyals and total expenditure of 85,875m. riyals. The overall deficit was 44,491m. riyals.

In 1995 the Government prepared a formal budget (approved by the legislature on 30 April) which provided for total expenditure of 111,128m. riyals and total revenue of 89,646m. riyals, leaving a deficit of 21,482m. riyals. It had previously been announced in December 1994 that capital spending in 1994 would total around 35,000m. riyals, of which 20,000m. riyals would be spent on post-war reconstruction and infrastructural development. The 1995 budget was preceded by a package of economic measures designed to limit the size of the budget deficit (which would otherwise have reached an estimated 60,000m. riyals). At the end of March the prices of a wide range of commodities and services were raised by between 50% and 100%

(petrol being one of the items that doubled in price), while public-sector pay and pensions were increased by between 20% for top grades and 50% (or a minimum of 1,000 riyals per month) for lower grades. Flour and wheat prices remained heavily subsidized, while imported medicines, milk and rice were exempted from increases in customs duties. Significant cuts were announced in expenditure on Yemen's diplomatic missions and official offices in other countries, while the armed forces were instructed to retire or discharge a total of 50,000 personnel. On 30 March a unified official exchange rate of 50 riyals per US dollar was introduced, and on 7 May local banks were authorized to carry out currency trading at prevailing free-market exchange rates (which remained far weaker than the new official rate).

Following talks with delegations from the World Bank and the IMF, the Government announced in late May 1995 that it was drawing up a five-year plan to restructure the economy over the period 1996–2000. The draft plan envisaged the flotation of the riyal within three years; progressive withdrawal of price subsidies on basic goods, including grain, rice and flour; liberalization of the food distribution system; far-reaching administrative reforms, including some decentralization measures; full harmonization of the northern and southern legal systems; and the introduction of a privatization programme (to be followed by the establishment of a stock market). Joint public-private sector ventures would be encouraged in infrastructural and other projects, and particular efforts would be made to secure high levels of private investment in labour-intensive projects. Seven publicly-owned companies in Aden (five of which were food-processing concerns) were earmarked for early privatization, as were a number of small-scale power generation facilities. The Government was expected to finalize the content of the five-year plan after further consultations with representatives of the Bretton Woods institutions, who were understood to favour a 50% reduction in public-sector employment and a two-year phasing-out period for all government price subsidies. The Yemen Government, for its part, was hoping that IMF/World Bank financial assistance for structural reforms would be complemented by measures to secure a reduction in Yemen's external indebtedness.

In July 1995 the Central Bank of Yemen raised its maximum deposit rate from 9% to 22% to stimulate savings in local currency, and used an estimated US $27m. of its foreign assets to support the free-market exchange rate of the riyal, which had declined in late June to its lowest ever level of 165 to the dollar (a level previously reached on the unofficial currency market in April, prior to the authorization of free-market currency dealing through the banking system). In mid-July Yemen's Prime Minister said that the public finances were currently showing a slightly smaller deficit than had been forecast in the 1995 budget, while a senior World Bank official expressed strong confidence in government economic policy and foresaw a tripling of World Bank assistance to Yemen if the Government moved quickly to implement key structural reforms. The free-market exchange rate per dollar strengthened to 55 riyals during August before declining to 114 riyals in November and 130 riyals in December. At the beginning of December the Central Bank held its first ever auction of treasury bills, having announced that it would be issuing short-dated bills with a total face value of 12,000m. riyals over the next six months with the aim of reducing excess liquidity in the country's economy.

In January 1996 the Government announced the immediate abolition of the official exchange rate of 50 riyals per dollar, while asserting its readiness to intervene in the currency market if the riyal's free-market value weakened beyond 'the real and practical rate'. (At the same time the so-called customs exchange rate—now the main indicator of current government estimates of the 'real and practical' value of the currency—was devalued to 100 riyals per dollar.) The Central Bank was authorized to use up to US $480m. of foreign reserves to support the riyal during the first 15 months of the floating exchange rate regime. Intervention by the Central Bank caused the exchange rate to strengthen to 100 riyals per dollar at some points during the first quarter of 1996. In April 1996, when the Central Bank did not intervene in the local currency market, the rate fell back to 134 riyals per dollar.

As well as abolishing the official exchange rate at the beginning of 1996, the Government reduced official price subsidies for many basic foodstuffs. Market prices rose sharply, and some commodities were in short supply for a time, as a result of hoarding prompted by expectations of future price increases. In January 1996 the Government announced that electricity prices were to rise by 50%–100% and water charges by 40%–60%, depending on consumption. Prices of oil products and domestic gas were also increased, although the price increase for diesel (originally 100%) was reduced to 33% after protest action by farmers.

The 1996 budget provided for expenditure of 181,416m. riyals (a 63.2% increase over the previous budget) and revenue of 155,886m. riyals (an increase of 73.9%), resulting in a deficit of 25,530m. riyals (19% less than the 1995 budget deficit). The spending allocations included 1,000m. riyals to alleviate the severity of economic reforms for the most vulnerable sections of the population. A January 1996 meeting of multilateral, regional and bilateral donors commended Yemen's current economic policies and pledged a total of US $500m. of new funding in 1996 ($350m. in support of structural reforms and $150m. to finance development projects). The Arab Monetary Fund was to provide $68m. under a loan agreement signed in November 1995. A 15-month stand-by credit of SDR 132m. (about $194m.) was formally approved by the IMF in March 1996, and the World Bank approved an $80m. structural reform programme in April, to be supplemented by further credits for a number of civil works projects designed to provide short-term employment for labourers. It was announced in late June that the Government was to set up a $20m. Social Development and Employment Fund, through which investment in job-creation and related programmes would be channelled.

In July 1996 the Government finalized its development plan for the period 1996–2000, which included a GDP growth target of 7.2% per annum. Oil and gas production was targeted to grow by 55% during the period of the plan. It was envisaged that total investment would amount to 818,000m. riyals (more than US $5,800m. at the prevailing exchange rate). Of this, nearly 390,000m. riyals represented foreign investment in the oil and gas sector (three-quarters of which was for the planned LNG export scheme). There were 207,000m. riyals of foreign aid, 121,600m. riyals of public investment and the balance (nearly 100,000m. riyals) came from private-sector investment.

As originally adopted, Yemen's 1997 budget provided for total expenditure of 313,985m. riyals and total revenue of 301,222m. riyals, leaving a deficit of 12,763m. riyals. However, additional expenditure of 12,610m. riyals was approved by the legislature in September 1997, increasing the final 1997 budget deficit to 25,373m. riyals. When capital items were excluded, the revised 1997 budget was in surplus by 2,690m. riyals on current account. The largest revenue sources in the 1997 budget were oil and gas (63%), taxation (11%), customs duties (10%) and foreign aid (6%), while the largest expenditure categories in the revised total were subsidies on food and energy prices (23%), defence (16%), education (16%), new investment (12%) and debt-servicing (10%). The Central Bank's foreign-exchange reserves increased from US $564m. at the end of 1995 to $969m. at the end of 1996 and stood at $1,072m. in mid-1997. The currency exchange rate averaged around 130 riyals to the dollar in the year to mid-1997. The Central Bank's minimum interest rate on riyal bank deposits (which had been 20% in April 1997) was reduced to 12% in August 1997 and 11% in December 1997.

In early June 1997 UNDP announced an allocation of US $200m. to support projects in Yemen over the next five years. The World Bank had previously announced $420m. of new loan allocations over a period of three years. In mid-June 1997 IMF officials held talks with Yemen's new Government to discuss the terms of a proposed three-year extended structural adjustment facility. Later that month a meeting of 26 donor bodies affirmed aid pledges to Yemen totalling $1,800m. over three years. In pursuance of its structural reform programme, the Government introduced substantial price increases for fuel, wheat and flour at the start of July 1997, while at the same time increasing public-sector wages by 10%. In September 1997 the Government announced its intention to establish an official stock exchange in early 1998 and to begin preparations to privatize the National Bank of Yemen (established in 1969

through the nationalization of foreign commercial banks' operations in the PDRY).

At the end of October 1997 the IMF approved a US $512m. loan and credit package in support of the Government's economic programme for the period 1997–2000. The package comprised SDR 264.8m. ($366m.) in loans under the IMF's Enhanced Structural Adjustment Facility, plus a credit of SDR 105.9m. ($146m.) under the Extended Fund Facility. The objectives of the medium-term strategy for 1997–2000 were to achieve average non-oil GDP growth of 6% per annum in real terms; to keep the core inflation rate at or below 5% per annum; to restrict the external current-account deficit to 2% of GDP; and to maintain sufficient foreign-exchange reserves to cover 4.5 months of imports. The budget deficit was to be limited to an average 2% of GDP. The structural adjustment process was to involve reorientating spending towards social sectors and infrastructure; reforming direct and indirect taxation; eliminating price subsidies; introducing administrative, civil service and financial sector reforms; implementing a 'rapidly moving and broad privatization programme'; and taking steps to 'enhance the competitive environment'. The World Bank approved two new loans in November 1997: SDR 58.9m. ($80m.) to assist the structural reform process in the financial and banking sector and SDR 17.7m. ($24.7m.) to support rural development in southern Yemen.

Yemen's 1998 budget provided for an 11.7% increase in total revenue, to 336,583m. riyals, while expenditure was set at 350,054m. riyals (7% higher than the revised 1997 total). The resultant deficit of 13,471m. riyals was wholly attributable to capital spending, as the current account was expected to show a surplus of 31,028m. riyals. The oil and gas sector was expected to contribute 61% of revenue in 1998, followed by taxation (13%), customs duties (9%) and foreign aid (6%). The main expenditure categories were education (18%), new investment (16%), defence (15%), subsidies on food and energy prices (14%) and debt servicing (10%). The central assumption in the 1998 revenue estimates was that crude oil prices would average US $18 per barrel in 1998. In practice, oil prices fell by around one-third in the opening months of 1998 (see Mining and Energy, above), with the result that Yemen's budget deficit stood at 36,200m. riyals, instead of an expected 4,400m. riyals, at the end of April 1998.

In April 1998 the Government announced forthcoming 40% increases in wheat and flour prices, and stated that it intended to phase out all subsidies on these items by the end of the century. In 1997 the annual cost of wheat and flour subsidies was 48,000m. riyals. Further price rises in mid-June 1998, affecting various subsidized commodities including gasoline, kerosene, bottled gas and basic foodstuffs, sparked protest demonstrations in San'a and several other urban centres. At least 34 deaths were reported as protesters clashed with security forces. The Government raised public-sector wages by 15% from the start of July 1998, having secured IMF approval for a higher 1998 budget deficit (5% of GDP) than had originally been targeted. There was an increase in 1998 in kidnappings of foreigners and government officials by armed tribesmen in rural areas, reportedly aimed at publicizing grievances over low levels of development spending. There was also a reported increase in petty damage to oil pipelines by disaffected tribesmen. Within the oil industry, employees of Yemen Hunt Oil threatened to take strike action unless their pay and conditions were improved.

Yemen made it known in 1998 that Saudi Arabia had begun to issue entry visas to Yemeni workers for the first time since the Gulf War, although Yemenis were now required to have Saudi sponsors and to obtain work and residence permits (requirements that had previously been waived for Yemenis). An estimated 400,000 Yemenis were already working in Saudi Arabia in early 1998. There was no expectation of a large-scale influx of Yemenis into Saudi Arabia at this time, not least because the Saudi economy was itself adversely affected by the sharp downturn in world oil prices.

The 1999 budget provided for expenditure of 335,500m. riyals (4.1% less than in 1998) and revenue of 294,400m. riyals, leaving a deficit of 41,100m. riyals. In contrast to the situation in 1998, when revenue fell far below budgeted levels because of depressed oil export prices, the outlook in mid-1999 was for above-budget revenue in the current year, reflecting the unexpectedly strong recovery of the oil market since the end of 1998. An IMF report issued in March 1999 noted the severe impact of reduced oil income on all sectors of Yemen's economy in 1998, the final fiscal deficit in 1998 being equivalent to about 6% of GDP, while the estimated 1998 inflation rate was around 11% and GDP growth was below 3%, in real terms. In July 1999 the IMF was forecasting a fiscal deficit of around 3% of GDP in 1999, coupled with inflation of less than 10% and real growth of 4% in non-oil GDP. By July 1999 a total of SDR 153m. (US $206m.) had been approved for disbursement under the October 1997 IMF support programme for Yemen.

In April 1999 the Government raised public-sector salaries while reducing some price subsidies. In the following month the prices of kerosene, fuel oil and bottled gas were increased. The currency exchange rate declined to 170 riyals per US dollar in early June 1999, necessitating an increase in the minimum interest rate for riyal bank deposits (which had been moving upwards since October 1998) to 20%—a level last seen in 1997. At the same time the minimum proportion of deposits that banks were required to hold in riyals was raised from 10% to 15%. In mid-August 1999 the currency exchange rate was 148 riyals per dollar. Against a background of strong improvement in the national finances, the benchmark interest rate was reduced in stages, standing at 13% in July 2000. In early August 2000 the exchange rate was 156 riyals per dollar. Yemen's budget for 2000 provided for expenditure of 422,250m. riyals and revenue of 388,950m. riyals, leaving a deficit of 33,300m. riyals. Oil revenue was expected to total around 246,520m. riyals in that year.

In March 2001 the IMF estimated that the actual 2000 budget out-turn was likely to show a surplus equivalent to 9% of GDP, compared with a deficit equivalent to 0.4% of GDP in 1999. While acknowledging that strong growth in oil export earnings was the main factor in the transformation of the public finances in 2000, the IMF welcomed the Yemeni authorities' efforts 'to restrain public expenditures in the face of rising pressures for a relaxation of the adjustment effort'. Yemen's budget for 2001 provided for expenditure of 501,882m. riyals and revenue of 487,843m. riyals, leaving a deficit of 14,039m. riyals. The budget's oil revenue projections reportedly assumed an average export price of US $22 per barrel in 2001. The Government rejected demands put forward in the legislature and the press for an additional 20,000m. riyals of expenditure (based on a higher oil price projection). In July 2001 the Government took the unpopular step of raising the price of diesel fuel from 10 riyals to 17 riyals per litre as part of its subsidy reduction programme.

The approved budget for 2002 provided for expenditure of 531,829m. riyals (a 6% increase over 2001) and revenue of 482,021m. riyals (1% less than in 2001), the resulting projected deficit of 49,808m. riyals being equivalent to 2.4% of anticipated GDP (compared with an outturn surplus of 2.8% in 2001). Priority was given to augmenting allocations for defence (to 104,844m. riyals) and internal security (to 26,300m. riyals) to finance Yemen's anti-terrorism endeavours, although the budget also provided for the implementation of outstanding economic reforms. About 20% of projected expenditure was transferred to newly-elected local councils to enable them to carry out their responsibilities for health, education and new development projects. Approval of the budget in January 2002 was accompanied by the enactment of a law on the introduction of a general sales tax (GST), although implementation was deferred pending a review of the indirect taxation system. The exchange rate in August 2002 was 176 riyals per dollar. The Central Bank's foreign exchange reserves stood at US $3,659m. at the end of April 2002 compared with $2,953m. at the end of January 2001.

FOREIGN TRADE AND BALANCE OF PAYMENTS

The official trade and payments statistics for Yemen, before and after unification, provide a broad outline of developments, based on recorded information. There is a deficiency of accurate and detailed information in several key areas, mostly relating to labour migration and workers' remittances, and some official trade figures give unrealistically low import totals (smuggling having been particularly widespread in the former YAR in the late 1970s and early 1980s). The blurring of such statistics

reflects the very high levels of economic inter-dependence that developed within the Arabian peninsula in the 1970s and 1980s, as Saudi Arabia and other oil-rich Gulf states provided mass employment opportunities for Yemeni workers. Insofar as they were used to offset the large deficits in the Yemeni states' basic commodity trade, the inflows of remittance income from the oil states strengthened the overall balance-of-payments positions of the YAR and PDRY. (In practice, significant amounts of remittance income were spent on imported consumer goods, particularly in the YAR.) However, remittance income did not eliminate either state's heavy dependence on foreign aid to finance development projects and budget deficits, nor did it represent a stable and predictable income source, being highly dependent on fluctuations in the host countries' economic cycles, which were closely linked to swings in world oil prices. In the 1990s unified Yemen benefited from a stronger export base as it developed its own oilfields. At the same time import demand was boosted, and remittance income cut, as the country absorbed the impact of the large repatriations of Yemeni workers arising from the 1990–91 Gulf crisis. Having become accustomed to modest rises in export earnings as oil production developed, Yemen was in 1998 adjusting to a major slump in world oil prices. In late 1997 Yemen secured substantial relief in respect of its major arrears of foreign debt (including debt stemming from the former PDRY's heavy reliance on Soviet aid).

Until the late 1980s the former YAR's merchandise exports covered less than 3% of the value of imports. World Bank statistics showed that in the period 1965–80 exports grew at an average annual rate of only 2.8%, whereas imports grew by 23.3% per year. In the period 1980–88, however, the average annual growth in exports was 35.6%, while imports declined by 10% per year. The improvement in export performance was attributable to the start of crude oil exports at the end of 1987. In 1987 YAR exports were worth only US $19m., against imports of $1,311m.; in 1988 exports rose sharply to $485m., against imports of $1,310m. In the early 1980s the YAR's official annual trade deficit ran at about $1,500m., falling to around $1,200m. per year in 1986 and 1987 and to $835m. in 1988. The estimated value of goods smuggled into the former YAR to avoid high import duties was $1,000m. in 1983. According to the World Bank, oil and other minerals accounted for 88% of YAR exports by value in 1988 (compared with 9% in 1965), manufactured goods for 11% (0% in 1965) and other primary commodities for 1% (91% in 1965). In the same year food accounted for 28% of total imports by value (compared with 41% in 1965), manufactured goods for 55% (47% in 1965), fuels for 8% (6% in 1965) and other primary commodities for 6% (6% in 1965).

According to the World Bank, the former PDRY's exports declined in value in the period 1965–80 by an annual average of 13.7%, while imports fell by 7.5% per year. In the period 1980–88, however, exports increased by an average of 1.9% per year and imports by 4.4% per year. In 1988 exports were worth US $80m., while imports reached $598m. The former PDRY's main export commodities (excluding refined petroleum products) were cotton, hides and skins, fish, rice and coffee. The chief imports (excluding crude oil) were manufactured goods for development projects, clothing, foodstuffs and livestock. Fuels and minerals accounted for 90% of total PDRY exports by value in 1988 (against 80% in 1965), other primary commodities for 9% (14% in 1965), and manufactured goods for 1% (8% in 1965).

Following unification, Yemen's external trade was temporarily disrupted by the UN embargo on trade with Iraq and Kuwait, which necessitated a diversion to the Aden refinery of Yemeni crude oil that would otherwise have gone for export (see Manufacturing and Industry, above). Yemen's merchandise exports in 1990 totalled 7,066m. riyals (including 6,188m. riyals from oil), whereas merchandise imports totalled 20,863m. riyals, producing a visible trade deficit of 13,795m. riyals, compared with a combined deficit for the YAR and PDRY in 1989 of 11,533m. riyals (exports 6,765m. riyals, imports 18,298m. riyals). There was a visible trade deficit of 18,238.4m. riyals in 1992 (exports 6,075.9m. riyals, imports 24,314.3m. riyals). The provisional trade figures for 1993 showed a deficit of 25,382.3m. riyals (exports 5,693.3m. riyals, imports 31,075.6m. riyals). In 1994 Yemen's merchandise trade was in surplus by US $302.1m. (exports $1,824m., imports $1,521.9m.). There were visible trade deficits of $11m. in 1995 and $30.8m. in 1996. In 1997 merchandise trade was in deficit by $132.5m. (exports $2,274m., imports $2,406.5m.), while in 1998 there was a sharply increased deficit of $726.8m., export earnings having fallen by 34%, to $1,500.1m., as a result of that year's downturn in world oil prices, whereas import spending was reduced by 7.4%, to $2,227.8m., in 1998. Official trade figures for 1999 showed a surplus of $357.8m. (exports $2,478.3m., imports $2,120.5m.), there having been a rise of more than 73% (from $1,228.7m. to $2,131.2m.) in the value of Yemen's oil exports. A further substantial rise in oil prices in 2000, combined with a 10.8% rise in the volume of Yemen's oil exports, boosted the provisional calculation of the visible trade surplus to $1,609.4m. (exports $4,093.8m., imports $2,484.4m.). Preliminary figures for 2001 indicated a reduced trade surplus of $609m. (exports $3,115m., imports $2,506m.).

Yemen had a current-account deficit of 1,711m. riyals in 1990, compared with a combined YAR and PDRY deficit of 9,853m. riyals in 1989. The services account showed receipts of 17,518m. riyals in 1990 (5,519m. riyals in 1989) exceeding payments of 5,432m. riyals (3,839m. riyals in 1989). The strong upturn in private remittances in 1990 was attributable to Yemeni nationals returning from Saudi Arabia because of the Gulf crisis. The World Bank assessed Yemen's net remittance income at US $800m. in 1991, and suggested that the current account was $20m. in surplus in that year. Prior to the 1990 Gulf crisis, remittance income had averaged around $2,000m. per year. According to World Bank estimates, a fall in Yemen's net remittance income to $340m. in 1992 was a contributory factor in an overall current-account deficit of $1,582m. in that year. In mid-1994 the Arab Monetary Fund extended a $47m. loan to Yemen to support the financing of the country's 1993 balance-of-payments deficit. Yemen had a current-account deficit of $1,248m. and an overall balance-of-payments deficit of $1,113m. in 1993. In 1994 there was a current-account surplus of $366m. and an estimated overall deficit of $653m. In 1995 Yemen received estimated remittance income of $1,120m. and recorded a surplus of $183m. on the current account. In 1996 Yemen received remittance income of $1,182m. and recorded a current-account deficit of $70m. In 1997 net current transfers totalling $1,255.3m. were received, producing a current-account surplus of $51.6m. when set against the merchandise trade deficit of $142.5m., a services deficit of $426.3m. (credits $207.6m., debits $633.9m.) and an invisible income deficit of $634.9m. (credits $69.6m., debits $704.5m.). In 1998 net remittance income was estimated to be virtually unchanged, at $1,256.3m., leaving the current account in deficit by $228.1m. when set against the merchandise trade deficit of $700.5m., a services deficit of $362m. (credits $207.5m., debits $569.5m.) and an invisible income deficit of $421.9m. (credits $65.5m., debits $487.4m.). The 30.8% reduction in outgoings on the invisibles account in 1998 was attributable, in part, to debt rescheduling agreements with overseas creditors. In 1999 the balance of payments showed a current-account surplus of $768.4m. and an overall surplus of $268.9m. Net remittance income in 1999 was $1,314m. Provisional figures for 2000 showed a current-account surplus of $1,539.7m. and an overall balance-of-payments surplus of $1,425.0m. According to preliminary figures, the current-account surplus fell to $770m. in 2001.

In June 1990 the World Bank confirmed that Yemen would be entitled to concessionary finance and that loan programmes and development projects under way in the YAR and the PDRY would continue in the unified country. Unified Yemen's receipts of official development aid amounted to US $405m. in 1990 and $313m. in 1991 (in which year it represented 3.9% of GNP).

Figures disclosed in July 1990 showed unified Yemen's total foreign debt as US $7,256m., equivalent to about 110% of current GNP and some 50% higher than the previous Western estimate of about $5,000m. Of the total, $4,366m. was debt attributable to the former PDRY (owed mainly to the USSR, China and eastern European countries) and $2,890m. to the former YAR. In September 1990 France agreed to cancel all of Yemen's outstanding debt to it—some $55m.—and Japan also granted debt-relief aid. According to the World Bank, Yemen's external debt totalled $6,598m. at the end of 1992. In December 1994 the Government said that it intended to negotiate with Russia for the cancellation of 90% of Yemen's debt to the former USSR. In mid-1995 Japan's cumulative debt-relief grants to

Yemen totalled $68.4m. In September 1996 the 'Paris Club' of official creditors agreed to recommend the rescheduling of about $100m. of Yemen's debt. In April 1997 the USA announced a rescheduling of Yemeni debt over a period of 40 years, including a 20-year exemption period.

Russia, which became a member of the 'Paris Club' in 1997, disclosed that it was owed US $400m. of commercial debt by Yemen, three-quarters of which was overdue for repayment. However, the bulk of the former Soviet Union's lending had been on non-commercial terms within the framework of bilateral co-operation agreements with the former PDRY and YAR. The total lending under these agreements was almost $6,700m., of which $6,500m. (including nearly $2,700m. of arrears) was still outstanding. Loan agreements had been denominated in roubles, with typical repayment periods of between five and 15 years and typical interest rates of 2% to 5%, and had usually specified repayment in hard currency by the YAR or 'in the national currency for subsequent purchase of goods' by the PDRY. The former Soviet Union had by 1988 acceded to 19 requests for postponement of debt repayments, the total value of all repayments received being less than 170m. roubles.

At a 'Paris Club' meeting in November 1997 Russia agreed to waive about US $5,360m. of Yemeni debt (80% of $6,700m.) and to apply so-called 'Naples conditions' (67% of debt written off and 33% rescheduled over a greatly extended period at very low interest rates) to the remainder. Yemen's debts to the other 'Paris Cub' countries were to be reviewed by each country with a view to rescheduling on 'Naples' terms. Total Yemeni indebtedness to foreign creditors other than Russia was estimated to be about $1,500m. in 1997. Yemen's Prime Minister stated after the November 1997 'Paris Club' meeting that creditor countries in two regions—the Arab world and eastern Europe—had not as yet discussed debt rescheduling with Yemen. In the case of eastern Europe, the amounts involved were relatively modest and were not considered a problem by Yemen. In the case of major Arab creditor countries, including Saudi Arabia, Kuwait and Iraq, the Yemen Government had requested rescheduling negotiations with a view to obtaining terms similar to those applied by 'Paris Club' countries. There had, however, been no response from any of the countries concerned, with the result that all debts to other Arab governments remained 'in place and frozen' at the end of 1997. In June 1999 it was reported that Yemen's current net outstanding debt to Russia totalled $426m. and was to be repaid over 33 years at an interest rate of 1.19%. A formal analysis of Yemen's end-1999 external debt position, carried out by the Government in collaboration with the IMF and the World Bank, concluded that the present debt was 'sustainable over the medium term'. Agreements were reported in December 2000 on the rescheduling of some of Yemen's debts to Saudi Arabia and Kuwait. The Saudi-Yemeni Co-operation Council (which had last met prior to the outbreak of the Gulf crisis of 1990–91) agreed that a resumption of Saudi funding for Yemeni development projects was to be based partly on the provision of new loans of up to $300m. and partly on a restructuring of earlier debt totalling more than $330m.

ECONOMIC PROSPECTS

Following its annual 'Article IV' consultations with the Government in August 2002, the IMF noted that Yemen's economic prospects appeared to be 'relatively stable' and applauded the authorities' efforts to meet the 'difficult challenges' posed by the transition to a market economy, diversification away from oil and the reduction of poverty. The Fund expressed concern, however, that in 2001 there had been a sharp increase in prices, a deterioration in the fiscal position (largely owing to public-sector wage increases and higher defence spending) and slow progress on structural reform. Stressing the importance of adherence to the reform programme in the shorter term, the IMF noted that 'private investment remains limited as a result of structural impediments—particularly poor governance and weak law enforcement' and called on the Government 'to address these issues more forcefully to strengthen private sector and donor confidence'. Over the medium term, the Fund warned that 'significant adjustment will be needed...to maintain stability in the face of a possible decline in oil revenues' and urged 'the adoption of a stronger budget aimed at reducing the non-oil deficit and improving the composition of expenditure'. It also recommended 'a cautious approach to fiscal decentralization

pending the establishment of effective monitoring and control of decentralized expenditures'.

Statistical Survey

Source (unless otherwise indicated): Republic of Yemen Central Statistical Organization, POB 13434, San'a; tel. (1) 250619; fax (1) 250664.

Area and Population

AREA, POPULATION AND DENSITY

Area (sq km)	536,869*
Population (census results)†	
16 December 1994	
Males	7,473,540
Females	7,114,267
Total	14,587,807
Population (official estimates at mid-year)	
1999	17,671,000
2000	18,261,000
2001	18,863,000
Density (per sq km) at mid-2001	35.1

* 207,286 sq miles.
† Excluding adjustment for underenumeration.

PRINCIPAL TOWNS
(estimated population for urban agglomerations at mid-1993)

San'a (capital)	926,595
Aden	400,783
Taiz	290,107
Hodeida	246,068

Source: UN, *Demographic Yearbook*.

Mid-2001 (UN estimate, incl. suburbs): San'a 1,410,000 (Source: UN, *World Urbanization Prospects: The 2001 Revision*).

BIRTHS, MARRIAGES AND DEATHS (UN estimates, annual averages)

	1985–90	1990–95	1995–2000
Birth rate (per 1,000) . .	49.3	52.6	51.4
Death rate (per 1,000) . .	13.8	12.5	9.9

Source: UN, *World Population Prospects: The 2000 Revision*.

Expectation of life (official estimates, years at birth, 2000): 60.7 (males 58.8; females 62.7).

2000: Registered live births 252,895; Birth rate (per 1,000) 38.9; Registered deaths 18,441; Death rate (per 1,000) 11.2; Marriages 1,834.

ECONOMICALLY ACTIVE POPULATION
(ISIC Major Divisions, '000 persons aged 15 years and over)

	1998	1999
Agriculture, forestry and fishing . . .	1,928	1,996
Mining and quarrying	13	13
Manufacturing	188	206
Electricity, gas and water.	21	21
Construction.	341	382
Trade, restaurants and hotels. . . .	415	440
Transport, storage and communication . .	196	210
Finance, insurance and real estate . .	47	49
Social and community services . . .	365	412
Public administration	405	389
Total labour force	3,919	4,119

Source: IMF, *Republic of Yemen: Selected Issues* (April 2001).

Health and Welfare

KEY INDICATORS

Fertility (births per woman, 2000)	7.6
Under-5 mortality rate (per 1,000 live births, 2000). .	117
HIV/AIDS (% of persons aged 15–49, 2001). . . .	0.12
Physicians (per 1,000 head, 1996)	0.23
Hospital beds (per 1,000 head, 1990)	0.60
Health expenditure (1998): US $ per head (PPP) . .	49
% of GDP	3.9
public (% of total) . . .	39.1
Access to water (% of persons, 2000)	69
Access to sanitation (% of persons, 2000) . . .	45
Human Development Index (2000): ranking . . .	144
value	0.479

For sources and definitions, see explanatory note on p. vi.

Agriculture

PRINCIPAL CROPS ('000 metric tons)

	1998	1999	2000
Wheat	167	140	142
Barley	56	43	42
Maize	62	47	48
Millet	74	65	65
Sorghum	474	399	375
Potatoes.	196	211	210
Pulses	77	63	63
Sesame seed. . . .	17	18	18
Cottonseed	24	25	28
Tomatoes	231	240	251
Onions (dry). . . .	72	68	75
Other vegetables. . . .	134	140	144
Watermelons	95	83	78
Melons	35	36	36
Grapes	155	156	156
Dates	27	29	30
Bananas	85	89	90
Oranges	150	156	158
Papayas.	63	67	68
Other fruit	76	83	89
Coffee (green)	11	11	11
Tobacco (leaves)	11	11	12
Cotton (lint)*	8	8	9

* Unofficial figures.
Source: FAO.

LIVESTOCK ('000 head, year ending September)

	1998	1999	2000
Horses*	3	3	3
Asses*	500	500	500
Cattle	1,263	1,282	1,339
Camels	183	185	190
Sheep	4,527	4,667	4,804
Goats	4,089	4,204	4,252
Chickens (million)*	27	28	30

* FAO estimates.
Source: FAO.

LIVESTOCK PRODUCTS ('000 metric tons)

	1998	1999	2000
Beef and veal	45	47	52
Mutton and lamb* . . .	23	24	24
Goat meat*	22	22	22
Poultry meat	61	63	67
Cows' milk	168	177	180
Sheep's milk.	15	16	16
Goats' milk	20	20	20
Cheese	11	11	11
Butter	4	4	5
Hen eggs†	31	31	31
Wool (greasy)†	4	4	4
Cattle hides	8	9	10

* FAO estimates.   † Unofficial figures.

Source: FAO.

Forestry

ROUNDWOOD REMOVALS ('000 cubic metres, excl. bark, estimates)

	1998	1999	2000
Total (all fuel wood) . . .	278	290	302

Source: FAO.

Fishing

('000 metric tons, live weight)

	1997	1998	1999
Demersal percomorphs* . .	5.3	5.9	5.7
Pelagic percomorphs* . . .	62.3	75.8	74.9
Indian oil sardine* . . .	4.3	4.9	4.7
Narrow-barred Spanish mackerel	3.7	3.6	3.6*
Sharks, rays and skates, etc.* .	5.0	5.8	5.6
Cuttlefish and bobtail squids .	8.7	5.1	4.2
Total catch (incl. others) . .	112.8	127.6	123.3

* Estimate(s).

Source: FAO, *Yearbook of Fishery Statistics*.

Mining

('000 metric tons, unless otherwise indicated)

	1998	1999	2000
Crude petroleum ('000 barrels) .	138,600	149,000	167,000
Natural gas (million cu m)* . .	15,000	16,000	18,000
Salt.	147	149	150*
Gypsum (crude)	102	103	100*

* Estimate(s).

Source: US Geological Survey.

Industry

SELECTED PRODUCTS ('000 barrels, unless otherwise indicated)

	1996	1997	1998
Motor spirit (petrol)	8,913	8,803	8,100
Kerosene	4,935	4,073	3,700
Distillate fuel oils . . .	10,525	10,530	6,900
Residual fuel oils* . . .	10,300	10,300	10,600
Cement ('000 metric tons) . .	1,028	1,235	1,201
Electricity (million kWh)* . .	2,457	2,482	2,633

* Estimates.

1999: Cement 1,231; Electricity 2,633.

Source: mainly US Geological Survey.

Finance

CURRENCY AND EXCHANGE RATES

Monetary Units
  100 fils = 1 Yemeni riyal.

Sterling, Dollar and Euro Equivalents (31 May 2002)
  £1 sterling = 256.80 riyals;
  US $1 = 175.09 riyals;
  €1 = 164.36 riyals;
  1,000 Yemeni riyals = £3.894 = $5.711 = €6.084.

Average Exchange Rate (Yemeni riyals per US $)
  1999   155.718
  2000   161.718
  2001   168.672

Note: The exchange rate of US $1 = 9.76 Yemeni riyals, established in the YAR in 1988, remained in force until February 1990, when a new rate of $1 = 12.01 riyals was introduced. Following the merger of the two Yemens in May 1990, the YAR's currency was adopted as the currency of the unified country. In March 1995 the official exchange rate was amended from 12.01 to 50.04 riyals per US dollar. The rate has since been adjusted. From mid-1996 data refer to a market-determined exchange rate, applicable to most private transactions.

GENERAL BUDGET (million riyals)

Revenue	1998	1999	2000*
Taxation	80,832	89,745	102,611
Direct.	28,868	32,139	44,025
Indirect	51,081	59,414	58,586
Other current revenue . .	140,890	236,244	482,257
Capital revenue . . .	439	427	677
Loans and aids	22,409	34,375	198
Total	244,570	360,791	585,743

Expenditure	1999	2000*
Services sector	99,977	142,642
General administration. . . .	47,147	90,048
Government subsidies . . .	26,930	25,068
Security and internal order . . .	25,900	36,526
Defence	67,602	75,508
Education	66,128	90,054
Health	13,897	18,611
Social services	7,722	10,055
Social insurance and labour. .	2,338	3,945
Youth and sports	686	747
Culture, information and tourism . .	4,699	5,363
Economic services	40,119	30,748
Construction and housing . .	16,640	19,266
Agriculture and fishing	7,581	9,274
Mining	1,150	788
Electricity	12,752	205
Communication	73	52
Transportation.	738	273
Economy and commerce . . .	1,185	890
Public sector debt	47,489	54,631
Total	342,934	422,249

* Provisional.

INTERNATIONAL RESERVES (US $ million at 31 December)

	1999	2000	2001
Gold*	15.3	14.4	14.6
IMF special drawing rights . .	176.3	84.6	18.5
Foreign exchange . . .	1,295.1	2,815.6	3,639.6
Total	1,486.7	2,914.6	3,672.7

* National valuation.

Source: IMF, *International Financial Statistics*.

MONEY SUPPLY (million riyals at 31 December)

	1999	2000	2001
Currency outside banks . .	166,924	197,123	212,795
Demand deposits at commercial banks	29,649	41,004	48,992
Total money (incl. others) . .	207,197	247,248	282,683

Source: IMF, *International Financial Statistics*.

COST OF LIVING
(Consumer price index for urban areas; base: 1994 = 100)

	1997	1998	1999
Food	199.6	231.6	257.3
Housing	248.1	269.2	296.4
Clothing	280.3	248.7	258.2
All items (incl. others) . . .	214.1	239.6	264.0

Source: IMF, *Republic of Yemen: Selected Issues*.
2000 (base: November 1999 = 100): All items 104.59.

NATIONAL ACCOUNTS (million riyals at current prices, provisional)
National Income and Product

	1998	1999	2000
Domestic factor incomes* . .	719,725	975,723	1,202,529
Consumption of fixed capital .	78,691	97,648	113,333
Gross domestic product (GDP) at factor cost	798,416	1,073,371	1,315,862
Indirect taxes, *less* subsidies . .	50,905	59,248	63,950
GDP in purchasers' values .	849,321	1,132,619	1,379,812
Net factor income from abroad .	−47,816	−105,676	−185,293
Gross national product (GNP) .	801,505	1,026,943	1,194,519
Less Consumption of fixed capital .	78,691	97,648	113,333
National income in market prices	722,814	929,295	1,081,186
Other current transfers received from abroad	164,822	195,762	245,183
Less Other current transfers paid abroad	2,269	576	−2,749
National disposable income .	885,367	1,124,481	1,323,620

* Compensation of employees and the operating surplus of enterprises.

Expenditure on the Gross Domestic Product*

	1998	1999	2000
Government final consumption expenditure	124,473	156,273	194,133
Private final consumption expenditure	576,227	770,168	797,196
Increase in stocks . . .	8,655	13,122	12,590
Gross fixed capital formation . .	267,810	265,371	251,684
Total domestic expenditure	977,165	1,204,934	1,255,603
Exports of goods and services . .	234,189	410,931	696,151
Less Imports of goods and services	362,033	483,246	571,942
GDP in purchasers' values .	849,321	1,132,619	1,379,812
GDP at constant 1995 prices .	167,382	172,290	215,507

* Provisional figures.

Gross Domestic Product by Economic Activity
(million riyals at current prices, provisional)

	1998	1999	2000
Agriculture, hunting, forestry and fishing	164,524	182,547	211,720
Mining and quarrying . . .	139,170	330,481	466,956
Manufacturing	86,697	92,793	103,078
Electricity, gas and water . . .	7,912	8,401	9,157
Construction	44,571	52,827	58,642
Trade, restaurants and hotels . .	94,950	101,790	119,345
Transport, storage and communications . . .	121,648	131,097	142,657
Finance, insurance, real estate and business services . .	84,635	101,949	107,493
Government services . . .	93,635	119,113	149,287
Other community, social and personal services . . .	9,053	10,325	11,328
Private non-profit services to households	738	830	940
Sub-total	847,533	1,132,153	1,380,603
Import duties	29,653	28,701	28,348
Less Imputed bank service charge	27,865	28,235	29,139
GDP in purchasers' values .	849,321	1,132,619	1,379,812

BALANCE OF PAYMENTS (US $ million)

	1998	1999	2000
Exports of goods f.o.b. . . .	1,503.7	2,478.3	4,093.8
Imports of goods f.o.b. . . .	−2,288.8	−2,120.4	−2,484.4
Trade balance	−785.1	357.9	1,609.4
Exports of services . . .	174.4	183.2	210.8
Imports of services . . .	−692.9	−718.6	−809.3
Balance on goods and services	−1,303.6	−177.5	462.9
Other income received . .	101.1	94.1	297.4
Other income paid . . .	−276.6	−570.9	−845.4
Balance on goods, services and income	−1,479.1	−654.3	462.9
Current transfers received . .	1,223.5	1,262.1	1,471.9
Current transfers paid . .	−47.7	−30.7	−72.4
Current balance . . .	−303.3	577.1	1,862.4
Direct investment from abroad .	−219.4	−194.3	−200.9
Other investment assets . .	10.1	−358.1	−508.9
Other investment liabilities . .	−263.6	−1.5	−203.4
Net errors and omissions . .	188.2	45.2	333.3
Overall balance . . .	−580.9	74.0	1,594.4

Source: IMF, *International Financial Statistics*.

External Trade

PRINCIPAL COMMODITIES
(distribution by SITC, million riyals at current prices)

Imports c.i.f.	1998	1999	2000
Food and live animals	83,667.5	103,400.2	111,136.6
Dairy products and birds' eggs	11,395.3	11,106.9	13,973.0
Cereals and cereal preparations	34,520.0	52,771.9	50,596.6
Sugar, sugar preparations and honey	13,399.5	14,618.3	17,454.6
Beverages and tobacco	5,920.6	6,304.5	6,297.4
Mineral fuels, lubricants, etc.	18,977.1	25,165.1	44,930.5
Petroleum, petroleum products, etc.	44,912.3	25,147.4	18,943.9
Animal and vegetable oils and fats	11,274.0	10,435.0	14,612.1
Vegetable oils and fats	13,553.6	9,482.7	11,139.7
Chemicals and related products	28,690.1	29,123.4	36,406.8
Medical and pharmaceutical	12,482.3	11,677.0	12,058.5
Basic manufactures	50,936.9	47,848.1	55,190.2
Iron and steel	15,738.1	14,978.2	16,193.8
Machinery and transport equipment	71,357.0	67,250.9	78,332.0
Machinery specialized in particular industries	13,620.1	16,474.3	14,193.5
Road vehicles	14,473.5	14,959.7	28,071.1
Miscellaneous manufactured articles	15,541.7	16,524.7	16,883.3
Total (incl. others)	294,509.7	312,749.4	375,782.9

Exports f.o.b.*	1998	1999	2000
Crude materials (inedible) except fuels	3,357.9	2,221.9	3,030.9
Mineral fuels, lubricants, etc.	186,151.9	359,104.7	636,503.1
Petroleum, petroleum products, etc.	185,611.0	358,153.0	633,745.5
Total (incl. others)	203,480.3	380,010.2	659,609.0

* Including re-exports (24,362.5 in 1998; 28,385.2 in 1999; 45,671.9 in 2000).

PRINCIPAL TRADING PARTNERS (million riyals at current prices)*

Imports c.i.f.	1998	1999	2000
Argentina	3,379.0	1,929.8	4,032.1
Australia	7,121.8	13,144.3	9,456.9
Belgium	6,260.6	3,405.7	2,729.8
Brazil	8,471.5	8,722.0	9,276.7
China, People's Republic	9,047.1	9,226.4	13,179.8
Djibouti	4,194.8	5,089.9	6,125.2
Egypt	3,493.4	3,970.7	6,185.1
France (incl. Monaco)	16,469.5	13,108.0	17,118.1
Germany	10,470.3	9,358.1	11,474.3
India	6,379.7	8,213.4	9,570.3
Italy	12,680.5	11,048.0	10,003.4
Japan	6,379.7	8,213.4	11,941.4
Korea, Republic	5,597.3	4,265.6	3,713.0
Kuwait	6,734.5	17,834.4	17,555.1
Malaysia	10,780.9	10,563.9	12,671.8
Netherlands	6,352.6	4,635.3	6,022.3
Saudi Arabia	34,451.1	36,424.7	51,737.1
Singapore	9,415.8	10,588.5	11,823.9
Somalia	4,845.0	5,447.1	3,396.9
Switzerland	8,084.8	6,832.5	17,476.2
Thailand	3,822.9	5,814.8	12,287.4
Turkey	8,150.3	6,860.6	8,328.4
United Arab Emirates	26,520.2	37,962.1	37,385.7
United Kingdom	14,876.3	12,972.8	11,970.9
USA	16,969.3	18,550.0	16,682.4
Total (incl. others)	294,509.7	312,749.4	375,782.9

Exports f.o.b.†	1998	1999	2000
Brazil	n.a.	n.a.	10,270.1
China, People's Republic	50,742.2	107,936.5	125,219.8
India	476.6	26,412.5	99,070.0
Italy	1,667.3	658.8	5,228.2
Japan	7,463.7	3,848.7	13,628.8
Korea, Republic	2,303.6	51,238.6	114,021.7
Malaysia	842.3	0.6‡	11,759.9‡
Saudi Arabia	4,550.4	6,657.7	7,746.9
Singapore	36,049.9	30,538.6	12,013.8
Thailand	45,049.7	95,457.9§	113,226.4
USA	5,506.1	2,284.6	40,551.7
Total (incl. others)	203,480.3	380,010.2	659,609.0

* Imports by country of first consignment; exports by country of last consignment.
† Including re-exports.
‡ Excluding domestic exports.
§ Excluding re-exports.

Transport

ROAD TRAFFIC (vehicles in use at 31 December)

	1994	1995	1996
Passenger cars	227,854	229,084	240,567
Buses and coaches	2,712	2,835	3,437
Goods vehicles	279,154	279,780	291,149

Source: IRF, *World Road Statistics*.

SHIPPING

Merchant Fleet (registered at 31 December)

	1999	2000	2001
Number of vessels	48	46	44
Total displacement ('000 grt)	30.9	28.3	73.8

Source: Lloyd's Register-Fairplay, *World Fleet Statistics*.

International Sea-borne Freight Traffic ('000 metric tons)

	1988	1989	1990
Goods loaded	1,836	1,883	1,936
Goods unloaded	7,189	7,151	7,829

Source: UN, *Monthly Bulletin of Statistics*.

CIVIL AVIATION (traffic on scheduled services)

	1996	1997	1998
Kilometres flown (million)	11	13	12
Passengers carried ('000)	588	707	765
Passenger-km (million)	849	1,076	1,104
Total ton-km (million)	86	115	120

Source: UN, *Statistical Yearbook*.

Tourism

TOURISM ARRIVALS

	1998	1999	2000
Africa	2,696	4,312	5,658
Sudan.	1,858	2,310	2,288
Americas	5,585	6,732	8,161
Asia.	6,743	4,444	8,342
Europe	54,164	22,201	24,825
France	11,590	4,500	4,535
Germany	11,109	5,810	4,194
Italy	7,006	2,572	4,748
Netherlands	3,864	976	1,014
Switzerland	2,742	368	502
United Kingdom . . .	6,626	2,759	4,342
Middle East	17,746	20,263	25,404
Egypt	1,990	2,632	3,355
Iraq	2,121	2,250	2,543
Jordan	2,263	2,744	2,352
Saudi Arabia	6,087	7,533	9,842
Syria	1,070	1,574	2,278
Total (incl. others)	87,628	58,370	72,836

Tourism receipts (US $ million): 84 in 1998; 61 in 1999; 76 in 2000.

Source: General Tourism Authority.

Education

(1999/2000, unless otherwise indicated)

	Schools	Teachers	Students		
			Males	Females	Total
Pre-primary* . .	42	532	3,274	2,822	6,156
Primary . . .	11,013†	113,812	1,832,822	955,459	2,788,281
Secondary. . .	n.a.	14,063	277,024	97,459	374,483
Higher* . . .	7	3,429	112,187	34,994	147,181

* Public education only.
† 1993/94 (Source: UNESCO, *Statistical Yearbook*.

Adult literacy rate (UNESCO estimates): 46.3% (males 67.5%; females 25.2%) in 2000 (Source: UNDP, *Human Development Report*).

Communications Media

	1999	2000	2001
Television receivers ('000 in use)	5,000	5,200	n.a.
Telephones ('000 main lines in use)*	372.0	417.1	423.1
Mobile cellular telephones ('000 subscribers)*	27.7	32.0	152.0
Personal computers ('000 in use)* .	30	35	37
Internet users ('000)*. . . .	10	15	17
Daily newspapers			
Number	n.a.	3	n.a.
Circulation ('000 copies) . .	n.a.	50	n.a.

* Source: International Telecommunication Union.

Radio receivers ('000 in use): 1,050 in 1997.

Facsimile machines ('000 in use, estimate): 2,784 in 1995.

Sources: UN, *Statistical Yearbook*; UNESCO, *Statistical Yearbook*.

Directory

The Constitution

A draft constitution for the united Republic of Yemen (based on that endorsed by the Yemen Arab Republic (YAR) and the People's Democratic Republic of Yemen (PDRY) in December 1981) was published in December 1989, and was approved by a popular referendum on 15–16 May 1991.

On 29 September 1994 52 articles were amended, 29 added and one cancelled, leaving a total of 159 articles in the Constitution. Further amendments to the Constitution were adopted by the House of Representatives in late November 2000 and approved in a national referendum on 20 February 2001.

The Constitution defines the Yemeni Republic as an independent and sovereign Arab and Islamic country. The document states that the Republic 'is an indivisible whole, and it is impermissible to concede any part of it. The Yemeni people are part of the Arab and Islamic nation.' The Islamic *Shari'a* is identified as the basis of all laws.

The revised Constitution provides for the election, by direct universal suffrage, of the President of the Republic; the President is elected for a seven-year term (increased from five years by the amendments approved in 2001). The President is empowered to appoint a Vice-President. The President of the Republic is, *ex officio*, Supreme Commander of the Armed Forces. The Constitution as amended in 2001 requires presidential candidates to obtain the endorsement of 5% of a combined vote of the appointed Consultative Council and the elected House of Representatives (in place of 10% of the latter chamber alone).

Legislative authority is vested in the 301-member House of Representatives, which is elected, by universal suffrage, for a six-year term (increased from four years by amendment in 2001). The role of the House of Representatives is defined as to 'monitor' the executive. The President is empowered to dissolve the legislature and call new elections within a period of 60 days.

The upper house of the legislature, the Consultative Council, has 111 members (increased from 59 by amendment in 2001), nominated by the President.

The President of the Republic appoints the Prime Minister and other members of the Government on the advice of the Prime Minister.

The Constitution delineates the separation of the powers of the organs of State, and guarantees the independence of the judiciary.

The existence of a multi-party political system is confirmed. Serving members of the police and armed forces are banned from political activity.

The Government

HEAD OF STATE

President: Field Marshal ALI ABDULLAH SALEH (took office 24 May 1990; re-elected 1 October 1994, 23 September 1999).

Vice-President: Maj.-Gen. ABD AR-RABBUH MANSUR HADI.

COUNCIL OF MINISTERS
(September 2002)

Prime Minister: ABD AL-QADIR BAJAMMAL.

Deputy Prime Minister and Minister of Finance: ALAWI SALIH AS-SALAMI.

Minister of Foreign Affairs: ABU BAKR AL-KURBI.

Minister of Defence: ABDULLAH ELEWA.

Minister of the Interior: RASHID AL-ALIMI.

Minister of Education: FADHL ABUGHANEM.

Minister of Petroleum and Mineral Resources: RASHID BARBAA.

Minister of Religious Endowments and Guidance: QASSIM AL-AAJAM.

Minister of Transport: ABD AL-MALIK AL-MOALLIMI.

Minister of Fisheries: ALI HASSAN AL-AHMADI.

Minister of Planning and Development: AHMAD MUHAMMAD SUFAN.

Minister of Supply and Trade: ABD AR-RAHMAN MUHAMMAD ALI OTHMAN.

Minister of Public Works and Urban Planning: ABDULLAH HUSSAIN AD-DAFI.

Minister of Marine Transport: SAID YAFAEE.

Minister of Culture: ABD AL-WAHAB AR-ROHANI.

Minister of Higher Education and Scientific Research: YAHYA MUHAMMAD ABDULLAH ASH-SHUAIBI.

Minister of Agriculture and Water Resources: AHMAD SALIM AL-JABALI.

Minister of Immigrants' Affairs: ABDO QUBATI.

Minister of Technical Education and Vocational Training: MUHAMMAD ABDULLAH AL-BATTANI.

Minister of Legal Affairs: ABDULLAH AHMAD GHANIM.

Minister of Youth and Sports: ABD AR-RAHMAN AL-AKWAA.

Minister of the Civil Service and Social Security: ABD AL-WAHAB RAWIH.

Minister of Tourism and the Environment: ABD AL-MALEK AL-IRYANI.

Minister of Labour and Social Affairs: ABD AL-KARIM AL-ARHABI.

Minister of Information: HUSSAIN AL-AWADHI.

Minister of Justice: AHMAD AQABAT.

Minister of Public Health and Demography: ABD AN-NASSER MUNAIBARI.

Minister of Electricity and Water: YAHYA AL-ABYADH.

Minister of State for Human Rights: WAHIBA FARE'E.

Ministers of State without Portfolio: MUHSIN AL-YUSOFI, KHALID ASH-SHARIF, MUHAMMAD YASSER.

Secretary-General for the Presidential Office: ABDULLAH AL-BASHIRI.

MINISTRIES

All ministries are in San'a.

Ministry of Communications: Airport Rd, al-Jiraf, POB 25237, San'a; tel. (1) 331456; fax (1) 331457.

Ministry of Immigrants' Affairs: San'a; internet www.y-mia.net.

Ministry of Information: San'a; tel. (1) 274008; fax (1) 282004; e-mail yemen-info@y.net.ye; internet www.yemeninfo.gov.ye.

Ministry of Oil and Mineral Resources: POB 81, San'a; tel. (1) 202313; internet www.momr.gov.ye.

Ministry of Planning and Development: POB 175, San'a; tel. (1) 250101; fax (1) 251503.

Ministry of Supply and Trade: POB 22210, San'a; tel. (1) 252363; fax (1) 252337; e-mail most@y.net.ye; internet www.most.org.ye.

President and Legislature

PRESIDENT
Presidential Election, 23 September 1999

Candidates	Votes	% of votes
Field Marshal Ali Abdullah Saleh . . .	3,445,608	96.3
Najib Qahtan ash-Sha'bi	132,532	3.7
Total	**3,577,960**	**100.0**

THE HOUSE OF REPRESENTATIVES

Speaker: Sheikh ABDULLAH BIN HUSSAIN AL-AHMAR.

General Election, 27 April 1997

Party	Seats
General People's Congress (GPC)	187
Yemeni Islah Party (YIP)	53
Independents	54
Baathist and Nasserite parties	7
Total	**301**

Political Organizations

In the former PDRY the YSP was the only legal political party until December 1989, when the formation of opposition parties was legalized. There were no political parties in the former YAR. The two leading parties that emerged in the unified Yemen were the GPC and the YSP. During 1990 an estimated 30 to 40 further political parties were reported to have been formed, and in 1991 a law was passed regulating the formation of political parties. Following the civil war from May to July 1994, President Saleh excluded the YSP from the new Government formed in October 1994. In 1995 43 parties were known to be in existence. The number of registered political parties was reported to be 22 in mid-2000.

Al-Haq: San'a; conservative Islamic party; Sec.-Gen. Sheikh AHMAD ASH-SHAMI.

Democratic Coalition of Opposition: San'a; f. 1995 as a coalition of 13 political parties and organizations, including a splinter faction of the YSP and the LSY.

General People's Congress (GPC): San'a; e-mail gpc@y.net.ye; internet www.gpc.org.ye; a broad grouping of supporters of President Saleh; Chair. Field Marshal ALI ABDULLAH SALEH; Vice-Chair. Maj.-Gen. ABD AR-RABBUH MANSUR HADI; Sec.-Gen. Dr ABD AL-KARIM AL-IRYANI.

League of the Sons of Yemen (LSY): Aden; represents interests of southern tribes; Leader ABD AR-RAHMAN AL-JIFRI; Sec.-Gen. MOHSEN FARID.

Nasserite Unionist Popular Organization: Aden; f. 1989 as a legal party.

National Opposition Co-ordination Council: San'a; f. 2001 as a coalition of opposition parties, including the YSP.

Yemen Socialist Party (YSP): San'a; f. 1978 to succeed the United Political Organization—National Front (UPO—NF); fmrly Marxist-Leninist 'vanguard' party based on 'scientific socialism'; has Political Bureau and Cen. Cttee; Sec.-Gen. ALI SALEH OBAD.

Yemeni Islah Party (YIP): POB 23090, San'a; tel. (1) 213281; fax (1) 213311; internet www.yemeniislahparty.com; f. 1990 by mems of the legislature and other political figures, and tribal leaders; seeks constitutional reform based on Islamic law; Leader Sheikh ABDULLAH BIN HUSSAIN AL-AHMAR; Sec.-Gen. Sheikh MUHAMMAD ALI AL-YADOUMI.

Yemeni Unionist Rally Party: Aden; f. 1990 by intellectuals and politicians from the fmr YAR and PDRY to safeguard human rights; Leader OMAR AL-JAWI.

Other parties in Yemen include the **Arab Socialist Baath Party**; the **Federation of Popular Forces**; the **Liberation Front Party**; the **Nasserite Democratic Party**; the **National Democratic Front**; the **National Social Party**; the **Popular Nasserite Reformation Party**; the **Social Green Party**; and the **Yemen League**.

Diplomatic Representation

EMBASSIES IN YEMEN

Algeria: POB 509, 67 Amman St, San'a; tel. (1) 209689; fax (1) 209688; Ambassador: BEN HADID CHADLI.

Bulgaria: POB 1518, St No. 22, San'a; tel. (1) 207924; Chargé d'affaires: ALEXI ALAXIEV.

China, People's Republic: az-Zubairy St, San'a; tel. (1) 275337; Ambassador: ZHOU GUOBIN.

Cuba: POB 15256, St No. 6B, San'a; tel. (1) 217304; fax (1) 217305; Ambassador: HÉCTOR ARGILES PÉREZ.

Czech Republic: POB 2501, Safiya Janoobia, San'a; tel. (1) 247946; fax (1) 244418; Ambassador: ILJA MAZANEK.

Egypt: POB 1134, Gamal Abd al-Nasser St, San'a; tel. (1) 275948; fax (1) 274196; Ambassador: Dr MAHMOUD MURTADA.

Eritrea: POB 11040, Western Safia Bldg, San'a; tel. (1) 209422; fax (1) 214088; Ambassador: MAHMOUD ALI JABRA.

Ethiopia: POB 234, Al-Hamadani St, San'a; tel. (1) 208833; fax (1) 213780; e-mail ethoembs@y.net.ye; Ambassador: TEKETEL FORSIDO.

France: POB 1286, Cnr Sts 2/21, San'a; tel. (1) 268888; fax (1) 269160; internet www.y.net.ye/ambafrancesanaa; Ambassador: PIERRE BOILLOT.

Germany: POB 41, Hadda Area, opposite Jamaa ar-Rahman, San'a; tel. (1) 413177; fax (1) 413179; Ambassador: Dr WERNER ZIMPRICH.

Hungary: POB 11558, As-Safiya Al-Gharbiyya, St No. 6B, San'a; tel. (1) 216250; fax (1) 216251; Ambassador: TIBOR SZATMARI.

India: POB 1154, San'a; tel. (1) 508084; fax (1) 508105; e-mail indiaemb@y.net.ye; Ambassador: M. S. SUMAN.

Indonesia: POB 19873, No. 15, St No. 16, Sixty Rd, Hadda Area, San'a; tel. (1) 217388; fax (1) 414383; Ambassador: AHMAD NOOR.

Iran: POB 1437, Haddah St, San'a; tel. (1) 413552; Chargé d'affaires: ABBAS ETRY.

Iraq: POB 498, South Airport Rd, San'a; tel. (1) 269574; Ambassador: MUHSIN KHALIL.

Italy: POB 1152, No. 5 Bldg, St No. 29, San'a; tel. (1) 265616; fax (1) 266137; e-mail italianembassy@y.net.ye; Ambassador: Dr VITALIANO NAPOLEONE.

Japan: POB 817, San'a; tel. (1) 207356; fax (1) 209531; Ambassador: SUSUMU AKIYAMA.

Jordan: POB 2152, San'a; tel. (1) 413279; Ambassador: FOUAD BATAYNEH.

Korea, Democratic People's Republic: POB 1209, al-Hasaba, Mazda Rd, San'a; tel. (1) 232340; Ambassador: CHANG MYONG SON.

Korea, Republic: San'a; tel. (1) 245959; Ambassador: PAK HI-JOO.

Kuwait: POB 3746, South Ring Rd, San'a; tel. (1) 268876; fax (1) 268875; Chargé d'affaires: MANSOUR AL-AWADI.

Lebanon: POB 2283, Haddah St, San'a; tel. (1) 203459; fax (1) 201120; Ambassador: HASSAN BERRO.

Libya: POB 1506, Ring Rd, St No. 8, House No. 145, San'a; Secretary of Libyan Brotherhood Office: A. U. HEFIANA.

Mauritania: POB 19383, No. 6, Algeria St, San'a; tel. (1) 216770; fax (1) 215926; Ambassador: AHMED OULD SIDY.

Morocco: POB 10236, West Safiya, San'a; tel. (1) 247964; fax (1) 247793; Ambassador: LAHCEN AZOULAY.

Netherlands: POB 463, off 14th October St, San'a; tel. (1) 421000; fax 421035; e-mail holland@y.net.ye; internet www.holland.com.ye; Ambassador: B. J. RONHAAR.

Oman: POB 105, Aser area, az-Zubairy St, San'a; tel. (1) 208933; Ambassador: ABDULLAH BIN HAMAD AL-BADI.

Pakistan: POB 2848, Ring Rd, San'a; tel. (1) 248814; fax (1) 248866; e-mail pakemb@y.net.ye; Ambassador: M. ASGHAR AFRIDI.

Poland: POB 16168, Hadda St, San'a; tel. (1) 412243; fax (1) 413647; Ambassador: KRZYSZTOF SUPROWICZ.

Romania: POB 2169, No. 22, St No. 21, Nouakchott Rd, San'a; tel. (1) 209003; fax (1) 214100; e-mail a.romana-sanaa@y.net.ye; Chargé d'affaires: GHEORGHE VILCU.

Russia: POB 1087, 26 September St, San'a; tel. (1) 278719; fax (1) 283142; Ambassador: IGOR G. IVASHENKO.

Saudi Arabia: POB 1184, Zuhara House, Hadda Rd, San'a; tel. (1) 240429; Ambassador: MUHAMMAD AL-QAHTANI.

Somalia: San'a; tel. (1) 208864; Ambassador: ABD AS-SALLAM MU'ALLIM ADAM.

Sudan: POB 2561, 82 Abou al-Hassan al-Hamadani St, San'a; tel. (1) 265231; fax (1) 265234; Ambassador: OMAR AS-SAID TAHA.

Syria: POB 494, Hadda Rd, Damascus St 1, San'a; tel. (1) 414891; Ambassador: Dr FAROUK TAHA.

Tunisia: POB 2561, Diplomatic area, St No. 22, San'a; tel. (1) 240458; Ambassador: ABBÈS MOHSEN.

Turkey: POB 18371, as-Safiya, San'a; tel. and fax (1) 241395; Ambassador: SANLI TOPÇUOĞLU.

United Arab Emirates: POB 2250, Ring Rd, San'a; tel. (1) 248777; Ambassador: SAIF BIN MAKTOOM AL-MANSOORY.

United Kingdom: POB 1287, 129 Hadda Rd, San'a; tel. (1) 264081; fax (1) 263059; Ambassador: FRANCES GUY.

USA: POB 22347, Sheraton Hotel District, San'a; tel. (1) 238843; fax (1) 251563; e-mail usembassy08@y.net.ye; internet www.usembassy.ye; Ambassador: EDMUND J. HULL.

Religion

ISLAM

The majority of the population are Muslims. Most are Sunni Muslims of the Shafi'a sect, except in the north-west of the country, where Zaidism (a moderate sect of the Shi'a order) is the dominant persuasion.

CHRISTIANITY

The Roman Catholic Church

Apostolic Vicariate of Arabia: POB 54, Abu Dhabi, United Arab Emirates; tel. (2) 4461895; fax (2) 4465177; e-mail apvicar@emirates.net.ae; responsible for a territory comprising most of the Arabian peninsula (including Saudi Arabia, the UAE, Oman, Qatar, Bahrain and Yemen), containing an estimated 1,300,000 Roman Catholics (31 December 1999); Vicar Apostolic GIOVANNI BERNARDO GREMOLI, Titular Bishop of Masuccaba (resident in the UAE); Vicar Delegate for Yemen Rev. GEORGE PUDUSSERY.

The Anglican Communion

Within the Episcopal Church in Jerusalem and the Middle East, Yemen forms part of the diocese of Cyprus and the Gulf. The Anglican congregations in San'a and Aden are entirely expatriate; the Bishop in Cyprus and the Gulf is resident in Cyprus, while the Archdeacon in the Gulf is resident in Qatar.

HINDUISM

There is a small Hindu community.

Judicial System

Yemen's Constitution guarantees the independence of the judiciary and identifies Islamic (*Shari'a*) as the basis of all laws.

Yemen is divided into 18 Governorates, each of which is further divided into Districts. Each District has a Court of First Instance in which all cases are heard by a single magistrate. Appeals against decisions of the Courts of First Instance are referred to a Court of Appeal. Each Governorate has a Court of Appeal with four divisions: Civil, Criminal, Matrimonial and Commercial, each of which consists of three judges.

The Supreme Court of the Republic, which sits in San'a, rules on matters concerning the Constitution, appeals against decisions of the Courts of Appeal and cases brought against members of the Legislature. The Supreme Court has eight divisions, each of which consists of five judges.

The Supreme Judicial Council supervises the proper function of the courts and its Chairman is the President of the Republic.

The Press

Legislation embodying the freedom of the press in the unified Republic of Yemen was enacted in May 1990. The lists below include publications which appeared in the YAR and the PDRY prior to their unification in May 1990.

DAILIES

Al-Jumhuriya: Taiz Information Office, Taiz; tel. (4) 216748; Arabic; circ. 100,000.

Ar-Rabi' 'Ashar Min Uktubar (14 October): POB 4227, Crater, Aden; f. 1968; not published on Saturdays; Arabic; Editorial Dir FAROUQ MUSTAFA RIFAT; Chief Editor MUHAMMAD HUSSAIN MUHAMMAD; circ. 20,000.

Ash-Sharara (The Spark): 14 October Corpn for Printing, Publishing, Distribution and Advertising, POB 4227, Crater, Aden; Arabic; circ. 6,000.

Ath-Thawra (The Revolution): POB 2195, San'a; tel. (1) 262626; fax (1) 274139; e-mail editor@althawara.gov.ye; internet www.althawra.gov.ae; Arabic; govt-owned; Editor MUHAMMAD AZ-ZORKAH; circ. 110,000.

WEEKLIES AND OTHERS

Attijarah (Trade): POB 3370, Hodeida; tel. (3) 213784; fax (3) 211528; e-mail hodcci@y.net.ye; monthly; Arabic; commercial.

Al-Ayyam: POB 648, al-Khalij al-Imami, Crater, Aden; tel. (2) 255170; fax (2) 255692; e-mail editor@al-ayyam-yemen.com; Editor HISHAM BASHRAHEEL.

Al-Bilad (The Country): POB 1438, San'a; weekly; Arabic; centre-right.

Dar as-Salam (Peace): POB 1790, San'a; tel. (1) 272946; f. 1948; weekly; Arabic; political, economic and general essays; Editor ABDULLAH MUKBOOL AS-SICGUL.

Al-Fanoon: Ministry of Culture and Tourism, POB 1187, Tawahi 102, Aden; tel. (2) 23831; f. 1980; Arabic; monthly arts review; Editor FAISAL SOFY; circ. 15,500.

Al-Gundi (The Soldier): Ministry of Defence, Madinat ash-Sha'ab; fortnightly; Arabic; circ. 8,500.

Al-Hares: Aden; fortnightly; Arabic; circ. 8,000.

Al-Hikma (Wisdom): POB 4227, Crater, Aden; monthly; Arabic; publ. by the Writers' Union; circ. 5,000.

Al-Ma'in (Spring): Ministry of Information, San'a; monthly; general interest.

Majallat al-Jaish (Army Magazine): POB 2182, San'a; tel. (1) 231181; monthly; publ. by Ministry of Defence.

Al-Maseerah (Journey): Ministry of Information, POB 2182, San'a; tel. (1) 231181; monthly; general interest.

Al-Mithaq (The Charter): San'a; internet www.gpc.org.ye/mathak; weekly; organ of the General People's Congress.

Ar-Ra'i al-'Am (Public Opinion): POB 293, San'a; tel. (1) 242090; weekly; independent; Editor ALI MUHAMMAD AL-OLAFI.

Ar-Risalah: POB 55777, 26 September St, Taiz; tel. (4) 214215; fax (4) 221164; e-mail alaws@y.net.ye; f. 1968; weekly; Arabic.

As-Sahwa (Awakening): POB 11126, Hadda Road, San'a; tel. (1) 247892; fax (1) 269218; weekly; Islamic fundamentalist; Editor MUHAMMAD AL-YADDOUMI.

As-Salam (Peace): POB 181, San'a; tel. (1) 272946; weekly.

San'a: POB 193, San'a; fortnightly; Arabic; inclined to left.

Sawt al-'Ummal (The Workers' Voice): POB 4227, Crater, Aden; weekly; Arabic.

Sawt al-Yemen (Voice of Yemen): POB 302, San'a; weekly; Arabic.

Ash-Shura: POB 15114, San'a; tel. (1) 213584; fax (1) 213468; e-mail shoura@y.net.ye; Editor ABDALLAH SA'AD; circ. 15,000.

At-Ta'awun (Co-operation): at-Ta'awun Bldg, az-Zubairy St, San'a; weekly; Arabic; supports co-operative societies.

Ath-Thawri (The Revolutionary): POB 4227, Crater, Aden; weekly; published on Saturday; Arabic; organ of Cen. Cttee of YSP; Editor Dr AHMAD ABDULLAH SALIH.

26 September: 26 September Publishing, POB 17, San'a; tel. (1) 262626; fax (1) 234129; e-mail webmaster@26september.com; internet www.y.net.ye/26september; armed forces weekly; circ. 25,000.

Al-Wahda al-Watani (National Unity): Al-Baath Printing House, POB 193, San'a; tel. (1) 77511; f. 1982; fmrly *Al-Omal*; monthly; Editor MUHAMMAD SALEM ALI; circ. 40,000.

Al-Yemen: Yemen Printing and Publishing Co, POB 1081, San'a; tel. (1) 72376; f. 1971; weekly; Arabic; centre-right; Editor MUHAMMAD AHMAD AS-SABAGH.

The Yemen Times: POB 2579, Hadda St, San'a; tel. (1) 268661; fax (1) 268276; e-mail yementimes@yementimes.com; internet www.yementimes.com; f. 1991; independent weekly; English; Editor-in-Chief WALID AS-SAQQAF; circ. 30,000.

Yemen Observer: POB 19183, Central Suites, Mujahid St, Sana'a; tel. (1) 248217; fax (1) 243222; e-mail info@yobserver.com; internet www.yobserver,com; f. 1996; independent weekly; English; Editor-in-Chief FARRIS SANABANI.

Yemeni Women: POB 4227, Crater, Aden; monthly; circ. 5,000.

NEWS AGENCIES

Aden News Agency (ANA): Ministry of Culture and Tourism, POB 1187, Tawahi 102, Aden; tel. (2) 24874; f. 1970; govt-owned; Dir-Gen. AHMAD MUHAMMAD IBRAHIM.

Saba News Agency: POB 881, San'a; tel. (1) 250078; fax (1) 250078; e-mail sabanews@y.net.ye; internet www.sabanews.gov.ye; f. 1970; Editor HUSEIN AL-AWADI.

Publishers

Armed Forces Printing Press: POB 17, San'a; tel. (1) 274240.

14 October Corpn for Printing, Publishing, Distribution and Advertising: POB 4227, Crater, Aden; under control of the Ministry of Information; Chair. and Gen. Man. SALIH AHMAD SALAH.

26 September Publishing: POB 17, San'a; tel. (1) 274240.

Ath-Thawrah Corpn: POB 2195, San'a; fax (1) 251505; Chair. M. R. AZ-ZURKAH.

Yemen Printing and Publishing Co: POB 1081, San'a; Chair. AHMAD MUHAMMAD HADI.

Broadcasting and Communications

TELECOMMUNICATIONS

Public Telecommunications Corpn: POB 17045, Airport Rd, al-Jiraf, San'a; tel. (1) 250040; Dir-Gen. MUHAMMAD AL-KASSOUS.

BROADCASTING

Yemen Radio and Television Corpn: POB 2182, San'a; tel. (1) 230654; fax (1) 230761; state-controlled; Gen. Man. AHMED T. SHAYANY.

Finance

(cap. = capital; res = reserves; dep. = deposits; m. = million; brs = branches; amounts in Yemeni riyals, unless otherwise indicated)

BANKING

Central Bank

Central Bank of Yemen: POB 59, Ali Abd al-Mughni St, San'a; tel. (1) 274310; fax (1) 274360; e-mail info@centralbank.gov.ye; internet www.centralbank.gov.ye; f. 1971; merged with Bank of Yemen in 1990; cap. and res 12,414.5m., dep. 249,998.6m. (Dec. 1996); Gov. AHMAD ABD AR-RAHMAN AS-SAMAWI; Dep. Gov. SALEM MUHAMMAD AL-ASHWALI; 20 brs.

Principal Banks

Arab Bank PLC (Jordan): POB 475, az-Zubairy St, San'a; tel. (1) 276585; fax (1) 276583; e-mail arabbank@y.net.ye; internet www.arabbank.com; f. 1972; Man. MAHDI ALAWI; 5 brs.

Co-operative and Agricultural Credit Bank: POB 2015, Banks Complex, az-Zubairy St, San'a; tel. (1) 220090; fax (1) 220088; e-mail cacbank@y.net.ye; f. 1976; cap. 293m., total assets 4,930m. (Dec. 2000); Chair. Dr MUHAMMAD H. AL-WADAN; Dir-Gen. YAHIA AS-SABRI; 27 brs.

Crédit Agricole Indosuez (France): POB 651, az-Zubairy St, San'a; tel. (1) 274370; fax (1) 274501; e-mail caindosuezye@y.net.ye; Regional Man. FRANÇOIS RIVIER; 6 brs.

Industrial Bank of Yemen: POB 323, Banks Complex, az-Zubairy St, San'a; tel. (1) 207381; fax (1) 207379; f. 1976; industrial investment; cap. 100m., total assets 269.8m. (1987); Chair. and Man. Dir ABBAS ABDU MUHAMMAD AL-KIRSHY; Gen. Man. ABD AL-KARIM ISMAIL AL-ARHABI.

International Bank of Yemen YSC: POB 4444, 106 az-Zubairy St, San'a; tel. (1) 273273; fax (1) 274127; e-mail a.t.alabsi@y.net.ye; internet www.iboyemen.com; f. 1980; commercial bank; cap. 906.4m., res 71.1m., dep. 11,042.2m. (Dec. 1999); Chair. ALI LUTF ATH-THOUR; Gen. Man. MUHAMMAD ABDULLAH M. AL-AMERY; 4 brs.

Islamic Bank of Yemen for Finance and Investment: POB 18452, Mareb Yemen Insurance Co Bldg, az-Zubairy St, San'a; tel. (1) 206117; fax (1) 205679; e-mail ibr-islbk-yesan@y.net.ye; internet www.islamicbankymn.com; f. 1996; commercial, investment and retail banking; cap. 1,030m., res 51.6m., dep. 5,720.4m. (Dec. 2000); Chair. A. KARIM AR-RAHMAN AL-ASWADI.

National Bank of Yemen: POB 5, Arwa Rd, Crater, Aden; tel. and fax (2) 253484; e-mail nby.ho@y.net.ye; f. 1970 as National Bank of South Yemen; reorg. 1971; cap. and res 2,856m., dep. 33,847m. (Dec. 2001); Chair. and Gen. Man. ABD AR-RAHMAN MUHAMMAD AL-KUHALI; 28 brs.

United Bank Ltd (Pakistan): POB 1295, Ali Abd al-Mughni St, San'a; tel. (1) 272424; fax (1) 274168; e-mail ublsana@y.net.ye; Vice-Pres. and Gen. Man. INAYATULLAH BUTT; 1 br.

Watani Bank for Trade and Investment: POB 3058, az-Zubairy St, San'a; tel. (1) 206613; fax (1) 205706; e-mail watanibank@y.net.ye; internet www.watanibank.com; f. 1998; cap. 1,000m., res 12.1m., dep. 7,071.5m. (Dec. 1999); Chair. Dr AHMAD ALI AL-HAMDANI; Gen. Man. SHABIH MEHDI NAQVI.

Yemen Bank for Reconstruction and Development (YBRD): POB 541, 26 September St, San'a; tel. (1) 270481; fax (1) 271684; e-mail ybrdho@y.net.ye; internet www.ybrd.com.ye; f. 1962; cap. 1,000m., res 367.5m., dep. 21,702.8m. (Dec. 1999); Chair. ABDULLAH SALIM AL-GIFRI; Gen. Man. HUSSAIN FADHLE MUHAMMAD; 13 brs.

Yemen Commercial Bank: POB 19845, az-Zubairy St, San'a; tel. (1) 284272; fax (1) 284656; e-mail ycbho@y.net.ye; internet www.ycbank.com; f. 1993; cap. 993.7m., res 191.2m., dep. 21,658.4m. (Dec. 2000); Chair. Sheikh Muhammad bin Yahya ar-Rowaishan; Chief Exec. and Gen. Man. Sikander Mahmoud; 8 brs.

INSURANCE

Aman Insurance Co (YSC): POB 1133, San'a; tel. (1) 214104; fax (1) 209452; e-mail aman-ins@y.net.ye; internet www.y.net.ye/amaninsurance; all classes of insurance; Gen. Man. Akil as-Sakkaf.

Mareb Yemen Insurance Co: POB 2284, az-Zubairy St, San'a; tel. (1) 206114; fax (1) 206118; e-mail maryinsco74@y.net.ye; internet www.marebinsurance.com.ye; f. 1974; all classes of insurance; cap. 150m.; Chair. and Gen. Man. Ali M. Hashim.

National Insurance and Re-insurance Co: POB 456, Aden; tel. (2) 51464; f. 1970; Lloyd's Agents; cap. 5m. Yemeni dinars; Gen. Man. Abubakr S. al-Qoti.

Saba Yemen Insurance Co: POB 19214, San'a; tel. (1) 240908; fax (1) 240943; e-mail sabains@yenet.com; internet www.sabainsurance.com; f. 1990; all classes of insurance; Gen. Man. Sabah Haddad.

Trust Yemen Insurance and Reinsurance Co: POB 18392, San'a; tel. (1) 264263; fax (1) 263234; all classes of insurance; Gen. Man. Daoud al-Khatib.

United Insurance Co: POB 1883, az-Zubairy St, San'a; tel. (1) 214232; fax (1) 214012; e-mail unitedinsurance@y.net.ye; internet www.unitedinsuranceyemen.com; f. 1981; all classes of general insurance and life; cap. 100m.; Gen. Man. Tarek A. Hayel Saeed.

Al-Watania Insurance Co (YSC): POB 15497, San'a; tel. (1) 272874; fax (1) 272924; e-mail alwatania@yenet.com; all classes of insurance.

Yemen General Insurance Co (SYC): POB 2709, YGI Bldg, 25 Algiers St, San'a; tel. (1) 442489; fax (1) 442492; e-mail ygi-san@y.net.ye; f. 1977; all classes of insurance; cap. 300m.; Chair. Abd al-Gabbar Thabet; Gen. Man. Mun'em al-Khafaji.

Yemen Insurance Co: POB 8437, San'a; tel. (1) 272805; fax (1) 274177; e-mail yemeninsurance@yenet.com; f. 1990; all classes of insurance; Deputy Gen. Man. Khalid Bashir Tahir.

Trade and Industry

GOVERNMENT AGENCIES

General Corpn for Foreign Trade and Grains: POB 77, San'a; tel. (1) 202345; fax (1) 209511; f. 1976; Dir-Gen. Abd ar-Rahman al-Madwahi.

General Corpn for Manufacturing and Marketing of Cement: POB 1920, San'a; tel. (1) 215691; fax (1) 263168; Chair. Amin Abd al-Wahid Ahmed.

National Co for Foreign Trade: POB 90, Crater, Aden; tel. (2) 42793; fax (2) 42631; f. 1969; incorporates main foreign trading businesses (nationalized in 1970) and arranges their supply to the National Co for Home Trade; Gen. Man. Ahmed Muhammad Saleh (acting).

National Co for Home Trade: POB 90, Crater, Aden; tel. (2) 41483; fax (2) 41226; f. 1969; marketing of general consumer goods, building materials, electrical goods, motor cars and spare parts, agricultural machinery etc.; Man. Dir Abd ar-Rahman as-Sailani.

National Dockyards Co: POB 1244, Tawahi, Aden; tel. (2) 23837; Man. Dir Saleh al-Muntasir Mehdi.

National Drug Corpn: Aden; tel. (2) 04912; fax (2) 21242; f. 1972; import of pharmaceutical products, chemicals, medical supplies, baby foods and scientific instruments; Chair. and Gen. Man. Dr Awadh Salam Issa Bamatraf.

Public Corpn for Building and Housing: POB 7022, al-Mansoura, Aden; tel. (2) 342296; fax (2) 345726; f. 1973; govt contractors and contractors of private housing projects; Dir-Gen. Hussain Muhammad al-Wali.

Public Corpn for Maritime Affairs (PCMA): POB 19396, San'a; tel. (1) 414412; fax (1) 414645; f. 1990; protection of the marine environment; registration of ships; implementation of international maritime conventions; Chair. Saeed Yafai.

Yemen Co for Industry and Commerce Ltd: POB 5423, Taiz; tel. (4) 218058; fax (4) 218054; Chair. Ali Muhammad Said.

Yemen Co for Investment and Finance Ltd: POB 2789, San'a; tel. (1) 276372; fax (1) 274178; f. 1981; cap. 100m.; Chair. and Gen. Man. Abdullah Ishaq.

Yemen Drug Co for Industry and Commerce: POB 40, San'a; tel. (1) 234250; fax (1) 234290; Chair. Muhammad Ali Muqbil; Man. Dir Abd ar-Rahman A. Ghaleb.

Yemen Economical Corpn: POB 1207, San'a; tel. (1) 262501; fax (1) 262508; Commercial Man. A. Karim Sayaghi.

Yemen Land Transport Corpn: POB 279, Taiz St, San'a; tel. (1) 268307; f. 1961; Chair. Abd al-Kadoos al-Massry; Gen. Man. Hamid Mukrid.

Yemen Trading and Construction Co: POB 1092, San'a; tel. (1) 264005; fax (1) 240624; e-mail ytcc@y.net.ye; f. 1979; intial cap. 100m. riyals.

DEVELOPMENT ORGANIZATIONS

Agricultural Research and Extension Authority: POB 87148 Dhamar; e-mail muharram@y.net.ye.

General Board for Development of Eastern Region: San'a.

General Board for Development of Tihama: San'a.

Yemen Free Zone Public Authority: Aden; tel. (2) 241210; fax (2) 221237; supervises creation of a free zone for industrial investment; Chair. Abd al-Qadir Ba-Jammal.

CHAMBERS OF COMMERCE

Chamber of Commerce and Industry—Aden: POB 473, Crater 101, Aden; tel. (2) 257376; fax (2) 255660; e-mail cciaden@y.net.ye; f. 1886; 5,000 mems; Pres. Muhammad Omer Bamashmus; Dir G. Ahmad Hadi Salem.

Federation of Chambers of Commerce: POB 16992, San'a; tel. (1) 211765; Dir Jamal Sharhan.

Hodeida Chamber of Commerce: POB 3370, 20 az-Zubairy St, Hodeida; tel. (3) 217401; fax (3) 211528; e-mail hodcci@y.net.ye; internet www.hodcci.com.ye; f. 1960; 6,500 mems; cap. 10m. riyals; Dir Nabil al-Wageeh.

San'a Chamber of Commerce and Industry: Airport Rd, al-Hasabah St, POB 195, San'a; tel. (1) 232361; fax (1) 232412; f. 1963; Pres. Al-Haj Hussain al-Watari; Gen. Man. Abdullah H. ar-Rubaidi.

Taiz Chamber of Commerce: POB 5029, Chamber St, Taiz; tel. (4) 210580; fax (4) 212335; e-mail taizchamber@y.net.ye; Dir Mofid A. Saif.

Yemen Chamber of Commerce and Industry: POB 16690, San'a; tel. (1) 223539; fax (1) 251555.

STATE HYDROCARBONS COMPANIES

General Corpn for Oil and Mineral Resources: San'a; f. 1990; state petroleum co; Pres. Ahmad Barakat.

Ministry of Oil and Mineral Resources: POB 81, San'a; tel. (1) 202313; internet www.momr.gov.ye; responsible for the refining and marketing of petroleum products, and for prospecting and exploitation of indigenous hydrocarbons and other minerals; subsidiaries include:

Aden Refinery Co: POB 3003, Aden 110; tel. (2) 76234; fax (2) 76600; f. 1952; operates petroleum refinery; capacity 8.6m. tons per year; output 4.2m. tons (1990); operates 1 oil tanker; Exec. Dir Muhammad Hussein al-Haj; Refinery Man. Ahmad Hassan al-Gifri.

Yemen National Oil Co: POB 5050, Maalla, Aden; sole petroleum concessionaire, importer and distributor of petroleum products; Gen. Man. Muhammad Abd Hussein.

UTILITIES

Electricity

Public Electricity Corpn: POB 11422, Government Complex, Haddah Rd, San'a; tel. (1) 264131; fax (1) 263115; Man. Dir Ahmad al-Aini.

Water

National Water and Sanitation Authority (NWSA): (Taiz Branch) POB 5283, Taiz; tel. (4) 222628; fax (4) 212323.

TRADE UNIONS

Agricultural Co-operatives Union: POB 649, San'a; tel. (1) 270685; fax (1) 274125.

General Confederation of Workers: POB 1162, Maalla, Aden; f. 1956; affiliated to WFTU and ICFTU; 35,000 mems; Pres. Rajeh Saleh Naji; Gen. Sec. Abd ar-Razak Shaif.

Trade Union Federation: San'a; Pres. Ali Saif Muqbil.

Transport

RAILWAYS

There are no railways in Yemen.

ROADS

In 1996 Yemen had a total road network of 64,725 km, including 5,234 km of main roads and 2,474 km of secondary roads. In 1999 there were an estimated 6,000 km of roads, 11.5% of which were paved.

General Corpn for Roads and Bridges: POB 1185, az-Zubairy St, Asir Rd, San'a; tel. (1) 202278; fax (1) 209571; e-mail gcrb@y.net.ye; responsible for maintenance and construction.

Yemen Land Transport Co: Aden; f. 1980; incorporates fmr Yemen Bus Co and all other public transport of the fmr PDRY; Chair. ABD AL-JALIL TAHIR BADR; Gen. Man. SALIH AWAD AL-AMUDI.

SHIPPING

Aden is the main port. Aden Main Harbour has 28 first-class berths. In addition there is ample room to accommodate vessels of light draught at anchor in the 18-foot dredged area. There is also 800 feet of cargo wharf accommodating vessels of 300 feet length and 18 feet draught. Aden Oil Harbour accommodates four tankers of 57,000 tons and up to 40 feet draught. In March 1999 work was completed on a US $580m. programme to expand container handling facilities at Aden, with the aim of establishing the port as a major transhipment centre. Hodeida port, on the Red Sea, was expanded with Soviet aid and now handles a considerable amount of traffic; there are also ports at Maalla, Mocha, Nishtun and Salif.

At 31 December 2001 Yemen's merchant fleet comprised 44 vessels, with a combined displacement of 73,757 grt.

Yemen Ports Authority: POB 1316, Steamer Point, Aden; tel. (2) 203521; fax (2) 202850; e-mail roy@y.net.ye; f. 1888; Harbour Master Capt. BARAKAT ALI DARWISH.

Principal Shipping Companies

Aden Refinery Co: POB 3003, Aden 110; tel. (2) 430743; fax (2) 376600; 2 general tankers and 1 chemical tanker; Exec.-Dir MUHAMMAD HUSSAIN AL-HAJ.

Arabian Gulf Navigation Co (Yemen) Ltd: POB 3740, Hodeida; tel. (3) 2442; 1 general cargo vessel.

Al-Katiri Shipping Corpn: POB 716, Aden; tel. (2) 255538; fax (2) 251152; 1 general cargo vessel.

Elkirshi Shipping and Stevedoring Co: POB 3813, al-Hamdi St, Hodeida; tel. (3) 224263; operates at ports of Hodeida, Mocha and Salif.

Hodeida Shipping and Transport Co Ltd: POB 3337, Hodeida; tel. (3) 238130; fax (3) 211533; e-mail hodship_1969@y.net.ye; internet www.hodship.com; shipping agents, stevedoring, Lloyd's agents; clearance, haulage land transportation, cargo and vessel surveys.

Middle East Shipping Co Ltd: POB 3700, Hodeida; tel. (3) 217276; fax (3) 211529; e-mail mideast@mideastshipping.com; internet www.mideastshipping.com; f. 1962; Chair. ABD AL-WASA HAYEL SAEED; Gen. Man. SAMEER AL-GALIL GAZEM; brs in Mocha, Aden, Taiz, Mukalla, San'a, Salif, Ras Isa, ash-Shihr.

National Shipping Co: POB 1228, Steamer Point, Aden; tel. (2) 204861; fax (2) 202644; shipping, bunkering, clearing and forwarding, and travel agents; Gen. Man. MUHAMMAD OTHMAN.

Yemen Navigation Line: POB 4190, Aden; tel. (2) 24861; fleet of 3 general cargo vessels.

Yemen Shipping Development Co Ltd: POB 3686, Hodeida; tel. (3) 224103; fax (3) 211584; 1 general cargo vessel; Shipping Man. FAHDLE A. KARIM.

Yeslam Salem Alshagga: POB 778, Aden; 1 general cargo vessel.

CIVIL AVIATION

There are six international airports—San'a International (13 km from the city), Aden Civil Airport (at Khormaksar, 11 km from the port of Aden), al-Ganad (at Taiz), Mukalla (Riyan), Seyoun and Hodeida Airport.

Yemen Airways (Yemenia): POB 1183, Airport Rd, San'a; tel. (1) 232380; fax (1) 252991; e-mail yemenia@y.net.ye; internet www .yemenia.com.ye; f. 1961 as Yemen Airlines; nationalized as Yemen Airways Corpn 1972; present name adopted 1978; merged with airlines of fmr PDRY in 1996; owned 51% by Yemeni Govt and 49% by Govt of Saudi Arabia; scheduled for privatization; supervised by a ministerial cttee under the Ministry of Transport; internal services and external services to more than 25 destinations in the Middle East, Asia, Africa, Europe and the USA; Chair. HASSAN ABDO SOHBI.

Tourism

The former YAR formed a joint tourism company with the PDRY in 1980. Yemen boasts areas of beautiful scenery, a favourable climate and towns of historic and architectural importance. UNESCO has named San'a and Shibam as World Heritage sites. However, the growth of tourism has, in recent years, been hampered by political instability. In 2000 some 72,836 tourists visited Yemen; tourist receipts for that year were estimated at US $76m.

Association of Yemen Tourism and Travel Agencies: San'a; internet www.aytta.org; Chair. YAHAYA M. A. SALEH.

General Authority of Tourism: POB 129, San'a; tel. (1) 252319, fax (1) 252316; e-mail mkt@yenet.com; Chair. ABD AR-RAHMAN MAH-YOUB.

Yemen Tourism Promotion Board: POB 5607, 48 Amman St, San'a; tel. (1) 264057; fax (1) 264284; e-mail yementpb@y.net.ye; Man. ABDU LUTF.

Defence

The armed forces of the former YAR and the PDRY were officially merged in May 1990, but by early 1994 the process had not been completed and in May civil war broke out between the forces of the two former states, culminating in victory for the North. In October President Saleh announced plans for the modernization of the armed forces, which would include the banning of party affiliation in the security services and armed forces, and in March 1995 the full merger of the armed forces was announced.

Supreme Commander of the Armed Forces: Field Marshal ALI ABDULLAH SALEH.

Chief of the General Staff: Brig.-Gen. ABDULLAH ALI ULAYWAH.

Estimated defence budget (2002): 104,844m. riyals.

Military Service: conscription (formerly three years) ended in May 2001.

Total Armed Forces (August 2001): 54,000: army 49,000; navy 1,500; air force 3,500. Reserves estimated at 40,000 (army).

Paramilitary Forces: an estimated 70,000-strong Ministry of the Interior Force, and at least 20,000 tribal levies.

Education

Primary education in the Yemen is compulsory between the ages of six and 15. Secondary education, beginning at 15, lasts for a further three years. In 1996 enrolment at primary schools was equivalent to 70% of children in the relevant age-group (boys 100%; girls 40%). Enrolment at secondary schools in that year was equivalent to just 34% of students in the appropriate age-group (males 53%; females 14%). In the 1993/94 academic year, 11,999 pupils were in pre-primary education. In 1996/97 2,699,788 pupils attended primary institutions. There were 354,288 pupils in secondary education in that year. In 1999/2000 some 147,181 students were enrolled at seven state-controlled institutes of higher education. In 2000 public expenditure on education was forecast at 90,054m. riyals, equivalent to 21.3% of total government spending.

Bibliography

Amin, Dr S. H. *Law and Justice in Contemporary Yemen.* Glasgow, Royston, 1987.

Ansaldi, C. *Il Yemen nella storia e nella leggenda.* Rome, 1933.

Attar, Mohamed Said El-. *Le sous-développement économique et social du Yémen.* Algiers, Editions Tiers-Monde, 1966.

Badeeb, Said M. *The Saudi–Egyptian Conflict over North Yemen 1962–70.* Colorado, Westview Press, 1986.

Balsan, François. *Inquiétant Yémen.* Paris, 1961.

Behbehari, Hashim S. H. London, KP1, 1985.

Bethmann, E. W. *Yemen on the Threshold. American Friends of the Middle East.* Washington, 1960.

Bidwell, Robin. *The Two Yemens.* London, Longman, 1983.

Brinton, J. Y. *Aden and the Federation of South Arabia.* Washington, DC, American Society of International Law, 1964.

Burrowes, Robert D. *The Yemen Arab Republic:* The Politics of Development 1962–1986. London, Croom Helm, 1987.

Historical Dictionary of Yemen. London, Scarecrow Press, 1995.

Carapico, Sheila. *Civil Society in Yemen: The Political Economy of Activism in Modern Arabia*. Cambridge University Press, 1998.

Central Office of Information. *Aden and South Arabia*. London, HMSO, 1965.

Chelhod, Joseph. *L'Arabie du Sud. Histoire et civilisation*; Vol. I: *Le peuple yéménite et ses racines*; Vol. II; Vol. III. Paris, Éditions Maisonneuve et Larose, 1985.

Colonial Office. *Accession of Aden to the Federation of South Arabia*. London, HMSO, 1962.

Aden and the Yemen. London, HMSO, 1960.

Treaty of Friendship and Protection between the United Kingdom and the Federation of South Arabia. London, HMSO, 1964.

Detalle, Renaud. *Tensions in Arabia—The Saudi–Yemeni Fault Line*. Baden-Baden, Nomos Verlagsgesellschaft, 2000.

Deutsch, Robert. *Der Yemen*. Vienna, 1914.

Doe, Brian. *Southern Arabia*. London, Thames and Hudson, 1972.

Dresch, Paul. *A History of Modern Yemen*. Cambridge University Press, 2001.

Enders, Klaus, Williams, Sherwyn E., Choueiri, Nada G., Sobolev, Yuri V., and Walliser, Jan. *Yemen in the 1990s: From Unification to Economic Reform* (IMF Occasional Paper). Washington, DC, IMF Publication Services, 2002.

Federation of South Arabia. *Conference on Constitutional Problems of South Arabia*. HMSO, 1964.

Freitag, Ulrike, and Clarence-Smith, William (Eds). *Hadhrami Traders, Scholars and Statesmen in the Indian Ocean, 1750s–1960s*. Leiden, Brill, 1997

Gavin, R. J. *Aden 1839–1967*. London, Hurst, 1973.

Gehrke, Dr Ulrich. *Südarabien, Südarabische Föderation oder Süd-Jemen?* Hamburg, Orient Magazine, German Near and Middle East Association, 1967.

Helfritz, H. *The Yemen: A Secret Journey*. London, Allen and Unwin, 1958.

Heyworth-Dunne, G. E. *Al-Yemen: Social, Political and Economic Survey*. Cairo, 1952.

Hickinbotham, Sir Tom. *Aden*. London, Constable, 1959.

Ingrams, Doreen. *A Survey of the Social and Economic Conditions of the Aden Protectorate*. London.

Ingrams, Doreen, and Ingrams, Leila (Eds), *The Records of Yemen 1798–1960*. London, Archive Editions, 1995.

Ingrams, Harold. *The Yemen; Imams, Rulers and Revolutions*. London, 1963.

Ingrams, W. H. *A Report on the Social, Economic and Political Conditions of the Hadhramaut, Aden Protectorate*. London, 1936.

Arabia and the Isles. London, Murray, 1947.

Ismail, Tareq Y., and Jacqueline S. *The People's Democratic Republic of Yemen. Politics, Economics and Society*. London, Pinter, 1986.

Jacob, Harold F. *Kings of Arabia*. London, 1923.

Jenner, Michael. *Yemen Rediscovered*. London, Longman, 1983.

Johnston, Charles. *The View from Steamer Point*. London, Collins, 1964.

Kennedy, Scott. *Yemen — A Pictorial Tour*. London, Motivate Publishing Ltd, 1998.

King, Gillian. *Imperial Outpost—Aden*. New York, Oxford University Press, 1964.

Knox-Mawer, June. *The Sultans Came to Tea*. London, Murray, 1961.

Kostiner, Joseph. *Yemen: The Tortuous Quest for Unity 1990–94*. London, The Royal Institute of International Affairs, 1996.

Kour, Z. H. *The History of Aden, 1839–1972*. London, Frank Cass, 1980.

Lackner, Helen. *The People's Democratic Republic of Yemen: Outpost of Socialist Development in Arabia*. London, Ithaca Press, 1985.

Ledger, David. *Shifting Sands: the British in South Arabia*. London, Peninsula Publishing, 1983.

Leveau, R., Mermier, F., and Steinbach, U. (Eds). *Le Yémen contemporain*. Paris, Éditions Karthala, 1999.

Little, Tom. *South Arabia*. London, Pall Mall Press, 1968.

Macro, Eric. *Bibliography of the Yemen, with Notes on Mocha*. University of Miami Press, 1959.

Yemen and the Western World since 1571. London, C. Hurst, and New York, Praeger, 1968.

Mallakh, Ragaie el-. *The Economic Development of the Yemen Arab Republic*. London, Croom Helm, 1986.

Mercier, Eric. *Aden: un parcours interrompu*. Tours, Centre Français d'Etudes Yéménites-URBAMA, 1997.

Naval Intelligence Division. *Western Arabia and the Red Sea*. (Admiralty Handbook) 1946.

O'Ballance, Edgar. *The War in the Yemen*. London, Faber, 1971.

Page, Stephen. *The Soviet Union and the Yemens: Influence in Assymetrical Relationships*. New York, Praeger, 1985.

Paget, Julian. *Last Post: Aden 1964–67*. London, Faber and Faber, 1969.

Pawelke, Gunther. *Der Yemen: Das Verbotene Land*. Düsseldorf, Econ. Verlag, 1959.

Peterson, J. E. *Yemen, the Search for a Modern State*. London, Croom Helm, 1981.

Pieragostini, Karl. *Britain, Aden and South Arabia*. London, Macmillan, 1992.

Pridham, B. R. (Ed.) *Contemporary Yemen: Politics and Historical Background*. London, Croom Helm, 1984.

Economy and Society and Culture in Contemporary Yemen. London, Croom Helm, 1985.

Qat Commission of Inquiry. *Report*. Aden, 1958.

Rouaud, Alain. *Le Yémen*. Brussels, Editions Complexe, 1979.

Schmidt, Dana Adams. *Yemen, the Unknown War*. London, Bodley Head, 1968.

Scott, H. *In the High Yemen*. London, Murray, 1942.

Serjeant, R. B. *The Portuguese off the South Arabian Coast*. Oxford, Clarendon, 1963; reprinted Beirut, 1974.

Serjeant, R. B., and Lwecokc, Ronald. *San'a: an Arabian Islamic City*. London, 1983.

Smith, G. Rex. *The Yemens*. Oxford, World Bibliographical Series, Clio Press, 1984.

Stookey, Robert W. *Yemen: The Politics of the Yemen Arab Republic*. Westview Press, 1978.

Suwaidi, Jamal S. al-. (Ed.) *The Yemeni War of 1994: Causes and Consequences*. Saqi Books, 1995.

Trevaskis, Sir Kennedy. *Shades of Amber, A South Arabian Episode*. London, Hutchinson, 1967.

Van der Meulen, Daniel. *Hadhramaut: Some of Its Mysteries Unveiled*. Leiden, 1932, reprinted 1964.

Waterfield, Gordon. *Sultans of Aden*. London, Murray, 1968.

Wenner, Manfred W. *Yemen: a selected Bibliography of Literature since 1960*. Washington, DC, Library of Congress Legislative Reference Service, 1965.

Modern Yemen, 1918–1966. Baltimore, Johns Hopkins Press, 1967.

PART THREE
Regional Information

REGIONAL ORGANIZATIONS

THE UNITED NATIONS IN THE MIDDLE EAST AND NORTH AFRICA

Address: United Nations Plaza, New York, NY 10017, USA.

Telephone: (212) 963-1234; **fax:** (212) 963-4879; **internet:** www.un.org.

The United Nations (UN) was founded on 24 October 1945. The organization, which has 191 member states, aims to maintain international peace and security and to develop international co-operation in addressing economic, social, cultural and humanitarian problems. The principal organs of the UN are the General Assembly, the Security Council, the Economic and Social Council (ECOSOC), the International Court of Justice and the Secretariat. The General Assembly, which meets for three months each year, comprises representatives of all UN member states. The Security Council investigates disputes between member countries, and may recommend ways and means of peaceful settlement: it comprises five permanent members (the People's Republic of China, France, Russia, the United Kingdom and the USA) and 10 other members elected by the General Assembly for a two-year period. The Economic and Social Council comprises representatives of 54 member states, elected by the General Assembly for a three-year period: it promotes co-operation on economic, social, cultural and humanitarian matters, acting as a central policy-making body and co-ordinating the activities of the UN's specialized agencies. The International Court of Justice comprises 15 judges of different nationalities, elected for nine-year terms by the General Assembly and the Security Council: it adjudicates in legal disputes between UN member states.

Secretary-General of the United Nations: KOFI ANNAN (Ghana) (1997–2006)

MEMBER STATES IN THE MIDDLE EAST AND NORTH AFRICA

(with assessments for percentage contributions to UN budget for 2003, and year of admission)

Algeria	0.07000	1962
Bahrain	0.01800	1971
Cyprus	0.03800	1960
Egypt	0.08100	1945
Iran	0.27200	1945
Iraq	0.13600	1945
Israel	0.41500	1949
Jordan	0.00800	1955
Kuwait	0.14700	1963
Lebanon	0.01200	1945
Libya	0.06700	1955
Morocco	0.04400	1956
Oman	0.06100	1971
Qatar	0.03400	1971
Saudi Arabia	0.55400	1945
Syria	0.08000	1945
Tunisia	0.03000	1956
Turkey	0.44000	1945
United Arab Emirates	0.20200	1971
Yemen	0.00600	1947/67*

* The Yemen Arab Republic became a member of the UN in 1947, and the People's Democratic Republic of Yemen was admitted in 1967. The two countries formed the Republic of Yemen in 1990.

PERMANENT MISSIONS TO THE UNITED NATIONS

(with Permanent Representatives—September 2002)

Algeria: 326 East 48th St, New York, NY 10017; tel. (212) 750-1960; fax (212) 759-9538; e-mail algeria@un.int; internet www.algeria-un.org; ABDELLAH BAALI.

Bahrain: 866 Second Ave, 14th/15th Floors, tel. (212) 223-6200; fax (212) 319-0687; e-mail bahrain@un.int; JASIM MUHAMMAD BUALLAY.

Cyprus: 13 East 40th St, New York, NY 10016; tel. (212) 481-6023; fax (212) 685-7316; e-mail cyprus@un.int; internet www.un.int/cyprus; SOTIRIOS ZACKHEOS.

Egypt: 304 East 44th St, New York, NY 10017; tel. (212) 503-0300; fax (212) 949-5999; e-mail egypt@un.int; AHMED ABOUL GHEIT.

Iran: 622 Third Ave, 34th Floor, New York, NY 10017; tel. (212) 687-2020; fax (212) 867-7086; e-mail iran@un.int; JAVAD ZARIF.

Iraq: 14 East 79th St, New York, NY 10021; tel. (212) 737-4434; fax (212) 772-1794; e-mail iraq@un.int; internet www.iraqi-mission.org; MOHAMMED A. ALDOURI.

Israel: 800 Second Ave, New York, NY 10017; tel. (212) 499-5510; fax (212) 499-5515; e-mail israel.un@israelfm.org; internet www.israel-un.org; YEHUDA LANCRY.

Jordan: 866 United Nations Plaza, Suite 552, New York, NY 10017; tel. (212) 832-9553; fax (212) 832-5346; e-mail jordan@un.int; Prince ZEID RA'AD ZEID AL-HUSSEIN.

Kuwait: 321 East 44th St, New York, NY 10017; tel. (212) 973-4300; fax (212) 370-1733; e-mail kuwait@un.int; internet www.kuwaitmission.org; MOHAMMAD A. ABULHASAN.

Lebanon: 866 United Nations Plaza, Room 531–533, New York, NY 10017; tel. (212) 355-5460; fax (212) 838-2819; e-mail lebanon@un.int; Chargé d'affaires a.i. Dr HICHAM HAMDAN.

Libya: 309–315 East 48th St, New York, NY 10017; tel. (212) 752-5775; fax (212) 593-4787; e-mail info@libya-un.org; internet www.libya-un.org; ABUZED OMAR DORDA.

Morocco: 866 Second Ave, 6th/7th Floors, New York, NY 10017; tel. (212) 421-1580; fax (212) 980-1512; e-mail morocco@un.int; internet www.un.int/morocco; MOHAMED BENNOUNA.

Oman: 866 United Nations Plaza, Suite 540, New York, NY 10017; tel. (212) 355-3505; fax (212) 644-0070; e-mail oman@un.int; FAUD MUBARAK AL-HINAI.

Qatar: 809 United Nations Plaza, 4th Floor, New York, NY 10017; tel. (212) 486-9335; fax (212) 758-4952; e-mail qatar@un.int; JAMAL NASSIR SULTAN AL-BADER.

Saudi Arabia: 405 Lexington Ave, 56th Floor, New York, NY 10017; tel. (212) 697-4830; fax (212) 983-4895; e-mail saudiarabia@un.int; internet www.saudi-un-ny.org; FAWZI BIN ABDUL MAJEED SHOBOKSHI.

Syria: 820 Second Ave, 15th Floor, New York, NY 10017; tel. (212) 661-1313; fax (212) 983-4439; e-mail syria@un.int; Dr MIKHAIL WEHBE.

Tunisia: 31 Beekman Pl., New York, NY 10022; tel. (212) 751-7503; fax (212) 751-0569; e-mail tunisia@un.int; internet www.tunisiaonline.com/tunisia-un/index.html; NOUREDDINE MEJDOUB.

Turkey: 821 United Nations Plaza, 10th Floor, New York, NY 10017; tel. (212) 949-0150; fax (212) 949-0086; e-mail turkey@un.int; internet www.un.int/turkey; MEHMET UMIT PAMIR.

United Arab Emirates: 747 Third Ave, 36th Floor, New York, NY 10017; tel. (212) 371-0480; fax (212) 371-4923; e-mail uae@un.int; ABDULAZIZ NASSER R. AL-SHAMSI.

Yemen: 413 East 51st St, New York, NY 10022; tel. (212) 355-1730; fax (212) 750-9613; e-mail yemen@un.int; ABDULLAH M. AS-SAIDI.

Observers

African Union: 346 East 50th St, New York, NY 10022; tel. (212) 319-5490; fax (212) 319-7135; AMADOU KÉBÉ.

Asian-African Legal Consultative Organization: 404 East 66th St, Apt 12C, New York, NY 10021; tel. (212) 734-7608; e-mail aalco@un.int; K. BHAGWAT-SINGH.

International Committee of the Red Cross: 801 Second Ave, 18th Floor, New York, NY 10017; tel. (212) 599-6021; fax (212) 599-6009; e-mail redcrosscommittee@un.int; SYLVIE JUNOD.

League of Arab States: 747 Third Ave, 35th Floor, New York, NY 10017; tel. (212) 838-8700; fax (212) 355-3909; e-mail las@un.int; Dr HUSSEIN A. HASSOUNA.

Organization of the Islamic Conference: 130 East 40th St, 5th Floor, New York, NY 10016; tel. (212) 883-0140; fax (212) 883-0143; e-mail oic@un.int; internet www.un.int/oic; MOKHTAR LAMANI.

Palestine: 115 East 65th St, New York, NY 10021; tel. (212) 288-8500; fax (212) 517-2377; e-mail mission@palestine-un.org; internet www.palestine-un.org; Dr NASSER AL-KIDWA.

The Economic Co-operation Organization and the Organization of the Black Sea Economic Co-operation are among a number of intergovernmental organizations that have a standing invitation to participate as Observers, but do not maintain permanent offices at the United Nations.

GENERAL ASSEMBLY COMMITTEES CONCERNED WITH THE MIDDLE EAST

Committee on the Exercise of the Inalienable Rights of the Palestinian People: f. 1975; 25 members, elected by the General Assembly.

Special Committee on Peace-keeping Operations: f. 1965; 34 appointed members.

In April 1997 the General Assembly convened an emergency special session on 'illegal Israel actions' in Palestinian territory; the session continues to be convened intermittently.

United Nations Information Centres

Algeria: BP 823, 9A rue Emile Payen, Hydra, Algiers; tel. (2) 691212; fax (2) 692315; e-mail unic.dz@undp.org; internet www.unic.org.dz.

Bahrain: POB 26004, Bldg 69, Rd 1901, Manama 319; tel. (973) 311-676; fax (973) 311-692; e-mail unic@batelco.com.bh (also covers Qatar and the United Arab Emirates).

Egypt: POB 982, World Trade Centre, 1191 Corniche El Nil, Boulak, Cairo; tel. (2) 5315593; fax (2) 3553705; e-mail info@unic-eg.org; internet www.unic-eg.org (also covers Saudi Arabia).

Iran: POB 15875-4557, Ghaem Magham Farahani Ave 185, Tehran 15868; tel. (21) 873-1534; fax (21) 204-4523; e-mail unic@unic.un.or.ir.

Lebanon: POB 11-8575, Riad es-Solh Sq., Chouran, Beirut; tel. (1) 981301; fax (1) 981516; e-mail friji@escwa.org.lb (also covers Jordan, Kuwait and Syria).

Libya: POB 286, Muzzafar Al-Aftas St, Hay el-Andalous, Tripoli; tel. (21) 4777885; fax (21) 4777343; e-mail fo.lby@undp.org.

Morocco: BP 601, Angle Charia Ibnouzaid 6, Rabat; tel. (7) 7686-33; fax (7) 7683-77; e-mail cinu@fusion.net.ma; internet www.cinu.org.ma.

Tunisia: BP 863, 61 blvd Bab-Benat, 1035 Tunis; tel. 71560203; fax 71568811; e-mail uni.tunis@planet.tn; internet www.unic-tunis.intl.tn.

Turkey: PK 407, 197 Atatürk Bul., Ankara; tel. (312) 4268113; fax (312) 4689719; e-mail unic@un.org.tr; internet www.org.tr/unic.html.

Yemen: POB 237, Handhal St, 4, Al-Boniya Area, San'a; tel. (1) 274000; fax (1) 274043; e-mail unicyem@y.net.ye.

Economic Commission for Africa—ECA

Address: Africa Hall, POB 3001, Addis Ababa, Ethiopia.
Telephone: (1) 517200; **fax:** (1) 514416; **e-mail:** ecainfo@uneca.org; **internet:** www.uneca.org.

The UN Economic Commission for Africa was founded in 1958 by a resolution of the UN Economic and Social Council (ECOSOC) to initiate and take part in measures for facilitating Africa's economic development.

MEMBERS

Algeria	Eritrea	Niger
Angola	Ethiopia	Nigeria
Benin	Gabon	Rwanda
Botswana	The Gambia	São Tomé and
Burkina Faso	Ghana	Príncipe
Burundi	Guinea	Senegal
Cameroon	Guinea-Bissau	Seychelles
Cape Verde	Kenya	Sierra Leone
Central African	Lesotho	Somalia
Republic	Liberia	South Africa
Chad	Libya	Sudan
Comoros	Madagascar	Swaziland
Congo, Democratic	Malawi	Tanzania
Republic	Mali	Togo
Congo, Republic	Mauritania	Tunisia
Côte d'Ivoire	Mauritius	Uganda
Djibouti	Morocco	Zambia
Egypt	Mozambique	Zimbabwe
Equatorial Guinea	Namibia	

Organization

(September 2002)

COMMISSION

The Commission may only act with the agreement of the government of the country concerned. It is also empowered to make recommendations on any matter within its competence directly to the government of the member or associate member concerned, to governments admitted in a consultative capacity, and to the UN Specialized Agencies. The Commission is required to submit for prior consideration by ECOSOC any of its proposals for actions that would be likely to have important effects on the international economy.

CONFERENCE OF MINISTERS

The Conference, which meets every two years, is attended by ministers responsible for economic or financial affairs, planning and development of governments of member states, and is the main deliberative body of the Commission.

The Commission's responsibility to promote concerted action for the economic and social development of Africa is vested primarily in the Conference, which considers matters of general policy and the priorities to be assigned to the Commission's programmes, considers inter-African and international economic policy, and makes recommendations to member states in connection with such matters.

OTHER POLICY-MAKING BODIES

A Conference of Ministers of Finance and a Conference of Ministers responsible for economic and social development and planning meet in alternate years to formulate policy recommendations. Each is served by a committee of experts. Five intergovernmental committees of experts attached to the Sub-regional Development Centres (see below) meet annually and report to the Commission through a Technical Preparatory Committee of the Whole, which was established in 1979 to deal with matters submitted for the consideration of the Conference.

Seven other committees meet regularly to consider issues relating to the following policy areas: women and development; development information; sustainable development; human development and civil society; industry and private sector development; natural resources and science and technology; and regional co-operation and integration.

SECRETARIAT

The Secretariat provides the services necessary for the meeting of the Conference of Ministers and the meetings of the Commission's subsidiary bodies, carries out the resolutions and implements the programmes adopted there. It comprises an Office of the Executive

Secretary, the African Centre for Women and the following eight divisions: Food Security and Sustainable Development; Development Management; Development Information Services; Regional Co-operation and Integration; Programme Planning, Finance and Evaluation; Economic and Social Policy; Human Resources and System Management; Conference and General Services.

Executive Secretary: KINGSLEY Y. AMOAKO (Ghana).

SUB-REGIONAL DEVELOPMENT CENTRES

Multinational Programming and Operational Centres (MULPOCs) were established, in 1977, to implement regional development programmes. In May 1997 the Commission decided to transform the MULPOCs into Sub-regional Development Centres (SRDCs) in order to enable member states to play a more effective role in the process of African integration and to facilitate the integration efforts of the other UN agencies active in the sub-regions. In addition, the SRDCs were to act as the operational arms of ECA at national and sub-regional levels: to ensure harmony between the objectives of sub-regional and regional programmes and those defined by the Commission; to provide advisory services; to facilitate sub-regional economic co-operation, integration and development; to collect and disseminate information; to stimulate policy dialogue; and to promote gender issues.

Central Africa: POB 836, Yaoundé, Cameroon; tel. 23-14-61; fax 23-31-85; e-mail casrdrc@un.cm; Dir ADDO IRO.

Eastern Africa: POB 4654, Kigali, Rwanda; tel. 86549; fax 86546; e-mail easrdc@rwandatel1.rwanda1.com; Dir HALIGOU OUDRAOGO.

Northern Africa: POB 316, Tangier, Morocco; tel. (39) 322346; fax (39) 340357; e-mail srdc-na@uneca.org; Dir ABDELOUAHAB REZIG.

Southern Africa: POB 30647, Lusaka, Zambia; tel. (1) 228502; fax (1) 236949; e-mail srdcsa.uneca@un.zm; Dir Dr ROBERT M. OKELLO.

West Africa: POB 744, Niamey, Niger; tel. 72-29-61; fax 72-28-94; e-mail srdcwest@uneca.org; Dir JEGGAN C. SENGHOR.

Activities

The Commission's activities are designed to encourage sustainable socio-economic development in Africa and to increase economic co-operation among African countries and between Africa and other parts of the world. The Secretariat has been guided in its efforts by major regional strategies including the Abuja Treaty establishing the African Economic Community signed under the aegis of the Organization of African Unity (OAU, now African Union—AU) in 1991, the UN System-wide Special Initiative on Africa (launched in 1996, see below), and the UN New Agenda for the Development of Africa covering the period 1991–2000. ECA was designated as the main body responsible for identifying and preparing programmes on economic and corporate governance under the New Partnership for Africa's Development (NEPAD), launched in October 2001 (see p. 1292). ECA's main programme areas for the period 1996–2001 were based on an Agenda for Action, which was announced by the OAU Council of Ministers in March 1995 and adopted by African heads of state in June, with the stated aim of 'relaunching Africa's economic and social development'. The five overall objectives were to facilitate economic and social policy analysis and implementation; to ensure food security and sustainable development; to strengthen development management; to harness information for development; and to promote regional co-operation and integration. In all its activities ECA aimed to promote the themes of capacity-building and of fostering leadership and the empowerment of women in Africa. In May 1998 ECA's African Centre for Women inaugurated a new Fund for African Women's Development to support capacity-building activities.

DEVELOPMENT INFORMATION SERVICES

The Development Information Services Division (DISD), established in 1997, has responsibility for co-ordinating the implementation of the Harnessing Information Technology for Africa project (in the context of the UN System-wide Special Initiative on Africa) and for implementing the African Information Society Initiative (AISI), a framework for creating an information and communications infrastructure; for overseeing quality enhancement and dissemination of statistical databases; for improving access to information by means of enhanced library and documentation services and output; and for strengthening geo-information systems for sustainable development. In addition, ECA encourages member governments to liberalize the telecommunications sector and stimulate imports of computers in order to enable the expansion of information technology throughout Africa. ECA manages the Information Technology Centre for Africa, based in Addis Ababa.

Regional statistical development activities are managed through the Co-ordinating Committee on African Statistical Development (CASD, established in 1992). The CASD facilitates the harmonization of statistical systems and methodologies at regional and national level; establishes mechanisms for the continuous exchange of information between governments, national agencies and regional and sub-regional bodies, and all bilateral and multilateral agencies; identifies and proposes new lines of action; and informs the Conference of African Planners, Statisticians and Population and Information Specialists on the progress of the Addis Ababa Plan of Action for Statistical Development in the 1990s (adopted in 1992). In May 1997 five task forces were established to undertake the CASD's activities; these covered the following areas: improving e-mail connectivity; monitoring the implementation of the Addis Ababa Plan of Action; strengthening statistical training programme for Africa (STPA) centres; assisting with the formation of census and household survey data service centres in up to five pilot countries, and with the establishment of a similar regional ECA service centre; and establishing live databases, comprising core macro and sectoral statistical indicators, initially as a pilot project, with eventual links to a regional database facility.

ECA assists its member states in (i) population data collection and data processing; (ii) analysis of demographic data obtained from censuses or surveys; (iii) training demographers at the Regional Institute for Population Studies (RIPS) in Accra, Ghana, and at the Institut de formation et de recherche démographiques (IFORD) in Yaoundé, Cameroon; (iv) formulation of population policies and integrating population variables in development planning, through advisory missions and through the organization of national seminars on population and development; and (v) dissemination of demographic information. The strengthening of national population policies was an important element of ECA's objective of ensuring food security in African countries.

In August 2000 ECA launched the Africa Knowledge Networks Forum (AKNF). The Forum, to be convened on an annual basis under ECA auspices, was to facilitate co-operation in information-sharing and research between professional research and development networks, and also between these and policy-makers, educators, civil society organizations and the private sector. It was to provide technical support to the ADF process (see below).

DEVELOPMENT MANAGEMENT

ECA aims to assist governments, public corporations, universities and the private sector in improving their financial management; strengthening policy-making and analytical capacities; adopting measures to redress skill shortages; enhancing human resources development and utilization; and promoting social development through programmes focusing on youth, people with disabilities and the elderly. The Secretariat organizes training workshops, seminars and conferences at national, subregional and regional levels for ministers, public administrators and senior policy-makers, as well as for private and non-governmental organizations. ECA aims to increase the participation of women in economic development and incorporates this objective into its administrative activities and work programmes.

Following the failure to implement many of the proposals under the UN Industrial Development Decade for Africa (IDDA, 1980–90) and the UN Programme of Action for African Economic Recovery and Development (1986–90), a second IDDA was adopted by the Conference of African Ministers of Industry in July 1991. The main objectives of IDDA II (1993–2003) included the consolidation and rehabilitation of existing industries, the expansion of new investments, and the promotion of small-scale industries and technological capabilities. In June 1996 a conference, organized by ECA, was held in Accra, Ghana, with the aim of reviving private investment in Africa in order to stimulate the private sector and promote future economic development. In October 1999 the first African Development Forum (ADF) was held in Addis Ababa, Ethiopia. The ADF process was initiated by ECA to formulate an agenda for effective, sustainable development in African countries through dialogue and partnership between governments, academics, the private sector, donor agencies etc. It was intended that the process would focus towards an annual meeting concerned with a specific development issue. The first Forum was convened on the theme 'The Challenge to Africa of Globalization and the Information Age'. It reviewed the AISI (see above) and formulated country action plans and work programmes. The four issues addressed were: strengthening Africa's information infrastructure; Africa and the information economy; information and communication technologies for improved governance; and democratizing access to the information society. The second ADF, convened in October 2000, in Addis Ababa, on the theme 'AIDS: the Greatest Leadership Challenge', addressed the impact on Africa of the HIV/AIDS epidemic and issued a Consensus and Plan of Action. The third ADF, held in March 2002, addressed the theme 'Defining Priorities for Regional Integration'.

In 1997 ECA hosted the first of a series of meetings on good governance, in the context of the UN System-wide Special Initiative on Africa. The second African Governance Forum (AGF II) was held in Accra, Ghana, in June 1998. The Forum focused on accountability and transparency, which participants agreed were essential elements in promoting development in Africa and should involve commitment from both governments and civil organizations. AGF III was convened in June 1999 in Bamako, Mali, to consider issues relating to conflict prevention, management and governance. The fourth AGF, which took place in Kampala, Uganda, in September 2000, focused on parliamentary processes and their role in consolidating good governance on the continent. AGF V, addressing the role of local government in reducing poverty in Africa, was held in Maputo, Mozambique, in May 2002.

ECONOMIC AND SOCIAL POLICY

The Economic and Social Policy division concentrates on the following areas: economic policy analysis, trade and debt, social policy and poverty analysis, and the co-ordination and monitoring of special issues and programmes. Monitoring economic and social trends in the African region and studying the development problems concerning it are among the fundamental tasks of the Commission, while the special issues programme updates legislative bodies regarding the progress made in the implementation of initiatives affecting the continent. Every year the Commission publishes the *Survey of Economic and Social Conditions in Africa* and the *Economic Report on Africa*.

The Commission gives assistance to governments in general economic analysis, fiscal, financial and monetary management, trade liberalization, regional integration and planning. ECA's work on economic planning has been broadened in recent years, in order to give more emphasis to macro-economic management in a mixed economy approach: a project is being undertaken to develop short-term forecasting and policy models to support economic management. The Commission has also undertaken a major study of the informal sector in African countries. Special assistance is given to least-developed, land-locked and island countries which have a much lower income level than other countries and which are faced with heavier constraints. Studies are also undertaken to assist longer-term planning.

In May 1994 ECA ministers of economic and social development and of planning, meeting in Addis Ababa, adopted a *Framework Agenda for Building and Utilizing Critical Capacities in Africa*. The agenda aimed to identify new priority areas to stimulate development by, for example, strengthening management structures, a more efficient use of a country's physical infrastructure and by expanding processing or manufacturing facilities.

ECA aims to strengthen African participation in international negotiations. To this end, assistance has been provided to member states in the ongoing multilateral trade negotiations under the World Trade Organization; in the annual conferences of the IMF and the World Bank; in negotiations with the EU; and in meetings related to economic co-operation among developing countries. Studies have been prepared on problems and prospects likely to arise for the African region from the implementation of the Common Fund for Commodities and the Generalized System of Trade Preferences (both supervised by UNCTAD); the impacts of exchange-rate fluctuations on the economies of African countries; and on the long-term implications of different debt arrangements for African economies. ECA assists individual member states by undertaking studies on domestic trade, expansion of intra-African trade, transnational corporations, integration of women in trade and development, and strengthening the capacities of state-trading organizations. ECA encourages the diversification of production, the liberalization of cross-border trade and the expansion of domestic trade structures, within regional economic groupings, in order to promote intra-African trade. ECA also helps to organize regional and 'All-Africa' trade fairs.

In March/April 1997 the Conference of African Ministers of Finance, meeting in Addis Ababa, reviewed a new initiative of the World Bank and IMF to assist the world's most heavily indebted poor countries (numbering 42 at mid-2002, of which 33 were in sub-Saharan Africa). While the Conference recognized the importance of the involvement of multilateral institutions in assisting African economies to achieve a sustainable level of development, it criticized aspects of the structural adjustment programmes imposed by the institutions and advocated more flexible criteria to determine eligibility for the new scheme.

ECA aims to improve the socio-economic prospects of women through the promotion of equal access to resources and opportunities and equal participation in decision-making.

FOOD SECURITY AND SUSTAINABLE DEVELOPMENT

In the early 1990s reports were compiled on the development, implementation and sound management of environmental programmes at national, sub-regional and regional levels. ECA members adopted a common African position for the UN Conference on Environment and Development, held in June 1992. In 1995 ECA published its first comprehensive report and statistical survey of human development issues in African countries. The *Human Development in Africa Report*, which was to be published every two years,

aimed to demonstrate levels of development attained, particularly in the education and child health sectors, to identify areas of concern and to encourage further action by policy-makers and development experts. ECA is actively involved in the promotion of food security in African countries through raising awareness of the relationship between population, food security, the environment and sustainable development; encouraging the advancement of science and technology in member states; and providing policy analysis support and technical advisory services.

PROGRAMME PLANNING, FINANCE AND EVALUATION

ECA provides guidance in the formulation of policies towards the achievement of Africa's development objectives to the policy-making organs of the UN and the AU. It contributes to the work of the General Assembly and other specialized agencies by providing an African perspective in the preparation of development strategies. In March 1996 the UN announced its System-wide Special Initiative on Africa to mobilize resources and to implement a series of political and economic development objectives over a 10-year period. ECA's Executive Secretary is the Co-Chair, with the Administrator of the UNDP, of the Steering Committee for the Initiative.

REGIONAL CO-OPERATION AND INTEGRATION

The Regional Co-operation and Integration Division administers the transport and communications and mineral and energy sectors, in addition to its activities concerning the Sub-regional Development Centres (SRDCs—see above), the integrated development of transboundary water resources, and facilitating and enhancing the process of regional economic integration. In June 2002 ECA issued its first *Annual Report on Regional Integration*.

ECA was appointed lead agency for the second United Nations Transport and Communications Decade in Africa (UNTACDA II), covering the period 1991–2000. The principal aim of UNTACDA II was the establishment of an efficient, integrated transport and communications system in Africa. The specific objectives of the programme included: (i) the removal of physical and non-physical barriers to intra-African trade and travel, and improvement in the road transport sector; (ii) improvement in the efficiency and financial viability of railways; (iii) development of Africa's shipping capacity and improvement in the performance of Africa's ports; (iv) development of integrated transport systems for each lake and river basin; (v) improvement of integration of all modes of transport in order to carry cargo in one chain of transport smoothly; (vi) integration of African airlines, and restructuring of civil aviation and airport management authorities; (vii) improvement in the quality and availability of transport in urban areas; (viii) development of integrated regional telecommunications networks; (ix) development of broadcasting services, with the aim of supporting socio-economic development; and (x) expansion of Africa's postal network. In April 2002 African ministers of transport and communications met to assess the outcome of UNCTADA II. ECA is the co-ordinator, with the World Bank, of a regional Road Management Initiative, which was launched in 1988. By early 1996 13 African countries were receiving assistance under the initiative, which sought to encourage a partnership between the public and private sectors to manage and maintain road infrastructure more efficiently and thus to improve country-wide communications and transportation activities. The third African road safety congress was held in April 1997, in Pretoria, South Africa. The congress, which was jointly organized by ECA and the OECD, aimed to increase awareness of the need to adopt an integrated approach to road safety problems. During 1998/99 transport activities included consideration of a new African air transport policy, workshops on port restructuring, and regional and country analyses of transport trends and reforms.

The Fourth Regional Conference on the Development and Utilization of Mineral Resources in Africa, held in March 1991, adopted an action plan that included the formulation of national mineral exploitation policies; and the promotion of the gemstone industry, small-scale mining and the iron and steel industry. ECA supports the Southern African Mineral Resources Development Centre in Dar-es-Salaam, Tanzania, and the Central African Mineral Development Centre in Brazzaville, Republic of the Congo, which provide advisory and laboratory services to their respective member states.

ECA's Energy Programme provides assistance to member states in the development of indigenous energy resources and the formulation of energy policies to extricate member states from continued energy crises. In 1997 ECA strengthened co-operation with the World Energy Council and agreed to help implement the Council's African Energy Programme.

ECA assists member states in the assessment and use of water resources and the development of river and lake basins common to more than one country. ECA encourages co-operation between countries with regard to water issues and collaborates with other UN agencies and regional organizations to promote technical and economic co-operation in this area. ECA has been particularly active in efforts to promote the integrated development of the water resources of the Zambezi river basin and of Lake Victoria.

In all of its activities ECA aims to strengthen institutional capacities in order to support the process of regional integration, and aims to assist countries to implement existing co-operative agreements, for example by promoting the harmonization of macroeconomic and taxation policies and the removal of non-tariff barriers to trade.

ASSOCIATED BODY

Information Technology Centre for Africa—ITCA: POB 3001, Addis Ababa, Ethiopia; tel. (1) 314520; fax (1) 515829; e-mail mfaye@uneca.org; internet www.uneca.org/itca; aims to strengthen the continent's communications infrastructure and promote the use of information and communications technologies in planning and policy-making; stages exhibitions and provides training facilities.

Finance

For the two-year period 2000–01 ECA's regular budget, an appropriation from the UN budget, was an estimated US $78.5m.

Publications

Africa in Figures.
African Statistical Yearbook.
African Trade Bulletin (2 a year).
African Women's Report (annually).
Africa's Population and Development Bulletin.
Annual Report on Regional Integration.
Compendium of Intra-African and Related Foreign Trade Statistics.
Directory of African Statisticians (every 2 years).
ECA Development Policy Review.
ECA Environment Newsletter (3 a year).
ECANews (monthly).
Economic Report on Africa (annually).
Focus on African Industry (2 a year).
GenderNet (annually).
Human Development in Africa Report (every 2 years).
Human Rights Education.
Report of the Executive Secretary (every 2 years).
Survey of Economic and Social Conditions in Africa (annually).
Country reports, policy and discussion papers, reports of conferences and meetings, training series, working paper series.

Economic and Social Commission for Western Asia—ESCWA

Address: Riad es-Solh Sq., POB 11-8575, Beirut, Lebanon.
Telephone: (1) 981301; **fax:** (1) 981510; **e-mail:** unescwa@escwa.org.lb; **internet:** www.escwa.org.lb.

The UN Economic Commission for Western Asia was established in 1974 by a resolution of the UN Economic and Social Council (ECOSOC), to provide facilities of a wider scope for those countries previously served by the UN Economic and Social Office in Beirut (UNESOB). The name 'Economic and Social Commission for Western Asia' (ESCWA) was adopted in 1985.

MEMBERS

Bahrain	Palestine
Egypt	Qatar
Iraq	Saudi Arabia
Jordan	Syria
Kuwait	United Arab Emirates
Lebanon	Yemen
Oman	

Organization

(September 2002)

COMMISSION

The sessions of the Commission (held every two years) are attended by delegates from member states. Representatives of UN bodies and specialized agencies, regional organizations, other UN member states, and non-governmental organizations having consultative status with ECOSOC may attend as observers.

PREPARATORY COMMITTEE

The Committee, formerly the Technical Committee, has the task of reviewing programming issues and presenting recommendations in that regard to the sessions of the Commission. It is the principal subsidiary body of the Commission and functions as its policy-making structure. Six specialized inter-governmental committees have been established to consider specific areas of activity, to report on these to the Preparatory Committee and to assist the Committee in formulating ESCWA's medium-term work programmes.

Statistics Committee: established in 1992; meets every two years.

Committee on Social Development: established in 1994; meets every two years.

Committee on Energy: established in 1995; meets every two years.

Committee on Water Resources: established in 1995; meets every two years.

Committee on Transport: established in 1997; meets annually.

Committee on Liberalization of Foreign Trade and Economic Globalization: established in 1997; meets every two years.

In addition, a Consultative Committee on Scientific Technological Development and Technological Innovation was established in 2001, and was to meet every two years, comprising experts from public institutions, the private sector, civil society and research centres.

SECRETARIAT

The Secretariat comprises an Executive Secretary, a Deputy Executive Secretary, a Senior Adviser and Secretary of the Commission, an Information Services Unit and divisions for administrative services and programme planning and technical co-operation. ESCWA's technical and substantive activities are undertaken by the following divisions: energy, natural resources and environment; social development issues and policies; economic development issues and policies; sectoral issues and policies; and statistics. The Secretariat administers the UN Regional Co-ordination Group for the ESCWA region, which was established in March 1999.

Executive Secretary: MERVAT M. TALLAWY (Egypt).

Activities

ESCWA is responsible for proposing policies and actions to support development and to further economic co-operation and integration in western Asia. ESCWA undertakes or sponsors studies of economic social and development issues of the region, collects and disseminates information, and provides advisory services to member states in various fields of economic and social development. It also organizes conferences and intergovernmental and export group meetings and sponsors training workshops and seminars.

Much of ESCWA's work is carried out in co-operation with other UN bodies, as well as with other international and regional organizations, for example the League of Arab States (q.v.) the Co-operation Council for the Arab States of the Gulf (q.v.) and the Organization of the Islamic Conference (OIC, q.v.). In April 2001 ESCWA convened an inaugural consultative meeting with representatives of more than 100 non-governmental organizations, in order to strengthen co-operation with civil society.

ESCWA works within the framework of medium-term plans, which are divided into two-year programmes of action and priorities. The Commission restructured its work programme in the mid-1990s, which focused ESCWA activities from 15 to five sub-programmes. A further reorganization of the sub-programmes was implemented in 1997 to provide the framework for activities in the medium-term period 1998–2001. In May 2001 the Commission approved a work programme for 2002–03 on the basis of the existing sub-programme structure.

MANAGEMENT OF NATURAL RESOURCES AND ENVIRONMENT

The main objective of the sub-programme is to promote regional co-ordination and co-operation in the management of natural resources, in particular water resources and energy, and the protection of the environment. Work in this area aims to counter the problem of an increasing shortage of freshwater resources and deterioration in water quality resulting from population growth, agricultural land-use and socio-economic development, by supporting measures for more rational use and conservation of water resources, and by promoting public awareness and community participation in water and environmental protection projects. In addition, ESCWA assists governments in the formulation and implementation of capacity-building programmes and the development of surface and ground-water resources. In 2002–03 ESCWA aimed to promote greater co-operation among member and non-member countries in the management and use of shared water resources.

ESCWA supports co-operation in the establishment of electricity distribution and supply networks throughout the region and promotes the use of alternative sources of energy and the development of new and renewable energy technologies. Similarly, ESCWA promotes the application of environmentally sound technologies in order to achieve sustainable development, as well as measures to recycle resources, minimize waste and reduce the environmental impact of transport operations and energy use. Under the sub-programme ESCWA collaborates with national, regional and international organizations in monitoring and reporting on emerging environmental issues and to pursue implementation of Agenda 21, which was adopted at the June 1992 UN Conference on Environment and Development, with particular regard to land and water resource management and conservation.

IMPROVEMENT OF THE QUALITY OF LIFE

ESCWA's key areas of activity in this sub-programme are population, sustainable human development, the advancement of women and gender equality, and human settlements. The sub-programme was designed to pursue the implementation of recommendations relevant to the region of the four UN world conferences held on these themes during the mid-1990s.

ESCWA's objectives with regard to population are to increase awareness and understanding of links between population factors and poverty, human rights and the environment, and to strengthen the capacities of member states to analyse and assess demographic trends and migration. In the area of human development ESCWA aims to further the alleviation of poverty and to generate a sustainable approach to development through, for example, greater involvement of community groups in decision-making and projects to strengthen production and income-generating capabilities. The sub-programme incorporates activities to ensure all gender-related recommendations of the four world conferences could be pursued in the region, including support for the role of the family and assistance to organizations for monitoring and promoting the advancement of women. With regard to human settlements, the objectives of the sub-programme are to monitor and identify problems resulting from rapid urbanization and social change, to promote understanding and awareness of the problems and needs of human settlements, and to strengthen the capacity of governments in the region in formulating appropriate policies and strategies for sustainable human settlement development. In 2002–03 ESCWA's priorities were to develop and promote social policies and strategies with the emphasis on family cohesion, the advancement of women, poverty reduction, disabled and ageing populations, population dynamics, and the security of tenure. It also aimed to promote transparent and accountable governance, based on greater participation of civil society. In February 2002 ESCWA organized a ministerial preparatory meeting for the World Assembly on Ageing, which was convened, in Madrid, Spain, in April. The meeting adopted an Arab Plan on the Elderly up to the Year 2012.

ECONOMIC DEVELOPMENT AND GLOBAL CHANGES

During the period 2002–03 ESCWA aimed to assist member states to achieve sustainable economic development in the region and to integrate more fully into the world economy. Under the sub-programme ESCWA aimed to assist member countries to identify the challenges and opportunities created by the World Trade Organ-

ization (WTO) and other regional groupings, in particular with regard to free trade areas, the liberalization and management of financial markets, and the promotion of foreign direct investment. It also intended to improve the analysis of economic developments and the formulation of economic management policies, as well as to provide guidance on alternative development strategies to reduce the dominance of the petroleum sector. In June 2002 ESCWA organized a workshop for the business community and an expert group meeting to discuss the outcome of the WTO ministerial conference, which was held in Doha, Qatar, in November 2001, and future trade negotiations under the agreed Development Agenda.

CO-ORDINATION OF POLICIES AND HARMONIZATION OF NORMS AND REGULATIONS FOR SECTORAL DEVELOPMENT

This sub-programme is concerned with the harmonization of standards throughout the region in the areas of transport, industry, agriculture and technology. ESCWA aims to promote co-operation among member states in transport and infrastructure policies and greater uniformity of safety and legal standards, the latter with a view to facilitating border crossings between countries in the region. ESCWA, similarly, aims to assist local industries to meet regional and international standards and regulations, as well as to improve the competitiveness of industries through the development of skills and policies and greater co-operation with other national and regional support institutions. In May 2001 ESCWA member states adopted an Agreement on International Transport System in the Arab Mashreq, which had been formulated by the Secretariat with the aim of establishing a unified transportation network linking all countries in the region. In 2002–03 ESCWA envisaged pursuing activities to promote the harmonization of norms and standards for sustainable development within the region. ESCWA also aimed to provide support for the co-ordination of sectoral policies, in particular with regard to poverty-related issues, and to develop and disseminate related statistics, information and electronic data.

CO-ORDINATION AND HARMONIZATION OF STATISTICS AND INFORMATION DEVELOPMENT

In the medium-term ESCWA intended to develop the statistical systems of member states in order to improve the relevance and accuracy of economic and social data, and to implement measures to make the information more accessible to planners and researchers. Priorities for the biennium 2002–03 included activities to improve human and institutional capacities, in particular in the use of statistical tools for data analysis, to expand the adoption and implementation of international statistical methods, and to promote co-operation to further the regional harmonization of statistics.

Finance

ESCWA's share of the UN budget for the two years 2000–01 was US $50.3m., compared with $49.5m. for the previous biennium.

Publications

All publications are annual, unless otherwise indicated.
Agriculture and Development in Western Asia.
ESCWA Update (monthly).
External Trade Bulletin of the ESCWA Region.
National Accounts Studies of the ESCWA Region.
Population Bulletin of the ESCWA Region.
Prices and Financial Statistics in the ESCWA Region.
Socio-economic Data Sheet (every 2 years).
Statistical Abstract of the ESCWA Region.
Survey of Economic and Social Developments in the ESCWA Region.
Transport Bulletin.
Weekly News.

United Nations Development Programme—UNDP

Address: One United Nations Plaza, New York, NY 10017, USA.
Telephone: (212) 906-5295; **fax:** (212) 906-5364; **e-mail:** hq@undp.org; **internet:** www.undp.org.

The Programme was established in 1965 by the UN General Assembly. Its central mission is to help countries eradicate poverty and achieve a sustainable level of human development, an approach to economic growth that encompasses individual well-being and choice, equitable distribution of the benefits of development, and conservation of the environment. UNDP advocates for a more inclusive global economy.

Organization

(September 2002)

UNDP is responsible to the UN General Assembly, to which it reports through the UN Economic and Social Council.

EXECUTIVE BOARD

The 36-member Executive Board is responsible for providing intergovernmental support to and supervision of the activities of UNDP and the UN Population Fund (UNFPA, of which UNDP is the governing body).

SECRETARIAT

In recent years UNDP has implemented a process aimed at restructuring and improving the efficiency of its administration. Offices and divisions at the Secretariat include: an Operations Support Group; Offices of the United Nations Development Group, the Human Development Report, Audit and Performance Review, and Communications; and Bureaux for Crisis Prevention and Recovery, Resources and Strategic Partnerships, Development Policy, and Management. Five regional bureaux, all headed by an assistant administrator, cover: Africa; Asia and the Pacific; the Arab states; Latin America and the Caribbean; and Europe and the Commonwealth of Independent States. There is also a Division for Global and Interregional Programmes.

Administrator: MARK MALLOCH BROWN (United Kingdom).

Assistant Administrator and Director of the Regional Bureau for Arab States: Dr RIMA KHALAF HUNAIDI.

COUNTRY OFFICES

In almost every country receiving UNDP assistance there is an office, headed by the UNDP Resident Representative, who usually also serves as the UN Resident Co-ordinator, responsible for the co-ordination of all UN technical assistance and operational development activities, advising the government on formulating the country programme, ensuring that field activities are carried out, and acting as the leader of the UN team of experts working in the country. The offices function as the primary presence of the UN in most developing countries.

OFFICES OF UNDP REPRESENTATIVES IN THE MIDDLE EAST AND NORTH AFRICA

Algeria: 9A rue Emile Payen Hydra, BP 823, Algiers 16000; tel. (2) 21-69-12-12; fax (2) 21-69-23-55; c mail registry.dz@undp.org; internet www.dz.undp.org.

Bahrain: 69 UN House, Rd 1901, Hoora 319, POB 26814, Manama; tel. 311600; fax 311500; e-mail registry@undp.org; internet www.undp.org.bh.

Egypt: World Trade Centre Bldg, 4th Floor, 1191 Corniche en-Nil St, Boulak, POB 982, Cairo; tel. (2) 5784840; fax (2) 5784847; e-mail fo.egy@undp.org; internet www.undp.org.eg.

Iran: United Nations Bldg, 185 Ghaem Magham Farahani Ave, POB 15875-4557, Tehran 15868; tel. (21) 8732812; fax (21) 8738864.

Iraq: Bldg No. 153, 102 Abi Nawas St, POB 2048 (Alwiyah), Baghdad; tel. (1) 907-6358; fax (1) 886-2523; e-mail regirq@un.org; internet www.iq.undp.org.

Jordan: Hirbawi Bldg, 'Obadah Ibn Al-Samet St, POB 941631, Amman; tel. (6) 566-8177; fax (6) 567-6582; e-mail registry.jo@undp.org; internet www.undp-jordan.org.

Kuwait: St No. 7, Block No. 12, Villa No. 8, Jabriya, POB 2993 Safat; tel. 5329870; fax 5325879; e-mail registry.kw@undp.org; internet www.undp-kuwait.org.

Lebanon: UN House, 7th Floor, Riad El-Solh Sq., POB 11–3216, Beirut; tel. (1) 981301; fax (1) 981521; e-mail registry@undp.org; internet www.undp.org.lb.

Libya: 67–71 Turkiya St, POB 358, Tripoli; tel. (21) 333-6297; fax (21) 333-0856.

Morocco: Immeuble de l'ONU, Angle ave Moulay Hassan et rue Assafi, Rabat; tel. (7) 37703555; fax (7) 37701566; e-mail registry.ma@undp.org; internet www.pnud.org.ma.

Qatar: Fariq Bin Omran (near English Speaking School and Doha Players' Theatre), Box 3233, Doha; tel. 863260; fax 861552.

Saudi Arabia: POB 558, King Faysal St, Riyadh 11421; tel. (1) 465-3157; fax (1) 465-2087; e-mail fo.san@undp.org.

Syria: Abou Roumaneh 28, al-Jala'a St, POB 2317, Damascus; tel. (11) 3332440; fax (11) 3327764.

Tunisia: 61 blvd Bab Bénat, BP 863, Tunis 1035; tel. (1) 564-011; fax (1) 560-094; e-mail registry.tn@undp.org; internet www.tn.undp.org.

Turkey: 197 Atatürk Bul., 06680 Kavaklıdere, PK 407, Ankara; tel. (312) 4268113; fax (312) 4261372; e-mail fo.tur@undp.org.

United Arab Emirates: Sheikh Khalifa bin Shakhbout St, West 17/1 Villa no. 41, POB 3490, Abu Dhabi; tel. (2) 655600; fax (2) 650818; e-mail undp@emirates.net.ae.

Yemen: Al-Khorashi Bldg, opposite Awqaf Housing Complex, Shar'a Siteen, POB 551, San'a; tel. (1) 415505; fax (1) 4125411; e-mail fo.yem@undp.org.

There is also a UNDP office in the 'Occupied Palestinian Territories' (POB 51359, 4A Ya'kubi St, Jerusalem 91513; tel. 2-6277337; fax 2-6280089).

Activities

As the world's largest source of grant-funded technical assistance for developing countries, UNDP provides advisory and support services to governments and UN teams. Assistance is mostly non-monetary, comprising the provision of experts' services, consultancies, equipment and training for local workers, including fellowships for advanced study abroad. UNDP supports programme countries in attracting aid and utilizing it efficiently. The Programme is committed to allocating some 88% of its regular resources to low-income developing countries. Developing countries themselves contribute significantly to the total project costs in terms of personnel, facilities, equipment and supplies.

Since the mid-1990s UNDP has strengthened its focus on results, streamlining its management practices and promoting clearly defined objectives for the advancement of sustainable human development. Under 'UNDP 2001', an extensive internal process of reform initiated during the late 1990s, UNDP placed increased emphasis on its activities in the field and on performance and accountability, focusing on the following priority areas: democratic governance; poverty reduction; crisis prevention and recovery; energy and environment; promotion of information and communications technology; and combating HIV/AIDS. In 2001 UNDP established six Thematic Trust Funds, covering each of these areas, to enable increased support of its programme activities. Gender equality and the provision of country-level aid co-ordination services are also important focus areas. In accordance with the more results-oriented approach developed under the 'UNDP 2001' process the Programme has introduced a new Multi-Year Funding Framework (MYFF), the first phase of which covers the period 2000–03. The MYFF outlines the country-driven goals around which funding is to be mobilized, integrating programme objectives, resources, budget and outcomes. It provides the basis for the Administrator's Business Plans for the same duration and enables policy coherence in the implementation of programmes at country, regional and global levels. A Results-Oriented Annual Report (ROAR) was produced for the first time in 2000 from data compiled by country offices and regional programmes. It was hoped that UNDP's greater focus on performance would generate increased voluntary contributions from donors, thereby strengthening the Programme's core resource base. In September the first ever Ministerial Meeting of ministers of development co-operation and foreign affairs and other senior officials from donor and programme countries, convened in New York, USA, endorsed UNDP's new orientation.

From the mid-1990s UNDP also determined to assume a more active and integrative role within the UN system-wide development framework. UNDP Resident Representatives—usually also serving as UN Resident Co-ordinators, with responsibility for managing inter-agency co-operation on sustainable human development initatives at country level—were to play a focal role in implementing this approach. In order to promote its co-ordinating function UNDP allocated increased resources to training and skill-sharing programmes. In late 1997 the UNDP Administrator was appointed to chair the UN Development Group (UNDG), which was established as part of a series of structural reform measures initiated by the UN Secretary-General, with the aim of strengthening collaboration between all UN funds, programmes and bodies concerned with development. The UNDG promotes coherent policy at country level through the system of UN Resident Co-ordinators (see above), the Common Country Assessment mechanism (CCA, a country-based process for evaluating national development situations), and the UN Development Assistance Framework (UNDAF, the foundation for planning and co-ordinating development operations at country level, based on the CCA). Within the framework of the Administrator's Business Plans for 2000–03 a new Bureau for Resources and Strategic Partnerships was established to build and strengthen working partnerships with other UN bodies, donor and programme countries, international financial institutions and development banks, civil society organizations and the private sector. The Bureau was also to serve UNDP's regional bureaux and country offices through the exchange of information and promotion of partnership strategies.

UNDP has a catalyst and co-ordinating function as the focus of UN system-wide efforts to achieve the so-called Millennium Goals, pledged by governments attending a summit meeting of the UN General Assembly in September 2000. The objectives included a reduction by 50% in the number of people with income of less than US $1 a day and those suffering from hunger and lack of safe drinking water by 2015. Other commitments made concerned equal access to education for girls and boys, the provision of universal primary education, the reduction of maternal mortality by 75%, and the reversal of the spread of HIV/AIDS and other diseases.

UNDP aims to help governments to reassess their development priorities and to design initiatives for sustainable human development. UNDP country offices support the formulation of national human development reports (NHDRs), which aim to facilitate activities such as policy-making, the allocation of resources and monitoring progress towards poverty eradiction and sustainable development. The first Arab Human Development Report was issued in July 2002. In addition, the preparation of Advisory Notes and Country Co-operation Frameworks by UNDP officials helps to highlight country-specific aspects of poverty eradiction and national strategic priorities. In January 1998 the Executive Board adopted eight guiding principles relating to sustainable human development that were to be implemented by all country offices, in order to ensure a focus to UNDP activities. A network of Sub-regional Resource Facilities (SURFs) has been established to strengthen and co-ordinate UNDP's technical assistance services. Since 1990 UNDP has published an annual global *Human Development Report*, incorporating a Human Development Index, which ranks countries in terms of human development, using three key indicators: life expectancy, adult literacy and basic income required for a decent standard of living. In 1997 a Human Poverty Index and a Gender-related Development Index, which assesses gender equality on the basis of life expectancy, education and income, were introduced into the Report for the first time.

UNDP's activities to facilitate poverty eradiction include support for capacity-building programmes and initiatives to generate sustainable livelihoods, for example by improving access to credit, land and technologies, and the promotion of strategies to improve education and health provision for the poorest elements of populations (with a focus on women and girls). In 1996 UNDP launched the Poverty Strategies Initiative (PSI) to strengthen national capacities to assess and monitor the extent of poverty and to combat the problem. All PSI projects were to involve representatives of governments, the private sector, social organizations and research institutions in policy debate and formulation. With the World Bank, UNDP helps governments of developing countries applying for international debt relief to draft Poverty Reduction Stategy Papers. In 1997 a UNDP scheme to support private-sector and community-based initiatives to generate employment opportunities, MicroStart, became operational.

Approximately one-quarter of all UNDP programme resources support national efforts to ensure efficient and accountable governance and to build effective relations between the state, the private sector and civil society, which are essential to achieving sustainable development. UNDP undertakes assessment missions to help ensure free and fair elections and works to promote human rights, a transparent and competent public sector, a competent judicial system and decentralized government and decision-making. In May/June 1999 a World Conference on Governance was held in Manila, the Philippines, attended by some 1,000 government officials and representatives of the private sector and non-governmental organizations. UNDP sponsored a series of meetings held on the subject of Building Capacities for Governance. In April UNDP and the Office of the High Commissioner for Human Rights launched a joint programme to strengthen capacity-building in order to promote the integration of human rights issues into activities concerned with sustainable human development. UNDP supports the Africa Governance Forum which convenes regularly to consider aspects of governance and development.

UNDP plays a role in developing the agenda for international co-operation on environmental and energy issues, focusing on the relationship between energy policies, environmental protection, poverty and development. UNDP supports the development of national programmes that emphasize the sustainable management of natural resources, for example through its Sustainable Energy Initiative, which promotes more efficient use of energy resources and the introduction of renewable alternatives to conventional fuels. UNDP is also concerned with forest management, the aquatic environment and sustainable agriculture and food security. Within UNDP's framework of urban development activities, the Local Initiative Facility for Urban Environment (LIFE) undertakes small-scale environmental projects in low-income communities, in collaboration with local authorities and community-based groups. Other initiatives include the Urban Management Programme and the Public-Private Partnerships Programme for the Urban Environment, which aim to generate funds, promote research and support new technologies to enhance sustainable environments in urban areas. Activities undertaken under the Urban Management Programme have included pollution and traffic control in the historic centre of Damascus, Syria. In 1996 UNDP initiated a process of collaboration between city authorities world-wide to promote implementations of the commitments made at the 1995 Copenhagen summit for social development (see below) and to help to combat aspects of poverty and other urban problems, such as poor housing, transport, the management of waste disposal, water supply and sanitation. The first Forum of the so-called World Alliance of Cities Against Poverty was convened in October 1998, in Lyon, France. The second Forum took place in April 2000 in Geneva, Switzerland, and the third Forum was held in April 2002 in Huy, Belgium.

UNDP is a co-sponsor, jointly with WHO, the World Bank, UNDCP, UNICEF, UNESCO, ILO and UNFPA, of the Joint UN Programme on HIV/AIDS, which became operational on 1 January 1996. UNDP also has responsibility for co-ordinating activities following global UN conferences. In March 1995 government representatives attending the World Summit for Social Development, which was held in Copenhagen, Denmark, approved initiatives to promote the eradication of poverty, to increase and reallocate official development assistance to basic social programmes and to promote equal access to education. The Programme of Action adopted at the meeting advocated that UNDP support the implementation of social development programmes, co-ordinate these efforts through its field offices and organize efforts on the part of the UN system to stimulate capacity-building at local, national and regional levels. By 1998 the multi-donor PSI (see above), introduced following the Summit, was being implemented in more than 80 countries. Other activities were directed towards strengthening the private sectors in developing countries, in particular through the provision of financing for micro-enterprises, and creating the capacity for sound economic management and good governance. A special session of the UN General Assembly to review implementation of the Summit's objectives was convened in June 2000. Following the UN Fourth World Conference on Women, held in Beijing, People's Republic of China, in September 1995, UNDP led inter-agency efforts to ensure the full participation of women in all economic, political and professional activities and assisted with further situation analysis and training activities. UNDP also created a Gender in Development Office to ensure that women participate more fully in UNDP-sponsored activities. In June 2000 a special session of the UN General Assembly was convened to review the conference, entitled Women 2000: Gender Equality, Development and Peace for the 21st Century (Beijing + 5). UNDP played an important role, at both national and international levels, in preparing for the second World Conference on Human Settlements (Habitat II), which was held in İstanbul, Turkey, in June 1996. At the conference UNDP announced the establishment of a new facility, which was designed to promote private-sector investment in urban infrastructure. A special session of the UN General Assembly, entitled Istanbul + 5, was held in June 2001 to report on the implementation of the recommendations of the Habitat II conference.

UNDP collaborates with other UN agencies in countries in crisis and with special circumstances to promote relief and development efforts, in order to secure the foundations for sustainable human development, and thereby increase national capabilities to prevent or pre-empt future crises. In particular, UNDP is concerned to achieve reconciliation, reintegration and reconstruction in affected countries, as well as to support emergency interventions and manage the delivery of programme aid. Special development initiatives undertaken include socio-economic rehabilitation in Lebanon and environmental improvements in areas of resettlement in Gaza and the West Bank UNDP has extended its Disaster Management Training Programme, in order, partly, to help countries meet the objectives of the International Decade for Natural Disaster Reduction (announced in 1990). UNDP is co-ordinating an Electricity Network Rehabilitation Programme in northern Iraq, funded under the ongoing oil-for-food programme. UNDP has established a mine action unit within its Bureau for Crisis Prevention and Recovery (formerly the Emergency Response Division), in order to strengthen national de-mining capabilities. UNDP is the focal point within the UN system for strengthening national capacities for natural disaster reduction (prevention, preparedness and mitigation relating to natural, environmental and technological hazards).

UNDP aims to ensure that, rather than creating an ever-widening 'digital divide', ongoing rapid advancements in information technology are harnessed by poorer countries to accelerate progress in achieving sustainable human development. UNDP advises governments on technology policy, promotes digital entrepreneurship in programme countries and works with private-sector partners to provide reliable and affordable communications networks. UNDP and the World Bank host the secretariat of the Digital Opportunity Task Force, a partnership between industrialized nations, developing countries, business and non-governmental organizations that was established in 2000. The Bureau for Development Policy operates the Information Technology for Development Programme, which aims to promote sustainable human development through increased utilization of information and communications technologies globally. The Programme aims to establish technology access centres in developing countries. A Sustainable Development Networking Programme focuses on expanding internet connectivity in poorer countries through building national capacities and supporting local internet sites. UNDP has used mobile internet units to train people in isolated rural areas.

In 1999 UNDP, in collaboration with an international communications company, Cisco Systems, and other partners, launched NetAid, an internet-based forum (accessible at www.netaid.org) for mobilizing and co-ordinating fundraising and other activities aimed at alleviating poverty and promoting sustainable development. With Cisco Systems and other partners, UNDP has worked to establish academies of information technology to support training and capacity-building in developing countries. By February 2002 70 academies had been established in 34 countries.

In 1996 UNDP implemented its first corporate communications and advocacy strategy, which aimed to generate public awareness of the activities of the UN system, to promote debate on development issues and to mobilize resources by increasing public and donor appreciation of UNDP. UNDP sponsors the International Day for the Eradication of Poverty, held annually on 17 October.

Finance

UNDP and its various funds and programmes are financed by the voluntary contributions of members of the United Nations and the Programme's participating agencies, as well as through cost-sharing by recipient governments and third-party donors. In 2000 total voluntary contributions amounted to US $2,400m., of which $634m. was for regular (core) resources (compared with $681m. in 1999). Donor co-finance, including trust funds and cost-sharing by third parties, amounted to $571m. in 2000, while cost-sharing by programme country governments amounted to more than $900m. It was hoped that the introduction of a new Multi-Year Funding Framework for the four-year period 2000–03 and of Results-Oriented Annual Reports from 2000 (see above) would increase UNDP's resource base by stimulating an increase in voluntary contributions. In 2000 field programme expenditure under UNDP's regular programme totalled $1,458m.

Publications

Annual Report of the Administrator.

Choices (quarterly).

Co-operation South (quarterly).

Global Public Goods: International Co-operation in the 21st Century.

Human Development Report (annually).

Poverty Report (annually).

Result-Oriented Annual Report.

Associated Funds and Programmes

UNDP is the central funding, planning and co-ordinating body for technical co-operation within the UN. Associated funds and programmes, financed separately by means of voluntary contributions, provide specific services through the UNDP network

CAPACITY 21

UNDP initiated Capacity 21 at the UN Conference on Environment and Development, which was held in June 1992, to support developing countries in preparing and implementing policies for sustainable development. Capacity 21 promotes new approaches to development, through national development strategies, community-based management and training programmes.

GLOBAL ENVIRONMENT FACILITY—GEF

The GEF, which is managed jointly by UNDP, the World Bank and UNEP, began operations in 1991 for an initial pilot phase covering 1991–94. Its aim is to support projects to conserve biological diversity, protect international waters, and reduce the depletion of the ozone layer in the atmosphere. UNDP is responsible for capacity-building, targeted research, pre-investment activities and technical assistance. UNDP also administers the Small Grants Programme of the GEF, which supports community-based activities by local non-governmental organizations. During the pilot phase of the GEF total funding was US $1,500m.. In 1994 representatives of 34 countries agreed to provide $2,000m. to replenish GEF funds. In 1998 36 donor countries pledged $2,750m. for the next replenishment of GEF funds (GEF-2) covering the period 1 July 1998–30 June 2002. At 30 June 2000 the GEF portfolio comprised 165 projects; 94 had been completed at that time. During 1991–99 some $939m. in funding was approved for the GEF-UNDP project portfolio.

PROGRAMME OF ASSISTANCE TO THE PALESTINIAN PEOPLE—PAPP

PAPP, established in 1978, is committed to strengthening newly-created institutions, to creating employment opportunities and to stimulating private and public investment in the area to enhance trade and export potential in the Israeli-occupied Territories and Palestinian autonomous areas. Examples of PAPP activities include the following: construction of sewage collection networks and systems in the northern Gaza Strip; provision of water to 500,000 people in rural and urban areas of the West Bank and Gaza; construction of schools, youth and health centres; support to vegetable and fish traders through the construction of cold-storage and packing facilities; and provision of loans to strengthen industry and commerce.

Internet: www.papp.undp.org.

UNITED NATIONS CAPITAL DEVELOPMENT FUND—UNCDF

The Fund was established in 1966 and became fully operational in 1974. It invests in poor communities in least-developed countries through local governance projects and microfinance operations, with the aim of increasing such communities' access to essential local infrastructure and services and thereby improving their productive capacities and self-reliance. UNCDF encourages participation by local people and local government in the planning, implementation and monitoring of projects. The Fund aims to promote the interests of women in community projects and to enhance their earning capacities. By 1999 56 countries world-wide had received UNCDF assistance. In 1998 UNCDF nominated 15 countries in which to concentrate subsequent programmes. A Special Unit for Microfinance (SUM), established in 1997 as a joint UNDP/UNCDF operation, was fully integrated into UNCDF in 1999. UNCDF's annual programming budget amounts to some US $40m.

Executive-Secretary: NORMAND LAUZON.

UNITED NATIONS DEVELOPMENT FUND FOR WOMEN—UNIFEM

UNIFEM, which became an associated fund of UNDP in 1985, is the UN's lead agency in addressing the issues relating to women in development and promoting the rights of women world-wide. The Fund provides direct financial and technical support to enable low-income women in developing countries to increase earnings, gain access to labour-saving technologies and otherwise improve the quality of their lives. It also funds activities that include women in decision-making related to mainstream development projects. In 2000 UNIFEM approved 77 new projects and continued to support some 159 ongoing programmes world-wide. UNIFEM has supported the preparation of national reports in 30 countries and used the priorities identified in these reports and in other regional initiatives to formulate a Women's Development Agenda for the 21st century. Through these efforts, UNIFEM played an active role in the preparation for the UN Fourth World Conference on Women, which was held in Beijing, People's Republic of China, in September 1995. UNIFEM participated in a special session of the UN General Assembly convened in June 2000 to review the conference, entitled Gender Equality, Development and Peace for the 21st Century (Beijing + 5). In March 2001 UNIFEM, in collaboration with International Alert, launched a Millennium Peace Prize for Women. Programme expenditure in 2000 totalled US $25.4m.

Director: NOELEEN HEYZER (Singapore).

UNDP DRYLANDS DEVELOPMENT CENTRE—DDC

The Centre, based in Nairobi, Kenya, was established in February 2002, superseding the former UN Office to Combat Desertification and Drought (UNSO). (UNSO had been established following the conclusion, in October 1994, of the UN Convention to Combat Desertification in Those Countries Experiencing Serious Drought and/or Desertification, Particularly in Africa; in turn, UNSO had replaced the former UN Sudano–Sahelian Office.) The DDC was to focus on the following areas: ensuring that national development planning takes account of the needs of dryland communities, particularly in proverty reduction strategies; helping countries to cope with the effects of climate variability, especially drought, and to prepare for future climate change; and addressing local issues affecting the utilization of resources.

Director: PHILIP DOBIE.

UNITED NATIONS VOLUNTEERS—UNV

The United Nations Volunteers is an important source of middle-level skills for the UN development system, supplied at modest cost, particularly in the least-developed countries. Volunteers expand the scope of UNDP project activities by supplementing the work of international and host country experts and by extending the influence of projects to local community levels. UNV also supports technical co-operation within and among the developing countries by encouraging volunteers from the countries themselves and by forming regional exchange teams made up of such volunteers. The UN Short-term Advisory (UNISTAR) Programme, which is the private-sector development arm of UNV, has increasingly focused its attention on countries in the process of economic transition. In addition to development activities UNV has become increasingly involved in areas such as peace-building, elections, human rights and community-based environmental programmes.

Since 1994 UNV has administered UNDP's Transfer of Knowledge Through Expatriate Nationals (TOKTEN) programme, which was initiated in 1977 to enable specialists and professionals from developing countries to contribute to development efforts in their countries of origin through short-term technical assignments.

By 31 January 2002 2,946 UNVs were serving in 132 countries. At that time the total number of people who had served under the initiative amounted to more than 30,000 in some 140 countries.

Executive Co-ordinator: SHARON CAPELING-ALAKIJA.

United Nations Environment Programme—UNEP

Address: POB 30552, Nairobi, Kenya.

Telephone: (20) 621234; **fax:** (20) 624489; **e-mail:** cpiinfo@unep.org; **internet:** www.unep.org.

The United Nations Environment Programme was established in 1972 by the UN General Assembly, following recommendations of the 1972 UN Conference on the Human Environment, in Stockholm, Sweden, to encourage international co-operation in matters relating to the human environment.

Organization

(September 2002)

GOVERNING COUNCIL

The main functions of the Governing Council, which meets every two years, are to promote international co-operation in the field of the environment and to provide general policy guide-lines for the direction and co-ordination of environmental programmes within the UN system. It comprises representatives of 58 states, elected by the UN General Assembly, for four-year terms, on a regional basis. The Council is assisted in its work by a Committee of Permanent Representatives.

HIGH-LEVEL COMMITTEE OF MINISTERS AND OFFICIALS IN CHARGE OF THE ENVIRONMENT

The Committee was established by the Governing Council in 1997, with a mandate to consider the international environmental agenda and to make recommendations to the Council on reform and policy issues. In addition, the Committee, comprising 36 elected members, was to provide guidance and advice to the Executive Director, to enhance UNEP's collaboration and co-operation with other multilateral bodies and to help to mobilize financial resources for UNEP.

SECRETARIAT

Offices and divisions at UNEP headquarters include the the Office of the Executive Director; the Secretariat for Governing Bodies; Offices for Evaluation and Oversight, Programme Co-ordination and Management, and Resource Mobilization; and divisions of communications and public information, early warning and assessment, policy development and law, policy implementation, technology and industry and economics, regional co-operation and representation, environmental conventions, and GEF co-ordination.

Executive Director: Dr KLAUS TÖPFER (Germany).

REGIONAL OFFICES

Africa: POB 30552, Nairobi, Kenya; tel. (20) 624283; fax (20) 623928; internet www.unep.org/roa.

Europe: CP 356, 15 chemin des Anémones, 1219 Châtelaine, Geneva, Switzerland; tel. (22) 9178279; fax (22) 9178024; e-mail roe@unep.ch; internet www.unep.ch.

West Asia: POB 10880, Manama; Villa 2113, Rd 2432, Block 324, Al-Juffair, Bahrain; tel. 276072; fax 276075; e-mail www.unep rowa@unep.org.bh; internet www.unep.org.bh.

OTHER OFFICES

Convention on International Trade in Endangered Species of Wild Fauna and Flora (CITES): CP 456, 15 chemin des Anémones, 1219 Châtelaine, Geneva, Switzerland; tel. (22) 9178139; fax (22) 7973417; e-mail cites@unep.ch; internet www.cites.org; Sec.-Gen. WILLEM WIJNSTEKERS.

Global Programme of Action for the Protection of the Marine Environment from Land-based Activities: POB 16227, 2500 The Hague, The Netherlands; tel. (70) 3114460; fax (70) 3456648; e-mail gpa@unep.nl; internet www.gpa.unep.org; Co-ordinator VEERLE VANDEWEERD.

Secretariat of the Basel Convention: 15 chemin des Anémones, 1219 Châtelaine, Geneva, Switzerland; tel. (22) 9178218; fax (22) 7973454; e-mail sbc@unep.ch; internet www.basel.int; Exec. Sec. SACHIKO KUWABARA-YAMAMOTO.

Secretariat of the Convention on Biological Diversity: World Trade Center, 393 St Jacques St, West Suite 300, Montréal, QC, Canada HR7 1N9; tel. (514) 288-2220; fax (514) 288-6588; e-mail secretariat@biodiv.org; internet www.biodiv.org; Exec. Sec. Dr HAMDALLAH ZEDAN.

Secretariat of the Multilateral Fund for the Implementation of the Montreal Protocol: 1800 McGill College Ave, 27th Floor, Montréal, QC, Canada H3A 3J6; tel. (514) 282-1122; fax (514) 282-0068; e-mail secretariat@unmfs.org; internet www.unmfs.org; Chief Dr OMAR EL-ARINI.

UNEP Arab League Liaison Office: POB 212, Cairo, Egypt; tel. (2) 3361349; fax (2) 3370658.

UNEP Chemicals: 11–13 chemin des Anémones, 1219 Châtelaine, Geneva, Switzerland; tel. (22) 9178111; fax (22) 7973460; e-mail opereira@unep.ch; internet www.chem.unep.ch; Dir JAMES B. WILLIS.

UNEP Co-ordinating Unit for the Mediterranean Action Plan (MEDU): Leoforos Vassileos Konstantinou 48, POB 18019, 11610 Athens, Greece; tel. (1) 7273100; fax (1) 7253196; e-mail unepmedu@unepmap.gr; internet www.unepmap.gr; Co-ordinator LUCIEN CHABASON.

UNEP Divison of Technology, Industry and Environment: Tour Mirabeau, 39–43, Quai André Citroën, 75739 Paris Cédex 15, France; tel. 1-44-37-14-41; fax 1-44-37-14-74; e-mail unep.tie@unep.fr; internet www.uneptie.org; Dir JACQUELINE ALOISI DE LARDEREL.

UNEP International Environmental Technology Centre: 2-110 Ryokuchi koen, Tsurumi-ku, Osaka 538-0036, Japan; tel. (6) 6915-4581; fax (6) 6915-0304; e-mail ietc@unep.or.jp; internet www.unep.or.jp; Dir STEVE HALLS.

UNEP Ozone Secretariat: POB 30552, Nairobi, Kenya; tel. (20) 623885; fax (20) 623913; e-mail jwillis@unep.org; internet www.unep.org/ozone; Officer-in-Charge MICHAEL GRABER.

UNEP Secretariat for the UN Scientific Committee on the Effects of Atomic Radiation: Vienna International Centre, Wagramerstrasse 5, 1400 Vienna, Austria; tel. (1) 26060-4330; fax (1) 26060-5902; e-mail norman.gentner@unvienna.un.or.at; internet www.unscear.org; Sec. NORMAN GENTNER.

UNEP/CMS (Convention on the Conservation of Migratory Species of Wild Animals) **Secretariat:** Martin-Luther-King-Str 8, 53175

Bonn, Germany; tel. (228) 8152402; fax (228) 8152449; e-mail cms@unep.de; internet www.wcmc.org.uk/cms; Exec. Sec. ARNULF MÜLLER-HELMBRECHT.

Activities

UNEP serves as a focal point for environmental action within the UN system. It aims to maintain a constant watch on the changing state of the environment; to analyse the trends; to assess the problems using a wide range of data and techniques; and to promote projects leading to environmentally sound development. It plays a catalytic and co-ordinating role within and beyond the UN system. Many UNEP projects are implemented in co-operation with other UN agencies, particularly UNDP, the World Bank group, FAO, UNESCO and WHO. About 45 intergovernmental organizations outside the UN system and 60 international non-governmental organizations have official observer status on UNEP's Governing Council, and, through the Environment Liaison Centre in Nairobi, UNEP is linked to more than 6,000 non-governmental bodies concerned with the environment. UNEP also sponsors international conferences, programmes, plans and agreements regarding all aspects of the environment.

In February 1997 the Governing Council, at its 19th session, adopted a ministerial declaration (the Nairobi Declaration) on UNEP's future role and mandate, which recognized the organization as the principal UN body working in the field of the environment and as the leading global environmental authority, setting and overseeing the international environmental agenda. In June a special session of the UN General Assembly, referred to as 'Rio + 5', was convened to review the state of the environment and progress achieved in implementing the objectives of the UN Conference on Environment and Development (UNCED) in Rio de Janeiro, Brazil, in June 1992. The meeting adopted a Programme for Further Implementation of Agenda 21 (a programme of activities to promote sustainable development, adopted by UNCED) in order to intensify efforts in areas such as energy, freshwater resources and technology transfer. The meeting confirmed UNEP's essential role in advancing the Programme and as a global authority promoting a coherent legal and political approach to the environmental challenges of sustainable development. An extensive process of restructuring and realignment of functions was subsequently initiated by UNEP, and a new organizational structure reflecting the decisions of the Nairobi Declaration was implemented during 1999. UNEP played a leading role in preparing for the World Summit on Sustainable Development (WSSD), held in August/September 2002 in Johannesburg, South Africa to assess strategies for strengthening the implementation of Agenda 21. Governments participating in the conference made commitments to attaining several objectives, including a reduction by one-half in the proportion of people world-wide lacking access to clean water or good sanitation by 2015, the restocking of depleted fisheries by 2015, a reduction in the ongoing loss in biodiversity by 2010, and the production and utilization of chemicals without causing harm to human beings and the environment by 2020. Participants also determined to increase usage of renewable energy sources. A large number of partnerships between governments, private sector interests and civil society groups were announced at the summit.

In May 2000 UNEP sponsored the first annual Global Ministerial Environment Forum (GMEF), held in Malmö, Sweden, and attended by environment ministers and other government delegates from more than 130 countries. Participants reviewed policy issues in the field of the environment and addressed issues such as the impact on the environment of population growth, the depletion of the earth's natural resources, climate change and the need for improved freshwater supplies. The Forum issued the Malmö Declaration which identified the effective implementation of international agreements on environmental matters at national level as the most pressing challenge for policy makers. The Declaration emphasized the importance of mobilizing domestic and international resources and urged increased co-operation from civil society and the private sector in achieving sustainable development. The second GMEF, held in Nairobi in February 2001, addressed means of strengthening international environmental governance, and established an Open-Ended Intergovernmental Group of Ministers or Their Representatives to prepare a report on possible reforms. GMEF-3, held in Cartagena, Colombia, in February 2002, considered UNEP's participation in the forthcoming WSSD, with a focus on environmental guidance issues.

ENVIRONMENTAL ASSESSMENT AND EARLY WARNING

The Nairobi Declaration resolved that the strengthening of UNEP's information, monitoring and assessment capabilities was a crucial element of the organization's restructuring, in order to help establish priorities for international, national and regional action, and to ensure the efficient and accurate dissemination of emerging environmental trends and emergencies.

In 1995 UNEP launched the Global Environment Outlook (GEO) process of environmental assessment. UNEP is assisted in its analysis of the state of the global environment by an extensive network of collaborating centres. Reports on the process are issued every two–three years. (The first *Global Environment Outlook, GEO-1*, was published in January 1997, the second, *GEO 2000*, in September 1999, and *GEO-3* in May 2002.) In July 2002 UNEP issued the first *Africa Environment Outlook*. During that year UNEP was conducting a detailed study of the environment of the Palestinian territories; the results were to be presented to the Governing Council in February 2003. UNEP is leading a major Global International Waters Assessment (GIWA) to consider all aspects of the world's water-related issues, in particular problems of shared transboundary waters, and of future sustainable management of water resources. UNEP is also a sponsoring agency of the Joint Group of Experts on the Scientific Aspects of Marine Environmental Pollution, and contributes to the preparation of reports on the state of the marine environment and on the impact of land-based activities on that environment. In November 1995 UNEP published a Global Biodiversity Assessment, which was the first comprehensive study of biological resources throughout the world. The UNEP-World Conservation Monitoring Centre (UNEP-WCMC), established in June 2000, provides biodiversity-related assessment. UNEP is a partner in the International Coral Reef Action Network—ICRAN, which was established in 2000 to manage and protect coral reefs world-wide. In June 2001 UNEP launched the Millennium Ecosystems Assessment, which is expected to be completed in 2004. Other major assessments under way in 2002 included GIWA; the Assessment of Impact and Adaptation to Climate Change; the Solar and Wind Energy Resource Assessment; the Regionally-Based Assessment of Persistent Toxic Substances; the Land Degradation Assessment in Drylands; and the Global Methodology for Mapping Human Impacts on the Biosphere (GLOBIO) project.

UNEP's environmental information network includes the Global Resource Information Database (GRID), which converts collected data into information usable by decision-makers. The INFOTERRA programme facilitates the exchange of environmental information through an extensive network of national 'focal points'. By early 2002 177 countries were participating in the network. Through INFOTERRA UNEP promotes public access to environmental information and also participation in environmental. UNEP aims to establish in every developing region an Environment and Natural Resource Information Network (ENRIN) in order to make available technical advice and manage environmental information and data for improved decision-making and action-planning in countries most in need of assistance. UNEP aims to integrate all its information resources in order further to improve access to information and to promote its international exchange. This has been pursued through UNEP.net, an internet-based interactive environmental information- and data-sharing facility, and Mercure, a telecommunications service using satellite technology to link a network of 16 earth stations throughout the world.

UNEP's information, monitoring and assessment structures also serve to enhance early-warning capabilities and to provide accurate information during an environmental emergency. In 2001 UNEP published *The Mesopotamian Marshlands: Demise of an Ecosystem*, charting the erosion of some 90% of Mesopotamian wetlands (located mainly in southern Iraq, at the confluence of the Tigris and Euphrates rivers) as a result of draining and damming activities.

POLICY DEVELOPMENT AND LAW

UNEP aims to promote the development of policy tools and guidelines in order to achieve the sustainable management of the world environment. At a national level it assists governments to develop and implement appropriate environmental instruments and aims to co-ordinate policy initiatives. Training workshops in various aspects of environmental law and its applications are conducted. UNEP supports the development of new legal, economic and other policy instruments to improve the effectiveness of existing environmental agreements.

UNEP was instrumental in the drafting of a Convention on Biological Diversity (CBD) to preserve the immense variety of plant and animal species, in particular those threatened with extinction. The Convention entered into force at the end of 1993; by March 2002 180 countries and the European Community were parties to the CBD. The CBD's Cartagena Protocol on Biosafety (so-called as it had been addressed at an extraordinary session of parties to the CBD convened in Cartagena, Colombia, in February 1999) was adopted at a meeting of parties to the CBD held in Montreal, Canada, in January 2000. The Protocol regulates the transboundary movement and use of living modified organisms resulting from biotechnology (such as genetically modified—GM—seeds and crops), in order to reduce any potential adverse effects on biodiversity and human health. It establishes an Advanced Informed Agreement procedure to govern the import of such organisms. By March 2002 the Protocol had been ratified by 13 states. In January 2002 UNEP launched a major project aimed at supporting developing countries with assessing the potential health and environmental risks and benefits of GM crops, in preparation for the Protocol's entry into force. In February the parties to the CBD and other partners convened a conference, in Montreal, to address ways in which the traditional knowledge and practices of local communities could be preserved and used to conserve highly-threatened species and ecosystems. In April the sixth conference of parties to the CBD adopted detailed global guide-lines on the management of genetic resources. UNEP supports co-operation for biodiversity assessment and management in selected developing regions and for the development of strategies for the conservation and sustainable exploitation of individual threatened species (e.g. the Global Tiger Action Plan). It also provides assistance for the preparation of individual country studies and strategies to strengthen national biodiversity management and research. UNEP administers the Convention on International Trade in Endangered Species of Wild Flora and Fauna (CITES), which entered into force in 1975.

In October 1994 87 countries, meeting under UN auspices, signed a Convention to Combat Desertification (see UNDP Drylands Development Centre, p. 1258), which aimed to provide a legal framework to counter the degradation of drylands. An estimated 75% of all drylands have suffered some land degradation, affecting approximately 1,000m. people in 110 countries. UNEP continues to support the implementation of the Convention, as part of its efforts to protect land resources. UNEP also aims to improve the assessment of dryland degradation and desertification in co-operation with governments and other international bodies, as well as identifying the causes of degradation and measures to overcome these.

UNEP is the lead UN agency for promoting environmentally sustainable water management. It regards the unsustainable use of water as the most urgent environmental and sustainable development issue, and estimates that two-thirds of the world's population will suffer chronic water shortages by 2025. This is attributed to rising demand for drinking water as a result of growing populations, decreasing quality of water because of pollution, and the increasing requirements of industries and agriculture. In 2000 UNEP adopted a new water policy and strategy, comprising assessment, management and co-ordination components. The Global International Waters Assessment (see above) is the primary framework for the assessment component. The management component includes the Global Programme of Action (GPA) for the Protection of the Marine Environment from Land-based Activities (adopted in November 1995), and UNEP's freshwater programme and regional seas programme. The GPA for the Protection of the Marine Environment for Land-based Activities focuses on the effects of activities such as pollution on freshwater resources, marine biodiversity and the coastal ecosystems of small-island developing states. UNEP aims to develop a similar global instrument to ensure the integrated management of freshwater resources. It promotes international co-operation in the management of river basins and coastal areas and for the development of tools and guide-lines to achieve the sustainable management of freshwater and coastal resources. UNEP provides scientific, technical and administrative support to facilitate the implementation and co-ordination of 14 regional seas conventions and 13 regional plans of action, and is developing a strategy to strengthen collaboration in their implementation. The new water policy and strategy emphasizes the need for improved co-ordination of existing activities. UNEP aims to play an enhanced role within relevant co-ordination mechanisms, such as the UN open-ended informal consultation process on oceans and the law of the sea.

In 1996 UNEP, in collaboration with FAO, began to work towards promoting and formulating a legally-binding international convention on prior informed consent (PIC) for hazardous chemicals and pesticides in international trade, extending a voluntary PIC procedure of information exchange undertaken by more than 100 governments since 1991. The Convention was adopted at a conference held in Rotterdam, Netherlands, in September 1998, and was to enter into force on being ratified by 50 signatory states. It aimed to reduce risks to human health and the environment by restricting the production, export and use of hazardous substances and enhancing information exchange procedures.

In conjunction with UN-Habitat, UNDP, the World Bank and other regional organizations and institutions, UNEP promotes environmental concerns in urban planning and management through the Sustainable Cities Programme, as well as regional workshops concerned with urban pollution and the impact of transportation systems. In 1994 UNEP inaugurated an International Environmental Technology Centre (IETC), with offices in Osaka and Shiga, Japan, in order to strengthen the capabilities of developing countries and countries with economies in transition to promote environmentally-sound management of cities and freshwater reservoirs through technology co-operation and partnerships.

UNEP has played a key role in global efforts to combat risks to the ozone layer, resultant climatic changes and atmospheric pollution. UNEP worked in collaboration with the World Meteorological Organization to formulate the UN Framework Convention on Climate Change (UNFCCC), with the aim of reducing the emission of gases that have a warming effect on the atmosphere, and has remained an active participant in the ongoing process to review and enforce its implementation. UNEP was the lead agency in formulating the 1987 Montreal Protocol to the Vienna Convention for the Protection of the Ozone Layer (1985), which provided for a 50% reduction in the production of chlorofluorocarbons (CFCs) by 2000. An amendment to the Protocol was adopted in 1990, which required complete cessation of the production of CFCs by 2000 in industrialized countries and by 2010 in developing countries; these deadlines were advanced to 1996 and 2006, respectively, in November 1992. In 1997 the ninth conference of the parties to the Vienna Convention adopted a further amendment which aimed to introduce a licensing system for all controlled substances. The eleventh conference of parties, meeting in Beijing, People's Republic of China, in November/December 1999, adopted the Beijing Amendment, which imposed tighter controls on the import and export of hydrochlorofluorocarbons, and on the production and consumption of bromochloromethane (Halon-1011, an industrial solvent and fire extinguisher). The Beijing Amendment entered into force in December 2001. A Multilateral Fund for the Implementation of the Montreal Protocol was established in June 1990 to promote the use of suitable technologies and the transfer of technologies to developing countries. UNEP, UNDP, the World Bank and UNIDO are the sponsors of the Fund, which by July 2001 had approved financing for some 3,850 projects in 124 developing countries at a cost of US $1,200m. Commitments of $440m. were made to the fourth replenishment of the Fund, covering the three-year period 2000–02.

POLICY IMPLEMENTATION

UNEP's Division of Environmental Policy Implementation incorporates two main functions: technical co-operation and response to environmental emergencies.

With the UN Office for the Co-ordination of Humanitarian Assistance, UNEP has established a Joint Environment Unit to mobilize and co-ordinate international assistance and expertise for countries facing environmental emergencies and natural disasters. In December 2001 UNEP established a new Post-conflict Assessment Unit.

UNEP, together with UNDP and the World Bank, is an implementing agency of the Global Environment Facility (GEF, q.v.), which was established in 1991 as a mechanism for international co-operation in projects concerned with biological diversity, climate change, international waters and depletion of the ozone layer. UNEP services the Scientific and Technical Advisory Panel, which was established to provide expert advice on GEF programmes and operational strategies.

TECHNOLOGY, INDUSTRY AND ECONOMICS

The use of inappropriate industrial technologies and the widespread adoption of unsustainable production and consumption patterns have been identified as being inefficient in the use of renewable resources and wasteful, in particular in the use of energy and water. UNEP aims to encourage governments and the private sector to develop and adopt policies and practices that are cleaner and safer, make efficient use of natural resources, incorporate environmental costs, ensure the environmentally sound management of chemicals, and reduce pollution and risks to human health and the environment. In collaboration with other organizations and agencies UNEP works to define and formulate international guide-lines and agreements to address these issues. UNEP also promotes the transfer of appropriate technologies and organizes conferences and training workshops to provide sustainable production practices. Relevant information is disseminated through the International Cleaner Production Information Clearing House. UNEP, together with UNIDO, has established eight National Cleaner Production Centres to promote a preventive approach to industrial pollution control. In October 1998 UNEP adopted an International Declaration on Cleaner Production, with a commitment to implement cleaner and more sustainable production methods and to monitor results; the Declaration had 267 signatories at December 2001, including representatives of 45 governments. In 1997 UNEP and the Coalition for Environmentally Responsible Economies launched the Global Reporting Initiative, which, with participation by corporations, business associations and other organizations and stakeholders, develops guide-lines for voluntary reporting by companies on their economic, environmental and social performance. In April 2002 UNEP launched the 'Life-Cycle Initiative', which aims to assist governments, businesses and other consumers with adopting environmentally-sound policies and practice, in view of the upward trend in global consumption patterns.

UNEP provides institutional servicing to the Basel Convention on the Control of Transboundary Movements of Hazardous Wastes and their Disposal, which was adopted in 1989 with the aim of preventing the disposal of wastes from industrialized countries in countries that have no processing facilities. In March 1994 the second meeting of parties to the Convention agreed to ban exportation of hazardous wastes between OECD and non-OECD countries by the end of 1997. The third meeting of parties to the Convention, held in September 1995, proposed that the ban should be incorporated into the Convention as an amendment. The resulting so-called Ban Amendment required ratification by three-quarters of the 62 signatory states present at the time of its adoption before it could enter into effect; by March 2002 the Ban Amendment had been ratified by 29 parties. The fourth full meeting of parties to the Convention, held in February 1998, attempted to clarify the classification and listing of hazardous wastes. At March 2002 the number of parties to the Convention totalled 149. In December 1999 132 states adopted a Protocol to the Convention to address issues relating to liability and compensation for damages from waste exports. The governments also agreed to establish a multilateral fund to finance immediate clean-up operations following any environmental accident. The first Continental Conference for Africa on Unwanted Stockpiles of Hazardous Wastes was held in Rabat, Morocco, in January 2001.

The UNEP Chemicals office was established to promote the sound management of hazardous substances, central to which was the International Register of Potentially Toxic Chemicals (IRPTC). UNEP aims to facilitate access to data on chemicals and hazardous wastes, in order to assess and control health and environmental risks, by using the IRPTC as a clearing house facility of relevant information and by publishing information and technical reports on the impact of the use of chemicals.

UNEP's OzonAction Programme works to promote information exchange, training and technological awareness. Its objective is to strengthen the capacity of governments and industry in developing countries to undertake measures towards the cost-effective phasing-out of ozone-depleting substances. UNEP also encourages the development of alternative and renewable sources of energy. To achieve this, UNEP is supporting the establishment of a network of centres to research and exchange information of environmentally-sound energy technology resources.

REGIONAL CO-OPERATION AND REPRESENTATION

UNEP maintains six regional offices. These work to initiate and promote UNEP objectives and to ensure that all programme fomulation and delivery meets the specific needs of countries and regions. They also provide a focal point for building national, sub-regional and regional partnership and enhancing local participation in UNEP initiatives. Following UNEP's reorganization a co-ordination office was established at headquarters to promote regional policy integration, to co-ordinate programme planning, and to provide necessary services to the regional offices.

UNEP provides administrative support to several regional conventions, organizes conferences, workshops and seminars at national and regional levels, and may extend advisory services or technical assistance to individual governments.

UNEP supports the environmental component of the New Partnership for Africa's Development (NEPAD, q.v.); the establishment of a Pan-African Environment Agency is under consideration by the initiative.

CONVENTIONS

UNEP aims to develop and promote international environmental legislation in order to pursue an integrated response to global environmental issues, to enhance collaboration among existing convention secretariats, and to co-ordinate support to implement the work programmes of international instruments.

UNEP has been an active participant in the formulation of several major conventions (see above). The division of Environmental Conventions is mandated to assist the Division of Policy Development and Law in the formulation of new agreements or protocols to existing conventions. Following the successful adoption of the Rotterdam Convention in September 1998, UNEP played a leading role

in formulating a multilateral agreement to reduce and ultimately eliminate the manufacture and use of Persistent Organic Pollutants (POPs), which are considered to be a major global environmental hazard. The agreement on POPs, concluded in December 2000 at a conference sponsored by UNEP in Johannesburg, South Africa, was adopted by 127 countries in May 2001.

UNEP has been designated to provide secretariat functions to a number of global and regional environmental conventions (see above for list of offices).

COMMUNICATIONS AND PUBLIC INFORMATION

UNEP's public education campaigns and outreach programmes promote community involvement in environmental issues. Further communication of environmental concerns is undertaken through the media, an information centre service and special promotional events, including World Environment Day, photograph competitions and the awarding of the Sasakawa Prize to recognize distinguished service to the environment by individuals and groups. In 1996 UNEP initiated a Global Environment Citizenship Programme to promote acknowledgement of the environmental responsibilities of all sectors of society.

Finance

UNEP derives its finances from the regular budget of the United Nations and from voluntary contributions to the Environment Fund. A budget of US $119.9m. was authorized for the two-year period 2002–03, of which $100m. was for programme activities (see below), $14.9m. for management and administration, and $5m. for fund programme reserves.

Publications

Africa Environment Outlook.
Annual Report.
APELL Newsletter (2 a year).
Cleaner Production Newsletter (2 a year).
Climate Change Bulletin (quarterly).
Connect (UNESCO-UNEP newsletter on environmental degradation, quarterly).
EarthViews (quarterly).
Environment Forum (quarterly).
Environmental Law Bulletin (2 a year).
Financial Services Initiative (2 a year).
GEF News (quarterly).
Global Environment Outlook.
Global Water Review.
GPA Newsletter.
IETC Insight (3 a year).
Industry and Environment Review (quarterly).
Leave it to Us (children's magazine, 2 a year).
Managing Hazardous Waste (2 a year).
Our Planet (6 a year).
OzonAction Newsletter (quarterly).
Tourism Focus (2 a year).
UNEP Chemicals Newsletter (2 a year).
UNEP Update (monthly).
World Atlas of Coral Reefs.
World Atlas of Desertification.
Studies, reports, legal texts, technical guide-lines, etc.

United Nations High Commissioner for Refugees—UNHCR

Address: CP 2500, 1211 Geneva 2 dépôt, Switzerland.
Telephone: (22) 7398111; **fax:** (22) 7397312; **e-mail:** unhcr@unhcr.ch; **internet:** www.unhcr.ch.

The Office of the High Commissioner was established in 1951 to provide international protection for refugees and to seek durable solutions to their problems.

Organization
(September 2002)

HIGH COMMISSIONER

The High Commissioner is elected by the United Nations General Assembly on the nomination of the Secretary-General, and is responsible to the General Assembly and to the UN Economic and Social Council (ECOSOC).

High Commissioner: RUUD LUBBERS (Netherlands).
Deputy High Commissioner: MARY ANN WYRSCH (USA).

EXECUTIVE COMMITTEE

The Executive Committee of the High Commissioner's Programme (ExCom), established by ECOSOC, gives the High Commissioner policy directives in respect of material assistance programmes and advice in the field of international protection. In addition, it oversees UNHCR's general policies and use of funds. ExCom, which comprises representatives of 57 states, both members and non-members of the UN, meets once a year.

ADMINISTRATION

Headquarters include the Executive Office, comprising the offices of the High Commissioner, the Deputy High Commissioner and the Assistant High Commissioner. There are separate offices for the Inspector General, the Special Envoy in the former Yugoslavia, the Director of the UNHCR liaison office in New York, and the Director of the Emergency Response Service. The other principal administrative units are the Division of Communication and Information, the Department of International Protection, the Division of Resource Management, and the Department of Operations, which is responsible for the five regional bureaux covering Africa; Asia and the Pacific; Europe; the Americas and the Caribbean; and Central Asia, South-West Asia, North Africa and the Middle East. At July 2002 there were 268 UNHCR field offices in 114 countries. At that time UNHCR employed 5,523 people, including short-term staff, of whom 84% were working in the field.

OFFICE IN THE MIDDLE EAST AND NORTH AFRICA

Regional Office for the Middle East: POB 1844, Cairo, Egypt; e-mail areca@unhcr.ch.

Activities

The competence of the High Commissioner extends to any person who, owing to well-founded fear of being persecuted for reasons of race, religion, nationality or political opinion, is outside the country of his or her nationality and is unable or, owing to such fear or for reasons other than personal convenience, remains unwilling to accept the protection of that country; or who, not having a nationality and being outside the country of former habitual residence, is unable or, owing to such fear or for reasons other than personal convenience, is unwilling to return to it. This competence may be extended, by resolutions of the UN General Assembly and decisions of ExCom, to cover certain other 'persons of concern', in addition to refugees meeting these criteria. Refugees who are assisted by other UN agencies, or who have the same rights or obligations as nationals of their country of residence, are outside the mandate of UNHCR.

In recent years there has been a significant shift in UNHCR's focus of activities. Increasingly UNHCR is called upon to support people who have been displaced within their own country, i.e. with similar needs to those of refugees but who have not crossed an international border, or those threatened with displacement as a result of armed conflict. Operations involving internally displaced populations may be undertaken only at the request of the UN Secretary-General or the General Assembly and with the consent of the country concerned. In addition, UNHCR is providing greater support to refugees who have returned to their country of origin, to assist their reintegration, and is working to enable the local

community to support the returnees, frequently through the implementation of Quick Impact Projects (QIPs). At December 2001 the refugee population world-wide provisionally totalled 12.1m. and UNHCR was concerned with an estimated further 940,800 asylum-seekers, 462,700 recently returned refugees and 6.3m. others (of whom an estimated 5.0m. were internally displaced persons—IDPs).

INTERNATIONAL PROTECTION

As laid down in the Statute of the Office, UNHCR's primary function is to extend international protection to refugees, and its second function is to seek durable solutions to their problems. In the exercise of its mandate UNHCR seeks to ensure that refugees and asylum-seekers are protected against *refoulement* (forcible return), that they receive asylum, and that they are treated according to internationally recognized standards of treatment. UNHCR pursues these objectives by a variety of means that include promoting the conclusion and ratification by states of international conventions for the protection of refugees, particularly the 1951 UN Convention relating to the Status of Refugees, extended by a Protocol adopted in 1967. The Convention defines the rights and duties of refugees and contains provisions dealing with a variety of matters which affect their day-to-day lives. UNHCR has also continued to encourage further accessions to the 1969 OAU (now AU) Convention Governing the Specific Aspects of Refugee Problems in Africa (to which 45 states—including Algeria, Egypt, Libya, Morocco and Tunisia—were party at February 2001).

UNHCR has actively encouraged states to accede to the 1951 UN Refugee Convention and the 1967 Protocol: 144 states had acceded to either or both of these basic refugee instruments by mid-2002. An increasing number of states have also adopted domestic legislation and/or administrative measures to implement the international instruments, particularly in the field of procedures for the determination of refugee status. UNHCR has sought to address the specific needs of refugee women and children, and has also attempted to deal with the problem of military attacks on refugee camps, by adopting and encouraging the acceptance of a set of principles to ensure the safety of refugees. In recent years it has formulated a strategy designed to address the fundamental causes of refugee flows. In 2001, in response to widespread concern about perceived high numbers of asylum-seekers and large-scale international economic migration and human trafficking, UNHCR initiated a series of Global Consultations on International Protection with the signatories to the 1951 Convention and 1967 Protocol, and other interested parties, with a view to strengthening both the application and scope of international refugee legislation. Following the major terrorist attacks perpetrated in September 2001 against targets in the USA, UNHCR issued a list of concerns relating to possible negative consequences for asylum-seekers and refugees, including the threat of increased xenophobia and discrimination. In addition, with the subsequent threat of action by a US-led global coalition against countries suspected of harbouring and promoting terrorist organizations, UNHCR reassessed its contingency plans for possible large-scale population displacement in the Middle East.

The first phase of an assistance operation uses UNHCR's capacity of emergency preparedness and response. This enables UNHCR to address the immediate needs of refugees at short notice, for example, by employing specially trained emergency teams and maintaining stockpiles of basic equipment, medical aid and materials. A significant proportion of UNHCR expenditure is allocated to the next phase of an operation, providing 'care and maintenance' in stable refugee circumstances. This assistance can take various forms, including the provision of food, shelter, medical care and essential supplies. Also covered in many instances are basic services, including education and counselling. Whenever possible, measures of this kind are accompanied by efforts to encourage maximum levels of self-reliance among the refugee population.

As far as possible, assistance is geared towards the identification and implementation of durable solutions to refugee problems, this being the second statutory responsibility of UNHCR. Such solutions generally take one of three forms: voluntary repatriation, local integration and resettlement. Where voluntary repatriation is feasible, the Office assists refugees to overcome obstacles preventing their return to their country of origin. This may be done through negotiations with governments involved, or by providing funds either for the physical movement of refugees or for the rehabilitation of returnees once back in their own country.

When voluntary repatriation is not feasible, efforts are made to assist refugees to integrate locally and to become self-supporting in their countries of asylum. In cases where resettlement through emigration is the only viable solution to a refugee problem, UNHCR negotiates with governments in an endeavour to obtain resettlement opportunities, to encourage liberalization of admission criteria and to draw up special immigration schemes.

In the early 1990s UNHCR aimed to consolidate efforts to integrate certain priorities into its programme planning and implementation, as a standard discipline in all phases of assistance. The considerations include awareness of specific problems confronting refugee women, the needs of refugee children, the environmental impact of refugee programmes and long-term development objectives. In an effort to improve the effectiveness of its programmes UNHCR has initiated a process of delegating authority, as well as responsibility for operational budgets, to its regional and field representatives, increasing flexibility and accountability. An Evaluation and Policy Analysis Unit, established in 1999, reviews systematically UNHCR's operational effectiveness.

REGIONAL ASSISTANCE

From 1979, as a result of civil strife in Afghanistan, there was a massive movement of refugees from that country into Pakistan and Iran, creating the world's largest refugee population, which reached a peak of almost 6.3m. in 1990. In April 1992, following the establishment of a new government in Afghanistan, refugees began to repatriate in substantial numbers (hitherto only a small proportion had returned), although large numbers of people continued to flee into Pakistan as a result of continuing insecurity. From October 1996 an escalation of hostilities resulted in further large-scale population displacement. During 1997 UNHCR operated a pilot scheme to organize group repatriations to specific areas in Afghanistan, under the protection of international observers; despite initial successes, however, the scheme was suspended in late 1998. In early 1998 UNHCR initiated a new monitoring system to evaluate the situation of returnees to Afghanistan. By the end of that year the total number of returnees from Iran and Pakistan since 1988 amounted to more than 4.2m. In recent years UNHCR, with other UN agencies, attempted to meet the immediate needs of IDPs and recent returnees through systematic monitoring and, for example, by initiating small-scale multi-sectoral QIPs to improve shelter, rural water supply, and local infrastructure, organizing income-generating and capacity-building activities, and providing food and tools. However, the ongoing civil conflict, as well as severe droughts and harsh winter conditions, caused renewed population displacement, precluding a settlement of the Afghan refugee situation and entailing immense difficulties in undertaking comprehensive relief efforts. Activities were disrupted by periodic withdrawals of UN international personnel owing to security concerns. In Iran UNHCR aimed to ensure the voluntary nature of repatriation, while in Pakistan it focused activities on strengthening refugees' capacity for self-sufficiency. In mid-2001 UNHCR warned that the food insecurity in the country was continuing to deteriorate, and that population movements were ongoing. In September, prompted by the threat of impending military action directed by a US-led global coalition against targets in the Taliban-administered areas of Afghanistan, UNHCR launched a US $252m. appeal to finance an emergency relief operation to cope with a potentially large further movement of Afghan refugees and IDPs. Although all surrounding countries imposed 'closed border' policies, it was envisaged that, were the security situation to deteriorate significantly, large numbers of Afghans might attempt to cross into the surrounding countries (mainly Iran and Pakistan) at unsecured points of entry. UNHCR urged the adoption of more liberal border policies and began substantially to reinforce its presence in Iran and Pakistan. Activities being undertaken included the supply of basic relief items such as tents and health and hygiene kits, assistance with the provision of community services such as education for school-age children, and preparations for the construction of new camps near the Pakistan-Afghanistan border and in Iran. In October (when air-strikes were initiated against Afghanistan) UNHCR opened a staging camp at a major crossing point on the Afghanistan-Pakistan border, and put in place a system for monitoring new refugee arrivals (implemented by local people rather than by UNHCR personnel). It was estimated that from October 2001–January 2002 about 50,000 Afghan refugees entered Pakistan officially, while an estimated 150,000 crossed into the country at unofficial border points; much smaller movements into Iran were reported. Spontaneous repatriations also occurred during that period (reportedly partly owing to the poor conditions at many camps in Pakistan), and UNHCR-assisted IDP returns were also undertaken. UNHCR resumed operations within Afghanistan in mid-November 2001, distributing supplies and implementing QIPs, for example aimed at providing warm winter clothing. From that month some 130,000 Afghan refugees in Pakistan were relocated from inadequate accommodation to new camps. At 31 December there were an estimated 1.48m. Afghan refugees in Iran. On 1 March 2002 UNHCR initiated, jointly with the new interim Afghan administration, an assisted repatriation programme. Each returning family was to receive food and basic household items, as well as information about security and mine-awareness. UNHCR also concluded tripartite accords on

repatriation with the Afghan authorities and with Iran and Pakistan. By early August more than 1.2m. Afghan refugees had registered to return under the programme, including some 150,000 from Iran, while an estimated 200,000 had returned spontaneously, of whom 41,000 were from Iran. UNHCR had assisted a further 200,000 IDPs to return to their home areas. In early August UNHCR signed a new agreement with the Iranian Government to grant access to Afghans in detention centres throughout that country and to undertake a screening programme for asylum-seekers, in order to deal with the problem of undocumented refugees. However, at the same time UNHCR expressed its concern at reports that the Iranian authorities were applying pressure on long-term refugees to return to Afghanistan involuntarily.

In March–May 1991, following the war against Iraq by a multinational force, and the subsequent Iraqi suppression of resistance in Kurdish areas in the north of the country, there was a massive movement of some 1.5m., mainly Kurdish, refugees into Iran and Turkey. UNHCR was designated the principal UN agency to attempt to alleviate the crisis. In May the refugees began to return to Iraq in huge numbers and UNHCR assisted in their repatriation, establishing relief stations along their routes from Iran and Turkey. Following the war to liberate Kuwait UNHCR gave protection and assistance to Iraqis, Bidoon (stateless people) and Palestinians who were forced to leave that country. In May 2000 the Kuwaiti authorities determined that all Bidoon still resident in the country should register officially with the national authorities by 27 June; while it was agreed that citizenship requirement restrictions would be eased for some 36,000 Bidoon who had been enumerated at a population census in 1965, the remaining stateless residents (numbering an estimated 75,000) were to be required to apply for short-term residency permits. At 31 December 2001 there were, provisionally, 1,255 registered refugees in Kuwait. However, it was estimated that an additional 138,000 people in Kuwait were of concern to UNHCR, mainly Bidoons, Iraqis and Palestinians.

In April 1994 UNHCR initiated a programme to provide food and relief assistance to Turkish Kurds who had fled into northern Iraq. In September 1996 fighting escalated among the Kurdish factions in northern Iraq. By the time a cease-fire agreement was concluded in November some 65,000 Iraqi Kurds had fled across the border into Iran. UNHCR, together with the Iranian Government, provided these new refugees with basic humanitarian supplies. By the end of the year, however, the majority of refugees had returned to Iraq, owing to poor conditions in the temporary settlements, security concerns at being located in the border region and pressure from the Iranian authorities. In December, UNHCR announced its intention to withdraw from the Atroush camp in northern Iraq, which housed an estimated 15,000 Turkish Kurds, following several breaches of security in the camp, and expressed its concern at the political vacuum in the region resulting from the factional conflict. UNHCR proceeded to transfer 3,500 people to other local settlements, and continued to provide humanitarian assistance to those refugees who had settled closer to Iraqi-controlled territory but who had been refused asylum. During 1997–2000 some 2,200 Turkish Kurds repatriated from Iraq with assistance from UNHCR. At 31 December 2001 the refugee population in Iraq amounted to an estimated 128,142, of whom about 39,200 were being assisted by UNHCR. The total refugee population included some 90,000 Palestinians, 23,680 Iranian Kurds, and 13,136 Kurds from Turkey. In addition, there were an estimated 1,968 returned refugees in Iraq of concern to UNHCR. At that time there was still a substantial Iraqi refugee population in the region, mainly comprising the 386,000 people in Iran. In March 2001 the Governments of Iran and Iraq concluded a bilateral accord on the voluntary repatriation of some 5,000 Iranians and 5,000 Iraqis; UNHCR was to assist with the implementation of the agreement. During 2002 UNHCR was providing counselling to those refugee families to enable them to make a decision on repatriation.

In June 1992 people fleeing the civil war and famine in Somalia began arriving in Yemen in large numbers. UNHCR set up camps to accommodate some 50,000 refugees, providing them with shelter, food, water and sanitation. As a result of civil conflict in Yemen in mid-1994, a large camp in the south of the country was demolished and other refugees had to be relocated, while the Yemen authorities initiated a campaign of forcible repatriation. During 1998–mid-2000 the refugee population in Yemen expanded, owing to an influx of Somalis fleeing civil conflict and, to a lesser extent, people displaced by the 1998–2000 Eritrea–Ethiopia border conflict. The relocation of refugees to a newly-constructed camp at al-Kharaz, central Yemen, commenced in late 2000. At December 2001 Yemen was hosting an estimated 69,468, mostly Somali, refugees.

UNHCR co-ordinates humanitarian assistance for the estimated 165,000 Sahrawis registered as refugees in four camps in the Tindouf area of Algeria. In September 1997 an agreement was reached on implementing the 1991 Settlement Plan for the Western Sahara. Accordingly, UNHCR was to help organize the registration and safe return of some 120,000 Sahrawi refugees provisionally identified as eligible to vote in the planned referendum on the future of the territory. In addition, UNHCR was to facilitate the reintegration of the returnees and monitor their rehabilitation. By early 2002, however little progress had been achieved towards the implementation of the Settlement Plan.

Persons of concern to UNHCR in the Middle East and North Africa (at 31 December 2001, '000, provisional figures)*

Country	Refugees	Asylum seekers	Returnees	Others of concern
Algeria . . .	169.4	—	—	—
Egypt . . .	7.2	15.7	—	—
Iran . . .	1,868.0	—	—	—
Iraq . . .	128.1	0.4	2.0	—
Kuwait. . .	1.3	—	—	138.0
Libya . . .	11.7	—	—	—
Syria . . .	3.4	0.6	—	—
Yemen . . .	69.5	2.4	0.2	—

* The table shows only those countries where the total number of persons of concern to UNHCR amounted to more than 10,000. The figures are provided mostly by governments, based on their own methods of estimation. The data do not include Palestinian refugees, who come under the care of UNRWA (q.v.).

CO-OPERATION WITH OTHER ORGANIZATIONS

UNHCR works closely with other UN agencies, intergovernmental organizations and non-governmental organizations (NGOs) to increase the scope and effectiveness of its operations. Within the UN system UNHCR co-operates, principally, with the World Food Programme in the distribution of food aid, UNICEF and the World Health Organization in the provision of family welfare and child immunization programmes, OCHA in the delivery of emergency humanitarian relief, UNDP in development-related activities and the preparation of guide-lines for the continuum of emergency

assistance to development programmes, and the Office of the UN High Commissioner for Human Rights. UNHCR also has close working relationships with the International Committee of the Red Cross and the International Organization for Migration. In 2001 UNHCR worked with 537 NGOs as 'implementing partners', enabling UNHCR to broaden the use of its resources while maintaining a co-ordinating role in the provision of assistance. UNHCR and the League of Arab States (q.v.) signed a co-operation agreement in June 2000.

Finance

The United Nations regular budget finances a proportion of UNHCR administrative expenditure. The majority of UNHCR's programme expenditure (about 98%) is funded by voluntary contributions, mainly from governments. The Private Sector and Public Affairs Service, established in 2001, aims to increase funding from non-governmental donor sources, for example by developing partnerships with foundations and corporations. UNHCR assistance activities are financed from the Unified Annual Programme Budget. Following approval of the Budget any subsequently-identified requirements are managed by Supplementary Programmes, financed by separate appeals. Of the total US $828.6m. approved under the programme budget for 2002, $7.1m. was allocated to North Africa and $16.6m. to the Middle East.

Publications

Refugees (quarterly, in English, French, German, Italian, Japanese and Spanish).
Refugee Survey Quarterly.
The State of the World's Refugees (every 2 years).
UNHCR Handbook for Emergencies.

United Nations Peace-keeping Operations

Address: Department of Peace-keeping Operations, Room S-3727-B, United Nations, New York, NY 10017, USA.

Telephone: (212) 963-8079; **fax:** (212) 963-9222; **internet:** www.un.org/Depts/dpko/.

United Nations peace-keeping operations have been conceived as instruments of conflict control. The UN has used these operations in various conflicts, with the consent of the parties involved, to maintain international peace and security, without prejudice to the positions or claims of parties, in order to facilitate the search for political settlements through peaceful means such as mediation and the good offices of the Secretary-General. Each operation has been established with a specific mandate, which requires periodic review by the Security Council. United Nations peace-keeping operations fall into two categories: peace-keeping forces and observer missions.

Peace-keeping forces are composed of contingents of military and civilian personnel made available by member states. These forces assist in preventing the recurrence of fighting, restoring and maintaining peace, and promoting a return to normal conditions. To this end, peace-keeping forces are authorized as necessary to undertake negotiations, persuasion, observation and fact-finding. They run patrols and interpose physically between the opposing parties. Peace-keeping forces are permitted to use their weapons only in self-defence.

Military observer missions are composed of officers (usually unarmed), who are made available, on the Secretary-General's request, by member states. A mission's function is to observe and report to the Secretary-General (who in turn informs the UN Security Council) on the maintenance of a cease-fire, to investigate violations and to do what it can to improve the situation.

Peace-keeping forces and observer missions must at all times maintain complete impartiality and avoid any action that might affect the claims or positions of the parties.

The UN's peace-keeping forces and observer missions are financed in most cases by assessed contributions from member states of the organization. In recent years a significant expansion in the UN's peace-keeping activities has been accompanied by a perpetual financial crisis within the organization, as a result of the increased financial burden and the failure of some member states to pay outstanding contributions. By 31 December 2001 unpaid assessed contributions to the peace-keeping budget amounted to US $1,900m.

UNITED NATIONS DISENGAGEMENT OBSERVER FORCE—UNDOF

Headquarters: Camp Faouar, Syria.

Commander: Maj.-Gen. Bo Wranker (Sweden).

UNDOF was established for an initial period of six months by a UN Security Council resolution in May 1974, following the signature in Geneva of a disengagement agreement between Syrian and Israeli forces. The mandate has since been extended by successive resolutions. The initial task of the Force was to take over territory evacuated in stages by the Israeli troops, in accordance with the disengagement agreement, to hand over territory to Syrian troops, and to establish an area of separation on the Golan Heights.

UNDOF continues to monitor the area of separation; it carries out inspections of the areas of limited armaments and forces; uses its best efforts to maintain the cease-fire; and undertakes activities of a humanitarian nature, such as arranging the transfer of prisoners and war-dead between Syria and Israel. The Force operates exclusively on Syrian territory.

At 31 July 2002 the Force comprised 1,027 troops; it is assisted by approximately 80 military observers of UNTSO's Observer Group Golan, and supported by 123 international and local civilian personnel. Further UNTSO military observers help UNDOF in the performance of its tasks, as required. The General Assembly appropriated US $40.8m. to cover the cost of the operation for the period 1 July 2002–30 June 2003.

UNITED NATIONS INTERIM FORCE IN LEBANON—UNIFIL

Headquarters: Naqoura, Lebanon.

Personal Representative of the UN Secretary-General for Southern Lebanon: Staffan de Mistura (Sweden).

Commander: Maj.-Gen. Lalit Mohan Tewari (India).

UNIFIL was established by UN Security Council Resolution 425 in March 1978, following an invasion of Lebanon by Israeli forces. The force was mandated to confirm the withdrawal of Israeli forces, to restore international peace and security, and to assist the Government of Lebanon in ensuring the return of its effective authority in southern Lebanon. UNIFIL also extended humanitarian assistance to the population of the area, particularly following the second Israeli invasion of Lebanon in 1982. UNIFIL has provided civilians with food, water, fuel; medical and dental services; and some veterinary assistance. In April 1992, in accordance with its mandate, UNIFIL completed the transfer of part of its zone of operations to the control of the Lebanese army.

In March 1998 the Israeli Government announced that it recognized Security Council Resolution 425, requiring the unconditional withdrawal of its forces from southern Lebanon. It stipulated, however, that any withdrawal of its troops must be conditional on receiving security guarantees from the Lebanese authorities. A formal decision to this effect, adopted on 1 April, was rejected by the Lebanese and Syrian Governments. In mid-April 2000 the Israeli Government formally notified the UN Secretary-General of its intention to comply forthwith and in full with Resolution 425. Later in that month the UN Secretary-General dispatched a team of experts to study the technical aspects of the impending implementation of Resolution 425, and sent a delegation, led by both his Special Co-ordinator for the Middle East Peace Process, Terje Roed-Larsen, and the Commander of UNIFIL, to consult with regional Governments and groupings. The withdrawal of Israeli troops commenced in mid-May, and the final contingent was reported to have left Lebanon on 24 May. Meanwhile, the Security Council endorsed an operational plan to enable UNIFIL to verify the withdrawal. All concerned parties were urged to co-operate with UNIFIL in order to ensure the full implementation of the resolution. In accordance with its mandate, UNIFIL was to be disbanded following the resumption by the Lebanese Government of effective authority and the normal responsibilities of a state throughout the area, including the re-establishment of law and order structures. In mid-June the UN Secretary-General confirmed that Israeli forces had been fully evacuated from southern Lebanon. Soon afterwards UNIFIL reported several Israeli violations of the line of withdrawal, the so-called Blue Line. The Israeli Government agreed to rectify these by the end of July, and on 24 July the UN Secretary-General confirmed that no serious violations remained. UNIFIL, reinforced with additional troops, patrolled the area vacated by the Israeli forces, monitored the line of withdrawal, undertook demining activities, and continued to provide humanitarian assistance. From August 2000 the Lebanese Government deployed a Joint Security Force to the area and began re-establishing local administrative structures and reintegrating basic services into the rest of the country. However, the authorities declined to deploy military personnel along the border zone, on the grounds that a comprehensive peace agreement with Israel would first need to be achieved. In November, following two serious violations of the Blue Line in the previous month by both Israeli troops and Hezbollah militia, the Security Council urged the Lebanese Government to take effective control of the whole area vacated by Israel and to assume international responsibilities. In January 2001 the UN Secretary-General reported that UNIFIL no longer exercised control over the area of operation, which remained relatively stable. The Security Council endorsed his proposals to reconfigure the Force in order to focus on its remaining mandate of maintaining and observing the cease-fire along the line of withdrawal. An initial reduction in the Force's strength to 4,550 troops was effected by July. During the year several incidents involving Hezbollah attacks on Israeli military positions and frequent violations of the area of withdrawal by Israeli military aircraft were reported. In response to an increase from early 2002 in incidents generating tension in the area of UNIFIL's operation, reportedly perpetrated by Hezbollah and other militants, and persistent Israeli air violations of the Blue Line, the UN Secretary-General's Personal Representative for Southern Lebanon and Terje Roed-Larsen (see above) undertook diplomatic efforts aimed at restoring stability, and, despite restrictions on its movements, UNIFIL increased its patrols. By the end of 2002 UNIFIL was expected to have a reduced force strength of some 2,000 troops. The Force's mandate was most recently extended until 31 January 2003.

At 31 July 2002 the Force comprised 3,426 troops, assisted by some 50 military observers of UNTSO's Observer Group Lebanon, and also by some 445 international and local civilian staff. The General Assembly appropriation for the operation for the period 1 July 2002–30 June 2003 amounted to US $117.1m.

UNITED NATIONS IRAQ-KUWAIT OBSERVATION MISSION—UNIKOM

Headquarters: Umm Qasr, Iraq.

Commander: Maj.-Gen. MIGUEL ANGEL MORENO (Argentina).

UNIKOM was established by a UN Security Council resolution (initially for a six-month period) in April 1991, to monitor a 200-km demilitarized zone along the border between Iraq and Kuwait. The task of the mission was to deter violations of the border, to monitor

the Khor Abdullah waterway between Iraq and Kuwait, and to prevent military activity within the zone. In February 1993 the Security Council adopted a resolution to strengthen UNIKOM, following incursions into Kuwaiti territory by Iraqi personnel. The resolution enabled the use of physical action to prevent or redress violations of the demilitarized zone or the newly-defined boundary between Iraq and Kuwait. UNIKOM assisted with the relocation of Iraqi citizens from Kuwait, which was completed in February 1994; has provided technical support to other UN operations in the area (especially the Iraq–Kuwait Boundary Demarcation Commission, which was terminated in 1993); and facilitates the humanitarian activities of the International Committee of the Red Cross. A maritime operation to monitor the Khor Abdullah waterway commenced in February 2000.

At 31 July 2002 UNIKOM comprised 904 troops and 195 military observers, assisted by some 226 international and local civilian support staff. The UN General Assembly appropriated US $52.9m. for the maintenance of the mission for the period 1 July 2002–30 June 2003; two-thirds of UNIKOM's total costs are funded by voluntary contributions from Kuwait.

UNITED NATIONS MISSION FOR THE REFERENDUM IN WESTERN SAHARA— MINURSO

Headquarters: el-Aaiún, Western Sahara.

Special Representative of the UN Secretary-General and Chief of Mission: WILLIAM LACY SWING (USA).

Personal Envoy of the UN Secretary-General: JAMES A. BAKER, III (USA).

Commander: Maj.-Gen. GYORGY SZARAZ (HUNGARY).

In April 1991 the UN Security Council endorsed the establishment of MINURSO to verify a cease-fire in the disputed territory of Western Sahara, which came into effect in September 1991, and to implement a settlement plan, involving the repatriation of Western Saharan refugees (in co-ordination with UNHCR), the release of all Sahrawi political prisoners, and the organization of a referendum on the future of the territory. Western Sahara is claimed by Morocco, the administering power since 1975, and by the Algerian-supported Frente Popular para la Liberación de Saguia el Hamra y Río de Oro—Frente Polisario. Although originally envisaged for January 1992, the referendum was postponed indefinitely. In 1992 and 1993 the UN Secretary-General's Special Representative organized negotiations between the Frente Polisario and the Moroccan Government, who were in serious disagreement regarding criteria for eligibility to vote in the plebiscite (in particular, the Moroccan Government insisted that more than 100,000 members of ethnic groups who had been forced to leave the territory under Spanish rule prior to the last official census in 1974, the results of which were to be used as a basis for voter registration, should be allowed to participate in the referendum). In March 1993 the Security Council advocated that further efforts should be made to compile a satisfactory electoral list and to resolve the outstanding differences on procedural issues. An Identification Commission was consequently established to begin the process of voter registration, although this was obstructed by the failure of the Moroccan Government and the Frente Polisario to pursue political dialogue. The identification and registration operation was formally initiated in August 1994; however, the process was complicated by the dispersed nature of the Western Saharan population. In December 1995 the UN Secretary-General reported that the identification of voters had stalled, owing to persistent obstruction of the process on the part of the Moroccan and Frente Polisario authorities; at the end of May 1996 the Security Council endorsed a recommendation of the Secretary-General to suspend the identification process until all sides demonstrate their willingness to co-operate with the mission. The Security Council decided that MINURSO's operational capacity should be reduced by 20%, with sufficient troops retained to monitor and verify the cease-fire.

In early 1997 the new Secretary-General of the UN, Kofi Annan, attempted to revive the possibility of an imminent resolution of the dispute, amid increasing concerns that the opposing authorities were preparing for a resumption of hostilities in the event of a collapse of the existing cease-fire, and appointed James Baker, a former US Secretary of State, as his Personal Envoy to the region. In June Baker obtained the support of Morocco and the Frente Polisario, as well as Algeria and Mauritania (which border the disputed territory), to conduct further negotiations in order to advance the referendum process. Direct talks between senior representatives of the Moroccan Government and the Frente Polisario authorities were initiated later in that month, in Lisbon, Portugal, under the auspices of the UN, and attended by Algeria and Mauritania in an observer capacity. In September the two sides concluded an agreement which aimed to resolve the outstanding issues of contention and enable the referendum to be conducted in late 1998. The agreement included a commitment by both parties to identify eligible Sahrawi voters on an individual basis, in accordance with the results of the 1974 census, and a code of conduct to ensure the impartiality of the poll. In October 1997 the Security Council endorsed a recommendation of the Secretary-General to increase the strength of the mission, to enable it to supervise nine identification centres. The process of voter identification resumed in December 1997. The agenda for the settlement plan envisaged that the identification process would be followed by a process of appeal, the publication of a final list of voters, and then by a transitional period, under UN authority, during which all Sahrawi refugees would be repatriated. The referendum was scheduled to be conducted in December 1998.

In January 1998 the Security Council approved the deployment of an engineering unit to support MINURSO in its demining activities. By early September 1998 the initial identification process had been completed, with a total of 147,350 voters identified, including 87,238 since December 1997. However, the controversial issue of the eligibility of 65,000 members of three Saharan tribal groups remained unresolved. In October the Security Council endorsed a series of measures proposed by the Secretary-General to advance the referendum, including a strengthened Identification Commission to consider requests from any applicant from the three disputed tribal groups on an individual basis. The proposals also incorporated the need for an agreement by both sides with UNHCR with regard to arrangements for the repatriation of refugees. In November, following a visit to the region by the Secretary-General, the Frente Polisario accepted the proposals, and in March 1999 the Moroccan Government signed an agreement with the UN to secure the legal basis of the MINURSO operation. In May the Moroccan Government and the Frente Polisario agreed in principle to a draft plan of action for cross-border confidence measures. A new timetable envisaged the referendum being held in July 2000. In July 1999 the UN published the first part of a provisional list of 84,251 qualified voters. The appeals process then commenced. In late November almost 200 Moroccan prisoners of war were released by the Frente Polisario, following a series of negotiations led by the Special Representative of the UN Secretary-General. The identification of applicants from the three disputed Saharan tribal groups was completed at the end of December. In January 2000 the second, final part of the provisional list of qualified voters was issued, and a six-week appeals process ensued. In December 1999 the Security Council acknowledged that persisting disagreements obstructing the implementation of the settlement plan (mainly concerning the processing and analysis of appeals, the release of remaining prisoners and the repatriation of refugees) precluded any possibility of conducting the planned referendum before 2002.

In June 2001 the Personal Envoy of the Secretary-General elaborated a draft Framework Agreement on the Status of Western Sahara, which envisaged the disputed area remaining part of Morocco, but with substantial devolution of authority. Any referendum would be postponed. The Security Council, when granting an extension of MINURSO's mandate until November, authorized Baker to discuss the proposals with all concerned parties. In November the Security Council, at the insistence of the Frente Polisario, requested the opinion of the UN Legal Counsel regarding the legality of two short-term reconnaissance licences granted by Morocco to international petroleum companies for operation in Western Sahara. In that month the Council extended MINURSO's mandate until the end of February 2002. In January the new Special Representative of the UN Secretary-General, William Lacy Swing, visited the region and met with leaders of both sides. He welcomed the release by the Frente Polisario of a further 115 Moroccan prisoners, but urged both sides to free all long-term detainees. Further visits to the region were undertaken by Lacy Swing during the year. MINURSO's mandate was extended for two and three month intervals, respectively, in February and April, and in July was extended to 31 January 2003, in support of the Special Representative's ongoing diplomatic efforts. In July 2002 the Frente Polisario released a further 101 Moroccan prisoners.

The mission has headquarters in the north and south of the disputed territory, and there is a liaison office in Tindouf, Algeria, which was established in order to maintain contact with the Frente Polisario (which is based in Algeria) and the Algerian Government. At 31 July 2002 MINURSO comprised 189 military observers, 27 troops and 25 civilian police observers, supported by 285 international and local civilian personnel. The General Assembly appropriation to cover the cost of the mission for the period 1 July 2002–30 June 2003 amounted to US $41.5m.

UNITED NATIONS PEACE-KEEPING FORCE IN CYPRUS—UNFICYP

Headquarters: Nicosia, Cyprus.

Special Adviser to the UN Secretary-General: ALVARO DE SOTO (Peru).

Acting Special Representative of the UN Secretary-General and Chief of Mission: ZBIGNIEW WLOSOWICZ (Poland).

Commander: Maj.-Gen. JIN HA HWANG (Republic of Korea).

UNFICYP was established in March 1964 by a UN Security Council resolution (initially for a three-month duration, subsequently periodically extended) to prevent a recurrence of fighting between the Greek and Turkish Cypriot communities, and to contribute to the maintenance of law and order and a return to normal conditions. The Force controls a 180-km buffer zone, established (following the Turkish intervention in 1974) between the cease-fire lines of the Turkish forces and the Cyprus National Guard. It is mandated to investigate and act upon all violations of the cease-fire and buffer zone. The Force also performs humanitarian functions, such as facilitating the supply of electricity and water across the cease-fire lines, and offering emergency medical services. In August 1996 serious hostilities between elements of the two communities in the UN-controlled buffer zone resulted in the deaths of two people and injuries to many others, including 12 UN personnel. Following further intercommunal violence, UNFICYP advocated the prohibition of all weapons and military posts along the length of the buffer zone. The Force also proposed additional humanitarian measures to improve the conditions of minority groups living in the two parts of the island. In reports to the Security Council, the UN Secretary-General has consistently recognized UNFICYP as being indispensable to maintaining calm on the island and to creating the best conditions for his good offices. In July 1997 a new series of direct negotiations between the leaders of the two communities was initiated, under the auspices of the UN Secretary-General's Special Adviser; however, the talks were suspended at the end of that year. In November 1999 the leaders of the two communities agreed to participate in proximity negotiations, to be mediated by the UN. The first round of these took place in New York, in December. A second and third round were convened in Geneva, Switzerland, in February and July 2000, respectively. A fourth round of proximity talks was held in New York in September and a fifth round in Geneva, in November. In December 2001 the leaders of the two communities met together, in the presence of the Special Adviser, and agreed to begin a series of direct talks in the following month. By September 2002 an intensive dialogue between the two sides was still ongoing. In May the UN Secretary-General visited Cyprus. In a report issued at the end of that month he noted that the two leaders had agreed to address the outstanding issue of missing persons, and also that a number of restrictions placed on the Force's activities during 2000 by the Turkish Cypriot authorities and Turkish forces remained in place.

At 1 July 2002 UNFICYP had an operational strength of 1,203 military personnel and 35 civilian police officers, supported by 146 international and local civilian staff. Over the period 1 July 2002–30 June 2003 the proposed cost of maintaining the force amounted to US $45.6m., including voluntary contributions from the Governments of Cyprus and of Greece amounting to $15.2m. and $6.5m., respectively.

UNITED NATIONS TRUCE SUPERVISION ORGANIZATION—UNTSO

Headquarters: Government House, Jerusalem.

Chief-of-Staff: Maj.-Gen. CARL A. DODD (Ireland).

UNTSO was established initially to supervise the truce called by the UN Security Council in Palestine in May 1948 and has assisted in the application of the 1949 Armistice Agreements. Its activities have evolved over the years, in response to developments in the Middle East and in accordance with the relevant resolutions of the Security Council. There is no periodic renewal procedure for UNTSO's mandate.

UNTSO observers assist UN peace-keeping forces in the Middle East, at present UNIFIL and UNDOF (see above). The mission maintains offices in Beirut, Lebanon and Damascus, Syria. In addition, UNTSO operates a number of outposts in the Sinai region of Egypt to maintain a UN presence there. UNTSO observers have been available at short notice to form the nucleus of new peace-keeping operations.

The operational strength of UNTSO at 31 March 2002 was 155 military observers, supported by 214 international and local civilian staff. UNTSO expenditures are covered by the regular budget of the United Nations. The cost of the operation in 2002 was estimated to be US $23.2m.

United Nations Relief and Works Agency for Palestine Refugees in the Near East—UNRWA

Addresses: Gamal Abd an-Nasser St, Gaza City; Bayader Wadi Seer, POB 140157, Amman 11814, Jordan.
Telephone (Gaza City): (7) 6777333; **fax:** (7) 6777555.
Telephone (Amman): (6) 5826171; **fax:** (6) 5826177.
E-mail: unrwapio@unrwa.org; **internet:** www.un.org/unrwa/.

UNRWA was established by the UN General Assembly to provide relief, health, education and welfare services for Palestine refugees in the Near East, initially on a short-term basis. UNRWA began operations in May 1950 and, in the absence of a solution to the refugee problem, its mandate has subsequently been extended by the General Assembly.

Organization

(September 2002)

UNRWA employs an international staff of about 120 and more than 22,500 local staff, mainly Palestine refugees. In mid-1996 the agency's headquarters were relocated, from Vienna, Austria, to Gaza and Jordan. The Commissioner-General is the head of all UNRWA operations and reports directly to the UN General Assembly. UNRWA has no governing body, but its activities are reviewed annually by a 10-member Advisory Commission comprising representatives of the governments of:

Belgium	Jordan	Turkey
Egypt	Lebanon	United Kingdom
France	Syria	USA
Japan		

Commissioner-General: PETER HANSEN (Denmark).

FIELD OFFICES

Each field office is headed by a director and has departments responsible for education, health and relief and social services programmes, finance, administration, supply and transport, legal affairs and public information.

Gaza: POB 61; Al Azhar Rd, Rimal Quarter, Gaza City; tel. (7) 2824508; fax (7) 6777444.
Jordan: POB 484; Al Zubeidi Bldg, Mustafa Bin Abdullah St, Tla'a Al-Ali, Amman; tel. (6) 5607194; fax (6) 5685476.
Lebanon: POB 11-0947, Beirut 1107 2060; Bir Hassan, Ghobeiri, Beirut; tel. (1) 822415; fax (1) 840469.
Syria: POB 4313; UN Compound, Mezzah Highway/Beirut Rd, Damascus; tel. (11) 6133035; fax (11) 6133047.
West Bank: POB 19149; Sheik Jarrah Qtr, East Jerusalem; tel. (2) 5890400; fax (2) 5322714.

LIAISON OFFICES

Egypt: 2 Dar-el-Shifa St, Garden City, POB 227, Cairo; tel. (2) 354-8502; fax (2) 354-8504.
Switzerland: Rm 92-93 Annexe Le Bocage, Palais des Nations, 1211 Geneva; tel. (22) 9171166; fax (22) 9170956.
USA: 2 United Nations Plaza, Room DC 2-1755, New York, NY 10017; tel. (212) 963-2255; fax (212) 935-7899.

Activities

ASSISTANCE ACTIVITIES

Since 1950 UNRWA has been the main provider of relief, health, education and social services for Palestine refugees in Lebanon, Syria, Jordan, the West Bank and the Gaza Strip. For UNRWA's purposes, a Palestine refugee is one whose normal residence was in Palestine for a minimum of two years before the 1948 conflict and who, as a result of the Arab–Israeli hostilities, lost his or her home and means of livelihood. To be eligible for assistance, a refugee must reside in one of the five areas in which UNRWA operates and be in need. A refugee's descendants who fulfil certain criteria are also eligible for UNRWA assistance. At 30 June 2002 UNRWA was providing essential services to 3,973,360 registered refugees (see table). Of these, an estimated 1,262,867 (32%) were living in 59 camps serviced by the Agency, while the remaining refugees had settled in the towns and villages already existing.

UNRWA's three principal areas of activity are education, health, and relief and social services. Some 89% of the Agency's 2002 general fund budget was devoted to these three operational programmes.

Education accounted for 52% of UNRWA's 2002 budget. In the 2001/2002 school year there were 486,020 pupils enrolled in 644 UNRWA schools, and 16,933 educational staff. UNRWA also operated eight vocational and teacher-training centres, which provided a total of 4,884 training places. UNRWA awarded 197 scholarships for study at Arab universities in 2001/02. Technical co-operation for the Agency's education programme is provided by UNESCO.

Health services accounted for 18% of UNRWA's 2002 general fund budget. At mid-2002 there were 122 primary health care units providing outpatient medical care, disease prevention and control, maternal and child health care and family planning services, of which 88 also offered dental care. At that time the number of health staff totalled 3,607. During 2001 patient visits to UNRWA medical units numbered 8.8m. UNRWA also operates a small hospital in the West Bank and offers assistance towards emergency and other secondary treatment, mainly through contractual agreements with non-governmental and private hospitals. Technical assistance for the health programme is provided by WHO.

Relief and social services accounted for 10% of UNRWA's general fund budget for 2002. These services comprise the distribution of food rations, the provision of emergency shelter and the organization of welfare programmes for the poorest refugees (at 30 June 2002 229,404 refugees, or 5.8% of the total registered refugee population, were eligible to receive special hardship assistance). In 2002 UNRWA provided technical and financial support to 71 women's programme centres, 27 youth activity centres and 36 community-based rehabilitation centres.

In order to encourage Palestinian self-reliance the Agency issues grants to ailing businesses and loans to families who qualify as special hardship cases. In 1991 UNRWA launched an income generation programme, which provides capital loans to small businesses and micro-enterprises with the objective of creating sustainable employment and eliminating poverty, particularly in the Occupied Territories. By 30 June 2002 53,036 loans, with a total estimated value of US $68.7m., had been issued to new and existing Palestinian-owned enterprises.

SPECIAL PROGRAMMES

Following the signing of the Declaration of Principles by the Palestine Liberation Organization and the Israeli Government in September 1993, UNRWA initiated a Peace Implementation Programme (PIP) to improve services and infrastructure for Palestinian refugees. In September 1994 the first phase of the programme (PIP I) was concluded after the receipt of US $93.2m. in pledged donations. PIP I projects included the construction of 33 schools and 24 classrooms and specialized education rooms, the rehabilitation of 4,700 shelters, the upgrading of solid waste disposal facilities throughout the Gaza Strip and feasibility studies for two sewerage systems. It was estimated that these projects created more than 5,500 jobs in the Gaza Strip for an average period of four months each. By the end of 2000 the total number of PIP projects, including those under the second phase of the programme (PIP II), amounted to 496, while funds received or pledged to the Programme totalled $255.6m.

Since 1993 UNRWA has been engaged in the construction, equipping and commissioning of a 232-bed hospital in the Gaza Strip, with funds from the European Union and its member states. The outpatient facilities opened in July 2000. The hospital and an affiliated nursing college were to be integrated into the health care system of the Palestinian (National) Authority (PA), once the process of commissioning had been completed.

AID TO DISPLACED PERSONS

After the renewal of Arab–Israeli hostilities in the Middle East in June 1967, hundreds of thousands of people fled from the fighting and from Israeli-occupied areas to east Jordan, Syria and Egypt. UNRWA provided emergency relief for displaced refugees and was additionally empowered by a UN General Assembly resolution to provide 'humanitarian assistance, as far as practicable, on an emergency basis and as a temporary measure' for those persons other than Palestine refugees who were newly displaced and in urgent need. In practice, UNRWA lacked the funds to aid the other displaced persons and the main burden of supporting them devolved on the Arab governments concerned. The Agency, as requested by the Government of Jordan in 1967 and on that Government's behalf, distributes rations to displaced persons in Jordan who are not registered refugees of 1948.

RECENT EMERGENCIES

In November 2000 UNRWA launched an emergency humanitarian appeal for US \$39.1m. in additional funds to assist Palestinian refugees affected by the most recent escalation of violence in the region and the Israeli-imposed blockade on PA-controlled territory. UNRWA became the lead agency with responsibility for the co-ordination and delivery of emergency assistance, as well as for monitoring the immediate needs of the local populations. A second appeal was made by the Agency in April 2001, for some \$37.2m., and a third emergency appeal, for \$77m., was issued in June to provide basic food and medical supplies until the end of the year. The additional resources were also required to fund a programme of emergency workdays, which aimed to provide employment and income for labourers with dependents, while improving the local infrastructure. In addition, UNRWA intended to provide extra schooling days to make up for those missed because of the fighting, trauma counselling for children, and post-injury rehabilitation. In mid-January 2002 UNRWA reacted immediately to assess the needs of refugees following the demolition of 54 shelters by Israeli forces, and provided emergency supplies, including tents, blankets, mats and food. A fourth emergency appeal, for some \$117.1m., was launched at the end of January to provide food aid, medical care, shelter reconstruction and emergency work programmes for refugees in the affected areas. In February the Commissioner-General protested at the Israeli bombing of Gaza City and at the damage caused by Israeli security forces in the Palestinian towns of Jenin and Nablus. In March the Commissioner-General expressed deep concern at the worsening humanitarian situation in the Palestinian territories, as well as his outrage at the death of an UNRWA staff member during an Israeli incursion into Tulkarem camp. Later in that month UNRWA assessed the damage inflicted against UNRWA infrastructure during March amounted to \$3.8m. In early April UNRWA efforts to deliver emergency food and medical supplies to Ramallah hospital and other areas in the West Bank were hindered by attacks and threats by Israeli troops. The Commissioner-General expressed concern at the deteriorating security and humanitarian situation and for the welfare of detained and besieged UN workers. In mid-April UNRWA was permitted limited access to Jenin refugee camp, which had experienced extensive fighting during a two-week period of occupation by Israeli forces. UNRWA delivered food and water and attempted to co-ordinate international efforts to send search and rescue teams into the camp. It also undertook to reintroduce essential services and to initiate the reconstruction of refugee homes. At the same time UNRWA noted with concern the entry restrictions imposed by Israel against the Gaza Strip, which were causing extreme food shortages. In May UNRWA organized a conference of 28 countries to highlight the need for an additional \$70m. to meet the humanitarian requirements resulting from the Israeli incursions. In July UNRWA requested \$55.7m. in additional aid, at meetings held in Jerusalem and Amman. Of the total amount, \$26m. was allocated for emergency shelter repair and reconstruction.

STATISTICS

Refugees Registered with UNRWA (30 June 2002)

Country	Number	% of total
Jordan	1,679,623	42.3
Gaza Strip	878,977	22.1
West Bank	626,532	15.8
Syria	401,185	10.1
Lebanon	387,043	9.7
Total	3,973,360	100.0

Finance

UNRWA is financed almost entirely by voluntary contributions from governments and the European Union, the remainder being provided by UN bodies, non-governmental organizations, business corporations and private sources, which also contribute to extra-budgetary activities. UNRWA's general fund budget for 2001 amounted to US \$330.7m., with an additional \$55.5m. in project financing. The total proposed budget for 2003 budget amounted to \$405.5m.

Publication

Annual Report of the Commissioner-General of UNRWA.

Food and Agriculture Organization—FAO

Address: Viale delle Terme di Caracalla, 00100 Rome, Italy.
Telephone: (06) 57051; **fax:** (06) 5705-3152; **e-mail:** fao-hq@fao.org; **internet:** www.fao.org.

FAO, the first specialized agency of the UN to be founded after the Second World War, aims to alleviate malnutrition and hunger, and serves as a co-ordinating agency for development programmes in the whole range of food and agriculture, including forestry and fisheries. It helps developing countries to promote educational and training facilities and the creation of appropriate institutions.

Organization

(September 2002)

CONFERENCE

The governing body is the FAO Conference of member nations, which meets every two years It formulates policy, determines the Organization's programme and budget on a biennial basis, and elects new members. It also elects the Director-General of the Secretariat and the Independent Chairman of the Council. Every second year, FAO also holds conferences in each of its five regions (designated the Near East, Asia and the Pacific, Africa, Latin America and the Caribbean, and Europe).

COUNCIL

The FAO Council is composed of representatives of 49 member nations, elected by the Conference for staggered three-year terms. It is the interim governing body of FAO between sessions of the Conference. The most important standing Committees of the Council are: the Finance and Programme Committees, the Committee on Commodity Problems, the Committee on Fisheries, the Committee on Agriculture and the Committee on Forestry.

SECRETARIAT

The total number of FAO staff in May 2002 was 3,700, of whom 1,500 were professional staff and 2,200 general service staff. About one-half of the Organization's staff were based at headquarters. Work is supervised by the following Departments: Administration and Finance; General Affairs and Information; Economic and Social Policy; Agriculture; Forestry; Fisheries; Sustainable Development; and Technical Co-operation.

Director-General: JACQUES DIOUF (Senegal).

REGIONAL OFFICES

Regional Office for the Near East: 11 el-Eslah el-Zerai St, POB 2223, Dokki, Cairo, Egypt; tel. (2) 3372229; fax (2) 3373419; e-mail fao-rne@field.fao.org; Regional Rep. ATIF Y. BUKHARI.

Sub-regional Office for North Africa: BP 300, Tunis, Tunisia; tel. (1) 847553; fax (1) 791859; e-mail fao-snea@field.fao.org; Sub-regional Rep. MUSTAPHA SINACEUR.

Activities

FAO aims to raise levels of nutrition and standards of living, by improving the production and distribution of food and other commodities derived from farms, fisheries and forests. FAO's ultimate objective is the achievement of world food security, 'Food for All'. The organization provides technical information, advice and assistance by disseminating information; acting as a neutral forum for discussion of food and agricultural issues; advising governments on policy and planning; and developing capacity directly in the field.

In November 1996 FAO hosted the World Food Summit, which was held in Rome and was attended by heads of state and senior government representatives of 186 countries. Participants approved the Rome Declaration on World Food Security and the World Food Summit Plan of Action, with the aim of halving the number of people afflicted by undernutrition, at that time estimated to total 828m. world-wide, by no later than 2015. A review conference, World Food Summit: Five Years Later, held in June 2002, reaffirmed commitment to this objective.

In November 1999 the FAO Conference approved a long-term Strategic Framework for the period 2000–15, which emphasized national and international co-operation in pursuing the goals of the 1996 World Food Summit. The Framework promoted interdisciplinarity and partnership, and defined three main global objectives: constant access by all people to sufficient nutritionally adequate and safe food, ensuring that levels of undernourishment were reduced by 50% by 2015; the continued contribution of sustainable agriculture and rural development to economic and social progress and well-being; and the conservation, improvement and sustainable use of natural resources. It identified five corporate strategies (each supported by several strategic objectives), covering the following areas: reducing food insecurity and rural poverty; ensuring enabling policy and regulatory frameworks for food, agriculture, fisheries and forestry; creating sustainable increases in the supply and availability of agricultural, fisheries and forestry products; conserving and enhancing sustainable use of the natural resource base; and generating knowledge. The November 2001 FAO Conference adopted a medium-term plan covering 2002–07 and a work programme for 2000–03, both on the basis of the Strategic Framework.

FAO organizes an annual series of fund-raising events, 'TeleFood', some of which are broadcast on television and the internet in order to raise public awareness of the problems of hunger and malnutrition. Since its inception in 1997 public donations to Tele-Food have exceeded US $9m., financing more than 1,000 'grass-roots' projects in more than 100 countries. The projects have provided tools, seeds and other essential supplies directly to small-scale farmers, and have been especially aimed at helping women.

In 1999 FAO signed a memorandum of understanding with UNAIDS on strengthening co-operation. In December 2001 FAO, IFAD and WFP determined to strengthen inter-agency collaboration in developing strategies to combat the threat posed by the HIV/AIDS epidemic to food security, nutrition and rural livelihoods. During that month experts from those organizations and UNAIDS held a technical consultation on means of mitigating the impact of HIV/AIDS on agriculture and rural communities in affected areas.

The Technical Cooperation Department has responsibility for FAO's operational activities, including policy development assistance to member countries; investment support; and the management of activities associated with the development and implementation of country, sub-regional and regional programmes. The Department manages the technical co-operation programme (TCP, which funds 13% of FAO's field programme expenditures), and mobilizes resources.

AGRICULTURE

FAO's Field Programme provides training and technical assistance to enable small farmers to increase crop production, by a number of methods, including improved seeds and fertilizer use, soil conservation and reafforestation, better water resource management, upgrading storage facilities, and improvements in processing and marketing. Governments are advised on the conservation of genetic resources, on improving the supply of seeds, and on crop protection.

Plant protection, weed control and animal health programmes form an important part of FAO's work as farming methods become more intensive, and pests more resistant to control methods. In 1985 the FAO Conference approved an International Code of Conduct on the Distribution and Use of Pesticides, and in 1989 adopted an additional clause concerning 'Prior Informed Consent' (PIC), whereby international shipments of newly banned or restricted pesticides should not proceed without the agreement of importing countries. Under the clause FAO aims to inform governments about the hazards of toxic chemicals and to encourage them to take proper measures to curb trade in highly toxic agrochemicals, while keeping the pesticides industry informed of control actions. In 1996 FAO publicized a new initiative which aimed to increase awareness of, and to promote international action on, obsolete and hazardous stocks of pesticides remaining throughout the world (estimated in 2001 to total some 500,000 metric tons). In September 1998 a new legally-binding treaty on trade in hazardous chemical and pesticides was adopted at an international conference held in Rotterdam, the Netherlands. The so-called Rotterdam Convention required that hazardous chemicals and pesticides banned or severely restricted in at least two countries should not be exported unless explicitly agreed by the importing country. It also identified certain pesticide formulations as too dangerous to be used by farmers in developing countries, and incorporated an obligation that countries halt national production of those hazardous compounds. The treaty was to enter into force on being ratified by 50 signatory states. FAO was co-operating with UNEP to provide an interim secretariat for the Convention. In July 1999 a conference on the Rotterdam Convention, held in Rome, established an Interim Chemical Review Committee with responsibility for recommending the inclusion of chemicals or pesticide formulations in the PIC procedure. By March 2002 the treaty had been ratified by 20 states. A central concept of FAO's plant protection programme is the Integrated Pest Management

(IPM) strategy, which aims to reduce over-reliance on pesticides. IPM principles include biological control methods, such as the introduction of natural predators (including spiders and wasps) to reduce pest infestation, crop rotation and the use of pest-resistant crop varieties. In 1995 FAO initiated a project, at the request of 16 Middle Eastern and North African Governments, to improve the development and use of IPM strategies at a local and national level throughout the region, and to improve their dissemination between the countries. In February 2001 FAO warned that some 30% of pesticides sold in developing countries did not meet internationally accepted quality standards.

In June 1996 representatives of more than 150 governments attending a conference in Leipzig, Germany, organized by FAO, adopted a Global Plan of Action to conserve and improve the use of plant genetic resources, in order to enhance food security throughout the world. The Plan included measures to strengthen the development of plant varieties and to promote the use and availability of local varieties and locally-adapted crops to farmers, in particular following a natural disaster, war or civil conflict. The conservation and sustainable use of plant and animal genetic resources are promoted by FAO's Global System for Plant Genetic Resources, which includes five databases, and the Global Strategy on the Management of Farm Animal Genetic Resources. An FAO programme supports the establishment of gene banks, designed to maintain the world's biological diversity by preserving animal and plant species threatened with extinction. FAO, jointly with UNEP, has published a document listing the current state of global livestock genetic diversity. In November 2001 the FAO Conference adopted the International Treaty on Plant Genetic Resources for Food and Agriculture, which was to provide a framework to ensure access to plant genetic resources and to related knowledge, technologies and funding. The Treaty was to enter into force once it had been ratified by 40 signatory states.

FAO's Joint Division with the International Atomic Energy Agency (IAEA) tests controlled-release formulas of pesticides and herbicides that can limit the amount of agrochemicals needed to protect crops. The Joint FAO-IAEA Division is engaged in exploring biotechnologies and in developing non-toxic fertilizers (especially those that are locally available) and improved strains of food crops (especially from indigenous varieties). In animal production and health, the Joint Division has developed progesterone-measuring and disease-diagnostic kits, thousands of which are delivered to developing countries every year.

An Emergency Prevention System for Transboundary Animal and Plant Pests and Diseases (EMPRES) was established in 1994 to strengthen FAO's activities in the prevention, control and, where possible, eradication of agricultural pests and of highly contagious livestock diseases (which the system categorizes as epidemic diseases of strategic importance, such as rinderpest or foot-and-mouth; diseases requiring tactical attention at international or regional level, e.g. Rift Valley fever; and emerging diseases, e.g. bovine spongiform encephalopathy—BSE). During 1994 EMPRES published guide-lines on all aspects of desert locust monitoring, commissioned an evaluation of recent control efforts and prepared a concept paper on desert locust management. FAO has assumed responsibility for technical leadership and co-ordination of the Global Rinderpest Eradication Campaign, which aims to eradicate the disease by 2010.

In November 1997 FAO initiated a Programme Against African Trypanosomiasis, which aimed to counter the parasitic disease, spread by the tsetse fly, which manifests itself as ngana in cattle and other animals and as sleeping sickness in humans, and is prevalent in almost one-third of Africa.

FAO's organic agriculture programme provides technical assistance and policy advice on the production, certification and trading of organic produce. In July 2001 the FAO/WHO Codex Alimentarius Commission adopted guide-lines on organic livestock production, covering organic breeding methods, the elimination of growth hormones and certain chemicals in veterinary medicines, and the use of good quality organic feed with no meat or bone meal content.

FISHERIES

FAO's Fisheries Department consists of a multi-disciplinary body of experts who are involved in every aspect of fisheries development from coastal surveys, conservation management and use of aquatic genetic resources, improvment of production, processing and storage, to the compilation and analysis of statistics, development of computer databases, improvement of fishing gear, institution building and training. In March 1995 a ministerial meeting of fisheries adopted the Rome Consensus on World Fisheries, which identified a need for immediate action to eliminate overfishing and to rebuild and enhance depleting fish stocks. In November the FAO Conference adopted a Code of Conduct for Responsible Fishing, which incorporated many global fisheries and aquaculture issues (including fisheries resource conservation and development, fish catches, seafood and fish processing, commercialization, trade and research) to promote the sustainable development of the sector.

FAO promotes aquaculture as a valuable source of animal protein, and as an income-generating activity for rural communities. In February 1999 the FAO Committee on Fisheries adopted new international measures, within the framework of the Code of Conduct, in order to reduce over-exploitation of the world's fish resources, as well as plans of action for the conservation and management of sharks and the reduction in the incidental catch of seabirds in longline fisheries. The voluntary measures were endorsed at a ministerial meeting, held in March and attended by representatives of some 126 countries, which issued a declaration to promote the implementation of the Code of Conduct and to achieve sustainable management of fisheries and aquaculture. In February 2000 FAO and the Network of Aquaculture Centres in Asia and the Pacific (NACA) jointly convened a Conference on Aquaculture in the Third Millennium, which was held in Bangkok, Thailand, and attended by participants representing more than 200 governmental and non-governmental organizations. The Conference debated global trends in aquaculture and future policy measures to ensure the sustainable development of the sector. It adopted the Bangkok Declaration and Strategy for Aquaculture Beyond 2000. In December 2001 FAO issued a report based on the technical proceedings of the conference. In March 2001 FAO adopted an international plan of action to address the problem of so-called illegal, unreported and unregulated fishing. In October FAO and the Icelandic Government jointly organized the Reykjavik Conference on Responsible Fisheries in the Marine Ecosystem, which adopted a declaration on pursuing responsible and sustainable fishing activities in the context of ecosystem-based fisheries management (EBFM). EBFM involves determining the boundaries of individual marine ecosystems, and maintaining or rebuilding the habitats and biodiversity of each of these so that all species will be supported at levels of maximum production.

FORESTRY

FAO focuses on the contribution of forestry to food security, on effective and responsible forest management and on maintaining a balance between the economic, ecological and social benefits of forest resources. FAO has helped to develop national forestry programmes and to promote the sustainable development of all types of forest. FAO administers the global Forests, Trees and People Programme, which promotes the sustainable management of tree and forest resources, based on local knowledge and management practices, in order to improve the livelihoods of rural people in developing countries. FAO's Strategic Plan for Forestry was approved in March 1999; its main objectives were to maintain the environmental diversity of forests, to realise the economic potential of forests and trees within a sustainable framework, and to expand access to information on forestry. During 1997 FAO helped to organize the Eleventh World Forestry Congress, which was held in Antalya, Turkey, in October.

PROCESSING AND MARKETING

An estimated 20% of all food harvested is lost before it can be consumed. FAO helps to reduce immediate post-harvest losses through the introduction of improved processing methods and storage systems. It also advises on the distribution and marketing of agricultural produce and on the selection and preparation of foods for optimum nutrition. Many of these activities form part of wider rural development projects. FAO continues to favour the elimination of export subsidies and related discriminatory practices, such as protectionist measures that hamper international trade in agricultural commodities. FAO has organized regional workshops and national projects in order to help member states to implement new World Trade Organization regulations, in particular with regard to agricultural policy, intellectual property rights, sanitary and phytosanitary measures, technical barriers to trade and the international standards of the Codex Alimentarius. FAO evaluates new market trends and helps to develop improved plant and animal quarantine procedures. In November 1997 the FAO Conference adopted new guide-lines on surveillance and export certification systems in order to harmonize plant quarantine standards. In August 1999 FAO announced the establishment of a new forum, PhAction, to promote post-harvest research and the development of effective post-harvest services and infrastructure.

ENVIRONMENT

At the UN Conference on Environment and Development, held in Rio de Janeiro in June 1992, FAO participated in several working parties and supported the adoption of Agenda 21, a programme of activities to promote sustainable development. FAO was subsequently designated as the UN agency responsible for the chapters of Agenda 21 concerned with water resources, forests, fragile mountain ecosystems and sustainable agriculture and rural development. FAO was designated by the UN General Assembly as the lead agency for co-ordinating the International Year of Mountains (2002), which aimed to raise awareness of mountain ecosystems and to promote the conservation and sustainable development of mountainous regions.

NUTRITION

In December 1992 an International Conference on Nutrition was held in Rome, administered jointly by FAO and WHO. The Conference approved a World Declaration on Nutrition and a Plan of Action, aimed at promoting efforts to combat malnutrition as a development priority. Since the conference, more than 100 countries have formulated national plans of action for nutrition, many of which were based on existing development plans such as comprehensive food security initiatives, national poverty alleviation programmes and action plans to attain the targets set by the World Summit for Children in September 1990. In January 2001 a joint team of FAO and WHO experts issued a report concerning the allergenicity of foods derived from biotechnology (i.e. genetically modified—GM foods). In July the Codex Alimentarius Commission agreed the first global principles for assessing the safety of GM foods, and approved a series of maximum levels of environmental contaminants in food. In April 2002 FAO and WHO announced a joint review of their food standards operations, including the activities of the Codex Alimentarius Commission.

FOOD SECURITY

FAO's food security policy aims to encourage the production of adequate food supplies, to maximize stability in the flow of supplies, and to ensure access on the part of those who need them. FAO's Special Programme for Food Security (SPFS), which was initiated in 1994, was designed to assist target countries, i.e. low-income countries with a food deficit, to increase food production and productivity as rapidly as possible. This was to be achieved primarily through the widespread adoption by farmers of available improved production technologies, with emphasis on areas of high potential. FAO was actively involved in the formulation of a Plan of Action on food security, adopted at the World Food Summit in November 1996, and was to be responsible for monitoring and promoting its implementation. In March 1999 FAO signed agreements with IFAD and the World Food Programme (WFP, q.v.), in order to increase co-operation under the framework of the SPFS. At May 2002 82 countries were categorized as 'low-income food-deficit', of which more than one-half were in Africa. The SPFS was operational in 69 countries. The SPFS promotes South-South co-operation to improve food security and the exchange of knowledge and experience. In 2002 26 bilateral co-operation agreements were in force.

FAO's Global Information and Early Warning System (GIEWS), which became operational in 1975, maintains a database on and monitors the crop and food outlook at global, regional, national and sub-national levels in order to detect emerging food supply difficulties and disasters and to ensure rapid intervention in countries experiencing food supply shortages. It publishes regular reports on the weather conditions and crop prospects in sub-Saharan Africa and in the Sahel region and issues special alerts which describe the situation in countries or sub-regions experiencing food difficulties and recommends an appropriate international response. In October 1999 FAO published the first *State of Food Insecurity in the World*, based on data compiled by a new Food Insecurity and Vulnerability Information and Mapping Systems programme. In April 2002 GIEWS issued an alert on the rapidly deteriorating food situation in the West Bank and Gaza Strip.

FAO INVESTMENT CENTRE

The Investment Centre was established in 1964 to help countries prepare viable investment projects that would attract external financing. The Centre focuses its evaluation of projects on two fundamental concerns: the promotion of sustainable activities for land management, forestry development and environmental protection; and the alleviation of rural poverty. In 2000–01 90 projects were approved, representing a total investment of some US $3,700m.

EMERGENCY RELIEF

FAO works to rehabilitate agricultural production following natural and man-made disasters by providing emergency seeds, tools, and technical and other assistance. New projects approved by FAO's Special Relief Operations Service in 2001 included emergency assistance to contain the spread of Rift Valley Fever in Iraq. Jointly with the United Nations, FAO is responsible for WFP (see below), which provides emergency food supplies and food aid in support of development projects.

INFORMATION

FAO functions as an information centre, collecting, analysing, interpreting and disseminating information through various media. It issues regular statistical reports, commodity studies, and technical manuals in local languages (see list of publications below). Other materials produced by the FAO include information booklets, reference papers, reports of meetings, training manuals and audiovisuals.

FAO's internet-based interactive World Agricultural Information Centre (WAICENT) offers access to agricultural publications, technical documentation, codes of conduct, data, statistics and multi-media resources. FAO compiles and co-ordinates an extensive range of international databases on agriculture, fisheries, forestry, food and statistics, the most important of these being AGRIS (the International Information System for the Agricultural Sciences and Technology) and CARIS (the Current Agricultural Research Information System). Statistical databases include the GLOBEFISH databank and electronic library, FISHDAB (the Fisheries Statistical Database), FORIS (Forest Resources Information System), and GIS (the Geographic Information System). In addition, FAOSTAT provides access to updated figures in six agriculture-related topics.

FAO REGIONAL COMMISSIONS

Commission for Controlling the Desert Locust in the Near East: f. 1965 to carry out all possible measures to control plagues of the desert locust within the region and to reduce crop damage. Mems: 13 states.

Commission for Controlling the Desert Locust in North-West Africa: f. 1971 to promote research on control of the desert locust. Mems: 4 states.

General Fisheries Council for the Mediterranean—GFCM: f. 1952 to develop aquatic resources, to encourage and co-ordinate research in the fishing and allied industries, to assemble and publish information, and to recommend the standardization of scientific equipment, techniques and nomenclature. Mems: 19 states.

Near East Forestry Commission: f. 1953 to advise on formulation of forest policy and review and co-ordinate its implementation throughout the region; to exchange information and advise on technical problems. Mems: 20 states.

Near East Regional Commission on Agriculture: f. 1983 to conduct periodic reviews of agricultural problems in the region; to promote the formulation and implementation of regional and national policies and programmes for improving production of crops and livestock; to strengthen the production and management of crops, livestock, supporting services and research; to promote the transfer of technology and regional technical co-operation; and to provide guidance on training and manpower development. Mems: 15 states.

Near East Regional Economic and Social Policy Commission: f. 1983 to review developments relating to food, agriculture and food security; to recommend policies on agrarian reform and rural development; and to review and exchange information on food and nutrition policies and on agricultural planning. Mems: 15 states.

Regional Commission on Land and Water Use in the Near East: f. 1967 to review the current situation with regard to land and water use in the region; to identify the main problems concerning the development of land and water resources which require research and study and to consider other related matters. Mems: 21 states.

Finance

FAO's Regular Programme, which is financed by contributions from the member governments, covers the cost of FAO's Secretariat, its Technical Co-operation Programme (TCP) and part of the cost of several special action programmes. The budget for the two years 2002–03 totalled US $651.8m.. Much of FAO's technical assistance programme is funded from extra-budgetary sources. The single largest contributor is the United Nations Development Programme (UNDP), which in 1999 accounted for $26m., or 8.5% of field project expenditures. More important are the trust funds that come mainly from donor countries and international financing institutions. In 1999 they totalled $228m., or 76.5% of field project expenditures. FAO's contribution under the TCP (FAO's regular budgetary funds for the Field Programme) was $39m., or 13% of field project expenditures in that year, while the Organization's contribution under the Special Programme for Food Security was $5m., or some 2% of the total $298m. In 2001 total field programme expenditure amounted to $367m.

World Food Programme—WFP

Address: Via Cesare Giulio Viola 68, Parco dei Medici, 00148 Rome, Italy.

Telephone: (06) 651-31; **fax:** (06) 651-328-40; **e-mail:** wfpinfo@wfp.org; **internet:** www.wfp.org.

WFP, which became operational in 1963, is the principal food aid agency of the UN. It aims to alleviate acute hunger by providing emergency relief following natural or man-made humanitarian disasters, to eradicate chronic undernourishment, and to support social development. Priority is given to vulnerable groups, such as children and pregnant women. During 2001 WFP benefited some 77m. people world-wide, of whom 20m. received aid through development projects,

43m. through emergency operations, and 14m. through rehabilitation programmes. Total food deliveries in that year amounted to 4.2m. metric tons in 82 countries.

Through its development activities, WFP aims to alleviate poverty in developing countries by promoting self-reliant families and communities. Food is supplied, for example, as an incentive in labour-intensive projects which provide employment and strengthen self-help capacity. WFP supports activities to boost agricultural production, to rehabilitate and improve local infrastructure, particularly transport systems, and to encourage education, training and health programmes. Some WFP projects are intended to alleviate the effects of structural adjustment programmes (particularly programmes which involve reductions in public expenditure and in subsidies for basic foods). During 2001 WFP supported 67 development projects and 30 'country programmes' in 55 countries world-wide, for which operational expenditure totalled US $225m. School feeding projects benefited 15m. children during that year. In 2001 WFP initiated a new Global School Feeding Campaign to strengthen international co-operation to expand educational opportunities for poor children and to improve the quality of the teaching environment.

In the early 1990s there was a substantial shift in the balance between emergency and development assistance provided by WFP, owing to the growing needs of refugees and displaced persons and victims of drought and other natural disasters. In addition, there was a noticeable increase in aid given to those in need as a result of civil war, compared with commitments for natural disaster victims. Following a comprehensive evaluation of its activities, WFP became increasingly focused on linking its relief and development activities to provide a continuum between short-term relief and longer-term rehabilitation and development. In order to achieve this objective, WFP has aimed to integrate elements that strengthen disaster mitigation into development projects, including soil conservation, reafforestation, irrigation infrastructure, and transport construction and rehabilitation, and to promote capacity-building elements within relief operations, e.g. training, income-generating activities and environmental protection measures. A new programme of emergency response training was inaugurated in 2000, while security concerns for personnel was incorporated as a new element into all general planning and training activities. In 1999 WFP adopted a new Food Aid and Development policy, which aims to use food assistance both to cover immediate requirements and to create conditions conducive to enhancing the long-term food security of vulnerable populations. During that year protracted relief and recovery operations (PRROs) were introduced, where the emphasis is on fostering stability, rehabilitation and long-term development after an emergency. In these operations, which are undertaken in collaboration with UNHCR and other international agencies, WFP is responsible for mobilizing basic food commodities and for related transport, handling and storage costs. The key elements of WFP's emergency response capacity are its strategic stores of food and logistics equipment, stand-by arrangements to enable the rapid deployment of personnel, communications and other essential equipment, and the Augmented Logistics Intervention Team for Emergencies (ALITE), which undertakes capacity assessments and contingency-planning. In 2000 a new UN Humanitarian Response Depot was opened in Brindisi, Italy, under the direction of WFP experts, for the storage of essential rapid response equipment. In that year WFP also led efforts, undertaken with other UN humanitarian agencies, for the design and application of local UN Joint Logistics Centre facilities, which aimed to co-ordinate resources in an emergency situation.

In 2001 WFP operational expenditure in the Middle East and North Africa amounted to an estimated US $54.0m. (3% of total operational expenditure in that year), including $3.0m. for emergency relief operations, $14.3m. for PRROs, and $12.2m. for agricultural, rural and human resource development projects. Examples of WFP projects under way in early 2002 included support for Afghan and Iraqi refugees in Iran, land improvement activities in Jordan, the provision of emergency food assistance to drought-affected farmers in Syria, the provision of emergency food assistance and land improvement support for communities affected by insecurity in the West Bank and Gaza, and food assistance and support for girls' education in Yemen. In addition, WFP was implementing a PRRO in Iraq aimed at supplementing the general ration distribution system provided for under UN Security Council Resolution 986, with a particular emphasis on providing vulnerable groups such as children and hospital patients with essential micronutrients. In 2000 WFP, FAO and WHO issued a report which determined that some 800,000 Iraqi children under the age of five were seriously malnourished.

WFP Executive Director: James T. Morris (USA).

FAO Publications

Animal Health Yearbook.
Commodity Review and Outlook (annually).

Environment and Energy Bulletin.
Fertilizer Yearbook.
Food Crops and Shortages (6 a year).
Food Outlook (5 a year).
Plant Protection Bulletin (quarterly).
Production Yearbook.
Quarterly Bulletin of Statistics.
The State of Food and Agriculture (annually).
The State of Food Insecurity in the World (annually).

The State of World Fisheries and Aquaculture (every 2 years).
The State of the World's Forests (every two years).
Technical Co-operation Among Developing Countries Newsletter.
Trade Yearbook.
Unasylva (quarterly).
World Animal Review (two a year).
World Watch List for Domestic Animal Diversity.
Yearbook of Fishery Statistics.
Yearbook of Forest Products.
Commodity reviews; studies; manuals.

International Bank for Reconstruction and Development—IBRD, and International Development Association—IDA (World Bank)

Address: 1818 H St, NW, Washington, DC 20433, USA.

Telephone: (202) 477-1234; **fax:** (202) 477-6391; **e-mail:** pic@worldbank.org; **internet:** www.worldbank.org.

The IBRD was established in December 1945. Initially it was concerned with post-war reconstruction in Europe; since then its aim has been to assist the economic development of member nations by making loans where private capital is not available on reasonable terms to finance productive investments. Loans are made either direct to governments, or to private enterprises with the guarantee of their governments. The 'World Bank', as it is commonly known, comprises the IBRD and the International Development Association (IDA), which was founded in 1960. The affiliated group of institutions, comprising the IBRD, the IDA, the International Finance Corporation (IFC, q.v.), the Multilateral Investment Guarantee Agency (MIGA, q.v.) and the International Centre for Settlement of Investment Disputes (ICSID) is referred to as the World Bank Group. Only members of the International Monetary Fund (IMF, q.v.) may be considered for membership in the Bank. Subscriptions to the capital stock of the Bank are based on each member's quota in the IMF, which is designed to reflect the country's relative economic strength. Voting rights are related to shareholdings.

Organization

(September 2002)

Officers and staff of the IBRD serve concurrently as officers and staff in the IDA. The World Bank has offices in New York, Paris (for Europe), Brussels, Frankfurt, Geneva, London and Tokyo, as well as in more than 100 countries of operation. Country Directors are located in some 28 country offices.

BOARD OF GOVERNORS

The Board of Governors consists of one Governor appointed by each member nation. Typically, a Governor is the country's finance minister, central bank governor, or a minister or an official of comparable rank. The Board normally meets once a year.

EXECUTIVE DIRECTORS

The general operations of the World Bank are conducted by a Board of 24 Executive Directors. Five Directors are appointed by the five members having the largest number of shares of capital stock, and the rest are elected by the Governors representing the other members. The President of the Bank is Chairman of the Board.

OFFICERS

President and Chairman of Executive Directors: JAMES D. WOL-FENSOHN (USA).

Vice-President, Middle East and North Africa Region: JEAN-LOUIS SARBIB.

Activities

FINANCIAL OPERATIONS

IBRD loans are usually for a period of 20 years or less. Loans are made to governments, or must be guaranteed by the government concerned. IDA assistance is aimed at the poorer developing countries (i.e. those with a gross national product per head of less than US $885 were eligible for assistance in 2000/01). Under IDA lending conditions,

credits can be extended to countries whose balance of payments could not sustain the burden of repayment required for IBRD loans. Terms are more favourable than those provided by the IBRD; credits are for a period of 35–40 years, with a 'grace' period of 10 years, and carry no interest charges.

The IBRD's capital is derived from members' subscriptions to capital shares, the calculation of which is based on their quotas in the IMF (q.v.). At 30 June 2001 the total subscribed capital of the IBRD was US $189,505m., of which the paid-in portion was $11,476m. (6.1%); the remainder is subject to call if required. Most of the IBRD's lendable funds come from its borrowing in world capital markets, and also from its retained earnings and the flow of repayments on its loans. Bank loans carry a variable interest rate, rather than a rate fixed at the time of borrowing.

IDA's development resources, consisting of members' subscriptions and supplementary resources (additional subscriptions and contributions), are replenished periodically by contributions from the more affluent member countries. In March 1996 representatives of more than 30 donor countries concluded negotiations for the 11th replenishment of IDA funds (and for a one-year interim fund), to finance the period July 1996–June 1999. New contributions over the three-year period were to amount to US $11,000m., while total funds available for lending, including past donor contributions, repayments of IDA credits and the World Bank's contributions, were to amount to $22,000m. In November 1998 representatives of 39 donor countries agreed to provide $11,600m. for the 12th replenishment of IDA funds, enabling total lending to amount to an estimated $20,500m. in the period July 1999–June 2002. The new IDA-12 resources were to be directed towards the following objectives: investing in people; promoting good governance; promoting broad-based growth; and protecting the environment. Discussions on the 13th replenishment of IDA resources were undertaken in 2001/02, and for the first time involved representatives of borrowing countries, civil society and other public groups. A final commitment, providing for some $23,000m. in resources for the period 1 July 2002–30 June 2005, was concluded in early July 2002.

During the year ending 30 June 2001 US $507.5m., or 3% of World Bank assistance approved, was for the Middle East and North Africa (excluding Turkey), compared with $920.1m. in the previous financial year. Of the total approved in 2000/01, $152.3m. was in the form of IDA credits and $355.2m. in IBRD loans. An additional $36.1m. was provided by the Trust Fund for Gaza and the West Bank. Some 32% of total Bank lending for the region was allocated to public sector management, 29% to infrastructure projects and 17% to human development activities.

The World Bank's primary objectives are the achievement of sustainable economic growth and the reduction of poverty in developing countries. In March 1997 the Board of Executive Directors endorsed a 'Strategic Compact', providing for a programme of reforms, to be implemented over a period of 30 months, to increase the effectiveness of the Bank in achieving its central objective of poverty reduction. The reforms included greater decentralization of decision-making, and investment in front-line operations, enhancing the administration of loans, and improving access to information and co-ordination of Bank activities through a knowledge management system comprising four thematic networks: the Human Development Network; the Environmentally and Socially Sustainable Development Network; the Finance, Private Sector and Infrastructure Development Network; and the Poverty Reduction and Economic Management Network. In 2000/01 the Bank adopted a new two-year Strategic Framework which emphasized two essential approaches for Bank support: strengthening the investment climate and prospects for sustainable development in a country, and supporting investment in the poor. In September 2001 the Bank announced that it was to join the UN as a full partner in implementing the so-called Millennium Development Goals, and was to make them central to its development agenda. The objectives, which were approved by governments attending a special session of the UN General Assembly in September 2000, included a reduction by 50% in the number of people with an income of less than US $1 a day and those suffering from hunger and lack of safe drinking water by 2015. The Bank was closely involved in preparations for the International Conference on Financing for Development, which was held in Monterrey, Mexico, in March 2002, and incorporated discussions on achieving the Millennium Goals.

The Bank's efforts to reduce poverty comprise two main elements: the compiling of country-specific assessments and the formulation of country assistance strategies (CASs) to review and guide the Bank's country programmes. Since August 1998 the Bank has published CASs, with the approval of the governments concerned. In 1998/99 the Bank's Executive Directors endorsed a Comprehensive Development Framework (CDF) to effect a new approach to development assistance based on partnerships and country responsibility, with an emphasis on the interdependence of the social, structural, human, governmental, economic and environmental elements of development. The Framework, which aimed to enhance the overall effectiveness of development assistance, was formulated after a series of consultative meetings, organized by the Bank and attended by representatives of governments, donor agencies, financial institutions, non-governmental organizations, the private sector and academics.

In December 1999 the Bank introduced a new approach to implementing the principles of the CDF, as part of its strategy to enhance the debt relief scheme for heavily indebted poor countries (see below). Applicant countries were requested to formulate a national strategy to reduce poverty, to be presented in the form of a Poverty Reduction Strategy Paper (PRSP). In cases where there might be some delay in issuing a full PRSP, it was permissible for a country to submit a less detailed 'interim' PRSP (I-PRSP) in order to secure the preliminary qualification for debt relief. During 2000/01 32 countries issued full and interim PRSPs for consideration by the Bank and IMF, compared with 12 in the previous year. During that year the Bank introduced a new Poverty Reduction Support Credit to help low-income countries to implement the policy and institutional reforms outlined in their PRSP. The first credits were approved for Uganda and Viet Nam in May and June respectively. It was envisaged that in 2001/02 each CAS presented for an IDA country would be based on a PRSP. In January 2002 a PRSP public review conference, attended by more than 200 representatives of donor agencies, civil society groups, and developing country organizations was held as part of an ongoing review of the scheme by the Bank and the IMF.

The Bank has played a major role in promoting and co-ordinating international efforts in support of the Middle East peace process and in enhancing economic development throughout the region. Following agreement, in May 1994, on the implementation of the Declaration of Principles between Palestine and Israel, the Bank issued a report outlining an investment programme to assist Palestine in its transitional period to autonomous government: the Emergency Assistance Programme for the Occupied Territories was to cover a three-year period, with an investment budget of US $1,200m. pledged by the international community. Under the Programme, a Trust Fund for Gaza and the West Bank was established, in order to finance, on IDA terms, projects for the reconstruction and improvement of infrastructure, in particular education and health services. The Bank acts as the secretariat for the *Ad Hoc* Liaison Committee for the West Bank and Gaza, and for the joint Israeli-Jordan steering committee for the Jordan Rift Valley Development Programme. The Bank hosts annual meetings of a Consultative Group for the West Bank and Gaza, attended by donor governments and institutions, which considers projects for funding and reviews their implementation.

In September 1996 the World Bank/IMF Development Committee endorsed a joint initiative to assist heavily indebted poor countries (HIPCs) to reduce their debt burden to a sustainable level, in order to make more resources available for poverty reduction and economic growth. A new Trust Fund was established by the World Bank in November to finance the initiative. The Fund, consisting of an initial allocation of US $500m. from the IBRD surplus and other contributions from multilateral creditors, was to be administered by IDA. Of the 41 HIPCs identified by the Bank, only one country, Yemen, was in the Middle East and North Africa region. In September 1999 the World Bank and IMF reached an agreement on an enhanced HIPC scheme to allow more countries to benefit from the initiative, to accelerate the process by which a country may qualify for assistance and to enhance the effectiveness of debt relief. Additional revenue was to be generated through the revaluation of a percentage of IMF gold reserves. Under the enhanced initiative it was agreed that, during the initial phase of the process to ensure suitability for debt relief, each applicant country should formulate a PRSP, and should demonstrate prudent financial management in the implementation of the strategy

for at least one year, with support from the IDA and IMF. At the pivotal 'decision point' of the process, having thus developed and successfully applied the poverty reduction strategy, applicant countries still deemed to have an unsustainable level of debt were to qualify for interim debt relief from the IMF and IDA, as well as relief on highly concessional terms from other official bilateral creditors and multilateral institutions. During the ensuing 'interim period' countries were required successfully to implement further economic and social development reforms, as a final demonstration of suitability for securing full debt relief at the 'completion point' of the scheme.

TECHNICAL ASSISTANCE

The provision of technical assistance to member countries is a major component of Bank activities. The economic and sector work (ESW) undertaken by the Bank is the vehicle for considerable technical assistance. In addition, project loans and credits may include funds designated specifically for feasibility studies, resource surveys, management or planning advice, and training. The Economic Development Institute has become one of the most important of the Bank's activities in technical assistance. It provides training in national economic management and project analysis for government officials at the middle and upper levels of responsibility. It also runs overseas courses aiming to build up local training capability, and administers a graduate scholarship programme.

In 1992 the Bank established an Institutional Development Fund (IDF) to provide rapid, small-scale financial assistance, to a maximum value of US $500,000, for capacity-building initiatives.

ECONOMIC RESEARCH AND STUDIES

In the 1990s the World Bank's research, conducted by its own research staff, was increasingly concerned with providing information to reinforce the Bank's expanding advisory role to developing countries. Consequently the principal areas of current research focus on issues such as maintaining sustainable growth while protecting the environment and the poorest sectors of society, encouraging the development of the private sector, and reducing and decentralizing government activities. The Bank, together with UNDP, UNEP and the FAO, sponsors the Consultative Group on International Agricultural Research (CGIAR), which was formed in 1971 to raise financial support for research on improving crops and animal production in developing countries. CGIAR supports 16 research centres.

CO-OPERATION WITH OTHER ORGANIZATIONS

The World Bank co-operates closely with other UN bodies through consultations, meetings, and joint activities; co-operation with UNDP and WHO, in their programmes to improve health, nutrition and sanitation, is especially important. It collaborates with the IMF in implementing economic adjustment programmes in developing countries. The Bank holds regular consultations with the European Community and OECD on development issues, and the Bank-NGO Committee provides an annual forum for discussion with non-governmental organizations (NGOs). The Bank chairs meetings of donor governments and organizations for the co-ordination of aid to particular countries. The Bank also conducts co-financing and aid co-ordination projects with official aid agencies, export credit agencies and commercial banks.

In 1997 a Partnerships Group was established to strengthen the Bank's work with development institutions, representatives of civil society and the private sector. The Group established a new Development Grant Facility, which became operational in October, to support partnership initiatives and to co-ordinate all of the Bank's grant-making activities. Also in 1997 the Bank, in partnership with the IMF, UNCTAD, UNDP, the World Trade Organization (WTO) and International Trade Commission, established an Integrated Framework for Trade-related Assistance to Least Developed Countries, at the request of the WTO, to assist those countries to integrate into the global trading system and improve basic trading capabilities. Strengthening co-operation with external partners was a fundamental element of the Comprehensive Development Framework, which was adopted in 1998/99 (see above). In March 2000 the Bank signed a Memorandum of Understanding with the African Development Bank providing for a strategic partnership between the two institutions, with a particular emphasis on capacity-building.

In June 1995 the World Bank joined other international donors (including regional development banks, other UN bodies, Canada, France, the Netherlands and the USA) in establishing a Consultative Group to Assist the Poorest (CGAP), which was to channel funds to the most needy through 'grass-roots' agencies. An initial credit of approximately US $200m. was committed by the donors. The Bank manages the CGAP Secretariat, which is responsible for the administration of external funding and for the evaluation and approval of project financing. In addition, the CGAP provides training and information services on microfinance for policy-makers and practitioners.

The Bank supports regional research networks and learning partnerships, for example the Mediterranean Development Forum, which brings together participants from government, academia and the private sector to discuss issues such as globalization, social protection, partnerships with civil society, and employment generation. In October 1996 the World Bank and the EU hosted an international conference, held in Istanbul, Turkey, to consider the privatization process in the Middle East and North Africa region and the participation of the private sector in major infrastructure projects. In the following month, at a regional economic 'summit' meeting, convened in Cairo, Egypt, the Bank declared its willingness to support the involvement of the private sector by reducing the perceived investment risks associated with such projects. In May 1997 the Bank sponsored a conference, held in Marrakech, Morocco, which aimed to promote economic development and regional competitiveness.

The Bank is a lead organization in providing reconstruction assistance following natural disasters or conflicts, usually in collaboration with other UN agencies or international organizations, and through special trust funds.

EVALUATION

The Bank's Operations Evaluation Department is an independent unit within the World Bank, which studies and publishes the results of projects after a loan has been fully disbursed, so as to identify problems and possible improvements in future activities. Internal auditing is also carried out, to monitor the effectiveness of the Bank's operations and management.

In September 1993 the Bank's Board of Executive Directors agreed to establish an Independent Inspection Panel, consistent with the Bank's objective of improving project implementation and accountability. The Panel, which became operational in September 1994, was to conduct independent investigations and report on complaints concerning the design, appraisal and implementation of development projects supported by the Bank. By the end of 2001 the panel had received 22 formal requests for inspection, and had undertaken 12 investigations.

IBRD INSTITUTIONS

World Bank Institute—WBI: founded in March 1999 by merger of the Bank's Learning and Leadership Centre, previously responsible for internal staff training, and the Economic Development Institute (EDI), which had been established in 1955 to train government officials concerned with development programmes and policies. The WBI aims to emphasize the Bank's priority areas through the provision of training courses and seminars relating to poverty, crisis response, good governance and anti-corruption strategies. The WBI also took the lead in co-ordinating a process of consultation and dialogue with researchers and other representatives of civil society to examine poverty for the 2000/01 *World Development Report*. During 1999/2000 the WBI expanded its programmes through distance learning, global knowledge networks, and use of new technologies. Under the EDI a World Links for Development programme was initiated to connect schools in developing countries with partner establishments in industrialized nations via the internet. A new initiative, Global Development Learning Network, aimed to expand access to information and learning opportunities through the internet, videoconferences and organized exchanges. Vice-Pres. FRANNIE LÉAUTIER (Tanzania/France).

International Centre for Settlement of Investment Disputes—ICSID: founded in 1966 under the Convention of the Settlement of Investment Disputes between States and Nationals of Other States. The Convention was designed to encourage the growth of private foreign investment for economic development, by creating the possibility, always subject to the consent of both parties, for a Contracting State and a foreign investor who is a national of another Contracting State to settle any legal dispute that might arise out of such an investment by conciliation and/or arbitration before an impartial, international forum. The governing body of the Centre is its Administrative Council, composed of one representative of each Contracting State, all of whom have equal voting power. The President of the World Bank is (*ex officio*) the non-voting Chairman of the Administrative Council.

At March 2002 134 states had ratified the Convention to become ICSID Contracting States. At the end of 2001 the number of cases registered with the Centre totalled 95. Sec.-Gen. KO-YUNG TUNG (Japan).

Publications

Abstracts of Current Studies: The World Bank Research Program (annually).

Annual Report on Operations Evaluation.

Annual Report on Portfolio Performance.

Global Development Finance (annually, also on CD-Rom and online).

Global Economic Prospects (annually).

ICSID Annual Report.

News from ICSID (2 a year).

Poverty Reduction Strategies Newsletter (quarterly).

Research News (quarterly).

Staff Working Papers.

Transition (every 2 months).

World Bank Annual Report.

World Bank Atlas (annually).

World Bank Economic Review (3 a year).

The World Bank and the Environment (annually).

World Bank Research Observer (2 a year).

World Development Indicators (annually, also on CD-Rom and online).

World Development Report (annually, also on CD-Rom).

WORLD BANK OPERATIONS IN THE MIDDLE EAST AND NORTH AFRICA

IBRD Loans Approved, July 2000–June 2001 (US $ million)

Country	Purpose	Amount
Algeria	Energy and mining technical assistance loan	18.0
	Budget systems modernization project	23.7
Jordan	Public sector reform loan I	120.0
Lebanon . . .	Community development project	20.0
Morocco . . .	Information infrastructure sector development loan	65.0
	Irrigation-based community development project	32.6
Tunisia	Agricultural support services project	21.3
	Cultural heritage project	17.0
	Transport sector investment project	37.6
Total		355.2

IDA Credits Approved, July 2000–June 2001 (US $ million)

Country	Purpose	Amount
Djibouti . . .	School access and improvement programme	10.0
Yemen . . .	Rural access programme	45.0
	Rural water supply and sanitation project	20.0
	Basic education expansion project	56.0
	Irrigation improvement project	21.3
Total		152.3

Source: *World Bank Annual Report 2001.*

International Finance Corporation—IFC

Address: 2121 Pennsylvania Ave, NW, Washington, DC 20433, USA.

Telephone: (202) 473-7711; **fax:** (202) 974-4384; **e-mail:** information@ifc.org; **internet:** www.ifc.org/.

IFC was founded in 1956 as an affiliate of the World Bank to stimulate economic growth in developing countries by financing private-sector investments, mobilizing capital in international financial markets, and providing technical assistance and advice to governments and businesses.

Organization

(September 2002)

IFC is a separate legal entity in the World Bank Group. Executive Directors of the World Bank also serve as Directors of IFC. The President of the World Bank is, *ex officio*, Chairman of the IFC Board of Directors, which has appointed him President of IFC. Subject to his overall supervision, the day-to-day operations of IFC are conducted by its staff under the direction of the Executive Vice-President.

PRINCIPAL OFFICERS

President: JAMES D. WOLFENSOHN (USA).
Executive Vice-President: PETER L. WOICKE (Germany).

REGIONAL MISSION

The Middle East and North Africa: World Trade Center, 1191 Corniche en-Nil, 12th Floor, Cairo, Egypt; tel. (2) 579-5353; fax (2) 579-2211; Resident Dir SAMI HADDAD.

Activities

IFC aims to promote economic development in developing member countries by assisting the growth of private enterprise and effective capital markets. It finances private sector projects, through loans, the purchase of equity, quasi-equity products, and risk management services, and assists governments to create conditions that stimulate the flow of domestic and foreign private savings and investment. IFC also mobilizes additional resources from other financial institutions, in particular through syndicated loans, thus providing access to international capital markets. IFC provides a range of advisory services to help to improve the investment climate in developing countries and offers technical assistance to private enterprises and governments.

IFC's authorized capital is US $2,450.0m. At 30 June 2001 IFC's paid-in capital was $2,360m. The World Bank is the principal source of borrowed funds, but IFC also borrows from private capital markets. In 2000/01 project financing approved amounted to $5,357m. for 240 projects, compared with $5,846m. for 259 projects in the previous year. Of the total approved, $3,742m. was for IFC's own account, while $1,615m. was used in loan syndications and underwriting of securities issues and investment funds by more than 100 participant banks and institutional investors. Generally, the IFC limits its financing to less than 25% of the total cost of a project, but may take up to a 35% stake in a venture (although never as a majority shareholder).

During the year ending 30 June 2001 IFC approved total financing of US $961m. for 15 projects in the Middle East and North Africa, compared with $85m. in the previous year. IFC activities were concerned with the development of infrastructure, for example power projects in Egypt, the financial sector and services for small and medium-sized enterprises, including investment in a regional trade finance facility, and support for new sectors and businesses, for example financing of an irrigation technology company in Syria and investment in a consulting and software development business in Egypt.

IFC administers, jointly with the IBRD, the Foreign Investment Advisory Service (FIAS), which provides advice to governments on attracting foreign investment and strengthening national investment frameworks. In addition, the Technical Assistance Trust Funds Program (TATF) manages resources contributed by various governments and agencies to provide finance for feasibility studies, project identification studies and other types of technical assistance relating to project preparation. In 1999/2000 IFC and the World bank combined their advisory services to create the Private Sector Advisory Services. FIAS was to operate within the framework of the new unit, alongside a Corporate Finance Services facility, which supports private-sector involvement in state-owned and -operated enterprises.

Publications

Annual Report.
Emerging Stock Markets Factbook (annually).
Impact (quarterly).
Lessons of Experience (series).
Results on the Ground (series).
Review of Small Businesses (annually)
Discussion papers and technical documents.

Multilateral Investment Guarantee Agency—MIGA

Address: 1818 H Street, NW, Washington, DC 20433, USA.
Telephone: (202) 473-6163; **fax:** (202) 522-2630; **internet:** www.miga.org/.

MIGA was founded in 1988, as an affiliate of the World Bank, to encourage the flow of foreign direct investment to, and among, developing member countries, through the provision of political risk insurance and investment marketing services to foreign investors and host governments, respectively.

Organization

(September 2002)

MIGA is legally and financially separate from the World Bank. It is supervised by a Council of Governors (comprising one Governor and one Alternate of each member country) and an elected Board of Directors (of no less than 12 members).

President: JAMES D. WOLFENSOHN (USA).
Executive Vice-President: MOTOMICHI IKAWA (Japan).

Activities

The convention establishing MIGA took effect in April 1988. Authorized capital amounted to US $1,082m. In April 1998 MIGA's

Board of Directors approved an increase in MIGA's capital base. A grant of $150m. was transferred from the IBRD as part of the package, while the capital increase (totalling $700m. callable capital and $150m. paid-in capital) was approved by MIGA's Council of Governors in April 1999. At 30 June 2001 total subscriptions to the capital stock amounted to $1,438m., of which $279m. was paid-in.

MIGA guarantees eligible investments against losses resulting from non-commercial risks, under four main categories:

transfer risk resulting from host government restrictions on currency conversion and transfer;

risk of loss resulting from legislative or administrative actions of the host government;

repudiation by the host government of contracts with investors in cases in which the investor has no access to a competent forum;

the risk of armed conflict and civil unrest.

Before guaranteeing any investment MIGA must ensure that it is commercially viable, contributes to the development process and will not be harmful to the environment. In 1998/99 MIGA and IFC appointed the first Compliance Advisor and Ombudsman to consider the concerns of local communities directly affected by MIGA or IFC sponsored projects. In February 1999 the Board of Directors approved an increase in the amount of political risk insurance available for each project, from US $75m. to $200m.

During the year to June 2001 MIGA issued 66 investment guarantee contracts for 46 projects in 28 countries, with a value of

US \$2,000m. The amount of direct investment associated with the contracts totalled approximately \$5,200m., bringing the total estimated investment facilitated since 1988 to \$41,200m.

MIGA also provides policy and advisory services to promote foreign investment in developing countries and in transitional economies, and to disseminate information on investment opportunities. In 1998 MIGA sponsored a special conference, entitled 'Safeguarding Investment in the West Bank and Gaza'. In June 1999 MIGA issued its first guarantee contract, valued at US \$5m., under a Trust Fund which had been established in 1997 to promote foreign investment in the West Bank and Gaza. In October 1995 MIGA established a new network on investment opportunities, which connected investment promotion agencies (IPAs) throughout the world on an electronic information network. The so-called IPA*net* aimed to encourage further investments among developing countries, to provide access to comprehensive information on investment laws and conditions and to strengthen communications between governmental, business and financial associations and investors. A new internet-based facility, 'PrivatizationLink', was launched in 1998 to provide information on investment opportunities resulting from the privatization of industries in developing economies. In April 2002 MIGA launched a new service, 'FDIXchange', to provide potential investors, advisers and financial institutions with up-to-date market analysis and information on foreign direct investment opportunities in emerging economies (accessible at www.fdixchange.com).

Publications

Annual Report.
Investment Promotion Quarterly (electronic news update).
MIGA News (quarterly).

International Fund for Agricultural Development—IFAD

Address: Via del Serafico 107, 00142 Rome, Italy.
Telephone: (06) 54591; **fax:** (06) 5043463; **e-mail:** ifad@ifad.org; **internet:** www.ifad.org.

IFAD was established in 1977 following a decision by the 1974 UN World Food Conference, with a mandate to combat hunger and eradicate poverty on a sustainable basis in the low-income, food-deficit regions of the world. Funding operations began in January 1978.

Organization

(September 2002)

GOVERNING COUNCIL

Each member state is represented in the Governing Council by a Governor and an Alternate. Sessions are held annually with special sessions convened as required. The Governing Council elects the President of the Fund (who also chairs the Executive Board) by a two-thirds majority for a four-year term. The President is eligible for re-election.

EXECUTIVE BOARD

The Board consists of 18 members and 18 alternates, elected by the Governing Council, who serve for three years. The Executive Board is responsible for the conduct and general operation of IFAD and approves loans and grants for projects; it holds three regular sessions a year.

Following agreement on the fourth replenishment of the Fund's resources in February 1997, the governance structure of the Fund was amended. Former Category I countries (i.e. industrialized donor countries) were reclassified as List A countries and were awarded a greater share of the 1,800 votes in the Governing Council and Executive Board, in order to reflect their financial contributions to the Fund. Former Category II countries (petroleum-exporting developing donor countries) were reclassified as List B countries, while recipient developing countries, formally Category III countries, were termed as List C countries, and divided into three regional Sub-Lists. Where previously each category was ensured equal representation on the Executive Board, the new allocation of seats was as follows: eight List A countries, four List B, and two of each Sub-List C group of countries.
President and Chairman of Executive Board: LENNART BÅGE (Sweden).
Vice-President: JOHN WESTLEY (USA).

Activities

The Fund's objective is to mobilize additional resources to be made available on concessionary terms for agricultural development in developing member states. IFAD provides financing primarily for projects and programmes specifically designed to introduce, expand or improve food production systems and to strengthen related policies, services and institutions within the framework of national priorities and strategies. In allocating resources IFAD is guided by: the need to increase food production in the poorest food-deficit countries; the potential for increasing food production in other developing countries; and the importance of improving the nutrition, health and education of the poorest people in developing countries, i.e. small-scale farmers, artisanal fishermen, nomadic pastoralists, indigenous populations, rural women, and the rural landless. All projects emphasize the participation of beneficiaries in development initiatives, both at the local and national level. IFAD is committed to achieving the so-called Millennium Goals, pledged by governments attending a special session of the UN General Assembly in September 2000, in particular to reduce by 50% the proportion of people living in extreme poverty by 2015. IFAD's Strategic Framework for 2002–06 reiterates its commitment to enabling the rural poor to overcome their poverty. Accordingly, the Fund's efforts were to focus on the following objectives: strengthening the capacity of the rural poor and their organizations; improving equitable access to productive natural resources and technology; and increasing access to financial services and markets. Within this Framework the Fund has also formulated regional strategies for rural poverty reduction. IFAD's strategic objectives for the Near East and North Africa region were to focus on the following four main themes: the empowerment of the rural poor; supporting means of income diversification; gender issues; and natural resource management. IFAD was to continue its efforts to support community development and institution-building, to promote appropriate technologies for marginal and dry-land areas, to facilitate rural infrastructure investments and to promote rural microenterprise development.

IFAD is empowered to make both grants and loans. Grants are limited to 7.5% of the resources committed in any one financial year. Loans are available on highly concessional, intermediate or ordinary terms. More than two-thirds of total IFAD lending is awarded on highly concessional terms, i.e. with no interest charges (although bearing an annual service charge of 0.75%) and a repayment period of 40 years, including a 10-year grace period. To avoid duplication of work, the administration of loans, for the purposes of disbursements and supervision of project implementation, is entrusted to competent international financial institutions, with the Fund retaining an active interest. During 2001 IFAD provided financing for some 41% of the costs of projects approved during that year, while the remainder was contributed by external donors, multilateral institutions and the recipient countries.

IFAD's development projects usually include a number of components, such as infrastructure (e.g. improvement of water supplies, small-scale irrigation and road construction); input supply (e.g. improved seeds, fertilizers and pesticides); institutional support (e.g. research, training and extension services); and producer incentives (e.g. pricing and marketing improvements). IFAD also attempts to enable the landless to acquire income-generating assets: by increasing the provision of credit for the rural poor, it seeks to free them from dependence on the capital market and to generate productive activities. The Fund supports projects that are concerned with environmental conservation, in an effort to alleviate poverty that results from the deterioration of natural resources. In addition to promoting small-scale irrigation (which has proved more economically and ecologically viable than large-scale systems), projects include low-cost anti-erosion measures, land improvement, soil conservation, agro-forestry systems, improved management of arid rangeland, and safe biological control of pests.

IFAD is a leading repository of knowledge, resources and expertise in the field of rural hunger and poverty alleviation. During 1995 a team established to review IFAD's activities focused on the Fund's role as an innovator, emphasizing the importance of pioneering practices and strategies that can be replicated, and of making its knowledge available to relevant agencies and governments. IFAD has developed a Livestock and Rangeland Knowledgebase, aiming to provide easy access to shared knowledge and experience, based on relevant case studies, in order to improve the design, direction and outcome of projects. During the late 1990s IFAD established several partnerships within the agribusiness sector, with a view to improving performance at project level, broadening access to capital markets, and encouraging the advancement of new technologies.

Through its technical assistance grants, IFAD aims to promote research and capacity-building in the agricultural sector, as well as the development of technologies to increase production and alleviate rural poverty. IFAD is financing efforts to improve the production of durum wheat in the dryland areas of West Asia and North Africa and is supporting the establishment of a regional animal surveillance and control network to identify and prevent outbreaks of livestock diseases in North Africa, the Middle East and the Arab Peninsula. In 1998 the Near East and North Africa Management Training in Agriculture programme was initiated, with the aim of strengthening national training capacities in the fields of agriculture and rural development.

During 2001 IFAD approved four projects in the Near East and North Africa region (which, according to IFAD's classification, includes parts of Central and Eastern Europe, Djibouti, Somalia and Sudan), amounting to some US $52.9m. in lending (13% of total IFAD lending in that year). In early 1998 the IFAD Governing Council approved the establishment of a Fund for Gaza and the West Bank which enabled the Fund to provide financial assistance to those territories.

In October 1997 IFAD was appointed to administer the Global Mechanism of the Convention to Combat Desertification in those Countries Experiencing Drought and Desertification, Particularly in Africa, which entered into force in December 1996. The Mechanism was envisaged as a means of mobilizing and channelling resources for implementation of the Convention. A series of collaborative institutional arrangements was to be concluded between IFAD, UNDP and the World Bank in order to facilitate the effective functioning of the Mechanism.

During 1999–2000 IFAD conducted a detailed study of rural poverty, the conclusions and recommendations of which were issued as the *Rural Poverty Report 2001*.

Finance

IFAD's programme of work for 2001 envisaged loans and grants totalling US $433.9m. The target for the fifth replenishment of IFAD funds, covering the period 2000–02, amounted to $460m. The replenishment became effective in September 2001. In 2001 the provisional budget for administrative expenses amounted to $53.6m.

Publications

Annual Report.
IFAD Update (2 a year).
Rural Poverty Report (annually).
Staff Working Papers (series).

International Monetary Fund—IMF

Address: 700 19th St, NW, Washington, DC 20431, USA.

Telephone: (202) 623-7430; **fax:** (202) 623-6220; **e-mail:** publicaffairs@imf.org; **internet:** www.imf.org.

The IMF was established at the same time as the World Bank in December 1945, to promote international monetary co-operation, to facilitate the expansion and balanced growth of international trade and to promote stability in foreign exchange.

Organization

(September 2002)

BOARD OF GOVERNORS

The highest authority of the Fund is exercised by the Board of Governors, on which each member country is represented by a Governor and an Alternate Governor. The Board normally meets annually. The International Monetary and Financial Committee (formerly the Interim Committee) advises and reports to the Board on matters relating to the management and adaptation of the international monetary and financial system, sudden disturbances that might threaten the system and proposals to amend the Articles of Agreement. The voting power of each country is related to its quota in the Fund.

BOARD OF EXECUTIVE DIRECTORS

The 24-member Board of Executive Directors is responsible for the day-to-day operations of the Fund. The USA, the United Kingdom, Germany, France and Japan each appoint one Executive Director. There is also one Executive Director each from the People's Republic of China, Russia and Saudi Arabia, while the remainder are appointed by groups of the remaining member countries.

OFFICERS

Managing Director: HORST KÖHLER (Germany).

First Deputy Managing Director: ANNE KRUEGER (USA).

Deputy Managing Directors: SHIGEMITSU SUGISAKI (Japan); EDUARDO ANINAT (Chile).

Director, African Department: ABDOULAYE BIO TCHANE (Benin).

Director, Middle Eastern Department: GEORGE ABED (Jordan).

Activities

The purposes of the IMF, as set out in the Articles of Agreement, are:

(i) To promote international monetary co-operation through a permanent institution which provides the machinery for consultation and collaboration on monetary problems.

(ii) To facilitate the expansion and balanced growth of international trade, and to contribute thereby to the promotion and maintenance of high levels of employment and real income and to the development of members' productive resources.

(iii) To promote exchange stability, to maintain orderly exchange arrangements among members, and to avoid competitive exchange depreciation.

(iv) To assist in the establishment of a multilateral system of payments in respect of current transactions between members and in the elimination of foreign exchange restrictions which hamper the growth of trade.

(v) To give confidence to members by making the general resources of the Fund temporarily available to them, under adequate safeguards, thus providing them with the opportunity to correct maladjustments in their balance of payments, without resorting to measures destructive of national or international prosperity.

(vi) In accordance with the above, to shorten the duration of and lessen the degree of disequilibrium in the international balances of payments of members.

In joining the Fund, each country agrees to co-operate with the above objectives, and the Fund monitors members' compliance by holding an annual consultation with each country, in order to survey the country's exchange rate policies and determine its need for assistance.

In accordance with its objective of facilitating the expansion of international trade, the IMF encourages its members to accept the obligations of Article VIII, Sections two, three and four, of the IMF Articles of Agreement. Members that accept Article VIII undertake to refrain from imposing restrictions on the making of payments and transfers for current international transactions and from engaging in discriminatory currency arrangements or multiple currency practices without IMF approval. By mid-2002 150 members had accepted Article VIII status.

In April 1998 the Executive Board, in order to refine discussions concerning the strengthening of the international monetary system, identified the following fundamental approaches: reinforcing international and domestic financial systems; strengthening IMF surveillance; promoting greater availability and transparency of information regarding member countries' economic data and policies; emphasizing the central role of the IMF in crisis management; and establishing effective procedures to involve the private sector in forestalling or resolving financial crises. During 1999/2000 the Fund implemented several measures in connection with its ongoing efforts to appraise and reinforce the global financial architecture, including, in March 2000, the adoption by the Executive Board of a strengthened framework to safeguard the use of IMF resources and, in April, approval by the Board of the establishment of an independent evaluation office to complement the Fund's internal and external evaluation activities. During 2000 the Fund established the IMF Center, in Washington, DC, which aimed to promote awareness and understanding of its activities. In September the Fund's new Managing Director announced his intention to focus and streamline the principles of 'conditionality' (which links Fund financing with the implementation of specific economic policies by the recipient countries) in order to strengthen the concept of national ownership and as part of the wider reform of the international financial system. The issue remained under discussion by the Executive Board, and was to be open to public comment. In 2000/01 the Fund established an International Capital Markets Department to improve its understanding of financial markets, and a separate Consultative Group on capital markets to serve as a forum for regular dialogue between the Fund and representatives of the private sector. In early 2002 a position of Director for Special Operations was created to enhance the Fund's ability to respond to critical situations affecting member countries.

RESOURCES

Members' subscriptions form the basic resource of the IMF. They are supplemented by borrowing. Under the General Arrangements to Borrow (GAB), established in 1962, the 'Group of Ten' industrialized nations (Belgium, Canada, France, Germany, Italy, Japan, the Netherlands, Sweden, the United Kingdom and the USA) and Switzerland (which became a member of the IMF in 1992, but which had been a full participant in the GAB from 1984) undertake to lend the Fund up to SDR 17,000m. in their own currencies, so as to help meet the balance-of-payments requirements of any member of the group, or to meet requests to the Fund from countries with balance-of-payments problems that could threaten the stability of the international monetary system. In July 1983 the Fund entered into an agreement with Saudi Arabia, in association with the GAB, making available SDR 1,500m., and other borrowing arrangements were completed in 1984 with the BIS, the Saudi Arabian Monetary Agency, Belgium and Japan, making available a further SDR 6,000m.

In May 1996 GAB participants concluded an agreement in principle to expand the resources available for borrowing to SDR 34,000m., by securing the support of other countries with the financial capacity to support the international monetary system. The so-called New Arrangements to Borrow (NAB) was approved by the Executive Board in January 1997. It was to enter into force, for an initial five-year period, as soon as the five largest potential creditors (of the anticipated 25 member countries and institutions participating in NAB) had approved the initiative and the total credit arrangement of participants endorsing the scheme had reached at least SDR 28,900m. While the GAB credit arrangement was to remain in effect, the NAB was expected to be the first facility to be activated in the event of the Fund requiring supplementary resources. In July 1998 the GAB was activated for the first time in more than 20 years in order to provide funds totalling US \$6,300m. in support of an IMF emergency assistance package for Russia (the first time the GAB had been used for a non-participant). The NAB became effective in November, and was used for the first time as part of an extensive programme of support for Brazil, which was adopted by the IMF in early December.

DRAWING ARRANGEMENTS

Exchange transactions within the Fund take the form of members' purchases (i.e. drawings) from the Fund of the currencies of other members for the equivalent amounts of their own currencies. Fund resources are available to eligible members on an essentially short-term and revolving basis to provide members with temporary assistance to contribute to the solution of their payments problems. Before making a purchase, a member must show that its balance of payments or reserve position make the purchase necessary. Apart from this requirement, reserve tranche purchases (i.e. purchases that do not bring the Fund's holdings of the member's currency to a level above its quota) are permitted unconditionally.

With further purchases, however, the Fund's policy of 'conditionality' means that a member requesting assistance must agree to adjust its economic policies, as stipulated by the IMF. All requests other than for use of the reserve tranche are examined by the Executive Board to determine whether the proposed use would be consistent with the Fund's policies, and a member must discuss its proposed adjustment programme (including fiscal, monetary, exchange and trade policies) with IMF staff. Purchases outside the

reserve tranche are made in four credit tranches, each equivalent to 25% of the member's quota; a member must reverse the transaction by repurchasing its own currency (with SDRs or currencies specified by the Fund) within a specified time. A credit tranche purchase is usually made under a 'Stand-by Arrangement' with the Fund, or under the Extended Fund Facility. A Stand-by Arrangement is normally of one or two years' duration, and the amount is made available in instalments, subject to the member's observance of 'performance criteria'; repurchases must be made within three-and-a-quarter to five years. An Extended Arrangement is normally of three years' duration, and the member must submit detailed economic programmes and progress reports for each year; repurchases must be made within four-and-a-half to 10 years. A member whose payments imbalance is large in relation to its quota may make use of temporary facilities established by the Fund using borrowed resources, namely the 'enlarged access policy' established in 1981, which helps to finance Stand-by and Extended Arrangements for such a member, up to a limit of between 90% and 110% of the member's quota annually. In October 1994 the Executive Board agreed to increase, for three years, the annual access limit under IMF regular tranche drawings, Stand-by Arrangements and Extended Fund Facility credits from 68% to 100% of a member's quota, with the cumulative access limit remaining at 300% of quota. The arrangements were extended, on a temporary basis, in November 1997.

In February 2002 a Stand-by Arrangement totalling SDR 12,821.2m., including amounts approved under the Supplemental Reserve Facility (see below), was concluded with Turkey, replacing a previous credit arrangement, approved in December 1999, under which some SDR 11,700m. was disbursed. At the end of the financial year 2001/02 an Extended Fund Facility remained in effect with Jordan, of which SDR 60.9m. was undrawn.

In addition, special-purpose arrangements have been introduced, all of which are subject to the member's co-operation with the Fund to find an appropriate solution to its difficulties. In January 2000 the Executive Board resolved to eliminate the contingency component of the former Compensatory and Contingency Financing Facility, established in 1988, reforming it as the Compensatory Financing Facility (CFF). The CCF provides compensation to members whose export earnings are reduced owing to circumstances beyond their control, or who are affected by excess costs of cereal imports. In December 1997 the Executive Board established a new Supplemental Reserve Facility (SRF) to provide short-term assistance to members experiencing exceptional balance-of-payments difficulties resulting from a sudden loss of market confidence. Repayments were to be made within one to one-and-a-half years of the purchase, unless otherwise extended by the Board. In April 1999 an additional facility, the Contingent Credit Lines (CCL), was established to provide short-term financing on similar terms to the SRF in order to prevent more stable economies being affected by adverse international financial developments and to maintain investor confidence. Under the CCL member countries were to have access to up to 500% of their quota, subject to meeting various economic criteria stipulated by the Fund.

In November 1999 the Fund's existing facility to provide balance-of-payments assistance on concessionary terms to low-income member countries, the Enhanced Structural Adjustment Facility, was reformulated as the Poverty Reduction and Growth Facility (PRGF) with greater emphasis on poverty reduction as a key element of growth-orientated economic strategies. Assistance under the PRGF, for which 77 countries were deemed eligible, was to be matched to specific national requirements, and based upon a national poverty reduction strategy, to be formulated in collaboration with non-governmental organizations, representatives of civil society, and bilateral and multilateral institutions and presented in a Poverty Reduction Strategy Paper. PRGF loans carry an interest rate of 0.5% per year and are repayable over 10 years, with a five-and-a-half-year grace period; each country is permitted to borrow up to 140% of its quotas (in exceptional circumstances the maximum access can be raised to 185%). A PGRF Trust replaced the former ESAF Trust.

The PRGF supports, through long-maturity loans and grants, IMF participation in a joint initiative, with the World Bank, to provide exceptional assistance to heavily indebted poor countries (HIPCs), in order to help them to achieve a sustainable level of debt management. The initiative was formally approved at the September 1996 meeting of the Interim Committee, having received the support of the 'Paris Club' of international creditors which agreed to increase the relief on official debt from 67% to 80%. Resources for the HIPC initiative are channelled through the PRGF Trust.

In early 1999 the IMF and World Bank initiated a comprehensive review of the HIPC scheme, in order to consider modifications of the initiative and to strengthen the link between debt relief and poverty reduction. A consensus emerged among the financial institutions and leading industrialized nations to enhance the scheme, in order to make it available to more countries, and to accelerate the process of providing debt relief. In September the IMF Board of

Governors expressed its commitment to undertaking an off-market transaction of a percentage of the Fund's gold reserves (i.e. a sale, at market prices, to central banks of member countries with repayment obligations to the Fund, which were then to be made in gold), as part of the funding arrangements of the enhanced HIPC scheme. This was undertaken during the period December 1999–April 2000. By July 2002 six countries had reached the 'completion point' of the process to assess eligibility for assistance, making available committed funds, while a further 21 eligible countries had reached their 'decision points' at which debt relief is

MEMBERSHIP AND QUOTAS IN THE MIDDLE EAST AND NORTH AFRICA (million SDR)*

Country	September 2002
Algeria	1,254.7
Bahrain	135.0
Cyprus	139.6
Egypt	943.7
Iran	1,497.2
Iraq†	(1,188.4) 504.0
Israel	928.2
Jordan	170.5
Kuwait	1,381.1
Lebanon	203.0
Libya	1,123.7
Morocco	588.2
Oman	194.0
Qatar	263.8
Saudi Arabia	6,985.5
Syria	293.6
Tunisia	286.5
Turkey	964.0
United Arab Emirates	611.7
Yemen	243.5

* The Special Drawing Right (SDR) was introduced in 1970 as a substitute for gold in international payments, and was intended eventually to become the principal reserve asset in the international monetary system. Its value (which was US $1.32713 at 5 August 2002 and averaged $1.27304 in 2001) is based on the currencies of the five largest exporting countries. Each member is assigned a quota related to its national income, monetary reserves, trade balance and other economic indicators; the quota approximately determines a member's voting power and the amount of foreign exchange it may purchase from the Fund. A member's subscription is equal to its quota. In January 1998 the Board of Governors adopted a resolution in support of an increase, under the Eleventh General Review, of some 45% in total quotas, subject to approval by member states constituting 85% of total quotas (as at December 1997). Sufficient consent had been granted by January 1999 to enable the overall increase in quotas to enter into effect. All members were then granted until 30 July to consent to the higher quotas. At August 2002 total quotas in the Fund amounted to SDR 212,657.9m.
† Iraq had overdue obligations and was therefore ineligible to consent to any increase. The figure listed is that determined under the Eighth General Review, while the figure in parentheses is the proposed Eleventh General Review quota.

approved. In that month IMF assistance under the scheme in net present value terms amounted to US $2,043m. of a total of $25,102m. of assistance committed. The estimated nominal debt relief value of assistance at that time totalled $41,520m.

SURVEILLANCE

Under its Articles of Agreement, the Fund is mandated to oversee the effective functioning of the international monetary system and to review the policies of individual member countries to ensure the stability of the exchange rate system. The Fund's main tools of surveillance are regular consultations with member countries conducted in accordance with Article IV of the Articles of Agreement, which cover fiscal and monetary policies, balance-of-payments and external debt developments, as well as policies that affect the economic performance of a country, such as the labour market, social and environmental issues and good governance and aspects of the country's capital accounts, and finance and banking sectors. In April 1997, in an effort to improve the value of surveillance by means of increased transparency, the Executive Board agreed to the voluntary issue of Press Information Notices (PINs) (on the internet and in *IMF Economic Reviews*), following each member's Article IV consultation with the Board, to those member countries wishing to make public the Fund's views. Other background papers providing information on and analysis of economic developments in individual countries continued to be made available. In addition, World Economic Outlook discussions are held, normally twice a

year, by the Executive Board to access policy implications from a multilateral perspective and to monitor global developments.

In April 1996 the IMF established the Special Data Dissemination Standard (SDDS), which was intended to improve access to reliable economic statistical information for member countries that have, or are seeking, access to international capital markets. In March 1999 the IMF undertook to strengthen the Standard by the introduction of a new reserves data template. By mid-2002 50 countries had subscribed to the Standard. The Fund maintains a Dissemination Standards Bulletin Board (accessible at dsbb.imf.org), which aims to ensure that information on SDDS subscribing countries is widely available. In December 1997 the Executive Board approved a new General Data Dissemination System (GDDS), to encourage all member countries to improve the production and dissemination of core economic data. The operational phase of the GDDS commenced in May 2000.

In April 1998 the then Interim Committee adopted a voluntary Code of Good Practices on Fiscal Transparency: Declaration of Principles, which aimed to increase the quality and promptness of official reports on economic indicators, and in September 1999 it adopted a Code of Good Practices on Transparency in Monetary and Financial Policies: Declaration of Principles. The IMF and World Bank jointly established a Financial Sector Assessment Programme in May 1999, initially as a pilot project, which aimed to promote greater global financial security through the preparation of confidential detailed evaluations of the financial sectors of countries. Assessments were undertaken of 12 industrialized countries, emerging market economies and developing countries. During 2000 the FSAP was extended to cover a further 24 countries. It remained under regular review by the Boards of Governors of the Fund and World Bank. As part of the FSAP, Fund staff may conclude a Financial System Stability Assessment (FSSA), addressing issues relating to macroeconomic stability and the strength of a country's financial system. A separate component of the FSAP are Reports on the Observance of Standards and Codes, which are compiled after an assessment of a country's implementation and observance of internationally recognized financial standards. In March 2000 the Executive Board adopted a strengthened framework to safeguard the use of IMF resources. All member countries making use of Fund resources were to be required to publish annual central bank statements audited in accordance with internationally accepted standards. It was also agreed that any instance of intentional misreporting of information by a member country should be publicized. In the following month the Executive Board approved the establishment of an Independent Evaluation Office to conduct objective evaluations of IMF policy and operations. In August the Executive Board adopted a Code of Conduct to guide its activities.

In April 2001 the Executive Board agreed on measures to enhance international efforts to counter money-laundering, in particular through the Fund's ongoing financial supervision activities and its programme of assessment of offshore financial centres. In November the IMFC, in response to the terrorist attacks against targets in the USA, which had occurred in September, resolved, *inter alia*, to strengthen the Fund's focus on surveillance, and, in particular, to extend measures to counter money-laundering to include the funds of terrorist organizations. It determined to accelerate efforts to assess offshore centres and to provide technical support to enable poorer countries to meet international financial standards.

TECHNICAL ASSISTANCE

Technical assistance is provided by special missions or resident representatives who advise members on every aspect of economic management; more specialized technical assistance is provided by the IMF's various departments. In 2000/01 the IMFC determined that technical assistance should be central to IMF's work in crisis prevention and management, in capacity-building for low-income countries, and in restoring macroeconomic stability in countries following a financial crisis. Technical assistance activities subsequently underwent a process of review and reorganization to align them more closely with IMF policy priorities and other initiatives, for example the Financial Stability Assessment Programme. The majority of technical assistance is provided by the Departments of Monetary and Exchange Affairs, of Fiscal Affairs and of Statistics, and by the IMF Institute. The Institute, founded in 1964, trains officials from member countries in financial analysis and policy, balance-of-payments methodology and public finance: it also gives assistance to national and regional training centres. The IMF is co-sponsor of the Joint Vienna Institute, which was opened in the Austrian capital in October 1992 and which trains officials from former centrally-planned economies in various aspects of economic management and public administration. In January 1999 the IMF, in co-operation with the African Development Bank and the World Bank, announced the establishment of a Joint Africa Institute, to be located in Abidjan, Côte d'Ivoire. The Institute was to provide training to officials from the region in economic policy and management, as well as in other development and governance issues.

Publications

Annual Report.

Balance of Payments Statistics Yearbook.

Direction of Trade Statistics (quarterly, with yearbook).

Finance and Development (quarterly, published jointly with the World Bank).

Global Financial Stability Report (quarterly).

Government Finance Statistics Yearbook.

IMF Economic Review, (3 a year).

IMF Survey (2 a month).

International Financial Statistics (monthly, with yearbook).

Joint BIS-IMF-OECD-World Bank Statistics on External Debt (quarterly).

Staff Papers (quarterly).

World Economic Outlook (2 a year).

Occasional papers, economic reviews, pamphlets, publications brochure.

United Nations Educational, Scientific and Cultural Organization—UNESCO

Address: 7 place de Fontenoy, 75352 Paris, France.

Telephone: 1-45-68-10-00; **fax:** 1-45-67-16-90; **internet:** www .unesco.org.

UNESCO was established in 1946 'for the purpose of advancing, through the educational, scientific and cultural relations of the peoples of the world, the objectives of international peace and the common welfare of mankind'.

Organization

(September 2002)

GENERAL CONFERENCE

The supreme governing body of the Organization, the Conference meets in ordinary session once in two years and is composed of representatives of the member states.

EXECUTIVE BOARD

The Board, comprising 58 members, prepares the programme to be submitted to the Conference and supervises its execution; it meets twice or sometimes three times a year.

SECRETARIAT

Director-General: KOICHIRO MATSUURA (Japan).

REGIONAL OFFICES

Regional Office for Education in the Arab States: POB 5244, Ave Cité Sportive, Beirut, Lebanon; tel. (1) 850075; fax (1) 824854; e-mail beirut@unesco.org; Dir VICTOR BILLEH.

Regional Office for Science and Technology in the Arab States—ROSTAS: 8 Abd ar-Rahman Fahmy St, Garden City, Cairo, Egypt; tel. (2) 7945599; fax (2) 7945296; e-mail cairo@unesco.org; internet www.unesco-cairo.org; also covers informatics; Dir MUHAMMAD ED-DEEK.

Regional Office for Social and Human Sciences in the Arab Region: POB 363, 12 rue de Rhodes-Notre Dame, 1002 Tunis, Tunisia; tel. (1) 790947; fax (1) 791588; e-mail tunis@unesco.org; liaison office with the Arab League Educational, Cultural and Scientific Organization; Dir FRANCISCO CARRILLO-MONTESINOS.

UNESCO International Institute for Capacity Building in Africa—UNESCO-IICBA: POB 2305, Addis Ababa, Ethiopia; tel. (1) 55-75-86; fax (1) 55-75-85; e-mail webmaster@unesco-iicba.org; internet www.unesco-iicba.org; f. 1999 to promote capacity building in the following areas: teacher education; curriculum development; educational policy, planning and management, and distance education; Dir Dr FAY KING CHUNG.

UNESCO Office—Amman: POB 2270, Wadi Saqra, Amman, Jordan; tel. (6) 5514234; fax (6) 5532183; e-mail amman@unesco.org; Dir NDEYE FALL.

UNESCO Office—Doha: POB 3945, Doha, Qatar; tel. 867707; fax 867644; e-mail doha@unesco.org; Dr ABDALLA BUBTANA.

UNESCO Office—Rabat: BP 1777, 35 ave du 16 Novembre, Agdal, Rabat, Morocco; tel. (7) 670374; fax (7) 670375; e-mail rabat@unesco .org; Dir ALEXIS POKROVSKY.

Activities in the Middle East and North Africa

In November 2001 the General Conference approved a medium-term strategy to guide UNESCO during the period 2002–07. The Conference adopted a new unifying theme for the organization: 'UNESCO contributing to peace and human development in an era of globalization through education, the sciences, culture and communication'. UNESCO's central mission as defined under the strategy was to contribute to peace and human development in the globalized world through its four programme domains (Education, Natural and Social and Human Sciences, Culture, and Communication and Information), incorporating the following three principal dimensions: developing universal principles and norms to meet emerging challenges and protect the 'common public good'; promoting pluralism and diversity; and promoting empowerment and participation in the emerging knowledge society through equitable access, capacity-building and knowledge-sharing. Programme activities were to be focused particularly on supporting disadvantaged and excluded groups or geographic regions. The organization aimed to decentralize its operations in order to ensure more country-driven programming. UNESCO's overall work programme for 2002–03 comprised the following major programmes: education; natural sciences; social and human sciences; culture; and communication and information. Basic education; fresh water resources and ecosystems; the ethics of science and technology; diversity, intercultural pluralism and dialogue; and universal access to information, especially in the public domain, were designated as the priority themes. The work programme incorporated two transdisciplinary projects—eradication of poverty, especially extreme poverty; and the contribution of information and communication technologies to the development of education, science and culture and the construction of a knowledge society. UNESCO aims to promote a culture of peace. The UN General Assembly designated UNESCO as the lead agency for co-ordinating the International Decade for a Culture of Peace and Non-Violence for the Children of the World (2001–10), with a focus on education. In the implementation of all its activities UNESCO aims to contribute to achieving the UN Millennium Goal of halving levels of extreme poverty by 2015.

In December 1993 UNESCO organized a meeting, held in Granada, Spain, of Israeli and Palestinian academics and experts. Under a process termed 'Granada II', UNESCO aimed to promote peace between the two sides through a series of co-operation projects. The process was formally inaugurated in January 1999 when representatives of the Israeli Government and the Palestinian authorities signed six agreements to collaborate on projects relating to medical research, joint music education, interfaith dialogue, and tourism and infrastructure.

Since the 1990s Africa has been a priority focus of UNESCO's activities. In November 2001 UNESCO organized an international seminar entitled *Forward-looking approaches and innovative strategies to promote the development of Africa in the 21st century,* which aimed to review UNESCO's strategy on Africa in the light of the recently-launched New Partnership on Africa's Development (q.v.).

EDUCATION

Since its establishment UNESCO has devoted itself to promoting education in accordance with principles based on democracy and respect for human rights.

In March 1990 UNESCO, with other UN agencies, sponsored the World Conference on Education for All. 'Education for All' was subsequently adopted as a guiding principle of UNESCO's contribution to development. UNESCO advocates 'Literacy for All' as a key component of 'Education for All', regarding literacy as essential to basic education and to social and human development. In April 2000 several UN agencies, including UNESCO and UNICEF, and other partners sponsored the World Education Forum, held in Dakar, Senegal, to assess international progress in achieving the goal of 'Education for All' and to adopt a strategy for further action (the

'Dakar Framework'), with the aim of ensuring universal basic education by 2015. The Forum launched the Global Initiative for Education for All. The Dakar Framework emphasized the role of improved access to education in the reduction of poverty and in diminishing inequalities within and between societies. UNESCO was appointed as the lead agency in the implementation of the Framework. UNESCO's role in pursuing the goals of the Dakar Forum was to focus on co-ordination, advocacy, mobilization of resources, and information-sharing at international, regional and national levels. It was to oversee national policy reforms, with a particular focus on the integration of 'Education for All' objectives into national education plans, which were to be produced by all member countries by 2002. UNESCO's work programme on Education for 2002–03 aimed to promote an effective follow-up to the Forum and comprised the following two main components: Basic Education for All: Meeting the Commitments of the Dakar World Education Forum; and Building Knowledge Societies through Quality Education and a Renewal of Education Systems. 'Basic Education for All', signifying the promotion of access to learning opportunities throughout the lives of all individuals, including the most disadvantaged, was designated as the principal theme of the programme and was deemed to require urgent action. The second part of the strategy was to improve the quality of educational provision and renew and diversify education systems, with a view to ensuring that educational needs at all levels were met. This component included updating curricular programmes in secondary education, strengthening science and technology activities and ensuring equal access to education for girls and women. (UNESCO supports the UN Girls' Education Initiative, established following the Dakar Forum.) The work programme focused on the importance of knowledge, information and communication in the increasingly globalized world, and the significance of education as a means of empowerment for the poor and of enhancing basic quality of life.

Within the UN system, UNESCO is responsible for providing technical assistance and educational services in the context of emergency situations. This includes providing education to refugees and displaced persons, as well as assistance for the rehabilitation of national education systems. In Palestine, UNESCO collaborates with UNRWA (q.v.) to assist with the training of teachers, educational planning and rehabilitation of schools. UNESCO also supports the Programme for Palestinian–European Academic Co-operation in Education (the 'Peace Programme'), which was initiated in late 1991 to support academic exchanges and to enable Palestinian students to study abroad. An office of the Peace Programme was established at UNESCO headquarters in 1995.

UNESCO is concerned with improving the quality, relevance and efficiency of higher education. It assists member states in reforming their national systems, organizes high-level conferences for Ministers of Education and other decision-makers, and disseminates research papers. A World Conference on Higher Education was convened in October 1998 in Paris, France. The Conference adopted a World Declaration on Higher Education for the 21st Century, incorporating proposals to reform higher education, with emphasis on access to education, and educating for individual development and active participation in society.

The UNESCO International Institute for Capacity Building in Africa, based in Addis Ababa, Ethiopia, promotes capacity building in teacher education, curriculum development, educational policy, planning and management, and distance education. The International Institute for Educational Planning and the International Bureau of Education undertake training, research and the exchange of information on aspects of education. A UNESCO Institute for Education, based in Hamburg, Germany, researches literacy activities and the evolution of adult learning systems. UNESCO aims to promote the use of new information and communication technologies in the expansion of learning opportunities. A joint UNESCO/ILO committee of experts has been established to consider strategies for enhancing the status of the teaching profession.

The April 2000 World Education Forum recognized the global HIV/AIDS pandemic to be a significant challenge to the attainment of 'Education for All'. UNESCO, as a co-sponsor of the Joint UN Programme on HIV/AIDS—UNAIDS, takes an active role in promoting formal and non-formal preventive health education.

NATURAL SCIENCES

In November 1999 the General Conference endorsed a Declaration on Science and the Use of Scientific Knowledge and an agenda for action, which had been adopted at the World Conference on Science, held in June/July 1999, in Budapest, Hungary. UNESCO was to co-ordinate the follow-up to the conference and, in conjunction with the International Council for Science (q.v.), to promote initiatives in international scientific partnership. The following were identified as priority areas of UNESCO's work programme on Natural Sciences for 2002–03: Science and Technology: Capacity-building and Management; and Sciences, Environment and Sustainable Development. Water Security in the 21st Century was designated as the principal theme, involving addressing threats to water resources

and their associated ecosystems. UNESCO was to be the lead UN agency involved in the preparation of the first *World Water Development Report*, due to be issued in 2003. The Science and Technology component of the programme focused on the follow-up of the World Conference on Science, involving the elaboration of national policies on science and technology; strengthening science education; improving university teaching and enhancing national research capacities; and reinforcing international co-operation in mathematics, physics, chemistry, biology, biotechnology and the engineering sciences. UNESCO aims to contribute to bridging the divide between community-held traditional knowledge and scientific knowledge.

UNESCO aims to improve the level of university teaching of the basic sciences through training courses, establishing national and regional networks and centres of excellence, and fostering co-operative research. In carrying out its mission, UNESCO relies on partnerships with non-governmental organizations and the world scientific communities. In 1996 UNESCO initiated a 10-year World Solar Programme, which aimed to promote the application of solar energy and to increase research, development and public awareness of all forms of ecologically-sustainable energy use.

UNESCO has established various forms of intergovernmental co-operation concerned with the environmental sciences and research on natural resources, in order to support the recommendations of the June 1992 UN Conference on Environment and Development and, in particular, the implementation of 'Agenda 21' to promote sustainable development. The International Geological Correlation Programme, undertaken jointly with the International Union of Geological Sciences, aims to improve and facilitate global research of geological processes. In the context of the International Decade for Natural Disaster Reduction (declared in 1990), UNESCO has conducted scientific studies of natural hazards and means of mitigating their effects and has organized several disaster-related workshops. The International Hydrological Programme considers scientific aspects of water resources assessment and management; and the Intergovernmental Oceanographic Commission (IOC) focuses on issues relating to oceans, shorelines and marine resources, in particular the role of the ocean in climate and global systems. The IOC has been actively involved in the establishment of a Global Coral Reef Monitoring Network. It is developing a Global Ocean Observing System. An initiative on Environment and Development in Coastal Regions and in Small Islands is concerned with ensuring environmentally-sound and sustainable development by strengthening management of the following key areas: freshwater resources; the mitigation of coastline instability; biological diversity; and coastal ecosystem productivity. UNESCO hosts the secretariat of the World Water Assessment Programme on freshwater resources.

UNESCO's Man and the Biosphere Programme supports a world-wide network of biosphere reserves (comprising 408 sites in 94 countries at May 2002), which aim to promote environmental conservation and research, education and training in biodiversity and problems of land use. Following the signing of the Convention to Combat Desertification in October 1994, UNESCO initiated an International Programme for Arid Land Crops, based on a network of existing institutions, to assist implementation of the Convention.

The Regional Office for Science and Technology (ROSTAS) organizes courses and studies on the teaching of basic science, computer science, hydrology, oceanography, geophysics, soil biology, geomorphology and seismology. It provides regional seminars, training courses and consultancy missions. As part of its programmes in arid zone research, UNESCO has helped to establish research institutes in Iraq and Saudi Arabia, and has given financial aid to Egypt's Desert Research Institute.

SOCIAL AND HUMAN SCIENCES

UNESCO is mandated to contribute to the world-wide development of the social and human sciences and philosophy, which it regards as of great importance in policy-making and maintaining ethical vigilance. The structure of UNESCO's Social and Human Sciences programme takes into account both an ethical and standard-setting dimension, and research, policy-making, action in the field and future-oriented activities. UNESCO's work programme for 2002–03 on Social and Human Sciences comprised three main components: The Ethics of Science and Technology; Promotion of Human Rights, Peace and Democratic Principles; and Improvement of Policies Relating to Social Transformations and Promotion of Anticipation and Prospective Studies. The priority Ethics of Science and Technology element aimed to reinforce UNESCO's role as an intellectual forum for ethical reflection on challenges related to the advance of science and technology; oversee the follow-up of the Universal Declaration on the Human Genome and Human Rights (see below); promote education in science and technology; ensure UNESCO's role in promoting good practices through encouraging the inclusion of ethical guiding principles in policy formulation and reinforcing international networks; and to promote international co-operation in human sciences and philosophy. The Social and Human Sciences programme had the main intellectual and conceptual responsibility for the transdisciplinary theme 'eradication of poverty, especially extreme poverty'.

UNESCO aims to promote and protect human rights and acts as an interdisciplinary, multicultural and pluralistic forum for reflection on issues relating to the ethical dimension of scientific advances, for example in biogenetics, new technology, and medicine. In May 1997 the International Bioethics Committee, a group of 36 specialists who meet under UNESCO auspices, approved a draft version of a Universal Declaration on the Human Genome and Human Rights, in an attempt to provide ethical guide-lines for developments in human genetics. The Declaration, which identified some 100,000 hereditary genes as 'common heritage', was adopted by the UNESCO General Conference in November and committed states to promoting the dissemination of relevant scientific knowledge and co-operating in genome research. The November Conference also resolved to establish an 18-member World Commission on the Ethics of Scientific Knowledge and Technology (COMEST) to serve as a forum for the exchange of information and ideas and to promote dialogue between scientific communities, decision-makers and the public. UNESCO hosts the secretariat of COMEST, which met for the first time in April 1999 in Oslo, Norway. Its second meeting, which took place in December 2001 in Berlin, Germany, focused on the ethics of energy, fresh water and outer space.

UNESCO aims to assist the building and consolidation of peaceful and democratic societies. An international network of institutions and centres involved in research on conflict resolution is being established to support the promotion of peace. Other training, workshop and research activities have been undertaken in countries which have suffered conflict. The Associated Schools Project (ASPnet—comprising more than 6,700 institutions in 166 countries in 2001) has, for nearly 50 years, promoted the principles of peace, human rights, democracy and international co-operation through education. An International Youth Clearing House and Information Service (INFOYOUTH) aims to increase and consolidate the information available on the situation of young people in society, and to heighten awareness of their needs, aspirations and potential among public and private decision-makers. UNESCO also focuses on the educational and cultural dimensions of physical education and sport and their capacity to preserve and improve health.

In 1994 UNESCO initiated an international social science research programme, the Management of Social Transformations (MOST), to promote capacity-building in social planning at all levels of decision-making. UNESCO sponsors several research fellowships in the social sciences. In other activities UNESCO promotes the rehabilitation of underprivileged urban areas, the research of sociocultural factors affecting demographic change and the study of family issues.

Fundamental to UNESCO's mission is the rejection of all forms of discrimination. It disseminates scientific information aimed at combating racial prejudice, works to improve the status of women and their access to education, and promotes equality between men and women.

CULTURE

In undertaking efforts to preserve the world's cultural and natural heritage UNESCO has attempted to emphasize the link between culture and development. In November 2001 the General Conference adopted the UNESCO Universal Declaration on Cultural Diversity, which affirmed the importance of intercultural dialogue in establishing a climate of peace. The work programme on Culture for 2002–03 included the following interrelated components: Reinforcing Normative Action in the Field of Culture; Protecting Cultural Diversity and Promoting Cultural Pluralism and Intercultural Dialogue; and Strengthening Links between Culture and Development. The focus was to be on all aspects of cultural heritage, and on the encouragement of cultural diversity and dialogue between cultures and civilizations. Under the 2002–03 programme UNESCO aimed to launch the Global Alliance on Cultural Diversity, a six-year initiative to promote partnerships between governments, non-governmental bodies and the private sector, with a view to supporting cultural diversity through the strengthening of cultural industries and the prevention of cultural piracy. UNESCO was designated as the lead agency for co-ordinating the UN Year for Cultural Heritage, celebrated in 2002.

UNESCO's World Heritage Programme, inaugurated in 1978, aims to protect historic sites and natural landmarks of outstanding universal significance, in accordance with the 1972 UNESCO Convention Concerning the Protection of the World Cultural and Natural Heritage, by providing financial aid for restoration, technical assistance, training and management planning. By December 2001 the 'World Heritage List' comprised 721 sites in 124 countries, of which 554 had cultural significance, 144 were natural landmarks, and 23 were of 'mixed' importance. UNESCO is assisting in the exploration of prehistoric sites in Libya, and in the preservation of sites and monuments in other countries, for example Carthage and Al-Qairawan in Tunisia, Fez in Morocco, Tyre in Lebanon and the Casbah of Algiers in Algeria. The Organization has assisted Iraq in

the establishment of a regional training centre for the conservation of cultural property in the Arab countries.

In 1992 a World Heritage Centre was established to enable rapid mobilization of international technical assistance for the preservation of cultural sites. In addition, UNESCO supports efforts for the collection and safeguarding of humanity's non-material 'intangible' heritage, including oral traditions, music, dance and medicine. UNESCO produces an *Atlas of the World's Languages in Danger of Disappearing*. The most recent edition, issued in February 2002, reported that, of some 6,000 languages spoken world-wide, about one-half were endangered.

The November 2001 General Conference adopted the Convention on the Protection of the Underwater Cultural Heritage, covering the protection from commercial exploitation of shipwrecks, submerged historical sites, etc. situated in the territorial waters of signatory states. UNESCO also administers the 1954 Hague Convention on the Protection of Cultural Property in the Event of Armed Conflict and the 1970 Convention on the Means of Prohibiting and Preventing the Illicit Import, Export and Transfer of Ownership of Cultural Property.

UNESCO encourages the translation and publication of literary works, publishes albums of art, and produces records, audiovisual programmes and travelling art exhibitions. It supports the development of book publishing and distribution, including the free flow of books and educational material across borders, and the training of editors and managers in publishing. UNESCO is active in preparing and encouraging the enforcement of international legislation on copyright.

In December 1992 UNESCO established the World Commission on Culture and Development, to strengthen links between culture and development and to prepare a report on the issue. UNESCO was the leading agency for implementing the UN's World Decade for Cultural Development (1988–97). In the framework of the World Decade UNESCO launched the Silk Roads Project, as a multidisciplinary study of the interactions among cultures and civilizations along the routes linking Asia and Europe. Other regional projects were undertaken to consider the dynamic process of dialogue and exchange in forming cultural identities, for example, a project to investigate the contributions of Arab culture to Latin American cultures through Spain and Portugal, and to promote creativity and cultural life.

COMMUNICATION AND INFORMATION

In 2001 UNESCO introduced a major programme, 'Information for All', as the principal policy-guiding framework for the Communication and Information sector. The organization works towards establishing an open, non-exclusive knowledge society based on information-sharing and incorporating the socio-cultural and ethical dimensions of sustainable development. It promotes the free flow of, and universal access to information, knowledge, data and best practices, through the development of communications infrastructures, the elimination of impediments to freedom of expression, and the promotion of the right to information; through encouraging international co-operation in maintaining libraries and archives; and through efforts to harness informatics for development purposes and strengthen member states' capacities in this field. Activities include assistance with the development of legislation and training programmes in countries where independent and pluralistic media are emerging; assistance in the monitoring of media independence, pluralism and diversity; promotion of exchange programmes and study tours; and improving access and opportunities for women in the media. UNESCO recognizes that the so-called global 'digital divide', in addition to other developmental differences between countries, generates exclusion and marginalization, and that increased participation in the democratic process can be attained through strengthening national communication and information capacities. UNESCO promotes the upholding of human rights in the use of cyberspace. The organization was to participate in the World Summit on the Information Society, scheduled to take place in Geneva, Switzerland, in December 2003. The work programme on Communication and Information for 2002–03 comprised the following components: Promoting Equitable Access to Information and Knowledge Especially in the Public Domain; and Promoting Freedom of Expression and Strengthening Communication Capacities. During 2002–03 UNESCO was to evaluate its interactive internet-based WebWorld Portal, which aims to provide global communication and information services at all levels of society. UNESCO's Memory of the World project aims to preserve in digital form, and thereby to promote wide access to, the world's documentary heritage.

In regions affected by conflict UNESCO supports efforts to establish and maintain an independent media service. This strategy is largely implemented through an International Programme for the Development of Communication (IPDC). IPDC provides support to communication and media development projects in the developing world, including the establishment of news agencies and newspapers and training editorial and technical staff. Since its establishment in 1982 IPDC has provided around US $85m. to finance some 900 projects. Since September 1993 UNESCO has provided assistance for the establishment of the Palestinian Broadcasting Corporation and the modernization of the Palestinian News Agency, largely through the IPDC. In December 1998 UNESCO helped to establish the Israeli-Palestinian Media Forum, which aimed to foster professional co-operation between Israeli and Palestinian journalists.

In March 1997 the first International Congress on Ethical, Legal and Societal Aspects of Digital Information ('InfoEthics') was held in Monte Carlo, Monaco. At the second 'InfoEthics' Congress, held in October 1998, experts discussed issues concerning privacy, confidentiality and security in the electronic transfer of information. UNESCO maintains an Observatory on the Information Society, which provides up-to-date information on the development of new information and communications technologies and analysis of major trends, and aims to raise awareness of related ethical, legal and societal issues. The UNESCO Institute for Information Technologies in Education was established in Moscow, Russia in 1998. In 2001 the UNESCO Institute for Statistics was established in Montréal, Canada.

Finance

UNESCO's activities are funded through a regular budget provided by contributions from member states and extrabudgetary funds from other sources, particularly UNDP, the World Bank, regional banks and other bilateral Funds-in-Trust arrangements. UNESCO co-operates with many other UN agencies and international non-governmental organizations.

UNESCO's Regular Programme budget for the two years 2002–03 was US $544.4m., the same as for the previous biennium. Extra-budgetary funds for 2002–03 were estimated at US $320m.

Publications

(mostly in English, French and Spanish editions; Arabic, Chinese and Russian versions are also available in many cases)

Atlas of the World's Languages in Danger of Disappearing.
Copyright Bulletin (quarterly).
International Review of Education (quarterly).
International Social Science Journal (quarterly).
Museum International (quarterly).
Nature and Resources (quarterly).
Prospects (quarterly review on education).
UNESCO Courier (monthly, in 27 languages).
UNESCO Sources (monthly).
UNESCO Statistical Yearbook.
World Communication Report.
World Educational Report (every 2 years).
World Heritage Review (quarterly).
World Information Report.
World Science Report (every 2 years).
Books, databases, video and radio documentaries, statistics, scientific maps and atlases.

World Health Organization—WHO

Address: ave Appia 20, 1211 Geneva 27, Switzerland.
Telephone: (22) 7912111; **fax:** (22) 7913111; **e-mail:** info@who.int; **internet:** www.who.int.
WHO was established in 1948 as the central agency directing international health work.

Organization

(September 2002)

WORLD HEALTH ASSEMBLY

The Assembly meets annually in Geneva; it is responsible for policy making, and the biennial programme and budget; it appoints the Director-General, admits new members and reviews budget contributions.

EXECUTIVE BOARD

The Board is composed of 32 health experts designated by, but not representing, their governments; they serve for three years, and the World Health Assembly elects 10–12 member states each year to the Board. It meets at least twice a year to review the Director-General's programme, which it forwards to the Assembly with any recommendations that seem necessary. It advises on questions referred to it by the Assembly and is responsible for putting into effect the decisions and policies of the Assembly. It is also empowered to take emergency measures in case of epidemics or disasters.
Chairman: Myriam Abel (Vanuatu).

SECRETARIAT

Director-General: Dr Gro Harlem Brundtland (Norway).
Executive Directors: Dr Anarfi Asamoa-Baah (Ghana) (Health Technology and Pharmaceuticals), Maryan Baquerot (General Management), Dr David L. Heymann (USA) (Communicable Diseases), Christopher Murray (Evidence and Information for Policy), Dr David Nabarro (United Kingdom) (Sustainable Development and Healthy Environments), Dr Tomris Türmen (Turkey) (Family and Community Health), Dr Derek Yach (South Africa) (Non-communicable Diseases and Mental Health); Nadia Younes (Egypt) (External Relations and Governing Bodies).
Chef de Cabinet (Office of the Director-General): Denis Aitkin (United Kingdom).

REGIONAL OFFICES

Africa: Cité du Djoue, BP 06, Brazzaville, Republic of the Congo; tel. and fax 83-91-00; e-mail regafro@whoafr.org; internet www.whoafr.org; Dir Dr Ebrahim Malick Samba (The Gambia).

Eastern Mediterranean: POB 1517, Alexandria 21563, Egypt; tel. (3) 4820223; fax (3) 4838916; e-mail webmaster@emro.who.int; internet: www.emro.who.int; Dir Dr Hussein Abd ar-Razzaq Gezairy.

Activities

WHO's objective is stated in the constitution as 'the attainment by all peoples of the highest possible level of health'. In November 2001 WHO issued the International Classification of Functioning, Disability and Health (ICF) to act as an international standard and guide-line for determining health and disability.

It acts as the central authority directing international health work, and establishes relations with professional groups and government health authorities on that basis.

It provides, on request from member states, technical and policy assistance in support of programmes to promote health, prevent and control health problems, control and eradicate disease, train health workers best suited to local needs and strengthen national health systems. Aid is provided in emergencies and natural disasters.

A global programme of collaborative research and exchange of scientific information is carried out in co-operation with about 1,200 leading national institutions. Particular stress is laid on the widespread communicable diseases of the tropics, and the countries directly concerned are assisted in developing their research capabilities.

It keeps diseases and other health problems under constant surveillance, promotes the exchange of information, formulates health regulations for international travel, and sets standards for the quality control of drugs, vaccines and other substances affecting health.

It collects and disseminates health data and carries out statistical analyses and comparative studies in such diseases as cancer, heart disease and mental illness.

It promotes improved environmental conditions, including housing, sanitation and working conditions. All available information on effects on human health of the pollutants in the environment is critically reviewed and published.

Co-operation among scientists and professional groups is encouraged. The organization negotiates and sustains national and global partnerships. It may propose international conventions and agreements, and develops and promotes international norms and standards. The organization promotes the development and testing of new technologies, tools and guide-lines. It assists in developing an informed public opinion on matters of health.

HEALTH FOR ALL

WHO's first global strategy for pursuing 'Health for all' was adopted in May 1981 by the 34th World Health Assembly. The objective of 'Health for all' was identified as the attainment by all citizens of the world of a level of health that would permit them to lead a socially and economically productive life, requiring fair distribution of available resources, universal access to essential health care, and the promotion of preventive health care. In May 1998 the 51st World Health Assembly renewed the initiative, adopting a global strategy in support of 'Health for all in the 21st century', to be effected through regional and national health policies. The new approach was to build on the primary health care approach of the initial strategy, but was to strengthen the emphasis on quality of life, equity in health and access to health services. The following have been identified as minimum requirements of 'Health for All':

Safe water in the home or within 15 minutes' walking distance, and adequate sanitary facilities in the home or immediate vicinity;

Immunization against diphtheria, pertussis, tetanus, poliomyelitis, measles and tuberculosis;

Local health care, including availability of essential drugs, within one hour's travel;

Trained personnel to attend childbirth, and to care for pregnant mothers and children up to at least one year old.

In July 1998 Dr Gro Harlem Brundtland officially took office as the new Director-General of WHO. She immediately announced an extensive reform of the organization, including restructuring the WHO technical programmes into the following groups, or 'clusters', each headed by an Executive Director (see above): Communicable Diseases; Non-communicable Diseases and Mental Health; Family and Community Health; Sustainable Development and Healthy Environments; Health Technology and Pharmaceuticals; Evidence and Information for Policy; External affairs and Governing Bodies; and General Management. The Office of the Director-General (including audit, oversight and legal activities) is headed by a Chef de Cabinet. In 2000 WHO adopted a new corporate strategy, entailing a stronger focus on performance and programme delivery through standardized plans of action, and increased consistency and efficiency throughout the organization.

The Tenth General Programme of Work, for the period 2002–05, defined a policy framework for pursuing the principal objectives of building healthy populations and combating ill health. The Programme took into account: increasing understanding of the social, economic, political and cultural factors involved in achieving better health and the role played by better health in poverty reduction; the increasing complexity of health systems; the importance of safeguarding health as a component of humanitarian action; and the need for greater co-ordination among development organizations. It incorporated four interrelated strategic directions: lessening excess mortality, morbidity and disability, especially in poor and marginalized populations; promoting healthy lifestyles and reducing risk factors to human health arising from environmental, economic, social and behavioural causes; developing equitable and financially fair health systems; and establishing an enabling policy and an institutional environment for the health sector and promoting an effective health dimension to social, economic, environmental and development policy.

COMMUNICABLE DISEASES

WHO identifies infectious and parasitic communicable diseases as a major obstacle to social and economic progress, particularly in developing countries, where, in addition to disabilities and loss of productivity and household earnings, they cause nearly one-half of all deaths. Emerging and re-emerging diseases, those likely to cause epidemics, increasing incidence of zoonoses (diseases passed from animals to humans either directly or by insects) attributable to environmental changes, outbreaks of unknown etiology, and the undermining of some drug therapies by the spread of antimicrobial resistance are main areas of concern. In recent years WHO has noted the global spread of communicable diseases through international travel, voluntary human migration and involuntary population displacement.

WHO's Communicable Diseases group works to reduce the impact of infectious diseases world-wide through surveillance and response; prevention, control and eradication strategies; and research and product development. Combating malaria and tuberculosis (TB) are organization-wide priorities and, as such, are supported not only by their own areas of work but also by activities undertaken in other areas. The group seeks to identify new technologies and tools, and to foster national development through strengthening health services and the better use of existing tools. It aims to strengthen global monitoring of important communicable disease problems. The group advocates a functional approach to disease control. It aims to create consensus and consolidate partnerships around targeted diseases and collaborates with other groups at all stages to provide an integrated response. In April 2000 WHO and several partner institutions in epidemic surveillance established a Global Outbreak Alert and Response Network. Through the Network WHO aims to maintain constant vigilance regarding outbreaks of disease and to link world-wide expertise to provide an immediate response capability. A Global Fund to Fight AIDS, TB and Malaria was established, with WHO participation, in 2001 (see below).

One of WHO's major achievements was the eradication of smallpox. Following a massive international campaign of vaccination and surveillance, begun in 1958 and intensified in 1967, the last case was detected in 1977 and the eradication of the disease was declared in 1980. In May 1996 the World Health Assembly resolved that, pending a final endorsement, all remaining known stocks of the smallpox virus were to be destroyed on 30 June 1999; in May 1999, however, it was agreed to retain existing stocks until 2002. In late 2001, in response to fears that illegally-held virus stocks could be used in acts of biological terrorism (see below), WHO reassembled a team of technical experts on smallpox. In January 2002 the Executive Board determined that stocks of the virus should continue to be retained, to enable research into more effective treatments and vaccines. In 1988 the World Health Assembly declared its commitment to the similar eradication of poliomyelitis and launched the Global Polio Eradication Initiative. By 2001 the number of reported polio cases world-wide had declined to 480, from 35,000 in 1988 (the actual number of cases in 1988 was estimated at around 350,000).

In 1995 WHO established a Global Tuberculosis Programme to address the challenges of the TB epidemic, which had been declared a global emergency by the Organization in 1993. According to WHO estimates, one-third of the world's population carries the TB bacillus, and 2m.–3m. people die from the disease each year. WHO provides technical support to all member countries, with special attention given to those with high TB prevalence, to establish effective national tuberculosis control programmes. WHO's strategy for TB control includes the use of DOTS (direct observation treatment, short-course), standardized treatment guide-lines, and result accountability through routine evaluation of treatment outcomes. Simultaneously, WHO is encouraging research with the aim of further disseminating DOTS, adapting DOTS for wider use, developing new tools for prevention, diagnosis and treatment, and containing new threats such as the HIV/TB co-epidemic. In March 1999 WHO announced the launch of a new initiative, 'Stop TB', in partnership with the World Bank, the US Government and a coalition of non-governmental organizations, which aimed to promote DOTS to ensure its use in 85% of cases by 2005 (compared with around one-quarter in 1999). However, inadequate control of DOTS in some areas, leading to partial and inconsistent treatments, has resulted in the development of drug-resistant and, often, incurable strains of the disease. The incidence of so-called multidrug-resistant TB (MDR-TB) strains, that are unresponsive to the two main anti-TB drugs, has risen in recent years. During 2001 WHO was developing and testing DOTS-Plus, a strategy for controlling the spread of MDR-TB in areas of high prevalence. In 2001 WHO estimated that more than 8m. new cases of TB were occurring world-wide each year, of which the largest concentration was in south-east Asia. It envisaged a substantial increase in new cases by 2005, mainly owing to the severity of the HIV/TB co-epidemic. TB is the principal cause of death for people infected with the HIV virus. In March 2001 the Global TB Drug Facility was launched under the 'Stop TB' initiative; this aimed to increase access to high-quality anti-TB drugs for sufferers in developing countries. In October the 'Stop TB' partnership announced a Global Plan to Stop TB, which envisaged the expansion of access to DOTS; the advancement of MDR-TB prevention measures; the development of anti-TB drugs entailing a shorter treatment period; and the implementation of new strategies for treating people with HIV and TB.

The Special Programme for Research and Training in Tropical Diseases, sponsored jointly by WHO, UNDP and the World Bank, was established in 1975, and comprises a world-wide network of about 5,000 scientists working on the development of vaccines, new drugs, diagnostic kits and preventive measures, and an applied field research on practical community issues affecting the target diseases. In January 1998 a new 20-year programme to eliminate lymphatic filariasis was initiated, with substantial funding and support from two major pharmaceutical companies, and in collaboration with the World Bank, the Arab Fund for Economic and Social Development and the governments of Japan, the United Kingdom and the USA. A Ministerial Conference on Malaria, organized by WHO in October 1992, adopted a Global Malaria Control Strategy specifying requirements for effective control of the disease, which kills an estimated 1m. people every year and affects a further 300m.–500m. WHO assists countries where malaria is endemic to prepare national plans of action for malaria control in accordance with the Strategy, which emphasizes strengthening local capabilities, for example through training for effective health control. In July 1998 WHO declared the control of malaria a priority concern, and in October formally launched the 'Roll Back Malaria' programme, in conjunction with UNICEF, the World Bank and UNDP. Emphasis was to be placed on strengthening local health systems and on the promotion of inexpensive preventative measures, including the use of bednets treated with insecticides. The global Roll Back Malaria partnership, linking governments, development agencies, and other partners, aims to mobilize resources and support for controlling the disease. WHO, with a number of private and public partners, also supports the development of more effective anti-malaria drugs and vaccines through the 'Medicines for Malaria' venture.

WHO is committed to the elimination of leprosy (the reduction of the prevalence of leprosy to less than one case per 10,000 population). The use of a highly effective combination of three drugs (known as multi-drug therapy—MDT) resulted in a reduction in the number of leprosy cases world-wide from 10m.–12m. in 1988 to 597,000 in 2000. The Global Alliance for the Elimination of Leprosy, launched in November 1999 by WHO, in collaboration with governments of affected countries and several private partners, including a major pharmaceutical company, aims to bring about the eradication of the disease by the end of 2005, through the continued use of MDT treatment. In July 1998 the Director-General of WHO and representatives of more than 20 countries, meeting in Yamoussoukro, Côte d'Ivoire, signed a declaration on the control of another mycobacterial disease, Buruli ulcer.

The objective of providing immunization for all children by 1990 was adopted by the World Health Assembly in 1977. Six diseases (measles, whooping cough, tetanus, poliomyelitis, tuberculosis and diphtheria) became the target of the Expanded Programme on Immunization (EPI), in which WHO, UNICEF and many other organizations collaborated. As a result of massive international and national efforts, the global immunization coverage increased from 20% in the early 1980s to the targeted rate of 80% by the end of 1990. This coverage signified that more than 100m. children in the developing world under the age of one had been successfully vaccinated against the targeted diseases, the lives of about 3m. children had been saved every year, and 500,000 annual cases of paralysis as a result of polio had been prevented. In 1992 the Assembly resolved to reach a new target of 90% immunization coverage with the six EPI vaccines; to introduce hepatitis B as a seventh vaccine (with the aim of an 80% reduction in the incidence of the disease in children by 2001); and to introduce the yellow fever vaccine in areas where it occurs endemically.

In June 2000 WHO released a report entitled 'Overcoming Antimicrobial Resistance', in which it warned that the misuse of antibiotics could render some common infectious illnesses unresponsive to treatment. At that time WHO issued guide-lines which aimed to mitigate the risks associated with the use of antimicrobials in livestock reared for human consumption.

NON-COMMUNICABLE DISEASES AND MENTAL HEALTH

The Non-communicable Diseases and Mental Health group comprises departments responsible for the surveillance, prevention and management of uninfectious diseases (such as those arising from an unhealthy diet), and departments for health promotion, disability, injury prevention and rehabilitation, mental health and substance abuse. Surveillance, prevention and management of non-communicable diseases; tobacco; and mental health are all organization-wide priorities.

Unhealthy diet, physical inactivity and tobacco use are regarded as common, preventable risk factors for the four most prominent non-communicable diseases: cardiovascular diseases, cancer, chronic respiratory disease and diabetes. WHO aims to monitor the global epidemiological situation of non-communicable diseases, to co-ordinate multinational research activities concerned with prevention and care, and to analyse determining factors such as gender and poverty. In mid-1998 the Organization adopted a resolution on measures to be taken to combat non-communicable diseases, the prevalence of which was anticipated to increase, particularly in developing countries, owing to rising life expectancy and changes in lifestyles. For example, between 1995 and 2025 the number of adults affected by diabetes was projected to increase from 135m. to 300m. In February 1999 WHO initiated a new programme, 'Vision 2020: the Right to Sight', which aimed to eliminate avoidable blindness (estimated to be as much as 80% of all cases) by 2020. Blindness was otherwise predicted to increase by as much as twofold, owing to the increased longevity of the global population. WHO's programmes for diabetes mellitus, chronic rheumatic diseases and asthma assist with the development of national initiatives, based upon goals and targets for the improvement of early detection, care and reduction of long-term complications.

WHO works to assess the impact of injuries, violence and sensory impairments on health. The health promotion division promotes decentralized and community-based health programmes and is concerned with developing new approaches to population ageing and encouraging healthy life-styles and self-care. It also seeks to relieve the negative impact of social changes such as urbanization, migration and changes in family structure upon health. WHO advocates a multi-sectoral approach—involving public health, legal and educational systems—to the prevention of injuries, which represent 16%

of the global burden of disease. It aims to support governments in developing suitable strategies to prevent and mitigate the consequences of violence, unintentional injury and disability. Several health promotion projects have been undertaken, in collaboration between WHO regional and country offices and other relevant organizations, including: the Global School Health Initiative, to bridge the sectors of health and education and to promote the health of school-age children; the Global Strategy for Occupational Health, to promote the health of the working population and the control of occupational health risks; Community-based Rehabilitation, aimed at providing a more enabling environment for people with disabilities; and a communication strategy to provide training and support for health communications personnel and initiatives. In 2000 WHO, UNESCO, the World Bank and UNICEF adopted the joint Focusing Resources for Effective School Health (FRESH Start) approach to promoting life skills among adolescents.

Mental health problems, which include unipolar and bipolar affective disorders, psychosis, epilepsy, dementia, Parkinson's disease, multiple sclerosis, drug and alcohol dependency, and neuropsychiatric disorders such as post-traumatic stress disorder, obsessive compulsive disorder and panic disorder, have been identified by WHO as significant global health problems. Although, overall, physical health has improved, mental, behavioural and social health problems are increasing, owing to extended life expectancy and improved child mortality rates, and factors such as war and poverty. WHO aims to address mental problems by increasing awareness of mental health issues and promoting improved mental health services and primary care. The Organization formulates guide-lines and protocols for the prevention and management of mental problems.

The Substance Abuse department is concerned with problems of alcohol, drugs and other substance abuse. Within its Programme on Substance Abuse (PSA), which was established in 1990 in response to the global increase in substance abuse, WHO provides technical support to assist countries in formulating policies with regard to the prevention and reduction of the health and social effects of psychoactive substance abuse. The PSA's sphere of activity includes epidemiological surveillance and risk assessment, advocacy and the dissemination of information, strengthening national and regional prevention and health promotion techniques and strategies, the development of cost-effective treatment and rehabilitation approaches, and also encompasses regulatory activities as required under the international drugs-control treaties in force.

The Tobacco or Health Programme aims to reduce the use of tobacco, by educating tobacco-users and preventing young people from adopting the habit. In 1996 WHO published its first report on the tobacco situation world-wide. According to WHO, about one-third of the world's population aged over 15 years smoke tobacco, which causes approximately 3.5m. deaths each year (through lung cancer, heart disease, chronic bronchitis and other effects). In 1998 the 'Tobacco Free Initiative', a major global anti-smoking campaign, was established. In May 1999 the World Health Assembly endorsed the formulation of a Framework Convention on Tobacco Control (FCTC) to help to combat the increase in tobacco use (although a number of tobacco growers expressed concerns about the effect of the convention on their livelihoods). It was envisaged that the Framework Convention would be adopted in 2003; a draft of the treaty was released in July 2002. The greatest increase in tobacco use is forecast to occur in developing countries.

FAMILY AND COMMUNITY HEALTH

WHO's Family and Community Health group addresses the following areas of work: child and adolescent health, research and programme development in reproductive health, making pregnancy safer, women's health, and HIV/AIDS. Making pregnancy safer and HIV/AIDS are organization-wide priorities. The group's aim is to improve access to sustainable health care for all by strengthening health systems and fostering individual, family and community development. Activities include newborn care; child health, including promoting and protecting the health and development of the child through such approaches as promotion of breast-feeding and use of the mother-baby package, as well as care of the sick child, including diarrhoeal and acute respiratory disease control and support to women and children in difficult circumstances; the promotion of safe motherhood and maternal health; adolescent health, including the promotion and development of young people and the prevention of specific health problems; women, health and development, including addressing issues of gender, sexual violence, and harmful traditional practices; and human reproduction, including research related to contraceptive technologies and effective methods. A regional workshop to strengthen national capabilities in mother and child health in the Eastern Mediterranean was convened in Cairo, Egypt, in April 1999, under a strengthened initiative to reduce maternal illness and mortality. In addition, WHO aims to provide technical leadership and co-ordination on reproductive health and to support countries in their efforts to ensure that people: experience healthy sexual development and maturation; have the capacity for healthy, equitable and responsible relationships; can achieve their reproductive intentions safely and healthily; avoid illnesses, diseases and injury related to sexuality and reproduction; and receive appropriate counselling, care and rehabilitation for diseases and conditions related to sexuality and reproduction.

WHO's Division of Diarrhoeal and Acute Respiratory Disease Control encourages national programmes aimed at reducing the estimated 3.5m. yearly childhood deaths as a result of diarrhoea, particularly through the use of oral rehydration therapy and preventive measures. The Division is also seeking to reduce deaths from pneumonia in infants through the use of a simple case-management strategy involving the recognition of danger signs and treatment with an appropriate antibiotic. In September 1997 WHO, in collaboration with UNICEF, formally launched a programme advocating the Integrated Management of Childhood Illness (IMCI), following successful regional trials in more than 20 developing countries during 1996–97. IMCI recognizes that pneumonia, diarrhoea, measles, malaria and malnutrition cause some 70% of the approximately 11m. childhood deaths each year, and recommends screening sick children for all five conditions, in order to enable health workers to reach a more accurate diagnosis than may be achieved from the results of a single assessment.

The HIV/AIDS epidemic represents a major threat to human well-being and socio-economic progress. WHO's Global Programme on AIDS, initiated in 1987, was concluded in December 1995. The Joint UN Programme on the Human Immunodeficiency Virus (HIV) and AIDS (UNAIDS) became operational on 1 January 1996, sponsored jointly by WHO, the World Bank, UNICEF, UNDP, UNESCO, UNFPA and ILO. The UNAIDS secretariat is based at WHO headquarters. WHO established an Office of HIV/AIDS and Sexually-Transmitted Diseases in order to ensure the continuity of its global response to the problem, which included support for national control and education plans, improving the safety of blood supplies and improving the care and support of AIDS patients. In addition, the Office was to liaise with UNAIDS and to make available WHO's research and technical expertise. WHO participates in the 'Accelerating Access' initiative, which aims to expand access to care, support and antiretroviral (ARV) treatments for people with HIV/AIDS. A WHO-UNAIDS HIV Vaccine Initiative was launched in 2000. In July 2001 a meeting of the Group of Seven industrialized nations and Russia (G-8), convened in Genoa, Italy, announced the formation of a new Global Fund to Fight AIDS, TB and Malaria (as previously proposed by the UN Secretary-General and recommended by the World Health Assembly). The Fund, a partnership between governments, UN bodies (including WHO) and other agencies, and private-sector interests, aimed to disburse US $700m.–$800m. in grants during 2002, thereby increasing annual global expenditure on combating those diseases by about 50%. In December 2001 an estimated 40m. adults and children world-wide were living with HIV/AIDS; of these, 5m. were estimated to have been infected during that year. Of those people reported to have been newly affected in 2001, 80,000 were in North Africa and the Middle East.

SUSTAINABLE DEVELOPMENT AND HEALTHY ENVIRONMENTS

The Sustainable Development and Healthy Environments group focuses on the following areas of work: health in sustainable development; nutrition; health and environment; food safety; and emergency preparedness and response. Food safety is an organization-wide priority.

WHO promotes recognition of good health status as one of the most important assets of the poor. The Sustainable Development and Healthy Environment group seeks to monitor the advantages and disadvantages for health, nutrition environment and development arising from the process of globalization; to integrate the issue of health into poverty reduction programmes; and to promote human rights and equality. Adequate and safe food and nutrition is a priority programme area. An estimated 780m. people world-wide cannot meet basic needs for energy and protein, more than 2,000m. people lack essential vitamins and minerals, and 170m. children are estimated to be malnourished. WHO collaborates with FAO, WFP, UNICEF and other UN agencies in its activities relating to nutrition and food safety. In December 1992 an International Conference on Nutrition, co-sponsored by FAO and WHO, adopted a World Declaration on Nutrition and a Plan of Action designed to make the fight against malnutrition a development priority. In pursuing the objectives of the Declaration WHO promotes the elaboration of national plans of action for nutrition and aims to identify and support countries with high levels of malnutrition, which includes protein energy deficiencies, and deficiencies of iron, vitamin A and iodine. A strategy of universal salt iodization was launched in 1993 (iodine deficiency has been found to be a cause of mental handicap). In collaboration with other international agencies, WHO is implementing a comprehensive strategy for promoting appropriate infant, young-child and maternal nutrition, and for dealing effectively with nutritional emergencies in large populations. Areas of emphasis include promoting health-care practices that enhance successful breast-feeding; appropriate complementary feeding; refining the use and interpretation of body measurements for assessing nutritional status; relevant information, education and training; and action to give effect to the 1981 International Code of Marketing of Breast-milk Substitutes. The Food Safety Programme aims to eliminate risks, such as biological contaminants in foods which are a major cause of diarrhoea and malnutrition in children. WHO, together with FAO, establishes food standards (through the work of the Codex Alimentarius Commission) and evaluates food additives, pesticide residues and other contaminants and their implications for health. In March 2002 an intergovernmental task force established by the Codex Alimentarius Commission finalized 'principles for the risk analysis of foods derived from biotechnology', which were to provide a framework for assessing the safety of genetically-modified—GM foods and plants. In the following month WHO and FAO announced a joint review of their food standards operations.

WHO's programme area on environment and health undertakes a wide range of initiatives to tackle the increasing threats to health and well-being from a changing environment, especially in relation to air pollution, control of monitoring of water quality, sanitation, protection against radiation, management of hazardous waste, chemical safety and housing hygiene. The major part of WHO's technical co-operation in environmental health in developing countries is concerned with community water supply and sanitation. The Programme also gives prominence to the assessment of health risks from chemical, physical and biological agents. To contribute to the solution of environmental health problems associated with the rapid urbanization of cities in the developing world, the Programme was promoting globally in the 1990s the Healthy City approach that had been initiated in Europe. WHO is also working with other agencies to consider the implications on human health of global climate change.

Following the major terrorist attacks perpetrated against targets in the USA in September 2001, WHO focused renewed attention on the potential deliberate use of infectious diseases, such as anthrax and smallpox, or of chemical agents, in acts of biological or chemical terrorism. In that month WHO issued draft guide-lines entitled 'Health Aspects of Biological and Chemical Weapons.'

Through its Division of Emergency and Humanitarian Action WHO acts as the 'health arm' of UN relief efforts in response to emergencies and natural disasters. Its emergency preparedness activities include co-ordination, policy-making and planning, awareness-building, technical advice, training, publication of standards and guide-lines, and research. Its emergency relief activities include organizational support, the provision of emergency drugs and supplies and conducting technical emergency assessment missions. The Division's objective is to strengthen the national capacity of member states to reduce the adverse health consequences of disasters. In responding to emergency situations, WHO aims to develop projects and activities that will assist the national authorities concerned in rebuilding or strengthening their own capacity to handle the impact of such situations.

WHO assists UNRWA (q.v.) in providing healthcare to Palestinians living in the Occupied Territories. In October 1993, following a peace accord reached by Israel and Palestine in September, WHO launched an appeal for US $10m. to finance a technical assistance programme that was to implement the transfer of health services to a Palestinian self-governing authority, and provide for primary health care projects in the Occupied Territories. In May 1994 the World Health Assembly adopted a resolution to support the programme and to allocate the necessary funds to meet the urgent health needs of the Palestinian people.

In March 1996 a survey of health conditions in Iraq, published by WHO, generated concern at the impact on the population of the ongoing international trade embargo and, in particular, the widespread incidence of nutritional deficiencies and increasing infant mortality rates. Under the terms of Resolution 986 of the UN Security Council, which permitted the limited sale of petroleum by the Iraqi authorities in order to facilitate the purchase of essential humanitarian supplies, WHO was responsible for distributing medicines and medical supplies, for supervising the distribution of medicines by the Iraqi authorities in central and southern Iraq and for implementing an epidemiological surveillance network in the northern Kurdish provinces of Iraq. The distribution of medicines to an anticipated 600 hospitals and health centres was initiated in May 1997.

HEALTH TECHNOLOGY AND PHARMACEUTICALS

WHO's Health Technology and Pharmaceuticals group, made up of the departments of essential drugs and other medicines, vaccines and other biologicals, and blood safety and clinical technology, covers the following areas of work: essential medicines—access, quality and rational use; immunization and vaccine development; and world-wide co-operation on blood safety and clinical technology. Blood safety and clinical technology are an organization-wide priority.

In January 1999 the Executive Board adopted a resolution on WHO's Revised Drug Strategy, which placed emphasis on the inequalities of access to pharmaceuticals, and also covered specific aspects of drugs policy, quality assurance, drug promotion, drug donation, independent drug information and rational drug use. Plans of action involving co-operation with member states and other international organizations in order to monitor and analyse the pharmaceutical and public health implications of international agreements, including trade agreements. In April 2001 experts from WHO and the World Trade Organization participated in a workshop to address ways of lowering the cost of medicines in less developed countries. In the following month the World Health Assembly adopted a resolution urging member states to promote equitable access to essential drugs, noting that this was denied to about one-third of the world's population. WHO participates with other partners in the 'Accelerating Access' initiative, which aims to expand access to antiretroviral drugs for people with HIV/AIDS (see above).

WHO reports that 2m. children die each year of diseases for which common vaccines exist. In September 1991 the Children's Vaccine Initiative (CVI) was launched, jointly sponsored by the Rockefeller Foundation, UNDP, UNICEF, WHO and the World Bank, to facilitate the development and provision of children's vaccines. The CVI has as its ultimate goal the development of a single oral immunization shortly after birth that will protect against all major childhood diseases. In 1998 the CVI reported that 4m. children die each year of diseases for which there are existing, common vaccines. In 1999 WHO, UNICEF, the World Bank and a number of public- and private-sector partners formed the Global Alliance for Vaccines and Immunization (GAVI), which aimed to expand the provision of existing vaccines and to accelerate the development and introduction of new vaccines and technologies, with the goal of protecting children of all nationalities and from all socio-economic backgrounds against vaccine-preventable diseases.

WHO supports states in ensuring access to safe blood, blood products, transfusions, injections, and health-care technologies.

EVIDENCE AND INFORMATION FOR HEALTH POLICY

The Evidence and Information for Health Policy group addresses the following areas of work: evidence for the development of health policy; health information management and dissemination; and research policy and the promotion and organization of health systems. The group aims to assist policy-makers assess health needs, choose intervention strategies, design policy and monitor performance, and thereby improve the performance of national health systems. The group also supports international and national dialogue on health policy.

In July 2001 WHO and six leading medical publishers announced an initiative to enable relevant authorities in developing countries to access nearly 1,000 biomedical journals through the internet at no or greatly reduced cost, in order to improve the world-wide circulation of scientific information.

Finance

WHO's regular budget is provided by assessment of member states and associate members. An additional fund for specific projects is provided by voluntary contributions from members and other sources. Funds are received from the UNDP and from UNFPA for population programmes. A regular budget of US $842.7m. was proposed for the 2002–03 biennium, of which $186.5m. (22% of the total) was allocated to Africa and $83.4m. (9.9%) to the eastern Mediterranean region.

Publications

Bulletin of WHO (monthly).
Environmental Health Criteria.
International Digest of Health Legislation (quarterly).
Model List of Essential Drugs (biennially).
Weekly Epidemiological Record.
WHO Drug Information (quarterly).
WHO Model Formulary.
World Health Report (annually).
World Health Statistics Annual.
Series of technical reports.

Other UN Organizations Active in the Middle East and North Africa

OFFICE FOR THE CO-ORDINATION OF HUMANITARIAN AFFAIRS

Address: United Nations Plaza, New York, NY10017, USA.
Telephone: (212) 963-1234; **fax:** (212) 963-1312; **e-mail:** ochany@un.org; **internet:** www.reliefweb.int/ocha-ol.
The Office was established in January 1998 as part of the UN Secretariat, with a mandate to co-ordinate international humanitarian assistance and to provide policy and other advice on humanitarian issues. It administers the Humanitarian Early Warning System, as well as Integrated Regional Information Networks to monitor the situation in different countries and a Disaster Response System
Under Secretary-General for Humanitarian Affairs and Emergency Relief Co-ordinator: KENZO OSHIMA (Japan).

OFFICE FOR DRUG CONTROL AND CRIME PREVENTION—ODCCP

Address: Vienna International Centre, POB 500, 1400 Vienna, Austria.
Telephone: (1) 26060-0; **fax:** (1) 26060-5866; **e-mail:** www.odccp.org; **internet:** www.odccp.org.
The Office was established on 1 November 1997 to strengthen the UN's integrated approach to issues relating to drug control, crime prevention and international terrorism. It comprises two principal components: the United Nations International Drug Control Programme (UNDCP) and the Centre for International Crime Prevention, both headed by the ODCCP Executive Director.
Executive Director: ANTONIO MARIA COSTA (Italy).

OFFICE OF THE IRAQ PROGRAMME

Address: United Nations, New York, NY10017, USA.
Telephone: (212) 963-4341; **internet:** www.un.org/Depts/oip.
The Office was established in October 1997 to assume responsibility for the implementation of Security Council Resolution 986, which was adopted in April 1995 to provide for the limited sale of Iraqi petroleum to enable the purchase of humanitarian supplies and the provision of contributions to the UN Compensation Committee (which had been established to settle claims against Iraq resulting from the Gulf War). Exports of petroleum up to a value of US $1,000m. every 90 days initially were to be permitted under the agreement; the Council was responsible for renewing the mandate of the agreement and for approving contracts for the sale of petroleum and the purchase of food and medical goods. In February 1998 the Council approved a resolution expanding the so-called oil-for-food programme to allow for sales of petroleum up to a value of $5,256m. every 180 days and in October 1999 the Council agreed to permit Iraq to generate a further $3,040m. in the next 180-day period of the oil-for-food agreement, accounting for the shortfall of authorized revenue that had not yet been generated. In mid-December the Council approved a six-month extension of the programme. A few days later it adopted a resolution establishing a new policy towards Iraq. The resolution provided for an unlimited ceiling on petroleum exports under the agreed humanitarian programme, and for a suspension of sanctions dependent upon Iraq's co-operation with a new arms inspection body, the UN Monitoring, Verification and Inspection Commission (UNMOVIC) that was to replace the UN Special Commission (UNSCOM), which had been established in 1991 to monitor the disposal of weapons. At the end of March 2000 the Council doubled the maximum permitted revenue that Iraq might use to purchase petroleum industry spare parts and other equipment under the ongoing programme. A new sanctions regime was discussed during 2001. This envisaged facilitating the transfer of civilian and humanitarian goods to Iraq, while tightening border checks for military or other illegal trading. Disagreements among Council members concerned the extra responsibility placed on Iraq's neighbouring countries and the compilation of a list of 'controlled' items requiring special approval to be imported into Iraq. The existing oil-for-food scheme was extended in early July after Russia confirmed that it would veto the new proposals. A further extension was granted in November; however, the Council

approved a draft list of goods for review which it intended to enter into effect on 30 May 2002. The Goods Review List was adopted in May, with new procedures for contracts for humanitarian supplies and equipment. The Office of the Iraq Programme was to co-operate closely with IAEA and UNMOVIC in the processing and evaluation of contract applications. At the end of May assistance totalling some $22,590m. had arrived in Iraq under the programme.

Executive Director: BENON V. SEVAN (Cyprus).

OFFICE OF THE UNITED NATIONS HIGH COMMISSIONER FOR HUMAN RIGHTS

Address: Palais Wilson, 52 rue de Paquis, 1201 Geneva, Switzerland.

Telephone: (22) 9179290; **fax:** (22) 9179022; **e-mail:** scrt.hchr@unog.ch; **internet:** www.unhchr.ch.

The Office is a body of the UN Secretariat and is the focal point for UN human rights activities. Since September 1997 it has incorporated the Centre for Human Rights.

High Commissioner: SERGIO VIEIRA DE MELLO (Brazil).

OFFICE OF THE UNITED NATIONS SPECIAL CO-ORDINATOR IN THE OCCUPIED TERRITORIES—UNSCO

Address: POB 490, Government House, Jerusalem 91004.

Telephone: (7) 2822746; **fax** (7) 2820966; **e-mail:** unsco@palnet.com.

UNSCO was established in June 1994 to support the Middle East peace process, in particular implementation of the Declaration of Principles with regard to interim arrangements for Palestinian self-rule (signed by the Israeli Government and the Palestine Liberation Organization in 1993), and to enhance the effectiveness of international donor assistance to the emerging autonomous areas. Since September 1999 the Special Co-ordinator has also acted as the Personal Representative of the UN Secretary-General to the Palestine Liberation Organization and the Palestinian (National) Authority. The Special Co-ordinator undertakes to co-ordinate UN programmes and agencies working in the region and organizes an annual inter-agency meeting. The Co-ordinator also co-chairs a Local Aid Co-ordination Committee to consider political and socio-economic developments affecting donor assistance and to identify priority areas for support. The Co-ordinator reports regularly on the Palestinian economy and has documented the confrontations, mobility restrictions and border closures which have affected the Palestinian people most recently since September 2001.

Special Co-ordinator: TERJE ROED-LARSEN (Norway).

UNITED NATIONS HUMAN SETTLEMENTS PROGRAMME—UN-Habitat

Address: POB 30030, Nairobi, Kenya.

Telephone: (20) 621234; **fax:** (20) 624266; **e-mail:** infohabitat@unhabitat.org; **internet:** www.unhabitat.org.

UN-Habitat was established, as the United Nations Centre for Human Settlements, in 1978 to service the inter-governmental Commission on Human Settlements. It became a full UN programme on 1 January 2002, serving as the focus for human settlements activities in the UN system. A Conference on Human Settlements (Habitat II) was held in İstanbul, Turkey, in June 1996.

Executive Director: ANNA KAJUMULO TABAIJUKA (Tanzania) .

UNITED NATIONS CHILDREN'S FUND—UNICEF

Address: 3 United Nations Plaza, New York, NY 10017, USA.

Telephone: (212) 326-7000; **fax:** (212) 888-7465; **e-mail:** netmaster@unicef.org; **internet:** www.unicef.org.

UNICEF was established in 1946 by the UN General Assembly as the UN International Children's Emergency Fund, to meet the emergency needs of children in post-war Europe and China. In 1950 its mandate was changed to emphasize programmes giving long-term benefits to children everywhere, particularly those in developing countries who are in the greatest need.

Executive Director: CAROL BELLAMY (USA).

Regional Office for the Middle East and North Africa: POB 1551, UNICEF House, Tl'a al-Ali al Dahak Bin Soufian St, 11821 Amman, Jordan; tel. (6) 5539977; fax (6) 5538880; e-mail menaro@unicef.org.jo.

UNITED NATIONS CONFERENCE ON TRADE AND DEVELOPMENT—UNCTAD

Address: Palais des Nations, 1211 Geneva 10, Switzerland.

Telephone: (22) 9071234; **fax:** (22) 9070057 **e-mail:** ers@unctad.org; **internet:** www.unctad.org.

UNCTAD was established in 1964. It is the principal organ of the UN General Assembly concerned with trade and development, and is the focal point within the UN system for integrated activities relating to trade, finance, technology, investment and sustainable development. It aims to maximize the trade and development opportunities of developing countries, in particular least-developed countries, and to assist them to adapt to the increasing globalization and liberalization of the world economy. UNCTAD undertakes consensus-building activities, research and policy analysis and technical co-operation.

Secretary-General: RUBENS RICÚPERO (Brazil).

UNITED NATIONS POPULATION FUND—UNFPA

Address: 220 East 42nd St, New York, NY 10017, USA.

Telephone: (212) 297-5020; **fax:** (212) 297-4911; **internet:** www.unfpa.org.

Created in 1967 as the Trust Fund for Population Activities, the UN Fund for Population Activities (UNFPA) was established as a Fund of the UN General Assembly in 1972 and was made a subsidiary organ of the UN General Assembly in 1979, with the UNDP Governing Council designated as its governing body. In 1987 UNFPA's name was changed to the United Nations Population Fund (retaining the same acronym).

Executive Director: THORAYA A. OBAID (Saudi Arabia).

UN Specialized Agencies

INTERNATIONAL ATOMIC ENERGY AGENCY—IAEA

Address: Wagramerstrasse 5, POB 100, 1400 Vienna, Austria.

Telephone: (1) 26000; **fax:** (1) 26007; **e-mail:** official.mail@iaea.org; **internet:** www.iaea.org/worldatom.

The Agency was founded in 1957 as an autonomous intergovernmental organization, although it is administratively part of the UN system and reports annually to the UN General Assembly. Its main objectives are to enlarge the contribution of atomic energy to peace, health and prosperity throughout the world, and to ensure that materials and services provided by the Agency are not used to further any military purpose.

Director-General: Dr MOHAMMAD EL-BARADEI (Egypt).

INTERNATIONAL CIVIL AVIATION ORGANIZATION—ICAO

Address: 999 University St, Montréal, QC H3C 5H7, Canada.

Telephone: (514) 954-8219; **fax:** (514) 954-6077; **e-mail:** icaohq@icao.org; **internet:** www.icao.int.

ICAO was founded in 1947, on the basis of the Convention on International Civil Aviation, signed in Chicago, in 1944, to develop the techniques of international air navigation and to help in the planning and improvement of international air transport.

Secretary-General: RENATO CLAUDIO COSTA PEREIRA (Brazil).

Regional Office for the Middle East: Egyptian Civil Aviation Complex, Cairo Airport Rd, 11776 Cairo, Egypt.

INTERNATIONAL LABOUR ORGANIZATION—ILO

Address: 4 route des Morillons, 1211 Geneva 22, Switzerland.

Telephone: (22) 7996111; **fax:** (22) 7988685; **e-mail:** ilo@ilo.org; **internet:** www.ilo.org.

ILO was founded in 1919 to work for social justice as a basis for lasting peace. It carries out this mandate by promoting decent living standards, satisfactory conditions of work and pay and adequate employment opportunities. Methods of action include the creation of international labour standards; the provision of technical co-operation services; and training, education, research and publishing activities to advance ILO objectives.

Director-General: JUAN O. SOMAVÍA (Chile).

Regional Office for Africa: BP 3960, Abidjan 01, Côte d'Ivoire; tel. 20-32-27-16.

Regional Office for Arab States: POB 11-4088, Beirut, Lebanon; tel. (1) 752400; fax (1) 752405; e-mail beirut@ilo.org.lb.

INTERNATIONAL MARITIME ORGANIZATION—IMO

Address: 4 Albert Embankment, London, SE1 7SR, United Kingdom.

Telephone: (20) 7735-7611; **fax:** (20) 7587-3210; **e-mail:** info@imo.org; **internet:** www.imo.org.

The Inter-Governmental Maritime Consultative Organization (IMCO) began operations in 1959, as a specialized agency of the UN to facilitate co-operation among governments on technical matters affecting international shipping. Its main aims are to improve the safety of international shipping, and to prevent pollution caused by ships. IMCO became IMO in 1982.

Secretary-General: WILLIAM A. O'NEIL (Canada).

INTERNATIONAL TELECOMMUNICATION UNION—ITU

Address: Place des Nations, 1211 Geneva 20, Switzerland.

Telephone: (22) 7305111; **fax:** (22) 7337256; **e-mail:** itumail@itu.int; **internet:** www.itu.int.

Founded in 1865, ITU became a specialized agency of the UN in 1947. It acts to encourage world co-operation for the improvement and use of telecommunications, to promote technical development, to harmonize national policies in the field, and to promote the extension of telecommunications throughout the world.

Secretary-General: YOSHIO UTSUMI (Japan).

UNITED NATIONS INDUSTRIAL DEVELOPMENT ORGANIZATION—UNIDO

Address: Vienna International Centre, POB 300, 1400 Vienna, Austria.

Telephone: (1) 260260; **fax:** (1) 2692669; **e-mail:** unido@unido.org; **internet:** www.unido.org.

UNIDO began operations in 1967 and became a specialized agency in 1985. Its objectives are to promote sustainable and socially equitable industrial development in developing countries and in countries with economies in transition. It aims to assist such countries to integrate fully into global economic system by mobilizing knowledge, skills, information and technology to promote productive employment, competitive economies and sound environment.

Director-General: CARLOS ALFREDO MAGARIÑOS (Argentina).

UNIVERSAL POSTAL UNION—UPU

Address: Weltpoststr., 3000 Berne 15, Switzerland.

Telephone: (31) 3503111; **fax:** (31) 3503110; **e-mail:** info@upu.int; **internet:** www.upu.int.

The General Postal Union was founded by the Treaty of Berne (1874), beginning operations in July 1875. Three years later its name was changed to the Universal Postal Union. In 1948 UPU became a specialized agency of the UN. It aims to develop and unify the international postal service, to study problems and to provide training.

Director-General: THOMAS E. LEAVEY (USA).

WORLD INTELLECTUAL PROPERTY ORGANIZATION—WIPO

Address: 34 chemin des Colombettes, 1211 Geneva 20, Switzerland.

Telephone: (22) 3389111; **fax:** (22) 7335428; **e-mail:** wipo.mail@wipo.int; **internet:** www.wipo.int.

WIPO was established in 1970. It became a specialized agency of the UN in 1974 concerned with the protection of intellectual property (e.g. industrial and technical patents and literary copyrights). WIPO formulates and administers treaties embodying international norms and standards of intellectual property, establishes model laws, and facilitates applications for the protection of inventions, trademarks etc. WIPO provides legal and technical assistance to developing countries and countries with economies in transition and advises countries on obligations under the World Trade Organization's agreement on Trade-Related Aspects of Intellectual Property Rights (TRIPS).

Director-General: Dr KAMIL IDRIS (Sudan).

WORLD METEOROLOGICAL ORGANIZATION—WMO

Address: 7 bis ave de la Paix, 1211 Geneva 2, Switzerland.

Telephone: (22) 7308111; **fax:** (22) 7308181; e-mail ipa@wmo.ch; **internet:** www.wmo.ch.

WMO was established in 1950 and was recognized as a Specialized Agency of the UN in 1951. It aims to improve the exchange of information in the fields of meteorology, climatology and operational hydrology, and its applications. WMO jointly implements the UN Framework Convention on Climate Change with UNEP.

Secretary-General: Prof. G.O.P. OBASI (Nigeria).

AFRICAN UNION—AU

Address: POB 3243, Addis Ababa, Ethiopia.
Telephone: (1) 51-7700; **fax:** (1) 51-2622; **e-mail:** tpst@africa
-union.org; **internet** www.africa-union.org.

In May 2001 the Constitutive Act of the African Union entered into force. In July 2002 the African Union (AU) became fully operational, replacing the Organization of African Unity (OAU), which had been founded in 1963. The AU aims to support unity, solidarity and peace among African states; to promote and defend African common positions on issues of shared interest; to encourage human rights, democratic principles and good governance; to advance the development of member states by encouraging research and by working to eradicate preventable diseases; and to promote sustainable development and political and socio-economic integration, including co-ordinating and harmonizing policy between the continent's various 'regional economic communities' (see below).

FORMATION

There were various attempts at establishing an inter-African organization from the 1950s. In November 1958 Ghana and Guinea (later joined by Mali) drafted a Charter that was to form the basis of a Union of African States. In January 1961 a conference was held at Casablanca, attended by the heads of state of Ghana, Guinea, Mali, Morocco, and representatives of Libya and of the provisional government of the Algerian Republic (GPRA). Tunisia, Nigeria, Liberia and Togo declined the invitation to attend. An African Charter was adopted and it was decided to set up an African Military Command and an African Common Market.

Between October 1960 and March 1961 three conferences were held by French-speaking African countries, at Abidjan, Brazzaville and Yaoundé, Cameroon. None of the 12 countries that attended these meetings had been present at the Casablanca Conference. These conferences led eventually to the signing in September 1961, at Tananarive, of a charter establishing the Union africaine et malgache, later the Organisation commune africaine et mauricienne (OCAM).

In May 1961 a conference was held at Monrovia, Liberia, attended by the heads of state or representatives of 19 countries: Cameroon, Central African Republic, Chad, Congo Republic (ex-French), Côte d'Ivoire, Dahomey, Ethiopia, Gabon, Liberia, Madagascar, Mauritania, Niger, Nigeria, Senegal, Sierra Leone, Somalia, Togo, Tunisia and Upper Volta. Meeting again (with the exception of Tunisia and with the addition of the ex-Belgian Congo Republic) in January 1962 at Lagos, Nigeria, they established a permanent secretariat and a standing committee of finance ministers, and accepted a draft charter for an Organization of Inter-African and Malagasy States.

It was the Conference of Addis Ababa, convened in 1963, which finally brought together African states despite the regional, political and linguistic differences that divided them. The foreign ministers of 32 African states attended the Preparatory Meeting held in mid-May: Algeria, Burundi, Cameroon, Central African Republic, Chad, Congo (Brazzaville) (now Republic of the Congo), Congo (Léopoldville) (now Democratic Republic of the Congo), Côte d'Ivoire, Dahomey (now Benin), Ethiopia, Gabon, Ghana, Guinea, Liberia, Libya, Madagascar, Mali, Mauritania, Morocco, Niger, Nigeria, Rwanda, Senegal, Sierra Leone, Somalia, Sudan, Tanganyika (now Tanzania), Togo, Tunisia, Uganda, the United Arab Republic (Egypt) and Upper Volta (now Burkina Faso).

The topics discussed by the meeting were: (i) creation of an Organization of African States; (ii) co-operation among African states in the following fields: economic and social; education, culture and science; collective defence; (iii) decolonization; (iv) apartheid and racial discrimination; (v) effects of economic grouping on the economic development of Africa; (vi) disarmament; (vii) creation of a Permanent Conciliation Commission; and (viii) Africa and the United Nations.

The Heads of State Conference that opened on 23 May 1963 drew up the Charter of the Organization of African Unity, which was then signed by the heads of 30 states on 25 May. The Charter was essentially functional and reflected a compromise between the concept of a loose association of states favoured by the Monrovia Group and the federal idea supported by the Casablanca Group, and in particular by Ghana.

In May 1994 the Abuja Treaty Establishing the African Economic Community (AEC, signed in June 1991) entered into force. The formation of the Community was expected to be a gradual process, to be completed by 2028.

An extraordinary summit meeting, convened in September 1999, in Sirte, Libya, at the request of the Libyan leader Col al-Qaddafi, determined to establish an African Union, based on the principles and objectives of the OAU and AEC, but furthering African co-operation, development and integration. Heads of state declared their commitment to accelerating the establishment of regional institutions, including a pan-African parliament, court of justice and central bank, as well as the implementation of economic and monetary union, as provided for by the Abuja Treaty Establishing the AEC. In July 2000 at the annual OAU summit meeting, held at Lomé, Togo, 27 heads of state and government signed the draft Constitutive Act of the African Union, which was to enter into force one month after ratification by two-thirds of member states' legislatures; this was achieved on 26 May 2001. The Union was inaugurated, replacing the OAU, on 9 July 2002, at a summit meeting of heads of state and government held in Durban, South Africa, following a transitional period of one year after the endorsement of the Act in July 2001. (During the transitional year, pending the transfer of all assets and liabilities to the Union, the OAU Charter remained in effect. A review of all OAU treaties was implemented, with those deemed relevant retained by the AU.) During an initial interim period, from July 2002–July 2003, the establishment of the AU's main policy organs and other institutions was to be finalized; the four key organs were launched in July 2002. Morocco is the only African country that is not a member of the AU (see below).

The AU aims to strengthen and advance the process of African political and socio-economic integration initiated by the OAU. The Union operates on the basis of both the Constitutive Act and the Abuja Treaty. It is envisaged that the process of implementing the Abuja Treaty will be accelerated. A protocol to the Treaty, establishing a Pan-African Parliament was opened for signature under the OAU in March 2001, and a protocol relating to the establishment of a Peace and Security Council was adopted at the July 2002 inaugural summit meeting of the AU.

MEMBERS*

Algeria	Eritrea	Nigeria
Angola	Ethiopia	Rwanda
Benin	Gabon	São Tomé and
Botswana	The Gambia	Príncipe
Burkina Faso	Ghana	Senegal
Burundi	Guinea	Seychelles
Cameroon	Guinea-Bissau	Sierra Leone
Cape Verde	Kenya	Somalia
Central African	Lesotho	South Africa
Republic	Liberia	Sudan
Chad	Libya	Swaziland
The Comoros	Madagascar†	Tanzania
Congo, Democratic	Malawi	Togo
Republic	Mali	Tunisia
Congo, Republic	Mauritania	Uganda
Côte d'Ivoire	Mauritius	Zambia
Djibouti	Mozambique	Zimbabwe
Egypt	Namibia	
Equatorial Guinea	Niger	

* The Sahrawi Arab Democratic Republic (SADR–Western Sahara) was admitted to the OAU in February 1982, following recognition by more than one-half of the member states, but its membership was disputed by Morocco and other states which claimed that a two-thirds majority was needed to admit a state whose existence was in question. Morocco withdrew from the OAU with effect from November 1985, and has not applied to join the AU. The SADR ratified the Constitutive Act in December 2000 and is a full member of the AU.

† Madagascar was suspended from meetings of the AU in July 2002 (having been suspended from the OAU in the previous month).

Note: The Constitutive Act stipulates that member states in which Governments accede to power by unconstitutional means are liable to suspension from participating in the Union's activities and to the imposition of sanctions by the Union.

Organization

(September 2002)

ASSEMBLY

The Assembly, comprising member countries' Heads of State and Government, is the supreme organ of the Union and meets at least once a year to determine and monitor the Union's priorities and common policies and to adopt its annual work programme. Resolutions are passed by a two-thirds majority, procedural matters by a simple majority. Extraordinary sessions may be convened at the request of a member state and on approval by a two-thirds majority. A chairperson is elected at each meeting from among the members, to hold office for one year. The Assembly ensures compliance by member states with decisions of the Union, adopts the biennial budget, will appoint judges of the planned Court of Justice, and hears and settles disputes between member states. The first Assembly meeting was held in Durban, South Africa, in July 2002. (July 2003: Maputo, Mozambique. Subsequently the Assembly was to meet in Addis Ababa, Ethiopia, in alternate years.)

Chairperson (2002/03): THABO MBEKI (Pres. of South Africa).

EXECUTIVE COUNCIL

Consists of ministers of foreign affairs and others and meets at least twice a year (in February and July), with provision for extraordinary sessions. The Council's Chairperson is the Minister of Foreign Affairs (or another competent authority) of the country that has provided the Chairperson of the Assembly. Prepares meetings of, and is responsible to, the Assembly. Determines the issues to be submitted to the Assembly for decision, co-ordinates and harmonizes the policies, activities and initiatives of the Union in areas of common interest to member states, monitors the implementation of policies and decisions of the Assembly.

PERMANENT REPRESENTATIVES COMMITTEE

The Committee, which comprises Ambassadors accredited to the AU and meets at least once a month, is responsible to, advises and prepares meetings of the Executive Council, including its agenda and draft decisions.

COMMISSION

(An Interim Commission was to be operational from July 2002–July 2003.) The Commission is permanent secretariat of the organization. It comprises a Chairperson (elected for a four-year term of office by the Assembly), Deputy Chairperson and eight Commissioners (responsible for: peace and security; political affairs; infrastructure and energy; social affairs; human resources, science and technology; trade and industry; rural economy and agriculture; and economic affairs) who are elected on the basis of equal geographical distribution. Members of the Commission serve a term of four years and may stand for re-election for one further term of office. Further support staff assist the smooth functioning of the Commission. The Commission represents the Union under the guidance of and as mandated by the Assembly and the Executive Council, and reports to the Executive Council. It deals with administrative issues, implements the decisions of the Union, and acts as the custodian of the Constitutive Act and Protocols, and other agreements. Its work covers the following domains: control of pandemics; disaster management; international crime and terrorism; environmental management; negotiations relating to external trade; negotiations relating to external debt; population, migration, refugees and displaced persons; food security; socio-economic integration; and all other areas where a common position has been established by Union member states. It has responsibility for the co-ordination of AU activities and meetings.

Interim Chairperson: AMARA ESSY (Côte d'Ivoire).

SPECIALIZED TECHNICAL COMMITTEES

There are specialized committees for monetary and financial affairs; rural economy and agricultural matters; trade, customs and immigration; industry, science and technology, energy, natural resources and environment; transport, communications and tourism; health, labour and social affairs; and education, culture and human resources. These have responsibility for implementing the Union's programmes and projects.

Note: In May 2002 a 15-member High Level Advisory Panel of Eminent Persons was formed to make recommendations on key aspects of the finalization of the OAU–AU transition process and on possible action by the AU during the 2002–03 interim period. The Panel was to be disbanded in late 2003. At mid-2002 several organs of the AU remained to be established, including a Pan-African Parliament comprising elected representatives from the Union's five principal regions (northern, eastern, southern, western and central); a Court of Justice, which was to pass judgment on alleged human rights abuses; an Economic, Social and Cultural Council, which was to have an advisory function and was to comprise representatives of civic and professional bodies; and a 15-country Peace and Security Council. In addition three financial instititions were to be inaugurated to manage the financing of programmes and projects: an African Central Bank, an African Monetary Fund, and an African Investment Bank.

Finance

At May 2002 some US $52m. was owed in arrears to the OAU. No final decisions on the AU's funding mechanisms had been taken at mid-2002.

Activities

The AU has the following areas of interest: peace and security; political affairs; infrastructure and energy; social affairs; human resources, science and technology; trade and industry; rural economy and agriculture; and economic affairs. In July 2001 the OAU adopted a New African Initiative, which was subsequently renamed the New Partnership for Africa's Development—NEPAD (see below). NEPAD, which was officially launched in October, represents a long-term strategy for socio-economic recovery in Africa and aims to promote the strengthening of democracy and economic management in the region. The heads of state of Algeria, Egypt, Nigeria, Senegal and South Africa have played leading roles in its preparation and management. In June 2002 NEPAD heads of state and government adopted a Declaration on Democracy, Political, Economic and Corporate Governance and announced the development of an African Peer Review Mechanism (whose secretariat was to be hosted by the UN Economic Commission for Africa, q.v.). Meeting during that month the Group of Seven industrialized nations and Russia (the G-8) welcomed the formation of NEPAD and adopted an Africa Action Plan in support of the initiative. NEPAD is ultimately answerable to the AU Assembly. The inaugural summit of the Assembly, held in Durban, South Africa, in July 2002, issued a Declaration on the Implementation of NEPAD, which urged all member states to adopt the Declaration on Democracy, Political, Economic and Corporate Governance and to participate in the peer-review process.

PEACE AND SECURITY

Pending the ratification and entry into force of the Protocol on the Peace and Security Council, adopted by the first AU summit of heads of state and government in July 2002, the 1993 Cairo Declaration on the OAU Mechanism for Conflict Prevention, Management and Resolution was to remain in effect. The Protocol provides for the inauguration of an AU collective security and early warning mechanism, comprising a 15-country Peace and Security Council, operational at the levels of heads of state and government, ministers of foreign affairs, and permanent representatives, to be supported by a five-member advisory Panel of the Wise, a Continental Early Warning System, an African Standby Force and a Peace Fund (superseding the OAU Peace Fund, which was established in June 1993 and had received contributions of US $42m. by March 2002). The activities of the Peace and Security Council were to include the promotion of peace, security and stability; early warning and preventive diplomacy; peace-making mediation; peace support operations and intervention; peace-building activities and post-conflict reconstruction; and humanitarian action and disaster management. The Council was to implement the common defence policy of the Union, and to ensure the implementation of the 1999 OAU Convention on the Prevention and Combating of Terrorism (which provided for the exchange of information to help counter terrorism and for signatory states to refrain from granting asylum to terrorists). Member states were to set aside standby troop contingents for the planned African Standby Force, which was mandated to undertake observation, monitoring and other peace-support missions; to deploy in member states as required to prevent the resurgence or escalation of violence; to intervene in member states as required to restore stability; to conduct post-conflict disarmament and demobilization and other peace-building activities; and to provide emergency humanitarian assistance. The Council was to harmonize and co-ordinate the activities of other regional security mechanisms.

The extraordinary OAU summit meeting convened in Sirte, Libya in September 1999 determined to hold a regular ministerial Conference on Security, Stability, Development and Cooperation in Africa (CSSDCA): the first CSSDCA took place in Abuja, Nigeria, in May 2000. The CSSDCA process provides a forum for the development of policies aimed at advancing the common values of the AU and AEC in the areas of peace, security and co-operation. In December 2000 OAU heads of state and government adopted the Bamako Declaration, concerning arresting the circulation of small arms on the continent.

In recent years the OAU was involved in peace-making and peace-building activities in several African countries and regions. Military observer missions were deployed in Rwanda (1991–93), Burundi (1993–96), the Comoros (1998–2002), the Democratic Republic of the Congo (from 1999) and Eritrea and Ethiopia (from 2000). In February 2002 the OAU mediated talks between President Didier Ratsiraka of Madagascar and the official opposition leader Marc Ravalomanana, who established a rival Madagascan government during that month, having also claimed victory at the presidential election held in that country in December 2001. In March 2002 the OAU held talks with each of the disputing sides in the Madagascan political crisis, facilitating the conclusion in mid-April of the so-called Dakar Agreement, providing for the formation of an interim government of national unity, pending the staging of a new presidential election. However, in the following month Ravalomanana was declared President by a Madagascan constitutional court. In view of significant opposition to this decision, the OAU determined not to recognize the Ravalomanana administration and, in June, suspended Madagascar from its meetings. In July the newly inaugurated AU upheld this decision, suspending the country from AU meetings pending the staging of free and fair elections leading to the establishment of a legitimate and democratic government.

INFRASTRUCTURE, ENERGY AND THE ENVIRONMENT

Meeting in Lomé, Togo, in July 2001, OAU heads of state and government authorized the establishment of an African Energy Commission—AFREC, which was to increase co-operation in energy matters between Africa and other regions. The convention establishing AFREC had six signatories at January 2002.

In 1964 the OAU adopted a Declaration on the Denuclearization of Africa, and in April 1996 it adopted the African Nuclear Weapons Free Zone Treaty (also known as the 'Pelindaba Treaty'), which identifies Africa as a nuclear weapon-free zone and promotes co-operation in the peaceful uses of nuclear energy.

In 1968 OAU member states adopted the African Convention on the Conservation of Nature and Natural Resources. The Bamako Convention on the Ban of the Import into Africa and the Control of Transboundary Movement and Management of Hazardous Wastes within Africa was adopted by OAU member states in 1991 and entered into force in April 1998.

POLITICAL AND SOCIAL AFFAIRS

The African Charter on Human and People's Rights, which was adopted by the OAU in 1981 and entered into force in October 1986, provided for the establishment of an 11-member African Commission on Human and People's Rights, based in Banjul, The Gambia. The African Charter on the Rights and Welfare of the Child was opened for signature in July 1990, but has not yet entered into force. In March 2001 the OAU adopted a Protocol to the Abuja Treaty Establishing the AEC relating to the Pan-African Parliament. Once established the Parliament was to have an advisory and consultative function.

The July 2002 inaugural summit meeting of AU heads of state and government adopted a Declaration Governing Democratic Elections in Africa, providing guide-lines for the conduct of national elections in member states and outlining the AU's electoral observation and monitoring role. In March an OAU observer team found the Zimbabwean presidential election, held in controversial circumstances during that month, to have been conducted freely and fairly. In recent years several large population displacements have occurred in Africa, mainly as a result of violent conflict. In 1969 OAU member states adopted the Convention Governing the Specific Aspects of Refugee Problems in Africa, which entered into force in June 1974. The Convention promotes close co-operation with UNHCR (q.v.). The AU maintains a Special Refugee Contingency Fund to provide relief assistance and to support repatriation activities, education projects, etc. for displaced people in Africa. The AU aims to address pressing health issues affecting member states, including the eradication of endemic parasitic and infectious diseases and improving access to medicines. An African Summit on HIV/AIDS, Tuberculosis and other related Infectious Diseases was convened, under OAU auspices, in March 2001. An AU Scientific, Technical and Research Commission is based in Lagos, Nigeria, and a Centre for Linguistic and Historical Studies by Oral Tradition is based in Niamey, Niger.

TRADE, INDUSTRY AND ECONOMIC CO-OPERATION

In October 1999 a conference on Industrial Partnerships and Investment in Africa was held in Dakar, Senegal, jointly organized by the OAU with UNIDO, the ECA, the African Development Bank and the Alliance for Africa's Industrialization. In June 1997 the first meeting between ministers of the OAU and the European Union (EU) was convened in New York, USA. In April 2000 the first EU–Africa summit of heads of state and government was held in Cairo, Egypt, under the auspices of the EU and OAU. The summit adopted the Cairo Plan of Action, which addressed areas including economic integration, trade and investment, private-sector development in Africa, human rights and good governance, peace and security, and development issues such as education, health and food security. A second EU–Africa summit meeting was to be held in April 2003, in Lisbon, Portugal. More than 200 business representatives participated in an AU Business Summit, convened in July 2002, in Durban, South Africa, alongside the inaugural AU summit of heads of state and government.

The AU aims to reduce obstacles to intra-African trade and to reverse the continuing disproportionate level of trade conducted by many African countries with their former colonial powers.

In June 1991 the OAU Assembly of Heads of State signed the Abuja Treaty Establishing the African Economic Community (AEC). The Treaty was to enter into force after ratification by two-thirds of member states. The Community was to be established by 2028, following a gradual six-phase process involving the co-ordination, harmonization and progressive integration of the activities of all existing and future sub-regional economic unions. (There are 14 so-

called 'regional economic communities'—RECs in Africa, including the following major RECs that are regarded as the five pillars, or building blocks, of the AEC: the Common Market for Eastern and Southern Africa—COMESA, the Communauté économique des états de l'Afrique centrale—CEEAC, the Economic Community of West African States—ECOWAS, the Southern African Development Community—SADC, and the Union of the Arab Maghreb (q.v.). The subsidiary RECs are: the Communauté économique et monétaire de l'Afrique centrale—CEMAC, the Community of Sahel-Saharan States—CEN-SAD (q.v.), the East African Community—EAC, the Economic Community of the Great Lakes Countries, the Intergovernmental Authority on Development—IGAD, the Indian Ocean Commission—IOC, the Mano River Union, the Southern African Customs Union, and the Union économique et monétaire ouest-africaine—UEMOA.) The main policy-making organ of the AEC was to be an Economic and Social Council. The Abuja Treaty entered into force on 12 May 1994, having been ratified by the requisite number of OAU member states. The inaugural meeting of the AEC took place in June 1997.

Specialized Agencies

African Accounting Council: POB 11223, Kinshasa, Democratic Republic of the Congo; tel. (12) 33567; f. 1979; provides assistance to institutions in member countries on standardization of accounting; promotes education, further training and research in accountancy and related areas of study. Publ. *Information and Liaison Bulletin* (every two months).

African Civil Aviation Commission—AFCAC: 15 blvd de la République, BP 2356, Dakar, Senegal; tel. 839-93-73; fax 823-26-61; e-mail cafac@sentoo.sn; internet www.afcac-cafac.sn; f. 1969 to encourage co-operation in all civil aviation activities; promotes co-ordination and better utilization and development of African air transport systems and the standardization of aircraft, flight equipment and training programmes for pilots and mechanics; organizes working groups and seminars, and compiles statistics. Pres. MAMDOUH HESHMAT (Egypt); Sec. CHARLES M. DIOP.

Pan-African Institution of Education for Development—PIED: 29 ave de la Justice, BP 1764, Kinshasa I, Democratic Republic of the Congo; tel. (12) 34527; e-mail baseeduc@hotmail.com; f. 1973, became specialized agency in 1986, present name adopted 2001; undertakes educational research and training, focuses on co-operation and problem-solving, acts as an observatory for education. Publs *Bulletin d'Information* (quarterly), *Revue africaine des sciences de l'éducation* (2 a year), *Répertoire africain des institutions de recherche* (annually).

Pan-African News Agency—PANAPRESS: BP 4650, Dakar, Senegal; tel. 824-14-10; fax 824-13-90; internet www.panapress.com; regional headquarters in Khartoum, Sudan; Lusaka, Zambia; Kinshasa, Democratic Republic of the Congo; Lagos, Nigeria; Tripoli, Libya; began operations in May 1983, restructured in late 1990s; receives information from national news agencies and circulates news in English and French. Dir-Gen. BABACAR FALL. Publ. *PANA Review*.

Pan-African Postal Union—PAPU: POB 6026, Arusha, Tanzania; tel. (27) 2508603; fax (27) 2503913; e-mail papu@habari.co.tz; f. 1980 to extend members' co-operation in the improvement of postal services. Sec.-Gen. JILANI BEN HADDADA. Publ. *PAPU Bulletin*.

Pan-African Railways Union: BP 687, Kinshasa, Democratic Republic of the Congo; tel. (12) 23861; f. 1972 to standardize, expand, co-ordinate and improve members' railway services; the ultimate aim is to link all systems; main organs: Gen. Assembly, Exec. Bd, Gen. Secr., five tech. cttees. Mems in 30 African countries.

Pan-African Telecommunications Union: POB 7248, Kinshasa, Democratic Republic of the Congo; f. 1977; co-ordinates devt of telecommunications networks and services in Africa.

Supreme Council for Sports in Africa: BP 1363, Yaoundé, Cameroon; tel. and fax 23-95-80; Sec.-Gen. Dr AWOTURE ELEYAE (Nigeria). Publs *SCSA News* (6 a year), *African Sports Movement Directory* (annually).

ASSOCIATED PARTNERSHIP

New Partnership for Africa's Development—NEPAD: POB 1234, Midrand, Halfway House, 1685 South Africa (secretariat); internet www.nepad.org; f. 2001 as a long-term strategy to promote socio-economic development in Africa; adopted Declaration on Democracy, Political, Economic and Corporate Governance and the African Peer Review Mechanism in June 2002; heads of state implementation cttee comprises representatives of 20 countries (four from each of the AU's five regions: northern, eastern, southern, western and central); steering cttee, comprising Algeria, Egypt, Nigeria, Senegal and South Africa, meets once a month; Implementation Cttee Chair. Gen. (retd) OLUSEGUN OBASANJO (Pres. of Nigeria); Steering Cttee Chair. Prof. WISEMAN NKUHLU (South Africa).

ARAB FUND FOR ECONOMIC AND SOCIAL DEVELOPMENT—AFESD

Address: POB 21923, Safat, 13080 Kuwait.

Telephone: 4844500; **fax:** 4815760; **e-mail:** hq@arabfund.org; **internet:** www.arabfund.org.

Established in 1968 by the Economic Council of the Arab League, the Fund began its operations in 1974. It participates in the financing of economic and social development projects in the Arab states.

MEMBERSHIP

Twenty-one members (see table of subscriptions below).

Organization

(September 2002)

BOARD OF GOVERNORS

The Board of Governors consists of a Governor and an Alternate Governor appointed by each member of the Fund. The Board of Governors is considered as the General Assembly of the Fund, and has all powers.

BOARD OF DIRECTORS

The Board of Directors is composed of eight Directors elected by the Board of Governors from among Arab citizens of recognized experience and competence. They are elected for a renewable term of two years.

The Board of Directors is charged with all the activities of the Fund and exercises the powers delegated to it by the Board of Governors.

Director-General and Chairman of the Board of Directors: ABDLATIF YOUSUF AL-HAMAD.

FINANCIAL STRUCTURE

In 1982 the authorized capital was increased from 400m. Kuwaiti dinars (KD) to KD 800m., divided into 80,000 shares having a value of KD 10,000 each. At the end of 2001 paid-up capital was KD 663.04m.

LOANS BY MEMBER, 2001

Member	Project	Amount (KD million)
Algeria . . .	Pumping and conveyance of water from Bani Haroun	31.0
Djibouti. . .	Development of the education sector	4.0
Egypt . . .	Cairo North power generation station	27.0
Lebanon .	Conveyance of water from Litani to Southern Lebanon	31.0
Mauritania .	Connecting Boghe to Manantali electrical grid	4.0
	Debt reduction	14.0
	Nouakchott–Nouadhibou road	16.0
Morocco. . .	Casablanca–el-Jadida motorway	15.0
Sudan . . .	Atbara-Haiya–Port Sudan road	25.0
Syria . . .	Expansion of Nasrieh power plant and conversion to combined cycle	25.0
Tunisia .	Tunis–Mjaz el-Bab motorway	25.0
	Developmental credit lines	11.0
Yemen . . .	Sayhat–Nishtun road	26.0
	San'a International Airport development	28.0
Total		**282.0**

SUBSCRIPTIONS (KD million, December 2001)*

Algeria.	. .	64.78	Oman	. . . .	17.28
Bahrain	. .	2.16	Palestine.	. . .	1.10
Djibouti	. .	0.02	Qatar	. . . .	6.75
Egypt .	. .	40.50	Saudi Arabia.	. .	159.07
Iraq	. . .	31.76	Somalia	. . . .	0.21
Jordan .	. .	17.30	Sudan	. . . .	11.06
Kuwait.	. .	169.70	Syria.	. . . .	24.00
Lebanon	. .	2.00	Tunisia	. . . .	6.16
Libya .	. .	59.85	United Arab Emirates .		28.00
Mauritania.	.	0.82	Yemen	. . . .	4.52
Morocco.	. .	16.00			
			Total	. . . . .	**663.04**

* 100 Kuwaiti dinars = US $315.6 (December 2001).

Activities

Pursuant to the Agreement Establishing the Fund (as amended in 1997 by the Board of Governors), the purpose of the Fund is to contribute to the financing of economic and social development projects in the Arab states and countries by:

1. Financing economic development projects of an investment character by means of loans granted on concessionary terms to governments and public enterprises and corporations, giving preference to projects which are vital to the Arab entity, as well as to joint Arab projects.

2. Financing private sector projects in member states by providing all forms of loans and guarantees to corporations and enterprises (possessing juridical personality), participating in their equity capital, and providing other forms of financing and the requisite financial, technical and advisory services, in accordance with such regulations and subject to such conditions as may be prescribed by the Board of Directors.

3. Forming or participating in the equity capital of corporations possessing juridical personality, for the implementation and financing of private sector projects in member states, including the provision and financing of technical, advisory and financial services.

4. Establishing and administering special funds with aims compatible with those of the Fund and with resources provided by the Fund or other sources.

5. Encouraging, directly or indirectly, the investment of public and private capital in a manner conducive to the development and growth of the Arab economy.

6. Providing expertise and technical assistance in the various fields of economic development.

The Fund co-operates with other Arab organizations such as the Arab Monetary Fund, the League of Arab States and OAPEC in preparing regional studies and conferences, for example in the areas of human resource development, demographic research and private sector financing of infrastructure projects. It also acts as the secretariat of the Co-ordination Group of Arab National and Regional Development Financing Institutions. These organizations also work together to produce a *Joint Arab Economic Report*, which considers economic and social developments in the Arab states.

During 2001 the Fund approved 14 new loans, totalling KD 282m., for projects in 10 member countries. At the end of that year total

LOANS BY SECTOR, 2001

Sector	Amount (KD million)	%
Agriculture and rural development . .	31.0	11.0
Energy and electricity	56.0	19.8
Industry and mining	11.0	3.9
Transport and telecommunications . .	135.0	47.9
Water and sewerage	31.0	11.0
Other	18.0	6.4
Total	**282.0**	**100.0**

lending since 1974 amounted to KD 3,855.7m., which helped to finance 417 projects in 17 Arab countries.

The total number of technical assistance grants provided by the end of 2000 was 678, with a value of KD 89.1m. During 2001 the Fund extended 28 new grants, totalling KD 5.0m., of which 63% was to enhance institution building and to support training in

specialized Arab scientific and research centres, while 24% was for general studies and other research activities.

In December 1997 AFESD initiated an Arab Fund Fellowships Programme, which aimed to provide grants to Arab academics to conduct university teaching or advanced research.

ARAB MONETARY FUND

Address: Arab Monetary Fund Bldg, Corniche Rd, POB 2818, Abu Dhabi, United Arab Emirates.

Telephone: (2) 215000; **fax:** (2) 326454; **e-mail:** centralmail@amfad .org.ae; **internet:** www.amf.org.ae.

The Agreement establishing the Arab Monetary Fund was approved by the Economic Council of Arab States in Rabat, Morocco, in April 1976 and entered into force on 2 February 1977.

MEMBERS

Algeria	Oman
Bahrain	Palestine
Djibouti	Qatar
Egypt	Saudi Arabia
Iraq*	Somalia*
Jordan	Sudan*
Kuwait	Syria
Lebanon	Tunisia
Libya	United Arab Emirates
Mauritania	Yemen
Morocco	

* From July 1993 loans to Iraq, Somalia and Sudan were suspended as a result of their failure to repay debts to the Fund totalling US $603m. By the end of 1998 the arrears amounted to AAD 197.3m. (or some $833.4m.). Sudan was readmitted in April 2000, having settled arrears of $214m.

Organization

(September 2002)

BOARD OF GOVERNORS

The Board of Governors is the highest authority of the Arab Monetary Fund. It formulates policies on Arab economic integration and liberalization of trade among member states. With certain exceptions, it may delegate to the Board of Executive Directors some of its powers. The Board of Governors is composed of a governor and a deputy governor appointed by each member state for a term of five years. It meets at least once a year; meetings may also be convened at the request of half the members, or of members holding half of the total voting power.

BOARD OF EXECUTIVE DIRECTORS

The Board of Executive Directors exercises all powers vested in it by the Board of Governors and may delegate to the Director-General such powers as it deems fit. It is composed of the Director-General and eight non-resident directors elected by the Board of Governors. Each director holds office for three years and may be re-elected.

DIRECTOR-GENERAL

The Director-General of the Fund is appointed by the Board of Governors for a renewable five-year term, and serves as Chairman of the Board of Executive Directors.

The Director-General supervises a Committee on Loans and a Committee on Investments to make recommendations on loan and investment policies to the Board of Executive Directors, and is required to submit an Annual Report to the Board of Governors.

Director-General and Chairman of the Board of Executive Directors: Dr JASSIM ABDULLAH AL-MANNAI.

FINANCE

The Arab Accounting Dinar (AAD) is a unit of account equivalent to three IMF Special Drawing Rights. (The average value of the SDR in 2001 was US $1.27304.)

Each member paid, in convertible currencies, 5% of the value of its shares at the time of its ratification of the Agreement and another 20% when the Agreement entered into force. In addition, each member paid 2% of the value of its shares in its national currency regardless of whether it is convertible. The second 25% of the capital

was to be subscribed by the end of September 1979, bringing the total paid-up capital in convertible currencies to AAD 131.5m. An increase in requests for loans led to a resolution by the Board of Governors in April 1981, giving members the option of paying the balance of their subscribed capital. This payment became obligatory in July 1981, when total approved loans exceeded 50% of the already paid-up capital in convertible currencies. In April 1983 the authorized capital of the Fund was increased from AAD 288m. to AAD 600m. The new capital stock comprised 12,000 shares, each having the value of AAD 50,000. At the end of 2000 total paid-up capital was AAD 324.1m.

CAPITAL SUBSCRIPTIONS
(million Arab Accounting Dinars, 31 December 2000)

Member	Paid-up capital
Algeria	42.40
Bahrain	5.00
Djibouti	0.25
Egypt	32.00
Iraq	42.40
Jordan	5.40
Kuwait	32.00
Lebanon	5.00
Libya	13.44
Mauritania	5.00
Morocco	15.00
Oman	5.00
Palestine	2.16
Qatar	10.00
Saudi Arabia	48.40
Somalia	4.00
Sudan	10.00
Syria	7.20
Tunisia	7.00
United Arab Emirates	19.20
Yemen	15.40
Total	324.09*

* Excluding Palestine's share, which was deferred by a Board of Governors' resolution in 1978.

Activities

The creation of the Arab Monetary Fund was seen as a step towards the goal of Arab economic integration. It assists member states in balance of payments difficulties, and also has a broad range of aims.

The Articles of Agreement define the Fund's aims as follows:

(*a*) to correct disequilibria in the balance of payments of member states;

(*b*) to promote the stability of exchange rates among Arab currencies, to render them mutually convertible, and to eliminate restrictions on current payments between member states;

(*c*) to establish policies and modes of monetary co-operation to accelerate Arab economic integration and economic development in the member states;

(*d*) to tender advice on the investment of member states' financial resources in foreign markets, whenever called upon to do so;

(*e*) to promote the development of Arab financial markets;

(*f*) to promote the use of the Arab dinar as a unit of account and to pave the way for the creation of a unified Arab currency;

(*g*) to co-ordinate the positions of member states in dealing with international monetary and economic problems; and

(*h*) to provide a mechanism for the settlement of current payments between member states in order to promote trade among them.

The Arab Monetary Fund functions both as a fund and a bank. It is empowered:

(*a*) to provide short- and medium-term loans to finance balance of payments deficits of member states;

(*b*) to issue guarantees to member states to strengthen their borrowing capabilities;

(*c*) to act as intermediary in the issuance of loans in Arab and international markets for the account of member states and under their guarantees;

(*d*) to co-ordinate the monetary policies of member states;

(*e*) to manage any funds placed under its charge by member states;

(*f*) to hold periodic consultations with member states on their economic conditions; and

(*g*) to provide technical assistance to banking and monetary institutions in member states.

Loans are intended to finance an overall balance of payments deficit and a member may draw up to 75% of its paid-up subscription, in convertible currencies, for this purpose unconditionally (automatic loans). A member may, however, obtain loans in excess of this limit, subject to agreement with the Fund on a programme aimed at reducing its balance of payments deficit (ordinary and extended loans, equivalent to 175% and 250% of its quota respectively). From 1981 a country receiving no extended loans was entitled to a loan under the Inter-Arab Trade Facility (discontinued in 1989) of up to 100% of its quota. In addition, a member has the right to borrow up to 50% of its paid-up capital in order to cope with an unexpected deficit in its balance of payments resulting from a decrease in its exports of goods and services or a large increase in its imports of agricultural products following a poor harvest (compensatory loans).

Automatic and compensatory loans are repayable within three years, while ordinary and extended loans are repayable within five

LOANS APPROVED, 1978–2000

Type of loan	Number of loans	Amount (AAD '000)
Automatic	55	266,625
Ordinary	11	104,566
Compensatory	12	79,885
Extended	19	223,451
Structural Adjustment Facility . . .	7	88,332
Inter-Arab Trade Facility (cancelled in 1989)	11	64,730
Total	115	827,589

LOANS APPROVED, 2000

Borrower	Type of loan	Amount (AAD million)
Djibouti	Extended	0.245
Egypt	Structural Adjustment Facility	23.152
Lebanon. . . .	Structural Adjustment Facility	3.602
Mauritania . . .	Extended	4.000
Morocco	Compensatory	7.400
Total		38.399

and seven years respectively. Loans are granted at concessionary and uniform rates of interest which increase with the length of the period of the loan. In 1988 the Fund's executive directors agreed to modify their policy on lending, placing an emphasis on the correction of economic imbalances in recipient countries. In 1996 the Fund established the Structural Adjustment Facility, providing up to 75% of a member's paid-up subscription. This may include a technical assistance component comprising a grant of up to 2% of the total loan.

Over the period 1978–2000 the Fund extended 115 loans amounting to AAD 827.6m. During 2000 the Fund approved five loans, amounting to AAD 38.4m., while loan disbursements amounted to AAD 47.2m.

The Fund's technical assistance activities are extended through either the provision of experts to the country concerned or in the form of specialized training of officials of member countries. In view of the increased importance of this type of assistance, the Fund established, in 1988, the Economic Policy Institute (EPI) which offers regular training courses and specialized seminars for middle-level and senior staff, respectively, of financial and monetary institutions of the Arab countries. On 1 April 1999 the Fund signed a memorandum of understanding with the International Monetary Fund to establish a joint regional training programme. During 2000 eight training courses and one workshop were organized by the EPI under this joint programme.

TRADE PROMOTION

Arab Trade Financing Program—ATFP: POB 26799, Arab Monetary Fund Bldg, 7th Floor, Corniche Rd, Abu Dhabi, United Arab Emirates; tel. (2) 6316999; fax (2) 6316793; e-mail atfphq@atfp.org.ae; internet www.atfp.org.ae; f. 1989 to develop and promote trade between Arab countries and to enhance the competitive ability of Arab exporters; operates by extending lines of credit to Arab exporters and importers through national agencies (some 121 agencies designated by the monetary authorities of 18 Arab countries at early 2001). The Arab Monetary Fund provided 50% of ATFP's authorized capital of US $500m.; participation was also invited from private and official Arab financial institutions and joint Arab/foreign institutions. ATFP administers the Inter-Arab Trade Information Network (IATIN), and organizes Buyers–Sellers meetings to promote Arab goods. Chair. and Chief Exec. Dr JASSIM ABDULLAH AL-MANNAI. Publs *Annual Report* (Arabic and English), *IATIN Quarterly Bulletin* (Arabic).

Publications

Annual Report.

AMDB Bulletin (quarterly).

Arab Countries: Economic Indicators (annually).

Balance of Payments and External Public Debt of Arab Countries (annually).

Foreign Trade of Arab Countries (annually).

Joint Arab Economic Report (annually).

Money and Credit in Arab Countries.

National Accounts of Arab Countries (annually).

Reports on commodity structure (by value and quantity) of member countries' imports from and exports to other Arab countries; other studies on economic, social, management and fiscal issues.

CO-OPERATION COUNCIL FOR THE ARAB STATES OF THE GULF

Address: POB 7153, Riyadh 11462, Saudi Arabia.

Telephone: (1) 482-7777; **fax:** (1) 482-9089; **internet:** www.gcc -sg.org.

More generally known as the Gulf Co-operation Council (GCC), the organization was established on 25 May 1981 by six Arab states.

MEMBERS

Bahrain	Oman	Saudi Arabia
Kuwait	Qatar	United Arab Emirates

Organization

(September 2002)

SUPREME COUNCIL

The Supreme Council is the highest authority of the GCC. It comprises the heads of member states and meets annually in ordinary session, and in emergency session if demanded by two or more members. The Council also convenes an annual consultative meeting. The Presidency of the Council is undertaken by each state in turn, in alphabetical order. The Supreme Council draws up the overall policy of the organization; it discusses recommendations and laws presented to it by the Ministerial Council and the Secretariat General in preparation for endorsement. The GCC's charter provided for the creation of a commission for the settlement of disputes between member states, to be attached to and appointed by the Supreme Council. The Supreme Council convenes the commission for the settlement of disputes on an *ad hoc* basis to address altercations between member states as they arise.

MINISTERIAL COUNCIL

The Ministerial Council consists of the foreign ministers of member states (or other ministers acting on their behalf), meeting every three months, and in emergency session if demanded by two or more members. It prepares for the meetings of the Supreme Council, and draws up policies, recommendations, studies and projects aimed at developing co-operation and co-ordination among member states in various spheres. GCC ministerial committees have been established in a number of areas of co-operation; sectoral ministerial meetings are held periodically.

CONSULTATIVE COMMISSION

The Consultative Commission comprising 30 members (five from each member state) nominated for a three-year period, acts as an advisory body, considering matters referred to it by the Supreme Council.

SECRETARIAT GENERAL

The Secretariat assists member states in implementing recommendations by the Supreme and Ministerial Councils, and prepares reports and studies, budgets and accounts. The Secretary-General is appointed by the Supreme Council for a three-year term renewable once. The position is rotated among member states in order to ensure equal representation. Assistant Secretary-Generals are appointed by the Ministerial Council upon the recommendation of the Secretary-General. The Secretariat comprises the following divisions and departments: political affairs; economic affairs; military affairs; human and environmental affairs; the Office of the Secretary-General, Finance and Administrative Affairs; a patent bureau; an administrative development unit; an internal auditing unit; an information centre; and a telecommunications bureau (based in Bahrain). All member states contribute in equal proportions towards the budget of the Secretariat.

Secretary-General: ABDUL RAHMAN BIN HAMAD AL-ATTIYA (Qatar).

Assistant Secretary-General for Political Affairs: Dr HAMAD ALI AS-SULAYTI (Bahrain).

Assistant Secretary-General for Economic Affairs: AJLAN BEN ALI AL-KUWARI (Qatar).

Assistant Secretary-General for Military Affairs: Maj.-Gen. ALI IBN SALEM AL MUAMARI (Oman).

Note: In December 2001 the Supreme Council admitted Yemen (which applied to join the organization as a full member in 1996) as a member of the GCC's Arab Bureau of Education for the Gulf States (see p. 1324), as a participant in meetings of GCC ministers

of health and of labour and social affairs, and, alongside the GCC member states, as a participant in the biennial Gulf Cup football tournament. The Council also authorized the establishment of a Supreme Defence Council. This was to be composed of defence ministers meeting on an annual basis to consider security matters and supervise the implementation of the organization's joint defence pact.

Activities

The GCC was established following a series of meetings of foreign ministers of the states concerned, culminating in an agreement on the basic details of its charter on 10 March 1981. The Charter was signed by the six heads of state on 25 May. It describes the organization as providing 'the means for realizing co-ordination, integration and co-operation' in all economic, social and cultural affairs.

ECONOMIC CO-OPERATION

In November 1981 GCC ministers drew up a 'unified economic agreement' covering freedom of movement of people and capital, the abolition of customs duties, technical co-operation, harmonization of banking regulations and financial and monetary co-ordination. At the same time GCC heads of state approved the formation of a Gulf Investment Corporation, to be based in Kuwait (see below). In March 1983 customs duties on domestic products of the Gulf states were abolished, and new regulations allowing free movement of workers and vehicles between member states were also introduced. A common minimum customs levy (of between 4% and 20%) on foreign imports was imposed in 1986. In February 1987 the governors of the member states' central banks agreed in principle to co-ordinate their rates of exchange, and this was approved by the Supreme Council in November. It was subsequently agreed to link the Gulf currencies to a 'basket' of other currencies. In April 1993 the Gulf central bank governors decided to allow Kuwait's currency to become part of the GCC monetary system that was established following Iraq's invasion of Kuwait in order to defend the Gulf currencies. In May 1992 GCC trade ministers announced the objective of establishing a GCC common market. Meeting in September GCC ministers reached agreement on the application of a unified system of tariffs by March 1993. A meeting of the Supreme Council, held in December 1992, however, decided to mandate GCC officials to formulate a plan for the introduction of common external tariffs, to be presented to the Council in December 1993. Only the tax on tobacco products was to be standardized from March 1993, at a rate of 50% (later increased to 70%). In April 1994 ministers of finance agreed to pursue a gradual approach to the unification of tariffs. A technical committee, which had been constituted to consider aspects of establishing a customs union, met for the first time in June 1998. In November 1999 the Supreme Council concluded an agreement to establish the customs union by 1 March 2005. However, in December 2001 the Supreme Council, meeting in Muscat, Oman, adopted a new agreement on regional economic union ('Economic Agreement Between the Arab GCC States'), which superseded the 1981 'unified economic agreement'. The new accord brought forward the deadline for the establishment of the proposed customs union to 1 January 2003 and provided for a standard tariff level of 5% for foreign imports (with the exception of 53 essential commodities previously exempted by the Supreme Council). The agreement also provided for the introduction, by 1 January 2010, of a GCC single currency, linked to the US dollar. The necessary economic performance measures for monetary union were to be established by the end of 2005. The Supreme Council also authorized the creation of a new independent authority for overseeing the unification of specifications and standards throughout member states.

In April 1993 GCC central bank governors agreed to establish a joint banking supervisory committee, in order to devise rules for GCC banks to operate in other member states. In December 1997 GCC heads of state authorized guide-lines to this effect. These were to apply only to banks established at least 10 years previously with a share capital of more than US $100m.

The first annual GCC Economic Forum was due to be held in Muscat, Oman, in November 2002.

TRADE AND INDUSTRY

In 1982 a ministerial committee was formed to co-ordinate trade policies and development in the region. Technical subcommittees were established to oversee a strategic food reserve for the member states, and joint trade exhibitions (which were generally held every year until responsibility was transferred to the private sector in 1996). In 1986 the Supreme Council approved a measure whereby citizens of GCC member states were enabled to undertake certain retail trade activities in any other member state, with effect from 1 March 1987. In September 2000 GCC ministers of commerce agreed to establish a technical committee to promote the development of electronic commerce and trade among member states.

In 1976 the GCC member states formed the Gulf Organization for Industrial Consulting (q.v.), based in Doha, Qatar, which promotes regional industrial development. In 1985 the Supreme Council endorsed a common industrial strategy for the Gulf states. It approved regulations stipulating that priority should be given to imports of GCC industrial products, and permitting GCC investors to obtain loans from GCC industrial development banks. In November 1986 resolutions were adopted on the protection of industrial products, and on the co-ordination of industrial projects, in order to avoid duplication. In 1989 the Ministerial Council approved the Unified GCC Foreign Capital Investment Regulations, which aimed to attract foreign investment and to co-ordinate investments amongst GCC countries. Further guide-lines to promote foreign investment in the region were formulated during 1997. In December 1999 the Supreme Council amended the conditions determining rules of origin on industrial products in order to promote direct investment and intra-Community trade. In December 1992 the Supreme Council endorsed Patent Regulations for GCC member states to facilitate regional scientific and technological research. A GCC Patent Office for the protection of intellectual property in the region, was established in 1998.

In December 1998 the Supreme Council approved a long-term strategy for regional development, covering the period 2000–25, which had been formulated by GCC ministers of planning. The strategy aimed to achieve integrated, sustainable development in all member states and the co-ordination of national development plans. The Supreme Council also approved a framework Gulf population strategy formulated by the ministers of planning. In December 2000 the Supreme Council agreed gradually to limit, by means of the imposition of quotas and deterrent taxation measures, the numbers of foreign workers admitted to member states, in order to redress the current demographic imbalance resulting from the large foreign population resident in the region (believed to comprise more than one-third of the overall population). Unified procedures and measures for facilitating the intra-regional movement of people and commercial traffic were adopted by the Supreme Council in December 2001, as well as unified standards in the areas of education and healthcare.

AGRICULTURE

A unified agricultural policy for GCC countries was endorsed by the Supreme Council in November 1985. Co-operation in the agricultural sector extends to consideration of the water resources in the region. Between 1983 and 1990 ministers also approved proposals for harmonizing legislation relating to water conservation, veterinary vaccines, insecticides, fertilizers, fisheries and seeds. A permanent committee on fisheries aims to co-ordinate national fisheries policies, to establish designated fishing periods and to undertake surveys of the fishing potential in the Arabian (Persian) Gulf. In February 2001 GCC ministers responsible for water and electricity determined to formulate a common water policy for the region, which experiences annual shortfalls of water. Unified agricultural quarantine laws were adopted by the Supreme Council in December 2001.

TRANSPORT, COMMUNICATIONS AND INFORMATION

During 1985 feasibility studies were undertaken on new rail and road links between member states, and on the establishment of a joint coastal transport company. A scheme to build a 1,700-km railway to link all the member states and Iraq (and thereby the European railway network) was postponed, owing to its high estimated cost. In November 1993 ministers agreed to request assistance from the International Telecommunication Union on the establishment of a joint telecommunications network, which had been approved by ministers in 1986. The region's telecommunications systems were to be integrated through underwater fibre-optic cables and a satellite-based mobile telephone network. In the mid-1990s GCC ministers of information began convening on a regular basis with a view to formulating a joint external information policy. In November 1997 GCC interior ministers approved a simplified passport system to facilitate travel between member countries.

ENERGY

In 1982 a ministerial committee was established to co-ordinate hydrocarbons policies and prices. Ministers adopted a petroleum security plan to safeguard individual members against a halt in their production, to form a stockpile of petroleum products, and to organize a boycott of any non-member country when appropriate. In December 1987 the Supreme Council adopted a plan whereby a member state whose petroleum production was disrupted could 'borrow' petroleum from other members, in order to fulfil its export obligations. GCC petroleum ministers hold occasional co-ordination meetings to discuss the agenda and policies of OPEC (q.v.), to which all six member states belong.

During the early 1990s proposals were formulated to integrate the electricity networks of the six member countries. In the first stage of the plan the networks of Saudi Arabia, Bahrain, Kuwait and Qatar would be integrated; those of the United Arab Emirates (UAE) and Oman would be interconnected and finally linked to the others in the second stage. In December 1997 GCC heads of state declared that work should commence on the first stage of the plan, under the management of an independent authority. The estimated cost of the project was more than US $6,000m. However, it was agreed not to invite private developers to participate in construction of the grid, but that the first phase of the project be financed by member states (to contribute 35% of the estimated $2,000m. required), and by loans from commercial banking and international monetary institutions. The Gulf Council Interconnection Authority was established in 1999, with its headquarters in Dammam, Saudi Arabia.

CULTURAL CO-OPERATION

The GCC Folklore Centre, based in Doha, Qatar, was established in 1983 to collect, document and classify the regional cultural heritage, publish research, sponsor and protect regional folklore, provide a database on Gulf folklore, and to promote traditional culture through education.

REGIONAL SECURITY

Although no mention of defence or security was made in the original charter, the summit meeting which ratified the charter also issued a statement rejecting any foreign military presence in the region. The Supreme Council meeting in November 1981 agreed to include defence co-operation in the activities of the organization: as a result, defence ministers met in January 1982 to discuss a common security policy, including a joint air defence system and standardization of weapons. In November 1984 member states agreed to form the Peninsula Shield Force for rapid deployment against external aggression, comprising units from the armed forces of each country under a central command to be based in north-eastern Saudi Arabia.

In October 1987 (following an Iranian missile attack on Kuwait, which supported Iraq in its war against Iran) GCC ministers of foreign affairs issued a statement declaring that aggression against one member state was regarded as aggression against them all. In December the Supreme Council approved a joint pact on regional co-operation in matters of security. In August 1990 the Ministerial Council condemned Iraq's invasion of Kuwait as a violation of sovereignty, and demanded the withdrawal of all Iraqi troops from Kuwait. The Peninsula Shield Force was not sufficiently developed to be deployed in defence of Kuwait. During the crisis and the ensuing war between Iraq and a multinational force which took place in January and February 1991, the GCC developed closer links with Egypt and Syria, which, together with Saudi Arabia, played the most active role among the Arab countries in the anti-Iraqi alliance. In March the six GCC nations, Egypt and Syria formulated the 'Declaration of Damascus', which announced plans to establish a regional peace-keeping force. The Declaration also urged the abolition of all weapons of mass destruction in the area, and recommended the resolution of the Palestinian question by an international conference. In June Egypt and Syria, whose troops were to have formed the largest proportion of the proposed peace-keeping force, announced their withdrawal from the project, reportedly as a result of disagreements with the GCC concerning the composition of the force and the remuneration involved. A meeting of ministers of foreign affairs of the eight countries took place in July, but agreed only to provide mutual military assistance when necessary. In September 1992 the signatories of the Damascus Declaration adopted a joint statement on regional questions, including the Middle East peace process and the dispute between the UAE and Iran (see below), but rejected an Egyptian proposal to establish a series of rapid deployment forces which could be called upon to defend the interests of any of the eight countries. A meeting of GCC ministers of defence in November agreed to maintain the Peninsula Shield Force. In November 1993 GCC ministers of defence approved a proposal for the significant expansion of the Force and for the incorporation of air and naval units. Ministers also agreed to strengthen the defence of the region by developing joint surveillance and early warning systems. A GCC military committee was established, and convened for the first time in April 1994, to discuss the implementation of the proposals. However, the expansion of the Peninsula Shield Force was not implemented. Joint military training exercises were conducted by troops from five GCC states (excluding

Qatar) in northern Kuwait in March 1996. In December 1997 the Supreme Council approved plans for linking the region's military telecommunications networks and establishing a common early warning system. In December 2000 GCC leaders adopted a joint defence pact aimed at enhancing the grouping's defence capability. The pact formally committed member states to defending any other member state from external attack, envisaging the expansion of the Peninsula Shield Force from 5,000 to 22,000 troops and the creation of a new rapid deployment function within the Force. In March 2001 the GCC member states inaugurated the first phase of the long-envisaged joint air defence system. In December GCC heads of state authorized the establishment of a supreme defence council, comprising member states' ministers of defence, to address security-related matters and supervise the implementation of the joint defence pact. The council was to convene on an annual basis.

In 1992 Iran extended its authority over the island of Abu Musa, which it had administered under a joint arrangement with the UAE since 1971. In September 1992 the GCC Ministerial Council condemned Iran's continued occupation of the island and efforts to consolidate its presence, and reiterated support of UAE sovereignty over Abu Musa, as well as the largely uninhabited Greater and Lesser Tunb islands (also claimed by Iran). All three islands are situated at the approach to the Strait of Hormuz, through which petroleum exports are transported. In December 1994 the GCC supported the UAE's request that the dispute be referred to the International Court of Justice (ICJ).

In September 1992 a rift within the GCC was caused by an incident on the disputed border between Saudi Arabia and Qatar. Qatar's threat to boycott a meeting of the Supreme Council in December was allayed at the last minute as a result of mediation efforts by the Egyptian President. At the meeting, which was held in UAE, Qatar and Saudi Arabia agreed to establish a joint technical committee to demarcate the disputed border. In November 1994 a security agreement, to counter regional crime and terrorism, was concluded by GCC states. The pact, however, was not signed by Kuwait, which claimed that a clause concerning the extradition of offenders was in contravention of its constitution; Qatar did not attend the meeting, held in Riyadh, owing to its ongoing dispute with Saudi Arabia. During 1995 the deterioration of relations between Qatar and other GCC states threatened to undermine the Council's solidarity. In December Qatar publicly displayed its dissatisfaction at the appointment, without a consensus agreement, of Saudi Arabia's nominee as the new Secretary-General by failing to attend the final session of the Supreme Council, held in Muscat, Oman. However, at a meeting of ministers of foreign affairs in March 1996, Qatar endorsed the new Secretary-General, following an agreement on future appointment procedures, and reasserted its commitment to the organization. In June Saudi Arabia and Qatar agreed to reactivate the joint technical committee in order to finalize the demarcation of their mutual border: border maps drafted by the committee were approved by both sides in December 1999. In December 1996 Qatar hosted the annual GCC summit meeting; however, Bahrain refused to attend, owing to Qatar's 'unfriendly attitude' and a long-standing dispute between the two countries (referred by Qatar to the ICJ in 1991) concerning the sovereignty of the Hawar islands, and of other islands, maritime and border areas. The issue dominated the meeting, which agreed to establish a four-member committee to resolve the conflicting sovereignty claims. In January 1997 the ministers of foreign affairs of Kuwait, Oman, Saudi Arabia and the UAE, meeting in Riyadh, formulated a seven-point memorandum of understanding to ease tensions between Bahrain and Qatar. The two countries refused to sign the agreement; however, in March both sides announced their intention to establish diplomatic relations at ambassadorial level. In March 2001 the ICJ ruled on the dispute between Bahrain and Qatar concerning the sovereignty of the Hawar Islands and other territorial boundaries, awarding Bahrain sovereignty of the Hawar islands, while supporting Qatar's sovereignty over other disputed territories. The GCC welcomed the judgement, which was accepted by the Governments of both countries.

In May 1997 the Ministerial Council, meeting in Riyadh, expressed concern at Turkey's cross-border military operation in northern Iraq and urged a withdrawal of Turkish troops from Iraqi territory. In December the Supreme Council reaffirmed the need to ensure the sovereignty and territorial integrity of Iraq. At the same time, however, the Council expressed concern at the escalation of tensions in the region, owing to Iraq's failure to co-operate with the UN Special Commission (UNSCOM). The Council also noted the opportunity to strengthen relations with Iran, in view of political developments in that country. In February 1998 the US Defense Secretary visited each of the GCC countries in order to generate regional support for any punitive military action against Iraq, given that country's obstruction of UN weapons inspectors. Kuwait was the only country to declare its support for the use of force (and to permit the use of its bases in military operations against Iraq), while other member states urged a diplomatic solution to the crisis. Qatar pursued a diplomatic initiative to negotiate directly with the

Iraqi authorities, and during February, the Qatari Minister of Foreign Affairs became the most senior GCC government official to visit Iraq since 1990. The GCC supported an agreement concluded between the UN Secretary-General and the Iraqi authorities at the end of February 1998, and urged Iraq to co-operate with UNSCOM in order to secure an end to the problem and a removal of the international embargo against the country. This position was subsequently reiterated by the Supreme Council. (In December 1999 UNSCOM was replaced by a new arms inspection body, the UN Monitoring, Verification and Inspection Commission—UNMOVIC.) In December 2000 Kuwait and Saudi Arabia rejected a proposal by the Qatari Government, supported by the UAE, that the GCC should soften its policy on Iraq and demand the immediate removal of the international embargo against that country. During that month the Supreme Council determined to establish a committee with the function of touring Arab states to explain the GCC's Iraq policy. In September 2002 the US Secretary of State met representatives of the GCC to discuss ongoing US pressure on the UN Security Council to draft a new resolution insisting that Iraq comply with previous UN demands, setting a time frame for such compliance and authorizing the use of force against Iraq in response to non-compliance.

The GCC has condemned repeated military exercises conducted by Iran in the waters around the disputed islands of Abu Musa and Greater and Lesser Tunb as a threat to regional security and a violation of the UAE's sovereignty. Nevertheless, member countries have pursued efforts to strengthen relations with Iran. In May 1999 President Khatami undertook a state visit to Qatar, Saudi Arabia and Syria, prompting concern on the part of the UAE that its support within the GCC and the solidarity of the grouping were being undermined. In June a meeting of GCC ministers of foreign affairs was adjourned, owing to reported disagreements between Saudi Arabia and the UAE. Diplomatic efforts secured commitments, issued by both countries later in that month, to co-operate fully within the GCC. In early July the Ministerial Council reasserted GCC support of the UAE's sovereignty claim over the three disputed islands and determined to establish a committee, comprising the ministers of foreign affairs of Oman, Qatar and Saudi Arabia and the GCC Secretary-General, to resolve the dispute. In December the Supreme Council extended the mandate of the committee to establish a mechanism for direct negotiations between UAE and Iran. Iran, however, refused to co-operate with the committee; consequently, the committee's mandate was terminated in January 2001. In March the Ministerial Council demanded that Iran cease the construction of buildings for settlement on the disputed islands, and reiterated its support for the UAE's sovereignty claim.

EXTERNAL RELATIONS

In June 1988 an agreement was signed by GCC and European Community (EC) ministers on economic co-operation; this took effect from January 1990. Under the accord a joint ministerial council (meeting on an annual basis) was established, and working groups were subsequently created to promote co-operation in several specific areas, including business, energy, the environment and industry. In October 1990 GCC and EC ministers of foreign affairs commenced negotiations on formulating a free-trade agreement. In October 1995 a conference was held in Muscat, Oman, which aimed to strengthen economic co-operation between European Union (EU, as the restructured EC was now known) and GCC member states, and to promote investment in both regions. GCC heads of state, meeting in December 1997, condemned statements issued by the European Parliament, as well as by other organizations, regarding human rights issues in member states and insisted they amounted to interference in GCC judicial systems. In December 2001 the GCC Supreme Council agreed to establish a customs union—a precondition of the proposed GCC-EU free-trade agreement—by 1 January 2003 (see above). Free-trade negotiations were continuing in 2002.

In September 1994 GCC ministers of foreign affairs decided to end the secondary and tertiary embargo on trade with Israel. In February 1995 a ministerial meeting of signatories of the Damascus Declaration adopted a common stand, criticizing Israel for its refusal to renew the nuclear non-proliferation treaty. In December 1996 the foreign ministers of the Damascus Declaration states, convened in Cairo, requested the USA to exert financial pressure on Israel to halt the construction of settlements on occupied Arab territory. In December 2001 GCC heads of state issued a statement holding Israeli government policy responsible for the escalating crisis in the Palestinian territories. The consultative meeting of heads of state held in May 2002 declared its support for a Saudi-proposed initiative aimed at achieving a peaceful resolution of the crisis.

In June 1997 ministers of foreign affairs of the Damascus Declaration states agreed to pursue efforts to establish a free-trade zone throughout the region, which they envisaged as the nucleus of a future Arab common market. (Meanwhile, the League of Arab States (q.v.) has also initiated efforts to create a Greater Arab Free Trade Area.)

The GCC-USA Economic Dialogue, which commenced in 1985, convenes periodically as a government forum to promote co-operation between the GCC economies and the USA. Since the late 1990s private-sector interests have been increasingly represented at sessions of the Dialogue. It was announced in March 2001 that a business forum was to be established under the auspices of the Dialogue, to act as a permanent means of facilitating trade and investment between the GCC countries and the USA.

The GCC Secretary-General denounced the major terrorist attacks that were perpetrated in September 2001 against targets in the USA. Meeting in an emergency session in mid-September, in Riyadh, Saudi Arabia, GCC foreign ministers agreed to support the aims of the developing international coalition against terrorism. Meanwhile, however, member states urged parallel international resolve to halt action by the Israeli security forces against Palestinians. In December the Supreme Council declared the organization's full co-operation with the anti-terrorism coalition.

INVESTMENT CORPORATION

Gulf Investment Corporation (GIC): Joint Banking Center, Kuwait Real Estate Bldg, POB 3402, Safat 13035, Kuwait; tel. 2431911; fax 2448894; e-mail gic@gic.com.kw; f. 1983 by the six member states of the GCC, each contributing US $350m. of the total

capital of $2,100m.; total assets $19,500m. (1999); investment chiefly in the Gulf region, financing industrial projects (including pharmaceuticals, chemicals, steel wire, aircraft engineering, aluminium, dairy produce and chicken-breeding). GIC provides merchant banking and financial advisory services, and in 1992 was appointed to advise the Kuwaiti Government on a programme of privatization. Chair. IBRAHIM ABDUL-KARIM; Gen. Man. HISHAM A. RAZZUQI. Publ. *The GIC Gazetteer* (annually).

Gulf International Bank: POB 1017, Al-Dowali Bldg, 3 Palace Ave, Manama 317, Bahrain; tel. 534000; fax 522633; e-mail info@gib.com.bh; internet www.gibonline.com; f. 1976 by the six GCC states and Iraq; became a wholly-owned subsidiary of the GIC (without Iraqi shareholdings) in 1991; in April 1999 a merger with Saudi Investment Bank was concluded; cap. US $1,000m., dep. $10,949.7m., total assets $15,232.0m. (Dec. 2001). Chair. EBRAHIM BIN KHALIFA AL-KHALIFA; CEO DR KHALED M. AL-FAYEZ.

Publications

GCC News (monthly).
At-Ta'awun (periodical).

COUNCIL OF ARAB ECONOMIC UNITY

Address: 1191 Corniche en-Nil, 12th Floor, POB 1, Mohammed Fareed, Cairo, Egypt.
Telephone: (2) 5755321; **fax:** (2) 5754090.
Established in 1957 by the Economic Council of the League of Arab States (q.v.). The first meeting of the Council was held in 1964.

MEMBERS

Egypt	Palestine
Iraq	Somalia
Jordan	Sudan
Libya	Syria
Mauritania	Yemen

Organization

(August 2002)

COUNCIL

The Council consists of representatives of member states, usually ministers of economy, finance and trade. It meets twice a year; meetings are chaired by the representative of each country for one year.

GENERAL SECRETARIAT

Entrusted with the implementation of the Council's decisions and with proposing work plans, including efforts to encourage participation by member states in the Arab Economic Unity Agreement. The Secretariat also compiles statistics, conducts research and publishes studies on Arab economic problems and on the effects of major world economic trends.
General Secretary: Dr AHMED GOWEILI (Egypt).

COMMITTEES

There are seven standing committees: preparatory, follow-up and Arab Common Market development; Permanent Delegates; budget; economic planning; fiscal and monetary matters; customs and trade planning and co-ordination; statistics. There are also seven *ad hoc* committees, including meetings of experts on tariffs, trade promotion and trade legislation.

Activities

The Council undertakes to co-ordinate measures leading to a customs union subject to a unified administration; conduct market and commodity studies; assist with the unification of statistical terminology and methods of data collection; conduct studies for the formation of new joint Arab companies and federations; and to formulate specific programmes for agricultural and industrial co-ordination and for improving road and railway networks.

ARAB COMMON MARKET

Based on a resolution passed by the Council in August 1964; its implementation was to be supervised by the Council. Customs duties

and other taxes on trade between the member countries were to be eliminated in stages prior to the adoption of a full customs union, and ultimately all restrictions on trade between the member countries, including quotas, and restrictions on residence, employment and transport, were to be abolished. In practice little progress was achieved in the development of an Arab common market during 1964–2000. However, efforts towards liberalizing intra-Arab trade were intensified in 2001. A meeting of Council ministers of economy and trade convened in Baghdad, Iraq, in June, issued the 'Baghdad Declaration' on establishing an, initially, quadripartite free-trade area comprising Egypt, Iraq, Libya and Syria; future participation by other member states was urged by the Council's General Secretary. The initiative was envisaged as a cornerstone of the Greater Arab Free Trade Area—GAFTA (q.v.), which was being implemented by the Arab League. The meeting also approved an executive programme for developing the common market and a 10-year strategy for joint Arab economic action, determined to establish a compensation fund to support the integration of the least developed Arab states into the regional economy, and agreed to provide technical assistance for Arab states aiming to join the WTO. It was reported in late 2001 that Palestine had also applied to join the free-trade area, and that consideration of its application would delay the zone's entry into force. In May Egypt, Jordan, Morocco and Tunisia (all participants in the Euro-Mediterranean Partnership—see European Union), meeting in Agadir, Morocco, had agreed to establish the Mediterranean Arab Free Trade Area (MAFTA) as a cornerstone of a planned larger Arab-Mediterranean free trade area. In 2002 the Council was considering a draft general framework for Arab economic action in the areas of investment, technology, trade and joint ventures (see below) covering the next 20 years.

JOINT VENTURES

A number of multilateral organizations in industry and agriculture have been formed on the principle that faster development and economies of scale may be achieved by combining the efforts of member states. In industries that are new to the member countries Arab Joint Companies are formed, while existing industries are co-ordinated by the setting up of Arab Specialized Unions. The unions are for closer co-operation on problems of production and marketing, and to help companies deal as a group in international markets. The companies are intended to be self-supporting on a purely commercial basis; they may issue shares to citizens of the participating countries. The joint ventures are:

Arab Joint Companies:

Arab Company for Drug Industries and Medical Appliances—ACDIMA: POB 925161, Amman 11190, Jordan; tel. (6) 5821618; fax (6) 5821649; e-mail acdima@go.com.jo; internet www.acdima.com; f. 1976.

Arab Company for Electronic Commerce; f. 2001.

Arab Company for Industrial Investment: POB 3385, Alwiyah, Baghdad, Iraq; tel. 718-9215; fax 718-0710.

Arab Company for Livestock Development: POB 5305, Damascus, Syria; tel. 666037.

Arab Mining Company: POB 20198, Amman, Jordan; tel. (6) 5663148; fax (6) 5684114; e-mail armico@go.com.jo; f. 1974.

Specialized Arab Unions and Federations:

Arab Co-operative Federation: POB 57640, Baghdad, Iraq; tel. (1) 888-8121; f. 1985.

Arab Federation for Paper, Printing and Packaging Industries: POB 5456, Baghdad, Iraq; tel. (1) 887-2384; fax (1) 886-9639; f. 1977; 250 mems.

Arab Federation of Chemical Fertilizers Producers: Cairo, Egypt; f. 1976.

Arab Federation of Engineering Industries: POB 509, Baghdad, Iraq; tel. (1) 776-1101; f. 1975.

Arab Federation of Leather Industries: POB 2188, Damascus, Syria; f. 1978; activities currently suspended.

Arab Federation of Shipping: POB 1161, Baghdad, Iraq; tel. (1) 717-4540; fax (1) 717-7243; f. 1979; 22 mems.

Arab Federation of Textile Industries: POB 620, Damascus, Syria; f. 1976; activities currently suspended.

Arab Federation of Travel Agents: POB 7090, Amman, Jordan.

Arab Seaports Federation: Alexandria, Egypt; f. 1977.

Arab Steel Union: Algiers, Algeria; f. 1972.

Arab Sugar Federation: POB 195, Khartoum, Sudan; f. 1977; activities currently suspended.

Arab Union for Cement and Building Materials: POB 9015, Damascus, Syria; tel. (11) 6118598; fax (11) 6111318; e-mail aucbm@net.sy; internet www.aucbm.org; f. 1977; 22 mem. countries, 100 mem. cos.

Arab Union for Information Technology.

Arab Union of Fish Producers: POB 15064, Baghdad, Iraq; tel. (1) 551-1261; f. 1976.

Arab Union of Food Industries: POB 13025, Baghdad, Iraq; f. 1976.

Arab Union of Hotels and Tourism: Beirut, Lebanon; f. 1994.

Arab Union of Land Transport: POB 926324, Amman 11110, Jordan; tel. (6) 5663153; fax (6) 5664232; f. 1978.

Arab Union of the Manufacturers of Pharmaceuticals and Medical Appliances: POB 81150, Amman 11181, Jordan; tel. (6) 4654306; fax (6) 4648141; f. 1986.

Arab Union of the Manufacturers of Tyres and Rubber Products: Alexandria, Egypt; f. 1993.

Arab Union of Railways: POB 6599, Aleppo, Syria; tel. (21)2667270; fax (21) 2686000; ; f. 1979.

General Arab Insurance Federation: POB 611, 11511 Cairo, Egypt; tel. (2) 5743177; fax (2) 5762310; f. 1964.

General Union of Arab Agricultural Workers and Co-operatives: Tripoli, Libya; f. 1993.

Union of Arab Contractors: Cairo, Egypt; f. 1995.

Union of Arab Investors: Cairo, Egypt; f. 1995.

Publications

Annual Bulletin for Arab Countries' Foreign Trade Statistics.

Annual Bulletin for Official Exchange Rates of Arab Currencies.

Arab Economic Unity Bulletin (2 a year).

Demographic Yearbook for Arab Countries.

Economic Report of the General Secretary (2 a year).

Guide to Studies prepared by Secretariat.

Progress Report (2 a year).

Statistical Yearbook for Arab Countries.

Yearbook for Intra-Arab Trade Statistics.

Yearbook of National Accounts for Arab Countries.

ECONOMIC CO-OPERATION ORGANIZATION—ECO

Address: 1 Golbou Alley, Kamranieh St, POB 14155-6176, Tehran, Iran.

Telephone: (21) 2831733; **fax:** (21) 2831732; **e-mail:** registry@ecosecretariat.org; **internet:** www.ecosecretariat.org.

The Economic Co-operation Organization (ECO) was established in 1985 as the successor to the Regional Co-operation for Development, founded in 1964.

MEMBERS

Afghanistan	Kyrgyzstan	Turkey
Azerbaijan	Pakistan	Turkmenistan
Iran	Tajikistan	Uzbekistan
Kazakhstan		

The 'Turkish Republic of Northern Cyprus' has been granted special guest status.

Organization

(September 2002)

SUMMIT MEETING

The first summit meeting of heads of state and of government of member countries was held in Tehran in February 1992. Summit meetings are generally held at least once every two years. The sixth summit meeting was convened in Tehran in June 2000. The seventh summit meeting was scheduled to be held in Turkey in October 2002.

COUNCIL OF MINISTERS

The Council of Ministers, comprising ministers of foreign affairs of member states, is the principal policy- and decision-making body of ECO. It meets at least once a year.

REGIONAL PLANNING COUNCIL

The Council, comprising senior planning officials or other representatives of member states, meets at least once a year. It is responsible for reviewing programmes of activity and evaluating results achieved, and for proposing future plans of action to the Council of Ministers.

COUNCIL OF PERMANENT REPRESENTATIVES

Permanent representatives or Ambassadors of member countries accredited to Iran meet regularly to formulate policy for consideration by the Council of Ministers and to promote implementation of decisions reached at ministerial or summit level.

SECRETARIAT

The Secretariat is headed by a Secretary-General, who is supported by two Deputy Secretaries-General. The following Directorates administer and co-ordinate the main areas of ECO activities: Trade and investment; Transport and communications; Energy, minerals and environment; Industry and agriculture (to be renamed Human Development); Project research; Economic research and statistics; and Co-ordination and international relations.

Secretary-General: SAYED MOJTABA ARASTOU (Iran).

Activities

The Regional Co-operation for Development (RCD) was established in 1964 as a tripartite arrangement between Iran, Pakistan and Turkey, which aimed to promote economic co-operation between member states. ECO replaced the RCD in 1985, and seven additional members were admitted to the Organization in November 1992. The main areas of co-operation are transport (including the building of road and rail links, of particular importance as seven member states are landlocked), telecommunications and post, trade and investment, energy (including the interconnection of power grids in the region), minerals, environmental issues, industry, and agriculture. ECO priorities and objectives for each sector are defined in the Quetta Plan of Action and the İstanbul Declaration; an Almaty Outline Plan, which was adopted in 1993, is specifically concerned with the development of regional transport and communication infrastructure. The period 1998–2007 has been designated as the ECO Decade of Transport and Communications.

In 1990 an ECO College of Insurance was inaugurated. A joint Chamber of Commerce and Industry was established in 1993. The third ECO summit meeting, held in Islamabad, Pakistan, in March 1995, concluded formal agreements on the establishment of several other regional institutes and agencies: an ECO Trade and Development Bank, in İstanbul, Turkey (with main branches in Tehran, Iran, and Islamabad, Pakistan), a joint shipping company, airline, and an ECO Cultural Institute, all to be based in Iran, and an ECO Reinsurance Company and an ECO Science Foundation, with headquarters in Pakistan. In addition, heads of state and of government endorsed the creation of an ECO eminent persons group and signed the following two agreements in order to enhance and facilitate trade throughout the region: the Transit Trade Agreement (which entered into force in December 1997) and the Agreement on the Simplification of Visa Procedures for Businessmen of ECO Countries (which came into effect in March 1998). The sixth ECO summit meeting, held in June 2000 in Tehran, urged the completion of the necessary formalities for the creation of the planned ECO Trade and Development Bank and ECO Reinsurance Company. In May 2001 the Council of Ministers agreed to terminate the ECO airline project, owing to its unsustainable cost, and to replace it with a framework agreement on co-operation in the field of air transport.

In September 1996, at an extraordinary meeting of the ECO Council of Ministers, held in Izmir, Turkey, member countries signed a revised Treaty of Izmir, the Organization's fundamental charter. An extraordinary summit meeting, held in Ashgabat, Turkmenistan, in May 1997, adopted the Ashgabat Declaration, emphasizing the importance of the development of the transport and communications infrastructure and the network of transnational petroleum and gas pipelines through bilateral and regional arrangements in the ECO area. In May 1998, at the fifth summit meeting, held in Almaty, Kazakhstan, ECO heads of state and of government signed a Transit Transport Framework Agreement and a memorandum of understanding to help combat the cross-border trafficking of illegal goods. The meeting also agreed to establish an ECO Educational Institute in Ankara, Turkey. In June 2000 the sixth ECO summit encouraged member states to participate in the development of information and communication technologies through the establishment of a database of regional educational and training institutions specializing in that field. The ECO heads of state and government also reconfirmed their commitment to the Ashgabat Declaration. In December 2001 ECO organized its first workshop on energy conservation and efficiency in Ankara.

Convening in conference for the first time in early March 2000, ECO ministers of trade signed a Framework Agreement on ECO Trade Co-operation (ECOFAT), which established a basis for the expansion of intra-regional trade. The Framework Agreement envis-aged the eventual adoption of an ECO Trade Agreement (ECOTA), providing for the gradual elimination of regional tariff and non-tariff barriers between member states. ECO and the International Trade Centre are jointly implementing a project on expanding intra-ECO trade. In November the first meeting of ECO ministers responsible for energy and petroleum, convened in Islamabad, adopted a plan of action for regional co-operation on energy and petroleum matters over the period 2001–05. The first meeting of ECO ministers of agriculture, convened in July 2002, in Islamabad, adopted a declaration on co-operation in the agricultural sector, which specified that member states would contribute to agricultural rehabilitation in Afghanistan, establishing a special fund for the purpose, and considered instigating a mechanism for the regional exchange of agricultural and cattle products.

ECO staged its third trade fair in Bandar Anzali, Iran, in July 1998. The fourth fair, scheduled to be held in Karachi, Pakistan, in May 2002, was postponed. The Organization maintains ECO TradeNet, an internet-based repository of regional trade information. ECO has co-operation agreements with several UN agencies and other international organizations in development-related activities. An ECO-UN International Drug Control Programme (UNDCP) Project on Drug Control and Co-ordination Unit commenced operations in Tehran in July 1999. ECO has been granted observer status at the UN, OIC and WTO.

In November 2001 the UN Secretary-General requested ECO to take an active role in efforts to restore stability in Afghanistan and to co-operate closely with his special representative in that country. In June 2002 the ECO Secretary-General participated in a tripartite ministerial conference on co-operation for development in Afghanistan that was convened under the auspices of the UN Development Programme and attended by representatives from Afghanistan, Iran and Pakistan.

Finance

Member states contribute to a centralized administrative budget.

Publication

ECO Annual Economic Report.
ECO Bulletin (quarterly).

THE EUROPEAN UNION

The Mediterranean Policy of the European Union*

In 1972 the European Community formulated a scheme to negotiate a series of parallel trade and co-operation agreements encompassing almost all of the non-member states on the coast of the Mediterranean. Association Agreements, intended to lead to customs union or the eventual full accession of the country concerned, had been signed with Greece in 1962, Turkey in 1963 and Malta in 1971; a fourth Agreement was signed with Cyprus in 1972. Simple trade agreements with Spain, Portugal and Yugoslavia were all effective by September 1973. (Greece became a member of the Community in 1981, and Portugal and Spain in 1986.) During the 1970s a series of agreements covering trade and economic co-operation were concluded with the Arab Mediterranean countries (the Maghreb countries—Algeria, Morocco and Tunisia, and the Mashreq countries—Egypt, Jordan, Lebanon and Syria) and Israel, all establishing free access to EC markets for most industrial products, either immediately or shortly afterwards. Access for agricultural products was facilitated, although some tariffs remained. For refined petroleum, cotton and phosphate fertilizers, the EC imposed quotas for a transitional period on some of the Mediterranean countries. The principle of reciprocity (the granting of preferences in return) was not applied immediately in all of the co-operation agreements; in the Association Agreements, and some others, there were provisions for its introduction in the medium or long-term, should the economic progress of the country concerned warrant this. In the event of a disturbance in a particular sector, or of economic decline in a particular region, the contracting party concerned was entitled to take protective action. Special organizations (Association or Co-operation Councils, comprising representatives of the Community and the respective countries) were instituted to supervise the implementation of the agreements for each country. Many of the agreements were accompanied by financial protocols stating the amount of aid each Mediterranean country would receive. Financial aid takes the form of direct grants, as well as loans from the European Investment Bank (EIB).

In 1982 the Commission formulated an integrated plan for the development of its own Mediterranean regions and recommended the adoption of a new policy towards the non-Community countries of the Mediterranean. This was to include greater emphasis on diversifying agriculture, in order to avoid surpluses of items such as citrus fruits, olive oil and wine (which the Mediterranean countries all wished to export to the Community) and to reduce these countries' dependence on imported food. The Commission also called for a return to the original principle of free access to the Community market for industrial goods from the Mediterranean countries, which had effectively been disregarded in the case of competitive imports of textiles, footwear and other goods, together with more efficient negotiating machinery to take action when problems arose. In 1985 the Commission negotiated modifications in agreements with non-member Mediterranean countries to ensure that their exports of agricultural produce to the EC would not be adversely affected by the accession of Portugal and Spain to the Community at the beginning of 1986.

In December 1990, as part of a new policy of providing greater financial assistance for the region, the European Council approved ECU 2,075m. in loans and grants for the Maghreb and Mashreq countries and Israel, over a five-year period from November 1991. This was to include support for structural adjustment programmes, undertaken in conjunction with the IMF and the World Bank. Particular emphasis was placed on increasing food production, promoting investment and the development of small and medium-sized businesses, and protecting the environment. From 1 January 1993 the majority of agricultural exports from Mediterranean non-Community countries were granted exemption from customs duties.

---

* The European Union was formally established on 1 November 1993 under the Treaty on European Union; prior to this it was known as the European Community (EC).

In June 1995 the European Council endorsed a programme to reform and strengthen the Mediterranean policy of the EU. The initiative envisaged the establishment of a Euro-Mediterranean Economic Area (EMEA), preceded by a gradual liberalization of trade within the region through bilateral and regional free-trade arrangements, and the adoption of financial and technical measures to support the implementation of structural reforms in Mediterranean partner countries. In November 1995 a conference of ministers of foreign affairs of the EU member states, 11 Mediterranean non-member countries (excluding Libya) and the Palestine authorities was convened in Barcelona, Spain. The conference endorsed the agreement on the EMEA and resolved to establish a permanent Euro-Mediterranean ministerial dialogue. It issued the 'Barcelona Declaration', endorsing commitments to uphold democratic principles and to pursue greater co-operation in the control of international crime, drugs-trafficking and illegal migration. The Declaration set the objective of establishing a Euro-Mediterranean free-trade area by 2010. The process of co-operation and dialogue under this agreement (the Euro-Mediterranean Partnership) became known as the Barcelona Process. The new approach involves increased political dialogue with partnership countries as well as further efforts to improve economic co-operation, security, democracy and human rights. The Process has three pillars (known as 'baskets'): Political and Security Partnership ('basket I'); Economic and Financial Partnership ('basket II'); and Cultural, Social and Human Partnership ('basket III'). Bilateral co-operation under the Process is mainly achieved through the implementation of Association Agreements, while overall regional co-operation is conducted within a framework of programmes, networks and fora. A Euro-Mediterranean Committee for the Barcelona Process, comprising high-level representatives of the EU and the Mediterranean partner countries, guides the Process, making preparations for ministerial conferences, etc. The Committee is chaired by the incumbent EU presidency.

A second Euro-Mediterranean Conference of foreign affairs ministers was held in April 1997, in Malta, to review implementation of the partnership strategy. Euro-Mediterranean foreign ministers convened for a third conference in April 1999, in Stuttgart, Germany. The Stuttgart conference agreed that Libya could in time become a partner in the process, following the withdrawal of UN sanctions on that country and acceptance of the full terms of the Barcelona Declaration. Libya has subsequently attended some meetings as an observer. A fourth conference took place in November 2000 in Marseilles, France, with Libya in attendance as a special guest. The conference focused on the adoption of a new common strategy for the Mediterranean, aimed at strengthening the Barcelona Process. The fifth conference of foreign ministers, convened in Valencia, Spain, in April 2002, noted the importance of consolidating the Barcelona Process in view of ongoing developments in the Middle East and, to this end, adopted the Valencia Action Plan, incorporating several measures designed to reinforce political dialogue, develop co-operation in economic, commercial and financial matters, and place increased focus on the social, cultural and human dimension. The conference urged the implementation of UN Security Council resolutions relevant to the Israel–Palestine crisis.

Several regional sectoral conferences have been organized within the framework of the Barcelona Process. The first Euro-Mediterranean Energy Forum was convened in May 1997 and a second Energy Forum was held in May 1998. The inaugural meeting of a Euro-Mediterranean Parliamentary Forum was convened in October 1998. The second meeting of the Forum took place in February 2001 and the third in November. Thereafter the meeting was to be held annually. Sectoral ministerial conferences have been held on culture, energy, the environment, health, industrial co-operation, information, trade and water.

The EU's primary financial instrument for the implementation of the Euro-Mediterranean Partnership is the MEDA programme, providing support for the reform of economic and social structures within partnership countries. Financial aid commitments under MEDA I (covering 1995–99) amounted to ECU 3,400m., out of a total of ECU 4,685.5m. approved by the Council for that period in assistance for the Maghreb and Mashreq countries, as well as for Israel, Palestine, Cyprus, Malta, Turkey and Libya. In 1999 the MEDA Regulation (the legal basis for the programme, adopted in July 1996) was reviewed and revised. The amended programme was named MEDA II. Under MEDA II, long-term strategy papers for the period 2000–06 have been drawn up at national and regional levels. Based on these papers, regional and national indicative programmes (of three years duration) have been developed, in conjunction with the EIB. The aim is to consolidate the resources available under MEDA, and make the process of disbursement more efficient. In 2000 some €879m. was committed under MEDA I, with €8.8m carried into 2001. The budget for MEDA II (2000–06) was €5,350m. To complement these grants, the EIB was to provide €6,400m. under its Euromed II lending mandate in 2000–07, and another €1,000m. from its own resources. In 2000 the EIB gave a total of €1,214m. to Euro-Mediterranean Partnership countries.

Agreements with Countries in the Middle East and North Africa

THE MAGHREB COUNTRIES

In June 1992 the EC approved a proposal to conclude new bilateral agreements with the Maghreb countries, incorporating the following components: political dialogue; financial, economic, technical and cultural co-operation; and the eventual establishment of a free-trade area. An Association Agreement with Tunisia was signed in July 1995, with the aim of eliminating duties and other trade barriers on most products over a transitional 12-year period and providing greater access to European funds for investment and economic and industrial restructuring. The Agreement was formally concluded in early 1998 and entered into force on 1 March; the first meeting of the EC–Tunisia Association Council was convened in July. Morocco applied to join the EC in 1987; however, its application was rejected on the grounds that it was not a European country. In 1988 the EC reached an agreement with Morocco concerning fishing rights for the Spanish and Portuguese fleets in Moroccan waters (formerly subject to bilateral treaties). A new four-year fisheries agreement entered into effect in 1992. In October 1994 the EU and Morocco agreed to terminate the agreement one year early (with effect from 30 April 1995), as a result of a dispute concerning fishing licences and other incidents involving Moroccan and EU (mainly Spanish and Portuguese) fishing vessels. In November 1995, following extensive negotiations, the two sides concluded a further four-year fisheries accord, which established new levels of compensation to the Moroccan fishing industry and catch quotas to enable EU fleets to operate again in Moroccan waters. The Moroccan Government did not renew the fisheries accord on its expiry on 30 November 1999; however, negotiations on a new agreement were subsequently held. In 1995 Morocco concluded negotiations with the EU on an Association Agreement that aims to eliminate trade barriers in the industrial and service sectors over a 12-year period. The Agreement was concluded in January 2000 and entered into force in March. It also provides for greater preferential access for certain agricultural products, including citrus fruits and tomatoes. The first meeting of the EU–Morocco Association Council was held in October 2000. Under MEDA II some €426m. was allocated in support of a national indicative programme for 2002–04 formulated in close co-operation with the Moroccan authorities. The EIB has funded projects related to road development, irrigation and the provision of drinking water. In July 2002 relations between the EU and Morocco were strained when the Moroccan Government briefly deployed a contingent of troops on, and reiterated a territorial claim to, the small Spanish-held Mediterranean island of Perejil. The European Commission urged bilateral dialogue between the two countries and, shortly afterwards, a consensus was reached to maintain the *status quo* existing prior to the incident.

The Community's relations with Algeria have been affected by political and civil instability in that country and by concerns regarding the government's respect for human rights and democratic principles. In March 1997 negotiations were initiated between the European Commission and representatives of the Algerian government on a Euro-Mediterranean Association Agreement that would incorporate political commitments relating to democracy and human rights: this was concluded in December 2001 and signed in April 2002. In 2000, under the EU's ECHO (European Community Humanitarian Office) programme, Algeria received emergency food aid for Sahrawi refugees of €4.9m. Algeria was allocated €90m. under MEDA II during 2000–01 to fund four projects. From 1996–2001 the EIB provided loans with a value of about €620m. for projects in the energy, transport, water resources management and environment sectors.

THE MASHREQ COUNTRIES

Following the Iraqi invasion of Kuwait in August 1990, additional financial aid was provided to Egypt and Jordan, which, together with Turkey, were the partner countries most directly affected by the regional crisis. In November 1994 the EU–Syria Co-operation Council convened for the first time since Syria's co-operation agreement was signed in 1977. At the same time the EU agreed to remove its embargo on the trade of armaments with Syria. Preliminary negotiations for the conclusion of an Association Agreement were initiated in July 1996, although formal authorization to the European Commission to conclude an Association Agreement was only granted by EU heads of government in December 1997. Negotiations on the Agreement were ongoing in 2002. Syria is one of the beneficiaries of the MEDA programme, but did not ratify the MEDA framework convention until July 2000.

Negotiations between representatives of the EU and Egypt on the establishment of an Association Agreement were initiated in January 1995. However, progress was affected by opposition on the part of the Egyptian authorities to EU protection of its farm and processed food products. A provisional agreement on the conclusion of a trade accord, which envisaged the removal of barriers to trade over a 12-year period, was eventually reached in June 1999. In early 2001, some 18 months after the conclusion of negotiations, the Egyptian Government decided to finalize the Association Agreement; this was signed in June. In May, Egypt, together with Jordan, Tunisia and Morocco, made the Agadir Declaration, providing for the establishment of a quadripartite free-trade area (the Mediterranean Arab Free Trade Area—MAFTA). The MAFTA initiative aims to support the Barcelona Process by providing a cornerstone of the planned Euro-Mediterranean free-trade area. EU aid to Egypt awarded under the MEDA programme has included €122.5m. to support phase I of a social development fund and, in collaboration with the World Bank, €155m. in support of phase II of the fund.

An Association Agreement was formally concluded with Jordan in November 1997, and received assent by the European Parliament in July 1998. The first EU–Jordan Association Council meeting was held in June 2002. An Association Agreement with Lebanon was signed during that month.Under MEDA II Lebanon was awarded €80m. in support of a national indicative programme covering the period 2002–04.

ISRAEL

In January 1989 the EC and Israel eliminated the last tariff barriers to full free trade for industrial products. A Euro-Mediterranean Association Agreement with Israel was signed in 1995, providing further trade concessions and stronger economic co-operation and establishing an institutional political dialogue between the two parties. The Agreement entered into force in June 2000, when the first meeting of the EU–Israel Association Council was also held. An agreement on scientific and technical co-operation, enabling Israel's access to the Community's fourth framework programme (1994–98) on research and technological development, was signed in October 1995. An agreement extending associated country status to Israel within the fifth framework programme (1999–2002), was signed in March 1999. Israel signed a framework agreement with the EIB in June 2000.

During 1998 diplomatic relations between Israel and the EU deteriorated, owing partly to Israel's inappropriate application of EU preferential trading arrangements by exporting agricultural products from Jewish settlements in the West Bank and Gaza, East Jerusalem and the Golan Heights (not recognized by the EU as part of Israel) under Israeli licence. In May the Israeli Prime Minister insisted that any EU role in the Middle East peace process would be unacceptable if the European Commission proceeded with a threat to ban the disputed products from being imported into the EU. Additionally, the European Commission was critical of Israel's perceived obstruction of Palestinian trade, which had impeded implementation of the interim agreement between the EU and the Palestinian (National) Authority (PA—see below). Bilateral relations between the EU and Israel improved following the election of a new Israeli administration in May 1999. However, the escalation of violence between Israel and the Palestinians from late September 2000 led to a worsening of EU–Israel relations. The European Parliament condemned the acts of provocation that sparked the new *intifada* (uprising), and called for a speedy resumption of the peace process. The EU adopted a more hardline stance on the issue of imports of disputed goods, as well as the expansion of Jewish settlements (to which it is opposed). The EU's position on these issues, together with its substantial financial contribution to the PA (see below), has resulted in the organization being viewed by Israel as an unsuitable mediator in the conflict.

YEMEN

A co-operation agreement with the former Yemen Arab Republic, covering commercial, economic and development co-operation, was signed in October 1984. The agreement entered into force in January 1985, initially for a five-year period. In May 1989 the EC decided to intensify and diversify its co-operation with the Yemen Arab Republic. In June 1992 the European Council agreed to extend the original co-operation agreement to include the whole of the new Republic of Yemen (formed by the unification of the Yemen Arab Republic with the People's Democratic Republic of Yemen in 1990). During 1994 food aid and other Community projects in Yemen were suspended owing to civil conflict in that country, although ECU 1.2m. of humanitarian aid was delivered. In March 1995 the EU-Yemen Joint Co-operation Council convened for the first time since early 1993. A new co-operation agreement, incorporating a political element (i.e. commitments to democratic principles and respect for human rights), and providing for 'most favoured nation' treatment was initialled by both sides in April 1997, and the draft agreement was signed in November. The agreement entered into force on 1 July 1998. In April 1997 the European Commission provided substantial technical and financial support to assist the electoral process in Yemen. Under the ECHO programme, Yemen received €1.74m. for refugees and other vulnerable groups in 2000.

CO-OPERATION COUNCIL FOR THE ARAB STATES OF THE GULF—GCC

A co-operation agreement with the GCC was signed in June 1988 and entered into force in January 1990. Negotiations on a full free-trade pact began in October, but it was expected that any agreement would involve transition periods of some 12 years for the reduction of European tariffs on 'sensitive products' (i.e. petrochemicals). In 1992–93 the agreement was jeopardized by the GCC's opposition to an EC proposal to introduce a supplementary tax on petroleum, in order to reduce the use of pollutant-releasing fossil fuels, as well as the failure of the GCC to adopt a unified tariff structure. While these issues continued to obstruct the conclusion of an accord, in July 1995 an EU-GCC ministerial meeting in Granada, Spain agreed to establish a committee to facilitate dialogue between the two sides and to promote co-operation in other areas, such as cultural and scientific activities. In December 2001 the GCC Supreme Council agreed to establish a customs union—a precondition of the proposed EU–GCC free-trade agreement—by 1 January 2003. Free-trade negotiations were continuing in 2002.

IRAN

Talks were held with Iran in April 1992 on the establishment of a co-operation accord. In December the Council of Ministers advocated that a 'critical dialogue' be pursued with Iran, owing to that country's importance to regional security. The two sides subsequently held regular meetings; however, the development of more extensive relations was hindered by the EU's concerns over Iran's stance on the Middle East peace process, international terrorism and human rights-in particular, the situation of minorities in Iran and the death warrant imposed on a British author in 1989. In April 1997 the EU suspended its critical dialogue with Iran, following a ruling by a German court that identified the Iranian authorities as having ordered the assassination of four Kurdish dissidents in Berlin in 1992. The German and Dutch Governments withdrew their ambassadors from Iran and urged other EU countries to do the same. At the end of April 1997 a meeting of ministers of foreign affairs of EU countries confirmed the suspension of the dialogue, but resolved that all diplomatic relations with Iran be upheld, in order to maintain the strong trading relationship between the two sides. This decision, however, was reversed when the Iranian government refused to permit the German and Dutch ambassadors to return to their posts in Tehran. In November, following the election in May of Dr Sayed Muhammad Khatami as president, Iran agreed to readmit all EU ambassadors. In February 1998 EU ministers of foreign affairs removed the ban on high-level contacts with the Iranian administration, with the aim of strengthening dialogue between the two sides. Foreign ministry officials conducted talks with the Iranian authorities in July, on the basis of a ministerial decision in June to initiate a 'comprehensive' dialogue with Iran. In November 2000 an EU–Iran working group on trade and investment met for the first time. The Commission adopted a communication on developing closer relations with Iran in February 2001, and in November the European Council mandated the Commission to negotiatiate a trade and co-operation agreement with that country. Dr Khatami's re-election to the presidency in June was welcomed by the EU.

CYPRUS

An Association Agreement with Cyprus came into effect in June 1973. Immediate tariff reductions were made by the EC of 70% in the industrial sector, 40% for citrus fruit and 100% for carob beans. From July 1977 the EC granted duty-free entry to industrial goods from Cyprus, limited by tariff quotas in respect of man-made textiles and some garments. From 1978 specific tariff reductions were granted on fruit and vegetables, while Cyprus applied 35% tariff reductions on most Community products. In December 1987 the European Council adopted a protocol providing for the establishment of a full customs union, to be completed in two phases.

In July 1990 Cyprus and Malta made formal applications to join the EC. In June 1993 the European Commission approved the eligibility of both to join the Community. In accordance with an agreement concluded in March 1995, accession negotiations were to commence six months after the conclusion of the 1996 EU inter-governmental conference. In June 1995 the EU-Cyprus Association Council agreed to pursue a 'structured dialogue' as part of the pre-accession negotiations, and approved a new financial protocol, amounting to ECU 74m., for the period 1996–98. The first joint ministerial meeting was held in September 1995. During 1996 and 1997 the EU, together with the USA, undertook intensive diplomatic activities to broker a peace settlement in the divided country, to facilitate Cyprus's accession to the EU as a single entity. In July 1997 the European Commission published a report entitled 'Agenda 2000', which presented the Commission's new 'reinforced pre-accession strategy', uniting all existing forms of support into a single 'Accession Partnership' (AP) programme for all candidate countries. These APs, approved by the Commission in March 1998, were designed to support each country's preparations for accession by identifying priority areas and providing financial assistance. Each AP was complemented by a 'National Programme for the Adoption of the Acquis' (NPAA). (The acquis communautaire is the entire body of legislation of the European Community.)

In December 1997 the European Council agreed that accession negotiations with Cyprus should commence in March 1998. Accordingly, talks were initiated on 30 March, with detailed negotiations commencing in November. The Turkish Cypriot authorities refused an invitation to participate in the talks unless the EU extended full diplomatic recognition to the 'Turkish Republic of Northern Cyprus' ('TRNC'). Negotiations therefore proceeded without the TRNC; the Turkish Cypriot community has, however, been referred to in all position papers adopted. In 1999 the European Council stated that while a political settlement would facilitate the accession of Cyprus to the EU, it was not a precondition. The first AP with Cyprus came into force in March 2000 and in August 2001 Cyprus produced a revised NPAA. By July 2002 negotiations with Cyprus on 28 of 30 chapters of the acquis communautaire had been provisionally concluded, and it was envisaged that the negotiations process would be completed by the end of that year, with Cyprus expected to be in the first wave of new entrants to the EU. Under the heading 'specific aid', Cyprus received €9m. from the EU in 2000; €5m. was granted for 'harmonization' projects. The Commission allocated preaccession aid of €57m. for 2000–04.

In November 1996 the Maltese Government announced its intention to suspend its application for EU membership. However, in September 1998, following the return to power of a nationalist government, Malta renewed its bid. In February 1999 the Commission recommended the initiation of accession negotiations; these commenced in February 2000. Malta's NPAA was adopted in September. By July 2002 negotiations with Malta had been provisionally concluded on 24 chapters of the acquis communautaire. Malta was to receive €38m. in pre-accession aid during 2000–04.

TURKEY

An Association Agreement with Turkey was signed in September 1963. The preparatory phase of the agreement lasted from 1964 to 1973, during which time preferences were given on agricultural products accounting for 40% of Turkey's exports to the EC: unmanufactured tobacco, dried raisins and figs, and nuts.

The transitional phase began in 1973, aiming to introduce a customs union by gradual stages over 12 to 22 years, depending on the product. The EC granted immediate duty- and quota-free access for industrial products, but placed restrictions on refined petroleum products and three textile products. The fourth financial protocol to the Association Agreement was to make available ECU 600m. for the period 1981–86 but, following the 1980 coup in Turkey, EC aid was suspended. A ministerial meeting was held in September 1986 to reactivate the Association Agreement.

In April 1987 Turkey applied for full membership of the EC. In 1989, however, the Commission stated that formal negotiations on Turkish membership could not take place until 1993, and that it would first be necessary for Turkey to restructure its economy, improve its observance of human rights and harmonize its relations with Greece. The Commission undertook, however, to increase the EC's financial assistance for Turkey. In 1990 and 1991 additional assistance was provided for Turkey, as one of the countries directly affected by the crisis that followed the Iraqi invasion of Kuwait in August 1990.

In June 1992 the European Council agreed that relations with Turkey should be upgraded and in November a framework programme was adopted for the conclusion of a customs union. Discussions on the issue were pursued in 1993–94, and the Turkish Government undertook domestic economic reforms to ensure that the customs union could enter into effect on 1 January 1995. In December 1994 the EU–Turkey Association Council agreed to postpone the customs union, owing to persistent concerns regarding the Turkish Government's record on human rights, democracy and the rule of law. Negotiations to conclude the agreement in early 1995 were initially blocked by Greek opposition. However, Greece removed its veto on the customs union after receiving assurance on the accession of Cyprus to the EU, and the agreement was signed at a meeting of the EU–Turkey Association Council in March. The customs union was ratified by the European Parliament in December, with a proviso that the human rights situation in Turkey, in particular the treatment of its Kurdish population, continue to be monitored. The union entered into effect on 1 January 1996. Under the accord, commercial barriers were to be eliminated and Turkey was to harmonize its laws to facilitate the flow of trade and investment between the two sides.

In April 1997 Turkey was assured that it would be considered on equal terms with any other country applying for membership of the EU, in spite of continuing concerns regarding human rights, the strength of influence of Islamic fundamentalism in the country and the situation in Cyprus. This policy was subsequently confirmed in 'Agenda 2000', published in July, and by the European Council meeting that was held in Luxembourg, in December. However, while

the Luxembourg meeting confirmed Turkey's eligibility to join the EU, it failed to nominate that country as a candidate for admission (a status granted to 11 other countries). The Turkish Government declared the decision to be discriminatory and resolved to end all further political dialogue with the EU until Turkey's status had been restored to an equal level with all other aspirant members. From August 1999, when a devastating earthquake struck northwestern Turkey, a *rapprochement* began to take place between Greece and Turkey. Greece lifted its long-standing veto on disbursements of aid to Turkey and the EU made a loan of ECU 600m. to the Turkish Government to assist with reconstruction. This improvement in relations culminated, at the Helsinki summit meeting of EU leaders in December, in a formal invitation to Turkey to present its candidacy for EU membership.

The EU's 2000 Progress Report on Turkey noted that concerns over human rights persisted. It stated that more work was needed on institutional reforms to guarantee democracy and the rule of law, and that substantial efforts were required in policy fields other than the customs union to improve the country's alignment with the 'acquis'. In December the European Council reached agreement on an initial AP with Turkey. At the same time, the Council approved a package of EIB loans totalling €450m. to help Turkey implement its customs agreement with the EU. Turkey's NPAA, published in May 2001, incorporated a package of significant constitutional reforms relating to guaranteeing freedom of expression and association and limiting capital punishment, with a view to meeting EU human rights standards. While welcoming this departure, the 2001 Progress Report reiterated its concerns over the human rights situation, urging the strict implementation of human rights legislation and the reform of many existing structures and practices, and also urging the Turkish authorities to abolish the death penalty.

In late 2000 the EU initiated progress towards establishing a rapid reaction force, with the aim of interlinking the operations of NATO and the EU in conflicts affecting EU member states. However, Turkey (a NATO member) initially refused to agree to allow the EU guaranteed access to NATO planning capability for missions in which NATO as a whole was not involved, obstructing the signing of a basic agreement between the EU and NATO in December. In December 2001 Turkey reportedly withdrew its objections, in view of reassurances from the EU that it would be consulted on a case-by-case basis.

In April 2001 the Commission proposed a regulation grouping the three existing mechanisms for financial assistance to Turkey into a single programme, with the aim of targeting assistance towards the implementation of the pre-accession strategy. It was envisaged that Turkey would be allocated €177m. annually during the period 2002–06.

Euro-Arab Dialogue

The 'Euro-Arab Dialogue' was initiated in 1973, initially to provide a forum for discussion of economic issues: the principal organ was a General Committee, and about 30 working groups were set up to discuss specific issues and prepare projects, such as the creation of a Euro-Arab Centre for the Transfer of Technology. After the Egypt-Israel peace agreement in 1979 all activity was suspended at the request of the Arab League.

In December 1989 a meeting of ministers of foreign affairs of Arab and EC countries agreed to reactivate the Dialogue, entrusting political discussions to an annual ministerial meeting, and economic, technical, social and cultural matters to the General Committee of the Dialogue. However, meetings were suspended as a result of Iraq's invasion of Kuwait in August 1990. Senior officials from the EC and Arab countries agreed in April 1992 to resume the Dialogue.

In 1992 the EC was involved in the Middle East peace negotiations, and participated in and chaired working groups on specific issues that formed part of the process. In September 1993, following the signing of a peace agreement between Israeli and the Palestine Liberation Organisation (PLO), the EC committed ECU 33m. in immediate humanitarian assistance for the provision of housing, education and the development of small businesses in Jericho and the Gaza Strip. In addition, a five-year assistance programme for the period 1994–98 was proposed, to comprise ECU 500m. in grants and loans to improve economic and social infrastructure in the Occupied Territories. Further assistance, totalling over ECU 100m., was disbursed during these years. In November 1998 an assistance programme totalling €250m. was approved for the period 1999–2003.

In October 1996 EU ministers of foreign affairs expressed concern at the adverse effect on the peace process of Israeli activities in East Jerusalem and agreed to appoint a special envoy to the Middle East to strengthen EU involvement in promoting a peaceful settlement. In November ministers endorsed the appointment of Miguel Angel Moratinos, at that time Spain's ambassador to Israel. In July 1997 Moratinos successfully negotiated a meeting of the PLO leader, Yasser Arafat, and the Israeli Minister of Foreign Affairs. The two agreed to revive the peace talks, which had been suspended earlier in the year. The EU continued in its attempts to facilitate the peace process during 1998–99, alongside the USA, the principal mediator in the region; however, its efforts were undermined by a deterioration in diplomatic relations with Israel (see above).

An Interim Euro-Mediterranean Agreement on Trade and Co-operation was signed with the Palestinian authorities in January 1997 and entered into force on 1 July. The Agreement confirmed existing trade concessions, further reduced tariff levels for Palestinian exports to the EU and provided for the implementation of a full Association Agreement within five years. A joint statement establishing regular political dialogue between the EU and the PLO was concluded at the same time. In April 1998 the EU and the PA signed a security co-operation agreement providing for regular meetings to promote joint efforts on security issues, in particular, in combating terrorism. In March 1999 EU heads of state and government urged Israel to fulfil within one year the 'unqualified Palestinian right' to independence. Israel was strongly critical of what it perceived as an ultimatum and stated that the EU had reduced its scope as a mediator in the Middle East peace process. In April the European Parliament demanded an investigation into the handling of Commission funds to Palestinian-controlled areas of the West Bank and Gaza. At that time the EU was the largest donor to the PA (and remains so). (It was subsequently announced that no evidence had been discovered related to the alleged misuse of the funds, although the implementation of economic and other reforms are increasingly a condition of EU assistance to the PA.) The EC–Palestinian Joint Committee, established under the Interim Agreement, met for the first time in May 2000. The committee discussed issues of free trade, customs co-operation and bilateral aid. Implementation of the Agreement has been slow, partly owing to Israeli obstruction of Palestinian trade. The EU provided a total of €155.6m. to the PA in 2000. Palestinian refugees in the Occupied Territories, southern Lebanon and Jordan were granted €18m.

Following the outbreak of the new *intifada* in late 2000, and the economic difficulties that ensued in the PA, the EU granted emergency loans to cover the Authority's running costs. From mid-2001 the EU granted €10m. per month in direct budgetary assistance to the PA; a decision was taken by the European Parliament in June 2002 to continue providing this support. In mid-2001 the EU's High Representative for Common Foreign and Security Policy, Javier Solana Madariaga, toured the region with the aim of encouraging a return to peace. Solana Madariaga had served on the Mitchell Committee, established in late 2000 to examine the causes of the violence and determine measures to arrest it. (The recommendations of the Committee were published in May 2001.) During 2001 ECHO provided assistance for emergency relief projects improving access to primary health care and drinking water in the West Bank and Gaza; emergency provision of food and other essential items and psychosocial support projects for children were also funded. In June 2002 the EU allocated €5m. to the PA to support the rehabilitation of its administrative structure, which had been seriously undermined since the launch of Israel's 'Operation Defensive Shield' in March, in order to enable it to provide adequate services to the Palestinian people. In April a so-called 'Quartet' meeting on the Middle East crisis, comprising envoys from the EU, USA, UN and Russia, held in Madrid, Spain, issued the 'Madrid Declaration', in which it demanded that Israel evacuate its forces from Palestinian cities and urged Arafat to act to prevent ongoing terrorist attacks being conducted by extremist Palestinians against Israeli citizens. The Quartet determined to continue close consultations on the situation. Meeting in July the Quartet agreed on the necessity of continuing international support for Palestinian economic and political reform and institution-building activities, and welcomed the establishment of an International Task Force on Reform (comprising delegates from the EU, USA, Russia, Japan, Norway, World Bank, IMF, and the UN Secretary-General), which, under Quartet auspices, was to develop an action plan for the implementation of such reforms.

In July 1994 representatives of the European Commission and the Arab League met to promote co-operation and good relations. During 1995 the Commission supported a Euro-Arab project to establish a central management training institute for business leaders in Granada, Spain. The Commission has undertaken co-operation projects with the Arab League and its specialized agencies in areas such as the environment, civil aviation, telecommunications, finance and management.

ISLAMIC DEVELOPMENT BANK

Address: POB 5925, Jeddah 21432, Saudi Arabia.

Telephone: (2) 6361400; **fax:** (2) 6366871; **e-mail:** idbarchives@isdb.org.sa; **internet:** www.isdb.org.

The Bank is an international financial institution that was established following a conference of Ministers of Finance of member countries of the Organization of the Islamic Conference (OIC, q.v.), held in Jeddah in December 1973. Its aim is to encourage the economic development and social progress of member countries and of Muslim communities in non-member countries, in accordance with the principles of the Islamic *Shari'a* (sacred law). The Bank formally opened in October 1975.

MEMBERS

There are 54 members.

Organization

(September 2002)

BOARD OF GOVERNORS

Each member country is represented by a governor, usually its Minister of Finance, and an alternate. The Board of Governors is the supreme authority of the Bank, and meets annually. The 27th Annual Meeting was scheduled to be held in Ouagadougou, Burkina Faso, in October 2002.

BOARD OF EXECUTIVE DIRECTORS

The Board consists of 14 members, seven of whom are appointed by the seven largest subscribers to the capital stock of the Bank; the remaining seven are elected by Governors representing the other subscribers. Members of the Board of Executive Directors are elected for three-year terms. The Board is responsible for the direction of the general operations of the Bank.

ADMINISTRATION

In addition to the President of the Bank, there are three Vice-Presidents, responsible for Operations, Trade and Policy, and Finance and Administration.

President of the Bank and Chairman of the Board of Executive Directors: Dr AHMED MOHAMED ALI.

Vice-President Operations: Dr AMADOU BOUBACAR CISSE.

Vice-President Trade and Policy: Dr SYED JAAFAR AZNAN.

Vice-President Finance and Administration: MUZAFAR AL HAJ MUZAFAR.

REGIONAL OFFICES

Kazakhstan: c/o Director, External Aid Co-ordination Dept, 93–95 Ablay-Khan Ave, 480091 Almaty; tel. (3272) 62-18-68; fax (3272) 69-61-52; Dir ZEINAL ABIDIN.

Malaysia: Level 11, Front Wing, Bank Industri, Jalan Sultan Ismail, POB 13671, 50818 Kuala Lumpur; tel. (3) 2946627; fax (3) 2946626; Dir SALEH AMRAN BIN JAMAN (acting).

Morocco: 177 Ave John Kennedy, Souissi 10105, POB 5003, Rabat; tel. (7) 757191; fax (7) 775726; Dir HANI SALIM SUNBUL.

FINANCIAL STRUCTURE

The authorized capital of the Bank is 6,000m. Islamic Dinars (divided into 600,000 shares, having a value of 10,000 Islamic Dinars each). The Islamic Dinar (ID) is the Bank's unit of account and is equivalent to the value of one Special Drawing Right of the IMF (SDR 1 = US $1.32713 at 5 August 2002).

Subscribed capital amounts to ID 4,000m.

Activities

The Bank adheres to the Islamic principle forbidding usury, and does not grant loans or credits for interest. Instead, its methods of project financing are: provision of interest-free loans (with a service fee), mainly for infrastructural projects which are expected to have a marked impact on long-term socio-economic development; provision of technical assistance (e.g. for feasibility studies); equity participation in industrial and agricultural projects; leasing operations, involving the leasing of equipment such as ships, and instalment sale financing; and profit-sharing operations. Funds not immediately needed for projects are used for foreign trade financing. Under the Import Trade Financing Operations (ITFO) scheme, funds

SUBSCRIPTIONS (million Islamic Dinars, as at 5 April 2000*)

Afghanistan . . .	5.00	Maldives	2.50
Albania . . .	2.50	Mali	4.92
Algeria . . .	124.26	Mauritania . . .	4.92
Azerbaijan . . .	4.92	Morocco	24.81
Bahrain	7.00	Mozambique . . .	2.50
Bangladesh . . .	49.29	Niger.	12.41
Benin	4.92	Oman	13.78
Brunei . . .	12.41	Pakistan . . .	124.26
Burkina Faso. . .	12.41	Palestine . . .	9.85
Cameroon . . .	12.41	Qatar. . . .	49.23
Chad	4.92	Saudi Arabia . .	997.17
Comoros . . .	2.50	Senegal . . .	12.42
Djibouti	2.50	Sierra Leone . . .	2.50
Egypt . . .	346.00	Somalia . . .	2.50
Gabon . . .	14.77	Sudan . . .	19.69
The Gambia . .	2.50	Suriname. . . .	2.50
Guinea . . .	12.41	Syria	5.00
Guinea-Bissau . .	2.50	Tajikistan . . .	2.50
Indonesia. . .	124.26	Togo	2.50
Iran	349.97	Tunisia . . .	9.85
Iraq	13.05	Turkey	315.47
Jordan . . .	19.89	Turkmenistan . .	2.50
Kazakhstan . . .	2.50	Uganda . . .	12.41
Kuwait . . .	496.64	United Arab	
Kyrgyzstan . . .	2.50	Emirates . .	283.03
Lebanon . . .	4.92	Yemen	24.81
Libya. . . .	400.00	**Total**. . . .	**4,060.54**
Malaysia . . .	79.56		

* Côte d'Ivoire became a member of the Bank after this date.

are used for importing commodities for development purposes (i.e. raw materials and intermediate industrial goods, rather than consumer goods), with priority given to the import of goods from other member countries (see table). The Longer-term Trade Financing Scheme (LTTFS) was introduced in 1987/88 to provide financing for the export of non-traditional and capital goods. During AH 1419 the LTTFS was renamed the Export Financing Scheme (EFS). A special programme under the EFS became operational in AH 1419, on the basis of a memorandum of understanding signed between the Bank and the Arab Bank for Economic Development in Africa (BADEA), to finance Arab exports to non-Arab League members of the OAU (now African Union, q.v.).

The Bank's Special Assistance programme was initiated in AH 1400 to support the economic and social development of Muslim communities in non-member countries, in particular in the education and health sectors. It also aimed to provide emergency aid in times of natural disasters, and to assist Muslim refugees throughout the world. Operations undertaken by the Bank are financed by the Waqf Fund (formerly the Special Assistance Account). Other assistance activities include scholarship programmes, technical co-operation projects and the sacrificial meat utilization project.

By 5 April 2000 the Bank had approved a total of ID 4,947.98m. for project financing and technical assistance, a total of ID 11,125.24m. for foreign trade financing, and ID 402.59m. for special assistance operations, excluding amounts for cancelled operations. During the Islamic year 1420 (17 April 1999 to 5 April 2000) the Bank approved a total of ID 1,522.80m., for 230 operations.

The Bank approved 39 loans in the year ending 5 April 2000, amounting to ID 179.70m. (compared with 38 loans, totalling ID 159.79m., in the previous year). These loans supported projects concerned with the construction and modernization of schools and health centres, infrastructural improvements, and agricultural developments. During the year ending 5 April 2000 the Bank's disbursements totalled ID 871m., bringing the total cumulative disbursements since the Bank began operations to ID 11,010m.

Operations approved, Islamic year 1420 (17 April 1999–5 April 2000)

Type of operation	Number of operations	Total amount (million Islamic Dinars)
Ordinary operations . . .	112	725.49
Project financing . . .	77	718.31
Technical assistance . . .	35	7.19
Trade financing operations* .	64	805.85
Waqf Fund operations . . .	54	21.46
Total†	**230**	**1,522.80**

* Including ITFO, the EFS, the Islamic Bank's Portfolio and the UIF.
† Excluding cancelled operations.

Project financing and technical assistance by sector, Islamic year 1420 (17 April 1999–5 April 2000)

Sector	Number of operations	Amount (million Islamic Dinars)	%
Agriculture and agro-industry	18	87.51	12.1
Industry and mining . .	4	71.40	9.8
Transport and communications . . .	17	99.25	13.7
Public utilities . . .	18	222.18	30.6
Social sectors	39	183.74	25.3
Financial services/Other* .	16	61.41	8.5
Total†	**112**	**725.49**	**100.0**

* Mainly approved amounts for Islamic banks.
† Excluding cancelled operations.

During AH 1420 the Bank approved 35 technical assistance operations for 19 countries (as well as six regional projects) in the form of grants and loans, amounting to ID 7.19m.

Import trade financing approved during the Islamic year 1420 amounted to ID 651.34m. for 39 operations in 12 member countries. By the end of that year cumulative import trade financing amounted to ID 9,480.37m., of which 37.4% was for imports of crude petroleum, 26.4% for intermediate industrial goods, 7.5% for vegetable oil and 6.4% for refined petroleum products. Export financing approved under the EFS amounted to ID 61.32m. for 15 operations in nine countries in AH 1420. In the same year the Bank's Portfolio for Investment and Development, established in AH 1407 (1986–87), approved eight operations amounting to US $106.6m. (or approximately ID 79.1m.). Since its introduction, the Portfolio has approved net financing operations amounting to $1,490.1m. (or ID 1,106.0m.).

The Bank's Unit Investment Fund (UIF) became operational in 1990, with the aim of mobilizing additional resources and providing a profitable channel for investments conforming to *Shari'a*. The initial issue of the UIF was US $100m., which has subsequently been increased to $325m. The Fund finances mainly private-sector industrial projects in middle-income countries. The UIF also finances short-term trade financing operations: two were approved in AH 1420, amounting to $19.0m. In October 1998 the Bank announced the establishment of a new fund to invest in infrastructure projects in member states. The Bank committed $250m. to the fund, which was to comprise $1,000m. equity capital and a $500m. Islamic financing facility. In September 1999 the Bank's Board of Executive Directors approved the establishment of an Islamic Corporation for the Development of the Private Sector, which aimed to identify opportunities in the private sector, provide financial products and services compatible with Islamic law, and expand access to Islamic capital markets for private companies in member countries. The Bank was to retain 50% of the authorized capital of $1,000m., with the remainder owned by member countries (30%) and public financial institutions (20%). In November 2001 the Bank signed an agreement with Malaysia, Bahrain, Indonesia and Sudan for the establishment of an Islamic financial market. In April 2002 the Bank, jointly with governors of central banks and the Accounting and Auditing Organization for Islamic Financial Institutions, concluded an agreement, under the auspices of the IMF, for the establishment of an Islamic Financial Services Board. The Board, which was to be located in Kuala Lumpur, Malaysia, was intended to elaborate and harmonize standards for best practices in the regulation and supervision of the Islamic financial services industry.

During AH 1420 the Bank approved 54 Waqf Fund operations, amounting to ID 21.5m. Of the total financing, 28 operations provided assistance for Muslim communities in 18 non-member countries.

By the end of AH 1420 the Bank's scholarships programme for Muslim communities in non-member countries had benefited some 5,343 students, at a cost of ID 27m., since it began in 1983. The Merit Scholarship Programme, initiated in AH 1412 (1991–92), aims to develop scientific, technological and research capacities in member countries through advanced studies and/or research. During the second five-year phase of the initiative, which commenced in January 1997, 20 scholars each year were expected to be placed in academic centres of excellence in Australia, Europe and the USA under the programme. In December 1997 the Board of Executive Directors approved a new scholarship programme designed specifically to assist scholars from 18 least-developed member countries to study for a masters degree in science and technology. A total of 190 scholarships were expected to have been awarded by AH 1423. The Bank's Programme for Technical Co-operation aims to mobilize technical capabilities among member countries and to promote the exchange of expertise, experience and skills through expert missions, training, seminars and workshops. During AH 1420 74 projects were implemented under the programme. The Bank also undertakes the distribution of meat sacrificed by

Muslim pilgrims: in AH 1420 meat from approximately 416,699 animals was distributed to the needy in 26 countries.

SUBSIDIARY ORGANS

Islamic Corporation for the Insurance of Investment and Export Credit—ICIEC: POB 15722, Jeddah 21454, Saudi Arabia; tel. (2) 6445666; fax (2) 6379504; e-mail idb.iciec@isdb.org.sa; internet www.iciec.org; f. 1994; aims to promote trade and the flow of investments among member countries of the OIC through the provision of export credit and investment insurance services; auth. cap. ID 100m., subscribed cap. ID 95.0m. (March 2001). Man. Dr ABDEL RAHMAN A. TAHA. Mems: 29 OIC member states.

Islamic Research and Training Institute: POB 9201, Jeddah 21413, Saudi Arabia; tel. (2) 6361400; fax (2) 6378927; e-mail mal jarhi@isdb.org.sa; internet www.irti.org; f. 1982 to undertake research enabling economic, financial and banking activities to conform to Islamic law, and to provide training for staff involved in development activities in the Bank's member countries. The Institute also organizes seminars and workshops, and holds training courses aimed at furthering the expertise of government and financial officials in Islamic developing countries. Dir Dr MABID ALI AL-JARHI. Publs *Annual Report, Journal of Islamic Economic Studies,* various research studies, monographs, reports.

Publication

Annual Report.

LEAGUE OF ARAB STATES

Address: POB 11642, Arab League Bldg, Tahrir Square, Cairo, Egypt.
Telephone: (2) 575-0511; **fax:** (2) 574-0331; **internet:** www.arableagueonline.org/arableague/index_en.jsp.

The League of Arab States (more generally known as the Arab League) is a voluntary association of sovereign Arab states, designed to strengthen the close ties linking them and to co-ordinate their policies and activities and direct them towards the common good of all the Arab countries. It was founded in March 1945.

MEMBERS

Algeria	Lebanon	Somalia
Bahrain	Libya	Sudan
Comoros	Mauritania	Syria
Djibouti	Morocco	Tunisia
Egypt	Oman	United Arab
Iraq	Palestine*	Emirates
Jordan	Qatar	Yemen
Kuwait	Saudi Arabia	

* Palestine is considered an independent state, and therefore a full member of the League.

Organization

(September 2002)

COUNCIL

The supreme organ of the Arab League, the Council consists of representatives of the member states, each of which has one vote, and a representative for Palestine. The Council meets ordinarily every March, normally at the League headquarters, at the level of heads of state ('kings, heads of state and emirs'), and in March and September at the level of foreign ministers. The summit-level meeting reviews all issues related to Arab national security strategies, co-ordinates supreme policies of the Arab states towards regional and international issues, reviews recommendations and reports submitted to it by meetings at foreign minister level, appoints the Secretary-General of the League, and is mandated to amend the League's Charter. Decisions of the summit-level Council are passed on a consensus basis. Foreign ministers' meetings assess the implementation of summit resolutions, prepare relevant reports, and make arrangements for subsequent summits. Committees comprising a smaller group of foreign ministers may be appointed to follow up closely summit resolutions. Extraordinary summit-level meetings may be held at the request of one member state or the Secretary-General, if approved by a two-thirds majority of member states. Extraordinary sessions of ministers of foreign affairs may, be held at the request of two member states or of the Secretary-General. The presidency of ordinary meetings is rotated in accordance with the alphabetical order of the League's member states. Unanimous decisions of the Council are binding upon all member states of the League; majority decisions are binding only on those states which have accepted them.

The Council is supported by technical and specialized committees advising on financial and administrative affairs, information affairs and legal affairs. In addition, specialized ministerial councils have been established to formulate common policies for the regulation and the advancement of co-operation in the following sectors: communications; electricity; environment; health; housing and construction; information; interior; justice; social affairs; tourism; transportation; and youth and sports.

GENERAL SECRETARIAT

The administrative and financial offices of the League. The Secretariat carries out the decisions of the Council, and provides financial and administrative services for the personnel of the League. General departments comprise: the Bureau of the Secretary-General, Arab Affairs, Economic Affairs, Information Affairs, Legal Affairs, Palestine Affairs, Political International Affairs, Military Affairs, Social Affairs, Administrative and Financial Affairs, and Internal Audit. In addition, there is a Documentation and Information Centre, an Arab League Centre in Tunis, an Arab Fund for Technical Assistance in African States, a Higher Arab Institute for Translation in Algiers, a Music Academy in Baghdad, and a Special Bureau for Boycotting Israel, based in Damascus, Syria (see below). The following bodies have also been established: an administrative court, an investment arbitration board and a higher auditing board.

The Secretary-General is appointed at summit meetings of the Council by a two-thirds' majority of the member states, for a five-year, renewable term. He appoints the Assistant Secretaries-General and principal officials, with the approval of the Council. He has the rank of ambassador, and the Assistant Secretaries-General have the rank of ministers plenipotentiary.

Secretary-General: AMR MUHAMMAD MOUSSA (Egypt).

DEFENCE AND ECONOMIC CO-OPERATION

Groups established under the Treaty of Joint Defence and Economic Co-operation, concluded in 1950 to complement the Charter of the League.

Arab Unified Military Command: f. 1964 to co-ordinate military policies for the liberation of Palestine.

Economic and Social Council: compares and co-ordinates the economic policies of the member states; supervises the activities of the Arab League's specialized agencies. The Council is composed of ministers of economic affairs or their deputies; decisions are taken by majority vote. The first meeting was held in 1953. In February 1997 the Economic and Social Council adopted the Executive Programme of the League's (1981) Agreement to Facilitate and Develop Trade Among Arab Countries, with a view to establishing a Greater Arab Free Trade Area (see below).

Joint Defence Council: supervises implementation of those aspects of the treaty concerned with common defence. Composed of foreign and defence ministers; decisions by a two-thirds' majority vote of members are binding on all.

Permanent Military Commission: established 1950; composed of representatives of army general staffs; main purpose: to draw up plans of joint defence for submission to the Joint Defence Council.

ARAB DETERRENT FORCE

Created in June 1976 by the Arab League Council to supervise successive attempts to cease hostilities in Lebanon, and afterwards to maintain the peace. The mandate of the Force has been successively renewed. The Arab League summit conference in October 1976 agreed that costs were to be paid in the following percentage contributions: Saudi Arabia and Kuwait 20% each, the United Arab Emirates 15%, Qatar 10% and other Arab states 35%.

OTHER INSTITUTIONS OF THE LEAGUE

Other bodies established by resolutions adopted by the Council of the League:

Administrative Tribunal of the Arab League: f. 1964; began operations 1966.

Arab Fund for Technical Assistance to African Countries: f. 1975 to provide technical assistance for development projects by providing African and Arab experts, grants for scholarships and training, and finance for technical studies.

Higher Auditing Board: comprises representatives of seven member states, elected every three years; undertakes financial and administrative auditing duties.

Investment Arbitration Board: examines disputes between member states relating to capital investments.

Special Bureau for Boycotting Israel: POB 437, Damascus, Syria; f. 1951 to prevent trade between Arab countries and Israel, and to enforce a boycott by Arab countries of companies outside the region that conduct trade with Israel.

SPECIALIZED AGENCIES

All member states of the Arab League are also members of the Specialized Agencies, which constitute an integral part of the Arab League. (See also entries on the Arab Fund for Economic and Social Development, the Arab Monetary Fund, the Council of Arab Economic Unity and the Organization of Arab Petroleum Exporting Countries.)

Arab Academy for Science, Technology and Maritime Transport—AASTMT: POB 1029, Alexandria, Egypt; tel. (3) 5602388; fax (3) 5622525; internet www.aast.edu/web/main.jsp; f. 1975 as Arab Maritime Transport Academy; provides specialized training in marine transport, engineering, technology and management. Dir-Gen. Dr GAMAL ED-DIN MOUKHTAR. Publs *Maritime Research Bulletin* (monthly), *Journal of the Arab Academy for Science, Technology and Maritime Transport* (2 a year).

Arab Administrative Development Organization—ARADO: POB 2692 Al-Horreia, Heliopolis, Cairo, Egypt; tel. (2) 4175401; fax (2) 4175407; e-mail arado@arado.org; internet www.arado.org; f. 1961 (as Arab Organization of Administrative Sciences), became operational in 1969; administration development, training, consultancy, research and studies, information, documentation; promotes Arab and international co-operation in administrative sciences; includes Arab Network of Administrative Information; 20 Arab state members; Library of 26,000 volumes, 400 periodicals. Dir-Gen. Dr MOHAMED IBRAHIM AL-TWEGRI. Publs *Arab Journal of Administration* (biannual), *Management Newsletter* (quarterly), research series, training manuals.

Arab Atomic Energy Agency—AAEA: POB 402, al-Manzah 1004, 1004 Tunis, Tunisia; tel. (71) 709464; fax (71) 711330; e-mail aaea@aaea.org.tn; f. 1988 to co-ordinate research into the peaceful uses of atomic energy. Dir-Gen. Prof. Dr MAHMOUD NASREDDINE (Lebanon). Publs *The Atom and Development* (quarterly), other publs in the field of nuclear sciences and their applications in industry, biology, medicine, agriculture, food irradiation and seawater desalination.

Arab Bank for Economic Development in Africa (Banque arabe pour le développement économique en Afrique—BADEA): Sayed Abd ar-Rahman el-Mahdi St, POB 2640, Khartoum 11111, Sudan; tel. (11) 773646; fax (11) 770600; e-mail badea@badea.org; internet www.badea.org; f. 1973 by Arab League; provides loans and grants to African countries to finance development projects; paid-up cap. US $1,500m. (Dec. 2001). In 2001 the Bank approved loans and grants totalling $124m. By the end of 2001 total loans and grants approved since funding activities began in 1975 amounted to $2,211.3m. Subscribing countries: all countries of Arab League, except the Comoros, Djibouti, Somalia and Yemen; recipient countries: all countries of the African Union (q.v.), except those belonging to the Arab League. Chair. AHMAD ABDALLAH AL-AKEIL (Saudi Arabia); Dir-Gen. MEDHAT SAMI LOTFY (Egypt). Publs *Annual Report, Co-operation for Development* (quarterly), Studies on Afro-Arab co-operation, periodic brochures.

Arab Centre for the Study of Arid Zones and Dry Lands—ACSAD: POB 2440, Damascus, Syria; tel. (11) 5743039; fax (11) 5743037; e-mail acsad@net.sy; internet www.acsad.org; f. 1971 to conduct regional research and development programmes related to water and soil resources, plant and animal production, agro-meteorology, and socio-economic studies of arid zones. The Centre holds conferences and training courses and encourages the exchange of information by Arab scientists. Dir-Gen. Dr ADEL SAFER.

Arab Industrial Development and Mining Organization: rue France, Zanagat Al Khatawat, POB 8019, Rabat, Morocco; tel. (7) 772600; fax (7) 772188; e-mail aidmo@arifonet.org.ma; internet www.arifonet.org.ma; f. 1990 by merger of Arab Industrial Development Organization, Arab Organization for Mineral Resources and Arab Organization for Standardization and Metrology. Comprises a 13-member Executive Council, a High Consultative Committee of Standardization, a High Committee of Mineral Resources and a Co-ordination Committee for Arab Industrial Research Centres; a Ministerial Council, of ministers of member states responsible for industry, meets every two years. Dir-Gen. TALA'AT BEN DAFER. Publs *Arab Industrial Development* (monthly and quarterly newsletters).

Arab Labour Organization: POB 814, Cairo, Egypt; f. 1965 for co-operation between member states in labour problems; unification of labour legislation and general conditions of work wherever possible; research; technical assistance; social insurance; training, etc.; the organization has a tripartite structure: governments, employers and workers. Dir-Gen. IBRAHIM GUDIR. Publs *ALO Bulletin* (monthly), *Arab Labour Review* (quarterly), *Legislative Bulletin* (annually), series of research reports and studies concerned with economic and social development issues in the Arab world.

Arab League Educational, Cultural and Scientific Organization—ALECSO: POB 1120, Tunis, Tunisia; tel. (71) 784-466; fax (71) 784-965; e-mail alecso@email.ati.tn; internet www.slis.uwm.edu/ALECSO/; f. 1970 to promote and co-ordinate educational, cultural and scientific activities in the Arab region. Regional units: Arab Centre for Arabization, Translation, Authorship, and Publication—Damascus, Syria; Institute of Arab Manuscript—Cairo, Egypt; Institute of Arab Research and Studies—Cairo, Egypt; Khartoum Institute for Arabic Language—Khartoum, Sudan; and the Arabization Coordination Bureau—Rabat, Morocco. Dir-Gen. Dr MONGI BOUSNINA. Publs *Arab Journal of Culture, Arab Journal of Science, Arab Bulletin of Publications, Statistical Yearbook, Journal of the Institute of Arab Manuscripts, Arab Magazine for Information Science.*

Arab Organization for Agricultural Development—AOAD: St no. 7, Al-Amarat, POB 474, Khartoum, Sudan; tel. (11) 472176; fax (11) 471402; e-mail aoad@sudanmail.net; internet www.aoad.org; f. 1970; began operations in 1972 to contribute to co-operation in agricultural activities, and in the development of natural and human resources for agriculture; compiles data, conducts studies, training and food security programmes; includes Arab Institute of Forestry and Range, Arab Centre for Information and Early Warning, and Arab Centre for Agricultural Documentation. Dir-Gen. Dr SALEM AL-LOZI. Publs *Agricultural Statistics Yearbook, Annual Report on Agricultural Development, the State of Arab Food Security* (annually), *Agriculture and Development in the Arab World* (quarterly), *Accession Bulletin* (every 2 months), *AOAD Newsletter* (monthly), *Arab Agricultural Research Journal, Arab Journal for Irrigation Water Management* (2 a year).

Arab Satellite Communications Organization—ARABSAT: King Fahd Express Rd (Ollaya St), POB 1038, Riyadh, 11431 Saudi Arabia; tel. (1) 4820000; fax (1) 4887999; e-mail albidnah@arabsat.com; internet www.arabsat.com; f. 1976; regional satellite telecommunications organization providing television, telephone and data exchange services to members and private users; operates three satellites, which cover all Arab and Mediterranean countries, controlled by a Primary Control Station in Dirab, Saudi Arabia, and a Secondary Control Facility, based in Dkhila, Tunisia. Dir-Gen. SAAD IBN ABD AL-AZIZ AL-BIDNAH (Saudi Arabia).

Arab States Broadcasting Union—ASBU: POB 250, 1080 Tunis Cedex; 6 rue des Entrepreneurs, zone industrielle Charguia 2, Ariana Aéroport, Tunisia; tel. (71) 703854; fax (71) 703855; e-mail asbu@asbu.intl.tn; internet www.asbu.org.tn; f. 1969 to promote Arab fraternity, co-ordinate and study broadcasting subjects, to exchange expertise and technical co-operation in broadcasting; conducts training and audience research. Mems: 21 Arab radio and TV stations and six foreign associates. Exec. Chair. Dr FAYEZ AL SAYEGH (Syria). Publ. *ASBU Review* (quarterly).

Inter-Arab Investment Guarantee Corporation: POB 23568, Safat 13096, Kuwait; tel. 4844500; fax 4815741; internet www.iaigc.org; f. 1975; insures Arab investors for non-commercial risks, and export credits for commercial and non-commercial risks; undertakes research and other activities to promote inter-Arab trade and investment; cap. p.u. US $81m., res $168m. (Dec. 2000). Mems: 22 Arab governments. Dir-Gen. MAMOUN IBRAHIM HASSAN. Publs *News Bulletin* (monthly), *Arab Investment Climate Report* (annually).

External Relations

ARAB LEAGUE OFFICES AND INFORMATION CENTRES ABROAD

Established by the Arab League to co-ordinate work at all levels among Arab embassies abroad.

Austria: Kärntner Ring 17, 1010 Vienna; e-mail arab.league.vienna@aon.at.

Belgium: 28 ave de l'Uruguay, 1000 Brussels; e-mail ligue.etats.arabes@skynet.be.

China, People's Republic: 1-14-2 Lian Ma He, Tayuan Diplomatic Building, Beijing 100600; e-mail lasj@a-a.net.cn.

Ethiopia: POB 5768, Addis Ababa; e-mail arague.et@telecom.net.et.

France: 36 rue Fortuny, 75017 Paris; e-mail leap@pelnet.com.

Germany: Markgrafenstr. 25, 10117 Berlin.

India: F.63 Poorvo MargVasant Vihar, New Delhi; e-mail las@mantraonline.com.

Italy: Piazzale delle Belle Arti 6, 001961 Rome; e-mail legaarab@shareware.it.

Russia: 28 Koniouch Kovskaya, 123242 Moscow; e-mail ligarab@granit.ru.

Spain: Paseo de la Castellana 180, 60°, 28046 Madrid; e-mail liga .arabe@terra.es.

Switzerland: 9 rue du Valais, 1202 Geneva; e-mail saad.alfarargi@ ties.itu.int.

United Kingdom: 52 Green St, London, W1Y 3RH; e-mail las@ jamia-uk.dmon.co.uk.

USA: 1100 17th St, NW, Suite 602, Washington, DC 20036; e-mail arableague@aol.com; 747 Third Ave, 35th Floor, New York, NY 10017 (UN Office).

Record of Events

1945   Pact of the Arab League signed, March.

1946   Cultural Treaty signed.

1950   Joint Defence and Economic Co-operation Treaty.

1952   Agreements on extradition, writs and letters of request, nationality of Arabs outside their country of origin.

1953   Formation of Economic and Social Council.
Convention on the privileges and immunities of the League.

1954   Nationality Agreement.

1956   Agreement on the adoption of a Common Tariff Nomenclature.

1962   Arab Economic Unity Agreement.

1964   First summit conference of Arab heads of state, Cairo, January. First meeting of Council of Arab Economic Unity, June. Arab Common Market Agreement endorsed by the Council, August. Second summit conference welcomed establishment of Palestine Liberation Organization (PLO), September.

1969   Fifth summit conference, Rabat. Call for mobilization of all Arab nations against Israel.

1977   Tripoli Declaration, December. Decision of Algeria, Iraq, Libya and Yemen PDR to boycott League meetings in Egypt in response to President Sadat's visit to Israel.

1979   Council meeting resolved to withdraw Arab ambassadors from Egypt; to recommend severance of political and diplomatic relations with Egypt; to suspend Egypt's membership of the League on the date of the signing of its formal peace treaty with Israel (26 March); to transfer the headquarters of the League to Tunis; to condemn US policy regarding its role in concluding the Camp David agreements (in September 1978) and the peace treaty; to halt all bank loans, deposits, guarantees or facilities, as well as all financial or technical contributions and aid to Egypt; to prohibit trade exchanges with the Egyptian state and with private establishments dealing with Israel.

1981   In November the 12th summit conference, held in Fez, Morocco, was suspended owing to disagreement over a Saudi Arabian proposal known as the Fahd Plan, which included not only the Arab demands on behalf of the Palestinians, as approved by the UN General Assembly, but also an implied *de facto* recognition of Israel.

1982   The 12th summit conference was reconvened in September. It adopted a peace plan, which demanded Israel's withdrawal from territories occupied in 1967, and removal of Israeli settlements in these areas; freedom of worship for all religions in the sacred places; the right of the Palestinian people to self-determination, under the leadership of the PLO; temporary supervision for the West Bank and the Gaza Strip; the creation of an independent Palestinian state, with Jerusalem as its capital; and a guarantee of peace for all the states of the region by the UN Security Council.

1983   The summit meeting due to be held in November was postponed owing to members' differences of opinion concerning Syria's opposition to Yasser Arafat's chairmanship of the PLO, and Syrian support of Iran in the war against Iraq.

1984   In March an emergency meeting established an Arab League committee to encourage international efforts to bring about a negotiated settlement of the Iran–Iraq war. In May ministers of foreign affairs adopted a resolution urging Iran to stop attacking non-belligerent ships and installations in the Gulf region: similar attacks by Iraq were not mentioned.

1985   In August an emergency summit conference was boycotted by Algeria, Lebanon, Libya, Syria and Yemen PDR, while of the other 16 members only nine were represented by their heads of state. Two commissions were set up to mediate in disagreements between Arab states (between Jordan and Syria, Iraq and Syria, Iraq and Libya, and Libya and the PLO).

1986   In July King Hassan of Morocco announced that he was resigning as chairman of the next League summit conference, after criticism by several Arab leaders of his meeting with the Israeli Prime Minister earlier that month. A ministerial meeting, held in October, condemned any attempt at direct negotiation with Israel.

1987   An extraordinary summit conference was held in November, mainly to discuss the war between Iran and Iraq. Contrary to expectations, the participants unanimously agreed on a statement expressing support for Iraq in its defence of its legitimate rights, and criticizing Iran for its procrastination in accepting the UN Security Council Resolution 598 of July, which had recommended a cease-fire and negotiations on a settlement of the conflict. The meeting also stated that the resumption of diplomatic relations with Egypt was a matter to be decided by individual states.

1988   In June a summit conference agreed to provide finance for the PLO to continue the Palestinian uprising in Israeli-occupied territories. It reiterated a demand for the convening of an international conference, attended by the PLO, to seek to bring about a peaceful settlement in the Middle East (thereby implicitly rejecting recent proposals by the US Government for a conference that would exclude the PLO).

1989   In January an Arab League group, comprising six ministers of foreign affairs, began discussions with the two rival Lebanese governments on the possibility of a political settlement in Lebanon. At a summit conference, held in May, Egypt was readmitted to the League. The Conference expressed support for the chairman of the PLO, Yasser Arafat, in his recent peace proposals made before the UN General Assembly, and reiterated the League's support for proposals that an international conference should be convened to discuss the rights of Palestinians: in so doing, it accepted UN Security Council Resolutions 242 and 338 on a peaceful settlement in the Middle East and thus gave tacit recognition to the State of Israel. The meeting also supported Arafat in rejecting Israeli proposals for elections in the Israeli-occupied territories of the West Bank and the Gaza Strip. A new mediation committee was established, with a six-month mandate to negotiate a cease-fire in Lebanon, and to reconvene the Lebanese legislature with the aim of holding a presidential election and restoring constitutional government in Lebanon. In September the principal factions in Lebanon agreed to observe a cease-fire, and the surviving members of the Lebanese legislature (originally elected in 1972) met at Ta'if, in Saudi Arabia, in October, and approved the League's proposed 'charter of national reconciliation'.

1990   In May a summit conference, held in Baghdad, Iraq (which was boycotted by Syria and Lebanon), criticized recent efforts by Western governments to prevent the development of advanced weapons technology in Iraq. In August an emergency summit conference was held to discuss the invasion and annexation of Kuwait by Iraq. Twelve members (Bahrain, Djibouti, Egypt, Kuwait, Lebanon, Morocco, Oman, Qatar, Saudi Arabia, Somalia, Syria and the United Arab Emirates) approved a resolution condemning Iraq's action, and demanding the withdrawal of Iraqi forces from Kuwait and the reinstatement of the Government. The 12 states expressed support for the Saudi Arabian Government's invitation to the USA to send forces to defend Saudi Arabia; they also agreed to impose economic sanctions on Iraq, and to provide troops for an Arab defensive force in Saudi Arabia. The remaining member states, however, condemned the presence of foreign troops in Saudi Arabia, and their ministers of foreign affairs refused to attend a meeting, held at the end of August, to discuss possible solutions to the crisis. The dissenting countries also rejected the decision, taken earlier in the year, to return the League's headquarters from Tunis to Cairo. None the less, the official transfer of the League's headquarters to Cairo took place at the end of October. In November King Hassan of Morocco urged the convening of an Arab summit conference, in an attempt to find an 'Arab solution' to Iraq's annexation of Kuwait. However, the divisions in the Arab world over the issue meant that conditions for such a meeting could not be agreed.

1991   The first meeting of the Arab League since August 1990 took place in March, attended by representatives of all 21 member nations, including Iraq. Discussion of the recently-ended war against Iraq was avoided, in an attempt to re-establish the unity of the League. In September, despite deep divisions between member states, it was agreed that a committee should be formed to co-ordinate Arab positions in preparation for the US-sponsored peace talks between Arab countries and Israel. (In the event, an *ad hoc* meeting, attended by Egypt, Jordan, Syria, the PLO, Saudi Arabia—representing the Gulf Co-operation Council (GCC), and Morocco—representing the Union of the Arab Maghreb, was held in October, prior to the start of the talks.) In December the League expressed solidarity with

Libya, which was under international pressure to extradite two government agents who were suspected of involvement in the explosion which destroyed a US passenger aircraft over Lockerbie, United Kingdom, in December 1988.

1992   The League attempted to mediate between the warring factions in Somalia. In March the League appointed a committee to seek to resolve the disputes between Libya and the USA, the United Kingdom and France over the Lockerbie bomb and the explosion which destroyed a French passenger aircraft over Niger in September 1989. The League condemned the UN's decision, at the end of March, to impose sanctions against Libya, and appealed for a negotiated solution. In September the League's Council issued a condemnation of Iran's alleged occupation of three islands in the Persian (Arabian) Gulf that were claimed by the United Arab Emirates, and decided to refer the issue to the UN.

1993   In April the Council approved the creation of a committee to consider the political and security aspects of water supply in Arab countries. In the same month the League pledged its commitment to the Middle East peace talks, but warned that Israel's continued refusal to repatriate the Palestinians based in Lebanon remained a major obstacle to the process. In September the Council admitted the Comoros as the 22nd member of the League. Following the signing of the Israeli-PLO peace accord in September the Council convened in emergency session, at which it approved the agreement, despite opposition from some members, notably Syria. In November it was announced that the League's boycott of commercial activity with Israel was to be maintained.

1994   The League condemned a decision of the GCC, announced in late September, to end the secondary and tertiary trade embargo against Israel, by which member states refuse to trade with international companies which have investments in Israel. A statement issued by the League insisted that the embargo could be removed only on the decision of the Council. Earlier in September the Council endorsed a recommendation that the UN conduct a census of Palestinian refugees, in the absence of any such action taken by the League.

1995   In March Arab ministers of foreign affairs approved a resolution urging Israel to renew the Nuclear Non-Proliferation Treaty (NPT). The resolution stipulated that failure by Israel to do so would cause Arab states to seek to protect legitimate Arab interests by alternative means. In May an extraordinary session of the Council condemned a decision by Israel to confiscate Arab-owned land in East Jerusalem for resettlement. The Israeli Government announced the suspension of its expropriation plans. In September the Council discussed plans for a regional court of justice and for an Arab Code of Honour to prevent the use of force in disputes between Arab states.

1996   In March, following protests by Syria and Iraq that extensive construction work in southern Turkey was restricting water supply in the region, the Council determined that the waters of the Euphrates and Tigris rivers be shared equitably between the three countries. In April an emergency meeting of the Council issued a further endorsement of Syria's position in the dispute with Turkey. The main objective of the meeting, which was convened at the request of Palestine, was to attract international attention to the problem of radiation from an Israeli nuclear reactor. The Council requested an immediate technical inspection of the site by the UN, and further demanded that Israel be obliged to sign the NPT to ensure the eradication of its nuclear weaponry. In June an extraordinary summit conference of League heads of state was convened, the first since 1990, in order to formulate a united Arab response to the election, in May, of a new government in Israel and to the prospects for peace in the Middle East. At the conference, which was attended by heads of state of 13 countries and senior representatives of seven others (Iraq was excluded from the meeting in order to ensure the attendance of the Gulf member states), Israel was urged to honour its undertaking to withdraw from the Occupied Territories, including Jerusalem, and to respect the establishment of an independent Palestinian state, in order to ensure the success of the peace process. A final communiqué of the meeting warned that Israeli co-operation was essential to prevent Arab states' reconsidering their participation in the peace process and the re-emergence of regional tensions. Meanwhile, there were concerns over increasing inter-Arab hostility, in particular between Syria and Jordan, owing to the latter's relations with Israel and allegations of Syrian involvement in recent terrorist attacks against Jordanian targets. In early September the League condemned US missile attacks against Iraq as an infringement of that country's sovereignty. In addition, it expressed concern at the impact on Iraqi territorial integrity of Turkish intervention

in the north of Iraq. Later in September the League met in emergency session, following an escalation of civil unrest in Jerusalem and the Occupied Territories. The League urged the UN Security Council to prevent further alleged Israeli aggression against the Palestinians. In November the League criticized Israel's settlement policy, and at the beginning of December convened in emergency session to consider measures to end any expansion of the Jewish population in the West Bank and Gaza.

1997   In March the Council met in emergency session, in response to the Israeli Government's decision to proceed with construction of a new settlement at Har Homa (Jabal Abu-Ghunaim) in East Jerusalem. The Council pledged its commitment to seeking a reversal of the decision and urged the international community to support this aim. At the end of March ministers of foreign affairs of Arab League states agreed to end all efforts to secure normal diplomatic relations with Israel (although binding agreements already in force with Egypt, Jordan and Palestine were exempt) and to close diplomatic offices and missions while construction work continued in East Jerusalem. In addition, ministers recommended reactivating the economic boycott against Israel until comprehensive peace was achieved in the region and suspending Arab participation in the multilateral talks that were initiated in 1991 to further the peace process. Earlier in the year, in February, the Economic and Social Council adopted the Executive Programme of the (1981) Agreement to Facilitate and Develop Trade Among Arab Countries, with a view to creating a Greater Arab Free Trade Area (GAFTA), which aimed to facilitate and develop inter-Arab trade through the reduction and eventual elimination of customs duties over a 10-year period (at a rate of 10% per year), with effect from 1 January 1998. (According to schedule the fifth 10% reduction was achieved in January 2002.) The Council agreed to supervise the implementation of the free trade agenda and formally to review its progress twice a year. In June the League condemned Turkey's military incursion into northern Iraq and demanded a withdrawal of Turkish troops from Iraqi territory. Meeting in September, ministers of foreign affairs of member states advocated a gradual removal of international sanctions against Libya, and agreed that member countries should permit international flights to leave Libya for specific humanitarian and religious purposes and when used for the purposes of transporting foreign nationals. Ministers also voted to pursue the decision, adopted in March, not to strengthen relations with Israel. Several countries urged a formal boycott of the forthcoming Middle East and North Africa economic conference, in protest at the lack of progress in the peace process (for which the League blamed Israel, which was due to participate in the conference). However, the meeting upheld a request by the Qatari Government, the host of the conference, that each member should decide individually whether to attend. In the event, only seven Arab League countries participated in the conference, which was held in Doha in mid-November, while the Secretary-General of the League decided not to attend as the organization's official representative. In November the League criticized the decision of the US Government to impose economic sanctions against Sudan. The League also expressed concern at the tensions arising from Iraq's decision not to co-operate fully with UN weapons inspectors, and held several meetings with representatives of the Iraqi administration in an effort to secure a peaceful conclusion to the impasse.

1998   In early 1998 the Secretary-General of the League condemned the use or threat of force against Iraq and continued to undertake diplomatic efforts to secure Iraq's compliance with UN Security Council resolutions. The League endorsed the agreement concluded between the UN Secretary-General and the Iraqi authorities in late February, and reaffirmed its commitment to facilitating the eventual removal of the international embargo against Iraq. A meeting of the Council in March, attended by ministers of foreign affairs of 16 member states, rejected Israel's proposal to withdraw from southern Lebanon, which was conditional on the deployment by the Lebanese Government of extra troops to secure Israeli territory from attack, and, additionally, urged international support to secure Israel's withdrawal from the Golan Heights. In April Arab League ministers of the interior and of justice adopted the Arab Convention for the Suppression of Terrorism, which incorporated security and judicial measures, such as extradition arrangements and the exchange of evidence. The agreement was to enter into effect 30 days after being ratified by at least seven member countries. (This was achieved in May 2000.) In August the League denounced terrorist bomb attacks against the US embassies in Kenya and Tanzania. Nevertheless, it condemned US retaliatory military action, a few days later, against suspected terrorist targets in Afghanistan and Sudan, and endorsed a request by the Sudanese Government that the Security Council investigate the incident. In the same month the USA and United Kingdom accepted a proposal of the Libyan Government, supported by the Arab League, that the suspects in the Lockerbie case be tried in The Hague, Netherlands, under Scottish law. Among items concluded by the Council at its meeting in September were condemnation of Turkey's military co-operation with Israel and a request that the UN dispatch a fact-finding mission to examine conditions in the Israeli-occupied territories and alleged violations of Palestinian property rights. In November, following an escalation of tensions between the Iraqi authorities and UN weapons inspectors, the Secretary-General reiterated the League's opposition to the use of force against Iraq, but urged Iraq to maintain a flexible approach in its relations with the UN. The League condemned the subsequent bombing of strategic targets in Iraq, conducted by US and British military aircraft from mid-December, and offered immediate medical assistance to victims of the attacks.

1999   An emergency meeting of ministers of foreign affairs, held in late January to formulate a unified Arab response to the aerial attacks on targets in Iraq and attended by representatives of 18 member states, expressed concern at the military response to the stand-off between Iraq and the UN, and agreed to establish a seven-member *ad hoc* committee to consider the removal of punitive measures against Iraq within the framework of UN resolutions. However the Iraqi delegation withdrew from the meeting in protest at the final statement, which included a request that Iraq recognize Kuwait's territorial integrity. In March the League's Council determined that member states would suspend sanctions imposed against Libya, once arrangements for the trial of the suspects in the Lockerbie case had been finalized. (The suspects were transferred to a detention centre in the Netherlands in early April, whereupon the UN Security Council suspended its sanctions against Libya.) The meeting also expressed support for a UN resolution convening an international conference to facilitate the implementation of agreements applying to Israel and the Occupied Territories, condemned Israel's refusal to withdraw from the Occupied Territories without a majority vote in favour from its legislature, as well as its refusal to resume the peace negotiations with Lebanon and Syria that had ended in 1996, and advocated the publication of evidence of Israeli violence against Palestinians. The Council considered other issues, including the need to prevent further Israeli expansion in Jerusalem and the problem of Palestinian refugees, and reiterated demands for international support to secure Israel's withdrawal from the Golan Heights. In May the League expressed its concern at the political situation in the Comoros, following the removal of the government and establishment of a new military regime in that country at the end of April. In June the League condemned an Israeli aerial attack on Beirut and southern Lebanon. In September Iraq chaired a meeting of the Ministerial Council for the first time since 1990. The meeting considered a range of issues, including the Middle East peace process, US military aid to Israel, and a dispute with the Walt Disney corporation regarding a forthcoming exhibition which appeared to depict Jerusalem as the capital of Israel. Later in September an extraordinary meeting of League senior media and information officials was convened to discuss the latter issue. Negotiations with representatives of Disney were pursued and the implied threat of an Arab boycott of the corporation was averted following assurances that the exhibition would be apolitical. In October the Secretary General of the League condemned the Mauritanian authorities for concluding an agreement with Israel to establish diplomatic relations. In November the League, in conjunction with the Arab Monetary Fund and the Palestinian Monetary Authority, convened a symposium on the planned issuance of a Palestinian currency. The League demanded that Israel compensate Palestinians for alleged losses incurred by their enforced use of the Israeli currency. In late December, prior to a short-lived resumption of Israeli-Syrian peace negotiations, the League reaffirmed its full support for Syria's position.

2000   In February the League strongly condemned an Israeli aerial attack on southern Lebanon; the League's Council changed the venue of its next meeting, in March, from its Cairo headquarters to Beirut as a gesture of solidarity with Lebanon. During March the Secretary-General of the League expressed regret over Iraq's failure to join the *ad hoc* committee established in early 1999 (see above) and also over Iraq's refusal to co-operate with the recently established UN Monitoring, Verification and Inspection Commission (UNMOVIC). The League welcomed the withdrawal of Israeli forces from southern Lebanon in May, although it subsequently condemned continuing territorial violations by the Israeli military. In June the League concluded

a co-operation accord with UNHCR; the two bodies agreed to exchange documents and data. At a meeting of the Council in early September, foreign ministers adopted an Appendix to the League's Charter, providing for the Council to meet ordinarily every March at the level of a summit conference of heads of state ('kings, heads of state and emirs'). The Council was to continue to meet at the level of foreign ministers every March and September. In addition, resolutions were passed urging international bodies to avoid participating in conferences in Jerusalem, reiterating a threatened boycott of a US chain of restaurants which was accused of operating a franchise in an Israeli settlement in the West Bank, and opposing an Israeli initiative for a Jewish emblem to be included as a symbol of the International Red Cross and Red Crescent Movement. At an emergency summit conference convened in late October in response to mounting insecurity in Jerusalem and the Occupied Territories, 15 Arab heads of state, senior officials from six countries and Yasser Arafat, the Palestinian National Authority leader, strongly rebuked Israel, which was accused of inciting the ongoing violent disturbances by stalling the progress of the peace process. The summit determined to 'freeze' co-operation with Israel, requested the formation of an international committee to conduct an impartial assessment of the situation, urged the UN Security Council to establish a mechanism to bring alleged Israeli 'war' criminals to trial, and requested the UN to approve the creation of an international force to protect Palestinians residing in the Occupied Territories. The summit also endorsed the establishment of an 'Al-Aqsa Fund', with a value of US $800m., which was to finance initiatives aimed at promoting the Arab and Islamic identity of Jerusalem, and a smaller 'Jerusalem Intifada Fund' to support the families of Palestinians killed in the unrest. A follow-up committee was subsequently established to implement the resolutions adopted by the emergency summit.

2001   In early January a meeting of League foreign ministers reviewed a proposed framework agreement, presented by outgoing President Clinton of the USA, which aimed to resolve the continuing extreme tension between the Israeli and Palestinian authorities. The meeting agreed that the issues dominating the stalled Middle East peace process should not be redefined, strongly objecting to a proposal that, in exchange for Palestinian assumption of control over Muslim holy sites in Jerusalem, Palestinians exiled at the time of the foundation of the Israeli state in 1948 should forgo their claimed right to return to their former homes. At the end of January, following the completion of the trial in The Hague, Netherlands, of the two Libyans accused of complicity in the Lockerbie case (one of whom was found guilty and one of whom was acquitted), the Secretary-General of the League urged the UN Security Council fully to terminate the sanctions against Libya that had been suspended in 1999. Meeting in mid-March the League's Council pledged that member states would not consider themselves bound by the (inactive) UN sanctions. The Council also reiterated the League's opposition to the economic sanctions maintained by the USA against Sudan, welcomed the political *rapprochement* achieved in the Comoros in February, and accused Iran of threatening regional security by conducting military manoeuvres on the three disputed islands in the Persian (Arabian) Gulf that were also claimed by the United Arab Emirates. In late March the League's first ordinary annual summit-level Council was convened, in Amman, Jordan. The summit issued the Amman Declaration, which emphasized the promotion of Arab unity, and demanded the reversal of Israel's 1967 occupation of Arab territories and the removal of the UN sanctions against Iraq. The Declaration also urged all member states to accelerate implementation of the GAFTA initiative. (It was reported prior to the summit that 15 of the League's 22 member states were making sufficient progress in realizing the requisite trade liberalization measures.) Heads of state attending the summit meeting requested that the League consider means of reactivating the now relaxed Arab economic boycott of Israel, and agreed that the Jordanian King should mediate contacts between Iraq and Kuwait. At the summit Amr Moussa, hitherto Egypt's minister of foreign affairs, was appointed as the League's new Secretary-General. In May a meeting of League ministers of foreign affairs determined that all political contacts with Israel should be suspended in protest at aerial attacks by Israel on Palestinian targets in the West Bank. In July representatives of 13 member countries met in Damascus, Syria, under the auspices of the Special Bureau for Boycotting Israel. The meeting declared unanimous support for reactivated trade measures against Israeli companies and foreign businesses dealing with Israel. In August an emergency meeting of ministers of foreign affairs of Arab League states was convened at the request of the Palestinian authorities to address the recent escalation of hostilities and Israel's seizure of institutions in East Jerusalem. The meeting, which was attended by the League's Secretary-General and the leader of the Palestinian (National) Authority (PA), Yasser Arafat, aimed to formulate a unified Arab response to the situation. The meeting followed an emergency gathering of information ministers of member countries, at which it was agreed to provide political and media support to the Palestinian position. An emergency meeting of the League's Council convened in mid-September in response to recent major terrorist attacks on the USA allegedly perpetrated by militant Islamist fundamentalists, condemned the atrocities, while urging respect for the rights of Arab and Muslim US citizens. The Secretary-General subsequently emphasized the need for co-ordinated global anti-terrorist action to have clearly defined goals and to be based on sufficient consultations and secure evidence. He also deplored anti-Islamic prejudice, stated that US-led military action against any Arab state would not be supported and that Israeli participation in an international anti-terrorism alliance would be unacceptable, and urged a review of the UN sanctions regime against Iraq and an accelerated settlement to the Palestinian-Israeli crisis. A meeting of League foreign ministers in Doha, in early October, condemned international terrorism but did not express support for retaliatory military action by the USA and its allies. In December a further emergency meeting of League foreign affairs ministers was held to discuss the deepening Middle East crisis.

2002   In January the League appointed a commissioner responsible for promoting dialogue between civilizations. The commissioner was mandated to encourage understanding in Western countries of Arab and Muslim civilization and viewpoints, with the aim of redressing perceived negative stereotypes (especially in view of the Islamist fundamentalist connection to the September 2001 terrorist atrocities). In early March a meeting of League foreign ministers agreed to support an initiative proposed by Crown Prince Abdullah of Saudi Arabia aimed at brokering a peaceful settlement to the by now critical Palestinian-Israeli crisis. The Saudi-backed plan—entailing the restoration of 'normal' Arab relations with Israel and acceptance of its right to exist in peace and security, in exchange for a full Israeli withdrawal from the Occupied Territories, the establishment of an independent Palestinian state with East Jerusalem as its capital, and the return of refugees—was unanimously endorsed, as the first ever pan-Arab Palestinian–Israeli peace initiative, by the summit-level Council held in Beirut in late March. The plan urged compliance with Security Council Resolution 194 concerning the return of Palestinian refugees to Israel, or appropriate compensation for their property; however, precise details of eligibility criteria for the proposed return, a contentious issue owing to the potentially huge numbers of refugees and descendants of refugees involved, were not elaborated. Conditions imposed by Israel on Yasser Arafat's freedom of movement deterred him from attending the summit. The Egyptian and Jordanian leaders failed to attend. The Arab leaders also agreed that external threats to the security of any Arab country (with particular reference to Iraq) would be regarded as an attack on the security of all Arab states, demanded respect for Iraq's sovereignty, and reiterated demands for the withdrawal of international sanctions against Iraq. A *rapprochement* between Iraq and Kuwait occurred at the summit meeting when the Iraqi envoy representing Saddam Hussain declared Iraq's respect for Kuwait's sovereignty and security. A committee of nine foreign ministers (representing Bahrain, Egypt, Jordan, Lebanon, Morocco, Palestine, Saudi Arabia, Syria and Yemen) was appointed to co-ordinate activities related to following up the summit's decisions (issued in its 'Beirut Declaration'). At the end of March the League's Secretary-General condemned the Israeli military's siege of Yasser Arafat's presidential compound in Ramallah (initiated in retaliation against a succession of Palestinian bomb attacks on Israeli civilians). An extraordinary ministerial Council meeting held in April at the request of Palestine to consider the 'unprecedented deterioration' of the situation in the Palestinian territories accused certain states (notably the USA) of implementing a pro-Israeli bias that enabled Israel to act outside the scope of

international law and to ignore relevant UN resolutions, and accused Israel of undermining international co-operation in combating terrorism by attempting to equate its actions towards the Palestinian people with recent anti-terrorism activities conducted by the USA. In April the Secretary-General of the League announced his support of a UN Security Council resolution mandating a fact-finding mission to investigate recent alleged Israeli atrocities perpetrated at the Jenin refugee camp in the West Bank; he later condemned Israel for obstructing the mission's activities. A meeting organized by the Special Bureau for Boycotting Israel at the end of the month in Damascus, Syria, was attended by representatives of all League member states except for Egypt, Jordan and Mauritania (which have relations with Israel). The meeting agreed to expand boycott measures and assessed the status of 17 companies believed to have interests in Israel. Israel's termination of its siege of Arafat's Ramallah compound in early May was welcomed by the Secretary-General. In early June the League appointed a special representative to Somalia to assist with the ongoing reconciliation efforts in that country. A meeting of Arab information ministers in mid-June launched a US $22.5m. campaign to combat Israel's Palestine policy through the international media. In mid-July the committee appointed to follow up the resolutions of the Beirut summit reiterated its support of the pan-Arab peace initiative. Soon afterwards the Secretary-General pledged support for Morocco in its territorial dispute with Spain over the small Mediterranean islet of Perejil. Following an aerial raid by the Israeli military on targets in Gaza in late July, the League urged a halt in the export of weaponry, particularly F-16 military aircraft, to Israel. In early August the Secretary-General expressed strong concern at US threats to attack Iraq in view of its failure to implement UN resolutions, stating that such action would seriously undermine regional stability. A ministerial Council meeting held in early September reiterated its complete opposition to the threat of aggression against any Arab country, including Iraq, and demanded the withdrawal of the sanctions against that country. The meeting agreed to intensify Arab efforts to expose Israeli atrocities against the Palestinians and urged the international community to provide protection and reparations for Palestinians. The Council authorized the establishment of a committee to address the welfare of imprisoned Palestinians and urged the USA and UK to reconsider their policies on exporting weaponry to Israel, while issuing a resolution concerning the danger posed by Israel's possession of weapons of mass destruction. The Council deplored the USA's continuing active imposition of sanctions against Libya and endorsed Libya's right to claim compensation in respect of these. In addition, a committee was established to encourage peace efforts in Sudan. In mid-September, following an ultimatum by the USA that military action against Iraq would ensue were the UN to fail within a short time limit to ensure the elimination of any Iraqi-held weapons of mass destruction, the League urged Iraq to negotiate the return of UN weapons inspectors and thereby avoid confrontation. Soon afterwards, after tripartite consultations between the Secretary-General of the League, the UN Secretary-General and the Iraqi foreign minister concerning the implementation of UN resolutions and eventual withdrawal of UN sanctions, Iraq agreed to admit UNMOVIC personnel. The League opposed ongoing US pressure on the Security Council to draft a new resolution establishing a stict time frame for Iraqi compliance with UN demands and authorizing the use of force against Iraq in response to non-compliance.

FINANCE

In September 2002 the Council approved a budget of US $35m. for the Secretariat in 2003.

Publications

Arab Perspectives—Sh'oun Arabiyya (monthly).
Journal of Arab Affairs (monthly).
Bulletins of treaties and agreements concluded among the member states, essays, regular publications circulated by regional offices.

ORGANIZATION OF ARAB PETROLEUM EXPORTING COUNTRIES—OAPEC

Address: POB 20501, Safat 13066, Kuwait.
Telephone: 4844500; **fax:** 4815747; **e-mail:** oapec@qualitynet.net; **internet:** www.oapecorg.org.

OAPEC was established in 1968 to safeguard the interests of members and to determine ways and means for their co-operation in various forms of economic activity in the petroleum industry. OAPEC member states accounted for 29.3% of total world petroleum production in 2000, and for 11.9% of total global natural gas output in 1999.

MEMBERS

Algeria	Kuwait	Saudi Arabia
Bahrain	Libya	Syria
Egypt	Qatar	United Arab Emirates
Iraq		

Organization

(September 2002)

MINISTERIAL COUNCIL

The Council consists normally of the ministers of petroleum of the member states, and forms the supreme authority of the Organization, responsible for drawing up its general policy, directing its activities and laying down its governing rules. It meets twice yearly, and may hold extraordinary sessions. Chairmanship is on an annual rotation basis.

EXECUTIVE BUREAU

Assists the Council to direct the management of the Organization, approves staff regulations, reviews the budget, and refers it to the Council, considers matters relating to the Organization's agreements and activities and draws up the agenda for the Council. The Bureau comprises one senior official from each member state. Chairmanship is by rotation on an annual basis, following the same order as the Ministerial Council chairmanship. The Bureau convenes at least three times a year.

GENERAL SECRETARIAT

Secretary-General: ABDULAZIZ A. AL-TURKI (Saudi Arabia).

Besides the Office of the Secretary-General, there are four departments: Finance and Administrative Affairs, Information and Library, Technical Affairs, and Economics. The last two form the Arab Centre for Energy Studies (which was established in 1983). At the end of 2000 there were 22 professional staff members and 29 general personnel at the General Secretariat.

JUDICIAL TRIBUNAL

The Tribunal comprises seven judges from Arab countries. Its task is to settle differences in interpretation and application of the OAPEC Agreement, arising between members and also between OAPEC and its affiliates; disputes among member countries on petroleum activities falling within OAPEC's jurisdiction and not under the sovereignty of member countries; and disputes that the Ministerial Council decides to submit to the Tribunal.

President: FARIS ABDUL AL-WAGAYAN.
Registrar: Dr RIAD RASHAD AL-DAOUDI.

Activities

OAPEC co-ordinates different aspects of the Arab petroleum industry through the joint undertakings described below. It co-operates with the League of Arab States and other Arab organizations, and attempts to link petroleum research institutes in the Arab states. It organizes or participates in conferences and seminars, many of which are held jointly with non-Arab organizations in order to enhance Arab and international co-operation. OAPEC collaborates with the AFESD, the Arab Monetary Fund and the League of Arab States in compiling the annual *Joint Arab Economic Report*, which is issued by the Arab Monetary Fund.

OAPEC provides training in technical matters and in documentation and information. The General Secretariat also conducts technical and feasibility studies and carries out market reviews. It provides information through a library, 'databank' and the publications listed below.

The invasion of Kuwait by Iraq in August 1990, and the subsequent international embargo on petroleum exports from Iraq and Kuwait, severely disrupted OAPEC's activities. In December the OAPEC Council decided to establish temporary headquarters in Cairo while Kuwait was under occupation. The Council resolved to reschedule overdue payments by Iraq and Syria over a 15-year period, and to postpone the Fifth Arab Energy Conference from mid-1992 to mid-1994. The Conference was held in Cairo, Egypt, in May 1994. In June OAPEC returned to its permanent headquarters in Kuwait. The Sixth Arab Energy Conference was held in Damascus, Syria, in May 1998, with the theme of 'Energy and Arab Co-operation'. The seventh conference, focusing on the same theme, was convened in May 2002, in Cairo, Egypt. It was attended by OAPEC ministers of petroleum and energy, senior officials from other Arab states, and representatives of invited institutions and organizations concerned with energy issues.

Finance

The General Secretariat's budget for 2001 amounted to 1,465,000 Kuwaiti dinars (KD). A budget of 117,200 KD was approved for the Judicial Tribunal.

Publications

Annual Statistical Report.
Energy Resources Monitor (quarterly, Arabic).
OAPEC Monthly Bulletin (Arabic and English editions).
Oil and Arab Co-operation (quarterly, Arabic).
Secretary-General's Annual Report (Arabic and English editions).
Papers, studies, conference proceedings.

OAPEC-Sponsored Ventures

Arab Maritime Petroleum Transport Company—AMPTC: POB 22525, Safat 13086, Kuwait; tel. 4844500; fax 4842996; f. 1973 to undertake transport of crude petroleum, gas, refined products and petro-chemicals, and thus to increase Arab participation in the tanker transport industry; auth. cap. US $200m.; Gen. Man. SULAYMAN AL-BASSAM.

Arab Petroleum Investments Corporation—APICORP: POB 9599, Dammam 31423, Saudi Arabia; tel. (3) 847-0444; fax (3) 847-0022; e-mail apicorp@apicorp-arabia.com; internet www.apicorp-arabia.com; f. 1975 to finance investments in petroleum and petrochemicals projects and related industries in the Arab world and in developing countries, with priority being given to Arab joint ventures. Projects financed include gas liquefaction plants, petrochemicals, tankers, oil refineries, pipelines, exploration, detergents, fertilizers and process control instrumentation; auth. cap. US $1,200m.; subs. cap. $460m. Shareholders: Kuwait, Saudi Arabia and United Arab Emirates (17% each), Libya (15%), Iraq and Qatar (10% each), Algeria (5%), Bahrain, Egypt and Syria (3% each). Chair. ABDULLAH A. AZ-ZAID (Saudi Arabia); Gen. Man. and CEO RASHEED AL-MARAJ.

Arab Detergent Chemicals Company—ARADET: POB 27864, el-Monsour, Baghdad, Iraq; tel. (1) 541-9893; f. 1981; produces and markets linear alkyl benzene; an additional project to construct a sodium tripolyphosphate plant has been suspended temporarily owing to the trade embargo against Iraq; APICORP and the Iraqi Government each hold 32% of shares in the co; auth. cap. 72m. Iraqi dinars; subs. cap. 60m. Iraqi dinars.

Arab Petroleum Services Company—APSCO: POB 12925, Tripoli, Libya; tel. (21) 45861; fax (21) 3331930; f. 1977 to provide petroleum services through the establishment of companies specializing in various activities, and to train specialized personnel; auth. cap. 100m. Libyan dinars; subs. cap. 15m. Libyan dinars. Chair. AYAD HUSSEIN AD-DALI; Gen. Man. ISMAIL AL-KORAITLI.

Arab Drilling and Workover Company: POB 680, Suani Rd, km 3.5, Tripoli, Libya; tel. (21) 800064; fax (21) 805945; f. 1980; 40%-owned by APSCO; auth. cap. 12m. Libyan dinars; Gen. Man. MUHAMMAD AHMAD ATTIGA.

Arab Geophysical Exploration Services Company—AGESCO: POB 84224, Airport Rd, Tripoli, Libya; tel. (21) 4804863; fax (21) 4803199; f. 1985; 40%-owned by APSCO; auth. cap. 12m. Libyan dinars; subs. cap. 4m. Libyan dinars; Gen. Man. AYAD HUSSEIN AD-DALI.

Arab Well Logging Company—AWLCO: POB 6225, Baghdad, Iraq; tel. (1) 541-8259; f. 1983; wholly-owned subsidiary of APSCO; provides well-logging services and data interpretation; auth. cap. 7m. Iraqi dinars.

Arab Petroleum Training Institute—APTI: POB 6037, Al-Tajeyat, Baghdad, Iraq; tel. (1) 523-4100; fax (1) 521-0526; f. 1978 to provide instruction in many technical and managerial aspects of the oil industry. From Dec. 1994 the Institute was placed under the trusteeship of the Iraqi Government; the arrangement was scheduled to come to an end in Dec. 1998. Dir HAZIM A. AS-SULTAN.

Arab Shipbuilding and Repair Yard Company—ASRY: POB 50110, Hidd, Bahrain; tel. 671111; fax 670236; e-mail asryco@batel co.com.bh; internet www.asry.net; f. 1974 to undertake repairs and servicing of vessels; operates a 500,000 dwt dry dock in Bahrain; two floating docks operational since 1992; has recently diversified it activities, e.g. into upgrading oil rigs; cap. (auth. and subs.) US \$340m.; Chair. EID ABDULLA YOUSIF (Bahrain); Chief Exec. MOHAMED M. AL-KHATEEB.

ORGANIZATION OF THE ISLAMIC CONFERENCE—OIC

Address: Kilo 6, Mecca Rd, POB 178, Jeddah 21411, Saudi Arabia.
Telephone: (2) 680-0800; **fax:** (2) 687-3568; **e-mail:** info@oic-oci.org; **internet:** www.oic-oci.org.

The Organization was formally established in May 1971, when its Secretariat became operational, following a summit meeting of Muslim heads of state at Rabat, Morocco, in September 1969, and the Islamic Foreign Ministers' Conference in Jeddah in March 1970, and in Karachi, Pakistan, in December 1970.

MEMBERS

Afghanistan*	Brunei	Egypt
Albania	Burkina Faso	Gabon
Algeria	Cameroon	The Gambia
Azerbaijan	Chad	Guinea
Bahrain	The Comoros	Guinea-Bissau
Bangladesh	Côte d'Ivoire	Guyana
Benin	Djibouti	Indonesia
Iran	Mozambique	Suriname
Iraq	Niger	Syria
Jordan	Nigeria†	Tajikistan
Kazakhstan	Oman	Togo
Kuwait	Pakistan	Tunisia
Kyrgyzstan	Palestine	Turkey
Lebanon	Qatar	Turkmenistan
Libya	Saudi Arabia	Uganda
Malaysia	Senegal	United Arab
Maldives	Sierra Leone	Emirates
Mali	Somalia	Uzbekistan
Mauritania	Sudan	Yemen
Morocco		

* Afghanistan's membership of the OIC was suspended in 1996; however, it was reported to have resumed full membership following the establishment of an interim authority in late 2001.

† Nigeria renounced its membership in May 1991; however, the OIC has not formally recognized this decision.

Note: Observer status has been granted to Bosnia and Herzegovina, the Central African Republic, Thailand, the Muslim community of the 'Turkish Republic of Northern Cyprus', the Moro National Liberation Front (MNLF) of the southern Philippines, the United Nations, the African Union, the Non-Aligned Movement, the League of Arab States, the Economic Co-operation Organization, the Union of the Arab Maghreb and the Co-operation Council for the Arab States of the Gulf.

Organization

(September 2002)

SUMMIT CONFERENCES

The supreme body of the Organization is the Conference of Heads of State, which met in 1969 at Rabat, Morocco, in 1974 at Lahore, Pakistan, and in January 1981 at Mecca, Saudi Arabia, when it was decided that summit conferences would be held every three years in future. Ninth Conference: Doha, Qatar, November 2000.

CONFERENCE OF MINISTERS OF FOREIGN AFFAIRS

Conferences take place annually, to consider the means for implementing the general policy of the Organization, although they may also be convened for extraordinary sessions.

SECRETARIAT

The executive organ of the Organization, headed by a Secretary-General (who is elected by the Conference of Ministers of Foreign Affairs for a four-year term, renewable only once) and four Assistant Secretaries-General (similarly appointed).

Secretary-General: Dr ABDELOUAHED BELKEZIZ (Morocco).

At the summit conference in January 1981 it was decided that an International Islamic Court of Justice should be established to adjudicate in disputes between Muslim countries. Experts met in January 1983 to draw up a constitution for the court; however, by 2002 it was not yet in operation.

STANDING COMMITTEES

Al-Quds Committee: f. 1975 to implement the resolutions of the Islamic Conference on the status of Jerusalem (Al-Quds); it meets at the level of foreign ministers; maintains the Al-Quds Fund; Chair. King MUHAMMAD VI of Morocco.

Standing Committee for Economic and Commercial Co-operation (COMCEC): f. 1981; Chair. AHMET NECDET SEZER (Pres. of Turkey).

Standing Committee for Information and Cultural Affairs (COMIAC): f. 1981. Chair. ABDOULAYE WADE (Pres. of Senegal).

Standing Committee for Scientific and Technological Co-operation (COMSTECH): f. 1981; Chair. Gen. PERVEZ MUSHARRAF (Pres. of Pakistan).

Other committees comprise the Islamic Peace Committee, the Permanent Finance Committee, the Committee of Islamic Solidarity with the Peoples of the Sahel, the Eight-Member Committee on the Situation of Muslims in the Philippines, the Six-Member Committee on Palestine, and the *ad hoc* Committee on Afghanistan. In addition, there is an Islamic Commission for Economic, Cultural and Social Affairs and OIC contact groups on Bosnia and Herzegovina, Kosovo, Jammu and Kashmir, and Sierra Leone.

Activities

The Organization's aims, as proclaimed in the Charter that was adopted in 1972, are:

(i) To promote Islamic solidarity among member states;

(ii) To consolidate co-operation among member states in the economic, social, cultural, scientific and other vital fields, and to arrange consultations among member states belonging to international organizations;

(iii) To endeavour to eliminate racial segregation and discrimination and to eradicate colonialism in all its forms;

(iv) To take necessary measures to support international peace and security founded on justice;

(v) To co-ordinate all efforts for the safeguard of the Holy Places and support of the struggle of the people of Palestine, and help them to regain their rights and liberate their land;

(vi) To strengthen the struggle of all Muslim people with a view to safeguarding their dignity, independence and national rights; and

(vii) To create a suitable atmosphere for the promotion of co-operation and understanding among member states and other countries.

The first summit conference of Islamic leaders (representing 24 states) took place in 1969 following the burning of the Al Aqsa Mosque in Jerusalem. At this conference it was decided that Islamic governments should 'consult together with a view to promoting close co-operation and mutual assistance in the economic, scientific, cultural and spiritual fields, inspired by the immortal teachings of

Islam'. Thereafter the foreign ministers of the countries concerned met annually, and adopted the Charter of the Organization of the Islamic Conference in 1972.

At the second Islamic summit conference (Lahore, Pakistan, 1974), the Islamic Solidarity Fund was established, together with a committee of representatives which later evolved into the Islamic Commission for Economic, Cultural and Social Affairs. Subsequently, numerous other subsidiary bodies have been set up (see below).

ECONOMIC CO-OPERATION

A general agreement for economic, technical and commercial co-operation came into force in 1981, providing for the establishment of joint investment projects and trade co-ordination. This was followed by an agreement on promotion, protection and guarantee of investments among member states. A plan of action to strengthen economic co-operation was adopted at the third Islamic summit conference in 1981, aiming to promote collective self-reliance and the development of joint ventures in all sectors. In 1994 the 1981 plan of action was revised; the reformulated plan placed greater emphasis on private-sector participation in its implementation. Although several meetings of experts were subsequently held to discuss some of the 10 priority focus areas of the plan, little progress was achieved in implementing it during the 1990s.

The fifth summit conference, held in 1987, approved proposals for joint development of modern technology, and for improving scientific and technical skills in the less developed Islamic countries. The first international Islamic trade fair was held in Jeddah, Saudi Arabia, in March 2001.

In 1991 22 OIC member states signed a framework agreement concerning the introduction of a system of trade preferences among member states. It was envisaged that, if implemented, this would represent the first step towards the eventual establishment of an Islamic common market. In May 2001 the OIC Secretary-General urged increased progress in the ratification of the framework agreement. An OIC group of experts was considering the implications of the proposed creation of such a common market.

CULTURAL CO-OPERATION

The Organization supports education in Muslim communities throughout the world, and was instrumental in the establishment of Islamic universities in Niger and Uganda (see below). It organizes seminars on various aspects of Islam, and encourages dialogue with the other monotheistic religions. Support is given to publications on Islam both in Muslim and Western countries. The OIC organizes meetings at ministerial level to consider aspects of information policy and new technologies.

HUMANITARIAN ASSISTANCE

Assistance is given to Muslim communities affected by wars and natural disasters, in co-operation with UN organizations, particularly UNHCR. The countries of the Sahel region (Burkina Faso, Cape Verde, Chad, The Gambia, Guinea, Guinea-Bissau, Mali, Mauritania, Niger and Senegal) receive particular attention as victims of drought. In April 1999 the OIC resolved to send humanitarian aid to assist the displaced ethnic Albanian population of Kosovo and Metohija, in southern Serbia. Several member states have provided humanitarian assistance to the Muslim population affected by the conflict in Chechnya. During 2001 the OIC was providing emergency assistance to Afghanistan, and in October established an Afghan People Assistance Fund. The OIC also administers a Trust Fund for the urgent return of refugees and the displaced to Bosnia and Herzegovina.

POLITICAL CO-OPERATION

Since its inception the OIC has called for vacation of Arab territories by Israel, recognition of the rights of Palestinians and of the Palestine Liberation Organization (PLO) as their sole legitimate representative, and the restoration of Jerusalem to Arab rule. The 1981 summit conference called for a *jihad* (holy war—though not necessarily in a military sense) 'for the liberation of Jerusalem and the occupied territories'; this was to include an Islamic economic boycott of Israel. In 1982 Islamic ministers of foreign affairs decided to establish Islamic offices for boycotting Israel and for military co-operation with the PLO. The 1984 summit conference agreed to reinstate Egypt (suspended following the peace treaty signed with Israel in 1979) as a member of the OIC, although the resolution was opposed by seven states.

In August 1990 a majority of ministers of foreign affairs condemned Iraq's recent invasion of Kuwait, and demanded the withdrawal of Iraqi forces. In August 1991 the Conference of Ministers of Foreign Affairs obstructed Iraq's attempt to propose a resolution demanding the repeal of economic sanctions against the country. The sixth summit conference, held in Senegal in December, reflected the divisions in the Arab world that resulted from Iraq's invasion of Kuwait and the ensuing war. Twelve heads of state did not attend,

reportedly to register protest at the presence of Jordan and the PLO at the conference, both of which had given support to Iraq. Disagreement also arose between the PLO and the majority of other OIC members when a proposal was adopted to cease the OIC's support for the PLO's *jihad* in the Arab territories occupied by Israel, in an attempt to further the Middle East peace negotiations.

In August 1992 the UN General Assembly approved a non-binding resolution, introduced by the OIC, that requested the UN Security Council to take increased action, including the use of force, in order to defend the non-Serbian population of Bosnia and Herzegovina (some 43% of Bosnians being Muslims) from Serbian aggression, and to restore its 'territorial integrity'. The OIC Conference of Ministers of Foreign Affairs, which was held in December, demanded anew that the UN Security Council take all necessary measures against Serbia and Montenegro, including military intervention, in order to protect the Bosnian Muslims.

A report by an OIC fact-finding mission, which in February 1993 visited Azad Kashmir while investigating allegations of repression of the largely Muslim population of the Indian state of Jammu and Kashmir by the Indian armed forces, was presented to the 1993 Conference. The meeting urged member states to take the necessary measures to persuade India to cease the 'massive human rights violations' in Jammu and Kashmir and to allow the Indian Kashmiris to 'exercise their inalienable right to self-determination'. In September 1994 ministers of foreign affairs, meeting in Islamabad, Pakistan, agreed to establish a contact group on Jammu and Kashmir, which was to provide a mechanism for promoting international awareness of the situation in that region and for seeking a peaceful solution to the dispute. In December OIC heads of state approved a resolution condemning reported human rights abuses by Indian security forces in Kashmir.

In July 1994 the OIC Secretary-General visited Afghanistan and proposed the establishment of a preparatory mechanism to promote national reconciliation in that country. In mid-1995 Saudi Arabia, acting as a representative of the OIC, pursued a peace initiative for Afghanistan and issued an invitation for leaders of the different factions to hold negotiations in Jeddah.

A special ministerial meeting on Bosnia and Herzegovina was held in July 1993, at which seven OIC countries committed themselves to making available up to 17,000 troops to serve in the UN Protection Force in the former Yugoslavia (UNPROFOR). The meeting also decided to dispatch immediately a ministerial mission to persuade influential governments to support the OIC's demands for the removal of the arms embargo on Bosnian Muslims and the convening of a restructured international conference to bring about a political solution to the conflict. In December 1994 OIC heads of state, convened in Morocco, proclaimed that the UN arms embargo on Bosnia and Herzegovina could not be applied to the Muslim authorities of that Republic. The Conference also resolved to review economic relations between OIC member states and any country that supported Serbian activities. An aid fund was established, to which member states were requested to contribute between US \$500,000 and \$5m., in order to provide further humanitarian and economic assistance to Bosnian Muslims. In relation to wider concerns the conference adopted a Code of Conduct for Combating International Terrorism, in an attempt to control Muslim extremist groups. The code commits states to ensuring that militant groups do not use their territory for planning or executing terrorist activity against other states, in addition to states refraining from direct support or participation in acts of terrorism. In a further resolution the OIC supported the decision by Iraq to recognize Kuwait, but advocated that Iraq comply with all UN Security Council decisions.

In July 1995 the OIC contact group on Bosnia and Herzegovina (at that time comprising Egypt, Iran, Malaysia, Morocco, Pakistan, Saudi Arabia, Senegal and Turkey), meeting in Geneva, declared the UN arms embargo against Bosnia and Herzegovina to be 'invalid'. Several Governments subsequently announced their willingness officially to supply weapons and other military assistance to the Bosnian Muslim forces. In September a meeting of all OIC ministers of defence and foreign affairs endorsed the establishment of an 'assistance mobilization group' which was to supply military, economic, legal and other assistance to Bosnia and Herzegovina. In a joint declaration the ministers also demanded the return of all territory seized by Bosnian Serb forces, the continued NATO bombing of Serb military targets, and that the city of Sarajevo be preserved under a Muslim-led Bosnian Government. In November the OIC Secretary-General endorsed the peace accord for the former Yugoslavia, which was concluded, in Dayton, USA, by leaders of all the conflicting factions, and reaffirmed the commitment of Islamic states to participate in efforts to implement the accord. In the following month the OIC Conference of Ministers of Foreign Affairs, convened in Conakry, Guinea, requested the full support of the international community to reconstruct Bosnia and Herzegovina through humanitarian aid as well as economic and technical co-operation. Ministers declared that Palestine and the establishment of fully-autonomous Palestinian control of Jerusalem were issues of central importance for the Muslim world. The Conference urged the removal of all aspects of occupation and the cessation of the construction of Israeli settlements in the occupied territories. In addition, the final statement of the meeting condemned Armenian aggression against Azerbaijan, registered concern at the persisting civil conflict in Afghanistan, demanded the elimination of all weapons of mass destruction and pledged support for Libya (affected by the US trade embargo). Ministers determined that an intergovernmental group of experts should be established in 1996 to address the situation of minority Muslim communities residing in non-OIC states.

In December 1996 OIC ministers of foreign affairs, meeting in Jakarta, Indonesia, urged the international community to apply pressure on Israel in order to ensure its implementation of the terms of the Middle East peace process. The ministers reaffirmed the importance of ensuring that the provisions of the Dayton Peace Agreement for the former Yugoslavia were fully implemented, called for a peaceful settlement of the Kashmir issue, demanded that Iraq fulfil its obligations for the establishment of security, peace and stability in the region and proposed that an international conference on peace and national reconciliation in Somalia be convened. The ministers elected a new Secretary-General who confirmed that the organization would continue to develop its role as an international mediator. In March 1997, at an extraordinary summit held in Pakistan, OIC heads of state and of government reiterated the organization's objective of increasing international pressure on Israel to ensure the full implementation of the terms of the Middle East peace process. An 'Islamabad Declaration' was also adopted, which pledged to increase co-operation between members of the OIC. In June the OIC condemned the decision by the US House of Representatives to recognize Jerusalem as the Israeli capital. The Secretary-General of the OIC issued a statement rejecting the US decision as counter to the role of the USA as sponsor of the Middle East peace plan.

In early 1998 the OIC appealed for an end to the threat of US-led military action against Iraq arising from a dispute regarding access granted to international weapons inspectors. The crisis was averted by an agreement concluded between the Iraqi authorities and the UN Secretary-General in February. In March OIC ministers of foreign affairs, meeting in Doha, Qatar, requested an end to the international sanctions against Iraq. Additionally, the ministers urged all states to end the process of restoring normal trading and diplomatic relations with Israel pending that country's withdrawal from the occupied territories and acceptance of an independent Palestinian state. In April the OIC, jointly with the UN, sponsored new peace negotiations between the main disputing factions in Afghanistan, which were conducted in Islamabad, Pakistan. In early May, however, the talks collapsed and were postponed indefinitely. In September the Secretaries-General of the OIC and UN agreed to establish a joint mission to counter the deteriorating security situation along the Afghan–Iranian border, following the large-scale deployment of Taliban troops in the region and consequent military manoeuvres by the Iranian authorities. They also reiterated the need to proceed with negotiations to conclude a peaceful settlement in Afghanistan. In December the OIC appealed for a diplomatic solution to the tensions arising from Iraq's withdrawal of co-operation with UN weapons inspectors, and criticized subsequent military air-strikes, led by the USA, as having been conducted without renewed UN authority. An OIC Convention on Combating International Terrorism was adopted in 1998. An OIC committee of experts responsible for formulating a plan of action for safeguarding the rights of Muslim communities and minorities met for the first time in 1998.

In early April 1999 ministers of foreign affairs of the countries comprising OIC's contact group met to consider the crisis in Kosovo. The meeting condemned Serbian atrocities being committed against the local Albanian population and urged the provision of international assistance for the thousands of people displaced by the conflict. The group resolved to establish a committee to co-ordinate relief aid provided by member states. The ministers also expressed their willingness to help to formulate a peaceful settlement and to participate in any subsequent implementation force. In June an OIC Parliamentary Union was inaugurated; its founding conference was convened in Tehran, Iran.

In early March 2000 the OIC mediated contacts between the parties to the conflict in Afghanistan, with a view to reviving peace negotiations. Talks, held under OIC auspices, ensued in May. In November OIC heads of state attended the ninth summit conference, held in Doha, Qatar. In view of the significant deterioration in relations between Israel and the Palestinian (National) Authority during late 2000, the summit issued a Declaration pledging solidarity with the Palestinian cause and accusing the Israeli authorities of implementing large-scale systematic violations of human rights against Palestinians. The summit also issued the Doha Declaration, which reaffirmed commitment to the OIC Charter and undertook to modernize the organization's organs and mechanisms. Both the elected Government of Afghanistan and the Taliban sent delegations to the Doha conference. The summit determined that Afghanistan's

official participation in the OIC, suspended in 1996, should not yet be reinstated. In early 2001 a high-level delegation from the OIC visited Afghanistan in an attempt to prevent further destruction of ancient statues by Taliban supporters.

In May 2001 the OIC convened an emergency meeting, following an escalation of Israeli-Palestinian violence. The meeting resolved to halt all diplomatic and political contacts with the Israeli government, while restrictions remained in force against Palestinian-controlled territories. In June the OIC condemned attacks and ongoing discrimination against the Muslim Community in Myanmar. In the same month the OIC Secretary-General undertook a tour of six African countries—Burkina Faso, The Gambia, Guinea, Mali, Niger and Senegal, to promote co-operation and to consider further OIC support for those states. In August the Secretary-General condemned Israel's seizure of several Palestinian institutions in East Jerusalem and aerial attacks against Palestinian settlements. The OIC initiated high-level diplomatic efforts to convene a meeting of the UN Security Council in order to discuss the situation.

In September 2001 the OIC Secretary-General strongly condemned major terrorist attacks perpetrated against targets in the USA. Soon afterwards the US authorities rejected a proposal by the Taliban regime that an OIC observer mission be deployed to monitor the activities of the Saudi Arabian-born exiled militant Islamist fundamentalist leader Osama bin Laden, who was accused by the US Government of having co-ordinated the attacks from alleged terrorist bases in the Taliban-administered area of Afghanistan. An extraordinary meeting of OIC ministers of foreign affairs, convened in early October, in Doha, Qatar, to consider the implications of the terrorist atrocities, condemned the attacks and declared its support for combating all manifestations of terrorism within the framework of a proposed collective initiative co-ordinated under the auspices of the UN. The meeting, which did not pronounce directly on the recently-initiated US-led military retaliation against targets in Afghanistan, urged that no Arab or Muslim state should be targeted under the pretext of eliminating terrorism. It determined to establish a fund to assist Afghan civilians. In February 2002 the Secretary-General expressed concern at statements of the US administration describing Iran and Iraq (as well as the Democratic People's Republic of Korea) as belonging to an 'axis of evil' involved in international terrorism and the development of weapons of mass destruction. In early April OIC foreign ministers convened an extraordinary session on terrorism, in Kuala Lumpur, Malaysia. The meeting issued the 'Kuala Lumpur Declaration', which reiterated member states' collective resolve to combat terrorism, recalling the organization's 1994 code of conduct and 1998 convention to this effect; condemned attempts to associate terrorist activities with Islamists or any other particular creed, civilization or nationality, and rejected attempts to associate Islamic states or the Palestinian struggle with terrorism; rejected the implementation of international action against any Muslim state on the pretext of combating terrorism; urged the organization of a global conference on international terrorism; and urged an examination of the root causes of international terrorism. In addition, the meeting strongly condemned Israel's ongoing military intervention in areas controlled by the Palestinian (National) Authority. The meeting adopted a plan of action on addressing the issues raised in the declaration. Its implementation was to be co-ordinated by a 13-member committee on international terrorism. Member states were encouraged to sign and ratify the Convention on Combating International Terrorism in order to accelerate its implementation. In June ministers of foreign affairs, meeting in Khartoum, Sudan, issued a declaration reiterating the OIC call for an international conference to be convened, under UN auspices, in order clearly to define terrorism and to agree on the international procedures and mechanisms for combating terrorism through the UN. The conference also repeated demands for the international community to exert pressure on Israel to withdraw from all Palestinian-controlled territories and for the establishment of an independent Palestinian state. It endorsed the peace plan for the region that had been adopted by the summit meeting of the League of Arab States in March (see p. 1312).

In June 2002 the OIC Secretary-General expressed his concern at the escalation of tensions between Pakistan and India regarding Kashmir. He urged both sides to withdraw their troops and to refrain from the use of force. In the following month the OIC pledged its support for Morocco in a territorial dispute with Spain over the small island of Perejil, but called for a negotiated settlement to resolve the issue.

Finance

The OIC's activities are financed by mandatory contributions from member states. The budget for 2002/03 totalled US $11.4m.

SUBSIDIARY ORGANS

Islamic Centre for the Development of Trade: Complexe Commercial des Habous, ave des FAR, BP 13545, Casablanca, Morocco; tel. (2) 314974; fax (2) 310110; e-mail icdt@icdt.org; internet www.icdt.org; f. 1983 to encourage regular commercial contacts, harmonize policies and promote investments among OIC mems. Dir-Gen. ALLAL RACHDI. Publs *Tijaris: International and Inter-Islamic Trade Magazine* (bi-monthly), *Inter-Islamic Trade Report* (annually).

Islamic Jurisprudence (Fiqh) Academy: POB 13917, Jeddah, Saudi Arabia; tel. (2) 667-1664; fax (2) 667-0873; internet www.fiqhacademy.org.sa; f. 1982. Sec.-Gen. Sheikh MOHAMED HABIB IBN AL-KHODHA.

Islamic Solidarity Fund: c/o OIC Secretariat, POB 178, Jeddah 21411, Saudi Arabia; tel. (2) 680-0800; fax (2) 687-3568; f. 1974 to meet the needs of Islamic communities by providing emergency aid and the finance to build mosques, Islamic centres, hospitals, schools and universities. Chair. Sheikh NASIR ABDULLAH BIN HAMDAN; Exec. Dir ABDULLAH HERSI.

Islamic University in Uganda: POB 2555, Mbale, Uganda; tel. (45) 33502; fax (45) 34452; e-mail iuiu@info.com.co.ug; Kampala Liaison Office: POB 7689, Kampala; tel. (41) 236874; fax (41) 254576; f. 1988 to meet the educational needs of Muslim populations in English-speaking African countries; mainly financed by OIC. Principal Officer Prof. MAHDI ADAMU.

Islamic University of Niger: BP 11507, Niamey, Niger; tel. 723903; fax 733796; f. 1984; provides courses of study in *Shari'a* (Islamic law) and Arabic language and literature; also offers courses in pedagogy and teacher training; receives grants from Islamic Solidarity Fund and contributions from OIC member states. Rector Prof. ABDELALI OUDHRIRI.

Islamic University of Technology—IUT: GPO Box 3003, Board-Bazar, Gazipur 1704, Dhaka, Bangladesh; tel. (2) 980-0960; fax (2) 980-0970; e-mail dg@iit.dhaka.edu; internet www.iitoic -dhaka.edu; f. 1981 as the Islamic Centre for Technical and Vocational Training and Resources, named changed to Islamic Institute of Technology in 1994, current name adopted in June 2001; aims to develop human resources in OIC mem. states, with special reference to engineering, technology, tech. and vocational education and research; 224 staff and 1,000 students; library of 23,000 vols. Vice-Chancellor Prof. Dr M. ANWAR HOSSAIN. Publs *News Bulletin* (annually), annual calendar and announcement for admission, reports, human resources development series.

Research Centre for Islamic History, Art and Culture—IRCICA: POB 24, Beşiktaş 80692, İstanbul, Turkey; tel. (212) 2591742; fax (212) 2584365; e-mail ircica@superonline.com; internet www.ircica.org; f. 1980; library of 50,000 vols. Dir-Gen. Prof. Dr EKMELEDDİN İHSANOĞLU. Publs *Newsletter* (3 a year), monographical studies.

Statistical, Economic and Social Research and Training Centre for the Islamic Countries: Attar Sok 4, GOP 06700, Ankara, Turkey; tel. (312) 4686172; fax (312) 4673458; e-mail oicankara@sesrtcic.org; internet www.sesrtcic.org; f. 1978. Dir-Gen. ERDİNÇ ERDÜN. Publs *Journal of Economic Co-operation among Islamic Countries* (quarterly), *InfoReport* (quarterly), *Statistical Yearbook* (annually).

SPECIALIZED INSTITUTIONS

International Islamic News Agency—IINA: King Khalid Palace, Madinah Rd, POB 5054, Jeddah, Saudi Arabia; tel. (2) 665-8561; fax (2) 665-9358; e-mail iina@ogertel.com; internet www.islamicnews .org; f. 1972; distributes news and reports daily on events in the Islamic world, in Arabic, English and French. Dir-Gen. ABDULWAHAB KASHIF.

Islamic Educational, Scientific and Cultural Organization—ISESCO: BP 755, Rabat 10104, Morocco; tel. (7) 772433; fax (7) 772058; e-mail cid@isesco.org.ma; internet www.isesco.org.ma; f. 1982. Dir-Gen. Dr ABDULAZIZ BIN OTHMAN AL-TWAIJRI. Publs *ISESCO Newsletter* (quarterly), *Islam Today* (2 a year), *ISESCO Triennial*.

Islamic States Broadcasting Organization—ISBO: POB 6351, Jeddah 21442, Saudi Arabia; tel. (2) 672-1121; fax (2) 672-2600; e-mail isbo@isbo.org; internet www.isbo.org; f. 1975. Sec.-Gen. HUSSEIN AL-ASKARY.

The Islamic Development Bank (see p. 1305) is also a Specialized Institution of the OIC.

AFFILIATED INSTITUTIONS

International Association of Islamic Banks—IAIB: King Abdulaziz St, Queen's Bldg, 23rd Floor, Al-Balad Dist, POB 9707, Jeddah 21423, Saudi Arabia; tel. (2) 651-6900; fax (2) 651-6552; f. 1977 to link financial institutions operating on Islamic banking principles; activities include training and research; mems: 192 banks and other financial institutions in 34 countries. Sec.-Gen. SAMIR A. SHAIKH.

Islamic Chamber of Commerce and Industry: POB 3831, Clifton, Karachi 75600, Pakistan; tel. (21) 5874756; fax (21) 5870765; e-mail icci@icci-oic.org; internet icci-oic.org; f. 1979 to promote trade and industry among member states; comprises nat. chambers or feds of chambers of commerce and industry. Sec.-Gen. AQEEL AHMAD AL-JASSEM.

Islamic Committee for the International Crescent: POB 17434, Benghazi, Libya; tel. (61) 95823; fax (61) 95829; f. 1979 to attempt to alleviate the suffering caused by natural disasters and war. Sec.-Gen. Dr AHMAD ABDALLAH CHERIF.

Islamic Solidarity Sports Federation: POB 5844, Riyadh 11442, Saudi Arabia; tel. and fax (1) 482-2145; f. 1981. Sec.-Gen. Dr MOHAMMAD SALEH GAZDAR.

Organization of Islamic Capitals and Cities—OICC: POB 13621, Jeddah 21414, Saudi Arabia; tel. (2) 698-2141; fax (2) 698-1053; e-mail secrtriat@oicc.org; internet www.oicc.org; f. 1980 to promote and develop co-operation among OICC mems, to preserve their character and heritage, to implement planning guide-lines for the growth of Islamic cities and to upgrade standards of public services and utilities in those cities. Sec.-Gen. OMAR ABDULLAH KADI.

Organization of the Islamic Shipowners' Association: POB 14900, Jeddah 21434, Saudi Arabia; tel. (2) 663-7882; fax (2) 660-4920; e-mail oisa@sbm.net.sa; f. 1981 to promote co-operation among maritime cos in Islamic countries. In 1998 mems approved the establishment of a new commercial venture, the Bakkah Shipping Company, to enhance sea transport in the region. Sec.-Gen. Dr ABDULLATIF A. SULTAN.

World Federation of Arab-Islamic Schools: POB 3446, Jeddah, Saudi Arabia; tel. (2) 670-0019; fax (2) 671-0823; f. 1976; supports Arab-Islamic schools world-wide and encourages co-operation between the institutions; promotes the dissemination of the Arabic language and Islamic culture; supports the training of personnel.

ORGANIZATION OF THE PETROLEUM EXPORTING COUNTRIES—OPEC

Address: Obere Donaustrasse 93, 1020 Vienna, Austria.

Telephone: (1) 211-12-279; **fax:** (1) 214-98-27; **e-mail:** info@opec .org; **internet:** www.opec.org.

OPEC was established in 1960 to link countries whose main source of export earnings is petroleum; it aims to unify and co-ordinate members' petroleum policies and to safeguard their interests generally. The OPEC Fund for International Development is described on p. 000.

OPEC's share of world petroleum production was 41.5% in 2000 (compared with 44.7% in 1980 and 54.7% in 1974). OPEC members were estimated to possess 79.3% of the world's known reserves of crude petroleum in 2000; about two-thirds of these were in the Middle East. In 2000 OPEC members possessed about 44.4% of known reserves of natural gas.

MEMBERS

Algeria	Kuwait	Saudi Arabia
Indonesia	Libya	United Arab Emirates
Iran	Nigeria	Venezuela
Iraq	Qatar	

Organization

(September 2002)

CONFERENCE

The Conference is the supreme authority of the Organization, responsible for the formulation of its general policy. It consists of representatives of member countries, who examine reports and recommendations submitted by the Board of Governors. It approves the appointment of Governors from each country and elects the Chairman of the Board of Governors. It works on the unanimity principle, and meets at least twice a year.

BOARD OF GOVERNORS

The Board directs the management of the Organization; it implements resolutions of the Conference and draws up an annual budget. It consists of one governor for each member country, and meets at least twice a year.

MINISTERIAL MONITORING COMMITTEE

The Committee (f. 1982) is responsible for monitoring price evolution and ensuring the stability of the world petroleum market. As such, it is charged with the preparation of long-term strategies, including the allocation of quotas to be presented to the Conference. The Committee consists of all national representatives, and is normally convened four times a year. A Ministerial Monitoring Sub-committee, reporting to the Committee on production and supply figures, was established in 1993.

ECONOMIC COMMISSION

A specialized body operating within the framework of the Secretariat, with a view to assisting the Organization in promoting stability in international prices for petroleum at equitable levels; consists of a Board, national representatives and a commission staff; meets at least twice a year.

SECRETARIAT

Secretary-General: Dr Alvaro Silva Calderon (Venezuela).

Research Division: comprises three departments:

Data Services Department: Maintains and expands information services to support the research activities of the Secretariat and those of member countries; collects, collates and analyses statistical information and provides essential data for forecasts and estimates necessary for OPEC medium- and long-term strategies.

Energy Studies Department: Energy Section monitors, forecasts and analyses developments in the energy and petrochemical industries and their implications for OPEC, and prepares forecasts of demands for OPEC petroleum and gas. Petroleum Section assists the Board of the Economic Commission in determining the relative values of OPEC crude petroleum and gases and in developing alternative methodologies for this purpose.

Petroleum Market Analysis Department: Monitors and analyses short-term oil market indicators and world economic developments, factors affecting the supply and demand balance, policy developments affecting prices and petroleum demand, crude oil and product market performance, stocks, spot price movements and refinery utilization.

Division Director: Dr Adnan Shihab-Eldin (Kuwait).

Administration and Human Resources Department: Responsible for all organization methods, provision of administrative services for all meetings, personnel matters, budgets, accounting and internal control; reviews general administrative policies and industrial relations practised throughout the oil industry; **Head:** S. J. Senussi.

Public Relations and Information Department: Concerned with communicating OPEC objectives, decisions and actions; produces and distributes a number of publications, films, slides and tapes; and disseminates news of general interest regarding the Organization and member countries on energy and other related issues. Operates a daily on-line news service, the OPEC News Agency (OPECNA). An OPEC Library contains an extensive collection of energy-related publications; **Head: (vacant).**

Legal Office: Provides legal advice, supervises the Secretariat's legal commitments, evaluates legal issues of concern to the Organization and member countries, and recommends appropriate action; **Legal Officer:** Dolores Dobarro de Torres (Venezuela).

Office of the Secretary-General: Provides the Secretary-General with executive assistance in maintaining contacts with governments, organizations and delegations, in matters of protocol and in the preparation for and co-ordination of meetings; **Officer-in-Charge:** Karin Chacin.

Note: In September 2000 the Conference agreed that regular meetings of heads of state or government should be convened every five years.

Record of Events

1960 The first OPEC Conference was held in Baghdad in September, attended by representatives from Iran, Iraq, Kuwait, Saudi Arabia and Venezuela.

1961 Second Conference, Caracas, January. Qatar was admitted to membership; a Board of Governors was formed and statutes agreed.

1962 Fourth Conference, Geneva, April and June. Protests were addressed to petroleum companies against price cuts introduced in August 1960. Indonesia and Libya were admitted to membership.

1965 In July the Conference reached agreement on a two-year joint production programme, implemented from 1965 to 1967, to limit annual growth in output to secure adequate prices.

1967 Abu Dhabi was admitted to membership.

1969 Algeria was admitted to membership.

1970 Twenty-first Conference, Caracas, December. Tax on income of petroleum companies was raised to 55%.

1971 A five-year agreement was concluded in February between the six producing countries in the Gulf and 23 international petroleum companies (Tehran Agreement). Nigeria was admitted to membership.

1972 In January petroleum companies agreed to adjust petroleum revenues of the largest producers after changes in currency exchange rates (Geneva Agreement).

1973 OPEC and petroleum companies concluded an agreement whereby posted prices of crude petroleum were raised by 11.9% and a mechanism was installed to make monthly adjustments to prices in future (Second Geneva Agreement). Negotiations with petroleum companies on revision of the Tehran Agreement collapsed in October, and the Gulf states unilaterally declared 70% increases in posted prices, from US $3.01 to $5.11 per barrel. In December the Conference resolved to increase the posted price by nearly 130%, to $11.65 per barrel, from 1 January 1974. Ecuador was admitted to full membership and Gabon became an associate member.

1974 As a result of Saudi opposition to the December price increase, prices were held at current level for first quarter (and subsequently for the remainder of 1974). Abu Dhabi's membership was transferred to the United Arab Emirates (UAE). A meeting in June increased royalties charged to petroleum companies from 12.5% to 14.5% in all member states except Saudi Arabia. A meeting in September increased governmental take by about 3.5% through further increases in royalties on equity crude to 16.67% and in taxes to 65.65%, except in Saudi Arabia.

1975 OPEC's first summit meeting of heads of state or government was held in Algiers in March. Gabon was admitted to full membership. A ministerial meeting in September agreed to raise prices by 10% for the period until June 1976.

1976 The OPEC Fund for International Development was created in May. In December 11 member states endorsed a rise in basic prices of 10% as of 1 January 1977, and a further 5% rise as of 1 July 1977. However, Saudi Arabia and the UAE decided to raise their prices by 5% only.

1977 Following an earlier waiver by nine members of the 5% second stage of the price increase, Saudi Arabia and the UAE announced in July that they would both raise their prices by 5%. As a result, a single level of prices throughout the organization was restored. Because of continued disagreements between the 'moderates', led by Saudi Arabia and Iran, and the 'radicals', led by Algeria, Libya and Iraq, the Conference, held in December, was unable to settle on an increase in prices.

1978 The June Conference agreed that price levels should remain stable until the end of the year. In December it was decided to raise prices in four instalments, in order to compensate for the effects of the depreciation of the US dollar. These would bring a rise of 14.5% over nine months, but an average increase of 10% for 1979.

1979 At an extraordinary meeting in March members decided to raise prices by 9%. In June the Conference agreed minimum and maximum prices that seemed likely to add between 15% and 20% to import bills of consumer countries. The December Conference agreed in principle to convert the OPEC Fund into a development agency with its own legal personality.

1980 In June the Conference decided to set the price for a marker crude at US $32 per barrel, and that the value differentials which could be added above this ceiling (on account of quality and geographical location) should not exceed $5 per barrel. The planned OPEC summit meeting in Baghdad in November was postponed indefinitely because of the Iran–Iraq war, but the scheduled ministerial meeting went ahead in Bali in December, with both Iranians and Iraqis present. A ceiling price of $41 per barrel was fixed for premium crudes.

1981 In May attempts to achieve price reunification were made, but Saudi Arabia refused to increase its US $32 per barrel price unless the higher prices charged by other countries were lowered. Most of the other OPEC countries agreed to cut production by 10% so as to reduce the surplus. An emergency meeting in Geneva in August again failed to unify prices, although Saudi Arabia agreed to reduce production by 1m. barrels per day (b/d). In October OPEC countries agreed to increase the Saudi marker price to $34 per barrel, with a ceiling price of $38 per barrel.

1982 In March an emergency meeting of petroleum ministers was held in Vienna and agreed (for the first time in OPEC's history) to defend the Organization's price structure by imposing an overall production ceiling of 18m. b/d. In December the Conference agreed to limit OPEC production to 18.5m. b/d in 1983 but postponed the allocation of national quotas pending consultations among the respective governments.

1983 In January an emergency meeting of petroleum ministers, fearing a collapse in world petroleum prices, decided to reduce the production ceiling to 17.5m. b/d, but failed to agree on individual production quotas or on adjustments to the differentials in prices charged for the high-quality crude petroleum produced by Algeria, Libya and Nigeria compared with that produced by the Gulf States. In February Nigeria cut its prices to US $30 per barrel, following a collapse in its production. To avoid a 'price war' OPEC set the official price of marker crude at $29 per barrel, and agreed to maintain existing price differentials at the level agreed on in March 1982, with the temporary exception that the differentials for Nigerian crudes should be $1 more than the price of the marker crude. It also agreed to maintain the production ceiling of 17.5m. b/d and allocated quotas for each member country except Saudi Arabia, which was to act as a 'swing producer' to supply the balancing quantities to meet market requirements.

1984 In October the production ceiling was lowered to 16m. b/d. In December price differentials for light (more expensive) and heavy (cheaper) crudes were slightly altered in an attempt to counteract price-cutting by non-OPEC producers, particularly Norway and the United Kingdom.

1985 In January members (except Algeria, Iran and Libya) effectively abandoned the marker price system. During the year production in excess of quotas by OPEC members, unofficial discounts and barter deals by members, and price cuts by non-members (such as Mexico, which had hitherto kept its prices in line with those of OPEC) contributed to a weakening of the market.

1986 During the first half of the year petroleum prices dropped to below US $10 per barrel. In April ministers agreed to set OPEC production at 16.7m. b/d for the third quarter of 1986 and at 17.3m. b/d for the fourth quarter. Algeria, Iran and Libya dissented. Discussions were also held with non-member countries (Angola, Egypt, Malaysia, Mexico and Oman), which agreed to co-operate in limiting production, although the United Kingdom declined. In August all members, with the exception of Iraq (which demanded to be allowed the same quota as Iran and, when this was denied it, refused to be a party to the agreement), agreed upon a return to production quotas, with the aim of cutting production to 14.8m. b/d (about 16.8m. b/d including Iraq's production) for the ensuing two months. This measure resulted in an increase in prices to about $15 per barrel, and was extended until the end of the year. In December members (with the exception of Iraq) agreed to return to a fixed pricing system at a level of $18 per barrel as the OPEC reference price, with effect from 1 February 1987. OPEC's total production for the first half of 1987 was not to exceed 15.8m. b/d.

1987 In June, with prices having stabilized, the Conference decided that production during the third and fourth quarters of the year should be limited to 16.6m. b/d (including Iraq's production). However, total production continued to exceed the agreed levels. In December ministers decided to extend the existing agreement for the first half of 1988, although Iraq, once more, refused to participate.

1988 By March prices had fallen below US $15 per barrel. In April non-OPEC producers offered to reduce the volume of their petroleum exports by 5% if OPEC members would do the same. Saudi Arabia, however, refused to accept further reductions in production, insisting that existing quotas should first be more strictly enforced. In June the previous production limit (15.06m. b/d, excluding Iraq's production) was again renewed for six months, in the hope that increasing demand would be sufficient to raise prices. By October, however, petroleum prices were below $12 per barrel. In November a new agreement was reached, limiting total production (including that of Iraq) to 18.5m. b/d, with effect from 1 January 1989. Identical quotas were agreed for Iran and Iraq.

1989 In June (when prices had returned to about US $18 per barrel) ministers agreed to increase the production limit to 19.5m. b/d for the second half of 1989. However, Kuwait and the UAE indicated that they would not feel bound to observe this limit. In September the production limit was again increased, to 20.5m. b/d, and in November the limit for the first half of 1990 was increased to 22m. b/d.

1990 In May members resolved to adhere more strictly to the agreed production quotas, in response to a sharp decline in prices. By late June, however, it was reported that total production had decreased by only 400,000 b/d, and prices remained at about US $14 per barrel. In July Iraq threatened to take military action against Kuwait unless it reduced its petroleum production. In the same month OPEC members agreed to limit output to 22.5m. b/d. In August Iraq invaded Kuwait, and petroleum exports by the two countries were halted by an international embargo. Petroleum prices immediately increased to exceed $25 per barrel. Later in the month an informal consultative meeting of OPEC ministers placed the July agreement in abeyance, and permitted a temporary increase in production of petroleum, of between 3m. and 3.5m. b/d (mostly by Saudi Arabia, the UAE and Venezuela). In September and October prices fluctuated in response to political developments in the Gulf region, reaching a point in excess of $40 per barrel in early October, but falling to about $25 per barrel by the end of the month. In December a meeting of OPEC members voted to maintain the high levels of production and to reinstate the quotas that had been agreed in July, once the Gulf crisis was over. During the period August 1990–February 1991 Saudi Arabia increased its petroleum output from 5.4m. to 8.5m. b/d. Seven of the other OPEC states also produced in excess of their agreed quotas.

1991 In March, in an attempt to reach the target of a minimum reference price of US $21 per barrel, ministers agreed to reduce production from 23m. b/d to 22.3m. b/d, although Saudi Arabia refused to return to its pre-August 1990 quota. In June ministers decided to maintain the level of 22.3m. b/d into the third quarter of the year, since Iraq and Kuwait were still unable to export their petroleum. In September it was agreed that OPEC members' production for the last quarter of 1991 should be raised to 23.65m. b/d, and in November the OPEC Conference decided to maintain the increased production ceiling during the first quarter of 1992. From early November, however, the price of petroleum declined sharply, owing to lower than anticipated demand.

1992 The Ministerial Monitoring Committee, meeting in February, decided to impose a production ceiling of 22.98m. b/d with immediate effect. In May ministers agreed to maintain the production restriction during the third quarter of 1992. Kuwait, which was resuming production in the wake of the extensive damage inflicted on its oil-wells by Iraq during the Gulf War, was granted a special dispensation to produce without a fixed quota. During the first half of 1992 member states' petroleum output consistently exceeded agreed levels, with Saudi Arabia and Iran the principal over-producers. In June, at the UN Conference on Environment and Development, OPEC's Secretary-General expressed its member countries' strong objections to the tax on fossil fuels (designed to reduce pollution) proposed by the EC. In September agreement was reached on a production ceiling of 24.2m. b/d for the final quarter of 1992, in an attempt to raise the price of crude petroleum to the OPEC target of US $21 per barrel. At the Conference, held in November, Ecuador formally resigned from OPEC, the first country ever to do so, citing as reasons the high membership fee and OPEC's refusal to increase Ecuador's quota. The meeting agreed to restrict production to 24.58m. b/d for the first quarter of 1993 (24.46m. b/d, excluding Ecuador).

1993 In February a quota was set for Kuwait for the first time since the onset of the Gulf crisis. Kuwait agreed to produce 1.6m. b/d (400,000 less than current output) from 1 March, on the understanding that this would be substantially increased in the third quarter of the year. The quota for overall production from 1 March was set at 23.58m. b/d. A Ministerial Monitoring Sub-committee was established to supervise compliance with quotas. In June OPEC ministers decided to 'roll over' the overall quota of 23.58m. b/d into the third quarter of the year. However, Kuwait rejected its new allocation of 1.76m. b/d, demanding a quota of at least 2m. In July discussions between Iraq and the UN on the possible supervised sale of Iraqi petroleum depressed petroleum prices to below US $16 per barrel. The Monitoring Sub-committee urged member states to adhere to their production quotas (which were exceeded by a total of 1m. b/d in July). At the end of September an extraordinary meeting of the Conference agreed on a raised production ceiling of 24.52m. b/d, to be effective for six months from 1 October. Kuwait accepted a quota of 2m. b/d, which brought the country back into the production ceiling mechanism. Iran agreed on an allocation of 3.6m. b/d, while Saudi Arabia consented to freeze production at current levels, in order to support petroleum prices which remained persistently low. In November the Conference rejected any further reduction in production. Prices subsequently fell below $14.

1994 In March OPEC ministers opted to maintain the output quotas agreed in September 1993 until the end of the year, and urged non-OPEC producers to freeze their production levels. (Iraq failed to endorse the agreement, recognizing only the production agreement adopted in July 1990.) At the meeting Saudi Arabia resisted a proposal from Iran and Nigeria, both severely affected by declines in petroleum revenue, to reduce its production by 1m. b/d in order to boost prices. In November ministers endorsed a proposal by Saudi Arabia to maintain the existing production quota (of 24.52m. b/d) until the end of 1995.

1995 In January it was reported that Gabon was reconsidering its membership of OPEC, owing to difficulties in meeting its budget contribution. During the first half of the year Gabon consistently exceeded its quota of 287,000 b/d, by 48,000 b/d, and the country failed to send a delegate to the ministerial Conference in June. At the Conference ministers expressed concern at OPEC's falling share of the world petroleum market. The Conference criticized the high level of North Sea production, by Norway and the United Kingdom, and urged collective production restraint in order to stimulate prices. In November the Conference agreed to extend the existing production quota (24.52m. b/d) for a further six months, in order to stabilize prices. During the year, however, output remained in excess of the production quotas, at some 25.58m. b/d.

1996 The possibility of a UN-Iraqi agreement permitting limited petroleum sales dominated OPEC concerns in the first half of the year and contributed to price fluctuations in the world markets. By early 1996 output by OPEC countries was estimated to be substantially in excess of quota levels; however, the price per barrel remained relatively buoyant (the average basket price reaching US $21 in March), owing largely to unseasonal cold weather in the northern hemisphere. In May a memorandum of understanding was signed between Iraq and the UN to allow the export of petroleum, up to a value of $2,000m. over a six-month period, in order to fund humanitarian relief efforts within that country. In June the Conference agreed to increase the overall output ceiling by 800,000 b/d, i.e. the anticipated level of exports from Iraq in the first six months of the agreement. Gabon's withdrawal from the Organization was confirmed at the meeting. As a result of these developments, the new production ceiling was set at 25.03m. b/d. Independent market observers expressed concern that, without any formal agreement to reduce overall production and given the actual widespread violation of the quota system, the renewed export of Iraqi petroleum would substantially depress petroleum prices. In September the Monitoring Sub-committee acknowledged that members were exceeding their production quotas, but declined to impose any punitive measures (owing to the steady increase in petroleum prices). In November the Conference agreed to maintain the existing production quota for a further six months. Also in that month, Iraq accepted certain disputed technical terms of the UN agreement, enabling the export of petroleum to commence in December.

1997 During the first half of the year petroleum prices declined, reaching a low of US $16.7 per barrel in early April, owing to the Iraqi exports, depressed world demand and persistent over-production. In June the Conference agreed to extend the existing production ceiling, of 25.03m. b/d, for a further six-month period. Member states resolved to adhere to their individual quotas in order to reduce the cumulative excess production of an estimated 2m. b/d; however, Venezuela, which (some sources claimed) was producing almost 800,000 b/d over its quota of 2.4m. b/d, declined to co-operate. An escalation in political tensions in the Gulf region in October, in particular Iraq's reluctance to co-operate with UN inspectors, prompted an increase in the price of crude petroleum to some $21.2 per barrel. Price fluctuations ensued, although there was a general downward trend. In November the OPEC Conference, meeting in Jakarta, approved a proposal by Saudi Arabia, to increase the overall production ceiling by some 10%, with effect from 1 January 1998, in order to meet the perceived stable world demand and to reflect more accurately current output levels. At the same time the Iranian Government announced its intention to increase its production

capacity and maintain its share of the quota by permitting foreign companies to conduct petroleum exploration in its territory.

1998 A decline in petroleum prices at the start of the year caused widespread concern, and speculation that this had resulted from the decision to increase production to 27.5m. b/d, coinciding with the prospect of a decline in demand from Asian economies that had been undermined by extreme financial difficulties and of a new Iraqi agreement with the UN with provision for increased petroleum exports. A meeting of the Monitoring Sub-committee, in late January, urged members to implement production restraint and resolved to send a monitoring team to member states to encourage compliance with the agreed quotas. (Venezuela remained OPEC's principal over-producer.) In February the UN Security Council approved a new agreement permitting Iraq to export petroleum valued at up to US $5,256m. every 180 days, although the Iraqi Government insisted that its production and export capacity was limited to $4,000m. In March Saudi Arabia, Venezuela and Mexico announced a joint agreement to reduce domestic production by 300,000 b/d, 200,000 b/d and 100,000 b/d respectively, with effect from 1 April, and agreed to co-operate in persuading other petroleum producing countries to commit to similar reductions. At the end of March an emergency ministerial meeting ratified the reduction proposals (the so-called 'Riyadh Pact'), which amounted to 1.245m. b/d pledged by OPEC members and 270,000 b/d by non-member states. Nevertheless, prices remained low, with over-production, together with lack of market confidence in member states' willingness to comply with the restricted quotas, an outstanding concern. In June Saudi Arabia, Venezuela and Mexico reached agreement on further reductions in output of some 450,000 b/d. Later in that month the Conference, having reviewed the market situation, agreed to implement a new reduction in total output of some 1.36m b/d, with effect from 1 July, reducing the total production target for OPEC members to 24.387m. b/d. Iran, which had been criticized for not adhering to the reductions agreed in March, confirmed that it would reduce output by 305,000 b/d. In early August petroleum prices fell below $12 per barrel. In September Iraq's petroleum production reached an estimated 2.4m. b/d, contributing to concerns of over-supply in the world market. In early November OPEC members attending a conference of the parties to the UN Framework Convention on Climate Change, held in Buenos Aires, Argentina, warned that they would claim compensation for any lost revenue resulting from initiatives to limit the emission of 'greenhouse gases' and reduce the consumption of petroleum. Later in November OPEC ministers, meeting in Vienna, resolved to maintain the existing production levels, but improve compliance. Subsequently, despite an escalation of tensions between the UN and Iraqi authorities, prices remained consistently around the level of $11 per barrel. Air-strikes initiated in December by the USA and United Kingdom against strategic targets in Iraq were not considered to have interrupted petroleum supplies and therefore had little impact on prices.

1999 In March ministers from Algeria, Iran, Mexico, Saudi Arabia and Venezuela, meeting in The Hague, Netherlands, agreed further to reduce petroleum production, owing to the continued weakness of the global market. Subsequently, petroleum prices rose by nearly 40%, after reaching the lowest price of US $9.9 per barrel in mid-February. Later in March OPEC confirmed a new reduction in output of 2.104m. b/d from 1 April, including commitments from non-OPEC members Mexico, Norway, Oman and Russia to decrease production by a total of 388,000 b/d. The agreement envisaged a total production target for OPEC member countries of 22.976m. b/d. By June total production by OPEC member states (excluding Iraq) had declined to a reported 23.25m. b/d (compared with 27.72m. in March). The evidence of almost 90% compliance with the new production quotas contributed to market confidence that stockpiles of petroleum would be reduced, and resulted in sustained price increases. In September OPEC ministers confirmed that the existing quotas would be maintained for a further six-month period. At the end of September the reference price for petroleum rose above $24, its highest level since January 1997. Prices remained buoyant during the rest of the year; however, there was increasing speculation at whether the situation was sustainable. At the end of November Iraq temporarily suspended its petroleum exports, totalling some 2.2m. b/d, pending agreement on a new phase of the 'oil-for-food' arrangement and concern at the lack of progress on the removal of international sanctions.

2000 In March petroleum prices attained their highest level since the 1990 Gulf crisis, with the the reference price briefly exceeding US \$34. At the end of that month OPEC ministers, meeting in Vienna, agreed to raise output by 1.45m. b/d, in order to ease supply shortages and thereby contain the surge in prices, with a view to restoring these to a more moderate level. A further increase in production, of 500,000 b/d, was approved by member states in June, to take effect from July (contingent on the reference price continuing to exceed \$28 for 20 consecutive days). Prices remained high, reaching \$34.6 in early September and leading to intense international pressure on OPEC to resolve the situation. OPEC ministers immediately announced that an increase in production of 800,000 b/d would take effect from 1 October and indicated that, were the reference price still to exceed \$28 at the end of that month, an additional increase in output would be implemented. It was noted that a target band of \$22–\$28 per barrel was envisaged as an acceptable price level. The production agreement was supported by five non-OPEC member countries: Angola, Mexico, Norway, Oman and Russia. In late September both the Group of Seven industrialized nations (G-7) and the IMF issued warnings about the potential economic and social consequences of sustained high petroleum prices. Meanwhile the US administration agreed to release part of its strategic petroleum reserve. Towards the end of the month OPEC heads of state or government, convened at their first summit since 1975, issued the so-called 'Caracas Declaration' in which they resolved to promote market stability by developing 'remunerative, stable and competitive' pricing policies in conjunction with implementing a production policy that would secure OPEC member states an equitable share of world supply; by strengthening co-operation between the organization and other oil-exporting nations; and by developing communication between petroleum producers and consumers. The declaration also affirmed the organization's commitment to environmentally sound practice and to promoting sustainable global economic growth, social development and the eradication of poverty; supported research in technical and scientific fields; expressed concern that government taxation policies significantly inflate the end cost of petroleum; and agreed to convene future heads of state summits at regular five-yearly intervals. By the end of September petroleum prices had declined to just above \$30 per barrel; this was attributed in part to an announcement by the Saudi Arabian Government that it would consider unilaterally raising output if prices were to remain at a high level. However, the decline in prices was short-lived, as the political crisis in the Middle East prompted a further series of increases: by 12 October the London Brent crude price exceeded \$35 per barrel. From 31 October an additional increase in production, of 500,000 b/d, was implemented, as planned for in early September. Meeting in mid-November the Conference appointed Dr Alí Rodríguez Araque as the new OPEC Secretary-General, with effect from January 2001. Addressing the Conference, Rodríguez identified the following contributory factors to the high level of petroleum prices other than the relationship between production and price levels: a decline in recent years in the refining capacity of the USA (the world's largest market), the high national taxes on consumption (particularly within the European Union), and price distortions deriving from speculation on futures markets. Attending the sixth conference of parties to the UN Framework Convention on Climate Change later in November OPEC reiterated its concern over the lost revenue that limits on 'greenhouse gas' emissions and reduced petroleum consumption would represent for member states, estimating this at \$63,000m. per year.

2001 In mid-January, with a view to stabilizing petroleum prices that by now had fallen back to around US \$25 per barrel, the Conference agreed to implement a reduction in production of 1.5m. b/d, to take effect on 1 February. A further reduction, of 1m. b/d, effective from 1 April, was approved by the Conference in mid-March, limiting overall production to 24.2m. b/d. In early June an extraordinary meeting of the Conference determined to maintain the production level, given that prices had stabilized within the agreed price range of \$22–\$28 per barrel, in spite of market reports forecasting reduced demand. A further extraordinary meeting was convened in early July, following Iraq's decision temporarily to suspend its petroleum exports under the UN programme,

which again resolved to make no adjustment to the output ceiling. Later in that month, however, OPEC responded to a gradual decline in petroleum prices, which reached \$22.78 in mid-July, by announcing a ministerial agreement to reduce production by 1m. b/d, with effect from 1 September. Meeting in late September the Conference addressed the repercussions of recent major terrorist attacks on targets in the USA, which had caused significant market uncertainty. OPEC's spot basket reference price had fallen back to around \$20 per barrel. The Conference declared its commitment to stabilizing the market and determined to leave production levels unchanged (at 23.2m. b/d) in order to ensure sufficient supplies. It agreed to establish an expert working group, comprising representatives of OPEC and non-OPEC producer countries, to evaluate future market developments and advance dialogue and co-operation. At a further meeting in December the Conference decided, in view of the prevailing global economic uncertainty and a decline in the average basket price level to \$17–\$18 in November and December, to prevent a further deterioration in petroleum prices by reducing output by a further 1.5m. b/d for six months from 1 January 2002, contingent upon the non-OPEC producers concurrently implementing a reduction in production amounting to 500,000 b/d. The Conference resolved to continue to develop contacts with the non-OPEC producer states. By the end of December 2001 the non-OPEC producers had committed themselves to a reduction in output totalling 462,500 b/d, which was considered by OPEC an adequate basis for lowering its own production ceiling to 21.70m. b/d from the start of 2002, as planned.

2002 Meeting in March the OPEC Conference welcomed a gradual improvement in the reference price (the spot basket price had averaged nearly \$19 in February), attributing this to a high level of compliance by member countries with their agreed production quotas and to ongoing support from non-OPEC producers. The latter were urged to maintain their voluntarily-imposed reductions in output. Six non-OPEC producers—Angola, Egypt, Mexico, Oman, Russia and Syria—attended the meeting as observers. Concern was expressed over the potentially destabilizing effects of the ongoing Middle East crisis. Prices rose significantly in early April following the imposition by Iraq of a one-month suspension of its oil exports in protest at the ongoing Israeli military intervention in areas controlled by the Palestinian (National) Authority. The ensuing reduction in global supply was compounded by constraints on Venezuelan production caused by a strike in the oil sector. It was reported at this time that the Iranian Government advocated the implementation of a general embargo by the Arab states on oil exports to Western countries perceived to be supporting Israeli actions. During April–early August the reference price stabilized at around \$25. Meeting in June the Conference determined to maintain the existing production quota (21.70 b/d) and appointed a new Secretary-General, Dr Alvaro Silva Calderon, hitherto the Venezuelan the minister of energy and mines. In September the Conference agreed to maintain existing production levels until the end of 2002, although the ongoing threat of US military action against Iraq had caused prices to exceed \$26 from August. At the end of September the average basket price stood at \$28.34, in excess of the target range of \$22–\$28.

Finance

The budget for 2002 amounted to €16.7m., of which €3.5m. was to be financed by transfer from the Reserve Fund and the balance was to be contributed by member states.

Publications

Annual Report.

Annual Statistical Bulletin.

Monthly Oil Market Report.

OPEC Bulletin (monthly).

OPEC Review (quarterly).

Reports, information papers, press releases.

OPEC FUND FOR INTERNATIONAL DEVELOPMENT

Address: POB 995, 1011 Vienna, Austria.
Telephone: (1) 515-64-0; **fax:** (1) 513-92-38; **e-mail:** info@opecfund
.org; **internet:** www.opecfund.org.
The Fund was established by OPEC member countries in 1976.

MEMBERS
Member countries of OPEC (q.v.).

Organization
(September 2002)

ADMINISTRATION
The Fund is administered by a Ministerial Council and a Governing Board. Each member country is represented on the Council by its minister of finance. The Board consists of one representative and one alternate for each member country.
Chairman, Ministerial Council: Dr YOUSEF H. AL-EBRAHEEM (Kuwait).
Chairman, Governing Board: Dr SALEH A. AL-OMAIR (Saudi Arabia).
Director-General of the Fund: Dr YESUFU SEYYID ABDULAI (Nigeria).

FINANCIAL STRUCTURE
The resources of the Fund, whose unit of account is the US dollar, consist of contributions by OPEC member countries, and income received from operations or otherwise accruing to the Fund.
The initial endowment of the Fund amounted to US $800m. Its resources have been replenished three times, and have been further increased by the profits accruing to seven OPEC member countries through the sales of gold held by the International Monetary Fund. The pledged contributions to the OPEC Fund amounted to $3,435m. at the end of 2001, and paid-in contributions totalled some $2,990m.

Activities

The OPEC Fund for International Development is a multilateral agency for financial co-operation and assistance. Its objective is to reinforce financial co-operation between OPEC member countries and other developing countries through the provision of financial support to the latter on appropriate terms, to assist them in their economic and social development. The Fund was conceived as a collective financial facility which would consolidate the assistance extended by its member countries; its resources are additional to those already made available through other bilateral and multilateral aid agencies of OPEC members. It is empowered to:

(*i*) Provide concessional loans for balance-of-payments support;

(*ii*) Provide concessional loans for the implementation of development projects and programmes;

(*iii*) Make contributions and/or provide loans to eligible international agencies; and

(*iv*) Finance technical assistance and research through grants.

The eligible beneficiaries of the Fund's assistance are the governments of developing countries other than OPEC member countries, and international development agencies whose beneficiaries are developing countries. The Fund gives priority to the countries with the lowest income.
The Fund may undertake technical, economic and financial appraisal of a project submitted to it, or entrust such an appraisal to an appropriate international development agency, the executing national agency of a member country, or any other qualified agency. Most projects financed by the Fund have been co-financed by other development finance agencies. In each such case, one of the co-financing agencies may be appointed to administer the Fund's loan in association with its own. This practice has enabled the Fund to extend its lending activities to 109 countries over a short period of time and in a simple way, with the aim of avoiding duplication and complications. As its experience grew, the Fund increasingly resorted to parallel, rather than joint financing, taking up separate project components to be financed according to its rules and policies. In addition, it started to finance some projects completely on its own. These trends necessitated the issuance in 1982 of guide-lines for the procurement of goods and services under the Fund's loans, allowing for a margin of preference for goods and services of local origin or originating in other developing countries: the general

OPEC FUND COMMITMENTS AND DISBURSEMENTS IN 2001 (US $ million)

	Commit- ments	Disburse- ments
Public-sector lending operations:	332.33	175.42
Project financing	273.83	159.82
Programme financing	—	6.00
HIPC initiative financing*	58.50	9.60
Private-sector lending operations	58.60	7.80
Grant Programme:	5.21	3.94
Technical assistance	3.04	2.93
Research and other activities	0.67	0.48
Emergency aid	1.50	0.54
Total	396.14	187.16

* Heavily Indebted Poor Countries initiative, jointly implemented by the International Monetary Fund and World Bank.

Project loans approved in 2001 (US $ million)

	Loans approved
Sector:	
Transportation	102.76
Agriculture and agro-industry	20.00
Education	60.89
Energy	16.90
Health	21.20
Telecommunications	2.50
Water supply and sewerage	26.30
Multisectoral	23.28
Total	273.83
Region*:	
Africa	162.29
Asia	92.24
Europe	2.70
Latin America and the Caribbean	16.60

* A total of 38 loans was approved for projects in 33 countries, benefiting 20 countries in Africa, nine in Asia, three in Latin America and the Caribbean, and one in Europe.

principle of competitive bidding is, however, followed by the Fund. The loans are not tied to procurement from Fund member countries or from any other countries. The margin of preference for goods and services obtainable in developing countries is allowed on the request of the borrower and within defined limits. Fund assistance in the form of programme loans has a broader coverage than project lending. Programme loans are used to stimulate an economic sector or sub-sector, and assist recipient countries in obtaining inputs, equipment and spare parts. Besides extending loans for project and programme financing and balance of payments support, the Fund also undertakes other operations, including grants in support of technical assistance and other activities (mainly research), and financial contributions to other international institutions. In 1998 the Fund began to extend lines of credit to support private-sector activities in beneficiary countries. The so-called Private-Sector Facility aims to encourage the growth of private enterprises, in particular small and medium-sized enterprises, and to support the development of local capital markets.
By the end of December 2001 the Fund had approved 913 loans since operations began in 1976, totalling US $4,873.7m., of which $3,698.3m. (or 75.9%) was for project financing, $724.2m. (14.9%) was for balance-of-payments support, $305.3m. (6.3%) was for programme financing and $145.8m. (3.0%) was allocated as financing for the Heavily Indebted Poor Countries (HIPC) initiative (see World Bank, p. 1273). Private sector operations totalled $111.7m. at that time. The Fund's 15th lending programme, approved for a three-year period, became effective on 1 January 2002.
Direct loans are supplemented by grants to support technical assistance, food aid and research. By the end of December 2001 568 grants, amounting to US $251.8m., had been extended, including $83.6m. to the Common Fund for Commodities (established by the UN Conference on Trade and Development—UNCTAD), $44.1m. in support of emergency relief operations, $99.1m. in technical

assistance often in co-operation with UN agencies or other development organizations, and a special contribution of $20m. to the International Fund for Agricultural Development (IFAD). In addition, the OPEC Fund had committed $971.8m. to other international institutions by the end of 2001, comprising OPEC members' contributions to the resources of IFAD, and irrevocable transfers in the name of its members to the IMF Trust Fund. By the end of 2001 66.2% of total commitments had been disbursed.

During the year ending 31 December 2001 the Fund's total commitments amounted to US $332.3m. (compared with $284.4m. in 2000). These commitments included 38 public sector project loans, amounting to $273.8m., and nine loans, totalling $58.5m., to finance debt-relief under the HIPC initiative. The largest proportion of project loans (37.5%) was to support improvements in the transportation sector in 12 countries and includedroad connections to remote rural areas in Benin, Cameroon, Chad, Malawi, Senegal and Tanzania, rehabilitation of major highways in Ethiopia, the Republic of Korea and Lebanon, the expansion of the international airport in Ethiopia and modernization of railways in Pakistan. The education sector received 22.2% of loans, which supported the construction and improvement of primary level facilities in Angola, Cote d'Ivoire,

Equatorial Guinea and Kenya, secondary education improvements in Mozambique and the expansion of a specialized technology institute in India. Four loans (9.6% of the total) were allocated to improve water supply and sewerage in Albania, Haiti, Honduras and Yemen. Five health sector loans accounted for 7.7% of the total and were allocated to fund hospital improvements in Lesotho and Zambia, HIV/AIDS activities in Chad and Djibouti, and laboratory facilities in Burkina Faso.

During 2001 the Fund approved US $5.21m. for 37 grants, of which $3.04m. was for technical assistance activities, $671,000 for research, and $1.50m. to support emergency humanitarian operations in El Salvador, India, Algeria, Cuba and Honduras, as well as other humanitarian activities in Mongolia, for Afghan refugees in Pakistan and for Palestinians receiving medical care in Austria.

Publications

Annual Report (in Arabic, English, French and Spanish).
OPEC Fund Newsletter (3 a year).
Occasional papers and documents.

OTHER REGIONAL ORGANIZATIONS

These organizations are arranged under the following sub-headings:

Agriculture	Industrial Relations	Social Sciences and Social
Commodities	Law	Welfare
Development and Economic Co-operation	Medicine and Health	Trade and Industry
Education, Arts and Sport	Post and Telecommunications	Transport
Finance and Economics	Religion and Welfare	
Government and Politics	Science and Technology	

(See also lists of subsidiary bodies in the chapters on the main regional organizations, e.g. Council of Arab Economic Unity, League of Arab States, OIC, etc.; and the list of Research Institutes, p. 1331.)

AGRICULTURE

Arab Authority for Agricultural Investment and Development—AAAID: POB 2102, Khartoum, Sudan; tel. 784914; fax 772600; e-mail aaarabi@emirates.net.ae; f. 1976 to accelerate agricultural development in the Arab world and to ensure food security; acts principally by equity participation in agricultural projects. Mems: Algeria, Egypt, Iraq, Jordan, Kuwait, Mauritania, Morocco, Oman, Qatar, Saudi Arabia, Somalia, Sudan, Syria, Tunisia, United Arab Emirates. Pres. ABDULKARIM AL-AMRI. Publs *Annual Report, Journal of Agricultural Investment.*

International Centre for Agricultural Research in the Dry Areas—ICARDA: POB 5466, Aleppo, Syria; tel. (21) 2213433; fax (21) 2213490; e-mail icarda@cgiar.org; internet www.icarda.cgiar .org; f. 1977; aims to improve the production of lentils, barley and faba beans throughout the developing world; supports the improvement of on-farm water-use efficiency, rangeland and small-ruminant production in all dry-area developing countries; within the West and Central Asia and North Africa region promotes the improvement of bread and durum wheat and chick-pea production and of farming systems. Undertakes research, training and dissemination of information, in co-operation with national, regional and international research institutes, universities and ministries of agriculture, in order to enhance production, alleviate poverty and promote sustainable natural resource management practices; member of the network of 16 agricultural research centres supported by the Consultative Group on International Agricultural Research (CGIAR). Dir-Gen. Dr ADEL EL-BELTAGY. Publs *Annual Report, Caravan Newsletter* (2 a year).

COMMODITIES

African Petroleum Producers' Association—APPA: BP 1097, Brazzaville, Republic of the Congo; tel. 83-64-38; fax 83-67-99; f. 1987 by African petroleum-producing countries to reinforce co-operation among regional producers and to stabilize prices; council of ministers responsible for the hydrocarbons sector of each country meets twice a year. First APPA Congress and Exhibition scheduled to be held in Tripoli, Libya, in March 2003. Mems: Algeria, Angola, Benin, Cameroon, the Dem. Repub. of the Congo, Repub. of the Congo, Côte d'Ivoire, Egypt, Equatorial Guinea, Gabon, Libya, Nigeria. Presidency rotates. Exec. Sec. MAXIME OBIANG-NZE. Publ. *APPA Bulletin* (2 a year).

International Grains Council: 1 Canada Sq., Canary Wharf, London, E14 5AE, United Kingdom; tel. (20) 7513-1122; fax (20) 7513-0630; e-mail igc@igc.org.uk; internet www.igc.org.uk; f. 1949

as International Wheat Council, present name adopted in 1995; responsible for the admin. of the International Grains Agreement (1995), comprising the Grain Trade Convention (GTC) and the Food Aid Convention (FAC); the GTC aims to further international co-operation in all aspects of trade in grains, to promote international trade in grains, and to secure the freest possible flow of this trade in the interests of mems, particularly developing mem. countries; and to contribute to the stability of the international grain market; under the FAC donors pledge specified minimum annual amounts of food aid for developing countries in the form of grain and other eligible products; the Council acts as forum for consultations between mems, and provides comprehensive information on the international grain market and factors affecting it. Mems: 29. Exec. Dir G. DENIS. Publs *World Grain Statistics* (annually), *Wheat and Coarse Grain Shipments* (annually), *Report for the Fiscal Year* (annually), *Grain Market Report* (monthly), *IGC Grain Market Indicators* (weekly).

International Olive Oil Council: Príncipe de Vergara 154, Madrid 28002, Spain; tel. (91) 5903638; fax (91) 5631263; e-mail iooc@inter nationaloliveoil.org; internet www.internationaloliveoil.org; f. 1959 to administer the International Agreement on Olive Oil and Table Olives, the objectives of which are as follows: to promote international co-operation in connection with problems of the world economy for olive products; to prevent the occurrence of any unfair competition in the world olive products trade; to encourage the production and consumption of, and international trade in, olive products, and to reduce the disadvantages due to fluctuations of supplies on the market. Mems of the 1986 Agreement (Fourth Agreement), as amended and extended, 1993: Algeria, Cyprus, Egypt, Israel, Lebanon, Morocco, Tunisia, Turkey, Yugoslavia (Serbia and Montenegro) and the 15 member countries of the EU. Dir FAUSTO LUCHETTI. Publs *Information Sheet* (fortnightly, French and Spanish), *OLIVAE* (5 a year, in English, French, Italian and Spanish), economic and technical studies, etc.

DEVELOPMENT AND ECONOMIC CO-OPERATION

African Training and Research Centre in Administration for Development (Centre africain de formation et de recherche administratives pour le développement—CAFRAD): ave Mohamed, BP 310, Tangiers, 90001 Morocco; tel. (212) 3942652; fax (212) 39325785; e-mail cafrad@cafrad.org; internet www.cafrad.org; f. 1964 by agreement between Morocco and UNESCO; undertakes research into administrative problems in Africa, documentation of results, provision of a consultation service for governments and organizations; holds frequent workshops for training of senior civil servants; prepares the Biennial Pan-African Conference of Ministers of the Civil Service . Mems: 37 African states. Chair. M'HAMED EL KAHLIFA; Dir-Gen. Prof. TIJJANI MUHAMMAD BANDE. Publs *African Administrative Studies* (2 a year), *Research Studies, CAFRAD News* (quarterly, in English, French and Arabic), *Collection: Etudes et Documents, Répertoire des Consultants, Répertoire des institutions de formation et de recherché en Afrique.*

Afro-Asian Housing Organization—AAHO: POB 5623, 28 Ramses Ave, Cairo, Egypt; f. 1965 to promote co-operation between African and Asian countries in housing, reconstruction, physical planning and related matters. Mems: 18 countries. Sec.-Gen. HASSAN M. HASSAN (Egypt).

Afro-Asian Rural Development Organization—AARDO: Plot No. 2, State Guest House Complex (Near Chanakyapuri Telephone Exchange), Chanakyapuri, New Delhi 110021, India; tel. (11) 4100475; fax (11) 4672045; e-mail aardohq@nde.vsnl.net.in; internet www.aardo.org; f. 1962 to act as catalyst for co-operative restructuring of rural life in Africa and Asia; to explore collectively opportunities for co-ordination of efforts for promoting welfare and eradicating hunger, thirst, disease, illiteracy and poverty amongst the rural people; and to assist the formation of organizations of farmers and other rural people. Activities include collaborative research on development issues; training; assistance in forming organizations of farmers and other rural people; the exchange of information; international conferences and seminars; and awarding 100 individual training fellowships at nine institutes in Egypt, India, Japan, the Republic of Korea and Taiwan. Mems: 12 African, 14 Asian and one African associate. Sec.-Gen. Dr BAHAR MUNIP. Publs *Annual Report, Afro-Asian Journal of Rural Development, AARDO Newsletter* (2 a year), conference and committee reports.

Arab Co-operation Council: POB 2640, Khartoum, Sudan; tel. (11)73646; f. 1989 to promote economic co-operation between member states, including free movement of workers, joint projects in transport, communications and agriculture, and eventual integration of trade and monetary policies. Mems: Egypt, Iraq, Jordan, Yemen.

Arab Gulf Programme for the United Nations Development Organizations—AGFUND: POB 18371, Riyadh 11415, Saudi Arabia; tel. (1) 441-8888; fax (1) 441-2962; e-mail info@agfund.org; internet www.agfund.org; f. 1981 to provide grants (not exceeding 50% of project costs) for projects in mother and child care undertaken by the United Nations, Arab non-governmental organizations and other international bodies, and to co-ordinate assistance by the nations of the Gulf. Mems: Bahrain, Iraq, Kuwait, Oman, Qatar, Saudi Arabia, United Arab Emirates. Pres. HRH Prince TALAL IBN ABD AL-AZIZ AS-SAUD.

Community of Sahel-Saharan States (Communauté des Etats Sahelo–Sahariens—CEN-SAD): POB 4041, Aljazaer Sq., Tripoli, Libya; tel. (21) 361-4832; fax (21) 333-2116; e-mail censad_sg@yahoo.com; f. 1998; fmrly known as COMESSA; aims to strengthen co-operation between signatory states in order to promote their economic, social and cultural integration and to facilitate conflict resolution and poverty alleviation; partnership agreements signed with many orgs, including the OAU (now AU), the UN and ECOWAS. Mems: Benin, Burkina Faso, Central African Republic, Chad, Djibouti, Egypt, Eritrea, The Gambia, Libya, Mali, Morocco, Niger, Nigeria, Senegal, Somalia, Sudan, Togo, Tunisia. Sec.-Gen. Dr MOHAMED AL-MADANI AL-AZHARI.

Developing Eight—D-8: Muṣir Fuad Paṣa Yalıısı, Eski Tersane, Emirgan, Cad. 90, İstanbul 80860, Turkey; tel. (212) 2775513; fax (212) 2775519; internet www.developing-8.net; inaugurated at a meeting of heads of state in June 1997; aims to foster economic co-operation between member states and to strengthen the role of developing countries in the global economy; project areas include trade and industry, agriculture, human resources, telecommunications, rural development, finance (incl. privatizations and banking), energy, environment and health. Third summit meeting, convened in Cairo, Egypt, in Feb. 2001, discussed reducing trade barriers amongst member states and considered the impact of external debt on member economies. Mems: Bangladesh, Egypt, Indonesia, Iran, Malaysia, Nigeria, Pakistan, Turkey. Exec. Dir AYHAN KAMEL.

Economic Research Forum for the Arab Countries, Iran and Turkey: 7 Boulos Hanna St, Dokki, Cairo, Egypt; tel. (2) 3370810; fax (2) 3485553; e-mail erf@idsc.gov.eg; internet erf.org.eg; f. 1993 to conduct in-depth economic research, compile an economic database for the region, and provide training. Dir Dr HEBA HANDOUSSA (Egypt). Publ. *ERF Newsletter* (quarterly).

Indian Ocean Rim Association for Regional Co-operation—IOR-ARC: Sorèce House, 14 Angus Rd, Vacoas, Mauritius; tel. 698-3979; fax 697-5390; e-mail iorarchq@intnet.mu; the first intergovernmental meeting of countries in the region to promote an Indian Ocean Rim initiative was convened in March 1995; charter to establish the Asscn was signed at a ministerial meeting in March 1997; aims to promote regional economic co-operation in the fields

of trade, investment, the environment, tourism, and science and technology. Third meeting of Council of Ministers held in Muscat, Oman, April 2001. Mems: Australia, Bangladesh, India, Indonesia, Iran, Kenya, Madagascar, Malaysia, Mauritius, Mozambique, Oman, Seychelles, Singapore, South Africa, Sri Lanka, Tanzania, Thailand, United Arab Emirates and Yemen. Dialogue countries: People's Republic of China, Egypt, Japan, United Kingdom. Chair. YOUSSOUF BIN ABDULLAH AL-ALAWI (Oman); Dir DEVDASLALL DUSORUTH (Mauritius).

Organization of the Black Sea Economic Co-operation—BSEC: İstinye Cad. Müşir Fuad Paşa Yalısı, Eski Tersane 80860 İstinye-İstanbul, Turkey; tel. (212) 229-63-30; fax (212) 229-63-36; e-mail bsec@turk.net; internet www.bsec-organization.org; f.1992 as the Black Sea Economic Co-operation (name changed on entry into force of BSEC Charter on 1 May 1999); aims to strengthen regional co-operation, particularly in the field of economic development. The following institutions have been established within the framework of BSEC: a Parliamentary Assembly (established in 1993), a Business Council (1992), a Black Sea Trade and Development Bank (inaugurated in 1998), a BSEC Co-ordination Centre, and a Black Sea International Studies Centre (opened in 1998). Mems: Albania, Armenia, Azerbaijan, Bulgaria, Georgia, Greece, Moldova, Romania, Russia, Turkey, Ukraine. Sec.-Gen. VALERI CHECHELASHVILI (Georgia).

Union of the Arab Maghreb (Union du Maghreb arabe—UMA): 14 rue Zalagh, Agdal, Rabat, Morocco; tel. (212) 37671274; fax (212) 37671253; e-mail sg.uma@maghrebarabe.org; internet www.maghrebarabe.org; f. 1989; aims to encourage joint ventures and to create a single market; structure comprises a council of heads of state (meeting annually), a council of ministers of foreign affairs, a follow-up committee, composed of ministers responsible for Maghreb affairs, a consultative council of 30 delegates from each country, a UMA judicial court, and four specialized ministerial commissions. Chairmanship rotates annually between heads of state. The UMA represents member countries' interests in negotiations with the EU, Arab and African regional organizations, as well as other international organizations. A Maghreb Investment and Foreign Trade Bank, funding joint agricultural and industrial projects, has been established and a customs union created. In May 1999 the follow-up committee convened to formulate a programme to reactivate the Union; a meeting of the council of ministers of foreign affairs was envisaged. Mems: Algeria, Libya, Mauritania, Morocco, Tunisia. Sec.-Gen. MOHAMED AMAMOU (Tunisia).

EDUCATION, ARTS AND SPORT

Afro-Asian Writers' Association: 'Al Ahram' Bldg, Al-Gala'a St, Cairo, Egypt; tel (2) 5747011; fax (2) 5747023; f. 1958. Mems: writers' orgs in 50 countries. Sec.-Gen. LOTFI EL-KHOLY. Publs *Lotus Magazine of Afro-Asian Writings* (quarterly in English, French and Arabic), *Afro-Asian Literature Series* (in English, French and Arabic).

Alliance israélite universelle: 45 rue La Bruyère, 75428 Paris Cedex 09, France; tel. 1-53-32-88-55; fax 1-48-74-51-33; e-mail info@aiu.org; internet www.aiu.org; f. 1860 to work for the emancipation and moral progress of the Jews; maintains 41 schools in the Mediterranean area and Canada; library of 120,000 vols. Mems: 8,000 in 16 countries. Pres. ADY STEG; Dir JEAN-JACQUES WAHL (France). Publs *Cahiers de l'Alliance Israélite Universelle* (3 a year), *The Alliance Review, Les Cahiers du Judaïsme* (quarterly).

Arab Bureau of Education for the Gulf States: POB 3908, Riyadh 11481, Saudi Arabia; tel. (1) 480-0555; fax (1) 480-2839; e-mail abegs@abegs.org; internet www.abegs.org; f. 1975; co-ordinates and promotes co-operation and integration among member countries in the fields of education, culture and science; aims to unify the educational systems of all Gulf Arab states. Specialized organs: Gulf Arab States' Educational Research Center (POB 25566, Safat, Kuwait), Council of Higher Education, Arabian Gulf University (opened in Bahrain in 1982). Mems: Governments of Bahrain, Kuwait, Oman, Qatar, Saudi Arabia, the United Arab Emirates and Yemen. Dir-Gen. Dr ALI M. AT-TOWAGRY. Publs *Risalat Ul-Khaleej al-Arabi* (quarterly), *Arab Gulf Journal of Scientific Research* (2 a year).

Arab Sports Confederation: POB 62997, Riyadh, Saudi Arabia; tel. (1) 482-4927; fax (1) 482-3196; f. 1976 to encourage regional co-operation in sport. Mems: 20 national Olympic Committees, 38 Arab sports federations. Pres. Prince FAISAL BIN FAHD BIN ABD AL-AZIZ; Sec.-Gen. OTHMAN M. AS-SAAD.

Association of African Sports Confederations: POB 1363, Yaoundé, Cameroon; tel. 23-95-80; fax 23-95-30; f. 1983 to promote co-operation among African sports confederations and to promote African sport at the international level. Mems: in 53 countries. Sec.-Gen. Dr AWOTURE ELEYAE.

Association of Arab Historians: POB 4085, Baghdad, Iraq; tel. (1) 443-8868; f. 1974. Mems: historians in 22 countries of the region. Sec.-Gen. Prof. MUSTAFA AN-NAJJAR. Publ. *Arab Historian.*

Association of Arab Universities: POB 401, Jubeyha, Amman, Jordan; tel. (6) 5345131; fax (6) 5332994; e-mail sec-gen@aaru.edu

.jo; internet www.aaru.edu.jo; f. 1964; a scientific conference is held every 3 years (2000: Beirut, Lebanon); council meetings held annually. Mems: 146 universities and institutes in 19 countries. Sec.-Gen. Dr MARWAN RASIM KAMAL. Publs *Journal of AARU* (2 a year), *Directory of Arab Universities, Directory of Teaching Staff of Arab Universities.*

European Union of Arabic and Islamic Scholars (Union européenne d'Arabisants et d'Islamisants—UEAI): c/o Dipartimento di studi e ricerche su Africa e Paesi Arabi, Istituto Universitario Orientale, Palazzo Corigliano, Piazza San Domenico Maggiore 12, 80134 Naples, Italy; tel. (081) 5517840; fax (081) 5515386; f. 1964 to organize Congresses of Arabic and Islamic Studies; holds congresses every two years. Mems: about 300 in 28 countries. Sec.-Gen. Prof. CARMELA BAFFIONI (Italy).

International Institute for Adult Education Methods: POB 19395/6194, 5th Floor, Golfam St, 19156 Tehran, Iran; tel. (21) 2220313; f. 1968 by UNESCO and the Government of Iran; collects, analyzes and distributes information concerning the methods, media and techniques used in adult education programmes; maintains documentation service and library on adult education; arranges seminars. Dir Dr MOHAMMAD REZA HAMIDIZADE. Publs *Selection of Adult Education Issues* (monthly), *Adult Education and Development* (quarterly), *New Library Holdings* (quarterly).

Islamic Academy of Sciences: POB 830036 Zahran, Amman, Jordan; tel. (6) 5522104; fax (6) 5511803; e-mail ias@go.com.jo; internet www.ias-worldwide.org; f. 1986; holds Annual Conference (2002: Doha, Qatar). Dir-Gen. MONEEF R. AL-ZOU'BI. Publ. *IAS Newsletter.*

FINANCE

Accounting and Auditing Organization for Islamic Financial Institutions—AAOIFI: POB 1176, Manama, Bahrain; tel. 244496; fax 250194; e-mail aaoifi@batelco.com.bh; internet aaoifi.com; f. 1990; aims to develop accounting, auditing and banking practices and to harmonize standards among member institutions. Sec.-Gen. Prof. RIFAAT ABDEL KARIM.

Arab Society of Certified Accountants: POB 96, Imbaba 12411, 51 el-Hegaz St, Mohandisseen, Cairo, Egypt; tel. (2) 3479952; fax (2) 3445729; e-mail info@ascasociety.org; internet www.ascasociety.org; f. 1984 as a professional body to supervise qualifications for Arab accountants and to maintain standards; organizes Arab International Accounting Conference (1998: Beirut, Lebanon). Mems in 21 countries. Sec.-Gen. SAMAR AL-LABBAD. Publs *Arab Certified Accountant* (monthly), *ASCA Information Guide, International Accountancy Standards, International Audit Standards, Abu-Ghazaleh Dictionary of Accountancy.*

Union of Arab Banks (UAB): POB 2416, Beirut, Lebanon; tel. (1) 863460; fax (1) 867925; e-mail uab@cyberianet; f. 1972; aims to foster co-operation between Arab banks and to increase their efficiency; prepares feasibility studies for projects; 2001 Arab Banking Conference: Beirut, Lebanon.

Union of Arab Stock Exchanges and Securities Commissions: POB 22235, Safat 13083, Kuwait; tel. 2412991; fax 2420778; f. 1982 to develop capital markets in the Arab world; Sec.-Gen. SAFIQ AR-RUKEIBI (Kuwait).

GOVERNMENT AND POLITICS

Afro-Asian Peoples' Solidarity Organization—AAPSO: 89 Abdel Aziz al-Saoud St, POB 11559-61 Manial el-Roda, Cairo, Egypt; tel. (2) 3636081; fax (2) 3637361; e-mail aapso@idsc.gov.eg; f. 1958 as the Organization for Afro-Asian Peoples' Solidarity; acts as a permanent liaison body between the peoples of Africa and Asia and aims to ensure their sovereignty, peace, disarmament and their economic, social and cultural development. Mems: 82 national committees and 10 European associates. Pres. Dr MOURAD GHALEB; Sec.-Gen. NOURI ABD AR-RAZZAK HUSSEIN (Iraq). Publs *Solidarity Bulletin, Human Rights Newsletter* (monthly), *Development and Socio-Economic Progress* (quarterly).

Arab Inter-Parliamentary Union: POB 4130, Damascus, Syria; tel. (11) 447654; fax (11) 234336; f. 1974; aims to strengthen dialogue between Arab parliamentarians to co-ordinate activities and representation at international forums. Mems from 15 countries. Chair. Dr MUHAMMAD JALAL ESSAID.

Parliamentary Association for Euro-Arab Co-operation: 10 ave de la Renaissance, 1000 Brussels, Belgium; tel. (2) 231-13-00; fax (2) 231-06-46; e-mail paeac@medea.be; internet www.medea.be; f. 1974 as an association of more than 650 parliamentarians of all parties from the national parliaments of 18 of the Council of Europe countries and from the European Parliament, to promote friendship and co-operation between Europe and the Arab world; Executive Committee (which has at least two members per country) holds annual meeting with Arab Inter-Parliamentary Union: the Euro-Arab Parliamentary Dialogue; works for the progress of the Euro-Arab Dialogue and a settlement in the Middle East which takes into account the national rights of the Palestinian people. Sec.-Gen. POL MARCK (Belgium).

INDUSTRIAL RELATIONS

Arab Federation of Petroleum, Mining and Chemicals Workers: POB 5339, Tripoli, Libya; tel. (21) 444-7597; fax (21) 444-9139; f. 1961 to establish proper industrial relations policies and procedures for the guidance of all affiliated unions; promotes establishment of trade unions in the relevant industries in countries where they do not exist. Publs *Arab Petroleum* (monthly, in English, Arabic and French editions), specialized publications and statistics.

International Confederation of Arab Trade Unions—ICATU: POB 3225, Samat at-Tahir, Damascus, Syria; tel. (11) 459544; fax (11) 420323; f. 1956. Holds General Congress every four years. Mems: trade unions in 18 countries, and 13 affiliate international federations. Sec.-Gen. HASSAN JEMAM. Publ. *Al-Amal al-Arab* (monthly).

LAW

Arab Organization for Human Rights: 91 al-Marghany St, Heliopolis, Cairo, Egypt; tel. (2) 4181396; fax (2) 4185346; e-mail aohr@link.com.eg; internet www.aohr.org; f. 1983 to defend fundamental freedoms of citizens of the Arab states; assists political prisoners and their families; has consultative status with UN Economic and Social Council. General Assembly convened every three years. Mems in 14 countries. Sec.-Gen. MOHAMMED FAYEK. Publs *Newsletter* (monthly), *Annual Report, The State of Human Rights in the Arab World, Nadwat Fikria* (series).

Asian-African Legal Consultative Organization—AALCO: 66 Vasant Marg, Vasant Vihar, New Delhi 110024, India; tel. (11) 6152251; fax (11) 6152041; e-mail aalco@ysnl.com; internet www.aalco.org; f. 1956 to consider legal problems referred to it by member countries and to serve as a forum for Asian-African co-operation in international law and economic relations; provides background material for conferences, prepares standard/model contract forms suited to the needs of the region; promotes arbitration as a means of settling international commercial disputes; trains officers of member states. Mems: 45 countries. Pres. Dr P. S. RAO (India); Sec.-Gen. Dr WAFIK Z. KAMIL (Egypt).

International Association of Jewish Lawyers and Jurists: 10 Daniel Frish St, Tel Aviv 64731, Israel; tel. (3) 691-0673; fax (3) 695-3855; e-mail iajlj@goldmail.net.il; internet www.intjewishlawyers.org; f. 1969; promotes human rights and the rule of law; studies issues of interest to Jewish communities within international and domestic law; international congress held every 3 years. Pres. Judge HADASSA BEN-ITTO; Exec. Dir. OPHRA KIDRON. Publ. *Justice* (quarterly).

Union of Arab Jurists: POB 6026, al-Mansour, Baghdad, Iraq; tel. (1) 5372371; fax (1) 53723693; f. 1975 to safeguard the Arab legislative and judicial heritage; to facilitate contacts between Arab lawyers; to encourage the study of Islamic jurisprudence; and to defend human rights. Mems: national jurists associations in 15 countries. Sec.-Gen. Dr SHIBIB LAZIM AL-MALIKI. Publs *Al-Hukuki al-Arabi* (Arab Jurist), documents and studies.

MEDICINE AND HEALTH

International Federation of Red Cross and Red Crescent Societies: 17 Chemin des Crêts, Petit-Saconnex, CP 372, 1211 Geneva 19, Switzerland; tel. (22) 7304222; fax (22) 7330395; e-mail secretariat@ifrc.org; internet www.ifrc.org; f. 1919 to prevent and alleviate human suffering and to promote humanitarian activities by national Red Cross and Red Crescent societies; conducts relief operations for refugees and victims of disasters, co-ordinates relief supplies and assists in disaster prevention; Pres. JUAN MANUEL SUÁREZ DEL TORO RIVERO (Spain); Sec.-Gen. DIDIER CHERPITEL (France). Publs *Annual Report, Red Cross Red Crescent* (quarterly), *Weekly News, World Disasters Report, Emergency Appeal.*

Middle East Neurosurgical Society: Neurosurgical Department, American University Medical Centre, POB 113-6044, Beirut, Lebanon; tel. (1) 353486; fax (1) 342517; e-mail gfhaddad@aub.edn.lb; f. 1958 to promote clinical advances and scientific research and to spread knowledge of neurosurgery and related fields among all members of the medical profession in the Middle East; Scientific Congress held every two years (2002: Syria). Mems in 17 countries. Pres. Dr GAMAL AZAB; Sec. Dr SHERIF IZZAT.

POST AND TELECOMMUNICATIONS

Arab Permanent Postal Commission: c/o Arab League Bldg, Tahrir Sq., Cairo, Egypt; tel. (2) 5750511; fax (2) 5775626; f. 1952; aims to establish stricter postal relations between the Arab countries than those laid down by the Universal Postal Union, and to pursue the development and modernization of postal services in member countries. Publs *APU Bulletin* (monthly), *APU Review* (quarterly), *APU News* (annually).

Arab Telecommunications Union: POB 2397, Baghdad, Iraq; tel. (1) 555-0642; f. 1953 to co-ordinate and develop telecommunications between member countries; to exchange technical aid and encourage research; promotes establishment of new cable telecommunications networks in the region. Sec.-Gen. ABDUL JAFFAR HASSAN KHALAF IBRAHIM AL-ANI. Publs *Arab Telecommunications Union Journal* (2 a year), *Economic and Technical Studies.*

RELIGION AND WELFARE

Bahá'í International Community: Bahá'í World Centre, POB 155, 31 001 Haifa, Israel; tel. (4) 8358394; fax (4) 8358522; e-mail opi@bwc.org; internet ww.bahai.org; f. 1844 in Persia to promote the unity of mankind and world peace through the teachings of the Bahá'í religion, which include the equality of men and women and the elimination of all forms of prejudice; maintains schools for children and adults throughout the world, operates educational and cultural radio stations in the Americas; there are 32 Bahá'í Publishing Trusts in countries world-wide. Governing body: The Universal House of Justice, consisting of nine members elected by 182 National Spiritual Assemblies. Mems: in 129,949 centres world-wide. The Association for Bahá'í Studies (Ottawa, Canada) has affiliates in 27 countries. Sec.-Gen. ALBERT LINCOLN (USA). Publs *The Bahá'í World* (annually), *La Pensée Bahá'íe* (quarterly), *World Order* (quarterly), *Opinioni Bahá'í* (quarterly), *One Country* (quarterly), *The Journal of Bahá'í Studies* (quarterly), *Herald of the South* (quarterly), *Bahá'í Briefe* (2 a year), *Andalib* (every 2 months).

Middle East Council of Churches: rue Makhoul, DEEB bldg, POB 5376, Beirut, Lebanon; tel. and fax (1) 344894; e-mail mecc@cyberia.net.lb; internet www.mecchurches.org; f. 1974. Mems: 28 churches in 12 countries. Pres Pope SHENOUDAH III, Patriarch PETROS VII, Rev. Dr SELIM SAHYOUNI, Archbishop KYRILLOS BUSTROS; Gen. Sec. Rev. Dr RIAD JARJOUR. Publs *MECC News Report* (monthly), *Al Montada News Bulletin* (quarterly, in Arabic), *Courrier oecuménique du moyen-Orient* (quarterly), *MECC Perspectives* (3 a year).

Muslim World League (Rabita al-Alam al-Islami): POB 537, Mecca, Saudi Arabia; tel. (2) 5422733; fax (2) 5436619; e-mail mwlhq@aol.com; internet www.arab.net/mwl; London office: 46 Goodge St, London W1, United Kingdom; tel. (20) 7636-7568; f. 1962; aims to advance Islamic unity and solidarity, and to promote world peace and respect for human rights; provides financial assistance for Islamic education, medical care and relief work; has 30 offices throughout the world. Sec.-Gen. Dr ABDULLAH BIN ABDULMOSHIN AL-TURKI. Publs *Majalla al-Rabita* (monthly, Arabic), *Akhbar al-Alam al Islami* (weekly, Arabic), *Muslim World League Journal* (monthly, English), *Dawat al-Haq* (monthly, Arabic).

World Jewish Congress (Congrès Juif Mondial): 501 Madison Ave, New York, NY 10022, USA; tel. (212) 755-5770; fax (212) 755-5883; internet www.wcj.org.il; f. 1936 as a voluntary asscn of representative Jewish communities and organizations throughout the world; aims to foster the unity of the Jewish people and to ensure the continuity and development of its religious, spiritual, cultural and social heritage. Leads the campaign for financial compensation to be paid to victims of the Nazi holocaust. Mems: Jewish communities in 84 countries. Pres. EDGAR M. BRONFMAN; Sec.-Gen. ISRAEL SINGER. Publs *WJC Report* (New York), *Gesher* (Hebrew quarterly), *Batfutstot* (Jerusalem), *Boletín Informativo OJI* (every 2 weeks, Buenos Aires).

SCIENCE AND TECHNOLOGY

African Organization of Cartography and Remote Sensing: 5 route de Bedjarah, BP 102, 16040 Hussein Dey, Algeria; tel. (21) 23-33-39; fax (21) 77-79-34; e-mail ooct@wissal.dz; f. 1988 by amalgamation of African Association of Cartography and African Council for Remote Sensing; aims to encourage the development of cartography and of remote-sensing by satellites; organizes confs and other meetings, promotes establishment of training insts; maintains regional training centres in Burkina Faso, Kenya, Nigeria and Tunisia. Mems: national cartographic institutions of 24 countries. Sec.-Gen. UNIS MUFTAH.

Federation of Arab Engineers: POB 6117, Baghdad, Iraq; tel. (1) 7762366; fax (1) 2434469; f. 1963 as Arab Engineering Union; a regional body of the World Federation of Engineering Organizations; co-operates with the Arab League, UNESCO and the other regional engineering federations. Holds a Pan-Arab conference on engineering studies every three years and annual symposia and seminars in different Arab countries. Mems: engineering asscns in 15 Arab countries; Sec.-Gen. GHASSAN A. RADHWAN.

Federation of Arab Scientific Research Councils: POB 13027, Al Karkh/Karadat Mariam, Baghdad, Iraq; tel. (1) 888-1709; fax (1) 886-6346; f. 1976 to encourage co-operation in scientific research, promote the establishment of new institutions and plan joint regional research projects. Mems: national science bodies of 15 countries. Sec.-Gen. Prof. TAHA AN-NUEIMI. Publs *Journal of Computer Research, Journal of Environment and Sustained Development,*

Journal of Biotechnology, reports from conferences, seminars and workshops.

SOCIAL SCIENCES AND SOCIAL WELFARE

Arab Towns Organization—ATO: POB 68160, Kaifan 71962, Kuwait; tel. 4849705; fax 4849322; e-mail ato@ato.net; internet www.ato.net; f. 1967; aims to promote co-operation and the exchange of expertise with regard to urban administration; works to improve the standard of municipal services and utilities in Arab towns and to preserve the character and heritage of Arab towns. Administers an Institute for Urban Development (AUDI), based in Riyadh, Saudi Arabia, which provides training and research for municipal officers; the Arab Towns Development Fund, to help member towns implement projects; and the ATO Award, to encourage the preservation of Arab architecture. Mems: 413 towns. Dir-Gen. MUHAMMAD ABD AL-HAMID AS-SAQR; Sec.-Gen. ABD AL-AZIZ Y. AL-ADSANI. Publ. *Al-Madinah Al-Arabiyah* (every 2 months).

Centre for Social Science Research and Documentation for the Arab Region: Zamalek PO, Cairo, Egypt; tel. (2) 3472099; fax (2) 3470019; f. 1978 to encourage co-operation between regional research bodies; Mems: Egypt, Iraq, Kuwait, Saudi Arabia, Tunisia; Dir-Gen. Dr AHMAD M. KHALIFA. Publs *Newsletter* (3 a year), *Arab Comnet* (3 a year).

International Planned Parenthood Federation: Regional Office for the Arab World, 2 pl. Virgile, Notre Dame 1082, Tunis, Tunisia; tel. 71787743; fax 71789934; aims to advance education in family planning, to promote the use of family planning services through local voluntary assns, and to organize the training of service delivery providers. Mem. assns in Algeria, Bahrain, Egypt, Iraq, Jordan, Lebanon, Mauritania, Morocco, Palestine, Somalia, Sudan, Syria, Tunisia, Yemen. Regional Dir Dr MOHAMED BOUZIDI.

International Union for Oriental and Asian Studies: Közraktar u. 12A 11/2, 1093 Budapest, Hungary; f. 1951 by the 22nd International Congress of Orientalists under the auspices of UNESCO, to promote contacts between orientalists throughout the world, and to organize congresses, research and publications. Mems: in 24 countries. Sec.-Gen. Prof. GEORG HAZAL. Publs *Philologiae Turcicae Fundamenta, Materalien zum Sumerischen Lexikon, Sanskrit Dictionary, Corpus Inscriptionum Iranicarum, Linguistic Atlas of Iran, Matériels des parlers iraniens, Turcology Annual, Bibliographieegyptologique.*

Third World Forum: 39 Dokki St, POB 43, Orman Giza, Cairo, Egypt; tel. (2) 7488092; fax (2) 7480668; e-mail 20sabry2@gega.net; internet www.egypt2020.org; f. 1973 to link social scientists and others from the developing countries, to discuss alternative development policies and encourage research; currently undertaking Egypt 2020 research project; maintains regional offices in Egypt, Mexico, Senegal and Sri Lanka. Mems: individuals in more than 50 countries. Chair. ISMAIL-SABRI ABDALLA. Publ. *TWF Newsletter.*

TRADE AND INDUSTRY

Arab Iron and Steel Union—AISU: BP 4, route de Chéraga, Algiers, Algeria; (21) 371580; fax (21) 371975; e-mail relex@solbar ab.com; internet www.solbarab.com; f. 1972 to develop commercial and technical aspects of Arab steel production by helping member associations to commercialize their production in Arab markets, guaranteeing them high quality materials and intermediary products, informing them of recent developments in the industry and organizing training sessions; also arranges two annual symposia. Mems: 80 companies in 15 Arab countries. Gen.-Sec. MUHAMMAD LAID LACHGAR. Publs *AISU Annual Statistical Bulletin, Arab Steel Review* (monthly), *News Steel World* (2 a month), *Information Bulletin* (2 a month).

General Union of Chambers of Commerce, Industry and Agriculture for Arab Countries—GUCCIAAC: POB 11-2837, Beirut, Lebanon; tel. (1) 814269; fax (1) 862841; e-mail gucciaac@destina tion.com.lb; internet www.gucciaac.org.lb; f. 1951 to enhance Arab economic development, integration and security through the co-ordination of industrial, agricultural and trade policies and legislation. Mems: chambers of commerce, industry and agriculture in 22 countries. Sec. Gen. Dr ELIAS GHANTOUS. Publs *Al-Omran al-Arabi* (every 2 months), *Arab Economic Report* (in Arabic and English), economic papers, proceedings of conferences and seminars.

Gulf Organization for Industrial Consulting—GOIC: POB 5114, Doha, Qatar; tel. 4858888; fax 4831465; e-mail goic@ goic.org.qa; internet www.goic.org.qa; f. 1976 by the Gulf Arab states to encourage industrial co-ordination among Gulf Arab states, to pool industrial expertise and to encourage joint regional projects; undertakes feasibility studies, market diagnosis, assistance in policy-making, legal consultancies, project promotion, promotion of small and medium industrial investment profiles and technical training; maintains industrial data bank. Mems: mem. states of the GCC (q.v.). Sec.-Gen. MOHAMED BIN ALI BIN ABDULLAH AL-MUSALLAM. Publs *GOIC Monthly Bulletin* (in Arabic), *Al Ta' awon al-Sina'e* (quarterly, in Arabic and English), *Annual Report*.

TRANSPORT

Arab Air Carriers' Organization—AACO: POB 13-5468, Beirut, Lebanon; tel. (1) 861297; fax (1) 863168; e-mail info@aaco.org; internet www.aaco.org; f. 1965 to promote co-operation in the activities of Arab airline companies. Mems: 20 Arab air carriers. Pres. AKBAR AL-BAKER (Qatar); Sec.-Gen. ABD AL-WAHAB TEFFAHA. Publs bulletins, reports and research documents on aviation in the Arab world.

CALENDARS, TIME RECKONING, AND WEIGHTS AND MEASURES

The Islamic Calendar

The Islamic era dates from 16 July 622, which was the beginning of the Arab year in which the *Hijra* ('flight' or migration) of the Prophet Muhammad (the founder of Islam), from Mecca to Medina (in modern Saudi Arabia), took place. The Islamic or *Hijri* Calendar is lunar, each year having 354 or 355 days, the extra day being intercalated 11 times every 30 years. Accordingly, the beginning of the *Hijri* year occurs earlier in the Gregorian Calendar by a few days each year. Dates are reckoned in terms of the *anno Hegirae* (AH) or year of the Hegira (*Hijra*). The Islamic year AH 1423 began on 15 March 2002.

The year is divided into the following months:

1. Muharram	30 days	7. Rajab	30 days
2. Safar	29 „	8. Shaaban	29 „
3. Rabia I	30 „	9. Ramadan	30 „
4. Rabia II	29 „	10. Shawwal	29 „
5. Jumada I	30 „	11. Dhu'l-Qa'da	30 „
6. Jumada II	29 „	12. Dhu'l-Hijja	29 or 30 days

The *Hijri* Calendar is used for religious purposes throughout the Islamic world and is the official calendar in Saudi Arabia. In most Arab countries it is used in conjunction with the Gregorian Calendar for official purposes, but in Turkey and Egypt the Gregorian Calendar has replaced it.

PRINCIPAL ISLAMIC FESTIVALS

New Year: 1st Muharram. The first 10 days of the year are regarded as holy, especially the 10th.

Ashoura: 10th Muharram. Celebrates the first meeting of Adam and Eve after leaving Paradise, also the ending of the Flood and the death of Husain, grandson of the Prophet Muhammad. The feast is celebrated with fairs and processions.

Mouloud or **Yum an-Nabi** (Birth of Muhammad): 12th Rabia I.

Leilat al-Meiraj (Ascension of Muhammad): 27th Rajab.

Ramadan (Month of Fasting).

Id al-Fitr or **Id as-Saghir** or **Küçük Bayram** (The Small Feast): Three days beginning 1st Shawwal. This celebration follows the constraint of the Ramadan fast.

Id al-Adha or **Id al-Kabir** or **Büyük Bayram** (The Great Feast, Feast of the Sacrifice): Four days beginning on 10th Dhu'l-Hijja. The principal Islamic festival, commemorating Abraham's sacrifice and coinciding with the pilgrimage to Mecca. Celebrated by the sacrifice of a sheep, by feasting and by donations to the poor.

Islamic Year	1422		1423		1424	
New Year	26 March	2001	15 March	2002	5 March	2003
Ashoura	4 April	2001	24 March	2002	14 March	2003
Mouloud	4 June	2001	24 May	2002	14 May	2003
Leilat al-Meiraj. . . .	15 Oct.	2001	4 Oct.	2002	24 Sept.	2003
Ramadan begins . . .	17 Nov.	2001	6 Nov.	2002	27 Oct.	2003
Id al-Fitr	17 Dec.	2001	6 Dec.	2002	26 Nov.	2003
Id al-Adha	23 Feb.	2002	12 Feb.	2003	2 Feb.	2004

Note: Local determinations may vary by one day from those given here.

The Iranian Calendar

The Iranian Calendar, introduced in 1925, was based on the Islamic Calendar, adapted to the solar year. Iranian New Year (*Now Ruz*) occurs at the vernal equinox, which usually falls on 21 March in the Gregorian Calendar. In Iran it was decided to base the calendar on the coronation of Cyrus the Great, in place of the *Hijra*, from 1976, and the year beginning 21 March 1976 became 2535. During 1978, however, it was decided to revert to the former system of dating. The year 1381 began on 21 March 2002.

The Iranian year is divided into the following months:

1. Favardine	31 days	7. Mehr	30 days
2. Ordibehecht	31 „	8. Aban	30 „
3. Khordad	31 „	9. Azar	30 „
4. Tir	31 „	10. Dey	30 „
5. Mordad	31 „	11. Bahman	30 „
6. Chariver	31 „	12. Esfand	29 or 30 days

The Iranian Calendar is used for all purposes in Iran, except the determining of Islamic religious festivals, for which the lunar Islamic Calendar is used.

The Hebrew Calendar

The Hebrew Calendar is solar with respect to the year but lunar with respect to the months. The normal year has 353–355 days in 12 lunar months, but seven times in each 19 years an extra month of 30 days (*Adar II*) is intercalated after the normal month of Adar to adjust the calendar to the solar year. New Year (*Rosh Hashanah*) usually falls in September of the Gregorian calendar, but the day varies considerably. The year 5763 began on 7 September 2002.

The months are as follows:

1. Tishri	30 days	7. Nisan	30 days
2. Marcheshvan	29 or 30 days	8. Iyyar	29 „
3. Kislev	29 or 30 „	9. Sivan	30 „
4. Tebeth	29 days	10. Tammuz	29 „
5. Shebat	30 „	11. Ab	30 „
6. Adar	29 „	12. Ellul	29 „
(Adar II)	30 „		

The Hebrew Calendar is used to determine the dates of Jewish religious festivals only. The civil year begins with the month Tishri, while the ecclesiastical year commences on the first day of Nisan.

Standard Time

The table shows zones of standard time, relative to Greenwich Mean Time (GMT). Many of the individual countries adopt daylight saving time at certain times of year.

Traditional Arabic time is still widely used by the local population in Saudi Arabia except in most of the Eastern Province. This system is based on the local time of sunset, when timepieces are all set to 12.

GMT	One hour ahead	Two hours ahead	Three hours ahead	Three and one-half hours ahead	Four hours ahead
Morocco	Algeria	Cyprus	Bahrain	Iran	Oman
	Libya	Egypt	Iraq		United Arab
	Spanish North	Israel	Kuwait		Emirates
	Africa	Jordan	Qatar		
	Tunisia	Lebanon	Saudi Arabia		
		Syria	Yemen		
		Turkey			

Weights and Measures

Principal weights and units of measurement in common use as alternatives to the metric and imperial systems.

WEIGHT

Unit	Country	Metric equivalent	Imperial equivalent
Hogga	Iraq	1.27 kg	2.8 lb
Maund	Yemen	37.29 kg	82.28 lb
	Saudi Arabia		
Qintar (Kantar) or Buhar	Cyprus	228.614 kg	504 lb
	Egypt	44.928 kg	99.05 lb
Ratl or Rotl	Saudi Arabia	0.449 kg	0.99 lb
	Egypt		
Uqqa or Oke	Cyprus	1.27 kg	2.8 lb
	Egypt	1.245 kg	2.751 lb
Yeni Okka	Turkey	1 kg	2.205 lb

LENGTH

Unit	Country	Metric equivalent	Imperial equivalent
Busa	Saudi Arabia	2.54 cm	1 in
Dirraa, Dra or Pic	Cyprus	60.96 cm	2 ft

CAPACITY

Unit	Country	Metric equivalent	Imperial equivalent
Ardabb or Ardeb	Saudi Arabia	198.024 litres	45.36 gallons
	Egypt		
Kadah	Egypt	2.063 litres	3.63 pints
	Cyprus	36.368 litres	1 pint
Keila	Egypt	16.502 litres	3.63 gallons

AREA

Unit	Country	Metric equivalent	Imperial equivalent
Donum or Dunum	Cyprus	1,335.8 sq m	0.33 acre
	Iraq	2,500 sq m	0.62 acre
	Israel	1,000 sq m	0.2471 acre
	Jordan		
	Syria	919.04 sq m	0.2272 acre
	Turkey		
Feddan	Saudi Arabia	4,201 sq m	1.038 acres
	Egypt		
Yeni Donum	Turkey	10,000 sq m (1 ha)	2.471 acres

Metric to Imperial Conversions

Metric units	Imperial units	To convert metric into imperial units multiply by:	To convert imperial into metric units multiply by:
Weight:			
Gram	Ounce (Avoirdupois)	0.035274	28.3495
Kilogram (kg)	Pound (lb)	2.204622	0.453592
Metric ton ('000 kg)	Short ton (2,000 lb)	1.102311	0.907185
	Long ton (2,240 lb)	0.984207	1.016047
	(The short ton is in general use in the USA, while the long ton is normally used in the United Kingdom and the Commonwealth.)		
Length			
Centimetre (cm)	Inch (in)	0.3937008	2.54
Metre (m)	Yard (=3 feet)	1.09361	0.9144
Kilometre (km)	Mile	0.62137	1.609344
Volume			
Cubic metre (cu m)	Cubic foot	35.315	0.0283
	Cubic yard	1.30795	0.764555
Capacity			
Litre	Gallon (=8 pints)	0.219969	4.54609
	Gallon (US)	0.264172	3.78541
Area			
Square metre (sq m)	Square yard	1.19599	0.836127
Hectare (ha)	Acre	2.47105	0.404686
Square kilometre (sq km)	Square mile	0.386102	2.589988

RESEARCH INSTITUTES

ASSOCIATIONS AND INSTITUTES STUDYING THE MIDDLE EAST AND NORTH AFRICA

(See also Regional Organizations—Education, Arts and Sport)

ALGERIA

Institut d'Etudes Arabes: Université d'Alger, 2 rue Didouche Mourad, Algiers.

Institut d'Etudes Orientales: Université d'Alger, 2 rue Didouche Mourad, Algiers; publ. *Annales*.

ARGENTINA

Sección Interdisciplinaria de Estudios de Asia y Africa: Universidad de Buenos Aires, Moreno 350, 1002 Buenos Aires; tel. and fax (11) 43458196; e-mail africayasia@yahoo.com.ar; f. 1982; research and lectures; Dir Prof. MARISA PINEAU; publs *Temas de Africa y Asia* (2 a year).

ARMENIA

Institute of Oriental Studies of the National Academy of Sciences of Armenia: Pr. Marshal Bagramyan 24G, Yerevan 375019; tel. (3741) 583382; e-mail nhovanes@sci.am; f. 1971; Dir N. H. HOVHANNISIAN.

AUSTRALIA AND NEW ZEALAND

Australasian Middle East Studies Association: POB 64, Footscray 3011, Australia; Department of Semitic Studies, University of Sydney, N.S.W. 2006; tel. (2) 6922190; Pres. Dr A. SHBOUL; Past Pres. NEIL TRUSCOTT; publ. *Conference Proceedings*.

Programme in Middle East Studies: University of Western Australia, Nedlands, Western Australia 6009; tel. (8) 93802926; fax (8) 93801016; e-mail rgabby@ecel.uwa.edu.au; f. 1975 to promote, encourage and facilitate teaching, research and the dissemination of information on the Middle East; Dir Prof. R. GABBAY.

AUSTRIA

Afro-Asiatisches Institut in Wien: Türkenstrasse 3, A-1090 Vienna; tel. (1) 3105145; e-mail office@aai-wien.at; internet www.aai-wien.at/aai-wien/; f. 1959 by the Roman Catholic Church in Vienna; seminars, scholarship programmes and other religious and cultural exchange between Africans and Asians in Vienna; Rector KONSTANTIN SPIEGELFELD; Dir Economics Programme GERHARD LANG.

Institut für Orientalistik der Universität Wien: Spitalgasse 2–4, A-1090 Vienna; tel. (1) 427743401; fax (1) 42779434; e-mail orientalistik@univie.ac.at; internet www.univie.ac.at/orientalistik; library of 26,200 vols; Dir Prof. Dr HERMANN HUNGER; publs *Wiener Zeitschrift für die Kunde des Morgenlandes* (annually), *Türkologischer Anzeiger* (annually), *Archiv für Orientforschung* (annually).

AZERBAIJAN

Institute of Oriental Studies: Academy of Sciences, Pr. Husain Javid 31, 370143 Baku; tel. (12) 392351; e-mail shorg@lan.ab.az; f. 1958; Dir GOVKHAR BAKHSHALIYEVA.

BELGIUM

Centre d'Etudes et de Recherches Arabes: Université de l'Etat à Mons, 24 ave Champ de Mars, 7000 Mons; tel. (65) 373615; fax (65) 840631; e-mail prof.h.safar@worldonline.be; f. 1978; library of 2,000 vols; Dir Prof. H. SAFAR.

Centre pour l'Etude des Problèmes du Monde Musulman Contemporain: 44 ave Jeanne, 1050 Brussels; tel. (2) 6423359; f. 1957; Dir A. DESTREE; publs *Correspondance d'Orient-Etudes* and collections *Correspondance d'Orient* and *Le monde musulman contemporain—Initiations*.

Departement Oosterse en Slavische Studies: Faculteit Letteren, Katholieke Universiteit te Leuven, Blijde Inkomststraat 21, 3000 Leuven; tel. (16) 324931; fax (16) 324932; e-mail oriental.studies@arts.kuleuven.ac.be; internet www.kuleuven .ac.be; f. 1936; Pres. Prof. K. VAN LERBERGHE; 80 mems; publs *Orientalia Lovaniensia Analecta, Orientalia Lovaniensia Periodica, Bibliothèque du Muséon* (1929–68), *Orientalia et Biblica Lovaniensia* (1957–68), *Inforient-Reeks*.

Fondation Egyptologique Reine Elisabeth: Parc du Cinquantenaire, 10, 1000 Brussels; tel. (2) 7417364; f. 1923 to encourage Egyptian studies; 480 mems; library of 90,000 vols; Pres. Comte D'ARSCHOT; Dirs M. AL. MARTIN and H. DE MEULENAERE; publs *Chronique d'Egypte, Bibliotheca Aegyptiaca, Papyrologica Bruxellensia, Bibliographie Papyrologique sur fiches, Monumenta Aegyptiaca, Rites égyptiens, Papyri Bruxellenses Graecae, Monographies Reine Elisabeth*.

Nederlands-Vlaams Instituut in Cairo: (see under Egypt).

CUBA

Centro de Estudios de Africa y del Medio Oriente (Centre for African and Middle Eastern Studies): Avda 3ra, No 1805, entre 18 y 20, Miramar, Playa, Havana.

CYPRUS

PLO Research Centre: POB 5614, 16 Artemidos St, Strovolos, Nicosia; tel. (2) 429396; fax (2) 312104; fmrly in Beirut, Lebanon; f. 1965; studies Palestine question; Dir SABRI JIRYIS; publs *Shu'un Filastiniya* (Palestine Affairs, monthly) and various books and pamphlets on aspects of the Palestine problem.

CZECH REPUBLIC

Orientální ústav AV ČR (Oriental Institute AS CR): 182 08 Prague 8, Pod vodárenskou věží 4; tel. (2) 66052492; fax (2) 86581897; e-mail orient@orient.cas.cz; f. 1922; internet www .orient.cas.cz; attached to Czech Academy of Sciences; Dir Dr JIŘÍ PROSECKÝ; publs *Archiv orientální* (quarterly), *Nový Orient* (monthly).

DENMARK

Center for Mellemøst-Studier (Centre for Contemporary Middle East Studies): University of Southern Denmark, Main Campus, Odense University, Campusvej 55, 5230 Odense M; tel. 65502183; fax 65502161; e-mail middle-east@hist.sdu.dk; internet http://middle-east.hum.sdu.dk; f. 1983; national centre for interdisciplinary research in cultures and societies of the contemporary Middle East; 10-member research team; library of 3,000 vols and 90 periodicals; Dir Prof. MARTIN HVIDT; publs *Mellemøst Information* (monthly in Danish), *Information om Indvandrere* (quarterly in Danish) and a monographical series via internet.

Orientalsk Forum (Orientalist Forum): University of Copenhagen, Carsten Niebuhr Institute of Near Eastern Studies, Snorresgade 17–19, 2300 Copenhagen S; tel. 35328900; fax 35328926; e-mail orientalsk@forum.dk; internet www.hum.ku.dk/cni; f. 1987 to undertake the study and further the understanding of the Middle East and North Africa region; 120 mems; Pres. JOHAN HERMANN RUMP; Vice-Pres. JAKOB SKOVGAARD-PETERSEN; publ. *Semiramis* (annual).

Orientalsk Samfund (Orientalist Association): Department of History, Njalsgade 80, 2300 Copenhagen S; tel. 35328296; e-mail littrup@hum.ku.dk; f. 1915 to undertake the study and further the understanding of Oriental cultures and civilizations; 20 mems; Pres. Dr LEIF LITTRUP; Sec. Prof. J. P. ASMUSSEN; publ. *Acta Orientalia* (annually).

EGYPT

Academy of the Arabic Language: 15 Aziz Abaza St, Zamalek, 11211 Cairo; tel. (2) 7355931; fax (2) 7362002; e-mail aal@idsc.net.eg; internet www.arabicacademy.org.eg; f. 1932; Pres. Dr AHMED SHAWKY DHEIF; library of 60,000 vols and periodicals; publs *Review* (2 a year), books on reviving Arabic heritage, council and conference proceedings, biographies of members of Academy, lexicons and directories of scientific and technical terms.

Al-Ahram Centre for Political and Strategic Studies (ACPSS): Al-Ahram Foundation, al-Galaa St, Cairo; tel. and fax (2) 5786037; e-mail acpss@ahram.org.eg; internet www .ahram.org.eg.acpss/; f. 1968; research into international relations, politics and economics; particular emphasis on Arab-Israeli relations; Dir Dr ABDEL MONEM SAID; publs incl. *The Arab Strategic Report* (annual), *Strategic Economic Directions* (annual), *The State of Religion in Egypt Report* (annual), *Strategic Papers* (monthly), *Al-Ahram Strategic File* (monthly), *Israeli Digest* (monthly), *Strategic Readings* (monthly), *Egyptian Affairs* (quarterly), *Iran Digest* (monthly).

American Research Center in Egypt Inc: 2 Midan Qasr ad-Dubarah, Garden City, Cairo; tel. (2) 3548239; fax (2) 3553052; and 30 East 20th St, Suite 401, New York, NY 10003-1310, tel. (212) 5296661; fax (212) 5296856; f. 1948 by American universities to promote research by US and Canadian scholars in all phases of Egyptian civilization, including archaeology, art history, humanities and social sciences; grants and fellowships available; 32 institutional mems and 1,250 individual mems; Pres. JANET JOHNSON; Vice-Pres. CHARLES D. SMITH; Cairo Dir MARK M. EASTON; New York Dir TERENCE WALZ; publs *Journal* (annually), *Newsletter* (quarterly).

Institut Dominicain d'Etudes Orientales: Priory of the Dominican Fathers, 1 Sharia Masna at-Tarabish, BP 18 Abbasiyah, 11381 Cairo; tel. (2) 4825509; fax (2) 6820682; e-mail ideo@ link.com.eg; internet www.ideo-cairo.org; f. 1953; Dir Père REGIS MORELON; publ. *Mélanges de L'Institut Dominicain d'Etudes Orientales* (*MIDEO* — every 18 months).

Institut d'Egypte: 13 Sharia Sheikh Rihane, Cairo; f. 1798; studies literary, artistic and scientific questions relating to Egypt and neighbouring countries; 60 mems, 50 assoc. mems, 50 corresp. mems; library of 160,000 vols; Pres. Dr SULAIMAN HAZIEN; Sec. Gen. P. GHALIOUNGU; publs *Bulletin* (annually), *Mémoires* (irregular).

Institut Français d'Archéologie Orientale: 37 rue Sheikh Ali Youssef, BP 11562, Cairo; tel. (2) 3548248; fax (2) 3544635; e-mail ngrimal@ifao.egnet.net; f. 1880; excavations, research and publications; library of 70,000 vols; Dir Prof. NICOLAS GRIMAL; publs *Bulletin de l'Institut Français d'Archéologie Orientale*, *Annales Islamologiques*, etc.

Institute of Arab Research and Studies: 1 Tolombat St, POB 229, Cairo (Garden City); tel. (2) 3551648; fax (2) 3562543; f. 1953; research and studies into contemporary Arab affairs; international relations; library service; affiliated to the Arab League Educational, Cultural and Scientific Organization—ALECSO; Dir Prof. AHMAD YOUSUF AHMAD; publ. *Bulletin of Arab Research and Studies* (annual).

Middle East Research Centre: el-Khalifa el-Mahmoun St, Ain Shams University; tel. (2) 821117; Dir Prof. Dr MUHAMMAD REDA EL-EDET.

National Centre for Middle East Studies: 1 Kasr el-Nile St, Bab el-Louk, POB 18, 11513 Cairo; tel. (2) 770041; fax (2) 770063; f. 1989; research into peace process, arms control and conflict resolutions; Dir R. AHMAD ISMAIL FAKHR; publ. *Middle East Papers* (3 per year).

Nederlands-Vlaams Instituut in Cairo (NVIC) (Netherlands-Flemish Institute in Cairo): 1 Dr Mahmoud Azmi St, POB 50, 11211 Zamalek, Cairo; tel. (2) 7382522; fax (2) 7382523; e-mail nvic@rite.com; internet www.leidenuniv.nl; f. 1971; fmrly Netherlands Institute for Archaeology and Arabic Studies in Cairo; Dir Dr JOHANNES DEN HEIJER; library and publs in the field of Arabic Studies, Egyptology, archaeology and Coptology.

Société Archéologique d'Alexandrie: POB 815, 6 Mahmoud Mokhtar St, 21111 Alexandria; tel. and fax (3) 4820650; f. 1893; 248 mems; Pres. A. M. SADEK; Vice-Pres. YOUSSEF EL-GHERIANI; Treas. K. EL-ADM; publs *Bulletins, Mémoires, Monuments de l'Egypte Gréco-Romaine, Cahiers, Publications Spéciales, Archaeological and Historical Studies.*

Société Egyptienne d'Economie Politique, de Statistique et de Législation: BP 732, 16 ave Ramses, Cairo; f. 1909; 1,550 mems; 3,018 mems; library of 18,259 vols; Pres. Dr ATIF SIDKY.

Sec.-Gen. Dr MAHMOUD HAFEZ GHANEM; Tech. Secs Dr FATHI EL-MASSAFAWI and Dr SAKR AHMAD SAKR; publ. *Revue* (quarterly in Arabic, French and English).

Society for Coptic Archaeology: 222 ave Ramses, Cairo; tel. (2) 4824252; f. 1934; 360 mems; library of 15,000 vols; Pres. WASSIF BOUTROS GHALI; Sec.-Gen. Dr A. KHATER; Treas. AMIN F. ABD EN-NOUR; publs *Bulletin* (annually), *Fouilles, Bibliothèque d'Art et d'Archéologie, Textes et Documents,* etc.

FINLAND

Suomen Itämainen Seura (Finnish Oriental Society): c/o Department of Asian and African Studies, Unioninkatu 38B, POB 59, 00014 University of Helsinki; fax (0) 19122094; e-mail kaj.ohrnberg.helsinki.fi; f. 1917; 187 mems; Pres. Prof. TAPANI HARVIAINEN; Sec. Phil. lic. KAJ ÖHRNBERG; publ. *Studia Orientalia.*

FRANCE

Centre Interdisciplinaire d'Etudes et de Recherches sur les Relations Internationales au Moyen-Orient (Centre of Interdisciplinary Studies and Research on International Relations in the Middle East): Université de Rennes II Haute Bretagne, 6 ave Gaston Berger, 35043 Rennes Cedex; tel. 2-99-33-52-52.

Fondation Nationale des Sciences Politiques: 27 rue Saint-Guillaume, 75337 Paris Cedex 07; tel. 1-45-49-50-50; fax 1-44-10-84-50; f. 1945; Pres. RENÉ RÉMOND; Administrator R. DESCOINGS; Arab world section has research team of 5 mems; publs include *Maghreb-Machrek* (quarterly).

Institut d'Etudes Arabes et Islamiques: Université de la Sorbonne Nouvelle (Paris III), 13 rue de Santeuil, 75231 Paris Cedex 05; tel. 1-45-87-41-39; Dir JEAN-PATRICK GUILLAUME.

Institut d'Etudes Iraniennes: Université de la Sorbonne Nouvelle (Paris III), 13 rue Santeuil, 75231 Paris Cedex 05; tel. (1) 45874069; fax (1) 45874170; e-mail iran@ivry.cmrs.fr; f. 1947; Dir YANN RICHARD; publs *Travaux, Travaux et Mémoires* (series), *Studia Iranica* (journal), *Abstracta Iranica* (annual bibliography).

Institut d'Etudes Sémitiques: Institut d'Etudes Sémitiques, Collège de France, 52 rue du Cardinal Lemoine, 75231 Paris Cedex 05; tel. (1) 44271051; fax (1) 44271603; e-mail etudes .semitiques@college-de-france.fr; f. 1930; Pres. J. TEIXIDOR: publ. *Semitica.*

Institut du Monde Arabe: 1 rue des Fossés Saint-Bernard, 75236 Paris Cedex 05; tel. 1-40-51-38-38; fax 1-43-54-76-45; e-mail scharif@imarabe.org; internet www.imarabe.org/; f. 1980; Pres. CAMILLE CABANA.

Institut de Recherches et d'Etudes sur le Monde Arabe et Musulman (Institute of Research and Studies on the Arab and Muslim World): Université d'Aix-Marseille I et III, Maison Méditerranéenne des Sciences de l'Homme, 5 rue du Château de l'Horloge, BP 647, 13094 Aix-en-Provence Cedex 2; tel. 4-42-23-85-00; fax 4-42-23-85-01; e-mail secretariat .iremam@mmshuniv_aix.fr.

Institut National des Langues et Civilisations Orientales: 2 rue de Lille, 75343 Paris Cedex 07; tel. 1-49-26-42-00; fax 1-49-26-42-99; internet www.inalco.fr; f. 1795; faculties of languages and civilizations of West Asia and Africa; the Far East, India and Oceania; Eastern Europe; North and Central America; library of 430,000 vols and 7,000 periodicals; c. 11,800 students, 300 teachers and lecturers; Pres. GILLES DELOUCHE; Vice-Pres. CLAUDE ALLIBERT; Sec. Gen. JOSETTE LE CALVEZ; High International Studies (DHEI), Department of International Business (CPEI), Automatic Languages Treatment (TAL), Multilingual Engineering (IM); publs *Livret de l'Etudiant* (annually), various Oriental studies and periodicals.

Institut de Papyrologie: Université de Paris-Sorbonne, 1 rue Victor-Cousin, 75005 Paris; tel. 1-40-46-26-45; Dir ALAIN BLANCHARD.

Société Asiatique: 3 rue Mazarine, 75006 Paris; tel. and fax 1-44-41-43-14; f. 1822; 800 mems; library of 100,000 vols; Pres. DANIEL GIMARET; Vice-Pres JEAN-MARIE MAHÉ, PIERRE FILLIOZAT; Secs J. L. BACQUE-GRAMMONT, PIERRE BORDREUIL, MARIE BOSCALS DE RÉALS; publs *Journal Asiatique* (2 a year), *Cahiers de la Société Asiatique.*

GEORGIA

Institute of Oriental Studies of the Academy of Sciences of Georgia: Ul. acad. G. Tsereteli 3, 380062 Tbilisi; tel. (32) 233885; fax (32) 233008; e-mail orientge@hotmail.com; f. 1960; researches languages, history and culture of Near, Middle and Far East; Dir Prof. T. V. GAMKRELIDZE.

GERMANY

Deutsche Arbeitsgemeinschaft Vorderer Orient (DAVO): Centre for Research on the Arab World (CERAW), Institute of Geography, University of Mainz, 55099 Mainz; tel. (6131) 3922701; fax (6131) 3924736; e-mail davo@geo .uni-mainz.de; internet www.davo-online.de; f. 1993; interdisciplinary association of more than 650 scholars, students and others interested in contemporary research on the Middle East and North Africa; Pres. Prof. Dr GÜNTER MEYER.

Deutsche Morgenländische Gesellschaft: 69120 Heidelberg, Im Neuenheimer Feld 330; tel. (6221) 548900; fax (6221) 544998; e-mail dmg@sai.uni-heidelberg.de; internet www.dmg -web.de; f. 1845; Sec. MANFRED HAKE; publs *Zeitschrift* (two a year), *Abhandlungen für die Kunde des Morgenlandes, Bibliotheca Islamica, Wörterbuch der Klassischen Arabischen Sprache, Beiruter Texte und Studien, Verzeichnis der orientalischen Handschriften in Deutschland,* etc.

Deutsches Orient-Institut: 20148 Hamburg, Mittelweg 150; tel. (40) 4132050; fax (40) 441484; e-mail doihh@uni-ham burg.de; internet www.doihh.de; f. 1960; affil. to Deutsches Übersee-Institut; devoted to research in politics, social sciences and economics of Near and Middle East; Dir Prof. Dr UDO STEINBACH; publs *Nahost Jahrbuch* (annually), *Orient* (quarterly), *Mitteilungen* (irregular), *Schriften* (irregular).

Freie Universität Berlin Institut für Altorientalistik: 14195 Berlin, Hüttenweg 7; tel. (30) 83853347; fax (30) 83853600; e-mail renger2@zedat.fu-berlin.de; f. 1950; Dir JOHANNES RENGER.

Internationale Gesellschaft für Orientforschung: Orientalisches Seminar, J. W. Goethe-Universität, Postfach 11-1932, 60054 Frankfurt/Main 11; f. 1948; 400 mems; Pres. Prof. R. SELLHEIM; publ. *Oriens* (annually).

Nah- und Mittelost Verein e.V. (German Near and Middle East Association): 20354 Hamburg, Große Theaterstrasse 1, Postfach 303909; tel. (40) 4503310; fax (40) 45033131; e-mail numov@numov.de; internet www.numov.de; f. 1934; 600 mems; Chair. WERNER SCHOELTZKE.

Seminar für Orientalische Sprachen: Nassestr. 2, 53113 Bonn; tel. (228) 738415; fax (228) 738446; e-mail uso010@ uni-bonn.de; f. 1959 (1887 Berlin); University of Bonn, Near East Department; Prof. Dr W. SCHMUCKER.

Zentrum für Türkeistudien: 45127 Essen, Altendorfer Str. 3; tel. (201) 31980; fax (201) 3198333; e-mail zft@uni-essen.de; internet www.uni-essen.de/zft/; f. 1985; Turkish studies; Dir Prof. Dr FARUK SEN.

INDIA

Asiatic Society of Bombay: Town Hall, Shahid Bhagatsingh, Mumbai 400 023; tel. 2660956; fax 2665139; e-mail asbl@bom2.vsnl.net.in; internet www.education.vsnl.com/asbl; f. 1804 as Bombay Literary Society; established the Dr P. V. Kane Research Institute for Oriental Studies (later renamed the Dr P. V. Kane Institute for Post Graduate Studies and Research—affiliated to the University of Bombay) in 1973; conducts doctorate programmes; promotes and publishes research in culture, art and literature of Asia; holds seminars and lectures on current, historical and cultural affairs; 2,464 mems; 243,590 vols; 2,434 MSS and 11,830 old coins; Pres. B. G. DESHMUKH; Hon. Sec. VIMAL SHAH; publs incl. annual *Journal,* reports, critical annotated texts of rare Sanskrit and Pali MSS.

IRAN

British Institute of Persian Studies: Kucheh Alvand, Khiaban Dr Ali Shariati, Gholhak, POB 11365-6844, Tehran 19396; f. 1961; cultural institute, with emphasis on history and archaeology; 650 individual mems; library of more than 10,000 vols; Hon. Sec. Dr CHARLES MELVILLE; publ. *Iran* (annually).

Institute for Political and International Studies—IPIS: Shaheed Bahonar Ave, Shaheed Aghaii St, Tajrish, Tehran; POB 19395/1793, Tehran; tel. (21) 2571010; fax (21) 2710964; e-mail ipis@www.dci.co.ir; f. 1983; research and information on Iran's foreign policy and international relations; emphasis on Middle East, Persian (Arabian) Gulf, Europe, South-East Asia and Central Asia; Dir Gen. Dr SAYED ABASS ARAGHCHI; publs *Central Asia and the Caucasus* (quarterly), *Iranian Journal of International Affairs* (quarterly), *Foreign Policy* (quarterly).

IRAQ

Centre for Arab Gulf Studies: University of Basrah, POB 49, Basrah; tel. (40) 314657; fax (40) 213235; f. 1974; research into economics, politics, strategic issues, geography, history and culture in the Persian (Arabian) Gulf region; Dir Dr MUHAMMAD ABDULLAH ALAZAWI; publ. *Arab Gulf Journal* (quarterly).

Deutsches Archäologisches Institut: Hay al-Maarife 821/ 63, POB 2105, Alwiya, Baghdad; tel. 5431353.

Instituto Hispano-Arabe de Cultura: Hurriya Sq, Hay Babil 925/25/80, POB 2256, Alwiyah; tel. 7766045; f. 1958; Dir JUAN M. CASADO RAMOS.

Iraq Academy: Academy of Sciences, Waziriyah, Baghdad; tel. (66) 4221733; f. 1947 to maintain the Arabic language, to undertake research into Arabic history, Islamic heritage and the history of Iraq, and to encourage research in the modern arts and sciences; Pres. Prof. Dr NAJIH M. KHALIL AR-RAWI; Sec.-Gen. Prof. Dr AHMAD MATLOUB; publ. *Journal of the Academy of Sciences* (quarterly, in Arabic) (2 a year, in Kurdish).

ISRAEL

The Academy of the Hebrew Language: POB 3449, Jerusalem 91034; tel. (2) 5632242; fax (2) 5617065; e-mail acad2u@vms.huji.ac.il; internet hebrew-academy.huji.ac.il; f. 1953; study and development of the Hebrew language and compilation of a historical dictionary; Pres. Prof. M. BAR-ASHER; publs *Zikhronot, Leshonenu* (quarterly), *Leshonenu La'am,* monographs and dictionaries.

W. F. Albright Institute of Archaeological Research in Jerusalem: POB 19096, 26 Salah ed-Din, Jerusalem 91190; tel. (2) 6282131; fax (2) 6264424; e-mail Director@Albright.org.il; internet www.WFAlbright.org; f. 1900 by American Schools of Oriental Research; research in Syro-Palestinian archaeology, Biblical studies, Near Eastern history and languages; sponsors excavations; Pres. S. W. CRAWFORD; Dir Dr S. GITIN.

Arab Studies Society: POB 20479, Jerusalem; tel. (2) 6273330; fax (2) 6286820; e-mail arabstudies@arabs.arabstudies; internet http://www.arabstudies.org; f. 1980 to promote Arabic culture in general and Palestinian thought and culture in particular; works undertaken by 8 centres with 14 departments; library of more than 16,000 vols on Palestine and the Middle East; Chair FAISAL HUSSEINI; Gen. Dir ISHAQ BUDEIRI; publs more than 100 books on culture and history of Jerusalem and Palestine.

Begin-Sadat Centre for Strategic Studies: Bar-Ilan University, Ramat-Gan 52900; tel. (3) 5318959; fax (3) 5359195; e-mail besa@mail.biu.ac.il; internet www.biu.ac.il/soc/besa; f. 1992; research on Middle Eastern security; conferences and workshops; Dir Prof. EFRAIM INBAR; publs *BESA Bulletin, BESA Colloquia on Strategy and Diplomacy, BESA Security and Policy Studies, BESA Studies, The Middle East Review of International Affairs (MERIA).*

The Ben-Zvi Institute for the Study of Jewish Communities in the East: POB 7660, 12 Abravanel St, Jerusalem 91076; tel. (2) 5398844; fax (2) 5612329; e-mail mahonzvi@h2.hum.huji .ac.il; internet www.ybz.org.il; f. 1948; sponsors research in the history and culture of Jewish communities in the East; library of MSS and printed books; Chair. Prof. HAGGAI BEN SHAMMAI; publs *Sefunot, Pe'amim* (quarterly), and monographs.

Council for British Research in the Levant (CBRL): POB 19283, Jerusalem; tel. (2) 5828101; fax (2) 5323844; f. 1920; e-mail cbrl@netvision.net.il; internet www.britac.ac.uk/institutes/ cbrl/index/html; fmrly British School of Archaeology in Jerusalem and British Institute at Amman for Archaeology and History; promotes study of arts and social sciences relevant to the Levant; hostel and library; Dir Dr BILL FINLAYSON.

Couvent Saint Etienne des Pères Dominicains, Ecole Biblique et Archéologique Française: POB 19053, Jerusalem 91190; tel. (2) 6264468; fax (2) 6282567; e-mail directeur@ebof .edu; f. 1890; research, Biblical and Oriental studies, exploration and excavation in Palestine and Jordan; Dir JEAN-MICHEL POFFET; library of 130,000 vols; publs *Revue Biblique, Etudes Bibliques, Cahiers annexes de la Bible de Jérusalem, Cahiers de la Revue Biblique, Bible de Jérusalem.*

Moshe Dayan Center for Middle Eastern and African Studies/Shiloah Institute: Tel-Aviv University, Ramat Aviv, Tel-Aviv 69978; tel. (3) 6409646; fax (3) 6415802; e-mail dayan cen@ccsg.tau.ac.il; internet www.dayan.org; f. 1959; Dir Prof. ASHER SUSSER; publs *Middle East Contemporary Survey* (annually), also monographs, teaching aids, studies and occasional papers, computerized database on the Middle East, electronic Current Contents on the Middle East and North Africa; library e-mail dayanlib@ccsg.tau.ac.il.

Historical Society of Israel: POB 4179, Jerusalem 91041; tel. (2) 5637171; fax (2) 5662135; e-mail shazar@shazar.org.il; f. 1925 to promote the study of Jewish history and general history; 1,000 mems; Chair. Prof. MICHAEL HEYD; Gen. Sec. ZVI YEKUTIEL; publ. *Zion* (quarterly), *Historia* (2 per year).

Institute of Asian and African Studies: Hebrew University, Mount Scopus, Jerusalem 91905; tel. (2) 5883516; fax (2) 5883658; e-mail AsiaAfrica@h2.hum.huji.ac.il; f. 1926; incorporates Max Schloessinger Memorial Foundation; studies of medieval and modern languages, culture and history of Middle East, Asia and Africa; Dir REUVEN AMITAI; publs incl. *Max Schloessinger Memorial Series, Collected Studies in Arabic and Islam Series, Jerusalem Studies in Arabic and Islam,* translation series and studies in classical Islam and Arabic language and literature, *Hebrew University Armenian Series.*

Israel Exploration Society: POB 7041, 5 Avida St, Jerusalem 91070; tel. (2) 6257991; fax (2) 6247772; e-mail ies@vms.huji .ac.il; internet www.hum.huji.ac.il/ies; f. 1913; excavations and historical research, congresses and lectures; 4,000 mems; Chair. Prof. A. BIRAN; Dir J. AVIRAM; publs *Eretz-Israel* (Hebrew and English, commemorative series), *Qadmoniot* (bi-annual), *Israel Exploration Journal* (English bi-annual), various books on archaeology (in Hebrew and English).

Israel Oriental Society: The Hebrew University, Jerusalem 91905; tel. (2) 5883633; f. 1949; lectures and symposia to study all aspects of contemporary Middle Eastern, Asian and African affairs; Pres. TEDDY KOLLEK; publs *Hamizrah Hehadash* (Hebrew—with English summary—annual), *Oriental Notes and Studies* (1951–71).

Jaffee Center for Strategic Studies—JCSS: Tel-Aviv University, Ramat-Aviv, Tel-Aviv 69978; tel. (3) 6409200; fax (3) 6422404; e-mail jcss2@post.tau.ac.il; internet www.tau.ac .il/jcss; f. 1977; research into Middle Eastern strategic affairs; Chair. MELVIN JAFFEE; Dir Prof. SHAI FELDMAN; publs *JCSS Bulletin* (2 a year), *The Middle East Military Balance* (annual), *Strategic Assessment* (quarterly).

Jerusalem University College: POB 1276 Mt Zion, Jerusalem 91012; tel. (2) 671-8628; fax (2) 673-2717; e-mail president@ juc.edu; internet www.juc.edu; f. 1957 as Institute of Holy Land Studies; Christian study centre, grad. and undergrad. in the history, languages, religions and cultures of Israel in the Middle Eastern Context; Pres. Dr SIDNEY DEWAAL; Academic Dean Dr PAUL WRIGHT.

Orientalisches Institut der Görres-Gesellschaft: Schmidt-Schule, POB 19424, Jerusalem; historical and archaeological studies.

Pontifical Biblical Institute: POB 497, 3 Paul Emile Botta St, Jerusalem 91004; tel. (2) 6252843; fax (2) 6241203; e-mail pbijer@netvision.net.il; f. 1927; study of Biblical languages and Biblical archaeology, history, topography; in conjunction with Hebrew University of Jerusalem; seminar for post-graduate students, student tours; Dir TOM FITZPATRICK.

Bertha von Suttner Research Program for Peace Studies and Conflict Resolution in the Middle East: University of Haifa, Mount Carmel, Haifa 31905; tel. (4) 8240111; fax (4) 8342104.

The Harry S. Truman Research Institute for the Advancement of Peace: Hebrew University, Mount Scopus, Jerusalem

91905; tel. (2) 5882300; fax (2) 5828076; e-mail mstruman@ mscc.huji.ac.il; f. 1966; conducts and sponsors social science and historical research, organizes conferences on developing and non-Western countries, with special emphasis on the Middle East; Dir Prof. AMNON COHEN; publs works on the Middle East, Africa, Asia and Latin America.

Wilfrid Israel Museum for Oriental Art and Studies: Kibbutz Hazorea, Mobile Post Ha'amakim 30060; tel. (4) 9899566; fax (4) 9590860; e-mail wilfrid@hazorea.org.il; f. 1947; opened 1951 in memory of late Wilfrid Israel; a cultural centre for reference, study and art exhbns; houses Wilfrid Israel collection of Near and Far Eastern art and cultural materials; local archaeological exhibits from neolithic to Byzantine times; science and art library; Dir EHUD DOR; Curator for Far and Middle Eastern Art ORNA MERON; Curator for Archaeology RUTH GOSHEN.

ITALY

Istituto di Studi del Vicino Oriente: Dipartimento di Scienze Storiche, Archeologiche ed Antropologiche dell'Antichità, Sezione Vicino Oriente, Università degli Studi di Roma 'La Sapienza', P.le Aldo Moro, 5-00100 Rome; Dir Prof. PAOLO MATTHIAE.

Istituto Italiano per l'Africa e l'Oriente (IsIAO): via Ulisse Aldrovandi 16, 00197 Rome; tel. (6) 3221258; fax (6) 3225348; e-mail info@isiao.it; internet www.isiao.it; f. 1906; absorbed Istituto Italiano per il Medio ed Estremo Oriente; Pres. Prof. GHERARDO GNOLI; Dir-Gen. Dott. GIANCARLO GARGARUTI.

Istituto per l'Oriente C. A. Nallino: Via A. Caroncini 19, 00197 Rome; tel. (06) 8084106; fax (06) 8079395; e-mail ipocan@ libero.it; f. 1921 as L'istituto per l'Oriente; adopted current name in 1982 in honour of one of its founders, Carlo Alfonso Nallino; under supervision of the Ministry of Foreign Affairs; research into all aspects of bilateral and multilateral relations between Italy and the countries of the Near and Middle East; particular emphasis on law, society and immigration; library service; organizes courses on Arabic and Islamic culture; Pres. Prof. FRANCESCO CASTRO; publ. *Oriente Moderno* (monographic essays and bibliographical reviews).

Istituto per le relazioni tra l'Italia e i paesi dell'Africa, America Latina e Medio Oriente: via del Tritone 62B, 00187 Rome; tel. (06) 6792321; fax (06) 6797849; f. 1971; Pres. GILBERTO BONALUMI; publ. *Politica Internazionale* (6 a year Italian edition).

JAPAN

Ajia Keizai Kenkyusho (Institute of Developing Economies): 42 Ichigaya-Hommura-cho, Shinjuku-ku, Tokyo 162-8442; tel. (3) 33534231; fax (3) 32268475; f. 1958; 254 mems; Chair. YŌTARŌ IIDA; Pres. KATSUHISA YAMADA; library of 351,595 vols; publs *Ajia Keizai* (Japanese, monthly), *The Developing Economies* (English, quarterly), occasional papers in English.

Chuto Chosakai (Middle East Institute of Japan): POB 1513, Shinjuku i-Land Tower, Tokyo 163-13; tel. (3) 53232145; fax (3) 53232148; f. 1960; Chair. WASUKE MIYAKE; publs *Chuto Kenkyu* (Journal of Middle Eastern Studies—monthly), *Chuto Nenkan* (Yearbook of Middle East and North Africa), *Newsletter.*

Nippon Oriento Gakkai (Society for Near Eastern Studies in Japan): Tokyo Tenrikyokan. 9, 1-chome, Kanda Nishiki-cho, Chiyoda-ku, Tokyo 101-0054; tel. and fax (3) 32917519; f. 1954; about 800 mems; Pres. KOJI KAMIOKA; publs *Oriento* (Japanese, 2 a year), *Orient* (European languages annual).

JORDAN

Centre for Strategic Studies: University of Jordan, Amman; tel. (6) 5355667; fax (6) 5355515; e-mail uojcss@go.com.jo; f. 1984; research on strategic, political, economic and social issues concerning Jordan and the Middle East; Dir Dr MUSTAFA B. HAMARNEH.

KYRGYZSTAN

Centre for Studies of Islam and Iran: Bishkek Humanities University, 720044 Bishkek, pr. Tynchtyk 27; tel. and fax (312) 48-40-35; internet bhu.freenet.kg; f. 2002.

LEBANON

Arab Institute for Research and Publishing: POB 11-5460; 3rd Floor, Carlton Tower Bldg, Saqiat el-Janzeer, Beirut; tel.

and fax (1) 807900; Gen. Man. MAHER KAYYALI; works in Arabic and English.

Centre d'Etudes et de Recherches sur le Moyen-Orient contemporain (CERMOC): BP 2691, rue de Damas, Beirut; tel. (1) 615841; fax (1) 615877; e-mail cermoc.adm@lb.refer.org; Ambassade de France au Liban, Valise Diplomatique, 128 bis, rue de l'Université, 75531 Paris, France; f. 1977; 4 research fellows and 9 contractual researchers; university research and documentation institution; library specializes in human and social sciences concerning the Middle East; Dir HENRI LAURENS; publs 67 books on contemporary Middle East.

Institut Français d'Archéologie du Proche Orient: rue de Damas, BP 11-1424, Beirut; tel. (1) 420298; fax (1) 615866; Jordanian Section: BP 5348, Amman, Jordan; tel. (6) 4611872; fax (6) 4643840; Syrian Section: BP 3694, Damascus, Syria; tel. (11) 3338727; fax (11) 3325013; e-mail ifapo@net.sy; f. 1946; library of 45,000 vols (Bibliothèque Henri Seyrig); Dir J. L. HUOT; publs *Syria, Revue d'Art et d'Archéologie* (annually), *Bibliothèque Archéologique et Historique*.

Institute for Palestine Studies, Publishing and Research Organization: POB 11-7164, Nsouli-Verdun St, Beirut; tel. and fax (1) 868387; e-mail ipsb10@calvacom.fr; 3501 M St, NW, POB 25301, Washington, DC 20007, USA; tel. (202) 3423990; fax (202) 3423927; e-mail jps@cais.com; 13 Hera St, POB 5658, Nicosia, Cyprus; tel. (2) 456165; fax (2) 456324; f. 1963; independent non-profit Arab research organization; to promote better understanding of the Palestine problem and the Arab-Israeli conflict; library of 30,000 vols, microfilm collection, private papers and archives; Hon. Chair. Dr CONSTANTINE ZURAYK; Chair. Dr HISHAM NASHABE; Exec. Sec. Prof. WALID KHALIDI; publs *Journal of Palestine Studies* (English, quarterly), *Revue d'études palestiniennes* (French, quarterly), *Majallat ad-Dirasat al-Filistiniyah* (Arabic, quarterly) and documentary series, reprints, research papers, etc.

Lebanese Center for Policy Studies—LCPS: Tayyar Center, Bloc C, 3rd Floor, Sin al-Fil, POB 55-215, Beirut; tel. (1) 490561; fax (1) 490375; e-mail info@lcps.org.lb; internet www.lcps-lebanon.org; f. 1989; research into political, social and economic development; library facilities; Pres. Dr ELIE A. SALEM; Gen. Dir Dr SALIM NASR; publs books and commissioned studies.

THE NETHERLANDS

Assyriologisch Instituut der Rijksuniversiteit: Rijksuniversiteit Leiden, POB 9515, 2300 RA Leiden; tel. (71) 5272260; fax (71) 5272615; e-mail K.R.Veenhof@let.leidenuniv.nl; Dir Prof. Emeritus Dr K. R. VEENHOF; publs *Altbabylonische Briefe in Umschrift und Übersetzung* (14 vols, continuing series), *Collection, Liagre Böhl Collection* (c. 3,000 cuneiform tablets) published in conjunction with the Netherlands Institute for the Near East, Leiden.

Middle East Research Associates: POB 10765, 1001 ET Amsterdam; tel. (20) 6201579; fax (20) 6264479; e-mail mera@xs4all.nl; internet http://www.xs4all.nl/~mera; Dir P. AARTS; publs *Occasional Papers* (quarterly).

Nederlands-Vlaams Instituut in Cairo (NVIC): POB 20061, 2500 EB The Hague (see under Egypt).

Netherlands Council for Trade Promotion (Netherlands Middle East Business Council): Bezuidenhoutseweg 181, POB 10, 2501 CA The Hague; tel. (70) 3441544; fax (070) 3853531; e-mail councils@nchnl.nl; f. 1949; publs *Middle East Newsletter, Jordan Newsletter*.

Netherlands Institute for the Near East (*Nederlands Instituut voor het Nabije Oosten*): Witte Singel 25, POB 9515, 2300 RA Leiden; tel. (71) 5272036; fax (71) 5272038; e-mail a.de.beurs@let.leidenuniv.nl; internet www.leidenuniv.nl/nino/nino.html; Dir Prof. Dr J. DE ROOS; library of c. 35,000 vols and 600 periodicals; publs *Anatolica, Studia Francisci Scholten Memoriae dicata, Scholae de Buck, Publications de l'Institut historique et archéologique néerlandais de Stamboul, Bibliotheca Orientalis, Tabulae de Liagre Böhl, Studia de Liagre Böhl, Egyptologische Uitgaven* (monographs), *Achaemenid History* (monographs).

PAKISTAN

Institute of Islamic Culture: 2 Club Rd, Lahore 3; tel. (42) 6363127; f. 1950; Dir RASHID AHMAD JULLUNDHRI; publs *Al-Ma'arif*

(quarterly) and about 200 publications on Islamic subjects in English and Urdu.

Islamic Research Institute: International Islamic University, Faisal Masjid, POB 1035, Islamabad 44000; tel. (51) 254874; fax (51) 853360; e-mail dg-iri@iri-iiu.sdnpk.undp.org; f. 1960; conducts research in Islamic studies; organizes seminars and conferences on various aspects of Islam; library of 120,000 books and periodicals, 610 microfilms, 260 MSS, 1,035 photostats, 220 audio cassettes; Dir-Gen. Dr ZAFAR ISHAQ ANSARI; publs *Ad-Dirasat al-Islamiyah* (Arabic, quarterly), *Islamic Studies* (English, quarterly), *Fikr O-Nazar* (Urdu, quarterly), also monographs, reports, etc.

POLAND

Zakład Archeologii Śródziemnomorskiej (Research Centre for Mediterranean Archaeology): Pałac Staszica, (Room 33), Nowy Świat 72,00-330 Warsaw; f. 1956; tel. (22) 6572791; fax 8266560; e-mail zaspan@zaspan.waw.pl; 18 mems; Research Institute of Academy of Sciences; documentation and publication of Polish excavations in the Middle East and antiquities in Polish museums; Prof. KAROL MYŚLIWIEC, Prof. ZSOLT KISS; publs *Travaux du Centre d'Archéologie Méditerranéenne, Palmyre, Nubia, Faras, Deir el-Bahari, Nea Paphos, Alexandrie, Corpus Vasorum Antiquorum, Corpus Signorum Imperii Romani, Tell Atrib*.

PORTUGAL

Instituto de Estudos Árabes e Islâmicos: Faculdade de Letras, Cidade Universitária, 1699 Lisbon; tel. (1) 7920000; fax (1) 7960063; f. 1966; library; 6 teachers; specializes in Arabic and Islamic studies; Dir A. DIAS FARINHA.

RUSSIA

Russian Centre for Strategic and International Studies: ul. Rozhdestvenka 12, 103753 Moscow; tel. (095) 9245150; fax (095) 4256237; f. 1991; research and training in international relations; Islamic studies, strategic and military studies, the Middle East and North Africa; Pres. VITALII V. NAUMKIN; Exec. Dir ALEKSANDR FILONIK.

SAUDI ARABIA

Arab Urban Development Institute: POB 6892, Riyadh 11452; tel. (1) 4802555; fax (1) 4802666; e-mail info@araburban.org; internet www.araburban.org; f. 1980; affiliated to the Arab Towns Organization (ATO); provides training, research, consultancy and documentation services to Arab cities and municipalities and members of ATO for improving the Arab city and preserving its original character and Islamic cultural heritage; Dir-Gen. Eng. AHMED AS-SALLOUM; library of 78,440 vols and 630 periodicals; publs books and research papers.

Centre for Research and Islamic Economics: King Abd al-Aziz University, POB 16711, Jeddah 21474; tel. (2) 6952128; fax (2) 6952066; f. 1977; research into all aspects of Islamic economics; Dir Dr GHAZIOBAID MODANI.

SLOVAKIA

Institute of Asian and African Studies: Slovak Academy of Sciences, Klemensova 19, 813 64 Bratislava; tel. and fax (7) 52926326; e-mail kabinet@klemens.savba.sk; internet http://klemens.savba.sk/kosav/enhlav.htm; f. 1960; 17 mems; Dir Institute Dr V. KRUPA; publ. *Asian and African Studies* (2 a year).

SPAIN

Asociación Española de Orientalistas: Universidad Autónoma, Edificio Rectorado, Canto Blanco, 28049 Madrid; tel. (91) 3974112; f. 1965; publs *Boletín* (annually), etc.

Instituto Egipcio de Estudios Islámicos: Francisco de Asis Méndez Casariego 1, Madrid 28002; tel. (91) 5639468; fax (91) 5638640; e-mail iegipcio@mundivia.es; internet www.mundivia.es/iegipcio; affiliated to Ministry of Higher Education, Cairo; f. 1950; Dir Dr MUHAMMAD MUHAMMAD ABD AL-ATTA; publs *Revista del Instituto Egipcio de Estudios Islámicos* and other books on Hispano-Arabic studies.

Instituto de Filología: Duque de Medinaceli 6, 28014 Madrid; tel. (91) 4290626; fax (91) 3690940; f. 1985 as a result of the amalgamation of four existing institutes (the Benito Arias Montano, Miguel Asin, Miguel de Cervantes and Antonio de Nebrija); six depts: Departamento de Estudios Arabes (four members), Departamento de Filología Biblica y de Oriente Antiguo (eight members), Departamento de Estudios Hebraicos (four members); Dir TERESA ORTEGA MONASTERIO; Sec. JULIO CÉSAR SUILS; publs *Sefarad* (review of Hebrew, Sephardic and Ancient Studies, 2 a year), *Alqantara* (review of Arab Studies, 2 a year) and books.

SWEDEN

Nordiska Afrikainstitutet (Nordic Africa Institute): POB 1703, 75147, Uppsala; tel. (18) 562200; fax (18) 562290; e-mail nai@nai.uu.se; internet www.nai.uu.se; f. 1962; research and documentation centre for contemporary African affairs, organizes seminars and publishes wide range of books and pamphlets in Swedish and English; library of 55,000 vols, 600 periodicals; Dir L. WOHLGEMUTH; publs *Seminar Proceedings, Research Reports, Discussion Papers, Annual Report, Current African Issues,* monographs and newsletters.

SWITZERLAND

Schweizerische Asiengesellschaft (Swiss Asia Society): Ostasiatisches Seminar der Universität Zürich, Zürichbergstr. 4, 8032 Zürich; tel. (1) 6343181; fax (1) 6344921; e-mail office@oas.unizh.ch; internet www.sagw.ch/dt/mitglieder/outer .asp?id=40; f. 1939; 202 mems; Pres. Prof. Dr E. KLOPFENSTEIN; publs *Asiatische Studien/Etudes Asiatiques* (4 a year), *Schweizer Asiatische Studien/Etudes Asiatiques Suisses* (Monographien und Studienhefte).

SYRIA

Institut Français d'Etudes Arabes: BP 344, Damascus; tel. (11) 3330214; fax (11) 3327887; e-mail ifead@net.sy; internet www.univ-aix.fr/ifead/ f. 1922; library of 55,000 vols, 980 periodicals; Dir DOMINIQUE MALLET; Head Librarian MICHEL NIETO; 48 scholars; publs *Bulletin d'Etudes Orientales* (annually, 52 vols published), monographs, translations and Arabic texts (158 vols published).

Near East Foundation: BP 427, Damascus.

TAJIKISTAN

Institute of Oriental Studies of Tajikistan: Ul. Parvin 8, Dushanbe; tel. (31) 243010; Dir AKBAR TURSONOV.

TUNISIA

Institut des Belles Lettres Arabes: 12 rue Jamâa el-Haoua, 1008 Tunis BM; tel. (71) 560133; fax (71) 572683; e-mail ibla@ gnet.tn; f. 1930; cultural centre; Dir R. ECHEVERRIA; publs *IBLA* (2 a year) and special studies.

TURKEY

British Institute of Archaeology at Ankara: Tahran Caddesi 24, Kavaklıdere, 06700 Ankara; tel. (312) 4275487; fax (312) 4280159; e-mail ingark-o@tr.net; f. 1948; archaeological research and excavation; Dir Dr HUGH ELTON; publs *Anatolian Studies* and *Anatolian Archaeology* (annually), *Occasional Publications.*

Deutsches Archäologisches Institut: Gümüşsuyu/Ayazpaşa Camii Sok. 48, TR-80090, İstanbul; tel. (212) 2440714; fax (212) 2523491; e-mail daiist@attglobal.net; f. 1929; Dir Prof. Dr-Ing. ADOLF HOFFMANN; publs *Istanbuler Mitteilungen* (annually), *Istanbuler Forschungen, Beihefte zu Istanbuler Mitteilungen.*

Institut Français d'Etudes Anatoliennes: Palais de France, PK 54, Beyoğlu, 80072 İstanbul; tel. (212) 2443327; fax (212) 2528091; f. 1930; 15 scientific mems; library of c. 30,000 vols; Dir PAUL DUMONT; publs *Collection IFEA, Collection Varia Turcica, Collection Varia Anatolica, Anatolia Antiqua, Anatolia Moderna.*

Institute for Research on Economic Relations in Turkey, Europe and the Middle East: Dept of Economics, University of Istanbul, Beyazit; tel. (212) 5221489; fax (212) 5205473; Dir. E. MANISALI.

Netherlands Historical Archaeological Institute: Istiklâl Caddesi 393, Beyoğlu, İstanbul; tel. (212) 2939283; fax (212) 2513846; e-mail nhaiist@superonline.com; f. 1958; library of 12,000 vols; Dir Dr H. E. LAGRO; publs *Publications de l'Institut Historique et Archéologique Néerlandais de Stamboul, Anatolica.*

Österreichisches Kulturforum Istanbul: Köybaşi Cad. 44, 80870 Yeniköy, İstanbul; tel. (212) 2237843; fax (212) 2233469; e-mail ako-ist@austriakult.org.tr; internet www.austriakult .org.tr; Dir Consul Dr ULRIKE OUTSCHAR.

Türk Dil Kurumu (Turkish Language Institute): Atatürk Bul. 217, 06680 Kavaklıdere Ankara; tel. (312) 4286100; fax (312) 4285288; 40 mems; library of 28,000 vols; Pres. Prof. Dr ŞÜKRÜ HALUK AKALIN; publs *Türk Dili* (monthly), *Türk Dili Araştırmaları Yıllığı-Belleten* (annually).

Türk Kültürünü Araştırma Enstitüsü (Institute for the Study of Turkish Culture): 17 Sokak No. 38, Bahçelievler, Ankara; tel. (312) 2133100; f. 1961; scholarly research into all aspects of Turkish culture; Dir Prof. Dr SÜKRÜ ELÇİN; publs *Türk Kültürü* (monthly), *Cultura Turcica* (annually), *Türk Kültürü Araştırmaları* (annually).

Türk Tarih Kurumu (Turkish Historical Society): Kızılay Sok. 1, 06100 Ankara; tel. (312) 3102368; fax (312) 3101698; e-mail ttkinfo@ttk.org.tr; internet www.ttk.org.tr; f. 1931; 40 mems; library of 216,960 vols; Pres. Prof. YUSUF HALAÇOĞLU; publs *Belleten* (3 a year), *Belgeler* (annually).

UNITED ARAB EMIRATES

Centre for Documentation and Research: Presidential Court, POB 5884, Abu Dhabi; tel. (2) 4445400; fax (2) 54445811; e-mail dg@cdr.gov.ae; f. 1968; attached to Ministry of Foreign Affairs; research, data collection and analysis on aspects of the Persian (Arabian) Gulf region; Dir Dr ABDULLAH AR-REYES; publ. *Arabian Gulf Research Review* (quarterly).

UNITED KINGDOM

Arab Research Centre: 5 Belgrave Sq., London, SW1X 8PH; tel. (20) 72357642; f. 1979; research into problems and issues concerning the Arab world; library of 27,000 vols; commissions writing of special papers; holds international symposia; Chair. ABD AL-MAJID FARID; Man. ALIA ARNALL.

British School of Archaeology in Iraq: 10 Carlton House Terrace, London, SW1Y 5AH; fax (20) 79695401; e-mail bsai@ britac.ac.uk; internet users.ox.ac.uk/~neareast/bsai.htm; f. 1932; Chair. H. E. W. CRAWFORD; Pres. Prof. DAVID OATES; publ. *Journal Iraq.*

British Society for Middle Eastern Studies (Brismes): administrative offices c/o Institute for Middle Eastern and Islamic Studies, Durham (see below); tel. (191) 3747989; fax (191) 3742830; e-mail a.l.haysey@durham.ac.uk; internet www.dur.ac.uk/brismes; publs incl. *British Journal of Middle Eastern Studies* (2 a year).

Centre for Lebanese Studies: 59 Observatory St, Oxford, OX2 6EP; tel. (1865) 558465; fax (1865) 514317; e-mail shehadi @sable.ox.ac.uk; internet www.lebanesestudies.com; Dir NADIM SHEHADI; Administrator ANNE-MARIE COCKBURN.

Centre of Middle Eastern and Islamic Studies: Faculty of Oriental Studies, Sidgwick Ave, Cambridge CB3 9DA; tel. and fax (1223) 335103; e-mail knb21@cam.ac.uk; internet www .cmeis.cam.ac.uk; f. 1960; Dir Dr AMIRA K. BENNISON.

Council for the Advancement of Arab-British Understanding (CAABU): Arab-British Centre, 1 Gough Square, London, EC4A 3DE; tel. (20) 78321310; fax (20) 78321319; e-mail caabu@caabu.org; internet www.caabu.org; f. 1967; Dir CHRIS DOYLE.

Egypt Exploration Society: 3 Doughty Mews, London, WC1N 2PG; tel. (20) 72421880; fax (20) 74046118; e-mail eeslondon@ talk21.com; internet www.ees.ac.uk; f. 1882; library of 4,500 vols; c. 3,000 mems; Chair. Prof. ALAN B. LLOYD; Sec.-Gen. Dr PATRICIA SPENCER; publs *Bulletin of the Egypt Exploration Society, Excavation Memoirs, Archaeological Survey, Graeco-Roman*

Memoirs, Journal of Egyptian Archaeology, Texts from Excavations, Egyptian Archaeology, etc.

Institute of Arab and Islamic Studies: University of Exeter, Stocker Rd, Exeter, EX4 4ND; tel. (1392) 264036; fax (1392) 264035; internet www.ex.ac.uk/iais; f. 1999 by amalgamation of Centre for Arab Gulf Studies and Dept of Middle Eastern Studies; multi-disciplinary centre for Arab and Islamic studies; extensive library and documentation unit; Dir Prof. TIM NIBLOCK.

Institute of Ismaili Studies: 42–44 Grosvenor Gdns, London SW1W 0EB; tel. (20) 78816000; fax (20) 78816040; e-mail info@iis.ac.uk; internet www.iis.ac.uk/; f. 1977 to promote scholarship and learning on Islam; library of printed and audiovisual materials and MSS; Dir Prof. AZIM NANJI.

Institute for Middle Eastern and Islamic Studies: University of Durham, The Al-Qasimi Bldg, Elvet Hill Rd, Durham, DH1 3TU; tel. (191) 3742822; fax (191) 3742830; e-mail p.g.starkey@durham.ac.uk; internet www.ac.uk/~dmeOwww; f. 1962; responsible for teaching undergraduate and postgraduate courses in Arabic, Persian, Turkish, political economy and international relations of the Middle East and North Africa, Middle Eastern and Islamic studies; organizes seminars, lectures and conferences; documentation unit f. 1970 to monitor economic, social and political devts in the region with some 200,000 documents; publication programme of research monographs, occasional papers and bibliographies; Chair. Dr P. STARKEY.

Islamic Cultural Centre (and London Central Mosque): 146 Park Rd, London, NW8 7RG; tel. (20) 77243363; e-mail islamic200@aol.com; internet www.Islamicculturalcentre.co.uk; f. 1944 to provide information and guidance on Islam and Islamic culture and to provide facilities for Muslims residing in Great Britain; library of 20,000 vols in Arabic, English, Urdu and Persian; Dir-Gen. Dr AHMAD AD-DUBAYAN.

Maghreb Studies Association: c/o The Executive Secretary, M. BEN-MADANI, 45 Burton St, London, WC1H 9AL; tel. (20) 73881840; f. 1981; independent; to promote the study of, and interest in, the Maghreb; organizes lectures and conferences; issues occasional publications and co-operates with the periodical *The Maghreb Review* (q.v.); Chair. Prof. HÉDI BOURAOUI.

Middle East Association: Bury House, 33 Bury St, London, SW1Y 6AX; tel. (20) 78392137; fax (20) 78396121; e-mail mail@the-mea.co.uk; internet www.the-mea.co.uk; f. 1961; an asscn for firms actively promoting UK trade with 20 Arab countries, plus Iran and Turkey; 400 mems; Dir-Gen. BRIAN CONSTANT; Sec. P. K. WILLINGTON.

Middle East Centre: St Antony's College, 68 Woodstock Rd, Oxford, OX2 6JF; tel. (1865) 284780; fax (1865) 311475; e-mail eugene.rogan@sant.ox.ac.uk; f. 1958; Dir Dr EUGENE ROGAN; library of 34,000 vols and archive of private papers and photographs; publs St Antony's Middle East monographs.

The Muslim Institute: 109 Fulham Palace Rd, London, W6 8JA; tel. (20) 85631995; fax (20) 85631993; e-mail musliminstitute@hotmail.com; internet www.musliminstitute.com; f. 1974; research and teaching programmes, academic and current affairs seminars, library of 6,000 vols; 800 mems; Dir Dr M. GHAYASUDDIN SIDDIQUI; supplies publications of the Muslim Parliament of Great Britain.

Oxford Centre for Islamic Studies: George St, Oxford OX1 2AR; tel. (1865) 278730; fax (1865) 248942; f. 1985; Dir Dr FARHAN A. NIZAMI; Reg. Dr DAVID G. BROWNING; publs *Journal of Islamic Studies* (3 a year).

Palestine Exploration Fund: 2 Hinde Mews, Marylebone Lane, London, W1U 2AA; tel. (20) 79355379; fax (20) 74867438; e-mail pefund@compuserve.com; internet www.pef.org.uk; f. 1865; 900 subscribers; Pres. The Archbishop of Canterbury; Chair. J. N. TUBB; Exec. Sec. Dr R. L. CHAPMAN, III; Hon. Sec. D. M. JACOBSON; publ. *Palestine Exploration Quarterly.*

Royal Asiatic Society of Great Britain and Ireland: 60 Queen's Gardens, London, W2 3AF; tel. (20) 77244741; fax (20) 77064008; e-mail info@royalasiaticsociety.org; internet www.royalasiaticsociety.org; f. 1823 for the study of the history, sociology, institutions, customs, languages and art of Asia; approx. 700 mems; approx. 700 subscribing libraries; library of 50,000 vols and 1,500 MSS; branches in various Asian cities;

Pres. Prof. A. STOCKWELL; publs *Journal, Storey Bibliography of Persian Literature* and monographs.

Royal Society for Asian Affairs: 2 Belgrave Square, London, SW1X 8PJ; tel. (20) 72355122; fax (20) 72596771; e-mail sec@rsaa.org.uk; internet www.rsaa.org.uk; f. 1901; 1,200 mems with past or present knowledge of the Near, Middle and Far East and Central Asia; library of more than 7,000 vols; Pres. Lord DENMAN; Chair. Sir HAROLD WALKER; Sec. N. J. M. CAMERON; publ. *Journal* (3 a year).

The Saudi-British Society: 21 Collingham Rd, London, SW5 0NU; tel. (20) 73738414; fax (20) 78352088; non-political; Chair. Lord DENMAN; Sec. WILLIAM FULLERTON.

School of Oriental and African Studies, University of London: Thornhaugh St, London, WC1H 0XG; tel. (20) 76372388; fax (20) 74363844; internet www.soas.ac.uk; f. 1916; library of over 750,000 vols and 2,750 MSS; Dir Prof. COLIN BUNDY.

UNITED STATES OF AMERICA

America-Mideast Educational & Training Services, Inc (AMIDEAST): Suite 1100, 1730 M St, NW, Washington, DC 20036-4505; tel. (202) 7769600; fax (202) 7767000; e-mail inquiries@amideast.org; internet www.amideast.org; f. 1951; a private, non-profit organization promoting understanding and co-operation between Americans and the people of the Middle East and North Africa through programmes of education, development and information; offices in Washington, DC, and Egypt, Israeli-occupied Territories, Jordan, Kuwait, Lebanon, Morocco, Syria, Tunisia and Yemen; Pres. and CEO WILLIAM A. RUGH; publs on education in the Middle East, *Advising Quarterly, AMIDEAST News* (quarterly), *Introduction to the Arab World* (educational videotape), and *Arab World Almanac* (three times per year).

American Oriental Society: Room 110D, Hatcher Graduate Library, University of Michigan, Ann Arbor, MI 48109-1205; tel. (734) 6474760; e-mail jrodgers@umich.edu; f. 1842; 1,350 mems; library of 23,500 vols; Pres. CHAUNCEY GOODRICH; Sec. JONATHAN RODGERS; publs *Journal* (quarterly), monograph series, essay series and offprint series.

American Schools of Oriental Research: 656 Beacon St, 5th Floor, Boston, MA 02215; tel. (617) 3536570; fax (617) 3536575; e-mail asor@bu.edu; internet www.asor.org; f. 1900; 1,500 mems; support activities of independent archaeological institutions abroad: The Albright Institute of Archaeological Research, Jerusalem, Israel, the American Center of Oriental Research in Amman, Jordan, and the Cyprus American Archaeological Research Institute in Nicosia, Cyprus; Pres. LAWRENCE T. GERATY; publs *Newsletter* (quarterly), *Near Eastern Archaeology* (quarterly), *Bulletin* (quarterly), *Journal of Cuneiform Studies* (quarterly), *Annual.*

Center for Contemporary Arab Studies: ICC 241, Box 571020, Georgetown University, Washington, DC 20057-1020; tel. (202) 6875793; fax (202) 6877001; e-mail ccasinfo@georgetown.edu; internet www.ccasonline.org; f. 1975; active in postgraduate education, public affairs, outreach to pre-college educators; Dir Dr BARBARA F. STOWASSER; Academic Dir Dr JUDITH TUCKER; publs on social, economic, political, cultural and development aspects of Arab World, newsletter (four a year).

Center for Middle Eastern and North African Studies: University of Michigan, 1080 South University Ave, Suite 4640, Social Work Bldg, Ann Arbor, MI 48109-1106; tel. (734) 7640350; fax (734) 7648523; e-mail cmenas@umich.edu; internet www.umich.edu/iinet/cmenas/; f. 1961; research into the ancient, medieval and modern cultures of the modern Middle East and North Africa, Near Eastern languages and literature; library includes 340,000 vols on Middle East and North Africa; Dir Dr MICHAEL BONNER.

Center for Middle Eastern Studies: University of Chicago, 5828 S. University Ave, Chicago, IL 60637; tel. (773) 7028297; fax (773) 7022587; f. 1965; e-mail cme@uchicago.edu; internet www.cmes.uchicago.edu; f. 1965; research into medieval and modern cultures of North Africa and Western and Central Asia; Dir JOHN E. WOODS.

Center for Middle Eastern Studies: Harvard University, Coolidge Hall, 1430 Massachusetts Ave, Cambridge, MA 02138;

tel. (617) 4954055; fax (617) 4968584; e-mail mideast@fas .harvard.edu; internet www.fas.harvard.edu/~mideast; research on Middle Eastern subjects and Islamic studies; Dir Prof. ÇEMAL KAFADAR; Publs *Middle East Monograph Series, Harvard Middle Eastern and Islamic Review.*

Center for Middle Eastern Studies: The University of Texas at Austin, Austin, TX 78712; tel. (512) 4713881; fax (512) 4717834; e-mail cmes@menic.utexas.edu; internet www.menic.utexas.edu; f. 1960; comprehensive interdisciplinary programme in area studies and languages of the Middle East, with some 50 affiliated faculties; offers graduate and undergraduate degrees in Middle Eastern studies; Dir Dr ABRAHAM MARCUS; publs books on the modern Middle East and translations of contemporary fiction and memoirs.

Department of Near Eastern Languages and Cultures: Indiana University, Bloomington, IN 47405; tel. (812) 8555993; fax (812) 8557841; e-mail nelcmesp@indiana.edu; internet www.indiana.edu/~nelcmesp/; graduate and undergraduate courses in Islamic studies, Middle Eastern literatures, religions, and cultures and civilizations, Byzantine studies, and Arabic language and linguistics.

Gustave E. von Grunebaum Center for Near Eastern Studies: POB 951480, University of California, Los Angeles, 10286 Bunche Hall, Los Angeles, CA 90095; tel. (310) 8251181; fax (310) 2062406; e-mail cnes@isop.ucla.edu; internet www .isop.ucla.edu/cnes; f. 1957; social sciences, culture and language studies of the Near East since the rise of Islam; a growing programme of Ancient Near Eastern Studies; library of more than 250,000 vols and MSS collection in Arabic, Armenian, Hebrew, Judaeo-Persian, Persian and Turkish; annual publication of series of colloquia and of Levi Della Vida Award Conference volumes; 100 associated faculty members; Dir Dr LEONARD BINDER.

Hoover Institution on War, Revolution and Peace: Stanford University, Stanford, CA 94305-6010; tel. (650) 7231754; fax (650) 7231687; e-mail jajko@hoover.stanford.edu; internet www.hoover.stanford.edu; f. 1919; library of 1.7 m. vols and 4,500 archives on 20th-century history includes important collection of 125,000 vols and 150 archives on Middle East and North Africa; Dir J. RAISIAN; Middle East Dep. Curator E. A. JAJKO; publs about 20 books each year.

Middle East Center: University of Utah, 260 s. Central Campus Dr., Rm 153, Salt Lake City, UT 84112-9157; tel. (801) 5816181; fax (801) 5816183; f. 1960; co-ordinates programme in Middle East languages and area studies in 12 academic departments; BA, MA and PhD in Middle East Studies with area of concentration in Arabic, Hebrew, Persian, Turkish, anthropology, history and political science; annual summer programme for Utah educators in the Middle East, research and exchange agreements with several universities; pre-doctoral and teaching fellowships in Middle Eastern languages; library of 150,000 vols; Dir Dr PETER SLUGETT.

Middle East Forum: Suite 1050, 1500 Walnut St, Philadelphia, PA 19102; tel. (215) 5465406; fax (215) 5465409; e-mail mef@meforum.org; internet www.MEForum.org; f. 1994; Dir DANIEL PIPES; Deputy Dir JANE MAESTRO; publs *Middle East Quarterly, Middle East Intelligence Bulletin.*

Middle East Institute: 1761 N St, NW, Washington, DC 20036; tel. (202) 7851141; fax (202) 3318861; e-mail members@ mideasti.org; internet www.mideasti.org; f. 1946; promotes American understanding of the Middle East, North Africa, the Caucasus and Central Asia; the MEI is a non-profit making independent resource centre that sponsors classes in Arabic, Hebrew, Persian and Turkish, co-ordinates cultural presentations and an annual garden series, convenes political and economic programmes and an annual conference and conducts scholar-in-residence and college internship programmes; Keiser Library 25,000 vols; 1,300 mems; Pres. Hon. ROSCOE S. SUDDARTH; publs *Middle East Journal* (quarterly) and occasional books.

Middle East Institute: Columbia University, International Affairs Bldg, New York, NY 10027; tel. (212) 8542584; fax (212) 8541413; f. 1954; a graduate training programme on the modern

Middle East for students seeking professional careers as regional specialists, research into problems of economics, government, law, and international relations of the Middle East countries, and their languages and history; library of more than 150,000 vols in Middle East vernaculars and equally rich in Western languages, including Russian; Dir GARY SICK.

Middle East Policy Council: Suite 512, 1730 M St, NW, Washington, DC 20036; tel. (202) 2966767; fax (202) 2965791; e-mail ajoyce@mepc.org; internet mepc.org; f. 1981; publ. *Middle East Policy* (quarterly).

Middle East Studies Association of North America: University of Arizona, 1643 E. Helen St, Tucson, AZ 85721; tel. (520) 6215850; fax (520) 6269095; e-mail mesana@u.arizona.edu; internet www.mesa.arizona.edu; f. 1966 to promote high standards of scholarship and instruction in Middle East studies, to facilitate communication among scholars through meetings and publications, and to foster co-operation among persons and organizations concerned with the scholarly study of the Middle East since the rise of Islam; 2,400 mems; Pres. (2001) R. STEPHEN HUMPHREYS, (2002) JOEL BEININ; Exec. Dir ANNE H. BETTERIDGE; publs *International Journal of Middle East Studies* (quarterly), *Bulletin* (2 a year), *Newsletter* (4 a year).

Middle East Studies Center: Portland State Univ., POB 751, Portland, OR 97207; tel. (503) 7254074; fax (503) 7255320; e-mail jon@sab.misc.pdx.edu; f. 1959; Middle East language and area studies, Arabic, Hebrew, Persian and Turkish languages and literatures; contemporary Turkish studies and Islamic studies programme; area classes in history, political science, geography, anthropology and sociology; extensive outreach activities; Dir JON MANDAVILLE; Assoc. Dir MARTA COLBURN.

Near East Foundation: 420 Lexington Ave, Suite 2516, New York, NY 10170-2599; tel. (212) 8670064; fax (212) 8670169; e-mail nef-hq@neareast.org; internet www.neareast.org; f. 1915; provides technical and financial assistance in support of locally-organized projects in agriculture and rural/community development in the Middle East and Africa; Chair. GEOFFREY A. THOMPSON; Pres. RICHARD C. ROBARTS; publs *Annual Report.*

Oriental Institute: 1155 East 58th St, Chicago, IL 60637; tel. (773) 7029514; fax (773) 702-9853; f. 1919; principally concerned with cultures and languages of the ancient Near East; extensive museum; affiliated to the University of Chicago; Dir GENE GRAGG.

Program in Near Eastern Studies: Princeton University, Jones Hall, Princeton, NJ 08544; tel. (609) 2584272; fax (609) 2581242; f. 1947; research in all aspects of the modern Near East and North Africa; library of 340,000 vols; Dir ANDRAS HAMORI; publs *Princeton Studies on the Near East* (irregular), *Princeton Papers: Inter-disciplinary Journal of Middle Eastern Studies* (semi-annual).

Semitic Museum: Harvard University, 6 Divinity Ave, Cambridge, MA 02138; tel. (617) 4954631; fax (617) 4968904; e-mail davis4@fas.harvard.edu; internet www.fas.harvard/~semitic; f. 1889; sponsors exploration and research in Western Asia; contains collection of exhibits from ancient Near East; research collections open by appointment, museum open to general public; Dir LAWRENCE E. STAGER.

Washington Institute for Near East Policy: Suite 1050, 1828 L St, NW, Washington, DC 20036; tel. (202) 4520650; fax (202) 2235364; e-mail info@washingtoninstitute.org; internet www.washingtoninstitute.org; f. 1985; promotes scholarly research and informed debate on the Middle East; Chair. BARBI WEINBERG; Exec. Dir ROBERT SATLOFF; publs incl. *Analytical Reports Series, Conference Proceedings, Policy Focus Series, Policy Paper Series,* also monographs.

VATICAN CITY

Pontificium Institutum Orientale (Pontifical Oriental Institute): 7 Piazza Santa Maria Maggiore, 00185 Rome; tel. (06) 4474170; fax (06) 4465576; f. 1917; library of 147,360 vols; Rector Rev. HÉCTOR VALL VILARDELL; Sec. Rev. JAKOV KULIČ; publs *Orientalia Christiana Periodica, Orientalia Christiana Analecta, Concilium Florentinum (Documenta et Scriptores), Anaphorae Syriacae, Kanonika.*

SELECT BIBLIOGRAPHY

Books on the Middle East

See also bibliographies at end of relevant chapters in Part Two.

Abdel Malek, A. *La pensée politique arabe contemporaine*. Paris, Editions du Seuil, 1970.

Abed, George T. (Ed.). *The Palestinian Economy: Studies in Development under Prolonged Occupation*. London, Routledge, 1988.

The Economic Viability of a Palestinian State. Washington, DC, Institute for Palestine State, 1990.

Abir, Mordechai. *Oil, Power and Politics: Conflict in Arabia, The Red Sea and The Gulf*. London, Frank Cass, 1974.

Abu Jaber, Kamel S. *The Arab Baath Socialist Party*. New York, Syracuse University Press, 1966.

Abu-Lughod, Ibrahim (Ed.). *The Transformation of Palestine: Essays on the Development of the Arab-Israeli Conflict*. Evanston, Ill, Northwestern University Press, 1971.

Abu-Zahra, Nadia. *The Pure and Powerful: Studies in Contemporary Muslim Society*. Reading, Ithaca Press, 1997.

Aburish, Said. *Cry Palestine: Inside the West Bank*. London, Bloomsbury, 1991.

Acharya, Amitar. *US Military Strategy in the Gulf*. London, Routledge, 1989.

Adams, Michael and Mayhew, Christopher. *Publish it Not. . .the Middle East Cover-up*. London, Longman, 1975.

Addas, Claude. *Quest for the Red Sulphur: The Life of Ibn 'Arabi*. Cambridge, Islamic Texts Society, 1995.

Adelson, Roger. *London and the Invention of the Middle East: Money, Power and War 1902–1922*. New Haven, Yale University Press, 1995.

Afkhami, Mahnaz. *Faith and Freedom: Women's Human Rights in the Muslim World*. London, I. B. Tauris, 1996.

Ahmed, Akbar S. *Discovering Islam: making Sense of Muslim History and Society*. London, Routledge, 1989.

Ajami, Fouad. *The Arab Predicament: Arab Political Thought and Practice since 1967*. Cambridge University Press, 2nd edn, 1992.

Alderson, A. D. *The Structure of the Ottoman Dynasty*. New York, Oxford University Press, 1956.

Algosaibi, Ghazi al-. *The Gulf crisis—an attempt to understand*. London, Kegan Paul International, 1993.

Ali, Tariq. *The Clash of Fundamentalisms: Crusades, Jihads and Modernity*. London, Verso, 2002.

Allan, Tony. *The Middle East Water Question: Hydropolitics and the Global Economy*. London, I. B. Tauris, 2001.

Allen, Richard. *Imperialism and Nationalism in the Fertile Crescent: Sources and Prospects of the Arab-Israeli Conflict*. London, Oxford University Press, 1975.

Alterman, Jon B. *New Media, New Politics? From Satellite Television to the Internet in the Arab World*. Washington Institute for Near East Policy, 1998.

Anderson, Jack, and Boyd, James. *Oil: The Real Story Behind the World Energy Crisis*. London, Sidgwick and Jackson, 1984.

Arberry, A. J. (Ed.). *Religion in the Middle East*—Volume I, *Judaism and Christianity*, Volume II, *Islam and General Summary*. Cambridge University Press, 1969.

Aruru, Naseer Hasan (Ed.). *Palestinian Refugees: the Right of Return*. London, Pluto Press, 2001.

Aruri, Naseer Hasan, and Shuraydi Mohammad A. (Eds). *Revising Culture, Reinventing Peace: The Influence of Edward W. Said*. Interlink Publishing Group, 2000.

Ashkenasi, Abraham (Ed.). *The Future of Jerusalem*. Frankfurt-am-Main, Peter Lang, 1999.

Ashtor, E. *A Social and Economic History of the Near East in the Middle Ages*. London, Collins, 1976.

Ateek, Nairn and Prior, Michael (Eds). *Holy Land Hollow Jubilee: God, Justice and the Palestinians*. Melisende, 1999.

Ayoob, M. (Ed.). *The Middle East in World Politics*. London, Croom Helm, 1981.

Ayubi, Nazih N. *Over-Stating the Arab State: Politics and Society in the Middle East*. London, I. B. Tauris, 1995.

Azzam, Salem (Ed.). *Islam and Contemporary Society: Islamic Council of Europe*. London, Longman, 1982.

Bailey, Sydney. *Four Arab-Israeli wars and the Peace Process*. London, Macmillan, 1990.

Barkey, Henri. *The Politics of Economic Reform in the Middle East*. London, Macmillan, 1993.

Barnaby, Frank. *The Invisible Bomb: The Nuclear Arms Race in the Middle East*. London, I. B. Tauris, 1989.

Baster, James. *The Introduction of Western Economic Institutions into the Middle East*. Royal Institute of International Affairs and Oxford University Press, 1960.

Behbehani, Hashim S. H. *China's Foreign Policy in the Arab World 1955–75*. Henley-on-Thames, Kegan Paul International, 1982.

Beinin, Joel. *Workers and Peasants in the Modern Middle East*. Cambridge University Press, 2001.

Beinin, Joel, and Stork, Joe (eds). *Political Islam: Essays from Middle East Report*. Berkeley, CA, University of California Press, 1996.

Bell, J. Bowyer. *The Long War, Israel and the Arabs since 1946*. Englewood Cliffs, NJ, 1969.

Ben-Zvi, Abraham. *Decade of Transition: Eisenhower, Kennedy, and the Origins of American-Israeli Alliance*. Columbia University Press, 1999.

Bennis, Phyllis, and Moushabeck, Michael (Eds). *Beyond the Storm: A Gulf Crisis Reader*. Edinburgh, Canongate Press, 1992.

Berberoglu, Berch (Ed.). *Power and Stability in the Middle East*. London, Zed Books, 1989.

Berque, Jacques. *L'Islam au défi*. Paris, Gallimard, 1980.

Berque, Jacques and Charnay, J.-P. *Normes et valeurs dans l'Islam contemporaine*. Paris, Payot, 1966.

Bethell, Nicholas. *The Palestine Triangle*. London, André Deutsch, 1979.

Bianquis, Th., Bosworth, C. E., Donzel, E. van, and Heinrichs, W. P. (Eds). *Encyclopaedia of Islam*. 10 Vols. Leiden, Brill Academic Publishers, 2000.

Bidwell, Robin (Ed.). *Dictionary of Modern Arab History*. London, Kegan Paul International, 1998.

Bill, J. and Springborg, R. *Politics in the Middle East*. London, HarperCollins, 4th edn, 1994.

Binder, Leonard. *The Ideological Revolution in the Middle East*. New York, 1964.

Biswas, Asit K. (Ed.). *Core and Periphery: A Comprehensive Approach to Middle Eastern Water*. Oxford University Press, 1998.

Blake, Gerald H., and Drysdale, Alasdair. *The Middle East and North Africa: A Political Geography*. Oxford University Press, 1985.

Bonine, Michael E. (Ed.). *Population, poverty and politics in Middle Eastern cities*. University Press of Florida, 1997.

Boulares, Habib. *Islam: the Fear and the Hope*. London, Zed Books, 1991.

Boyd, Douglas A. *Broadcasting in the Arab World: A Survey of Radio and Television in the Middle East*. Philadelphia, Temple University Press, 1982.

Bregman, Ahron and El-Tahri, Jihan. *The Fifty Years War: Israel and the Arabs*. London, Penguin and BBC Books, 1998.

Brenchley, Frank. *Britain and the Middle East: an economic history, 1945–1987*. London, Lester Crook Academic Publishing, 1989.

Breslauer, George W. (Ed.). *Soviet Strategy in the Middle East*. London, Routledge, 1989.

Brittain, Victoria (Ed.). *The Gulf Between Us: The Gulf War and Beyond*. London, Virago, 1991.

Brockelmann, C. *History of the Islamic Peoples*. New York and London, 1947–48.

Brooks, Geraldine. *Nine Parts of Desire: The Hidden World of Islamic Women*. London, Hamish Hamilton, 1995.

Brown, Daniel. *Rethinking Tradition in Modern Islamic Thought*. Cambridge University Press, 1996.

Brown, L. Carl. *Diplomacy in the Middle East*. London, I. B. Tauris, 2001.

Brown, L. Carl, and Gordon, Matthew S. (Eds). *Franco-Arab Encounters*. American University of Beirut, 1996.

Brown, Malcolm. *The Letters of T.E. Lawrence*. Oxford University Press, 1991.

Buchanan, Andrew S. *Peace with Justice: A History of the Israeli-Palestinian Declaration of Principles on Interim Self-Government Arrangements*. Basingstoke, St Martin's Press, 2000.

Bull, Gen. Odd. *War and Peace in the Middle East: the Experience and Views of a UN Observer*. London, Leo Cooper, 1976.

Bullard, Sir R. *Britain and the Middle East from the earliest times until 1952*. London, 1952.

Bulloch, John. *The Making of a War: The Middle East from 1967–1973*. London, Longman, 1974.

Bulloch, John, and Morris, Harvey. *The Gulf War*. London, Methuen, 1990.

    Saddam's War. London, Faber & Faber, 1991.

Burgat, François. *Face to Face with Political Islam*. London, I. B. Tauris, 1997.

Burke, Edmond. *Struggle for Survival in the Modern Middle East*. London, I. B. Tauris, 1994.

Burrows, Bernard. *Footnotes in the Sand: the Gulf in Transition*. London, Michael Russell, 1991.

Butt, Gerald. *A Rock and a Hard Place: origins of Arab-Western conflict in the Middle East*. London, Harper Collins, 1994.

    The Arabs: Myth and Reality. London, I. B. Tauris, 1998.

Butterworth, Charles E., and Zartman, I. William (Eds). *Between the State and Islam*. Cambridge University Press, 2001.

Calabrese, John. *China's changing relations with the Middle East*. London, Pinter, 1990.

Carré, Olivier. *L'Idéologie palestinienne de résistance*. Paris, Armand Colin, 1972.

    Mystique et Politique. Paris, Presses de la Fondation nationale des sciences politiques and Editions du Cerf, 1984.

Carrère d'Encausse, Hélène. *La politique soviétique au Moyen-Orient, 1955–1975*. Paris, Presses de la Fondation Nationale des Sciences Politiques, 1976.

Cattan, Henry. *Palestine and International Law: The Legal Aspects of the Arab-Israeli Conflict*. London, Longman, 1973.

    Jerusalem. London, Croom Helm, 1981 (Reissued, Gregg Revivals, 1994).

Cattan, J. *Evolution of Oil Concessions in the Middle East and North Africa*. New York, Oceana, Dobbs Ferry, 1967.

Celasun, Merih (Ed.). *State-Owned Enterprises in the Middle East and North Africa: Privatization, Performance and Reform*. London, Routledge, 2000.

Chaliand, Gérard. *People Without a Country: The Kurds and Kurdistan*. London, Zed Press, 2nd edn, 1992.

Chevallier, Dominique, Guellouz, Azzedine and Miquel, André. *Les arabes, l'islam et l'europe*. Paris, Flammarion, 1991.

Chomsky, Noam. *Peace in the Middle East?: Reflections on Justice and Nationhood*. London, Collins, 1976.

    The Fateful Triangle: The United States, Israel and the Palestinians. London, Pluto Press, 1983.

    Pirates and Emperors: International Terrorism in the Real World. Armana Books, USA, 1990.

Chomsky, Noam, and Said, Edward. *Acts of Aggression: Policing Rogue States*. New York, Seven Stories Press, 2002.

Choudhury, Masudul Alam. *Reforming The Muslim World*. London, Kegan Paul International, 1998.

Choueiri, Youssef M. *Arab History and the Nation-State: A Study in Modern Arab Historiography 1820–1980*. London, Routledge, 1980.

    Arab Nationalism: A History. Oxford, Blackwell, 2001.

    Islamic Fundamentalism. London, Continuum, 2002.

Clarke, John I., and Fisher, W. B. (Ed.). *Populations of the Middle East and North Africa*. University of London Press, 1972.

Cleveland, William L. *A History of the Modern Middle East*. Oxford, Westview Press, 1994.

Cobban, Helena. *The Palestinian Liberation Organization: People, Power and Politics*. Cambridge University Press, 1984.

Cohen, Michael J. *Palestine: Retreat from the Mandate*. London, Elek Books, 1978.

Cole, Juan R. I. *Modernity and The Millennium: The Genesis of the Bahá'í Faith in the Nineteenth Century*. Columbia University Press, 1998.

Conrad, Lawrence J. (Ed.). *The Formation and Perception of the Modern Arab World, Studies by Marwan R. Buheiry*. Princeton, The Darwin Press, 1989.

Cook, M. A. (Ed.). *Studies in the Economic History of the Middle East*. Oxford University Press, 1970.

Cooley, John K. *Green March, Black September: The Story of the Palestinian Arabs*. London, Frank Cass, 1973.

    Payback: America's Long War in the Middle East. London, Brassey's UK, 1992.

Coon, C. S. *Caravan: the Story of the Middle East*. New York, 1951, and London, 1952.

    The Impact of the West on Social Institutions. New York, 1952.

Corbin, Henry. *History of Islamic Philosophy*. London, Kegan Paul International, 1992.

Cordesman, Anthony. *Weapons of mass destruction in the Middle East*. London, Brasseys, 1991.

Corm, Georges. *Fragmentation of the Middle East: the last thirty years*. London, Unwin Hyman, 1988.

Costello, V. F. *Urbanisation in the Middle East*. Cambridge University Press, 1977.

Courbage, Youssef and Fargues, Philippe. *Christians and Jews under Islam*. London, I. B. Tauris, 1997.

Craig, Sir James Shemlan. *A History of the Middle East Centre for Arab Studies*. London, Macmillan, 1998.

Crone, Patricia. *Meccan Trade and the Rise of Islam*. Oxford, Basil Blackwell, 1987.

Cudsi, Alexander, and Dessouki, Ali E. Hillal (Eds). *Islam and Power*. London, Croom Helm, 1981.

Cursetjee, Manockjee Cursetjee. *The Land of the Date*. Reading, Garnet, 1999.

Curtiss, Richard H. *Stealth PACs: how Israel's American lobby took control of US-Middle East policy*. Washington, American Educational Trust, 1990.

Daftary, Farhad. *The Assassin Legends: Myths of the Isma'lis*. London, I. B. Tauris, 1995.

    A Short History of the Isma'lis: Traditions of a Muslim Community. Edinburgh University Press, 1999.

Damiani, Anita. *Enlightened Observers: British Travellers to the Middle East 1715–1850*. American University of Beirut, 1979.

Daniel, Norman. *Islam and the West: The Making of an Image*. One World Publications, revised edn, 1993.

    Islam, Europe and Empire. Edinburgh University Press, 1964.

Decobert, Christian. *Le mendiant et le combattant: l'institution de l'islam*. Paris, Editions du Seuil, 1991.

Dekmejian, R. H. *Islam in Revolution: fundamentalism in the Arab World*. New York, Syracuse University Press, 1995.

De la Billière, Peter. *Storm Command: a personal account of the Gulf War*. London, Harper Collins, 1992.

De Vore, Ronald M. (Ed.). *The Arab–Israeli Conflict: A Historical, Political, Social and Military Bibliography*. Oxford, Clio Press, 1977.

Dimbleby, Jonathan, and McCullin, Donald. *The Palestinians.* London, Quartet, 1970.

Dowek, Ephraim. *Israeli–Egyptian Relations, 1980–2000.* London, Frank Cass, 2001.

Dupuy, Trevor N. *Elusive Victory: The Arab-Israeli Wars 1947–1974.* London, MacDonald and Jane's, 1979.

Easterman, Daniel. *New Jerusalems—reflections on Islam, fundamentalism and the Rushdie affair.* London, Grafton Books, 1992.

Efrat, Moshe, and Bercovitch, Jacob. *Superpowers and Client States in the Middle East: The Imbalance of Influence.* London, Routledge, 1991.

Ehteshami, Anoushiravan, and Hinnebusch, Raymond. *Syria and Iran: Middle Powers in a Penetrated Regional System.* London, Routledge, 1997.

Ehteshami, Anoushiravan, and Nonneman, Gerd. *War and Peace in the Gulf: Domestic Politics and Regional Relations into the 1990s.* Reading, Ithaca Press, 1991.

Elon, Amos. A Blood-Dimmed Tide: *Dispatches from the Middle East.* London, Allen Lane, 2000.

Enayat, Hamid. *Modern Islamic Political Thought: The Response of the Shi'i and Sunni Muslims to the Twentieth Century.* London, Macmillan, 1982.

Enderlin, Charles. *Le Rêve brisé: Histoire de l'échec du processus de paix au Proche-Orient (1995–2002).* Paris, Fayard, 2002.

Esposito, John L. (Ed.). *Voices of Resurgent Islam.* New York, Oxford University Press, 1983.

The Islamic Threat, Myth or Reality? New York, Oxford University Press Inc., 1992.

The Oxford History of Islam. New York, Oxford University Press, Inc., 2000.

Unholy War: Terror in the Name of Islam. New York, Oxford University Press, Inc., 2002.

Esmail, Aziz. *Reason, Interpretation and Islam: Essays in the Philosophy of Religion.* Richmond, Curzon Press, 1999.

Ettinghausen, Richard. Books and Periodicals in Western Languages dealing with the Near and Middle East. Washington, Middle East Institute, 1952.

Fahmy, Mansour. *La condition de la femme en islam.* Paris, Editions Allia, 1991.

Faqir, Fadia (Ed.). *In The House of Silence.* Reading, Garnet, 1998.

Field, Henry. *Bibliography on Southwestern Asia: VII, A Seventh Compilation.* University of Miami, 1962.

Field, Michael. *$100,000,000 a Day—Inside the World of Middle East Money.* London, Sidgwick and Jackson, 1975.

Inside the Arab World. London, John Murray, 1994.

Findlay, Allan M. *The Arab World.* London, Routledge, 1996.

Fisher, S. N. *Social Forces in the Middle East.* Ithaca, NY, Cornell University Press, 3rd edn, 1977.

The Middle East: A History. New York, McGraw-Hill, 4th edn, 1990.

Fisher, W. B. *The Middle East—a Physical, Social and Regional Geography.* London, 7th edn, 1978.

Frangi, Abdallah. *The PLO and Palestine.* London, Zed Press, 1984.

Freedman, Robert O. *Soviet Policy toward the Middle East since 1970.* New York, Praeger, 3rd edn, 1983.

Friedman, Thomas. *From Beirut to Jerusalem.* New York, Farrar, Straus and Giroux, 1989.

Frye, R. N. (Ed.). *The Near East and the Great Powers.* Cambridge, Mass, Harvard University Press, 1951; London, New York and Toronto, Oxford University Press, 1952.

Fuller, Graham E., and Lesser, Jan O. *A Sense of Siege: The Geopolitics of Islam and the West.* Boulder, CO, Westview Press, 1995.

Gallagher, Nancy Elizabeth (Ed.). *Approaches to the History of the Middle East: Interviews with leading Middle East historians.* Reading, Garnet, 1995.

Gee, John. *Unequal Conflict.* London, Pluto Press, 1998.

Gelber, Yoav. Palestine 1948: *War, Escape and the Emergence of the Palestinian Refugee Problem.* Brighton, Sussex Academic Press, 2001.

Gerner, Deborah J. *Understanding the Contemporary Middle East.* Boulder, CO, Lynne Rienner, 2000.

Gershoni, Israel, and Jankowski, James (Eds). *Rethinking Nationalism in the Arab Middle East.* New York, Columbia University Press, 1998.

Gershoni, Israel, Erdem, Hakan, and Woköck, Ursula (Eds). *Histories of the Modern Middle East: New Directions.* Boulder, CO, Lynn Rienner, 2002.

Ghareeb, Edmund and Khadduri, Majid. *War in the Gulf, 1990–91: The Iraq-Kuwait Conflict and its Implications.* Oxford University Press, 1997.

Giacaman, George and Dag Jrund Lonning. *After Oslo: New Realities, Old Problems.* Pluto Press, 1998.

Gibb, H. A. R. *Mohammedanism.* London, 1949.

Modern Trends in Islam. Chicago, 1947.

Studies on the Civilisation of Islam. London, 1962.

Gibb, H. A. R., and Bowen, Harold. *Islamic Society and the West.* London, 2 vols, 1950, 1957.

Gilbar, Gad. *Population Dilemmas in the Middle East.* London, Frank Cass, 1997.

Gilbert, Martin. *The Arab-Israeli Conflict: Its History in Maps.* London, Weidenfeld and Nicolson, 1974 (reissued, Dent: International Publishing Services, 1993).

Gilmour, David. *The Dispossessed: The Ordeal of the Palestinians 1917–80.* London, Sidgwick & Jackson, 1980.

Gilsenan, Michael. *Recognizing Islam: Religion and Society in the Modern Middle East.* London, I. B. Tauris, 1990.

Gittings, John (Ed.). *Beyond the Gulf War: The Middle East and the New World Order.* London, Catholic Institute for International Relations, 1991.

Glassé, Cyril. *The Concise Encyclopedia of Islam.* London, revised edn, Stacey International, 2001.

Glubb, Lt-Gen. Sir John. *A Short History of the Arab Peoples.* London, Hodder and Stoughton, 1969.

Golan, Galia. *The Soviet Union and the Middle East Crisis.* Cambridge University Press, 1977.

Gomaa, Ahmed M. *The Foundation of the League of Arab States.* London, Longman, 1977.

Goodwin, Godfrey. *The Janissaries.* London, Saqi Books, 1997.

Gowers, Andrew, and Walter, Tony. *Behind the Myth: Yasir Arafat and the Palestinian revolution.* London, W.H. Allen, 1990.

Graz, Liesl. *The Turbulent Gulf.* London, I.B. Tauris, 1990.

Gresh, Alain, and Vidal, Dominique. *A–Z of the Middle East.* London, Zed Books, 1991.

Grossman, Mark. *Encyclopaedia of the Persian Gulf War.* Santa Barbara, California, ABC-Clio, 1996.

Grundwald, K., and Ronall, J. O. *Industrialisation in the Middle East.* New York, Council for Middle East Affairs, 1960.

Grunebaum, Gustave E. von (Ed.). *Unity and Variety in Muslim Civilisation.* Chicago, 1955.

Islam: Essays on the Nature and Growth of a Cultural Tradition. London, Routledge and Kegan Paul, 1961.

Modern Islam: the Search for Cultural Identity. London, 1962.

Guazzone, Laura. *The Islamist Dilemma.* Reading, Ithaca Press, 1995.

Guyatt, Nicholas. *The Absence of Peace: Understanding The Israeli-Palestinian Conflict.* London, Zed Press, 1998.

Hakimian, Hassan, and Moshaver, Ziba (Eds). *The State and Global Change: The Political Economy of Change in the Middle East and North Africa.* Richmond, Curzon, 2001.

Halliday, Fred. *Nation and Religion in the Middle East.* Boulder, CO, Lynne Rienner, 2000.

Islam and the Myth of Confrontation: Religion and Politics in the Middle East. London, I. B. Tauris, revised edn, 2002.

Halm, Heinz. *The Fatimids and their Traditions of Learning.* London, I. B. Tauris, 1997.

Halpern, Manfred. *The Politics of Social Change in the Middle East and North Africa*. New York, Princeton University Press, 1963.

Hansen, Birte. *Unipolarity and the Middle East*. Richmond, Curzon Press, 1999.

Hardy, Roger. *Arabia after the Storm: internal stability of the Gulf Arab states*. London, Royal Institute of International Affairs, 1992.

Hare, William. *The Struggle for the Holy Land*. London, Madison Publishing, 1998.

Harris, Lillian Craig. *China Considers the Middle East*. London, I. B. Tauris, 1994.

Hart, Alan. *Arafat—Terrorist or Peacemaker?* London, Sidgwick and Jackson, 2nd edn, 1994.

Hartshorn, J. E. *Oil Companies and Governments*. London, Faber, 1962.

Hassan bin Talal, Crown Prince of Jordan. *A Study on Jerusalem*. London, Longman, 1980.

Hatem, M. Abdel-Kader. *Information and the Arab Cause*. London, Longman, 1974.

Hayes, J. R. (Ed.). *The Genius of Arab Civilisation: Source of Renaissance*. New York University Press, 3rd edn, 1992.

Hazard. *Atlas of Islamic History*. Oxford University Press, 1951.

Heikal, Mohammed. *Illusions of Triumph: An Arab View of the Gulf War*. London, Harper Collins, 1992.

Hershlag, Z. Y. *Introduction to the Modern Economic History of the Middle East*. Leiden, E. J. Brill, 2nd edn, 1980.

Herzog, Maj.-Gen. Chaim. *The War of Atonement*. London, Weidenfeld and Nicolson, 1975.

   The Arab-Israeli Wars. London, Arms and Armour Press, 1982.

Hewedy, Amin. *Militarisation and Security in the Middle East*. London, Pinter, 1989.

Higgins, Rosalyn. *United Nations Peacekeeping 1946–67: Documents and Commentary*, Volume I, *The Middle East*. Oxford University Press, 1969.

Hiro, Dilip. *Inside the Middle East*. London, Routledge and Kegan Paul, 1981.

   Islamic Fundamentalism. London, Paladin, 1988.

   The Longest War. London, Grafton Books, 1990.

   Dictionary of the Middle East. London, Macmillan, 1996.

   Sharing the Promised Land. An Interwoven Tale of Israelis and Palestinians. London, Hodder & Stoughton, 1996.

   War Without End: The Rise Of Islamist Terrorism And Global Response. London, Routledge, 2002.

Hirst, David. *Oil and Public Opinion in the Middle East*. New York, Praeger, 1966.

   The Gun and the Olive Branch: the Roots of Violence in the Middle East. London, Faber, 1977.

Hirszowicz, Lukasz. *The Third Reich and the Arab East*. London, Routledge and Kegan Paul, 1966.

   A Short History of the Near East. New York, 1966.

   Makers of Arab History. London, Macmillan, 1968.

   Islam. A Way of Life. London, Oxford University Press, 1971.

Hoare, Ian and Tayar, Graham (Eds). *The Arabs. A handbook on the politics and economics of the contemporary Arab world*. London, BBC Publications, 1971.

Hodgkin, E. C. *The Arabs*. Modern World Series, Oxford University Press, 1966.

   (Ed.). *Two Kings in Arabia: Sir Reader Bullard's Letters from Jeddah*. Reading, Ithaca Press, 1999.

Holt, P. M. *Studies in the History of the Near East*. London, Frank Cass, 1973.

Holt, P. M., Lambton, A. K. S., and Lewis, B. (Eds.). *The Cambridge History of Islam*. Vol. I, *The Central Islamic Lands*. Cambridge University Press, 1970; Vol. II, *The Further Islamic Lands, Islamic Society and Civilization*. Cambridge University Press, 1971.

Hopwood, Derek (Ed.). *Studies in Arab History*. London, Macmillan, 1990.

Hourani, A. H. *Minorities in the Arab World*. London, 1947.

   A Vision of History. Beirut, 1961.

   Arabic Thought in the Liberal Age 1798–1939. Oxford University Press, 1962.

   Europe and the Middle East. London, Macmillan, 1980.

   The Emergence of the Modern Middle East. London, Macmillan, 1981.

   A History of the Arab Peoples. London, Faber and Faber, 1991.

   Islam in European Thought. Cambridge University Press, 1991.

Hoveyda, Fereydoun. *Que veulent les arabes?* Paris, Editions First, 1991.

Hudson, Michael C. *Arab Politics: The Search for Legitimacy*. New Haven and London, Yale University Press, 1977/78.

Hurewitz, J. C. *Unity and Disunity in the Middle East*. New York, Carnegie Endowment for International Peace, 1952.

   Middle East Dilemmas. New York, 1953.

   Diplomacy in the Near and Middle East. Vol. I, *1535–1914*; Vol. II, *1914–56*. Van Nostrand, 1956.

   Soviet-American Rivalry in the Middle East (Ed.). London, Pall Mall Press, and New York, Praeger, 1969.

   Middle East Politics: The Military Dimension. London, Pall Mall Press, 1969.

Husari, Khaldun S Al-. *Three Reformers; A Study in Modern Arab Political Thought*. Beirut, Khayats, 1966.

Hussein, Mahmoud. *Les Arabes au présent*. Paris, Editions Seuil, 1974.

Ibrahim, Saad Eddin. *The New Arab Social Order: A Study of the Social Impact of Oil Wealth*. Boulder, CO, Westview Press, 1982.

International Institute for Strategic Studies. *Sources of Conflict in the Middle East*. London, Adelphi Papers, International Institute for Strategic Studies, 1966.

   Domestic Politics and Regional Security: Jordan, Syria and Israel. London, Gower, International Institute for Strategic Studies, 1989.

Ionides, Michael. *Divide and Lose: the Arab Revolt 1955–58*. London, Bles, 1960.

Irwin, I. J. *Islam in the Modern National State*. Cambridge University Press, 1965.

Isaak, David T., and Fesharaki, F. *OPEC, the Gulf and the World Petroleum Market*. London, Croom Helm, 1983.

Issawi, Charles. *An Economic History of the Middle East and North Africa*. London, Methuen, 1982.

Isstaif, Abdul-Nabi. *Towards a New Orientalism: A Cross-Cultural Encounter*. Richmond, Curzon Press, 1999.

Izzard, Molly. *The Gulf*. London, John Murray, 1979.

Jabbor, Suhayl J., and Conrad, Lawrence I. (Eds). *The Bedouins and the Desert: Aspects of Nomadic Life in the Arab East*. Albany, State University of New York Press, 1996.

Jaber, Faleh A. (Ed.) *Post-Marxism and the Middle East*. London, Saqi Books, 1997.

Janin, R. *Les églises orientales et les rites orientaux*. Paris, 1926.

Jansen, G. H. *Non-Alignment and the Afro-Asian States*. New York, Praeger, 1966.

   Militant Islam. London, Pan Books, 1979.

Jansen, Johannes J. G. *The Dual Nature of Islamic Fundamentalism*. Ithaca, N.Y., Cornell University Press, 1997.

Jawad, Haifaa A. *The Middle East in the New World Order*. London, Macmillan, 1996.

Jerichow, A. and Simonsen, J. B. (Eds). *Islam in a Changing World and the Middle East*. Richmond, Surrey, Curzon Press, 1997.

Johnson, Nels. *Islam and the Politics of Meaning in Palestinian Nationalism*. Henley-on-Thames, Kegan Paul International, 1983.

Jones, David. *The Arab World*. New York, Hilary House, 1967.

Kandiyoti, Deniz (Ed.). *Gendering the Middle East: Emerging Perspectives*. London, I. B. Tauris, 1996.

Kapiszewski, Andrzej. *Nationals and Expatriates: Population and Labour Dilemmas of the Gulf Cooperation Council States.* Reading, Ithaca Press, 2000.

Karpat, Kemal H. *Political and Social Thought in the Contemporary Middle East.* London, Pall Mall Press, 1968.

Katz, Mark N. *Russia and Arabia: Soviet Foreign Policy toward the Arabian Peninsula.* Baltimore and London, Johns Hopkins University Press, 1986.

Kayal, Alawi D. *The Control of Oil: East–West Rivalry in the Persian Gulf.* London, Kegan Paul, 2002.

Kaye, Dalia Dassa. *Beyond the Handshake: Multilateral Cooperation in the Arab-Israeli Peace Process, 1991–96.* New York, Columbia University Press, 2001.

Keay, John. *The Arabs: A Living History.* London, Harvill, 1983.

Kedourie, Elie. *England and the Middle East.* London, 1956.

The Chatham House Version and other Middle-Eastern Studies. London, Weidenfeld and Nicolson, 1970.

Arabic Political Memoirs and Other Studies. London, Frank Cass, 1974.

In the Anglo-Arab Labyrinth. 1976.

Islam in the Modern World and Other Studies. London, Mansell, 1980.

Towards a Modern Iran. 1980.

Kelly, J. B. *Eastern Arabian Frontiers.* London, Faber, 1963.

Arabia, the Gulf and the West: A Critical View of the Arabs and their Oil Policy. London, Weidenfeld and Nicolson, 1980.

Kemp, Geoffrey and Harkavy, Robert. *The Strategic Geography of the Changing Middle East.* Washington, DC, The Brookings Institution, 1996.

Kemp, Geoffrey and Pressman, Jeremy. *Point of No Return: The Deadly Struggle for Middle East Peace.* Washington, DC, The Brookings Institution, 1997.

Kepel, Gilles (trans. Antony Roberts). *Jihad: The Trail of Political Islam.* London, I. B. Tauris, 2002.

Kerr, Malcolm. *The Arab Cold War 1958-1964.* Oxford University Press, 1965.

Khadouri, M. *Political Trends in the Arab World.* Baltimore, Johns Hopkins Press, 1970.

Khadouri, M., and Lievesny, H. J. (Eds) *Law in the Middle East,* Vol. I, Washington, 1955.

Khalil, Muhammad. *The Arab States and the Arab League (historical documents).* Beirut, Khayats.

Khan, Sarfraz. *Muslim Reformist Political Thought: Revivalists, Modernists and Free Will.* Richmond, Curzon Press, 1999.

Khouri, Fred J. *The Arab-Israeli Dilemma.* Syracuse/New York, 1968.

Khuri, Fuad I. *Imams and Emirs: state, religion and sects in Islam.* London, Saqi Books, 1990.

Tents and Pyramids. London, Saqi Books, 1992.

Kingsbury, R. C., and Pounds, N. J. G. *An Atlas of Middle Eastern Affairs.* New York, 1963.

Kingston, Paul W. T. *Britain and the Politics of Modernization in the Middle East, 1945-1958.* Cambridge University Press, 1996.

Kirk, George E. *The Middle East in the War.* London, 1953.

A Short History of the Middle East: from the Rise of Islam to Modern Times. New York, 1955.

Klein, Menachem. *Jerusalem: The Contested City.* New York University Press, 2001.

Kliot, Norit. *Water Resources and Conflict in the Middle East.* London, Routledge, 1994.

Koch, Christopher. *Gulf Security in the Twenty-First Century.* London, I. B. Tauris, 1997.

Kreyenbroek, Philip G., and Sperl, Stefan (Eds). *The Kurds: a contemporary overview.* London, Routledge, 1992.

Kreutz, Andrej. *Vatican Policy on the Palestinian—Israeli Conflict: the struggle for the Holy Land.* London, Greenwood Press, 1990.

Kumar, Ravinder. *India and the Persian Gulf Region.* London, 1965.

Kurzman, Dan. *Genesis 1948: The First Arab/Israeli War.* London, Vallentine, Mitchell, 1972.

Kutschera, Chris. *Le mouvement national kurde.* Paris, Flammarion, 1979.

La Guardia, Anton. *Holy Land, Unholy War: Israelis and Palestinians.* London, John Murray, 2001.

Lall, Arthur. *The UN and the Middle East Crisis.* New York/London, 1968.

Lapidus, Ira M. *A History of Islamic Societies.* Cambridge University Press, 1989.

Laqueur, W. Z. *Communism and Nationalism in the Middle East.* London and New York, 1957.

A History of Zionism. London, Weidenfeld and Nicolson, 1972.

The Struggle for the Middle East: The Soviet Union and the Middle East 1958–68. London, Routledge and Kegan Paul, 1969.

Confrontation: The Middle-East War and World Politics. London, Wildwood, 1974.

(Ed.) *The Middle East in Transition.* London, Routledge and Kegan Paul, 1958.

(Ed.) *The Israel-Arab Reader.* New York/London, Penguin Books, 4th edn, 1984.

Lemarchand, Philippe (Ed.). *The Crescent of Crises: A Geopolitical Atlas of the Middle East and the Arab World.* Paris, Editions Complexe, 1995.

Lenczowski, George. *The Middle East in World Affairs.* Ithaca, N.Y., Cornell University Press, 4th edn, 1980.

Oil and State in the Middle East. Cornell University Press, 1960.

Lesch, David W. (Ed.). *The Middle East and the United States: A Historical and Political Reassessment.* Boulder, Colorado, Westview Press, 1996.

Lewis, Bernard. *The Arabs in History.* Oxford University Press, 6th edn, 1993.

Shaping of the Modern Middle East. New York, Oxford University Press, 1994.

Race and Colour in Islam. London, 1971.

Islam in History. Open Court Publishing Co., 2nd edn, 1992.

Islam to 1453. London, 1974.

The Middle East: 2000 Years of History from the Rise of Christianity to the Present Day. London, Phoenix Press, revised edn, 2000.

What Went Wrong?: Western Impact and Middle Eastern Response. New York, Oxford University Press, 2001.

Lieden, Karl. (Ed.). *The conflict of traditionalism and modernism in the Muslim Middle East.* Austin, Texas, 1969.

Lippman, Thomas W. *Understanding Islam: An Introduction to the Moslem World.* New York, New American Library, 1982.

Lloyd, Selwyn. *Suez 1956: A Personal Account.* London, Jonathan Cape, 1978.

Logan, William S. and White, Paul J. (Eds). *Remaking the Middle East.* Oxford, Berg, 1997.

Longrigg, S. H. *Oil in the Middle East.* London, 1954, 3rd edn, London 1968.

The Middle East: a Social Geography. London, 2nd revised edn, 1970.

Louis, William Roger. *The British Empire in the Middle East 1945–51.* Oxford University Press, 1984.

Maalouf, Amin. *The Crusades Through Arab Eyes.* Saqi Books, 1984.

Mabro, Judy (Ed.). *Veiled Half-Truths: Western Travellers' Perceptions of Middle Eastern Women.* London, I. B. Tauris, 1992.

McCarthy, Justin. *The Population of Palestine.* New York, Columbia University Press, 1991.

Macdonald, Robert W. *The League of Arab States.* Princeton, Princeton University Press, 1965.

McDowall, David. *The Kurds: a nation denied.* London, Minority Rights Group, 1992.

Europe and the Arabs: discord and symbiosis. London, Royal Institute of International Affairs, 1992.

A Modern History of the Kurds. London, I. B. Tauris, 1997.

Maddy-Weitzmann, Bruce, and Inbar, Efraim (Eds). *Religious Radicalism in the Greater Middle East.* London, Frank Cass, 1997.

Mallat, Chibli. *The Middle East into the Twenty-First Century: The Japan Lectures and other studies on the Arab-Israeli conflict, the Gulf crisis and political Islam.* Reading, Ithaca Press, 1996.

Mannin, Ethel. *A Lance for the Arabs.* London, 1973.

Mansfield, Peter. *The Ottoman Empire and Its Successors.* London, Macmillan, 1973.

(Ed.). *The Middle East: A Political and Economic Survey.* London, Oxford University Press, 5th edn, 1980.

The Arabs. Penguin, 5th edn, 1992.

Marlow, Louise. *Hierarchy and Egalitarianism in Islamic Thought.* Cambridge University Press, 1996.

Martin Muqoz, Gema (Ed.). *Islam, Modernism and the West: Cultural and Political Relations at the end of the Millennium.* London, I. B. Tauris, 1997.

Mattar, Philip (Ed.). *Encyclopedia of the Palestinians.* London, Fitzroy Dearborn, 2000.

Maull, Hanns, and Pick, Otto (Eds). *The Gulf War.* London, Pinter Publishers, 1989.

Meijer, Roel (Ed.). *Cosmopolitanism, Identity and Authenticity in the Middle East.* Richmond, Curzon Press, 1999.

Meisami, J. S., and Starkey, Paul. *Encyclopaedia of Arabic Literature.* London, Routledge, 1995.

Menashiri, David (Ed.). *Central Asia meets the Middle East.* London, Frank Cass, 1998.

Mendelsohn, Everett. *A Compassionate Peace: a future for Israel, Palestine and the Middle East.* New York, The Noonday Press, 1989.

Meskell, Lynn. *Archaeology Under Fire: Nationalism, politics and heritage in the Eastern Mediterranean and Middle East.* London, Routledge, 1998.

Mikdashi, Zuhayr. *The Community of Oil Exporting Countries.* London, George Allen and Unwin, 1972.

Miller, Davina. *Subverting Policy: British Arms Sales to Iran and Iraq.* London, Cassell, 1996.

Milton-Edwards, Beverley, and Hinchliffe, Peter. *Conflicts in the Middle East since 1945.* London, Routledge, 2001.

Miquel, André. *Islam et sa civilisation.* Paris, 1968.

Mojtahed-zadeh, Pirouz. *Security and Territoriality in the Persian Gulf: A Maritime Political Geography.* Richmond, Curzon Press, 1999.

Moller, Bjorn (Ed.). *Oil and Water: Co-operative Security in the Persian Gulf.* London, I. B. Tauris, 2001.

Momen, Moojan. *An Introduction to Shi'i Islam.* London, Yale University Press, revised edn, 1987.

Mommer, Bernard. *Global Oil and the Nation State.* New York, Oxford University Press, Inc. 2002.

Monroe, Elizabeth. *Britain's Moment in the Middle East 1914–71.* London, Chatto and Windus, new edn 1981.

Philby of Arabia. Reading, Ithaca Press, 1998.

Moore, John Norton. *The Arab-Israeli Conflict.* 4 vols. Princeton, Readings and Documents, 1976–92.

Morris, Claud. *The Last Inch: A Middle East Odyssey.* London, Kegan Paul International, 1996.

Mortimer, Edward. *Faith and Power: The Politics of Islam.* London, Faber, 1982.

Morzellec, Joëlle Le. *La question de Jérusalem devant l'Organisation des Nations Unies.* Brussels, Emile Bruylant, S.A., 1979.

Mosley, Leonard. *Power Play: The Tumultuous World of Middle East Oil 1890–1973.* London, Weidenfeld and Nicolson, 1973.

Mostyn, T. *Major Political Events in Iran, Iraq and the Arabian Peninsula 1945–1990.* Oxford/New York, Facts on File, 1991.

Munson, Henry Jr. *Islam and Revolution in the Middle East.* New Haven and London, Yale University Press, 1988.

Murakami, Masahiro. *Managing Water for Peace in the Middle East: Alternative Strategies.* Tokyo, United Nations University Press, 1996.

Murden, Simon W. Murden. *Islam, the Middle East, and the New Global Hegemony.* Boulder, CO, Lynne Rienner, 2002

Nasr, Seyyed Hossein. *Science and Civilization in Islam.* Harvard (1968), revised edn, 1987.

Navias, Martin. *Going Ballistic: the build-up of missiles in the Middle East.* London, Brassey's, 1993.

Nevakivi, Jukka. *Britain, France and the Arab Middle East 1914–20.* Athlone Press, University of London, 1969.

Niblock, Tim. *'Pariah' States and Sanctions in the Middle East: Iraq, Libya, Sudan.* Boulder, CO, Lynne Rienner, 2001.

Niblock, Tim, and Murphy, Emma. *Economic and Political Liberalism in the Middle East.* London, British Academic Press, 1993.

Nizameddin, Talal. *Russia and the Middle East.* London, C. Hurst & Co, 1999.

Nonneman, Gerd. *Development, Administration and Aid in the Middle East.* London, Routledge, 1988.

(Ed.) *The Middle East and Europe: The Search for Stability and Integration.* London, Federal Trust, 1993.

Nutting, Anthony. *The Arabs.* London, Hollis and Carter, 1965.

No End of a Lesson, The Story of Suez. London, Constable, 1967.

Nydell, Margaret K. *Understanding Arabs: A Guide for Westerners.* Yarmouth, Maine, Intercultural Press, 1992.

O'Ballance, Edgar. *The Third Arab-Israeli War.* London, Faber and Faber, 1972.

The Gulf War. London, Brassey's Defence Publishers, 1990.

Odell, Peter. *Oil and World Power.* London, Penguin, 1983.

Oren, Michael B. *Six Days of War: June 1967 and the Making of the Modern Middle East.* London/New York, Oxford University Press, 2002.

Owen, Roger. *The Middle East in the World Economy 1800–1914.* London, I. B. Tauris (1972), revised edn, 1993.

State, Power and Politics in the Making of the Modern Middle East. London, Routledge, 2nd edn, 2000.

A History of Middle East Economies in the 20th Century. London, I. B. Tauris, 1998.

Palmer, Alan. *The Decline and Fall of the Ottoman Empire.* London, John Murray, 1992.

Palumbo, Michael. *The Palestinian Catastrophe.* London, Faber, 1987.

Pantelides, Veronica S. *Arab Education 1956–1978: A Bibliography.* London, Mansell, 1982.

Parker, Richard B. *The October War—A Retrospective.* Gainesville, FL, University Press of Florida, 2001.

Pennar, Jaan. *The USSR and the Arabs: The Ideological Dimension.* London, Hurst, 1973.

Persson, Magnus. *Great Britain, the United States and the Security of the Middle East: The Formation of the Baghdad Pact.* Lund University Press (Sweden), 1998.

Peters, F. E. *The Hajj: The Muslim pilgrimage to Mecca and the holy places.* Princeton University Press, 1995.

Piscatori, James P. (Ed.). *Islam in the Political Process.* Cambridge University Press, 1983.

Islam in a World of Nation-States. Cambridge University Press, 1986.

Playfair, Ian S. O. *The Mediterranean and the Middle East.* London, History of the Second World War, HMSO, 1966.

Poliak, A. N. *Feudalism in Egypt, Syria, Palestine and the Lebanon, 1250–1900.* London, Luzac, for the Royal Asiatic Society, 1939.

Polk, W. R. *The Arab World Today.* Harvard University Press, 1991.

(Ed. with Chambers, R. L.) *Beginnings of Modernization in the Middle East: the Nineteenth Century.* University of Chicago Press, 1969.

The Elusive Peace: The Middle East in the Twentieth Century. London, Frank Cass, 1980.

Porath, Y. *The Emergence of the Palestinian Arab National Movement 1918–1929.* London, Frank Cass, 1974.

Quandt, William B. *Peace Process: American Diplomacy and the Arab–Israeli Conflict since 1967.* Berkeley, CA, University of California Press, 2001.

Qubain, Fahim I. *Education and Science in the Arab World.* Baltimore, Johns Hopkins Press, 1967.

Raufer, Xavier. *Atlas Mondial de l'Islam Activiste.* Paris, Editions de la Table Ronde, 1991.

Richards, A. and Waterbury, J. *A Political Economy of the Middle East.* Boulder, CO, Westview Press (1990), 2nd edn (revised), 1996.

Ridgeway, James (Ed.). *The March to War.* New York, Four Walls Eight Windows, 1991.

Rikhye, Maj.-Gen. I. J. *The Sinai Blunder.* London, Frank Cass, 1980.

Rivlin, B., and Szyliowicz, J. S. (Eds). *The Contemporary Middle East—Tradition and Innovation.* New York, Random House, 1965.

Roberts, D. S. *Islam: A Concise Introduction.* New York, Harper and Row, 1982.

Robinson, Francis. *Atlas of the Islamic World since 1500.* London, Phaidon, 1983.

(Ed.) *The Cambridge Illustrated History of the Islamic World.* Cambridge University Press, 1996.

Robinson, Neal. *Islam: A Concise Introduction.* Richmond, Curzon Press, 1999.

Rodinson, Maxime. *Islam and Capitalism.* France, 1965, England, 1974.

Muhammad. London, Penguin, 1974.

La fascination de l'Islam. Paris, Maspero, 1980.

The Arabs. University of Chicago Press (1981), revised edn, 1989.

Israel and the Arabs. London, Penguin, 1982.

Europe and the Mystique of Islam. London, I. B. Tauris, 1989.

Rogan, Eugene L., and Shlaim, Avi (Eds). *The War for Palestine: Rewriting the History of 1948.* Cambridge University Press, 2001.

Ro'i, Ya'acov. *The Limits of Power: Soviet Policy in the Middle East.* London, Croom Helm, 1978.

Ronart, Stephan and Nandy. *Concise Encyclopaedia of Arabic Civilization.* Amsterdam, 1966.

Rondot, Pierre. *The Destiny of the Middle East.* London, Chatto & Windus, 1960.

L'Islam. Paris, Prismes, 1965.

Rouhani, Fuad. *A History of OPEC.* London, Pall Mall Press, 1972.

Roy, Olivier. *The Failure of Political Islam.* London, I. B. Tauris, 1995.

Rubin, Barry M. *The Arab States and the Palestine Conflict.* New York, Syracuse University Press, 1981.

Ruthven, Malise. *Islam in the World.* Harmondsworth, Penguin (1984), revised edn, 1991.

A Satanic Affair: Salman Rushdie and the Rage of Islam. London, Chatto and Windus, 1990.

A Fury for God: The Islamist Attack on America. London, Granta Books, 2002.

Sachar, Howard M. *Europe Leaves the Middle East 1936–1954.* London, Allen Lane, 1973.

Said, Edward W. *The Question of Palestine.* London, Routledge, 1979 (reissued, Vintage, 1992).

Covering Islam. London, Routledge, 1982.

The End of the Peace Process: Oslo and After. New York, Pantheon Books, 2000.

Salame, G. *Democracy without Democrats? The Renewal of Politics in the Muslim World.* London/New York, I. B. Tauris, 1994.

Salem, Paul (Ed.). *Conflict Resolution in the Arab World: Selected Essays.* American University of Beirut, 1997.

Sardar, Ziauddin (Ed.). *Science and Technology in the Middle East.* Harlow, Longman, 1982.

Sauvaget, J. *Introduction à l'histoire de l'orient musulman.* Paris, 1943. 2nd edn re-cast by C. Cahen, University of California Press, 1965.

Savory, R. M. *Introduction to Islamic Civilization.* Cambridge University Press, 1976.

Sayigh, Fatallah. *Le Désert et la Gloire.* Paris, Editions Gallimard, 1993.

Sayigh, Yusif A. *The Determinants of Arab Economic Development.* London, Croom Helm, 1977.

The Economies of the Arab World. London, Croom Helm, 1978.

Arab Oil Policies in the 1970s. London, Croom Helm, 1983.

Elusive Development: From Dependence to Self-Reliance in the Arab Region. London, Routledge, 1991.

Schimmel, Annemarie. *Islam: An Introduction.* State University of New York Press, 1992.

Shulze, Reinhard. *A Modern History of the Islamic World.* London, I. B. Tauris, 2002.

Scott Appleby, R. (Ed.). *Spokesmen for the Despised: Fundamentalist Leaders of the Middle East.* University of Chicago Press, 1997.

Seale, Patrick. *Abu Nidal: A Gun for Hire.* London, Hutchinson, 1992.

Searight, Sarah. *The British in the Middle East.* London, Weidenfeld and Nicolson, 1969.

Shaban, M. A. *The Abbasid Revolution.* Cambridge University Press, 1970.

Islamic History: A New Interpretation. 2 vols. Cambridge University Press, 1976–78.

Shadid, Muhammad K. *The United States and the Palestinians.* London, Croom Helm, 1981.

Shafik, Nemat. *Prospects for Middle East and North African Economies.* Basingstoke, Macmillan Press, 1997.

Shapland, Gregory. *Rivers of Discord: International Water Disputes in the Middle East.* London, C. Hurst and Co, 1997.

Sharabi, H. B. *Governments and Politics of the Middle East in the Twentieth Century.* London, Greenwood Press (1962), revised edn, 1987.

Nationalism and Revolution in the Arab World. New York, Van Nostrand, 1966.

Palestine and Israel: The Lethal Dilemma. New York, Pegasus Press, 1969.

Shiloah, Amnon. *Music in the World of Islam: A Socio-Cultural Study.* Aldershot, Scolar Press, 1995.

Shlaim, Avi. *War and Peace in the Middle East.* New York/London, Penguin Books, 1995.

Shlaim, Avi. and Sayigh, Y. (Eds). *The Cold War and The Middle East.* Oxford University Press, 1998.

Sid-Ahmad, Abd as-Salam, and Ehteshami, Anoushiravan (Eds). *Islamic Fundamentalism.* Boulder, Colorado, Westview Press, 1996.

Sid-Ahmad, Muhammad. *After the Guns Fell Silent.* London, Croom Helm, 1976.

Sivan, Emmanuel. *Radical Islam: Medieval Theology and Modern Politics.* Yale University Press, 1991.

Smith, W. Cantwell. *Islam and Modern History.* Toronto, 1957.

Sourdel, Dominique. *Medieval Islam.* London, Routledge and Kegan Paul, 1984.

Southern, R. W. *Western Views of Islam in the Middle Ages.* Oxford, 1957.

Stark, Freya. *Dust in the Lion's Paw.* London and New York, 1961.

Stevens, Georgina G. (Ed.). *The United States and the Middle East.* Englewood Cliffs, NJ, Prentice-Hall, 1964.

Stewart, Desmond. *The Middle East: Temple of Janus.* London, Hamish Hamilton, 1972.

Stewart, P. J. *Unfolding Islam.* Reading, Ithaca Press, 1995.

Stickley, Thomas (Ed.). *Man, Food and Agriculture in the Middle East.* American University of Beirut, 1969.

Stocking, G. W. *Middle East Oil. A Study in Political and Economic Controversy.* Nashville, Vanderbilt University Press, 1979.

Sumner, B. H. *Tsardom and Imperialism in the Far East and Middle East.* London, Oxford University Press, 1940.

Susser, Asher, and Shmuelevitz, Aryeh (Eds). *The Hashemites in the Modern Arab World: essays in honour of the late Professor Uriel Dann.* London, Frank Cass, 1995.

Taylor, Alan R. *The Arab Balance of Power.* New York, Syracuse University Press, 1982.

Taylor, Trevor. *The Middle East in the International System: Lessons from Europe and Implications for Europe.* London, Royal Institute of International Affairs, 1997.

Thayer, P. W. (Ed.). *Tensions in the Middle East.* Baltimore, 1958.

Thomas, L. V., and Frye, R. N. *The United States and Turkey and Iran.* Cambridge, Massachusetts, 1951.

Tillman, Seth P. *The United States in the Middle East.* Hemel Hempstead, Indiana University Press, 1982.

Trevelyan, Humphrey (Lord). *The Middle East in Revolution.* London, Macmillan, 1970.

Trimingham, J. Spencer. *The Sufi Orders in Islam.* Oxford, Clarendon Press, 1971.

Tschirgi, Dan. *The American Search for Mideast Peace.* New York, Praeger, 1989.

Usher, Graham. *Dispatches from Palestine.* London, Pluto Press, 1999.

Vassiliev, Alexei. *Russian Policy in the Middle East: from messianism to pragmatism.* Reading, Ithaca Press, 1993.

Vatikiotis, P. J. *Conflict in the Middle East.* London, George Allen and Unwin, 1971.

Islam and the State. London, Routledge, 1991.

Viorst, Milton. *Reaching for the Olive Branch: UNRWA and peace in the Middle East.* Washington, Middle East Institute, 1989.

Wadsman, P., and Teissedre, R.-F. *Nos politiciens face au conflict israélo arabe.* Paris, 1969.

Waines, David. *The Unholy War.* Wilmette, Medina Press, 1971.

An Introduction to Islam. Cambridge University Press, 1995.

Walker, Christopher J. *Armenia: The Survival of a Nation.* London, Croom Helm, 1980.

Warriner, Doreen. *Land and Poverty in the Middle East.* London, 1948.

Land Reform and Development in the Middle East: Study of Egypt, Syria and Iraq. London, 1962.

Wasserstein, Bernard. *Divided Jerusalem: The Struggle for the Holy City.* London, Profile, 2001.

Watkins, Eric (Ed.). *The Middle East Environment: selected papers of the 1995 Conference of the British Society for Middle Eastern Studies.* Cambridge, St. Malo Press, 1995.

Watt, W. Montgomery. *Muhammad at Mecca.* Oxford, Clarendon Press, 1953.

Muhammad at Medina. Oxford, Clarendon Press (1956), revised edn, 1991.

Muhammad: Prophet and Statesman. Oxford University Press (1961), revised edn, 1974.

Muslim Intellectual—Al Ghazari. Edinburgh University Press, 1962.

Islamic Philosophy and Theology: an Extended Survey. Edinburgh University Press (1963), revised edn, 1995.

Islamic Political Thought: The Basic Concepts. Edinburgh University Press (1968), revised edn, 1987.

What is Islam? London, Longman, 2nd edn, 1979.

Weidenfeld, Werner and Janning, Josef and Behrendt, Sven. *Transformation in the Middle East and North Africa.* Gütersloh, Bertelsmann Foundation, 1997.

Wilson, Rodney. *Trade and Investment in the Middle East.* Macmillan Press, 1977.

Economic Development in the Middle East. London, Routledge, 1995.

Wolf, Aaron T. *Hydropolitics Along the Jordan River: Scarce Water and its Impact on the Arab-Israeli Conflict.* Tokyo, United Nations University Press, 1996.

Woolfson, Marion. *Prophets in Babylon: Jews in the Arab World.* London, Faber, 1980.

Wright, Clifford A. *Facts and Fables: the Arab Israeli conflict.* London, Kegan Paul International, 1989.

Wright, J. W., Jr (Ed.). *The Political Economy of Middle East Peace: The Impact of Competing Arab and Israeli Trade.* London, Routledge, 1999.

Wright, J. W., Jr, and Drake, Laura (Eds). *Economic and Political Impediments to Middle East Peace: Critical Questions and Alternative Scenarios.* New York, St. Martin's Press, 1999.

Yamani, Mai (Ed.). *Feminism and Islam: Legal and Literary Perspectives.* Reading, Ithaca Press, 1996.

Yapp, M. E. *The Near East since the First World War.* London, Longman, 1991.

Yergin, Daniel. *The Prize: the Epic Quest for Oil, Money and Power.* New York, Simon and Schuster (1990), revised edn, 1993.

Yousef, Ahmed and Keeble, Caroline F. *The Agent: The Truth Behind the Anti-Muslim Campaign in America.* Annandale (Virginia), UASR, 1999.

Zahlan, Rosemarie Said. *The Making of the Modern Gulf States.* Reading, Ithaca Press, revised edn, 1999.

Zeine, Z. N. *The Struggle for Arab Independence.* Beirut, 1960.

Zouilaï, Kaddour. *Des voiles et des serrures: de la fermeture en islam.* Paris, L'Harmattan, 1991.

Books on North Africa

See also bibliographies at end of relevant chapters in Part Two.

Abun-Nasr, Jamil M. *A History of the Maghreb.* Cambridge University Press, 1972.

Allal El-Fassi (trans. H. Z. Nuseibeh). *The Independence Movements in Arab North Africa.* Washington, DC, 1954.

Amin, Samir. *L'Economie du Maghreb.* 2 vols Paris, Editions du Minuit, 1966.

The Maghreb in the Modern World. London, Penguin Books, 1971.

Balta, Paul. *Le Grand Maghreb.* Paris, Editions La Découverte, 1990.

Balta, Paul, and Rulleau, Claudine. *L'Algérie des algériens.* Paris, Editions Ouvrières, 1982.

Berque, Jacques. *Le Maghreb entre deux guerres.* Paris, Editions du Seuil, 2nd edn, 1967.

Bonnefous, Marc. *Le Maghreb: repères et rappels.* Editions du Centre des Hautes Etudes sur l'Afrique et l'Asie modernes de Paris, 1991.

Brace, R. M. *Morocco, Algeria, Tunisia.* Englewood Cliffs, N.J., Prentice-Hall, 1964.

Brown, Leon Carl (Ed.). *State and Society in Independent North Africa.* Washington, Middle East Institute, 1966.

Burgat, François. *The Islamic Movement in North Africa.* University of Texas, 1993.

Capot-Rey, R. *Le Sahara français.* Paris, 1953.

Centre d'Etudes des Relations Internationales. *Le Maghreb et la communauté économique européenne.* Paris, Editions FNSP, 1965.

Charbonneau, J. (Ed.). *Le Sahara français.* Paris, Cahiers Charles de Foucauld, No. 38, 1955.

Clancy-Smith, Julia. *North Africa, Islam and the Mediterranean World.* London, Frank Cass, 2001.

Collinson, Sarah. *Shore to Shore: The Politics of Migration in Euro-Maghreb Relations.* London, Royal Institute of International Affairs, 1997.

Damis, John. *Conflict in Northwest Africa: The Western Sahara Dispute.* Stanford University, California, Hoover Institute Press, 1983.

Duclos, J., Leca, J., and Duvignaud, J. *Les nationalismes maghrébins.* Paris, Centre d'Etudes des Relations Internationales, 1966.

Economic Commission for Africa. *Main Problems of Economic Co-operation in North Africa.* Tangier, 1966.

Evers Rasander, E and Westerlund, David (Eds). *African Islam and Islam in Africa: Encounters Between Sufis and Islamists.* London, C. Hurst and Co, 1997.

Furlonge, Sir Geoffrey. *The Lands of Barbary.* London, John Murray, 1966.

Gallagher, C. F. *The US and North Africa.* Cambridge, Massachusetts, 1964.

Gardi, René. *Sahara, Monographie einer grossen Wüste.* Berne, Kummerley and Frey, 1967.

Gautier, E. F. *Le Passé de l'Afrique du Nord.* Paris, 1937.

Germidis, Dimitri, with the help of Delapierre, Michel. *Le Maghreb, la France et l'enjeu technologique.* Paris, Editions Cujas, 1976.

Gordon, D. C. *North Africa's French Legacy 1954–62.* Harvard, 1962.

Hahn, Lorna. *North Africa: from Nationalism to Nationhood.* Washington, 1960.

Hermassi, Elbaki. *Leadership and National Development in North Africa.* University of California Press, 1973.

Heseltine, N. *From Libyan Sands to Chad.* Leiden, 1960.

Joffé, E. G. H. (Ed.). *North Africa: Nation, State and Region.* London, Routledge/University of London, 1993.

Julien, Ch.-A. *Histoire de l'Afrique du nord.* 2 vols, Paris, 2nd edn, 1951–52.

L'Afrique du nord en marche. Paris, 1953.

History of North Africa: From the Arab Conquest to 1830. Revised by R. Le Tourneau. Ed. C. C. Stewart. London, Routledge and Kegan Paul, 1970.

Khaldoun, Ibn. *History of the Berbers.* Translated into French by Slane. 4 vols, Algiers, 1852–56.

Knapp, Wilfrid. *North West Africa: A Political and Economic Survey.* Oxford University Press, 3rd edn, 1977.

Le Tourneau, Roger. *Evolution politique de l'Afrique du nord musulmane.* Paris, 1962.

Liska, G. *The Greater Maghreb: From Independence to Unity?* Washington, DC, Center of Foreign Policy Research, 1963.

Marçais, G. *La Berberie musulmane et l'Orient au moyen age.* Paris, 1946.

Moore, C. H. *Politics in North Africa.* Boston, MA, Little, Brown, 1970.

Mortimer, Edward. *France and the Africans, 1944–1960.* London, Faber, 1969.

Muzikár, Joseph. *Les perspectives de l'intégration des pays maghrébins et leur attitude vis-à-vis du marché commun.* Nancy, 1968.

Nickerson, Jane S. *Short History of North Africa.* New York, 1961.

Parrinder, Geoffrey. *Religion in Africa.* London, Pall Mall Press, 1970.

Polk, William R. (Ed.). *Developmental Revolution: North Africa, Middle East, South Asia.* Washington, DC, Middle East Institute, 1963.

Raven, Susan. *Rome in Africa.* London, Evans Brothers, 1970 (reissued, Routledge, 1993).

Robana, Abderrahma. *The Prospects for an Economic Community in North Africa.* London, Pall Mall, 1973.

Sahli, Mohamed Cherif. *Décoloniser l'histoire; introduction à l'histoire du Maghreb.* Paris, Maspero, 1965.

Schramm, Josef. *Die Westsahara.* Freilassing, Paunonia Verlag, 1969.

Shahin, Emad. *Political Ascent: Contemporary Islamic Movements in North Africa.* Boulder, Colorado, Westview Press, 1996.

Steel, R. (Ed.). *North Africa.* New York, Wilson, 1967.

Toynbee, Sir Arnold. *Between Niger and Nile.* Oxford University Press, 1965.

Trimingham, J. S. *The influence of Islam upon Africa.* London, Longmans, and Beirut, Librairie du Liban, 1968.

UNESCO. *Arid Zone Research*, Vol. XIX: *Nomades et Nomadisme au Sahara.* UNESCO, 1963.

Warren, Cline and Santmyer, C. *Agriculture of Northern Africa.* Washington, US Department of Agriculture, 1965.

White, Gregory. *A Comparative Political Economy of Tunisia and Morocco: On the Outside of Europe Looking In.* Albany NY, State University of New York Press, 2001.

Zartman, I. William. *Government and Politics in North Africa.* London, Greenwood Press, revised edn, 1978.

(Ed.) *Man, State and Society in the Contemporary Maghreb.* London, Pall Mall, 1973.

SELECT BIBLIOGRAPHY (PERIODICALS)

Al-Abhath. Published by American University of Beirut, POB 11-0236/31, Beirut, Lebanon; tel. (1) 340460; fax (1) 361091; e-mail publications@aub.edu.lb; f. 1948; Editor Assad Khairallah; English and Arabic; annual on Middle East studies.

Acta Orientalia. c/o Orientalsk Samfund, Department of History, Njalsgade 80, 2300 Copenhagen S, Denmark; tel. 35328296; f. 1922; publ. under auspices of the Oriental Societies of Denmark, Finland, Norway, and Sweden; history, language, archaeology and religions of the Near and Far East; Editor Prof. Per Kvaerne; annually.

Acta Orientalia Academiae Scientiarum Hungaricae. H-1363 Budapest, POB 24, Hungary; f. 1950; text in English, French, German or Russian; Editor A. Sárközi; 3 a year.

Africa Contemporary Record. Africana Publishing Co, Holmes & Meier Publishers Inc, IUB Building, 30 Irving Place, New York, NY 10003, USA; tel. (212) 2544100; fax (212) 2544104; annual surveys, special essays and indices.

Africa Quarterly. Indian Council for Cultural Relations, Azad Bhavan, Indraprastha Estate, New Delhi 110002, India; tel. 3379309; fax 3378639; e-mail iccr@vsml.com; f. 1961; Editor T. G. Ramamurthi; circ. 700.

Africa Research Bulletins. Blackwell Publishers, 108 Cowley Road, Oxford, OX4 1JF, England; tel. (1865) 791100; fax (1865) 791347; e-mail poconner@blackwellpublishers.co.uk; internet www.africa-research-bulletin.com; f. 1964; monthly bulletins on (*a*) political and (*b*) economic subjects; Eds Pita Adams, Virginia Baily, Veronica Hoskins, Elizabeth Oliver.

Africa Review. World of Information, 2 Market St, Saffron Walden, Essex, CB10 1HZ, England; tel. (1799) 521150; fax (1799) 524805; e-mail info@worldinformation.com; internet www.worldinformation.com; f. 1977; political and economic analysis; Editor D. Brett; annually.

Akhbar al-Alam al-Islami: Press and Publications Department, Muslim World League, POB 537, Mecca al-Mukarramah, Saudi Arabia; tel. (2) 5422733; fax (2) 5436619; internet www.arab.net/mwl; Arabic; weekly.

Alam Attijarat (The World of Business). Johnston International Publishing Corpn (New York), Beirut, Lebanon; Arabic; business; Editor Nadim Makdisi; 10 a year.

Anatolian Studies. BIAA, Senate House, Malet St, London, WC1E 7HU, England; tel. and fax (20) 78628734; f. 1948; annual of the British Institute of Archaeology at Ankara; Editor Dr Stephen Hill.

Anatolica. Netherlands Historical Archaeological Institute at İstanbul, Istiklâl Caddesi 393, İstanbul-Beyoğlu, Turkey; tel. 2939283; fax 2513846; e-mail nhaiist@superonline.com; f. 1967; Editors B. Flemming, H. E. Lagro, J. J. Roodenberg, J. de Roos, D. J. W. Meijer, M. Özdoğan; annually.

Annales archéologiques Arabes Syriennes. Direction Générale des Antiquités et des Musées, University St, Damascus, Syria; tel. 2214854; f. 1951; archaeological and historical review; Dir-Gen. Dr Sultan Moheisen; annually.

Annuaire de l'Afrique du Nord. Edited by the Institut de recherches et d'études sur le Monde Arabe et Musulman, 3–5 ave Pasteur, 13617 Aix-en-Provence Cedex 1; tel. 4-42-23-85-00; fax 4-42-23-85-01; e-mail adiremam@univ-aix.fr; published by the Centre National de la Recherche Scientifique, CNRS Editions, 15 rue Malebranche, 75005 Paris, France; f. 1962; year-book contains special studies on current affairs and political science, report on a collective programme of social sciences research on North Africa (Algeria, Egypt, Libya, Mauritania, Morocco, Tunisia), chronologies, chronicles, documentation and book reviews; Editor Jean-Noël Ferrié.

The Arab Economist. Centre for Economic, Financial and Social Research and Documentation SAL, Gefinor Tower, Clemenceau St, Bloc B-POB 11-6068, Beirut, Lebanon; f. 1969; Chair. Dr Chafic Akhras; monthly; circ. 7,300.

Arab Oil and Gas / Le Pétrole et Le Gaz Arabes. The Arab Petroleum Research Centre, 7 ave Ingrès, 75016 Paris, France; tel. 1-45-24-33-10; fax 1-45-20-16-85; f. 1971; petroleum and gas; English and French edns; Editor Dr Nicolas Sarkis; fortnightly.

Arab Political Documents. publ. by American University of Beirut, Beirut, Lebanon; f. 1963; Editor Yousuf Khoury; Arabic; compiles important political documents of the year in various Arab countries; annually.

Arab Studies Quarterly. Association of Arab-American University Graduates, Inc. (AAUG), 4201 Connecticut Ave NSW, Suite 303, Washington, DC 20008, USA; tel. (202) 2378312; fax (202) 2378313; internet www.aaug.org/asq.htm; f. 1976; Editor Jamal R. Nassar.

Arabia: The Islamic World Review. Crown House, Crown Lane, East Burnham, Bucks, SL2 3SG, England; tel. (12814) 5177; monthly.

Arabica (Revue d'Etudes Arabes et Islamiques): Université Paris III, 13 rue de Santeuil, 75231 Paris Cédex 05, France; tel. 1-45-87-41-39; Dir (Scientifique) Mohammed Arkoun; Editor Leiden Brill; quarterly.

Aramco World. Aramco Services Co, Box 2106, Houston, TX 77252-2106, USA; non-political information—culture, natural history, economics, etc.—of the Middle East; Editor Robert Arndt; bimonthly.

Archiv für Orientforschung. c/o Institut für Orientalistik der Universität Wien, Spitalgasse 2, 1090 Vienna, Austria; tel. (1) 427743401; fax (1) 42779434; e-mail gebhard-selz@univie.ac.at; internet www.univie.ac.at/orientalistik; f. 1923; Editors Gebhard J. Selz, Hermann Hunger; annually.

Armenian Review. The Armenian Review Inc., 80 Bigelow Ave, Watertown, MA 02472, USA; tel. (617) 9264037; fax (617) 9261750; f. 1948; Editor Dr Hayg Oshagan; quarterly.

Asian Affairs. Royal Society for Asian Affairs, 2 Belgrave Square, London, SW1X 8PJ, England; tel. (20) 72355122; fax (20) 72596771; e-mail sec@rsaa.org.uk; internet www.rsaa.org.uk; f. 1901; 3 a year.

L'Asie nouvelle. 94 rue St Lazare, 75442 Paris Cédex 09, France; tel. 1-45-26-67-01; weekly and special issues; Dir André Roux.

Awad: Cahiers d'études berbères. Paris; f. 1985; Dir Tassadit Yacine.

Belleten. Türk Tarih Kurumu, Kızılay Sokak no. 1, 06100 Ankara, Turkey; tel. 3102368; fax 3101698; e-mail ttkinfo@ttk.gov.tr; internet www.ttk.org.tr; f. 1937; history and archaeology of Turkey; Editor Prof. Dr Yusuf Halaçoğlu; 3 a year.

The Bibliography of the Middle East. Publisher L. Farès, BP 2712, Damascus, Syria; annually.

Bibliotheca Orientalis. Published by Netherlands Institute for the Near East, Witte Singel 25, POB 9515, 2300 RA Leiden, Netherlands; tel. (71) 5272036; fax (71) 5272038; e-mail a.de.beurs@let.leidenuniv.nl; internet www.leidenuniv.nl/nino/nino.html; f. 1943; edited by J. de Roos, D. J. W. Meijer, H. J. A. de Meulenaere, A. van der Kooij, C. Nijland, J. J. Roodenberg, M. Stol; 3 double issues a year.

British Journal of Middle Eastern Studies. BRISMES Administrative Office, IMEIS, University of Durham, South Road, Durham DH1 3TG, England; tel. (191) 3747989; fax (191) 3742830; f. 1974 (as *British Society of Middle Eastern Studies Bulletin*); Editor Prof. Ian Netton, Dept of Arabic and Middle Eastern Studies, University of Leeds, Leeds LS2 9JT; tel. (113) 2333420; fax (113) 2333426; e-mail i.r.netton@leeds.ac.uk; 2 a year.

Bulletin d'études orientales. Institut français d'études arabes, BP 344, Damascus, Syria; tel. (11) 3330214; fax (11) 3327887; e-mail ifead@net.sy; internet www.ifead.org; f. 1922; annually (52 vols published).

Bulletin of the School of Oriental and African Studies. School of Oriental and African Studies, University of London, Thornhaugh Street, Russell Sq., London, WC1H 0XG, England; tel. (20) 78984064; fax (20) 78984849; e-mail bulletin@soas.ac.uk; publ. by Cambridge University Press; 3 a year.

Les Cahiers de l'Orient. 60 rue des Cévennes, 75015 Paris, France; tel. 1-40-60-73-11; f. 1986; published by CERPO (Centre of Near East Studies); review of Islamic and Arab affairs; quarterly.

Les Cahiers de Tunisie. Publ. by Faculté des sciences humaines et sociales de Tunis, 94 blvd de 9 Avril 1938, 1007 Tunis, Tunisia; tel. 260858; f. 1953; research in humanities; Dir Hédi Cherif; Editor-in-Chief Hassan Annabi; every six months.

Chuto Kenkyu (Journal of Middle Eastern Studies). The Middle East Institute of Japan, POB 1513, Shinjuku i-Land Tower, 163-13 Tokyo, Japan; tel. (3) 53232145; fax (3) 53232148; f. 1960; Editor Wasuke Miyake; monthly.

Le Commerce du Levant. Achrafieh-Accaoui, Media Centre, 3rd Floor, BP 90-1397 Jdeideh, Beirut, Lebanon; tel. (1) 561406; fax (1) 561900; e-mail lecommerce@inco.com.lb; internet www.lecommercedulevant.com; monthly.

Comunità Mediterranea. Lungotevere Flaminio 34, Rome, Italy; law and political science relating to Mediterranean countries; Pres. E. Bussi.

Crescent International. 300 Steelcase Rd West, Unit 8, Markham, ON L3R 2W2, Canada; tel. (905) 4749292; fax (905) 4749293; e-mail crescent@inforamp.net; f. 1980; deals with Islamic movement throughout the world; 2 a month.

Dawat al-Haq. Muslim World League, POB 537, Mecca al-Mukarramah, Saudi Arabia; tel. (2) 5422733; fax (2) 5436619; internet arab.net/mwl; Arabic; monthly.

Deutsche Morgenländische Gesellschaft; Zeitschrift. Seminar für Sinologie, Humboldt University, Unter den Linden 6, 10099 Berlin, Germany; tel. (3) 20936611; f. 1847; covers the history, languages and literature of the Orient; Editor Prof. Dr Florian C. Reiter; 2 a year.

Developing Economies. Nihon Boeki Shinkokai Ajia Keizai Kenkyusho (Institute of Developing Economies, Japan External Trade Organization), 3-2-2 Wakaba, Mihama-ku, Chiba-shi 261-8545, Japan; tel. (043) 2999500; fax (043) 2999724; e-mail info@ide.go.ip; internet www.ide.go.ip; f. 1962; English; quarterly.

L'Economiste Arabe. Centre d'études et de documentation économiques, financières et sociales, SAL, BP 6068, Beirut, Lebanon; Pres. Dr Chafic Akhras, Dir-Gen. Dr Sabbah al-Haj; monthly.

Europe Outremer. 178 quai L. Blériot, 75016 Paris, France; tel. 1-46-47-78-44; f. 1923; economic and political material on French-speaking states of Africa; monthly.

France-Pays Arabes. 14 rue Augereau, 75007 Paris, France; tel. 145552752; fax 145512726; f. 1968; politics, economics and culture of the Arab world; Dir Lucien Bitterlin; monthly.

Grand Maghreb. BP 45, 38402 Saint-Martin-d'Hères, France; monthly.

Hamizrah Hehadash. Israel Oriental Society. The Hebrew University, Jerusalem, Israel; e-mail ios49@hotmail.com; f. 1949; Hebrew with English summary; Middle Eastern, Asian and African affairs; Editors Haim Gerber, Elie Padeh.

Hesperis-Tamuda. Faculté des Lettres et des Sciences Humaines, Université Muhammad V, BP 1040, Rabat, Morocco; tel. (212) 7771989; fax (212) 7772068; f. 1921; history, anthropology, civilization of Maghreb and Western Islam, special reference to bibliography; Chief Editor B. Boutaleb; annually; circ. 2,000.

Ibla. Institut des belles lettres arabes, 12 rue Jamâa el-Haoua, 1008 Tunis BM, Tunisia; tel. (71) 560133; fax (71) 572683; e-mail ibla@gnet.tn; f. 1937; 2 a year.

Indo-Iranian Journal. Kluwer Academic Publishers, POB 17, 3300 AA Dordrecht, Netherlands; tel. (78) 6392392; e-mail services@wkap.nl; internet www.wkap.nl; f. 1957; Editors H. W. Bodewitz and O. van Hinübek; quarterly.

Indo-Iranica. Iran Society, 12 Dr M. Ishaque Road, Kolkata 700016, India; tel. 2269899; f. 1946; promotion of Persian studies and Indo-Iranian cultural relations; Gen. Sec. and Man. Editor M. A. Majid; quarterly.

International Journal of Middle East Studies. Cambridge University Press, The Edinburgh Bldg, Shaftesbury Road, Cambridge, CB2 2RU, England; tel. (1223) 326070; fax (1223) 315052; e-mail journals_marketing@cambridge.org; internet journals.cambridge.org; Journal of the Middle East Studies Association of North America; first issue Jan. 1970; Editor Juan Cole, University of Michigan, USA; 4 a year.

Iraq. British School of Archaeology in Iraq, 10 Carlton House Terrace, London, SW1Y 5AH, England; fax (20) 79695401; e-mail bsai@britac.ac.uk; f. 1932; annually.

Der Islam. D-20148 Hamburg, Rothenbaumchaussee 36, Germany; tel. (040) 41233180; fax (040) 41235674; e-mail der_islam@uni-hamburg.de; 2 a year.

Islamic and Comparative Law Review. Dept of Law, Hamdard University, Tughlaqabad, New Delhi 110062, India; tel. (11) 6439685; f. 1981; Founder-Editor Tahir Mahmood; two a year.

Islamic Quarterly. The Islamic Cultural Centre, 146 Park Road, London, NW8 7RG, England; tel (20) 77243363; fax (20) 77240493; e-mail islamic200@aol.com; f. 1954; Editor Dr Hamad al-Majed; quarterly.

Israel and Palestine. POB 3349, Tel-Aviv 61033, Israel; tel. (3) 5239391; fax (3) 5290348; f. 1971; Editor Maxim Ghilan; International Secretariat of the International Jewish Peace Union (IJPU); approx. 20 a year.

Jeune Afrique/L'Intelligent. Groupe Jeune Afrique, 57 bis rue d'Auteuil, 75016 Paris, France; tel. 1-44-30-19-60; fax 1-44-30-19-30; e-mail mailbox@jeuneafrique.com; internet www.jeuneafrique.com; f. 1960; Publisher Bechir ben Yahmed; weekly.

Journal of the American Oriental Society. American Oriental Society, 329 Sterling Memorial Library, Box 208236, Yale Station, New Haven, CT 06520, USA; tel. (313) 7474760; f. 1842; Ancient Near East, Inner Asia, South and Southeast Asia, Islamic Near East, and Far East; quarterly.

Journal Asiatique. Journal de la société asiatique, 3 rue Mazarine, 75006 Paris, France; f. 1822; Dir Anna Scherrer-Schaub; covers all phases of Oriental research; 2 a year.

Journal of Muslim Minority Affairs. Institute of Muslim Minority Affairs, 46 Goodge St, London, W1T 4LU, England; tel. (20) 76366740; fax (20) 72551473; f. 1976; Man. Editor Dr Saleha Mahmood; 2 a year.

Journal of Near Eastern Studies. Oriental Institute, University of Chicago, 1155 East 58th Street, Chicago, IL 60637, USA; tel (773) 7029540; fax (773) 7029853; e-mail r-biggs@uchicago.edu; devoted to the Ancient and Medieval Near and Middle East, archaeology, languages, history, Islam; Editor R. Biggs.

Journal of North African Studies. Frank Cass & Co Ltd, Crown House, 47 Chase Side, Southgate, London, N14 5BP; tel. (20) 89202100; fax (20) 84478548; e-mail info@frankcass.com; internet www.frankcass.com; f. 1996; quarterly; Editors John P. Entelis, George Joffé.

Journal of Palestine Studies. 3501 M St, NW, Washington, DC 20007, USA; tel. (202) 3423990; fax (202) 3423927; e-mail jps@ipsjps.org; internet http://www.ipsjps.org; f. 1971; publ. by the University of California Press for the Inst. for Palestine Studies, Washington, DC; Palestinian affairs and the Arab–Israeli conflict; Editor Hisham Sharabi; Assoc. Editor Philip Mattar; circ. 3,600; quarterly.

The Maghreb Review. 45 Burton St, London, WC1H 9AL, England; tel. (20) 73881840; f. 1976; North Africa and its historical geopolitical and environment, and sub-Saharan African, Middle Eastern and Islamic studies from earliest times to the present; Editor Muhammad ben Madani; quarterly.

Maghreb-Sélection. IC Publications, 10 rue Vineuse, 75784 Paris Cédex 16, France; tel. 1-44-30-81-00; fax 1-44-30-81-11; e-mail benyeddor@wanadoo.fr; f. 1979; economic information about North Africa; weekly.

Majallat a-Rabita. Press and Publications Department, Muslim World League, POB 537, Mecca al-Mukarramah, Saudi Arabia; tel. (2) 5422733; fax (2) 5436619; internet arab.net/mwl; Arabic; monthly.

Marchés Arabes. IC Publications, 10 rue Vineuse, 75784 Paris Cédex 16, France; tel. 1-44-30-81-00; fax 1-44-30-81-11; e-mail rosenwald@wanadoo.fr; f. 1978; economic information about the Middle East; fortnightly.

Marchés Tropicaux et Mediterranéens. 190 blvd Malesherbes, 75017 Paris, France; tel. 1-43-18-87-00; f. 1945; African economics; Publr Moreux SA; Editor Sébastien de Dianous; weekly.

MEN Weekly. Middle East News Agency, Sharia Hoda Sharawi, Cairo, Egypt; tel. (2) 3933000; fax (2) 3935055; internet mena.org.eg; f. 1962; weekly news bulletin.

Le Message de l'Islam. BP 14155, 3899 Tehran, Iran; theoretical review of Iranian Islam; monthly.

The Middle East. 7 Coldbath Sq., London, EC1R 4LQ, England; tel. (20) 77137711; fax (20) 77137970; e-mail icpubs@africasia.com; internet www.africasia.com; f. 1974; political, economic and cultural; Editor Pat Lancaster; Publr Ahmed Afif Ben Yedder; circ. 18,463; monthly.

Middle East Business Intelligence. 717 D St, NW, Suite 300, Washington, DC 20004, USA; tel. (202) 6286900; fax (202) 6286618; newsletter of business and sales opportunities and market information; Publr William C. Hearn; 2 a month.

Middle East Contemporary Survey. Moshe Dayan Centre for Middle Eastern and African Studies, c/o Westview Press, 5500 Central Ave, Boulder, CO 80301, USA; tel. (303) 4443541; fax (303) 4493356; 12 Hid's Copse Rd, Cumnor Hill, Oxford, OX2 9JJ, England; tel. (1865) 865466; fax (1865) 862763; annual record of political developments, country surveys, special essays, maps, tables, notes, indices; Editors Ami Ayalon, Bruce Maddy-Weitzman.

Middle East Economic Digest. MEED Ltd, 33–39 Bowling Green Lane, London, EC1R 0DA, England; tel. (20) 74706200; fax (20) 78319537; e-mail david-butter@meed.com; internet www.meed.com; f. 1957; weekly report on economic, business and political developments; Editor-in-Chief Edmund O'Sullivan; Editor David Butter.

Middle East Economic Survey. Middle East Petroleum and Economic Publications (Cyprus), POB 24940, 1355 Nicosia, Cyprus; tel. (22) 665431; fax (22) 671988; e-mail info@mees.com; internet www.mees.com; f. 1957 (in Beirut); weekly review and analysis of petroleum, finance and banking, and political developments; Publr Basim W. Itayim; Editor Walid Khadduri.

Middle East Events Bulletin. Centre of Near and Middle Eastern Studies, School of Oriental and African Studies—SOAS, University of London, Thornhaugh St, Russell Sq., London, WC1H 0XG, England; tel. (20) 78984330; fax (20) 78984329; e-mail mepub@soas.ac.uk; internet www.soas.ac.uk/cnmes; English; Editor Fiona McLean; monthly.

Middle East Executive Reports. 717 D Street, NW, Suite 300, Washington, DC 20004, USA; tel. (202) 6286900; fax (202) 6286618; legal and practical business guide to the Middle East; Publr William C. Hearn; monthly.

Middle East Focus. Canadian Academic Foundation for Peace in the Middle East, 1057 Steeles Ave West, POB 81509, North York, ON M2R 3X1, Canada; tel. (416) 9639477; f. 1978; contemporary Middle Eastern issues; English; Editor Irving Abella; quarterly.

Middle East Insight. Suite 500, 1156 15th St, NW, Washington, DC 20036, USA; tel. (202) 4662146; fax (202) 4662147; e-mail comments@mideastinsight.org; internet www.mideastinsight.org; f. 1980; politics, economics and culture; English; Editor George Nader; 6 a year.

Middle East International. 21 Collingham Road, London, SW5 0NU, England; tel. (20) 73735228; fax (20) 73705956; f. 1971; fortnightly; political and economic developments, book reviews; Editor Michael Wall.

The Middle East Journal. Middle East Institute, 1761 N Street, NW, Washington, DC 20036, USA; tel. (202) 7850191; fax (202) 3318861; e-mail mej@mideasti.org; internet www.mideasti.org; journal in English devoted to the study of the modern Near East; f. 1947; Editor Michael Collins Dunn; circ. 4,000; quarterly.

Middle East Military Balance. Jaffee Center for Strategic Studies, Tel-Aviv University, Ramat-Aviv, Tel-Aviv 69978, Israel; tel. (3) 6409926; fax (3) 6422404; e-mail jcss2@post.tau.ac.il;

internet www.tau.ac.il/jcss; English; Editor Dr Ephraim Kam; annual.

Middle East Monitor. Business Monitor International Ltd, Queen Victoria St, London, EC4V 4DU, England; tel. (20) 72480468; fax (20) 72480467; monthly; economic and political brief; Editor John Roberts.

The Middle East Observer. 41 Sherif St, Cairo, Egypt; tel. (2) 3926919; fax (2) 3939732; e-mail meo@soficom.com.eg; internet www.meobserver.com; f. 1954; economics; English; Editor Hesham A. Raouf; Publr Ahmad Foda; weekly.

Middle East Policy. Middle East Policy Council, 1730 M Street, NW, Suite 512, Washington, DC 20036, USA; tel. (202) 2966767; fax (202) 2965791; e-mail ajoyce@mepc.org; internet www.mepc.org; policy analysis; quarterly; Editor Anne Joyce.

Middle East Quarterly. Middle East Forum, Suite 1050, 1500 Walnut St, Philadelphia, PA 19102, USA; tel. (215) 5465406; fax (215) 5465409; e-mail meq@MEForum.org; internet www.MEForum.org; f. 1994; English; Editor Martin Kramer; quarterly.

Middle East Report. Middle East Research and Information Project, 1500 Mass Ave NW, Suite 119, Washington, DC 20005, USA; tel. (202) 2233677; fax (202) 22336054; e-mail ctoensing@merip.org; Editor Chris Oensing; quarterly.

Middle East Review. World of Information, 2 Market St, Saffron Walden, Essex, CB10 1HZ, England; tel. (1799) 521150; fax (1799) 524805; e-mail info@worldinformation.com; internet www.worldinformation.com; f. 1974; political and economic analysis; Man. Editor D. Brett; annually.

Middle East Studies Association Bulletin. 200 LCI, Catholic University of America, Washington, DC 20064, USA; tel. (202) 3195999; fax (202) 3196267; Editor Jon Anderson; 2 a year.

Middle Eastern Studies. Frank Cass & Co Ltd, Crown House, 47 Chase Side, Southgate, London, N14 5BP; tel. (20) 89202100; fax (20) 84478548; e-mail info@frankcass.com; internet www.frankcass.com; f. 1964; Editor Sylvia Kedourie; 4 a year.

Mideast Report. 60 East 42nd Street, Suite 1433, New York, NY 10017, USA; political analysis, oil and finance and business intelligence.

Monde-Arabe-Maghreb-Machrek. Direction de la Documentation, Secrétariat général du gouvernement, La documentation française, 29–31 quai Voltaire, 75344 Paris Cédex 07, France; tel. 1-40-15-71-68; fax 1-40-15-72-30; e-mail magmac@ladocfrancaise.gouv.fr; internet http://www.ladocfrancaise.gouv.fr; f. 1964; published with the assistance of the Fondation nationale des Sciences politiques and the Centre d'étude de l'Orient contemporain (University of Paris III); quarterly.

The Muslim World. 77 Sherman Street, Hartford, CT 06105, USA; tel. (860) 509-9500; fax (860) 509-9539; f. 1911; Islamic studies in general and Muslim-Christian relations in past and present; Editors Ibrahim Abu-Rabi' and Jane I. Smith; 2 a year.

The Muslim World League Journal. Press and Publications Department, Muslim World League, POB 537, Mecca al-Mukarramah, Saudi Arabia; tel. (2) 5441622; fax (2) 5441622; internet arab.net/mwl; Chief Editor Hamid Hassan ar-Raddadi; monthly in English.

Near East Report. 440 First St, NW, Suite 607, Washington, DC 20001, USA; tel. (202) 6395200; fax (202) 3474916; e-mail ner@aipac.org; internet www.aipac.org; f. 1957; analyses US policy in the Middle East; Editor Raphael Danziger; circ. 55,000; bi-weekly.

Oil and Gas Journal. Penn Well Publishing Co, 1421 S. Sheridan, Tulsa, Oklahoma 74101, USA; tel. (918) 8353161; fax (918) 8329295; f. 1902; petroleum industry and business weekly; Editor John L. Kennedy; circ. 42,000.

Orient. Journal for Politics and Economics of the Middle East, D-20148, 2 Hamburg, Mittelweg 150, Germany; tel. (40) 4132050; fax (40) 441484; e-mail doihh@uni-hamburg.de; internet www.doihh.de; f. 1960; current affairs articles in German and English; documents, book reviews and bibliographies; Editor Prof. Dr Udo Steinbach; quarterly.

Oriente Moderno. Istituto per l'Oriente C.A. Nallino, via A. Caroncini 19, 00197 Rome, Italy; tel. (6) 8084106; fax (6) 8079395; e-mail ipocan@libero.it; f. 1921; articles, book reviews.

Palestine Affairs. POB 1691, Beirut, Lebanon; studies of Palestine problem; f. 1971; monthly in Arabic; Editor Bilal El-Hassan.

Persica. Dutch-Iranian Society; University of Leiden, Dept of Persian Studies, Witte Singel 24, POB 9515, 2300 RA Leiden, Netherlands; e-mail Persica@Let.Leidenuniv.nl; f. 1963; Publr Peeters, Bondgenotenlaan 153, 3000 Leuven, Belgium; Editors J. de Bruijn, J. G. J. ter Haar, C. Hillenbrand, R. Hillenbrand, B. Radtke, W. J. Vogelsang; annually.

Petroleum Economist. POB 105, Baird House, 15/17 St. Cross St, London, EC1N 8UN, England; tel. (20) 78315588; fax (20) 78314567; internet www.petroleum-economist.com; f. 1934; monthly in English; Editor Derek Bamber; circ. 5,500.

Petroleum Times Energy Report. Nexus Media Ltd, Nexos House, Azalea Drive, Swanley, Kent, BR8 8HY, England.

Politica Internazionale. Via del Tritone 62B, 00187 Rome, Italy; tel. (6) 6792321; fax (6) 6797849; publ. by Istituto per le relazioni tra Italia e i Paesi dell' Africa, America Latina e Medio Oriente; Italian edition (6 a year).

Pour la Palestine. 21 rue Voltaire, 75011 Paris, France; tel. 1-43-72-15-79; fax 1-43-72-07-25; e-mail amfpafp@club-internet.fr; f. 1979; monthly.

Revue d'assyriologie et d'archéologie orientale. Presses universitaires de France, 12 rue Jean-de-Beauvais, 75005 Paris, France; f. 1923; Dirs Paul Garelli, Pierre Amiet; 2 a year.

Revue des études islamiques. Librairie Orientaliste Paul Geuthner SA, 12 rue Vavin, 75006 Paris, France; f. 1927.

Revue d'études Palestiniennes. Published by Institute for Palestine Studies (see *Journal of Palestine Studies*); distributed by Les Editions de Minuit, 7 rue Bernard Palissy, 75006 Paris, France; tel. 1-44-39-39-20; fax 1-45-44-82-36; f. 1981; Chief Editor Elias Sanbar; quarterly.

Rivista Degli Studi Orientali. Dipartimento di Studi Orientali, Facoltà di Lettere, Università Degli Studi, 'La Sapienza', Rome, Italy; tel. (6) 49913562; fax (6) 4451209; e-mail studiorient@axrma.uniroma1.it; Publr Istituti Editoriali e Poligrafici Internazionali; quarterly.

Rocznik Orientalistyczny. Instytut Orientalistyczny, Uniwersytet Warszawski, 00-927 Warszawa 64, Poland; e-mail mmdziekan@poczta.onet.pl; f. 1915; Editor-in-Chief Edward Tryjarski; Sec. Marek M. Dziekan; 2 a year.

Royal Asiatic Society of Great Britain and Ireland Journal. 60 Queen's Gardens, London W2 3AF, England; tel. (20) 77244742; fax (20) 77064008; e-mail info@royalasiaticsociety.org; internet www.royalasiaticsociety.org; f. 1823; covers all aspects of Oriental research; Pres. Prof. A. Stockwell; Editor Dr Sarah Ansari; 3 a year.

Studia Arabistyczne i Islamistyczne. Zakład Arabistyki i Islamistyki, Instytut Orientalistyczny, Uniwersytet Warszawski, 00-927 Warszawa 64, Poland; e-mail mmdziekan@poczta.onet.pl; f. 1993; Editor-in-Chief Janusz Danecki; Sec. Marek M. Dziekan; annually.

Studia Islamica, G. P. Maisonneuve et Larose, 15 rue Victor-Cousin, 75005 Paris, France; tel. 1-44-41-49-30; fax 1-43-25-77-41; f. 1953; Editors A. L. Udovitch and A. M. Turki; 2 a year.

Studies in Islam. Indian Institute of Islamic Studies, Panchkuin Road, New Delhi 110001, India; f. 1964; quarterly.

Sumer. State Antiquities and Heritage Organization, Karkh, Salihiya, Jamal abd an-Nasr St, Baghdad, Iraq; tel. 5376121; f. 1945; archaeological and historical; Chair. Editorial Bd Dr M. Said; annually.

At-Tijara al-Arabiya al-Inkleezya (World Arab Trade). Sahara Publications, 38 Greyhound Rd, London, W6 8NX, England; tel. (20) 76101387; fax (20) 76100078; e-mail a.h.n@btinternet.com; www.saharapublications.com; f. 1947; Arabic; 6 a year.

Turcica. Publ. by Université des sciences humaines, Strasbourg, and Association pour le développement des études turques, EHESS, 54 blvd Raspail, 75006 Paris, France; tel. 1-49-54-23-01; fax 1-49-54-26-72; e-mail Etudes-turques@ehess.fr; internet www.ehess.fr/centres/chdt/page_acceuil.html; f. 1971; all aspects of Turkish and Turkic culture; annually; Eds Prof. Gilles Veinstein and Paul Dumont.

Türk Kültürü Araştırmaları. T. K. Araştırma Enstitüsü, 17 Sokak No. 38 Bahçelievler, Ankara, Turkey; tel. (312) 2133100; f. 1964; scholarly articles in Turkish; Editor Dr Şükrü Elçin; annually.

Turkish Studies. Frank Cass & Co, Crown House, 47 Chase Side, London, N14 5BP; tel. (20) 89202100; fax (20) 84478548; e-mail info@frankcass.com; internet www.frankcass.com; f. 2000; three a year; Editor Barry Rubin.

Türkologischer Anzeiger (Turkology Annual). Oriental Institute of the University of Vienna; A-1090 Vienna, Spitalgasse 2, Hof 4, Austria; tel. (1) 427743401; fax (1) 42779434; annually.

Al-Urdun al-jadid (New Jordan). POB 4856, Nicosia, Cyprus; Arabic; quarterly.

Vostok (Oriens). Russian Academy of Sciences, 103031 Moscow, ul. Rozhdestvenka 12, Russia: tel. 9255146; f. 1955; Afro-Asian Societies past and present; Editor-in-Chief Dr V. V. Naumkin; 6 a year.

The Washington Report on Middle East Affairs. POB 53062, Washington, DC 20009, USA; tel. (202) 9396050; fax (202) 2654574; e-mail wrmea@aol.com; internet http://www.washington-report.org; f. 1982; 8 a year.

Die Welt des Islams. (International Journal for the Study of Modern Islam.) Published by Brill Academic Publishers, postbus 9000, 2300 PA, Leiden, Netherlands; tel. (71) 5353500; fax (71) 5317532; Orientalisches Seminar der Universität, Regina-Pacis-Weg 7, 53113 Bonn, Federal Republic of Germany; tel. (228) 737462; fax (228) 735601; f. 1913; contains articles in German, English and French on the contemporary Muslim world with special reference to literature; Editors Prof. Dr S. Wild (University of Bonn), Prof. Dr W. Ende (University of Freiburg), Prof. Dr M. Ursinus (University of Heidelberg).

Wiener Zeitschrift für die Kunde des Morgenlandes. Oriental Institute of the University of Vienna, Spitalgasse 2, Hof. 4, A-1090 Vienna, Austria; tel. (1) 427743431; fax (1) 42779434; e-mail univie.ac.at/orientalistik; internet www.univie.ac.at/orientalistik; Editors O. Prof. Dr Arne A. Ambros, O. Prof. Dr Gebhard J. Selz, O. Prof. Dr Markus Köhbach; annually.

INDEX OF REGIONAL ORGANIZATIONS

(main references only)

Europa's Regional Surveys of the World

A unique series of regularly revised reference titles aimed at businesses, libraries, universities, government departments, embassies, newspapers and international organizations

'Europa's Regional Surveys of the World are justly renowned for their exceptionally high levels of production, content and accuracy.' Reference Reviews

South America, Central America and the Caribbean

- An incomparable source of factual and statistical information for this vast region
- Reflects the very latest political and economic developments
- Includes contributions from over 30 leading authorities on Latin American and Caribbean affairs
- Provides a systematic survey of each country
- Enlightened commentary on topical issues, such as international trade and the banana war, the environment and the drug crisis

Africa South of the Sahara

- A one-volume library of essential data on all the countries of Sub-Saharan Africa
- Over 1,200 pages of economic and demographic statistics, wide-ranging directory material and authoritative articles
- Contributions from 50 leading experts on African affairs
- Incisive analysis and the latest available information
- Includes details of international organizations active in the region

Central and South Eastern Europe

- This title is one of the two new successor volumes to Europa's award-winning Eastern Europe and the Commonwealth of Independent States
- Includes country-by-country surveys, political, economic and social information
- Detailed articles by acknowledged experts cover issues of regional importance such as integration with the West, social policy and religion, the Macedonian Question
- Coverage of regional organizations, research institutes and periodicals
- A select bibliography and a political profile section

Western Europe

- Over 660 pages of statistics, directory and analytical information
- Introductory essays on the region cover political, economic and social issues ranging from the impact of the European Union to Western Europe's environmental politics and its relations with the wider world
- Acknowledged authorities write on regional and country-specific topics
- Chronologies detailing the history of each country

Eastern Europe, Russia and Central Asia

- This title is one of the two successor volumes to the award-winning Eastern Europe and the Commonwealth of Independent States
- Includes country-by-country surveys, political, economic and social information
- Articles by acknowledged authorities covering regional issues such as the politics of energy and the environment
- Coverage of regional organizations, institutes and periodicals
- A select bibliography and a political profile section

The Middle East and North Africa

- Covers the Middle Eastern world from Algeria to Yemen
- Draws together the events of the past twelve months
- Provides comprehensive information on the United Nations and all major international organizations operating in the area
- A detailed calendar of events, expert articles, up to date statistics and directory information
- An invaluable reference source in business matters relating to the area

The Far East and Australasia

- A systematic survey of all the countries of East Asia, South Asia, South-East Asia, Australasia and the Pacific Islands
- Essential for anyone with a professional interest in this part of the world, the book keeps you up to date with current economic and political developments
- Presents over 1,400 pages of statistics, directory information and expert analysis
- Provides details of all major international organizations active in the region

The USA and Canada

- Invaluable reference guide to the political, economic and social affairs of these two powerful North American nations
- Contributions from over 30 acknowledged authorities
- Specially commissioned articles cover issues such as the USA and the United Nations, Aboriginal Peoples in North America, the Canadian Economy
- Includes wide-ranging statistics and directory information
- Provides geographical and historical introductions to each state/province, data on the economies, and a comprehensive governmental and legislative directory section

For further information on any of the above titles contact our marketing department on:

tel. + 44 (0) 20 7842 2110   fax. + 44 (0) 20 7842 2249

e-mail info.europa@tandf.co.uk   www.europapublications.co.uk